Comparative Guide to American Elementary & Secondary Schools

2005

Third Edition

Comparative Guide to American Elementary & Secondary Schools

All Public School Districts Serving 1,500 or More Students

A Universal Reference Book

PUBLISHER: Leslie Mackenzie
EDITOR: David Garoogian
EDITORIAL DIRECTOR: Laura Mars-Proietti
MARKETING DIRECTOR: Jessica Moody

A Universal Reference Book
Grey House Publishing, Inc.
185 Millerton Road
Millerton, NY 12546
518.789.8700
FAX 518.789.0545
www.greyhouse.com
e-mail: books @greyhouse.com

First edition 1996
Third edition 2004

Printed in the USA

Publisher's Cataloging-In-Publication Data
(Prepared by The Donohue Group, Inc.)

The comparative guide to American elementary & secondary schools : covers all public school districts serving 1,500 or more students. -- 3rd ed. --

p. ; cm.
Includes index.
ISBN: 1-59237-047-0

1. School districts--United States--States--Statistics. 2. School districts--United States--States--Directories. 3. Public schools--United States--States--Statistics. 4. Elementary schools--United States--States--Statistics. 5. High schools--United States--States--Statistics.

LB2817.3 .C66 2005
371.01/0973/021

Table of Contents

Introduction

Welcome to the third edition of *The Comparative Guide to American Elementary & Secondary Schools,* published by Universal Reference Publications, an imprint of Grey House Publishing. This remarkable resource brings together pertinent evaluative and demographic statistics from a wide range of sources for 5,874 public school districts in the United States - all districts with 1,500 or more students. These districts contain and represent nearly 80% of all the public schools in the country.

These demographics and statistics are organized into a highly readable format that saves hours of research time. The logical and consistent format makes important comparative projects possible and easier than ever. Reviewers agree on the wide-ranging usefulness of this resource.

"Extremely useful for school district comparisons..."
Choice

"...Valuable for academic and large public library collections."
ARBA

This 2005 edition of *The Comparative Guide to American Elementary & Secondary Schools* is a comprehensive compilation with even more details, more test scores, and more ranking data than previous editions. The data is arranged in state chapters with three sections in each chapter:

Section One — State Educational Profile

This section has doubled to two full pages per state. The first page includes the following categories: Schools, Students, Diploma Recipients, High School Drop-out Rate, Staff, Student/Staff Ratios, Current Spending and College Entrance Exam Scores.

Page two of the Profile section includes test scores from the *National Assessment of Educational Progress.* Users will find reading and mathematics scores for both 4th grade and 8th grade levels, broken down by gender, race, ethnicity, and class size.

Section Two — School District Profiles

This section is arranged alphabetically by county, then by name of school district. Each profile includes basic information, including name, address, phone, and web site, and offers data on 9 categories: Grade Span; District Type; Number and Type of Schools; Number of Teachers; Number of Librarians/Media Specialists and Guidance Counselors; Current Spending; Enrollment, Drop-out Rates and Diploma Recipients by Race/Ethnicity. **Brand new** to this edition is **male/female ratio** within each district, as well as number of **high school diploma recipients by race**.

Section Three — School District Rankings

This section ranks 16 pieces of data, including the newly added male/female ratios and high school diploma recipients by race.

Following the 50 state chapters is an expanded **National Ranking** section where you can compare, state by state, each piece of criteria found in the **School District Profiles**.

To further facilitate research, *The Comparative Guide to American Elementary & Secondary Schools* includes two indexes:

- **School District Index:** an alphabetical listing of all school districts in this edition, including the city they are located in, and the page number of their detailed profile.
- **City Index:** an alphabetical listing of all cities represented by the school districts profiled in this Guide, and the page number of the school district profile it is included in.

Many sources were used to compile the valuable data in this edition. Please refer to the **User's Guide** for a detailed explanation of the sources of the data in this reference work, as well as definitions of terms used.

As always, we welcome comments and suggestions.

USER'S GUIDE

School District Profile

Shown below is a fictitious listing illustrating the kind of information that is or might be included in a School District Profile. Each numbered item of information is described in the paragraphs following the example. Both the State and National Rankings utilize the same criteria and follow the same guidelines.

❶ **Anniston City SD**
1425 Woodstock Ave • Anniston, AL 36207
Mailing Address: PO Box 432 • Anniston, AL 36207-5432
(256) 231-5000 • http://www.anniston.k12.fl.us
❷ **Grade Span:** KG-12; ❸ **Agency Type:** 4
❹ **Schools:** 10
6 Primary; 1 Middle; 2 High; 1 Other Level
8 Regular; 0 Special Education; 0 Vocational; 2 Alternative
1 Magnet; 0 Charter; 7 Title I Eligible; 6 School-wide Title I
❺ **Students:** 2,839 (52.1% male; 47.9% female)
Individual Education Program: 508 (17.9%)
English Language Learner: 17 (0.6%); Migrant: 0 (0.0%)
Eligible for Free Lunch Program: 2,063 (72.7%)
Eligible for Reduced-Price Lunch Program: 163 (5.7%)
❻ **Teachers:** 194.2 (15.1 to 1)
❼ **Librarians/Media Specialists:** 8.0 (354.9 to 1)
❽ **Guidance Counselors:** 8.1 (350.5 to 1)
❾ **Current Spending:** ($ per student per year)
Total: $6,136; Instruction: $3,625; Support Services: $2,037
❿ **Enrollment, Drop-out Rates, Diploma Recipients by Race/Eth.**

Category	Total	White	Black	Asian	AIAN	Hisp.
Enrollment (%)	100.0	8.3	90.3	0.1	0.0	1.1
Drop-out Rate (%)	7.4	5.8	8.6	1.3	n/a	2.0
H.S. Diplomas (#)	154	19	129	1	0	5

❶ **Name/Address/Phone/Web Site:** *Source: U.S. Department of Education, National Center for Education Statistics, Common Core of Data, Local Education Agency (School District) Universe Survey: School Year 2003-2003.* Web site addresses were researched by the editors. Abbreviations used: SD=School District; RD=Regional District; UD=Unified District; ED=Elementary District; ESD=Elementary School District; HSD=High School District; USD=Unified School District; ISD=Independent School District; CSD=Community School District; JSD=Joint School District; MSD=Municipal School District; PSD=Public School District; CCD=Community Consolidated District; CUD=Community Unit District; CISD=Consolidated Independent School District; UFSD=Unified School District; JUSD=Joint Unified School District; CUSD=Community Unit School District; CHSD=Community High School District; UHSD=Unified High School District; ICSD=Independent Community School District; JUHSD=Joint Union High School District; JUESD=Joint Union Elementary School District

❷ **Grade Span:** The span of grades intended to be served by this school or agency, whether or not there are students currently enrolled in all grades. If a high school also has a prekindergarten program, the grade span of the high school is reported as a high school, not as a PK-12 school. For example, if a school has PK, 9, 10, 11, and 12 grades, the grade span will be reported as Grades 9 through 12 (9-12). Also, the ungraded designation (UG) cannot be used in a grade span unless the whole school is ungraded students, and in this case the grade span is reported as UGUG. *Source: U.S. Department of Education, National Center for Education Statistics, Common Core of Data, Local Education Agency (School District) Universe Survey: School Year 2002-2003.*

❸ **Agency Type:**

1 = Local school district that is not a component of a supervisory union.
2 = Local school district component of a supervisory union sharing a superintendent and administrative services with other local school districts.
3 = Supervisory union administrative center, or a county superintendent serving the same purpose. Type 3 agencies generally do not report student membership, although Massachusetts and Vermont are exceptions.
4 = Regional education services agency, or a county superintendent serving the same purpose.
5 = State-operated institution charged, at least in part, with providing elementary and/or secondary instruction or services to a special need population.
6 = Federally-operated institution charged, at least in part, with providing elementary and/or secondary instruction or services to a special need population.
7 = Other education agencies that do not fit into the first six categories.
Source: U.S. Department of Education, National Center for Education Statistics, Common Core of Data, Local Education Agency (School District) Universe Survey: School Year 2002-2003.

❹ **Schools:** Total number of schools in the district. *Source: U.S. Department of Education, National Center for Education Statistics, Common Core of Data, Public Elementary/Secondary School Universe Survey: School Year 2002-2003.*

Grade Levels:

Primary: Low grade - prekindergarten through 3; high grade - prekindergarten through 8
Middle: Low grade - 4 through 7; high grade - 4 through 9
High: Low grade - 7 through 12; high grade - 12 only
Other Level: Any configuration not falling within the previous three, including ungraded schools

Curriculum:

Regular: A regular school is defined as a public elementary/secondary school that does not focus primarily on vocational, special, or alternative education.

Special Education: A special education school is defined as a public elementary/secondary school that focuses primarily on special education, including instruction for any of the following: autism, deaf-blindness, developmental delay, hearing impairment, mental retardation, multiple disabilities, orthopedic impairment, serious emotional disturbance, specific learning disability, speech or language impairment, traumatic brain injury, visually impaired, and other health impairments. These schools adapt curriculum, materials or instruction for students served.

Vocational: A vocational educational school is defined as a public elementary/secondary school that focuses primarily on providing formal preparation for semi-skilled, skilled, technical, or professional occupations for high school-aged students who have opted to develop or expand their employment opportunities, often in lieu of preparing for college entry.

Alternative: A public elementary/secondary school that addresses needs of students which typically cannot be met in a regular school; provides nontraditional education; serves as an adjunct to a regular school; and falls outside of the categories of regular, special education, or vocational education.

Type:

Magnet: A special school or program designed to attract students of different racial/ethnic backgrounds for the purpose of reducing, preventing or eliminating racial isolation (50 percent or more minority enrollment); and/or to provide an academic or social focus on a particular theme (e.g., science/math, performing arts, gifted/talented, or foreign language).

Charter: A school providing free public elementary and/or secondary education to eligible students under a specific charter granted by the state legislature or other appropriate authority, and designated by such authority to be a charter school.

Title I Eligible: A school designated under appropriate state and federal regulations as being eligible for participation in programs authorized by Title I of Public Law 103-382.

School-wide Title I: A school in which all the pupils in a school are designated under appropriate state and federal regulations as being eligible for participation in programs authorized by Title I of Public Law 103-382.

❺ **Students:** A student is an individual for whom instruction is provided in an elementary or secondary education program that is not an adult education program and is under the jurisdiction of a school, school system, or other education institution. The gender breakdown is shown in parentheses. *Sources: U.S. Department of Education, National Center for Education Statistics, Common Core of Data, Local Education Agency (School District) Universe Survey: School Year 2002-2003 and Public Elementary/Secondary School Universe Survey: School Year 2002-2003*

For the following five categories, the first value shown is the number of students, the second value (in parentheses) is the percent of the entire student population.

Individual Education Program (IEP): A written instructional plan for students with disabilities designated as special education students under IDEA-Part B. The written instructional plan includes a statement of present levels of educational performance of a child; statement of annual goals, including short-term instructional objectives; statement of specific educational services to be provided and the extent to which the child will be able to participate in regular educational programs; the projected date for initiation and anticipated duration of services; the appropriate objectives, criteria and evaluation procedures; and the schedules for determining, on at least an annual basis, whether instructional objectives are being achieved. *Source: U.S. Department of Education, National Center for Education Statistics, Common Core of Data, Local Education Agency (School District) Universe Survey: School Year 2002-2003*

English Language Learner (ELL): Formerly referred to as Limited English Proficient (LEP). Students being served in appropriate programs of language assistance (e.g., English as a Second Language, High Intensity Language Training, bilingual education). Does not include pupils enrolled in a class to learn a language other than English. Also Limited-English-Proficient students are individuals who were not born in the United States or whose native language is a language other than English; or individuals who come from environments where a language other than English is dominant; or individuals who are American Indians and Alaskan Natives and who come from environments where a language other than English has had a significant impact on their level of English language proficiency; and who, by reason thereof, have sufficient difficulty speaking, reading, writing, or understanding the English language, to deny such individuals the opportunity to learn successfully in classrooms where the language of instruction is English or to participate fully in our society. *Source: U.S. Department of Education, National Center for Education Statistics, Common Core of Data, Local Education Agency (School District) Universe Survey: School Year 2002-2003*

Migrant: A migrant student as defined under federal regulation 34 CFR 200.40: 1) (a) Is younger than 22 (and has not graduated from high school or does not hold a high school equivalency certificate), but (b), if the child is too young to attend school-sponsored educational programs, is old enough to benefit from an organized instructional program; and 2) A migrant agricultural worker or a migrant fisher or has a parent, spouse, or guardian who is a migrant agricultural worker or a migrant fisher; and 3) Performs, or has a parent, spouse, or guardian who performs qualifying agricultural or fishing employment as a principal means of livelihood; and 4) Has moved within the preceding 36 months to obtain or to accompany or join a parent, spouse, or guardian to obtain, temporary or seasonal employment in agricultural or fishing work; and 5) Has moved from one school district to another; or in a state that is comprised of a single school district, has moved from one administrative area to another within such district; or resides in a school district of more than 15,000 square miles, and migrates a distance of 20 miles or more to a temporary residence to engage in a fishing activity. Provision 5 currently applies only to Alaska. *Source: U.S. Department of Education, National Center for Education Statistics, Common Core of Data, Public Elementary/Secondary School Universe Survey: School Year 2002-2003*

Eligible for Free Lunch Program: The free lunch program is defined as a program under the National School Lunch Act that provides cash subsidies for free lunches to students based on family size and income criteria. *Source: U.S. Department of Education, National Center for Education Statistics, Common Core of Data, Public Elementary/Secondary School Universe Survey: School Year 2002-2003*

Eligible for Reduced-Price Lunch Program: A student who is eligible to participate in the Reduced-Price Lunch Program under the National School Lunch Act. *Source: U.S. Department of Education, National Center for Education Statistics, Common Core of Data, Public Elementary/Secondary School Universe Survey: School Year 2002-2003*

❻ **Teachers:** Teachers are defined as individuals who provide instruction to pre-kindergarten, kindergarten, grades 1 through 12, or ungraded classes, or individuals who teach in an environment other than a classroom setting, and who maintain daily student attendance records. Numbers reported are full-time equivalents. The students per teacher ratio is shown in parentheses. *Source: U.S. Department of Education, National Center for Education Statistics, Common Core of Data, Local Education Agency (School District) Universe Survey: School Year 2002-2003.*

❼ **Librarians/Media Specialists:** Library and media support staff are defined as staff members who render other professional library and media services; also includes library aides and those involved in library/media support. Their duties include selecting, preparing, caring for, and making available to instructional staff, equipment, films, filmstrips, transparencies, tapes, TV programs, and similar materials maintained separately or as part of an instructional materials center. Also included are activities in the audio-visual center, TV studio, related-work-study areas, and services provided by audio-visual personnel. Numbers reported are full-time equivalents. The students per librarian/media specialist ratio is shown in parentheses. *Source: U.S. Department of Education, National Center for Education Statistics, Common Core of Data, Local Education Agency (School District) Universe Survey: School Year 2002-2003.*

❽ **Guidance Counselors:** Professional staff assigned specific duties and school time for any of the following activities in an elementary or secondary setting: counseling with students and parents; consulting with other staff members on learning problems; evaluating student abilities; assisting students in making educational and career choices; assisting students in personal and social development; providing referral assistance; and/or working with other staff members in planning and conducting guidance programs for students. The state applies its own standards in apportioning the aggregate of guidance counselors/directors into the elementary and secondary level components. Numbers reported are full-time equivalents. The students per guidance counselor ratio is shown in parentheses. *Source: U.S. Department of Education, National Center for Education Statistics, Common Core of Data, Local Education Agency (School District) Universe Survey: School Year 2002-2003.*

⑨ Current Spending

Total: Expenditure for Instruction, Support Services, and Other Elementary/Secondary Programs. Includes salaries, employee benefits, purchased services, and supplies, as well as payments made by states on behalf of school districts. Also includes transfers made by school districts into their own retirement system. Excludes expenditure for Non-Elementary/Secondary Programs, debt service, capital outlay, and transfers to other governments or school districts. This item is formally called "Current Expenditures for Public Elementary/Secondary Education."

Instruction: Includes payments from all funds for salaries, employee benefits, supplies, materials, and contractual services for elementary/secondary instruction. It excludes capital outlay, debt service, and interfund transfers for elementary/secondary instruction. Instruction covers regular, special, and vocational programs offered in both the regular school year and summer school. It excludes instructional support activities as well as adult education and community services. Instruction salaries includes salaries for teachers and teacher aides and assistants.

Support Services: Relates to support services functions (series 2000) defined in Financial Accounting for Local and State School Systems (National Center for Education Statistics 2000). Includes payments from all funds for salaries, employee benefits, supplies, materials, and contractual services. It excludes capital outlay, debt service, and interfund transfers. It includes expenditure for the following functions:

- Business/Central/Other Support Services
- General Administration
- Instructional Staff Support
- Operation and Maintenance
- Pupil Support Services
- Pupil Transportation Services
- School Administration
- Nonspecified Support Services

Values shown are dollars per pupil per year. They were calculated by dividing the total dollar amounts by the fall membership. Fall membership is comprised of the total student enrollment on October 1 (or the closest school day to October 1) for all grade levels (including prekindergarten and kindergarten) and ungraded pupils. Membership includes students both present and absent on the measurement day. *Source: U.S. Department of Education, National Center for Education Statistics, Common Core of Data, School District Finance Survey (F-33), Fiscal Year 2001.*

⑩ Enrollment, Drop-out Rates, and Diploma Recipients by Race/Ethnicity:

Enrollment: Breakdown of student enrollment by race. *Source: U.S. Department of Education, National Center for Education Statistics, Common Core of Data, Public Elementary/Secondary School Universe Survey: School Year 2002-2003.*

Drop-out: A dropout is a student who was enrolled in school at some time during the previous school year; was not enrolled at the beginning of the current school year; has not graduated from high school or completed a state or district approved educational program; and does not meet any of the following exclusionary conditions: has transferred to another public school district, private school, or state- or district-approved educational program; is temporarily absent due to suspension or school-approved illness; or has died. The values shown are drop-out rates by race and cover grades 9 through 12. *Source: U.S. Department of Education, National Center for Education Statistics, Common Core of Data, Local Education Agency Universe Dropout File: School Year 2000-2001*

H.S. Diplomas: A student who has received a diploma during the previous school year or subsequent summer school. This category includes regular diploma recipients and other diploma recipients. A High School Diploma is a formal document certifying the successful completion of a secondary school program prescribed by the state education agency or other appropriate body. The values shown are the number of high school diploma recipients by race. *Source: U.S. Department of Education, National Center for Education Statistics, Common Core of Data, Local Education Agency (School District) Universe Survey: School Year 2002-2003.*

Race/Ethnicity:

White: A person having origins in any of the original peoples of Europe, North Africa, or the Middle East. Figures include non-Hispanic whites only.

Black: A person having origins in any of the black racial groups of Africa. Figures include non-Hispanic blacks only.

Asian (Asian/Pacific Islander): A person having origins in any of the original peoples of the Far east, Southeast Asia, the Indian subcontinent, or the Pacific Islands. This includes, for example, China, India, Japan, Korea, the Philippine Islands, and Samoa.

AIAN (American Indian/Alaskan Native): A person having origins in any of the original peoples of North America, and who maintains cultural identification through tribal affiliation or community recognition.

Hispanic: A person of Mexican, Puerto Rican, Cuban, Central or South American, or other Spanish culture or origin, regardless of race.

Figures exclude schools that did not report race/ethnicity data.

Note: n/a indicates data not available.

State and National Educational Profiles

Please refer to the District Profile section in the front of this User's Guide for an explanation of data for all items except for the following:

Average Salary: The average teacher salary in 2002-2003. *Source: American Federation of Teachers, 2003 Survey & Analysis of Teacher Salary Trends*

College Entrance Exam Scores:

Scholastic Aptitude Test (SAT). *Source: The College Board, Mean SAT I Verbal and Math Scores by State (The College Board strongly discourages the comparison or ranking of states on the basis of SAT scores alone)*

American College Testing Program (ACT). *ACT, 2003 ACT National and State Scores*

State and National NAEP Test Scores

The National Assessment of Educational Progress (NAEP), also known as "the Nation's Report Card," is the only nationally representative and continuing assessment of what America's students know and can do in various subject areas.

The NAEP 2003 reading and mathematics assessments were administered to representative samples of fourth- and eighth-graders in participating states and other jurisdictions. In 2003, 50 states and 3 jurisdictions at grade 4 and grade 8 participated in both assessments and met student and school participation criteria for reporting results. Approximately 343,000 students from 13,000 schools were assessed. The national results reflect the performance of students attending both public and nonpublic schools, while the state and jurisdiction results reflect only the performance of students attending public schools.

The results of student performance are presented in two ways: as average scores on the NAEP mathematics/reading scale and as the percentages of students attaining NAEP mathematics/reading achievement levels. The average scale scores represent how students performed on the assessment. The achievement levels (basic, proficient, advanced) represent how that performance measured up against set expectations for achievement. Thus, the average scale scores represent what students know and can do, while the achievement-level results indicate the degree to which student performance meets expectations of what they should know and be able to do.

Mathematics

Average mathematics scale score results are based on the NAEP mathematics scale, which ranges from 0 to 500. The NAEP mathematics assessment is a composite combining separate scales for each of the mathematics content strands: (1) number sense, properties and operations; (2) measurement; (3) geometry and spatial sense; (4) data analysis, statistics and probability; and (5) algebra and functions. Average scale scores are computed for groups, not for individual students. The average scores are based on analyses of the percentages of students who answered each item successfully. While the score ranges at each grade in mathematics are identical, the scale was derived independently at each grade. Therefore, average scale scores across grades cannot be compared. For example, equal scale scores on the grade 4 and grade 8 scales do not imply equal levels of mathematics achievement.

Reading

Average reading scale score results are based on the NAEP reading scale, which ranges from 0 to 500. The NAEP reading assessment scale is a composite combining separate scales for each reading context specified by the reading framework (at grade 4, reading for literary experience and reading for information, and at grade 8, those contexts and reading to perform a task). Average scale scores are computed for groups, not for individual students. The average scores are based on analyses of the percentages of students who answered each item successfully. While the score ranges at each grade in reading are identical, the scale was derived independently at each grade. Therefore, average scale scores across grades cannot be compared. For example, equal scale scores on the grade 4 and grade 8 scales do not imply equal levels of reading achievement.

Standard Error

The average scores and percentages presented in this publication are estimates because they are based on representative samples of students rather than on the entire population of students. Moreover, the collection of subject-area questions used at each grade level is but a sample of the many questions that could have been asked. As such, NAEP results are subject to a measure of uncertainty, reflected in the standard error of the estimates (appears in parentheses).

Rank

The state ranking appears in the column labeled Rank. In most cases, 50 states and the District of Columbia are ranked. However in cases where data was not available, fewer than 51 states may be ranked. For example, a ranking of 32/41 indicates that the state ranked number 32 out of the 41 states with available data. All rankings represent their corresponding values sorted in descending order.

Caution

Readers are cautioned against interpreting NAEP results as implying causal relations. Inferences related to subgroup performance or to the effectiveness of public and nonpublic schools, for example, should take into consideration the many socioeconomic and educational factors that may also impact performance. *Source: U.S. Department of Education, National Center for Education Statistics, The Nation's Report Card*

Alabama

Alabama Public School Educational Profile

Category	Value	Category	Value
Schools *(2002-2003)*	1,537	**Diploma Recipients** *(2002-2003)*	35,887
Instructional Level		White, Non-Hispanic	23,462
Primary	723	Black, Non-Hispanic	11,374
Middle	235	Asian/Pacific Islander	347
High	362	American Indian/Alaskan Native	459
Other Level	217	Hispanic	245
Curriculum		**High School Drop-out Rate** (%) *(2000-2001)*	4.1
Regular	1,359	White, Non-Hispanic	4.2
Special Education	26	Black, Non-Hispanic	4.0
Vocational	75	Asian/Pacific Islander	2.5
Alternative	77	American Indian/Alaskan Native	2.6
Type		Hispanic	5.5
Magnet	40	**Staff** *(2002-2003)*	88,106.7
Charter	0	Teachers	46,325.0
Title I Eligible	874	Average Salary ($)	39,524
School-wide Title I	638	Librarians/Media Specialists	1,358.9
Students *(2002-2003)*	729,067	Guidance Counselors	1,696.1
Gender (%)		**Ratios** *(2002-2003)*	
Male	51.7	Student/Teacher Ratio	15.7 to 1
Female	48.3	Student/Librarian Ratio	536.5 to 1
Race/Ethnicity (%)		Student/Counselor Ratio	429.8 to 1
White, Non-Hispanic	60.2	**Current Spending** *($ per student in FY 2001)*	6,028
Black, Non-Hispanic	36.3	Instruction	3,691
Asian/Pacific Islander	0.9	Support Services	1,919
American Indian/Alaskan Native	0.8	**College Entrance Exam Scores** *(2003)*	
Hispanic	1.8	Scholastic Aptitude Test (SAT)	
Classification (%)		Participation Rate (%)	10
Individual Education Program (IEP)	13.0	Mean SAT I Verbal Score	559
Migrant	1.1	Mean SAT I Math Score	552
English Language Learner (ELL)	1.5	American College Testing Program (ACT)	
Eligible for Free Lunch Program	41.8	Participation Rate (%)	73
Eligible for Reduced-Price Lunch Program	8.3	Average Composite Score	20.1

Note: *For an explanation of data, please refer to the User's Guide in the front of the book; n/a indicates data not available*

Alabama NAEP 2003 Test Scores

Reading		
Grade/Category	Value	Rank
4th Grade		
Average Proficiency	*207.1 (1.7)*	45/51
Proficiency by Gender/Race/Ethnicity		
Male	203.7 (2.0)	44/51
Female	*210.7 (1.8)*	46/51
White, Non-Hispanic	218.6 (1.5)	50/51
Black, Non-Hispanic	188.2 (2.5)	40/42
Asian, Non-Hispanic	n/a	n/a
American Indian, Non-Hispanic	n/a	n/a
Hispanic	n/a	n/a
Proficiency by Class Size		
Less than 16 Students	153.5 (5.6)	45/45
16 to 18 Students	*204.8 (5.3)*	40/48
19 to 20 Students	212.5 (4.2)	39/50
21 to 25 Students	209.7 (2.3)	44/51
Greater than 25 Students	208.5 (3.0)	41/49
Percent Attaining Achievement Levels		
Below Basic	47.5 (1.8)	7/51
Basic or Above	52.5 (1.8)	45/51
Proficient or Above	22.2 (1.6)	44/51
Advanced or Above	4.5 (0.7)	44/51
8th Grade		
Average Proficiency	253.2 (1.5)	46/51
Proficiency by Gender/Race/Ethnicity		
Male	245.8 (1.5)	49/51
Female	260.5 (2.0)	43/51
White, Non-Hispanic	262.4 (1.5)	47/50
Black, Non-Hispanic	236.9 (2.0)	37/41
Asian, Non-Hispanic	n/a	n/a
American Indian, Non-Hispanic	n/a	n/a
Hispanic	n/a	n/a
Proficiency by Parents Highest Level of Ed.		
Did Not Finish High School	238.2 (3.0)	45/50
Graduated High School	245.7 (1.9)	46/50
Some Education After High School	262.5 (1.9)	43/50
Graduated College	261.6 (2.4)	45/50
Percent Attaining Achievement Levels		
Below Basic	35.4 (1.6)	7/51
Basic or Above	64.6 (1.6)	45/51
Proficient or Above	22.3 (1.7)	45/51
Advanced or Above	1.6 (0.4)	44/51

Mathematics		
Grade/Category	Value	Rank
4th Grade		
Average Proficiency	223.3 (1.2)	48/51
Proficiency by Gender/Race/Ethnicity		
Male	223.3 (1.3)	49/51
Female	223.4 (1.3)	48/51
White, Non-Hispanic	232.3 (1.3)	49/51
Black, Non-Hispanic	207.9 (1.2)	39/42
Asian, Non-Hispanic	n/a	n/a
American Indian, Non-Hispanic	n/a	n/a
Hispanic	n/a	n/a
Proficiency by Class Size		
Less than 16 Students	194.3 (5.3)	47/47
16 to 18 Students	*226.3 (5.2)*	35/48
19 to 20 Students	231.2 (3.2)	36/50
21 to 25 Students	223.0 (1.8)	50/51
Greater than 25 Students	222.7 (3.0)	46/49
Percent Attaining Achievement Levels		
Below Basic	35.4 (1.7)	4/51
Basic or Above	64.6 (1.7)	48/51
Proficient or Above	18.8 (1.5)	48/51
Advanced or Above	1.2 (0.2)	47/51
8th Grade		
Average Proficiency	261.9 (1.5)	49/51
Proficiency by Gender/Race/Ethnicity		
Male	262.6 (1.8)	49/51
Female	261.2 (1.6)	49/51
White, Non-Hispanic	274.4 (1.5)	48/50
Black, Non-Hispanic	240.3 (1.6)	39/41
Asian, Non-Hispanic	n/a	n/a
American Indian, Non-Hispanic	n/a	n/a
Hispanic	n/a	n/a
Proficiency by Parents Highest Level of Ed.		
Did Not Finish High School	248.9 (2.7)	47/50
Graduated High School	252.7 (1.7)	49/50
Some Education After High School	266.8 (2.0)	49/50
Graduated College	270.5 (2.2)	48/50
Percent Attaining Achievement Levels		
Below Basic	47.1 (1.7)	4/51
Basic or Above	52.9 (1.7)	48/51
Proficient or Above	15.7 (1.4)	48/51
Advanced or Above	1.9 (0.5)	46/51

Note: *For an explanation of data, please refer to the User's Guide in the front of the book; values in italics indicate that the nature of the sample does not allow accurate determination of the variability of the statistic; n/a indicates data not available*

Autauga County

Autauga County SD

153 W 4th St • Prattville, AL 36067-3011
(334) 365-5706 • http://www.autaugacountyschool.org/
Grade Span: KG-12; **Agency Type:** 1
Schools: 13
4 Primary; 2 Middle; 3 High; 4 Other Level
11 Regular; 0 Special Education; 1 Vocational; 1 Alternative
0 Magnet; 0 Charter; 7 Title I Eligible; 3 School-wide Title I
Students: 8,940 (51.8% male; 48.2% female)
Individual Education Program: 974 (10.9%);
English Language Learner: 27 (0.3%); Migrant: 0 (0.0%)
Eligible for Free Lunch Program: 2,702 (30.2%)
Eligible for Reduced-Price Lunch Program: 661 (7.4%)
Teachers: 537.5 (16.6 to 1)
Librarians/Media Specialists: 10.0 (894.0 to 1)
Guidance Counselors: 17.5 (510.9 to 1)
Current Spending: ($ per student per year):
Total: $5,077; Instruction: $3,235; Support Services: $1,528

Enrollment, Drop-out Rates and Diploma Recipients by Race/Ethnicity

Category	Total	White	Black	Asian	AIAN	Hisp.
Enrollment (%)	100.0	75.1	22.9	0.7	0.2	1.1
Drop-out Rate (%)	4.2	4.1	4.5	10.5	33.3	0.0
H.S. Diplomas (#)	405	317	79	3	1	5

Baldwin County

Baldwin County SD

2600-A N Hand Ave • Bay Minette, AL 36507-4180
(334) 937-0306 • http://www.bcbe.org/
Grade Span: KG-12; **Agency Type:** 1
Schools: 46
26 Primary; 10 Middle; 8 High; 2 Other Level
42 Regular; 0 Special Education; 2 Vocational; 2 Alternative
0 Magnet; 0 Charter; 18 Title I Eligible; 18 School-wide Title I
Students: 23,411 (52.0% male; 48.0% female)
Individual Education Program: 3,780 (16.1%);
English Language Learner: 241 (1.0%); Migrant: 111 (0.5%)
Eligible for Free Lunch Program: 5,805 (24.8%)
Eligible for Reduced-Price Lunch Program: 1,745 (7.5%)
Teachers: 1,550.7 (15.1 to 1)
Librarians/Media Specialists: 42.5 (550.8 to 1)
Guidance Counselors: 59.2 (395.5 to 1)
Current Spending: ($ per student per year):
Total: $5,893; Instruction: $3,719; Support Services: $1,856

Enrollment, Drop-out Rates and Diploma Recipients by Race/Ethnicity

Category	Total	White	Black	Asian	AIAN	Hisp.
Enrollment (%)	100.0	80.8	16.6	0.5	0.4	1.8
Drop-out Rate (%)	3.6	3.5	4.0	0.0	9.1	10.2
H.S. Diplomas (#)	1,093	961	109	8	4	11

Barbour County

Eufaula City SD

420 Sanford Ave • Eufaula, AL 36027-1450
(334) 687-1100 • http://www.ecs.k12.al.us/
Grade Span: PK-12; **Agency Type:** 1
Schools: 5
3 Primary; 1 Middle; 1 High; 0 Other Level
5 Regular; 0 Special Education; 0 Vocational; 0 Alternative
0 Magnet; 0 Charter; 3 Title I Eligible; 3 School-wide Title I
Students: 2,883 (51.6% male; 48.4% female)
Individual Education Program: 351 (12.2%);
English Language Learner: 13 (0.5%); Migrant: 0 (0.0%)
Eligible for Free Lunch Program: 1,457 (50.5%)
Eligible for Reduced-Price Lunch Program: 232 (8.0%)
Teachers: 191.2 (15.1 to 1)
Librarians/Media Specialists: 5.0 (576.6 to 1)
Guidance Counselors: 7.0 (411.9 to 1)
Current Spending: ($ per student per year):
Total: $5,649; Instruction: $3,566; Support Services: $1,671

Enrollment, Drop-out Rates and Diploma Recipients by Race/Ethnicity

Category	Total	White	Black	Asian	AIAN	Hisp.
Enrollment (%)	100.0	46.2	52.4	0.4	0.1	0.9
Drop-out Rate (%)	3.9	3.4	4.6	0.0	0.0	0.0
H.S. Diplomas (#)	154	70	82	0	0	2

Bibb County

Bibb County SD

157 SW Davidson Dr • Centreville, AL 35042-2277
(205) 926-9881 • http://www.bibbed.org/
Grade Span: KG-12; **Agency Type:** 1
Schools: 10
5 Primary; 1 Middle; 2 High; 2 Other Level
9 Regular; 0 Special Education; 1 Vocational; 0 Alternative
0 Magnet; 0 Charter; 9 Title I Eligible; 5 School-wide Title I
Students: 3,600 (51.7% male; 48.3% female)
Individual Education Program: 596 (16.6%);
English Language Learner: 11 (0.3%); Migrant: 0 (0.0%)
Eligible for Free Lunch Program: 1,777 (49.4%)
Eligible for Reduced-Price Lunch Program: 458 (12.7%)
Teachers: 224.7 (16.0 to 1)
Librarians/Media Specialists: 8.5 (423.5 to 1)
Guidance Counselors: 9.5 (378.9 to 1)
Current Spending: ($ per student per year):
Total: $5,619; Instruction: $3,509; Support Services: $1,675

Enrollment, Drop-out Rates and Diploma Recipients by Race/Ethnicity

Category	Total	White	Black	Asian	AIAN	Hisp.
Enrollment (%)	100.0	70.6	28.7	0.1	0.1	0.6
Drop-out Rate (%)	4.1	4.2	3.9	n/a	n/a	0.0
H.S. Diplomas (#)	131	103	27	0	0	1

Blount County

Blount County SD

204 2nd Ave E • Oneonta, AL 35121-0007
Mailing Address: PO Box 578 • Oneonta, AL 35121-0007
(205) 625-4102 • http://blountcountyschools.net/
Grade Span: PK-12; **Agency Type:** 1
Schools: 16
6 Primary; 1 Middle; 6 High; 3 Other Level
13 Regular; 1 Special Education; 1 Vocational; 1 Alternative
0 Magnet; 0 Charter; 9 Title I Eligible; 9 School-wide Title I
Students: 7,549 (51.7% male; 48.3% female)
Individual Education Program: 1,082 (14.3%);
English Language Learner: 482 (6.4%); Migrant: 210 (2.8%)
Eligible for Free Lunch Program: 2,297 (30.4%)
Eligible for Reduced-Price Lunch Program: 693 (9.2%)
Teachers: 427.9 (17.6 to 1)
Librarians/Media Specialists: 13.0 (580.7 to 1)
Guidance Counselors: 14.0 (539.2 to 1)
Current Spending: ($ per student per year):
Total: $5,127; Instruction: $3,146; Support Services: $1,577

Enrollment, Drop-out Rates and Diploma Recipients by Race/Ethnicity

Category	Total	White	Black	Asian	AIAN	Hisp.
Enrollment (%)	100.0	92.5	0.3	0.2	0.2	6.8
Drop-out Rate (%)	6.0	6.0	0.0	0.0	33.3	5.2
H.S. Diplomas (#)	313	306	0	0	1	6

Bullock County

Bullock County SD

108 Hardaway Ave W • Union Springs, AL 36089-0231
Mailing Address: PO Box 231 • Union Springs, AL 36089-0231
(334) 738-2860 • http://bullock.k12.al.us/
Grade Span: KG-12; **Agency Type:** 1
Schools: 5
2 Primary; 1 Middle; 2 High; 0 Other Level
4 Regular; 0 Special Education; 1 Vocational; 0 Alternative
0 Magnet; 0 Charter; 4 Title I Eligible; 4 School-wide Title I
Students: 1,893 (51.7% male; 48.3% female)
Individual Education Program: 239 (12.6%);
English Language Learner: 13 (0.7%); Migrant: 0 (0.0%)
Eligible for Free Lunch Program: 1,570 (82.9%)
Eligible for Reduced-Price Lunch Program: 142 (7.5%)
Teachers: 127.0 (14.9 to 1)
Librarians/Media Specialists: 4.0 (473.3 to 1)
Guidance Counselors: 5.0 (378.6 to 1)
Current Spending: ($ per student per year):
Total: $5,938; Instruction: $3,466; Support Services: $1,968

Enrollment, Drop-out Rates and Diploma Recipients by Race/Ethnicity

Category	Total	White	Black	Asian	AIAN	Hisp.
Enrollment (%)	100.0	0.3	98.5	0.0	0.0	1.2
Drop-out Rate (%)	3.8	0.0	3.8	n/a	n/a	0.0
H.S. Diplomas (#)	110	0	110	0	0	0

Butler County

Butler County SD

215 Administrative Dr • Greenville, AL 36037-1833
(334) 382-2665 • http://www.butlerco.k12.al.us/
Grade Span: KG-12; **Agency Type:** 1
Schools: 8
3 Primary; 1 Middle; 2 High; 2 Other Level
7 Regular; 0 Special Education; 1 Vocational; 0 Alternative
0 Magnet; 0 Charter; 7 Title I Eligible; 7 School-wide Title I
Students: 3,526 (51.5% male; 48.5% female)
Individual Education Program: 538 (15.3%);

English Language Learner: 3 (0.1%); Migrant: 0 (0.0%)
Eligible for Free Lunch Program: 2,273 (64.5%)
Eligible for Reduced-Price Lunch Program: 429 (12.2%)
Teachers: 212.8 (16.6 to 1)
Librarians/Media Specialists: 6.0 (587.7 to 1)
Guidance Counselors: 9.0 (391.8 to 1)
Current Spending: ($ per student per year):
Total: $5,910; Instruction: $3,647; Support Services: $1,861
Enrollment, Drop-out Rates and Diploma Recipients by Race/Ethnicity

Category	Total	White	Black	Asian	AIAN	Hisp.
Enrollment (%)	100.0	38.6	61.1	0.2	0.1	0.1
Drop-out Rate (%)	5.6	5.8	5.4	25.0	n/a	0.0
H.S. Diplomas (#)	168	85	81	2	0	0

Calhoun County

Anniston City SD
1425 Woodstock Ave • Anniston, AL 36207
Mailing Address: PO Box 1500 • Anniston, AL 36202-1500
(256) 231-5000 • http://www.anniston-k12.org/
Grade Span: PK-12; **Agency Type:** 1
Schools: 9
5 Primary; 0 Middle; 1 High; 3 Other Level
7 Regular; 0 Special Education; 0 Vocational; 2 Alternative
0 Magnet; 0 Charter; 7 Title I Eligible; 4 School-wide Title I
Students: 2,668 (49.8% male; 50.2% female)
Individual Education Program: 461 (17.3%);
English Language Learner: 34 (1.3%); Migrant: 0 (0.0%)
Eligible for Free Lunch Program: 2,109 (79.0%)
Eligible for Reduced-Price Lunch Program: 162 (6.1%)
Teachers: 159.6 (16.7 to 1)
Librarians/Media Specialists: 7.0 (381.1 to 1)
Guidance Counselors: 6.0 (444.7 to 1)
Current Spending: ($ per student per year):
Total: $6,578; Instruction: $3,699; Support Services: $2,246
Enrollment, Drop-out Rates and Diploma Recipients by Race/Ethnicity

Category	Total	White	Black	Asian	AIAN	Hisp.
Enrollment (%)	100.0	6.3	92.2	0.0	0.0	1.4
Drop-out Rate (%)	8.9	29.2	8.2	n/a	n/a	0.0
H.S. Diplomas (#)	77	1	74	1	0	1

Calhoun County SD
4400 Mccellan Blvd • Anniston, AL 36201
Mailing Address: PO Box 2084 • Anniston, AL 36202-2084
(256) 236-7641 • http://www.calhoun.k12.al.us/
Grade Span: PK-12; **Agency Type:** 1
Schools: 20
8 Primary; 1 Middle; 4 High; 7 Other Level
17 Regular; 0 Special Education; 1 Vocational; 2 Alternative
0 Magnet; 0 Charter; 11 Title I Eligible; 10 School-wide Title I
Students: 9,471 (52.4% male; 47.6% female)
Individual Education Program: 1,354 (14.3%);
English Language Learner: 39 (0.4%); Migrant: 0 (0.0%)
Eligible for Free Lunch Program: 3,518 (37.1%)
Eligible for Reduced-Price Lunch Program: 964 (10.2%)
Teachers: 552.9 (17.1 to 1)
Librarians/Media Specialists: 18.0 (526.2 to 1)
Guidance Counselors: 20.0 (473.6 to 1)
Current Spending: ($ per student per year):
Total: $5,606; Instruction: $3,224; Support Services: $1,967
Enrollment, Drop-out Rates and Diploma Recipients by Race/Ethnicity

Category	Total	White	Black	Asian	AIAN	Hisp.
Enrollment (%)	100.0	85.6	12.5	0.7	0.2	1.1
Drop-out Rate (%)	4.4	4.9	1.5	5.3	0.0	0.0
H.S. Diplomas (#)	451	399	43	3	0	6

Jacksonville City SD
123 College St SW • Jacksonville, AL 36265-2165
(256) 782-5682 • http://www.jacksonville.k12.al.us/
Grade Span: KG-12; **Agency Type:** 1
Schools: 2
1 Primary; 0 Middle; 1 High; 0 Other Level
2 Regular; 0 Special Education; 0 Vocational; 0 Alternative
0 Magnet; 0 Charter; 1 Title I Eligible; 0 School-wide Title I
Students: 1,702 (53.6% male; 46.4% female)
Individual Education Program: 184 (10.8%);
English Language Learner: 23 (1.4%); Migrant: 0 (0.0%)
Eligible for Free Lunch Program: 518 (30.4%)
Eligible for Reduced-Price Lunch Program: 116 (6.8%)
Teachers: 103.0 (16.5 to 1)
Librarians/Media Specialists: 1.8 (945.6 to 1)
Guidance Counselors: 3.5 (486.3 to 1)
Current Spending: ($ per student per year):
Total: $5,480; Instruction: $3,548; Support Services: $1,583
Enrollment, Drop-out Rates and Diploma Recipients by Race/Ethnicity

Category	Total	White	Black	Asian	AIAN	Hisp.
Enrollment (%)	100.0	74.4	21.9	1.6	0.3	1.8
Drop-out Rate (%)	1.7	1.6	1.1	6.7	0.0	0.0
H.S. Diplomas (#)	90	72	11	6	0	1

Oxford City SD
310 E 2nd St • Oxford, AL 36203-1704
(256) 831-0243 • http://www.oxford.k12.al.us/
Grade Span: PK-12; **Agency Type:** 1
Schools: 5
2 Primary; 1 Middle; 2 High; 0 Other Level
4 Regular; 0 Special Education; 1 Vocational; 0 Alternative
0 Magnet; 0 Charter; 1 Title I Eligible; 0 School-wide Title I
Students: 3,177 (51.4% male; 48.6% female)
Individual Education Program: 330 (10.4%);
English Language Learner: 82 (2.6%); Migrant: 0 (0.0%)
Eligible for Free Lunch Program: 843 (26.5%)
Eligible for Reduced-Price Lunch Program: 208 (6.5%)
Teachers: 198.5 (16.0 to 1)
Librarians/Media Specialists: 4.0 (794.3 to 1)
Guidance Counselors: 6.3 (504.3 to 1)
Current Spending: ($ per student per year):
Total: $5,596; Instruction: $3,531; Support Services: $1,627
Enrollment, Drop-out Rates and Diploma Recipients by Race/Ethnicity

Category	Total	White	Black	Asian	AIAN	Hisp.
Enrollment (%)	100.0	74.5	21.2	0.9	0.0	3.5
Drop-out Rate (%)	3.0	2.8	4.2	0.0	n/a	0.0
H.S. Diplomas (#)	185	145	35	5	0	0

Chambers County

Chambers County SD
202 1st Ave SE • Lafayette, AL 36862-2102
Mailing Address: Box 408D • Lafayette, AL 36862-0408
(334) 864-9343 • http://www.chambersk12.org/
Grade Span: KG-12; **Agency Type:** 1
Schools: 11
6 Primary; 1 Middle; 3 High; 1 Other Level
10 Regular; 0 Special Education; 1 Vocational; 0 Alternative
0 Magnet; 0 Charter; 7 Title I Eligible; 7 School-wide Title I
Students: 4,374 (51.2% male; 48.8% female)
Individual Education Program: 543 (12.4%);
English Language Learner: 12 (0.3%); Migrant: 0 (0.0%)
Eligible for Free Lunch Program: 2,431 (55.6%)
Eligible for Reduced-Price Lunch Program: 410 (9.4%)
Teachers: 264.1 (16.6 to 1)
Librarians/Media Specialists: 10.0 (437.4 to 1)
Guidance Counselors: 8.5 (514.6 to 1)
Current Spending: ($ per student per year):
Total: $5,509; Instruction: $3,365; Support Services: $1,746
Enrollment, Drop-out Rates and Diploma Recipients by Race/Ethnicity

Category	Total	White	Black	Asian	AIAN	Hisp.
Enrollment (%)	100.0	47.4	52.2	0.2	0.0	0.2
Drop-out Rate (%)	5.4	6.8	4.2	0.0	n/a	n/a
H.S. Diplomas (#)	199	87	112	0	0	0

Cherokee County

Cherokee County SD
130 E Main St • Centre, AL 35960-1517
(256) 927-3362 • http://www.tiger.org/
Grade Span: KG-12; **Agency Type:** 1
Schools: 8
1 Primary; 1 Middle; 2 High; 4 Other Level
7 Regular; 0 Special Education; 1 Vocational; 0 Alternative
0 Magnet; 0 Charter; 6 Title I Eligible; 5 School-wide Title I
Students: 4,101 (53.2% male; 46.8% female)
Individual Education Program: 606 (14.8%);
English Language Learner: 6 (0.1%); Migrant: 0 (0.0%)
Eligible for Free Lunch Program: 1,390 (33.9%)
Eligible for Reduced-Price Lunch Program: 425 (10.4%)
Teachers: 251.3 (16.3 to 1)
Librarians/Media Specialists: 6.8 (603.1 to 1)
Guidance Counselors: 9.0 (455.7 to 1)
Current Spending: ($ per student per year):
Total: $5,905; Instruction: $3,687; Support Services: $1,729
Enrollment, Drop-out Rates and Diploma Recipients by Race/Ethnicity

Category	Total	White	Black	Asian	AIAN	Hisp.
Enrollment (%)	100.0	92.8	6.2	0.2	0.2	0.6
Drop-out Rate (%)	6.0	6.0	6.0	0.0	0.0	0.0
H.S. Diplomas (#)	167	158	8	0	0	1

Chilton County

Chilton County SD

1705 Lay Dam Rd • Clanton, AL 35045-2032
(205) 280-3000 • http://www.chiltonschools.org/
Grade Span: PK-12; **Agency Type:** 1
Schools: 12
3 Primary; 2 Middle; 3 High; 4 Other Level
11 Regular; 0 Special Education; 1 Vocational; 0 Alternative
0 Magnet; 0 Charter; 9 Title I Eligible; 0 School-wide Title I
Students: 6,995 (51.8% male; 48.2% female)
Individual Education Program: 1,196 (17.1%);
English Language Learner: 159 (2.3%); Migrant: 14 (0.2%)
Eligible for Free Lunch Program: 2,241 (32.0%)
Eligible for Reduced-Price Lunch Program: 954 (13.6%)
Teachers: 443.6 (15.8 to 1)
Librarians/Media Specialists: 13.5 (518.1 to 1)
Guidance Counselors: 14.4 (485.8 to 1)
Current Spending: ($ per student per year):
Total: $5,546; Instruction: $3,346; Support Services: $1,798
Enrollment, Drop-out Rates and Diploma Recipients by Race/Ethnicity

Category	Total	White	Black	Asian	AIAN	Hisp.
Enrollment (%)	100.0	81.2	15.0	0.2	0.0	3.5
Drop-out Rate (%)	4.4	4.6	2.9	0.0	n/a	9.5
H.S. Diplomas (#)	329	287	42	0	0	0

Choctaw County

Choctaw County SD

107 Tom Orr Dr • Butler, AL 36904-0839
(205) 459-3031 • http://choctawboe.k12.al.us/
Grade Span: KG-12; **Agency Type:** 1
Schools: 8
4 Primary; 0 Middle; 3 High; 1 Other Level
6 Regular; 0 Special Education; 1 Vocational; 1 Alternative
0 Magnet; 0 Charter; 6 Title I Eligible; 6 School-wide Title I
Students: 2,204 (52.4% male; 47.6% female)
Individual Education Program: 290 (13.2%);
English Language Learner: 0 (0.0%); Migrant: 0 (0.0%)
Eligible for Free Lunch Program: 1,466 (66.5%)
Eligible for Reduced-Price Lunch Program: 232 (10.5%)
Teachers: 139.1 (15.8 to 1)
Librarians/Media Specialists: 5.5 (400.7 to 1)
Guidance Counselors: 4.5 (489.8 to 1)
Current Spending: ($ per student per year):
Total: $6,312; Instruction: $3,718; Support Services: $2,102
Enrollment, Drop-out Rates and Diploma Recipients by Race/Ethnicity

Category	Total	White	Black	Asian	AIAN	Hisp.
Enrollment (%)	100.0	26.3	73.4	0.1	0.2	0.0
Drop-out Rate (%)	8.5	17.5	5.4	n/a	0.0	n/a
H.S. Diplomas (#)	104	21	83	0	0	0

Clarke County

Clarke County SD

155 W Cobb St • Grove Hill, AL 36451-0936
Mailing Address: Box 936 • Grove Hill, AL 36451-0936
(334) 275-3255
Grade Span: PK-12; **Agency Type:** 1
Schools: 9
4 Primary; 2 Middle; 3 High; 0 Other Level
9 Regular; 0 Special Education; 0 Vocational; 0 Alternative
0 Magnet; 0 Charter; 7 Title I Eligible; 7 School-wide Title I
Students: 3,605 (50.3% male; 49.7% female)
Individual Education Program: 493 (13.7%);
English Language Learner: 0 (0.0%); Migrant: 0 (0.0%)
Eligible for Free Lunch Program: 1,997 (55.4%)
Eligible for Reduced-Price Lunch Program: 312 (8.7%)
Teachers: 224.9 (16.0 to 1)
Librarians/Media Specialists: 6.7 (538.1 to 1)
Guidance Counselors: 7.2 (500.7 to 1)
Current Spending: ($ per student per year):
Total: $5,986; Instruction: $3,465; Support Services: $1,999
Enrollment, Drop-out Rates and Diploma Recipients by Race/Ethnicity

Category	Total	White	Black	Asian	AIAN	Hisp.
Enrollment (%)	100.0	35.6	64.0	0.1	0.2	0.1
Drop-out Rate (%)	0.7	0.6	0.8	0.0	0.0	0.0
H.S. Diplomas (#)	176	63	113	0	0	0

Thomasville City SD

3001 Gates Dr • Thomasville, AL 36784-0458
Mailing Address: PO Box 458 • Thomasville, AL 36784-0458
(334) 636-9955 • http://www.thomasvilleschools.org/
Grade Span: KG-12; **Agency Type:** 1
Schools: 3
1 Primary; 1 Middle; 1 High; 0 Other Level
3 Regular; 0 Special Education; 0 Vocational; 0 Alternative
0 Magnet; 0 Charter; 2 Title I Eligible; 1 School-wide Title I
Students: 1,645 (51.5% male; 48.5% female)
Individual Education Program: 174 (10.6%);
English Language Learner: 4 (0.2%); Migrant: 0 (0.0%)
Eligible for Free Lunch Program: 695 (42.2%)
Eligible for Reduced-Price Lunch Program: 127 (7.7%)
Teachers: 107.8 (15.3 to 1)
Librarians/Media Specialists: 3.0 (548.3 to 1)
Guidance Counselors: 4.0 (411.3 to 1)
Current Spending: ($ per student per year):
Total: $5,472; Instruction: $3,633; Support Services: $1,531
Enrollment, Drop-out Rates and Diploma Recipients by Race/Ethnicity

Category	Total	White	Black	Asian	AIAN	Hisp.
Enrollment (%)	100.0	55.0	44.4	0.4	0.0	0.2
Drop-out Rate (%)	1.3	1.8	0.6	n/a	n/a	0.0
H.S. Diplomas (#)	87	57	29	0	0	1

Clay County

Clay County SD

121 2nd Ave N • Ashland, AL 36251-0278
Mailing Address: PO Box 278 • Ashland, AL 36251-0278
(256) 354-5414
Grade Span: KG-12; **Agency Type:** 1
Schools: 6
2 Primary; 0 Middle; 2 High; 2 Other Level
6 Regular; 0 Special Education; 0 Vocational; 0 Alternative
0 Magnet; 0 Charter; 4 Title I Eligible; 3 School-wide Title I
Students: 2,330 (51.7% male; 48.3% female)
Individual Education Program: 334 (14.3%);
English Language Learner: 0 (0.0%); Migrant: 0 (0.0%)
Eligible for Free Lunch Program: 1,021 (43.8%)
Eligible for Reduced-Price Lunch Program: 301 (12.9%)
Teachers: 146.4 (15.9 to 1)
Librarians/Media Specialists: 2.5 (932.0 to 1)
Guidance Counselors: 5.5 (423.6 to 1)
Current Spending: ($ per student per year):
Total: $5,554; Instruction: $3,528; Support Services: $1,601
Enrollment, Drop-out Rates and Diploma Recipients by Race/Ethnicity

Category	Total	White	Black	Asian	AIAN	Hisp.
Enrollment (%)	100.0	75.4	22.4	0.1	0.5	1.6
Drop-out Rate (%)	2.4	2.1	3.0	n/a	0.0	14.3
H.S. Diplomas (#)	149	112	35	0	1	1

Cleburne County

Cleburne County SD

93 Education St • Heflin, AL 36264-2207
(256) 463-5624 • http://cleburneschools.net/
Grade Span: PK-12; **Agency Type:** 1
Schools: 8
4 Primary; 0 Middle; 3 High; 1 Other Level
6 Regular; 0 Special Education; 1 Vocational; 1 Alternative
0 Magnet; 0 Charter; 4 Title I Eligible; 1 School-wide Title I
Students: 2,643 (50.8% male; 49.2% female)
Individual Education Program: 428 (16.2%);
English Language Learner: 17 (0.6%); Migrant: 0 (0.0%)
Eligible for Free Lunch Program: 1,106 (41.8%)
Eligible for Reduced-Price Lunch Program: 279 (10.6%)
Teachers: 163.1 (16.2 to 1)
Librarians/Media Specialists: 5.5 (480.5 to 1)
Guidance Counselors: 5.0 (528.6 to 1)
Current Spending: ($ per student per year):
Total: $5,570; Instruction: $3,432; Support Services: $1,663
Enrollment, Drop-out Rates and Diploma Recipients by Race/Ethnicity

Category	Total	White	Black	Asian	AIAN	Hisp.
Enrollment (%)	100.0	94.4	4.4	0.2	0.2	0.9
Drop-out Rate (%)	5.6	5.8	2.3	n/a	n/a	0.0
H.S. Diplomas (#)	124	121	3	0	0	0

Coffee County

Coffee County SD

400 Reddoch Hill Rd • Elba, AL 36323-1661
(334) 897-5016 • http://www.coffeecounty.k12.al.us/
Grade Span: KG-12; **Agency Type:** 1
Schools: 4
1 Primary; 0 Middle; 1 High; 2 Other Level
4 Regular; 0 Special Education; 0 Vocational; 0 Alternative
0 Magnet; 0 Charter; 2 Title I Eligible; 2 School-wide Title I
Students: 1,960 (51.9% male; 48.1% female)
Individual Education Program: 278 (14.2%);
English Language Learner: 4 (0.2%); Migrant: 243 (12.4%)

Eligible for Free Lunch Program: 731 (37.3%)
Eligible for Reduced-Price Lunch Program: 233 (11.9%)
Teachers: 117.5 (16.7 to 1)
Librarians/Media Specialists: 3.0 (653.3 to 1)
Guidance Counselors: 5.5 (356.4 to 1)
Current Spending: ($ per student per year):
Total: $5,988; Instruction: $3,702; Support Services: $1,891
Enrollment, Drop-out Rates and Diploma Recipients by Race/Ethnicity

Category	Total	White	Black	Asian	AIAN	Hisp.
Enrollment (%)	100.0	89.0	7.2	0.4	3.2	0.1
Drop-out Rate (%)	5.7	5.9	4.9	0.0	0.0	n/a
H.S. Diplomas (#)	105	96	8	0	1	0

Enterprise City SD
502 E Watts St • Enterprise, AL 36330-1860
Mailing Address: PO Box 311790 • Enterprise, AL 36331-1790
(334) 347-9531 • http://enterpriseschools.net/
Grade Span: KG-12; **Agency Type:** 1
Schools: 10
6 Primary; 1 Middle; 1 High; 2 Other Level
10 Regular; 0 Special Education; 0 Vocational; 0 Alternative
0 Magnet; 0 Charter; 5 Title I Eligible; 0 School-wide Title I
Students: 5,256 (51.4% male; 48.6% female)
Individual Education Program: 558 (10.6%);
English Language Learner: 96 (1.8%); Migrant: 251 (4.8%)
Eligible for Free Lunch Program: 1,670 (31.8%)
Eligible for Reduced-Price Lunch Program: 373 (7.1%)
Teachers: 337.4 (15.6 to 1)
Librarians/Media Specialists: 11.0 (477.8 to 1)
Guidance Counselors: 12.4 (423.9 to 1)
Current Spending: ($ per student per year):
Total: $6,029; Instruction: $3,663; Support Services: $1,978
Enrollment, Drop-out Rates and Diploma Recipients by Race/Ethnicity

Category	Total	White	Black	Asian	AIAN	Hisp.
Enrollment (%)	100.0	64.5	27.6	2.4	0.3	5.2
Drop-out Rate (%)	4.4	4.0	5.9	7.0	0.0	0.0
H.S. Diplomas (#)	318	228	67	11	1	11

Colbert County

Colbert County SD
1101 Hwy 72 E • Tuscumbia, AL 35674-2412
(256) 386-8565 • http://www.colbertcountyschools.org/
Grade Span: PK-12; **Agency Type:** 1
Schools: 9
4 Primary; 1 Middle; 3 High; 1 Other Level
9 Regular; 0 Special Education; 0 Vocational; 0 Alternative
0 Magnet; 0 Charter; 5 Title I Eligible; 5 School-wide Title I
Students: 3,271 (54.8% male; 45.2% female)
Individual Education Program: 512 (15.7%);
English Language Learner: 20 (0.6%); Migrant: 9 (0.3%)
Eligible for Free Lunch Program: 1,587 (48.5%)
Eligible for Reduced-Price Lunch Program: 383 (11.7%)
Teachers: 216.8 (15.1 to 1)
Librarians/Media Specialists: 8.5 (384.8 to 1)
Guidance Counselors: 9.0 (363.4 to 1)
Current Spending: ($ per student per year):
Total: $6,266; Instruction: $3,744; Support Services: $2,087
Enrollment, Drop-out Rates and Diploma Recipients by Race/Ethnicity

Category	Total	White	Black	Asian	AIAN	Hisp.
Enrollment (%)	100.0	81.4	17.4	0.1	0.2	0.9
Drop-out Rate (%)	4.2	5.1	1.1	0.0	n/a	0.0
H.S. Diplomas (#)	116	97	19	0	0	0

Muscle Shoals City SD
3200 S Wilson Dam Rd • Muscle Shoals, AL 35661
Mailing Address: PO Box 2610 • Muscle Shoals, AL 35662-2610
(256) 389-2600 • http://www.mscs.k12.al.us/
Grade Span: KG-12; **Agency Type:** 1
Schools: 7
4 Primary; 1 Middle; 2 High; 0 Other Level
6 Regular; 0 Special Education; 1 Vocational; 0 Alternative
0 Magnet; 0 Charter; 3 Title I Eligible; 0 School-wide Title I
Students: 2,470 (50.8% male; 49.2% female)
Individual Education Program: 144 (5.8%);
English Language Learner: 15 (0.6%); Migrant: 0 (0.0%)
Eligible for Free Lunch Program: 375 (15.2%)
Eligible for Reduced-Price Lunch Program: 146 (5.9%)
Teachers: 158.0 (15.6 to 1)
Librarians/Media Specialists: 4.0 (617.5 to 1)
Guidance Counselors: 6.0 (411.7 to 1)
Current Spending: ($ per student per year):
Total: $6,615; Instruction: $3,942; Support Services: $2,194
Enrollment, Drop-out Rates and Diploma Recipients by Race/Ethnicity

Category	Total	White	Black	Asian	AIAN	Hisp.
Enrollment (%)	100.0	83.2	15.0	0.9	0.1	0.9
Drop-out Rate (%)	1.0	1.2	0.0	0.0	0.0	0.0
H.S. Diplomas (#)	137	116	20	1	0	0

Conecuh County

Conecuh County SD
100 Jackson St • Evergreen, AL 36401-2843
(334) 578-1752
Grade Span: PK-12; **Agency Type:** 1
Schools: 8
4 Primary; 1 Middle; 2 High; 1 Other Level
7 Regular; 0 Special Education; 1 Vocational; 0 Alternative
0 Magnet; 0 Charter; 5 Title I Eligible; 4 School-wide Title I
Students: 1,991 (52.8% male; 47.2% female)
Individual Education Program: 353 (17.7%);
English Language Learner: 0 (0.0%); Migrant: 0 (0.0%)
Eligible for Free Lunch Program: 1,476 (74.1%)
Eligible for Reduced-Price Lunch Program: 179 (9.0%)
Teachers: 125.7 (15.8 to 1)
Librarians/Media Specialists: 5.5 (362.0 to 1)
Guidance Counselors: 5.0 (398.2 to 1)
Current Spending: ($ per student per year):
Total: $5,970; Instruction: $3,506; Support Services: $1,912
Enrollment, Drop-out Rates and Diploma Recipients by Race/Ethnicity

Category	Total	White	Black	Asian	AIAN	Hisp.
Enrollment (%)	100.0	21.6	78.3	0.0	0.1	0.1
Drop-out Rate (%)	7.9	13.8	6.4	n/a	0.0	0.0
H.S. Diplomas (#)	58	16	42	0	0	0

Coosa County

Coosa County SD
Main St • Rockford, AL 35136-0037
Mailing Address: PO Box 37 • Rockford, AL 35136-0037
(256) 377-4913 • http://coosaschools.k12.al.us/
Grade Span: KG-12; **Agency Type:** 1
Schools: 6
4 Primary; 0 Middle; 2 High; 0 Other Level
5 Regular; 0 Special Education; 1 Vocational; 0 Alternative
0 Magnet; 0 Charter; 3 Title I Eligible; 3 School-wide Title I
Students: 1,708 (51.3% male; 48.7% female)
Individual Education Program: 243 (14.2%);
English Language Learner: 6 (0.4%); Migrant: 0 (0.0%)
Eligible for Free Lunch Program: 864 (50.6%)
Eligible for Reduced-Price Lunch Program: 221 (12.9%)
Teachers: 104.5 (16.3 to 1)
Librarians/Media Specialists: 4.0 (427.0 to 1)
Guidance Counselors: 6.0 (284.7 to 1)
Current Spending: ($ per student per year):
Total: $5,546; Instruction: $3,126; Support Services: $1,983
Enrollment, Drop-out Rates and Diploma Recipients by Race/Ethnicity

Category	Total	White	Black	Asian	AIAN	Hisp.
Enrollment (%)	100.0	49.4	49.8	0.1	0.4	0.4
Drop-out Rate (%)	4.4	4.5	4.3	n/a	0.0	0.0
H.S. Diplomas (#)	73	38	35	0	0	0

Covington County

Andalusia City SD
122 6th Ave • Andalusia, AL 36420-3152
(334) 222-3186
Grade Span: KG-12; **Agency Type:** 1
Schools: 3
1 Primary; 1 Middle; 0 High; 1 Other Level
3 Regular; 0 Special Education; 0 Vocational; 0 Alternative
0 Magnet; 0 Charter; 2 Title I Eligible; 2 School-wide Title I
Students: 1,745 (50.9% male; 49.1% female)
Individual Education Program: 176 (10.1%);
English Language Learner: 2 (0.1%); Migrant: 0 (0.0%)
Eligible for Free Lunch Program: 655 (37.5%)
Eligible for Reduced-Price Lunch Program: 130 (7.4%)
Teachers: 116.0 (15.0 to 1)
Librarians/Media Specialists: 4.0 (436.3 to 1)
Guidance Counselors: 4.0 (436.3 to 1)
Current Spending: ($ per student per year):
Total: $5,754; Instruction: $3,764; Support Services: $1,596
Enrollment, Drop-out Rates and Diploma Recipients by Race/Ethnicity

Category	Total	White	Black	Asian	AIAN	Hisp.
Enrollment (%)	100.0	67.7	31.1	0.5	0.3	0.4
Drop-out Rate (%)	3.1	3.4	2.2	n/a	0.0	0.0
H.S. Diplomas (#)	113	82	30	0	0	1

Covington County SD

807 C C Baker Ave • Andalusia, AL 36420-0460
Mailing Address: PO Box 460 • Andalusia, AL 36420-0460
(334) 222-7571 • http://www.covingtoncountyschools.net/
Grade Span: PK-12; **Agency Type:** 1
Schools: 8
3 Primary; 1 Middle; 2 High; 2 Other Level
8 Regular; 0 Special Education; 0 Vocational; 0 Alternative
0 Magnet; 0 Charter; 8 Title I Eligible; 8 School-wide Title I
Students: 3,242 (52.4% male; 47.6% female)
Individual Education Program: 484 (14.9%);
English Language Learner: 5 (0.2%); Migrant: 346 (10.7%)
Eligible for Free Lunch Program: 1,380 (42.6%)
Eligible for Reduced-Price Lunch Program: 338 (10.4%)
Teachers: 194.9 (16.6 to 1)
Librarians/Media Specialists: 5.8 (559.0 to 1)
Guidance Counselors: 7.5 (432.3 to 1)
Current Spending: ($ per student per year):
Total: $5,662; Instruction: $3,489; Support Services: $1,787
Enrollment, Drop-out Rates and Diploma Recipients by Race/Ethnicity

Category	Total	White	Black	Asian	AIAN	Hisp.
Enrollment (%)	100.0	88.9	10.2	0.2	0.5	0.3
Drop-out Rate (%)	6.9	7.6	1.9	n/a	0.0	0.0
H.S. Diplomas (#)	132	116	14	0	1	1

Crenshaw County

Crenshaw County SD

183 Votec Dr • Luverne, AL 36049-0072
(334) 335-6519
Grade Span: PK-12; **Agency Type:** 1
Schools: 4
0 Primary; 0 Middle; 1 High; 3 Other Level
3 Regular; 0 Special Education; 1 Vocational; 0 Alternative
0 Magnet; 0 Charter; 3 Title I Eligible; 3 School-wide Title I
Students: 2,348 (54.3% male; 45.7% female)
Individual Education Program: 293 (12.5%);
English Language Learner: 0 (0.0%); Migrant: 0 (0.0%)
Eligible for Free Lunch Program: 1,215 (51.7%)
Eligible for Reduced-Price Lunch Program: 310 (13.2%)
Teachers: 152.5 (15.4 to 1)
Librarians/Media Specialists: 4.0 (587.0 to 1)
Guidance Counselors: 6.0 (391.3 to 1)
Current Spending: ($ per student per year):
Total: $5,497; Instruction: $3,388; Support Services: $1,711
Enrollment, Drop-out Rates and Diploma Recipients by Race/Ethnicity

Category	Total	White	Black	Asian	AIAN	Hisp.
Enrollment (%)	100.0	65.9	33.0	0.2	0.3	0.6
Drop-out Rate (%)	3.8	3.3	4.6	n/a	0.0	n/a
H.S. Diplomas (#)	129	82	44	2	1	0

Cullman County

Cullman City SD

222 2nd Ave SE • Cullman, AL 35055-3514
Mailing Address: 301 1st St NE Ste 100 • Cullman, AL 35055-3514
(256) 734-2233 • http://www.cullmancats.net/
Grade Span: KG-12; **Agency Type:** 1
Schools: 6
3 Primary; 1 Middle; 2 High; 0 Other Level
5 Regular; 0 Special Education; 1 Vocational; 0 Alternative
0 Magnet; 0 Charter; 3 Title I Eligible; 0 School-wide Title I
Students: 2,643 (53.1% male; 46.9% female)
Individual Education Program: 297 (11.2%);
English Language Learner: 140 (5.3%); Migrant: 21 (0.8%)
Eligible for Free Lunch Program: 523 (19.8%)
Eligible for Reduced-Price Lunch Program: 149 (5.6%)
Teachers: 157.7 (16.8 to 1)
Librarians/Media Specialists: 5.0 (528.6 to 1)
Guidance Counselors: 6.0 (440.5 to 1)
Current Spending: ($ per student per year):
Total: $5,233; Instruction: $3,443; Support Services: $1,403
Enrollment, Drop-out Rates and Diploma Recipients by Race/Ethnicity

Category	Total	White	Black	Asian	AIAN	Hisp.
Enrollment (%)	100.0	92.8	0.3	0.7	0.1	6.2
Drop-out Rate (%)	0.7	0.7	0.0	0.0	0.0	0.0
H.S. Diplomas (#)	181	178	0	2	1	0

Cullman County SD

402 Arnold St NE • Cullman, AL 35055-1964
Mailing Address: PO Box 1590 • Cullman, AL 35056-1590
(256) 734-2933 • http://www.ccboe.org/
Grade Span: PK-12; **Agency Type:** 1
Schools: 27
13 Primary; 5 Middle; 8 High; 1 Other Level
25 Regular; 1 Special Education; 1 Vocational; 0 Alternative
0 Magnet; 0 Charter; 13 Title I Eligible; 1 School-wide Title I
Students: 9,622 (51.7% male; 48.3% female)
Individual Education Program: 1,259 (13.1%);
English Language Learner: 240 (2.5%); Migrant: 655 (6.8%)
Eligible for Free Lunch Program: 3,480 (36.2%)
Eligible for Reduced-Price Lunch Program: 1,241 (12.9%)
Teachers: 585.4 (16.4 to 1)
Librarians/Media Specialists: 17.0 (566.0 to 1)
Guidance Counselors: 16.8 (572.7 to 1)
Current Spending: ($ per student per year):
Total: $5,532; Instruction: $3,377; Support Services: $1,729
Enrollment, Drop-out Rates and Diploma Recipients by Race/Ethnicity

Category	Total	White	Black	Asian	AIAN	Hisp.
Enrollment (%)	100.0	96.6	1.3	0.1	0.1	1.9
Drop-out Rate (%)	6.9	7.0	2.8	0.0	0.0	4.2
H.S. Diplomas (#)	465	459	4	1	0	1

Dale County

Dale County SD

111 W Reynolds St • Ozark, AL 36360-1438
Mailing Address: PO Box 948 • Ozark, AL 36361-0948
(334) 774-2355 • http://www.dalecountyboe.org/
Grade Span: KG-12; **Agency Type:** 1
Schools: 7
3 Primary; 1 Middle; 2 High; 1 Other Level
7 Regular; 0 Special Education; 0 Vocational; 0 Alternative
0 Magnet; 0 Charter; 5 Title I Eligible; 5 School-wide Title I
Students: 2,654 (54.2% male; 45.8% female)
Individual Education Program: 341 (12.8%);
English Language Learner: 0 (0.0%); Migrant: 0 (0.0%)
Eligible for Free Lunch Program: 1,094 (41.2%)
Eligible for Reduced-Price Lunch Program: 271 (10.2%)
Teachers: 170.3 (15.6 to 1)
Librarians/Media Specialists: 5.2 (510.4 to 1)
Guidance Counselors: 4.0 (663.5 to 1)
Current Spending: ($ per student per year):
Total: $5,686; Instruction: $3,615; Support Services: $1,735
Enrollment, Drop-out Rates and Diploma Recipients by Race/Ethnicity

Category	Total	White	Black	Asian	AIAN	Hisp.
Enrollment (%)	100.0	79.3	19.8	0.3	0.3	0.2
Drop-out Rate (%)	6.4	7.4	2.6	0.0	n/a	0.0
H.S. Diplomas (#)	140	116	23	0	0	1

Daleville City SD

626 N Daleville Ave • Daleville, AL 36322-2006
(334) 598-2456 • http://www.daleville.k12.al.us/
Grade Span: KG-12; **Agency Type:** 1
Schools: 4
1 Primary; 1 Middle; 1 High; 1 Other Level
3 Regular; 0 Special Education; 0 Vocational; 1 Alternative
0 Magnet; 0 Charter; 2 Title I Eligible; 2 School-wide Title I
Students: 1,671 (53.7% male; 46.3% female)
Individual Education Program: 206 (12.3%);
English Language Learner: 6 (0.4%); Migrant: 0 (0.0%)
Eligible for Free Lunch Program: 595 (35.6%)
Eligible for Reduced-Price Lunch Program: 159 (9.5%)
Teachers: 105.3 (15.9 to 1)
Librarians/Media Specialists: 3.0 (557.0 to 1)
Guidance Counselors: 3.0 (557.0 to 1)
Current Spending: ($ per student per year):
Total: $5,615; Instruction: $3,560; Support Services: $1,681
Enrollment, Drop-out Rates and Diploma Recipients by Race/Ethnicity

Category	Total	White	Black	Asian	AIAN	Hisp.
Enrollment (%)	100.0	58.0	33.5	2.0	0.5	6.1
Drop-out Rate (%)	3.7	3.0	3.4	7.7	50.0	5.7
H.S. Diplomas (#)	90	45	32	4	0	9

Ozark City SD

928 E Andrews Ave • Ozark, AL 36360-1739
Mailing Address: 1044 Andrews Ave • Ozark, AL 36360-1739
(334) 774-5197 • http://www.ocbe.k12.al.us/
Grade Span: KG-12; **Agency Type:** 1
Schools: 8
3 Primary; 2 Middle; 3 High; 0 Other Level
6 Regular; 0 Special Education; 1 Vocational; 1 Alternative
0 Magnet; 0 Charter; 4 Title I Eligible; 0 School-wide Title I
Students: 2,818 (51.6% male; 48.4% female)
Individual Education Program: 388 (13.8%);
English Language Learner: 14 (0.5%); Migrant: 0 (0.0%)
Eligible for Free Lunch Program: 1,167 (41.4%)
Eligible for Reduced-Price Lunch Program: 234 (8.3%)
Teachers: 179.3 (15.7 to 1)
Librarians/Media Specialists: 5.5 (512.4 to 1)
Guidance Counselors: 8.0 (352.3 to 1)

Current Spending: ($ per student per year):
Total: $5,840; Instruction: $3,509; Support Services: $1,949
Enrollment, Drop-out Rates and Diploma Recipients by Race/Ethnicity

Category	Total	White	Black	Asian	AIAN	Hisp.
Enrollment (%)	100.0	56.2	41.4	0.8	0.4	1.2
Drop-out Rate (%)	3.6	3.5	3.6	0.0	11.1	7.7
H.S. Diplomas (#)	161	103	50	0	3	5

Dallas County

Dallas County SD
429 Lauderdale St • Selma, AL 36701-4581
Mailing Address: PO Box 1056 • Selma, AL 36702-1056
(334) 875-3440 • http://www.dallask12.org/
Grade Span: KG-12; **Agency Type:** 1
Schools: 14
7 Primary; 2 Middle; 4 High; 1 Other Level
13 Regular; 0 Special Education; 1 Vocational; 0 Alternative
0 Magnet; 0 Charter; 9 Title I Eligible; 9 School-wide Title I
Students: 4,536 (50.2% male; 49.8% female)
Individual Education Program: 628 (13.8%);
English Language Learner: 0 (0.0%); Migrant: 0 (0.0%)
Eligible for Free Lunch Program: 3,299 (72.7%)
Eligible for Reduced-Price Lunch Program: 313 (6.9%)
Teachers: 299.0 (15.2 to 1)
Librarians/Media Specialists: 11.0 (412.4 to 1)
Guidance Counselors: 11.6 (391.0 to 1)
Current Spending: ($ per student per year):
Total: $5,778; Instruction: $3,448; Support Services: $1,910
Enrollment, Drop-out Rates and Diploma Recipients by Race/Ethnicity

Category	Total	White	Black	Asian	AIAN	Hisp.
Enrollment (%)	100.0	23.1	76.6	0.3	0.0	0.0
Drop-out Rate (%)	3.5	7.5	2.3	0.0	0.0	n/a
H.S. Diplomas (#)	229	51	177	1	0	0

Selma City SD
300 Washington St • Selma, AL 36701-4454
Mailing Address: PO Box 350 • Selma, AL 36702-0350
(334) 874-1600 •
http://www.myaasite.com/programs/schools/districtView.asp?District=:;: %3CCA:
Grade Span: PK-12; **Agency Type:** 1
Schools: 13
8 Primary; 2 Middle; 2 High; 1 Other Level
11 Regular; 0 Special Education; 1 Vocational; 1 Alternative
0 Magnet; 0 Charter; 8 Title I Eligible; 6 School-wide Title I
Students: 4,096 (49.1% male; 50.9% female)
Individual Education Program: 435 (10.6%);
English Language Learner: 6 (0.1%); Migrant: 0 (0.0%)
Eligible for Free Lunch Program: 3,211 (78.4%)
Eligible for Reduced-Price Lunch Program: 287 (7.0%)
Teachers: 246.2 (16.6 to 1)
Librarians/Media Specialists: 11.0 (372.4 to 1)
Guidance Counselors: 11.3 (362.5 to 1)
Current Spending: ($ per student per year):
Total: $5,699; Instruction: $3,446; Support Services: $1,775
Enrollment, Drop-out Rates and Diploma Recipients by Race/Ethnicity

Category	Total	White	Black	Asian	AIAN	Hisp.
Enrollment (%)	100.0	5.0	94.4	0.4	0.0	0.1
Drop-out Rate (%)	0.2	0.0	0.2	0.0	n/a	n/a
H.S. Diplomas (#)	164	0	164	0	0	0

De Kalb County

Dekalb County SD
306 Main St W • Rainsville, AL 35968-1668
Mailing Address: PO Box 1668 • Rainsville, AL 35986-1668
(256) 638-6921
Grade Span: KG-12; **Agency Type:** 1
Schools: 14
3 Primary; 0 Middle; 1 High; 10 Other Level
11 Regular; 1 Special Education; 1 Vocational; 1 Alternative
0 Magnet; 0 Charter; 8 Title I Eligible; 6 School-wide Title I
Students: 7,978 (52.1% male; 47.9% female)
Individual Education Program: 1,116 (14.0%);
English Language Learner: 595 (7.5%); Migrant: 790 (9.9%)
Eligible for Free Lunch Program: 3,271 (41.0%)
Eligible for Reduced-Price Lunch Program: 932 (11.7%)
Teachers: 532.7 (15.0 to 1)
Librarians/Media Specialists: 16.5 (483.5 to 1)
Guidance Counselors: 19.5 (409.1 to 1)
Current Spending: ($ per student per year):
Total: $5,948; Instruction: $3,664; Support Services: $1,840

Enrollment, Drop-out Rates and Diploma Recipients by Race/Ethnicity

Category	Total	White	Black	Asian	AIAN	Hisp.
Enrollment (%)	100.0	76.6	1.1	0.2	12.8	9.3
Drop-out Rate (%)	5.6	6.8	0.0	0.0	1.8	4.8
H.S. Diplomas (#)	372	255	3	0	109	5

Fort Payne City SD
205 45th St NE • Fort Payne, AL 35967
Mailing Address: PO Box 681029 • Fort Payne, AL 35968-1611
(256) 845-0915 • http://www.ftpayk12.org/
Grade Span: KG-12; **Agency Type:** 1
Schools: 4
2 Primary; 1 Middle; 1 High; 0 Other Level
4 Regular; 0 Special Education; 0 Vocational; 0 Alternative
0 Magnet; 0 Charter; 2 Title I Eligible; 0 School-wide Title I
Students: 2,691 (51.8% male; 48.2% female)
Individual Education Program: 271 (10.1%);
English Language Learner: 430 (16.0%); Migrant: 73 (2.7%)
Eligible for Free Lunch Program: 939 (34.9%)
Eligible for Reduced-Price Lunch Program: 213 (7.9%)
Teachers: 163.9 (16.4 to 1)
Librarians/Media Specialists: 5.0 (538.2 to 1)
Guidance Counselors: 5.0 (538.2 to 1)
Current Spending: ($ per student per year):
Total: $5,550; Instruction: $3,509; Support Services: $1,543
Enrollment, Drop-out Rates and Diploma Recipients by Race/Ethnicity

Category	Total	White	Black	Asian	AIAN	Hisp.
Enrollment (%)	100.0	75.5	5.9	0.7	0.1	17.8
Drop-out Rate (%)	7.7	6.7	9.8	16.7	8.3	14.1
H.S. Diplomas (#)	136	118	4	1	12	1

Elmore County

Elmore County SD
203 Hill St • Wetumpka, AL 36092-2722
Mailing Address: PO Box 817 • Wetumpka, AL 36092-0014
(334) 567-1200 • http://www.elmoreco.com/
Grade Span: PK-12; **Agency Type:** 1
Schools: 15
6 Primary; 3 Middle; 5 High; 1 Other Level
14 Regular; 0 Special Education; 1 Vocational; 0 Alternative
0 Magnet; 0 Charter; 10 Title I Eligible; 0 School-wide Title I
Students: 10,038 (51.9% male; 48.1% female)
Individual Education Program: 1,251 (12.5%);
English Language Learner: 74 (0.7%); Migrant: 0 (0.0%)
Eligible for Free Lunch Program: 3,136 (31.2%)
Eligible for Reduced-Price Lunch Program: 886 (8.8%)
Teachers: 579.5 (17.3 to 1)
Librarians/Media Specialists: 14.0 (717.0 to 1)
Guidance Counselors: 22.0 (456.3 to 1)
Current Spending: ($ per student per year):
Total: $5,414; Instruction: $3,518; Support Services: $1,589
Enrollment, Drop-out Rates and Diploma Recipients by Race/Ethnicity

Category	Total	White	Black	Asian	AIAN	Hisp.
Enrollment (%)	100.0	71.0	27.3	0.6	0.1	1.0
Drop-out Rate (%)	5.5	5.2	6.2	0.0	25.0	21.4
H.S. Diplomas (#)	430	342	84	3	0	1

Tallassee City SD
308 King St • Tallassee, AL 36078-1316
(334) 283-6864
Grade Span: KG-12; **Agency Type:** 1
Schools: 3
1 Primary; 1 Middle; 1 High; 0 Other Level
3 Regular; 0 Special Education; 0 Vocational; 0 Alternative
0 Magnet; 0 Charter; 1 Title I Eligible; 0 School-wide Title I
Students: 1,884 (51.4% male; 48.6% female)
Individual Education Program: 218 (11.6%);
English Language Learner: 22 (1.2%); Migrant: 0 (0.0%)
Eligible for Free Lunch Program: 715 (38.0%)
Eligible for Reduced-Price Lunch Program: 156 (8.3%)
Teachers: 115.0 (16.4 to 1)
Librarians/Media Specialists: 3.0 (628.0 to 1)
Guidance Counselors: 3.5 (538.3 to 1)
Current Spending: ($ per student per year):
Total: $5,109; Instruction: $3,424; Support Services: $1,261
Enrollment, Drop-out Rates and Diploma Recipients by Race/Ethnicity

Category	Total	White	Black	Asian	AIAN	Hisp.
Enrollment (%)	100.0	72.2	26.3	0.4	0.2	0.9
Drop-out Rate (%)	5.1	5.0	5.8	0.0	0.0	0.0
H.S. Diplomas (#)	94	69	25	0	0	0

Escambia County

Escambia County SD

301 Belleville Ave • Brewton, AL 36426-2042
Mailing Address: PO Box 307 • Brewton, AL 36427-0307
(334) 867-6251 • http://www.escambiak12.net/
Grade Span: PK-12; **Agency Type:** 1
Schools: 14
6 Primary; 2 Middle; 5 High; 1 Other Level
11 Regular; 0 Special Education; 1 Vocational; 2 Alternative
0 Magnet; 0 Charter; 9 Title I Eligible; 8 School-wide Title I
Students: 4,724 (51.9% male; 48.1% female)
Individual Education Program: 617 (13.1%);
English Language Learner: 11 (0.2%); Migrant: 0 (0.0%)
Eligible for Free Lunch Program: 2,615 (55.4%)
Eligible for Reduced-Price Lunch Program: 602 (12.7%)
Teachers: 305.2 (15.5 to 1)
Librarians/Media Specialists: 10.5 (449.9 to 1)
Guidance Counselors: 13.0 (363.4 to 1)
Current Spending: ($ per student per year):
Total: $6,374; Instruction: $3,757; Support Services: $2,177
Enrollment, Drop-out Rates and Diploma Recipients by Race/Ethnicity

Category	Total	White	Black	Asian	AIAN	Hisp.
Enrollment (%)	100.0	55.0	38.7	0.2	5.3	0.8
Drop-out Rate (%)	4.5	4.8	4.0	0.0	5.5	0.0
H.S. Diplomas (#)	230	138	81	0	11	0

Etowah County

Attalla City SD

101 Case Ave • Attalla, AL 35954-3404
(256) 538-8051 • http://www.attalla.k12.al.us/
Grade Span: PK-12; **Agency Type:** 1
Schools: 4
1 Primary; 1 Middle; 1 High; 1 Other Level
4 Regular; 0 Special Education; 0 Vocational; 0 Alternative
0 Magnet; 0 Charter; 2 Title I Eligible; 2 School-wide Title I
Students: 1,856 (53.4% male; 46.6% female)
Individual Education Program: 345 (18.6%);
English Language Learner: 47 (2.5%); Migrant: 0 (0.0%)
Eligible for Free Lunch Program: 812 (43.8%)
Eligible for Reduced-Price Lunch Program: 231 (12.4%)
Teachers: 119.8 (15.5 to 1)
Librarians/Media Specialists: 3.8 (488.4 to 1)
Guidance Counselors: 5.0 (371.2 to 1)
Current Spending: ($ per student per year):
Total: $5,922; Instruction: $3,793; Support Services: $1,694
Enrollment, Drop-out Rates and Diploma Recipients by Race/Ethnicity

Category	Total	White	Black	Asian	AIAN	Hisp.
Enrollment (%)	100.0	82.1	14.1	0.2	0.2	3.4
Drop-out Rate (%)	6.6	7.1	3.2	0.0	0.0	0.0
H.S. Diplomas (#)	109	98	8	0	1	2

Etowah County SD

3200 W Meighan Blvd • Gadsden, AL 35904-1732
(256) 549-7578 • http://www.ecboe.org/
Grade Span: PK-12; **Agency Type:** 1
Schools: 22
9 Primary; 3 Middle; 6 High; 4 Other Level
19 Regular; 1 Special Education; 1 Vocational; 1 Alternative
0 Magnet; 0 Charter; 13 Title I Eligible; 7 School-wide Title I
Students: 8,480 (51.6% male; 48.4% female)
Individual Education Program: 1,226 (14.5%);
English Language Learner: 84 (1.0%); Migrant: 0 (0.0%)
Eligible for Free Lunch Program: 2,284 (26.9%)
Eligible for Reduced-Price Lunch Program: 913 (10.8%)
Teachers: 541.4 (15.7 to 1)
Librarians/Media Specialists: 19.1 (444.0 to 1)
Guidance Counselors: 19.0 (446.3 to 1)
Current Spending: ($ per student per year):
Total: $5,387; Instruction: $3,445; Support Services: $1,596
Enrollment, Drop-out Rates and Diploma Recipients by Race/Ethnicity

Category	Total	White	Black	Asian	AIAN	Hisp.
Enrollment (%)	100.0	97.2	1.4	0.4	0.1	0.9
Drop-out Rate (%)	4.6	4.6	0.0	0.0	n/a	18.2
H.S. Diplomas (#)	436	424	4	4	0	4

Gadsden City SD

1026 Chestnut St • Gadsden, AL 35901
Mailing Address: PO Box 184 • Gadsden, AL 35902-0184
(256) 543-3512 • http://www.gcs.k12.al.us/
Grade Span: PK-12; **Agency Type:** 1
Schools: 17
9 Primary; 3 Middle; 4 High; 1 Other Level
15 Regular; 0 Special Education; 1 Vocational; 1 Alternative
0 Magnet; 0 Charter; 11 Title I Eligible; 10 School-wide Title I
Students: 5,471 (51.2% male; 48.8% female)
Individual Education Program: 929 (17.0%);
English Language Learner: 158 (2.9%); Migrant: 110 (2.0%)
Eligible for Free Lunch Program: 3,244 (59.3%)
Eligible for Reduced-Price Lunch Program: 423 (7.7%)
Teachers: 368.3 (14.9 to 1)
Librarians/Media Specialists: 13.7 (399.3 to 1)
Guidance Counselors: 12.2 (448.4 to 1)
Current Spending: ($ per student per year):
Total: $6,226; Instruction: $3,737; Support Services: $2,036
Enrollment, Drop-out Rates and Diploma Recipients by Race/Ethnicity

Category	Total	White	Black	Asian	AIAN	Hisp.
Enrollment (%)	100.0	40.2	55.1	0.9	0.3	3.5
Drop-out Rate (%)	6.3	7.7	5.5	0.0	0.0	0.0
H.S. Diplomas (#)	257	121	133	1	0	2

Fayette County

Fayette County SD

103 First Ave NW • Fayette, AL 35555-0599
Mailing Address: PO Box 686 • Fayette, AL 35555-0599
(205) 932-4611 • http://www.fayette.k12.al.us/
Grade Span: KG-12; **Agency Type:** 1
Schools: 6
2 Primary; 1 Middle; 1 High; 2 Other Level
6 Regular; 0 Special Education; 0 Vocational; 0 Alternative
0 Magnet; 0 Charter; 5 Title I Eligible; 1 School-wide Title I
Students: 2,688 (51.4% male; 48.6% female)
Individual Education Program: 337 (12.5%);
English Language Learner: 0 (0.0%); Migrant: 0 (0.0%)
Eligible for Free Lunch Program: 941 (35.0%)
Eligible for Reduced-Price Lunch Program: 260 (9.7%)
Teachers: 172.6 (15.6 to 1)
Librarians/Media Specialists: 6.0 (448.0 to 1)
Guidance Counselors: 6.0 (448.0 to 1)
Current Spending: ($ per student per year):
Total: $5,640; Instruction: $3,475; Support Services: $1,738
Enrollment, Drop-out Rates and Diploma Recipients by Race/Ethnicity

Category	Total	White	Black	Asian	AIAN	Hisp.
Enrollment (%)	100.0	81.7	17.8	0.1	0.0	0.4
Drop-out Rate (%)	3.8	4.2	2.2	0.0	n/a	0.0
H.S. Diplomas (#)	145	120	25	0	0	0

Franklin County

Franklin County SD

500 N Coffee Ave • Russellville, AL 35653-0610
Mailing Address: PO Box 610 • Russellville, AL 35653-0610
(256) 332-1360 • http://www.franklin.k12.al.us/
Grade Span: KG-12; **Agency Type:** 1
Schools: 7
0 Primary; 0 Middle; 1 High; 6 Other Level
6 Regular; 0 Special Education; 1 Vocational; 0 Alternative
0 Magnet; 0 Charter; 6 Title I Eligible; 1 School-wide Title I
Students: 3,036 (51.9% male; 48.1% female)
Individual Education Program: 387 (12.7%);
English Language Learner: 122 (4.0%); Migrant: 134 (4.4%)
Eligible for Free Lunch Program: 1,365 (45.0%)
Eligible for Reduced-Price Lunch Program: 439 (14.5%)
Teachers: 202.1 (15.0 to 1)
Librarians/Media Specialists: 6.0 (506.0 to 1)
Guidance Counselors: 5.4 (562.2 to 1)
Current Spending: ($ per student per year):
Total: $5,867; Instruction: $3,628; Support Services: $1,809
Enrollment, Drop-out Rates and Diploma Recipients by Race/Ethnicity

Category	Total	White	Black	Asian	AIAN	Hisp.
Enrollment (%)	100.0	94.8	0.4	0.0	0.1	4.7
Drop-out Rate (%)	4.8	4.7	0.0	0.0	0.0	12.5
H.S. Diplomas (#)	132	128	1	0	1	2

Russellville City SD

1945 Waterloo Rd • Russellville, AL 35653-0880
Mailing Address: PO Box 880 • Russellville, AL 35653-0880
(256) 332-8440 • http://www.rcs.k12.al.us/
Grade Span: KG-12; **Agency Type:** 1
Schools: 4
2 Primary; 0 Middle; 1 High; 1 Other Level
4 Regular; 0 Special Education; 0 Vocational; 0 Alternative
0 Magnet; 0 Charter; 4 Title I Eligible; 0 School-wide Title I
Students: 2,342 (51.5% male; 48.5% female)
Individual Education Program: 214 (9.1%);
English Language Learner: 197 (8.4%); Migrant: 120 (5.1%)
Eligible for Free Lunch Program: 1,012 (43.2%)
Eligible for Reduced-Price Lunch Program: 212 (9.1%)

Teachers: 145.4 (16.1 to 1)
Librarians/Media Specialists: 4.0 (585.5 to 1)
Guidance Counselors: 4.0 (585.5 to 1)
Current Spending: ($ per student per year):
Total: $5,853; Instruction: $3,757; Support Services: $1,659
Enrollment, Drop-out Rates and Diploma Recipients by Race/Ethnicity

Category	Total	White	Black	Asian	AIAN	Hisp.
Enrollment (%)	100.0	72.5	10.8	0.2	0.0	16.4
Drop-out Rate (%)	2.5	2.0	0.0	n/a	n/a	12.0
H.S. Diplomas (#)	110	94	15	0	0	1

Geneva County

Geneva County SD
Courthouse • Geneva, AL 36340-0250
Mailing Address: PO Box 250 • Geneva, AL 36340-0250
(334) 684-5690
Grade Span: KG-12; **Agency Type:** 1
Schools: 9
3 Primary; 3 Middle; 3 High; 0 Other Level
9 Regular; 0 Special Education; 0 Vocational; 0 Alternative
0 Magnet; 0 Charter; 3 Title I Eligible; 3 School-wide Title I
Students: 2,715 (52.8% male; 47.2% female)
Individual Education Program: 339 (12.5%);
English Language Learner: 40 (1.5%); Migrant: 65 (2.4%)
Eligible for Free Lunch Program: 1,260 (46.4%)
Eligible for Reduced-Price Lunch Program: 218 (8.0%)
Teachers: 167.0 (16.3 to 1)
Librarians/Media Specialists: 6.0 (452.5 to 1)
Guidance Counselors: 6.0 (452.5 to 1)
Current Spending: ($ per student per year):
Total: $5,435; Instruction: $3,381; Support Services: $1,625
Enrollment, Drop-out Rates and Diploma Recipients by Race/Ethnicity

Category	Total	White	Black	Asian	AIAN	Hisp.
Enrollment (%)	100.0	80.7	16.6	0.4	0.3	2.0
Drop-out Rate (%)	2.3	1.9	3.4	0.0	0.0	6.7
H.S. Diplomas (#)	143	123	18	0	0	2

Greene County

Greene County SD
220 Main St • Eutaw, AL 35462-0569
Mailing Address: PO Box 569 • Eutaw, AL 35462-0569
(205) 372-3114
Grade Span: KG-12; **Agency Type:** 1
Schools: 5
2 Primary; 1 Middle; 2 High; 0 Other Level
4 Regular; 0 Special Education; 1 Vocational; 0 Alternative
0 Magnet; 0 Charter; 4 Title I Eligible; 4 School-wide Title I
Students: 1,754 (51.9% male; 48.1% female)
Individual Education Program: 220 (12.5%);
English Language Learner: 0 (0.0%); Migrant: 0 (0.0%)
Eligible for Free Lunch Program: 1,479 (84.3%)
Eligible for Reduced-Price Lunch Program: 139 (7.9%)
Teachers: 116.8 (15.0 to 1)
Librarians/Media Specialists: 4.0 (438.5 to 1)
Guidance Counselors: 4.0 (438.5 to 1)
Current Spending: ($ per student per year):
Total: $7,122; Instruction: $3,904; Support Services: $2,467
Enrollment, Drop-out Rates and Diploma Recipients by Race/Ethnicity

Category	Total	White	Black	Asian	AIAN	Hisp.
Enrollment (%)	100.0	0.1	99.9	0.0	0.0	0.0
Drop-out Rate (%)	6.0	0.0	6.0	n/a	n/a	n/a
H.S. Diplomas (#)	68	0	68	0	0	0

Hale County

Hale County SD
1115 Powers St • Greensboro, AL 36744-0360
Mailing Address: PO Box 360 • Greensboro, AL 36744-0360
(334) 624-8836 • http://www.halek12.org/
Grade Span: PK-12; **Agency Type:** 1
Schools: 10
4 Primary; 0 Middle; 5 High; 1 Other Level
9 Regular; 0 Special Education; 1 Vocational; 0 Alternative
0 Magnet; 0 Charter; 9 Title I Eligible; 9 School-wide Title I
Students: 3,348 (51.5% male; 48.5% female)
Individual Education Program: 356 (10.6%);
English Language Learner: 0 (0.0%); Migrant: 0 (0.0%)
Eligible for Free Lunch Program: 2,244 (67.0%)
Eligible for Reduced-Price Lunch Program: 290 (8.7%)
Teachers: 221.4 (15.1 to 1)
Librarians/Media Specialists: 8.0 (418.5 to 1)
Guidance Counselors: 7.4 (452.4 to 1)
Current Spending: ($ per student per year):
Total: $5,837; Instruction: $3,624; Support Services: $1,743
Enrollment, Drop-out Rates and Diploma Recipients by Race/Ethnicity

Category	Total	White	Black	Asian	AIAN	Hisp.
Enrollment (%)	100.0	25.7	73.8	0.1	0.1	0.3
Drop-out Rate (%)	4.0	4.8	3.7	n/a	n/a	0.0
H.S. Diplomas (#)	162	40	120	0	0	2

Henry County

Henry County SD
101a Doswell St • Abbeville, AL 36310-0635
Mailing Address: PO Box 635 • Abbeville, AL 36310-0635
(334) 585-2206 • http://www.familyeducation.com/al/henry
Grade Span: PK-12; **Agency Type:** 1
Schools: 7
2 Primary; 2 Middle; 2 High; 1 Other Level
6 Regular; 0 Special Education; 0 Vocational; 1 Alternative
0 Magnet; 0 Charter; 3 Title I Eligible; 2 School-wide Title I
Students: 2,707 (50.5% male; 49.5% female)
Individual Education Program: 338 (12.5%);
English Language Learner: 32 (1.2%); Migrant: 1 (<0.1%)
Eligible for Free Lunch Program: 1,368 (50.5%)
Eligible for Reduced-Price Lunch Program: 416 (15.4%)
Teachers: 169.0 (16.0 to 1)
Librarians/Media Specialists: 5.5 (492.2 to 1)
Guidance Counselors: 6.0 (451.2 to 1)
Current Spending: ($ per student per year):
Total: $5,806; Instruction: $3,626; Support Services: $1,662
Enrollment, Drop-out Rates and Diploma Recipients by Race/Ethnicity

Category	Total	White	Black	Asian	AIAN	Hisp.
Enrollment (%)	100.0	51.6	46.6	0.1	0.1	1.6
Drop-out Rate (%)	6.6	6.7	6.2	n/a	n/a	25.0
H.S. Diplomas (#)	124	78	46	0	0	0

Houston County

Dothan City SD
500 Dusy St • Dothan, AL 36301-2500
(334) 794-1407 • http://www.dothan.k12.al.us/
Grade Span: PK-12; **Agency Type:** 1
Schools: 19
11 Primary; 4 Middle; 3 High; 1 Other Level
17 Regular; 0 Special Education; 1 Vocational; 1 Alternative
0 Magnet; 0 Charter; 11 Title I Eligible; 9 School-wide Title I
Students: 8,743 (51.3% male; 48.7% female)
Individual Education Program: 1,196 (13.7%);
English Language Learner: 79 (0.9%); Migrant: 0 (0.0%)
Eligible for Free Lunch Program: 3,772 (43.1%)
Eligible for Reduced-Price Lunch Program: 576 (6.6%)
Teachers: 502.3 (17.4 to 1)
Librarians/Media Specialists: 19.0 (460.2 to 1)
Guidance Counselors: 21.0 (416.3 to 1)
Current Spending: ($ per student per year):
Total: $6,248; Instruction: $3,652; Support Services: $2,144
Enrollment, Drop-out Rates and Diploma Recipients by Race/Ethnicity

Category	Total	White	Black	Asian	AIAN	Hisp.
Enrollment (%)	100.0	47.1	50.6	1.0	0.2	1.2
Drop-out Rate (%)	6.1	4.2	8.8	4.3	0.0	5.9
H.S. Diplomas (#)	462	304	142	8	1	7

Houston County SD
404 W Washington St • Dothan, AL 36301-2520
Mailing Address: PO Box 1688 • Dothan, AL 36302-1688
(334) 792-8331 • http://www.hcboe.org/
Grade Span: KG-12; **Agency Type:** 1
Schools: 9
2 Primary; 0 Middle; 3 High; 4 Other Level
7 Regular; 0 Special Education; 1 Vocational; 1 Alternative
0 Magnet; 0 Charter; 3 Title I Eligible; 3 School-wide Title I
Students: 6,150 (51.5% male; 48.5% female)
Individual Education Program: 794 (12.9%);
English Language Learner: 34 (0.6%); Migrant: 5 (0.1%)
Eligible for Free Lunch Program: 1,866 (30.3%)
Eligible for Reduced-Price Lunch Program: 600 (9.8%)
Teachers: 383.3 (16.0 to 1)
Librarians/Media Specialists: 10.2 (602.9 to 1)
Guidance Counselors: 13.2 (465.9 to 1)
Current Spending: ($ per student per year):
Total: $5,515; Instruction: $3,464; Support Services: $1,618
Enrollment, Drop-out Rates and Diploma Recipients by Race/Ethnicity

Category	Total	White	Black	Asian	AIAN	Hisp.
Enrollment (%)	100.0	80.6	18.4	0.2	0.1	0.6
Drop-out Rate (%)	3.6	3.9	2.5	0.0	0.0	0.0
H.S. Diplomas (#)	323	271	41	1	2	8

Jackson County

Jackson County SD

16003 Al Hwy 35 • Scottsboro, AL 35768-0490
Mailing Address: PO Box 490 • Scottsboro, AL 35768-0490
(256) 259-9500 • http://www.jackson.k12.al.us/
Grade Span: PK-12; **Agency Type:** 1
Schools: 19
8 Primary; 2 Middle; 2 High; 7 Other Level
17 Regular; 0 Special Education; 1 Vocational; 1 Alternative
0 Magnet; 0 Charter; 16 Title I Eligible; 16 School-wide Title I
Students: 6,094 (51.8% male; 48.2% female)
Individual Education Program: 649 (10.6%);
English Language Learner: 61 (1.0%); Migrant: 0 (0.0%)
Eligible for Free Lunch Program: 2,661 (43.7%)
Eligible for Reduced-Price Lunch Program: 845 (13.9%)
Teachers: 394.2 (15.5 to 1)
Librarians/Media Specialists: 14.5 (420.3 to 1)
Guidance Counselors: 13.0 (468.8 to 1)
Current Spending: ($ per student per year):
Total: $6,119; Instruction: $3,633; Support Services: $1,968
Enrollment, Drop-out Rates and Diploma Recipients by Race/Ethnicity

Category	Total	White	Black	Asian	AIAN	Hisp.
Enrollment (%)	100.0	85.0	4.2	0.2	9.1	1.5
Drop-out Rate (%)	4.0	4.3	4.1	0.0	2.8	0.0
H.S. Diplomas (#)	277	198	9	1	69	0

Scottsboro City SD

906 S Scott St • Scottsboro, AL 35768-2642
(256) 218-2100 • http://www.scottsboropower.com/~jopat/
Grade Span: PK-12; **Agency Type:** 1
Schools: 6
3 Primary; 2 Middle; 1 High; 0 Other Level
6 Regular; 0 Special Education; 0 Vocational; 0 Alternative
0 Magnet; 0 Charter; 5 Title I Eligible; 0 School-wide Title I
Students: 2,709 (51.0% male; 49.0% female)
Individual Education Program: 340 (12.6%);
English Language Learner: 24 (0.9%); Migrant: 0 (0.0%)
Eligible for Free Lunch Program: 849 (31.3%)
Eligible for Reduced-Price Lunch Program: 243 (9.0%)
Teachers: 180.3 (15.0 to 1)
Librarians/Media Specialists: 6.0 (451.5 to 1)
Guidance Counselors: 7.0 (387.0 to 1)
Current Spending: ($ per student per year):
Total: $6,500; Instruction: $3,929; Support Services: $2,049
Enrollment, Drop-out Rates and Diploma Recipients by Race/Ethnicity

Category	Total	White	Black	Asian	AIAN	Hisp.
Enrollment (%)	100.0	90.6	7.9	0.3	0.0	1.3
Drop-out Rate (%)	3.6	3.4	7.3	0.0	n/a	0.0
H.S. Diplomas (#)	149	138	11	0	0	0

Jefferson County

Bessemer City SD

1621 5th Ave N • Bessemer, AL 35020
Mailing Address: PO Box 1230 • Bessemer, AL 35021-1230
(205) 481-9800 • http://www.bessk12.org/
Grade Span: KG-12; **Agency Type:** 1
Schools: 9
5 Primary; 1 Middle; 2 High; 1 Other Level
7 Regular; 0 Special Education; 1 Vocational; 1 Alternative
0 Magnet; 0 Charter; 7 Title I Eligible; 6 School-wide Title I
Students: 4,249 (51.2% male; 48.8% female)
Individual Education Program: 533 (12.5%);
English Language Learner: 27 (0.6%); Migrant: 0 (0.0%)
Eligible for Free Lunch Program: 2,942 (69.2%)
Eligible for Reduced-Price Lunch Program: 308 (7.2%)
Teachers: 282.5 (15.0 to 1)
Librarians/Media Specialists: 7.0 (607.0 to 1)
Guidance Counselors: 8.0 (531.1 to 1)
Current Spending: ($ per student per year):
Total: $5,773; Instruction: $3,412; Support Services: $1,920
Enrollment, Drop-out Rates and Diploma Recipients by Race/Ethnicity

Category	Total	White	Black	Asian	AIAN	Hisp.
Enrollment (%)	100.0	2.7	96.1	0.1	0.0	1.1
Drop-out Rate (%)	4.0	9.5	3.8	0.0	n/a	n/a
H.S. Diplomas (#)	109	3	106	0	0	0

Birmingham City SD

2015 N Park Pl • Birmingham, AL 35203-2762
Mailing Address: PO Box 10007 • Birmingham, AL 35202-0007
(205) 297-9226 • http://www.bhm.k12.al.us/
Grade Span: PK-12; **Agency Type:** 1
Schools: 92
52 Primary; 19 Middle; 19 High; 2 Other Level
74 Regular; 4 Special Education; 1 Vocational; 13 Alternative
11 Magnet; 0 Charter; 59 Title I Eligible; 56 School-wide Title I
Students: 36,133 (50.7% male; 49.3% female)
Individual Education Program: 5,056 (14.0%);
English Language Learner: 342 (0.9%); Migrant: 0 (0.0%)
Eligible for Free Lunch Program: 24,343 (67.4%)
Eligible for Reduced-Price Lunch Program: 2,602 (7.2%)
Teachers: 2,320.0 (15.6 to 1)
Librarians/Media Specialists: 75.0 (481.8 to 1)
Guidance Counselors: 90.2 (400.6 to 1)
Current Spending: ($ per student per year):
Total: $6,587; Instruction: $3,752; Support Services: $2,448
Enrollment, Drop-out Rates and Diploma Recipients by Race/Ethnicity

Category	Total	White	Black	Asian	AIAN	Hisp.
Enrollment (%)	100.0	2.3	96.4	0.3	0.0	1.1
Drop-out Rate (%)	2.3	0.4	2.4	0.0	n/a	0.0
H.S. Diplomas (#)	1,706	13	1,685	5	0	3

Fairfield City SD

6405 Ave D • Fairfield, AL 35064-0110
(205) 783-6850 • http://www.fairfield.k12.al.us/
Grade Span: KG-12; **Agency Type:** 1
Schools: 7
3 Primary; 1 Middle; 2 High; 1 Other Level
5 Regular; 0 Special Education; 1 Vocational; 1 Alternative
0 Magnet; 0 Charter; 3 Title I Eligible; 3 School-wide Title I
Students: 2,274 (50.1% male; 49.9% female)
Individual Education Program: 243 (10.7%);
English Language Learner: 16 (0.7%); Migrant: 0 (0.0%)
Eligible for Free Lunch Program: 1,388 (61.0%)
Eligible for Reduced-Price Lunch Program: 163 (7.2%)
Teachers: 155.5 (14.6 to 1)
Librarians/Media Specialists: 5.0 (454.8 to 1)
Guidance Counselors: 5.3 (429.1 to 1)
Current Spending: ($ per student per year):
Total: $5,598; Instruction: $3,357; Support Services: $1,781
Enrollment, Drop-out Rates and Diploma Recipients by Race/Ethnicity

Category	Total	White	Black	Asian	AIAN	Hisp.
Enrollment (%)	100.0	0.1	99.3	0.0	0.0	0.5
Drop-out Rate (%)	2.3	n/a	1.9	n/a	n/a	0.0
H.S. Diplomas (#)	130	0	129	0	0	1

Homewood City SD

7 Hollywood Blvd • Homewood, AL 35209
Mailing Address: PO Box 59366 • Homewood, AL 35259-9366
(205) 870-4203 • http://www.homewood.k12.al.us/
Grade Span: PK-12; **Agency Type:** 1
Schools: 5
3 Primary; 1 Middle; 1 High; 0 Other Level
5 Regular; 0 Special Education; 0 Vocational; 0 Alternative
0 Magnet; 0 Charter; 3 Title I Eligible; 0 School-wide Title I
Students: 3,220 (52.8% male; 47.2% female)
Individual Education Program: 348 (10.8%);
English Language Learner: 197 (6.1%); Migrant: 0 (0.0%)
Eligible for Free Lunch Program: 467 (14.5%)
Eligible for Reduced-Price Lunch Program: 181 (5.6%)
Teachers: 250.2 (12.9 to 1)
Librarians/Media Specialists: 5.0 (644.0 to 1)
Guidance Counselors: 10.0 (322.0 to 1)
Current Spending: ($ per student per year):
Total: $8,191; Instruction: $5,187; Support Services: $2,564
Enrollment, Drop-out Rates and Diploma Recipients by Race/Ethnicity

Category	Total	White	Black	Asian	AIAN	Hisp.
Enrollment (%)	100.0	66.6	26.5	3.0	0.2	3.7
Drop-out Rate (%)	0.6	0.4	1.4	0.0	n/a	0.0
H.S. Diplomas (#)	231	183	41	5	0	2

Hoover City SD

100 Municipal Dr Ste 200 • Hoover, AL 35216-5500
Mailing Address: 2810 Metropolitan Way • Hoover, AL 35243-5500
(205) 439-1015 • http://www.hoover.k12.al.us/
Grade Span: PK-12; **Agency Type:** 1
Schools: 14
9 Primary; 2 Middle; 1 High; 2 Other Level
14 Regular; 0 Special Education; 0 Vocational; 0 Alternative
0 Magnet; 0 Charter; 2 Title I Eligible; 0 School-wide Title I
Students: 10,722 (51.2% male; 48.8% female)
Individual Education Program: 911 (8.5%);
English Language Learner: 308 (2.9%); Migrant: 0 (0.0%)
Eligible for Free Lunch Program: 866 (8.1%)
Eligible for Reduced-Price Lunch Program: 359 (3.3%)
Teachers: 746.7 (14.4 to 1)
Librarians/Media Specialists: 15.0 (714.8 to 1)
Guidance Counselors: 25.5 (420.5 to 1)
Current Spending: ($ per student per year):
Total: $7,341; Instruction: $4,390; Support Services: $2,469

Enrollment, Drop-out Rates and Diploma Recipients by Race/Ethnicity

Category	Total	White	Black	Asian	AIAN	Hisp.
Enrollment (%)	100.0	77.8	13.6	5.0	0.1	3.6
Drop-out Rate (%)	1.7	1.7	1.4	0.0	0.0	8.3
H.S. Diplomas (#)	660	566	60	23	0	11

Jefferson County SD

2100 18th St S • Birmingham, AL 35209-1848
(205) 379-2000 • http://www.jefcoed.com/
Grade Span: KG-12; **Agency Type:** 1
Schools: 64
33 Primary; 8 Middle; 14 High; 9 Other Level
59 Regular; 2 Special Education; 1 Vocational; 2 Alternative
0 Magnet; 0 Charter; 20 Title I Eligible; 16 School-wide Title I
Students: 40,060 (52.1% male; 47.9% female)
Individual Education Program: 5,375 (13.4%);
English Language Learner: 512 (1.3%); Migrant: 0 (0.0%)
Eligible for Free Lunch Program: 8,984 (22.4%)
Eligible for Reduced-Price Lunch Program: 3,085 (7.7%)
Teachers: 2,511.7 (15.9 to 1)
Librarians/Media Specialists: 60.0 (667.7 to 1)
Guidance Counselors: 86.5 (463.1 to 1)
Current Spending: ($ per student per year):
Total: $5,651; Instruction: $3,608; Support Services: $1,691

Enrollment, Drop-out Rates and Diploma Recipients by Race/Ethnicity

Category	Total	White	Black	Asian	AIAN	Hisp.
Enrollment (%)	100.0	72.1	25.8	0.5	0.1	1.4
Drop-out Rate (%)	4.9	4.9	4.6	3.1	25.0	12.5
H.S. Diplomas (#)	2,278	1,799	459	15	1	4

Mountain Brook City SD

3 Church St • Mountain Brook, AL 35213-0040
Mailing Address: PO Box 130040 • Mountain Brook, AL 35213-0040
(205) 871-4608
Grade Span: KG-12; **Agency Type:** 1
Schools: 6
4 Primary; 1 Middle; 1 High; 0 Other Level
6 Regular; 0 Special Education; 0 Vocational; 0 Alternative
0 Magnet; 0 Charter; 1 Title I Eligible; 0 School-wide Title I
Students: 4,060 (51.0% male; 49.0% female)
Individual Education Program: 361 (8.9%);
English Language Learner: 5 (0.1%); Migrant: 0 (0.0%)
Eligible for Free Lunch Program: 0 (0.0%)
Eligible for Reduced-Price Lunch Program: 0 (0.0%)
Teachers: 317.1 (12.8 to 1)
Librarians/Media Specialists: 7.0 (580.0 to 1)
Guidance Counselors: 12.0 (338.3 to 1)
Current Spending: ($ per student per year):
Total: $8,088; Instruction: $5,148; Support Services: $2,618

Enrollment, Drop-out Rates and Diploma Recipients by Race/Ethnicity

Category	Total	White	Black	Asian	AIAN	Hisp.
Enrollment (%)	100.0	98.6	0.1	0.9	0.0	0.4
Drop-out Rate (%)	0.4	0.4	0.0	0.0	n/a	0.0
H.S. Diplomas (#)	262	260	1	1	0	0

Vestavia Hills City SD

1204 Montgomery Hwy • Birmingham, AL 35216
Mailing Address: PO Box 660826 • Birmingham, AL 35266-0826
(205) 402-5100 • http://www.vestavia.k12.al.us/
Grade Span: KG-12; **Agency Type:** 1
Schools: 6
3 Primary; 2 Middle; 1 High; 0 Other Level
6 Regular; 0 Special Education; 0 Vocational; 0 Alternative
0 Magnet; 0 Charter; 1 Title I Eligible; 0 School-wide Title I
Students: 4,709 (52.4% male; 47.6% female)
Individual Education Program: 413 (8.8%);
English Language Learner: 35 (0.7%); Migrant: 0 (0.0%)
Eligible for Free Lunch Program: 92 (2.0%)
Eligible for Reduced-Price Lunch Program: 18 (0.4%)
Teachers: 314.3 (15.0 to 1)
Librarians/Media Specialists: 7.0 (672.7 to 1)
Guidance Counselors: 12.0 (392.4 to 1)
Current Spending: ($ per student per year):
Total: $6,348; Instruction: $4,223; Support Services: $1,824

Enrollment, Drop-out Rates and Diploma Recipients by Race/Ethnicity

Category	Total	White	Black	Asian	AIAN	Hisp.
Enrollment (%)	100.0	89.8	5.9	3.1	0.1	1.0
Drop-out Rate (%)	0.7	0.6	1.5	1.8	0.0	9.1
H.S. Diplomas (#)	343	315	11	12	0	5

Lamar County

Lamar County SD

150 Butler Cir • Vernon, AL 35592-1379
Mailing Address: PO Box 1379 • Vernon, AL 35592-1379
(205) 695-7615
Grade Span: KG-12; **Agency Type:** 1
Schools: 5
0 Primary; 0 Middle; 1 High; 4 Other Level
4 Regular; 0 Special Education; 1 Vocational; 0 Alternative
0 Magnet; 0 Charter; 4 Title I Eligible; 1 School-wide Title I
Students: 2,594 (50.3% male; 49.7% female)
Individual Education Program: 261 (10.1%);
English Language Learner: 0 (0.0%); Migrant: 0 (0.0%)
Eligible for Free Lunch Program: 987 (38.0%)
Eligible for Reduced-Price Lunch Program: 201 (7.7%)
Teachers: 166.3 (15.6 to 1)
Librarians/Media Specialists: 5.0 (518.8 to 1)
Guidance Counselors: 7.0 (370.6 to 1)
Current Spending: ($ per student per year):
Total: $5,792; Instruction: $3,334; Support Services: $1,979

Enrollment, Drop-out Rates and Diploma Recipients by Race/Ethnicity

Category	Total	White	Black	Asian	AIAN	Hisp.
Enrollment (%)	100.0	81.3	18.0	0.1	0.0	0.6
Drop-out Rate (%)	2.8	2.8	2.5	n/a	n/a	0.0
H.S. Diplomas (#)	144	129	15	0	0	0

Lauderdale County

Florence City SD

541 Riverview Dr • Florence, AL 35630-6024
(256) 768-3015 • http://www.fcs.k12.al.us/
Grade Span: PK-12; **Agency Type:** 1
Schools: 9
5 Primary; 2 Middle; 2 High; 0 Other Level
8 Regular; 1 Special Education; 0 Vocational; 0 Alternative
0 Magnet; 0 Charter; 7 Title I Eligible; 0 School-wide Title I
Students: 4,237 (51.0% male; 49.0% female)
Individual Education Program: 479 (11.3%);
English Language Learner: 108 (2.5%); Migrant: 0 (0.0%)
Eligible for Free Lunch Program: 1,981 (46.8%)
Eligible for Reduced-Price Lunch Program: 245 (5.8%)
Teachers: 287.6 (14.7 to 1)
Librarians/Media Specialists: 8.0 (529.6 to 1)
Guidance Counselors: 11.5 (368.4 to 1)
Current Spending: ($ per student per year):
Total: $7,357; Instruction: $4,562; Support Services: $2,393

Enrollment, Drop-out Rates and Diploma Recipients by Race/Ethnicity

Category	Total	White	Black	Asian	AIAN	Hisp.
Enrollment (%)	100.0	58.8	37.8	1.0	0.1	2.3
Drop-out Rate (%)	5.2	4.7	6.2	9.1	0.0	0.0
H.S. Diplomas (#)	277	202	71	2	0	2

Lauderdale County SD

355 County Rd 61 • Florence, AL 35634
Mailing Address: PO Box 278 • Florence, AL 35631-0278
(256) 760-1300 • http://www.lcschools.org/
Grade Span: KG-12; **Agency Type:** 1
Schools: 13
3 Primary; 0 Middle; 2 High; 8 Other Level
12 Regular; 0 Special Education; 1 Vocational; 0 Alternative
0 Magnet; 0 Charter; 6 Title I Eligible; 2 School-wide Title I
Students: 8,843 (52.0% male; 48.0% female)
Individual Education Program: 963 (10.9%);
English Language Learner: 26 (0.3%); Migrant: 0 (0.0%)
Eligible for Free Lunch Program: 2,211 (25.0%)
Eligible for Reduced-Price Lunch Program: 685 (7.7%)
Teachers: 540.5 (16.4 to 1)
Librarians/Media Specialists: 14.5 (609.9 to 1)
Guidance Counselors: 22.0 (402.0 to 1)
Current Spending: ($ per student per year):
Total: $5,699; Instruction: $3,594; Support Services: $1,728

Enrollment, Drop-out Rates and Diploma Recipients by Race/Ethnicity

Category	Total	White	Black	Asian	AIAN	Hisp.
Enrollment (%)	100.0	96.2	3.0	0.1	0.1	0.6
Drop-out Rate (%)	2.7	2.8	1.2	0.0	0.0	0.0
H.S. Diplomas (#)	513	493	13	5	1	1

Lawrence County

Lawrence County SD

14131 Market St • Moulton, AL 35650-1407
(256) 905-2400 • http://www.lawrenceal.org/
Grade Span: KG-12; **Agency Type:** 1
Schools: 16

5 Primary; 2 Middle; 7 High; 2 Other Level
14 Regular; 0 Special Education; 1 Vocational; 1 Alternative
0 Magnet; 0 Charter; 11 Title I Eligible; 11 School-wide Title I
Students: 5,892 (52.4% male; 47.6% female)
Individual Education Program: 610 (10.4%);
English Language Learner: 47 (0.8%); Migrant: 303 (5.1%)
Eligible for Free Lunch Program: 2,407 (40.9%)
Eligible for Reduced-Price Lunch Program: 724 (12.3%)
Teachers: 365.3 (16.1 to 1)
Librarians/Media Specialists: 12.0 (491.0 to 1)
Guidance Counselors: 13.0 (453.2 to 1)
Current Spending: ($ per student per year):
Total: $6,113; Instruction: $3,720; Support Services: $1,956
Enrollment, Drop-out Rates and Diploma Recipients by Race/Ethnicity

Category	Total	White	Black	Asian	AIAN	Hisp.
Enrollment (%)	100.0	61.5	17.4	0.1	20.2	0.8
Drop-out Rate (%)	3.4	4.5	3.0	0.0	0.5	11.1
H.S. Diplomas (#)	343	179	64	0	98	2

Lee County

Auburn City SD
855 E Samford Ave • Auburn, AL 36830
Mailing Address: PO Box 3270 • Auburn, AL 36831-3270
(334) 887-2100 • http://www.auburnschools.org/
Grade Span: KG-12; **Agency Type:** 1
Schools: 10
6 Primary; 1 Middle; 1 High; 2 Other Level
9 Regular; 0 Special Education; 1 Vocational; 0 Alternative
0 Magnet; 0 Charter; 6 Title I Eligible; 1 School-wide Title I
Students: 4,573 (49.4% male; 50.6% female)
Individual Education Program: 474 (10.4%);
English Language Learner: 65 (1.4%); Migrant: 0 (0.0%)
Eligible for Free Lunch Program: 1,115 (24.4%)
Eligible for Reduced-Price Lunch Program: 269 (5.9%)
Teachers: 299.6 (15.3 to 1)
Librarians/Media Specialists: 10.0 (457.3 to 1)
Guidance Counselors: 11.0 (415.7 to 1)
Current Spending: ($ per student per year):
Total: $6,523; Instruction: $3,952; Support Services: $2,195
Enrollment, Drop-out Rates and Diploma Recipients by Race/Ethnicity

Category	Total	White	Black	Asian	AIAN	Hisp.
Enrollment (%)	100.0	60.7	32.5	5.3	0.2	1.3
Drop-out Rate (%)	1.0	0.6	1.6	1.9	0.0	0.0
H.S. Diplomas (#)	268	184	68	14	0	2

Lee County SD
215 S 9th St • Opelika, AL 36803-0120
Mailing Address: PO Box 120 • Opelika, AL 36803-0120
(334) 745-9770 • http://www.lee.k12.al.us/indexie.html
Grade Span: PK-12; **Agency Type:** 1
Schools: 12
5 Primary; 3 Middle; 4 High; 0 Other Level
12 Regular; 0 Special Education; 0 Vocational; 0 Alternative
0 Magnet; 0 Charter; 5 Title I Eligible; 4 School-wide Title I
Students: 9,216 (51.5% male; 48.5% female)
Individual Education Program: 765 (8.3%);
English Language Learner: 6 (0.1%); Migrant: 0 (0.0%)
Eligible for Free Lunch Program: 3,041 (33.0%)
Eligible for Reduced-Price Lunch Program: 857 (9.3%)
Teachers: 600.5 (15.3 to 1)
Librarians/Media Specialists: 12.0 (768.0 to 1)
Guidance Counselors: 19.5 (472.6 to 1)
Current Spending: ($ per student per year):
Total: $5,645; Instruction: $3,548; Support Services: $1,703
Enrollment, Drop-out Rates and Diploma Recipients by Race/Ethnicity

Category	Total	White	Black	Asian	AIAN	Hisp.
Enrollment (%)	100.0	74.3	23.8	0.6	0.1	1.2
Drop-out Rate (%)	3.3	2.7	5.6	0.0	0.0	0.0
H.S. Diplomas (#)	402	295	96	1	1	9

Opelika City SD
300 Simmons St • Opelika, AL 36803-2469
Mailing Address: PO Box 2469 • Opelika, AL 36803-2469
(334) 745-9700 • http://www.opelikaschools.org/
Grade Span: PK-12; **Agency Type:** 1
Schools: 9
6 Primary; 1 Middle; 1 High; 1 Other Level
8 Regular; 0 Special Education; 0 Vocational; 1 Alternative
0 Magnet; 0 Charter; 6 Title I Eligible; 6 School-wide Title I
Students: 4,323 (51.5% male; 48.5% female)
Individual Education Program: 444 (10.3%);
English Language Learner: 81 (1.9%); Migrant: 0 (0.0%)
Eligible for Free Lunch Program: 2,214 (51.2%)
Eligible for Reduced-Price Lunch Program: 260 (6.0%)
Teachers: 286.7 (15.1 to 1)
Librarians/Media Specialists: 9.0 (480.3 to 1)
Guidance Counselors: 9.0 (480.3 to 1)
Current Spending: ($ per student per year):
Total: $6,241; Instruction: $3,909; Support Services: $1,923
Enrollment, Drop-out Rates and Diploma Recipients by Race/Ethnicity

Category	Total	White	Black	Asian	AIAN	Hisp.
Enrollment (%)	100.0	35.3	62.3	1.6	0.1	0.8
Drop-out Rate (%)	0.7	0.6	0.8	0.0	0.0	0.0
H.S. Diplomas (#)	218	106	108	1	0	3

Limestone County

Athens City SD
313 E Washington St • Athens, AL 35611-2653
(256) 233-6600 • http://www.acs-k12.org/
Grade Span: KG-12; **Agency Type:** 1
Schools: 7
4 Primary; 1 Middle; 1 High; 1 Other Level
7 Regular; 0 Special Education; 0 Vocational; 0 Alternative
0 Magnet; 0 Charter; 3 Title I Eligible; 0 School-wide Title I
Students: 2,807 (51.2% male; 48.8% female)
Individual Education Program: 290 (10.3%);
English Language Learner: 140 (5.0%); Migrant: 247 (8.8%)
Eligible for Free Lunch Program: 796 (28.4%)
Eligible for Reduced-Price Lunch Program: 185 (6.6%)
Teachers: 186.3 (15.1 to 1)
Librarians/Media Specialists: 6.0 (467.8 to 1)
Guidance Counselors: 9.0 (311.9 to 1)
Current Spending: ($ per student per year):
Total: $7,137; Instruction: $4,639; Support Services: $2,098
Enrollment, Drop-out Rates and Diploma Recipients by Race/Ethnicity

Category	Total	White	Black	Asian	AIAN	Hisp.
Enrollment (%)	100.0	66.9	24.4	1.2	0.0	7.5
Drop-out Rate (%)	5.2	4.7	5.9	0.0	n/a	14.3
H.S. Diplomas (#)	147	111	31	3	0	2

Limestone County SD
300 S Jefferson St • Athens, AL 35611-2549
(256) 232-5353 •
http://limestone.schoolinsites.com/websites/LimestoneCountySchools/LimestoneCounty/
Grade Span: KG-12; **Agency Type:** 1
Schools: 12
5 Primary; 0 Middle; 1 High; 6 Other Level
11 Regular; 0 Special Education; 1 Vocational; 0 Alternative
0 Magnet; 0 Charter; 6 Title I Eligible; 1 School-wide Title I
Students: 7,987 (51.5% male; 48.5% female)
Individual Education Program: 896 (11.2%);
English Language Learner: 150 (1.9%); Migrant: 47 (0.6%)
Eligible for Free Lunch Program: 2,296 (28.7%)
Eligible for Reduced-Price Lunch Program: 618 (7.7%)
Teachers: 516.6 (15.5 to 1)
Librarians/Media Specialists: 14.0 (570.5 to 1)
Guidance Counselors: 18.5 (431.7 to 1)
Current Spending: ($ per student per year):
Total: $6,064; Instruction: $3,899; Support Services: $1,587
Enrollment, Drop-out Rates and Diploma Recipients by Race/Ethnicity

Category	Total	White	Black	Asian	AIAN	Hisp.
Enrollment (%)	100.0	86.1	10.5	0.3	0.1	3.0
Drop-out Rate (%)	6.9	6.6	7.9	12.5	0.0	23.5
H.S. Diplomas (#)	384	336	44	2	1	1

Lowndes County

Lowndes County SD
105 E Tuskeena St • Hayneville, AL 36040-0755
Mailing Address: PO Box 755 • Hayneville, AL 36040-0755
(334) 548-2131 • http://www.lowndesboe.org/
Grade Span: KG-12; **Agency Type:** 1
Schools: 9
4 Primary; 2 Middle; 3 High; 0 Other Level
8 Regular; 0 Special Education; 1 Vocational; 0 Alternative
0 Magnet; 0 Charter; 8 Title I Eligible; 6 School-wide Title I
Students: 2,544 (50.5% male; 49.5% female)
Individual Education Program: 413 (16.2%);
English Language Learner: 0 (0.0%); Migrant: 0 (0.0%)
Eligible for Free Lunch Program: 2,192 (86.2%)
Eligible for Reduced-Price Lunch Program: 144 (5.7%)
Teachers: 158.8 (16.0 to 1)
Librarians/Media Specialists: 8.0 (318.0 to 1)
Guidance Counselors: 9.0 (282.7 to 1)
Current Spending: ($ per student per year):
Total: $6,556; Instruction: $3,512; Support Services: $2,366

Enrollment, Drop-out Rates and Diploma Recipients by Race/Ethnicity

Category	Total	White	Black	Asian	AIAN	Hisp.
Enrollment (%)	100.0	0.7	99.2	0.1	0.0	0.0
Drop-out Rate (%)	2.7	0.0	2.7	n/a	n/a	n/a
H.S. Diplomas (#)	131	0	131	0	0	0

Macon County

Macon County SD

501 S School St • Tuskegee, AL 36083-0090
Mailing Address: PO Box 830090 • Tuskegee, AL 36083-0090
(334) 727-1600 • http://www.maconk12.org/
Grade Span: PK-12; **Agency Type:** 1
Schools: 8
5 Primary; 1 Middle; 1 High; 1 Other Level
8 Regular; 0 Special Education; 0 Vocational; 0 Alternative
0 Magnet; 0 Charter; 7 Title I Eligible; 7 School-wide Title I
Students: 3,898 (50.7% male; 49.3% female)
Individual Education Program: 426 (10.9%);
English Language Learner: 0 (0.0%); Migrant: 0 (0.0%)
Eligible for Free Lunch Program: 2,809 (72.1%)
Eligible for Reduced-Price Lunch Program: 342 (8.8%)
Teachers: 233.0 (16.7 to 1)
Librarians/Media Specialists: 7.0 (556.9 to 1)
Guidance Counselors: 8.0 (487.3 to 1)
Current Spending: ($ per student per year):
Total: $5,845; Instruction: $3,545; Support Services: $1,889

Enrollment, Drop-out Rates and Diploma Recipients by Race/Ethnicity

Category	Total	White	Black	Asian	AIAN	Hisp.
Enrollment (%)	100.0	3.3	96.6	0.0	0.0	0.1
Drop-out Rate (%)	3.8	0.0	4.0	n/a	n/a	n/a
H.S. Diplomas (#)	153	7	146	0	0	0

Madison County

Huntsville City SD

200 White St • Huntsville, AL 35801-4152
Mailing Address: PO Box 1256 • Huntsville, AL 35807-4801
(256) 428-6810 • http://www.hsv.k12.al.us/
Grade Span: PK-12; **Agency Type:** 1
Schools: 48
27 Primary; 9 Middle; 7 High; 5 Other Level
43 Regular; 1 Special Education; 1 Vocational; 3 Alternative
5 Magnet; 0 Charter; 20 Title I Eligible; 20 School-wide Title I
Students: 22,643 (51.3% male; 48.7% female)
Individual Education Program: 2,839 (12.5%);
English Language Learner: 283 (1.2%); Migrant: 0 (0.0%)
Eligible for Free Lunch Program: 7,879 (34.8%)
Eligible for Reduced-Price Lunch Program: 1,431 (6.3%)
Teachers: 1,508.1 (15.0 to 1)
Librarians/Media Specialists: 44.0 (514.6 to 1)
Guidance Counselors: 67.0 (338.0 to 1)
Current Spending: ($ per student per year):
Total: $6,814; Instruction: $4,262; Support Services: $2,196

Enrollment, Drop-out Rates and Diploma Recipients by Race/Ethnicity

Category	Total	White	Black	Asian	AIAN	Hisp.
Enrollment (%)	100.0	51.5	43.0	2.6	0.4	2.5
Drop-out Rate (%)	1.9	1.7	2.4	1.0	0.0	1.0
H.S. Diplomas (#)	1,146	737	339	39	13	18

Madison City SD

4192 Sullivan St • Madison, AL 35758-1615
(256) 464-8370 • http://www.madisoncity.k12.al.us/
Grade Span: KG-12; **Agency Type:** 1
Schools: 8
5 Primary; 2 Middle; 1 High; 0 Other Level
8 Regular; 0 Special Education; 0 Vocational; 0 Alternative
0 Magnet; 0 Charter; 2 Title I Eligible; 0 School-wide Title I
Students: 6,657 (52.1% male; 47.9% female)
Individual Education Program: 721 (10.8%);
English Language Learner: 340 (5.1%); Migrant: 0 (0.0%)
Eligible for Free Lunch Program: 769 (11.6%)
Eligible for Reduced-Price Lunch Program: 204 (3.1%)
Teachers: 395.3 (16.8 to 1)
Librarians/Media Specialists: 9.0 (739.7 to 1)
Guidance Counselors: 13.1 (508.2 to 1)
Current Spending: ($ per student per year):
Total: $5,476; Instruction: $3,389; Support Services: $1,769

Enrollment, Drop-out Rates and Diploma Recipients by Race/Ethnicity

Category	Total	White	Black	Asian	AIAN	Hisp.
Enrollment (%)	100.0	72.6	19.5	4.5	1.2	2.3
Drop-out Rate (%)	0.7	0.7	0.3	0.0	3.8	0.0
H.S. Diplomas (#)	409	316	63	17	8	5

Madison County SD

1275f Jordan Rd Bldg B • Huntsville, AL 35811
Mailing Address: PO Box 226 • Huntsville, AL 35804-0226
(256) 852-2557 • http://www.madison.k12.al.us/
Grade Span: PK-12; **Agency Type:** 1
Schools: 24
13 Primary; 4 Middle; 6 High; 1 Other Level
22 Regular; 0 Special Education; 1 Vocational; 1 Alternative
0 Magnet; 0 Charter; 7 Title I Eligible; 6 School-wide Title I
Students: 16,564 (51.8% male; 48.2% female)
Individual Education Program: 1,745 (10.5%);
English Language Learner: 170 (1.0%); Migrant: 33 (0.2%)
Eligible for Free Lunch Program: 3,087 (18.6%)
Eligible for Reduced-Price Lunch Program: 1,135 (6.9%)
Teachers: 972.9 (17.0 to 1)
Librarians/Media Specialists: 24.0 (690.2 to 1)
Guidance Counselors: 39.0 (424.7 to 1)
Current Spending: ($ per student per year):
Total: $5,577; Instruction: $3,445; Support Services: $1,828

Enrollment, Drop-out Rates and Diploma Recipients by Race/Ethnicity

Category	Total	White	Black	Asian	AIAN	Hisp.
Enrollment (%)	100.0	78.3	14.4	0.8	5.3	1.2
Drop-out Rate (%)	4.2	4.4	4.5	4.2	1.5	2.7
H.S. Diplomas (#)	813	637	109	3	62	2

Marengo County

Demopolis City SD

609 S Cedar St • Demopolis, AL 36732-0759
Mailing Address: PO Box 759 • Demopolis, AL 36732-0759
(334) 289-1670 • http://www.westal.net/dcs/index.htm
Grade Span: PK-12; **Agency Type:** 1
Schools: 4
1 Primary; 0 Middle; 1 High; 2 Other Level
4 Regular; 0 Special Education; 0 Vocational; 0 Alternative
0 Magnet; 0 Charter; 2 Title I Eligible; 2 School-wide Title I
Students: 2,355 (51.3% male; 48.7% female)
Individual Education Program: 200 (8.5%);
English Language Learner: 0 (0.0%); Migrant: 0 (0.0%)
Eligible for Free Lunch Program: 1,168 (49.6%)
Eligible for Reduced-Price Lunch Program: 180 (7.6%)
Teachers: 143.2 (16.4 to 1)
Librarians/Media Specialists: 4.5 (523.3 to 1)
Guidance Counselors: 4.5 (523.3 to 1)
Current Spending: ($ per student per year):
Total: $5,504; Instruction: $3,602; Support Services: $1,473

Enrollment, Drop-out Rates and Diploma Recipients by Race/Ethnicity

Category	Total	White	Black	Asian	AIAN	Hisp.
Enrollment (%)	100.0	46.4	52.0	0.3	0.0	1.2
Drop-out Rate (%)	3.9	3.2	4.8	n/a	n/a	0.0
H.S. Diplomas (#)	106	57	49	0	0	0

Marengo County SD

101 E Coats Ave • Linden, AL 36748-0339
Mailing Address: PO Box 480339 • Linden, AL 36748-0339
(334) 295-4123
Grade Span: KG-12; **Agency Type:** 1
Schools: 4
0 Primary; 0 Middle; 0 High; 4 Other Level
4 Regular; 0 Special Education; 0 Vocational; 0 Alternative
0 Magnet; 0 Charter; 4 Title I Eligible; 4 School-wide Title I
Students: 1,707 (53.7% male; 46.3% female)
Individual Education Program: 184 (10.8%);
English Language Learner: 0 (0.0%); Migrant: 0 (0.0%)
Eligible for Free Lunch Program: 1,385 (81.1%)
Eligible for Reduced-Price Lunch Program: 105 (6.2%)
Teachers: 111.5 (15.3 to 1)
Librarians/Media Specialists: 2.9 (588.6 to 1)
Guidance Counselors: 4.3 (397.0 to 1)
Current Spending: ($ per student per year):
Total: $6,167; Instruction: $3,593; Support Services: $1,965

Enrollment, Drop-out Rates and Diploma Recipients by Race/Ethnicity

Category	Total	White	Black	Asian	AIAN	Hisp.
Enrollment (%)	100.0	14.4	85.3	0.1	0.1	0.2
Drop-out Rate (%)	3.1	3.5	3.0	n/a	0.0	0.0
H.S. Diplomas (#)	88	21	67	0	0	0

Marion County

Marion County SD

188 Winchester Dr • Hamilton, AL 35570-6626
(205) 921-9319 • http://server.mcbe.net/
Grade Span: PK-12; **Agency Type:** 1
Schools: 11
4 Primary; 1 Middle; 3 High; 3 Other Level

10 Regular; 0 Special Education; 0 Vocational; 1 Alternative
0 Magnet; 0 Charter; 5 Title I Eligible; 0 School-wide Title I
Students: 3,765 (52.5% male; 47.5% female)
Individual Education Program: 478 (12.7%);
English Language Learner: 20 (0.5%); Migrant: 0 (0.0%)
Eligible for Free Lunch Program: 1,399 (37.2%)
Eligible for Reduced-Price Lunch Program: 399 (10.6%)
Teachers: 237.5 (15.9 to 1)
Librarians/Media Specialists: 8.0 (470.6 to 1)
Guidance Counselors: 8.5 (442.9 to 1)
Current Spending: ($ per student per year):
Total: $5,572; Instruction: $3,635; Support Services: $1,596
Enrollment, Drop-out Rates and Diploma Recipients by Race/Ethnicity

Category	Total	White	Black	Asian	AIAN	Hisp.
Enrollment (%)	100.0	94.8	4.0	0.2	0.1	0.9
Drop-out Rate (%)	5.6	5.8	2.9	0.0	n/a	0.0
H.S. Diplomas (#)	190	186	3	0	0	1

Marshall County

Albertville City SD
107 W Main St • Albertville, AL 35950-0025
(256) 891-1183 • http://www.albertk12.org/
Grade Span: KG-12; **Agency Type:** 1
Schools: 5
2 Primary; 2 Middle; 1 High; 0 Other Level
5 Regular; 0 Special Education; 0 Vocational; 0 Alternative
0 Magnet; 0 Charter; 4 Title I Eligible; 3 School-wide Title I
Students: 3,576 (51.0% male; 49.0% female)
Individual Education Program: 327 (9.1%);
English Language Learner: 601 (16.8%); Migrant: 652 (18.2%)
Eligible for Free Lunch Program: 1,464 (40.9%)
Eligible for Reduced-Price Lunch Program: 279 (7.8%)
Teachers: 227.2 (15.7 to 1)
Librarians/Media Specialists: 7.0 (510.9 to 1)
Guidance Counselors: 7.0 (510.9 to 1)
Current Spending: ($ per student per year):
Total: $5,764; Instruction: $3,685; Support Services: $1,714
Enrollment, Drop-out Rates and Diploma Recipients by Race/Ethnicity

Category	Total	White	Black	Asian	AIAN	Hisp.
Enrollment (%)	100.0	78.7	2.1	0.3	0.0	18.9
Drop-out Rate (%)	4.2	4.4	0.0	0.0	0.0	1.7
H.S. Diplomas (#)	140	132	2	1	0	5

Arab City SD
750 Arabian Dr NE • Arab, AL 35016-0740
(256) 586-6011 • http://www.arabcityschools.org/
Grade Span: PK-12; **Agency Type:** 1
Schools: 4
2 Primary; 1 Middle; 1 High; 0 Other Level
4 Regular; 0 Special Education; 0 Vocational; 0 Alternative
0 Magnet; 0 Charter; 2 Title I Eligible; 0 School-wide Title I
Students: 2,704 (52.0% male; 48.0% female)
Individual Education Program: 285 (10.5%);
English Language Learner: 33 (1.2%); Migrant: 0 (0.0%)
Eligible for Free Lunch Program: 435 (16.1%)
Eligible for Reduced-Price Lunch Program: 129 (4.8%)
Teachers: 167.5 (16.1 to 1)
Librarians/Media Specialists: 5.0 (540.8 to 1)
Guidance Counselors: 6.0 (450.7 to 1)
Current Spending: ($ per student per year):
Total: $5,488; Instruction: $3,432; Support Services: $1,704
Enrollment, Drop-out Rates and Diploma Recipients by Race/Ethnicity

Category	Total	White	Black	Asian	AIAN	Hisp.
Enrollment (%)	100.0	99.0	0.0	0.3	0.1	0.6
Drop-out Rate (%)	4.8	4.8	n/a	0.0	0.0	33.3
H.S. Diplomas (#)	191	191	0	0	0	0

Guntersville City SD
2208 Ringold St • Guntersville, AL 35976-0129
Mailing Address: PO Box 129 • Guntersville, AL 35976-0129
(256) 582-3159 • http://www.guntersvilleboe.com/
Grade Span: KG-12; **Agency Type:** 1
Schools: 4
1 Primary; 1 Middle; 1 High; 1 Other Level
4 Regular; 0 Special Education; 0 Vocational; 0 Alternative
0 Magnet; 0 Charter; 3 Title I Eligible; 1 School-wide Title I
Students: 1,814 (51.8% male; 48.2% female)
Individual Education Program: 181 (10.0%);
English Language Learner: 24 (1.3%); Migrant: 0 (0.0%)
Eligible for Free Lunch Program: 581 (32.0%)
Eligible for Reduced-Price Lunch Program: 106 (5.8%)
Teachers: 122.6 (14.8 to 1)
Librarians/Media Specialists: 4.0 (453.5 to 1)
Guidance Counselors: 5.0 (362.8 to 1)
Current Spending: ($ per student per year):
Total: $6,298; Instruction: $3,845; Support Services: $1,987
Enrollment, Drop-out Rates and Diploma Recipients by Race/Ethnicity

Category	Total	White	Black	Asian	AIAN	Hisp.
Enrollment (%)	100.0	85.5	12.4	0.6	0.0	1.5
Drop-out Rate (%)	5.2	5.1	7.1	0.0	n/a	0.0
H.S. Diplomas (#)	93	81	9	1	0	2

Marshall County SD
12380 US Hwy 431 S • Guntersville, AL 35976-9351
(256) 582-3171 • http://www.marshallk12.org/
Grade Span: PK-12; **Agency Type:** 1
Schools: 19
8 Primary; 4 Middle; 4 High; 3 Other Level
18 Regular; 0 Special Education; 0 Vocational; 1 Alternative
0 Magnet; 0 Charter; 14 Title I Eligible; 11 School-wide Title I
Students: 7,011 (53.0% male; 47.0% female)
Individual Education Program: 876 (12.5%);
English Language Learner: 322 (4.6%); Migrant: 102 (1.5%)
Eligible for Free Lunch Program: 2,946 (42.0%)
Eligible for Reduced-Price Lunch Program: 767 (10.9%)
Teachers: 411.2 (17.1 to 1)
Librarians/Media Specialists: 16.0 (438.2 to 1)
Guidance Counselors: 18.0 (389.5 to 1)
Current Spending: ($ per student per year):
Total: $6,200; Instruction: $3,504; Support Services: $2,199
Enrollment, Drop-out Rates and Diploma Recipients by Race/Ethnicity

Category	Total	White	Black	Asian	AIAN	Hisp.
Enrollment (%)	100.0	94.0	0.4	0.3	0.1	5.3
Drop-out Rate (%)	6.3	6.4	0.0	0.0	0.0	3.8
H.S. Diplomas (#)	281	278	1	0	0	2

Mobile County

Mobile County SD
504 Government St • Mobile, AL 36602-2098
Mailing Address: PO Box 1327 • Mobile, AL 36633-1327
(334) 690-8227 • http://www.mcpss.com/
Grade Span: PK-12; **Agency Type:** 1
Schools: 103
59 Primary; 21 Middle; 17 High; 6 Other Level
94 Regular; 2 Special Education; 2 Vocational; 5 Alternative
8 Magnet; 0 Charter; 78 Title I Eligible; 70 School-wide Title I
Students: 64,058 (51.7% male; 48.3% female)
Individual Education Program: 9,506 (14.8%);
English Language Learner: 685 (1.1%); Migrant: 1,623 (2.5%)
Eligible for Free Lunch Program: 36,766 (57.4%)
Eligible for Reduced-Price Lunch Program: 6,146 (9.6%)
Teachers: 4,050.7 (15.8 to 1)
Librarians/Media Specialists: 108.3 (591.5 to 1)
Guidance Counselors: 138.0 (464.2 to 1)
Current Spending: ($ per student per year):
Total: $5,404; Instruction: $3,390; Support Services: $1,629
Enrollment, Drop-out Rates and Diploma Recipients by Race/Ethnicity

Category	Total	White	Black	Asian	AIAN	Hisp.
Enrollment (%)	100.0	46.5	50.0	2.0	0.9	0.6
Drop-out Rate (%)	5.0	4.8	5.2	4.0	15.8	5.6
H.S. Diplomas (#)	2,854	1,415	1,343	65	23	8

Monroe County

Monroe County SD
Courthouse Room 127 • Monroeville, AL 36460
Mailing Address: Box 967 • Monroeville, AL 36461-0967
(334) 575-2168 • http://www.monroe.k12.al.us/
Grade Span: PK-12; **Agency Type:** 1
Schools: 13
4 Primary; 1 Middle; 4 High; 4 Other Level
11 Regular; 0 Special Education; 1 Vocational; 1 Alternative
0 Magnet; 0 Charter; 11 Title I Eligible; 8 School-wide Title I
Students: 4,388 (52.0% male; 48.0% female)
Individual Education Program: 455 (10.4%);
English Language Learner: 4 (0.1%); Migrant: 0 (0.0%)
Eligible for Free Lunch Program: 2,397 (54.6%)
Eligible for Reduced-Price Lunch Program: 406 (9.3%)
Teachers: 278.6 (15.8 to 1)
Librarians/Media Specialists: 9.0 (487.6 to 1)
Guidance Counselors: 9.0 (487.6 to 1)
Current Spending: ($ per student per year):
Total: $5,726; Instruction: $3,624; Support Services: $1,701
Enrollment, Drop-out Rates and Diploma Recipients by Race/Ethnicity

Category	Total	White	Black	Asian	AIAN	Hisp.
Enrollment (%)	100.0	41.2	56.6	1.2	0.8	0.2
Drop-out Rate (%)	4.7	6.1	3.6	0.0	12.5	0.0
H.S. Diplomas (#)	248	111	135	1	1	0

Montgomery County

Montgomery County SD
307 S Decatur St • Montgomery, AL 36104
Mailing Address: PO Box 1991 • Montgomery, AL 36102-1991
(334) 223-6710 • http://www.mps.k12.al.us/
Grade Span: PK-12; **Agency Type:** 1
Schools: 62
36 Primary; 12 Middle; 9 High; 5 Other Level
55 Regular; 3 Special Education; 0 Vocational; 4 Alternative
10 Magnet; 0 Charter; 32 Title I Eligible; 26 School-wide Title I
Students: 32,912 (51.4% male; 48.6% female)
Individual Education Program: 3,991 (12.1%);
English Language Learner: 403 (1.2%); Migrant: 0 (0.0%)
Eligible for Free Lunch Program: 19,199 (58.3%)
Eligible for Reduced-Price Lunch Program: 2,388 (7.3%)
Teachers: 2,131.9 (15.4 to 1)
Librarians/Media Specialists: 59.0 (557.8 to 1)
Guidance Counselors: 79.0 (416.6 to 1)
Current Spending: ($ per student per year):
Total: $5,728; Instruction: $3,475; Support Services: $1,874
Enrollment, Drop-out Rates and Diploma Recipients by Race/Ethnicity

Category	Total	White	Black	Asian	AIAN	Hisp.
Enrollment (%)	100.0	23.1	74.5	1.4	0.1	0.9
Drop-out Rate (%)	4.6	4.0	4.9	4.1	0.0	0.0
H.S. Diplomas (#)	1,607	473	1,101	17	4	12

Morgan County

Decatur City SD
302 4th Ave NE • Decatur, AL 35601-1972
(256) 552-3000 • http://www.dcs.edu/
Grade Span: PK-12; **Agency Type:** 1
Schools: 17
12 Primary; 3 Middle; 2 High; 0 Other Level
17 Regular; 0 Special Education; 0 Vocational; 0 Alternative
2 Magnet; 0 Charter; 5 Title I Eligible; 5 School-wide Title I
Students: 8,831 (50.1% male; 49.9% female)
Individual Education Program: 1,055 (11.9%);
English Language Learner: 489 (5.5%); Migrant: 387 (4.4%)
Eligible for Free Lunch Program: 3,258 (36.9%)
Eligible for Reduced-Price Lunch Program: 503 (5.7%)
Teachers: 592.0 (14.9 to 1)
Librarians/Media Specialists: 20.0 (441.6 to 1)
Guidance Counselors: 30.0 (294.4 to 1)
Current Spending: ($ per student per year):
Total: $6,755; Instruction: $4,096; Support Services: $2,226
Enrollment, Drop-out Rates and Diploma Recipients by Race/Ethnicity

Category	Total	White	Black	Asian	AIAN	Hisp.
Enrollment (%)	100.0	58.6	32.1	0.7	0.3	8.2
Drop-out Rate (%)	2.8	2.4	3.0	0.0	0.0	7.9
H.S. Diplomas (#)	406	307	90	4	0	5

Hartselle City SD
305 College St NE • Hartselle, AL 35640-2357
(256) 773-5419 • http://www.hcs.k12.al.us/
Grade Span: PK-12; **Agency Type:** 1
Schools: 6
3 Primary; 1 Middle; 2 High; 0 Other Level
5 Regular; 0 Special Education; 1 Vocational; 0 Alternative
0 Magnet; 0 Charter; 2 Title I Eligible; 0 School-wide Title I
Students: 3,067 (52.7% male; 47.3% female)
Individual Education Program: 391 (12.7%);
English Language Learner: 31 (1.0%); Migrant: 29 (0.9%)
Eligible for Free Lunch Program: 513 (16.7%)
Eligible for Reduced-Price Lunch Program: 144 (4.7%)
Teachers: 194.3 (15.8 to 1)
Librarians/Media Specialists: 5.0 (613.4 to 1)
Guidance Counselors: 7.0 (438.1 to 1)
Current Spending: ($ per student per year):
Total: $6,058; Instruction: $3,816; Support Services: $1,878
Enrollment, Drop-out Rates and Diploma Recipients by Race/Ethnicity

Category	Total	White	Black	Asian	AIAN	Hisp.
Enrollment (%)	100.0	92.3	5.7	0.2	0.4	1.4
Drop-out Rate (%)	3.1	3.1	4.2	0.0	0.0	0.0
H.S. Diplomas (#)	171	161	7	2	0	1

Morgan County SD
1325 Point Mallard Pkwy SE • Decatur, AL 35601-6542
(256) 353-6442 • http://www.morgank12.org/
Grade Span: PK-12; **Agency Type:** 1
Schools: 18
9 Primary; 1 Middle; 5 High; 3 Other Level
16 Regular; 0 Special Education; 1 Vocational; 1 Alternative
0 Magnet; 0 Charter; 9 Title I Eligible; 3 School-wide Title I
Students: 7,414 (52.0% male; 48.0% female)
Individual Education Program: 1,234 (16.6%);
English Language Learner: 45 (0.6%); Migrant: 308 (4.2%)
Eligible for Free Lunch Program: 2,234 (30.1%)
Eligible for Reduced-Price Lunch Program: 642 (8.7%)
Teachers: 509.1 (14.6 to 1)
Librarians/Media Specialists: 14.5 (511.3 to 1)
Guidance Counselors: 17.4 (426.1 to 1)
Current Spending: ($ per student per year):
Total: $6,627; Instruction: $3,853; Support Services: $2,304
Enrollment, Drop-out Rates and Diploma Recipients by Race/Ethnicity

Category	Total	White	Black	Asian	AIAN	Hisp.
Enrollment (%)	100.0	95.3	3.0	0.3	0.5	1.0
Drop-out Rate (%)	3.6	3.6	1.8	12.5	0.0	0.0
H.S. Diplomas (#)	381	370	7	1	1	2

Perry County

Perry County SD
200 Monroe St • Marion, AL 36756-0900
Mailing Address: PO Box 900 • Marion, AL 36756-0900
(334) 683-6528
Grade Span: KG-12; **Agency Type:** 1
Schools: 4
2 Primary; 0 Middle; 2 High; 0 Other Level
4 Regular; 0 Special Education; 0 Vocational; 0 Alternative
0 Magnet; 0 Charter; 4 Title I Eligible; 4 School-wide Title I
Students: 2,204 (51.3% male; 48.7% female)
Individual Education Program: 302 (13.7%);
English Language Learner: 0 (0.0%); Migrant: 0 (0.0%)
Eligible for Free Lunch Program: 2,005 (91.0%)
Eligible for Reduced-Price Lunch Program: 89 (4.0%)
Teachers: 142.7 (15.4 to 1)
Librarians/Media Specialists: 4.0 (551.0 to 1)
Guidance Counselors: 4.0 (551.0 to 1)
Current Spending: ($ per student per year):
Total: $5,833; Instruction: $3,543; Support Services: $1,783
Enrollment, Drop-out Rates and Diploma Recipients by Race/Ethnicity

Category	Total	White	Black	Asian	AIAN	Hisp.
Enrollment (%)	100.0	0.8	99.2	0.0	0.0	0.0
Drop-out Rate (%)	6.8	0.0	6.9	n/a	n/a	n/a
H.S. Diplomas (#)	120	2	118	0	0	0

Pickens County

Pickens County SD
50 Court Square • Carrollton, AL 35447-0032
Mailing Address: PO Box 32 • Carrollton, AL 35447-0032
(205) 367-2080 • http://www.pickens.k12.al.us/
Grade Span: PK-12; **Agency Type:** 1
Schools: 10
3 Primary; 1 Middle; 4 High; 2 Other Level
8 Regular; 0 Special Education; 1 Vocational; 1 Alternative
0 Magnet; 0 Charter; 8 Title I Eligible; 7 School-wide Title I
Students: 3,364 (50.8% male; 49.2% female)
Individual Education Program: 408 (12.1%);
English Language Learner: 0 (0.0%); Migrant: 0 (0.0%)
Eligible for Free Lunch Program: 2,022 (60.1%)
Eligible for Reduced-Price Lunch Program: 363 (10.8%)
Teachers: 222.8 (15.1 to 1)
Librarians/Media Specialists: 8.0 (420.5 to 1)
Guidance Counselors: 9.1 (369.7 to 1)
Current Spending: ($ per student per year):
Total: $6,039; Instruction: $3,722; Support Services: $1,877
Enrollment, Drop-out Rates and Diploma Recipients by Race/Ethnicity

Category	Total	White	Black	Asian	AIAN	Hisp.
Enrollment (%)	100.0	34.7	64.9	0.1	0.0	0.3
Drop-out Rate (%)	5.5	6.2	5.1	0.0	n/a	0.0
H.S. Diplomas (#)	214	85	129	0	0	0

Pike County

Pike County SD
101 W Love St • Troy, AL 36081-4231
(334) 566-1850 • http://www.pikecountyschools.com/
Grade Span: KG-12; **Agency Type:** 1
Schools: 6
3 Primary; 0 Middle; 2 High; 1 Other Level
5 Regular; 0 Special Education; 1 Vocational; 0 Alternative
0 Magnet; 0 Charter; 5 Title I Eligible; 5 School-wide Title I
Students: 2,124 (54.4% male; 45.6% female)
Individual Education Program: 364 (17.1%);
English Language Learner: 7 (0.3%); Migrant: 323 (15.2%)
Eligible for Free Lunch Program: 1,510 (71.1%)
Eligible for Reduced-Price Lunch Program: 269 (12.7%)

Teachers: 132.5 (16.0 to 1)
Librarians/Media Specialists: 5.0 (424.8 to 1)
Guidance Counselors: 5.0 (424.8 to 1)
Current Spending: ($ per student per year):
Total: $6,782; Instruction: $3,547; Support Services: $2,786
Enrollment, Drop-out Rates and Diploma Recipients by Race/Ethnicity

Category	Total	White	Black	Asian	AIAN	Hisp.
Enrollment (%)	100.0	44.0	55.0	0.2	0.5	0.3
Drop-out Rate (%)	6.9	8.9	5.6	0.0	0.0	0.0
H.S. Diplomas (#)	80	39	40	0	0	1

Troy City SD
500 Elm St • Troy, AL 36081-0529
Mailing Address: PO Box 529 • Troy, AL 36081-0529
(334) 566-3741 • http://www.troyschools.net/
Grade Span: KG-12; **Agency Type:** 1
Schools: 5
1 Primary; 1 Middle; 2 High; 1 Other Level
3 Regular; 0 Special Education; 1 Vocational; 1 Alternative
0 Magnet; 0 Charter; 2 Title I Eligible; 2 School-wide Title I
Students: 2,349 (52.2% male; 47.8% female)
Individual Education Program: 270 (11.5%);
English Language Learner: 15 (0.6%); Migrant: 14 (0.6%)
Eligible for Free Lunch Program: 1,154 (49.1%)
Eligible for Reduced-Price Lunch Program: 117 (5.0%)
Teachers: 147.9 (15.9 to 1)
Librarians/Media Specialists: 3.0 (783.0 to 1)
Guidance Counselors: 6.0 (391.5 to 1)
Current Spending: ($ per student per year):
Total: $5,523; Instruction: $3,418; Support Services: $1,700
Enrollment, Drop-out Rates and Diploma Recipients by Race/Ethnicity

Category	Total	White	Black	Asian	AIAN	Hisp.
Enrollment (%)	100.0	42.3	56.3	0.9	0.1	0.3
Drop-out Rate (%)	2.1	1.8	2.4	0.0	0.0	0.0
H.S. Diplomas (#)	107	36	69	1	1	0

Randolph County

Randolph County SD
2 Main St N • Wedowee, AL 36278-0288
Mailing Address: PO Box 288 • Wedowee, AL 36278-0288
(256) 357-4611 • http://www.randolph.k12.al.us/
Grade Span: KG-12; **Agency Type:** 1
Schools: 6
1 Primary; 0 Middle; 1 High; 4 Other Level
5 Regular; 0 Special Education; 1 Vocational; 0 Alternative
0 Magnet; 0 Charter; 4 Title I Eligible; 3 School-wide Title I
Students: 2,287 (51.8% male; 48.2% female)
Individual Education Program: 268 (11.7%);
English Language Learner: 16 (0.7%); Migrant: 0 (0.0%)
Eligible for Free Lunch Program: 952 (41.6%)
Eligible for Reduced-Price Lunch Program: 250 (10.9%)
Teachers: 143.2 (16.0 to 1)
Librarians/Media Specialists: 4.0 (571.8 to 1)
Guidance Counselors: 6.5 (351.8 to 1)
Current Spending: ($ per student per year):
Total: $5,470; Instruction: $3,329; Support Services: $1,756
Enrollment, Drop-out Rates and Diploma Recipients by Race/Ethnicity

Category	Total	White	Black	Asian	AIAN	Hisp.
Enrollment (%)	100.0	78.3	20.0	0.1	0.0	1.5
Drop-out Rate (%)	4.8	4.5	5.4	n/a	n/a	n/a
H.S. Diplomas (#)	84	66	18	0	0	0

Russell County

Phenix City City SD
1212 9th Ave • Phenix City, AL 36867
Mailing Address: PO Box 460 • Phenix City, AL 36868-0460
(334) 298-0534 • http://www.pcboe.net/
Grade Span: KG-12; **Agency Type:** 1
Schools: 9
6 Primary; 2 Middle; 1 High; 0 Other Level
9 Regular; 0 Special Education; 0 Vocational; 0 Alternative
1 Magnet; 0 Charter; 7 Title I Eligible; 5 School-wide Title I
Students: 5,062 (51.2% male; 48.8% female)
Individual Education Program: 599 (11.8%);
English Language Learner: 0 (0.0%); Migrant: 0 (0.0%)
Eligible for Free Lunch Program: 2,824 (55.8%)
Eligible for Reduced-Price Lunch Program: 365 (7.2%)
Teachers: 296.5 (17.1 to 1)
Librarians/Media Specialists: 9.0 (562.4 to 1)
Guidance Counselors: 12.0 (421.8 to 1)
Current Spending: ($ per student per year):
Total: $6,048; Instruction: $3,429; Support Services: $2,087
Enrollment, Drop-out Rates and Diploma Recipients by Race/Ethnicity

Category	Total	White	Black	Asian	AIAN	Hisp.
Enrollment (%)	100.0	35.9	62.7	0.4	0.0	0.9
Drop-out Rate (%)	3.3	3.3	3.3	0.0	n/a	0.0
H.S. Diplomas (#)	146	70	71	1	0	4

Russell County SD
506 14th St • Phenix City, AL 36867
Mailing Address: PO Box 400 • Phenix City, AL 36868-0400
(334) 298-8791 • http://www.russellcountyschools.org/
Grade Span: PK-12; **Agency Type:** 1
Schools: 11
6 Primary; 1 Middle; 3 High; 1 Other Level
8 Regular; 1 Special Education; 1 Vocational; 1 Alternative
0 Magnet; 0 Charter; 7 Title I Eligible; 7 School-wide Title I
Students: 3,725 (51.3% male; 48.7% female)
Individual Education Program: 344 (9.2%);
English Language Learner: 15 (0.4%); Migrant: 0 (0.0%)
Eligible for Free Lunch Program: 2,175 (58.4%)
Eligible for Reduced-Price Lunch Program: 387 (10.4%)
Teachers: 236.8 (15.7 to 1)
Librarians/Media Specialists: 7.0 (532.1 to 1)
Guidance Counselors: 9.0 (413.9 to 1)
Current Spending: ($ per student per year):
Total: $5,780; Instruction: $3,412; Support Services: $1,866
Enrollment, Drop-out Rates and Diploma Recipients by Race/Ethnicity

Category	Total	White	Black	Asian	AIAN	Hisp.
Enrollment (%)	100.0	56.2	41.4	0.8	0.1	1.5
Drop-out Rate (%)	8.9	11.0	6.8	0.0	n/a	8.3
H.S. Diplomas (#)	121	56	62	0	0	3

Shelby County

Shelby County SD
410 E College St • Columbiana, AL 35051-0429
Mailing Address: PO Box 1910 • Columbiana, AL 35051-0429
(205) 682-7000 • http://www.shelbyed.k12.al.us/
Grade Span: KG-12; **Agency Type:** 1
Schools: 34
16 Primary; 7 Middle; 8 High; 3 Other Level
31 Regular; 1 Special Education; 2 Vocational; 0 Alternative
0 Magnet; 0 Charter; 10 Title I Eligible; 7 School-wide Title I
Students: 21,629 (52.2% male; 47.8% female)
Individual Education Program: 2,747 (12.7%);
English Language Learner: 573 (2.6%); Migrant: 0 (0.0%)
Eligible for Free Lunch Program: 3,641 (16.8%)
Eligible for Reduced-Price Lunch Program: 1,102 (5.1%)
Teachers: 1,445.2 (15.0 to 1)
Librarians/Media Specialists: 34.0 (636.1 to 1)
Guidance Counselors: 51.0 (424.1 to 1)
Current Spending: ($ per student per year):
Total: $6,409; Instruction: $3,840; Support Services: $2,118
Enrollment, Drop-out Rates and Diploma Recipients by Race/Ethnicity

Category	Total	White	Black	Asian	AIAN	Hisp.
Enrollment (%)	100.0	84.0	11.4	1.4	0.1	3.0
Drop-out Rate (%)	3.1	3.1	2.8	0.0	0.0	7.5
H.S. Diplomas (#)	1,040	915	103	12	2	8

St. Clair County

Pell City City SD
25 Williamson Dr • Pell City, AL 35125-1227
(205) 884-4440 • http://www.pell.k12.al.us/
Grade Span: PK-12; **Agency Type:** 1
Schools: 7
4 Primary; 2 Middle; 1 High; 0 Other Level
7 Regular; 0 Special Education; 0 Vocational; 0 Alternative
0 Magnet; 0 Charter; 4 Title I Eligible; 3 School-wide Title I
Students: 3,913 (52.4% male; 47.6% female)
Individual Education Program: 679 (17.4%);
English Language Learner: 14 (0.4%); Migrant: 0 (0.0%)
Eligible for Free Lunch Program: 1,408 (36.0%)
Eligible for Reduced-Price Lunch Program: 330 (8.4%)
Teachers: 236.3 (16.6 to 1)
Librarians/Media Specialists: 8.0 (489.1 to 1)
Guidance Counselors: 8.0 (489.1 to 1)
Current Spending: ($ per student per year):
Total: $5,530; Instruction: $3,439; Support Services: $1,668
Enrollment, Drop-out Rates and Diploma Recipients by Race/Ethnicity

Category	Total	White	Black	Asian	AIAN	Hisp.
Enrollment (%)	100.0	85.4	12.9	0.2	0.2	1.2
Drop-out Rate (%)	7.1	7.4	5.4	0.0	0.0	11.1
H.S. Diplomas (#)	185	170	14	1	0	0

Saint Clair County SD

33205 US Hwy 231 • Ashville, AL 35953-0248
(205) 594-7131 • http://www.stclaircountyschools.net/
Grade Span: PK-12; **Agency Type:** 1
Schools: 17
5 Primary; 5 Middle; 5 High; 2 Other Level
15 Regular; 0 Special Education; 1 Vocational; 1 Alternative
0 Magnet; 0 Charter; 6 Title I Eligible; 4 School-wide Title I
Students: 7,144 (53.9% male; 46.1% female)
Individual Education Program: 915 (12.8%);
English Language Learner: 49 (0.7%); Migrant: 276 (3.9%)
Eligible for Free Lunch Program: 2,038 (28.5%)
Eligible for Reduced-Price Lunch Program: 686 (9.6%)
Teachers: 434.8 (16.4 to 1)
Librarians/Media Specialists: 14.0 (510.3 to 1)
Guidance Counselors: 16.3 (438.3 to 1)
Current Spending: ($ per student per year):
Total: $4,892; Instruction: $3,201; Support Services: $1,365
Enrollment, Drop-out Rates and Diploma Recipients by Race/Ethnicity

Category	Total	White	Black	Asian	AIAN	Hisp.
Enrollment (%)	100.0	89.6	8.3	0.3	0.4	1.5
Drop-out Rate (%)	4.1	3.9	7.1	0.0	0.0	0.0
H.S. Diplomas (#)	330	302	25	1	1	1

Sumter County

Sumter County SD

Hwy 28 To Country Club Dr • Livingston, AL 35470-0010
Mailing Address: PO Box 10 • Livingston, AL 35470-0010
(205) 652-9605
Grade Span: PK-12; **Agency Type:** 1
Schools: 7
3 Primary; 0 Middle; 3 High; 1 Other Level
6 Regular; 0 Special Education; 1 Vocational; 0 Alternative
0 Magnet; 0 Charter; 6 Title I Eligible; 6 School-wide Title I
Students: 2,705 (51.5% male; 48.5% female)
Individual Education Program: 371 (13.7%);
English Language Learner: 3 (0.1%); Migrant: 0 (0.0%)
Eligible for Free Lunch Program: 2,413 (89.2%)
Eligible for Reduced-Price Lunch Program: 168 (6.2%)
Teachers: 169.3 (16.0 to 1)
Librarians/Media Specialists: 6.2 (436.3 to 1)
Guidance Counselors: 6.0 (450.8 to 1)
Current Spending: ($ per student per year):
Total: $6,571; Instruction: $4,006; Support Services: $2,039
Enrollment, Drop-out Rates and Diploma Recipients by Race/Ethnicity

Category	Total	White	Black	Asian	AIAN	Hisp.
Enrollment (%)	100.0	0.1	99.7	0.0	0.0	0.1
Drop-out Rate (%)	0.4	0.0	0.4	n/a	0.0	n/a
H.S. Diplomas (#)	143	0	143	0	0	0

Talladega County

Sylacauga City SD

605 W 4th St • Sylacauga, AL 35150-1941
(256) 245-5256 • http://www.sylacauga.k12.al.us/
Grade Span: KG-12; **Agency Type:** 1
Schools: 6
2 Primary; 2 Middle; 2 High; 0 Other Level
5 Regular; 0 Special Education; 0 Vocational; 1 Alternative
0 Magnet; 0 Charter; 3 Title I Eligible; 2 School-wide Title I
Students: 2,290 (49.7% male; 50.3% female)
Individual Education Program: 269 (11.7%);
English Language Learner: 0 (0.0%); Migrant: 0 (0.0%)
Eligible for Free Lunch Program: 884 (38.6%)
Eligible for Reduced-Price Lunch Program: 161 (7.0%)
Teachers: 146.6 (15.6 to 1)
Librarians/Media Specialists: 5.0 (458.0 to 1)
Guidance Counselors: 6.0 (381.7 to 1)
Current Spending: ($ per student per year):
Total: $6,344; Instruction: $3,927; Support Services: $1,977
Enrollment, Drop-out Rates and Diploma Recipients by Race/Ethnicity

Category	Total	White	Black	Asian	AIAN	Hisp.
Enrollment (%)	100.0	61.6	37.1	0.6	0.1	0.6
Drop-out Rate (%)	1.2	1.6	0.4	0.0	0.0	0.0
H.S. Diplomas (#)	128	87	40	1	0	0

Talladega City SD

501 S St E • Talladega, AL 35160-2532
(256) 315-5600
Grade Span: KG-12; **Agency Type:** 1
Schools: 9
4 Primary; 1 Middle; 2 High; 2 Other Level
8 Regular; 0 Special Education; 1 Vocational; 0 Alternative
0 Magnet; 0 Charter; 5 Title I Eligible; 4 School-wide Title I
Students: 2,885 (50.9% male; 49.1% female)
Individual Education Program: 428 (14.8%);
English Language Learner: 0 (0.0%); Migrant: 0 (0.0%)
Eligible for Free Lunch Program: 1,609 (55.8%)
Eligible for Reduced-Price Lunch Program: 290 (10.1%)
Teachers: 183.6 (15.7 to 1)
Librarians/Media Specialists: 7.0 (412.1 to 1)
Guidance Counselors: 7.0 (412.1 to 1)
Current Spending: ($ per student per year):
Total: $6,288; Instruction: $3,858; Support Services: $1,959
Enrollment, Drop-out Rates and Diploma Recipients by Race/Ethnicity

Category	Total	White	Black	Asian	AIAN	Hisp.
Enrollment (%)	100.0	44.6	54.9	0.1	0.1	0.3
Drop-out Rate (%)	4.9	5.1	4.9	0.0	0.0	0.0
H.S. Diplomas (#)	150	80	70	0	0	0

Talladega County SD

106 W S St • Talladega, AL 35160-2455
Mailing Address: PO Box 887 • Talladega, AL 35161-0887
(256) 315-5100 • http://www.tcboe.org/
Grade Span: KG-12; **Agency Type:** 1
Schools: 18
7 Primary; 2 Middle; 6 High; 3 Other Level
16 Regular; 0 Special Education; 1 Vocational; 1 Alternative
0 Magnet; 0 Charter; 12 Title I Eligible; 11 School-wide Title I
Students: 7,773 (51.8% male; 48.2% female)
Individual Education Program: 910 (11.7%);
English Language Learner: 29 (0.4%); Migrant: 0 (0.0%)
Eligible for Free Lunch Program: 3,948 (50.8%)
Eligible for Reduced-Price Lunch Program: 1,019 (13.1%)
Teachers: 443.8 (17.5 to 1)
Librarians/Media Specialists: 15.0 (518.2 to 1)
Guidance Counselors: 16.0 (485.8 to 1)
Current Spending: ($ per student per year):
Total: $5,746; Instruction: $3,219; Support Services: $2,079
Enrollment, Drop-out Rates and Diploma Recipients by Race/Ethnicity

Category	Total	White	Black	Asian	AIAN	Hisp.
Enrollment (%)	100.0	58.1	41.1	0.2	0.1	0.5
Drop-out Rate (%)	4.6	5.7	3.1	n/a	n/a	0.0
H.S. Diplomas (#)	341	202	137	1	0	1

Tallapoosa County

Alexander City City SD

368 Wilson St • Alexander City, AL 35010-2053
Mailing Address: PO Box 1205 • Alexander City, AL 35011-1205
(256) 234-5074 • http://www.alex.k12.al.us/
Grade Span: KG-12; **Agency Type:** 1
Schools: 6
2 Primary; 1 Middle; 2 High; 1 Other Level
5 Regular; 0 Special Education; 1 Vocational; 0 Alternative
0 Magnet; 0 Charter; 5 Title I Eligible; 0 School-wide Title I
Students: 3,543 (51.2% male; 48.8% female)
Individual Education Program: 444 (12.5%);
English Language Learner: 21 (0.6%); Migrant: 0 (0.0%)
Eligible for Free Lunch Program: 1,342 (37.9%)
Eligible for Reduced-Price Lunch Program: 208 (5.9%)
Teachers: 240.8 (14.7 to 1)
Librarians/Media Specialists: 5.0 (708.6 to 1)
Guidance Counselors: 9.8 (361.5 to 1)
Current Spending: ($ per student per year):
Total: $5,779; Instruction: $3,736; Support Services: $1,746
Enrollment, Drop-out Rates and Diploma Recipients by Race/Ethnicity

Category	Total	White	Black	Asian	AIAN	Hisp.
Enrollment (%)	100.0	59.0	39.3	0.5	0.0	1.1
Drop-out Rate (%)	4.6	4.3	5.4	0.0	n/a	0.0
H.S. Diplomas (#)	168	114	51	2	0	1

Tallapoosa County SD

125 N Broadnax St, Rm 113 • Dadeville, AL 36853-1371
(256) 825-1020 • http://www2.webshoppe.net./users/tapcobord/index.html
Grade Span: KG-12; **Agency Type:** 1
Schools: 7
2 Primary; 0 Middle; 2 High; 3 Other Level
6 Regular; 0 Special Education; 1 Vocational; 0 Alternative
0 Magnet; 0 Charter; 4 Title I Eligible; 3 School-wide Title I
Students: 3,369 (52.3% male; 47.7% female)
Individual Education Program: 539 (16.0%);
English Language Learner: 0 (0.0%); Migrant: 0 (0.0%)
Eligible for Free Lunch Program: 1,614 (47.9%)
Eligible for Reduced-Price Lunch Program: 248 (7.4%)
Teachers: 224.7 (15.0 to 1)
Librarians/Media Specialists: 5.5 (612.5 to 1)
Guidance Counselors: 6.5 (518.3 to 1)
Current Spending: ($ per student per year):
Total: $5,968; Instruction: $3,779; Support Services: $1,726

Enrollment, Drop-out Rates and Diploma Recipients by Race/Ethnicity

Category	Total	White	Black	Asian	AIAN	Hisp.
Enrollment (%)	100.0	60.7	38.7	0.2	0.1	0.3
Drop-out Rate (%)	5.6	6.7	3.6	0.0	0.0	100.0
H.S. Diplomas (#)	177	123	50	0	0	4

Tuscaloosa County

Tuscaloosa City SD

1210 21st Ave • Tuscaloosa, AL 35401-2934
Mailing Address: PO Box 038991 • Tuscaloosa, AL 35403-8991
(205) 759-3530 • http://www.tusc.k12.al.us/
Grade Span: PK-12; **Agency Type:** 1
Schools: 21
12 Primary; 3 Middle; 3 High; 3 Other Level
17 Regular; 1 Special Education; 1 Vocational; 2 Alternative
3 Magnet; 0 Charter; 11 Title I Eligible; 9 School-wide Title I
Students: 9,772 (50.9% male; 49.1% female)
Individual Education Program: 1,359 (13.9%);
English Language Learner: 139 (1.4%); Migrant: 0 (0.0%)
Eligible for Free Lunch Program: 5,556 (56.9%)
Eligible for Reduced-Price Lunch Program: 724 (7.4%)
Teachers: 653.1 (15.0 to 1)
Librarians/Media Specialists: 20.0 (488.6 to 1)
Guidance Counselors: 27.0 (361.9 to 1)
Current Spending: ($ per student per year):
Total: $6,443; Instruction: $3,966; Support Services: $2,041

Enrollment, Drop-out Rates and Diploma Recipients by Race/Ethnicity

Category	Total	White	Black	Asian	AIAN	Hisp.
Enrollment (%)	100.0	25.4	72.3	1.2	0.0	1.1
Drop-out Rate (%)	5.7	1.5	7.7	0.0	0.0	0.0
H.S. Diplomas (#)	383	149	224	9	0	1

Tuscaloosa County SD

2314 Ninth St • Tuscaloosa, AL 35401-2319
Mailing Address: PO Drawer 2568 • Tuscaloosa, AL 35403-2568
(205) 758-0411 • http://www.tcss.net/
Grade Span: PK-12; **Agency Type:** 1
Schools: 29
16 Primary; 5 Middle; 6 High; 2 Other Level
26 Regular; 1 Special Education; 0 Vocational; 2 Alternative
0 Magnet; 0 Charter; 9 Title I Eligible; 8 School-wide Title I
Students: 15,863 (51.5% male; 48.5% female)
Individual Education Program: 1,944 (12.3%);
English Language Learner: 123 (0.8%); Migrant: 0 (0.0%)
Eligible for Free Lunch Program: 4,953 (31.2%)
Eligible for Reduced-Price Lunch Program: 1,348 (8.5%)
Teachers: 976.9 (16.2 to 1)
Librarians/Media Specialists: 28.0 (566.5 to 1)
Guidance Counselors: 33.0 (480.7 to 1)
Current Spending: ($ per student per year):
Total: $5,794; Instruction: $3,725; Support Services: $1,637

Enrollment, Drop-out Rates and Diploma Recipients by Race/Ethnicity

Category	Total	White	Black	Asian	AIAN	Hisp.
Enrollment (%)	100.0	74.5	24.1	0.4	0.1	0.9
Drop-out Rate (%)	4.6	4.6	4.8	0.0	0.0	0.0
H.S. Diplomas (#)	753	607	139	2	1	4

Walker County

Jasper City SD

110 W 17th St • Jasper, AL 35501
Mailing Address: PO Box 500 • Jasper, AL 35502-0500
(205) 384-6021 • http://www.jasper.k12.al.us/
Grade Span: PK-12; **Agency Type:** 1
Schools: 6
3 Primary; 1 Middle; 1 High; 1 Other Level
5 Regular; 1 Special Education; 0 Vocational; 0 Alternative
0 Magnet; 0 Charter; 3 Title I Eligible; 0 School-wide Title I
Students: 2,690 (51.2% male; 48.8% female)
Individual Education Program: 340 (12.6%);
English Language Learner: 1 (<0.1%); Migrant: 0 (0.0%)
Eligible for Free Lunch Program: 751 (27.9%)
Eligible for Reduced-Price Lunch Program: 144 (5.4%)
Teachers: 169.2 (15.9 to 1)
Librarians/Media Specialists: 5.0 (538.0 to 1)
Guidance Counselors: 8.0 (336.3 to 1)
Current Spending: ($ per student per year):
Total: $6,331; Instruction: $3,830; Support Services: $2,094

Enrollment, Drop-out Rates and Diploma Recipients by Race/Ethnicity

Category	Total	White	Black	Asian	AIAN	Hisp.
Enrollment (%)	100.0	79.4	18.3	1.0	0.1	1.2
Drop-out Rate (%)	2.8	3.1	0.7	20.0	0.0	14.3
H.S. Diplomas (#)	167	140	26	1	0	0

Walker County SD

1000 Viking Dr • Jasper, AL 35501-4966
Mailing Address: PO Box 311 • Jasper, AL 35502-0311
(205) 387-0555 • http://www.walkercountyschools.com/
Grade Span: KG-12; **Agency Type:** 1
Schools: 24
13 Primary; 2 Middle; 7 High; 2 Other Level
21 Regular; 0 Special Education; 1 Vocational; 2 Alternative
0 Magnet; 0 Charter; 13 Title I Eligible; 13 School-wide Title I
Students: 8,069 (52.2% male; 47.8% female)
Individual Education Program: 1,294 (16.0%);
English Language Learner: 8 (0.1%); Migrant: 0 (0.0%)
Eligible for Free Lunch Program: 3,461 (42.9%)
Eligible for Reduced-Price Lunch Program: 962 (11.9%)
Teachers: 527.5 (15.3 to 1)
Librarians/Media Specialists: 18.4 (438.5 to 1)
Guidance Counselors: 16.8 (480.3 to 1)
Current Spending: ($ per student per year):
Total: $6,081; Instruction: $3,607; Support Services: $1,997

Enrollment, Drop-out Rates and Diploma Recipients by Race/Ethnicity

Category	Total	White	Black	Asian	AIAN	Hisp.
Enrollment (%)	100.0	92.9	6.6	0.0	0.1	0.3
Drop-out Rate (%)	3.7	3.7	3.9	0.0	0.0	0.0
H.S. Diplomas (#)	344	317	26	0	0	1

Washington County

Washington County SD

Granade St • Chatom, AL 36518-1359
Mailing Address: PO Box 1359 • Chatom, AL 36518-1359
(334) 847-2401
Grade Span: KG-12; **Agency Type:** 1
Schools: 8
2 Primary; 0 Middle; 1 High; 5 Other Level
7 Regular; 0 Special Education; 1 Vocational; 0 Alternative
0 Magnet; 0 Charter; 7 Title I Eligible; 5 School-wide Title I
Students: 3,587 (53.1% male; 46.9% female)
Individual Education Program: 343 (9.6%);
English Language Learner: 0 (0.0%); Migrant: 163 (4.5%)
Eligible for Free Lunch Program: 1,737 (48.4%)
Eligible for Reduced-Price Lunch Program: 393 (11.0%)
Teachers: 223.8 (16.0 to 1)
Librarians/Media Specialists: 7.0 (512.4 to 1)
Guidance Counselors: 7.0 (512.4 to 1)
Current Spending: ($ per student per year):
Total: $5,822; Instruction: $3,690; Support Services: $1,756

Enrollment, Drop-out Rates and Diploma Recipients by Race/Ethnicity

Category	Total	White	Black	Asian	AIAN	Hisp.
Enrollment (%)	100.0	58.2	33.8	0.3	7.7	0.1
Drop-out Rate (%)	0.9	0.7	1.4	0.0	0.0	0.0
H.S. Diplomas (#)	200	107	77	0	16	0

Wilcox County

Wilcox County SD

2210 Hwy 221 • Camden, AL 36726-0160
Mailing Address: PO Box 160 • Camden, AL 36726-0160
(334) 682-4716
Grade Span: PK-12; **Agency Type:** 1
Schools: 7
4 Primary; 1 Middle; 1 High; 1 Other Level
6 Regular; 0 Special Education; 0 Vocational; 1 Alternative
0 Magnet; 0 Charter; 6 Title I Eligible; 5 School-wide Title I
Students: 2,485 (52.3% male; 47.7% female)
Individual Education Program: 277 (11.1%);
English Language Learner: 0 (0.0%); Migrant: 0 (0.0%)
Eligible for Free Lunch Program: 2,362 (95.1%)
Eligible for Reduced-Price Lunch Program: 29 (1.2%)
Teachers: 167.5 (14.8 to 1)
Librarians/Media Specialists: 6.0 (414.2 to 1)
Guidance Counselors: 6.0 (414.2 to 1)
Current Spending: ($ per student per year):
Total: $6,600; Instruction: $3,775; Support Services: $2,292

Enrollment, Drop-out Rates and Diploma Recipients by Race/Ethnicity

Category	Total	White	Black	Asian	AIAN	Hisp.
Enrollment (%)	100.0	0.3	99.6	0.0	0.0	0.1
Drop-out Rate (%)	4.3	100.0	4.2	n/a	n/a	n/a
H.S. Diplomas (#)	126	0	126	0	0	0

Winston County

Haleyville City SD

2011 20th St • Haleyville, AL 35565-1959
(205) 486-9231 • http://www.havc.k12.al.us/
Grade Span: PK-12; **Agency Type:** 1
Schools: 3
1 Primary; 0 Middle; 2 High; 0 Other Level
2 Regular; 0 Special Education; 1 Vocational; 0 Alternative
0 Magnet; 0 Charter; 1 Title I Eligible; 1 School-wide Title I
Students: 1,725 (53.2% male; 46.8% female)
Individual Education Program: 226 (13.1%);
English Language Learner: 41 (2.4%); Migrant: 0 (0.0%)
Eligible for Free Lunch Program: 650 (37.7%)
Eligible for Reduced-Price Lunch Program: 172 (10.0%)
Teachers: 115.0 (15.0 to 1)
Librarians/Media Specialists: 2.0 (862.5 to 1)
Guidance Counselors: 3.0 (575.0 to 1)
Current Spending: ($ per student per year):
Total: $5,383; Instruction: $3,677; Support Services: $1,292
Enrollment, Drop-out Rates and Diploma Recipients by Race/Ethnicity

Category	Total	White	Black	Asian	AIAN	Hisp.
Enrollment (%)	100.0	95.5	1.0	0.2	0.1	3.2
Drop-out Rate (%)	5.2	5.3	0.0	0.0	n/a	0.0
H.S. Diplomas (#)	104	102	1	1	0	0

Winston County SD

25125 Hwy 195 • Double Springs, AL 35553-0009
Mailing Address: PO Box 9 • Double Springs, AL 35553-0009
(205) 489-5018 • http://www.winstonk12.org/
Grade Span: KG-12; **Agency Type:** 1
Schools: 10
4 Primary; 1 Middle; 5 High; 0 Other Level
9 Regular; 0 Special Education; 1 Vocational; 0 Alternative
0 Magnet; 0 Charter; 5 Title I Eligible; 1 School-wide Title I
Students: 2,824 (51.6% male; 48.4% female)
Individual Education Program: 440 (15.6%);
English Language Learner: 0 (0.0%); Migrant: 0 (0.0%)
Eligible for Free Lunch Program: 1,218 (43.1%)
Eligible for Reduced-Price Lunch Program: 399 (14.1%)
Teachers: 188.2 (15.0 to 1)
Librarians/Media Specialists: 8.0 (353.0 to 1)
Guidance Counselors: 7.8 (362.1 to 1)
Current Spending: ($ per student per year):
Total: $6,206; Instruction: $3,649; Support Services: $2,102
Enrollment, Drop-out Rates and Diploma Recipients by Race/Ethnicity

Category	Total	White	Black	Asian	AIAN	Hisp.
Enrollment (%)	100.0	99.6	0.1	0.1	0.0	0.2
Drop-out Rate (%)	3.5	3.6	n/a	n/a	0.0	n/a
H.S. Diplomas (#)	160	159	0	0	1	0

Number of Schools

Rank	Number	District Name	City
1	103	Mobile County SD	Mobile
2	92	Birmingham City SD	Birmingham
3	64	Jefferson County SD	Birmingham
4	62	Montgomery County SD	Montgomery
5	48	Huntsville City SD	Huntsville
6	46	Baldwin County SD	Bay Minette
7	34	Shelby County SD	Columbiana
8	29	Tuscaloosa County SD	Tuscaloosa
9	27	Cullman County SD	Cullman
10	24	Madison County SD	Huntsville
10	24	Walker County SD	Jasper
12	22	Etowah County SD	Gadsden
13	21	Tuscaloosa City SD	Tuscaloosa
14	20	Calhoun County SD	Anniston
15	19	Dothan City SD	Dothan
15	19	Jackson County SD	Scottsboro
15	19	Marshall County SD	Guntersville
18	18	Morgan County SD	Decatur
18	18	Talladega County SD	Talladega
20	17	Decatur City SD	Decatur
20	17	Gadsden City SD	Gadsden
20	17	Saint Clair County SD	Ashville
23	16	Blount County SD	Oneonta
23	16	Lawrence County SD	Moulton
25	15	Elmore County SD	Wetumpka
26	14	Dallas County SD	Selma
26	14	Dekalb County SD	Rainsville
26	14	Escambia County SD	Brewton
26	14	Hoover City SD	Hoover
30	13	Autauga County SD	Prattville
30	13	Lauderdale County SD	Florence
30	13	Monroe County SD	Monroeville
30	13	Selma City SD	Selma
34	12	Chilton County SD	Clanton
34	12	Lee County SD	Opelika
34	12	Limestone County SD	Athens
37	11	Chambers County SD	Lafayette
37	11	Marion County SD	Hamilton
37	11	Russell County SD	Phenix City
40	10	Auburn City SD	Auburn
40	10	Bibb County SD	Centreville
40	10	Enterprise City SD	Enterprise
40	10	Hale County SD	Greensboro
40	10	Pickens County SD	Carrollton
40	10	Winston County SD	Double Springs
46	9	Anniston City SD	Anniston
46	9	Bessemer City SD	Bessemer
46	9	Clarke County SD	Grove Hill
46	9	Colbert County SD	Tuscumbia
46	9	Florence City SD	Florence
46	9	Geneva County SD	Geneva
46	9	Houston County SD	Dothan
46	9	Lowndes County SD	Hayneville
46	9	Opelika City SD	Opelika
46	9	Phenix City City SD	Phenix City
46	9	Talladega City SD	Talladega
57	8	Butler County SD	Greenville
57	8	Cherokee County SD	Centre
57	8	Choctaw County SD	Butler
57	8	Cleburne County SD	Heflin
57	8	Conecuh County SD	Evergreen
57	8	Covington County SD	Andalusia
57	8	Macon County SD	Tuskegee
57	8	Madison City SD	Madison
57	8	Ozark City SD	Ozark
57	8	Washington County SD	Chatom
67	7	Athens City SD	Athens
67	7	Dale County SD	Ozark
67	7	Fairfield City SD	Fairfield
67	7	Franklin County SD	Russellville
67	7	Henry County SD	Abbeville
67	7	Muscle Shoals City SD	Muscle Shoals
67	7	Pell City City SD	Pell City
67	7	Sumter County SD	Livingston
67	7	Tallapoosa County SD	Dadeville
67	7	Wilcox County SD	Camden
77	6	Alexander City City SD	Alexander City
77	6	Clay County SD	Ashland
77	6	Coosa County SD	Rockford
77	6	Cullman City SD	Cullman
77	6	Fayette County SD	Fayette
77	6	Hartselle City SD	Hartselle
77	6	Jasper City SD	Jasper
77	6	Mountain Brook City SD	Mountain Brook
77	6	Pike County SD	Troy
77	6	Randolph County SD	Wedowee
77	6	Scottsboro City SD	Scottsboro
77	6	Sylacauga City SD	Sylacauga
77	6	Vestavia Hills City SD	Birmingham
90	5	Albertville City SD	Albertville
90	5	Bullock County SD	Union Springs
90	5	Eufaula City SD	Eufaula
90	5	Greene County SD	Eutaw
90	5	Homewood City SD	Homewood
90	5	Lamar County SD	Vernon
90	5	Oxford City SD	Oxford
90	5	Troy City SD	Troy
98	4	Arab City SD	Arab
98	4	Attalla City SD	Attalla
98	4	Coffee County SD	Elba
98	4	Crenshaw County SD	Luverne
98	4	Daleville City SD	Daleville
98	4	Demopolis City SD	Demopolis
98	4	Fort Payne City SD	Fort Payne
98	4	Guntersville City SD	Guntersville
98	4	Marengo County SD	Linden
98	4	Perry County SD	Marion
98	4	Russellville City SD	Russellville
109	3	Andalusia City SD	Andalusia
109	3	Haleyville City SD	Haleyville
109	3	Tallassee City SD	Tallassee
109	3	Thomasville City SD	Thomasville
113	2	Jacksonville City SD	Jacksonville

Number of Teachers

Rank	Number	District Name	City
1	4,050	Mobile County SD	Mobile
2	2,511	Jefferson County SD	Birmingham
3	2,320	Birmingham City SD	Birmingham
4	2,131	Montgomery County SD	Montgomery
5	1,550	Baldwin County SD	Bay Minette
6	1,508	Huntsville City SD	Huntsville
7	1,445	Shelby County SD	Columbiana
8	976	Tuscaloosa County SD	Tuscaloosa
9	972	Madison County SD	Huntsville
10	746	Hoover City SD	Hoover
11	653	Tuscaloosa City SD	Tuscaloosa
12	600	Lee County SD	Opelika
13	592	Decatur City SD	Decatur
14	585	Cullman County SD	Cullman
15	579	Elmore County SD	Wetumpka
16	552	Calhoun County SD	Anniston
17	541	Etowah County SD	Gadsden
18	540	Lauderdale County SD	Florence
19	537	Autauga County SD	Prattville
20	532	Dekalb County SD	Rainsville
21	527	Walker County SD	Jasper
22	516	Limestone County SD	Athens
23	509	Morgan County SD	Decatur
24	502	Dothan City SD	Dothan
25	443	Talladega County SD	Talladega
26	443	Chilton County SD	Clanton
27	434	Saint Clair County SD	Ashville
28	427	Blount County SD	Oneonta
29	411	Marshall County SD	Guntersville
30	395	Madison City SD	Madison
31	394	Jackson County SD	Scottsboro
32	383	Houston County SD	Dothan
33	368	Gadsden City SD	Gadsden
34	365	Lawrence County SD	Moulton
35	337	Enterprise City SD	Enterprise
36	317	Mountain Brook City SD	Mountain Brook
37	314	Vestavia Hills City SD	Birmingham
38	305	Escambia County SD	Brewton
39	299	Auburn City SD	Auburn
40	299	Dallas County SD	Selma
41	296	Phenix City City SD	Phenix City
42	287	Florence City SD	Florence
43	286	Opelika City SD	Opelika
44	282	Bessemer City SD	Bessemer
45	278	Monroe County SD	Monroeville
46	264	Chambers County SD	Lafayette
47	251	Cherokee County SD	Centre
48	250	Homewood City SD	Homewood
49	246	Selma City SD	Selma
50	240	Alexander City City SD	Alexander City
51	237	Marion County SD	Hamilton
52	236	Russell County SD	Phenix City
53	236	Pell City City SD	Pell City
54	233	Macon County SD	Tuskegee
55	227	Albertville City SD	Albertville
56	224	Clarke County SD	Grove Hill
57	224	Bibb County SD	Centreville
57	224	Tallapoosa County SD	Dadeville
59	223	Washington County SD	Chatom
60	222	Pickens County SD	Carrollton
61	221	Hale County SD	Greensboro
62	216	Colbert County SD	Tuscumbia
63	212	Butler County SD	Greenville
64	202	Franklin County SD	Russellville
65	198	Oxford City SD	Oxford
66	194	Covington County SD	Andalusia
67	194	Hartselle City SD	Hartselle
68	191	Eufaula City SD	Eufaula
69	188	Winston County SD	Double Springs
70	186	Athens City SD	Athens
71	183	Talladega City SD	Talladega
72	180	Scottsboro City SD	Scottsboro
73	179	Ozark City SD	Ozark
74	172	Fayette County SD	Fayette
75	170	Dale County SD	Ozark
76	169	Sumter County SD	Livingston
77	169	Jasper City SD	Jasper
78	169	Henry County SD	Abbeville
79	167	Arab City SD	Arab
79	167	Wilcox County SD	Camden
81	167	Geneva County SD	Geneva
82	166	Lamar County SD	Vernon
83	163	Fort Payne City SD	Fort Payne
84	163	Cleburne County SD	Heflin
85	159	Anniston City SD	Anniston
86	158	Lowndes County SD	Hayneville
87	158	Muscle Shoals City SD	Muscle Shoals
88	157	Cullman City SD	Cullman
89	155	Fairfield City SD	Fairfield
90	152	Crenshaw County SD	Luverne
91	147	Troy City SD	Troy
92	146	Sylacauga City SD	Sylacauga
93	146	Clay County SD	Ashland
94	145	Russellville City SD	Russellville
95	143	Demopolis City SD	Demopolis
95	143	Randolph County SD	Wedowee
97	142	Perry County SD	Marion
98	139	Choctaw County SD	Butler
99	132	Pike County SD	Troy
100	127	Bullock County SD	Union Springs
101	125	Conecuh County SD	Evergreen
102	122	Guntersville City SD	Guntersville
103	119	Attalla City SD	Attalla
104	117	Coffee County SD	Elba
105	116	Greene County SD	Eutaw
106	116	Andalusia City SD	Andalusia
107	115	Haleyville City SD	Haleyville
107	115	Tallassee City SD	Tallassee
109	111	Marengo County SD	Linden
110	107	Thomasville City SD	Thomasville
111	105	Daleville City SD	Daleville
112	104	Coosa County SD	Rockford
113	103	Jacksonville City SD	Jacksonville

Number of Students

Rank	Number	District Name	City
1	64,058	Mobile County SD	Mobile
2	40,060	Jefferson County SD	Birmingham
3	36,133	Birmingham City SD	Birmingham
4	32,912	Montgomery County SD	Montgomery
5	23,411	Baldwin County SD	Bay Minette
6	22,643	Huntsville City SD	Huntsville
7	21,629	Shelby County SD	Columbiana
8	16,564	Madison County SD	Huntsville
9	15,863	Tuscaloosa County SD	Tuscaloosa
10	10,722	Hoover City SD	Hoover
11	10,038	Elmore County SD	Wetumpka
12	9,772	Tuscaloosa City SD	Tuscaloosa
13	9,622	Cullman County SD	Cullman
14	9,471	Calhoun County SD	Anniston
15	9,216	Lee County SD	Opelika
16	8,940	Autauga County SD	Prattville
17	8,843	Lauderdale County SD	Florence
18	8,831	Decatur City SD	Decatur
19	8,743	Dothan City SD	Dothan
20	8,480	Etowah County SD	Gadsden
21	8,069	Walker County SD	Jasper
22	7,987	Limestone County SD	Athens
23	7,978	Dekalb County SD	Rainsville
24	7,773	Talladega County SD	Talladega
25	7,549	Blount County SD	Oneonta
26	7,414	Morgan County SD	Decatur
27	7,144	Saint Clair County SD	Ashville
28	7,011	Marshall County SD	Guntersville
29	6,995	Chilton County SD	Clanton
30	6,657	Madison City SD	Madison
31	6,150	Houston County SD	Dothan
32	6,094	Jackson County SD	Scottsboro
33	5,892	Lawrence County SD	Moulton
34	5,471	Gadsden City SD	Gadsden
35	5,256	Enterprise City SD	Enterprise
36	5,062	Phenix City City SD	Phenix City
37	4,724	Escambia County SD	Brewton
38	4,709	Vestavia Hills City SD	Birmingham
39	4,573	Auburn City SD	Auburn
40	4,536	Dallas County SD	Selma
41	4,388	Monroe County SD	Monroeville
42	4,374	Chambers County SD	Lafayette

43	4,323	Opelika City SD	Opelika
44	4,249	Bessemer City SD	Bessemer
45	4,237	Florence City SD	Florence
46	4,101	Cherokee County SD	Centre
47	4,096	Selma City SD	Selma
48	4,060	Mountain Brook City SD	Mountain Brook
49	3,913	Pell City City SD	Pell City
50	3,898	Macon County SD	Tuskegee
51	3,765	Marion County SD	Hamilton
52	3,725	Russell County SD	Phenix City
53	3,605	Clarke County SD	Grove Hill
54	3,600	Bibb County SD	Centreville
55	3,587	Washington County SD	Chatom
56	3,576	Albertville City SD	Albertville
57	3,543	Alexander City City SD	Alexander City
58	3,526	Butler County SD	Greenville
59	3,369	Tallapoosa County SD	Dadeville
60	3,364	Pickens County SD	Carrollton
61	3,348	Hale County SD	Greensboro
62	3,271	Colbert County SD	Tuscumbia
63	3,242	Covington County SD	Andalusia
64	3,220	Homewood City SD	Homewood
65	3,177	Oxford City SD	Oxford
66	3,067	Hartselle City SD	Hartselle
67	3,036	Franklin County SD	Russellville
68	2,885	Talladega City SD	Talladega
69	2,883	Eufaula City SD	Eufaula
70	2,824	Winston County SD	Double Springs
71	2,818	Ozark City SD	Ozark
72	2,807	Athens City SD	Athens
73	2,715	Geneva County SD	Geneva
74	2,709	Scottsboro City SD	Scottsboro
75	2,707	Henry County SD	Abbeville
76	2,705	Sumter County SD	Livingston
77	2,704	Arab City SD	Arab
78	2,691	Fort Payne City SD	Fort Payne
79	2,690	Jasper City SD	Jasper
80	2,688	Fayette County SD	Fayette
81	2,668	Anniston City SD	Anniston
82	2,654	Dale County SD	Ozark
83	2,643	Cleburne County SD	Heflin
83	2,643	Cullman City SD	Cullman
85	2,594	Lamar County SD	Vernon
86	2,544	Lowndes County SD	Hayneville
87	2,485	Wilcox County SD	Camden
88	2,470	Muscle Shoals City SD	Muscle Shoals
89	2,355	Demopolis City SD	Demopolis
90	2,349	Troy City SD	Troy
91	2,348	Crenshaw County SD	Luverne
92	2,342	Russellville City SD	Russellville
93	2,330	Clay County SD	Ashland
94	2,290	Sylacauga City SD	Sylacauga
95	2,287	Randolph County SD	Wedowee
96	2,274	Fairfield City SD	Fairfield
97	2,204	Choctaw County SD	Butler
97	2,204	Perry County SD	Marion
99	2,124	Pike County SD	Troy
100	1,991	Conecuh County SD	Evergreen
101	1,960	Coffee County SD	Elba
102	1,893	Bullock County SD	Union Springs
103	1,884	Tallassee City SD	Tallassee
104	1,856	Attalla City SD	Attalla
105	1,814	Guntersville City SD	Guntersville
106	1,754	Greene County SD	Eutaw
107	1,745	Andalusia City SD	Andalusia
108	1,725	Haleyville City SD	Haleyville
109	1,708	Coosa County SD	Rockford
110	1,707	Marengo County SD	Linden
111	1,702	Jacksonville City SD	Jacksonville
112	1,671	Daleville City SD	Daleville
113	1,645	Thomasville City SD	Thomasville

Male Students

Rank	Percent	District Name	City
1	54.8	Colbert County SD	Tuscumbia
2	54.4	Pike County SD	Troy
3	54.3	Crenshaw County SD	Luverne
4	54.2	Dale County SD	Ozark
5	53.9	Saint Clair County SD	Ashville
6	53.7	Daleville City SD	Daleville
6	53.7	Marengo County SD	Linden
8	53.6	Jacksonville City SD	Jacksonville
9	53.4	Attalla City SD	Attalla
10	53.2	Cherokee County SD	Centre
10	53.2	Haleyville City SD	Haleyville
12	53.1	Cullman City SD	Cullman
12	53.1	Washington County SD	Chatom
14	53.0	Marshall County SD	Guntersville
15	52.8	Conecuh County SD	Evergreen
15	52.8	Geneva County SD	Geneva
15	52.8	Homewood City SD	Homewood
18	52.7	Hartselle City SD	Hartselle
19	52.5	Marion County SD	Hamilton
20	52.4	Calhoun County SD	Anniston
20	52.4	Choctaw County SD	Butler
20	52.4	Covington County SD	Andalusia
20	52.4	Lawrence County SD	Moulton
20	52.4	Pell City City SD	Pell City
20	52.4	Vestavia Hills City SD	Birmingham
26	52.3	Tallapoosa County SD	Dadeville
26	52.3	Wilcox County SD	Camden
28	52.2	Shelby County SD	Columbiana
28	52.2	Troy City SD	Troy
28	52.2	Walker County SD	Jasper
31	52.1	Dekalb County SD	Rainsville
31	52.1	Jefferson County SD	Birmingham
31	52.1	Madison City SD	Madison
34	52.0	Arab City SD	Arab
34	52.0	Baldwin County SD	Bay Minette
34	52.0	Lauderdale County SD	Florence
34	52.0	Monroe County SD	Monroeville
34	52.0	Morgan County SD	Decatur
39	51.9	Coffee County SD	Elba
39	51.9	Elmore County SD	Wetumpka
39	51.9	Escambia County SD	Brewton
39	51.9	Franklin County SD	Russellville
39	51.9	Greene County SD	Eutaw
44	51.8	Autauga County SD	Prattville
44	51.8	Chilton County SD	Clanton
44	51.8	Fort Payne City SD	Fort Payne
44	51.8	Guntersville City SD	Guntersville
44	51.8	Jackson County SD	Scottsboro
44	51.8	Madison County SD	Huntsville
44	51.8	Randolph County SD	Wedowee
44	51.8	Talladega County SD	Talladega
52	51.7	Bibb County SD	Centreville
52	51.7	Blount County SD	Oneonta
52	51.7	Bullock County SD	Union Springs
52	51.7	Clay County SD	Ashland
52	51.7	Cullman County SD	Cullman
52	51.7	Mobile County SD	Mobile
58	51.6	Etowah County SD	Gadsden
58	51.6	Eufaula City SD	Eufaula
58	51.6	Ozark City SD	Ozark
58	51.6	Winston County SD	Double Springs
62	51.5	Butler County SD	Greenville
62	51.5	Hale County SD	Greensboro
62	51.5	Houston County SD	Dothan
62	51.5	Lee County SD	Opelika
62	51.5	Limestone County SD	Athens
62	51.5	Opelika City SD	Opelika
62	51.5	Russellville City SD	Russellville
62	51.5	Sumter County SD	Livingston
62	51.5	Thomasville City SD	Thomasville
62	51.5	Tuscaloosa County SD	Tuscaloosa
72	51.4	Enterprise City SD	Enterprise
72	51.4	Fayette County SD	Fayette
72	51.4	Montgomery County SD	Montgomery
72	51.4	Oxford City SD	Oxford
72	51.4	Tallassee City SD	Tallassee
77	51.3	Coosa County SD	Rockford
77	51.3	Demopolis City SD	Demopolis
77	51.3	Dothan City SD	Dothan
77	51.3	Huntsville City SD	Huntsville
77	51.3	Perry County SD	Marion
77	51.3	Russell County SD	Phenix City
83	51.2	Alexander City City SD	Alexander City
83	51.2	Athens City SD	Athens
83	51.2	Bessemer City SD	Bessemer
83	51.2	Chambers County SD	Lafayette
83	51.2	Gadsden City SD	Gadsden
83	51.2	Hoover City SD	Hoover
83	51.2	Jasper City SD	Jasper
83	51.2	Phenix City City SD	Phenix City
91	51.0	Albertville City SD	Albertville
91	51.0	Florence City SD	Florence
91	51.0	Mountain Brook City SD	Mountain Brook
91	51.0	Scottsboro City SD	Scottsboro
95	50.9	Andalusia City SD	Andalusia
95	50.9	Talladega City SD	Talladega
95	50.9	Tuscaloosa City SD	Tuscaloosa
98	50.8	Cleburne County SD	Heflin
98	50.8	Muscle Shoals City SD	Muscle Shoals
98	50.8	Pickens County SD	Carrollton
101	50.7	Birmingham City SD	Birmingham
101	50.7	Macon County SD	Tuskegee
103	50.5	Henry County SD	Abbeville
103	50.5	Lowndes County SD	Hayneville
105	50.3	Clarke County SD	Grove Hill
105	50.3	Lamar County SD	Vernon
107	50.2	Dallas County SD	Selma
108	50.1	Decatur City SD	Decatur
108	50.1	Fairfield City SD	Fairfield
110	49.8	Anniston City SD	Anniston
111	49.7	Sylacauga City SD	Sylacauga
112	49.4	Auburn City SD	Auburn
113	49.1	Selma City SD	Selma

Female Students

Rank	Percent	District Name	City
1	50.9	Selma City SD	Selma
2	50.6	Auburn City SD	Auburn
3	50.3	Sylacauga City SD	Sylacauga
4	50.2	Anniston City SD	Anniston
5	49.9	Decatur City SD	Decatur
5	49.9	Fairfield City SD	Fairfield
7	49.8	Dallas County SD	Selma
8	49.7	Clarke County SD	Grove Hill
8	49.7	Lamar County SD	Vernon
10	49.5	Henry County SD	Abbeville
10	49.5	Lowndes County SD	Hayneville
12	49.3	Birmingham City SD	Birmingham
12	49.3	Macon County SD	Tuskegee
14	49.2	Cleburne County SD	Heflin
14	49.2	Muscle Shoals City SD	Muscle Shoals
14	49.2	Pickens County SD	Carrollton
17	49.1	Andalusia City SD	Andalusia
17	49.1	Talladega City SD	Talladega
17	49.1	Tuscaloosa City SD	Tuscaloosa
20	49.0	Albertville City SD	Albertville
20	49.0	Florence City SD	Florence
20	49.0	Mountain Brook City SD	Mountain Brook
20	49.0	Scottsboro City SD	Scottsboro
24	48.8	Alexander City City SD	Alexander City
24	48.8	Athens City SD	Athens
24	48.8	Bessemer City SD	Bessemer
24	48.8	Chambers County SD	Lafayette
24	48.8	Gadsden City SD	Gadsden
24	48.8	Hoover City SD	Hoover
24	48.8	Jasper City SD	Jasper
24	48.8	Phenix City City SD	Phenix City
32	48.7	Coosa County SD	Rockford
32	48.7	Demopolis City SD	Demopolis
32	48.7	Dothan City SD	Dothan
32	48.7	Huntsville City SD	Huntsville
32	48.7	Perry County SD	Marion
32	48.7	Russell County SD	Phenix City
38	48.6	Enterprise City SD	Enterprise
38	48.6	Fayette County SD	Fayette
38	48.6	Montgomery County SD	Montgomery
38	48.6	Oxford City SD	Oxford
38	48.6	Tallassee City SD	Tallassee
43	48.5	Butler County SD	Greenville
43	48.5	Hale County SD	Greensboro
43	48.5	Houston County SD	Dothan
43	48.5	Lee County SD	Opelika
43	48.5	Limestone County SD	Athens
43	48.5	Opelika City SD	Opelika
43	48.5	Russellville City SD	Russellville
43	48.5	Sumter County SD	Livingston
43	48.5	Thomasville City SD	Thomasville
43	48.5	Tuscaloosa County SD	Tuscaloosa
53	48.4	Etowah County SD	Gadsden
53	48.4	Eufaula City SD	Eufaula
53	48.4	Ozark City SD	Ozark
53	48.4	Winston County SD	Double Springs
57	48.3	Bibb County SD	Centreville
57	48.3	Blount County SD	Oneonta
57	48.3	Bullock County SD	Union Springs
57	48.3	Clay County SD	Ashland
57	48.3	Cullman County SD	Cullman
57	48.3	Mobile County SD	Mobile
63	48.2	Autauga County SD	Prattville
63	48.2	Chilton County SD	Clanton
63	48.2	Fort Payne City SD	Fort Payne
63	48.2	Guntersville City SD	Guntersville
63	48.2	Jackson County SD	Scottsboro
63	48.2	Madison County SD	Huntsville
63	48.2	Randolph County SD	Wedowee
63	48.2	Talladega County SD	Talladega
71	48.1	Coffee County SD	Elba
71	48.1	Elmore County SD	Wetumpka
71	48.1	Escambia County SD	Brewton
71	48.1	Franklin County SD	Russellville
71	48.1	Greene County SD	Eutaw
76	48.0	Arab City SD	Arab
76	48.0	Baldwin County SD	Bay Minette
76	48.0	Lauderdale County SD	Florence
76	48.0	Monroe County SD	Monroeville
76	48.0	Morgan County SD	Decatur
81	47.9	Dekalb County SD	Rainsville
81	47.9	Jefferson County SD	Birmingham
81	47.9	Madison City SD	Madison
84	47.8	Shelby County SD	Columbiana
84	47.8	Troy City SD	Troy
84	47.8	Walker County SD	Jasper

87	47.7	Tallapoosa County SD	Dadeville
87	47.7	Wilcox County SD	Camden
89	47.6	Calhoun County SD	Anniston
89	47.6	Choctaw County SD	Butler
89	47.6	Covington County SD	Andalusia
89	47.6	Lawrence County SD	Moulton
89	47.6	Pell City City SD	Pell City
89	47.6	Vestavia Hills City SD	Birmingham
95	47.5	Marion County SD	Hamilton
96	47.3	Hartselle City SD	Hartselle
97	47.2	Conecuh County SD	Evergreen
97	47.2	Geneva County SD	Geneva
97	47.2	Homewood City SD	Homewood
100	47.0	Marshall County SD	Guntersville
101	46.9	Cullman City SD	Cullman
101	46.9	Washington County SD	Chatom
103	46.8	Cherokee County SD	Centre
103	46.8	Haleyville City SD	Haleyville
105	46.6	Attalla City SD	Attalla
106	46.4	Jacksonville City SD	Jacksonville
107	46.3	Daleville City SD	Daleville
107	46.3	Marengo County SD	Linden
109	46.1	Saint Clair County SD	Ashville
110	45.8	Dale County SD	Ozark
111	45.7	Crenshaw County SD	Luverne
112	45.6	Pike County SD	Troy
113	45.2	Colbert County SD	Tuscumbia

Individual Education Program Students

Rank	Percent	District Name	City
1	18.6	Attalla City SD	Attalla
2	17.7	Conecuh County SD	Evergreen
3	17.4	Pell City City SD	Pell City
4	17.3	Anniston City SD	Anniston
5	17.1	Chilton County SD	Clanton
5	17.1	Pike County SD	Troy
7	17.0	Gadsden City SD	Gadsden
8	16.6	Bibb County SD	Centreville
8	16.6	Morgan County SD	Decatur
10	16.2	Cleburne County SD	Heflin
10	16.2	Lowndes County SD	Hayneville
12	16.1	Baldwin County SD	Bay Minette
13	16.0	Tallapoosa County SD	Dadeville
13	16.0	Walker County SD	Jasper
15	15.7	Colbert County SD	Tuscumbia
16	15.6	Winston County SD	Double Springs
17	15.3	Butler County SD	Greenville
18	14.9	Covington County SD	Andalusia
19	14.8	Cherokee County SD	Centre
19	14.8	Mobile County SD	Mobile
19	14.8	Talladega City SD	Talladega
22	14.5	Etowah County SD	Gadsden
23	14.3	Blount County SD	Oneonta
23	14.3	Calhoun County SD	Anniston
23	14.3	Clay County SD	Ashland
26	14.2	Coffee County SD	Elba
26	14.2	Coosa County SD	Rockford
28	14.0	Birmingham City SD	Birmingham
28	14.0	Dekalb County SD	Rainsville
30	13.9	Tuscaloosa City SD	Tuscaloosa
31	13.8	Dallas County SD	Selma
31	13.8	Ozark City SD	Ozark
33	13.7	Clarke County SD	Grove Hill
33	13.7	Dothan City SD	Dothan
33	13.7	Perry County SD	Marion
33	13.7	Sumter County SD	Livingston
37	13.4	Jefferson County SD	Birmingham
38	13.2	Choctaw County SD	Butler
39	13.1	Cullman County SD	Cullman
39	13.1	Escambia County SD	Brewton
39	13.1	Haleyville City SD	Haleyville
42	12.9	Houston County SD	Dothan
43	12.8	Dale County SD	Ozark
43	12.8	Saint Clair County SD	Ashville
45	12.7	Franklin County SD	Russellville
45	12.7	Hartselle City SD	Hartselle
45	12.7	Marion County SD	Hamilton
45	12.7	Shelby County SD	Columbiana
49	12.6	Bullock County SD	Union Springs
49	12.6	Jasper City SD	Jasper
49	12.6	Scottsboro City SD	Scottsboro
52	12.5	Alexander City City SD	Alexander City
52	12.5	Bessemer City SD	Bessemer
52	12.5	Crenshaw County SD	Luverne
52	12.5	Elmore County SD	Wetumpka
52	12.5	Fayette County SD	Fayette
52	12.5	Geneva County SD	Geneva
52	12.5	Greene County SD	Eutaw
52	12.5	Henry County SD	Abbeville
52	12.5	Huntsville City SD	Huntsville
52	12.5	Marshall County SD	Guntersville
62	12.4	Chambers County SD	Lafayette
63	12.3	Daleville City SD	Daleville
63	12.3	Tuscaloosa County SD	Tuscaloosa
65	12.2	Eufaula City SD	Eufaula
66	12.1	Montgomery County SD	Montgomery
66	12.1	Pickens County SD	Carrollton
68	11.9	Decatur City SD	Decatur
69	11.8	Phenix City City SD	Phenix City
70	11.7	Randolph County SD	Wedowee
70	11.7	Sylacauga City SD	Sylacauga
70	11.7	Talladega County SD	Talladega
73	11.6	Tallassee City SD	Tallassee
74	11.5	Troy City SD	Troy
75	11.3	Florence City SD	Florence
76	11.2	Cullman City SD	Cullman
76	11.2	Limestone County SD	Athens
78	11.1	Wilcox County SD	Camden
79	10.9	Autauga County SD	Prattville
79	10.9	Lauderdale County SD	Florence
79	10.9	Macon County SD	Tuskegee
82	10.8	Homewood City SD	Homewood
82	10.8	Jacksonville City SD	Jacksonville
82	10.8	Madison City SD	Madison
82	10.8	Marengo County SD	Linden
86	10.7	Fairfield City SD	Fairfield
87	10.6	Enterprise City SD	Enterprise
87	10.6	Hale County SD	Greensboro
87	10.6	Jackson County SD	Scottsboro
87	10.6	Selma City SD	Selma
87	10.6	Thomasville City SD	Thomasville
92	10.5	Arab City SD	Arab
92	10.5	Madison County SD	Huntsville
94	10.4	Auburn City SD	Auburn
94	10.4	Lawrence County SD	Moulton
94	10.4	Monroe County SD	Monroeville
94	10.4	Oxford City SD	Oxford
98	10.3	Athens City SD	Athens
98	10.3	Opelika City SD	Opelika
100	10.1	Andalusia City SD	Andalusia
100	10.1	Fort Payne City SD	Fort Payne
100	10.1	Lamar County SD	Vernon
103	10.0	Guntersville City SD	Guntersville
104	9.6	Washington County SD	Chatom
105	9.2	Russell County SD	Phenix City
106	9.1	Albertville City SD	Albertville
106	9.1	Russellville City SD	Russellville
108	8.9	Mountain Brook City SD	Mountain Brook
109	8.8	Vestavia Hills City SD	Birmingham
110	8.5	Demopolis City SD	Demopolis
110	8.5	Hoover City SD	Hoover
112	8.3	Lee County SD	Opelika
113	5.8	Muscle Shoals City SD	Muscle Shoals

English Language Learner Students

Rank	Percent	District Name	City
1	16.8	Albertville City SD	Albertville
2	16.0	Fort Payne City SD	Fort Payne
3	8.4	Russellville City SD	Russellville
4	7.5	Dekalb County SD	Rainsville
5	6.4	Blount County SD	Oneonta
6	6.1	Homewood City SD	Homewood
7	5.5	Decatur City SD	Decatur
8	5.3	Cullman City SD	Cullman
9	5.1	Madison City SD	Madison
10	5.0	Athens City SD	Athens
11	4.6	Marshall County SD	Guntersville
12	4.0	Franklin County SD	Russellville
13	2.9	Gadsden City SD	Gadsden
13	2.9	Hoover City SD	Hoover
15	2.6	Oxford City SD	Oxford
15	2.6	Shelby County SD	Columbiana
17	2.5	Attalla City SD	Attalla
17	2.5	Cullman County SD	Cullman
17	2.5	Florence City SD	Florence
20	2.4	Haleyville City SD	Haleyville
21	2.3	Chilton County SD	Clanton
22	1.9	Limestone County SD	Athens
22	1.9	Opelika City SD	Opelika
24	1.8	Enterprise City SD	Enterprise
25	1.5	Geneva County SD	Geneva
26	1.4	Auburn City SD	Auburn
26	1.4	Jacksonville City SD	Jacksonville
26	1.4	Tuscaloosa City SD	Tuscaloosa
29	1.3	Anniston City SD	Anniston
29	1.3	Guntersville City SD	Guntersville
29	1.3	Jefferson County SD	Birmingham
32	1.2	Arab City SD	Arab
32	1.2	Henry County SD	Abbeville
32	1.2	Huntsville City SD	Huntsville
32	1.2	Montgomery County SD	Montgomery
32	1.2	Tallassee City SD	Tallassee
37	1.1	Mobile County SD	Mobile
38	1.0	Baldwin County SD	Bay Minette
38	1.0	Etowah County SD	Gadsden
38	1.0	Hartselle City SD	Hartselle
38	1.0	Jackson County SD	Scottsboro
38	1.0	Madison County SD	Huntsville
43	0.9	Birmingham City SD	Birmingham
43	0.9	Dothan City SD	Dothan
43	0.9	Scottsboro City SD	Scottsboro
46	0.8	Lawrence County SD	Moulton
46	0.8	Tuscaloosa County SD	Tuscaloosa
48	0.7	Bullock County SD	Union Springs
48	0.7	Elmore County SD	Wetumpka
48	0.7	Fairfield City SD	Fairfield
48	0.7	Randolph County SD	Wedowee
48	0.7	Saint Clair County SD	Ashville
48	0.7	Vestavia Hills City SD	Birmingham
54	0.6	Alexander City City SD	Alexander City
54	0.6	Bessemer City SD	Bessemer
54	0.6	Cleburne County SD	Heflin
54	0.6	Colbert County SD	Tuscumbia
54	0.6	Houston County SD	Dothan
54	0.6	Morgan County SD	Decatur
54	0.6	Muscle Shoals City SD	Muscle Shoals
54	0.6	Troy City SD	Troy
62	0.5	Eufaula City SD	Eufaula
62	0.5	Marion County SD	Hamilton
62	0.5	Ozark City SD	Ozark
65	0.4	Calhoun County SD	Anniston
65	0.4	Coosa County SD	Rockford
65	0.4	Daleville City SD	Daleville
65	0.4	Pell City City SD	Pell City
65	0.4	Russell County SD	Phenix City
65	0.4	Talladega County SD	Talladega
71	0.3	Autauga County SD	Prattville
71	0.3	Bibb County SD	Centreville
71	0.3	Chambers County SD	Lafayette
71	0.3	Lauderdale County SD	Florence
71	0.3	Pike County SD	Troy
76	0.2	Coffee County SD	Elba
76	0.2	Covington County SD	Andalusia
76	0.2	Escambia County SD	Brewton
76	0.2	Thomasville City SD	Thomasville
80	0.1	Andalusia City SD	Andalusia
80	0.1	Butler County SD	Greenville
80	0.1	Cherokee County SD	Centre
80	0.1	Lee County SD	Opelika
80	0.1	Monroe County SD	Monroeville
80	0.1	Mountain Brook City SD	Mountain Brook
80	0.1	Selma City SD	Selma
80	0.1	Sumter County SD	Livingston
80	0.1	Walker County SD	Jasper
89	0.0	Jasper City SD	Jasper
90	0.0	Choctaw County SD	Butler
90	0.0	Clarke County SD	Grove Hill
90	0.0	Clay County SD	Ashland
90	0.0	Conecuh County SD	Evergreen
90	0.0	Crenshaw County SD	Luverne
90	0.0	Dale County SD	Ozark
90	0.0	Dallas County SD	Selma
90	0.0	Demopolis City SD	Demopolis
90	0.0	Fayette County SD	Fayette
90	0.0	Greene County SD	Eutaw
90	0.0	Hale County SD	Greensboro
90	0.0	Lamar County SD	Vernon
90	0.0	Lowndes County SD	Hayneville
90	0.0	Macon County SD	Tuskegee
90	0.0	Marengo County SD	Linden
90	0.0	Perry County SD	Marion
90	0.0	Phenix City City SD	Phenix City
90	0.0	Pickens County SD	Carrollton
90	0.0	Sylacauga City SD	Sylacauga
90	0.0	Talladega City SD	Talladega
90	0.0	Tallapoosa County SD	Dadeville
90	0.0	Washington County SD	Chatom
90	0.0	Wilcox County SD	Camden
90	0.0	Winston County SD	Double Springs

Migrant Students

Rank	Percent	District Name	City
1	18.2	Albertville City SD	Albertville
2	15.2	Pike County SD	Troy
3	12.4	Coffee County SD	Elba
4	10.7	Covington County SD	Andalusia
5	9.9	Dekalb County SD	Rainsville
6	8.8	Athens City SD	Athens
7	6.8	Cullman County SD	Cullman
8	5.1	Lawrence County SD	Moulton
8	5.1	Russellville City SD	Russellville
10	4.8	Enterprise City SD	Enterprise
11	4.5	Washington County SD	Chatom
12	4.4	Decatur City SD	Decatur
12	4.4	Franklin County SD	Russellville
14	4.2	Morgan County SD	Decatur

Rank	Percent	District Name	City
15	3.9	Saint Clair County SD	Ashville
16	2.8	Blount County SD	Oneonta
17	2.7	Fort Payne City SD	Fort Payne
18	2.5	Mobile County SD	Mobile
19	2.4	Geneva County SD	Geneva
20	2.0	Gadsden City SD	Gadsden
21	1.5	Marshall County SD	Guntersville
22	0.9	Hartselle City SD	Hartselle
23	0.8	Cullman City SD	Cullman
24	0.6	Limestone County SD	Athens
24	0.6	Troy City SD	Troy
26	0.5	Baldwin County SD	Bay Minette
27	0.3	Colbert County SD	Tuscumbia
28	0.2	Chilton County SD	Clanton
28	0.2	Madison County SD	Huntsville
30	0.1	Houston County SD	Dothan
31	0.0	Henry County SD	Abbeville
32	0.0	Alexander City SD	Alexander City
32	0.0	Andalusia City SD	Andalusia
32	0.0	Anniston City SD	Anniston
32	0.0	Arab City SD	Arab
32	0.0	Attalla City SD	Attalla
32	0.0	Auburn City SD	Auburn
32	0.0	Autauga County SD	Prattville
32	0.0	Bessemer City SD	Bessemer
32	0.0	Bibb County SD	Centreville
32	0.0	Birmingham City SD	Birmingham
32	0.0	Bullock County SD	Union Springs
32	0.0	Butler County SD	Greenville
32	0.0	Calhoun County SD	Anniston
32	0.0	Chambers County SD	Lafayette
32	0.0	Cherokee County SD	Centre
32	0.0	Choctaw County SD	Butler
32	0.0	Clarke County SD	Grove Hill
32	0.0	Clay County SD	Ashland
32	0.0	Cleburne County SD	Heflin
32	0.0	Conecuh County SD	Evergreen
32	0.0	Coosa County SD	Rockford
32	0.0	Crenshaw County SD	Luverne
32	0.0	Dale County SD	Ozark
32	0.0	Daleville City SD	Daleville
32	0.0	Dallas County SD	Selma
32	0.0	Demopolis City SD	Demopolis
32	0.0	Dothan City SD	Dothan
32	0.0	Elmore County SD	Wetumpka
32	0.0	Escambia County SD	Brewton
32	0.0	Etowah County SD	Gadsden
32	0.0	Eufaula City SD	Eufaula
32	0.0	Fairfield City SD	Fairfield
32	0.0	Fayette County SD	Fayette
32	0.0	Florence City SD	Florence
32	0.0	Greene County SD	Eutaw
32	0.0	Guntersville City SD	Guntersville
32	0.0	Hale County SD	Greensboro
32	0.0	Haleyville City SD	Haleyville
32	0.0	Homewood City SD	Homewood
32	0.0	Hoover City SD	Hoover
32	0.0	Huntsville City SD	Huntsville
32	0.0	Jackson County SD	Scottsboro
32	0.0	Jacksonville City SD	Jacksonville
32	0.0	Jasper City SD	Jasper
32	0.0	Jefferson County SD	Birmingham
32	0.0	Lamar County SD	Vernon
32	0.0	Lauderdale County SD	Florence
32	0.0	Lee County SD	Opelika
32	0.0	Lowndes County SD	Hayneville
32	0.0	Macon County SD	Tuskegee
32	0.0	Madison City SD	Madison
32	0.0	Marengo County SD	Linden
32	0.0	Marion County SD	Hamilton
32	0.0	Monroe County SD	Monroeville
32	0.0	Montgomery County SD	Montgomery
32	0.0	Mountain Brook City SD	Mountain Brook
32	0.0	Muscle Shoals City SD	Muscle Shoals
32	0.0	Opelika City SD	Opelika
32	0.0	Oxford City SD	Oxford
32	0.0	Ozark City SD	Ozark
32	0.0	Pell City City SD	Pell City
32	0.0	Perry County SD	Marion
32	0.0	Phenix City City SD	Phenix City
32	0.0	Pickens County SD	Carrollton
32	0.0	Randolph County SD	Wedowee
32	0.0	Russell County SD	Phenix City
32	0.0	Scottsboro City SD	Scottsboro
32	0.0	Selma City SD	Selma
32	0.0	Shelby County SD	Columbiana
32	0.0	Sumter County SD	Livingston
32	0.0	Sylacauga City SD	Sylacauga
32	0.0	Talladega City SD	Talladega
32	0.0	Talladega County SD	Talladega
32	0.0	Tallapoosa County SD	Dadeville
32	0.0	Tallassee City SD	Tallassee
32	0.0	Thomasville City SD	Thomasville
32	0.0	Tuscaloosa City SD	Tuscaloosa
32	0.0	Tuscaloosa County SD	Tuscaloosa
32	0.0	Vestavia Hills City SD	Birmingham
32	0.0	Walker County SD	Jasper
32	0.0	Wilcox County SD	Camden
32	0.0	Winston County SD	Double Springs

Students Eligible for Free Lunch

Rank	Percent	District Name	City
1	95.1	Wilcox County SD	Camden
2	91.0	Perry County SD	Marion
3	89.2	Sumter County SD	Livingston
4	86.2	Lowndes County SD	Hayneville
5	84.3	Greene County SD	Eutaw
6	82.9	Bullock County SD	Union Springs
7	81.1	Marengo County SD	Linden
8	79.0	Anniston City SD	Anniston
9	78.4	Selma City SD	Selma
10	74.1	Conecuh County SD	Evergreen
11	72.7	Dallas County SD	Selma
12	72.1	Macon County SD	Tuskegee
13	71.1	Pike County SD	Troy
14	69.2	Bessemer City SD	Bessemer
15	67.4	Birmingham City SD	Birmingham
16	67.0	Hale County SD	Greensboro
17	66.5	Choctaw County SD	Butler
18	64.5	Butler County SD	Greenville
19	61.0	Fairfield City SD	Fairfield
20	60.1	Pickens County SD	Carrollton
21	59.3	Gadsden City SD	Gadsden
22	58.4	Russell County SD	Phenix City
23	58.3	Montgomery County SD	Montgomery
24	57.4	Mobile County SD	Mobile
25	56.9	Tuscaloosa City SD	Tuscaloosa
26	55.8	Phenix City City SD	Phenix City
26	55.8	Talladega City SD	Talladega
28	55.6	Chambers County SD	Lafayette
29	55.4	Clarke County SD	Grove Hill
29	55.4	Escambia County SD	Brewton
31	54.6	Monroe County SD	Monroeville
32	51.7	Crenshaw County SD	Luverne
33	51.2	Opelika City SD	Opelika
34	50.8	Talladega County SD	Talladega
35	50.6	Coosa County SD	Rockford
36	50.5	Eufaula City SD	Eufaula
36	50.5	Henry County SD	Abbeville
38	49.6	Demopolis City SD	Demopolis
39	49.4	Bibb County SD	Centreville
40	49.1	Troy City SD	Troy
41	48.5	Colbert County SD	Tuscumbia
42	48.4	Washington County SD	Chatom
43	47.9	Tallapoosa County SD	Dadeville
44	46.8	Florence City SD	Florence
45	46.4	Geneva County SD	Geneva
46	45.0	Franklin County SD	Russellville
47	43.8	Attalla City SD	Attalla
47	43.8	Clay County SD	Ashland
49	43.7	Jackson County SD	Scottsboro
50	43.2	Russellville City SD	Russellville
51	43.1	Dothan City SD	Dothan
51	43.1	Winston County SD	Double Springs
53	42.9	Walker County SD	Jasper
54	42.6	Covington County SD	Andalusia
55	42.2	Thomasville City SD	Thomasville
56	42.0	Marshall County SD	Guntersville
57	41.8	Cleburne County SD	Heflin
58	41.6	Randolph County SD	Wedowee
59	41.4	Ozark City SD	Ozark
60	41.2	Dale County SD	Ozark
61	41.0	Dekalb County SD	Rainsville
62	40.9	Albertville City SD	Albertville
62	40.9	Lawrence County SD	Moulton
64	38.6	Sylacauga City SD	Sylacauga
65	38.0	Lamar County SD	Vernon
65	38.0	Tallassee City SD	Tallassee
67	37.9	Alexander City City SD	Alexander City
68	37.7	Haleyville City SD	Haleyville
69	37.5	Andalusia City SD	Andalusia
70	37.3	Coffee County SD	Elba
71	37.2	Marion County SD	Hamilton
72	37.1	Calhoun County SD	Anniston
73	36.9	Decatur City SD	Decatur
74	36.2	Cullman County SD	Cullman
75	36.0	Pell City City SD	Pell City
76	35.6	Daleville City SD	Daleville
77	35.0	Fayette County SD	Fayette
78	34.9	Fort Payne City SD	Fort Payne
79	34.8	Huntsville City SD	Huntsville
80	33.9	Cherokee County SD	Centre
81	33.0	Lee County SD	Opelika
82	32.0	Chilton County SD	Clanton
82	32.0	Guntersville City SD	Guntersville
84	31.8	Enterprise City SD	Enterprise
85	31.3	Scottsboro City SD	Scottsboro
86	31.2	Elmore County SD	Wetumpka
86	31.2	Tuscaloosa County SD	Tuscaloosa
88	30.4	Blount County SD	Oneonta
88	30.4	Jacksonville City SD	Jacksonville
90	30.3	Houston County SD	Dothan
91	30.2	Autauga County SD	Prattville
92	30.1	Morgan County SD	Decatur
93	28.7	Limestone County SD	Athens
94	28.5	Saint Clair County SD	Ashville
95	28.4	Athens City SD	Athens
96	27.9	Jasper City SD	Jasper
97	26.9	Etowah County SD	Gadsden
98	26.5	Oxford City SD	Oxford
99	25.0	Lauderdale County SD	Florence
100	24.8	Baldwin County SD	Bay Minette
101	24.4	Auburn City SD	Auburn
102	22.4	Jefferson County SD	Birmingham
103	19.8	Cullman City SD	Cullman
104	18.6	Madison County SD	Huntsville
105	16.8	Shelby County SD	Columbiana
106	16.7	Hartselle City SD	Hartselle
107	16.1	Arab City SD	Arab
108	15.2	Muscle Shoals City SD	Muscle Shoals
109	14.5	Homewood City SD	Homewood
110	11.6	Madison City SD	Madison
111	8.1	Hoover City SD	Hoover
112	2.0	Vestavia Hills City SD	Birmingham
113	0.0	Mountain Brook City SD	Mountain Brook

Students Eligible for Reduced-Price Lunch

Rank	Percent	District Name	City
1	15.4	Henry County SD	Abbeville
2	14.5	Franklin County SD	Russellville
3	14.1	Winston County SD	Double Springs
4	13.9	Jackson County SD	Scottsboro
5	13.6	Chilton County SD	Clanton
6	13.2	Crenshaw County SD	Luverne
7	13.1	Talladega County SD	Talladega
8	12.9	Clay County SD	Ashland
8	12.9	Coosa County SD	Rockford
8	12.9	Cullman County SD	Cullman
11	12.7	Bibb County SD	Centreville
11	12.7	Escambia County SD	Brewton
11	12.7	Pike County SD	Troy
14	12.4	Attalla City SD	Attalla
15	12.3	Lawrence County SD	Moulton
16	12.2	Butler County SD	Greenville
17	11.9	Coffee County SD	Elba
17	11.9	Walker County SD	Jasper
19	11.7	Colbert County SD	Tuscumbia
19	11.7	Dekalb County SD	Rainsville
21	11.0	Washington County SD	Chatom
22	10.9	Marshall County SD	Guntersville
22	10.9	Randolph County SD	Wedowee
24	10.8	Etowah County SD	Gadsden
24	10.8	Pickens County SD	Carrollton
26	10.6	Cleburne County SD	Heflin
26	10.6	Marion County SD	Hamilton
28	10.5	Choctaw County SD	Butler
29	10.4	Cherokee County SD	Centre
29	10.4	Covington County SD	Andalusia
29	10.4	Russell County SD	Phenix City
32	10.2	Calhoun County SD	Anniston
32	10.2	Dale County SD	Ozark
34	10.1	Talladega City SD	Talladega
35	10.0	Haleyville City SD	Haleyville
36	9.8	Houston County SD	Dothan
37	9.7	Fayette County SD	Fayette
38	9.6	Mobile County SD	Mobile
38	9.6	Saint Clair County SD	Ashville
40	9.5	Daleville City SD	Daleville
41	9.4	Chambers County SD	Lafayette
42	9.3	Lee County SD	Opelika
42	9.3	Monroe County SD	Monroeville
44	9.2	Blount County SD	Oneonta
45	9.1	Russellville City SD	Russellville
46	9.0	Conecuh County SD	Evergreen
46	9.0	Scottsboro City SD	Scottsboro
48	8.8	Elmore County SD	Wetumpka
48	8.8	Macon County SD	Tuskegee
50	8.7	Clarke County SD	Grove Hill
50	8.7	Hale County SD	Greensboro
50	8.7	Morgan County SD	Decatur
53	8.5	Tuscaloosa County SD	Tuscaloosa
54	8.4	Pell City City SD	Pell City
55	8.3	Ozark City SD	Ozark
55	8.3	Tallassee City SD	Tallassee
57	8.0	Eufaula City SD	Eufaula

57	8.0	Geneva County SD	Geneva
59	7.9	Fort Payne City SD	Fort Payne
59	7.9	Greene County SD	Eutaw
61	7.8	Albertville City SD	Albertville
62	7.7	Gadsden City SD	Gadsden
62	7.7	Jefferson County SD	Birmingham
62	7.7	Lamar County SD	Vernon
62	7.7	Lauderdale County SD	Florence
62	7.7	Limestone County SD	Athens
62	7.7	Thomasville City SD	Thomasville
68	7.6	Demopolis City SD	Demopolis
69	7.5	Baldwin County SD	Bay Minette
69	7.5	Bullock County SD	Union Springs
71	7.4	Andalusia City SD	Andalusia
71	7.4	Autauga County SD	Prattville
71	7.4	Tallapoosa County SD	Dadeville
71	7.4	Tuscaloosa City SD	Tuscaloosa
75	7.3	Montgomery County SD	Montgomery
76	7.2	Bessemer City SD	Bessemer
76	7.2	Birmingham City SD	Birmingham
76	7.2	Fairfield City SD	Fairfield
76	7.2	Phenix City City SD	Phenix City
80	7.1	Enterprise City SD	Enterprise
81	7.0	Selma City SD	Selma
81	7.0	Sylacauga City SD	Sylacauga
83	6.9	Dallas County SD	Selma
83	6.9	Madison County SD	Huntsville
85	6.8	Jacksonville City SD	Jacksonville
86	6.6	Athens City SD	Athens
86	6.6	Dothan City SD	Dothan
88	6.5	Oxford City SD	Oxford
89	6.3	Huntsville City SD	Huntsville
90	6.2	Marengo County SD	Linden
90	6.2	Sumter County SD	Livingston
92	6.1	Anniston City SD	Anniston
93	6.0	Opelika City SD	Opelika
94	5.9	Alexander City City SD	Alexander City
94	5.9	Auburn City SD	Auburn
94	5.9	Muscle Shoals City SD	Muscle Shoals
97	5.8	Florence City SD	Florence
97	5.8	Guntersville City SD	Guntersville
99	5.7	Decatur City SD	Decatur
99	5.7	Lowndes County SD	Hayneville
101	5.6	Cullman City SD	Cullman
101	5.6	Homewood City SD	Homewood
103	5.4	Jasper City SD	Jasper
104	5.1	Shelby County SD	Columbiana
105	5.0	Troy City SD	Troy
106	4.8	Arab City SD	Arab
107	4.7	Hartselle City SD	Hartselle
108	4.0	Perry County SD	Marion
109	3.3	Hoover City SD	Hoover
110	3.1	Madison City SD	Madison
111	1.2	Wilcox County SD	Camden
112	0.4	Vestavia Hills City SD	Birmingham
113	0.0	Mountain Brook City SD	Mountain Brook

Student/Teacher Ratio

Rank	Ratio	District Name	City
1	17.6	Blount County SD	Oneonta
2	17.5	Talladega County SD	Talladega
3	17.4	Dothan City SD	Dothan
4	17.3	Elmore County SD	Wetumpka
5	17.1	Calhoun County SD	Anniston
5	17.1	Marshall County SD	Guntersville
5	17.1	Phenix City City SD	Phenix City
8	17.0	Madison County SD	Huntsville
9	16.8	Cullman City SD	Cullman
9	16.8	Madison City SD	Madison
11	16.7	Anniston City SD	Anniston
11	16.7	Coffee County SD	Elba
11	16.7	Macon County SD	Tuskegee
14	16.6	Autauga County SD	Prattville
14	16.6	Butler County SD	Greenville
14	16.6	Chambers County SD	Lafayette
14	16.6	Covington County SD	Andalusia
14	16.6	Pell City City SD	Pell City
14	16.6	Selma City SD	Selma
20	16.5	Jacksonville City SD	Jacksonville
21	16.4	Cullman County SD	Cullman
21	16.4	Demopolis City SD	Demopolis
21	16.4	Fort Payne City SD	Fort Payne
21	16.4	Lauderdale County SD	Florence
21	16.4	Saint Clair County SD	Ashville
21	16.4	Tallassee City SD	Tallassee
27	16.3	Cherokee County SD	Centre
27	16.3	Coosa County SD	Rockford
27	16.3	Geneva County SD	Geneva
30	16.2	Cleburne County SD	Heflin
30	16.2	Tuscaloosa County SD	Tuscaloosa
32	16.1	Arab City SD	Arab
32	16.1	Lawrence County SD	Moulton
32	16.1	Russellville City SD	Russellville
35	16.0	Bibb County SD	Centreville
35	16.0	Clarke County SD	Grove Hill
35	16.0	Henry County SD	Abbeville
35	16.0	Houston County SD	Dothan
35	16.0	Lowndes County SD	Hayneville
35	16.0	Oxford City SD	Oxford
35	16.0	Pike County SD	Troy
35	16.0	Randolph County SD	Wedowee
35	16.0	Sumter County SD	Livingston
35	16.0	Washington County SD	Chatom
45	15.9	Clay County SD	Ashland
45	15.9	Daleville City SD	Daleville
45	15.9	Jasper City SD	Jasper
45	15.9	Jefferson County SD	Birmingham
45	15.9	Marion County SD	Hamilton
45	15.9	Troy City SD	Troy
51	15.8	Chilton County SD	Clanton
51	15.8	Choctaw County SD	Butler
51	15.8	Conecuh County SD	Evergreen
51	15.8	Hartselle City SD	Hartselle
51	15.8	Mobile County SD	Mobile
51	15.8	Monroe County SD	Monroeville
57	15.7	Albertville City SD	Albertville
57	15.7	Etowah County SD	Gadsden
57	15.7	Ozark City SD	Ozark
57	15.7	Russell County SD	Phenix City
57	15.7	Talladega City SD	Talladega
62	15.6	Birmingham City SD	Birmingham
62	15.6	Dale County SD	Ozark
62	15.6	Enterprise City SD	Enterprise
62	15.6	Fayette County SD	Fayette
62	15.6	Lamar County SD	Vernon
62	15.6	Muscle Shoals City SD	Muscle Shoals
62	15.6	Sylacauga City SD	Sylacauga
69	15.5	Attalla City SD	Attalla
69	15.5	Escambia County SD	Brewton
69	15.5	Jackson County SD	Scottsboro
69	15.5	Limestone County SD	Athens
73	15.4	Crenshaw County SD	Luverne
73	15.4	Montgomery County SD	Montgomery
73	15.4	Perry County SD	Marion
76	15.3	Auburn City SD	Auburn
76	15.3	Lee County SD	Opelika
76	15.3	Marengo County SD	Linden
76	15.3	Thomasville City SD	Thomasville
76	15.3	Walker County SD	Jasper
81	15.2	Dallas County SD	Selma
82	15.1	Athens City SD	Athens
82	15.1	Baldwin County SD	Bay Minette
82	15.1	Colbert County SD	Tuscumbia
82	15.1	Eufaula City SD	Eufaula
82	15.1	Hale County SD	Greensboro
82	15.1	Opelika City SD	Opelika
82	15.1	Pickens County SD	Carrollton
89	15.0	Andalusia City SD	Andalusia
89	15.0	Bessemer City SD	Bessemer
89	15.0	Dekalb County SD	Rainsville
89	15.0	Franklin County SD	Russellville
89	15.0	Greene County SD	Eutaw
89	15.0	Haleyville City SD	Haleyville
89	15.0	Huntsville City SD	Huntsville
89	15.0	Scottsboro City SD	Scottsboro
89	15.0	Shelby County SD	Columbiana
89	15.0	Tallapoosa County SD	Dadeville
89	15.0	Tuscaloosa City SD	Tuscaloosa
89	15.0	Vestavia Hills City SD	Birmingham
89	15.0	Winston County SD	Double Springs
102	14.9	Bullock County SD	Union Springs
102	14.9	Decatur City SD	Decatur
102	14.9	Gadsden City SD	Gadsden
105	14.8	Guntersville City SD	Guntersville
105	14.8	Wilcox County SD	Camden
107	14.7	Alexander City City SD	Alexander City
107	14.7	Florence City SD	Florence
109	14.6	Fairfield City SD	Fairfield
109	14.6	Morgan County SD	Decatur
111	14.4	Hoover City SD	Hoover
112	12.9	Homewood City SD	Homewood
113	12.8	Mountain Brook City SD	Mountain Brook

Student/Librarian Ratio

Rank	Ratio	District Name	City
1	945.6	Jacksonville City SD	Jacksonville
2	932.0	Clay County SD	Ashland
3	894.0	Autauga County SD	Prattville
4	862.5	Haleyville City SD	Haleyville
5	794.3	Oxford City SD	Oxford
6	783.0	Troy City SD	Troy
7	768.0	Lee County SD	Opelika
8	739.7	Madison City SD	Madison
9	717.0	Elmore County SD	Wetumpka
10	714.8	Hoover City SD	Hoover
11	708.6	Alexander City City SD	Alexander City
12	690.2	Madison County SD	Huntsville
13	672.7	Vestavia Hills City SD	Birmingham
14	667.7	Jefferson County SD	Birmingham
15	653.3	Coffee County SD	Elba
16	644.0	Homewood City SD	Homewood
17	636.1	Shelby County SD	Columbiana
18	628.0	Tallassee City SD	Tallassee
19	617.5	Muscle Shoals City SD	Muscle Shoals
20	613.4	Hartselle City SD	Hartselle
21	612.5	Tallapoosa County SD	Dadeville
22	609.9	Lauderdale County SD	Florence
23	607.0	Bessemer City SD	Bessemer
24	603.1	Cherokee County SD	Centre
25	602.9	Houston County SD	Dothan
26	591.5	Mobile County SD	Mobile
27	588.6	Marengo County SD	Linden
28	587.7	Butler County SD	Greenville
29	587.0	Crenshaw County SD	Luverne
30	585.5	Russellville City SD	Russellville
31	580.7	Blount County SD	Oneonta
32	580.0	Mountain Brook City SD	Mountain Brook
33	576.6	Eufaula City SD	Eufaula
34	571.8	Randolph County SD	Wedowee
35	570.5	Limestone County SD	Athens
36	566.5	Tuscaloosa County SD	Tuscaloosa
37	566.0	Cullman County SD	Cullman
38	562.4	Phenix City City SD	Phenix City
39	559.0	Covington County SD	Andalusia
40	557.8	Montgomery County SD	Montgomery
41	557.0	Daleville City SD	Daleville
42	556.9	Macon County SD	Tuskegee
43	551.0	Perry County SD	Marion
44	550.8	Baldwin County SD	Bay Minette
45	548.3	Thomasville City SD	Thomasville
46	540.8	Arab City SD	Arab
47	538.2	Fort Payne City SD	Fort Payne
48	538.1	Clarke County SD	Grove Hill
49	538.0	Jasper City SD	Jasper
50	532.1	Russell County SD	Phenix City
51	529.6	Florence City SD	Florence
52	528.6	Cullman City SD	Cullman
53	526.2	Calhoun County SD	Anniston
54	523.3	Demopolis City SD	Demopolis
55	518.8	Lamar County SD	Vernon
56	518.2	Talladega County SD	Talladega
57	518.1	Chilton County SD	Clanton
58	514.6	Huntsville City SD	Huntsville
59	512.4	Ozark City SD	Ozark
59	512.4	Washington County SD	Chatom
61	511.3	Morgan County SD	Decatur
62	510.9	Albertville City SD	Albertville
63	510.4	Dale County SD	Ozark
64	510.3	Saint Clair County SD	Ashville
65	506.0	Franklin County SD	Russellville
66	492.2	Henry County SD	Abbeville
67	491.0	Lawrence County SD	Moulton
68	489.1	Pell City City SD	Pell City
69	488.6	Tuscaloosa City SD	Tuscaloosa
70	488.4	Attalla City SD	Attalla
71	487.6	Monroe County SD	Monroeville
72	483.5	Dekalb County SD	Rainsville
73	481.8	Birmingham City SD	Birmingham
74	480.5	Cleburne County SD	Heflin
75	480.3	Opelika City SD	Opelika
76	477.8	Enterprise City SD	Enterprise
77	473.3	Bullock County SD	Union Springs
78	470.6	Marion County SD	Hamilton
79	467.8	Athens City SD	Athens
80	460.2	Dothan City SD	Dothan
81	458.0	Sylacauga City SD	Sylacauga
82	457.3	Auburn City SD	Auburn
83	454.8	Fairfield City SD	Fairfield
84	453.5	Guntersville City SD	Guntersville
85	452.5	Geneva County SD	Geneva
86	451.5	Scottsboro City SD	Scottsboro
87	449.9	Escambia County SD	Brewton
88	448.0	Fayette County SD	Fayette
89	444.0	Etowah County SD	Gadsden
90	441.6	Decatur City SD	Decatur
91	438.5	Greene County SD	Eutaw
91	438.5	Walker County SD	Jasper
93	438.2	Marshall County SD	Guntersville
94	437.4	Chambers County SD	Lafayette
95	436.3	Andalusia City SD	Andalusia
95	436.3	Sumter County SD	Livingston
97	427.0	Coosa County SD	Rockford
98	424.8	Pike County SD	Troy
99	423.5	Bibb County SD	Centreville
100	420.5	Pickens County SD	Carrollton
101	420.3	Jackson County SD	Scottsboro
102	418.5	Hale County SD	Greensboro

103	414.2	Wilcox County SD	Camden
104	412.4	Dallas County SD	Selma
105	412.1	Talladega City SD	Talladega
106	400.7	Choctaw County SD	Butler
107	399.3	Gadsden City SD	Gadsden
108	384.8	Colbert County SD	Tuscumbia
109	381.1	Anniston City SD	Anniston
110	372.4	Selma City SD	Selma
111	362.0	Conecuh County SD	Evergreen
112	353.0	Winston County SD	Double Springs
113	318.0	Lowndes County SD	Hayneville

Student/Counselor Ratio

Rank	Ratio	District Name	City
1	663.5	Dale County SD	Ozark
2	585.5	Russellville City SD	Russellville
3	575.0	Haleyville City SD	Haleyville
4	572.7	Cullman County SD	Cullman
5	562.2	Franklin County SD	Russellville
6	557.0	Daleville City SD	Daleville
7	551.0	Perry County SD	Marion
8	539.2	Blount County SD	Oneonta
9	538.3	Tallassee City SD	Tallassee
10	538.2	Fort Payne City SD	Fort Payne
11	531.1	Bessemer City SD	Bessemer
12	528.6	Cleburne County SD	Heflin
13	523.3	Demopolis City SD	Demopolis
14	518.3	Tallapoosa County SD	Dadeville
15	514.6	Chambers County SD	Lafayette
16	512.4	Washington County SD	Chatom
17	510.9	Albertville City SD	Albertville
17	510.9	Autauga County SD	Prattville
19	508.2	Madison City SD	Madison
20	504.3	Oxford City SD	Oxford
21	500.7	Clarke County SD	Grove Hill
22	489.8	Choctaw County SD	Butler
23	489.1	Pell City City SD	Pell City
24	487.6	Monroe County SD	Monroeville
25	487.3	Macon County SD	Tuskegee
26	486.3	Jacksonville City SD	Jacksonville
27	485.8	Chilton County SD	Clanton
27	485.8	Talladega County SD	Talladega
29	480.7	Tuscaloosa County SD	Tuscaloosa
30	480.3	Opelika City SD	Opelika
30	480.3	Walker County SD	Jasper
32	473.6	Calhoun County SD	Anniston
33	472.6	Lee County SD	Opelika
34	468.8	Jackson County SD	Scottsboro
35	465.9	Houston County SD	Dothan
36	464.2	Mobile County SD	Mobile
37	463.1	Jefferson County SD	Birmingham
38	456.3	Elmore County SD	Wetumpka
39	455.7	Cherokee County SD	Centre
40	453.2	Lawrence County SD	Moulton
41	452.5	Geneva County SD	Geneva
42	452.4	Hale County SD	Greensboro
43	451.2	Henry County SD	Abbeville
44	450.8	Sumter County SD	Livingston
45	450.7	Arab City SD	Arab
46	448.4	Gadsden City SD	Gadsden
47	448.0	Fayette County SD	Fayette
48	446.3	Etowah County SD	Gadsden
49	444.7	Anniston City SD	Anniston
50	442.9	Marion County SD	Hamilton
51	440.5	Cullman City SD	Cullman
52	438.5	Greene County SD	Eutaw
53	438.3	Saint Clair County SD	Ashville
54	438.1	Hartselle City SD	Hartselle
55	436.3	Andalusia City SD	Andalusia
56	432.3	Covington County SD	Andalusia
57	431.7	Limestone County SD	Athens
58	429.1	Fairfield City SD	Fairfield
59	426.1	Morgan County SD	Decatur
60	424.8	Pike County SD	Troy
61	424.7	Madison County SD	Huntsville
62	424.1	Shelby County SD	Columbiana
63	423.9	Enterprise City SD	Enterprise
64	423.6	Clay County SD	Ashland
65	421.8	Phenix City City SD	Phenix City
66	420.5	Hoover City SD	Hoover
67	416.6	Montgomery County SD	Montgomery
68	416.3	Dothan City SD	Dothan
69	415.7	Auburn City SD	Auburn
70	414.2	Wilcox County SD	Camden
71	413.9	Russell County SD	Phenix City
72	412.1	Talladega City SD	Talladega
73	411.9	Eufaula City SD	Eufaula
74	411.7	Muscle Shoals City SD	Muscle Shoals
75	411.3	Thomasville City SD	Thomasville
76	409.1	Dekalb County SD	Rainsville
77	402.0	Lauderdale County SD	Florence
78	400.6	Birmingham City SD	Birmingham
79	398.2	Conecuh County SD	Evergreen
80	397.0	Marengo County SD	Linden
81	395.5	Baldwin County SD	Bay Minette
82	392.4	Vestavia Hills City SD	Birmingham
83	391.8	Butler County SD	Greenville
84	391.5	Troy City SD	Troy
85	391.3	Crenshaw County SD	Luverne
86	391.0	Dallas County SD	Selma
87	389.5	Marshall County SD	Guntersville
88	387.0	Scottsboro City SD	Scottsboro
89	381.7	Sylacauga City SD	Sylacauga
90	378.9	Bibb County SD	Centreville
91	378.6	Bullock County SD	Union Springs
92	371.2	Attalla City SD	Attalla
93	370.6	Lamar County SD	Vernon
94	369.7	Pickens County SD	Carrollton
95	368.4	Florence City SD	Florence
96	363.4	Colbert County SD	Tuscumbia
96	363.4	Escambia County SD	Brewton
98	362.8	Guntersville City SD	Guntersville
99	362.5	Selma City SD	Selma
100	362.1	Winston County SD	Double Springs
101	361.9	Tuscaloosa City SD	Tuscaloosa
102	361.5	Alexander City City SD	Alexander City
103	356.4	Coffee County SD	Elba
104	352.3	Ozark City SD	Ozark
105	351.8	Randolph County SD	Wedowee
106	338.3	Mountain Brook City SD	Mountain Brook
107	338.0	Huntsville City SD	Huntsville
108	336.3	Jasper City SD	Jasper
109	322.0	Homewood City SD	Homewood
110	311.9	Athens City SD	Athens
111	294.4	Decatur City SD	Decatur
112	284.7	Coosa County SD	Rockford
113	282.7	Lowndes County SD	Hayneville

Current Spending per Student in FY2001

Rank	Dollars	District Name	City
1	8,191	Homewood City SD	Homewood
2	8,088	Mountain Brook City SD	Mountain Brook
3	7,357	Florence City SD	Florence
4	7,341	Hoover City SD	Hoover
5	7,137	Athens City SD	Athens
6	7,122	Greene County SD	Eutaw
7	6,814	Huntsville City SD	Huntsville
8	6,782	Pike County SD	Troy
9	6,755	Decatur City SD	Decatur
10	6,627	Morgan County SD	Decatur
11	6,615	Muscle Shoals City SD	Muscle Shoals
12	6,600	Wilcox County SD	Camden
13	6,587	Birmingham City SD	Birmingham
14	6,578	Anniston City SD	Anniston
15	6,571	Sumter County SD	Livingston
16	6,556	Lowndes County SD	Hayneville
17	6,523	Auburn City SD	Auburn
18	6,500	Scottsboro City SD	Scottsboro
19	6,443	Tuscaloosa City SD	Tuscaloosa
20	6,409	Shelby County SD	Columbiana
21	6,374	Escambia County SD	Brewton
22	6,348	Vestavia Hills City SD	Birmingham
23	6,344	Sylacauga City SD	Sylacauga
24	6,331	Jasper City SD	Jasper
25	6,312	Choctaw County SD	Butler
26	6,298	Guntersville City SD	Guntersville
27	6,288	Talladega City SD	Talladega
28	6,266	Colbert County SD	Tuscumbia
29	6,248	Dothan City SD	Dothan
30	6,241	Opelika City SD	Opelika
31	6,226	Gadsden City SD	Gadsden
32	6,206	Winston County SD	Double Springs
33	6,200	Marshall County SD	Guntersville
34	6,167	Marengo County SD	Linden
35	6,119	Jackson County SD	Scottsboro
36	6,113	Lawrence County SD	Moulton
37	6,081	Walker County SD	Jasper
38	6,064	Limestone County SD	Athens
39	6,058	Hartselle City SD	Hartselle
40	6,048	Phenix City City SD	Phenix City
41	6,039	Pickens County SD	Carrollton
42	6,029	Enterprise City SD	Enterprise
43	5,988	Coffee County SD	Elba
44	5,986	Clarke County SD	Grove Hill
45	5,970	Conecuh County SD	Evergreen
46	5,968	Tallapoosa County SD	Dadeville
47	5,948	Dekalb County SD	Rainsville
48	5,938	Bullock County SD	Union Springs
49	5,922	Attalla City SD	Attalla
50	5,910	Butler County SD	Greenville
51	5,905	Cherokee County SD	Centre
52	5,893	Baldwin County SD	Bay Minette
53	5,867	Franklin County SD	Russellville
54	5,853	Russellville City SD	Russellville
55	5,845	Macon County SD	Tuskegee
56	5,840	Ozark City SD	Ozark
57	5,837	Hale County SD	Greensboro
58	5,833	Perry County SD	Marion
59	5,822	Washington County SD	Chatom
60	5,806	Henry County SD	Abbeville
61	5,794	Tuscaloosa County SD	Tuscaloosa
62	5,792	Lamar County SD	Vernon
63	5,780	Russell County SD	Phenix City
64	5,779	Alexander City City SD	Alexander City
65	5,778	Dallas County SD	Selma
66	5,773	Bessemer City SD	Bessemer
67	5,764	Albertville City SD	Albertville
68	5,754	Andalusia City SD	Andalusia
69	5,746	Talladega County SD	Talladega
70	5,728	Montgomery County SD	Montgomery
71	5,726	Monroe County SD	Monroeville
72	5,699	Lauderdale County SD	Florence
72	5,699	Selma City SD	Selma
74	5,686	Dale County SD	Ozark
75	5,662	Covington County SD	Andalusia
76	5,651	Jefferson County SD	Birmingham
77	5,649	Eufaula City SD	Eufaula
78	5,645	Lee County SD	Opelika
79	5,640	Fayette County SD	Fayette
80	5,619	Bibb County SD	Centreville
81	5,615	Daleville City SD	Daleville
82	5,606	Calhoun County SD	Anniston
83	5,598	Fairfield City SD	Fairfield
84	5,596	Oxford City SD	Oxford
85	5,577	Madison County SD	Huntsville
86	5,572	Marion County SD	Hamilton
87	5,570	Cleburne County SD	Heflin
88	5,554	Clay County SD	Ashland
89	5,550	Fort Payne City SD	Fort Payne
90	5,546	Chilton County SD	Clanton
90	5,546	Coosa County SD	Rockford
92	5,532	Cullman County SD	Cullman
93	5,530	Pell City City SD	Pell City
94	5,523	Troy City SD	Troy
95	5,515	Houston County SD	Dothan
96	5,509	Chambers County SD	Lafayette
97	5,504	Demopolis City SD	Demopolis
98	5,497	Crenshaw County SD	Luverne
99	5,488	Arab City SD	Arab
100	5,480	Jacksonville City SD	Jacksonville
101	5,476	Madison City SD	Madison
102	5,472	Thomasville City SD	Thomasville
103	5,470	Randolph County SD	Wedowee
104	5,435	Geneva County SD	Geneva
105	5,414	Elmore County SD	Wetumpka
106	5,404	Mobile County SD	Mobile
107	5,387	Etowah County SD	Gadsden
108	5,383	Haleyville City SD	Haleyville
109	5,233	Cullman City SD	Cullman
110	5,127	Blount County SD	Oneonta
111	5,109	Tallassee City SD	Tallassee
112	5,077	Autauga County SD	Prattville
113	4,892	Saint Clair County SD	Ashville

Number of Diploma Recipients

Rank	Number	District Name	City
1	2,854	Mobile County SD	Mobile
2	2,278	Jefferson County SD	Birmingham
3	1,706	Birmingham City SD	Birmingham
4	1,607	Montgomery County SD	Montgomery
5	1,146	Huntsville City SD	Huntsville
6	1,093	Baldwin County SD	Bay Minette
7	1,040	Shelby County SD	Columbiana
8	813	Madison County SD	Huntsville
9	753	Tuscaloosa County SD	Tuscaloosa
10	660	Hoover City SD	Hoover
11	513	Lauderdale County SD	Florence
12	465	Cullman County SD	Cullman
13	462	Dothan City SD	Dothan
14	451	Calhoun County SD	Anniston
15	436	Etowah County SD	Gadsden
16	430	Elmore County SD	Wetumpka
17	409	Madison City SD	Madison
18	406	Decatur City SD	Decatur
19	405	Autauga County SD	Prattville
20	402	Lee County SD	Opelika
21	384	Limestone County SD	Athens
22	383	Tuscaloosa City SD	Tuscaloosa
23	381	Morgan County SD	Decatur
24	372	Dekalb County SD	Rainsville
25	344	Walker County SD	Jasper
26	343	Lawrence County SD	Moulton
26	343	Vestavia Hills City SD	Birmingham
28	341	Talladega County SD	Talladega
29	330	Saint Clair County SD	Ashville
30	329	Chilton County SD	Clanton

31	323	Houston County SD	Dothan
32	318	Enterprise City SD	Enterprise
33	313	Blount County SD	Oneonta
34	281	Marshall County SD	Guntersville
35	277	Florence City SD	Florence
35	277	Jackson County SD	Scottsboro
37	268	Auburn City SD	Auburn
38	262	Mountain Brook City SD	Mountain Brook
39	257	Gadsden City SD	Gadsden
40	248	Monroe County SD	Monroeville
41	231	Homewood City SD	Homewood
42	230	Escambia County SD	Brewton
43	229	Dallas County SD	Selma
44	218	Opelika City SD	Opelika
45	214	Pickens County SD	Carrollton
46	200	Washington County SD	Chatom
47	199	Chambers County SD	Lafayette
48	191	Arab City SD	Arab
49	190	Marion County SD	Hamilton
50	185	Oxford City SD	Oxford
50	185	Pell City City SD	Pell City
52	181	Cullman City SD	Cullman
53	177	Tallapoosa County SD	Dadeville
54	176	Clarke County SD	Grove Hill
55	171	Hartselle City SD	Hartselle
56	168	Alexander City City SD	Alexander City
56	168	Butler County SD	Greenville
58	167	Cherokee County SD	Centre
58	167	Jasper City SD	Jasper
60	164	Selma City SD	Selma
61	162	Hale County SD	Greensboro
62	161	Ozark City SD	Ozark
63	160	Winston County SD	Double Springs
64	154	Eufaula City SD	Eufaula
65	153	Macon County SD	Tuskegee
66	150	Talladega City SD	Talladega
67	149	Clay County SD	Ashland
67	149	Scottsboro City SD	Scottsboro
69	147	Athens City SD	Athens
70	146	Phenix City City SD	Phenix City
71	145	Fayette County SD	Fayette
72	144	Lamar County SD	Vernon
73	143	Geneva County SD	Geneva
73	143	Sumter County SD	Livingston
75	140	Albertville City SD	Albertville
75	140	Dale County SD	Ozark
77	137	Muscle Shoals City SD	Muscle Shoals
78	136	Fort Payne City SD	Fort Payne
79	132	Covington County SD	Andalusia
79	132	Franklin County SD	Russellville
81	131	Bibb County SD	Centreville
81	131	Lowndes County SD	Hayneville
83	130	Fairfield City SD	Fairfield
84	129	Crenshaw County SD	Luverne
85	128	Sylacauga City SD	Sylacauga
86	126	Wilcox County SD	Camden
87	124	Cleburne County SD	Heflin
87	124	Henry County SD	Abbeville
89	121	Russell County SD	Phenix City
90	120	Perry County SD	Marion
91	116	Colbert County SD	Tuscumbia
92	113	Andalusia City SD	Andalusia
93	110	Bullock County SD	Union Springs
93	110	Russellville City SD	Russellville
95	109	Attalla City SD	Attalla
95	109	Bessemer City SD	Bessemer
97	107	Troy City SD	Troy
98	106	Demopolis City SD	Demopolis
99	105	Coffee County SD	Elba
100	104	Choctaw County SD	Butler
100	104	Haleyville City SD	Haleyville
102	94	Tallassee City SD	Tallassee
103	93	Guntersville City SD	Guntersville
104	90	Daleville City SD	Daleville
104	90	Jacksonville City SD	Jacksonville
106	88	Marengo County SD	Linden
107	87	Thomasville City SD	Thomasville
108	84	Randolph County SD	Wedowee
109	80	Pike County SD	Troy
110	77	Anniston City SD	Anniston
111	73	Coosa County SD	Rockford
112	68	Greene County SD	Eutaw
113	58	Conecuh County SD	Evergreen

High School Drop-out Rate

Rank	Percent	District Name	City
1	8.9	Anniston City SD	Anniston
1	8.9	Russell County SD	Phenix City
3	8.5	Choctaw County SD	Butler
4	7.9	Conecuh County SD	Evergreen
5	7.7	Fort Payne City SD	Fort Payne
6	7.1	Pell City City SD	Pell City
7	6.9	Covington County SD	Andalusia
7	6.9	Cullman County SD	Cullman
7	6.9	Limestone County SD	Athens
7	6.9	Pike County SD	Troy
11	6.8	Perry County SD	Marion
12	6.6	Attalla City SD	Attalla
12	6.6	Henry County SD	Abbeville
14	6.4	Dale County SD	Ozark
15	6.3	Gadsden City SD	Gadsden
15	6.3	Marshall County SD	Guntersville
17	6.1	Dothan City SD	Dothan
18	6.0	Blount County SD	Oneonta
18	6.0	Cherokee County SD	Centre
18	6.0	Greene County SD	Eutaw
21	5.7	Coffee County SD	Elba
21	5.7	Tuscaloosa City SD	Tuscaloosa
23	5.6	Butler County SD	Greenville
23	5.6	Cleburne County SD	Heflin
23	5.6	Dekalb County SD	Rainsville
23	5.6	Marion County SD	Hamilton
23	5.6	Tallapoosa County SD	Dadeville
28	5.5	Elmore County SD	Wetumpka
28	5.5	Pickens County SD	Carrollton
30	5.4	Chambers County SD	Lafayette
31	5.2	Athens City SD	Athens
31	5.2	Florence City SD	Florence
31	5.2	Guntersville City SD	Guntersville
31	5.2	Haleyville City SD	Haleyville
35	5.1	Tallassee City SD	Tallassee
36	5.0	Mobile County SD	Mobile
37	4.9	Jefferson County SD	Birmingham
37	4.9	Talladega City SD	Talladega
39	4.8	Arab City SD	Arab
39	4.8	Franklin County SD	Russellville
39	4.8	Randolph County SD	Wedowee
42	4.7	Monroe County SD	Monroeville
43	4.6	Alexander City City SD	Alexander City
43	4.6	Etowah County SD	Gadsden
43	4.6	Montgomery County SD	Montgomery
43	4.6	Talladega County SD	Talladega
43	4.6	Tuscaloosa County SD	Tuscaloosa
48	4.5	Escambia County SD	Brewton
49	4.4	Calhoun County SD	Anniston
49	4.4	Chilton County SD	Clanton
49	4.4	Coosa County SD	Rockford
49	4.4	Enterprise City SD	Enterprise
53	4.3	Wilcox County SD	Camden
54	4.2	Albertville City SD	Albertville
54	4.2	Autauga County SD	Prattville
54	4.2	Colbert County SD	Tuscumbia
54	4.2	Madison County SD	Huntsville
58	4.1	Bibb County SD	Centreville
58	4.1	Saint Clair County SD	Ashville
60	4.0	Bessemer City SD	Bessemer
60	4.0	Hale County SD	Greensboro
60	4.0	Jackson County SD	Scottsboro
63	3.9	Demopolis City SD	Demopolis
63	3.9	Eufaula City SD	Eufaula
65	3.8	Bullock County SD	Union Springs
65	3.8	Crenshaw County SD	Luverne
65	3.8	Fayette County SD	Fayette
65	3.8	Macon County SD	Tuskegee
69	3.7	Daleville City SD	Daleville
69	3.7	Walker County SD	Jasper
71	3.6	Baldwin County SD	Bay Minette
71	3.6	Houston County SD	Dothan
71	3.6	Morgan County SD	Decatur
71	3.6	Ozark City SD	Ozark
71	3.6	Scottsboro City SD	Scottsboro
76	3.5	Dallas County SD	Selma
76	3.5	Winston County SD	Double Springs
78	3.4	Lawrence County SD	Moulton
79	3.3	Lee County SD	Opelika
79	3.3	Phenix City City SD	Phenix City
81	3.1	Andalusia City SD	Andalusia
81	3.1	Hartselle City SD	Hartselle
81	3.1	Marengo County SD	Linden
81	3.1	Shelby County SD	Columbiana
85	3.0	Oxford City SD	Oxford
86	2.8	Decatur City SD	Decatur
86	2.8	Jasper City SD	Jasper
86	2.8	Lamar County SD	Vernon
89	2.7	Lauderdale County SD	Florence
89	2.7	Lowndes County SD	Hayneville
91	2.5	Russellville City SD	Russellville
92	2.4	Clay County SD	Ashland
93	2.3	Birmingham City SD	Birmingham
93	2.3	Fairfield City SD	Fairfield
93	2.3	Geneva County SD	Geneva
96	2.1	Troy City SD	Troy
97	1.9	Huntsville City SD	Huntsville
98	1.7	Hoover City SD	Hoover
98	1.7	Jacksonville City SD	Jacksonville
100	1.3	Thomasville City SD	Thomasville
101	1.2	Sylacauga City SD	Sylacauga
102	1.0	Auburn City SD	Auburn
102	1.0	Muscle Shoals City SD	Muscle Shoals
104	0.9	Washington County SD	Chatom
105	0.7	Clarke County SD	Grove Hill
105	0.7	Cullman City SD	Cullman
105	0.7	Madison City SD	Madison
105	0.7	Opelika City SD	Opelika
105	0.7	Vestavia Hills City SD	Birmingham
110	0.6	Homewood City SD	Homewood
111	0.4	Mountain Brook City SD	Mountain Brook
111	0.4	Sumter County SD	Livingston
113	0.2	Selma City SD	Selma

Alaska

Alaska Public School Educational Profile

Category	Value	Category	Value
Schools *(2002-2003)*	518	**Diploma Recipients** *(2002-2003)*	6,945
Instructional Level		White, Non-Hispanic	4,734
Primary	178	Black, Non-Hispanic	252
Middle	36	Asian/Pacific Islander	422
High	69	American Indian/Alaskan Native	1,340
Other Level	235	Hispanic	197
Curriculum		**High School Drop-out Rate** (%) *(2000-2001)*	8.2
Regular	483	White, Non-Hispanic	6.3
Special Education	2	Black, Non-Hispanic	11.4
Vocational	2	Asian/Pacific Islander	8.6
Alternative	31	American Indian/Alaskan Native	12.7
Type		Hispanic	11.0
Magnet	18	**Staff** *(2002-2003)*	16,935.7
Charter	15	Teachers	8,083.7
Title I Eligible	318	Average Salary ($)	49,694
School-wide Title I	82	Librarians/Media Specialists	160.8
Students *(2002-2003)*	134,364	Guidance Counselors	289.9
Gender (%)		**Ratios** *(2002-2003)*	
Male	51.6	Student/Teacher Ratio	16.6 to 1
Female	48.4	Student/Librarian Ratio	835.6 to 1
Race/Ethnicity (%)		Student/Counselor Ratio	463.5 to 1
White, Non-Hispanic	59.4	**Current Spending** *($ per student in FY 2001)*	9,563
Black, Non-Hispanic	4.7	Instruction	5,617
Asian/Pacific Islander	6.3	Support Services	3,627
American Indian/Alaskan Native	25.9	**College Entrance Exam Scores** *(2003)*	
Hispanic	3.7	Scholastic Aptitude Test (SAT)	
Classification (%)		Participation Rate (%)	55
Individual Education Program (IEP)	13.5	Mean SAT I Verbal Score	518
Migrant	7.6	Mean SAT I Math Score	518
English Language Learner (ELL)	12.2	American College Testing Program (ACT)	
Eligible for Free Lunch Program	19.2	Participation Rate (%)	32
Eligible for Reduced-Price Lunch Program	6.8	Average Composite Score	21.1

Note: *For an explanation of data, please refer to the User's Guide in the front of the book; n/a indicates data not available*

Alaska NAEP 2003 Test Scores

Reading		
Grade/Category	Value	Rank
4th Grade		
Average Proficiency	211.5 (1.6)	42/51
Proficiency by Gender/Race/Ethnicity		
Male	205.2 (1.9)	43/51
Female	218.2 (2.0)	38/51
White, Non-Hispanic	226.4 (1.2)	22/51
Black, Non-Hispanic	208.9 (3.5)	4/42
Asian, Non-Hispanic	209.2 (3.0)	9/41
American Indian, Non-Hispanic	207.0 (4.5)	23/25
Hispanic	184.4 (2.5)	10/12
Proficiency by Class Size		
Less than 16 Students	179.3 (5.7)	44/45
16 to 18 Students	*188.7 (9.3)*	47/48
19 to 20 Students	*209.3 (5.8)*	43/50
21 to 25 Students	219.1 (2.1)	34/51
Greater than 25 Students	221.7 (2.2)	18/49
Percent Attaining Achievement Levels		
Below Basic	42.3 (1.8)	11/51
Basic or Above	57.7 (1.8)	41/51
Proficient or Above	27.7 (1.6)	37/51
Advanced or Above	6.0 (0.8)	37/51
8th Grade		
Average Proficiency	256.4 (1.1)	42/51
Proficiency by Gender/Race/Ethnicity		
Male	250.3 (1.8)	43/51
Female	262.9 (1.4)	39/51
White, Non-Hispanic	267.9 (1.0)	35/50
Black, Non-Hispanic	248.9 (3.6)	5/41
Asian, Non-Hispanic	246.4 (3.6)	18/37
American Indian, Non-Hispanic	253.5 (3.5)	20/23
Hispanic	234.9 (2.7)	10/10
Proficiency by Parents Highest Level of Ed.		
Did Not Finish High School	n/a	n/a
Graduated High School	n/a	n/a
Some Education After High School	n/a	n/a
Graduated College	n/a	n/a
Percent Attaining Achievement Levels		
Below Basic	33.3 (1.2)	10/51
Basic or Above	66.7 (1.2)	42/51
Proficient or Above	26.8 (1.3)	35/51
Advanced or Above	2.7 (0.5)	21/51

Mathematics		
Grade/Category	Value	Rank
4th Grade		
Average Proficiency	233.0 (0.8)	34/51
Proficiency by Gender/Race/Ethnicity		
Male	234.5 (0.9)	34/51
Female	231.3 (1.1)	35/51
White, Non-Hispanic	242.0 (0.9)	26/51
Black, Non-Hispanic	221.5 (2.5)	9/42
Asian, Non-Hispanic	227.9 (3.1)	9/43
American Indian, Non-Hispanic	230.3 (2.3)	21/26
Hispanic	217.6 (1.7)	6/12
Proficiency by Class Size		
Less than 16 Students	216.1 (3.0)	37/47
16 to 18 Students	*229.3 (5.1)*	31/48
19 to 20 Students	*227.6 (4.0)*	42/50
21 to 25 Students	236.0 (1.4)	31/51
Greater than 25 Students	239.6 (1.8)	12/49
Percent Attaining Achievement Levels		
Below Basic	25.2 (1.2)	18/51
Basic or Above	74.8 (1.2)	34/51
Proficient or Above	30.2 (1.1)	34/51
Advanced or Above	3.6 (0.5)	22/51
8th Grade		
Average Proficiency	279.0 (0.9)	26/51
Proficiency by Gender/Race/Ethnicity		
Male	280.2 (1.3)	27/51
Female	277.8 (1.2)	26/51
White, Non-Hispanic	290.3 (0.9)	9/50
Black, Non-Hispanic	263.1 (3.0)	2/41
Asian, Non-Hispanic	263.0 (3.7)	11/37
American Indian, Non-Hispanic	279.9 (3.0)	18/23
Hispanic	259.1 (1.9)	7/11
Proficiency by Parents Highest Level of Ed.		
Did Not Finish High School	n/a	n/a
Graduated High School	n/a	n/a
Some Education After High School	n/a	n/a
Graduated College	n/a	n/a
Percent Attaining Achievement Levels		
Below Basic	30.3 (1.4)	25/51
Basic or Above	69.7 (1.4)	27/51
Proficient or Above	30.0 (1.1)	24/51
Advanced or Above	5.7 (0.6)	17/51

***Note:** For an explanation of data, please refer to the User's Guide in the front of the book; values in italics indicate that the nature of the sample does not allow accurate determination of the variability of the statistic; n/a indicates data not available*

Anchorage Borough

Anchorage SD

4600 Debarr Ave • Anchorage, AK 99519-6614
Mailing Address: PO Box 196614 • Anchorage, AK 99519-6614
(907) 742-4312 • http://www.asdk12.org/
Grade Span: PK-12; **Agency Type:** 1
Schools: 98
64 Primary; 9 Middle; 15 High; 10 Other Level
83 Regular; 2 Special Education; 1 Vocational; 12 Alternative
10 Magnet; 3 Charter; 28 Title I Eligible; 13 School-wide Title I
Students: 50,055 (51.8% male; 48.2% female)
Individual Education Program: 7,201 (14.4%);
English Language Learner: 5,504 (11.0%); Migrant: 1,283 (2.6%)
Eligible for Free Lunch Program: 7,271 (14.5%)
Eligible for Reduced-Price Lunch Program: 2,752 (5.5%)
Teachers: 2,889.8 (17.3 to 1)
Librarians/Media Specialists: 73.5 (681.0 to 1)
Guidance Counselors: 103.1 (485.5 to 1)
Current Spending: ($ per student per year):
Total: $7,399; Instruction: $4,071; Support Services: $3,117
Enrollment, Drop-out Rates and Diploma Recipients by Race/Ethnicity

Category	Total	White	Black	Asian	AIAN	Hisp.
Enrollment (%)	100.0	60.0	8.9	11.1	13.7	6.3
Drop-out Rate (%)	9.3	6.7	12.5	11.4	20.5	12.1
H.S. Diplomas (#)	2,505	1,763	174	255	196	117

Bethel Borough

Lower Kuskokwim SD

1004 Ron Edwards Way • Bethel, AK 99559-0305
Mailing Address: PO Box 305 • Bethel, AK 99559-0305
(907) 543-4810 • http://www.lksd.org/
Grade Span: PK-12; **Agency Type:** 1
Schools: 28
3 Primary; 0 Middle; 2 High; 23 Other Level
26 Regular; 0 Special Education; 0 Vocational; 2 Alternative
1 Magnet; 1 Charter; 27 Title I Eligible; 0 School-wide Title I
Students: 3,726 (51.4% male; 48.6% female)
Individual Education Program: 512 (13.7%);
English Language Learner: 2,202 (59.1%); Migrant: 1,013 (27.2%)
Eligible for Free Lunch Program: 1,942 (52.1%)
Eligible for Reduced-Price Lunch Program: 318 (8.5%)
Teachers: 265.5 (14.0 to 1)
Librarians/Media Specialists: 4.0 (931.5 to 1)
Guidance Counselors: 3.0 (1,242.0 to 1)
Current Spending: ($ per student per year):
Total: $16,135; Instruction: $9,542; Support Services: $5,786
Enrollment, Drop-out Rates and Diploma Recipients by Race/Ethnicity

Category	Total	White	Black	Asian	AIAN	Hisp.
Enrollment (%)	100.0	4.8	0.4	0.5	94.0	0.3
Drop-out Rate (%)	18.5	3.5	0.0	0.0	19.8	0.0
H.S. Diplomas (#)	118	11	0	3	104	0

Fairbanks North Star Borough

Fairbanks North Star Boro SD

520 Fifth Ave • Fairbanks, AK 99701-4756
(907) 452-2000 • http://www.northstar.k12.ak.us/
Grade Span: PK-12; **Agency Type:** 1
Schools: 33
20 Primary; 4 Middle; 6 High; 3 Other Level
30 Regular; 0 Special Education; 1 Vocational; 2 Alternative
1 Magnet; 1 Charter; 9 Title I Eligible; 5 School-wide Title I
Students: 15,412 (51.5% male; 48.5% female)
Individual Education Program: 2,186 (14.2%);
English Language Learner: 501 (3.3%); Migrant: 241 (1.6%)
Eligible for Free Lunch Program: 2,307 (15.0%)
Eligible for Reduced-Price Lunch Program: 1,498 (9.7%)
Teachers: 882.0 (17.5 to 1)
Librarians/Media Specialists: 9.0 (1,712.4 to 1)
Guidance Counselors: 43.5 (354.3 to 1)
Current Spending: ($ per student per year):
Total: $8,470; Instruction: $5,137; Support Services: $3,069
Enrollment, Drop-out Rates and Diploma Recipients by Race/Ethnicity

Category	Total	White	Black	Asian	AIAN	Hisp.
Enrollment (%)	100.0	70.6	8.2	3.3	13.8	4.0
Drop-out Rate (%)	10.5	8.7	9.3	4.1	23.4	15.3
H.S. Diplomas (#)	785	637	45	29	60	14

Juneau Borough

Juneau Borough Schs

1208 Glacier Ave • Juneau, AK 99801
Mailing Address: 10014 Crazy Horse Dr • Juneau, AK 99801
(907) 463-1700 • http://www.jsd.k12.ak.us/
Grade Span: PK-12; **Agency Type:** 1
Schools: 12
7 Primary; 2 Middle; 1 High; 2 Other Level
11 Regular; 0 Special Education; 0 Vocational; 1 Alternative
1 Magnet; 1 Charter; 4 Title I Eligible; 0 School-wide Title I
Students: 5,543 (51.3% male; 48.7% female)
Individual Education Program: 736 (13.3%);
English Language Learner: 717 (12.9%); Migrant: 0 (0.0%)
Eligible for Free Lunch Program: 495 (8.9%)
Eligible for Reduced-Price Lunch Program: 101 (1.8%)
Teachers: 325.8 (17.0 to 1)
Librarians/Media Specialists: 6.0 (923.8 to 1)
Guidance Counselors: 10.6 (522.9 to 1)
Current Spending: ($ per student per year):
Total: $8,160; Instruction: $4,958; Support Services: $3,143
Enrollment, Drop-out Rates and Diploma Recipients by Race/Ethnicity

Category	Total	White	Black	Asian	AIAN	Hisp.
Enrollment (%)	100.0	63.1	1.1	9.1	23.3	3.5
Drop-out Rate (%)	9.2	6.4	5.3	3.3	21.2	20.6
H.S. Diplomas (#)	333	249	1	27	48	8

Kenai Peninsula Borough

Kenai Peninsula Borough Schs

148 N Binkley St • Soldotna, AK 99669
(907) 262-5846 • http://www.kpbsd.k12.ak.us/
Grade Span: PK-12; **Agency Type:** 1
Schools: 43
19 Primary; 4 Middle; 9 High; 11 Other Level
39 Regular; 0 Special Education; 0 Vocational; 4 Alternative
3 Magnet; 3 Charter; 23 Title I Eligible; 0 School-wide Title I
Students: 9,750 (51.7% male; 48.3% female)
Individual Education Program: 1,299 (13.3%);
English Language Learner: 224 (2.3%); Migrant: 642 (6.6%)
Eligible for Free Lunch Program: 1,678 (17.2%)
Eligible for Reduced-Price Lunch Program: 786 (8.1%)
Teachers: 603.8 (16.1 to 1)
Librarians/Media Specialists: 17.3 (563.6 to 1)
Guidance Counselors: 17.1 (570.2 to 1)
Current Spending: ($ per student per year):
Total: $8,732; Instruction: $5,101; Support Services: $3,394
Enrollment, Drop-out Rates and Diploma Recipients by Race/Ethnicity

Category	Total	White	Black	Asian	AIAN	Hisp.
Enrollment (%)	100.0	83.9	0.6	1.7	12.0	1.7
Drop-out Rate (%)	7.4	7.0	7.4	1.5	10.6	12.0
H.S. Diplomas (#)	669	564	15	18	65	7

Ketchikan Gateway Borough

Ketchikan Gateway Borough SD

2610 Fourth Ave • Ketchikan, AK 99901-6278
Mailing Address: 333 Schoenbar Rd • Ketchikan, AK 99901-6278
(907) 225-2118 • http://www.kgbsd.org/
Grade Span: PK-12; **Agency Type:** 1
Schools: 10
5 Primary; 1 Middle; 2 High; 2 Other Level
8 Regular; 0 Special Education; 0 Vocational; 2 Alternative
0 Magnet; 1 Charter; 7 Title I Eligible; 0 School-wide Title I
Students: 2,391 (50.9% male; 49.1% female)
Individual Education Program: 329 (13.8%);
English Language Learner: 58 (2.4%); Migrant: 103 (4.3%)
Eligible for Free Lunch Program: 393 (16.4%)
Eligible for Reduced-Price Lunch Program: 103 (4.3%)
Teachers: 141.5 (16.9 to 1)
Librarians/Media Specialists: 3.0 (797.0 to 1)
Guidance Counselors: 2.0 (1,195.5 to 1)
Current Spending: ($ per student per year):
Total: $8,161; Instruction: $4,800; Support Services: $3,217
Enrollment, Drop-out Rates and Diploma Recipients by Race/Ethnicity

Category	Total	White	Black	Asian	AIAN	Hisp.
Enrollment (%)	100.0	62.7	1.0	5.9	28.3	2.1
Drop-out Rate (%)	9.4	6.3	12.5	14.6	18.6	5.0
H.S. Diplomas (#)	128	104	3	11	9	1

Kodiak Island Borough

Kodiak Island Borough SD

722 Mill Bay Rd • Kodiak, AK 99615
(907) 486-9210 • http://www.kodiak.k12.ak.us/
Grade Span: PK-12; **Agency Type:** 1
Schools: 16
4 Primary; 1 Middle; 2 High; 9 Other Level
15 Regular; 0 Special Education; 0 Vocational; 1 Alternative
0 Magnet; 0 Charter; 7 Title I Eligible; 0 School-wide Title I
Students: 2,754 (52.4% male; 47.6% female)
Individual Education Program: 413 (15.0%);
English Language Learner: 205 (7.4%); Migrant: 484 (17.6%)
Eligible for Free Lunch Program: 611 (22.2%)
Eligible for Reduced-Price Lunch Program: 301 (10.9%)
Teachers: 190.2 (14.5 to 1)
Librarians/Media Specialists: 1.0 (2,754.0 to 1)
Guidance Counselors: 6.0 (459.0 to 1)
Current Spending: ($ per student per year):
Total: $9,522; Instruction: $5,677; Support Services: $3,580
Enrollment, Drop-out Rates and Diploma Recipients by Race/Ethnicity

Category	Total	White	Black	Asian	AIAN	Hisp.
Enrollment (%)	100.0	47.9	1.1	22.6	22.5	5.9
Drop-out Rate (%)	4.5	3.9	18.2	3.9	6.7	0.0
H.S. Diplomas (#)	184	96	1	38	45	4

Matanuska-Susitna Borough

Matanuska-Susitna Borough Schs

125 W Evergreen • Palmer, AK 99645
(907) 746-9255 • http://www.mat-su.k12.ak.us/schdist
Grade Span: PK-12; **Agency Type:** 1
Schools: 36
18 Primary; 5 Middle; 8 High; 5 Other Level
33 Regular; 0 Special Education; 0 Vocational; 3 Alternative
0 Magnet; 2 Charter; 18 Title I Eligible; 6 School-wide Title I
Students: 13,870 (52.2% male; 47.8% female)
Individual Education Program: 2,115 (15.2%);
English Language Learner: 433 (3.1%); Migrant: 425 (3.1%)
Eligible for Free Lunch Program: 2,432 (17.5%)
Eligible for Reduced-Price Lunch Program: 1,093 (7.9%)
Teachers: 802.2 (17.3 to 1)
Librarians/Media Specialists: 22.0 (630.5 to 1)
Guidance Counselors: 22.8 (608.3 to 1)
Current Spending: ($ per student per year):
Total: $8,316; Instruction: $4,547; Support Services: $3,549
Enrollment, Drop-out Rates and Diploma Recipients by Race/Ethnicity

Category	Total	White	Black	Asian	AIAN	Hisp.
Enrollment (%)	100.0	84.5	1.0	1.0	11.5	1.9
Drop-out Rate (%)	4.7	4.8	12.9	0.0	4.5	4.2
H.S. Diplomas (#)	830	739	8	8	54	21

Nome Borough

Bering Strait SD

225 Main St • Unalakleet, AK 99684-0225
Mailing Address: PO Box 225 • Unalakleet, AK 99684-0225
(907) 624-3611 • http://www.bssd.org/
Grade Span: PK-12; **Agency Type:** 1
Schools: 15
0 Primary; 0 Middle; 0 High; 15 Other Level
15 Regular; 0 Special Education; 0 Vocational; 0 Alternative
0 Magnet; 0 Charter; 15 Title I Eligible; 15 School-wide Title I
Students: 1,753 (51.1% male; 48.9% female)
Individual Education Program: 263 (15.0%);
English Language Learner: 943 (53.8%); Migrant: 631 (36.0%)
Eligible for Free Lunch Program: 1,032 (58.9%)
Eligible for Reduced-Price Lunch Program: 208 (11.9%)
Teachers: 169.5 (10.3 to 1)
Librarians/Media Specialists: 1.0 (1,753.0 to 1)
Guidance Counselors: 8.0 (219.1 to 1)
Current Spending: ($ per student per year):
Total: $17,509; Instruction: $11,309; Support Services: $5,305
Enrollment, Drop-out Rates and Diploma Recipients by Race/Ethnicity

Category	Total	White	Black	Asian	AIAN	Hisp.
Enrollment (%)	100.0	1.5	0.0	0.2	98.3	0.0
Drop-out Rate (%)	9.1	0.0	n/a	0.0	9.3	n/a
H.S. Diplomas (#)	47	2	0	1	44	0

North Slope Borough

North Slope Borough SD

829 Aivak St • Barrow, AK 99723-0169
Mailing Address: PO Box 169 • Barrow, AK 99723-0169
(907) 852-5311 • http://www.nsbsd.k12.ak.us/
Grade Span: PK-12; **Agency Type:** 1
Schools: 10
1 Primary; 1 Middle; 1 High; 7 Other Level
10 Regular; 0 Special Education; 0 Vocational; 0 Alternative
0 Magnet; 0 Charter; 4 Title I Eligible; 0 School-wide Title I
Students: 2,115 (51.4% male; 48.6% female)
Individual Education Program: 219 (10.4%);
English Language Learner: 1,127 (53.3%); Migrant: 591 (27.9%)
Eligible for Free Lunch Program: 286 (13.5%)
Eligible for Reduced-Price Lunch Program: 268 (12.7%)
Teachers: 196.2 (10.8 to 1)
Librarians/Media Specialists: 3.0 (705.0 to 1)
Guidance Counselors: 8.9 (237.6 to 1)
Current Spending: ($ per student per year):
Total: $22,085; Instruction: $11,356; Support Services: $9,086
Enrollment, Drop-out Rates and Diploma Recipients by Race/Ethnicity

Category	Total	White	Black	Asian	AIAN	Hisp.
Enrollment (%)	100.0	7.8	0.9	6.4	84.3	0.7
Drop-out Rate (%)	13.2	1.4	16.7	3.0	15.9	0.0
H.S. Diplomas (#)	133	11	0	5	115	2

Northwest Arctic Borough

Northwest Arctic SD

776 Third Ave • Kotzebue, AK 99752
Mailing Address: PO Box 51 • Kotzebue, AK 99752
(907) 442-3472 • http://www.nwabsd.schoolzone.net/
Grade Span: PK-12; **Agency Type:** 1
Schools: 13
2 Primary; 0 Middle; 0 High; 11 Other Level
13 Regular; 0 Special Education; 0 Vocational; 0 Alternative
0 Magnet; 0 Charter; 13 Title I Eligible; 10 School-wide Title I
Students: 2,172 (50.5% male; 49.5% female)
Individual Education Program: 222 (10.2%);
English Language Learner: 296 (13.6%); Migrant: 836 (38.5%)
Eligible for Free Lunch Program: 1,069 (49.2%)
Eligible for Reduced-Price Lunch Program: 196 (9.0%)
Teachers: 164.3 (13.2 to 1)
Librarians/Media Specialists: 2.0 (1,086.0 to 1)
Guidance Counselors: 8.0 (271.5 to 1)
Current Spending: ($ per student per year):
Total: $16,073; Instruction: $8,250; Support Services: $6,939
Enrollment, Drop-out Rates and Diploma Recipients by Race/Ethnicity

Category	Total	White	Black	Asian	AIAN	Hisp.
Enrollment (%)	100.0	3.9	0.1	0.6	95.2	0.1
Drop-out Rate (%)	13.8	0.0	n/a	0.0	14.5	n/a
H.S. Diplomas (#)	68	5	0	1	62	0

Sitka Borough

Sitka Borough SD

300 Kostrometinoff St • Sitka, AK 99835-0179
Mailing Address: PO Box 179 • Sitka, AK 99835-0179
(907) 747-8622 • http://www.ssd.k12.ak.us/
Grade Span: PK-12; **Agency Type:** 1
Schools: 6
2 Primary; 1 Middle; 2 High; 1 Other Level
6 Regular; 0 Special Education; 0 Vocational; 0 Alternative
0 Magnet; 0 Charter; 4 Title I Eligible; 0 School-wide Title I
Students: 1,582 (50.4% male; 49.6% female)
Individual Education Program: 260 (16.4%);
English Language Learner: 32 (2.0%); Migrant: 108 (6.8%)
Eligible for Free Lunch Program: 270 (17.1%)
Eligible for Reduced-Price Lunch Program: 144 (9.1%)
Teachers: 109.5 (14.4 to 1)
Librarians/Media Specialists: 3.0 (527.3 to 1)
Guidance Counselors: 5.0 (316.4 to 1)
Current Spending: ($ per student per year):
Total: $8,540; Instruction: $5,695; Support Services: $2,685
Enrollment, Drop-out Rates and Diploma Recipients by Race/Ethnicity

Category	Total	White	Black	Asian	AIAN	Hisp.
Enrollment (%)	100.0	58.8	1.3	6.9	30.5	2.6
Drop-out Rate (%)	8.8	6.2	0.0	3.7	14.6	17.6
H.S. Diplomas (#)	89	52	1	5	29	2

Wade Hampton Borough

Lower Yukon SD

1st Bldg Airport Rd • Mountain Village, AK 99632-0089
Mailing Address: PO Box 32089 • Mountain Village, AK 99632-0089
(907) 591-2411 • http://www.lysd.gcisa.net/lysd/default.htm
Grade Span: PK-12; **Agency Type:** 1
Schools: 11
0 Primary; 0 Middle; 0 High; 11 Other Level
11 Regular; 0 Special Education; 0 Vocational; 0 Alternative
0 Magnet; 0 Charter; 11 Title I Eligible; 11 School-wide Title I
Students: 2,037 (51.8% male; 48.2% female)
Individual Education Program: 224 (11.0%);
English Language Learner: 1,585 (77.8%); Migrant: 729 (35.8%)
Eligible for Free Lunch Program: 1,537 (75.5%)
Eligible for Reduced-Price Lunch Program: 213 (10.5%)
Teachers: 144.9 (14.1 to 1)
Librarians/Media Specialists: 0.0 (0.0 to 1)
Guidance Counselors: 7.0 (291.0 to 1)
Current Spending: ($ per student per year):
Total: $13,342; Instruction: $7,348; Support Services: $4,928

Enrollment, Drop-out Rates and Diploma Recipients by Race/Ethnicity

Category	Total	White	Black	Asian	AIAN	Hisp.
Enrollment (%)	100.0	1.2	0.0	0.0	98.8	0.0
Drop-out Rate (%)	0.0	n/a	n/a	n/a	0.0	n/a
H.S. Diplomas (#)	50	0	0	0	50	0

Yukon-Koyukuk Borough

Galena City SD

299 Antoski Ave • Galena, AK 99741-0299
Mailing Address: PO Box 299 • Galena, AK 99741-0299
(907) 656-1205 • http://www.galenaalaska.org/
Grade Span: PK-12; **Agency Type:** 1
Schools: 4
1 Primary; 0 Middle; 2 High; 1 Other Level
4 Regular; 0 Special Education; 0 Vocational; 0 Alternative
1 Magnet; 0 Charter; 2 Title I Eligible; 0 School-wide Title I
Students: 3,889 (50.5% male; 49.5% female)
Individual Education Program: 106 (2.7%);
English Language Learner: 17 (0.4%); Migrant: 39 (1.0%)
Eligible for Free Lunch Program: 34 (0.9%)
Eligible for Reduced-Price Lunch Program: 12 (0.3%)
Teachers: 63.4 (61.3 to 1)
Librarians/Media Specialists: 2.2 (1,767.7 to 1)
Guidance Counselors: 4.5 (864.2 to 1)
Current Spending: ($ per student per year):
Total: $4,903; Instruction: $2,981; Support Services: $1,866

Enrollment, Drop-out Rates and Diploma Recipients by Race/Ethnicity

Category	Total	White	Black	Asian	AIAN	Hisp.
Enrollment (%)	100.0	84.5	2.3	1.7	10.5	1.0
Drop-out Rate (%)	0.1	0.2	0.0	0.0	0.0	0.0
H.S. Diplomas (#)	131	97	1	2	28	3

Number of Schools

Rank	Number	District Name	City
1	98	Anchorage SD	Anchorage
2	43	Kenai Peninsula Borough Schs	Soldotna
3	36	Matanuska-Susitna Borough Schs	Palmer
4	33	Fairbanks North Star Boro SD	Fairbanks
5	28	Lower Kuskokwim SD	Bethel
6	16	Kodiak Island Borough SD	Kodiak
7	15	Bering Strait SD	Unalakleet
8	13	Northwest Arctic SD	Kotzebue
9	12	Juneau Borough Schs	Juneau
10	11	Lower Yukon SD	Mountain Vlg
11	10	Ketchikan Gateway Borough SD	Ketchikan
11	10	North Slope Borough SD	Barrow
13	6	Sitka Borough SD	Sitka
14	4	Galena City SD	Galena

Number of Teachers

Rank	Number	District Name	City
1	2,889	Anchorage SD	Anchorage
2	882	Fairbanks North Star Boro SD	Fairbanks
3	802	Matanuska-Susitna Borough Schs	Palmer
4	603	Kenai Peninsula Borough Schs	Soldotna
5	325	Juneau Borough Schs	Juneau
6	265	Lower Kuskokwim SD	Bethel
7	196	North Slope Borough SD	Barrow
8	190	Kodiak Island Borough SD	Kodiak
9	169	Bering Strait SD	Unalakleet
10	164	Northwest Arctic SD	Kotzebue
11	144	Lower Yukon SD	Mountain Vlg
12	141	Ketchikan Gateway Borough SD	Ketchikan
13	109	Sitka Borough SD	Sitka
14	63	Galena City SD	Galena

Number of Students

Rank	Number	District Name	City
1	50,055	Anchorage SD	Anchorage
2	15,412	Fairbanks North Star Boro SD	Fairbanks
3	13,870	Matanuska-Susitna Borough Schs	Palmer
4	9,750	Kenai Peninsula Borough Schs	Soldotna
5	5,543	Juneau Borough Schs	Juneau
6	3,889	Galena City SD	Galena
7	3,726	Lower Kuskokwim SD	Bethel
8	2,754	Kodiak Island Borough SD	Kodiak
9	2,391	Ketchikan Gateway Borough SD	Ketchikan
10	2,172	Northwest Arctic SD	Kotzebue
11	2,115	North Slope Borough SD	Barrow
12	2,037	Lower Yukon SD	Mountain Vlg
13	1,753	Bering Strait SD	Unalakleet
14	1,582	Sitka Borough SD	Sitka

Male Students

Rank	Percent	District Name	City
1	52.4	Kodiak Island Borough SD	Kodiak
2	52.2	Matanuska-Susitna Borough Schs	Palmer
3	51.8	Anchorage SD	Anchorage
3	51.8	Lower Yukon SD	Mountain Vlg
5	51.7	Kenai Peninsula Borough Schs	Soldotna
6	51.5	Fairbanks North Star Boro SD	Fairbanks
7	51.4	Lower Kuskokwim SD	Bethel
7	51.4	North Slope Borough SD	Barrow
9	51.3	Juneau Borough Schs	Juneau
10	51.1	Bering Strait SD	Unalakleet
11	50.9	Ketchikan Gateway Borough SD	Ketchikan
12	50.5	Galena City SD	Galena
12	50.5	Northwest Arctic SD	Kotzebue
14	50.4	Sitka Borough SD	Sitka

Female Students

Rank	Percent	District Name	City
1	49.6	Sitka Borough SD	Sitka
2	49.5	Galena City SD	Galena
2	49.5	Northwest Arctic SD	Kotzebue
4	49.1	Ketchikan Gateway Borough SD	Ketchikan
5	48.9	Bering Strait SD	Unalakleet
6	48.7	Juneau Borough Schs	Juneau
7	48.6	Lower Kuskokwim SD	Bethel
7	48.6	North Slope Borough SD	Barrow
9	48.5	Fairbanks North Star Boro SD	Fairbanks
10	48.3	Kenai Peninsula Borough Schs	Soldotna
11	48.2	Anchorage SD	Anchorage
11	48.2	Lower Yukon SD	Mountain Vlg
13	47.8	Matanuska-Susitna Borough Schs	Palmer
14	47.6	Kodiak Island Borough SD	Kodiak

Individual Education Program Students

Rank	Percent	District Name	City
1	16.4	Sitka Borough SD	Sitka
2	15.2	Matanuska-Susitna Borough Schs	Palmer
3	15.0	Bering Strait SD	Unalakleet
3	15.0	Kodiak Island Borough SD	Kodiak
5	14.4	Anchorage SD	Anchorage
6	14.2	Fairbanks North Star Boro SD	Fairbanks
7	13.8	Ketchikan Gateway Borough SD	Ketchikan
8	13.7	Lower Kuskokwim SD	Bethel
9	13.3	Juneau Borough Schs	Juneau
9	13.3	Kenai Peninsula Borough Schs	Soldotna
11	11.0	Lower Yukon SD	Mountain Vlg
12	10.4	North Slope Borough SD	Barrow
13	10.2	Northwest Arctic SD	Kotzebue
14	2.7	Galena City SD	Galena

English Language Learner Students

Rank	Percent	District Name	City
1	77.8	Lower Yukon SD	Mountain Vlg
2	59.1	Lower Kuskokwim SD	Bethel
3	53.8	Bering Strait SD	Unalakleet
4	53.3	North Slope Borough SD	Barrow
5	13.6	Northwest Arctic SD	Kotzebue
6	12.9	Juneau Borough Schs	Juneau
7	11.0	Anchorage SD	Anchorage
8	7.4	Kodiak Island Borough SD	Kodiak
9	3.3	Fairbanks North Star Boro SD	Fairbanks
10	3.1	Matanuska-Susitna Borough Schs	Palmer
11	2.4	Ketchikan Gateway Borough SD	Ketchikan
12	2.3	Kenai Peninsula Borough Schs	Soldotna
13	2.0	Sitka Borough SD	Sitka
14	0.4	Galena City SD	Galena

Migrant Students

Rank	Percent	District Name	City
1	38.5	Northwest Arctic SD	Kotzebue
2	36.0	Bering Strait SD	Unalakleet
3	35.8	Lower Yukon SD	Mountain Vlg
4	27.9	North Slope Borough SD	Barrow
5	27.2	Lower Kuskokwim SD	Bethel
6	17.6	Kodiak Island Borough SD	Kodiak
7	6.8	Sitka Borough SD	Sitka
8	6.6	Kenai Peninsula Borough Schs	Soldotna
9	4.3	Ketchikan Gateway Borough SD	Ketchikan
10	3.1	Matanuska-Susitna Borough Schs	Palmer
11	2.6	Anchorage SD	Anchorage
12	1.6	Fairbanks North Star Boro SD	Fairbanks
13	1.0	Galena City SD	Galena
14	0.0	Juneau Borough Schs	Juneau

Students Eligible for Free Lunch

Rank	Percent	District Name	City
1	75.5	Lower Yukon SD	Mountain Vlg
2	58.9	Bering Strait SD	Unalakleet
3	52.1	Lower Kuskokwim SD	Bethel
4	49.2	Northwest Arctic SD	Kotzebue
5	22.2	Kodiak Island Borough SD	Kodiak
6	17.5	Matanuska-Susitna Borough Schs	Palmer
7	17.2	Kenai Peninsula Borough Schs	Soldotna
8	17.1	Sitka Borough SD	Sitka
9	16.4	Ketchikan Gateway Borough SD	Ketchikan
10	15.0	Fairbanks North Star Boro SD	Fairbanks
11	14.5	Anchorage SD	Anchorage
12	13.5	North Slope Borough SD	Barrow
13	8.9	Juneau Borough Schs	Juneau
14	0.9	Galena City SD	Galena

Students Eligible for Reduced-Price Lunch

Rank	Percent	District Name	City
1	12.7	North Slope Borough SD	Barrow
2	11.9	Bering Strait SD	Unalakleet
3	10.9	Kodiak Island Borough SD	Kodiak
4	10.5	Lower Yukon SD	Mountain Vlg
5	9.7	Fairbanks North Star Boro SD	Fairbanks
6	9.1	Sitka Borough SD	Sitka
7	9.0	Northwest Arctic SD	Kotzebue
8	8.5	Lower Kuskokwim SD	Bethel
9	8.1	Kenai Peninsula Borough Schs	Soldotna
10	7.9	Matanuska-Susitna Borough Schs	Palmer
11	5.5	Anchorage SD	Anchorage
12	4.3	Ketchikan Gateway Borough SD	Ketchikan
13	1.8	Juneau Borough Schs	Juneau
14	0.3	Galena City SD	Galena

Student/Teacher Ratio

Rank	Ratio	District Name	City
1	61.3	Galena City SD	Galena
2	17.5	Fairbanks North Star Boro SD	Fairbanks
3	17.3	Anchorage SD	Anchorage
3	17.3	Matanuska-Susitna Borough Schs	Palmer
5	17.0	Juneau Borough Schs	Juneau
6	16.9	Ketchikan Gateway Borough SD	Ketchikan
7	16.1	Kenai Peninsula Borough Schs	Soldotna
8	14.5	Kodiak Island Borough SD	Kodiak
9	14.4	Sitka Borough SD	Sitka
10	14.1	Lower Yukon SD	Mountain Vlg
11	14.0	Lower Kuskokwim SD	Bethel
12	13.2	Northwest Arctic SD	Kotzebue
13	10.8	North Slope Borough SD	Barrow
14	10.3	Bering Strait SD	Unalakleet

Student/Librarian Ratio

Rank	Ratio	District Name	City
1	2,754.0	Kodiak Island Borough SD	Kodiak
2	1,767.7	Galena City SD	Galena
3	1,753.0	Bering Strait SD	Unalakleet
4	1,712.4	Fairbanks North Star Boro SD	Fairbanks
5	1,086.0	Northwest Arctic SD	Kotzebue
6	931.5	Lower Kuskokwim SD	Bethel
7	923.8	Juneau Borough Schs	Juneau
8	797.0	Ketchikan Gateway Borough SD	Ketchikan
9	705.0	North Slope Borough SD	Barrow
10	681.0	Anchorage SD	Anchorage
11	630.5	Matanuska-Susitna Borough Schs	Palmer
12	563.6	Kenai Peninsula Borough Schs	Soldotna
13	527.3	Sitka Borough SD	Sitka
14	0.0	Lower Yukon SD	Mountain Vlg

Student/Counselor Ratio

Rank	Ratio	District Name	City
1	1,242.0	Lower Kuskokwim SD	Bethel
2	1,195.5	Ketchikan Gateway Borough SD	Ketchikan
3	864.2	Galena City SD	Galena
4	608.3	Matanuska-Susitna Borough Schs	Palmer
5	570.2	Kenai Peninsula Borough Schs	Soldotna
6	522.9	Juneau Borough Schs	Juneau
7	485.5	Anchorage SD	Anchorage
8	459.0	Kodiak Island Borough SD	Kodiak
9	354.3	Fairbanks North Star Boro SD	Fairbanks
10	316.4	Sitka Borough SD	Sitka
11	291.0	Lower Yukon SD	Mountain Vlg
12	271.5	Northwest Arctic SD	Kotzebue
13	237.6	North Slope Borough SD	Barrow
14	219.1	Bering Strait SD	Unalakleet

Current Spending per Student in FY2001

Rank	Dollars	District Name	City
1	22,085	North Slope Borough SD	Barrow
2	17,509	Bering Strait SD	Unalakleet
3	16,135	Lower Kuskokwim SD	Bethel
4	16,073	Northwest Arctic SD	Kotzebue
5	13,342	Lower Yukon SD	Mountain Vlg
6	9,522	Kodiak Island Borough SD	Kodiak
7	8,732	Kenai Peninsula Borough Schs	Soldotna
8	8,540	Sitka Borough SD	Sitka
9	8,470	Fairbanks North Star Boro SD	Fairbanks
10	8,316	Matanuska-Susitna Borough Schs	Palmer
11	8,161	Ketchikan Gateway Borough SD	Ketchikan
12	8,160	Juneau Borough Schs	Juneau
13	7,399	Anchorage SD	Anchorage
14	4,903	Galena City SD	Galena

Number of Diploma Recipients

Rank	Number	District Name	City
1	2,505	Anchorage SD	Anchorage
2	830	Matanuska-Susitna Borough Schs	Palmer
3	785	Fairbanks North Star Boro SD	Fairbanks
4	669	Kenai Peninsula Borough Schs	Soldotna
5	333	Juneau Borough Schs	Juneau
6	184	Kodiak Island Borough SD	Kodiak
7	133	North Slope Borough SD	Barrow
8	131	Galena City SD	Galena
9	128	Ketchikan Gateway Borough SD	Ketchikan
10	118	Lower Kuskokwim SD	Bethel
11	89	Sitka Borough SD	Sitka
12	68	Northwest Arctic SD	Kotzebue
13	50	Lower Yukon SD	Mountain Vlg
14	47	Bering Strait SD	Unalakleet

High School Drop-out Rate

Rank	Percent	District Name	City
1	18.5	Lower Kuskokwim SD	Bethel
2	13.8	Northwest Arctic SD	Kotzebue
3	13.2	North Slope Borough SD	Barrow
4	10.5	Fairbanks North Star Boro SD	Fairbanks
5	9.4	Ketchikan Gateway Borough SD	Ketchikan

6	9.3	Anchorage SD	Anchorage
7	9.2	Juneau Borough Schs	Juneau
8	9.1	Bering Strait SD	Unalakleet
9	8.8	Sitka Borough SD	Sitka
10	7.4	Kenai Peninsula Borough Schs	Soldotna
11	4.7	Matanuska-Susitna Borough Schs	Palmer
12	4.5	Kodiak Island Borough SD	Kodiak
13	0.1	Galena City SD	Galena
14	0.0	Lower Yukon SD	Mountain Vlg

Arizona

Arizona Public School Educational Profile

Category	Value	Category	Value
Schools *(2002-2003)*	1,942	**Diploma Recipients** *(2002-2003)*	47,175
Instructional Level		White, Non-Hispanic	28,640
Primary	1,080	Black, Non-Hispanic	2,008
Middle	248	Asian/Pacific Islander	1,286
High	420	American Indian/Alaskan Native	2,762
Other Level	194	Hispanic	12,479
Curriculum		**High School Drop-out Rate** (%) *(2000-2001)*	10.9
Regular	1,813	White, Non-Hispanic	7.1
Special Education	11	Black, Non-Hispanic	13.9
Vocational	46	Asian/Pacific Islander	5.0
Alternative	72	American Indian/Alaskan Native	17.0
Type		Hispanic	16.8
Magnet	0	**Staff** *(2002-2003)*	95,760.7
Charter	325	Teachers	46,627.7
Title I Eligible	1,038	Average Salary ($)	39,955
School-wide Title I	519	Librarians/Media Specialists	847.0
Students *(2002-2003)*	962,252	Guidance Counselors	1,225.5
Gender (%)		**Ratios** *(2002-2003)*	
Male	51.5	Student/Teacher Ratio	20.6 to 1
Female	48.5	Student/Librarian Ratio	1,136.1 to 1
Race/Ethnicity (%)		Student/Counselor Ratio	785.2 to 1
White, Non-Hispanic	50.1	**Current Spending** *($ per student in FY 2001)*	5,964
Black, Non-Hispanic	4.8	Instruction	3,387
Asian/Pacific Islander	2.1	Support Services	2,201
American Indian/Alaskan Native	6.6	**College Entrance Exam Scores** *(2003)*	
Hispanic	36.5	Scholastic Aptitude Test (SAT)	
Classification (%)		Participation Rate (%)	38
Individual Education Program (IEP)	10.9	Mean SAT I Verbal Score	524
Migrant	0.2	Mean SAT I Math Score	525
English Language Learner (ELL)	15.5	American College Testing Program (ACT)	
Eligible for Free Lunch Program	9.1	Participation Rate (%)	27
Eligible for Reduced-Price Lunch Program	3.0	Average Composite Score	21.4

Note: *For an explanation of data, please refer to the User's Guide in the front of the book; n/a indicates data not available*

Arizona NAEP 2003 Test Scores

Reading			Mathematics		
Grade/Category	**Value**	**Rank**	**Grade/Category**	**Value**	**Rank**
4th Grade			**4th Grade**		
Average Proficiency	208.9 (1.2)	43/51	Average Proficiency	228.9 (1.1)	41/51
Proficiency by Gender/Race/Ethnicity			Proficiency by Gender/Race/Ethnicity		
Male	206.1 (1.4)	42/51	Male	230.7 (1.2)	39/51
Female	211.6 (1.5)	44/51	Female	227.2 (1.1)	42/51
White, Non-Hispanic	223.2 (1.4)	38/51	White, Non-Hispanic	240.5 (1.1)	33/51
Black, Non-Hispanic	195.8 (3.4)	29/42	Black, Non-Hispanic	214.9 (3.2)	24/42
Asian, Non-Hispanic	195.1 (1.9)	37/41	Asian, Non-Hispanic	217.5 (1.3)	33/43
American Indian, Non-Hispanic	224.6 (4.9)	14/25	American Indian, Non-Hispanic	244.4 (2.9)	17/26
Hispanic	182.3 (2.5)	11/12	Hispanic	210.1 (3.2)	12/12
Proficiency by Class Size			Proficiency by Class Size		
Less than 16 Students	n/a	n/a	Less than 16 Students	*226.4 (7.3)*	19/47
16 to 18 Students	*207.2 (8.5)*	36/48	16 to 18 Students	*223.1 (6.9)*	40/48
19 to 20 Students	*203.4 (5.3)*	47/50	19 to 20 Students	*225.9 (3.3)*	44/50
21 to 25 Students	207.2 (2.1)	46/51	21 to 25 Students	225.8 (1.8)	47/51
Greater than 25 Students	213.4 (2.5)	37/49	Greater than 25 Students	233.7 (1.9)	30/49
Percent Attaining Achievement Levels			Percent Attaining Achievement Levels		
Below Basic	45.8 (1.5)	9/51	Below Basic	30.0 (1.5)	10/51
Basic or Above	54.2 (1.5)	43/51	Basic or Above	70.0 (1.5)	42/51
Proficient or Above	23.5 (1.1)	43/51	Proficient or Above	25.4 (1.4)	39/51
Advanced or Above	4.5 (0.5)	44/51	Advanced or Above	2.2 (0.3)	41/51
8th Grade			**8th Grade**		
Average Proficiency	255.3 (1.4)	43/51	Average Proficiency	271.2 (1.2)	39/51
Proficiency by Gender/Race/Ethnicity			Proficiency by Gender/Race/Ethnicity		
Male	250.6 (1.5)	42/51	Male	271.2 (1.3)	39/51
Female	260.1 (1.7)	45/51	Female	271.2 (1.4)	38/51
White, Non-Hispanic	268.4 (1.2)	31/50	White, Non-Hispanic	283.9 (1.2)	34/50
Black, Non-Hispanic	244.8 (4.0)	18/41	Black, Non-Hispanic	256.4 (3.6)	12/41
Asian, Non-Hispanic	240.0 (1.9)	33/37	Asian, Non-Hispanic	257.7 (1.6)	23/37
American Indian, Non-Hispanic	n/a	n/a	American Indian, Non-Hispanic	n/a	n/a
Hispanic	*238.5 (5.0)*	9/10	Hispanic	254.3 (3.0)	10/11
Proficiency by Parents Highest Level of Ed.			Proficiency by Parents Highest Level of Ed.		
Did Not Finish High School	237.8 (2.5)	46/50	Did Not Finish High School	256.8 (2.1)	26/50
Graduated High School	248.2 (2.1)	44/50	Graduated High School	265.9 (1.7)	34/50
Some Education After High School	264.2 (1.8)	40/50	Some Education After High School	276.6 (1.8)	37/50
Graduated College	267.5 (1.7)	36/50	Graduated College	283.7 (1.3)	35/50
Percent Attaining Achievement Levels			Percent Attaining Achievement Levels		
Below Basic	33.7 (1.4)	9/51	Below Basic	38.5 (1.6)	12/51
Basic or Above	66.3 (1.4)	43/51	Basic or Above	61.5 (1.6)	40/51
Proficient or Above	24.9 (1.6)	41/51	Proficient or Above	20.9 (1.2)	41/51
Advanced or Above	1.6 (0.3)	44/51	Advanced or Above	2.7 (0.3)	42/51

Note: *For an explanation of data, please refer to the User's Guide in the front of the book; values in italics indicate that the nature of the sample does not allow accurate determination of the variability of the statistic; n/a indicates data not available*

Apache County

Chinle Agency

PO Box 6003 • Chinle, AZ 86503
(520) 674-5130 • http://www.Chinleusd.k12.az.us/
Grade Span: KG-12; **Agency Type:** 6
Schools: 10
6 Primary; 0 Middle; 1 High; 3 Other Level
10 Regular; 0 Special Education; 0 Vocational; 0 Alternative
0 Magnet; 0 Charter; 10 Title I Eligible; 10 School-wide Title I
Students: 2,929 (n/a% male; n/a% female)
Individual Education Program: n/a;
English Language Learner: n/a; Migrant: n/a
Eligible for Free Lunch Program: n/a
Eligible for Reduced-Price Lunch Program: n/a
Teachers: n/a
Librarians/Media Specialists: n/a
Guidance Counselors: n/a
Current Spending: ($ per student per year):
Total: n/a; Instruction: n/a; Support Services: n/a
Enrollment, Drop-out Rates and Diploma Recipients by Race/Ethnicity

Category	Total	White	Black	Asian	AIAN	Hisp.
Enrollment (%)	100.0	0.0	0.0	0.0	100.0	0.0
Drop-out Rate (%)	n/a	n/a	n/a	n/a	n/a	n/a
H.S. Diplomas (#)	n/a	n/a	n/a	n/a	n/a	n/a

Chinle Unified District

Navajo Rte 7 & State Hwy 191 • Chinle, AZ 86503-0587
Mailing Address: PO Box 587 • Chinle, AZ 86503-0587
(928) 674-9630 • http://www.chinleusd.k12.az.us/
Grade Span: PK-12; **Agency Type:** 1
Schools: 8
4 Primary; 2 Middle; 2 High; 0 Other Level
7 Regular; 0 Special Education; 0 Vocational; 1 Alternative
0 Magnet; 0 Charter; 7 Title I Eligible; 0 School-wide Title I
Students: 4,196 (50.3% male; 49.7% female)
Individual Education Program: 460 (11.0%);
English Language Learner: 2,417 (57.6%); Migrant: 0 (0.0%)
Eligible for Free Lunch Program: n/a
Eligible for Reduced-Price Lunch Program: n/a
Teachers: 268.7 (15.6 to 1)
Librarians/Media Specialists: 5.0 (839.2 to 1)
Guidance Counselors: 9.0 (466.2 to 1)
Current Spending: ($ per student per year):
Total: $7,440; Instruction: $3,549; Support Services: $3,453
Enrollment, Drop-out Rates and Diploma Recipients by Race/Ethnicity

Category	Total	White	Black	Asian	AIAN	Hisp.
Enrollment (%)	100.0	1.2	0.0	0.1	98.5	0.2
Drop-out Rate (%)	2.0	0.0	n/a	n/a	2.0	0.0
H.S. Diplomas (#)	222	2	0	0	219	1

Fort Defiance Agency

PO Box 110 • Fort Defiance, AZ 86504-0110
(520) 729-7255
Grade Span: KG-12; **Agency Type:** 6
Schools: 11
9 Primary; 0 Middle; 2 High; 0 Other Level
11 Regular; 0 Special Education; 0 Vocational; 0 Alternative
0 Magnet; 0 Charter; 11 Title I Eligible; 11 School-wide Title I
Students: 2,088 (n/a% male; n/a% female)
Individual Education Program: n/a;
English Language Learner: n/a; Migrant: n/a
Eligible for Free Lunch Program: n/a
Eligible for Reduced-Price Lunch Program: n/a
Teachers: n/a
Librarians/Media Specialists: n/a
Guidance Counselors: n/a
Current Spending: ($ per student per year):
Total: n/a; Instruction: n/a; Support Services: n/a
Enrollment, Drop-out Rates and Diploma Recipients by Race/Ethnicity

Category	Total	White	Black	Asian	AIAN	Hisp.
Enrollment (%)	100.0	0.0	0.0	0.0	100.0	0.0
Drop-out Rate (%)	n/a	n/a	n/a	n/a	n/a	n/a
H.S. Diplomas (#)	n/a	n/a	n/a	n/a	n/a	n/a

Ganado Unified District

Hwy 264 • Ganado, AZ 86505-1757
Mailing Address: PO Box 1757 • Ganado, AZ 86505-1757
(928) 755-1099 • http://www.ganado.k12.az.us/
Grade Span: PK-12; **Agency Type:** 1
Schools: 4
2 Primary; 1 Middle; 1 High; 0 Other Level
4 Regular; 0 Special Education; 0 Vocational; 0 Alternative
0 Magnet; 0 Charter; 4 Title I Eligible; 4 School-wide Title I
Students: 2,043 (51.0% male; 49.0% female)
Individual Education Program: 152 (7.4%);
English Language Learner: 1,358 (66.5%); Migrant: 0 (0.0%)
Eligible for Free Lunch Program: n/a
Eligible for Reduced-Price Lunch Program: n/a
Teachers: 127.7 (16.0 to 1)
Librarians/Media Specialists: 3.0 (681.0 to 1)
Guidance Counselors: 6.4 (319.2 to 1)
Current Spending: ($ per student per year):
Total: $9,832; Instruction: $4,079; Support Services: $5,376
Enrollment, Drop-out Rates and Diploma Recipients by Race/Ethnicity

Category	Total	White	Black	Asian	AIAN	Hisp.
Enrollment (%)	100.0	1.0	0.0	0.1	98.7	0.1
Drop-out Rate (%)	3.0	0.0	n/a	0.0	3.1	0.0
H.S. Diplomas (#)	133	1	0	0	132	0

Window Rock Unified District

Navajo Rte 12 • Fort Defiance, AZ 86504-0559
Mailing Address: PO Box 559 • Fort Defiance, AZ 86504-0559
(928) 729-7505 • http://www.wrschool.net/
Grade Span: PK-12; **Agency Type:** 1
Schools: 6
4 Primary; 1 Middle; 1 High; 0 Other Level
6 Regular; 0 Special Education; 0 Vocational; 0 Alternative
0 Magnet; 0 Charter; 5 Title I Eligible; 0 School-wide Title I
Students: 2,953 (51.4% male; 48.6% female)
Individual Education Program: 324 (11.0%);
English Language Learner: 1,539 (52.1%); Migrant: 0 (0.0%)
Eligible for Free Lunch Program: n/a
Eligible for Reduced-Price Lunch Program: n/a
Teachers: 200.4 (14.7 to 1)
Librarians/Media Specialists: 4.0 (738.3 to 1)
Guidance Counselors: 7.0 (421.9 to 1)
Current Spending: ($ per student per year):
Total: $7,836; Instruction: $3,663; Support Services: $2,791
Enrollment, Drop-out Rates and Diploma Recipients by Race/Ethnicity

Category	Total	White	Black	Asian	AIAN	Hisp.
Enrollment (%)	100.0	0.6	0.0	0.1	99.3	0.0
Drop-out Rate (%)	7.0	16.7	n/a	0.0	7.0	n/a
H.S. Diplomas (#)	128	0	0	1	127	0

Cochise County

Douglas Unified District

1132 12th St • Douglas, AZ 85607
(520) 364-2447 • http://www.dusd.k12.az.us/
Grade Span: PK-12; **Agency Type:** 1
Schools: 12
7 Primary; 2 Middle; 2 High; 1 Other Level
12 Regular; 0 Special Education; 0 Vocational; 0 Alternative
0 Magnet; 0 Charter; 10 Title I Eligible; 0 School-wide Title I
Students: 4,104 (52.4% male; 47.6% female)
Individual Education Program: 414 (10.1%);
English Language Learner: 0 (0.0%); Migrant: 142 (3.5%)
Eligible for Free Lunch Program: n/a
Eligible for Reduced-Price Lunch Program: n/a
Teachers: 215.0 (19.1 to 1)
Librarians/Media Specialists: 3.0 (1,368.0 to 1)
Guidance Counselors: 7.4 (554.6 to 1)
Current Spending: ($ per student per year):
Total: $4,789; Instruction: $2,981; Support Services: $1,528
Enrollment, Drop-out Rates and Diploma Recipients by Race/Ethnicity

Category	Total	White	Black	Asian	AIAN	Hisp.
Enrollment (%)	100.0	4.2	0.3	0.2	0.1	95.3
Drop-out Rate (%)	9.3	4.8	0.0	0.0	n/a	9.6
H.S. Diplomas (#)	226	12	0	1	0	213

Sierra Vista Unified District

3555 Fry Blvd • Sierra Vista, AZ 85635-2972
(520) 515-2700 • http://www.sierravistapublicschools.com/
Grade Span: PK-12; **Agency Type:** 1
Schools: 8
5 Primary; 2 Middle; 1 High; 0 Other Level
8 Regular; 0 Special Education; 0 Vocational; 0 Alternative
0 Magnet; 0 Charter; 4 Title I Eligible; 2 School-wide Title I
Students: 6,832 (51.2% male; 48.8% female)
Individual Education Program: 759 (11.1%);
English Language Learner: 0 (0.0%); Migrant: 0 (0.0%)
Eligible for Free Lunch Program: 1,936 (28.3%)
Eligible for Reduced-Price Lunch Program: 578 (8.5%)
Teachers: 350.2 (19.5 to 1)
Librarians/Media Specialists: 6.0 (1,138.7 to 1)
Guidance Counselors: 11.0 (621.1 to 1)
Current Spending: ($ per student per year):
Total: $4,912; Instruction: $2,611; Support Services: $2,026

Enrollment, Drop-out Rates and Diploma Recipients by Race/Ethnicity

Category	Total	White	Black	Asian	AIAN	Hisp.
Enrollment (%)	100.0	57.5	10.7	5.1	1.1	25.5
Drop-out Rate (%)	7.4	6.7	8.0	3.4	5.3	10.9
H.S. Diplomas (#)	572	360	57	45	4	106

Coconino County

Flagstaff Unified District

3285 E Sparrow Ave • Flagstaff, AZ 86004-7795
(928) 527-6000 • http://www.flagstaff.k12.az.us/
Grade Span: PK-12; **Agency Type:** 1
Schools: 21
13 Primary; 3 Middle; 5 High; 0 Other Level
20 Regular; 0 Special Education; 0 Vocational; 1 Alternative
0 Magnet; 0 Charter; 12 Title I Eligible; 8 School-wide Title I
Students: 11,497 (51.7% male; 48.3% female)
Individual Education Program: 1,753 (15.2%);
English Language Learner: 1,742 (15.2%); Migrant: 0 (0.0%)
Eligible for Free Lunch Program: n/a
Eligible for Reduced-Price Lunch Program: n/a
Teachers: 723.5 (15.9 to 1)
Librarians/Media Specialists: 17.0 (676.3 to 1)
Guidance Counselors: 27.3 (421.1 to 1)
Current Spending: ($ per student per year):
Total: $6,048; Instruction: $3,518; Support Services: $2,342
Enrollment, Drop-out Rates and Diploma Recipients by Race/Ethnicity

Category	Total	White	Black	Asian	AIAN	Hisp.
Enrollment (%)	100.0	56.0	2.5	1.2	22.8	17.6
Drop-out Rate (%)	6.7	3.6	4.8	1.7	11.3	14.4
H.S. Diplomas (#)	741	490	6	14	135	96

Page Unified District

500 S Navajo Dr • Page, AZ 86040-1927
Mailing Address: PO Box 1927 • Page, AZ 86040-1927
(928) 608-4100 • http://www.pageud.k12.az.us/
Grade Span: PK-12; **Agency Type:** 1
Schools: 4
2 Primary; 1 Middle; 1 High; 0 Other Level
4 Regular; 0 Special Education; 0 Vocational; 0 Alternative
0 Magnet; 0 Charter; 4 Title I Eligible; 4 School-wide Title I
Students: 3,096 (53.8% male; 46.2% female)
Individual Education Program: 512 (16.5%);
English Language Learner: 985 (31.8%); Migrant: 0 (0.0%)
Eligible for Free Lunch Program: n/a
Eligible for Reduced-Price Lunch Program: n/a
Teachers: 202.0 (15.3 to 1)
Librarians/Media Specialists: 1.0 (3,096.0 to 1)
Guidance Counselors: 1.0 (3,096.0 to 1)
Current Spending: ($ per student per year):
Total: $5,872; Instruction: $3,317; Support Services: $2,210
Enrollment, Drop-out Rates and Diploma Recipients by Race/Ethnicity

Category	Total	White	Black	Asian	AIAN	Hisp.
Enrollment (%)	100.0	25.9	0.4	0.5	70.7	2.6
Drop-out Rate (%)	16.8	14.6	0.0	0.0	17.9	16.7
H.S. Diplomas (#)	168	61	0	1	105	1

Tuba City Unified District

E Fir St • Tuba City, AZ 86045-0067
Mailing Address: PO Box 67 • Tuba City, AZ 86045-0067
(928) 283-4211 •
http://www.tcusd.k12.az.us/education/district/district.php?sectionid=1
Grade Span: PK-12; **Agency Type:** 1
Schools: 7
4 Primary; 1 Middle; 2 High; 0 Other Level
6 Regular; 0 Special Education; 0 Vocational; 1 Alternative
0 Magnet; 0 Charter; 7 Title I Eligible; 7 School-wide Title I
Students: 2,573 (50.6% male; 49.4% female)
Individual Education Program: 314 (12.2%);
English Language Learner: 1,129 (43.9%); Migrant: 0 (0.0%)
Eligible for Free Lunch Program: n/a
Eligible for Reduced-Price Lunch Program: n/a
Teachers: 163.4 (15.7 to 1)
Librarians/Media Specialists: 4.0 (643.3 to 1)
Guidance Counselors: 9.4 (273.7 to 1)
Current Spending: ($ per student per year):
Total: $7,408; Instruction: $3,507; Support Services: $3,598
Enrollment, Drop-out Rates and Diploma Recipients by Race/Ethnicity

Category	Total	White	Black	Asian	AIAN	Hisp.
Enrollment (%)	100.0	2.2	0.1	0.2	97.2	0.3
Drop-out Rate (%)	17.5	0.0	n/a	n/a	17.7	0.0
H.S. Diplomas (#)	149	3	0	0	146	0

Western Navajo Agency

PO Box 746 • Tuba City, AZ 86045
(520) 283-2218
Grade Span: KG-12; **Agency Type:** 6
Schools: 15
10 Primary; 0 Middle; 3 High; 2 Other Level
15 Regular; 0 Special Education; 0 Vocational; 0 Alternative
0 Magnet; 0 Charter; 15 Title I Eligible; 15 School-wide Title I
Students: 4,188 (n/a% male; n/a% female)
Individual Education Program: n/a;
English Language Learner: n/a; Migrant: n/a
Eligible for Free Lunch Program: n/a
Eligible for Reduced-Price Lunch Program: n/a
Teachers: n/a
Librarians/Media Specialists: n/a
Guidance Counselors: n/a
Current Spending: ($ per student per year):
Total: n/a; Instruction: n/a; Support Services: n/a
Enrollment, Drop-out Rates and Diploma Recipients by Race/Ethnicity

Category	Total	White	Black	Asian	AIAN	Hisp.
Enrollment (%)	100.0	0.0	0.0	0.0	100.0	0.0
Drop-out Rate (%)	n/a	n/a	n/a	n/a	n/a	n/a
H.S. Diplomas (#)	n/a	n/a	n/a	n/a	n/a	n/a

Gila County

Globe Unified District

501 E Ash St • Globe, AZ 85501-2295
Mailing Address: 455 N Willow • Globe, AZ 85501-2295
(928) 425-3211 • http://www.globe.k12.az.us/
Grade Span: PK-12; **Agency Type:** 1
Schools: 4
1 Primary; 2 Middle; 1 High; 0 Other Level
4 Regular; 0 Special Education; 0 Vocational; 0 Alternative
0 Magnet; 0 Charter; 3 Title I Eligible; 2 School-wide Title I
Students: 2,195 (51.4% male; 48.6% female)
Individual Education Program: 339 (15.4%);
English Language Learner: 0 (0.0%); Migrant: 0 (0.0%)
Eligible for Free Lunch Program: n/a
Eligible for Reduced-Price Lunch Program: n/a
Teachers: 109.9 (20.0 to 1)
Librarians/Media Specialists: 3.0 (731.7 to 1)
Guidance Counselors: 2.0 (1,097.5 to 1)
Current Spending: ($ per student per year):
Total: $3,999; Instruction: $2,284; Support Services: $1,715
Enrollment, Drop-out Rates and Diploma Recipients by Race/Ethnicity

Category	Total	White	Black	Asian	AIAN	Hisp.
Enrollment (%)	100.0	48.9	0.5	0.5	21.4	28.7
Drop-out Rate (%)	8.1	5.2	0.0	0.0	12.3	11.4
H.S. Diplomas (#)	105	60	1	1	15	28

Payson Unified District

514 W Wade Ln • Payson, AZ 85541
Mailing Address: PO Box 919 • Payson, AZ 85547-0919
(928) 474-2070 • http://www.pusd.k12.az.us
Grade Span: PK-12; **Agency Type:** 1
Schools: 6
3 Primary; 1 Middle; 2 High; 0 Other Level
6 Regular; 0 Special Education; 0 Vocational; 0 Alternative
0 Magnet; 0 Charter; 3 Title I Eligible; 0 School-wide Title I
Students: 2,875 (52.4% male; 47.6% female)
Individual Education Program: 336 (11.7%);
English Language Learner: 6 (0.2%); Migrant: 0 (0.0%)
Eligible for Free Lunch Program: 1,047 (36.4%)
Eligible for Reduced-Price Lunch Program: 277 (9.6%)
Teachers: 158.5 (18.1 to 1)
Librarians/Media Specialists: 4.5 (638.9 to 1)
Guidance Counselors: 5.0 (575.0 to 1)
Current Spending: ($ per student per year):
Total: $5,178; Instruction: $2,949; Support Services: $2,052
Enrollment, Drop-out Rates and Diploma Recipients by Race/Ethnicity

Category	Total	White	Black	Asian	AIAN	Hisp.
Enrollment (%)	100.0	86.0	0.7	0.7	3.3	9.4
Drop-out Rate (%)	10.7	10.8	0.0	20.0	18.2	5.9
H.S. Diplomas (#)	157	138	0	2	6	11

Graham County

Safford Unified District

734 11th St • Safford, AZ 85546-2967
(928) 348-7000 • http://www.saffordusd.k12.az.us/
Grade Span: PK-12; **Agency Type:** 1
Schools: 6
2 Primary; 1 Middle; 2 High; 1 Other Level
6 Regular; 0 Special Education; 0 Vocational; 0 Alternative

0 Magnet; 0 Charter; 3 Title I Eligible; 0 School-wide Title I
Students: 2,856 (50.8% male; 49.2% female)
Individual Education Program: 389 (13.6%);
English Language Learner: 0 (0.0%); Migrant: 0 (0.0%)
Eligible for Free Lunch Program: n/a
Eligible for Reduced-Price Lunch Program: n/a
Teachers: 148.9 (19.2 to 1)
Librarians/Media Specialists: 4.0 (714.0 to 1)
Guidance Counselors: 7.0 (408.0 to 1)
Current Spending: ($ per student per year):
Total: $4,929; Instruction: $2,847; Support Services: $1,941
Enrollment, Drop-out Rates and Diploma Recipients by Race/Ethnicity

Category	Total	White	Black	Asian	AIAN	Hisp.
Enrollment (%)	100.0	52.6	2.3	0.6	1.5	43.1
Drop-out Rate (%)	5.1	5.5	0.0	0.0	0.0	5.0
H.S. Diplomas (#)	162	93	3	2	4	60

La Paz County

Parker Unified SD
1608 Laguna Ave • Parker, AZ 85344-1090
Mailing Address: PO Box 1090 • Parker, AZ 85344-1090
(928) 669-9244 • http://www.parkerusd.k12.az.us/
Grade Span: PK-12; **Agency Type:** 1
Schools: 6
2 Primary; 2 Middle; 1 High; 1 Other Level
6 Regular; 0 Special Education; 0 Vocational; 0 Alternative
0 Magnet; 0 Charter; 2 Title I Eligible; 0 School-wide Title I
Students: 2,057 (51.2% male; 48.8% female)
Individual Education Program: 347 (16.9%);
English Language Learner: 202 (9.8%); Migrant: 1 (<0.1%)
Eligible for Free Lunch Program: n/a
Eligible for Reduced-Price Lunch Program: n/a
Teachers: 126.1 (16.3 to 1)
Librarians/Media Specialists: 2.0 (1,028.5 to 1)
Guidance Counselors: 3.0 (685.7 to 1)
Current Spending: ($ per student per year):
Total: $5,725; Instruction: $3,189; Support Services: $2,309
Enrollment, Drop-out Rates and Diploma Recipients by Race/Ethnicity

Category	Total	White	Black	Asian	AIAN	Hisp.
Enrollment (%)	100.0	29.1	1.3	0.6	37.0	31.9
Drop-out Rate (%)	16.7	13.1	30.0	14.3	26.4	12.4
H.S. Diplomas (#)	116	49	3	1	25	38

Maricopa County

Agua Fria Union High SD
750 E Riley Dr • Avondale, AZ 85323-2154
(623) 932-7000 • http://www.aguafria.org/
Grade Span: 09-12; **Agency Type:** 1
Schools: 3
0 Primary; 0 Middle; 3 High; 0 Other Level
3 Regular; 0 Special Education; 0 Vocational; 0 Alternative
0 Magnet; 0 Charter; 2 Title I Eligible; 0 School-wide Title I
Students: 3,101 (51.4% male; 48.6% female)
Individual Education Program: 279 (9.0%);
English Language Learner: 156 (5.0%); Migrant: 16 (0.5%)
Eligible for Free Lunch Program: n/a
Eligible for Reduced-Price Lunch Program: n/a
Teachers: 140.8 (22.0 to 1)
Librarians/Media Specialists: 2.2 (1,409.5 to 1)
Guidance Counselors: 8.5 (364.8 to 1)
Current Spending: ($ per student per year):
Total: $5,976; Instruction: $3,155; Support Services: $2,505
Enrollment, Drop-out Rates and Diploma Recipients by Race/Ethnicity

Category	Total	White	Black	Asian	AIAN	Hisp.
Enrollment (%)	100.0	50.3	7.7	3.6	1.4	37.0
Drop-out Rate (%)	4.4	3.9	3.4	0.0	3.8	5.5
H.S. Diplomas (#)	425	244	28	15	7	131

Alhambra Elementary District
4510 N 37th Ave • Phoenix, AZ 85019
(602) 336-2920 • http://www.alhambra.k12.az.us/
Grade Span: PK-08; **Agency Type:** 1
Schools: 15
12 Primary; 3 Middle; 0 High; 0 Other Level
15 Regular; 0 Special Education; 0 Vocational; 0 Alternative
0 Magnet; 0 Charter; 14 Title I Eligible; 14 School-wide Title I
Students: 14,608 (51.7% male; 48.3% female)
Individual Education Program: 1,480 (10.1%);
English Language Learner: 7,375 (50.5%); Migrant: 0 (0.0%)
Eligible for Free Lunch Program: n/a
Eligible for Reduced-Price Lunch Program: n/a
Teachers: 717.7 (20.4 to 1)
Librarians/Media Specialists: 14.0 (1,043.4 to 1)
Guidance Counselors: 9.5 (1,537.7 to 1)
Current Spending: ($ per student per year):
Total: $4,452; Instruction: $2,693; Support Services: $1,413
Enrollment, Drop-out Rates and Diploma Recipients by Race/Ethnicity

Category	Total	White	Black	Asian	AIAN	Hisp.
Enrollment (%)	100.0	16.8	8.0	3.0	3.9	68.3
Drop-out Rate (%)	n/a	n/a	n/a	n/a	n/a	n/a
H.S. Diplomas (#)	n/a	n/a	n/a	n/a	n/a	n/a

Avondale Elementary District
235 W Western Ave • Avondale, AZ 85323-1848
(623) 772-5013 • http://www.avondale.k12.az.us/
Grade Span: PK-08; **Agency Type:** 1
Schools: 7
5 Primary; 2 Middle; 0 High; 0 Other Level
7 Regular; 0 Special Education; 0 Vocational; 0 Alternative
0 Magnet; 0 Charter; 4 Title I Eligible; 4 School-wide Title I
Students: 4,130 (53.5% male; 46.5% female)
Individual Education Program: 339 (8.2%);
English Language Learner: 1,131 (27.4%); Migrant: 10 (0.2%)
Eligible for Free Lunch Program: n/a
Eligible for Reduced-Price Lunch Program: n/a
Teachers: 203.5 (20.3 to 1)
Librarians/Media Specialists: 5.0 (826.0 to 1)
Guidance Counselors: 4.0 (1,032.5 to 1)
Current Spending: ($ per student per year):
Total: $4,447; Instruction: $2,681; Support Services: $1,459
Enrollment, Drop-out Rates and Diploma Recipients by Race/Ethnicity

Category	Total	White	Black	Asian	AIAN	Hisp.
Enrollment (%)	100.0	29.1	6.6	0.5	1.5	62.3
Drop-out Rate (%)	n/a	n/a	n/a	n/a	n/a	n/a
H.S. Diplomas (#)	n/a	n/a	n/a	n/a	n/a	n/a

Balsz Elementary District
4825 E Roosevelt • Phoenix, AZ 85008-5917
(602) 629-6400 • http://www.balsz.k12.az.us/
Grade Span: PK-08; **Agency Type:** 1
Schools: 4
4 Primary; 0 Middle; 0 High; 0 Other Level
4 Regular; 0 Special Education; 0 Vocational; 0 Alternative
0 Magnet; 0 Charter; 0 Title I Eligible; 0 School-wide Title I
Students: 3,265 (51.8% male; 48.2% female)
Individual Education Program: 318 (9.7%);
English Language Learner: 1,429 (43.8%); Migrant: 0 (0.0%)
Eligible for Free Lunch Program: n/a
Eligible for Reduced-Price Lunch Program: n/a
Teachers: 181.3 (18.0 to 1)
Librarians/Media Specialists: 4.0 (816.3 to 1)
Guidance Counselors: 4.0 (816.3 to 1)
Current Spending: ($ per student per year):
Total: $4,956; Instruction: $2,753; Support Services: $1,822
Enrollment, Drop-out Rates and Diploma Recipients by Race/Ethnicity

Category	Total	White	Black	Asian	AIAN	Hisp.
Enrollment (%)	100.0	12.1	10.0	1.3	6.0	70.6
Drop-out Rate (%)	n/a	n/a	n/a	n/a	n/a	n/a
H.S. Diplomas (#)	n/a	n/a	n/a	n/a	n/a	n/a

Cartwright Elementary District
3401 N 67th Ave • Phoenix, AZ 85033-4599
(623) 691-4009 • http://www.cartwright.k12.az.us/
Grade Span: PK-08; **Agency Type:** 1
Schools: 23
19 Primary; 4 Middle; 0 High; 0 Other Level
21 Regular; 2 Special Education; 0 Vocational; 0 Alternative
0 Magnet; 0 Charter; 20 Title I Eligible; 20 School-wide Title I
Students: 19,780 (51.3% male; 48.7% female)
Individual Education Program: 2,204 (11.1%);
English Language Learner: 7,771 (39.3%); Migrant: 0 (0.0%)
Eligible for Free Lunch Program: n/a
Eligible for Reduced-Price Lunch Program: n/a
Teachers: 963.8 (20.5 to 1)
Librarians/Media Specialists: 5.0 (3,956.0 to 1)
Guidance Counselors: 8.0 (2,472.5 to 1)
Current Spending: ($ per student per year):
Total: $4,697; Instruction: $3,111; Support Services: $1,308
Enrollment, Drop-out Rates and Diploma Recipients by Race/Ethnicity

Category	Total	White	Black	Asian	AIAN	Hisp.
Enrollment (%)	100.0	12.2	6.7	0.8	1.2	79.1
Drop-out Rate (%)	n/a	n/a	n/a	n/a	n/a	n/a
H.S. Diplomas (#)	n/a	n/a	n/a	n/a	n/a	n/a

Cave Creek Unified District

33606 N 60th St • Cave Creek, AZ 85262-5243
Mailing Address: PO Box 426 • Cave Creek, AZ 85327
(480) 575-2000 • http://www.ccusd.k12.az.us/
Grade Span: PK-12; **Agency Type:** 7
Schools: 7
4 Primary; 2 Middle; 1 High; 0 Other Level
7 Regular; 0 Special Education; 0 Vocational; 0 Alternative
0 Magnet; 0 Charter; 2 Title I Eligible; 0 School-wide Title I
Students: 5,112 (50.9% male; 49.1% female)
Individual Education Program: 431 (8.4%);
English Language Learner: 23 (0.4%); Migrant: 0 (0.0%)
Eligible for Free Lunch Program: 268 (5.2%)
Eligible for Reduced-Price Lunch Program: 56 (1.1%)
Teachers: n/a
Librarians/Media Specialists: n/a
Guidance Counselors: n/a
Current Spending: ($ per student per year):
Total: $5,337; Instruction: $2,672; Support Services: $2,400
Enrollment, Drop-out Rates and Diploma Recipients by Race/Ethnicity

Category	Total	White	Black	Asian	AIAN	Hisp.
Enrollment (%)	100.0	90.8	1.3	1.4	0.3	6.1
Drop-out Rate (%)	2.9	2.6	0.0	0.0	0.0	11.4
H.S. Diplomas (#)	198	187	0	2	1	8

Chandler Unified District

1525 W Frye Rd • Chandler, AZ 85224-6178
(480) 812-7000 • http://www.chandler.k12.az.us/
Grade Span: PK-12; **Agency Type:** 1
Schools: 28
19 Primary; 3 Middle; 3 High; 2 Other Level
26 Regular; 0 Special Education; 0 Vocational; 1 Alternative
0 Magnet; 0 Charter; 7 Title I Eligible; 4 School-wide Title I
Students: 24,497 (n/a% male; n/a% female)
Individual Education Program: 2,423 (9.9%);
English Language Learner: 3,629 (14.8%); Migrant: 52 (0.2%)
Eligible for Free Lunch Program: 4,943 (20.2%)
Eligible for Reduced-Price Lunch Program: 1,063 (4.3%)
Teachers: 1,244.7 (19.7 to 1)
Librarians/Media Specialists: 23.0 (1,065.1 to 1)
Guidance Counselors: 37.0 (662.1 to 1)
Current Spending: ($ per student per year):
Total: $4,740; Instruction: $2,842; Support Services: $1,628
Enrollment, Drop-out Rates and Diploma Recipients by Race/Ethnicity

Category	Total	White	Black	Asian	AIAN	Hisp.
Enrollment (%)	100.0	n/a	n/a	n/a	n/a	n/a
Drop-out Rate (%)	3.1	1.7	2.7	1.8	7.1	6.5
H.S. Diplomas (#)	1,021	647	70	50	22	232

Creighton Elementary District

2702 E Flower St • Phoenix, AZ 85016-7498
(602) 381-6000 • http://www.creighton.k12.az.us/
Grade Span: PK-12; **Agency Type:** 1
Schools: 10
9 Primary; 0 Middle; 0 High; 1 Other Level
10 Regular; 0 Special Education; 0 Vocational; 0 Alternative
0 Magnet; 0 Charter; 9 Title I Eligible; 9 School-wide Title I
Students: 8,383 (50.2% male; 49.8% female)
Individual Education Program: 803 (9.6%);
English Language Learner: 5,073 (60.5%); Migrant: 0 (0.0%)
Eligible for Free Lunch Program: n/a
Eligible for Reduced-Price Lunch Program: n/a
Teachers: 453.8 (18.5 to 1)
Librarians/Media Specialists: 6.0 (1,397.2 to 1)
Guidance Counselors: 0.0 (0.0 to 1)
Current Spending: ($ per student per year):
Total: $5,338; Instruction: $3,028; Support Services: $1,963
Enrollment, Drop-out Rates and Diploma Recipients by Race/Ethnicity

Category	Total	White	Black	Asian	AIAN	Hisp.
Enrollment (%)	100.0	10.3	4.3	0.6	3.5	81.3
Drop-out Rate (%)	n/a	n/a	n/a	n/a	n/a	n/a
H.S. Diplomas (#)	0	0	0	0	0	0

Deer Valley Unified District

20402 N 15th Ave • Phoenix, AZ 85027-3699
(623) 445-5000 • http://www.dvusd.k12.az.us/
Grade Span: PK-12; **Agency Type:** 1
Schools: 32
23 Primary; 3 Middle; 4 High; 2 Other Level
31 Regular; 0 Special Education; 1 Vocational; 0 Alternative
0 Magnet; 0 Charter; 7 Title I Eligible; 3 School-wide Title I
Students: 30,049 (51.3% male; 48.7% female)
Individual Education Program: 3,466 (11.5%);
English Language Learner: 1,255 (4.2%); Migrant: 0 (0.0%)
Eligible for Free Lunch Program: 4,312 (14.3%)
Eligible for Reduced-Price Lunch Program: 1,753 (5.8%)
Teachers: 1,568.4 (19.2 to 1)
Librarians/Media Specialists: 30.0 (1,001.6 to 1)
Guidance Counselors: 40.6 (740.1 to 1)
Current Spending: ($ per student per year):
Total: $4,783; Instruction: $2,926; Support Services: $1,626
Enrollment, Drop-out Rates and Diploma Recipients by Race/Ethnicity

Category	Total	White	Black	Asian	AIAN	Hisp.
Enrollment (%)	100.0	81.4	3.0	3.1	0.9	11.6
Drop-out Rate (%)	5.0	4.5	7.7	4.7	6.9	8.8
H.S. Diplomas (#)	1,320	1,115	27	45	9	124

Dysart Unified District

11405 N Dysart Rd • El Mirage, AZ 85335
(623) 876-7000 • http://dysart.org/
Grade Span: PK-12; **Agency Type:** 1
Schools: 9
7 Primary; 0 Middle; 1 High; 1 Other Level
9 Regular; 0 Special Education; 0 Vocational; 0 Alternative
0 Magnet; 0 Charter; 7 Title I Eligible; 4 School-wide Title I
Students: 8,982 (51.6% male; 48.4% female)
Individual Education Program: 962 (10.7%);
English Language Learner: 1,717 (19.1%); Migrant: 41 (0.5%)
Eligible for Free Lunch Program: n/a
Eligible for Reduced-Price Lunch Program: n/a
Teachers: 446.9 (20.1 to 1)
Librarians/Media Specialists: 1.0 (8,982.0 to 1)
Guidance Counselors: 11.6 (774.3 to 1)
Current Spending: ($ per student per year):
Total: $4,966; Instruction: $2,495; Support Services: $2,133
Enrollment, Drop-out Rates and Diploma Recipients by Race/Ethnicity

Category	Total	White	Black	Asian	AIAN	Hisp.
Enrollment (%)	100.0	42.1	7.8	1.7	1.0	47.4
Drop-out Rate (%)	26.2	21.2	24.4	18.8	50.0	28.4
H.S. Diplomas (#)	189	46	17	4	0	122

East Valley Institute of Technology

1601 W Main St • Mesa, AZ 85201-6910
(480) 461-4094
Grade Span: 09-12; **Agency Type:** 7
Schools: 10
0 Primary; 0 Middle; 10 High; 0 Other Level
0 Regular; 0 Special Education; 10 Vocational; 0 Alternative
0 Magnet; 0 Charter; 1 Title I Eligible; 0 School-wide Title I
Students: 12,666 (57.2% male; 42.8% female)
Individual Education Program: 0 (0.0%);
English Language Learner: 0 (0.0%); Migrant: 1 (<0.1%)
Eligible for Free Lunch Program: n/a
Eligible for Reduced-Price Lunch Program: n/a
Teachers: n/a
Librarians/Media Specialists: n/a
Guidance Counselors: n/a
Current Spending: ($ per student per year):
Total: n/a; Instruction: n/a; Support Services: n/a
Enrollment, Drop-out Rates and Diploma Recipients by Race/Ethnicity

Category	Total	White	Black	Asian	AIAN	Hisp.
Enrollment (%)	100.0	68.0	5.0	3.4	2.5	21.0
Drop-out Rate (%)	n/a	n/a	n/a	n/a	n/a	n/a
H.S. Diplomas (#)	0	0	0	0	0	0

Fountain Hills Unified District

16000 E Palisades Blvd • Fountain Hills, AZ 85268-2441
(480) 664-5000 • http://www.fhusd.org/
Grade Span: PK-12; **Agency Type:** 1
Schools: 4
2 Primary; 1 Middle; 1 High; 0 Other Level
4 Regular; 0 Special Education; 0 Vocational; 0 Alternative
0 Magnet; 0 Charter; 2 Title I Eligible; 0 School-wide Title I
Students: 2,549 (53.0% male; 47.0% female)
Individual Education Program: 213 (8.4%);
English Language Learner: 17 (0.7%); Migrant: 0 (0.0%)
Eligible for Free Lunch Program: 91 (3.6%)
Eligible for Reduced-Price Lunch Program: 24 (0.9%)
Teachers: 133.5 (19.1 to 1)
Librarians/Media Specialists: 3.0 (849.7 to 1)
Guidance Counselors: 4.0 (637.3 to 1)
Current Spending: ($ per student per year):
Total: $4,826; Instruction: $2,721; Support Services: $1,869
Enrollment, Drop-out Rates and Diploma Recipients by Race/Ethnicity

Category	Total	White	Black	Asian	AIAN	Hisp.
Enrollment (%)	100.0	87.2	0.7	1.8	5.8	4.5
Drop-out Rate (%)	5.3	3.7	33.3	0.0	25.5	5.9
H.S. Diplomas (#)	176	164	1	2	5	4

Fowler Elementary District

1617 S 67th Ave • Phoenix, AZ 85043-7717
(623) 707-4500 • http://www.fesd.org/
Grade Span: PK-08; **Agency Type:** 1
Schools: 4
3 Primary; 1 Middle; 0 High; 0 Other Level
4 Regular; 0 Special Education; 0 Vocational; 0 Alternative
0 Magnet; 0 Charter; 3 Title I Eligible; 3 School-wide Title I
Students: 2,759 (50.8% male; 49.2% female)
Individual Education Program: 310 (11.2%);
English Language Learner: 1,079 (39.1%); Migrant: 9 (0.3%)
Eligible for Free Lunch Program: n/a
Eligible for Reduced-Price Lunch Program: n/a
Teachers: 139.9 (19.7 to 1)
Librarians/Media Specialists: 2.0 (1,379.5 to 1)
Guidance Counselors: 1.0 (2,759.0 to 1)
Current Spending: ($ per student per year):
Total: $4,600; Instruction: $2,636; Support Services: $1,616
Enrollment, Drop-out Rates and Diploma Recipients by Race/Ethnicity

Category	Total	White	Black	Asian	AIAN	Hisp.
Enrollment (%)	100.0	14.5	7.6	0.6	1.3	76.0
Drop-out Rate (%)	n/a	n/a	n/a	n/a	n/a	n/a
H.S. Diplomas (#)	n/a	n/a	n/a	n/a	n/a	n/a

Gilbert Unified District

140 S Gilbert Rd • Gilbert, AZ 85296-1014
(480) 497-3452 • http://www.gilbert.k12.az.us/index.html
Grade Span: PK-12; **Agency Type:** 1
Schools: 36
24 Primary; 5 Middle; 6 High; 1 Other Level
34 Regular; 0 Special Education; 0 Vocational; 2 Alternative
0 Magnet; 0 Charter; 6 Title I Eligible; 0 School-wide Title I
Students: 33,256 (51.9% male; 48.1% female)
Individual Education Program: 3,156 (9.5%);
English Language Learner: 880 (2.6%); Migrant: 27 (0.1%)
Eligible for Free Lunch Program: 2,738 (8.2%)
Eligible for Reduced-Price Lunch Program: 1,135 (3.4%)
Teachers: 1,826.8 (18.2 to 1)
Librarians/Media Specialists: 32.0 (1,039.3 to 1)
Guidance Counselors: 31.0 (1,072.8 to 1)
Current Spending: ($ per student per year):
Total: $4,752; Instruction: $2,737; Support Services: $1,782
Enrollment, Drop-out Rates and Diploma Recipients by Race/Ethnicity

Category	Total	White	Black	Asian	AIAN	Hisp.
Enrollment (%)	100.0	78.6	3.6	3.5	0.9	13.4
Drop-out Rate (%)	2.5	2.3	2.7	1.1	4.0	4.0
H.S. Diplomas (#)	1,817	1,507	40	78	8	184

Glendale Elementary District

7301 N 58th Ave • Glendale, AZ 85301-1893
(623) 842-8100 • http://www.gesd.k12.az.us/
Grade Span: PK-12; **Agency Type:** 1
Schools: 17
15 Primary; 1 Middle; 0 High; 1 Other Level
14 Regular; 0 Special Education; 1 Vocational; 2 Alternative
0 Magnet; 0 Charter; 15 Title I Eligible; 14 School-wide Title I
Students: 13,075 (51.5% male; 48.5% female)
Individual Education Program: 1,505 (11.5%);
English Language Learner: 3,931 (30.1%); Migrant: 128 (1.0%)
Eligible for Free Lunch Program: n/a
Eligible for Reduced-Price Lunch Program: n/a
Teachers: 672.6 (19.4 to 1)
Librarians/Media Specialists: 15.0 (871.7 to 1)
Guidance Counselors: 2.0 (6,537.5 to 1)
Current Spending: ($ per student per year):
Total: $4,560; Instruction: $2,829; Support Services: $1,462
Enrollment, Drop-out Rates and Diploma Recipients by Race/Ethnicity

Category	Total	White	Black	Asian	AIAN	Hisp.
Enrollment (%)	100.0	24.1	9.8	2.4	2.7	61.1
Drop-out Rate (%)	n/a	n/a	n/a	n/a	n/a	n/a
H.S. Diplomas (#)	0	0	0	0	0	0

Glendale Union High SD

7650 N 43rd Ave • Glendale, AZ 85301-1661
(623) 435-6000 • http://guhsdns1.guhsd.k12.az.us/
Grade Span: 09-12; **Agency Type:** 1
Schools: 12
0 Primary; 0 Middle; 12 High; 0 Other Level
9 Regular; 0 Special Education; 0 Vocational; 3 Alternative
0 Magnet; 0 Charter; 6 Title I Eligible; 1 School-wide Title I
Students: 14,228 (51.1% male; 48.9% female)
Individual Education Program: 1,316 (9.2%);
English Language Learner: 770 (5.4%); Migrant: 49 (0.3%)
Eligible for Free Lunch Program: n/a
Eligible for Reduced-Price Lunch Program: n/a
Teachers: 672.4 (21.2 to 1)
Librarians/Media Specialists: 9.0 (1,580.9 to 1)
Guidance Counselors: 32.0 (444.6 to 1)
Current Spending: ($ per student per year):
Total: $5,649; Instruction: $3,209; Support Services: $2,232
Enrollment, Drop-out Rates and Diploma Recipients by Race/Ethnicity

Category	Total	White	Black	Asian	AIAN	Hisp.
Enrollment (%)	100.0	56.5	6.7	3.0	2.5	31.4
Drop-out Rate (%)	5.9	4.8	6.1	5.0	12.2	8.1
H.S. Diplomas (#)	2,609	1,705	152	111	45	596

Higley Unified District

15201 S Higley Rd • Higley, AZ 85236-9715
(480) 279-7000 • http://www.husd.org/
Grade Span: PK-12; **Agency Type:** 1
Schools: 12
6 Primary; 0 Middle; 2 High; 4 Other Level
12 Regular; 0 Special Education; 0 Vocational; 0 Alternative
0 Magnet; 0 Charter; 6 Title I Eligible; 0 School-wide Title I
Students: 3,835 (50.5% male; 49.5% female)
Individual Education Program: 424 (11.1%);
English Language Learner: 46 (1.2%); Migrant: 13 (0.3%)
Eligible for Free Lunch Program: 184 (4.8%)
Eligible for Reduced-Price Lunch Program: 133 (3.5%)
Teachers: 161.0 (23.8 to 1)
Librarians/Media Specialists: 3.5 (1,095.7 to 1)
Guidance Counselors: 1.4 (2,739.3 to 1)
Current Spending: ($ per student per year):
Total: $8,381; Instruction: $5,782; Support Services: $2,472
Enrollment, Drop-out Rates and Diploma Recipients by Race/Ethnicity

Category	Total	White	Black	Asian	AIAN	Hisp.
Enrollment (%)	100.0	69.9	3.8	1.9	5.2	19.1
Drop-out Rate (%)	13.6	14.6	26.7	0.0	18.2	8.8
H.S. Diplomas (#)	129	86	8	2	6	27

Isaac Elementary District

3348 W Mcdowell Rd • Phoenix, AZ 85009-2390
(602) 455-6700 • http://isaaceld.org/index.htm
Grade Span: PK-08; **Agency Type:** 1
Schools: 13
10 Primary; 3 Middle; 0 High; 0 Other Level
13 Regular; 0 Special Education; 0 Vocational; 0 Alternative
0 Magnet; 0 Charter; 12 Title I Eligible; 12 School-wide Title I
Students: 8,545 (50.2% male; 49.8% female)
Individual Education Program: 855 (10.0%);
English Language Learner: 5,141 (60.2%); Migrant: 7 (0.1%)
Eligible for Free Lunch Program: n/a
Eligible for Reduced-Price Lunch Program: n/a
Teachers: 465.0 (18.4 to 1)
Librarians/Media Specialists: 6.0 (1,424.2 to 1)
Guidance Counselors: 5.0 (1,709.0 to 1)
Current Spending: ($ per student per year):
Total: $5,006; Instruction: $2,804; Support Services: $1,835
Enrollment, Drop-out Rates and Diploma Recipients by Race/Ethnicity

Category	Total	White	Black	Asian	AIAN	Hisp.
Enrollment (%)	100.0	3.4	2.3	0.3	0.9	93.1
Drop-out Rate (%)	n/a	n/a	n/a	n/a	n/a	n/a
H.S. Diplomas (#)	n/a	n/a	n/a	n/a	n/a	n/a

Kyrene Elementary District

8700 S Kyrene Rd • Tempe, AZ 85284-2197
(480) 783-4000 • http://www.kyrene.k12.az.us/
Grade Span: PK-08; **Agency Type:** 1
Schools: 26
20 Primary; 6 Middle; 0 High; 0 Other Level
25 Regular; 0 Special Education; 0 Vocational; 1 Alternative
0 Magnet; 0 Charter; 4 Title I Eligible; 0 School-wide Title I
Students: 18,803 (51.1% male; 48.9% female)
Individual Education Program: 1,635 (8.7%);
English Language Learner: 466 (2.5%); Migrant: 0 (0.0%)
Eligible for Free Lunch Program: 1,474 (7.8%)
Eligible for Reduced-Price Lunch Program: 699 (3.7%)
Teachers: 1,005.5 (18.7 to 1)
Librarians/Media Specialists: 28.0 (671.5 to 1)
Guidance Counselors: 8.0 (2,350.4 to 1)
Current Spending: ($ per student per year):
Total: $4,607; Instruction: $2,762; Support Services: $1,599
Enrollment, Drop-out Rates and Diploma Recipients by Race/Ethnicity

Category	Total	White	Black	Asian	AIAN	Hisp.
Enrollment (%)	100.0	71.0	6.2	7.4	2.0	13.4
Drop-out Rate (%)	n/a	n/a	n/a	n/a	n/a	n/a
H.S. Diplomas (#)	n/a	n/a	n/a	n/a	n/a	n/a

Laveen Elementary District

9401 S 51st Ave • Laveen, AZ 85339-0029
Mailing Address: PO Box 29 • Laveen, AZ 85339-0029
(602) 237-9100 • http://laveeneld.k12.az.us/
Grade Span: PK-08; **Agency Type:** 1
Schools: 3
2 Primary; 1 Middle; 0 High; 0 Other Level
3 Regular; 0 Special Education; 0 Vocational; 0 Alternative
0 Magnet; 0 Charter; 3 Title I Eligible; 3 School-wide Title I
Students: 1,699 (50.0% male; 50.0% female)
Individual Education Program: 234 (13.8%);
English Language Learner: 576 (33.9%); Migrant: 0 (0.0%)
Eligible for Free Lunch Program: n/a
Eligible for Reduced-Price Lunch Program: n/a
Teachers: 88.5 (19.2 to 1)
Librarians/Media Specialists: 3.0 (566.3 to 1)
Guidance Counselors: 2.0 (849.5 to 1)
Current Spending: ($ per student per year):
Total: $4,964; Instruction: $2,570; Support Services: $2,100
Enrollment, Drop-out Rates and Diploma Recipients by Race/Ethnicity

Category	Total	White	Black	Asian	AIAN	Hisp.
Enrollment (%)	100.0	17.0	4.2	0.5	11.6	66.7
Drop-out Rate (%)	n/a	n/a	n/a	n/a	n/a	n/a
H.S. Diplomas (#)	n/a	n/a	n/a	n/a	n/a	n/a

Liberty Elementary District

19818 W Hwy 85 • Buckeye, AZ 85326-9258
(623) 386-2940
Grade Span: PK-08; **Agency Type:** 1
Schools: 3
3 Primary; 0 Middle; 0 High; 0 Other Level
3 Regular; 0 Special Education; 0 Vocational; 0 Alternative
0 Magnet; 0 Charter; 1 Title I Eligible; 0 School-wide Title I
Students: 1,842 (50.6% male; 49.4% female)
Individual Education Program: 302 (16.4%);
English Language Learner: 80 (4.3%); Migrant: 19 (1.0%)
Eligible for Free Lunch Program: 484 (26.3%)
Eligible for Reduced-Price Lunch Program: 144 (7.8%)
Teachers: 102.8 (17.9 to 1)
Librarians/Media Specialists: 2.0 (921.0 to 1)
Guidance Counselors: 0.0 (0.0 to 1)
Current Spending: ($ per student per year):
Total: $4,758; Instruction: $2,848; Support Services: $1,693
Enrollment, Drop-out Rates and Diploma Recipients by Race/Ethnicity

Category	Total	White	Black	Asian	AIAN	Hisp.
Enrollment (%)	100.0	68.5	2.7	0.7	1.1	27.0
Drop-out Rate (%)	n/a	n/a	n/a	n/a	n/a	n/a
H.S. Diplomas (#)	n/a	n/a	n/a	n/a	n/a	n/a

Litchfield Elementary District

553 Plaza Circle • Litchfield Park, AZ 85340-4996
(623) 535-6000 • http://www.lesd.k12.az.us/
Grade Span: PK-08; **Agency Type:** 1
Schools: 8
6 Primary; 2 Middle; 0 High; 0 Other Level
8 Regular; 0 Special Education; 0 Vocational; 0 Alternative
0 Magnet; 0 Charter; 2 Title I Eligible; 0 School-wide Title I
Students: 5,209 (50.9% male; 49.1% female)
Individual Education Program: 535 (10.3%);
English Language Learner: 338 (6.5%); Migrant: 8 (0.2%)
Eligible for Free Lunch Program: 782 (15.0%)
Eligible for Reduced-Price Lunch Program: 361 (6.9%)
Teachers: 247.5 (21.0 to 1)
Librarians/Media Specialists: 4.5 (1,157.6 to 1)
Guidance Counselors: 5.0 (1,041.8 to 1)
Current Spending: ($ per student per year):
Total: $4,976; Instruction: $2,868; Support Services: $1,830
Enrollment, Drop-out Rates and Diploma Recipients by Race/Ethnicity

Category	Total	White	Black	Asian	AIAN	Hisp.
Enrollment (%)	100.0	61.6	6.5	3.8	1.1	26.9
Drop-out Rate (%)	n/a	n/a	n/a	n/a	n/a	n/a
H.S. Diplomas (#)	n/a	n/a	n/a	n/a	n/a	n/a

Littleton Elementary District

1252 S 115th Ave • Cashion, AZ 85329-0280
Mailing Address: PO Box 280 • Cashion, AZ 85329-0280
(623) 478-5610
Grade Span: PK-08; **Agency Type:** 1
Schools: 3
2 Primary; 1 Middle; 0 High; 0 Other Level
3 Regular; 0 Special Education; 0 Vocational; 0 Alternative
0 Magnet; 0 Charter; 2 Title I Eligible; 2 School-wide Title I
Students: 1,824 (52.5% male; 47.5% female)
Individual Education Program: 231 (12.7%);
English Language Learner: 514 (28.2%); Migrant: 16 (0.9%)
Eligible for Free Lunch Program: n/a
Eligible for Reduced-Price Lunch Program: n/a
Teachers: 82.3 (22.2 to 1)
Librarians/Media Specialists: 0.0 (0.0 to 1)
Guidance Counselors: 0.0 (0.0 to 1)
Current Spending: ($ per student per year):
Total: $5,898; Instruction: $2,858; Support Services: $2,676
Enrollment, Drop-out Rates and Diploma Recipients by Race/Ethnicity

Category	Total	White	Black	Asian	AIAN	Hisp.
Enrollment (%)	100.0	22.0	3.3	0.8	1.0	72.9
Drop-out Rate (%)	n/a	n/a	n/a	n/a	n/a	n/a
H.S. Diplomas (#)	n/a	n/a	n/a	n/a	n/a	n/a

Madison Elementary District

5601 N 16th St • Phoenix, AZ 85016-2903
(602) 664-7900 • http://www.msd38.k12.az.us/
Grade Span: PK-12; **Agency Type:** 1
Schools: 9
5 Primary; 2 Middle; 0 High; 1 Other Level
8 Regular; 0 Special Education; 0 Vocational; 0 Alternative
0 Magnet; 0 Charter; 4 Title I Eligible; 2 School-wide Title I
Students: 5,195 (51.8% male; 48.2% female)
Individual Education Program: 523 (10.1%);
English Language Learner: 723 (13.9%); Migrant: 0 (0.0%)
Eligible for Free Lunch Program: 1,693 (32.6%)
Eligible for Reduced-Price Lunch Program: 450 (8.7%)
Teachers: 301.0 (17.3 to 1)
Librarians/Media Specialists: 6.0 (865.8 to 1)
Guidance Counselors: 1.0 (5,195.0 to 1)
Current Spending: ($ per student per year):
Total: $5,701; Instruction: $3,076; Support Services: $2,325
Enrollment, Drop-out Rates and Diploma Recipients by Race/Ethnicity

Category	Total	White	Black	Asian	AIAN	Hisp.
Enrollment (%)	100.0	58.1	5.5	1.8	5.7	28.9
Drop-out Rate (%)	n/a	n/a	n/a	n/a	n/a	n/a
H.S. Diplomas (#)	0	0	0	0	0	0

Maricopa County Regional District

358 N 5th Ave • Phoenix, AZ 85003
(602) 452-4700 • http://www.musd20.org/
Grade Span: PK-12; **Agency Type:** 1
Schools: 13
3 Primary; 0 Middle; 5 High; 4 Other Level
6 Regular; 0 Special Education; 0 Vocational; 6 Alternative
0 Magnet; 0 Charter; 7 Title I Eligible; 2 School-wide Title I
Students: 2,400 (57.3% male; 42.7% female)
Individual Education Program: 178 (7.4%);
English Language Learner: 91 (3.8%); Migrant: 0 (0.0%)
Eligible for Free Lunch Program: n/a
Eligible for Reduced-Price Lunch Program: n/a
Teachers: 89.6 (26.8 to 1)
Librarians/Media Specialists: 0.0 (0.0 to 1)
Guidance Counselors: 0.8 (3,000.0 to 1)
Current Spending: ($ per student per year):
Total: $6,038; Instruction: $2,481; Support Services: $3,524
Enrollment, Drop-out Rates and Diploma Recipients by Race/Ethnicity

Category	Total	White	Black	Asian	AIAN	Hisp.
Enrollment (%)	100.0	38.1	16.1	0.7	8.5	36.7
Drop-out Rate (%)	50.6	49.2	45.5	0.0	22.1	59.0
H.S. Diplomas (#)	139	71	9	1	3	55

Mesa Unified District

63 E Main Street • Mesa, AZ 85201-7422
(480) 472-0155 • http://www.mpsaz.org/
Grade Span: PK-12; **Agency Type:** 1
Schools: 91
59 Primary; 16 Middle; 12 High; 3 Other Level
84 Regular; 1 Special Education; 0 Vocational; 5 Alternative
0 Magnet; 0 Charter; 36 Title I Eligible; 28 School-wide Title I
Students: 75,269 (51.5% male; 48.5% female)
Individual Education Program: 6,480 (8.6%);
English Language Learner: 6,094 (8.1%); Migrant: 192 (0.3%)
Eligible for Free Lunch Program: 23,134 (30.7%)
Eligible for Reduced-Price Lunch Program: 7,124 (9.5%)
Teachers: 3,682.0 (20.4 to 1)
Librarians/Media Specialists: 70.5 (1,067.6 to 1)
Guidance Counselors: 89.7 (839.1 to 1)
Current Spending: ($ per student per year):
Total: $5,015; Instruction: $3,078; Support Services: $1,673
Enrollment, Drop-out Rates and Diploma Recipients by Race/Ethnicity

Category	Total	White	Black	Asian	AIAN	Hisp.
Enrollment (%)	100.0	62.7	3.7	2.2	3.8	27.6
Drop-out Rate (%)	4.1	3.0	4.6	2.3	11.0	7.3
H.S. Diplomas (#)	4,014	3,099	103	89	104	619

Murphy Elementary District

2615 W Buckeye Rd • Phoenix, AZ 85009-5783
(602) 353-5000 • http://msd.k12.az.us/
Grade Span: PK-08; **Agency Type:** 1
Schools: 4
4 Primary; 0 Middle; 0 High; 0 Other Level
4 Regular; 0 Special Education; 0 Vocational; 0 Alternative
0 Magnet; 0 Charter; 4 Title I Eligible; 4 School-wide Title I
Students: 2,731 (52.0% male; 48.0% female)
Individual Education Program: 353 (12.9%);
English Language Learner: 1,672 (61.2%); Migrant: 2 (0.1%)
Eligible for Free Lunch Program: n/a
Eligible for Reduced-Price Lunch Program: n/a
Teachers: 145.4 (18.8 to 1)
Librarians/Media Specialists: 2.0 (1,365.5 to 1)
Guidance Counselors: 1.0 (2,731.0 to 1)
Current Spending: ($ per student per year):
Total: $6,186; Instruction: $2,915; Support Services: $2,549
Enrollment, Drop-out Rates and Diploma Recipients by Race/Ethnicity

Category	Total	White	Black	Asian	AIAN	Hisp.
Enrollment (%)	100.0	3.0	2.1	0.3	0.6	94.0
Drop-out Rate (%)	n/a	n/a	n/a	n/a	n/a	n/a
H.S. Diplomas (#)	n/a	n/a	n/a	n/a	n/a	n/a

Osborn Elementary District

1226 W Osborn Rd • Phoenix, AZ 85013-3618
(602) 707-2000 • http://www.osbornnet.org/
Grade Span: PK-08; **Agency Type:** 1
Schools: 6
4 Primary; 2 Middle; 0 High; 0 Other Level
2 Regular; 0 Special Education; 0 Vocational; 4 Alternative
0 Magnet; 0 Charter; 6 Title I Eligible; 6 School-wide Title I
Students: 4,177 (51.2% male; 48.8% female)
Individual Education Program: 446 (10.7%);
English Language Learner: 1,756 (42.0%); Migrant: 0 (0.0%)
Eligible for Free Lunch Program: n/a
Eligible for Reduced-Price Lunch Program: n/a
Teachers: 251.5 (16.6 to 1)
Librarians/Media Specialists: 2.5 (1,670.8 to 1)
Guidance Counselors: 2.5 (1,670.8 to 1)
Current Spending: ($ per student per year):
Total: $5,611; Instruction: $2,969; Support Services: $2,259
Enrollment, Drop-out Rates and Diploma Recipients by Race/Ethnicity

Category	Total	White	Black	Asian	AIAN	Hisp.
Enrollment (%)	100.0	19.4	10.5	2.4	10.5	57.2
Drop-out Rate (%)	n/a	n/a	n/a	n/a	n/a	n/a
H.S. Diplomas (#)	n/a	n/a	n/a	n/a	n/a	n/a

Paradise Valley Unified District

15002 N 32nd St • Phoenix, AZ 85032-4441
(602) 867-5235 • http://www.pvusd.k12.az.us/
Grade Span: PK-12; **Agency Type:** 1
Schools: 49
30 Primary; 10 Middle; 9 High; 0 Other Level
47 Regular; 0 Special Education; 1 Vocational; 1 Alternative
0 Magnet; 0 Charter; 7 Title I Eligible; 1 School-wide Title I
Students: 35,073 (51.7% male; 48.3% female)
Individual Education Program: 3,600 (10.3%);
English Language Learner: 3,329 (9.5%); Migrant: 0 (0.0%)
Eligible for Free Lunch Program: 5,419 (15.5%)
Eligible for Reduced-Price Lunch Program: 1,920 (5.5%)
Teachers: 1,872.8 (18.7 to 1)
Librarians/Media Specialists: 37.5 (935.3 to 1)
Guidance Counselors: 37.9 (925.4 to 1)
Current Spending: ($ per student per year):
Total: $4,790; Instruction: $2,998; Support Services: $1,594
Enrollment, Drop-out Rates and Diploma Recipients by Race/Ethnicity

Category	Total	White	Black	Asian	AIAN	Hisp.
Enrollment (%)	100.0	77.2	3.1	2.7	1.1	16.0
Drop-out Rate (%)	4.6	3.8	6.4	2.7	12.5	10.9
H.S. Diplomas (#)	2,136	1,843	49	62	9	173

Pendergast Elementary District

3802 N 91st Ave • Phoenix, AZ 85037-2368
(623) 772-2215 • http://pendergast.k12.az.us/
Grade Span: PK-08; **Agency Type:** 1
Schools: 11
11 Primary; 0 Middle; 0 High; 0 Other Level
11 Regular; 0 Special Education; 0 Vocational; 0 Alternative
0 Magnet; 0 Charter; 3 Title I Eligible; 3 School-wide Title I
Students: 9,615 (51.6% male; 48.4% female)
Individual Education Program: 1,078 (11.2%);
English Language Learner: 1,799 (18.7%); Migrant: 12 (0.1%)
Eligible for Free Lunch Program: 2,582 (26.9%)
Eligible for Reduced-Price Lunch Program: 794 (8.3%)
Teachers: 506.4 (19.0 to 1)
Librarians/Media Specialists: 10.0 (961.5 to 1)
Guidance Counselors: 9.5 (1,012.1 to 1)
Current Spending: ($ per student per year):
Total: $4,645; Instruction: $2,684; Support Services: $1,742
Enrollment, Drop-out Rates and Diploma Recipients by Race/Ethnicity

Category	Total	White	Black	Asian	AIAN	Hisp.
Enrollment (%)	100.0	36.3	10.1	2.3	1.6	49.7
Drop-out Rate (%)	n/a	n/a	n/a	n/a	n/a	n/a
H.S. Diplomas (#)	n/a	n/a	n/a	n/a	n/a	n/a

Peoria Unified SD

6330 W Thunderbird Rd • Glendale, AZ 85306
Mailing Address: PO Box 39 • Peoria, AZ 85380-0039
(623) 486-6032 • http://www.peoriaud.k12.az.us/
Grade Span: PK-12; **Agency Type:** 1
Schools: 36
28 Primary; 0 Middle; 5 High; 3 Other Level
35 Regular; 0 Special Education; 0 Vocational; 1 Alternative
0 Magnet; 0 Charter; 6 Title I Eligible; 0 School-wide Title I
Students: 35,178 (51.7% male; 48.3% female)
Individual Education Program: 3,937 (11.2%);
English Language Learner: 1,447 (4.1%); Migrant: 70 (0.2%)
Eligible for Free Lunch Program: 4,071 (11.6%)
Eligible for Reduced-Price Lunch Program: 1,760 (5.0%)
Teachers: 1,827.6 (19.2 to 1)
Librarians/Media Specialists: 32.0 (1,099.3 to 1)
Guidance Counselors: 58.0 (606.5 to 1)
Current Spending: ($ per student per year):
Total: $4,751; Instruction: $2,930; Support Services: $1,605
Enrollment, Drop-out Rates and Diploma Recipients by Race/Ethnicity

Category	Total	White	Black	Asian	AIAN	Hisp.
Enrollment (%)	100.0	71.0	4.8	3.0	1.2	20.0
Drop-out Rate (%)	5.1	4.3	6.9	2.3	18.6	8.2
H.S. Diplomas (#)	1,990	1,559	76	65	5	285

Phoenix Elementary District

1817 N 7th St • Phoenix, AZ 85006
(602) 257-3755 • http://www.phxelem.k12.az.us/
Grade Span: PK-08; **Agency Type:** 1
Schools: 20
17 Primary; 2 Middle; 0 High; 1 Other Level
18 Regular; 0 Special Education; 0 Vocational; 2 Alternative
0 Magnet; 0 Charter; 15 Title I Eligible; 14 School-wide Title I
Students: 8,588 (50.2% male; 49.8% female)
Individual Education Program: 965 (11.2%);
English Language Learner: 4,532 (52.8%); Migrant: 16 (0.2%)
Eligible for Free Lunch Program: n/a
Eligible for Reduced-Price Lunch Program: n/a
Teachers: 506.9 (16.9 to 1)
Librarians/Media Specialists: 4.0 (2,147.0 to 1)
Guidance Counselors: 3.0 (2,862.7 to 1)
Current Spending: ($ per student per year):
Total: $6,685; Instruction: $3,614; Support Services: $2,622
Enrollment, Drop-out Rates and Diploma Recipients by Race/Ethnicity

Category	Total	White	Black	Asian	AIAN	Hisp.
Enrollment (%)	100.0	5.0	5.9	0.8	2.9	85.4
Drop-out Rate (%)	n/a	n/a	n/a	n/a	n/a	n/a
H.S. Diplomas (#)	n/a	n/a	n/a	n/a	n/a	n/a

Phoenix Union High SD

4502 N Central Ave • Phoenix, AZ 85012
(602) 764-1500 •
http://www.phxhs.k12.az.us/education/district/district.php?sectionid=1
Grade Span: 09-12; **Agency Type:** 1
Schools: 14
0 Primary; 0 Middle; 14 High; 0 Other Level
10 Regular; 1 Special Education; 1 Vocational; 2 Alternative
0 Magnet; 0 Charter; 11 Title I Eligible; 11 School-wide Title I
Students: 23,616 (50.8% male; 49.2% female)
Individual Education Program: 2,320 (9.8%);
English Language Learner: 4,330 (18.3%); Migrant: 63 (0.3%)
Eligible for Free Lunch Program: n/a
Eligible for Reduced-Price Lunch Program: n/a
Teachers: 1,275.5 (18.5 to 1)
Librarians/Media Specialists: 10.0 (2,361.6 to 1)
Guidance Counselors: 84.0 (281.1 to 1)
Current Spending: ($ per student per year):
Total: $7,402; Instruction: $3,806; Support Services: $3,383
Enrollment, Drop-out Rates and Diploma Recipients by Race/Ethnicity

Category	Total	White	Black	Asian	AIAN	Hisp.
Enrollment (%)	100.0	13.7	10.4	1.5	3.2	71.2
Drop-out Rate (%)	12.5	11.3	10.5	8.7	19.9	13.0
H.S. Diplomas (#)	3,534	675	396	91	113	2,259

Queen Creek Unified District

20740 S Ellsworth Rd • Queen Creek, AZ 85242-9314
(480) 987-5935
Grade Span: PK-12; **Agency Type:** 1
Schools: 5
3 Primary; 1 Middle; 1 High; 0 Other Level
5 Regular; 0 Special Education; 0 Vocational; 0 Alternative
0 Magnet; 0 Charter; 4 Title I Eligible; 1 School-wide Title I
Students: 2,155 (52.4% male; 47.6% female)
Individual Education Program: 222 (10.3%);
English Language Learner: 219 (10.2%); Migrant: 122 (5.7%)
Eligible for Free Lunch Program: 678 (31.5%)
Eligible for Reduced-Price Lunch Program: 137 (6.4%)
Teachers: 114.2 (18.9 to 1)
Librarians/Media Specialists: 1.0 (2,155.0 to 1)
Guidance Counselors: 2.9 (743.1 to 1)
Current Spending: ($ per student per year):
Total: $5,311; Instruction: $2,648; Support Services: $2,205
Enrollment, Drop-out Rates and Diploma Recipients by Race/Ethnicity

Category	Total	White	Black	Asian	AIAN	Hisp.
Enrollment (%)	100.0	65.2	0.8	0.6	1.2	32.2
Drop-out Rate (%)	6.8	3.4	0.0	0.0	0.0	12.8
H.S. Diplomas (#)	84	52	0	0	0	32

Roosevelt Elementary District

6000 S 7th St • Phoenix, AZ 85042-4294
(602) 243-2605 • http://www.rsd.k12.az.us/
Grade Span: PK-08; **Agency Type:** 1
Schools: 22
21 Primary; 0 Middle; 0 High; 0 Other Level
19 Regular; 1 Special Education; 0 Vocational; 1 Alternative
0 Magnet; 0 Charter; 20 Title I Eligible; 20 School-wide Title I
Students: 11,442 (50.3% male; 49.7% female)
Individual Education Program: 1,154 (10.1%);
English Language Learner: 4,030 (35.2%); Migrant: 12 (0.1%)
Eligible for Free Lunch Program: n/a
Eligible for Reduced-Price Lunch Program: n/a
Teachers: 621.0 (18.4 to 1)
Librarians/Media Specialists: 18.0 (635.7 to 1)
Guidance Counselors: 1.0 (11,442.0 to 1)
Current Spending: ($ per student per year):
Total: $6,913; Instruction: $3,776; Support Services: $2,714
Enrollment, Drop-out Rates and Diploma Recipients by Race/Ethnicity

Category	Total	White	Black	Asian	AIAN	Hisp.
Enrollment (%)	100.0	3.6	15.6	0.1	0.9	79.7
Drop-out Rate (%)	n/a	n/a	n/a	n/a	n/a	n/a
H.S. Diplomas (#)	n/a	n/a	n/a	n/a	n/a	n/a

Scottsdale Unified District

3811 N 44th St • Phoenix, AZ 85018-5489
(480) 484-6100 • http://www.susd.org/
Grade Span: PK-12; **Agency Type:** 1
Schools: 34
21 Primary; 6 Middle; 4 High; 3 Other Level
34 Regular; 0 Special Education; 0 Vocational; 0 Alternative
0 Magnet; 0 Charter; 5 Title I Eligible; 2 School-wide Title I
Students: 27,245 (51.6% male; 48.4% female)
Individual Education Program: 2,488 (9.1%);
English Language Learner: 2,041 (7.5%); Migrant: 0 (0.0%)
Eligible for Free Lunch Program: 2,979 (10.9%)
Eligible for Reduced-Price Lunch Program: 977 (3.6%)
Teachers: 1,529.8 (17.8 to 1)
Librarians/Media Specialists: 25.0 (1,089.8 to 1)
Guidance Counselors: 40.3 (676.1 to 1)
Current Spending: ($ per student per year):
Total: $5,128; Instruction: $2,986; Support Services: $1,951
Enrollment, Drop-out Rates and Diploma Recipients by Race/Ethnicity

Category	Total	White	Black	Asian	AIAN	Hisp.
Enrollment (%)	100.0	82.1	2.1	3.1	1.2	11.4
Drop-out Rate (%)	1.6	1.4	2.4	1.2	2.7	3.3
H.S. Diplomas (#)	1,708	1,513	33	67	9	86

Tempe Elementary District

3205 S Rural Rd • Tempe, AZ 85282
Mailing Address: PO Box 27708 • Tempe, AZ 85285-7708
(480) 730-7102 • http://www.tempe3.k12.az.us/
Grade Span: PK-12; **Agency Type:** 1
Schools: 26
20 Primary; 5 Middle; 0 High; 1 Other Level
25 Regular; 0 Special Education; 0 Vocational; 1 Alternative
0 Magnet; 0 Charter; 17 Title I Eligible; 17 School-wide Title I
Students: 13,394 (51.4% male; 48.6% female)
Individual Education Program: 1,639 (12.2%);
English Language Learner: 3,483 (26.0%); Migrant: 0 (0.0%)
Eligible for Free Lunch Program: n/a
Eligible for Reduced-Price Lunch Program: n/a
Teachers: 825.2 (16.2 to 1)
Librarians/Media Specialists: 17.0 (787.9 to 1)
Guidance Counselors: 23.8 (562.8 to 1)
Current Spending: ($ per student per year):
Total: $5,758; Instruction: $3,220; Support Services: $2,257
Enrollment, Drop-out Rates and Diploma Recipients by Race/Ethnicity

Category	Total	White	Black	Asian	AIAN	Hisp.
Enrollment (%)	100.0	33.9	10.5	3.8	8.4	43.4
Drop-out Rate (%)	n/a	n/a	n/a	n/a	n/a	n/a
H.S. Diplomas (#)	0	0	0	0	0	0

Tempe Union High SD

500 W Guadalupe Rd • Tempe, AZ 85283-3599
(480) 839-0292 • http://www.tuhsd.k12.az.us/
Grade Span: 09-12; **Agency Type:** 1
Schools: 8
0 Primary; 0 Middle; 7 High; 0 Other Level
7 Regular; 0 Special Education; 0 Vocational; 0 Alternative
0 Magnet; 0 Charter; 4 Title I Eligible; 0 School-wide Title I
Students: 13,163 (51.5% male; 48.5% female)
Individual Education Program: 1,122 (8.5%);
English Language Learner: 0 (0.0%); Migrant: 0 (0.0%)
Eligible for Free Lunch Program: n/a
Eligible for Reduced-Price Lunch Program: n/a
Teachers: 652.0 (20.2 to 1)
Librarians/Media Specialists: 19.0 (692.8 to 1)
Guidance Counselors: 35.7 (368.7 to 1)
Current Spending: ($ per student per year):
Total: $5,237; Instruction: $2,929; Support Services: $2,001
Enrollment, Drop-out Rates and Diploma Recipients by Race/Ethnicity

Category	Total	White	Black	Asian	AIAN	Hisp.
Enrollment (%)	100.0	63.3	7.8	5.8	3.0	20.1
Drop-out Rate (%)	4.2	2.9	4.4	2.1	11.2	8.1
H.S. Diplomas (#)	2,678	1,850	197	142	61	428

Tolleson Elementary District

9401 W Garfield Rd • Tolleson, AZ 85353-2941
Mailing Address: 9261 W Van Buren • Tolleson, AZ 85353-2941
(623) 936-9740
Grade Span: PK-08; **Agency Type:** 1
Schools: 3
3 Primary; 0 Middle; 0 High; 0 Other Level
3 Regular; 0 Special Education; 0 Vocational; 0 Alternative
0 Magnet; 0 Charter; 3 Title I Eligible; 0 School-wide Title I
Students: 1,877 (50.7% male; 49.3% female)
Individual Education Program: 164 (8.7%);
English Language Learner: 545 (29.0%); Migrant: 0 (0.0%)
Eligible for Free Lunch Program: n/a
Eligible for Reduced-Price Lunch Program: n/a
Teachers: 102.0 (18.4 to 1)
Librarians/Media Specialists: 2.0 (938.5 to 1)
Guidance Counselors: 0.0 (0.0 to 1)
Current Spending: ($ per student per year):
Total: $5,026; Instruction: $2,775; Support Services: $1,925
Enrollment, Drop-out Rates and Diploma Recipients by Race/Ethnicity

Category	Total	White	Black	Asian	AIAN	Hisp.
Enrollment (%)	100.0	14.1	7.1	1.1	1.4	76.2
Drop-out Rate (%)	n/a	n/a	n/a	n/a	n/a	n/a
H.S. Diplomas (#)	n/a	n/a	n/a	n/a	n/a	n/a

Tolleson Union High SD

9419 W Van Buren St • Tolleson, AZ 85353-2898
(623) 478-4000 • http://www.tuhsd.org/
Grade Span: 09-12; **Agency Type:** 1
Schools: 3
0 Primary; 0 Middle; 3 High; 0 Other Level
3 Regular; 0 Special Education; 0 Vocational; 0 Alternative
0 Magnet; 0 Charter; 2 Title I Eligible; 2 School-wide Title I
Students: 4,993 (51.3% male; 48.7% female)
Individual Education Program: 512 (10.3%);
English Language Learner: 299 (6.0%); Migrant: 76 (1.5%)
Eligible for Free Lunch Program: 1,079 (21.6%)
Eligible for Reduced-Price Lunch Program: 309 (6.2%)
Teachers: 245.4 (20.3 to 1)
Librarians/Media Specialists: 3.0 (1,664.3 to 1)
Guidance Counselors: 12.0 (416.1 to 1)
Current Spending: ($ per student per year):
Total: $5,326; Instruction: $2,755; Support Services: $2,239
Enrollment, Drop-out Rates and Diploma Recipients by Race/Ethnicity

Category	Total	White	Black	Asian	AIAN	Hisp.
Enrollment (%)	100.0	32.8	9.5	2.8	2.3	52.7
Drop-out Rate (%)	10.8	9.1	8.8	4.9	17.1	12.6
H.S. Diplomas (#)	742	352	55	20	13	302

Washington Elementary District

8610 N 19th Ave • Phoenix, AZ 85021-4294
(602) 347-2615 • http://www.wesd.k12.az.us/
Grade Span: PK-08; **Agency Type:** 1
Schools: 32
28 Primary; 4 Middle; 0 High; 0 Other Level
32 Regular; 0 Special Education; 0 Vocational; 0 Alternative
0 Magnet; 0 Charter; 20 Title I Eligible; 10 School-wide Title I
Students: 24,506 (52.4% male; 47.6% female)
Individual Education Program: 3,336 (13.6%);
English Language Learner: 5,215 (21.3%); Migrant: 0 (0.0%)
Eligible for Free Lunch Program: 7,623 (31.1%)
Eligible for Reduced-Price Lunch Program: 2,485 (10.1%)
Teachers: 1,346.5 (18.2 to 1)
Librarians/Media Specialists: 20.7 (1,183.9 to 1)
Guidance Counselors: 10.0 (2,450.6 to 1)
Current Spending: ($ per student per year):
Total: $5,000; Instruction: $3,216; Support Services: $1,494
Enrollment, Drop-out Rates and Diploma Recipients by Race/Ethnicity

Category	Total	White	Black	Asian	AIAN	Hisp.
Enrollment (%)	100.0	52.1	6.2	3.0	3.3	35.4
Drop-out Rate (%)	n/a	n/a	n/a	n/a	n/a	n/a
H.S. Diplomas (#)	n/a	n/a	n/a	n/a	n/a	n/a

Wickenburg Unified District

40 W Yavapai St • Wickenburg, AZ 85390-9999
(928) 668-5350 • http://www.wickenburg.k12.az.us/
Grade Span: PK-12; **Agency Type:** 1
Schools: 5
2 Primary; 1 Middle; 1 High; 1 Other Level
5 Regular; 0 Special Education; 0 Vocational; 0 Alternative
0 Magnet; 0 Charter; 4 Title I Eligible; 0 School-wide Title I
Students: 1,503 (50.7% male; 49.3% female)
Individual Education Program: 170 (11.3%);
English Language Learner: 129 (8.6%); Migrant: 0 (0.0%)
Eligible for Free Lunch Program: 512 (34.1%)
Eligible for Reduced-Price Lunch Program: 126 (8.4%)
Teachers: 86.2 (17.4 to 1)
Librarians/Media Specialists: 1.2 (1,252.5 to 1)
Guidance Counselors: 2.1 (715.7 to 1)
Current Spending: ($ per student per year):
Total: $5,327; Instruction: $2,945; Support Services: $2,130
Enrollment, Drop-out Rates and Diploma Recipients by Race/Ethnicity

Category	Total	White	Black	Asian	AIAN	Hisp.
Enrollment (%)	100.0	77.4	0.9	0.5	1.7	19.6
Drop-out Rate (%)	11.4	10.2	75.0	0.0	37.5	12.7
H.S. Diplomas (#)	89	77	1	1	0	10

Mohave County

Bullhead City Elementary District

1004 Hancock Rd • Bullhead City, AZ 86442-5901
(928) 758-3961 • http://www.bullhead.apscc.k12.az.us/
Grade Span: PK-08; **Agency Type:** 1
Schools: 7
5 Primary; 2 Middle; 0 High; 0 Other Level
7 Regular; 0 Special Education; 0 Vocational; 0 Alternative
0 Magnet; 0 Charter; 3 Title I Eligible; 0 School-wide Title I
Students: 3,918 (53.3% male; 46.7% female)
Individual Education Program: 359 (9.2%);
English Language Learner: 643 (16.4%); Migrant: 0 (0.0%)
Eligible for Free Lunch Program: n/a
Eligible for Reduced-Price Lunch Program: n/a
Teachers: 211.1 (18.6 to 1)
Librarians/Media Specialists: 7.0 (559.7 to 1)
Guidance Counselors: 3.0 (1,306.0 to 1)
Current Spending: ($ per student per year):
Total: $4,035; Instruction: $2,580; Support Services: $1,246
Enrollment, Drop-out Rates and Diploma Recipients by Race/Ethnicity

Category	Total	White	Black	Asian	AIAN	Hisp.
Enrollment (%)	100.0	59.6	2.5	1.0	1.3	35.5
Drop-out Rate (%)	n/a	n/a	n/a	n/a	n/a	n/a
H.S. Diplomas (#)	n/a	n/a	n/a	n/a	n/a	n/a

Colorado River Union High SD

5221 Hwy 95 • Fort Mojave, AZ 86426
Mailing Address: PO Box 21479 • Bullhead City, AZ 86439-1479
(928) 768-1665 • http://www.cruhsd.org
Grade Span: 09-12; **Agency Type:** 1
Schools: 2
0 Primary; 0 Middle; 2 High; 0 Other Level
2 Regular; 0 Special Education; 0 Vocational; 0 Alternative
0 Magnet; 0 Charter; 2 Title I Eligible; 0 School-wide Title I
Students: 2,033 (51.8% male; 48.2% female)
Individual Education Program: 237 (11.7%);
English Language Learner: 12 (0.6%); Migrant: 0 (0.0%)
Eligible for Free Lunch Program: n/a
Eligible for Reduced-Price Lunch Program: n/a
Teachers: 50.0 (40.7 to 1)
Librarians/Media Specialists: 1.0 (2,033.0 to 1)
Guidance Counselors: 2.0 (1,016.5 to 1)
Current Spending: ($ per student per year):
Total: $4,380; Instruction: $2,185; Support Services: $1,890
Enrollment, Drop-out Rates and Diploma Recipients by Race/Ethnicity

Category	Total	White	Black	Asian	AIAN	Hisp.
Enrollment (%)	100.0	71.0	1.2	1.0	2.8	24.0
Drop-out Rate (%)	19.2	16.8	35.7	11.1	28.9	26.1
H.S. Diplomas (#)	320	247	3	7	10	53

Kingman Unified SD

3033 Macdonald Ave • Kingman, AZ 86401
(928) 753-5678
Grade Span: PK-12; **Agency Type:** 1
Schools: 11
6 Primary; 1 Middle; 3 High; 1 Other Level
11 Regular; 0 Special Education; 0 Vocational; 0 Alternative
0 Magnet; 0 Charter; 7 Title I Eligible; 0 School-wide Title I
Students: 7,198 (51.8% male; 48.2% female)
Individual Education Program: 954 (13.3%);
English Language Learner: 0 (0.0%); Migrant: 0 (0.0%)
Eligible for Free Lunch Program: n/a
Eligible for Reduced-Price Lunch Program: n/a
Teachers: 375.6 (19.2 to 1)
Librarians/Media Specialists: 8.5 (846.8 to 1)
Guidance Counselors: 8.1 (888.6 to 1)
Current Spending: ($ per student per year):
Total: n/a; Instruction: n/a; Support Services: n/a
Enrollment, Drop-out Rates and Diploma Recipients by Race/Ethnicity

Category	Total	White	Black	Asian	AIAN	Hisp.
Enrollment (%)	100.0	83.8	1.0	1.0	2.6	11.6
Drop-out Rate (%)	n/a	n/a	n/a	n/a	n/a	n/a
H.S. Diplomas (#)	442	377	3	11	9	42

Lake Havasu Unified District

2200 Havasupai Blvd • Lake Havasu City, AZ 86403-3798
(928) 855-8466 • http://www.havasu.k12.az.us/
Grade Span: PK-12; **Agency Type:** 1
Schools: 9
5 Primary; 2 Middle; 1 High; 1 Other Level
9 Regular; 0 Special Education; 0 Vocational; 0 Alternative
0 Magnet; 0 Charter; 5 Title I Eligible; 5 School-wide Title I
Students: 6,312 (51.3% male; 48.7% female)
Individual Education Program: 660 (10.5%);
English Language Learner: 232 (3.7%); Migrant: 0 (0.0%)
Eligible for Free Lunch Program: n/a
Eligible for Reduced-Price Lunch Program: n/a
Teachers: 312.3 (20.2 to 1)
Librarians/Media Specialists: 2.0 (3,156.0 to 1)
Guidance Counselors: 4.6 (1,372.2 to 1)
Current Spending: ($ per student per year):
Total: $4,646; Instruction: $2,595; Support Services: $1,765
Enrollment, Drop-out Rates and Diploma Recipients by Race/Ethnicity

Category	Total	White	Black	Asian	AIAN	Hisp.
Enrollment (%)	100.0	81.2	0.6	1.2	1.1	15.8
Drop-out Rate (%)	6.3	5.4	10.0	4.2	4.0	13.5
H.S. Diplomas (#)	316	273	2	6	2	33

Mohave Valley Elementary District

8450 S Olive • Mohave Valley, AZ 86440-5070
Mailing Address: PO Box 5070 • Mohave Valley, AZ 86446
(928) 768-2507 • http://www.mvesd16.org/
Grade Span: PK-08; **Agency Type:** 1
Schools: 4
3 Primary; 1 Middle; 0 High; 0 Other Level
4 Regular; 0 Special Education; 0 Vocational; 0 Alternative
0 Magnet; 0 Charter; 3 Title I Eligible; 1 School-wide Title I
Students: 1,752 (51.0% male; 49.0% female)
Individual Education Program: 309 (17.6%);
English Language Learner: 47 (2.7%); Migrant: 0 (0.0%)
Eligible for Free Lunch Program: 839 (47.9%)
Eligible for Reduced-Price Lunch Program: 316 (18.0%)
Teachers: 77.5 (22.6 to 1)
Librarians/Media Specialists: 1.0 (1,752.0 to 1)
Guidance Counselors: 0.0 (0.0 to 1)
Current Spending: ($ per student per year):
Total: $4,856; Instruction: $2,533; Support Services: $2,053

Enrollment, Drop-out Rates and Diploma Recipients by Race/Ethnicity

Category	Total	White	Black	Asian	AIAN	Hisp.
Enrollment (%)	100.0	71.9	1.2	1.4	8.8	16.8
Drop-out Rate (%)	n/a	n/a	n/a	n/a	n/a	n/a
H.S. Diplomas (#)	n/a	n/a	n/a	n/a	n/a	n/a

Peach Springs Unified District

16500 E Hwy 66 • Peach Springs, AZ 86403-0360
Mailing Address: PO Box 360 • Peach Springs, AZ 86434-0138
(928) 769-2202
Grade Span: PK-12; **Agency Type:** 1
Schools: 32
22 Primary; 1 Middle; 1 High; 5 Other Level
29 Regular; 0 Special Education; 0 Vocational; 0 Alternative
0 Magnet; 0 Charter; 15 Title I Eligible; 3 School-wide Title I
Students: 2,157 (52.4% male; 47.6% female)
Individual Education Program: 218 (10.1%);
English Language Learner: 119 (5.5%); Migrant: 0 (0.0%)
Eligible for Free Lunch Program: n/a
Eligible for Reduced-Price Lunch Program: n/a
Teachers: 24.8 (87.0 to 1)
Librarians/Media Specialists: 0.0 (0.0 to 1)
Guidance Counselors: 0.0 (0.0 to 1)
Current Spending: ($ per student per year):
Total: $6,361; Instruction: $4,714; Support Services: $1,532

Enrollment, Drop-out Rates and Diploma Recipients by Race/Ethnicity

Category	Total	White	Black	Asian	AIAN	Hisp.
Enrollment (%)	100.0	57.9	7.6	2.9	18.1	13.5
Drop-out Rate (%)	44.1	41.2	50.0	0.0	43.2	91.7
H.S. Diplomas (#)	47	31	1	0	5	10

Navajo County

Blue Ridge Unified District

1200 W White Mountain Blvd • Lakeside, AZ 85929-0885
(928) 368-6126 • http://www.brusd.k12.az.us/
Grade Span: PK-12; **Agency Type:** 1
Schools: 4
1 Primary; 2 Middle; 1 High; 0 Other Level
4 Regular; 0 Special Education; 0 Vocational; 0 Alternative
0 Magnet; 0 Charter; 2 Title I Eligible; 0 School-wide Title I
Students: 2,548 (50.8% male; 49.2% female)
Individual Education Program: 316 (12.4%);
English Language Learner: 110 (4.3%); Migrant: 0 (0.0%)
Eligible for Free Lunch Program: 1,086 (42.6%)
Eligible for Reduced-Price Lunch Program: 217 (8.5%)
Teachers: 146.3 (17.4 to 1)
Librarians/Media Specialists: 1.0 (2,548.0 to 1)
Guidance Counselors: 4.6 (553.9 to 1)
Current Spending: ($ per student per year):
Total: $5,553; Instruction: $3,262; Support Services: $2,068

Enrollment, Drop-out Rates and Diploma Recipients by Race/Ethnicity

Category	Total	White	Black	Asian	AIAN	Hisp.
Enrollment (%)	100.0	75.5	0.9	0.6	9.3	13.6
Drop-out Rate (%)	9.1	6.4	20.0	0.0	32.0	15.0
H.S. Diplomas (#)	145	116	0	3	6	20

Holbrook Unified District

1000 N 8th Ave • Holbrook, AZ 86025-0640
Mailing Address: PO Box 640 • Holbrook, AZ 86025-0640
(928) 524-6144 • http://www.holbrook.k12.az.us/
Grade Span: PK-12; **Agency Type:** 1
Schools: 5
3 Primary; 1 Middle; 1 High; 0 Other Level
5 Regular; 0 Special Education; 0 Vocational; 0 Alternative
0 Magnet; 0 Charter; 4 Title I Eligible; 4 School-wide Title I
Students: 2,045 (51.7% male; 48.3% female)
Individual Education Program: 240 (11.7%);
English Language Learner: 442 (21.6%); Migrant: 0 (0.0%)
Eligible for Free Lunch Program: n/a
Eligible for Reduced-Price Lunch Program: n/a
Teachers: 132.1 (15.5 to 1)
Librarians/Media Specialists: 1.0 (2,045.0 to 1)
Guidance Counselors: 5.0 (409.0 to 1)
Current Spending: ($ per student per year):
Total: $5,918; Instruction: $3,358; Support Services: $2,226

Enrollment, Drop-out Rates and Diploma Recipients by Race/Ethnicity

Category	Total	White	Black	Asian	AIAN	Hisp.
Enrollment (%)	100.0	28.9	1.8	0.6	54.7	14.0
Drop-out Rate (%)	11.6	5.6	6.7	0.0	15.1	10.0
H.S. Diplomas (#)	139	42	5	2	77	13

Hopi Agency

PO Box 568 • Kearns Canyon, AZ 86034
(520) 738-2262 • http://www.susd.org/schools/elem/Hopi/index.htm
Grade Span: KG-12; **Agency Type:** 6
Schools: 8
6 Primary; 0 Middle; 1 High; 1 Other Level
8 Regular; 0 Special Education; 0 Vocational; 0 Alternative
0 Magnet; 0 Charter; 8 Title I Eligible; 8 School-wide Title I
Students: 1,725 (n/a% male; n/a% female)
Individual Education Program: n/a;
English Language Learner: n/a; Migrant: n/a
Eligible for Free Lunch Program: n/a
Eligible for Reduced-Price Lunch Program: n/a
Teachers: n/a
Librarians/Media Specialists: n/a
Guidance Counselors: n/a
Current Spending: ($ per student per year):
Total: n/a; Instruction: n/a; Support Services: n/a

Enrollment, Drop-out Rates and Diploma Recipients by Race/Ethnicity

Category	Total	White	Black	Asian	AIAN	Hisp.
Enrollment (%)	100.0	0.0	0.0	0.0	100.0	0.0
Drop-out Rate (%)	n/a	n/a	n/a	n/a	n/a	n/a
H.S. Diplomas (#)	n/a	n/a	n/a	n/a	n/a	n/a

Kayenta Unified District

N Hwy 163 • Kayenta, AZ 86033-0337
Mailing Address: PO Box 337 • Kayenta, AZ 86033-0337
(928) 697-2012 • http://www.kayenta.k12.az.us/
Grade Span: PK-12; **Agency Type:** 1
Schools: 5
2 Primary; 1 Middle; 1 High; 0 Other Level
4 Regular; 0 Special Education; 0 Vocational; 0 Alternative
0 Magnet; 0 Charter; 4 Title I Eligible; 3 School-wide Title I
Students: 2,463 (51.2% male; 48.8% female)
Individual Education Program: 222 (9.0%);
English Language Learner: 1,776 (72.1%); Migrant: 0 (0.0%)
Eligible for Free Lunch Program: n/a
Eligible for Reduced-Price Lunch Program: n/a
Teachers: 152.8 (16.1 to 1)
Librarians/Media Specialists: 4.5 (547.3 to 1)
Guidance Counselors: 6.6 (373.2 to 1)
Current Spending: ($ per student per year):
Total: $7,361; Instruction: $4,022; Support Services: $2,991

Enrollment, Drop-out Rates and Diploma Recipients by Race/Ethnicity

Category	Total	White	Black	Asian	AIAN	Hisp.
Enrollment (%)	100.0	1.6	0.0	0.0	98.2	0.2
Drop-out Rate (%)	7.0	8.3	n/a	n/a	6.9	n/a
H.S. Diplomas (#)	188	2	0	0	186	0

Show Low Unified District

1350 N Central Ave • Show Low, AZ 85901-4645
Mailing Address: 500 W Old Linden Rd • Show Low, AZ 85901-4645
(928) 537-6001 • http://www.show-low.k12.az.us/
Grade Span: PK-12; **Agency Type:** 1
Schools: 9
3 Primary; 3 Middle; 2 High; 0 Other Level
8 Regular; 0 Special Education; 0 Vocational; 0 Alternative
0 Magnet; 0 Charter; 5 Title I Eligible; 5 School-wide Title I
Students: 2,561 (52.3% male; 47.7% female)
Individual Education Program: 307 (12.0%);
English Language Learner: 50 (2.0%); Migrant: 0 (0.0%)
Eligible for Free Lunch Program: n/a
Eligible for Reduced-Price Lunch Program: n/a
Teachers: 134.5 (19.0 to 1)
Librarians/Media Specialists: 1.0 (2,561.0 to 1)
Guidance Counselors: 4.0 (640.3 to 1)
Current Spending: ($ per student per year):
Total: $4,865; Instruction: $2,565; Support Services: $2,017

Enrollment, Drop-out Rates and Diploma Recipients by Race/Ethnicity

Category	Total	White	Black	Asian	AIAN	Hisp.
Enrollment (%)	100.0	84.7	0.6	0.7	4.6	9.4
Drop-out Rate (%)	4.9	4.0	0.0	0.0	15.6	11.6
H.S. Diplomas (#)	198	174	0	1	7	16

Snowflake Unified District

682 School Bus Ln • Snowflake, AZ 85937-1100
(928) 536-4156 • http://www.snowflake.k12.az.us/
Grade Span: PK-12; **Agency Type:** 1
Schools: 7
3 Primary; 3 Middle; 1 High; 0 Other Level
7 Regular; 0 Special Education; 0 Vocational; 0 Alternative
0 Magnet; 0 Charter; 5 Title I Eligible; 2 School-wide Title I
Students: 3,303 (52.3% male; 47.7% female)
Individual Education Program: 385 (11.7%);
English Language Learner: 0 (0.0%); Migrant: 0 (0.0%)

Eligible for Free Lunch Program: n/a
Eligible for Reduced-Price Lunch Program: n/a
Teachers: 135.0 (24.5 to 1)
Librarians/Media Specialists: 3.0 (1,101.0 to 1)
Guidance Counselors: 2.0 (1,651.5 to 1)
Current Spending: ($ per student per year):
Total: $5,936; Instruction: $2,958; Support Services: $2,848
Enrollment, Drop-out Rates and Diploma Recipients by Race/Ethnicity

Category	Total	White	Black	Asian	AIAN	Hisp.
Enrollment (%)	100.0	81.3	0.5	0.5	8.2	9.5
Drop-out Rate (%)	8.3	6.8	0.0	20.0	15.2	16.4
H.S. Diplomas (#)	139	122	1	0	8	8

Whiteriver Unified District
200 Cemetery Rd • Whiteriver, AZ 85941-0190
Mailing Address: PO Box 190 • Whiteriver, AZ 85941-0190
(928) 338-4842 • http://www.wusd.k12.az.us/
Grade Span: PK-12; **Agency Type:** 1
Schools: 5
3 Primary; 1 Middle; 1 High; 0 Other Level
5 Regular; 0 Special Education; 0 Vocational; 0 Alternative
0 Magnet; 0 Charter; 5 Title I Eligible; 0 School-wide Title I
Students: 2,480 (50.7% male; 49.3% female)
Individual Education Program: 391 (15.8%);
English Language Learner: 1,792 (72.3%); Migrant: 0 (0.0%)
Eligible for Free Lunch Program: n/a
Eligible for Reduced-Price Lunch Program: n/a
Teachers: 168.4 (14.7 to 1)
Librarians/Media Specialists: 3.0 (826.7 to 1)
Guidance Counselors: 7.0 (354.3 to 1)
Current Spending: ($ per student per year):
Total: $6,601; Instruction: $3,433; Support Services: $2,827
Enrollment, Drop-out Rates and Diploma Recipients by Race/Ethnicity

Category	Total	White	Black	Asian	AIAN	Hisp.
Enrollment (%)	100.0	0.4	0.0	0.0	99.4	0.1
Drop-out Rate (%)	29.3	0.0	n/a	0.0	29.6	0.0
H.S. Diplomas (#)	116	2	0	1	112	1

Winslow Unified District
800 Apache Ave • Winslow, AZ 86047-0580
Mailing Address: PO Box 580 • Winslow, AZ 86047-0580
(928) 289-3375 • http://www.winslowsd.k12.az.us/
Grade Span: PK-12; **Agency Type:** 1
Schools: 5
3 Primary; 1 Middle; 1 High; 0 Other Level
5 Regular; 0 Special Education; 0 Vocational; 0 Alternative
0 Magnet; 0 Charter; 5 Title I Eligible; 0 School-wide Title I
Students: 2,615 (50.0% male; 50.0% female)
Individual Education Program: 384 (14.7%);
English Language Learner: 157 (6.0%); Migrant: 0 (0.0%)
Eligible for Free Lunch Program: n/a
Eligible for Reduced-Price Lunch Program: n/a
Teachers: 152.0 (17.2 to 1)
Librarians/Media Specialists: 3.0 (871.7 to 1)
Guidance Counselors: 4.5 (581.1 to 1)
Current Spending: ($ per student per year):
Total: $5,112; Instruction: $2,771; Support Services: $2,127
Enrollment, Drop-out Rates and Diploma Recipients by Race/Ethnicity

Category	Total	White	Black	Asian	AIAN	Hisp.
Enrollment (%)	100.0	26.9	3.3	1.2	45.5	23.1
Drop-out Rate (%)	11.0	5.2	15.0	0.0	12.8	15.6
H.S. Diplomas (#)	148	49	4	1	75	19

Pima County

Amphitheater Unified District
701 W Wetmore • Tucson, AZ 85705-1547
(520) 696-5130 • http://www.amphi.com/
Grade Span: PK-12; **Agency Type:** 1
Schools: 22
13 Primary; 3 Middle; 4 High; 2 Other Level
20 Regular; 1 Special Education; 0 Vocational; 1 Alternative
0 Magnet; 0 Charter; 11 Title I Eligible; 8 School-wide Title I
Students: 3,254 (51.0% male; 49.0% female)
Individual Education Program: 2,250 (69.1%);
English Language Learner: 1,415 (43.5%); Migrant: 0 (0.0%)
Eligible for Free Lunch Program: n/a
Eligible for Reduced-Price Lunch Program: n/a
Teachers: 893.6 (3.6 to 1)
Librarians/Media Specialists: 9.5 (342.5 to 1)
Guidance Counselors: 20.8 (156.4 to 1)
Current Spending: ($ per student per year):
Total: $4,739; Instruction: $2,623; Support Services: $1,866
Enrollment, Drop-out Rates and Diploma Recipients by Race/Ethnicity

Category	Total	White	Black	Asian	AIAN	Hisp.
Enrollment (%)	100.0	57.3	4.5	3.1	2.2	32.9
Drop-out Rate (%)	4.1	3.3	2.0	2.5	5.6	6.2
H.S. Diplomas (#)	947	669	20	37	11	210

Catalina Foothills Unified District
2101 E River Rd • Tucson, AZ 85718-6597
(520) 299-6446 • http://www.cfsd.k12.az.us/
Grade Span: PK-12; **Agency Type:** 1
Schools: 8
5 Primary; 2 Middle; 1 High; 0 Other Level
8 Regular; 0 Special Education; 0 Vocational; 0 Alternative
0 Magnet; 0 Charter; 4 Title I Eligible; 0 School-wide Title I
Students: 5,012 (51.5% male; 48.5% female)
Individual Education Program: 494 (9.9%);
English Language Learner: 88 (1.8%); Migrant: 0 (0.0%)
Eligible for Free Lunch Program: n/a
Eligible for Reduced-Price Lunch Program: n/a
Teachers: 297.6 (16.8 to 1)
Librarians/Media Specialists: 8.0 (626.5 to 1)
Guidance Counselors: 12.2 (410.8 to 1)
Current Spending: ($ per student per year):
Total: $5,148; Instruction: $2,871; Support Services: $1,968
Enrollment, Drop-out Rates and Diploma Recipients by Race/Ethnicity

Category	Total	White	Black	Asian	AIAN	Hisp.
Enrollment (%)	100.0	80.1	1.5	8.0	0.4	9.9
Drop-out Rate (%)	1.3	1.2	0.0	0.9	33.3	2.8
H.S. Diplomas (#)	431	351	4	32	1	43

Flowing Wells Unified District
1556 W Prince Rd • Tucson, AZ 85705-3024
(520) 690-2212 • http://www.flowingwells.k12.az.us/
Grade Span: PK-12; **Agency Type:** 1
Schools: 11
7 Primary; 1 Middle; 2 High; 1 Other Level
10 Regular; 0 Special Education; 0 Vocational; 1 Alternative
0 Magnet; 0 Charter; 5 Title I Eligible; 0 School-wide Title I
Students: 6,089 (50.7% male; 49.3% female)
Individual Education Program: 733 (12.0%);
English Language Learner: 169 (2.8%); Migrant: 0 (0.0%)
Eligible for Free Lunch Program: n/a
Eligible for Reduced-Price Lunch Program: n/a
Teachers: 304.7 (20.0 to 1)
Librarians/Media Specialists: 2.0 (3,044.5 to 1)
Guidance Counselors: 15.0 (405.9 to 1)
Current Spending: ($ per student per year):
Total: $5,038; Instruction: $2,903; Support Services: $1,773
Enrollment, Drop-out Rates and Diploma Recipients by Race/Ethnicity

Category	Total	White	Black	Asian	AIAN	Hisp.
Enrollment (%)	100.0	56.4	1.9	1.6	2.0	38.2
Drop-out Rate (%)	8.9	8.6	5.9	0.0	14.7	10.0
H.S. Diplomas (#)	363	247	12	6	4	94

Marana Unified District
11279 W Grier Rd Ste 115a • Marana, AZ 85653-9776
(520) 682-4749 • http://maranausd.org/
Grade Span: PK-12; **Agency Type:** 1
Schools: 17
9 Primary; 3 Middle; 4 High; 0 Other Level
15 Regular; 0 Special Education; 0 Vocational; 1 Alternative
0 Magnet; 0 Charter; 5 Title I Eligible; 1 School-wide Title I
Students: 12,363 (51.6% male; 48.4% female)
Individual Education Program: 1,521 (12.3%);
English Language Learner: 359 (2.9%); Migrant: 26 (0.2%)
Eligible for Free Lunch Program: 2,195 (17.8%)
Eligible for Reduced-Price Lunch Program: 1,102 (8.9%)
Teachers: 648.4 (19.1 to 1)
Librarians/Media Specialists: 14.0 (883.1 to 1)
Guidance Counselors: 24.9 (496.5 to 1)
Current Spending: ($ per student per year):
Total: $4,624; Instruction: $2,479; Support Services: $1,941
Enrollment, Drop-out Rates and Diploma Recipients by Race/Ethnicity

Category	Total	White	Black	Asian	AIAN	Hisp.
Enrollment (%)	100.0	72.0	3.2	1.9	1.7	21.4
Drop-out Rate (%)	5.0	4.4	10.2	5.0	3.8	6.4
H.S. Diplomas (#)	683	513	22	21	9	118

Sahuarita Unified District
350 W Sahuarita Rd • Sahuarita, AZ 85629-9522
(520) 625-3502 • http://www.sahuarita.k12.az.us/
Grade Span: PK-12; **Agency Type:** 1
Schools: 5
3 Primary; 1 Middle; 1 High; 0 Other Level
5 Regular; 0 Special Education; 0 Vocational; 0 Alternative

0 Magnet; 0 Charter; 5 Title I Eligible; 0 School-wide Title I
Students: 2,250 (49.6% male; 50.4% female)
Individual Education Program: 303 (13.5%);
English Language Learner: 221 (9.8%); Migrant: 0 (0.0%)
Eligible for Free Lunch Program: n/a
Eligible for Reduced-Price Lunch Program: n/a
Teachers: 129.5 (17.4 to 1)
Librarians/Media Specialists: 1.0 (2,250.0 to 1)
Guidance Counselors: 4.0 (562.5 to 1)
Current Spending: ($ per student per year):
Total: $5,615; Instruction: $2,807; Support Services: $2,506
Enrollment, Drop-out Rates and Diploma Recipients by Race/Ethnicity

Category	Total	White	Black	Asian	AIAN	Hisp.
Enrollment (%)	100.0	46.8	0.9	1.1	1.2	50.0
Drop-out Rate (%)	5.7	3.4	16.7	0.0	12.5	8.7
H.S. Diplomas (#)	121	72	1	0	1	47

Sunnyside Unified District

2238 E Ginter Rd • Tucson, AZ 85706-5806
(520) 545-2000 • http://www.sunnysideud.k12.az.us/
Grade Span: PK-12; **Agency Type:** 1
Schools: 23
14 Primary; 4 Middle; 2 High; 3 Other Level
23 Regular; 0 Special Education; 0 Vocational; 0 Alternative
0 Magnet; 0 Charter; 17 Title I Eligible; 17 School-wide Title I
Students: 15,602 (51.6% male; 48.4% female)
Individual Education Program: 2,204 (14.1%);
English Language Learner: 5,781 (37.1%); Migrant: 0 (0.0%)
Eligible for Free Lunch Program: n/a
Eligible for Reduced-Price Lunch Program: n/a
Teachers: 874.3 (17.8 to 1)
Librarians/Media Specialists: 19.0 (821.2 to 1)
Guidance Counselors: 22.7 (687.3 to 1)
Current Spending: ($ per student per year):
Total: $5,546; Instruction: $3,047; Support Services: $2,178
Enrollment, Drop-out Rates and Diploma Recipients by Race/Ethnicity

Category	Total	White	Black	Asian	AIAN	Hisp.
Enrollment (%)	100.0	7.5	2.3	0.6	4.2	85.3
Drop-out Rate (%)	17.0	14.4	12.0	0.0	25.0	17.2
H.S. Diplomas (#)	580	73	15	3	16	473

Tucson Unified District

1010 E 10th St • Tucson, AZ 85719
Mailing Address: PO Box 40400 • Tucson, AZ 85717-0400
(520) 225-6000 • http://www.tusd.k12.az.us/
Grade Span: PK-12; **Agency Type:** 1
Schools: 125
79 Primary; 21 Middle; 22 High; 3 Other Level
117 Regular; 1 Special Education; 0 Vocational; 7 Alternative
0 Magnet; 0 Charter; 35 Title I Eligible; 27 School-wide Title I
Students: 61,958 (51.3% male; 48.7% female)
Individual Education Program: 7,361 (11.9%);
English Language Learner: 9,727 (15.7%); Migrant: 0 (0.0%)
Eligible for Free Lunch Program: n/a
Eligible for Reduced-Price Lunch Program: n/a
Teachers: 3,463.5 (17.9 to 1)
Librarians/Media Specialists: 103.6 (598.1 to 1)
Guidance Counselors: 148.2 (418.1 to 1)
Current Spending: ($ per student per year):
Total: $5,709; Instruction: $2,997; Support Services: $2,381
Enrollment, Drop-out Rates and Diploma Recipients by Race/Ethnicity

Category	Total	White	Black	Asian	AIAN	Hisp.
Enrollment (%)	100.0	37.8	6.5	2.6	4.1	49.0
Drop-out Rate (%)	6.1	3.5	5.6	2.5	11.7	9.2
H.S. Diplomas (#)	3,309	1,691	201	117	97	1,203

Vail Unified District

13801 E Benson Hwy • Vail, AZ 85641-0800
Mailing Address: PO Box 800 • Vail, AZ 85641-0800
(520) 762-2040 • http://www.vail.k12.az.us/
Grade Span: PK-12; **Agency Type:** 1
Schools: 10
6 Primary; 1 Middle; 2 High; 1 Other Level
10 Regular; 0 Special Education; 0 Vocational; 0 Alternative
0 Magnet; 0 Charter; 2 Title I Eligible; 0 School-wide Title I
Students: 5,102 (52.1% male; 47.9% female)
Individual Education Program: 592 (11.6%);
English Language Learner: 0 (0.0%); Migrant: 0 (0.0%)
Eligible for Free Lunch Program: 514 (10.1%)
Eligible for Reduced-Price Lunch Program: 311 (6.1%)
Teachers: 301.2 (16.9 to 1)
Librarians/Media Specialists: 6.0 (850.3 to 1)
Guidance Counselors: 1.9 (2,685.3 to 1)
Current Spending: ($ per student per year):
Total: $6,445; Instruction: $4,017; Support Services: $2,192
Enrollment, Drop-out Rates and Diploma Recipients by Race/Ethnicity

Category	Total	White	Black	Asian	AIAN	Hisp.
Enrollment (%)	100.0	72.7	5.5	2.2	1.1	18.5
Drop-out Rate (%)	4.7	4.8	0.0	0.0	0.0	6.7
H.S. Diplomas (#)	58	42	3	5	0	8

Pinal County

Apache Junction Unified District

1575 W Southern Ave • Apache Junction, AZ 85220
(480) 982-1110 • http://www.ajusd.org/
Grade Span: PK-12; **Agency Type:** 1
Schools: 9
5 Primary; 3 Middle; 1 High; 0 Other Level
8 Regular; 0 Special Education; 0 Vocational; 1 Alternative
0 Magnet; 0 Charter; 5 Title I Eligible; 0 School-wide Title I
Students: 5,846 (51.6% male; 48.4% female)
Individual Education Program: 679 (11.6%);
English Language Learner: 0 (0.0%); Migrant: 0 (0.0%)
Eligible for Free Lunch Program: n/a
Eligible for Reduced-Price Lunch Program: n/a
Teachers: 289.2 (20.2 to 1)
Librarians/Media Specialists: 7.0 (835.1 to 1)
Guidance Counselors: 13.0 (449.7 to 1)
Current Spending: ($ per student per year):
Total: $5,645; Instruction: $2,679; Support Services: $2,721
Enrollment, Drop-out Rates and Diploma Recipients by Race/Ethnicity

Category	Total	White	Black	Asian	AIAN	Hisp.
Enrollment (%)	100.0	80.8	1.4	1.4	1.5	15.0
Drop-out Rate (%)	4.0	4.4	0.0	0.0	0.0	2.2
H.S. Diplomas (#)	242	208	3	4	2	25

Casa Grande Elementary District

1460 N Pinal Ave • Casa Grande, AZ 85222-3397
(520) 836-2111 • http://www.cgelem.k12.az.us/
Grade Span: PK-08; **Agency Type:** 1
Schools: 10
8 Primary; 2 Middle; 0 High; 0 Other Level
10 Regular; 0 Special Education; 0 Vocational; 0 Alternative
0 Magnet; 0 Charter; 7 Title I Eligible; 1 School-wide Title I
Students: 5,574 (51.8% male; 48.2% female)
Individual Education Program: 757 (13.6%);
English Language Learner: 586 (10.5%); Migrant: 41 (0.7%)
Eligible for Free Lunch Program: n/a
Eligible for Reduced-Price Lunch Program: n/a
Teachers: 329.2 (16.9 to 1)
Librarians/Media Specialists: 9.0 (619.3 to 1)
Guidance Counselors: 3.0 (1,858.0 to 1)
Current Spending: ($ per student per year):
Total: $5,056; Instruction: $2,874; Support Services: $1,941
Enrollment, Drop-out Rates and Diploma Recipients by Race/Ethnicity

Category	Total	White	Black	Asian	AIAN	Hisp.
Enrollment (%)	100.0	35.0	6.1	0.5	6.9	51.5
Drop-out Rate (%)	n/a	n/a	n/a	n/a	n/a	n/a
H.S. Diplomas (#)	n/a	n/a	n/a	n/a	n/a	n/a

Casa Grande Union High SD

2730 N Trekell Rd • Casa Grande, AZ 85222-4193
Mailing Address: 1362 N Casa Grande Ave • Casa Grande, AZ 85222-4193
(520) 316-3360
Grade Span: 09-12; **Agency Type:** 1
Schools: 3
0 Primary; 0 Middle; 3 High; 0 Other Level
3 Regular; 0 Special Education; 0 Vocational; 0 Alternative
0 Magnet; 0 Charter; 1 Title I Eligible; 0 School-wide Title I
Students: 2,840 (49.9% male; 50.1% female)
Individual Education Program: 366 (12.9%);
English Language Learner: 0 (0.0%); Migrant: 5 (0.2%)
Eligible for Free Lunch Program: n/a
Eligible for Reduced-Price Lunch Program: n/a
Teachers: 130.6 (21.7 to 1)
Librarians/Media Specialists: 2.0 (1,420.0 to 1)
Guidance Counselors: 7.0 (405.7 to 1)
Current Spending: ($ per student per year):
Total: $5,351; Instruction: $2,796; Support Services: $2,096
Enrollment, Drop-out Rates and Diploma Recipients by Race/Ethnicity

Category	Total	White	Black	Asian	AIAN	Hisp.
Enrollment (%)	100.0	38.5	4.7	0.5	12.5	43.8
Drop-out Rate (%)	n/a	n/a	n/a	n/a	n/a	n/a
H.S. Diplomas (#)	387	181	8	5	34	159

Central Arizona Valley Inst of Tech
8470 N Overfield Rd • Coolidge, AZ 85228
(520) 423-1944
Grade Span: 09-12; **Agency Type:** 7
Schools: 6
0 Primary; 0 Middle; 6 High; 0 Other Level
0 Regular; 0 Special Education; 6 Vocational; 0 Alternative
0 Magnet; 0 Charter; 0 Title I Eligible; 0 School-wide Title I
Students: 3,111 (50.2% male; 49.8% female)
Individual Education Program: 0 (0.0%);
English Language Learner: 0 (0.0%); Migrant: 0 (0.0%)
Eligible for Free Lunch Program: n/a
Eligible for Reduced-Price Lunch Program: n/a
Teachers: n/a
Librarians/Media Specialists: n/a
Guidance Counselors: n/a
Current Spending: ($ per student per year):
Total: n/a; Instruction: n/a; Support Services: n/a
Enrollment, Drop-out Rates and Diploma Recipients by Race/Ethnicity

Category	Total	White	Black	Asian	AIAN	Hisp.
Enrollment (%)	100.0	36.1	4.8	0.3	14.0	44.7
Drop-out Rate (%)	n/a	n/a	n/a	n/a	n/a	n/a
H.S. Diplomas (#)	0	0	0	0	0	0

Coolidge Unified District
221 W Central Ave • Coolidge, AZ 85228-4109
(520) 723-2045 • http://www.cusd.k12.az.us/
Grade Span: PK-12; **Agency Type:** 1
Schools: 8
2 Primary; 3 Middle; 2 High; 0 Other Level
6 Regular; 0 Special Education; 0 Vocational; 1 Alternative
0 Magnet; 0 Charter; 5 Title I Eligible; 2 School-wide Title I
Students: 2,986 (50.9% male; 49.1% female)
Individual Education Program: 438 (14.7%);
English Language Learner: 0 (0.0%); Migrant: 5 (0.2%)
Eligible for Free Lunch Program: n/a
Eligible for Reduced-Price Lunch Program: n/a
Teachers: 166.1 (18.0 to 1)
Librarians/Media Specialists: 3.0 (995.3 to 1)
Guidance Counselors: 3.0 (995.3 to 1)
Current Spending: ($ per student per year):
Total: $5,522; Instruction: $2,963; Support Services: $2,295
Enrollment, Drop-out Rates and Diploma Recipients by Race/Ethnicity

Category	Total	White	Black	Asian	AIAN	Hisp.
Enrollment (%)	100.0	28.3	9.5	0.3	22.2	39.6
Drop-out Rate (%)	13.6	8.3	14.5	0.0	22.9	12.9
H.S. Diplomas (#)	138	56	15	1	18	48

Florence Unified SD
350 S Main St • Florence, AZ 85232-0829
Mailing Address: PO Box 2850 • Florence, AZ 85232-0829
(520) 866-3500
Grade Span: PK-12; **Agency Type:** 1
Schools: 5
3 Primary; 1 Middle; 1 High; 0 Other Level
5 Regular; 0 Special Education; 0 Vocational; 0 Alternative
0 Magnet; 0 Charter; 4 Title I Eligible; 1 School-wide Title I
Students: 1,963 (50.3% male; 49.7% female)
Individual Education Program: 189 (9.6%);
English Language Learner: 0 (0.0%); Migrant: 21 (1.1%)
Eligible for Free Lunch Program: 746 (38.0%)
Eligible for Reduced-Price Lunch Program: 265 (13.5%)
Teachers: 136.8 (14.3 to 1)
Librarians/Media Specialists: 1.0 (1,963.0 to 1)
Guidance Counselors: 2.0 (981.5 to 1)
Current Spending: ($ per student per year):
Total: $4,863; Instruction: $2,725; Support Services: $2,027
Enrollment, Drop-out Rates and Diploma Recipients by Race/Ethnicity

Category	Total	White	Black	Asian	AIAN	Hisp.
Enrollment (%)	100.0	60.9	4.2	0.5	2.9	31.5
Drop-out Rate (%)	6.9	7.1	4.2	0.0	10.0	7.0
H.S. Diplomas (#)	78	54	4	0	1	19

Santa Cruz County

Nogales Unified District
310 W Plum St • Nogales, AZ 85621-2611
(520) 375-7800 • http://www.nusd.k12.az.us/
Grade Span: PK-12; **Agency Type:** 1
Schools: 11
5 Primary; 2 Middle; 2 High; 1 Other Level
8 Regular; 1 Special Education; 0 Vocational; 1 Alternative
0 Magnet; 0 Charter; 9 Title I Eligible; 9 School-wide Title I
Students: 6,309 (51.4% male; 48.6% female)
Individual Education Program: 555 (8.8%);
English Language Learner: 1,695 (26.9%); Migrant: 0 (0.0%)
Eligible for Free Lunch Program: n/a
Eligible for Reduced-Price Lunch Program: n/a
Teachers: 331.6 (19.0 to 1)
Librarians/Media Specialists: 4.0 (1,577.3 to 1)
Guidance Counselors: 15.0 (420.6 to 1)
Current Spending: ($ per student per year):
Total: $4,093; Instruction: $2,199; Support Services: $1,571
Enrollment, Drop-out Rates and Diploma Recipients by Race/Ethnicity

Category	Total	White	Black	Asian	AIAN	Hisp.
Enrollment (%)	100.0	1.8	0.1	0.1	0.1	97.8
Drop-out Rate (%)	8.0	6.4	0.0	0.0	n/a	8.1
H.S. Diplomas (#)	353	9	1	1	0	342

Santa Cruz Valley Unified District
1374 W Frontage Rd • Rio Rico, AZ 85648-2006
(520) 281-8282 • http://www.scvuhs.org/
Grade Span: PK-12; **Agency Type:** 1
Schools: 4
2 Primary; 1 Middle; 1 High; 0 Other Level
4 Regular; 0 Special Education; 0 Vocational; 0 Alternative
0 Magnet; 0 Charter; 4 Title I Eligible; 0 School-wide Title I
Students: 2,862 (53.0% male; 47.0% female)
Individual Education Program: 211 (7.4%);
English Language Learner: 1,303 (45.5%); Migrant: 0 (0.0%)
Eligible for Free Lunch Program: n/a
Eligible for Reduced-Price Lunch Program: n/a
Teachers: 133.3 (21.5 to 1)
Librarians/Media Specialists: 2.0 (1,431.0 to 1)
Guidance Counselors: 4.0 (715.5 to 1)
Current Spending: ($ per student per year):
Total: $4,609; Instruction: $2,691; Support Services: $1,563
Enrollment, Drop-out Rates and Diploma Recipients by Race/Ethnicity

Category	Total	White	Black	Asian	AIAN	Hisp.
Enrollment (%)	100.0	10.7	0.3	0.5	0.1	88.4
Drop-out Rate (%)	14.9	3.7	0.0	0.0	n/a	16.7
H.S. Diplomas (#)	101	9	0	2	1	89

Yavapai County

Chino Valley Unified District
115 N Hwy 89 • Chino Valley, AZ 86323-0225
Mailing Address: PO Box 225 • Chino Valley, AZ 86323-0225
(928) 636-2458 • http://www.chinleusd.k12.az.us/
Grade Span: PK-12; **Agency Type:** 1
Schools: 4
2 Primary; 1 Middle; 1 High; 0 Other Level
4 Regular; 0 Special Education; 0 Vocational; 0 Alternative
0 Magnet; 0 Charter; 2 Title I Eligible; 0 School-wide Title I
Students: 2,604 (53.4% male; 46.6% female)
Individual Education Program: 383 (14.7%);
English Language Learner: 201 (7.7%); Migrant: 0 (0.0%)
Eligible for Free Lunch Program: n/a
Eligible for Reduced-Price Lunch Program: n/a
Teachers: 141.8 (18.4 to 1)
Librarians/Media Specialists: 1.0 (2,604.0 to 1)
Guidance Counselors: 3.6 (723.3 to 1)
Current Spending: ($ per student per year):
Total: $4,290; Instruction: $2,574; Support Services: $1,451
Enrollment, Drop-out Rates and Diploma Recipients by Race/Ethnicity

Category	Total	White	Black	Asian	AIAN	Hisp.
Enrollment (%)	100.0	82.8	0.7	0.5	1.2	14.8
Drop-out Rate (%)	5.5	4.6	0.0	50.0	0.0	15.4
H.S. Diplomas (#)	144	132	1	0	1	10

Cottonwood-Oak Creek Elementary Dist
1 N Willard St • Cottonwood, AZ 86326-0057
(928) 634-2288 • http://www.cocsd.k12.az.us/
Grade Span: PK-08; **Agency Type:** 1
Schools: 4
3 Primary; 1 Middle; 0 High; 0 Other Level
4 Regular; 0 Special Education; 0 Vocational; 0 Alternative
0 Magnet; 0 Charter; 4 Title I Eligible; 1 School-wide Title I
Students: 2,541 (52.7% male; 47.3% female)
Individual Education Program: 224 (8.8%);
English Language Learner: 339 (13.3%); Migrant: 0 (0.0%)
Eligible for Free Lunch Program: n/a
Eligible for Reduced-Price Lunch Program: n/a
Teachers: 135.0 (18.8 to 1)
Librarians/Media Specialists: 2.0 (1,270.5 to 1)
Guidance Counselors: 0.0 (0.0 to 1)
Current Spending: ($ per student per year):
Total: $5,049; Instruction: $2,545; Support Services: $2,158

Enrollment, Drop-out Rates and Diploma Recipients by Race/Ethnicity

Category	Total	White	Black	Asian	AIAN	Hisp.
Enrollment (%)	100.0	71.6	0.6	0.7	1.5	25.6
Drop-out Rate (%)	n/a	n/a	n/a	n/a	n/a	n/a
H.S. Diplomas (#)	n/a	n/a	n/a	n/a	n/a	n/a

Humboldt Unified District

8766 E Hwy 69 • Prescott Valley, AZ 86314
(928) 759-4000
Grade Span: PK-12; **Agency Type:** 1
Schools: 9
5 Primary; 2 Middle; 1 High; 0 Other Level
8 Regular; 0 Special Education; 0 Vocational; 0 Alternative
0 Magnet; 0 Charter; 4 Title I Eligible; 0 School-wide Title I
Students: 4,908 (51.1% male; 48.9% female)
Individual Education Program: 728 (14.8%);
English Language Learner: 324 (6.6%); Migrant: 0 (0.0%)
Eligible for Free Lunch Program: 1,529 (31.2%)
Eligible for Reduced-Price Lunch Program: 640 (13.0%)
Teachers: 256.0 (19.2 to 1)
Librarians/Media Specialists: 2.2 (2,230.9 to 1)
Guidance Counselors: 6.8 (721.8 to 1)
Current Spending: ($ per student per year):
Total: $4,937; Instruction: $2,713; Support Services: $1,994
Enrollment, Drop-out Rates and Diploma Recipients by Race/Ethnicity

Category	Total	White	Black	Asian	AIAN	Hisp.
Enrollment (%)	100.0	78.5	0.8	1.3	1.3	18.2
Drop-out Rate (%)	6.3	5.4	16.7	8.7	7.7	12.1
H.S. Diplomas (#)	281	238	2	2	4	35

Prescott Unified District

146 S Granite St • Prescott, AZ 86303-4786
(928) 445-5400 • http://www.prescott.k12.az.us/
Grade Span: PK-12; **Agency Type:** 1
Schools: 12
5 Primary; 2 Middle; 1 High; 0 Other Level
8 Regular; 0 Special Education; 0 Vocational; 0 Alternative
0 Magnet; 0 Charter; 2 Title I Eligible; 0 School-wide Title I
Students: 5,114 (51.6% male; 48.4% female)
Individual Education Program: 611 (11.9%);
English Language Learner: 165 (3.2%); Migrant: 0 (0.0%)
Eligible for Free Lunch Program: 889 (17.4%)
Eligible for Reduced-Price Lunch Program: 269 (5.3%)
Teachers: 274.6 (18.6 to 1)
Librarians/Media Specialists: 1.0 (5,114.0 to 1)
Guidance Counselors: 8.0 (639.3 to 1)
Current Spending: ($ per student per year):
Total: $4,656; Instruction: $2,674; Support Services: $1,579
Enrollment, Drop-out Rates and Diploma Recipients by Race/Ethnicity

Category	Total	White	Black	Asian	AIAN	Hisp.
Enrollment (%)	100.0	83.9	1.1	1.6	2.6	10.8
Drop-out Rate (%)	5.3	4.5	0.0	0.0	17.2	12.2
H.S. Diplomas (#)	326	289	2	3	4	28

Yuma County

Crane Elementary District

4250 W 16th St • Yuma, AZ 85364-4099
(928) 373-3400 • http://familyeducation.com/az/crane_elementary
Grade Span: PK-08; **Agency Type:** 1
Schools: 7
5 Primary; 2 Middle; 0 High; 0 Other Level
7 Regular; 0 Special Education; 0 Vocational; 0 Alternative
0 Magnet; 0 Charter; 6 Title I Eligible; 5 School-wide Title I
Students: 5,599 (51.4% male; 48.6% female)
Individual Education Program: 695 (12.4%);
English Language Learner: 2,035 (36.3%); Migrant: 85 (1.5%)
Eligible for Free Lunch Program: n/a
Eligible for Reduced-Price Lunch Program: n/a
Teachers: 288.7 (19.4 to 1)
Librarians/Media Specialists: 0.8 (6,998.8 to 1)
Guidance Counselors: 8.0 (699.9 to 1)
Current Spending: ($ per student per year):
Total: $5,264; Instruction: $2,797; Support Services: $2,160
Enrollment, Drop-out Rates and Diploma Recipients by Race/Ethnicity

Category	Total	White	Black	Asian	AIAN	Hisp.
Enrollment (%)	100.0	26.0	1.9	1.8	0.9	69.3
Drop-out Rate (%)	n/a	n/a	n/a	n/a	n/a	n/a
H.S. Diplomas (#)	n/a	n/a	n/a	n/a	n/a	n/a

Gadsden Elementary District

1453 N Main St • San Luis, AZ 85349
Mailing Address: PO Box 6870 • San Luis, AZ 85349
(928) 627-6540 • http://www.gesd32.org/district/html/
Grade Span: PK-08; **Agency Type:** 1
Schools: 5
3 Primary; 1 Middle; 0 High; 0 Other Level
4 Regular; 0 Special Education; 0 Vocational; 0 Alternative
0 Magnet; 0 Charter; 3 Title I Eligible; 3 School-wide Title I
Students: 4,046 (49.5% male; 50.5% female)
Individual Education Program: 208 (5.1%);
English Language Learner: 3,628 (89.7%); Migrant: 52 (1.3%)
Eligible for Free Lunch Program: n/a
Eligible for Reduced-Price Lunch Program: n/a
Teachers: 157.2 (25.7 to 1)
Librarians/Media Specialists: 4.0 (1,011.5 to 1)
Guidance Counselors: 4.3 (940.9 to 1)
Current Spending: ($ per student per year):
Total: $4,828; Instruction: $2,656; Support Services: $1,796
Enrollment, Drop-out Rates and Diploma Recipients by Race/Ethnicity

Category	Total	White	Black	Asian	AIAN	Hisp.
Enrollment (%)	100.0	0.3	0.0	0.0	0.0	99.7
Drop-out Rate (%)	n/a	n/a	n/a	n/a	n/a	n/a
H.S. Diplomas (#)	n/a	n/a	n/a	n/a	n/a	n/a

Somerton Elementary District

215 N Carlisle Ave • Somerton, AZ 85350-3200
Mailing Address: PO Box 3200 • Somerton, AZ 85350-3200
(928) 341-6000 • http://www.somerton.k12.az.us/
Grade Span: PK-08; **Agency Type:** 1
Schools: 4
3 Primary; 1 Middle; 0 High; 0 Other Level
4 Regular; 0 Special Education; 0 Vocational; 0 Alternative
0 Magnet; 0 Charter; 4 Title I Eligible; 4 School-wide Title I
Students: 2,467 (51.6% male; 48.4% female)
Individual Education Program: 354 (14.3%);
English Language Learner: 1,600 (64.9%); Migrant: 80 (3.2%)
Eligible for Free Lunch Program: n/a
Eligible for Reduced-Price Lunch Program: n/a
Teachers: 126.1 (19.6 to 1)
Librarians/Media Specialists: 2.0 (1,233.5 to 1)
Guidance Counselors: 2.0 (1,233.5 to 1)
Current Spending: ($ per student per year):
Total: $4,983; Instruction: $2,488; Support Services: $2,078
Enrollment, Drop-out Rates and Diploma Recipients by Race/Ethnicity

Category	Total	White	Black	Asian	AIAN	Hisp.
Enrollment (%)	100.0	1.2	0.2	0.1	5.6	92.9
Drop-out Rate (%)	n/a	n/a	n/a	n/a	n/a	n/a
H.S. Diplomas (#)	n/a	n/a	n/a	n/a	n/a	n/a

Yuma Elementary District

4th Ave and 6th St • Yuma, AZ 85364-2973
Mailing Address: 450 6th St • Yuma, AZ 85364-2973
(928) 782-6581 • http://www.yuma.org/
Grade Span: PK-08; **Agency Type:** 1
Schools: 17
12 Primary; 5 Middle; 0 High; 0 Other Level
17 Regular; 0 Special Education; 0 Vocational; 0 Alternative
0 Magnet; 0 Charter; 16 Title I Eligible; 13 School-wide Title I
Students: 10,814 (51.4% male; 48.6% female)
Individual Education Program: 973 (9.0%);
English Language Learner: 3,044 (28.1%); Migrant: 140 (1.3%)
Eligible for Free Lunch Program: n/a
Eligible for Reduced-Price Lunch Program: n/a
Teachers: 562.4 (19.2 to 1)
Librarians/Media Specialists: 14.0 (772.4 to 1)
Guidance Counselors: 15.0 (720.9 to 1)
Current Spending: ($ per student per year):
Total: $4,904; Instruction: $2,807; Support Services: $1,696
Enrollment, Drop-out Rates and Diploma Recipients by Race/Ethnicity

Category	Total	White	Black	Asian	AIAN	Hisp.
Enrollment (%)	100.0	30.4	3.4	0.9	1.2	64.0
Drop-out Rate (%)	n/a	n/a	n/a	n/a	n/a	n/a
H.S. Diplomas (#)	n/a	n/a	n/a	n/a	n/a	n/a

Yuma Union High SD

3150 Ave • Yuma, AZ 85364-7998
(928) 726-1731 • http://www.yuma.org/
Grade Span: 09-12; **Agency Type:** 1
Schools: 4
0 Primary; 0 Middle; 4 High; 0 Other Level
3 Regular; 0 Special Education; 0 Vocational; 1 Alternative
0 Magnet; 0 Charter; 4 Title I Eligible; 3 School-wide Title I
Students: 9,426 (51.3% male; 48.7% female)
Individual Education Program: 834 (8.8%);

English Language Learner: 613 (6.5%); Migrant: 195 (2.1%)
Eligible for Free Lunch Program: n/a
Eligible for Reduced-Price Lunch Program: n/a

Teachers: 420.3 (22.4 to 1)
Librarians/Media Specialists: 6.0 (1,571.0 to 1)
Guidance Counselors: 25.4 (371.1 to 1)
Current Spending: ($ per student per year):
Total: $5,552; Instruction: $2,813; Support Services: $2,422

Enrollment, Drop-out Rates and Diploma Recipients by Race/Ethnicity

Category	Total	White	Black	Asian	AIAN	Hisp.
Enrollment (%)	100.0	26.1	2.0	1.2	1.1	69.6
Drop-out Rate (%)	6.9	5.2	7.0	5.8	10.0	7.5
H.S. Diplomas (#)	1,389	415	26	13	5	930

Number of Schools

Rank	Number	District Name	City
1	125	Tucson Unified District	Tucson
2	91	Mesa Unified District	Mesa
3	49	Paradise Valley Unified District	Phoenix
4	36	Gilbert Unified District	Gilbert
4	36	Peoria Unified SD	Glendale
6	34	Scottsdale Unified District	Phoenix
7	32	Deer Valley Unified District	Phoenix
7	32	Peach Springs Unified District	Peach Springs
7	32	Washington Elementary District	Phoenix
10	28	Chandler Unified District	Chandler
11	26	Kyrene Elementary District	Tempe
11	26	Tempe Elementary District	Tempe
13	23	Cartwright Elementary District	Phoenix
13	23	Sunnyside Unified District	Tucson
15	22	Amphitheater Unified District	Tucson
15	22	Roosevelt Elementary District	Phoenix
17	21	Flagstaff Unified District	Flagstaff
18	20	Phoenix Elementary District	Phoenix
19	17	Glendale Elementary District	Glendale
19	17	Marana Unified District	Marana
19	17	Yuma Elementary District	Yuma
22	15	Alhambra Elementary District	Phoenix
22	15	Western Navajo Agency	Tuba City
24	14	Phoenix Union High SD	Phoenix
25	13	Isaac Elementary District	Phoenix
25	13	Maricopa County Regional District	Phoenix
27	12	Douglas Unified District	Douglas
27	12	Glendale Union High SD	Glendale
27	12	Higley Unified District	Higley
27	12	Prescott Unified District	Prescott
31	11	Flowing Wells Unified District	Tucson
31	11	Fort Defiance Agency	Fort Defiance
31	11	Kingman Unified SD	Kingman
31	11	Nogales Unified District	Nogales
31	11	Pendergast Elementary District	Phoenix
36	10	Casa Grande Elementary District	Casa Grande
36	10	Chinle Agency	Chinle
36	10	Creighton Elementary District	Phoenix
36	10	East Valley Institute of Tech	Mesa
36	10	Vail Unified District	Vail
41	9	Apache Junction Unified District	Apache Junction
41	9	Dysart Unified District	El Mirage
41	9	Humboldt Unified District	Prescott Valley
41	9	Lake Havasu Unified District	Lk Havasu City
41	9	Madison Elementary District	Phoenix
41	9	Show Low Unified District	Show Low
47	8	Catalina Foothills Unified Dist	Tucson
47	8	Chinle Unified District	Chinle
47	8	Coolidge Unified District	Coolidge
47	8	Hopi Agency	Kearns Canyon
47	8	Litchfield Elementary District	Litchfield Park
47	8	Sierra Vista Unified District	Sierra Vista
47	8	Tempe Union High SD	Tempe
54	7	Avondale Elementary District	Avondale
54	7	Bullhead City Elementary District	Bullhead City
54	7	Cave Creek Unified District	Cave Creek
54	7	Crane Elementary District	Yuma
54	7	Snowflake Unified District	Snowflake
54	7	Tuba City Unified District	Tuba City
60	6	Central Ariz Valley Inst of Tech	Coolidge
60	6	Osborn Elementary District	Phoenix
60	6	Parker Unified SD	Parker
60	6	Payson Unified District	Payson
60	6	Safford Unified District	Safford
60	6	Window Rock Unified District	Fort Defiance
66	5	Florence Unified SD	Florence
66	5	Gadsden Elementary District	San Luis
66	5	Holbrook Unified District	Holbrook
66	5	Kayenta Unified District	Kayenta
66	5	Queen Creek Unified District	Queen Creek
66	5	Sahuarita Unified District	Sahuarita
66	5	Whiteriver Unified District	Whiteriver
66	5	Wickenburg Unified District	Wickenburg
66	5	Winslow Unified District	Winslow
75	4	Balsz Elementary District	Phoenix
75	4	Blue Ridge Unified District	Lakeside
75	4	Chino Valley Unified District	Chino Valley
75	4	Cottonwood-Oak Creek Elem Dist	Cottonwood
75	4	Fountain Hills Unified District	Fountain Hills
75	4	Fowler Elementary District	Phoenix
75	4	Ganado Unified District	Ganado
75	4	Globe Unified District	Globe
75	4	Mohave Valley Elementary District	Mohave Valley
75	4	Murphy Elementary District	Phoenix
75	4	Page Unified District	Page
75	4	Santa Cruz Valley Unified District	Rio Rico
75	4	Somerton Elementary District	Somerton
75	4	Yuma Union High SD	Yuma
89	3	Agua Fria Union High SD	Avondale
89	3	Casa Grande Union High SD	Casa Grande
89	3	Laveen Elementary District	Laveen
89	3	Liberty Elementary District	Buckeye
89	3	Littleton Elementary District	Cashion
89	3	Tolleson Elementary District	Tolleson
89	3	Tolleson Union High SD	Tolleson
96	2	Colorado River Union High SD	Fort Mojave

Number of Teachers

Rank	Number	District Name	City
1	3,682	Mesa Unified District	Mesa
2	3,463	Tucson Unified District	Tucson
3	1,872	Paradise Valley Unified District	Phoenix
4	1,827	Peoria Unified SD	Glendale
5	1,826	Gilbert Unified District	Gilbert
6	1,568	Deer Valley Unified District	Phoenix
7	1,529	Scottsdale Unified District	Phoenix
8	1,346	Washington Elementary District	Phoenix
9	1,275	Phoenix Union High SD	Phoenix
10	1,244	Chandler Unified District	Chandler
11	1,005	Kyrene Elementary District	Tempe
12	963	Cartwright Elementary District	Phoenix
13	893	Amphitheater Unified District	Tucson
14	874	Sunnyside Unified District	Tucson
15	825	Tempe Elementary District	Tempe
16	723	Flagstaff Unified District	Flagstaff
17	717	Alhambra Elementary District	Phoenix
18	672	Glendale Elementary District	Glendale
19	672	Glendale Union High SD	Glendale
20	652	Tempe Union High SD	Tempe
21	648	Marana Unified District	Marana
22	621	Roosevelt Elementary District	Phoenix
23	562	Yuma Elementary District	Yuma
24	506	Phoenix Elementary District	Phoenix
25	506	Pendergast Elementary District	Phoenix
26	465	Isaac Elementary District	Phoenix
27	453	Creighton Elementary District	Phoenix
28	446	Dysart Unified District	El Mirage
29	420	Yuma Union High SD	Yuma
30	375	Kingman Unified SD	Kingman
31	350	Sierra Vista Unified District	Sierra Vista
32	331	Nogales Unified District	Nogales
33	329	Casa Grande Elementary District	Casa Grande
34	312	Lake Havasu Unified District	Lk Havasu City
35	304	Flowing Wells Unified District	Tucson
36	301	Vail Unified District	Vail
37	301	Madison Elementary District	Phoenix
38	297	Catalina Foothills Unified Dist	Tucson
39	289	Apache Junction Unified District	Apache Junction
40	288	Crane Elementary District	Yuma
41	274	Prescott Unified District	Prescott
42	268	Chinle Unified District	Chinle
43	256	Humboldt Unified District	Prescott Valley
44	251	Osborn Elementary District	Phoenix
45	247	Litchfield Elementary District	Litchfield Park
46	245	Tolleson Union High SD	Tolleson
47	215	Douglas Unified District	Douglas
48	211	Bullhead City Elementary District	Bullhead City
49	203	Avondale Elementary District	Avondale
50	202	Page Unified District	Page
51	200	Window Rock Unified District	Fort Defiance
52	181	Balsz Elementary District	Phoenix
53	168	Whiteriver Unified District	Whiteriver
54	166	Coolidge Unified District	Coolidge
55	163	Tuba City Unified District	Tuba City
56	161	Higley Unified District	Higley
57	158	Payson Unified District	Payson
58	157	Gadsden Elementary District	San Luis
59	152	Kayenta Unified District	Kayenta
60	152	Winslow Unified District	Winslow
61	148	Safford Unified District	Safford
62	146	Blue Ridge Unified District	Lakeside
63	145	Murphy Elementary District	Phoenix
64	141	Chino Valley Unified District	Chino Valley
65	140	Agua Fria Union High SD	Avondale
66	139	Fowler Elementary District	Phoenix
67	136	Florence Unified SD	Florence
68	135	Cottonwood-Oak Creek Elem Dist	Cottonwood
68	135	Snowflake Unified District	Snowflake
70	134	Show Low Unified District	Show Low
71	133	Fountain Hills Unified District	Fountain Hills
72	133	Santa Cruz Valley Unified District	Rio Rico
73	132	Holbrook Unified District	Holbrook
74	130	Casa Grande Union High SD	Casa Grande
75	129	Sahuarita Unified District	Sahuarita
76	127	Ganado Unified District	Ganado
77	126	Parker Unified SD	Parker
77	126	Somerton Elementary District	Somerton
79	114	Queen Creek Unified District	Queen Creek
80	109	Globe Unified District	Globe
81	102	Liberty Elementary District	Buckeye
82	102	Tolleson Elementary District	Tolleson
83	89	Maricopa County Regional District	Phoenix
84	88	Laveen Elementary District	Laveen
85	86	Wickenburg Unified District	Wickenburg
86	82	Littleton Elementary District	Cashion
87	77	Mohave Valley Elementary District	Mohave Valley
88	50	Colorado River Union High SD	Fort Mojave
89	24	Peach Springs Unified District	Peach Springs
90	n/a	Cave Creek Unified District	Cave Creek
90	n/a	Central Ariz Valley Inst of Tech	Coolidge
90	n/a	Chinle Agency	Chinle
90	n/a	East Valley Institute of Tech	Mesa
90	n/a	Fort Defiance Agency	Fort Defiance
90	n/a	Hopi Agency	Kearns Canyon
90	n/a	Western Navajo Agency	Tuba City

Number of Students

Rank	Number	District Name	City
1	75,269	Mesa Unified District	Mesa
2	61,958	Tucson Unified District	Tucson
3	35,178	Peoria Unified SD	Glendale
4	35,073	Paradise Valley Unified District	Phoenix
5	33,256	Gilbert Unified District	Gilbert
6	30,049	Deer Valley Unified District	Phoenix
7	27,245	Scottsdale Unified District	Phoenix
8	24,506	Washington Elementary District	Phoenix
9	24,497	Chandler Unified District	Chandler
10	23,616	Phoenix Union High SD	Phoenix
11	19,780	Cartwright Elementary District	Phoenix
12	18,803	Kyrene Elementary District	Tempe
13	15,602	Sunnyside Unified District	Tucson
14	14,608	Alhambra Elementary District	Phoenix
15	14,228	Glendale Union High SD	Glendale
16	13,394	Tempe Elementary District	Tempe
17	13,163	Tempe Union High SD	Tempe
18	13,075	Glendale Elementary District	Glendale
19	12,666	East Valley Institute of Tech	Mesa
20	12,363	Marana Unified District	Marana
21	11,497	Flagstaff Unified District	Flagstaff
22	11,442	Roosevelt Elementary District	Phoenix
23	10,814	Yuma Elementary District	Yuma
24	9,615	Pendergast Elementary District	Phoenix
25	9,426	Yuma Union High SD	Yuma
26	8,982	Dysart Unified District	El Mirage
27	8,588	Phoenix Elementary District	Phoenix
28	8,545	Isaac Elementary District	Phoenix
29	8,383	Creighton Elementary District	Phoenix
30	7,198	Kingman Unified SD	Kingman
31	6,832	Sierra Vista Unified District	Sierra Vista
32	6,312	Lake Havasu Unified District	Lk Havasu City
33	6,309	Nogales Unified District	Nogales
34	6,089	Flowing Wells Unified District	Tucson
35	5,846	Apache Junction Unified District	Apache Junction
36	5,599	Crane Elementary District	Yuma
37	5,574	Casa Grande Elementary District	Casa Grande
38	5,209	Litchfield Elementary District	Litchfield Park
39	5,195	Madison Elementary District	Phoenix
40	5,114	Prescott Unified District	Prescott
41	5,112	Cave Creek Unified District	Cave Creek
42	5,102	Vail Unified District	Vail
43	5,012	Catalina Foothills Unified Dist	Tucson
44	4,993	Tolleson Union High SD	Tolleson
45	4,908	Humboldt Unified District	Prescott Valley
46	4,196	Chinle Unified District	Chinle
47	4,188	Western Navajo Agency	Tuba City
48	4,177	Osborn Elementary District	Phoenix
49	4,130	Avondale Elementary District	Avondale
50	4,104	Douglas Unified District	Douglas
51	4,046	Gadsden Elementary District	San Luis
52	3,918	Bullhead City Elementary District	Bullhead City
53	3,835	Higley Unified District	Higley
54	3,303	Snowflake Unified District	Snowflake
55	3,265	Balsz Elementary District	Phoenix
56	3,254	Amphitheater Unified District	Tucson
57	3,111	Central Ariz Valley Inst of Tech	Coolidge
58	3,101	Agua Fria Union High SD	Avondale
59	3,096	Page Unified District	Page
60	2,986	Coolidge Unified District	Coolidge
61	2,953	Window Rock Unified District	Fort Defiance
62	2,929	Chinle Agency	Chinle
63	2,875	Payson Unified District	Payson
64	2,862	Santa Cruz Valley Unified District	Rio Rico
65	2,856	Safford Unified District	Safford
66	2,840	Casa Grande Union High SD	Casa Grande
67	2,759	Fowler Elementary District	Phoenix
68	2,731	Murphy Elementary District	Phoenix
69	2,615	Winslow Unified District	Winslow
70	2,604	Chino Valley Unified District	Chino Valley
71	2,573	Tuba City Unified District	Tuba City
72	2,561	Show Low Unified District	Show Low
73	2,549	Fountain Hills Unified District	Fountain Hills
74	2,548	Blue Ridge Unified District	Lakeside
75	2,541	Cottonwood-Oak Creek Elem Dist	Cottonwood
76	2,480	Whiteriver Unified District	Whiteriver

77	2,467	Somerton Elementary District	Somerton
78	2,463	Kayenta Unified District	Kayenta
79	2,400	Maricopa County Regional District	Phoenix
80	2,250	Sahuarita Unified District	Sahuarita
81	2,195	Globe Unified District	Globe
82	2,157	Peach Springs Unified District	Peach Springs
83	2,155	Queen Creek Unified District	Queen Creek
84	2,088	Fort Defiance Agency	Fort Defiance
85	2,057	Parker Unified SD	Parker
86	2,045	Holbrook Unified District	Holbrook
87	2,043	Ganado Unified District	Ganado
88	2,033	Colorado River Union High SD	Fort Mojave
89	1,963	Florence Unified SD	Florence
90	1,877	Tolleson Elementary District	Tolleson
91	1,842	Liberty Elementary District	Buckeye
92	1,824	Littleton Elementary District	Cashion
93	1,752	Mohave Valley Elementary District	Mohave Valley
94	1,725	Hopi Agency	Kearns Canyon
95	1,699	Laveen Elementary District	Laveen
96	1,503	Wickenburg Unified District	Wickenburg

Male Students

Rank	Percent	District Name	City
1	57.3	Maricopa County Regional District	Phoenix
2	57.2	East Valley Institute of Tech	Mesa
3	53.8	Page Unified District	Page
4	53.5	Avondale Elementary District	Avondale
5	53.4	Chino Valley Unified District	Chino Valley
6	53.3	Bullhead City Elementary District	Bullhead City
7	53.0	Fountain Hills Unified District	Fountain Hills
7	53.0	Santa Cruz Valley Unified District	Rio Rico
9	52.7	Cottonwood-Oak Creek Elem Dist	Cottonwood
10	52.5	Littleton Elementary District	Cashion
11	52.4	Douglas Unified District	Douglas
11	52.4	Payson Unified District	Payson
11	52.4	Peach Springs Unified District	Peach Springs
11	52.4	Queen Creek Unified District	Queen Creek
11	52.4	Washington Elementary District	Phoenix
16	52.3	Show Low Unified District	Show Low
16	52.3	Snowflake Unified District	Snowflake
18	52.1	Vail Unified District	Vail
19	52.0	Murphy Elementary District	Phoenix
20	51.9	Gilbert Unified District	Gilbert
21	51.8	Balsz Elementary District	Phoenix
21	51.8	Casa Grande Elementary District	Casa Grande
21	51.8	Colorado River Union High SD	Fort Mojave
21	51.8	Kingman Unified SD	Kingman
21	51.8	Madison Elementary District	Phoenix
26	51.7	Alhambra Elementary District	Phoenix
26	51.7	Flagstaff Unified District	Flagstaff
26	51.7	Holbrook Unified District	Holbrook
26	51.7	Paradise Valley Unified District	Phoenix
26	51.7	Peoria Unified SD	Glendale
31	51.6	Apache Junction Unified District	Apache Junction
31	51.6	Dysart Unified District	El Mirage
31	51.6	Marana Unified District	Marana
31	51.6	Pendergast Elementary District	Phoenix
31	51.6	Prescott Unified District	Prescott
31	51.6	Scottsdale Unified District	Phoenix
31	51.6	Somerton Elementary District	Somerton
31	51.6	Sunnyside Unified District	Tucson
39	51.5	Catalina Foothills Unified Dist	Tucson
39	51.5	Glendale Elementary District	Glendale
39	51.5	Mesa Unified District	Mesa
39	51.5	Tempe Union High SD	Tempe
43	51.4	Agua Fria Union High SD	Avondale
43	51.4	Crane Elementary District	Yuma
43	51.4	Globe Unified District	Globe
43	51.4	Nogales Unified District	Nogales
43	51.4	Tempe Elementary District	Tempe
43	51.4	Window Rock Unified District	Fort Defiance
43	51.4	Yuma Elementary District	Yuma
50	51.3	Cartwright Elementary District	Phoenix
50	51.3	Deer Valley Unified District	Phoenix
50	51.3	Lake Havasu Unified District	Lk Havasu City
50	51.3	Tolleson Union High SD	Tolleson
50	51.3	Tucson Unified District	Tucson
50	51.3	Yuma Union High SD	Yuma
56	51.2	Kayenta Unified District	Kayenta
56	51.2	Osborn Elementary District	Phoenix
56	51.2	Parker Unified SD	Parker
56	51.2	Sierra Vista Unified District	Sierra Vista
60	51.1	Glendale Union High SD	Glendale
60	51.1	Humboldt Unified District	Prescott Valley
60	51.1	Kyrene Elementary District	Tempe
63	51.0	Amphitheater Unified District	Tucson
63	51.0	Ganado Unified District	Ganado
63	51.0	Mohave Valley Elementary District	Mohave Valley
66	50.9	Cave Creek Unified District	Cave Creek
66	50.9	Coolidge Unified District	Coolidge
66	50.9	Litchfield Elementary District	Litchfield Park
69	50.8	Blue Ridge Unified District	Lakeside
69	50.8	Fowler Elementary District	Phoenix
69	50.8	Phoenix Union High SD	Phoenix
69	50.8	Safford Unified District	Safford
73	50.7	Flowing Wells Unified District	Tucson
73	50.7	Tolleson Elementary District	Tolleson
73	50.7	Whiteriver Unified District	Whiteriver
73	50.7	Wickenburg Unified District	Wickenburg
77	50.6	Liberty Elementary District	Buckeye
77	50.6	Tuba City Unified District	Tuba City
79	50.5	Higley Unified District	Higley
80	50.3	Chinle Unified District	Chinle
80	50.3	Florence Unified SD	Florence
80	50.3	Roosevelt Elementary District	Phoenix
83	50.2	Central Ariz Valley Inst of Tech	Coolidge
83	50.2	Creighton Elementary District	Phoenix
83	50.2	Isaac Elementary District	Phoenix
83	50.2	Phoenix Elementary District	Phoenix
87	50.0	Laveen Elementary District	Laveen
87	50.0	Winslow Unified District	Winslow
89	49.9	Casa Grande Union High SD	Casa Grande
90	49.6	Sahuarita Unified District	Sahuarita
91	49.5	Gadsden Elementary District	San Luis
92	n/a	Chandler Unified District	Chandler
92	n/a	Chinle Agency	Chinle
92	n/a	Fort Defiance Agency	Fort Defiance
92	n/a	Hopi Agency	Kearns Canyon
92	n/a	Western Navajo Agency	Tuba City

Female Students

Rank	Percent	District Name	City
1	50.5	Gadsden Elementary District	San Luis
2	50.4	Sahuarita Unified District	Sahuarita
3	50.1	Casa Grande Union High SD	Casa Grande
4	50.0	Laveen Elementary District	Laveen
4	50.0	Winslow Unified District	Winslow
6	49.8	Central Ariz Valley Inst of Tech	Coolidge
6	49.8	Creighton Elementary District	Phoenix
6	49.8	Isaac Elementary District	Phoenix
6	49.8	Phoenix Elementary District	Phoenix
10	49.7	Chinle Unified District	Chinle
10	49.7	Florence Unified SD	Florence
10	49.7	Roosevelt Elementary District	Phoenix
13	49.5	Higley Unified District	Higley
14	49.4	Liberty Elementary District	Buckeye
14	49.4	Tuba City Unified District	Tuba City
16	49.3	Flowing Wells Unified District	Tucson
16	49.3	Tolleson Elementary District	Tolleson
16	49.3	Whiteriver Unified District	Whiteriver
16	49.3	Wickenburg Unified District	Wickenburg
20	49.2	Blue Ridge Unified District	Lakeside
20	49.2	Fowler Elementary District	Phoenix
20	49.2	Phoenix Union High SD	Phoenix
20	49.2	Safford Unified District	Safford
24	49.1	Cave Creek Unified District	Cave Creek
24	49.1	Coolidge Unified District	Coolidge
24	49.1	Litchfield Elementary District	Litchfield Park
27	49.0	Amphitheater Unified District	Tucson
27	49.0	Ganado Unified District	Ganado
27	49.0	Mohave Valley Elementary District	Mohave Valley
30	48.9	Glendale Union High SD	Glendale
30	48.9	Humboldt Unified District	Prescott Valley
30	48.9	Kyrene Elementary District	Tempe
33	48.8	Kayenta Unified District	Kayenta
33	48.8	Osborn Elementary District	Phoenix
33	48.8	Parker Unified SD	Parker
33	48.8	Sierra Vista Unified District	Sierra Vista
37	48.7	Cartwright Elementary District	Phoenix
37	48.7	Deer Valley Unified District	Phoenix
37	48.7	Lake Havasu Unified District	Lk Havasu City
37	48.7	Tolleson Union High SD	Tolleson
37	48.7	Tucson Unified District	Tucson
37	48.7	Yuma Union High SD	Yuma
43	48.6	Agua Fria Union High SD	Avondale
43	48.6	Crane Elementary District	Yuma
43	48.6	Globe Unified District	Globe
43	48.6	Nogales Unified District	Nogales
43	48.6	Tempe Elementary District	Tempe
43	48.6	Window Rock Unified District	Fort Defiance
43	48.6	Yuma Elementary District	Yuma
50	48.5	Catalina Foothills Unified Dist	Tucson
50	48.5	Glendale Elementary District	Glendale
50	48.5	Mesa Unified District	Mesa
50	48.5	Tempe Union High SD	Tempe
54	48.4	Apache Junction Unified District	Apache Junction
54	48.4	Dysart Unified District	El Mirage
54	48.4	Marana Unified District	Marana
54	48.4	Pendergast Elementary District	Phoenix
54	48.4	Prescott Unified District	Prescott
54	48.4	Scottsdale Unified District	Phoenix
54	48.4	Somerton Elementary District	Somerton
54	48.4	Sunnyside Unified District	Tucson
62	48.3	Alhambra Elementary District	Phoenix
62	48.3	Flagstaff Unified District	Flagstaff
62	48.3	Holbrook Unified District	Holbrook
62	48.3	Paradise Valley Unified District	Phoenix
62	48.3	Peoria Unified SD	Glendale
67	48.2	Balsz Elementary District	Phoenix
67	48.2	Casa Grande Elementary District	Casa Grande
67	48.2	Colorado River Union High SD	Fort Mojave
67	48.2	Kingman Unified SD	Kingman
67	48.2	Madison Elementary District	Phoenix
72	48.1	Gilbert Unified District	Gilbert
73	48.0	Murphy Elementary District	Phoenix
74	47.9	Vail Unified District	Vail
75	47.7	Show Low Unified District	Show Low
75	47.7	Snowflake Unified District	Snowflake
77	47.6	Douglas Unified District	Douglas
77	47.6	Payson Unified District	Payson
77	47.6	Peach Springs Unified District	Peach Springs
77	47.6	Queen Creek Unified District	Queen Creek
77	47.6	Washington Elementary District	Phoenix
82	47.5	Littleton Elementary District	Cashion
83	47.3	Cottonwood-Oak Creek Elem Dist	Cottonwood
84	47.0	Fountain Hills Unified District	Fountain Hills
84	47.0	Santa Cruz Valley Unified District	Rio Rico
86	46.7	Bullhead City Elementary District	Bullhead City
87	46.6	Chino Valley Unified District	Chino Valley
88	46.5	Avondale Elementary District	Avondale
89	46.2	Page Unified District	Page
90	42.8	East Valley Institute of Tech	Mesa
91	42.7	Maricopa County Regional District	Phoenix
92	n/a	Chandler Unified District	Chandler
92	n/a	Chinle Agency	Chinle
92	n/a	Fort Defiance Agency	Fort Defiance
92	n/a	Hopi Agency	Kearns Canyon
92	n/a	Western Navajo Agency	Tuba City

Individual Education Program Students

Rank	Percent	District Name	City
1	69.1	Amphitheater Unified District	Tucson
2	17.6	Mohave Valley Elementary District	Mohave Valley
3	16.9	Parker Unified SD	Parker
4	16.5	Page Unified District	Page
5	16.4	Liberty Elementary District	Buckeye
6	15.8	Whiteriver Unified District	Whiteriver
7	15.4	Globe Unified District	Globe
8	15.2	Flagstaff Unified District	Flagstaff
9	14.8	Humboldt Unified District	Prescott Valley
10	14.7	Chino Valley Unified District	Chino Valley
10	14.7	Coolidge Unified District	Coolidge
10	14.7	Winslow Unified District	Winslow
13	14.3	Somerton Elementary District	Somerton
14	14.1	Sunnyside Unified District	Tucson
15	13.8	Laveen Elementary District	Laveen
16	13.6	Casa Grande Elementary District	Casa Grande
16	13.6	Safford Unified District	Safford
16	13.6	Washington Elementary District	Phoenix
19	13.5	Sahuarita Unified District	Sahuarita
20	13.3	Kingman Unified SD	Kingman
21	12.9	Casa Grande Union High SD	Casa Grande
21	12.9	Murphy Elementary District	Phoenix
23	12.7	Littleton Elementary District	Cashion
24	12.4	Blue Ridge Unified District	Lakeside
24	12.4	Crane Elementary District	Yuma
26	12.3	Marana Unified District	Marana
27	12.2	Tempe Elementary District	Tempe
27	12.2	Tuba City Unified District	Tuba City
29	12.0	Flowing Wells Unified District	Tucson
29	12.0	Show Low Unified District	Show Low
31	11.9	Prescott Unified District	Prescott
31	11.9	Tucson Unified District	Tucson
33	11.7	Colorado River Union High SD	Fort Mojave
33	11.7	Holbrook Unified District	Holbrook
33	11.7	Payson Unified District	Payson
33	11.7	Snowflake Unified District	Snowflake
37	11.6	Apache Junction Unified District	Apache Junction
37	11.6	Vail Unified District	Vail
39	11.5	Deer Valley Unified District	Phoenix
39	11.5	Glendale Elementary District	Glendale
41	11.3	Wickenburg Unified District	Wickenburg
42	11.2	Fowler Elementary District	Phoenix
42	11.2	Pendergast Elementary District	Phoenix
42	11.2	Peoria Unified SD	Glendale
42	11.2	Phoenix Elementary District	Phoenix
46	11.1	Cartwright Elementary District	Phoenix
46	11.1	Higley Unified District	Higley
46	11.1	Sierra Vista Unified District	Sierra Vista
49	11.0	Chinle Unified District	Chinle
49	11.0	Window Rock Unified District	Fort Defiance
51	10.7	Dysart Unified District	El Mirage
51	10.7	Osborn Elementary District	Phoenix
53	10.5	Lake Havasu Unified District	Lk Havasu City
54	10.3	Litchfield Elementary District	Litchfield Park
54	10.3	Paradise Valley Unified District	Phoenix

Rank	Percent	District Name	City
54	10.3	Queen Creek Unified District	Queen Creek
54	10.3	Tolleson Union High SD	Tolleson
58	10.1	Alhambra Elementary District	Phoenix
58	10.1	Douglas Unified District	Douglas
58	10.1	Madison Elementary District	Phoenix
58	10.1	Peach Springs Unified District	Peach Springs
58	10.1	Roosevelt Elementary District	Phoenix
63	10.0	Isaac Elementary District	Phoenix
64	9.9	Catalina Foothills Unified Dist	Tucson
64	9.9	Chandler Unified District	Chandler
66	9.8	Phoenix Union High SD	Phoenix
67	9.7	Balsz Elementary District	Phoenix
68	9.6	Creighton Elementary District	Phoenix
68	9.6	Florence Unified SD	Florence
70	9.5	Gilbert Unified District	Gilbert
71	9.2	Bullhead City Elementary District	Bullhead City
71	9.2	Glendale Union High SD	Glendale
73	9.1	Scottsdale Unified District	Phoenix
74	9.0	Agua Fria Union High SD	Avondale
74	9.0	Kayenta Unified District	Kayenta
74	9.0	Yuma Elementary District	Yuma
77	8.8	Cottonwood-Oak Creek Elem Dist	Cottonwood
77	8.8	Nogales Unified District	Nogales
77	8.8	Yuma Union High SD	Yuma
80	8.7	Kyrene Elementary District	Tempe
80	8.7	Tolleson Elementary District	Tolleson
82	8.6	Mesa Unified District	Mesa
83	8.5	Tempe Union High SD	Tempe
84	8.4	Cave Creek Unified District	Cave Creek
84	8.4	Fountain Hills Unified District	Fountain Hills
86	8.2	Avondale Elementary District	Avondale
87	7.4	Ganado Unified District	Ganado
87	7.4	Maricopa County Regional District	Phoenix
87	7.4	Santa Cruz Valley Unified District	Rio Rico
90	5.1	Gadsden Elementary District	San Luis
91	0.0	Central Ariz Valley Inst of Tech	Coolidge
91	0.0	East Valley Institute of Tech	Mesa
93	n/a	Chinle Agency	Chinle
93	n/a	Fort Defiance Agency	Fort Defiance
93	n/a	Hopi Agency	Kearns Canyon
93	n/a	Western Navajo Agency	Tuba City

English Language Learner Students

Rank	Percent	District Name	City
1	89.7	Gadsden Elementary District	San Luis
2	72.3	Whiteriver Unified District	Whiteriver
3	72.1	Kayenta Unified District	Kayenta
4	66.5	Ganado Unified District	Ganado
5	64.9	Somerton Elementary District	Somerton
6	61.2	Murphy Elementary District	Phoenix
7	60.5	Creighton Elementary District	Phoenix
8	60.2	Isaac Elementary District	Phoenix
9	57.6	Chinle Unified District	Chinle
10	52.8	Phoenix Elementary District	Phoenix
11	52.1	Window Rock Unified District	Fort Defiance
12	50.5	Alhambra Elementary District	Phoenix
13	45.5	Santa Cruz Valley Unified District	Rio Rico
14	43.9	Tuba City Unified District	Tuba City
15	43.8	Balsz Elementary District	Phoenix
16	43.5	Amphitheater Unified District	Tucson
17	42.0	Osborn Elementary District	Phoenix
18	39.3	Cartwright Elementary District	Phoenix
19	39.1	Fowler Elementary District	Phoenix
20	37.1	Sunnyside Unified District	Tucson
21	36.3	Crane Elementary District	Yuma
22	35.2	Roosevelt Elementary District	Phoenix
23	33.9	Laveen Elementary District	Laveen
24	31.8	Page Unified District	Page
25	30.1	Glendale Elementary District	Glendale
26	29.0	Tolleson Elementary District	Tolleson
27	28.2	Littleton Elementary District	Cashion
28	28.1	Yuma Elementary District	Yuma
29	27.4	Avondale Elementary District	Avondale
30	26.9	Nogales Unified District	Nogales
31	26.0	Tempe Elementary District	Tempe
32	21.6	Holbrook Unified District	Holbrook
33	21.3	Washington Elementary District	Phoenix
34	19.1	Dysart Unified District	El Mirage
35	18.7	Pendergast Elementary District	Phoenix
36	18.3	Phoenix Union High SD	Phoenix
37	16.4	Bullhead City Elementary District	Bullhead City
38	15.7	Tucson Unified District	Tucson
39	15.2	Flagstaff Unified District	Flagstaff
40	14.8	Chandler Unified District	Chandler
41	13.9	Madison Elementary District	Phoenix
42	13.3	Cottonwood-Oak Creek Elem Dist	Cottonwood
43	10.5	Casa Grande Elementary District	Casa Grande
44	10.2	Queen Creek Unified District	Queen Creek
45	9.8	Parker Unified SD	Parker
45	9.8	Sahuarita Unified District	Sahuarita
47	9.5	Paradise Valley Unified District	Phoenix
48	8.6	Wickenburg Unified District	Wickenburg
49	8.1	Mesa Unified District	Mesa
50	7.7	Chino Valley Unified District	Chino Valley
51	7.5	Scottsdale Unified District	Phoenix
52	6.6	Humboldt Unified District	Prescott Valley
53	6.5	Litchfield Elementary District	Litchfield Park
53	6.5	Yuma Union High SD	Yuma
55	6.0	Tolleson Union High SD	Tolleson
55	6.0	Winslow Unified District	Winslow
57	5.5	Peach Springs Unified District	Peach Springs
58	5.4	Glendale Union High SD	Glendale
59	5.0	Agua Fria Union High SD	Avondale
60	4.3	Blue Ridge Unified District	Lakeside
60	4.3	Liberty Elementary District	Buckeye
62	4.2	Deer Valley Unified District	Phoenix
63	4.1	Peoria Unified SD	Glendale
64	3.8	Maricopa County Regional District	Phoenix
65	3.7	Lake Havasu Unified District	Lk Havasu City
66	3.2	Prescott Unified District	Prescott
67	2.9	Marana Unified District	Marana
68	2.8	Flowing Wells Unified District	Tucson
69	2.7	Mohave Valley Elementary District	Mohave Valley
70	2.6	Gilbert Unified District	Gilbert
71	2.5	Kyrene Elementary District	Tempe
72	2.0	Show Low Unified District	Show Low
73	1.8	Catalina Foothills Unified Dist	Tucson
74	1.2	Higley Unified District	Higley
75	0.7	Fountain Hills Unified District	Fountain Hills
76	0.6	Colorado River Union High SD	Fort Mojave
77	0.4	Cave Creek Unified District	Cave Creek
78	0.2	Payson Unified District	Payson
79	0.0	Apache Junction Unified District	Apache Junction
79	0.0	Casa Grande Union High SD	Casa Grande
79	0.0	Central Ariz Valley Inst of Tech	Coolidge
79	0.0	Coolidge Unified District	Coolidge
79	0.0	Douglas Unified District	Douglas
79	0.0	East Valley Institute of Tech	Mesa
79	0.0	Florence Unified SD	Florence
79	0.0	Globe Unified District	Globe
79	0.0	Kingman Unified SD	Kingman
79	0.0	Safford Unified District	Safford
79	0.0	Sierra Vista Unified District	Sierra Vista
79	0.0	Snowflake Unified District	Snowflake
79	0.0	Tempe Union High SD	Tempe
79	0.0	Vail Unified District	Vail
93	n/a	Chinle Agency	Chinle
93	n/a	Fort Defiance Agency	Fort Defiance
93	n/a	Hopi Agency	Kearns Canyon
93	n/a	Western Navajo Agency	Tuba City

Migrant Students

Rank	Percent	District Name	City
1	5.7	Queen Creek Unified District	Queen Creek
2	3.5	Douglas Unified District	Douglas
3	3.2	Somerton Elementary District	Somerton
4	2.1	Yuma Union High SD	Yuma
5	1.5	Crane Elementary District	Yuma
5	1.5	Tolleson Union High SD	Tolleson
7	1.3	Gadsden Elementary District	San Luis
7	1.3	Yuma Elementary District	Yuma
9	1.1	Florence Unified SD	Florence
10	1.0	Glendale Elementary District	Glendale
10	1.0	Liberty Elementary District	Buckeye
12	0.9	Littleton Elementary District	Cashion
13	0.7	Casa Grande Elementary District	Casa Grande
14	0.5	Agua Fria Union High SD	Avondale
14	0.5	Dysart Unified District	El Mirage
16	0.3	Fowler Elementary District	Phoenix
16	0.3	Glendale Union High SD	Glendale
16	0.3	Higley Unified District	Higley
16	0.3	Mesa Unified District	Mesa
16	0.3	Phoenix Union High SD	Phoenix
21	0.2	Avondale Elementary District	Avondale
21	0.2	Casa Grande Union High SD	Casa Grande
21	0.2	Chandler Unified District	Chandler
21	0.2	Coolidge Unified District	Coolidge
21	0.2	Litchfield Elementary District	Litchfield Park
21	0.2	Marana Unified District	Marana
21	0.2	Peoria Unified SD	Glendale
21	0.2	Phoenix Elementary District	Phoenix
29	0.1	Gilbert Unified District	Gilbert
29	0.1	Isaac Elementary District	Phoenix
29	0.1	Murphy Elementary District	Phoenix
29	0.1	Pendergast Elementary District	Phoenix
29	0.1	Roosevelt Elementary District	Phoenix
34	0.0	East Valley Institute of Tech	Mesa
34	0.0	Parker Unified SD	Parker
36	0.0	Alhambra Elementary District	Phoenix
36	0.0	Amphitheater Unified District	Tucson
36	0.0	Apache Junction Unified District	Apache Junction
36	0.0	Balsz Elementary District	Phoenix
36	0.0	Blue Ridge Unified District	Lakeside
36	0.0	Bullhead City Elementary District	Bullhead City
36	0.0	Cartwright Elementary District	Phoenix
36	0.0	Catalina Foothills Unified Dist	Tucson
36	0.0	Cave Creek Unified District	Cave Creek
36	0.0	Central Ariz Valley Inst of Tech	Coolidge
36	0.0	Chinle Unified District	Chinle
36	0.0	Chino Valley Unified District	Chino Valley
36	0.0	Colorado River Union High SD	Fort Mojave
36	0.0	Cottonwood-Oak Creek Elem Dist	Cottonwood
36	0.0	Creighton Elementary District	Phoenix
36	0.0	Deer Valley Unified District	Phoenix
36	0.0	Flagstaff Unified District	Flagstaff
36	0.0	Flowing Wells Unified District	Tucson
36	0.0	Fountain Hills Unified District	Fountain Hills
36	0.0	Ganado Unified District	Ganado
36	0.0	Globe Unified District	Globe
36	0.0	Holbrook Unified District	Holbrook
36	0.0	Humboldt Unified District	Prescott Valley
36	0.0	Kayenta Unified District	Kayenta
36	0.0	Kingman Unified SD	Kingman
36	0.0	Kyrene Elementary District	Tempe
36	0.0	Lake Havasu Unified District	Lk Havasu City
36	0.0	Laveen Elementary District	Laveen
36	0.0	Madison Elementary District	Phoenix
36	0.0	Maricopa County Regional District	Phoenix
36	0.0	Mohave Valley Elementary District	Mohave Valley
36	0.0	Nogales Unified District	Nogales
36	0.0	Osborn Elementary District	Phoenix
36	0.0	Page Unified District	Page
36	0.0	Paradise Valley Unified District	Phoenix
36	0.0	Payson Unified District	Payson
36	0.0	Peach Springs Unified District	Peach Springs
36	0.0	Prescott Unified District	Prescott
36	0.0	Safford Unified District	Safford
36	0.0	Sahuarita Unified District	Sahuarita
36	0.0	Santa Cruz Valley Unified District	Rio Rico
36	0.0	Scottsdale Unified District	Phoenix
36	0.0	Show Low Unified District	Show Low
36	0.0	Sierra Vista Unified District	Sierra Vista
36	0.0	Snowflake Unified District	Snowflake
36	0.0	Sunnyside Unified District	Tucson
36	0.0	Tempe Elementary District	Tempe
36	0.0	Tempe Union High SD	Tempe
36	0.0	Tolleson Elementary District	Tolleson
36	0.0	Tuba City Unified District	Tuba City
36	0.0	Tucson Unified District	Tucson
36	0.0	Vail Unified District	Vail
36	0.0	Washington Elementary District	Phoenix
36	0.0	Whiteriver Unified District	Whiteriver
36	0.0	Wickenburg Unified District	Wickenburg
36	0.0	Window Rock Unified District	Fort Defiance
36	0.0	Winslow Unified District	Winslow
93	n/a	Chinle Agency	Chinle
93	n/a	Fort Defiance Agency	Fort Defiance
93	n/a	Hopi Agency	Kearns Canyon
93	n/a	Western Navajo Agency	Tuba City

Students Eligible for Free Lunch

Rank	Percent	District Name	City
1	47.9	Mohave Valley Elementary District	Mohave Valley
2	42.6	Blue Ridge Unified District	Lakeside
3	38.0	Florence Unified SD	Florence
4	36.4	Payson Unified District	Payson
5	34.1	Wickenburg Unified District	Wickenburg
6	32.6	Madison Elementary District	Phoenix
7	31.5	Queen Creek Unified District	Queen Creek
8	31.2	Humboldt Unified District	Prescott Valley
9	31.1	Washington Elementary District	Phoenix
10	30.7	Mesa Unified District	Mesa
11	28.3	Sierra Vista Unified District	Sierra Vista
12	26.9	Pendergast Elementary District	Phoenix
13	26.3	Liberty Elementary District	Buckeye
14	21.6	Tolleson Union High SD	Tolleson
15	20.2	Chandler Unified District	Chandler
16	17.8	Marana Unified District	Marana
17	17.4	Prescott Unified District	Prescott
18	15.5	Paradise Valley Unified District	Phoenix
19	15.0	Litchfield Elementary District	Litchfield Park
20	14.3	Deer Valley Unified District	Phoenix
21	11.6	Peoria Unified SD	Glendale
22	10.9	Scottsdale Unified District	Phoenix
23	10.1	Vail Unified District	Vail
24	8.2	Gilbert Unified District	Gilbert
25	7.8	Kyrene Elementary District	Tempe
26	5.2	Cave Creek Unified District	Cave Creek
27	4.8	Higley Unified District	Higley
28	3.6	Fountain Hills Unified District	Fountain Hills
29	n/a	Agua Fria Union High SD	Avondale
29	n/a	Alhambra Elementary District	Phoenix
29	n/a	Amphitheater Unified District	Tucson
29	n/a	Apache Junction Unified District	Apache Junction
29	n/a	Avondale Elementary District	Avondale
29	n/a	Balsz Elementary District	Phoenix

29	n/a	Bullhead City Elementary District	Bullhead City
29	n/a	Cartwright Elementary District	Phoenix
29	n/a	Casa Grande Elementary District	Casa Grande
29	n/a	Casa Grande Union High SD	Casa Grande
29	n/a	Catalina Foothills Unified Dist	Tucson
29	n/a	Central Ariz Valley Inst of Tech	Coolidge
29	n/a	Chinle Agency	Chinle
29	n/a	Chinle Unified District	Chinle
29	n/a	Chino Valley Unified District	Chino Valley
29	n/a	Colorado River Union High SD	Fort Mojave
29	n/a	Coolidge Unified District	Coolidge
29	n/a	Cottonwood-Oak Creek Elem Dist	Cottonwood
29	n/a	Crane Elementary District	Yuma
29	n/a	Creighton Elementary District	Phoenix
29	n/a	Douglas Unified District	Douglas
29	n/a	Dysart Unified District	El Mirage
29	n/a	East Valley Institute of Tech	Mesa
29	n/a	Flagstaff Unified District	Flagstaff
29	n/a	Flowing Wells Unified District	Tucson
29	n/a	Fort Defiance Agency	Fort Defiance
29	n/a	Fowler Elementary District	Phoenix
29	n/a	Gadsden Elementary District	San Luis
29	n/a	Ganado Unified District	Ganado
29	n/a	Glendale Elementary District	Glendale
29	n/a	Glendale Union High SD	Glendale
29	n/a	Globe Unified District	Globe
29	n/a	Holbrook Unified District	Holbrook
29	n/a	Hopi Agency	Kearns Canyon
29	n/a	Isaac Elementary District	Phoenix
29	n/a	Kayenta Unified District	Kayenta
29	n/a	Kingman Unified SD	Kingman
29	n/a	Lake Havasu Unified District	Lk Havasu City
29	n/a	Laveen Elementary District	Laveen
29	n/a	Littleton Elementary District	Cashion
29	n/a	Maricopa County Regional District	Phoenix
29	n/a	Murphy Elementary District	Phoenix
29	n/a	Nogales Unified District	Nogales
29	n/a	Osborn Elementary District	Phoenix
29	n/a	Page Unified District	Page
29	n/a	Parker Unified SD	Parker
29	n/a	Peach Springs Unified District	Peach Springs
29	n/a	Phoenix Elementary District	Phoenix
29	n/a	Phoenix Union High SD	Phoenix
29	n/a	Roosevelt Elementary District	Phoenix
29	n/a	Safford Unified District	Safford
29	n/a	Sahuarita Unified District	Sahuarita
29	n/a	Santa Cruz Valley Unified District	Rio Rico
29	n/a	Show Low Unified District	Show Low
29	n/a	Snowflake Unified District	Snowflake
29	n/a	Somerton Elementary District	Somerton
29	n/a	Sunnyside Unified District	Tucson
29	n/a	Tempe Elementary District	Tempe
29	n/a	Tempe Union High SD	Tempe
29	n/a	Tolleson Elementary District	Tolleson
29	n/a	Tuba City Unified District	Tuba City
29	n/a	Tucson Unified District	Tucson
29	n/a	Western Navajo Agency	Tuba City
29	n/a	Whiteriver Unified District	Whiteriver
29	n/a	Window Rock Unified District	Fort Defiance
29	n/a	Winslow Unified District	Winslow
29	n/a	Yuma Elementary District	Yuma
29	n/a	Yuma Union High SD	Yuma

Students Eligible for Reduced-Price Lunch

Rank	Percent	District Name	City
1	18.0	Mohave Valley Elementary District	Mohave Valley
2	13.5	Florence Unified SD	Florence
3	13.0	Humboldt Unified District	Prescott Valley
4	10.1	Washington Elementary District	Phoenix
5	9.6	Payson Unified District	Payson
6	9.5	Mesa Unified District	Mesa
7	8.9	Marana Unified District	Marana
8	8.7	Madison Elementary District	Phoenix
9	8.5	Blue Ridge Unified District	Lakeside
9	8.5	Sierra Vista Unified District	Sierra Vista
11	8.4	Wickenburg Unified District	Wickenburg
12	8.3	Pendergast Elementary District	Phoenix
13	7.8	Liberty Elementary District	Buckeye
14	6.9	Litchfield Elementary District	Litchfield Park
15	6.4	Queen Creek Unified District	Queen Creek
16	6.2	Tolleson Union High SD	Tolleson
17	6.1	Vail Unified District	Vail
18	5.8	Deer Valley Unified District	Phoenix
19	5.5	Paradise Valley Unified District	Phoenix
20	5.3	Prescott Unified District	Prescott
21	5.0	Peoria Unified SD	Glendale
22	4.3	Chandler Unified District	Chandler
23	3.7	Kyrene Elementary District	Tempe
24	3.6	Scottsdale Unified District	Phoenix
25	3.5	Higley Unified District	Higley
26	3.4	Gilbert Unified District	Gilbert
27	1.1	Cave Creek Unified District	Cave Creek
28	0.9	Fountain Hills Unified District	Fountain Hills
29	n/a	Agua Fria Union High SD	Avondale
29	n/a	Alhambra Elementary District	Phoenix
29	n/a	Amphitheater Unified District	Tucson
29	n/a	Apache Junction Unified District	Apache Junction
29	n/a	Avondale Elementary District	Avondale
29	n/a	Balsz Elementary District	Phoenix
29	n/a	Bullhead City Elementary District	Bullhead City
29	n/a	Cartwright Elementary District	Phoenix
29	n/a	Casa Grande Elementary District	Casa Grande
29	n/a	Casa Grande Union High SD	Casa Grande
29	n/a	Catalina Foothills Unified Dist	Tucson
29	n/a	Central Ariz Valley Inst of Tech	Coolidge
29	n/a	Chinle Agency	Chinle
29	n/a	Chinle Unified District	Chinle
29	n/a	Chino Valley Unified District	Chino Valley
29	n/a	Colorado River Union High SD	Fort Mojave
29	n/a	Coolidge Unified District	Coolidge
29	n/a	Cottonwood-Oak Creek Elem Dist	Cottonwood
29	n/a	Crane Elementary District	Yuma
29	n/a	Creighton Elementary District	Phoenix
29	n/a	Douglas Unified District	Douglas
29	n/a	Dysart Unified District	El Mirage
29	n/a	East Valley Institute of Tech	Mesa
29	n/a	Flagstaff Unified District	Flagstaff
29	n/a	Flowing Wells Unified District	Tucson
29	n/a	Fort Defiance Agency	Fort Defiance
29	n/a	Fowler Elementary District	Phoenix
29	n/a	Gadsden Elementary District	San Luis
29	n/a	Ganado Unified District	Ganado
29	n/a	Glendale Elementary District	Glendale
29	n/a	Glendale Union High SD	Glendale
29	n/a	Globe Unified District	Globe
29	n/a	Holbrook Unified District	Holbrook
29	n/a	Hopi Agency	Kearns Canyon
29	n/a	Isaac Elementary District	Phoenix
29	n/a	Kayenta Unified District	Kayenta
29	n/a	Kingman Unified SD	Kingman
29	n/a	Lake Havasu Unified District	Lk Havasu City
29	n/a	Laveen Elementary District	Laveen
29	n/a	Littleton Elementary District	Cashion
29	n/a	Maricopa County Regional District	Phoenix
29	n/a	Murphy Elementary District	Phoenix
29	n/a	Nogales Unified District	Nogales
29	n/a	Osborn Elementary District	Phoenix
29	n/a	Page Unified District	Page
29	n/a	Parker Unified SD	Parker
29	n/a	Peach Springs Unified District	Peach Springs
29	n/a	Phoenix Elementary District	Phoenix
29	n/a	Phoenix Union High SD	Phoenix
29	n/a	Roosevelt Elementary District	Phoenix
29	n/a	Safford Unified District	Safford
29	n/a	Sahuarita Unified District	Sahuarita
29	n/a	Santa Cruz Valley Unified District	Rio Rico
29	n/a	Show Low Unified District	Show Low
29	n/a	Snowflake Unified District	Snowflake
29	n/a	Somerton Elementary District	Somerton
29	n/a	Sunnyside Unified District	Tucson
29	n/a	Tempe Elementary District	Tempe
29	n/a	Tempe Union High SD	Tempe
29	n/a	Tolleson Elementary District	Tolleson
29	n/a	Tuba City Unified District	Tuba City
29	n/a	Tucson Unified District	Tucson
29	n/a	Western Navajo Agency	Tuba City
29	n/a	Whiteriver Unified District	Whiteriver
29	n/a	Window Rock Unified District	Fort Defiance
29	n/a	Winslow Unified District	Winslow
29	n/a	Yuma Elementary District	Yuma
29	n/a	Yuma Union High SD	Yuma

Student/Teacher Ratio

Rank	Ratio	District Name	City
1	87.0	Peach Springs Unified District	Peach Springs
2	40.7	Colorado River Union High SD	Fort Mojave
3	26.8	Maricopa County Regional District	Phoenix
4	25.7	Gadsden Elementary District	San Luis
5	24.5	Snowflake Unified District	Snowflake
6	23.8	Higley Unified District	Higley
7	22.6	Mohave Valley Elementary District	Mohave Valley
8	22.4	Yuma Union High SD	Yuma
9	22.2	Littleton Elementary District	Cashion
10	22.0	Agua Fria Union High SD	Avondale
11	21.7	Casa Grande Union High SD	Casa Grande
12	21.5	Santa Cruz Valley Unified District	Rio Rico
13	21.2	Glendale Union High SD	Glendale
14	21.0	Litchfield Elementary District	Litchfield Park
15	20.5	Cartwright Elementary District	Phoenix
16	20.4	Alhambra Elementary District	Phoenix
16	20.4	Mesa Unified District	Mesa
18	20.3	Avondale Elementary District	Avondale
18	20.3	Tolleson Union High SD	Tolleson
20	20.2	Apache Junction Unified District	Apache Junction
20	20.2	Lake Havasu Unified District	Lk Havasu City
20	20.2	Tempe Union High SD	Tempe
23	20.1	Dysart Unified District	El Mirage
24	20.0	Flowing Wells Unified District	Tucson
24	20.0	Globe Unified District	Globe
26	19.7	Chandler Unified District	Chandler
26	19.7	Fowler Elementary District	Phoenix
28	19.6	Somerton Elementary District	Somerton
29	19.5	Sierra Vista Unified District	Sierra Vista
30	19.4	Crane Elementary District	Yuma
30	19.4	Glendale Elementary District	Glendale
32	19.2	Deer Valley Unified District	Phoenix
32	19.2	Humboldt Unified District	Prescott Valley
32	19.2	Kingman Unified SD	Kingman
32	19.2	Laveen Elementary District	Laveen
32	19.2	Peoria Unified SD	Glendale
32	19.2	Safford Unified District	Safford
32	19.2	Yuma Elementary District	Yuma
39	19.1	Douglas Unified District	Douglas
39	19.1	Fountain Hills Unified District	Fountain Hills
39	19.1	Marana Unified District	Marana
42	19.0	Nogales Unified District	Nogales
42	19.0	Pendergast Elementary District	Phoenix
42	19.0	Show Low Unified District	Show Low
45	18.9	Queen Creek Unified District	Queen Creek
46	18.8	Cottonwood-Oak Creek Elem Dist	Cottonwood
46	18.8	Murphy Elementary District	Phoenix
48	18.7	Kyrene Elementary District	Tempe
48	18.7	Paradise Valley Unified District	Phoenix
50	18.6	Bullhead City Elementary District	Bullhead City
50	18.6	Prescott Unified District	Prescott
52	18.5	Creighton Elementary District	Phoenix
52	18.5	Phoenix Union High SD	Phoenix
54	18.4	Chino Valley Unified District	Chino Valley
54	18.4	Isaac Elementary District	Phoenix
54	18.4	Roosevelt Elementary District	Phoenix
54	18.4	Tolleson Elementary District	Tolleson
58	18.2	Gilbert Unified District	Gilbert
58	18.2	Washington Elementary District	Phoenix
60	18.1	Payson Unified District	Payson
61	18.0	Balsz Elementary District	Phoenix
61	18.0	Coolidge Unified District	Coolidge
63	17.9	Liberty Elementary District	Buckeye
63	17.9	Tucson Unified District	Tucson
65	17.8	Scottsdale Unified District	Phoenix
65	17.8	Sunnyside Unified District	Tucson
67	17.4	Blue Ridge Unified District	Lakeside
67	17.4	Sahuarita Unified District	Sahuarita
67	17.4	Wickenburg Unified District	Wickenburg
70	17.3	Madison Elementary District	Phoenix
71	17.2	Winslow Unified District	Winslow
72	16.9	Casa Grande Elementary District	Casa Grande
72	16.9	Phoenix Elementary District	Phoenix
72	16.9	Vail Unified District	Vail
75	16.8	Catalina Foothills Unified Dist	Tucson
76	16.6	Osborn Elementary District	Phoenix
77	16.3	Parker Unified SD	Parker
78	16.2	Tempe Elementary District	Tempe
79	16.1	Kayenta Unified District	Kayenta
80	16.0	Ganado Unified District	Ganado
81	15.9	Flagstaff Unified District	Flagstaff
82	15.7	Tuba City Unified District	Tuba City
83	15.6	Chinle Unified District	Chinle
84	15.5	Holbrook Unified District	Holbrook
85	15.3	Page Unified District	Page
86	14.7	Whiteriver Unified District	Whiteriver
86	14.7	Window Rock Unified District	Fort Defiance
88	14.3	Florence Unified SD	Florence
89	3.6	Amphitheater Unified District	Tucson
90	n/a	Cave Creek Unified District	Cave Creek
90	n/a	Central Ariz Valley Inst of Tech	Coolidge
90	n/a	Chinle Agency	Chinle
90	n/a	East Valley Institute of Tech	Mesa
90	n/a	Fort Defiance Agency	Fort Defiance
90	n/a	Hopi Agency	Kearns Canyon
90	n/a	Western Navajo Agency	Tuba City

Student/Librarian Ratio

Rank	Ratio	District Name	City
1	8,982.0	Dysart Unified District	El Mirage
2	6,998.8	Crane Elementary District	Yuma
3	5,114.0	Prescott Unified District	Prescott
4	3,956.0	Cartwright Elementary District	Phoenix
5	3,156.0	Lake Havasu Unified District	Lk Havasu City
6	3,096.0	Page Unified District	Page
7	3,044.5	Flowing Wells Unified District	Tucson
8	2,604.0	Chino Valley Unified District	Chino Valley
9	2,561.0	Show Low Unified District	Show Low
10	2,548.0	Blue Ridge Unified District	Lakeside
11	2,361.6	Phoenix Union High SD	Phoenix

12	2,250.0	Sahuarita Unified District	Sahuarita
13	2,230.9	Humboldt Unified District	Prescott Valley
14	2,155.0	Queen Creek Unified District	Queen Creek
15	2,147.0	Phoenix Elementary District	Phoenix
16	2,045.0	Holbrook Unified District	Holbrook
17	2,033.0	Colorado River Union High SD	Fort Mojave
18	1,963.0	Florence Unified SD	Florence
19	1,752.0	Mohave Valley Elementary District	Mohave Valley
20	1,670.8	Osborn Elementary District	Phoenix
21	1,664.3	Tolleson Union High SD	Tolleson
22	1,580.9	Glendale Union High SD	Glendale
23	1,577.3	Nogales Unified District	Nogales
24	1,571.0	Yuma Union High SD	Yuma
25	1,431.0	Santa Cruz Valley Unified District	Rio Rico
26	1,424.2	Isaac Elementary District	Phoenix
27	1,420.0	Casa Grande Union High SD	Casa Grande
28	1,409.5	Agua Fria Union High SD	Avondale
29	1,397.2	Creighton Elementary District	Phoenix
30	1,379.5	Fowler Elementary District	Phoenix
31	1,368.0	Douglas Unified District	Douglas
32	1,365.5	Murphy Elementary District	Phoenix
33	1,270.5	Cottonwood-Oak Creek Elem Dist	Cottonwood
34	1,252.5	Wickenburg Unified District	Wickenburg
35	1,233.5	Somerton Elementary District	Somerton
36	1,183.9	Washington Elementary District	Phoenix
37	1,157.6	Litchfield Elementary District	Litchfield Park
38	1,138.7	Sierra Vista Unified District	Sierra Vista
39	1,101.0	Snowflake Unified District	Snowflake
40	1,099.3	Peoria Unified SD	Glendale
41	1,095.7	Higley Unified District	Higley
42	1,089.8	Scottsdale Unified District	Phoenix
43	1,067.6	Mesa Unified District	Mesa
44	1,065.1	Chandler Unified District	Chandler
45	1,043.4	Alhambra Elementary District	Phoenix
46	1,039.3	Gilbert Unified District	Gilbert
47	1,028.5	Parker Unified SD	Parker
48	1,011.5	Gadsden Elementary District	San Luis
49	1,001.6	Deer Valley Unified District	Phoenix
50	995.3	Coolidge Unified District	Coolidge
51	961.5	Pendergast Elementary District	Phoenix
52	938.5	Tolleson Elementary District	Tolleson
53	935.3	Paradise Valley Unified District	Phoenix
54	921.0	Liberty Elementary District	Buckeye
55	883.1	Marana Unified District	Marana
56	871.7	Glendale Elementary District	Glendale
56	871.7	Winslow Unified District	Winslow
58	865.8	Madison Elementary District	Phoenix
59	850.3	Vail Unified District	Vail
60	849.7	Fountain Hills Unified District	Fountain Hills
61	846.8	Kingman Unified SD	Kingman
62	839.2	Chinle Unified District	Chinle
63	835.1	Apache Junction Unified District	Apache Junction
64	826.7	Whiteriver Unified District	Whiteriver
65	826.0	Avondale Elementary District	Avondale
66	821.2	Sunnyside Unified District	Tucson
67	816.3	Balsz Elementary District	Phoenix
68	787.9	Tempe Elementary District	Tempe
69	772.4	Yuma Elementary District	Yuma
70	738.3	Window Rock Unified District	Fort Defiance
71	731.7	Globe Unified District	Globe
72	714.0	Safford Unified District	Safford
73	692.8	Tempe Union High SD	Tempe
74	681.0	Ganado Unified District	Ganado
75	676.3	Flagstaff Unified District	Flagstaff
76	671.5	Kyrene Elementary District	Tempe
77	643.3	Tuba City Unified District	Tuba City
78	638.9	Payson Unified District	Payson
79	635.7	Roosevelt Elementary District	Phoenix
80	626.5	Catalina Foothills Unified Dist	Tucson
81	619.3	Casa Grande Elementary District	Casa Grande
82	598.1	Tucson Unified District	Tucson
83	566.3	Laveen Elementary District	Laveen
84	559.7	Bullhead City Elementary District	Bullhead City
85	547.3	Kayenta Unified District	Kayenta
86	342.5	Amphitheater Unified District	Tucson
87	0.0	Littleton Elementary District	Cashion
87	0.0	Maricopa County Regional District	Phoenix
87	0.0	Peach Springs Unified District	Peach Springs
90	n/a	Cave Creek Unified District	Cave Creek
90	n/a	Central Ariz Valley Inst of Tech	Coolidge
90	n/a	Chinle Agency	Chinle
90	n/a	East Valley Institute of Tech	Mesa
90	n/a	Fort Defiance Agency	Fort Defiance
90	n/a	Hopi Agency	Keams Canyon
90	n/a	Western Navajo Agency	Tuba City

Student/Counselor Ratio

Rank	Ratio	District Name	City
1	11,442.0	Roosevelt Elementary District	Phoenix
2	6,537.5	Glendale Elementary District	Glendale
3	5,195.0	Madison Elementary District	Phoenix
4	3,096.0	Page Unified District	Page
5	3,000.0	Maricopa County Regional District	Phoenix
6	2,862.7	Phoenix Elementary District	Phoenix
7	2,759.0	Fowler Elementary District	Phoenix
8	2,739.3	Higley Unified District	Higley
9	2,731.0	Murphy Elementary District	Phoenix
10	2,685.3	Vail Unified District	Vail
11	2,472.5	Cartwright Elementary District	Phoenix
12	2,450.6	Washington Elementary District	Phoenix
13	2,350.4	Kyrene Elementary District	Tempe
14	1,858.0	Casa Grande Elementary District	Casa Grande
15	1,709.0	Isaac Elementary District	Phoenix
16	1,670.8	Osborn Elementary District	Phoenix
17	1,651.5	Snowflake Unified District	Snowflake
18	1,537.7	Alhambra Elementary District	Phoenix
19	1,372.2	Lake Havasu Unified District	Lk Havasu City
20	1,306.0	Bullhead City Elementary District	Bullhead City
21	1,233.5	Somerton Elementary District	Somerton
22	1,097.5	Globe Unified District	Globe
23	1,072.8	Gilbert Unified District	Gilbert
24	1,041.8	Litchfield Elementary District	Litchfield Park
25	1,032.5	Avondale Elementary District	Avondale
26	1,016.5	Colorado River Union High SD	Fort Mojave
27	1,012.1	Pendergast Elementary District	Phoenix
28	995.3	Coolidge Unified District	Coolidge
29	981.5	Florence Unified SD	Florence
30	940.9	Gadsden Elementary District	San Luis
31	925.4	Paradise Valley Unified District	Phoenix
32	888.6	Kingman Unified SD	Kingman
33	849.5	Laveen Elementary District	Laveen
34	839.1	Mesa Unified District	Mesa
35	816.3	Balsz Elementary District	Phoenix
36	774.3	Dysart Unified District	El Mirage
37	743.1	Queen Creek Unified District	Queen Creek
38	740.1	Deer Valley Unified District	Phoenix
39	723.3	Chino Valley Unified District	Chino Valley
40	721.8	Humboldt Unified District	Prescott Valley
41	720.9	Yuma Elementary District	Yuma
42	715.7	Wickenburg Unified District	Wickenburg
43	715.5	Santa Cruz Valley Unified District	Rio Rico
44	699.9	Crane Elementary District	Yuma
45	687.3	Sunnyside Unified District	Tucson
46	685.7	Parker Unified SD	Parker
47	676.1	Scottsdale Unified District	Phoenix
48	662.1	Chandler Unified District	Chandler
49	640.3	Show Low Unified District	Show Low
50	639.3	Prescott Unified District	Prescott
51	637.3	Fountain Hills Unified District	Fountain Hills
52	621.1	Sierra Vista Unified District	Sierra Vista
53	606.5	Peoria Unified SD	Glendale
54	581.1	Winslow Unified District	Winslow
55	575.0	Payson Unified District	Payson
56	562.8	Tempe Elementary District	Tempe
57	562.5	Sahuarita Unified District	Sahuarita
58	554.6	Douglas Unified District	Douglas
59	553.9	Blue Ridge Unified District	Lakeside
60	496.5	Marana Unified District	Marana
61	466.2	Chinle Unified District	Chinle
62	449.7	Apache Junction Unified District	Apache Junction
63	444.6	Glendale Union High SD	Glendale
64	421.9	Window Rock Unified District	Fort Defiance
65	421.1	Flagstaff Unified District	Flagstaff
66	420.6	Nogales Unified District	Nogales
67	418.1	Tucson Unified District	Tucson
68	416.1	Tolleson Union High SD	Tolleson
69	410.8	Catalina Foothills Unified Dist	Tucson
70	409.0	Holbrook Unified District	Holbrook
71	408.0	Safford Unified District	Safford
72	405.9	Flowing Wells Unified District	Tucson
73	405.7	Casa Grande Union High SD	Casa Grande
74	373.2	Kayenta Unified District	Kayenta
75	371.1	Yuma Union High SD	Yuma
76	368.7	Tempe Union High SD	Tempe
77	364.8	Agua Fria Union High SD	Avondale
78	354.3	Whiteriver Unified District	Whiteriver
79	319.2	Ganado Unified District	Ganado
80	281.1	Phoenix Union High SD	Phoenix
81	273.7	Tuba City Unified District	Tuba City
82	156.4	Amphitheater Unified District	Tucson
83	0.0	Cottonwood-Oak Creek Elem Dist	Cottonwood
83	0.0	Creighton Elementary District	Phoenix
83	0.0	Liberty Elementary District	Buckeye
83	0.0	Littleton Elementary District	Cashion
83	0.0	Mohave Valley Elementary District	Mohave Valley
83	0.0	Peach Springs Unified District	Peach Springs
83	0.0	Tolleson Elementary District	Tolleson
90	n/a	Cave Creek Unified District	Cave Creek
90	n/a	Central Ariz Valley Inst of Tech	Coolidge
90	n/a	Chinle Agency	Chinle
90	n/a	East Valley Institute of Tech	Mesa
90	n/a	Fort Defiance Agency	Fort Defiance
90	n/a	Hopi Agency	Keams Canyon
90	n/a	Western Navajo Agency	Tuba City

Current Spending per Student in FY2001

Rank	Dollars	District Name	City
1	9,832	Ganado Unified District	Ganado
2	8,381	Higley Unified District	Higley
3	7,836	Window Rock Unified District	Fort Defiance
4	7,440	Chinle Unified District	Chinle
5	7,408	Tuba City Unified District	Tuba City
6	7,402	Phoenix Union High SD	Phoenix
7	7,361	Kayenta Unified District	Kayenta
8	6,913	Roosevelt Elementary District	Phoenix
9	6,685	Phoenix Elementary District	Phoenix
10	6,601	Whiteriver Unified District	Whiteriver
11	6,445	Vail Unified District	Vail
12	6,361	Peach Springs Unified District	Peach Springs
13	6,186	Murphy Elementary District	Phoenix
14	6,048	Flagstaff Unified District	Flagstaff
15	6,038	Maricopa County Regional District	Phoenix
16	5,976	Agua Fria Union High SD	Avondale
17	5,936	Snowflake Unified District	Snowflake
18	5,918	Holbrook Unified District	Holbrook
19	5,898	Littleton Elementary District	Cashion
20	5,872	Page Unified District	Page
21	5,758	Tempe Elementary District	Tempe
22	5,725	Parker Unified SD	Parker
23	5,709	Tucson Unified District	Tucson
24	5,701	Madison Elementary District	Phoenix
25	5,649	Glendale Union High SD	Glendale
26	5,645	Apache Junction Unified District	Apache Junction
27	5,615	Sahuarita Unified District	Sahuarita
28	5,611	Osborn Elementary District	Phoenix
29	5,553	Blue Ridge Unified District	Lakeside
30	5,552	Yuma Union High SD	Yuma
31	5,546	Sunnyside Unified District	Tucson
32	5,522	Coolidge Unified District	Coolidge
33	5,351	Casa Grande Union High SD	Casa Grande
34	5,338	Creighton Elementary District	Phoenix
35	5,337	Cave Creek Unified District	Cave Creek
36	5,327	Wickenburg Unified District	Wickenburg
37	5,326	Tolleson Union High SD	Tolleson
38	5,311	Queen Creek Unified District	Queen Creek
39	5,264	Crane Elementary District	Yuma
40	5,237	Tempe Union High SD	Tempe
41	5,178	Payson Unified District	Payson
42	5,148	Catalina Foothills Unified Dist	Tucson
43	5,128	Scottsdale Unified District	Phoenix
44	5,112	Winslow Unified District	Winslow
45	5,056	Casa Grande Elementary District	Casa Grande
46	5,049	Cottonwood-Oak Creek Elem Dist	Cottonwood
47	5,038	Flowing Wells Unified District	Tucson
48	5,026	Tolleson Elementary District	Tolleson
49	5,015	Mesa Unified District	Mesa
50	5,006	Isaac Elementary District	Phoenix
51	5,000	Washington Elementary District	Phoenix
52	4,983	Somerton Elementary District	Somerton
53	4,976	Litchfield Elementary District	Litchfield Park
54	4,966	Dysart Unified District	El Mirage
55	4,964	Laveen Elementary District	Laveen
56	4,956	Balsz Elementary District	Phoenix
57	4,937	Humboldt Unified District	Prescott Valley
58	4,929	Safford Unified District	Safford
59	4,912	Sierra Vista Unified District	Sierra Vista
60	4,904	Yuma Elementary District	Yuma
61	4,865	Show Low Unified District	Show Low
62	4,863	Florence Unified SD	Florence
63	4,856	Mohave Valley Elementary District	Mohave Valley
64	4,828	Gadsden Elementary District	San Luis
65	4,826	Fountain Hills Unified District	Fountain Hills
66	4,790	Paradise Valley Unified District	Phoenix
67	4,789	Douglas Unified District	Douglas
68	4,783	Deer Valley Unified District	Phoenix
69	4,758	Liberty Elementary District	Buckeye
70	4,752	Gilbert Unified District	Gilbert
71	4,751	Peoria Unified SD	Glendale
72	4,740	Chandler Unified District	Chandler
73	4,739	Amphitheater Unified District	Tucson
74	4,697	Cartwright Elementary District	Phoenix
75	4,656	Prescott Unified District	Prescott
76	4,646	Lake Havasu Unified District	Lk Havasu City
77	4,645	Pendergast Elementary District	Phoenix
78	4,624	Marana Unified District	Marana
79	4,609	Santa Cruz Valley Unified District	Rio Rico
80	4,607	Kyrene Elementary District	Tempe
81	4,600	Fowler Elementary District	Phoenix
82	4,560	Glendale Elementary District	Glendale
83	4,452	Alhambra Elementary District	Phoenix
84	4,447	Avondale Elementary District	Avondale
85	4,380	Colorado River Union High SD	Fort Mojave
86	4,290	Chino Valley Unified District	Chino Valley
87	4,093	Nogales Unified District	Nogales
88	4,035	Bullhead City Elementary District	Bullhead City
89	3,999	Globe Unified District	Globe
90	n/a	Central Ariz Valley Inst of Tech	Coolidge

90	n/a	Chinle Agency	Chinle
90	n/a	East Valley Institute of Tech	Mesa
90	n/a	Fort Defiance Agency	Fort Defiance
90	n/a	Hopi Agency	Kearns Canyon
90	n/a	Kingman Unified SD	Kingman
90	n/a	Western Navajo Agency	Tuba City

Number of Diploma Recipients

Rank	Number	District Name	City
1	4,014	Mesa Unified District	Mesa
2	3,534	Phoenix Union High SD	Phoenix
3	3,309	Tucson Unified District	Tucson
4	2,678	Tempe Union High SD	Tempe
5	2,609	Glendale Union High SD	Glendale
6	2,136	Paradise Valley Unified District	Phoenix
7	1,990	Peoria Unified SD	Glendale
8	1,817	Gilbert Unified District	Gilbert
9	1,708	Scottsdale Unified District	Phoenix
10	1,389	Yuma Union High SD	Yuma
11	1,320	Deer Valley Unified District	Phoenix
12	1,021	Chandler Unified District	Chandler
13	947	Amphitheater Unified District	Tucson
14	742	Tolleson Union High SD	Tolleson
15	741	Flagstaff Unified District	Flagstaff
16	683	Marana Unified District	Marana
17	580	Sunnyside Unified District	Tucson
18	572	Sierra Vista Unified District	Sierra Vista
19	442	Kingman Unified SD	Kingman
20	431	Catalina Foothills Unified Dist	Tucson
21	425	Agua Fria Union High SD	Avondale
22	387	Casa Grande Union High SD	Casa Grande
23	363	Flowing Wells Unified District	Tucson
24	353	Nogales Unified District	Nogales
25	326	Prescott Unified District	Prescott
26	320	Colorado River Union High SD	Fort Mojave
27	316	Lake Havasu Unified District	Lk Havasu City
28	281	Humboldt Unified District	Prescott Valley
29	242	Apache Junction Unified District	Apache Junction
30	226	Douglas Unified District	Douglas
31	222	Chinle Unified District	Chinle
32	198	Cave Creek Unified District	Cave Creek
32	198	Show Low Unified District	Show Low
34	189	Dysart Unified District	El Mirage
35	188	Kayenta Unified District	Kayenta
36	176	Fountain Hills Unified District	Fountain Hills
37	168	Page Unified District	Page
38	162	Safford Unified District	Safford
39	157	Payson Unified District	Payson
40	149	Tuba City Unified District	Tuba City
41	148	Winslow Unified District	Winslow
42	145	Blue Ridge Unified District	Lakeside
43	144	Chino Valley Unified District	Chino Valley
44	139	Holbrook Unified District	Holbrook
44	139	Maricopa County Regional District	Phoenix
44	139	Snowflake Unified District	Snowflake
47	138	Coolidge Unified District	Coolidge
48	133	Ganado Unified District	Ganado
49	129	Higley Unified District	Higley
50	128	Window Rock Unified District	Fort Defiance
51	121	Sahuarita Unified District	Sahuarita
52	116	Parker Unified SD	Parker
52	116	Whiteriver Unified District	Whiteriver
54	105	Globe Unified District	Globe
55	101	Santa Cruz Valley Unified District	Rio Rico
56	89	Wickenburg Unified District	Wickenburg
57	84	Queen Creek Unified District	Queen Creek
58	78	Florence Unified SD	Florence
59	58	Vail Unified District	Vail
60	47	Peach Springs Unified District	Peach Springs
61	0	Central Ariz Valley Inst of Tech	Coolidge
61	0	Creighton Elementary District	Phoenix
61	0	East Valley Institute of Tech	Mesa
61	0	Glendale Elementary District	Glendale
61	0	Madison Elementary District	Phoenix
61	0	Tempe Elementary District	Tempe
67	n/a	Alhambra Elementary District	Phoenix
67	n/a	Avondale Elementary District	Avondale
67	n/a	Balsz Elementary District	Phoenix
67	n/a	Bullhead City Elementary District	Bullhead City
67	n/a	Cartwright Elementary District	Phoenix
67	n/a	Casa Grande Elementary District	Casa Grande
67	n/a	Chinle Agency	Chinle
67	n/a	Cottonwood-Oak Creek Elem Dist	Cottonwood
67	n/a	Crane Elementary District	Yuma
67	n/a	Fort Defiance Agency	Fort Defiance
67	n/a	Fowler Elementary District	Phoenix
67	n/a	Gadsden Elementary District	San Luis
67	n/a	Hopi Agency	Kearns Canyon
67	n/a	Isaac Elementary District	Phoenix
67	n/a	Kyrene Elementary District	Tempe
67	n/a	Laveen Elementary District	Laveen
67	n/a	Liberty Elementary District	Buckeye
67	n/a	Litchfield Elementary District	Litchfield Park
67	n/a	Littleton Elementary District	Cashion
67	n/a	Mohave Valley Elementary District	Mohave Valley
67	n/a	Murphy Elementary District	Phoenix
67	n/a	Osborn Elementary District	Phoenix
67	n/a	Pendergast Elementary District	Phoenix
67	n/a	Phoenix Elementary District	Phoenix
67	n/a	Roosevelt Elementary District	Phoenix
67	n/a	Somerton Elementary District	Somerton
67	n/a	Tolleson Elementary District	Tolleson
67	n/a	Washington Elementary District	Phoenix
67	n/a	Western Navajo Agency	Tuba City
67	n/a	Yuma Elementary District	Yuma

High School Drop-out Rate

Rank	Percent	District Name	City
1	50.6	Maricopa County Regional District	Phoenix
2	44.1	Peach Springs Unified District	Peach Springs
3	29.3	Whiteriver Unified District	Whiteriver
4	26.2	Dysart Unified District	El Mirage
5	19.2	Colorado River Union High SD	Fort Mojave
6	17.5	Tuba City Unified District	Tuba City
7	17.0	Sunnyside Unified District	Tucson
8	16.8	Page Unified District	Page
9	16.7	Parker Unified SD	Parker
10	14.9	Santa Cruz Valley Unified District	Rio Rico
11	13.6	Coolidge Unified District	Coolidge
11	13.6	Higley Unified District	Higley
13	12.5	Phoenix Union High SD	Phoenix
14	11.6	Holbrook Unified District	Holbrook
15	11.4	Wickenburg Unified District	Wickenburg
16	11.0	Winslow Unified District	Winslow
17	10.8	Tolleson Union High SD	Tolleson
18	10.7	Payson Unified District	Payson
19	9.3	Douglas Unified District	Douglas
20	9.1	Blue Ridge Unified District	Lakeside
21	8.9	Flowing Wells Unified District	Tucson
22	8.3	Snowflake Unified District	Snowflake
23	8.1	Globe Unified District	Globe
24	8.0	Nogales Unified District	Nogales
25	7.4	Sierra Vista Unified District	Sierra Vista
26	7.0	Kayenta Unified District	Kayenta
26	7.0	Window Rock Unified District	Fort Defiance
28	6.9	Florence Unified SD	Florence
28	6.9	Yuma Union High SD	Yuma
30	6.8	Queen Creek Unified District	Queen Creek
31	6.7	Flagstaff Unified District	Flagstaff
32	6.3	Humboldt Unified District	Prescott Valley
32	6.3	Lake Havasu Unified District	Lk Havasu City
34	6.1	Tucson Unified District	Tucson
35	5.9	Glendale Union High SD	Glendale
36	5.7	Sahuarita Unified District	Sahuarita
37	5.5	Chino Valley Unified District	Chino Valley
38	5.3	Fountain Hills Unified District	Fountain Hills
38	5.3	Prescott Unified District	Prescott
40	5.1	Peoria Unified SD	Glendale
40	5.1	Safford Unified District	Safford
42	5.0	Deer Valley Unified District	Phoenix
42	5.0	Marana Unified District	Marana
44	4.9	Show Low Unified District	Show Low
45	4.7	Vail Unified District	Vail
46	4.6	Paradise Valley Unified District	Phoenix
47	4.4	Agua Fria Union High SD	Avondale
48	4.2	Tempe Union High SD	Tempe
49	4.1	Amphitheater Unified District	Tucson
49	4.1	Mesa Unified District	Mesa
51	4.0	Apache Junction Unified District	Apache Junction
52	3.1	Chandler Unified District	Chandler
53	3.0	Ganado Unified District	Ganado
54	2.9	Cave Creek Unified District	Cave Creek
55	2.5	Gilbert Unified District	Gilbert
56	2.0	Chinle Unified District	Chinle
57	1.6	Scottsdale Unified District	Phoenix
58	1.3	Catalina Foothills Unified Dist	Tucson
59	n/a	Alhambra Elementary District	Phoenix
59	n/a	Avondale Elementary District	Avondale
59	n/a	Balsz Elementary District	Phoenix
59	n/a	Bullhead City Elementary District	Bullhead City
59	n/a	Cartwright Elementary District	Phoenix
59	n/a	Casa Grande Elementary District	Casa Grande
59	n/a	Casa Grande Union High SD	Casa Grande
59	n/a	Central Ariz Valley Inst of Tech	Coolidge
59	n/a	Chinle Agency	Chinle
59	n/a	Cottonwood-Oak Creek Elem Dist	Cottonwood
59	n/a	Crane Elementary District	Yuma
59	n/a	Creighton Elementary District	Phoenix
59	n/a	East Valley Institute of Tech	Mesa
59	n/a	Fort Defiance Agency	Fort Defiance
59	n/a	Fowler Elementary District	Phoenix
59	n/a	Gadsden Elementary District	San Luis
59	n/a	Glendale Elementary District	Glendale
59	n/a	Hopi Agency	Kearns Canyon
59	n/a	Isaac Elementary District	Phoenix
59	n/a	Kingman Unified SD	Kingman
59	n/a	Kyrene Elementary District	Tempe
59	n/a	Laveen Elementary District	Laveen
59	n/a	Liberty Elementary District	Buckeye
59	n/a	Litchfield Elementary District	Litchfield Park
59	n/a	Littleton Elementary District	Cashion
59	n/a	Madison Elementary District	Phoenix
59	n/a	Mohave Valley Elementary District	Mohave Valley
59	n/a	Murphy Elementary District	Phoenix
59	n/a	Osborn Elementary District	Phoenix
59	n/a	Pendergast Elementary District	Phoenix
59	n/a	Phoenix Elementary District	Phoenix
59	n/a	Roosevelt Elementary District	Phoenix
59	n/a	Somerton Elementary District	Somerton
59	n/a	Tempe Elementary District	Tempe
59	n/a	Tolleson Elementary District	Tolleson
59	n/a	Washington Elementary District	Phoenix
59	n/a	Western Navajo Agency	Tuba City
59	n/a	Yuma Elementary District	Yuma

Arkansas

Arkansas Public School Educational Profile

Category	Value	Category	Value
Schools *(2002-2003)*	1,150	**Diploma Recipients** *(2002-2003)*	26,984
Instructional Level		White, Non-Hispanic	20,138
Primary	571	Black, Non-Hispanic	5,779
Middle	199	Asian/Pacific Islander	323
High	345	American Indian/Alaskan Native	118
Other Level	35	Hispanic	626
Curriculum		**High School Drop-out Rate** (%) *(2000-2001)*	5.3
Regular	1,122	White, Non-Hispanic	4.8
Special Education	4	Black, Non-Hispanic	6.5
Vocational	19	Asian/Pacific Islander	3.7
Alternative	5	American Indian/Alaskan Native	7.5
Type		Hispanic	8.6
Magnet	7	**Staff** *(2002-2003)*	63,815.0
Charter	7	Teachers	30,330.0
Title I Eligible	814	Average Salary ($)	37,536
School-wide Title I	432	Librarians/Media Specialists	1,012.0
Students *(2002-2003)*	450,985	Guidance Counselors	1,436.0
Gender (%)		**Ratios** *(2002-2003)*	
Male	51.3	Student/Teacher Ratio	14.9 to 1
Female	48.7	Student/Librarian Ratio	445.6 to 1
Race/Ethnicity (%)		Student/Counselor Ratio	314.1 to 1
White, Non-Hispanic	70.5	**Current Spending** *($ per student in FY 2001)*	6,276
Black, Non-Hispanic	23.2	Instruction	3,867
Asian/Pacific Islander	1.0	Support Services	2,088
American Indian/Alaskan Native	0.5	**College Entrance Exam Scores** *(2003)*	
Hispanic	4.8	Scholastic Aptitude Test (SAT)	
Classification (%)		Participation Rate (%)	6
Individual Education Program (IEP)	12.7	Mean SAT I Verbal Score	564
Migrant	2.0	Mean SAT I Math Score	554
English Language Learner (ELL)	3.4	American College Testing Program (ACT)	
Eligible for Free Lunch Program	39.6	Participation Rate (%)	73
Eligible for Reduced-Price Lunch Program	8.8	Average Composite Score	20.3

Note: *For an explanation of data, please refer to the User's Guide in the front of the book; n/a indicates data not available*

Arkansas NAEP 2003 Test Scores

Reading			Mathematics		
Grade/Category	**Value**	**Rank**	**Grade/Category**	**Value**	**Rank**
4th Grade			**4th Grade**		
Average Proficiency	213.6 (1.4)	38/51	Average Proficiency	229.0 (0.9)	40/51
Proficiency by Gender/Race/Ethnicity			Proficiency by Gender/Race/Ethnicity		
Male	208.8 (1.8)	40/51	Male	228.4 (1.2)	44/51
Female	218.4 (1.4)	37/51	Female	229.6 (1.0)	37/51
White, Non-Hispanic	222.6 (1.3)	40/51	White, Non-Hispanic	237.2 (0.8)	43/51
Black, Non-Hispanic	189.8 (2.3)	37/42	Black, Non-Hispanic	206.1 (1.4)	41/42
Asian, Non-Hispanic	*203.8 (4.1)*	23/41	Asian, Non-Hispanic	220.9 (3.0)	24/43
American Indian, Non-Hispanic	n/a	n/a	American Indian, Non-Hispanic	n/a	n/a
Hispanic	n/a	n/a	Hispanic	n/a	n/a
Proficiency by Class Size			Proficiency by Class Size		
Less than 16 Students	*198.8 (8.9)*	30/45	Less than 16 Students	*218.1 (4.7)*	34/47
16 to 18 Students	206.9 (4.6)	37/48	16 to 18 Students	224.3 (4.1)	37/48
19 to 20 Students	217.1 (2.7)	31/50	19 to 20 Students	227.9 (2.6)	41/50
21 to 25 Students	213.9 (2.0)	41/51	21 to 25 Students	230.3 (1.7)	41/51
Greater than 25 Students	*222.4 (4.3)*	15/49	Greater than 25 Students	*237.2 (2.5)*	19/49
Percent Attaining Achievement Levels			Percent Attaining Achievement Levels		
Below Basic	40.4 (1.7)	15/51	Below Basic	28.8 (1.3)	11/51
Basic or Above	59.6 (1.7)	37/51	Basic or Above	71.2 (1.3)	41/51
Proficient or Above	28.1 (1.5)	36/51	Proficient or Above	26.2 (1.1)	38/51
Advanced or Above	6.2 (0.7)	34/51	Advanced or Above	2.3 (0.4)	39/51
8th Grade			**8th Grade**		
Average Proficiency	258.0 (1.3)	39/51	Average Proficiency	265.8 (1.2)	46/51
Proficiency by Gender/Race/Ethnicity			Proficiency by Gender/Race/Ethnicity		
Male	253.5 (1.3)	36/51	Male	264.9 (1.5)	47/51
Female	262.6 (1.7)	42/51	Female	266.8 (1.4)	44/51
White, Non-Hispanic	265.6 (1.2)	44/50	White, Non-Hispanic	275.3 (1.1)	46/50
Black, Non-Hispanic	232.3 (2.1)	41/41	Black, Non-Hispanic	239.5 (2.1)	41/41
Asian, Non-Hispanic	256.8 (4.8)	4/37	Asian, Non-Hispanic	*248.5 (5.5)*	35/37
American Indian, Non-Hispanic	n/a	n/a	American Indian, Non-Hispanic	n/a	n/a
Hispanic	n/a	n/a	Hispanic	n/a	n/a
Proficiency by Parents Highest Level of Ed.			Proficiency by Parents Highest Level of Ed.		
Did Not Finish High School	247.5 (3.3)	18/50	Did Not Finish High School	252.7 (3.1)	42/50
Graduated High School	250.5 (2.0)	38/50	Graduated High School	259.2 (1.8)	42/50
Some Education After High School	265.8 (1.8)	30/50	Some Education After High School	275.1 (1.8)	40/50
Graduated College	266.7 (1.6)	38/50	Graduated College	273.7 (2.1)	45/50
Percent Attaining Achievement Levels			Percent Attaining Achievement Levels		
Below Basic	29.9 (1.4)	15/51	Below Basic	42.1 (1.6)	8/51
Basic or Above	70.1 (1.4)	37/51	Basic or Above	57.9 (1.6)	44/51
Proficient or Above	26.8 (1.4)	35/51	Proficient or Above	18.6 (1.2)	45/51
Advanced or Above	1.9 (0.4)	38/51	Advanced or Above	2.2 (0.4)	44/51

***Note:** For an explanation of data, please refer to the User's Guide in the front of the book; values in italics indicate that the nature of the sample does not allow accurate determination of the variability of the statistic; n/a indicates data not available*

Arkansas County

Stuttgart SD

2501 S Main • Stuttgart, AR 72160-0928
(870) 673-3561 • http://sps.k12.ar.us/
Grade Span: KG-12; **Agency Type:** 1
Schools: 6
2 Primary; 2 Middle; 1 High; 1 Other Level
6 Regular; 0 Special Education; 0 Vocational; 0 Alternative
0 Magnet; 0 Charter; 5 Title I Eligible; 4 School-wide Title I
Students: 1,868 (51.6% male; 48.4% female)
Individual Education Program: 184 (9.9%);
English Language Learner: 11 (0.6%); Migrant: 22 (1.2%)
Eligible for Free Lunch Program: 942 (50.4%)
Eligible for Reduced-Price Lunch Program: 160 (8.6%)
Teachers: 133.0 (14.0 to 1)
Librarians/Media Specialists: 6.0 (311.3 to 1)
Guidance Counselors: 6.0 (311.3 to 1)
Current Spending: ($ per student per year):
Total: $5,245; Instruction: $3,153; Support Services: $1,756
Enrollment, Drop-out Rates and Diploma Recipients by Race/Ethnicity

Category	Total	White	Black	Asian	AIAN	Hisp.
Enrollment (%)	100.0	50.5	48.7	0.3	0.0	0.5
Drop-out Rate (%)	10.0	5.0	17.4	0.0	n/a	0.0
H.S. Diplomas (#)	134	86	46	0	0	2

Ashley County

Crossett SD

219 Main • Crossett, AR 71635-3323
(870) 364-3112 • http://csd1.sesc.k12.ar.us/
Grade Span: PK-12; **Agency Type:** 1
Schools: 7
3 Primary; 2 Middle; 2 High; 0 Other Level
6 Regular; 0 Special Education; 0 Vocational; 1 Alternative
0 Magnet; 0 Charter; 4 Title I Eligible; 0 School-wide Title I
Students: 2,445 (49.6% male; 50.4% female)
Individual Education Program: 216 (8.8%);
English Language Learner: 29 (1.2%); Migrant: 1 (<0.1%)
Eligible for Free Lunch Program: 911 (37.3%)
Eligible for Reduced-Price Lunch Program: 153 (6.3%)
Teachers: 160.0 (15.3 to 1)
Librarians/Media Specialists: 6.0 (407.5 to 1)
Guidance Counselors: 7.0 (349.3 to 1)
Current Spending: ($ per student per year):
Total: $5,414; Instruction: $3,270; Support Services: $1,832
Enrollment, Drop-out Rates and Diploma Recipients by Race/Ethnicity

Category	Total	White	Black	Asian	AIAN	Hisp.
Enrollment (%)	100.0	61.8	36.9	0.2	0.0	1.0
Drop-out Rate (%)	4.8	3.9	6.5	n/a	0.0	0.0
H.S. Diplomas (#)	126	88	37	0	1	0

Hamburg SD

521 E Lincoln • Hamburg, AR 71646-3303
(870) 853-9851 • http://se.sesc.k12.ar.us/hamburg/
Grade Span: PK-12; **Agency Type:** 1
Schools: 6
3 Primary; 2 Middle; 1 High; 0 Other Level
6 Regular; 0 Special Education; 0 Vocational; 0 Alternative
0 Magnet; 0 Charter; 4 Title I Eligible; 4 School-wide Title I
Students: 1,614 (49.9% male; 50.1% female)
Individual Education Program: 197 (12.2%);
English Language Learner: 97 (6.0%); Migrant: 45 (2.8%)
Eligible for Free Lunch Program: 1,124 (69.6%)
Eligible for Reduced-Price Lunch Program: 38 (2.4%)
Teachers: 113.0 (14.3 to 1)
Librarians/Media Specialists: 5.0 (322.8 to 1)
Guidance Counselors: 5.0 (322.8 to 1)
Current Spending: ($ per student per year):
Total: $6,110; Instruction: $3,753; Support Services: $1,892
Enrollment, Drop-out Rates and Diploma Recipients by Race/Ethnicity

Category	Total	White	Black	Asian	AIAN	Hisp.
Enrollment (%)	100.0	55.5	37.1	0.1	0.0	7.4
Drop-out Rate (%)	5.9	4.8	6.4	n/a	n/a	13.0
H.S. Diplomas (#)	116	65	47	0	0	4

Baxter County

Mountain Home SD

1230 S Maple • Mountain Home, AR 72653-4840
(870) 425-1201 • http://bombers.k12.ar.us/
Grade Span: KG-12; **Agency Type:** 1
Schools: 6
2 Primary; 2 Middle; 1 High; 1 Other Level
6 Regular; 0 Special Education; 0 Vocational; 0 Alternative
0 Magnet; 0 Charter; 6 Title I Eligible; 5 School-wide Title I
Students: 3,786 (52.0% male; 48.0% female)
Individual Education Program: 456 (12.0%);
English Language Learner: 10 (0.3%); Migrant: 0 (0.0%)
Eligible for Free Lunch Program: 1,100 (29.1%)
Eligible for Reduced-Price Lunch Program: 308 (8.1%)
Teachers: 223.0 (17.0 to 1)
Librarians/Media Specialists: 6.0 (631.0 to 1)
Guidance Counselors: 9.0 (420.7 to 1)
Current Spending: ($ per student per year):
Total: $5,307; Instruction: $3,412; Support Services: $1,640
Enrollment, Drop-out Rates and Diploma Recipients by Race/Ethnicity

Category	Total	White	Black	Asian	AIAN	Hisp.
Enrollment (%)	100.0	98.1	0.1	0.7	0.5	0.6
Drop-out Rate (%)	4.3	4.4	0.0	0.0	0.0	0.0
H.S. Diplomas (#)	240	240	0	0	0	0

Benton County

Bentonville SD

400 NW Second St • Bentonville, AR 72712-5238
(479) 254-5000 • http://www.bentonville.k12.ar.us/bps/scripts/home.asp
Grade Span: KG-12; **Agency Type:** 1
Schools: 10
5 Primary; 4 Middle; 1 High; 0 Other Level
10 Regular; 0 Special Education; 0 Vocational; 0 Alternative
0 Magnet; 0 Charter; 5 Title I Eligible; 1 School-wide Title I
Students: 7,721 (51.0% male; 49.0% female)
Individual Education Program: 860 (11.1%);
English Language Learner: 196 (2.5%); Migrant: 138 (1.8%)
Eligible for Free Lunch Program: 1,295 (16.8%)
Eligible for Reduced-Price Lunch Program: 595 (7.7%)
Teachers: 483.0 (16.0 to 1)
Librarians/Media Specialists: 10.0 (772.1 to 1)
Guidance Counselors: 17.0 (454.2 to 1)
Current Spending: ($ per student per year):
Total: $5,627; Instruction: $3,386; Support Services: $1,922
Enrollment, Drop-out Rates and Diploma Recipients by Race/Ethnicity

Category	Total	White	Black	Asian	AIAN	Hisp.
Enrollment (%)	100.0	89.5	1.3	2.0	1.1	6.1
Drop-out Rate (%)	6.8	6.1	5.9	8.6	40.0	16.7
H.S. Diplomas (#)	392	367	3	6	2	14

Rogers SD

212 S Third St • Rogers, AR 72756-4547
(501) 636-3910 • http://icu.nwsc.k12.ar.us/
Grade Span: PK-12; **Agency Type:** 1
Schools: 18
12 Primary; 2 Middle; 1 High; 3 Other Level
18 Regular; 0 Special Education; 0 Vocational; 0 Alternative
0 Magnet; 0 Charter; 8 Title I Eligible; 5 School-wide Title I
Students: 11,853 (51.3% male; 48.7% female)
Individual Education Program: 1,454 (12.3%);
English Language Learner: 2,449 (20.7%); Migrant: 1,023 (8.6%)
Eligible for Free Lunch Program: 3,733 (31.5%)
Eligible for Reduced-Price Lunch Program: 1,173 (9.9%)
Teachers: 687.0 (17.3 to 1)
Librarians/Media Specialists: 18.0 (658.5 to 1)
Guidance Counselors: 29.0 (408.7 to 1)
Current Spending: ($ per student per year):
Total: $5,220; Instruction: $3,376; Support Services: $1,556
Enrollment, Drop-out Rates and Diploma Recipients by Race/Ethnicity

Category	Total	White	Black	Asian	AIAN	Hisp.
Enrollment (%)	100.0	70.8	0.6	1.4	0.5	26.8
Drop-out Rate (%)	3.6	2.8	0.0	1.9	10.5	6.9
H.S. Diplomas (#)	596	487	3	16	3	87

Siloam Springs SD

847 S Dogwood • Siloam Springs, AR 72761-0798
Mailing Address: PO Box 798 • Siloam Springs, AR 72761-0798
(479) 524-3191 • http://pride.nwsc.k12.ar.us/index.html
Grade Span: KG-12; **Agency Type:** 1
Schools: 5
2 Primary; 2 Middle; 1 High; 0 Other Level
5 Regular; 0 Special Education; 0 Vocational; 0 Alternative
0 Magnet; 0 Charter; 5 Title I Eligible; 0 School-wide Title I
Students: 2,972 (52.0% male; 48.0% female)
Individual Education Program: 230 (7.7%);
English Language Learner: 264 (8.9%); Migrant: 202 (6.8%)
Eligible for Free Lunch Program: 842 (28.3%)
Eligible for Reduced-Price Lunch Program: 379 (12.8%)
Teachers: 184.0 (16.2 to 1)
Librarians/Media Specialists: 5.0 (594.4 to 1)
Guidance Counselors: 7.0 (424.6 to 1)
Current Spending: ($ per student per year):
Total: $5,713; Instruction: $3,648; Support Services: $1,782

Enrollment, Drop-out Rates and Diploma Recipients by Race/Ethnicity

Category	Total	White	Black	Asian	AIAN	Hisp.
Enrollment (%)	100.0	76.5	0.2	0.9	6.0	16.3
Drop-out Rate (%)	1.4	1.2	0.0	0.0	0.0	3.5
H.S. Diplomas (#)	222	191	0	3	6	22

Boone County

Harrison SD

400 S Sycamore St • Harrison, AR 72601-5293
(870) 741-7600 • http://taurus.oursc.k12.ar.us/
Grade Span: KG-12; **Agency Type:** 1
Schools: 7
4 Primary; 1 Middle; 2 High; 0 Other Level
7 Regular; 0 Special Education; 0 Vocational; 0 Alternative
0 Magnet; 0 Charter; 4 Title I Eligible; 1 School-wide Title I
Students: 2,796 (51.6% male; 48.4% female)
Individual Education Program: 303 (10.8%);
English Language Learner: 2 (0.1%); Migrant: 0 (0.0%)
Eligible for Free Lunch Program: 790 (28.3%)
Eligible for Reduced-Price Lunch Program: 250 (8.9%)
Teachers: 174.0 (16.1 to 1)
Librarians/Media Specialists: 7.0 (399.4 to 1)
Guidance Counselors: 9.0 (310.7 to 1)
Current Spending: ($ per student per year):
Total: $5,137; Instruction: $3,123; Support Services: $1,688
Enrollment, Drop-out Rates and Diploma Recipients by Race/Ethnicity

Category	Total	White	Black	Asian	AIAN	Hisp.
Enrollment (%)	100.0	98.1	0.0	0.3	0.5	1.0
Drop-out Rate (%)	4.0	4.0	n/a	0.0	0.0	0.0
H.S. Diplomas (#)	194	190	2	2	0	0

Bradley County

Warren SD

803 N Walnut • Warren, AR 71671-2008
Mailing Address: PO Box 1210 • Warren, AR 71671-2008
(870) 226-6738 • http://zebra.wsc.k12.ar.us/~wbulldog/
Grade Span: KG-12; **Agency Type:** 1
Schools: 5
1 Primary; 2 Middle; 2 High; 0 Other Level
4 Regular; 0 Special Education; 1 Vocational; 0 Alternative
0 Magnet; 0 Charter; 3 Title I Eligible; 3 School-wide Title I
Students: 1,571 (51.4% male; 48.6% female)
Individual Education Program: 157 (10.0%);
English Language Learner: 54 (3.4%); Migrant: 85 (5.4%)
Eligible for Free Lunch Program: 791 (50.4%)
Eligible for Reduced-Price Lunch Program: 169 (10.8%)
Teachers: 111.0 (14.2 to 1)
Librarians/Media Specialists: 4.0 (392.8 to 1)
Guidance Counselors: 5.0 (314.2 to 1)
Current Spending: ($ per student per year):
Total: $6,033; Instruction: $3,826; Support Services: $1,882
Enrollment, Drop-out Rates and Diploma Recipients by Race/Ethnicity

Category	Total	White	Black	Asian	AIAN	Hisp.
Enrollment (%)	100.0	49.4	42.1	0.1	0.1	8.3
Drop-out Rate (%)	3.6	3.0	4.3	n/a	0.0	4.8
H.S. Diplomas (#)	102	57	39	0	0	6

Carroll County

Berryville SD

PO Box 408 • Berryville, AR 72616-0408
(870) 423-7065 • http://bobcat.oursc.k12.ar.us/
Grade Span: KG-12; **Agency Type:** 1
Schools: 3
1 Primary; 1 Middle; 1 High; 0 Other Level
3 Regular; 0 Special Education; 0 Vocational; 0 Alternative
0 Magnet; 0 Charter; 2 Title I Eligible; 0 School-wide Title I
Students: 1,692 (51.7% male; 48.3% female)
Individual Education Program: 182 (10.8%);
English Language Learner: 199 (11.8%); Migrant: 177 (10.5%)
Eligible for Free Lunch Program: 601 (35.5%)
Eligible for Reduced-Price Lunch Program: 180 (10.6%)
Teachers: 111.0 (15.2 to 1)
Librarians/Media Specialists: 3.0 (564.0 to 1)
Guidance Counselors: 4.0 (423.0 to 1)
Current Spending: ($ per student per year):
Total: $5,289; Instruction: $3,267; Support Services: $1,747
Enrollment, Drop-out Rates and Diploma Recipients by Race/Ethnicity

Category	Total	White	Black	Asian	AIAN	Hisp.
Enrollment (%)	100.0	81.7	0.1	0.2	0.4	17.7
Drop-out Rate (%)	3.0	3.1	n/a	n/a	33.3	0.0
H.S. Diplomas (#)	100	93	0	0	0	7

Clark County

Arkadelphia SD

234 N 11th • Arkadelphia, AR 71923-4903
(870) 246-5564 • http://apsd.k12.ar.us/
Grade Span: PK-12; **Agency Type:** 1
Schools: 5
2 Primary; 2 Middle; 1 High; 0 Other Level
5 Regular; 0 Special Education; 0 Vocational; 0 Alternative
0 Magnet; 0 Charter; 4 Title I Eligible; 3 School-wide Title I
Students: 2,276 (51.4% male; 48.6% female)
Individual Education Program: 306 (13.4%);
English Language Learner: 0 (0.0%); Migrant: 0 (0.0%)
Eligible for Free Lunch Program: 792 (34.8%)
Eligible for Reduced-Price Lunch Program: 202 (8.9%)
Teachers: 150.0 (15.2 to 1)
Librarians/Media Specialists: 5.0 (455.2 to 1)
Guidance Counselors: 8.0 (284.5 to 1)
Current Spending: ($ per student per year):
Total: $6,139; Instruction: $3,885; Support Services: $1,985
Enrollment, Drop-out Rates and Diploma Recipients by Race/Ethnicity

Category	Total	White	Black	Asian	AIAN	Hisp.
Enrollment (%)	100.0	59.8	35.6	1.1	0.1	3.3
Drop-out Rate (%)	2.8	3.1	2.2	0.0	0.0	7.7
H.S. Diplomas (#)	164	99	59	3	0	3

Cleburne County

Heber Springs SD

800 W Moore • Heber Springs, AR 72543-2402
(501) 362-6712 • http://hssdweb.afsc.k12.ar.us/
Grade Span: KG-12; **Agency Type:** 1
Schools: 3
1 Primary; 1 Middle; 1 High; 0 Other Level
3 Regular; 0 Special Education; 0 Vocational; 0 Alternative
0 Magnet; 0 Charter; 3 Title I Eligible; 3 School-wide Title I
Students: 1,696 (50.9% male; 49.1% female)
Individual Education Program: 290 (17.1%);
English Language Learner: 11 (0.6%); Migrant: 0 (0.0%)
Eligible for Free Lunch Program: 541 (31.9%)
Eligible for Reduced-Price Lunch Program: 144 (8.5%)
Teachers: 120.0 (14.1 to 1)
Librarians/Media Specialists: 3.0 (565.3 to 1)
Guidance Counselors: 5.0 (339.2 to 1)
Current Spending: ($ per student per year):
Total: $5,691; Instruction: $3,662; Support Services: $1,701
Enrollment, Drop-out Rates and Diploma Recipients by Race/Ethnicity

Category	Total	White	Black	Asian	AIAN	Hisp.
Enrollment (%)	100.0	97.9	0.3	0.5	0.2	1.1
Drop-out Rate (%)	6.8	6.5	n/a	33.3	n/a	0.0
H.S. Diplomas (#)	95	94	0	1	0	0

Columbia County

Magnolia SD

1400 High School Dr • Magnolia, AR 71754-0649
Mailing Address: PO Box 649 • Magnolia, AR 71754-0649
(870) 234-4933
Grade Span: KG-12; **Agency Type:** 1
Schools: 4
1 Primary; 2 Middle; 1 High; 0 Other Level
4 Regular; 0 Special Education; 0 Vocational; 0 Alternative
0 Magnet; 0 Charter; 4 Title I Eligible; 0 School-wide Title I
Students: 2,771 (50.3% male; 49.7% female)
Individual Education Program: 252 (9.1%);
English Language Learner: 17 (0.6%); Migrant: 5 (0.2%)
Eligible for Free Lunch Program: 1,156 (41.7%)
Eligible for Reduced-Price Lunch Program: 180 (6.5%)
Teachers: 174.0 (15.9 to 1)
Librarians/Media Specialists: 4.0 (692.8 to 1)
Guidance Counselors: 8.0 (346.4 to 1)
Current Spending: ($ per student per year):
Total: $5,068; Instruction: $3,162; Support Services: $1,659
Enrollment, Drop-out Rates and Diploma Recipients by Race/Ethnicity

Category	Total	White	Black	Asian	AIAN	Hisp.
Enrollment (%)	100.0	53.4	45.1	0.4	0.1	1.0
Drop-out Rate (%)	4.5	2.8	7.1	0.0	n/a	20.0
H.S. Diplomas (#)	209	143	66	0	0	0

Conway County

South Conway County SD

704 E Church St • Morrilton, AR 72110-3559
(501) 354-9400 • http://mdd.k12.ar.us/
Grade Span: KG-12; **Agency Type:** 1
Schools: 6
3 Primary; 1 Middle; 2 High; 0 Other Level
5 Regular; 0 Special Education; 1 Vocational; 0 Alternative
0 Magnet; 0 Charter; 4 Title I Eligible; 3 School-wide Title I
Students: 2,406 (49.9% male; 50.1% female)
Individual Education Program: 347 (14.4%);
English Language Learner: 41 (1.7%); Migrant: 0 (0.0%)
Eligible for Free Lunch Program: 1,119 (46.5%)
Eligible for Reduced-Price Lunch Program: 234 (9.7%)
Teachers: 166.0 (14.5 to 1)
Librarians/Media Specialists: 6.0 (401.0 to 1)
Guidance Counselors: 8.0 (300.8 to 1)
Current Spending: ($ per student per year):
Total: $5,638; Instruction: $3,430; Support Services: $1,885
Enrollment, Drop-out Rates and Diploma Recipients by Race/Ethnicity

Category	Total	White	Black	Asian	AIAN	Hisp.
Enrollment (%)	100.0	69.9	25.4	0.7	0.4	3.6
Drop-out Rate (%)	3.9	3.0	6.4	0.0	0.0	6.3
H.S. Diplomas (#)	166	121	44	0	0	1

Craighead County

Jonesboro SD

1307 Flint St • Jonesboro, AR 72401-3968
(870) 933-5800 • http://www.jps.k12.ar.us/
Grade Span: KG-12; **Agency Type:** 1
Schools: 10
5 Primary; 3 Middle; 2 High; 0 Other Level
9 Regular; 0 Special Education; 1 Vocational; 0 Alternative
0 Magnet; 0 Charter; 6 Title I Eligible; 2 School-wide Title I
Students: 4,753 (50.0% male; 50.0% female)
Individual Education Program: 515 (10.8%);
English Language Learner: 114 (2.4%); Migrant: 93 (2.0%)
Eligible for Free Lunch Program: 2,094 (44.1%)
Eligible for Reduced-Price Lunch Program: 300 (6.3%)
Teachers: 271.0 (17.5 to 1)
Librarians/Media Specialists: 9.0 (528.1 to 1)
Guidance Counselors: 14.0 (339.5 to 1)
Current Spending: ($ per student per year):
Total: $5,612; Instruction: $3,348; Support Services: $1,929
Enrollment, Drop-out Rates and Diploma Recipients by Race/Ethnicity

Category	Total	White	Black	Asian	AIAN	Hisp.
Enrollment (%)	100.0	65.9	29.0	0.9	0.1	4.1
Drop-out Rate (%)	3.5	2.7	5.3	5.6	0.0	8.6
H.S. Diplomas (#)	315	216	84	6	1	8

Nettleton SD

2616 Progress Dr • Jonesboro, AR 72401-7639
Mailing Address: 4109 Race St • Jonesboro, AR 72401-7639
(870) 910-7800 • http://nettleton.crsc.k12.ar.us/
Grade Span: KG-12; **Agency Type:** 1
Schools: 6
3 Primary; 2 Middle; 1 High; 0 Other Level
6 Regular; 0 Special Education; 0 Vocational; 0 Alternative
0 Magnet; 0 Charter; 4 Title I Eligible; 0 School-wide Title I
Students: 2,623 (50.6% male; 49.4% female)
Individual Education Program: 340 (13.0%);
English Language Learner: 45 (1.7%); Migrant: 6 (0.2%)
Eligible for Free Lunch Program: 730 (27.8%)
Eligible for Reduced-Price Lunch Program: 169 (6.4%)
Teachers: 166.0 (15.8 to 1)
Librarians/Media Specialists: 6.0 (437.2 to 1)
Guidance Counselors: 7.0 (374.7 to 1)
Current Spending: ($ per student per year):
Total: $5,485; Instruction: $3,428; Support Services: $1,762
Enrollment, Drop-out Rates and Diploma Recipients by Race/Ethnicity

Category	Total	White	Black	Asian	AIAN	Hisp.
Enrollment (%)	100.0	80.3	16.2	0.9	0.2	2.4
Drop-out Rate (%)	3.7	3.7	3.0	0.0	0.0	14.3
H.S. Diplomas (#)	152	137	9	5	0	1

Westside CSD

1630 Hwy 91 W • Jonesboro, AR 72404-9284
(870) 935-7503 • http://crowleys.crsc.k12.ar.us/~westside/
Grade Span: KG-12; **Agency Type:** 1
Schools: 3
1 Primary; 1 Middle; 1 High; 0 Other Level
3 Regular; 0 Special Education; 0 Vocational; 0 Alternative
0 Magnet; 0 Charter; 3 Title I Eligible; 0 School-wide Title I
Students: 1,659 (51.1% male; 48.9% female)
Individual Education Program: 227 (13.7%);
English Language Learner: 1 (0.1%); Migrant: 15 (0.9%)
Eligible for Free Lunch Program: 405 (24.4%)
Eligible for Reduced-Price Lunch Program: 126 (7.6%)
Teachers: 109.0 (15.2 to 1)
Librarians/Media Specialists: 3.0 (553.0 to 1)
Guidance Counselors: 5.0 (331.8 to 1)
Current Spending: ($ per student per year):
Total: $5,162; Instruction: $3,029; Support Services: $1,829
Enrollment, Drop-out Rates and Diploma Recipients by Race/Ethnicity

Category	Total	White	Black	Asian	AIAN	Hisp.
Enrollment (%)	100.0	98.8	0.2	0.0	0.0	1.0
Drop-out Rate (%)	5.0	4.6	0.0	n/a	n/a	200.0
H.S. Diplomas (#)	91	91	0	0	0	0

Crawford County

Alma SD

916 Hwy 64 E • Alma, AR 72921-2359
Mailing Address: PO Box 2359 • Alma, AR 72921-2359
(479) 632-4791 • http://alma.wsc.k12.ar.us/
Grade Span: KG-12; **Agency Type:** 1
Schools: 4
2 Primary; 1 Middle; 1 High; 0 Other Level
4 Regular; 0 Special Education; 0 Vocational; 0 Alternative
0 Magnet; 0 Charter; 4 Title I Eligible; 0 School-wide Title I
Students: 2,916 (52.1% male; 47.9% female)
Individual Education Program: 386 (13.2%);
English Language Learner: 6 (0.2%); Migrant: 79 (2.7%)
Eligible for Free Lunch Program: 862 (29.6%)
Eligible for Reduced-Price Lunch Program: 297 (10.2%)
Teachers: 181.0 (16.1 to 1)
Librarians/Media Specialists: 4.0 (729.0 to 1)
Guidance Counselors: 7.0 (416.6 to 1)
Current Spending: ($ per student per year):
Total: $5,427; Instruction: $3,422; Support Services: $1,667
Enrollment, Drop-out Rates and Diploma Recipients by Race/Ethnicity

Category	Total	White	Black	Asian	AIAN	Hisp.
Enrollment (%)	100.0	96.3	1.0	0.5	0.1	2.1
Drop-out Rate (%)	3.2	3.1	12.5	0.0	20.0	0.0
H.S. Diplomas (#)	188	183	1	2	1	1

Van Buren SD

2221 Pointer Tr • Van Buren, AR 72956-2336
(479) 474-7942 • http://vbschools.k12.ar.us/
Grade Span: PK-12; **Agency Type:** 1
Schools: 11
6 Primary; 4 Middle; 1 High; 0 Other Level
11 Regular; 0 Special Education; 0 Vocational; 0 Alternative
0 Magnet; 0 Charter; 4 Title I Eligible; 3 School-wide Title I
Students: 5,537 (51.0% male; 49.0% female)
Individual Education Program: 689 (12.4%);
English Language Learner: 237 (4.3%); Migrant: 213 (3.8%)
Eligible for Free Lunch Program: 1,822 (32.9%)
Eligible for Reduced-Price Lunch Program: 529 (9.6%)
Teachers: 367.0 (15.1 to 1)
Librarians/Media Specialists: 11.0 (503.4 to 1)
Guidance Counselors: 15.0 (369.1 to 1)
Current Spending: ($ per student per year):
Total: $5,533; Instruction: $3,557; Support Services: $1,657
Enrollment, Drop-out Rates and Diploma Recipients by Race/Ethnicity

Category	Total	White	Black	Asian	AIAN	Hisp.
Enrollment (%)	100.0	85.5	1.5	3.3	1.5	8.2
Drop-out Rate (%)	6.1	6.1	14.3	4.4	3.1	4.8
H.S. Diplomas (#)	300	247	8	19	4	22

Crittenden County

Marion SD

200 Manor St • Marion, AR 72364-1909
(870) 739-5100 • http://marion.crsc.k12.ar.us/
Grade Span: KG-12; **Agency Type:** 1
Schools: 6
2 Primary; 2 Middle; 1 High; 1 Other Level
6 Regular; 0 Special Education; 0 Vocational; 0 Alternative
0 Magnet; 0 Charter; 0 Title I Eligible; 0 School-wide Title I
Students: 3,296 (51.2% male; 48.8% female)
Individual Education Program: 359 (10.9%);
English Language Learner: 5 (0.2%); Migrant: 37 (1.1%)
Eligible for Free Lunch Program: 1,054 (32.0%)
Eligible for Reduced-Price Lunch Program: 348 (10.6%)
Teachers: 183.0 (18.0 to 1)
Librarians/Media Specialists: 6.0 (549.3 to 1)
Guidance Counselors: 8.0 (412.0 to 1)

Current Spending: ($ per student per year):
Total: $5,351; Instruction: $3,311; Support Services: $1,710
Enrollment, Drop-out Rates and Diploma Recipients by Race/Ethnicity

Category	Total	White	Black	Asian	AIAN	Hisp.
Enrollment (%)	100.0	71.7	25.8	0.7	0.2	1.6
Drop-out Rate (%)	6.6	4.2	14.6	0.0	n/a	0.0
H.S. Diplomas (#)	158	123	32	3	0	0

West Memphis SD

301 S Avalon • West Memphis, AR 72301
Mailing Address: PO Box 826 • West Memphis, AR 72303-0826
(870) 735-1915 • http://west.grsc.k12.ar.us/
Grade Span: PK-12; **Agency Type:** 1
Schools: 12
8 Primary; 3 Middle; 1 High; 0 Other Level
12 Regular; 0 Special Education; 0 Vocational; 0 Alternative
0 Magnet; 0 Charter; 8 Title I Eligible; 8 School-wide Title I
Students: 6,109 (50.4% male; 49.6% female)
Individual Education Program: 749 (12.3%);
English Language Learner: 0 (0.0%); Migrant: 0 (0.0%)
Eligible for Free Lunch Program: 3,972 (65.0%)
Eligible for Reduced-Price Lunch Program: 320 (5.2%)
Teachers: 388.0 (15.7 to 1)
Librarians/Media Specialists: 12.0 (509.1 to 1)
Guidance Counselors: 17.0 (359.4 to 1)
Current Spending: ($ per student per year):
Total: $5,119; Instruction: $3,368; Support Services: $1,427
Enrollment, Drop-out Rates and Diploma Recipients by Race/Ethnicity

Category	Total	White	Black	Asian	AIAN	Hisp.
Enrollment (%)	100.0	18.5	80.8	0.2	0.0	0.5
Drop-out Rate (%)	6.0	5.2	6.2	0.0	n/a	0.0
H.S. Diplomas (#)	260	53	205	1	0	1

Cross County

Wynne SD

1300 N Falls Blvd • Wynne, AR 72396-0069
Mailing Address: PO Box 69 • Wynne, AR 72396-0069
(870) 238-5000 • http://wynne.k12.ar.us
Grade Span: KG-12; **Agency Type:** 1
Schools: 4
2 Primary; 1 Middle; 1 High; 0 Other Level
4 Regular; 0 Special Education; 0 Vocational; 0 Alternative
0 Magnet; 0 Charter; 2 Title I Eligible; 0 School-wide Title I
Students: 2,843 (51.8% male; 48.2% female)
Individual Education Program: 339 (11.9%);
English Language Learner: 2 (0.1%); Migrant: 40 (1.4%)
Eligible for Free Lunch Program: 1,236 (43.5%)
Eligible for Reduced-Price Lunch Program: 189 (6.6%)
Teachers: 184.0 (15.5 to 1)
Librarians/Media Specialists: 4.0 (710.8 to 1)
Guidance Counselors: 9.0 (315.9 to 1)
Current Spending: ($ per student per year):
Total: $5,165; Instruction: $3,348; Support Services: $1,519
Enrollment, Drop-out Rates and Diploma Recipients by Race/Ethnicity

Category	Total	White	Black	Asian	AIAN	Hisp.
Enrollment (%)	100.0	68.9	30.1	0.5	0.1	0.5
Drop-out Rate (%)	4.5	3.5	6.6	0.0	n/a	0.0
H.S. Diplomas (#)	196	128	65	1	0	2

Desha County

Dumas SD

213 Adams St • Dumas, AR 71639
(870) 382-4571 • http://wwwdumas.sesc.k12.ar.us/
Grade Span: PK-12; **Agency Type:** 1
Schools: 4
2 Primary; 1 Middle; 1 High; 0 Other Level
4 Regular; 0 Special Education; 0 Vocational; 0 Alternative
0 Magnet; 0 Charter; 3 Title I Eligible; 3 School-wide Title I
Students: 1,607 (50.5% male; 49.5% female)
Individual Education Program: 229 (14.3%);
English Language Learner: 57 (3.5%); Migrant: 13 (0.8%)
Eligible for Free Lunch Program: 1,070 (66.6%)
Eligible for Reduced-Price Lunch Program: 134 (8.3%)
Teachers: 124.0 (13.0 to 1)
Librarians/Media Specialists: 4.0 (401.8 to 1)
Guidance Counselors: 6.0 (267.8 to 1)
Current Spending: ($ per student per year):
Total: $6,098; Instruction: $3,934; Support Services: $1,832
Enrollment, Drop-out Rates and Diploma Recipients by Race/Ethnicity

Category	Total	White	Black	Asian	AIAN	Hisp.
Enrollment (%)	100.0	29.0	65.0	0.2	0.1	5.7
Drop-out Rate (%)	4.3	5.8	3.2	n/a	n/a	10.7
H.S. Diplomas (#)	116	27	83	0	0	6

Drew County

Monticello SD

935 Scogin Dr • Monticello, AR 71655-5733
(870) 367-4000 • http://msd.sesc.k12.ar.us/
Grade Span: KG-12; **Agency Type:** 1
Schools: 6
2 Primary; 1 Middle; 2 High; 0 Other Level
4 Regular; 0 Special Education; 1 Vocational; 0 Alternative
0 Magnet; 0 Charter; 3 Title I Eligible; 2 School-wide Title I
Students: 2,102 (51.0% male; 49.0% female)
Individual Education Program: 240 (11.4%);
English Language Learner: 0 (0.0%); Migrant: 0 (0.0%)
Eligible for Free Lunch Program: 869 (41.3%)
Eligible for Reduced-Price Lunch Program: 122 (5.8%)
Teachers: 132.0 (15.9 to 1)
Librarians/Media Specialists: 4.0 (525.5 to 1)
Guidance Counselors: 6.0 (350.3 to 1)
Current Spending: ($ per student per year):
Total: $5,293; Instruction: $3,104; Support Services: $1,872
Enrollment, Drop-out Rates and Diploma Recipients by Race/Ethnicity

Category	Total	White	Black	Asian	AIAN	Hisp.
Enrollment (%)	100.0	61.7	36.7	0.4	0.1	1.1
Drop-out Rate (%)	1.6	1.5	1.9	0.0	n/a	0.0
H.S. Diplomas (#)	151	97	51	3	0	0

Faulkner County

Conway SD

2220 Prince St • Conway, AR 72034
(501) 450-4800 • http://www.conwayschools.afsc.k12.ar.us/
Grade Span: KG-12; **Agency Type:** 1
Schools: 13
8 Primary; 2 Middle; 2 High; 1 Other Level
12 Regular; 0 Special Education; 1 Vocational; 0 Alternative
0 Magnet; 0 Charter; 5 Title I Eligible; 1 School-wide Title I
Students: 8,109 (51.3% male; 48.7% female)
Individual Education Program: 1,123 (13.8%);
English Language Learner: 97 (1.2%); Migrant: 17 (0.2%)
Eligible for Free Lunch Program: 2,053 (25.3%)
Eligible for Reduced-Price Lunch Program: 534 (6.6%)
Teachers: 488.0 (16.6 to 1)
Librarians/Media Specialists: 11.0 (737.2 to 1)
Guidance Counselors: 19.0 (426.8 to 1)
Current Spending: ($ per student per year):
Total: $5,385; Instruction: $3,283; Support Services: $1,863
Enrollment, Drop-out Rates and Diploma Recipients by Race/Ethnicity

Category	Total	White	Black	Asian	AIAN	Hisp.
Enrollment (%)	100.0	74.3	21.5	0.9	0.3	3.0
Drop-out Rate (%)	5.5	5.5	4.9	0.0	16.7	11.1
H.S. Diplomas (#)	446	371	66	6	0	3

Greenbrier SD

4 School Dr • Greenbrier, AR 72058-9206
(501) 679-4808 • http://gps.k12.ar.us/
Grade Span: PK-12; **Agency Type:** 1
Schools: 5
2 Primary; 1 Middle; 1 High; 1 Other Level
5 Regular; 0 Special Education; 0 Vocational; 0 Alternative
0 Magnet; 0 Charter; 5 Title I Eligible; 0 School-wide Title I
Students: 2,397 (51.5% male; 48.5% female)
Individual Education Program: 359 (15.0%);
English Language Learner: 1 (<0.1%); Migrant: 2 (0.1%)
Eligible for Free Lunch Program: 618 (25.8%)
Eligible for Reduced-Price Lunch Program: 267 (11.1%)
Teachers: 162.0 (14.8 to 1)
Librarians/Media Specialists: 5.0 (479.4 to 1)
Guidance Counselors: 6.0 (399.5 to 1)
Current Spending: ($ per student per year):
Total: $5,331; Instruction: $3,425; Support Services: $1,615
Enrollment, Drop-out Rates and Diploma Recipients by Race/Ethnicity

Category	Total	White	Black	Asian	AIAN	Hisp.
Enrollment (%)	100.0	97.2	0.7	0.3	0.5	1.4
Drop-out Rate (%)	3.5	3.3	0.0	0.0	0.0	25.0
H.S. Diplomas (#)	143	139	0	1	0	3

Vilonia SD

11 Eagle St • Vilonia, AR 72173-0160
Mailing Address: PO Box 160 • Vilonia, AR 72173-0160
(501) 796-2113 • http://www.byers-soft.com/vilonia/
Grade Span: KG-12; **Agency Type:** 1
Schools: 5
2 Primary; 1 Middle; 1 High; 1 Other Level
5 Regular; 0 Special Education; 0 Vocational; 0 Alternative
0 Magnet; 0 Charter; 3 Title I Eligible; 0 School-wide Title I

Students: 2,588 (51.8% male; 48.2% female)
Individual Education Program: 374 (14.5%);
English Language Learner: 2 (0.1%); Migrant: 0 (0.0%)
Eligible for Free Lunch Program: 502 (19.4%)
Eligible for Reduced-Price Lunch Program: 241 (9.3%)
Teachers: 145.0 (17.8 to 1)
Librarians/Media Specialists: 4.0 (647.0 to 1)
Guidance Counselors: 7.0 (369.7 to 1)
Current Spending: ($ per student per year):
Total: $5,081; Instruction: $3,258; Support Services: $1,532
Enrollment, Drop-out Rates and Diploma Recipients by Race/Ethnicity

Category	Total	White	Black	Asian	AIAN	Hisp.
Enrollment (%)	100.0	98.1	0.2	0.2	0.5	1.0
Drop-out Rate (%)	2.0	1.9	0.0	0.0	0.0	12.5
H.S. Diplomas (#)	171	164	2	2	0	3

Franklin County

Ozark SD
1609 Walden Dr • Ozark, AR 72949-0135
Mailing Address: PO Box 135 • Ozark, AR 72949-0135
(479) 667-4118
Grade Span: KG-12; **Agency Type:** 1
Schools: 3
1 Primary; 1 Middle; 1 High; 0 Other Level
3 Regular; 0 Special Education; 0 Vocational; 0 Alternative
0 Magnet; 0 Charter; 2 Title I Eligible; 0 School-wide Title I
Students: 1,633 (52.2% male; 47.8% female)
Individual Education Program: 162 (9.9%);
English Language Learner: 5 (0.3%); Migrant: 9 (0.6%)
Eligible for Free Lunch Program: 490 (30.0%)
Eligible for Reduced-Price Lunch Program: 158 (9.7%)
Teachers: 104.0 (15.7 to 1)
Librarians/Media Specialists: 3.0 (544.3 to 1)
Guidance Counselors: 4.0 (408.3 to 1)
Current Spending: ($ per student per year):
Total: $4,891; Instruction: $2,989; Support Services: $1,633
Enrollment, Drop-out Rates and Diploma Recipients by Race/Ethnicity

Category	Total	White	Black	Asian	AIAN	Hisp.
Enrollment (%)	100.0	96.4	0.9	0.7	1.0	1.0
Drop-out Rate (%)	4.5	4.4	0.0	0.0	0.0	n/a
H.S. Diplomas (#)	138	124	10	0	2	2

Garland County

Hot Springs SD
400 Linwood St • Hot Springs, AR 71913
(501) 624-3372 • http://hsprings.dsc.k12.ar.us/
Grade Span: PK-12; **Agency Type:** 1
Schools: 6
4 Primary; 0 Middle; 1 High; 1 Other Level
6 Regular; 0 Special Education; 0 Vocational; 0 Alternative
0 Magnet; 0 Charter; 5 Title I Eligible; 5 School-wide Title I
Students: 3,401 (52.0% male; 48.0% female)
Individual Education Program: 503 (14.8%);
English Language Learner: 158 (4.6%); Migrant: 2 (0.1%)
Eligible for Free Lunch Program: 2,105 (61.9%)
Eligible for Reduced-Price Lunch Program: 290 (8.5%)
Teachers: 257.0 (13.2 to 1)
Librarians/Media Specialists: 6.0 (566.8 to 1)
Guidance Counselors: 9.0 (377.9 to 1)
Current Spending: ($ per student per year):
Total: $6,526; Instruction: $3,991; Support Services: $2,167
Enrollment, Drop-out Rates and Diploma Recipients by Race/Ethnicity

Category	Total	White	Black	Asian	AIAN	Hisp.
Enrollment (%)	100.0	49.3	42.6	1.3	0.4	6.4
Drop-out Rate (%)	11.3	14.2	8.9	0.0	n/a	3.0
H.S. Diplomas (#)	152	78	66	4	0	4

Lake Hamilton SD
205 Wolf St • Pearcy, AR 71964
(501) 767-2306 • http://wolves.dsc.k12.ar.us/
Grade Span: KG-12; **Agency Type:** 1
Schools: 6
2 Primary; 2 Middle; 1 High; 1 Other Level
6 Regular; 0 Special Education; 0 Vocational; 0 Alternative
0 Magnet; 0 Charter; 3 Title I Eligible; 0 School-wide Title I
Students: 3,773 (52.8% male; 47.2% female)
Individual Education Program: 525 (13.9%);
English Language Learner: 33 (0.9%); Migrant: 0 (0.0%)
Eligible for Free Lunch Program: 901 (23.9%)
Eligible for Reduced-Price Lunch Program: 383 (10.2%)
Teachers: 205.0 (18.4 to 1)
Librarians/Media Specialists: 6.0 (628.8 to 1)
Guidance Counselors: 14.0 (269.5 to 1)
Current Spending: ($ per student per year):
Total: $5,318; Instruction: $3,244; Support Services: $1,681
Enrollment, Drop-out Rates and Diploma Recipients by Race/Ethnicity

Category	Total	White	Black	Asian	AIAN	Hisp.
Enrollment (%)	100.0	94.3	2.6	1.1	0.0	2.0
Drop-out Rate (%)	0.5	0.5	4.3	0.0	0.0	0.0
H.S. Diplomas (#)	212	202	5	3	0	2

Lakeside SD
2837 Malvern Ave • Hot Springs, AR 71901-8321
(501) 262-1880 • http://se.sesc.k12.ar.us/lakeside/
Grade Span: KG-12; **Agency Type:** 1
Schools: 5
2 Primary; 1 Middle; 1 High; 1 Other Level
5 Regular; 0 Special Education; 0 Vocational; 0 Alternative
0 Magnet; 0 Charter; 5 Title I Eligible; 0 School-wide Title I
Students: 2,517 (51.0% male; 49.0% female)
Individual Education Program: 298 (11.8%);
English Language Learner: 117 (4.6%); Migrant: 0 (0.0%)
Eligible for Free Lunch Program: 442 (17.6%)
Eligible for Reduced-Price Lunch Program: 147 (5.8%)
Teachers: 158.0 (15.9 to 1)
Librarians/Media Specialists: 5.0 (503.4 to 1)
Guidance Counselors: 6.0 (419.5 to 1)
Current Spending: ($ per student per year):
Total: $5,677; Instruction: $3,393; Support Services: $2,040
Enrollment, Drop-out Rates and Diploma Recipients by Race/Ethnicity

Category	Total	White	Black	Asian	AIAN	Hisp.
Enrollment (%)	100.0	91.1	3.8	1.6	0.6	2.8
Drop-out Rate (%)	2.3	2.5	0.0	0.0	0.0	0.0
H.S. Diplomas (#)	155	140	11	1	1	2

Grant County

Sheridan SD
400 N Rock • Sheridan, AR 72150-2228
(870) 942-3135 • http://jackets.arsc.k12.ar.us/
Grade Span: KG-12; **Agency Type:** 1
Schools: 6
2 Primary; 3 Middle; 1 High; 0 Other Level
6 Regular; 0 Special Education; 0 Vocational; 0 Alternative
0 Magnet; 0 Charter; 6 Title I Eligible; 0 School-wide Title I
Students: 4,099 (50.9% male; 49.1% female)
Individual Education Program: 475 (11.6%);
English Language Learner: 10 (0.2%); Migrant: 0 (0.0%)
Eligible for Free Lunch Program: 960 (23.4%)
Eligible for Reduced-Price Lunch Program: 444 (10.8%)
Teachers: 249.0 (16.5 to 1)
Librarians/Media Specialists: 6.0 (683.2 to 1)
Guidance Counselors: 10.0 (409.9 to 1)
Current Spending: ($ per student per year):
Total: $4,972; Instruction: $3,244; Support Services: $1,435
Enrollment, Drop-out Rates and Diploma Recipients by Race/Ethnicity

Category	Total	White	Black	Asian	AIAN	Hisp.
Enrollment (%)	100.0	96.5	1.9	0.6	0.1	0.8
Drop-out Rate (%)	4.3	4.4	2.9	0.0	0.0	0.0
H.S. Diplomas (#)	246	238	5	2	1	0

Greene County

Greene County Tech SD
5413 W Kingshighway • Paragould, AR 72450-3368
(870) 236-2762 • http://gctsd.nesc.k12.ar.us/
Grade Span: KG-12; **Agency Type:** 1
Schools: 4
1 Primary; 2 Middle; 1 High; 0 Other Level
4 Regular; 0 Special Education; 0 Vocational; 0 Alternative
0 Magnet; 0 Charter; 4 Title I Eligible; 0 School-wide Title I
Students: 2,891 (52.3% male; 47.7% female)
Individual Education Program: 398 (13.8%);
English Language Learner: 7 (0.2%); Migrant: 12 (0.4%)
Eligible for Free Lunch Program: 803 (27.8%)
Eligible for Reduced-Price Lunch Program: 280 (9.7%)
Teachers: 180.0 (16.1 to 1)
Librarians/Media Specialists: 5.0 (578.2 to 1)
Guidance Counselors: 7.0 (413.0 to 1)
Current Spending: ($ per student per year):
Total: $5,163; Instruction: $3,133; Support Services: $1,723
Enrollment, Drop-out Rates and Diploma Recipients by Race/Ethnicity

Category	Total	White	Black	Asian	AIAN	Hisp.
Enrollment (%)	100.0	98.9	0.4	0.1	0.1	0.6
Drop-out Rate (%)	4.3	4.3	n/a	0.0	0.0	0.0
H.S. Diplomas (#)	154	151	0	0	0	3

Paragould SD

631 W Court St • Paragould, AR 72450-4248
(870) 239-2105 • http://rams.nesd.k12.ar.us/
Grade Span: KG-12; **Agency Type:** 1
Schools: 6
3 Primary; 2 Middle; 1 High; 0 Other Level
6 Regular; 0 Special Education; 0 Vocational; 0 Alternative
0 Magnet; 0 Charter; 4 Title I Eligible; 2 School-wide Title I
Students: 2,651 (50.8% male; 49.2% female)
Individual Education Program: 470 (17.7%);
English Language Learner: 5 (0.2%); Migrant: 10 (0.4%)
Eligible for Free Lunch Program: 1,026 (38.7%)
Eligible for Reduced-Price Lunch Program: 249 (9.4%)
Teachers: 171.0 (15.5 to 1)
Librarians/Media Specialists: 7.0 (378.7 to 1)
Guidance Counselors: 7.0 (378.7 to 1)
Current Spending: ($ per student per year):
Total: $5,431; Instruction: $3,531; Support Services: $1,638
Enrollment, Drop-out Rates and Diploma Recipients by Race/Ethnicity

Category	Total	White	Black	Asian	AIAN	Hisp.
Enrollment (%)	100.0	97.2	0.9	0.3	0.1	1.6
Drop-out Rate (%)	6.9	6.8	16.7	0.0	0.0	10.0
H.S. Diplomas (#)	132	129	0	0	0	3

Hempstead County

Hope SD

117 E Second St • Hope, AR 71801-4402
(870) 722-2700 • http://hhs.swsc.k12.ar.us/
Grade Span: PK-12; **Agency Type:** 1
Schools: 5
1 Primary; 2 Middle; 2 High; 0 Other Level
5 Regular; 0 Special Education; 0 Vocational; 0 Alternative
0 Magnet; 0 Charter; 5 Title I Eligible; 0 School-wide Title I
Students: 2,754 (52.0% male; 48.0% female)
Individual Education Program: 279 (10.1%);
English Language Learner: 209 (7.6%); Migrant: 131 (4.8%)
Eligible for Free Lunch Program: 1,520 (55.2%)
Eligible for Reduced-Price Lunch Program: 173 (6.3%)
Teachers: 183.0 (15.0 to 1)
Librarians/Media Specialists: 5.0 (550.8 to 1)
Guidance Counselors: 8.0 (344.3 to 1)
Current Spending: ($ per student per year):
Total: $5,879; Instruction: $3,797; Support Services: $1,759
Enrollment, Drop-out Rates and Diploma Recipients by Race/Ethnicity

Category	Total	White	Black	Asian	AIAN	Hisp.
Enrollment (%)	100.0	35.7	50.3	0.4	0.1	13.5
Drop-out Rate (%)	7.0	5.6	7.6	0.0	0.0	14.3
H.S. Diplomas (#)	178	73	91	1	0	13

Hot Spring County

Malvern SD

1517 S Main St • Malvern, AR 72104-5231
(501) 332-7500 • http://malvern.dsc.k12.ar.us/
Grade Span: KG-12; **Agency Type:** 1
Schools: 6
3 Primary; 2 Middle; 1 High; 0 Other Level
6 Regular; 0 Special Education; 0 Vocational; 0 Alternative
0 Magnet; 0 Charter; 5 Title I Eligible; 0 School-wide Title I
Students: 2,200 (50.9% male; 49.1% female)
Individual Education Program: 303 (13.8%);
English Language Learner: 0 (0.0%); Migrant: 1 (<0.1%)
Eligible for Free Lunch Program: 922 (41.9%)
Eligible for Reduced-Price Lunch Program: 275 (12.5%)
Teachers: 144.0 (15.3 to 1)
Librarians/Media Specialists: 6.0 (366.7 to 1)
Guidance Counselors: 7.0 (314.3 to 1)
Current Spending: ($ per student per year):
Total: $5,708; Instruction: $3,627; Support Services: $1,767
Enrollment, Drop-out Rates and Diploma Recipients by Race/Ethnicity

Category	Total	White	Black	Asian	AIAN	Hisp.
Enrollment (%)	100.0	65.9	32.0	0.5	0.2	1.4
Drop-out Rate (%)	5.5	5.1	5.6	0.0	0.0	66.7
H.S. Diplomas (#)	139	93	43	1	0	2

Howard County

Nashville SD

600 N Fourth • Nashville, AR 71852-3911
(870) 845-3425 • http://nsd.dmsc.k12.ar.us/
Grade Span: KG-12; **Agency Type:** 1
Schools: 4
1 Primary; 2 Middle; 1 High; 0 Other Level
4 Regular; 0 Special Education; 0 Vocational; 0 Alternative
0 Magnet; 0 Charter; 3 Title I Eligible; 1 School-wide Title I
Students: 1,757 (51.8% male; 48.2% female)
Individual Education Program: 203 (11.6%);
English Language Learner: 87 (5.0%); Migrant: 62 (3.5%)
Eligible for Free Lunch Program: 745 (42.4%)
Eligible for Reduced-Price Lunch Program: 199 (11.3%)
Teachers: 130.0 (13.5 to 1)
Librarians/Media Specialists: 4.0 (439.3 to 1)
Guidance Counselors: 5.0 (351.4 to 1)
Current Spending: ($ per student per year):
Total: $5,115; Instruction: $3,285; Support Services: $1,525
Enrollment, Drop-out Rates and Diploma Recipients by Race/Ethnicity

Category	Total	White	Black	Asian	AIAN	Hisp.
Enrollment (%)	100.0	64.5	26.4	1.3	0.1	7.7
Drop-out Rate (%)	3.8	2.8	5.8	12.5	0.0	0.0
H.S. Diplomas (#)	105	70	29	0	2	4

Independence County

Batesville SD

330 E College • Batesville, AR 72501-5624
(870) 793-6831 • http://bsd.ncsc.k12.ar.us/
Grade Span: KG-12; **Agency Type:** 1
Schools: 7
4 Primary; 2 Middle; 1 High; 0 Other Level
7 Regular; 0 Special Education; 0 Vocational; 0 Alternative
0 Magnet; 0 Charter; 4 Title I Eligible; 4 School-wide Title I
Students: 2,099 (51.2% male; 48.8% female)
Individual Education Program: 346 (16.5%);
English Language Learner: 83 (4.0%); Migrant: 144 (6.9%)
Eligible for Free Lunch Program: 725 (34.5%)
Eligible for Reduced-Price Lunch Program: 180 (8.6%)
Teachers: 141.0 (14.9 to 1)
Librarians/Media Specialists: 6.0 (349.8 to 1)
Guidance Counselors: 7.0 (299.9 to 1)
Current Spending: ($ per student per year):
Total: $5,732; Instruction: $3,604; Support Services: $1,836
Enrollment, Drop-out Rates and Diploma Recipients by Race/Ethnicity

Category	Total	White	Black	Asian	AIAN	Hisp.
Enrollment (%)	100.0	83.4	9.2	2.0	0.2	5.2
Drop-out Rate (%)	7.3	7.8	4.3	0.0	0.0	0.0
H.S. Diplomas (#)	129	121	7	0	1	0

Jackson County

Newport SD

406 Wilkerson Dr • Newport, AR 72112-3949
(870) 523-1375 • http://newport.crsc.k12.ar.us/1024/Index.htm
Grade Span: KG-12; **Agency Type:** 1
Schools: 4
1 Primary; 2 Middle; 1 High; 0 Other Level
4 Regular; 0 Special Education; 0 Vocational; 0 Alternative
0 Magnet; 0 Charter; 3 Title I Eligible; 3 School-wide Title I
Students: 1,625 (51.9% male; 48.1% female)
Individual Education Program: 220 (13.5%);
English Language Learner: 21 (1.3%); Migrant: 22 (1.4%)
Eligible for Free Lunch Program: 848 (52.2%)
Eligible for Reduced-Price Lunch Program: 188 (11.6%)
Teachers: 128.0 (12.7 to 1)
Librarians/Media Specialists: 4.0 (406.3 to 1)
Guidance Counselors: 5.0 (325.0 to 1)
Current Spending: ($ per student per year):
Total: $6,139; Instruction: $3,645; Support Services: $2,107
Enrollment, Drop-out Rates and Diploma Recipients by Race/Ethnicity

Category	Total	White	Black	Asian	AIAN	Hisp.
Enrollment (%)	100.0	64.2	33.5	0.6	0.1	1.7
Drop-out Rate (%)	8.9	9.0	8.0	n/a	50.0	0.0
H.S. Diplomas (#)	120	67	52	0	1	0

Jefferson County

Dollarway SD

4900 Dollarway Rd • Pine Bluff, AR 71602-4006
(870) 534-7003 • http://www.dollarway.org/
Grade Span: KG-12; **Agency Type:** 1
Schools: 5
2 Primary; 2 Middle; 1 High; 0 Other Level
5 Regular; 0 Special Education; 0 Vocational; 0 Alternative
0 Magnet; 0 Charter; 4 Title I Eligible; 4 School-wide Title I
Students: 1,538 (52.2% male; 47.8% female)
Individual Education Program: 184 (12.0%);
English Language Learner: 0 (0.0%); Migrant: 0 (0.0%)
Eligible for Free Lunch Program: 1,159 (75.4%)
Eligible for Reduced-Price Lunch Program: 101 (6.6%)
Teachers: 107.0 (14.4 to 1)

Librarians/Media Specialists: 4.0 (384.5 to 1)
Guidance Counselors: 5.0 (307.6 to 1)
Current Spending: ($ per student per year):
Total: $5,847; Instruction: $3,576; Support Services: $1,889
Enrollment, Drop-out Rates and Diploma Recipients by Race/Ethnicity

Category	Total	White	Black	Asian	AIAN	Hisp.
Enrollment (%)	100.0	12.5	87.4	0.1	0.0	0.1
Drop-out Rate (%)	7.9	7.3	8.1	n/a	n/a	0.0
H.S. Diplomas (#)	96	14	82	0	0	0

Pine Bluff SD
1215 W Pullen • Pine Bluff, AR 71601
(870) 543-4200 • http://pbweb.arsc.k12.ar.us/
Grade Span: KG-12; **Agency Type:** 1
Schools: 14
7 Primary; 5 Middle; 1 High; 1 Other Level
14 Regular; 0 Special Education; 0 Vocational; 0 Alternative
0 Magnet; 0 Charter; 11 Title I Eligible; 11 School-wide Title I
Students: 6,158 (50.2% male; 49.8% female)
Individual Education Program: 641 (10.4%);
English Language Learner: 17 (0.3%); Migrant: 1 (<0.1%)
Eligible for Free Lunch Program: 3,601 (58.5%)
Eligible for Reduced-Price Lunch Program: 451 (7.3%)
Teachers: 420.0 (14.7 to 1)
Librarians/Media Specialists: 12.0 (513.2 to 1)
Guidance Counselors: 15.0 (410.5 to 1)
Current Spending: ($ per student per year):
Total: $5,443; Instruction: $3,108; Support Services: $2,101
Enrollment, Drop-out Rates and Diploma Recipients by Race/Ethnicity

Category	Total	White	Black	Asian	AIAN	Hisp.
Enrollment (%)	100.0	6.6	92.8	0.2	0.0	0.3
Drop-out Rate (%)	10.9	8.0	11.3	0.0	n/a	0.0
H.S. Diplomas (#)	319	47	268	2	0	2

Watson Chapel SD
4100 Camden Rd • Pine Bluff, AR 71603-9096
(870) 879-0220 • http://watson2.arsc.k12.ar.us/
Grade Span: KG-12; **Agency Type:** 1
Schools: 5
2 Primary; 2 Middle; 1 High; 0 Other Level
5 Regular; 0 Special Education; 0 Vocational; 0 Alternative
0 Magnet; 0 Charter; 4 Title I Eligible; 3 School-wide Title I
Students: 3,168 (50.3% male; 49.7% female)
Individual Education Program: 315 (9.9%);
English Language Learner: 1 (<0.1%); Migrant: 0 (0.0%)
Eligible for Free Lunch Program: 1,455 (45.9%)
Eligible for Reduced-Price Lunch Program: 227 (7.2%)
Teachers: 187.0 (16.9 to 1)
Librarians/Media Specialists: 6.0 (528.0 to 1)
Guidance Counselors: 8.0 (396.0 to 1)
Current Spending: ($ per student per year):
Total: $5,118; Instruction: $3,272; Support Services: $1,606
Enrollment, Drop-out Rates and Diploma Recipients by Race/Ethnicity

Category	Total	White	Black	Asian	AIAN	Hisp.
Enrollment (%)	100.0	40.2	59.5	0.2	0.0	0.1
Drop-out Rate (%)	2.5	1.7	3.1	0.0	n/a	0.0
H.S. Diplomas (#)	225	106	118	0	0	1

White Hall SD
1020 W Holland Ave • White Hall, AR 71602-9572
(870) 247-2002 • http://pinebluff.dina.org/education/whpublic.html
Grade Span: KG-12; **Agency Type:** 1
Schools: 7
4 Primary; 2 Middle; 1 High; 0 Other Level
7 Regular; 0 Special Education; 0 Vocational; 0 Alternative
0 Magnet; 0 Charter; 4 Title I Eligible; 0 School-wide Title I
Students: 3,057 (51.8% male; 48.2% female)
Individual Education Program: 333 (10.9%);
English Language Learner: 0 (0.0%); Migrant: 0 (0.0%)
Eligible for Free Lunch Program: 586 (19.2%)
Eligible for Reduced-Price Lunch Program: 197 (6.4%)
Teachers: 179.0 (17.1 to 1)
Librarians/Media Specialists: 7.0 (436.7 to 1)
Guidance Counselors: 9.0 (339.7 to 1)
Current Spending: ($ per student per year):
Total: $5,189; Instruction: $3,308; Support Services: $1,621
Enrollment, Drop-out Rates and Diploma Recipients by Race/Ethnicity

Category	Total	White	Black	Asian	AIAN	Hisp.
Enrollment (%)	100.0	90.9	6.6	1.0	0.4	1.1
Drop-out Rate (%)	3.2	3.2	1.8	0.0	0.0	14.3
H.S. Diplomas (#)	184	162	14	4	1	3

Johnson County

Clarksville SD
1701 Clark Rd • Clarksville, AR 72830-3915
(479) 754-8454 • http://panthernet.wsc.k12.ar.us/
Grade Span: KG-12; **Agency Type:** 1
Schools: 5
2 Primary; 2 Middle; 1 High; 0 Other Level
5 Regular; 0 Special Education; 0 Vocational; 0 Alternative
0 Magnet; 0 Charter; 4 Title I Eligible; 0 School-wide Title I
Students: 2,178 (51.3% male; 48.7% female)
Individual Education Program: 253 (11.6%);
English Language Learner: 253 (11.6%); Migrant: 222 (10.2%)
Eligible for Free Lunch Program: 993 (45.6%)
Eligible for Reduced-Price Lunch Program: 245 (11.2%)
Teachers: 146.0 (14.9 to 1)
Librarians/Media Specialists: 5.0 (435.6 to 1)
Guidance Counselors: 5.0 (435.6 to 1)
Current Spending: ($ per student per year):
Total: $5,409; Instruction: $3,507; Support Services: $1,599
Enrollment, Drop-out Rates and Diploma Recipients by Race/Ethnicity

Category	Total	White	Black	Asian	AIAN	Hisp.
Enrollment (%)	100.0	78.9	3.9	0.2	0.2	16.7
Drop-out Rate (%)	6.6	7.0	0.0	0.0	100.0	6.0
H.S. Diplomas (#)	102	85	4	1	0	12

Lee County

Lee County SD
188 W Chestnut St • Marianna, AR 72360-2002
(870) 295-7100 • http://lcsd1.grsc.k12.ar.us/
Grade Span: KG-12; **Agency Type:** 1
Schools: 4
2 Primary; 1 Middle; 1 High; 0 Other Level
4 Regular; 0 Special Education; 0 Vocational; 0 Alternative
0 Magnet; 0 Charter; 0 Title I Eligible; 0 School-wide Title I
Students: 1,622 (49.3% male; 50.7% female)
Individual Education Program: 212 (13.1%);
English Language Learner: 1 (0.1%); Migrant: 0 (0.0%)
Eligible for Free Lunch Program: 1,361 (83.9%)
Eligible for Reduced-Price Lunch Program: 117 (7.2%)
Teachers: 103.0 (15.7 to 1)
Librarians/Media Specialists: 4.0 (405.5 to 1)
Guidance Counselors: 5.0 (324.4 to 1)
Current Spending: ($ per student per year):
Total: $6,387; Instruction: $3,650; Support Services: $2,318
Enrollment, Drop-out Rates and Diploma Recipients by Race/Ethnicity

Category	Total	White	Black	Asian	AIAN	Hisp.
Enrollment (%)	100.0	9.4	89.3	0.0	0.0	1.3
Drop-out Rate (%)	4.3	8.3	4.1	n/a	n/a	0.0
H.S. Diplomas (#)	117	2	115	0	0	0

Lincoln County

Star City SD
206 Cleveland St • Star City, AR 71667-5218
(870) 628-4237 • http://se.sesc.k12.ar.us/starcity/
Grade Span: KG-12; **Agency Type:** 1
Schools: 3
1 Primary; 0 Middle; 1 High; 1 Other Level
3 Regular; 0 Special Education; 0 Vocational; 0 Alternative
0 Magnet; 0 Charter; 2 Title I Eligible; 1 School-wide Title I
Students: 1,520 (51.8% male; 48.2% female)
Individual Education Program: 229 (15.1%);
English Language Learner: 23 (1.5%); Migrant: 14 (0.9%)
Eligible for Free Lunch Program: 569 (37.4%)
Eligible for Reduced-Price Lunch Program: 116 (7.6%)
Teachers: 101.0 (15.0 to 1)
Librarians/Media Specialists: 3.0 (506.7 to 1)
Guidance Counselors: 4.0 (380.0 to 1)
Current Spending: ($ per student per year):
Total: $4,956; Instruction: $3,275; Support Services: $1,425
Enrollment, Drop-out Rates and Diploma Recipients by Race/Ethnicity

Category	Total	White	Black	Asian	AIAN	Hisp.
Enrollment (%)	100.0	80.1	18.0	0.2	0.1	1.6
Drop-out Rate (%)	5.1	4.3	6.3	0.0	n/a	40.0
H.S. Diplomas (#)	90	69	20	0	0	1

Little River County

Ashdown SD
511 N Second • Ashdown, AR 71822-2706
(870) 898-3208 • http://nexus.dmsc.k12.ar.us/schools/ashdown.htm
Grade Span: KG-12; **Agency Type:** 1
Schools: 5

2 Primary; 2 Middle; 1 High; 0 Other Level
5 Regular; 0 Special Education; 0 Vocational; 0 Alternative
0 Magnet; 0 Charter; 2 Title I Eligible; 1 School-wide Title I
Students: 1,656 (52.5% male; 47.5% female)
Individual Education Program: 206 (12.4%);
English Language Learner: 14 (0.8%); Migrant: 0 (0.0%)
Eligible for Free Lunch Program: 602 (36.4%)
Eligible for Reduced-Price Lunch Program: 173 (10.4%)
Teachers: 121.0 (13.7 to 1)
Librarians/Media Specialists: 5.0 (331.2 to 1)
Guidance Counselors: 5.0 (331.2 to 1)
Current Spending: ($ per student per year):
Total: $5,491; Instruction: $3,309; Support Services: $1,926
Enrollment, Drop-out Rates and Diploma Recipients by Race/Ethnicity

Category	Total	White	Black	Asian	AIAN	Hisp.
Enrollment (%)	100.0	65.9	30.7	0.2	1.1	2.1
Drop-out Rate (%)	3.9	2.9	6.8	0.0	0.0	0.0
H.S. Diplomas (#)	100	71	27	0	0	2

Lonoke County

Cabot SD

602 No Lincoln • Cabot, AR 72023-2540
(501) 843-3363 • http://cabot.wmsc.k12.ar.us/
Grade Span: KG-12; **Agency Type:** 1
Schools: 12
7 Primary; 4 Middle; 0 High; 1 Other Level
12 Regular; 0 Special Education; 0 Vocational; 0 Alternative
0 Magnet; 0 Charter; 11 Title I Eligible; 2 School-wide Title I
Students: 7,496 (51.4% male; 48.6% female)
Individual Education Program: 1,036 (13.8%);
English Language Learner: 31 (0.4%); Migrant: 6 (0.1%)
Eligible for Free Lunch Program: 1,535 (20.5%)
Eligible for Reduced-Price Lunch Program: 459 (6.1%)
Teachers: 466.0 (16.1 to 1)
Librarians/Media Specialists: 12.0 (624.7 to 1)
Guidance Counselors: 18.0 (416.4 to 1)
Current Spending: ($ per student per year):
Total: $5,159; Instruction: $3,329; Support Services: $1,624
Enrollment, Drop-out Rates and Diploma Recipients by Race/Ethnicity

Category	Total	White	Black	Asian	AIAN	Hisp.
Enrollment (%)	100.0	96.3	0.7	0.9	0.6	1.5
Drop-out Rate (%)	5.4	5.3	22.2	5.3	0.0	14.3
H.S. Diplomas (#)	450	440	0	5	1	4

Lonoke SD

401 W Holly St • Lonoke, AR 72086-0740
Mailing Address: PO Box 740 • Lonoke, AR 72086-0740
(501) 676-2042 • http://170.211.188.150/
Grade Span: KG-12; **Agency Type:** 1
Schools: 4
2 Primary; 1 Middle; 1 High; 0 Other Level
4 Regular; 0 Special Education; 0 Vocational; 0 Alternative
0 Magnet; 0 Charter; 4 Title I Eligible; 0 School-wide Title I
Students: 1,763 (52.1% male; 47.9% female)
Individual Education Program: 266 (15.1%);
English Language Learner: 34 (1.9%); Migrant: 27 (1.5%)
Eligible for Free Lunch Program: 630 (35.7%)
Eligible for Reduced-Price Lunch Program: 139 (7.9%)
Teachers: 111.0 (15.9 to 1)
Librarians/Media Specialists: 4.0 (440.8 to 1)
Guidance Counselors: 4.0 (440.8 to 1)
Current Spending: ($ per student per year):
Total: $5,617; Instruction: $3,321; Support Services: $1,943
Enrollment, Drop-out Rates and Diploma Recipients by Race/Ethnicity

Category	Total	White	Black	Asian	AIAN	Hisp.
Enrollment (%)	100.0	76.3	20.8	0.1	0.2	2.6
Drop-out Rate (%)	4.8	5.0	4.5	0.0	0.0	0.0
H.S. Diplomas (#)	104	75	29	0	0	0

Madison County

Huntsville SD

104-B W War Eagle Dr • Huntsville, AR 72740-0160
(479) 738-2011 • http://eagle.nwsc.k12.ar.us/
Grade Span: KG-12; **Agency Type:** 1
Schools: 4
2 Primary; 1 Middle; 1 High; 0 Other Level
4 Regular; 0 Special Education; 0 Vocational; 0 Alternative
0 Magnet; 0 Charter; 4 Title I Eligible; 0 School-wide Title I
Students: 2,085 (51.8% male; 48.2% female)
Individual Education Program: 249 (11.9%);
English Language Learner: 69 (3.3%); Migrant: 75 (3.6%)
Eligible for Free Lunch Program: 682 (32.7%)
Eligible for Reduced-Price Lunch Program: 144 (6.9%)
Teachers: 118.0 (17.7 to 1)
Librarians/Media Specialists: 4.0 (521.3 to 1)
Guidance Counselors: 6.0 (347.5 to 1)
Current Spending: ($ per student per year):
Total: $4,706; Instruction: $2,857; Support Services: $1,568
Enrollment, Drop-out Rates and Diploma Recipients by Race/Ethnicity

Category	Total	White	Black	Asian	AIAN	Hisp.
Enrollment (%)	100.0	93.4	0.3	0.7	0.3	5.2
Drop-out Rate (%)	7.6	7.7	0.0	0.0	0.0	7.1
H.S. Diplomas (#)	123	118	0	1	1	3

Miller County

Texarkana SD

3512 Grand Ave • Texarkana, AR 71854
(870) 772-3371 • http://darkstar.swsc.k12.ar.us/
Grade Span: KG-12; **Agency Type:** 1
Schools: 9
5 Primary; 2 Middle; 2 High; 0 Other Level
8 Regular; 0 Special Education; 1 Vocational; 0 Alternative
0 Magnet; 0 Charter; 8 Title I Eligible; 8 School-wide Title I
Students: 4,592 (53.1% male; 46.9% female)
Individual Education Program: 738 (16.1%);
English Language Learner: 16 (0.3%); Migrant: 9 (0.2%)
Eligible for Free Lunch Program: 2,400 (52.3%)
Eligible for Reduced-Price Lunch Program: 309 (6.7%)
Teachers: 316.0 (14.5 to 1)
Librarians/Media Specialists: 8.0 (574.0 to 1)
Guidance Counselors: 14.0 (328.0 to 1)
Current Spending: ($ per student per year):
Total: $6,077; Instruction: $3,896; Support Services: $1,790
Enrollment, Drop-out Rates and Diploma Recipients by Race/Ethnicity

Category	Total	White	Black	Asian	AIAN	Hisp.
Enrollment (%)	100.0	50.3	47.7	0.1	0.2	1.6
Drop-out Rate (%)	12.9	12.5	13.6	0.0	0.0	7.1
H.S. Diplomas (#)	217	106	109	1	0	1

Mississippi County

Blytheville SD

405 W Park St • Blytheville, AR 72315
Mailing Address: PO Box 1169 • Blytheville, AR 72316-1169
(870) 762-2053 • http://crowleys.crsc.k12.ar.us/~blythev/
Grade Span: KG-12; **Agency Type:** 1
Schools: 7
3 Primary; 2 Middle; 2 High; 0 Other Level
7 Regular; 0 Special Education; 0 Vocational; 0 Alternative
0 Magnet; 1 Charter; 7 Title I Eligible; 7 School-wide Title I
Students: 3,386 (50.6% male; 49.4% female)
Individual Education Program: 479 (14.1%);
English Language Learner: 17 (0.5%); Migrant: 15 (0.4%)
Eligible for Free Lunch Program: 2,327 (68.7%)
Eligible for Reduced-Price Lunch Program: 261 (7.7%)
Teachers: 224.0 (15.1 to 1)
Librarians/Media Specialists: 6.0 (564.3 to 1)
Guidance Counselors: 10.0 (338.6 to 1)
Current Spending: ($ per student per year):
Total: $5,613; Instruction: $3,312; Support Services: $1,930
Enrollment, Drop-out Rates and Diploma Recipients by Race/Ethnicity

Category	Total	White	Black	Asian	AIAN	Hisp.
Enrollment (%)	100.0	22.7	75.9	0.3	0.0	1.1
Drop-out Rate (%)	10.6	11.0	10.6	0.0	0.0	0.0
H.S. Diplomas (#)	163	48	112	1	0	2

Osceola SD

2750 W Semmes • Osceola, AR 72370-0628
(870) 563-2561 • http://crowleys.crsc.k12.ar.us/~osceola/
Grade Span: PK-12; **Agency Type:** 1
Schools: 6
2 Primary; 3 Middle; 1 High; 0 Other Level
6 Regular; 0 Special Education; 0 Vocational; 0 Alternative
0 Magnet; 1 Charter; 6 Title I Eligible; 5 School-wide Title I
Students: 1,751 (54.1% male; 45.9% female)
Individual Education Program: 262 (15.0%);
English Language Learner: 2 (0.1%); Migrant: 3 (0.2%)
Eligible for Free Lunch Program: 1,245 (71.1%)
Eligible for Reduced-Price Lunch Program: 180 (10.3%)
Teachers: 118.0 (14.8 to 1)
Librarians/Media Specialists: 5.0 (350.2 to 1)
Guidance Counselors: 5.0 (350.2 to 1)
Current Spending: ($ per student per year):
Total: $6,217; Instruction: $4,005; Support Services: $1,758

Enrollment, Drop-out Rates and Diploma Recipients by Race/Ethnicity

Category	Total	White	Black	Asian	AIAN	Hisp.
Enrollment (%)	100.0	25.8	73.2	0.1	0.0	0.9
Drop-out Rate (%)	6.4	2.3	7.5	0.0	n/a	50.0
H.S. Diplomas (#)	124	34	90	0	0	0

Ouachita County

Camden Fairview SD

625 Clifton St • Camden, AR 71701-3327
(870) 836-4193 • http://cfpsd.scsc.k12.ar.us/
Grade Span: KG-12; **Agency Type:** 1
Schools: 7
3 Primary; 2 Middle; 1 High; 1 Other Level
6 Regular; 0 Special Education; 0 Vocational; 1 Alternative
0 Magnet; 0 Charter; 4 Title I Eligible; 1 School-wide Title I
Students: 3,159 (50.6% male; 49.4% female)
Individual Education Program: 356 (11.3%);
English Language Learner: 2 (0.1%); Migrant: 0 (0.0%)
Eligible for Free Lunch Program: 1,649 (52.2%)
Eligible for Reduced-Price Lunch Program: 192 (6.1%)
Teachers: 203.0 (15.6 to 1)
Librarians/Media Specialists: 6.0 (526.5 to 1)
Guidance Counselors: 9.0 (351.0 to 1)
Current Spending: ($ per student per year):
Total: $5,966; Instruction: $3,706; Support Services: $1,906

Enrollment, Drop-out Rates and Diploma Recipients by Race/Ethnicity

Category	Total	White	Black	Asian	AIAN	Hisp.
Enrollment (%)	100.0	38.1	60.6	0.7	0.2	0.5
Drop-out Rate (%)	5.1	3.9	6.0	0.0	n/a	0.0
H.S. Diplomas (#)	230	103	126	0	0	1

Phillips County

Helena-West Helena SD

PO Box 369 • Helena, AR 72342-0369
(870) 338-4425 • http://hwh.grsc.k12.ar.us/
Grade Span: KG-12; **Agency Type:** 1
Schools: 6
3 Primary; 2 Middle; 1 High; 0 Other Level
6 Regular; 0 Special Education; 0 Vocational; 0 Alternative
0 Magnet; 0 Charter; 6 Title I Eligible; 6 School-wide Title I
Students: 3,419 (49.9% male; 50.1% female)
Individual Education Program: 396 (11.6%);
English Language Learner: 1 (<0.1%); Migrant: 0 (0.0%)
Eligible for Free Lunch Program: 2,801 (81.9%)
Eligible for Reduced-Price Lunch Program: 180 (5.3%)
Teachers: 222.0 (15.4 to 1)
Librarians/Media Specialists: 7.0 (488.4 to 1)
Guidance Counselors: 8.0 (427.4 to 1)
Current Spending: ($ per student per year):
Total: $6,341; Instruction: $3,673; Support Services: $2,243

Enrollment, Drop-out Rates and Diploma Recipients by Race/Ethnicity

Category	Total	White	Black	Asian	AIAN	Hisp.
Enrollment (%)	100.0	7.1	92.3	0.3	0.0	0.4
Drop-out Rate (%)	12.7	24.4	11.8	0.0	0.0	0.0
H.S. Diplomas (#)	183	9	171	0	1	2

Poinsett County

Trumann SD

221 Pine Ave • Trumann, AR 72472-2700
(870) 483-6444 • http://wildcat.crsc.k12.ar.us/
Grade Span: KG-12; **Agency Type:** 1
Schools: 3
1 Primary; 1 Middle; 1 High; 0 Other Level
3 Regular; 0 Special Education; 0 Vocational; 0 Alternative
0 Magnet; 0 Charter; 2 Title I Eligible; 2 School-wide Title I
Students: 1,723 (50.1% male; 49.9% female)
Individual Education Program: 311 (18.0%);
English Language Learner: 13 (0.8%); Migrant: 70 (4.1%)
Eligible for Free Lunch Program: 828 (48.1%)
Eligible for Reduced-Price Lunch Program: 167 (9.7%)
Teachers: 115.0 (15.0 to 1)
Librarians/Media Specialists: 3.0 (574.3 to 1)
Guidance Counselors: 5.0 (344.6 to 1)
Current Spending: ($ per student per year):
Total: $5,201; Instruction: $3,252; Support Services: $1,631

Enrollment, Drop-out Rates and Diploma Recipients by Race/Ethnicity

Category	Total	White	Black	Asian	AIAN	Hisp.
Enrollment (%)	100.0	90.4	7.6	0.1	0.3	1.7
Drop-out Rate (%)	8.0	7.7	13.8	n/a	n/a	0.0
H.S. Diplomas (#)	81	80	1	0	0	0

Polk County

Mena SD

501 Hickory Ave • Mena, AR 71953-1945
(479) 394-1710 • http://170.211.34.2/Mena%20Public%202000/index.htm
Grade Span: KG-12; **Agency Type:** 1
Schools: 4
2 Primary; 1 Middle; 1 High; 0 Other Level
4 Regular; 0 Special Education; 0 Vocational; 0 Alternative
0 Magnet; 0 Charter; 2 Title I Eligible; 2 School-wide Title I
Students: 1,886 (51.7% male; 48.3% female)
Individual Education Program: 175 (9.3%);
English Language Learner: 0 (0.0%); Migrant: 0 (0.0%)
Eligible for Free Lunch Program: 755 (40.0%)
Eligible for Reduced-Price Lunch Program: 216 (11.5%)
Teachers: 120.0 (15.7 to 1)
Librarians/Media Specialists: 4.0 (471.5 to 1)
Guidance Counselors: 6.0 (314.3 to 1)
Current Spending: ($ per student per year):
Total: $5,459; Instruction: $3,510; Support Services: $1,636

Enrollment, Drop-out Rates and Diploma Recipients by Race/Ethnicity

Category	Total	White	Black	Asian	AIAN	Hisp.
Enrollment (%)	100.0	97.3	0.0	0.7	0.6	1.4
Drop-out Rate (%)	4.1	3.7	n/a	50.0	16.7	14.3
H.S. Diplomas (#)	117	115	0	1	1	0

Pope County

Russellville SD

220 W 10th St • Russellville, AR 72811-0928
Mailing Address: PO Box 928 • Russellville, AR 72811-0928
(479) 968-1306 • http://rsd.afsc.k12.ar.us/
Grade Span: KG-12; **Agency Type:** 1
Schools: 11
6 Primary; 2 Middle; 2 High; 1 Other Level
10 Regular; 0 Special Education; 1 Vocational; 0 Alternative
0 Magnet; 0 Charter; 5 Title I Eligible; 2 School-wide Title I
Students: 5,179 (51.6% male; 48.4% female)
Individual Education Program: 558 (10.8%);
English Language Learner: 121 (2.3%); Migrant: 165 (3.2%)
Eligible for Free Lunch Program: 1,763 (34.0%)
Eligible for Reduced-Price Lunch Program: 361 (7.0%)
Teachers: 330.0 (15.7 to 1)
Librarians/Media Specialists: 11.0 (470.8 to 1)
Guidance Counselors: 16.0 (323.7 to 1)
Current Spending: ($ per student per year):
Total: $6,224; Instruction: $4,029; Support Services: $1,917

Enrollment, Drop-out Rates and Diploma Recipients by Race/Ethnicity

Category	Total	White	Black	Asian	AIAN	Hisp.
Enrollment (%)	100.0	85.5	6.7	1.7	0.7	5.4
Drop-out Rate (%)	6.1	5.6	10.4	0.0	9.1	13.2
H.S. Diplomas (#)	324	288	23	3	2	8

Pulaski County

Little Rock SD

810 W Markham St • Little Rock, AR 72201-1306
(501) 447-1002 • http://www.lrsd.org/
Grade Span: PK-12; **Agency Type:** 1
Schools: 52
34 Primary; 8 Middle; 8 High; 2 Other Level
49 Regular; 0 Special Education; 1 Vocational; 2 Alternative
7 Magnet; 0 Charter; 34 Title I Eligible; 26 School-wide Title I
Students: 25,526 (49.9% male; 50.1% female)
Individual Education Program: 2,689 (10.5%);
English Language Learner: 785 (3.1%); Migrant: 0 (0.0%)
Eligible for Free Lunch Program: 11,812 (46.3%)
Eligible for Reduced-Price Lunch Program: 1,758 (6.9%)
Teachers: 1,744.0 (14.6 to 1)
Librarians/Media Specialists: 50.0 (510.5 to 1)
Guidance Counselors: 83.0 (307.5 to 1)
Current Spending: ($ per student per year):
Total: $7,391; Instruction: $4,260; Support Services: $2,847

Enrollment, Drop-out Rates and Diploma Recipients by Race/Ethnicity

Category	Total	White	Black	Asian	AIAN	Hisp.
Enrollment (%)	100.0	25.6	68.9	1.6	0.2	3.7
Drop-out Rate (%)	4.4	3.2	4.7	2.2	0.0	11.0
H.S. Diplomas (#)	1,334	428	865	17	2	22

North Little Rock SD

2700 Poplar St • North Little Rock, AR 72114
(501) 771-8000 • http://www.nlrsd.k12.ar.us/
Grade Span: PK-12; **Agency Type:** 1
Schools: 20
14 Primary; 4 Middle; 0 High; 2 Other Level

20 Regular; 0 Special Education; 0 Vocational; 0 Alternative
0 Magnet; 0 Charter; 17 Title I Eligible; 8 School-wide Title I
Students: 8,812 (50.8% male; 49.2% female)
Individual Education Program: 0 (0.0%);
English Language Learner: 88 (1.0%); Migrant: 0 (0.0%)
Eligible for Free Lunch Program: 4,405 (50.0%)
Eligible for Reduced-Price Lunch Program: 426 (4.8%)
Teachers: 604.0 (14.6 to 1)
Librarians/Media Specialists: 16.0 (550.8 to 1)
Guidance Counselors: 25.0 (352.5 to 1)
Current Spending: ($ per student per year):
Total: $6,880; Instruction: $3,927; Support Services: $2,630
Enrollment, Drop-out Rates and Diploma Recipients by Race/Ethnicity

Category	Total	White	Black	Asian	AIAN	Hisp.
Enrollment (%)	100.0	38.7	57.7	0.4	0.1	3.0
Drop-out Rate (%)	0.5	0.5	0.5	0.0	0.0	3.8
H.S. Diplomas (#)	508	261	222	9	2	14

Pulaski County Special SD
925 E Dixon Rd • Little Rock, AR 72216-4199
Mailing Address: PO Box 8601 • Little Rock, AR 72216-8601
(501) 490-2000 • http://pcssdweb.k12.ar.us/
Grade Span: PK-12; **Agency Type:** 1
Schools: 36
24 Primary; 5 Middle; 6 High; 1 Other Level
36 Regular; 0 Special Education; 0 Vocational; 0 Alternative
0 Magnet; 0 Charter; 21 Title I Eligible; 13 School-wide Title I
Students: 18,323 (52.3% male; 47.7% female)
Individual Education Program: 2,551 (13.9%);
English Language Learner: 92 (0.5%); Migrant: 0 (0.0%)
Eligible for Free Lunch Program: 6,466 (35.3%)
Eligible for Reduced-Price Lunch Program: 1,755 (9.6%)
Teachers: 1,213.0 (15.1 to 1)
Librarians/Media Specialists: 36.0 (509.0 to 1)
Guidance Counselors: 61.0 (300.4 to 1)
Current Spending: ($ per student per year):
Total: $6,673; Instruction: $3,870; Support Services: $2,499
Enrollment, Drop-out Rates and Diploma Recipients by Race/Ethnicity

Category	Total	White	Black	Asian	AIAN	Hisp.
Enrollment (%)	100.0	59.6	37.8	0.7	0.2	1.6
Drop-out Rate (%)	7.3	6.7	8.8	2.2	0.0	9.1
H.S. Diplomas (#)	816	539	260	8	0	9

Randolph County

Pocahontas SD
2300 N Park • Pocahontas, AR 72455-1306
(870) 892-4573 • http://www.nesc.k12.ar.us/
Grade Span: KG-12; **Agency Type:** 1
Schools: 4
2 Primary; 1 Middle; 1 High; 0 Other Level
4 Regular; 0 Special Education; 0 Vocational; 0 Alternative
0 Magnet; 0 Charter; 2 Title I Eligible; 0 School-wide Title I
Students: 1,771 (52.9% male; 47.1% female)
Individual Education Program: 237 (13.4%);
English Language Learner: 6 (0.3%); Migrant: 4 (0.2%)
Eligible for Free Lunch Program: 643 (36.3%)
Eligible for Reduced-Price Lunch Program: 287 (16.2%)
Teachers: 108.0 (16.4 to 1)
Librarians/Media Specialists: 4.0 (442.8 to 1)
Guidance Counselors: 8.0 (221.4 to 1)
Current Spending: ($ per student per year):
Total: $5,262; Instruction: $3,487; Support Services: $1,527
Enrollment, Drop-out Rates and Diploma Recipients by Race/Ethnicity

Category	Total	White	Black	Asian	AIAN	Hisp.
Enrollment (%)	100.0	97.2	1.0	0.2	0.2	1.4
Drop-out Rate (%)	4.5	4.5	25.0	0.0	0.0	0.0
H.S. Diplomas (#)	110	106	0	0	1	3

Saline County

Benton SD
PO Box 939 • Benton, AR 72018
(501) 778-4861 • http://www.bentonark.com/sindex.html
Grade Span: KG-12; **Agency Type:** 1
Schools: 7
4 Primary; 1 Middle; 1 High; 1 Other Level
7 Regular; 0 Special Education; 0 Vocational; 0 Alternative
0 Magnet; 0 Charter; 0 Title I Eligible; 0 School-wide Title I
Students: 4,150 (51.9% male; 48.1% female)
Individual Education Program: 431 (10.4%);
English Language Learner: 72 (1.7%); Migrant: 3 (0.1%)
Eligible for Free Lunch Program: 764 (18.4%)
Eligible for Reduced-Price Lunch Program: 231 (5.6%)
Teachers: 263.0 (15.8 to 1)
Librarians/Media Specialists: 7.0 (592.9 to 1)
Guidance Counselors: 10.0 (415.0 to 1)
Current Spending: ($ per student per year):
Total: $5,462; Instruction: $3,543; Support Services: $1,654
Enrollment, Drop-out Rates and Diploma Recipients by Race/Ethnicity

Category	Total	White	Black	Asian	AIAN	Hisp.
Enrollment (%)	100.0	91.7	4.9	0.6	0.5	2.4
Drop-out Rate (%)	4.1	2.9	20.4	10.0	16.7	23.5
H.S. Diplomas (#)	274	259	9	3	0	3

Bryant SD
200 NW 4th St • Bryant, AR 72022-3424
(501) 847-5600 • http://bryant.dsc.k12.ar.us/
Grade Span: KG-12; **Agency Type:** 1
Schools: 8
5 Primary; 1 Middle; 1 High; 1 Other Level
8 Regular; 0 Special Education; 0 Vocational; 0 Alternative
0 Magnet; 0 Charter; 6 Title I Eligible; 0 School-wide Title I
Students: 5,967 (51.6% male; 48.4% female)
Individual Education Program: 891 (14.9%);
English Language Learner: 66 (1.1%); Migrant: 0 (0.0%)
Eligible for Free Lunch Program: 1,109 (18.6%)
Eligible for Reduced-Price Lunch Program: 357 (6.0%)
Teachers: 345.0 (17.3 to 1)
Librarians/Media Specialists: 8.0 (745.9 to 1)
Guidance Counselors: 14.0 (426.2 to 1)
Current Spending: ($ per student per year):
Total: $5,053; Instruction: $3,443; Support Services: $1,409
Enrollment, Drop-out Rates and Diploma Recipients by Race/Ethnicity

Category	Total	White	Black	Asian	AIAN	Hisp.
Enrollment (%)	100.0	95.4	1.9	0.9	0.4	1.5
Drop-out Rate (%)	4.4	4.2	10.3	0.0	0.0	7.7
H.S. Diplomas (#)	388	380	3	2	0	3

Scott County

Waldron SD
570 Hwy 71 S • Waldron, AR 72958-1397
(479) 637-3179 • http://zebra.wsc.k12.ar.us/~wbulldog/
Grade Span: KG-12; **Agency Type:** 1
Schools: 3
1 Primary; 1 Middle; 1 High; 0 Other Level
3 Regular; 0 Special Education; 0 Vocational; 0 Alternative
0 Magnet; 0 Charter; 2 Title I Eligible; 2 School-wide Title I
Students: 1,658 (50.5% male; 49.5% female)
Individual Education Program: 201 (12.1%);
English Language Learner: 64 (3.9%); Migrant: 160 (9.7%)
Eligible for Free Lunch Program: 704 (42.5%)
Eligible for Reduced-Price Lunch Program: 159 (9.6%)
Teachers: 113.0 (14.7 to 1)
Librarians/Media Specialists: 3.0 (552.7 to 1)
Guidance Counselors: 5.0 (331.6 to 1)
Current Spending: ($ per student per year):
Total: $4,825; Instruction: $2,956; Support Services: $1,591
Enrollment, Drop-out Rates and Diploma Recipients by Race/Ethnicity

Category	Total	White	Black	Asian	AIAN	Hisp.
Enrollment (%)	100.0	89.4	0.4	1.6	1.3	7.4
Drop-out Rate (%)	3.4	2.7	n/a	0.0	0.0	26.7
H.S. Diplomas (#)	110	106	0	1	1	2

Sebastian County

Fort Smith SD
3205 Jenny Lind Rd • Fort Smith, AR 72901
Mailing Address: PO Box 1948 • Fort Smith, AR 72902-1948
(501) 785-2501 • http://clx.fssc.k12.ar.us/
Grade Span: KG-12; **Agency Type:** 1
Schools: 26
19 Primary; 4 Middle; 3 High; 0 Other Level
25 Regular; 0 Special Education; 0 Vocational; 1 Alternative
0 Magnet; 0 Charter; 16 Title I Eligible; 14 School-wide Title I
Students: 12,844 (50.9% male; 49.1% female)
Individual Education Program: 1,758 (13.7%);
English Language Learner: 1,601 (12.5%); Migrant: 728 (5.7%)
Eligible for Free Lunch Program: 5,479 (42.7%)
Eligible for Reduced-Price Lunch Program: 987 (7.7%)
Teachers: 820.0 (15.7 to 1)
Librarians/Media Specialists: 24.0 (535.2 to 1)
Guidance Counselors: 35.0 (367.0 to 1)
Current Spending: ($ per student per year):
Total: $6,118; Instruction: $3,725; Support Services: $2,063

Enrollment, Drop-out Rates and Diploma Recipients by Race/Ethnicity

Category	Total	White	Black	Asian	AIAN	Hisp.
Enrollment (%)	100.0	61.0	14.6	6.5	3.0	14.9
Drop-out Rate (%)	5.5	4.7	6.7	3.4	7.4	12.7
H.S. Diplomas (#)	822	554	108	86	25	49

Greenwood SD

420 N Main • Greenwood, AR 72936-7016
(479) 996-4142 • http://greenwood.k12.ar.us/
Grade Span: KG-12; **Agency Type:** 1
Schools: 5
2 Primary; 1 Middle; 1 High; 1 Other Level
5 Regular; 0 Special Education; 0 Vocational; 0 Alternative
0 Magnet; 0 Charter; 5 Title I Eligible; 0 School-wide Title I
Students: 3,169 (51.5% male; 48.5% female)
Individual Education Program: 407 (12.8%);
English Language Learner: 13 (0.4%); Migrant: 1 (<0.1%)
Eligible for Free Lunch Program: 448 (14.1%)
Eligible for Reduced-Price Lunch Program: 212 (6.7%)
Teachers: 184.0 (17.2 to 1)
Librarians/Media Specialists: 5.0 (633.8 to 1)
Guidance Counselors: 8.0 (396.1 to 1)
Current Spending: ($ per student per year):
Total: $5,213; Instruction: $3,298; Support Services: $1,686
Enrollment, Drop-out Rates and Diploma Recipients by Race/Ethnicity

Category	Total	White	Black	Asian	AIAN	Hisp.
Enrollment (%)	100.0	95.3	0.3	0.9	2.1	1.4
Drop-out Rate (%)	2.9	2.8	0.0	0.0	6.7	12.5
H.S. Diplomas (#)	227	221	0	3	2	1

Sevier County

Dequeen SD

PO Box 950 • De Queen, AR 71832-0950
(870) 584-4312 • http://leopards.k12.ar.us/
Grade Span: KG-12; **Agency Type:** 1
Schools: 4
2 Primary; 1 Middle; 1 High; 0 Other Level
4 Regular; 0 Special Education; 0 Vocational; 0 Alternative
0 Magnet; 0 Charter; 3 Title I Eligible; 2 School-wide Title I
Students: 1,886 (52.4% male; 47.6% female)
Individual Education Program: 177 (9.4%);
English Language Learner: 757 (40.1%); Migrant: 526 (27.9%)
Eligible for Free Lunch Program: 1,019 (54.0%)
Eligible for Reduced-Price Lunch Program: 164 (8.7%)
Teachers: 121.0 (15.6 to 1)
Librarians/Media Specialists: 4.0 (471.5 to 1)
Guidance Counselors: 6.0 (314.3 to 1)
Current Spending: ($ per student per year):
Total: $4,876; Instruction: $2,827; Support Services: $1,676
Enrollment, Drop-out Rates and Diploma Recipients by Race/Ethnicity

Category	Total	White	Black	Asian	AIAN	Hisp.
Enrollment (%)	100.0	47.1	6.3	0.2	2.2	44.2
Drop-out Rate (%)	6.8	6.4	9.7	0.0	7.7	6.8
H.S. Diplomas (#)	81	57	1	0	3	20

Sharp County

Highland SD

1 Rebel Circle • Hardy, AR 72542-0419
Mailing Address: PO Box 419 • Hardy, AR 72542-0419
(870) 856-3275
Grade Span: KG-12; **Agency Type:** 1
Schools: 3
1 Primary; 1 Middle; 1 High; 0 Other Level
3 Regular; 0 Special Education; 0 Vocational; 0 Alternative
0 Magnet; 0 Charter; 3 Title I Eligible; 3 School-wide Title I
Students: 1,539 (52.8% male; 47.2% female)
Individual Education Program: 222 (14.4%);
English Language Learner: 0 (0.0%); Migrant: 1 (0.1%)
Eligible for Free Lunch Program: 718 (46.7%)
Eligible for Reduced-Price Lunch Program: 143 (9.3%)
Teachers: 95.0 (16.2 to 1)
Librarians/Media Specialists: 3.0 (513.0 to 1)
Guidance Counselors: 4.0 (384.8 to 1)
Current Spending: ($ per student per year):
Total: $5,153; Instruction: $3,148; Support Services: $1,689
Enrollment, Drop-out Rates and Diploma Recipients by Race/Ethnicity

Category	Total	White	Black	Asian	AIAN	Hisp.
Enrollment (%)	100.0	97.4	0.7	0.3	0.5	1.1
Drop-out Rate (%)	5.8	5.6	n/a	n/a	0.0	50.0
H.S. Diplomas (#)	83	82	0	0	0	1

St. Francis County

Forrest City SD

845 N Rosser • Forrest City, AR 72335-2364
(870) 633-1485 • http://mustang.grsc.k12.ar.us/
Grade Span: KG-12; **Agency Type:** 1
Schools: 8
5 Primary; 1 Middle; 1 High; 1 Other Level
8 Regular; 0 Special Education; 0 Vocational; 0 Alternative
0 Magnet; 0 Charter; 8 Title I Eligible; 8 School-wide Title I
Students: 4,045 (51.4% male; 48.6% female)
Individual Education Program: 532 (13.2%);
English Language Learner: 1 (<0.1%); Migrant: 48 (1.2%)
Eligible for Free Lunch Program: 2,643 (65.3%)
Eligible for Reduced-Price Lunch Program: 407 (10.1%)
Teachers: 248.0 (16.3 to 1)
Librarians/Media Specialists: 7.0 (577.9 to 1)
Guidance Counselors: 10.0 (404.5 to 1)
Current Spending: ($ per student per year):
Total: $7,362; Instruction: $4,315; Support Services: $2,520
Enrollment, Drop-out Rates and Diploma Recipients by Race/Ethnicity

Category	Total	White	Black	Asian	AIAN	Hisp.
Enrollment (%)	100.0	25.2	74.1	0.2	0.0	0.4
Drop-out Rate (%)	10.4	12.0	9.6	0.0	0.0	n/a
H.S. Diplomas (#)	236	51	181	2	2	0

Union County

El Dorado SD

200 W Oak St • El Dorado, AR 71730-5618
(870) 864-5001 • http://www.scsc.k12.ar.us/eldorado/
Grade Span: KG-12; **Agency Type:** 1
Schools: 10
7 Primary; 2 Middle; 1 High; 0 Other Level
10 Regular; 0 Special Education; 0 Vocational; 0 Alternative
0 Magnet; 1 Charter; 9 Title I Eligible; 7 School-wide Title I
Students: 4,416 (52.5% male; 47.5% female)
Individual Education Program: 416 (9.4%);
English Language Learner: 76 (1.7%); Migrant: 0 (0.0%)
Eligible for Free Lunch Program: 1,982 (44.9%)
Eligible for Reduced-Price Lunch Program: 311 (7.0%)
Teachers: 287.0 (15.4 to 1)
Librarians/Media Specialists: 9.0 (490.7 to 1)
Guidance Counselors: 14.0 (315.4 to 1)
Current Spending: ($ per student per year):
Total: $5,387; Instruction: $3,356; Support Services: $1,734
Enrollment, Drop-out Rates and Diploma Recipients by Race/Ethnicity

Category	Total	White	Black	Asian	AIAN	Hisp.
Enrollment (%)	100.0	40.7	55.4	0.6	0.0	3.2
Drop-out Rate (%)	2.8	1.1	4.1	0.0	0.0	16.7
H.S. Diplomas (#)	308	135	167	3	0	3

Washington County

Farmington SD

42 S Double Springs Rd • Farmington, AR 72730-2707
(479) 266-1805 • http://farmington.k12.ar.us/
Grade Span: KG-12; **Agency Type:** 1
Schools: 3
1 Primary; 1 Middle; 1 High; 0 Other Level
3 Regular; 0 Special Education; 0 Vocational; 0 Alternative
0 Magnet; 0 Charter; 1 Title I Eligible; 0 School-wide Title I
Students: 1,759 (49.8% male; 50.2% female)
Individual Education Program: 149 (8.5%);
English Language Learner: 39 (2.2%); Migrant: 0 (0.0%)
Eligible for Free Lunch Program: 334 (19.0%)
Eligible for Reduced-Price Lunch Program: 163 (9.3%)
Teachers: 127.0 (13.9 to 1)
Librarians/Media Specialists: 3.0 (586.3 to 1)
Guidance Counselors: 5.0 (351.8 to 1)
Current Spending: ($ per student per year):
Total: $5,277; Instruction: $3,177; Support Services: $1,823
Enrollment, Drop-out Rates and Diploma Recipients by Race/Ethnicity

Category	Total	White	Black	Asian	AIAN	Hisp.
Enrollment (%)	100.0	94.1	1.4	0.5	0.6	3.5
Drop-out Rate (%)	2.7	2.6	0.0	0.0	0.0	16.7
H.S. Diplomas (#)	98	95	0	0	2	1

Fayetteville SD

1000 W Stone St • Fayetteville, AR 72701
(479) 444-3000 • http://www.fayar.net/
Grade Span: PK-12; **Agency Type:** 1
Schools: 15
9 Primary; 2 Middle; 2 High; 2 Other Level
15 Regular; 0 Special Education; 0 Vocational; 0 Alternative

0 Magnet; 0 Charter; 0 Title I Eligible; 0 School-wide Title I
Students: 8,005 (50.5% male; 49.5% female)
Individual Education Program: 1,089 (13.6%);
English Language Learner: 529 (6.6%); Migrant: 158 (2.0%)
Eligible for Free Lunch Program: 1,929 (24.1%)
Eligible for Reduced-Price Lunch Program: 454 (5.7%)
Teachers: 498.0 (16.1 to 1)
Librarians/Media Specialists: 16.0 (500.3 to 1)
Guidance Counselors: 24.0 (333.5 to 1)
Current Spending: ($ per student per year):
Total: $6,336; Instruction: $3,637; Support Services: $2,430
Enrollment, Drop-out Rates and Diploma Recipients by Race/Ethnicity

Category	Total	White	Black	Asian	AIAN	Hisp.
Enrollment (%)	100.0	80.4	8.3	3.4	1.1	6.8
Drop-out Rate (%)	6.7	6.3	5.6	3.0	30.8	12.1
H.S. Diplomas (#)	539	472	23	16	3	25

Springdale SD

PO Box 8 • Springdale, AR 72765-0008
(479) 750-8800 • http://www.sadmin.jonesnet.org/
Grade Span: KG-12; **Agency Type:** 1
Schools: 16
11 Primary; 2 Middle; 0 High; 3 Other Level
16 Regular; 0 Special Education; 0 Vocational; 0 Alternative
0 Magnet; 0 Charter; 6 Title I Eligible; 6 School-wide Title I
Students: 12,839 (51.6% male; 48.4% female)
Individual Education Program: 1,424 (11.1%);
English Language Learner: 3,838 (29.9%); Migrant: 1,200 (9.3%)
Eligible for Free Lunch Program: 4,264 (33.2%)
Eligible for Reduced-Price Lunch Program: 984 (7.7%)
Teachers: 684.0 (18.8 to 1)
Librarians/Media Specialists: 17.0 (755.2 to 1)
Guidance Counselors: 27.0 (475.5 to 1)
Current Spending: ($ per student per year):
Total: $5,477; Instruction: $3,616; Support Services: $1,577
Enrollment, Drop-out Rates and Diploma Recipients by Race/Ethnicity

Category	Total	White	Black	Asian	AIAN	Hisp.
Enrollment (%)	100.0	66.7	1.1	6.0	0.7	25.6
Drop-out Rate (%)	6.5	5.9	25.0	6.6	6.7	9.9
H.S. Diplomas (#)	554	469	3	25	0	57

White County

Beebe SD

1201 W Center St • Beebe, AR 72012-3103
(501) 882-5463 • http://thor.k12.ar.us/
Grade Span: KG-12; **Agency Type:** 1
Schools: 6
2 Primary; 2 Middle; 1 High; 1 Other Level
6 Regular; 0 Special Education; 0 Vocational; 0 Alternative
0 Magnet; 0 Charter; 3 Title I Eligible; 0 School-wide Title I
Students: 2,370 (52.3% male; 47.7% female)
Individual Education Program: 312 (13.2%);
English Language Learner: 2 (0.1%); Migrant: 4 (0.2%)
Eligible for Free Lunch Program: 655 (27.6%)
Eligible for Reduced-Price Lunch Program: 186 (7.8%)
Teachers: 141.0 (16.8 to 1)
Librarians/Media Specialists: 5.0 (474.0 to 1)
Guidance Counselors: 6.0 (395.0 to 1)
Current Spending: ($ per student per year):
Total: $5,321; Instruction: $3,284; Support Services: $1,726
Enrollment, Drop-out Rates and Diploma Recipients by Race/Ethnicity

Category	Total	White	Black	Asian	AIAN	Hisp.
Enrollment (%)	100.0	94.5	3.7	0.8	0.3	0.8
Drop-out Rate (%)	4.3	4.0	10.3	0.0	0.0	0.0
H.S. Diplomas (#)	118	110	5	1	2	0

Searcy SD

801 N Elm • Searcy, AR 72143-3640
(501) 268-3517 • http://ssweb.wmsc.k12.ar.us/
Grade Span: KG-12; **Agency Type:** 1
Schools: 6
3 Primary; 2 Middle; 1 High; 0 Other Level
6 Regular; 0 Special Education; 0 Vocational; 0 Alternative
0 Magnet; 0 Charter; 3 Title I Eligible; 0 School-wide Title I
Students: 3,666 (50.3% male; 49.7% female)
Individual Education Program: 374 (10.2%);
English Language Learner: 35 (1.0%); Migrant: 70 (1.9%)
Eligible for Free Lunch Program: 889 (24.2%)
Eligible for Reduced-Price Lunch Program: 292 (8.0%)
Teachers: 217.0 (16.9 to 1)
Librarians/Media Specialists: 6.0 (611.0 to 1)
Guidance Counselors: 10.0 (366.6 to 1)
Current Spending: ($ per student per year):
Total: $4,886; Instruction: $3,085; Support Services: $1,506
Enrollment, Drop-out Rates and Diploma Recipients by Race/Ethnicity

Category	Total	White	Black	Asian	AIAN	Hisp.
Enrollment (%)	100.0	89.1	8.2	0.5	0.2	2.0
Drop-out Rate (%)	4.4	3.8	10.5	12.5	100.0	0.0
H.S. Diplomas (#)	214	193	17	1	0	3

Yell County

Dardanelle SD

209 Cedar St • Dardanelle, AR 72834-3215
(479) 229-4111 • http://lizardlink.afsc.k12.ar.us/
Grade Span: KG-12; **Agency Type:** 1
Schools: 4
2 Primary; 1 Middle; 1 High; 0 Other Level
4 Regular; 0 Special Education; 0 Vocational; 0 Alternative
0 Magnet; 0 Charter; 4 Title I Eligible; 4 School-wide Title I
Students: 1,764 (52.6% male; 47.4% female)
Individual Education Program: 228 (12.9%);
English Language Learner: 232 (13.2%); Migrant: 181 (10.3%)
Eligible for Free Lunch Program: 769 (43.6%)
Eligible for Reduced-Price Lunch Program: 229 (13.0%)
Teachers: 113.0 (15.6 to 1)
Librarians/Media Specialists: 4.0 (441.0 to 1)
Guidance Counselors: 4.0 (441.0 to 1)
Current Spending: ($ per student per year):
Total: $4,853; Instruction: $3,030; Support Services: $1,536
Enrollment, Drop-out Rates and Diploma Recipients by Race/Ethnicity

Category	Total	White	Black	Asian	AIAN	Hisp.
Enrollment (%)	100.0	78.7	3.7	1.1	0.3	16.2
Drop-out Rate (%)	3.6	3.6	7.1	0.0	0.0	2.5
H.S. Diplomas (#)	101	89	4	0	2	6

Number of Schools

Rank	Number	District Name	City
1	52	Little Rock SD	Little Rock
2	36	Pulaski County Special SD	Little Rock
3	26	Fort Smith SD	Fort Smith
4	20	North Little Rock SD	N Little Rock
5	18	Rogers SD	Rogers
6	16	Springdale SD	Springdale
7	15	Fayetteville SD	Fayetteville
8	14	Pine Bluff SD	Pine Bluff
9	13	Conway SD	Conway
10	12	Cabot SD	Cabot
10	12	West Memphis SD	West Memphis
12	11	Russellville SD	Russellville
12	11	Van Buren SD	Van Buren
14	10	Bentonville SD	Bentonville
14	10	El Dorado SD	El Dorado
14	10	Jonesboro SD	Jonesboro
17	9	Texarkana SD	Texarkana
18	8	Bryant SD	Bryant
18	8	Forrest City SD	Forrest City
20	7	Batesville SD	Batesville
20	7	Benton SD	Benton
20	7	Blytheville SD	Blytheville
20	7	Camden Fairview SD	Camden
20	7	Crossett SD	Crossett
20	7	Harrison SD	Harrison
20	7	White Hall SD	White Hall
27	6	Beebe SD	Beebe
27	6	Hamburg SD	Hamburg
27	6	Helena-West Helena SD	Helena
27	6	Hot Springs SD	Hot Springs
27	6	Lake Hamilton SD	Pearcy
27	6	Malvern SD	Malvern
27	6	Marion SD	Marion
27	6	Monticello SD	Monticello
27	6	Mountain Home SD	Mountain Home
27	6	Nettleton SD	Jonesboro
27	6	Osceola SD	Osceola
27	6	Paragould SD	Paragould
27	6	Searcy SD	Searcy
27	6	Sheridan SD	Sheridan
27	6	South Conway County SD	Morrilton
27	6	Stuttgart SD	Stuttgart
43	5	Arkadelphia SD	Arkadelphia
43	5	Ashdown SD	Ashdown
43	5	Clarksville SD	Clarksville
43	5	Dollarway SD	Pine Bluff
43	5	Greenbrier SD	Greenbrier
43	5	Greenwood SD	Greenwood
43	5	Hope SD	Hope
43	5	Lakeside SD	Hot Springs
43	5	Siloam Springs SD	Siloam Springs
43	5	Vilonia SD	Vilonia
43	5	Warren SD	Warren
43	5	Watson Chapel SD	Pine Bluff
55	4	Alma SD	Alma
55	4	Dardanelle SD	Dardanelle
55	4	Dequeen SD	De Queen
55	4	Dumas SD	Dumas
55	4	Greene County Tech SD	Paragould
55	4	Huntsville SD	Huntsville
55	4	Lee County SD	Marianna
55	4	Lonoke SD	Lonoke
55	4	Magnolia SD	Magnolia
55	4	Mena SD	Mena
55	4	Nashville SD	Nashville
55	4	Newport SD	Newport
55	4	Pocahontas SD	Pocahontas
55	4	Wynne SD	Wynne
69	3	Berryville SD	Berryville
69	3	Farmington SD	Farmington
69	3	Heber Springs SD	Heber Springs
69	3	Highland SD	Hardy
69	3	Ozark SD	Ozark
69	3	Star City SD	Star City
69	3	Trumann SD	Trumann
69	3	Waldron SD	Waldron
69	3	Westside CSD	Jonesboro

Number of Teachers

Rank	Number	District Name	City
1	1,744	Little Rock SD	Little Rock
2	1,213	Pulaski County Special SD	Little Rock
3	820	Fort Smith SD	Fort Smith
4	687	Rogers SD	Rogers
5	684	Springdale SD	Springdale
6	604	North Little Rock SD	N Little Rock
7	498	Fayetteville SD	Fayetteville
8	488	Conway SD	Conway
9	483	Bentonville SD	Bentonville
10	466	Cabot SD	Cabot
11	420	Pine Bluff SD	Pine Bluff
12	388	West Memphis SD	West Memphis
13	367	Van Buren SD	Van Buren
14	345	Bryant SD	Bryant
15	330	Russellville SD	Russellville
16	316	Texarkana SD	Texarkana
17	287	El Dorado SD	El Dorado
18	271	Jonesboro SD	Jonesboro
19	263	Benton SD	Benton
20	257	Hot Springs SD	Hot Springs
21	249	Sheridan SD	Sheridan
22	248	Forrest City SD	Forrest City
23	224	Blytheville SD	Blytheville
24	223	Mountain Home SD	Mountain Home
25	222	Helena-West Helena SD	Helena
26	217	Searcy SD	Searcy
27	205	Lake Hamilton SD	Pearcy
28	203	Camden Fairview SD	Camden
29	187	Watson Chapel SD	Pine Bluff
30	184	Greenwood SD	Greenwood
30	184	Siloam Springs SD	Siloam Springs
30	184	Wynne SD	Wynne
33	183	Hope SD	Hope
33	183	Marion SD	Marion
35	181	Alma SD	Alma
36	180	Greene County Tech SD	Paragould
37	179	White Hall SD	White Hall
38	174	Harrison SD	Harrison
38	174	Magnolia SD	Magnolia
40	171	Paragould SD	Paragould
41	166	Nettleton SD	Jonesboro
41	166	South Conway County SD	Morrilton
43	162	Greenbrier SD	Greenbrier
44	160	Crossett SD	Crossett
45	158	Lakeside SD	Hot Springs
46	150	Arkadelphia SD	Arkadelphia
47	146	Clarksville SD	Clarksville
48	145	Vilonia SD	Vilonia
49	144	Malvern SD	Malvern
50	141	Batesville SD	Batesville
50	141	Beebe SD	Beebe
52	133	Stuttgart SD	Stuttgart
53	132	Monticello SD	Monticello
54	130	Nashville SD	Nashville
55	128	Newport SD	Newport
56	127	Farmington SD	Farmington
57	124	Dumas SD	Dumas
58	121	Ashdown SD	Ashdown
58	121	Dequeen SD	De Queen
60	120	Heber Springs SD	Heber Springs
60	120	Mena SD	Mena
62	118	Huntsville SD	Huntsville
62	118	Osceola SD	Osceola
64	115	Trumann SD	Trumann
65	113	Dardanelle SD	Dardanelle
65	113	Hamburg SD	Hamburg
65	113	Waldron SD	Waldron
68	111	Berryville SD	Berryville
68	111	Lonoke SD	Lonoke
68	111	Warren SD	Warren
71	109	Westside CSD	Jonesboro
72	108	Pocahontas SD	Pocahontas
73	107	Dollarway SD	Pine Bluff
74	104	Ozark SD	Ozark
75	103	Lee County SD	Marianna
76	101	Star City SD	Star City
77	95	Highland SD	Hardy

Number of Students

Rank	Number	District Name	City
1	25,526	Little Rock SD	Little Rock
2	18,323	Pulaski County Special SD	Little Rock
3	12,844	Fort Smith SD	Fort Smith
4	12,839	Springdale SD	Springdale
5	11,853	Rogers SD	Rogers
6	8,812	North Little Rock SD	N Little Rock
7	8,109	Conway SD	Conway
8	8,005	Fayetteville SD	Fayetteville
9	7,721	Bentonville SD	Bentonville
10	7,496	Cabot SD	Cabot
11	6,158	Pine Bluff SD	Pine Bluff
12	6,109	West Memphis SD	West Memphis
13	5,967	Bryant SD	Bryant
14	5,537	Van Buren SD	Van Buren
15	5,179	Russellville SD	Russellville
16	4,753	Jonesboro SD	Jonesboro
17	4,592	Texarkana SD	Texarkana
18	4,416	El Dorado SD	El Dorado
19	4,150	Benton SD	Benton
20	4,099	Sheridan SD	Sheridan
21	4,045	Forrest City SD	Forrest City
22	3,786	Mountain Home SD	Mountain Home
23	3,773	Lake Hamilton SD	Pearcy
24	3,666	Searcy SD	Searcy
25	3,419	Helena-West Helena SD	Helena
26	3,401	Hot Springs SD	Hot Springs
27	3,386	Blytheville SD	Blytheville
28	3,296	Marion SD	Marion
29	3,169	Greenwood SD	Greenwood
30	3,168	Watson Chapel SD	Pine Bluff
31	3,159	Camden Fairview SD	Camden
32	3,057	White Hall SD	White Hall
33	2,972	Siloam Springs SD	Siloam Springs
34	2,916	Alma SD	Alma
35	2,891	Greene County Tech SD	Paragould
36	2,843	Wynne SD	Wynne
37	2,796	Harrison SD	Harrison
38	2,771	Magnolia SD	Magnolia
39	2,754	Hope SD	Hope
40	2,651	Paragould SD	Paragould
41	2,623	Nettleton SD	Jonesboro
42	2,588	Vilonia SD	Vilonia
43	2,517	Lakeside SD	Hot Springs
44	2,445	Crossett SD	Crossett
45	2,406	South Conway County SD	Morrilton
46	2,397	Greenbrier SD	Greenbrier
47	2,370	Beebe SD	Beebe
48	2,276	Arkadelphia SD	Arkadelphia
49	2,200	Malvern SD	Malvern
50	2,178	Clarksville SD	Clarksville
51	2,102	Monticello SD	Monticello
52	2,099	Batesville SD	Batesville
53	2,085	Huntsville SD	Huntsville
54	1,886	Dequeen SD	De Queen
54	1,886	Mena SD	Mena
56	1,868	Stuttgart SD	Stuttgart
57	1,771	Pocahontas SD	Pocahontas
58	1,764	Dardanelle SD	Dardanelle
59	1,763	Lonoke SD	Lonoke
60	1,759	Farmington SD	Farmington
61	1,757	Nashville SD	Nashville
62	1,751	Osceola SD	Osceola
63	1,723	Trumann SD	Trumann
64	1,696	Heber Springs SD	Heber Springs
65	1,692	Berryville SD	Berryville
66	1,659	Westside CSD	Jonesboro
67	1,658	Waldron SD	Waldron
68	1,656	Ashdown SD	Ashdown
69	1,633	Ozark SD	Ozark
70	1,625	Newport SD	Newport
71	1,622	Lee County SD	Marianna
72	1,614	Hamburg SD	Hamburg
73	1,607	Dumas SD	Dumas
74	1,571	Warren SD	Warren
75	1,539	Highland SD	Hardy
76	1,538	Dollarway SD	Pine Bluff
77	1,520	Star City SD	Star City

Male Students

Rank	Percent	District Name	City
1	54.1	Osceola SD	Osceola
2	53.1	Texarkana SD	Texarkana
3	52.9	Pocahontas SD	Pocahontas
4	52.8	Highland SD	Hardy
4	52.8	Lake Hamilton SD	Pearcy
6	52.6	Dardanelle SD	Dardanelle
7	52.5	Ashdown SD	Ashdown
7	52.5	El Dorado SD	El Dorado
9	52.4	Dequeen SD	De Queen
10	52.3	Beebe SD	Beebe
10	52.3	Greene County Tech SD	Paragould
10	52.3	Pulaski County Special SD	Little Rock
13	52.2	Dollarway SD	Pine Bluff
13	52.2	Ozark SD	Ozark
15	52.1	Alma SD	Alma
15	52.1	Lonoke SD	Lonoke
17	52.0	Hope SD	Hope
17	52.0	Hot Springs SD	Hot Springs
17	52.0	Mountain Home SD	Mountain Home
17	52.0	Siloam Springs SD	Siloam Springs
21	51.9	Benton SD	Benton
21	51.9	Newport SD	Newport
23	51.8	Huntsville SD	Huntsville
23	51.8	Nashville SD	Nashville
23	51.8	Star City SD	Star City
23	51.8	Vilonia SD	Vilonia
23	51.8	White Hall SD	White Hall
23	51.8	Wynne SD	Wynne
29	51.7	Berryville SD	Berryville
29	51.7	Mena SD	Mena
31	51.6	Bryant SD	Bryant
31	51.6	Harrison SD	Harrison
31	51.6	Russellville SD	Russellville

31	51.6	Springdale SD	Springdale
31	51.6	Stuttgart SD	Stuttgart
36	51.5	Greenbrier SD	Greenbrier
36	51.5	Greenwood SD	Greenwood
38	51.4	Arkadelphia SD	Arkadelphia
38	51.4	Cabot SD	Cabot
38	51.4	Forrest City SD	Forrest City
38	51.4	Warren SD	Warren
42	51.3	Clarksville SD	Clarksville
42	51.3	Conway SD	Conway
42	51.3	Rogers SD	Rogers
45	51.2	Batesville SD	Batesville
45	51.2	Marion SD	Marion
47	51.1	Westside CSD	Jonesboro
48	51.0	Bentonville SD	Bentonville
48	51.0	Lakeside SD	Hot Springs
48	51.0	Monticello SD	Monticello
48	51.0	Van Buren SD	Van Buren
52	50.9	Fort Smith SD	Fort Smith
52	50.9	Heber Springs SD	Heber Springs
52	50.9	Malvern SD	Malvern
52	50.9	Sheridan SD	Sheridan
56	50.8	North Little Rock SD	N Little Rock
56	50.8	Paragould SD	Paragould
58	50.6	Blytheville SD	Blytheville
58	50.6	Camden Fairview SD	Camden
58	50.6	Nettleton SD	Jonesboro
61	50.5	Dumas SD	Dumas
61	50.5	Fayetteville SD	Fayetteville
61	50.5	Waldron SD	Waldron
64	50.4	West Memphis SD	West Memphis
65	50.3	Magnolia SD	Magnolia
65	50.3	Searcy SD	Searcy
65	50.3	Watson Chapel SD	Pine Bluff
68	50.2	Pine Bluff SD	Pine Bluff
69	50.1	Trumann SD	Trumann
70	50.0	Jonesboro SD	Jonesboro
71	49.9	Hamburg SD	Hamburg
71	49.9	Helena-West Helena SD	Helena
71	49.9	Little Rock SD	Little Rock
71	49.9	South Conway County SD	Morrilton
75	49.8	Farmington SD	Farmington
76	49.6	Crossett SD	Crossett
77	49.3	Lee County SD	Marianna

Female Students

Rank	Percent	District Name	City
1	50.7	Lee County SD	Marianna
2	50.4	Crossett SD	Crossett
3	50.2	Farmington SD	Farmington
4	50.1	Hamburg SD	Hamburg
4	50.1	Helena-West Helena SD	Helena
4	50.1	Little Rock SD	Little Rock
4	50.1	South Conway County SD	Morrilton
8	50.0	Jonesboro SD	Jonesboro
9	49.9	Trumann SD	Trumann
10	49.8	Pine Bluff SD	Pine Bluff
11	49.7	Magnolia SD	Magnolia
11	49.7	Searcy SD	Searcy
11	49.7	Watson Chapel SD	Pine Bluff
14	49.6	West Memphis SD	West Memphis
15	49.5	Dumas SD	Dumas
15	49.5	Fayetteville SD	Fayetteville
15	49.5	Waldron SD	Waldron
18	49.4	Blytheville SD	Blytheville
18	49.4	Camden Fairview SD	Camden
18	49.4	Nettleton SD	Jonesboro
21	49.2	North Little Rock SD	N Little Rock
21	49.2	Paragould SD	Paragould
23	49.1	Fort Smith SD	Fort Smith
23	49.1	Heber Springs SD	Heber Springs
23	49.1	Malvern SD	Malvern
23	49.1	Sheridan SD	Sheridan
27	49.0	Bentonville SD	Bentonville
27	49.0	Lakeside SD	Hot Springs
27	49.0	Monticello SD	Monticello
27	49.0	Van Buren SD	Van Buren
31	48.9	Westside CSD	Jonesboro
32	48.8	Batesville SD	Batesville
32	48.8	Marion SD	Marion
34	48.7	Clarksville SD	Clarksville
34	48.7	Conway SD	Conway
34	48.7	Rogers SD	Rogers
37	48.6	Arkadelphia SD	Arkadelphia
37	48.6	Cabot SD	Cabot
37	48.6	Forrest City SD	Forrest City
37	48.6	Warren SD	Warren
41	48.5	Greenbrier SD	Greenbrier
41	48.5	Greenwood SD	Greenwood
43	48.4	Bryant SD	Bryant
43	48.4	Harrison SD	Harrison
43	48.4	Russellville SD	Russellville
43	48.4	Springdale SD	Springdale
43	48.4	Stuttgart SD	Stuttgart
48	48.3	Berryville SD	Berryville
48	48.3	Mena SD	Mena
50	48.2	Huntsville SD	Huntsville
50	48.2	Nashville SD	Nashville
50	48.2	Star City SD	Star City
50	48.2	Vilonia SD	Vilonia
50	48.2	White Hall SD	White Hall
50	48.2	Wynne SD	Wynne
56	48.1	Benton SD	Benton
56	48.1	Newport SD	Newport
58	48.0	Hope SD	Hope
58	48.0	Hot Springs SD	Hot Springs
58	48.0	Mountain Home SD	Mountain Home
58	48.0	Siloam Springs SD	Siloam Springs
62	47.9	Alma SD	Alma
62	47.9	Lonoke SD	Lonoke
64	47.8	Dollarway SD	Pine Bluff
64	47.8	Ozark SD	Ozark
66	47.7	Beebe SD	Beebe
66	47.7	Greene County Tech SD	Paragould
66	47.7	Pulaski County Special SD	Little Rock
69	47.6	Dequeen SD	De Queen
70	47.5	Ashdown SD	Ashdown
70	47.5	El Dorado SD	El Dorado
72	47.4	Dardanelle SD	Dardanelle
73	47.2	Highland SD	Hardy
73	47.2	Lake Hamilton SD	Pearcy
75	47.1	Pocahontas SD	Pocahontas
76	46.9	Texarkana SD	Texarkana
77	45.9	Osceola SD	Osceola

Individual Education Program Students

Rank	Percent	District Name	City
1	18.0	Trumann SD	Trumann
2	17.7	Paragould SD	Paragould
3	17.1	Heber Springs SD	Heber Springs
4	16.5	Batesville SD	Batesville
5	16.1	Texarkana SD	Texarkana
6	15.1	Lonoke SD	Lonoke
6	15.1	Star City SD	Star City
8	15.0	Greenbrier SD	Greenbrier
8	15.0	Osceola SD	Osceola
10	14.9	Bryant SD	Bryant
11	14.8	Hot Springs SD	Hot Springs
12	14.5	Vilonia SD	Vilonia
13	14.4	Highland SD	Hardy
13	14.4	South Conway County SD	Morrilton
15	14.3	Dumas SD	Dumas
16	14.1	Blytheville SD	Blytheville
17	13.9	Lake Hamilton SD	Pearcy
17	13.9	Pulaski County Special SD	Little Rock
19	13.8	Cabot SD	Cabot
19	13.8	Conway SD	Conway
19	13.8	Greene County Tech SD	Paragould
19	13.8	Malvern SD	Malvern
23	13.7	Fort Smith SD	Fort Smith
23	13.7	Westside CSD	Jonesboro
25	13.6	Fayetteville SD	Fayetteville
26	13.5	Newport SD	Newport
27	13.4	Arkadelphia SD	Arkadelphia
27	13.4	Pocahontas SD	Pocahontas
29	13.2	Alma SD	Alma
29	13.2	Beebe SD	Beebe
29	13.2	Forrest City SD	Forrest City
32	13.1	Lee County SD	Marianna
33	13.0	Nettleton SD	Jonesboro
34	12.9	Dardanelle SD	Dardanelle
35	12.8	Greenwood SD	Greenwood
36	12.4	Ashdown SD	Ashdown
36	12.4	Van Buren SD	Van Buren
38	12.3	Rogers SD	Rogers
38	12.3	West Memphis SD	West Memphis
40	12.2	Hamburg SD	Hamburg
41	12.1	Waldron SD	Waldron
42	12.0	Dollarway SD	Pine Bluff
42	12.0	Mountain Home SD	Mountain Home
44	11.9	Huntsville SD	Huntsville
44	11.9	Wynne SD	Wynne
46	11.8	Lakeside SD	Hot Springs
47	11.6	Clarksville SD	Clarksville
47	11.6	Helena-West Helena SD	Helena
47	11.6	Nashville SD	Nashville
47	11.6	Sheridan SD	Sheridan
51	11.4	Monticello SD	Monticello
52	11.3	Camden Fairview SD	Camden
53	11.1	Bentonville SD	Bentonville
53	11.1	Springdale SD	Springdale
55	10.9	Marion SD	Marion
55	10.9	White Hall SD	White Hall
57	10.8	Berryville SD	Berryville
57	10.8	Harrison SD	Harrison
57	10.8	Jonesboro SD	Jonesboro
57	10.8	Russellville SD	Russellville
61	10.5	Little Rock SD	Little Rock
62	10.4	Benton SD	Benton
62	10.4	Pine Bluff SD	Pine Bluff
64	10.2	Searcy SD	Searcy
65	10.1	Hope SD	Hope
66	10.0	Warren SD	Warren
67	9.9	Ozark SD	Ozark
67	9.9	Stuttgart SD	Stuttgart
67	9.9	Watson Chapel SD	Pine Bluff
70	9.4	Dequeen SD	De Queen
70	9.4	El Dorado SD	El Dorado
72	9.3	Mena SD	Mena
73	9.1	Magnolia SD	Magnolia
74	8.8	Crossett SD	Crossett
75	8.5	Farmington SD	Farmington
76	7.7	Siloam Springs SD	Siloam Springs
77	0.0	North Little Rock SD	N Little Rock

English Language Learner Students

Rank	Percent	District Name	City
1	40.1	Dequeen SD	De Queen
2	29.9	Springdale SD	Springdale
3	20.7	Rogers SD	Rogers
4	13.2	Dardanelle SD	Dardanelle
5	12.5	Fort Smith SD	Fort Smith
6	11.8	Berryville SD	Berryville
7	11.6	Clarksville SD	Clarksville
8	8.9	Siloam Springs SD	Siloam Springs
9	7.6	Hope SD	Hope
10	6.6	Fayetteville SD	Fayetteville
11	6.0	Hamburg SD	Hamburg
12	5.0	Nashville SD	Nashville
13	4.6	Hot Springs SD	Hot Springs
13	4.6	Lakeside SD	Hot Springs
15	4.3	Van Buren SD	Van Buren
16	4.0	Batesville SD	Batesville
17	3.9	Waldron SD	Waldron
18	3.5	Dumas SD	Dumas
19	3.4	Warren SD	Warren
20	3.3	Huntsville SD	Huntsville
21	3.1	Little Rock SD	Little Rock
22	2.5	Bentonville SD	Bentonville
23	2.4	Jonesboro SD	Jonesboro
24	2.3	Russellville SD	Russellville
25	2.2	Farmington SD	Farmington
26	1.9	Lonoke SD	Lonoke
27	1.7	Benton SD	Benton
27	1.7	El Dorado SD	El Dorado
27	1.7	Nettleton SD	Jonesboro
27	1.7	South Conway County SD	Morrilton
31	1.5	Star City SD	Star City
32	1.3	Newport SD	Newport
33	1.2	Conway SD	Conway
33	1.2	Crossett SD	Crossett
35	1.1	Bryant SD	Bryant
36	1.0	North Little Rock SD	N Little Rock
36	1.0	Searcy SD	Searcy
38	0.9	Lake Hamilton SD	Pearcy
39	0.8	Ashdown SD	Ashdown
39	0.8	Trumann SD	Trumann
41	0.6	Heber Springs SD	Heber Springs
41	0.6	Magnolia SD	Magnolia
41	0.6	Stuttgart SD	Stuttgart
44	0.5	Blytheville SD	Blytheville
44	0.5	Pulaski County Special SD	Little Rock
46	0.4	Cabot SD	Cabot
46	0.4	Greenwood SD	Greenwood
48	0.3	Mountain Home SD	Mountain Home
48	0.3	Ozark SD	Ozark
48	0.3	Pine Bluff SD	Pine Bluff
48	0.3	Pocahontas SD	Pocahontas
48	0.3	Texarkana SD	Texarkana
53	0.2	Alma SD	Alma
53	0.2	Greene County Tech SD	Paragould
53	0.2	Marion SD	Marion
53	0.2	Paragould SD	Paragould
53	0.2	Sheridan SD	Sheridan
58	0.1	Beebe SD	Beebe
58	0.1	Camden Fairview SD	Camden
58	0.1	Harrison SD	Harrison
58	0.1	Lee County SD	Marianna
58	0.1	Osceola SD	Osceola
58	0.1	Vilonia SD	Vilonia
58	0.1	Westside CSD	Jonesboro
58	0.1	Wynne SD	Wynne
66	0.0	Forrest City SD	Forrest City
66	0.0	Greenbrier SD	Greenbrier
66	0.0	Helena-West Helena SD	Helena
66	0.0	Watson Chapel SD	Pine Bluff

Rank	Percent	District Name	City
70	0.0	Arkadelphia SD	Arkadelphia
70	0.0	Dollarway SD	Pine Bluff
70	0.0	Highland SD	Hardy
70	0.0	Malvern SD	Malvern
70	0.0	Mena SD	Mena
70	0.0	Monticello SD	Monticello
70	0.0	West Memphis SD	West Memphis
70	0.0	White Hall SD	White Hall

Migrant Students

Rank	Percent	District Name	City
1	27.9	Dequeen SD	De Queen
2	10.5	Berryville SD	Berryville
3	10.3	Dardanelle SD	Dardanelle
4	10.2	Clarksville SD	Clarksville
5	9.7	Waldron SD	Waldron
6	9.3	Springdale SD	Springdale
7	8.6	Rogers SD	Rogers
8	6.9	Batesville SD	Batesville
9	6.8	Siloam Springs SD	Siloam Springs
10	5.7	Fort Smith SD	Fort Smith
11	5.4	Warren SD	Warren
12	4.8	Hope SD	Hope
13	4.1	Trumann SD	Trumann
14	3.8	Van Buren SD	Van Buren
15	3.6	Huntsville SD	Huntsville
16	3.5	Nashville SD	Nashville
17	3.2	Russellville SD	Russellville
18	2.8	Hamburg SD	Hamburg
19	2.7	Alma SD	Alma
20	2.0	Fayetteville SD	Fayetteville
20	2.0	Jonesboro SD	Jonesboro
22	1.9	Searcy SD	Searcy
23	1.8	Bentonville SD	Bentonville
24	1.5	Lonoke SD	Lonoke
25	1.4	Newport SD	Newport
25	1.4	Wynne SD	Wynne
27	1.2	Forrest City SD	Forrest City
27	1.2	Stuttgart SD	Stuttgart
29	1.1	Marion SD	Marion
30	0.9	Star City SD	Star City
30	0.9	Westside CSD	Jonesboro
32	0.8	Dumas SD	Dumas
33	0.6	Ozark SD	Ozark
34	0.4	Blytheville SD	Blytheville
34	0.4	Greene County Tech SD	Paragould
34	0.4	Paragould SD	Paragould
37	0.2	Beebe SD	Beebe
37	0.2	Conway SD	Conway
37	0.2	Magnolia SD	Magnolia
37	0.2	Nettleton SD	Jonesboro
37	0.2	Osceola SD	Osceola
37	0.2	Pocahontas SD	Pocahontas
37	0.2	Texarkana SD	Texarkana
44	0.1	Benton SD	Benton
44	0.1	Cabot SD	Cabot
44	0.1	Greenbrier SD	Greenbrier
44	0.1	Highland SD	Hardy
44	0.1	Hot Springs SD	Hot Springs
49	0.0	Crossett SD	Crossett
49	0.0	Greenwood SD	Greenwood
49	0.0	Malvern SD	Malvern
49	0.0	Pine Bluff SD	Pine Bluff
53	0.0	Arkadelphia SD	Arkadelphia
53	0.0	Ashdown SD	Ashdown
53	0.0	Bryant SD	Bryant
53	0.0	Camden Fairview SD	Camden
53	0.0	Dollarway SD	Pine Bluff
53	0.0	El Dorado SD	El Dorado
53	0.0	Farmington SD	Farmington
53	0.0	Harrison SD	Harrison
53	0.0	Heber Springs SD	Heber Springs
53	0.0	Helena-West Helena SD	Helena
53	0.0	Lake Hamilton SD	Pearcy
53	0.0	Lakeside SD	Hot Springs
53	0.0	Lee County SD	Marianna
53	0.0	Little Rock SD	Little Rock
53	0.0	Mena SD	Mena
53	0.0	Monticello SD	Monticello
53	0.0	Mountain Home SD	Mountain Home
53	0.0	North Little Rock SD	N Little Rock
53	0.0	Pulaski County Special SD	Little Rock
53	0.0	Sheridan SD	Sheridan
53	0.0	South Conway County SD	Morrilton
53	0.0	Vilonia SD	Vilonia
53	0.0	Watson Chapel SD	Pine Bluff
53	0.0	West Memphis SD	West Memphis
53	0.0	White Hall SD	White Hall

Students Eligible for Free Lunch

Rank	Percent	District Name	City
1	83.9	Lee County SD	Marianna
2	81.9	Helena-West Helena SD	Helena
3	75.4	Dollarway SD	Pine Bluff
4	71.1	Osceola SD	Osceola
5	69.6	Hamburg SD	Hamburg
6	68.7	Blytheville SD	Blytheville
7	66.6	Dumas SD	Dumas
8	65.3	Forrest City SD	Forrest City
9	65.0	West Memphis SD	West Memphis
10	61.9	Hot Springs SD	Hot Springs
11	58.5	Pine Bluff SD	Pine Bluff
12	55.2	Hope SD	Hope
13	54.0	Dequeen SD	De Queen
14	52.3	Texarkana SD	Texarkana
15	52.2	Camden Fairview SD	Camden
15	52.2	Newport SD	Newport
17	50.4	Stuttgart SD	Stuttgart
17	50.4	Warren SD	Warren
19	50.0	North Little Rock SD	N Little Rock
20	48.1	Trumann SD	Trumann
21	46.7	Highland SD	Hardy
22	46.5	South Conway County SD	Morrilton
23	46.3	Little Rock SD	Little Rock
24	45.9	Watson Chapel SD	Pine Bluff
25	45.6	Clarksville SD	Clarksville
26	44.9	El Dorado SD	El Dorado
27	44.1	Jonesboro SD	Jonesboro
28	43.6	Dardanelle SD	Dardanelle
29	43.5	Wynne SD	Wynne
30	42.7	Fort Smith SD	Fort Smith
31	42.5	Waldron SD	Waldron
32	42.4	Nashville SD	Nashville
33	41.9	Malvern SD	Malvern
34	41.7	Magnolia SD	Magnolia
35	41.3	Monticello SD	Monticello
36	40.0	Mena SD	Mena
37	38.7	Paragould SD	Paragould
38	37.4	Star City SD	Star City
39	37.3	Crossett SD	Crossett
40	36.4	Ashdown SD	Ashdown
41	36.3	Pocahontas SD	Pocahontas
42	35.7	Lonoke SD	Lonoke
43	35.5	Berryville SD	Berryville
44	35.3	Pulaski County Special SD	Little Rock
45	34.8	Arkadelphia SD	Arkadelphia
46	34.5	Batesville SD	Batesville
47	34.0	Russellville SD	Russellville
48	33.2	Springdale SD	Springdale
49	32.9	Van Buren SD	Van Buren
50	32.7	Huntsville SD	Huntsville
51	32.0	Marion SD	Marion
52	31.9	Heber Springs SD	Heber Springs
53	31.5	Rogers SD	Rogers
54	30.0	Ozark SD	Ozark
55	29.6	Alma SD	Alma
56	29.1	Mountain Home SD	Mountain Home
57	28.3	Harrison SD	Harrison
57	28.3	Siloam Springs SD	Siloam Springs
59	27.8	Greene County Tech SD	Paragould
59	27.8	Nettleton SD	Jonesboro
61	27.6	Beebe SD	Beebe
62	25.8	Greenbrier SD	Greenbrier
63	25.3	Conway SD	Conway
64	24.4	Westside CSD	Jonesboro
65	24.2	Searcy SD	Searcy
66	24.1	Fayetteville SD	Fayetteville
67	23.9	Lake Hamilton SD	Pearcy
68	23.4	Sheridan SD	Sheridan
69	20.5	Cabot SD	Cabot
70	19.4	Vilonia SD	Vilonia
71	19.2	White Hall SD	White Hall
72	19.0	Farmington SD	Farmington
73	18.6	Bryant SD	Bryant
74	18.4	Benton SD	Benton
75	17.6	Lakeside SD	Hot Springs
76	16.8	Bentonville SD	Bentonville
77	14.1	Greenwood SD	Greenwood

Students Eligible for Reduced-Price Lunch

Rank	Percent	District Name	City
1	16.2	Pocahontas SD	Pocahontas
2	13.0	Dardanelle SD	Dardanelle
3	12.8	Siloam Springs SD	Siloam Springs
4	12.5	Malvern SD	Malvern
5	11.6	Newport SD	Newport
6	11.5	Mena SD	Mena
7	11.3	Nashville SD	Nashville
8	11.2	Clarksville SD	Clarksville
9	11.1	Greenbrier SD	Greenbrier
10	10.8	Sheridan SD	Sheridan
10	10.8	Warren SD	Warren
12	10.6	Berryville SD	Berryville
12	10.6	Marion SD	Marion
14	10.4	Ashdown SD	Ashdown
15	10.3	Osceola SD	Osceola
16	10.2	Alma SD	Alma
16	10.2	Lake Hamilton SD	Pearcy
18	10.1	Forrest City SD	Forrest City
19	9.9	Rogers SD	Rogers
20	9.7	Greene County Tech SD	Paragould
20	9.7	Ozark SD	Ozark
20	9.7	South Conway County SD	Morrilton
20	9.7	Trumann SD	Trumann
24	9.6	Pulaski County Special SD	Little Rock
24	9.6	Van Buren SD	Van Buren
24	9.6	Waldron SD	Waldron
27	9.4	Paragould SD	Paragould
28	9.3	Farmington SD	Farmington
28	9.3	Highland SD	Hardy
28	9.3	Vilonia SD	Vilonia
31	8.9	Arkadelphia SD	Arkadelphia
31	8.9	Harrison SD	Harrison
33	8.7	Dequeen SD	De Queen
34	8.6	Batesville SD	Batesville
34	8.6	Stuttgart SD	Stuttgart
36	8.5	Heber Springs SD	Heber Springs
36	8.5	Hot Springs SD	Hot Springs
38	8.3	Dumas SD	Dumas
39	8.1	Mountain Home SD	Mountain Home
40	8.0	Searcy SD	Searcy
41	7.9	Lonoke SD	Lonoke
42	7.8	Beebe SD	Beebe
43	7.7	Bentonville SD	Bentonville
43	7.7	Blytheville SD	Blytheville
43	7.7	Fort Smith SD	Fort Smith
43	7.7	Springdale SD	Springdale
47	7.6	Star City SD	Star City
47	7.6	Westside CSD	Jonesboro
49	7.3	Pine Bluff SD	Pine Bluff
50	7.2	Lee County SD	Marianna
50	7.2	Watson Chapel SD	Pine Bluff
52	7.0	El Dorado SD	El Dorado
52	7.0	Russellville SD	Russellville
54	6.9	Huntsville SD	Huntsville
54	6.9	Little Rock SD	Little Rock
56	6.7	Greenwood SD	Greenwood
56	6.7	Texarkana SD	Texarkana
58	6.6	Conway SD	Conway
58	6.6	Dollarway SD	Pine Bluff
58	6.6	Wynne SD	Wynne
61	6.5	Magnolia SD	Magnolia
62	6.4	Nettleton SD	Jonesboro
62	6.4	White Hall SD	White Hall
64	6.3	Crossett SD	Crossett
64	6.3	Hope SD	Hope
64	6.3	Jonesboro SD	Jonesboro
67	6.1	Cabot SD	Cabot
67	6.1	Camden Fairview SD	Camden
69	6.0	Bryant SD	Bryant
70	5.8	Lakeside SD	Hot Springs
70	5.8	Monticello SD	Monticello
72	5.7	Fayetteville SD	Fayetteville
73	5.6	Benton SD	Benton
74	5.3	Helena-West Helena SD	Helena
75	5.2	West Memphis SD	West Memphis
76	4.8	North Little Rock SD	N Little Rock
77	2.4	Hamburg SD	Hamburg

Student/Teacher Ratio

Rank	Ratio	District Name	City
1	18.8	Springdale SD	Springdale
2	18.4	Lake Hamilton SD	Pearcy
3	18.0	Marion SD	Marion
4	17.8	Vilonia SD	Vilonia
5	17.7	Huntsville SD	Huntsville
6	17.5	Jonesboro SD	Jonesboro
7	17.3	Bryant SD	Bryant
7	17.3	Rogers SD	Rogers
9	17.2	Greenwood SD	Greenwood
10	17.1	White Hall SD	White Hall
11	17.0	Mountain Home SD	Mountain Home
12	16.9	Searcy SD	Searcy
12	16.9	Watson Chapel SD	Pine Bluff
14	16.8	Beebe SD	Beebe
15	16.6	Conway SD	Conway
16	16.5	Sheridan SD	Sheridan
17	16.4	Pocahontas SD	Pocahontas
18	16.3	Forrest City SD	Forrest City
19	16.2	Highland SD	Hardy
19	16.2	Siloam Springs SD	Siloam Springs
21	16.1	Alma SD	Alma
21	16.1	Cabot SD	Cabot

21	16.1	Fayetteville SD	Fayetteville
21	16.1	Greene County Tech SD	Paragould
21	16.1	Harrison SD	Harrison
26	16.0	Bentonville SD	Bentonville
27	15.9	Lakeside SD	Hot Springs
27	15.9	Lonoke SD	Lonoke
27	15.9	Magnolia SD	Magnolia
27	15.9	Monticello SD	Monticello
31	15.8	Benton SD	Benton
31	15.8	Nettleton SD	Jonesboro
33	15.7	Fort Smith SD	Fort Smith
33	15.7	Lee County SD	Marianna
33	15.7	Mena SD	Mena
33	15.7	Ozark SD	Ozark
33	15.7	Russellville SD	Russellville
33	15.7	West Memphis SD	West Memphis
39	15.6	Camden Fairview SD	Camden
39	15.6	Dardanelle SD	Dardanelle
39	15.6	Dequeen SD	De Queen
42	15.5	Paragould SD	Paragould
42	15.5	Wynne SD	Wynne
44	15.4	El Dorado SD	El Dorado
44	15.4	Helena-West Helena SD	Helena
46	15.3	Crossett SD	Crossett
46	15.3	Malvern SD	Malvern
48	15.2	Arkadelphia SD	Arkadelphia
48	15.2	Berryville SD	Berryville
48	15.2	Westside CSD	Jonesboro
51	15.1	Blytheville SD	Blytheville
51	15.1	Pulaski County Special SD	Little Rock
51	15.1	Van Buren SD	Van Buren
54	15.0	Hope SD	Hope
54	15.0	Star City SD	Star City
54	15.0	Trumann SD	Trumann
57	14.9	Batesville SD	Batesville
57	14.9	Clarksville SD	Clarksville
59	14.8	Greenbrier SD	Greenbrier
59	14.8	Osceola SD	Osceola
61	14.7	Pine Bluff SD	Pine Bluff
61	14.7	Waldron SD	Waldron
63	14.6	Little Rock SD	Little Rock
63	14.6	North Little Rock SD	N Little Rock
65	14.5	South Conway County SD	Morrilton
65	14.5	Texarkana SD	Texarkana
67	14.4	Dollarway SD	Pine Bluff
68	14.3	Hamburg SD	Hamburg
69	14.2	Warren SD	Warren
70	14.1	Heber Springs SD	Heber Springs
71	14.0	Stuttgart SD	Stuttgart
72	13.9	Farmington SD	Farmington
73	13.7	Ashdown SD	Ashdown
74	13.5	Nashville SD	Nashville
75	13.2	Hot Springs SD	Hot Springs
76	13.0	Dumas SD	Dumas
77	12.7	Newport SD	Newport

Student/Librarian Ratio

Rank	Ratio	District Name	City
1	772.1	Bentonville SD	Bentonville
2	755.2	Springdale SD	Springdale
3	745.9	Bryant SD	Bryant
4	737.2	Conway SD	Conway
5	729.0	Alma SD	Alma
6	710.8	Wynne SD	Wynne
7	692.8	Magnolia SD	Magnolia
8	683.2	Sheridan SD	Sheridan
9	658.5	Rogers SD	Rogers
10	647.0	Vilonia SD	Vilonia
11	633.8	Greenwood SD	Greenwood
12	631.0	Mountain Home SD	Mountain Home
13	628.8	Lake Hamilton SD	Pearcy
14	624.7	Cabot SD	Cabot
15	611.0	Searcy SD	Searcy
16	594.4	Siloam Springs SD	Siloam Springs
17	592.9	Benton SD	Benton
18	586.3	Farmington SD	Farmington
19	578.2	Greene County Tech SD	Paragould
20	577.9	Forrest City SD	Forrest City
21	574.3	Trumann SD	Trumann
22	574.0	Texarkana SD	Texarkana
23	566.8	Hot Springs SD	Hot Springs
24	565.3	Heber Springs SD	Heber Springs
25	564.3	Blytheville SD	Blytheville
26	564.0	Berryville SD	Berryville
27	553.0	Westside CSD	Jonesboro
28	552.7	Waldron SD	Waldron
29	550.8	Hope SD	Hope
29	550.8	North Little Rock SD	N Little Rock
31	549.3	Marion SD	Marion
32	544.3	Ozark SD	Ozark
33	535.2	Fort Smith SD	Fort Smith
34	528.1	Jonesboro SD	Jonesboro
35	528.0	Watson Chapel SD	Pine Bluff
36	526.5	Camden Fairview SD	Camden
37	525.5	Monticello SD	Monticello
38	521.3	Huntsville SD	Huntsville
39	513.2	Pine Bluff SD	Pine Bluff
40	513.0	Highland SD	Hardy
41	510.5	Little Rock SD	Little Rock
42	509.1	West Memphis SD	West Memphis
43	509.0	Pulaski County Special SD	Little Rock
44	506.7	Star City SD	Star City
45	503.4	Lakeside SD	Hot Springs
45	503.4	Van Buren SD	Van Buren
47	500.3	Fayetteville SD	Fayetteville
48	490.7	El Dorado SD	El Dorado
49	488.4	Helena-West Helena SD	Helena
50	479.4	Greenbrier SD	Greenbrier
51	474.0	Beebe SD	Beebe
52	471.5	Dequeen SD	De Queen
52	471.5	Mena SD	Mena
54	470.8	Russellville SD	Russellville
55	455.2	Arkadelphia SD	Arkadelphia
56	442.8	Pocahontas SD	Pocahontas
57	441.0	Dardanelle SD	Dardanelle
58	440.8	Lonoke SD	Lonoke
59	439.3	Nashville SD	Nashville
60	437.2	Nettleton SD	Jonesboro
61	436.7	White Hall SD	White Hall
62	435.6	Clarksville SD	Clarksville
63	407.5	Crossett SD	Crossett
64	406.3	Newport SD	Newport
65	405.5	Lee County SD	Marianna
66	401.8	Dumas SD	Dumas
67	401.0	South Conway County SD	Morrilton
68	399.4	Harrison SD	Harrison
69	392.8	Warren SD	Warren
70	384.5	Dollarway SD	Pine Bluff
71	378.7	Paragould SD	Paragould
72	366.7	Malvern SD	Malvern
73	350.2	Osceola SD	Osceola
74	349.8	Batesville SD	Batesville
75	331.2	Ashdown SD	Ashdown
76	322.8	Hamburg SD	Hamburg
77	311.3	Stuttgart SD	Stuttgart

Student/Counselor Ratio

Rank	Ratio	District Name	City
1	475.5	Springdale SD	Springdale
2	454.2	Bentonville SD	Bentonville
3	441.0	Dardanelle SD	Dardanelle
4	440.8	Lonoke SD	Lonoke
5	435.6	Clarksville SD	Clarksville
6	427.4	Helena-West Helena SD	Helena
7	426.8	Conway SD	Conway
8	426.2	Bryant SD	Bryant
9	424.6	Siloam Springs SD	Siloam Springs
10	423.0	Berryville SD	Berryville
11	420.7	Mountain Home SD	Mountain Home
12	419.5	Lakeside SD	Hot Springs
13	416.6	Alma SD	Alma
14	416.4	Cabot SD	Cabot
15	415.0	Benton SD	Benton
16	413.0	Greene County Tech SD	Paragould
17	412.0	Marion SD	Marion
18	410.5	Pine Bluff SD	Pine Bluff
19	409.9	Sheridan SD	Sheridan
20	408.7	Rogers SD	Rogers
21	408.3	Ozark SD	Ozark
22	404.5	Forrest City SD	Forrest City
23	399.5	Greenbrier SD	Greenbrier
24	396.1	Greenwood SD	Greenwood
25	396.0	Watson Chapel SD	Pine Bluff
26	395.0	Beebe SD	Beebe
27	384.8	Highland SD	Hardy
28	380.0	Star City SD	Star City
29	378.7	Paragould SD	Paragould
30	377.9	Hot Springs SD	Hot Springs
31	374.7	Nettleton SD	Jonesboro
32	369.7	Vilonia SD	Vilonia
33	369.1	Van Buren SD	Van Buren
34	367.0	Fort Smith SD	Fort Smith
35	366.6	Searcy SD	Searcy
36	359.4	West Memphis SD	West Memphis
37	352.5	North Little Rock SD	N Little Rock
38	351.8	Farmington SD	Farmington
39	351.4	Nashville SD	Nashville
40	351.0	Camden Fairview SD	Camden
41	350.3	Monticello SD	Monticello
42	350.2	Osceola SD	Osceola
43	349.3	Crossett SD	Crossett
44	347.5	Huntsville SD	Huntsville
45	346.4	Magnolia SD	Magnolia
46	344.6	Trumann SD	Trumann
47	344.3	Hope SD	Hope
48	339.7	White Hall SD	White Hall
49	339.5	Jonesboro SD	Jonesboro
50	339.2	Heber Springs SD	Heber Springs
51	338.6	Blytheville SD	Blytheville
52	333.5	Fayetteville SD	Fayetteville
53	331.8	Westside CSD	Jonesboro
54	331.6	Waldron SD	Waldron
55	331.2	Ashdown SD	Ashdown
56	328.0	Texarkana SD	Texarkana
57	325.0	Newport SD	Newport
58	324.4	Lee County SD	Marianna
59	323.7	Russellville SD	Russellville
60	322.8	Hamburg SD	Hamburg
61	315.9	Wynne SD	Wynne
62	315.4	El Dorado SD	El Dorado
63	314.3	Dequeen SD	De Queen
63	314.3	Malvern SD	Malvern
63	314.3	Mena SD	Mena
66	314.2	Warren SD	Warren
67	311.3	Stuttgart SD	Stuttgart
68	310.7	Harrison SD	Harrison
69	307.6	Dollarway SD	Pine Bluff
70	307.5	Little Rock SD	Little Rock
71	300.8	South Conway County SD	Morrilton
72	300.4	Pulaski County Special SD	Little Rock
73	299.9	Batesville SD	Batesville
74	284.5	Arkadelphia SD	Arkadelphia
75	269.5	Lake Hamilton SD	Pearcy
76	267.8	Dumas SD	Dumas
77	221.4	Pocahontas SD	Pocahontas

Current Spending per Student in FY2001

Rank	Dollars	District Name	City
1	7,391	Little Rock SD	Little Rock
2	7,362	Forrest City SD	Forrest City
3	6,880	North Little Rock SD	N Little Rock
4	6,673	Pulaski County Special SD	Little Rock
5	6,526	Hot Springs SD	Hot Springs
6	6,387	Lee County SD	Marianna
7	6,341	Helena-West Helena SD	Helena
8	6,336	Fayetteville SD	Fayetteville
9	6,224	Russellville SD	Russellville
10	6,217	Osceola SD	Osceola
11	6,139	Arkadelphia SD	Arkadelphia
11	6,139	Newport SD	Newport
13	6,118	Fort Smith SD	Fort Smith
14	6,110	Hamburg SD	Hamburg
15	6,098	Dumas SD	Dumas
16	6,077	Texarkana SD	Texarkana
17	6,033	Warren SD	Warren
18	5,966	Camden Fairview SD	Camden
19	5,879	Hope SD	Hope
20	5,847	Dollarway SD	Pine Bluff
21	5,732	Batesville SD	Batesville
22	5,713	Siloam Springs SD	Siloam Springs
23	5,708	Malvern SD	Malvern
24	5,691	Heber Springs SD	Heber Springs
25	5,677	Lakeside SD	Hot Springs
26	5,638	South Conway County SD	Morrilton
27	5,627	Bentonville SD	Bentonville
28	5,617	Lonoke SD	Lonoke
29	5,613	Blytheville SD	Blytheville
30	5,612	Jonesboro SD	Jonesboro
31	5,533	Van Buren SD	Van Buren
32	5,491	Ashdown SD	Ashdown
33	5,485	Nettleton SD	Jonesboro
34	5,477	Springdale SD	Springdale
35	5,462	Benton SD	Benton
36	5,459	Mena SD	Mena
37	5,443	Pine Bluff SD	Pine Bluff
38	5,431	Paragould SD	Paragould
39	5,427	Alma SD	Alma
40	5,414	Crossett SD	Crossett
41	5,409	Clarksville SD	Clarksville
42	5,387	El Dorado SD	El Dorado
43	5,385	Conway SD	Conway
44	5,351	Marion SD	Marion
45	5,331	Greenbrier SD	Greenbrier
46	5,321	Beebe SD	Beebe
47	5,318	Lake Hamilton SD	Pearcy
48	5,307	Mountain Home SD	Mountain Home
49	5,293	Monticello SD	Monticello
50	5,289	Berryville SD	Berryville
51	5,277	Farmington SD	Farmington
52	5,262	Pocahontas SD	Pocahontas
53	5,245	Stuttgart SD	Stuttgart
54	5,220	Rogers SD	Rogers
55	5,213	Greenwood SD	Greenwood
56	5,201	Trumann SD	Trumann
57	5,189	White Hall SD	White Hall
58	5,165	Wynne SD	Wynne

59	5,163	Greene County Tech SD	Paragould
60	5,162	Westside CSD	Jonesboro
61	5,159	Cabot SD	Cabot
62	5,153	Highland SD	Hardy
63	5,137	Harrison SD	Harrison
64	5,119	West Memphis SD	West Memphis
65	5,118	Watson Chapel SD	Pine Bluff
66	5,115	Nashville SD	Nashville
67	5,081	Vilonia SD	Vilonia
68	5,068	Magnolia SD	Magnolia
69	5,053	Bryant SD	Bryant
70	4,972	Sheridan SD	Sheridan
71	4,956	Star City SD	Star City
72	4,891	Ozark SD	Ozark
73	4,886	Searcy SD	Searcy
74	4,876	Dequeen SD	De Queen
75	4,853	Dardanelle SD	Dardanelle
76	4,825	Waldron SD	Waldron
77	4,706	Huntsville SD	Huntsville

Number of Diploma Recipients

Rank	Number	District Name	City
1	1,334	Little Rock SD	Little Rock
2	822	Fort Smith SD	Fort Smith
3	816	Pulaski County Special SD	Little Rock
4	596	Rogers SD	Rogers
5	554	Springdale SD	Springdale
6	539	Fayetteville SD	Fayetteville
7	508	North Little Rock SD	N Little Rock
8	450	Cabot SD	Cabot
9	446	Conway SD	Conway
10	392	Bentonville SD	Bentonville
11	388	Bryant SD	Bryant
12	324	Russellville SD	Russellville
13	319	Pine Bluff SD	Pine Bluff
14	315	Jonesboro SD	Jonesboro
15	308	El Dorado SD	El Dorado
16	300	Van Buren SD	Van Buren
17	274	Benton SD	Benton
18	260	West Memphis SD	West Memphis
19	246	Sheridan SD	Sheridan
20	240	Mountain Home SD	Mountain Home
21	236	Forrest City SD	Forrest City
22	230	Camden Fairview SD	Camden
23	227	Greenwood SD	Greenwood
24	225	Watson Chapel SD	Pine Bluff
25	222	Siloam Springs SD	Siloam Springs
26	217	Texarkana SD	Texarkana
27	214	Searcy SD	Searcy
28	212	Lake Hamilton SD	Pearcy
29	209	Magnolia SD	Magnolia
30	196	Wynne SD	Wynne
31	194	Harrison SD	Harrison
32	188	Alma SD	Alma
33	184	White Hall SD	White Hall
34	183	Helena-West Helena SD	Helena
35	178	Hope SD	Hope
36	171	Vilonia SD	Vilonia
37	166	South Conway County SD	Morrilton
38	164	Arkadelphia SD	Arkadelphia
39	163	Blytheville SD	Blytheville
40	158	Marion SD	Marion
41	155	Lakeside SD	Hot Springs
42	154	Greene County Tech SD	Paragould
43	152	Hot Springs SD	Hot Springs
43	152	Nettleton SD	Jonesboro
45	151	Monticello SD	Monticello
46	143	Greenbrier SD	Greenbrier
47	139	Malvern SD	Malvern
48	138	Ozark SD	Ozark
49	134	Stuttgart SD	Stuttgart
50	132	Paragould SD	Paragould
51	129	Batesville SD	Batesville
52	126	Crossett SD	Crossett
53	124	Osceola SD	Osceola
54	123	Huntsville SD	Huntsville
55	120	Newport SD	Newport
56	118	Beebe SD	Beebe
57	117	Lee County SD	Marianna
57	117	Mena SD	Mena
59	116	Dumas SD	Dumas
59	116	Hamburg SD	Hamburg
61	110	Pocahontas SD	Pocahontas
61	110	Waldron SD	Waldron
63	105	Nashville SD	Nashville
64	104	Lonoke SD	Lonoke
65	102	Clarksville SD	Clarksville
65	102	Warren SD	Warren
67	101	Dardanelle SD	Dardanelle
68	100	Ashdown SD	Ashdown
68	100	Berryville SD	Berryville
70	98	Farmington SD	Farmington
71	96	Dollarway SD	Pine Bluff
72	95	Heber Springs SD	Heber Springs
73	91	Westside CSD	Jonesboro
74	90	Star City SD	Star City
75	83	Highland SD	Hardy
76	81	Dequeen SD	De Queen
76	81	Trumann SD	Trumann

High School Drop-out Rate

Rank	Percent	District Name	City
1	12.9	Texarkana SD	Texarkana
2	12.7	Helena-West Helena SD	Helena
3	11.3	Hot Springs SD	Hot Springs
4	10.9	Pine Bluff SD	Pine Bluff
5	10.6	Blytheville SD	Blytheville
6	10.4	Forrest City SD	Forrest City
7	10.0	Stuttgart SD	Stuttgart
8	8.9	Newport SD	Newport
9	8.0	Trumann SD	Trumann
10	7.9	Dollarway SD	Pine Bluff
11	7.6	Huntsville SD	Huntsville
12	7.3	Batesville SD	Batesville
12	7.3	Pulaski County Special SD	Little Rock
14	7.0	Hope SD	Hope
15	6.9	Paragould SD	Paragould
16	6.8	Bentonville SD	Bentonville
16	6.8	Dequeen SD	De Queen
16	6.8	Heber Springs SD	Heber Springs
19	6.7	Fayetteville SD	Fayetteville
20	6.6	Clarksville SD	Clarksville
20	6.6	Marion SD	Marion
22	6.5	Springdale SD	Springdale
23	6.4	Osceola SD	Osceola
24	6.1	Russellville SD	Russellville
24	6.1	Van Buren SD	Van Buren
26	6.0	West Memphis SD	West Memphis
27	5.9	Hamburg SD	Hamburg
28	5.8	Highland SD	Hardy
29	5.5	Conway SD	Conway
29	5.5	Fort Smith SD	Fort Smith
29	5.5	Malvern SD	Malvern
32	5.4	Cabot SD	Cabot
33	5.1	Camden Fairview SD	Camden
33	5.1	Star City SD	Star City
35	5.0	Westside CSD	Jonesboro
36	4.8	Crossett SD	Crossett
36	4.8	Lonoke SD	Lonoke
38	4.5	Magnolia SD	Magnolia
38	4.5	Ozark SD	Ozark
38	4.5	Pocahontas SD	Pocahontas
38	4.5	Wynne SD	Wynne
42	4.4	Bryant SD	Bryant
42	4.4	Little Rock SD	Little Rock
42	4.4	Searcy SD	Searcy
45	4.3	Beebe SD	Beebe
45	4.3	Dumas SD	Dumas
45	4.3	Greene County Tech SD	Paragould
45	4.3	Lee County SD	Marianna
45	4.3	Mountain Home SD	Mountain Home
45	4.3	Sheridan SD	Sheridan
51	4.1	Benton SD	Benton
51	4.1	Mena SD	Mena
53	4.0	Harrison SD	Harrison
54	3.9	Ashdown SD	Ashdown
54	3.9	South Conway County SD	Morrilton
56	3.8	Nashville SD	Nashville
57	3.7	Nettleton SD	Jonesboro
58	3.6	Dardanelle SD	Dardanelle
58	3.6	Rogers SD	Rogers
58	3.6	Warren SD	Warren
61	3.5	Greenbrier SD	Greenbrier
61	3.5	Jonesboro SD	Jonesboro
63	3.4	Waldron SD	Waldron
64	3.2	Alma SD	Alma
64	3.2	White Hall SD	White Hall
66	3.0	Berryville SD	Berryville
67	2.9	Greenwood SD	Greenwood
68	2.8	Arkadelphia SD	Arkadelphia
68	2.8	El Dorado SD	El Dorado
70	2.7	Farmington SD	Farmington
71	2.5	Watson Chapel SD	Pine Bluff
72	2.3	Lakeside SD	Hot Springs
73	2.0	Vilonia SD	Vilonia
74	1.6	Monticello SD	Monticello
75	1.4	Siloam Springs SD	Siloam Springs
76	0.5	Lake Hamilton SD	Pearcy
76	0.5	North Little Rock SD	N Little Rock

California

California Public School Educational Profile

Category	Value	Category	Value
Schools *(2002-2003)*	9,101	**Diploma Recipients** *(2002-2003)*	325,895
Instructional Level		White, Non-Hispanic	140,421
Primary	5,552	Black, Non-Hispanic	23,451
Middle	1,306	Asian/Pacific Islander	48,206
High	1,795	American Indian/Alaskan Native	3,036
Other Level	448	Hispanic	109,038
Curriculum		**High School Drop-out Rate** (%) *(2000-2001)*	n/a
Regular	7,788	White, Non-Hispanic	n/a
Special Education	127	Black, Non-Hispanic	n/a
Vocational	0	Asian/Pacific Islander	n/a
Alternative	1,186	American Indian/Alaskan Native	n/a
Type		Hispanic	n/a
Magnet	438	**Staff** *(2002-2003)*	574,965.0
Charter	409	Teachers	301,003.0
Title I Eligible	5,490	Average Salary ($)	55,693
School-wide Title I	2,289	Librarians/Media Specialists	1,387.5
Students *(2002-2003)*	6,244,403	Guidance Counselors	6,681.0
Gender (%)		**Ratios** *(2002-2003)*	
Male	51.4	Student/Teacher Ratio	20.7 to 1
Female	48.6	Student/Librarian Ratio	4,500.5 to 1
Race/Ethnicity (%)		Student/Counselor Ratio	934.7 to 1
White, Non-Hispanic	33.7	**Current Spending** *($ per student in FY 2001)*	7,404
Black, Non-Hispanic	8.3	Instruction	4,572
Asian/Pacific Islander	11.2	Support Services	2,554
American Indian/Alaskan Native	0.9	**College Entrance Exam Scores** *(2003)*	
Hispanic	45.2	Scholastic Aptitude Test (SAT)	
Classification (%)		Participation Rate (%)	54
Individual Education Program (IEP)	10.8	Mean SAT I Verbal Score	499
Migrant	3.7	Mean SAT I Math Score	519
English Language Learner (ELL)	25.6	American College Testing Program (ACT)	
Eligible for Free Lunch Program	39.1	Participation Rate (%)	15
Eligible for Reduced-Price Lunch Program	9.0	Average Composite Score	21.5

Note: *For an explanation of data, please refer to the User's Guide in the front of the book; n/a indicates data not available*

California NAEP 2003 Test Scores

Reading		
Grade/Category	**Value**	**Rank**
4th Grade		
Average Proficiency	205.6 (1.2)	47/51
Proficiency by Gender/Race/Ethnicity		
Male	202.0 (1.4)	47/51
Female	209.2 (1.4)	48/51
White, Non-Hispanic	223.8 (1.7)	36/51
Black, Non-Hispanic	192.8 (3.1)	33/42
Asian, Non-Hispanic	190.7 (1.3)	40/41
American Indian, Non-Hispanic	223.6 (3.2)	16/25
Hispanic	n/a	n/a
Proficiency by Class Size		
Less than 16 Students	*192.3 (9.9)*	35/45
16 to 18 Students	*218.0 (11.6)*	19/48
19 to 20 Students	*205.1 (9.7)*	44/50
21 to 25 Students	*204.8 (6.5)*	50/51
Greater than 25 Students	206.3 (1.4)	46/49
Percent Attaining Achievement Levels		
Below Basic	50.4 (1.6)	5/51
Basic or Above	49.6 (1.6)	47/51
Proficient or Above	21.1 (1.1)	46/51
Advanced or Above	5.0 (0.5)	42/51
8th Grade		
Average Proficiency	251.0 (1.3)	50/51
Proficiency by Gender/Race/Ethnicity		
Male	247.2 (1.5)	46/51
Female	255.0 (1.5)	50/51
White, Non-Hispanic	265.2 (1.7)	45/50
Black, Non-Hispanic	239.2 (2.5)	32/41
Asian, Non-Hispanic	236.5 (1.6)	37/37
American Indian, Non-Hispanic	266.4 (2.4)	13/23
Hispanic	n/a	n/a
Proficiency by Parents Highest Level of Ed.		
Did Not Finish High School	237.0 (2.0)	48/50
Graduated High School	245.1 (2.6)	47/50
Some Education After High School	256.8 (2.0)	47/50
Graduated College	265.2 (1.7)	41/50
Percent Attaining Achievement Levels		
Below Basic	38.8 (1.3)	3/51
Basic or Above	61.2 (1.3)	49/51
Proficient or Above	22.4 (1.4)	44/51
Advanced or Above	2.0 (0.3)	35/51

Mathematics		
Grade/Category	**Value**	**Rank**
4th Grade		
Average Proficiency	227.5 (0.9)	44/51
Proficiency by Gender/Race/Ethnicity		
Male	229.4 (1.1)	42/51
Female	225.4 (1.1)	47/51
White, Non-Hispanic	242.8 (1.2)	22/51
Black, Non-Hispanic	212.7 (2.0)	30/42
Asian, Non-Hispanic	215.8 (0.8)	38/43
American Indian, Non-Hispanic	245.7 (3.2)	15/26
Hispanic	n/a	n/a
Proficiency by Class Size		
Less than 16 Students	*225.9 (7.5)*	22/47
16 to 18 Students	*235.0 (11.8)*	21/48
19 to 20 Students	*221.4 (6.9)*	48/50
21 to 25 Students	*231.1 (4.5)*	39/51
Greater than 25 Students	227.8 (1.2)	40/49
Percent Attaining Achievement Levels		
Below Basic	32.9 (1.1)	6/51
Basic or Above	67.1 (1.1)	46/51
Proficient or Above	24.7 (1.3)	40/51
Advanced or Above	3.0 (0.5)	30/51
8th Grade		
Average Proficiency	267.0 (1.2)	44/51
Proficiency by Gender/Race/Ethnicity		
Male	268.0 (1.5)	43/51
Female	266.1 (1.3)	45/51
White, Non-Hispanic	282.9 (1.5)	37/50
Black, Non-Hispanic	245.8 (2.3)	34/41
Asian, Non-Hispanic	249.8 (1.4)	32/37
American Indian, Non-Hispanic	287.1 (3.8)	12/23
Hispanic	n/a	n/a
Proficiency by Parents Highest Level of Ed.		
Did Not Finish High School	245.9 (1.8)	49/50
Graduated High School	255.4 (1.6)	46/50
Some Education After High School	274.9 (1.9)	41/50
Graduated College	281.6 (1.8)	38/50
Percent Attaining Achievement Levels		
Below Basic	44.3 (1.3)	5/51
Basic or Above	55.7 (1.3)	46/51
Proficient or Above	21.7 (1.1)	38/51
Advanced or Above	4.4 (0.7)	30/51

Note: *For an explanation of data, please refer to the User's Guide in the front of the book; values in italics indicate that the nature of the sample does not allow accurate determination of the variability of the statistic; n/a indicates data not available*

Alameda County

Alameda City Unified

2200 Central Ave • Alameda, CA 94501-4450
(510) 337-7060 • http://www.alameda.k12.ca.us/
Grade Span: KG-12; **Agency Type:** 1
Schools: 20
12 Primary; 3 Middle; 5 High; 0 Other Level
19 Regular; 0 Special Education; 0 Vocational; 1 Alternative
0 Magnet; 2 Charter; 6 Title I Eligible; 0 School-wide Title I
Students: 10,615 (50.7% male; 49.3% female)
Individual Education Program: 1,150 (10.8%);
English Language Learner: 2,180 (20.5%); Migrant: 1 (<0.1%)
Eligible for Free Lunch Program: 2,380 (22.4%)
Eligible for Reduced-Price Lunch Program: 817 (7.7%)
Teachers: 514.8 (20.6 to 1)
Librarians/Media Specialists: 12.0 (884.6 to 1)
Guidance Counselors: 11.7 (907.3 to 1)
Current Spending: ($ per student per year):
Total: $6,513; Instruction: $4,173; Support Services: $2,155
Enrollment, Drop-out Rates and Diploma Recipients by Race/Ethnicity

Category	Total	White	Black	Asian	AIAN	Hisp.
Enrollment (%)	100.0	32.0	14.2	37.5	1.0	11.0
Drop-out Rate (%)	n/a	n/a	n/a	n/a	n/a	n/a
H.S. Diplomas (#)	645	201	84	277	4	66

Albany City Unified

904 Talbot Ave • Albany, CA 94706-2020
(510) 558-3750 • http://www.albany.k12.ca.us/
Grade Span: KG-12; **Agency Type:** 1
Schools: 6
3 Primary; 1 Middle; 2 High; 0 Other Level
5 Regular; 0 Special Education; 0 Vocational; 1 Alternative
0 Magnet; 0 Charter; 3 Title I Eligible; 0 School-wide Title I
Students: 3,145 (51.1% male; 48.9% female)
Individual Education Program: 322 (10.2%);
English Language Learner: 344 (10.9%); Migrant: 0 (0.0%)
Eligible for Free Lunch Program: 309 (9.8%)
Eligible for Reduced-Price Lunch Program: 124 (3.9%)
Teachers: 154.5 (20.4 to 1)
Librarians/Media Specialists: 1.3 (2,419.2 to 1)
Guidance Counselors: 5.2 (604.8 to 1)
Current Spending: ($ per student per year):
Total: $7,596; Instruction: $4,943; Support Services: $2,450
Enrollment, Drop-out Rates and Diploma Recipients by Race/Ethnicity

Category	Total	White	Black	Asian	AIAN	Hisp.
Enrollment (%)	100.0	44.6	7.8	31.2	0.3	9.8
Drop-out Rate (%)	n/a	n/a	n/a	n/a	n/a	n/a
H.S. Diplomas (#)	181	85	14	55	0	20

Berkeley Unified

2134 Martin Luther King, Jr W • Berkeley, CA 94704-1109
(510) 644-6147 • http://www.berkeley.k12.ca.us/
Grade Span: KG-12; **Agency Type:** 1
Schools: 15
11 Primary; 3 Middle; 1 High; 0 Other Level
15 Regular; 0 Special Education; 0 Vocational; 0 Alternative
4 Magnet; 0 Charter; 14 Title I Eligible; 5 School-wide Title I
Students: 9,060 (50.6% male; 49.4% female)
Individual Education Program: 1,020 (11.3%);
English Language Learner: 1,301 (14.4%); Migrant: 0 (0.0%)
Eligible for Free Lunch Program: 2,591 (28.6%)
Eligible for Reduced-Price Lunch Program: 673 (7.4%)
Teachers: 498.0 (18.2 to 1)
Librarians/Media Specialists: 3.8 (2,384.2 to 1)
Guidance Counselors: 9.8 (924.5 to 1)
Current Spending: ($ per student per year):
Total: $9,116; Instruction: $5,612; Support Services: $3,295
Enrollment, Drop-out Rates and Diploma Recipients by Race/Ethnicity

Category	Total	White	Black	Asian	AIAN	Hisp.
Enrollment (%)	100.0	29.2	33.5	7.8	0.2	15.2
Drop-out Rate (%)	n/a	n/a	n/a	n/a	n/a	n/a
H.S. Diplomas (#)	673	265	217	69	1	65

Castro Valley Unified

4430 Alma Ave • Castro Valley, CA 94546-0146
Mailing Address: PO Box 2146 • Castro Valley, CA 94546-0146
(510) 537-3000 • http://www.cv.k12.ca.us/
Grade Span: KG-12; **Agency Type:** 1
Schools: 14
9 Primary; 2 Middle; 3 High; 0 Other Level
12 Regular; 1 Special Education; 0 Vocational; 1 Alternative
0 Magnet; 0 Charter; 3 Title I Eligible; 0 School-wide Title I
Students: 8,211 (50.4% male; 49.6% female)
Individual Education Program: 836 (10.2%);
English Language Learner: 473 (5.8%); Migrant: 0 (0.0%)
Eligible for Free Lunch Program: 750 (9.1%)
Eligible for Reduced-Price Lunch Program: 325 (4.0%)
Teachers: 378.6 (21.7 to 1)
Librarians/Media Specialists: 2.0 (4,105.5 to 1)
Guidance Counselors: 11.4 (720.3 to 1)
Current Spending: ($ per student per year):
Total: $6,169; Instruction: $4,019; Support Services: $1,932
Enrollment, Drop-out Rates and Diploma Recipients by Race/Ethnicity

Category	Total	White	Black	Asian	AIAN	Hisp.
Enrollment (%)	100.0	57.2	4.8	23.1	1.2	13.4
Drop-out Rate (%)	n/a	n/a	n/a	n/a	n/a	n/a
H.S. Diplomas (#)	551	355	17	124	6	48

Dublin Unified

7471 Larkdale Ave • Dublin, CA 94568-1500
(925) 828-2551 • http://www.dublin.k12.ca.us/
Grade Span: KG-12; **Agency Type:** 1
Schools: 8
5 Primary; 1 Middle; 2 High; 0 Other Level
7 Regular; 0 Special Education; 0 Vocational; 1 Alternative
0 Magnet; 0 Charter; 5 Title I Eligible; 0 School-wide Title I
Students: 4,338 (51.1% male; 48.9% female)
Individual Education Program: 411 (9.5%);
English Language Learner: 138 (3.2%); Migrant: 0 (0.0%)
Eligible for Free Lunch Program: 315 (7.3%)
Eligible for Reduced-Price Lunch Program: 134 (3.1%)
Teachers: 220.8 (19.6 to 1)
Librarians/Media Specialists: 1.0 (4,338.0 to 1)
Guidance Counselors: 3.4 (1,275.9 to 1)
Current Spending: ($ per student per year):
Total: $7,256; Instruction: $4,663; Support Services: $2,363
Enrollment, Drop-out Rates and Diploma Recipients by Race/Ethnicity

Category	Total	White	Black	Asian	AIAN	Hisp.
Enrollment (%)	100.0	58.8	5.4	17.7	1.2	12.2
Drop-out Rate (%)	n/a	n/a	n/a	n/a	n/a	n/a
H.S. Diplomas (#)	250	161	16	42	3	28

Fremont Unified

4210 Technology Dr • Fremont, CA 94537-5008
Mailing Address: PO Box 5008 • Fremont, CA 94537-5008
(510) 657-2350 • http://www.fremont.k12.ca.us/
Grade Span: KG-12; **Agency Type:** 1
Schools: 41
28 Primary; 5 Middle; 6 High; 2 Other Level
39 Regular; 0 Special Education; 0 Vocational; 2 Alternative
0 Magnet; 1 Charter; 6 Title I Eligible; 2 School-wide Title I
Students: 31,452 (52.2% male; 47.8% female)
Individual Education Program: 2,755 (8.8%);
English Language Learner: 4,952 (15.7%); Migrant: 277 (0.9%)
Eligible for Free Lunch Program: 2,902 (9.2%)
Eligible for Reduced-Price Lunch Program: 1,355 (4.3%)
Teachers: 1,493.5 (21.1 to 1)
Librarians/Media Specialists: 3.6 (8,736.7 to 1)
Guidance Counselors: 31.9 (986.0 to 1)
Current Spending: ($ per student per year):
Total: $6,183; Instruction: $4,229; Support Services: $1,796
Enrollment, Drop-out Rates and Diploma Recipients by Race/Ethnicity

Category	Total	White	Black	Asian	AIAN	Hisp.
Enrollment (%)	100.0	32.7	5.5	45.9	1.1	14.3
Drop-out Rate (%)	n/a	n/a	n/a	n/a	n/a	n/a
H.S. Diplomas (#)	1,972	865	58	827	8	214

Hayward Unified

24411 Amador St • Hayward, CA 94540-0001
Mailing Address: PO Box 5000 • Hayward, CA 94540-0001
(510) 784-2600 • http://www.husd.k12.ca.us/
Grade Span: KG-12; **Agency Type:** 1
Schools: 33
23 Primary; 6 Middle; 3 High; 1 Other Level
32 Regular; 0 Special Education; 0 Vocational; 1 Alternative
0 Magnet; 0 Charter; 18 Title I Eligible; 13 School-wide Title I
Students: 24,051 (51.6% male; 48.4% female)
Individual Education Program: 2,472 (10.3%);
English Language Learner: 8,072 (33.6%); Migrant: 690 (2.9%)
Eligible for Free Lunch Program: 8,663 (36.0%)
Eligible for Reduced-Price Lunch Program: 2,679 (11.1%)
Teachers: 1,203.2 (20.0 to 1)
Librarians/Media Specialists: 19.8 (1,214.7 to 1)
Guidance Counselors: 23.0 (1,045.7 to 1)
Current Spending: ($ per student per year):
Total: $6,665; Instruction: $4,392; Support Services: $2,040

Enrollment, Drop-out Rates and Diploma Recipients by Race/Ethnicity

Category	Total	White	Black	Asian	AIAN	Hisp.
Enrollment (%)	100.0	15.0	15.8	21.3	0.7	47.1
Drop-out Rate (%)	n/a	n/a	n/a	n/a	n/a	n/a
H.S. Diplomas (#)	1,264	253	209	350	11	441

Livermore Valley Joint Unified

685 E Jack London Blvd • Livermore, CA 94550-1800
(925) 606-3200 • http://www.lvjusd.k12.ca.us/
Grade Span: KG-12; **Agency Type:** 1
Schools: 21
12 Primary; 4 Middle; 4 High; 1 Other Level
18 Regular; 0 Special Education; 0 Vocational; 3 Alternative
0 Magnet; 0 Charter; 0 Title I Eligible; 0 School-wide Title I
Students: 13,978 (50.9% male; 49.1% female)
Individual Education Program: 1,553 (11.1%);
English Language Learner: 1,461 (10.5%); Migrant: 238 (1.7%)
Eligible for Free Lunch Program: 1,432 (10.2%)
Eligible for Reduced-Price Lunch Program: 386 (2.8%)
Teachers: 614.4 (22.8 to 1)
Librarians/Media Specialists: 0.0 (0.0 to 1)
Guidance Counselors: 4.8 (2,912.1 to 1)
Current Spending: ($ per student per year):
Total: $6,516; Instruction: $4,201; Support Services: $2,159

Enrollment, Drop-out Rates and Diploma Recipients by Race/Ethnicity

Category	Total	White	Black	Asian	AIAN	Hisp.
Enrollment (%)	100.0	69.8	2.9	8.5	0.5	18.1
Drop-out Rate (%)	n/a	n/a	n/a	n/a	n/a	n/a
H.S. Diplomas (#)	918	693	22	67	5	125

New Haven Unified

34200 Alvarado-Niles Rd • Union City, CA 94587-4402
(510) 471-1100 • http://www.nhusd.k12.ca.us/
Grade Span: KG-12; **Agency Type:** 1
Schools: 12
8 Primary; 3 Middle; 1 High; 0 Other Level
12 Regular; 0 Special Education; 0 Vocational; 0 Alternative
0 Magnet; 0 Charter; 7 Title I Eligible; 0 School-wide Title I
Students: 13,582 (52.5% male; 47.5% female)
Individual Education Program: 1,229 (9.0%);
English Language Learner: 3,455 (25.4%); Migrant: 358 (2.6%)
Eligible for Free Lunch Program: 3,078 (22.7%)
Eligible for Reduced-Price Lunch Program: 1,003 (7.4%)
Teachers: 660.0 (20.6 to 1)
Librarians/Media Specialists: 10.7 (1,269.3 to 1)
Guidance Counselors: 17.4 (780.6 to 1)
Current Spending: ($ per student per year):
Total: $6,866; Instruction: $4,479; Support Services: $2,188

Enrollment, Drop-out Rates and Diploma Recipients by Race/Ethnicity

Category	Total	White	Black	Asian	AIAN	Hisp.
Enrollment (%)	100.0	16.8	10.5	42.2	0.4	30.2
Drop-out Rate (%)	n/a	n/a	n/a	n/a	n/a	n/a
H.S. Diplomas (#)	828	170	83	397	0	178

Newark Unified

5715 Musick Ave • Newark, CA 94560-0385
Mailing Address: PO Box 385 • Newark, CA 94560-0385
(510) 818-4103 • http://www.nusd.k12.ca.us/
Grade Span: KG-12; **Agency Type:** 1
Schools: 14
8 Primary; 2 Middle; 3 High; 1 Other Level
10 Regular; 0 Special Education; 0 Vocational; 4 Alternative
1 Magnet; 0 Charter; 3 Title I Eligible; 0 School-wide Title I
Students: 7,401 (52.2% male; 47.8% female)
Individual Education Program: 772 (10.4%);
English Language Learner: 1,502 (20.3%); Migrant: 153 (2.1%)
Eligible for Free Lunch Program: 1,391 (18.8%)
Eligible for Reduced-Price Lunch Program: 444 (6.0%)
Teachers: 383.9 (19.3 to 1)
Librarians/Media Specialists: 1.0 (7,401.0 to 1)
Guidance Counselors: 5.6 (1,321.6 to 1)
Current Spending: ($ per student per year):
Total: $6,894; Instruction: $4,121; Support Services: $2,581

Enrollment, Drop-out Rates and Diploma Recipients by Race/Ethnicity

Category	Total	White	Black	Asian	AIAN	Hisp.
Enrollment (%)	100.0	29.6	6.0	25.6	0.5	38.4
Drop-out Rate (%)	n/a	n/a	n/a	n/a	n/a	n/a
H.S. Diplomas (#)	520	180	24	146	6	164

Oakland Unified

1025 Second Ave • Oakland, CA 94606-2212
(510) 879-8100 • http://www.ousd.k12.ca.us/
Grade Span: KG-12; **Agency Type:** 1
Schools: 110
68 Primary; 22 Middle; 14 High; 6 Other Level
100 Regular; 2 Special Education; 0 Vocational; 8 Alternative
4 Magnet; 13 Charter; 89 Title I Eligible; 44 School-wide Title I
Students: 52,501 (50.7% male; 49.3% female)
Individual Education Program: 5,690 (10.8%);
English Language Learner: 17,538 (33.4%); Migrant: 668 (1.3%)
Eligible for Free Lunch Program: 29,931 (57.0%)
Eligible for Reduced-Price Lunch Program: 4,564 (8.7%)
Teachers: 2,888.0 (18.2 to 1)
Librarians/Media Specialists: 9.8 (5,357.2 to 1)
Guidance Counselors: 59.7 (879.4 to 1)
Current Spending: ($ per student per year):
Total: $7,928; Instruction: $5,184; Support Services: $2,421

Enrollment, Drop-out Rates and Diploma Recipients by Race/Ethnicity

Category	Total	White	Black	Asian	AIAN	Hisp.
Enrollment (%)	100.0	5.8	43.3	17.3	0.5	32.2
Drop-out Rate (%)	n/a	n/a	n/a	n/a	n/a	n/a
H.S. Diplomas (#)	1,617	88	687	519	6	311

Piedmont City Unified

760 Magnolia Ave • Piedmont, CA 94611-4047
(510) 594-2600 • http://www.piedmont.k12.ca.us/
Grade Span: KG-12; **Agency Type:** 1
Schools: 6
3 Primary; 1 Middle; 2 High; 0 Other Level
5 Regular; 0 Special Education; 0 Vocational; 1 Alternative
0 Magnet; 0 Charter; 0 Title I Eligible; 0 School-wide Title I
Students: 2,566 (51.5% male; 48.5% female)
Individual Education Program: 299 (11.7%);
English Language Learner: 77 (3.0%); Migrant: 0 (0.0%)
Eligible for Free Lunch Program: 0 (0.0%)
Eligible for Reduced-Price Lunch Program: 0 (0.0%)
Teachers: 152.4 (16.8 to 1)
Librarians/Media Specialists: 4.0 (641.5 to 1)
Guidance Counselors: 7.9 (324.8 to 1)
Current Spending: ($ per student per year):
Total: $7,275; Instruction: $4,653; Support Services: $2,611

Enrollment, Drop-out Rates and Diploma Recipients by Race/Ethnicity

Category	Total	White	Black	Asian	AIAN	Hisp.
Enrollment (%)	100.0	70.0	3.2	20.4	0.2	3.5
Drop-out Rate (%)	n/a	n/a	n/a	n/a	n/a	n/a
H.S. Diplomas (#)	241	166	14	50	2	8

Pleasanton Unified

4665 Bernal Ave • Pleasanton, CA 94566-7449
(925) 462-5500 • http://www.pleasanton.k12.ca.us/
Grade Span: KG-12; **Agency Type:** 1
Schools: 15
9 Primary; 3 Middle; 3 High; 0 Other Level
14 Regular; 0 Special Education; 0 Vocational; 1 Alternative
0 Magnet; 0 Charter; 3 Title I Eligible; 0 School-wide Title I
Students: 13,729 (50.6% male; 49.4% female)
Individual Education Program: 1,524 (11.1%);
English Language Learner: 552 (4.0%); Migrant: 0 (0.0%)
Eligible for Free Lunch Program: 379 (2.8%)
Eligible for Reduced-Price Lunch Program: 175 (1.3%)
Teachers: 682.0 (20.1 to 1)
Librarians/Media Specialists: 3.0 (4,576.3 to 1)
Guidance Counselors: 17.5 (784.5 to 1)
Current Spending: ($ per student per year):
Total: $7,384; Instruction: $4,775; Support Services: $2,293

Enrollment, Drop-out Rates and Diploma Recipients by Race/Ethnicity

Category	Total	White	Black	Asian	AIAN	Hisp.
Enrollment (%)	100.0	70.1	1.9	18.3	0.8	7.6
Drop-out Rate (%)	n/a	n/a	n/a	n/a	n/a	n/a
H.S. Diplomas (#)	910	712	20	109	9	54

San Leandro Unified

14735 Juniper St • San Leandro, CA 94579-1222
(510) 667-3500 • http://www.sanleandro.k12.ca.us/
Grade Span: KG-12; **Agency Type:** 1
Schools: 13
9 Primary; 2 Middle; 2 High; 0 Other Level
12 Regular; 0 Special Education; 0 Vocational; 1 Alternative
0 Magnet; 1 Charter; 5 Title I Eligible; 0 School-wide Title I
Students: 8,749 (52.0% male; 48.0% female)
Individual Education Program: 920 (10.5%);
English Language Learner: 2,193 (25.1%); Migrant: 6 (0.1%)
Eligible for Free Lunch Program: 1,828 (20.9%)
Eligible for Reduced-Price Lunch Program: 913 (10.4%)
Teachers: 435.7 (20.1 to 1)
Librarians/Media Specialists: 2.6 (3,365.0 to 1)
Guidance Counselors: 11.7 (747.8 to 1)
Current Spending: ($ per student per year):
Total: $6,022; Instruction: $3,948; Support Services: $1,827

Enrollment, Drop-out Rates and Diploma Recipients by Race/Ethnicity

Category	Total	White	Black	Asian	AIAN	Hisp.
Enrollment (%)	100.0	21.4	16.5	26.8	0.9	33.9
Drop-out Rate (%)	n/a	n/a	n/a	n/a	n/a	n/a
H.S. Diplomas (#)	454	127	79	129	5	113

San Lorenzo Unified

15510 Usher St • San Lorenzo, CA 94580-0037
Mailing Address: PO Box 37 • San Lorenzo, CA 94580-0037
(510) 317-4600 • http://www.slzusd.k12.ca.us/
Grade Span: KG-12; **Agency Type:** 1
Schools: 15
9 Primary; 3 Middle; 2 High; 1 Other Level
14 Regular; 0 Special Education; 0 Vocational; 1 Alternative
0 Magnet; 0 Charter; 5 Title I Eligible; 0 School-wide Title I
Students: 11,684 (51.7% male; 48.3% female)
Individual Education Program: 1,311 (11.2%);
English Language Learner: 2,620 (22.4%); Migrant: 204 (1.7%)
Eligible for Free Lunch Program: 2,906 (24.9%)
Eligible for Reduced-Price Lunch Program: 1,074 (9.2%)
Teachers: 593.7 (19.7 to 1)
Librarians/Media Specialists: 5.0 (2,336.8 to 1)
Guidance Counselors: 13.8 (846.7 to 1)
Current Spending: ($ per student per year):
Total: $6,654; Instruction: $4,160; Support Services: $2,214

Enrollment, Drop-out Rates and Diploma Recipients by Race/Ethnicity

Category	Total	White	Black	Asian	AIAN	Hisp.
Enrollment (%)	100.0	25.2	14.1	20.5	0.9	39.3
Drop-out Rate (%)	n/a	n/a	n/a	n/a	n/a	n/a
H.S. Diplomas (#)	660	241	91	137	8	183

Amador County

Amador County Unified

217 Rex Ave, #7 • Jackson, CA 95642-2020
(209) 223-1750 • http://www.teachnet.k12.ca.us/
Grade Span: KG-12; **Agency Type:** 1
Schools: 12
6 Primary; 2 Middle; 3 High; 1 Other Level
10 Regular; 0 Special Education; 0 Vocational; 2 Alternative
0 Magnet; 0 Charter; 7 Title I Eligible; 0 School-wide Title I
Students: 4,664 (51.2% male; 48.8% female)
Individual Education Program: 658 (14.1%);
English Language Learner: 55 (1.2%); Migrant: 0 (0.0%)
Eligible for Free Lunch Program: 945 (20.3%)
Eligible for Reduced-Price Lunch Program: 455 (9.8%)
Teachers: 200.7 (23.2 to 1)
Librarians/Media Specialists: 0.0 (0.0 to 1)
Guidance Counselors: 7.0 (666.3 to 1)
Current Spending: ($ per student per year):
Total: $5,500; Instruction: $3,262; Support Services: $2,084

Enrollment, Drop-out Rates and Diploma Recipients by Race/Ethnicity

Category	Total	White	Black	Asian	AIAN	Hisp.
Enrollment (%)	100.0	84.6	0.8	1.4	3.9	8.8
Drop-out Rate (%)	n/a	n/a	n/a	n/a	n/a	n/a
H.S. Diplomas (#)	343	294	2	3	11	26

Butte County

Chico Unified

1163 E Seventh St • Chico, CA 95928-5999
(530) 891-3000 • http://www.cusd.chico.k12.ca.us/
Grade Span: KG-12; **Agency Type:** 1
Schools: 26
17 Primary; 3 Middle; 3 High; 3 Other Level
23 Regular; 0 Special Education; 0 Vocational; 3 Alternative
0 Magnet; 1 Charter; 15 Title I Eligible; 5 School-wide Title I
Students: 14,011 (51.8% male; 48.2% female)
Individual Education Program: 1,727 (12.3%);
English Language Learner: 1,773 (12.7%); Migrant: 298 (2.1%)
Eligible for Free Lunch Program: 4,084 (29.1%)
Eligible for Reduced-Price Lunch Program: 933 (6.7%)
Teachers: 693.9 (20.2 to 1)
Librarians/Media Specialists: 5.5 (2,547.5 to 1)
Guidance Counselors: 19.0 (737.4 to 1)
Current Spending: ($ per student per year):
Total: $5,951; Instruction: $3,888; Support Services: $1,849

Enrollment, Drop-out Rates and Diploma Recipients by Race/Ethnicity

Category	Total	White	Black	Asian	AIAN	Hisp.
Enrollment (%)	100.0	72.2	3.4	7.1	1.4	15.0
Drop-out Rate (%)	n/a	n/a	n/a	n/a	n/a	n/a
H.S. Diplomas (#)	967	736	21	72	12	126

Gridley Unified

429 Magnolia St • Gridley, CA 95948-2533
(530) 846-4721 • http://www.bcoe.butte.k12.ca.us/persdir/gridley.htm
Grade Span: KG-12; **Agency Type:** 1
Schools: 7
3 Primary; 1 Middle; 3 High; 0 Other Level
4 Regular; 0 Special Education; 0 Vocational; 3 Alternative
0 Magnet; 0 Charter; 4 Title I Eligible; 0 School-wide Title I
Students: 2,123 (51.7% male; 48.3% female)
Individual Education Program: 181 (8.5%);
English Language Learner: 520 (24.5%); Migrant: 365 (17.2%)
Eligible for Free Lunch Program: 1,100 (51.8%)
Eligible for Reduced-Price Lunch Program: 139 (6.5%)
Teachers: 113.5 (18.7 to 1)
Librarians/Media Specialists: 1.0 (2,123.0 to 1)
Guidance Counselors: 4.5 (471.8 to 1)
Current Spending: ($ per student per year):
Total: $6,667; Instruction: $4,288; Support Services: $2,059

Enrollment, Drop-out Rates and Diploma Recipients by Race/Ethnicity

Category	Total	White	Black	Asian	AIAN	Hisp.
Enrollment (%)	100.0	48.6	0.4	5.6	0.7	44.3
Drop-out Rate (%)	n/a	n/a	n/a	n/a	n/a	n/a
H.S. Diplomas (#)	148	92	0	9	0	47

Oroville City Elementary

2795 Yard St • Oroville, CA 95966-5113
(530) 532-3000 • http://www.bcoe.butte.k12.ca.us/persdir/oroelem.htm
Grade Span: KG-08; **Agency Type:** 1
Schools: 7
6 Primary; 1 Middle; 0 High; 0 Other Level
7 Regular; 0 Special Education; 0 Vocational; 0 Alternative
0 Magnet; 0 Charter; 7 Title I Eligible; 6 School-wide Title I
Students: 3,367 (51.3% male; 48.7% female)
Individual Education Program: 535 (15.9%);
English Language Learner: 454 (13.5%); Migrant: 140 (4.2%)
Eligible for Free Lunch Program: 2,102 (62.4%)
Eligible for Reduced-Price Lunch Program: 386 (11.5%)
Teachers: 174.0 (19.4 to 1)
Librarians/Media Specialists: 1.0 (3,367.0 to 1)
Guidance Counselors: 2.0 (1,683.5 to 1)
Current Spending: ($ per student per year):
Total: $6,277; Instruction: $4,054; Support Services: $1,897

Enrollment, Drop-out Rates and Diploma Recipients by Race/Ethnicity

Category	Total	White	Black	Asian	AIAN	Hisp.
Enrollment (%)	100.0	63.7	5.9	12.8	5.7	7.1
Drop-out Rate (%)	n/a	n/a	n/a	n/a	n/a	n/a
H.S. Diplomas (#)	n/a	n/a	n/a	n/a	n/a	n/a

Oroville Union High

2211 Washington Ave • Oroville, CA 95966-5440
(530) 538-2300 • http://www.ouhsd.org/
Grade Span: 09-12; **Agency Type:** 1
Schools: 5
0 Primary; 0 Middle; 5 High; 0 Other Level
3 Regular; 0 Special Education; 0 Vocational; 2 Alternative
0 Magnet; 1 Charter; 5 Title I Eligible; 0 School-wide Title I
Students: 2,927 (51.3% male; 48.7% female)
Individual Education Program: 363 (12.4%);
English Language Learner: 193 (6.6%); Migrant: 163 (5.6%)
Eligible for Free Lunch Program: 1,094 (37.4%)
Eligible for Reduced-Price Lunch Program: 191 (6.5%)
Teachers: 131.1 (22.3 to 1)
Librarians/Media Specialists: 2.0 (1,463.5 to 1)
Guidance Counselors: 5.0 (585.4 to 1)
Current Spending: ($ per student per year):
Total: $6,342; Instruction: $3,881; Support Services: $2,222

Enrollment, Drop-out Rates and Diploma Recipients by Race/Ethnicity

Category	Total	White	Black	Asian	AIAN	Hisp.
Enrollment (%)	100.0	65.7	3.5	15.9	5.5	9.4
Drop-out Rate (%)	n/a	n/a	n/a	n/a	n/a	n/a
H.S. Diplomas (#)	489	315	17	78	34	45

Paradise Unified

6696 Clark Rd • Paradise, CA 95969-2834
(530) 872-6400 • http://www.paradise.k12.ca.us/
Grade Span: KG-12; **Agency Type:** 1
Schools: 13
5 Primary; 3 Middle; 3 High; 2 Other Level
10 Regular; 0 Special Education; 0 Vocational; 3 Alternative
0 Magnet; 4 Charter; 8 Title I Eligible; 0 School-wide Title I
Students: 5,295 (51.4% male; 48.6% female)
Individual Education Program: 582 (11.0%);
English Language Learner: 24 (0.5%); Migrant: 0 (0.0%)
Eligible for Free Lunch Program: 1,516 (28.6%)
Eligible for Reduced-Price Lunch Program: 401 (7.6%)

Teachers: 282.9 (18.7 to 1)
Librarians/Media Specialists: 2.5 (2,118.0 to 1)
Guidance Counselors: 7.6 (696.7 to 1)
Current Spending: ($ per student per year):
Total: $6,116; Instruction: $4,112; Support Services: $1,778
Enrollment, Drop-out Rates and Diploma Recipients by Race/Ethnicity

Category	Total	White	Black	Asian	AIAN	Hisp.
Enrollment (%)	100.0	89.9	0.6	1.6	1.6	6.0
Drop-out Rate (%)	n/a	n/a	n/a	n/a	n/a	n/a
H.S. Diplomas (#)	373	333	2	8	6	24

Thermalito Union Elementary
400 Grand Ave • Oroville, CA 95965-4007
(530) 538-2900 • http://www.bcoe.butte.k12.ca.us/thermal.htm
Grade Span: KG-08; **Agency Type:** 1
Schools: 4
3 Primary; 1 Middle; 0 High; 0 Other Level
3 Regular; 0 Special Education; 0 Vocational; 1 Alternative
0 Magnet; 0 Charter; 3 Title I Eligible; 3 School-wide Title I
Students: 1,566 (51.2% male; 48.8% female)
Individual Education Program: 132 (8.4%);
English Language Learner: 423 (27.0%); Migrant: 147 (9.4%)
Eligible for Free Lunch Program: 1,336 (85.3%)
Eligible for Reduced-Price Lunch Program: 95 (6.1%)
Teachers: 86.9 (18.0 to 1)
Librarians/Media Specialists: 0.1 (15,660.0 to 1)
Guidance Counselors: 2.3 (680.9 to 1)
Current Spending: ($ per student per year):
Total: $7,247; Instruction: $4,351; Support Services: $2,453
Enrollment, Drop-out Rates and Diploma Recipients by Race/Ethnicity

Category	Total	White	Black	Asian	AIAN	Hisp.
Enrollment (%)	100.0	54.5	2.6	31.6	4.5	5.9
Drop-out Rate (%)	n/a	n/a	n/a	n/a	n/a	n/a
H.S. Diplomas (#)	n/a	n/a	n/a	n/a	n/a	n/a

Calaveras County

Calaveras Unified
501 Gold Strike Rd • San Andreas, CA 95249-0788
Mailing Address: PO Box 788 • San Andreas, CA 95249-0788
(209) 754-3504 • http://www.calaveras.k12.ca.us/
Grade Span: KG-12; **Agency Type:** 1
Schools: 13
6 Primary; 1 Middle; 5 High; 1 Other Level
8 Regular; 0 Special Education; 0 Vocational; 5 Alternative
0 Magnet; 0 Charter; 5 Title I Eligible; 2 School-wide Title I
Students: 3,731 (49.9% male; 50.1% female)
Individual Education Program: 463 (12.4%);
English Language Learner: 35 (0.9%); Migrant: 0 (0.0%)
Eligible for Free Lunch Program: 815 (21.8%)
Eligible for Reduced-Price Lunch Program: 308 (8.3%)
Teachers: 188.2 (19.8 to 1)
Librarians/Media Specialists: 0.0 (0.0 to 1)
Guidance Counselors: 2.0 (1,865.5 to 1)
Current Spending: ($ per student per year):
Total: $6,488; Instruction: $3,907; Support Services: $2,476
Enrollment, Drop-out Rates and Diploma Recipients by Race/Ethnicity

Category	Total	White	Black	Asian	AIAN	Hisp.
Enrollment (%)	100.0	86.2	1.2	1.3	2.7	8.1
Drop-out Rate (%)	n/a	n/a	n/a	n/a	n/a	n/a
H.S. Diplomas (#)	236	218	2	1	2	13

Colusa County

Colusa Unified
745 Tenth St • Colusa, CA 95932-2220
(530) 458-7791 •
http://www.colusa.k12.ca.us/education/district/district.php?sectionid=1
Grade Span: KG-12; **Agency Type:** 1
Schools: 5
1 Primary; 1 Middle; 1 High; 2 Other Level
3 Regular; 0 Special Education; 0 Vocational; 2 Alternative
0 Magnet; 0 Charter; 3 Title I Eligible; 2 School-wide Title I
Students: 1,538 (50.8% male; 49.2% female)
Individual Education Program: 0 (0.0%);
English Language Learner: 584 (38.0%); Migrant: 220 (14.3%)
Eligible for Free Lunch Program: 671 (43.6%)
Eligible for Reduced-Price Lunch Program: 133 (8.6%)
Teachers: 83.3 (18.5 to 1)
Librarians/Media Specialists: 1.0 (1,538.0 to 1)
Guidance Counselors: 2.0 (769.0 to 1)
Current Spending: ($ per student per year):
Total: $6,599; Instruction: $4,170; Support Services: $2,165
Enrollment, Drop-out Rates and Diploma Recipients by Race/Ethnicity

Category	Total	White	Black	Asian	AIAN	Hisp.
Enrollment (%)	100.0	46.9	0.9	2.5	2.9	43.2
Drop-out Rate (%)	n/a	n/a	n/a	n/a	n/a	n/a
H.S. Diplomas (#)	87	46	0	1	1	39

Contra Costa County

Acalanes Union High
1212 Pleasant Hill Rd • Lafayette, CA 94549-2623
(925) 935-2800 • http://www.acalanes.acalanes.k12.ca.us/
Grade Span: 09-12; **Agency Type:** 1
Schools: 5
0 Primary; 0 Middle; 5 High; 0 Other Level
4 Regular; 0 Special Education; 0 Vocational; 1 Alternative
0 Magnet; 0 Charter; 1 Title I Eligible; 0 School-wide Title I
Students: 5,744 (51.4% male; 48.6% female)
Individual Education Program: 433 (7.5%);
English Language Learner: 90 (1.6%); Migrant: 0 (0.0%)
Eligible for Free Lunch Program: 25 (0.4%)
Eligible for Reduced-Price Lunch Program: 7 (0.1%)
Teachers: 264.4 (21.7 to 1)
Librarians/Media Specialists: 4.0 (1,436.0 to 1)
Guidance Counselors: 13.2 (435.2 to 1)
Current Spending: ($ per student per year):
Total: $6,763; Instruction: $4,069; Support Services: $2,555
Enrollment, Drop-out Rates and Diploma Recipients by Race/Ethnicity

Category	Total	White	Black	Asian	AIAN	Hisp.
Enrollment (%)	100.0	79.1	1.2	13.9	0.2	5.1
Drop-out Rate (%)	n/a	n/a	n/a	n/a	n/a	n/a
H.S. Diplomas (#)	1,279	1,047	13	165	7	41

Antioch Unified
510 G St • Antioch, CA 94509-0904
Mailing Address: PO Box 768 • Antioch, CA 94509-0904
(925) 706-4100 • http://www.antioch.k12.ca.us/
Grade Span: KG-12; **Agency Type:** 1
Schools: 21
12 Primary; 3 Middle; 4 High; 2 Other Level
18 Regular; 0 Special Education; 0 Vocational; 3 Alternative
0 Magnet; 1 Charter; 7 Title I Eligible; 6 School-wide Title I
Students: 21,136 (50.7% male; 49.3% female)
Individual Education Program: 2,109 (10.0%);
English Language Learner: 1,568 (7.4%); Migrant: 0 (0.0%)
Eligible for Free Lunch Program: 4,844 (22.9%)
Eligible for Reduced-Price Lunch Program: 1,816 (8.6%)
Teachers: 995.5 (21.2 to 1)
Librarians/Media Specialists: 3.0 (7,045.3 to 1)
Guidance Counselors: 5.3 (3,987.9 to 1)
Current Spending: ($ per student per year):
Total: $5,843; Instruction: $3,883; Support Services: $1,730
Enrollment, Drop-out Rates and Diploma Recipients by Race/Ethnicity

Category	Total	White	Black	Asian	AIAN	Hisp.
Enrollment (%)	100.0	41.3	14.5	10.4	1.1	25.2
Drop-out Rate (%)	n/a	n/a	n/a	n/a	n/a	n/a
H.S. Diplomas (#)	1,254	599	152	150	15	285

Brentwood Union Elementary
255 Guthrie Ln • Brentwood, CA 94513-1610
(925) 634-1168 • http://www.brentwood.k12.ca.us/
Grade Span: KG-08; **Agency Type:** 1
Schools: 7
5 Primary; 2 Middle; 0 High; 0 Other Level
7 Regular; 0 Special Education; 0 Vocational; 0 Alternative
0 Magnet; 0 Charter; 3 Title I Eligible; 0 School-wide Title I
Students: 5,343 (51.2% male; 48.8% female)
Individual Education Program: 658 (12.3%);
English Language Learner: 780 (14.6%); Migrant: 275 (5.1%)
Eligible for Free Lunch Program: 1,038 (19.4%)
Eligible for Reduced-Price Lunch Program: 306 (5.7%)
Teachers: 272.7 (19.6 to 1)
Librarians/Media Specialists: 0.0 (0.0 to 1)
Guidance Counselors: 5.9 (905.6 to 1)
Current Spending: ($ per student per year):
Total: $6,464; Instruction: $4,368; Support Services: $1,873
Enrollment, Drop-out Rates and Diploma Recipients by Race/Ethnicity

Category	Total	White	Black	Asian	AIAN	Hisp.
Enrollment (%)	100.0	61.4	3.3	5.0	0.8	29.5
Drop-out Rate (%)	n/a	n/a	n/a	n/a	n/a	n/a
H.S. Diplomas (#)	n/a	n/a	n/a	n/a	n/a	n/a

John Swett Unified

341 #B (Selby) • Crockett, CA 94525
(510) 787-1141 • http://www.jsusd.k12.ca.us/
Grade Span: KG-12; **Agency Type:** 1
Schools: 4
1 Primary; 1 Middle; 1 High; 1 Other Level
3 Regular; 0 Special Education; 0 Vocational; 1 Alternative
0 Magnet; 0 Charter; 2 Title I Eligible; 0 School-wide Title I
Students: 1,827 (52.1% male; 47.9% female)
Individual Education Program: 211 (11.5%);
English Language Learner: 243 (13.3%); Migrant: 0 (0.0%)
Eligible for Free Lunch Program: 508 (27.8%)
Eligible for Reduced-Price Lunch Program: 106 (5.8%)
Teachers: 95.9 (19.1 to 1)
Librarians/Media Specialists: 0.6 (3,045.0 to 1)
Guidance Counselors: 2.6 (702.7 to 1)
Current Spending: ($ per student per year):
Total: $6,612; Instruction: $4,153; Support Services: $2,274
Enrollment, Drop-out Rates and Diploma Recipients by Race/Ethnicity

Category	Total	White	Black	Asian	AIAN	Hisp.
Enrollment (%)	100.0	38.5	21.7	18.8	0.8	19.9
Drop-out Rate (%)	n/a	n/a	n/a	n/a	n/a	n/a
H.S. Diplomas (#)	145	59	22	40	2	22

Lafayette Elementary

3477 School St • Lafayette, CA 94549-1029
Mailing Address: PO Box 1029 • Lafayette, CA 94549-1029
(925) 284-7011 • http://www.lafsd.k12.ca.us/
Grade Span: KG-08; **Agency Type:** 1
Schools: 5
4 Primary; 1 Middle; 0 High; 0 Other Level
5 Regular; 0 Special Education; 0 Vocational; 0 Alternative
0 Magnet; 0 Charter; 2 Title I Eligible; 0 School-wide Title I
Students: 3,425 (52.3% male; 47.7% female)
Individual Education Program: 282 (8.2%);
English Language Learner: 52 (1.5%); Migrant: 0 (0.0%)
Eligible for Free Lunch Program: 5 (0.1%)
Eligible for Reduced-Price Lunch Program: 0 (0.0%)
Teachers: 180.8 (18.9 to 1)
Librarians/Media Specialists: 1.0 (3,425.0 to 1)
Guidance Counselors: 1.6 (2,140.6 to 1)
Current Spending: ($ per student per year):
Total: $6,213; Instruction: $4,418; Support Services: $1,795
Enrollment, Drop-out Rates and Diploma Recipients by Race/Ethnicity

Category	Total	White	Black	Asian	AIAN	Hisp.
Enrollment (%)	100.0	80.3	0.9	10.2	0.2	2.7
Drop-out Rate (%)	n/a	n/a	n/a	n/a	n/a	n/a
H.S. Diplomas (#)	n/a	n/a	n/a	n/a	n/a	n/a

Liberty Union High

20 Oak St • Brentwood, CA 94513-1379
(925) 634-2166 • http://www.libertyuhsd.k12.ca.us/
Grade Span: 09-12; **Agency Type:** 1
Schools: 4
0 Primary; 0 Middle; 4 High; 0 Other Level
2 Regular; 0 Special Education; 0 Vocational; 2 Alternative
0 Magnet; 0 Charter; 1 Title I Eligible; 0 School-wide Title I
Students: 4,467 (50.5% male; 49.5% female)
Individual Education Program: 475 (10.6%);
English Language Learner: 415 (9.3%); Migrant: 235 (5.3%)
Eligible for Free Lunch Program: 334 (7.5%)
Eligible for Reduced-Price Lunch Program: 61 (1.4%)
Teachers: 183.4 (24.4 to 1)
Librarians/Media Specialists: 2.0 (2,233.5 to 1)
Guidance Counselors: 8.5 (525.5 to 1)
Current Spending: ($ per student per year):
Total: $6,625; Instruction: $3,569; Support Services: $2,872
Enrollment, Drop-out Rates and Diploma Recipients by Race/Ethnicity

Category	Total	White	Black	Asian	AIAN	Hisp.
Enrollment (%)	100.0	64.0	3.2	4.3	1.0	27.3
Drop-out Rate (%)	n/a	n/a	n/a	n/a	n/a	n/a
H.S. Diplomas (#)	794	555	22	32	4	181

Martinez Unified

921 Susana St • Martinez, CA 94553-1848
(925) 313-0480 • http://www.cccoe.k12.ca.us/cccoe/schools.htm
Grade Span: KG-12; **Agency Type:** 1
Schools: 8
4 Primary; 1 Middle; 1 High; 2 Other Level
6 Regular; 0 Special Education; 0 Vocational; 2 Alternative
0 Magnet; 0 Charter; 4 Title I Eligible; 3 School-wide Title I
Students: 4,338 (51.4% male; 48.6% female)
Individual Education Program: 611 (14.1%);
English Language Learner: 216 (5.0%); Migrant: 0 (0.0%)
Eligible for Free Lunch Program: 500 (11.5%)
Eligible for Reduced-Price Lunch Program: 231 (5.3%)
Teachers: 213.3 (20.3 to 1)
Librarians/Media Specialists: 2.0 (2,169.0 to 1)
Guidance Counselors: 4.0 (1,084.5 to 1)
Current Spending: ($ per student per year):
Total: $6,271; Instruction: $4,109; Support Services: $1,980
Enrollment, Drop-out Rates and Diploma Recipients by Race/Ethnicity

Category	Total	White	Black	Asian	AIAN	Hisp.
Enrollment (%)	100.0	70.9	4.2	5.1	2.8	16.9
Drop-out Rate (%)	n/a	n/a	n/a	n/a	n/a	n/a
H.S. Diplomas (#)	315	224	12	12	21	46

Moraga Elementary

1540 School St • Moraga, CA 94556-0158
Mailing Address: PO Box 158 • Moraga, CA 94556-0158
(925) 376-5943 • http://www.moraga.k12.ca.us/
Grade Span: KG-08; **Agency Type:** 1
Schools: 4
3 Primary; 1 Middle; 0 High; 0 Other Level
4 Regular; 0 Special Education; 0 Vocational; 0 Alternative
0 Magnet; 0 Charter; 4 Title I Eligible; 0 School-wide Title I
Students: 1,829 (53.4% male; 46.6% female)
Individual Education Program: 159 (8.7%);
English Language Learner: 21 (1.1%); Migrant: 0 (0.0%)
Eligible for Free Lunch Program: 14 (0.8%)
Eligible for Reduced-Price Lunch Program: 0 (0.0%)
Teachers: 94.1 (19.4 to 1)
Librarians/Media Specialists: 0.0 (0.0 to 1)
Guidance Counselors: 0.3 (6,096.7 to 1)
Current Spending: ($ per student per year):
Total: $6,504; Instruction: $4,191; Support Services: $2,309
Enrollment, Drop-out Rates and Diploma Recipients by Race/Ethnicity

Category	Total	White	Black	Asian	AIAN	Hisp.
Enrollment (%)	100.0	78.8	0.8	16.4	0.2	3.0
Drop-out Rate (%)	n/a	n/a	n/a	n/a	n/a	n/a
H.S. Diplomas (#)	n/a	n/a	n/a	n/a	n/a	n/a

Mount Diablo Unified

1936 Carlotta Dr • Concord, CA 94519-1358
(925) 682-8000 • http://www.mdusd.k12.ca.us/
Grade Span: KG-12; **Agency Type:** 1
Schools: 55
30 Primary; 10 Middle; 13 High; 2 Other Level
45 Regular; 1 Special Education; 0 Vocational; 9 Alternative
7 Magnet; 1 Charter; 9 Title I Eligible; 7 School-wide Title I
Students: 36,891 (51.5% male; 48.5% female)
Individual Education Program: 4,871 (13.2%);
English Language Learner: 5,795 (15.7%); Migrant: 11 (<0.1%)
Eligible for Free Lunch Program: 7,561 (20.5%)
Eligible for Reduced-Price Lunch Program: 2,335 (6.3%)
Teachers: 1,850.2 (19.9 to 1)
Librarians/Media Specialists: 31.6 (1,167.4 to 1)
Guidance Counselors: 0.0 (0.0 to 1)
Current Spending: ($ per student per year):
Total: $6,030; Instruction: $3,948; Support Services: $1,866
Enrollment, Drop-out Rates and Diploma Recipients by Race/Ethnicity

Category	Total	White	Black	Asian	AIAN	Hisp.
Enrollment (%)	100.0	59.0	5.0	12.4	0.4	23.1
Drop-out Rate (%)	n/a	n/a	n/a	n/a	n/a	n/a
H.S. Diplomas (#)	2,161	1,405	80	321	17	338

Oakley Union Elementary

91 Mercedes Ln • Oakley, CA 94561-0007
(925) 625-0700 • http://www.ouesd.k12.ca.us/
Grade Span: KG-08; **Agency Type:** 1
Schools: 6
4 Primary; 2 Middle; 0 High; 0 Other Level
6 Regular; 0 Special Education; 0 Vocational; 0 Alternative
0 Magnet; 0 Charter; 2 Title I Eligible; 0 School-wide Title I
Students: 4,354 (50.5% male; 49.5% female)
Individual Education Program: 643 (14.8%);
English Language Learner: 391 (9.0%); Migrant: 134 (3.1%)
Eligible for Free Lunch Program: 722 (16.6%)
Eligible for Reduced-Price Lunch Program: 285 (6.5%)
Teachers: 219.7 (19.8 to 1)
Librarians/Media Specialists: 0.0 (0.0 to 1)
Guidance Counselors: 2.0 (2,177.0 to 1)
Current Spending: ($ per student per year):
Total: $5,995; Instruction: $3,983; Support Services: $1,853
Enrollment, Drop-out Rates and Diploma Recipients by Race/Ethnicity

Category	Total	White	Black	Asian	AIAN	Hisp.
Enrollment (%)	100.0	57.2	5.4	4.5	1.1	30.3
Drop-out Rate (%)	n/a	n/a	n/a	n/a	n/a	n/a
H.S. Diplomas (#)	n/a	n/a	n/a	n/a	n/a	n/a

Orinda Union Elementary

8 Altarinda Rd • Orinda, CA 94563-2603
(925) 254-4901 • http://www.orinda.k12.ca.us/
Grade Span: KG-08; **Agency Type:** 1
Schools: 5
4 Primary; 1 Middle; 0 High; 0 Other Level
5 Regular; 0 Special Education; 0 Vocational; 0 Alternative
0 Magnet; 0 Charter; 3 Title I Eligible; 0 School-wide Title I
Students: 2,410 (51.4% male; 48.6% female)
Individual Education Program: 196 (8.1%);
English Language Learner: 26 (1.1%); Migrant: 0 (0.0%)
Eligible for Free Lunch Program: 8 (0.3%)
Eligible for Reduced-Price Lunch Program: 0 (0.0%)
Teachers: 131.4 (18.3 to 1)
Librarians/Media Specialists: 4.2 (573.8 to 1)
Guidance Counselors: 2.0 (1,205.0 to 1)
Current Spending: ($ per student per year):
Total: $6,685; Instruction: $4,312; Support Services: $2,372
Enrollment, Drop-out Rates and Diploma Recipients by Race/Ethnicity

Category	Total	White	Black	Asian	AIAN	Hisp.
Enrollment (%)	100.0	77.5	0.9	14.5	0.2	2.7
Drop-out Rate (%)	n/a	n/a	n/a	n/a	n/a	n/a
H.S. Diplomas (#)	n/a	n/a	n/a	n/a	n/a	n/a

Pittsburg Unified

2000 Railroad Ave • Pittsburg, CA 94565-3830
(925) 473-4231 • http://www.pittsburg.k12.ca.us/
Grade Span: KG-12; **Agency Type:** 1
Schools: 11
7 Primary; 2 Middle; 1 High; 1 Other Level
10 Regular; 0 Special Education; 0 Vocational; 1 Alternative
0 Magnet; 0 Charter; 11 Title I Eligible; 10 School-wide Title I
Students: 9,542 (52.3% male; 47.7% female)
Individual Education Program: 1,036 (10.9%);
English Language Learner: 2,876 (30.1%); Migrant: 0 (0.0%)
Eligible for Free Lunch Program: 3,928 (41.2%)
Eligible for Reduced-Price Lunch Program: 1,766 (18.5%)
Teachers: 448.8 (21.3 to 1)
Librarians/Media Specialists: 1.0 (9,542.0 to 1)
Guidance Counselors: 10.0 (954.2 to 1)
Current Spending: ($ per student per year):
Total: $6,298; Instruction: $3,914; Support Services: $2,095
Enrollment, Drop-out Rates and Diploma Recipients by Race/Ethnicity

Category	Total	White	Black	Asian	AIAN	Hisp.
Enrollment (%)	100.0	13.3	25.3	12.7	0.7	44.8
Drop-out Rate (%)	n/a	n/a	n/a	n/a	n/a	n/a
H.S. Diplomas (#)	428	103	110	78	1	130

San Ramon Valley Unified

699 Old Orchard Dr • Danville, CA 94526-4331
(925) 552-5500 • http://www.srvusd.k12.ca.us/
Grade Span: KG-12; **Agency Type:** 1
Schools: 28
17 Primary; 6 Middle; 4 High; 1 Other Level
26 Regular; 0 Special Education; 0 Vocational; 2 Alternative
3 Magnet; 0 Charter; 9 Title I Eligible; 0 School-wide Title I
Students: 21,561 (50.7% male; 49.3% female)
Individual Education Program: 2,317 (10.7%);
English Language Learner: 355 (1.6%); Migrant: 0 (0.0%)
Eligible for Free Lunch Program: 145 (0.7%)
Eligible for Reduced-Price Lunch Program: 114 (0.5%)
Teachers: 1,005.7 (21.4 to 1)
Librarians/Media Specialists: 9.0 (2,395.7 to 1)
Guidance Counselors: 23.0 (937.4 to 1)
Current Spending: ($ per student per year):
Total: $6,400; Instruction: $4,081; Support Services: $2,127
Enrollment, Drop-out Rates and Diploma Recipients by Race/Ethnicity

Category	Total	White	Black	Asian	AIAN	Hisp.
Enrollment (%)	100.0	78.1	1.8	15.3	0.7	4.0
Drop-out Rate (%)	n/a	n/a	n/a	n/a	n/a	n/a
H.S. Diplomas (#)	1,491	1,127	25	245	18	76

Walnut Creek Elementary

960 Ygnacio Valley Rd • Walnut Creek, CA 94597
(925) 944-6850 • http://www.wcsd.k12.ca.us/
Grade Span: KG-08; **Agency Type:** 1
Schools: 6
5 Primary; 1 Middle; 0 High; 0 Other Level
6 Regular; 0 Special Education; 0 Vocational; 0 Alternative
0 Magnet; 0 Charter; 2 Title I Eligible; 0 School-wide Title I
Students: 3,340 (52.0% male; 48.0% female)
Individual Education Program: 356 (10.7%);
English Language Learner: 257 (7.7%); Migrant: 0 (0.0%)
Eligible for Free Lunch Program: 145 (4.3%)
Eligible for Reduced-Price Lunch Program: 76 (2.3%)
Teachers: 174.3 (19.2 to 1)
Librarians/Media Specialists: 0.0 (0.0 to 1)
Guidance Counselors: 1.4 (2,385.7 to 1)
Current Spending: ($ per student per year):
Total: $6,034; Instruction: $3,746; Support Services: $2,081
Enrollment, Drop-out Rates and Diploma Recipients by Race/Ethnicity

Category	Total	White	Black	Asian	AIAN	Hisp.
Enrollment (%)	100.0	74.3	2.3	12.9	0.5	9.1
Drop-out Rate (%)	n/a	n/a	n/a	n/a	n/a	n/a
H.S. Diplomas (#)	n/a	n/a	n/a	n/a	n/a	n/a

West Contra Costa Unified

1108 Bissell Ave • Richmond, CA 94801-3135
(510) 234-3825 • http://www.wccusd.k12.ca.us/
Grade Span: KG-12; **Agency Type:** 1
Schools: 63
40 Primary; 7 Middle; 14 High; 2 Other Level
54 Regular; 1 Special Education; 0 Vocational; 8 Alternative
1 Magnet; 2 Charter; 29 Title I Eligible; 24 School-wide Title I
Students: 34,940 (51.8% male; 48.2% female)
Individual Education Program: 4,945 (14.2%);
English Language Learner: 9,811 (28.1%); Migrant: 2 (<0.1%)
Eligible for Free Lunch Program: 12,678 (36.3%)
Eligible for Reduced-Price Lunch Program: 3,861 (11.1%)
Teachers: 1,799.2 (19.4 to 1)
Librarians/Media Specialists: 9.0 (3,882.2 to 1)
Guidance Counselors: 33.2 (1,052.4 to 1)
Current Spending: ($ per student per year):
Total: $6,920; Instruction: $4,508; Support Services: $2,193
Enrollment, Drop-out Rates and Diploma Recipients by Race/Ethnicity

Category	Total	White	Black	Asian	AIAN	Hisp.
Enrollment (%)	100.0	14.9	29.4	17.2	0.3	36.0
Drop-out Rate (%)	n/a	n/a	n/a	n/a	n/a	n/a
H.S. Diplomas (#)	1,770	391	487	442	2	443

Del Norte County

Del Norte County Unified

301 W Washington Blvd • Crescent City, CA 95531-8340
(707) 464-6141 • http://www.delnorte.k12.ca.us/
Grade Span: KG-12; **Agency Type:** 1
Schools: 11
8 Primary; 1 Middle; 2 High; 0 Other Level
10 Regular; 0 Special Education; 0 Vocational; 1 Alternative
0 Magnet; 0 Charter; 6 Title I Eligible; 6 School-wide Title I
Students: 4,330 (51.9% male; 48.1% female)
Individual Education Program: 585 (13.5%);
English Language Learner: 341 (7.9%); Migrant: 73 (1.7%)
Eligible for Free Lunch Program: 2,380 (55.0%)
Eligible for Reduced-Price Lunch Program: 392 (9.1%)
Teachers: 228.0 (19.0 to 1)
Librarians/Media Specialists: 0.0 (0.0 to 1)
Guidance Counselors: 4.0 (1,082.5 to 1)
Current Spending: ($ per student per year):
Total: $7,345; Instruction: $4,599; Support Services: $2,446
Enrollment, Drop-out Rates and Diploma Recipients by Race/Ethnicity

Category	Total	White	Black	Asian	AIAN	Hisp.
Enrollment (%)	100.0	65.7	0.6	7.2	13.8	12.8
Drop-out Rate (%)	n/a	n/a	n/a	n/a	n/a	n/a
H.S. Diplomas (#)	289	212	4	27	24	22

El Dorado County

Black Oak Mine Unified

6540 Wentworth Springs Rd • Georgetown, CA 95634-9001
Mailing Address: PO Box 4510 • Georgetown, CA 95634-9001
(530) 333-8300 • http://bomusd.k12.ca.us/
Grade Span: KG-12; **Agency Type:** 1
Schools: 7
4 Primary; 0 Middle; 3 High; 0 Other Level
5 Regular; 0 Special Education; 0 Vocational; 2 Alternative
0 Magnet; 0 Charter; 4 Title I Eligible; 0 School-wide Title I
Students: 2,022 (53.7% male; 46.3% female)
Individual Education Program: 169 (8.4%);
English Language Learner: 18 (0.9%); Migrant: 1 (<0.1%)
Eligible for Free Lunch Program: 426 (21.1%)
Eligible for Reduced-Price Lunch Program: 139 (6.9%)
Teachers: 100.2 (20.2 to 1)
Librarians/Media Specialists: 0.6 (3,370.0 to 1)
Guidance Counselors: 1.5 (1,348.0 to 1)
Current Spending: ($ per student per year):
Total: $6,369; Instruction: $3,938; Support Services: $2,250

Enrollment, Drop-out Rates and Diploma Recipients by Race/Ethnicity

Category	Total	White	Black	Asian	AIAN	Hisp.
Enrollment (%)	100.0	90.2	0.5	1.4	2.8	4.3
Drop-out Rate (%)	n/a	n/a	n/a	n/a	n/a	n/a
H.S. Diplomas (#)	150	146	0	2	0	2

Buckeye Union Elementary

4560 Buckeye Rd • Shingle Springs, CA 95682-0547
Mailing Address: PO Box 547 • Shingle Springs, CA 95682-0547
(530) 677-2261 • http://buckeye.k12.ca.us/
Grade Span: KG-08; **Agency Type:** 1
Schools: 6
4 Primary; 2 Middle; 0 High; 0 Other Level
6 Regular; 0 Special Education; 0 Vocational; 0 Alternative
0 Magnet; 0 Charter; 1 Title I Eligible; 0 School-wide Title I
Students: 4,213 (49.7% male; 50.3% female)
Individual Education Program: 212 (5.0%);
English Language Learner: 26 (0.6%); Migrant: 0 (0.0%)
Eligible for Free Lunch Program: 199 (4.7%)
Eligible for Reduced-Price Lunch Program: 95 (2.3%)
Teachers: 200.0 (21.1 to 1)
Librarians/Media Specialists: 1.0 (4,213.0 to 1)
Guidance Counselors: 3.9 (1,080.3 to 1)
Current Spending: ($ per student per year):
Total: $5,795; Instruction: $3,881; Support Services: $1,885

Enrollment, Drop-out Rates and Diploma Recipients by Race/Ethnicity

Category	Total	White	Black	Asian	AIAN	Hisp.
Enrollment (%)	100.0	86.4	1.2	5.7	1.3	4.9
Drop-out Rate (%)	n/a	n/a	n/a	n/a	n/a	n/a
H.S. Diplomas (#)	n/a	n/a	n/a	n/a	n/a	n/a

El Dorado Union High

4675 Missouri Flat Rd • Placerville, CA 95619-1450
Mailing Address: PO Box 1450 • Diamond Springs, CA 95619-1450
(530) 622-5081 • http://www.eduhsd.k12.ca.us/
Grade Span: 09-12; **Agency Type:** 1
Schools: 9
0 Primary; 0 Middle; 9 High; 0 Other Level
5 Regular; 0 Special Education; 0 Vocational; 4 Alternative
0 Magnet; 1 Charter; 4 Title I Eligible; 0 School-wide Title I
Students: 6,858 (51.0% male; 49.0% female)
Individual Education Program: 613 (8.9%);
English Language Learner: 36 (0.5%); Migrant: 9 (0.1%)
Eligible for Free Lunch Program: 433 (6.3%)
Eligible for Reduced-Price Lunch Program: 190 (2.8%)
Teachers: 319.6 (21.5 to 1)
Librarians/Media Specialists: 4.4 (1,558.6 to 1)
Guidance Counselors: 15.4 (445.3 to 1)
Current Spending: ($ per student per year):
Total: $6,688; Instruction: $3,845; Support Services: $2,650

Enrollment, Drop-out Rates and Diploma Recipients by Race/Ethnicity

Category	Total	White	Black	Asian	AIAN	Hisp.
Enrollment (%)	100.0	86.5	0.9	2.4	2.6	6.7
Drop-out Rate (%)	n/a	n/a	n/a	n/a	n/a	n/a
H.S. Diplomas (#)	1,488	1,320	12	37	38	80

Lake Tahoe Unified

1021 Al Tahoe Blvd • South Lake Tahoe, CA 96150-4426
(530) 541-2850 • http://tahoe.ltusd.k12.ca.us/
Grade Span: KG-12; **Agency Type:** 1
Schools: 9
5 Primary; 1 Middle; 2 High; 1 Other Level
7 Regular; 0 Special Education; 0 Vocational; 2 Alternative
0 Magnet; 0 Charter; 5 Title I Eligible; 0 School-wide Title I
Students: 5,238 (51.7% male; 48.3% female)
Individual Education Program: 695 (13.3%);
English Language Learner: 1,132 (21.6%); Migrant: 0 (0.0%)
Eligible for Free Lunch Program: 1,550 (29.6%)
Eligible for Reduced-Price Lunch Program: 696 (13.3%)
Teachers: 251.9 (20.8 to 1)
Librarians/Media Specialists: 1.0 (5,238.0 to 1)
Guidance Counselors: 6.5 (805.8 to 1)
Current Spending: ($ per student per year):
Total: $6,261; Instruction: $4,036; Support Services: $2,000

Enrollment, Drop-out Rates and Diploma Recipients by Race/Ethnicity

Category	Total	White	Black	Asian	AIAN	Hisp.
Enrollment (%)	100.0	53.4	0.5	5.6	0.5	30.3
Drop-out Rate (%)	n/a	n/a	n/a	n/a	n/a	n/a
H.S. Diplomas (#)	308	212	2	12	4	78

Mother Lode Union Elementary

3783 Forni Rd • Placerville, CA 95667-6207
(530) 622-6464 • http://www.mlusd.k12.ca.us/
Grade Span: KG-08; **Agency Type:** 1
Schools: 3
2 Primary; 1 Middle; 0 High; 0 Other Level
3 Regular; 0 Special Education; 0 Vocational; 0 Alternative
0 Magnet; 0 Charter; 1 Title I Eligible; 0 School-wide Title I
Students: 1,611 (50.5% male; 49.5% female)
Individual Education Program: 113 (7.0%);
English Language Learner: 31 (1.9%); Migrant: 12 (0.7%)
Eligible for Free Lunch Program: 308 (19.1%)
Eligible for Reduced-Price Lunch Program: 153 (9.5%)
Teachers: 85.3 (18.9 to 1)
Librarians/Media Specialists: 0.0 (0.0 to 1)
Guidance Counselors: 0.9 (1,790.0 to 1)
Current Spending: ($ per student per year):
Total: $6,269; Instruction: $4,134; Support Services: $1,957

Enrollment, Drop-out Rates and Diploma Recipients by Race/Ethnicity

Category	Total	White	Black	Asian	AIAN	Hisp.
Enrollment (%)	100.0	81.6	0.7	1.0	4.5	12.2
Drop-out Rate (%)	n/a	n/a	n/a	n/a	n/a	n/a
H.S. Diplomas (#)	n/a	n/a	n/a	n/a	n/a	n/a

Rescue Union Elementary

2390 Bass Lake Rd • Rescue, CA 95672-9608
(916) 933-0129 • http://rescue.k12.ca.us/
Grade Span: KG-08; **Agency Type:** 1
Schools: 5
4 Primary; 1 Middle; 0 High; 0 Other Level
5 Regular; 0 Special Education; 0 Vocational; 0 Alternative
0 Magnet; 0 Charter; 2 Title I Eligible; 0 School-wide Title I
Students: 3,529 (52.1% male; 47.9% female)
Individual Education Program: 279 (7.9%);
English Language Learner: 61 (1.7%); Migrant: 0 (0.0%)
Eligible for Free Lunch Program: 232 (6.6%)
Eligible for Reduced-Price Lunch Program: 91 (2.6%)
Teachers: 170.7 (20.7 to 1)
Librarians/Media Specialists: 0.0 (0.0 to 1)
Guidance Counselors: 2.0 (1,764.5 to 1)
Current Spending: ($ per student per year):
Total: $5,626; Instruction: $3,681; Support Services: $1,835

Enrollment, Drop-out Rates and Diploma Recipients by Race/Ethnicity

Category	Total	White	Black	Asian	AIAN	Hisp.
Enrollment (%)	100.0	88.1	0.9	4.7	0.9	5.4
Drop-out Rate (%)	n/a	n/a	n/a	n/a	n/a	n/a
H.S. Diplomas (#)	n/a	n/a	n/a	n/a	n/a	n/a

Fresno County

Central Unified

4605 N Polk Ave • Fresno, CA 93722-5334
(559) 276-5206
Grade Span: KG-12; **Agency Type:** 1
Schools: 16
11 Primary; 2 Middle; 2 High; 1 Other Level
14 Regular; 0 Special Education; 0 Vocational; 2 Alternative
0 Magnet; 0 Charter; 11 Title I Eligible; 2 School-wide Title I
Students: 11,289 (51.3% male; 48.7% female)
Individual Education Program: 1,210 (10.7%);
English Language Learner: 1,950 (17.3%); Migrant: 401 (3.6%)
Eligible for Free Lunch Program: 3,868 (34.3%)
Eligible for Reduced-Price Lunch Program: 1,180 (10.5%)
Teachers: 575.5 (19.6 to 1)
Librarians/Media Specialists: 5.0 (2,257.8 to 1)
Guidance Counselors: 7.2 (1,567.9 to 1)
Current Spending: ($ per student per year):
Total: $6,212; Instruction: $3,478; Support Services: $2,405

Enrollment, Drop-out Rates and Diploma Recipients by Race/Ethnicity

Category	Total	White	Black	Asian	AIAN	Hisp.
Enrollment (%)	100.0	30.7	9.2	14.9	0.7	42.9
Drop-out Rate (%)	n/a	n/a	n/a	n/a	n/a	n/a
H.S. Diplomas (#)	605	219	38	95	5	247

Clovis Unified

1450 Herndon Ave • Clovis, CA 93611-0567
(559) 397-9000 • http://www.clovisusd.k12.ca.us/
Grade Span: KG-12; **Agency Type:** 1
Schools: 38
27 Primary; 4 Middle; 6 High; 1 Other Level
35 Regular; 0 Special Education; 0 Vocational; 3 Alternative
0 Magnet; 0 Charter; 11 Title I Eligible; 8 School-wide Title I
Students: 34,031 (50.6% male; 49.4% female)
Individual Education Program: 3,450 (10.1%);
English Language Learner: 3,024 (8.9%); Migrant: 711 (2.1%)
Eligible for Free Lunch Program: 7,006 (20.6%)
Eligible for Reduced-Price Lunch Program: 2,433 (7.1%)
Teachers: 1,538.7 (22.1 to 1)
Librarians/Media Specialists: 11.2 (3,038.5 to 1)
Guidance Counselors: 63.9 (532.6 to 1)

Current Spending: ($ per student per year):
Total: $6,656; Instruction: $3,854; Support Services: $2,546
Enrollment, Drop-out Rates and Diploma Recipients by Race/Ethnicity

Category	Total	White	Black	Asian	AIAN	Hisp.
Enrollment (%)	100.0	59.6	3.7	13.9	1.3	21.0
Drop-out Rate (%)	n/a	n/a	n/a	n/a	n/a	n/a
H.S. Diplomas (#)	2,052	1,341	58	277	29	345

Coalinga-Huron Joint Unified
657 Sunset St • Coalinga, CA 93210-2927
(559) 935-7500 • http://www.chusd.k12.ca.us/chusd/
Grade Span: KG-12; **Agency Type:** 1
Schools: 11
5 Primary; 2 Middle; 4 High; 0 Other Level
8 Regular; 0 Special Education; 0 Vocational; 3 Alternative
0 Magnet; 0 Charter; 8 Title I Eligible; 6 School-wide Title I
Students: 4,231 (52.6% male; 47.4% female)
Individual Education Program: 389 (9.2%);
English Language Learner: 1,355 (32.0%); Migrant: 1,519 (35.9%)
Eligible for Free Lunch Program: 2,451 (57.9%)
Eligible for Reduced-Price Lunch Program: 362 (8.6%)
Teachers: 186.8 (22.6 to 1)
Librarians/Media Specialists: 0.0 (0.0 to 1)
Guidance Counselors: 5.0 (846.2 to 1)
Current Spending: ($ per student per year):
Total: $6,543; Instruction: $3,864; Support Services: $2,373
Enrollment, Drop-out Rates and Diploma Recipients by Race/Ethnicity

Category	Total	White	Black	Asian	AIAN	Hisp.
Enrollment (%)	100.0	22.9	0.9	0.9	0.1	74.3
Drop-out Rate (%)	n/a	n/a	n/a	n/a	n/a	n/a
H.S. Diplomas (#)	223	56	2	5	1	157

Firebaugh-Las Deltas Joint Unified
1976 Morris Kyle Dr • Firebaugh, CA 93622-9711
(559) 659-1476
Grade Span: KG-12; **Agency Type:** 1
Schools: 6
1 Primary; 2 Middle; 3 High; 0 Other Level
4 Regular; 0 Special Education; 0 Vocational; 2 Alternative
0 Magnet; 0 Charter; 3 Title I Eligible; 3 School-wide Title I
Students: 2,459 (51.6% male; 48.4% female)
Individual Education Program: 230 (9.4%);
English Language Learner: 914 (37.2%); Migrant: 1,722 (70.0%)
Eligible for Free Lunch Program: 1,762 (71.7%)
Eligible for Reduced-Price Lunch Program: 298 (12.1%)
Teachers: 129.3 (19.0 to 1)
Librarians/Media Specialists: 1.0 (2,459.0 to 1)
Guidance Counselors: 3.2 (768.4 to 1)
Current Spending: ($ per student per year):
Total: $6,699; Instruction: $3,860; Support Services: $2,403
Enrollment, Drop-out Rates and Diploma Recipients by Race/Ethnicity

Category	Total	White	Black	Asian	AIAN	Hisp.
Enrollment (%)	100.0	6.3	1.0	0.2	0.0	92.5
Drop-out Rate (%)	n/a	n/a	n/a	n/a	n/a	n/a
H.S. Diplomas (#)	103	7	1	0	0	95

Fowler Unified
658 E Adams Ave • Fowler, CA 93625-2111
(559) 834-2591 • http://www.fowler.k12.ca.us/
Grade Span: KG-12; **Agency Type:** 1
Schools: 6
3 Primary; 1 Middle; 2 High; 0 Other Level
5 Regular; 0 Special Education; 0 Vocational; 1 Alternative
0 Magnet; 0 Charter; 4 Title I Eligible; 0 School-wide Title I
Students: 2,136 (52.3% male; 47.7% female)
Individual Education Program: 267 (12.5%);
English Language Learner: 500 (23.4%); Migrant: 243 (11.4%)
Eligible for Free Lunch Program: 1,431 (67.0%)
Eligible for Reduced-Price Lunch Program: 228 (10.7%)
Teachers: 105.0 (20.3 to 1)
Librarians/Media Specialists: 1.0 (2,136.0 to 1)
Guidance Counselors: 2.0 (1,068.0 to 1)
Current Spending: ($ per student per year):
Total: $6,338; Instruction: $3,848; Support Services: $2,166
Enrollment, Drop-out Rates and Diploma Recipients by Race/Ethnicity

Category	Total	White	Black	Asian	AIAN	Hisp.
Enrollment (%)	100.0	19.1	0.7	5.9	0.2	74.1
Drop-out Rate (%)	n/a	n/a	n/a	n/a	n/a	n/a
H.S. Diplomas (#)	143	32	1	12	0	98

Fresno County Office of Ed
1111 Van Ness Ave • Fresno, CA 93721-2002
(559) 265-3000 • http://www.fcoe.k12.ca.us/
Grade Span: KG-12; **Agency Type:** 4
Schools: 5
1 Primary; 0 Middle; 1 High; 3 Other Level
1 Regular; 1 Special Education; 0 Vocational; 3 Alternative
0 Magnet; 1 Charter; 0 Title I Eligible; 0 School-wide Title I
Students: 2,190 (67.4% male; 32.6% female)
Individual Education Program: 1,541 (70.4%);
English Language Learner: 475 (21.7%); Migrant: 15 (0.7%)
Eligible for Free Lunch Program: 329 (15.0%)
Eligible for Reduced-Price Lunch Program: 15 (0.7%)
Teachers: 204.4 (10.7 to 1)
Librarians/Media Specialists: 1.0 (2,190.0 to 1)
Guidance Counselors: 0.5 (4,380.0 to 1)
Current Spending: ($ per student per year):
Total: $26,743; Instruction: $12,102; Support Services: $14,495
Enrollment, Drop-out Rates and Diploma Recipients by Race/Ethnicity

Category	Total	White	Black	Asian	AIAN	Hisp.
Enrollment (%)	100.0	18.7	22.2	8.0	1.0	49.9
Drop-out Rate (%)	n/a	n/a	n/a	n/a	n/a	n/a
H.S. Diplomas (#)	109	32	10	30	2	35

Fresno Unified
Ed Center, Tulare & M Sts • Fresno, CA 93721-2287
(559) 457-3000 • http://www.fresno.k12.ca.us/
Grade Span: KG-12; **Agency Type:** 1
Schools: 103
64 Primary; 16 Middle; 20 High; 3 Other Level
91 Regular; 3 Special Education; 0 Vocational; 9 Alternative
12 Magnet; 7 Charter; 91 Title I Eligible; 58 School-wide Title I
Students: 81,222 (50.9% male; 49.1% female)
Individual Education Program: 8,417 (10.4%);
English Language Learner: 26,212 (32.3%); Migrant: 11,390 (14.0%)
Eligible for Free Lunch Program: 56,518 (69.6%)
Eligible for Reduced-Price Lunch Program: 5,305 (6.5%)
Teachers: 3,938.3 (20.6 to 1)
Librarians/Media Specialists: 23.0 (3,531.4 to 1)
Guidance Counselors: 77.6 (1,046.7 to 1)
Current Spending: ($ per student per year):
Total: $7,252; Instruction: $4,675; Support Services: $2,285
Enrollment, Drop-out Rates and Diploma Recipients by Race/Ethnicity

Category	Total	White	Black	Asian	AIAN	Hisp.
Enrollment (%)	100.0	18.4	11.6	17.1	0.8	52.2
Drop-out Rate (%)	n/a	n/a	n/a	n/a	n/a	n/a
H.S. Diplomas (#)	3,721	974	368	896	27	1,455

Golden Plains Unified
22000 Nevada St • San Joaquin, CA 93660-0520
Mailing Address: PO Box 937 • San Joaquin, CA 93660-0520
(559) 693-1115 • http://www.gpusd.k12.ca.us/
Grade Span: KG-12; **Agency Type:** 1
Schools: 6
4 Primary; 0 Middle; 2 High; 0 Other Level
5 Regular; 0 Special Education; 0 Vocational; 1 Alternative
0 Magnet; 0 Charter; 6 Title I Eligible; 2 School-wide Title I
Students: 1,957 (51.3% male; 48.7% female)
Individual Education Program: 66 (3.4%);
English Language Learner: 1,135 (58.0%); Migrant: 1,094 (55.9%)
Eligible for Free Lunch Program: 1,712 (87.5%)
Eligible for Reduced-Price Lunch Program: 123 (6.3%)
Teachers: 100.2 (19.5 to 1)
Librarians/Media Specialists: 0.0 (0.0 to 1)
Guidance Counselors: 5.0 (391.4 to 1)
Current Spending: ($ per student per year):
Total: $8,864; Instruction: $4,909; Support Services: $3,522
Enrollment, Drop-out Rates and Diploma Recipients by Race/Ethnicity

Category	Total	White	Black	Asian	AIAN	Hisp.
Enrollment (%)	100.0	4.3	0.1	1.5	0.0	93.4
Drop-out Rate (%)	n/a	n/a	n/a	n/a	n/a	n/a
H.S. Diplomas (#)	104	4	0	2	0	98

Kerman Unified
151 S First St • Kerman, CA 93630-1029
(559) 846-5383 • http://www.kermanusd.k12.ca.us/
Grade Span: KG-12; **Agency Type:** 1
Schools: 7
2 Primary; 2 Middle; 3 High; 0 Other Level
5 Regular; 0 Special Education; 0 Vocational; 2 Alternative
0 Magnet; 0 Charter; 7 Title I Eligible; 0 School-wide Title I
Students: 3,655 (50.7% male; 49.3% female)
Individual Education Program: 392 (10.7%);
English Language Learner: 1,277 (34.9%); Migrant: 1,131 (30.9%)
Eligible for Free Lunch Program: 2,152 (58.9%)
Eligible for Reduced-Price Lunch Program: 552 (15.1%)
Teachers: 183.9 (19.9 to 1)
Librarians/Media Specialists: 1.3 (2,811.5 to 1)
Guidance Counselors: 0.0 (0.0 to 1)
Current Spending: ($ per student per year):
Total: $6,912; Instruction: $4,034; Support Services: $2,573

Enrollment, Drop-out Rates and Diploma Recipients by Race/Ethnicity

Category	Total	White	Black	Asian	AIAN	Hisp.
Enrollment (%)	100.0	17.2	0.2	6.8	0.5	75.2
Drop-out Rate (%)	n/a	n/a	n/a	n/a	n/a	n/a
H.S. Diplomas (#)	199	51	0	20	0	127

Kings Canyon Joint Unified

675 W Manning Ave • Reedley, CA 93654-2427
(559) 637-1210 • http://www.kc-usd.k12.ca.us/
Grade Span: KG-12; **Agency Type:** 1
Schools: 16
10 Primary; 3 Middle; 2 High; 1 Other Level
14 Regular; 0 Special Education; 0 Vocational; 2 Alternative
0 Magnet; 0 Charter; 13 Title I Eligible; 8 School-wide Title I
Students: 8,839 (51.0% male; 49.0% female)
Individual Education Program: 937 (10.6%);
English Language Learner: 3,446 (39.0%); Migrant: 1,190 (13.5%)
Eligible for Free Lunch Program: 5,799 (65.6%)
Eligible for Reduced-Price Lunch Program: 959 (10.8%)
Teachers: 424.3 (20.8 to 1)
Librarians/Media Specialists: 2.4 (3,682.9 to 1)
Guidance Counselors: 5.7 (1,550.7 to 1)
Current Spending: ($ per student per year):
Total: $6,311; Instruction: $4,029; Support Services: $1,980
Enrollment, Drop-out Rates and Diploma Recipients by Race/Ethnicity

Category	Total	White	Black	Asian	AIAN	Hisp.
Enrollment (%)	100.0	18.7	0.7	2.0	0.7	77.9
Drop-out Rate (%)	n/a	n/a	n/a	n/a	n/a	n/a
H.S. Diplomas (#)	510	139	2	21	3	344

Kingsburg Elementary Charter

1310 Stroud Ave • Kingsburg, CA 93631-1000
(559) 897-2331 • http://www.kingsburg-elem.k12.ca.us/
Grade Span: KG-08; **Agency Type:** 1
Schools: 5
3 Primary; 2 Middle; 0 High; 0 Other Level
4 Regular; 0 Special Education; 0 Vocational; 1 Alternative
0 Magnet; 5 Charter; 4 Title I Eligible; 0 School-wide Title I
Students: 2,114 (51.1% male; 48.9% female)
Individual Education Program: 277 (13.1%);
English Language Learner: 144 (6.8%); Migrant: 10 (0.5%)
Eligible for Free Lunch Program: 607 (28.7%)
Eligible for Reduced-Price Lunch Program: 243 (11.5%)
Teachers: 103.5 (20.4 to 1)
Librarians/Media Specialists: 1.0 (2,114.0 to 1)
Guidance Counselors: 1.0 (2,114.0 to 1)
Current Spending: ($ per student per year):
Total: $6,274; Instruction: $3,806; Support Services: $2,160
Enrollment, Drop-out Rates and Diploma Recipients by Race/Ethnicity

Category	Total	White	Black	Asian	AIAN	Hisp.
Enrollment (%)	100.0	51.0	0.3	3.9	0.5	42.6
Drop-out Rate (%)	n/a	n/a	n/a	n/a	n/a	n/a
H.S. Diplomas (#)	n/a	n/a	n/a	n/a	n/a	n/a

Mendota Unified

115 Mccabe Ave • Mendota, CA 93640-2000
(559) 655-4942 • http://www.mendotausd.k12.ca.us/
Grade Span: KG-12; **Agency Type:** 1
Schools: 6
2 Primary; 1 Middle; 3 High; 0 Other Level
4 Regular; 0 Special Education; 0 Vocational; 2 Alternative
0 Magnet; 0 Charter; 5 Title I Eligible; 4 School-wide Title I
Students: 2,130 (52.7% male; 47.3% female)
Individual Education Program: 130 (6.1%);
English Language Learner: 1,513 (71.0%); Migrant: 1,183 (55.5%)
Eligible for Free Lunch Program: 1,893 (88.9%)
Eligible for Reduced-Price Lunch Program: 59 (2.8%)
Teachers: 105.9 (20.1 to 1)
Librarians/Media Specialists: 1.0 (2,130.0 to 1)
Guidance Counselors: 2.0 (1,065.0 to 1)
Current Spending: ($ per student per year):
Total: $6,870; Instruction: $3,898; Support Services: $2,591
Enrollment, Drop-out Rates and Diploma Recipients by Race/Ethnicity

Category	Total	White	Black	Asian	AIAN	Hisp.
Enrollment (%)	100.0	0.9	0.1	0.4	0.0	98.5
Drop-out Rate (%)	n/a	n/a	n/a	n/a	n/a	n/a
H.S. Diplomas (#)	92	0	0	0	0	92

Parlier Unified

900 Newmark Ave • Parlier, CA 93648-2034
(559) 646-2731 • http://www.parlier.k12.ca.us/
Grade Span: KG-12; **Agency Type:** 1
Schools: 6
3 Primary; 1 Middle; 2 High; 0 Other Level
5 Regular; 0 Special Education; 0 Vocational; 1 Alternative
0 Magnet; 0 Charter; 6 Title I Eligible; 1 School-wide Title I
Students: 3,317 (50.5% male; 49.5% female)
Individual Education Program: 209 (6.3%);
English Language Learner: 2,106 (63.5%); Migrant: 1,374 (41.4%)
Eligible for Free Lunch Program: 3,240 (97.7%)
Eligible for Reduced-Price Lunch Program: 0 (0.0%)
Teachers: 176.4 (18.8 to 1)
Librarians/Media Specialists: 0.0 (0.0 to 1)
Guidance Counselors: 3.0 (1,105.7 to 1)
Current Spending: ($ per student per year):
Total: $6,959; Instruction: $3,976; Support Services: $2,588
Enrollment, Drop-out Rates and Diploma Recipients by Race/Ethnicity

Category	Total	White	Black	Asian	AIAN	Hisp.
Enrollment (%)	100.0	0.3	0.3	0.5	0.0	98.8
Drop-out Rate (%)	n/a	n/a	n/a	n/a	n/a	n/a
H.S. Diplomas (#)	99	0	0	0	0	99

Riverdale Joint Unified

3086 W Mt Whitney • Riverdale, CA 93656-1058
Mailing Address: PO Box 1058 • Riverdale, CA 93656-1058
(559) 867-8200 • http://www.riverdale.k12.ca.us/
Grade Span: KG-12; **Agency Type:** 1
Schools: 5
1 Primary; 1 Middle; 3 High; 0 Other Level
3 Regular; 0 Special Education; 0 Vocational; 2 Alternative
0 Magnet; 0 Charter; 3 Title I Eligible; 3 School-wide Title I
Students: 1,577 (50.7% male; 49.3% female)
Individual Education Program: 92 (5.8%);
English Language Learner: 476 (30.2%); Migrant: 748 (47.4%)
Eligible for Free Lunch Program: 974 (61.8%)
Eligible for Reduced-Price Lunch Program: 194 (12.3%)
Teachers: 80.8 (19.5 to 1)
Librarians/Media Specialists: 1.0 (1,577.0 to 1)
Guidance Counselors: 1.3 (1,213.1 to 1)
Current Spending: ($ per student per year):
Total: $5,896; Instruction: $3,539; Support Services: $1,983
Enrollment, Drop-out Rates and Diploma Recipients by Race/Ethnicity

Category	Total	White	Black	Asian	AIAN	Hisp.
Enrollment (%)	100.0	25.9	2.3	0.8	0.1	70.9
Drop-out Rate (%)	n/a	n/a	n/a	n/a	n/a	n/a
H.S. Diplomas (#)	100	30	3	2	0	65

Sanger Unified

1905 Seventh St • Sanger, CA 93657-2806
(559) 875-6521 • http://www.sanger.k12.ca.us/
Grade Span: KG-12; **Agency Type:** 1
Schools: 18
12 Primary; 1 Middle; 3 High; 2 Other Level
15 Regular; 0 Special Education; 0 Vocational; 3 Alternative
0 Magnet; 3 Charter; 14 Title I Eligible; 4 School-wide Title I
Students: 8,213 (51.3% male; 48.7% female)
Individual Education Program: 647 (7.9%);
English Language Learner: 2,168 (26.4%); Migrant: 362 (4.4%)
Eligible for Free Lunch Program: 4,574 (55.7%)
Eligible for Reduced-Price Lunch Program: 844 (10.3%)
Teachers: 433.1 (19.0 to 1)
Librarians/Media Specialists: 1.5 (5,475.3 to 1)
Guidance Counselors: 9.4 (873.7 to 1)
Current Spending: ($ per student per year):
Total: $6,591; Instruction: $3,834; Support Services: $2,398
Enrollment, Drop-out Rates and Diploma Recipients by Race/Ethnicity

Category	Total	White	Black	Asian	AIAN	Hisp.
Enrollment (%)	100.0	20.3	0.8	5.2	0.4	72.4
Drop-out Rate (%)	n/a	n/a	n/a	n/a	n/a	n/a
H.S. Diplomas (#)	497	138	2	33	0	324

Selma Unified

3036 Thompson Ave • Selma, CA 93662-2497
(559) 898-6500 • http://www.selma.k12.ca.us/
Grade Span: KG-12; **Agency Type:** 1
Schools: 12
8 Primary; 1 Middle; 3 High; 0 Other Level
10 Regular; 0 Special Education; 0 Vocational; 2 Alternative
0 Magnet; 0 Charter; 9 Title I Eligible; 8 School-wide Title I
Students: 5,948 (52.2% male; 47.8% female)
Individual Education Program: 733 (12.3%);
English Language Learner: 2,009 (33.8%); Migrant: 581 (9.8%)
Eligible for Free Lunch Program: 3,344 (56.2%)
Eligible for Reduced-Price Lunch Program: 654 (11.0%)
Teachers: 296.9 (20.0 to 1)
Librarians/Media Specialists: 1.0 (5,948.0 to 1)
Guidance Counselors: 1.4 (4,248.6 to 1)
Current Spending: ($ per student per year):
Total: $6,465; Instruction: $3,866; Support Services: $2,248

Enrollment, Drop-out Rates and Diploma Recipients by Race/Ethnicity

Category	Total	White	Black	Asian	AIAN	Hisp.
Enrollment (%)	100.0	13.0	0.8	4.8	0.9	78.6
Drop-out Rate (%)	n/a	n/a	n/a	n/a	n/a	n/a
H.S. Diplomas (#)	289	51	2	11	3	216

Sierra Unified

31975 Lodge Rd • Auberry, CA 93602-9753
(559) 855-3662 • http://www.sierra.k12.ca.us/
Grade Span: KG-12; **Agency Type:** 1
Schools: 11
6 Primary; 1 Middle; 3 High; 1 Other Level
7 Regular; 0 Special Education; 0 Vocational; 4 Alternative
0 Magnet; 1 Charter; 4 Title I Eligible; 0 School-wide Title I
Students: 2,432 (50.7% male; 49.3% female)
Individual Education Program: 270 (11.1%);
English Language Learner: 44 (1.8%); Migrant: 0 (0.0%)
Eligible for Free Lunch Program: 588 (24.2%)
Eligible for Reduced-Price Lunch Program: 205 (8.4%)
Teachers: 135.9 (17.9 to 1)
Librarians/Media Specialists: 2.7 (900.7 to 1)
Guidance Counselors: 4.6 (528.7 to 1)
Current Spending: ($ per student per year):
Total: $8,249; Instruction: $4,854; Support Services: $3,042

Enrollment, Drop-out Rates and Diploma Recipients by Race/Ethnicity

Category	Total	White	Black	Asian	AIAN	Hisp.
Enrollment (%)	100.0	73.2	1.2	2.7	11.1	9.0
Drop-out Rate (%)	n/a	n/a	n/a	n/a	n/a	n/a
H.S. Diplomas (#)	212	173	3	0	21	15

Glenn County

Orland Joint Unified

1320 Sixth St • Orland, CA 95963-1641
(530) 865-1200 • http://www.glenn-co.k12.ca.us/orlandschools.htm
Grade Span: KG-12; **Agency Type:** 1
Schools: 6
2 Primary; 1 Middle; 3 High; 0 Other Level
4 Regular; 0 Special Education; 0 Vocational; 2 Alternative
1 Magnet; 0 Charter; 4 Title I Eligible; 1 School-wide Title I
Students: 2,403 (49.5% male; 50.5% female)
Individual Education Program: 238 (9.9%);
English Language Learner: 389 (16.2%); Migrant: 302 (12.6%)
Eligible for Free Lunch Program: 1,080 (44.9%)
Eligible for Reduced-Price Lunch Program: 264 (11.0%)
Teachers: 123.3 (19.5 to 1)
Librarians/Media Specialists: 2.0 (1,201.5 to 1)
Guidance Counselors: 4.0 (600.8 to 1)
Current Spending: ($ per student per year):
Total: $6,093; Instruction: $3,828; Support Services: $1,974

Enrollment, Drop-out Rates and Diploma Recipients by Race/Ethnicity

Category	Total	White	Black	Asian	AIAN	Hisp.
Enrollment (%)	100.0	52.2	0.6	1.9	1.3	43.1
Drop-out Rate (%)	n/a	n/a	n/a	n/a	n/a	n/a
H.S. Diplomas (#)	167	101	2	1	0	63

Willows Unified

334 W Sycamore St • Willows, CA 95988-2830
(530) 934-6600 • http://www.wunif.k12.ca.us/
Grade Span: KG-12; **Agency Type:** 1
Schools: 7
2 Primary; 2 Middle; 3 High; 0 Other Level
3 Regular; 0 Special Education; 0 Vocational; 4 Alternative
0 Magnet; 0 Charter; 4 Title I Eligible; 0 School-wide Title I
Students: 1,825 (51.9% male; 48.1% female)
Individual Education Program: 0 (0.0%);
English Language Learner: 297 (16.3%); Migrant: 238 (13.0%)
Eligible for Free Lunch Program: 854 (46.8%)
Eligible for Reduced-Price Lunch Program: 159 (8.7%)
Teachers: 87.4 (20.9 to 1)
Librarians/Media Specialists: 0.0 (0.0 to 1)
Guidance Counselors: 2.7 (675.9 to 1)
Current Spending: ($ per student per year):
Total: $6,427; Instruction: $4,014; Support Services: $2,093

Enrollment, Drop-out Rates and Diploma Recipients by Race/Ethnicity

Category	Total	White	Black	Asian	AIAN	Hisp.
Enrollment (%)	100.0	54.9	1.3	10.7	2.5	30.5
Drop-out Rate (%)	n/a	n/a	n/a	n/a	n/a	n/a
H.S. Diplomas (#)	106	70	1	13	3	19

Humboldt County

Eureka City Unified

3200 Walford Ave • Eureka, CA 95503-4887
(707) 441-2400 • http://www.eurekacityschools.org/
Grade Span: KG-12; **Agency Type:** 1
Schools: 14
7 Primary; 2 Middle; 5 High; 0 Other Level
10 Regular; 1 Special Education; 0 Vocational; 3 Alternative
0 Magnet; 0 Charter; 8 Title I Eligible; 0 School-wide Title I
Students: 5,247 (51.7% male; 48.3% female)
Individual Education Program: 688 (13.1%);
English Language Learner: 477 (9.1%); Migrant: 0 (0.0%)
Eligible for Free Lunch Program: 2,097 (40.0%)
Eligible for Reduced-Price Lunch Program: 472 (9.0%)
Teachers: 281.7 (18.6 to 1)
Librarians/Media Specialists: 3.0 (1,749.0 to 1)
Guidance Counselors: 7.3 (718.8 to 1)
Current Spending: ($ per student per year):
Total: $7,204; Instruction: $4,329; Support Services: $2,585

Enrollment, Drop-out Rates and Diploma Recipients by Race/Ethnicity

Category	Total	White	Black	Asian	AIAN	Hisp.
Enrollment (%)	100.0	67.7	3.3	8.0	12.1	8.9
Drop-out Rate (%)	n/a	n/a	n/a	n/a	n/a	n/a
H.S. Diplomas (#)	419	332	6	30	31	20

Northern Humboldt Union High

2755 Mckinleyville Ave • Mc Kinleyville, CA 95521-3400
(707) 839-6470
Grade Span: 09-12; **Agency Type:** 1
Schools: 5
0 Primary; 0 Middle; 5 High; 0 Other Level
2 Regular; 0 Special Education; 0 Vocational; 3 Alternative
0 Magnet; 0 Charter; 2 Title I Eligible; 0 School-wide Title I
Students: 1,944 (51.5% male; 48.5% female)
Individual Education Program: 223 (11.5%);
English Language Learner: 6 (0.3%); Migrant: 0 (0.0%)
Eligible for Free Lunch Program: 132 (6.8%)
Eligible for Reduced-Price Lunch Program: 7 (0.4%)
Teachers: 94.2 (20.6 to 1)
Librarians/Media Specialists: 2.2 (883.6 to 1)
Guidance Counselors: 5.0 (388.8 to 1)
Current Spending: ($ per student per year):
Total: $5,971; Instruction: $3,694; Support Services: $2,265

Enrollment, Drop-out Rates and Diploma Recipients by Race/Ethnicity

Category	Total	White	Black	Asian	AIAN	Hisp.
Enrollment (%)	100.0	82.9	0.9	1.7	8.6	4.4
Drop-out Rate (%)	n/a	n/a	n/a	n/a	n/a	n/a
H.S. Diplomas (#)	402	342	4	7	27	22

Imperial County

Brawley Elementary

261 D St • Brawley, CA 92227-1912
(760) 344-2330 • http://www.icoe.k12.ca.us/besd/besd.htm
Grade Span: KG-08; **Agency Type:** 1
Schools: 5
4 Primary; 1 Middle; 0 High; 0 Other Level
5 Regular; 0 Special Education; 0 Vocational; 0 Alternative
0 Magnet; 0 Charter; 5 Title I Eligible; 2 School-wide Title I
Students: 3,760 (52.3% male; 47.7% female)
Individual Education Program: 273 (7.3%);
English Language Learner: 1,174 (31.2%); Migrant: 783 (20.8%)
Eligible for Free Lunch Program: 2,180 (58.0%)
Eligible for Reduced-Price Lunch Program: 431 (11.5%)
Teachers: 190.0 (19.8 to 1)
Librarians/Media Specialists: 0.0 (0.0 to 1)
Guidance Counselors: 2.0 (1,880.0 to 1)
Current Spending: ($ per student per year):
Total: $6,429; Instruction: $4,250; Support Services: $1,970

Enrollment, Drop-out Rates and Diploma Recipients by Race/Ethnicity

Category	Total	White	Black	Asian	AIAN	Hisp.
Enrollment (%)	100.0	11.4	3.1	0.8	0.1	84.6
Drop-out Rate (%)	n/a	n/a	n/a	n/a	n/a	n/a
H.S. Diplomas (#)	n/a	n/a	n/a	n/a	n/a	n/a

Brawley Union High

480 N Imperial Ave • Brawley, CA 92227-1625
(760) 312-5819 • http://www.brawleyhigh.org/
Grade Span: 07-12; **Agency Type:** 1
Schools: 3
0 Primary; 0 Middle; 3 High; 0 Other Level
1 Regular; 0 Special Education; 0 Vocational; 2 Alternative
0 Magnet; 0 Charter; 3 Title I Eligible; 1 School-wide Title I
Students: 1,797 (49.1% male; 50.9% female)

Individual Education Program: 172 (9.6%);
English Language Learner: 597 (33.2%); Migrant: 422 (23.5%)
Eligible for Free Lunch Program: 673 (37.5%)
Eligible for Reduced-Price Lunch Program: 128 (7.1%)
Teachers: 80.7 (22.3 to 1)
Librarians/Media Specialists: 0.0 (0.0 to 1)
Guidance Counselors: 7.0 (256.7 to 1)
Current Spending: ($ per student per year):
Total: $7,882; Instruction: $4,235; Support Services: $2,886
Enrollment, Drop-out Rates and Diploma Recipients by Race/Ethnicity

Category	Total	White	Black	Asian	AIAN	Hisp.
Enrollment (%)	100.0	13.6	1.5	0.9	0.6	82.7
Drop-out Rate (%)	n/a	n/a	n/a	n/a	n/a	n/a
H.S. Diplomas (#)	321	62	4	2	0	253

Calexico Unified
901 Andrade Ave • Calexico, CA 92232-0792
Mailing Address: PO Box 792 • Calexico, CA 92232-0792
(760) 768-3888 • http://bordernet.calexico.k12.ca.us/
Grade Span: KG-12; **Agency Type:** 1
Schools: 10
6 Primary; 2 Middle; 2 High; 0 Other Level
9 Regular; 0 Special Education; 0 Vocational; 1 Alternative
0 Magnet; 0 Charter; 10 Title I Eligible; 7 School-wide Title I
Students: 8,668 (50.8% male; 49.2% female)
Individual Education Program: 582 (6.7%);
English Language Learner: 6,622 (76.4%); Migrant: 1,893 (21.8%)
Eligible for Free Lunch Program: 5,301 (61.2%)
Eligible for Reduced-Price Lunch Program: 1,500 (17.3%)
Teachers: 431.8 (20.1 to 1)
Librarians/Media Specialists: 0.0 (0.0 to 1)
Guidance Counselors: 16.0 (541.8 to 1)
Current Spending: ($ per student per year):
Total: $6,388; Instruction: $4,319; Support Services: $1,691
Enrollment, Drop-out Rates and Diploma Recipients by Race/Ethnicity

Category	Total	White	Black	Asian	AIAN	Hisp.
Enrollment (%)	100.0	0.7	0.0	1.0	0.0	98.0
Drop-out Rate (%)	n/a	n/a	n/a	n/a	n/a	n/a
H.S. Diplomas (#)	476	7	1	12	0	456

Central Union High
1001 Brighton Ave • El Centro, CA 92243-3110
(760) 336-4500 • http://www.cuhsd.net/
Grade Span: 09-12; **Agency Type:** 1
Schools: 3
0 Primary; 0 Middle; 3 High; 0 Other Level
2 Regular; 0 Special Education; 0 Vocational; 1 Alternative
0 Magnet; 0 Charter; 3 Title I Eligible; 2 School-wide Title I
Students: 3,816 (50.7% male; 49.3% female)
Individual Education Program: 299 (7.8%);
English Language Learner: 1,620 (42.5%); Migrant: 628 (16.5%)
Eligible for Free Lunch Program: 1,771 (46.4%)
Eligible for Reduced-Price Lunch Program: 386 (10.1%)
Teachers: 176.6 (21.6 to 1)
Librarians/Media Specialists: 1.0 (3,816.0 to 1)
Guidance Counselors: 11.0 (346.9 to 1)
Current Spending: ($ per student per year):
Total: $7,206; Instruction: $4,151; Support Services: $2,728
Enrollment, Drop-out Rates and Diploma Recipients by Race/Ethnicity

Category	Total	White	Black	Asian	AIAN	Hisp.
Enrollment (%)	100.0	10.6	2.0	2.0	0.1	85.3
Drop-out Rate (%)	n/a	n/a	n/a	n/a	n/a	n/a
H.S. Diplomas (#)	683	104	6	19	0	554

El Centro Elementary
1256 Broadway • El Centro, CA 92243-2317
(760) 352-5712 • http://www.ecsd.k12.ca.us/
Grade Span: KG-08; **Agency Type:** 1
Schools: 11
9 Primary; 2 Middle; 0 High; 0 Other Level
11 Regular; 0 Special Education; 0 Vocational; 0 Alternative
0 Magnet; 0 Charter; 11 Title I Eligible; 10 School-wide Title I
Students: 6,223 (51.3% male; 48.7% female)
Individual Education Program: 555 (8.9%);
English Language Learner: 2,907 (46.7%); Migrant: 930 (14.9%)
Eligible for Free Lunch Program: 3,780 (60.7%)
Eligible for Reduced-Price Lunch Program: 714 (11.5%)
Teachers: 290.2 (21.4 to 1)
Librarians/Media Specialists: 0.0 (0.0 to 1)
Guidance Counselors: 4.0 (1,555.8 to 1)
Current Spending: ($ per student per year):
Total: $6,434; Instruction: $4,549; Support Services: $1,589
Enrollment, Drop-out Rates and Diploma Recipients by Race/Ethnicity

Category	Total	White	Black	Asian	AIAN	Hisp.
Enrollment (%)	100.0	7.6	2.7	2.5	0.1	87.1
Drop-out Rate (%)	n/a	n/a	n/a	n/a	n/a	n/a
H.S. Diplomas (#)	n/a	n/a	n/a	n/a	n/a	n/a

Holtville Unified
621 E Sixth St • Holtville, CA 92250-1450
(760) 356-2974 • http://www.holtville.k12.ca.us/
Grade Span: KG-12; **Agency Type:** 1
Schools: 5
2 Primary; 1 Middle; 2 High; 0 Other Level
4 Regular; 0 Special Education; 0 Vocational; 1 Alternative
0 Magnet; 0 Charter; 5 Title I Eligible; 0 School-wide Title I
Students: 1,924 (52.0% male; 48.0% female)
Individual Education Program: 191 (9.9%);
English Language Learner: 884 (45.9%); Migrant: 524 (27.2%)
Eligible for Free Lunch Program: 1,073 (55.8%)
Eligible for Reduced-Price Lunch Program: 163 (8.5%)
Teachers: 95.4 (20.2 to 1)
Librarians/Media Specialists: 0.0 (0.0 to 1)
Guidance Counselors: 2.0 (962.0 to 1)
Current Spending: ($ per student per year):
Total: $6,459; Instruction: $3,976; Support Services: $2,175
Enrollment, Drop-out Rates and Diploma Recipients by Race/Ethnicity

Category	Total	White	Black	Asian	AIAN	Hisp.
Enrollment (%)	100.0	20.9	0.6	1.3	0.4	76.9
Drop-out Rate (%)	n/a	n/a	n/a	n/a	n/a	n/a
H.S. Diplomas (#)	133	36	1	4	1	91

Imperial Unified
219 NE St • Imperial, CA 92251-1176
(760) 355-3200 • http://www.icoe.k12.ca.us/iusd/
Grade Span: KG-12; **Agency Type:** 1
Schools: 6
3 Primary; 1 Middle; 2 High; 0 Other Level
5 Regular; 0 Special Education; 0 Vocational; 1 Alternative
0 Magnet; 0 Charter; 3 Title I Eligible; 0 School-wide Title I
Students: 2,634 (50.6% male; 49.4% female)
Individual Education Program: 208 (7.9%);
English Language Learner: 623 (23.7%); Migrant: 107 (4.1%)
Eligible for Free Lunch Program: 626 (23.8%)
Eligible for Reduced-Price Lunch Program: 233 (8.8%)
Teachers: 132.8 (19.8 to 1)
Librarians/Media Specialists: 0.0 (0.0 to 1)
Guidance Counselors: 3.5 (752.6 to 1)
Current Spending: ($ per student per year):
Total: $5,982; Instruction: $3,718; Support Services: $2,056
Enrollment, Drop-out Rates and Diploma Recipients by Race/Ethnicity

Category	Total	White	Black	Asian	AIAN	Hisp.
Enrollment (%)	100.0	28.5	1.9	1.7	0.1	67.7
Drop-out Rate (%)	n/a	n/a	n/a	n/a	n/a	n/a
H.S. Diplomas (#)	152	59	5	4	1	82

Inyo County

Bishop Union Elementary
800 W Elm St • Bishop, CA 93514
(760) 872-1060
Grade Span: KG-08; **Agency Type:** 1
Schools: 3
2 Primary; 1 Middle; 0 High; 0 Other Level
3 Regular; 0 Special Education; 0 Vocational; 0 Alternative
0 Magnet; 0 Charter; 3 Title I Eligible; 0 School-wide Title I
Students: 1,516 (48.7% male; 51.3% female)
Individual Education Program: 112 (7.4%);
English Language Learner: 184 (12.1%); Migrant: 0 (0.0%)
Eligible for Free Lunch Program: 438 (28.9%)
Eligible for Reduced-Price Lunch Program: 169 (11.1%)
Teachers: 73.0 (20.8 to 1)
Librarians/Media Specialists: 0.0 (0.0 to 1)
Guidance Counselors: 1.5 (1,010.7 to 1)
Current Spending: ($ per student per year):
Total: $6,639; Instruction: $4,323; Support Services: $2,028
Enrollment, Drop-out Rates and Diploma Recipients by Race/Ethnicity

Category	Total	White	Black	Asian	AIAN	Hisp.
Enrollment (%)	100.0	61.7	0.5	1.8	15.8	19.5
Drop-out Rate (%)	n/a	n/a	n/a	n/a	n/a	n/a
H.S. Diplomas (#)	n/a	n/a	n/a	n/a	n/a	n/a

Kern County

Arvin Union Elementary

737 Bear Mountain Blvd • Arvin, CA 93203-1413
(661) 854-6500 • http://frontpage.lightspeed.net/ausd/
Grade Span: KG-08; **Agency Type:** 1
Schools: 3
2 Primary; 1 Middle; 0 High; 0 Other Level
3 Regular; 0 Special Education; 0 Vocational; 0 Alternative
0 Magnet; 0 Charter; 3 Title I Eligible; 3 School-wide Title I
Students: 2,845 (51.1% male; 48.9% female)
Individual Education Program: 261 (9.2%);
English Language Learner: 1,963 (69.0%); Migrant: 1,618 (56.9%)
Eligible for Free Lunch Program: 2,362 (83.0%)
Eligible for Reduced-Price Lunch Program: 263 (9.2%)
Teachers: 139.7 (20.4 to 1)
Librarians/Media Specialists: 0.0 (0.0 to 1)
Guidance Counselors: 0.0 (0.0 to 1)
Current Spending: ($ per student per year):
Total: $6,332; Instruction: $4,011; Support Services: $1,889
Enrollment, Drop-out Rates and Diploma Recipients by Race/Ethnicity

Category	Total	White	Black	Asian	AIAN	Hisp.
Enrollment (%)	100.0	4.0	0.8	0.6	0.0	94.6
Drop-out Rate (%)	n/a	n/a	n/a	n/a	n/a	n/a
H.S. Diplomas (#)	n/a	n/a	n/a	n/a	n/a	n/a

Bakersfield City Elementary

1300 Baker St • Bakersfield, CA 93305-4326
(661) 631-4600 • http://www.bcsd.k12.ca.us/
Grade Span: KG-08; **Agency Type:** 1
Schools: 43
33 Primary; 10 Middle; 0 High; 0 Other Level
40 Regular; 1 Special Education; 0 Vocational; 2 Alternative
7 Magnet; 0 Charter; 29 Title I Eligible; 28 School-wide Title I
Students: 28,179 (50.9% male; 49.1% female)
Individual Education Program: 2,729 (9.7%);
English Language Learner: 7,433 (26.4%); Migrant: 5,092 (18.1%)
Eligible for Free Lunch Program: 21,750 (77.2%)
Eligible for Reduced-Price Lunch Program: 2,571 (9.1%)
Teachers: 1,511.4 (18.6 to 1)
Librarians/Media Specialists: 8.0 (3,522.4 to 1)
Guidance Counselors: 35.5 (793.8 to 1)
Current Spending: ($ per student per year):
Total: $7,048; Instruction: $4,576; Support Services: $2,101
Enrollment, Drop-out Rates and Diploma Recipients by Race/Ethnicity

Category	Total	White	Black	Asian	AIAN	Hisp.
Enrollment (%)	100.0	17.8	13.2	1.9	1.2	65.8
Drop-out Rate (%)	n/a	n/a	n/a	n/a	n/a	n/a
H.S. Diplomas (#)	n/a	n/a	n/a	n/a	n/a	n/a

Beardsley Elementary

1001 Roberts Ln • Bakersfield, CA 93308-4503
(661) 393-8550 • http://webup.web.kern.org/districts/beardsley/
Grade Span: KG-08; **Agency Type:** 1
Schools: 3
1 Primary; 2 Middle; 0 High; 0 Other Level
3 Regular; 0 Special Education; 0 Vocational; 0 Alternative
0 Magnet; 0 Charter; 3 Title I Eligible; 2 School-wide Title I
Students: 1,758 (49.9% male; 50.1% female)
Individual Education Program: 198 (11.3%);
English Language Learner: 119 (6.8%); Migrant: 5 (0.3%)
Eligible for Free Lunch Program: 1,096 (62.3%)
Eligible for Reduced-Price Lunch Program: 254 (14.4%)
Teachers: 86.5 (20.3 to 1)
Librarians/Media Specialists: 0.0 (0.0 to 1)
Guidance Counselors: 0.0 (0.0 to 1)
Current Spending: ($ per student per year):
Total: $6,490; Instruction: $4,094; Support Services: $2,068
Enrollment, Drop-out Rates and Diploma Recipients by Race/Ethnicity

Category	Total	White	Black	Asian	AIAN	Hisp.
Enrollment (%)	100.0	73.3	1.2	1.0	2.0	20.4
Drop-out Rate (%)	n/a	n/a	n/a	n/a	n/a	n/a
H.S. Diplomas (#)	n/a	n/a	n/a	n/a	n/a	n/a

Delano Joint Union High

1747 Princeton St • Delano, CA 93215-1501
(661) 725-4000 • http://www.delanohighschool.org/
Grade Span: 09-12; **Agency Type:** 1
Schools: 3
0 Primary; 0 Middle; 3 High; 0 Other Level
1 Regular; 0 Special Education; 0 Vocational; 2 Alternative
0 Magnet; 0 Charter; 2 Title I Eligible; 2 School-wide Title I
Students: 3,630 (51.5% male; 48.5% female)
Individual Education Program: 300 (8.3%);
English Language Learner: 1,792 (49.4%); Migrant: 1,182 (32.6%)
Eligible for Free Lunch Program: 1,998 (55.0%)
Eligible for Reduced-Price Lunch Program: 601 (16.6%)
Teachers: 156.0 (23.3 to 1)
Librarians/Media Specialists: 0.0 (0.0 to 1)
Guidance Counselors: 7.0 (518.6 to 1)
Current Spending: ($ per student per year):
Total: $6,888; Instruction: $4,100; Support Services: $2,564
Enrollment, Drop-out Rates and Diploma Recipients by Race/Ethnicity

Category	Total	White	Black	Asian	AIAN	Hisp.
Enrollment (%)	100.0	2.9	1.2	16.3	0.0	79.6
Drop-out Rate (%)	n/a	n/a	n/a	n/a	n/a	n/a
H.S. Diplomas (#)	655	22	9	98	1	525

Delano Union Elementary

1405 12th Ave • Delano, CA 93215-2416
(661) 721-5000 • http://www.duesd.org/
Grade Span: KG-08; **Agency Type:** 1
Schools: 10
7 Primary; 3 Middle; 0 High; 0 Other Level
9 Regular; 0 Special Education; 0 Vocational; 1 Alternative
0 Magnet; 0 Charter; 10 Title I Eligible; 1 School-wide Title I
Students: 7,097 (50.5% male; 49.5% female)
Individual Education Program: 582 (8.2%);
English Language Learner: 4,039 (56.9%); Migrant: 3,274 (46.1%)
Eligible for Free Lunch Program: 6,619 (93.3%)
Eligible for Reduced-Price Lunch Program: 0 (0.0%)
Teachers: 331.0 (21.4 to 1)
Librarians/Media Specialists: 0.0 (0.0 to 1)
Guidance Counselors: 1.0 (7,097.0 to 1)
Current Spending: ($ per student per year):
Total: $6,133; Instruction: $3,766; Support Services: $2,013
Enrollment, Drop-out Rates and Diploma Recipients by Race/Ethnicity

Category	Total	White	Black	Asian	AIAN	Hisp.
Enrollment (%)	100.0	2.5	1.8	14.2	0.1	80.9
Drop-out Rate (%)	n/a	n/a	n/a	n/a	n/a	n/a
H.S. Diplomas (#)	n/a	n/a	n/a	n/a	n/a	n/a

Fruitvale Elementary

7311 Rosedale Hwy • Bakersfield, CA 93308-5738
(661) 589-3830 • http://www.fruitvale.k12.ca.us/
Grade Span: KG-08; **Agency Type:** 1
Schools: 5
4 Primary; 1 Middle; 0 High; 0 Other Level
5 Regular; 0 Special Education; 0 Vocational; 0 Alternative
0 Magnet; 0 Charter; 4 Title I Eligible; 0 School-wide Title I
Students: 3,047 (49.4% male; 50.6% female)
Individual Education Program: 334 (11.0%);
English Language Learner: 42 (1.4%); Migrant: 0 (0.0%)
Eligible for Free Lunch Program: 339 (11.1%)
Eligible for Reduced-Price Lunch Program: 329 (10.8%)
Teachers: 147.7 (20.6 to 1)
Librarians/Media Specialists: 0.0 (0.0 to 1)
Guidance Counselors: 1.0 (3,047.0 to 1)
Current Spending: ($ per student per year):
Total: $5,918; Instruction: $3,892; Support Services: $1,826
Enrollment, Drop-out Rates and Diploma Recipients by Race/Ethnicity

Category	Total	White	Black	Asian	AIAN	Hisp.
Enrollment (%)	100.0	71.6	3.9	4.8	1.0	18.4
Drop-out Rate (%)	n/a	n/a	n/a	n/a	n/a	n/a
H.S. Diplomas (#)	n/a	n/a	n/a	n/a	n/a	n/a

Greenfield Union Elementary

1624 Fairview Rd • Bakersfield, CA 93307-5512
(661) 837-6000 • http://www.greenfield.k12.ca.us/
Grade Span: KG-08; **Agency Type:** 1
Schools: 9
7 Primary; 2 Middle; 0 High; 0 Other Level
9 Regular; 0 Special Education; 0 Vocational; 0 Alternative
0 Magnet; 0 Charter; 9 Title I Eligible; 9 School-wide Title I
Students: 7,140 (51.1% male; 48.9% female)
Individual Education Program: 682 (9.6%);
English Language Learner: 1,933 (27.1%); Migrant: 1,671 (23.4%)
Eligible for Free Lunch Program: 4,549 (63.7%)
Eligible for Reduced-Price Lunch Program: 1,118 (15.7%)
Teachers: 346.9 (20.6 to 1)
Librarians/Media Specialists: 0.0 (0.0 to 1)
Guidance Counselors: 3.0 (2,380.0 to 1)
Current Spending: ($ per student per year):
Total: $6,094; Instruction: $3,799; Support Services: $2,010
Enrollment, Drop-out Rates and Diploma Recipients by Race/Ethnicity

Category	Total	White	Black	Asian	AIAN	Hisp.
Enrollment (%)	100.0	18.8	12.1	4.0	0.9	63.4
Drop-out Rate (%)	n/a	n/a	n/a	n/a	n/a	n/a
H.S. Diplomas (#)	n/a	n/a	n/a	n/a	n/a	n/a

Kern County Office of Ed

1300 17th St, City Centre • Bakersfield, CA 93301-4504
(661) 636-4000 • http://www.kern.org/
Grade Span: KG-12; **Agency Type:** 4
Schools: 5
0 Primary; 0 Middle; 0 High; 5 Other Level
1 Regular; 1 Special Education; 0 Vocational; 3 Alternative
0 Magnet; 1 Charter; 0 Title I Eligible; 0 School-wide Title I
Students: 2,510 (66.9% male; 33.1% female)
Individual Education Program: 1,410 (56.2%);
English Language Learner: 326 (13.0%); Migrant: 5 (0.2%)
Eligible for Free Lunch Program: 1,121 (44.7%)
Eligible for Reduced-Price Lunch Program: 152 (6.1%)
Teachers: 194.2 (12.9 to 1)
Librarians/Media Specialists: 0.0 (0.0 to 1)
Guidance Counselors: 2.0 (1,255.0 to 1)
Current Spending: ($ per student per year):
Total: $39,805; Instruction: $11,335; Support Services: $26,508

Enrollment, Drop-out Rates and Diploma Recipients by Race/Ethnicity

Category	Total	White	Black	Asian	AIAN	Hisp.
Enrollment (%)	100.0	44.2	10.7	0.9	0.6	43.0
Drop-out Rate (%)	n/a	n/a	n/a	n/a	n/a	n/a
H.S. Diplomas (#)	160	84	17	1	0	58

Kern Union High

5801 Sundale Ave • Bakersfield, CA 93309-2924
(661) 827-3100 • http://www.khsd.k12.ca.us/
Grade Span: 09-12; **Agency Type:** 1
Schools: 22
0 Primary; 0 Middle; 22 High; 0 Other Level
14 Regular; 2 Special Education; 0 Vocational; 6 Alternative
0 Magnet; 1 Charter; 16 Title I Eligible; 0 School-wide Title I
Students: 30,953 (50.4% male; 49.6% female)
Individual Education Program: 2,605 (8.4%);
English Language Learner: 3,344 (10.8%); Migrant: 3,227 (10.4%)
Eligible for Free Lunch Program: 11,255 (36.4%)
Eligible for Reduced-Price Lunch Program: 1,745 (5.6%)
Teachers: 1,348.4 (23.0 to 1)
Librarians/Media Specialists: 14.0 (2,210.9 to 1)
Guidance Counselors: 70.1 (441.6 to 1)
Current Spending: ($ per student per year):
Total: $6,244; Instruction: $3,489; Support Services: $2,482

Enrollment, Drop-out Rates and Diploma Recipients by Race/Ethnicity

Category	Total	White	Black	Asian	AIAN	Hisp.
Enrollment (%)	100.0	41.6	8.1	3.6	0.9	45.9
Drop-out Rate (%)	n/a	n/a	n/a	n/a	n/a	n/a
H.S. Diplomas (#)	5,741	2,674	372	321	58	2,316

Lamont Elementary

8201 Palm Ave • Lamont, CA 93241-2118
(661) 845-0751 • http://www.lamontschooldistrict.org/
Grade Span: KG-08; **Agency Type:** 1
Schools: 4
2 Primary; 2 Middle; 0 High; 0 Other Level
4 Regular; 0 Special Education; 0 Vocational; 0 Alternative
0 Magnet; 0 Charter; 4 Title I Eligible; 4 School-wide Title I
Students: 2,719 (50.5% male; 49.5% female)
Individual Education Program: 270 (9.9%);
English Language Learner: 2,002 (73.6%); Migrant: 1,332 (49.0%)
Eligible for Free Lunch Program: 2,171 (79.8%)
Eligible for Reduced-Price Lunch Program: 347 (12.8%)
Teachers: 125.2 (21.7 to 1)
Librarians/Media Specialists: 1.0 (2,719.0 to 1)
Guidance Counselors: 2.0 (1,359.5 to 1)
Current Spending: ($ per student per year):
Total: $6,854; Instruction: $4,646; Support Services: $1,804

Enrollment, Drop-out Rates and Diploma Recipients by Race/Ethnicity

Category	Total	White	Black	Asian	AIAN	Hisp.
Enrollment (%)	100.0	5.4	0.3	1.3	0.0	93.0
Drop-out Rate (%)	n/a	n/a	n/a	n/a	n/a	n/a
H.S. Diplomas (#)	n/a	n/a	n/a	n/a	n/a	n/a

Mcfarland Unified

601 Second St • Mcfarland, CA 93250-1121
(661) 792-3081
Grade Span: KG-12; **Agency Type:** 1
Schools: 6
2 Primary; 1 Middle; 3 High; 0 Other Level
4 Regular; 0 Special Education; 0 Vocational; 2 Alternative
0 Magnet; 0 Charter; 5 Title I Eligible; 0 School-wide Title I
Students: 2,829 (50.4% male; 49.6% female)
Individual Education Program: 279 (9.9%);
English Language Learner: 1,074 (38.0%); Migrant: 1,294 (45.7%)
Eligible for Free Lunch Program: 2,010 (71.0%)
Eligible for Reduced-Price Lunch Program: 163 (5.8%)
Teachers: 148.4 (19.1 to 1)
Librarians/Media Specialists: 1.0 (2,829.0 to 1)
Guidance Counselors: 3.1 (912.6 to 1)
Current Spending: ($ per student per year):
Total: $7,329; Instruction: $4,372; Support Services: $2,580

Enrollment, Drop-out Rates and Diploma Recipients by Race/Ethnicity

Category	Total	White	Black	Asian	AIAN	Hisp.
Enrollment (%)	100.0	4.0	0.4	0.4	0.2	95.0
Drop-out Rate (%)	n/a	n/a	n/a	n/a	n/a	n/a
H.S. Diplomas (#)	194	15	1	1	1	176

Mojave Unified

3500 Douglas Ave • Mojave, CA 93501-1143
(661) 824-4001 • http://www.mojave.k12.ca.us/
Grade Span: KG-12; **Agency Type:** 1
Schools: 9
3 Primary; 3 Middle; 2 High; 1 Other Level
6 Regular; 0 Special Education; 0 Vocational; 3 Alternative
0 Magnet; 0 Charter; 5 Title I Eligible; 0 School-wide Title I
Students: 2,618 (52.0% male; 48.0% female)
Individual Education Program: 230 (8.8%);
English Language Learner: 302 (11.5%); Migrant: 10 (0.4%)
Eligible for Free Lunch Program: 1,236 (47.2%)
Eligible for Reduced-Price Lunch Program: 160 (6.1%)
Teachers: 115.8 (22.6 to 1)
Librarians/Media Specialists: 0.0 (0.0 to 1)
Guidance Counselors: 3.2 (818.1 to 1)
Current Spending: ($ per student per year):
Total: $6,444; Instruction: $3,759; Support Services: $2,404

Enrollment, Drop-out Rates and Diploma Recipients by Race/Ethnicity

Category	Total	White	Black	Asian	AIAN	Hisp.
Enrollment (%)	100.0	49.6	17.2	3.1	1.0	28.0
Drop-out Rate (%)	n/a	n/a	n/a	n/a	n/a	n/a
H.S. Diplomas (#)	169	94	24	7	2	41

Muroc Joint Unified

17100 Foothill Ave • North Edwards, CA 93523-0833
Mailing Address: PO Box 833 • North Edwards, CA 93523-0833
(760) 769-4821 • http://www.muroc.k12.ca.us/
Grade Span: KG-12; **Agency Type:** 1
Schools: 7
3 Primary; 1 Middle; 2 High; 1 Other Level
6 Regular; 0 Special Education; 0 Vocational; 1 Alternative
0 Magnet; 0 Charter; 2 Title I Eligible; 0 School-wide Title I
Students: 2,434 (50.6% male; 49.4% female)
Individual Education Program: 265 (10.9%);
English Language Learner: 23 (0.9%); Migrant: 0 (0.0%)
Eligible for Free Lunch Program: 328 (13.5%)
Eligible for Reduced-Price Lunch Program: 231 (9.5%)
Teachers: 121.4 (20.0 to 1)
Librarians/Media Specialists: 0.0 (0.0 to 1)
Guidance Counselors: 3.0 (811.3 to 1)
Current Spending: ($ per student per year):
Total: $8,839; Instruction: $5,067; Support Services: $3,478

Enrollment, Drop-out Rates and Diploma Recipients by Race/Ethnicity

Category	Total	White	Black	Asian	AIAN	Hisp.
Enrollment (%)	100.0	67.4	12.7	8.3	1.1	10.2
Drop-out Rate (%)	n/a	n/a	n/a	n/a	n/a	n/a
H.S. Diplomas (#)	135	109	9	12	0	5

Norris Elementary

6940 Calloway Dr • Bakersfield, CA 93312-9005
(661) 387-7000
Grade Span: KG-08; **Agency Type:** 1
Schools: 4
3 Primary; 1 Middle; 0 High; 0 Other Level
4 Regular; 0 Special Education; 0 Vocational; 0 Alternative
0 Magnet; 0 Charter; 0 Title I Eligible; 0 School-wide Title I
Students: 1,852 (52.8% male; 47.2% female)
Individual Education Program: 125 (6.7%);
English Language Learner: 17 (0.9%); Migrant: 0 (0.0%)
Eligible for Free Lunch Program: 114 (6.2%)
Eligible for Reduced-Price Lunch Program: 92 (5.0%)
Teachers: 91.2 (20.3 to 1)
Librarians/Media Specialists: 1.0 (1,852.0 to 1)
Guidance Counselors: 1.8 (1,028.9 to 1)
Current Spending: ($ per student per year):
Total: $5,665; Instruction: $3,650; Support Services: $1,798

Enrollment, Drop-out Rates and Diploma Recipients by Race/Ethnicity

Category	Total	White	Black	Asian	AIAN	Hisp.
Enrollment (%)	100.0	78.9	1.8	2.0	0.5	12.3
Drop-out Rate (%)	n/a	n/a	n/a	n/a	n/a	n/a
H.S. Diplomas (#)	n/a	n/a	n/a	n/a	n/a	n/a

Panama Buena Vista Union Elementary

4200 Ashe Rd • Bakersfield, CA 93313-2029
(661) 831-8331 • http://www.pbvusd.k12.ca.us/
Grade Span: KG-08; **Agency Type:** 1
Schools: 20
16 Primary; 4 Middle; 0 High; 0 Other Level
20 Regular; 0 Special Education; 0 Vocational; 0 Alternative
0 Magnet; 0 Charter; 7 Title I Eligible; 0 School-wide Title I
Students: 13,450 (50.9% male; 49.1% female)
Individual Education Program: 1,082 (8.0%);
English Language Learner: 696 (5.2%); Migrant: 71 (0.5%)
Eligible for Free Lunch Program: 4,037 (30.0%)
Eligible for Reduced-Price Lunch Program: 1,580 (11.7%)
Teachers: 676.1 (19.9 to 1)
Librarians/Media Specialists: 1.0 (13,450.0 to 1)
Guidance Counselors: 4.0 (3,362.5 to 1)
Current Spending: ($ per student per year):
Total: $6,155; Instruction: $4,118; Support Services: $1,814
Enrollment, Drop-out Rates and Diploma Recipients by Race/Ethnicity

Category	Total	White	Black	Asian	AIAN	Hisp.
Enrollment (%)	100.0	49.8	11.7	6.8	0.8	31.0
Drop-out Rate (%)	n/a	n/a	n/a	n/a	n/a	n/a
H.S. Diplomas (#)	n/a	n/a	n/a	n/a	n/a	n/a

Richland SD

331 Shafter Ave • Shafter, CA 93263-1999
(661) 746-8600
Grade Span: KG-08; **Agency Type:** 1
Schools: 3
2 Primary; 1 Middle; 0 High; 0 Other Level
3 Regular; 0 Special Education; 0 Vocational; 0 Alternative
0 Magnet; 0 Charter; 3 Title I Eligible; 0 School-wide Title I
Students: 2,824 (51.2% male; 48.8% female)
Individual Education Program: 299 (10.6%);
English Language Learner: 1,476 (52.3%); Migrant: 1,400 (49.6%)
Eligible for Free Lunch Program: 2,347 (83.1%)
Eligible for Reduced-Price Lunch Program: 162 (5.7%)
Teachers: 136.5 (20.7 to 1)
Librarians/Media Specialists: 1.0 (2,824.0 to 1)
Guidance Counselors: 0.5 (5,648.0 to 1)
Current Spending: ($ per student per year):
Total: $6,455; Instruction: $4,097; Support Services: $1,940
Enrollment, Drop-out Rates and Diploma Recipients by Race/Ethnicity

Category	Total	White	Black	Asian	AIAN	Hisp.
Enrollment (%)	100.0	10.7	0.4	0.5	0.1	87.5
Drop-out Rate (%)	n/a	n/a	n/a	n/a	n/a	n/a
H.S. Diplomas (#)	n/a	n/a	n/a	n/a	n/a	n/a

Rosedale Union Elementary

2553 Old Farm Rd • Bakersfield, CA 93312-3531
(661) 588-6000 • http://www.rosedale.k12.ca.us/schools.htm
Grade Span: KG-08; **Agency Type:** 1
Schools: 8
6 Primary; 2 Middle; 0 High; 0 Other Level
8 Regular; 0 Special Education; 0 Vocational; 0 Alternative
0 Magnet; 0 Charter; 3 Title I Eligible; 0 School-wide Title I
Students: 4,085 (51.2% male; 48.8% female)
Individual Education Program: 344 (8.4%);
English Language Learner: 72 (1.8%); Migrant: 6 (0.1%)
Eligible for Free Lunch Program: 354 (8.7%)
Eligible for Reduced-Price Lunch Program: 223 (5.5%)
Teachers: 192.5 (21.2 to 1)
Librarians/Media Specialists: 1.0 (4,085.0 to 1)
Guidance Counselors: 2.0 (2,042.5 to 1)
Current Spending: ($ per student per year):
Total: $5,576; Instruction: $3,729; Support Services: $1,704
Enrollment, Drop-out Rates and Diploma Recipients by Race/Ethnicity

Category	Total	White	Black	Asian	AIAN	Hisp.
Enrollment (%)	100.0	77.3	2.8	3.1	0.2	15.6
Drop-out Rate (%)	n/a	n/a	n/a	n/a	n/a	n/a
H.S. Diplomas (#)	n/a	n/a	n/a	n/a	n/a	n/a

Sierra Sands Unified

113 Felspar • Ridgecrest, CA 93555-3520
(760) 375-3363 • http://www.ssusd.org/
Grade Span: KG-12; **Agency Type:** 1
Schools: 11
7 Primary; 2 Middle; 2 High; 0 Other Level
10 Regular; 0 Special Education; 0 Vocational; 1 Alternative
0 Magnet; 0 Charter; 4 Title I Eligible; 3 School-wide Title I
Students: 5,567 (51.3% male; 48.7% female)
Individual Education Program: 611 (11.0%);
English Language Learner: 540 (9.7%); Migrant: 0 (0.0%)
Eligible for Free Lunch Program: 1,662 (29.9%)
Eligible for Reduced-Price Lunch Program: 450 (8.1%)
Teachers: 275.5 (20.2 to 1)
Librarians/Media Specialists: 1.0 (5,567.0 to 1)
Guidance Counselors: 7.6 (732.5 to 1)
Current Spending: ($ per student per year):
Total: $6,535; Instruction: $3,871; Support Services: $2,416
Enrollment, Drop-out Rates and Diploma Recipients by Race/Ethnicity

Category	Total	White	Black	Asian	AIAN	Hisp.
Enrollment (%)	100.0	72.3	5.5	4.7	1.3	14.0
Drop-out Rate (%)	n/a	n/a	n/a	n/a	n/a	n/a
H.S. Diplomas (#)	361	292	14	15	5	33

Southern Kern Unified

3082 Glendower St • Rosamond, CA 93560-0640
Mailing Address: PO Drawer CC • Rosamond, CA 93560-0640
(661) 256-5000 • http://www.skusd.k12.ca.us/
Grade Span: KG-12; **Agency Type:** 1
Schools: 6
2 Primary; 1 Middle; 2 High; 1 Other Level
4 Regular; 0 Special Education; 0 Vocational; 2 Alternative
0 Magnet; 0 Charter; 2 Title I Eligible; 0 School-wide Title I
Students: 3,220 (51.1% male; 48.9% female)
Individual Education Program: 298 (9.3%);
English Language Learner: 313 (9.7%); Migrant: 167 (5.2%)
Eligible for Free Lunch Program: 1,281 (39.8%)
Eligible for Reduced-Price Lunch Program: 335 (10.4%)
Teachers: 140.3 (23.0 to 1)
Librarians/Media Specialists: 0.0 (0.0 to 1)
Guidance Counselors: 0.0 (0.0 to 1)
Current Spending: ($ per student per year):
Total: $6,127; Instruction: $3,845; Support Services: $2,045
Enrollment, Drop-out Rates and Diploma Recipients by Race/Ethnicity

Category	Total	White	Black	Asian	AIAN	Hisp.
Enrollment (%)	100.0	50.6	9.0	2.6	1.3	36.2
Drop-out Rate (%)	n/a	n/a	n/a	n/a	n/a	n/a
H.S. Diplomas (#)	151	88	5	9	0	49

Standard Elementary

1200 N Chester Ave • Bakersfield, CA 93308-3521
(661) 392-2110
Grade Span: KG-08; **Agency Type:** 1
Schools: 4
3 Primary; 1 Middle; 0 High; 0 Other Level
4 Regular; 0 Special Education; 0 Vocational; 0 Alternative
0 Magnet; 0 Charter; 4 Title I Eligible; 2 School-wide Title I
Students: 2,584 (51.9% male; 48.1% female)
Individual Education Program: 291 (11.3%);
English Language Learner: 43 (1.7%); Migrant: 2 (0.1%)
Eligible for Free Lunch Program: 1,006 (38.9%)
Eligible for Reduced-Price Lunch Program: 400 (15.5%)
Teachers: 129.2 (20.0 to 1)
Librarians/Media Specialists: 0.0 (0.0 to 1)
Guidance Counselors: 2.0 (1,292.0 to 1)
Current Spending: ($ per student per year):
Total: $6,953; Instruction: $4,295; Support Services: $2,190
Enrollment, Drop-out Rates and Diploma Recipients by Race/Ethnicity

Category	Total	White	Black	Asian	AIAN	Hisp.
Enrollment (%)	100.0	84.9	0.7	0.6	1.1	12.4
Drop-out Rate (%)	n/a	n/a	n/a	n/a	n/a	n/a
H.S. Diplomas (#)	n/a	n/a	n/a	n/a	n/a	n/a

Taft City Elementary

820 N Sixth St • Taft, CA 93268-2306
(661) 763-1521 • http://www.taftcity.k12.ca.us/
Grade Span: KG-08; **Agency Type:** 1
Schools: 7
4 Primary; 3 Middle; 0 High; 0 Other Level
6 Regular; 0 Special Education; 0 Vocational; 1 Alternative
0 Magnet; 0 Charter; 6 Title I Eligible; 5 School-wide Title I
Students: 2,127 (52.3% male; 47.7% female)
Individual Education Program: 256 (12.0%);
English Language Learner: 377 (17.7%); Migrant: 421 (19.8%)
Eligible for Free Lunch Program: 1,127 (53.0%)
Eligible for Reduced-Price Lunch Program: 264 (12.4%)
Teachers: 112.5 (18.9 to 1)
Librarians/Media Specialists: 0.0 (0.0 to 1)
Guidance Counselors: 2.9 (733.4 to 1)
Current Spending: ($ per student per year):
Total: $6,714; Instruction: $4,123; Support Services: $2,246
Enrollment, Drop-out Rates and Diploma Recipients by Race/Ethnicity

Category	Total	White	Black	Asian	AIAN	Hisp.
Enrollment (%)	100.0	70.1	0.6	2.3	0.0	26.8
Drop-out Rate (%)	n/a	n/a	n/a	n/a	n/a	n/a
H.S. Diplomas (#)	n/a	n/a	n/a	n/a	n/a	n/a

Tehachapi Unified

400 S Snyder • Tehachapi, CA 93561-1519
(661) 822-2100 • http://www.teh.k12.ca.us/
Grade Span: KG-12; **Agency Type:** 1
Schools: 7
4 Primary; 1 Middle; 2 High; 0 Other Level
6 Regular; 0 Special Education; 0 Vocational; 1 Alternative
0 Magnet; 0 Charter; 3 Title I Eligible; 0 School-wide Title I
Students: 4,907 (52.4% male; 47.6% female)
Individual Education Program: 585 (11.9%);
English Language Learner: 405 (8.3%); Migrant: 228 (4.6%)
Eligible for Free Lunch Program: 1,156 (23.6%)
Eligible for Reduced-Price Lunch Program: 713 (14.5%)
Teachers: 225.2 (21.8 to 1)
Librarians/Media Specialists: 1.0 (4,907.0 to 1)
Guidance Counselors: 2.0 (2,453.5 to 1)
Current Spending: ($ per student per year):
Total: $6,302; Instruction: $4,063; Support Services: $2,068
Enrollment, Drop-out Rates and Diploma Recipients by Race/Ethnicity

Category	Total	White	Black	Asian	AIAN	Hisp.
Enrollment (%)	100.0	74.0	2.5	1.3	1.3	20.4
Drop-out Rate (%)	n/a	n/a	n/a	n/a	n/a	n/a
H.S. Diplomas (#)	304	247	2	3	4	45

Wasco Union Elementary

639 Broadway • Wasco, CA 93280-1899
(661) 758-7100 • http://www.wasco.k12.ca.us/
Grade Span: KG-08; **Agency Type:** 1
Schools: 4
2 Primary; 2 Middle; 0 High; 0 Other Level
4 Regular; 0 Special Education; 0 Vocational; 0 Alternative
0 Magnet; 0 Charter; 4 Title I Eligible; 0 School-wide Title I
Students: 2,849 (51.6% male; 48.4% female)
Individual Education Program: 223 (7.8%);
English Language Learner: 1,398 (49.1%); Migrant: 1,811 (63.6%)
Eligible for Free Lunch Program: 2,163 (75.9%)
Eligible for Reduced-Price Lunch Program: 320 (11.2%)
Teachers: 140.5 (20.3 to 1)
Librarians/Media Specialists: 0.0 (0.0 to 1)
Guidance Counselors: 0.0 (0.0 to 1)
Current Spending: ($ per student per year):
Total: $6,640; Instruction: $4,093; Support Services: $2,089
Enrollment, Drop-out Rates and Diploma Recipients by Race/Ethnicity

Category	Total	White	Black	Asian	AIAN	Hisp.
Enrollment (%)	100.0	9.2	4.9	0.6	0.1	85.3
Drop-out Rate (%)	n/a	n/a	n/a	n/a	n/a	n/a
H.S. Diplomas (#)	n/a	n/a	n/a	n/a	n/a	n/a

Kings County

Central Union Elementary

15783 18th Ave • Lemoore, CA 93245-9742
(559) 924-3405 • http://www.kings.k12.ca.us/central/
Grade Span: KG-08; **Agency Type:** 1
Schools: 4
4 Primary; 0 Middle; 0 High; 0 Other Level
4 Regular; 0 Special Education; 0 Vocational; 0 Alternative
0 Magnet; 0 Charter; 2 Title I Eligible; 2 School-wide Title I
Students: 1,996 (51.3% male; 48.7% female)
Individual Education Program: 183 (9.2%);
English Language Learner: 193 (9.7%); Migrant: 146 (7.3%)
Eligible for Free Lunch Program: 619 (31.0%)
Eligible for Reduced-Price Lunch Program: 366 (18.3%)
Teachers: 114.0 (17.5 to 1)
Librarians/Media Specialists: 0.0 (0.0 to 1)
Guidance Counselors: 1.0 (1,996.0 to 1)
Current Spending: ($ per student per year):
Total: $8,601; Instruction: $5,458; Support Services: $2,864
Enrollment, Drop-out Rates and Diploma Recipients by Race/Ethnicity

Category	Total	White	Black	Asian	AIAN	Hisp.
Enrollment (%)	100.0	41.5	12.7	10.5	6.6	28.7
Drop-out Rate (%)	n/a	n/a	n/a	n/a	n/a	n/a
H.S. Diplomas (#)	n/a	n/a	n/a	n/a	n/a	n/a

Corcoran Joint Unified

1520 Patterson Ave • Corcoran, CA 93212-1722
(559) 992-3104 • http://www.kings.k12.ca.us/corcoran/
Grade Span: KG-12; **Agency Type:** 1
Schools: 6
3 Primary; 1 Middle; 2 High; 0 Other Level
5 Regular; 0 Special Education; 0 Vocational; 1 Alternative
0 Magnet; 0 Charter; 4 Title I Eligible; 4 School-wide Title I
Students: 3,177 (51.0% male; 49.0% female)
Individual Education Program: 198 (6.2%);
English Language Learner: 835 (26.3%); Migrant: 1,363 (42.9%)
Eligible for Free Lunch Program: 2,057 (64.7%)
Eligible for Reduced-Price Lunch Program: 265 (8.3%)
Teachers: 158.8 (20.0 to 1)
Librarians/Media Specialists: 0.7 (4,538.6 to 1)
Guidance Counselors: 3.0 (1,059.0 to 1)
Current Spending: ($ per student per year):
Total: $6,603; Instruction: $4,286; Support Services: $1,981
Enrollment, Drop-out Rates and Diploma Recipients by Race/Ethnicity

Category	Total	White	Black	Asian	AIAN	Hisp.
Enrollment (%)	100.0	13.5	3.7	0.8	0.2	81.8
Drop-out Rate (%)	n/a	n/a	n/a	n/a	n/a	n/a
H.S. Diplomas (#)	121	18	7	0	0	96

Hanford Elementary

714 N White St • Hanford, CA 93232
Mailing Address: PO Box G-1067 • Hanford, CA 93232
(559) 585-2265 • http://www.hesd.k12.ca.us/
Grade Span: KG-08; **Agency Type:** 1
Schools: 11
9 Primary; 2 Middle; 0 High; 0 Other Level
10 Regular; 0 Special Education; 0 Vocational; 1 Alternative
0 Magnet; 0 Charter; 11 Title I Eligible; 7 School-wide Title I
Students: 5,262 (51.9% male; 48.1% female)
Individual Education Program: 285 (5.4%);
English Language Learner: 1,099 (20.9%); Migrant: 1,006 (19.1%)
Eligible for Free Lunch Program: 3,070 (58.3%)
Eligible for Reduced-Price Lunch Program: 694 (13.2%)
Teachers: 257.5 (20.4 to 1)
Librarians/Media Specialists: 0.0 (0.0 to 1)
Guidance Counselors: 0.0 (0.0 to 1)
Current Spending: ($ per student per year):
Total: $6,470; Instruction: $3,646; Support Services: $2,567
Enrollment, Drop-out Rates and Diploma Recipients by Race/Ethnicity

Category	Total	White	Black	Asian	AIAN	Hisp.
Enrollment (%)	100.0	31.2	8.0	2.7	0.5	57.7
Drop-out Rate (%)	n/a	n/a	n/a	n/a	n/a	n/a
H.S. Diplomas (#)	n/a	n/a	n/a	n/a	n/a	n/a

Hanford Joint Union High

120 E Grangeville Rd • Hanford, CA 93230-3067
(559) 582-4401 • http://www.kings.k12.ca.us/huhsd/
Grade Span: 09-12; **Agency Type:** 1
Schools: 5
0 Primary; 0 Middle; 5 High; 0 Other Level
2 Regular; 0 Special Education; 0 Vocational; 3 Alternative
0 Magnet; 0 Charter; 4 Title I Eligible; 0 School-wide Title I
Students: 3,601 (51.1% male; 48.9% female)
Individual Education Program: 281 (7.8%);
English Language Learner: 137 (3.8%); Migrant: 150 (4.2%)
Eligible for Free Lunch Program: 639 (17.7%)
Eligible for Reduced-Price Lunch Program: 104 (2.9%)
Teachers: 148.8 (24.2 to 1)
Librarians/Media Specialists: 2.0 (1,800.5 to 1)
Guidance Counselors: 9.0 (400.1 to 1)
Current Spending: ($ per student per year):
Total: $6,019; Instruction: $3,440; Support Services: $2,434
Enrollment, Drop-out Rates and Diploma Recipients by Race/Ethnicity

Category	Total	White	Black	Asian	AIAN	Hisp.
Enrollment (%)	100.0	42.4	6.9	4.4	0.6	44.2
Drop-out Rate (%)	n/a	n/a	n/a	n/a	n/a	n/a
H.S. Diplomas (#)	533	280	31	23	2	197

Lemoore Union Elementary

100 Vine St • Lemoore, CA 93245-3418
(559) 924-6800 • http://www.luhsd.k12.ca.us/
Grade Span: KG-08; **Agency Type:** 1
Schools: 5
4 Primary; 1 Middle; 0 High; 0 Other Level
5 Regular; 0 Special Education; 0 Vocational; 0 Alternative
0 Magnet; 0 Charter; 5 Title I Eligible; 0 School-wide Title I
Students: 3,181 (51.4% male; 48.6% female)
Individual Education Program: 308 (9.7%);
English Language Learner: 579 (18.2%); Migrant: 703 (22.1%)
Eligible for Free Lunch Program: 1,446 (45.5%)
Eligible for Reduced-Price Lunch Program: 381 (12.0%)
Teachers: 158.6 (20.1 to 1)
Librarians/Media Specialists: 0.0 (0.0 to 1)
Guidance Counselors: 2.0 (1,590.5 to 1)
Current Spending: ($ per student per year):
Total: $5,669; Instruction: $3,705; Support Services: $1,724
Enrollment, Drop-out Rates and Diploma Recipients by Race/Ethnicity

Category	Total	White	Black	Asian	AIAN	Hisp.
Enrollment (%)	100.0	35.3	9.2	8.6	1.8	45.1
Drop-out Rate (%)	n/a	n/a	n/a	n/a	n/a	n/a
H.S. Diplomas (#)	n/a	n/a	n/a	n/a	n/a	n/a

Lemoore Union High
101 E Bush St • Lemoore, CA 93245-3601
(559) 924-6610 • http://tigger.luhsd.k12.ca.us/
Grade Span: 09-12; **Agency Type:** 1
Schools: 3
0 Primary; 0 Middle; 3 High; 0 Other Level
1 Regular; 0 Special Education; 0 Vocational; 2 Alternative
0 Magnet; 0 Charter; 2 Title I Eligible; 0 School-wide Title I
Students: 2,155 (50.7% male; 49.3% female)
Individual Education Program: 193 (9.0%);
English Language Learner: 52 (2.4%); Migrant: 265 (12.3%)
Eligible for Free Lunch Program: 455 (21.1%)
Eligible for Reduced-Price Lunch Program: 191 (8.9%)
Teachers: 95.1 (22.7 to 1)
Librarians/Media Specialists: 0.3 (7,183.3 to 1)
Guidance Counselors: 5.3 (406.6 to 1)
Current Spending: ($ per student per year):
Total: $7,504; Instruction: $3,850; Support Services: $3,364
Enrollment, Drop-out Rates and Diploma Recipients by Race/Ethnicity

Category	Total	White	Black	Asian	AIAN	Hisp.
Enrollment (%)	100.0	44.3	8.4	9.4	2.3	35.4
Drop-out Rate (%)	n/a	n/a	n/a	n/a	n/a	n/a
H.S. Diplomas (#)	381	204	32	46	4	94

Reef-Sunset Unified
205 N Park Ave • Avenal, CA 93204-1425
(559) 386-9083 • http://www.kings.k12.ca.us/rsusd/
Grade Span: KG-12; **Agency Type:** 1
Schools: 9
4 Primary; 1 Middle; 4 High; 0 Other Level
5 Regular; 0 Special Education; 0 Vocational; 4 Alternative
0 Magnet; 0 Charter; 7 Title I Eligible; 4 School-wide Title I
Students: 2,422 (52.6% male; 47.4% female)
Individual Education Program: 289 (11.9%);
English Language Learner: 1,585 (65.4%); Migrant: 1,291 (53.3%)
Eligible for Free Lunch Program: 2,395 (98.9%)
Eligible for Reduced-Price Lunch Program: 0 (0.0%)
Teachers: 127.5 (19.0 to 1)
Librarians/Media Specialists: 0.0 (0.0 to 1)
Guidance Counselors: 3.0 (807.3 to 1)
Current Spending: ($ per student per year):
Total: $6,954; Instruction: $4,117; Support Services: $2,453
Enrollment, Drop-out Rates and Diploma Recipients by Race/Ethnicity

Category	Total	White	Black	Asian	AIAN	Hisp.
Enrollment (%)	100.0	5.1	0.7	0.1	0.1	93.9
Drop-out Rate (%)	n/a	n/a	n/a	n/a	n/a	n/a
H.S. Diplomas (#)	101	6	2	0	0	93

Lake County

Kelseyville Unified
4325 Main St • Kelseyville, CA 95451-8953
(707) 279-1511 • http://www.kusd.lake.k12.ca.us/
Grade Span: KG-12; **Agency Type:** 1
Schools: 8
2 Primary; 2 Middle; 4 High; 0 Other Level
6 Regular; 0 Special Education; 0 Vocational; 2 Alternative
0 Magnet; 0 Charter; 4 Title I Eligible; 1 School-wide Title I
Students: 1,967 (52.3% male; 47.7% female)
Individual Education Program: 231 (11.7%);
English Language Learner: 253 (12.9%); Migrant: 382 (19.4%)
Eligible for Free Lunch Program: 874 (44.4%)
Eligible for Reduced-Price Lunch Program: 181 (9.2%)
Teachers: 101.9 (19.3 to 1)
Librarians/Media Specialists: 0.0 (0.0 to 1)
Guidance Counselors: 3.0 (655.7 to 1)
Current Spending: ($ per student per year):
Total: $6,523; Instruction: $3,934; Support Services: $2,297
Enrollment, Drop-out Rates and Diploma Recipients by Race/Ethnicity

Category	Total	White	Black	Asian	AIAN	Hisp.
Enrollment (%)	100.0	67.7	1.8	1.4	3.0	25.7
Drop-out Rate (%)	n/a	n/a	n/a	n/a	n/a	n/a
H.S. Diplomas (#)	157	125	0	1	3	28

Konocti Unified
9430 Lake St • Lower Lake, CA 95457-5000
Mailing Address: PO Box 5000 • Lower Lake, CA 95457-5000
(707) 994-6475 • http://www.konoctiusd.lake.k12.ca.us/kusd/kusd1.html
Grade Span: KG-12; **Agency Type:** 1
Schools: 9
5 Primary; 0 Middle; 2 High; 2 Other Level
6 Regular; 0 Special Education; 0 Vocational; 3 Alternative
0 Magnet; 0 Charter; 8 Title I Eligible; 5 School-wide Title I
Students: 3,356 (50.4% male; 49.6% female)
Individual Education Program: 436 (13.0%);
English Language Learner: 332 (9.9%); Migrant: 140 (4.2%)
Eligible for Free Lunch Program: 2,128 (63.4%)
Eligible for Reduced-Price Lunch Program: 340 (10.1%)
Teachers: 172.0 (19.5 to 1)
Librarians/Media Specialists: 0.0 (0.0 to 1)
Guidance Counselors: 6.0 (559.3 to 1)
Current Spending: ($ per student per year):
Total: $7,071; Instruction: $4,175; Support Services: $2,520
Enrollment, Drop-out Rates and Diploma Recipients by Race/Ethnicity

Category	Total	White	Black	Asian	AIAN	Hisp.
Enrollment (%)	100.0	68.8	7.1	1.9	5.9	16.2
Drop-out Rate (%)	n/a	n/a	n/a	n/a	n/a	n/a
H.S. Diplomas (#)	145	113	8	1	6	17

Lakeport Unified
100 Lange St • Lakeport, CA 95453-3297
(707) 262-3000 • http://www.lakeport.k12.ca.us/
Grade Span: KG-12; **Agency Type:** 1
Schools: 5
1 Primary; 1 Middle; 2 High; 1 Other Level
3 Regular; 0 Special Education; 0 Vocational; 2 Alternative
0 Magnet; 0 Charter; 2 Title I Eligible; 1 School-wide Title I
Students: 1,910 (50.9% male; 49.1% female)
Individual Education Program: 135 (7.1%);
English Language Learner: 131 (6.9%); Migrant: 196 (10.3%)
Eligible for Free Lunch Program: 730 (38.2%)
Eligible for Reduced-Price Lunch Program: 163 (8.5%)
Teachers: 99.9 (19.1 to 1)
Librarians/Media Specialists: 0.0 (0.0 to 1)
Guidance Counselors: 2.7 (707.4 to 1)
Current Spending: ($ per student per year):
Total: $6,127; Instruction: $3,877; Support Services: $2,014
Enrollment, Drop-out Rates and Diploma Recipients by Race/Ethnicity

Category	Total	White	Black	Asian	AIAN	Hisp.
Enrollment (%)	100.0	73.0	1.6	1.1	5.0	17.7
Drop-out Rate (%)	n/a	n/a	n/a	n/a	n/a	n/a
H.S. Diplomas (#)	134	112	4	2	3	13

Middletown Unified
20932 Big Canyon Rd • Middletown, CA 95461-0338
Mailing Address: PO Box 338 • Middletown, CA 95461-0338
(707) 987-4100 • http://www.musd.lake.k12.ca.us/
Grade Span: KG-12; **Agency Type:** 1
Schools: 8
4 Primary; 1 Middle; 3 High; 0 Other Level
5 Regular; 0 Special Education; 0 Vocational; 3 Alternative
0 Magnet; 0 Charter; 3 Title I Eligible; 0 School-wide Title I
Students: 1,749 (52.6% male; 47.4% female)
Individual Education Program: 211 (12.1%);
English Language Learner: 84 (4.8%); Migrant: 50 (2.9%)
Eligible for Free Lunch Program: 247 (14.1%)
Eligible for Reduced-Price Lunch Program: 118 (6.7%)
Teachers: 93.3 (18.7 to 1)
Librarians/Media Specialists: 0.0 (0.0 to 1)
Guidance Counselors: 1.5 (1,166.0 to 1)
Current Spending: ($ per student per year):
Total: $6,172; Instruction: $3,816; Support Services: $2,118
Enrollment, Drop-out Rates and Diploma Recipients by Race/Ethnicity

Category	Total	White	Black	Asian	AIAN	Hisp.
Enrollment (%)	100.0	83.3	1.5	1.9	1.3	10.5
Drop-out Rate (%)	n/a	n/a	n/a	n/a	n/a	n/a
H.S. Diplomas (#)	130	107	0	6	5	12

Lassen County

Westwood Unified
Fifth and Delwood Sts • Westwood, CA 96137-1225
Mailing Address: PO Box 1225 • Westwood, CA 96137-1225
(530) 256-2311
Grade Span: KG-12; **Agency Type:** 1
Schools: 6
2 Primary; 0 Middle; 3 High; 1 Other Level
3 Regular; 0 Special Education; 0 Vocational; 3 Alternative
0 Magnet; 1 Charter; 2 Title I Eligible; 1 School-wide Title I
Students: 2,156 (51.5% male; 48.5% female)
Individual Education Program: 0 (0.0%);
English Language Learner: 48 (2.2%); Migrant: 0 (0.0%)
Eligible for Free Lunch Program: 296 (13.7%)
Eligible for Reduced-Price Lunch Program: 91 (4.2%)
Teachers: 76.0 (28.4 to 1)
Librarians/Media Specialists: 0.0 (0.0 to 1)
Guidance Counselors: 0.0 (0.0 to 1)
Current Spending: ($ per student per year):
Total: $8,163; Instruction: $5,337; Support Services: $2,634

Enrollment, Drop-out Rates and Diploma Recipients by Race/Ethnicity

Category	Total	White	Black	Asian	AIAN	Hisp.
Enrollment (%)	100.0	32.2	23.5	4.6	1.4	20.3
Drop-out Rate (%)	n/a	n/a	n/a	n/a	n/a	n/a
H.S. Diplomas (#)	45	39	0	0	1	2

Los Angeles County

ABC Unified

16700 Norwalk Blvd • Cerritos, CA 90703-1838
(562) 926-5566 • http://www.abcusd.k12.ca.us/
Grade Span: KG-12; **Agency Type:** 1
Schools: 30
19 Primary; 5 Middle; 6 High; 0 Other Level
28 Regular; 0 Special Education; 0 Vocational; 2 Alternative
1 Magnet; 0 Charter; 13 Title I Eligible; 8 School-wide Title I
Students: 22,332 (52.2% male; 47.8% female)
Individual Education Program: 2,138 (9.6%);
English Language Learner: 4,806 (21.5%); Migrant: 1,160 (5.2%)
Eligible for Free Lunch Program: 6,260 (28.0%)
Eligible for Reduced-Price Lunch Program: 1,568 (7.0%)
Teachers: 1,000.8 (22.3 to 1)
Librarians/Media Specialists: 0.0 (0.0 to 1)
Guidance Counselors: 18.7 (1,194.2 to 1)
Current Spending: ($ per student per year):
Total: $6,345; Instruction: $4,393; Support Services: $1,686

Enrollment, Drop-out Rates and Diploma Recipients by Race/Ethnicity

Category	Total	White	Black	Asian	AIAN	Hisp.
Enrollment (%)	100.0	11.9	9.6	40.7	0.3	37.4
Drop-out Rate (%)	n/a	n/a	n/a	n/a	n/a	n/a
H.S. Diplomas (#)	1,636	250	174	768	4	440

Acton-Agua Dulce Unified

32248 N Crown Valley Rd • Acton, CA 93510-0068
Mailing Address: PO Box 68 • Acton, CA 93510-0068
(661) 269-5999 • http://aadusd.k12.ca.us/
Grade Span: KG-12; **Agency Type:** 1
Schools: 5
3 Primary; 1 Middle; 1 High; 0 Other Level
5 Regular; 0 Special Education; 0 Vocational; 0 Alternative
0 Magnet; 0 Charter; 2 Title I Eligible; 0 School-wide Title I
Students: 2,078 (50.8% male; 49.2% female)
Individual Education Program: 301 (14.5%);
English Language Learner: 99 (4.8%); Migrant: 9 (0.4%)
Eligible for Free Lunch Program: 300 (14.4%)
Eligible for Reduced-Price Lunch Program: 85 (4.1%)
Teachers: 89.0 (23.3 to 1)
Librarians/Media Specialists: 0.0 (0.0 to 1)
Guidance Counselors: 2.0 (1,039.0 to 1)
Current Spending: ($ per student per year):
Total: $5,691; Instruction: $3,728; Support Services: $1,963

Enrollment, Drop-out Rates and Diploma Recipients by Race/Ethnicity

Category	Total	White	Black	Asian	AIAN	Hisp.
Enrollment (%)	100.0	78.8	1.1	2.0	0.6	16.0
Drop-out Rate (%)	n/a	n/a	n/a	n/a	n/a	n/a
H.S. Diplomas (#)	98	82	1	4	0	11

Alhambra City Elementary

15 W Alhambra Rd • Alhambra, CA 91802-2110
Mailing Address: PO Box 110 • Alhambra, CA 91802-2110
(626) 308-2200 • http://www.alhambra.k12.ca.us/
Grade Span: KG-08; **Agency Type:** 2
Schools: 13
13 Primary; 0 Middle; 0 High; 0 Other Level
13 Regular; 0 Special Education; 0 Vocational; 0 Alternative
0 Magnet; 0 Charter; 13 Title I Eligible; 8 School-wide Title I
Students: 11,434 (50.7% male; 49.3% female)
Individual Education Program: 1,059 (9.3%);
English Language Learner: 5,143 (45.0%); Migrant: 181 (1.6%)
Eligible for Free Lunch Program: 5,808 (50.8%)
Eligible for Reduced-Price Lunch Program: 1,749 (15.3%)
Teachers: 554.7 (20.6 to 1)
Librarians/Media Specialists: 0.0 (0.0 to 1)
Guidance Counselors: 0.9 (12,704.4 to 1)
Current Spending: ($ per student per year):
Total: $6,813; Instruction: $4,283; Support Services: $2,265

Enrollment, Drop-out Rates and Diploma Recipients by Race/Ethnicity

Category	Total	White	Black	Asian	AIAN	Hisp.
Enrollment (%)	100.0	8.1	1.0	48.5	0.0	42.4
Drop-out Rate (%)	n/a	n/a	n/a	n/a	n/a	n/a
H.S. Diplomas (#)	n/a	n/a	n/a	n/a	n/a	n/a

Alhambra City High

15 W Alhambra Rd • Alhambra, CA 91802-2110
Mailing Address: PO Box 110 • Alhambra, CA 91802-2110
(626) 308-2200 • http://www.alhambra.k12.ca.us/
Grade Span: 07-12; **Agency Type:** 2
Schools: 6
0 Primary; 0 Middle; 6 High; 0 Other Level
3 Regular; 0 Special Education; 0 Vocational; 3 Alternative
0 Magnet; 0 Charter; 5 Title I Eligible; 4 School-wide Title I
Students: 8,352 (51.8% male; 48.2% female)
Individual Education Program: 642 (7.7%);
English Language Learner: 3,063 (36.7%); Migrant: 124 (1.5%)
Eligible for Free Lunch Program: 4,311 (51.6%)
Eligible for Reduced-Price Lunch Program: 927 (11.1%)
Teachers: 356.1 (23.5 to 1)
Librarians/Media Specialists: 3.0 (2,784.0 to 1)
Guidance Counselors: 16.4 (509.3 to 1)
Current Spending: ($ per student per year):
Total: n/a; Instruction: n/a; Support Services: n/a

Enrollment, Drop-out Rates and Diploma Recipients by Race/Ethnicity

Category	Total	White	Black	Asian	AIAN	Hisp.
Enrollment (%)	100.0	6.5	0.8	54.7	0.1	37.9
Drop-out Rate (%)	n/a	n/a	n/a	n/a	n/a	n/a
H.S. Diplomas (#)	1,641	93	5	1,059	3	481

Antelope Valley Union High

44811 N Sierra Hwy • Lancaster, CA 93534-3226
(661) 948-7655 • http://www.avdistrict.org/navpage.html
Grade Span: KG-12; **Agency Type:** 1
Schools: 11
0 Primary; 0 Middle; 10 High; 1 Other Level
8 Regular; 0 Special Education; 0 Vocational; 3 Alternative
0 Magnet; 2 Charter; 5 Title I Eligible; 0 School-wide Title I
Students: 21,067 (50.5% male; 49.5% female)
Individual Education Program: 2,767 (13.1%);
English Language Learner: 2,230 (10.6%); Migrant: 222 (1.1%)
Eligible for Free Lunch Program: 5,668 (26.9%)
Eligible for Reduced-Price Lunch Program: 1,288 (6.1%)
Teachers: 831.1 (25.3 to 1)
Librarians/Media Specialists: 1.7 (12,392.4 to 1)
Guidance Counselors: 40.4 (521.5 to 1)
Current Spending: ($ per student per year):
Total: $6,255; Instruction: $3,840; Support Services: $2,215

Enrollment, Drop-out Rates and Diploma Recipients by Race/Ethnicity

Category	Total	White	Black	Asian	AIAN	Hisp.
Enrollment (%)	100.0	40.5	20.2	3.9	0.7	34.1
Drop-out Rate (%)	n/a	n/a	n/a	n/a	n/a	n/a
H.S. Diplomas (#)	2,992	1,511	482	154	24	804

Arcadia Unified

234 Campus Dr • Arcadia, CA 91007-6902
(626) 821-8300 • http://www.ausd.k12.ca.us/
Grade Span: KG-12; **Agency Type:** 1
Schools: 11
6 Primary; 3 Middle; 1 High; 1 Other Level
10 Regular; 0 Special Education; 0 Vocational; 1 Alternative
0 Magnet; 0 Charter; 7 Title I Eligible; 0 School-wide Title I
Students: 9,942 (51.2% male; 48.8% female)
Individual Education Program: 839 (8.4%);
English Language Learner: 1,373 (13.8%); Migrant: 1 (<0.1%)
Eligible for Free Lunch Program: 545 (5.5%)
Eligible for Reduced-Price Lunch Program: 386 (3.9%)
Teachers: 435.2 (22.8 to 1)
Librarians/Media Specialists: 1.0 (9,942.0 to 1)
Guidance Counselors: 13.5 (736.4 to 1)
Current Spending: ($ per student per year):
Total: $5,970; Instruction: $4,058; Support Services: $1,684

Enrollment, Drop-out Rates and Diploma Recipients by Race/Ethnicity

Category	Total	White	Black	Asian	AIAN	Hisp.
Enrollment (%)	100.0	26.3	1.2	62.0	0.2	10.2
Drop-out Rate (%)	n/a	n/a	n/a	n/a	n/a	n/a
H.S. Diplomas (#)	832	268	7	495	3	59

Azusa Unified

546 S Citrus Ave • Azusa, CA 91702-0500
Mailing Address: PO Box 500 • Azusa, CA 91702-0500
(626) 967-6211 • http://www.azusausd.k12.ca.us/
Grade Span: KG-12; **Agency Type:** 1
Schools: 18
12 Primary; 3 Middle; 3 High; 0 Other Level
17 Regular; 0 Special Education; 0 Vocational; 1 Alternative
0 Magnet; 0 Charter; 12 Title I Eligible; 12 School-wide Title I
Students: 12,164 (51.1% male; 48.9% female)
Individual Education Program: 1,165 (9.6%);
English Language Learner: 4,941 (40.6%); Migrant: 107 (0.9%)

Eligible for Free Lunch Program: 6,281 (51.6%)
Eligible for Reduced-Price Lunch Program: 2,146 (17.6%)
Teachers: 574.8 (21.2 to 1)
Librarians/Media Specialists: 0.0 (0.0 to 1)
Guidance Counselors: 10.2 (1,192.5 to 1)
Current Spending: ($ per student per year):
Total: $6,396; Instruction: $4,139; Support Services: $1,952
Enrollment, Drop-out Rates and Diploma Recipients by Race/Ethnicity

Category	Total	White	Black	Asian	AIAN	Hisp.
Enrollment (%)	100.0	10.5	2.4	2.9	0.1	84.0
Drop-out Rate (%)	n/a	n/a	n/a	n/a	n/a	n/a
H.S. Diplomas (#)	529	76	16	28	0	409

Baldwin Park Unified
3699 N Holly Ave • Baldwin Park, CA 91706-5397
(626) 962-3311 • http://www.bpusd.net/templates/home.asp?pid=494
Grade Span: KG-12; **Agency Type:** 1
Schools: 22
13 Primary; 4 Middle; 3 High; 2 Other Level
20 Regular; 0 Special Education; 0 Vocational; 2 Alternative
0 Magnet; 1 Charter; 17 Title I Eligible; 17 School-wide Title I
Students: 19,163 (51.3% male; 48.7% female)
Individual Education Program: 1,513 (7.9%);
English Language Learner: 6,739 (35.2%); Migrant: 467 (2.4%)
Eligible for Free Lunch Program: 11,304 (59.0%)
Eligible for Reduced-Price Lunch Program: 2,711 (14.1%)
Teachers: 847.9 (22.6 to 1)
Librarians/Media Specialists: 3.4 (5,636.2 to 1)
Guidance Counselors: 12.0 (1,596.9 to 1)
Current Spending: ($ per student per year):
Total: $6,180; Instruction: $3,950; Support Services: $1,955
Enrollment, Drop-out Rates and Diploma Recipients by Race/Ethnicity

Category	Total	White	Black	Asian	AIAN	Hisp.
Enrollment (%)	100.0	5.3	1.8	5.8	0.3	85.7
Drop-out Rate (%)	n/a	n/a	n/a	n/a	n/a	n/a
H.S. Diplomas (#)	713	37	26	61	14	574

Bassett Unified
904 N Willow Ave • La Puente, CA 91746-1615
(626) 931-3000 • http://www.bassett.k12.ca.us/
Grade Span: KG-12; **Agency Type:** 1
Schools: 8
5 Primary; 1 Middle; 2 High; 0 Other Level
7 Regular; 0 Special Education; 0 Vocational; 1 Alternative
0 Magnet; 0 Charter; 8 Title I Eligible; 5 School-wide Title I
Students: 6,129 (50.5% male; 49.5% female)
Individual Education Program: 647 (10.6%);
English Language Learner: 2,024 (33.0%); Migrant: 22 (0.4%)
Eligible for Free Lunch Program: 3,993 (65.1%)
Eligible for Reduced-Price Lunch Program: 959 (15.6%)
Teachers: 281.2 (21.8 to 1)
Librarians/Media Specialists: 0.0 (0.0 to 1)
Guidance Counselors: 7.5 (817.2 to 1)
Current Spending: ($ per student per year):
Total: $6,751; Instruction: $4,217; Support Services: $2,193
Enrollment, Drop-out Rates and Diploma Recipients by Race/Ethnicity

Category	Total	White	Black	Asian	AIAN	Hisp.
Enrollment (%)	100.0	2.4	1.7	3.1	0.5	92.0
Drop-out Rate (%)	n/a	n/a	n/a	n/a	n/a	n/a
H.S. Diplomas (#)	308	8	1	14	1	276

Bellflower Unified
16703 S Clark Ave • Bellflower, CA 90706-5203
(562) 866-9011 • http://www.citywd.com/bellflower/sch_1.htm
Grade Span: KG-12; **Agency Type:** 1
Schools: 15
11 Primary; 0 Middle; 3 High; 1 Other Level
13 Regular; 0 Special Education; 0 Vocational; 2 Alternative
0 Magnet; 0 Charter; 9 Title I Eligible; 0 School-wide Title I
Students: 15,421 (51.5% male; 48.5% female)
Individual Education Program: 990 (6.4%);
English Language Learner: 2,706 (17.5%); Migrant: 0 (0.0%)
Eligible for Free Lunch Program: 5,684 (36.9%)
Eligible for Reduced-Price Lunch Program: 2,251 (14.6%)
Teachers: 691.3 (22.3 to 1)
Librarians/Media Specialists: 3.2 (4,819.1 to 1)
Guidance Counselors: 9.0 (1,713.4 to 1)
Current Spending: ($ per student per year):
Total: $5,976; Instruction: $3,956; Support Services: $1,713
Enrollment, Drop-out Rates and Diploma Recipients by Race/Ethnicity

Category	Total	White	Black	Asian	AIAN	Hisp.
Enrollment (%)	100.0	24.7	17.0	10.0	0.4	47.5
Drop-out Rate (%)	n/a	n/a	n/a	n/a	n/a	n/a
H.S. Diplomas (#)	780	234	156	109	3	278

Beverly Hills Unified
255 S Lasky Dr • Beverly Hills, CA 90212-3644
(310) 551-5100 • http://www.beverlyhills.k12.ca.us/
Grade Span: KG-12; **Agency Type:** 1
Schools: 6
4 Primary; 0 Middle; 2 High; 0 Other Level
5 Regular; 0 Special Education; 0 Vocational; 1 Alternative
0 Magnet; 0 Charter; 2 Title I Eligible; 0 School-wide Title I
Students: 5,232 (50.6% male; 49.4% female)
Individual Education Program: 589 (11.3%);
English Language Learner: 311 (5.9%); Migrant: 0 (0.0%)
Eligible for Free Lunch Program: 209 (4.0%)
Eligible for Reduced-Price Lunch Program: 138 (2.6%)
Teachers: 286.6 (18.3 to 1)
Librarians/Media Specialists: 3.0 (1,744.0 to 1)
Guidance Counselors: 12.0 (436.0 to 1)
Current Spending: ($ per student per year):
Total: $8,183; Instruction: $5,157; Support Services: $2,861
Enrollment, Drop-out Rates and Diploma Recipients by Race/Ethnicity

Category	Total	White	Black	Asian	AIAN	Hisp.
Enrollment (%)	100.0	76.4	4.6	13.7	0.0	4.1
Drop-out Rate (%)	n/a	n/a	n/a	n/a	n/a	n/a
H.S. Diplomas (#)	472	363	24	65	0	20

Bonita Unified
115 W Allen Ave • San Dimas, CA 91773-1437
(909) 971-8200 • http://www.bonita.k12.ca.us/
Grade Span: KG-12; **Agency Type:** 1
Schools: 14
8 Primary; 2 Middle; 3 High; 1 Other Level
12 Regular; 0 Special Education; 0 Vocational; 2 Alternative
0 Magnet; 0 Charter; 3 Title I Eligible; 0 School-wide Title I
Students: 10,178 (51.0% male; 49.0% female)
Individual Education Program: 1,265 (12.4%);
English Language Learner: 189 (1.9%); Migrant: 12 (0.1%)
Eligible for Free Lunch Program: 1,912 (18.8%)
Eligible for Reduced-Price Lunch Program: 600 (5.9%)
Teachers: 442.3 (23.0 to 1)
Librarians/Media Specialists: 2.0 (5,089.0 to 1)
Guidance Counselors: 12.1 (841.2 to 1)
Current Spending: ($ per student per year):
Total: $6,094; Instruction: $4,060; Support Services: $1,904
Enrollment, Drop-out Rates and Diploma Recipients by Race/Ethnicity

Category	Total	White	Black	Asian	AIAN	Hisp.
Enrollment (%)	100.0	53.1	4.9	8.0	0.9	31.4
Drop-out Rate (%)	n/a	n/a	n/a	n/a	n/a	n/a
H.S. Diplomas (#)	761	434	50	62	7	202

Burbank Unified
1900 W Olive Ave • Burbank, CA 91506-2460
(818) 729-4400 • http://www.burbank.k12.ca.us/
Grade Span: KG-12; **Agency Type:** 1
Schools: 20
11 Primary; 3 Middle; 4 High; 2 Other Level
16 Regular; 1 Special Education; 0 Vocational; 3 Alternative
0 Magnet; 1 Charter; 5 Title I Eligible; 5 School-wide Title I
Students: 16,747 (51.0% male; 49.0% female)
Individual Education Program: 1,667 (10.0%);
English Language Learner: 3,195 (19.1%); Migrant: 0 (0.0%)
Eligible for Free Lunch Program: 4,450 (26.6%)
Eligible for Reduced-Price Lunch Program: 1,114 (6.7%)
Teachers: 788.3 (21.2 to 1)
Librarians/Media Specialists: 0.0 (0.0 to 1)
Guidance Counselors: 18.8 (890.8 to 1)
Current Spending: ($ per student per year):
Total: $6,327; Instruction: $4,184; Support Services: $1,927
Enrollment, Drop-out Rates and Diploma Recipients by Race/Ethnicity

Category	Total	White	Black	Asian	AIAN	Hisp.
Enrollment (%)	100.0	50.8	2.7	8.8	0.1	36.5
Drop-out Rate (%)	n/a	n/a	n/a	n/a	n/a	n/a
H.S. Diplomas (#)	1,094	551	23	98	0	383

Castaic Union Elementary
28131 Livingston Ave • Valencia, CA 91355-3359
(661) 257-4500 • http://www.castaic.k12.ca.us/
Grade Span: KG-08; **Agency Type:** 1
Schools: 3
2 Primary; 1 Middle; 0 High; 0 Other Level
3 Regular; 0 Special Education; 0 Vocational; 0 Alternative
0 Magnet; 0 Charter; 1 Title I Eligible; 0 School-wide Title I
Students: 3,403 (51.2% male; 48.8% female)
Individual Education Program: 336 (9.9%);
English Language Learner: 263 (7.7%); Migrant: 0 (0.0%)
Eligible for Free Lunch Program: 354 (10.4%)
Eligible for Reduced-Price Lunch Program: 107 (3.1%)

Teachers: 159.9 (21.3 to 1)
Librarians/Media Specialists: 0.0 (0.0 to 1)
Guidance Counselors: 2.9 (1,173.4 to 1)
Current Spending: ($ per student per year):
Total: $5,486; Instruction: $3,799; Support Services: $1,666

Enrollment, Drop-out Rates and Diploma Recipients by Race/Ethnicity

Category	Total	White	Black	Asian	AIAN	Hisp.
Enrollment (%)	100.0	65.2	3.0	6.9	0.1	22.6
Drop-out Rate (%)	n/a	n/a	n/a	n/a	n/a	n/a
H.S. Diplomas (#)	n/a	n/a	n/a	n/a	n/a	n/a

Centinela Valley Union High

14901 S Inglewood Ave • Lawndale, CA 90260-1251
(310) 263-3200 • http://www.centinela.k12.ca.us/
Grade Span: 09-12; **Agency Type:** 1
Schools: 4
0 Primary; 0 Middle; 4 High; 0 Other Level
3 Regular; 0 Special Education; 0 Vocational; 1 Alternative
0 Magnet; 0 Charter; 4 Title I Eligible; 0 School-wide Title I
Students: 7,476 (51.9% male; 48.1% female)
Individual Education Program: 852 (11.4%);
English Language Learner: 2,150 (28.8%); Migrant: 0 (0.0%)
Eligible for Free Lunch Program: 3,145 (42.1%)
Eligible for Reduced-Price Lunch Program: 670 (9.0%)
Teachers: 288.7 (25.9 to 1)
Librarians/Media Specialists: 0.0 (0.0 to 1)
Guidance Counselors: 18.0 (415.3 to 1)
Current Spending: ($ per student per year):
Total: $6,205; Instruction: $3,649; Support Services: $2,208

Enrollment, Drop-out Rates and Diploma Recipients by Race/Ethnicity

Category	Total	White	Black	Asian	AIAN	Hisp.
Enrollment (%)	100.0	4.8	21.7	6.2	0.2	65.9
Drop-out Rate (%)	n/a	n/a	n/a	n/a	n/a	n/a
H.S. Diplomas (#)	1,107	53	194	117	3	722

Charter Oak Unified

20240 Cienega Ave • Covina, CA 91723-0009
Mailing Address: PO Box 9 • Covina, CA 91723-0009
(626) 966-8331 • http://www.cousd.k12.ca.us/
Grade Span: KG-12; **Agency Type:** 1
Schools: 10
5 Primary; 1 Middle; 2 High; 2 Other Level
7 Regular; 0 Special Education; 0 Vocational; 3 Alternative
0 Magnet; 0 Charter; 5 Title I Eligible; 0 School-wide Title I
Students: 7,026 (51.3% male; 48.7% female)
Individual Education Program: 631 (9.0%);
English Language Learner: 638 (9.1%); Migrant: 4 (0.1%)
Eligible for Free Lunch Program: 1,339 (19.1%)
Eligible for Reduced-Price Lunch Program: 472 (6.7%)
Teachers: 243.0 (28.9 to 1)
Librarians/Media Specialists: 0.0 (0.0 to 1)
Guidance Counselors: 0.0 (0.0 to 1)
Current Spending: ($ per student per year):
Total: $5,679; Instruction: $3,761; Support Services: $1,713

Enrollment, Drop-out Rates and Diploma Recipients by Race/Ethnicity

Category	Total	White	Black	Asian	AIAN	Hisp.
Enrollment (%)	100.0	42.0	4.5	8.2	0.3	43.7
Drop-out Rate (%)	n/a	n/a	n/a	n/a	n/a	n/a
H.S. Diplomas (#)	407	188	17	44	3	155

Claremont Unified

2080 N Mountain Ave • Claremont, CA 91711-2643
(909) 398-0600 • http://www.cusd.claremont.edu/
Grade Span: KG-12; **Agency Type:** 1
Schools: 12
8 Primary; 1 Middle; 3 High; 0 Other Level
9 Regular; 1 Special Education; 0 Vocational; 2 Alternative
0 Magnet; 0 Charter; 6 Title I Eligible; 0 School-wide Title I
Students: 6,866 (50.5% male; 49.5% female)
Individual Education Program: 784 (11.4%);
English Language Learner: 604 (8.8%); Migrant: 4 (0.1%)
Eligible for Free Lunch Program: 1,110 (16.2%)
Eligible for Reduced-Price Lunch Program: 370 (5.4%)
Teachers: 314.8 (21.8 to 1)
Librarians/Media Specialists: 1.0 (6,866.0 to 1)
Guidance Counselors: 7.0 (980.9 to 1)
Current Spending: ($ per student per year):
Total: $6,774; Instruction: $4,363; Support Services: $2,143

Enrollment, Drop-out Rates and Diploma Recipients by Race/Ethnicity

Category	Total	White	Black	Asian	AIAN	Hisp.
Enrollment (%)	100.0	50.2	9.6	13.1	0.7	26.0
Drop-out Rate (%)	n/a	n/a	n/a	n/a	n/a	n/a
H.S. Diplomas (#)	585	321	54	99	2	109

Compton Unified

604 S Tamarind Ave • Compton, CA 90220-3826
(310) 639-4321 • http://www.compton.k12.ca.us/
Grade Span: KG-12; **Agency Type:** 1
Schools: 39
23 Primary; 9 Middle; 6 High; 1 Other Level
35 Regular; 0 Special Education; 0 Vocational; 4 Alternative
1 Magnet; 0 Charter; 36 Title I Eligible; 35 School-wide Title I
Students: 32,550 (50.9% male; 49.1% female)
Individual Education Program: 1,545 (4.7%);
English Language Learner: 17,229 (52.9%); Migrant: 6 (<0.1%)
Eligible for Free Lunch Program: 26,724 (82.1%)
Eligible for Reduced-Price Lunch Program: 1,445 (4.4%)
Teachers: 1,416.3 (23.0 to 1)
Librarians/Media Specialists: 3.0 (10,850.0 to 1)
Guidance Counselors: 41.5 (784.3 to 1)
Current Spending: ($ per student per year):
Total: $6,358; Instruction: $3,996; Support Services: $2,048

Enrollment, Drop-out Rates and Diploma Recipients by Race/Ethnicity

Category	Total	White	Black	Asian	AIAN	Hisp.
Enrollment (%)	100.0	0.3	30.3	1.1	0.1	67.8
Drop-out Rate (%)	n/a	n/a	n/a	n/a	n/a	n/a
H.S. Diplomas (#)	902	2	398	8	3	491

Covina-Valley Unified

519 E Badillo St • Covina, CA 91723-0269
Mailing Address: PO Box 269 • Covina, CA 91723-0269
(626) 974-7000 • http://www.cvusd.k12.ca.us/
Grade Span: KG-12; **Agency Type:** 1
Schools: 20
12 Primary; 3 Middle; 4 High; 1 Other Level
18 Regular; 0 Special Education; 0 Vocational; 2 Alternative
0 Magnet; 0 Charter; 10 Title I Eligible; 7 School-wide Title I
Students: 14,718 (51.1% male; 48.9% female)
Individual Education Program: 1,714 (11.6%);
English Language Learner: 1,858 (12.6%); Migrant: 107 (0.7%)
Eligible for Free Lunch Program: 5,176 (35.2%)
Eligible for Reduced-Price Lunch Program: 1,692 (11.5%)
Teachers: 671.9 (21.9 to 1)
Librarians/Media Specialists: 2.0 (7,359.0 to 1)
Guidance Counselors: 15.0 (981.2 to 1)
Current Spending: ($ per student per year):
Total: $6,008; Instruction: $3,703; Support Services: $2,057

Enrollment, Drop-out Rates and Diploma Recipients by Race/Ethnicity

Category	Total	White	Black	Asian	AIAN	Hisp.
Enrollment (%)	100.0	22.8	5.4	10.7	0.4	58.4
Drop-out Rate (%)	n/a	n/a	n/a	n/a	n/a	n/a
H.S. Diplomas (#)	979	318	58	117	5	478

Culver City Unified

4034 Irving Pl • Culver City, CA 90232-2810
(310) 842-4220 • http://www.ccusd.k12.ca.us/
Grade Span: KG-12; **Agency Type:** 1
Schools: 10
5 Primary; 1 Middle; 3 High; 1 Other Level
7 Regular; 0 Special Education; 0 Vocational; 3 Alternative
0 Magnet; 0 Charter; 4 Title I Eligible; 0 School-wide Title I
Students: 6,671 (51.7% male; 48.3% female)
Individual Education Program: 608 (9.1%);
English Language Learner: 1,212 (18.2%); Migrant: 0 (0.0%)
Eligible for Free Lunch Program: 1,574 (23.6%)
Eligible for Reduced-Price Lunch Program: 667 (10.0%)
Teachers: 316.5 (21.1 to 1)
Librarians/Media Specialists: 1.0 (6,671.0 to 1)
Guidance Counselors: 8.5 (784.8 to 1)
Current Spending: ($ per student per year):
Total: $7,312; Instruction: $4,434; Support Services: $2,625

Enrollment, Drop-out Rates and Diploma Recipients by Race/Ethnicity

Category	Total	White	Black	Asian	AIAN	Hisp.
Enrollment (%)	100.0	27.0	19.4	13.6	0.3	39.0
Drop-out Rate (%)	n/a	n/a	n/a	n/a	n/a	n/a
H.S. Diplomas (#)	307	88	53	58	0	108

Downey Unified

11627 Brookshire Ave • Downey, CA 90241-7017
Mailing Address: PO Box 7017 • Downey, CA 90241-7017
(562) 904-3500 • http://www.dusd.net/
Grade Span: KG-12; **Agency Type:** 1
Schools: 22
13 Primary; 5 Middle; 3 High; 1 Other Level
20 Regular; 1 Special Education; 0 Vocational; 1 Alternative
0 Magnet; 0 Charter; 14 Title I Eligible; 0 School-wide Title I
Students: 22,298 (51.2% male; 48.8% female)
Individual Education Program: 2,414 (10.8%);
English Language Learner: 5,492 (24.6%); Migrant: 5 (<0.1%)

Eligible for Free Lunch Program: 7,376 (33.1%)
Eligible for Reduced-Price Lunch Program: 4,246 (19.0%)
Teachers: 977.8 (22.8 to 1)
Librarians/Media Specialists: 6.0 (3,716.3 to 1)
Guidance Counselors: 21.6 (1,032.3 to 1)
Current Spending: ($ per student per year):
Total: $5,497; Instruction: $3,639; Support Services: $1,584
Enrollment, Drop-out Rates and Diploma Recipients by Race/Ethnicity

Category	Total	White	Black	Asian	AIAN	Hisp.
Enrollment (%)	100.0	15.5	4.0	6.0	0.4	74.1
Drop-out Rate (%)	n/a	n/a	n/a	n/a	n/a	n/a
H.S. Diplomas (#)	1,292	318	61	114	3	796

Duarte Unified
1620 Huntington Dr • Duarte, CA 91010-2534
(626) 358-1191 • http://www.duarte.k12.ca.us/
Grade Span: KG-12; **Agency Type:** 1
Schools: 8
5 Primary; 1 Middle; 2 High; 0 Other Level
7 Regular; 0 Special Education; 0 Vocational; 1 Alternative
0 Magnet; 0 Charter; 8 Title I Eligible; 3 School-wide Title I
Students: 4,693 (51.4% male; 48.6% female)
Individual Education Program: 391 (8.3%);
English Language Learner: 872 (18.6%); Migrant: 179 (3.8%)
Eligible for Free Lunch Program: 2,285 (48.7%)
Eligible for Reduced-Price Lunch Program: 693 (14.8%)
Teachers: 213.0 (22.0 to 1)
Librarians/Media Specialists: 0.0 (0.0 to 1)
Guidance Counselors: 1.8 (2,607.2 to 1)
Current Spending: ($ per student per year):
Total: $6,403; Instruction: $3,637; Support Services: $2,406
Enrollment, Drop-out Rates and Diploma Recipients by Race/Ethnicity

Category	Total	White	Black	Asian	AIAN	Hisp.
Enrollment (%)	100.0	13.6	10.1	6.5	0.1	67.6
Drop-out Rate (%)	n/a	n/a	n/a	n/a	n/a	n/a
H.S. Diplomas (#)	320	51	37	29	0	202

East Whittier City Elementary
14535 E Whittier Blvd • Whittier, CA 90605-2130
(562) 698-0351 • http://www.ewcsd.k12.ca.us/
Grade Span: KG-08; **Agency Type:** 1
Schools: 13
10 Primary; 3 Middle; 0 High; 0 Other Level
13 Regular; 0 Special Education; 0 Vocational; 0 Alternative
0 Magnet; 0 Charter; 7 Title I Eligible; 3 School-wide Title I
Students: 9,409 (51.7% male; 48.3% female)
Individual Education Program: 1,128 (12.0%);
English Language Learner: 1,876 (19.9%); Migrant: 6 (0.1%)
Eligible for Free Lunch Program: 2,366 (25.1%)
Eligible for Reduced-Price Lunch Program: 801 (8.5%)
Teachers: 450.9 (20.9 to 1)
Librarians/Media Specialists: 0.0 (0.0 to 1)
Guidance Counselors: 4.2 (2,240.2 to 1)
Current Spending: ($ per student per year):
Total: $6,204; Instruction: $4,171; Support Services: $1,830
Enrollment, Drop-out Rates and Diploma Recipients by Race/Ethnicity

Category	Total	White	Black	Asian	AIAN	Hisp.
Enrollment (%)	100.0	25.4	3.1	3.8	0.6	66.6
Drop-out Rate (%)	n/a	n/a	n/a	n/a	n/a	n/a
H.S. Diplomas (#)	n/a	n/a	n/a	n/a	n/a	n/a

Eastside Union Elementary
45006 30th St E • Lancaster, CA 93535-7849
(661) 952-1200 • http://www.lacoe.edu/sch-dist/eastside/
Grade Span: KG-08; **Agency Type:** 1
Schools: 4
3 Primary; 1 Middle; 0 High; 0 Other Level
4 Regular; 0 Special Education; 0 Vocational; 0 Alternative
0 Magnet; 0 Charter; 4 Title I Eligible; 2 School-wide Title I
Students: 2,621 (49.7% male; 50.3% female)
Individual Education Program: 268 (10.2%);
English Language Learner: 605 (23.1%); Migrant: 186 (7.1%)
Eligible for Free Lunch Program: 1,493 (57.0%)
Eligible for Reduced-Price Lunch Program: 381 (14.5%)
Teachers: 120.2 (21.8 to 1)
Librarians/Media Specialists: 3.0 (873.7 to 1)
Guidance Counselors: 0.0 (0.0 to 1)
Current Spending: ($ per student per year):
Total: $6,041; Instruction: $3,733; Support Services: $2,071
Enrollment, Drop-out Rates and Diploma Recipients by Race/Ethnicity

Category	Total	White	Black	Asian	AIAN	Hisp.
Enrollment (%)	100.0	33.5	24.1	2.0	0.4	39.5
Drop-out Rate (%)	n/a	n/a	n/a	n/a	n/a	n/a
H.S. Diplomas (#)	n/a	n/a	n/a	n/a	n/a	n/a

El Monte City Elementary
3540 N Lexington Ave • El Monte, CA 91731-2684
(626) 453-3700
Grade Span: KG-08; **Agency Type:** 1
Schools: 19
19 Primary; 0 Middle; 0 High; 0 Other Level
18 Regular; 1 Special Education; 0 Vocational; 0 Alternative
0 Magnet; 0 Charter; 19 Title I Eligible; 16 School-wide Title I
Students: 11,951 (51.4% male; 48.6% female)
Individual Education Program: 1,203 (10.1%);
English Language Learner: 5,541 (46.4%); Migrant: 292 (2.4%)
Eligible for Free Lunch Program: 8,670 (72.5%)
Eligible for Reduced-Price Lunch Program: 1,141 (9.5%)
Teachers: 577.4 (20.7 to 1)
Librarians/Media Specialists: 0.0 (0.0 to 1)
Guidance Counselors: 0.0 (0.0 to 1)
Current Spending: ($ per student per year):
Total: $6,636; Instruction: $4,505; Support Services: $1,760
Enrollment, Drop-out Rates and Diploma Recipients by Race/Ethnicity

Category	Total	White	Black	Asian	AIAN	Hisp.
Enrollment (%)	100.0	4.7	0.6	14.8	0.1	79.4
Drop-out Rate (%)	n/a	n/a	n/a	n/a	n/a	n/a
H.S. Diplomas (#)	n/a	n/a	n/a	n/a	n/a	n/a

El Monte Union High
3537 Johnson Ave • El Monte, CA 91731-3290
(626) 444-9005 • http://www.emuhsd.k12.ca.us/
Grade Span: 09-12; **Agency Type:** 1
Schools: 7
0 Primary; 0 Middle; 7 High; 0 Other Level
5 Regular; 0 Special Education; 0 Vocational; 2 Alternative
0 Magnet; 0 Charter; 7 Title I Eligible; 2 School-wide Title I
Students: 10,111 (50.5% male; 49.5% female)
Individual Education Program: 894 (8.8%);
English Language Learner: 3,309 (32.7%); Migrant: 284 (2.8%)
Eligible for Free Lunch Program: 5,382 (53.2%)
Eligible for Reduced-Price Lunch Program: 1,083 (10.7%)
Teachers: 412.6 (24.5 to 1)
Librarians/Media Specialists: 2.8 (3,611.1 to 1)
Guidance Counselors: 24.0 (421.3 to 1)
Current Spending: ($ per student per year):
Total: $6,284; Instruction: $3,816; Support Services: $2,206
Enrollment, Drop-out Rates and Diploma Recipients by Race/Ethnicity

Category	Total	White	Black	Asian	AIAN	Hisp.
Enrollment (%)	100.0	4.3	0.7	18.4	0.1	76.4
Drop-out Rate (%)	n/a	n/a	n/a	n/a	n/a	n/a
H.S. Diplomas (#)	1,705	77	9	368	1	1,248

El Rancho Unified
9333 Loch Lomond Dr • Pico Rivera, CA 90660-2913
(562) 942-1500 • http://www.erusd.k12.ca.us/
Grade Span: KG-12; **Agency Type:** 1
Schools: 17
12 Primary; 3 Middle; 2 High; 0 Other Level
16 Regular; 0 Special Education; 0 Vocational; 1 Alternative
0 Magnet; 0 Charter; 17 Title I Eligible; 0 School-wide Title I
Students: 12,333 (51.0% male; 49.0% female)
Individual Education Program: 1,208 (9.8%);
English Language Learner: 4,089 (33.2%); Migrant: 90 (0.7%)
Eligible for Free Lunch Program: 6,040 (49.0%)
Eligible for Reduced-Price Lunch Program: 1,853 (15.0%)
Teachers: 584.9 (21.1 to 1)
Librarians/Media Specialists: 0.0 (0.0 to 1)
Guidance Counselors: 9.0 (1,370.3 to 1)
Current Spending: ($ per student per year):
Total: $6,497; Instruction: $4,191; Support Services: $2,026
Enrollment, Drop-out Rates and Diploma Recipients by Race/Ethnicity

Category	Total	White	Black	Asian	AIAN	Hisp.
Enrollment (%)	100.0	2.4	0.5	1.2	0.2	95.6
Drop-out Rate (%)	n/a	n/a	n/a	n/a	n/a	n/a
H.S. Diplomas (#)	596	21	6	18	2	549

El Segundo Unified
641 Sheldon St • El Segundo, CA 90245-3036
(310) 615-2650 • http://www.elsegundousd.com/policies/gate.htm
Grade Span: KG-12; **Agency Type:** 1
Schools: 5
2 Primary; 1 Middle; 2 High; 0 Other Level
4 Regular; 0 Special Education; 0 Vocational; 1 Alternative
0 Magnet; 0 Charter; 1 Title I Eligible; 0 School-wide Title I
Students: 3,044 (50.7% male; 49.3% female)
Individual Education Program: 243 (8.0%);
English Language Learner: 202 (6.6%); Migrant: 0 (0.0%)
Eligible for Free Lunch Program: 194 (6.4%)
Eligible for Reduced-Price Lunch Program: 118 (3.9%)

Teachers: 145.4 (20.9 to 1)
Librarians/Media Specialists: 1.0 (3,044.0 to 1)
Guidance Counselors: 2.6 (1,170.8 to 1)
Current Spending: ($ per student per year):
Total: $7,015; Instruction: $4,343; Support Services: $2,449
Enrollment, Drop-out Rates and Diploma Recipients by Race/Ethnicity

Category	Total	White	Black	Asian	AIAN	Hisp.
Enrollment (%)	100.0	69.0	4.4	9.9	0.3	16.4
Drop-out Rate (%)	n/a	n/a	n/a	n/a	n/a	n/a
H.S. Diplomas (#)	247	159	11	33	2	42

Garvey Elementary
2730 N Del Mar • Rosemead, CA 91770-3026
(626) 307-3400 • http://www.garvey.k12.ca.us/
Grade Span: KG-08; **Agency Type:** 1
Schools: 13
11 Primary; 2 Middle; 0 High; 0 Other Level
13 Regular; 0 Special Education; 0 Vocational; 0 Alternative
0 Magnet; 0 Charter; 13 Title I Eligible; 0 School-wide Title I
Students: 6,859 (51.0% male; 49.0% female)
Individual Education Program: 735 (10.7%);
English Language Learner: 3,190 (46.5%); Migrant: 237 (3.5%)
Eligible for Free Lunch Program: 4,948 (72.1%)
Eligible for Reduced-Price Lunch Program: 840 (12.2%)
Teachers: 328.7 (20.9 to 1)
Librarians/Media Specialists: 2.9 (2,365.2 to 1)
Guidance Counselors: 0.6 (11,431.7 to 1)
Current Spending: ($ per student per year):
Total: $6,913; Instruction: $4,290; Support Services: $2,213
Enrollment, Drop-out Rates and Diploma Recipients by Race/Ethnicity

Category	Total	White	Black	Asian	AIAN	Hisp.
Enrollment (%)	100.0	2.3	0.4	50.0	0.1	47.3
Drop-out Rate (%)	n/a	n/a	n/a	n/a	n/a	n/a
H.S. Diplomas (#)	n/a	n/a	n/a	n/a	n/a	n/a

Glendale Unified
223 N Jackson St • Glendale, CA 91206-4334
(818) 241-3111 • http://www.glendale.k12.ca.us/
Grade Span: KG-12; **Agency Type:** 1
Schools: 32
20 Primary; 4 Middle; 6 High; 2 Other Level
28 Regular; 1 Special Education; 0 Vocational; 3 Alternative
0 Magnet; 0 Charter; 17 Title I Eligible; 16 School-wide Title I
Students: 29,749 (50.8% male; 49.2% female)
Individual Education Program: 2,690 (9.0%);
English Language Learner: 10,697 (36.0%); Migrant: 3 (<0.1%)
Eligible for Free Lunch Program: 10,814 (36.4%)
Eligible for Reduced-Price Lunch Program: 2,666 (9.0%)
Teachers: 1,423.0 (20.9 to 1)
Librarians/Media Specialists: 0.0 (0.0 to 1)
Guidance Counselors: 27.8 (1,070.1 to 1)
Current Spending: ($ per student per year):
Total: $6,554; Instruction: $4,432; Support Services: $1,886
Enrollment, Drop-out Rates and Diploma Recipients by Race/Ethnicity

Category	Total	White	Black	Asian	AIAN	Hisp.
Enrollment (%)	100.0	57.3	1.1	18.6	0.1	22.6
Drop-out Rate (%)	n/a	n/a	n/a	n/a	n/a	n/a
H.S. Diplomas (#)	2,002	1,278	14	392	5	313

Glendora Unified
500 N Loraine Ave • Glendora, CA 91741-2964
(626) 963-1611 • http://www.glendora.k12.ca.us/
Grade Span: KG-12; **Agency Type:** 1
Schools: 10
6 Primary; 2 Middle; 2 High; 0 Other Level
9 Regular; 0 Special Education; 0 Vocational; 1 Alternative
0 Magnet; 0 Charter; 5 Title I Eligible; 0 School-wide Title I
Students: 7,996 (50.5% male; 49.5% female)
Individual Education Program: 793 (9.9%);
English Language Learner: 246 (3.1%); Migrant: 4 (0.1%)
Eligible for Free Lunch Program: 868 (10.9%)
Eligible for Reduced-Price Lunch Program: 346 (4.3%)
Teachers: 349.7 (22.9 to 1)
Librarians/Media Specialists: 1.0 (7,996.0 to 1)
Guidance Counselors: 8.0 (999.5 to 1)
Current Spending: ($ per student per year):
Total: $5,685; Instruction: $3,707; Support Services: $1,782
Enrollment, Drop-out Rates and Diploma Recipients by Race/Ethnicity

Category	Total	White	Black	Asian	AIAN	Hisp.
Enrollment (%)	100.0	70.8	2.0	6.3	0.4	20.5
Drop-out Rate (%)	n/a	n/a	n/a	n/a	n/a	n/a
H.S. Diplomas (#)	577	405	7	53	4	95

Gorman Elementary
49847 Gorman School Rd • Gorman, CA 93243-0104
Mailing Address: PO Box 104 • Gorman, CA 93243-0104
(661) 248-6816
Grade Span: KG-12; **Agency Type:** 1
Schools: 4
1 Primary; 1 Middle; 1 High; 1 Other Level
4 Regular; 0 Special Education; 0 Vocational; 0 Alternative
0 Magnet; 3 Charter; 4 Title I Eligible; 0 School-wide Title I
Students: 1,771 (48.3% male; 51.7% female)
Individual Education Program: 85 (4.8%);
English Language Learner: 77 (4.3%); Migrant: 0 (0.0%)
Eligible for Free Lunch Program: 294 (16.6%)
Eligible for Reduced-Price Lunch Program: 399 (22.5%)
Teachers: 65.8 (26.9 to 1)
Librarians/Media Specialists: 0.0 (0.0 to 1)
Guidance Counselors: 2.0 (885.5 to 1)
Current Spending: ($ per student per year):
Total: $5,376; Instruction: $4,133; Support Services: $1,201
Enrollment, Drop-out Rates and Diploma Recipients by Race/Ethnicity

Category	Total	White	Black	Asian	AIAN	Hisp.
Enrollment (%)	100.0	50.8	15.2	4.9	0.8	21.5
Drop-out Rate (%)	n/a	n/a	n/a	n/a	n/a	n/a
H.S. Diplomas (#)	28	21	3	1	0	2

Hacienda La Puente Unified
15959 E Gale Ave • City Of Industry, CA 91716-0002
Mailing Address: PO Box 60002 • City Of Industry, CA 91716-0002
(626) 933-1000
Grade Span: KG-12; **Agency Type:** 1
Schools: 37
24 Primary; 5 Middle; 5 High; 3 Other Level
34 Regular; 1 Special Education; 0 Vocational; 2 Alternative
0 Magnet; 1 Charter; 23 Title I Eligible; 16 School-wide Title I
Students: 25,184 (51.2% male; 48.8% female)
Individual Education Program: 2,498 (9.9%);
English Language Learner: 6,905 (27.4%); Migrant: 610 (2.4%)
Eligible for Free Lunch Program: 13,131 (52.1%)
Eligible for Reduced-Price Lunch Program: 4,262 (16.9%)
Teachers: 1,144.9 (22.0 to 1)
Librarians/Media Specialists: 0.0 (0.0 to 1)
Guidance Counselors: 23.9 (1,053.7 to 1)
Current Spending: ($ per student per year):
Total: $5,905; Instruction: $3,684; Support Services: $1,941
Enrollment, Drop-out Rates and Diploma Recipients by Race/Ethnicity

Category	Total	White	Black	Asian	AIAN	Hisp.
Enrollment (%)	100.0	8.1	2.8	17.3	0.4	71.1
Drop-out Rate (%)	n/a	n/a	n/a	n/a	n/a	n/a
H.S. Diplomas (#)	1,345	139	55	359	4	768

Hawthorne Elementary
14120 S Hawthorne Blvd • Hawthorne, CA 90250-5210
(310) 676-2276 • http://www.hawthorne.k12.ca.us/
Grade Span: KG-08; **Agency Type:** 1
Schools: 11
8 Primary; 3 Middle; 0 High; 0 Other Level
11 Regular; 0 Special Education; 0 Vocational; 0 Alternative
0 Magnet; 0 Charter; 11 Title I Eligible; 10 School-wide Title I
Students: 9,835 (51.3% male; 48.7% female)
Individual Education Program: 931 (9.5%);
English Language Learner: 4,564 (46.4%); Migrant: 0 (0.0%)
Eligible for Free Lunch Program: 6,771 (68.8%)
Eligible for Reduced-Price Lunch Program: 1,459 (14.8%)
Teachers: 471.5 (20.9 to 1)
Librarians/Media Specialists: 0.0 (0.0 to 1)
Guidance Counselors: 9.0 (1,092.8 to 1)
Current Spending: ($ per student per year):
Total: $6,348; Instruction: $3,939; Support Services: $2,019
Enrollment, Drop-out Rates and Diploma Recipients by Race/Ethnicity

Category	Total	White	Black	Asian	AIAN	Hisp.
Enrollment (%)	100.0	3.1	29.3	6.1	0.2	59.9
Drop-out Rate (%)	n/a	n/a	n/a	n/a	n/a	n/a
H.S. Diplomas (#)	n/a	n/a	n/a	n/a	n/a	n/a

Inglewood Unified
401 S Inglewood Ave • Inglewood, CA 90301-2501
(310) 419-2700 • http://inglewood.k12.ca.us/
Grade Span: KG-12; **Agency Type:** 1
Schools: 19
13 Primary; 2 Middle; 4 High; 0 Other Level
18 Regular; 0 Special Education; 0 Vocational; 1 Alternative
6 Magnet; 0 Charter; 18 Title I Eligible; 15 School-wide Title I
Students: 17,741 (51.2% male; 48.8% female)
Individual Education Program: 1,272 (7.2%);
English Language Learner: 6,011 (33.9%); Migrant: 0 (0.0%)

Eligible for Free Lunch Program: 7,891 (44.5%)
Eligible for Reduced-Price Lunch Program: 1,610 (9.1%)
Teachers: 823.9 (21.5 to 1)
Librarians/Media Specialists: 3.0 (5,913.7 to 1)
Guidance Counselors: 15.0 (1,182.7 to 1)
Current Spending: ($ per student per year):
Total: $6,311; Instruction: $4,076; Support Services: $1,963
Enrollment, Drop-out Rates and Diploma Recipients by Race/Ethnicity

Category	Total	White	Black	Asian	AIAN	Hisp.
Enrollment (%)	100.0	0.7	40.5	1.0	0.0	57.8
Drop-out Rate (%)	n/a	n/a	n/a	n/a	n/a	n/a
H.S. Diplomas (#)	666	4	284	7	0	371

Keppel Union Elementary

34004 128th St, E • Pearblossom, CA 93553-0186
Mailing Address: PO Box 186 • Pearblossom, CA 93553-0186
(661) 944-2155 • http://www.keppel.k12.ca.us/
Grade Span: KG-08; **Agency Type:** 1
Schools: 6
5 Primary; 1 Middle; 0 High; 0 Other Level
6 Regular; 0 Special Education; 0 Vocational; 0 Alternative
0 Magnet; 0 Charter; 3 Title I Eligible; 0 School-wide Title I
Students: 2,924 (51.8% male; 48.2% female)
Individual Education Program: 353 (12.1%);
English Language Learner: 589 (20.1%); Migrant: 344 (11.8%)
Eligible for Free Lunch Program: 1,701 (58.2%)
Eligible for Reduced-Price Lunch Program: 383 (13.1%)
Teachers: 134.2 (21.8 to 1)
Librarians/Media Specialists: 0.0 (0.0 to 1)
Guidance Counselors: 1.0 (2,924.0 to 1)
Current Spending: ($ per student per year):
Total: $6,213; Instruction: $3,961; Support Services: $1,914
Enrollment, Drop-out Rates and Diploma Recipients by Race/Ethnicity

Category	Total	White	Black	Asian	AIAN	Hisp.
Enrollment (%)	100.0	33.7	12.4	1.2	1.2	50.2
Drop-out Rate (%)	n/a	n/a	n/a	n/a	n/a	n/a
H.S. Diplomas (#)	n/a	n/a	n/a	n/a	n/a	n/a

La Canada Unified

5039 Palm Dr • La Canada, CA 91011-1518
(818) 952-8300 • http://www.lcusd.net/
Grade Span: KG-12; **Agency Type:** 1
Schools: 5
3 Primary; 0 Middle; 1 High; 1 Other Level
4 Regular; 1 Special Education; 0 Vocational; 0 Alternative
0 Magnet; 0 Charter; 0 Title I Eligible; 0 School-wide Title I
Students: 4,363 (51.4% male; 48.6% female)
Individual Education Program: 396 (9.1%);
English Language Learner: 104 (2.4%); Migrant: 0 (0.0%)
Eligible for Free Lunch Program: 18 (0.4%)
Eligible for Reduced-Price Lunch Program: 13 (0.3%)
Teachers: 193.9 (22.5 to 1)
Librarians/Media Specialists: 1.0 (4,363.0 to 1)
Guidance Counselors: 6.0 (727.2 to 1)
Current Spending: ($ per student per year):
Total: $6,530; Instruction: $4,266; Support Services: $2,116
Enrollment, Drop-out Rates and Diploma Recipients by Race/Ethnicity

Category	Total	White	Black	Asian	AIAN	Hisp.
Enrollment (%)	100.0	71.1	0.2	24.3	0.0	3.3
Drop-out Rate (%)	n/a	n/a	n/a	n/a	n/a	n/a
H.S. Diplomas (#)	325	212	2	104	0	3

Lancaster Elementary

44711 N Cedar Ave • Lancaster, CA 93534-3210
(661) 948-4661 • http://www.lancaster.k12.ca.us/
Grade Span: KG-08; **Agency Type:** 1
Schools: 18
14 Primary; 4 Middle; 0 High; 0 Other Level
16 Regular; 0 Special Education; 0 Vocational; 2 Alternative
0 Magnet; 0 Charter; 17 Title I Eligible; 9 School-wide Title I
Students: 15,576 (51.0% male; 49.0% female)
Individual Education Program: 2,116 (13.6%);
English Language Learner: 2,061 (13.2%); Migrant: 407 (2.6%)
Eligible for Free Lunch Program: 8,009 (51.4%)
Eligible for Reduced-Price Lunch Program: 1,581 (10.2%)
Teachers: 729.5 (21.4 to 1)
Librarians/Media Specialists: 0.0 (0.0 to 1)
Guidance Counselors: 0.0 (0.0 to 1)
Current Spending: ($ per student per year):
Total: $6,057; Instruction: $3,983; Support Services: $1,827
Enrollment, Drop-out Rates and Diploma Recipients by Race/Ethnicity

Category	Total	White	Black	Asian	AIAN	Hisp.
Enrollment (%)	100.0	33.1	27.7	3.3	0.8	35.0
Drop-out Rate (%)	n/a	n/a	n/a	n/a	n/a	n/a
H.S. Diplomas (#)	n/a	n/a	n/a	n/a	n/a	n/a

Las Virgenes Unified

4111 N Las Virgenes Rd • Calabasas, CA 91302-1929
(818) 880-4000 • http://www.lvusd.k12.ca.us/
Grade Span: KG-12; **Agency Type:** 1
Schools: 13
8 Primary; 2 Middle; 3 High; 0 Other Level
12 Regular; 0 Special Education; 0 Vocational; 1 Alternative
0 Magnet; 0 Charter; 0 Title I Eligible; 0 School-wide Title I
Students: 12,119 (51.3% male; 48.7% female)
Individual Education Program: 1,268 (10.5%);
English Language Learner: 556 (4.6%); Migrant: 0 (0.0%)
Eligible for Free Lunch Program: 187 (1.5%)
Eligible for Reduced-Price Lunch Program: 172 (1.4%)
Teachers: 538.3 (22.5 to 1)
Librarians/Media Specialists: 4.8 (2,524.8 to 1)
Guidance Counselors: 13.1 (925.1 to 1)
Current Spending: ($ per student per year):
Total: $6,092; Instruction: $4,108; Support Services: $1,854
Enrollment, Drop-out Rates and Diploma Recipients by Race/Ethnicity

Category	Total	White	Black	Asian	AIAN	Hisp.
Enrollment (%)	100.0	84.3	1.6	7.6	0.2	5.3
Drop-out Rate (%)	n/a	n/a	n/a	n/a	n/a	n/a
H.S. Diplomas (#)	861	754	12	64	1	27

Lawndale Elementary

4161 W 147th St • Lawndale, CA 90260-1709
(310) 973-1300 • http://www.lawndale.k12.ca.us/
Grade Span: KG-12; **Agency Type:** 1
Schools: 8
6 Primary; 1 Middle; 1 High; 0 Other Level
8 Regular; 0 Special Education; 0 Vocational; 0 Alternative
0 Magnet; 1 Charter; 8 Title I Eligible; 7 School-wide Title I
Students: 6,394 (52.0% male; 48.0% female)
Individual Education Program: 804 (12.6%);
English Language Learner: 2,580 (40.4%); Migrant: 0 (0.0%)
Eligible for Free Lunch Program: 3,647 (57.0%)
Eligible for Reduced-Price Lunch Program: 1,107 (17.3%)
Teachers: 307.1 (20.8 to 1)
Librarians/Media Specialists: 1.3 (4,918.5 to 1)
Guidance Counselors: 2.9 (2,204.8 to 1)
Current Spending: ($ per student per year):
Total: $6,770; Instruction: $4,483; Support Services: $1,949
Enrollment, Drop-out Rates and Diploma Recipients by Race/Ethnicity

Category	Total	White	Black	Asian	AIAN	Hisp.
Enrollment (%)	100.0	8.4	14.8	9.0	0.4	67.2
Drop-out Rate (%)	n/a	n/a	n/a	n/a	n/a	n/a
H.S. Diplomas (#)	0	0	0	0	0	0

Lennox Elementary

10319 S Firmona Ave • Lennox, CA 90304-1419
(310) 330-4950 • http://www.lennox.k12.ca.us/
Grade Span: KG-12; **Agency Type:** 1
Schools: 7
5 Primary; 1 Middle; 1 High; 0 Other Level
7 Regular; 0 Special Education; 0 Vocational; 0 Alternative
0 Magnet; 1 Charter; 7 Title I Eligible; 5 School-wide Title I
Students: 7,521 (51.3% male; 48.7% female)
Individual Education Program: 635 (8.4%);
English Language Learner: 5,357 (71.2%); Migrant: 0 (0.0%)
Eligible for Free Lunch Program: 6,295 (83.7%)
Eligible for Reduced-Price Lunch Program: 773 (10.3%)
Teachers: 347.3 (21.7 to 1)
Librarians/Media Specialists: 0.0 (0.0 to 1)
Guidance Counselors: 12.5 (601.7 to 1)
Current Spending: ($ per student per year):
Total: $6,209; Instruction: $4,385; Support Services: $1,438
Enrollment, Drop-out Rates and Diploma Recipients by Race/Ethnicity

Category	Total	White	Black	Asian	AIAN	Hisp.
Enrollment (%)	100.0	0.5	2.3	1.1	0.1	95.6
Drop-out Rate (%)	n/a	n/a	n/a	n/a	n/a	n/a
H.S. Diplomas (#)	0	0	0	0	0	0

Little Lake City Elementary

10515 S Pioneer Blvd • Santa Fe Springs, CA 90670-3703
(562) 868-8241 • http://www.littlelake.k12.ca.us/
Grade Span: KG-08; **Agency Type:** 1
Schools: 9
7 Primary; 2 Middle; 0 High; 0 Other Level
9 Regular; 0 Special Education; 0 Vocational; 0 Alternative
0 Magnet; 0 Charter; 5 Title I Eligible; 0 School-wide Title I
Students: 5,226 (51.6% male; 48.4% female)
Individual Education Program: 619 (11.8%);
English Language Learner: 1,230 (23.5%); Migrant: 87 (1.7%)
Eligible for Free Lunch Program: 2,232 (42.7%)
Eligible for Reduced-Price Lunch Program: 1,047 (20.0%)

Teachers: 243.4 (21.5 to 1)
Librarians/Media Specialists: 0.0 (0.0 to 1)
Guidance Counselors: 2.0 (2,613.0 to 1)
Current Spending: ($ per student per year):
Total: $6,848; Instruction: $4,660; Support Services: $1,870
Enrollment, Drop-out Rates and Diploma Recipients by Race/Ethnicity

Category	Total	White	Black	Asian	AIAN	Hisp.
Enrollment (%)	100.0	10.4	3.1	4.2	0.3	82.0
Drop-out Rate (%)	n/a	n/a	n/a	n/a	n/a	n/a
H.S. Diplomas (#)	n/a	n/a	n/a	n/a	n/a	n/a

Long Beach Unified

1515 Hughes Way • Long Beach, CA 90810-1839
(562) 997-8000 • http://www.lbusd.k12.ca.us/
Grade Span: KG-12; **Agency Type:** 1
Schools: 89
60 Primary; 15 Middle; 11 High; 3 Other Level
86 Regular; 0 Special Education; 0 Vocational; 3 Alternative
44 Magnet; 4 Charter; 71 Title I Eligible; 59 School-wide Title I
Students: 97,212 (50.8% male; 49.2% female)
Individual Education Program: 7,660 (7.9%);
English Language Learner: 31,852 (32.8%); Migrant: 2,906 (3.0%)
Eligible for Free Lunch Program: 52,563 (54.1%)
Eligible for Reduced-Price Lunch Program: 10,953 (11.3%)
Teachers: 4,520.8 (21.5 to 1)
Librarians/Media Specialists: 63.8 (1,523.7 to 1)
Guidance Counselors: 158.2 (614.5 to 1)
Current Spending: ($ per student per year):
Total: $6,840; Instruction: $4,409; Support Services: $2,126
Enrollment, Drop-out Rates and Diploma Recipients by Race/Ethnicity

Category	Total	White	Black	Asian	AIAN	Hisp.
Enrollment (%)	100.0	17.1	18.8	15.6	0.3	48.1
Drop-out Rate (%)	n/a	n/a	n/a	n/a	n/a	n/a
H.S. Diplomas (#)	4,664	1,006	928	1,174	21	1,535

Los Angeles County Office of Ed

9300 Imperial Hwy • Downey, CA 90242-2813
(562) 922-6127 • http://www.lacoe.edu/
Grade Span: KG-12; **Agency Type:** 4
Schools: 14
1 Primary; 0 Middle; 7 High; 6 Other Level
3 Regular; 1 Special Education; 0 Vocational; 10 Alternative
0 Magnet; 2 Charter; 1 Title I Eligible; 0 School-wide Title I
Students: 11,441 (68.0% male; 32.0% female)
Individual Education Program: 7,192 (62.9%);
English Language Learner: 3,570 (31.2%); Migrant: 114 (1.0%)
Eligible for Free Lunch Program: 2,879 (25.2%)
Eligible for Reduced-Price Lunch Program: 203 (1.8%)
Teachers: 1,011.0 (11.3 to 1)
Librarians/Media Specialists: 1.0 (11,441.0 to 1)
Guidance Counselors: 29.2 (391.8 to 1)
Current Spending: ($ per student per year):
Total: $31,095; Instruction: $17,101; Support Services: $13,993
Enrollment, Drop-out Rates and Diploma Recipients by Race/Ethnicity

Category	Total	White	Black	Asian	AIAN	Hisp.
Enrollment (%)	100.0	14.5	25.3	6.6	0.5	51.5
Drop-out Rate (%)	n/a	n/a	n/a	n/a	n/a	n/a
H.S. Diplomas (#)	851	76	224	96	22	417

Los Angeles Unified

333 S Beaudry Ave • Los Angeles, CA 90017
(213) 241-1000 • http://www.lausd.k12.ca.us/
Grade Span: KG-12; **Agency Type:** 1
Schools: 677
463 Primary; 78 Middle; 108 High; 28 Other Level
597 Regular; 18 Special Education; 0 Vocational; 62 Alternative
130 Magnet; 49 Charter; 570 Title I Eligible; 279 School-wide Title I
Students: 746,852 (51.0% male; 49.0% female)
Individual Education Program: 85,529 (11.5%);
English Language Learner: 320,594 (42.9%); Migrant: 3,540 (0.5%)
Eligible for Free Lunch Program: 501,670 (67.2%)
Eligible for Reduced-Price Lunch Program: 53,447 (7.2%)
Teachers: 35,483.0 (21.0 to 1)
Librarians/Media Specialists: 88.2 (8,467.7 to 1)
Guidance Counselors: 894.7 (834.8 to 1)
Current Spending: ($ per student per year):
Total: $7,384; Instruction: $4,790; Support Services: $2,254
Enrollment, Drop-out Rates and Diploma Recipients by Race/Ethnicity

Category	Total	White	Black	Asian	AIAN	Hisp.
Enrollment (%)	100.0	9.4	12.1	6.3	0.3	71.9
Drop-out Rate (%)	n/a	n/a	n/a	n/a	n/a	n/a
H.S. Diplomas (#)	27,720	4,285	3,836	3,037	90	16,472

Los Nietos Elementary

8324 S Westman Ave • Whittier, CA 90606-2405
Mailing Address: PO Box 2405 • Whittier, CA 90606-2405
(562) 692-0271 • http://www.losnietos.k12.ca.us/
Grade Span: KG-08; **Agency Type:** 1
Schools: 4
3 Primary; 1 Middle; 0 High; 0 Other Level
4 Regular; 0 Special Education; 0 Vocational; 0 Alternative
0 Magnet; 0 Charter; 4 Title I Eligible; 4 School-wide Title I
Students: 2,350 (51.2% male; 48.8% female)
Individual Education Program: 255 (10.9%);
English Language Learner: 833 (35.4%); Migrant: 81 (3.4%)
Eligible for Free Lunch Program: 2,338 (99.5%)
Eligible for Reduced-Price Lunch Program: 0 (0.0%)
Teachers: 116.0 (20.3 to 1)
Librarians/Media Specialists: 0.0 (0.0 to 1)
Guidance Counselors: 1.0 (2,350.0 to 1)
Current Spending: ($ per student per year):
Total: $6,271; Instruction: $4,057; Support Services: $1,921
Enrollment, Drop-out Rates and Diploma Recipients by Race/Ethnicity

Category	Total	White	Black	Asian	AIAN	Hisp.
Enrollment (%)	100.0	4.2	0.9	0.7	0.2	94.1
Drop-out Rate (%)	n/a	n/a	n/a	n/a	n/a	n/a
H.S. Diplomas (#)	n/a	n/a	n/a	n/a	n/a	n/a

Lowell Joint

11019 Valley Home Ave • Whittier, CA 90603-3042
(562) 943-0211 • http://www.ljsd.k12.ca.us/
Grade Span: KG-08; **Agency Type:** 1
Schools: 6
5 Primary; 1 Middle; 0 High; 0 Other Level
6 Regular; 0 Special Education; 0 Vocational; 0 Alternative
0 Magnet; 0 Charter; 3 Title I Eligible; 0 School-wide Title I
Students: 3,384 (51.2% male; 48.8% female)
Individual Education Program: 361 (10.7%);
English Language Learner: 332 (9.8%); Migrant: 0 (0.0%)
Eligible for Free Lunch Program: 409 (12.1%)
Eligible for Reduced-Price Lunch Program: 163 (4.8%)
Teachers: 151.8 (22.3 to 1)
Librarians/Media Specialists: 0.0 (0.0 to 1)
Guidance Counselors: 0.0 (0.0 to 1)
Current Spending: ($ per student per year):
Total: $6,084; Instruction: $3,740; Support Services: $2,168
Enrollment, Drop-out Rates and Diploma Recipients by Race/Ethnicity

Category	Total	White	Black	Asian	AIAN	Hisp.
Enrollment (%)	100.0	51.1	1.7	4.3	0.1	39.5
Drop-out Rate (%)	n/a	n/a	n/a	n/a	n/a	n/a
H.S. Diplomas (#)	n/a	n/a	n/a	n/a	n/a	n/a

Lynwood Unified

11321 Bullis Rd • Lynwood, CA 90262-3600
(310) 886-1600 • http://www.lynwood.k12.ca.us
Grade Span: KG-12; **Agency Type:** 1
Schools: 15
10 Primary; 2 Middle; 3 High; 0 Other Level
14 Regular; 0 Special Education; 0 Vocational; 1 Alternative
1 Magnet; 0 Charter; 15 Title I Eligible; 2 School-wide Title I
Students: 19,464 (50.8% male; 49.2% female)
Individual Education Program: 778 (4.0%);
English Language Learner: 9,864 (50.7%); Migrant: 587 (3.0%)
Eligible for Free Lunch Program: 10,981 (56.4%)
Eligible for Reduced-Price Lunch Program: 1,025 (5.3%)
Teachers: 771.0 (25.2 to 1)
Librarians/Media Specialists: 2.0 (9,732.0 to 1)
Guidance Counselors: 17.0 (1,144.9 to 1)
Current Spending: ($ per student per year):
Total: $5,652; Instruction: $3,672; Support Services: $1,757
Enrollment, Drop-out Rates and Diploma Recipients by Race/Ethnicity

Category	Total	White	Black	Asian	AIAN	Hisp.
Enrollment (%)	100.0	0.3	10.3	1.4	0.1	87.4
Drop-out Rate (%)	n/a	n/a	n/a	n/a	n/a	n/a
H.S. Diplomas (#)	824	1	142	21	0	660

Manhattan Beach Unified

1230 Rosecrans Ste 400 • Manhattan Beach, CA 90266-2478
(310) 725-9050 • http://www.manhattan.k12.ca.us/
Grade Span: KG-12; **Agency Type:** 1
Schools: 7
5 Primary; 1 Middle; 1 High; 0 Other Level
7 Regular; 0 Special Education; 0 Vocational; 0 Alternative
0 Magnet; 0 Charter; 1 Title I Eligible; 0 School-wide Title I
Students: 6,465 (51.8% male; 48.2% female)
Individual Education Program: 658 (10.2%);
English Language Learner: 109 (1.7%); Migrant: 0 (0.0%)
Eligible for Free Lunch Program: 204 (3.2%)

Eligible for Reduced-Price Lunch Program: 82 (1.3%)
Teachers: 320.9 (20.1 to 1)
Librarians/Media Specialists: 1.0 (6,465.0 to 1)
Guidance Counselors: 11.0 (587.7 to 1)
Current Spending: ($ per student per year):
Total: $7,417; Instruction: $4,688; Support Services: $2,419
Enrollment, Drop-out Rates and Diploma Recipients by Race/Ethnicity

Category	Total	White	Black	Asian	AIAN	Hisp.
Enrollment (%)	100.0	77.2	1.7	9.6	0.3	8.2
Drop-out Rate (%)	n/a	n/a	n/a	n/a	n/a	n/a
H.S. Diplomas (#)	502	390	16	33	0	63

Monrovia Unified

325 E Huntington Dr • Monrovia, CA 91016-3585
(626) 471-2000 • http://www.monroviaschools.net/home.html
Grade Span: KG-12; **Agency Type:** 1
Schools: 11
6 Primary; 2 Middle; 2 High; 1 Other Level
10 Regular; 0 Special Education; 0 Vocational; 1 Alternative
0 Magnet; 0 Charter; 6 Title I Eligible; 0 School-wide Title I
Students: 6,695 (51.3% male; 48.7% female)
Individual Education Program: 507 (7.6%);
English Language Learner: 1,250 (18.7%); Migrant: 26 (0.4%)
Eligible for Free Lunch Program: 2,742 (41.0%)
Eligible for Reduced-Price Lunch Program: 1,018 (15.2%)
Teachers: 323.2 (20.7 to 1)
Librarians/Media Specialists: 0.0 (0.0 to 1)
Guidance Counselors: 6.5 (1,030.0 to 1)
Current Spending: ($ per student per year):
Total: $6,526; Instruction: $4,183; Support Services: $2,074
Enrollment, Drop-out Rates and Diploma Recipients by Race/Ethnicity

Category	Total	White	Black	Asian	AIAN	Hisp.
Enrollment (%)	100.0	28.1	12.8	4.9	0.7	51.8
Drop-out Rate (%)	n/a	n/a	n/a	n/a	n/a	n/a
H.S. Diplomas (#)	366	151	50	16	1	148

Montebello Unified

123 S Montebello Blvd • Montebello, CA 90640-4729
(323) 887-7900 • http://www.montebello.k12.ca.us/
Grade Span: KG-12; **Agency Type:** 1
Schools: 29
18 Primary; 6 Middle; 5 High; 0 Other Level
27 Regular; 0 Special Education; 0 Vocational; 2 Alternative
0 Magnet; 0 Charter; 29 Title I Eligible; 28 School-wide Title I
Students: 35,590 (50.7% male; 49.3% female)
Individual Education Program: 2,941 (8.3%);
English Language Learner: 16,295 (45.8%); Migrant: 16 (<0.1%)
Eligible for Free Lunch Program: 21,342 (60.0%)
Eligible for Reduced-Price Lunch Program: 4,911 (13.8%)
Teachers: 1,487.5 (23.9 to 1)
Librarians/Media Specialists: 10.0 (3,559.0 to 1)
Guidance Counselors: 39.0 (912.6 to 1)
Current Spending: ($ per student per year):
Total: $6,426; Instruction: $4,077; Support Services: $2,081
Enrollment, Drop-out Rates and Diploma Recipients by Race/Ethnicity

Category	Total	White	Black	Asian	AIAN	Hisp.
Enrollment (%)	100.0	2.7	0.4	4.1	0.1	92.6
Drop-out Rate (%)	n/a	n/a	n/a	n/a	n/a	n/a
H.S. Diplomas (#)	1,543	53	6	148	1	1,335

Mountain View Elementary

3320 Gilman Rd • El Monte, CA 91732-3226
(626) 652-4000 • http://www.mvsd.k12.ca.us/index.htm
Grade Span: KG-08; **Agency Type:** 1
Schools: 12
10 Primary; 2 Middle; 0 High; 0 Other Level
12 Regular; 0 Special Education; 0 Vocational; 0 Alternative
0 Magnet; 0 Charter; 12 Title I Eligible; 0 School-wide Title I
Students: 10,497 (51.7% male; 48.3% female)
Individual Education Program: 942 (9.0%);
English Language Learner: 6,471 (61.6%); Migrant: 386 (3.7%)
Eligible for Free Lunch Program: 7,910 (75.4%)
Eligible for Reduced-Price Lunch Program: 363 (3.5%)
Teachers: 485.3 (21.6 to 1)
Librarians/Media Specialists: 1.0 (10,497.0 to 1)
Guidance Counselors: 2.0 (5,248.5 to 1)
Current Spending: ($ per student per year):
Total: $6,567; Instruction: $4,597; Support Services: $1,517
Enrollment, Drop-out Rates and Diploma Recipients by Race/Ethnicity

Category	Total	White	Black	Asian	AIAN	Hisp.
Enrollment (%)	100.0	1.2	0.3	6.8	0.0	91.4
Drop-out Rate (%)	n/a	n/a	n/a	n/a	n/a	n/a
H.S. Diplomas (#)	n/a	n/a	n/a	n/a	n/a	n/a

Newhall Elementary

25375 Orchard Village, Ste 20 • Valencia, CA 91355-3055
(661) 286-2200 • http://www.newhall.k12.ca.us/
Grade Span: KG-06; **Agency Type:** 1
Schools: 7
7 Primary; 0 Middle; 0 High; 0 Other Level
7 Regular; 0 Special Education; 0 Vocational; 0 Alternative
0 Magnet; 0 Charter; 4 Title I Eligible; 0 School-wide Title I
Students: 6,555 (51.3% male; 48.7% female)
Individual Education Program: 577 (8.8%);
English Language Learner: 1,218 (18.6%); Migrant: 0 (0.0%)
Eligible for Free Lunch Program: 1,539 (23.5%)
Eligible for Reduced-Price Lunch Program: 343 (5.2%)
Teachers: 297.5 (22.0 to 1)
Librarians/Media Specialists: 0.0 (0.0 to 1)
Guidance Counselors: 1.9 (3,450.0 to 1)
Current Spending: ($ per student per year):
Total: $5,742; Instruction: $3,800; Support Services: $1,942
Enrollment, Drop-out Rates and Diploma Recipients by Race/Ethnicity

Category	Total	White	Black	Asian	AIAN	Hisp.
Enrollment (%)	100.0	56.7	2.7	8.2	0.1	32.3
Drop-out Rate (%)	n/a	n/a	n/a	n/a	n/a	n/a
H.S. Diplomas (#)	n/a	n/a	n/a	n/a	n/a	n/a

Norwalk-La Mirada Unified

12820 Pioneer Blvd • Norwalk, CA 90650-2894
(562) 868-0431 • http://www.nlmusd.k12.ca.us/
Grade Span: KG-12; **Agency Type:** 1
Schools: 29
18 Primary; 7 Middle; 4 High; 0 Other Level
28 Regular; 0 Special Education; 0 Vocational; 1 Alternative
0 Magnet; 0 Charter; 11 Title I Eligible; 5 School-wide Title I
Students: 24,093 (51.6% male; 48.4% female)
Individual Education Program: 2,417 (10.0%);
English Language Learner: 4,818 (20.0%); Migrant: 1,161 (4.8%)
Eligible for Free Lunch Program: 9,847 (40.9%)
Eligible for Reduced-Price Lunch Program: 2,196 (9.1%)
Teachers: 1,091.1 (22.1 to 1)
Librarians/Media Specialists: 1.8 (13,385.0 to 1)
Guidance Counselors: 26.6 (905.8 to 1)
Current Spending: ($ per student per year):
Total: $6,546; Instruction: $4,039; Support Services: $2,240
Enrollment, Drop-out Rates and Diploma Recipients by Race/Ethnicity

Category	Total	White	Black	Asian	AIAN	Hisp.
Enrollment (%)	100.0	17.7	4.5	8.1	0.4	69.1
Drop-out Rate (%)	n/a	n/a	n/a	n/a	n/a	n/a
H.S. Diplomas (#)	1,192	276	67	133	5	711

Palmdale Elementary

39139 10th St E • Palmdale, CA 93550-3419
(661) 947-7191 • http://www.psd.k12.ca.us/
Grade Span: KG-08; **Agency Type:** 1
Schools: 25
22 Primary; 3 Middle; 0 High; 0 Other Level
23 Regular; 0 Special Education; 0 Vocational; 2 Alternative
1 Magnet; 1 Charter; 23 Title I Eligible; 14 School-wide Title I
Students: 22,524 (51.4% male; 48.6% female)
Individual Education Program: 3,078 (13.7%);
English Language Learner: 5,420 (24.1%); Migrant: 384 (1.7%)
Eligible for Free Lunch Program: 11,529 (51.2%)
Eligible for Reduced-Price Lunch Program: 3,545 (15.7%)
Teachers: 1,047.5 (21.5 to 1)
Librarians/Media Specialists: 0.0 (0.0 to 1)
Guidance Counselors: 3.0 (7,508.0 to 1)
Current Spending: ($ per student per year):
Total: $6,817; Instruction: $4,467; Support Services: $2,024
Enrollment, Drop-out Rates and Diploma Recipients by Race/Ethnicity

Category	Total	White	Black	Asian	AIAN	Hisp.
Enrollment (%)	100.0	23.1	23.2	3.8	0.8	48.2
Drop-out Rate (%)	n/a	n/a	n/a	n/a	n/a	n/a
H.S. Diplomas (#)	n/a	n/a	n/a	n/a	n/a	n/a

Palos Verdes Peninsula Unified

3801 Via La Selva • Palos Verdes Estates, CA 90274-1119
(310) 378-9966
Grade Span: KG-12; **Agency Type:** 1
Schools: 17
11 Primary; 3 Middle; 2 High; 1 Other Level
16 Regular; 0 Special Education; 0 Vocational; 1 Alternative
0 Magnet; 0 Charter; 7 Title I Eligible; 0 School-wide Title I
Students: 11,223 (51.2% male; 48.8% female)
Individual Education Program: 1,206 (10.7%);
English Language Learner: 731 (6.5%); Migrant: 0 (0.0%)
Eligible for Free Lunch Program: 163 (1.5%)
Eligible for Reduced-Price Lunch Program: 65 (0.6%)

Teachers: 523.7 (21.4 to 1)
Librarians/Media Specialists: 1.0 (11,223.0 to 1)
Guidance Counselors: 15.4 (728.8 to 1)
Current Spending: ($ per student per year):
Total: $6,149; Instruction: $3,960; Support Services: $1,815
Enrollment, Drop-out Rates and Diploma Recipients by Race/Ethnicity

Category	Total	White	Black	Asian	AIAN	Hisp.
Enrollment (%)	100.0	66.7	1.6	27.8	0.1	3.8
Drop-out Rate (%)	n/a	n/a	n/a	n/a	n/a	n/a
H.S. Diplomas (#)	736	440	15	250	1	30

Paramount Unified
15110 California Ave • Paramount, CA 90723-4320
(562) 602-6000 • http://www.paramount.k12.ca.us/index.html
Grade Span: KG-12; **Agency Type:** 1
Schools: 18
14 Primary; 0 Middle; 4 High; 0 Other Level
16 Regular; 0 Special Education; 0 Vocational; 2 Alternative
1 Magnet; 0 Charter; 18 Title I Eligible; 12 School-wide Title I
Students: 17,229 (50.1% male; 49.9% female)
Individual Education Program: 1,372 (8.0%);
English Language Learner: 7,662 (44.5%); Migrant: 313 (1.8%)
Eligible for Free Lunch Program: 12,431 (72.2%)
Eligible for Reduced-Price Lunch Program: 2,285 (13.3%)
Teachers: 779.6 (22.1 to 1)
Librarians/Media Specialists: 0.0 (0.0 to 1)
Guidance Counselors: 25.8 (667.8 to 1)
Current Spending: ($ per student per year):
Total: $6,265; Instruction: $3,947; Support Services: $2,000
Enrollment, Drop-out Rates and Diploma Recipients by Race/Ethnicity

Category	Total	White	Black	Asian	AIAN	Hisp.
Enrollment (%)	100.0	3.4	11.7	3.2	0.2	81.5
Drop-out Rate (%)	n/a	n/a	n/a	n/a	n/a	n/a
H.S. Diplomas (#)	593	22	57	33	1	480

Pasadena Unified
351 S Hudson Ave • Pasadena, CA 91101-3507
(626) 795-6981 • http://www.pasadena.k12.ca.us/
Grade Span: KG-12; **Agency Type:** 1
Schools: 32
23 Primary; 3 Middle; 4 High; 2 Other Level
31 Regular; 0 Special Education; 0 Vocational; 1 Alternative
2 Magnet; 0 Charter; 24 Title I Eligible; 22 School-wide Title I
Students: 23,282 (51.3% male; 48.7% female)
Individual Education Program: 2,898 (12.4%);
English Language Learner: 6,160 (26.5%); Migrant: 127 (0.5%)
Eligible for Free Lunch Program: 12,518 (53.8%)
Eligible for Reduced-Price Lunch Program: 1,964 (8.4%)
Teachers: 1,129.1 (20.6 to 1)
Librarians/Media Specialists: 6.0 (3,880.3 to 1)
Guidance Counselors: 29.5 (789.2 to 1)
Current Spending: ($ per student per year):
Total: $7,931; Instruction: $4,675; Support Services: $2,935
Enrollment, Drop-out Rates and Diploma Recipients by Race/Ethnicity

Category	Total	White	Black	Asian	AIAN	Hisp.
Enrollment (%)	100.0	15.9	27.5	3.8	0.2	52.5
Drop-out Rate (%)	n/a	n/a	n/a	n/a	n/a	n/a
H.S. Diplomas (#)	970	165	351	37	4	413

Pomona Unified
800 S Garey Ave • Pomona, CA 91769-2900
Mailing Address: PO Box 2900 • Pomona, CA 91769-2900
(909) 397-4800 • http://www.pomona.k12.ca.us/
Grade Span: KG-12; **Agency Type:** 1
Schools: 40
27 Primary; 6 Middle; 6 High; 1 Other Level
37 Regular; 0 Special Education; 0 Vocational; 3 Alternative
0 Magnet; 0 Charter; 31 Title I Eligible; 19 School-wide Title I
Students: 35,427 (51.1% male; 48.9% female)
Individual Education Program: 3,490 (9.9%);
English Language Learner: 16,613 (46.9%); Migrant: 362 (1.0%)
Eligible for Free Lunch Program: 20,044 (56.6%)
Eligible for Reduced-Price Lunch Program: 4,426 (12.5%)
Teachers: 1,716.5 (20.6 to 1)
Librarians/Media Specialists: 4.0 (8,856.8 to 1)
Guidance Counselors: 24.0 (1,476.1 to 1)
Current Spending: ($ per student per year):
Total: $6,794; Instruction: $4,256; Support Services: $2,242
Enrollment, Drop-out Rates and Diploma Recipients by Race/Ethnicity

Category	Total	White	Black	Asian	AIAN	Hisp.
Enrollment (%)	100.0	7.6	8.5	6.9	0.1	76.8
Drop-out Rate (%)	n/a	n/a	n/a	n/a	n/a	n/a
H.S. Diplomas (#)	1,410	158	146	159	1	946

Redondo Beach Unified
1401 Inglewood Ave • Redondo Beach, CA 90278-3912
(310) 379-5449 • http://www.beachnet.gen.ca.us/rbsd/
Grade Span: KG-12; **Agency Type:** 1
Schools: 12
8 Primary; 2 Middle; 2 High; 0 Other Level
11 Regular; 0 Special Education; 0 Vocational; 1 Alternative
0 Magnet; 0 Charter; 4 Title I Eligible; 0 School-wide Title I
Students: 7,993 (51.4% male; 48.6% female)
Individual Education Program: 993 (12.4%);
English Language Learner: 856 (10.7%); Migrant: 0 (0.0%)
Eligible for Free Lunch Program: 1,190 (14.9%)
Eligible for Reduced-Price Lunch Program: 490 (6.1%)
Teachers: 383.9 (20.8 to 1)
Librarians/Media Specialists: 1.0 (7,993.0 to 1)
Guidance Counselors: 12.8 (624.5 to 1)
Current Spending: ($ per student per year):
Total: $6,975; Instruction: $4,288; Support Services: $2,431
Enrollment, Drop-out Rates and Diploma Recipients by Race/Ethnicity

Category	Total	White	Black	Asian	AIAN	Hisp.
Enrollment (%)	100.0	54.6	8.8	12.2	1.1	22.9
Drop-out Rate (%)	n/a	n/a	n/a	n/a	n/a	n/a
H.S. Diplomas (#)	440	274	11	55	0	100

Rosemead Elementary
3907 Rosemead Blvd • Rosemead, CA 91770-2041
(626) 312-2900 • http://www.rosemead.k12.ca.us/
Grade Span: KG-08; **Agency Type:** 1
Schools: 5
4 Primary; 1 Middle; 0 High; 0 Other Level
5 Regular; 0 Special Education; 0 Vocational; 0 Alternative
0 Magnet; 0 Charter; 5 Title I Eligible; 0 School-wide Title I
Students: 3,403 (51.6% male; 48.4% female)
Individual Education Program: 266 (7.8%);
English Language Learner: 1,219 (35.8%); Migrant: 325 (9.6%)
Eligible for Free Lunch Program: 1,921 (56.5%)
Eligible for Reduced-Price Lunch Program: 695 (20.4%)
Teachers: 164.5 (20.7 to 1)
Librarians/Media Specialists: 0.0 (0.0 to 1)
Guidance Counselors: 0.0 (0.0 to 1)
Current Spending: ($ per student per year):
Total: $6,194; Instruction: $3,972; Support Services: $1,872
Enrollment, Drop-out Rates and Diploma Recipients by Race/Ethnicity

Category	Total	White	Black	Asian	AIAN	Hisp.
Enrollment (%)	100.0	5.2	0.7	44.4	0.1	49.1
Drop-out Rate (%)	n/a	n/a	n/a	n/a	n/a	n/a
H.S. Diplomas (#)	n/a	n/a	n/a	n/a	n/a	n/a

Rowland Unified
1830 Nogales St • Rowland Heights, CA 91748-0490
(626) 965-2541 • http://www.rowland-unified.org/main.htm
Grade Span: KG-12; **Agency Type:** 1
Schools: 22
15 Primary; 3 Middle; 4 High; 0 Other Level
20 Regular; 0 Special Education; 0 Vocational; 2 Alternative
0 Magnet; 0 Charter; 15 Title I Eligible; 12 School-wide Title I
Students: 18,739 (51.6% male; 48.4% female)
Individual Education Program: 1,833 (9.8%);
English Language Learner: 5,837 (31.1%); Migrant: 30 (0.2%)
Eligible for Free Lunch Program: 7,762 (41.4%)
Eligible for Reduced-Price Lunch Program: 2,504 (13.4%)
Teachers: 861.2 (21.8 to 1)
Librarians/Media Specialists: 2.0 (9,369.5 to 1)
Guidance Counselors: 13.0 (1,441.5 to 1)
Current Spending: ($ per student per year):
Total: $6,557; Instruction: $4,069; Support Services: $2,184
Enrollment, Drop-out Rates and Diploma Recipients by Race/Ethnicity

Category	Total	White	Black	Asian	AIAN	Hisp.
Enrollment (%)	100.0	6.5	4.4	28.8	0.1	58.4
Drop-out Rate (%)	n/a	n/a	n/a	n/a	n/a	n/a
H.S. Diplomas (#)	1,072	110	62	435	1	464

San Gabriel Unified
102 E Broadway • San Gabriel, CA 91776-4500
(626) 451-5400
Grade Span: KG-12; **Agency Type:** 1
Schools: 9
5 Primary; 1 Middle; 2 High; 1 Other Level
7 Regular; 0 Special Education; 0 Vocational; 2 Alternative
0 Magnet; 1 Charter; 3 Title I Eligible; 1 School-wide Title I
Students: 6,188 (52.0% male; 48.0% female)
Individual Education Program: 480 (7.8%);
English Language Learner: 2,112 (34.1%); Migrant: 14 (0.2%)
Eligible for Free Lunch Program: 2,596 (42.0%)
Eligible for Reduced-Price Lunch Program: 702 (11.3%)

Teachers: 286.0 (21.6 to 1)
Librarians/Media Specialists: 2.0 (3,094.0 to 1)
Guidance Counselors: 7.5 (825.1 to 1)
Current Spending: ($ per student per year):
Total: $6,518; Instruction: $4,094; Support Services: $1,985
Enrollment, Drop-out Rates and Diploma Recipients by Race/Ethnicity

Category	Total	White	Black	Asian	AIAN	Hisp.
Enrollment (%)	100.0	14.4	1.4	42.4	0.3	39.7
Drop-out Rate (%)	n/a	n/a	n/a	n/a	n/a	n/a
H.S. Diplomas (#)	416	73	5	173	3	157

San Marino Unified

1665 W Dr • San Marino, CA 91108-2594
(626) 299-7000 • http://www.san-marino.k12.ca.us/
Grade Span: KG-12; **Agency Type:** 1
Schools: 4
2 Primary; 1 Middle; 1 High; 0 Other Level
4 Regular; 0 Special Education; 0 Vocational; 0 Alternative
0 Magnet; 0 Charter; 0 Title I Eligible; 0 School-wide Title I
Students: 3,190 (52.5% male; 47.5% female)
Individual Education Program: 321 (10.1%);
English Language Learner: 229 (7.2%); Migrant: 0 (0.0%)
Eligible for Free Lunch Program: 18 (0.6%)
Eligible for Reduced-Price Lunch Program: 4 (0.1%)
Teachers: 157.7 (20.2 to 1)
Librarians/Media Specialists: 1.0 (3,190.0 to 1)
Guidance Counselors: 5.0 (638.0 to 1)
Current Spending: ($ per student per year):
Total: $7,177; Instruction: $4,355; Support Services: $2,629
Enrollment, Drop-out Rates and Diploma Recipients by Race/Ethnicity

Category	Total	White	Black	Asian	AIAN	Hisp.
Enrollment (%)	100.0	31.2	0.2	64.7	0.1	3.7
Drop-out Rate (%)	n/a	n/a	n/a	n/a	n/a	n/a
H.S. Diplomas (#)	280	59	2	206	0	11

Santa Monica-Malibu Unified

1651 16th St • Santa Monica, CA 90404-3891
(310) 450-8338 • http://www.smmusd.org/
Grade Span: KG-12; **Agency Type:** 1
Schools: 16
11 Primary; 2 Middle; 2 High; 1 Other Level
14 Regular; 0 Special Education; 0 Vocational; 2 Alternative
1 Magnet; 1 Charter; 4 Title I Eligible; 0 School-wide Title I
Students: 12,789 (51.3% male; 48.7% female)
Individual Education Program: 1,538 (12.0%);
English Language Learner: 1,635 (12.8%); Migrant: 0 (0.0%)
Eligible for Free Lunch Program: 2,251 (17.6%)
Eligible for Reduced-Price Lunch Program: 756 (5.9%)
Teachers: 608.8 (21.0 to 1)
Librarians/Media Specialists: 6.0 (2,131.5 to 1)
Guidance Counselors: 23.5 (544.2 to 1)
Current Spending: ($ per student per year):
Total: $7,178; Instruction: $4,657; Support Services: $2,279
Enrollment, Drop-out Rates and Diploma Recipients by Race/Ethnicity

Category	Total	White	Black	Asian	AIAN	Hisp.
Enrollment (%)	100.0	58.0	8.1	6.4	0.3	27.2
Drop-out Rate (%)	n/a	n/a	n/a	n/a	n/a	n/a
H.S. Diplomas (#)	852	458	78	62	0	254

Saugus Union Elementary

24930 Ave Stanford • Santa Clarita, CA 91355-1272
(661) 294-7500 • http://www.saugus.k12.ca.us/
Grade Span: KG-06; **Agency Type:** 1
Schools: 14
14 Primary; 0 Middle; 0 High; 0 Other Level
14 Regular; 0 Special Education; 0 Vocational; 0 Alternative
0 Magnet; 0 Charter; 2 Title I Eligible; 0 School-wide Title I
Students: 10,060 (50.7% male; 49.3% female)
Individual Education Program: 1,068 (10.6%);
English Language Learner: 427 (4.2%); Migrant: 0 (0.0%)
Eligible for Free Lunch Program: 748 (7.4%)
Eligible for Reduced-Price Lunch Program: 394 (3.9%)
Teachers: 480.1 (21.0 to 1)
Librarians/Media Specialists: 0.0 (0.0 to 1)
Guidance Counselors: 0.5 (20,120.0 to 1)
Current Spending: ($ per student per year):
Total: $5,768; Instruction: $4,041; Support Services: $1,368
Enrollment, Drop-out Rates and Diploma Recipients by Race/Ethnicity

Category	Total	White	Black	Asian	AIAN	Hisp.
Enrollment (%)	100.0	72.8	2.9	7.4	0.0	16.8
Drop-out Rate (%)	n/a	n/a	n/a	n/a	n/a	n/a
H.S. Diplomas (#)	n/a	n/a	n/a	n/a	n/a	n/a

South Pasadena Unified

1020 El Centro St • South Pasadena, CA 91030-3118
(626) 441-5810 • http://www.spusd.k12.ca.us/
Grade Span: KG-12; **Agency Type:** 1
Schools: 5
3 Primary; 1 Middle; 1 High; 0 Other Level
5 Regular; 0 Special Education; 0 Vocational; 0 Alternative
0 Magnet; 0 Charter; 3 Title I Eligible; 0 School-wide Title I
Students: 4,100 (50.7% male; 49.3% female)
Individual Education Program: 360 (8.8%);
English Language Learner: 280 (6.8%); Migrant: 0 (0.0%)
Eligible for Free Lunch Program: 208 (5.1%)
Eligible for Reduced-Price Lunch Program: 127 (3.1%)
Teachers: 179.6 (22.8 to 1)
Librarians/Media Specialists: 2.0 (2,050.0 to 1)
Guidance Counselors: 7.5 (546.7 to 1)
Current Spending: ($ per student per year):
Total: $6,561; Instruction: $4,185; Support Services: $2,190
Enrollment, Drop-out Rates and Diploma Recipients by Race/Ethnicity

Category	Total	White	Black	Asian	AIAN	Hisp.
Enrollment (%)	100.0	36.8	3.3	35.7	0.2	17.3
Drop-out Rate (%)	n/a	n/a	n/a	n/a	n/a	n/a
H.S. Diplomas (#)	301	97	10	143	1	41

South Whittier Elementary

10120 Painter Ave • Whittier, CA 90605-0037
Mailing Address: PO Box 3037 • Whittier, CA 90605-0037
(562) 944-6231
Grade Span: KG-08; **Agency Type:** 1
Schools: 8
7 Primary; 1 Middle; 0 High; 0 Other Level
8 Regular; 0 Special Education; 0 Vocational; 0 Alternative
0 Magnet; 0 Charter; 8 Title I Eligible; 8 School-wide Title I
Students: 4,604 (50.1% male; 49.9% female)
Individual Education Program: 405 (8.8%);
English Language Learner: 1,165 (25.3%); Migrant: 129 (2.8%)
Eligible for Free Lunch Program: 1,943 (42.2%)
Eligible for Reduced-Price Lunch Program: 572 (12.4%)
Teachers: 218.6 (21.1 to 1)
Librarians/Media Specialists: 0.0 (0.0 to 1)
Guidance Counselors: 0.0 (0.0 to 1)
Current Spending: ($ per student per year):
Total: $6,522; Instruction: $4,370; Support Services: $1,814
Enrollment, Drop-out Rates and Diploma Recipients by Race/Ethnicity

Category	Total	White	Black	Asian	AIAN	Hisp.
Enrollment (%)	100.0	5.6	1.0	2.1	0.6	90.7
Drop-out Rate (%)	n/a	n/a	n/a	n/a	n/a	n/a
H.S. Diplomas (#)	n/a	n/a	n/a	n/a	n/a	n/a

Sulphur Springs Union Elementary

17866 Sierra Hwy • Canyon Country, CA 91351-1671
(661) 252-5131 • http://www.sssd.k12.ca.us/
Grade Span: KG-06; **Agency Type:** 1
Schools: 8
8 Primary; 0 Middle; 0 High; 0 Other Level
8 Regular; 0 Special Education; 0 Vocational; 0 Alternative
0 Magnet; 0 Charter; 3 Title I Eligible; 2 School-wide Title I
Students: 5,455 (52.9% male; 47.1% female)
Individual Education Program: 514 (9.4%);
English Language Learner: 645 (11.8%); Migrant: 0 (0.0%)
Eligible for Free Lunch Program: 1,184 (21.7%)
Eligible for Reduced-Price Lunch Program: 412 (7.6%)
Teachers: 262.6 (20.8 to 1)
Librarians/Media Specialists: 0.0 (0.0 to 1)
Guidance Counselors: 0.0 (0.0 to 1)
Current Spending: ($ per student per year):
Total: $5,911; Instruction: $4,067; Support Services: $1,844
Enrollment, Drop-out Rates and Diploma Recipients by Race/Ethnicity

Category	Total	White	Black	Asian	AIAN	Hisp.
Enrollment (%)	100.0	60.5	5.1	5.8	0.5	28.1
Drop-out Rate (%)	n/a	n/a	n/a	n/a	n/a	n/a
H.S. Diplomas (#)	n/a	n/a	n/a	n/a	n/a	n/a

Temple City Unified

9700 Las Tunas Dr • Temple City, CA 91780-1610
(626) 548-5000 • http://www.templecity.k12.ca.us/
Grade Span: KG-12; **Agency Type:** 1
Schools: 8
3 Primary; 2 Middle; 2 High; 1 Other Level
6 Regular; 0 Special Education; 0 Vocational; 2 Alternative
0 Magnet; 0 Charter; 4 Title I Eligible; 0 School-wide Title I
Students: 5,689 (51.6% male; 48.4% female)
Individual Education Program: 473 (8.3%);
English Language Learner: 775 (13.6%); Migrant: 2 (<0.1%)
Eligible for Free Lunch Program: 1,368 (24.0%)

Eligible for Reduced-Price Lunch Program: 564 (9.9%)
Teachers: 263.5 (21.6 to 1)
Librarians/Media Specialists: 0.8 (7,111.3 to 1)
Guidance Counselors: 7.0 (812.7 to 1)
Current Spending: ($ per student per year):
Total: $6,263; Instruction: $4,114; Support Services: $1,957
Enrollment, Drop-out Rates and Diploma Recipients by Race/Ethnicity

Category	Total	White	Black	Asian	AIAN	Hisp.
Enrollment (%)	100.0	26.5	1.1	52.6	0.3	19.2
Drop-out Rate (%)	n/a	n/a	n/a	n/a	n/a	n/a
H.S. Diplomas (#)	395	133	4	201	0	56

Torrance Unified
2335 Plaza Del Amo • Torrance, CA 90501-3420
(310) 972-6500 • http://www.tusd.org/
Grade Span: KG-12; **Agency Type:** 1
Schools: 30
17 Primary; 8 Middle; 5 High; 0 Other Level
29 Regular; 0 Special Education; 0 Vocational; 1 Alternative
0 Magnet; 0 Charter; 7 Title I Eligible; 0 School-wide Title I
Students: 24,876 (51.6% male; 48.4% female)
Individual Education Program: 2,680 (10.8%);
English Language Learner: 2,889 (11.6%); Migrant: 0 (0.0%)
Eligible for Free Lunch Program: 2,832 (11.4%)
Eligible for Reduced-Price Lunch Program: 1,219 (4.9%)
Teachers: 1,197.3 (20.8 to 1)
Librarians/Media Specialists: 4.0 (6,219.0 to 1)
Guidance Counselors: 34.0 (731.6 to 1)
Current Spending: ($ per student per year):
Total: $5,978; Instruction: $3,941; Support Services: $1,816
Enrollment, Drop-out Rates and Diploma Recipients by Race/Ethnicity

Category	Total	White	Black	Asian	AIAN	Hisp.
Enrollment (%)	100.0	43.0	4.0	34.5	0.9	17.7
Drop-out Rate (%)	n/a	n/a	n/a	n/a	n/a	n/a
H.S. Diplomas (#)	1,813	783	89	590	96	255

Walnut Valley Unified
880 S Lemon Ave • Walnut, CA 91789-2931
(909) 595-1261 • http://www.walnutvalley.k12.ca.us/
Grade Span: KG-12; **Agency Type:** 1
Schools: 16
9 Primary; 3 Middle; 4 High; 0 Other Level
14 Regular; 0 Special Education; 0 Vocational; 2 Alternative
1 Magnet; 0 Charter; 4 Title I Eligible; 0 School-wide Title I
Students: 15,334 (51.5% male; 48.5% female)
Individual Education Program: 1,034 (6.7%);
English Language Learner: 1,109 (7.2%); Migrant: 1 (<0.1%)
Eligible for Free Lunch Program: 843 (5.5%)
Eligible for Reduced-Price Lunch Program: 479 (3.1%)
Teachers: 689.4 (22.2 to 1)
Librarians/Media Specialists: 0.0 (0.0 to 1)
Guidance Counselors: 19.0 (807.1 to 1)
Current Spending: ($ per student per year):
Total: $5,748; Instruction: $3,628; Support Services: $1,991
Enrollment, Drop-out Rates and Diploma Recipients by Race/Ethnicity

Category	Total	White	Black	Asian	AIAN	Hisp.
Enrollment (%)	100.0	19.7	4.7	56.4	0.8	18.4
Drop-out Rate (%)	n/a	n/a	n/a	n/a	n/a	n/a
H.S. Diplomas (#)	1,288	290	73	733	1	191

West Covina Unified
1717 W Merced Ave • West Covina, CA 91790-3406
(626) 939-4600 • http://www.wcusd.k12.ca.us/
Grade Span: KG-12; **Agency Type:** 1
Schools: 13
8 Primary; 2 Middle; 2 High; 1 Other Level
12 Regular; 0 Special Education; 0 Vocational; 1 Alternative
0 Magnet; 1 Charter; 11 Title I Eligible; 8 School-wide Title I
Students: 10,563 (51.2% male; 48.8% female)
Individual Education Program: 560 (5.3%);
English Language Learner: 1,337 (12.7%); Migrant: 29 (0.3%)
Eligible for Free Lunch Program: 2,990 (28.3%)
Eligible for Reduced-Price Lunch Program: 1,777 (16.8%)
Teachers: 487.8 (21.7 to 1)
Librarians/Media Specialists: 0.0 (0.0 to 1)
Guidance Counselors: 10.0 (1,056.3 to 1)
Current Spending: ($ per student per year):
Total: $5,671; Instruction: $3,738; Support Services: $1,692
Enrollment, Drop-out Rates and Diploma Recipients by Race/Ethnicity

Category	Total	White	Black	Asian	AIAN	Hisp.
Enrollment (%)	100.0	12.5	6.7	14.7	0.4	65.6
Drop-out Rate (%)	n/a	n/a	n/a	n/a	n/a	n/a
H.S. Diplomas (#)	587	97	40	119	1	330

Westside Union Elementary
46809 N 70th St W • Lancaster, CA 93535-7836
(661) 948-2669 • http://www.westside.k12.ca.us/
Grade Span: KG-08; **Agency Type:** 1
Schools: 9
7 Primary; 2 Middle; 0 High; 0 Other Level
9 Regular; 0 Special Education; 0 Vocational; 0 Alternative
0 Magnet; 0 Charter; 4 Title I Eligible; 0 School-wide Title I
Students: 7,104 (50.5% male; 49.5% female)
Individual Education Program: 770 (10.8%);
English Language Learner: 121 (1.7%); Migrant: 21 (0.3%)
Eligible for Free Lunch Program: 1,256 (17.7%)
Eligible for Reduced-Price Lunch Program: 384 (5.4%)
Teachers: 323.6 (22.0 to 1)
Librarians/Media Specialists: 0.0 (0.0 to 1)
Guidance Counselors: 3.8 (1,869.5 to 1)
Current Spending: ($ per student per year):
Total: $5,597; Instruction: $3,768; Support Services: $1,663
Enrollment, Drop-out Rates and Diploma Recipients by Race/Ethnicity

Category	Total	White	Black	Asian	AIAN	Hisp.
Enrollment (%)	100.0	65.6	9.9	4.6	0.9	17.8
Drop-out Rate (%)	n/a	n/a	n/a	n/a	n/a	n/a
H.S. Diplomas (#)	n/a	n/a	n/a	n/a	n/a	n/a

Whittier City Elementary
7211 S Whittier Ave • Whittier, CA 90602-1123
(562) 789-3000 • http://www.whittiercity.k12.ca.us/
Grade Span: KG-08; **Agency Type:** 1
Schools: 13
11 Primary; 2 Middle; 0 High; 0 Other Level
13 Regular; 0 Special Education; 0 Vocational; 0 Alternative
0 Magnet; 0 Charter; 13 Title I Eligible; 8 School-wide Title I
Students: 7,387 (51.6% male; 48.4% female)
Individual Education Program: 801 (10.8%);
English Language Learner: 1,908 (25.8%); Migrant: 6 (0.1%)
Eligible for Free Lunch Program: 3,389 (45.9%)
Eligible for Reduced-Price Lunch Program: 1,393 (18.9%)
Teachers: 347.8 (21.2 to 1)
Librarians/Media Specialists: 0.0 (0.0 to 1)
Guidance Counselors: 6.2 (1,191.5 to 1)
Current Spending: ($ per student per year):
Total: $6,347; Instruction: $4,117; Support Services: $1,931
Enrollment, Drop-out Rates and Diploma Recipients by Race/Ethnicity

Category	Total	White	Black	Asian	AIAN	Hisp.
Enrollment (%)	100.0	8.8	1.0	1.7	0.4	86.9
Drop-out Rate (%)	n/a	n/a	n/a	n/a	n/a	n/a
H.S. Diplomas (#)	n/a	n/a	n/a	n/a	n/a	n/a

Whittier Union High
9401 S Painter Ave • Whittier, CA 90605-2798
(562) 698-8121 • http://www.wuhsd.k12.ca.us/
Grade Span: 09-12; **Agency Type:** 1
Schools: 7
0 Primary; 0 Middle; 7 High; 0 Other Level
5 Regular; 0 Special Education; 0 Vocational; 2 Alternative
0 Magnet; 0 Charter; 4 Title I Eligible; 0 School-wide Title I
Students: 12,202 (51.4% male; 48.6% female)
Individual Education Program: 1,044 (8.6%);
English Language Learner: 1,866 (15.3%); Migrant: 108 (0.9%)
Eligible for Free Lunch Program: 2,900 (23.8%)
Eligible for Reduced-Price Lunch Program: 935 (7.7%)
Teachers: 488.7 (25.0 to 1)
Librarians/Media Specialists: 1.0 (12,202.0 to 1)
Guidance Counselors: 31.5 (387.4 to 1)
Current Spending: ($ per student per year):
Total: $7,028; Instruction: $4,278; Support Services: $2,481
Enrollment, Drop-out Rates and Diploma Recipients by Race/Ethnicity

Category	Total	White	Black	Asian	AIAN	Hisp.
Enrollment (%)	100.0	18.7	1.5	2.7	0.5	76.5
Drop-out Rate (%)	n/a	n/a	n/a	n/a	n/a	n/a
H.S. Diplomas (#)	2,093	495	32	101	8	1,454

William S Hart Union High
21515 Redview Dr • Santa Clarita, CA 91350-2948
(661) 259-0033 • http://www.hart.k12.ca.us/
Grade Span: 07-12; **Agency Type:** 1
Schools: 12
0 Primary; 4 Middle; 8 High; 0 Other Level
10 Regular; 0 Special Education; 0 Vocational; 2 Alternative
0 Magnet; 1 Charter; 5 Title I Eligible; 0 School-wide Title I
Students: 20,058 (51.6% male; 48.4% female)
Individual Education Program: 2,239 (11.2%);
English Language Learner: 1,332 (6.6%); Migrant: 0 (0.0%)
Eligible for Free Lunch Program: 1,673 (8.3%)
Eligible for Reduced-Price Lunch Program: 397 (2.0%)

Teachers: 816.2 (24.6 to 1)
Librarians/Media Specialists: 10.0 (2,005.8 to 1)
Guidance Counselors: 42.2 (475.3 to 1)
Current Spending: ($ per student per year):
Total: $6,385; Instruction: $3,961; Support Services: $2,280
Enrollment, Drop-out Rates and Diploma Recipients by Race/Ethnicity

Category	Total	White	Black	Asian	AIAN	Hisp.
Enrollment (%)	100.0	63.8	4.1	7.5	0.4	23.7
Drop-out Rate (%)	n/a	n/a	n/a	n/a	n/a	n/a
H.S. Diplomas (#)	2,393	1,682	87	165	14	440

Wilsona Elementary
18050 E Ave O • Palmdale, CA 93591-3800
(661) 264-1111 • http://www.theav.com/schools/wilsona.htm
Grade Span: KG-08; **Agency Type:** 1
Schools: 4
3 Primary; 1 Middle; 0 High; 0 Other Level
3 Regular; 0 Special Education; 0 Vocational; 1 Alternative
0 Magnet; 0 Charter; 3 Title I Eligible; 3 School-wide Title I
Students: 2,091 (52.7% male; 47.3% female)
Individual Education Program: 320 (15.3%);
English Language Learner: 527 (25.2%); Migrant: 68 (3.3%)
Eligible for Free Lunch Program: 1,305 (62.4%)
Eligible for Reduced-Price Lunch Program: 218 (10.4%)
Teachers: 95.4 (21.9 to 1)
Librarians/Media Specialists: 0.0 (0.0 to 1)
Guidance Counselors: 1.0 (2,091.0 to 1)
Current Spending: ($ per student per year):
Total: $6,661; Instruction: $4,402; Support Services: $1,936
Enrollment, Drop-out Rates and Diploma Recipients by Race/Ethnicity

Category	Total	White	Black	Asian	AIAN	Hisp.
Enrollment (%)	100.0	28.3	22.4	1.0	2.1	46.2
Drop-out Rate (%)	n/a	n/a	n/a	n/a	n/a	n/a
H.S. Diplomas (#)	n/a	n/a	n/a	n/a	n/a	n/a

Wiseburn Elementary
13530 Aviation Blvd • Hawthorne, CA 90250-6462
(310) 643-3025 • http://www.wiseburn.k12.ca.us/
Grade Span: KG-08; **Agency Type:** 1
Schools: 4
3 Primary; 1 Middle; 0 High; 0 Other Level
4 Regular; 0 Special Education; 0 Vocational; 0 Alternative
0 Magnet; 0 Charter; 1 Title I Eligible; 0 School-wide Title I
Students: 1,930 (53.4% male; 46.6% female)
Individual Education Program: 165 (8.5%);
English Language Learner: 197 (10.2%); Migrant: 0 (0.0%)
Eligible for Free Lunch Program: 448 (23.2%)
Eligible for Reduced-Price Lunch Program: 294 (15.2%)
Teachers: 94.0 (20.5 to 1)
Librarians/Media Specialists: 0.0 (0.0 to 1)
Guidance Counselors: 0.6 (3,216.7 to 1)
Current Spending: ($ per student per year):
Total: $6,040; Instruction: $3,875; Support Services: $1,982
Enrollment, Drop-out Rates and Diploma Recipients by Race/Ethnicity

Category	Total	White	Black	Asian	AIAN	Hisp.
Enrollment (%)	100.0	27.0	13.5	8.4	0.2	50.8
Drop-out Rate (%)	n/a	n/a	n/a	n/a	n/a	n/a
H.S. Diplomas (#)	n/a	n/a	n/a	n/a	n/a	n/a

Madera County

Chowchilla Elementary
355 N Fifth St • Chowchilla, CA 93610-0907
Mailing Address: PO Box 910 • Chowchilla, CA 93610-0910
(559) 665-8000 • http://www.chowchillaelem.k12.ca.us/
Grade Span: KG-08; **Agency Type:** 1
Schools: 4
3 Primary; 1 Middle; 0 High; 0 Other Level
4 Regular; 0 Special Education; 0 Vocational; 0 Alternative
0 Magnet; 0 Charter; 4 Title I Eligible; 4 School-wide Title I
Students: 1,707 (53.6% male; 46.4% female)
Individual Education Program: 45 (2.6%);
English Language Learner: 539 (31.6%); Migrant: 129 (7.6%)
Eligible for Free Lunch Program: 1,140 (66.8%)
Eligible for Reduced-Price Lunch Program: 198 (11.6%)
Teachers: 83.0 (20.6 to 1)
Librarians/Media Specialists: 0.0 (0.0 to 1)
Guidance Counselors: 0.0 (0.0 to 1)
Current Spending: ($ per student per year):
Total: $6,009; Instruction: $3,648; Support Services: $2,053
Enrollment, Drop-out Rates and Diploma Recipients by Race/Ethnicity

Category	Total	White	Black	Asian	AIAN	Hisp.
Enrollment (%)	100.0	45.2	2.2	2.2	1.7	48.3
Drop-out Rate (%)	n/a	n/a	n/a	n/a	n/a	n/a
H.S. Diplomas (#)	n/a	n/a	n/a	n/a	n/a	n/a

Madera Unified
1902 Howard Rd • Madera, CA 93637-5123
(559) 675-4500 • http://www.madera.k12.ca.us/
Grade Span: KG-12; **Agency Type:** 1
Schools: 19
14 Primary; 2 Middle; 2 High; 1 Other Level
17 Regular; 0 Special Education; 0 Vocational; 2 Alternative
0 Magnet; 0 Charter; 19 Title I Eligible; 8 School-wide Title I
Students: 16,855 (50.9% male; 49.1% female)
Individual Education Program: 1,143 (6.8%);
English Language Learner: 6,951 (41.2%); Migrant: 2,430 (14.4%)
Eligible for Free Lunch Program: 10,578 (62.8%)
Eligible for Reduced-Price Lunch Program: 2,074 (12.3%)
Teachers: 813.5 (20.7 to 1)
Librarians/Media Specialists: 2.0 (8,427.5 to 1)
Guidance Counselors: 14.0 (1,203.9 to 1)
Current Spending: ($ per student per year):
Total: $6,308; Instruction: $3,791; Support Services: $2,222
Enrollment, Drop-out Rates and Diploma Recipients by Race/Ethnicity

Category	Total	White	Black	Asian	AIAN	Hisp.
Enrollment (%)	100.0	18.4	3.3	1.3	0.2	76.5
Drop-out Rate (%)	n/a	n/a	n/a	n/a	n/a	n/a
H.S. Diplomas (#)	796	236	29	15	0	516

Marin County

Dixie Elementary
380 Nova Albion Way • San Rafael, CA 94903-3523
(415) 492-3700 • http://dixiesd.marin.k12.ca.us/dixieschool/
Grade Span: KG-08; **Agency Type:** 1
Schools: 4
3 Primary; 1 Middle; 0 High; 0 Other Level
4 Regular; 0 Special Education; 0 Vocational; 0 Alternative
0 Magnet; 0 Charter; 0 Title I Eligible; 0 School-wide Title I
Students: 1,855 (49.8% male; 50.2% female)
Individual Education Program: 213 (11.5%);
English Language Learner: 24 (1.3%); Migrant: 0 (0.0%)
Eligible for Free Lunch Program: 61 (3.3%)
Eligible for Reduced-Price Lunch Program: 9 (0.5%)
Teachers: 100.2 (18.5 to 1)
Librarians/Media Specialists: 1.0 (1,855.0 to 1)
Guidance Counselors: 1.0 (1,855.0 to 1)
Current Spending: ($ per student per year):
Total: $7,096; Instruction: $4,396; Support Services: $2,642
Enrollment, Drop-out Rates and Diploma Recipients by Race/Ethnicity

Category	Total	White	Black	Asian	AIAN	Hisp.
Enrollment (%)	100.0	79.3	3.1	10.2	0.3	6.4
Drop-out Rate (%)	n/a	n/a	n/a	n/a	n/a	n/a
H.S. Diplomas (#)	n/a	n/a	n/a	n/a	n/a	n/a

Mill Valley Elementary
411 Sycamore Ave • Mill Valley, CA 94941-2231
(415) 389-7700 • http://www.mvschools.org/
Grade Span: KG-08; **Agency Type:** 1
Schools: 6
5 Primary; 1 Middle; 0 High; 0 Other Level
6 Regular; 0 Special Education; 0 Vocational; 0 Alternative
0 Magnet; 0 Charter; 3 Title I Eligible; 0 School-wide Title I
Students: 2,288 (51.1% male; 48.9% female)
Individual Education Program: 232 (10.1%);
English Language Learner: 57 (2.5%); Migrant: 0 (0.0%)
Eligible for Free Lunch Program: 37 (1.6%)
Eligible for Reduced-Price Lunch Program: 18 (0.8%)
Teachers: 128.3 (17.8 to 1)
Librarians/Media Specialists: 4.5 (508.4 to 1)
Guidance Counselors: 3.9 (586.7 to 1)
Current Spending: ($ per student per year):
Total: $8,248; Instruction: $5,324; Support Services: $2,908
Enrollment, Drop-out Rates and Diploma Recipients by Race/Ethnicity

Category	Total	White	Black	Asian	AIAN	Hisp.
Enrollment (%)	100.0	79.0	2.5	11.0	0.4	5.4
Drop-out Rate (%)	n/a	n/a	n/a	n/a	n/a	n/a
H.S. Diplomas (#)	n/a	n/a	n/a	n/a	n/a	n/a

Novato Unified
1015 Seventh St • Novato, CA 94945-2205
(415) 897-4201 • http://www.novato.ca.us/nusd/
Grade Span: KG-12; **Agency Type:** 1
Schools: 16
9 Primary; 3 Middle; 3 High; 1 Other Level
14 Regular; 0 Special Education; 0 Vocational; 2 Alternative
0 Magnet; 1 Charter; 8 Title I Eligible; 0 School-wide Title I
Students: 7,794 (51.6% male; 48.4% female)
Individual Education Program: 890 (11.4%);
English Language Learner: 772 (9.9%); Migrant: 2 (<0.1%)

Eligible for Free Lunch Program: 726 (9.3%)
Eligible for Reduced-Price Lunch Program: 375 (4.8%)
Teachers: 390.4 (20.0 to 1)
Librarians/Media Specialists: 9.0 (866.0 to 1)
Guidance Counselors: 9.0 (866.0 to 1)
Current Spending: ($ per student per year):
Total: $6,442; Instruction: $4,149; Support Services: $2,145
Enrollment, Drop-out Rates and Diploma Recipients by Race/Ethnicity

Category	Total	White	Black	Asian	AIAN	Hisp.
Enrollment (%)	100.0	71.2	2.8	7.0	0.2	16.8
Drop-out Rate (%)	n/a	n/a	n/a	n/a	n/a	n/a
H.S. Diplomas (#)	481	380	9	39	1	51

Ross Valley Elementary
110 Show Dr • San Anselmo, CA 94960-1112
(415) 454-2162
Grade Span: KG-08; **Agency Type:** 1
Schools: 4
3 Primary; 1 Middle; 0 High; 0 Other Level
4 Regular; 0 Special Education; 0 Vocational; 0 Alternative
1 Magnet; 0 Charter; 2 Title I Eligible; 0 School-wide Title I
Students: 1,790 (50.3% male; 49.7% female)
Individual Education Program: 236 (13.2%);
English Language Learner: 71 (4.0%); Migrant: 0 (0.0%)
Eligible for Free Lunch Program: 93 (5.2%)
Eligible for Reduced-Price Lunch Program: 27 (1.5%)
Teachers: 97.9 (18.3 to 1)
Librarians/Media Specialists: 0.0 (0.0 to 1)
Guidance Counselors: 1.0 (1,790.0 to 1)
Current Spending: ($ per student per year):
Total: $7,060; Instruction: $4,435; Support Services: $2,536
Enrollment, Drop-out Rates and Diploma Recipients by Race/Ethnicity

Category	Total	White	Black	Asian	AIAN	Hisp.
Enrollment (%)	100.0	85.4	1.7	5.0	0.2	6.4
Drop-out Rate (%)	n/a	n/a	n/a	n/a	n/a	n/a
H.S. Diplomas (#)	n/a	n/a	n/a	n/a	n/a	n/a

San Rafael City Elementary
310 Nova Albion Way • San Rafael, CA 94903-3523
(415) 492-3233 • http://mcoeweb.marin.k12.ca.us/
Grade Span: KG-08; **Agency Type:** 2
Schools: 8
7 Primary; 1 Middle; 0 High; 0 Other Level
8 Regular; 0 Special Education; 0 Vocational; 0 Alternative
0 Magnet; 0 Charter; 6 Title I Eligible; 1 School-wide Title I
Students: 3,566 (53.0% male; 47.0% female)
Individual Education Program: 534 (15.0%);
English Language Learner: 1,564 (43.9%); Migrant: 0 (0.0%)
Eligible for Free Lunch Program: 1,459 (40.9%)
Eligible for Reduced-Price Lunch Program: 329 (9.2%)
Teachers: 184.3 (19.3 to 1)
Librarians/Media Specialists: 0.6 (5,943.3 to 1)
Guidance Counselors: 3.4 (1,048.8 to 1)
Current Spending: ($ per student per year):
Total: $6,767; Instruction: $4,248; Support Services: $2,294
Enrollment, Drop-out Rates and Diploma Recipients by Race/Ethnicity

Category	Total	White	Black	Asian	AIAN	Hisp.
Enrollment (%)	100.0	36.5	5.7	7.7	0.3	48.2
Drop-out Rate (%)	n/a	n/a	n/a	n/a	n/a	n/a
H.S. Diplomas (#)	n/a	n/a	n/a	n/a	n/a	n/a

San Rafael City High
310 Nova Albione • San Rafael, CA 94903-3500
(415) 492-3233
Grade Span: 09-12; **Agency Type:** 2
Schools: 3
0 Primary; 0 Middle; 3 High; 0 Other Level
2 Regular; 0 Special Education; 0 Vocational; 1 Alternative
0 Magnet; 0 Charter; 2 Title I Eligible; 0 School-wide Title I
Students: 2,091 (52.3% male; 47.7% female)
Individual Education Program: 225 (10.8%);
English Language Learner: 300 (14.3%); Migrant: 0 (0.0%)
Eligible for Free Lunch Program: 225 (10.8%)
Eligible for Reduced-Price Lunch Program: 71 (3.4%)
Teachers: 100.1 (20.9 to 1)
Librarians/Media Specialists: 1.0 (2,091.0 to 1)
Guidance Counselors: 5.0 (418.2 to 1)
Current Spending: ($ per student per year):
Total: $7,363; Instruction: $3,878; Support Services: $2,934
Enrollment, Drop-out Rates and Diploma Recipients by Race/Ethnicity

Category	Total	White	Black	Asian	AIAN	Hisp.
Enrollment (%)	100.0	57.7	3.9	8.3	0.6	29.2
Drop-out Rate (%)	n/a	n/a	n/a	n/a	n/a	n/a
H.S. Diplomas (#)	407	259	12	42	1	91

Tamalpais Union High
395 Doherty Dr • Larkspur, CA 94977-0605
Mailing Address: PO Box 605 • Larkspur, CA 94977-0605
(415) 945-3737 • http://www.tamdistrict.org/
Grade Span: KG-12; **Agency Type:** 1
Schools: 5
0 Primary; 0 Middle; 5 High; 0 Other Level
3 Regular; 0 Special Education; 0 Vocational; 2 Alternative
0 Magnet; 0 Charter; 2 Title I Eligible; 0 School-wide Title I
Students: 3,782 (52.0% male; 48.0% female)
Individual Education Program: 22 (0.6%);
English Language Learner: 43 (1.1%); Migrant: 1 (<0.1%)
Eligible for Free Lunch Program: 54 (1.4%)
Eligible for Reduced-Price Lunch Program: 23 (0.6%)
Teachers: 203.2 (18.6 to 1)
Librarians/Media Specialists: 3.0 (1,260.7 to 1)
Guidance Counselors: 11.8 (320.5 to 1)
Current Spending: ($ per student per year):
Total: $9,029; Instruction: $5,155; Support Services: $3,723
Enrollment, Drop-out Rates and Diploma Recipients by Race/Ethnicity

Category	Total	White	Black	Asian	AIAN	Hisp.
Enrollment (%)	100.0	78.9	2.9	5.1	0.6	4.6
Drop-out Rate (%)	n/a	n/a	n/a	n/a	n/a	n/a
H.S. Diplomas (#)	827	693	20	48	5	52

Mariposa County

Mariposa County Unified
5082 Old Hwy N • Mariposa, CA 95338-0008
Mailing Address: PO Box 8 • Mariposa, CA 95338-0008
(209) 742-0250 • http://www.mariposa.k12.ca.us/
Grade Span: KG-12; **Agency Type:** 1
Schools: 14
7 Primary; 1 Middle; 5 High; 1 Other Level
11 Regular; 0 Special Education; 0 Vocational; 3 Alternative
0 Magnet; 0 Charter; 11 Title I Eligible; 1 School-wide Title I
Students: 2,560 (50.0% male; 50.0% female)
Individual Education Program: 365 (14.3%);
English Language Learner: 17 (0.7%); Migrant: 0 (0.0%)
Eligible for Free Lunch Program: 721 (28.2%)
Eligible for Reduced-Price Lunch Program: 208 (8.1%)
Teachers: 133.6 (19.2 to 1)
Librarians/Media Specialists: 0.0 (0.0 to 1)
Guidance Counselors: 5.0 (512.0 to 1)
Current Spending: ($ per student per year):
Total: $7,104; Instruction: $3,828; Support Services: $3,091
Enrollment, Drop-out Rates and Diploma Recipients by Race/Ethnicity

Category	Total	White	Black	Asian	AIAN	Hisp.
Enrollment (%)	100.0	81.4	2.0	1.6	7.0	6.1
Drop-out Rate (%)	n/a	n/a	n/a	n/a	n/a	n/a
H.S. Diplomas (#)	194	159	2	9	13	10

Mendocino County

Fort Bragg Unified
312 S Lincoln St • Fort Bragg, CA 95437-4416
(707) 961-2850 • http://www.fortbragg.k12.ca.us
Grade Span: KG-12; **Agency Type:** 1
Schools: 8
3 Primary; 2 Middle; 3 High; 0 Other Level
5 Regular; 0 Special Education; 0 Vocational; 3 Alternative
0 Magnet; 0 Charter; 5 Title I Eligible; 0 School-wide Title I
Students: 2,084 (53.3% male; 46.7% female)
Individual Education Program: 251 (12.0%);
English Language Learner: 468 (22.5%); Migrant: 327 (15.7%)
Eligible for Free Lunch Program: 897 (43.0%)
Eligible for Reduced-Price Lunch Program: 245 (11.8%)
Teachers: 125.1 (16.7 to 1)
Librarians/Media Specialists: 1.0 (2,084.0 to 1)
Guidance Counselors: 3.0 (694.7 to 1)
Current Spending: ($ per student per year):
Total: $7,492; Instruction: $4,832; Support Services: $2,382
Enrollment, Drop-out Rates and Diploma Recipients by Race/Ethnicity

Category	Total	White	Black	Asian	AIAN	Hisp.
Enrollment (%)	100.0	64.9	1.4	2.8	1.4	28.9
Drop-out Rate (%)	n/a	n/a	n/a	n/a	n/a	n/a
H.S. Diplomas (#)	144	110	0	4	2	26

Ukiah Unified
925 N State St • Ukiah, CA 95482-3411
(707) 463-5211 • http://www.uusd.net/
Grade Span: KG-12; **Agency Type:** 1
Schools: 17
7 Primary; 2 Middle; 4 High; 4 Other Level
16 Regular; 0 Special Education; 0 Vocational; 1 Alternative

0 Magnet; 6 Charter; 15 Title I Eligible; 0 School-wide Title I
Students: 6,855 (51.5% male; 48.5% female)
Individual Education Program: 1,009 (14.7%);
English Language Learner: 1,549 (22.6%); Migrant: 1,307 (19.1%)
Eligible for Free Lunch Program: 3,214 (46.9%)
Eligible for Reduced-Price Lunch Program: 777 (11.3%)
Teachers: 365.0 (18.8 to 1)
Librarians/Media Specialists: 1.0 (6,855.0 to 1)
Guidance Counselors: 8.0 (856.9 to 1)
Current Spending: ($ per student per year):
Total: $7,053; Instruction: $4,480; Support Services: $2,256
Enrollment, Drop-out Rates and Diploma Recipients by Race/Ethnicity

Category	Total	White	Black	Asian	AIAN	Hisp.
Enrollment (%)	100.0	59.3	1.1	2.0	6.4	31.2
Drop-out Rate (%)	n/a	n/a	n/a	n/a	n/a	n/a
H.S. Diplomas (#)	509	364	9	18	20	98

Willits Unified
618 S Main St • Willits, CA 95490-3007
(707) 459-5314 • http://ntap.k12.ca.us/wusd/index.shtml
Grade Span: KG-12; **Agency Type:** 1
Schools: 10
3 Primary; 2 Middle; 3 High; 2 Other Level
6 Regular; 0 Special Education; 0 Vocational; 4 Alternative
0 Magnet; 1 Charter; 5 Title I Eligible; 0 School-wide Title I
Students: 2,346 (53.2% male; 46.8% female)
Individual Education Program: 301 (12.8%);
English Language Learner: 205 (8.7%); Migrant: 170 (7.2%)
Eligible for Free Lunch Program: 937 (39.9%)
Eligible for Reduced-Price Lunch Program: 256 (10.9%)
Teachers: 132.5 (17.7 to 1)
Librarians/Media Specialists: 1.0 (2,346.0 to 1)
Guidance Counselors: 2.9 (809.0 to 1)
Current Spending: ($ per student per year):
Total: $6,897; Instruction: $4,479; Support Services: $2,173
Enrollment, Drop-out Rates and Diploma Recipients by Race/Ethnicity

Category	Total	White	Black	Asian	AIAN	Hisp.
Enrollment (%)	100.0	73.5	0.9	1.6	6.6	16.5
Drop-out Rate (%)	n/a	n/a	n/a	n/a	n/a	n/a
H.S. Diplomas (#)	165	143	1	5	4	11

Merced County

Atwater Elementary
1401 Broadway Ave • Atwater, CA 95301-3535
(209) 357-6100 • http://www.aesd.k12.ca.us/
Grade Span: KG-08; **Agency Type:** 1
Schools: 8
7 Primary; 1 Middle; 0 High; 0 Other Level
8 Regular; 0 Special Education; 0 Vocational; 0 Alternative
0 Magnet; 0 Charter; 8 Title I Eligible; 5 School-wide Title I
Students: 4,736 (51.1% male; 48.9% female)
Individual Education Program: 403 (8.5%);
English Language Learner: 1,695 (35.8%); Migrant: 421 (8.9%)
Eligible for Free Lunch Program: 2,658 (56.1%)
Eligible for Reduced-Price Lunch Program: 629 (13.3%)
Teachers: 238.6 (19.8 to 1)
Librarians/Media Specialists: 1.0 (4,736.0 to 1)
Guidance Counselors: 2.6 (1,821.5 to 1)
Current Spending: ($ per student per year):
Total: $6,259; Instruction: $3,993; Support Services: $1,908
Enrollment, Drop-out Rates and Diploma Recipients by Race/Ethnicity

Category	Total	White	Black	Asian	AIAN	Hisp.
Enrollment (%)	100.0	31.6	6.0	8.1	0.5	53.8
Drop-out Rate (%)	n/a	n/a	n/a	n/a	n/a	n/a
H.S. Diplomas (#)	n/a	n/a	n/a	n/a	n/a	n/a

Delhi Unified
9716 Hinton Ave • Delhi, CA 95315-0338
(209) 668-6130 • http://www.delhi.k12.ca.us/
Grade Span: KG-12; **Agency Type:** 1
Schools: 5
2 Primary; 1 Middle; 2 High; 0 Other Level
4 Regular; 0 Special Education; 0 Vocational; 1 Alternative
0 Magnet; 0 Charter; 3 Title I Eligible; 2 School-wide Title I
Students: 2,488 (51.6% male; 48.4% female)
Individual Education Program: 282 (11.3%);
English Language Learner: 1,179 (47.4%); Migrant: 251 (10.1%)
Eligible for Free Lunch Program: 1,358 (54.6%)
Eligible for Reduced-Price Lunch Program: 268 (10.8%)
Teachers: 124.5 (20.0 to 1)
Librarians/Media Specialists: 1.0 (2,488.0 to 1)
Guidance Counselors: 1.0 (2,488.0 to 1)
Current Spending: ($ per student per year):
Total: $5,907; Instruction: $3,858; Support Services: $1,818

Enrollment, Drop-out Rates and Diploma Recipients by Race/Ethnicity

Category	Total	White	Black	Asian	AIAN	Hisp.
Enrollment (%)	100.0	23.2	2.4	2.4	0.4	71.6
Drop-out Rate (%)	n/a	n/a	n/a	n/a	n/a	n/a
H.S. Diplomas (#)	80	14	1	1	0	64

Dos Palos Oro Loma Joint Unified
2041 Almond St • Dos Palos, CA 93620-2303
(209) 392-6101 • http://www.dpol.k12.ca.us/
Grade Span: KG-12; **Agency Type:** 1
Schools: 7
3 Primary; 1 Middle; 3 High; 0 Other Level
6 Regular; 0 Special Education; 0 Vocational; 1 Alternative
1 Magnet; 0 Charter; 4 Title I Eligible; 0 School-wide Title I
Students: 2,734 (51.4% male; 48.6% female)
Individual Education Program: 341 (12.5%);
English Language Learner: 1,015 (37.1%); Migrant: 534 (19.5%)
Eligible for Free Lunch Program: 1,676 (61.3%)
Eligible for Reduced-Price Lunch Program: 165 (6.0%)
Teachers: 145.5 (18.8 to 1)
Librarians/Media Specialists: 2.0 (1,367.0 to 1)
Guidance Counselors: 3.9 (701.0 to 1)
Current Spending: ($ per student per year):
Total: $6,694; Instruction: $3,950; Support Services: $2,423
Enrollment, Drop-out Rates and Diploma Recipients by Race/Ethnicity

Category	Total	White	Black	Asian	AIAN	Hisp.
Enrollment (%)	100.0	25.7	4.4	0.2	0.1	68.8
Drop-out Rate (%)	n/a	n/a	n/a	n/a	n/a	n/a
H.S. Diplomas (#)	171	67	14	1	1	88

Gustine Unified
1500 Meredith Ave • Gustine, CA 95322-1127
(209) 854-3784 • http://www.gustine.k12.ca.us/
Grade Span: KG-12; **Agency Type:** 1
Schools: 5
2 Primary; 1 Middle; 2 High; 0 Other Level
4 Regular; 0 Special Education; 0 Vocational; 1 Alternative
0 Magnet; 0 Charter; 3 Title I Eligible; 1 School-wide Title I
Students: 1,792 (52.7% male; 47.3% female)
Individual Education Program: 159 (8.9%);
English Language Learner: 658 (36.7%); Migrant: 385 (21.5%)
Eligible for Free Lunch Program: 827 (46.1%)
Eligible for Reduced-Price Lunch Program: 187 (10.4%)
Teachers: 102.0 (17.6 to 1)
Librarians/Media Specialists: 0.0 (0.0 to 1)
Guidance Counselors: 1.0 (1,792.0 to 1)
Current Spending: ($ per student per year):
Total: $6,068; Instruction: $3,957; Support Services: $1,870
Enrollment, Drop-out Rates and Diploma Recipients by Race/Ethnicity

Category	Total	White	Black	Asian	AIAN	Hisp.
Enrollment (%)	100.0	35.9	0.7	1.1	0.2	62.1
Drop-out Rate (%)	n/a	n/a	n/a	n/a	n/a	n/a
H.S. Diplomas (#)	117	61	0	2	0	54

Hilmar Unified
7807 N Lander Ave • Hilmar, CA 95324-9398
(209) 667-5701 • http://www.hilmar.k12.ca.us/
Grade Span: KG-12; **Agency Type:** 1
Schools: 6
2 Primary; 1 Middle; 3 High; 0 Other Level
4 Regular; 0 Special Education; 0 Vocational; 2 Alternative
0 Magnet; 0 Charter; 3 Title I Eligible; 0 School-wide Title I
Students: 2,410 (50.9% male; 49.1% female)
Individual Education Program: 240 (10.0%);
English Language Learner: 561 (23.3%); Migrant: 96 (4.0%)
Eligible for Free Lunch Program: 665 (27.6%)
Eligible for Reduced-Price Lunch Program: 223 (9.3%)
Teachers: 123.7 (19.5 to 1)
Librarians/Media Specialists: 0.0 (0.0 to 1)
Guidance Counselors: 1.0 (2,410.0 to 1)
Current Spending: ($ per student per year):
Total: $6,506; Instruction: $4,235; Support Services: $2,017
Enrollment, Drop-out Rates and Diploma Recipients by Race/Ethnicity

Category	Total	White	Black	Asian	AIAN	Hisp.
Enrollment (%)	100.0	75.0	0.6	2.0	0.2	22.2
Drop-out Rate (%)	n/a	n/a	n/a	n/a	n/a	n/a
H.S. Diplomas (#)	174	142	1	1	1	29

Livingston Union Elementary
922 B St • Livingston, CA 95334-1150
(209) 394-5400 • http://www.lusd.k12.ca.us/
Grade Span: KG-08; **Agency Type:** 1
Schools: 4
3 Primary; 1 Middle; 0 High; 0 Other Level
4 Regular; 0 Special Education; 0 Vocational; 0 Alternative

0 Magnet; 0 Charter; 4 Title I Eligible; 3 School-wide Title I
Students: 2,433 (50.6% male; 49.4% female)
Individual Education Program: 230 (9.5%);
English Language Learner: 1,668 (68.6%); Migrant: 359 (14.8%)
Eligible for Free Lunch Program: 1,741 (71.6%)
Eligible for Reduced-Price Lunch Program: 386 (15.9%)
Teachers: 118.6 (20.5 to 1)
Librarians/Media Specialists: 1.0 (2,433.0 to 1)
Guidance Counselors: 0.5 (4,866.0 to 1)
Current Spending: ($ per student per year):
Total: $6,147; Instruction: $4,145; Support Services: $1,679
Enrollment, Drop-out Rates and Diploma Recipients by Race/Ethnicity

Category	Total	White	Black	Asian	AIAN	Hisp.
Enrollment (%)	100.0	8.8	1.0	12.4	0.1	77.7
Drop-out Rate (%)	n/a	n/a	n/a	n/a	n/a	n/a
H.S. Diplomas (#)	n/a	n/a	n/a	n/a	n/a	n/a

Los Banos Unified
1717 S 11th St • Los Banos, CA 93635-4800
(209) 826-3801 • http://www.losbanosusd.k12.ca.us/
Grade Span: KG-12; **Agency Type:** 1
Schools: 10
5 Primary; 2 Middle; 3 High; 0 Other Level
8 Regular; 0 Special Education; 0 Vocational; 2 Alternative
0 Magnet; 0 Charter; 6 Title I Eligible; 1 School-wide Title I
Students: 7,844 (51.9% male; 48.1% female)
Individual Education Program: 375 (4.8%);
English Language Learner: 2,036 (26.0%); Migrant: 495 (6.3%)
Eligible for Free Lunch Program: 3,188 (40.6%)
Eligible for Reduced-Price Lunch Program: 1,007 (12.8%)
Teachers: 366.9 (21.4 to 1)
Librarians/Media Specialists: 3.4 (2,307.1 to 1)
Guidance Counselors: 0.0 (0.0 to 1)
Current Spending: ($ per student per year):
Total: $5,498; Instruction: $3,374; Support Services: $1,882
Enrollment, Drop-out Rates and Diploma Recipients by Race/Ethnicity

Category	Total	White	Black	Asian	AIAN	Hisp.
Enrollment (%)	100.0	27.5	4.0	3.1	0.6	63.1
Drop-out Rate (%)	n/a	n/a	n/a	n/a	n/a	n/a
H.S. Diplomas (#)	424	166	20	21	0	215

Merced City Elementary
444 W 23rd St • Merced, CA 95340-3723
(209) 385-6600 • http://www.mcsd.k12.ca.us/
Grade Span: KG-08; **Agency Type:** 1
Schools: 17
13 Primary; 4 Middle; 0 High; 0 Other Level
16 Regular; 0 Special Education; 0 Vocational; 1 Alternative
0 Magnet; 1 Charter; 16 Title I Eligible; 16 School-wide Title I
Students: 11,384 (50.9% male; 49.1% female)
Individual Education Program: 1,186 (10.4%);
English Language Learner: 3,446 (30.3%); Migrant: 591 (5.2%)
Eligible for Free Lunch Program: 6,948 (61.0%)
Eligible for Reduced-Price Lunch Program: 1,223 (10.7%)
Teachers: 551.1 (20.7 to 1)
Librarians/Media Specialists: 16.0 (711.5 to 1)
Guidance Counselors: 8.7 (1,308.5 to 1)
Current Spending: ($ per student per year):
Total: $6,697; Instruction: $4,457; Support Services: $1,933
Enrollment, Drop-out Rates and Diploma Recipients by Race/Ethnicity

Category	Total	White	Black	Asian	AIAN	Hisp.
Enrollment (%)	100.0	24.9	7.6	18.8	0.2	48.5
Drop-out Rate (%)	n/a	n/a	n/a	n/a	n/a	n/a
H.S. Diplomas (#)	n/a	n/a	n/a	n/a	n/a	n/a

Merced Union High
3430 A St • Atwater, CA 95301
Mailing Address: PO Box 2147 • Merced, CA 95344-0147
(209) 385-6412
Grade Span: 09-12; **Agency Type:** 1
Schools: 7
0 Primary; 0 Middle; 6 High; 1 Other Level
5 Regular; 0 Special Education; 0 Vocational; 2 Alternative
0 Magnet; 0 Charter; 7 Title I Eligible; 5 School-wide Title I
Students: 9,621 (49.9% male; 50.1% female)
Individual Education Program: 1,143 (11.9%);
English Language Learner: 1,975 (20.5%); Migrant: 635 (6.6%)
Eligible for Free Lunch Program: 6,062 (63.0%)
Eligible for Reduced-Price Lunch Program: 1,187 (12.3%)
Teachers: 419.4 (22.9 to 1)
Librarians/Media Specialists: 5.4 (1,781.7 to 1)
Guidance Counselors: 18.9 (509.0 to 1)
Current Spending: ($ per student per year):
Total: $6,467; Instruction: $3,919; Support Services: $2,292
Enrollment, Drop-out Rates and Diploma Recipients by Race/Ethnicity

Category	Total	White	Black	Asian	AIAN	Hisp.
Enrollment (%)	100.0	30.7	5.2	16.9	0.8	46.3
Drop-out Rate (%)	n/a	n/a	n/a	n/a	n/a	n/a
H.S. Diplomas (#)	1,951	695	93	367	14	779

Weaver Union Elementary
3076 E Childs Ave • Merced, CA 95340-9583
(209) 723-7606
Grade Span: KG-08; **Agency Type:** 1
Schools: 2
1 Primary; 1 Middle; 0 High; 0 Other Level
2 Regular; 0 Special Education; 0 Vocational; 0 Alternative
0 Magnet; 0 Charter; 2 Title I Eligible; 2 School-wide Title I
Students: 1,591 (51.3% male; 48.7% female)
Individual Education Program: 163 (10.2%);
English Language Learner: 572 (36.0%); Migrant: 132 (8.3%)
Eligible for Free Lunch Program: 823 (51.7%)
Eligible for Reduced-Price Lunch Program: 154 (9.7%)
Teachers: 90.1 (17.7 to 1)
Librarians/Media Specialists: 1.5 (1,060.7 to 1)
Guidance Counselors: 2.0 (795.5 to 1)
Current Spending: ($ per student per year):
Total: $6,278; Instruction: $4,257; Support Services: $1,698
Enrollment, Drop-out Rates and Diploma Recipients by Race/Ethnicity

Category	Total	White	Black	Asian	AIAN	Hisp.
Enrollment (%)	100.0	27.3	8.0	15.2	0.1	49.5
Drop-out Rate (%)	n/a	n/a	n/a	n/a	n/a	n/a
H.S. Diplomas (#)	n/a	n/a	n/a	n/a	n/a	n/a

Winton Elementary
7000 N Center St • Winton, CA 95388-0008
Mailing Address: PO Box 8 • Winton, CA 95388-0008
(209) 357-6175
Grade Span: KG-08; **Agency Type:** 1
Schools: 3
2 Primary; 1 Middle; 0 High; 0 Other Level
3 Regular; 0 Special Education; 0 Vocational; 0 Alternative
0 Magnet; 0 Charter; 3 Title I Eligible; 3 School-wide Title I
Students: 1,793 (52.0% male; 48.0% female)
Individual Education Program: 126 (7.0%);
English Language Learner: 1,072 (59.8%); Migrant: 266 (14.8%)
Eligible for Free Lunch Program: 1,784 (99.5%)
Eligible for Reduced-Price Lunch Program: 0 (0.0%)
Teachers: 92.4 (19.4 to 1)
Librarians/Media Specialists: 0.0 (0.0 to 1)
Guidance Counselors: 1.0 (1,793.0 to 1)
Current Spending: ($ per student per year):
Total: $6,932; Instruction: $4,454; Support Services: $2,078
Enrollment, Drop-out Rates and Diploma Recipients by Race/Ethnicity

Category	Total	White	Black	Asian	AIAN	Hisp.
Enrollment (%)	100.0	12.3	3.0	7.8	0.2	76.7
Drop-out Rate (%)	n/a	n/a	n/a	n/a	n/a	n/a
H.S. Diplomas (#)	n/a	n/a	n/a	n/a	n/a	n/a

Monterey County

Alisal Union Elementary
1205 E Market St • Salinas, CA 93905-2831
(831) 753-5700 • http://www.monterey.k12.ca.us/~alisaldo/
Grade Span: KG-08; **Agency Type:** 1
Schools: 12
11 Primary; 1 Middle; 0 High; 0 Other Level
12 Regular; 0 Special Education; 0 Vocational; 0 Alternative
0 Magnet; 1 Charter; 11 Title I Eligible; 7 School-wide Title I
Students: 7,903 (51.7% male; 48.3% female)
Individual Education Program: 527 (6.7%);
English Language Learner: 5,635 (71.3%); Migrant: 4,307 (54.5%)
Eligible for Free Lunch Program: 5,400 (68.3%)
Eligible for Reduced-Price Lunch Program: 1,487 (18.8%)
Teachers: 338.5 (23.3 to 1)
Librarians/Media Specialists: 1.0 (7,903.0 to 1)
Guidance Counselors: 0.0 (0.0 to 1)
Current Spending: ($ per student per year):
Total: $6,478; Instruction: $4,118; Support Services: $2,034
Enrollment, Drop-out Rates and Diploma Recipients by Race/Ethnicity

Category	Total	White	Black	Asian	AIAN	Hisp.
Enrollment (%)	100.0	5.6	1.2	3.6	0.2	89.1
Drop-out Rate (%)	n/a	n/a	n/a	n/a	n/a	n/a
H.S. Diplomas (#)	n/a	n/a	n/a	n/a	n/a	n/a

Carmel Unified

4380 Carmel Valley Rd • Carmel, CA 93922-2700
Mailing Address: PO Box 222700 • Carmel, CA 93922-2700
(831) 624-1546 • http://schools.monterey.k12.ca.us/~carmeldo/
Grade Span: KG-12; **Agency Type:** 1
Schools: 6
3 Primary; 1 Middle; 2 High; 0 Other Level
5 Regular; 0 Special Education; 0 Vocational; 1 Alternative
0 Magnet; 0 Charter; 2 Title I Eligible; 0 School-wide Title I
Students: 2,199 (52.3% male; 47.7% female)
Individual Education Program: 214 (9.7%);
English Language Learner: 100 (4.5%); Migrant: 0 (0.0%)
Eligible for Free Lunch Program: 143 (6.5%)
Eligible for Reduced-Price Lunch Program: 92 (4.2%)
Teachers: 133.0 (16.5 to 1)
Librarians/Media Specialists: 2.0 (1,099.5 to 1)
Guidance Counselors: 7.0 (314.1 to 1)
Current Spending: ($ per student per year):
Total: $9,858; Instruction: $5,692; Support Services: $3,990
Enrollment, Drop-out Rates and Diploma Recipients by Race/Ethnicity

Category	Total	White	Black	Asian	AIAN	Hisp.
Enrollment (%)	100.0	81.0	0.6	3.7	0.8	8.8
Drop-out Rate (%)	n/a	n/a	n/a	n/a	n/a	n/a
H.S. Diplomas (#)	177	151	1	9	1	13

Gonzales Unified

600 Elko St • Gonzales, CA 93926-3033
Mailing Address: PO Drawer G • Gonzales, CA 93926-3033
(831) 675-0100 • http://schools.monterey.k12.ca.us/~gonzunif/
Grade Span: KG-12; **Agency Type:** 1
Schools: 3
1 Primary; 1 Middle; 1 High; 0 Other Level
3 Regular; 0 Special Education; 0 Vocational; 0 Alternative
0 Magnet; 0 Charter; 3 Title I Eligible; 3 School-wide Title I
Students: 2,375 (50.4% male; 49.6% female)
Individual Education Program: 209 (8.8%);
English Language Learner: 1,534 (64.6%); Migrant: 1,334 (56.2%)
Eligible for Free Lunch Program: 1,232 (51.9%)
Eligible for Reduced-Price Lunch Program: 355 (14.9%)
Teachers: 111.1 (21.4 to 1)
Librarians/Media Specialists: 0.8 (2,968.8 to 1)
Guidance Counselors: 3.0 (791.7 to 1)
Current Spending: ($ per student per year):
Total: $8,059; Instruction: $4,756; Support Services: $2,996
Enrollment, Drop-out Rates and Diploma Recipients by Race/Ethnicity

Category	Total	White	Black	Asian	AIAN	Hisp.
Enrollment (%)	100.0	5.5	0.8	2.7	0.3	90.4
Drop-out Rate (%)	n/a	n/a	n/a	n/a	n/a	n/a
H.S. Diplomas (#)	147	6	6	2	0	133

Greenfield Union Elementary

493 El Camino Real • Greenfield, CA 93927-0097
(831) 674-2840 • http://www.greenfield.k12.ca.us/
Grade Span: KG-08; **Agency Type:** 1
Schools: 4
4 Primary; 0 Middle; 0 High; 0 Other Level
4 Regular; 0 Special Education; 0 Vocational; 0 Alternative
0 Magnet; 0 Charter; 4 Title I Eligible; 4 School-wide Title I
Students: 2,561 (48.7% male; 51.3% female)
Individual Education Program: 286 (11.2%);
English Language Learner: 1,486 (58.0%); Migrant: 1,068 (41.7%)
Eligible for Free Lunch Program: 1,405 (54.9%)
Eligible for Reduced-Price Lunch Program: 442 (17.3%)
Teachers: 129.2 (19.8 to 1)
Librarians/Media Specialists: 0.5 (5,122.0 to 1)
Guidance Counselors: 4.0 (640.3 to 1)
Current Spending: ($ per student per year):
Total: $7,102; Instruction: $4,167; Support Services: $2,526
Enrollment, Drop-out Rates and Diploma Recipients by Race/Ethnicity

Category	Total	White	Black	Asian	AIAN	Hisp.
Enrollment (%)	100.0	3.9	0.7	0.9	0.0	94.2
Drop-out Rate (%)	n/a	n/a	n/a	n/a	n/a	n/a
H.S. Diplomas (#)	n/a	n/a	n/a	n/a	n/a	n/a

King City Joint Union High

800 Broadway • King City, CA 93930-3326
(831) 385-0606 • http://www.kingcity.k12.ca.us/
Grade Span: 09-12; **Agency Type:** 1
Schools: 4
0 Primary; 0 Middle; 4 High; 0 Other Level
2 Regular; 0 Special Education; 0 Vocational; 2 Alternative
0 Magnet; 0 Charter; 2 Title I Eligible; 0 School-wide Title I
Students: 2,162 (50.1% male; 49.9% female)
Individual Education Program: 243 (11.2%);
English Language Learner: 287 (13.3%); Migrant: 1,169 (54.1%)
Eligible for Free Lunch Program: 1,035 (47.9%)
Eligible for Reduced-Price Lunch Program: 321 (14.8%)
Teachers: 86.7 (24.9 to 1)
Librarians/Media Specialists: 1.0 (2,162.0 to 1)
Guidance Counselors: 4.1 (527.3 to 1)
Current Spending: ($ per student per year):
Total: $6,430; Instruction: $3,864; Support Services: $2,566
Enrollment, Drop-out Rates and Diploma Recipients by Race/Ethnicity

Category	Total	White	Black	Asian	AIAN	Hisp.
Enrollment (%)	100.0	13.9	0.9	0.8	0.6	83.3
Drop-out Rate (%)	n/a	n/a	n/a	n/a	n/a	n/a
H.S. Diplomas (#)	340	64	1	1	2	269

King City Union Elementary

800 Broadway • King City, CA 93930-2984
(831) 385-1144 • http://www.kingcity.k12.ca.us/
Grade Span: KG-08; **Agency Type:** 1
Schools: 3
2 Primary; 1 Middle; 0 High; 0 Other Level
3 Regular; 0 Special Education; 0 Vocational; 0 Alternative
0 Magnet; 0 Charter; 3 Title I Eligible; 0 School-wide Title I
Students: 2,627 (52.6% male; 47.4% female)
Individual Education Program: 221 (8.4%);
English Language Learner: 1,461 (55.6%); Migrant: 1,042 (39.7%)
Eligible for Free Lunch Program: 1,463 (55.7%)
Eligible for Reduced-Price Lunch Program: 466 (17.7%)
Teachers: 133.6 (19.7 to 1)
Librarians/Media Specialists: 0.0 (0.0 to 1)
Guidance Counselors: 1.0 (2,627.0 to 1)
Current Spending: ($ per student per year):
Total: $6,234; Instruction: $4,193; Support Services: $1,607
Enrollment, Drop-out Rates and Diploma Recipients by Race/Ethnicity

Category	Total	White	Black	Asian	AIAN	Hisp.
Enrollment (%)	100.0	14.1	0.2	1.2	0.2	82.9
Drop-out Rate (%)	n/a	n/a	n/a	n/a	n/a	n/a
H.S. Diplomas (#)	n/a	n/a	n/a	n/a	n/a	n/a

Monterey Peninsula Unified

700 Pacific St • Monterey, CA 93942-1031
(831) 645-1200 • http://www.mpusd.k12.ca.us/
Grade Span: KG-12; **Agency Type:** 1
Schools: 23
14 Primary; 4 Middle; 4 High; 1 Other Level
22 Regular; 0 Special Education; 0 Vocational; 1 Alternative
0 Magnet; 3 Charter; 10 Title I Eligible; 7 School-wide Title I
Students: 12,312 (51.1% male; 48.9% female)
Individual Education Program: 1,475 (12.0%);
English Language Learner: 3,169 (25.7%); Migrant: 446 (3.6%)
Eligible for Free Lunch Program: 4,107 (33.4%)
Eligible for Reduced-Price Lunch Program: 1,236 (10.0%)
Teachers: 588.5 (20.9 to 1)
Librarians/Media Specialists: 4.0 (3,078.0 to 1)
Guidance Counselors: 12.0 (1,026.0 to 1)
Current Spending: ($ per student per year):
Total: $6,239; Instruction: $4,301; Support Services: $1,686
Enrollment, Drop-out Rates and Diploma Recipients by Race/Ethnicity

Category	Total	White	Black	Asian	AIAN	Hisp.
Enrollment (%)	100.0	34.3	11.9	16.2	0.7	34.4
Drop-out Rate (%)	n/a	n/a	n/a	n/a	n/a	n/a
H.S. Diplomas (#)	611	265	84	144	3	115

North Monterey County Unified

8142 Moss Landing Rd • Moss Landing, CA 95039-0049
(831) 633-3343 • http://www.nmcusd.org/
Grade Span: KG-12; **Agency Type:** 1
Schools: 12
4 Primary; 2 Middle; 4 High; 2 Other Level
8 Regular; 0 Special Education; 0 Vocational; 4 Alternative
0 Magnet; 1 Charter; 9 Title I Eligible; 0 School-wide Title I
Students: 6,109 (50.3% male; 49.7% female)
Individual Education Program: 420 (6.9%);
English Language Learner: 1,614 (26.4%); Migrant: 2,107 (34.5%)
Eligible for Free Lunch Program: 2,669 (43.7%)
Eligible for Reduced-Price Lunch Program: 697 (11.4%)
Teachers: 301.8 (20.2 to 1)
Librarians/Media Specialists: 1.0 (6,109.0 to 1)
Guidance Counselors: 7.0 (872.7 to 1)
Current Spending: ($ per student per year):
Total: $7,386; Instruction: $4,497; Support Services: $2,682
Enrollment, Drop-out Rates and Diploma Recipients by Race/Ethnicity

Category	Total	White	Black	Asian	AIAN	Hisp.
Enrollment (%)	100.0	38.6	1.4	3.7	0.5	53.3
Drop-out Rate (%)	n/a	n/a	n/a	n/a	n/a	n/a
H.S. Diplomas (#)	415	236	7	21	1	148

Pacific Grove Unified

555 Sinex Ave • Pacific Grove, CA 93950-4320
(831) 646-6520 • http://www.pgusd.org/
Grade Span: KG-12; **Agency Type:** 1
Schools: 5
2 Primary; 1 Middle; 2 High; 0 Other Level
4 Regular; 0 Special Education; 0 Vocational; 1 Alternative
0 Magnet; 0 Charter; 2 Title I Eligible; 0 School-wide Title I
Students: 1,952 (52.0% male; 48.0% female)
Individual Education Program: 285 (14.6%);
English Language Learner: 66 (3.4%); Migrant: 0 (0.0%)
Eligible for Free Lunch Program: 138 (7.1%)
Eligible for Reduced-Price Lunch Program: 40 (2.0%)
Teachers: 96.2 (20.3 to 1)
Librarians/Media Specialists: 1.8 (1,084.4 to 1)
Guidance Counselors: 3.8 (513.7 to 1)
Current Spending: ($ per student per year):
Total: $7,604; Instruction: $4,750; Support Services: $2,682
Enrollment, Drop-out Rates and Diploma Recipients by Race/Ethnicity

Category	Total	White	Black	Asian	AIAN	Hisp.
Enrollment (%)	100.0	79.4	1.9	7.6	0.4	9.9
Drop-out Rate (%)	n/a	n/a	n/a	n/a	n/a	n/a
H.S. Diplomas (#)	174	139	3	17	3	12

Salinas City Elementary

431 W Alisal St • Salinas, CA 93901-1624
(831) 753-5600 • http://schools.monterey.k12.ca.us/~salcity/
Grade Span: KG-06; **Agency Type:** 1
Schools: 14
14 Primary; 0 Middle; 0 High; 0 Other Level
13 Regular; 0 Special Education; 0 Vocational; 1 Alternative
0 Magnet; 0 Charter; 9 Title I Eligible; 8 School-wide Title I
Students: 9,079 (50.5% male; 49.5% female)
Individual Education Program: 525 (5.8%);
English Language Learner: 4,134 (45.5%); Migrant: 4,546 (50.1%)
Eligible for Free Lunch Program: 4,715 (51.9%)
Eligible for Reduced-Price Lunch Program: 1,745 (19.2%)
Teachers: 457.2 (19.9 to 1)
Librarians/Media Specialists: 0.0 (0.0 to 1)
Guidance Counselors: 0.0 (0.0 to 1)
Current Spending: ($ per student per year):
Total: $5,948; Instruction: $4,314; Support Services: $1,324
Enrollment, Drop-out Rates and Diploma Recipients by Race/Ethnicity

Category	Total	White	Black	Asian	AIAN	Hisp.
Enrollment (%)	100.0	15.3	3.0	5.7	0.3	74.5
Drop-out Rate (%)	n/a	n/a	n/a	n/a	n/a	n/a
H.S. Diplomas (#)	n/a	n/a	n/a	n/a	n/a	n/a

Salinas Union High

431 W Alisal St • Salinas, CA 93901-1624
(831) 796-7000 • http://www.salinas.k12.ca.us/
Grade Span: 07-12; **Agency Type:** 1
Schools: 10
0 Primary; 5 Middle; 5 High; 0 Other Level
8 Regular; 0 Special Education; 0 Vocational; 2 Alternative
0 Magnet; 0 Charter; 8 Title I Eligible; 0 School-wide Title I
Students: 13,599 (50.6% male; 49.4% female)
Individual Education Program: 1,149 (8.4%);
English Language Learner: 5,411 (39.8%); Migrant: 4,619 (34.0%)
Eligible for Free Lunch Program: 4,989 (36.7%)
Eligible for Reduced-Price Lunch Program: 1,949 (14.3%)
Teachers: 600.6 (22.6 to 1)
Librarians/Media Specialists: 3.8 (3,578.7 to 1)
Guidance Counselors: 30.2 (450.3 to 1)
Current Spending: ($ per student per year):
Total: $6,281; Instruction: $3,838; Support Services: $2,236
Enrollment, Drop-out Rates and Diploma Recipients by Race/Ethnicity

Category	Total	White	Black	Asian	AIAN	Hisp.
Enrollment (%)	100.0	16.7	2.2	6.8	0.4	73.7
Drop-out Rate (%)	n/a	n/a	n/a	n/a	n/a	n/a
H.S. Diplomas (#)	1,443	331	43	113	8	948

Santa Rita Union Elementary

57 Russell Rd • Salinas, CA 93906-4325
(831) 443-7200 • http://www.santaritaschools.org/home.html
Grade Span: KG-08; **Agency Type:** 1
Schools: 4
3 Primary; 1 Middle; 0 High; 0 Other Level
4 Regular; 0 Special Education; 0 Vocational; 0 Alternative
0 Magnet; 0 Charter; 3 Title I Eligible; 1 School-wide Title I
Students: 2,995 (51.1% male; 48.9% female)
Individual Education Program: 226 (7.5%);
English Language Learner: 978 (32.7%); Migrant: 404 (13.5%)
Eligible for Free Lunch Program: 914 (30.5%)
Eligible for Reduced-Price Lunch Program: 501 (16.7%)
Teachers: 148.5 (20.2 to 1)
Librarians/Media Specialists: 0.0 (0.0 to 1)
Guidance Counselors: 1.0 (2,995.0 to 1)
Current Spending: ($ per student per year):
Total: $5,804; Instruction: $3,888; Support Services: $1,675
Enrollment, Drop-out Rates and Diploma Recipients by Race/Ethnicity

Category	Total	White	Black	Asian	AIAN	Hisp.
Enrollment (%)	100.0	17.4	3.6	9.6	0.8	67.6
Drop-out Rate (%)	n/a	n/a	n/a	n/a	n/a	n/a
H.S. Diplomas (#)	n/a	n/a	n/a	n/a	n/a	n/a

Soledad Unified

1261 Metz Rd • Soledad, CA 93960-0186
Mailing Address: PO Box 186 • Soledad, CA 93960-0186
(831) 678-3987 • http://mainst.monterey.k12.ca.us/
Grade Span: KG-12; **Agency Type:** 1
Schools: 7
3 Primary; 1 Middle; 3 High; 0 Other Level
5 Regular; 0 Special Education; 0 Vocational; 2 Alternative
0 Magnet; 0 Charter; 7 Title I Eligible; 3 School-wide Title I
Students: 3,655 (52.1% male; 47.9% female)
Individual Education Program: 235 (6.4%);
English Language Learner: 2,118 (57.9%); Migrant: 1,424 (39.0%)
Eligible for Free Lunch Program: 3,032 (83.0%)
Eligible for Reduced-Price Lunch Program: 278 (7.6%)
Teachers: 163.8 (22.3 to 1)
Librarians/Media Specialists: 1.0 (3,655.0 to 1)
Guidance Counselors: 4.0 (913.8 to 1)
Current Spending: ($ per student per year):
Total: $6,139; Instruction: $3,717; Support Services: $2,028
Enrollment, Drop-out Rates and Diploma Recipients by Race/Ethnicity

Category	Total	White	Black	Asian	AIAN	Hisp.
Enrollment (%)	100.0	4.2	1.1	1.9	0.2	91.8
Drop-out Rate (%)	n/a	n/a	n/a	n/a	n/a	n/a
H.S. Diplomas (#)	150	4	0	7	0	136

Napa County

Napa Valley Unified

2425 Jefferson St • Napa, CA 94558-4931
(707) 253-3715 • http://www.nvusd.k12.ca.us/
Grade Span: KG-12; **Agency Type:** 1
Schools: 36
24 Primary; 5 Middle; 5 High; 2 Other Level
27 Regular; 0 Special Education; 0 Vocational; 9 Alternative
4 Magnet; 4 Charter; 16 Title I Eligible; 5 School-wide Title I
Students: 16,881 (51.4% male; 48.6% female)
Individual Education Program: 1,913 (11.3%);
English Language Learner: 4,518 (26.8%); Migrant: 1,102 (6.5%)
Eligible for Free Lunch Program: 4,198 (24.9%)
Eligible for Reduced-Price Lunch Program: 1,758 (10.4%)
Teachers: 840.2 (20.1 to 1)
Librarians/Media Specialists: 4.6 (3,669.8 to 1)
Guidance Counselors: 14.8 (1,140.6 to 1)
Current Spending: ($ per student per year):
Total: $6,360; Instruction: $4,130; Support Services: $2,011
Enrollment, Drop-out Rates and Diploma Recipients by Race/Ethnicity

Category	Total	White	Black	Asian	AIAN	Hisp.
Enrollment (%)	100.0	52.9	2.2	5.0	2.0	37.7
Drop-out Rate (%)	n/a	n/a	n/a	n/a	n/a	n/a
H.S. Diplomas (#)	998	681	22	63	12	210

Saint Helena Unified

465 Main St • Saint Helena, CA 94574-2159
(707) 967-2708 • http://www.sthelena.k12.ca.us/
Grade Span: KG-12; **Agency Type:** 1
Schools: 5
2 Primary; 1 Middle; 2 High; 0 Other Level
4 Regular; 0 Special Education; 0 Vocational; 1 Alternative
0 Magnet; 0 Charter; 5 Title I Eligible; 0 School-wide Title I
Students: 1,500 (50.7% male; 49.3% female)
Individual Education Program: 0 (0.0%);
English Language Learner: 385 (25.7%); Migrant: 202 (13.5%)
Eligible for Free Lunch Program: 347 (23.1%)
Eligible for Reduced-Price Lunch Program: 186 (12.4%)
Teachers: 82.0 (18.3 to 1)
Librarians/Media Specialists: 0.0 (0.0 to 1)
Guidance Counselors: 4.0 (375.0 to 1)
Current Spending: ($ per student per year):
Total: $7,404; Instruction: $4,405; Support Services: $2,739
Enrollment, Drop-out Rates and Diploma Recipients by Race/Ethnicity

Category	Total	White	Black	Asian	AIAN	Hisp.
Enrollment (%)	100.0	54.3	0.3	0.7	0.1	43.2
Drop-out Rate (%)	n/a	n/a	n/a	n/a	n/a	n/a
H.S. Diplomas (#)	116	76	0	2	0	38

Nevada County

Grass Valley Elementary

10840 Gilmore Way • Grass Valley, CA 95945-5409
(530) 273-4483 • http://www.gvsd.k12.ca.us/
Grade Span: KG-08; **Agency Type:** 1
Schools: 7
5 Primary; 2 Middle; 0 High; 0 Other Level
4 Regular; 0 Special Education; 0 Vocational; 3 Alternative
0 Magnet; 1 Charter; 3 Title I Eligible; 0 School-wide Title I
Students: 1,932 (52.3% male; 47.7% female)
Individual Education Program: 217 (11.2%);
English Language Learner: 44 (2.3%); Migrant: 0 (0.0%)
Eligible for Free Lunch Program: 482 (24.9%)
Eligible for Reduced-Price Lunch Program: 220 (11.4%)
Teachers: 101.8 (19.0 to 1)
Librarians/Media Specialists: 0.2 (9,660.0 to 1)
Guidance Counselors: 1.5 (1,288.0 to 1)
Current Spending: ($ per student per year):
Total: $7,061; Instruction: $4,479; Support Services: $1,930
Enrollment, Drop-out Rates and Diploma Recipients by Race/Ethnicity

Category	Total	White	Black	Asian	AIAN	Hisp.
Enrollment (%)	100.0	82.2	1.4	1.9	2.4	8.0
Drop-out Rate (%)	n/a	n/a	n/a	n/a	n/a	n/a
H.S. Diplomas (#)	n/a	n/a	n/a	n/a	n/a	n/a

Nevada Joint Union High

11645 Ridge Rd • Grass Valley, CA 95945-5024
(530) 273-3351 •
http://www.nuhsd.k12.ca.us/scripts/page.pl?p=dist_scl.htm
Grade Span: 08-12; **Agency Type:** 1
Schools: 9
0 Primary; 0 Middle; 9 High; 0 Other Level
2 Regular; 0 Special Education; 0 Vocational; 7 Alternative
0 Magnet; 0 Charter; 2 Title I Eligible; 0 School-wide Title I
Students: 4,354 (53.5% male; 46.5% female)
Individual Education Program: 370 (8.5%);
English Language Learner: 24 (0.6%); Migrant: 0 (0.0%)
Eligible for Free Lunch Program: 247 (5.7%)
Eligible for Reduced-Price Lunch Program: 94 (2.2%)
Teachers: 204.6 (21.3 to 1)
Librarians/Media Specialists: 1.9 (2,291.6 to 1)
Guidance Counselors: 10.5 (414.7 to 1)
Current Spending: ($ per student per year):
Total: $6,977; Instruction: $4,128; Support Services: $2,675
Enrollment, Drop-out Rates and Diploma Recipients by Race/Ethnicity

Category	Total	White	Black	Asian	AIAN	Hisp.
Enrollment (%)	100.0	91.8	0.7	1.5	1.8	4.1
Drop-out Rate (%)	n/a	n/a	n/a	n/a	n/a	n/a
H.S. Diplomas (#)	907	821	12	21	11	42

Pleasant Ridge Union Elementary

22580 Kingston Ln • Grass Valley, CA 95949-7706
(530) 268-2800 • http://www.pleasantridge.k12.ca.us/
Grade Span: KG-08; **Agency Type:** 1
Schools: 4
4 Primary; 0 Middle; 0 High; 0 Other Level
4 Regular; 0 Special Education; 0 Vocational; 0 Alternative
0 Magnet; 0 Charter; 4 Title I Eligible; 0 School-wide Title I
Students: 2,071 (51.6% male; 48.4% female)
Individual Education Program: 165 (8.0%);
English Language Learner: 3 (0.1%); Migrant: 0 (0.0%)
Eligible for Free Lunch Program: 185 (8.9%)
Eligible for Reduced-Price Lunch Program: 110 (5.3%)
Teachers: 103.2 (20.1 to 1)
Librarians/Media Specialists: 0.0 (0.0 to 1)
Guidance Counselors: 1.0 (2,071.0 to 1)
Current Spending: ($ per student per year):
Total: $5,876; Instruction: $4,209; Support Services: $1,571
Enrollment, Drop-out Rates and Diploma Recipients by Race/Ethnicity

Category	Total	White	Black	Asian	AIAN	Hisp.
Enrollment (%)	100.0	91.3	0.9	1.7	1.1	4.5
Drop-out Rate (%)	n/a	n/a	n/a	n/a	n/a	n/a
H.S. Diplomas (#)	n/a	n/a	n/a	n/a	n/a	n/a

Twin Ridges Elementary

18847 Oak Tree Rd • North San Juan, CA 95960-0529
Mailing Address: PO Box 529 • North San Juan, CA 95960-0529
(530) 292-4221
Grade Span: KG-12; **Agency Type:** 1
Schools: 13
11 Primary; 0 Middle; 1 High; 1 Other Level
12 Regular; 0 Special Education; 0 Vocational; 1 Alternative
0 Magnet; 11 Charter; 4 Title I Eligible; 2 School-wide Title I
Students: 1,854 (49.4% male; 50.6% female)
Individual Education Program: 164 (8.8%);
English Language Learner: 0 (0.0%); Migrant: 0 (0.0%)
Eligible for Free Lunch Program: 4 (0.2%)
Eligible for Reduced-Price Lunch Program: 496 (26.8%)
Teachers: 99.2 (18.7 to 1)
Librarians/Media Specialists: 0.0 (0.0 to 1)
Guidance Counselors: 0.2 (9,270.0 to 1)
Current Spending: ($ per student per year):
Total: $7,131; Instruction: $4,170; Support Services: $2,911
Enrollment, Drop-out Rates and Diploma Recipients by Race/Ethnicity

Category	Total	White	Black	Asian	AIAN	Hisp.
Enrollment (%)	100.0	84.3	1.8	1.9	2.1	7.1
Drop-out Rate (%)	n/a	n/a	n/a	n/a	n/a	n/a
H.S. Diplomas (#)	33	28	1	1	0	1

Orange County

Anaheim Elementary

1001 SE St • Anaheim, CA 92805-5749
(714) 517-7500 • http://www.acsd.k12.ca.us/
Grade Span: KG-06; **Agency Type:** 1
Schools: 23
23 Primary; 0 Middle; 0 High; 0 Other Level
23 Regular; 0 Special Education; 0 Vocational; 0 Alternative
0 Magnet; 0 Charter; 23 Title I Eligible; 10 School-wide Title I
Students: 22,375 (51.1% male; 48.9% female)
Individual Education Program: 2,184 (9.8%);
English Language Learner: 14,359 (64.2%); Migrant: 175 (0.8%)
Eligible for Free Lunch Program: 14,352 (64.1%)
Eligible for Reduced-Price Lunch Program: 4,446 (19.9%)
Teachers: 1,038.5 (21.5 to 1)
Librarians/Media Specialists: 0.0 (0.0 to 1)
Guidance Counselors: 1.0 (22,375.0 to 1)
Current Spending: ($ per student per year):
Total: $5,975; Instruction: $3,856; Support Services: $2,111
Enrollment, Drop-out Rates and Diploma Recipients by Race/Ethnicity

Category	Total	White	Black	Asian	AIAN	Hisp.
Enrollment (%)	100.0	8.6	1.9	6.4	0.3	82.1
Drop-out Rate (%)	n/a	n/a	n/a	n/a	n/a	n/a
H.S. Diplomas (#)	n/a	n/a	n/a	n/a	n/a	n/a

Anaheim Union High

501 Crescent Way • Anaheim, CA 92803-3520
Mailing Address: PO Box 3520 • Anaheim, CA 92803-3520
(714) 999-3511 • http://www.auhsd.k12.ca.us/
Grade Span: 07-12; **Agency Type:** 1
Schools: 21
0 Primary; 8 Middle; 12 High; 1 Other Level
17 Regular; 1 Special Education; 0 Vocational; 3 Alternative
0 Magnet; 0 Charter; 9 Title I Eligible; 6 School-wide Title I
Students: 31,338 (51.2% male; 48.8% female)
Individual Education Program: 3,682 (11.7%);
English Language Learner: 8,847 (28.2%); Migrant: 235 (0.7%)
Eligible for Free Lunch Program: 10,087 (32.2%)
Eligible for Reduced-Price Lunch Program: 3,628 (11.6%)
Teachers: 1,278.0 (24.5 to 1)
Librarians/Media Specialists: 13.0 (2,410.6 to 1)
Guidance Counselors: 63.0 (497.4 to 1)
Current Spending: ($ per student per year):
Total: $6,681; Instruction: $4,003; Support Services: $2,155
Enrollment, Drop-out Rates and Diploma Recipients by Race/Ethnicity

Category	Total	White	Black	Asian	AIAN	Hisp.
Enrollment (%)	100.0	26.0	3.4	16.3	0.5	53.7
Drop-out Rate (%)	n/a	n/a	n/a	n/a	n/a	n/a
H.S. Diplomas (#)	3,688	1,103	150	735	22	1,678

Brea-Olinda Unified

Number One Civic Center • Brea, CA 92821-9990
Mailing Address: PO Box 300 • Brea, CA 92821-9990
(714) 990-7800 • http://www.bousd.k12.ca.us/
Grade Span: KG-12; **Agency Type:** 1
Schools: 9
6 Primary; 1 Middle; 2 High; 0 Other Level
8 Regular; 0 Special Education; 0 Vocational; 1 Alternative
0 Magnet; 0 Charter; 4 Title I Eligible; 0 School-wide Title I
Students: 6,123 (51.5% male; 48.5% female)
Individual Education Program: 599 (9.8%);
English Language Learner: 643 (10.5%); Migrant: 0 (0.0%)
Eligible for Free Lunch Program: 681 (11.1%)
Eligible for Reduced-Price Lunch Program: 441 (7.2%)
Teachers: 285.7 (21.4 to 1)
Librarians/Media Specialists: 0.0 (0.0 to 1)
Guidance Counselors: 5.2 (1,177.5 to 1)
Current Spending: ($ per student per year):
Total: $6,198; Instruction: $3,792; Support Services: $2,137

Enrollment, Drop-out Rates and Diploma Recipients by Race/Ethnicity

Category	Total	White	Black	Asian	AIAN	Hisp.
Enrollment (%)	100.0	60.2	1.7	13.4	0.3	24.1
Drop-out Rate (%)	n/a	n/a	n/a	n/a	n/a	n/a
H.S. Diplomas (#)	487	288	7	80	3	84

Buena Park Elementary

6885 Orangethorpe Ave • Buena Park, CA 90620-1348
(714) 522-8412 • http://www.ocde.k12.ca.us/bpsd/
Grade Span: KG-08; **Agency Type:** 1
Schools: 7
6 Primary; 1 Middle; 0 High; 0 Other Level
7 Regular; 0 Special Education; 0 Vocational; 0 Alternative
0 Magnet; 0 Charter; 7 Title I Eligible; 3 School-wide Title I
Students: 6,384 (50.1% male; 49.9% female)
Individual Education Program: 739 (11.6%);
English Language Learner: 2,768 (43.4%); Migrant: 5 (0.1%)
Eligible for Free Lunch Program: 3,206 (50.2%)
Eligible for Reduced-Price Lunch Program: 1,016 (15.9%)
Teachers: 298.0 (21.4 to 1)
Librarians/Media Specialists: 0.0 (0.0 to 1)
Guidance Counselors: 0.0 (0.0 to 1)
Current Spending: ($ per student per year):
Total: $6,337; Instruction: $4,137; Support Services: $1,898

Enrollment, Drop-out Rates and Diploma Recipients by Race/Ethnicity

Category	Total	White	Black	Asian	AIAN	Hisp.
Enrollment (%)	100.0	19.7	6.1	17.5	0.2	56.2
Drop-out Rate (%)	n/a	n/a	n/a	n/a	n/a	n/a
H.S. Diplomas (#)	n/a	n/a	n/a	n/a	n/a	n/a

Capistrano Unified

32972 Calle Perfecto • San Juan Capistrano, CA 92675-4706
(949) 489-7000 • http://www.capousd.k12.ca.us/
Grade Span: KG-12; **Agency Type:** 1
Schools: 51
36 Primary; 8 Middle; 7 High; 0 Other Level
48 Regular; 1 Special Education; 0 Vocational; 2 Alternative
0 Magnet; 1 Charter; 16 Title I Eligible; 3 School-wide Title I
Students: 48,608 (51.6% male; 48.4% female)
Individual Education Program: 4,544 (9.3%);
English Language Learner: 6,882 (14.2%); Migrant: 189 (0.4%)
Eligible for Free Lunch Program: 2,276 (4.7%)
Eligible for Reduced-Price Lunch Program: 6,299 (13.0%)
Teachers: 2,141.8 (22.7 to 1)
Librarians/Media Specialists: 1.0 (48,608.0 to 1)
Guidance Counselors: 8.0 (6,076.0 to 1)
Current Spending: ($ per student per year):
Total: $6,135; Instruction: $4,027; Support Services: $1,916

Enrollment, Drop-out Rates and Diploma Recipients by Race/Ethnicity

Category	Total	White	Black	Asian	AIAN	Hisp.
Enrollment (%)	100.0	69.6	1.3	6.6	0.4	18.1
Drop-out Rate (%)	n/a	n/a	n/a	n/a	n/a	n/a
H.S. Diplomas (#)	2,644	1,951	26	152	8	292

Centralia Elementary

6625 La Palma Ave • Buena Park, CA 90620-2859
(714) 228-3100 • http://www.cesd.k12.ca.us/main.htm
Grade Span: KG-06; **Agency Type:** 1
Schools: 9
9 Primary; 0 Middle; 0 High; 0 Other Level
9 Regular; 0 Special Education; 0 Vocational; 0 Alternative
0 Magnet; 0 Charter; 3 Title I Eligible; 1 School-wide Title I
Students: 5,352 (51.8% male; 48.2% female)
Individual Education Program: 494 (9.2%);
English Language Learner: 1,537 (28.7%); Migrant: 4 (0.1%)
Eligible for Free Lunch Program: 1,803 (33.7%)
Eligible for Reduced-Price Lunch Program: 578 (10.8%)
Teachers: 248.4 (21.5 to 1)
Librarians/Media Specialists: 0.0 (0.0 to 1)
Guidance Counselors: 5.1 (1,049.4 to 1)
Current Spending: ($ per student per year):
Total: $6,117; Instruction: $3,758; Support Services: $2,102

Enrollment, Drop-out Rates and Diploma Recipients by Race/Ethnicity

Category	Total	White	Black	Asian	AIAN	Hisp.
Enrollment (%)	100.0	28.1	4.7	23.2	0.6	41.9
Drop-out Rate (%)	n/a	n/a	n/a	n/a	n/a	n/a
H.S. Diplomas (#)	n/a	n/a	n/a	n/a	n/a	n/a

Cypress Elementary

9470 Moody St • Cypress, CA 90630-2919
(714) 220-6900 • http://www.cypsd.k12.ca.us/
Grade Span: KG-06; **Agency Type:** 1
Schools: 10
10 Primary; 0 Middle; 0 High; 0 Other Level
10 Regular; 0 Special Education; 0 Vocational; 0 Alternative
0 Magnet; 0 Charter; 2 Title I Eligible; 0 School-wide Title I
Students: 4,815 (52.5% male; 47.5% female)
Individual Education Program: 514 (10.7%);
English Language Learner: 593 (12.3%); Migrant: 0 (0.0%)
Eligible for Free Lunch Program: 910 (18.9%)
Eligible for Reduced-Price Lunch Program: 472 (9.8%)
Teachers: 247.7 (19.4 to 1)
Librarians/Media Specialists: 0.0 (0.0 to 1)
Guidance Counselors: 0.0 (0.0 to 1)
Current Spending: ($ per student per year):
Total: $6,274; Instruction: $4,230; Support Services: $1,801

Enrollment, Drop-out Rates and Diploma Recipients by Race/Ethnicity

Category	Total	White	Black	Asian	AIAN	Hisp.
Enrollment (%)	100.0	45.8	4.9	28.2	0.8	19.8
Drop-out Rate (%)	n/a	n/a	n/a	n/a	n/a	n/a
H.S. Diplomas (#)	n/a	n/a	n/a	n/a	n/a	n/a

Fountain Valley Elementary

17210 Oak St • Fountain Valley, CA 92708-3405
(714) 843-3200 • http://www.fvsd.k12.ca.us/
Grade Span: KG-08; **Agency Type:** 1
Schools: 11
8 Primary; 3 Middle; 0 High; 0 Other Level
11 Regular; 0 Special Education; 0 Vocational; 0 Alternative
0 Magnet; 0 Charter; 5 Title I Eligible; 0 School-wide Title I
Students: 6,320 (51.2% male; 48.8% female)
Individual Education Program: 621 (9.8%);
English Language Learner: 460 (7.3%); Migrant: 3 (<0.1%)
Eligible for Free Lunch Program: 450 (7.1%)
Eligible for Reduced-Price Lunch Program: 263 (4.2%)
Teachers: 285.2 (22.2 to 1)
Librarians/Media Specialists: 1.0 (6,320.0 to 1)
Guidance Counselors: 0.4 (15,800.0 to 1)
Current Spending: ($ per student per year):
Total: $6,620; Instruction: $4,256; Support Services: $2,220

Enrollment, Drop-out Rates and Diploma Recipients by Race/Ethnicity

Category	Total	White	Black	Asian	AIAN	Hisp.
Enrollment (%)	100.0	61.1	1.1	24.3	0.8	12.0
Drop-out Rate (%)	n/a	n/a	n/a	n/a	n/a	n/a
H.S. Diplomas (#)	n/a	n/a	n/a	n/a	n/a	n/a

Fullerton Elementary

1401 W Valencia Dr • Fullerton, CA 92633-3938
(714) 447-7400 • http://www.fsd.k12.ca.us/
Grade Span: KG-08; **Agency Type:** 1
Schools: 19
16 Primary; 3 Middle; 0 High; 0 Other Level
19 Regular; 0 Special Education; 0 Vocational; 0 Alternative
2 Magnet; 0 Charter; 9 Title I Eligible; 5 School-wide Title I
Students: 13,554 (51.2% male; 48.8% female)
Individual Education Program: 1,386 (10.2%);
English Language Learner: 4,279 (31.6%); Migrant: 58 (0.4%)
Eligible for Free Lunch Program: 3,941 (29.1%)
Eligible for Reduced-Price Lunch Program: 1,129 (8.3%)
Teachers: 601.8 (22.5 to 1)
Librarians/Media Specialists: 1.2 (11,295.0 to 1)
Guidance Counselors: 3.8 (3,566.8 to 1)
Current Spending: ($ per student per year):
Total: $6,008; Instruction: $3,824; Support Services: $1,931

Enrollment, Drop-out Rates and Diploma Recipients by Race/Ethnicity

Category	Total	White	Black	Asian	AIAN	Hisp.
Enrollment (%)	100.0	33.6	2.4	18.7	0.2	45.2
Drop-out Rate (%)	n/a	n/a	n/a	n/a	n/a	n/a
H.S. Diplomas (#)	n/a	n/a	n/a	n/a	n/a	n/a

Fullerton Joint Union High

1051 W Bastanchury Rd • Fullerton, CA 92833-2247
(714) 870-2800 • http://www.fjuhsd.k12.ca.us/
Grade Span: 09-12; **Agency Type:** 1
Schools: 8
0 Primary; 0 Middle; 8 High; 0 Other Level
6 Regular; 0 Special Education; 0 Vocational; 2 Alternative
2 Magnet; 0 Charter; 3 Title I Eligible; 0 School-wide Title I
Students: 16,195 (49.5% male; 50.5% female)
Individual Education Program: 1,106 (6.8%);
English Language Learner: 4,874 (30.1%); Migrant: 5 (<0.1%)
Eligible for Free Lunch Program: 847 (5.2%)
Eligible for Reduced-Price Lunch Program: 117 (0.7%)
Teachers: 555.3 (29.2 to 1)
Librarians/Media Specialists: 5.0 (3,239.0 to 1)
Guidance Counselors: 15.0 (1,079.7 to 1)
Current Spending: ($ per student per year):
Total: $5,889; Instruction: $3,575; Support Services: $2,203

Enrollment, Drop-out Rates and Diploma Recipients by Race/Ethnicity

Category	Total	White	Black	Asian	AIAN	Hisp.
Enrollment (%)	100.0	29.0	2.4	19.8	0.3	48.1
Drop-out Rate (%)	n/a	n/a	n/a	n/a	n/a	n/a
H.S. Diplomas (#)	2,670	1,071	79	618	7	894

Garden Grove Unified

10331 Stanford Ave • Garden Grove, CA 92840-6351
(714) 663-6000 • http://www.ggusd.k12.ca.us/
Grade Span: KG-12; **Agency Type:** 1
Schools: 67
47 Primary; 10 Middle; 10 High; 0 Other Level
63 Regular; 2 Special Education; 0 Vocational; 2 Alternative
0 Magnet; 0 Charter; 55 Title I Eligible; 26 School-wide Title I
Students: 50,066 (51.0% male; 49.0% female)
Individual Education Program: 5,035 (10.1%);
English Language Learner: 26,407 (52.7%); Migrant: 14 (<0.1%)
Eligible for Free Lunch Program: 23,253 (46.4%)
Eligible for Reduced-Price Lunch Program: 6,830 (13.6%)
Teachers: 2,197.0 (22.8 to 1)
Librarians/Media Specialists: 15.0 (3,337.7 to 1)
Guidance Counselors: 35.0 (1,430.5 to 1)
Current Spending: ($ per student per year):
Total: $6,336; Instruction: $4,129; Support Services: $1,940

Enrollment, Drop-out Rates and Diploma Recipients by Race/Ethnicity

Category	Total	White	Black	Asian	AIAN	Hisp.
Enrollment (%)	100.0	17.7	1.2	30.0	0.3	50.8
Drop-out Rate (%)	n/a	n/a	n/a	n/a	n/a	n/a
H.S. Diplomas (#)	2,738	643	25	1,095	4	971

Huntington Beach City Elementary

20451 Craimer Ln • Huntington Beach, CA 92646-0071
(714) 964-8888 • http://hbuhsd.k12.ca.us/
Grade Span: KG-08; **Agency Type:** 1
Schools: 10
8 Primary; 2 Middle; 0 High; 0 Other Level
10 Regular; 0 Special Education; 0 Vocational; 0 Alternative
0 Magnet; 0 Charter; 4 Title I Eligible; 0 School-wide Title I
Students: 6,998 (51.8% male; 48.2% female)
Individual Education Program: 729 (10.4%);
English Language Learner: 527 (7.5%); Migrant: 0 (0.0%)
Eligible for Free Lunch Program: 711 (10.2%)
Eligible for Reduced-Price Lunch Program: 235 (3.4%)
Teachers: 308.3 (22.7 to 1)
Librarians/Media Specialists: 0.0 (0.0 to 1)
Guidance Counselors: 0.0 (0.0 to 1)
Current Spending: ($ per student per year):
Total: $6,139; Instruction: $4,126; Support Services: $1,815

Enrollment, Drop-out Rates and Diploma Recipients by Race/Ethnicity

Category	Total	White	Black	Asian	AIAN	Hisp.
Enrollment (%)	100.0	73.3	1.2	11.0	1.2	12.9
Drop-out Rate (%)	n/a	n/a	n/a	n/a	n/a	n/a
H.S. Diplomas (#)	n/a	n/a	n/a	n/a	n/a	n/a

Huntington Beach Union High

10251 Yorktown Ave • Huntington Beach, CA 92646-2999
(714) 964-3339 • http://www2.hbuhsd.org/
Grade Span: 09-12; **Agency Type:** 1
Schools: 8
0 Primary; 0 Middle; 8 High; 0 Other Level
6 Regular; 0 Special Education; 0 Vocational; 2 Alternative
1 Magnet; 0 Charter; 3 Title I Eligible; 1 School-wide Title I
Students: 14,668 (51.7% male; 48.3% female)
Individual Education Program: 1,515 (10.3%);
English Language Learner: 1,661 (11.3%); Migrant: 3 (<0.1%)
Eligible for Free Lunch Program: 1,875 (12.8%)
Eligible for Reduced-Price Lunch Program: 351 (2.4%)
Teachers: 582.1 (25.2 to 1)
Librarians/Media Specialists: 1.0 (14,668.0 to 1)
Guidance Counselors: 1.0 (14,668.0 to 1)
Current Spending: ($ per student per year):
Total: $6,587; Instruction: $3,757; Support Services: $2,628

Enrollment, Drop-out Rates and Diploma Recipients by Race/Ethnicity

Category	Total	White	Black	Asian	AIAN	Hisp.
Enrollment (%)	100.0	50.3	1.2	24.8	5.7	18.0
Drop-out Rate (%)	n/a	n/a	n/a	n/a	n/a	n/a
H.S. Diplomas (#)	2,905	1,449	36	788	212	418

Irvine Unified

5050 Barranca Pkwy • Irvine, CA 92604-4652
(949) 936-5000 • http://www.iusd.k12.ca.us/
Grade Span: KG-12; **Agency Type:** 1
Schools: 34
22 Primary; 5 Middle; 5 High; 2 Other Level
31 Regular; 0 Special Education; 0 Vocational; 3 Alternative
0 Magnet; 0 Charter; 9 Title I Eligible; 0 School-wide Title I
Students: 24,771 (51.6% male; 48.4% female)
Individual Education Program: 2,070 (8.4%);
English Language Learner: 3,201 (12.9%); Migrant: 0 (0.0%)
Eligible for Free Lunch Program: 1,113 (4.5%)
Eligible for Reduced-Price Lunch Program: 611 (2.5%)
Teachers: 1,057.6 (23.4 to 1)
Librarians/Media Specialists: 8.6 (2,880.3 to 1)
Guidance Counselors: 19.6 (1,263.8 to 1)
Current Spending: ($ per student per year):
Total: $6,317; Instruction: $4,173; Support Services: $1,996

Enrollment, Drop-out Rates and Diploma Recipients by Race/Ethnicity

Category	Total	White	Black	Asian	AIAN	Hisp.
Enrollment (%)	100.0	51.6	2.5	36.0	0.5	7.2
Drop-out Rate (%)	n/a	n/a	n/a	n/a	n/a	n/a
H.S. Diplomas (#)	1,838	1,081	29	628	1	94

La Habra City Elementary

500 N Walnut St • La Habra, CA 90633-0307
Mailing Address: PO Box 307 • La Habra, CA 90633-0307
(562) 690-2300 • http://www.lhcsd.k12.ca.us/
Grade Span: KG-08; **Agency Type:** 1
Schools: 9
7 Primary; 2 Middle; 0 High; 0 Other Level
9 Regular; 0 Special Education; 0 Vocational; 0 Alternative
0 Magnet; 0 Charter; 7 Title I Eligible; 3 School-wide Title I
Students: 6,456 (50.7% male; 49.3% female)
Individual Education Program: 555 (8.6%);
English Language Learner: 3,012 (46.7%); Migrant: 0 (0.0%)
Eligible for Free Lunch Program: 3,502 (54.2%)
Eligible for Reduced-Price Lunch Program: 862 (13.4%)
Teachers: 327.1 (19.7 to 1)
Librarians/Media Specialists: 0.0 (0.0 to 1)
Guidance Counselors: 0.0 (0.0 to 1)
Current Spending: ($ per student per year):
Total: $6,402; Instruction: $4,179; Support Services: $1,900

Enrollment, Drop-out Rates and Diploma Recipients by Race/Ethnicity

Category	Total	White	Black	Asian	AIAN	Hisp.
Enrollment (%)	100.0	22.2	1.6	3.0	0.0	73.2
Drop-out Rate (%)	n/a	n/a	n/a	n/a	n/a	n/a
H.S. Diplomas (#)	n/a	n/a	n/a	n/a	n/a	n/a

Laguna Beach Unified

550 Blumont St • Laguna Beach, CA 92651-2356
(949) 497-7700 • http://www.lagunabeachschools.org/
Grade Span: KG-12; **Agency Type:** 1
Schools: 4
2 Primary; 1 Middle; 1 High; 0 Other Level
4 Regular; 0 Special Education; 0 Vocational; 0 Alternative
0 Magnet; 0 Charter; 3 Title I Eligible; 0 School-wide Title I
Students: 2,700 (50.9% male; 49.1% female)
Individual Education Program: 208 (7.7%);
English Language Learner: 76 (2.8%); Migrant: 0 (0.0%)
Eligible for Free Lunch Program: 186 (6.9%)
Eligible for Reduced-Price Lunch Program: 56 (2.1%)
Teachers: 122.5 (22.0 to 1)
Librarians/Media Specialists: 0.0 (0.0 to 1)
Guidance Counselors: 3.0 (900.0 to 1)
Current Spending: ($ per student per year):
Total: $7,414; Instruction: $4,821; Support Services: $2,385

Enrollment, Drop-out Rates and Diploma Recipients by Race/Ethnicity

Category	Total	White	Black	Asian	AIAN	Hisp.
Enrollment (%)	100.0	83.6	1.1	3.6	0.5	9.6
Drop-out Rate (%)	n/a	n/a	n/a	n/a	n/a	n/a
H.S. Diplomas (#)	195	168	1	7	0	18

Los Alamitos Unified

10293 Bloomfield St • Los Alamitos, CA 90720-2264
(562) 799-4700 • http://www.losalusd.k12.ca.us/
Grade Span: KG-12; **Agency Type:** 1
Schools: 10
6 Primary; 2 Middle; 2 High; 0 Other Level
9 Regular; 0 Special Education; 0 Vocational; 1 Alternative
0 Magnet; 0 Charter; 3 Title I Eligible; 0 School-wide Title I
Students: 9,087 (51.0% male; 49.0% female)
Individual Education Program: 777 (8.6%);
English Language Learner: 200 (2.2%); Migrant: 0 (0.0%)
Eligible for Free Lunch Program: 521 (5.7%)
Eligible for Reduced-Price Lunch Program: 278 (3.1%)
Teachers: 397.2 (22.9 to 1)
Librarians/Media Specialists: 9.8 (927.2 to 1)
Guidance Counselors: 7.0 (1,298.1 to 1)
Current Spending: ($ per student per year):
Total: $6,711; Instruction: $4,512; Support Services: $1,992

Enrollment, Drop-out Rates and Diploma Recipients by Race/Ethnicity

Category	Total	White	Black	Asian	AIAN	Hisp.
Enrollment (%)	100.0	68.9	3.0	13.1	0.5	12.4
Drop-out Rate (%)	n/a	n/a	n/a	n/a	n/a	n/a
H.S. Diplomas (#)	657	469	27	79	2	79

Magnolia Elementary

2705 W Orange Ave • Anaheim, CA 92804-3203
(714) 761-5533 • http://www.msd.k12.ca.us/
Grade Span: KG-06; **Agency Type:** 1
Schools: 9
9 Primary; 0 Middle; 0 High; 0 Other Level
9 Regular; 0 Special Education; 0 Vocational; 0 Alternative
0 Magnet; 0 Charter; 9 Title I Eligible; 8 School-wide Title I
Students: 6,989 (50.8% male; 49.2% female)
Individual Education Program: 671 (9.6%);
English Language Learner: 3,478 (49.8%); Migrant: 34 (0.5%)
Eligible for Free Lunch Program: 3,984 (57.0%)
Eligible for Reduced-Price Lunch Program: 1,138 (16.3%)
Teachers: 352.1 (19.8 to 1)
Librarians/Media Specialists: 0.0 (0.0 to 1)
Guidance Counselors: 2.0 (3,494.5 to 1)
Current Spending: ($ per student per year):
Total: $6,401; Instruction: $4,257; Support Services: $1,823
Enrollment, Drop-out Rates and Diploma Recipients by Race/Ethnicity

Category	Total	White	Black	Asian	AIAN	Hisp.
Enrollment (%)	100.0	16.8	3.8	14.2	0.4	64.8
Drop-out Rate (%)	n/a	n/a	n/a	n/a	n/a	n/a
H.S. Diplomas (#)	n/a	n/a	n/a	n/a	n/a	n/a

Newport-Mesa Unified

2985-A Bear St • Costa Mesa, CA 92626
Mailing Address: PO Box 1368 • Newport Beach, CA 92663-0368
(714) 424-5000 • http://www.nmusd.k12.ca.us/
Grade Span: KG-12; **Agency Type:** 1
Schools: 31
20 Primary; 4 Middle; 7 High; 0 Other Level
29 Regular; 0 Special Education; 0 Vocational; 2 Alternative
0 Magnet; 0 Charter; 14 Title I Eligible; 4 School-wide Title I
Students: 22,275 (51.7% male; 48.3% female)
Individual Education Program: 2,443 (11.0%);
English Language Learner: 6,212 (27.9%); Migrant: 171 (0.8%)
Eligible for Free Lunch Program: 7,049 (31.6%)
Eligible for Reduced-Price Lunch Program: 1,482 (6.7%)
Teachers: 1,091.1 (20.4 to 1)
Librarians/Media Specialists: 6.8 (3,275.7 to 1)
Guidance Counselors: 24.2 (920.5 to 1)
Current Spending: ($ per student per year):
Total: $6,648; Instruction: $4,248; Support Services: $2,131
Enrollment, Drop-out Rates and Diploma Recipients by Race/Ethnicity

Category	Total	White	Black	Asian	AIAN	Hisp.
Enrollment (%)	100.0	53.7	1.2	6.0	0.3	38.7
Drop-out Rate (%)	n/a	n/a	n/a	n/a	n/a	n/a
H.S. Diplomas (#)	1,118	740	7	105	4	262

Ocean View Elementary

17200 Pinehurst Ln • Huntington Beach, CA 92647-5569
(714) 847-2551 • http://www.ovsd.org/
Grade Span: KG-08; **Agency Type:** 1
Schools: 15
11 Primary; 4 Middle; 0 High; 0 Other Level
15 Regular; 0 Special Education; 0 Vocational; 0 Alternative
0 Magnet; 0 Charter; 6 Title I Eligible; 0 School-wide Title I
Students: 10,180 (52.1% male; 47.9% female)
Individual Education Program: 1,016 (10.0%);
English Language Learner: 2,179 (21.4%); Migrant: 2 (<0.1%)
Eligible for Free Lunch Program: 2,636 (25.9%)
Eligible for Reduced-Price Lunch Program: 777 (7.6%)
Teachers: 488.9 (20.8 to 1)
Librarians/Media Specialists: 0.0 (0.0 to 1)
Guidance Counselors: 0.0 (0.0 to 1)
Current Spending: ($ per student per year):
Total: $6,316; Instruction: $4,360; Support Services: $1,769
Enrollment, Drop-out Rates and Diploma Recipients by Race/Ethnicity

Category	Total	White	Black	Asian	AIAN	Hisp.
Enrollment (%)	100.0	54.5	1.6	13.0	1.0	29.2
Drop-out Rate (%)	n/a	n/a	n/a	n/a	n/a	n/a
H.S. Diplomas (#)	n/a	n/a	n/a	n/a	n/a	n/a

Orange County Office of Ed

200 Kalmus Dr • Costa Mesa, CA 92628-9050
Mailing Address: PO Box 9050 • Costa Mesa, CA 92628-9050
(714) 966-4000 • http://www.ocde.k12.ca.us/
Grade Span: KG-12; **Agency Type:** 4
Schools: 4
0 Primary; 0 Middle; 0 High; 4 Other Level
1 Regular; 1 Special Education; 0 Vocational; 2 Alternative
0 Magnet; 0 Charter; 0 Title I Eligible; 0 School-wide Title I
Students: 8,271 (60.1% male; 39.9% female)
Individual Education Program: 1,135 (13.7%);
English Language Learner: 1,977 (23.9%); Migrant: 0 (0.0%)
Eligible for Free Lunch Program: 144 (1.7%)
Eligible for Reduced-Price Lunch Program: 11 (0.1%)
Teachers: 459.4 (18.0 to 1)
Librarians/Media Specialists: 1.0 (8,271.0 to 1)
Guidance Counselors: 2.0 (4,135.5 to 1)
Current Spending: ($ per student per year):
Total: $14,858; Instruction: $6,883; Support Services: $7,943
Enrollment, Drop-out Rates and Diploma Recipients by Race/Ethnicity

Category	Total	White	Black	Asian	AIAN	Hisp.
Enrollment (%)	100.0	37.0	3.1	5.8	0.6	49.2
Drop-out Rate (%)	n/a	n/a	n/a	n/a	n/a	n/a
H.S. Diplomas (#)	1,066	419	43	96	5	494

Orange Unified

1401 N Handy St • Orange, CA 92856-8122
Mailing Address: PO Box 11022 • Orange, CA 92856-8122
(714) 997-6100 • http://www.orangeusd.k12.ca.us/
Grade Span: KG-12; **Agency Type:** 1
Schools: 42
29 Primary; 6 Middle; 4 High; 3 Other Level
40 Regular; 1 Special Education; 0 Vocational; 1 Alternative
7 Magnet; 2 Charter; 16 Title I Eligible; 11 School-wide Title I
Students: 31,823 (51.6% male; 48.4% female)
Individual Education Program: 3,191 (10.0%);
English Language Learner: 6,741 (21.2%); Migrant: 168 (0.5%)
Eligible for Free Lunch Program: 8,763 (27.5%)
Eligible for Reduced-Price Lunch Program: 2,025 (6.4%)
Teachers: 1,506.4 (21.1 to 1)
Librarians/Media Specialists: 9.5 (3,349.8 to 1)
Guidance Counselors: 31.7 (1,003.9 to 1)
Current Spending: ($ per student per year):
Total: $5,939; Instruction: $3,784; Support Services: $1,936
Enrollment, Drop-out Rates and Diploma Recipients by Race/Ethnicity

Category	Total	White	Black	Asian	AIAN	Hisp.
Enrollment (%)	100.0	42.8	1.7	12.5	0.8	41.3
Drop-out Rate (%)	n/a	n/a	n/a	n/a	n/a	n/a
H.S. Diplomas (#)	2,065	1,015	74	389	15	564

Placentia-Yorba Linda Unified

1301 E Orangethorpe Ave • Placentia, CA 92670-5302
(714) 996-2550 • http://www.pylusd.k12.ca.us/
Grade Span: KG-12; **Agency Type:** 1
Schools: 30
21 Primary; 4 Middle; 5 High; 0 Other Level
27 Regular; 1 Special Education; 0 Vocational; 2 Alternative
4 Magnet; 0 Charter; 6 Title I Eligible; 5 School-wide Title I
Students: 26,464 (51.7% male; 48.3% female)
Individual Education Program: 2,870 (10.8%);
English Language Learner: 4,441 (16.8%); Migrant: 372 (1.4%)
Eligible for Free Lunch Program: 5,222 (19.7%)
Eligible for Reduced-Price Lunch Program: 1,648 (6.2%)
Teachers: 1,177.1 (22.5 to 1)
Librarians/Media Specialists: 3.0 (8,821.3 to 1)
Guidance Counselors: 19.8 (1,336.6 to 1)
Current Spending: ($ per student per year):
Total: $6,218; Instruction: $3,991; Support Services: $2,048
Enrollment, Drop-out Rates and Diploma Recipients by Race/Ethnicity

Category	Total	White	Black	Asian	AIAN	Hisp.
Enrollment (%)	100.0	59.3	1.7	9.2	0.4	29.3
Drop-out Rate (%)	n/a	n/a	n/a	n/a	n/a	n/a
H.S. Diplomas (#)	1,656	1,107	16	197	7	329

Saddleback Valley Unified

25631 Peter A Hartman Way • Mission Viejo, CA 92691-3199
(949) 586-1234 • http://www.svusd.k12.ca.us/
Grade Span: KG-12; **Agency Type:** 1
Schools: 37
26 Primary; 4 Middle; 6 High; 1 Other Level
34 Regular; 1 Special Education; 0 Vocational; 2 Alternative
0 Magnet; 1 Charter; 11 Title I Eligible; 0 School-wide Title I
Students: 35,566 (51.5% male; 48.5% female)
Individual Education Program: 3,122 (8.8%);
English Language Learner: 2,798 (7.9%); Migrant: 2 (<0.1%)
Eligible for Free Lunch Program: 3,202 (9.0%)
Eligible for Reduced-Price Lunch Program: 1,283 (3.6%)
Teachers: 1,566.9 (22.7 to 1)
Librarians/Media Specialists: 4.0 (8,891.5 to 1)
Guidance Counselors: 14.4 (2,469.9 to 1)
Current Spending: ($ per student per year):
Total: $6,119; Instruction: $4,225; Support Services: $1,743

Enrollment, Drop-out Rates and Diploma Recipients by Race/Ethnicity

Category	Total	White	Black	Asian	AIAN	Hisp.
Enrollment (%)	100.0	68.1	2.1	10.5	0.4	18.9
Drop-out Rate (%)	n/a	n/a	n/a	n/a	n/a	n/a
H.S. Diplomas (#)	2,157	1,576	37	252	9	283

Santa Ana Unified

1601 E Chestnut Ave • Santa Ana, CA 92701-6322
(714) 558-5501 • http://www.sausd.k12.ca.us/
Grade Span: KG-12; **Agency Type:** 1
Schools: 55
36 Primary; 9 Middle; 10 High; 0 Other Level
51 Regular; 0 Special Education; 0 Vocational; 4 Alternative
1 Magnet; 3 Charter; 49 Title I Eligible; 43 School-wide Title I
Students: 63,610 (50.1% male; 49.9% female)
Individual Education Program: 5,711 (9.0%);
English Language Learner: 40,400 (63.5%); Migrant: 1,145 (1.8%)
Eligible for Free Lunch Program: 37,540 (59.0%)
Eligible for Reduced-Price Lunch Program: 10,095 (15.9%)
Teachers: 2,938.7 (21.6 to 1)
Librarians/Media Specialists: 4.0 (15,902.5 to 1)
Guidance Counselors: 50.7 (1,254.6 to 1)
Current Spending: ($ per student per year):
Total: $6,403; Instruction: $4,457; Support Services: $1,649

Enrollment, Drop-out Rates and Diploma Recipients by Race/Ethnicity

Category	Total	White	Black	Asian	AIAN	Hisp.
Enrollment (%)	100.0	3.5	0.8	3.3	0.1	92.1
Drop-out Rate (%)	n/a	n/a	n/a	n/a	n/a	n/a
H.S. Diplomas (#)	2,484	131	30	185	2	2,131

Savanna Elementary

1330 S Knott Ave • Anaheim, CA 92804-4711
(714) 236-3800 • http://www.savsd.k12.ca.us/
Grade Span: KG-06; **Agency Type:** 1
Schools: 4
4 Primary; 0 Middle; 0 High; 0 Other Level
4 Regular; 0 Special Education; 0 Vocational; 0 Alternative
0 Magnet; 0 Charter; 3 Title I Eligible; 1 School-wide Title I
Students: 2,486 (53.6% male; 46.4% female)
Individual Education Program: 245 (9.9%);
English Language Learner: 810 (32.6%); Migrant: 3 (0.1%)
Eligible for Free Lunch Program: 991 (39.9%)
Eligible for Reduced-Price Lunch Program: 353 (14.2%)
Teachers: 121.2 (20.5 to 1)
Librarians/Media Specialists: 0.0 (0.0 to 1)
Guidance Counselors: 0.6 (4,143.3 to 1)
Current Spending: ($ per student per year):
Total: $6,359; Instruction: $4,405; Support Services: $1,705

Enrollment, Drop-out Rates and Diploma Recipients by Race/Ethnicity

Category	Total	White	Black	Asian	AIAN	Hisp.
Enrollment (%)	100.0	25.3	5.7	17.5	0.3	50.0
Drop-out Rate (%)	n/a	n/a	n/a	n/a	n/a	n/a
H.S. Diplomas (#)	n/a	n/a	n/a	n/a	n/a	n/a

Tustin Unified

300 S C St • Tustin, CA 92780-3695
(714) 730-7301 • http://www.tustin.k12.ca.us/
Grade Span: KG-12; **Agency Type:** 1
Schools: 26
17 Primary; 5 Middle; 4 High; 0 Other Level
24 Regular; 0 Special Education; 0 Vocational; 2 Alternative
1 Magnet; 0 Charter; 10 Title I Eligible; 0 School-wide Title I
Students: 18,518 (51.2% male; 48.8% female)
Individual Education Program: 1,930 (10.4%);
English Language Learner: 5,446 (29.4%); Migrant: 4 (<0.1%)
Eligible for Free Lunch Program: 4,589 (24.8%)
Eligible for Reduced-Price Lunch Program: 1,632 (8.8%)
Teachers: 837.7 (22.1 to 1)
Librarians/Media Specialists: 2.0 (9,259.0 to 1)
Guidance Counselors: 19.0 (974.6 to 1)
Current Spending: ($ per student per year):
Total: $6,090; Instruction: $4,053; Support Services: $1,816

Enrollment, Drop-out Rates and Diploma Recipients by Race/Ethnicity

Category	Total	White	Black	Asian	AIAN	Hisp.
Enrollment (%)	100.0	38.2	3.0	14.0	0.3	43.8
Drop-out Rate (%)	n/a	n/a	n/a	n/a	n/a	n/a
H.S. Diplomas (#)	944	439	36	148	4	315

Westminster Elementary

14121 Cedarwood Ave • Westminster, CA 92683-4482
(714) 894-7311 • http://www.wsd.k12.ca.us/
Grade Span: KG-08; **Agency Type:** 1
Schools: 17
13 Primary; 4 Middle; 0 High; 0 Other Level
16 Regular; 0 Special Education; 0 Vocational; 1 Alternative
0 Magnet; 0 Charter; 12 Title I Eligible; 11 School-wide Title I
Students: 10,113 (51.5% male; 48.5% female)
Individual Education Program: 1,103 (10.9%);
English Language Learner: 4,337 (42.9%); Migrant: 1 (<0.1%)
Eligible for Free Lunch Program: 4,939 (48.8%)
Eligible for Reduced-Price Lunch Program: 1,327 (13.1%)
Teachers: 511.5 (19.8 to 1)
Librarians/Media Specialists: 0.0 (0.0 to 1)
Guidance Counselors: 5.0 (2,022.6 to 1)
Current Spending: ($ per student per year):
Total: $6,645; Instruction: $4,639; Support Services: $1,734

Enrollment, Drop-out Rates and Diploma Recipients by Race/Ethnicity

Category	Total	White	Black	Asian	AIAN	Hisp.
Enrollment (%)	100.0	22.5	1.2	35.1	1.0	37.9
Drop-out Rate (%)	n/a	n/a	n/a	n/a	n/a	n/a
H.S. Diplomas (#)	n/a	n/a	n/a	n/a	n/a	n/a

Placer County

Auburn Union Elementary

55 College Way • Auburn, CA 95603-5001
(530) 885-7242 • http://www.auesd.k12.ca.us/
Grade Span: KG-08; **Agency Type:** 1
Schools: 5
4 Primary; 1 Middle; 0 High; 0 Other Level
5 Regular; 0 Special Education; 0 Vocational; 0 Alternative
0 Magnet; 0 Charter; 2 Title I Eligible; 0 School-wide Title I
Students: 2,708 (50.6% male; 49.4% female)
Individual Education Program: 285 (10.5%);
English Language Learner: 187 (6.9%); Migrant: 6 (0.2%)
Eligible for Free Lunch Program: 688 (25.4%)
Eligible for Reduced-Price Lunch Program: 338 (12.5%)
Teachers: 126.9 (21.3 to 1)
Librarians/Media Specialists: 0.0 (0.0 to 1)
Guidance Counselors: 2.7 (1,003.0 to 1)
Current Spending: ($ per student per year):
Total: $6,242; Instruction: $4,233; Support Services: $1,785

Enrollment, Drop-out Rates and Diploma Recipients by Race/Ethnicity

Category	Total	White	Black	Asian	AIAN	Hisp.
Enrollment (%)	100.0	83.5	1.7	3.7	0.6	10.3
Drop-out Rate (%)	n/a	n/a	n/a	n/a	n/a	n/a
H.S. Diplomas (#)	n/a	n/a	n/a	n/a	n/a	n/a

Dry Creek Joint Elementary

9707 Cook Riolo Rd • Roseville, CA 95747-9793
(916) 771-0646 • http://web.drycreek.k12.ca.us/
Grade Span: KG-08; **Agency Type:** 1
Schools: 8
6 Primary; 2 Middle; 0 High; 0 Other Level
8 Regular; 0 Special Education; 0 Vocational; 0 Alternative
0 Magnet; 0 Charter; 3 Title I Eligible; 0 School-wide Title I
Students: 6,386 (50.8% male; 49.2% female)
Individual Education Program: 570 (8.9%);
English Language Learner: 430 (6.7%); Migrant: 0 (0.0%)
Eligible for Free Lunch Program: 663 (10.4%)
Eligible for Reduced-Price Lunch Program: 467 (7.3%)
Teachers: 300.3 (21.3 to 1)
Librarians/Media Specialists: 0.0 (0.0 to 1)
Guidance Counselors: 4.5 (1,419.1 to 1)
Current Spending: ($ per student per year):
Total: $5,526; Instruction: $3,787; Support Services: $1,739

Enrollment, Drop-out Rates and Diploma Recipients by Race/Ethnicity

Category	Total	White	Black	Asian	AIAN	Hisp.
Enrollment (%)	100.0	72.1	5.9	9.6	0.7	9.3
Drop-out Rate (%)	n/a	n/a	n/a	n/a	n/a	n/a
H.S. Diplomas (#)	n/a	n/a	n/a	n/a	n/a	n/a

Eureka Union Elementary

5477 Eureka Rd • Granite Bay, CA 95746-8808
(916) 791-4939 • http://www.eurekacityschools.org/
Grade Span: KG-08; **Agency Type:** 1
Schools: 8
3 Primary; 5 Middle; 0 High; 0 Other Level
8 Regular; 0 Special Education; 0 Vocational; 0 Alternative
0 Magnet; 0 Charter; 3 Title I Eligible; 0 School-wide Title I
Students: 4,243 (52.1% male; 47.9% female)
Individual Education Program: 385 (9.1%);
English Language Learner: 50 (1.2%); Migrant: 0 (0.0%)
Eligible for Free Lunch Program: 127 (3.0%)
Eligible for Reduced-Price Lunch Program: 53 (1.2%)
Teachers: 202.8 (20.9 to 1)
Librarians/Media Specialists: 0.0 (0.0 to 1)
Guidance Counselors: 1.0 (4,243.0 to 1)
Current Spending: ($ per student per year):
Total: $5,542; Instruction: $3,736; Support Services: $1,754

Enrollment, Drop-out Rates and Diploma Recipients by Race/Ethnicity

Category	Total	White	Black	Asian	AIAN	Hisp.
Enrollment (%)	100.0	83.3	1.1	7.8	0.8	4.7
Drop-out Rate (%)	n/a	n/a	n/a	n/a	n/a	n/a
H.S. Diplomas (#)	n/a	n/a	n/a	n/a	n/a	n/a

Loomis Union Elementary

3290 Humphrey Rd • Loomis, CA 95650-9043
(916) 652-1800 • http://www.loomis-usd.k12.ca.us/
Grade Span: KG-08; **Agency Type:** 1
Schools: 4
4 Primary; 0 Middle; 0 High; 0 Other Level
4 Regular; 0 Special Education; 0 Vocational; 0 Alternative
0 Magnet; 0 Charter; 2 Title I Eligible; 0 School-wide Title I
Students: 1,934 (50.9% male; 49.1% female)
Individual Education Program: 175 (9.0%);
English Language Learner: 11 (0.6%); Migrant: 0 (0.0%)
Eligible for Free Lunch Program: 122 (6.3%)
Eligible for Reduced-Price Lunch Program: 119 (6.2%)
Teachers: 95.0 (20.4 to 1)
Librarians/Media Specialists: 0.0 (0.0 to 1)
Guidance Counselors: 0.0 (0.0 to 1)
Current Spending: ($ per student per year):
Total: $5,669; Instruction: $3,765; Support Services: $1,856

Enrollment, Drop-out Rates and Diploma Recipients by Race/Ethnicity

Category	Total	White	Black	Asian	AIAN	Hisp.
Enrollment (%)	100.0	88.5	0.4	2.9	1.7	5.1
Drop-out Rate (%)	n/a	n/a	n/a	n/a	n/a	n/a
H.S. Diplomas (#)	n/a	n/a	n/a	n/a	n/a	n/a

Placer Union High

13000 New Airport Rd • Auburn, CA 95604-5048
Mailing Address: PO Box 5048 • Auburn, CA 95604-5048
(530) 886-4400 • http://www.puhsd.k12.ca.us/
Grade Span: 09-12; **Agency Type:** 1
Schools: 6
0 Primary; 0 Middle; 6 High; 0 Other Level
3 Regular; 1 Special Education; 0 Vocational; 2 Alternative
0 Magnet; 0 Charter; 3 Title I Eligible; 0 School-wide Title I
Students: 4,706 (51.7% male; 48.3% female)
Individual Education Program: 460 (9.8%);
English Language Learner: 29 (0.6%); Migrant: 0 (0.0%)
Eligible for Free Lunch Program: 288 (6.1%)
Eligible for Reduced-Price Lunch Program: 168 (3.6%)
Teachers: 212.4 (22.2 to 1)
Librarians/Media Specialists: 1.0 (4,706.0 to 1)
Guidance Counselors: 10.3 (456.9 to 1)
Current Spending: ($ per student per year):
Total: $6,633; Instruction: $3,699; Support Services: $2,575

Enrollment, Drop-out Rates and Diploma Recipients by Race/Ethnicity

Category	Total	White	Black	Asian	AIAN	Hisp.
Enrollment (%)	100.0	89.3	0.6	2.6	1.7	5.1
Drop-out Rate (%)	n/a	n/a	n/a	n/a	n/a	n/a
H.S. Diplomas (#)	936	839	8	29	9	49

Rocklin Unified

2615 Sierra Meadows Dr • Rocklin, CA 95677-2811
(916) 624-2428 • http://www.rocklin.k12.ca.us/
Grade Span: KG-12; **Agency Type:** 1
Schools: 15
10 Primary; 2 Middle; 2 High; 1 Other Level
13 Regular; 0 Special Education; 0 Vocational; 2 Alternative
0 Magnet; 1 Charter; 5 Title I Eligible; 0 School-wide Title I
Students: 8,615 (51.5% male; 48.5% female)
Individual Education Program: 889 (10.3%);
English Language Learner: 189 (2.2%); Migrant: 0 (0.0%)
Eligible for Free Lunch Program: 610 (7.1%)
Eligible for Reduced-Price Lunch Program: 372 (4.3%)
Teachers: 413.8 (20.8 to 1)
Librarians/Media Specialists: 3.0 (2,871.7 to 1)
Guidance Counselors: 6.7 (1,285.8 to 1)
Current Spending: ($ per student per year):
Total: $5,896; Instruction: $3,864; Support Services: $1,833

Enrollment, Drop-out Rates and Diploma Recipients by Race/Ethnicity

Category	Total	White	Black	Asian	AIAN	Hisp.
Enrollment (%)	100.0	80.5	1.6	7.0	0.9	7.1
Drop-out Rate (%)	n/a	n/a	n/a	n/a	n/a	n/a
H.S. Diplomas (#)	446	368	4	34	3	27

Roseville City Elementary

1000 Darling Way • Roseville, CA 95678-4341
(916) 786-5090 • http://www.rcsdk8.org/
Grade Span: KG-08; **Agency Type:** 1
Schools: 14
11 Primary; 3 Middle; 0 High; 0 Other Level
14 Regular; 0 Special Education; 0 Vocational; 0 Alternative
0 Magnet; 0 Charter; 5 Title I Eligible; 1 School-wide Title I
Students: 7,114 (50.0% male; 50.0% female)
Individual Education Program: 747 (10.5%);
English Language Learner: 549 (7.7%); Migrant: 0 (0.0%)
Eligible for Free Lunch Program: 1,116 (15.7%)
Eligible for Reduced-Price Lunch Program: 537 (7.5%)
Teachers: 342.6 (20.8 to 1)
Librarians/Media Specialists: 0.0 (0.0 to 1)
Guidance Counselors: 0.6 (11,856.7 to 1)
Current Spending: ($ per student per year):
Total: $6,274; Instruction: $4,072; Support Services: $1,872

Enrollment, Drop-out Rates and Diploma Recipients by Race/Ethnicity

Category	Total	White	Black	Asian	AIAN	Hisp.
Enrollment (%)	100.0	71.2	2.7	7.4	0.9	17.2
Drop-out Rate (%)	n/a	n/a	n/a	n/a	n/a	n/a
H.S. Diplomas (#)	n/a	n/a	n/a	n/a	n/a	n/a

Roseville Joint Union High

1750 Cirby Way • Roseville, CA 95661-5520
(916) 786-2051 • http://www.rjuhsd.k12.ca.us/
Grade Span: 09-12; **Agency Type:** 1
Schools: 7
0 Primary; 0 Middle; 7 High; 0 Other Level
4 Regular; 0 Special Education; 0 Vocational; 3 Alternative
0 Magnet; 0 Charter; 4 Title I Eligible; 0 School-wide Title I
Students: 7,724 (50.4% male; 49.6% female)
Individual Education Program: 612 (7.9%);
English Language Learner: 95 (1.2%); Migrant: 0 (0.0%)
Eligible for Free Lunch Program: 551 (7.1%)
Eligible for Reduced-Price Lunch Program: 19 (0.2%)
Teachers: 347.9 (22.2 to 1)
Librarians/Media Specialists: 3.0 (2,574.7 to 1)
Guidance Counselors: 19.3 (400.2 to 1)
Current Spending: ($ per student per year):
Total: $6,335; Instruction: $3,607; Support Services: $2,536

Enrollment, Drop-out Rates and Diploma Recipients by Race/Ethnicity

Category	Total	White	Black	Asian	AIAN	Hisp.
Enrollment (%)	100.0	76.0	3.7	8.3	0.5	11.4
Drop-out Rate (%)	n/a	n/a	n/a	n/a	n/a	n/a
H.S. Diplomas (#)	1,585	1,273	57	102	18	135

Tahoe-Truckee Joint Unified

11839 Donner Pass Rd • Truckee, CA 96161-4951
(530) 582-2500
Grade Span: KG-12; **Agency Type:** 1
Schools: 13
6 Primary; 2 Middle; 3 High; 2 Other Level
10 Regular; 0 Special Education; 0 Vocational; 3 Alternative
1 Magnet; 1 Charter; 6 Title I Eligible; 0 School-wide Title I
Students: 5,342 (50.5% male; 49.5% female)
Individual Education Program: 579 (10.8%);
English Language Learner: 922 (17.3%); Migrant: 0 (0.0%)
Eligible for Free Lunch Program: 877 (16.4%)
Eligible for Reduced-Price Lunch Program: 316 (5.9%)
Teachers: 295.0 (18.1 to 1)
Librarians/Media Specialists: 2.0 (2,671.0 to 1)
Guidance Counselors: 9.2 (580.7 to 1)
Current Spending: ($ per student per year):
Total: $6,819; Instruction: $4,295; Support Services: $2,375

Enrollment, Drop-out Rates and Diploma Recipients by Race/Ethnicity

Category	Total	White	Black	Asian	AIAN	Hisp.
Enrollment (%)	100.0	73.6	0.8	1.0	0.8	21.2
Drop-out Rate (%)	n/a	n/a	n/a	n/a	n/a	n/a
H.S. Diplomas (#)	379	281	4	3	2	64

Western Placer Unified

810 J St • Lincoln, CA 95648-1825
(916) 645-6350 • http://www.wpusd.k12.ca.us/
Grade Span: KG-12; **Agency Type:** 1
Schools: 9
3 Primary; 1 Middle; 3 High; 2 Other Level
7 Regular; 0 Special Education; 0 Vocational; 2 Alternative
0 Magnet; 5 Charter; 7 Title I Eligible; 0 School-wide Title I
Students: 7,280 (50.1% male; 49.9% female)
Individual Education Program: 646 (8.9%);
English Language Learner: 580 (8.0%); Migrant: 0 (0.0%)
Eligible for Free Lunch Program: 865 (11.9%)
Eligible for Reduced-Price Lunch Program: 375 (5.2%)
Teachers: 365.1 (19.9 to 1)
Librarians/Media Specialists: 0.0 (0.0 to 1)
Guidance Counselors: 4.0 (1,820.0 to 1)
Current Spending: ($ per student per year):
Total: $6,442; Instruction: $4,131; Support Services: $2,167

Enrollment, Drop-out Rates and Diploma Recipients by Race/Ethnicity

Category	Total	White	Black	Asian	AIAN	Hisp.
Enrollment (%)	100.0	74.6	2.0	1.9	0.9	15.5
Drop-out Rate (%)	n/a	n/a	n/a	n/a	n/a	n/a
H.S. Diplomas (#)	581	435	19	10	8	87

Plumas County

Plumas Unified

50 Church St • Quincy, CA 95971-6009
(530) 283-6500 • http://www.pcoe.k12.ca.us/
Grade Span: KG-12; **Agency Type:** 1
Schools: 16
6 Primary; 1 Middle; 8 High; 1 Other Level
11 Regular; 0 Special Education; 0 Vocational; 5 Alternative
0 Magnet; 1 Charter; 15 Title I Eligible; 0 School-wide Title I
Students: 3,213 (52.3% male; 47.7% female)
Individual Education Program: 409 (12.7%);
English Language Learner: 94 (2.9%); Migrant: 0 (0.0%)
Eligible for Free Lunch Program: 853 (26.5%)
Eligible for Reduced-Price Lunch Program: 301 (9.4%)
Teachers: 176.8 (18.2 to 1)
Librarians/Media Specialists: 0.0 (0.0 to 1)
Guidance Counselors: 3.3 (973.6 to 1)
Current Spending: ($ per student per year):
Total: $7,876; Instruction: $4,731; Support Services: $2,890
Enrollment, Drop-out Rates and Diploma Recipients by Race/Ethnicity

Category	Total	White	Black	Asian	AIAN	Hisp.
Enrollment (%)	100.0	79.6	1.4	1.7	6.9	9.8
Drop-out Rate (%)	n/a	n/a	n/a	n/a	n/a	n/a
H.S. Diplomas (#)	264	225	3	8	10	18

Riverside County

Alvord Unified

10365 Keller Ave • Riverside, CA 92505-1349
(909) 509-5000 • http://www.alvord.k12.ca.us/
Grade Span: KG-12; **Agency Type:** 1
Schools: 19
12 Primary; 4 Middle; 3 High; 0 Other Level
18 Regular; 0 Special Education; 0 Vocational; 1 Alternative
0 Magnet; 0 Charter; 10 Title I Eligible; 4 School-wide Title I
Students: 19,122 (52.0% male; 48.0% female)
Individual Education Program: 1,853 (9.7%);
English Language Learner: 7,076 (37.0%); Migrant: 3 (<0.1%)
Eligible for Free Lunch Program: 7,493 (39.2%)
Eligible for Reduced-Price Lunch Program: 2,676 (14.0%)
Teachers: 832.3 (23.0 to 1)
Librarians/Media Specialists: 7.0 (2,731.7 to 1)
Guidance Counselors: 17.4 (1,099.0 to 1)
Current Spending: ($ per student per year):
Total: $5,878; Instruction: $3,908; Support Services: $1,766
Enrollment, Drop-out Rates and Diploma Recipients by Race/Ethnicity

Category	Total	White	Black	Asian	AIAN	Hisp.
Enrollment (%)	100.0	26.6	5.9	5.1	0.5	61.5
Drop-out Rate (%)	n/a	n/a	n/a	n/a	n/a	n/a
H.S. Diplomas (#)	837	305	49	73	2	408

Banning Unified

161 W Williams St • Banning, CA 92220-4746
(909) 922-0201 • http://www.banning.k12.ca.us/
Grade Span: KG-12; **Agency Type:** 1
Schools: 9
4 Primary; 2 Middle; 2 High; 1 Other Level
7 Regular; 0 Special Education; 0 Vocational; 2 Alternative
0 Magnet; 0 Charter; 6 Title I Eligible; 6 School-wide Title I
Students: 4,655 (51.2% male; 48.8% female)
Individual Education Program: 461 (9.9%);
English Language Learner: 1,076 (23.1%); Migrant: 0 (0.0%)
Eligible for Free Lunch Program: 2,819 (60.6%)
Eligible for Reduced-Price Lunch Program: 708 (15.2%)
Teachers: 211.7 (22.0 to 1)
Librarians/Media Specialists: 0.0 (0.0 to 1)
Guidance Counselors: 3.0 (1,551.7 to 1)
Current Spending: ($ per student per year):
Total: $6,770; Instruction: $4,095; Support Services: $2,304
Enrollment, Drop-out Rates and Diploma Recipients by Race/Ethnicity

Category	Total	White	Black	Asian	AIAN	Hisp.
Enrollment (%)	100.0	23.2	11.4	9.6	5.3	47.2
Drop-out Rate (%)	n/a	n/a	n/a	n/a	n/a	n/a
H.S. Diplomas (#)	217	57	36	44	10	66

Beaumont Unified

500 Grace Ave • Beaumont, CA 92223-0187
Mailing Address: PO Box 187 • Beaumont, CA 92223-0187
(909) 845-1631 • http://www.beaumontusd.k12.ca.us/
Grade Span: KG-12; **Agency Type:** 1
Schools: 9
4 Primary; 1 Middle; 2 High; 2 Other Level
5 Regular; 0 Special Education; 0 Vocational; 4 Alternative
0 Magnet; 0 Charter; 4 Title I Eligible; 3 School-wide Title I
Students: 4,356 (50.5% male; 49.5% female)
Individual Education Program: 353 (8.1%);
English Language Learner: 673 (15.5%); Migrant: 0 (0.0%)
Eligible for Free Lunch Program: 1,760 (40.4%)
Eligible for Reduced-Price Lunch Program: 736 (16.9%)
Teachers: 196.0 (22.2 to 1)
Librarians/Media Specialists: 0.5 (8,712.0 to 1)
Guidance Counselors: 3.5 (1,244.6 to 1)
Current Spending: ($ per student per year):
Total: $6,230; Instruction: $3,567; Support Services: $2,372
Enrollment, Drop-out Rates and Diploma Recipients by Race/Ethnicity

Category	Total	White	Black	Asian	AIAN	Hisp.
Enrollment (%)	100.0	48.9	3.4	3.1	2.0	41.8
Drop-out Rate (%)	n/a	n/a	n/a	n/a	n/a	n/a
H.S. Diplomas (#)	161	102	3	3	2	51

Coachella Valley Unified

87-225 Church St • Thermal, CA 92274-0847
Mailing Address: PO Box 847 • Thermal, CA 92274-0847
(760) 399-5137 • http://www.coachella.k12.ca.us/
Grade Span: KG-12; **Agency Type:** 1
Schools: 17
11 Primary; 2 Middle; 3 High; 1 Other Level
15 Regular; 0 Special Education; 0 Vocational; 2 Alternative
0 Magnet; 0 Charter; 16 Title I Eligible; 6 School-wide Title I
Students: 13,867 (51.5% male; 48.5% female)
Individual Education Program: 1,147 (8.3%);
English Language Learner: 9,699 (69.9%); Migrant: 3,331 (24.0%)
Eligible for Free Lunch Program: 10,462 (75.4%)
Eligible for Reduced-Price Lunch Program: 1,607 (11.6%)
Teachers: 640.2 (21.7 to 1)
Librarians/Media Specialists: 1.0 (13,867.0 to 1)
Guidance Counselors: 11.0 (1,260.6 to 1)
Current Spending: ($ per student per year):
Total: $6,481; Instruction: $3,926; Support Services: $2,177
Enrollment, Drop-out Rates and Diploma Recipients by Race/Ethnicity

Category	Total	White	Black	Asian	AIAN	Hisp.
Enrollment (%)	100.0	1.6	0.3	0.3	0.4	97.3
Drop-out Rate (%)	n/a	n/a	n/a	n/a	n/a	n/a
H.S. Diplomas (#)	558	17	0	2	0	539

Corona-Norco Unified

2820 Clark Ave • Norco, CA 91760-1903
(909) 736-5000 • http://www.cnusd.k12.ca.us/
Grade Span: KG-12; **Agency Type:** 1
Schools: 39
23 Primary; 5 Middle; 9 High; 2 Other Level
32 Regular; 1 Special Education; 0 Vocational; 6 Alternative
2 Magnet; 0 Charter; 12 Title I Eligible; 6 School-wide Title I
Students: 41,977 (51.2% male; 48.8% female)
Individual Education Program: 4,381 (10.4%);
English Language Learner: 6,472 (15.4%); Migrant: 185 (0.4%)
Eligible for Free Lunch Program: 10,826 (25.8%)
Eligible for Reduced-Price Lunch Program: 5,327 (12.7%)
Teachers: 1,982.2 (21.2 to 1)
Librarians/Media Specialists: 4.0 (10,494.3 to 1)
Guidance Counselors: 40.0 (1,049.4 to 1)
Current Spending: ($ per student per year):
Total: $6,018; Instruction: $3,864; Support Services: $1,901
Enrollment, Drop-out Rates and Diploma Recipients by Race/Ethnicity

Category	Total	White	Black	Asian	AIAN	Hisp.
Enrollment (%)	100.0	42.8	6.0	6.3	0.5	44.4
Drop-out Rate (%)	n/a	n/a	n/a	n/a	n/a	n/a
H.S. Diplomas (#)	2,170	1,050	139	173	4	804

Desert Sands Unified

47-950 Dune Palms Rd • La Quinta, CA 92253-4000
(760) 777-4200 • http://www.dsusd.k12.ca.us/
Grade Span: KG-12; **Agency Type:** 1
Schools: 27
16 Primary; 6 Middle; 4 High; 1 Other Level
26 Regular; 0 Special Education; 0 Vocational; 1 Alternative
0 Magnet; 1 Charter; 16 Title I Eligible; 8 School-wide Title I
Students: 25,180 (50.8% male; 49.2% female)
Individual Education Program: 2,118 (8.4%);
English Language Learner: 7,585 (30.1%); Migrant: 596 (2.4%)

Eligible for Free Lunch Program: 10,399 (41.3%)
Eligible for Reduced-Price Lunch Program: 2,972 (11.8%)
Teachers: 1,177.0 (21.4 to 1)
Librarians/Media Specialists: 4.0 (6,295.0 to 1)
Guidance Counselors: 37.0 (680.5 to 1)
Current Spending: ($ per student per year):
Total: $6,335; Instruction: $3,966; Support Services: $2,084
Enrollment, Drop-out Rates and Diploma Recipients by Race/Ethnicity

Category	Total	White	Black	Asian	AIAN	Hisp.
Enrollment (%)	100.0	30.8	2.1	2.0	0.5	63.5
Drop-out Rate (%)	n/a	n/a	n/a	n/a	n/a	n/a
H.S. Diplomas (#)	1,394	571	25	30	7	756

Hemet Unified

2350 W Latham Ave • Hemet, CA 92545-3632
(909) 765-5100 • http://www.hemetusd.k12.ca.us/
Grade Span: KG-12; **Agency Type:** 1
Schools: 20
11 Primary; 3 Middle; 4 High; 2 Other Level
17 Regular; 0 Special Education; 0 Vocational; 3 Alternative
0 Magnet; 0 Charter; 19 Title I Eligible; 8 School-wide Title I
Students: 18,931 (50.7% male; 49.3% female)
Individual Education Program: 2,146 (11.3%);
English Language Learner: 2,348 (12.4%); Migrant: 0 (0.0%)
Eligible for Free Lunch Program: 7,809 (41.2%)
Eligible for Reduced-Price Lunch Program: 3,240 (17.1%)
Teachers: 883.6 (21.4 to 1)
Librarians/Media Specialists: 6.0 (3,155.2 to 1)
Guidance Counselors: 28.0 (676.1 to 1)
Current Spending: ($ per student per year):
Total: $6,185; Instruction: $3,968; Support Services: $1,931
Enrollment, Drop-out Rates and Diploma Recipients by Race/Ethnicity

Category	Total	White	Black	Asian	AIAN	Hisp.
Enrollment (%)	100.0	57.4	4.6	2.2	1.2	34.2
Drop-out Rate (%)	n/a	n/a	n/a	n/a	n/a	n/a
H.S. Diplomas (#)	995	699	30	29	5	232

Jurupa Unified

4850 Pedley Rd • Riverside, CA 92509-6611
(909) 360-4100 • http://www.jusd.k12.ca.us/
Grade Span: KG-12; **Agency Type:** 1
Schools: 24
16 Primary; 3 Middle; 5 High; 0 Other Level
21 Regular; 0 Special Education; 0 Vocational; 3 Alternative
0 Magnet; 0 Charter; 17 Title I Eligible; 5 School-wide Title I
Students: 20,469 (51.2% male; 48.8% female)
Individual Education Program: 1,938 (9.5%);
English Language Learner: 5,466 (26.7%); Migrant: 3 (<0.1%)
Eligible for Free Lunch Program: 9,017 (44.1%)
Eligible for Reduced-Price Lunch Program: 2,555 (12.5%)
Teachers: 940.8 (21.8 to 1)
Librarians/Media Specialists: 0.0 (0.0 to 1)
Guidance Counselors: 18.0 (1,137.2 to 1)
Current Spending: ($ per student per year):
Total: $6,326; Instruction: $3,966; Support Services: $2,088
Enrollment, Drop-out Rates and Diploma Recipients by Race/Ethnicity

Category	Total	White	Black	Asian	AIAN	Hisp.
Enrollment (%)	100.0	28.4	4.7	2.2	0.4	64.3
Drop-out Rate (%)	n/a	n/a	n/a	n/a	n/a	n/a
H.S. Diplomas (#)	797	339	43	19	2	392

Lake Elsinore Unified

545 Chaney St • Lake Elsinore, CA 92530-2723
(909) 674-7731 • http://www.leusd.k12.ca.us/
Grade Span: KG-12; **Agency Type:** 1
Schools: 22
13 Primary; 4 Middle; 3 High; 2 Other Level
19 Regular; 0 Special Education; 0 Vocational; 3 Alternative
1 Magnet; 0 Charter; 12 Title I Eligible; 2 School-wide Title I
Students: 18,933 (51.4% male; 48.6% female)
Individual Education Program: 2,425 (12.8%);
English Language Learner: 2,859 (15.1%); Migrant: 0 (0.0%)
Eligible for Free Lunch Program: 5,289 (27.9%)
Eligible for Reduced-Price Lunch Program: 2,424 (12.8%)
Teachers: 832.9 (22.7 to 1)
Librarians/Media Specialists: 0.0 (0.0 to 1)
Guidance Counselors: 19.5 (970.9 to 1)
Current Spending: ($ per student per year):
Total: $6,094; Instruction: $3,961; Support Services: $1,897
Enrollment, Drop-out Rates and Diploma Recipients by Race/Ethnicity

Category	Total	White	Black	Asian	AIAN	Hisp.
Enrollment (%)	100.0	52.4	4.8	3.4	0.8	37.2
Drop-out Rate (%)	n/a	n/a	n/a	n/a	n/a	n/a
H.S. Diplomas (#)	900	547	37	48	5	256

Menifee Union Elementary

30205 Menifee Rd • Menifee, CA 92584-8109
(909) 672-1851 • http://www.menifeeusd.k12.ca.us/
Grade Span: KG-08; **Agency Type:** 1
Schools: 6
4 Primary; 2 Middle; 0 High; 0 Other Level
6 Regular; 0 Special Education; 0 Vocational; 0 Alternative
0 Magnet; 0 Charter; 1 Title I Eligible; 1 School-wide Title I
Students: 5,407 (50.6% male; 49.4% female)
Individual Education Program: 450 (8.3%);
English Language Learner: 731 (13.5%); Migrant: 0 (0.0%)
Eligible for Free Lunch Program: 968 (17.9%)
Eligible for Reduced-Price Lunch Program: 327 (6.0%)
Teachers: 245.5 (22.0 to 1)
Librarians/Media Specialists: 0.0 (0.0 to 1)
Guidance Counselors: 0.0 (0.0 to 1)
Current Spending: ($ per student per year):
Total: $5,803; Instruction: $3,905; Support Services: $1,673
Enrollment, Drop-out Rates and Diploma Recipients by Race/Ethnicity

Category	Total	White	Black	Asian	AIAN	Hisp.
Enrollment (%)	100.0	59.2	2.9	3.6	0.9	31.8
Drop-out Rate (%)	n/a	n/a	n/a	n/a	n/a	n/a
H.S. Diplomas (#)	n/a	n/a	n/a	n/a	n/a	n/a

Moreno Valley Unified

25634 Alessandro Blvd • Moreno Valley, CA 92553-4306
Mailing Address: 13911 Perris Blvd • Moreno Valley, CA 92553-4306
(909) 485-5600 • http://www.mvusd.k12.ca.us/
Grade Span: KG-12; **Agency Type:** 1
Schools: 33
19 Primary; 6 Middle; 6 High; 2 Other Level
30 Regular; 0 Special Education; 0 Vocational; 3 Alternative
8 Magnet; 1 Charter; 21 Title I Eligible; 17 School-wide Title I
Students: 34,176 (50.9% male; 49.1% female)
Individual Education Program: 3,660 (10.7%);
English Language Learner: 9,534 (27.9%); Migrant: 2 (<0.1%)
Eligible for Free Lunch Program: 15,387 (45.0%)
Eligible for Reduced-Price Lunch Program: 4,916 (14.4%)
Teachers: 1,533.3 (22.3 to 1)
Librarians/Media Specialists: 0.0 (0.0 to 1)
Guidance Counselors: 61.9 (552.1 to 1)
Current Spending: ($ per student per year):
Total: $6,166; Instruction: $4,110; Support Services: $1,807
Enrollment, Drop-out Rates and Diploma Recipients by Race/Ethnicity

Category	Total	White	Black	Asian	AIAN	Hisp.
Enrollment (%)	100.0	22.9	23.1	5.6	0.4	46.7
Drop-out Rate (%)	n/a	n/a	n/a	n/a	n/a	n/a
H.S. Diplomas (#)	1,694	635	363	152	3	538

Murrieta Valley Unified

41870 Mcalby Ct • Murrieta, CA 92562-7021
(909) 696-1600 • http://www.murrieta.k12.ca.us/
Grade Span: KG-12; **Agency Type:** 1
Schools: 13
8 Primary; 3 Middle; 2 High; 0 Other Level
12 Regular; 0 Special Education; 0 Vocational; 1 Alternative
0 Magnet; 0 Charter; 5 Title I Eligible; 0 School-wide Title I
Students: 15,434 (50.9% male; 49.1% female)
Individual Education Program: 1,368 (8.9%);
English Language Learner: 442 (2.9%); Migrant: 0 (0.0%)
Eligible for Free Lunch Program: 1,381 (8.9%)
Eligible for Reduced-Price Lunch Program: 1,025 (6.6%)
Teachers: 674.9 (22.9 to 1)
Librarians/Media Specialists: 2.0 (7,717.0 to 1)
Guidance Counselors: 14.5 (1,064.4 to 1)
Current Spending: ($ per student per year):
Total: $6,081; Instruction: $3,849; Support Services: $2,060
Enrollment, Drop-out Rates and Diploma Recipients by Race/Ethnicity

Category	Total	White	Black	Asian	AIAN	Hisp.
Enrollment (%)	100.0	64.5	5.9	7.1	0.7	20.0
Drop-out Rate (%)	n/a	n/a	n/a	n/a	n/a	n/a
H.S. Diplomas (#)	690	520	29	26	1	102

Palm Springs Unified

333 S Farrell Dr • Palm Springs, CA 92262-7905
(760) 416-6000 • http://www.psusd.k12.ca.us/
Grade Span: KG-12; **Agency Type:** 1
Schools: 24
14 Primary; 4 Middle; 5 High; 1 Other Level
22 Regular; 0 Special Education; 0 Vocational; 2 Alternative
0 Magnet; 0 Charter; 24 Title I Eligible; 0 School-wide Title I
Students: 22,067 (51.2% male; 48.8% female)
Individual Education Program: 2,001 (9.1%);
English Language Learner: 6,955 (31.5%); Migrant: 217 (1.0%)
Eligible for Free Lunch Program: 11,868 (53.8%)

Eligible for Reduced-Price Lunch Program: 3,354 (15.2%)
Teachers: 1,085.4 (20.3 to 1)
Librarians/Media Specialists: 7.0 (3,152.4 to 1)
Guidance Counselors: 19.6 (1,125.9 to 1)
Current Spending: ($ per student per year):
Total: $6,310; Instruction: $3,952; Support Services: $2,106
Enrollment, Drop-out Rates and Diploma Recipients by Race/Ethnicity

Category	Total	White	Black	Asian	AIAN	Hisp.
Enrollment (%)	100.0	27.7	5.1	3.6	0.9	62.6
Drop-out Rate (%)	n/a	n/a	n/a	n/a	n/a	n/a
H.S. Diplomas (#)	950	420	41	49	9	431

Palo Verde Unified

295 N First St • Blythe, CA 92225-1703
(760) 922-4164 • http://www.pvusd-bly.k12.ca.us/
Grade Span: KG-12; **Agency Type:** 1
Schools: 6
3 Primary; 1 Middle; 2 High; 0 Other Level
5 Regular; 0 Special Education; 0 Vocational; 1 Alternative
0 Magnet; 0 Charter; 6 Title I Eligible; 1 School-wide Title I
Students: 3,686 (51.7% male; 48.3% female)
Individual Education Program: 295 (8.0%);
English Language Learner: 601 (16.3%); Migrant: 366 (9.9%)
Eligible for Free Lunch Program: 1,768 (48.0%)
Eligible for Reduced-Price Lunch Program: 300 (8.1%)
Teachers: 175.6 (21.0 to 1)
Librarians/Media Specialists: 0.0 (0.0 to 1)
Guidance Counselors: 2.0 (1,843.0 to 1)
Current Spending: ($ per student per year):
Total: $6,738; Instruction: $3,890; Support Services: $2,559
Enrollment, Drop-out Rates and Diploma Recipients by Race/Ethnicity

Category	Total	White	Black	Asian	AIAN	Hisp.
Enrollment (%)	100.0	34.0	10.9	1.0	0.6	53.5
Drop-out Rate (%)	n/a	n/a	n/a	n/a	n/a	n/a
H.S. Diplomas (#)	185	58	15	3	0	109

Perris Elementary

143 E First St • Perris, CA 92570-2113
(909) 657-3118 • http://www.perris.k12.ca.us/
Grade Span: KG-06; **Agency Type:** 1
Schools: 7
7 Primary; 0 Middle; 0 High; 0 Other Level
7 Regular; 0 Special Education; 0 Vocational; 0 Alternative
0 Magnet; 0 Charter; 6 Title I Eligible; 6 School-wide Title I
Students: 4,969 (51.5% male; 48.5% female)
Individual Education Program: 507 (10.2%);
English Language Learner: 2,203 (44.3%); Migrant: 132 (2.7%)
Eligible for Free Lunch Program: 3,481 (70.1%)
Eligible for Reduced-Price Lunch Program: 951 (19.1%)
Teachers: 249.0 (20.0 to 1)
Librarians/Media Specialists: 0.0 (0.0 to 1)
Guidance Counselors: 0.0 (0.0 to 1)
Current Spending: ($ per student per year):
Total: $6,087; Instruction: $3,634; Support Services: $2,020
Enrollment, Drop-out Rates and Diploma Recipients by Race/Ethnicity

Category	Total	White	Black	Asian	AIAN	Hisp.
Enrollment (%)	100.0	9.5	15.2	1.8	0.5	72.7
Drop-out Rate (%)	n/a	n/a	n/a	n/a	n/a	n/a
H.S. Diplomas (#)	n/a	n/a	n/a	n/a	n/a	n/a

Perris Union High

155 E Fourth St • Perris, CA 92570-2124
(909) 943-6369 • http://www.puhsd.org/
Grade Span: 07-12; **Agency Type:** 1
Schools: 6
0 Primary; 1 Middle; 5 High; 0 Other Level
3 Regular; 0 Special Education; 0 Vocational; 3 Alternative
0 Magnet; 1 Charter; 4 Title I Eligible; 1 School-wide Title I
Students: 6,976 (50.6% male; 49.4% female)
Individual Education Program: 551 (7.9%);
English Language Learner: 703 (10.1%); Migrant: 45 (0.6%)
Eligible for Free Lunch Program: 2,594 (37.2%)
Eligible for Reduced-Price Lunch Program: 587 (8.4%)
Teachers: 300.1 (23.2 to 1)
Librarians/Media Specialists: 3.0 (2,325.3 to 1)
Guidance Counselors: 12.0 (581.3 to 1)
Current Spending: ($ per student per year):
Total: $5,931; Instruction: $3,607; Support Services: $2,201
Enrollment, Drop-out Rates and Diploma Recipients by Race/Ethnicity

Category	Total	White	Black	Asian	AIAN	Hisp.
Enrollment (%)	100.0	34.1	11.2	2.6	0.8	50.2
Drop-out Rate (%)	n/a	n/a	n/a	n/a	n/a	n/a
H.S. Diplomas (#)	994	423	90	29	12	430

Riverside County Office of Ed

3939 13th St • Riverside, CA 92502-0868
Mailing Address: PO Box 868 • Riverside, CA 92502-0868
(909) 826-6530 • http://www.rcoe.k12.ca.us/
Grade Span: KG-12; **Agency Type:** 4
Schools: 5
0 Primary; 0 Middle; 0 High; 5 Other Level
1 Regular; 1 Special Education; 0 Vocational; 3 Alternative
0 Magnet; 1 Charter; 1 Title I Eligible; 0 School-wide Title I
Students: 3,744 (59.0% male; 41.0% female)
Individual Education Program: 2,658 (71.0%);
English Language Learner: 751 (20.1%); Migrant: 1 (<0.1%)
Eligible for Free Lunch Program: 8 (0.2%)
Eligible for Reduced-Price Lunch Program: 4 (0.1%)
Teachers: 300.6 (12.5 to 1)
Librarians/Media Specialists: 1.0 (3,744.0 to 1)
Guidance Counselors: 0.0 (0.0 to 1)
Current Spending: ($ per student per year):
Total: $36,699; Instruction: $16,757; Support Services: $19,449
Enrollment, Drop-out Rates and Diploma Recipients by Race/Ethnicity

Category	Total	White	Black	Asian	AIAN	Hisp.
Enrollment (%)	100.0	32.5	11.8	2.1	0.8	52.3
Drop-out Rate (%)	n/a	n/a	n/a	n/a	n/a	n/a
H.S. Diplomas (#)	285	122	36	10	3	114

Riverside Unified

3380 14th St • Riverside, CA 92516-2800
Mailing Address: PO Box 2800 • Riverside, CA 92516-2800
(909) 788-7134 • http://www.rusd.k12.ca.us/
Grade Span: KG-12; **Agency Type:** 1
Schools: 45
28 Primary; 6 Middle; 9 High; 2 Other Level
39 Regular; 1 Special Education; 0 Vocational; 5 Alternative
0 Magnet; 0 Charter; 21 Title I Eligible; 14 School-wide Title I
Students: 40,888 (51.0% male; 49.0% female)
Individual Education Program: 4,362 (10.7%);
English Language Learner: 6,611 (16.2%); Migrant: 0 (0.0%)
Eligible for Free Lunch Program: 14,879 (36.4%)
Eligible for Reduced-Price Lunch Program: 4,818 (11.8%)
Teachers: 1,765.2 (23.2 to 1)
Librarians/Media Specialists: 11.0 (3,717.1 to 1)
Guidance Counselors: 46.3 (883.1 to 1)
Current Spending: ($ per student per year):
Total: $6,698; Instruction: $4,092; Support Services: $2,373
Enrollment, Drop-out Rates and Diploma Recipients by Race/Ethnicity

Category	Total	White	Black	Asian	AIAN	Hisp.
Enrollment (%)	100.0	39.1	9.8	4.8	0.5	45.8
Drop-out Rate (%)	n/a	n/a	n/a	n/a	n/a	n/a
H.S. Diplomas (#)	2,251	1,110	223	156	10	752

Romoland Elementary

25900 Leon Rd • Homeland, CA 92548
(909) 926-9244
Grade Span: KG-08; **Agency Type:** 1
Schools: 2
2 Primary; 0 Middle; 0 High; 0 Other Level
2 Regular; 0 Special Education; 0 Vocational; 0 Alternative
0 Magnet; 0 Charter; 2 Title I Eligible; 2 School-wide Title I
Students: 1,690 (51.7% male; 48.3% female)
Individual Education Program: 144 (8.5%);
English Language Learner: 693 (41.0%); Migrant: 4 (0.2%)
Eligible for Free Lunch Program: 1,000 (59.2%)
Eligible for Reduced-Price Lunch Program: 254 (15.0%)
Teachers: 78.0 (21.7 to 1)
Librarians/Media Specialists: 0.0 (0.0 to 1)
Guidance Counselors: 0.0 (0.0 to 1)
Current Spending: ($ per student per year):
Total: $6,446; Instruction: $4,010; Support Services: $2,057
Enrollment, Drop-out Rates and Diploma Recipients by Race/Ethnicity

Category	Total	White	Black	Asian	AIAN	Hisp.
Enrollment (%)	100.0	34.9	1.9	0.7	0.4	61.8
Drop-out Rate (%)	n/a	n/a	n/a	n/a	n/a	n/a
H.S. Diplomas (#)	n/a	n/a	n/a	n/a	n/a	n/a

San Jacinto Unified

2045 S San Jacinto Ave • San Jacinto, CA 92583-5626
(909) 929-7700 • http://www.sanjacinto.k12.ca.us/
Grade Span: KG-12; **Agency Type:** 1
Schools: 9
5 Primary; 2 Middle; 2 High; 0 Other Level
8 Regular; 0 Special Education; 0 Vocational; 1 Alternative
0 Magnet; 1 Charter; 4 Title I Eligible; 0 School-wide Title I
Students: 6,682 (51.5% male; 48.5% female)
Individual Education Program: 812 (12.2%);
English Language Learner: 1,730 (25.9%); Migrant: 0 (0.0%)

Eligible for Free Lunch Program: 3,608 (54.0%)
Eligible for Reduced-Price Lunch Program: 882 (13.2%)
Teachers: 297.4 (22.5 to 1)
Librarians/Media Specialists: 0.0 (0.0 to 1)
Guidance Counselors: 5.0 (1,336.4 to 1)
Current Spending: ($ per student per year):
Total: $5,980; Instruction: $3,553; Support Services: $2,166
Enrollment, Drop-out Rates and Diploma Recipients by Race/Ethnicity

Category	Total	White	Black	Asian	AIAN	Hisp.
Enrollment (%)	100.0	33.2	5.1	2.2	3.1	54.2
Drop-out Rate (%)	n/a	n/a	n/a	n/a	n/a	n/a
H.S. Diplomas (#)	260	109	4	3	9	134

Temecula Valley Unified
31350 Rancho Vista Rd • Temecula, CA 92592-6202
(909) 676-2661 • http://www.tvusd.k12.ca.us/
Grade Span: KG-12; **Agency Type:** 1
Schools: 22
13 Primary; 4 Middle; 4 High; 1 Other Level
19 Regular; 0 Special Education; 0 Vocational; 3 Alternative
0 Magnet; 2 Charter; 4 Title I Eligible; 0 School-wide Title I
Students: 21,998 (50.6% male; 49.4% female)
Individual Education Program: 2,180 (9.9%);
English Language Learner: 1,190 (5.4%); Migrant: 0 (0.0%)
Eligible for Free Lunch Program: 1,988 (9.0%)
Eligible for Reduced-Price Lunch Program: 1,095 (5.0%)
Teachers: 1,054.6 (20.9 to 1)
Librarians/Media Specialists: 3.0 (7,332.7 to 1)
Guidance Counselors: 19.5 (1,128.1 to 1)
Current Spending: ($ per student per year):
Total: $5,921; Instruction: $4,141; Support Services: $1,642
Enrollment, Drop-out Rates and Diploma Recipients by Race/Ethnicity

Category	Total	White	Black	Asian	AIAN	Hisp.
Enrollment (%)	100.0	66.2	4.9	7.6	1.3	18.7
Drop-out Rate (%)	n/a	n/a	n/a	n/a	n/a	n/a
H.S. Diplomas (#)	1,049	771	57	81	4	135

Val Verde Unified
975 E Morgan Rd • Perris, CA 92571-3103
(909) 940-6100 • http://www.valverde.edu/
Grade Span: KG-12; **Agency Type:** 1
Schools: 12
7 Primary; 2 Middle; 3 High; 0 Other Level
11 Regular; 0 Special Education; 0 Vocational; 1 Alternative
0 Magnet; 0 Charter; 6 Title I Eligible; 5 School-wide Title I
Students: 12,450 (51.5% male; 48.5% female)
Individual Education Program: 1,030 (8.3%);
English Language Learner: 3,363 (27.0%); Migrant: 2 (<0.1%)
Eligible for Free Lunch Program: 6,037 (48.5%)
Eligible for Reduced-Price Lunch Program: 1,962 (15.8%)
Teachers: 496.2 (25.1 to 1)
Librarians/Media Specialists: 0.0 (0.0 to 1)
Guidance Counselors: 9.0 (1,383.3 to 1)
Current Spending: ($ per student per year):
Total: $6,196; Instruction: $3,857; Support Services: $2,108
Enrollment, Drop-out Rates and Diploma Recipients by Race/Ethnicity

Category	Total	White	Black	Asian	AIAN	Hisp.
Enrollment (%)	100.0	14.8	20.7	3.7	0.3	60.4
Drop-out Rate (%)	n/a	n/a	n/a	n/a	n/a	n/a
H.S. Diplomas (#)	558	116	127	39	2	274

Sacramento County

Center Joint Unified
8408 Watt Ave • Antelope, CA 95843-9116
(916) 338-6330
Grade Span: KG-12; **Agency Type:** 1
Schools: 9
4 Primary; 1 Middle; 2 High; 2 Other Level
8 Regular; 0 Special Education; 0 Vocational; 1 Alternative
0 Magnet; 1 Charter; 2 Title I Eligible; 1 School-wide Title I
Students: 5,904 (50.9% male; 49.1% female)
Individual Education Program: 640 (10.8%);
English Language Learner: 595 (10.1%); Migrant: 0 (0.0%)
Eligible for Free Lunch Program: 1,189 (20.1%)
Eligible for Reduced-Price Lunch Program: 504 (8.5%)
Teachers: 312.8 (18.9 to 1)
Librarians/Media Specialists: 2.0 (2,952.0 to 1)
Guidance Counselors: 5.4 (1,093.3 to 1)
Current Spending: ($ per student per year):
Total: $6,232; Instruction: $3,905; Support Services: $2,130
Enrollment, Drop-out Rates and Diploma Recipients by Race/Ethnicity

Category	Total	White	Black	Asian	AIAN	Hisp.
Enrollment (%)	100.0	57.5	13.4	12.4	1.1	11.5
Drop-out Rate (%)	n/a	n/a	n/a	n/a	n/a	n/a
H.S. Diplomas (#)	324	191	45	54	4	30

Del Paso Heights Elementary
3780 Rosin Court, Ste 270 • Sacramento, CA 95834-1646
(916) 641-5300 •
http://webpages.grant.k12.ca.us/education/school/school.php?sectionid=1256
Grade Span: KG-06; **Agency Type:** 1
Schools: 5
5 Primary; 0 Middle; 0 High; 0 Other Level
5 Regular; 0 Special Education; 0 Vocational; 0 Alternative
0 Magnet; 0 Charter; 5 Title I Eligible; 0 School-wide Title I
Students: 2,155 (51.6% male; 48.4% female)
Individual Education Program: 175 (8.1%);
English Language Learner: 936 (43.4%); Migrant: 1 (<0.1%)
Eligible for Free Lunch Program: 1,960 (91.0%)
Eligible for Reduced-Price Lunch Program: 135 (6.3%)
Teachers: 115.0 (18.7 to 1)
Librarians/Media Specialists: 0.0 (0.0 to 1)
Guidance Counselors: 3.0 (718.3 to 1)
Current Spending: ($ per student per year):
Total: $7,741; Instruction: $4,724; Support Services: $2,363
Enrollment, Drop-out Rates and Diploma Recipients by Race/Ethnicity

Category	Total	White	Black	Asian	AIAN	Hisp.
Enrollment (%)	100.0	11.1	32.3	34.9	0.4	19.6
Drop-out Rate (%)	n/a	n/a	n/a	n/a	n/a	n/a
H.S. Diplomas (#)	n/a	n/a	n/a	n/a	n/a	n/a

Elk Grove Unified
9510 Elk Grove-Florin Rd • Elk Grove, CA 95624-1801
(916) 686-7700 • http://www.egusd.k12.ca.us/
Grade Span: KG-12; **Agency Type:** 1
Schools: 55
33 Primary; 6 Middle; 13 High; 3 Other Level
45 Regular; 1 Special Education; 0 Vocational; 9 Alternative
0 Magnet; 1 Charter; 12 Title I Eligible; 3 School-wide Title I
Students: 52,418 (51.6% male; 48.4% female)
Individual Education Program: 4,760 (9.1%);
English Language Learner: 10,232 (19.5%); Migrant: 96 (0.2%)
Eligible for Free Lunch Program: 15,285 (29.2%)
Eligible for Reduced-Price Lunch Program: 5,046 (9.6%)
Teachers: 2,600.9 (20.2 to 1)
Librarians/Media Specialists: 12.0 (4,368.2 to 1)
Guidance Counselors: 62.2 (842.7 to 1)
Current Spending: ($ per student per year):
Total: $6,692; Instruction: $4,299; Support Services: $2,073
Enrollment, Drop-out Rates and Diploma Recipients by Race/Ethnicity

Category	Total	White	Black	Asian	AIAN	Hisp.
Enrollment (%)	100.0	35.4	18.6	25.3	1.3	19.4
Drop-out Rate (%)	n/a	n/a	n/a	n/a	n/a	n/a
H.S. Diplomas (#)	2,728	1,108	455	773	20	371

Folsom-Cordova Unified
125 E Bidwell St • Folsom, CA 95630-3241
(916) 355-1111 • http://www.fcusd.k12.ca.us/
Grade Span: KG-12; **Agency Type:** 1
Schools: 30
18 Primary; 4 Middle; 5 High; 3 Other Level
24 Regular; 1 Special Education; 0 Vocational; 5 Alternative
0 Magnet; 0 Charter; 8 Title I Eligible; 5 School-wide Title I
Students: 17,614 (50.9% male; 49.1% female)
Individual Education Program: 2,281 (12.9%);
English Language Learner: 1,981 (11.2%); Migrant: 2 (<0.1%)
Eligible for Free Lunch Program: 4,076 (23.1%)
Eligible for Reduced-Price Lunch Program: 945 (5.4%)
Teachers: 820.3 (21.5 to 1)
Librarians/Media Specialists: 3.0 (5,871.3 to 1)
Guidance Counselors: 20.4 (863.4 to 1)
Current Spending: ($ per student per year):
Total: $6,327; Instruction: $3,890; Support Services: $2,165
Enrollment, Drop-out Rates and Diploma Recipients by Race/Ethnicity

Category	Total	White	Black	Asian	AIAN	Hisp.
Enrollment (%)	100.0	67.9	9.2	10.0	0.6	12.0
Drop-out Rate (%)	n/a	n/a	n/a	n/a	n/a	n/a
H.S. Diplomas (#)	898	655	68	85	7	82

Galt Joint Union Elementary
1018 C St Ste 210 • Galt, CA 95632-1733
(209) 744-4545 • http://www.galt.k12.ca.us/
Grade Span: KG-08; **Agency Type:** 1
Schools: 5

4 Primary; 1 Middle; 0 High; 0 Other Level
5 Regular; 0 Special Education; 0 Vocational; 0 Alternative
0 Magnet; 0 Charter; 3 Title I Eligible; 0 School-wide Title I
Students: 4,257 (50.1% male; 49.9% female)
Individual Education Program: 513 (12.1%);
English Language Learner: 1,073 (25.2%); Migrant: 704 (16.5%)
Eligible for Free Lunch Program: 1,516 (35.6%)
Eligible for Reduced-Price Lunch Program: 500 (11.7%)
Teachers: 228.9 (18.6 to 1)
Librarians/Media Specialists: 0.0 (0.0 to 1)
Guidance Counselors: 0.0 (0.0 to 1)
Current Spending: ($ per student per year):
Total: $6,149; Instruction: $4,024; Support Services: $1,859
Enrollment, Drop-out Rates and Diploma Recipients by Race/Ethnicity

Category	Total	White	Black	Asian	AIAN	Hisp.
Enrollment (%)	100.0	50.9	1.9	3.3	1.3	42.6
Drop-out Rate (%)	n/a	n/a	n/a	n/a	n/a	n/a
H.S. Diplomas (#)	n/a	n/a	n/a	n/a	n/a	n/a

Galt Joint Union High
145 N Lincoln Way • Galt, CA 95632-1720
(209) 745-3061 • http://www.ghsd.k12.ca.us/
Grade Span: 09-12; **Agency Type:** 1
Schools: 2
0 Primary; 0 Middle; 2 High; 0 Other Level
1 Regular; 0 Special Education; 0 Vocational; 1 Alternative
0 Magnet; 0 Charter; 2 Title I Eligible; 0 School-wide Title I
Students: 2,074 (51.9% male; 48.1% female)
Individual Education Program: 188 (9.1%);
English Language Learner: 346 (16.7%); Migrant: 303 (14.6%)
Eligible for Free Lunch Program: 449 (21.6%)
Eligible for Reduced-Price Lunch Program: 66 (3.2%)
Teachers: 98.2 (21.1 to 1)
Librarians/Media Specialists: 0.0 (0.0 to 1)
Guidance Counselors: 3.0 (691.3 to 1)
Current Spending: ($ per student per year):
Total: $6,292; Instruction: $3,717; Support Services: $2,374
Enrollment, Drop-out Rates and Diploma Recipients by Race/Ethnicity

Category	Total	White	Black	Asian	AIAN	Hisp.
Enrollment (%)	100.0	58.0	1.8	4.1	1.5	33.4
Drop-out Rate (%)	n/a	n/a	n/a	n/a	n/a	n/a
H.S. Diplomas (#)	366	231	2	10	9	114

Grant Joint Union High
1333 Grand Ave • Sacramento, CA 95838-3697
(916) 286-4800 • http://www.grant.k12.ca.us/
Grade Span: KG-12; **Agency Type:** 1
Schools: 14
0 Primary; 6 Middle; 8 High; 0 Other Level
9 Regular; 1 Special Education; 0 Vocational; 4 Alternative
2 Magnet; 0 Charter; 6 Title I Eligible; 4 School-wide Title I
Students: 12,682 (52.4% male; 47.6% female)
Individual Education Program: 1,601 (12.6%);
English Language Learner: 2,976 (23.5%); Migrant: 22 (0.2%)
Eligible for Free Lunch Program: 5,270 (41.6%)
Eligible for Reduced-Price Lunch Program: 1,262 (10.0%)
Teachers: 572.7 (22.1 to 1)
Librarians/Media Specialists: 4.0 (3,170.5 to 1)
Guidance Counselors: 28.2 (449.7 to 1)
Current Spending: ($ per student per year):
Total: $7,153; Instruction: $3,839; Support Services: $3,136
Enrollment, Drop-out Rates and Diploma Recipients by Race/Ethnicity

Category	Total	White	Black	Asian	AIAN	Hisp.
Enrollment (%)	100.0	36.4	19.0	16.0	1.9	21.2
Drop-out Rate (%)	n/a	n/a	n/a	n/a	n/a	n/a
H.S. Diplomas (#)	1,345	549	213	292	12	237

Natomas Unified
1901 Arena Blvd • Sacramento, CA 95834-1905
(916) 567-5400 • http://www.natomas.k12.ca.us/
Grade Span: KG-12; **Agency Type:** 1
Schools: 10
5 Primary; 2 Middle; 2 High; 1 Other Level
8 Regular; 0 Special Education; 0 Vocational; 2 Alternative
0 Magnet; 1 Charter; 4 Title I Eligible; 1 School-wide Title I
Students: 7,653 (51.0% male; 49.0% female)
Individual Education Program: 678 (8.9%);
English Language Learner: 911 (11.9%); Migrant: 2 (<0.1%)
Eligible for Free Lunch Program: 1,548 (20.2%)
Eligible for Reduced-Price Lunch Program: 675 (8.8%)
Teachers: 386.0 (19.8 to 1)
Librarians/Media Specialists: 1.0 (7,653.0 to 1)
Guidance Counselors: 9.0 (850.3 to 1)
Current Spending: ($ per student per year):
Total: $6,671; Instruction: $4,094; Support Services: $2,320
Enrollment, Drop-out Rates and Diploma Recipients by Race/Ethnicity

Category	Total	White	Black	Asian	AIAN	Hisp.
Enrollment (%)	100.0	29.0	25.0	16.1	1.0	26.1
Drop-out Rate (%)	n/a	n/a	n/a	n/a	n/a	n/a
H.S. Diplomas (#)	386	125	89	74	2	93

North Sacramento Elementary
670 Dixieanne Ave • Sacramento, CA 95815-3023
(916) 263-8287 • http://www.nssd.k12.ca.us/
Grade Span: KG-06; **Agency Type:** 1
Schools: 11
11 Primary; 0 Middle; 0 High; 0 Other Level
10 Regular; 0 Special Education; 0 Vocational; 1 Alternative
0 Magnet; 0 Charter; 11 Title I Eligible; 10 School-wide Title I
Students: 5,552 (51.3% male; 48.7% female)
Individual Education Program: 592 (10.7%);
English Language Learner: 1,958 (35.3%); Migrant: 57 (1.0%)
Eligible for Free Lunch Program: 3,862 (69.6%)
Eligible for Reduced-Price Lunch Program: 645 (11.6%)
Teachers: 299.5 (18.5 to 1)
Librarians/Media Specialists: 0.0 (0.0 to 1)
Guidance Counselors: 10.9 (509.4 to 1)
Current Spending: ($ per student per year):
Total: $7,394; Instruction: $4,337; Support Services: $2,660
Enrollment, Drop-out Rates and Diploma Recipients by Race/Ethnicity

Category	Total	White	Black	Asian	AIAN	Hisp.
Enrollment (%)	100.0	21.6	19.7	14.0	1.2	42.2
Drop-out Rate (%)	n/a	n/a	n/a	n/a	n/a	n/a
H.S. Diplomas (#)	n/a	n/a	n/a	n/a	n/a	n/a

Rio Linda Union Elementary
627 L St • Rio Linda, CA 95673-3430
(916) 991-1704 • http://www.rlusd.com/
Grade Span: KG-08; **Agency Type:** 1
Schools: 23
22 Primary; 1 Middle; 0 High; 0 Other Level
22 Regular; 0 Special Education; 0 Vocational; 1 Alternative
0 Magnet; 1 Charter; 19 Title I Eligible; 13 School-wide Title I
Students: 10,134 (51.0% male; 49.0% female)
Individual Education Program: 1,163 (11.5%);
English Language Learner: 1,977 (19.5%); Migrant: 6 (0.1%)
Eligible for Free Lunch Program: 4,521 (44.6%)
Eligible for Reduced-Price Lunch Program: 1,247 (12.3%)
Teachers: 555.1 (18.3 to 1)
Librarians/Media Specialists: 1.0 (10,134.0 to 1)
Guidance Counselors: 5.0 (2,026.8 to 1)
Current Spending: ($ per student per year):
Total: $6,596; Instruction: $4,459; Support Services: $1,853
Enrollment, Drop-out Rates and Diploma Recipients by Race/Ethnicity

Category	Total	White	Black	Asian	AIAN	Hisp.
Enrollment (%)	100.0	56.3	16.1	6.8	1.1	19.7
Drop-out Rate (%)	n/a	n/a	n/a	n/a	n/a	n/a
H.S. Diplomas (#)	n/a	n/a	n/a	n/a	n/a	n/a

River Delta Joint Unified
445 Montezuma • Rio Vista, CA 94571-1651
(707) 374-6381 • http://www.riverdelta.k12.ca.us/
Grade Span: KG-12; **Agency Type:** 1
Schools: 10
5 Primary; 1 Middle; 3 High; 1 Other Level
8 Regular; 0 Special Education; 0 Vocational; 2 Alternative
0 Magnet; 0 Charter; 4 Title I Eligible; 3 School-wide Title I
Students: 2,490 (49.3% male; 50.7% female)
Individual Education Program: 305 (12.2%);
English Language Learner: 753 (30.2%); Migrant: 679 (27.3%)
Eligible for Free Lunch Program: 803 (32.2%)
Eligible for Reduced-Price Lunch Program: 118 (4.7%)
Teachers: 122.2 (20.4 to 1)
Librarians/Media Specialists: 0.0 (0.0 to 1)
Guidance Counselors: 5.4 (461.1 to 1)
Current Spending: ($ per student per year):
Total: $6,590; Instruction: $3,884; Support Services: $2,483
Enrollment, Drop-out Rates and Diploma Recipients by Race/Ethnicity

Category	Total	White	Black	Asian	AIAN	Hisp.
Enrollment (%)	100.0	53.6	0.9	3.4	0.5	41.2
Drop-out Rate (%)	n/a	n/a	n/a	n/a	n/a	n/a
H.S. Diplomas (#)	178	113	0	9	0	56

Robla Elementary
5248 Rose St • Sacramento, CA 95838-1633
(916) 991-1728 • http://www.robla.k12.ca.us/
Grade Span: KG-06; **Agency Type:** 1
Schools: 5
5 Primary; 0 Middle; 0 High; 0 Other Level
5 Regular; 0 Special Education; 0 Vocational; 0 Alternative

0 Magnet; 0 Charter; 5 Title I Eligible; 5 School-wide Title I
Students: 2,323 (51.8% male; 48.2% female)
Individual Education Program: 356 (15.3%);
English Language Learner: 933 (40.2%); Migrant: 0 (0.0%)
Eligible for Free Lunch Program: 1,306 (56.2%)
Eligible for Reduced-Price Lunch Program: 352 (15.2%)
Teachers: 117.2 (19.8 to 1)
Librarians/Media Specialists: 0.0 (0.0 to 1)
Guidance Counselors: 0.0 (0.0 to 1)
Current Spending: ($ per student per year):
Total: $6,808; Instruction: $4,425; Support Services: $2,020
Enrollment, Drop-out Rates and Diploma Recipients by Race/Ethnicity

Category	Total	White	Black	Asian	AIAN	Hisp.
Enrollment (%)	100.0	32.8	16.8	20.7	0.6	28.8
Drop-out Rate (%)	n/a	n/a	n/a	n/a	n/a	n/a
H.S. Diplomas (#)	n/a	n/a	n/a	n/a	n/a	n/a

Sacramento City Unified
5735 47th Ave • Sacramento, CA 95824-6870
Mailing Address: PO Box 246870 • Sacramento, CA 95824-6870
(916) 643-9000 • http://www.scusd.edu/
Grade Span: KG-12; **Agency Type:** 1
Schools: 80
62 Primary; 8 Middle; 8 High; 2 Other Level
75 Regular; 0 Special Education; 0 Vocational; 5 Alternative
12 Magnet; 1 Charter; 65 Title I Eligible; 39 School-wide Title I
Students: 52,850 (51.1% male; 48.9% female)
Individual Education Program: 6,460 (12.2%);
English Language Learner: 15,875 (30.0%); Migrant: 1,047 (2.0%)
Eligible for Free Lunch Program: 29,560 (55.9%)
Eligible for Reduced-Price Lunch Program: 2,910 (5.5%)
Teachers: 2,489.8 (21.2 to 1)
Librarians/Media Specialists: 16.2 (3,262.3 to 1)
Guidance Counselors: 32.2 (1,641.3 to 1)
Current Spending: ($ per student per year):
Total: $7,414; Instruction: $4,453; Support Services: $2,550
Enrollment, Drop-out Rates and Diploma Recipients by Race/Ethnicity

Category	Total	White	Black	Asian	AIAN	Hisp.
Enrollment (%)	100.0	22.6	22.1	24.8	1.5	27.6
Drop-out Rate (%)	n/a	n/a	n/a	n/a	n/a	n/a
H.S. Diplomas (#)	2,237	515	357	886	32	441

San Juan Unified
3738 Walnut Ave • Carmichael, CA 95609-0477
Mailing Address: PO Box 477 • Carmichael, CA 95609-0477
(916) 971-7700 • http://www.sanjuan.edu/
Grade Span: KG-12; **Agency Type:** 1
Schools: 84
52 Primary; 10 Middle; 14 High; 8 Other Level
75 Regular; 3 Special Education; 0 Vocational; 6 Alternative
2 Magnet; 4 Charter; 33 Title I Eligible; 14 School-wide Title I
Students: 52,212 (50.9% male; 49.1% female)
Individual Education Program: 4,802 (9.2%);
English Language Learner: 4,122 (7.9%); Migrant: 7 (<0.1%)
Eligible for Free Lunch Program: 3,453 (6.6%)
Eligible for Reduced-Price Lunch Program: 6,905 (13.2%)
Teachers: 2,522.1 (20.7 to 1)
Librarians/Media Specialists: 5.0 (10,442.4 to 1)
Guidance Counselors: 57.6 (906.5 to 1)
Current Spending: ($ per student per year):
Total: $7,144; Instruction: $4,486; Support Services: $2,448
Enrollment, Drop-out Rates and Diploma Recipients by Race/Ethnicity

Category	Total	White	Black	Asian	AIAN	Hisp.
Enrollment (%)	100.0	72.6	7.1	6.2	2.3	11.8
Drop-out Rate (%)	n/a	n/a	n/a	n/a	n/a	n/a
H.S. Diplomas (#)	3,556	2,804	171	244	54	277

San Benito County

Hollister SD
2690 Cienega Rd • Hollister, CA 95023-4570
(831) 634-2000 • http://www.hollister.goleta.k12.ca.us/
Grade Span: KG-08; **Agency Type:** 1
Schools: 8
6 Primary; 2 Middle; 0 High; 0 Other Level
8 Regular; 0 Special Education; 0 Vocational; 0 Alternative
0 Magnet; 0 Charter; 6 Title I Eligible; 0 School-wide Title I
Students: 6,280 (52.3% male; 47.7% female)
Individual Education Program: 763 (12.1%);
English Language Learner: 1,722 (27.4%); Migrant: 1,846 (29.4%)
Eligible for Free Lunch Program: 1,918 (30.5%)
Eligible for Reduced-Price Lunch Program: 867 (13.8%)
Teachers: 304.4 (20.6 to 1)
Librarians/Media Specialists: 0.0 (0.0 to 1)
Guidance Counselors: 1.0 (6,280.0 to 1)
Current Spending: ($ per student per year):
Total: $6,329; Instruction: $4,277; Support Services: $1,865
Enrollment, Drop-out Rates and Diploma Recipients by Race/Ethnicity

Category	Total	White	Black	Asian	AIAN	Hisp.
Enrollment (%)	100.0	33.4	1.1	2.5	0.5	61.9
Drop-out Rate (%)	n/a	n/a	n/a	n/a	n/a	n/a
H.S. Diplomas (#)	n/a	n/a	n/a	n/a	n/a	n/a

San Benito High
1220 Monterey St • Hollister, CA 95023-4708
(831) 637-5831 • http://www.sbhsd.k12.ca.us/
Grade Span: 09-12; **Agency Type:** 1
Schools: 2
0 Primary; 0 Middle; 2 High; 0 Other Level
1 Regular; 0 Special Education; 0 Vocational; 1 Alternative
0 Magnet; 0 Charter; 2 Title I Eligible; 0 School-wide Title I
Students: 2,902 (51.6% male; 48.4% female)
Individual Education Program: 294 (10.1%);
English Language Learner: 207 (7.1%); Migrant: 939 (32.4%)
Eligible for Free Lunch Program: 247 (8.5%)
Eligible for Reduced-Price Lunch Program: 66 (2.3%)
Teachers: 124.4 (23.3 to 1)
Librarians/Media Specialists: 1.0 (2,902.0 to 1)
Guidance Counselors: 5.7 (509.1 to 1)
Current Spending: ($ per student per year):
Total: $6,697; Instruction: $3,829; Support Services: $2,684
Enrollment, Drop-out Rates and Diploma Recipients by Race/Ethnicity

Category	Total	White	Black	Asian	AIAN	Hisp.
Enrollment (%)	100.0	41.7	0.9	2.7	0.2	54.2
Drop-out Rate (%)	n/a	n/a	n/a	n/a	n/a	n/a
H.S. Diplomas (#)	604	270	8	13	1	311

San Bernardino County

Adelanto Elementary
11824 Air Expressway • Adelanto, CA 92301-0070
Mailing Address: PO Box 70 • Adelanto, CA 92301-0070
(760) 246-8691 • http://www.adelanto.k12.ca.us/
Grade Span: KG-08; **Agency Type:** 1
Schools: 9
7 Primary; 2 Middle; 0 High; 0 Other Level
9 Regular; 0 Special Education; 0 Vocational; 0 Alternative
0 Magnet; 0 Charter; 7 Title I Eligible; 6 School-wide Title I
Students: 5,548 (50.9% male; 49.1% female)
Individual Education Program: 611 (11.0%);
English Language Learner: 1,419 (25.6%); Migrant: 0 (0.0%)
Eligible for Free Lunch Program: 2,965 (53.4%)
Eligible for Reduced-Price Lunch Program: 764 (13.8%)
Teachers: 260.5 (21.3 to 1)
Librarians/Media Specialists: 0.0 (0.0 to 1)
Guidance Counselors: 2.0 (2,774.0 to 1)
Current Spending: ($ per student per year):
Total: $6,235; Instruction: $3,994; Support Services: $1,889
Enrollment, Drop-out Rates and Diploma Recipients by Race/Ethnicity

Category	Total	White	Black	Asian	AIAN	Hisp.
Enrollment (%)	100.0	29.0	19.4	2.5	0.8	48.3
Drop-out Rate (%)	n/a	n/a	n/a	n/a	n/a	n/a
H.S. Diplomas (#)	n/a	n/a	n/a	n/a	n/a	n/a

Alta Loma Elementary
9340 Baseline Rd • Alta Loma, CA 91701-5821
(909) 484-5151 • http://www.alsd.k12.ca.us/
Grade Span: KG-08; **Agency Type:** 1
Schools: 10
8 Primary; 2 Middle; 0 High; 0 Other Level
10 Regular; 0 Special Education; 0 Vocational; 0 Alternative
0 Magnet; 0 Charter; 4 Title I Eligible; 0 School-wide Title I
Students: 7,609 (50.8% male; 49.2% female)
Individual Education Program: 633 (8.3%);
English Language Learner: 250 (3.3%); Migrant: 0 (0.0%)
Eligible for Free Lunch Program: 759 (10.0%)
Eligible for Reduced-Price Lunch Program: 451 (5.9%)
Teachers: 317.7 (24.0 to 1)
Librarians/Media Specialists: 0.0 (0.0 to 1)
Guidance Counselors: 0.0 (0.0 to 1)
Current Spending: ($ per student per year):
Total: $5,711; Instruction: $3,975; Support Services: $1,556
Enrollment, Drop-out Rates and Diploma Recipients by Race/Ethnicity

Category	Total	White	Black	Asian	AIAN	Hisp.
Enrollment (%)	100.0	59.5	8.9	6.1	0.4	22.9
Drop-out Rate (%)	n/a	n/a	n/a	n/a	n/a	n/a
H.S. Diplomas (#)	n/a	n/a	n/a	n/a	n/a	n/a

Apple Valley Unified

22974 Bear Valley Rd • Apple Valley, CA 92308-7423
(760) 247-8001 • http://www.avstc.org/stchtml/schools/avusd_m.htm
Grade Span: KG-12; **Agency Type:** 1
Schools: 16
9 Primary; 2 Middle; 3 High; 2 Other Level
14 Regular; 0 Special Education; 0 Vocational; 2 Alternative
0 Magnet; 1 Charter; 13 Title I Eligible; 6 School-wide Title I
Students: 13,850 (50.7% male; 49.3% female)
Individual Education Program: 1,845 (13.3%);
English Language Learner: 431 (3.1%); Migrant: 0 (0.0%)
Eligible for Free Lunch Program: 4,790 (34.6%)
Eligible for Reduced-Price Lunch Program: 1,548 (11.2%)
Teachers: 642.0 (21.6 to 1)
Librarians/Media Specialists: 0.0 (0.0 to 1)
Guidance Counselors: 14.0 (989.3 to 1)
Current Spending: ($ per student per year):
Total: $6,487; Instruction: $4,171; Support Services: $2,089
Enrollment, Drop-out Rates and Diploma Recipients by Race/Ethnicity

Category	Total	White	Black	Asian	AIAN	Hisp.
Enrollment (%)	100.0	60.9	11.5	3.0	0.6	23.4
Drop-out Rate (%)	n/a	n/a	n/a	n/a	n/a	n/a
H.S. Diplomas (#)	855	574	61	40	6	172

Barstow Unified

551 S Ave H • Barstow, CA 92311-2500
(760) 255-6000 • http://www.barstow.k12.ca.us/
Grade Span: KG-12; **Agency Type:** 1
Schools: 12
8 Primary; 2 Middle; 1 High; 1 Other Level
11 Regular; 0 Special Education; 0 Vocational; 1 Alternative
0 Magnet; 0 Charter; 12 Title I Eligible; 7 School-wide Title I
Students: 6,816 (51.5% male; 48.5% female)
Individual Education Program: 784 (11.5%);
English Language Learner: 597 (8.8%); Migrant: 0 (0.0%)
Eligible for Free Lunch Program: 3,331 (48.9%)
Eligible for Reduced-Price Lunch Program: 669 (9.8%)
Teachers: 324.7 (21.0 to 1)
Librarians/Media Specialists: 1.0 (6,816.0 to 1)
Guidance Counselors: 12.0 (568.0 to 1)
Current Spending: ($ per student per year):
Total: $6,517; Instruction: $3,913; Support Services: $2,288
Enrollment, Drop-out Rates and Diploma Recipients by Race/Ethnicity

Category	Total	White	Black	Asian	AIAN	Hisp.
Enrollment (%)	100.0	39.8	14.6	2.9	2.4	40.3
Drop-out Rate (%)	n/a	n/a	n/a	n/a	n/a	n/a
H.S. Diplomas (#)	365	171	43	18	16	117

Bear Valley Unified

42271 Moonridge Rd • Big Bear Lake, CA 92315-1529
Mailing Address: Box 1529 • Big Bear Lake, CA 92315-1529
(909) 866-4631 • http://www.bigbear.k12.ca.us/
Grade Span: KG-12; **Agency Type:** 1
Schools: 8
4 Primary; 1 Middle; 2 High; 1 Other Level
7 Regular; 0 Special Education; 0 Vocational; 1 Alternative
0 Magnet; 1 Charter; 6 Title I Eligible; 0 School-wide Title I
Students: 3,390 (52.1% male; 47.9% female)
Individual Education Program: 350 (10.3%);
English Language Learner: 214 (6.3%); Migrant: 0 (0.0%)
Eligible for Free Lunch Program: 1,012 (29.9%)
Eligible for Reduced-Price Lunch Program: 265 (7.8%)
Teachers: 159.1 (21.3 to 1)
Librarians/Media Specialists: 0.6 (5,650.0 to 1)
Guidance Counselors: 3.0 (1,130.0 to 1)
Current Spending: ($ per student per year):
Total: $6,118; Instruction: $3,882; Support Services: $1,990
Enrollment, Drop-out Rates and Diploma Recipients by Race/Ethnicity

Category	Total	White	Black	Asian	AIAN	Hisp.
Enrollment (%)	100.0	79.5	1.4	1.3	0.9	16.8
Drop-out Rate (%)	n/a	n/a	n/a	n/a	n/a	n/a
H.S. Diplomas (#)	220	191	4	1	0	24

Central Elementary

10601 Church St, Ste 112 • Rancho Cucamonga, CA 91730-6863
(909) 989-8541 • http://www.centralusd.k12.ca.us/
Grade Span: KG-08; **Agency Type:** 1
Schools: 7
5 Primary; 2 Middle; 0 High; 0 Other Level
7 Regular; 0 Special Education; 0 Vocational; 0 Alternative
0 Magnet; 0 Charter; 2 Title I Eligible; 0 School-wide Title I
Students: 5,231 (50.3% male; 49.7% female)
Individual Education Program: 493 (9.4%);
English Language Learner: 552 (10.6%); Migrant: 0 (0.0%)
Eligible for Free Lunch Program: 1,122 (21.4%)
Eligible for Reduced-Price Lunch Program: 560 (10.7%)
Teachers: 236.8 (22.1 to 1)
Librarians/Media Specialists: 1.0 (5,231.0 to 1)
Guidance Counselors: 4.0 (1,307.8 to 1)
Current Spending: ($ per student per year):
Total: $5,951; Instruction: $4,020; Support Services: $1,715
Enrollment, Drop-out Rates and Diploma Recipients by Race/Ethnicity

Category	Total	White	Black	Asian	AIAN	Hisp.
Enrollment (%)	100.0	35.3	10.3	5.1	1.3	33.9
Drop-out Rate (%)	n/a	n/a	n/a	n/a	n/a	n/a
H.S. Diplomas (#)	n/a	n/a	n/a	n/a	n/a	n/a

Chaffey Joint Union High

211 W Fifth St • Ontario, CA 91762-1698
(909) 988-8511 • http://www.cjuhsd.k12.ca.us/
Grade Span: 09-12; **Agency Type:** 1
Schools: 11
0 Primary; 0 Middle; 11 High; 0 Other Level
8 Regular; 0 Special Education; 0 Vocational; 3 Alternative
0 Magnet; 0 Charter; 5 Title I Eligible; 1 School-wide Title I
Students: 21,981 (50.9% male; 49.1% female)
Individual Education Program: 2,292 (10.4%);
English Language Learner: 3,497 (15.9%); Migrant: 2 (<0.1%)
Eligible for Free Lunch Program: 3,199 (14.6%)
Eligible for Reduced-Price Lunch Program: 788 (3.6%)
Teachers: 907.8 (24.2 to 1)
Librarians/Media Specialists: 8.0 (2,747.6 to 1)
Guidance Counselors: 55.1 (398.9 to 1)
Current Spending: ($ per student per year):
Total: $6,271; Instruction: $3,985; Support Services: $2,135
Enrollment, Drop-out Rates and Diploma Recipients by Race/Ethnicity

Category	Total	White	Black	Asian	AIAN	Hisp.
Enrollment (%)	100.0	32.0	10.9	6.0	0.5	50.3
Drop-out Rate (%)	n/a	n/a	n/a	n/a	n/a	n/a
H.S. Diplomas (#)	3,873	1,481	435	282	11	1,659

Chino Valley Unified

5130 Riverside Dr • Chino, CA 91710-4130
(909) 628-1201 • http://www.chino.k12.ca.us/
Grade Span: KG-12; **Agency Type:** 1
Schools: 32
20 Primary; 5 Middle; 7 High; 0 Other Level
29 Regular; 0 Special Education; 0 Vocational; 3 Alternative
1 Magnet; 0 Charter; 15 Title I Eligible; 5 School-wide Title I
Students: 32,916 (51.3% male; 48.7% female)
Individual Education Program: 2,812 (8.5%);
English Language Learner: 3,797 (11.5%); Migrant: 2 (<0.1%)
Eligible for Free Lunch Program: 6,673 (20.3%)
Eligible for Reduced-Price Lunch Program: 2,612 (7.9%)
Teachers: 1,445.9 (22.8 to 1)
Librarians/Media Specialists: 4.0 (8,229.0 to 1)
Guidance Counselors: 23.0 (1,431.1 to 1)
Current Spending: ($ per student per year):
Total: $5,768; Instruction: $3,861; Support Services: $1,726
Enrollment, Drop-out Rates and Diploma Recipients by Race/Ethnicity

Category	Total	White	Black	Asian	AIAN	Hisp.
Enrollment (%)	100.0	37.8	5.0	12.3	0.2	44.7
Drop-out Rate (%)	n/a	n/a	n/a	n/a	n/a	n/a
H.S. Diplomas (#)	1,865	860	120	206	2	677

Colton Joint Unified

1212 Valencia Dr • Colton, CA 92324-1798
(909) 580-5000 • http://www.colton.k12.ca.us/
Grade Span: KG-12; **Agency Type:** 1
Schools: 26
18 Primary; 4 Middle; 3 High; 1 Other Level
24 Regular; 0 Special Education; 0 Vocational; 2 Alternative
4 Magnet; 0 Charter; 11 Title I Eligible; 11 School-wide Title I
Students: 24,018 (51.3% male; 48.7% female)
Individual Education Program: 2,247 (9.4%);
English Language Learner: 4,398 (18.3%); Migrant: 0 (0.0%)
Eligible for Free Lunch Program: 9,195 (38.3%)
Eligible for Reduced-Price Lunch Program: 2,878 (12.0%)
Teachers: 1,109.2 (21.7 to 1)
Librarians/Media Specialists: 4.5 (5,337.3 to 1)
Guidance Counselors: 25.0 (960.7 to 1)
Current Spending: ($ per student per year):
Total: $5,978; Instruction: $3,667; Support Services: $2,024
Enrollment, Drop-out Rates and Diploma Recipients by Race/Ethnicity

Category	Total	White	Black	Asian	AIAN	Hisp.
Enrollment (%)	100.0	16.7	9.6	3.8	0.5	68.4
Drop-out Rate (%)	n/a	n/a	n/a	n/a	n/a	n/a
H.S. Diplomas (#)	789	200	51	37	2	497

Cucamonga Elementary

8776 Archibald Ave • Rancho Cucamonga, CA 91730-4698
(909) 987-8942 • http://www.cuca.k12.ca.us/
Grade Span: KG-08; **Agency Type:** 1
Schools: 4
3 Primary; 1 Middle; 0 High; 0 Other Level
4 Regular; 0 Special Education; 0 Vocational; 0 Alternative
0 Magnet; 0 Charter; 4 Title I Eligible; 0 School-wide Title I
Students: 2,892 (53.3% male; 46.7% female)
Individual Education Program: 256 (8.9%);
English Language Learner: 782 (27.0%); Migrant: 0 (0.0%)
Eligible for Free Lunch Program: 1,396 (48.3%)
Eligible for Reduced-Price Lunch Program: 453 (15.7%)
Teachers: 129.0 (22.4 to 1)
Librarians/Media Specialists: 0.0 (0.0 to 1)
Guidance Counselors: 0.0 (0.0 to 1)
Current Spending: ($ per student per year):
Total: $6,453; Instruction: $4,090; Support Services: $2,046
Enrollment, Drop-out Rates and Diploma Recipients by Race/Ethnicity

Category	Total	White	Black	Asian	AIAN	Hisp.
Enrollment (%)	100.0	16.5	16.1	5.6	0.6	60.9
Drop-out Rate (%)	n/a	n/a	n/a	n/a	n/a	n/a
H.S. Diplomas (#)	n/a	n/a	n/a	n/a	n/a	n/a

Etiwanda Elementary

6061 E Ave • Etiwanda, CA 91739-0248
(909) 899-2451 • http://etiwanda.k12.ca.us/eh/ehhome.htm
Grade Span: KG-08; **Agency Type:** 1
Schools: 13
10 Primary; 3 Middle; 0 High; 0 Other Level
13 Regular; 0 Special Education; 0 Vocational; 0 Alternative
0 Magnet; 0 Charter; 4 Title I Eligible; 0 School-wide Title I
Students: 10,287 (51.5% male; 48.5% female)
Individual Education Program: 896 (8.7%);
English Language Learner: 233 (2.3%); Migrant: 0 (0.0%)
Eligible for Free Lunch Program: 1,268 (12.3%)
Eligible for Reduced-Price Lunch Program: 817 (7.9%)
Teachers: 461.5 (22.3 to 1)
Librarians/Media Specialists: 0.3 (34,290.0 to 1)
Guidance Counselors: 0.0 (0.0 to 1)
Current Spending: ($ per student per year):
Total: $4,837; Instruction: $3,402; Support Services: $1,287
Enrollment, Drop-out Rates and Diploma Recipients by Race/Ethnicity

Category	Total	White	Black	Asian	AIAN	Hisp.
Enrollment (%)	100.0	39.4	17.0	10.5	0.4	31.8
Drop-out Rate (%)	n/a	n/a	n/a	n/a	n/a	n/a
H.S. Diplomas (#)	n/a	n/a	n/a	n/a	n/a	n/a

Fontana Unified

9680 Citrus Ave • Fontana, CA 92335-5571
(909) 357-5000 • http://www.fontana.k12.ca.us/
Grade Span: KG-12; **Agency Type:** 1
Schools: 37
25 Primary; 7 Middle; 4 High; 1 Other Level
35 Regular; 0 Special Education; 0 Vocational; 2 Alternative
0 Magnet; 0 Charter; 31 Title I Eligible; 29 School-wide Title I
Students: 40,168 (51.0% male; 49.0% female)
Individual Education Program: 4,253 (10.6%);
English Language Learner: 14,674 (36.5%); Migrant: 0 (0.0%)
Eligible for Free Lunch Program: 20,478 (51.0%)
Eligible for Reduced-Price Lunch Program: 5,812 (14.5%)
Teachers: 1,807.5 (22.2 to 1)
Librarians/Media Specialists: 1.0 (40,168.0 to 1)
Guidance Counselors: 47.5 (845.6 to 1)
Current Spending: ($ per student per year):
Total: $6,402; Instruction: $3,864; Support Services: $2,263
Enrollment, Drop-out Rates and Diploma Recipients by Race/Ethnicity

Category	Total	White	Black	Asian	AIAN	Hisp.
Enrollment (%)	100.0	11.2	9.3	2.0	0.5	77.1
Drop-out Rate (%)	n/a	n/a	n/a	n/a	n/a	n/a
H.S. Diplomas (#)	1,793	353	177	61	5	1,197

Hesperia Unified

9144 Third St • Hesperia, CA 92345-3643
(760) 244-4411 • http://163.150.128.65/
Grade Span: KG-12; **Agency Type:** 1
Schools: 21
13 Primary; 2 Middle; 5 High; 1 Other Level
18 Regular; 0 Special Education; 0 Vocational; 3 Alternative
0 Magnet; 1 Charter; 14 Title I Eligible; 11 School-wide Title I
Students: 16,195 (50.6% male; 49.4% female)
Individual Education Program: 1,591 (9.8%);
English Language Learner: 2,065 (12.8%); Migrant: 0 (0.0%)
Eligible for Free Lunch Program: 6,607 (40.8%)
Eligible for Reduced-Price Lunch Program: 2,251 (13.9%)
Teachers: 723.8 (22.4 to 1)
Librarians/Media Specialists: 0.0 (0.0 to 1)
Guidance Counselors: 13.5 (1,199.6 to 1)
Current Spending: ($ per student per year):
Total: $6,008; Instruction: $3,919; Support Services: $1,849
Enrollment, Drop-out Rates and Diploma Recipients by Race/Ethnicity

Category	Total	White	Black	Asian	AIAN	Hisp.
Enrollment (%)	100.0	51.6	5.8	1.4	0.7	37.2
Drop-out Rate (%)	n/a	n/a	n/a	n/a	n/a	n/a
H.S. Diplomas (#)	857	511	58	18	7	248

Morongo Unified

5715 Utah Tr • Twentynine Palms, CA 92277-0980
Mailing Address: PO Box 1209 • Twentynine Palms, CA 92277-0980
(760) 367-9191 • http://www.morongo.k12.ca.us/
Grade Span: KG-12; **Agency Type:** 1
Schools: 17
11 Primary; 2 Middle; 4 High; 0 Other Level
15 Regular; 0 Special Education; 0 Vocational; 2 Alternative
0 Magnet; 0 Charter; 17 Title I Eligible; 9 School-wide Title I
Students: 9,467 (51.6% male; 48.4% female)
Individual Education Program: 1,384 (14.6%);
English Language Learner: 162 (1.7%); Migrant: 0 (0.0%)
Eligible for Free Lunch Program: 2,249 (23.8%)
Eligible for Reduced-Price Lunch Program: 1,118 (11.8%)
Teachers: 465.6 (20.3 to 1)
Librarians/Media Specialists: 2.0 (4,733.5 to 1)
Guidance Counselors: 8.0 (1,183.4 to 1)
Current Spending: ($ per student per year):
Total: $6,881; Instruction: $4,251; Support Services: $2,347
Enrollment, Drop-out Rates and Diploma Recipients by Race/Ethnicity

Category	Total	White	Black	Asian	AIAN	Hisp.
Enrollment (%)	100.0	67.5	8.5	4.9	1.4	16.6
Drop-out Rate (%)	n/a	n/a	n/a	n/a	n/a	n/a
H.S. Diplomas (#)	456	328	33	39	3	53

Mountain View Elementary

2585 S Archibald Ave • Ontario, CA 91761-8146
(909) 947-2205 • http://www.mvsd.k12.ca.us/index.htm
Grade Span: KG-08; **Agency Type:** 1
Schools: 4
3 Primary; 1 Middle; 0 High; 0 Other Level
4 Regular; 0 Special Education; 0 Vocational; 0 Alternative
0 Magnet; 0 Charter; 2 Title I Eligible; 0 School-wide Title I
Students: 3,439 (50.6% male; 49.4% female)
Individual Education Program: 340 (9.9%);
English Language Learner: 438 (12.7%); Migrant: 1 (<0.1%)
Eligible for Free Lunch Program: 815 (23.7%)
Eligible for Reduced-Price Lunch Program: 465 (13.5%)
Teachers: 166.1 (20.7 to 1)
Librarians/Media Specialists: 0.0 (0.0 to 1)
Guidance Counselors: 1.0 (3,439.0 to 1)
Current Spending: ($ per student per year):
Total: $5,953; Instruction: $4,142; Support Services: $1,577
Enrollment, Drop-out Rates and Diploma Recipients by Race/Ethnicity

Category	Total	White	Black	Asian	AIAN	Hisp.
Enrollment (%)	100.0	24.9	14.1	6.0	0.3	50.8
Drop-out Rate (%)	n/a	n/a	n/a	n/a	n/a	n/a
H.S. Diplomas (#)	n/a	n/a	n/a	n/a	n/a	n/a

Ontario-Montclair Elementary

950 W D St • Ontario, CA 91762-3026
(909) 459-2500 • http://www.omsd.k12.ca.us/
Grade Span: KG-08; **Agency Type:** 1
Schools: 32
26 Primary; 6 Middle; 0 High; 0 Other Level
31 Regular; 1 Special Education; 0 Vocational; 0 Alternative
0 Magnet; 0 Charter; 32 Title I Eligible; 23 School-wide Title I
Students: 27,270 (51.2% male; 48.8% female)
Individual Education Program: 2,494 (9.1%);
English Language Learner: 14,377 (52.7%); Migrant: 0 (0.0%)
Eligible for Free Lunch Program: 17,634 (64.7%)
Eligible for Reduced-Price Lunch Program: 3,255 (11.9%)
Teachers: 1,298.7 (21.0 to 1)
Librarians/Media Specialists: 0.0 (0.0 to 1)
Guidance Counselors: 6.0 (4,545.0 to 1)
Current Spending: ($ per student per year):
Total: $6,573; Instruction: $4,249; Support Services: $1,915
Enrollment, Drop-out Rates and Diploma Recipients by Race/Ethnicity

Category	Total	White	Black	Asian	AIAN	Hisp.
Enrollment (%)	100.0	9.8	5.0	3.1	0.4	81.6
Drop-out Rate (%)	n/a	n/a	n/a	n/a	n/a	n/a
H.S. Diplomas (#)	n/a	n/a	n/a	n/a	n/a	n/a

Oro Grande Elementary

19175 Third St • Oro Grande, CA 92368-0386
Mailing Address: PO Box 386 • Oro Grande, CA 92368-0386
(760) 245-9260
Grade Span: KG-12; **Agency Type:** 1
Schools: 2
1 Primary; 0 Middle; 0 High; 1 Other Level
2 Regular; 0 Special Education; 0 Vocational; 0 Alternative
0 Magnet; 1 Charter; 2 Title I Eligible; 0 School-wide Title I
Students: 2,846 (51.0% male; 49.0% female)
Individual Education Program: 11 (0.4%);
English Language Learner: 327 (11.5%); Migrant: 0 (0.0%)
Eligible for Free Lunch Program: 118 (4.1%)
Eligible for Reduced-Price Lunch Program: 11 (0.4%)
Teachers: 105.0 (27.1 to 1)
Librarians/Media Specialists: 0.0 (0.0 to 1)
Guidance Counselors: 0.0 (0.0 to 1)
Current Spending: ($ per student per year):
Total: $12,915; Instruction: $8,547; Support Services: $3,575
Enrollment, Drop-out Rates and Diploma Recipients by Race/Ethnicity

Category	Total	White	Black	Asian	AIAN	Hisp.
Enrollment (%)	100.0	44.2	18.9	2.4	0.7	33.7
Drop-out Rate (%)	n/a	n/a	n/a	n/a	n/a	n/a
H.S. Diplomas (#)	100	41	2	1	1	55

Redlands Unified

20 W Lugonia • Redlands, CA 92373-1508
Mailing Address: PO Box 3008 • Redlands, CA 92373-1508
(909) 307-5300 • http://www.redlands.k12.ca.us/
Grade Span: KG-12; **Agency Type:** 1
Schools: 21
14 Primary; 3 Middle; 4 High; 0 Other Level
20 Regular; 0 Special Education; 0 Vocational; 1 Alternative
0 Magnet; 1 Charter; 13 Title I Eligible; 7 School-wide Title I
Students: 20,285 (50.1% male; 49.9% female)
Individual Education Program: 1,939 (9.6%);
English Language Learner: 2,114 (10.4%); Migrant: 0 (0.0%)
Eligible for Free Lunch Program: 6,292 (31.0%)
Eligible for Reduced-Price Lunch Program: 2,338 (11.5%)
Teachers: 922.9 (22.0 to 1)
Librarians/Media Specialists: 5.0 (4,057.0 to 1)
Guidance Counselors: 30.2 (671.7 to 1)
Current Spending: ($ per student per year):
Total: $6,179; Instruction: $3,880; Support Services: $2,089
Enrollment, Drop-out Rates and Diploma Recipients by Race/Ethnicity

Category	Total	White	Black	Asian	AIAN	Hisp.
Enrollment (%)	100.0	46.0	8.4	10.8	0.9	33.4
Drop-out Rate (%)	n/a	n/a	n/a	n/a	n/a	n/a
H.S. Diplomas (#)	1,313	682	85	171	13	356

Rialto Unified

182 E Walnut Ave • Rialto, CA 92376-3530
(909) 820-7700 • http://www.rialto.k12.ca.us/
Grade Span: KG-12; **Agency Type:** 1
Schools: 27
17 Primary; 5 Middle; 5 High; 0 Other Level
25 Regular; 0 Special Education; 0 Vocational; 2 Alternative
0 Magnet; 1 Charter; 19 Title I Eligible; 16 School-wide Title I
Students: 30,172 (50.7% male; 49.3% female)
Individual Education Program: 2,410 (8.0%);
English Language Learner: 7,045 (23.3%); Migrant: 0 (0.0%)
Eligible for Free Lunch Program: 16,176 (53.6%)
Eligible for Reduced-Price Lunch Program: 2,954 (9.8%)
Teachers: 1,383.2 (21.8 to 1)
Librarians/Media Specialists: 8.0 (3,771.5 to 1)
Guidance Counselors: 35.0 (862.1 to 1)
Current Spending: ($ per student per year):
Total: $6,065; Instruction: $3,659; Support Services: $2,160
Enrollment, Drop-out Rates and Diploma Recipients by Race/Ethnicity

Category	Total	White	Black	Asian	AIAN	Hisp.
Enrollment (%)	100.0	10.2	24.5	2.9	0.2	62.2
Drop-out Rate (%)	n/a	n/a	n/a	n/a	n/a	n/a
H.S. Diplomas (#)	1,392	207	370	79	0	736

Rim of The World Unified

27614 Hwy 18 • Lake Arrowhead, CA 92352-0430
Mailing Address: PO Box 430 • Lake Arrowhead, CA 92352-0430
(909) 336-2031 • http://www.rimsd.k12.ca.us/
Grade Span: KG-12; **Agency Type:** 1
Schools: 8
4 Primary; 2 Middle; 2 High; 0 Other Level
7 Regular; 0 Special Education; 0 Vocational; 1 Alternative
0 Magnet; 0 Charter; 5 Title I Eligible; 0 School-wide Title I
Students: 5,780 (51.1% male; 48.9% female)
Individual Education Program: 578 (10.0%);
English Language Learner: 297 (5.1%); Migrant: 0 (0.0%)
Eligible for Free Lunch Program: 1,375 (23.8%)
Eligible for Reduced-Price Lunch Program: 334 (5.8%)
Teachers: 248.9 (23.2 to 1)
Librarians/Media Specialists: 2.0 (2,890.0 to 1)
Guidance Counselors: 7.0 (825.7 to 1)
Current Spending: ($ per student per year):
Total: $6,236; Instruction: $3,840; Support Services: $2,232
Enrollment, Drop-out Rates and Diploma Recipients by Race/Ethnicity

Category	Total	White	Black	Asian	AIAN	Hisp.
Enrollment (%)	100.0	79.7	1.3	1.4	0.8	15.1
Drop-out Rate (%)	n/a	n/a	n/a	n/a	n/a	n/a
H.S. Diplomas (#)	394	336	2	14	1	38

San Bernardino City Unified

777 N F St • San Bernardino, CA 92410-3017
(909) 381-1100 • http://www.sbcusd.k12.ca.us/
Grade Span: KG-12; **Agency Type:** 1
Schools: 65
44 Primary; 8 Middle; 10 High; 3 Other Level
55 Regular; 3 Special Education; 0 Vocational; 7 Alternative
23 Magnet; 1 Charter; 61 Title I Eligible; 47 School-wide Title I
Students: 56,096 (50.8% male; 49.2% female)
Individual Education Program: 6,517 (11.6%);
English Language Learner: 15,258 (27.2%); Migrant: 0 (0.0%)
Eligible for Free Lunch Program: 37,477 (66.8%)
Eligible for Reduced-Price Lunch Program: 7,664 (13.7%)
Teachers: 2,645.8 (21.2 to 1)
Librarians/Media Specialists: 4.8 (11,686.7 to 1)
Guidance Counselors: 84.5 (663.9 to 1)
Current Spending: ($ per student per year):
Total: $6,699; Instruction: $3,868; Support Services: $2,504
Enrollment, Drop-out Rates and Diploma Recipients by Race/Ethnicity

Category	Total	White	Black	Asian	AIAN	Hisp.
Enrollment (%)	100.0	17.5	20.3	3.2	1.1	57.7
Drop-out Rate (%)	n/a	n/a	n/a	n/a	n/a	n/a
H.S. Diplomas (#)	1,933	526	345	132	22	905

San Bernardino County Supt.

601 NE St • San Bernardino, CA 92404-2310
(909) 386-2400 • http://www.sbcss.k12.ca.us/sbcss/
Grade Span: KG-12; **Agency Type:** 4
Schools: 6
0 Primary; 0 Middle; 1 High; 5 Other Level
0 Regular; 2 Special Education; 0 Vocational; 4 Alternative
0 Magnet; 0 Charter; 0 Title I Eligible; 0 School-wide Title I
Students: 3,223 (71.9% male; 28.1% female)
Individual Education Program: n/a;
English Language Learner: 285 (8.8%); Migrant: 0 (0.0%)
Eligible for Free Lunch Program: 934 (29.0%)
Eligible for Reduced-Price Lunch Program: 33 (1.0%)
Teachers: 314.7 (10.2 to 1)
Librarians/Media Specialists: 0.5 (6,446.0 to 1)
Guidance Counselors: 3.0 (1,074.3 to 1)
Current Spending: ($ per student per year):
Total: $37,660; Instruction: $18,146; Support Services: $19,514
Enrollment, Drop-out Rates and Diploma Recipients by Race/Ethnicity

Category	Total	White	Black	Asian	AIAN	Hisp.
Enrollment (%)	100.0	36.2	17.5	3.3	0.9	41.7
Drop-out Rate (%)	n/a	n/a	n/a	n/a	n/a	n/a
H.S. Diplomas (#)	0	0	0	0	0	0

Silver Valley Unified

35320 Daggett Yermo Rd • Yermo, CA 92398-0847
Mailing Address: PO Box 847 • Yermo, CA 92398-0847
(760) 254-2916 • http://www.silvervalley.k12.ca.us/
Grade Span: KG-12; **Agency Type:** 1
Schools: 8
3 Primary; 2 Middle; 2 High; 1 Other Level
6 Regular; 0 Special Education; 0 Vocational; 2 Alternative
0 Magnet; 0 Charter; 3 Title I Eligible; 0 School-wide Title I
Students: 2,670 (51.2% male; 48.8% female)
Individual Education Program: 279 (10.4%);
English Language Learner: 86 (3.2%); Migrant: 0 (0.0%)
Eligible for Free Lunch Program: 651 (24.4%)
Eligible for Reduced-Price Lunch Program: 432 (16.2%)
Teachers: 147.5 (18.1 to 1)
Librarians/Media Specialists: 0.0 (0.0 to 1)
Guidance Counselors: 4.0 (667.5 to 1)
Current Spending: ($ per student per year):
Total: $9,099; Instruction: $4,960; Support Services: $3,714

Enrollment, Drop-out Rates and Diploma Recipients by Race/Ethnicity

Category	Total	White	Black	Asian	AIAN	Hisp.
Enrollment (%)	100.0	46.3	15.1	4.0	1.2	16.5
Drop-out Rate (%)	n/a	n/a	n/a	n/a	n/a	n/a
H.S. Diplomas (#)	83	49	9	12	2	10

Snowline Joint Unified

4075 Nielson Rd • Phelan, CA 92329-6000
Mailing Address: PO Box 296000 • Phelan, CA 92329-6000
(760) 868-5817 • http://www.snowline.k12.ca.us/
Grade Span: KG-12; **Agency Type:** 1
Schools: 13
5 Primary; 2 Middle; 3 High; 3 Other Level
10 Regular; 0 Special Education; 0 Vocational; 3 Alternative
0 Magnet; 2 Charter; 9 Title I Eligible; 2 School-wide Title I
Students: 8,785 (51.7% male; 48.3% female)
Individual Education Program: 951 (10.8%);
English Language Learner: 480 (5.5%); Migrant: 0 (0.0%)
Eligible for Free Lunch Program: 1,791 (20.4%)
Eligible for Reduced-Price Lunch Program: 509 (5.8%)
Teachers: 424.9 (20.7 to 1)
Librarians/Media Specialists: 0.0 (0.0 to 1)
Guidance Counselors: 9.0 (976.1 to 1)
Current Spending: ($ per student per year):
Total: $6,643; Instruction: $4,418; Support Services: $2,050
Enrollment, Drop-out Rates and Diploma Recipients by Race/Ethnicity

Category	Total	White	Black	Asian	AIAN	Hisp.
Enrollment (%)	100.0	66.9	5.9	1.8	0.9	23.8
Drop-out Rate (%)	n/a	n/a	n/a	n/a	n/a	n/a
H.S. Diplomas (#)	685	358	62	17	3	240

Upland Unified

390 N Euclid Ave • Upland, CA 91785-1239
Mailing Address: PO Box 1239 • Upland, CA 91785-1239
(909) 985-1864 • http://www.upland.k12.ca.us/
Grade Span: KG-12; **Agency Type:** 1
Schools: 15
10 Primary; 2 Middle; 2 High; 1 Other Level
13 Regular; 0 Special Education; 0 Vocational; 2 Alternative
0 Magnet; 1 Charter; 7 Title I Eligible; 5 School-wide Title I
Students: 13,237 (50.5% male; 49.5% female)
Individual Education Program: 1,021 (7.7%);
English Language Learner: 1,425 (10.8%); Migrant: 0 (0.0%)
Eligible for Free Lunch Program: 3,398 (25.7%)
Eligible for Reduced-Price Lunch Program: 903 (6.8%)
Teachers: 594.9 (22.3 to 1)
Librarians/Media Specialists: 1.0 (13,237.0 to 1)
Guidance Counselors: 13.0 (1,018.2 to 1)
Current Spending: ($ per student per year):
Total: $5,720; Instruction: $3,905; Support Services: $1,598
Enrollment, Drop-out Rates and Diploma Recipients by Race/Ethnicity

Category	Total	White	Black	Asian	AIAN	Hisp.
Enrollment (%)	100.0	43.6	9.6	6.3	0.6	32.3
Drop-out Rate (%)	n/a	n/a	n/a	n/a	n/a	n/a
H.S. Diplomas (#)	912	481	84	95	1	244

Victor Elementary

15579 Eighth St • Victorville, CA 92392-3348
(760) 245-1691 • http://www.vesd.org/
Grade Span: KG-06; **Agency Type:** 1
Schools: 15
15 Primary; 0 Middle; 0 High; 0 Other Level
15 Regular; 0 Special Education; 0 Vocational; 0 Alternative
0 Magnet; 3 Charter; 10 Title I Eligible; 1 School-wide Title I
Students: 9,442 (50.2% male; 49.8% female)
Individual Education Program: 708 (7.5%);
English Language Learner: 1,084 (11.5%); Migrant: 0 (0.0%)
Eligible for Free Lunch Program: 4,348 (46.0%)
Eligible for Reduced-Price Lunch Program: 1,089 (11.5%)
Teachers: 413.7 (22.8 to 1)
Librarians/Media Specialists: 0.0 (0.0 to 1)
Guidance Counselors: 3.0 (3,147.3 to 1)
Current Spending: ($ per student per year):
Total: $5,715; Instruction: $3,802; Support Services: $1,692
Enrollment, Drop-out Rates and Diploma Recipients by Race/Ethnicity

Category	Total	White	Black	Asian	AIAN	Hisp.
Enrollment (%)	100.0	38.8	15.6	2.8	0.7	40.5
Drop-out Rate (%)	n/a	n/a	n/a	n/a	n/a	n/a
H.S. Diplomas (#)	n/a	n/a	n/a	n/a	n/a	n/a

Victor Valley Union High

16350 Mojave Dr • Victorville, CA 92392-3655
(760) 955-3200 • http://www.vvuhsd.k12.ca.us/
Grade Span: 07-12; **Agency Type:** 1
Schools: 8
0 Primary; 3 Middle; 5 High; 0 Other Level
5 Regular; 0 Special Education; 0 Vocational; 3 Alternative
1 Magnet; 2 Charter; 6 Title I Eligible; 3 School-wide Title I
Students: 10,424 (50.7% male; 49.3% female)
Individual Education Program: 1,214 (11.6%);
English Language Learner: 531 (5.1%); Migrant: 0 (0.0%)
Eligible for Free Lunch Program: 4,061 (39.0%)
Eligible for Reduced-Price Lunch Program: 957 (9.2%)
Teachers: 402.1 (25.9 to 1)
Librarians/Media Specialists: 3.0 (3,474.7 to 1)
Guidance Counselors: 16.9 (616.8 to 1)
Current Spending: ($ per student per year):
Total: $6,566; Instruction: $3,827; Support Services: $2,497
Enrollment, Drop-out Rates and Diploma Recipients by Race/Ethnicity

Category	Total	White	Black	Asian	AIAN	Hisp.
Enrollment (%)	100.0	36.1	17.1	3.8	1.0	39.0
Drop-out Rate (%)	n/a	n/a	n/a	n/a	n/a	n/a
H.S. Diplomas (#)	1,145	489	147	63	11	388

Yucaipa-Calimesa Joint Unified

12797 Third St • Yucaipa, CA 92399-4544
(909) 797-0174 • http://www.ycjusd.k12.ca.us/
Grade Span: KG-12; **Agency Type:** 1
Schools: 11
6 Primary; 2 Middle; 2 High; 1 Other Level
10 Regular; 0 Special Education; 0 Vocational; 1 Alternative
0 Magnet; 0 Charter; 4 Title I Eligible; 0 School-wide Title I
Students: 9,242 (51.9% male; 48.1% female)
Individual Education Program: 889 (9.6%);
English Language Learner: 649 (7.0%); Migrant: 0 (0.0%)
Eligible for Free Lunch Program: 2,296 (24.8%)
Eligible for Reduced-Price Lunch Program: 854 (9.2%)
Teachers: 399.8 (23.1 to 1)
Librarians/Media Specialists: 1.0 (9,242.0 to 1)
Guidance Counselors: 10.0 (924.2 to 1)
Current Spending: ($ per student per year):
Total: $5,883; Instruction: $3,869; Support Services: $1,790
Enrollment, Drop-out Rates and Diploma Recipients by Race/Ethnicity

Category	Total	White	Black	Asian	AIAN	Hisp.
Enrollment (%)	100.0	71.0	1.3	1.5	0.8	24.2
Drop-out Rate (%)	n/a	n/a	n/a	n/a	n/a	n/a
H.S. Diplomas (#)	635	508	3	12	6	105

San Diego County

Alpine Union Elementary

1323 Administration Way • Alpine, CA 91901-2104
(619) 445-3236 • http://alpineschooldistrict.net/
Grade Span: KG-08; **Agency Type:** 1
Schools: 7
5 Primary; 2 Middle; 0 High; 0 Other Level
5 Regular; 0 Special Education; 0 Vocational; 2 Alternative
0 Magnet; 0 Charter; 5 Title I Eligible; 0 School-wide Title I
Students: 2,428 (50.9% male; 49.1% female)
Individual Education Program: 304 (12.5%);
English Language Learner: 78 (3.2%); Migrant: 0 (0.0%)
Eligible for Free Lunch Program: 265 (10.9%)
Eligible for Reduced-Price Lunch Program: 124 (5.1%)
Teachers: 121.3 (20.0 to 1)
Librarians/Media Specialists: 0.0 (0.0 to 1)
Guidance Counselors: 1.0 (2,428.0 to 1)
Current Spending: ($ per student per year):
Total: $6,362; Instruction: $4,326; Support Services: $1,840
Enrollment, Drop-out Rates and Diploma Recipients by Race/Ethnicity

Category	Total	White	Black	Asian	AIAN	Hisp.
Enrollment (%)	100.0	77.7	0.9	2.6	4.5	13.4
Drop-out Rate (%)	n/a	n/a	n/a	n/a	n/a	n/a
H.S. Diplomas (#)	n/a	n/a	n/a	n/a	n/a	n/a

Bonsall Union Elementary

31505 Old River Rd • Bonsall, CA 92003-5112
(760) 631-5200 • http://www.nctimes.net/~busd/welcome.html
Grade Span: KG-12; **Agency Type:** 1
Schools: 5
3 Primary; 1 Middle; 0 High; 1 Other Level
5 Regular; 0 Special Education; 0 Vocational; 0 Alternative
0 Magnet; 3 Charter; 2 Title I Eligible; 0 School-wide Title I
Students: 1,740 (50.6% male; 49.4% female)
Individual Education Program: 160 (9.2%);
English Language Learner: 454 (26.1%); Migrant: 300 (17.2%)
Eligible for Free Lunch Program: 509 (29.3%)
Eligible for Reduced-Price Lunch Program: 154 (8.9%)
Teachers: 85.2 (20.4 to 1)
Librarians/Media Specialists: 0.0 (0.0 to 1)
Guidance Counselors: 0.6 (2,900.0 to 1)

Current Spending: ($ per student per year):
Total: $6,642; Instruction: $4,153; Support Services: $2,179

Enrollment, Drop-out Rates and Diploma Recipients by Race/Ethnicity

Category	Total	White	Black	Asian	AIAN	Hisp.
Enrollment (%)	100.0	51.7	1.5	2.9	7.5	35.3
Drop-out Rate (%)	n/a	n/a	n/a	n/a	n/a	n/a
H.S. Diplomas (#)	0	0	0	0	0	0

Cajon Valley Union Elementary

189 Roanoke Rd • El Cajon, CA 92022-1007
Mailing Address: PO Box 1007 • El Cajon, CA 92022-1007
(619) 588-3000 • http://www.cajon.k12.ca.us/schools/index.htm
Grade Span: KG-08; **Agency Type:** 1
Schools: 28
22 Primary; 6 Middle; 0 High; 0 Other Level
26 Regular; 0 Special Education; 0 Vocational; 2 Alternative
3 Magnet; 0 Charter; 17 Title I Eligible; 13 School-wide Title I
Students: 18,653 (51.3% male; 48.7% female)
Individual Education Program: 2,567 (13.8%);
English Language Learner: 3,724 (20.0%); Migrant: 4 (<0.1%)
Eligible for Free Lunch Program: 6,935 (37.2%)
Eligible for Reduced-Price Lunch Program: 2,237 (12.0%)
Teachers: 882.8 (21.1 to 1)
Librarians/Media Specialists: 1.0 (18,653.0 to 1)
Guidance Counselors: 13.0 (1,434.8 to 1)
Current Spending: ($ per student per year):
Total: $6,473; Instruction: $4,295; Support Services: $1,912

Enrollment, Drop-out Rates and Diploma Recipients by Race/Ethnicity

Category	Total	White	Black	Asian	AIAN	Hisp.
Enrollment (%)	100.0	61.6	7.1	3.1	1.0	27.0
Drop-out Rate (%)	n/a	n/a	n/a	n/a	n/a	n/a
H.S. Diplomas (#)	n/a	n/a	n/a	n/a	n/a	n/a

Carlsbad Unified

801 Pine Ave • Carlsbad, CA 92008-2430
(760) 729-9291 • http://www.carlsbadusd.k12.ca.us/
Grade Span: KG-12; **Agency Type:** 1
Schools: 13
8 Primary; 2 Middle; 2 High; 1 Other Level
11 Regular; 0 Special Education; 0 Vocational; 2 Alternative
0 Magnet; 0 Charter; 5 Title I Eligible; 2 School-wide Title I
Students: 9,940 (51.8% male; 48.2% female)
Individual Education Program: 1,055 (10.6%);
English Language Learner: 933 (9.4%); Migrant: 252 (2.5%)
Eligible for Free Lunch Program: 1,348 (13.6%)
Eligible for Reduced-Price Lunch Program: 567 (5.7%)
Teachers: 473.0 (21.0 to 1)
Librarians/Media Specialists: 3.0 (3,313.3 to 1)
Guidance Counselors: 7.0 (1,420.0 to 1)
Current Spending: ($ per student per year):
Total: $6,276; Instruction: $4,058; Support Services: $2,014

Enrollment, Drop-out Rates and Diploma Recipients by Race/Ethnicity

Category	Total	White	Black	Asian	AIAN	Hisp.
Enrollment (%)	100.0	65.3	2.1	6.1	0.5	24.7
Drop-out Rate (%)	n/a	n/a	n/a	n/a	n/a	n/a
H.S. Diplomas (#)	602	440	17	33	4	108

Chula Vista Elementary

84 E J St • Chula Vista, CA 91910-6115
(619) 425-9600 • http://www.cvesd.k12.ca.us/
Grade Span: KG-06; **Agency Type:** 1
Schools: 39
39 Primary; 0 Middle; 0 High; 0 Other Level
39 Regular; 0 Special Education; 0 Vocational; 0 Alternative
0 Magnet; 6 Charter; 21 Title I Eligible; 2 School-wide Title I
Students: 24,587 (51.8% male; 48.2% female)
Individual Education Program: 2,682 (10.9%);
English Language Learner: 8,898 (36.2%); Migrant: 17 (0.1%)
Eligible for Free Lunch Program: 6,619 (26.9%)
Eligible for Reduced-Price Lunch Program: 3,905 (15.9%)
Teachers: 1,256.0 (19.6 to 1)
Librarians/Media Specialists: 20.0 (1,229.4 to 1)
Guidance Counselors: 4.0 (6,146.8 to 1)
Current Spending: ($ per student per year):
Total: $6,666; Instruction: $4,408; Support Services: $1,998

Enrollment, Drop-out Rates and Diploma Recipients by Race/Ethnicity

Category	Total	White	Black	Asian	AIAN	Hisp.
Enrollment (%)	100.0	18.2	5.1	12.6	0.5	63.6
Drop-out Rate (%)	n/a	n/a	n/a	n/a	n/a	n/a
H.S. Diplomas (#)	n/a	n/a	n/a	n/a	n/a	n/a

Coronado Unified

555 D Ave • Coronado, CA 92118-1714
(619) 522-8900 • http://www.coronado.k12.ca.us/
Grade Span: KG-12; **Agency Type:** 1
Schools: 5
2 Primary; 1 Middle; 2 High; 0 Other Level
4 Regular; 0 Special Education; 0 Vocational; 1 Alternative
0 Magnet; 0 Charter; 1 Title I Eligible; 0 School-wide Title I
Students: 2,791 (49.8% male; 50.2% female)
Individual Education Program: 349 (12.5%);
English Language Learner: 44 (1.6%); Migrant: 0 (0.0%)
Eligible for Free Lunch Program: 79 (2.8%)
Eligible for Reduced-Price Lunch Program: 142 (5.1%)
Teachers: 149.9 (18.6 to 1)
Librarians/Media Specialists: 0.0 (0.0 to 1)
Guidance Counselors: 4.0 (697.8 to 1)
Current Spending: ($ per student per year):
Total: $7,092; Instruction: $4,567; Support Services: $2,340

Enrollment, Drop-out Rates and Diploma Recipients by Race/Ethnicity

Category	Total	White	Black	Asian	AIAN	Hisp.
Enrollment (%)	100.0	75.5	3.1	6.7	0.7	12.2
Drop-out Rate (%)	n/a	n/a	n/a	n/a	n/a	n/a
H.S. Diplomas (#)	248	204	4	15	0	24

Del Mar Union Elementary

225 Ninth St • Del Mar, CA 92014-2716
(858) 755-9301 • http://delmarschools.com/
Grade Span: KG-06; **Agency Type:** 1
Schools: 6
6 Primary; 0 Middle; 0 High; 0 Other Level
6 Regular; 0 Special Education; 0 Vocational; 0 Alternative
0 Magnet; 0 Charter; 0 Title I Eligible; 0 School-wide Title I
Students: 3,324 (53.1% male; 46.9% female)
Individual Education Program: 354 (10.6%);
English Language Learner: 128 (3.9%); Migrant: 1 (<0.1%)
Eligible for Free Lunch Program: 55 (1.7%)
Eligible for Reduced-Price Lunch Program: 21 (0.6%)
Teachers: 189.7 (17.5 to 1)
Librarians/Media Specialists: 0.0 (0.0 to 1)
Guidance Counselors: 0.0 (0.0 to 1)
Current Spending: ($ per student per year):
Total: $6,778; Instruction: $4,709; Support Services: $2,052

Enrollment, Drop-out Rates and Diploma Recipients by Race/Ethnicity

Category	Total	White	Black	Asian	AIAN	Hisp.
Enrollment (%)	100.0	74.7	1.2	20.4	0.1	3.6
Drop-out Rate (%)	n/a	n/a	n/a	n/a	n/a	n/a
H.S. Diplomas (#)	n/a	n/a	n/a	n/a	n/a	n/a

Encinitas Union Elementary

101 S Rancho Santa Fe Rd • Encinitas, CA 92024-4308
(760) 944-4300 • http://www.eusd.k12.ca.us/default.htm
Grade Span: KG-06; **Agency Type:** 1
Schools: 10
10 Primary; 0 Middle; 0 High; 0 Other Level
10 Regular; 0 Special Education; 0 Vocational; 0 Alternative
0 Magnet; 0 Charter; 4 Title I Eligible; 0 School-wide Title I
Students: 5,624 (52.0% male; 48.0% female)
Individual Education Program: 500 (8.9%);
English Language Learner: 714 (12.7%); Migrant: 136 (2.4%)
Eligible for Free Lunch Program: 673 (12.0%)
Eligible for Reduced-Price Lunch Program: 207 (3.7%)
Teachers: 268.2 (21.0 to 1)
Librarians/Media Specialists: 0.0 (0.0 to 1)
Guidance Counselors: 0.6 (9,373.3 to 1)
Current Spending: ($ per student per year):
Total: $6,291; Instruction: $4,089; Support Services: $2,068

Enrollment, Drop-out Rates and Diploma Recipients by Race/Ethnicity

Category	Total	White	Black	Asian	AIAN	Hisp.
Enrollment (%)	100.0	74.9	0.8	5.7	0.3	18.3
Drop-out Rate (%)	n/a	n/a	n/a	n/a	n/a	n/a
H.S. Diplomas (#)	n/a	n/a	n/a	n/a	n/a	n/a

Escondido Union Elementary

1330 E Grand Ave • Escondido, CA 92027-3099
(760) 432-2400 • http://www.escusd.k12.ca.us/
Grade Span: KG-12; **Agency Type:** 1
Schools: 21
16 Primary; 4 Middle; 0 High; 1 Other Level
20 Regular; 1 Special Education; 0 Vocational; 0 Alternative
0 Magnet; 1 Charter; 13 Title I Eligible; 5 School-wide Title I
Students: 20,201 (50.9% male; 49.1% female)
Individual Education Program: 2,359 (11.7%);
English Language Learner: 8,535 (42.3%); Migrant: 717 (3.5%)
Eligible for Free Lunch Program: 9,622 (47.6%)
Eligible for Reduced-Price Lunch Program: 2,844 (14.1%)

Teachers: 1,041.3 (19.4 to 1)
Librarians/Media Specialists: 0.4 (50,502.5 to 1)
Guidance Counselors: 9.0 (2,244.6 to 1)
Current Spending: ($ per student per year):
Total: $6,233; Instruction: $4,013; Support Services: $1,956
Enrollment, Drop-out Rates and Diploma Recipients by Race/Ethnicity

Category	Total	White	Black	Asian	AIAN	Hisp.
Enrollment (%)	100.0	33.3	3.0	4.3	0.5	58.4
Drop-out Rate (%)	n/a	n/a	n/a	n/a	n/a	n/a
H.S. Diplomas (#)	0	0	0	0	0	0

Escondido Union High
302 N Midway Dr • Escondido, CA 92027-2741
(760) 291-3200 • http://www.escusd.k12.ca.us/
Grade Span: 09-12; **Agency Type:** 1
Schools: 6
0 Primary; 0 Middle; 6 High; 0 Other Level
4 Regular; 0 Special Education; 0 Vocational; 2 Alternative
0 Magnet; 1 Charter; 4 Title I Eligible; 0 School-wide Title I
Students: 8,363 (51.2% male; 48.8% female)
Individual Education Program: 786 (9.4%);
English Language Learner: 1,423 (17.0%); Migrant: 218 (2.6%)
Eligible for Free Lunch Program: 783 (9.4%)
Eligible for Reduced-Price Lunch Program: 236 (2.8%)
Teachers: 374.9 (22.3 to 1)
Librarians/Media Specialists: 0.0 (0.0 to 1)
Guidance Counselors: 16.0 (522.7 to 1)
Current Spending: ($ per student per year):
Total: $6,727; Instruction: $4,011; Support Services: $2,552
Enrollment, Drop-out Rates and Diploma Recipients by Race/Ethnicity

Category	Total	White	Black	Asian	AIAN	Hisp.
Enrollment (%)	100.0	49.1	2.5	4.8	0.7	42.8
Drop-out Rate (%)	n/a	n/a	n/a	n/a	n/a	n/a
H.S. Diplomas (#)	1,556	849	57	93	13	542

Fallbrook Union Elementary
321 N Iowa St • Fallbrook, CA 92088-0698
Mailing Address: PO Box 698 • Fallbrook, CA 92088-0698
(760) 723-7000 • http://www.fuesd.k12.ca.us/
Grade Span: KG-08; **Agency Type:** 1
Schools: 9
7 Primary; 2 Middle; 0 High; 0 Other Level
8 Regular; 0 Special Education; 0 Vocational; 1 Alternative
0 Magnet; 0 Charter; 3 Title I Eligible; 0 School-wide Title I
Students: 5,871 (51.6% male; 48.4% female)
Individual Education Program: 575 (9.8%);
English Language Learner: 1,776 (30.3%); Migrant: 604 (10.3%)
Eligible for Free Lunch Program: 1,939 (33.0%)
Eligible for Reduced-Price Lunch Program: 556 (9.5%)
Teachers: 280.5 (20.9 to 1)
Librarians/Media Specialists: 0.0 (0.0 to 1)
Guidance Counselors: 4.8 (1,223.1 to 1)
Current Spending: ($ per student per year):
Total: $6,956; Instruction: $4,503; Support Services: $2,232
Enrollment, Drop-out Rates and Diploma Recipients by Race/Ethnicity

Category	Total	White	Black	Asian	AIAN	Hisp.
Enrollment (%)	100.0	45.5	4.0	2.5	0.5	43.4
Drop-out Rate (%)	n/a	n/a	n/a	n/a	n/a	n/a
H.S. Diplomas (#)	n/a	n/a	n/a	n/a	n/a	n/a

Fallbrook Union High
S Mission Rd & Stage Coach • Fallbrook, CA 92088-0368
Mailing Address: PO Box 368 • Fallbrook, CA 92088-0368
(760) 723-6332
Grade Span: 09-12; **Agency Type:** 1
Schools: 3
0 Primary; 0 Middle; 3 High; 0 Other Level
1 Regular; 0 Special Education; 0 Vocational; 2 Alternative
0 Magnet; 0 Charter; 1 Title I Eligible; 0 School-wide Title I
Students: 3,079 (51.0% male; 49.0% female)
Individual Education Program: 332 (10.8%);
English Language Learner: 535 (17.4%); Migrant: 252 (8.2%)
Eligible for Free Lunch Program: 786 (25.5%)
Eligible for Reduced-Price Lunch Program: 224 (7.3%)
Teachers: 138.2 (22.3 to 1)
Librarians/Media Specialists: 0.0 (0.0 to 1)
Guidance Counselors: 4.5 (684.2 to 1)
Current Spending: ($ per student per year):
Total: $7,295; Instruction: $4,372; Support Services: $2,687
Enrollment, Drop-out Rates and Diploma Recipients by Race/Ethnicity

Category	Total	White	Black	Asian	AIAN	Hisp.
Enrollment (%)	100.0	54.2	2.3	3.3	2.4	37.1
Drop-out Rate (%)	n/a	n/a	n/a	n/a	n/a	n/a
H.S. Diplomas (#)	595	359	14	23	18	180

Grossmont Union High
1100 Murray Dr • La Mesa, CA 91944-1043
Mailing Address: PO Box 1043 • La Mesa, CA 91944-1043
(619) 644-8000 • http://www.grossmont.k12.ca.us/
Grade Span: 08-12; **Agency Type:** 1
Schools: 18
0 Primary; 0 Middle; 18 High; 0 Other Level
11 Regular; 3 Special Education; 0 Vocational; 4 Alternative
0 Magnet; 1 Charter; 6 Title I Eligible; 2 School-wide Title I
Students: 24,447 (51.0% male; 49.0% female)
Individual Education Program: 2,994 (12.2%);
English Language Learner: 1,494 (6.1%); Migrant: 5 (<0.1%)
Eligible for Free Lunch Program: 3,588 (14.7%)
Eligible for Reduced-Price Lunch Program: 1,278 (5.2%)
Teachers: 1,028.9 (23.8 to 1)
Librarians/Media Specialists: 11.4 (2,144.5 to 1)
Guidance Counselors: 39.3 (622.1 to 1)
Current Spending: ($ per student per year):
Total: $7,080; Instruction: $4,307; Support Services: $2,578
Enrollment, Drop-out Rates and Diploma Recipients by Race/Ethnicity

Category	Total	White	Black	Asian	AIAN	Hisp.
Enrollment (%)	100.0	61.7	7.9	5.8	2.1	20.1
Drop-out Rate (%)	n/a	n/a	n/a	n/a	n/a	n/a
H.S. Diplomas (#)	4,387	2,996	247	236	99	688

Jamul-Dulzura Union Elementary
14581 Lyons Valley Rd • Jamul, CA 91935-3324
(619) 669-7700
Grade Span: KG-09; **Agency Type:** 1
Schools: 4
1 Primary; 2 Middle; 0 High; 1 Other Level
4 Regular; 0 Special Education; 0 Vocational; 0 Alternative
0 Magnet; 1 Charter; 1 Title I Eligible; 0 School-wide Title I
Students: 1,710 (51.5% male; 48.5% female)
Individual Education Program: 153 (8.9%);
English Language Learner: 234 (13.7%); Migrant: 0 (0.0%)
Eligible for Free Lunch Program: 67 (3.9%)
Eligible for Reduced-Price Lunch Program: 82 (4.8%)
Teachers: 74.0 (23.1 to 1)
Librarians/Media Specialists: 0.0 (0.0 to 1)
Guidance Counselors: 1.0 (1,710.0 to 1)
Current Spending: ($ per student per year):
Total: $6,653; Instruction: $3,954; Support Services: $2,513
Enrollment, Drop-out Rates and Diploma Recipients by Race/Ethnicity

Category	Total	White	Black	Asian	AIAN	Hisp.
Enrollment (%)	100.0	70.9	1.8	1.4	1.3	21.8
Drop-out Rate (%)	n/a	n/a	n/a	n/a	n/a	n/a
H.S. Diplomas (#)	n/a	n/a	n/a	n/a	n/a	n/a

Julian Union Elementary
1704 Hwy 78 • Julian, CA 92036-0337
Mailing Address: PO Box 337 • Julian, CA 92036-0337
(760) 765-0661
Grade Span: KG-12; **Agency Type:** 1
Schools: 3
1 Primary; 1 Middle; 0 High; 1 Other Level
3 Regular; 0 Special Education; 0 Vocational; 0 Alternative
0 Magnet; 1 Charter; 3 Title I Eligible; 0 School-wide Title I
Students: 1,640 (47.8% male; 52.2% female)
Individual Education Program: 134 (8.2%);
English Language Learner: 35 (2.1%); Migrant: 0 (0.0%)
Eligible for Free Lunch Program: 145 (8.8%)
Eligible for Reduced-Price Lunch Program: 113 (6.9%)
Teachers: 66.5 (24.7 to 1)
Librarians/Media Specialists: 0.0 (0.0 to 1)
Guidance Counselors: 0.4 (4,100.0 to 1)
Current Spending: ($ per student per year):
Total: $6,708; Instruction: $4,442; Support Services: $2,185
Enrollment, Drop-out Rates and Diploma Recipients by Race/Ethnicity

Category	Total	White	Black	Asian	AIAN	Hisp.
Enrollment (%)	100.0	72.2	4.5	2.7	4.6	13.5
Drop-out Rate (%)	n/a	n/a	n/a	n/a	n/a	n/a
H.S. Diplomas (#)	33	17	0	1	0	6

Julian Union High
1656 Hwy 78 • Julian, CA 92036-0417
Mailing Address: PO Box 417 • Julian, CA 92036-0417
(760) 765-3208
Grade Span: KG-12; **Agency Type:** 1
Schools: 3
0 Primary; 0 Middle; 2 High; 1 Other Level
2 Regular; 0 Special Education; 0 Vocational; 1 Alternative
0 Magnet; 1 Charter; 2 Title I Eligible; 0 School-wide Title I
Students: 2,020 (52.6% male; 47.4% female)
Individual Education Program: 67 (3.3%);

English Language Learner: 156 (7.7%); Migrant: 0 (0.0%)
Eligible for Free Lunch Program: 47 (2.3%)
Eligible for Reduced-Price Lunch Program: 14 (0.7%)
Teachers: 83.7 (24.1 to 1)
Librarians/Media Specialists: 0.0 (0.0 to 1)
Guidance Counselors: 0.0 (0.0 to 1)
Current Spending: ($ per student per year):
Total: $10,717; Instruction: $6,283; Support Services: $4,434
Enrollment, Drop-out Rates and Diploma Recipients by Race/Ethnicity

Category	Total	White	Black	Asian	AIAN	Hisp.
Enrollment (%)	100.0	59.0	5.9	1.9	1.9	17.9
Drop-out Rate (%)	n/a	n/a	n/a	n/a	n/a	n/a
H.S. Diplomas (#)	109	68	4	6	5	25

La Mesa-Spring Valley
4750 Date Ave • La Mesa, CA 91941-5214
(619) 668-5700 • http://www.lmsvsd.k12.ca.us/
Grade Span: KG-08; **Agency Type:** 1
Schools: 22
18 Primary; 4 Middle; 0 High; 0 Other Level
22 Regular; 0 Special Education; 0 Vocational; 0 Alternative
0 Magnet; 0 Charter; 9 Title I Eligible; 4 School-wide Title I
Students: 14,548 (50.9% male; 49.1% female)
Individual Education Program: 1,816 (12.5%);
English Language Learner: 2,524 (17.3%); Migrant: 4 (<0.1%)
Eligible for Free Lunch Program: 4,265 (29.3%)
Eligible for Reduced-Price Lunch Program: 1,737 (11.9%)
Teachers: 697.0 (20.9 to 1)
Librarians/Media Specialists: 4.0 (3,637.0 to 1)
Guidance Counselors: 27.6 (527.1 to 1)
Current Spending: ($ per student per year):
Total: $6,253; Instruction: $3,818; Support Services: $2,179
Enrollment, Drop-out Rates and Diploma Recipients by Race/Ethnicity

Category	Total	White	Black	Asian	AIAN	Hisp.
Enrollment (%)	100.0	43.2	11.5	7.3	1.4	29.5
Drop-out Rate (%)	n/a	n/a	n/a	n/a	n/a	n/a
H.S. Diplomas (#)	n/a	n/a	n/a	n/a	n/a	n/a

Lakeside Union Elementary
12335 Woodside Ave • Lakeside, CA 92040-0578
Mailing Address: PO Box 578 • Lakeside, CA 92040-0578
(619) 390-2600 • http://www.lsschools.k12.ca.us/lakeside/default.htm
Grade Span: KG-12; **Agency Type:** 1
Schools: 11
8 Primary; 2 Middle; 1 High; 0 Other Level
11 Regular; 0 Special Education; 0 Vocational; 0 Alternative
0 Magnet; 2 Charter; 6 Title I Eligible; 0 School-wide Title I
Students: 4,974 (51.1% male; 48.9% female)
Individual Education Program: 791 (15.9%);
English Language Learner: 329 (6.6%); Migrant: 2 (<0.1%)
Eligible for Free Lunch Program: 945 (19.0%)
Eligible for Reduced-Price Lunch Program: 526 (10.6%)
Teachers: 240.0 (20.7 to 1)
Librarians/Media Specialists: 0.0 (0.0 to 1)
Guidance Counselors: 4.0 (1,243.5 to 1)
Current Spending: ($ per student per year):
Total: $6,517; Instruction: $4,422; Support Services: $1,904
Enrollment, Drop-out Rates and Diploma Recipients by Race/Ethnicity

Category	Total	White	Black	Asian	AIAN	Hisp.
Enrollment (%)	100.0	76.8	3.4	2.1	2.7	14.7
Drop-out Rate (%)	n/a	n/a	n/a	n/a	n/a	n/a
H.S. Diplomas (#)	13	12	1	0	0	0

Lemon Grove Elementary
8025 Lincoln St • Lemon Grove, CA 91945-2515
(619) 825-5600 • http://www.lgsd.k12.ca.us/
Grade Span: KG-08; **Agency Type:** 1
Schools: 8
6 Primary; 2 Middle; 0 High; 0 Other Level
8 Regular; 0 Special Education; 0 Vocational; 0 Alternative
0 Magnet; 0 Charter; 4 Title I Eligible; 1 School-wide Title I
Students: 4,441 (49.9% male; 50.1% female)
Individual Education Program: 533 (12.0%);
English Language Learner: 784 (17.7%); Migrant: 3 (0.1%)
Eligible for Free Lunch Program: 1,808 (40.7%)
Eligible for Reduced-Price Lunch Program: 816 (18.4%)
Teachers: 221.8 (20.0 to 1)
Librarians/Media Specialists: 0.0 (0.0 to 1)
Guidance Counselors: 0.0 (0.0 to 1)
Current Spending: ($ per student per year):
Total: $6,762; Instruction: $4,341; Support Services: $2,012
Enrollment, Drop-out Rates and Diploma Recipients by Race/Ethnicity

Category	Total	White	Black	Asian	AIAN	Hisp.
Enrollment (%)	100.0	29.2	23.6	9.8	1.0	36.4
Drop-out Rate (%)	n/a	n/a	n/a	n/a	n/a	n/a
H.S. Diplomas (#)	n/a	n/a	n/a	n/a	n/a	n/a

Mountain Empire Unified
3291 Buckman Springs Rd • Pine Valley, CA 91962-4003
(619) 473-9022 • http://www.meusd.k12.ca.us/
Grade Span: KG-12; **Agency Type:** 1
Schools: 12
6 Primary; 1 Middle; 5 High; 0 Other Level
8 Regular; 0 Special Education; 0 Vocational; 4 Alternative
0 Magnet; 0 Charter; 11 Title I Eligible; 7 School-wide Title I
Students: 1,822 (51.9% male; 48.1% female)
Individual Education Program: 183 (10.0%);
English Language Learner: 252 (13.8%); Migrant: 13 (0.7%)
Eligible for Free Lunch Program: 735 (40.3%)
Eligible for Reduced-Price Lunch Program: 163 (8.9%)
Teachers: 95.1 (19.2 to 1)
Librarians/Media Specialists: 1.0 (1,822.0 to 1)
Guidance Counselors: 2.5 (728.8 to 1)
Current Spending: ($ per student per year):
Total: $7,438; Instruction: $4,332; Support Services: $2,841
Enrollment, Drop-out Rates and Diploma Recipients by Race/Ethnicity

Category	Total	White	Black	Asian	AIAN	Hisp.
Enrollment (%)	100.0	59.3	1.9	1.2	9.2	28.3
Drop-out Rate (%)	n/a	n/a	n/a	n/a	n/a	n/a
H.S. Diplomas (#)	108	74	1	0	3	30

National Elementary
1500 N Ave • National City, CA 91950-4827
(619) 336-7500 • http://www.sdcoe.k12.ca.us/districts/national/index.html
Grade Span: KG-06; **Agency Type:** 1
Schools: 10
10 Primary; 0 Middle; 0 High; 0 Other Level
10 Regular; 0 Special Education; 0 Vocational; 0 Alternative
0 Magnet; 0 Charter; 4 Title I Eligible; 0 School-wide Title I
Students: 6,590 (51.9% male; 48.1% female)
Individual Education Program: 697 (10.6%);
English Language Learner: 3,605 (54.7%); Migrant: 70 (1.1%)
Eligible for Free Lunch Program: 6,560 (99.5%)
Eligible for Reduced-Price Lunch Program: 0 (0.0%)
Teachers: 295.9 (22.3 to 1)
Librarians/Media Specialists: 0.0 (0.0 to 1)
Guidance Counselors: 2.8 (2,353.6 to 1)
Current Spending: ($ per student per year):
Total: $6,796; Instruction: $4,440; Support Services: $2,001
Enrollment, Drop-out Rates and Diploma Recipients by Race/Ethnicity

Category	Total	White	Black	Asian	AIAN	Hisp.
Enrollment (%)	100.0	3.4	3.6	14.1	0.4	78.5
Drop-out Rate (%)	n/a	n/a	n/a	n/a	n/a	n/a
H.S. Diplomas (#)	n/a	n/a	n/a	n/a	n/a	n/a

Oceanside Unified
2111 Mission Ave • Oceanside, CA 92054-2326
(760) 757-2560 • http://gsh.org/ousdweb/
Grade Span: KG-12; **Agency Type:** 1
Schools: 28
19 Primary; 3 Middle; 4 High; 2 Other Level
25 Regular; 0 Special Education; 0 Vocational; 3 Alternative
2 Magnet; 1 Charter; 19 Title I Eligible; 0 School-wide Title I
Students: 22,482 (50.9% male; 49.1% female)
Individual Education Program: 2,411 (10.7%);
English Language Learner: 6,044 (26.9%); Migrant: 1,024 (4.6%)
Eligible for Free Lunch Program: 8,055 (35.8%)
Eligible for Reduced-Price Lunch Program: 2,861 (12.7%)
Teachers: 1,150.9 (19.5 to 1)
Librarians/Media Specialists: 4.0 (5,620.5 to 1)
Guidance Counselors: 21.0 (1,070.6 to 1)
Current Spending: ($ per student per year):
Total: $6,696; Instruction: $4,106; Support Services: $2,351
Enrollment, Drop-out Rates and Diploma Recipients by Race/Ethnicity

Category	Total	White	Black	Asian	AIAN	Hisp.
Enrollment (%)	100.0	31.2	10.7	8.3	0.8	49.1
Drop-out Rate (%)	n/a	n/a	n/a	n/a	n/a	n/a
H.S. Diplomas (#)	957	340	144	113	4	356

Poway Unified
13626 Twin Peaks Rd • Poway, CA 92064-3034
(858) 748-0010 • http://powayusd.sdcoe.k12.ca.us/
Grade Span: KG-12; **Agency Type:** 1
Schools: 31
21 Primary; 5 Middle; 5 High; 0 Other Level
30 Regular; 0 Special Education; 0 Vocational; 1 Alternative

0 Magnet; 0 Charter; 5 Title I Eligible; 0 School-wide Title I
Students: 32,754 (51.5% male; 48.5% female)
Individual Education Program: 3,231 (9.9%);
English Language Learner: 2,337 (7.1%); Migrant: 0 (0.0%)
Eligible for Free Lunch Program: 1,850 (5.6%)
Eligible for Reduced-Price Lunch Program: 820 (2.5%)
Teachers: 1,525.2 (21.5 to 1)
Librarians/Media Specialists: 7.5 (4,367.2 to 1)
Guidance Counselors: 40.1 (816.8 to 1)
Current Spending: ($ per student per year):
Total: $6,557; Instruction: $4,178; Support Services: $2,029
Enrollment, Drop-out Rates and Diploma Recipients by Race/Ethnicity

Category	Total	White	Black	Asian	AIAN	Hisp.
Enrollment (%)	100.0	65.3	3.3	19.0	0.5	9.4
Drop-out Rate (%)	n/a	n/a	n/a	n/a	n/a	n/a
H.S. Diplomas (#)	2,230	1,571	54	412	14	166

Ramona City Unified
720 Ninth St • Ramona, CA 92065-2348
(760) 788-5000 • http://www.ramona.k12.ca.us/
Grade Span: KG-12; **Agency Type:** 1
Schools: 11
5 Primary; 1 Middle; 3 High; 2 Other Level
9 Regular; 0 Special Education; 0 Vocational; 2 Alternative
0 Magnet; 1 Charter; 5 Title I Eligible; 1 School-wide Title I
Students: 7,359 (51.2% male; 48.8% female)
Individual Education Program: 955 (13.0%);
English Language Learner: 935 (12.7%); Migrant: 271 (3.7%)
Eligible for Free Lunch Program: 1,562 (21.2%)
Eligible for Reduced-Price Lunch Program: 554 (7.5%)
Teachers: 321.9 (22.9 to 1)
Librarians/Media Specialists: 1.0 (7,359.0 to 1)
Guidance Counselors: 6.8 (1,082.2 to 1)
Current Spending: ($ per student per year):
Total: $6,387; Instruction: $4,093; Support Services: $2,059
Enrollment, Drop-out Rates and Diploma Recipients by Race/Ethnicity

Category	Total	White	Black	Asian	AIAN	Hisp.
Enrollment (%)	100.0	71.3	1.3	1.8	1.2	24.4
Drop-out Rate (%)	n/a	n/a	n/a	n/a	n/a	n/a
H.S. Diplomas (#)	483	383	3	2	5	90

San Diego County Office of Ed
6401 Linda Vista Rd • San Diego, CA 92111-7319
(858) 292-3500 • http://www.sdcoe.k12.ca.us/
Grade Span: KG-12; **Agency Type:** 4
Schools: 10
1 Primary; 0 Middle; 3 High; 6 Other Level
1 Regular; 2 Special Education; 0 Vocational; 7 Alternative
0 Magnet; 1 Charter; 1 Title I Eligible; 0 School-wide Title I
Students: 3,378 (60.1% male; 39.9% female)
Individual Education Program: 854 (25.3%);
English Language Learner: 450 (13.3%); Migrant: 0 (0.0%)
Eligible for Free Lunch Program: 2,707 (80.1%)
Eligible for Reduced-Price Lunch Program: 151 (4.5%)
Teachers: 231.4 (14.6 to 1)
Librarians/Media Specialists: 1.4 (2,412.9 to 1)
Guidance Counselors: 1.0 (3,378.0 to 1)
Current Spending: ($ per student per year):
Total: $44,947; Instruction: $17,919; Support Services: $26,720
Enrollment, Drop-out Rates and Diploma Recipients by Race/Ethnicity

Category	Total	White	Black	Asian	AIAN	Hisp.
Enrollment (%)	100.0	32.6	17.3	4.9	1.5	42.3
Drop-out Rate (%)	n/a	n/a	n/a	n/a	n/a	n/a
H.S. Diplomas (#)	214	78	40	15	2	79

San Diego Unified
4100 Normal St • San Diego, CA 92103-2653
(619) 725-8000 • http://www.sdcs.k12.ca.us/
Grade Span: KG-12; **Agency Type:** 1
Schools: 185
128 Primary; 26 Middle; 23 High; 8 Other Level
177 Regular; 1 Special Education; 0 Vocational; 7 Alternative
29 Magnet; 20 Charter; 143 Title I Eligible; 79 School-wide Title I
Students: 140,753 (51.3% male; 48.7% female)
Individual Education Program: 17,011 (12.1%);
English Language Learner: 40,351 (28.7%); Migrant: 97 (0.1%)
Eligible for Free Lunch Program: 64,688 (46.0%)
Eligible for Reduced-Price Lunch Program: 15,017 (10.7%)
Teachers: 7,494.8 (18.8 to 1)
Librarians/Media Specialists: 49.2 (2,860.8 to 1)
Guidance Counselors: 288.2 (488.4 to 1)
Current Spending: ($ per student per year):
Total: $7,508; Instruction: $4,744; Support Services: $2,492
Enrollment, Drop-out Rates and Diploma Recipients by Race/Ethnicity

Category	Total	White	Black	Asian	AIAN	Hisp.
Enrollment (%)	100.0	26.2	15.0	17.4	0.5	40.9
Drop-out Rate (%)	n/a	n/a	n/a	n/a	n/a	n/a
H.S. Diplomas (#)	6,504	2,230	877	1,632	44	1,721

San Dieguito Union High
710 Encinitas Blvd • Encinitas, CA 92024-3357
(760) 753-6491 • http://www.sduhsd.k12.ca.us/
Grade Span: 07-12; **Agency Type:** 1
Schools: 9
0 Primary; 4 Middle; 5 High; 0 Other Level
7 Regular; 0 Special Education; 0 Vocational; 2 Alternative
0 Magnet; 0 Charter; 3 Title I Eligible; 0 School-wide Title I
Students: 11,337 (52.9% male; 47.1% female)
Individual Education Program: 1,232 (10.9%);
English Language Learner: 511 (4.5%); Migrant: 133 (1.2%)
Eligible for Free Lunch Program: 522 (4.6%)
Eligible for Reduced-Price Lunch Program: 181 (1.6%)
Teachers: 504.2 (22.5 to 1)
Librarians/Media Specialists: 6.0 (1,889.5 to 1)
Guidance Counselors: 25.6 (442.9 to 1)
Current Spending: ($ per student per year):
Total: $6,983; Instruction: $3,890; Support Services: $2,883
Enrollment, Drop-out Rates and Diploma Recipients by Race/Ethnicity

Category	Total	White	Black	Asian	AIAN	Hisp.
Enrollment (%)	100.0	78.9	0.8	8.6	0.2	11.2
Drop-out Rate (%)	n/a	n/a	n/a	n/a	n/a	n/a
H.S. Diplomas (#)	1,533	1,250	8	120	4	148

San Marcos Unified
1 Civic Center Dr, Ste 300 • San Marcos, CA 92069-2952
(760) 744-4776 • http://www.smusd.org/
Grade Span: KG-12; **Agency Type:** 1
Schools: 14
9 Primary; 2 Middle; 2 High; 1 Other Level
12 Regular; 0 Special Education; 0 Vocational; 2 Alternative
0 Magnet; 0 Charter; 9 Title I Eligible; 0 School-wide Title I
Students: 13,910 (51.4% male; 48.6% female)
Individual Education Program: 1,554 (11.2%);
English Language Learner: 3,777 (27.2%); Migrant: 462 (3.3%)
Eligible for Free Lunch Program: 4,169 (30.0%)
Eligible for Reduced-Price Lunch Program: 1,270 (9.1%)
Teachers: 658.9 (21.1 to 1)
Librarians/Media Specialists: 1.0 (13,910.0 to 1)
Guidance Counselors: 11.2 (1,242.0 to 1)
Current Spending: ($ per student per year):
Total: $5,835; Instruction: $3,679; Support Services: $1,940
Enrollment, Drop-out Rates and Diploma Recipients by Race/Ethnicity

Category	Total	White	Black	Asian	AIAN	Hisp.
Enrollment (%)	100.0	42.4	3.1	6.2	0.8	47.5
Drop-out Rate (%)	n/a	n/a	n/a	n/a	n/a	n/a
H.S. Diplomas (#)	594	313	15	33	2	231

San Ysidro Elementary
4350 Otay Mesa Rd • San Ysidro, CA 92173-1617
(619) 428-4476 • http://www.sysd.k12.ca.us/
Grade Span: KG-08; **Agency Type:** 1
Schools: 9
7 Primary; 2 Middle; 0 High; 0 Other Level
7 Regular; 1 Special Education; 0 Vocational; 1 Alternative
0 Magnet; 0 Charter; 9 Title I Eligible; 0 School-wide Title I
Students: 5,025 (52.4% male; 47.6% female)
Individual Education Program: 467 (9.3%);
English Language Learner: 3,649 (72.6%); Migrant: 212 (4.2%)
Eligible for Free Lunch Program: 3,936 (78.3%)
Eligible for Reduced-Price Lunch Program: 673 (13.4%)
Teachers: 252.5 (19.9 to 1)
Librarians/Media Specialists: 0.0 (0.0 to 1)
Guidance Counselors: 3.0 (1,675.0 to 1)
Current Spending: ($ per student per year):
Total: $7,195; Instruction: $4,522; Support Services: $2,293
Enrollment, Drop-out Rates and Diploma Recipients by Race/Ethnicity

Category	Total	White	Black	Asian	AIAN	Hisp.
Enrollment (%)	100.0	2.4	2.2	2.6	0.2	92.5
Drop-out Rate (%)	n/a	n/a	n/a	n/a	n/a	n/a
H.S. Diplomas (#)	n/a	n/a	n/a	n/a	n/a	n/a

Santee Elementary
9625 Cuyamaca St • Santee, CA 92071-2674
(619) 258-2300 • http://www.santee.k12.ca.us/
Grade Span: KG-08; **Agency Type:** 1
Schools: 12
12 Primary; 0 Middle; 0 High; 0 Other Level
10 Regular; 0 Special Education; 0 Vocational; 2 Alternative

0 Magnet; 0 Charter; 5 Title I Eligible; 0 School-wide Title I
Students: 7,345 (51.9% male; 48.1% female)
Individual Education Program: 1,064 (14.5%);
English Language Learner: 529 (7.2%); Migrant: 0 (0.0%)
Eligible for Free Lunch Program: 1,157 (15.8%)
Eligible for Reduced-Price Lunch Program: 606 (8.3%)
Teachers: 346.0 (21.2 to 1)
Librarians/Media Specialists: 2.0 (3,672.5 to 1)
Guidance Counselors: 0.0 (0.0 to 1)
Current Spending: ($ per student per year):
Total: $5,889; Instruction: $3,911; Support Services: $1,835
Enrollment, Drop-out Rates and Diploma Recipients by Race/Ethnicity

Category	Total	White	Black	Asian	AIAN	Hisp.
Enrollment (%)	100.0	82.1	1.9	2.8	0.4	12.8
Drop-out Rate (%)	n/a	n/a	n/a	n/a	n/a	n/a
H.S. Diplomas (#)	n/a	n/a	n/a	n/a	n/a	n/a

Solana Beach Elementary
309 N Rios Ave • Solana Beach, CA 92075-1241
(858) 794-3900 • http://www.sbsd.k12.ca.us/
Grade Span: KG-06; **Agency Type:** 1
Schools: 5
5 Primary; 0 Middle; 0 High; 0 Other Level
5 Regular; 0 Special Education; 0 Vocational; 0 Alternative
0 Magnet; 0 Charter; 2 Title I Eligible; 0 School-wide Title I
Students: 2,654 (52.3% male; 47.7% female)
Individual Education Program: 373 (14.1%);
English Language Learner: 264 (9.9%); Migrant: 50 (1.9%)
Eligible for Free Lunch Program: 184 (6.9%)
Eligible for Reduced-Price Lunch Program: 57 (2.1%)
Teachers: 156.6 (16.9 to 1)
Librarians/Media Specialists: 0.0 (0.0 to 1)
Guidance Counselors: 0.0 (0.0 to 1)
Current Spending: ($ per student per year):
Total: $7,344; Instruction: $5,109; Support Services: $2,073
Enrollment, Drop-out Rates and Diploma Recipients by Race/Ethnicity

Category	Total	White	Black	Asian	AIAN	Hisp.
Enrollment (%)	100.0	75.2	0.9	13.0	0.1	10.9
Drop-out Rate (%)	n/a	n/a	n/a	n/a	n/a	n/a
H.S. Diplomas (#)	n/a	n/a	n/a	n/a	n/a	n/a

South Bay Union Elementary
601 Elm Ave • Imperial Beach, CA 91932-2029
(619) 628-1600 • http://sbusd.k12.ca.us/sbusd/index.htm
Grade Span: KG-06; **Agency Type:** 1
Schools: 12
12 Primary; 0 Middle; 0 High; 0 Other Level
12 Regular; 0 Special Education; 0 Vocational; 0 Alternative
0 Magnet; 0 Charter; 12 Title I Eligible; 0 School-wide Title I
Students: 9,424 (51.4% male; 48.6% female)
Individual Education Program: 980 (10.4%);
English Language Learner: 4,079 (43.3%); Migrant: 10 (0.1%)
Eligible for Free Lunch Program: 4,059 (43.1%)
Eligible for Reduced-Price Lunch Program: 1,740 (18.5%)
Teachers: 467.8 (20.1 to 1)
Librarians/Media Specialists: 0.0 (0.0 to 1)
Guidance Counselors: 0.0 (0.0 to 1)
Current Spending: ($ per student per year):
Total: $7,272; Instruction: $4,693; Support Services: $2,284
Enrollment, Drop-out Rates and Diploma Recipients by Race/Ethnicity

Category	Total	White	Black	Asian	AIAN	Hisp.
Enrollment (%)	100.0	11.8	4.5	8.0	0.4	75.0
Drop-out Rate (%)	n/a	n/a	n/a	n/a	n/a	n/a
H.S. Diplomas (#)	n/a	n/a	n/a	n/a	n/a	n/a

Sweetwater Union High
1130 Fifth Ave • Chula Vista, CA 91911-2812
(619) 691-5500 • http://www.suhsd.k12.ca.us/
Grade Span: 07-12; **Agency Type:** 1
Schools: 26
0 Primary; 11 Middle; 15 High; 0 Other Level
21 Regular; 1 Special Education; 0 Vocational; 4 Alternative
8 Magnet; 1 Charter; 15 Title I Eligible; 9 School-wide Title I
Students: 37,878 (51.3% male; 48.7% female)
Individual Education Program: 4,274 (11.3%);
English Language Learner: 9,925 (26.2%); Migrant: 100 (0.3%)
Eligible for Free Lunch Program: 12,823 (33.9%)
Eligible for Reduced-Price Lunch Program: 4,620 (12.2%)
Teachers: 1,770.8 (21.4 to 1)
Librarians/Media Specialists: 20.0 (1,893.9 to 1)
Guidance Counselors: 118.1 (320.7 to 1)
Current Spending: ($ per student per year):
Total: $6,607; Instruction: $3,851; Support Services: $2,573
Enrollment, Drop-out Rates and Diploma Recipients by Race/Ethnicity

Category	Total	White	Black	Asian	AIAN	Hisp.
Enrollment (%)	100.0	14.9	4.6	12.0	0.5	67.9
Drop-out Rate (%)	n/a	n/a	n/a	n/a	n/a	n/a
H.S. Diplomas (#)	4,768	804	195	667	20	3,082

Valley Center-Pauma Unified
28751 Cole Grade Rd • Valley Center, CA 92082-6599
(760) 749-0464
Grade Span: KG-12; **Agency Type:** 1
Schools: 10
4 Primary; 3 Middle; 2 High; 1 Other Level
9 Regular; 0 Special Education; 0 Vocational; 1 Alternative
0 Magnet; 1 Charter; 6 Title I Eligible; 0 School-wide Title I
Students: 4,740 (52.3% male; 47.7% female)
Individual Education Program: 594 (12.5%);
English Language Learner: 951 (20.1%); Migrant: 683 (14.4%)
Eligible for Free Lunch Program: 1,220 (25.7%)
Eligible for Reduced-Price Lunch Program: 389 (8.2%)
Teachers: 247.6 (19.1 to 1)
Librarians/Media Specialists: 0.0 (0.0 to 1)
Guidance Counselors: 4.0 (1,185.0 to 1)
Current Spending: ($ per student per year):
Total: $6,645; Instruction: $4,411; Support Services: $2,003
Enrollment, Drop-out Rates and Diploma Recipients by Race/Ethnicity

Category	Total	White	Black	Asian	AIAN	Hisp.
Enrollment (%)	100.0	56.7	0.4	1.4	10.8	30.7
Drop-out Rate (%)	n/a	n/a	n/a	n/a	n/a	n/a
H.S. Diplomas (#)	330	218	1	6	30	75

Vista Unified
1234 Arcadia Ave • Vista, CA 92084-3404
(760) 726-2170 • http://www.vusd.k12.ca.us/
Grade Span: KG-12; **Agency Type:** 1
Schools: 27
15 Primary; 4 Middle; 5 High; 3 Other Level
22 Regular; 2 Special Education; 0 Vocational; 3 Alternative
1 Magnet; 2 Charter; 13 Title I Eligible; 4 School-wide Title I
Students: 27,709 (51.1% male; 48.9% female)
Individual Education Program: 3,417 (12.3%);
English Language Learner: 6,420 (23.2%); Migrant: 718 (2.6%)
Eligible for Free Lunch Program: 8,367 (30.2%)
Eligible for Reduced-Price Lunch Program: 3,068 (11.1%)
Teachers: 1,262.7 (21.9 to 1)
Librarians/Media Specialists: 6.2 (4,469.2 to 1)
Guidance Counselors: 26.6 (1,041.7 to 1)
Current Spending: ($ per student per year):
Total: $7,017; Instruction: $4,663; Support Services: $2,123
Enrollment, Drop-out Rates and Diploma Recipients by Race/Ethnicity

Category	Total	White	Black	Asian	AIAN	Hisp.
Enrollment (%)	100.0	42.2	5.5	5.6	0.7	44.1
Drop-out Rate (%)	n/a	n/a	n/a	n/a	n/a	n/a
H.S. Diplomas (#)	1,996	844	182	169	14	739

San Francisco County

San Francisco Unified
555 Franklin St Room 102 • San Francisco, CA 94102-5207
(415) 241-6000 • http://nisus.sfusd.k12.ca.us/
Grade Span: KG-12; **Agency Type:** 1
Schools: 114
77 Primary; 17 Middle; 20 High; 0 Other Level
111 Regular; 0 Special Education; 0 Vocational; 3 Alternative
5 Magnet; 6 Charter; 73 Title I Eligible; 44 School-wide Title I
Students: 58,216 (51.7% male; 48.3% female)
Individual Education Program: 6,755 (11.6%);
English Language Learner: 16,269 (27.9%); Migrant: 409 (0.7%)
Eligible for Free Lunch Program: 24,879 (42.7%)
Eligible for Reduced-Price Lunch Program: 9,353 (16.1%)
Teachers: 3,362.0 (17.3 to 1)
Librarians/Media Specialists: 29.1 (2,000.5 to 1)
Guidance Counselors: 106.8 (545.1 to 1)
Current Spending: ($ per student per year):
Total: $6,611; Instruction: $4,086; Support Services: $2,281
Enrollment, Drop-out Rates and Diploma Recipients by Race/Ethnicity

Category	Total	White	Black	Asian	AIAN	Hisp.
Enrollment (%)	100.0	10.0	14.7	51.2	0.6	21.4
Drop-out Rate (%)	n/a	n/a	n/a	n/a	n/a	n/a
H.S. Diplomas (#)	3,399	382	339	2,132	18	520

San Joaquin County

Escalon Unified

1520 Yosemite Ave • Escalon, CA 95320-1753
(209) 838-3591 • http://www.escalonusd.org/
Grade Span: KG-12; **Agency Type:** 1
Schools: 8
4 Primary; 2 Middle; 2 High; 0 Other Level
6 Regular; 0 Special Education; 0 Vocational; 2 Alternative
0 Magnet; 0 Charter; 5 Title I Eligible; 0 School-wide Title I
Students: 3,112 (52.4% male; 47.6% female)
Individual Education Program: 336 (10.8%);
English Language Learner: 509 (16.4%); Migrant: 943 (30.3%)
Eligible for Free Lunch Program: 861 (27.7%)
Eligible for Reduced-Price Lunch Program: 230 (7.4%)
Teachers: 138.8 (22.4 to 1)
Librarians/Media Specialists: 0.0 (0.0 to 1)
Guidance Counselors: 4.6 (676.5 to 1)
Current Spending: ($ per student per year):
Total: $5,871; Instruction: $3,805; Support Services: $1,861
Enrollment, Drop-out Rates and Diploma Recipients by Race/Ethnicity

Category	Total	White	Black	Asian	AIAN	Hisp.
Enrollment (%)	100.0	65.6	0.6	1.4	0.7	31.7
Drop-out Rate (%)	n/a	n/a	n/a	n/a	n/a	n/a
H.S. Diplomas (#)	216	161	1	6	4	44

Jefferson Elementary

7500 W Linne Rd • Tracy, CA 95376-9278
(209) 836-3388
Grade Span: KG-08; **Agency Type:** 1
Schools: 3
2 Primary; 1 Middle; 0 High; 0 Other Level
3 Regular; 0 Special Education; 0 Vocational; 0 Alternative
0 Magnet; 0 Charter; 3 Title I Eligible; 0 School-wide Title I
Students: 1,520 (51.3% male; 48.7% female)
Individual Education Program: 94 (6.2%);
English Language Learner: 159 (10.5%); Migrant: 11 (0.7%)
Eligible for Free Lunch Program: 143 (9.4%)
Eligible for Reduced-Price Lunch Program: 44 (2.9%)
Teachers: 77.5 (19.6 to 1)
Librarians/Media Specialists: 0.0 (0.0 to 1)
Guidance Counselors: 0.0 (0.0 to 1)
Current Spending: ($ per student per year):
Total: $5,942; Instruction: $3,896; Support Services: $1,784
Enrollment, Drop-out Rates and Diploma Recipients by Race/Ethnicity

Category	Total	White	Black	Asian	AIAN	Hisp.
Enrollment (%)	100.0	56.7	6.1	16.6	0.9	19.6
Drop-out Rate (%)	n/a	n/a	n/a	n/a	n/a	n/a
H.S. Diplomas (#)	n/a	n/a	n/a	n/a	n/a	n/a

Lincoln Unified

2010 W Swain Rd • Stockton, CA 95207-4055
(209) 953-8700 • http://www.lincolnusd.k12.ca.us/
Grade Span: KG-12; **Agency Type:** 1
Schools: 14
10 Primary; 1 Middle; 3 High; 0 Other Level
11 Regular; 0 Special Education; 0 Vocational; 3 Alternative
0 Magnet; 0 Charter; 9 Title I Eligible; 0 School-wide Title I
Students: 8,939 (50.7% male; 49.3% female)
Individual Education Program: 828 (9.3%);
English Language Learner: 1,563 (17.5%); Migrant: 45 (0.5%)
Eligible for Free Lunch Program: 2,425 (27.1%)
Eligible for Reduced-Price Lunch Program: 671 (7.5%)
Teachers: 437.3 (20.4 to 1)
Librarians/Media Specialists: 1.8 (4,966.1 to 1)
Guidance Counselors: 16.0 (558.7 to 1)
Current Spending: ($ per student per year):
Total: $6,314; Instruction: $4,143; Support Services: $1,950
Enrollment, Drop-out Rates and Diploma Recipients by Race/Ethnicity

Category	Total	White	Black	Asian	AIAN	Hisp.
Enrollment (%)	100.0	42.3	12.2	20.3	0.7	24.0
Drop-out Rate (%)	n/a	n/a	n/a	n/a	n/a	n/a
H.S. Diplomas (#)	476	225	39	122	2	87

Linden Unified

18527 E Main St • Linden, CA 95236
(209) 887-3894 • http://www.sjcoe.k12.ca.us/LUSD/D.O..html
Grade Span: KG-12; **Agency Type:** 1
Schools: 6
3 Primary; 1 Middle; 2 High; 0 Other Level
5 Regular; 0 Special Education; 0 Vocational; 1 Alternative
0 Magnet; 0 Charter; 3 Title I Eligible; 0 School-wide Title I
Students: 2,509 (49.6% male; 50.4% female)
Individual Education Program: 245 (9.8%);
English Language Learner: 506 (20.2%); Migrant: 765 (30.5%)
Eligible for Free Lunch Program: 811 (32.3%)
Eligible for Reduced-Price Lunch Program: 186 (7.4%)
Teachers: 130.7 (19.2 to 1)
Librarians/Media Specialists: 0.0 (0.0 to 1)
Guidance Counselors: 2.4 (1,045.4 to 1)
Current Spending: ($ per student per year):
Total: $6,467; Instruction: $3,961; Support Services: $2,250
Enrollment, Drop-out Rates and Diploma Recipients by Race/Ethnicity

Category	Total	White	Black	Asian	AIAN	Hisp.
Enrollment (%)	100.0	57.9	1.0	2.9	0.7	37.6
Drop-out Rate (%)	n/a	n/a	n/a	n/a	n/a	n/a
H.S. Diplomas (#)	150	96	0	7	0	44

Lodi Unified

1305 E Vine St • Lodi, CA 95240-3148
(209) 331-7000 • http://www.lodiusd.net/
Grade Span: KG-12; **Agency Type:** 1
Schools: 43
31 Primary; 4 Middle; 7 High; 1 Other Level
37 Regular; 0 Special Education; 0 Vocational; 6 Alternative
0 Magnet; 3 Charter; 18 Title I Eligible; 13 School-wide Title I
Students: 28,396 (51.3% male; 48.7% female)
Individual Education Program: 3,385 (11.9%);
English Language Learner: 7,925 (27.9%); Migrant: 2,801 (9.9%)
Eligible for Free Lunch Program: 14,537 (51.2%)
Eligible for Reduced-Price Lunch Program: 2,514 (8.9%)
Teachers: 1,464.2 (19.4 to 1)
Librarians/Media Specialists: 4.3 (6,603.7 to 1)
Guidance Counselors: 40.2 (706.4 to 1)
Current Spending: ($ per student per year):
Total: $6,306; Instruction: $4,116; Support Services: $2,003
Enrollment, Drop-out Rates and Diploma Recipients by Race/Ethnicity

Category	Total	White	Black	Asian	AIAN	Hisp.
Enrollment (%)	100.0	38.8	7.4	22.6	0.7	30.4
Drop-out Rate (%)	n/a	n/a	n/a	n/a	n/a	n/a
H.S. Diplomas (#)	1,456	703	88	382	2	281

Manteca Unified

2901 E Louise Ave • Manteca, CA 95336-0032
Mailing Address: PO Box 32 • Manteca, CA 95336-0032
(209) 825-3200 • http://www.mantecausd.net/
Grade Span: KG-12; **Agency Type:** 1
Schools: 23
18 Primary; 0 Middle; 5 High; 0 Other Level
20 Regular; 0 Special Education; 0 Vocational; 3 Alternative
0 Magnet; 0 Charter; 10 Title I Eligible; 2 School-wide Title I
Students: 21,052 (51.0% male; 49.0% female)
Individual Education Program: 1,837 (8.7%);
English Language Learner: 2,803 (13.3%); Migrant: 1,147 (5.4%)
Eligible for Free Lunch Program: 5,008 (23.8%)
Eligible for Reduced-Price Lunch Program: 1,955 (9.3%)
Teachers: 994.1 (21.2 to 1)
Librarians/Media Specialists: 3.0 (7,017.3 to 1)
Guidance Counselors: 18.5 (1,137.9 to 1)
Current Spending: ($ per student per year):
Total: $6,052; Instruction: $3,931; Support Services: $1,938
Enrollment, Drop-out Rates and Diploma Recipients by Race/Ethnicity

Category	Total	White	Black	Asian	AIAN	Hisp.
Enrollment (%)	100.0	43.6	7.6	10.5	1.5	36.6
Drop-out Rate (%)	n/a	n/a	n/a	n/a	n/a	n/a
H.S. Diplomas (#)	1,061	563	67	124	19	288

Ripon Unified

304 N Acacia Ave • Ripon, CA 95366-2404
(209) 599-2131 • http://www.riponusd.net/
Grade Span: KG-12; **Agency Type:** 1
Schools: 6
4 Primary; 0 Middle; 2 High; 0 Other Level
5 Regular; 0 Special Education; 0 Vocational; 1 Alternative
0 Magnet; 0 Charter; 2 Title I Eligible; 0 School-wide Title I
Students: 2,773 (51.8% male; 48.2% female)
Individual Education Program: 235 (8.5%);
English Language Learner: 237 (8.5%); Migrant: 326 (11.8%)
Eligible for Free Lunch Program: 359 (12.9%)
Eligible for Reduced-Price Lunch Program: 131 (4.7%)
Teachers: 137.8 (20.1 to 1)
Librarians/Media Specialists: 0.0 (0.0 to 1)
Guidance Counselors: 1.5 (1,848.7 to 1)
Current Spending: ($ per student per year):
Total: $5,482; Instruction: $3,828; Support Services: $1,442
Enrollment, Drop-out Rates and Diploma Recipients by Race/Ethnicity

Category	Total	White	Black	Asian	AIAN	Hisp.
Enrollment (%)	100.0	68.6	1.2	2.4	0.6	26.8
Drop-out Rate (%)	n/a	n/a	n/a	n/a	n/a	n/a
H.S. Diplomas (#)	154	124	0	2	1	27

San Joaquin County Office of Ed

2901 Arch-Airport Rd • Stockton, CA 95213-9030
Mailing Address: PO Box 213030 • Stockton, CA 95213-9030
(209) 468-4800 • http://www.sjcoe.k12.ca.us/
Grade Span: KG-12; **Agency Type:** 4
Schools: 4
0 Primary; 0 Middle; 0 High; 4 Other Level
1 Regular; 1 Special Education; 0 Vocational; 2 Alternative
0 Magnet; 1 Charter; 0 Title I Eligible; 0 School-wide Title I
Students: 2,223 (63.8% male; 36.2% female)
Individual Education Program: 637 (28.7%);
English Language Learner: 87 (3.9%); Migrant: 28 (1.3%)
Eligible for Free Lunch Program: 1,084 (48.8%)
Eligible for Reduced-Price Lunch Program: 138 (6.2%)
Teachers: 153.6 (14.5 to 1)
Librarians/Media Specialists: 0.0 (0.0 to 1)
Guidance Counselors: 5.0 (444.6 to 1)
Current Spending: ($ per student per year):
Total: $26,729; Instruction: $10,390; Support Services: $16,174
Enrollment, Drop-out Rates and Diploma Recipients by Race/Ethnicity

Category	Total	White	Black	Asian	AIAN	Hisp.
Enrollment (%)	100.0	34.2	13.9	9.3	1.8	37.5
Drop-out Rate (%)	n/a	n/a	n/a	n/a	n/a	n/a
H.S. Diplomas (#)	130	45	13	26	0	46

Stockton City Unified

701 N Madison St • Stockton, CA 95202-1634
(209) 953-4050 • http://www.stockton.k12.ca.us/
Grade Span: KG-12; **Agency Type:** 1
Schools: 48
35 Primary; 4 Middle; 6 High; 3 Other Level
42 Regular; 2 Special Education; 0 Vocational; 4 Alternative
9 Magnet; 1 Charter; 42 Title I Eligible; 34 School-wide Title I
Students: 39,421 (50.8% male; 49.2% female)
Individual Education Program: 3,969 (10.1%);
English Language Learner: 9,321 (23.6%); Migrant: 6,825 (17.3%)
Eligible for Free Lunch Program: 22,744 (57.7%)
Eligible for Reduced-Price Lunch Program: 1,929 (4.9%)
Teachers: 1,974.7 (20.0 to 1)
Librarians/Media Specialists: 9.0 (4,380.1 to 1)
Guidance Counselors: 74.0 (532.7 to 1)
Current Spending: ($ per student per year):
Total: $6,788; Instruction: $4,218; Support Services: $2,288
Enrollment, Drop-out Rates and Diploma Recipients by Race/Ethnicity

Category	Total	White	Black	Asian	AIAN	Hisp.
Enrollment (%)	100.0	12.7	14.4	20.5	2.7	49.6
Drop-out Rate (%)	n/a	n/a	n/a	n/a	n/a	n/a
H.S. Diplomas (#)	1,309	155	199	408	37	510

Tracy Joint Unified

315 E Eleventh St • Tracy, CA 95376-4095
(209) 830-3200 • http://www.tracy.k12.ca.us/
Grade Span: KG-12; **Agency Type:** 1
Schools: 21
11 Primary; 4 Middle; 6 High; 0 Other Level
17 Regular; 0 Special Education; 0 Vocational; 4 Alternative
2 Magnet; 1 Charter; 7 Title I Eligible; 1 School-wide Title I
Students: 15,252 (50.9% male; 49.1% female)
Individual Education Program: 1,324 (8.7%);
English Language Learner: 2,289 (15.0%); Migrant: 627 (4.1%)
Eligible for Free Lunch Program: 2,537 (16.6%)
Eligible for Reduced-Price Lunch Program: 780 (5.1%)
Teachers: 760.1 (20.1 to 1)
Librarians/Media Specialists: 3.9 (3,910.8 to 1)
Guidance Counselors: 16.0 (953.3 to 1)
Current Spending: ($ per student per year):
Total: $6,014; Instruction: $3,771; Support Services: $2,055
Enrollment, Drop-out Rates and Diploma Recipients by Race/Ethnicity

Category	Total	White	Black	Asian	AIAN	Hisp.
Enrollment (%)	100.0	44.1	7.6	14.4	1.2	32.7
Drop-out Rate (%)	n/a	n/a	n/a	n/a	n/a	n/a
H.S. Diplomas (#)	927	505	69	110	10	233

San Luis Obispo County

Atascadero Unified

5601 W Mall • Atascadero, CA 93422-4234
(805) 462-4200 • http://www.atas.k12.ca.us/
Grade Span: KG-12; **Agency Type:** 1
Schools: 12
7 Primary; 2 Middle; 2 High; 1 Other Level
10 Regular; 0 Special Education; 0 Vocational; 2 Alternative
0 Magnet; 0 Charter; 9 Title I Eligible; 0 School-wide Title I
Students: 5,791 (52.3% male; 47.7% female)
Individual Education Program: 642 (11.1%);
English Language Learner: 179 (3.1%); Migrant: 34 (0.6%)
Eligible for Free Lunch Program: 774 (13.4%)
Eligible for Reduced-Price Lunch Program: 433 (7.5%)
Teachers: 292.8 (19.8 to 1)
Librarians/Media Specialists: 1.0 (5,791.0 to 1)
Guidance Counselors: 10.3 (562.2 to 1)
Current Spending: ($ per student per year):
Total: $6,049; Instruction: $3,887; Support Services: $1,962
Enrollment, Drop-out Rates and Diploma Recipients by Race/Ethnicity

Category	Total	White	Black	Asian	AIAN	Hisp.
Enrollment (%)	100.0	83.4	1.8	1.6	0.5	12.7
Drop-out Rate (%)	n/a	n/a	n/a	n/a	n/a	n/a
H.S. Diplomas (#)	397	351	4	12	2	28

Lucia Mar Unified

602 Orchard St • Arroyo Grande, CA 93420-4000
(805) 474-3000 • http://www.luciamar.k12.ca.us/
Grade Span: KG-12; **Agency Type:** 1
Schools: 16
10 Primary; 3 Middle; 3 High; 0 Other Level
15 Regular; 0 Special Education; 0 Vocational; 1 Alternative
0 Magnet; 0 Charter; 12 Title I Eligible; 0 School-wide Title I
Students: 10,916 (51.7% male; 48.3% female)
Individual Education Program: 1,173 (10.7%);
English Language Learner: 1,237 (11.3%); Migrant: 702 (6.4%)
Eligible for Free Lunch Program: 3,600 (33.0%)
Eligible for Reduced-Price Lunch Program: 1,281 (11.7%)
Teachers: 533.4 (20.5 to 1)
Librarians/Media Specialists: 2.0 (5,458.0 to 1)
Guidance Counselors: 10.0 (1,091.6 to 1)
Current Spending: ($ per student per year):
Total: $5,992; Instruction: $3,940; Support Services: $1,821
Enrollment, Drop-out Rates and Diploma Recipients by Race/Ethnicity

Category	Total	White	Black	Asian	AIAN	Hisp.
Enrollment (%)	100.0	61.6	1.6	3.6	0.6	32.1
Drop-out Rate (%)	n/a	n/a	n/a	n/a	n/a	n/a
H.S. Diplomas (#)	691	472	5	26	4	184

Paso Robles Joint Unified

800 Niblick Rd • Paso Robles, CA 93447-7010
Mailing Address: PO Box 7010 • Paso Robles, CA 93447-7010
(805) 238-2222 • http://king.prps.k12.ca.us/
Grade Span: KG-12; **Agency Type:** 1
Schools: 14
6 Primary; 3 Middle; 4 High; 1 Other Level
10 Regular; 0 Special Education; 0 Vocational; 4 Alternative
0 Magnet; 1 Charter; 11 Title I Eligible; 3 School-wide Title I
Students: 6,900 (52.7% male; 47.3% female)
Individual Education Program: 732 (10.6%);
English Language Learner: 1,341 (19.4%); Migrant: 578 (8.4%)
Eligible for Free Lunch Program: 1,846 (26.8%)
Eligible for Reduced-Price Lunch Program: 630 (9.1%)
Teachers: 359.2 (19.2 to 1)
Librarians/Media Specialists: 4.0 (1,725.0 to 1)
Guidance Counselors: 11.8 (584.7 to 1)
Current Spending: ($ per student per year):
Total: $6,984; Instruction: $4,405; Support Services: $2,322
Enrollment, Drop-out Rates and Diploma Recipients by Race/Ethnicity

Category	Total	White	Black	Asian	AIAN	Hisp.
Enrollment (%)	100.0	59.4	4.1	1.8	0.9	33.7
Drop-out Rate (%)	n/a	n/a	n/a	n/a	n/a	n/a
H.S. Diplomas (#)	423	298	17	16	2	87

San Luis Coastal Unified

261 Cuesta Dr • San Luis Obispo, CA 93405-3099
(805) 549-1200 • http://www.slcusd.org/
Grade Span: KG-12; **Agency Type:** 1
Schools: 16
10 Primary; 3 Middle; 3 High; 0 Other Level
15 Regular; 0 Special Education; 0 Vocational; 1 Alternative
3 Magnet; 1 Charter; 5 Title I Eligible; 2 School-wide Title I
Students: 7,945 (51.0% male; 49.0% female)
Individual Education Program: 715 (9.0%);
English Language Learner: 598 (7.5%); Migrant: 231 (2.9%)
Eligible for Free Lunch Program: 1,333 (16.8%)
Eligible for Reduced-Price Lunch Program: 628 (7.9%)
Teachers: 382.8 (20.8 to 1)
Librarians/Media Specialists: 4.0 (1,986.3 to 1)
Guidance Counselors: 15.7 (506.1 to 1)
Current Spending: ($ per student per year):
Total: $6,432; Instruction: $3,958; Support Services: $2,274

Enrollment, Drop-out Rates and Diploma Recipients by Race/Ethnicity

Category	Total	White	Black	Asian	AIAN	Hisp.
Enrollment (%)	100.0	75.0	1.8	4.4	0.6	16.9
Drop-out Rate (%)	n/a	n/a	n/a	n/a	n/a	n/a
H.S. Diplomas (#)	541	458	7	21	3	50

Templeton Unified

960 Old County Rd • Templeton, CA 93465-9419
(805) 434-5800 • http://www.tusdnet.k12.ca.us/
Grade Span: KG-12; **Agency Type:** 1
Schools: 8
3 Primary; 1 Middle; 3 High; 1 Other Level
4 Regular; 0 Special Education; 0 Vocational; 4 Alternative
0 Magnet; 0 Charter; 5 Title I Eligible; 0 School-wide Title I
Students: 2,684 (49.7% male; 50.3% female)
Individual Education Program: 166 (6.2%);
English Language Learner: 77 (2.9%); Migrant: 16 (0.6%)
Eligible for Free Lunch Program: 205 (7.6%)
Eligible for Reduced-Price Lunch Program: 118 (4.4%)
Teachers: 131.2 (20.5 to 1)
Librarians/Media Specialists: 0.0 (0.0 to 1)
Guidance Counselors: 3.0 (894.7 to 1)
Current Spending: ($ per student per year):
Total: $5,963; Instruction: $3,929; Support Services: $1,840
Enrollment, Drop-out Rates and Diploma Recipients by Race/Ethnicity

Category	Total	White	Black	Asian	AIAN	Hisp.
Enrollment (%)	100.0	84.5	0.9	1.6	1.2	11.7
Drop-out Rate (%)	n/a	n/a	n/a	n/a	n/a	n/a
H.S. Diplomas (#)	192	167	2	8	3	12

San Mateo County

Belmont-Redwood Shores Elementary

2960 Hallmark Dr • Belmont, CA 94002-2943
(650) 637-4800 • http://www.belmont.gov/educ/district/
Grade Span: KG-08; **Agency Type:** 1
Schools: 6
5 Primary; 1 Middle; 0 High; 0 Other Level
6 Regular; 0 Special Education; 0 Vocational; 0 Alternative
0 Magnet; 0 Charter; 2 Title I Eligible; 0 School-wide Title I
Students: 2,541 (51.8% male; 48.2% female)
Individual Education Program: 1,274 (50.1%);
English Language Learner: 100 (3.9%); Migrant: 0 (0.0%)
Eligible for Free Lunch Program: 80 (3.1%)
Eligible for Reduced-Price Lunch Program: 0 (0.0%)
Teachers: 140.3 (18.1 to 1)
Librarians/Media Specialists: 0.0 (0.0 to 1)
Guidance Counselors: 0.8 (3,176.3 to 1)
Current Spending: ($ per student per year):
Total: $6,175; Instruction: $4,213; Support Services: $1,944
Enrollment, Drop-out Rates and Diploma Recipients by Race/Ethnicity

Category	Total	White	Black	Asian	AIAN	Hisp.
Enrollment (%)	100.0	58.3	2.8	22.6	0.5	8.9
Drop-out Rate (%)	n/a	n/a	n/a	n/a	n/a	n/a
H.S. Diplomas (#)	n/a	n/a	n/a	n/a	n/a	n/a

Burlingame Elementary

1825 Trousdale Dr • Burlingame, CA 94010-4509
(650) 259-3800 • http://www.burlingameschools.com/
Grade Span: KG-08; **Agency Type:** 1
Schools: 6
5 Primary; 1 Middle; 0 High; 0 Other Level
6 Regular; 0 Special Education; 0 Vocational; 0 Alternative
0 Magnet; 0 Charter; 3 Title I Eligible; 0 School-wide Title I
Students: 2,327 (51.5% male; 48.5% female)
Individual Education Program: 190 (8.2%);
English Language Learner: 303 (13.0%); Migrant: 0 (0.0%)
Eligible for Free Lunch Program: 75 (3.2%)
Eligible for Reduced-Price Lunch Program: 38 (1.6%)
Teachers: 118.2 (19.7 to 1)
Librarians/Media Specialists: 3.6 (646.4 to 1)
Guidance Counselors: 1.5 (1,551.3 to 1)
Current Spending: ($ per student per year):
Total: $6,295; Instruction: $4,250; Support Services: $2,031
Enrollment, Drop-out Rates and Diploma Recipients by Race/Ethnicity

Category	Total	White	Black	Asian	AIAN	Hisp.
Enrollment (%)	100.0	58.8	0.9	20.8	0.0	11.9
Drop-out Rate (%)	n/a	n/a	n/a	n/a	n/a	n/a
H.S. Diplomas (#)	n/a	n/a	n/a	n/a	n/a	n/a

Cabrillo Unified

498 Kelly Ave • Half Moon Bay, CA 94019-1636
(650) 712-7100 • http://www.coastside.net/cusd/
Grade Span: KG-12; **Agency Type:** 1
Schools: 7
4 Primary; 1 Middle; 2 High; 0 Other Level
6 Regular; 0 Special Education; 0 Vocational; 1 Alternative
0 Magnet; 0 Charter; 3 Title I Eligible; 0 School-wide Title I
Students: 3,649 (49.6% male; 50.4% female)
Individual Education Program: 369 (10.1%);
English Language Learner: 938 (25.7%); Migrant: 388 (10.6%)
Eligible for Free Lunch Program: 626 (17.2%)
Eligible for Reduced-Price Lunch Program: 262 (7.2%)
Teachers: 178.1 (20.5 to 1)
Librarians/Media Specialists: 1.0 (3,649.0 to 1)
Guidance Counselors: 4.8 (760.2 to 1)
Current Spending: ($ per student per year):
Total: $6,602; Instruction: $3,743; Support Services: $2,703
Enrollment, Drop-out Rates and Diploma Recipients by Race/Ethnicity

Category	Total	White	Black	Asian	AIAN	Hisp.
Enrollment (%)	100.0	57.2	0.5	4.1	0.3	35.2
Drop-out Rate (%)	n/a	n/a	n/a	n/a	n/a	n/a
H.S. Diplomas (#)	259	188	2	10	1	58

Jefferson Elementary

101 Lincoln Ave • Daly City, CA 94015-3934
(650) 991-1000 • http://www.smcoe.k12.ca.us/jesd/
Grade Span: KG-08; **Agency Type:** 1
Schools: 17
12 Primary; 5 Middle; 0 High; 0 Other Level
16 Regular; 0 Special Education; 0 Vocational; 1 Alternative
0 Magnet; 0 Charter; 6 Title I Eligible; 0 School-wide Title I
Students: 6,852 (50.9% male; 49.1% female)
Individual Education Program: 576 (8.4%);
English Language Learner: 1,928 (28.1%); Migrant: 0 (0.0%)
Eligible for Free Lunch Program: 2,089 (30.5%)
Eligible for Reduced-Price Lunch Program: 1,222 (17.8%)
Teachers: 322.4 (21.3 to 1)
Librarians/Media Specialists: 3.0 (2,284.0 to 1)
Guidance Counselors: 0.0 (0.0 to 1)
Current Spending: ($ per student per year):
Total: $6,163; Instruction: $4,203; Support Services: $1,713
Enrollment, Drop-out Rates and Diploma Recipients by Race/Ethnicity

Category	Total	White	Black	Asian	AIAN	Hisp.
Enrollment (%)	100.0	7.2	5.0	46.9	0.4	32.3
Drop-out Rate (%)	n/a	n/a	n/a	n/a	n/a	n/a
H.S. Diplomas (#)	n/a	n/a	n/a	n/a	n/a	n/a

Jefferson Union High

699 Serramonte Blvd, Ste 100 • Daly City, CA 94015-4132
(650) 550-7900 • http://www.juhsd.k12.ca.us/
Grade Span: 09-12; **Agency Type:** 1
Schools: 5
0 Primary; 0 Middle; 5 High; 0 Other Level
3 Regular; 0 Special Education; 0 Vocational; 2 Alternative
0 Magnet; 0 Charter; 2 Title I Eligible; 0 School-wide Title I
Students: 5,375 (52.4% male; 47.6% female)
Individual Education Program: 370 (6.9%);
English Language Learner: 420 (7.8%); Migrant: 0 (0.0%)
Eligible for Free Lunch Program: 757 (14.1%)
Eligible for Reduced-Price Lunch Program: 427 (7.9%)
Teachers: 244.3 (22.0 to 1)
Librarians/Media Specialists: 4.0 (1,343.8 to 1)
Guidance Counselors: 10.6 (507.1 to 1)
Current Spending: ($ per student per year):
Total: $6,538; Instruction: $3,652; Support Services: $2,725
Enrollment, Drop-out Rates and Diploma Recipients by Race/Ethnicity

Category	Total	White	Black	Asian	AIAN	Hisp.
Enrollment (%)	100.0	25.0	5.2	43.7	0.4	25.5
Drop-out Rate (%)	n/a	n/a	n/a	n/a	n/a	n/a
H.S. Diplomas (#)	1,085	317	68	457	6	237

Laguna Salada Union Elementary

375 Reina Del Mar • Pacifica, CA 94044-3052
(650) 738-6600 • http://www.lsusd.k12.ca.us/
Grade Span: KG-08; **Agency Type:** 1
Schools: 7
6 Primary; 1 Middle; 0 High; 0 Other Level
7 Regular; 0 Special Education; 0 Vocational; 0 Alternative
4 Magnet; 0 Charter; 2 Title I Eligible; 0 School-wide Title I
Students: 3,153 (51.4% male; 48.6% female)
Individual Education Program: 343 (10.9%);
English Language Learner: 181 (5.7%); Migrant: 0 (0.0%)
Eligible for Free Lunch Program: 312 (9.9%)
Eligible for Reduced-Price Lunch Program: 209 (6.6%)
Teachers: 146.3 (21.6 to 1)
Librarians/Media Specialists: 1.0 (3,153.0 to 1)
Guidance Counselors: 1.0 (3,153.0 to 1)
Current Spending: ($ per student per year):
Total: $6,087; Instruction: $3,621; Support Services: $2,219

Enrollment, Drop-out Rates and Diploma Recipients by Race/Ethnicity

Category	Total	White	Black	Asian	AIAN	Hisp.
Enrollment (%)	100.0	59.2	4.2	17.9	1.1	16.0
Drop-out Rate (%)	n/a	n/a	n/a	n/a	n/a	n/a
H.S. Diplomas (#)	n/a	n/a	n/a	n/a	n/a	n/a

Menlo Park City Elementary

181 Encinal Ave • Atherton, CA 94027-3102
(650) 321-7140 • http://www.mpcsd.k12.ca.us/
Grade Span: KG-08; **Agency Type:** 1
Schools: 4
3 Primary; 1 Middle; 0 High; 0 Other Level
4 Regular; 0 Special Education; 0 Vocational; 0 Alternative
0 Magnet; 0 Charter; 0 Title I Eligible; 0 School-wide Title I
Students: 2,039 (54.2% male; 45.8% female)
Individual Education Program: 267 (13.1%);
English Language Learner: 137 (6.7%); Migrant: 0 (0.0%)
Eligible for Free Lunch Program: 46 (2.3%)
Eligible for Reduced-Price Lunch Program: 18 (0.9%)
Teachers: 130.2 (15.7 to 1)
Librarians/Media Specialists: 3.4 (599.7 to 1)
Guidance Counselors: 2.9 (703.1 to 1)
Current Spending: ($ per student per year):
Total: $7,658; Instruction: $5,434; Support Services: $2,206
Enrollment, Drop-out Rates and Diploma Recipients by Race/Ethnicity

Category	Total	White	Black	Asian	AIAN	Hisp.
Enrollment (%)	100.0	70.4	3.0	8.7	0.1	10.7
Drop-out Rate (%)	n/a	n/a	n/a	n/a	n/a	n/a
H.S. Diplomas (#)	n/a	n/a	n/a	n/a	n/a	n/a

Millbrae Elementary

555 Richmond Dr • Millbrae, CA 94030-1600
(650) 697-5693 • http://www.smcoe.k12.ca.us/msd/do/do.htm
Grade Span: KG-08; **Agency Type:** 1
Schools: 5
4 Primary; 1 Middle; 0 High; 0 Other Level
5 Regular; 0 Special Education; 0 Vocational; 0 Alternative
0 Magnet; 0 Charter; 2 Title I Eligible; 0 School-wide Title I
Students: 2,151 (50.2% male; 49.8% female)
Individual Education Program: 181 (8.4%);
English Language Learner: 517 (24.0%); Migrant: 0 (0.0%)
Eligible for Free Lunch Program: 95 (4.4%)
Eligible for Reduced-Price Lunch Program: 87 (4.0%)
Teachers: 108.9 (19.8 to 1)
Librarians/Media Specialists: 0.6 (3,585.0 to 1)
Guidance Counselors: 1.0 (2,151.0 to 1)
Current Spending: ($ per student per year):
Total: $6,283; Instruction: $3,891; Support Services: $2,197
Enrollment, Drop-out Rates and Diploma Recipients by Race/Ethnicity

Category	Total	White	Black	Asian	AIAN	Hisp.
Enrollment (%)	100.0	33.8	2.2	40.3	0.1	16.1
Drop-out Rate (%)	n/a	n/a	n/a	n/a	n/a	n/a
H.S. Diplomas (#)	n/a	n/a	n/a	n/a	n/a	n/a

Ravenswood City Elementary

2160 Euclid Ave • East Palo Alto, CA 94303-1703
(650) 329-2800 • http://www.ravenswood.k12.ca.us/
Grade Span: KG-12; **Agency Type:** 1
Schools: 12
9 Primary; 2 Middle; 1 High; 0 Other Level
12 Regular; 0 Special Education; 0 Vocational; 0 Alternative
0 Magnet; 4 Charter; 12 Title I Eligible; 8 School-wide Title I
Students: 5,168 (50.8% male; 49.2% female)
Individual Education Program: 476 (9.2%);
English Language Learner: 3,473 (67.2%); Migrant: 383 (7.4%)
Eligible for Free Lunch Program: 2,926 (56.6%)
Eligible for Reduced-Price Lunch Program: 683 (13.2%)
Teachers: 283.1 (18.3 to 1)
Librarians/Media Specialists: 0.0 (0.0 to 1)
Guidance Counselors: 1.0 (5,168.0 to 1)
Current Spending: ($ per student per year):
Total: $7,371; Instruction: $4,144; Support Services: $2,838
Enrollment, Drop-out Rates and Diploma Recipients by Race/Ethnicity

Category	Total	White	Black	Asian	AIAN	Hisp.
Enrollment (%)	100.0	0.7	19.3	9.9	0.1	68.7
Drop-out Rate (%)	n/a	n/a	n/a	n/a	n/a	n/a
H.S. Diplomas (#)	0	0	0	0	0	0

Redwood City Elementary

750 Bradford St • Redwood City, CA 94063-1727
(650) 423-2200 • http://www.rcsd.k12.ca.us/
Grade Span: KG-12; **Agency Type:** 1
Schools: 17
14 Primary; 2 Middle; 1 High; 0 Other Level
16 Regular; 0 Special Education; 0 Vocational; 1 Alternative
16 Magnet; 2 Charter; 12 Title I Eligible; 4 School-wide Title I
Students: 8,813 (52.1% male; 47.9% female)
Individual Education Program: 978 (11.1%);
English Language Learner: 4,461 (50.6%); Migrant: 456 (5.2%)
Eligible for Free Lunch Program: 3,461 (39.3%)
Eligible for Reduced-Price Lunch Program: 1,244 (14.1%)
Teachers: 532.0 (16.6 to 1)
Librarians/Media Specialists: 0.0 (0.0 to 1)
Guidance Counselors: 1.0 (8,813.0 to 1)
Current Spending: ($ per student per year):
Total: $7,668; Instruction: $4,967; Support Services: $2,475
Enrollment, Drop-out Rates and Diploma Recipients by Race/Ethnicity

Category	Total	White	Black	Asian	AIAN	Hisp.
Enrollment (%)	100.0	27.5	2.6	6.2	0.4	63.2
Drop-out Rate (%)	n/a	n/a	n/a	n/a	n/a	n/a
H.S. Diplomas (#)	3	3	0	0	0	0

San Bruno Park Elementary

500 Acacia Ave • San Bruno, CA 94066-4298
(650) 624-3100 • http://sbpsd.k12.ca.us/
Grade Span: KG-08; **Agency Type:** 1
Schools: 8
7 Primary; 1 Middle; 0 High; 0 Other Level
8 Regular; 0 Special Education; 0 Vocational; 0 Alternative
0 Magnet; 0 Charter; 2 Title I Eligible; 0 School-wide Title I
Students: 2,800 (51.5% male; 48.5% female)
Individual Education Program: 247 (8.8%);
English Language Learner: 349 (12.5%); Migrant: 0 (0.0%)
Eligible for Free Lunch Program: 569 (20.3%)
Eligible for Reduced-Price Lunch Program: 289 (10.3%)
Teachers: 135.1 (20.7 to 1)
Librarians/Media Specialists: 0.0 (0.0 to 1)
Guidance Counselors: 2.5 (1,120.0 to 1)
Current Spending: ($ per student per year):
Total: $5,870; Instruction: $3,840; Support Services: $1,840
Enrollment, Drop-out Rates and Diploma Recipients by Race/Ethnicity

Category	Total	White	Black	Asian	AIAN	Hisp.
Enrollment (%)	100.0	39.0	2.8	24.7	0.5	33.0
Drop-out Rate (%)	n/a	n/a	n/a	n/a	n/a	n/a
H.S. Diplomas (#)	n/a	n/a	n/a	n/a	n/a	n/a

San Carlos Elementary

826 Chestnut St • San Carlos, CA 94070-3802
(650) 508-7333 • http://scsd.sancarlos.k12.ca.us/
Grade Span: KG-08; **Agency Type:** 1
Schools: 7
5 Primary; 2 Middle; 0 High; 0 Other Level
7 Regular; 0 Special Education; 0 Vocational; 0 Alternative
0 Magnet; 6 Charter; 2 Title I Eligible; 0 School-wide Title I
Students: 2,580 (53.3% male; 46.7% female)
Individual Education Program: 209 (8.1%);
English Language Learner: 51 (2.0%); Migrant: 0 (0.0%)
Eligible for Free Lunch Program: 45 (1.7%)
Eligible for Reduced-Price Lunch Program: 15 (0.6%)
Teachers: 136.7 (18.9 to 1)
Librarians/Media Specialists: 0.0 (0.0 to 1)
Guidance Counselors: 2.0 (1,290.0 to 1)
Current Spending: ($ per student per year):
Total: $9,137; Instruction: $7,253; Support Services: $1,870
Enrollment, Drop-out Rates and Diploma Recipients by Race/Ethnicity

Category	Total	White	Black	Asian	AIAN	Hisp.
Enrollment (%)	100.0	77.2	2.0	8.1	0.4	9.6
Drop-out Rate (%)	n/a	n/a	n/a	n/a	n/a	n/a
H.S. Diplomas (#)	n/a	n/a	n/a	n/a	n/a	n/a

San Mateo Union High

650 N Delaware St • San Mateo, CA 94401-1795
(650) 762-0200 • http://www.smuhsd.k12.ca.us/
Grade Span: 09-12; **Agency Type:** 1
Schools: 8
0 Primary; 0 Middle; 8 High; 0 Other Level
6 Regular; 0 Special Education; 0 Vocational; 2 Alternative
0 Magnet; 0 Charter; 4 Title I Eligible; 0 School-wide Title I
Students: 8,250 (52.3% male; 47.7% female)
Individual Education Program: 941 (11.4%);
English Language Learner: 1,144 (13.9%); Migrant: 0 (0.0%)
Eligible for Free Lunch Program: 322 (3.9%)
Eligible for Reduced-Price Lunch Program: 143 (1.7%)
Teachers: 396.6 (20.8 to 1)
Librarians/Media Specialists: 6.0 (1,375.0 to 1)
Guidance Counselors: 17.6 (468.7 to 1)
Current Spending: ($ per student per year):
Total: $8,411; Instruction: $4,560; Support Services: $3,598

Enrollment, Drop-out Rates and Diploma Recipients by Race/Ethnicity

Category	Total	White	Black	Asian	AIAN	Hisp.
Enrollment (%)	100.0	47.2	2.6	28.2	0.3	21.7
Drop-out Rate (%)	n/a	n/a	n/a	n/a	n/a	n/a
H.S. Diplomas (#)	1,763	882	32	549	7	293

San Mateo-Foster City Elementary

300 28th Ave • San Mateo, CA 94402-0058
Mailing Address: PO Box K • San Mateo, CA 94402-0058
(650) 312-7700 • http://www.smfc.k12.ca.us/
Grade Span: KG-08; **Agency Type:** 1
Schools: 21
16 Primary; 5 Middle; 0 High; 0 Other Level
20 Regular; 0 Special Education; 0 Vocational; 1 Alternative
6 Magnet; 0 Charter; 8 Title I Eligible; 0 School-wide Title I
Students: 10,087 (50.9% male; 49.1% female)
Individual Education Program: 1,174 (11.6%);
English Language Learner: 2,418 (24.0%); Migrant: 0 (0.0%)
Eligible for Free Lunch Program: 2,016 (20.0%)
Eligible for Reduced-Price Lunch Program: 864 (8.6%)
Teachers: 524.9 (19.2 to 1)
Librarians/Media Specialists: 4.0 (2,521.8 to 1)
Guidance Counselors: 8.0 (1,260.9 to 1)
Current Spending: ($ per student per year):
Total: $6,503; Instruction: $4,377; Support Services: $1,798

Enrollment, Drop-out Rates and Diploma Recipients by Race/Ethnicity

Category	Total	White	Black	Asian	AIAN	Hisp.
Enrollment (%)	100.0	42.1	3.7	25.6	0.2	27.6
Drop-out Rate (%)	n/a	n/a	n/a	n/a	n/a	n/a
H.S. Diplomas (#)	n/a	n/a	n/a	n/a	n/a	n/a

Sequoia Union High

480 James Ave • Redwood City, CA 94062-1041
(650) 369-1411 • http://www.seq.org/
Grade Span: 09-12; **Agency Type:** 1
Schools: 6
0 Primary; 0 Middle; 6 High; 0 Other Level
4 Regular; 0 Special Education; 0 Vocational; 2 Alternative
0 Magnet; 0 Charter; 3 Title I Eligible; 0 School-wide Title I
Students: 7,680 (51.7% male; 48.3% female)
Individual Education Program: 879 (11.4%);
English Language Learner: 2,185 (28.5%); Migrant: 330 (4.3%)
Eligible for Free Lunch Program: 1,214 (15.8%)
Eligible for Reduced-Price Lunch Program: 367 (4.8%)
Teachers: 376.4 (20.4 to 1)
Librarians/Media Specialists: 3.8 (2,021.1 to 1)
Guidance Counselors: 22.0 (349.1 to 1)
Current Spending: ($ per student per year):
Total: $8,248; Instruction: $4,356; Support Services: $3,594

Enrollment, Drop-out Rates and Diploma Recipients by Race/Ethnicity

Category	Total	White	Black	Asian	AIAN	Hisp.
Enrollment (%)	100.0	41.9	6.2	9.8	0.2	41.9
Drop-out Rate (%)	n/a	n/a	n/a	n/a	n/a	n/a
H.S. Diplomas (#)	1,197	567	79	120	0	431

South San Francisco Unified

398 B St • South San Francisco, CA 94080-4423
(650) 877-8700
Grade Span: KG-12; **Agency Type:** 1
Schools: 16
10 Primary; 3 Middle; 3 High; 0 Other Level
15 Regular; 0 Special Education; 0 Vocational; 1 Alternative
0 Magnet; 0 Charter; 6 Title I Eligible; 2 School-wide Title I
Students: 9,563 (52.1% male; 47.9% female)
Individual Education Program: 1,062 (11.1%);
English Language Learner: 1,733 (18.1%); Migrant: 193 (2.0%)
Eligible for Free Lunch Program: 1,997 (20.9%)
Eligible for Reduced-Price Lunch Program: 804 (8.4%)
Teachers: 457.2 (20.9 to 1)
Librarians/Media Specialists: 2.0 (4,781.5 to 1)
Guidance Counselors: 12.8 (747.1 to 1)
Current Spending: ($ per student per year):
Total: $6,094; Instruction: $3,634; Support Services: $2,179

Enrollment, Drop-out Rates and Diploma Recipients by Race/Ethnicity

Category	Total	White	Black	Asian	AIAN	Hisp.
Enrollment (%)	100.0	19.7	3.8	39.1	0.3	37.1
Drop-out Rate (%)	n/a	n/a	n/a	n/a	n/a	n/a
H.S. Diplomas (#)	633	153	26	279	1	174

Santa Barbara County

Carpinteria Unified

1400 Lindon Ave • Carpinteria, CA 93013-1414
(805) 684-4511 • http://www.cusd.net/home/
Grade Span: KG-12; **Agency Type:** 1
Schools: 8
4 Primary; 1 Middle; 3 High; 0 Other Level
6 Regular; 0 Special Education; 0 Vocational; 2 Alternative
0 Magnet; 0 Charter; 4 Title I Eligible; 0 School-wide Title I
Students: 3,018 (51.8% male; 48.2% female)
Individual Education Program: 310 (10.3%);
English Language Learner: 1,161 (38.5%); Migrant: 632 (20.9%)
Eligible for Free Lunch Program: 952 (31.5%)
Eligible for Reduced-Price Lunch Program: 365 (12.1%)
Teachers: 146.8 (20.6 to 1)
Librarians/Media Specialists: 0.0 (0.0 to 1)
Guidance Counselors: 3.0 (1,006.0 to 1)
Current Spending: ($ per student per year):
Total: $6,484; Instruction: $3,922; Support Services: $2,310

Enrollment, Drop-out Rates and Diploma Recipients by Race/Ethnicity

Category	Total	White	Black	Asian	AIAN	Hisp.
Enrollment (%)	100.0	33.7	1.1	2.8	0.3	62.0
Drop-out Rate (%)	n/a	n/a	n/a	n/a	n/a	n/a
H.S. Diplomas (#)	203	97	2	5	1	98

Goleta Union Elementary

401 N Fairview Ave • Goleta, CA 93117-1732
(805) 681-1200 • http://www.goleta.k12.ca.us/
Grade Span: KG-06; **Agency Type:** 1
Schools: 10
10 Primary; 0 Middle; 0 High; 0 Other Level
10 Regular; 0 Special Education; 0 Vocational; 0 Alternative
0 Magnet; 0 Charter; 5 Title I Eligible; 1 School-wide Title I
Students: 4,110 (50.6% male; 49.4% female)
Individual Education Program: 422 (10.3%);
English Language Learner: 1,167 (28.4%); Migrant: 92 (2.2%)
Eligible for Free Lunch Program: 845 (20.6%)
Eligible for Reduced-Price Lunch Program: 446 (10.9%)
Teachers: 208.1 (19.8 to 1)
Librarians/Media Specialists: 0.0 (0.0 to 1)
Guidance Counselors: 0.5 (8,220.0 to 1)
Current Spending: ($ per student per year):
Total: $6,264; Instruction: $3,884; Support Services: $2,184

Enrollment, Drop-out Rates and Diploma Recipients by Race/Ethnicity

Category	Total	White	Black	Asian	AIAN	Hisp.
Enrollment (%)	100.0	48.7	1.8	7.9	0.7	40.9
Drop-out Rate (%)	n/a	n/a	n/a	n/a	n/a	n/a
H.S. Diplomas (#)	n/a	n/a	n/a	n/a	n/a	n/a

Lompoc Unified

1301 N A St • Lompoc, CA 93438-8000
Mailing Address: PO Box 8000 • Lompoc, CA 93438-8000
(805) 736-2371 • http://www1.lusd.org/index.jsp
Grade Span: KG-12; **Agency Type:** 1
Schools: 16
10 Primary; 3 Middle; 3 High; 0 Other Level
15 Regular; 0 Special Education; 0 Vocational; 1 Alternative
0 Magnet; 0 Charter; 11 Title I Eligible; 6 School-wide Title I
Students: 11,617 (51.7% male; 48.3% female)
Individual Education Program: 842 (7.2%);
English Language Learner: 2,094 (18.0%); Migrant: 1,114 (9.6%)
Eligible for Free Lunch Program: 3,879 (33.4%)
Eligible for Reduced-Price Lunch Program: 1,281 (11.0%)
Teachers: 615.1 (18.9 to 1)
Librarians/Media Specialists: 2.0 (5,808.5 to 1)
Guidance Counselors: 12.0 (968.1 to 1)
Current Spending: ($ per student per year):
Total: $5,793; Instruction: $3,860; Support Services: $1,799

Enrollment, Drop-out Rates and Diploma Recipients by Race/Ethnicity

Category	Total	White	Black	Asian	AIAN	Hisp.
Enrollment (%)	100.0	42.9	7.2	5.0	1.6	43.2
Drop-out Rate (%)	n/a	n/a	n/a	n/a	n/a	n/a
H.S. Diplomas (#)	568	305	47	40	10	166

Orcutt Union Elementary

Soares & Dyer Sts • Orcutt, CA 93457-2310
Mailing Address: PO Box 2310 • Orcutt, CA 93457-2310
(805) 938-8900 • http://www.orcutt-schools.net/public/
Grade Span: KG-08; **Agency Type:** 1
Schools: 8
6 Primary; 2 Middle; 0 High; 0 Other Level
8 Regular; 0 Special Education; 0 Vocational; 0 Alternative
0 Magnet; 0 Charter; 1 Title I Eligible; 0 School-wide Title I
Students: 5,032 (52.5% male; 47.5% female)

Individual Education Program: 403 (8.0%);
English Language Learner: 290 (5.8%); Migrant: 8 (0.2%)
Eligible for Free Lunch Program: 777 (15.4%)
Eligible for Reduced-Price Lunch Program: 442 (8.8%)
Teachers: 238.3 (21.1 to 1)
Librarians/Media Specialists: 0.2 (25,160.0 to 1)
Guidance Counselors: 0.0 (0.0 to 1)
Current Spending: ($ per student per year):
Total: $6,005; Instruction: $3,820; Support Services: $2,022
Enrollment, Drop-out Rates and Diploma Recipients by Race/Ethnicity

Category	Total	White	Black	Asian	AIAN	Hisp.
Enrollment (%)	100.0	65.7	2.2	5.4	1.3	25.2
Drop-out Rate (%)	n/a	n/a	n/a	n/a	n/a	n/a
H.S. Diplomas (#)	n/a	n/a	n/a	n/a	n/a	n/a

Santa Barbara Elementary
720 Santa Barbara St • Santa Barbara, CA 93101-3167
(805) 963-4331 • http://www.sbceo.k12.ca.us/~sbsdweb/
Grade Span: KG-08; **Agency Type:** 2
Schools: 13
13 Primary; 0 Middle; 0 High; 0 Other Level
13 Regular; 0 Special Education; 0 Vocational; 0 Alternative
3 Magnet; 3 Charter; 10 Title I Eligible; 5 School-wide Title I
Students: 6,093 (51.5% male; 48.5% female)
Individual Education Program: 671 (11.0%);
English Language Learner: 2,576 (42.3%); Migrant: 66 (1.1%)
Eligible for Free Lunch Program: 2,612 (42.9%)
Eligible for Reduced-Price Lunch Program: 1,139 (18.7%)
Teachers: 308.4 (19.8 to 1)
Librarians/Media Specialists: 8.2 (743.0 to 1)
Guidance Counselors: 0.0 (0.0 to 1)
Current Spending: ($ per student per year):
Total: $7,459; Instruction: $4,958; Support Services: $1,896
Enrollment, Drop-out Rates and Diploma Recipients by Race/Ethnicity

Category	Total	White	Black	Asian	AIAN	Hisp.
Enrollment (%)	100.0	24.5	2.3	2.1	1.0	69.7
Drop-out Rate (%)	n/a	n/a	n/a	n/a	n/a	n/a
H.S. Diplomas (#)	n/a	n/a	n/a	n/a	n/a	n/a

Santa Barbara High
720 Santa Barbara St • Santa Barbara, CA 93101-3167
(805) 963-4331 • http://www.sbceo.k12.ca.us/districts/sbhighsd/
Grade Span: 06-12; **Agency Type:** 2
Schools: 13
0 Primary; 6 Middle; 7 High; 0 Other Level
8 Regular; 0 Special Education; 0 Vocational; 5 Alternative
0 Magnet; 1 Charter; 4 Title I Eligible; 1 School-wide Title I
Students: 10,392 (51.5% male; 48.5% female)
Individual Education Program: 1,050 (10.1%);
English Language Learner: 1,955 (18.8%); Migrant: 136 (1.3%)
Eligible for Free Lunch Program: 1,659 (16.0%)
Eligible for Reduced-Price Lunch Program: 702 (6.8%)
Teachers: 474.3 (21.9 to 1)
Librarians/Media Specialists: 7.0 (1,484.6 to 1)
Guidance Counselors: 23.6 (440.3 to 1)
Current Spending: ($ per student per year):
Total: $6,032; Instruction: $3,858; Support Services: $2,144
Enrollment, Drop-out Rates and Diploma Recipients by Race/Ethnicity

Category	Total	White	Black	Asian	AIAN	Hisp.
Enrollment (%)	100.0	48.9	2.0	4.7	1.2	43.1
Drop-out Rate (%)	n/a	n/a	n/a	n/a	n/a	n/a
H.S. Diplomas (#)	1,358	745	35	60	8	510

Santa Maria Joint Union High
2560 Skyway Dr • Santa Maria, CA 93455-6112
(805) 922-4573 • http://www.smjuhsd.k12.ca.us/
Grade Span: 09-12; **Agency Type:** 1
Schools: 3
0 Primary; 0 Middle; 3 High; 0 Other Level
2 Regular; 0 Special Education; 0 Vocational; 1 Alternative
0 Magnet; 0 Charter; 3 Title I Eligible; 1 School-wide Title I
Students: 6,429 (50.8% male; 49.2% female)
Individual Education Program: 530 (8.2%);
English Language Learner: 1,618 (25.2%); Migrant: 1,582 (24.6%)
Eligible for Free Lunch Program: 1,304 (20.3%)
Eligible for Reduced-Price Lunch Program: 322 (5.0%)
Teachers: 257.9 (24.9 to 1)
Librarians/Media Specialists: 0.6 (10,715.0 to 1)
Guidance Counselors: 3.3 (1,948.2 to 1)
Current Spending: ($ per student per year):
Total: $6,069; Instruction: $3,632; Support Services: $2,260
Enrollment, Drop-out Rates and Diploma Recipients by Race/Ethnicity

Category	Total	White	Black	Asian	AIAN	Hisp.
Enrollment (%)	100.0	32.4	0.5	7.0	0.7	58.7
Drop-out Rate (%)	n/a	n/a	n/a	n/a	n/a	n/a
H.S. Diplomas (#)	1,093	451	4	56	10	570

Santa Maria-Bonita Elementary
708 S Miller St • Santa Maria, CA 93454-6230
(805) 928-1783 • http://www.sbceo.k12.ca.us/districts/smbonitasd/
Grade Span: KG-08; **Agency Type:** 1
Schools: 16
13 Primary; 3 Middle; 0 High; 0 Other Level
16 Regular; 0 Special Education; 0 Vocational; 0 Alternative
0 Magnet; 0 Charter; 16 Title I Eligible; 13 School-wide Title I
Students: 12,034 (52.1% male; 47.9% female)
Individual Education Program: 830 (6.9%);
English Language Learner: 6,532 (54.3%); Migrant: 3,677 (30.6%)
Eligible for Free Lunch Program: 8,090 (67.2%)
Eligible for Reduced-Price Lunch Program: 1,750 (14.5%)
Teachers: 586.5 (20.5 to 1)
Librarians/Media Specialists: 0.5 (24,068.0 to 1)
Guidance Counselors: 6.0 (2,005.7 to 1)
Current Spending: ($ per student per year):
Total: $6,784; Instruction: $4,540; Support Services: $1,909
Enrollment, Drop-out Rates and Diploma Recipients by Race/Ethnicity

Category	Total	White	Black	Asian	AIAN	Hisp.
Enrollment (%)	100.0	11.1	1.5	3.8	0.6	83.0
Drop-out Rate (%)	n/a	n/a	n/a	n/a	n/a	n/a
H.S. Diplomas (#)	n/a	n/a	n/a	n/a	n/a	n/a

Santa Clara County

Alum Rock Union Elementary
2930 Gay Ave • San Jose, CA 95127-2322
(408) 928-6800 • http://www.alumrock.k12.ca.us/home.htm
Grade Span: KG-08; **Agency Type:** 1
Schools: 25
19 Primary; 6 Middle; 0 High; 0 Other Level
25 Regular; 0 Special Education; 0 Vocational; 0 Alternative
0 Magnet; 0 Charter; 16 Title I Eligible; 13 School-wide Title I
Students: 14,416 (51.1% male; 48.9% female)
Individual Education Program: 1,498 (10.4%);
English Language Learner: 7,971 (55.3%); Migrant: 1,103 (7.7%)
Eligible for Free Lunch Program: 8,129 (56.4%)
Eligible for Reduced-Price Lunch Program: 2,226 (15.4%)
Teachers: 721.1 (20.0 to 1)
Librarians/Media Specialists: 1.0 (14,416.0 to 1)
Guidance Counselors: 12.0 (1,201.3 to 1)
Current Spending: ($ per student per year):
Total: $7,029; Instruction: $4,654; Support Services: $2,055
Enrollment, Drop-out Rates and Diploma Recipients by Race/Ethnicity

Category	Total	White	Black	Asian	AIAN	Hisp.
Enrollment (%)	100.0	3.9	2.2	19.0	0.9	74.1
Drop-out Rate (%)	n/a	n/a	n/a	n/a	n/a	n/a
H.S. Diplomas (#)	n/a	n/a	n/a	n/a	n/a	n/a

Berryessa Union Elementary
1376 Piedmont Rd • San Jose, CA 95132-2427
(408) 923-1800 • http://www.berryessa.k12.ca.us/index.html
Grade Span: KG-08; **Agency Type:** 1
Schools: 14
11 Primary; 3 Middle; 0 High; 0 Other Level
13 Regular; 0 Special Education; 0 Vocational; 1 Alternative
0 Magnet; 0 Charter; 9 Title I Eligible; 0 School-wide Title I
Students: 8,427 (51.9% male; 48.1% female)
Individual Education Program: 749 (8.9%);
English Language Learner: 3,001 (35.6%); Migrant: 0 (0.0%)
Eligible for Free Lunch Program: 1,570 (18.6%)
Eligible for Reduced-Price Lunch Program: 693 (8.2%)
Teachers: 405.0 (20.8 to 1)
Librarians/Media Specialists: 0.0 (0.0 to 1)
Guidance Counselors: 7.0 (1,203.9 to 1)
Current Spending: ($ per student per year):
Total: $6,324; Instruction: $4,313; Support Services: $1,805
Enrollment, Drop-out Rates and Diploma Recipients by Race/Ethnicity

Category	Total	White	Black	Asian	AIAN	Hisp.
Enrollment (%)	100.0	12.3	3.7	63.7	0.4	19.8
Drop-out Rate (%)	n/a	n/a	n/a	n/a	n/a	n/a
H.S. Diplomas (#)	n/a	n/a	n/a	n/a	n/a	n/a

Cambrian Elementary
4115 Jacksol Dr • San Jose, CA 95124-3312
(408) 377-2103 • http://www.cambrian.k12.ca.us/
Grade Span: KG-08; **Agency Type:** 1
Schools: 6

4 Primary; 2 Middle; 0 High; 0 Other Level
5 Regular; 0 Special Education; 0 Vocational; 1 Alternative
0 Magnet; 0 Charter; 2 Title I Eligible; 0 School-wide Title I
Students: 2,807 (51.1% male; 48.9% female)
Individual Education Program: 212 (7.6%);
English Language Learner: 140 (5.0%); Migrant: 0 (0.0%)
Eligible for Free Lunch Program: 363 (12.9%)
Eligible for Reduced-Price Lunch Program: 161 (5.7%)
Teachers: 138.3 (20.3 to 1)
Librarians/Media Specialists: 0.0 (0.0 to 1)
Guidance Counselors: 1.0 (2,807.0 to 1)
Current Spending: ($ per student per year):
Total: $5,881; Instruction: $3,964; Support Services: $1,917
Enrollment, Drop-out Rates and Diploma Recipients by Race/Ethnicity

Category	Total	White	Black	Asian	AIAN	Hisp.
Enrollment (%)	100.0	60.2	4.2	13.3	0.9	21.2
Drop-out Rate (%)	n/a	n/a	n/a	n/a	n/a	n/a
H.S. Diplomas (#)	n/a	n/a	n/a	n/a	n/a	n/a

Campbell Union Elementary
155 N Third St • Campbell, CA 95008-2044
(408) 364-4200 • http://www.campbellusd.k12.ca.us/
Grade Span: KG-08; **Agency Type:** 1
Schools: 12
9 Primary; 3 Middle; 0 High; 0 Other Level
12 Regular; 0 Special Education; 0 Vocational; 0 Alternative
0 Magnet; 1 Charter; 7 Title I Eligible; 0 School-wide Title I
Students: 7,483 (52.5% male; 47.5% female)
Individual Education Program: 717 (9.6%);
English Language Learner: 2,236 (29.9%); Migrant: 3 (<0.1%)
Eligible for Free Lunch Program: 1,865 (24.9%)
Eligible for Reduced-Price Lunch Program: 582 (7.8%)
Teachers: 388.2 (19.3 to 1)
Librarians/Media Specialists: 0.0 (0.0 to 1)
Guidance Counselors: 3.0 (2,494.3 to 1)
Current Spending: ($ per student per year):
Total: $6,414; Instruction: $4,483; Support Services: $1,772
Enrollment, Drop-out Rates and Diploma Recipients by Race/Ethnicity

Category	Total	White	Black	Asian	AIAN	Hisp.
Enrollment (%)	100.0	43.6	5.2	16.4	0.6	34.1
Drop-out Rate (%)	n/a	n/a	n/a	n/a	n/a	n/a
H.S. Diplomas (#)	n/a	n/a	n/a	n/a	n/a	n/a

Campbell Union High
3235 Union Ave • San Jose, CA 95124-2009
(408) 371-0960 • http://www.cuhsd.org/
Grade Span: 09-12; **Agency Type:** 1
Schools: 7
0 Primary; 0 Middle; 7 High; 0 Other Level
6 Regular; 0 Special Education; 0 Vocational; 1 Alternative
0 Magnet; 0 Charter; 2 Title I Eligible; 0 School-wide Title I
Students: 7,527 (52.0% male; 48.0% female)
Individual Education Program: 782 (10.4%);
English Language Learner: 401 (5.3%); Migrant: 0 (0.0%)
Eligible for Free Lunch Program: 390 (5.2%)
Eligible for Reduced-Price Lunch Program: 140 (1.9%)
Teachers: 319.6 (23.6 to 1)
Librarians/Media Specialists: 2.5 (3,010.8 to 1)
Guidance Counselors: 12.0 (627.3 to 1)
Current Spending: ($ per student per year):
Total: $6,460; Instruction: $3,802; Support Services: $2,459
Enrollment, Drop-out Rates and Diploma Recipients by Race/Ethnicity

Category	Total	White	Black	Asian	AIAN	Hisp.
Enrollment (%)	100.0	58.4	3.8	13.8	0.7	19.1
Drop-out Rate (%)	n/a	n/a	n/a	n/a	n/a	n/a
H.S. Diplomas (#)	1,414	909	48	217	10	202

Cupertino Union School
10301 Vista Dr • Cupertino, CA 95014-2091
(408) 252-3000 • http://www.cupertino.k12.ca.us/
Grade Span: KG-08; **Agency Type:** 1
Schools: 24
20 Primary; 4 Middle; 0 High; 0 Other Level
24 Regular; 0 Special Education; 0 Vocational; 0 Alternative
0 Magnet; 0 Charter; 3 Title I Eligible; 0 School-wide Title I
Students: 15,873 (51.5% male; 48.5% female)
Individual Education Program: 1,055 (6.6%);
English Language Learner: 1,707 (10.8%); Migrant: 1 (<0.1%)
Eligible for Free Lunch Program: 505 (3.2%)
Eligible for Reduced-Price Lunch Program: 209 (1.3%)
Teachers: 734.5 (21.6 to 1)
Librarians/Media Specialists: 0.0 (0.0 to 1)
Guidance Counselors: 4.0 (3,968.3 to 1)
Current Spending: ($ per student per year):
Total: $6,137; Instruction: $4,037; Support Services: $1,940
Enrollment, Drop-out Rates and Diploma Recipients by Race/Ethnicity

Category	Total	White	Black	Asian	AIAN	Hisp.
Enrollment (%)	100.0	36.2	1.1	58.2	0.2	4.1
Drop-out Rate (%)	n/a	n/a	n/a	n/a	n/a	n/a
H.S. Diplomas (#)	n/a	n/a	n/a	n/a	n/a	n/a

East Side Union High
830 N Capitol Ave • San Jose, CA 95133-1316
(408) 347-5000 • http://www.esuhsd.k12.ca.us/
Grade Span: KG-12; **Agency Type:** 1
Schools: 21
0 Primary; 0 Middle; 19 High; 2 Other Level
15 Regular; 0 Special Education; 0 Vocational; 6 Alternative
11 Magnet; 4 Charter; 7 Title I Eligible; 0 School-wide Title I
Students: 24,409 (51.8% male; 48.2% female)
Individual Education Program: 2,514 (10.3%);
English Language Learner: 6,020 (24.7%); Migrant: 370 (1.5%)
Eligible for Free Lunch Program: 6,056 (24.8%)
Eligible for Reduced-Price Lunch Program: 883 (3.6%)
Teachers: 1,158.5 (21.1 to 1)
Librarians/Media Specialists: 12.3 (1,984.5 to 1)
Guidance Counselors: 41.5 (588.2 to 1)
Current Spending: ($ per student per year):
Total: $7,477; Instruction: $4,208; Support Services: $3,110
Enrollment, Drop-out Rates and Diploma Recipients by Race/Ethnicity

Category	Total	White	Black	Asian	AIAN	Hisp.
Enrollment (%)	100.0	15.2	4.6	37.6	0.4	42.2
Drop-out Rate (%)	n/a	n/a	n/a	n/a	n/a	n/a
H.S. Diplomas (#)	4,467	772	178	2,040	19	1,457

Evergreen Elementary
3188 Quimby Rd • San Jose, CA 95148-3022
(408) 270-6800 • http://www.do.esd.k12.ca.us/
Grade Span: KG-08; **Agency Type:** 1
Schools: 17
14 Primary; 3 Middle; 0 High; 0 Other Level
17 Regular; 0 Special Education; 0 Vocational; 0 Alternative
0 Magnet; 0 Charter; 7 Title I Eligible; 5 School-wide Title I
Students: 12,621 (51.3% male; 48.7% female)
Individual Education Program: 1,010 (8.0%);
English Language Learner: 3,949 (31.3%); Migrant: 240 (1.9%)
Eligible for Free Lunch Program: 2,752 (21.8%)
Eligible for Reduced-Price Lunch Program: 881 (7.0%)
Teachers: 586.7 (21.5 to 1)
Librarians/Media Specialists: 9.3 (1,357.1 to 1)
Guidance Counselors: 0.0 (0.0 to 1)
Current Spending: ($ per student per year):
Total: $5,896; Instruction: $4,009; Support Services: $1,695
Enrollment, Drop-out Rates and Diploma Recipients by Race/Ethnicity

Category	Total	White	Black	Asian	AIAN	Hisp.
Enrollment (%)	100.0	12.1	4.3	50.7	0.5	32.3
Drop-out Rate (%)	n/a	n/a	n/a	n/a	n/a	n/a
H.S. Diplomas (#)	n/a	n/a	n/a	n/a	n/a	n/a

Franklin-Mckinley Elementary
645 Wool Creek Dr • San Jose, CA 95112-2617
(408) 283-6000 • http://www.fmsd.k12.ca.us/
Grade Span: KG-08; **Agency Type:** 1
Schools: 14
12 Primary; 2 Middle; 0 High; 0 Other Level
14 Regular; 0 Special Education; 0 Vocational; 0 Alternative
0 Magnet; 0 Charter; 10 Title I Eligible; 6 School-wide Title I
Students: 9,953 (50.4% male; 49.6% female)
Individual Education Program: 856 (8.6%);
English Language Learner: 5,500 (55.3%); Migrant: 917 (9.2%)
Eligible for Free Lunch Program: 5,255 (52.8%)
Eligible for Reduced-Price Lunch Program: 1,400 (14.1%)
Teachers: 514.7 (19.3 to 1)
Librarians/Media Specialists: 2.0 (4,976.5 to 1)
Guidance Counselors: 5.0 (1,990.6 to 1)
Current Spending: ($ per student per year):
Total: $6,806; Instruction: $4,201; Support Services: $2,253
Enrollment, Drop-out Rates and Diploma Recipients by Race/Ethnicity

Category	Total	White	Black	Asian	AIAN	Hisp.
Enrollment (%)	100.0	3.6	2.4	33.9	0.4	59.6
Drop-out Rate (%)	n/a	n/a	n/a	n/a	n/a	n/a
H.S. Diplomas (#)	n/a	n/a	n/a	n/a	n/a	n/a

Fremont Union High
589 W Fremont Ave • Sunnyvale, CA 94087
Mailing Address: PO Box F • Sunnyvale, CA 94087
(408) 522-2200 • http://www.fuhsd.org/
Grade Span: 09-12; **Agency Type:** 1
Schools: 6
0 Primary; 0 Middle; 6 High; 0 Other Level

5 Regular; 0 Special Education; 0 Vocational; 1 Alternative
0 Magnet; 0 Charter; 1 Title I Eligible; 0 School-wide Title I
Students: 9,138 (51.1% male; 48.9% female)
Individual Education Program: 764 (8.4%);
English Language Learner: 1,050 (11.5%); Migrant: 26 (0.3%)
Eligible for Free Lunch Program: 281 (3.1%)
Eligible for Reduced-Price Lunch Program: 84 (0.9%)
Teachers: 421.3 (21.7 to 1)
Librarians/Media Specialists: 5.8 (1,575.5 to 1)
Guidance Counselors: 11.4 (801.6 to 1)
Current Spending: ($ per student per year):
Total: $7,011; Instruction: $4,403; Support Services: $2,401
Enrollment, Drop-out Rates and Diploma Recipients by Race/Ethnicity

Category	Total	White	Black	Asian	AIAN	Hisp.
Enrollment (%)	100.0	37.4	2.0	48.2	0.3	12.0
Drop-out Rate (%)	n/a	n/a	n/a	n/a	n/a	n/a
H.S. Diplomas (#)	1,985	741	52	997	6	189

Gilroy Unified

7810 Arroyo Circle • Gilroy, CA 95020-7313
(408) 847-2700 • http://www.gusd.k12.ca.us/
Grade Span: KG-12; **Agency Type:** 1
Schools: 14
9 Primary; 1 Middle; 4 High; 0 Other Level
12 Regular; 0 Special Education; 0 Vocational; 2 Alternative
0 Magnet; 1 Charter; 14 Title I Eligible; 0 School-wide Title I
Students: 9,630 (51.1% male; 48.9% female)
Individual Education Program: 923 (9.6%);
English Language Learner: 2,952 (30.7%); Migrant: 1,059 (11.0%)
Eligible for Free Lunch Program: 3,556 (36.9%)
Eligible for Reduced-Price Lunch Program: 761 (7.9%)
Teachers: 483.8 (19.9 to 1)
Librarians/Media Specialists: 1.0 (9,630.0 to 1)
Guidance Counselors: 8.0 (1,203.8 to 1)
Current Spending: ($ per student per year):
Total: $6,309; Instruction: $3,865; Support Services: $2,125
Enrollment, Drop-out Rates and Diploma Recipients by Race/Ethnicity

Category	Total	White	Black	Asian	AIAN	Hisp.
Enrollment (%)	100.0	26.7	1.7	4.6	0.6	65.7
Drop-out Rate (%)	n/a	n/a	n/a	n/a	n/a	n/a
H.S. Diplomas (#)	446	170	13	35	2	226

Los Altos Elementary

201 Covington Rd • Los Altos, CA 94024-4030
(650) 947-1150 • http://www.sccoe.k12.ca.us/district/4320home.html
Grade Span: KG-08; **Agency Type:** 1
Schools: 8
6 Primary; 2 Middle; 0 High; 0 Other Level
8 Regular; 0 Special Education; 0 Vocational; 0 Alternative
0 Magnet; 0 Charter; 0 Title I Eligible; 0 School-wide Title I
Students: 4,032 (51.0% male; 49.0% female)
Individual Education Program: 351 (8.7%);
English Language Learner: 203 (5.0%); Migrant: 0 (0.0%)
Eligible for Free Lunch Program: 55 (1.4%)
Eligible for Reduced-Price Lunch Program: 1 (<0.1%)
Teachers: 201.3 (20.0 to 1)
Librarians/Media Specialists: 0.0 (0.0 to 1)
Guidance Counselors: 1.0 (4,032.0 to 1)
Current Spending: ($ per student per year):
Total: $7,068; Instruction: $4,867; Support Services: $2,192
Enrollment, Drop-out Rates and Diploma Recipients by Race/Ethnicity

Category	Total	White	Black	Asian	AIAN	Hisp.
Enrollment (%)	100.0	70.8	1.0	25.3	0.0	2.9
Drop-out Rate (%)	n/a	n/a	n/a	n/a	n/a	n/a
H.S. Diplomas (#)	n/a	n/a	n/a	n/a	n/a	n/a

Los Gatos Union Elementary

15766 Poppy Ln • Los Gatos, CA 95030-3228
(408) 335-2000 • http://www.lgusd.k12.ca.us/
Grade Span: KG-08; **Agency Type:** 1
Schools: 5
4 Primary; 1 Middle; 0 High; 0 Other Level
5 Regular; 0 Special Education; 0 Vocational; 0 Alternative
0 Magnet; 0 Charter; 2 Title I Eligible; 0 School-wide Title I
Students: 2,652 (50.9% male; 49.1% female)
Individual Education Program: 263 (9.9%);
English Language Learner: 44 (1.7%); Migrant: 0 (0.0%)
Eligible for Free Lunch Program: 41 (1.5%)
Eligible for Reduced-Price Lunch Program: 20 (0.8%)
Teachers: 140.1 (18.9 to 1)
Librarians/Media Specialists: 1.0 (2,652.0 to 1)
Guidance Counselors: 1.0 (2,652.0 to 1)
Current Spending: ($ per student per year):
Total: $6,958; Instruction: $4,651; Support Services: $2,125
Enrollment, Drop-out Rates and Diploma Recipients by Race/Ethnicity

Category	Total	White	Black	Asian	AIAN	Hisp.
Enrollment (%)	100.0	79.5	0.8	13.7	0.2	4.4
Drop-out Rate (%)	n/a	n/a	n/a	n/a	n/a	n/a
H.S. Diplomas (#)	n/a	n/a	n/a	n/a	n/a	n/a

Los Gatos-Saratoga Joint Union High

17421 Farley Rd W • Los Gatos, CA 95030-3308
(408) 354-2520 • http://www.eduniverse.com/members/schools
Grade Span: 09-12; **Agency Type:** 1
Schools: 2
0 Primary; 0 Middle; 2 High; 0 Other Level
2 Regular; 0 Special Education; 0 Vocational; 0 Alternative
0 Magnet; 0 Charter; 1 Title I Eligible; 0 School-wide Title I
Students: 2,873 (52.9% male; 47.1% female)
Individual Education Program: 234 (8.1%);
English Language Learner: 12 (0.4%); Migrant: 0 (0.0%)
Eligible for Free Lunch Program: 14 (0.5%)
Eligible for Reduced-Price Lunch Program: 0 (0.0%)
Teachers: 130.2 (22.1 to 1)
Librarians/Media Specialists: 2.0 (1,436.5 to 1)
Guidance Counselors: 3.6 (798.1 to 1)
Current Spending: ($ per student per year):
Total: $8,538; Instruction: $4,900; Support Services: $3,433
Enrollment, Drop-out Rates and Diploma Recipients by Race/Ethnicity

Category	Total	White	Black	Asian	AIAN	Hisp.
Enrollment (%)	100.0	64.4	0.5	27.1	0.5	4.5
Drop-out Rate (%)	n/a	n/a	n/a	n/a	n/a	n/a
H.S. Diplomas (#)	651	452	3	174	3	17

Milpitas Unified

1331 E Calaveras Blvd • Milpitas, CA 95035-5707
(408) 945-2300 • http://www.milpitas.k12.ca.us/
Grade Span: KG-12; **Agency Type:** 1
Schools: 14
9 Primary; 2 Middle; 3 High; 0 Other Level
12 Regular; 0 Special Education; 0 Vocational; 2 Alternative
0 Magnet; 0 Charter; 6 Title I Eligible; 0 School-wide Title I
Students: 9,516 (51.9% male; 48.1% female)
Individual Education Program: 903 (9.5%);
English Language Learner: 2,292 (24.1%); Migrant: 0 (0.0%)
Eligible for Free Lunch Program: 2,063 (21.7%)
Eligible for Reduced-Price Lunch Program: 877 (9.2%)
Teachers: 448.6 (21.2 to 1)
Librarians/Media Specialists: 2.3 (4,137.4 to 1)
Guidance Counselors: 8.8 (1,081.4 to 1)
Current Spending: ($ per student per year):
Total: $6,255; Instruction: $3,954; Support Services: $2,044
Enrollment, Drop-out Rates and Diploma Recipients by Race/Ethnicity

Category	Total	White	Black	Asian	AIAN	Hisp.
Enrollment (%)	100.0	16.9	4.8	58.5	0.4	19.4
Drop-out Rate (%)	n/a	n/a	n/a	n/a	n/a	n/a
H.S. Diplomas (#)	710	165	36	380	2	127

Moreland Elementary

4710 Campbell Ave • San Jose, CA 95130-1709
(408) 874-2900 • http://www.moreland.k12.ca.us/
Grade Span: KG-08; **Agency Type:** 1
Schools: 10
7 Primary; 3 Middle; 0 High; 0 Other Level
9 Regular; 0 Special Education; 0 Vocational; 1 Alternative
0 Magnet; 0 Charter; 3 Title I Eligible; 1 School-wide Title I
Students: 4,413 (52.2% male; 47.8% female)
Individual Education Program: 384 (8.7%);
English Language Learner: 857 (19.4%); Migrant: 0 (0.0%)
Eligible for Free Lunch Program: 724 (16.4%)
Eligible for Reduced-Price Lunch Program: 323 (7.3%)
Teachers: 235.2 (18.8 to 1)
Librarians/Media Specialists: 0.0 (0.0 to 1)
Guidance Counselors: 2.0 (2,206.5 to 1)
Current Spending: ($ per student per year):
Total: $6,763; Instruction: $4,216; Support Services: $2,315
Enrollment, Drop-out Rates and Diploma Recipients by Race/Ethnicity

Category	Total	White	Black	Asian	AIAN	Hisp.
Enrollment (%)	100.0	46.9	4.8	26.2	0.7	21.4
Drop-out Rate (%)	n/a	n/a	n/a	n/a	n/a	n/a
H.S. Diplomas (#)	n/a	n/a	n/a	n/a	n/a	n/a

Morgan Hill Unified

15600 Concord Circle • Morgan Hill, CA 95037-7110
(408) 201-6023 • http://www.mhu.k12.ca.us/
Grade Span: KG-12; **Agency Type:** 1
Schools: 15
10 Primary; 3 Middle; 2 High; 0 Other Level
14 Regular; 0 Special Education; 0 Vocational; 1 Alternative

0 Magnet; 1 Charter; 7 Title I Eligible; 1 School-wide Title I
Students: 8,809 (51.0% male; 49.0% female)
Individual Education Program: 912 (10.4%);
English Language Learner: 1,446 (16.4%); Migrant: 843 (9.6%)
Eligible for Free Lunch Program: 1,642 (18.6%)
Eligible for Reduced-Price Lunch Program: 433 (4.9%)
Teachers: 407.3 (21.6 to 1)
Librarians/Media Specialists: 1.8 (4,893.9 to 1)
Guidance Counselors: 6.5 (1,355.2 to 1)
Current Spending: ($ per student per year):
Total: $5,950; Instruction: $3,905; Support Services: $1,856

Enrollment, Drop-out Rates and Diploma Recipients by Race/Ethnicity

Category	Total	White	Black	Asian	AIAN	Hisp.
Enrollment (%)	100.0	49.1	2.3	8.4	0.5	36.2
Drop-out Rate (%)	n/a	n/a	n/a	n/a	n/a	n/a
H.S. Diplomas (#)	615	365	10	56	1	183

Mount Pleasant Elementary

3434 Marten Ave • San Jose, CA 95148-1300
(408) 223-3700 • http://www.sccoe.k12.ca.us/district/4328home.html
Grade Span: KG-08; **Agency Type:** 1
Schools: 5
3 Primary; 2 Middle; 0 High; 0 Other Level
5 Regular; 0 Special Education; 0 Vocational; 0 Alternative
1 Magnet; 0 Charter; 2 Title I Eligible; 2 School-wide Title I
Students: 2,849 (54.5% male; 45.5% female)
Individual Education Program: 288 (10.1%);
English Language Learner: 1,454 (51.0%); Migrant: 193 (6.8%)
Eligible for Free Lunch Program: 1,199 (42.1%)
Eligible for Reduced-Price Lunch Program: 461 (16.2%)
Teachers: 145.0 (19.6 to 1)
Librarians/Media Specialists: 0.0 (0.0 to 1)
Guidance Counselors: 1.0 (2,849.0 to 1)
Current Spending: ($ per student per year):
Total: $6,986; Instruction: $4,110; Support Services: $2,587

Enrollment, Drop-out Rates and Diploma Recipients by Race/Ethnicity

Category	Total	White	Black	Asian	AIAN	Hisp.
Enrollment (%)	100.0	8.3	5.2	20.4	0.0	65.6
Drop-out Rate (%)	n/a	n/a	n/a	n/a	n/a	n/a
H.S. Diplomas (#)	n/a	n/a	n/a	n/a	n/a	n/a

Mountain View-Los Altos Union High

1299 Bryant Ave • Mountain View, CA 94040-4527
(650) 940-4650 • http://www.mvla.k12.ca.us/
Grade Span: 09-12; **Agency Type:** 1
Schools: 5
0 Primary; 0 Middle; 5 High; 0 Other Level
3 Regular; 0 Special Education; 0 Vocational; 2 Alternative
0 Magnet; 1 Charter; 4 Title I Eligible; 0 School-wide Title I
Students: 3,263 (51.3% male; 48.7% female)
Individual Education Program: 271 (8.3%);
English Language Learner: 250 (7.7%); Migrant: 16 (0.5%)
Eligible for Free Lunch Program: 309 (9.5%)
Eligible for Reduced-Price Lunch Program: 71 (2.2%)
Teachers: 155.5 (21.0 to 1)
Librarians/Media Specialists: 2.0 (1,631.5 to 1)
Guidance Counselors: 8.2 (397.9 to 1)
Current Spending: ($ per student per year):
Total: $9,647; Instruction: $5,496; Support Services: $3,941

Enrollment, Drop-out Rates and Diploma Recipients by Race/Ethnicity

Category	Total	White	Black	Asian	AIAN	Hisp.
Enrollment (%)	100.0	53.7	3.2	20.8	0.5	18.8
Drop-out Rate (%)	n/a	n/a	n/a	n/a	n/a	n/a
H.S. Diplomas (#)	639	357	28	141	1	100

Mountain View-Whisman Elementary

750 A San Pierre Way • Mountain View, CA 94043
(650) 526-3500 • http://www.mvsd.k12.ca.us/index.htm
Grade Span: KG-08; **Agency Type:** 1
Schools: 9
7 Primary; 2 Middle; 0 High; 0 Other Level
9 Regular; 0 Special Education; 0 Vocational; 0 Alternative
0 Magnet; 0 Charter; 4 Title I Eligible; 0 School-wide Title I
Students: 4,486 (50.8% male; 49.2% female)
Individual Education Program: 483 (10.8%);
English Language Learner: 1,714 (38.2%); Migrant: 2 (<0.1%)
Eligible for Free Lunch Program: 1,223 (27.3%)
Eligible for Reduced-Price Lunch Program: 420 (9.4%)
Teachers: 216.8 (20.7 to 1)
Librarians/Media Specialists: 0.0 (0.0 to 1)
Guidance Counselors: 0.3 (14,953.3 to 1)
Current Spending: ($ per student per year):
Total: $6,895; Instruction: $4,298; Support Services: $2,302

Enrollment, Drop-out Rates and Diploma Recipients by Race/Ethnicity

Category	Total	White	Black	Asian	AIAN	Hisp.
Enrollment (%)	100.0	36.7	5.3	17.3	0.3	39.9
Drop-out Rate (%)	n/a	n/a	n/a	n/a	n/a	n/a
H.S. Diplomas (#)	n/a	n/a	n/a	n/a	n/a	n/a

Oak Grove Elementary

6578 Santa Teresa Blvd • San Jose, CA 95119-1204
(408) 227-8300 • http://www.ogsd.k12.ca.us/
Grade Span: KG-08; **Agency Type:** 1
Schools: 22
18 Primary; 4 Middle; 0 High; 0 Other Level
21 Regular; 0 Special Education; 0 Vocational; 1 Alternative
0 Magnet; 0 Charter; 5 Title I Eligible; 5 School-wide Title I
Students: 11,613 (51.5% male; 48.5% female)
Individual Education Program: 1,152 (9.9%);
English Language Learner: 3,100 (26.7%); Migrant: 278 (2.4%)
Eligible for Free Lunch Program: 3,085 (26.6%)
Eligible for Reduced-Price Lunch Program: 1,183 (10.2%)
Teachers: 571.2 (20.3 to 1)
Librarians/Media Specialists: 0.5 (23,226.0 to 1)
Guidance Counselors: 7.2 (1,612.9 to 1)
Current Spending: ($ per student per year):
Total: $6,640; Instruction: $4,372; Support Services: $2,029

Enrollment, Drop-out Rates and Diploma Recipients by Race/Ethnicity

Category	Total	White	Black	Asian	AIAN	Hisp.
Enrollment (%)	100.0	30.6	6.0	21.4	0.6	35.8
Drop-out Rate (%)	n/a	n/a	n/a	n/a	n/a	n/a
H.S. Diplomas (#)	n/a	n/a	n/a	n/a	n/a	n/a

Palo Alto Unified

25 Churchill Ave • Palo Alto, CA 94306-1005
(650) 329-3700 • http://www.pausd.palo-alto.ca.us/
Grade Span: KG-12; **Agency Type:** 1
Schools: 19
13 Primary; 3 Middle; 2 High; 1 Other Level
18 Regular; 0 Special Education; 0 Vocational; 1 Alternative
0 Magnet; 0 Charter; 3 Title I Eligible; 0 School-wide Title I
Students: 10,129 (51.5% male; 48.5% female)
Individual Education Program: 1,159 (11.4%);
English Language Learner: 724 (7.1%); Migrant: 0 (0.0%)
Eligible for Free Lunch Program: 380 (3.8%)
Eligible for Reduced-Price Lunch Program: 205 (2.0%)
Teachers: 619.2 (16.4 to 1)
Librarians/Media Specialists: 12.5 (810.3 to 1)
Guidance Counselors: 12.9 (785.2 to 1)
Current Spending: ($ per student per year):
Total: $9,077; Instruction: $6,069; Support Services: $2,838

Enrollment, Drop-out Rates and Diploma Recipients by Race/Ethnicity

Category	Total	White	Black	Asian	AIAN	Hisp.
Enrollment (%)	100.0	64.0	4.1	21.7	0.2	7.5
Drop-out Rate (%)	n/a	n/a	n/a	n/a	n/a	n/a
H.S. Diplomas (#)	709	486	19	166	3	35

San Jose Unified

855 Lenzen Ave • San Jose, CA 95126-2736
(408) 535-6000 • http://www.sjusd.k12.ca.us/
Grade Span: KG-12; **Agency Type:** 1
Schools: 57
32 Primary; 7 Middle; 17 High; 1 Other Level
46 Regular; 0 Special Education; 0 Vocational; 11 Alternative
5 Magnet; 1 Charter; 22 Title I Eligible; 11 School-wide Title I
Students: 32,612 (50.8% male; 49.2% female)
Individual Education Program: 3,685 (11.3%);
English Language Learner: 8,565 (26.3%); Migrant: 1,336 (4.1%)
Eligible for Free Lunch Program: 10,209 (31.3%)
Eligible for Reduced-Price Lunch Program: 3,249 (10.0%)
Teachers: 1,755.8 (18.6 to 1)
Librarians/Media Specialists: 32.0 (1,019.1 to 1)
Guidance Counselors: 26.4 (1,235.3 to 1)
Current Spending: ($ per student per year):
Total: $7,463; Instruction: $4,771; Support Services: $2,455

Enrollment, Drop-out Rates and Diploma Recipients by Race/Ethnicity

Category	Total	White	Black	Asian	AIAN	Hisp.
Enrollment (%)	100.0	29.1	3.5	15.1	1.7	50.4
Drop-out Rate (%)	n/a	n/a	n/a	n/a	n/a	n/a
H.S. Diplomas (#)	1,740	632	57	387	20	644

Santa Clara County Office of Ed

1290 Ridder Park Dr • San Jose, CA 95131-2398
(408) 453-6500 • http://www.sccoe.k12.ca.us/
Grade Span: KG-12; **Agency Type:** 4
Schools: 5
0 Primary; 0 Middle; 2 High; 3 Other Level
0 Regular; 1 Special Education; 0 Vocational; 4 Alternative

0 Magnet; 0 Charter; 0 Title I Eligible; 0 School-wide Title I
Students: 2,240 (69.0% male; 31.0% female)
Individual Education Program: 2,048 (91.4%);
English Language Learner: 270 (12.1%); Migrant: 3 (0.1%)
Eligible for Free Lunch Program: 121 (5.4%)
Eligible for Reduced-Price Lunch Program: 23 (1.0%)
Teachers: 243.0 (9.2 to 1)
Librarians/Media Specialists: 1.0 (2,240.0 to 1)
Guidance Counselors: 5.0 (448.0 to 1)
Current Spending: ($ per student per year):
Total: $34,409; Instruction: $21,852; Support Services: $12,261
Enrollment, Drop-out Rates and Diploma Recipients by Race/Ethnicity

Category	Total	White	Black	Asian	AIAN	Hisp.
Enrollment (%)	100.0	27.1	5.4	18.7	0.4	45.4
Drop-out Rate (%)	n/a	n/a	n/a	n/a	n/a	n/a
H.S. Diplomas (#)	128	29	12	26	5	50

Santa Clara Unified
1889 Lawrence Rd • Santa Clara, CA 95052-0397
Mailing Address: PO Box 397 • Santa Clara, CA 95052-0397
(408) 423-2000 • http://www.scu.k12.ca.us/
Grade Span: KG-12; **Agency Type:** 1
Schools: 23
16 Primary; 3 Middle; 3 High; 1 Other Level
21 Regular; 0 Special Education; 0 Vocational; 2 Alternative
0 Magnet; 0 Charter; 7 Title I Eligible; 0 School-wide Title I
Students: 13,623 (51.5% male; 48.5% female)
Individual Education Program: 1,591 (11.7%);
English Language Learner: 3,038 (22.3%); Migrant: 733 (5.4%)
Eligible for Free Lunch Program: 3,545 (26.0%)
Eligible for Reduced-Price Lunch Program: 1,671 (12.3%)
Teachers: 679.5 (20.0 to 1)
Librarians/Media Specialists: 7.0 (1,946.1 to 1)
Guidance Counselors: 14.0 (973.1 to 1)
Current Spending: ($ per student per year):
Total: $7,162; Instruction: $4,661; Support Services: $2,243
Enrollment, Drop-out Rates and Diploma Recipients by Race/Ethnicity

Category	Total	White	Black	Asian	AIAN	Hisp.
Enrollment (%)	100.0	37.1	4.3	29.7	0.9	26.6
Drop-out Rate (%)	n/a	n/a	n/a	n/a	n/a	n/a
H.S. Diplomas (#)	804	339	34	257	5	169

Saratoga Union Elementary
20460 Forrest Hills Dr • Saratoga, CA 95070-6020
(408) 867-3424 • http://www.susd.k12.ca.us/
Grade Span: KG-08; **Agency Type:** 1
Schools: 4
3 Primary; 1 Middle; 0 High; 0 Other Level
4 Regular; 0 Special Education; 0 Vocational; 0 Alternative
0 Magnet; 0 Charter; 0 Title I Eligible; 0 School-wide Title I
Students: 2,417 (51.9% male; 48.1% female)
Individual Education Program: 205 (8.5%);
English Language Learner: 48 (2.0%); Migrant: 0 (0.0%)
Eligible for Free Lunch Program: 11 (0.5%)
Eligible for Reduced-Price Lunch Program: 2 (0.1%)
Teachers: 130.7 (18.5 to 1)
Librarians/Media Specialists: 1.0 (2,417.0 to 1)
Guidance Counselors: 1.8 (1,342.8 to 1)
Current Spending: ($ per student per year):
Total: $6,454; Instruction: $4,318; Support Services: $1,995
Enrollment, Drop-out Rates and Diploma Recipients by Race/Ethnicity

Category	Total	White	Black	Asian	AIAN	Hisp.
Enrollment (%)	100.0	51.2	0.1	41.7	0.1	2.7
Drop-out Rate (%)	n/a	n/a	n/a	n/a	n/a	n/a
H.S. Diplomas (#)	n/a	n/a	n/a	n/a	n/a	n/a

Sunnyvale Elementary
819 W Iowa Ave • Sunnyvale, CA 94088-3217
Mailing Address: PO Box 3217 • Sunnyvale, CA 94088-3217
(408) 522-8200 • http://www.sesd.org/index.html
Grade Span: KG-08; **Agency Type:** 1
Schools: 11
8 Primary; 3 Middle; 0 High; 0 Other Level
10 Regular; 0 Special Education; 0 Vocational; 1 Alternative
0 Magnet; 0 Charter; 7 Title I Eligible; 0 School-wide Title I
Students: 5,931 (51.4% male; 48.6% female)
Individual Education Program: 565 (9.5%);
English Language Learner: 1,875 (31.6%); Migrant: 34 (0.6%)
Eligible for Free Lunch Program: 1,509 (25.4%)
Eligible for Reduced-Price Lunch Program: 649 (10.9%)
Teachers: 304.0 (19.5 to 1)
Librarians/Media Specialists: 1.0 (5,931.0 to 1)
Guidance Counselors: 0.0 (0.0 to 1)
Current Spending: ($ per student per year):
Total: $7,086; Instruction: $4,644; Support Services: $2,173

Enrollment, Drop-out Rates and Diploma Recipients by Race/Ethnicity

Category	Total	White	Black	Asian	AIAN	Hisp.
Enrollment (%)	100.0	25.3	3.6	30.4	0.9	38.8
Drop-out Rate (%)	n/a	n/a	n/a	n/a	n/a	n/a
H.S. Diplomas (#)	n/a	n/a	n/a	n/a	n/a	n/a

Union Elementary
5175 Union Ave • San Jose, CA 95124-5434
(408) 377-8010 • http://www.unionsd.k12.ca.us/
Grade Span: KG-08; **Agency Type:** 1
Schools: 10
8 Primary; 2 Middle; 0 High; 0 Other Level
10 Regular; 0 Special Education; 0 Vocational; 0 Alternative
0 Magnet; 0 Charter; 3 Title I Eligible; 0 School-wide Title I
Students: 4,637 (51.5% male; 48.5% female)
Individual Education Program: 533 (11.5%);
English Language Learner: 261 (5.6%); Migrant: 0 (0.0%)
Eligible for Free Lunch Program: 445 (9.6%)
Eligible for Reduced-Price Lunch Program: 167 (3.6%)
Teachers: 229.1 (20.2 to 1)
Librarians/Media Specialists: 0.0 (0.0 to 1)
Guidance Counselors: 2.0 (2,318.5 to 1)
Current Spending: ($ per student per year):
Total: $6,411; Instruction: $4,296; Support Services: $1,934
Enrollment, Drop-out Rates and Diploma Recipients by Race/Ethnicity

Category	Total	White	Black	Asian	AIAN	Hisp.
Enrollment (%)	100.0	71.5	2.7	11.4	0.6	12.7
Drop-out Rate (%)	n/a	n/a	n/a	n/a	n/a	n/a
H.S. Diplomas (#)	n/a	n/a	n/a	n/a	n/a	n/a

Santa Cruz County

Live Oak Elementary
984-1 Bostwick Ln • Santa Cruz, CA 95062-1756
(831) 475-6333 • http://www.lodo.santacruz.k12.ca.us/
Grade Span: KG-08; **Agency Type:** 1
Schools: 5
4 Primary; 1 Middle; 0 High; 0 Other Level
5 Regular; 0 Special Education; 0 Vocational; 0 Alternative
0 Magnet; 0 Charter; 4 Title I Eligible; 0 School-wide Title I
Students: 1,948 (51.8% male; 48.2% female)
Individual Education Program: 295 (15.1%);
English Language Learner: 540 (27.7%); Migrant: 35 (1.8%)
Eligible for Free Lunch Program: 535 (27.5%)
Eligible for Reduced-Price Lunch Program: 227 (11.7%)
Teachers: 97.9 (19.9 to 1)
Librarians/Media Specialists: 0.3 (6,493.3 to 1)
Guidance Counselors: 2.5 (779.2 to 1)
Current Spending: ($ per student per year):
Total: $6,987; Instruction: $4,231; Support Services: $2,524
Enrollment, Drop-out Rates and Diploma Recipients by Race/Ethnicity

Category	Total	White	Black	Asian	AIAN	Hisp.
Enrollment (%)	100.0	51.3	3.1	3.6	0.9	38.9
Drop-out Rate (%)	n/a	n/a	n/a	n/a	n/a	n/a
H.S. Diplomas (#)	n/a	n/a	n/a	n/a	n/a	n/a

Pajaro Valley Unified School
294 Green Valley Rd • Watsonville, CA 95076
Mailing Address: PO Box 50010 • Watsonville, CA 95077-5010
(831) 786-2100 • http://www.pvusd.santacruz.k12.ca.us/
Grade Span: KG-12; **Agency Type:** 1
Schools: 30
19 Primary; 5 Middle; 5 High; 1 Other Level
26 Regular; 0 Special Education; 0 Vocational; 4 Alternative
0 Magnet; 5 Charter; 18 Title I Eligible; 11 School-wide Title I
Students: 19,661 (50.7% male; 49.3% female)
Individual Education Program: 2,271 (11.6%);
English Language Learner: 9,116 (46.4%); Migrant: 8,654 (44.0%)
Eligible for Free Lunch Program: 9,175 (46.7%)
Eligible for Reduced-Price Lunch Program: 1,962 (10.0%)
Teachers: 1,082.9 (18.2 to 1)
Librarians/Media Specialists: 0.0 (0.0 to 1)
Guidance Counselors: 18.5 (1,062.8 to 1)
Current Spending: ($ per student per year):
Total: $7,245; Instruction: $4,253; Support Services: $2,706
Enrollment, Drop-out Rates and Diploma Recipients by Race/Ethnicity

Category	Total	White	Black	Asian	AIAN	Hisp.
Enrollment (%)	100.0	21.1	0.5	2.1	0.3	75.8
Drop-out Rate (%)	n/a	n/a	n/a	n/a	n/a	n/a
H.S. Diplomas (#)	1,009	309	3	32	5	656

San Lorenzo Valley Unified

6134 Hwy 9 • Felton, CA 95018-9704
(831) 335-7488 • http://www.slvdo.santacruz.k12.ca.us/index.html
Grade Span: KG-12; **Agency Type:** 1
Schools: 9
5 Primary; 1 Middle; 2 High; 1 Other Level
7 Regular; 0 Special Education; 0 Vocational; 2 Alternative
0 Magnet; 2 Charter; 4 Title I Eligible; 0 School-wide Title I
Students: 3,869 (51.3% male; 48.7% female)
Individual Education Program: 490 (12.7%);
English Language Learner: 36 (0.9%); Migrant: 0 (0.0%)
Eligible for Free Lunch Program: 313 (8.1%)
Eligible for Reduced-Price Lunch Program: 154 (4.0%)
Teachers: 182.6 (21.2 to 1)
Librarians/Media Specialists: 0.0 (0.0 to 1)
Guidance Counselors: 3.2 (1,209.1 to 1)
Current Spending: ($ per student per year):
Total: $6,758; Instruction: $4,464; Support Services: $2,116
Enrollment, Drop-out Rates and Diploma Recipients by Race/Ethnicity

Category	Total	White	Black	Asian	AIAN	Hisp.
Enrollment (%)	100.0	87.3	1.7	2.5	1.0	5.7
Drop-out Rate (%)	n/a	n/a	n/a	n/a	n/a	n/a
H.S. Diplomas (#)	303	274	3	8	4	14

Santa Cruz City Elementary

2931 Mission St • Santa Cruz, CA 95060-5709
(831) 429-3800 • http://www.sccs.santacruz.k12.ca.us/
Grade Span: KG-08; **Agency Type:** 2
Schools: 7
7 Primary; 0 Middle; 0 High; 0 Other Level
6 Regular; 0 Special Education; 0 Vocational; 1 Alternative
0 Magnet; 0 Charter; 3 Title I Eligible; 0 School-wide Title I
Students: 2,636 (52.7% male; 47.3% female)
Individual Education Program: 485 (18.4%);
English Language Learner: 650 (24.7%); Migrant: 74 (2.8%)
Eligible for Free Lunch Program: 787 (29.9%)
Eligible for Reduced-Price Lunch Program: 250 (9.5%)
Teachers: 140.3 (18.8 to 1)
Librarians/Media Specialists: 6.0 (439.3 to 1)
Guidance Counselors: 0.0 (0.0 to 1)
Current Spending: ($ per student per year):
Total: $7,049; Instruction: $3,952; Support Services: $2,718
Enrollment, Drop-out Rates and Diploma Recipients by Race/Ethnicity

Category	Total	White	Black	Asian	AIAN	Hisp.
Enrollment (%)	100.0	52.7	2.2	4.4	0.3	34.5
Drop-out Rate (%)	n/a	n/a	n/a	n/a	n/a	n/a
H.S. Diplomas (#)	n/a	n/a	n/a	n/a	n/a	n/a

Santa Cruz City High

2931 Mission St • Santa Cruz, CA 95060-5709
(831) 429-3800 • http://www.sccs.santacruz.k12.ca.us/
Grade Span: KG-12; **Agency Type:** 2
Schools: 10
0 Primary; 3 Middle; 6 High; 1 Other Level
7 Regular; 0 Special Education; 0 Vocational; 3 Alternative
0 Magnet; 2 Charter; 6 Title I Eligible; 0 School-wide Title I
Students: 5,157 (53.2% male; 46.8% female)
Individual Education Program: 586 (11.4%);
English Language Learner: 369 (7.2%); Migrant: 49 (1.0%)
Eligible for Free Lunch Program: 562 (10.9%)
Eligible for Reduced-Price Lunch Program: 152 (2.9%)
Teachers: 215.7 (23.9 to 1)
Librarians/Media Specialists: 5.0 (1,031.4 to 1)
Guidance Counselors: 12.2 (422.7 to 1)
Current Spending: ($ per student per year):
Total: n/a; Instruction: n/a; Support Services: n/a
Enrollment, Drop-out Rates and Diploma Recipients by Race/Ethnicity

Category	Total	White	Black	Asian	AIAN	Hisp.
Enrollment (%)	100.0	68.0	2.1	4.5	0.6	20.5
Drop-out Rate (%)	n/a	n/a	n/a	n/a	n/a	n/a
H.S. Diplomas (#)	1,051	804	31	54	3	151

Scotts Valley Unified

4444 Scotts Valley Dr, Ste 5B • Scotts Valley, CA 95066-4529
(831) 438-1820 • http://www.svusd.santacruz.k12.ca.us/
Grade Span: KG-12; **Agency Type:** 1
Schools: 4
2 Primary; 1 Middle; 1 High; 0 Other Level
4 Regular; 0 Special Education; 0 Vocational; 0 Alternative
0 Magnet; 0 Charter; 1 Title I Eligible; 0 School-wide Title I
Students: 2,713 (51.0% male; 49.0% female)
Individual Education Program: 234 (8.6%);
English Language Learner: 43 (1.6%); Migrant: 0 (0.0%)
Eligible for Free Lunch Program: 88 (3.2%)
Eligible for Reduced-Price Lunch Program: 34 (1.3%)
Teachers: 130.9 (20.7 to 1)
Librarians/Media Specialists: 0.0 (0.0 to 1)
Guidance Counselors: 4.6 (589.8 to 1)
Current Spending: ($ per student per year):
Total: $5,997; Instruction: $4,185; Support Services: $1,685
Enrollment, Drop-out Rates and Diploma Recipients by Race/Ethnicity

Category	Total	White	Black	Asian	AIAN	Hisp.
Enrollment (%)	100.0	86.7	1.0	5.9	0.5	5.6
Drop-out Rate (%)	n/a	n/a	n/a	n/a	n/a	n/a
H.S. Diplomas (#)	0	0	0	0	0	0

Soquel Union Elementary

620 Monterey Ave • Capitola, CA 95010-3618
(831) 464-5630 • http://www.soqueldo.santacruz.k12.ca.us/
Grade Span: KG-08; **Agency Type:** 1
Schools: 5
5 Primary; 0 Middle; 0 High; 0 Other Level
5 Regular; 0 Special Education; 0 Vocational; 0 Alternative
0 Magnet; 0 Charter; 3 Title I Eligible; 0 School-wide Title I
Students: 2,112 (51.4% male; 48.6% female)
Individual Education Program: 225 (10.7%);
English Language Learner: 212 (10.0%); Migrant: 0 (0.0%)
Eligible for Free Lunch Program: 378 (17.9%)
Eligible for Reduced-Price Lunch Program: 171 (8.1%)
Teachers: 106.7 (19.8 to 1)
Librarians/Media Specialists: 0.0 (0.0 to 1)
Guidance Counselors: 1.0 (2,112.0 to 1)
Current Spending: ($ per student per year):
Total: $6,720; Instruction: $4,410; Support Services: $2,080
Enrollment, Drop-out Rates and Diploma Recipients by Race/Ethnicity

Category	Total	White	Black	Asian	AIAN	Hisp.
Enrollment (%)	100.0	69.8	2.5	3.9	0.5	23.0
Drop-out Rate (%)	n/a	n/a	n/a	n/a	n/a	n/a
H.S. Diplomas (#)	n/a	n/a	n/a	n/a	n/a	n/a

Shasta County

Anderson Union High

1469 Ferry St • Anderson, CA 96007-3313
(530) 378-0568 • http://forest.anderson.k12.ca.us/
Grade Span: 09-12; **Agency Type:** 1
Schools: 6
0 Primary; 0 Middle; 6 High; 0 Other Level
3 Regular; 0 Special Education; 0 Vocational; 3 Alternative
0 Magnet; 1 Charter; 4 Title I Eligible; 0 School-wide Title I
Students: 2,458 (50.2% male; 49.8% female)
Individual Education Program: 185 (7.5%);
English Language Learner: 17 (0.7%); Migrant: 11 (0.4%)
Eligible for Free Lunch Program: 753 (30.6%)
Eligible for Reduced-Price Lunch Program: 497 (20.2%)
Teachers: 109.1 (22.5 to 1)
Librarians/Media Specialists: 2.0 (1,229.0 to 1)
Guidance Counselors: 7.0 (351.1 to 1)
Current Spending: ($ per student per year):
Total: $6,379; Instruction: $3,706; Support Services: $2,425
Enrollment, Drop-out Rates and Diploma Recipients by Race/Ethnicity

Category	Total	White	Black	Asian	AIAN	Hisp.
Enrollment (%)	100.0	82.1	0.7	2.9	6.3	8.0
Drop-out Rate (%)	n/a	n/a	n/a	n/a	n/a	n/a
H.S. Diplomas (#)	475	409	3	16	21	26

Cascade Union Elementary

1645 W Mill St • Anderson, CA 96007-3226
(530) 378-7000 • http://www.shastalink.k12.ca.us/cascade
Grade Span: KG-08; **Agency Type:** 1
Schools: 5
3 Primary; 2 Middle; 0 High; 0 Other Level
4 Regular; 0 Special Education; 0 Vocational; 1 Alternative
0 Magnet; 0 Charter; 5 Title I Eligible; 2 School-wide Title I
Students: 1,604 (55.4% male; 44.6% female)
Individual Education Program: 190 (11.8%);
English Language Learner: 47 (2.9%); Migrant: 23 (1.4%)
Eligible for Free Lunch Program: 924 (57.6%)
Eligible for Reduced-Price Lunch Program: 265 (16.5%)
Teachers: 84.0 (19.1 to 1)
Librarians/Media Specialists: 0.0 (0.0 to 1)
Guidance Counselors: 1.0 (1,604.0 to 1)
Current Spending: ($ per student per year):
Total: $7,355; Instruction: $4,532; Support Services: $2,404
Enrollment, Drop-out Rates and Diploma Recipients by Race/Ethnicity

Category	Total	White	Black	Asian	AIAN	Hisp.
Enrollment (%)	100.0	71.8	2.2	2.6	13.1	8.7
Drop-out Rate (%)	n/a	n/a	n/a	n/a	n/a	n/a
H.S. Diplomas (#)	n/a	n/a	n/a	n/a	n/a	n/a

Enterprise Elementary

1155 Mistletoe Ln • Redding, CA 96002-0749
(530) 224-4100 • http://www.enterprise.k12.ca.us/
Grade Span: KG-10; **Agency Type:** 1
Schools: 9
7 Primary; 1 Middle; 0 High; 1 Other Level
8 Regular; 0 Special Education; 0 Vocational; 1 Alternative
0 Magnet; 1 Charter; 8 Title I Eligible; 5 School-wide Title I
Students: 3,814 (51.7% male; 48.3% female)
Individual Education Program: 360 (9.4%);
English Language Learner: 358 (9.4%); Migrant: 25 (0.7%)
Eligible for Free Lunch Program: 1,598 (41.9%)
Eligible for Reduced-Price Lunch Program: 611 (16.0%)
Teachers: 197.9 (19.3 to 1)
Librarians/Media Specialists: 1.0 (3,814.0 to 1)
Guidance Counselors: 1.0 (3,814.0 to 1)
Current Spending: ($ per student per year):
Total: $6,600; Instruction: $4,509; Support Services: $1,788
Enrollment, Drop-out Rates and Diploma Recipients by Race/Ethnicity

Category	Total	White	Black	Asian	AIAN	Hisp.
Enrollment (%)	100.0	75.5	2.9	8.2	3.9	7.5
Drop-out Rate (%)	n/a	n/a	n/a	n/a	n/a	n/a
H.S. Diplomas (#)	n/a	n/a	n/a	n/a	n/a	n/a

Gateway Unified

4411 Mountain Lakes Blvd • Redding, CA 96003-1446
(530) 245-7900 • http://www.gsd.k12.ca.us/
Grade Span: KG-12; **Agency Type:** 1
Schools: 11
5 Primary; 2 Middle; 3 High; 1 Other Level
8 Regular; 0 Special Education; 0 Vocational; 3 Alternative
0 Magnet; 1 Charter; 6 Title I Eligible; 4 School-wide Title I
Students: 3,738 (52.7% male; 47.3% female)
Individual Education Program: 416 (11.1%);
English Language Learner: 144 (3.9%); Migrant: 10 (0.3%)
Eligible for Free Lunch Program: 1,610 (43.1%)
Eligible for Reduced-Price Lunch Program: 381 (10.2%)
Teachers: 198.7 (18.8 to 1)
Librarians/Media Specialists: 1.0 (3,738.0 to 1)
Guidance Counselors: 3.0 (1,246.0 to 1)
Current Spending: ($ per student per year):
Total: $7,040; Instruction: $4,395; Support Services: $2,342
Enrollment, Drop-out Rates and Diploma Recipients by Race/Ethnicity

Category	Total	White	Black	Asian	AIAN	Hisp.
Enrollment (%)	100.0	79.3	1.2	3.4	10.0	5.9
Drop-out Rate (%)	n/a	n/a	n/a	n/a	n/a	n/a
H.S. Diplomas (#)	259	206	1	4	28	20

Redding Elementary

5885 E Bonnyview Rd • Redding, CA 96099-2418
Mailing Address: PO Box 992418 • Redding, CA 96099-2418
(530) 225-0011 • http://redding.echalk.com/
Grade Span: KG-12; **Agency Type:** 1
Schools: 15
10 Primary; 1 Middle; 2 High; 2 Other Level
14 Regular; 0 Special Education; 0 Vocational; 1 Alternative
0 Magnet; 7 Charter; 7 Title I Eligible; 5 School-wide Title I
Students: 4,126 (52.3% male; 47.7% female)
Individual Education Program: 369 (8.9%);
English Language Learner: 94 (2.3%); Migrant: 8 (0.2%)
Eligible for Free Lunch Program: 1,382 (33.5%)
Eligible for Reduced-Price Lunch Program: 412 (10.0%)
Teachers: 203.2 (20.3 to 1)
Librarians/Media Specialists: 0.0 (0.0 to 1)
Guidance Counselors: 3.0 (1,375.3 to 1)
Current Spending: ($ per student per year):
Total: $6,182; Instruction: $3,994; Support Services: $1,865
Enrollment, Drop-out Rates and Diploma Recipients by Race/Ethnicity

Category	Total	White	Black	Asian	AIAN	Hisp.
Enrollment (%)	100.0	83.8	2.5	4.1	3.8	5.5
Drop-out Rate (%)	n/a	n/a	n/a	n/a	n/a	n/a
H.S. Diplomas (#)	3	3	0	0	0	0

Shasta Union High

2200 Eureka Way Ste B • Redding, CA 96001-1012
(530) 241-3261 • http://www.suhsd.net/
Grade Span: KG-12; **Agency Type:** 1
Schools: 11
1 Primary; 0 Middle; 9 High; 1 Other Level
5 Regular; 0 Special Education; 0 Vocational; 6 Alternative
0 Magnet; 2 Charter; 2 Title I Eligible; 0 School-wide Title I
Students: 5,748 (50.8% male; 49.2% female)
Individual Education Program: 417 (7.3%);
English Language Learner: 75 (1.3%); Migrant: 25 (0.4%)
Eligible for Free Lunch Program: 631 (11.0%)
Eligible for Reduced-Price Lunch Program: 183 (3.2%)
Teachers: 253.8 (22.6 to 1)
Librarians/Media Specialists: 1.0 (5,748.0 to 1)
Guidance Counselors: 14.8 (388.4 to 1)
Current Spending: ($ per student per year):
Total: $6,232; Instruction: $3,785; Support Services: $2,247
Enrollment, Drop-out Rates and Diploma Recipients by Race/Ethnicity

Category	Total	White	Black	Asian	AIAN	Hisp.
Enrollment (%)	100.0	84.0	1.3	6.0	3.2	4.5
Drop-out Rate (%)	n/a	n/a	n/a	n/a	n/a	n/a
H.S. Diplomas (#)	1,055	893	13	62	39	47

Solano County

Benicia Unified

350 E K St • Benicia, CA 94510-3437
(707) 747-8300 • http://www.benicia.k12.ca.us/
Grade Span: KG-12; **Agency Type:** 1
Schools: 9
5 Primary; 1 Middle; 2 High; 1 Other Level
7 Regular; 0 Special Education; 0 Vocational; 2 Alternative
0 Magnet; 0 Charter; 4 Title I Eligible; 0 School-wide Title I
Students: 5,423 (51.7% male; 48.3% female)
Individual Education Program: 573 (10.6%);
English Language Learner: 100 (1.8%); Migrant: 0 (0.0%)
Eligible for Free Lunch Program: 353 (6.5%)
Eligible for Reduced-Price Lunch Program: 188 (3.5%)
Teachers: 273.3 (19.8 to 1)
Librarians/Media Specialists: 0.0 (0.0 to 1)
Guidance Counselors: 5.8 (935.0 to 1)
Current Spending: ($ per student per year):
Total: $6,282; Instruction: $4,186; Support Services: $1,911
Enrollment, Drop-out Rates and Diploma Recipients by Race/Ethnicity

Category	Total	White	Black	Asian	AIAN	Hisp.
Enrollment (%)	100.0	68.8	8.0	12.2	0.7	10.3
Drop-out Rate (%)	n/a	n/a	n/a	n/a	n/a	n/a
H.S. Diplomas (#)	416	285	24	53	3	50

Dixon Unified

305 N Almond St • Dixon, CA 95620-2702
(707) 678-5582 • http://www.dixonusd.org/
Grade Span: KG-12; **Agency Type:** 1
Schools: 7
4 Primary; 1 Middle; 2 High; 0 Other Level
6 Regular; 0 Special Education; 0 Vocational; 1 Alternative
0 Magnet; 0 Charter; 2 Title I Eligible; 0 School-wide Title I
Students: 3,933 (51.8% male; 48.2% female)
Individual Education Program: 441 (11.2%);
English Language Learner: 747 (19.0%); Migrant: 669 (17.0%)
Eligible for Free Lunch Program: 1,171 (29.8%)
Eligible for Reduced-Price Lunch Program: 405 (10.3%)
Teachers: 201.7 (19.5 to 1)
Librarians/Media Specialists: 0.8 (4,916.3 to 1)
Guidance Counselors: 6.1 (644.8 to 1)
Current Spending: ($ per student per year):
Total: $5,970; Instruction: $4,006; Support Services: $1,760
Enrollment, Drop-out Rates and Diploma Recipients by Race/Ethnicity

Category	Total	White	Black	Asian	AIAN	Hisp.
Enrollment (%)	100.0	47.9	2.9	3.1	0.6	44.6
Drop-out Rate (%)	n/a	n/a	n/a	n/a	n/a	n/a
H.S. Diplomas (#)	200	108	10	7	1	74

Fairfield-Suisun Unified

1975 Pennsylvania Ave • Fairfield, CA 94533-3643
(707) 399-5000 • http://www.fsusd.k12.ca.us/
Grade Span: KG-12; **Agency Type:** 1
Schools: 28
18 Primary; 5 Middle; 5 High; 0 Other Level
25 Regular; 0 Special Education; 0 Vocational; 3 Alternative
0 Magnet; 0 Charter; 9 Title I Eligible; 5 School-wide Title I
Students: 22,972 (50.7% male; 49.3% female)
Individual Education Program: 2,569 (11.2%);
English Language Learner: 2,864 (12.5%); Migrant: 288 (1.3%)
Eligible for Free Lunch Program: 5,908 (25.7%)
Eligible for Reduced-Price Lunch Program: 1,952 (8.5%)
Teachers: 1,119.5 (20.5 to 1)
Librarians/Media Specialists: 9.9 (2,320.4 to 1)
Guidance Counselors: 20.7 (1,109.8 to 1)
Current Spending: ($ per student per year):
Total: $5,827; Instruction: $3,675; Support Services: $1,969
Enrollment, Drop-out Rates and Diploma Recipients by Race/Ethnicity

Category	Total	White	Black	Asian	AIAN	Hisp.
Enrollment (%)	100.0	36.2	22.2	15.6	1.0	25.0
Drop-out Rate (%)	n/a	n/a	n/a	n/a	n/a	n/a
H.S. Diplomas (#)	1,106	470	225	232	10	169

Travis Unified

2751 De Ronde Dr • Travis Afb, CA 94533-9710
(707) 437-4604 • http://www.travisusd.k12.ca.us/
Grade Span: KG-12; **Agency Type:** 1
Schools: 10
5 Primary; 1 Middle; 3 High; 1 Other Level
7 Regular; 0 Special Education; 0 Vocational; 3 Alternative
3 Magnet; 0 Charter; 3 Title I Eligible; 0 School-wide Title I
Students: 5,363 (51.5% male; 48.5% female)
Individual Education Program: 584 (10.9%);
English Language Learner: 173 (3.2%); Migrant: 1 (<0.1%)
Eligible for Free Lunch Program: 467 (8.7%)
Eligible for Reduced-Price Lunch Program: 644 (12.0%)
Teachers: 292.8 (18.3 to 1)
Librarians/Media Specialists: 3.8 (1,411.3 to 1)
Guidance Counselors: 6.0 (893.8 to 1)
Current Spending: ($ per student per year):
Total: $6,780; Instruction: $4,233; Support Services: $2,354
Enrollment, Drop-out Rates and Diploma Recipients by Race/Ethnicity

Category	Total	White	Black	Asian	AIAN	Hisp.
Enrollment (%)	100.0	55.0	16.9	13.6	1.2	12.5
Drop-out Rate (%)	n/a	n/a	n/a	n/a	n/a	n/a
H.S. Diplomas (#)	292	146	64	42	0	40

Vacaville Unified

751 School St • Vacaville, CA 95688-3945
(707) 453-6100 • http://www.vusd.solanocoe.k12.ca.us/
Grade Span: KG-12; **Agency Type:** 1
Schools: 19
13 Primary; 2 Middle; 3 High; 1 Other Level
17 Regular; 0 Special Education; 0 Vocational; 2 Alternative
0 Magnet; 1 Charter; 6 Title I Eligible; 2 School-wide Title I
Students: 14,806 (51.3% male; 48.7% female)
Individual Education Program: 1,600 (10.8%);
English Language Learner: 1,341 (9.1%); Migrant: 280 (1.9%)
Eligible for Free Lunch Program: 2,666 (18.0%)
Eligible for Reduced-Price Lunch Program: 1,012 (6.8%)
Teachers: 747.3 (19.8 to 1)
Librarians/Media Specialists: 5.0 (2,961.2 to 1)
Guidance Counselors: 12.4 (1,194.0 to 1)
Current Spending: ($ per student per year):
Total: $6,183; Instruction: $3,867; Support Services: $2,123
Enrollment, Drop-out Rates and Diploma Recipients by Race/Ethnicity

Category	Total	White	Black	Asian	AIAN	Hisp.
Enrollment (%)	100.0	62.0	7.5	7.2	1.2	21.3
Drop-out Rate (%)	n/a	n/a	n/a	n/a	n/a	n/a
H.S. Diplomas (#)	1,035	688	74	72	15	149

Vallejo City Unified

211 Valle Vista • Vallejo, CA 94590-3256
(707) 556-8921 • http://www.vallejo.k12.ca.us/
Grade Span: KG-12; **Agency Type:** 1
Schools: 28
17 Primary; 5 Middle; 5 High; 1 Other Level
26 Regular; 1 Special Education; 0 Vocational; 1 Alternative
0 Magnet; 2 Charter; 15 Title I Eligible; 6 School-wide Title I
Students: 19,872 (51.5% male; 48.5% female)
Individual Education Program: 2,337 (11.8%);
English Language Learner: 2,846 (14.3%); Migrant: 0 (0.0%)
Eligible for Free Lunch Program: 6,213 (31.3%)
Eligible for Reduced-Price Lunch Program: 1,877 (9.4%)
Teachers: 961.8 (20.7 to 1)
Librarians/Media Specialists: 7.0 (2,838.9 to 1)
Guidance Counselors: 26.0 (764.3 to 1)
Current Spending: ($ per student per year):
Total: $6,755; Instruction: $4,297; Support Services: $2,212
Enrollment, Drop-out Rates and Diploma Recipients by Race/Ethnicity

Category	Total	White	Black	Asian	AIAN	Hisp.
Enrollment (%)	100.0	16.4	34.4	25.0	0.6	22.6
Drop-out Rate (%)	n/a	n/a	n/a	n/a	n/a	n/a
H.S. Diplomas (#)	1,099	180	344	405	14	144

Sonoma County

Bellevue Union Elementary

3223 Primrose Ave • Santa Rosa, CA 95407-7723
(707) 542-5197
Grade Span: KG-06; **Agency Type:** 1
Schools: 3
3 Primary; 0 Middle; 0 High; 0 Other Level
3 Regular; 0 Special Education; 0 Vocational; 0 Alternative
0 Magnet; 0 Charter; 3 Title I Eligible; 0 School-wide Title I
Students: 1,699 (49.6% male; 50.4% female)
Individual Education Program: 199 (11.7%);
English Language Learner: 1,059 (62.3%); Migrant: 108 (6.4%)
Eligible for Free Lunch Program: 1,134 (66.7%)
Eligible for Reduced-Price Lunch Program: 277 (16.3%)
Teachers: 92.8 (18.3 to 1)
Librarians/Media Specialists: 0.0 (0.0 to 1)
Guidance Counselors: 0.0 (0.0 to 1)
Current Spending: ($ per student per year):
Total: $7,543; Instruction: $5,445; Support Services: $1,710
Enrollment, Drop-out Rates and Diploma Recipients by Race/Ethnicity

Category	Total	White	Black	Asian	AIAN	Hisp.
Enrollment (%)	100.0	23.1	3.8	6.9	2.1	63.3
Drop-out Rate (%)	n/a	n/a	n/a	n/a	n/a	n/a
H.S. Diplomas (#)	n/a	n/a	n/a	n/a	n/a	n/a

Cloverdale Unified

97 School St • Cloverdale, CA 95425-3244
(707) 894-1920 • http://www.cusd.org/district/schools.html
Grade Span: KG-12; **Agency Type:** 1
Schools: 4
1 Primary; 1 Middle; 2 High; 0 Other Level
3 Regular; 0 Special Education; 0 Vocational; 1 Alternative
0 Magnet; 0 Charter; 2 Title I Eligible; 0 School-wide Title I
Students: 1,597 (52.5% male; 47.5% female)
Individual Education Program: 173 (10.8%);
English Language Learner: 199 (12.5%); Migrant: 281 (17.6%)
Eligible for Free Lunch Program: 513 (32.1%)
Eligible for Reduced-Price Lunch Program: 129 (8.1%)
Teachers: 85.7 (18.6 to 1)
Librarians/Media Specialists: 0.0 (0.0 to 1)
Guidance Counselors: 1.0 (1,597.0 to 1)
Current Spending: ($ per student per year):
Total: $6,396; Instruction: $4,473; Support Services: $1,768
Enrollment, Drop-out Rates and Diploma Recipients by Race/Ethnicity

Category	Total	White	Black	Asian	AIAN	Hisp.
Enrollment (%)	100.0	61.6	0.7	0.6	1.4	35.8
Drop-out Rate (%)	n/a	n/a	n/a	n/a	n/a	n/a
H.S. Diplomas (#)	103	78	0	1	2	22

Cotati-Rohnert Park Unified

1601 E Cotati Ave • Rohnert Park, CA 94928-3606
(707) 792-4722 • http://www.crpusd.sonoma.edu/
Grade Span: KG-12; **Agency Type:** 1
Schools: 15
8 Primary; 3 Middle; 4 High; 0 Other Level
11 Regular; 0 Special Education; 0 Vocational; 4 Alternative
1 Magnet; 0 Charter; 5 Title I Eligible; 1 School-wide Title I
Students: 7,678 (52.2% male; 47.8% female)
Individual Education Program: 895 (11.7%);
English Language Learner: 894 (11.6%); Migrant: 110 (1.4%)
Eligible for Free Lunch Program: 867 (11.3%)
Eligible for Reduced-Price Lunch Program: 487 (6.3%)
Teachers: 344.5 (22.3 to 1)
Librarians/Media Specialists: 2.0 (3,839.0 to 1)
Guidance Counselors: 10.4 (738.3 to 1)
Current Spending: ($ per student per year):
Total: $6,434; Instruction: $4,377; Support Services: $1,854
Enrollment, Drop-out Rates and Diploma Recipients by Race/Ethnicity

Category	Total	White	Black	Asian	AIAN	Hisp.
Enrollment (%)	100.0	68.2	3.3	8.0	1.4	18.3
Drop-out Rate (%)	n/a	n/a	n/a	n/a	n/a	n/a
H.S. Diplomas (#)	487	364	13	39	4	66

Healdsburg Unified

925 University St • Healdsburg, CA 95448-3528
(707) 431-3117 • http://www.husd.com/
Grade Span: KG-12; **Agency Type:** 1
Schools: 6
3 Primary; 1 Middle; 2 High; 0 Other Level
5 Regular; 0 Special Education; 0 Vocational; 1 Alternative
0 Magnet; 0 Charter; 3 Title I Eligible; 0 School-wide Title I
Students: 2,789 (52.1% male; 47.9% female)
Individual Education Program: 180 (6.5%);
English Language Learner: 618 (22.2%); Migrant: 470 (16.9%)
Eligible for Free Lunch Program: 725 (26.0%)
Eligible for Reduced-Price Lunch Program: 220 (7.9%)
Teachers: 137.3 (20.3 to 1)
Librarians/Media Specialists: 0.0 (0.0 to 1)
Guidance Counselors: 6.2 (449.8 to 1)
Current Spending: ($ per student per year):
Total: $6,836; Instruction: $4,307; Support Services: $2,211
Enrollment, Drop-out Rates and Diploma Recipients by Race/Ethnicity

Category	Total	White	Black	Asian	AIAN	Hisp.
Enrollment (%)	100.0	55.1	0.5	0.9	0.6	41.4
Drop-out Rate (%)	n/a	n/a	n/a	n/a	n/a	n/a
H.S. Diplomas (#)	203	148	1	1	2	51

Mark West Union Elementary
305 Mark W Springs Rd • Santa Rosa, CA 95404-1101
(707) 524-2970
Grade Span: KG-06; **Agency Type:** 1
Schools: 3
3 Primary; 0 Middle; 0 High; 0 Other Level
3 Regular; 0 Special Education; 0 Vocational; 0 Alternative
0 Magnet; 0 Charter; 0 Title I Eligible; 0 School-wide Title I
Students: 1,551 (51.4% male; 48.6% female)
Individual Education Program: 145 (9.3%);
English Language Learner: 63 (4.1%); Migrant: 7 (0.5%)
Eligible for Free Lunch Program: 172 (11.1%)
Eligible for Reduced-Price Lunch Program: 83 (5.4%)
Teachers: 80.7 (19.2 to 1)
Librarians/Media Specialists: 0.0 (0.0 to 1)
Guidance Counselors: 1.5 (1,034.0 to 1)
Current Spending: ($ per student per year):
Total: $6,210; Instruction: $4,422; Support Services: $1,659
Enrollment, Drop-out Rates and Diploma Recipients by Race/Ethnicity

Category	Total	White	Black	Asian	AIAN	Hisp.
Enrollment (%)	100.0	78.4	2.5	4.4	1.0	11.2
Drop-out Rate (%)	n/a	n/a	n/a	n/a	n/a	n/a
H.S. Diplomas (#)	n/a	n/a	n/a	n/a	n/a	n/a

Old Adobe Union Elementary
845 Crinella Dr • Petaluma, CA 94954-4450
(707) 765-4321
Grade Span: KG-06; **Agency Type:** 1
Schools: 5
5 Primary; 0 Middle; 0 High; 0 Other Level
5 Regular; 0 Special Education; 0 Vocational; 0 Alternative
0 Magnet; 0 Charter; 2 Title I Eligible; 0 School-wide Title I
Students: 1,976 (50.2% male; 49.8% female)
Individual Education Program: 168 (8.5%);
English Language Learner: 389 (19.7%); Migrant: 46 (2.3%)
Eligible for Free Lunch Program: 265 (13.4%)
Eligible for Reduced-Price Lunch Program: 132 (6.7%)
Teachers: 97.3 (20.3 to 1)
Librarians/Media Specialists: 0.0 (0.0 to 1)
Guidance Counselors: 0.0 (0.0 to 1)
Current Spending: ($ per student per year):
Total: $6,536; Instruction: $4,288; Support Services: $2,091
Enrollment, Drop-out Rates and Diploma Recipients by Race/Ethnicity

Category	Total	White	Black	Asian	AIAN	Hisp.
Enrollment (%)	100.0	70.3	1.6	6.8	0.8	20.5
Drop-out Rate (%)	n/a	n/a	n/a	n/a	n/a	n/a
H.S. Diplomas (#)	n/a	n/a	n/a	n/a	n/a	n/a

Petaluma City Elementary
200 Douglas St • Petaluma, CA 94952-2575
(707) 778-4604 • http://www.petalumacityschools.org/
Grade Span: KG-08; **Agency Type:** 2
Schools: 9
9 Primary; 0 Middle; 0 High; 0 Other Level
8 Regular; 0 Special Education; 0 Vocational; 1 Alternative
0 Magnet; 2 Charter; 3 Title I Eligible; 0 School-wide Title I
Students: 2,268 (50.6% male; 49.4% female)
Individual Education Program: 253 (11.2%);
English Language Learner: 515 (22.7%); Migrant: 54 (2.4%)
Eligible for Free Lunch Program: 443 (19.5%)
Eligible for Reduced-Price Lunch Program: 128 (5.6%)
Teachers: 124.0 (18.3 to 1)
Librarians/Media Specialists: 0.0 (0.0 to 1)
Guidance Counselors: 0.0 (0.0 to 1)
Current Spending: ($ per student per year):
Total: $6,674; Instruction: $4,328; Support Services: $2,122
Enrollment, Drop-out Rates and Diploma Recipients by Race/Ethnicity

Category	Total	White	Black	Asian	AIAN	Hisp.
Enrollment (%)	100.0	68.4	1.5	3.7	0.7	25.0
Drop-out Rate (%)	n/a	n/a	n/a	n/a	n/a	n/a
H.S. Diplomas (#)	n/a	n/a	n/a	n/a	n/a	n/a

Petaluma Joint Union High
200 Douglas St • Petaluma, CA 94952-2575
(707) 778-4604
Grade Span: KG-12; **Agency Type:** 2
Schools: 10
1 Primary; 3 Middle; 5 High; 1 Other Level
5 Regular; 0 Special Education; 0 Vocational; 5 Alternative
0 Magnet; 1 Charter; 3 Title I Eligible; 0 School-wide Title I
Students: 5,771 (50.7% male; 49.3% female)
Individual Education Program: 594 (10.3%);
English Language Learner: 588 (10.2%); Migrant: 83 (1.4%)
Eligible for Free Lunch Program: 468 (8.1%)
Eligible for Reduced-Price Lunch Program: 106 (1.8%)
Teachers: 262.5 (22.0 to 1)
Librarians/Media Specialists: 4.0 (1,442.8 to 1)
Guidance Counselors: 13.4 (430.7 to 1)
Current Spending: ($ per student per year):
Total: n/a; Instruction: n/a; Support Services: n/a
Enrollment, Drop-out Rates and Diploma Recipients by Race/Ethnicity

Category	Total	White	Black	Asian	AIAN	Hisp.
Enrollment (%)	100.0	77.1	1.3	4.6	0.6	16.4
Drop-out Rate (%)	n/a	n/a	n/a	n/a	n/a	n/a
H.S. Diplomas (#)	691	568	5	22	3	93

Piner-Olivet Union Elementary
3450 Coffey Ln • Santa Rosa, CA 95403-1919
(707) 522-3000 • http://www.pousd.k12.ca.us/
Grade Span: KG-08; **Agency Type:** 1
Schools: 4
3 Primary; 1 Middle; 0 High; 0 Other Level
4 Regular; 0 Special Education; 0 Vocational; 0 Alternative
0 Magnet; 1 Charter; 3 Title I Eligible; 0 School-wide Title I
Students: 1,706 (53.2% male; 46.8% female)
Individual Education Program: 153 (9.0%);
English Language Learner: 230 (13.5%); Migrant: 16 (0.9%)
Eligible for Free Lunch Program: 249 (14.6%)
Eligible for Reduced-Price Lunch Program: 189 (11.1%)
Teachers: 85.4 (20.0 to 1)
Librarians/Media Specialists: 0.0 (0.0 to 1)
Guidance Counselors: 0.0 (0.0 to 1)
Current Spending: ($ per student per year):
Total: $6,581; Instruction: $4,619; Support Services: $1,791
Enrollment, Drop-out Rates and Diploma Recipients by Race/Ethnicity

Category	Total	White	Black	Asian	AIAN	Hisp.
Enrollment (%)	100.0	68.3	4.9	8.4	1.2	16.7
Drop-out Rate (%)	n/a	n/a	n/a	n/a	n/a	n/a
H.S. Diplomas (#)	n/a	n/a	n/a	n/a	n/a	n/a

Rincon Valley Union Elementary
1000 Yulupa Ave • Santa Rosa, CA 95405-7020
(707) 542-7375
Grade Span: KG-06; **Agency Type:** 1
Schools: 8
8 Primary; 0 Middle; 0 High; 0 Other Level
8 Regular; 0 Special Education; 0 Vocational; 0 Alternative
0 Magnet; 0 Charter; 5 Title I Eligible; 0 School-wide Title I
Students: 2,744 (51.4% male; 48.6% female)
Individual Education Program: 300 (10.9%);
English Language Learner: 127 (4.6%); Migrant: 10 (0.4%)
Eligible for Free Lunch Program: 393 (14.3%)
Eligible for Reduced-Price Lunch Program: 211 (7.7%)
Teachers: 141.8 (19.4 to 1)
Librarians/Media Specialists: 0.0 (0.0 to 1)
Guidance Counselors: 0.0 (0.0 to 1)
Current Spending: ($ per student per year):
Total: $7,110; Instruction: $4,561; Support Services: $2,285
Enrollment, Drop-out Rates and Diploma Recipients by Race/Ethnicity

Category	Total	White	Black	Asian	AIAN	Hisp.
Enrollment (%)	100.0	76.0	3.3	6.3	1.3	13.1
Drop-out Rate (%)	n/a	n/a	n/a	n/a	n/a	n/a
H.S. Diplomas (#)	n/a	n/a	n/a	n/a	n/a	n/a

Santa Rosa Elementary
211 Ridgway Ave • Santa Rosa, CA 95401-4320
(707) 528-5352 • http://www.srcs.k12.ca.us/
Grade Span: KG-08; **Agency Type:** 2
Schools: 13
13 Primary; 0 Middle; 0 High; 0 Other Level
13 Regular; 0 Special Education; 0 Vocational; 0 Alternative
0 Magnet; 2 Charter; 9 Title I Eligible; 4 School-wide Title I
Students: 4,720 (52.7% male; 47.3% female)
Individual Education Program: 586 (12.4%);
English Language Learner: 1,998 (42.3%); Migrant: 362 (7.7%)
Eligible for Free Lunch Program: 1,847 (39.1%)
Eligible for Reduced-Price Lunch Program: 700 (14.8%)
Teachers: 305.9 (15.4 to 1)
Librarians/Media Specialists: 1.0 (4,720.0 to 1)
Guidance Counselors: 7.3 (646.6 to 1)
Current Spending: ($ per student per year):
Total: $6,951; Instruction: $4,420; Support Services: $2,245
Enrollment, Drop-out Rates and Diploma Recipients by Race/Ethnicity

Category	Total	White	Black	Asian	AIAN	Hisp.
Enrollment (%)	100.0	40.7	3.6	5.4	1.8	45.2
Drop-out Rate (%)	n/a	n/a	n/a	n/a	n/a	n/a
H.S. Diplomas (#)	n/a	n/a	n/a	n/a	n/a	n/a

Santa Rosa High

211 Ridgway Ave • Santa Rosa, CA 95401-4320
(707) 528-5181 • http://www.srcs.k12.ca.us/
Grade Span: 07-12; **Agency Type:** 2
Schools: 16
0 Primary; 6 Middle; 10 High; 0 Other Level
11 Regular; 0 Special Education; 0 Vocational; 5 Alternative
0 Magnet; 1 Charter; 8 Title I Eligible; 0 School-wide Title I
Students: 13,029 (51.1% male; 48.9% female)
Individual Education Program: 1,556 (11.9%);
English Language Learner: 1,887 (14.5%); Migrant: 304 (2.3%)
Eligible for Free Lunch Program: 1,596 (12.2%)
Eligible for Reduced-Price Lunch Program: 630 (4.8%)
Teachers: 588.8 (22.1 to 1)
Librarians/Media Specialists: 10.0 (1,302.9 to 1)
Guidance Counselors: 36.6 (356.0 to 1)
Current Spending: ($ per student per year):
Total: n/a; Instruction: n/a; Support Services: n/a
Enrollment, Drop-out Rates and Diploma Recipients by Race/Ethnicity

Category	Total	White	Black	Asian	AIAN	Hisp.
Enrollment (%)	100.0	61.5	3.0	6.5	1.9	23.9
Drop-out Rate (%)	n/a	n/a	n/a	n/a	n/a	n/a
H.S. Diplomas (#)	1,506	1,045	49	127	16	242

Sonoma Valley Unified

17850 Railroad Ave • Sonoma, CA 95476-6412
(707) 935-6000 • http://www.sonomavly.k12.ca.us/
Grade Span: KG-12; **Agency Type:** 1
Schools: 11
6 Primary; 2 Middle; 3 High; 0 Other Level
9 Regular; 0 Special Education; 0 Vocational; 2 Alternative
0 Magnet; 1 Charter; 7 Title I Eligible; 2 School-wide Title I
Students: 4,936 (52.1% male; 47.9% female)
Individual Education Program: 543 (11.0%);
English Language Learner: 1,311 (26.6%); Migrant: 311 (6.3%)
Eligible for Free Lunch Program: 1,329 (26.9%)
Eligible for Reduced-Price Lunch Program: 386 (7.8%)
Teachers: 240.3 (20.5 to 1)
Librarians/Media Specialists: 1.0 (4,936.0 to 1)
Guidance Counselors: 9.8 (503.7 to 1)
Current Spending: ($ per student per year):
Total: $6,247; Instruction: $4,361; Support Services: $1,706
Enrollment, Drop-out Rates and Diploma Recipients by Race/Ethnicity

Category	Total	White	Black	Asian	AIAN	Hisp.
Enrollment (%)	100.0	61.2	0.6	1.7	0.3	34.9
Drop-out Rate (%)	n/a	n/a	n/a	n/a	n/a	n/a
H.S. Diplomas (#)	287	212	4	5	0	65

West Sonoma County Union High

462 Johnson St • Sebastopol, CA 95472-3401
(707) 824-6403 • http://www.wscuhsd.k12.ca.us/
Grade Span: 07-12; **Agency Type:** 1
Schools: 6
0 Primary; 0 Middle; 6 High; 0 Other Level
3 Regular; 0 Special Education; 0 Vocational; 3 Alternative
0 Magnet; 1 Charter; 1 Title I Eligible; 0 School-wide Title I
Students: 2,687 (51.2% male; 48.8% female)
Individual Education Program: 386 (14.4%);
English Language Learner: 126 (4.7%); Migrant: 47 (1.7%)
Eligible for Free Lunch Program: 226 (8.4%)
Eligible for Reduced-Price Lunch Program: 95 (3.5%)
Teachers: 128.1 (21.0 to 1)
Librarians/Media Specialists: 0.0 (0.0 to 1)
Guidance Counselors: 8.9 (301.9 to 1)
Current Spending: ($ per student per year):
Total: $6,713; Instruction: $4,525; Support Services: $1,986
Enrollment, Drop-out Rates and Diploma Recipients by Race/Ethnicity

Category	Total	White	Black	Asian	AIAN	Hisp.
Enrollment (%)	100.0	80.4	1.2	1.6	1.4	10.3
Drop-out Rate (%)	n/a	n/a	n/a	n/a	n/a	n/a
H.S. Diplomas (#)	590	507	4	19	8	44

Windsor Unified

9291 Old Redwood Hwy #300 C • Windsor, CA 95492-9217
(707) 837-7700 • http://www.scoe.org/clients/wusd/
Grade Span: KG-12; **Agency Type:** 1
Schools: 7
4 Primary; 1 Middle; 2 High; 0 Other Level
6 Regular; 0 Special Education; 0 Vocational; 1 Alternative
0 Magnet; 1 Charter; 1 Title I Eligible; 0 School-wide Title I
Students: 4,602 (49.9% male; 50.1% female)
Individual Education Program: 330 (7.2%);
English Language Learner: 991 (21.5%); Migrant: 255 (5.5%)
Eligible for Free Lunch Program: 1,088 (23.6%)
Eligible for Reduced-Price Lunch Program: 457 (9.9%)
Teachers: 220.7 (20.9 to 1)
Librarians/Media Specialists: 0.0 (0.0 to 1)
Guidance Counselors: 6.9 (667.0 to 1)
Current Spending: ($ per student per year):
Total: $6,114; Instruction: $4,025; Support Services: $1,892
Enrollment, Drop-out Rates and Diploma Recipients by Race/Ethnicity

Category	Total	White	Black	Asian	AIAN	Hisp.
Enrollment (%)	100.0	61.6	1.2	3.1	1.8	32.2
Drop-out Rate (%)	n/a	n/a	n/a	n/a	n/a	n/a
H.S. Diplomas (#)	193	135	4	6	1	47

Stanislaus County

Ceres Unified

2503 Lawrence St • Ceres, CA 95307-0307
Mailing Address: PO Box 307 • Ceres, CA 95307-0307
(209) 538-0141 • http://www.ceres.k12.ca.us/default.htm
Grade Span: KG-12; **Agency Type:** 1
Schools: 13
7 Primary; 2 Middle; 2 High; 2 Other Level
11 Regular; 0 Special Education; 0 Vocational; 2 Alternative
0 Magnet; 1 Charter; 11 Title I Eligible; 7 School-wide Title I
Students: 10,028 (50.3% male; 49.7% female)
Individual Education Program: 1,050 (10.5%);
English Language Learner: 1,778 (17.7%); Migrant: 1,317 (13.1%)
Eligible for Free Lunch Program: 4,527 (45.1%)
Eligible for Reduced-Price Lunch Program: 1,122 (11.2%)
Teachers: 474.0 (21.2 to 1)
Librarians/Media Specialists: 2.0 (5,014.0 to 1)
Guidance Counselors: 8.0 (1,253.5 to 1)
Current Spending: ($ per student per year):
Total: $5,995; Instruction: $3,894; Support Services: $1,827
Enrollment, Drop-out Rates and Diploma Recipients by Race/Ethnicity

Category	Total	White	Black	Asian	AIAN	Hisp.
Enrollment (%)	100.0	39.3	2.7	5.7	1.8	49.3
Drop-out Rate (%)	n/a	n/a	n/a	n/a	n/a	n/a
H.S. Diplomas (#)	578	250	15	10	4	259

Empire Union Elementary

116 N Mcclure Rd • Modesto, CA 95357-1329
(209) 521-2800 • http://www.empire.k12.ca.us/
Grade Span: KG-08; **Agency Type:** 1
Schools: 6
5 Primary; 1 Middle; 0 High; 0 Other Level
6 Regular; 0 Special Education; 0 Vocational; 0 Alternative
0 Magnet; 0 Charter; 6 Title I Eligible; 3 School-wide Title I
Students: 4,244 (52.7% male; 47.3% female)
Individual Education Program: 503 (11.9%);
English Language Learner: 1,001 (23.6%); Migrant: 259 (6.1%)
Eligible for Free Lunch Program: 1,735 (40.9%)
Eligible for Reduced-Price Lunch Program: 644 (15.2%)
Teachers: 197.6 (21.5 to 1)
Librarians/Media Specialists: 1.0 (4,244.0 to 1)
Guidance Counselors: 6.1 (695.7 to 1)
Current Spending: ($ per student per year):
Total: $6,234; Instruction: $4,055; Support Services: $1,831
Enrollment, Drop-out Rates and Diploma Recipients by Race/Ethnicity

Category	Total	White	Black	Asian	AIAN	Hisp.
Enrollment (%)	100.0	43.6	5.7	9.0	0.8	39.1
Drop-out Rate (%)	n/a	n/a	n/a	n/a	n/a	n/a
H.S. Diplomas (#)	n/a	n/a	n/a	n/a	n/a	n/a

Hughson Unified

7419 E Whitmore Ave • Hughson, CA 95326
Mailing Address: PO Box 99 • Hughson, CA 95326
(209) 883-4428 • http://stan-co.k12.ca.us/hughson/do/welcome.html
Grade Span: KG-12; **Agency Type:** 1
Schools: 4
1 Primary; 1 Middle; 2 High; 0 Other Level
3 Regular; 0 Special Education; 0 Vocational; 1 Alternative
0 Magnet; 0 Charter; 3 Title I Eligible; 1 School-wide Title I
Students: 2,007 (51.1% male; 48.9% female)
Individual Education Program: 163 (8.1%);
English Language Learner: 379 (18.9%); Migrant: 563 (28.1%)
Eligible for Free Lunch Program: 678 (33.8%)
Eligible for Reduced-Price Lunch Program: 201 (10.0%)
Teachers: 98.3 (20.4 to 1)
Librarians/Media Specialists: 0.0 (0.0 to 1)
Guidance Counselors: 1.9 (1,056.3 to 1)
Current Spending: ($ per student per year):
Total: $6,447; Instruction: $3,967; Support Services: $2,101

Enrollment, Drop-out Rates and Diploma Recipients by Race/Ethnicity

Category	Total	White	Black	Asian	AIAN	Hisp.
Enrollment (%)	100.0	60.9	1.3	1.8	0.2	35.5
Drop-out Rate (%)	n/a	n/a	n/a	n/a	n/a	n/a
H.S. Diplomas (#)	191	141	0	3	0	46

Keyes Union Elementary

5465 Seventh St • Keyes, CA 95328-0549
Mailing Address: PO Box 549 • Keyes, CA 95328-0549
(209) 669-2921
Grade Span: KG-12; **Agency Type:** 1
Schools: 6
3 Primary; 1 Middle; 0 High; 2 Other Level
6 Regular; 0 Special Education; 0 Vocational; 0 Alternative
0 Magnet; 4 Charter; 3 Title I Eligible; 1 School-wide Title I
Students: 1,868 (53.4% male; 46.6% female)
Individual Education Program: 198 (10.6%);
English Language Learner: 353 (18.9%); Migrant: 161 (8.6%)
Eligible for Free Lunch Program: 619 (33.1%)
Eligible for Reduced-Price Lunch Program: 79 (4.2%)
Teachers: 90.3 (20.7 to 1)
Librarians/Media Specialists: 0.0 (0.0 to 1)
Guidance Counselors: 0.0 (0.0 to 1)
Current Spending: ($ per student per year):
Total: $5,178; Instruction: $3,378; Support Services: $1,537

Enrollment, Drop-out Rates and Diploma Recipients by Race/Ethnicity

Category	Total	White	Black	Asian	AIAN	Hisp.
Enrollment (%)	100.0	53.1	2.6	3.6	0.5	36.6
Drop-out Rate (%)	n/a	n/a	n/a	n/a	n/a	n/a
H.S. Diplomas (#)	1	1	0	0	0	0

Modesto City Elementary

426 Locust St • Modesto, CA 95351-2631
(209) 576-4011 • http://www.monet.k12.ca.us/
Grade Span: KG-08; **Agency Type:** 2
Schools: 27
23 Primary; 4 Middle; 0 High; 0 Other Level
27 Regular; 0 Special Education; 0 Vocational; 0 Alternative
0 Magnet; 0 Charter; 24 Title I Eligible; 14 School-wide Title I
Students: 18,954 (51.7% male; 48.3% female)
Individual Education Program: 2,498 (13.2%);
English Language Learner: 6,165 (32.5%); Migrant: 1,648 (8.7%)
Eligible for Free Lunch Program: 11,683 (61.6%)
Eligible for Reduced-Price Lunch Program: 2,110 (11.1%)
Teachers: 947.7 (20.0 to 1)
Librarians/Media Specialists: 17.0 (1,114.9 to 1)
Guidance Counselors: 0.0 (0.0 to 1)
Current Spending: ($ per student per year):
Total: $6,289; Instruction: $4,107; Support Services: $1,911

Enrollment, Drop-out Rates and Diploma Recipients by Race/Ethnicity

Category	Total	White	Black	Asian	AIAN	Hisp.
Enrollment (%)	100.0	30.1	5.5	7.9	1.0	55.5
Drop-out Rate (%)	n/a	n/a	n/a	n/a	n/a	n/a
H.S. Diplomas (#)	n/a	n/a	n/a	n/a	n/a	n/a

Modesto City High

426 Locust St • Modesto, CA 95351-2631
(209) 576-4011 • http://www.monet.k12.ca.us/
Grade Span: 07-12; **Agency Type:** 2
Schools: 6
0 Primary; 0 Middle; 6 High; 0 Other Level
5 Regular; 0 Special Education; 0 Vocational; 1 Alternative
0 Magnet; 0 Charter; 2 Title I Eligible; 0 School-wide Title I
Students: 15,544 (49.5% male; 50.5% female)
Individual Education Program: 1,684 (10.8%);
English Language Learner: 2,338 (15.0%); Migrant: 641 (4.1%)
Eligible for Free Lunch Program: 3,902 (25.1%)
Eligible for Reduced-Price Lunch Program: 662 (4.3%)
Teachers: 601.8 (25.8 to 1)
Librarians/Media Specialists: 5.0 (3,108.8 to 1)
Guidance Counselors: 32.1 (484.2 to 1)
Current Spending: ($ per student per year):
Total: n/a; Instruction: n/a; Support Services: n/a

Enrollment, Drop-out Rates and Diploma Recipients by Race/Ethnicity

Category	Total	White	Black	Asian	AIAN	Hisp.
Enrollment (%)	100.0	47.2	5.3	11.2	0.9	35.3
Drop-out Rate (%)	n/a	n/a	n/a	n/a	n/a	n/a
H.S. Diplomas (#)	2,815	1,476	117	350	28	844

Newman-Crows Landing Unified

890 O St • Newman, CA 95360-1199
(209) 862-2933 • http://nclusd.k12.ca.us/
Grade Span: KG-12; **Agency Type:** 1
Schools: 7
2 Primary; 2 Middle; 2 High; 1 Other Level
4 Regular; 0 Special Education; 0 Vocational; 3 Alternative
0 Magnet; 0 Charter; 5 Title I Eligible; 3 School-wide Title I
Students: 2,308 (53.3% male; 46.7% female)
Individual Education Program: 248 (10.7%);
English Language Learner: 743 (32.2%); Migrant: 531 (23.0%)
Eligible for Free Lunch Program: 963 (41.7%)
Eligible for Reduced-Price Lunch Program: 277 (12.0%)
Teachers: 112.2 (20.6 to 1)
Librarians/Media Specialists: 0.0 (0.0 to 1)
Guidance Counselors: 1.0 (2,308.0 to 1)
Current Spending: ($ per student per year):
Total: $5,472; Instruction: $3,445; Support Services: $1,779

Enrollment, Drop-out Rates and Diploma Recipients by Race/Ethnicity

Category	Total	White	Black	Asian	AIAN	Hisp.
Enrollment (%)	100.0	34.5	2.0	1.9	0.5	58.5
Drop-out Rate (%)	n/a	n/a	n/a	n/a	n/a	n/a
H.S. Diplomas (#)	146	51	2	4	0	89

Oakdale Joint Unified

168 S Third Ave • Oakdale, CA 95361-3935
(209) 848-4884 • http://www.oakdale.k12.ca.us/
Grade Span: KG-12; **Agency Type:** 1
Schools: 8
3 Primary; 1 Middle; 4 High; 0 Other Level
5 Regular; 0 Special Education; 0 Vocational; 3 Alternative
0 Magnet; 1 Charter; 4 Title I Eligible; 0 School-wide Title I
Students: 4,910 (50.4% male; 49.6% female)
Individual Education Program: 516 (10.5%);
English Language Learner: 420 (8.6%); Migrant: 556 (11.3%)
Eligible for Free Lunch Program: 1,404 (28.6%)
Eligible for Reduced-Price Lunch Program: 373 (7.6%)
Teachers: 231.1 (21.2 to 1)
Librarians/Media Specialists: 0.0 (0.0 to 1)
Guidance Counselors: 5.0 (982.0 to 1)
Current Spending: ($ per student per year):
Total: $5,996; Instruction: $3,752; Support Services: $2,040

Enrollment, Drop-out Rates and Diploma Recipients by Race/Ethnicity

Category	Total	White	Black	Asian	AIAN	Hisp.
Enrollment (%)	100.0	73.1	0.9	1.5	0.5	22.5
Drop-out Rate (%)	n/a	n/a	n/a	n/a	n/a	n/a
H.S. Diplomas (#)	357	293	0	6	2	52

Patterson Joint Unified

200 N Seventh St • Patterson, CA 95363-0547
Mailing Address: PO Box 547 • Patterson, CA 95363-0547
(209) 892-3700 • http://www.stan-co.k12.ca.us/Patterson/welcome.htm
Grade Span: KG-12; **Agency Type:** 1
Schools: 8
4 Primary; 2 Middle; 2 High; 0 Other Level
7 Regular; 0 Special Education; 0 Vocational; 1 Alternative
0 Magnet; 1 Charter; 6 Title I Eligible; 2 School-wide Title I
Students: 4,251 (50.3% male; 49.7% female)
Individual Education Program: 494 (11.6%);
English Language Learner: 1,806 (42.5%); Migrant: 1,237 (29.1%)
Eligible for Free Lunch Program: 2,298 (54.1%)
Eligible for Reduced-Price Lunch Program: 650 (15.3%)
Teachers: 202.4 (21.0 to 1)
Librarians/Media Specialists: 1.0 (4,251.0 to 1)
Guidance Counselors: 4.0 (1,062.8 to 1)
Current Spending: ($ per student per year):
Total: $6,023; Instruction: $3,697; Support Services: $2,039

Enrollment, Drop-out Rates and Diploma Recipients by Race/Ethnicity

Category	Total	White	Black	Asian	AIAN	Hisp.
Enrollment (%)	100.0	25.4	2.7	3.0	0.7	68.2
Drop-out Rate (%)	n/a	n/a	n/a	n/a	n/a	n/a
H.S. Diplomas (#)	211	76	5	3	0	127

Riverbank Unified

6715 7th St • Riverbank, CA 95367-2345
(209) 869-2538 • http://stan-co.k12.ca.us/riverbank/
Grade Span: KG-12; **Agency Type:** 1
Schools: 5
3 Primary; 1 Middle; 1 High; 0 Other Level
5 Regular; 0 Special Education; 0 Vocational; 0 Alternative
0 Magnet; 0 Charter; 5 Title I Eligible; 1 School-wide Title I
Students: 3,193 (52.5% male; 47.5% female)
Individual Education Program: 290 (9.1%);
English Language Learner: 1,334 (41.8%); Migrant: 870 (27.2%)
Eligible for Free Lunch Program: 1,603 (50.2%)
Eligible for Reduced-Price Lunch Program: 416 (13.0%)
Teachers: 158.1 (20.2 to 1)
Librarians/Media Specialists: 0.0 (0.0 to 1)
Guidance Counselors: 4.0 (798.3 to 1)
Current Spending: ($ per student per year):
Total: $5,995; Instruction: $3,673; Support Services: $2,019

Enrollment, Drop-out Rates and Diploma Recipients by Race/Ethnicity

Category	Total	White	Black	Asian	AIAN	Hisp.
Enrollment (%)	100.0	31.3	1.8	0.9	0.9	64.5
Drop-out Rate (%)	n/a	n/a	n/a	n/a	n/a	n/a
H.S. Diplomas (#)	201	78	1	1	1	120

Salida Union Elementary

5250 Tamara Way • Salida, CA 95368-9226
(209) 545-0339 • http://www.salida.k12.ca.us/
Grade Span: KG-08; **Agency Type:** 1
Schools: 5
4 Primary; 1 Middle; 0 High; 0 Other Level
5 Regular; 0 Special Education; 0 Vocational; 0 Alternative
0 Magnet; 0 Charter; 4 Title I Eligible; 0 School-wide Title I
Students: 3,473 (51.4% male; 48.6% female)
Individual Education Program: 367 (10.6%);
English Language Learner: 556 (16.0%); Migrant: 253 (7.3%)
Eligible for Free Lunch Program: 720 (20.7%)
Eligible for Reduced-Price Lunch Program: 353 (10.2%)
Teachers: 180.8 (19.2 to 1)
Librarians/Media Specialists: 0.0 (0.0 to 1)
Guidance Counselors: 2.0 (1,736.5 to 1)
Current Spending: ($ per student per year):
Total: $5,492; Instruction: $3,401; Support Services: $1,804
Enrollment, Drop-out Rates and Diploma Recipients by Race/Ethnicity

Category	Total	White	Black	Asian	AIAN	Hisp.
Enrollment (%)	100.0	44.1	6.1	7.0	0.6	41.1
Drop-out Rate (%)	n/a	n/a	n/a	n/a	n/a	n/a
H.S. Diplomas (#)	n/a	n/a	n/a	n/a	n/a	n/a

Stanislaus Union Elementary

3601 Carver Rd • Modesto, CA 95356-0926
(209) 529-9546 • http://www.stanunion.k12.ca.us/
Grade Span: KG-08; **Agency Type:** 1
Schools: 6
5 Primary; 1 Middle; 0 High; 0 Other Level
6 Regular; 0 Special Education; 0 Vocational; 0 Alternative
0 Magnet; 0 Charter; 5 Title I Eligible; 1 School-wide Title I
Students: 3,309 (51.2% male; 48.8% female)
Individual Education Program: 371 (11.2%);
English Language Learner: 559 (16.9%); Migrant: 114 (3.4%)
Eligible for Free Lunch Program: 1,376 (41.6%)
Eligible for Reduced-Price Lunch Program: 289 (8.7%)
Teachers: 152.5 (21.7 to 1)
Librarians/Media Specialists: 0.0 (0.0 to 1)
Guidance Counselors: 0.0 (0.0 to 1)
Current Spending: ($ per student per year):
Total: $5,579; Instruction: $3,723; Support Services: $1,678
Enrollment, Drop-out Rates and Diploma Recipients by Race/Ethnicity

Category	Total	White	Black	Asian	AIAN	Hisp.
Enrollment (%)	100.0	40.7	7.9	12.4	0.6	35.9
Drop-out Rate (%)	n/a	n/a	n/a	n/a	n/a	n/a
H.S. Diplomas (#)	n/a	n/a	n/a	n/a	n/a	n/a

Sylvan Union Elementary

605 Sylvan Ave • Modesto, CA 95350-1517
(209) 574-5000 • http://www.sylvan.k12.ca.us/stockard.html
Grade Span: KG-08; **Agency Type:** 1
Schools: 10
8 Primary; 2 Middle; 0 High; 0 Other Level
10 Regular; 0 Special Education; 0 Vocational; 0 Alternative
0 Magnet; 0 Charter; 5 Title I Eligible; 1 School-wide Title I
Students: 7,377 (50.5% male; 49.5% female)
Individual Education Program: 851 (11.5%);
English Language Learner: 680 (9.2%); Migrant: 9 (0.1%)
Eligible for Free Lunch Program: 1,718 (23.3%)
Eligible for Reduced-Price Lunch Program: 669 (9.1%)
Teachers: 370.3 (19.9 to 1)
Librarians/Media Specialists: 3.0 (2,459.0 to 1)
Guidance Counselors: 5.0 (1,475.4 to 1)
Current Spending: ($ per student per year):
Total: $5,660; Instruction: $3,749; Support Services: $1,643
Enrollment, Drop-out Rates and Diploma Recipients by Race/Ethnicity

Category	Total	White	Black	Asian	AIAN	Hisp.
Enrollment (%)	100.0	59.0	5.8	6.9	0.9	26.6
Drop-out Rate (%)	n/a	n/a	n/a	n/a	n/a	n/a
H.S. Diplomas (#)	n/a	n/a	n/a	n/a	n/a	n/a

Turlock Joint Elementary

1574 E Canal Dr • Turlock, CA 95381-1105
Mailing Address: PO Box 1105 • Turlock, CA 95381-1105
(209) 667-0645 • http://www.turlock.k12.ca.us/
Grade Span: KG-08; **Agency Type:** 2
Schools: 11
9 Primary; 2 Middle; 0 High; 0 Other Level
11 Regular; 0 Special Education; 0 Vocational; 0 Alternative
1 Magnet; 0 Charter; 8 Title I Eligible; 4 School-wide Title I
Students: 8,933 (51.2% male; 48.8% female)
Individual Education Program: 1,026 (11.5%);
English Language Learner: 2,533 (28.4%); Migrant: 404 (4.5%)
Eligible for Free Lunch Program: 4,312 (48.3%)
Eligible for Reduced-Price Lunch Program: 795 (8.9%)
Teachers: 447.7 (20.0 to 1)
Librarians/Media Specialists: 0.0 (0.0 to 1)
Guidance Counselors: 5.5 (1,624.2 to 1)
Current Spending: ($ per student per year):
Total: $6,098; Instruction: $4,134; Support Services: $1,691
Enrollment, Drop-out Rates and Diploma Recipients by Race/Ethnicity

Category	Total	White	Black	Asian	AIAN	Hisp.
Enrollment (%)	100.0	45.7	1.6	5.4	0.9	46.3
Drop-out Rate (%)	n/a	n/a	n/a	n/a	n/a	n/a
H.S. Diplomas (#)	n/a	n/a	n/a	n/a	n/a	n/a

Turlock Joint Union High

1574 E Canal Dr • Turlock, CA 95381-1105
Mailing Address: PO Box 810913 • Turlock, CA 95381-9013
(209) 667-0645 • http://www.turlock.k12.ca.us/
Grade Span: 09-12; **Agency Type:** 2
Schools: 4
0 Primary; 0 Middle; 4 High; 0 Other Level
2 Regular; 0 Special Education; 0 Vocational; 2 Alternative
0 Magnet; 0 Charter; 3 Title I Eligible; 0 School-wide Title I
Students: 4,340 (49.3% male; 50.7% female)
Individual Education Program: 457 (10.5%);
English Language Learner: 649 (15.0%); Migrant: 179 (4.1%)
Eligible for Free Lunch Program: 948 (21.8%)
Eligible for Reduced-Price Lunch Program: 192 (4.4%)
Teachers: 187.8 (23.1 to 1)
Librarians/Media Specialists: 0.0 (0.0 to 1)
Guidance Counselors: 9.8 (442.9 to 1)
Current Spending: ($ per student per year):
Total: $6,255; Instruction: $3,707; Support Services: $2,308
Enrollment, Drop-out Rates and Diploma Recipients by Race/Ethnicity

Category	Total	White	Black	Asian	AIAN	Hisp.
Enrollment (%)	100.0	53.5	1.8	6.3	0.9	36.9
Drop-out Rate (%)	n/a	n/a	n/a	n/a	n/a	n/a
H.S. Diplomas (#)	801	478	10	71	10	232

Waterford Unified

12420 Bentley St • Waterford, CA 95386-9158
(209) 874-1809
Grade Span: KG-12; **Agency Type:** 1
Schools: 4
1 Primary; 1 Middle; 1 High; 1 Other Level
4 Regular; 0 Special Education; 0 Vocational; 0 Alternative
0 Magnet; 1 Charter; 3 Title I Eligible; 1 School-wide Title I
Students: 2,946 (50.4% male; 49.6% female)
Individual Education Program: 268 (9.1%);
English Language Learner: 504 (17.1%); Migrant: 375 (12.7%)
Eligible for Free Lunch Program: 871 (29.6%)
Eligible for Reduced-Price Lunch Program: 208 (7.1%)
Teachers: 140.3 (21.0 to 1)
Librarians/Media Specialists: 0.0 (0.0 to 1)
Guidance Counselors: 1.0 (2,946.0 to 1)
Current Spending: ($ per student per year):
Total: $6,827; Instruction: $4,356; Support Services: $2,141
Enrollment, Drop-out Rates and Diploma Recipients by Race/Ethnicity

Category	Total	White	Black	Asian	AIAN	Hisp.
Enrollment (%)	100.0	56.0	2.7	1.8	1.2	33.5
Drop-out Rate (%)	n/a	n/a	n/a	n/a	n/a	n/a
H.S. Diplomas (#)	32	14	0	2	0	16

Sutter County

Live Oak Unified

2201 Pennington Rd • Live Oak, CA 95953-2469
(530) 695-5400 • http://www.hs.lousd.k12.ca.us/lousd/lousd.htm
Grade Span: KG-12; **Agency Type:** 1
Schools: 6
2 Primary; 1 Middle; 2 High; 1 Other Level
4 Regular; 0 Special Education; 0 Vocational; 2 Alternative
0 Magnet; 0 Charter; 5 Title I Eligible; 4 School-wide Title I
Students: 1,860 (50.8% male; 49.2% female)
Individual Education Program: 90 (4.8%);
English Language Learner: 472 (25.4%); Migrant: 396 (21.3%)
Eligible for Free Lunch Program: 1,231 (66.2%)
Eligible for Reduced-Price Lunch Program: 304 (16.3%)
Teachers: 89.6 (20.8 to 1)
Librarians/Media Specialists: 0.0 (0.0 to 1)
Guidance Counselors: 1.0 (1,860.0 to 1)

Current Spending: ($ per student per year):
Total: $5,740; Instruction: $3,649; Support Services: $1,787
Enrollment, Drop-out Rates and Diploma Recipients by Race/Ethnicity

Category	Total	White	Black	Asian	AIAN	Hisp.
Enrollment (%)	100.0	33.1	0.3	12.0	1.3	52.7
Drop-out Rate (%)	n/a	n/a	n/a	n/a	n/a	n/a
H.S. Diplomas (#)	104	43	0	14	5	42

Yuba City Unified

750 Palora Ave • Yuba City, CA 95991-3627
(530) 822-5200 • http://www.ycusd.k12.ca.us/
Grade Span: KG-12; **Agency Type:** 1
Schools: 17
11 Primary; 2 Middle; 2 High; 2 Other Level
15 Regular; 0 Special Education; 0 Vocational; 2 Alternative
0 Magnet; 1 Charter; 15 Title I Eligible; 9 School-wide Title I
Students: 11,579 (52.1% male; 47.9% female)
Individual Education Program: 847 (7.3%);
English Language Learner: 2,426 (21.0%); Migrant: 1,904 (16.4%)
Eligible for Free Lunch Program: 4,317 (37.3%)
Eligible for Reduced-Price Lunch Program: 1,189 (10.3%)
Teachers: 582.6 (19.9 to 1)
Librarians/Media Specialists: 5.0 (2,315.8 to 1)
Guidance Counselors: 21.2 (546.2 to 1)
Current Spending: ($ per student per year):
Total: $6,325; Instruction: $4,062; Support Services: $2,025
Enrollment, Drop-out Rates and Diploma Recipients by Race/Ethnicity

Category	Total	White	Black	Asian	AIAN	Hisp.
Enrollment (%)	100.0	48.2	3.3	16.9	1.6	29.6
Drop-out Rate (%)	n/a	n/a	n/a	n/a	n/a	n/a
H.S. Diplomas (#)	681	357	8	130	12	174

Tehama County

Corning Union Elementary

1590 S St • Corning, CA 96021-2934
(530) 824-7700 • http://www.cuesd.tehama.k12.ca.us/
Grade Span: KG-08; **Agency Type:** 1
Schools: 5
4 Primary; 1 Middle; 0 High; 0 Other Level
4 Regular; 0 Special Education; 0 Vocational; 1 Alternative
0 Magnet; 0 Charter; 4 Title I Eligible; 1 School-wide Title I
Students: 1,964 (51.9% male; 48.1% female)
Individual Education Program: 117 (6.0%);
English Language Learner: 535 (27.2%); Migrant: 128 (6.5%)
Eligible for Free Lunch Program: 1,220 (62.1%)
Eligible for Reduced-Price Lunch Program: 188 (9.6%)
Teachers: 104.8 (18.7 to 1)
Librarians/Media Specialists: 0.6 (3,273.3 to 1)
Guidance Counselors: 1.0 (1,964.0 to 1)
Current Spending: ($ per student per year):
Total: $6,809; Instruction: $4,508; Support Services: $1,935
Enrollment, Drop-out Rates and Diploma Recipients by Race/Ethnicity

Category	Total	White	Black	Asian	AIAN	Hisp.
Enrollment (%)	100.0	52.4	0.9	0.9	1.0	44.7
Drop-out Rate (%)	n/a	n/a	n/a	n/a	n/a	n/a
H.S. Diplomas (#)	n/a	n/a	n/a	n/a	n/a	n/a

Red Bluff Joint Union High

1525 Douglass St • Red Bluff, CA 96080-2599
Mailing Address: PO Box 1507 • Red Bluff, CA 96080-2599
(530) 529-8700 • http://www.rbuhsd.k12.ca.us/
Grade Span: 09-12; **Agency Type:** 1
Schools: 4
0 Primary; 0 Middle; 4 High; 0 Other Level
1 Regular; 0 Special Education; 0 Vocational; 3 Alternative
0 Magnet; 0 Charter; 4 Title I Eligible; 2 School-wide Title I
Students: 2,059 (51.0% male; 49.0% female)
Individual Education Program: 188 (9.1%);
English Language Learner: 43 (2.1%); Migrant: 19 (0.9%)
Eligible for Free Lunch Program: 655 (31.8%)
Eligible for Reduced-Price Lunch Program: 116 (5.6%)
Teachers: 95.0 (21.7 to 1)
Librarians/Media Specialists: 0.0 (0.0 to 1)
Guidance Counselors: 4.0 (514.8 to 1)
Current Spending: ($ per student per year):
Total: $7,182; Instruction: $3,848; Support Services: $2,843
Enrollment, Drop-out Rates and Diploma Recipients by Race/Ethnicity

Category	Total	White	Black	Asian	AIAN	Hisp.
Enrollment (%)	100.0	74.8	1.2	1.6	3.4	14.8
Drop-out Rate (%)	n/a	n/a	n/a	n/a	n/a	n/a
H.S. Diplomas (#)	440	358	4	9	14	55

Red Bluff Union Elementary

1755 Airport Rd • Red Bluff, CA 96080-4514
(530) 527-7200 • http://www.rbuhsd.k12.ca.us/
Grade Span: KG-12; **Agency Type:** 1
Schools: 6
3 Primary; 2 Middle; 0 High; 1 Other Level
5 Regular; 0 Special Education; 0 Vocational; 1 Alternative
0 Magnet; 1 Charter; 4 Title I Eligible; 3 School-wide Title I
Students: 2,331 (51.7% male; 48.3% female)
Individual Education Program: 175 (7.5%);
English Language Learner: 297 (12.7%); Migrant: 66 (2.8%)
Eligible for Free Lunch Program: 920 (39.5%)
Eligible for Reduced-Price Lunch Program: 247 (10.6%)
Teachers: 114.2 (20.4 to 1)
Librarians/Media Specialists: 0.5 (4,662.0 to 1)
Guidance Counselors: 1.6 (1,456.9 to 1)
Current Spending: ($ per student per year):
Total: $6,716; Instruction: $4,382; Support Services: $2,088
Enrollment, Drop-out Rates and Diploma Recipients by Race/Ethnicity

Category	Total	White	Black	Asian	AIAN	Hisp.
Enrollment (%)	100.0	74.9	1.1	1.2	2.1	19.5
Drop-out Rate (%)	n/a	n/a	n/a	n/a	n/a	n/a
H.S. Diplomas (#)	0	0	0	0	0	0

Tulare County

Burton Elementary

264 N Westwood St • Porterville, CA 93257-2542
(559) 781-8020 • http://burton.davis.k12.ut.us/
Grade Span: KG-08; **Agency Type:** 1
Schools: 5
3 Primary; 2 Middle; 0 High; 0 Other Level
5 Regular; 0 Special Education; 0 Vocational; 0 Alternative
0 Magnet; 0 Charter; 4 Title I Eligible; 2 School-wide Title I
Students: 2,657 (51.9% male; 48.1% female)
Individual Education Program: 131 (4.9%);
English Language Learner: 364 (13.7%); Migrant: 75 (2.8%)
Eligible for Free Lunch Program: 1,065 (40.1%)
Eligible for Reduced-Price Lunch Program: 495 (18.6%)
Teachers: 131.9 (20.1 to 1)
Librarians/Media Specialists: 1.0 (2,657.0 to 1)
Guidance Counselors: 2.0 (1,328.5 to 1)
Current Spending: ($ per student per year):
Total: $6,084; Instruction: $3,935; Support Services: $1,779
Enrollment, Drop-out Rates and Diploma Recipients by Race/Ethnicity

Category	Total	White	Black	Asian	AIAN	Hisp.
Enrollment (%)	100.0	44.4	1.0	5.6	0.9	48.1
Drop-out Rate (%)	n/a	n/a	n/a	n/a	n/a	n/a
H.S. Diplomas (#)	n/a	n/a	n/a	n/a	n/a	n/a

Cutler-Orosi Joint Unified

41855 Rd 128 • Orosi, CA 93647-2008
(559) 528-4763 • http://www.cojusd.org/
Grade Span: KG-12; **Agency Type:** 1
Schools: 11
5 Primary; 1 Middle; 5 High; 0 Other Level
7 Regular; 0 Special Education; 0 Vocational; 4 Alternative
0 Magnet; 0 Charter; 11 Title I Eligible; 0 School-wide Title I
Students: 3,981 (52.3% male; 47.7% female)
Individual Education Program: 111 (2.8%);
English Language Learner: 2,366 (59.4%); Migrant: 581 (14.6%)
Eligible for Free Lunch Program: 2,424 (60.9%)
Eligible for Reduced-Price Lunch Program: 192 (4.8%)
Teachers: 197.5 (20.2 to 1)
Librarians/Media Specialists: 0.0 (0.0 to 1)
Guidance Counselors: 1.5 (2,654.0 to 1)
Current Spending: ($ per student per year):
Total: $6,919; Instruction: $4,395; Support Services: $2,164
Enrollment, Drop-out Rates and Diploma Recipients by Race/Ethnicity

Category	Total	White	Black	Asian	AIAN	Hisp.
Enrollment (%)	100.0	2.2	0.5	4.3	0.0	92.7
Drop-out Rate (%)	n/a	n/a	n/a	n/a	n/a	n/a
H.S. Diplomas (#)	194	7	0	18	0	168

Dinuba Unified

1327 E El Monte Way • Dinuba, CA 93618-1800
(559) 595-7200
Grade Span: KG-12; **Agency Type:** 1
Schools: 8
5 Primary; 1 Middle; 2 High; 0 Other Level
7 Regular; 0 Special Education; 0 Vocational; 1 Alternative
0 Magnet; 0 Charter; 8 Title I Eligible; 0 School-wide Title I
Students: 5,310 (52.1% male; 47.9% female)
Individual Education Program: 432 (8.1%);
English Language Learner: 1,599 (30.1%); Migrant: 911 (17.2%)

Eligible for Free Lunch Program: 3,377 (63.6%)
Eligible for Reduced-Price Lunch Program: 636 (12.0%)
Teachers: 260.3 (20.4 to 1)
Librarians/Media Specialists: 1.0 (5,310.0 to 1)
Guidance Counselors: 7.9 (672.2 to 1)
Current Spending: ($ per student per year):
Total: $6,305; Instruction: $4,027; Support Services: $1,982
Enrollment, Drop-out Rates and Diploma Recipients by Race/Ethnicity

Category	Total	White	Black	Asian	AIAN	Hisp.
Enrollment (%)	100.0	12.0	0.8	1.6	0.3	85.3
Drop-out Rate (%)	n/a	n/a	n/a	n/a	n/a	n/a
H.S. Diplomas (#)	299	53	0	6	0	240

Earlimart Elementary
785 E Center Ave • Earlimart, CA 93219-1970
Mailing Address: PO Box 11970 • Earlimart, CA 93219-1970
(661) 849-3386 • http://www.earlimart.k12.ca.us/
Grade Span: KG-08; **Agency Type:** 1
Schools: 3
2 Primary; 1 Middle; 0 High; 0 Other Level
3 Regular; 0 Special Education; 0 Vocational; 0 Alternative
0 Magnet; 0 Charter; 3 Title I Eligible; 2 School-wide Title I
Students: 1,828 (51.4% male; 48.6% female)
Individual Education Program: 94 (5.1%);
English Language Learner: 1,531 (83.8%); Migrant: 502 (27.5%)
Eligible for Free Lunch Program: 1,518 (83.0%)
Eligible for Reduced-Price Lunch Program: 206 (11.3%)
Teachers: 92.0 (19.9 to 1)
Librarians/Media Specialists: 0.0 (0.0 to 1)
Guidance Counselors: 0.0 (0.0 to 1)
Current Spending: ($ per student per year):
Total: $5,936; Instruction: $3,551; Support Services: $2,039
Enrollment, Drop-out Rates and Diploma Recipients by Race/Ethnicity

Category	Total	White	Black	Asian	AIAN	Hisp.
Enrollment (%)	100.0	2.4	0.8	3.1	0.1	93.7
Drop-out Rate (%)	n/a	n/a	n/a	n/a	n/a	n/a
H.S. Diplomas (#)	n/a	n/a	n/a	n/a	n/a	n/a

Exeter Union Elementary
134 SE St • Exeter, CA 93221-1731
(559) 592-9421
Grade Span: KG-08; **Agency Type:** 1
Schools: 4
2 Primary; 2 Middle; 0 High; 0 Other Level
3 Regular; 0 Special Education; 0 Vocational; 1 Alternative
0 Magnet; 0 Charter; 4 Title I Eligible; 3 School-wide Title I
Students: 1,923 (51.9% male; 48.1% female)
Individual Education Program: 105 (5.5%);
English Language Learner: 367 (19.1%); Migrant: 299 (15.5%)
Eligible for Free Lunch Program: 949 (49.4%)
Eligible for Reduced-Price Lunch Program: 230 (12.0%)
Teachers: 102.1 (18.8 to 1)
Librarians/Media Specialists: 0.0 (0.0 to 1)
Guidance Counselors: 0.0 (0.0 to 1)
Current Spending: ($ per student per year):
Total: $6,530; Instruction: $4,403; Support Services: $1,819
Enrollment, Drop-out Rates and Diploma Recipients by Race/Ethnicity

Category	Total	White	Black	Asian	AIAN	Hisp.
Enrollment (%)	100.0	51.2	0.4	1.1	0.6	46.5
Drop-out Rate (%)	n/a	n/a	n/a	n/a	n/a	n/a
H.S. Diplomas (#)	n/a	n/a	n/a	n/a	n/a	n/a

Farmersville Unified
281 S Farmersville Blvd • Farmersville, CA 93223-1833
(559) 747-0776 • http://www.farmersville.k12.ca.us/
Grade Span: KG-12; **Agency Type:** 1
Schools: 5
2 Primary; 1 Middle; 2 High; 0 Other Level
4 Regular; 0 Special Education; 0 Vocational; 1 Alternative
0 Magnet; 0 Charter; 4 Title I Eligible; 3 School-wide Title I
Students: 2,321 (49.1% male; 50.9% female)
Individual Education Program: 140 (6.0%);
English Language Learner: 1,152 (49.6%); Migrant: 722 (31.1%)
Eligible for Free Lunch Program: 1,677 (72.3%)
Eligible for Reduced-Price Lunch Program: 286 (12.3%)
Teachers: 124.4 (18.7 to 1)
Librarians/Media Specialists: 0.0 (0.0 to 1)
Guidance Counselors: 2.6 (892.7 to 1)
Current Spending: ($ per student per year):
Total: $6,756; Instruction: $4,276; Support Services: $2,142
Enrollment, Drop-out Rates and Diploma Recipients by Race/Ethnicity

Category	Total	White	Black	Asian	AIAN	Hisp.
Enrollment (%)	100.0	12.7	0.3	0.6	0.4	85.2
Drop-out Rate (%)	n/a	n/a	n/a	n/a	n/a	n/a
H.S. Diplomas (#)	118	7	2	0	0	109

Lindsay Unified
519 E Honolulu St • Lindsay, CA 93247-2143
(559) 562-5111 • http://www.lindsay.k12.ca.us/
Grade Span: KG-12; **Agency Type:** 1
Schools: 7
3 Primary; 1 Middle; 3 High; 0 Other Level
5 Regular; 0 Special Education; 0 Vocational; 2 Alternative
0 Magnet; 0 Charter; 7 Title I Eligible; 5 School-wide Title I
Students: 3,555 (49.8% male; 50.2% female)
Individual Education Program: 139 (3.9%);
English Language Learner: 2,065 (58.1%); Migrant: 1,272 (35.8%)
Eligible for Free Lunch Program: 2,471 (69.5%)
Eligible for Reduced-Price Lunch Program: 301 (8.5%)
Teachers: 181.5 (19.6 to 1)
Librarians/Media Specialists: 1.0 (3,555.0 to 1)
Guidance Counselors: 8.5 (418.2 to 1)
Current Spending: ($ per student per year):
Total: $7,223; Instruction: $4,050; Support Services: $2,755
Enrollment, Drop-out Rates and Diploma Recipients by Race/Ethnicity

Category	Total	White	Black	Asian	AIAN	Hisp.
Enrollment (%)	100.0	9.4	0.3	0.9	0.1	88.6
Drop-out Rate (%)	n/a	n/a	n/a	n/a	n/a	n/a
H.S. Diplomas (#)	207	27	0	6	0	174

Porterville Unified
600 W Grand Ave • Porterville, CA 93257-2029
(559) 793-2455 • http://porterville.k12.ca.us/dist/Home.html
Grade Span: KG-12; **Agency Type:** 1
Schools: 17
9 Primary; 2 Middle; 5 High; 1 Other Level
14 Regular; 0 Special Education; 0 Vocational; 3 Alternative
0 Magnet; 0 Charter; 17 Title I Eligible; 9 School-wide Title I
Students: 12,487 (51.2% male; 48.8% female)
Individual Education Program: 688 (5.5%);
English Language Learner: 2,626 (21.0%); Migrant: 1,368 (11.0%)
Eligible for Free Lunch Program: 8,798 (70.5%)
Eligible for Reduced-Price Lunch Program: 973 (7.8%)
Teachers: 611.1 (20.4 to 1)
Librarians/Media Specialists: 3.4 (3,672.6 to 1)
Guidance Counselors: 8.0 (1,560.9 to 1)
Current Spending: ($ per student per year):
Total: $6,540; Instruction: $4,370; Support Services: $1,863
Enrollment, Drop-out Rates and Diploma Recipients by Race/Ethnicity

Category	Total	White	Black	Asian	AIAN	Hisp.
Enrollment (%)	100.0	27.9	1.1	4.0	2.9	62.8
Drop-out Rate (%)	n/a	n/a	n/a	n/a	n/a	n/a
H.S. Diplomas (#)	972	375	9	73	20	493

Tulare City Elementary
600 N Cherry Ave • Tulare, CA 93274-2920
(559) 685-7200 • http://www.tcsd.k12.ca.us/
Grade Span: KG-08; **Agency Type:** 1
Schools: 13
9 Primary; 4 Middle; 0 High; 0 Other Level
12 Regular; 0 Special Education; 0 Vocational; 1 Alternative
0 Magnet; 0 Charter; 13 Title I Eligible; 8 School-wide Title I
Students: 7,861 (50.0% male; 50.0% female)
Individual Education Program: 606 (7.7%);
English Language Learner: 1,581 (20.1%); Migrant: 1,362 (17.3%)
Eligible for Free Lunch Program: 4,674 (59.5%)
Eligible for Reduced-Price Lunch Program: 951 (12.1%)
Teachers: 398.6 (19.7 to 1)
Librarians/Media Specialists: 0.0 (0.0 to 1)
Guidance Counselors: 3.0 (2,620.3 to 1)
Current Spending: ($ per student per year):
Total: $5,554; Instruction: $3,902; Support Services: $1,322
Enrollment, Drop-out Rates and Diploma Recipients by Race/Ethnicity

Category	Total	White	Black	Asian	AIAN	Hisp.
Enrollment (%)	100.0	28.7	7.8	2.7	0.5	60.0
Drop-out Rate (%)	n/a	n/a	n/a	n/a	n/a	n/a
H.S. Diplomas (#)	n/a	n/a	n/a	n/a	n/a	n/a

Tulare Joint Union High
426 N Blackstone • Tulare, CA 93274-4449
(559) 688-2021 • http://www.tulare.k12.ca.us/
Grade Span: 09-12; **Agency Type:** 1
Schools: 5
0 Primary; 0 Middle; 5 High; 0 Other Level
2 Regular; 0 Special Education; 0 Vocational; 3 Alternative
1 Magnet; 0 Charter; 5 Title I Eligible; 5 School-wide Title I
Students: 4,230 (50.6% male; 49.4% female)
Individual Education Program: 313 (7.4%);
English Language Learner: 291 (6.9%); Migrant: 470 (11.1%)
Eligible for Free Lunch Program: 1,380 (32.6%)
Eligible for Reduced-Price Lunch Program: 133 (3.1%)

Teachers: 173.8 (24.3 to 1)
Librarians/Media Specialists: 2.0 (2,115.0 to 1)
Guidance Counselors: 14.3 (295.8 to 1)
Current Spending: ($ per student per year):
Total: $6,382; Instruction: $3,703; Support Services: $2,325
Enrollment, Drop-out Rates and Diploma Recipients by Race/Ethnicity

Category	Total	White	Black	Asian	AIAN	Hisp.
Enrollment (%)	100.0	34.9	5.3	2.2	0.4	50.9
Drop-out Rate (%)	n/a	n/a	n/a	n/a	n/a	n/a
H.S. Diplomas (#)	870	376	50	18	5	404

Visalia Unified

5000 W Cypress Ave • Visalia, CA 93277-8300
(559) 730-7300 • http://www2.visalia.k12.ca.us/
Grade Span: KG-12; **Agency Type:** 1
Schools: 33
21 Primary; 4 Middle; 6 High; 2 Other Level
30 Regular; 1 Special Education; 0 Vocational; 2 Alternative
0 Magnet; 3 Charter; 16 Title I Eligible; 10 School-wide Title I
Students: 24,962 (50.8% male; 49.2% female)
Individual Education Program: 2,280 (9.1%);
English Language Learner: 5,407 (21.7%); Migrant: 1,266 (5.1%)
Eligible for Free Lunch Program: 10,207 (40.9%)
Eligible for Reduced-Price Lunch Program: 1,894 (7.6%)
Teachers: 1,190.7 (21.0 to 1)
Librarians/Media Specialists: 4.0 (6,240.5 to 1)
Guidance Counselors: 13.9 (1,795.8 to 1)
Current Spending: ($ per student per year):
Total: $6,140; Instruction: $4,080; Support Services: $1,838
Enrollment, Drop-out Rates and Diploma Recipients by Race/Ethnicity

Category	Total	White	Black	Asian	AIAN	Hisp.
Enrollment (%)	100.0	39.6	2.6	6.4	1.0	50.3
Drop-out Rate (%)	n/a	n/a	n/a	n/a	n/a	n/a
H.S. Diplomas (#)	1,310	706	19	112	12	461

Woodlake Union Elementary

300 W Whitney Ave • Woodlake, CA 93286-1238
(559) 564-8081
Grade Span: KG-08; **Agency Type:** 2
Schools: 3
2 Primary; 1 Middle; 0 High; 0 Other Level
3 Regular; 0 Special Education; 0 Vocational; 0 Alternative
0 Magnet; 0 Charter; 3 Title I Eligible; 3 School-wide Title I
Students: 1,600 (51.9% male; 48.1% female)
Individual Education Program: 86 (5.4%);
English Language Learner: 632 (39.5%); Migrant: 552 (34.5%)
Eligible for Free Lunch Program: 1,259 (78.7%)
Eligible for Reduced-Price Lunch Program: 105 (6.6%)
Teachers: 81.0 (19.8 to 1)
Librarians/Media Specialists: 0.0 (0.0 to 1)
Guidance Counselors: 0.0 (0.0 to 1)
Current Spending: ($ per student per year):
Total: $7,597; Instruction: $4,524; Support Services: $2,571
Enrollment, Drop-out Rates and Diploma Recipients by Race/Ethnicity

Category	Total	White	Black	Asian	AIAN	Hisp.
Enrollment (%)	100.0	13.1	0.5	0.5	0.0	85.9
Drop-out Rate (%)	n/a	n/a	n/a	n/a	n/a	n/a
H.S. Diplomas (#)	n/a	n/a	n/a	n/a	n/a	n/a

Tuolumne County

Sonora Union High

251 S Barretta St • Sonora, CA 95370-5042
(209) 533-8510 • http://www.sonorahs.k12.ca.us/district/
Grade Span: 09-12; **Agency Type:** 1
Schools: 4
0 Primary; 0 Middle; 4 High; 0 Other Level
1 Regular; 0 Special Education; 0 Vocational; 3 Alternative
0 Magnet; 0 Charter; 1 Title I Eligible; 0 School-wide Title I
Students: 1,720 (50.9% male; 49.1% female)
Individual Education Program: 147 (8.5%);
English Language Learner: 5 (0.3%); Migrant: 0 (0.0%)
Eligible for Free Lunch Program: 268 (15.6%)
Eligible for Reduced-Price Lunch Program: 50 (2.9%)
Teachers: 73.5 (23.4 to 1)
Librarians/Media Specialists: 1.0 (1,720.0 to 1)
Guidance Counselors: 4.0 (430.0 to 1)
Current Spending: ($ per student per year):
Total: $6,780; Instruction: $3,731; Support Services: $2,722
Enrollment, Drop-out Rates and Diploma Recipients by Race/Ethnicity

Category	Total	White	Black	Asian	AIAN	Hisp.
Enrollment (%)	100.0	82.4	0.7	1.4	3.0	8.3
Drop-out Rate (%)	n/a	n/a	n/a	n/a	n/a	n/a
H.S. Diplomas (#)	359	345	1	1	2	8

Ventura County

Conejo Valley Unified

1400 E Janss Rd • Thousand Oaks, CA 91362-2133
(805) 497-9511 • http://www.conejo.k12.ca.us/
Grade Span: KG-12; **Agency Type:** 1
Schools: 29
20 Primary; 4 Middle; 5 High; 0 Other Level
27 Regular; 0 Special Education; 0 Vocational; 2 Alternative
1 Magnet; 0 Charter; 6 Title I Eligible; 0 School-wide Title I
Students: 21,855 (52.0% male; 48.0% female)
Individual Education Program: 2,154 (9.9%);
English Language Learner: 1,748 (8.0%); Migrant: 0 (0.0%)
Eligible for Free Lunch Program: 1,899 (8.7%)
Eligible for Reduced-Price Lunch Program: 864 (4.0%)
Teachers: 979.0 (22.3 to 1)
Librarians/Media Specialists: 3.0 (7,285.0 to 1)
Guidance Counselors: 28.7 (761.5 to 1)
Current Spending: ($ per student per year):
Total: $5,973; Instruction: $4,053; Support Services: $1,755
Enrollment, Drop-out Rates and Diploma Recipients by Race/Ethnicity

Category	Total	White	Black	Asian	AIAN	Hisp.
Enrollment (%)	100.0	73.4	1.5	7.7	0.7	16.5
Drop-out Rate (%)	n/a	n/a	n/a	n/a	n/a	n/a
H.S. Diplomas (#)	1,413	1,137	12	114	3	146

Fillmore Unified

627 Sespe Ave • Fillmore, CA 93016-0697
Mailing Address: PO Box 697 • Fillmore, CA 93016-0697
(805) 524-6000 • http://www.fillmore.k12.ca.us/
Grade Span: KG-12; **Agency Type:** 1
Schools: 6
3 Primary; 1 Middle; 2 High; 0 Other Level
5 Regular; 0 Special Education; 0 Vocational; 1 Alternative
0 Magnet; 0 Charter; 6 Title I Eligible; 5 School-wide Title I
Students: 3,869 (50.0% male; 50.0% female)
Individual Education Program: 452 (11.7%);
English Language Learner: 1,525 (39.4%); Migrant: 1,188 (30.7%)
Eligible for Free Lunch Program: 1,869 (48.3%)
Eligible for Reduced-Price Lunch Program: 422 (10.9%)
Teachers: 186.8 (20.7 to 1)
Librarians/Media Specialists: 0.0 (0.0 to 1)
Guidance Counselors: 4.0 (967.3 to 1)
Current Spending: ($ per student per year):
Total: $6,467; Instruction: $3,962; Support Services: $2,245
Enrollment, Drop-out Rates and Diploma Recipients by Race/Ethnicity

Category	Total	White	Black	Asian	AIAN	Hisp.
Enrollment (%)	100.0	17.3	0.4	0.7	0.7	80.5
Drop-out Rate (%)	n/a	n/a	n/a	n/a	n/a	n/a
H.S. Diplomas (#)	233	58	0	3	2	170

Hueneme Elementary

205 N Ventura Rd • Port Hueneme, CA 93041-3065
(805) 488-3588 • http://www.huensd.k12.ca.us/
Grade Span: KG-08; **Agency Type:** 1
Schools: 11
9 Primary; 2 Middle; 0 High; 0 Other Level
11 Regular; 0 Special Education; 0 Vocational; 0 Alternative
0 Magnet; 0 Charter; 10 Title I Eligible; 3 School-wide Title I
Students: 8,648 (50.8% male; 49.2% female)
Individual Education Program: 780 (9.0%);
English Language Learner: 3,826 (44.2%); Migrant: 2,087 (24.1%)
Eligible for Free Lunch Program: 4,609 (53.3%)
Eligible for Reduced-Price Lunch Program: 1,422 (16.4%)
Teachers: 416.8 (20.7 to 1)
Librarians/Media Specialists: 0.0 (0.0 to 1)
Guidance Counselors: 2.0 (4,324.0 to 1)
Current Spending: ($ per student per year):
Total: $6,273; Instruction: $4,314; Support Services: $1,716
Enrollment, Drop-out Rates and Diploma Recipients by Race/Ethnicity

Category	Total	White	Black	Asian	AIAN	Hisp.
Enrollment (%)	100.0	12.7	4.0	8.9	0.7	73.8
Drop-out Rate (%)	n/a	n/a	n/a	n/a	n/a	n/a
H.S. Diplomas (#)	n/a	n/a	n/a	n/a	n/a	n/a

Moorpark Unified

30 Flory Ave • Moorpark, CA 93021-1862
(805) 378-6300 • http://www.mrpk.k12.ca.us/
Grade Span: KG-12; **Agency Type:** 1
Schools: 11
5 Primary; 3 Middle; 3 High; 0 Other Level
10 Regular; 0 Special Education; 0 Vocational; 1 Alternative
0 Magnet; 0 Charter; 6 Title I Eligible; 0 School-wide Title I
Students: 7,824 (50.8% male; 49.2% female)
Individual Education Program: 868 (11.1%);

English Language Learner: 1,374 (17.6%); Migrant: 425 (5.4%)
Eligible for Free Lunch Program: 1,739 (22.2%)
Eligible for Reduced-Price Lunch Program: 431 (5.5%)
Teachers: 375.8 (20.8 to 1)
Librarians/Media Specialists: 0.0 (0.0 to 1)
Guidance Counselors: 9.7 (806.6 to 1)
Current Spending: ($ per student per year):
Total: $6,023; Instruction: $3,861; Support Services: $1,965
Enrollment, Drop-out Rates and Diploma Recipients by Race/Ethnicity

Category	Total	White	Black	Asian	AIAN	Hisp.
Enrollment (%)	100.0	59.8	1.8	5.2	1.0	31.0
Drop-out Rate (%)	n/a	n/a	n/a	n/a	n/a	n/a
H.S. Diplomas (#)	569	364	12	45	5	143

Oak Park Unified
5801 E Conifer St • Oak Park, CA 91301-1002
(626) 735-3200 • http://www.opusd.k12.ca.us/
Grade Span: KG-12; **Agency Type:** 1
Schools: 6
3 Primary; 1 Middle; 2 High; 0 Other Level
5 Regular; 0 Special Education; 0 Vocational; 1 Alternative
0 Magnet; 0 Charter; 3 Title I Eligible; 0 School-wide Title I
Students: 3,752 (51.4% male; 48.6% female)
Individual Education Program: 332 (8.8%);
English Language Learner: 78 (2.1%); Migrant: 0 (0.0%)
Eligible for Free Lunch Program: 37 (1.0%)
Eligible for Reduced-Price Lunch Program: 20 (0.5%)
Teachers: 173.3 (21.7 to 1)
Librarians/Media Specialists: 0.0 (0.0 to 1)
Guidance Counselors: 5.0 (750.4 to 1)
Current Spending: ($ per student per year):
Total: $6,375; Instruction: $4,184; Support Services: $2,043
Enrollment, Drop-out Rates and Diploma Recipients by Race/Ethnicity

Category	Total	White	Black	Asian	AIAN	Hisp.
Enrollment (%)	100.0	86.0	1.2	9.5	0.0	3.4
Drop-out Rate (%)	n/a	n/a	n/a	n/a	n/a	n/a
H.S. Diplomas (#)	232	208	4	13	0	7

Ocean View Elementary
2382 Etting Rd • Oxnard, CA 93033-6864
(805) 488-4441 • http://www.ovsd.k12.ca.us/
Grade Span: KG-08; **Agency Type:** 1
Schools: 4
3 Primary; 1 Middle; 0 High; 0 Other Level
4 Regular; 0 Special Education; 0 Vocational; 0 Alternative
0 Magnet; 0 Charter; 2 Title I Eligible; 0 School-wide Title I
Students: 2,633 (51.7% male; 48.3% female)
Individual Education Program: 220 (8.4%);
English Language Learner: 1,294 (49.1%); Migrant: 729 (27.7%)
Eligible for Free Lunch Program: 1,419 (53.9%)
Eligible for Reduced-Price Lunch Program: 530 (20.1%)
Teachers: 132.0 (19.9 to 1)
Librarians/Media Specialists: 0.0 (0.0 to 1)
Guidance Counselors: 2.0 (1,316.5 to 1)
Current Spending: ($ per student per year):
Total: $7,010; Instruction: $4,315; Support Services: $2,389
Enrollment, Drop-out Rates and Diploma Recipients by Race/Ethnicity

Category	Total	White	Black	Asian	AIAN	Hisp.
Enrollment (%)	100.0	13.7	5.0	7.4	0.3	73.5
Drop-out Rate (%)	n/a	n/a	n/a	n/a	n/a	n/a
H.S. Diplomas (#)	n/a	n/a	n/a	n/a	n/a	n/a

Ojai Unified
414 E Ojai Ave • Ojai, CA 93024-0878
Mailing Address: PO Box 878 • Ojai, CA 93024-0878
(805) 640-4300 • http://www.ojai.k12.ca.us/
Grade Span: KG-12; **Agency Type:** 1
Schools: 9
5 Primary; 1 Middle; 2 High; 1 Other Level
8 Regular; 0 Special Education; 0 Vocational; 1 Alternative
0 Magnet; 1 Charter; 4 Title I Eligible; 0 School-wide Title I
Students: 3,915 (51.3% male; 48.7% female)
Individual Education Program: 394 (10.1%);
English Language Learner: 481 (12.3%); Migrant: 0 (0.0%)
Eligible for Free Lunch Program: 658 (16.8%)
Eligible for Reduced-Price Lunch Program: 249 (6.4%)
Teachers: 187.0 (20.9 to 1)
Librarians/Media Specialists: 0.0 (0.0 to 1)
Guidance Counselors: 4.0 (978.8 to 1)
Current Spending: ($ per student per year):
Total: $6,184; Instruction: $3,816; Support Services: $2,163
Enrollment, Drop-out Rates and Diploma Recipients by Race/Ethnicity

Category	Total	White	Black	Asian	AIAN	Hisp.
Enrollment (%)	100.0	71.6	0.9	2.5	0.8	23.4
Drop-out Rate (%)	n/a	n/a	n/a	n/a	n/a	n/a
H.S. Diplomas (#)	274	209	2	6	4	53

Oxnard Elementary
1051 S A St • Oxnard, CA 93030-7442
(805) 487-3918 • http://www.oxnardsd.org/
Grade Span: KG-08; **Agency Type:** 1
Schools: 20
16 Primary; 4 Middle; 0 High; 0 Other Level
19 Regular; 1 Special Education; 0 Vocational; 0 Alternative
0 Magnet; 0 Charter; 18 Title I Eligible; 14 School-wide Title I
Students: 16,625 (50.4% male; 49.6% female)
Individual Education Program: 1,548 (9.3%);
English Language Learner: 7,879 (47.4%); Migrant: 1,226 (7.4%)
Eligible for Free Lunch Program: 9,843 (59.2%)
Eligible for Reduced-Price Lunch Program: 2,567 (15.4%)
Teachers: 777.8 (21.4 to 1)
Librarians/Media Specialists: 0.0 (0.0 to 1)
Guidance Counselors: 0.0 (0.0 to 1)
Current Spending: ($ per student per year):
Total: $6,452; Instruction: $4,271; Support Services: $1,869
Enrollment, Drop-out Rates and Diploma Recipients by Race/Ethnicity

Category	Total	White	Black	Asian	AIAN	Hisp.
Enrollment (%)	100.0	9.2	3.0	3.3	0.4	83.5
Drop-out Rate (%)	n/a	n/a	n/a	n/a	n/a	n/a
H.S. Diplomas (#)	n/a	n/a	n/a	n/a	n/a	n/a

Oxnard Union High
309 S K St • Oxnard, CA 93030-5212
(805) 385-2500 • http://www.ouhsd.k12.ca.us/
Grade Span: KG-12; **Agency Type:** 1
Schools: 9
0 Primary; 0 Middle; 9 High; 0 Other Level
6 Regular; 0 Special Education; 0 Vocational; 3 Alternative
0 Magnet; 0 Charter; 8 Title I Eligible; 0 School-wide Title I
Students: 15,370 (51.3% male; 48.7% female)
Individual Education Program: 1,554 (10.1%);
English Language Learner: 3,461 (22.5%); Migrant: 2,390 (15.5%)
Eligible for Free Lunch Program: 4,435 (28.9%)
Eligible for Reduced-Price Lunch Program: 872 (5.7%)
Teachers: 633.8 (24.3 to 1)
Librarians/Media Specialists: 6.0 (2,561.7 to 1)
Guidance Counselors: 39.0 (394.1 to 1)
Current Spending: ($ per student per year):
Total: $6,108; Instruction: $3,872; Support Services: $2,004
Enrollment, Drop-out Rates and Diploma Recipients by Race/Ethnicity

Category	Total	White	Black	Asian	AIAN	Hisp.
Enrollment (%)	100.0	23.9	3.6	7.7	1.6	62.5
Drop-out Rate (%)	n/a	n/a	n/a	n/a	n/a	n/a
H.S. Diplomas (#)	2,529	717	98	272	50	1,392

Pleasant Valley School
600 Temple Ave • Camarillo, CA 93010-4835
(805) 482-2763 • http://www.pvsd.k12.ca.us/
Grade Span: KG-08; **Agency Type:** 1
Schools: 13
11 Primary; 2 Middle; 0 High; 0 Other Level
13 Regular; 0 Special Education; 0 Vocational; 0 Alternative
1 Magnet; 1 Charter; 4 Title I Eligible; 0 School-wide Title I
Students: 7,389 (51.6% male; 48.4% female)
Individual Education Program: 764 (10.3%);
English Language Learner: 680 (9.2%); Migrant: 67 (0.9%)
Eligible for Free Lunch Program: 756 (10.2%)
Eligible for Reduced-Price Lunch Program: 395 (5.3%)
Teachers: 353.5 (20.9 to 1)
Librarians/Media Specialists: 1.0 (7,389.0 to 1)
Guidance Counselors: 4.0 (1,847.3 to 1)
Current Spending: ($ per student per year):
Total: $5,686; Instruction: $3,793; Support Services: $1,830
Enrollment, Drop-out Rates and Diploma Recipients by Race/Ethnicity

Category	Total	White	Black	Asian	AIAN	Hisp.
Enrollment (%)	100.0	61.4	2.6	10.5	0.8	24.7
Drop-out Rate (%)	n/a	n/a	n/a	n/a	n/a	n/a
H.S. Diplomas (#)	n/a	n/a	n/a	n/a	n/a	n/a

Rio Elementary
3300 Cortez St • Oxnard, CA 93036-1309
(805) 485-3111 • http://www.rio.k12.ca.us/
Grade Span: KG-08; **Agency Type:** 1
Schools: 7
6 Primary; 1 Middle; 0 High; 0 Other Level
7 Regular; 0 Special Education; 0 Vocational; 0 Alternative

0 Magnet; 0 Charter; 7 Title I Eligible; 0 School-wide Title I
Students: 3,929 (50.6% male; 49.4% female)
Individual Education Program: 427 (10.9%);
English Language Learner: 1,833 (46.7%); Migrant: 1,314 (33.4%)
Eligible for Free Lunch Program: 1,695 (43.1%)
Eligible for Reduced-Price Lunch Program: 625 (15.9%)
Teachers: 182.0 (21.6 to 1)
Librarians/Media Specialists: 0.0 (0.0 to 1)
Guidance Counselors: 0.0 (0.0 to 1)
Current Spending: ($ per student per year):
Total: $5,824; Instruction: $3,812; Support Services: $1,697
Enrollment, Drop-out Rates and Diploma Recipients by Race/Ethnicity

Category	Total	White	Black	Asian	AIAN	Hisp.
Enrollment (%)	100.0	9.9	3.1	6.0	0.6	80.0
Drop-out Rate (%)	n/a	n/a	n/a	n/a	n/a	n/a
H.S. Diplomas (#)	n/a	n/a	n/a	n/a	n/a	n/a

Santa Paula Elementary
201 S Steckel Dr • Santa Paula, CA 93060
(805) 933-5342 • http://www.spesd.org/main/
Grade Span: KG-08; **Agency Type:** 1
Schools: 7
6 Primary; 1 Middle; 0 High; 0 Other Level
7 Regular; 0 Special Education; 0 Vocational; 0 Alternative
6 Magnet; 0 Charter; 7 Title I Eligible; 0 School-wide Title I
Students: 4,149 (50.9% male; 49.1% female)
Individual Education Program: 392 (9.4%);
English Language Learner: 2,141 (51.6%); Migrant: 1,113 (26.8%)
Eligible for Free Lunch Program: 2,201 (53.0%)
Eligible for Reduced-Price Lunch Program: 1,004 (24.2%)
Teachers: 200.7 (20.7 to 1)
Librarians/Media Specialists: 0.0 (0.0 to 1)
Guidance Counselors: 8.0 (518.6 to 1)
Current Spending: ($ per student per year):
Total: $6,816; Instruction: $4,174; Support Services: $2,308
Enrollment, Drop-out Rates and Diploma Recipients by Race/Ethnicity

Category	Total	White	Black	Asian	AIAN	Hisp.
Enrollment (%)	100.0	13.0	0.5	0.5	0.2	85.9
Drop-out Rate (%)	n/a	n/a	n/a	n/a	n/a	n/a
H.S. Diplomas (#)	n/a	n/a	n/a	n/a	n/a	n/a

Santa Paula Union High
500 E Santa Barbara St • Santa Paula, CA 93060-2633
(805) 525-0988 • http://www.spuhsd.k12.ca.us/front.html
Grade Span: 09-12; **Agency Type:** 1
Schools: 2
0 Primary; 0 Middle; 2 High; 0 Other Level
1 Regular; 0 Special Education; 0 Vocational; 1 Alternative
0 Magnet; 0 Charter; 1 Title I Eligible; 0 School-wide Title I
Students: 1,725 (51.5% male; 48.5% female)
Individual Education Program: 149 (8.6%);
English Language Learner: 204 (11.8%); Migrant: 334 (19.4%)
Eligible for Free Lunch Program: 636 (36.9%)
Eligible for Reduced-Price Lunch Program: 200 (11.6%)
Teachers: 62.7 (27.5 to 1)
Librarians/Media Specialists: 0.0 (0.0 to 1)
Guidance Counselors: 2.0 (862.5 to 1)
Current Spending: ($ per student per year):
Total: $6,081; Instruction: $3,455; Support Services: $2,441
Enrollment, Drop-out Rates and Diploma Recipients by Race/Ethnicity

Category	Total	White	Black	Asian	AIAN	Hisp.
Enrollment (%)	100.0	16.9	0.6	0.4	0.1	81.9
Drop-out Rate (%)	n/a	n/a	n/a	n/a	n/a	n/a
H.S. Diplomas (#)	286	41	1	2	0	242

Simi Valley Unified
875 E Cochran • Simi Valley, CA 93065-0999
(805) 520-6500 • http://www.simi.k12.ca.us/
Grade Span: KG-12; **Agency Type:** 1
Schools: 29
21 Primary; 3 Middle; 4 High; 1 Other Level
27 Regular; 0 Special Education; 0 Vocational; 2 Alternative
0 Magnet; 0 Charter; 4 Title I Eligible; 0 School-wide Title I
Students: 21,673 (51.5% male; 48.5% female)
Individual Education Program: 2,253 (10.4%);
English Language Learner: 1,630 (7.5%); Migrant: 0 (0.0%)
Eligible for Free Lunch Program: 2,570 (11.9%)
Eligible for Reduced-Price Lunch Program: 1,173 (5.4%)
Teachers: 945.0 (22.9 to 1)
Librarians/Media Specialists: 1.0 (21,673.0 to 1)
Guidance Counselors: 18.0 (1,204.1 to 1)
Current Spending: ($ per student per year):
Total: $5,745; Instruction: $3,849; Support Services: $1,758
Enrollment, Drop-out Rates and Diploma Recipients by Race/Ethnicity

Category	Total	White	Black	Asian	AIAN	Hisp.
Enrollment (%)	100.0	70.3	1.6	7.7	1.0	19.3
Drop-out Rate (%)	n/a	n/a	n/a	n/a	n/a	n/a
H.S. Diplomas (#)	1,148	831	21	111	18	167

Ventura Unified
120 E Santa Clara St • Ventura, CA 93001-2716
(805) 641-5000 • http://www.ventura.k12.ca.us
Grade Span: KG-12; **Agency Type:** 1
Schools: 29
18 Primary; 4 Middle; 6 High; 1 Other Level
24 Regular; 0 Special Education; 0 Vocational; 5 Alternative
2 Magnet; 0 Charter; 12 Title I Eligible; 7 School-wide Title I
Students: 17,744 (51.3% male; 48.7% female)
Individual Education Program: 1,779 (10.0%);
English Language Learner: 2,594 (14.6%); Migrant: 798 (4.5%)
Eligible for Free Lunch Program: 4,171 (23.5%)
Eligible for Reduced-Price Lunch Program: 2,024 (11.4%)
Teachers: 770.2 (23.0 to 1)
Librarians/Media Specialists: 7.2 (2,464.4 to 1)
Guidance Counselors: 29.4 (603.5 to 1)
Current Spending: ($ per student per year):
Total: $5,865; Instruction: $3,728; Support Services: $1,833
Enrollment, Drop-out Rates and Diploma Recipients by Race/Ethnicity

Category	Total	White	Black	Asian	AIAN	Hisp.
Enrollment (%)	100.0	55.3	2.4	3.4	1.2	37.6
Drop-out Rate (%)	n/a	n/a	n/a	n/a	n/a	n/a
H.S. Diplomas (#)	1,024	672	24	35	11	275

Yolo County

Davis Joint Unified
526 B St • Davis, CA 95616-3811
(530) 757-5300 • http://www.djusd.k12.ca.us/District/
Grade Span: KG-12; **Agency Type:** 1
Schools: 14
9 Primary; 2 Middle; 2 High; 1 Other Level
12 Regular; 0 Special Education; 0 Vocational; 2 Alternative
1 Magnet; 0 Charter; 6 Title I Eligible; 0 School-wide Title I
Students: 8,827 (50.4% male; 49.6% female)
Individual Education Program: 704 (8.0%);
English Language Learner: 839 (9.5%); Migrant: 99 (1.1%)
Eligible for Free Lunch Program: 703 (8.0%)
Eligible for Reduced-Price Lunch Program: 259 (2.9%)
Teachers: 438.2 (20.1 to 1)
Librarians/Media Specialists: 5.0 (1,765.4 to 1)
Guidance Counselors: 14.4 (613.0 to 1)
Current Spending: ($ per student per year):
Total: $6,322; Instruction: $4,064; Support Services: $2,139
Enrollment, Drop-out Rates and Diploma Recipients by Race/Ethnicity

Category	Total	White	Black	Asian	AIAN	Hisp.
Enrollment (%)	100.0	67.8	4.1	14.4	0.8	12.3
Drop-out Rate (%)	n/a	n/a	n/a	n/a	n/a	n/a
H.S. Diplomas (#)	576	420	9	84	5	56

Washington Unified
930 W Acres Rd • West Sacramento, CA 95691-3224
(916) 375-7600 • http://www.wusd.k12.ca.us/
Grade Span: KG-12; **Agency Type:** 1
Schools: 13
9 Primary; 1 Middle; 2 High; 1 Other Level
10 Regular; 0 Special Education; 0 Vocational; 3 Alternative
0 Magnet; 0 Charter; 9 Title I Eligible; 7 School-wide Title I
Students: 6,876 (51.1% male; 48.9% female)
Individual Education Program: 741 (10.8%);
English Language Learner: 1,859 (27.0%); Migrant: 1 (<0.1%)
Eligible for Free Lunch Program: 3,610 (52.5%)
Eligible for Reduced-Price Lunch Program: 813 (11.8%)
Teachers: 369.2 (18.6 to 1)
Librarians/Media Specialists: 1.0 (6,876.0 to 1)
Guidance Counselors: 7.3 (941.9 to 1)
Current Spending: ($ per student per year):
Total: $6,629; Instruction: $4,011; Support Services: $2,306
Enrollment, Drop-out Rates and Diploma Recipients by Race/Ethnicity

Category	Total	White	Black	Asian	AIAN	Hisp.
Enrollment (%)	100.0	41.2	5.2	13.9	2.4	37.1
Drop-out Rate (%)	n/a	n/a	n/a	n/a	n/a	n/a
H.S. Diplomas (#)	327	155	7	48	9	108

Winters Joint Unified
710 Railroad Ave • Winters, CA 95694-1646
(530) 795-6100 • http://winters.k12.ca.us/
Grade Span: KG-12; **Agency Type:** 1
Schools: 6

2 Primary; 2 Middle; 2 High; 0 Other Level
5 Regular; 0 Special Education; 0 Vocational; 1 Alternative
0 Magnet; 0 Charter; 4 Title I Eligible; 0 School-wide Title I
Students: 2,038 (53.1% male; 46.9% female)
Individual Education Program: 216 (10.6%);
English Language Learner: 670 (32.9%); Migrant: 397 (19.5%)
Eligible for Free Lunch Program: 754 (37.0%)
Eligible for Reduced-Price Lunch Program: 199 (9.8%)
Teachers: 109.1 (18.7 to 1)
Librarians/Media Specialists: 1.0 (2,038.0 to 1)
Guidance Counselors: 4.6 (443.0 to 1)
Current Spending: ($ per student per year):
Total: $6,430; Instruction: $3,767; Support Services: $2,495
Enrollment, Drop-out Rates and Diploma Recipients by Race/Ethnicity

Category	Total	White	Black	Asian	AIAN	Hisp.
Enrollment (%)	100.0	44.6	0.5	1.4	0.6	52.4
Drop-out Rate (%)	n/a	n/a	n/a	n/a	n/a	n/a
H.S. Diplomas (#)	122	59	0	6	3	54

Woodland Joint Unified
630 Cottonwood St • Woodland, CA 95695-3615
(530) 662-0201 • http://www.wjusd.k12.ca.us/
Grade Span: KG-12; **Agency Type:** 1
Schools: 17
13 Primary; 2 Middle; 2 High; 0 Other Level
15 Regular; 0 Special Education; 0 Vocational; 2 Alternative
0 Magnet; 0 Charter; 10 Title I Eligible; 7 School-wide Title I
Students: 10,445 (51.8% male; 48.2% female)
Individual Education Program: 1,121 (10.7%);
English Language Learner: 2,910 (27.9%); Migrant: 1,181 (11.3%)
Eligible for Free Lunch Program: 2,834 (27.1%)
Eligible for Reduced-Price Lunch Program: 983 (9.4%)
Teachers: 529.9 (19.7 to 1)
Librarians/Media Specialists: 1.0 (10,445.0 to 1)
Guidance Counselors: 10.6 (985.4 to 1)
Current Spending: ($ per student per year):
Total: $6,012; Instruction: $3,555; Support Services: $2,238
Enrollment, Drop-out Rates and Diploma Recipients by Race/Ethnicity

Category	Total	White	Black	Asian	AIAN	Hisp.
Enrollment (%)	100.0	41.3	1.6	5.0	0.7	51.1
Drop-out Rate (%)	n/a	n/a	n/a	n/a	n/a	n/a
H.S. Diplomas (#)	550	273	7	33	3	234

Yuba County

Marysville Joint Unified
1919 B St • Marysville, CA 95901-3731
(530) 741-6000 • http://www.mjusd.k12.ca.us/
Grade Span: KG-12; **Agency Type:** 1
Schools: 23
13 Primary; 4 Middle; 5 High; 1 Other Level
20 Regular; 0 Special Education; 0 Vocational; 3 Alternative
0 Magnet; 1 Charter; 19 Title I Eligible; 15 School-wide Title I
Students: 9,793 (51.2% male; 48.8% female)
Individual Education Program: 934 (9.5%);
English Language Learner: 2,200 (22.5%); Migrant: 538 (5.5%)
Eligible for Free Lunch Program: 6,396 (65.3%)
Eligible for Reduced-Price Lunch Program: 1,101 (11.2%)
Teachers: 493.5 (19.8 to 1)
Librarians/Media Specialists: 0.3 (32,643.3 to 1)
Guidance Counselors: 2.5 (3,917.2 to 1)
Current Spending: ($ per student per year):
Total: $6,663; Instruction: $4,248; Support Services: $2,104
Enrollment, Drop-out Rates and Diploma Recipients by Race/Ethnicity

Category	Total	White	Black	Asian	AIAN	Hisp.
Enrollment (%)	100.0	47.7	3.6	16.0	6.6	24.6
Drop-out Rate (%)	n/a	n/a	n/a	n/a	n/a	n/a
H.S. Diplomas (#)	421	201	9	106	36	69

Wheatland Elementary
711 W Olive • Wheatland, CA 95692-0818
Mailing Address: PO Box 818 • Wheatland, CA 95692-0818
(530) 633-3130 • http://www.wheatland.k12.ca.us/
Grade Span: KG-12; **Agency Type:** 1
Schools: 6
2 Primary; 2 Middle; 0 High; 2 Other Level
6 Regular; 0 Special Education; 0 Vocational; 0 Alternative
0 Magnet; 2 Charter; 2 Title I Eligible; 0 School-wide Title I
Students: 2,436 (52.0% male; 48.0% female)
Individual Education Program: 136 (5.6%);
English Language Learner: 97 (4.0%); Migrant: 7 (0.3%)
Eligible for Free Lunch Program: 518 (21.3%)
Eligible for Reduced-Price Lunch Program: 600 (24.6%)
Teachers: 121.3 (20.1 to 1)
Librarians/Media Specialists: 1.0 (2,436.0 to 1)
Guidance Counselors: 0.0 (0.0 to 1)
Current Spending: ($ per student per year):
Total: $7,575; Instruction: $4,630; Support Services: $2,579
Enrollment, Drop-out Rates and Diploma Recipients by Race/Ethnicity

Category	Total	White	Black	Asian	AIAN	Hisp.
Enrollment (%)	100.0	65.9	9.6	9.4	2.2	12.6
Drop-out Rate (%)	n/a	n/a	n/a	n/a	n/a	n/a
H.S. Diplomas (#)	0	0	0	0	0	0

Number of Schools

Rank	Number	District Name	City
1	677	Los Angeles Unified	Los Angeles
2	185	San Diego Unified	San Diego
3	114	San Francisco Unified	San Francisco
4	110	Oakland Unified	Oakland
5	103	Fresno Unified	Fresno
6	89	Long Beach Unified	Long Beach
7	84	San Juan Unified	Carmichael
8	80	Sacramento City Unified	Sacramento
9	67	Garden Grove Unified	Garden Grove
10	65	San Bernardino City Unified	San Bernardino
11	63	West Contra Costa Unified	Richmond
12	57	San Jose Unified	San Jose
13	55	Elk Grove Unified	Elk Grove
13	55	Mount Diablo Unified	Concord
13	55	Santa Ana Unified	Santa Ana
16	51	Capistrano Unified	San Juan Capis
17	48	Stockton City Unified	Stockton
18	45	Riverside Unified	Riverside
19	43	Bakersfield City Elementary	Bakersfield
19	43	Lodi Unified	Lodi
21	42	Orange Unified	Orange
22	41	Fremont Unified	Fremont
23	40	Pomona Unified	Pomona
24	39	Chula Vista Elementary	Chula Vista
24	39	Compton Unified	Compton
24	39	Corona-Norco Unified	Norco
27	38	Clovis Unified	Clovis
28	37	Fontana Unified	Fontana
28	37	Hacienda La Puente Unified	City of Industry
28	37	Saddleback Valley Unified	Mission Viejo
31	36	Napa Valley Unified	Napa
32	34	Irvine Unified	Irvine
33	33	Hayward Unified	Hayward
33	33	Moreno Valley Unified	Moreno Valley
33	33	Visalia Unified	Visalia
36	32	Chino Valley Unified	Chino
36	32	Glendale Unified	Glendale
36	32	Ontario-Montclair Elementary	Ontario
36	32	Pasadena Unified	Pasadena
40	31	Newport-Mesa Unified	Costa Mesa
40	31	Poway Unified	Poway
42	30	ABC Unified	Cerritos
42	30	Folsom-Cordova Unified	Folsom
42	30	Pajaro Valley Unified School	Watsonville
42	30	Placentia-Yorba Linda Unified	Placentia
42	30	Torrance Unified	Torrance
47	29	Conejo Valley Unified	Thousand Oaks
47	29	Montebello Unified	Montebello
47	29	Norwalk-La Mirada Unified	Norwalk
47	29	Simi Valley Unified	Simi Valley
47	29	Ventura Unified	Ventura
52	28	Cajon Valley Union Elementary	El Cajon
52	28	Fairfield-Suisun Unified	Fairfield
52	28	Oceanside Unified	Oceanside
52	28	San Ramon Valley Unified	Danville
52	28	Vallejo City Unified	Vallejo
57	27	Desert Sands Unified	La Quinta
57	27	Modesto City Elementary	Modesto
57	27	Rialto Unified	Rialto
57	27	Vista Unified	Vista
61	26	Chico Unified	Chico
61	26	Colton Joint Unified	Colton
61	26	Sweetwater Union High	Chula Vista
61	26	Tustin Unified	Tustin
65	25	Alum Rock Union Elementary	San Jose
65	25	Palmdale Elementary	Palmdale
67	24	Cupertino Union School	Cupertino
67	24	Jurupa Unified	Riverside
67	24	Palm Springs Unified	Palm Springs
70	23	Anaheim Elementary	Anaheim
70	23	Manteca Unified	Manteca
70	23	Marysville Joint Unified	Marysville
70	23	Monterey Peninsula Unified	Monterey
70	23	Rio Linda Union Elementary	Rio Linda
70	23	Santa Clara Unified	Santa Clara
76	22	Baldwin Park Unified	Baldwin Park
76	22	Downey Unified	Downey
76	22	Kern Union High	Bakersfield
76	22	La Mesa-Spring Valley	La Mesa
76	22	Lake Elsinore Unified	Lake Elsinore
76	22	Oak Grove Elementary	San Jose
76	22	Rowland Unified	Rowland Heights
76	22	Temecula Valley Unified	Temecula
84	21	Anaheim Union High	Anaheim
84	21	Antioch Unified	Antioch
84	21	East Side Union High	San Jose
84	21	Escondido Union Elementary	Escondido
84	21	Hesperia Unified	Hesperia
84	21	Livermore Valley Joint Unified	Livermore
84	21	Redlands Unified	Redlands
84	21	San Mateo-Foster City Elementary	San Mateo
84	21	Tracy Joint Unified	Tracy
93	20	Alameda City Unified	Alameda
93	20	Burbank Unified	Burbank
93	20	Covina-Valley Unified	Covina
93	20	Hemet Unified	Hemet
93	20	Oxnard Elementary	Oxnard
93	20	Panama Buena Vista Union Elem	Bakersfield
99	19	Alvord Unified	Riverside
99	19	El Monte City Elementary	El Monte
99	19	Fullerton Elementary	Fullerton
99	19	Inglewood Unified	Inglewood
99	19	Madera Unified	Madera
99	19	Palo Alto Unified	Palo Alto
99	19	Vacaville Unified	Vacaville
106	18	Azusa Unified	Azusa
106	18	Grossmont Union High	La Mesa
106	18	Lancaster Elementary	Lancaster
106	18	Paramount Unified	Paramount
106	18	Sanger Unified	Sanger
111	17	Coachella Valley Unified	Thermal
111	17	El Rancho Unified	Pico Rivera
111	17	Evergreen Elementary	San Jose
111	17	Jefferson Elementary	Daly City
111	17	Merced City Elementary	Merced
111	17	Morongo Unified	Twentynine Plms
111	17	Palos Verdes Peninsula Unified	Palos Verdes Est
111	17	Porterville Unified	Porterville
111	17	Redwood City Elementary	Redwood City
111	17	Ukiah Unified	Ukiah
111	17	Westminster Elementary	Westminster
111	17	Woodland Joint Unified	Woodland
111	17	Yuba City Unified	Yuba City
124	16	Apple Valley Unified	Apple Valley
124	16	Central Unified	Fresno
124	16	Kings Canyon Joint Unified	Reedley
124	16	Lompoc Unified	Lompoc
124	16	Lucia Mar Unified	Arroyo Grande
124	16	Novato Unified	Novato
124	16	Plumas Unified	Quincy
124	16	San Luis Coastal Unified	San Luis Obispo
124	16	Santa Maria-Bonita Elementary	Santa Maria
124	16	Santa Monica-Malibu Unified	Santa Monica
124	16	Santa Rosa High	Santa Rosa
124	16	South San Francisco Unified	S San Francisco
124	16	Walnut Valley Unified	Walnut
137	15	Bellflower Unified	Bellflower
137	15	Berkeley Unified	Berkeley
137	15	Cotati-Rohnert Park Unified	Rohnert Park
137	15	Lynwood Unified	Lynwood
137	15	Morgan Hill Unified	Morgan Hill
137	15	Ocean View Elementary	Huntington Bch
137	15	Pleasanton Unified	Pleasanton
137	15	Redding Elementary	Redding
137	15	Rocklin Unified	Rocklin
137	15	San Lorenzo Unified	San Lorenzo
137	15	Upland Unified	Upland
137	15	Victor Elementary	Victorville
149	14	Berryessa Union Elementary	San Jose
149	14	Bonita Unified	San Dimas
149	14	Castro Valley Unified	Castro Valley
149	14	Davis Joint Unified	Davis
149	14	Eureka City Unified	Eureka
149	14	Franklin-Mckinley Elementary	San Jose
149	14	Gilroy Unified	Gilroy
149	14	Grant Joint Union High	Sacramento
149	14	Lincoln Unified	Stockton
149	14	Los Angeles County Office of Ed	Downey
149	14	Mariposa County Unified	Mariposa
149	14	Milpitas Unified	Milpitas
149	14	Newark Unified	Newark
149	14	Paso Robles Joint Unified	Paso Robles
149	14	Roseville City Elementary	Roseville
149	14	Salinas City Elementary	Salinas
149	14	San Marcos Unified	San Marcos
149	14	Saugus Union Elementary	Santa Clarita
167	13	Alhambra City Elementary	Alhambra
167	13	Calaveras Unified	San Andreas
167	13	Carlsbad Unified	Carlsbad
167	13	Ceres Unified	Ceres
167	13	East Whittier City Elementary	Whittier
167	13	Etiwanda Elementary	Etiwanda
167	13	Garvey Elementary	Rosemead
167	13	Las Virgenes Unified	Calabasas
167	13	Murrieta Valley Unified	Murrieta
167	13	Paradise Unified	Paradise
167	13	Pleasant Valley School	Camarillo
167	13	San Leandro Unified	San Leandro
167	13	Santa Barbara Elementary	Santa Barbara
167	13	Santa Barbara High	Santa Barbara
167	13	Santa Rosa Elementary	Santa Rosa
167	13	Snowline Joint Unified	Phelan
167	13	Tahoe-Truckee Joint Unified	Truckee
167	13	Tulare City Elementary	Tulare
167	13	Twin Ridges Elementary	North San Juan
167	13	Washington Unified	West Sacramento
167	13	West Covina Unified	West Covina
167	13	Whittier City Elementary	Whittier
189	12	Alisal Union Elementary	Salinas
189	12	Amador County Unified	Jackson
189	12	Atascadero Unified	Atascadero
189	12	Barstow Unified	Barstow
189	12	Campbell Union Elementary	Campbell
189	12	Claremont Unified	Claremont
189	12	Mountain Empire Unified	Pine Valley
189	12	Mountain View Elementary	El Monte
189	12	New Haven Unified	Union City
189	12	North Monterey County Unified	Moss Landing
189	12	Ravenswood City Elementary	East Palo Alto
189	12	Redondo Beach Unified	Redondo Beach
189	12	Santee Elementary	Santee
189	12	Selma Unified	Selma
189	12	South Bay Union Elementary	Imperial Beach
189	12	Val Verde Unified	Perris
189	12	William S Hart Union High	Santa Clarita
206	11	Antelope Valley Union High	Lancaster
206	11	Arcadia Unified	Arcadia
206	11	Chaffey Joint Union High	Ontario
206	11	Coalinga-Huron Joint Unified	Coalinga
206	11	Cutler-Orosi Joint Unified	Orosi
206	11	Del Norte County Unified	Crescent City
206	11	El Centro Elementary	El Centro
206	11	Fountain Valley Elementary	Fountain Valley
206	11	Gateway Unified	Redding
206	11	Hanford Elementary	Hanford
206	11	Hawthorne Elementary	Hawthorne
206	11	Hueneme Elementary	Port Hueneme
206	11	Lakeside Union Elementary	Lakeside
206	11	Monrovia Unified	Monrovia
206	11	Moorpark Unified	Moorpark
206	11	North Sacramento Elementary	Sacramento
206	11	Pittsburg Unified	Pittsburg
206	11	Ramona City Unified	Ramona
206	11	Shasta Union High	Redding
206	11	Sierra Sands Unified	Ridgecrest
206	11	Sierra Unified	Auberry
206	11	Sonoma Valley Unified	Sonoma
206	11	Sunnyvale Elementary	Sunnyvale
206	11	Turlock Joint Elementary	Turlock
206	11	Yucaipa-Calimesa Joint Unified	Yucaipa
231	10	Alta Loma Elementary	Alta Loma
231	10	Calexico Unified	Calexico
231	10	Charter Oak Unified	Covina
231	10	Culver City Unified	Culver City
231	10	Cypress Elementary	Cypress
231	10	Delano Union Elementary	Delano
231	10	Encinitas Union Elementary	Encinitas
231	10	Glendora Unified	Glendora
231	10	Goleta Union Elementary	Goleta
231	10	Huntington Beach City Elementary	Huntington Bch
231	10	Los Alamitos Unified	Los Alamitos
231	10	Los Banos Unified	Los Banos
231	10	Moreland Elementary	San Jose
231	10	National Elementary	National City
231	10	Natomas Unified	Sacramento
231	10	Petaluma Joint Union High	Petaluma
231	10	River Delta Joint Unified	Rio Vista
231	10	Salinas Union High	Salinas
231	10	San Diego County Office of Ed	San Diego
231	10	Santa Cruz City High	Santa Cruz
231	10	Sylvan Union Elementary	Modesto
231	10	Travis Unified	Travis Afb
231	10	Union Elementary	San Jose
231	10	Valley Center-Pauma Unified	Valley Center
231	10	Willits Unified	Willits
256	9	Adelanto Elementary	Adelanto
256	9	Banning Unified	Banning
256	9	Beaumont Unified	Beaumont
256	9	Benicia Unified	Benicia
256	9	Brea-Olinda Unified	Brea
256	9	Center Joint Unified	Antelope
256	9	Centralia Elementary	Buena Park
256	9	El Dorado Union High	Placerville
256	9	Enterprise Elementary	Redding
256	9	Fallbrook Union Elementary	Fallbrook
256	9	Greenfield Union Elementary	Bakersfield
256	9	Konocti Unified	Lower Lake
256	9	La Habra City Elementary	La Habra
256	9	Lake Tahoe Unified	S Lake Tahoe
256	9	Little Lake City Elementary	Santa Fe Spgs
256	9	Magnolia Elementary	Anaheim
256	9	Mojave Unified	Mojave
256	9	Mountain View-Whisman Elementary	Mountain View
256	9	Nevada Joint Union High	Grass Valley
256	9	Ojai Unified	Ojai

256	9	Oxnard Union High	Oxnard
256	9	Petaluma City Elementary	Petaluma
256	9	Reef-Sunset Unified	Avenal
256	9	San Dieguito Union High	Encinitas
256	9	San Gabriel Unified	San Gabriel
256	9	San Jacinto Unified	San Jacinto
256	9	San Lorenzo Valley Unified	Felton
256	9	San Ysidro Elementary	San Ysidro
256	9	Western Placer Unified	Lincoln
256	9	Westside Union Elementary	Lancaster
286	8	Atwater Elementary	Atwater
286	8	Bassett Unified	La Puente
286	8	Bear Valley Unified	Big Bear Lake
286	8	Carpinteria Unified	Carpinteria
286	8	Dinuba Unified	Dinuba
286	8	Dry Creek Joint Elementary	Roseville
286	8	Duarte Unified	Duarte
286	8	Dublin Unified	Dublin
286	8	Escalon Unified	Escalon
286	8	Eureka Union Elementary	Granite Bay
286	8	Fort Bragg Unified	Fort Bragg
286	8	Fullerton Joint Union High	Fullerton
286	8	Hollister SD	Hollister
286	8	Huntington Beach Union High	Huntington Bch
286	8	Kelseyville Unified	Kelseyville
286	8	Lawndale Elementary	Lawndale
286	8	Lemon Grove Elementary	Lemon Grove
286	8	Los Altos Elementary	Los Altos
286	8	Martinez Unified	Martinez
286	8	Middletown Unified	Middletown
286	8	Oakdale Joint Unified	Oakdale
286	8	Orcutt Union Elementary	Orcutt
286	8	Patterson Joint Unified	Patterson
286	8	Rim of The World Unified	Lake Arrowhead
286	8	Rincon Valley Union Elementary	Santa Rosa
286	8	Rosedale Union Elementary	Bakersfield
286	8	San Bruno Park Elementary	San Bruno
286	8	San Mateo Union High	San Mateo
286	8	San Rafael City Elementary	San Rafael
286	8	Silver Valley Unified	Yermo
286	8	South Whittier Elementary	Whittier
286	8	Sulphur Springs Union Elementary	Canyon Country
286	8	Temple City Unified	Temple City
286	8	Templeton Unified	Templeton
286	8	Victor Valley Union High	Victorville
321	7	Alpine Union Elementary	Alpine
321	7	Black Oak Mine Unified	Georgetown
321	7	Brentwood Union Elementary	Brentwood
321	7	Buena Park Elementary	Buena Park
321	7	Cabrillo Unified	Half Moon Bay
321	7	Campbell Union High	San Jose
321	7	Central Elementary	Rcho Cucamong
321	7	Dixon Unified	Dixon
321	7	Dos Palos Oro Loma Joint Unified	Dos Palos
321	7	El Monte Union High	El Monte
321	7	Grass Valley Elementary	Grass Valley
321	7	Gridley Unified	Gridley
321	7	Kerman Unified	Kerman
321	7	Laguna Salada Union Elementary	Pacifica
321	7	Lennox Elementary	Lennox
321	7	Lindsay Unified	Lindsay
321	7	Manhattan Beach Unified	Manhattan Beach
321	7	Merced Union High	Atwater
321	7	Muroc Joint Unified	North Edwards
321	7	Newhall Elementary	Valencia
321	7	Newman-Crows Landing Unified	Newman
321	7	Oroville City Elementary	Oroville
321	7	Perris Elementary	Perris
321	7	Rio Elementary	Oxnard
321	7	Roseville Joint Union High	Roseville
321	7	San Carlos Elementary	San Carlos
321	7	Santa Cruz City Elementary	Santa Cruz
321	7	Santa Paula Elementary	Santa Paula
321	7	Soledad Unified	Soledad
321	7	Taft City Elementary	Taft
321	7	Tehachapi Unified	Tehachapi
321	7	Whittier Union High	Whittier
321	7	Willows Unified	Willows
321	7	Windsor Unified	Windsor
355	6	Albany City Unified	Albany
355	6	Alhambra City High	Alhambra
355	6	Anderson Union High	Anderson
355	6	Belmont-Redwood Shores Elementary	Belmont
355	6	Beverly Hills Unified	Beverly Hills
355	6	Buckeye Union Elementary	Shingle Springs
355	6	Burlingame Elementary	Burlingame
355	6	Cambrian Elementary	San Jose
355	6	Carmel Unified	Carmel
355	6	Corcoran Joint Unified	Corcoran
355	6	Del Mar Union Elementary	Del Mar
355	6	Empire Union Elementary	Modesto
355	6	Escondido Union High	Escondido
355	6	Fillmore Unified	Fillmore
355	6	Firebaugh-Las Deltas Joint Unified	Firebaugh
355	6	Fowler Unified	Fowler
355	6	Fremont Union High	Sunnyvale
355	6	Golden Plains Unified	San Joaquin
355	6	Healdsburg Unified	Healdsburg
355	6	Hilmar Unified	Hilmar
355	6	Imperial Unified	Imperial
355	6	Keppel Union Elementary	Pearblossom
355	6	Keyes Union Elementary	Keyes
355	6	Linden Unified	Linden
355	6	Live Oak Unified	Live Oak
355	6	Lowell Joint	Whittier
355	6	Mcfarland Unified	Mcfarland
355	6	Mendota Unified	Mendota
355	6	Menifee Union Elementary	Menifee
355	6	Mill Valley Elementary	Mill Valley
355	6	Modesto City High	Modesto
355	6	Oak Park Unified	Oak Park
355	6	Oakley Union Elementary	Oakley
355	6	Orland Joint Unified	Orland
355	6	Palo Verde Unified	Blythe
355	6	Parlier Unified	Parlier
355	6	Perris Union High	Perris
355	6	Piedmont City Unified	Piedmont
355	6	Placer Union High	Auburn
355	6	Red Bluff Union Elementary	Red Bluff
355	6	Ripon Unified	Ripon
355	6	San Bernardino County Supt.	San Bernardino
355	6	Sequoia Union High	Redwood City
355	6	Southern Kern Unified	Rosamond
355	6	Stanislaus Union Elementary	Modesto
355	6	Walnut Creek Elementary	Walnut Creek
355	6	West Sonoma County Union High	Sebastopol
355	6	Westwood Unified	Westwood
355	6	Wheatland Elementary	Wheatland
355	6	Winters Joint Unified	Winters
405	5	Acalanes Union High	Lafayette
405	5	Acton-Agua Dulce Unified	Acton
405	5	Auburn Union Elementary	Auburn
405	5	Bonsall Union Elementary	Bonsall
405	5	Brawley Elementary	Brawley
405	5	Burton Elementary	Porterville
405	5	Cascade Union Elementary	Anderson
405	5	Colusa Unified	Colusa
405	5	Corning Union Elementary	Corning
405	5	Coronado Unified	Coronado
405	5	Del Paso Heights Elementary	Sacramento
405	5	Delhi Unified	Delhi
405	5	El Segundo Unified	El Segundo
405	5	Farmersville Unified	Farmersville
405	5	Fresno County Office of Ed	Fresno
405	5	Fruitvale Elementary	Bakersfield
405	5	Galt Joint Union Elementary	Galt
405	5	Gustine Unified	Gustine
405	5	Hanford Joint Union High	Hanford
405	5	Holtville Unified	Holtville
405	5	Jefferson Union High	Daly City
405	5	Kern County Office of Ed	Bakersfield
405	5	Kingsburg Elementary Charter	Kingsburg
405	5	La Canada Unified	La Canada
405	5	Lafayette Elementary	Lafayette
405	5	Lakeport Unified	Lakeport
405	5	Lemoore Union Elementary	Lemoore
405	5	Live Oak Elementary	Santa Cruz
405	5	Los Gatos Union Elementary	Los Gatos
405	5	Millbrae Elementary	Millbrae
405	5	Mount Pleasant Elementary	San Jose
405	5	Mountain View-Los Altos Union High	Mountain View
405	5	Northern Humboldt Union High	McKinleyville
405	5	Old Adobe Union Elementary	Petaluma
405	5	Orinda Union Elementary	Orinda
405	5	Oroville Union High	Oroville
405	5	Pacific Grove Unified	Pacific Grove
405	5	Rescue Union Elementary	Rescue
405	5	Riverbank Unified	Riverbank
405	5	Riverdale Joint Unified	Riverdale
405	5	Riverside County Office of Ed	Riverside
405	5	Robla Elementary	Sacramento
405	5	Rosemead Elementary	Rosemead
405	5	Saint Helena Unified	Saint Helena
405	5	Salida Union Elementary	Salida
405	5	Santa Clara County Office of Ed	San Jose
405	5	Solana Beach Elementary	Solana Beach
405	5	Soquel Union Elementary	Capitola
405	5	South Pasadena Unified	South Pasadena
405	5	Tamalpais Union High	Larkspur
405	5	Tulare Joint Union High	Tulare
456	4	Centinela Valley Union High	Lawndale
456	4	Central Union Elementary	Lemoore
456	4	Chowchilla Elementary	Chowchilla
456	4	Cloverdale Unified	Cloverdale
456	4	Cucamonga Elementary	Rcho Cucamong
456	4	Dixie Elementary	San Rafael
456	4	Eastside Union Elementary	Lancaster
456	4	Exeter Union Elementary	Exeter
456	4	Gorman Elementary	Gorman
456	4	Greenfield Union Elementary	Greenfield
456	4	Hughson Unified	Hughson
456	4	Jamul-Dulzura Union Elementary	Jamul
456	4	John Swett Unified	Crockett
456	4	King City Joint Union High	King City
456	4	Laguna Beach Unified	Laguna Beach
456	4	Lamont Elementary	Lamont
456	4	Liberty Union High	Brentwood
456	4	Livingston Union Elementary	Livingston
456	4	Loomis Union Elementary	Loomis
456	4	Los Nietos Elementary	Whittier
456	4	Menlo Park City Elementary	Atherton
456	4	Moraga Elementary	Moraga
456	4	Mountain View Elementary	Ontario
456	4	Norris Elementary	Bakersfield
456	4	Ocean View Elementary	Oxnard
456	4	Orange County Office of Ed	Costa Mesa
456	4	Piner-Olivet Union Elementary	Santa Rosa
456	4	Pleasant Ridge Union Elementary	Grass Valley
456	4	Red Bluff Joint Union High	Red Bluff
456	4	Ross Valley Elementary	San Anselmo
456	4	San Joaquin County Office of Ed	Stockton
456	4	San Marino Unified	San Marino
456	4	Santa Rita Union Elementary	Salinas
456	4	Saratoga Union Elementary	Saratoga
456	4	Savanna Elementary	Anaheim
456	4	Scotts Valley Unified	Scotts Valley
456	4	Sonora Union High	Sonora
456	4	Standard Elementary	Bakersfield
456	4	Thermalito Union Elementary	Oroville
456	4	Turlock Joint Union High	Turlock
456	4	Wasco Union Elementary	Wasco
456	4	Waterford Unified	Waterford
456	4	Wilsona Elementary	Palmdale
456	4	Wiseburn Elementary	Hawthorne
500	3	Arvin Union Elementary	Arvin
500	3	Beardsley Elementary	Bakersfield
500	3	Bellevue Union Elementary	Santa Rosa
500	3	Bishop Union Elementary	Bishop
500	3	Brawley Union High	Brawley
500	3	Castaic Union Elementary	Valencia
500	3	Central Union High	El Centro
500	3	Delano Joint Union High	Delano
500	3	Earlimart Elementary	Earlimart
500	3	Fallbrook Union High	Fallbrook
500	3	Gonzales Unified	Gonzales
500	3	Jefferson Elementary	Tracy
500	3	Julian Union Elementary	Julian
500	3	Julian Union High	Julian
500	3	King City Union Elementary	King City
500	3	Lemoore Union High	Lemoore
500	3	Mark West Union Elementary	Santa Rosa
500	3	Mother Lode Union Elementary	Placerville
500	3	Richland SD	Shafter
500	3	San Rafael City High	San Rafael
500	3	Santa Maria Joint Union High	Santa Maria
500	3	Winton Elementary	Winton
500	3	Woodlake Union Elementary	Woodlake
523	2	Galt Joint Union High	Galt
523	2	Los Gatos-Saratoga Jt Union High	Los Gatos
523	2	Oro Grande Elementary	Oro Grande
523	2	Romoland Elementary	Homeland
523	2	San Benito High	Hollister
523	2	Santa Paula Union High	Santa Paula
523	2	Weaver Union Elementary	Merced

Number of Teachers

Rank	Number	District Name	City
1	35,483	Los Angeles Unified	Los Angeles
2	7,494	San Diego Unified	San Diego
3	4,520	Long Beach Unified	Long Beach
4	3,938	Fresno Unified	Fresno
5	3,362	San Francisco Unified	San Francisco
6	2,938	Santa Ana Unified	Santa Ana
7	2,888	Oakland Unified	Oakland
8	2,645	San Bernardino City Unified	San Bernardino
9	2,600	Elk Grove Unified	Elk Grove
10	2,522	San Juan Unified	Carmichael
11	2,489	Sacramento City Unified	Sacramento
12	2,197	Garden Grove Unified	Garden Grove
13	2,141	Capistrano Unified	San Juan Capis
14	1,982	Corona-Norco Unified	Norco
15	1,974	Stockton City Unified	Stockton
16	1,850	Mount Diablo Unified	Concord
17	1,807	Fontana Unified	Fontana
18	1,799	West Contra Costa Unified	Richmond
19	1,770	Sweetwater Union High	Chula Vista
20	1,765	Riverside Unified	Riverside

Rank	Number	District	City
21	1,755	San Jose Unified	San Jose
22	1,716	Pomona Unified	Pomona
23	1,566	Saddleback Valley Unified	Mission Viejo
24	1,538	Clovis Unified	Clovis
25	1,533	Moreno Valley Unified	Moreno Valley
26	1,525	Poway Unified	Poway
27	1,511	Bakersfield City Elementary	Bakersfield
28	1,506	Orange Unified	Orange
29	1,493	Fremont Unified	Fremont
30	1,487	Montebello Unified	Montebello
31	1,464	Lodi Unified	Lodi
32	1,445	Chino Valley Unified	Chino
33	1,423	Glendale Unified	Glendale
34	1,416	Compton Unified	Compton
35	1,383	Rialto Unified	Rialto
36	1,348	Kern Union High	Bakersfield
37	1,298	Ontario-Montclair Elementary	Ontario
38	1,278	Anaheim Union High	Anaheim
39	1,262	Vista Unified	Vista
40	1,256	Chula Vista Elementary	Chula Vista
41	1,203	Hayward Unified	Hayward
42	1,197	Torrance Unified	Torrance
43	1,190	Visalia Unified	Visalia
44	1,177	Placentia-Yorba Linda Unified	Placentia
45	1,177	Desert Sands Unified	La Quinta
46	1,158	East Side Union High	San Jose
47	1,150	Oceanside Unified	Oceanside
48	1,144	Hacienda La Puente Unified	City of Industry
49	1,129	Pasadena Unified	Pasadena
50	1,119	Fairfield-Suisun Unified	Fairfield
51	1,109	Colton Joint Unified	Colton
52	1,091	Newport-Mesa Unified	Costa Mesa
52	1,091	Norwalk-La Mirada Unified	Norwalk
54	1,085	Palm Springs Unified	Palm Springs
55	1,082	Pajaro Valley Unified School	Watsonville
56	1,057	Irvine Unified	Irvine
57	1,054	Temecula Valley Unified	Temecula
58	1,047	Palmdale Elementary	Palmdale
59	1,041	Escondido Union Elementary	Escondido
60	1,038	Anaheim Elementary	Anaheim
61	1,028	Grossmont Union High	La Mesa
62	1,011	Los Angeles County Office of Ed	Downey
63	1,005	San Ramon Valley Unified	Danville
64	1,000	ABC Unified	Cerritos
65	995	Antioch Unified	Antioch
66	994	Manteca Unified	Manteca
67	979	Conejo Valley Unified	Thousand Oaks
68	977	Downey Unified	Downey
69	961	Vallejo City Unified	Vallejo
70	947	Modesto City Elementary	Modesto
71	945	Simi Valley Unified	Simi Valley
72	940	Jurupa Unified	Riverside
73	922	Redlands Unified	Redlands
74	907	Chaffey Joint Union High	Ontario
75	883	Hemet Unified	Hemet
76	882	Cajon Valley Union Elementary	El Cajon
77	861	Rowland Unified	Rowland Heights
78	847	Baldwin Park Unified	Baldwin Park
79	840	Napa Valley Unified	Napa
80	837	Tustin Unified	Tustin
81	832	Lake Elsinore Unified	Lake Elsinore
82	832	Alvord Unified	Riverside
83	831	Antelope Valley Union High	Lancaster
84	823	Inglewood Unified	Inglewood
85	820	Folsom-Cordova Unified	Folsom
86	816	William S Hart Union High	Santa Clarita
87	813	Madera Unified	Madera
88	788	Burbank Unified	Burbank
89	779	Paramount Unified	Paramount
90	777	Oxnard Elementary	Oxnard
91	771	Lynwood Unified	Lynwood
92	770	Ventura Unified	Ventura
93	760	Tracy Joint Unified	Tracy
94	747	Vacaville Unified	Vacaville
95	734	Cupertino Union School	Cupertino
96	729	Lancaster Elementary	Lancaster
97	723	Hesperia Unified	Hesperia
98	721	Alum Rock Union Elementary	San Jose
99	697	La Mesa-Spring Valley	La Mesa
100	693	Chico Unified	Chico
101	691	Bellflower Unified	Bellflower
102	689	Walnut Valley Unified	Walnut
103	682	Pleasanton Unified	Pleasanton
104	679	Santa Clara Unified	Santa Clara
105	676	Panama Buena Vista Union Elem	Bakersfield
106	674	Murrieta Valley Unified	Murrieta
107	671	Covina-Valley Unified	Covina
108	660	New Haven Unified	Union City
109	658	San Marcos Unified	San Marcos
110	642	Apple Valley Unified	Apple Valley
111	640	Coachella Valley Unified	Thermal
112	633	Oxnard Union High	Oxnard
113	619	Palo Alto Unified	Palo Alto
114	615	Lompoc Unified	Lompoc
115	614	Livermore Valley Joint Unified	Livermore
116	611	Porterville Unified	Porterville
117	608	Santa Monica-Malibu Unified	Santa Monica
118	601	Fullerton Elementary	Fullerton
118	601	Modesto City High	Modesto
120	600	Salinas Union High	Salinas
121	594	Upland Unified	Upland
122	593	San Lorenzo Unified	San Lorenzo
123	588	Santa Rosa High	Santa Rosa
124	588	Monterey Peninsula Unified	Monterey
125	586	Evergreen Elementary	San Jose
126	586	Santa Maria-Bonita Elementary	Santa Maria
127	584	El Rancho Unified	Pico Rivera
128	582	Yuba City Unified	Yuba City
129	582	Huntington Beach Union High	Huntington Bch
130	577	El Monte City Elementary	El Monte
131	575	Central Unified	Fresno
132	574	Azusa Unified	Azusa
133	572	Grant Joint Union High	Sacramento
134	571	Oak Grove Elementary	San Jose
135	555	Fullerton Joint Union High	Fullerton
136	555	Rio Linda Union Elementary	Rio Linda
137	554	Alhambra City Elementary	Alhambra
138	551	Merced City Elementary	Merced
139	538	Las Virgenes Unified	Calabasas
140	533	Lucia Mar Unified	Arroyo Grande
141	532	Redwood City Elementary	Redwood City
142	529	Woodland Joint Unified	Woodland
143	524	San Mateo-Foster City Elementary	San Mateo
144	523	Palos Verdes Peninsula Unified	Palos Verdes Est
145	514	Alameda City Unified	Alameda
146	514	Franklin-Mckinley Elementary	San Jose
147	511	Westminster Elementary	Westminster
148	504	San Dieguito Union High	Encinitas
149	498	Berkeley Unified	Berkeley
150	496	Val Verde Unified	Perris
151	493	Marysville Joint Unified	Marysville
152	488	Ocean View Elementary	Huntington Bch
153	488	Whittier Union High	Whittier
154	487	West Covina Unified	West Covina
155	485	Mountain View Elementary	El Monte
156	483	Gilroy Unified	Gilroy
157	480	Saugus Union Elementary	Santa Clarita
158	474	Santa Barbara High	Santa Barbara
159	474	Ceres Unified	Ceres
160	473	Carlsbad Unified	Carlsbad
161	471	Hawthorne Elementary	Hawthorne
162	467	South Bay Union Elementary	Imperial Beach
163	465	Morongo Unified	Twentynine Plms
164	461	Etiwanda Elementary	Etiwanda
165	459	Orange County Office of Ed	Costa Mesa
166	457	Salinas City Elementary	Salinas
166	457	South San Francisco Unified	S San Francisco
168	450	East Whittier City Elementary	Whittier
169	448	Pittsburg Unified	Pittsburg
170	448	Milpitas Unified	Milpitas
171	447	Turlock Joint Elementary	Turlock
172	442	Bonita Unified	San Dimas
173	438	Davis Joint Unified	Davis
174	437	Lincoln Unified	Stockton
175	435	San Leandro Unified	San Leandro
176	435	Arcadia Unified	Arcadia
177	433	Sanger Unified	Sanger
178	431	Calexico Unified	Calexico
179	424	Snowline Joint Unified	Phelan
180	424	Kings Canyon Joint Unified	Reedley
181	421	Fremont Union High	Sunnyvale
182	419	Merced Union High	Atwater
183	416	Hueneme Elementary	Port Hueneme
184	413	Rocklin Unified	Rocklin
185	413	Victor Elementary	Victorville
186	412	El Monte Union High	El Monte
187	407	Morgan Hill Unified	Morgan Hill
188	405	Berryessa Union Elementary	San Jose
189	402	Victor Valley Union High	Victorville
190	399	Yucaipa-Calimesa Joint Unified	Yucaipa
191	398	Tulare City Elementary	Tulare
192	397	Los Alamitos Unified	Los Alamitos
193	396	San Mateo Union High	San Mateo
194	390	Novato Unified	Novato
195	388	Campbell Union Elementary	Campbell
196	386	Natomas Unified	Sacramento
197	383	Newark Unified	Newark
197	383	Redondo Beach Unified	Redondo Beach
199	382	San Luis Coastal Unified	San Luis Obispo
200	378	Castro Valley Unified	Castro Valley
201	376	Sequoia Union High	Redwood City
202	375	Moorpark Unified	Moorpark
203	374	Escondido Union High	Escondido
204	370	Sylvan Union Elementary	Modesto
205	369	Washington Unified	West Sacramento
206	366	Los Banos Unified	Los Banos
207	365	Western Placer Unified	Lincoln
208	365	Ukiah Unified	Ukiah
209	359	Paso Robles Joint Unified	Paso Robles
210	356	Alhambra City High	Alhambra
211	353	Pleasant Valley School	Camarillo
212	352	Magnolia Elementary	Anaheim
213	349	Glendora Unified	Glendora
214	347	Roseville Joint Union High	Roseville
215	347	Whittier City Elementary	Whittier
216	347	Lennox Elementary	Lennox
217	346	Greenfield Union Elementary	Bakersfield
218	346	Santee Elementary	Santee
219	344	Cotati-Rohnert Park Unified	Rohnert Park
220	342	Roseville City Elementary	Roseville
221	338	Alisal Union Elementary	Salinas
222	331	Delano Union Elementary	Delano
223	328	Garvey Elementary	Rosemead
224	327	La Habra City Elementary	La Habra
225	324	Barstow Unified	Barstow
226	323	Westside Union Elementary	Lancaster
227	323	Monrovia Unified	Monrovia
228	322	Jefferson Elementary	Daly City
229	321	Ramona City Unified	Ramona
230	320	Manhattan Beach Unified	Manhattan Beach
231	319	Campbell Union High	San Jose
231	319	El Dorado Union High	Placerville
233	317	Alta Loma Elementary	Alta Loma
234	316	Culver City Unified	Culver City
235	314	Claremont Unified	Claremont
236	314	San Bernardino County Supt.	San Bernardino
237	312	Center Joint Unified	Antelope
238	308	Santa Barbara Elementary	Santa Barbara
239	308	Huntington Beach City Elementary	Huntington Bch
240	307	Lawndale Elementary	Lawndale
241	305	Santa Rosa Elementary	Santa Rosa
242	304	Hollister SD	Hollister
243	304	Sunnyvale Elementary	Sunnyvale
244	301	North Monterey County Unified	Moss Landing
245	300	Riverside County Office of Ed	Riverside
246	300	Dry Creek Joint Elementary	Roseville
247	300	Perris Union High	Perris
248	299	North Sacramento Elementary	Sacramento
249	298	Buena Park Elementary	Buena Park
250	297	Newhall Elementary	Valencia
251	297	San Jacinto Unified	San Jacinto
252	296	Selma Unified	Selma
253	295	National Elementary	National City
254	295	Tahoe-Truckee Joint Unified	Truckee
255	292	Atascadero Unified	Atascadero
255	292	Travis Unified	Travis Afb
257	290	El Centro Elementary	El Centro
258	288	Centinela Valley Union High	Lawndale
259	286	Beverly Hills Unified	Beverly Hills
260	286	San Gabriel Unified	San Gabriel
261	285	Brea-Olinda Unified	Brea
262	285	Fountain Valley Elementary	Fountain Valley
263	283	Ravenswood City Elementary	East Palo Alto
264	282	Paradise Unified	Paradise
265	281	Eureka City Unified	Eureka
266	281	Bassett Unified	La Puente
267	280	Fallbrook Union Elementary	Fallbrook
268	275	Sierra Sands Unified	Ridgecrest
269	273	Benicia Unified	Benicia
270	272	Brentwood Union Elementary	Brentwood
271	268	Encinitas Union Elementary	Encinitas
272	264	Acalanes Union High	Lafayette
273	263	Temple City Unified	Temple City
274	262	Sulphur Springs Union Elementary	Canyon Country
275	262	Petaluma Joint Union High	Petaluma
276	260	Adelanto Elementary	Adelanto
277	260	Dinuba Unified	Dinuba
278	257	Santa Maria Joint Union High	Santa Maria
279	257	Hanford Elementary	Hanford
280	253	Shasta Union High	Redding
281	252	San Ysidro Elementary	San Ysidro
282	251	Lake Tahoe Unified	S Lake Tahoe
283	249	Perris Elementary	Perris
284	248	Rim of The World Unified	Lake Arrowhead
285	248	Centralia Elementary	Buena Park
286	247	Cypress Elementary	Cypress
287	247	Valley Center-Pauma Unified	Valley Center
288	245	Menifee Union Elementary	Menifee
289	244	Jefferson Union High	Daly City
290	243	Little Lake City Elementary	Santa Fe Spgs
291	243	Charter Oak Unified	Covina
291	243	Santa Clara County Office of Ed	San Jose
293	240	Sonoma Valley Unified	Sonoma
294	240	Lakeside Union Elementary	Lakeside
295	238	Atwater Elementary	Atwater
296	238	Orcutt Union Elementary	Orcutt
297	236	Central Elementary	Rcho Cucamong
298	235	Moreland Elementary	San Jose

299	231	San Diego County Office of Ed	San Diego
300	231	Oakdale Joint Unified	Oakdale
301	229	Union Elementary	San Jose
302	228	Galt Joint Union Elementary	Galt
303	228	Del Norte County Unified	Crescent City
304	225	Tehachapi Unified	Tehachapi
305	221	Lemon Grove Elementary	Lemon Grove
306	220	Dublin Unified	Dublin
307	220	Windsor Unified	Windsor
308	219	Oakley Union Elementary	Oakley
309	218	South Whittier Elementary	Whittier
310	216	Mountain View-Whisman Elementary	Mountain View
311	215	Santa Cruz City High	Santa Cruz
312	213	Martinez Unified	Martinez
313	213	Duarte Unified	Duarte
314	212	Placer Union High	Auburn
315	211	Banning Unified	Banning
316	208	Goleta Union Elementary	Goleta
317	204	Nevada Joint Union High	Grass Valley
318	204	Fresno County Office of Ed	Fresno
319	203	Redding Elementary	Redding
319	203	Tamalpais Union High	Larkspur
321	202	Eureka Union Elementary	Granite Bay
322	202	Patterson Joint Unified	Patterson
323	201	Dixon Unified	Dixon
324	201	Los Altos Elementary	Los Altos
325	200	Amador County Unified	Jackson
325	200	Santa Paula Elementary	Santa Paula
327	200	Buckeye Union Elementary	Shingle Springs
328	198	Gateway Unified	Redding
329	197	Enterprise Elementary	Redding
330	197	Empire Union Elementary	Modesto
331	197	Cutler-Orosi Joint Unified	Orosi
332	196	Beaumont Unified	Beaumont
333	194	Kern County Office of Ed	Bakersfield
334	193	La Canada Unified	La Canada
335	192	Rosedale Union Elementary	Bakersfield
336	190	Brawley Elementary	Brawley
337	189	Del Mar Union Elementary	Del Mar
338	188	Calaveras Unified	San Andreas
339	187	Turlock Joint Union High	Turlock
340	187	Ojai Unified	Ojai
341	186	Coalinga-Huron Joint Unified	Coalinga
341	186	Fillmore Unified	Fillmore
343	184	San Rafael City Elementary	San Rafael
344	183	Kerman Unified	Kerman
345	183	Liberty Union High	Brentwood
346	182	San Lorenzo Valley Unified	Felton
347	182	Rio Elementary	Oxnard
348	181	Lindsay Unified	Lindsay
349	180	Lafayette Elementary	Lafayette
349	180	Salida Union Elementary	Salida
351	179	South Pasadena Unified	South Pasadena
352	178	Cabrillo Unified	Half Moon Bay
353	176	Plumas Unified	Quincy
354	176	Central Union High	El Centro
355	176	Parlier Unified	Parlier
356	175	Palo Verde Unified	Blythe
357	174	Walnut Creek Elementary	Walnut Creek
358	174	Oroville City Elementary	Oroville
359	173	Tulare Joint Union High	Tulare
360	173	Oak Park Unified	Oak Park
361	172	Konocti Unified	Lower Lake
362	170	Rescue Union Elementary	Rescue
363	166	Mountain View Elementary	Ontario
364	164	Rosemead Elementary	Rosemead
365	163	Soledad Unified	Soledad
366	159	Castaic Union Elementary	Valencia
367	159	Bear Valley Unified	Big Bear Lake
368	158	Corcoran Joint Unified	Corcoran
369	158	Lemoore Union Elementary	Lemoore
370	158	Riverbank Unified	Riverbank
371	157	San Marino Unified	San Marino
372	156	Solana Beach Elementary	Solana Beach
373	156	Delano Joint Union High	Delano
374	155	Mountain View-Los Altos Union High	Mountain View
375	154	Albany City Unified	Albany
376	153	San Joaquin County Office of Ed	Stockton
377	152	Stanislaus Union Elementary	Modesto
378	152	Piedmont City Unified	Piedmont
379	151	Lowell Joint	Whittier
380	149	Coronado Unified	Coronado
381	148	Hanford Joint Union High	Hanford
382	148	Santa Rita Union Elementary	Salinas
383	148	Mcfarland Unified	Mcfarland
384	147	Fruitvale Elementary	Bakersfield
385	147	Silver Valley Unified	Yermo
386	146	Carpinteria Unified	Carpinteria
387	146	Laguna Salada Union Elementary	Pacifica
388	145	Dos Palos Oro Loma Joint Unified	Dos Palos
389	145	El Segundo Unified	El Segundo
390	145	Mount Pleasant Elementary	San Jose
391	141	Rincon Valley Union Elementary	Santa Rosa
392	140	Wasco Union Elementary	Wasco
393	140	Belmont-Redwood Shores Elementary	Belmont
393	140	Santa Cruz City Elementary	Santa Cruz
393	140	Southern Kern Unified	Rosamond
393	140	Waterford Unified	Waterford
397	140	Los Gatos Union Elementary	Los Gatos
398	139	Arvin Union Elementary	Arvin
399	138	Escalon Unified	Escalon
400	138	Cambrian Elementary	San Jose
401	138	Fallbrook Union High	Fallbrook
402	137	Ripon Unified	Ripon
403	137	Healdsburg Unified	Healdsburg
404	136	San Carlos Elementary	San Carlos
405	136	Richland SD	Shafter
406	135	Sierra Unified	Auberry
407	135	San Bruno Park Elementary	San Bruno
408	134	Keppel Union Elementary	Pearblossom
409	133	King City Union Elementary	King City
409	133	Mariposa County Unified	Mariposa
411	133	Carmel Unified	Carmel
412	132	Imperial Unified	Imperial
413	132	Willits Unified	Willits
414	132	Ocean View Elementary	Oxnard
415	131	Burton Elementary	Porterville
416	131	Orinda Union Elementary	Orinda
417	131	Templeton Unified	Templeton
418	131	Oroville Union High	Oroville
419	130	Scotts Valley Unified	Scotts Valley
420	130	Linden Unified	Linden
420	130	Saratoga Union Elementary	Saratoga
422	130	Los Gatos-Saratoga Jt Union High	Los Gatos
422	130	Menlo Park City Elementary	Atherton
424	129	Firebaugh-Las Deltas Joint Unified	Firebaugh
425	129	Greenfield Union Elementary	Greenfield
425	129	Standard Elementary	Bakersfield
427	129	Cucamonga Elementary	Rcho Cucamong
428	128	Mill Valley Elementary	Mill Valley
429	128	West Sonoma County Union High	Sebastopol
430	127	Reef-Sunset Unified	Avenal
431	126	Auburn Union Elementary	Auburn
432	125	Lamont Elementary	Lamont
433	125	Fort Bragg Unified	Fort Bragg
434	124	Delhi Unified	Delhi
435	124	Farmersville Unified	Farmersville
435	124	San Benito High	Hollister
437	124	Petaluma City Elementary	Petaluma
438	123	Hilmar Unified	Hilmar
439	123	Orland Joint Unified	Orland
440	122	Laguna Beach Unified	Laguna Beach
441	122	River Delta Joint Unified	Rio Vista
442	121	Muroc Joint Unified	North Edwards
443	121	Alpine Union Elementary	Alpine
443	121	Wheatland Elementary	Wheatland
445	121	Savanna Elementary	Anaheim
446	120	Eastside Union Elementary	Lancaster
447	118	Livingston Union Elementary	Livingston
448	118	Burlingame Elementary	Burlingame
449	117	Robla Elementary	Sacramento
450	116	Los Nietos Elementary	Whittier
451	115	Mojave Unified	Mojave
452	115	Del Paso Heights Elementary	Sacramento
453	114	Red Bluff Union Elementary	Red Bluff
454	114	Central Union Elementary	Lemoore
455	113	Gridley Unified	Gridley
456	112	Taft City Elementary	Taft
457	112	Newman-Crows Landing Unified	Newman
458	111	Gonzales Unified	Gonzales
459	109	Anderson Union High	Anderson
459	109	Winters Joint Unified	Winters
461	108	Millbrae Elementary	Millbrae
462	106	Soquel Union Elementary	Capitola
463	105	Mendota Unified	Mendota
464	105	Fowler Unified	Fowler
464	105	Oro Grande Elementary	Oro Grande
466	104	Corning Union Elementary	Corning
467	103	Kingsburg Elementary Charter	Kingsburg
468	103	Pleasant Ridge Union Elementary	Grass Valley
469	102	Exeter Union Elementary	Exeter
470	102	Gustine Unified	Gustine
471	101	Kelseyville Unified	Kelseyville
472	101	Grass Valley Elementary	Grass Valley
473	100	Black Oak Mine Unified	Georgetown
473	100	Dixie Elementary	San Rafael
473	100	Golden Plains Unified	San Joaquin
476	100	San Rafael City High	San Rafael
477	99	Lakeport Unified	Lakeport
478	99	Twin Ridges Elementary	North San Juan
479	98	Hughson Unified	Hughson
480	98	Galt Joint Union High	Galt
481	97	Live Oak Elementary	Santa Cruz
481	97	Ross Valley Elementary	San Anselmo
483	97	Old Adobe Union Elementary	Petaluma
484	96	Pacific Grove Unified	Pacific Grove
485	95	John Swett Unified	Crockett
486	95	Holtville Unified	Holtville
486	95	Wilsona Elementary	Palmdale
488	95	Lemoore Union High	Lemoore
488	95	Mountain Empire Unified	Pine Valley
490	95	Loomis Union Elementary	Loomis
490	95	Red Bluff Joint Union High	Red Bluff
492	94	Northern Humboldt Union High	McKinleyville
493	94	Moraga Elementary	Moraga
494	94	Wiseburn Elementary	Hawthorne
495	93	Middletown Unified	Middletown
496	92	Bellevue Union Elementary	Santa Rosa
497	92	Winton Elementary	Winton
498	92	Earlimart Elementary	Earlimart
499	91	Norris Elementary	Bakersfield
500	90	Keyes Union Elementary	Keyes
501	90	Weaver Union Elementary	Merced
502	89	Live Oak Unified	Live Oak
503	89	Acton-Agua Dulce Unified	Acton
504	87	Willows Unified	Willows
505	86	Thermalito Union Elementary	Oroville
506	86	King City Joint Union High	King City
507	86	Beardsley Elementary	Bakersfield
508	85	Cloverdale Unified	Cloverdale
509	85	Piner-Olivet Union Elementary	Santa Rosa
510	85	Mother Lode Union Elementary	Placerville
511	85	Bonsall Union Elementary	Bonsall
512	84	Cascade Union Elementary	Anderson
513	83	Julian Union High	Julian
514	83	Colusa Unified	Colusa
515	83	Chowchilla Elementary	Chowchilla
516	82	Saint Helena Unified	Saint Helena
517	81	Woodlake Union Elementary	Woodlake
518	80	Riverdale Joint Unified	Riverdale
519	80	Brawley Union High	Brawley
519	80	Mark West Union Elementary	Santa Rosa
521	78	Romoland Elementary	Homeland
522	77	Jefferson Elementary	Tracy
523	76	Westwood Unified	Westwood
524	74	Jamul-Dulzura Union Elementary	Jamul
525	73	Sonora Union High	Sonora
526	73	Bishop Union Elementary	Bishop
527	66	Julian Union Elementary	Julian
528	65	Gorman Elementary	Gorman
529	62	Santa Paula Union High	Santa Paula

Number of Students

Rank	Number	District Name	City
1	746,852	Los Angeles Unified	Los Angeles
2	140,753	San Diego Unified	San Diego
3	97,212	Long Beach Unified	Long Beach
4	81,222	Fresno Unified	Fresno
5	63,610	Santa Ana Unified	Santa Ana
6	58,216	San Francisco Unified	San Francisco
7	56,096	San Bernardino City Unified	San Bernardino
8	52,850	Sacramento City Unified	Sacramento
9	52,501	Oakland Unified	Oakland
10	52,418	Elk Grove Unified	Elk Grove
11	52,212	San Juan Unified	Carmichael
12	50,066	Garden Grove Unified	Garden Grove
13	48,608	Capistrano Unified	San Juan Capis
14	41,977	Corona-Norco Unified	Norco
15	40,888	Riverside Unified	Riverside
16	40,168	Fontana Unified	Fontana
17	39,421	Stockton City Unified	Stockton
18	37,878	Sweetwater Union High	Chula Vista
19	36,891	Mount Diablo Unified	Concord
20	35,590	Montebello Unified	Montebello
21	35,566	Saddleback Valley Unified	Mission Viejo
22	35,427	Pomona Unified	Pomona
23	34,940	West Contra Costa Unified	Richmond
24	34,176	Moreno Valley Unified	Moreno Valley
25	34,031	Clovis Unified	Clovis
26	32,870	Chino Valley Unified	Chino
27	32,754	Poway Unified	Poway
28	32,612	San Jose Unified	San Jose
29	32,550	Compton Unified	Compton
30	31,823	Orange Unified	Orange
31	31,452	Fremont Unified	Fremont
32	31,338	Anaheim Union High	Anaheim
33	30,953	Kern Union High	Bakersfield
34	30,172	Rialto Unified	Rialto
35	29,749	Glendale Unified	Glendale
36	28,396	Lodi Unified	Lodi
37	28,179	Bakersfield City Elementary	Bakersfield
38	27,709	Vista Unified	Vista
39	27,270	Ontario-Montclair Elementary	Ontario
40	26,464	Placentia-Yorba Linda Unified	Placentia
41	25,184	Hacienda La Puente Unified	City of Industry
42	25,180	Desert Sands Unified	La Quinta

43	24,962	Visalia Unified	Visalia
44	24,876	Torrance Unified	Torrance
45	24,771	Irvine Unified	Irvine
46	24,587	Chula Vista Elementary	Chula Vista
47	24,447	Grossmont Union High	La Mesa
48	24,409	East Side Union High	San Jose
49	24,093	Norwalk-La Mirada Unified	Norwalk
50	24,051	Hayward Unified	Hayward
51	24,018	Colton Joint Unified	Colton
52	23,282	Pasadena Unified	Pasadena
53	22,972	Fairfield-Suisun Unified	Fairfield
54	22,524	Palmdale Elementary	Palmdale
55	22,482	Oceanside Unified	Oceanside
56	22,375	Anaheim Elementary	Anaheim
57	22,332	ABC Unified	Cerritos
58	22,298	Downey Unified	Downey
59	22,275	Newport-Mesa Unified	Costa Mesa
60	22,067	Palm Springs Unified	Palm Springs
61	21,998	Temecula Valley Unified	Temecula
62	21,981	Chaffey Joint Union High	Ontario
63	21,855	Conejo Valley Unified	Thousand Oaks
64	21,673	Simi Valley Unified	Simi Valley
65	21,561	San Ramon Valley Unified	Danville
66	21,136	Antioch Unified	Antioch
67	21,067	Antelope Valley Union High	Lancaster
68	21,052	Manteca Unified	Manteca
69	20,469	Jurupa Unified	Riverside
70	20,285	Redlands Unified	Redlands
71	20,201	Escondido Union Elementary	Escondido
72	20,058	William S Hart Union High	Santa Clarita
73	19,872	Vallejo City Unified	Vallejo
74	19,661	Pajaro Valley Unified School	Watsonville
75	19,464	Lynwood Unified	Lynwood
76	19,163	Baldwin Park Unified	Baldwin Park
77	19,122	Alvord Unified	Riverside
78	18,954	Modesto City Elementary	Modesto
79	18,933	Lake Elsinore Unified	Lake Elsinore
80	18,931	Hemet Unified	Hemet
81	18,739	Rowland Unified	Rowland Heights
82	18,653	Cajon Valley Union Elementary	El Cajon
83	18,518	Tustin Unified	Tustin
84	17,744	Ventura Unified	Ventura
85	17,741	Inglewood Unified	Inglewood
86	17,614	Folsom-Cordova Unified	Folsom
87	17,229	Paramount Unified	Paramount
88	16,881	Napa Valley Unified	Napa
89	16,855	Madera Unified	Madera
90	16,747	Burbank Unified	Burbank
91	16,625	Oxnard Elementary	Oxnard
92	16,195	Fullerton Joint Union High	Fullerton
92	16,195	Hesperia Unified	Hesperia
94	15,873	Cupertino Union School	Cupertino
95	15,576	Lancaster Elementary	Lancaster
96	15,544	Modesto City High	Modesto
97	15,434	Murrieta Valley Unified	Murrieta
98	15,421	Bellflower Unified	Bellflower
99	15,370	Oxnard Union High	Oxnard
100	15,334	Walnut Valley Unified	Walnut
101	15,252	Tracy Joint Unified	Tracy
102	14,806	Vacaville Unified	Vacaville
103	14,718	Covina-Valley Unified	Covina
104	14,668	Huntington Beach Union High	Huntington Bch
105	14,548	La Mesa-Spring Valley	La Mesa
106	14,416	Alum Rock Union Elementary	San Jose
107	14,011	Chico Unified	Chico
108	13,978	Livermore Valley Joint Unified	Livermore
109	13,910	San Marcos Unified	San Marcos
110	13,867	Coachella Valley Unified	Thermal
111	13,850	Apple Valley Unified	Apple Valley
112	13,729	Pleasanton Unified	Pleasanton
113	13,623	Santa Clara Unified	Santa Clara
114	13,599	Salinas Union High	Salinas
115	13,582	New Haven Unified	Union City
116	13,554	Fullerton Elementary	Fullerton
117	13,450	Panama Buena Vista Union Elem	Bakersfield
118	13,237	Upland Unified	Upland
119	13,029	Santa Rosa High	Santa Rosa
120	12,789	Santa Monica-Malibu Unified	Santa Monica
121	12,682	Grant Joint Union High	Sacramento
122	12,621	Evergreen Elementary	San Jose
123	12,487	Porterville Unified	Porterville
124	12,450	Val Verde Unified	Perris
125	12,333	El Rancho Unified	Pico Rivera
126	12,312	Monterey Peninsula Unified	Monterey
127	12,202	Whittier Union High	Whittier
128	12,164	Azusa Unified	Azusa
129	12,119	Las Virgenes Unified	Calabasas
130	12,034	Santa Maria-Bonita Elementary	Santa Maria
131	11,951	El Monte City Elementary	El Monte
132	11,684	San Lorenzo Unified	San Lorenzo
133	11,617	Lompoc Unified	Lompoc
134	11,613	Oak Grove Elementary	San Jose
135	11,579	Yuba City Unified	Yuba City
136	11,441	Los Angeles County Office of Ed	Downey
137	11,434	Alhambra City Elementary	Alhambra
138	11,384	Merced City Elementary	Merced
139	11,337	San Dieguito Union High	Encinitas
140	11,289	Central Unified	Fresno
141	11,223	Palos Verdes Peninsula Unified	Palos Verdes Est
142	10,916	Lucia Mar Unified	Arroyo Grande
143	10,615	Alameda City Unified	Alameda
144	10,563	West Covina Unified	West Covina
145	10,497	Mountain View Elementary	El Monte
146	10,445	Woodland Joint Unified	Woodland
147	10,424	Victor Valley Union High	Victorville
148	10,392	Santa Barbara High	Santa Barbara
149	10,287	Etiwanda Elementary	Etiwanda
150	10,180	Ocean View Elementary	Huntington Bch
151	10,178	Bonita Unified	San Dimas
152	10,134	Rio Linda Union Elementary	Rio Linda
153	10,129	Palo Alto Unified	Palo Alto
154	10,113	Westminster Elementary	Westminster
155	10,111	El Monte Union High	El Monte
156	10,087	San Mateo-Foster City Elementary	San Mateo
157	10,060	Saugus Union Elementary	Santa Clarita
158	10,028	Ceres Unified	Ceres
159	9,953	Franklin-Mckinley Elementary	San Jose
160	9,942	Arcadia Unified	Arcadia
161	9,940	Carlsbad Unified	Carlsbad
162	9,835	Hawthorne Elementary	Hawthorne
163	9,793	Marysville Joint Unified	Marysville
164	9,630	Gilroy Unified	Gilroy
165	9,621	Merced Union High	Atwater
166	9,563	South San Francisco Unified	S San Francisco
167	9,542	Pittsburg Unified	Pittsburg
168	9,516	Milpitas Unified	Milpitas
169	9,467	Morongo Unified	Twentynine Plms
170	9,442	Victor Elementary	Victorville
171	9,424	South Bay Union Elementary	Imperial Beach
172	9,409	East Whittier City Elementary	Whittier
173	9,242	Yucaipa-Calimesa Joint Unified	Yucaipa
174	9,138	Fremont Union High	Sunnyvale
175	9,087	Los Alamitos Unified	Los Alamitos
176	9,079	Salinas City Elementary	Salinas
177	9,060	Berkeley Unified	Berkeley
178	8,939	Lincoln Unified	Stockton
179	8,933	Turlock Joint Elementary	Turlock
180	8,839	Kings Canyon Joint Unified	Reedley
181	8,827	Davis Joint Unified	Davis
182	8,813	Redwood City Elementary	Redwood City
183	8,809	Morgan Hill Unified	Morgan Hill
184	8,785	Snowline Joint Unified	Phelan
185	8,749	San Leandro Unified	San Leandro
186	8,668	Calexico Unified	Calexico
187	8,648	Hueneme Elementary	Port Hueneme
188	8,615	Rocklin Unified	Rocklin
189	8,427	Berryessa Union Elementary	San Jose
190	8,363	Escondido Union High	Escondido
191	8,352	Alhambra City High	Alhambra
192	8,271	Orange County Office of Ed	Costa Mesa
193	8,250	San Mateo Union High	San Mateo
194	8,213	Sanger Unified	Sanger
195	8,211	Castro Valley Unified	Castro Valley
196	7,996	Glendora Unified	Glendora
197	7,993	Redondo Beach Unified	Redondo Beach
198	7,945	San Luis Coastal Unified	San Luis Obispo
199	7,903	Alisal Union Elementary	Salinas
200	7,861	Tulare City Elementary	Tulare
201	7,844	Los Banos Unified	Los Banos
202	7,824	Moorpark Unified	Moorpark
203	7,794	Novato Unified	Novato
204	7,724	Roseville Joint Union High	Roseville
205	7,680	Sequoia Union High	Redwood City
206	7,678	Cotati-Rohnert Park Unified	Rohnert Park
207	7,653	Natomas Unified	Sacramento
208	7,609	Alta Loma Elementary	Alta Loma
209	7,527	Campbell Union High	San Jose
210	7,521	Lennox Elementary	Lennox
211	7,483	Campbell Union Elementary	Campbell
212	7,476	Centinela Valley Union High	Lawndale
213	7,401	Newark Unified	Newark
214	7,389	Pleasant Valley School	Camarillo
215	7,387	Whittier City Elementary	Whittier
216	7,377	Sylvan Union Elementary	Modesto
217	7,359	Ramona City Unified	Ramona
218	7,345	Santee Elementary	Santee
219	7,280	Western Placer Unified	Lincoln
220	7,140	Greenfield Union Elementary	Bakersfield
221	7,114	Roseville City Elementary	Roseville
222	7,104	Westside Union Elementary	Lancaster
223	7,097	Delano Union Elementary	Delano
224	7,026	Charter Oak Unified	Covina
225	6,998	Huntington Beach City Elementary	Huntington Bch
226	6,989	Magnolia Elementary	Anaheim
227	6,976	Perris Union High	Perris
228	6,900	Paso Robles Joint Unified	Paso Robles
229	6,876	Washington Unified	West Sacramento
230	6,866	Claremont Unified	Claremont
231	6,859	Garvey Elementary	Rosemead
232	6,858	El Dorado Union High	Placerville
233	6,855	Ukiah Unified	Ukiah
234	6,852	Jefferson Elementary	Daly City
235	6,816	Barstow Unified	Barstow
236	6,695	Monrovia Unified	Monrovia
237	6,682	San Jacinto Unified	San Jacinto
238	6,671	Culver City Unified	Culver City
239	6,590	National Elementary	National City
240	6,555	Newhall Elementary	Valencia
241	6,465	Manhattan Beach Unified	Manhattan Beach
242	6,456	La Habra City Elementary	La Habra
243	6,429	Santa Maria Joint Union High	Santa Maria
244	6,394	Lawndale Elementary	Lawndale
245	6,386	Dry Creek Joint Elementary	Roseville
246	6,384	Buena Park Elementary	Buena Park
247	6,320	Fountain Valley Elementary	Fountain Valley
248	6,280	Hollister SD	Hollister
249	6,223	El Centro Elementary	El Centro
250	6,188	San Gabriel Unified	San Gabriel
251	6,129	Bassett Unified	La Puente
252	6,123	Brea-Olinda Unified	Brea
253	6,109	North Monterey County Unified	Moss Landing
254	6,093	Santa Barbara Elementary	Santa Barbara
255	5,948	Selma Unified	Selma
256	5,931	Sunnyvale Elementary	Sunnyvale
257	5,904	Center Joint Unified	Antelope
258	5,871	Fallbrook Union Elementary	Fallbrook
259	5,791	Atascadero Unified	Atascadero
260	5,780	Rim of The World Unified	Lake Arrowhead
261	5,771	Petaluma Joint Union High	Petaluma
262	5,748	Shasta Union High	Redding
263	5,744	Acalanes Union High	Lafayette
264	5,689	Temple City Unified	Temple City
265	5,624	Encinitas Union Elementary	Encinitas
266	5,567	Sierra Sands Unified	Ridgecrest
267	5,552	North Sacramento Elementary	Sacramento
268	5,548	Adelanto Elementary	Adelanto
269	5,455	Sulphur Springs Union Elementary	Canyon Country
270	5,423	Benicia Unified	Benicia
271	5,407	Menifee Union Elementary	Menifee
272	5,375	Jefferson Union High	Daly City
273	5,363	Travis Unified	Travis Afb
274	5,352	Centralia Elementary	Buena Park
275	5,343	Brentwood Union Elementary	Brentwood
276	5,342	Tahoe-Truckee Joint Unified	Truckee
277	5,310	Dinuba Unified	Dinuba
278	5,295	Paradise Unified	Paradise
279	5,262	Hanford Elementary	Hanford
280	5,247	Eureka City Unified	Eureka
281	5,238	Lake Tahoe Unified	S Lake Tahoe
282	5,232	Beverly Hills Unified	Beverly Hills
283	5,231	Central Elementary	Rcho Cucamong
284	5,226	Little Lake City Elementary	Santa Fe Spgs
285	5,168	Ravenswood City Elementary	East Palo Alto
286	5,157	Santa Cruz City High	Santa Cruz
287	5,032	Orcutt Union Elementary	Orcutt
288	5,025	San Ysidro Elementary	San Ysidro
289	4,974	Lakeside Union Elementary	Lakeside
290	4,969	Perris Elementary	Perris
291	4,936	Sonoma Valley Unified	Sonoma
292	4,910	Oakdale Joint Unified	Oakdale
293	4,907	Tehachapi Unified	Tehachapi
294	4,815	Cypress Elementary	Cypress
295	4,740	Valley Center-Pauma Unified	Valley Center
296	4,736	Atwater Elementary	Atwater
297	4,720	Santa Rosa Elementary	Santa Rosa
298	4,706	Placer Union High	Auburn
299	4,693	Duarte Unified	Duarte
300	4,664	Amador County Unified	Jackson
301	4,655	Banning Unified	Banning
302	4,637	Union Elementary	San Jose
303	4,604	South Whittier Elementary	Whittier
304	4,602	Windsor Unified	Windsor
305	4,486	Mountain View-Whisman Elementary	Mountain View
306	4,467	Liberty Union High	Brentwood
307	4,441	Lemon Grove Elementary	Lemon Grove
308	4,413	Moreland Elementary	San Jose
309	4,363	La Canada Unified	La Canada
310	4,356	Beaumont Unified	Beaumont
311	4,354	Nevada Joint Union High	Grass Valley
311	4,354	Oakley Union Elementary	Oakley
313	4,340	Turlock Joint Union High	Turlock
314	4,338	Dublin Unified	Dublin
314	4,338	Martinez Unified	Martinez
316	4,330	Del Norte County Unified	Crescent City
317	4,257	Galt Joint Union Elementary	Galt
318	4,251	Patterson Joint Unified	Patterson
319	4,244	Empire Union Elementary	Modesto

Rank	Number	District Name	City
320	4,243	Eureka Union Elementary	Granite Bay
321	4,231	Coalinga-Huron Joint Unified	Coalinga
322	4,230	Tulare Joint Union High	Tulare
323	4,213	Buckeye Union Elementary	Shingle Springs
324	4,149	Santa Paula Elementary	Santa Paula
325	4,126	Redding Elementary	Redding
326	4,110	Goleta Union Elementary	Goleta
327	4,100	South Pasadena Unified	South Pasadena
328	4,085	Rosedale Union Elementary	Bakersfield
329	4,032	Los Altos Elementary	Los Altos
330	3,981	Cutler-Orosi Joint Unified	Orosi
331	3,933	Dixon Unified	Dixon
332	3,929	Rio Elementary	Oxnard
333	3,915	Ojai Unified	Ojai
334	3,869	Fillmore Unified	Fillmore
334	3,869	San Lorenzo Valley Unified	Felton
336	3,816	Central Union High	El Centro
337	3,814	Enterprise Elementary	Redding
338	3,782	Tamalpais Union High	Larkspur
339	3,760	Brawley Elementary	Brawley
340	3,752	Oak Park Unified	Oak Park
341	3,744	Riverside County Office of Ed	Riverside
342	3,738	Gateway Unified	Redding
343	3,731	Calaveras Unified	San Andreas
344	3,686	Palo Verde Unified	Blythe
345	3,655	Kerman Unified	Kerman
345	3,655	Soledad Unified	Soledad
347	3,649	Cabrillo Unified	Half Moon Bay
348	3,630	Delano Joint Union High	Delano
349	3,601	Hanford Joint Union High	Hanford
350	3,566	San Rafael City Elementary	San Rafael
351	3,555	Lindsay Unified	Lindsay
352	3,529	Rescue Union Elementary	Rescue
353	3,473	Salida Union Elementary	Salida
354	3,439	Mountain View Elementary	Ontario
355	3,425	Lafayette Elementary	Lafayette
356	3,403	Castaic Union Elementary	Valencia
356	3,403	Rosemead Elementary	Rosemead
358	3,390	Bear Valley Unified	Big Bear Lake
359	3,384	Lowell Joint	Whittier
360	3,378	San Diego County Office of Ed	San Diego
361	3,367	Oroville City Elementary	Oroville
362	3,356	Konocti Unified	Lower Lake
363	3,340	Walnut Creek Elementary	Walnut Creek
364	3,324	Del Mar Union Elementary	Del Mar
365	3,317	Parlier Unified	Parlier
366	3,309	Stanislaus Union Elementary	Modesto
367	3,263	Mountain View-Los Altos Union High	Mountain View
368	3,223	San Bernardino County Supt.	San Bernardino
369	3,220	Southern Kern Unified	Rosamond
370	3,213	Plumas Unified	Quincy
371	3,193	Riverbank Unified	Riverbank
372	3,190	San Marino Unified	San Marino
373	3,181	Lemoore Union Elementary	Lemoore
374	3,177	Corcoran Joint Unified	Corcoran
375	3,153	Laguna Salada Union Elementary	Pacifica
376	3,145	Albany City Unified	Albany
377	3,112	Escalon Unified	Escalon
378	3,079	Fallbrook Union High	Fallbrook
379	3,047	Fruitvale Elementary	Bakersfield
380	3,044	El Segundo Unified	El Segundo
381	3,018	Carpinteria Unified	Carpinteria
382	2,995	Santa Rita Union Elementary	Salinas
383	2,946	Waterford Unified	Waterford
384	2,927	Oroville Union High	Oroville
385	2,924	Keppel Union Elementary	Pearblossom
386	2,902	San Benito High	Hollister
387	2,892	Cucamonga Elementary	Rcho Cucamong
388	2,873	Los Gatos-Saratoga Jt Union High	Los Gatos
389	2,849	Mount Pleasant Elementary	San Jose
389	2,849	Wasco Union Elementary	Wasco
391	2,846	Oro Grande Elementary	Oro Grande
392	2,845	Arvin Union Elementary	Arvin
393	2,829	Mcfarland Unified	Mcfarland
394	2,824	Richland SD	Shafter
395	2,807	Cambrian Elementary	San Jose
396	2,800	San Bruno Park Elementary	San Bruno
397	2,791	Coronado Unified	Coronado
398	2,789	Healdsburg Unified	Healdsburg
399	2,773	Ripon Unified	Ripon
400	2,744	Rincon Valley Union Elementary	Santa Rosa
401	2,734	Dos Palos Oro Loma Joint Unified	Dos Palos
402	2,719	Lamont Elementary	Lamont
403	2,713	Scotts Valley Unified	Scotts Valley
404	2,708	Auburn Union Elementary	Auburn
405	2,700	Laguna Beach Unified	Laguna Beach
406	2,687	West Sonoma County Union High	Sebastopol
407	2,684	Templeton Unified	Templeton
408	2,670	Silver Valley Unified	Yermo
409	2,657	Burton Elementary	Porterville
410	2,654	Solana Beach Elementary	Solana Beach
411	2,652	Los Gatos Union Elementary	Los Gatos
412	2,636	Santa Cruz City Elementary	Santa Cruz
413	2,634	Imperial Unified	Imperial
414	2,633	Ocean View Elementary	Oxnard
415	2,627	King City Union Elementary	King City
416	2,621	Eastside Union Elementary	Lancaster
417	2,618	Mojave Unified	Mojave
418	2,584	Standard Elementary	Bakersfield
419	2,580	San Carlos Elementary	San Carlos
420	2,566	Piedmont City Unified	Piedmont
421	2,561	Greenfield Union Elementary	Greenfield
422	2,560	Mariposa County Unified	Mariposa
423	2,541	Belmont-Redwood Shores Elementary	Belmont
424	2,510	Kern County Office of Ed	Bakersfield
425	2,509	Linden Unified	Linden
426	2,490	River Delta Joint Unified	Rio Vista
427	2,488	Delhi Unified	Delhi
428	2,486	Savanna Elementary	Anaheim
429	2,459	Firebaugh-Las Deltas Joint Unified	Firebaugh
430	2,458	Anderson Union High	Anderson
431	2,436	Wheatland Elementary	Wheatland
432	2,434	Muroc Joint Unified	North Edwards
433	2,433	Livingston Union Elementary	Livingston
434	2,432	Sierra Unified	Auberry
435	2,428	Alpine Union Elementary	Alpine
436	2,422	Reef-Sunset Unified	Avenal
437	2,417	Saratoga Union Elementary	Saratoga
438	2,410	Hilmar Unified	Hilmar
438	2,410	Orinda Union Elementary	Orinda
440	2,403	Orland Joint Unified	Orland
441	2,375	Gonzales Unified	Gonzales
442	2,350	Los Nietos Elementary	Whittier
443	2,346	Willits Unified	Willits
444	2,331	Red Bluff Union Elementary	Red Bluff
445	2,327	Burlingame Elementary	Burlingame
446	2,323	Robla Elementary	Sacramento
447	2,321	Farmersville Unified	Farmersville
448	2,308	Newman-Crows Landing Unified	Newman
449	2,288	Mill Valley Elementary	Mill Valley
450	2,268	Petaluma City Elementary	Petaluma
451	2,240	Santa Clara County Office of Ed	San Jose
452	2,223	San Joaquin County Office of Ed	Stockton
453	2,199	Carmel Unified	Carmel
454	2,190	Fresno County Office of Ed	Fresno
455	2,162	King City Joint Union High	King City
456	2,156	Westwood Unified	Westwood
457	2,155	Del Paso Heights Elementary	Sacramento
457	2,155	Lemoore Union High	Lemoore
459	2,151	Millbrae Elementary	Millbrae
460	2,136	Fowler Unified	Fowler
461	2,130	Mendota Unified	Mendota
462	2,127	Taft City Elementary	Taft
463	2,123	Gridley Unified	Gridley
464	2,114	Kingsburg Elementary Charter	Kingsburg
465	2,112	Soquel Union Elementary	Capitola
466	2,091	San Rafael City High	San Rafael
466	2,091	Wilsona Elementary	Palmdale
468	2,084	Fort Bragg Unified	Fort Bragg
469	2,078	Acton-Agua Dulce Unified	Acton
470	2,074	Galt Joint Union High	Galt
471	2,071	Pleasant Ridge Union Elementary	Grass Valley
472	2,059	Red Bluff Joint Union High	Red Bluff
473	2,039	Menlo Park City Elementary	Atherton
474	2,038	Winters Joint Unified	Winters
475	2,022	Black Oak Mine Unified	Georgetown
476	2,020	Julian Union High	Julian
477	2,007	Hughson Unified	Hughson
478	1,996	Central Union Elementary	Lemoore
479	1,976	Old Adobe Union Elementary	Petaluma
480	1,967	Kelseyville Unified	Kelseyville
481	1,964	Corning Union Elementary	Corning
482	1,957	Golden Plains Unified	San Joaquin
483	1,952	Pacific Grove Unified	Pacific Grove
484	1,948	Live Oak Elementary	Santa Cruz
485	1,944	Northern Humboldt Union High	McKinleyville
486	1,934	Loomis Union Elementary	Loomis
487	1,932	Grass Valley Elementary	Grass Valley
488	1,930	Wiseburn Elementary	Hawthorne
489	1,924	Holtville Unified	Holtville
490	1,923	Exeter Union Elementary	Exeter
491	1,910	Lakeport Unified	Lakeport
492	1,868	Keyes Union Elementary	Keyes
493	1,860	Live Oak Unified	Live Oak
494	1,855	Dixie Elementary	San Rafael
495	1,854	Twin Ridges Elementary	North San Juan
496	1,852	Norris Elementary	Bakersfield
497	1,829	Moraga Elementary	Moraga
498	1,828	Earlimart Elementary	Earlimart
499	1,827	John Swett Unified	Crockett
500	1,825	Willows Unified	Willows
501	1,822	Mountain Empire Unified	Pine Valley
502	1,797	Brawley Union High	Brawley
503	1,793	Winton Elementary	Winton
504	1,792	Gustine Unified	Gustine
505	1,790	Ross Valley Elementary	San Anselmo
506	1,771	Gorman Elementary	Gorman
507	1,758	Beardsley Elementary	Bakersfield
508	1,749	Middletown Unified	Middletown
509	1,740	Bonsall Union Elementary	Bonsall
510	1,725	Santa Paula Union High	Santa Paula
511	1,720	Sonora Union High	Sonora
512	1,710	Jamul-Dulzura Union Elementary	Jamul
513	1,707	Chowchilla Elementary	Chowchilla
514	1,706	Piner-Olivet Union Elementary	Santa Rosa
515	1,699	Bellevue Union Elementary	Santa Rosa
516	1,690	Romoland Elementary	Homeland
517	1,640	Julian Union Elementary	Julian
518	1,611	Mother Lode Union Elementary	Placerville
519	1,604	Cascade Union Elementary	Anderson
520	1,600	Woodlake Union Elementary	Woodlake
521	1,597	Cloverdale Unified	Cloverdale
522	1,591	Weaver Union Elementary	Merced
523	1,577	Riverdale Joint Unified	Riverdale
524	1,566	Thermalito Union Elementary	Oroville
525	1,551	Mark West Union Elementary	Santa Rosa
526	1,538	Colusa Unified	Colusa
527	1,520	Jefferson Elementary	Tracy
528	1,516	Bishop Union Elementary	Bishop
529	1,500	Saint Helena Unified	Saint Helena

Male Students

Rank	Percent	District Name	City
1	71.9	San Bernardino County Supt.	San Bernardino
2	69.0	Santa Clara County Office of Ed	San Jose
3	68.0	Los Angeles County Office of Ed	Downey
4	67.4	Fresno County Office of Ed	Fresno
5	66.9	Kern County Office of Ed	Bakersfield
6	63.8	San Joaquin County Office of Ed	Stockton
7	60.1	Orange County Office of Ed	Costa Mesa
7	60.1	San Diego County Office of Ed	San Diego
9	59.0	Riverside County Office of Ed	Riverside
10	55.4	Cascade Union Elementary	Anderson
11	54.5	Mount Pleasant Elementary	San Jose
12	54.2	Menlo Park City Elementary	Atherton
13	53.7	Black Oak Mine Unified	Georgetown
14	53.6	Chowchilla Elementary	Chowchilla
14	53.6	Savanna Elementary	Anaheim
16	53.5	Nevada Joint Union High	Grass Valley
17	53.4	Keyes Union Elementary	Keyes
17	53.4	Moraga Elementary	Moraga
17	53.4	Wiseburn Elementary	Hawthorne
20	53.3	Cucamonga Elementary	Rcho Cucamong
20	53.3	Fort Bragg Unified	Fort Bragg
20	53.3	Newman-Crows Landing Unified	Newman
20	53.3	San Carlos Elementary	San Carlos
24	53.2	Piner-Olivet Union Elementary	Santa Rosa
24	53.2	Santa Cruz City High	Santa Cruz
24	53.2	Willits Unified	Willits
27	53.1	Del Mar Union Elementary	Del Mar
27	53.1	Winters Joint Unified	Winters
29	53.0	San Rafael City Elementary	San Rafael
30	52.9	Los Gatos-Saratoga Jt Union High	Los Gatos
30	52.9	San Dieguito Union High	Encinitas
30	52.9	Sulphur Springs Union Elementary	Canyon Country
33	52.8	Norris Elementary	Bakersfield
34	52.7	Empire Union Elementary	Modesto
34	52.7	Gateway Unified	Redding
34	52.7	Gustine Unified	Gustine
34	52.7	Mendota Unified	Mendota
34	52.7	Paso Robles Joint Unified	Paso Robles
34	52.7	Santa Cruz City Elementary	Santa Cruz
34	52.7	Santa Rosa Elementary	Santa Rosa
34	52.7	Wilsona Elementary	Palmdale
42	52.6	Coalinga-Huron Joint Unified	Coalinga
42	52.6	Julian Union High	Julian
42	52.6	King City Union Elementary	King City
42	52.6	Middletown Unified	Middletown
42	52.6	Reef-Sunset Unified	Avenal
47	52.5	Campbell Union Elementary	Campbell
47	52.5	Cloverdale Unified	Cloverdale
47	52.5	Cypress Elementary	Cypress
47	52.5	New Haven Unified	Union City
47	52.5	Orcutt Union Elementary	Orcutt
47	52.5	Riverbank Unified	Riverbank
47	52.5	San Marino Unified	San Marino
54	52.4	Escalon Unified	Escalon
54	52.4	Grant Joint Union High	Sacramento
54	52.4	Jefferson Union High	Daly City
54	52.4	San Ysidro Elementary	San Ysidro
54	52.4	Tehachapi Unified	Tehachapi
59	52.3	Atascadero Unified	Atascadero
59	52.3	Brawley Elementary	Brawley
59	52.3	Carmel Unified	Carmel
59	52.3	Cutler-Orosi Joint Unified	Orosi
59	52.3	Fowler Unified	Fowler
59	52.3	Grass Valley Elementary	Grass Valley

59	52.3	Hollister SD	Hollister
59	52.3	Kelseyville Unified	Kelseyville
59	52.3	Lafayette Elementary	Lafayette
59	52.3	Pittsburg Unified	Pittsburg
59	52.3	Plumas Unified	Quincy
59	52.3	Redding Elementary	Redding
59	52.3	San Mateo Union High	San Mateo
59	52.3	San Rafael City High	San Rafael
59	52.3	Solana Beach Elementary	Solana Beach
59	52.3	Taft City Elementary	Taft
59	52.3	Valley Center-Pauma Unified	Valley Center
76	52.2	ABC Unified	Cerritos
76	52.2	Cotati-Rohnert Park Unified	Rohnert Park
76	52.2	Fremont Unified	Fremont
76	52.2	Moreland Elementary	San Jose
76	52.2	Newark Unified	Newark
76	52.2	Selma Unified	Selma
82	52.1	Bear Valley Unified	Big Bear Lake
82	52.1	Dinuba Unified	Dinuba
82	52.1	Eureka Union Elementary	Granite Bay
82	52.1	Healdsburg Unified	Healdsburg
82	52.1	John Swett Unified	Crockett
82	52.1	Ocean View Elementary	Huntington Bch
82	52.1	Redwood City Elementary	Redwood City
82	52.1	Rescue Union Elementary	Rescue
82	52.1	Santa Maria-Bonita Elementary	Santa Maria
82	52.1	Soledad Unified	Soledad
82	52.1	Sonoma Valley Unified	Sonoma
82	52.1	South San Francisco Unified	S San Francisco
82	52.1	Yuba City Unified	Yuba City
95	52.0	Alvord Unified	Riverside
95	52.0	Campbell Union High	San Jose
95	52.0	Conejo Valley Unified	Thousand Oaks
95	52.0	Encinitas Union Elementary	Encinitas
95	52.0	Holtville Unified	Holtville
95	52.0	Lawndale Elementary	Lawndale
95	52.0	Mojave Unified	Mojave
95	52.0	Pacific Grove Unified	Pacific Grove
95	52.0	San Gabriel Unified	San Gabriel
95	52.0	San Leandro Unified	San Leandro
95	52.0	Tamalpais Union High	Larkspur
95	52.0	Walnut Creek Elementary	Walnut Creek
95	52.0	Wheatland Elementary	Wheatland
95	52.0	Winton Elementary	Winton
109	51.9	Berryessa Union Elementary	San Jose
109	51.9	Burton Elementary	Porterville
109	51.9	Centinela Valley Union High	Lawndale
109	51.9	Corning Union Elementary	Corning
109	51.9	Del Norte County Unified	Crescent City
109	51.9	Exeter Union Elementary	Exeter
109	51.9	Galt Joint Union High	Galt
109	51.9	Hanford Elementary	Hanford
109	51.9	Los Banos Unified	Los Banos
109	51.9	Milpitas Unified	Milpitas
109	51.9	Mountain Empire Unified	Pine Valley
109	51.9	National Elementary	National City
109	51.9	Santee Elementary	Santee
109	51.9	Saratoga Union Elementary	Saratoga
109	51.9	Standard Elementary	Bakersfield
109	51.9	Willows Unified	Willows
109	51.9	Woodlake Union Elementary	Woodlake
109	51.9	Yucaipa-Calimesa Joint Unified	Yucaipa
127	51.8	Alhambra City High	Alhambra
127	51.8	Belmont-Redwood Shores Elementary	Belmont
127	51.8	Carlsbad Unified	Carlsbad
127	51.8	Carpinteria Unified	Carpinteria
127	51.8	Centralia Elementary	Buena Park
127	51.8	Chico Unified	Chico
127	51.8	Chula Vista Elementary	Chula Vista
127	51.8	Dixon Unified	Dixon
127	51.8	East Side Union High	San Jose
127	51.8	Huntington Beach City Elementary	Huntington Bch
127	51.8	Keppel Union Elementary	Pearblossom
127	51.8	Live Oak Elementary	Santa Cruz
127	51.8	Manhattan Beach Unified	Manhattan Beach
127	51.8	Ripon Unified	Ripon
127	51.8	Robla Elementary	Sacramento
127	51.8	West Contra Costa Unified	Richmond
127	51.8	Woodland Joint Unified	Woodland
144	51.7	Alisal Union Elementary	Salinas
144	51.7	Benicia Unified	Benicia
144	51.7	Culver City Unified	Culver City
144	51.7	East Whittier City Elementary	Whittier
144	51.7	Enterprise Elementary	Redding
144	51.7	Eureka City Unified	Eureka
144	51.7	Gridley Unified	Gridley
144	51.7	Huntington Beach Union High	Huntington Bch
144	51.7	Lake Tahoe Unified	S Lake Tahoe
144	51.7	Lompoc Unified	Lompoc
144	51.7	Lucia Mar Unified	Arroyo Grande
144	51.7	Modesto City Elementary	Modesto
144	51.7	Mountain View Elementary	El Monte
144	51.7	Newport-Mesa Unified	Costa Mesa
144	51.7	Ocean View Elementary	Oxnard
144	51.7	Palo Verde Unified	Blythe
144	51.7	Placentia-Yorba Linda Unified	Placentia
144	51.7	Placer Union High	Auburn
144	51.7	Red Bluff Union Elementary	Red Bluff
144	51.7	Romoland Elementary	Homeland
144	51.7	San Francisco Unified	San Francisco
144	51.7	San Lorenzo Unified	San Lorenzo
144	51.7	Sequoia Union High	Redwood City
144	51.7	Snowline Joint Unified	Phelan
168	51.6	Capistrano Unified	San Juan Capis
168	51.6	Del Paso Heights Elementary	Sacramento
168	51.6	Delhi Unified	Delhi
168	51.6	Elk Grove Unified	Elk Grove
168	51.6	Fallbrook Union Elementary	Fallbrook
168	51.6	Firebaugh-Las Deltas Joint Unified	Firebaugh
168	51.6	Hayward Unified	Hayward
168	51.6	Irvine Unified	Irvine
168	51.6	Little Lake City Elementary	Santa Fe Spgs
168	51.6	Morongo Unified	Twentynine Plms
168	51.6	Norwalk-La Mirada Unified	Norwalk
168	51.6	Novato Unified	Novato
168	51.6	Orange Unified	Orange
168	51.6	Pleasant Ridge Union Elementary	Grass Valley
168	51.6	Pleasant Valley School	Camarillo
168	51.6	Rosemead Elementary	Rosemead
168	51.6	Rowland Unified	Rowland Heights
168	51.6	San Benito High	Hollister
168	51.6	Temple City Unified	Temple City
168	51.6	Torrance Unified	Torrance
168	51.6	Wasco Union Elementary	Wasco
168	51.6	Whittier City Elementary	Whittier
168	51.6	William S Hart Union High	Santa Clarita
191	51.5	Barstow Unified	Barstow
191	51.5	Bellflower Unified	Bellflower
191	51.5	Brea-Olinda Unified	Brea
191	51.5	Burlingame Elementary	Burlingame
191	51.5	Coachella Valley Unified	Thermal
191	51.5	Cupertino Union School	Cupertino
191	51.5	Delano Joint Union High	Delano
191	51.5	Etiwanda Elementary	Etiwanda
191	51.5	Jamul-Dulzura Union Elementary	Jamul
191	51.5	Mount Diablo Unified	Concord
191	51.5	Northern Humboldt Union High	McKinleyville
191	51.5	Oak Grove Elementary	San Jose
191	51.5	Palo Alto Unified	Palo Alto
191	51.5	Perris Elementary	Perris
191	51.5	Piedmont City Unified	Piedmont
191	51.5	Poway Unified	Poway
191	51.5	Rocklin Unified	Rocklin
191	51.5	Saddleback Valley Unified	Mission Viejo
191	51.5	San Bruno Park Elementary	San Bruno
191	51.5	San Jacinto Unified	San Jacinto
191	51.5	Santa Barbara Elementary	Santa Barbara
191	51.5	Santa Barbara High	Santa Barbara
191	51.5	Santa Clara Unified	Santa Clara
191	51.5	Santa Paula Union High	Santa Paula
191	51.5	Simi Valley Unified	Simi Valley
191	51.5	Travis Unified	Travis Afb
191	51.5	Ukiah Unified	Ukiah
191	51.5	Union Elementary	San Jose
191	51.5	Val Verde Unified	Perris
191	51.5	Vallejo City Unified	Vallejo
191	51.5	Walnut Valley Unified	Walnut
191	51.5	Westminster Elementary	Westminster
191	51.5	Westwood Unified	Westwood
224	51.4	Acalanes Union High	Lafayette
224	51.4	Dos Palos Oro Loma Joint Unified	Dos Palos
224	51.4	Duarte Unified	Duarte
224	51.4	Earlimart Elementary	Earlimart
224	51.4	El Monte City Elementary	El Monte
224	51.4	La Canada Unified	La Canada
224	51.4	Laguna Salada Union Elementary	Pacifica
224	51.4	Lake Elsinore Unified	Lake Elsinore
224	51.4	Lemoore Union Elementary	Lemoore
224	51.4	Mark West Union Elementary	Santa Rosa
224	51.4	Martinez Unified	Martinez
224	51.4	Napa Valley Unified	Napa
224	51.4	Oak Park Unified	Oak Park
224	51.4	Orinda Union Elementary	Orinda
224	51.4	Palmdale Elementary	Palmdale
224	51.4	Paradise Unified	Paradise
224	51.4	Redondo Beach Unified	Redondo Beach
224	51.4	Rincon Valley Union Elementary	Santa Rosa
224	51.4	Salida Union Elementary	Salida
224	51.4	San Marcos Unified	San Marcos
224	51.4	Soquel Union Elementary	Capitola
224	51.4	South Bay Union Elementary	Imperial Beach
224	51.4	Sunnyvale Elementary	Sunnyvale
224	51.4	Whittier Union High	Whittier
248	51.3	Baldwin Park Unified	Baldwin Park
248	51.3	Cajon Valley Union Elementary	El Cajon
248	51.3	Central Unified	Fresno
248	51.3	Central Union Elementary	Lemoore
248	51.3	Charter Oak Unified	Covina
248	51.3	Chino Valley Unified	Chino
248	51.3	Colton Joint Unified	Colton
248	51.3	El Centro Elementary	El Centro
248	51.3	Evergreen Elementary	San Jose
248	51.3	Golden Plains Unified	San Joaquin
248	51.3	Hawthorne Elementary	Hawthorne
248	51.3	Jefferson Elementary	Tracy
248	51.3	Las Virgenes Unified	Calabasas
248	51.3	Lennox Elementary	Lennox
248	51.3	Lodi Unified	Lodi
248	51.3	Monrovia Unified	Monrovia
248	51.3	Mountain View-Los Altos Union High	Mountain View
248	51.3	Newhall Elementary	Valencia
248	51.3	North Sacramento Elementary	Sacramento
248	51.3	Ojai Unified	Ojai
248	51.3	Oroville City Elementary	Oroville
248	51.3	Oroville Union High	Oroville
248	51.3	Oxnard Union High	Oxnard
248	51.3	Pasadena Unified	Pasadena
248	51.3	San Diego Unified	San Diego
248	51.3	San Lorenzo Valley Unified	Felton
248	51.3	Sanger Unified	Sanger
248	51.3	Santa Monica-Malibu Unified	Santa Monica
248	51.3	Sierra Sands Unified	Ridgecrest
248	51.3	Sweetwater Union High	Chula Vista
248	51.3	Vacaville Unified	Vacaville
248	51.3	Ventura Unified	Ventura
248	51.3	Weaver Union Elementary	Merced
281	51.2	Amador County Unified	Jackson
281	51.2	Anaheim Union High	Anaheim
281	51.2	Arcadia Unified	Arcadia
281	51.2	Banning Unified	Banning
281	51.2	Brentwood Union Elementary	Brentwood
281	51.2	Castaic Union Elementary	Valencia
281	51.2	Corona-Norco Unified	Norco
281	51.2	Downey Unified	Downey
281	51.2	Escondido Union High	Escondido
281	51.2	Fountain Valley Elementary	Fountain Valley
281	51.2	Fullerton Elementary	Fullerton
281	51.2	Hacienda La Puente Unified	City of Industry
281	51.2	Inglewood Unified	Inglewood
281	51.2	Jurupa Unified	Riverside
281	51.2	Los Nietos Elementary	Whittier
281	51.2	Lowell Joint	Whittier
281	51.2	Marysville Joint Unified	Marysville
281	51.2	Ontario-Montclair Elementary	Ontario
281	51.2	Palm Springs Unified	Palm Springs
281	51.2	Palos Verdes Peninsula Unified	Palos Verdes Est
281	51.2	Porterville Unified	Porterville
281	51.2	Ramona City Unified	Ramona
281	51.2	Richland SD	Shafter
281	51.2	Rosedale Union Elementary	Bakersfield
281	51.2	Silver Valley Unified	Yermo
281	51.2	Stanislaus Union Elementary	Modesto
281	51.2	Thermalito Union Elementary	Oroville
281	51.2	Turlock Joint Elementary	Turlock
281	51.2	Tustin Unified	Tustin
281	51.2	West Covina Unified	West Covina
281	51.2	West Sonoma County Union High	Sebastopol
312	51.1	Albany City Unified	Albany
312	51.1	Alum Rock Union Elementary	San Jose
312	51.1	Anaheim Elementary	Anaheim
312	51.1	Arvin Union Elementary	Arvin
312	51.1	Atwater Elementary	Atwater
312	51.1	Azusa Unified	Azusa
312	51.1	Cambrian Elementary	San Jose
312	51.1	Covina-Valley Unified	Covina
312	51.1	Dublin Unified	Dublin
312	51.1	Fremont Union High	Sunnyvale
312	51.1	Gilroy Unified	Gilroy
312	51.1	Greenfield Union Elementary	Bakersfield
312	51.1	Hanford Joint Union High	Hanford
312	51.1	Hughson Unified	Hughson
312	51.1	Kingsburg Elementary Charter	Kingsburg
312	51.1	Lakeside Union Elementary	Lakeside
312	51.1	Mill Valley Elementary	Mill Valley
312	51.1	Monterey Peninsula Unified	Monterey
312	51.1	Pomona Unified	Pomona
312	51.1	Rim of The World Unified	Lake Arrowhead
312	51.1	Sacramento City Unified	Sacramento
312	51.1	Santa Rita Union Elementary	Salinas
312	51.1	Santa Rosa High	Santa Rosa
312	51.1	Southern Kern Unified	Rosamond
312	51.1	Vista Unified	Vista
312	51.1	Washington Unified	West Sacramento
338	51.0	Bonita Unified	San Dimas
338	51.0	Burbank Unified	Burbank
338	51.0	Corcoran Joint Unified	Corcoran
338	51.0	El Dorado Union High	Placerville

338	51.0	El Rancho Unified	Pico Rivera
338	51.0	Fallbrook Union High	Fallbrook
338	51.0	Fontana Unified	Fontana
338	51.0	Garden Grove Unified	Garden Grove
338	51.0	Garvey Elementary	Rosemead
338	51.0	Grossmont Union High	La Mesa
338	51.0	Kings Canyon Joint Unified	Reedley
338	51.0	Lancaster Elementary	Lancaster
338	51.0	Los Alamitos Unified	Los Alamitos
338	51.0	Los Altos Elementary	Los Altos
338	51.0	Los Angeles Unified	Los Angeles
338	51.0	Manteca Unified	Manteca
338	51.0	Morgan Hill Unified	Morgan Hill
338	51.0	Natomas Unified	Sacramento
338	51.0	Oro Grande Elementary	Oro Grande
338	51.0	Red Bluff Joint Union High	Red Bluff
338	51.0	Rio Linda Union Elementary	Rio Linda
338	51.0	Riverside Unified	Riverside
338	51.0	San Luis Coastal Unified	San Luis Obispo
338	51.0	Scotts Valley Unified	Scotts Valley
362	50.9	Adelanto Elementary	Adelanto
362	50.9	Alpine Union Elementary	Alpine
362	50.9	Bakersfield City Elementary	Bakersfield
362	50.9	Center Joint Unified	Antelope
362	50.9	Chaffey Joint Union High	Ontario
362	50.9	Compton Unified	Compton
362	50.9	Escondido Union Elementary	Escondido
362	50.9	Folsom-Cordova Unified	Folsom
362	50.9	Fresno Unified	Fresno
362	50.9	Hilmar Unified	Hilmar
362	50.9	Jefferson Elementary	Daly City
362	50.9	La Mesa-Spring Valley	La Mesa
362	50.9	Laguna Beach Unified	Laguna Beach
362	50.9	Lakeport Unified	Lakeport
362	50.9	Livermore Valley Joint Unified	Livermore
362	50.9	Loomis Union Elementary	Loomis
362	50.9	Los Gatos Union Elementary	Los Gatos
362	50.9	Madera Unified	Madera
362	50.9	Merced City Elementary	Merced
362	50.9	Moreno Valley Unified	Moreno Valley
362	50.9	Murrieta Valley Unified	Murrieta
362	50.9	Oceanside Unified	Oceanside
362	50.9	Panama Buena Vista Union Elem	Bakersfield
362	50.9	San Juan Unified	Carmichael
362	50.9	San Mateo-Foster City Elementary	San Mateo
362	50.9	Santa Paula Elementary	Santa Paula
362	50.9	Sonora Union High	Sonora
362	50.9	Tracy Joint Unified	Tracy
390	50.8	Acton-Agua Dulce Unified	Acton
390	50.8	Alta Loma Elementary	Alta Loma
390	50.8	Calexico Unified	Calexico
390	50.8	Colusa Unified	Colusa
390	50.8	Desert Sands Unified	La Quinta
390	50.8	Dry Creek Joint Elementary	Roseville
390	50.8	Glendale Unified	Glendale
390	50.8	Hueneme Elementary	Port Hueneme
390	50.8	Live Oak Unified	Live Oak
390	50.8	Long Beach Unified	Long Beach
390	50.8	Lynwood Unified	Lynwood
390	50.8	Magnolia Elementary	Anaheim
390	50.8	Moorpark Unified	Moorpark
390	50.8	Mountain View-Whisman Elementary	Mountain View
390	50.8	Ravenswood City Elementary	East Palo Alto
390	50.8	San Bernardino City Unified	San Bernardino
390	50.8	San Jose Unified	San Jose
390	50.8	Santa Maria Joint Union High	Santa Maria
390	50.8	Shasta Union High	Redding
390	50.8	Stockton City Unified	Stockton
390	50.8	Visalia Unified	Visalia
411	50.7	Alameda City Unified	Alameda
411	50.7	Alhambra City Elementary	Alhambra
411	50.7	Antioch Unified	Antioch
411	50.7	Apple Valley Unified	Apple Valley
411	50.7	Central Union High	El Centro
411	50.7	El Segundo Unified	El Segundo
411	50.7	Fairfield-Suisun Unified	Fairfield
411	50.7	Hemet Unified	Hemet
411	50.7	Kerman Unified	Kerman
411	50.7	La Habra City Elementary	La Habra
411	50.7	Lemoore Union High	Lemoore
411	50.7	Lincoln Unified	Stockton
411	50.7	Montebello Unified	Montebello
411	50.7	Oakland Unified	Oakland
411	50.7	Pajaro Valley Unified School	Watsonville
411	50.7	Petaluma Joint Union High	Petaluma
411	50.7	Rialto Unified	Rialto
411	50.7	Riverdale Joint Unified	Riverdale
411	50.7	Saint Helena Unified	Saint Helena
411	50.7	San Ramon Valley Unified	Danville
411	50.7	Saugus Union Elementary	Santa Clarita
411	50.7	Sierra Unified	Auberry
411	50.7	South Pasadena Unified	South Pasadena
411	50.7	Victor Valley Union High	Victorville
435	50.6	Auburn Union Elementary	Auburn
435	50.6	Berkeley Unified	Berkeley
435	50.6	Beverly Hills Unified	Beverly Hills
435	50.6	Bonsall Union Elementary	Bonsall
435	50.6	Clovis Unified	Clovis
435	50.6	Goleta Union Elementary	Goleta
435	50.6	Hesperia Unified	Hesperia
435	50.6	Imperial Unified	Imperial
435	50.6	Livingston Union Elementary	Livingston
435	50.6	Menifee Union Elementary	Menifee
435	50.6	Mountain View Elementary	Ontario
435	50.6	Muroc Joint Unified	North Edwards
435	50.6	Perris Union High	Perris
435	50.6	Petaluma City Elementary	Petaluma
435	50.6	Pleasanton Unified	Pleasanton
435	50.6	Rio Elementary	Oxnard
435	50.6	Salinas Union High	Salinas
435	50.6	Temecula Valley Unified	Temecula
435	50.6	Tulare Joint Union High	Tulare
454	50.5	Antelope Valley Union High	Lancaster
454	50.5	Bassett Unified	La Puente
454	50.5	Beaumont Unified	Beaumont
454	50.5	Claremont Unified	Claremont
454	50.5	Delano Union Elementary	Delano
454	50.5	El Monte Union High	El Monte
454	50.5	Glendora Unified	Glendora
454	50.5	Lamont Elementary	Lamont
454	50.5	Liberty Union High	Brentwood
454	50.5	Mother Lode Union Elementary	Placerville
454	50.5	Oakley Union Elementary	Oakley
454	50.5	Parlier Unified	Parlier
454	50.5	Salinas City Elementary	Salinas
454	50.5	Sylvan Union Elementary	Modesto
454	50.5	Tahoe-Truckee Joint Unified	Truckee
454	50.5	Upland Unified	Upland
454	50.5	Westside Union Elementary	Lancaster
471	50.4	Castro Valley Unified	Castro Valley
471	50.4	Davis Joint Unified	Davis
471	50.4	Franklin-Mckinley Elementary	San Jose
471	50.4	Gonzales Unified	Gonzales
471	50.4	Kern Union High	Bakersfield
471	50.4	Konocti Unified	Lower Lake
471	50.4	Mcfarland Unified	Mcfarland
471	50.4	Oakdale Joint Unified	Oakdale
471	50.4	Oxnard Elementary	Oxnard
471	50.4	Roseville Joint Union High	Roseville
471	50.4	Waterford Unified	Waterford
482	50.3	Central Elementary	Rcho Cucamong
482	50.3	Ceres Unified	Ceres
482	50.3	North Monterey County Unified	Moss Landing
482	50.3	Patterson Joint Unified	Patterson
482	50.3	Ross Valley Elementary	San Anselmo
487	50.2	Anderson Union High	Anderson
487	50.2	Millbrae Elementary	Millbrae
487	50.2	Old Adobe Union Elementary	Petaluma
487	50.2	Victor Elementary	Victorville
491	50.1	Buena Park Elementary	Buena Park
491	50.1	Galt Joint Union Elementary	Galt
491	50.1	King City Joint Union High	King City
491	50.1	Paramount Unified	Paramount
491	50.1	Redlands Unified	Redlands
491	50.1	Santa Ana Unified	Santa Ana
491	50.1	South Whittier Elementary	Whittier
491	50.1	Western Placer Unified	Lincoln
499	50.0	Fillmore Unified	Fillmore
499	50.0	Mariposa County Unified	Mariposa
499	50.0	Roseville City Elementary	Roseville
499	50.0	Tulare City Elementary	Tulare
503	49.9	Beardsley Elementary	Bakersfield
503	49.9	Calaveras Unified	San Andreas
503	49.9	Lemon Grove Elementary	Lemon Grove
503	49.9	Merced Union High	Atwater
503	49.9	Windsor Unified	Windsor
508	49.8	Coronado Unified	Coronado
508	49.8	Dixie Elementary	San Rafael
508	49.8	Lindsay Unified	Lindsay
511	49.7	Buckeye Union Elementary	Shingle Springs
511	49.7	Eastside Union Elementary	Lancaster
511	49.7	Templeton Unified	Templeton
514	49.6	Bellevue Union Elementary	Santa Rosa
514	49.6	Cabrillo Unified	Half Moon Bay
514	49.6	Linden Unified	Linden
517	49.5	Fullerton Joint Union High	Fullerton
517	49.5	Modesto City High	Modesto
517	49.5	Orland Joint Unified	Orland
520	49.4	Fruitvale Elementary	Bakersfield
520	49.4	Twin Ridges Elementary	North San Juan
522	49.3	River Delta Joint Unified	Rio Vista
522	49.3	Turlock Joint Union High	Turlock
524	49.1	Brawley Union High	Brawley
524	49.1	Farmersville Unified	Farmersville
526	48.7	Bishop Union Elementary	Bishop
526	48.7	Greenfield Union Elementary	Greenfield
528	48.3	Gorman Elementary	Gorman
529	47.8	Julian Union Elementary	Julian

Female Students

Rank	Percent	District Name	City
1	52.2	Julian Union Elementary	Julian
2	51.7	Gorman Elementary	Gorman
3	51.3	Bishop Union Elementary	Bishop
3	51.3	Greenfield Union Elementary	Greenfield
5	50.9	Brawley Union High	Brawley
5	50.9	Farmersville Unified	Farmersville
7	50.7	River Delta Joint Unified	Rio Vista
7	50.7	Turlock Joint Union High	Turlock
9	50.6	Fruitvale Elementary	Bakersfield
9	50.6	Twin Ridges Elementary	North San Juan
11	50.5	Fullerton Joint Union High	Fullerton
11	50.5	Modesto City High	Modesto
11	50.5	Orland Joint Unified	Orland
14	50.4	Bellevue Union Elementary	Santa Rosa
14	50.4	Cabrillo Unified	Half Moon Bay
14	50.4	Linden Unified	Linden
17	50.3	Buckeye Union Elementary	Shingle Springs
17	50.3	Eastside Union Elementary	Lancaster
17	50.3	Templeton Unified	Templeton
20	50.2	Coronado Unified	Coronado
20	50.2	Dixie Elementary	San Rafael
20	50.2	Lindsay Unified	Lindsay
23	50.1	Beardsley Elementary	Bakersfield
23	50.1	Calaveras Unified	San Andreas
23	50.1	Lemon Grove Elementary	Lemon Grove
23	50.1	Merced Union High	Atwater
23	50.1	Windsor Unified	Windsor
28	50.0	Fillmore Unified	Fillmore
28	50.0	Mariposa County Unified	Mariposa
28	50.0	Roseville City Elementary	Roseville
28	50.0	Tulare City Elementary	Tulare
32	49.9	Buena Park Elementary	Buena Park
32	49.9	Galt Joint Union Elementary	Galt
32	49.9	King City Joint Union High	King City
32	49.9	Paramount Unified	Paramount
32	49.9	Redlands Unified	Redlands
32	49.9	Santa Ana Unified	Santa Ana
32	49.9	South Whittier Elementary	Whittier
32	49.9	Western Placer Unified	Lincoln
40	49.8	Anderson Union High	Anderson
40	49.8	Millbrae Elementary	Millbrae
40	49.8	Old Adobe Union Elementary	Petaluma
40	49.8	Victor Elementary	Victorville
44	49.7	Central Elementary	Rcho Cucamong
44	49.7	Ceres Unified	Ceres
44	49.7	North Monterey County Unified	Moss Landing
44	49.7	Patterson Joint Unified	Patterson
44	49.7	Ross Valley Elementary	San Anselmo
49	49.6	Castro Valley Unified	Castro Valley
49	49.6	Davis Joint Unified	Davis
49	49.6	Franklin-Mckinley Elementary	San Jose
49	49.6	Gonzales Unified	Gonzales
49	49.6	Kern Union High	Bakersfield
49	49.6	Konocti Unified	Lower Lake
49	49.6	Mcfarland Unified	Mcfarland
49	49.6	Oakdale Joint Unified	Oakdale
49	49.6	Oxnard Elementary	Oxnard
49	49.6	Roseville Joint Union High	Roseville
49	49.6	Waterford Unified	Waterford
60	49.5	Antelope Valley Union High	Lancaster
60	49.5	Bassett Unified	La Puente
60	49.5	Beaumont Unified	Beaumont
60	49.5	Claremont Unified	Claremont
60	49.5	Delano Union Elementary	Delano
60	49.5	El Monte Union High	El Monte
60	49.5	Glendora Unified	Glendora
60	49.5	Lamont Elementary	Lamont
60	49.5	Liberty Union High	Brentwood
60	49.5	Mother Lode Union Elementary	Placerville
60	49.5	Oakley Union Elementary	Oakley
60	49.5	Parlier Unified	Parlier
60	49.5	Salinas City Elementary	Salinas
60	49.5	Sylvan Union Elementary	Modesto
60	49.5	Tahoe-Truckee Joint Unified	Truckee
60	49.5	Upland Unified	Upland
60	49.5	Westside Union Elementary	Lancaster
77	49.4	Auburn Union Elementary	Auburn
77	49.4	Berkeley Unified	Berkeley
77	49.4	Beverly Hills Unified	Beverly Hills
77	49.4	Bonsall Union Elementary	Bonsall
77	49.4	Clovis Unified	Clovis
77	49.4	Goleta Union Elementary	Goleta
77	49.4	Hesperia Unified	Hesperia
77	49.4	Imperial Unified	Imperial
77	49.4	Livingston Union Elementary	Livingston
77	49.4	Menifee Union Elementary	Menifee

77	49.4	Mountain View Elementary	Ontario
77	49.4	Muroc Joint Unified	North Edwards
77	49.4	Perris Union High	Perris
77	49.4	Petaluma City Elementary	Petaluma
77	49.4	Pleasanton Unified	Pleasanton
77	49.4	Rio Elementary	Oxnard
77	49.4	Salinas Union High	Salinas
77	49.4	Temecula Valley Unified	Temecula
77	49.4	Tulare Joint Union High	Tulare
96	49.3	Alameda City Unified	Alameda
96	49.3	Alhambra City Elementary	Alhambra
96	49.3	Antioch Unified	Antioch
96	49.3	Apple Valley Unified	Apple Valley
96	49.3	Central Union High	El Centro
96	49.3	El Segundo Unified	El Segundo
96	49.3	Fairfield-Suisun Unified	Fairfield
96	49.3	Hemet Unified	Hemet
96	49.3	Kerman Unified	Kerman
96	49.3	La Habra City Elementary	La Habra
96	49.3	Lemoore Union High	Lemoore
96	49.3	Lincoln Unified	Stockton
96	49.3	Montebello Unified	Montebello
96	49.3	Oakland Unified	Oakland
96	49.3	Pajaro Valley Unified School	Watsonville
96	49.3	Petaluma Joint Union High	Petaluma
96	49.3	Rialto Unified	Rialto
96	49.3	Riverdale Joint Unified	Riverdale
96	49.3	Saint Helena Unified	Saint Helena
96	49.3	San Ramon Valley Unified	Danville
96	49.3	Saugus Union Elementary	Santa Clarita
96	49.3	Sierra Unified	Auberry
96	49.3	South Pasadena Unified	South Pasadena
96	49.3	Victor Valley Union High	Victorville
120	49.2	Acton-Agua Dulce Unified	Acton
120	49.2	Alta Loma Elementary	Alta Loma
120	49.2	Calexico Unified	Calexico
120	49.2	Colusa Unified	Colusa
120	49.2	Desert Sands Unified	La Quinta
120	49.2	Dry Creek Joint Elementary	Roseville
120	49.2	Glendale Unified	Glendale
120	49.2	Hueneme Elementary	Port Hueneme
120	49.2	Live Oak Unified	Live Oak
120	49.2	Long Beach Unified	Long Beach
120	49.2	Lynwood Unified	Lynwood
120	49.2	Magnolia Elementary	Anaheim
120	49.2	Moorpark Unified	Moorpark
120	49.2	Mountain View-Whisman Elementary	Mountain View
120	49.2	Ravenswood City Elementary	East Palo Alto
120	49.2	San Bernardino City Unified	San Bernardino
120	49.2	San Jose Unified	San Jose
120	49.2	Santa Maria Joint Union High	Santa Maria
120	49.2	Shasta Union High	Redding
120	49.2	Stockton City Unified	Stockton
120	49.2	Visalia Unified	Visalia
141	49.1	Adelanto Elementary	Adelanto
141	49.1	Alpine Union Elementary	Alpine
141	49.1	Bakersfield City Elementary	Bakersfield
141	49.1	Center Joint Unified	Antelope
141	49.1	Chaffey Joint Union High	Ontario
141	49.1	Compton Unified	Compton
141	49.1	Escondido Union Elementary	Escondido
141	49.1	Folsom-Cordova Unified	Folsom
141	49.1	Fresno Unified	Fresno
141	49.1	Hilmar Unified	Hilmar
141	49.1	Jefferson Elementary	Daly City
141	49.1	La Mesa-Spring Valley	La Mesa
141	49.1	Laguna Beach Unified	Laguna Beach
141	49.1	Lakeport Unified	Lakeport
141	49.1	Livermore Valley Joint Unified	Livermore
141	49.1	Loomis Union Elementary	Loomis
141	49.1	Los Gatos Union Elementary	Los Gatos
141	49.1	Madera Unified	Madera
141	49.1	Merced City Elementary	Merced
141	49.1	Moreno Valley Unified	Moreno Valley
141	49.1	Murrieta Valley Unified	Murrieta
141	49.1	Oceanside Unified	Oceanside
141	49.1	Panama Buena Vista Union Elem	Bakersfield
141	49.1	San Juan Unified	Carmichael
141	49.1	San Mateo-Foster City Elementary	San Mateo
141	49.1	Santa Paula Elementary	Santa Paula
141	49.1	Sonora Union High	Sonora
141	49.1	Tracy Joint Unified	Tracy
169	49.0	Bonita Unified	San Dimas
169	49.0	Burbank Unified	Burbank
169	49.0	Corcoran Joint Unified	Corcoran
169	49.0	El Dorado Union High	Placerville
169	49.0	El Rancho Unified	Pico Rivera
169	49.0	Fallbrook Union High	Fallbrook
169	49.0	Fontana Unified	Fontana
169	49.0	Garden Grove Unified	Garden Grove
169	49.0	Garvey Elementary	Rosemead
169	49.0	Grossmont Union High	La Mesa
169	49.0	Kings Canyon Joint Unified	Reedley
169	49.0	Lancaster Elementary	Lancaster
169	49.0	Los Alamitos Unified	Los Alamitos
169	49.0	Los Altos Elementary	Los Altos
169	49.0	Los Angeles Unified	Los Angeles
169	49.0	Manteca Unified	Manteca
169	49.0	Morgan Hill Unified	Morgan Hill
169	49.0	Natomas Unified	Sacramento
169	49.0	Oro Grande Elementary	Oro Grande
169	49.0	Red Bluff Joint Union High	Red Bluff
169	49.0	Rio Linda Union Elementary	Rio Linda
169	49.0	Riverside Unified	Riverside
169	49.0	San Luis Coastal Unified	San Luis Obispo
169	49.0	Scotts Valley Unified	Scotts Valley
193	48.9	Albany City Unified	Albany
193	48.9	Alum Rock Union Elementary	San Jose
193	48.9	Anaheim Elementary	Anaheim
193	48.9	Arvin Union Elementary	Arvin
193	48.9	Atwater Elementary	Atwater
193	48.9	Azusa Unified	Azusa
193	48.9	Cambrian Elementary	San Jose
193	48.9	Covina-Valley Unified	Covina
193	48.9	Dublin Unified	Dublin
193	48.9	Fremont Union High	Sunnyvale
193	48.9	Gilroy Unified	Gilroy
193	48.9	Greenfield Union Elementary	Bakersfield
193	48.9	Hanford Joint Union High	Hanford
193	48.9	Hughson Unified	Hughson
193	48.9	Kingsburg Elementary Charter	Kingsburg
193	48.9	Lakeside Union Elementary	Lakeside
193	48.9	Mill Valley Elementary	Mill Valley
193	48.9	Monterey Peninsula Unified	Monterey
193	48.9	Pomona Unified	Pomona
193	48.9	Rim of The World Unified	Lake Arrowhead
193	48.9	Sacramento City Unified	Sacramento
193	48.9	Santa Rita Union Elementary	Salinas
193	48.9	Santa Rosa High	Santa Rosa
193	48.9	Southern Kern Unified	Rosamond
193	48.9	Vista Unified	Vista
193	48.9	Washington Unified	West Sacramento
219	48.8	Amador County Unified	Jackson
219	48.8	Anaheim Union High	Anaheim
219	48.8	Arcadia Unified	Arcadia
219	48.8	Banning Unified	Banning
219	48.8	Brentwood Union Elementary	Brentwood
219	48.8	Castaic Union Elementary	Valencia
219	48.8	Corona-Norco Unified	Norco
219	48.8	Downey Unified	Downey
219	48.8	Escondido Union High	Escondido
219	48.8	Fountain Valley Elementary	Fountain Valley
219	48.8	Fullerton Elementary	Fullerton
219	48.8	Hacienda La Puente Unified	City of Industry
219	48.8	Inglewood Unified	Inglewood
219	48.8	Jurupa Unified	Riverside
219	48.8	Los Nietos Elementary	Whittier
219	48.8	Lowell Joint	Whittier
219	48.8	Marysville Joint Unified	Marysville
219	48.8	Ontario-Montclair Elementary	Ontario
219	48.8	Palm Springs Unified	Palm Springs
219	48.8	Palos Verdes Peninsula Unified	Palos Verdes Est
219	48.8	Porterville Unified	Porterville
219	48.8	Ramona City Unified	Ramona
219	48.8	Richland SD	Shafter
219	48.8	Rosedale Union Elementary	Bakersfield
219	48.8	Silver Valley Unified	Yermo
219	48.8	Stanislaus Union Elementary	Modesto
219	48.8	Thermalito Union Elementary	Oroville
219	48.8	Turlock Joint Elementary	Turlock
219	48.8	Tustin Unified	Tustin
219	48.8	West Covina Unified	West Covina
219	48.8	West Sonoma County Union High	Sebastopol
250	48.7	Baldwin Park Unified	Baldwin Park
250	48.7	Cajon Valley Union Elementary	El Cajon
250	48.7	Central Unified	Fresno
250	48.7	Central Union Elementary	Lemoore
250	48.7	Charter Oak Unified	Covina
250	48.7	Chino Valley Unified	Chino
250	48.7	Colton Joint Unified	Colton
250	48.7	El Centro Elementary	El Centro
250	48.7	Evergreen Elementary	San Jose
250	48.7	Golden Plains Unified	San Joaquin
250	48.7	Hawthorne Elementary	Hawthorne
250	48.7	Jefferson Elementary	Tracy
250	48.7	Las Virgenes Unified	Calabasas
250	48.7	Lennox Elementary	Lennox
250	48.7	Lodi Unified	Lodi
250	48.7	Monrovia Unified	Monrovia
250	48.7	Mountain View-Los Altos Union High	Mountain View
250	48.7	Newhall Elementary	Valencia
250	48.7	North Sacramento Elementary	Sacramento
250	48.7	Ojai Unified	Ojai
250	48.7	Oroville City Elementary	Oroville
250	48.7	Oroville Union High	Oroville
250	48.7	Oxnard Union High	Oxnard
250	48.7	Pasadena Unified	Pasadena
250	48.7	San Diego Unified	San Diego
250	48.7	San Lorenzo Valley Unified	Felton
250	48.7	Sanger Unified	Sanger
250	48.7	Santa Monica-Malibu Unified	Santa Monica
250	48.7	Sierra Sands Unified	Ridgecrest
250	48.7	Sweetwater Union High	Chula Vista
250	48.7	Vacaville Unified	Vacaville
250	48.7	Ventura Unified	Ventura
250	48.7	Weaver Union Elementary	Merced
283	48.6	Acalanes Union High	Lafayette
283	48.6	Dos Palos Oro Loma Joint Unified	Dos Palos
283	48.6	Duarte Unified	Duarte
283	48.6	Earlimart Elementary	Earlimart
283	48.6	El Monte City Elementary	El Monte
283	48.6	La Canada Unified	La Canada
283	48.6	Laguna Salada Union Elementary	Pacifica
283	48.6	Lake Elsinore Unified	Lake Elsinore
283	48.6	Lemoore Union Elementary	Lemoore
283	48.6	Mark West Union Elementary	Santa Rosa
283	48.6	Martinez Unified	Martinez
283	48.6	Napa Valley Unified	Napa
283	48.6	Oak Park Unified	Oak Park
283	48.6	Orinda Union Elementary	Orinda
283	48.6	Palmdale Elementary	Palmdale
283	48.6	Paradise Unified	Paradise
283	48.6	Redondo Beach Unified	Redondo Beach
283	48.6	Rincon Valley Union Elementary	Santa Rosa
283	48.6	Salida Union Elementary	Salida
283	48.6	San Marcos Unified	San Marcos
283	48.6	Soquel Union Elementary	Capitola
283	48.6	South Bay Union Elementary	Imperial Beach
283	48.6	Sunnyvale Elementary	Sunnyvale
283	48.6	Whittier Union High	Whittier
307	48.5	Barstow Unified	Barstow
307	48.5	Bellflower Unified	Bellflower
307	48.5	Brea-Olinda Unified	Brea
307	48.5	Burlingame Elementary	Burlingame
307	48.5	Coachella Valley Unified	Thermal
307	48.5	Cupertino Union School	Cupertino
307	48.5	Delano Joint Union High	Delano
307	48.5	Etiwanda Elementary	Etiwanda
307	48.5	Jamul-Dulzura Union Elementary	Jamul
307	48.5	Mount Diablo Unified	Concord
307	48.5	Northern Humboldt Union High	McKinleyville
307	48.5	Oak Grove Elementary	San Jose
307	48.5	Palo Alto Unified	Palo Alto
307	48.5	Perris Elementary	Perris
307	48.5	Piedmont City Unified	Piedmont
307	48.5	Poway Unified	Poway
307	48.5	Rocklin Unified	Rocklin
307	48.5	Saddleback Valley Unified	Mission Viejo
307	48.5	San Bruno Park Elementary	San Bruno
307	48.5	San Jacinto Unified	San Jacinto
307	48.5	Santa Barbara Elementary	Santa Barbara
307	48.5	Santa Barbara High	Santa Barbara
307	48.5	Santa Clara Unified	Santa Clara
307	48.5	Santa Paula Union High	Santa Paula
307	48.5	Simi Valley Unified	Simi Valley
307	48.5	Travis Unified	Travis Afb
307	48.5	Ukiah Unified	Ukiah
307	48.5	Union Elementary	San Jose
307	48.5	Val Verde Unified	Perris
307	48.5	Vallejo City Unified	Vallejo
307	48.5	Walnut Valley Unified	Walnut
307	48.5	Westminster Elementary	Westminster
307	48.5	Westwood Unified	Westwood
340	48.4	Capistrano Unified	San Juan Capis
340	48.4	Del Paso Heights Elementary	Sacramento
340	48.4	Delhi Unified	Delhi
340	48.4	Elk Grove Unified	Elk Grove
340	48.4	Fallbrook Union Elementary	Fallbrook
340	48.4	Firebaugh-Las Deltas Joint Unified	Firebaugh
340	48.4	Hayward Unified	Hayward
340	48.4	Irvine Unified	Irvine
340	48.4	Little Lake City Elementary	Santa Fe Spgs
340	48.4	Morongo Unified	Twentynine Plms
340	48.4	Norwalk-La Mirada Unified	Norwalk
340	48.4	Novato Unified	Novato
340	48.4	Orange Unified	Orange
340	48.4	Pleasant Ridge Union Elementary	Grass Valley
340	48.4	Pleasant Valley School	Camarillo
340	48.4	Rosemead Elementary	Rosemead
340	48.4	Rowland Unified	Rowland Heights
340	48.4	San Benito High	Hollister
340	48.4	Temple City Unified	Temple City
340	48.4	Torrance Unified	Torrance
340	48.4	Wasco Union Elementary	Wasco
340	48.4	Whittier City Elementary	Whittier
340	48.4	William S Hart Union High	Santa Clarita
363	48.3	Alisal Union Elementary	Salinas
363	48.3	Benicia Unified	Benicia

363	48.3	Culver City Unified	Culver City
363	48.3	East Whittier City Elementary	Whittier
363	48.3	Enterprise Elementary	Redding
363	48.3	Eureka City Unified	Eureka
363	48.3	Gridley Unified	Gridley
363	48.3	Huntington Beach Union High	Huntington Bch
363	48.3	Lake Tahoe Unified	S Lake Tahoe
363	48.3	Lompoc Unified	Lompoc
363	48.3	Lucia Mar Unified	Arroyo Grande
363	48.3	Modesto City Elementary	Modesto
363	48.3	Mountain View Elementary	El Monte
363	48.3	Newport-Mesa Unified	Costa Mesa
363	48.3	Ocean View Elementary	Oxnard
363	48.3	Palo Verde Unified	Blythe
363	48.3	Placentia-Yorba Linda Unified	Placentia
363	48.3	Placer Union High	Auburn
363	48.3	Red Bluff Union Elementary	Red Bluff
363	48.3	Romoland Elementary	Homeland
363	48.3	San Francisco Unified	San Francisco
363	48.3	San Lorenzo Unified	San Lorenzo
363	48.3	Sequoia Union High	Redwood City
363	48.3	Snowline Joint Unified	Phelan
387	48.2	Alhambra City High	Alhambra
387	48.2	Belmont-Redwood Shores Elementary	Belmont
387	48.2	Carlsbad Unified	Carlsbad
387	48.2	Carpinteria Unified	Carpinteria
387	48.2	Centralia Elementary	Buena Park
387	48.2	Chico Unified	Chico
387	48.2	Chula Vista Elementary	Chula Vista
387	48.2	Dixon Unified	Dixon
387	48.2	East Side Union High	San Jose
387	48.2	Huntington Beach City Elementary	Huntington Bch
387	48.2	Keppel Union Elementary	Pearblossom
387	48.2	Live Oak Elementary	Santa Cruz
387	48.2	Manhattan Beach Unified	Manhattan Beach
387	48.2	Ripon Unified	Ripon
387	48.2	Robla Elementary	Sacramento
387	48.2	West Contra Costa Unified	Richmond
387	48.2	Woodland Joint Unified	Woodland
404	48.1	Berryessa Union Elementary	San Jose
404	48.1	Burton Elementary	Porterville
404	48.1	Centinela Valley Union High	Lawndale
404	48.1	Corning Union Elementary	Corning
404	48.1	Del Norte County Unified	Crescent City
404	48.1	Exeter Union Elementary	Exeter
404	48.1	Galt Joint Union High	Galt
404	48.1	Hanford Elementary	Hanford
404	48.1	Los Banos Unified	Los Banos
404	48.1	Milpitas Unified	Milpitas
404	48.1	Mountain Empire Unified	Pine Valley
404	48.1	National Elementary	National City
404	48.1	Santee Elementary	Santee
404	48.1	Saratoga Union Elementary	Saratoga
404	48.1	Standard Elementary	Bakersfield
404	48.1	Willows Unified	Willows
404	48.1	Woodlake Union Elementary	Woodlake
404	48.1	Yucaipa-Calimesa Joint Unified	Yucaipa
422	48.0	Alvord Unified	Riverside
422	48.0	Campbell Union High	San Jose
422	48.0	Conejo Valley Unified	Thousand Oaks
422	48.0	Encinitas Union Elementary	Encinitas
422	48.0	Holtville Unified	Holtville
422	48.0	Lawndale Elementary	Lawndale
422	48.0	Mojave Unified	Mojave
422	48.0	Pacific Grove Unified	Pacific Grove
422	48.0	San Gabriel Unified	San Gabriel
422	48.0	San Leandro Unified	San Leandro
422	48.0	Tamalpais Union High	Larkspur
422	48.0	Walnut Creek Elementary	Walnut Creek
422	48.0	Wheatland Elementary	Wheatland
422	48.0	Winton Elementary	Winton
436	47.9	Bear Valley Unified	Big Bear Lake
436	47.9	Dinuba Unified	Dinuba
436	47.9	Eureka Union Elementary	Granite Bay
436	47.9	Healdsburg Unified	Healdsburg
436	47.9	John Swett Unified	Crockett
436	47.9	Ocean View Elementary	Huntington Bch
436	47.9	Redwood City Elementary	Redwood City
436	47.9	Rescue Union Elementary	Rescue
436	47.9	Santa Maria-Bonita Elementary	Santa Maria
436	47.9	Soledad Unified	Soledad
436	47.9	Sonoma Valley Unified	Sonoma
436	47.9	South San Francisco Unified	S San Francisco
436	47.9	Yuba City Unified	Yuba City
449	47.8	ABC Unified	Cerritos
449	47.8	Cotati-Rohnert Park Unified	Rohnert Park
449	47.8	Fremont Unified	Fremont
449	47.8	Moreland Elementary	San Jose
449	47.8	Newark Unified	Newark
449	47.8	Selma Unified	Selma
455	47.7	Atascadero Unified	Atascadero
455	47.7	Brawley Elementary	Brawley
455	47.7	Carmel Unified	Carmel
455	47.7	Cutler-Orosi Joint Unified	Orosi
455	47.7	Fowler Unified	Fowler
455	47.7	Grass Valley Elementary	Grass Valley
455	47.7	Hollister SD	Hollister
455	47.7	Kelseyville Unified	Kelseyville
455	47.7	Lafayette Elementary	Lafayette
455	47.7	Pittsburg Unified	Pittsburg
455	47.7	Plumas Unified	Quincy
455	47.7	Redding Elementary	Redding
455	47.7	San Mateo Union High	San Mateo
455	47.7	San Rafael City High	San Rafael
455	47.7	Solana Beach Elementary	Solana Beach
455	47.7	Taft City Elementary	Taft
455	47.7	Valley Center-Pauma Unified	Valley Center
472	47.6	Escalon Unified	Escalon
472	47.6	Grant Joint Union High	Sacramento
472	47.6	Jefferson Union High	Daly City
472	47.6	San Ysidro Elementary	San Ysidro
472	47.6	Tehachapi Unified	Tehachapi
477	47.5	Campbell Union Elementary	Campbell
477	47.5	Cloverdale Unified	Cloverdale
477	47.5	Cypress Elementary	Cypress
477	47.5	New Haven Unified	Union City
477	47.5	Orcutt Union Elementary	Orcutt
477	47.5	Riverbank Unified	Riverbank
477	47.5	San Marino Unified	San Marino
484	47.4	Coalinga-Huron Joint Unified	Coalinga
484	47.4	Julian Union High	Julian
484	47.4	King City Union Elementary	King City
484	47.4	Middletown Unified	Middletown
484	47.4	Reef-Sunset Unified	Avenal
489	47.3	Empire Union Elementary	Modesto
489	47.3	Gateway Unified	Redding
489	47.3	Gustine Unified	Gustine
489	47.3	Mendota Unified	Mendota
489	47.3	Paso Robles Joint Unified	Paso Robles
489	47.3	Santa Cruz City Elementary	Santa Cruz
489	47.3	Santa Rosa Elementary	Santa Rosa
489	47.3	Wilsona Elementary	Palmdale
497	47.2	Norris Elementary	Bakersfield
498	47.1	Los Gatos-Saratoga Jt Union High	Los Gatos
498	47.1	San Dieguito Union High	Encinitas
498	47.1	Sulphur Springs Union Elementary	Canyon Country
501	47.0	San Rafael City Elementary	San Rafael
502	46.9	Del Mar Union Elementary	Del Mar
502	46.9	Winters Joint Unified	Winters
504	46.8	Piner-Olivet Union Elementary	Santa Rosa
504	46.8	Santa Cruz City High	Santa Cruz
504	46.8	Willits Unified	Willits
507	46.7	Cucamonga Elementary	Rcho Cucamong
507	46.7	Fort Bragg Unified	Fort Bragg
507	46.7	Newman-Crows Landing Unified	Newman
507	46.7	San Carlos Elementary	San Carlos
511	46.6	Keyes Union Elementary	Keyes
511	46.6	Moraga Elementary	Moraga
511	46.6	Wiseburn Elementary	Hawthorne
514	46.5	Nevada Joint Union High	Grass Valley
515	46.4	Chowchilla Elementary	Chowchilla
515	46.4	Savanna Elementary	Anaheim
517	46.3	Black Oak Mine Unified	Georgetown
518	45.8	Menlo Park City Elementary	Atherton
519	45.5	Mount Pleasant Elementary	San Jose
520	44.6	Cascade Union Elementary	Anderson
521	41.0	Riverside County Office of Ed	Riverside
522	39.9	Orange County Office of Ed	Costa Mesa
522	39.9	San Diego County Office of Ed	San Diego
524	36.2	San Joaquin County Office of Ed	Stockton
525	33.1	Kern County Office of Ed	Bakersfield
526	32.6	Fresno County Office of Ed	Fresno
527	32.0	Los Angeles County Office of Ed	Downey
528	31.0	Santa Clara County Office of Ed	San Jose
529	28.1	San Bernardino County Supt.	San Bernardino

Individual Education Program Students

Rank	Percent	District Name	City
1	91.4	Santa Clara County Office of Ed	San Jose
2	71.0	Riverside County Office of Ed	Riverside
3	70.4	Fresno County Office of Ed	Fresno
4	62.9	Los Angeles County Office of Ed	Downey
5	56.2	Kern County Office of Ed	Bakersfield
6	50.1	Belmont-Redwood Shores Elementary	Belmont
7	28.7	San Joaquin County Office of Ed	Stockton
8	25.3	San Diego County Office of Ed	San Diego
9	18.4	Santa Cruz City Elementary	Santa Cruz
10	15.9	Lakeside Union Elementary	Lakeside
10	15.9	Oroville City Elementary	Oroville
12	15.3	Robla Elementary	Sacramento
12	15.3	Wilsona Elementary	Palmdale
14	15.1	Live Oak Elementary	Santa Cruz
15	15.0	San Rafael City Elementary	San Rafael
16	14.8	Oakley Union Elementary	Oakley
17	14.7	Ukiah Unified	Ukiah
18	14.6	Morongo Unified	Twentynine Plms
18	14.6	Pacific Grove Unified	Pacific Grove
20	14.5	Acton-Agua Dulce Unified	Acton
20	14.5	Santee Elementary	Santee
22	14.4	West Sonoma County Union High	Sebastopol
23	14.3	Mariposa County Unified	Mariposa
24	14.2	West Contra Costa Unified	Richmond
25	14.1	Amador County Unified	Jackson
25	14.1	Martinez Unified	Martinez
25	14.1	Solana Beach Elementary	Solana Beach
28	13.8	Cajon Valley Union Elementary	El Cajon
29	13.7	Orange County Office of Ed	Costa Mesa
29	13.7	Palmdale Elementary	Palmdale
31	13.6	Lancaster Elementary	Lancaster
32	13.5	Del Norte County Unified	Crescent City
33	13.3	Apple Valley Unified	Apple Valley
33	13.3	Lake Tahoe Unified	S Lake Tahoe
35	13.2	Modesto City Elementary	Modesto
35	13.2	Mount Diablo Unified	Concord
35	13.2	Ross Valley Elementary	San Anselmo
38	13.1	Antelope Valley Union High	Lancaster
38	13.1	Eureka City Unified	Eureka
38	13.1	Kingsburg Elementary Charter	Kingsburg
38	13.1	Menlo Park City Elementary	Atherton
42	13.0	Konocti Unified	Lower Lake
42	13.0	Ramona City Unified	Ramona
44	12.9	Folsom-Cordova Unified	Folsom
45	12.8	Lake Elsinore Unified	Lake Elsinore
45	12.8	Willits Unified	Willits
47	12.7	Plumas Unified	Quincy
47	12.7	San Lorenzo Valley Unified	Felton
49	12.6	Grant Joint Union High	Sacramento
49	12.6	Lawndale Elementary	Lawndale
51	12.5	Alpine Union Elementary	Alpine
51	12.5	Coronado Unified	Coronado
51	12.5	Dos Palos Oro Loma Joint Unified	Dos Palos
51	12.5	Fowler Unified	Fowler
51	12.5	La Mesa-Spring Valley	La Mesa
51	12.5	Valley Center-Pauma Unified	Valley Center
57	12.4	Bonita Unified	San Dimas
57	12.4	Calaveras Unified	San Andreas
57	12.4	Oroville Union High	Oroville
57	12.4	Pasadena Unified	Pasadena
57	12.4	Redondo Beach Unified	Redondo Beach
57	12.4	Santa Rosa Elementary	Santa Rosa
63	12.3	Brentwood Union Elementary	Brentwood
63	12.3	Chico Unified	Chico
63	12.3	Selma Unified	Selma
63	12.3	Vista Unified	Vista
67	12.2	Grossmont Union High	La Mesa
67	12.2	River Delta Joint Unified	Rio Vista
67	12.2	Sacramento City Unified	Sacramento
67	12.2	San Jacinto Unified	San Jacinto
71	12.1	Galt Joint Union Elementary	Galt
71	12.1	Hollister SD	Hollister
71	12.1	Keppel Union Elementary	Pearblossom
71	12.1	Middletown Unified	Middletown
71	12.1	San Diego Unified	San Diego
76	12.0	East Whittier City Elementary	Whittier
76	12.0	Fort Bragg Unified	Fort Bragg
76	12.0	Lemon Grove Elementary	Lemon Grove
76	12.0	Monterey Peninsula Unified	Monterey
76	12.0	Santa Monica-Malibu Unified	Santa Monica
76	12.0	Taft City Elementary	Taft
82	11.9	Empire Union Elementary	Modesto
82	11.9	Lodi Unified	Lodi
82	11.9	Merced Union High	Atwater
82	11.9	Reef-Sunset Unified	Avenal
82	11.9	Santa Rosa High	Santa Rosa
82	11.9	Tehachapi Unified	Tehachapi
88	11.8	Cascade Union Elementary	Anderson
88	11.8	Little Lake City Elementary	Santa Fe Spgs
88	11.8	Vallejo City Unified	Vallejo
91	11.7	Anaheim Union High	Anaheim
91	11.7	Bellevue Union Elementary	Santa Rosa
91	11.7	Cotati-Rohnert Park Unified	Rohnert Park
91	11.7	Escondido Union Elementary	Escondido
91	11.7	Fillmore Unified	Fillmore
91	11.7	Kelseyville Unified	Kelseyville
91	11.7	Piedmont City Unified	Piedmont
91	11.7	Santa Clara Unified	Santa Clara
99	11.6	Buena Park Elementary	Buena Park
99	11.6	Covina-Valley Unified	Covina
99	11.6	Pajaro Valley Unified School	Watsonville
99	11.6	Patterson Joint Unified	Patterson
99	11.6	San Bernardino City Unified	San Bernardino
99	11.6	San Francisco Unified	San Francisco
99	11.6	San Mateo-Foster City Elementary	San Mateo
99	11.6	Victor Valley Union High	Victorville
107	11.5	Barstow Unified	Barstow
107	11.5	Dixie Elementary	San Rafael

Rank	Score	District	City
107	11.5	John Swett Unified	Crockett
107	11.5	Los Angeles Unified	Los Angeles
107	11.5	Northern Humboldt Union High	McKinleyville
107	11.5	Rio Linda Union Elementary	Rio Linda
107	11.5	Sylvan Union Elementary	Modesto
107	11.5	Turlock Joint Elementary	Turlock
107	11.5	Union Elementary	San Jose
116	11.4	Centinela Valley Union High	Lawndale
116	11.4	Claremont Unified	Claremont
116	11.4	Novato Unified	Novato
116	11.4	Palo Alto Unified	Palo Alto
116	11.4	San Mateo Union High	San Mateo
116	11.4	Santa Cruz City High	Santa Cruz
116	11.4	Sequoia Union High	Redwood City
123	11.3	Beardsley Elementary	Bakersfield
123	11.3	Berkeley Unified	Berkeley
123	11.3	Beverly Hills Unified	Beverly Hills
123	11.3	Delhi Unified	Delhi
123	11.3	Hemet Unified	Hemet
123	11.3	Napa Valley Unified	Napa
123	11.3	San Jose Unified	San Jose
123	11.3	Standard Elementary	Bakersfield
123	11.3	Sweetwater Union High	Chula Vista
132	11.2	Dixon Unified	Dixon
132	11.2	Fairfield-Suisun Unified	Fairfield
132	11.2	Grass Valley Elementary	Grass Valley
132	11.2	Greenfield Union Elementary	Greenfield
132	11.2	King City Joint Union High	King City
132	11.2	Petaluma City Elementary	Petaluma
132	11.2	San Lorenzo Unified	San Lorenzo
132	11.2	San Marcos Unified	San Marcos
132	11.2	Stanislaus Union Elementary	Modesto
132	11.2	William S Hart Union High	Santa Clarita
142	11.1	Atascadero Unified	Atascadero
142	11.1	Gateway Unified	Redding
142	11.1	Livermore Valley Joint Unified	Livermore
142	11.1	Moorpark Unified	Moorpark
142	11.1	Pleasanton Unified	Pleasanton
142	11.1	Redwood City Elementary	Redwood City
142	11.1	Sierra Unified	Auberry
142	11.1	South San Francisco Unified	S San Francisco
150	11.0	Adelanto Elementary	Adelanto
150	11.0	Fruitvale Elementary	Bakersfield
150	11.0	Newport-Mesa Unified	Costa Mesa
150	11.0	Paradise Unified	Paradise
150	11.0	Santa Barbara Elementary	Santa Barbara
150	11.0	Sierra Sands Unified	Ridgecrest
150	11.0	Sonoma Valley Unified	Sonoma
157	10.9	Chula Vista Elementary	Chula Vista
157	10.9	Laguna Salada Union Elementary	Pacifica
157	10.9	Los Nietos Elementary	Whittier
157	10.9	Muroc Joint Unified	North Edwards
157	10.9	Pittsburg Unified	Pittsburg
157	10.9	Rincon Valley Union Elementary	Santa Rosa
157	10.9	Rio Elementary	Oxnard
157	10.9	San Dieguito Union High	Encinitas
157	10.9	Travis Unified	Travis Afb
157	10.9	Westminster Elementary	Westminster
167	10.8	Alameda City Unified	Alameda
167	10.8	Center Joint Unified	Antelope
167	10.8	Cloverdale Unified	Cloverdale
167	10.8	Downey Unified	Downey
167	10.8	Escalon Unified	Escalon
167	10.8	Fallbrook Union High	Fallbrook
167	10.8	Modesto City High	Modesto
167	10.8	Mountain View-Whisman Elementary	Mountain View
167	10.8	Oakland Unified	Oakland
167	10.8	Placentia-Yorba Linda Unified	Placentia
167	10.8	San Rafael City High	San Rafael
167	10.8	Snowline Joint Unified	Phelan
167	10.8	Tahoe-Truckee Joint Unified	Truckee
167	10.8	Torrance Unified	Torrance
167	10.8	Vacaville Unified	Vacaville
167	10.8	Washington Unified	West Sacramento
167	10.8	Westside Union Elementary	Lancaster
167	10.8	Whittier City Elementary	Whittier
185	10.7	Central Unified	Fresno
185	10.7	Cypress Elementary	Cypress
185	10.7	Garvey Elementary	Rosemead
185	10.7	Kerman Unified	Kerman
185	10.7	Lowell Joint	Whittier
185	10.7	Lucia Mar Unified	Arroyo Grande
185	10.7	Moreno Valley Unified	Moreno Valley
185	10.7	Newman-Crows Landing Unified	Newman
185	10.7	North Sacramento Elementary	Sacramento
185	10.7	Oceanside Unified	Oceanside
185	10.7	Palos Verdes Peninsula Unified	Palos Verdes Est
185	10.7	Riverside Unified	Riverside
185	10.7	San Ramon Valley Unified	Danville
185	10.7	Soquel Union Elementary	Capitola
185	10.7	Walnut Creek Elementary	Walnut Creek
185	10.7	Woodland Joint Unified	Woodland
201	10.6	Bassett Unified	La Puente
201	10.6	Benicia Unified	Benicia
201	10.6	Carlsbad Unified	Carlsbad
201	10.6	Del Mar Union Elementary	Del Mar
201	10.6	Fontana Unified	Fontana
201	10.6	Keyes Union Elementary	Keyes
201	10.6	Kings Canyon Joint Unified	Reedley
201	10.6	Liberty Union High	Brentwood
201	10.6	National Elementary	National City
201	10.6	Paso Robles Joint Unified	Paso Robles
201	10.6	Richland SD	Shafter
201	10.6	Salida Union Elementary	Salida
201	10.6	Saugus Union Elementary	Santa Clarita
201	10.6	Winters Joint Unified	Winters
215	10.5	Auburn Union Elementary	Auburn
215	10.5	Ceres Unified	Ceres
215	10.5	Las Virgenes Unified	Calabasas
215	10.5	Oakdale Joint Unified	Oakdale
215	10.5	Roseville City Elementary	Roseville
215	10.5	San Leandro Unified	San Leandro
215	10.5	Turlock Joint Union High	Turlock
222	10.4	Alum Rock Union Elementary	San Jose
222	10.4	Campbell Union High	San Jose
222	10.4	Chaffey Joint Union High	Ontario
222	10.4	Corona-Norco Unified	Norco
222	10.4	Fresno Unified	Fresno
222	10.4	Huntington Beach City Elementary	Huntington Bch
222	10.4	Merced City Elementary	Merced
222	10.4	Morgan Hill Unified	Morgan Hill
222	10.4	Newark Unified	Newark
222	10.4	Silver Valley Unified	Yermo
222	10.4	Simi Valley Unified	Simi Valley
222	10.4	South Bay Union Elementary	Imperial Beach
222	10.4	Tustin Unified	Tustin
235	10.3	Bear Valley Unified	Big Bear Lake
235	10.3	Carpinteria Unified	Carpinteria
235	10.3	East Side Union High	San Jose
235	10.3	Goleta Union Elementary	Goleta
235	10.3	Hayward Unified	Hayward
235	10.3	Huntington Beach Union High	Huntington Bch
235	10.3	Petaluma Joint Union High	Petaluma
235	10.3	Pleasant Valley School	Camarillo
235	10.3	Rocklin Unified	Rocklin
244	10.2	Albany City Unified	Albany
244	10.2	Castro Valley Unified	Castro Valley
244	10.2	Eastside Union Elementary	Lancaster
244	10.2	Fullerton Elementary	Fullerton
244	10.2	Manhattan Beach Unified	Manhattan Beach
244	10.2	Perris Elementary	Perris
244	10.2	Weaver Union Elementary	Merced
251	10.1	Cabrillo Unified	Half Moon Bay
251	10.1	Clovis Unified	Clovis
251	10.1	El Monte City Elementary	El Monte
251	10.1	Garden Grove Unified	Garden Grove
251	10.1	Mill Valley Elementary	Mill Valley
251	10.1	Mount Pleasant Elementary	San Jose
251	10.1	Ojai Unified	Ojai
251	10.1	Oxnard Union High	Oxnard
251	10.1	San Benito High	Hollister
251	10.1	San Marino Unified	San Marino
251	10.1	Santa Barbara High	Santa Barbara
251	10.1	Stockton City Unified	Stockton
263	10.0	Antioch Unified	Antioch
263	10.0	Burbank Unified	Burbank
263	10.0	Hilmar Unified	Hilmar
263	10.0	Mountain Empire Unified	Pine Valley
263	10.0	Norwalk-La Mirada Unified	Norwalk
263	10.0	Ocean View Elementary	Huntington Bch
263	10.0	Orange Unified	Orange
263	10.0	Rim of The World Unified	Lake Arrowhead
263	10.0	Ventura Unified	Ventura
272	9.9	Banning Unified	Banning
272	9.9	Castaic Union Elementary	Valencia
272	9.9	Conejo Valley Unified	Thousand Oaks
272	9.9	Glendora Unified	Glendora
272	9.9	Hacienda La Puente Unified	City of Industry
272	9.9	Holtville Unified	Holtville
272	9.9	Lamont Elementary	Lamont
272	9.9	Los Gatos Union Elementary	Los Gatos
272	9.9	Mcfarland Unified	Mcfarland
272	9.9	Mountain View Elementary	Ontario
272	9.9	Oak Grove Elementary	San Jose
272	9.9	Orland Joint Unified	Orland
272	9.9	Pomona Unified	Pomona
272	9.9	Poway Unified	Poway
272	9.9	Savanna Elementary	Anaheim
272	9.9	Temecula Valley Unified	Temecula
288	9.8	Anaheim Elementary	Anaheim
288	9.8	Brea-Olinda Unified	Brea
288	9.8	El Rancho Unified	Pico Rivera
288	9.8	Fallbrook Union Elementary	Fallbrook
288	9.8	Fountain Valley Elementary	Fountain Valley
288	9.8	Hesperia Unified	Hesperia
288	9.8	Linden Unified	Linden
288	9.8	Placer Union High	Auburn
288	9.8	Rowland Unified	Rowland Heights
297	9.7	Alvord Unified	Riverside
297	9.7	Bakersfield City Elementary	Bakersfield
297	9.7	Carmel Unified	Carmel
297	9.7	Lemoore Union Elementary	Lemoore
301	9.6	ABC Unified	Cerritos
301	9.6	Azusa Unified	Azusa
301	9.6	Brawley Union High	Brawley
301	9.6	Campbell Union Elementary	Campbell
301	9.6	Gilroy Unified	Gilroy
301	9.6	Greenfield Union Elementary	Bakersfield
301	9.6	Magnolia Elementary	Anaheim
301	9.6	Redlands Unified	Redlands
301	9.6	Yucaipa-Calimesa Joint Unified	Yucaipa
310	9.5	Dublin Unified	Dublin
310	9.5	Hawthorne Elementary	Hawthorne
310	9.5	Jurupa Unified	Riverside
310	9.5	Livingston Union Elementary	Livingston
310	9.5	Marysville Joint Unified	Marysville
310	9.5	Milpitas Unified	Milpitas
310	9.5	Sunnyvale Elementary	Sunnyvale
317	9.4	Central Elementary	Rcho Cucamong
317	9.4	Colton Joint Unified	Colton
317	9.4	Enterprise Elementary	Redding
317	9.4	Escondido Union High	Escondido
317	9.4	Firebaugh-Las Deltas Joint Unified	Firebaugh
317	9.4	Santa Paula Elementary	Santa Paula
317	9.4	Sulphur Springs Union Elementary	Canyon Country
324	9.3	Alhambra City Elementary	Alhambra
324	9.3	Capistrano Unified	San Juan Capis
324	9.3	Lincoln Unified	Stockton
324	9.3	Mark West Union Elementary	Santa Rosa
324	9.3	Oxnard Elementary	Oxnard
324	9.3	San Ysidro Elementary	San Ysidro
324	9.3	Southern Kern Unified	Rosamond
331	9.2	Arvin Union Elementary	Arvin
331	9.2	Bonsall Union Elementary	Bonsall
331	9.2	Central Union Elementary	Lemoore
331	9.2	Centralia Elementary	Buena Park
331	9.2	Coalinga-Huron Joint Unified	Coalinga
331	9.2	Ravenswood City Elementary	East Palo Alto
331	9.2	San Juan Unified	Carmichael
338	9.1	Culver City Unified	Culver City
338	9.1	Elk Grove Unified	Elk Grove
338	9.1	Eureka Union Elementary	Granite Bay
338	9.1	Galt Joint Union High	Galt
338	9.1	La Canada Unified	La Canada
338	9.1	Ontario-Montclair Elementary	Ontario
338	9.1	Palm Springs Unified	Palm Springs
338	9.1	Red Bluff Joint Union High	Red Bluff
338	9.1	Riverbank Unified	Riverbank
338	9.1	Visalia Unified	Visalia
338	9.1	Waterford Unified	Waterford
349	9.0	Charter Oak Unified	Covina
349	9.0	Glendale Unified	Glendale
349	9.0	Hueneme Elementary	Port Hueneme
349	9.0	Lemoore Union High	Lemoore
349	9.0	Loomis Union Elementary	Loomis
349	9.0	Mountain View Elementary	El Monte
349	9.0	New Haven Unified	Union City
349	9.0	Piner-Olivet Union Elementary	Santa Rosa
349	9.0	San Luis Coastal Unified	San Luis Obispo
349	9.0	Santa Ana Unified	Santa Ana
359	8.9	Berryessa Union Elementary	San Jose
359	8.9	Cucamonga Elementary	Rcho Cucamong
359	8.9	Dry Creek Joint Elementary	Roseville
359	8.9	El Centro Elementary	El Centro
359	8.9	El Dorado Union High	Placerville
359	8.9	Encinitas Union Elementary	Encinitas
359	8.9	Gustine Unified	Gustine
359	8.9	Jamul-Dulzura Union Elementary	Jamul
359	8.9	Murrieta Valley Unified	Murrieta
359	8.9	Natomas Unified	Sacramento
359	8.9	Redding Elementary	Redding
359	8.9	Western Placer Unified	Lincoln
371	8.8	El Monte Union High	El Monte
371	8.8	Fremont Unified	Fremont
371	8.8	Gonzales Unified	Gonzales
371	8.8	Mojave Unified	Mojave
371	8.8	Newhall Elementary	Valencia
371	8.8	Oak Park Unified	Oak Park
371	8.8	Saddleback Valley Unified	Mission Viejo
371	8.8	San Bruno Park Elementary	San Bruno
371	8.8	South Pasadena Unified	South Pasadena
371	8.8	South Whittier Elementary	Whittier
371	8.8	Twin Ridges Elementary	North San Juan
382	8.7	Etiwanda Elementary	Etiwanda
382	8.7	Los Altos Elementary	Los Altos
382	8.7	Manteca Unified	Manteca
382	8.7	Moraga Elementary	Moraga

382	8.7	Moreland Elementary	San Jose
382	8.7	Tracy Joint Unified	Tracy
388	8.6	Franklin-Mckinley Elementary	San Jose
388	8.6	La Habra City Elementary	La Habra
388	8.6	Los Alamitos Unified	Los Alamitos
388	8.6	Santa Paula Union High	Santa Paula
388	8.6	Scotts Valley Unified	Scotts Valley
388	8.6	Whittier Union High	Whittier
394	8.5	Atwater Elementary	Atwater
394	8.5	Chino Valley Unified	Chino
394	8.5	Gridley Unified	Gridley
394	8.5	Nevada Joint Union High	Grass Valley
394	8.5	Old Adobe Union Elementary	Petaluma
394	8.5	Ripon Unified	Ripon
394	8.5	Romoland Elementary	Homeland
394	8.5	Saratoga Union Elementary	Saratoga
394	8.5	Sonora Union High	Sonora
394	8.5	Wiseburn Elementary	Hawthorne
404	8.4	Arcadia Unified	Arcadia
404	8.4	Black Oak Mine Unified	Georgetown
404	8.4	Desert Sands Unified	La Quinta
404	8.4	Fremont Union High	Sunnyvale
404	8.4	Irvine Unified	Irvine
404	8.4	Jefferson Elementary	Daly City
404	8.4	Kern Union High	Bakersfield
404	8.4	King City Union Elementary	King City
404	8.4	Lennox Elementary	Lennox
404	8.4	Millbrae Elementary	Millbrae
404	8.4	Ocean View Elementary	Oxnard
404	8.4	Rosedale Union Elementary	Bakersfield
404	8.4	Salinas Union High	Salinas
404	8.4	Thermalito Union Elementary	Oroville
418	8.3	Alta Loma Elementary	Alta Loma
418	8.3	Coachella Valley Unified	Thermal
418	8.3	Delano Joint Union High	Delano
418	8.3	Duarte Unified	Duarte
418	8.3	Menifee Union Elementary	Menifee
418	8.3	Montebello Unified	Montebello
418	8.3	Mountain View-Los Altos Union High	Mountain View
418	8.3	Temple City Unified	Temple City
418	8.3	Val Verde Unified	Perris
427	8.2	Burlingame Elementary	Burlingame
427	8.2	Delano Union Elementary	Delano
427	8.2	Julian Union Elementary	Julian
427	8.2	Lafayette Elementary	Lafayette
427	8.2	Santa Maria Joint Union High	Santa Maria
432	8.1	Beaumont Unified	Beaumont
432	8.1	Del Paso Heights Elementary	Sacramento
432	8.1	Dinuba Unified	Dinuba
432	8.1	Hughson Unified	Hughson
432	8.1	Los Gatos-Saratoga Jt Union High	Los Gatos
432	8.1	Orinda Union Elementary	Orinda
432	8.1	San Carlos Elementary	San Carlos
439	8.0	Davis Joint Unified	Davis
439	8.0	El Segundo Unified	El Segundo
439	8.0	Evergreen Elementary	San Jose
439	8.0	Orcutt Union Elementary	Orcutt
439	8.0	Palo Verde Unified	Blythe
439	8.0	Panama Buena Vista Union Elem	Bakersfield
439	8.0	Paramount Unified	Paramount
439	8.0	Pleasant Ridge Union Elementary	Grass Valley
439	8.0	Rialto Unified	Rialto
448	7.9	Baldwin Park Unified	Baldwin Park
448	7.9	Imperial Unified	Imperial
448	7.9	Long Beach Unified	Long Beach
448	7.9	Perris Union High	Perris
448	7.9	Rescue Union Elementary	Rescue
448	7.9	Roseville Joint Union High	Roseville
448	7.9	Sanger Unified	Sanger
455	7.8	Central Union High	El Centro
455	7.8	Hanford Joint Union High	Hanford
455	7.8	Rosemead Elementary	Rosemead
455	7.8	San Gabriel Unified	San Gabriel
455	7.8	Wasco Union Elementary	Wasco
460	7.7	Alhambra City High	Alhambra
460	7.7	Laguna Beach Unified	Laguna Beach
460	7.7	Tulare City Elementary	Tulare
460	7.7	Upland Unified	Upland
464	7.6	Cambrian Elementary	San Jose
464	7.6	Monrovia Unified	Monrovia
466	7.5	Acalanes Union High	Lafayette
466	7.5	Anderson Union High	Anderson
466	7.5	Red Bluff Union Elementary	Red Bluff
466	7.5	Santa Rita Union Elementary	Salinas
466	7.5	Victor Elementary	Victorville
471	7.4	Bishop Union Elementary	Bishop
471	7.4	Tulare Joint Union High	Tulare
473	7.3	Brawley Elementary	Brawley
473	7.3	Shasta Union High	Redding
473	7.3	Yuba City Unified	Yuba City
476	7.2	Inglewood Unified	Inglewood
476	7.2	Lompoc Unified	Lompoc
476	7.2	Windsor Unified	Windsor
479	7.1	Lakeport Unified	Lakeport
480	7.0	Mother Lode Union Elementary	Placerville
480	7.0	Winton Elementary	Winton
482	6.9	Jefferson Union High	Daly City
482	6.9	North Monterey County Unified	Moss Landing
482	6.9	Santa Maria-Bonita Elementary	Santa Maria
485	6.8	Fullerton Joint Union High	Fullerton
485	6.8	Madera Unified	Madera
487	6.7	Alisal Union Elementary	Salinas
487	6.7	Calexico Unified	Calexico
487	6.7	Norris Elementary	Bakersfield
487	6.7	Walnut Valley Unified	Walnut
491	6.6	Cupertino Union School	Cupertino
492	6.5	Healdsburg Unified	Healdsburg
493	6.4	Bellflower Unified	Bellflower
493	6.4	Soledad Unified	Soledad
495	6.3	Parlier Unified	Parlier
496	6.2	Corcoran Joint Unified	Corcoran
496	6.2	Jefferson Elementary	Tracy
496	6.2	Templeton Unified	Templeton
499	6.1	Mendota Unified	Mendota
500	6.0	Corning Union Elementary	Corning
500	6.0	Farmersville Unified	Farmersville
502	5.8	Riverdale Joint Unified	Riverdale
502	5.8	Salinas City Elementary	Salinas
504	5.6	Wheatland Elementary	Wheatland
505	5.5	Exeter Union Elementary	Exeter
505	5.5	Porterville Unified	Porterville
507	5.4	Hanford Elementary	Hanford
507	5.4	Woodlake Union Elementary	Woodlake
509	5.3	West Covina Unified	West Covina
510	5.1	Earlimart Elementary	Earlimart
511	5.0	Buckeye Union Elementary	Shingle Springs
512	4.9	Burton Elementary	Porterville
513	4.8	Gorman Elementary	Gorman
513	4.8	Live Oak Unified	Live Oak
513	4.8	Los Banos Unified	Los Banos
516	4.7	Compton Unified	Compton
517	4.0	Lynwood Unified	Lynwood
518	3.9	Lindsay Unified	Lindsay
519	3.4	Golden Plains Unified	San Joaquin
520	3.3	Julian Union High	Julian
521	2.8	Cutler-Orosi Joint Unified	Orosi
522	2.6	Chowchilla Elementary	Chowchilla
523	0.6	Tamalpais Union High	Larkspur
524	0.4	Oro Grande Elementary	Oro Grande
525	0.0	Colusa Unified	Colusa
525	0.0	Saint Helena Unified	Saint Helena
525	0.0	Westwood Unified	Westwood
525	0.0	Willows Unified	Willows
529	n/a	San Bernardino County Supt.	San Bernardino

English Language Learner Students

Rank	Percent	District Name	City
1	83.8	Earlimart Elementary	Earlimart
2	76.4	Calexico Unified	Calexico
3	73.6	Lamont Elementary	Lamont
4	72.6	San Ysidro Elementary	San Ysidro
5	71.3	Alisal Union Elementary	Salinas
6	71.2	Lennox Elementary	Lennox
7	71.0	Mendota Unified	Mendota
8	69.9	Coachella Valley Unified	Thermal
9	69.0	Arvin Union Elementary	Arvin
10	68.6	Livingston Union Elementary	Livingston
11	67.2	Ravenswood City Elementary	East Palo Alto
12	65.4	Reef-Sunset Unified	Avenal
13	64.6	Gonzales Unified	Gonzales
14	64.2	Anaheim Elementary	Anaheim
15	63.5	Parlier Unified	Parlier
15	63.5	Santa Ana Unified	Santa Ana
17	62.3	Bellevue Union Elementary	Santa Rosa
18	61.6	Mountain View Elementary	El Monte
19	59.8	Winton Elementary	Winton
20	59.4	Cutler-Orosi Joint Unified	Orosi
21	58.1	Lindsay Unified	Lindsay
22	58.0	Golden Plains Unified	San Joaquin
22	58.0	Greenfield Union Elementary	Greenfield
24	57.9	Soledad Unified	Soledad
25	56.9	Delano Union Elementary	Delano
26	55.6	King City Union Elementary	King City
27	55.3	Alum Rock Union Elementary	San Jose
27	55.3	Franklin-Mckinley Elementary	San Jose
29	54.7	National Elementary	National City
30	54.3	Santa Maria-Bonita Elementary	Santa Maria
31	52.9	Compton Unified	Compton
32	52.7	Garden Grove Unified	Garden Grove
32	52.7	Ontario-Montclair Elementary	Ontario
34	52.3	Richland SD	Shafter
35	51.6	Santa Paula Elementary	Santa Paula
36	51.0	Mount Pleasant Elementary	San Jose
37	50.7	Lynwood Unified	Lynwood
38	50.6	Redwood City Elementary	Redwood City

39	49.8	Magnolia Elementary	Anaheim
40	49.6	Farmersville Unified	Farmersville
41	49.4	Delano Joint Union High	Delano
42	49.1	Ocean View Elementary	Oxnard
42	49.1	Wasco Union Elementary	Wasco
44	47.4	Delhi Unified	Delhi
44	47.4	Oxnard Elementary	Oxnard
46	46.9	Pomona Unified	Pomona
47	46.7	El Centro Elementary	El Centro
47	46.7	La Habra City Elementary	La Habra
47	46.7	Rio Elementary	Oxnard
50	46.5	Garvey Elementary	Rosemead
51	46.4	El Monte City Elementary	El Monte
51	46.4	Hawthorne Elementary	Hawthorne
51	46.4	Pajaro Valley Unified School	Watsonville
54	45.9	Holtville Unified	Holtville
55	45.8	Montebello Unified	Montebello
56	45.5	Salinas City Elementary	Salinas
57	45.0	Alhambra City Elementary	Alhambra
58	44.5	Paramount Unified	Paramount
59	44.3	Perris Elementary	Perris
60	44.2	Hueneme Elementary	Port Hueneme
61	43.9	San Rafael City Elementary	San Rafael
62	43.4	Buena Park Elementary	Buena Park
62	43.4	Del Paso Heights Elementary	Sacramento
64	43.3	South Bay Union Elementary	Imperial Beach
65	42.9	Los Angeles Unified	Los Angeles
65	42.9	Westminster Elementary	Westminster
67	42.5	Central Union High	El Centro
67	42.5	Patterson Joint Unified	Patterson
69	42.3	Escondido Union Elementary	Escondido
69	42.3	Santa Barbara Elementary	Santa Barbara
69	42.3	Santa Rosa Elementary	Santa Rosa
72	41.8	Riverbank Unified	Riverbank
73	41.2	Madera Unified	Madera
74	41.0	Romoland Elementary	Homeland
75	40.6	Azusa Unified	Azusa
76	40.4	Lawndale Elementary	Lawndale
77	40.2	Robla Elementary	Sacramento
78	39.8	Salinas Union High	Salinas
79	39.5	Woodlake Union Elementary	Woodlake
80	39.4	Fillmore Unified	Fillmore
81	39.0	Kings Canyon Joint Unified	Reedley
82	38.5	Carpinteria Unified	Carpinteria
83	38.2	Mountain View-Whisman Elementary	Mountain View
84	38.0	Colusa Unified	Colusa
84	38.0	Mcfarland Unified	Mcfarland
86	37.2	Firebaugh-Las Deltas Joint Unified	Firebaugh
87	37.1	Dos Palos Oro Loma Joint Unified	Dos Palos
88	37.0	Alvord Unified	Riverside
89	36.7	Alhambra City High	Alhambra
89	36.7	Gustine Unified	Gustine
91	36.5	Fontana Unified	Fontana
92	36.2	Chula Vista Elementary	Chula Vista
93	36.0	Glendale Unified	Glendale
93	36.0	Weaver Union Elementary	Merced
95	35.8	Atwater Elementary	Atwater
95	35.8	Rosemead Elementary	Rosemead
97	35.6	Berryessa Union Elementary	San Jose
98	35.4	Los Nietos Elementary	Whittier
99	35.3	North Sacramento Elementary	Sacramento
100	35.2	Baldwin Park Unified	Baldwin Park
101	34.9	Kerman Unified	Kerman
102	34.1	San Gabriel Unified	San Gabriel
103	33.9	Inglewood Unified	Inglewood
104	33.8	Selma Unified	Selma
105	33.6	Hayward Unified	Hayward
106	33.4	Oakland Unified	Oakland
107	33.2	Brawley Union High	Brawley
107	33.2	El Rancho Unified	Pico Rivera
109	33.0	Bassett Unified	La Puente
110	32.9	Winters Joint Unified	Winters
111	32.8	Long Beach Unified	Long Beach
112	32.7	El Monte Union High	El Monte
112	32.7	Santa Rita Union Elementary	Salinas
114	32.6	Savanna Elementary	Anaheim
115	32.5	Modesto City Elementary	Modesto
116	32.3	Fresno Unified	Fresno
117	32.2	Newman-Crows Landing Unified	Newman
118	32.0	Coalinga-Huron Joint Unified	Coalinga
119	31.6	Chowchilla Elementary	Chowchilla
119	31.6	Fullerton Elementary	Fullerton
119	31.6	Sunnyvale Elementary	Sunnyvale
122	31.5	Palm Springs Unified	Palm Springs
123	31.3	Evergreen Elementary	San Jose
124	31.2	Brawley Elementary	Brawley
124	31.2	Los Angeles County Office of Ed	Downey
126	31.1	Rowland Unified	Rowland Heights
127	30.7	Gilroy Unified	Gilroy
128	30.3	Fallbrook Union Elementary	Fallbrook
128	30.3	Merced City Elementary	Merced
130	30.2	River Delta Joint Unified	Rio Vista
130	30.2	Riverdale Joint Unified	Riverdale

132	30.1	Desert Sands Unified	La Quinta
132	30.1	Dinuba Unified	Dinuba
132	30.1	Fullerton Joint Union High	Fullerton
132	30.1	Pittsburg Unified	Pittsburg
136	30.0	Sacramento City Unified	Sacramento
137	29.9	Campbell Union Elementary	Campbell
138	29.4	Tustin Unified	Tustin
139	28.8	Centinela Valley Union High	Lawndale
140	28.7	Centralia Elementary	Buena Park
140	28.7	San Diego Unified	San Diego
142	28.5	Sequoia Union High	Redwood City
143	28.4	Goleta Union Elementary	Goleta
143	28.4	Turlock Joint Elementary	Turlock
145	28.2	Anaheim Union High	Anaheim
146	28.1	Jefferson Elementary	Daly City
146	28.1	West Contra Costa Unified	Richmond
148	27.9	Lodi Unified	Lodi
148	27.9	Moreno Valley Unified	Moreno Valley
148	27.9	Newport-Mesa Unified	Costa Mesa
148	27.9	San Francisco Unified	San Francisco
148	27.9	Woodland Joint Unified	Woodland
153	27.7	Live Oak Elementary	Santa Cruz
154	27.4	Hacienda La Puente Unified	City of Industry
154	27.4	Hollister SD	Hollister
156	27.2	Corning Union Elementary	Corning
156	27.2	San Bernardino City Unified	San Bernardino
156	27.2	San Marcos Unified	San Marcos
159	27.1	Greenfield Union Elementary	Bakersfield
160	27.0	Cucamonga Elementary	Rcho Cucamong
160	27.0	Thermalito Union Elementary	Oroville
160	27.0	Val Verde Unified	Perris
160	27.0	Washington Unified	West Sacramento
164	26.9	Oceanside Unified	Oceanside
165	26.8	Napa Valley Unified	Napa
166	26.7	Jurupa Unified	Riverside
166	26.7	Oak Grove Elementary	San Jose
168	26.6	Sonoma Valley Unified	Sonoma
169	26.5	Pasadena Unified	Pasadena
170	26.4	Bakersfield City Elementary	Bakersfield
170	26.4	North Monterey County Unified	Moss Landing
170	26.4	Sanger Unified	Sanger
173	26.3	Corcoran Joint Unified	Corcoran
173	26.3	San Jose Unified	San Jose
175	26.2	Sweetwater Union High	Chula Vista
176	26.1	Bonsall Union Elementary	Bonsall
177	26.0	Los Banos Unified	Los Banos
178	25.9	San Jacinto Unified	San Jacinto
179	25.8	Whittier City Elementary	Whittier
180	25.7	Cabrillo Unified	Half Moon Bay
180	25.7	Monterey Peninsula Unified	Monterey
180	25.7	Saint Helena Unified	Saint Helena
183	25.6	Adelanto Elementary	Adelanto
184	25.4	Live Oak Unified	Live Oak
184	25.4	New Haven Unified	Union City
186	25.3	South Whittier Elementary	Whittier
187	25.2	Galt Joint Union Elementary	Galt
187	25.2	Santa Maria Joint Union High	Santa Maria
187	25.2	Wilsona Elementary	Palmdale
190	25.1	San Leandro Unified	San Leandro
191	24.7	East Side Union High	San Jose
191	24.7	Santa Cruz City Elementary	Santa Cruz
193	24.6	Downey Unified	Downey
194	24.5	Gridley Unified	Gridley
195	24.1	Milpitas Unified	Milpitas
195	24.1	Palmdale Elementary	Palmdale
197	24.0	Millbrae Elementary	Millbrae
197	24.0	San Mateo-Foster City Elementary	San Mateo
199	23.9	Orange County Office of Ed	Costa Mesa
200	23.7	Imperial Unified	Imperial
201	23.6	Empire Union Elementary	Modesto
201	23.6	Stockton City Unified	Stockton
203	23.5	Grant Joint Union High	Sacramento
203	23.5	Little Lake City Elementary	Santa Fe Spgs
205	23.4	Fowler Unified	Fowler
206	23.3	Hilmar Unified	Hilmar
206	23.3	Rialto Unified	Rialto
208	23.2	Vista Unified	Vista
209	23.1	Banning Unified	Banning
209	23.1	Eastside Union Elementary	Lancaster
211	22.7	Petaluma City Elementary	Petaluma
212	22.6	Ukiah Unified	Ukiah
213	22.5	Fort Bragg Unified	Fort Bragg
213	22.5	Marysville Joint Unified	Marysville
213	22.5	Oxnard Union High	Oxnard
216	22.4	San Lorenzo Unified	San Lorenzo
217	22.3	Santa Clara Unified	Santa Clara
218	22.2	Healdsburg Unified	Healdsburg
219	21.7	Fresno County Office of Ed	Fresno
219	21.7	Visalia Unified	Visalia
221	21.6	Lake Tahoe Unified	S Lake Tahoe
222	21.5	ABC Unified	Cerritos
222	21.5	Windsor Unified	Windsor
224	21.4	Ocean View Elementary	Huntington Bch
225	21.2	Orange Unified	Orange
226	21.0	Porterville Unified	Porterville
226	21.0	Yuba City Unified	Yuba City
228	20.9	Hanford Elementary	Hanford
229	20.5	Alameda City Unified	Alameda
229	20.5	Merced Union High	Atwater
231	20.3	Newark Unified	Newark
232	20.2	Linden Unified	Linden
233	20.1	Keppel Union Elementary	Pearblossom
233	20.1	Riverside County Office of Ed	Riverside
233	20.1	Tulare City Elementary	Tulare
233	20.1	Valley Center-Pauma Unified	Valley Center
237	20.0	Cajon Valley Union Elementary	El Cajon
237	20.0	Norwalk-La Mirada Unified	Norwalk
239	19.9	East Whittier City Elementary	Whittier
240	19.7	Old Adobe Union Elementary	Petaluma
241	19.5	Elk Grove Unified	Elk Grove
241	19.5	Rio Linda Union Elementary	Rio Linda
243	19.4	Moreland Elementary	San Jose
243	19.4	Paso Robles Joint Unified	Paso Robles
245	19.1	Burbank Unified	Burbank
245	19.1	Exeter Union Elementary	Exeter
247	19.0	Dixon Unified	Dixon
248	18.9	Hughson Unified	Hughson
248	18.9	Keyes Union Elementary	Keyes
250	18.8	Santa Barbara High	Santa Barbara
251	18.7	Monrovia Unified	Monrovia
252	18.6	Duarte Unified	Duarte
252	18.6	Newhall Elementary	Valencia
254	18.3	Colton Joint Unified	Colton
255	18.2	Culver City Unified	Culver City
255	18.2	Lemoore Union Elementary	Lemoore
257	18.1	South San Francisco Unified	S San Francisco
258	18.0	Lompoc Unified	Lompoc
259	17.7	Ceres Unified	Ceres
259	17.7	Lemon Grove Elementary	Lemon Grove
259	17.7	Taft City Elementary	Taft
262	17.6	Moorpark Unified	Moorpark
263	17.5	Bellflower Unified	Bellflower
263	17.5	Lincoln Unified	Stockton
265	17.4	Fallbrook Union High	Fallbrook
266	17.3	Central Unified	Fresno
266	17.3	La Mesa-Spring Valley	La Mesa
266	17.3	Tahoe-Truckee Joint Unified	Truckee
269	17.1	Waterford Unified	Waterford
270	17.0	Escondido Union High	Escondido
271	16.9	Stanislaus Union Elementary	Modesto
272	16.8	Placentia-Yorba Linda Unified	Placentia
273	16.7	Galt Joint Union High	Galt
274	16.4	Escalon Unified	Escalon
274	16.4	Morgan Hill Unified	Morgan Hill
276	16.3	Palo Verde Unified	Blythe
276	16.3	Willows Unified	Willows
278	16.2	Orland Joint Unified	Orland
278	16.2	Riverside Unified	Riverside
280	16.0	Salida Union Elementary	Salida
281	15.9	Chaffey Joint Union High	Ontario
282	15.7	Fremont Unified	Fremont
282	15.7	Mount Diablo Unified	Concord
284	15.5	Beaumont Unified	Beaumont
285	15.4	Corona-Norco Unified	Norco
286	15.3	Whittier Union High	Whittier
287	15.1	Lake Elsinore Unified	Lake Elsinore
288	15.0	Modesto City High	Modesto
288	15.0	Tracy Joint Unified	Tracy
288	15.0	Turlock Joint Union High	Turlock
291	14.6	Brentwood Union Elementary	Brentwood
291	14.6	Ventura Unified	Ventura
293	14.5	Santa Rosa High	Santa Rosa
294	14.4	Berkeley Unified	Berkeley
295	14.3	San Rafael City High	San Rafael
295	14.3	Vallejo City Unified	Vallejo
297	14.2	Capistrano Unified	San Juan Capis
298	13.9	San Mateo Union High	San Mateo
299	13.8	Arcadia Unified	Arcadia
299	13.8	Mountain Empire Unified	Pine Valley
301	13.7	Burton Elementary	Porterville
301	13.7	Jamul-Dulzura Union Elementary	Jamul
303	13.6	Temple City Unified	Temple City
304	13.5	Menifee Union Elementary	Menifee
304	13.5	Oroville City Elementary	Oroville
304	13.5	Piner-Olivet Union Elementary	Santa Rosa
307	13.3	John Swett Unified	Crockett
307	13.3	King City Joint Union High	King City
307	13.3	Manteca Unified	Manteca
307	13.3	San Diego County Office of Ed	San Diego
311	13.2	Lancaster Elementary	Lancaster
312	13.0	Burlingame Elementary	Burlingame
312	13.0	Kern County Office of Ed	Bakersfield
314	12.9	Irvine Unified	Irvine
314	12.9	Kelseyville Unified	Kelseyville
316	12.8	Hesperia Unified	Hesperia
316	12.8	Santa Monica-Malibu Unified	Santa Monica
318	12.7	Chico Unified	Chico
318	12.7	Encinitas Union Elementary	Encinitas
318	12.7	Mountain View Elementary	Ontario
318	12.7	Ramona City Unified	Ramona
318	12.7	Red Bluff Union Elementary	Red Bluff
318	12.7	West Covina Unified	West Covina
324	12.6	Covina-Valley Unified	Covina
325	12.5	Cloverdale Unified	Cloverdale
325	12.5	Fairfield-Suisun Unified	Fairfield
325	12.5	San Bruno Park Elementary	San Bruno
328	12.4	Hemet Unified	Hemet
329	12.3	Cypress Elementary	Cypress
329	12.3	Ojai Unified	Ojai
331	12.1	Bishop Union Elementary	Bishop
331	12.1	Santa Clara County Office of Ed	San Jose
333	11.9	Natomas Unified	Sacramento
334	11.8	Santa Paula Union High	Santa Paula
334	11.8	Sulphur Springs Union Elementary	Canyon Country
336	11.6	Cotati-Rohnert Park Unified	Rohnert Park
336	11.6	Torrance Unified	Torrance
338	11.5	Chino Valley Unified	Chino
338	11.5	Fremont Union High	Sunnyvale
338	11.5	Mojave Unified	Mojave
338	11.5	Oro Grande Elementary	Oro Grande
338	11.5	Victor Elementary	Victorville
343	11.3	Huntington Beach Union High	Huntington Bch
343	11.3	Lucia Mar Unified	Arroyo Grande
345	11.2	Folsom-Cordova Unified	Folsom
346	10.9	Albany City Unified	Albany
347	10.8	Cupertino Union School	Cupertino
347	10.8	Kern Union High	Bakersfield
347	10.8	Upland Unified	Upland
350	10.7	Redondo Beach Unified	Redondo Beach
351	10.6	Antelope Valley Union High	Lancaster
351	10.6	Central Elementary	Rcho Cucamong
353	10.5	Brea-Olinda Unified	Brea
353	10.5	Jefferson Elementary	Tracy
353	10.5	Livermore Valley Joint Unified	Livermore
356	10.4	Redlands Unified	Redlands
357	10.2	Petaluma Joint Union High	Petaluma
357	10.2	Wiseburn Elementary	Hawthorne
359	10.1	Center Joint Unified	Antelope
359	10.1	Perris Union High	Perris
361	10.0	Soquel Union Elementary	Capitola
362	9.9	Konocti Unified	Lower Lake
362	9.9	Novato Unified	Novato
362	9.9	Solana Beach Elementary	Solana Beach
365	9.8	Lowell Joint	Whittier
366	9.7	Central Union Elementary	Lemoore
366	9.7	Sierra Sands Unified	Ridgecrest
366	9.7	Southern Kern Unified	Rosamond
369	9.5	Davis Joint Unified	Davis
370	9.4	Carlsbad Unified	Carlsbad
370	9.4	Enterprise Elementary	Redding
372	9.3	Liberty Union High	Brentwood
373	9.2	Pleasant Valley School	Camarillo
373	9.2	Sylvan Union Elementary	Modesto
375	9.1	Charter Oak Unified	Covina
375	9.1	Eureka City Unified	Eureka
375	9.1	Vacaville Unified	Vacaville
378	9.0	Oakley Union Elementary	Oakley
379	8.9	Clovis Unified	Clovis
380	8.8	Barstow Unified	Barstow
380	8.8	Claremont Unified	Claremont
380	8.8	San Bernardino County Supt.	San Bernardino
383	8.7	Willits Unified	Willits
384	8.6	Oakdale Joint Unified	Oakdale
385	8.5	Ripon Unified	Ripon
386	8.3	Tehachapi Unified	Tehachapi
387	8.0	Conejo Valley Unified	Thousand Oaks
387	8.0	Western Placer Unified	Lincoln
389	7.9	Del Norte County Unified	Crescent City
389	7.9	Saddleback Valley Unified	Mission Viejo
389	7.9	San Juan Unified	Carmichael
392	7.8	Jefferson Union High	Daly City
393	7.7	Castaic Union Elementary	Valencia
393	7.7	Julian Union High	Julian
393	7.7	Mountain View-Los Altos Union High	Mountain View
393	7.7	Roseville City Elementary	Roseville
393	7.7	Walnut Creek Elementary	Walnut Creek
398	7.5	Huntington Beach City Elementary	Huntington Bch
398	7.5	San Luis Coastal Unified	San Luis Obispo
398	7.5	Simi Valley Unified	Simi Valley
401	7.4	Antioch Unified	Antioch
402	7.3	Fountain Valley Elementary	Fountain Valley
403	7.2	San Marino Unified	San Marino
403	7.2	Santa Cruz City High	Santa Cruz
403	7.2	Santee Elementary	Santee
403	7.2	Walnut Valley Unified	Walnut
407	7.1	Palo Alto Unified	Palo Alto
407	7.1	Poway Unified	Poway

407	7.1	San Benito High	Hollister
410	7.0	Yucaipa-Calimesa Joint Unified	Yucaipa
411	6.9	Auburn Union Elementary	Auburn
411	6.9	Lakeport Unified	Lakeport
411	6.9	Tulare Joint Union High	Tulare
414	6.8	Beardsley Elementary	Bakersfield
414	6.8	Kingsburg Elementary Charter	Kingsburg
414	6.8	South Pasadena Unified	South Pasadena
417	6.7	Dry Creek Joint Elementary	Roseville
417	6.7	Menlo Park City Elementary	Atherton
419	6.6	El Segundo Unified	El Segundo
419	6.6	Lakeside Union Elementary	Lakeside
419	6.6	Oroville Union High	Oroville
419	6.6	William S Hart Union High	Santa Clarita
423	6.5	Palos Verdes Peninsula Unified	Palos Verdes Est
424	6.3	Bear Valley Unified	Big Bear Lake
425	6.1	Grossmont Union High	La Mesa
426	5.9	Beverly Hills Unified	Beverly Hills
427	5.8	Castro Valley Unified	Castro Valley
427	5.8	Orcutt Union Elementary	Orcutt
429	5.7	Laguna Salada Union Elementary	Pacifica
430	5.6	Union Elementary	San Jose
431	5.5	Snowline Joint Unified	Phelan
432	5.4	Temecula Valley Unified	Temecula
433	5.3	Campbell Union High	San Jose
434	5.2	Panama Buena Vista Union Elem	Bakersfield
435	5.1	Rim of The World Unified	Lake Arrowhead
435	5.1	Victor Valley Union High	Victorville
437	5.0	Cambrian Elementary	San Jose
437	5.0	Los Altos Elementary	Los Altos
437	5.0	Martinez Unified	Martinez
440	4.8	Acton-Agua Dulce Unified	Acton
440	4.8	Middletown Unified	Middletown
442	4.7	West Sonoma County Union High	Sebastopol
443	4.6	Las Virgenes Unified	Calabasas
443	4.6	Rincon Valley Union Elementary	Santa Rosa
445	4.5	Carmel Unified	Carmel
445	4.5	San Dieguito Union High	Encinitas
447	4.3	Gorman Elementary	Gorman
448	4.2	Saugus Union Elementary	Santa Clarita
449	4.1	Mark West Union Elementary	Santa Rosa
450	4.0	Pleasanton Unified	Pleasanton
450	4.0	Ross Valley Elementary	San Anselmo
450	4.0	Wheatland Elementary	Wheatland
453	3.9	Belmont-Redwood Shores Elementary	Belmont
453	3.9	Del Mar Union Elementary	Del Mar
453	3.9	Gateway Unified	Redding
453	3.9	San Joaquin County Office of Ed	Stockton
457	3.8	Hanford Joint Union High	Hanford
458	3.4	Pacific Grove Unified	Pacific Grove
459	3.3	Alta Loma Elementary	Alta Loma
460	3.2	Alpine Union Elementary	Alpine
460	3.2	Dublin Unified	Dublin
460	3.2	Silver Valley Unified	Yermo
460	3.2	Travis Unified	Travis Afb
464	3.1	Apple Valley Unified	Apple Valley
464	3.1	Atascadero Unified	Atascadero
464	3.1	Glendora Unified	Glendora
467	3.0	Piedmont City Unified	Piedmont
468	2.9	Cascade Union Elementary	Anderson
468	2.9	Murrieta Valley Unified	Murrieta
468	2.9	Plumas Unified	Quincy
468	2.9	Templeton Unified	Templeton
472	2.8	Laguna Beach Unified	Laguna Beach
473	2.5	Mill Valley Elementary	Mill Valley
474	2.4	La Canada Unified	La Canada
474	2.4	Lemoore Union High	Lemoore
476	2.3	Etiwanda Elementary	Etiwanda
476	2.3	Grass Valley Elementary	Grass Valley
476	2.3	Redding Elementary	Redding
479	2.2	Los Alamitos Unified	Los Alamitos
479	2.2	Rocklin Unified	Rocklin
479	2.2	Westwood Unified	Westwood
482	2.1	Julian Union Elementary	Julian
482	2.1	Oak Park Unified	Oak Park
482	2.1	Red Bluff Joint Union High	Red Bluff
485	2.0	San Carlos Elementary	San Carlos
485	2.0	Saratoga Union Elementary	Saratoga
487	1.9	Bonita Unified	San Dimas
487	1.9	Mother Lode Union Elementary	Placerville
489	1.8	Benicia Unified	Benicia
489	1.8	Rosedale Union Elementary	Bakersfield
489	1.8	Sierra Unified	Auberry
492	1.7	Los Gatos Union Elementary	Los Gatos
492	1.7	Manhattan Beach Unified	Manhattan Beach
492	1.7	Morongo Unified	Twentynine Plms
492	1.7	Rescue Union Elementary	Rescue
492	1.7	Standard Elementary	Bakersfield
492	1.7	Westside Union Elementary	Lancaster
498	1.6	Acalanes Union High	Lafayette
498	1.6	Coronado Unified	Coronado
498	1.6	San Ramon Valley Unified	Danville
498	1.6	Scotts Valley Unified	Scotts Valley
502	1.5	Lafayette Elementary	Lafayette
503	1.4	Fruitvale Elementary	Bakersfield
504	1.3	Dixie Elementary	San Rafael
504	1.3	Shasta Union High	Redding
506	1.2	Amador County Unified	Jackson
506	1.2	Eureka Union Elementary	Granite Bay
506	1.2	Roseville Joint Union High	Roseville
509	1.1	Moraga Elementary	Moraga
509	1.1	Orinda Union Elementary	Orinda
509	1.1	Tamalpais Union High	Larkspur
512	0.9	Black Oak Mine Unified	Georgetown
512	0.9	Calaveras Unified	San Andreas
512	0.9	Muroc Joint Unified	North Edwards
512	0.9	Norris Elementary	Bakersfield
512	0.9	San Lorenzo Valley Unified	Felton
517	0.7	Anderson Union High	Anderson
517	0.7	Mariposa County Unified	Mariposa
519	0.6	Buckeye Union Elementary	Shingle Springs
519	0.6	Loomis Union Elementary	Loomis
519	0.6	Nevada Joint Union High	Grass Valley
519	0.6	Placer Union High	Auburn
523	0.5	El Dorado Union High	Placerville
523	0.5	Paradise Unified	Paradise
525	0.4	Los Gatos-Saratoga Jt Union High	Los Gatos
526	0.3	Northern Humboldt Union High	McKinleyville
526	0.3	Sonora Union High	Sonora
528	0.1	Pleasant Ridge Union Elementary	Grass Valley
529	0.0	Twin Ridges Elementary	North San Juan

Migrant Students

Rank	Percent	District Name	City
1	70.0	Firebaugh-Las Deltas Joint Unified	Firebaugh
2	63.6	Wasco Union Elementary	Wasco
3	56.9	Arvin Union Elementary	Arvin
4	56.2	Gonzales Unified	Gonzales
5	55.9	Golden Plains Unified	San Joaquin
6	55.5	Mendota Unified	Mendota
7	54.5	Alisal Union Elementary	Salinas
8	54.1	King City Joint Union High	King City
9	53.3	Reef-Sunset Unified	Avenal
10	50.1	Salinas City Elementary	Salinas
11	49.6	Richland SD	Shafter
12	49.0	Lamont Elementary	Lamont
13	47.4	Riverdale Joint Unified	Riverdale
14	46.1	Delano Union Elementary	Delano
15	45.7	Mcfarland Unified	Mcfarland
16	44.0	Pajaro Valley Unified School	Watsonville
17	42.9	Corcoran Joint Unified	Corcoran
18	41.7	Greenfield Union Elementary	Greenfield
19	41.4	Parlier Unified	Parlier
20	39.7	King City Union Elementary	King City
21	39.0	Soledad Unified	Soledad
22	35.9	Coalinga-Huron Joint Unified	Coalinga
23	35.8	Lindsay Unified	Lindsay
24	34.5	North Monterey County Unified	Moss Landing
24	34.5	Woodlake Union Elementary	Woodlake
26	34.0	Salinas Union High	Salinas
27	33.4	Rio Elementary	Oxnard
28	32.6	Delano Joint Union High	Delano
29	32.4	San Benito High	Hollister
30	31.1	Farmersville Unified	Farmersville
31	30.9	Kerman Unified	Kerman
32	30.7	Fillmore Unified	Fillmore
33	30.6	Santa Maria-Bonita Elementary	Santa Maria
34	30.5	Linden Unified	Linden
35	30.3	Escalon Unified	Escalon
36	29.4	Hollister SD	Hollister
37	29.1	Patterson Joint Unified	Patterson
38	28.1	Hughson Unified	Hughson
39	27.7	Ocean View Elementary	Oxnard
40	27.5	Earlimart Elementary	Earlimart
41	27.3	River Delta Joint Unified	Rio Vista
42	27.2	Holtville Unified	Holtville
42	27.2	Riverbank Unified	Riverbank
44	26.8	Santa Paula Elementary	Santa Paula
45	24.6	Santa Maria Joint Union High	Santa Maria
46	24.1	Hueneme Elementary	Port Hueneme
47	24.0	Coachella Valley Unified	Thermal
48	23.5	Brawley Union High	Brawley
49	23.4	Greenfield Union Elementary	Bakersfield
50	23.0	Newman-Crows Landing Unified	Newman
51	22.1	Lemoore Union Elementary	Lemoore
52	21.8	Calexico Unified	Calexico
53	21.5	Gustine Unified	Gustine
54	21.3	Live Oak Unified	Live Oak
55	20.9	Carpinteria Unified	Carpinteria
56	20.8	Brawley Elementary	Brawley
57	19.8	Taft City Elementary	Taft
58	19.5	Dos Palos Oro Loma Joint Unified	Dos Palos
58	19.5	Winters Joint Unified	Winters
60	19.4	Kelseyville Unified	Kelseyville
60	19.4	Santa Paula Union High	Santa Paula
62	19.1	Hanford Elementary	Hanford
62	19.1	Ukiah Unified	Ukiah
64	18.1	Bakersfield City Elementary	Bakersfield
65	17.6	Cloverdale Unified	Cloverdale
66	17.3	Stockton City Unified	Stockton
66	17.3	Tulare City Elementary	Tulare
68	17.2	Bonsall Union Elementary	Bonsall
68	17.2	Dinuba Unified	Dinuba
68	17.2	Gridley Unified	Gridley
71	17.0	Dixon Unified	Dixon
72	16.9	Healdsburg Unified	Healdsburg
73	16.5	Central Union High	El Centro
73	16.5	Galt Joint Union Elementary	Galt
75	16.4	Yuba City Unified	Yuba City
76	15.7	Fort Bragg Unified	Fort Bragg
77	15.5	Exeter Union Elementary	Exeter
77	15.5	Oxnard Union High	Oxnard
79	14.9	El Centro Elementary	El Centro
80	14.8	Livingston Union Elementary	Livingston
80	14.8	Winton Elementary	Winton
82	14.6	Cutler-Orosi Joint Unified	Orosi
82	14.6	Galt Joint Union High	Galt
84	14.4	Madera Unified	Madera
84	14.4	Valley Center-Pauma Unified	Valley Center
86	14.3	Colusa Unified	Colusa
87	14.0	Fresno Unified	Fresno
88	13.5	Kings Canyon Joint Unified	Reedley
88	13.5	Saint Helena Unified	Saint Helena
88	13.5	Santa Rita Union Elementary	Salinas
91	13.1	Ceres Unified	Ceres
92	13.0	Willows Unified	Willows
93	12.7	Waterford Unified	Waterford
94	12.6	Orland Joint Unified	Orland
95	12.3	Lemoore Union High	Lemoore
96	11.8	Keppel Union Elementary	Pearblossom
96	11.8	Ripon Unified	Ripon
98	11.4	Fowler Unified	Fowler
99	11.3	Oakdale Joint Unified	Oakdale
99	11.3	Woodland Joint Unified	Woodland
101	11.1	Tulare Joint Union High	Tulare
102	11.0	Gilroy Unified	Gilroy
102	11.0	Porterville Unified	Porterville
104	10.6	Cabrillo Unified	Half Moon Bay
105	10.4	Kern Union High	Bakersfield
106	10.3	Fallbrook Union Elementary	Fallbrook
106	10.3	Lakeport Unified	Lakeport
108	10.1	Delhi Unified	Delhi
109	9.9	Lodi Unified	Lodi
109	9.9	Palo Verde Unified	Blythe
111	9.8	Selma Unified	Selma
112	9.6	Lompoc Unified	Lompoc
112	9.6	Morgan Hill Unified	Morgan Hill
112	9.6	Rosemead Elementary	Rosemead
115	9.4	Thermalito Union Elementary	Oroville
116	9.2	Franklin-Mckinley Elementary	San Jose
117	8.9	Atwater Elementary	Atwater
118	8.7	Modesto City Elementary	Modesto
119	8.6	Keyes Union Elementary	Keyes
120	8.4	Paso Robles Joint Unified	Paso Robles
121	8.3	Weaver Union Elementary	Merced
122	8.2	Fallbrook Union High	Fallbrook
123	7.7	Alum Rock Union Elementary	San Jose
123	7.7	Santa Rosa Elementary	Santa Rosa
125	7.6	Chowchilla Elementary	Chowchilla
126	7.4	Oxnard Elementary	Oxnard
126	7.4	Ravenswood City Elementary	East Palo Alto
128	7.3	Central Union Elementary	Lemoore
128	7.3	Salida Union Elementary	Salida
130	7.2	Willits Unified	Willits
131	7.1	Eastside Union Elementary	Lancaster
132	6.8	Mount Pleasant Elementary	San Jose
133	6.6	Merced Union High	Atwater
134	6.5	Corning Union Elementary	Corning
134	6.5	Napa Valley Unified	Napa
136	6.4	Bellevue Union Elementary	Santa Rosa
136	6.4	Lucia Mar Unified	Arroyo Grande
138	6.3	Los Banos Unified	Los Banos
138	6.3	Sonoma Valley Unified	Sonoma
140	6.1	Empire Union Elementary	Modesto
141	5.6	Oroville Union High	Oroville
142	5.5	Marysville Joint Unified	Marysville
142	5.5	Windsor Unified	Windsor
144	5.4	Manteca Unified	Manteca
144	5.4	Moorpark Unified	Moorpark
144	5.4	Santa Clara Unified	Santa Clara
147	5.3	Liberty Union High	Brentwood
148	5.2	ABC Unified	Cerritos
148	5.2	Merced City Elementary	Merced
148	5.2	Redwood City Elementary	Redwood City
148	5.2	Southern Kern Unified	Rosamond
152	5.1	Brentwood Union Elementary	Brentwood

Rank	Value	District	City
152	5.1	Visalia Unified	Visalia
154	4.8	Norwalk-La Mirada Unified	Norwalk
155	4.6	Oceanside Unified	Oceanside
155	4.6	Tehachapi Unified	Tehachapi
157	4.5	Turlock Joint Elementary	Turlock
157	4.5	Ventura Unified	Ventura
159	4.4	Sanger Unified	Sanger
160	4.3	Sequoia Union High	Redwood City
161	4.2	Hanford Joint Union High	Hanford
161	4.2	Konocti Unified	Lower Lake
161	4.2	Oroville City Elementary	Oroville
161	4.2	San Ysidro Elementary	San Ysidro
165	4.1	Imperial Unified	Imperial
165	4.1	Modesto City High	Modesto
165	4.1	San Jose Unified	San Jose
165	4.1	Tracy Joint Unified	Tracy
165	4.1	Turlock Joint Union High	Turlock
170	4.0	Hilmar Unified	Hilmar
171	3.8	Duarte Unified	Duarte
172	3.7	Mountain View Elementary	El Monte
172	3.7	Ramona City Unified	Ramona
174	3.6	Central Unified	Fresno
174	3.6	Monterey Peninsula Unified	Monterey
176	3.5	Escondido Union Elementary	Escondido
176	3.5	Garvey Elementary	Rosemead
178	3.4	Los Nietos Elementary	Whittier
178	3.4	Stanislaus Union Elementary	Modesto
180	3.3	San Marcos Unified	San Marcos
180	3.3	Wilsona Elementary	Palmdale
182	3.1	Oakley Union Elementary	Oakley
183	3.0	Long Beach Unified	Long Beach
183	3.0	Lynwood Unified	Lynwood
185	2.9	Hayward Unified	Hayward
185	2.9	Middletown Unified	Middletown
185	2.9	San Luis Coastal Unified	San Luis Obispo
188	2.8	Burton Elementary	Porterville
188	2.8	El Monte Union High	El Monte
188	2.8	Red Bluff Union Elementary	Red Bluff
188	2.8	Santa Cruz City Elementary	Santa Cruz
188	2.8	South Whittier Elementary	Whittier
193	2.7	Perris Elementary	Perris
194	2.6	Escondido Union High	Escondido
194	2.6	Lancaster Elementary	Lancaster
194	2.6	New Haven Unified	Union City
194	2.6	Vista Unified	Vista
198	2.5	Carlsbad Unified	Carlsbad
199	2.4	Baldwin Park Unified	Baldwin Park
199	2.4	Desert Sands Unified	La Quinta
199	2.4	El Monte City Elementary	El Monte
199	2.4	Encinitas Union Elementary	Encinitas
199	2.4	Hacienda La Puente Unified	City of Industry
199	2.4	Oak Grove Elementary	San Jose
199	2.4	Petaluma City Elementary	Petaluma
206	2.3	Old Adobe Union Elementary	Petaluma
206	2.3	Santa Rosa High	Santa Rosa
208	2.2	Goleta Union Elementary	Goleta
209	2.1	Chico Unified	Chico
209	2.1	Clovis Unified	Clovis
209	2.1	Newark Unified	Newark
212	2.0	Sacramento City Unified	Sacramento
212	2.0	South San Francisco Unified	S San Francisco
214	1.9	Evergreen Elementary	San Jose
214	1.9	Solana Beach Elementary	Solana Beach
214	1.9	Vacaville Unified	Vacaville
217	1.8	Live Oak Elementary	Santa Cruz
217	1.8	Paramount Unified	Paramount
217	1.8	Santa Ana Unified	Santa Ana
220	1.7	Del Norte County Unified	Crescent City
220	1.7	Little Lake City Elementary	Santa Fe Spgs
220	1.7	Livermore Valley Joint Unified	Livermore
220	1.7	Palmdale Elementary	Palmdale
220	1.7	San Lorenzo Unified	San Lorenzo
220	1.7	West Sonoma County Union High	Sebastopol
226	1.6	Alhambra City Elementary	Alhambra
227	1.5	Alhambra City High	Alhambra
227	1.5	East Side Union High	San Jose
229	1.4	Cascade Union Elementary	Anderson
229	1.4	Cotati-Rohnert Park Unified	Rohnert Park
229	1.4	Petaluma Joint Union High	Petaluma
229	1.4	Placentia-Yorba Linda Unified	Placentia
233	1.3	Fairfield-Suisun Unified	Fairfield
233	1.3	Oakland Unified	Oakland
233	1.3	San Joaquin County Office of Ed	Stockton
233	1.3	Santa Barbara High	Santa Barbara
237	1.2	San Dieguito Union High	Encinitas
238	1.1	Antelope Valley Union High	Lancaster
238	1.1	Davis Joint Unified	Davis
238	1.1	National Elementary	National City
238	1.1	Santa Barbara Elementary	Santa Barbara
242	1.0	Los Angeles County Office of Ed	Downey
242	1.0	North Sacramento Elementary	Sacramento
242	1.0	Palm Springs Unified	Palm Springs
242	1.0	Pomona Unified	Pomona
242	1.0	Santa Cruz City High	Santa Cruz
247	0.9	Azusa Unified	Azusa
247	0.9	Fremont Unified	Fremont
247	0.9	Piner-Olivet Union Elementary	Santa Rosa
247	0.9	Pleasant Valley School	Camarillo
247	0.9	Red Bluff Joint Union High	Red Bluff
247	0.9	Whittier Union High	Whittier
253	0.8	Anaheim Elementary	Anaheim
253	0.8	Newport-Mesa Unified	Costa Mesa
255	0.7	Anaheim Union High	Anaheim
255	0.7	Covina-Valley Unified	Covina
255	0.7	El Rancho Unified	Pico Rivera
255	0.7	Enterprise Elementary	Redding
255	0.7	Fresno County Office of Ed	Fresno
255	0.7	Jefferson Elementary	Tracy
255	0.7	Mother Lode Union Elementary	Placerville
255	0.7	Mountain Empire Unified	Pine Valley
255	0.7	San Francisco Unified	San Francisco
264	0.6	Atascadero Unified	Atascadero
264	0.6	Perris Union High	Perris
264	0.6	Sunnyvale Elementary	Sunnyvale
264	0.6	Templeton Unified	Templeton
268	0.5	Kingsburg Elementary Charter	Kingsburg
268	0.5	Lincoln Unified	Stockton
268	0.5	Los Angeles Unified	Los Angeles
268	0.5	Magnolia Elementary	Anaheim
268	0.5	Mark West Union Elementary	Santa Rosa
268	0.5	Mountain View-Los Altos Union High	Mountain View
268	0.5	Orange Unified	Orange
268	0.5	Panama Buena Vista Union Elem	Bakersfield
268	0.5	Pasadena Unified	Pasadena
277	0.4	Acton-Agua Dulce Unified	Acton
277	0.4	Anderson Union High	Anderson
277	0.4	Bassett Unified	La Puente
277	0.4	Capistrano Unified	San Juan Capis
277	0.4	Corona-Norco Unified	Norco
277	0.4	Fullerton Elementary	Fullerton
277	0.4	Mojave Unified	Mojave
277	0.4	Monrovia Unified	Monrovia
277	0.4	Rincon Valley Union Elementary	Santa Rosa
277	0.4	Shasta Union High	Redding
287	0.3	Beardsley Elementary	Bakersfield
287	0.3	Fremont Union High	Sunnyvale
287	0.3	Gateway Unified	Redding
287	0.3	Sweetwater Union High	Chula Vista
287	0.3	West Covina Unified	West Covina
287	0.3	Westside Union Elementary	Lancaster
287	0.3	Wheatland Elementary	Wheatland
294	0.2	Auburn Union Elementary	Auburn
294	0.2	Elk Grove Unified	Elk Grove
294	0.2	Grant Joint Union High	Sacramento
294	0.2	Kern County Office of Ed	Bakersfield
294	0.2	Orcutt Union Elementary	Orcutt
294	0.2	Redding Elementary	Redding
294	0.2	Romoland Elementary	Homeland
294	0.2	Rowland Unified	Rowland Heights
294	0.2	San Gabriel Unified	San Gabriel
303	0.1	Bonita Unified	San Dimas
303	0.1	Buena Park Elementary	Buena Park
303	0.1	Centralia Elementary	Buena Park
303	0.1	Charter Oak Unified	Covina
303	0.1	Chula Vista Elementary	Chula Vista
303	0.1	Claremont Unified	Claremont
303	0.1	East Whittier City Elementary	Whittier
303	0.1	El Dorado Union High	Placerville
303	0.1	Glendora Unified	Glendora
303	0.1	Lemon Grove Elementary	Lemon Grove
303	0.1	Rio Linda Union Elementary	Rio Linda
303	0.1	Rosedale Union Elementary	Bakersfield
303	0.1	San Diego Unified	San Diego
303	0.1	San Leandro Unified	San Leandro
303	0.1	Santa Clara County Office of Ed	San Jose
303	0.1	Savanna Elementary	Anaheim
303	0.1	South Bay Union Elementary	Imperial Beach
303	0.1	Standard Elementary	Bakersfield
303	0.1	Sylvan Union Elementary	Modesto
303	0.1	Whittier City Elementary	Whittier
323	0.0	Alameda City Unified	Alameda
323	0.0	Alvord Unified	Riverside
323	0.0	Arcadia Unified	Arcadia
323	0.0	Black Oak Mine Unified	Georgetown
323	0.0	Cajon Valley Union Elementary	El Cajon
323	0.0	Campbell Union Elementary	Campbell
323	0.0	Chaffey Joint Union High	Ontario
323	0.0	Chino Valley Unified	Chino
323	0.0	Compton Unified	Compton
323	0.0	Cupertino Union School	Cupertino
323	0.0	Del Mar Union Elementary	Del Mar
323	0.0	Del Paso Heights Elementary	Sacramento
323	0.0	Downey Unified	Downey
323	0.0	Folsom-Cordova Unified	Folsom
323	0.0	Fountain Valley Elementary	Fountain Valley
323	0.0	Fullerton Joint Union High	Fullerton
323	0.0	Garden Grove Unified	Garden Grove
323	0.0	Glendale Unified	Glendale
323	0.0	Grossmont Union High	La Mesa
323	0.0	Huntington Beach Union High	Huntington Bch
323	0.0	Jurupa Unified	Riverside
323	0.0	La Mesa-Spring Valley	La Mesa
323	0.0	Lakeside Union Elementary	Lakeside
323	0.0	Montebello Unified	Montebello
323	0.0	Moreno Valley Unified	Moreno Valley
323	0.0	Mount Diablo Unified	Concord
323	0.0	Mountain View Elementary	Ontario
323	0.0	Mountain View-Whisman Elementary	Mountain View
323	0.0	Natomas Unified	Sacramento
323	0.0	Novato Unified	Novato
323	0.0	Ocean View Elementary	Huntington Bch
323	0.0	Riverside County Office of Ed	Riverside
323	0.0	Saddleback Valley Unified	Mission Viejo
323	0.0	San Juan Unified	Carmichael
323	0.0	Tamalpais Union High	Larkspur
323	0.0	Temple City Unified	Temple City
323	0.0	Travis Unified	Travis Afb
323	0.0	Tustin Unified	Tustin
323	0.0	Val Verde Unified	Perris
323	0.0	Walnut Valley Unified	Walnut
323	0.0	Washington Unified	West Sacramento
323	0.0	West Contra Costa Unified	Richmond
323	0.0	Westminster Elementary	Westminster
366	0.0	Acalanes Union High	Lafayette
366	0.0	Adelanto Elementary	Adelanto
366	0.0	Albany City Unified	Albany
366	0.0	Alpine Union Elementary	Alpine
366	0.0	Alta Loma Elementary	Alta Loma
366	0.0	Amador County Unified	Jackson
366	0.0	Antioch Unified	Antioch
366	0.0	Apple Valley Unified	Apple Valley
366	0.0	Banning Unified	Banning
366	0.0	Barstow Unified	Barstow
366	0.0	Bear Valley Unified	Big Bear Lake
366	0.0	Beaumont Unified	Beaumont
366	0.0	Bellflower Unified	Bellflower
366	0.0	Belmont-Redwood Shores Elementary	Belmont
366	0.0	Benicia Unified	Benicia
366	0.0	Berkeley Unified	Berkeley
366	0.0	Berryessa Union Elementary	San Jose
366	0.0	Beverly Hills Unified	Beverly Hills
366	0.0	Bishop Union Elementary	Bishop
366	0.0	Brea-Olinda Unified	Brea
366	0.0	Buckeye Union Elementary	Shingle Springs
366	0.0	Burbank Unified	Burbank
366	0.0	Burlingame Elementary	Burlingame
366	0.0	Calaveras Unified	San Andreas
366	0.0	Cambrian Elementary	San Jose
366	0.0	Campbell Union High	San Jose
366	0.0	Carmel Unified	Carmel
366	0.0	Castaic Union Elementary	Valencia
366	0.0	Castro Valley Unified	Castro Valley
366	0.0	Center Joint Unified	Antelope
366	0.0	Centinela Valley Union High	Lawndale
366	0.0	Central Elementary	Rcho Cucamong
366	0.0	Colton Joint Unified	Colton
366	0.0	Conejo Valley Unified	Thousand Oaks
366	0.0	Coronado Unified	Coronado
366	0.0	Cucamonga Elementary	Rcho Cucamong
366	0.0	Culver City Unified	Culver City
366	0.0	Cypress Elementary	Cypress
366	0.0	Dixie Elementary	San Rafael
366	0.0	Dry Creek Joint Elementary	Roseville
366	0.0	Dublin Unified	Dublin
366	0.0	El Segundo Unified	El Segundo
366	0.0	Etiwanda Elementary	Etiwanda
366	0.0	Eureka City Unified	Eureka
366	0.0	Eureka Union Elementary	Granite Bay
366	0.0	Fontana Unified	Fontana
366	0.0	Fruitvale Elementary	Bakersfield
366	0.0	Gorman Elementary	Gorman
366	0.0	Grass Valley Elementary	Grass Valley
366	0.0	Hawthorne Elementary	Hawthorne
366	0.0	Hemet Unified	Hemet
366	0.0	Hesperia Unified	Hesperia
366	0.0	Huntington Beach City Elementary	Huntington Bch
366	0.0	Inglewood Unified	Inglewood
366	0.0	Irvine Unified	Irvine
366	0.0	Jamul-Dulzura Union Elementary	Jamul
366	0.0	Jefferson Elementary	Daly City
366	0.0	Jefferson Union High	Daly City
366	0.0	John Swett Unified	Crockett
366	0.0	Julian Union Elementary	Julian
366	0.0	Julian Union High	Julian
366	0.0	La Canada Unified	La Canada
366	0.0	La Habra City Elementary	La Habra
366	0.0	Lafayette Elementary	Lafayette
366	0.0	Laguna Beach Unified	Laguna Beach

366	0.0	Laguna Salada Union Elementary	Pacifica
366	0.0	Lake Elsinore Unified	Lake Elsinore
366	0.0	Lake Tahoe Unified	S Lake Tahoe
366	0.0	Las Virgenes Unified	Calabasas
366	0.0	Lawndale Elementary	Lawndale
366	0.0	Lennox Elementary	Lennox
366	0.0	Loomis Union Elementary	Loomis
366	0.0	Los Alamitos Unified	Los Alamitos
366	0.0	Los Altos Elementary	Los Altos
366	0.0	Los Gatos Union Elementary	Los Gatos
366	0.0	Los Gatos-Saratoga Jt Union High	Los Gatos
366	0.0	Lowell Joint	Whittier
366	0.0	Manhattan Beach Unified	Manhattan Beach
366	0.0	Mariposa County Unified	Mariposa
366	0.0	Martinez Unified	Martinez
366	0.0	Menifee Union Elementary	Menifee
366	0.0	Menlo Park City Elementary	Atherton
366	0.0	Mill Valley Elementary	Mill Valley
366	0.0	Millbrae Elementary	Millbrae
366	0.0	Milpitas Unified	Milpitas
366	0.0	Moraga Elementary	Moraga
366	0.0	Moreland Elementary	San Jose
366	0.0	Morongo Unified	Twentynine Plms
366	0.0	Muroc Joint Unified	North Edwards
366	0.0	Murrieta Valley Unified	Murrieta
366	0.0	Nevada Joint Union High	Grass Valley
366	0.0	Newhall Elementary	Valencia
366	0.0	Norris Elementary	Bakersfield
366	0.0	Northern Humboldt Union High	McKinleyville
366	0.0	Oak Park Unified	Oak Park
366	0.0	Ojai Unified	Ojai
366	0.0	Ontario-Montclair Elementary	Ontario
366	0.0	Orange County Office of Ed	Costa Mesa
366	0.0	Orinda Union Elementary	Orinda
366	0.0	Oro Grande Elementary	Oro Grande
366	0.0	Pacific Grove Unified	Pacific Grove
366	0.0	Palo Alto Unified	Palo Alto
366	0.0	Palos Verdes Peninsula Unified	Palos Verdes Est
366	0.0	Paradise Unified	Paradise
366	0.0	Piedmont City Unified	Piedmont
366	0.0	Pittsburg Unified	Pittsburg
366	0.0	Placer Union High	Auburn
366	0.0	Pleasant Ridge Union Elementary	Grass Valley
366	0.0	Pleasanton Unified	Pleasanton
366	0.0	Plumas Unified	Quincy
366	0.0	Poway Unified	Poway
366	0.0	Redlands Unified	Redlands
366	0.0	Redondo Beach Unified	Redondo Beach
366	0.0	Rescue Union Elementary	Rescue
366	0.0	Rialto Unified	Rialto
366	0.0	Rim of The World Unified	Lake Arrowhead
366	0.0	Riverside Unified	Riverside
366	0.0	Robla Elementary	Sacramento
366	0.0	Rocklin Unified	Rocklin
366	0.0	Roseville City Elementary	Roseville
366	0.0	Roseville Joint Union High	Roseville
366	0.0	Ross Valley Elementary	San Anselmo
366	0.0	San Bernardino City Unified	San Bernardino
366	0.0	San Bernardino County Supt.	San Bernardino
366	0.0	San Bruno Park Elementary	San Bruno
366	0.0	San Carlos Elementary	San Carlos
366	0.0	San Diego County Office of Ed	San Diego
366	0.0	San Jacinto Unified	San Jacinto
366	0.0	San Lorenzo Valley Unified	Felton
366	0.0	San Marino Unified	San Marino
366	0.0	San Mateo Union High	San Mateo
366	0.0	San Mateo-Foster City Elementary	San Mateo
366	0.0	San Rafael City Elementary	San Rafael
366	0.0	San Rafael City High	San Rafael
366	0.0	San Ramon Valley Unified	Danville
366	0.0	Santa Monica-Malibu Unified	Santa Monica
366	0.0	Santee Elementary	Santee
366	0.0	Saratoga Union Elementary	Saratoga
366	0.0	Saugus Union Elementary	Santa Clarita
366	0.0	Scotts Valley Unified	Scotts Valley
366	0.0	Sierra Sands Unified	Ridgecrest
366	0.0	Sierra Unified	Auberry
366	0.0	Silver Valley Unified	Yermo
366	0.0	Simi Valley Unified	Simi Valley
366	0.0	Snowline Joint Unified	Phelan
366	0.0	Sonora Union High	Sonora
366	0.0	Soquel Union Elementary	Capitola
366	0.0	South Pasadena Unified	South Pasadena
366	0.0	Sulphur Springs Union Elementary	Canyon Country
366	0.0	Tahoe-Truckee Joint Unified	Truckee
366	0.0	Temecula Valley Unified	Temecula
366	0.0	Torrance Unified	Torrance
366	0.0	Twin Ridges Elementary	North San Juan
366	0.0	Union Elementary	San Jose
366	0.0	Upland Unified	Upland
366	0.0	Vallejo City Unified	Vallejo
366	0.0	Victor Elementary	Victorville
366	0.0	Victor Valley Union High	Victorville
366	0.0	Walnut Creek Elementary	Walnut Creek
366	0.0	Western Placer Unified	Lincoln
366	0.0	Westwood Unified	Westwood
366	0.0	William S Hart Union High	Santa Clarita
366	0.0	Wiseburn Elementary	Hawthorne
366	0.0	Yucaipa-Calimesa Joint Unified	Yucaipa

Students Eligible for Free Lunch

Rank	Percent	District Name	City
1	99.5	Los Nietos Elementary	Whittier
1	99.5	National Elementary	National City
1	99.5	Winton Elementary	Winton
4	98.9	Reef-Sunset Unified	Avenal
5	97.7	Parlier Unified	Parlier
6	93.3	Delano Union Elementary	Delano
7	91.0	Del Paso Heights Elementary	Sacramento
8	88.9	Mendota Unified	Mendota
9	87.5	Golden Plains Unified	San Joaquin
10	85.3	Thermalito Union Elementary	Oroville
11	83.7	Lennox Elementary	Lennox
12	83.1	Richland SD	Shafter
13	83.0	Arvin Union Elementary	Arvin
13	83.0	Earlimart Elementary	Earlimart
13	83.0	Soledad Unified	Soledad
16	82.1	Compton Unified	Compton
17	80.1	San Diego County Office of Ed	San Diego
18	79.8	Lamont Elementary	Lamont
19	78.7	Woodlake Union Elementary	Woodlake
20	78.3	San Ysidro Elementary	San Ysidro
21	77.2	Bakersfield City Elementary	Bakersfield
22	75.9	Wasco Union Elementary	Wasco
23	75.4	Coachella Valley Unified	Thermal
23	75.4	Mountain View Elementary	El Monte
25	72.5	El Monte City Elementary	El Monte
26	72.3	Farmersville Unified	Farmersville
27	72.2	Paramount Unified	Paramount
28	72.1	Garvey Elementary	Rosemead
29	71.7	Firebaugh-Las Deltas Joint Unified	Firebaugh
30	71.6	Livingston Union Elementary	Livingston
31	71.0	Mcfarland Unified	Mcfarland
32	70.5	Porterville Unified	Porterville
33	70.1	Perris Elementary	Perris
34	69.6	Fresno Unified	Fresno
34	69.6	North Sacramento Elementary	Sacramento
36	69.5	Lindsay Unified	Lindsay
37	68.8	Hawthorne Elementary	Hawthorne
38	68.3	Alisal Union Elementary	Salinas
39	67.2	Los Angeles Unified	Los Angeles
39	67.2	Santa Maria-Bonita Elementary	Santa Maria
41	67.0	Fowler Unified	Fowler
42	66.8	Chowchilla Elementary	Chowchilla
42	66.8	San Bernardino City Unified	San Bernardino
44	66.7	Bellevue Union Elementary	Santa Rosa
45	66.2	Live Oak Unified	Live Oak
46	65.6	Kings Canyon Joint Unified	Reedley
47	65.3	Marysville Joint Unified	Marysville
48	65.1	Bassett Unified	La Puente
49	64.7	Corcoran Joint Unified	Corcoran
49	64.7	Ontario-Montclair Elementary	Ontario
51	64.1	Anaheim Elementary	Anaheim
52	63.7	Greenfield Union Elementary	Bakersfield
53	63.6	Dinuba Unified	Dinuba
54	63.4	Konocti Unified	Lower Lake
55	63.0	Merced Union High	Atwater
56	62.8	Madera Unified	Madera
57	62.4	Oroville City Elementary	Oroville
57	62.4	Wilsona Elementary	Palmdale
59	62.3	Beardsley Elementary	Bakersfield
60	62.1	Corning Union Elementary	Corning
61	61.8	Riverdale Joint Unified	Riverdale
62	61.6	Modesto City Elementary	Modesto
63	61.3	Dos Palos Oro Loma Joint Unified	Dos Palos
64	61.2	Calexico Unified	Calexico
65	61.0	Merced City Elementary	Merced
66	60.9	Cutler-Orosi Joint Unified	Orosi
67	60.7	El Centro Elementary	El Centro
68	60.6	Banning Unified	Banning
69	60.0	Montebello Unified	Montebello
70	59.5	Tulare City Elementary	Tulare
71	59.2	Oxnard Elementary	Oxnard
71	59.2	Romoland Elementary	Homeland
73	59.0	Baldwin Park Unified	Baldwin Park
73	59.0	Santa Ana Unified	Santa Ana
75	58.9	Kerman Unified	Kerman
76	58.3	Hanford Elementary	Hanford
77	58.2	Keppel Union Elementary	Pearblossom
78	58.0	Brawley Elementary	Brawley
79	57.9	Coalinga-Huron Joint Unified	Coalinga
80	57.7	Stockton City Unified	Stockton
81	57.6	Cascade Union Elementary	Anderson
82	57.0	Eastside Union Elementary	Lancaster
82	57.0	Lawndale Elementary	Lawndale
82	57.0	Magnolia Elementary	Anaheim
82	57.0	Oakland Unified	Oakland
86	56.6	Pomona Unified	Pomona
86	56.6	Ravenswood City Elementary	East Palo Alto
88	56.5	Rosemead Elementary	Rosemead
89	56.4	Alum Rock Union Elementary	San Jose
89	56.4	Lynwood Unified	Lynwood
91	56.2	Robla Elementary	Sacramento
91	56.2	Selma Unified	Selma
93	56.1	Atwater Elementary	Atwater
94	55.9	Sacramento City Unified	Sacramento
95	55.8	Holtville Unified	Holtville
96	55.7	King City Union Elementary	King City
96	55.7	Sanger Unified	Sanger
98	55.0	Del Norte County Unified	Crescent City
98	55.0	Delano Joint Union High	Delano
100	54.9	Greenfield Union Elementary	Greenfield
101	54.6	Delhi Unified	Delhi
102	54.2	La Habra City Elementary	La Habra
103	54.1	Long Beach Unified	Long Beach
103	54.1	Patterson Joint Unified	Patterson
105	54.0	San Jacinto Unified	San Jacinto
106	53.9	Ocean View Elementary	Oxnard
107	53.8	Palm Springs Unified	Palm Springs
107	53.8	Pasadena Unified	Pasadena
109	53.6	Rialto Unified	Rialto
110	53.4	Adelanto Elementary	Adelanto
111	53.3	Hueneme Elementary	Port Hueneme
112	53.2	El Monte Union High	El Monte
113	53.0	Santa Paula Elementary	Santa Paula
113	53.0	Taft City Elementary	Taft
115	52.8	Franklin-Mckinley Elementary	San Jose
116	52.5	Washington Unified	West Sacramento
117	52.1	Hacienda La Puente Unified	City of Industry
118	51.9	Gonzales Unified	Gonzales
118	51.9	Salinas City Elementary	Salinas
120	51.8	Gridley Unified	Gridley
121	51.7	Weaver Union Elementary	Merced
122	51.6	Alhambra City High	Alhambra
122	51.6	Azusa Unified	Azusa
124	51.4	Lancaster Elementary	Lancaster
125	51.2	Lodi Unified	Lodi
125	51.2	Palmdale Elementary	Palmdale
127	51.0	Fontana Unified	Fontana
128	50.8	Alhambra City Elementary	Alhambra
129	50.2	Buena Park Elementary	Buena Park
129	50.2	Riverbank Unified	Riverbank
131	49.4	Exeter Union Elementary	Exeter
132	49.0	El Rancho Unified	Pico Rivera
133	48.9	Barstow Unified	Barstow
134	48.8	San Joaquin County Office of Ed	Stockton
134	48.8	Westminster Elementary	Westminster
136	48.7	Duarte Unified	Duarte
137	48.5	Val Verde Unified	Perris
138	48.3	Cucamonga Elementary	Rcho Cucamong
138	48.3	Fillmore Unified	Fillmore
138	48.3	Turlock Joint Elementary	Turlock
141	48.0	Palo Verde Unified	Blythe
142	47.9	King City Joint Union High	King City
143	47.6	Escondido Union Elementary	Escondido
144	47.2	Mojave Unified	Mojave
145	46.9	Ukiah Unified	Ukiah
146	46.8	Willows Unified	Willows
147	46.7	Pajaro Valley Unified School	Watsonville
148	46.4	Central Union High	El Centro
148	46.4	Garden Grove Unified	Garden Grove
150	46.1	Gustine Unified	Gustine
151	46.0	San Diego Unified	San Diego
151	46.0	Victor Elementary	Victorville
153	45.9	Whittier City Elementary	Whittier
154	45.5	Lemoore Union Elementary	Lemoore
155	45.1	Ceres Unified	Ceres
156	45.0	Moreno Valley Unified	Moreno Valley
157	44.9	Orland Joint Unified	Orland
158	44.7	Kern County Office of Ed	Bakersfield
159	44.6	Rio Linda Union Elementary	Rio Linda
160	44.5	Inglewood Unified	Inglewood
161	44.4	Kelseyville Unified	Kelseyville
162	44.1	Jurupa Unified	Riverside
163	43.7	North Monterey County Unified	Moss Landing
164	43.6	Colusa Unified	Colusa
165	43.1	Gateway Unified	Redding
165	43.1	Rio Elementary	Oxnard
165	43.1	South Bay Union Elementary	Imperial Beach
168	43.0	Fort Bragg Unified	Fort Bragg
169	42.9	Santa Barbara Elementary	Santa Barbara
170	42.7	Little Lake City Elementary	Santa Fe Spgs
170	42.7	San Francisco Unified	San Francisco
172	42.2	South Whittier Elementary	Whittier
173	42.1	Centinela Valley Union High	Lawndale
173	42.1	Mount Pleasant Elementary	San Jose

Rank	Score	District	City
175	42.0	San Gabriel Unified	San Gabriel
176	41.9	Enterprise Elementary	Redding
177	41.7	Newman-Crows Landing Unified	Newman
178	41.6	Grant Joint Union High	Sacramento
178	41.6	Stanislaus Union Elementary	Modesto
180	41.4	Rowland Unified	Rowland Heights
181	41.3	Desert Sands Unified	La Quinta
182	41.2	Hemet Unified	Hemet
182	41.2	Pittsburg Unified	Pittsburg
184	41.0	Monrovia Unified	Monrovia
185	40.9	Empire Union Elementary	Modesto
185	40.9	Norwalk-La Mirada Unified	Norwalk
185	40.9	San Rafael City Elementary	San Rafael
185	40.9	Visalia Unified	Visalia
189	40.8	Hesperia Unified	Hesperia
190	40.7	Lemon Grove Elementary	Lemon Grove
191	40.6	Los Banos Unified	Los Banos
192	40.4	Beaumont Unified	Beaumont
193	40.3	Mountain Empire Unified	Pine Valley
194	40.1	Burton Elementary	Porterville
195	40.0	Eureka City Unified	Eureka
196	39.9	Savanna Elementary	Anaheim
196	39.9	Willits Unified	Willits
198	39.8	Southern Kern Unified	Rosamond
199	39.5	Red Bluff Union Elementary	Red Bluff
200	39.3	Redwood City Elementary	Redwood City
201	39.2	Alvord Unified	Riverside
202	39.1	Santa Rosa Elementary	Santa Rosa
203	39.0	Victor Valley Union High	Victorville
204	38.9	Standard Elementary	Bakersfield
205	38.3	Colton Joint Unified	Colton
206	38.2	Lakeport Unified	Lakeport
207	37.5	Brawley Union High	Brawley
208	37.4	Oroville Union High	Oroville
209	37.3	Yuba City Unified	Yuba City
210	37.2	Cajon Valley Union Elementary	El Cajon
210	37.2	Perris Union High	Perris
212	37.0	Winters Joint Unified	Winters
213	36.9	Bellflower Unified	Bellflower
213	36.9	Gilroy Unified	Gilroy
213	36.9	Santa Paula Union High	Santa Paula
216	36.7	Salinas Union High	Salinas
217	36.4	Glendale Unified	Glendale
217	36.4	Kern Union High	Bakersfield
217	36.4	Riverside Unified	Riverside
220	36.3	West Contra Costa Unified	Richmond
221	36.0	Hayward Unified	Hayward
222	35.8	Oceanside Unified	Oceanside
223	35.6	Galt Joint Union Elementary	Galt
224	35.2	Covina-Valley Unified	Covina
225	34.6	Apple Valley Unified	Apple Valley
226	34.3	Central Unified	Fresno
227	33.9	Sweetwater Union High	Chula Vista
228	33.8	Hughson Unified	Hughson
229	33.7	Centralia Elementary	Buena Park
230	33.5	Redding Elementary	Redding
231	33.4	Lompoc Unified	Lompoc
231	33.4	Monterey Peninsula Unified	Monterey
233	33.1	Downey Unified	Downey
233	33.1	Keyes Union Elementary	Keyes
235	33.0	Fallbrook Union Elementary	Fallbrook
235	33.0	Lucia Mar Unified	Arroyo Grande
237	32.6	Tulare Joint Union High	Tulare
238	32.3	Linden Unified	Linden
239	32.2	Anaheim Union High	Anaheim
239	32.2	River Delta Joint Unified	Rio Vista
241	32.1	Cloverdale Unified	Cloverdale
242	31.8	Red Bluff Joint Union High	Red Bluff
243	31.6	Newport-Mesa Unified	Costa Mesa
244	31.5	Carpinteria Unified	Carpinteria
245	31.3	San Jose Unified	San Jose
245	31.3	Vallejo City Unified	Vallejo
247	31.0	Central Union Elementary	Lemoore
247	31.0	Redlands Unified	Redlands
249	30.6	Anderson Union High	Anderson
250	30.5	Hollister SD	Hollister
250	30.5	Jefferson Elementary	Daly City
250	30.5	Santa Rita Union Elementary	Salinas
253	30.2	Vista Unified	Vista
254	30.0	Panama Buena Vista Union Elem	Bakersfield
254	30.0	San Marcos Unified	San Marcos
256	29.9	Bear Valley Unified	Big Bear Lake
256	29.9	Santa Cruz City Elementary	Santa Cruz
256	29.9	Sierra Sands Unified	Ridgecrest
259	29.8	Dixon Unified	Dixon
260	29.6	Lake Tahoe Unified	S Lake Tahoe
260	29.6	Waterford Unified	Waterford
262	29.3	Bonsall Union Elementary	Bonsall
262	29.3	La Mesa-Spring Valley	La Mesa
264	29.2	Elk Grove Unified	Elk Grove
265	29.1	Chico Unified	Chico
265	29.1	Fullerton Elementary	Fullerton
267	29.0	San Bernardino County Supt.	San Bernardino
268	28.9	Bishop Union Elementary	Bishop
268	28.9	Oxnard Union High	Oxnard
270	28.7	Kingsburg Elementary Charter	Kingsburg
271	28.6	Berkeley Unified	Berkeley
271	28.6	Oakdale Joint Unified	Oakdale
271	28.6	Paradise Unified	Paradise
274	28.3	West Covina Unified	West Covina
275	28.2	Mariposa County Unified	Mariposa
276	28.0	ABC Unified	Cerritos
277	27.9	Lake Elsinore Unified	Lake Elsinore
278	27.8	John Swett Unified	Crockett
279	27.7	Escalon Unified	Escalon
280	27.6	Hilmar Unified	Hilmar
281	27.5	Live Oak Elementary	Santa Cruz
281	27.5	Orange Unified	Orange
283	27.3	Mountain View-Whisman Elementary	Mountain View
284	27.1	Lincoln Unified	Stockton
284	27.1	Woodland Joint Unified	Woodland
286	26.9	Antelope Valley Union High	Lancaster
286	26.9	Chula Vista Elementary	Chula Vista
286	26.9	Sonoma Valley Unified	Sonoma
289	26.8	Paso Robles Joint Unified	Paso Robles
290	26.6	Burbank Unified	Burbank
290	26.6	Oak Grove Elementary	San Jose
292	26.5	Plumas Unified	Quincy
293	26.0	Healdsburg Unified	Healdsburg
293	26.0	Santa Clara Unified	Santa Clara
295	25.9	Ocean View Elementary	Huntington Bch
296	25.8	Corona-Norco Unified	Norco
297	25.7	Fairfield-Suisun Unified	Fairfield
297	25.7	Upland Unified	Upland
297	25.7	Valley Center-Pauma Unified	Valley Center
300	25.5	Fallbrook Union High	Fallbrook
301	25.4	Auburn Union Elementary	Auburn
301	25.4	Sunnyvale Elementary	Sunnyvale
303	25.2	Los Angeles County Office of Ed	Downey
304	25.1	East Whittier City Elementary	Whittier
304	25.1	Modesto City High	Modesto
306	24.9	Campbell Union Elementary	Campbell
306	24.9	Grass Valley Elementary	Grass Valley
306	24.9	Napa Valley Unified	Napa
306	24.9	San Lorenzo Unified	San Lorenzo
310	24.8	East Side Union High	San Jose
310	24.8	Tustin Unified	Tustin
310	24.8	Yucaipa-Calimesa Joint Unified	Yucaipa
313	24.4	Silver Valley Unified	Yermo
314	24.2	Sierra Unified	Auberry
315	24.0	Temple City Unified	Temple City
316	23.8	Imperial Unified	Imperial
316	23.8	Manteca Unified	Manteca
316	23.8	Morongo Unified	Twentynine Plms
316	23.8	Rim of The World Unified	Lake Arrowhead
316	23.8	Whittier Union High	Whittier
321	23.7	Mountain View Elementary	Ontario
322	23.6	Culver City Unified	Culver City
322	23.6	Tehachapi Unified	Tehachapi
322	23.6	Windsor Unified	Windsor
325	23.5	Newhall Elementary	Valencia
325	23.5	Ventura Unified	Ventura
327	23.3	Sylvan Union Elementary	Modesto
328	23.2	Wiseburn Elementary	Hawthorne
329	23.1	Folsom-Cordova Unified	Folsom
329	23.1	Saint Helena Unified	Saint Helena
331	22.9	Antioch Unified	Antioch
332	22.7	New Haven Unified	Union City
333	22.4	Alameda City Unified	Alameda
334	22.2	Moorpark Unified	Moorpark
335	21.8	Calaveras Unified	San Andreas
335	21.8	Evergreen Elementary	San Jose
335	21.8	Turlock Joint Union High	Turlock
338	21.7	Milpitas Unified	Milpitas
338	21.7	Sulphur Springs Union Elementary	Canyon Country
340	21.6	Galt Joint Union High	Galt
341	21.4	Central Elementary	Rcho Cucamong
342	21.3	Wheatland Elementary	Wheatland
343	21.2	Ramona City Unified	Ramona
344	21.1	Black Oak Mine Unified	Georgetown
344	21.1	Lemoore Union High	Lemoore
346	20.9	San Leandro Unified	San Leandro
346	20.9	South San Francisco Unified	S San Francisco
348	20.7	Salida Union Elementary	Salida
349	20.6	Clovis Unified	Clovis
349	20.6	Goleta Union Elementary	Goleta
351	20.5	Mount Diablo Unified	Concord
352	20.4	Snowline Joint Unified	Phelan
353	20.3	Amador County Unified	Jackson
353	20.3	Chino Valley Unified	Chino
353	20.3	San Bruno Park Elementary	San Bruno
353	20.3	Santa Maria Joint Union High	Santa Maria
357	20.2	Natomas Unified	Sacramento
358	20.1	Center Joint Unified	Antelope
359	20.0	San Mateo-Foster City Elementary	San Mateo
360	19.7	Placentia-Yorba Linda Unified	Placentia
361	19.5	Petaluma City Elementary	Petaluma
362	19.4	Brentwood Union Elementary	Brentwood
363	19.1	Charter Oak Unified	Covina
363	19.1	Mother Lode Union Elementary	Placerville
365	19.0	Lakeside Union Elementary	Lakeside
366	18.9	Cypress Elementary	Cypress
367	18.8	Bonita Unified	San Dimas
367	18.8	Newark Unified	Newark
369	18.6	Berryessa Union Elementary	San Jose
369	18.6	Morgan Hill Unified	Morgan Hill
371	18.0	Vacaville Unified	Vacaville
372	17.9	Menifee Union Elementary	Menifee
372	17.9	Soquel Union Elementary	Capitola
374	17.7	Hanford Joint Union High	Hanford
374	17.7	Westside Union Elementary	Lancaster
376	17.6	Santa Monica-Malibu Unified	Santa Monica
377	17.2	Cabrillo Unified	Half Moon Bay
378	16.8	Ojai Unified	Ojai
378	16.8	San Luis Coastal Unified	San Luis Obispo
380	16.6	Gorman Elementary	Gorman
380	16.6	Oakley Union Elementary	Oakley
380	16.6	Tracy Joint Unified	Tracy
383	16.4	Moreland Elementary	San Jose
383	16.4	Tahoe-Truckee Joint Unified	Truckee
385	16.2	Claremont Unified	Claremont
386	16.0	Santa Barbara High	Santa Barbara
387	15.8	Santee Elementary	Santee
387	15.8	Sequoia Union High	Redwood City
389	15.7	Roseville City Elementary	Roseville
390	15.6	Sonora Union High	Sonora
391	15.4	Orcutt Union Elementary	Orcutt
392	15.0	Fresno County Office of Ed	Fresno
393	14.9	Redondo Beach Unified	Redondo Beach
394	14.7	Grossmont Union High	La Mesa
395	14.6	Chaffey Joint Union High	Ontario
395	14.6	Piner-Olivet Union Elementary	Santa Rosa
397	14.4	Acton-Agua Dulce Unified	Acton
398	14.3	Rincon Valley Union Elementary	Santa Rosa
399	14.1	Jefferson Union High	Daly City
399	14.1	Middletown Unified	Middletown
401	13.7	Westwood Unified	Westwood
402	13.6	Carlsbad Unified	Carlsbad
403	13.5	Muroc Joint Unified	North Edwards
404	13.4	Atascadero Unified	Atascadero
404	13.4	Old Adobe Union Elementary	Petaluma
406	12.9	Cambrian Elementary	San Jose
406	12.9	Ripon Unified	Ripon
408	12.8	Huntington Beach Union High	Huntington Bch
409	12.3	Etiwanda Elementary	Etiwanda
410	12.2	Santa Rosa High	Santa Rosa
411	12.1	Lowell Joint	Whittier
412	12.0	Encinitas Union Elementary	Encinitas
413	11.9	Simi Valley Unified	Simi Valley
413	11.9	Western Placer Unified	Lincoln
415	11.5	Martinez Unified	Martinez
416	11.4	Torrance Unified	Torrance
417	11.3	Cotati-Rohnert Park Unified	Rohnert Park
418	11.1	Brea-Olinda Unified	Brea
418	11.1	Fruitvale Elementary	Bakersfield
418	11.1	Mark West Union Elementary	Santa Rosa
421	11.0	Shasta Union High	Redding
422	10.9	Alpine Union Elementary	Alpine
422	10.9	Glendora Unified	Glendora
422	10.9	Santa Cruz City High	Santa Cruz
425	10.8	San Rafael City High	San Rafael
426	10.4	Castaic Union Elementary	Valencia
426	10.4	Dry Creek Joint Elementary	Roseville
428	10.2	Huntington Beach City Elementary	Huntington Bch
428	10.2	Livermore Valley Joint Unified	Livermore
428	10.2	Pleasant Valley School	Camarillo
431	10.0	Alta Loma Elementary	Alta Loma
432	9.9	Laguna Salada Union Elementary	Pacifica
433	9.8	Albany City Unified	Albany
434	9.6	Union Elementary	San Jose
435	9.5	Mountain View-Los Altos Union High	Mountain View
436	9.4	Escondido Union High	Escondido
436	9.4	Jefferson Elementary	Tracy
438	9.3	Novato Unified	Novato
439	9.2	Fremont Unified	Fremont
440	9.1	Castro Valley Unified	Castro Valley
441	9.0	Saddleback Valley Unified	Mission Viejo
441	9.0	Temecula Valley Unified	Temecula
443	8.9	Murrieta Valley Unified	Murrieta
443	8.9	Pleasant Ridge Union Elementary	Grass Valley
445	8.8	Julian Union Elementary	Julian
446	8.7	Conejo Valley Unified	Thousand Oaks
446	8.7	Rosedale Union Elementary	Bakersfield
446	8.7	Travis Unified	Travis Afb
449	8.5	San Benito High	Hollister
450	8.4	West Sonoma County Union High	Sebastopol
451	8.3	William S Hart Union High	Santa Clarita

452	8.1	Petaluma Joint Union High	Petaluma
452	8.1	San Lorenzo Valley Unified	Felton
454	8.0	Davis Joint Unified	Davis
455	7.6	Templeton Unified	Templeton
456	7.5	Liberty Union High	Brentwood
457	7.4	Saugus Union Elementary	Santa Clarita
458	7.3	Dublin Unified	Dublin
459	7.1	Fountain Valley Elementary	Fountain Valley
459	7.1	Pacific Grove Unified	Pacific Grove
459	7.1	Rocklin Unified	Rocklin
459	7.1	Roseville Joint Union High	Roseville
463	6.9	Laguna Beach Unified	Laguna Beach
463	6.9	Solana Beach Elementary	Solana Beach
465	6.8	Northern Humboldt Union High	McKinleyville
466	6.6	Rescue Union Elementary	Rescue
466	6.6	San Juan Unified	Carmichael
468	6.5	Benicia Unified	Benicia
468	6.5	Carmel Unified	Carmel
470	6.4	El Segundo Unified	El Segundo
471	6.3	El Dorado Union High	Placerville
471	6.3	Loomis Union Elementary	Loomis
473	6.2	Norris Elementary	Bakersfield
474	6.1	Placer Union High	Auburn
475	5.7	Los Alamitos Unified	Los Alamitos
475	5.7	Nevada Joint Union High	Grass Valley
477	5.6	Poway Unified	Poway
478	5.5	Arcadia Unified	Arcadia
478	5.5	Walnut Valley Unified	Walnut
480	5.4	Santa Clara County Office of Ed	San Jose
481	5.2	Campbell Union High	San Jose
481	5.2	Fullerton Joint Union High	Fullerton
481	5.2	Ross Valley Elementary	San Anselmo
484	5.1	South Pasadena Unified	South Pasadena
485	4.7	Buckeye Union Elementary	Shingle Springs
485	4.7	Capistrano Unified	San Juan Capis
487	4.6	San Dieguito Union High	Encinitas
488	4.5	Irvine Unified	Irvine
489	4.4	Millbrae Elementary	Millbrae
490	4.3	Walnut Creek Elementary	Walnut Creek
491	4.1	Oro Grande Elementary	Oro Grande
492	4.0	Beverly Hills Unified	Beverly Hills
493	3.9	Jamul-Dulzura Union Elementary	Jamul
493	3.9	San Mateo Union High	San Mateo
495	3.8	Palo Alto Unified	Palo Alto
496	3.3	Dixie Elementary	San Rafael
497	3.2	Burlingame Elementary	Burlingame
497	3.2	Cupertino Union School	Cupertino
497	3.2	Manhattan Beach Unified	Manhattan Beach
497	3.2	Scotts Valley Unified	Scotts Valley
501	3.1	Belmont-Redwood Shores Elementary	Belmont
501	3.1	Fremont Union High	Sunnyvale
503	3.0	Eureka Union Elementary	Granite Bay
504	2.8	Coronado Unified	Coronado
504	2.8	Pleasanton Unified	Pleasanton
506	2.3	Julian Union High	Julian
506	2.3	Menlo Park City Elementary	Atherton
508	1.7	Del Mar Union Elementary	Del Mar
508	1.7	Orange County Office of Ed	Costa Mesa
508	1.7	San Carlos Elementary	San Carlos
511	1.6	Mill Valley Elementary	Mill Valley
512	1.5	Las Virgenes Unified	Calabasas
512	1.5	Los Gatos Union Elementary	Los Gatos
512	1.5	Palos Verdes Peninsula Unified	Palos Verdes Est
515	1.4	Los Altos Elementary	Los Altos
515	1.4	Tamalpais Union High	Larkspur
517	1.0	Oak Park Unified	Oak Park
518	0.8	Moraga Elementary	Moraga
519	0.7	San Ramon Valley Unified	Danville
520	0.6	San Marino Unified	San Marino
521	0.5	Los Gatos-Saratoga Jt Union High	Los Gatos
521	0.5	Saratoga Union Elementary	Saratoga
523	0.4	Acalanes Union High	Lafayette
523	0.4	La Canada Unified	La Canada
525	0.3	Orinda Union Elementary	Orinda
526	0.2	Riverside County Office of Ed	Riverside
526	0.2	Twin Ridges Elementary	North San Juan
528	0.1	Lafayette Elementary	Lafayette
529	0.0	Piedmont City Unified	Piedmont

Students Eligible for Reduced-Price Lunch

Rank	Percent	District Name	City
1	26.8	Twin Ridges Elementary	North San Juan
2	24.6	Wheatland Elementary	Wheatland
3	24.2	Santa Paula Elementary	Santa Paula
4	22.5	Gorman Elementary	Gorman
5	20.4	Rosemead Elementary	Rosemead
6	20.2	Anderson Union High	Anderson
7	20.1	Ocean View Elementary	Oxnard
8	20.0	Little Lake City Elementary	Santa Fe Spgs
9	19.9	Anaheim Elementary	Anaheim
10	19.2	Salinas City Elementary	Salinas
11	19.1	Perris Elementary	Perris
12	19.0	Downey Unified	Downey
13	18.9	Whittier City Elementary	Whittier
14	18.8	Alisal Union Elementary	Salinas
15	18.7	Santa Barbara Elementary	Santa Barbara
16	18.6	Burton Elementary	Porterville
17	18.5	Pittsburg Unified	Pittsburg
17	18.5	South Bay Union Elementary	Imperial Beach
19	18.4	Lemon Grove Elementary	Lemon Grove
20	18.3	Central Union Elementary	Lemoore
21	17.8	Jefferson Elementary	Daly City
22	17.7	King City Union Elementary	King City
23	17.6	Azusa Unified	Azusa
24	17.3	Calexico Unified	Calexico
24	17.3	Greenfield Union Elementary	Greenfield
24	17.3	Lawndale Elementary	Lawndale
27	17.1	Hemet Unified	Hemet
28	16.9	Beaumont Unified	Beaumont
28	16.9	Hacienda La Puente Unified	City of Industry
30	16.8	West Covina Unified	West Covina
31	16.7	Santa Rita Union Elementary	Salinas
32	16.6	Delano Joint Union High	Delano
33	16.5	Cascade Union Elementary	Anderson
34	16.4	Hueneme Elementary	Port Hueneme
35	16.3	Bellevue Union Elementary	Santa Rosa
35	16.3	Live Oak Unified	Live Oak
35	16.3	Magnolia Elementary	Anaheim
38	16.2	Mount Pleasant Elementary	San Jose
38	16.2	Silver Valley Unified	Yermo
40	16.1	San Francisco Unified	San Francisco
41	16.0	Enterprise Elementary	Redding
42	15.9	Buena Park Elementary	Buena Park
42	15.9	Chula Vista Elementary	Chula Vista
42	15.9	Livingston Union Elementary	Livingston
42	15.9	Rio Elementary	Oxnard
42	15.9	Santa Ana Unified	Santa Ana
47	15.8	Val Verde Unified	Perris
48	15.7	Cucamonga Elementary	Rcho Cucamong
48	15.7	Greenfield Union Elementary	Bakersfield
48	15.7	Palmdale Elementary	Palmdale
51	15.6	Bassett Unified	La Puente
52	15.5	Standard Elementary	Bakersfield
53	15.4	Alum Rock Union Elementary	San Jose
53	15.4	Oxnard Elementary	Oxnard
55	15.3	Alhambra City Elementary	Alhambra
55	15.3	Patterson Joint Unified	Patterson
57	15.2	Banning Unified	Banning
57	15.2	Empire Union Elementary	Modesto
57	15.2	Monrovia Unified	Monrovia
57	15.2	Palm Springs Unified	Palm Springs
57	15.2	Robla Elementary	Sacramento
57	15.2	Wiseburn Elementary	Hawthorne
63	15.1	Kerman Unified	Kerman
64	15.0	El Rancho Unified	Pico Rivera
64	15.0	Romoland Elementary	Homeland
66	14.9	Gonzales Unified	Gonzales
67	14.8	Duarte Unified	Duarte
67	14.8	Hawthorne Elementary	Hawthorne
67	14.8	King City Joint Union High	King City
67	14.8	Santa Rosa Elementary	Santa Rosa
71	14.6	Bellflower Unified	Bellflower
72	14.5	Eastside Union Elementary	Lancaster
72	14.5	Fontana Unified	Fontana
72	14.5	Santa Maria-Bonita Elementary	Santa Maria
72	14.5	Tehachapi Unified	Tehachapi
76	14.4	Beardsley Elementary	Bakersfield
76	14.4	Moreno Valley Unified	Moreno Valley
78	14.3	Salinas Union High	Salinas
79	14.2	Savanna Elementary	Anaheim
80	14.1	Baldwin Park Unified	Baldwin Park
80	14.1	Escondido Union Elementary	Escondido
80	14.1	Franklin-Mckinley Elementary	San Jose
80	14.1	Redwood City Elementary	Redwood City
84	14.0	Alvord Unified	Riverside
85	13.9	Hesperia Unified	Hesperia
86	13.8	Adelanto Elementary	Adelanto
86	13.8	Hollister SD	Hollister
86	13.8	Montebello Unified	Montebello
89	13.7	San Bernardino City Unified	San Bernardino
90	13.6	Garden Grove Unified	Garden Grove
91	13.5	Mountain View Elementary	Ontario
92	13.4	La Habra City Elementary	La Habra
92	13.4	Rowland Unified	Rowland Heights
92	13.4	San Ysidro Elementary	San Ysidro
95	13.3	Atwater Elementary	Atwater
95	13.3	Lake Tahoe Unified	S Lake Tahoe
95	13.3	Paramount Unified	Paramount
98	13.2	Hanford Elementary	Hanford
98	13.2	Ravenswood City Elementary	East Palo Alto
98	13.2	San Jacinto Unified	San Jacinto
98	13.2	San Juan Unified	Carmichael
102	13.1	Keppel Union Elementary	Pearblossom
102	13.1	Westminster Elementary	Westminster
104	13.0	Capistrano Unified	San Juan Capis
104	13.0	Riverbank Unified	Riverbank
106	12.8	Lake Elsinore Unified	Lake Elsinore
106	12.8	Lamont Elementary	Lamont
106	12.8	Los Banos Unified	Los Banos
109	12.7	Corona-Norco Unified	Norco
109	12.7	Oceanside Unified	Oceanside
111	12.5	Auburn Union Elementary	Auburn
111	12.5	Jurupa Unified	Riverside
111	12.5	Pomona Unified	Pomona
114	12.4	Saint Helena Unified	Saint Helena
114	12.4	South Whittier Elementary	Whittier
114	12.4	Taft City Elementary	Taft
117	12.3	Farmersville Unified	Farmersville
117	12.3	Madera Unified	Madera
117	12.3	Merced Union High	Atwater
117	12.3	Rio Linda Union Elementary	Rio Linda
117	12.3	Riverdale Joint Unified	Riverdale
117	12.3	Santa Clara Unified	Santa Clara
123	12.2	Garvey Elementary	Rosemead
123	12.2	Sweetwater Union High	Chula Vista
125	12.1	Carpinteria Unified	Carpinteria
125	12.1	Firebaugh-Las Deltas Joint Unified	Firebaugh
125	12.1	Tulare City Elementary	Tulare
128	12.0	Cajon Valley Union Elementary	El Cajon
128	12.0	Colton Joint Unified	Colton
128	12.0	Dinuba Unified	Dinuba
128	12.0	Exeter Union Elementary	Exeter
128	12.0	Lemoore Union Elementary	Lemoore
128	12.0	Newman-Crows Landing Unified	Newman
128	12.0	Travis Unified	Travis Afb
135	11.9	La Mesa-Spring Valley	La Mesa
135	11.9	Ontario-Montclair Elementary	Ontario
137	11.8	Desert Sands Unified	La Quinta
137	11.8	Fort Bragg Unified	Fort Bragg
137	11.8	Morongo Unified	Twentynine Plms
137	11.8	Riverside Unified	Riverside
137	11.8	Washington Unified	West Sacramento
142	11.7	Galt Joint Union Elementary	Galt
142	11.7	Live Oak Elementary	Santa Cruz
142	11.7	Lucia Mar Unified	Arroyo Grande
142	11.7	Panama Buena Vista Union Elem	Bakersfield
146	11.6	Anaheim Union High	Anaheim
146	11.6	Chowchilla Elementary	Chowchilla
146	11.6	Coachella Valley Unified	Thermal
146	11.6	North Sacramento Elementary	Sacramento
146	11.6	Santa Paula Union High	Santa Paula
151	11.5	Brawley Elementary	Brawley
151	11.5	Covina-Valley Unified	Covina
151	11.5	El Centro Elementary	El Centro
151	11.5	Kingsburg Elementary Charter	Kingsburg
151	11.5	Oroville City Elementary	Oroville
151	11.5	Redlands Unified	Redlands
151	11.5	Victor Elementary	Victorville
158	11.4	Grass Valley Elementary	Grass Valley
158	11.4	North Monterey County Unified	Moss Landing
158	11.4	Ventura Unified	Ventura
161	11.3	Earlimart Elementary	Earlimart
161	11.3	Long Beach Unified	Long Beach
161	11.3	San Gabriel Unified	San Gabriel
161	11.3	Ukiah Unified	Ukiah
165	11.2	Apple Valley Unified	Apple Valley
165	11.2	Ceres Unified	Ceres
165	11.2	Marysville Joint Unified	Marysville
165	11.2	Wasco Union Elementary	Wasco
169	11.1	Alhambra City High	Alhambra
169	11.1	Bishop Union Elementary	Bishop
169	11.1	Hayward Unified	Hayward
169	11.1	Modesto City Elementary	Modesto
169	11.1	Piner-Olivet Union Elementary	Santa Rosa
169	11.1	Vista Unified	Vista
169	11.1	West Contra Costa Unified	Richmond
176	11.0	Lompoc Unified	Lompoc
176	11.0	Orland Joint Unified	Orland
176	11.0	Selma Unified	Selma
179	10.9	Fillmore Unified	Fillmore
179	10.9	Goleta Union Elementary	Goleta
179	10.9	Sunnyvale Elementary	Sunnyvale
179	10.9	Willits Unified	Willits
183	10.8	Centralia Elementary	Buena Park
183	10.8	Delhi Unified	Delhi
183	10.8	Fruitvale Elementary	Bakersfield
183	10.8	Kings Canyon Joint Unified	Reedley
187	10.7	Central Elementary	Rcho Cucamong
187	10.7	El Monte Union High	El Monte
187	10.7	Fowler Unified	Fowler
187	10.7	Merced City Elementary	Merced
187	10.7	San Diego Unified	San Diego
192	10.6	Lakeside Union Elementary	Lakeside
192	10.6	Red Bluff Union Elementary	Red Bluff
194	10.5	Central Unified	Fresno

Rank	Score	District	City
195	10.4	Gustine Unified	Gustine
195	10.4	Napa Valley Unified	Napa
195	10.4	San Leandro Unified	San Leandro
195	10.4	Southern Kern Unified	Rosamond
195	10.4	Wilsona Elementary	Palmdale
200	10.3	Dixon Unified	Dixon
200	10.3	Lennox Elementary	Lennox
200	10.3	San Bruno Park Elementary	San Bruno
200	10.3	Sanger Unified	Sanger
200	10.3	Yuba City Unified	Yuba City
205	10.2	Gateway Unified	Redding
205	10.2	Lancaster Elementary	Lancaster
205	10.2	Oak Grove Elementary	San Jose
205	10.2	Salida Union Elementary	Salida
209	10.1	Central Union High	El Centro
209	10.1	Konocti Unified	Lower Lake
211	10.0	Culver City Unified	Culver City
211	10.0	Grant Joint Union High	Sacramento
211	10.0	Hughson Unified	Hughson
211	10.0	Monterey Peninsula Unified	Monterey
211	10.0	Pajaro Valley Unified School	Watsonville
211	10.0	Redding Elementary	Redding
211	10.0	San Jose Unified	San Jose
218	9.9	Temple City Unified	Temple City
218	9.9	Windsor Unified	Windsor
220	9.8	Amador County Unified	Jackson
220	9.8	Barstow Unified	Barstow
220	9.8	Cypress Elementary	Cypress
220	9.8	Rialto Unified	Rialto
220	9.8	Winters Joint Unified	Winters
225	9.7	Weaver Union Elementary	Merced
226	9.6	Corning Union Elementary	Corning
226	9.6	Elk Grove Unified	Elk Grove
228	9.5	El Monte City Elementary	El Monte
228	9.5	Fallbrook Union Elementary	Fallbrook
228	9.5	Mother Lode Union Elementary	Placerville
228	9.5	Muroc Joint Unified	North Edwards
228	9.5	Santa Cruz City Elementary	Santa Cruz
233	9.4	Mountain View-Whisman Elementary	Mountain View
233	9.4	Plumas Unified	Quincy
233	9.4	Vallejo City Unified	Vallejo
233	9.4	Woodland Joint Unified	Woodland
237	9.3	Hilmar Unified	Hilmar
237	9.3	Manteca Unified	Manteca
239	9.2	Arvin Union Elementary	Arvin
239	9.2	Kelseyville Unified	Kelseyville
239	9.2	Milpitas Unified	Milpitas
239	9.2	San Lorenzo Unified	San Lorenzo
239	9.2	San Rafael City Elementary	San Rafael
239	9.2	Victor Valley Union High	Victorville
239	9.2	Yucaipa-Calimesa Joint Unified	Yucaipa
246	9.1	Bakersfield City Elementary	Bakersfield
246	9.1	Del Norte County Unified	Crescent City
246	9.1	Inglewood Unified	Inglewood
246	9.1	Norwalk-La Mirada Unified	Norwalk
246	9.1	Paso Robles Joint Unified	Paso Robles
246	9.1	San Marcos Unified	San Marcos
246	9.1	Sylvan Union Elementary	Modesto
253	9.0	Centinela Valley Union High	Lawndale
253	9.0	Eureka City Unified	Eureka
253	9.0	Glendale Unified	Glendale
256	8.9	Bonsall Union Elementary	Bonsall
256	8.9	Lemoore Union High	Lemoore
256	8.9	Lodi Unified	Lodi
256	8.9	Mountain Empire Unified	Pine Valley
256	8.9	Turlock Joint Elementary	Turlock
261	8.8	Imperial Unified	Imperial
261	8.8	Natomas Unified	Sacramento
261	8.8	Orcutt Union Elementary	Orcutt
261	8.8	Tustin Unified	Tustin
265	8.7	Oakland Unified	Oakland
265	8.7	Stanislaus Union Elementary	Modesto
265	8.7	Willows Unified	Willows
268	8.6	Antioch Unified	Antioch
268	8.6	Coalinga-Huron Joint Unified	Coalinga
268	8.6	Colusa Unified	Colusa
268	8.6	San Mateo-Foster City Elementary	San Mateo
272	8.5	Center Joint Unified	Antelope
272	8.5	East Whittier City Elementary	Whittier
272	8.5	Fairfield-Suisun Unified	Fairfield
272	8.5	Holtville Unified	Holtville
272	8.5	Lakeport Unified	Lakeport
272	8.5	Lindsay Unified	Lindsay
278	8.4	Pasadena Unified	Pasadena
278	8.4	Perris Union High	Perris
278	8.4	Sierra Unified	Auberry
278	8.4	South San Francisco Unified	S San Francisco
282	8.3	Calaveras Unified	San Andreas
282	8.3	Corcoran Joint Unified	Corcoran
282	8.3	Fullerton Elementary	Fullerton
282	8.3	Santee Elementary	Santee
286	8.2	Berryessa Union Elementary	San Jose
286	8.2	Valley Center-Pauma Unified	Valley Center
288	8.1	Cloverdale Unified	Cloverdale
288	8.1	Mariposa County Unified	Mariposa
288	8.1	Palo Verde Unified	Blythe
288	8.1	Sierra Sands Unified	Ridgecrest
288	8.1	Soquel Union Elementary	Capitola
293	7.9	Chino Valley Unified	Chino
293	7.9	Etiwanda Elementary	Etiwanda
293	7.9	Gilroy Unified	Gilroy
293	7.9	Healdsburg Unified	Healdsburg
293	7.9	Jefferson Union High	Daly City
293	7.9	San Luis Coastal Unified	San Luis Obispo
299	7.8	Bear Valley Unified	Big Bear Lake
299	7.8	Campbell Union Elementary	Campbell
299	7.8	Porterville Unified	Porterville
299	7.8	Sonoma Valley Unified	Sonoma
303	7.7	Alameda City Unified	Alameda
303	7.7	Rincon Valley Union Elementary	Santa Rosa
303	7.7	Whittier Union High	Whittier
306	7.6	Oakdale Joint Unified	Oakdale
306	7.6	Ocean View Elementary	Huntington Bch
306	7.6	Paradise Unified	Paradise
306	7.6	Soledad Unified	Soledad
306	7.6	Sulphur Springs Union Elementary	Canyon Country
306	7.6	Visalia Unified	Visalia
312	7.5	Atascadero Unified	Atascadero
312	7.5	Lincoln Unified	Stockton
312	7.5	Ramona City Unified	Ramona
312	7.5	Roseville City Elementary	Roseville
316	7.4	Berkeley Unified	Berkeley
316	7.4	Escalon Unified	Escalon
316	7.4	Linden Unified	Linden
316	7.4	New Haven Unified	Union City
320	7.3	Dry Creek Joint Elementary	Roseville
320	7.3	Fallbrook Union High	Fallbrook
320	7.3	Moreland Elementary	San Jose
323	7.2	Brea-Olinda Unified	Brea
323	7.2	Cabrillo Unified	Half Moon Bay
323	7.2	Los Angeles Unified	Los Angeles
326	7.1	Brawley Union High	Brawley
326	7.1	Clovis Unified	Clovis
326	7.1	Waterford Unified	Waterford
329	7.0	ABC Unified	Cerritos
329	7.0	Evergreen Elementary	San Jose
331	6.9	Black Oak Mine Unified	Georgetown
331	6.9	Julian Union Elementary	Julian
333	6.8	Santa Barbara High	Santa Barbara
333	6.8	Upland Unified	Upland
333	6.8	Vacaville Unified	Vacaville
336	6.7	Burbank Unified	Burbank
336	6.7	Charter Oak Unified	Covina
336	6.7	Chico Unified	Chico
336	6.7	Middletown Unified	Middletown
336	6.7	Newport-Mesa Unified	Costa Mesa
336	6.7	Old Adobe Union Elementary	Petaluma
342	6.6	Laguna Salada Union Elementary	Pacifica
342	6.6	Murrieta Valley Unified	Murrieta
342	6.6	Woodlake Union Elementary	Woodlake
345	6.5	Fresno Unified	Fresno
345	6.5	Gridley Unified	Gridley
345	6.5	Oakley Union Elementary	Oakley
345	6.5	Oroville Union High	Oroville
349	6.4	Ojai Unified	Ojai
349	6.4	Orange Unified	Orange
351	6.3	Cotati-Rohnert Park Unified	Rohnert Park
351	6.3	Del Paso Heights Elementary	Sacramento
351	6.3	Golden Plains Unified	San Joaquin
351	6.3	Mount Diablo Unified	Concord
355	6.2	Loomis Union Elementary	Loomis
355	6.2	Placentia-Yorba Linda Unified	Placentia
355	6.2	San Joaquin County Office of Ed	Stockton
358	6.1	Antelope Valley Union High	Lancaster
358	6.1	Kern County Office of Ed	Bakersfield
358	6.1	Mojave Unified	Mojave
358	6.1	Redondo Beach Unified	Redondo Beach
358	6.1	Thermalito Union Elementary	Oroville
363	6.0	Dos Palos Oro Loma Joint Unified	Dos Palos
363	6.0	Menifee Union Elementary	Menifee
363	6.0	Newark Unified	Newark
366	5.9	Alta Loma Elementary	Alta Loma
366	5.9	Bonita Unified	San Dimas
366	5.9	Santa Monica-Malibu Unified	Santa Monica
366	5.9	Tahoe-Truckee Joint Unified	Truckee
370	5.8	John Swett Unified	Crockett
370	5.8	Mcfarland Unified	Mcfarland
370	5.8	Rim of The World Unified	Lake Arrowhead
370	5.8	Snowline Joint Unified	Phelan
374	5.7	Brentwood Union Elementary	Brentwood
374	5.7	Cambrian Elementary	San Jose
374	5.7	Carlsbad Unified	Carlsbad
374	5.7	Oxnard Union High	Oxnard
374	5.7	Richland SD	Shafter
379	5.6	Kern Union High	Bakersfield
379	5.6	Petaluma City Elementary	Petaluma
379	5.6	Red Bluff Joint Union High	Red Bluff
382	5.5	Moorpark Unified	Moorpark
382	5.5	Rosedale Union Elementary	Bakersfield
382	5.5	Sacramento City Unified	Sacramento
385	5.4	Claremont Unified	Claremont
385	5.4	Folsom-Cordova Unified	Folsom
385	5.4	Mark West Union Elementary	Santa Rosa
385	5.4	Simi Valley Unified	Simi Valley
385	5.4	Westside Union Elementary	Lancaster
390	5.3	Lynwood Unified	Lynwood
390	5.3	Martinez Unified	Martinez
390	5.3	Pleasant Ridge Union Elementary	Grass Valley
390	5.3	Pleasant Valley School	Camarillo
394	5.2	Grossmont Union High	La Mesa
394	5.2	Newhall Elementary	Valencia
394	5.2	Western Placer Unified	Lincoln
397	5.1	Alpine Union Elementary	Alpine
397	5.1	Coronado Unified	Coronado
397	5.1	Tracy Joint Unified	Tracy
400	5.0	Norris Elementary	Bakersfield
400	5.0	Santa Maria Joint Union High	Santa Maria
400	5.0	Temecula Valley Unified	Temecula
403	4.9	Morgan Hill Unified	Morgan Hill
403	4.9	Stockton City Unified	Stockton
403	4.9	Torrance Unified	Torrance
406	4.8	Cutler-Orosi Joint Unified	Orosi
406	4.8	Jamul-Dulzura Union Elementary	Jamul
406	4.8	Lowell Joint	Whittier
406	4.8	Novato Unified	Novato
406	4.8	Santa Rosa High	Santa Rosa
406	4.8	Sequoia Union High	Redwood City
412	4.7	Ripon Unified	Ripon
412	4.7	River Delta Joint Unified	Rio Vista
414	4.5	San Diego County Office of Ed	San Diego
415	4.4	Compton Unified	Compton
415	4.4	Templeton Unified	Templeton
415	4.4	Turlock Joint Union High	Turlock
418	4.3	Fremont Unified	Fremont
418	4.3	Glendora Unified	Glendora
418	4.3	Modesto City High	Modesto
418	4.3	Rocklin Unified	Rocklin
422	4.2	Carmel Unified	Carmel
422	4.2	Fountain Valley Elementary	Fountain Valley
422	4.2	Keyes Union Elementary	Keyes
422	4.2	Westwood Unified	Westwood
426	4.1	Acton-Agua Dulce Unified	Acton
427	4.0	Castro Valley Unified	Castro Valley
427	4.0	Conejo Valley Unified	Thousand Oaks
427	4.0	Millbrae Elementary	Millbrae
427	4.0	San Lorenzo Valley Unified	Felton
431	3.9	Albany City Unified	Albany
431	3.9	Arcadia Unified	Arcadia
431	3.9	El Segundo Unified	El Segundo
431	3.9	Saugus Union Elementary	Santa Clarita
435	3.7	Encinitas Union Elementary	Encinitas
436	3.6	Chaffey Joint Union High	Ontario
436	3.6	East Side Union High	San Jose
436	3.6	Placer Union High	Auburn
436	3.6	Saddleback Valley Unified	Mission Viejo
436	3.6	Union Elementary	San Jose
441	3.5	Benicia Unified	Benicia
441	3.5	Mountain View Elementary	El Monte
441	3.5	West Sonoma County Union High	Sebastopol
444	3.4	Huntington Beach City Elementary	Huntington Bch
444	3.4	San Rafael City High	San Rafael
446	3.2	Galt Joint Union High	Galt
446	3.2	Shasta Union High	Redding
448	3.1	Castaic Union Elementary	Valencia
448	3.1	Dublin Unified	Dublin
448	3.1	Los Alamitos Unified	Los Alamitos
448	3.1	South Pasadena Unified	South Pasadena
448	3.1	Tulare Joint Union High	Tulare
448	3.1	Walnut Valley Unified	Walnut
454	2.9	Davis Joint Unified	Davis
454	2.9	Hanford Joint Union High	Hanford
454	2.9	Jefferson Elementary	Tracy
454	2.9	Santa Cruz City High	Santa Cruz
454	2.9	Sonora Union High	Sonora
459	2.8	El Dorado Union High	Placerville
459	2.8	Escondido Union High	Escondido
459	2.8	Livermore Valley Joint Unified	Livermore
459	2.8	Mendota Unified	Mendota
463	2.6	Beverly Hills Unified	Beverly Hills
463	2.6	Rescue Union Elementary	Rescue
465	2.5	Irvine Unified	Irvine
465	2.5	Poway Unified	Poway
467	2.4	Huntington Beach Union High	Huntington Bch
468	2.3	Buckeye Union Elementary	Shingle Springs
468	2.3	San Benito High	Hollister
468	2.3	Walnut Creek Elementary	Walnut Creek
471	2.2	Mountain View-Los Altos Union High	Mountain View
471	2.2	Nevada Joint Union High	Grass Valley

473	2.1	Laguna Beach Unified	Laguna Beach
473	2.1	Solana Beach Elementary	Solana Beach
475	2.0	Pacific Grove Unified	Pacific Grove
475	2.0	Palo Alto Unified	Palo Alto
475	2.0	William S Hart Union High	Santa Clarita
478	1.9	Campbell Union High	San Jose
479	1.8	Los Angeles County Office of Ed	Downey
479	1.8	Petaluma Joint Union High	Petaluma
481	1.7	San Mateo Union High	San Mateo
482	1.6	Burlingame Elementary	Burlingame
482	1.6	San Dieguito Union High	Encinitas
484	1.5	Ross Valley Elementary	San Anselmo
485	1.4	Las Virgenes Unified	Calabasas
485	1.4	Liberty Union High	Brentwood
487	1.3	Cupertino Union School	Cupertino
487	1.3	Manhattan Beach Unified	Manhattan Beach
487	1.3	Pleasanton Unified	Pleasanton
487	1.3	Scotts Valley Unified	Scotts Valley
491	1.2	Eureka Union Elementary	Granite Bay
492	1.0	San Bernardino County Supt.	San Bernardino
492	1.0	Santa Clara County Office of Ed	San Jose
494	0.9	Fremont Union High	Sunnyvale
494	0.9	Menlo Park City Elementary	Atherton
496	0.8	Los Gatos Union Elementary	Los Gatos
496	0.8	Mill Valley Elementary	Mill Valley
498	0.7	Fresno County Office of Ed	Fresno
498	0.7	Fullerton Joint Union High	Fullerton
498	0.7	Julian Union High	Julian
501	0.6	Del Mar Union Elementary	Del Mar
501	0.6	Palos Verdes Peninsula Unified	Palos Verdes Est
501	0.6	San Carlos Elementary	San Carlos
501	0.6	Tamalpais Union High	Larkspur
505	0.5	Dixie Elementary	San Rafael
505	0.5	Oak Park Unified	Oak Park
505	0.5	San Ramon Valley Unified	Danville
508	0.4	Northern Humboldt Union High	McKinleyville
508	0.4	Oro Grande Elementary	Oro Grande
510	0.3	La Canada Unified	La Canada
511	0.2	Roseville Joint Union High	Roseville
512	0.1	Acalanes Union High	Lafayette
512	0.1	Orange County Office of Ed	Costa Mesa
512	0.1	Riverside County Office of Ed	Riverside
512	0.1	San Marino Unified	San Marino
512	0.1	Saratoga Union Elementary	Saratoga
517	0.0	Los Altos Elementary	Los Altos
518	0.0	Belmont-Redwood Shores Elementary	Belmont
518	0.0	Delano Union Elementary	Delano
518	0.0	Lafayette Elementary	Lafayette
518	0.0	Los Gatos-Saratoga Jt Union High	Los Gatos
518	0.0	Los Nietos Elementary	Whittier
518	0.0	Moraga Elementary	Moraga
518	0.0	National Elementary	National City
518	0.0	Orinda Union Elementary	Orinda
518	0.0	Parlier Unified	Parlier
518	0.0	Piedmont City Unified	Piedmont
518	0.0	Reef-Sunset Unified	Avenal
518	0.0	Winton Elementary	Winton

Student/Teacher Ratio

Rank	Ratio	District Name	City
1	29.2	Fullerton Joint Union High	Fullerton
2	28.9	Charter Oak Unified	Covina
3	28.4	Westwood Unified	Westwood
4	27.5	Santa Paula Union High	Santa Paula
5	27.1	Oro Grande Elementary	Oro Grande
6	26.9	Gorman Elementary	Gorman
7	25.9	Centinela Valley Union High	Lawndale
7	25.9	Victor Valley Union High	Victorville
9	25.8	Modesto City High	Modesto
10	25.3	Antelope Valley Union High	Lancaster
11	25.2	Huntington Beach Union High	Huntington Bch
11	25.2	Lynwood Unified	Lynwood
13	25.1	Val Verde Unified	Perris
14	25.0	Whittier Union High	Whittier
15	24.9	King City Joint Union High	King City
15	24.9	Santa Maria Joint Union High	Santa Maria
17	24.7	Julian Union Elementary	Julian
18	24.6	William S Hart Union High	Santa Clarita
19	24.5	Anaheim Union High	Anaheim
19	24.5	El Monte Union High	El Monte
21	24.4	Liberty Union High	Brentwood
22	24.3	Oxnard Union High	Oxnard
22	24.3	Tulare Joint Union High	Tulare
24	24.2	Chaffey Joint Union High	Ontario
24	24.2	Hanford Joint Union High	Hanford
26	24.1	Julian Union High	Julian
27	24.0	Alta Loma Elementary	Alta Loma
28	23.9	Montebello Unified	Montebello
28	23.9	Santa Cruz City High	Santa Cruz
30	23.8	Grossmont Union High	La Mesa
31	23.6	Campbell Union High	San Jose
32	23.5	Alhambra City High	Alhambra
33	23.4	Irvine Unified	Irvine
33	23.4	Sonora Union High	Sonora
35	23.3	Acton-Agua Dulce Unified	Acton
35	23.3	Alisal Union Elementary	Salinas
35	23.3	Delano Joint Union High	Delano
35	23.3	San Benito High	Hollister
39	23.2	Amador County Unified	Jackson
39	23.2	Perris Union High	Perris
39	23.2	Rim of The World Unified	Lake Arrowhead
39	23.2	Riverside Unified	Riverside
43	23.1	Jamul-Dulzura Union Elementary	Jamul
43	23.1	Turlock Joint Union High	Turlock
43	23.1	Yucaipa-Calimesa Joint Unified	Yucaipa
46	23.0	Alvord Unified	Riverside
46	23.0	Bonita Unified	San Dimas
46	23.0	Compton Unified	Compton
46	23.0	Kern Union High	Bakersfield
46	23.0	Southern Kern Unified	Rosamond
46	23.0	Ventura Unified	Ventura
52	22.9	Glendora Unified	Glendora
52	22.9	Los Alamitos Unified	Los Alamitos
52	22.9	Merced Union High	Atwater
52	22.9	Murrieta Valley Unified	Murrieta
52	22.9	Ramona City Unified	Ramona
52	22.9	Simi Valley Unified	Simi Valley
58	22.8	Arcadia Unified	Arcadia
58	22.8	Chino Valley Unified	Chino
58	22.8	Downey Unified	Downey
58	22.8	Garden Grove Unified	Garden Grove
58	22.8	Livermore Valley Joint Unified	Livermore
58	22.8	South Pasadena Unified	South Pasadena
58	22.8	Victor Elementary	Victorville
65	22.7	Capistrano Unified	San Juan Capis
65	22.7	Huntington Beach City Elementary	Huntington Bch
65	22.7	Lake Elsinore Unified	Lake Elsinore
65	22.7	Lemoore Union High	Lemoore
65	22.7	Saddleback Valley Unified	Mission Viejo
70	22.6	Baldwin Park Unified	Baldwin Park
70	22.6	Coalinga-Huron Joint Unified	Coalinga
70	22.6	Mojave Unified	Mojave
70	22.6	Salinas Union High	Salinas
70	22.6	Shasta Union High	Redding
75	22.5	Anderson Union High	Anderson
75	22.5	Fullerton Elementary	Fullerton
75	22.5	La Canada Unified	La Canada
75	22.5	Las Virgenes Unified	Calabasas
75	22.5	Placentia-Yorba Linda Unified	Placentia
75	22.5	San Dieguito Union High	Encinitas
75	22.5	San Jacinto Unified	San Jacinto
82	22.4	Cucamonga Elementary	Rcho Cucamong
82	22.4	Escalon Unified	Escalon
82	22.4	Hesperia Unified	Hesperia
85	22.3	ABC Unified	Cerritos
85	22.3	Bellflower Unified	Bellflower
85	22.3	Brawley Union High	Brawley
85	22.3	Conejo Valley Unified	Thousand Oaks
85	22.3	Cotati-Rohnert Park Unified	Rohnert Park
85	22.3	Escondido Union High	Escondido
85	22.3	Etiwanda Elementary	Etiwanda
85	22.3	Fallbrook Union High	Fallbrook
85	22.3	Lowell Joint	Whittier
85	22.3	Moreno Valley Unified	Moreno Valley
85	22.3	National Elementary	National City
85	22.3	Oroville Union High	Oroville
85	22.3	Soledad Unified	Soledad
85	22.3	Upland Unified	Upland
99	22.2	Beaumont Unified	Beaumont
99	22.2	Fontana Unified	Fontana
99	22.2	Fountain Valley Elementary	Fountain Valley
99	22.2	Placer Union High	Auburn
99	22.2	Roseville Joint Union High	Roseville
99	22.2	Walnut Valley Unified	Walnut
105	22.1	Central Elementary	Rcho Cucamong
105	22.1	Clovis Unified	Clovis
105	22.1	Grant Joint Union High	Sacramento
105	22.1	Los Gatos-Saratoga Jt Union High	Los Gatos
105	22.1	Norwalk-La Mirada Unified	Norwalk
105	22.1	Paramount Unified	Paramount
105	22.1	Santa Rosa High	Santa Rosa
105	22.1	Tustin Unified	Tustin
113	22.0	Banning Unified	Banning
113	22.0	Duarte Unified	Duarte
113	22.0	Hacienda La Puente Unified	City of Industry
113	22.0	Jefferson Union High	Daly City
113	22.0	Laguna Beach Unified	Laguna Beach
113	22.0	Menifee Union Elementary	Menifee
113	22.0	Newhall Elementary	Valencia
113	22.0	Petaluma Joint Union High	Petaluma
113	22.0	Redlands Unified	Redlands
113	22.0	Westside Union Elementary	Lancaster
123	21.9	Covina-Valley Unified	Covina
123	21.9	Santa Barbara High	Santa Barbara
123	21.9	Vista Unified	Vista
123	21.9	Wilsona Elementary	Palmdale
127	21.8	Bassett Unified	La Puente
127	21.8	Claremont Unified	Claremont
127	21.8	Eastside Union Elementary	Lancaster
127	21.8	Jurupa Unified	Riverside
127	21.8	Keppel Union Elementary	Pearblossom
127	21.8	Rialto Unified	Rialto
127	21.8	Rowland Unified	Rowland Heights
127	21.8	Tehachapi Unified	Tehachapi
135	21.7	Acalanes Union High	Lafayette
135	21.7	Castro Valley Unified	Castro Valley
135	21.7	Coachella Valley Unified	Thermal
135	21.7	Colton Joint Unified	Colton
135	21.7	Fremont Union High	Sunnyvale
135	21.7	Lamont Elementary	Lamont
135	21.7	Lennox Elementary	Lennox
135	21.7	Oak Park Unified	Oak Park
135	21.7	Red Bluff Joint Union High	Red Bluff
135	21.7	Romoland Elementary	Homeland
135	21.7	Stanislaus Union Elementary	Modesto
135	21.7	West Covina Unified	West Covina
147	21.6	Apple Valley Unified	Apple Valley
147	21.6	Central Union High	El Centro
147	21.6	Cupertino Union School	Cupertino
147	21.6	Laguna Salada Union Elementary	Pacifica
147	21.6	Morgan Hill Unified	Morgan Hill
147	21.6	Mountain View Elementary	El Monte
147	21.6	Rio Elementary	Oxnard
147	21.6	San Gabriel Unified	San Gabriel
147	21.6	Santa Ana Unified	Santa Ana
147	21.6	Temple City Unified	Temple City
157	21.5	Anaheim Elementary	Anaheim
157	21.5	Centralia Elementary	Buena Park
157	21.5	El Dorado Union High	Placerville
157	21.5	Empire Union Elementary	Modesto
157	21.5	Evergreen Elementary	San Jose
157	21.5	Folsom-Cordova Unified	Folsom
157	21.5	Inglewood Unified	Inglewood
157	21.5	Little Lake City Elementary	Santa Fe Spgs
157	21.5	Long Beach Unified	Long Beach
157	21.5	Palmdale Elementary	Palmdale
157	21.5	Poway Unified	Poway
168	21.4	Brea-Olinda Unified	Brea
168	21.4	Buena Park Elementary	Buena Park
168	21.4	Delano Union Elementary	Delano
168	21.4	Desert Sands Unified	La Quinta
168	21.4	El Centro Elementary	El Centro
168	21.4	Gonzales Unified	Gonzales
168	21.4	Hemet Unified	Hemet
168	21.4	Lancaster Elementary	Lancaster
168	21.4	Los Banos Unified	Los Banos
168	21.4	Oxnard Elementary	Oxnard
168	21.4	Palos Verdes Peninsula Unified	Palos Verdes Est
168	21.4	San Ramon Valley Unified	Danville
168	21.4	Sweetwater Union High	Chula Vista
181	21.3	Adelanto Elementary	Adelanto
181	21.3	Auburn Union Elementary	Auburn
181	21.3	Bear Valley Unified	Big Bear Lake
181	21.3	Castaic Union Elementary	Valencia
181	21.3	Dry Creek Joint Elementary	Roseville
181	21.3	Jefferson Elementary	Daly City
181	21.3	Nevada Joint Union High	Grass Valley
181	21.3	Pittsburg Unified	Pittsburg
189	21.2	Antioch Unified	Antioch
189	21.2	Azusa Unified	Azusa
189	21.2	Burbank Unified	Burbank
189	21.2	Ceres Unified	Ceres
189	21.2	Corona-Norco Unified	Norco
189	21.2	Manteca Unified	Manteca
189	21.2	Milpitas Unified	Milpitas
189	21.2	Oakdale Joint Unified	Oakdale
189	21.2	Rosedale Union Elementary	Bakersfield
189	21.2	Sacramento City Unified	Sacramento
189	21.2	San Bernardino City Unified	San Bernardino
189	21.2	San Lorenzo Valley Unified	Felton
189	21.2	Santee Elementary	Santee
189	21.2	Whittier City Elementary	Whittier
203	21.1	Buckeye Union Elementary	Shingle Springs
203	21.1	Cajon Valley Union Elementary	El Cajon
203	21.1	Culver City Unified	Culver City
203	21.1	East Side Union High	San Jose
203	21.1	El Rancho Unified	Pico Rivera
203	21.1	Fremont Unified	Fremont
203	21.1	Galt Joint Union High	Galt
203	21.1	Orange Unified	Orange
203	21.1	Orcutt Union Elementary	Orcutt
203	21.1	San Marcos Unified	San Marcos
203	21.1	South Whittier Elementary	Whittier
214	21.0	Barstow Unified	Barstow
214	21.0	Carlsbad Unified	Carlsbad
214	21.0	Encinitas Union Elementary	Encinitas
214	21.0	Los Angeles Unified	Los Angeles

214	21.0	Mountain View-Los Altos Union High	Mountain View
214	21.0	Ontario-Montclair Elementary	Ontario
214	21.0	Palo Verde Unified	Blythe
214	21.0	Patterson Joint Unified	Patterson
214	21.0	Santa Monica-Malibu Unified	Santa Monica
214	21.0	Saugus Union Elementary	Santa Clarita
214	21.0	Visalia Unified	Visalia
214	21.0	Waterford Unified	Waterford
214	21.0	West Sonoma County Union High	Sebastopol
227	20.9	East Whittier City Elementary	Whittier
227	20.9	El Segundo Unified	El Segundo
227	20.9	Eureka Union Elementary	Granite Bay
227	20.9	Fallbrook Union Elementary	Fallbrook
227	20.9	Garvey Elementary	Rosemead
227	20.9	Glendale Unified	Glendale
227	20.9	Hawthorne Elementary	Hawthorne
227	20.9	La Mesa-Spring Valley	La Mesa
227	20.9	Monterey Peninsula Unified	Monterey
227	20.9	Ojai Unified	Ojai
227	20.9	Pleasant Valley School	Camarillo
227	20.9	San Rafael City High	San Rafael
227	20.9	South San Francisco Unified	S San Francisco
227	20.9	Temecula Valley Unified	Temecula
227	20.9	Willows Unified	Willows
227	20.9	Windsor Unified	Windsor
243	20.8	Berryessa Union Elementary	San Jose
243	20.8	Bishop Union Elementary	Bishop
243	20.8	Kings Canyon Joint Unified	Reedley
243	20.8	Lake Tahoe Unified	S Lake Tahoe
243	20.8	Lawndale Elementary	Lawndale
243	20.8	Live Oak Unified	Live Oak
243	20.8	Moorpark Unified	Moorpark
243	20.8	Ocean View Elementary	Huntington Bch
243	20.8	Redondo Beach Unified	Redondo Beach
243	20.8	Rocklin Unified	Rocklin
243	20.8	Roseville City Elementary	Roseville
243	20.8	San Luis Coastal Unified	San Luis Obispo
243	20.8	San Mateo Union High	San Mateo
243	20.8	Sulphur Springs Union Elementary	Canyon Country
243	20.8	Torrance Unified	Torrance
258	20.7	El Monte City Elementary	El Monte
258	20.7	Fillmore Unified	Fillmore
258	20.7	Hueneme Elementary	Port Hueneme
258	20.7	Keyes Union Elementary	Keyes
258	20.7	Lakeside Union Elementary	Lakeside
258	20.7	Madera Unified	Madera
258	20.7	Merced City Elementary	Merced
258	20.7	Monrovia Unified	Monrovia
258	20.7	Mountain View Elementary	Ontario
258	20.7	Mountain View-Whisman Elementary	Mountain View
258	20.7	Rescue Union Elementary	Rescue
258	20.7	Richland SD	Shafter
258	20.7	Rosemead Elementary	Rosemead
258	20.7	San Bruno Park Elementary	San Bruno
258	20.7	San Juan Unified	Carmichael
258	20.7	Santa Paula Elementary	Santa Paula
258	20.7	Scotts Valley Unified	Scotts Valley
258	20.7	Snowline Joint Unified	Phelan
258	20.7	Vallejo City Unified	Vallejo
277	20.6	Alameda City Unified	Alameda
277	20.6	Alhambra City Elementary	Alhambra
277	20.6	Carpinteria Unified	Carpinteria
277	20.6	Chowchilla Elementary	Chowchilla
277	20.6	Fresno Unified	Fresno
277	20.6	Fruitvale Elementary	Bakersfield
277	20.6	Greenfield Union Elementary	Bakersfield
277	20.6	Hollister SD	Hollister
277	20.6	New Haven Unified	Union City
277	20.6	Newman-Crows Landing Unified	Newman
277	20.6	Northern Humboldt Union High	McKinleyville
277	20.6	Pasadena Unified	Pasadena
277	20.6	Pomona Unified	Pomona
290	20.5	Cabrillo Unified	Half Moon Bay
290	20.5	Fairfield-Suisun Unified	Fairfield
290	20.5	Livingston Union Elementary	Livingston
290	20.5	Lucia Mar Unified	Arroyo Grande
290	20.5	Santa Maria-Bonita Elementary	Santa Maria
290	20.5	Savanna Elementary	Anaheim
290	20.5	Sonoma Valley Unified	Sonoma
290	20.5	Templeton Unified	Templeton
290	20.5	Wiseburn Elementary	Hawthorne
299	20.4	Albany City Unified	Albany
299	20.4	Arvin Union Elementary	Arvin
299	20.4	Bonsall Union Elementary	Bonsall
299	20.4	Dinuba Unified	Dinuba
299	20.4	Hanford Elementary	Hanford
299	20.4	Hughson Unified	Hughson
299	20.4	Kingsburg Elementary Charter	Kingsburg
299	20.4	Lincoln Unified	Stockton
299	20.4	Loomis Union Elementary	Loomis
299	20.4	Newport-Mesa Unified	Costa Mesa
299	20.4	Porterville Unified	Porterville
299	20.4	Red Bluff Union Elementary	Red Bluff
299	20.4	River Delta Joint Unified	Rio Vista
299	20.4	Sequoia Union High	Redwood City
313	20.3	Beardsley Elementary	Bakersfield
313	20.3	Cambrian Elementary	San Jose
313	20.3	Fowler Unified	Fowler
313	20.3	Healdsburg Unified	Healdsburg
313	20.3	Los Nietos Elementary	Whittier
313	20.3	Martinez Unified	Martinez
313	20.3	Morongo Unified	Twentynine Plms
313	20.3	Norris Elementary	Bakersfield
313	20.3	Oak Grove Elementary	San Jose
313	20.3	Old Adobe Union Elementary	Petaluma
313	20.3	Pacific Grove Unified	Pacific Grove
313	20.3	Palm Springs Unified	Palm Springs
313	20.3	Redding Elementary	Redding
313	20.3	Wasco Union Elementary	Wasco
327	20.2	Black Oak Mine Unified	Georgetown
327	20.2	Chico Unified	Chico
327	20.2	Cutler-Orosi Joint Unified	Orosi
327	20.2	Elk Grove Unified	Elk Grove
327	20.2	Holtville Unified	Holtville
327	20.2	North Monterey County Unified	Moss Landing
327	20.2	Riverbank Unified	Riverbank
327	20.2	San Marino Unified	San Marino
327	20.2	Santa Rita Union Elementary	Salinas
327	20.2	Sierra Sands Unified	Ridgecrest
327	20.2	Union Elementary	San Jose
338	20.1	Burton Elementary	Porterville
338	20.1	Calexico Unified	Calexico
338	20.1	Davis Joint Unified	Davis
338	20.1	Lemoore Union Elementary	Lemoore
338	20.1	Manhattan Beach Unified	Manhattan Beach
338	20.1	Mendota Unified	Mendota
338	20.1	Napa Valley Unified	Napa
338	20.1	Pleasant Ridge Union Elementary	Grass Valley
338	20.1	Pleasanton Unified	Pleasanton
338	20.1	Ripon Unified	Ripon
338	20.1	San Leandro Unified	San Leandro
338	20.1	South Bay Union Elementary	Imperial Beach
338	20.1	Tracy Joint Unified	Tracy
338	20.1	Wheatland Elementary	Wheatland
352	20.0	Alpine Union Elementary	Alpine
352	20.0	Alum Rock Union Elementary	San Jose
352	20.0	Corcoran Joint Unified	Corcoran
352	20.0	Delhi Unified	Delhi
352	20.0	Hayward Unified	Hayward
352	20.0	Lemon Grove Elementary	Lemon Grove
352	20.0	Los Altos Elementary	Los Altos
352	20.0	Modesto City Elementary	Modesto
352	20.0	Muroc Joint Unified	North Edwards
352	20.0	Novato Unified	Novato
352	20.0	Perris Elementary	Perris
352	20.0	Piner-Olivet Union Elementary	Santa Rosa
352	20.0	Santa Clara Unified	Santa Clara
352	20.0	Selma Unified	Selma
352	20.0	Standard Elementary	Bakersfield
352	20.0	Stockton City Unified	Stockton
352	20.0	Turlock Joint Elementary	Turlock
369	19.9	Earlimart Elementary	Earlimart
369	19.9	Gilroy Unified	Gilroy
369	19.9	Kerman Unified	Kerman
369	19.9	Live Oak Elementary	Santa Cruz
369	19.9	Mount Diablo Unified	Concord
369	19.9	Ocean View Elementary	Oxnard
369	19.9	Panama Buena Vista Union Elem	Bakersfield
369	19.9	Salinas City Elementary	Salinas
369	19.9	San Ysidro Elementary	San Ysidro
369	19.9	Sylvan Union Elementary	Modesto
369	19.9	Western Placer Unified	Lincoln
369	19.9	Yuba City Unified	Yuba City
381	19.8	Atascadero Unified	Atascadero
381	19.8	Atwater Elementary	Atwater
381	19.8	Benicia Unified	Benicia
381	19.8	Brawley Elementary	Brawley
381	19.8	Calaveras Unified	San Andreas
381	19.8	Goleta Union Elementary	Goleta
381	19.8	Greenfield Union Elementary	Greenfield
381	19.8	Imperial Unified	Imperial
381	19.8	Magnolia Elementary	Anaheim
381	19.8	Marysville Joint Unified	Marysville
381	19.8	Millbrae Elementary	Millbrae
381	19.8	Natomas Unified	Sacramento
381	19.8	Oakley Union Elementary	Oakley
381	19.8	Robla Elementary	Sacramento
381	19.8	Santa Barbara Elementary	Santa Barbara
381	19.8	Soquel Union Elementary	Capitola
381	19.8	Vacaville Unified	Vacaville
381	19.8	Westminster Elementary	Westminster
381	19.8	Woodlake Union Elementary	Woodlake
400	19.7	Burlingame Elementary	Burlingame
400	19.7	King City Union Elementary	King City
400	19.7	La Habra City Elementary	La Habra
400	19.7	San Lorenzo Unified	San Lorenzo
400	19.7	Tulare City Elementary	Tulare
400	19.7	Woodland Joint Unified	Woodland
406	19.6	Brentwood Union Elementary	Brentwood
406	19.6	Central Unified	Fresno
406	19.6	Chula Vista Elementary	Chula Vista
406	19.6	Dublin Unified	Dublin
406	19.6	Jefferson Elementary	Tracy
406	19.6	Lindsay Unified	Lindsay
406	19.6	Mount Pleasant Elementary	San Jose
413	19.5	Dixon Unified	Dixon
413	19.5	Golden Plains Unified	San Joaquin
413	19.5	Hilmar Unified	Hilmar
413	19.5	Konocti Unified	Lower Lake
413	19.5	Oceanside Unified	Oceanside
413	19.5	Orland Joint Unified	Orland
413	19.5	Riverdale Joint Unified	Riverdale
413	19.5	Sunnyvale Elementary	Sunnyvale
421	19.4	Cypress Elementary	Cypress
421	19.4	Escondido Union Elementary	Escondido
421	19.4	Lodi Unified	Lodi
421	19.4	Moraga Elementary	Moraga
421	19.4	Oroville City Elementary	Oroville
421	19.4	Rincon Valley Union Elementary	Santa Rosa
421	19.4	West Contra Costa Unified	Richmond
421	19.4	Winton Elementary	Winton
429	19.3	Campbell Union Elementary	Campbell
429	19.3	Enterprise Elementary	Redding
429	19.3	Franklin-Mckinley Elementary	San Jose
429	19.3	Kelseyville Unified	Kelseyville
429	19.3	Newark Unified	Newark
429	19.3	San Rafael City Elementary	San Rafael
435	19.2	Linden Unified	Linden
435	19.2	Mariposa County Unified	Mariposa
435	19.2	Mark West Union Elementary	Santa Rosa
435	19.2	Mountain Empire Unified	Pine Valley
435	19.2	Paso Robles Joint Unified	Paso Robles
435	19.2	Salida Union Elementary	Salida
435	19.2	San Mateo-Foster City Elementary	San Mateo
435	19.2	Walnut Creek Elementary	Walnut Creek
443	19.1	Cascade Union Elementary	Anderson
443	19.1	John Swett Unified	Crockett
443	19.1	Lakeport Unified	Lakeport
443	19.1	Mcfarland Unified	Mcfarland
443	19.1	Valley Center-Pauma Unified	Valley Center
448	19.0	Del Norte County Unified	Crescent City
448	19.0	Firebaugh-Las Deltas Joint Unified	Firebaugh
448	19.0	Grass Valley Elementary	Grass Valley
448	19.0	Reef-Sunset Unified	Avenal
448	19.0	Sanger Unified	Sanger
453	18.9	Center Joint Unified	Antelope
453	18.9	Lafayette Elementary	Lafayette
453	18.9	Lompoc Unified	Lompoc
453	18.9	Los Gatos Union Elementary	Los Gatos
453	18.9	Mother Lode Union Elementary	Placerville
453	18.9	San Carlos Elementary	San Carlos
453	18.9	Taft City Elementary	Taft
460	18.8	Dos Palos Oro Loma Joint Unified	Dos Palos
460	18.8	Exeter Union Elementary	Exeter
460	18.8	Gateway Unified	Redding
460	18.8	Moreland Elementary	San Jose
460	18.8	Parlier Unified	Parlier
460	18.8	San Diego Unified	San Diego
460	18.8	Santa Cruz City Elementary	Santa Cruz
460	18.8	Ukiah Unified	Ukiah
468	18.7	Corning Union Elementary	Corning
468	18.7	Del Paso Heights Elementary	Sacramento
468	18.7	Farmersville Unified	Farmersville
468	18.7	Gridley Unified	Gridley
468	18.7	Middletown Unified	Middletown
468	18.7	Paradise Unified	Paradise
468	18.7	Twin Ridges Elementary	North San Juan
468	18.7	Winters Joint Unified	Winters
476	18.6	Bakersfield City Elementary	Bakersfield
476	18.6	Cloverdale Unified	Cloverdale
476	18.6	Coronado Unified	Coronado
476	18.6	Eureka City Unified	Eureka
476	18.6	Galt Joint Union Elementary	Galt
476	18.6	San Jose Unified	San Jose
476	18.6	Tamalpais Union High	Larkspur
476	18.6	Washington Unified	West Sacramento
484	18.5	Colusa Unified	Colusa
484	18.5	Dixie Elementary	San Rafael
484	18.5	North Sacramento Elementary	Sacramento
484	18.5	Saratoga Union Elementary	Saratoga
488	18.3	Bellevue Union Elementary	Santa Rosa
488	18.3	Beverly Hills Unified	Beverly Hills
488	18.3	Orinda Union Elementary	Orinda
488	18.3	Petaluma City Elementary	Petaluma
488	18.3	Ravenswood City Elementary	East Palo Alto
488	18.3	Rio Linda Union Elementary	Rio Linda
488	18.3	Ross Valley Elementary	San Anselmo

Rank	Ratio	District Name	City
488	18.3	Saint Helena Unified	Saint Helena
488	18.3	Travis Unified	Travis Afb
497	18.2	Berkeley Unified	Berkeley
497	18.2	Oakland Unified	Oakland
497	18.2	Pajaro Valley Unified School	Watsonville
497	18.2	Plumas Unified	Quincy
501	18.1	Belmont-Redwood Shores Elementary	Belmont
501	18.1	Silver Valley Unified	Yermo
501	18.1	Tahoe-Truckee Joint Unified	Truckee
504	18.0	Orange County Office of Ed	Costa Mesa
504	18.0	Thermalito Union Elementary	Oroville
506	17.9	Sierra Unified	Auberry
507	17.8	Mill Valley Elementary	Mill Valley
508	17.7	Weaver Union Elementary	Merced
508	17.7	Willits Unified	Willits
510	17.6	Gustine Unified	Gustine
511	17.5	Central Union Elementary	Lemoore
511	17.5	Del Mar Union Elementary	Del Mar
513	17.3	San Francisco Unified	San Francisco
514	16.9	Solana Beach Elementary	Solana Beach
515	16.8	Piedmont City Unified	Piedmont
516	16.7	Fort Bragg Unified	Fort Bragg
517	16.6	Redwood City Elementary	Redwood City
518	16.5	Carmel Unified	Carmel
519	16.4	Palo Alto Unified	Palo Alto
520	15.7	Menlo Park City Elementary	Atherton
521	15.4	Santa Rosa Elementary	Santa Rosa
522	14.6	San Diego County Office of Ed	San Diego
523	14.5	San Joaquin County Office of Ed	Stockton
524	12.9	Kern County Office of Ed	Bakersfield
525	12.5	Riverside County Office of Ed	Riverside
526	11.3	Los Angeles County Office of Ed	Downey
527	10.7	Fresno County Office of Ed	Fresno
528	10.2	San Bernardino County Supt.	San Bernardino
529	9.2	Santa Clara County Office of Ed	San Jose

Student/Librarian Ratio

Rank	Ratio	District Name	City
1	50,502.5	Escondido Union Elementary	Escondido
2	48,608.0	Capistrano Unified	San Juan Capis
3	40,168.0	Fontana Unified	Fontana
4	34,290.0	Etiwanda Elementary	Etiwanda
5	32,643.3	Marysville Joint Unified	Marysville
6	25,160.0	Orcutt Union Elementary	Orcutt
7	24,068.0	Santa Maria-Bonita Elementary	Santa Maria
8	23,226.0	Oak Grove Elementary	San Jose
9	21,673.0	Simi Valley Unified	Simi Valley
10	18,653.0	Cajon Valley Union Elementary	El Cajon
11	15,902.5	Santa Ana Unified	Santa Ana
12	15,660.0	Thermalito Union Elementary	Oroville
13	14,668.0	Huntington Beach Union High	Huntington Bch
14	14,416.0	Alum Rock Union Elementary	San Jose
15	13,910.0	San Marcos Unified	San Marcos
16	13,867.0	Coachella Valley Unified	Thermal
17	13,450.0	Panama Buena Vista Union Elem	Bakersfield
18	13,385.0	Norwalk-La Mirada Unified	Norwalk
19	13,237.0	Upland Unified	Upland
20	12,392.4	Antelope Valley Union High	Lancaster
21	12,202.0	Whittier Union High	Whittier
22	11,686.7	San Bernardino City Unified	San Bernardino
23	11,441.0	Los Angeles County Office of Ed	Downey
24	11,295.0	Fullerton Elementary	Fullerton
25	11,223.0	Palos Verdes Peninsula Unified	Palos Verdes Est
26	10,850.0	Compton Unified	Compton
27	10,715.0	Santa Maria Joint Union High	Santa Maria
28	10,497.0	Mountain View Elementary	El Monte
29	10,494.3	Corona-Norco Unified	Norco
30	10,445.0	Woodland Joint Unified	Woodland
31	10,442.4	San Juan Unified	Carmichael
32	10,134.0	Rio Linda Union Elementary	Rio Linda
33	9,942.0	Arcadia Unified	Arcadia
34	9,732.0	Lynwood Unified	Lynwood
35	9,660.0	Grass Valley Elementary	Grass Valley
36	9,630.0	Gilroy Unified	Gilroy
37	9,542.0	Pittsburg Unified	Pittsburg
38	9,369.5	Rowland Unified	Rowland Heights
39	9,259.0	Tustin Unified	Tustin
40	9,242.0	Yucaipa-Calimesa Joint Unified	Yucaipa
41	8,891.5	Saddleback Valley Unified	Mission Viejo
42	8,856.8	Pomona Unified	Pomona
43	8,821.3	Placentia-Yorba Linda Unified	Placentia
44	8,736.7	Fremont Unified	Fremont
45	8,712.0	Beaumont Unified	Beaumont
46	8,467.7	Los Angeles Unified	Los Angeles
47	8,427.5	Madera Unified	Madera
48	8,271.0	Orange County Office of Ed	Costa Mesa
49	8,229.0	Chino Valley Unified	Chino
50	7,996.0	Glendora Unified	Glendora
51	7,993.0	Redondo Beach Unified	Redondo Beach
52	7,903.0	Alisal Union Elementary	Salinas
53	7,717.0	Murrieta Valley Unified	Murrieta
54	7,653.0	Natomas Unified	Sacramento
55	7,401.0	Newark Unified	Newark
56	7,389.0	Pleasant Valley School	Camarillo
57	7,359.0	Covina-Valley Unified	Covina
57	7,359.0	Ramona City Unified	Ramona
59	7,332.7	Temecula Valley Unified	Temecula
60	7,285.0	Conejo Valley Unified	Thousand Oaks
61	7,183.3	Lemoore Union High	Lemoore
62	7,111.3	Temple City Unified	Temple City
63	7,045.3	Antioch Unified	Antioch
64	7,017.3	Manteca Unified	Manteca
65	6,876.0	Washington Unified	West Sacramento
66	6,866.0	Claremont Unified	Claremont
67	6,855.0	Ukiah Unified	Ukiah
68	6,816.0	Barstow Unified	Barstow
69	6,671.0	Culver City Unified	Culver City
70	6,603.7	Lodi Unified	Lodi
71	6,493.3	Live Oak Elementary	Santa Cruz
72	6,465.0	Manhattan Beach Unified	Manhattan Beach
73	6,446.0	San Bernardino County Supt.	San Bernardino
74	6,320.0	Fountain Valley Elementary	Fountain Valley
75	6,295.0	Desert Sands Unified	La Quinta
76	6,240.5	Visalia Unified	Visalia
77	6,219.0	Torrance Unified	Torrance
78	6,109.0	North Monterey County Unified	Moss Landing
79	5,948.0	Selma Unified	Selma
80	5,943.3	San Rafael City Elementary	San Rafael
81	5,931.0	Sunnyvale Elementary	Sunnyvale
82	5,913.7	Inglewood Unified	Inglewood
83	5,871.3	Folsom-Cordova Unified	Folsom
84	5,808.5	Lompoc Unified	Lompoc
85	5,791.0	Atascadero Unified	Atascadero
86	5,748.0	Shasta Union High	Redding
87	5,650.0	Bear Valley Unified	Big Bear Lake
88	5,636.2	Baldwin Park Unified	Baldwin Park
89	5,620.5	Oceanside Unified	Oceanside
90	5,567.0	Sierra Sands Unified	Ridgecrest
91	5,475.3	Sanger Unified	Sanger
92	5,458.0	Lucia Mar Unified	Arroyo Grande
93	5,357.2	Oakland Unified	Oakland
94	5,337.3	Colton Joint Unified	Colton
95	5,310.0	Dinuba Unified	Dinuba
96	5,238.0	Lake Tahoe Unified	S Lake Tahoe
97	5,231.0	Central Elementary	Rcho Cucamong
98	5,122.0	Greenfield Union Elementary	Greenfield
99	5,089.0	Bonita Unified	San Dimas
100	5,014.0	Ceres Unified	Ceres
101	4,976.5	Franklin-Mckinley Elementary	San Jose
102	4,966.1	Lincoln Unified	Stockton
103	4,936.0	Sonoma Valley Unified	Sonoma
104	4,918.5	Lawndale Elementary	Lawndale
105	4,916.3	Dixon Unified	Dixon
106	4,907.0	Tehachapi Unified	Tehachapi
107	4,893.9	Morgan Hill Unified	Morgan Hill
108	4,819.1	Bellflower Unified	Bellflower
109	4,781.5	South San Francisco Unified	S San Francisco
110	4,736.0	Atwater Elementary	Atwater
111	4,733.5	Morongo Unified	Twentynine Plms
112	4,720.0	Santa Rosa Elementary	Santa Rosa
113	4,706.0	Placer Union High	Auburn
114	4,662.0	Red Bluff Union Elementary	Red Bluff
115	4,576.3	Pleasanton Unified	Pleasanton
116	4,538.6	Corcoran Joint Unified	Corcoran
117	4,469.2	Vista Unified	Vista
118	4,380.1	Stockton City Unified	Stockton
119	4,368.2	Elk Grove Unified	Elk Grove
120	4,367.2	Poway Unified	Poway
121	4,363.0	La Canada Unified	La Canada
122	4,338.0	Dublin Unified	Dublin
123	4,251.0	Patterson Joint Unified	Patterson
124	4,244.0	Empire Union Elementary	Modesto
125	4,213.0	Buckeye Union Elementary	Shingle Springs
126	4,137.4	Milpitas Unified	Milpitas
127	4,105.5	Castro Valley Unified	Castro Valley
128	4,085.0	Rosedale Union Elementary	Bakersfield
129	4,057.0	Redlands Unified	Redlands
130	3,910.8	Tracy Joint Unified	Tracy
131	3,882.2	West Contra Costa Unified	Richmond
132	3,880.3	Pasadena Unified	Pasadena
133	3,839.0	Cotati-Rohnert Park Unified	Rohnert Park
134	3,816.0	Central Union High	El Centro
135	3,814.0	Enterprise Elementary	Redding
136	3,771.5	Rialto Unified	Rialto
137	3,744.0	Riverside County Office of Ed	Riverside
138	3,738.0	Gateway Unified	Redding
139	3,717.1	Riverside Unified	Riverside
140	3,716.3	Downey Unified	Downey
141	3,682.9	Kings Canyon Joint Unified	Reedley
142	3,679.4	Porterville Unified	Porterville
143	3,672.5	Santee Elementary	Santee
144	3,669.8	Napa Valley Unified	Napa
145	3,655.0	Soledad Unified	Soledad
146	3,649.0	Cabrillo Unified	Half Moon Bay
147	3,637.0	La Mesa-Spring Valley	La Mesa
148	3,611.1	El Monte Union High	El Monte
149	3,585.0	Millbrae Elementary	Millbrae
150	3,578.7	Salinas Union High	Salinas
151	3,559.0	Montebello Unified	Montebello
152	3,555.0	Lindsay Unified	Lindsay
153	3,531.4	Fresno Unified	Fresno
154	3,522.4	Bakersfield City Elementary	Bakersfield
155	3,474.7	Victor Valley Union High	Victorville
156	3,425.0	Lafayette Elementary	Lafayette
157	3,370.0	Black Oak Mine Unified	Georgetown
158	3,367.0	Oroville City Elementary	Oroville
159	3,365.0	San Leandro Unified	San Leandro
160	3,349.8	Orange Unified	Orange
161	3,337.7	Garden Grove Unified	Garden Grove
162	3,313.3	Carlsbad Unified	Carlsbad
163	3,275.7	Newport-Mesa Unified	Costa Mesa
164	3,273.3	Corning Union Elementary	Corning
165	3,262.3	Sacramento City Unified	Sacramento
166	3,239.0	Fullerton Joint Union High	Fullerton
167	3,190.0	San Marino Unified	San Marino
168	3,170.5	Grant Joint Union High	Sacramento
169	3,155.2	Hemet Unified	Hemet
170	3,153.0	Laguna Salada Union Elementary	Pacifica
171	3,152.4	Palm Springs Unified	Palm Springs
172	3,108.8	Modesto City High	Modesto
173	3,094.0	San Gabriel Unified	San Gabriel
174	3,078.0	Monterey Peninsula Unified	Monterey
175	3,045.0	John Swett Unified	Crockett
176	3,044.0	El Segundo Unified	El Segundo
177	3,038.5	Clovis Unified	Clovis
178	3,010.8	Campbell Union High	San Jose
179	2,968.8	Gonzales Unified	Gonzales
180	2,961.2	Vacaville Unified	Vacaville
181	2,952.0	Center Joint Unified	Antelope
182	2,902.0	San Benito High	Hollister
183	2,890.0	Rim of The World Unified	Lake Arrowhead
184	2,880.3	Irvine Unified	Irvine
185	2,871.7	Rocklin Unified	Rocklin
186	2,860.8	San Diego Unified	San Diego
187	2,838.9	Vallejo City Unified	Vallejo
188	2,829.0	Mcfarland Unified	Mcfarland
189	2,824.0	Richland SD	Shafter
190	2,811.5	Kerman Unified	Kerman
191	2,784.0	Alhambra City High	Alhambra
192	2,747.6	Chaffey Joint Union High	Ontario
193	2,731.7	Alvord Unified	Riverside
194	2,719.0	Lamont Elementary	Lamont
195	2,671.0	Tahoe-Truckee Joint Unified	Truckee
196	2,657.0	Burton Elementary	Porterville
197	2,652.0	Los Gatos Union Elementary	Los Gatos
198	2,574.7	Roseville Joint Union High	Roseville
199	2,561.7	Oxnard Union High	Oxnard
200	2,547.5	Chico Unified	Chico
201	2,524.8	Las Virgenes Unified	Calabasas
202	2,521.8	San Mateo-Foster City Elementary	San Mateo
203	2,488.0	Delhi Unified	Delhi
204	2,464.4	Ventura Unified	Ventura
205	2,459.0	Firebaugh-Las Deltas Joint Unified	Firebaugh
205	2,459.0	Sylvan Union Elementary	Modesto
207	2,436.0	Wheatland Elementary	Wheatland
208	2,433.0	Livingston Union Elementary	Livingston
209	2,419.2	Albany City Unified	Albany
210	2,417.0	Saratoga Union Elementary	Saratoga
211	2,412.9	San Diego County Office of Ed	San Diego
212	2,410.6	Anaheim Union High	Anaheim
213	2,395.7	San Ramon Valley Unified	Danville
214	2,384.2	Berkeley Unified	Berkeley
215	2,365.2	Garvey Elementary	Rosemead
216	2,346.0	Willits Unified	Willits
217	2,336.8	San Lorenzo Unified	San Lorenzo
218	2,325.3	Perris Union High	Perris
219	2,320.4	Fairfield-Suisun Unified	Fairfield
220	2,315.8	Yuba City Unified	Yuba City
221	2,307.1	Los Banos Unified	Los Banos
222	2,291.6	Nevada Joint Union High	Grass Valley
223	2,284.0	Jefferson Elementary	Daly City
224	2,257.8	Central Unified	Fresno
225	2,240.0	Santa Clara County Office of Ed	San Jose
226	2,233.5	Liberty Union High	Brentwood
227	2,210.9	Kern Union High	Bakersfield
228	2,190.0	Fresno County Office of Ed	Fresno
229	2,169.0	Martinez Unified	Martinez
230	2,162.0	King City Joint Union High	King City
231	2,144.5	Grossmont Union High	La Mesa
232	2,136.0	Fowler Unified	Fowler
233	2,131.5	Santa Monica-Malibu Unified	Santa Monica
234	2,130.0	Mendota Unified	Mendota
235	2,123.0	Gridley Unified	Gridley
236	2,118.0	Paradise Unified	Paradise
237	2,115.0	Tulare Joint Union High	Tulare
238	2,114.0	Kingsburg Elementary Charter	Kingsburg
239	2,091.0	San Rafael City High	San Rafael

Rank	Value	District	City
240	2,084.0	Fort Bragg Unified	Fort Bragg
241	2,050.0	South Pasadena Unified	South Pasadena
242	2,038.0	Winters Joint Unified	Winters
243	2,021.1	Sequoia Union High	Redwood City
244	2,005.8	William S Hart Union High	Santa Clarita
245	2,000.5	San Francisco Unified	San Francisco
246	1,986.3	San Luis Coastal Unified	San Luis Obispo
247	1,984.5	East Side Union High	San Jose
248	1,946.1	Santa Clara Unified	Santa Clara
249	1,893.9	Sweetwater Union High	Chula Vista
250	1,889.5	San Dieguito Union High	Encinitas
251	1,855.0	Dixie Elementary	San Rafael
252	1,852.0	Norris Elementary	Bakersfield
253	1,822.0	Mountain Empire Unified	Pine Valley
254	1,800.5	Hanford Joint Union High	Hanford
255	1,781.7	Merced Union High	Atwater
256	1,765.4	Davis Joint Unified	Davis
257	1,749.0	Eureka City Unified	Eureka
258	1,744.0	Beverly Hills Unified	Beverly Hills
259	1,725.0	Paso Robles Joint Unified	Paso Robles
260	1,720.0	Sonora Union High	Sonora
261	1,631.5	Mountain View-Los Altos Union High	Mountain View
262	1,577.0	Riverdale Joint Unified	Riverdale
263	1,575.5	Fremont Union High	Sunnyvale
264	1,558.6	El Dorado Union High	Placerville
265	1,538.0	Colusa Unified	Colusa
266	1,523.7	Long Beach Unified	Long Beach
267	1,484.6	Santa Barbara High	Santa Barbara
268	1,463.5	Oroville Union High	Oroville
269	1,442.8	Petaluma Joint Union High	Petaluma
270	1,436.5	Los Gatos-Saratoga Jt Union High	Los Gatos
271	1,436.0	Acalanes Union High	Lafayette
272	1,411.3	Travis Unified	Travis Afb
273	1,375.0	San Mateo Union High	San Mateo
274	1,367.0	Dos Palos Oro Loma Joint Unified	Dos Palos
275	1,357.1	Evergreen Elementary	San Jose
276	1,343.8	Jefferson Union High	Daly City
277	1,302.9	Santa Rosa High	Santa Rosa
278	1,269.3	New Haven Unified	Union City
279	1,260.7	Tamalpais Union High	Larkspur
280	1,229.4	Chula Vista Elementary	Chula Vista
281	1,229.0	Anderson Union High	Anderson
282	1,214.7	Hayward Unified	Hayward
283	1,201.5	Orland Joint Unified	Orland
284	1,167.4	Mount Diablo Unified	Concord
285	1,114.9	Modesto City Elementary	Modesto
286	1,099.5	Carmel Unified	Carmel
287	1,084.4	Pacific Grove Unified	Pacific Grove
288	1,060.7	Weaver Union Elementary	Merced
289	1,031.4	Santa Cruz City High	Santa Cruz
290	1,019.1	San Jose Unified	San Jose
291	927.2	Los Alamitos Unified	Los Alamitos
292	900.7	Sierra Unified	Auberry
293	884.6	Alameda City Unified	Alameda
294	883.6	Northern Humboldt Union High	McKinleyville
295	873.7	Eastside Union Elementary	Lancaster
296	866.0	Novato Unified	Novato
297	810.3	Palo Alto Unified	Palo Alto
298	743.0	Santa Barbara Elementary	Santa Barbara
299	711.5	Merced City Elementary	Merced
300	646.4	Burlingame Elementary	Burlingame
301	641.5	Piedmont City Unified	Piedmont
302	599.7	Menlo Park City Elementary	Atherton
303	573.8	Orinda Union Elementary	Orinda
304	508.4	Mill Valley Elementary	Mill Valley
305	439.3	Santa Cruz City Elementary	Santa Cruz
306	0.0	ABC Unified	Cerritos
306	0.0	Acton-Agua Dulce Unified	Acton
306	0.0	Adelanto Elementary	Adelanto
306	0.0	Alhambra City Elementary	Alhambra
306	0.0	Alpine Union Elementary	Alpine
306	0.0	Alta Loma Elementary	Alta Loma
306	0.0	Amador County Unified	Jackson
306	0.0	Anaheim Elementary	Anaheim
306	0.0	Apple Valley Unified	Apple Valley
306	0.0	Arvin Union Elementary	Arvin
306	0.0	Auburn Union Elementary	Auburn
306	0.0	Azusa Unified	Azusa
306	0.0	Banning Unified	Banning
306	0.0	Bassett Unified	La Puente
306	0.0	Beardsley Elementary	Bakersfield
306	0.0	Bellevue Union Elementary	Santa Rosa
306	0.0	Belmont-Redwood Shores Elementary	Belmont
306	0.0	Benicia Unified	Benicia
306	0.0	Berryessa Union Elementary	San Jose
306	0.0	Bishop Union Elementary	Bishop
306	0.0	Bonsall Union Elementary	Bonsall
306	0.0	Brawley Elementary	Brawley
306	0.0	Brawley Union High	Brawley
306	0.0	Brea-Olinda Unified	Brea
306	0.0	Brentwood Union Elementary	Brentwood
306	0.0	Buena Park Elementary	Buena Park
306	0.0	Burbank Unified	Burbank
306	0.0	Calaveras Unified	San Andreas
306	0.0	Calexico Unified	Calexico
306	0.0	Cambrian Elementary	San Jose
306	0.0	Campbell Union Elementary	Campbell
306	0.0	Carpinteria Unified	Carpinteria
306	0.0	Cascade Union Elementary	Anderson
306	0.0	Castaic Union Elementary	Valencia
306	0.0	Centinela Valley Union High	Lawndale
306	0.0	Central Union Elementary	Lemoore
306	0.0	Centralia Elementary	Buena Park
306	0.0	Charter Oak Unified	Covina
306	0.0	Chowchilla Elementary	Chowchilla
306	0.0	Cloverdale Unified	Cloverdale
306	0.0	Coalinga-Huron Joint Unified	Coalinga
306	0.0	Coronado Unified	Coronado
306	0.0	Cucamonga Elementary	Rcho Cucamong
306	0.0	Cupertino Union School	Cupertino
306	0.0	Cutler-Orosi Joint Unified	Orosi
306	0.0	Cypress Elementary	Cypress
306	0.0	Del Mar Union Elementary	Del Mar
306	0.0	Del Norte County Unified	Crescent City
306	0.0	Del Paso Heights Elementary	Sacramento
306	0.0	Delano Joint Union High	Delano
306	0.0	Delano Union Elementary	Delano
306	0.0	Dry Creek Joint Elementary	Roseville
306	0.0	Duarte Unified	Duarte
306	0.0	Earlimart Elementary	Earlimart
306	0.0	East Whittier City Elementary	Whittier
306	0.0	El Centro Elementary	El Centro
306	0.0	El Monte City Elementary	El Monte
306	0.0	El Rancho Unified	Pico Rivera
306	0.0	Encinitas Union Elementary	Encinitas
306	0.0	Escalon Unified	Escalon
306	0.0	Escondido Union High	Escondido
306	0.0	Eureka Union Elementary	Granite Bay
306	0.0	Exeter Union Elementary	Exeter
306	0.0	Fallbrook Union Elementary	Fallbrook
306	0.0	Fallbrook Union High	Fallbrook
306	0.0	Farmersville Unified	Farmersville
306	0.0	Fillmore Unified	Fillmore
306	0.0	Fruitvale Elementary	Bakersfield
306	0.0	Galt Joint Union Elementary	Galt
306	0.0	Galt Joint Union High	Galt
306	0.0	Glendale Unified	Glendale
306	0.0	Golden Plains Unified	San Joaquin
306	0.0	Goleta Union Elementary	Goleta
306	0.0	Gorman Elementary	Gorman
306	0.0	Greenfield Union Elementary	Bakersfield
306	0.0	Gustine Unified	Gustine
306	0.0	Hacienda La Puente Unified	City of Industry
306	0.0	Hanford Elementary	Hanford
306	0.0	Hawthorne Elementary	Hawthorne
306	0.0	Healdsburg Unified	Healdsburg
306	0.0	Hesperia Unified	Hesperia
306	0.0	Hilmar Unified	Hilmar
306	0.0	Hollister SD	Hollister
306	0.0	Holtville Unified	Holtville
306	0.0	Hueneme Elementary	Port Hueneme
306	0.0	Hughson Unified	Hughson
306	0.0	Huntington Beach City Elementary	Huntington Bch
306	0.0	Imperial Unified	Imperial
306	0.0	Jamul-Dulzura Union Elementary	Jamul
306	0.0	Jefferson Elementary	Tracy
306	0.0	Julian Union Elementary	Julian
306	0.0	Julian Union High	Julian
306	0.0	Jurupa Unified	Riverside
306	0.0	Kelseyville Unified	Kelseyville
306	0.0	Keppel Union Elementary	Pearblossom
306	0.0	Kern County Office of Ed	Bakersfield
306	0.0	Keyes Union Elementary	Keyes
306	0.0	King City Union Elementary	King City
306	0.0	Konocti Unified	Lower Lake
306	0.0	La Habra City Elementary	La Habra
306	0.0	Laguna Beach Unified	Laguna Beach
306	0.0	Lake Elsinore Unified	Lake Elsinore
306	0.0	Lakeport Unified	Lakeport
306	0.0	Lakeside Union Elementary	Lakeside
306	0.0	Lancaster Elementary	Lancaster
306	0.0	Lemon Grove Elementary	Lemon Grove
306	0.0	Lemoore Union Elementary	Lemoore
306	0.0	Lennox Elementary	Lennox
306	0.0	Linden Unified	Linden
306	0.0	Little Lake City Elementary	Santa Fe Spgs
306	0.0	Live Oak Unified	Live Oak
306	0.0	Livermore Valley Joint Unified	Livermore
306	0.0	Loomis Union Elementary	Loomis
306	0.0	Los Altos Elementary	Los Altos
306	0.0	Los Nietos Elementary	Whittier
306	0.0	Lowell Joint	Whittier
306	0.0	Magnolia Elementary	Anaheim
306	0.0	Mariposa County Unified	Mariposa
306	0.0	Mark West Union Elementary	Santa Rosa
306	0.0	Menifee Union Elementary	Menifee
306	0.0	Middletown Unified	Middletown
306	0.0	Mojave Unified	Mojave
306	0.0	Monrovia Unified	Monrovia
306	0.0	Moorpark Unified	Moorpark
306	0.0	Moraga Elementary	Moraga
306	0.0	Moreland Elementary	San Jose
306	0.0	Moreno Valley Unified	Moreno Valley
306	0.0	Mother Lode Union Elementary	Placerville
306	0.0	Mount Pleasant Elementary	San Jose
306	0.0	Mountain View Elementary	Ontario
306	0.0	Mountain View-Whisman Elementary	Mountain View
306	0.0	Muroc Joint Unified	North Edwards
306	0.0	National Elementary	National City
306	0.0	Newhall Elementary	Valencia
306	0.0	Newman-Crows Landing Unified	Newman
306	0.0	North Sacramento Elementary	Sacramento
306	0.0	Oak Park Unified	Oak Park
306	0.0	Oakdale Joint Unified	Oakdale
306	0.0	Oakley Union Elementary	Oakley
306	0.0	Ocean View Elementary	Huntington Bch
306	0.0	Ocean View Elementary	Oxnard
306	0.0	Ojai Unified	Ojai
306	0.0	Old Adobe Union Elementary	Petaluma
306	0.0	Ontario-Montclair Elementary	Ontario
306	0.0	Oro Grande Elementary	Oro Grande
306	0.0	Oxnard Elementary	Oxnard
306	0.0	Pajaro Valley Unified School	Watsonville
306	0.0	Palmdale Elementary	Palmdale
306	0.0	Palo Verde Unified	Blythe
306	0.0	Paramount Unified	Paramount
306	0.0	Parlier Unified	Parlier
306	0.0	Perris Elementary	Perris
306	0.0	Petaluma City Elementary	Petaluma
306	0.0	Piner-Olivet Union Elementary	Santa Rosa
306	0.0	Pleasant Ridge Union Elementary	Grass Valley
306	0.0	Plumas Unified	Quincy
306	0.0	Ravenswood City Elementary	East Palo Alto
306	0.0	Red Bluff Joint Union High	Red Bluff
306	0.0	Redding Elementary	Redding
306	0.0	Redwood City Elementary	Redwood City
306	0.0	Reef-Sunset Unified	Avenal
306	0.0	Rescue Union Elementary	Rescue
306	0.0	Rincon Valley Union Elementary	Santa Rosa
306	0.0	Rio Elementary	Oxnard
306	0.0	Ripon Unified	Ripon
306	0.0	River Delta Joint Unified	Rio Vista
306	0.0	Riverbank Unified	Riverbank
306	0.0	Robla Elementary	Sacramento
306	0.0	Romoland Elementary	Homeland
306	0.0	Rosemead Elementary	Rosemead
306	0.0	Roseville City Elementary	Roseville
306	0.0	Ross Valley Elementary	San Anselmo
306	0.0	Saint Helena Unified	Saint Helena
306	0.0	Salida Union Elementary	Salida
306	0.0	Salinas City Elementary	Salinas
306	0.0	San Bruno Park Elementary	San Bruno
306	0.0	San Carlos Elementary	San Carlos
306	0.0	San Jacinto Unified	San Jacinto
306	0.0	San Joaquin County Office of Ed	Stockton
306	0.0	San Lorenzo Valley Unified	Felton
306	0.0	San Ysidro Elementary	San Ysidro
306	0.0	Santa Paula Elementary	Santa Paula
306	0.0	Santa Paula Union High	Santa Paula
306	0.0	Santa Rita Union Elementary	Salinas
306	0.0	Saugus Union Elementary	Santa Clarita
306	0.0	Savanna Elementary	Anaheim
306	0.0	Scotts Valley Unified	Scotts Valley
306	0.0	Silver Valley Unified	Yermo
306	0.0	Snowline Joint Unified	Phelan
306	0.0	Solana Beach Elementary	Solana Beach
306	0.0	Soquel Union Elementary	Capitola
306	0.0	South Bay Union Elementary	Imperial Beach
306	0.0	South Whittier Elementary	Whittier
306	0.0	Southern Kern Unified	Rosamond
306	0.0	Standard Elementary	Bakersfield
306	0.0	Stanislaus Union Elementary	Modesto
306	0.0	Sulphur Springs Union Elementary	Canyon Country
306	0.0	Taft City Elementary	Taft
306	0.0	Templeton Unified	Templeton
306	0.0	Tulare City Elementary	Tulare
306	0.0	Turlock Joint Elementary	Turlock
306	0.0	Turlock Joint Union High	Turlock
306	0.0	Twin Ridges Elementary	North San Juan
306	0.0	Union Elementary	San Jose
306	0.0	Val Verde Unified	Perris
306	0.0	Valley Center-Pauma Unified	Valley Center
306	0.0	Victor Elementary	Victorville
306	0.0	Walnut Creek Elementary	Walnut Creek
306	0.0	Walnut Valley Unified	Walnut
306	0.0	Wasco Union Elementary	Wasco
306	0.0	Waterford Unified	Waterford

306	0.0	West Covina Unified	West Covina
306	0.0	West Sonoma County Union High	Sebastopol
306	0.0	Western Placer Unified	Lincoln
306	0.0	Westminster Elementary	Westminster
306	0.0	Westside Union Elementary	Lancaster
306	0.0	Westwood Unified	Westwood
306	0.0	Whittier City Elementary	Whittier
306	0.0	Willows Unified	Willows
306	0.0	Wilsona Elementary	Palmdale
306	0.0	Windsor Unified	Windsor
306	0.0	Winton Elementary	Winton
306	0.0	Wiseburn Elementary	Hawthorne
306	0.0	Woodlake Union Elementary	Woodlake

Student/Counselor Ratio

Rank	Ratio	District Name	City
1	22,375.0	Anaheim Elementary	Anaheim
2	20,120.0	Saugus Union Elementary	Santa Clarita
3	15,800.0	Fountain Valley Elementary	Fountain Valley
4	14,953.3	Mountain View-Whisman Elementary	Mountain View
5	14,668.0	Huntington Beach Union High	Huntington Bch
6	12,704.4	Alhambra City Elementary	Alhambra
7	11,856.7	Roseville City Elementary	Roseville
8	11,431.7	Garvey Elementary	Rosemead
9	9,373.3	Encinitas Union Elementary	Encinitas
10	9,270.0	Twin Ridges Elementary	North San Juan
11	8,813.0	Redwood City Elementary	Redwood City
12	8,220.0	Goleta Union Elementary	Goleta
13	7,508.0	Palmdale Elementary	Palmdale
14	7,097.0	Delano Union Elementary	Delano
15	6,280.0	Hollister SD	Hollister
16	6,146.8	Chula Vista Elementary	Chula Vista
17	6,096.7	Moraga Elementary	Moraga
18	6,076.0	Capistrano Unified	San Juan Capis
19	5,648.0	Richland SD	Shafter
20	5,248.5	Mountain View Elementary	El Monte
21	5,168.0	Ravenswood City Elementary	East Palo Alto
22	4,866.0	Livingston Union Elementary	Livingston
23	4,545.0	Ontario-Montclair Elementary	Ontario
24	4,380.0	Fresno County Office of Ed	Fresno
25	4,324.0	Hueneme Elementary	Port Hueneme
26	4,248.6	Selma Unified	Selma
27	4,243.0	Eureka Union Elementary	Granite Bay
28	4,143.3	Savanna Elementary	Anaheim
29	4,135.5	Orange County Office of Ed	Costa Mesa
30	4,100.0	Julian Union Elementary	Julian
31	4,032.0	Los Altos Elementary	Los Altos
32	3,987.9	Antioch Unified	Antioch
33	3,968.3	Cupertino Union School	Cupertino
34	3,917.2	Marysville Joint Unified	Marysville
35	3,814.0	Enterprise Elementary	Redding
36	3,566.8	Fullerton Elementary	Fullerton
37	3,494.5	Magnolia Elementary	Anaheim
38	3,450.0	Newhall Elementary	Valencia
39	3,439.0	Mountain View Elementary	Ontario
40	3,378.0	San Diego County Office of Ed	San Diego
41	3,362.5	Panama Buena Vista Union Elem	Bakersfield
42	3,216.7	Wiseburn Elementary	Hawthorne
43	3,176.3	Belmont-Redwood Shores Elementary	Belmont
44	3,153.0	Laguna Salada Union Elementary	Pacifica
45	3,147.3	Victor Elementary	Victorville
46	3,047.0	Fruitvale Elementary	Bakersfield
47	2,995.0	Santa Rita Union Elementary	Salinas
48	2,946.0	Waterford Unified	Waterford
49	2,924.0	Keppel Union Elementary	Pearblossom
50	2,912.1	Livermore Valley Joint Unified	Livermore
51	2,900.0	Bonsall Union Elementary	Bonsall
52	2,849.0	Mount Pleasant Elementary	San Jose
53	2,807.0	Cambrian Elementary	San Jose
54	2,774.0	Adelanto Elementary	Adelanto
55	2,654.0	Cutler-Orosi Joint Unified	Orosi
56	2,652.0	Los Gatos Union Elementary	Los Gatos
57	2,627.0	King City Union Elementary	King City
58	2,620.3	Tulare City Elementary	Tulare
59	2,613.0	Little Lake City Elementary	Santa Fe Spgs
60	2,607.2	Duarte Unified	Duarte
61	2,494.3	Campbell Union Elementary	Campbell
62	2,488.0	Delhi Unified	Delhi
63	2,469.9	Saddleback Valley Unified	Mission Viejo
64	2,453.5	Tehachapi Unified	Tehachapi
65	2,428.0	Alpine Union Elementary	Alpine
66	2,410.0	Hilmar Unified	Hilmar
67	2,385.7	Walnut Creek Elementary	Walnut Creek
68	2,380.0	Greenfield Union Elementary	Bakersfield
69	2,353.6	National Elementary	National City
70	2,350.0	Los Nietos Elementary	Whittier
71	2,318.5	Union Elementary	San Jose
72	2,308.0	Newman-Crows Landing Unified	Newman
73	2,244.6	Escondido Union Elementary	Escondido
74	2,240.2	East Whittier City Elementary	Whittier
75	2,206.5	Moreland Elementary	San Jose
76	2,204.8	Lawndale Elementary	Lawndale
77	2,177.0	Oakley Union Elementary	Oakley
78	2,151.0	Millbrae Elementary	Millbrae
79	2,140.6	Lafayette Elementary	Lafayette
80	2,114.0	Kingsburg Elementary Charter	Kingsburg
81	2,112.0	Soquel Union Elementary	Capitola
82	2,091.0	Wilsona Elementary	Palmdale
83	2,071.0	Pleasant Ridge Union Elementary	Grass Valley
84	2,042.5	Rosedale Union Elementary	Bakersfield
85	2,026.8	Rio Linda Union Elementary	Rio Linda
86	2,022.6	Westminster Elementary	Westminster
87	2,005.7	Santa Maria-Bonita Elementary	Santa Maria
88	1,996.0	Central Union Elementary	Lemoore
89	1,990.6	Franklin-Mckinley Elementary	San Jose
90	1,964.0	Corning Union Elementary	Corning
91	1,948.2	Santa Maria Joint Union High	Santa Maria
92	1,880.0	Brawley Elementary	Brawley
93	1,869.5	Westside Union Elementary	Lancaster
94	1,865.5	Calaveras Unified	San Andreas
95	1,860.0	Live Oak Unified	Live Oak
96	1,855.0	Dixie Elementary	San Rafael
97	1,848.7	Ripon Unified	Ripon
98	1,847.3	Pleasant Valley School	Camarillo
99	1,843.0	Palo Verde Unified	Blythe
100	1,821.5	Atwater Elementary	Atwater
101	1,820.0	Western Placer Unified	Lincoln
102	1,795.8	Visalia Unified	Visalia
103	1,793.0	Winton Elementary	Winton
104	1,792.0	Gustine Unified	Gustine
105	1,790.0	Mother Lode Union Elementary	Placerville
105	1,790.0	Ross Valley Elementary	San Anselmo
107	1,764.5	Rescue Union Elementary	Rescue
108	1,736.5	Salida Union Elementary	Salida
109	1,713.4	Bellflower Unified	Bellflower
110	1,710.0	Jamul-Dulzura Union Elementary	Jamul
111	1,683.5	Oroville City Elementary	Oroville
112	1,675.0	San Ysidro Elementary	San Ysidro
113	1,641.3	Sacramento City Unified	Sacramento
114	1,624.2	Turlock Joint Elementary	Turlock
115	1,612.9	Oak Grove Elementary	San Jose
116	1,604.0	Cascade Union Elementary	Anderson
117	1,597.0	Cloverdale Unified	Cloverdale
118	1,596.9	Baldwin Park Unified	Baldwin Park
119	1,590.5	Lemoore Union Elementary	Lemoore
120	1,567.9	Central Unified	Fresno
121	1,560.9	Porterville Unified	Porterville
122	1,555.8	El Centro Elementary	El Centro
123	1,551.7	Banning Unified	Banning
124	1,551.3	Burlingame Elementary	Burlingame
125	1,550.7	Kings Canyon Joint Unified	Reedley
126	1,476.1	Pomona Unified	Pomona
127	1,475.4	Sylvan Union Elementary	Modesto
128	1,456.9	Red Bluff Union Elementary	Red Bluff
129	1,441.5	Rowland Unified	Rowland Heights
130	1,434.8	Cajon Valley Union Elementary	El Cajon
131	1,431.1	Chino Valley Unified	Chino
132	1,430.5	Garden Grove Unified	Garden Grove
133	1,420.0	Carlsbad Unified	Carlsbad
134	1,419.1	Dry Creek Joint Elementary	Roseville
135	1,383.3	Val Verde Unified	Perris
136	1,375.3	Redding Elementary	Redding
137	1,370.3	El Rancho Unified	Pico Rivera
138	1,359.5	Lamont Elementary	Lamont
139	1,355.2	Morgan Hill Unified	Morgan Hill
140	1,348.0	Black Oak Mine Unified	Georgetown
141	1,342.8	Saratoga Union Elementary	Saratoga
142	1,336.6	Placentia-Yorba Linda Unified	Placentia
143	1,336.4	San Jacinto Unified	San Jacinto
144	1,328.5	Burton Elementary	Porterville
145	1,321.6	Newark Unified	Newark
146	1,316.5	Ocean View Elementary	Oxnard
147	1,308.5	Merced City Elementary	Merced
148	1,307.8	Central Elementary	Rcho Cucamong
149	1,298.1	Los Alamitos Unified	Los Alamitos
150	1,292.0	Standard Elementary	Bakersfield
151	1,290.0	San Carlos Elementary	San Carlos
152	1,288.0	Grass Valley Elementary	Grass Valley
153	1,285.8	Rocklin Unified	Rocklin
154	1,275.9	Dublin Unified	Dublin
155	1,263.8	Irvine Unified	Irvine
156	1,260.9	San Mateo-Foster City Elementary	San Mateo
157	1,260.6	Coachella Valley Unified	Thermal
158	1,255.0	Kern County Office of Ed	Bakersfield
159	1,254.6	Santa Ana Unified	Santa Ana
160	1,253.5	Ceres Unified	Ceres
161	1,246.0	Gateway Unified	Redding
162	1,244.6	Beaumont Unified	Beaumont
163	1,243.5	Lakeside Union Elementary	Lakeside
164	1,242.0	San Marcos Unified	San Marcos
165	1,235.3	San Jose Unified	San Jose
166	1,223.1	Fallbrook Union Elementary	Fallbrook
167	1,213.1	Riverdale Joint Unified	Riverdale
168	1,209.1	San Lorenzo Valley Unified	Felton
169	1,205.0	Orinda Union Elementary	Orinda
170	1,204.1	Simi Valley Unified	Simi Valley
171	1,203.9	Berryessa Union Elementary	San Jose
171	1,203.9	Madera Unified	Madera
173	1,203.8	Gilroy Unified	Gilroy
174	1,201.3	Alum Rock Union Elementary	San Jose
175	1,199.6	Hesperia Unified	Hesperia
176	1,194.2	ABC Unified	Cerritos
177	1,194.0	Vacaville Unified	Vacaville
178	1,192.5	Azusa Unified	Azusa
179	1,191.5	Whittier City Elementary	Whittier
180	1,185.0	Valley Center-Pauma Unified	Valley Center
181	1,183.4	Morongo Unified	Twentynine Plms
182	1,182.7	Inglewood Unified	Inglewood
183	1,177.5	Brea-Olinda Unified	Brea
184	1,173.4	Castaic Union Elementary	Valencia
185	1,170.8	El Segundo Unified	El Segundo
186	1,166.0	Middletown Unified	Middletown
187	1,144.9	Lynwood Unified	Lynwood
188	1,140.6	Napa Valley Unified	Napa
189	1,137.9	Manteca Unified	Manteca
190	1,137.2	Jurupa Unified	Riverside
191	1,130.0	Bear Valley Unified	Big Bear Lake
192	1,128.1	Temecula Valley Unified	Temecula
193	1,125.9	Palm Springs Unified	Palm Springs
194	1,120.0	San Bruno Park Elementary	San Bruno
195	1,109.8	Fairfield-Suisun Unified	Fairfield
196	1,105.7	Parlier Unified	Parlier
197	1,099.0	Alvord Unified	Riverside
198	1,093.3	Center Joint Unified	Antelope
199	1,092.8	Hawthorne Elementary	Hawthorne
200	1,091.6	Lucia Mar Unified	Arroyo Grande
201	1,084.5	Martinez Unified	Martinez
202	1,082.5	Del Norte County Unified	Crescent City
203	1,082.2	Ramona City Unified	Ramona
204	1,081.4	Milpitas Unified	Milpitas
205	1,080.3	Buckeye Union Elementary	Shingle Springs
206	1,079.7	Fullerton Joint Union High	Fullerton
207	1,074.3	San Bernardino County Supt.	San Bernardino
208	1,070.6	Oceanside Unified	Oceanside
209	1,070.1	Glendale Unified	Glendale
210	1,068.0	Fowler Unified	Fowler
211	1,065.0	Mendota Unified	Mendota
212	1,064.4	Murrieta Valley Unified	Murrieta
213	1,062.8	Pajaro Valley Unified School	Watsonville
213	1,062.8	Patterson Joint Unified	Patterson
215	1,059.0	Corcoran Joint Unified	Corcoran
216	1,056.3	Hughson Unified	Hughson
216	1,056.3	West Covina Unified	West Covina
218	1,053.7	Hacienda La Puente Unified	City of Industry
219	1,052.4	West Contra Costa Unified	Richmond
220	1,049.4	Centralia Elementary	Buena Park
220	1,049.4	Corona-Norco Unified	Norco
222	1,048.8	San Rafael City Elementary	San Rafael
223	1,046.7	Fresno Unified	Fresno
224	1,045.7	Hayward Unified	Hayward
225	1,045.4	Linden Unified	Linden
226	1,041.7	Vista Unified	Vista
227	1,039.0	Acton-Agua Dulce Unified	Acton
228	1,034.0	Mark West Union Elementary	Santa Rosa
229	1,032.3	Downey Unified	Downey
230	1,030.0	Monrovia Unified	Monrovia
231	1,028.9	Norris Elementary	Bakersfield
232	1,026.0	Monterey Peninsula Unified	Monterey
233	1,018.2	Upland Unified	Upland
234	1,010.7	Bishop Union Elementary	Bishop
235	1,006.0	Carpinteria Unified	Carpinteria
236	1,003.9	Orange Unified	Orange
237	1,003.0	Auburn Union Elementary	Auburn
238	999.5	Glendora Unified	Glendora
239	989.3	Apple Valley Unified	Apple Valley
240	986.0	Fremont Unified	Fremont
241	985.4	Woodland Joint Unified	Woodland
242	982.0	Oakdale Joint Unified	Oakdale
243	981.2	Covina-Valley Unified	Covina
244	980.9	Claremont Unified	Claremont
245	978.8	Ojai Unified	Ojai
246	976.1	Snowline Joint Unified	Phelan
247	974.6	Tustin Unified	Tustin
248	973.6	Plumas Unified	Quincy
249	973.1	Santa Clara Unified	Santa Clara
250	970.9	Lake Elsinore Unified	Lake Elsinore
251	968.1	Lompoc Unified	Lompoc
252	967.3	Fillmore Unified	Fillmore
253	962.0	Holtville Unified	Holtville
254	960.7	Colton Joint Unified	Colton
255	954.2	Pittsburg Unified	Pittsburg
256	953.3	Tracy Joint Unified	Tracy
257	941.9	Washington Unified	West Sacramento
258	937.4	San Ramon Valley Unified	Danville
259	935.0	Benicia Unified	Benicia
260	925.1	Las Virgenes Unified	Calabasas

261	924.5	Berkeley Unified	Berkeley
262	924.2	Yucaipa-Calimesa Joint Unified	Yucaipa
263	920.5	Newport-Mesa Unified	Costa Mesa
264	913.8	Soledad Unified	Soledad
265	912.6	Mcfarland Unified	Mcfarland
265	912.6	Montebello Unified	Montebello
267	907.3	Alameda City Unified	Alameda
268	906.5	San Juan Unified	Carmichael
269	905.8	Norwalk-La Mirada Unified	Norwalk
270	905.6	Brentwood Union Elementary	Brentwood
271	900.0	Laguna Beach Unified	Laguna Beach
272	894.7	Templeton Unified	Templeton
273	893.8	Travis Unified	Travis Afb
274	892.7	Farmersville Unified	Farmersville
275	890.8	Burbank Unified	Burbank
276	885.5	Gorman Elementary	Gorman
277	883.1	Riverside Unified	Riverside
278	879.4	Oakland Unified	Oakland
279	873.7	Sanger Unified	Sanger
280	872.7	North Monterey County Unified	Moss Landing
281	866.0	Novato Unified	Novato
282	863.4	Folsom-Cordova Unified	Folsom
283	862.5	Santa Paula Union High	Santa Paula
284	862.1	Rialto Unified	Rialto
285	856.9	Ukiah Unified	Ukiah
286	850.3	Natomas Unified	Sacramento
287	846.7	San Lorenzo Unified	San Lorenzo
288	846.2	Coalinga-Huron Joint Unified	Coalinga
289	845.6	Fontana Unified	Fontana
290	842.7	Elk Grove Unified	Elk Grove
291	841.2	Bonita Unified	San Dimas
292	834.8	Los Angeles Unified	Los Angeles
293	825.7	Rim of The World Unified	Lake Arrowhead
294	825.1	San Gabriel Unified	San Gabriel
295	818.1	Mojave Unified	Mojave
296	817.2	Bassett Unified	La Puente
297	816.8	Poway Unified	Poway
298	812.7	Temple City Unified	Temple City
299	811.3	Muroc Joint Unified	North Edwards
300	809.0	Willits Unified	Willits
301	807.3	Reef-Sunset Unified	Avenal
302	807.1	Walnut Valley Unified	Walnut
303	806.6	Moorpark Unified	Moorpark
304	805.8	Lake Tahoe Unified	S Lake Tahoe
305	801.6	Fremont Union High	Sunnyvale
306	798.3	Riverbank Unified	Riverbank
307	798.1	Los Gatos-Saratoga Jt Union High	Los Gatos
308	795.5	Weaver Union Elementary	Merced
309	793.8	Bakersfield City Elementary	Bakersfield
310	791.7	Gonzales Unified	Gonzales
311	789.2	Pasadena Unified	Pasadena
312	785.2	Palo Alto Unified	Palo Alto
313	784.8	Culver City Unified	Culver City
314	784.5	Pleasanton Unified	Pleasanton
315	784.3	Compton Unified	Compton
316	780.6	New Haven Unified	Union City
317	779.2	Live Oak Elementary	Santa Cruz
318	769.0	Colusa Unified	Colusa
319	768.4	Firebaugh-Las Deltas Joint Unified	Firebaugh
320	764.3	Vallejo City Unified	Vallejo
321	761.5	Conejo Valley Unified	Thousand Oaks
322	760.2	Cabrillo Unified	Half Moon Bay
323	752.6	Imperial Unified	Imperial
324	750.4	Oak Park Unified	Oak Park
325	747.8	San Leandro Unified	San Leandro
326	747.1	South San Francisco Unified	S San Francisco
327	738.3	Cotati-Rohnert Park Unified	Rohnert Park
328	737.4	Chico Unified	Chico
329	736.4	Arcadia Unified	Arcadia
330	733.4	Taft City Elementary	Taft
331	732.5	Sierra Sands Unified	Ridgecrest
332	731.6	Torrance Unified	Torrance
333	728.8	Mountain Empire Unified	Pine Valley
333	728.8	Palos Verdes Peninsula Unified	Palos Verdes Est
335	727.2	La Canada Unified	La Canada
336	720.3	Castro Valley Unified	Castro Valley
337	718.8	Eureka City Unified	Eureka
338	718.3	Del Paso Heights Elementary	Sacramento
339	707.4	Lakeport Unified	Lakeport
340	706.4	Lodi Unified	Lodi
341	703.1	Menlo Park City Elementary	Atherton
342	702.7	John Swett Unified	Crockett
343	701.0	Dos Palos Oro Loma Joint Unified	Dos Palos
344	697.8	Coronado Unified	Coronado
345	696.7	Paradise Unified	Paradise
346	695.7	Empire Union Elementary	Modesto
347	694.7	Fort Bragg Unified	Fort Bragg
348	691.3	Galt Joint Union High	Galt
349	684.2	Fallbrook Union High	Fallbrook
350	680.9	Thermalito Union Elementary	Oroville
351	680.5	Desert Sands Unified	La Quinta
352	676.5	Escalon Unified	Escalon
353	676.1	Hemet Unified	Hemet
354	675.9	Willows Unified	Willows
355	672.2	Dinuba Unified	Dinuba
356	671.7	Redlands Unified	Redlands
357	667.8	Paramount Unified	Paramount
358	667.5	Silver Valley Unified	Yermo
359	667.0	Windsor Unified	Windsor
360	666.3	Amador County Unified	Jackson
361	663.9	San Bernardino City Unified	San Bernardino
362	655.7	Kelseyville Unified	Kelseyville
363	646.6	Santa Rosa Elementary	Santa Rosa
364	644.8	Dixon Unified	Dixon
365	640.3	Greenfield Union Elementary	Greenfield
366	638.0	San Marino Unified	San Marino
367	627.3	Campbell Union High	San Jose
368	624.5	Redondo Beach Unified	Redondo Beach
369	622.1	Grossmont Union High	La Mesa
370	616.8	Victor Valley Union High	Victorville
371	614.5	Long Beach Unified	Long Beach
372	613.0	Davis Joint Unified	Davis
373	604.8	Albany City Unified	Albany
374	603.5	Ventura Unified	Ventura
375	601.7	Lennox Elementary	Lennox
376	600.8	Orland Joint Unified	Orland
377	589.8	Scotts Valley Unified	Scotts Valley
378	588.2	East Side Union High	San Jose
379	587.7	Manhattan Beach Unified	Manhattan Beach
380	586.7	Mill Valley Elementary	Mill Valley
381	585.4	Oroville Union High	Oroville
382	584.7	Paso Robles Joint Unified	Paso Robles
383	581.3	Perris Union High	Perris
384	580.7	Tahoe-Truckee Joint Unified	Truckee
385	568.0	Barstow Unified	Barstow
386	562.2	Atascadero Unified	Atascadero
387	559.3	Konocti Unified	Lower Lake
388	558.7	Lincoln Unified	Stockton
389	552.1	Moreno Valley Unified	Moreno Valley
390	546.7	South Pasadena Unified	South Pasadena
391	546.2	Yuba City Unified	Yuba City
392	545.1	San Francisco Unified	San Francisco
393	544.2	Santa Monica-Malibu Unified	Santa Monica
394	541.8	Calexico Unified	Calexico
395	532.7	Stockton City Unified	Stockton
396	532.6	Clovis Unified	Clovis
397	528.7	Sierra Unified	Auberry
398	527.3	King City Joint Union High	King City
399	527.1	La Mesa-Spring Valley	La Mesa
400	525.5	Liberty Union High	Brentwood
401	522.7	Escondido Union High	Escondido
402	521.5	Antelope Valley Union High	Lancaster
403	518.6	Delano Joint Union High	Delano
403	518.6	Santa Paula Elementary	Santa Paula
405	514.8	Red Bluff Joint Union High	Red Bluff
406	513.7	Pacific Grove Unified	Pacific Grove
407	512.0	Mariposa County Unified	Mariposa
408	509.4	North Sacramento Elementary	Sacramento
409	509.3	Alhambra City High	Alhambra
410	509.1	San Benito High	Hollister
411	509.0	Merced Union High	Atwater
412	507.1	Jefferson Union High	Daly City
413	506.1	San Luis Coastal Unified	San Luis Obispo
414	503.7	Sonoma Valley Unified	Sonoma
415	497.4	Anaheim Union High	Anaheim
416	488.4	San Diego Unified	San Diego
417	484.2	Modesto City High	Modesto
418	475.3	William S Hart Union High	Santa Clarita
419	471.8	Gridley Unified	Gridley
420	468.7	San Mateo Union High	San Mateo
421	461.1	River Delta Joint Unified	Rio Vista
422	456.9	Placer Union High	Auburn
423	450.3	Salinas Union High	Salinas
424	449.8	Healdsburg Unified	Healdsburg
425	449.7	Grant Joint Union High	Sacramento
426	448.0	Santa Clara County Office of Ed	San Jose
427	445.3	El Dorado Union High	Placerville
428	444.6	San Joaquin County Office of Ed	Stockton
429	443.0	Winters Joint Unified	Winters
430	442.9	San Dieguito Union High	Encinitas
430	442.9	Turlock Joint Union High	Turlock
432	441.6	Kern Union High	Bakersfield
433	440.3	Santa Barbara High	Santa Barbara
434	436.0	Beverly Hills Unified	Beverly Hills
435	435.2	Acalanes Union High	Lafayette
436	430.7	Petaluma Joint Union High	Petaluma
437	430.0	Sonora Union High	Sonora
438	422.7	Santa Cruz City High	Santa Cruz
439	421.3	El Monte Union High	El Monte
440	418.2	Lindsay Unified	Lindsay
440	418.2	San Rafael City High	San Rafael
442	415.3	Centinela Valley Union High	Lawndale
443	414.7	Nevada Joint Union High	Grass Valley
444	406.6	Lemoore Union High	Lemoore
445	400.2	Roseville Joint Union High	Roseville
446	400.1	Hanford Joint Union High	Hanford
447	398.9	Chaffey Joint Union High	Ontario
448	397.9	Mountain View-Los Altos Union High	Mountain View
449	394.1	Oxnard Union High	Oxnard
450	391.8	Los Angeles County Office of Ed	Downey
451	391.4	Golden Plains Unified	San Joaquin
452	388.8	Northern Humboldt Union High	McKinleyville
453	388.4	Shasta Union High	Redding
454	387.4	Whittier Union High	Whittier
455	375.0	Saint Helena Unified	Saint Helena
456	356.0	Santa Rosa High	Santa Rosa
457	351.1	Anderson Union High	Anderson
458	349.1	Sequoia Union High	Redwood City
459	346.9	Central Union High	El Centro
460	324.8	Piedmont City Unified	Piedmont
461	320.7	Sweetwater Union High	Chula Vista
462	320.5	Tamalpais Union High	Larkspur
463	314.1	Carmel Unified	Carmel
464	301.9	West Sonoma County Union High	Sebastopol
465	295.8	Tulare Joint Union High	Tulare
466	256.7	Brawley Union High	Brawley
467	0.0	Alisal Union Elementary	Salinas
467	0.0	Alta Loma Elementary	Alta Loma
467	0.0	Arvin Union Elementary	Arvin
467	0.0	Beardsley Elementary	Bakersfield
467	0.0	Bellevue Union Elementary	Santa Rosa
467	0.0	Buena Park Elementary	Buena Park
467	0.0	Charter Oak Unified	Covina
467	0.0	Chowchilla Elementary	Chowchilla
467	0.0	Cucamonga Elementary	Rcho Cucamong
467	0.0	Cypress Elementary	Cypress
467	0.0	Del Mar Union Elementary	Del Mar
467	0.0	Earlimart Elementary	Earlimart
467	0.0	Eastside Union Elementary	Lancaster
467	0.0	El Monte City Elementary	El Monte
467	0.0	Etiwanda Elementary	Etiwanda
467	0.0	Evergreen Elementary	San Jose
467	0.0	Exeter Union Elementary	Exeter
467	0.0	Galt Joint Union Elementary	Galt
467	0.0	Hanford Elementary	Hanford
467	0.0	Huntington Beach City Elementary	Huntington Bch
467	0.0	Jefferson Elementary	Tracy
467	0.0	Jefferson Elementary	Daly City
467	0.0	Julian Union High	Julian
467	0.0	Kerman Unified	Kerman
467	0.0	Keyes Union Elementary	Keyes
467	0.0	La Habra City Elementary	La Habra
467	0.0	Lancaster Elementary	Lancaster
467	0.0	Lemon Grove Elementary	Lemon Grove
467	0.0	Loomis Union Elementary	Loomis
467	0.0	Los Banos Unified	Los Banos
467	0.0	Lowell Joint	Whittier
467	0.0	Menifee Union Elementary	Menifee
467	0.0	Modesto City Elementary	Modesto
467	0.0	Mount Diablo Unified	Concord
467	0.0	Ocean View Elementary	Huntington Bch
467	0.0	Old Adobe Union Elementary	Petaluma
467	0.0	Orcutt Union Elementary	Orcutt
467	0.0	Oro Grande Elementary	Oro Grande
467	0.0	Oxnard Elementary	Oxnard
467	0.0	Perris Elementary	Perris
467	0.0	Petaluma City Elementary	Petaluma
467	0.0	Piner-Olivet Union Elementary	Santa Rosa
467	0.0	Rincon Valley Union Elementary	Santa Rosa
467	0.0	Rio Elementary	Oxnard
467	0.0	Riverside County Office of Ed	Riverside
467	0.0	Robla Elementary	Sacramento
467	0.0	Romoland Elementary	Homeland
467	0.0	Rosemead Elementary	Rosemead
467	0.0	Salinas City Elementary	Salinas
467	0.0	Santa Barbara Elementary	Santa Barbara
467	0.0	Santa Cruz City Elementary	Santa Cruz
467	0.0	Santee Elementary	Santee
467	0.0	Solana Beach Elementary	Solana Beach
467	0.0	South Bay Union Elementary	Imperial Beach
467	0.0	South Whittier Elementary	Whittier
467	0.0	Southern Kern Unified	Rosamond
467	0.0	Stanislaus Union Elementary	Modesto
467	0.0	Sulphur Springs Union Elementary	Canyon Country
467	0.0	Sunnyvale Elementary	Sunnyvale
467	0.0	Wasco Union Elementary	Wasco
467	0.0	Westwood Unified	Westwood
467	0.0	Wheatland Elementary	Wheatland
467	0.0	Woodlake Union Elementary	Woodlake

Current Spending per Student in FY2001

Rank	Dollars	District Name	City
1	44,947	San Diego County Office of Ed	San Diego
2	39,805	Kern County Office of Ed	Bakersfield
3	37,660	San Bernardino County Supt.	San Bernardino
4	36,699	Riverside County Office of Ed	Riverside
5	34,409	Santa Clara County Office of Ed	San Jose

6	31,095	Los Angeles County Office of Ed	Downey
7	26,743	Fresno County Office of Ed	Fresno
8	26,729	San Joaquin County Office of Ed	Stockton
9	14,858	Orange County Office of Ed	Costa Mesa
10	12,915	Oro Grande Elementary	Oro Grande
11	10,717	Julian Union High	Julian
12	9,858	Carmel Unified	Carmel
13	9,647	Mountain View-Los Altos Union High	Mountain View
14	9,137	San Carlos Elementary	San Carlos
15	9,116	Berkeley Unified	Berkeley
16	9,099	Silver Valley Unified	Yermo
17	9,077	Palo Alto Unified	Palo Alto
18	9,029	Tamalpais Union High	Larkspur
19	8,864	Golden Plains Unified	San Joaquin
20	8,839	Muroc Joint Unified	North Edwards
21	8,601	Central Union Elementary	Lemoore
22	8,538	Los Gatos-Saratoga Jt Union High	Los Gatos
23	8,411	San Mateo Union High	San Mateo
24	8,249	Sierra Unified	Auberry
25	8,248	Mill Valley Elementary	Mill Valley
25	8,248	Sequoia Union High	Redwood City
27	8,183	Beverly Hills Unified	Beverly Hills
28	8,163	Westwood Unified	Westwood
29	8,059	Gonzales Unified	Gonzales
30	7,931	Pasadena Unified	Pasadena
31	7,928	Oakland Unified	Oakland
32	7,882	Brawley Union High	Brawley
33	7,876	Plumas Unified	Quincy
34	7,741	Del Paso Heights Elementary	Sacramento
35	7,668	Redwood City Elementary	Redwood City
36	7,658	Menlo Park City Elementary	Atherton
37	7,604	Pacific Grove Unified	Pacific Grove
38	7,597	Woodlake Union Elementary	Woodlake
39	7,596	Albany City Unified	Albany
40	7,575	Wheatland Elementary	Wheatland
41	7,543	Bellevue Union Elementary	Santa Rosa
42	7,508	San Diego Unified	San Diego
43	7,504	Lemoore Union High	Lemoore
44	7,492	Fort Bragg Unified	Fort Bragg
45	7,477	East Side Union High	San Jose
46	7,463	San Jose Unified	San Jose
47	7,459	Santa Barbara Elementary	Santa Barbara
48	7,438	Mountain Empire Unified	Pine Valley
49	7,417	Manhattan Beach Unified	Manhattan Beach
50	7,414	Laguna Beach Unified	Laguna Beach
50	7,414	Sacramento City Unified	Sacramento
52	7,404	Saint Helena Unified	Saint Helena
53	7,394	North Sacramento Elementary	Sacramento
54	7,386	North Monterey County Unified	Moss Landing
55	7,384	Los Angeles Unified	Los Angeles
55	7,384	Pleasanton Unified	Pleasanton
57	7,371	Ravenswood City Elementary	East Palo Alto
58	7,363	San Rafael City High	San Rafael
59	7,355	Cascade Union Elementary	Anderson
60	7,345	Del Norte County Unified	Crescent City
61	7,344	Solana Beach Elementary	Solana Beach
62	7,329	Mcfarland Unified	Mcfarland
63	7,312	Culver City Unified	Culver City
64	7,295	Fallbrook Union High	Fallbrook
65	7,275	Piedmont City Unified	Piedmont
66	7,272	South Bay Union Elementary	Imperial Beach
67	7,256	Dublin Unified	Dublin
68	7,252	Fresno Unified	Fresno
69	7,247	Thermalito Union Elementary	Oroville
70	7,245	Pajaro Valley Unified School	Watsonville
71	7,223	Lindsay Unified	Lindsay
72	7,206	Central Union High	El Centro
73	7,204	Eureka City Unified	Eureka
74	7,195	San Ysidro Elementary	San Ysidro
75	7,182	Red Bluff Joint Union High	Red Bluff
76	7,178	Santa Monica-Malibu Unified	Santa Monica
77	7,177	San Marino Unified	San Marino
78	7,162	Santa Clara Unified	Santa Clara
79	7,153	Grant Joint Union High	Sacramento
80	7,144	San Juan Unified	Carmichael
81	7,131	Twin Ridges Elementary	North San Juan
82	7,110	Rincon Valley Union Elementary	Santa Rosa
83	7,104	Mariposa County Unified	Mariposa
84	7,102	Greenfield Union Elementary	Greenfield
85	7,096	Dixie Elementary	San Rafael
86	7,092	Coronado Unified	Coronado
87	7,086	Sunnyvale Elementary	Sunnyvale
88	7,080	Grossmont Union High	La Mesa
89	7,071	Konocti Unified	Lower Lake
90	7,068	Los Altos Elementary	Los Altos
91	7,061	Grass Valley Elementary	Grass Valley
92	7,060	Ross Valley Elementary	San Anselmo
93	7,053	Ukiah Unified	Ukiah
94	7,049	Santa Cruz City Elementary	Santa Cruz
95	7,048	Bakersfield City Elementary	Bakersfield
96	7,040	Gateway Unified	Redding
97	7,029	Alum Rock Union Elementary	San Jose
98	7,028	Whittier Union High	Whittier
99	7,017	Vista Unified	Vista
100	7,015	El Segundo Unified	El Segundo
101	7,011	Fremont Union High	Sunnyvale
102	7,010	Ocean View Elementary	Oxnard
103	6,987	Live Oak Elementary	Santa Cruz
104	6,986	Mount Pleasant Elementary	San Jose
105	6,984	Paso Robles Joint Unified	Paso Robles
106	6,983	San Dieguito Union High	Encinitas
107	6,977	Nevada Joint Union High	Grass Valley
108	6,975	Redondo Beach Unified	Redondo Beach
109	6,959	Parlier Unified	Parlier
110	6,958	Los Gatos Union Elementary	Los Gatos
111	6,956	Fallbrook Union Elementary	Fallbrook
112	6,954	Reef-Sunset Unified	Avenal
113	6,953	Standard Elementary	Bakersfield
114	6,951	Santa Rosa Elementary	Santa Rosa
115	6,932	Winton Elementary	Winton
116	6,920	West Contra Costa Unified	Richmond
117	6,919	Cutler-Orosi Joint Unified	Orosi
118	6,913	Garvey Elementary	Rosemead
119	6,912	Kerman Unified	Kerman
120	6,897	Willits Unified	Willits
121	6,895	Mountain View-Whisman Elementary	Mountain View
122	6,894	Newark Unified	Newark
123	6,888	Delano Joint Union High	Delano
124	6,881	Morongo Unified	Twentynine Plms
125	6,870	Mendota Unified	Mendota
126	6,866	New Haven Unified	Union City
127	6,854	Lamont Elementary	Lamont
128	6,848	Little Lake City Elementary	Santa Fe Spgs
129	6,840	Long Beach Unified	Long Beach
130	6,836	Healdsburg Unified	Healdsburg
131	6,827	Waterford Unified	Waterford
132	6,819	Tahoe-Truckee Joint Unified	Truckee
133	6,817	Palmdale Elementary	Palmdale
134	6,816	Santa Paula Elementary	Santa Paula
135	6,813	Alhambra City Elementary	Alhambra
136	6,809	Corning Union Elementary	Corning
137	6,808	Robla Elementary	Sacramento
138	6,806	Franklin-Mckinley Elementary	San Jose
139	6,796	National Elementary	National City
140	6,794	Pomona Unified	Pomona
141	6,788	Stockton City Unified	Stockton
142	6,784	Santa Maria-Bonita Elementary	Santa Maria
143	6,780	Sonora Union High	Sonora
143	6,780	Travis Unified	Travis Afb
145	6,778	Del Mar Union Elementary	Del Mar
146	6,774	Claremont Unified	Claremont
147	6,770	Banning Unified	Banning
147	6,770	Lawndale Elementary	Lawndale
149	6,767	San Rafael City Elementary	San Rafael
150	6,763	Acalanes Union High	Lafayette
150	6,763	Moreland Elementary	San Jose
152	6,762	Lemon Grove Elementary	Lemon Grove
153	6,758	San Lorenzo Valley Unified	Felton
154	6,756	Farmersville Unified	Farmersville
155	6,755	Vallejo City Unified	Vallejo
156	6,751	Bassett Unified	La Puente
157	6,738	Palo Verde Unified	Blythe
158	6,727	Escondido Union High	Escondido
159	6,720	Soquel Union Elementary	Capitola
160	6,716	Red Bluff Union Elementary	Red Bluff
161	6,714	Taft City Elementary	Taft
162	6,713	West Sonoma County Union High	Sebastopol
163	6,711	Los Alamitos Unified	Los Alamitos
164	6,708	Julian Union Elementary	Julian
165	6,699	Firebaugh-Las Deltas Joint Unified	Firebaugh
165	6,699	San Bernardino City Unified	San Bernardino
167	6,698	Riverside Unified	Riverside
168	6,697	Merced City Elementary	Merced
168	6,697	San Benito High	Hollister
170	6,696	Oceanside Unified	Oceanside
171	6,694	Dos Palos Oro Loma Joint Unified	Dos Palos
172	6,692	Elk Grove Unified	Elk Grove
173	6,688	El Dorado Union High	Placerville
174	6,685	Orinda Union Elementary	Orinda
175	6,681	Anaheim Union High	Anaheim
176	6,674	Petaluma City Elementary	Petaluma
177	6,671	Natomas Unified	Sacramento
178	6,667	Gridley Unified	Gridley
179	6,666	Chula Vista Elementary	Chula Vista
180	6,665	Hayward Unified	Hayward
181	6,663	Marysville Joint Unified	Marysville
182	6,661	Wilsona Elementary	Palmdale
183	6,656	Clovis Unified	Clovis
184	6,654	San Lorenzo Unified	San Lorenzo
185	6,653	Jamul-Dulzura Union Elementary	Jamul
186	6,648	Newport-Mesa Unified	Costa Mesa
187	6,645	Valley Center-Pauma Unified	Valley Center
187	6,645	Westminster Elementary	Westminster
189	6,643	Snowline Joint Unified	Phelan
190	6,642	Bonsall Union Elementary	Bonsall
191	6,640	Oak Grove Elementary	San Jose
191	6,640	Wasco Union Elementary	Wasco
193	6,639	Bishop Union Elementary	Bishop
194	6,636	El Monte City Elementary	El Monte
195	6,633	Placer Union High	Auburn
196	6,629	Washington Unified	West Sacramento
197	6,625	Liberty Union High	Brentwood
198	6,620	Fountain Valley Elementary	Fountain Valley
199	6,612	John Swett Unified	Crockett
200	6,611	San Francisco Unified	San Francisco
201	6,607	Sweetwater Union High	Chula Vista
202	6,603	Corcoran Joint Unified	Corcoran
203	6,602	Cabrillo Unified	Half Moon Bay
204	6,600	Enterprise Elementary	Redding
205	6,599	Colusa Unified	Colusa
206	6,596	Rio Linda Union Elementary	Rio Linda
207	6,591	Sanger Unified	Sanger
208	6,590	River Delta Joint Unified	Rio Vista
209	6,587	Huntington Beach Union High	Huntington Bch
210	6,581	Piner-Olivet Union Elementary	Santa Rosa
211	6,573	Ontario-Montclair Elementary	Ontario
212	6,567	Mountain View Elementary	El Monte
213	6,566	Victor Valley Union High	Victorville
214	6,561	South Pasadena Unified	South Pasadena
215	6,557	Poway Unified	Poway
215	6,557	Rowland Unified	Rowland Heights
217	6,554	Glendale Unified	Glendale
218	6,546	Norwalk-La Mirada Unified	Norwalk
219	6,543	Coalinga-Huron Joint Unified	Coalinga
220	6,540	Porterville Unified	Porterville
221	6,538	Jefferson Union High	Daly City
222	6,536	Old Adobe Union Elementary	Petaluma
223	6,535	Sierra Sands Unified	Ridgecrest
224	6,530	Exeter Union Elementary	Exeter
224	6,530	La Canada Unified	La Canada
226	6,526	Monrovia Unified	Monrovia
227	6,523	Kelseyville Unified	Kelseyville
228	6,522	South Whittier Elementary	Whittier
229	6,518	San Gabriel Unified	San Gabriel
230	6,517	Barstow Unified	Barstow
230	6,517	Lakeside Union Elementary	Lakeside
232	6,516	Livermore Valley Joint Unified	Livermore
233	6,513	Alameda City Unified	Alameda
234	6,506	Hilmar Unified	Hilmar
235	6,504	Moraga Elementary	Moraga
236	6,503	San Mateo-Foster City Elementary	San Mateo
237	6,497	El Rancho Unified	Pico Rivera
238	6,490	Beardsley Elementary	Bakersfield
239	6,488	Calaveras Unified	San Andreas
240	6,487	Apple Valley Unified	Apple Valley
241	6,484	Carpinteria Unified	Carpinteria
242	6,481	Coachella Valley Unified	Thermal
243	6,478	Alisal Union Elementary	Salinas
244	6,473	Cajon Valley Union Elementary	El Cajon
245	6,470	Hanford Elementary	Hanford
246	6,467	Fillmore Unified	Fillmore
246	6,467	Linden Unified	Linden
246	6,467	Merced Union High	Atwater
249	6,465	Selma Unified	Selma
250	6,464	Brentwood Union Elementary	Brentwood
251	6,460	Campbell Union High	San Jose
252	6,459	Holtville Unified	Holtville
253	6,455	Richland SD	Shafter
254	6,454	Saratoga Union Elementary	Saratoga
255	6,453	Cucamonga Elementary	Rcho Cucamong
256	6,452	Oxnard Elementary	Oxnard
257	6,447	Hughson Unified	Hughson
258	6,446	Romoland Elementary	Homeland
259	6,444	Mojave Unified	Mojave
260	6,442	Novato Unified	Novato
260	6,442	Western Placer Unified	Lincoln
262	6,434	Cotati-Rohnert Park Unified	Rohnert Park
262	6,434	El Centro Elementary	El Centro
264	6,432	San Luis Coastal Unified	San Luis Obispo
265	6,430	King City Joint Union High	King City
265	6,430	Winters Joint Unified	Winters
267	6,429	Brawley Elementary	Brawley
268	6,427	Willows Unified	Willows
269	6,426	Montebello Unified	Montebello
270	6,414	Campbell Union Elementary	Campbell
271	6,411	Union Elementary	San Jose
272	6,403	Duarte Unified	Duarte
272	6,403	Santa Ana Unified	Santa Ana
274	6,402	Fontana Unified	Fontana
274	6,402	La Habra City Elementary	La Habra
276	6,401	Magnolia Elementary	Anaheim
277	6,400	San Ramon Valley Unified	Danville
278	6,396	Azusa Unified	Azusa
278	6,396	Cloverdale Unified	Cloverdale
280	6,388	Calexico Unified	Calexico
281	6,387	Ramona City Unified	Ramona
282	6,385	William S Hart Union High	Santa Clarita

283	6,382	Tulare Joint Union High	Tulare
284	6,379	Anderson Union High	Anderson
285	6,375	Oak Park Unified	Oak Park
286	6,369	Black Oak Mine Unified	Georgetown
287	6,362	Alpine Union Elementary	Alpine
288	6,360	Napa Valley Unified	Napa
289	6,359	Savanna Elementary	Anaheim
290	6,358	Compton Unified	Compton
291	6,348	Hawthorne Elementary	Hawthorne
292	6,347	Whittier City Elementary	Whittier
293	6,345	ABC Unified	Cerritos
294	6,342	Oroville Union High	Oroville
295	6,338	Fowler Unified	Fowler
296	6,337	Buena Park Elementary	Buena Park
297	6,336	Garden Grove Unified	Garden Grove
298	6,335	Desert Sands Unified	La Quinta
298	6,335	Roseville Joint Union High	Roseville
300	6,332	Arvin Union Elementary	Arvin
301	6,329	Hollister SD	Hollister
302	6,327	Burbank Unified	Burbank
302	6,327	Folsom-Cordova Unified	Folsom
304	6,326	Jurupa Unified	Riverside
305	6,325	Yuba City Unified	Yuba City
306	6,324	Berryessa Union Elementary	San Jose
307	6,322	Davis Joint Unified	Davis
308	6,317	Irvine Unified	Irvine
309	6,316	Ocean View Elementary	Huntington Bch
310	6,314	Lincoln Unified	Stockton
311	6,311	Inglewood Unified	Inglewood
311	6,311	Kings Canyon Joint Unified	Reedley
313	6,310	Palm Springs Unified	Palm Springs
314	6,309	Gilroy Unified	Gilroy
315	6,308	Madera Unified	Madera
316	6,306	Lodi Unified	Lodi
317	6,305	Dinuba Unified	Dinuba
318	6,302	Tehachapi Unified	Tehachapi
319	6,298	Pittsburg Unified	Pittsburg
320	6,295	Burlingame Elementary	Burlingame
321	6,292	Galt Joint Union High	Galt
322	6,291	Encinitas Union Elementary	Encinitas
323	6,289	Modesto City Elementary	Modesto
324	6,284	El Monte Union High	El Monte
325	6,283	Millbrae Elementary	Millbrae
326	6,282	Benicia Unified	Benicia
327	6,281	Salinas Union High	Salinas
328	6,278	Weaver Union Elementary	Merced
329	6,277	Oroville City Elementary	Oroville
330	6,276	Carlsbad Unified	Carlsbad
331	6,274	Cypress Elementary	Cypress
331	6,274	Kingsburg Elementary Charter	Kingsburg
331	6,274	Roseville City Elementary	Roseville
334	6,273	Hueneme Elementary	Port Hueneme
335	6,271	Chaffey Joint Union High	Ontario
335	6,271	Los Nietos Elementary	Whittier
335	6,271	Martinez Unified	Martinez
338	6,269	Mother Lode Union Elementary	Placerville
339	6,265	Paramount Unified	Paramount
340	6,264	Goleta Union Elementary	Goleta
341	6,263	Temple City Unified	Temple City
342	6,261	Lake Tahoe Unified	S Lake Tahoe
343	6,259	Atwater Elementary	Atwater
344	6,255	Antelope Valley Union High	Lancaster
344	6,255	Milpitas Unified	Milpitas
344	6,255	Turlock Joint Union High	Turlock
347	6,253	La Mesa-Spring Valley	La Mesa
348	6,247	Sonoma Valley Unified	Sonoma
349	6,244	Kern Union High	Bakersfield
350	6,242	Auburn Union Elementary	Auburn
351	6,239	Monterey Peninsula Unified	Monterey
352	6,236	Rim of The World Unified	Lake Arrowhead
353	6,235	Adelanto Elementary	Adelanto
354	6,234	Empire Union Elementary	Modesto
354	6,234	King City Union Elementary	King City
356	6,233	Escondido Union Elementary	Escondido
357	6,232	Center Joint Unified	Antelope
357	6,232	Shasta Union High	Redding
359	6,230	Beaumont Unified	Beaumont
360	6,218	Placentia-Yorba Linda Unified	Placentia
361	6,213	Keppel Union Elementary	Pearblossom
361	6,213	Lafayette Elementary	Lafayette
363	6,212	Central Unified	Fresno
364	6,210	Mark West Union Elementary	Santa Rosa
365	6,209	Lennox Elementary	Lennox
366	6,205	Centinela Valley Union High	Lawndale
367	6,204	East Whittier City Elementary	Whittier
368	6,198	Brea-Olinda Unified	Brea
369	6,196	Val Verde Unified	Perris
370	6,194	Rosemead Elementary	Rosemead
371	6,185	Hemet Unified	Hemet
372	6,184	Ojai Unified	Ojai
373	6,183	Fremont Unified	Fremont
373	6,183	Vacaville Unified	Vacaville
375	6,182	Redding Elementary	Redding
376	6,180	Baldwin Park Unified	Baldwin Park
377	6,179	Redlands Unified	Redlands
378	6,175	Belmont-Redwood Shores Elementary	Belmont
379	6,172	Middletown Unified	Middletown
380	6,169	Castro Valley Unified	Castro Valley
381	6,166	Moreno Valley Unified	Moreno Valley
382	6,163	Jefferson Elementary	Daly City
383	6,155	Panama Buena Vista Union Elem	Bakersfield
384	6,149	Galt Joint Union Elementary	Galt
384	6,149	Palos Verdes Peninsula Unified	Palos Verdes Est
386	6,147	Livingston Union Elementary	Livingston
387	6,140	Visalia Unified	Visalia
388	6,139	Huntington Beach City Elementary	Huntington Bch
388	6,139	Soledad Unified	Soledad
390	6,137	Cupertino Union School	Cupertino
391	6,135	Capistrano Unified	San Juan Capis
392	6,133	Delano Union Elementary	Delano
393	6,127	Lakeport Unified	Lakeport
393	6,127	Southern Kern Unified	Rosamond
395	6,119	Saddleback Valley Unified	Mission Viejo
396	6,118	Bear Valley Unified	Big Bear Lake
397	6,117	Centralia Elementary	Buena Park
398	6,116	Paradise Unified	Paradise
399	6,114	Windsor Unified	Windsor
400	6,108	Oxnard Union High	Oxnard
401	6,098	Turlock Joint Elementary	Turlock
402	6,094	Bonita Unified	San Dimas
402	6,094	Greenfield Union Elementary	Bakersfield
402	6,094	Lake Elsinore Unified	Lake Elsinore
402	6,094	South San Francisco Unified	S San Francisco
406	6,093	Orland Joint Unified	Orland
407	6,092	Las Virgenes Unified	Calabasas
408	6,090	Tustin Unified	Tustin
409	6,087	Laguna Salada Union Elementary	Pacifica
409	6,087	Perris Elementary	Perris
411	6,084	Burton Elementary	Porterville
411	6,084	Lowell Joint	Whittier
413	6,081	Murrieta Valley Unified	Murrieta
413	6,081	Santa Paula Union High	Santa Paula
415	6,069	Santa Maria Joint Union High	Santa Maria
416	6,068	Gustine Unified	Gustine
417	6,065	Rialto Unified	Rialto
418	6,057	Lancaster Elementary	Lancaster
419	6,052	Manteca Unified	Manteca
420	6,049	Atascadero Unified	Atascadero
421	6,041	Eastside Union Elementary	Lancaster
422	6,040	Wiseburn Elementary	Hawthorne
423	6,034	Walnut Creek Elementary	Walnut Creek
424	6,032	Santa Barbara High	Santa Barbara
425	6,030	Mount Diablo Unified	Concord
426	6,023	Moorpark Unified	Moorpark
426	6,023	Patterson Joint Unified	Patterson
428	6,022	San Leandro Unified	San Leandro
429	6,019	Hanford Joint Union High	Hanford
430	6,018	Corona-Norco Unified	Norco
431	6,014	Tracy Joint Unified	Tracy
432	6,012	Woodland Joint Unified	Woodland
433	6,009	Chowchilla Elementary	Chowchilla
434	6,008	Covina-Valley Unified	Covina
434	6,008	Fullerton Elementary	Fullerton
434	6,008	Hesperia Unified	Hesperia
437	6,005	Orcutt Union Elementary	Orcutt
438	5,997	Scotts Valley Unified	Scotts Valley
439	5,996	Oakdale Joint Unified	Oakdale
440	5,995	Ceres Unified	Ceres
440	5,995	Oakley Union Elementary	Oakley
440	5,995	Riverbank Unified	Riverbank
443	5,992	Lucia Mar Unified	Arroyo Grande
444	5,982	Imperial Unified	Imperial
445	5,980	San Jacinto Unified	San Jacinto
446	5,978	Colton Joint Unified	Colton
446	5,978	Torrance Unified	Torrance
448	5,976	Bellflower Unified	Bellflower
449	5,975	Anaheim Elementary	Anaheim
450	5,973	Conejo Valley Unified	Thousand Oaks
451	5,971	Northern Humboldt Union High	McKinleyville
452	5,970	Arcadia Unified	Arcadia
452	5,970	Dixon Unified	Dixon
454	5,963	Templeton Unified	Templeton
455	5,953	Mountain View Elementary	Ontario
456	5,951	Central Elementary	Rcho Cucamong
456	5,951	Chico Unified	Chico
458	5,950	Morgan Hill Unified	Morgan Hill
459	5,948	Salinas City Elementary	Salinas
460	5,942	Jefferson Elementary	Tracy
461	5,939	Orange Unified	Orange
462	5,936	Earlimart Elementary	Earlimart
463	5,931	Perris Union High	Perris
464	5,921	Temecula Valley Unified	Temecula
465	5,918	Fruitvale Elementary	Bakersfield
466	5,911	Sulphur Springs Union Elementary	Canyon Country
467	5,907	Delhi Unified	Delhi
468	5,905	Hacienda La Puente Unified	City of Industry
469	5,896	Evergreen Elementary	San Jose
469	5,896	Riverdale Joint Unified	Riverdale
469	5,896	Rocklin Unified	Rocklin
472	5,889	Fullerton Joint Union High	Fullerton
472	5,889	Santee Elementary	Santee
474	5,883	Yucaipa-Calimesa Joint Unified	Yucaipa
475	5,881	Cambrian Elementary	San Jose
476	5,878	Alvord Unified	Riverside
477	5,876	Pleasant Ridge Union Elementary	Grass Valley
478	5,871	Escalon Unified	Escalon
479	5,870	San Bruno Park Elementary	San Bruno
480	5,865	Ventura Unified	Ventura
481	5,843	Antioch Unified	Antioch
482	5,835	San Marcos Unified	San Marcos
483	5,827	Fairfield-Suisun Unified	Fairfield
484	5,824	Rio Elementary	Oxnard
485	5,804	Santa Rita Union Elementary	Salinas
486	5,803	Menifee Union Elementary	Menifee
487	5,795	Buckeye Union Elementary	Shingle Springs
488	5,793	Lompoc Unified	Lompoc
489	5,768	Chino Valley Unified	Chino
489	5,768	Saugus Union Elementary	Santa Clarita
491	5,748	Walnut Valley Unified	Walnut
492	5,745	Simi Valley Unified	Simi Valley
493	5,742	Newhall Elementary	Valencia
494	5,740	Live Oak Unified	Live Oak
495	5,720	Upland Unified	Upland
496	5,715	Victor Elementary	Victorville
497	5,711	Alta Loma Elementary	Alta Loma
498	5,691	Acton-Agua Dulce Unified	Acton
499	5,686	Pleasant Valley School	Camarillo
500	5,685	Glendora Unified	Glendora
501	5,679	Charter Oak Unified	Covina
502	5,671	West Covina Unified	West Covina
503	5,669	Lemoore Union Elementary	Lemoore
503	5,669	Loomis Union Elementary	Loomis
505	5,665	Norris Elementary	Bakersfield
506	5,660	Sylvan Union Elementary	Modesto
507	5,652	Lynwood Unified	Lynwood
508	5,626	Rescue Union Elementary	Rescue
509	5,597	Westside Union Elementary	Lancaster
510	5,579	Stanislaus Union Elementary	Modesto
511	5,576	Rosedale Union Elementary	Bakersfield
512	5,554	Tulare City Elementary	Tulare
513	5,542	Eureka Union Elementary	Granite Bay
514	5,526	Dry Creek Joint Elementary	Roseville
515	5,500	Amador County Unified	Jackson
516	5,498	Los Banos Unified	Los Banos
517	5,497	Downey Unified	Downey
518	5,492	Salida Union Elementary	Salida
519	5,486	Castaic Union Elementary	Valencia
520	5,482	Ripon Unified	Ripon
521	5,472	Newman-Crows Landing Unified	Newman
522	5,376	Gorman Elementary	Gorman
523	5,178	Keyes Union Elementary	Keyes
524	4,837	Etiwanda Elementary	Etiwanda
525	n/a	Alhambra City High	Alhambra
525	n/a	Modesto City High	Modesto
525	n/a	Petaluma Joint Union High	Petaluma
525	n/a	Santa Cruz City High	Santa Cruz
525	n/a	Santa Rosa High	Santa Rosa

Number of Diploma Recipients

Rank	Number	District Name	City
1	27,720	Los Angeles Unified	Los Angeles
2	6,504	San Diego Unified	San Diego
3	5,741	Kern Union High	Bakersfield
4	4,768	Sweetwater Union High	Chula Vista
5	4,664	Long Beach Unified	Long Beach
6	4,467	East Side Union High	San Jose
7	4,387	Grossmont Union High	La Mesa
8	3,873	Chaffey Joint Union High	Ontario
9	3,721	Fresno Unified	Fresno
10	3,688	Anaheim Union High	Anaheim
11	3,556	San Juan Unified	Carmichael
12	3,399	San Francisco Unified	San Francisco
13	2,992	Antelope Valley Union High	Lancaster
14	2,905	Huntington Beach Union High	Huntington Bch
15	2,815	Modesto City High	Modesto
16	2,738	Garden Grove Unified	Garden Grove
17	2,728	Elk Grove Unified	Elk Grove
18	2,670	Fullerton Joint Union High	Fullerton
19	2,644	Capistrano Unified	San Juan Capis
20	2,529	Oxnard Union High	Oxnard
21	2,484	Santa Ana Unified	Santa Ana
22	2,393	William S Hart Union High	Santa Clarita
23	2,251	Riverside Unified	Riverside
24	2,237	Sacramento City Unified	Sacramento
25	2,230	Poway Unified	Poway
26	2,170	Corona-Norco Unified	Norco
27	2,161	Mount Diablo Unified	Concord

Rank	Number	District	City
28	2,157	Saddleback Valley Unified	Mission Viejo
29	2,093	Whittier Union High	Whittier
30	2,065	Orange Unified	Orange
31	2,052	Clovis Unified	Clovis
32	2,002	Glendale Unified	Glendale
33	1,996	Vista Unified	Vista
34	1,985	Fremont Union High	Sunnyvale
35	1,972	Fremont Unified	Fremont
36	1,951	Merced Union High	Atwater
37	1,933	San Bernardino City Unified	San Bernardino
38	1,865	Chino Valley Unified	Chino
39	1,838	Irvine Unified	Irvine
40	1,813	Torrance Unified	Torrance
41	1,793	Fontana Unified	Fontana
42	1,770	West Contra Costa Unified	Richmond
43	1,763	San Mateo Union High	San Mateo
44	1,740	San Jose Unified	San Jose
45	1,705	El Monte Union High	El Monte
46	1,694	Moreno Valley Unified	Moreno Valley
47	1,656	Placentia-Yorba Linda Unified	Placentia
48	1,641	Alhambra City High	Alhambra
49	1,636	ABC Unified	Cerritos
50	1,617	Oakland Unified	Oakland
51	1,585	Roseville Joint Union High	Roseville
52	1,556	Escondido Union High	Escondido
53	1,543	Montebello Unified	Montebello
54	1,533	San Dieguito Union High	Encinitas
55	1,506	Santa Rosa High	Santa Rosa
56	1,491	San Ramon Valley Unified	Danville
57	1,488	El Dorado Union High	Placerville
58	1,456	Lodi Unified	Lodi
59	1,443	Salinas Union High	Salinas
60	1,414	Campbell Union High	San Jose
61	1,413	Conejo Valley Unified	Thousand Oaks
62	1,410	Pomona Unified	Pomona
63	1,394	Desert Sands Unified	La Quinta
64	1,392	Rialto Unified	Rialto
65	1,358	Santa Barbara High	Santa Barbara
66	1,345	Grant Joint Union High	Sacramento
66	1,345	Hacienda La Puente Unified	City of Industry
68	1,313	Redlands Unified	Redlands
69	1,310	Visalia Unified	Visalia
70	1,309	Stockton City Unified	Stockton
71	1,292	Downey Unified	Downey
72	1,288	Walnut Valley Unified	Walnut
73	1,279	Acalanes Union High	Lafayette
74	1,264	Hayward Unified	Hayward
75	1,254	Antioch Unified	Antioch
76	1,197	Sequoia Union High	Redwood City
77	1,192	Norwalk-La Mirada Unified	Norwalk
78	1,148	Simi Valley Unified	Simi Valley
79	1,145	Victor Valley Union High	Victorville
80	1,118	Newport-Mesa Unified	Costa Mesa
81	1,107	Centinela Valley Union High	Lawndale
82	1,106	Fairfield-Suisun Unified	Fairfield
83	1,099	Vallejo City Unified	Vallejo
84	1,094	Burbank Unified	Burbank
85	1,093	Santa Maria Joint Union High	Santa Maria
86	1,085	Jefferson Union High	Daly City
87	1,072	Rowland Unified	Rowland Heights
88	1,066	Orange County Office of Ed	Costa Mesa
89	1,061	Manteca Unified	Manteca
90	1,055	Shasta Union High	Redding
91	1,051	Santa Cruz City High	Santa Cruz
92	1,049	Temecula Valley Unified	Temecula
93	1,035	Vacaville Unified	Vacaville
94	1,024	Ventura Unified	Ventura
95	1,009	Pajaro Valley Unified School	Watsonville
96	998	Napa Valley Unified	Napa
97	995	Hemet Unified	Hemet
98	994	Perris Union High	Perris
99	979	Covina-Valley Unified	Covina
100	972	Porterville Unified	Porterville
101	970	Pasadena Unified	Pasadena
102	967	Chico Unified	Chico
103	957	Oceanside Unified	Oceanside
104	950	Palm Springs Unified	Palm Springs
105	944	Tustin Unified	Tustin
106	936	Placer Union High	Auburn
107	927	Tracy Joint Unified	Tracy
108	918	Livermore Valley Joint Unified	Livermore
109	912	Upland Unified	Upland
110	910	Pleasanton Unified	Pleasanton
111	907	Nevada Joint Union High	Grass Valley
112	902	Compton Unified	Compton
113	900	Lake Elsinore Unified	Lake Elsinore
114	898	Folsom-Cordova Unified	Folsom
115	870	Tulare Joint Union High	Tulare
116	861	Las Virgenes Unified	Calabasas
117	857	Hesperia Unified	Hesperia
118	855	Apple Valley Unified	Apple Valley
119	852	Santa Monica-Malibu Unified	Santa Monica
120	851	Los Angeles County Office of Ed	Downey
121	837	Alvord Unified	Riverside
122	832	Arcadia Unified	Arcadia
123	828	New Haven Unified	Union City
124	827	Tamalpais Union High	Larkspur
125	824	Lynwood Unified	Lynwood
126	804	Santa Clara Unified	Santa Clara
127	801	Turlock Joint Union High	Turlock
128	797	Jurupa Unified	Riverside
129	796	Madera Unified	Madera
130	794	Liberty Union High	Brentwood
131	789	Colton Joint Unified	Colton
132	780	Bellflower Unified	Bellflower
133	761	Bonita Unified	San Dimas
134	736	Palos Verdes Peninsula Unified	Palos Verdes Est
135	713	Baldwin Park Unified	Baldwin Park
136	710	Milpitas Unified	Milpitas
137	709	Palo Alto Unified	Palo Alto
138	691	Lucia Mar Unified	Arroyo Grande
138	691	Petaluma Joint Union High	Petaluma
140	690	Murrieta Valley Unified	Murrieta
141	685	Snowline Joint Unified	Phelan
142	683	Central Union High	El Centro
143	681	Yuba City Unified	Yuba City
144	673	Berkeley Unified	Berkeley
145	666	Inglewood Unified	Inglewood
146	660	San Lorenzo Unified	San Lorenzo
147	657	Los Alamitos Unified	Los Alamitos
148	655	Delano Joint Union High	Delano
149	651	Los Gatos-Saratoga Jt Union High	Los Gatos
150	645	Alameda City Unified	Alameda
151	639	Mountain View-Los Altos Union High	Mountain View
152	635	Yucaipa-Calimesa Joint Unified	Yucaipa
153	633	South San Francisco Unified	S San Francisco
154	615	Morgan Hill Unified	Morgan Hill
155	611	Monterey Peninsula Unified	Monterey
156	605	Central Unified	Fresno
157	604	San Benito High	Hollister
158	602	Carlsbad Unified	Carlsbad
159	596	El Rancho Unified	Pico Rivera
160	595	Fallbrook Union High	Fallbrook
161	594	San Marcos Unified	San Marcos
162	593	Paramount Unified	Paramount
163	590	West Sonoma County Union High	Sebastopol
164	587	West Covina Unified	West Covina
165	585	Claremont Unified	Claremont
166	581	Western Placer Unified	Lincoln
167	578	Ceres Unified	Ceres
168	577	Glendora Unified	Glendora
169	576	Davis Joint Unified	Davis
170	569	Moorpark Unified	Moorpark
171	568	Lompoc Unified	Lompoc
172	558	Coachella Valley Unified	Thermal
172	558	Val Verde Unified	Perris
174	551	Castro Valley Unified	Castro Valley
175	550	Woodland Joint Unified	Woodland
176	541	San Luis Coastal Unified	San Luis Obispo
177	533	Hanford Joint Union High	Hanford
178	529	Azusa Unified	Azusa
179	520	Newark Unified	Newark
180	510	Kings Canyon Joint Unified	Reedley
181	509	Ukiah Unified	Ukiah
182	502	Manhattan Beach Unified	Manhattan Beach
183	497	Sanger Unified	Sanger
184	489	Oroville Union High	Oroville
185	487	Brea-Olinda Unified	Brea
185	487	Cotati-Rohnert Park Unified	Rohnert Park
187	483	Ramona City Unified	Ramona
188	481	Novato Unified	Novato
189	476	Calexico Unified	Calexico
189	476	Lincoln Unified	Stockton
191	475	Anderson Union High	Anderson
192	472	Beverly Hills Unified	Beverly Hills
193	456	Morongo Unified	Twentynine Plms
194	454	San Leandro Unified	San Leandro
195	446	Gilroy Unified	Gilroy
195	446	Rocklin Unified	Rocklin
197	440	Red Bluff Joint Union High	Red Bluff
197	440	Redondo Beach Unified	Redondo Beach
199	428	Pittsburg Unified	Pittsburg
200	424	Los Banos Unified	Los Banos
201	423	Paso Robles Joint Unified	Paso Robles
202	421	Marysville Joint Unified	Marysville
203	419	Eureka City Unified	Eureka
204	416	Benicia Unified	Benicia
204	416	San Gabriel Unified	San Gabriel
206	415	North Monterey County Unified	Moss Landing
207	407	Charter Oak Unified	Covina
207	407	San Rafael City High	San Rafael
209	402	Northern Humboldt Union High	McKinleyville
210	397	Atascadero Unified	Atascadero
211	395	Temple City Unified	Temple City
212	394	Rim of The World Unified	Lake Arrowhead
213	386	Natomas Unified	Sacramento
214	381	Lemoore Union High	Lemoore
215	379	Tahoe-Truckee Joint Unified	Truckee
216	373	Paradise Unified	Paradise
217	366	Galt Joint Union High	Galt
217	366	Monrovia Unified	Monrovia
219	365	Barstow Unified	Barstow
220	361	Sierra Sands Unified	Ridgecrest
221	359	Sonora Union High	Sonora
222	357	Oakdale Joint Unified	Oakdale
223	343	Amador County Unified	Jackson
224	340	King City Joint Union High	King City
225	330	Valley Center-Pauma Unified	Valley Center
226	327	Washington Unified	West Sacramento
227	325	La Canada Unified	La Canada
228	324	Center Joint Unified	Antelope
229	321	Brawley Union High	Brawley
230	320	Duarte Unified	Duarte
231	315	Martinez Unified	Martinez
232	308	Bassett Unified	La Puente
232	308	Lake Tahoe Unified	S Lake Tahoe
234	307	Culver City Unified	Culver City
235	304	Tehachapi Unified	Tehachapi
236	303	San Lorenzo Valley Unified	Felton
237	301	South Pasadena Unified	South Pasadena
238	299	Dinuba Unified	Dinuba
239	292	Travis Unified	Travis Afb
240	289	Del Norte County Unified	Crescent City
240	289	Selma Unified	Selma
242	287	Sonoma Valley Unified	Sonoma
243	286	Santa Paula Union High	Santa Paula
244	285	Riverside County Office of Ed	Riverside
245	280	San Marino Unified	San Marino
246	274	Ojai Unified	Ojai
247	264	Plumas Unified	Quincy
248	260	San Jacinto Unified	San Jacinto
249	259	Cabrillo Unified	Half Moon Bay
249	259	Gateway Unified	Redding
251	250	Dublin Unified	Dublin
252	248	Coronado Unified	Coronado
253	247	El Segundo Unified	El Segundo
254	241	Piedmont City Unified	Piedmont
255	236	Calaveras Unified	San Andreas
256	233	Fillmore Unified	Fillmore
257	232	Oak Park Unified	Oak Park
258	223	Coalinga-Huron Joint Unified	Coalinga
259	220	Bear Valley Unified	Big Bear Lake
260	217	Banning Unified	Banning
261	216	Escalon Unified	Escalon
262	214	San Diego County Office of Ed	San Diego
263	212	Sierra Unified	Auberry
264	211	Patterson Joint Unified	Patterson
265	207	Lindsay Unified	Lindsay
266	203	Carpinteria Unified	Carpinteria
266	203	Healdsburg Unified	Healdsburg
268	201	Riverbank Unified	Riverbank
269	200	Dixon Unified	Dixon
270	199	Kerman Unified	Kerman
271	195	Laguna Beach Unified	Laguna Beach
272	194	Cutler-Orosi Joint Unified	Orosi
272	194	Mariposa County Unified	Mariposa
272	194	Mcfarland Unified	Mcfarland
275	193	Windsor Unified	Windsor
276	192	Templeton Unified	Templeton
277	191	Hughson Unified	Hughson
278	185	Palo Verde Unified	Blythe
279	181	Albany City Unified	Albany
280	178	River Delta Joint Unified	Rio Vista
281	177	Carmel Unified	Carmel
282	174	Hilmar Unified	Hilmar
282	174	Pacific Grove Unified	Pacific Grove
284	171	Dos Palos Oro Loma Joint Unified	Dos Palos
285	169	Mojave Unified	Mojave
286	167	Orland Joint Unified	Orland
287	165	Willits Unified	Willits
288	161	Beaumont Unified	Beaumont
289	160	Kern County Office of Ed	Bakersfield
290	157	Kelseyville Unified	Kelseyville
291	154	Ripon Unified	Ripon
292	152	Imperial Unified	Imperial
293	151	Southern Kern Unified	Rosamond
294	150	Black Oak Mine Unified	Georgetown
294	150	Linden Unified	Linden
294	150	Soledad Unified	Soledad
297	148	Gridley Unified	Gridley
298	147	Gonzales Unified	Gonzales
299	146	Newman-Crows Landing Unified	Newman
300	145	John Swett Unified	Crockett
300	145	Konocti Unified	Lower Lake
302	144	Fort Bragg Unified	Fort Bragg
303	143	Fowler Unified	Fowler
304	135	Muroc Joint Unified	North Edwards
305	134	Lakeport Unified	Lakeport

306	133	Holtville Unified	Holtville
307	130	Middletown Unified	Middletown
307	130	San Joaquin County Office of Ed	Stockton
309	128	Santa Clara County Office of Ed	San Jose
310	122	Winters Joint Unified	Winters
311	121	Corcoran Joint Unified	Corcoran
312	118	Farmersville Unified	Farmersville
313	117	Gustine Unified	Gustine
314	116	Saint Helena Unified	Saint Helena
315	109	Fresno County Office of Ed	Fresno
315	109	Julian Union High	Julian
317	108	Mountain Empire Unified	Pine Valley
318	106	Willows Unified	Willows
319	104	Golden Plains Unified	San Joaquin
319	104	Live Oak Unified	Live Oak
321	103	Cloverdale Unified	Cloverdale
321	103	Firebaugh-Las Deltas Joint Unified	Firebaugh
323	101	Reef-Sunset Unified	Avenal
324	100	Oro Grande Elementary	Oro Grande
324	100	Riverdale Joint Unified	Riverdale
326	99	Parlier Unified	Parlier
327	98	Acton-Agua Dulce Unified	Acton
328	92	Mendota Unified	Mendota
329	87	Colusa Unified	Colusa
330	83	Silver Valley Unified	Yermo
331	80	Delhi Unified	Delhi
332	45	Westwood Unified	Westwood
333	33	Julian Union Elementary	Julian
333	33	Twin Ridges Elementary	North San Juan
335	32	Waterford Unified	Waterford
336	28	Gorman Elementary	Gorman
337	13	Lakeside Union Elementary	Lakeside
338	3	Redding Elementary	Redding
338	3	Redwood City Elementary	Redwood City
340	1	Keyes Union Elementary	Keyes
341	0	Bonsall Union Elementary	Bonsall
341	0	Escondido Union Elementary	Escondido
341	0	Lawndale Elementary	Lawndale
341	0	Lennox Elementary	Lennox
341	0	Ravenswood City Elementary	East Palo Alto
341	0	Red Bluff Union Elementary	Red Bluff
341	0	San Bernardino County Supt.	San Bernardino
341	0	Scotts Valley Unified	Scotts Valley
341	0	Wheatland Elementary	Wheatland
350	n/a	Adelanto Elementary	Adelanto
350	n/a	Alhambra City Elementary	Alhambra
350	n/a	Alisal Union Elementary	Salinas
350	n/a	Alpine Union Elementary	Alpine
350	n/a	Alta Loma Elementary	Alta Loma
350	n/a	Alum Rock Union Elementary	San Jose
350	n/a	Anaheim Elementary	Anaheim
350	n/a	Arvin Union Elementary	Arvin
350	n/a	Atwater Elementary	Atwater
350	n/a	Auburn Union Elementary	Auburn
350	n/a	Bakersfield City Elementary	Bakersfield
350	n/a	Beardsley Elementary	Bakersfield
350	n/a	Bellevue Union Elementary	Santa Rosa
350	n/a	Belmont-Redwood Shores Elementary	Belmont
350	n/a	Berryessa Union Elementary	San Jose
350	n/a	Bishop Union Elementary	Bishop
350	n/a	Brawley Elementary	Brawley
350	n/a	Brentwood Union Elementary	Brentwood
350	n/a	Buckeye Union Elementary	Shingle Springs
350	n/a	Buena Park Elementary	Buena Park
350	n/a	Burlingame Elementary	Burlingame
350	n/a	Burton Elementary	Porterville
350	n/a	Cajon Valley Union Elementary	El Cajon
350	n/a	Cambrian Elementary	San Jose
350	n/a	Campbell Union Elementary	Campbell
350	n/a	Cascade Union Elementary	Anderson
350	n/a	Castaic Union Elementary	Valencia
350	n/a	Central Elementary	Rcho Cucamong
350	n/a	Central Union Elementary	Lemoore
350	n/a	Centralia Elementary	Buena Park
350	n/a	Chowchilla Elementary	Chowchilla
350	n/a	Chula Vista Elementary	Chula Vista
350	n/a	Corning Union Elementary	Corning
350	n/a	Cucamonga Elementary	Rcho Cucamong
350	n/a	Cupertino Union School	Cupertino
350	n/a	Cypress Elementary	Cypress
350	n/a	Del Mar Union Elementary	Del Mar
350	n/a	Del Paso Heights Elementary	Sacramento
350	n/a	Delano Union Elementary	Delano
350	n/a	Dixie Elementary	San Rafael
350	n/a	Dry Creek Joint Elementary	Roseville
350	n/a	Earlimart Elementary	Earlimart
350	n/a	East Whittier City Elementary	Whittier
350	n/a	Eastside Union Elementary	Lancaster
350	n/a	El Centro Elementary	El Centro
350	n/a	El Monte City Elementary	El Monte
350	n/a	Empire Union Elementary	Modesto
350	n/a	Encinitas Union Elementary	Encinitas
350	n/a	Enterprise Elementary	Redding
350	n/a	Etiwanda Elementary	Etiwanda
350	n/a	Eureka Union Elementary	Granite Bay
350	n/a	Evergreen Elementary	San Jose
350	n/a	Exeter Union Elementary	Exeter
350	n/a	Fallbrook Union Elementary	Fallbrook
350	n/a	Fountain Valley Elementary	Fountain Valley
350	n/a	Franklin-Mckinley Elementary	San Jose
350	n/a	Fruitvale Elementary	Bakersfield
350	n/a	Fullerton Elementary	Fullerton
350	n/a	Galt Joint Union Elementary	Galt
350	n/a	Garvey Elementary	Rosemead
350	n/a	Goleta Union Elementary	Goleta
350	n/a	Grass Valley Elementary	Grass Valley
350	n/a	Greenfield Union Elementary	Bakersfield
350	n/a	Greenfield Union Elementary	Greenfield
350	n/a	Hanford Elementary	Hanford
350	n/a	Hawthorne Elementary	Hawthorne
350	n/a	Hollister SD	Hollister
350	n/a	Hueneme Elementary	Port Hueneme
350	n/a	Huntington Beach City Elementary	Huntington Bch
350	n/a	Jamul-Dulzura Union Elementary	Jamul
350	n/a	Jefferson Elementary	Daly City
350	n/a	Jefferson Elementary	Tracy
350	n/a	Keppel Union Elementary	Pearblossom
350	n/a	King City Union Elementary	King City
350	n/a	Kingsburg Elementary Charter	Kingsburg
350	n/a	La Habra City Elementary	La Habra
350	n/a	La Mesa-Spring Valley	La Mesa
350	n/a	Lafayette Elementary	Lafayette
350	n/a	Laguna Salada Union Elementary	Pacifica
350	n/a	Lamont Elementary	Lamont
350	n/a	Lancaster Elementary	Lancaster
350	n/a	Lemon Grove Elementary	Lemon Grove
350	n/a	Lemoore Union Elementary	Lemoore
350	n/a	Little Lake City Elementary	Santa Fe Spgs
350	n/a	Live Oak Elementary	Santa Cruz
350	n/a	Livingston Union Elementary	Livingston
350	n/a	Loomis Union Elementary	Loomis
350	n/a	Los Altos Elementary	Los Altos
350	n/a	Los Gatos Union Elementary	Los Gatos
350	n/a	Los Nietos Elementary	Whittier
350	n/a	Lowell Joint	Whittier
350	n/a	Magnolia Elementary	Anaheim
350	n/a	Mark West Union Elementary	Santa Rosa
350	n/a	Menifee Union Elementary	Menifee
350	n/a	Menlo Park City Elementary	Atherton
350	n/a	Merced City Elementary	Merced
350	n/a	Mill Valley Elementary	Mill Valley
350	n/a	Millbrae Elementary	Millbrae
350	n/a	Modesto City Elementary	Modesto
350	n/a	Moraga Elementary	Moraga
350	n/a	Moreland Elementary	San Jose
350	n/a	Mother Lode Union Elementary	Placerville
350	n/a	Mount Pleasant Elementary	San Jose
350	n/a	Mountain View Elementary	Ontario
350	n/a	Mountain View Elementary	El Monte
350	n/a	Mountain View-Whisman Elementary	Mountain View
350	n/a	National Elementary	National City
350	n/a	Newhall Elementary	Valencia
350	n/a	Norris Elementary	Bakersfield
350	n/a	North Sacramento Elementary	Sacramento
350	n/a	Oak Grove Elementary	San Jose
350	n/a	Oakley Union Elementary	Oakley
350	n/a	Ocean View Elementary	Oxnard
350	n/a	Ocean View Elementary	Huntington Bch
350	n/a	Old Adobe Union Elementary	Petaluma
350	n/a	Ontario-Montclair Elementary	Ontario
350	n/a	Orcutt Union Elementary	Orcutt
350	n/a	Orinda Union Elementary	Orinda
350	n/a	Oroville City Elementary	Oroville
350	n/a	Oxnard Elementary	Oxnard
350	n/a	Palmdale Elementary	Palmdale
350	n/a	Panama Buena Vista Union Elem	Bakersfield
350	n/a	Perris Elementary	Perris
350	n/a	Petaluma City Elementary	Petaluma
350	n/a	Piner-Olivet Union Elementary	Santa Rosa
350	n/a	Pleasant Ridge Union Elementary	Grass Valley
350	n/a	Pleasant Valley School	Camarillo
350	n/a	Rescue Union Elementary	Rescue
350	n/a	Richland SD	Shafter
350	n/a	Rincon Valley Union Elementary	Santa Rosa
350	n/a	Rio Elementary	Oxnard
350	n/a	Rio Linda Union Elementary	Rio Linda
350	n/a	Robla Elementary	Sacramento
350	n/a	Romoland Elementary	Homeland
350	n/a	Rosedale Union Elementary	Bakersfield
350	n/a	Rosemead Elementary	Rosemead
350	n/a	Roseville City Elementary	Roseville
350	n/a	Ross Valley Elementary	San Anselmo
350	n/a	Salida Union Elementary	Salida
350	n/a	Salinas City Elementary	Salinas
350	n/a	San Bruno Park Elementary	San Bruno
350	n/a	San Carlos Elementary	San Carlos
350	n/a	San Mateo-Foster City Elementary	San Mateo
350	n/a	San Rafael City Elementary	San Rafael
350	n/a	San Ysidro Elementary	San Ysidro
350	n/a	Santa Barbara Elementary	Santa Barbara
350	n/a	Santa Cruz City Elementary	Santa Cruz
350	n/a	Santa Maria-Bonita Elementary	Santa Maria
350	n/a	Santa Paula Elementary	Santa Paula
350	n/a	Santa Rita Union Elementary	Salinas
350	n/a	Santa Rosa Elementary	Santa Rosa
350	n/a	Santee Elementary	Santee
350	n/a	Saratoga Union Elementary	Saratoga
350	n/a	Saugus Union Elementary	Santa Clarita
350	n/a	Savanna Elementary	Anaheim
350	n/a	Solana Beach Elementary	Solana Beach
350	n/a	Soquel Union Elementary	Capitola
350	n/a	South Bay Union Elementary	Imperial Beach
350	n/a	South Whittier Elementary	Whittier
350	n/a	Standard Elementary	Bakersfield
350	n/a	Stanislaus Union Elementary	Modesto
350	n/a	Sulphur Springs Union Elementary	Canyon Country
350	n/a	Sunnyvale Elementary	Sunnyvale
350	n/a	Sylvan Union Elementary	Modesto
350	n/a	Taft City Elementary	Taft
350	n/a	Thermalito Union Elementary	Oroville
350	n/a	Tulare City Elementary	Tulare
350	n/a	Turlock Joint Elementary	Turlock
350	n/a	Union Elementary	San Jose
350	n/a	Victor Elementary	Victorville
350	n/a	Walnut Creek Elementary	Walnut Creek
350	n/a	Wasco Union Elementary	Wasco
350	n/a	Weaver Union Elementary	Merced
350	n/a	Westminster Elementary	Westminster
350	n/a	Westside Union Elementary	Lancaster
350	n/a	Whittier City Elementary	Whittier
350	n/a	Wilsona Elementary	Palmdale
350	n/a	Winton Elementary	Winton
350	n/a	Wiseburn Elementary	Hawthorne
350	n/a	Woodlake Union Elementary	Woodlake

High School Drop-out Rate

Rank	Percent	District Name	City
1	n/a	ABC Unified	Cerritos
1	n/a	Acalanes Union High	Lafayette
1	n/a	Acton-Agua Dulce Unified	Acton
1	n/a	Adelanto Elementary	Adelanto
1	n/a	Alameda City Unified	Alameda
1	n/a	Albany City Unified	Albany
1	n/a	Alhambra City Elementary	Alhambra
1	n/a	Alhambra City High	Alhambra
1	n/a	Alisal Union Elementary	Salinas
1	n/a	Alpine Union Elementary	Alpine
1	n/a	Alta Loma Elementary	Alta Loma
1	n/a	Alum Rock Union Elementary	San Jose
1	n/a	Alvord Unified	Riverside
1	n/a	Amador County Unified	Jackson
1	n/a	Anaheim Elementary	Anaheim
1	n/a	Anaheim Union High	Anaheim
1	n/a	Anderson Union High	Anderson
1	n/a	Antelope Valley Union High	Lancaster
1	n/a	Antioch Unified	Antioch
1	n/a	Apple Valley Unified	Apple Valley
1	n/a	Arcadia Unified	Arcadia
1	n/a	Arvin Union Elementary	Arvin
1	n/a	Atascadero Unified	Atascadero
1	n/a	Atwater Elementary	Atwater
1	n/a	Auburn Union Elementary	Auburn
1	n/a	Azusa Unified	Azusa
1	n/a	Bakersfield City Elementary	Bakersfield
1	n/a	Baldwin Park Unified	Baldwin Park
1	n/a	Banning Unified	Banning
1	n/a	Barstow Unified	Barstow
1	n/a	Bassett Unified	La Puente
1	n/a	Bear Valley Unified	Big Bear Lake
1	n/a	Beardsley Elementary	Bakersfield
1	n/a	Beaumont Unified	Beaumont
1	n/a	Bellevue Union Elementary	Santa Rosa
1	n/a	Bellflower Unified	Bellflower
1	n/a	Belmont-Redwood Shores Elementary	Belmont
1	n/a	Benicia Unified	Benicia
1	n/a	Berkeley Unified	Berkeley
1	n/a	Berryessa Union Elementary	San Jose
1	n/a	Beverly Hills Unified	Beverly Hills
1	n/a	Bishop Union Elementary	Bishop
1	n/a	Black Oak Mine Unified	Georgetown
1	n/a	Bonita Unified	San Dimas
1	n/a	Bonsall Union Elementary	Bonsall
1	n/a	Brawley Elementary	Brawley
1	n/a	Brawley Union High	Brawley
1	n/a	Brea-Olinda Unified	Brea
1	n/a	Brentwood Union Elementary	Brentwood
1	n/a	Buckeye Union Elementary	Shingle Springs

1	n/a	Buena Park Elementary	Buena Park
1	n/a	Burbank Unified	Burbank
1	n/a	Burlingame Elementary	Burlingame
1	n/a	Burton Elementary	Porterville
1	n/a	Cabrillo Unified	Half Moon Bay
1	n/a	Cajon Valley Union Elementary	El Cajon
1	n/a	Calaveras Unified	San Andreas
1	n/a	Calexico Unified	Calexico
1	n/a	Cambrian Elementary	San Jose
1	n/a	Campbell Union Elementary	Campbell
1	n/a	Campbell Union High	San Jose
1	n/a	Capistrano Unified	San Juan Capis
1	n/a	Carlsbad Unified	Carlsbad
1	n/a	Carmel Unified	Carmel
1	n/a	Carpinteria Unified	Carpinteria
1	n/a	Cascade Union Elementary	Anderson
1	n/a	Castaic Union Elementary	Valencia
1	n/a	Castro Valley Unified	Castro Valley
1	n/a	Center Joint Unified	Antelope
1	n/a	Centinela Valley Union High	Lawndale
1	n/a	Central Elementary	Rcho Cucamong
1	n/a	Central Unified	Fresno
1	n/a	Central Union Elementary	Lemoore
1	n/a	Central Union High	El Centro
1	n/a	Centralia Elementary	Buena Park
1	n/a	Ceres Unified	Ceres
1	n/a	Chaffey Joint Union High	Ontario
1	n/a	Charter Oak Unified	Covina
1	n/a	Chico Unified	Chico
1	n/a	Chino Valley Unified	Chino
1	n/a	Chowchilla Elementary	Chowchilla
1	n/a	Chula Vista Elementary	Chula Vista
1	n/a	Claremont Unified	Claremont
1	n/a	Cloverdale Unified	Cloverdale
1	n/a	Clovis Unified	Clovis
1	n/a	Coachella Valley Unified	Thermal
1	n/a	Coalinga-Huron Joint Unified	Coalinga
1	n/a	Colton Joint Unified	Colton
1	n/a	Colusa Unified	Colusa
1	n/a	Compton Unified	Compton
1	n/a	Conejo Valley Unified	Thousand Oaks
1	n/a	Corcoran Joint Unified	Corcoran
1	n/a	Corning Union Elementary	Corning
1	n/a	Corona-Norco Unified	Norco
1	n/a	Coronado Unified	Coronado
1	n/a	Cotati-Rohnert Park Unified	Rohnert Park
1	n/a	Covina-Valley Unified	Covina
1	n/a	Cucamonga Elementary	Rcho Cucamong
1	n/a	Culver City Unified	Culver City
1	n/a	Cupertino Union School	Cupertino
1	n/a	Cutler-Orosi Joint Unified	Orosi
1	n/a	Cypress Elementary	Cypress
1	n/a	Davis Joint Unified	Davis
1	n/a	Del Mar Union Elementary	Del Mar
1	n/a	Del Norte County Unified	Crescent City
1	n/a	Del Paso Heights Elementary	Sacramento
1	n/a	Delano Joint Union High	Delano
1	n/a	Delano Union Elementary	Delano
1	n/a	Delhi Unified	Delhi
1	n/a	Desert Sands Unified	La Quinta
1	n/a	Dinuba Unified	Dinuba
1	n/a	Dixie Elementary	San Rafael
1	n/a	Dixon Unified	Dixon
1	n/a	Dos Palos Oro Loma Joint Unified	Dos Palos
1	n/a	Downey Unified	Downey
1	n/a	Dry Creek Joint Elementary	Roseville
1	n/a	Duarte Unified	Duarte
1	n/a	Dublin Unified	Dublin
1	n/a	Earlimart Elementary	Earlimart
1	n/a	East Side Union High	San Jose
1	n/a	East Whittier City Elementary	Whittier
1	n/a	Eastside Union Elementary	Lancaster
1	n/a	El Centro Elementary	El Centro
1	n/a	El Dorado Union High	Placerville
1	n/a	El Monte City Elementary	El Monte
1	n/a	El Monte Union High	El Monte
1	n/a	El Rancho Unified	Pico Rivera
1	n/a	El Segundo Unified	El Segundo
1	n/a	Elk Grove Unified	Elk Grove
1	n/a	Empire Union Elementary	Modesto
1	n/a	Encinitas Union Elementary	Encinitas
1	n/a	Enterprise Elementary	Redding
1	n/a	Escalon Unified	Escalon
1	n/a	Escondido Union Elementary	Escondido
1	n/a	Escondido Union High	Escondido
1	n/a	Etiwanda Elementary	Etiwanda
1	n/a	Eureka City Unified	Eureka
1	n/a	Eureka Union Elementary	Granite Bay
1	n/a	Evergreen Elementary	San Jose
1	n/a	Exeter Union Elementary	Exeter
1	n/a	Fairfield-Suisun Unified	Fairfield
1	n/a	Fallbrook Union Elementary	Fallbrook
1	n/a	Fallbrook Union High	Fallbrook
1	n/a	Farmersville Unified	Farmersville
1	n/a	Fillmore Unified	Fillmore
1	n/a	Firebaugh-Las Deltas Joint Unified	Firebaugh
1	n/a	Folsom-Cordova Unified	Folsom
1	n/a	Fontana Unified	Fontana
1	n/a	Fort Bragg Unified	Fort Bragg
1	n/a	Fountain Valley Elementary	Fountain Valley
1	n/a	Fowler Unified	Fowler
1	n/a	Franklin-Mckinley Elementary	San Jose
1	n/a	Fremont Unified	Fremont
1	n/a	Fremont Union High	Sunnyvale
1	n/a	Fresno County Office of Ed	Fresno
1	n/a	Fresno Unified	Fresno
1	n/a	Fruitvale Elementary	Bakersfield
1	n/a	Fullerton Elementary	Fullerton
1	n/a	Fullerton Joint Union High	Fullerton
1	n/a	Galt Joint Union Elementary	Galt
1	n/a	Galt Joint Union High	Galt
1	n/a	Garden Grove Unified	Garden Grove
1	n/a	Garvey Elementary	Rosemead
1	n/a	Gateway Unified	Redding
1	n/a	Gilroy Unified	Gilroy
1	n/a	Glendale Unified	Glendale
1	n/a	Glendora Unified	Glendora
1	n/a	Golden Plains Unified	San Joaquin
1	n/a	Goleta Union Elementary	Goleta
1	n/a	Gonzales Unified	Gonzales
1	n/a	Gorman Elementary	Gorman
1	n/a	Grant Joint Union High	Sacramento
1	n/a	Grass Valley Elementary	Grass Valley
1	n/a	Greenfield Union Elementary	Bakersfield
1	n/a	Greenfield Union Elementary	Greenfield
1	n/a	Gridley Unified	Gridley
1	n/a	Grossmont Union High	La Mesa
1	n/a	Gustine Unified	Gustine
1	n/a	Hacienda La Puente Unified	City of Industry
1	n/a	Hanford Elementary	Hanford
1	n/a	Hanford Joint Union High	Hanford
1	n/a	Hawthorne Elementary	Hawthorne
1	n/a	Hayward Unified	Hayward
1	n/a	Healdsburg Unified	Healdsburg
1	n/a	Hemet Unified	Hemet
1	n/a	Hesperia Unified	Hesperia
1	n/a	Hilmar Unified	Hilmar
1	n/a	Hollister SD	Hollister
1	n/a	Holtville Unified	Holtville
1	n/a	Hueneme Elementary	Port Hueneme
1	n/a	Hughson Unified	Hughson
1	n/a	Huntington Beach City Elementary	Huntington Bch
1	n/a	Huntington Beach Union High	Huntington Bch
1	n/a	Imperial Unified	Imperial
1	n/a	Inglewood Unified	Inglewood
1	n/a	Irvine Unified	Irvine
1	n/a	Jamul-Dulzura Union Elementary	Jamul
1	n/a	Jefferson Elementary	Tracy
1	n/a	Jefferson Elementary	Daly City
1	n/a	Jefferson Union High	Daly City
1	n/a	John Swett Unified	Crockett
1	n/a	Julian Union Elementary	Julian
1	n/a	Julian Union High	Julian
1	n/a	Jurupa Unified	Riverside
1	n/a	Kelseyville Unified	Kelseyville
1	n/a	Keppel Union Elementary	Pearblossom
1	n/a	Kerman Unified	Kerman
1	n/a	Kern County Office of Ed	Bakersfield
1	n/a	Kern Union High	Bakersfield
1	n/a	Keyes Union Elementary	Keyes
1	n/a	King City Joint Union High	King City
1	n/a	King City Union Elementary	King City
1	n/a	Kings Canyon Joint Unified	Reedley
1	n/a	Kingsburg Elementary Charter	Kingsburg
1	n/a	Konocti Unified	Lower Lake
1	n/a	La Canada Unified	La Canada
1	n/a	La Habra City Elementary	La Habra
1	n/a	La Mesa-Spring Valley	La Mesa
1	n/a	Lafayette Elementary	Lafayette
1	n/a	Laguna Beach Unified	Laguna Beach
1	n/a	Laguna Salada Union Elementary	Pacifica
1	n/a	Lake Elsinore Unified	Lake Elsinore
1	n/a	Lake Tahoe Unified	S Lake Tahoe
1	n/a	Lakeport Unified	Lakeport
1	n/a	Lakeside Union Elementary	Lakeside
1	n/a	Lamont Elementary	Lamont
1	n/a	Lancaster Elementary	Lancaster
1	n/a	Las Virgenes Unified	Calabasas
1	n/a	Lawndale Elementary	Lawndale
1	n/a	Lemon Grove Elementary	Lemon Grove
1	n/a	Lemoore Union Elementary	Lemoore
1	n/a	Lemoore Union High	Lemoore
1	n/a	Lennox Elementary	Lennox
1	n/a	Liberty Union High	Brentwood
1	n/a	Lincoln Unified	Stockton
1	n/a	Linden Unified	Linden
1	n/a	Lindsay Unified	Lindsay
1	n/a	Little Lake City Elementary	Santa Fe Spgs
1	n/a	Live Oak Elementary	Santa Cruz
1	n/a	Live Oak Unified	Live Oak
1	n/a	Livermore Valley Joint Unified	Livermore
1	n/a	Livingston Union Elementary	Livingston
1	n/a	Lodi Unified	Lodi
1	n/a	Lompoc Unified	Lompoc
1	n/a	Long Beach Unified	Long Beach
1	n/a	Loomis Union Elementary	Loomis
1	n/a	Los Alamitos Unified	Los Alamitos
1	n/a	Los Altos Elementary	Los Altos
1	n/a	Los Angeles County Office of Ed	Downey
1	n/a	Los Angeles Unified	Los Angeles
1	n/a	Los Banos Unified	Los Banos
1	n/a	Los Gatos Union Elementary	Los Gatos
1	n/a	Los Gatos-Saratoga Jt Union High	Los Gatos
1	n/a	Los Nietos Elementary	Whittier
1	n/a	Lowell Joint	Whittier
1	n/a	Lucia Mar Unified	Arroyo Grande
1	n/a	Lynwood Unified	Lynwood
1	n/a	Madera Unified	Madera
1	n/a	Magnolia Elementary	Anaheim
1	n/a	Manhattan Beach Unified	Manhattan Beach
1	n/a	Manteca Unified	Manteca
1	n/a	Mariposa County Unified	Mariposa
1	n/a	Mark West Union Elementary	Santa Rosa
1	n/a	Martinez Unified	Martinez
1	n/a	Marysville Joint Unified	Marysville
1	n/a	Mcfarland Unified	Mcfarland
1	n/a	Mendota Unified	Mendota
1	n/a	Menifee Union Elementary	Menifee
1	n/a	Menlo Park City Elementary	Atherton
1	n/a	Merced City Elementary	Merced
1	n/a	Merced Union High	Atwater
1	n/a	Middletown Unified	Middletown
1	n/a	Mill Valley Elementary	Mill Valley
1	n/a	Millbrae Elementary	Millbrae
1	n/a	Milpitas Unified	Milpitas
1	n/a	Modesto City Elementary	Modesto
1	n/a	Modesto City High	Modesto
1	n/a	Mojave Unified	Mojave
1	n/a	Monrovia Unified	Monrovia
1	n/a	Montebello Unified	Montebello
1	n/a	Monterey Peninsula Unified	Monterey
1	n/a	Moorpark Unified	Moorpark
1	n/a	Moraga Elementary	Moraga
1	n/a	Moreland Elementary	San Jose
1	n/a	Moreno Valley Unified	Moreno Valley
1	n/a	Morgan Hill Unified	Morgan Hill
1	n/a	Morongo Unified	Twentynine Plms
1	n/a	Mother Lode Union Elementary	Placerville
1	n/a	Mount Diablo Unified	Concord
1	n/a	Mount Pleasant Elementary	San Jose
1	n/a	Mountain Empire Unified	Pine Valley
1	n/a	Mountain View Elementary	El Monte
1	n/a	Mountain View Elementary	Ontario
1	n/a	Mountain View-Los Altos Union High	Mountain View
1	n/a	Mountain View-Whisman Elementary	Mountain View
1	n/a	Muroc Joint Unified	North Edwards
1	n/a	Murrieta Valley Unified	Murrieta
1	n/a	Napa Valley Unified	Napa
1	n/a	National Elementary	National City
1	n/a	Natomas Unified	Sacramento
1	n/a	Nevada Joint Union High	Grass Valley
1	n/a	New Haven Unified	Union City
1	n/a	Newark Unified	Newark
1	n/a	Newhall Elementary	Valencia
1	n/a	Newman-Crows Landing Unified	Newman
1	n/a	Newport-Mesa Unified	Costa Mesa
1	n/a	Norris Elementary	Bakersfield
1	n/a	North Monterey County Unified	Moss Landing
1	n/a	North Sacramento Elementary	Sacramento
1	n/a	Northern Humboldt Union High	McKinleyville
1	n/a	Norwalk-La Mirada Unified	Norwalk
1	n/a	Novato Unified	Novato
1	n/a	Oak Grove Elementary	San Jose
1	n/a	Oak Park Unified	Oak Park
1	n/a	Oakdale Joint Unified	Oakdale
1	n/a	Oakland Unified	Oakland
1	n/a	Oakley Union Elementary	Oakley
1	n/a	Ocean View Elementary	Oxnard
1	n/a	Ocean View Elementary	Huntington Bch
1	n/a	Oceanside Unified	Oceanside
1	n/a	Ojai Unified	Ojai
1	n/a	Old Adobe Union Elementary	Petaluma
1	n/a	Ontario-Montclair Elementary	Ontario
1	n/a	Orange County Office of Ed	Costa Mesa
1	n/a	Orange Unified	Orange
1	n/a	Orcutt Union Elementary	Orcutt
1	n/a	Orinda Union Elementary	Orinda
1	n/a	Orland Joint Unified	Orland

1	n/a	Oro Grande Elementary	Oro Grande
1	n/a	Oroville City Elementary	Oroville
1	n/a	Oroville Union High	Oroville
1	n/a	Oxnard Elementary	Oxnard
1	n/a	Oxnard Union High	Oxnard
1	n/a	Pacific Grove Unified	Pacific Grove
1	n/a	Pajaro Valley Unified School	Watsonville
1	n/a	Palm Springs Unified	Palm Springs
1	n/a	Palmdale Elementary	Palmdale
1	n/a	Palo Alto Unified	Palo Alto
1	n/a	Palo Verde Unified	Blythe
1	n/a	Palos Verdes Peninsula Unified	Palos Verdes Est
1	n/a	Panama Buena Vista Union Elem	Bakersfield
1	n/a	Paradise Unified	Paradise
1	n/a	Paramount Unified	Paramount
1	n/a	Parlier Unified	Parlier
1	n/a	Pasadena Unified	Pasadena
1	n/a	Paso Robles Joint Unified	Paso Robles
1	n/a	Patterson Joint Unified	Patterson
1	n/a	Perris Elementary	Perris
1	n/a	Perris Union High	Perris
1	n/a	Petaluma City Elementary	Petaluma
1	n/a	Petaluma Joint Union High	Petaluma
1	n/a	Piedmont City Unified	Piedmont
1	n/a	Piner-Olivet Union Elementary	Santa Rosa
1	n/a	Pittsburg Unified	Pittsburg
1	n/a	Placentia-Yorba Linda Unified	Placentia
1	n/a	Placer Union High	Auburn
1	n/a	Pleasant Ridge Union Elementary	Grass Valley
1	n/a	Pleasant Valley School	Camarillo
1	n/a	Pleasanton Unified	Pleasanton
1	n/a	Plumas Unified	Quincy
1	n/a	Pomona Unified	Pomona
1	n/a	Porterville Unified	Porterville
1	n/a	Poway Unified	Poway
1	n/a	Ramona City Unified	Ramona
1	n/a	Ravenswood City Elementary	East Palo Alto
1	n/a	Red Bluff Joint Union High	Red Bluff
1	n/a	Red Bluff Union Elementary	Red Bluff
1	n/a	Redding Elementary	Redding
1	n/a	Redlands Unified	Redlands
1	n/a	Redondo Beach Unified	Redondo Beach
1	n/a	Redwood City Elementary	Redwood City
1	n/a	Reef-Sunset Unified	Avenal
1	n/a	Rescue Union Elementary	Rescue
1	n/a	Rialto Unified	Rialto
1	n/a	Richland SD	Shafter
1	n/a	Rim of The World Unified	Lake Arrowhead
1	n/a	Rincon Valley Union Elementary	Santa Rosa
1	n/a	Rio Elementary	Oxnard
1	n/a	Rio Linda Union Elementary	Rio Linda
1	n/a	Ripon Unified	Ripon
1	n/a	River Delta Joint Unified	Rio Vista
1	n/a	Riverbank Unified	Riverbank
1	n/a	Riverdale Joint Unified	Riverdale
1	n/a	Riverside County Office of Ed	Riverside
1	n/a	Riverside Unified	Riverside
1	n/a	Robla Elementary	Sacramento
1	n/a	Rocklin Unified	Rocklin
1	n/a	Romoland Elementary	Homeland
1	n/a	Rosedale Union Elementary	Bakersfield
1	n/a	Rosemead Elementary	Rosemead
1	n/a	Roseville City Elementary	Roseville
1	n/a	Roseville Joint Union High	Roseville
1	n/a	Ross Valley Elementary	San Anselmo
1	n/a	Rowland Unified	Rowland Heights
1	n/a	Sacramento City Unified	Sacramento
1	n/a	Saddleback Valley Unified	Mission Viejo
1	n/a	Saint Helena Unified	Saint Helena
1	n/a	Salida Union Elementary	Salida
1	n/a	Salinas City Elementary	Salinas
1	n/a	Salinas Union High	Salinas
1	n/a	San Benito High	Hollister
1	n/a	San Bernardino City Unified	San Bernardino
1	n/a	San Bernardino County Supt.	San Bernardino
1	n/a	San Bruno Park Elementary	San Bruno
1	n/a	San Carlos Elementary	San Carlos
1	n/a	San Diego County Office of Ed	San Diego
1	n/a	San Diego Unified	San Diego
1	n/a	San Dieguito Union High	Encinitas
1	n/a	San Francisco Unified	San Francisco
1	n/a	San Gabriel Unified	San Gabriel
1	n/a	San Jacinto Unified	San Jacinto
1	n/a	San Joaquin County Office of Ed	Stockton
1	n/a	San Jose Unified	San Jose
1	n/a	San Juan Unified	Carmichael
1	n/a	San Leandro Unified	San Leandro
1	n/a	San Lorenzo Unified	San Lorenzo
1	n/a	San Lorenzo Valley Unified	Felton
1	n/a	San Luis Coastal Unified	San Luis Obispo
1	n/a	San Marcos Unified	San Marcos
1	n/a	San Marino Unified	San Marino
1	n/a	San Mateo Union High	San Mateo
1	n/a	San Mateo-Foster City Elementary	San Mateo
1	n/a	San Rafael City Elementary	San Rafael
1	n/a	San Rafael City High	San Rafael
1	n/a	San Ramon Valley Unified	Danville
1	n/a	San Ysidro Elementary	San Ysidro
1	n/a	Sanger Unified	Sanger
1	n/a	Santa Ana Unified	Santa Ana
1	n/a	Santa Barbara Elementary	Santa Barbara
1	n/a	Santa Barbara High	Santa Barbara
1	n/a	Santa Clara County Office of Ed	San Jose
1	n/a	Santa Clara Unified	Santa Clara
1	n/a	Santa Cruz City Elementary	Santa Cruz
1	n/a	Santa Cruz City High	Santa Cruz
1	n/a	Santa Maria Joint Union High	Santa Maria
1	n/a	Santa Maria-Bonita Elementary	Santa Maria
1	n/a	Santa Monica-Malibu Unified	Santa Monica
1	n/a	Santa Paula Elementary	Santa Paula
1	n/a	Santa Paula Union High	Santa Paula
1	n/a	Santa Rita Union Elementary	Salinas
1	n/a	Santa Rosa Elementary	Santa Rosa
1	n/a	Santa Rosa High	Santa Rosa
1	n/a	Santee Elementary	Santee
1	n/a	Saratoga Union Elementary	Saratoga
1	n/a	Saugus Union Elementary	Santa Clarita
1	n/a	Savanna Elementary	Anaheim
1	n/a	Scotts Valley Unified	Scotts Valley
1	n/a	Selma Unified	Selma
1	n/a	Sequoia Union High	Redwood City
1	n/a	Shasta Union High	Redding
1	n/a	Sierra Sands Unified	Ridgecrest
1	n/a	Sierra Unified	Auberry
1	n/a	Silver Valley Unified	Yermo
1	n/a	Simi Valley Unified	Simi Valley
1	n/a	Snowline Joint Unified	Phelan
1	n/a	Solana Beach Elementary	Solana Beach
1	n/a	Soledad Unified	Soledad
1	n/a	Sonoma Valley Unified	Sonoma
1	n/a	Sonora Union High	Sonora
1	n/a	Soquel Union Elementary	Capitola
1	n/a	South Bay Union Elementary	Imperial Beach
1	n/a	South Pasadena Unified	South Pasadena
1	n/a	South San Francisco Unified	S San Francisco
1	n/a	South Whittier Elementary	Whittier
1	n/a	Southern Kern Unified	Rosamond
1	n/a	Standard Elementary	Bakersfield
1	n/a	Stanislaus Union Elementary	Modesto
1	n/a	Stockton City Unified	Stockton
1	n/a	Sulphur Springs Union Elementary	Canyon Country
1	n/a	Sunnyvale Elementary	Sunnyvale
1	n/a	Sweetwater Union High	Chula Vista
1	n/a	Sylvan Union Elementary	Modesto
1	n/a	Taft City Elementary	Taft
1	n/a	Tahoe-Truckee Joint Unified	Truckee
1	n/a	Tamalpais Union High	Larkspur
1	n/a	Tehachapi Unified	Tehachapi
1	n/a	Temecula Valley Unified	Temecula
1	n/a	Temple City Unified	Temple City
1	n/a	Templeton Unified	Templeton
1	n/a	Thermalito Union Elementary	Oroville
1	n/a	Torrance Unified	Torrance
1	n/a	Tracy Joint Unified	Tracy
1	n/a	Travis Unified	Travis Afb
1	n/a	Tulare City Elementary	Tulare
1	n/a	Tulare Joint Union High	Tulare
1	n/a	Turlock Joint Elementary	Turlock
1	n/a	Turlock Joint Union High	Turlock
1	n/a	Tustin Unified	Tustin
1	n/a	Twin Ridges Elementary	North San Juan
1	n/a	Ukiah Unified	Ukiah
1	n/a	Union Elementary	San Jose
1	n/a	Upland Unified	Upland
1	n/a	Vacaville Unified	Vacaville
1	n/a	Val Verde Unified	Perris
1	n/a	Vallejo City Unified	Vallejo
1	n/a	Valley Center-Pauma Unified	Valley Center
1	n/a	Ventura Unified	Ventura
1	n/a	Victor Elementary	Victorville
1	n/a	Victor Valley Union High	Victorville
1	n/a	Visalia Unified	Visalia
1	n/a	Vista Unified	Vista
1	n/a	Walnut Creek Elementary	Walnut Creek
1	n/a	Walnut Valley Unified	Walnut
1	n/a	Wasco Union Elementary	Wasco
1	n/a	Washington Unified	West Sacramento
1	n/a	Waterford Unified	Waterford
1	n/a	Weaver Union Elementary	Merced
1	n/a	West Contra Costa Unified	Richmond
1	n/a	West Covina Unified	West Covina
1	n/a	West Sonoma County Union High	Sebastopol
1	n/a	Western Placer Unified	Lincoln
1	n/a	Westminster Elementary	Westminster
1	n/a	Westside Union Elementary	Lancaster
1	n/a	Westwood Unified	Westwood
1	n/a	Wheatland Elementary	Wheatland
1	n/a	Whittier City Elementary	Whittier
1	n/a	Whittier Union High	Whittier
1	n/a	William S Hart Union High	Santa Clarita
1	n/a	Willits Unified	Willits
1	n/a	Willows Unified	Willows
1	n/a	Wilsona Elementary	Palmdale
1	n/a	Windsor Unified	Windsor
1	n/a	Winters Joint Unified	Winters
1	n/a	Winton Elementary	Winton
1	n/a	Wiseburn Elementary	Hawthorne
1	n/a	Woodlake Union Elementary	Woodlake
1	n/a	Woodland Joint Unified	Woodland
1	n/a	Yuba City Unified	Yuba City
1	n/a	Yucaipa-Calimesa Joint Unified	Yucaipa

Colorado

Colorado Public School Educational Profile

Category	Value	Category	Value
Schools *(2002-2003)*	1,690	**Diploma Recipients** *(2002-2003)*	40,760
Instructional Level		White, Non-Hispanic	31,506
Primary	967	Black, Non-Hispanic	1,798
Middle	292	Asian/Pacific Islander	1,442
High	350	American Indian/Alaskan Native	314
Other Level	81	Hispanic	5,700
Curriculum		**High School Drop-out Rate** (%) *(2000-2001)*	n/a
Regular	1,574	White, Non-Hispanic	n/a
Special Education	21	Black, Non-Hispanic	n/a
Vocational	7	Asian/Pacific Islander	n/a
Alternative	88	American Indian/Alaskan Native	n/a
Type		Hispanic	n/a
Magnet	2	**Staff** *(2002-2003)*	90,398.0
Charter	93	Teachers	45,401.0
Title I Eligible	859	Average Salary ($)	42,679
School-wide Title I	289	Librarians/Media Specialists	847.4
Students *(2002-2003)*	751,862	Guidance Counselors	1,390.3
Gender (%)		**Ratios** *(2002-2003)*	
Male	51.4	Student/Teacher Ratio	16.6 to 1
Female	48.6	Student/Librarian Ratio	887.3 to 1
Race/Ethnicity (%)		Student/Counselor Ratio	540.8 to 1
White, Non-Hispanic	65.7	**Current Spending** *($ per student in FY 2001)*	6,941
Black, Non-Hispanic	5.7	Instruction	4,010
Asian/Pacific Islander	3.0	Support Services	2,683
American Indian/Alaskan Native	1.2	**College Entrance Exam Scores** *(2003)*	
Hispanic	24.3	Scholastic Aptitude Test (SAT)	
Classification (%)		Participation Rate (%)	27
Individual Education Program (IEP)	10.1	Mean SAT I Verbal Score	551
Migrant	1.7	Mean SAT I Math Score	553
English Language Learner (ELL)	11.5	American College Testing Program (ACT)	
Eligible for Free Lunch Program	22.0	Participation Rate (%)	100
Eligible for Reduced-Price Lunch Program	6.6	Average Composite Score	20.1

Note: *For an explanation of data, please refer to the User's Guide in the front of the book; n/a indicates data not available*

Colorado NAEP 2003 Test Scores

Reading			Mathematics		
Grade/Category	**Value**	**Rank**	**Grade/Category**	**Value**	**Rank**
4th Grade			**4th Grade**		
Average Proficiency	223.7 (1.2)	8/51	Average Proficiency	235.2 (1.0)	28/51
Proficiency by Gender/Race/Ethnicity			Proficiency by Gender/Race/Ethnicity		
Male	220.4 (1.5)	8/51	Male	237.0 (1.2)	26/51
Female	227.0 (1.3)	9/51	Female	233.4 (1.1)	28/51
White, Non-Hispanic	231.6 (1.2)	7/51	White, Non-Hispanic	243.5 (0.9)	17/51
Black, Non-Hispanic	208.1 (2.6)	5/42	Black, Non-Hispanic	217.0 (2.4)	17/42
Asian, Non-Hispanic	204.8 (1.6)	21/41	Asian, Non-Hispanic	217.0 (1.8)	35/43
American Indian, Non-Hispanic	224.5 (3.7)	15/25	American Indian, Non-Hispanic	242.4 (4.3)	19/26
Hispanic	n/a	n/a	Hispanic	n/a	n/a
Proficiency by Class Size			Proficiency by Class Size		
Less than 16 Students	*209.2 (6.0)*	12/45	Less than 16 Students	*225.1 (5.9)*	24/47
16 to 18 Students	*213.8 (3.8)*	25/48	16 to 18 Students	*224.0 (3.6)*	39/48
19 to 20 Students	*221.4 (4.5)*	19/50	19 to 20 Students	*233.1 (4.4)*	31/50
21 to 25 Students	226.0 (1.6)	8/51	21 to 25 Students	237.6 (1.3)	26/51
Greater than 25 Students	225.0 (2.9)	7/49	Greater than 25 Students	236.5 (2.4)	23/49
Percent Attaining Achievement Levels			Percent Attaining Achievement Levels		
Below Basic	30.6 (1.4)	42/51	Below Basic	23.0 (1.3)	21/51
Basic or Above	69.4 (1.4)	9/51	Basic or Above	77.0 (1.3)	30/51
Proficient or Above	36.8 (1.7)	6/51	Proficient or Above	33.9 (1.5)	19/51
Advanced or Above	8.9 (0.9)	6/51	Advanced or Above	4.2 (0.5)	15/51
8th Grade			**8th Grade**		
Average Proficiency	267.6 (1.2)	11/51	Average Proficiency	283.4 (1.1)	13/51
Proficiency by Gender/Race/Ethnicity			Proficiency by Gender/Race/Ethnicity		
Male	261.5 (1.5)	14/51	Male	283.7 (1.4)	13/51
Female	273.9 (1.5)	10/51	Female	283.1 (1.2)	10/51
White, Non-Hispanic	274.6 (1.4)	7/50	White, Non-Hispanic	292.3 (1.2)	6/50
Black, Non-Hispanic	248.6 (3.2)	7/41	Black, Non-Hispanic	255.0 (2.9)	15/41
Asian, Non-Hispanic	247.4 (2.1)	15/37	Asian, Non-Hispanic	259.5 (1.9)	19/37
American Indian, Non-Hispanic	275.0 (3.6)	7/23	American Indian, Non-Hispanic	290.3 (4.0)	10/23
Hispanic	n/a	n/a	Hispanic	n/a	n/a
Proficiency by Parents Highest Level of Ed.			Proficiency by Parents Highest Level of Ed.		
Did Not Finish High School	248.1 (3.5)	15/50	Did Not Finish High School	254.2 (2.2)	36/50
Graduated High School	257.1 (2.1)	20/50	Graduated High School	269.7 (1.8)	24/50
Some Education After High School	271.6 (1.8)	7/50	Some Education After High School	281.7 (1.7)	21/50
Graduated College	276.8 (1.4)	5/50	Graduated College	295.0 (1.2)	3/50
Percent Attaining Achievement Levels			Percent Attaining Achievement Levels		
Below Basic	22.3 (1.3)	36/51	Below Basic	26.2 (1.1)	37/51
Basic or Above	77.7 (1.3)	16/51	Basic or Above	73.8 (1.1)	15/51
Proficient or Above	36.0 (1.6)	12/51	Proficient or Above	34.4 (1.3)	10/51
Advanced or Above	4.2 (0.8)	3/51	Advanced or Above	7.5 (0.8)	4/51

Note: *For an explanation of data, please refer to the User's Guide in the front of the book; values in italics indicate that the nature of the sample does not allow accurate determination of the variability of the statistic; n/a indicates data not available*

Adams County

Adams County 14

4720 E 69th Ave • Commerce City, CO 80022-2358
(303) 289-3950 • http://www.acsd14.k12.co.us/
Grade Span: PK-12; **Agency Type:** 1
Schools: 12
8 Primary; 2 Middle; 2 High; 0 Other Level
11 Regular; 0 Special Education; 0 Vocational; 1 Alternative
0 Magnet; 0 Charter; 9 Title I Eligible; 7 School-wide Title I
Students: 6,698 (50.9% male; 49.1% female)
Individual Education Program: 677 (10.1%);
English Language Learner: 2,112 (31.5%); Migrant: 667 (10.0%)
Eligible for Free Lunch Program: 3,626 (54.1%)
Eligible for Reduced-Price Lunch Program: 644 (9.6%)
Teachers: 375.5 (17.8 to 1)
Librarians/Media Specialists: 4.9 (1,366.9 to 1)
Guidance Counselors: 9.5 (705.1 to 1)
Current Spending: ($ per student per year):
Total: $6,803; Instruction: $3,861; Support Services: $2,701
Enrollment, Drop-out Rates and Diploma Recipients by Race/Ethnicity

Category	Total	White	Black	Asian	AIAN	Hisp.
Enrollment (%)	100.0	25.5	3.5	0.5	2.2	68.4
Drop-out Rate (%)	n/a	n/a	n/a	n/a	n/a	n/a
H.S. Diplomas (#)	236	105	3	0	3	125

Brighton 27J

630 S Eighth St • Brighton, CO 80601-3295
(303) 655-2900 • http://www.brightonps27j.k12.co.us/
Grade Span: PK-12; **Agency Type:** 1
Schools: 12
7 Primary; 2 Middle; 2 High; 1 Other Level
11 Regular; 0 Special Education; 0 Vocational; 1 Alternative
0 Magnet; 2 Charter; 5 Title I Eligible; 0 School-wide Title I
Students: 7,277 (51.1% male; 48.9% female)
Individual Education Program: 671 (9.2%);
English Language Learner: 1,470 (20.2%); Migrant: 297 (4.1%)
Eligible for Free Lunch Program: 1,561 (21.5%)
Eligible for Reduced-Price Lunch Program: 490 (6.7%)
Teachers: 414.9 (17.5 to 1)
Librarians/Media Specialists: 2.0 (3,638.5 to 1)
Guidance Counselors: 9.7 (750.2 to 1)
Current Spending: ($ per student per year):
Total: $6,053; Instruction: $3,321; Support Services: $2,455
Enrollment, Drop-out Rates and Diploma Recipients by Race/Ethnicity

Category	Total	White	Black	Asian	AIAN	Hisp.
Enrollment (%)	100.0	55.6	1.2	1.5	0.7	41.1
Drop-out Rate (%)	n/a	n/a	n/a	n/a	n/a	n/a
H.S. Diplomas (#)	271	180	1	8	1	81

Mapleton 1

591 E 80th Ave • Denver, CO 80229-5806
(303) 853-1000 • http://www.acsd1.k12.co.us/
Grade Span: PK-12; **Agency Type:** 1
Schools: 11
7 Primary; 2 Middle; 2 High; 0 Other Level
10 Regular; 0 Special Education; 0 Vocational; 1 Alternative
0 Magnet; 0 Charter; 6 Title I Eligible; 3 School-wide Title I
Students: 5,623 (51.3% male; 48.7% female)
Individual Education Program: 518 (9.2%);
English Language Learner: 1,379 (24.5%); Migrant: 218 (3.9%)
Eligible for Free Lunch Program: 1,467 (26.1%)
Eligible for Reduced-Price Lunch Program: 665 (11.8%)
Teachers: 278.7 (20.2 to 1)
Librarians/Media Specialists: 3.0 (1,874.3 to 1)
Guidance Counselors: 8.0 (702.9 to 1)
Current Spending: ($ per student per year):
Total: $5,573; Instruction: $3,318; Support Services: $2,078
Enrollment, Drop-out Rates and Diploma Recipients by Race/Ethnicity

Category	Total	White	Black	Asian	AIAN	Hisp.
Enrollment (%)	100.0	41.5	2.4	3.1	2.0	51.0
Drop-out Rate (%)	n/a	n/a	n/a	n/a	n/a	n/a
H.S. Diplomas (#)	210	124	4	7	2	73

Northglenn-Thornton 12

1500 E 128th Ave • Thornton, CO 80241
(720) 972-4000
Grade Span: PK-12; **Agency Type:** 1
Schools: 46
29 Primary; 8 Middle; 7 High; 2 Other Level
43 Regular; 0 Special Education; 1 Vocational; 2 Alternative
0 Magnet; 3 Charter; 20 Title I Eligible; 5 School-wide Title I
Students: 33,522 (50.5% male; 49.5% female)
Individual Education Program: 3,423 (10.2%);
English Language Learner: 2,279 (6.8%); Migrant: 320 (1.0%)
Eligible for Free Lunch Program: 5,420 (16.2%)
Eligible for Reduced-Price Lunch Program: 2,105 (6.3%)
Teachers: 1,725.2 (19.4 to 1)
Librarians/Media Specialists: 42.6 (786.9 to 1)
Guidance Counselors: 44.5 (753.3 to 1)
Current Spending: ($ per student per year):
Total: $5,784; Instruction: $3,675; Support Services: $1,939
Enrollment, Drop-out Rates and Diploma Recipients by Race/Ethnicity

Category	Total	White	Black	Asian	AIAN	Hisp.
Enrollment (%)	100.0	66.2	2.6	4.8	1.2	25.2
Drop-out Rate (%)	n/a	n/a	n/a	n/a	n/a	n/a
H.S. Diplomas (#)	1,566	1,156	36	81	8	285

Westminster 50

4476 W 68th Ave • Westminster, CO 80030-5898
(303) 428-3511 • http://www.adams50.k12.co.us/
Grade Span: PK-12; **Agency Type:** 1
Schools: 25
17 Primary; 4 Middle; 4 High; 0 Other Level
23 Regular; 0 Special Education; 1 Vocational; 1 Alternative
0 Magnet; 1 Charter; 15 Title I Eligible; 8 School-wide Title I
Students: 11,012 (51.1% male; 48.9% female)
Individual Education Program: 1,028 (9.3%);
English Language Learner: 2,894 (26.3%); Migrant: 247 (2.2%)
Eligible for Free Lunch Program: 3,965 (36.0%)
Eligible for Reduced-Price Lunch Program: 1,383 (12.6%)
Teachers: 655.1 (16.8 to 1)
Librarians/Media Specialists: 6.0 (1,835.3 to 1)
Guidance Counselors: 16.0 (688.3 to 1)
Current Spending: ($ per student per year):
Total: $5,912; Instruction: $3,555; Support Services: $2,149
Enrollment, Drop-out Rates and Diploma Recipients by Race/Ethnicity

Category	Total	White	Black	Asian	AIAN	Hisp.
Enrollment (%)	100.0	37.0	2.4	9.2	1.3	50.2
Drop-out Rate (%)	n/a	n/a	n/a	n/a	n/a	n/a
H.S. Diplomas (#)	498	272	8	57	10	151

Alamosa County

Alamosa RE-11J

209 Victoria Ave • Alamosa, CO 81101-4204
(719) 587-1600 • http://www.alamosa.k12.co.us/
Grade Span: PK-12; **Agency Type:** 1
Schools: 6
2 Primary; 2 Middle; 2 High; 0 Other Level
5 Regular; 0 Special Education; 0 Vocational; 1 Alternative
0 Magnet; 0 Charter; 5 Title I Eligible; 3 School-wide Title I
Students: 2,280 (53.2% male; 46.8% female)
Individual Education Program: 279 (12.2%);
English Language Learner: 167 (7.3%); Migrant: 260 (11.4%)
Eligible for Free Lunch Program: 1,009 (44.3%)
Eligible for Reduced-Price Lunch Program: 198 (8.7%)
Teachers: 146.6 (15.6 to 1)
Librarians/Media Specialists: 3.0 (760.0 to 1)
Guidance Counselors: 9.1 (250.5 to 1)
Current Spending: ($ per student per year):
Total: $5,572; Instruction: $3,276; Support Services: $2,102
Enrollment, Drop-out Rates and Diploma Recipients by Race/Ethnicity

Category	Total	White	Black	Asian	AIAN	Hisp.
Enrollment (%)	100.0	42.0	0.7	0.9	0.9	55.6
Drop-out Rate (%)	n/a	n/a	n/a	n/a	n/a	n/a
H.S. Diplomas (#)	132	72	0	4	0	56

Arapahoe County

Adams-Arapahoe 28J

1085 Peoria St • Aurora, CO 80011-6297
(303) 344-8060 • http://www.aps.k12.co.us/
Grade Span: PK-12; **Agency Type:** 1
Schools: 51
36 Primary; 7 Middle; 7 High; 1 Other Level
46 Regular; 1 Special Education; 1 Vocational; 3 Alternative
0 Magnet; 1 Charter; 24 Title I Eligible; 8 School-wide Title I
Students: 32,253 (51.8% male; 48.2% female)
Individual Education Program: 3,484 (10.8%);
English Language Learner: 11,479 (35.6%); Migrant: 1,004 (3.1%)
Eligible for Free Lunch Program: 11,355 (35.2%)
Eligible for Reduced-Price Lunch Program: 2,244 (7.0%)
Teachers: 1,740.9 (18.5 to 1)
Librarians/Media Specialists: 25.4 (1,269.8 to 1)
Guidance Counselors: 53.0 (608.5 to 1)
Current Spending: ($ per student per year):
Total: $6,164; Instruction: $3,682; Support Services: $2,275

Enrollment, Drop-out Rates and Diploma Recipients by Race/Ethnicity

Category	Total	White	Black	Asian	AIAN	Hisp.
Enrollment (%)	100.0	34.1	22.2	4.1	1.0	38.6
Drop-out Rate (%)	n/a	n/a	n/a	n/a	n/a	n/a
H.S. Diplomas (#)	1,120	569	233	95	11	212

Cherry Creek 5

4700 S Yosemite St • Greenwood Village, CO 80111-1394
(303) 773-1184
Grade Span: PK-12; **Agency Type:** 1
Schools: 53
37 Primary; 9 Middle; 6 High; 1 Other Level
51 Regular; 0 Special Education; 0 Vocational; 2 Alternative
1 Magnet; 1 Charter; 18 Title I Eligible; 0 School-wide Title I
Students: 45,738 (51.1% male; 48.9% female)
Individual Education Program: 5,096 (11.1%);
English Language Learner: 5,694 (12.4%); Migrant: 5 (<0.1%)
Eligible for Free Lunch Program: 3,636 (7.9%)
Eligible for Reduced-Price Lunch Program: 1,989 (4.3%)
Teachers: 2,715.0 (16.8 to 1)
Librarians/Media Specialists: 57.2 (799.6 to 1)
Guidance Counselors: 63.8 (716.9 to 1)
Current Spending: ($ per student per year):
Total: $6,784; Instruction: $4,221; Support Services: $2,153

Enrollment, Drop-out Rates and Diploma Recipients by Race/Ethnicity

Category	Total	White	Black	Asian	AIAN	Hisp.
Enrollment (%)	100.0	72.8	10.7	6.7	0.5	9.3
Drop-out Rate (%)	n/a	n/a	n/a	n/a	n/a	n/a
H.S. Diplomas (#)	2,922	2,368	221	193	5	135

Englewood 1

4101 S Bannock St • Englewood, CO 80110-4600
(303) 761-7050 • http://www.englewoodschools.org/
Grade Span: PK-12; **Agency Type:** 1
Schools: 11
6 Primary; 3 Middle; 2 High; 0 Other Level
10 Regular; 0 Special Education; 0 Vocational; 1 Alternative
0 Magnet; 0 Charter; 8 Title I Eligible; 0 School-wide Title I
Students: 4,200 (52.7% male; 47.3% female)
Individual Education Program: 497 (11.8%);
English Language Learner: 196 (4.7%); Migrant: 3 (0.1%)
Eligible for Free Lunch Program: 822 (19.6%)
Eligible for Reduced-Price Lunch Program: 288 (6.9%)
Teachers: 235.1 (17.9 to 1)
Librarians/Media Specialists: 3.0 (1,400.0 to 1)
Guidance Counselors: 13.0 (323.1 to 1)
Current Spending: ($ per student per year):
Total: $6,317; Instruction: $3,901; Support Services: $2,245

Enrollment, Drop-out Rates and Diploma Recipients by Race/Ethnicity

Category	Total	White	Black	Asian	AIAN	Hisp.
Enrollment (%)	100.0	69.0	4.1	1.7	2.2	22.9
Drop-out Rate (%)	n/a	n/a	n/a	n/a	n/a	n/a
H.S. Diplomas (#)	290	223	11	5	2	49

Littleton 6

5776 S Crocker St • Littleton, CO 80120-2012
(303) 347-3300 • http://www.lps.k12.co.us/
Grade Span: PK-12; **Agency Type:** 1
Schools: 27
18 Primary; 4 Middle; 5 High; 0 Other Level
25 Regular; 0 Special Education; 0 Vocational; 2 Alternative
0 Magnet; 2 Charter; 12 Title I Eligible; 0 School-wide Title I
Students: 16,408 (50.8% male; 49.2% female)
Individual Education Program: 1,660 (10.1%);
English Language Learner: 782 (4.8%); Migrant: 2 (<0.1%)
Eligible for Free Lunch Program: 1,162 (7.1%)
Eligible for Reduced-Price Lunch Program: 402 (2.5%)
Teachers: 975.9 (16.8 to 1)
Librarians/Media Specialists: 13.7 (1,197.7 to 1)
Guidance Counselors: 32.8 (500.2 to 1)
Current Spending: ($ per student per year):
Total: $6,326; Instruction: $3,963; Support Services: $2,064

Enrollment, Drop-out Rates and Diploma Recipients by Race/Ethnicity

Category	Total	White	Black	Asian	AIAN	Hisp.
Enrollment (%)	100.0	86.7	1.7	2.8	0.7	8.1
Drop-out Rate (%)	n/a	n/a	n/a	n/a	n/a	n/a
H.S. Diplomas (#)	1,223	1,127	14	37	2	43

Sheridan 2

4000 S Lowell Blvd • Sheridan, CO 80236
Mailing Address: PO Box 1198 • Englewood, CO 80150-1198
(720) 833-6991
Grade Span: PK-12; **Agency Type:** 1
Schools: 5
3 Primary; 1 Middle; 1 High; 0 Other Level
5 Regular; 0 Special Education; 0 Vocational; 0 Alternative
0 Magnet; 0 Charter; 3 Title I Eligible; 0 School-wide Title I
Students: 1,936 (52.3% male; 47.7% female)
Individual Education Program: 257 (13.3%);
English Language Learner: 492 (25.4%); Migrant: 10 (0.5%)
Eligible for Free Lunch Program: 938 (48.5%)
Eligible for Reduced-Price Lunch Program: 191 (9.9%)
Teachers: 126.7 (15.3 to 1)
Librarians/Media Specialists: 3.7 (523.2 to 1)
Guidance Counselors: 5.0 (387.2 to 1)
Current Spending: ($ per student per year):
Total: $6,957; Instruction: $4,226; Support Services: $2,472

Enrollment, Drop-out Rates and Diploma Recipients by Race/Ethnicity

Category	Total	White	Black	Asian	AIAN	Hisp.
Enrollment (%)	100.0	36.4	4.1	3.8	1.4	54.3
Drop-out Rate (%)	n/a	n/a	n/a	n/a	n/a	n/a
H.S. Diplomas (#)	76	46	2	3	1	24

Archuleta County

Archuleta County 50 Joint

309 Lewis St • Pagosa Springs, CO 81147-1498
Mailing Address: PO Box 1498 • Pagosa Springs, CO 81147-1498
(970) 264-2228 • http://www.pagosa.k12.co.us/
Grade Span: KG-12; **Agency Type:** 1
Schools: 4
1 Primary; 2 Middle; 1 High; 0 Other Level
4 Regular; 0 Special Education; 0 Vocational; 0 Alternative
0 Magnet; 0 Charter; 3 Title I Eligible; 0 School-wide Title I
Students: 1,588 (53.1% male; 46.9% female)
Individual Education Program: 129 (8.1%);
English Language Learner: 34 (2.1%); Migrant: 0 (0.0%)
Eligible for Free Lunch Program: 361 (22.7%)
Eligible for Reduced-Price Lunch Program: 165 (10.4%)
Teachers: 92.2 (17.2 to 1)
Librarians/Media Specialists: 3.1 (512.3 to 1)
Guidance Counselors: 4.0 (397.0 to 1)
Current Spending: ($ per student per year):
Total: $5,766; Instruction: $3,310; Support Services: $1,781

Enrollment, Drop-out Rates and Diploma Recipients by Race/Ethnicity

Category	Total	White	Black	Asian	AIAN	Hisp.
Enrollment (%)	100.0	77.5	1.0	0.4	1.3	19.8
Drop-out Rate (%)	n/a	n/a	n/a	n/a	n/a	n/a
H.S. Diplomas (#)	100	80	0	0	0	20

Boulder County

Boulder Valley RE-2

6500 Arapahoe Ave • Boulder, CO 80303
Mailing Address: PO Box 9011 • Boulder, CO 80301-9011
(303) 447-1010 • http://www.bvsd.k12.co.us/
Grade Span: PK-12; **Agency Type:** 1
Schools: 58
35 Primary; 11 Middle; 9 High; 3 Other Level
56 Regular; 1 Special Education; 1 Vocational; 0 Alternative
0 Magnet; 5 Charter; 22 Title I Eligible; 8 School-wide Title I
Students: 27,764 (51.0% male; 49.0% female)
Individual Education Program: 3,195 (11.5%);
English Language Learner: 2,756 (9.9%); Migrant: 371 (1.3%)
Eligible for Free Lunch Program: 2,652 (9.6%)
Eligible for Reduced-Price Lunch Program: 729 (2.6%)
Teachers: 1,712.2 (16.2 to 1)
Librarians/Media Specialists: 38.1 (728.7 to 1)
Guidance Counselors: 54.2 (512.3 to 1)
Current Spending: ($ per student per year):
Total: $6,413; Instruction: $4,095; Support Services: $2,152

Enrollment, Drop-out Rates and Diploma Recipients by Race/Ethnicity

Category	Total	White	Black	Asian	AIAN	Hisp.
Enrollment (%)	100.0	79.5	1.7	5.7	0.7	12.5
Drop-out Rate (%)	n/a	n/a	n/a	n/a	n/a	n/a
H.S. Diplomas (#)	1,810	1,536	29	95	9	141

Saint Vrain Valley RE-1J

395 S Pratt Pkwy • Longmont, CO 80501-6436
(303) 776-6200 • http://www.stvrain.k12.co.us/
Grade Span: PK-12; **Agency Type:** 1
Schools: 37
21 Primary; 6 Middle; 7 High; 3 Other Level
35 Regular; 0 Special Education; 0 Vocational; 2 Alternative
0 Magnet; 2 Charter; 13 Title I Eligible; 0 School-wide Title I
Students: 21,335 (51.6% male; 48.4% female)
Individual Education Program: 1,644 (7.7%);
English Language Learner: 3,507 (16.4%); Migrant: 332 (1.6%)
Eligible for Free Lunch Program: 3,303 (15.5%)
Eligible for Reduced-Price Lunch Program: 756 (3.5%)

Teachers: 1,244.1 (17.1 to 1)
Librarians/Media Specialists: 16.4 (1,300.9 to 1)
Guidance Counselors: 47.0 (453.9 to 1)
Current Spending: ($ per student per year):
Total: $5,944; Instruction: $3,554; Support Services: $2,200
Enrollment, Drop-out Rates and Diploma Recipients by Race/Ethnicity

Category	Total	White	Black	Asian	AIAN	Hisp.
Enrollment (%)	100.0	71.3	1.0	2.9	0.8	23.9
Drop-out Rate (%)	n/a	n/a	n/a	n/a	n/a	n/a
H.S. Diplomas (#)	1,134	970	6	29	13	116

Delta County

Delta County 50(J)
7655 2075 Rd • Delta, CO 81416-8390
(970) 874-4438 • http://www.delta.k12.co.us/
Grade Span: PK-12; **Agency Type:** 1
Schools: 15
6 Primary; 4 Middle; 4 High; 1 Other Level
15 Regular; 0 Special Education; 0 Vocational; 0 Alternative
0 Magnet; 0 Charter; 7 Title I Eligible; 5 School-wide Title I
Students: 5,116 (52.2% male; 47.8% female)
Individual Education Program: 648 (12.7%);
English Language Learner: 202 (3.9%); Migrant: 182 (3.6%)
Eligible for Free Lunch Program: 1,419 (27.7%)
Eligible for Reduced-Price Lunch Program: 527 (10.3%)
Teachers: 283.8 (18.0 to 1)
Librarians/Media Specialists: 0.0 (0.0 to 1)
Guidance Counselors: 8.0 (639.5 to 1)
Current Spending: ($ per student per year):
Total: $6,387; Instruction: $3,471; Support Services: $2,679
Enrollment, Drop-out Rates and Diploma Recipients by Race/Ethnicity

Category	Total	White	Black	Asian	AIAN	Hisp.
Enrollment (%)	100.0	82.3	0.5	0.5	0.8	15.8
Drop-out Rate (%)	n/a	n/a	n/a	n/a	n/a	n/a
H.S. Diplomas (#)	306	274	1	4	2	25

Denver County

Denver County 1
900 Grant St • Denver, CO 80203-2996
(303) 764-3200 • http://dpsnet.denver.k12.co.us/
Grade Span: PK-12; **Agency Type:** 1
Schools: 144
97 Primary; 22 Middle; 18 High; 7 Other Level
136 Regular; 0 Special Education; 1 Vocational; 7 Alternative
0 Magnet; 10 Charter; 85 Title I Eligible; 59 School-wide Title I
Students: 71,972 (51.0% male; 49.0% female)
Individual Education Program: 7,811 (10.9%);
English Language Learner: 21,203 (29.5%); Migrant: 836 (1.2%)
Eligible for Free Lunch Program: 38,044 (52.9%)
Eligible for Reduced-Price Lunch Program: 6,400 (8.9%)
Teachers: 4,471.5 (16.1 to 1)
Librarians/Media Specialists: 104.2 (690.7 to 1)
Guidance Counselors: 69.3 (1,038.6 to 1)
Current Spending: ($ per student per year):
Total: $7,148; Instruction: $3,754; Support Services: $3,160
Enrollment, Drop-out Rates and Diploma Recipients by Race/Ethnicity

Category	Total	White	Black	Asian	AIAN	Hisp.
Enrollment (%)	100.0	20.3	19.1	3.3	1.2	56.1
Drop-out Rate (%)	n/a	n/a	n/a	n/a	n/a	n/a
H.S. Diplomas (#)	2,612	882	566	155	13	996

Douglas County

Douglas County RE-1
620 Wilcox St • Castle Rock, CO 80104-1739
(303) 387-0030 • http://www.dcsd.k12.co.us/
Grade Span: PK-12; **Agency Type:** 1
Schools: 58
40 Primary; 8 Middle; 9 High; 1 Other Level
54 Regular; 1 Special Education; 0 Vocational; 3 Alternative
0 Magnet; 5 Charter; 22 Title I Eligible; 0 School-wide Title I
Students: 40,511 (51.0% male; 49.0% female)
Individual Education Program: 3,566 (8.8%);
English Language Learner: 822 (2.0%); Migrant: 9 (<0.1%)
Eligible for Free Lunch Program: 629 (1.6%)
Eligible for Reduced-Price Lunch Program: 455 (1.1%)
Teachers: 2,301.8 (17.6 to 1)
Librarians/Media Specialists: 14.0 (2,893.6 to 1)
Guidance Counselors: 47.0 (861.9 to 1)
Current Spending: ($ per student per year):
Total: $6,464; Instruction: $3,756; Support Services: $2,442
Enrollment, Drop-out Rates and Diploma Recipients by Race/Ethnicity

Category	Total	White	Black	Asian	AIAN	Hisp.
Enrollment (%)	100.0	88.6	1.6	3.4	0.6	5.8
Drop-out Rate (%)	n/a	n/a	n/a	n/a	n/a	n/a
H.S. Diplomas (#)	1,898	1,689	29	68	12	100

Eagle County

Eagle County RE-50
757 E 3rd St • Eagle, CO 81631-0740
Mailing Address: PO Box 740 • Eagle, CO 81631-0740
(970) 328-6321 • http://ecsd2.re50j.k12.co.us/ECSD/
Grade Span: PK-12; **Agency Type:** 1
Schools: 16
9 Primary; 4 Middle; 3 High; 0 Other Level
15 Regular; 0 Special Education; 0 Vocational; 1 Alternative
0 Magnet; 1 Charter; 10 Title I Eligible; 0 School-wide Title I
Students: 4,958 (51.5% male; 48.5% female)
Individual Education Program: 443 (8.9%);
English Language Learner: 1,254 (25.3%); Migrant: 8 (0.2%)
Eligible for Free Lunch Program: 700 (14.1%)
Eligible for Reduced-Price Lunch Program: 277 (5.6%)
Teachers: 345.2 (14.4 to 1)
Librarians/Media Specialists: 10.7 (463.4 to 1)
Guidance Counselors: 12.0 (413.2 to 1)
Current Spending: ($ per student per year):
Total: $7,015; Instruction: $3,970; Support Services: $2,820
Enrollment, Drop-out Rates and Diploma Recipients by Race/Ethnicity

Category	Total	White	Black	Asian	AIAN	Hisp.
Enrollment (%)	100.0	58.7	0.4	0.8	0.5	39.7
Drop-out Rate (%)	n/a	n/a	n/a	n/a	n/a	n/a
H.S. Diplomas (#)	237	185	1	4	0	47

El Paso County

Academy 20
7610 N Union Blvd • Colorado Springs, CO 80920-3899
(719) 598-2566 • http://www.d20.co.edu/
Grade Span: PK-12; **Agency Type:** 1
Schools: 27
16 Primary; 4 Middle; 5 High; 2 Other Level
26 Regular; 0 Special Education; 0 Vocational; 1 Alternative
0 Magnet; 3 Charter; 12 Title I Eligible; 2 School-wide Title I
Students: 18,698 (51.8% male; 48.2% female)
Individual Education Program: 1,298 (6.9%);
English Language Learner: 250 (1.3%); Migrant: 0 (0.0%)
Eligible for Free Lunch Program: 509 (2.7%)
Eligible for Reduced-Price Lunch Program: 396 (2.1%)
Teachers: 1,167.3 (16.0 to 1)
Librarians/Media Specialists: 11.2 (1,669.5 to 1)
Guidance Counselors: 45.1 (414.6 to 1)
Current Spending: ($ per student per year):
Total: $5,541; Instruction: $3,544; Support Services: $1,866
Enrollment, Drop-out Rates and Diploma Recipients by Race/Ethnicity

Category	Total	White	Black	Asian	AIAN	Hisp.
Enrollment (%)	100.0	85.5	3.8	4.0	0.8	6.0
Drop-out Rate (%)	n/a	n/a	n/a	n/a	n/a	n/a
H.S. Diplomas (#)	1,205	1,069	42	30	15	49

Cheyenne Mountain 12
1118 W Cheyenne Rd • Colorado Springs, CO 80906-2497
(719) 475-6100 • http://www.cmsd.k12.co.us/
Grade Span: PK-12; **Agency Type:** 1
Schools: 9
7 Primary; 1 Middle; 1 High; 0 Other Level
9 Regular; 0 Special Education; 0 Vocational; 0 Alternative
0 Magnet; 1 Charter; 4 Title I Eligible; 0 School-wide Title I
Students: 4,342 (50.4% male; 49.6% female)
Individual Education Program: 203 (4.7%);
English Language Learner: 251 (5.8%); Migrant: 0 (0.0%)
Eligible for Free Lunch Program: 165 (3.8%)
Eligible for Reduced-Price Lunch Program: 82 (1.9%)
Teachers: 271.8 (16.0 to 1)
Librarians/Media Specialists: 7.0 (620.3 to 1)
Guidance Counselors: 13.5 (321.6 to 1)
Current Spending: ($ per student per year):
Total: $5,142; Instruction: $3,059; Support Services: $1,944
Enrollment, Drop-out Rates and Diploma Recipients by Race/Ethnicity

Category	Total	White	Black	Asian	AIAN	Hisp.
Enrollment (%)	100.0	83.5	2.6	5.1	0.8	8.0
Drop-out Rate (%)	n/a	n/a	n/a	n/a	n/a	n/a
H.S. Diplomas (#)	316	282	7	13	2	12

Colorado Springs 11

1115 N El Paso St • Colorado Springs, CO 80903-2599
(719) 520-2000 • http://www.cssd11.k12.co.us/
Grade Span: PK-12; **Agency Type:** 1
Schools: 65
40 Primary; 10 Middle; 11 High; 4 Other Level
57 Regular; 2 Special Education; 0 Vocational; 6 Alternative
0 Magnet; 5 Charter; 34 Title I Eligible; 17 School-wide Title I
Students: 32,368 (51.3% male; 48.7% female)
Individual Education Program: 2,849 (8.8%);
English Language Learner: 920 (2.8%); Migrant: 121 (0.4%)
Eligible for Free Lunch Program: 7,760 (24.0%)
Eligible for Reduced-Price Lunch Program: 2,955 (9.1%)
Teachers: 1,917.7 (16.9 to 1)
Librarians/Media Specialists: 58.6 (552.4 to 1)
Guidance Counselors: 40.9 (791.4 to 1)
Current Spending: ($ per student per year):
Total: $6,910; Instruction: $3,648; Support Services: $3,077
Enrollment, Drop-out Rates and Diploma Recipients by Race/Ethnicity

Category	Total	White	Black	Asian	AIAN	Hisp.
Enrollment (%)	100.0	67.8	9.6	2.7	1.4	18.4
Drop-out Rate (%)	n/a	n/a	n/a	n/a	n/a	n/a
H.S. Diplomas (#)	1,816	1,350	154	63	25	224

Falcon 49

10850 E Woodmen Rd • Falcon, CO 80831-8127
(719) 495-3601 • http://d49.org/
Grade Span: PK-12; **Agency Type:** 1
Schools: 12
7 Primary; 3 Middle; 2 High; 0 Other Level
12 Regular; 0 Special Education; 0 Vocational; 0 Alternative
0 Magnet; 0 Charter; 4 Title I Eligible; 2 School-wide Title I
Students: 7,854 (51.8% male; 48.2% female)
Individual Education Program: 729 (9.3%);
English Language Learner: 58 (0.7%); Migrant: 2 (<0.1%)
Eligible for Free Lunch Program: 673 (8.6%)
Eligible for Reduced-Price Lunch Program: 460 (5.9%)
Teachers: 468.3 (16.8 to 1)
Librarians/Media Specialists: 11.7 (671.3 to 1)
Guidance Counselors: 19.3 (406.9 to 1)
Current Spending: ($ per student per year):
Total: $5,239; Instruction: $2,894; Support Services: $2,181
Enrollment, Drop-out Rates and Diploma Recipients by Race/Ethnicity

Category	Total	White	Black	Asian	AIAN	Hisp.
Enrollment (%)	100.0	75.0	7.5	4.5	2.1	10.9
Drop-out Rate (%)	n/a	n/a	n/a	n/a	n/a	n/a
H.S. Diplomas (#)	327	242	37	20	3	25

Fountain 8

425 W Alabama Ave • Fountain, CO 80817-1703
(719) 382-1300 • http://www.ffc8.org/
Grade Span: PK-12; **Agency Type:** 1
Schools: 10
6 Primary; 2 Middle; 2 High; 0 Other Level
9 Regular; 0 Special Education; 0 Vocational; 1 Alternative
0 Magnet; 0 Charter; 6 Title I Eligible; 3 School-wide Title I
Students: 5,545 (51.9% male; 48.1% female)
Individual Education Program: 532 (9.6%);
English Language Learner: 94 (1.7%); Migrant: 17 (0.3%)
Eligible for Free Lunch Program: 971 (17.5%)
Eligible for Reduced-Price Lunch Program: 707 (12.8%)
Teachers: 320.6 (17.3 to 1)
Librarians/Media Specialists: 6.2 (894.4 to 1)
Guidance Counselors: 12.0 (462.1 to 1)
Current Spending: ($ per student per year):
Total: $5,644; Instruction: $3,213; Support Services: $2,185
Enrollment, Drop-out Rates and Diploma Recipients by Race/Ethnicity

Category	Total	White	Black	Asian	AIAN	Hisp.
Enrollment (%)	100.0	59.3	19.4	3.5	2.1	15.7
Drop-out Rate (%)	n/a	n/a	n/a	n/a	n/a	n/a
H.S. Diplomas (#)	184	114	39	7	1	23

Harrison 2

1060 Harrison Rd • Colorado Springs, CO 80906-3586
(719) 579-2000 • http://www.harrison.k12.co.us/
Grade Span: PK-12; **Agency Type:** 1
Schools: 23
13 Primary; 3 Middle; 7 High; 0 Other Level
20 Regular; 0 Special Education; 0 Vocational; 3 Alternative
0 Magnet; 2 Charter; 17 Title I Eligible; 13 School-wide Title I
Students: 10,810 (50.8% male; 49.2% female)
Individual Education Program: 1,042 (9.6%);
English Language Learner: 851 (7.9%); Migrant: 29 (0.3%)
Eligible for Free Lunch Program: 4,520 (41.8%)
Eligible for Reduced-Price Lunch Program: 1,380 (12.8%)
Teachers: 719.1 (15.0 to 1)
Librarians/Media Specialists: 7.0 (1,544.3 to 1)
Guidance Counselors: 31.0 (348.7 to 1)
Current Spending: ($ per student per year):
Total: $6,201; Instruction: $3,643; Support Services: $2,290
Enrollment, Drop-out Rates and Diploma Recipients by Race/Ethnicity

Category	Total	White	Black	Asian	AIAN	Hisp.
Enrollment (%)	100.0	36.9	25.6	4.9	1.9	30.8
Drop-out Rate (%)	n/a	n/a	n/a	n/a	n/a	n/a
H.S. Diplomas (#)	400	162	123	34	2	79

Lewis-Palmer 38

146 Jefferson St • Monument, CO 80132-0040
Mailing Address: PO Box 40 • Monument, CO 80132-0040
(719) 488-4700 • http://www.lpsd.k12.co.us/
Grade Span: PK-12; **Agency Type:** 1
Schools: 9
5 Primary; 2 Middle; 1 High; 1 Other Level
9 Regular; 0 Special Education; 0 Vocational; 0 Alternative
0 Magnet; 1 Charter; 4 Title I Eligible; 0 School-wide Title I
Students: 5,179 (52.2% male; 47.8% female)
Individual Education Program: 402 (7.8%);
English Language Learner: 38 (0.7%); Migrant: 0 (0.0%)
Eligible for Free Lunch Program: 152 (2.9%)
Eligible for Reduced-Price Lunch Program: 81 (1.6%)
Teachers: 280.3 (18.5 to 1)
Librarians/Media Specialists: 3.0 (1,726.3 to 1)
Guidance Counselors: 15.1 (343.0 to 1)
Current Spending: ($ per student per year):
Total: $4,908; Instruction: $3,063; Support Services: $1,716
Enrollment, Drop-out Rates and Diploma Recipients by Race/Ethnicity

Category	Total	White	Black	Asian	AIAN	Hisp.
Enrollment (%)	100.0	91.9	1.2	2.2	0.7	3.9
Drop-out Rate (%)	n/a	n/a	n/a	n/a	n/a	n/a
H.S. Diplomas (#)	295	286	1	2	0	6

Widefield 3

1820 Main St • Colorado Springs, CO 80911-1152
(719) 391-3000 • http://www.wsd3.k12.co.us/
Grade Span: PK-12; **Agency Type:** 1
Schools: 17
11 Primary; 3 Middle; 3 High; 0 Other Level
16 Regular; 0 Special Education; 0 Vocational; 1 Alternative
0 Magnet; 1 Charter; 12 Title I Eligible; 2 School-wide Title I
Students: 8,606 (51.7% male; 48.3% female)
Individual Education Program: 1,090 (12.7%);
English Language Learner: 234 (2.7%); Migrant: 2 (<0.1%)
Eligible for Free Lunch Program: 1,132 (13.2%)
Eligible for Reduced-Price Lunch Program: 616 (7.2%)
Teachers: 493.6 (17.4 to 1)
Librarians/Media Specialists: 5.8 (1,483.8 to 1)
Guidance Counselors: 25.8 (333.6 to 1)
Current Spending: ($ per student per year):
Total: $5,365; Instruction: $3,304; Support Services: $1,862
Enrollment, Drop-out Rates and Diploma Recipients by Race/Ethnicity

Category	Total	White	Black	Asian	AIAN	Hisp.
Enrollment (%)	100.0	63.5	15.7	4.0	1.5	15.3
Drop-out Rate (%)	n/a	n/a	n/a	n/a	n/a	n/a
H.S. Diplomas (#)	532	354	66	39	5	68

Elbert County

Elizabeth C-1

634 S Elbert St • Elizabeth, CO 80107-0610
Mailing Address: PO Box 610 • Elizabeth, CO 80107-0610
(303) 646-4441 • http://www.elizabeth.k12.co.us/
Grade Span: PK-12; **Agency Type:** 1
Schools: 8
5 Primary; 1 Middle; 2 High; 0 Other Level
8 Regular; 0 Special Education; 0 Vocational; 0 Alternative
0 Magnet; 1 Charter; 2 Title I Eligible; 0 School-wide Title I
Students: 2,904 (52.0% male; 48.0% female)
Individual Education Program: 307 (10.6%);
English Language Learner: 1 (<0.1%); Migrant: 0 (0.0%)
Eligible for Free Lunch Program: 91 (3.1%)
Eligible for Reduced-Price Lunch Program: 26 (0.9%)
Teachers: 173.4 (16.7 to 1)
Librarians/Media Specialists: 0.9 (3,226.7 to 1)
Guidance Counselors: 5.0 (580.8 to 1)
Current Spending: ($ per student per year):
Total: $6,268; Instruction: $3,358; Support Services: $2,640

Enrollment, Drop-out Rates and Diploma Recipients by Race/Ethnicity

Category	Total	White	Black	Asian	AIAN	Hisp.
Enrollment (%)	100.0	90.8	1.4	1.2	0.9	5.7
Drop-out Rate (%)	n/a	n/a	n/a	n/a	n/a	n/a
H.S. Diplomas (#)	215	194	3	2	4	12

Fremont County

Canon City RE-1

101 N 14th St • Canon City, CO 81212-3564
(719) 276-5700 • http://www.canoncityschools.org/profile.htm
Grade Span: KG-12; **Agency Type:** 1
Schools: 10
7 Primary; 1 Middle; 2 High; 0 Other Level
9 Regular; 0 Special Education; 0 Vocational; 1 Alternative
0 Magnet; 1 Charter; 6 Title I Eligible; 5 School-wide Title I
Students: 4,215 (51.0% male; 49.0% female)
Individual Education Program: 459 (10.9%);
English Language Learner: 10 (0.2%); Migrant: 0 (0.0%)
Eligible for Free Lunch Program: 1,179 (28.0%)
Eligible for Reduced-Price Lunch Program: 399 (9.5%)
Teachers: 249.8 (16.9 to 1)
Librarians/Media Specialists: 3.0 (1,405.0 to 1)
Guidance Counselors: 7.7 (547.4 to 1)
Current Spending: ($ per student per year):
Total: $5,694; Instruction: $3,435; Support Services: $2,087

Enrollment, Drop-out Rates and Diploma Recipients by Race/Ethnicity

Category	Total	White	Black	Asian	AIAN	Hisp.
Enrollment (%)	100.0	90.0	0.7	1.0	0.7	7.6
Drop-out Rate (%)	n/a	n/a	n/a	n/a	n/a	n/a
H.S. Diplomas (#)	279	255	3	2	8	11

Florence RE-2

403 W 5th St • Florence, CO 81226-1103
(719) 784-6312
Grade Span: KG-12; **Agency Type:** 1
Schools: 6
2 Primary; 3 Middle; 1 High; 0 Other Level
6 Regular; 0 Special Education; 0 Vocational; 0 Alternative
0 Magnet; 0 Charter; 4 Title I Eligible; 2 School-wide Title I
Students: 1,915 (53.2% male; 46.8% female)
Individual Education Program: 261 (13.6%);
English Language Learner: 4 (0.2%); Migrant: 2 (0.1%)
Eligible for Free Lunch Program: 514 (26.8%)
Eligible for Reduced-Price Lunch Program: 193 (10.1%)
Teachers: 117.9 (16.2 to 1)
Librarians/Media Specialists: 1.0 (1,915.0 to 1)
Guidance Counselors: 5.5 (348.2 to 1)
Current Spending: ($ per student per year):
Total: $5,806; Instruction: $3,804; Support Services: $1,808

Enrollment, Drop-out Rates and Diploma Recipients by Race/Ethnicity

Category	Total	White	Black	Asian	AIAN	Hisp.
Enrollment (%)	100.0	86.7	0.8	0.4	1.0	11.1
Drop-out Rate (%)	n/a	n/a	n/a	n/a	n/a	n/a
H.S. Diplomas (#)	87	76	0	1	0	10

Garfield County

Garfield RE-2

839 Whiteriver • Rifle, CO 81650-3500
(970) 625-7600 • http://www.garfieldre2.k12.co.us/
Grade Span: PK-12; **Agency Type:** 1
Schools: 7
4 Primary; 2 Middle; 1 High; 0 Other Level
7 Regular; 0 Special Education; 0 Vocational; 0 Alternative
0 Magnet; 0 Charter; 6 Title I Eligible; 4 School-wide Title I
Students: 3,695 (51.8% male; 48.2% female)
Individual Education Program: 301 (8.1%);
English Language Learner: 636 (17.2%); Migrant: 61 (1.7%)
Eligible for Free Lunch Program: 660 (17.9%)
Eligible for Reduced-Price Lunch Program: 267 (7.2%)
Teachers: 215.6 (17.1 to 1)
Librarians/Media Specialists: 2.0 (1,847.5 to 1)
Guidance Counselors: 9.0 (410.6 to 1)
Current Spending: ($ per student per year):
Total: $5,045; Instruction: $3,020; Support Services: $1,813

Enrollment, Drop-out Rates and Diploma Recipients by Race/Ethnicity

Category	Total	White	Black	Asian	AIAN	Hisp.
Enrollment (%)	100.0	72.3	0.5	0.5	0.8	25.9
Drop-out Rate (%)	n/a	n/a	n/a	n/a	n/a	n/a
H.S. Diplomas (#)	156	146	0	2	4	4

Roaring Fork RE-1

1405 Grand Ave • Glenwood Springs, CO 81601-3807
(970) 384-6000 • http://www.rfsd.k12.co.us/
Grade Span: PK-12; **Agency Type:** 1
Schools: 14
6 Primary; 3 Middle; 5 High; 0 Other Level
12 Regular; 0 Special Education; 1 Vocational; 1 Alternative
0 Magnet; 1 Charter; 7 Title I Eligible; 5 School-wide Title I
Students: 4,864 (52.1% male; 47.9% female)
Individual Education Program: 300 (6.2%);
English Language Learner: 1,234 (25.4%); Migrant: 10 (0.2%)
Eligible for Free Lunch Program: 670 (13.8%)
Eligible for Reduced-Price Lunch Program: 299 (6.1%)
Teachers: 341.4 (14.2 to 1)
Librarians/Media Specialists: 8.0 (608.0 to 1)
Guidance Counselors: 10.6 (458.9 to 1)
Current Spending: ($ per student per year):
Total: $6,005; Instruction: $3,907; Support Services: $1,938

Enrollment, Drop-out Rates and Diploma Recipients by Race/Ethnicity

Category	Total	White	Black	Asian	AIAN	Hisp.
Enrollment (%)	100.0	65.6	0.3	0.9	0.3	32.8
Drop-out Rate (%)	n/a	n/a	n/a	n/a	n/a	n/a
H.S. Diplomas (#)	311	276	0	5	0	30

Gunnison County

Gunnison Watershed RE1J

800 N Blvd • Gunnison, CO 81230-2604
(970) 641-7760 • http://tomichi.ghs.gunnison.k12.co.us/
Grade Span: PK-12; **Agency Type:** 1
Schools: 6
2 Primary; 0 Middle; 2 High; 2 Other Level
5 Regular; 0 Special Education; 0 Vocational; 1 Alternative
0 Magnet; 1 Charter; 1 Title I Eligible; 0 School-wide Title I
Students: 1,644 (51.0% male; 49.0% female)
Individual Education Program: 143 (8.7%);
English Language Learner: 51 (3.1%); Migrant: 16 (1.0%)
Eligible for Free Lunch Program: 170 (10.3%)
Eligible for Reduced-Price Lunch Program: 60 (3.6%)
Teachers: 124.4 (13.2 to 1)
Librarians/Media Specialists: 1.9 (865.3 to 1)
Guidance Counselors: 4.9 (335.5 to 1)
Current Spending: ($ per student per year):
Total: $6,066; Instruction: $3,464; Support Services: $2,149

Enrollment, Drop-out Rates and Diploma Recipients by Race/Ethnicity

Category	Total	White	Black	Asian	AIAN	Hisp.
Enrollment (%)	100.0	87.5	0.2	0.9	2.5	8.9
Drop-out Rate (%)	n/a	n/a	n/a	n/a	n/a	n/a
H.S. Diplomas (#)	109	103	1	1	0	4

Jefferson County

Jefferson County R-1

1829 Denver W Dr, Bldg 27 • Golden, CO 80401-0001
Mailing Address: PO Box 4001 • Golden, CO 80401-0001
(303) 982-6500 • http://jeffco.k12.co.us/
Grade Span: PK-12; **Agency Type:** 1
Schools: 169
108 Primary; 23 Middle; 27 High; 11 Other Level
156 Regular; 6 Special Education; 1 Vocational; 6 Alternative
0 Magnet; 14 Charter; 62 Title I Eligible; 13 School-wide Title I
Students: 87,925 (51.4% male; 48.6% female)
Individual Education Program: 8,227 (9.4%);
English Language Learner: 5,057 (5.8%); Migrant: 996 (1.1%)
Eligible for Free Lunch Program: 10,001 (11.4%)
Eligible for Reduced-Price Lunch Program: 4,114 (4.7%)
Teachers: 4,857.4 (18.1 to 1)
Librarians/Media Specialists: 137.5 (639.5 to 1)
Guidance Counselors: 128.6 (683.7 to 1)
Current Spending: ($ per student per year):
Total: $7,340; Instruction: $3,720; Support Services: $3,407

Enrollment, Drop-out Rates and Diploma Recipients by Race/Ethnicity

Category	Total	White	Black	Asian	AIAN	Hisp.
Enrollment (%)	100.0	79.9	1.6	3.4	1.0	14.1
Drop-out Rate (%)	n/a	n/a	n/a	n/a	n/a	n/a
H.S. Diplomas (#)	5,334	4,614	66	197	29	428

La Plata County

Durango 9-R

201 E 12th St • Durango, CO 81301
(970) 247-5411 • http://www.durango.k12.co.us/
Grade Span: PK-12; **Agency Type:** 1
Schools: 12
7 Primary; 2 Middle; 1 High; 2 Other Level

11 Regular; 0 Special Education; 0 Vocational; 1 Alternative
0 Magnet; 1 Charter; 8 Title I Eligible; 0 School-wide Title I
Students: 4,761 (52.0% male; 48.0% female)
Individual Education Program: 506 (10.6%);
English Language Learner: 113 (2.4%); Migrant: 0 (0.0%)
Eligible for Free Lunch Program: 687 (14.4%)
Eligible for Reduced-Price Lunch Program: 302 (6.3%)
Teachers: 317.8 (15.0 to 1)
Librarians/Media Specialists: 10.3 (462.2 to 1)
Guidance Counselors: 18.4 (258.8 to 1)
Current Spending: ($ per student per year):
Total: $6,057; Instruction: $3,714; Support Services: $2,114
Enrollment, Drop-out Rates and Diploma Recipients by Race/Ethnicity

Category	Total	White	Black	Asian	AIAN	Hisp.
Enrollment (%)	100.0	82.4	0.7	1.0	4.3	11.7
Drop-out Rate (%)	n/a	n/a	n/a	n/a	n/a	n/a
H.S. Diplomas (#)	319	300	2	2	3	12

Larimer County

Poudre R-1
2407 La Porte Ave • Fort Collins, CO 80521-2297
(970) 482-7420 • http://www.psd.k12.co.us/
Grade Span: PK-12; **Agency Type:** 1
Schools: 53
31 Primary; 10 Middle; 9 High; 3 Other Level
46 Regular; 1 Special Education; 0 Vocational; 6 Alternative
0 Magnet; 3 Charter; 24 Title I Eligible; 2 School-wide Title I
Students: 24,538 (51.5% male; 48.5% female)
Individual Education Program: 2,002 (8.2%);
English Language Learner: 2,682 (10.9%); Migrant: 198 (0.8%)
Eligible for Free Lunch Program: 2,834 (11.5%)
Eligible for Reduced-Price Lunch Program: 890 (3.6%)
Teachers: 1,459.9 (16.8 to 1)
Librarians/Media Specialists: 33.6 (730.3 to 1)
Guidance Counselors: 56.8 (432.0 to 1)
Current Spending: ($ per student per year):
Total: $6,546; Instruction: $3,433; Support Services: $2,935
Enrollment, Drop-out Rates and Diploma Recipients by Race/Ethnicity

Category	Total	White	Black	Asian	AIAN	Hisp.
Enrollment (%)	100.0	80.9	2.0	3.2	1.1	12.8
Drop-out Rate (%)	n/a	n/a	n/a	n/a	n/a	n/a
H.S. Diplomas (#)	1,503	1,310	13	50	12	118

Thompson R-2J
535 N Douglas Ave • Loveland, CO 80537-5396
(970) 613-5000 • http://www.thompson.k12.co.us/
Grade Span: PK-12; **Agency Type:** 1
Schools: 28
18 Primary; 5 Middle; 5 High; 0 Other Level
27 Regular; 0 Special Education; 0 Vocational; 1 Alternative
0 Magnet; 0 Charter; 15 Title I Eligible; 3 School-wide Title I
Students: 14,974 (51.6% male; 48.4% female)
Individual Education Program: 1,653 (11.0%);
English Language Learner: 392 (2.6%); Migrant: 168 (1.1%)
Eligible for Free Lunch Program: 2,187 (14.6%)
Eligible for Reduced-Price Lunch Program: 901 (6.0%)
Teachers: 864.5 (17.3 to 1)
Librarians/Media Specialists: 9.0 (1,663.8 to 1)
Guidance Counselors: 37.1 (403.6 to 1)
Current Spending: ($ per student per year):
Total: $5,860; Instruction: $3,558; Support Services: $2,105
Enrollment, Drop-out Rates and Diploma Recipients by Race/Ethnicity

Category	Total	White	Black	Asian	AIAN	Hisp.
Enrollment (%)	100.0	86.4	0.9	1.2	0.9	10.6
Drop-out Rate (%)	n/a	n/a	n/a	n/a	n/a	n/a
H.S. Diplomas (#)	924	842	5	20	6	51

Logan County

Valley RE-1
415 Beattie St • Sterling, CO 80751-0910
(970) 522-0792 • http://www.re1valleyschools.com/
Grade Span: PK-12; **Agency Type:** 1
Schools: 9
5 Primary; 1 Middle; 3 High; 0 Other Level
8 Regular; 0 Special Education; 0 Vocational; 1 Alternative
0 Magnet; 0 Charter; 7 Title I Eligible; 2 School-wide Title I
Students: 2,860 (51.5% male; 48.5% female)
Individual Education Program: 471 (16.5%);
English Language Learner: 152 (5.3%); Migrant: 22 (0.8%)
Eligible for Free Lunch Program: 711 (24.9%)
Eligible for Reduced-Price Lunch Program: 237 (8.3%)
Teachers: 171.7 (16.7 to 1)
Librarians/Media Specialists: 2.0 (1,430.0 to 1)
Guidance Counselors: 2.7 (1,059.3 to 1)
Current Spending: ($ per student per year):
Total: $5,939; Instruction: $3,334; Support Services: $2,365
Enrollment, Drop-out Rates and Diploma Recipients by Race/Ethnicity

Category	Total	White	Black	Asian	AIAN	Hisp.
Enrollment (%)	100.0	83.8	1.0	0.1	0.0	15.0
Drop-out Rate (%)	n/a	n/a	n/a	n/a	n/a	n/a
H.S. Diplomas (#)	168	146	0	0	1	21

Mesa County

Mesa County Valley 51
2115 Grand Ave • Grand Junction, CO 81501-8063
(970) 254-5100 • http://www.mesa.k12.co.us/
Grade Span: PK-12; **Agency Type:** 1
Schools: 39
23 Primary; 8 Middle; 6 High; 2 Other Level
36 Regular; 1 Special Education; 0 Vocational; 2 Alternative
0 Magnet; 0 Charter; 19 Title I Eligible; 7 School-wide Title I
Students: 20,084 (51.3% male; 48.7% female)
Individual Education Program: 2,474 (12.3%);
English Language Learner: 770 (3.8%); Migrant: 464 (2.3%)
Eligible for Free Lunch Program: 5,792 (28.8%)
Eligible for Reduced-Price Lunch Program: 1,986 (9.9%)
Teachers: 1,164.0 (17.3 to 1)
Librarians/Media Specialists: 13.4 (1,498.8 to 1)
Guidance Counselors: 41.1 (488.7 to 1)
Current Spending: ($ per student per year):
Total: $5,663; Instruction: $3,630; Support Services: $1,836
Enrollment, Drop-out Rates and Diploma Recipients by Race/Ethnicity

Category	Total	White	Black	Asian	AIAN	Hisp.
Enrollment (%)	100.0	81.6	1.1	0.9	1.2	15.2
Drop-out Rate (%)	n/a	n/a	n/a	n/a	n/a	n/a
H.S. Diplomas (#)	1,179	1,042	4	21	11	101

Moffat County

Moffat County RE-1
775 Yampa Ave • Craig, CO 81625-2532
(970) 824-3268 • http://www.moffat.k12.co.us/
Grade Span: PK-12; **Agency Type:** 1
Schools: 9
6 Primary; 2 Middle; 1 High; 0 Other Level
9 Regular; 0 Special Education; 0 Vocational; 0 Alternative
0 Magnet; 0 Charter; 6 Title I Eligible; 0 School-wide Title I
Students: 2,585 (50.3% male; 49.7% female)
Individual Education Program: 318 (12.3%);
English Language Learner: 120 (4.6%); Migrant: 0 (0.0%)
Eligible for Free Lunch Program: 470 (18.2%)
Eligible for Reduced-Price Lunch Program: 157 (6.1%)
Teachers: 149.5 (17.3 to 1)
Librarians/Media Specialists: 2.1 (1,231.0 to 1)
Guidance Counselors: 6.1 (423.8 to 1)
Current Spending: ($ per student per year):
Total: $6,923; Instruction: $4,026; Support Services: $2,708
Enrollment, Drop-out Rates and Diploma Recipients by Race/Ethnicity

Category	Total	White	Black	Asian	AIAN	Hisp.
Enrollment (%)	100.0	85.9	0.4	0.7	1.6	11.3
Drop-out Rate (%)	n/a	n/a	n/a	n/a	n/a	n/a
H.S. Diplomas (#)	165	151	0	2	0	12

Montezuma County

Montezuma-Cortez RE-1
121 E First St • Cortez, CO 81321-0708
Mailing Address: Drawer R • Cortez, CO 81321-0708
(970) 565-7282 • http://www.cortez.k12.co.us/
Grade Span: PK-12; **Agency Type:** 1
Schools: 13
10 Primary; 1 Middle; 2 High; 0 Other Level
12 Regular; 0 Special Education; 0 Vocational; 1 Alternative
0 Magnet; 2 Charter; 7 Title I Eligible; 4 School-wide Title I
Students: 3,380 (52.5% male; 47.5% female)
Individual Education Program: 413 (12.2%);
English Language Learner: 1,128 (33.4%); Migrant: 0 (0.0%)
Eligible for Free Lunch Program: 1,277 (37.8%)
Eligible for Reduced-Price Lunch Program: 390 (11.5%)
Teachers: 218.6 (15.5 to 1)
Librarians/Media Specialists: 2.0 (1,690.0 to 1)
Guidance Counselors: 9.7 (348.5 to 1)
Current Spending: ($ per student per year):
Total: $5,914; Instruction: $3,690; Support Services: $2,016

Enrollment, Drop-out Rates and Diploma Recipients by Race/Ethnicity

Category	Total	White	Black	Asian	AIAN	Hisp.
Enrollment (%)	100.0	61.6	0.6	0.5	24.3	13.0
Drop-out Rate (%)	n/a	n/a	n/a	n/a	n/a	n/a
H.S. Diplomas (#)	164	116	1	2	22	23

Montrose County

Montrose County RE-1J

126 S 5th St • Montrose, CO 81401
Mailing Address: PO Box 10000 • Montrose, CO 81402-9701
(970) 249-7726 • http://www.mcsd.org/
Grade Span: PK-12; **Agency Type:** 1
Schools: 14
7 Primary; 2 Middle; 4 High; 1 Other Level
12 Regular; 0 Special Education; 0 Vocational; 2 Alternative
0 Magnet; 1 Charter; 9 Title I Eligible; 3 School-wide Title I
Students: 5,581 (50.6% male; 49.4% female)
Individual Education Program: 653 (11.7%);
English Language Learner: 468 (8.4%); Migrant: 460 (8.2%)
Eligible for Free Lunch Program: 1,680 (30.1%)
Eligible for Reduced-Price Lunch Program: 505 (9.0%)
Teachers: 328.9 (17.0 to 1)
Librarians/Media Specialists: 4.1 (1,361.2 to 1)
Guidance Counselors: 9.6 (581.4 to 1)
Current Spending: ($ per student per year):
Total: $6,060; Instruction: $3,341; Support Services: $2,510
Enrollment, Drop-out Rates and Diploma Recipients by Race/Ethnicity

Category	Total	White	Black	Asian	AIAN	Hisp.
Enrollment (%)	100.0	72.9	0.5	0.8	0.8	24.9
Drop-out Rate (%)	n/a	n/a	n/a	n/a	n/a	n/a
H.S. Diplomas (#)	348	300	0	2	2	44

Morgan County

Brush RE-2(J)

527 Industrial Park Rd • Brush, CO 80723-0585
Mailing Address: PO Box 585 • Brush, CO 80723-0585
(970) 842-5176 • http://brushschools.org/
Grade Span: PK-12; **Agency Type:** 1
Schools: 4
2 Primary; 1 Middle; 1 High; 0 Other Level
4 Regular; 0 Special Education; 0 Vocational; 0 Alternative
0 Magnet; 0 Charter; 2 Title I Eligible; 0 School-wide Title I
Students: 1,531 (49.2% male; 50.8% female)
Individual Education Program: 172 (11.2%);
English Language Learner: 384 (25.1%); Migrant: 139 (9.1%)
Eligible for Free Lunch Program: 460 (30.0%)
Eligible for Reduced-Price Lunch Program: 195 (12.7%)
Teachers: 109.8 (13.9 to 1)
Librarians/Media Specialists: 0.9 (1,701.1 to 1)
Guidance Counselors: 4.1 (373.4 to 1)
Current Spending: ($ per student per year):
Total: $5,861; Instruction: $3,505; Support Services: $2,082
Enrollment, Drop-out Rates and Diploma Recipients by Race/Ethnicity

Category	Total	White	Black	Asian	AIAN	Hisp.
Enrollment (%)	100.0	59.1	0.7	0.3	0.3	39.6
Drop-out Rate (%)	n/a	n/a	n/a	n/a	n/a	n/a
H.S. Diplomas (#)	94	76	0	0	0	18

Fort Morgan RE-3

230 Walnut St • Fort Morgan, CO 80701-2640
(970) 867-5633 • http://www.morgan.k12.co.us/
Grade Span: PK-12; **Agency Type:** 1
Schools: 8
4 Primary; 2 Middle; 2 High; 0 Other Level
7 Regular; 0 Special Education; 0 Vocational; 1 Alternative
0 Magnet; 0 Charter; 6 Title I Eligible; 4 School-wide Title I
Students: 3,309 (51.0% male; 49.0% female)
Individual Education Program: 381 (11.5%);
English Language Learner: 408 (12.3%); Migrant: 465 (14.1%)
Eligible for Free Lunch Program: 1,337 (40.4%)
Eligible for Reduced-Price Lunch Program: 380 (11.5%)
Teachers: 201.5 (16.4 to 1)
Librarians/Media Specialists: 2.5 (1,323.6 to 1)
Guidance Counselors: 7.3 (453.3 to 1)
Current Spending: ($ per student per year):
Total: $6,147; Instruction: $3,545; Support Services: $2,326
Enrollment, Drop-out Rates and Diploma Recipients by Race/Ethnicity

Category	Total	White	Black	Asian	AIAN	Hisp.
Enrollment (%)	100.0	48.3	0.2	0.3	0.2	50.9
Drop-out Rate (%)	n/a	n/a	n/a	n/a	n/a	n/a
H.S. Diplomas (#)	157	119	1	2	0	35

Otero County

East Otero R-1

1802 Colorado Ave Ste 200 • La Junta, CO 81050-3381
(719) 384-6900 • http://lajunta.k12.co.us/
Grade Span: PK-12; **Agency Type:** 1
Schools: 5
2 Primary; 1 Middle; 2 High; 0 Other Level
4 Regular; 0 Special Education; 0 Vocational; 1 Alternative
0 Magnet; 0 Charter; 2 Title I Eligible; 2 School-wide Title I
Students: 1,820 (50.1% male; 49.9% female)
Individual Education Program: 222 (12.2%);
English Language Learner: 17 (0.9%); Migrant: 12 (0.7%)
Eligible for Free Lunch Program: 746 (41.0%)
Eligible for Reduced-Price Lunch Program: 236 (13.0%)
Teachers: 119.0 (15.3 to 1)
Librarians/Media Specialists: 1.0 (1,820.0 to 1)
Guidance Counselors: 5.2 (350.0 to 1)
Current Spending: ($ per student per year):
Total: $6,475; Instruction: $3,878; Support Services: $2,315
Enrollment, Drop-out Rates and Diploma Recipients by Race/Ethnicity

Category	Total	White	Black	Asian	AIAN	Hisp.
Enrollment (%)	100.0	43.8	1.5	0.8	1.6	52.3
Drop-out Rate (%)	n/a	n/a	n/a	n/a	n/a	n/a
H.S. Diplomas (#)	128	59	3	1	0	65

Pitkin County

Aspen 1

0235 High School Rd • Aspen, CO 81611-3357
(970) 925-3760
Grade Span: PK-12; **Agency Type:** 1
Schools: 4
2 Primary; 1 Middle; 1 High; 0 Other Level
4 Regular; 0 Special Education; 0 Vocational; 0 Alternative
0 Magnet; 1 Charter; 2 Title I Eligible; 0 School-wide Title I
Students: 1,542 (52.6% male; 47.4% female)
Individual Education Program: 75 (4.9%);
English Language Learner: 144 (9.3%); Migrant: 0 (0.0%)
Eligible for Free Lunch Program: 0 (0.0%)
Eligible for Reduced-Price Lunch Program: 14 (0.9%)
Teachers: 123.1 (12.5 to 1)
Librarians/Media Specialists: 0.4 (3,855.0 to 1)
Guidance Counselors: 4.8 (321.3 to 1)
Current Spending: ($ per student per year):
Total: $9,199; Instruction: $6,434; Support Services: $2,765
Enrollment, Drop-out Rates and Diploma Recipients by Race/Ethnicity

Category	Total	White	Black	Asian	AIAN	Hisp.
Enrollment (%)	100.0	85.7	0.3	2.0	0.2	11.9
Drop-out Rate (%)	n/a	n/a	n/a	n/a	n/a	n/a
H.S. Diplomas (#)	95	90	1	0	0	4

Prowers County

Lamar RE-2

210 W Pearl • Lamar, CO 81052-3173
(719) 336-3251 • http://www.lamar.k12.co.us/
Grade Span: PK-12; **Agency Type:** 1
Schools: 7
4 Primary; 1 Middle; 2 High; 0 Other Level
6 Regular; 0 Special Education; 0 Vocational; 1 Alternative
0 Magnet; 1 Charter; 3 Title I Eligible; 2 School-wide Title I
Students: 1,832 (52.6% male; 47.4% female)
Individual Education Program: 182 (9.9%);
English Language Learner: 259 (14.1%); Migrant: 170 (9.3%)
Eligible for Free Lunch Program: 827 (45.1%)
Eligible for Reduced-Price Lunch Program: 189 (10.3%)
Teachers: 120.4 (15.2 to 1)
Librarians/Media Specialists: 2.0 (916.0 to 1)
Guidance Counselors: 4.0 (458.0 to 1)
Current Spending: ($ per student per year):
Total: $5,129; Instruction: $3,293; Support Services: $1,619
Enrollment, Drop-out Rates and Diploma Recipients by Race/Ethnicity

Category	Total	White	Black	Asian	AIAN	Hisp.
Enrollment (%)	100.0	52.4	0.7	0.3	0.9	45.8
Drop-out Rate (%)	n/a	n/a	n/a	n/a	n/a	n/a
H.S. Diplomas (#)	90	71	0	2	0	17

Pueblo County

Pueblo City 60

315 W 11th St • Pueblo, CO 81003-2804
(719) 549-7100 • http://www.pueblo60.k12.co.us/
Grade Span: PK-12; **Agency Type:** 1
Schools: 41

26 Primary; 6 Middle; 6 High; 3 Other Level
39 Regular; 1 Special Education; 0 Vocational; 1 Alternative
0 Magnet; 3 Charter; 23 Title I Eligible; 19 School-wide Title I
Students: 17,875 (51.6% male; 48.4% female)
Individual Education Program: 1,946 (10.9%);
English Language Learner: 1,448 (8.1%); Migrant: 318 (1.8%)
Eligible for Free Lunch Program: 7,494 (41.9%)
Eligible for Reduced-Price Lunch Program: 2,106 (11.8%)
Teachers: 1,114.4 (16.0 to 1)
Librarians/Media Specialists: 34.3 (521.1 to 1)
Guidance Counselors: 52.0 (343.8 to 1)
Current Spending: ($ per student per year):
Total: $5,918; Instruction: $3,294; Support Services: $2,388
Enrollment, Drop-out Rates and Diploma Recipients by Race/Ethnicity

Category	Total	White	Black	Asian	AIAN	Hisp.
Enrollment (%)	100.0	39.3	2.4	0.6	1.8	55.9
Drop-out Rate (%)	n/a	n/a	n/a	n/a	n/a	n/a
H.S. Diplomas (#)	907	475	24	8	12	388

Pueblo County Rural 70
24951 E Hwy 50 • Pueblo, CO 81006
(719) 542-0220 • http://www.dist70.k12.co.us/
Grade Span: PK-12; **Agency Type:** 1
Schools: 22
10 Primary; 7 Middle; 4 High; 1 Other Level
21 Regular; 0 Special Education; 0 Vocational; 1 Alternative
0 Magnet; 2 Charter; 10 Title I Eligible; 1 School-wide Title I
Students: 7,827 (51.5% male; 48.5% female)
Individual Education Program: 815 (10.4%);
English Language Learner: 113 (1.4%); Migrant: 110 (1.4%)
Eligible for Free Lunch Program: 1,488 (19.0%)
Eligible for Reduced-Price Lunch Program: 656 (8.4%)
Teachers: 425.7 (18.4 to 1)
Librarians/Media Specialists: 0.0 (0.0 to 1)
Guidance Counselors: 23.3 (335.9 to 1)
Current Spending: ($ per student per year):
Total: $5,108; Instruction: $2,955; Support Services: $1,935
Enrollment, Drop-out Rates and Diploma Recipients by Race/Ethnicity

Category	Total	White	Black	Asian	AIAN	Hisp.
Enrollment (%)	100.0	72.1	1.2	0.7	0.8	25.2
Drop-out Rate (%)	n/a	n/a	n/a	n/a	n/a	n/a
H.S. Diplomas (#)	349	271	3	2	4	69

Routt County

Steamboat Springs RE-2
325 7th St • Steamboat Springs, CO 80487
Mailing Address: PO Box 774368 • Steamboat Springs, CO 80477-4368
(970) 879-1530 • http://sailors.steamboat.k12.co.us/
Grade Span: KG-12; **Agency Type:** 1
Schools: 5
3 Primary; 1 Middle; 1 High; 0 Other Level
5 Regular; 0 Special Education; 0 Vocational; 0 Alternative
0 Magnet; 1 Charter; 3 Title I Eligible; 0 School-wide Title I
Students: 1,933 (52.7% male; 47.3% female)
Individual Education Program: 211 (10.9%);
English Language Learner: 21 (1.1%); Migrant: 1 (0.1%)
Eligible for Free Lunch Program: 55 (2.8%)
Eligible for Reduced-Price Lunch Program: 41 (2.1%)
Teachers: 137.1 (14.1 to 1)
Librarians/Media Specialists: 4.0 (483.3 to 1)
Guidance Counselors: 5.9 (327.6 to 1)
Current Spending: ($ per student per year):
Total: $7,508; Instruction: $4,295; Support Services: $2,938
Enrollment, Drop-out Rates and Diploma Recipients by Race/Ethnicity

Category	Total	White	Black	Asian	AIAN	Hisp.
Enrollment (%)	100.0	95.6	0.6	1.1	0.3	2.5
Drop-out Rate (%)	n/a	n/a	n/a	n/a	n/a	n/a
H.S. Diplomas (#)	132	127	0	1	0	4

Summit County

Summit RE-1
0150 School Rd • Frisco, CO 80443-0007
Mailing Address: PO Box 7 • Frisco, CO 80443-0007
(970) 668-3011 • http://summit.k12.co.us/
Grade Span: PK-12; **Agency Type:** 1
Schools: 8
6 Primary; 1 Middle; 1 High; 0 Other Level
8 Regular; 0 Special Education; 0 Vocational; 0 Alternative
0 Magnet; 0 Charter; 3 Title I Eligible; 0 School-wide Title I
Students: 2,775 (52.9% male; 47.1% female)
Individual Education Program: 272 (9.8%);
English Language Learner: 470 (16.9%); Migrant: 0 (0.0%)
Eligible for Free Lunch Program: 241 (8.7%)
Eligible for Reduced-Price Lunch Program: 111 (4.0%)
Teachers: 212.2 (13.1 to 1)
Librarians/Media Specialists: 8.0 (346.9 to 1)
Guidance Counselors: 9.8 (283.2 to 1)
Current Spending: ($ per student per year):
Total: $7,285; Instruction: $4,164; Support Services: $2,942
Enrollment, Drop-out Rates and Diploma Recipients by Race/Ethnicity

Category	Total	White	Black	Asian	AIAN	Hisp.
Enrollment (%)	100.0	80.4	0.3	1.5	0.2	17.6
Drop-out Rate (%)	n/a	n/a	n/a	n/a	n/a	n/a
H.S. Diplomas (#)	165	150	0	5	0	10

Teller County

Woodland Park RE-2
211 N Baldwin St • Woodland Park, CO 80866-0099
Mailing Address: PO Box 99 • Woodland Park, CO 80866-0099
(719) 687-6048 • http://www.wpsdk12.org/
Grade Span: PK-12; **Agency Type:** 1
Schools: 5
3 Primary; 1 Middle; 1 High; 0 Other Level
5 Regular; 0 Special Education; 0 Vocational; 0 Alternative
0 Magnet; 0 Charter; 3 Title I Eligible; 0 School-wide Title I
Students: 3,276 (52.4% male; 47.6% female)
Individual Education Program: 352 (10.7%);
English Language Learner: 22 (0.7%); Migrant: 0 (0.0%)
Eligible for Free Lunch Program: 307 (9.4%)
Eligible for Reduced-Price Lunch Program: 126 (3.8%)
Teachers: 190.5 (17.2 to 1)
Librarians/Media Specialists: 5.0 (655.2 to 1)
Guidance Counselors: 8.0 (409.5 to 1)
Current Spending: ($ per student per year):
Total: $5,082; Instruction: $2,958; Support Services: $1,987
Enrollment, Drop-out Rates and Diploma Recipients by Race/Ethnicity

Category	Total	White	Black	Asian	AIAN	Hisp.
Enrollment (%)	100.0	92.2	1.0	1.1	1.2	4.5
Drop-out Rate (%)	n/a	n/a	n/a	n/a	n/a	n/a
H.S. Diplomas (#)	210	194	3	0	4	9

Weld County

Eaton RE-2
200 Park Ave • Eaton, CO 80615-3528
(970) 454-3402
Grade Span: KG-12; **Agency Type:** 1
Schools: 4
2 Primary; 1 Middle; 1 High; 0 Other Level
4 Regular; 0 Special Education; 0 Vocational; 0 Alternative
0 Magnet; 0 Charter; 3 Title I Eligible; 0 School-wide Title I
Students: 1,533 (50.9% male; 49.1% female)
Individual Education Program: 144 (9.4%);
English Language Learner: 147 (9.6%); Migrant: 112 (7.3%)
Eligible for Free Lunch Program: 271 (17.7%)
Eligible for Reduced-Price Lunch Program: 99 (6.5%)
Teachers: 94.2 (16.3 to 1)
Librarians/Media Specialists: 1.9 (806.8 to 1)
Guidance Counselors: 3.9 (393.1 to 1)
Current Spending: ($ per student per year):
Total: $5,646; Instruction: $3,388; Support Services: $2,031
Enrollment, Drop-out Rates and Diploma Recipients by Race/Ethnicity

Category	Total	White	Black	Asian	AIAN	Hisp.
Enrollment (%)	100.0	77.5	0.3	0.5	0.4	21.3
Drop-out Rate (%)	n/a	n/a	n/a	n/a	n/a	n/a
H.S. Diplomas (#)	79	62	1	1	0	15

Greeley 6
1025 9th Ave • Greeley, CO 80631-4686
(970) 348-6000 • http://www.greeleyschools.org/
Grade Span: PK-12; **Agency Type:** 1
Schools: 32
15 Primary; 6 Middle; 7 High; 4 Other Level
25 Regular; 3 Special Education; 0 Vocational; 4 Alternative
1 Magnet; 3 Charter; 18 Title I Eligible; 8 School-wide Title I
Students: 17,131 (51.9% male; 48.1% female)
Individual Education Program: 1,844 (10.8%);
English Language Learner: 3,426 (20.0%); Migrant: 1,386 (8.1%)
Eligible for Free Lunch Program: 6,729 (39.3%)
Eligible for Reduced-Price Lunch Program: 1,499 (8.8%)
Teachers: 1,019.9 (16.8 to 1)
Librarians/Media Specialists: 0.0 (0.0 to 1)
Guidance Counselors: 29.8 (574.9 to 1)
Current Spending: ($ per student per year):
Total: $6,570; Instruction: $4,320; Support Services: $2,021

Enrollment, Drop-out Rates and Diploma Recipients by Race/Ethnicity

Category	Total	White	Black	Asian	AIAN	Hisp.
Enrollment (%)	100.0	50.3	1.2	1.0	0.6	47.0
Drop-out Rate (%)	n/a	n/a	n/a	n/a	n/a	n/a
H.S. Diplomas (#)	870	603	6	11	3	247

Johnstown-Milliken RE-5J

110 S Centennial Dr, Ste 1 • Milliken, CO 80543
(970) 587-2336
Grade Span: PK-12; **Agency Type:** 1
Schools: 5
3 Primary; 1 Middle; 1 High; 0 Other Level
5 Regular; 0 Special Education; 0 Vocational; 0 Alternative
0 Magnet; 1 Charter; 2 Title I Eligible; 0 School-wide Title I
Students: 1,916 (51.9% male; 48.1% female)
Individual Education Program: 213 (11.1%);
English Language Learner: 369 (19.3%); Migrant: 127 (6.6%)
Eligible for Free Lunch Program: 348 (18.2%)
Eligible for Reduced-Price Lunch Program: 158 (8.2%)
Teachers: 123.2 (15.6 to 1)
Librarians/Media Specialists: 3.0 (638.7 to 1)
Guidance Counselors: 3.1 (618.1 to 1)
Current Spending: ($ per student per year):
Total: $5,399; Instruction: $3,392; Support Services: $1,736

Enrollment, Drop-out Rates and Diploma Recipients by Race/Ethnicity

Category	Total	White	Black	Asian	AIAN	Hisp.
Enrollment (%)	100.0	63.4	0.5	0.5	0.2	35.5
Drop-out Rate (%)	n/a	n/a	n/a	n/a	n/a	n/a
H.S. Diplomas (#)	89	59	0	0	0	30

Keenesburg RE-3(J)

95 W Broadway • Keenesburg, CO 80643-0269
Mailing Address: PO Box 269 • Keenesburg, CO 80643-0269
(303) 536-2000 • http://www.rebel-net.tec.co.us/admin/index.asp
Grade Span: PK-12; **Agency Type:** 1
Schools: 8
6 Primary; 1 Middle; 1 High; 0 Other Level
8 Regular; 0 Special Education; 0 Vocational; 0 Alternative
0 Magnet; 1 Charter; 3 Title I Eligible; 0 School-wide Title I
Students: 1,925 (52.6% male; 47.4% female)
Individual Education Program: 251 (13.0%);
English Language Learner: 208 (10.8%); Migrant: 149 (7.7%)
Eligible for Free Lunch Program: 451 (23.4%)
Eligible for Reduced-Price Lunch Program: 181 (9.4%)
Teachers: 122.9 (15.7 to 1)
Librarians/Media Specialists: 0.9 (2,138.9 to 1)
Guidance Counselors: 2.0 (962.5 to 1)
Current Spending: ($ per student per year):
Total: $5,894; Instruction: $3,534; Support Services: $2,075

Enrollment, Drop-out Rates and Diploma Recipients by Race/Ethnicity

Category	Total	White	Black	Asian	AIAN	Hisp.
Enrollment (%)	100.0	69.6	0.6	0.8	0.1	28.9
Drop-out Rate (%)	n/a	n/a	n/a	n/a	n/a	n/a
H.S. Diplomas (#)	85	74	0	1	0	10

Weld County RE-1

14827 WCR 42 • Gilcrest, CO 80623-0157
Mailing Address: PO Box 157 • Gilcrest, CO 80623-0157
(970) 737-2403 • http://www.weld-re1.k12.co.us/
Grade Span: PK-12; **Agency Type:** 1
Schools: 6
3 Primary; 2 Middle; 1 High; 0 Other Level
6 Regular; 0 Special Education; 0 Vocational; 0 Alternative
0 Magnet; 0 Charter; 3 Title I Eligible; 0 School-wide Title I
Students: 1,916 (50.1% male; 49.9% female)
Individual Education Program: 224 (11.7%);
English Language Learner: 292 (15.2%); Migrant: 303 (15.8%)
Eligible for Free Lunch Program: 609 (31.8%)
Eligible for Reduced-Price Lunch Program: 156 (8.1%)
Teachers: 146.6 (13.1 to 1)
Librarians/Media Specialists: 0.3 (6,386.7 to 1)
Guidance Counselors: 5.0 (383.2 to 1)
Current Spending: ($ per student per year):
Total: $5,973; Instruction: $3,628; Support Services: $2,084

Enrollment, Drop-out Rates and Diploma Recipients by Race/Ethnicity

Category	Total	White	Black	Asian	AIAN	Hisp.
Enrollment (%)	100.0	51.5	0.9	0.6	0.7	46.3
Drop-out Rate (%)	n/a	n/a	n/a	n/a	n/a	n/a
H.S. Diplomas (#)	105	68	2	0	0	35

Weld County SD RE-8

301 Reynolds St • Fort Lupton, CO 80621-1329
(303) 857-3200 • http://www.weld-re1.k12.co.us/
Grade Span: PK-12; **Agency Type:** 1
Schools: 4
2 Primary; 1 Middle; 1 High; 0 Other Level
4 Regular; 0 Special Education; 0 Vocational; 0 Alternative
0 Magnet; 0 Charter; 4 Title I Eligible; 4 School-wide Title I
Students: 2,622 (52.9% male; 47.1% female)
Individual Education Program: 303 (11.6%);
English Language Learner: 1,188 (45.3%); Migrant: 343 (13.1%)
Eligible for Free Lunch Program: 1,162 (44.3%)
Eligible for Reduced-Price Lunch Program: 279 (10.6%)
Teachers: 177.4 (14.8 to 1)
Librarians/Media Specialists: 4.9 (535.1 to 1)
Guidance Counselors: 9.0 (291.3 to 1)
Current Spending: ($ per student per year):
Total: $6,255; Instruction: $3,654; Support Services: $2,309

Enrollment, Drop-out Rates and Diploma Recipients by Race/Ethnicity

Category	Total	White	Black	Asian	AIAN	Hisp.
Enrollment (%)	100.0	42.8	0.6	0.7	0.2	55.7
Drop-out Rate (%)	n/a	n/a	n/a	n/a	n/a	n/a
H.S. Diplomas (#)	143	72	0	3	1	67

Windsor RE-4

1020 Main St • Windsor, CO 80550-4776
Mailing Address: PO Box 609 • Windsor, CO 80550-4776
(970) 686-7411 • http://www.windsor.k12.co.us/
Grade Span: PK-12; **Agency Type:** 1
Schools: 6
4 Primary; 1 Middle; 1 High; 0 Other Level
6 Regular; 0 Special Education; 0 Vocational; 0 Alternative
0 Magnet; 1 Charter; 4 Title I Eligible; 0 School-wide Title I
Students: 2,943 (52.5% male; 47.5% female)
Individual Education Program: 251 (8.5%);
English Language Learner: 80 (2.7%); Migrant: 29 (1.0%)
Eligible for Free Lunch Program: 185 (6.3%)
Eligible for Reduced-Price Lunch Program: 121 (4.1%)
Teachers: 183.5 (16.0 to 1)
Librarians/Media Specialists: 5.0 (588.6 to 1)
Guidance Counselors: 6.0 (490.5 to 1)
Current Spending: ($ per student per year):
Total: $5,306; Instruction: $3,083; Support Services: $2,021

Enrollment, Drop-out Rates and Diploma Recipients by Race/Ethnicity

Category	Total	White	Black	Asian	AIAN	Hisp.
Enrollment (%)	100.0	85.3	0.7	1.2	0.9	11.9
Drop-out Rate (%)	n/a	n/a	n/a	n/a	n/a	n/a
H.S. Diplomas (#)	158	125	0	1	2	30

Number of Schools

Rank	Number	District Name	City
1	169	Jefferson County R-1	Golden
2	144	Denver County 1	Denver
3	65	Colorado Springs 11	Colorado Spgs
4	58	Boulder Valley RE-2	Boulder
4	58	Douglas County RE-1	Castle Rock
6	53	Cherry Creek 5	Greenwood Vlg
6	53	Poudre R-1	Fort Collins
8	51	Adams-Arapahoe 28J	Aurora
9	46	Northglenn-Thornton 12	Thornton
10	41	Pueblo City 60	Pueblo
11	39	Mesa County Valley 51	Grand Junction
12	37	Saint Vrain Valley RE-1J	Longmont
13	32	Greeley 6	Greeley
14	28	Thompson R-2J	Loveland
15	27	Academy 20	Colorado Spgs
15	27	Littleton 6	Littleton
17	25	Westminster 50	Westminster
18	23	Harrison 2	Colorado Spgs
19	22	Pueblo County Rural 70	Pueblo
20	17	Widefield 3	Colorado Spgs
21	16	Eagle County RE-50	Eagle
22	15	Delta County 50(J)	Delta
23	14	Montrose County RE-1J	Montrose
23	14	Roaring Fork RE-1	Glenwood Spgs
25	13	Montezuma-Cortez RE-1	Cortez
26	12	Adams County 14	Commerce City
26	12	Brighton 27J	Brighton
26	12	Durango 9-R	Durango
26	12	Falcon 49	Falcon
30	11	Englewood 1	Englewood
30	11	Mapleton 1	Denver
32	10	Canon City RE-1	Canon City
32	10	Fountain 8	Fountain
34	9	Cheyenne Mountain 12	Colorado Spgs
34	9	Lewis-Palmer 38	Monument
34	9	Moffat County RE-1	Craig
34	9	Valley RE-1	Sterling
38	8	Elizabeth C-1	Elizabeth
38	8	Fort Morgan RE-3	Fort Morgan
38	8	Keenesburg RE-3(J)	Keenesburg
38	8	Summit RE-1	Frisco
42	7	Garfield RE-2	Rifle
42	7	Lamar RE-2	Lamar
44	6	Alamosa RE-11J	Alamosa
44	6	Florence RE-2	Florence
44	6	Gunnison Watershed RE1J	Gunnison
44	6	Weld County RE-1	Gilcrest
44	6	Windsor RE-4	Windsor
49	5	East Otero R-1	La Junta
49	5	Johnstown-Milliken RE-5J	Milliken
49	5	Sheridan 2	Sheridan
49	5	Steamboat Springs RE-2	Steamboat Spgs
49	5	Woodland Park RE-2	Woodland Park
54	4	Archuleta County 50 Joint	Pagosa Springs
54	4	Aspen 1	Aspen
54	4	Brush RE-2(J)	Brush
54	4	Eaton RE-2	Eaton
54	4	Weld County SD RE-8	Fort Lupton

Number of Teachers

Rank	Number	District Name	City
1	4,857	Jefferson County R-1	Golden
2	4,471	Denver County 1	Denver
3	2,715	Cherry Creek 5	Greenwood Vlg
4	2,301	Douglas County RE-1	Castle Rock
5	1,917	Colorado Springs 11	Colorado Spgs
6	1,740	Adams-Arapahoe 28J	Aurora
7	1,725	Northglenn-Thornton 12	Thornton
8	1,712	Boulder Valley RE-2	Boulder
9	1,459	Poudre R-1	Fort Collins
10	1,244	Saint Vrain Valley RE-1J	Longmont
11	1,167	Academy 20	Colorado Spgs
12	1,164	Mesa County Valley 51	Grand Junction
13	1,114	Pueblo City 60	Pueblo
14	1,019	Greeley 6	Greeley
15	975	Littleton 6	Littleton
16	864	Thompson R-2J	Loveland
17	719	Harrison 2	Colorado Spgs
18	655	Westminster 50	Westminster
19	493	Widefield 3	Colorado Spgs
20	468	Falcon 49	Falcon
21	425	Pueblo County Rural 70	Pueblo
22	414	Brighton 27J	Brighton
23	375	Adams County 14	Commerce City
24	345	Eagle County RE-50	Eagle
25	341	Roaring Fork RE-1	Glenwood Spgs
26	328	Montrose County RE-1J	Montrose
27	320	Fountain 8	Fountain
28	317	Durango 9-R	Durango
29	283	Delta County 50(J)	Delta
30	280	Lewis-Palmer 38	Monument
31	278	Mapleton 1	Denver
32	271	Cheyenne Mountain 12	Colorado Spgs
33	249	Canon City RE-1	Canon City
34	235	Englewood 1	Englewood
35	218	Montezuma-Cortez RE-1	Cortez
36	215	Garfield RE-2	Rifle
37	212	Summit RE-1	Frisco
38	201	Fort Morgan RE-3	Fort Morgan
39	190	Woodland Park RE-2	Woodland Park
40	183	Windsor RE-4	Windsor
41	177	Weld County SD RE-8	Fort Lupton
42	173	Elizabeth C-1	Elizabeth
43	171	Valley RE-1	Sterling
44	149	Moffat County RE-1	Craig
45	146	Alamosa RE-11J	Alamosa
45	146	Weld County RE-1	Gilcrest
47	137	Steamboat Springs RE-2	Steamboat Spgs
48	126	Sheridan 2	Sheridan
49	124	Gunnison Watershed RE1J	Gunnison
50	123	Johnstown-Milliken RE-5J	Milliken
51	123	Aspen 1	Aspen
52	122	Keenesburg RE-3(J)	Keenesburg
53	120	Lamar RE-2	Lamar
54	119	East Otero R-1	La Junta
55	117	Florence RE-2	Florence
56	109	Brush RE-2(J)	Brush
57	94	Eaton RE-2	Eaton
58	92	Archuleta County 50 Joint	Pagosa Springs

Number of Students

Rank	Number	District Name	City
1	87,925	Jefferson County R-1	Golden
2	71,972	Denver County 1	Denver
3	45,738	Cherry Creek 5	Greenwood Vlg
4	40,511	Douglas County RE-1	Castle Rock
5	33,522	Northglenn-Thornton 12	Thornton
6	32,368	Colorado Springs 11	Colorado Spgs
7	32,253	Adams-Arapahoe 28J	Aurora
8	27,764	Boulder Valley RE-2	Boulder
9	24,538	Poudre R-1	Fort Collins
10	21,335	Saint Vrain Valley RE-1J	Longmont
11	20,084	Mesa County Valley 51	Grand Junction
12	18,698	Academy 20	Colorado Spgs
13	17,875	Pueblo City 60	Pueblo
14	17,131	Greeley 6	Greeley
15	16,408	Littleton 6	Littleton
16	14,974	Thompson R-2J	Loveland
17	11,012	Westminster 50	Westminster
18	10,810	Harrison 2	Colorado Spgs
19	8,606	Widefield 3	Colorado Spgs
20	7,854	Falcon 49	Falcon
21	7,827	Pueblo County Rural 70	Pueblo
22	7,277	Brighton 27J	Brighton
23	6,698	Adams County 14	Commerce City
24	5,623	Mapleton 1	Denver
25	5,581	Montrose County RE-1J	Montrose
26	5,545	Fountain 8	Fountain
27	5,179	Lewis-Palmer 38	Monument
28	5,116	Delta County 50(J)	Delta
29	4,958	Eagle County RE-50	Eagle
30	4,864	Roaring Fork RE-1	Glenwood Spgs
31	4,761	Durango 9-R	Durango
32	4,342	Cheyenne Mountain 12	Colorado Spgs
33	4,215	Canon City RE-1	Canon City
34	4,200	Englewood 1	Englewood
35	3,695	Garfield RE-2	Rifle
36	3,380	Montezuma-Cortez RE-1	Cortez
37	3,309	Fort Morgan RE-3	Fort Morgan
38	3,276	Woodland Park RE-2	Woodland Park
39	2,943	Windsor RE-4	Windsor
40	2,904	Elizabeth C-1	Elizabeth
41	2,860	Valley RE-1	Sterling
42	2,775	Summit RE-1	Frisco
43	2,622	Weld County SD RE-8	Fort Lupton
44	2,585	Moffat County RE-1	Craig
45	2,280	Alamosa RE-11J	Alamosa
46	1,936	Sheridan 2	Sheridan
47	1,933	Steamboat Springs RE-2	Steamboat Spgs
48	1,925	Keenesburg RE-3(J)	Keenesburg
49	1,916	Johnstown-Milliken RE-5J	Milliken
49	1,916	Weld County RE-1	Gilcrest
51	1,915	Florence RE-2	Florence
52	1,832	Lamar RE-2	Lamar
53	1,820	East Otero R-1	La Junta
54	1,644	Gunnison Watershed RE1J	Gunnison
55	1,588	Archuleta County 50 Joint	Pagosa Springs
56	1,542	Aspen 1	Aspen
57	1,533	Eaton RE-2	Eaton
58	1,531	Brush RE-2(J)	Brush

Male Students

Rank	Percent	District Name	City
1	53.2	Alamosa RE-11J	Alamosa
1	53.2	Florence RE-2	Florence
3	53.1	Archuleta County 50 Joint	Pagosa Springs
4	52.9	Summit RE-1	Frisco
4	52.9	Weld County SD RE-8	Fort Lupton
6	52.7	Englewood 1	Englewood
6	52.7	Steamboat Springs RE-2	Steamboat Spgs
8	52.6	Aspen 1	Aspen
8	52.6	Keenesburg RE-3(J)	Keenesburg
8	52.6	Lamar RE-2	Lamar
11	52.5	Montezuma-Cortez RE-1	Cortez
11	52.5	Windsor RE-4	Windsor
13	52.4	Woodland Park RE-2	Woodland Park
14	52.3	Sheridan 2	Sheridan
15	52.2	Delta County 50(J)	Delta
15	52.2	Lewis-Palmer 38	Monument
17	52.1	Roaring Fork RE-1	Glenwood Spgs
18	52.0	Durango 9-R	Durango
18	52.0	Elizabeth C-1	Elizabeth
20	51.9	Fountain 8	Fountain
20	51.9	Greeley 6	Greeley
20	51.9	Johnstown-Milliken RE-5J	Milliken
23	51.8	Academy 20	Colorado Spgs
23	51.8	Adams-Arapahoe 28J	Aurora
23	51.8	Falcon 49	Falcon
23	51.8	Garfield RE-2	Rifle
27	51.7	Widefield 3	Colorado Spgs
28	51.6	Pueblo City 60	Pueblo
28	51.6	Saint Vrain Valley RE-1J	Longmont
28	51.6	Thompson R-2J	Loveland
31	51.5	Eagle County RE-50	Eagle
31	51.5	Poudre R-1	Fort Collins
31	51.5	Pueblo County Rural 70	Pueblo
31	51.5	Valley RE-1	Sterling
35	51.4	Jefferson County R-1	Golden
36	51.3	Colorado Springs 11	Colorado Spgs
36	51.3	Mapleton 1	Denver
36	51.3	Mesa County Valley 51	Grand Junction
39	51.1	Brighton 27J	Brighton
39	51.1	Cherry Creek 5	Greenwood Vlg
39	51.1	Westminster 50	Westminster
42	51.0	Boulder Valley RE-2	Boulder
42	51.0	Canon City RE-1	Canon City
42	51.0	Denver County 1	Denver
42	51.0	Douglas County RE-1	Castle Rock
42	51.0	Fort Morgan RE-3	Fort Morgan
42	51.0	Gunnison Watershed RE1J	Gunnison
48	50.9	Adams County 14	Commerce City
48	50.9	Eaton RE-2	Eaton
50	50.8	Harrison 2	Colorado Spgs
50	50.8	Littleton 6	Littleton
52	50.6	Montrose County RE-1J	Montrose
53	50.5	Northglenn-Thornton 12	Thornton
54	50.4	Cheyenne Mountain 12	Colorado Spgs
55	50.3	Moffat County RE-1	Craig
56	50.1	East Otero R-1	La Junta
56	50.1	Weld County RE-1	Gilcrest
58	49.2	Brush RE-2(J)	Brush

Female Students

Rank	Percent	District Name	City
1	50.8	Brush RE-2(J)	Brush
2	49.9	East Otero R-1	La Junta
2	49.9	Weld County RE-1	Gilcrest
4	49.7	Moffat County RE-1	Craig
5	49.6	Cheyenne Mountain 12	Colorado Spgs
6	49.5	Northglenn-Thornton 12	Thornton
7	49.4	Montrose County RE-1J	Montrose
8	49.2	Harrison 2	Colorado Spgs
8	49.2	Littleton 6	Littleton
10	49.1	Adams County 14	Commerce City
10	49.1	Eaton RE-2	Eaton
12	49.0	Boulder Valley RE-2	Boulder
12	49.0	Canon City RE-1	Canon City
12	49.0	Denver County 1	Denver
12	49.0	Douglas County RE-1	Castle Rock
12	49.0	Fort Morgan RE-3	Fort Morgan
12	49.0	Gunnison Watershed RE1J	Gunnison
18	48.9	Brighton 27J	Brighton
18	48.9	Cherry Creek 5	Greenwood Vlg
18	48.9	Westminster 50	Westminster
21	48.7	Colorado Springs 11	Colorado Spgs
21	48.7	Mapleton 1	Denver
21	48.7	Mesa County Valley 51	Grand Junction
24	48.6	Jefferson County R-1	Golden
25	48.5	Eagle County RE-50	Eagle
25	48.5	Poudre R-1	Fort Collins
25	48.5	Pueblo County Rural 70	Pueblo
25	48.5	Valley RE-1	Sterling

29	48.4	Pueblo City 60	Pueblo
29	48.4	Saint Vrain Valley RE-1J	Longmont
29	48.4	Thompson R-2J	Loveland
32	48.3	Widefield 3	Colorado Spgs
33	48.2	Academy 20	Colorado Spgs
33	48.2	Adams-Arapahoe 28J	Aurora
33	48.2	Falcon 49	Falcon
33	48.2	Garfield RE-2	Rifle
37	48.1	Fountain 8	Fountain
37	48.1	Greeley 6	Greeley
37	48.1	Johnstown-Milliken RE-5J	Milliken
40	48.0	Durango 9-R	Durango
40	48.0	Elizabeth C-1	Elizabeth
42	47.9	Roaring Fork RE-1	Glenwood Spgs
43	47.8	Delta County 50(J)	Delta
43	47.8	Lewis-Palmer 38	Monument
45	47.7	Sheridan 2	Sheridan
46	47.6	Woodland Park RE-2	Woodland Park
47	47.5	Montezuma-Cortez RE-1	Cortez
47	47.5	Windsor RE-4	Windsor
49	47.4	Aspen 1	Aspen
49	47.4	Keenesburg RE-3(J)	Keenesburg
49	47.4	Lamar RE-2	Lamar
52	47.3	Englewood 1	Englewood
52	47.3	Steamboat Springs RE-2	Steamboat Spgs
54	47.1	Summit RE-1	Frisco
54	47.1	Weld County SD RE-8	Fort Lupton
56	46.9	Archuleta County 50 Joint	Pagosa Springs
57	46.8	Alamosa RE-11J	Alamosa
57	46.8	Florence RE-2	Florence

Individual Education Program Students

Rank	Percent	District Name	City
1	16.5	Valley RE-1	Sterling
2	13.6	Florence RE-2	Florence
3	13.3	Sheridan 2	Sheridan
4	13.0	Keenesburg RE-3(J)	Keenesburg
5	12.7	Delta County 50(J)	Delta
5	12.7	Widefield 3	Colorado Spgs
7	12.3	Mesa County Valley 51	Grand Junction
7	12.3	Moffat County RE-1	Craig
9	12.2	Alamosa RE-11J	Alamosa
9	12.2	East Otero R-1	La Junta
9	12.2	Montezuma-Cortez RE-1	Cortez
12	11.8	Englewood 1	Englewood
13	11.7	Montrose County RE-1J	Montrose
13	11.7	Weld County RE-1	Gilcrest
15	11.6	Weld County SD RE-8	Fort Lupton
16	11.5	Boulder Valley RE-2	Boulder
16	11.5	Fort Morgan RE-3	Fort Morgan
18	11.2	Brush RE-2(J)	Brush
19	11.1	Cherry Creek 5	Greenwood Vlg
19	11.1	Johnstown-Milliken RE-5J	Milliken
21	11.0	Thompson R-2J	Loveland
22	10.9	Canon City RE-1	Canon City
22	10.9	Denver County 1	Denver
22	10.9	Pueblo City 60	Pueblo
22	10.9	Steamboat Springs RE-2	Steamboat Spgs
26	10.8	Adams-Arapahoe 28J	Aurora
26	10.8	Greeley 6	Greeley
28	10.7	Woodland Park RE-2	Woodland Park
29	10.6	Durango 9-R	Durango
29	10.6	Elizabeth C-1	Elizabeth
31	10.4	Pueblo County Rural 70	Pueblo
32	10.2	Northglenn-Thornton 12	Thornton
33	10.1	Adams County 14	Commerce City
33	10.1	Littleton 6	Littleton
35	9.9	Lamar RE-2	Lamar
36	9.8	Summit RE-1	Frisco
37	9.6	Fountain 8	Fountain
37	9.6	Harrison 2	Colorado Spgs
39	9.4	Eaton RE-2	Eaton
39	9.4	Jefferson County R-1	Golden
41	9.3	Falcon 49	Falcon
41	9.3	Westminster 50	Westminster
43	9.2	Brighton 27J	Brighton
43	9.2	Mapleton 1	Denver
45	8.9	Eagle County RE-50	Eagle
46	8.8	Colorado Springs 11	Colorado Spgs
46	8.8	Douglas County RE-1	Castle Rock
48	8.7	Gunnison Watershed RE1J	Gunnison
49	8.5	Windsor RE-4	Windsor
50	8.2	Poudre R-1	Fort Collins
51	8.1	Archuleta County 50 Joint	Pagosa Springs
51	8.1	Garfield RE-2	Rifle
53	7.8	Lewis-Palmer 38	Monument
54	7.7	Saint Vrain Valley RE-1J	Longmont
55	6.9	Academy 20	Colorado Spgs
56	6.2	Roaring Fork RE-1	Glenwood Spgs
57	4.9	Aspen 1	Aspen
58	4.7	Cheyenne Mountain 12	Colorado Spgs

English Language Learner Students

Rank	Percent	District Name	City
1	45.3	Weld County SD RE-8	Fort Lupton
2	35.6	Adams-Arapahoe 28J	Aurora
3	33.4	Montezuma-Cortez RE-1	Cortez
4	31.5	Adams County 14	Commerce City
5	29.5	Denver County 1	Denver
6	26.3	Westminster 50	Westminster
7	25.4	Roaring Fork RE-1	Glenwood Spgs
7	25.4	Sheridan 2	Sheridan
9	25.3	Eagle County RE-50	Eagle
10	25.1	Brush RE-2(J)	Brush
11	24.5	Mapleton 1	Denver
12	20.2	Brighton 27J	Brighton
13	20.0	Greeley 6	Greeley
14	19.3	Johnstown-Milliken RE-5J	Milliken
15	17.2	Garfield RE-2	Rifle
16	16.9	Summit RE-1	Frisco
17	16.4	Saint Vrain Valley RE-1J	Longmont
18	15.2	Weld County RE-1	Gilcrest
19	14.1	Lamar RE-2	Lamar
20	12.4	Cherry Creek 5	Greenwood Vlg
21	12.3	Fort Morgan RE-3	Fort Morgan
22	10.9	Poudre R-1	Fort Collins
23	10.8	Keenesburg RE-3(J)	Keenesburg
24	9.9	Boulder Valley RE-2	Boulder
25	9.6	Eaton RE-2	Eaton
26	9.3	Aspen 1	Aspen
27	8.4	Montrose County RE-1J	Montrose
28	8.1	Pueblo City 60	Pueblo
29	7.9	Harrison 2	Colorado Spgs
30	7.3	Alamosa RE-11J	Alamosa
31	6.8	Northglenn-Thornton 12	Thornton
32	5.8	Cheyenne Mountain 12	Colorado Spgs
32	5.8	Jefferson County R-1	Golden
34	5.3	Valley RE-1	Sterling
35	4.8	Littleton 6	Littleton
36	4.7	Englewood 1	Englewood
37	4.6	Moffat County RE-1	Craig
38	3.9	Delta County 50(J)	Delta
39	3.8	Mesa County Valley 51	Grand Junction
40	3.1	Gunnison Watershed RE1J	Gunnison
41	2.8	Colorado Springs 11	Colorado Spgs
42	2.7	Widefield 3	Colorado Spgs
42	2.7	Windsor RE-4	Windsor
44	2.6	Thompson R-2J	Loveland
45	2.4	Durango 9-R	Durango
46	2.1	Archuleta County 50 Joint	Pagosa Springs
47	2.0	Douglas County RE-1	Castle Rock
48	1.7	Fountain 8	Fountain
49	1.4	Pueblo County Rural 70	Pueblo
50	1.3	Academy 20	Colorado Spgs
51	1.1	Steamboat Springs RE-2	Steamboat Spgs
52	0.9	East Otero R-1	La Junta
53	0.7	Falcon 49	Falcon
53	0.7	Lewis-Palmer 38	Monument
53	0.7	Woodland Park RE-2	Woodland Park
56	0.2	Canon City RE-1	Canon City
56	0.2	Florence RE-2	Florence
58	0.0	Elizabeth C-1	Elizabeth

Migrant Students

Rank	Percent	District Name	City
1	15.8	Weld County RE-1	Gilcrest
2	14.1	Fort Morgan RE-3	Fort Morgan
3	13.1	Weld County SD RE-8	Fort Lupton
4	11.4	Alamosa RE-11J	Alamosa
5	10.0	Adams County 14	Commerce City
6	9.3	Lamar RE-2	Lamar
7	9.1	Brush RE-2(J)	Brush
8	8.2	Montrose County RE-1J	Montrose
9	8.1	Greeley 6	Greeley
10	7.7	Keenesburg RE-3(J)	Keenesburg
11	7.3	Eaton RE-2	Eaton
12	6.6	Johnstown-Milliken RE-5J	Milliken
13	4.1	Brighton 27J	Brighton
14	3.9	Mapleton 1	Denver
15	3.6	Delta County 50(J)	Delta
16	3.1	Adams-Arapahoe 28J	Aurora
17	2.3	Mesa County Valley 51	Grand Junction
18	2.2	Westminster 50	Westminster
19	1.8	Pueblo City 60	Pueblo
20	1.7	Garfield RE-2	Rifle
21	1.6	Saint Vrain Valley RE-1J	Longmont
22	1.4	Pueblo County Rural 70	Pueblo
23	1.3	Boulder Valley RE-2	Boulder
24	1.2	Denver County 1	Denver
25	1.1	Jefferson County R-1	Golden
25	1.1	Thompson R-2J	Loveland
27	1.0	Gunnison Watershed RE1J	Gunnison
27	1.0	Northglenn-Thornton 12	Thornton
27	1.0	Windsor RE-4	Windsor
30	0.8	Poudre R-1	Fort Collins
30	0.8	Valley RE-1	Sterling
32	0.7	East Otero R-1	La Junta
33	0.5	Sheridan 2	Sheridan
34	0.4	Colorado Springs 11	Colorado Spgs
35	0.3	Fountain 8	Fountain
35	0.3	Harrison 2	Colorado Spgs
37	0.2	Eagle County RE-50	Eagle
37	0.2	Roaring Fork RE-1	Glenwood Spgs
39	0.1	Englewood 1	Englewood
39	0.1	Florence RE-2	Florence
39	0.1	Steamboat Springs RE-2	Steamboat Spgs
42	0.0	Cherry Creek 5	Greenwood Vlg
42	0.0	Douglas County RE-1	Castle Rock
42	0.0	Falcon 49	Falcon
42	0.0	Littleton 6	Littleton
42	0.0	Widefield 3	Colorado Spgs
47	0.0	Academy 20	Colorado Spgs
47	0.0	Archuleta County 50 Joint	Pagosa Springs
47	0.0	Aspen 1	Aspen
47	0.0	Canon City RE-1	Canon City
47	0.0	Cheyenne Mountain 12	Colorado Spgs
47	0.0	Durango 9-R	Durango
47	0.0	Elizabeth C-1	Elizabeth
47	0.0	Lewis-Palmer 38	Monument
47	0.0	Moffat County RE-1	Craig
47	0.0	Montezuma-Cortez RE-1	Cortez
47	0.0	Summit RE-1	Frisco
47	0.0	Woodland Park RE-2	Woodland Park

Students Eligible for Free Lunch

Rank	Percent	District Name	City
1	54.1	Adams County 14	Commerce City
2	52.9	Denver County 1	Denver
3	48.5	Sheridan 2	Sheridan
4	45.1	Lamar RE-2	Lamar
5	44.3	Alamosa RE-11J	Alamosa
5	44.3	Weld County SD RE-8	Fort Lupton
7	41.9	Pueblo City 60	Pueblo
8	41.8	Harrison 2	Colorado Spgs
9	41.0	East Otero R-1	La Junta
10	40.4	Fort Morgan RE-3	Fort Morgan
11	39.3	Greeley 6	Greeley
12	37.8	Montezuma-Cortez RE-1	Cortez
13	36.0	Westminster 50	Westminster
14	35.2	Adams-Arapahoe 28J	Aurora
15	31.8	Weld County RE-1	Gilcrest
16	30.1	Montrose County RE-1J	Montrose
17	30.0	Brush RE-2(J)	Brush
18	28.8	Mesa County Valley 51	Grand Junction
19	28.0	Canon City RE-1	Canon City
20	27.7	Delta County 50(J)	Delta
21	26.8	Florence RE-2	Florence
22	26.1	Mapleton 1	Denver
23	24.9	Valley RE-1	Sterling
24	24.0	Colorado Springs 11	Colorado Spgs
25	23.4	Keenesburg RE-3(J)	Keenesburg
26	22.7	Archuleta County 50 Joint	Pagosa Springs
27	21.5	Brighton 27J	Brighton
28	19.6	Englewood 1	Englewood
29	19.0	Pueblo County Rural 70	Pueblo
30	18.2	Johnstown-Milliken RE-5J	Milliken
30	18.2	Moffat County RE-1	Craig
32	17.9	Garfield RE-2	Rifle
33	17.7	Eaton RE-2	Eaton
34	17.5	Fountain 8	Fountain
35	16.2	Northglenn-Thornton 12	Thornton
36	15.5	Saint Vrain Valley RE-1J	Longmont
37	14.6	Thompson R-2J	Loveland
38	14.4	Durango 9-R	Durango
39	14.1	Eagle County RE-50	Eagle
40	13.8	Roaring Fork RE-1	Glenwood Spgs
41	13.2	Widefield 3	Colorado Spgs
42	11.5	Poudre R-1	Fort Collins
43	11.4	Jefferson County R-1	Golden
44	10.3	Gunnison Watershed RE1J	Gunnison
45	9.6	Boulder Valley RE-2	Boulder
46	9.4	Woodland Park RE-2	Woodland Park
47	8.7	Summit RE-1	Frisco
48	8.6	Falcon 49	Falcon
49	7.9	Cherry Creek 5	Greenwood Vlg
50	7.1	Littleton 6	Littleton
51	6.3	Windsor RE-4	Windsor
52	3.8	Cheyenne Mountain 12	Colorado Spgs
53	3.1	Elizabeth C-1	Elizabeth
54	2.9	Lewis-Palmer 38	Monument
55	2.8	Steamboat Springs RE-2	Steamboat Spgs
56	2.7	Academy 20	Colorado Spgs
57	1.6	Douglas County RE-1	Castle Rock
58	0.0	Aspen 1	Aspen

Students Eligible for Reduced-Price Lunch

Rank	Percent	District Name	City
1	13.0	East Otero R-1	La Junta
2	12.8	Fountain 8	Fountain
2	12.8	Harrison 2	Colorado Spgs
4	12.7	Brush RE-2(J)	Brush
5	12.6	Westminster 50	Westminster
6	11.8	Mapleton 1	Denver
6	11.8	Pueblo City 60	Pueblo
8	11.5	Fort Morgan RE-3	Fort Morgan
8	11.5	Montezuma-Cortez RE-1	Cortez
10	10.6	Weld County SD RE-8	Fort Lupton
11	10.4	Archuleta County 50 Joint	Pagosa Springs
12	10.3	Delta County 50(J)	Delta
12	10.3	Lamar RE-2	Lamar
14	10.1	Florence RE-2	Florence
15	9.9	Mesa County Valley 51	Grand Junction
15	9.9	Sheridan 2	Sheridan
17	9.6	Adams County 14	Commerce City
18	9.5	Canon City RE-1	Canon City
19	9.4	Keenesburg RE-3(J)	Keenesburg
20	9.1	Colorado Springs 11	Colorado Spgs
21	9.0	Montrose County RE-1J	Montrose
22	8.9	Denver County 1	Denver
23	8.8	Greeley 6	Greeley
24	8.7	Alamosa RE-11J	Alamosa
25	8.4	Pueblo County Rural 70	Pueblo
26	8.3	Valley RE-1	Sterling
27	8.2	Johnstown-Milliken RE-5J	Milliken
28	8.1	Weld County RE-1	Gilcrest
29	7.2	Garfield RE-2	Rifle
29	7.2	Widefield 3	Colorado Spgs
31	7.0	Adams-Arapahoe 28J	Aurora
32	6.9	Englewood 1	Englewood
33	6.7	Brighton 27J	Brighton
34	6.5	Eaton RE-2	Eaton
35	6.3	Durango 9-R	Durango
35	6.3	Northglenn-Thornton 12	Thornton
37	6.1	Moffat County RE-1	Craig
37	6.1	Roaring Fork RE-1	Glenwood Spgs
39	6.0	Thompson R-2J	Loveland
40	5.9	Falcon 49	Falcon
41	5.6	Eagle County RE-50	Eagle
42	4.7	Jefferson County R-1	Golden
43	4.3	Cherry Creek 5	Greenwood Vlg
44	4.1	Windsor RE-4	Windsor
45	4.0	Summit RE-1	Frisco
46	3.8	Woodland Park RE-2	Woodland Park
47	3.6	Gunnison Watershed RE1J	Gunnison
47	3.6	Poudre R-1	Fort Collins
49	3.5	Saint Vrain Valley RE-1J	Longmont
50	2.6	Boulder Valley RE-2	Boulder
51	2.5	Littleton 6	Littleton
52	2.1	Academy 20	Colorado Spgs
52	2.1	Steamboat Springs RE-2	Steamboat Spgs
54	1.9	Cheyenne Mountain 12	Colorado Spgs
55	1.6	Lewis-Palmer 38	Monument
56	1.1	Douglas County RE-1	Castle Rock
57	0.9	Aspen 1	Aspen
57	0.9	Elizabeth C-1	Elizabeth

Student/Teacher Ratio

Rank	Ratio	District Name	City
1	20.2	Mapleton 1	Denver
2	19.4	Northglenn-Thornton 12	Thornton
3	18.5	Adams-Arapahoe 28J	Aurora
3	18.5	Lewis-Palmer 38	Monument
5	18.4	Pueblo County Rural 70	Pueblo
6	18.1	Jefferson County R-1	Golden
7	18.0	Delta County 50(J)	Delta
8	17.9	Englewood 1	Englewood
9	17.8	Adams County 14	Commerce City
10	17.6	Douglas County RE-1	Castle Rock
11	17.5	Brighton 27J	Brighton
12	17.4	Widefield 3	Colorado Spgs
13	17.3	Fountain 8	Fountain
13	17.3	Mesa County Valley 51	Grand Junction
13	17.3	Moffat County RE-1	Craig
13	17.3	Thompson R-2J	Loveland
17	17.2	Archuleta County 50 Joint	Pagosa Springs
17	17.2	Woodland Park RE-2	Woodland Park
19	17.1	Garfield RE-2	Rifle
19	17.1	Saint Vrain Valley RE-1J	Longmont
21	17.0	Montrose County RE-1J	Montrose
22	16.9	Canon City RE-1	Canon City
22	16.9	Colorado Springs 11	Colorado Spgs
24	16.8	Cherry Creek 5	Greenwood Vlg
24	16.8	Falcon 49	Falcon
24	16.8	Greeley 6	Greeley
24	16.8	Littleton 6	Littleton
24	16.8	Poudre R-1	Fort Collins
24	16.8	Westminster 50	Westminster
30	16.7	Elizabeth C-1	Elizabeth
30	16.7	Valley RE-1	Sterling
32	16.4	Fort Morgan RE-3	Fort Morgan
33	16.3	Eaton RE-2	Eaton
34	16.2	Boulder Valley RE-2	Boulder
34	16.2	Florence RE-2	Florence
36	16.1	Denver County 1	Denver
37	16.0	Academy 20	Colorado Spgs
37	16.0	Cheyenne Mountain 12	Colorado Spgs
37	16.0	Pueblo City 60	Pueblo
37	16.0	Windsor RE-4	Windsor
41	15.7	Keenesburg RE-3(J)	Keenesburg
42	15.6	Alamosa RE-11J	Alamosa
42	15.6	Johnstown-Milliken RE-5J	Milliken
44	15.5	Montezuma-Cortez RE-1	Cortez
45	15.3	East Otero R-1	La Junta
45	15.3	Sheridan 2	Sheridan
47	15.2	Lamar RE-2	Lamar
48	15.0	Durango 9-R	Durango
48	15.0	Harrison 2	Colorado Spgs
50	14.8	Weld County SD RE-8	Fort Lupton
51	14.4	Eagle County RE-50	Eagle
52	14.2	Roaring Fork RE-1	Glenwood Spgs
53	14.1	Steamboat Springs RE-2	Steamboat Spgs
54	13.9	Brush RE-2(J)	Brush
55	13.2	Gunnison Watershed RE1J	Gunnison
56	13.1	Summit RE-1	Frisco
56	13.1	Weld County RE-1	Gilcrest
58	12.5	Aspen 1	Aspen

Student/Librarian Ratio

Rank	Ratio	District Name	City
1	6,386.7	Weld County RE-1	Gilcrest
2	3,855.0	Aspen 1	Aspen
3	3,638.5	Brighton 27J	Brighton
4	3,226.7	Elizabeth C-1	Elizabeth
5	2,893.6	Douglas County RE-1	Castle Rock
6	2,138.9	Keenesburg RE-3(J)	Keenesburg
7	1,915.0	Florence RE-2	Florence
8	1,874.3	Mapleton 1	Denver
9	1,847.5	Garfield RE-2	Rifle
10	1,835.3	Westminster 50	Westminster
11	1,820.0	East Otero R-1	La Junta
12	1,726.3	Lewis-Palmer 38	Monument
13	1,701.1	Brush RE-2(J)	Brush
14	1,690.0	Montezuma-Cortez RE-1	Cortez
15	1,669.5	Academy 20	Colorado Spgs
16	1,663.8	Thompson R-2J	Loveland
17	1,544.3	Harrison 2	Colorado Spgs
18	1,498.8	Mesa County Valley 51	Grand Junction
19	1,483.8	Widefield 3	Colorado Spgs
20	1,430.0	Valley RE-1	Sterling
21	1,405.0	Canon City RE-1	Canon City
22	1,400.0	Englewood 1	Englewood
23	1,366.9	Adams County 14	Commerce City
24	1,361.2	Montrose County RE-1J	Montrose
25	1,323.6	Fort Morgan RE-3	Fort Morgan
26	1,300.9	Saint Vrain Valley RE-1J	Longmont
27	1,269.8	Adams-Arapahoe 28J	Aurora
28	1,231.0	Moffat County RE-1	Craig
29	1,197.7	Littleton 6	Littleton
30	916.0	Lamar RE-2	Lamar
31	894.4	Fountain 8	Fountain
32	865.3	Gunnison Watershed RE1J	Gunnison
33	806.8	Eaton RE-2	Eaton
34	799.6	Cherry Creek 5	Greenwood Vlg
35	786.9	Northglenn-Thornton 12	Thornton
36	760.0	Alamosa RE-11J	Alamosa
37	730.3	Poudre R-1	Fort Collins
38	728.7	Boulder Valley RE-2	Boulder
39	690.7	Denver County 1	Denver
40	671.3	Falcon 49	Falcon
41	655.2	Woodland Park RE-2	Woodland Park
42	639.5	Jefferson County R-1	Golden
43	638.7	Johnstown-Milliken RE-5J	Milliken
44	620.3	Cheyenne Mountain 12	Colorado Spgs
45	608.0	Roaring Fork RE-1	Glenwood Spgs
46	588.6	Windsor RE-4	Windsor
47	552.4	Colorado Springs 11	Colorado Spgs
48	535.1	Weld County SD RE-8	Fort Lupton
49	523.2	Sheridan 2	Sheridan
50	521.1	Pueblo City 60	Pueblo
51	512.3	Archuleta County 50 Joint	Pagosa Springs
52	483.3	Steamboat Springs RE-2	Steamboat Spgs
53	463.4	Eagle County RE-50	Eagle
54	462.2	Durango 9-R	Durango
55	346.9	Summit RE-1	Frisco
56	0.0	Delta County 50(J)	Delta
56	0.0	Greeley 6	Greeley
56	0.0	Pueblo County Rural 70	Pueblo

Student/Counselor Ratio

Rank	Ratio	District Name	City
1	1,059.3	Valley RE-1	Sterling
2	1,038.6	Denver County 1	Denver
3	962.5	Keenesburg RE-3(J)	Keenesburg
4	861.9	Douglas County RE-1	Castle Rock
5	791.4	Colorado Springs 11	Colorado Spgs
6	753.3	Northglenn-Thornton 12	Thornton
7	750.2	Brighton 27J	Brighton
8	716.9	Cherry Creek 5	Greenwood Vlg
9	705.1	Adams County 14	Commerce City
10	702.9	Mapleton 1	Denver
11	688.3	Westminster 50	Westminster
12	683.7	Jefferson County R-1	Golden
13	639.5	Delta County 50(J)	Delta
14	618.1	Johnstown-Milliken RE-5J	Milliken
15	608.5	Adams-Arapahoe 28J	Aurora
16	581.4	Montrose County RE-1J	Montrose
17	580.8	Elizabeth C-1	Elizabeth
18	574.9	Greeley 6	Greeley
19	547.4	Canon City RE-1	Canon City
20	512.3	Boulder Valley RE-2	Boulder
21	500.2	Littleton 6	Littleton
22	490.5	Windsor RE-4	Windsor
23	488.7	Mesa County Valley 51	Grand Junction
24	462.1	Fountain 8	Fountain
25	458.9	Roaring Fork RE-1	Glenwood Spgs
26	458.0	Lamar RE-2	Lamar
27	453.9	Saint Vrain Valley RE-1J	Longmont
28	453.3	Fort Morgan RE-3	Fort Morgan
29	432.0	Poudre R-1	Fort Collins
30	423.8	Moffat County RE-1	Craig
31	414.6	Academy 20	Colorado Spgs
32	413.2	Eagle County RE-50	Eagle
33	410.6	Garfield RE-2	Rifle
34	409.5	Woodland Park RE-2	Woodland Park
35	406.9	Falcon 49	Falcon
36	403.6	Thompson R-2J	Loveland
37	397.0	Archuleta County 50 Joint	Pagosa Springs
38	393.1	Eaton RE-2	Eaton
39	387.2	Sheridan 2	Sheridan
40	383.2	Weld County RE-1	Gilcrest
41	373.4	Brush RE-2(J)	Brush
42	350.0	East Otero R-1	La Junta
43	348.7	Harrison 2	Colorado Spgs
44	348.5	Montezuma-Cortez RE-1	Cortez
45	348.2	Florence RE-2	Florence
46	343.8	Pueblo City 60	Pueblo
47	343.0	Lewis-Palmer 38	Monument
48	335.9	Pueblo County Rural 70	Pueblo
49	335.5	Gunnison Watershed RE1J	Gunnison
50	333.6	Widefield 3	Colorado Spgs
51	327.6	Steamboat Springs RE-2	Steamboat Spgs
52	323.1	Englewood 1	Englewood
53	321.6	Cheyenne Mountain 12	Colorado Spgs
54	321.3	Aspen 1	Aspen
55	291.3	Weld County SD RE-8	Fort Lupton
56	283.2	Summit RE-1	Frisco
57	258.8	Durango 9-R	Durango
58	250.5	Alamosa RE-11J	Alamosa

Current Spending per Student in FY2001

Rank	Dollars	District Name	City
1	9,199	Aspen 1	Aspen
2	7,508	Steamboat Springs RE-2	Steamboat Spgs
3	7,340	Jefferson County R-1	Golden
4	7,285	Summit RE-1	Frisco
5	7,148	Denver County 1	Denver
6	7,015	Eagle County RE-50	Eagle
7	6,957	Sheridan 2	Sheridan
8	6,923	Moffat County RE-1	Craig
9	6,910	Colorado Springs 11	Colorado Spgs
10	6,803	Adams County 14	Commerce City
11	6,784	Cherry Creek 5	Greenwood Vlg
12	6,570	Greeley 6	Greeley
13	6,546	Poudre R-1	Fort Collins
14	6,475	East Otero R-1	La Junta
15	6,464	Douglas County RE-1	Castle Rock
16	6,413	Boulder Valley RE-2	Boulder
17	6,387	Delta County 50(J)	Delta
18	6,326	Littleton 6	Littleton
19	6,317	Englewood 1	Englewood
20	6,268	Elizabeth C-1	Elizabeth
21	6,255	Weld County SD RE-8	Fort Lupton
22	6,201	Harrison 2	Colorado Spgs
23	6,164	Adams-Arapahoe 28J	Aurora
24	6,147	Fort Morgan RE-3	Fort Morgan
25	6,066	Gunnison Watershed RE1J	Gunnison
26	6,060	Montrose County RE-1J	Montrose
27	6,057	Durango 9-R	Durango
28	6,053	Brighton 27J	Brighton

29	6,005	Roaring Fork RE-1	Glenwood Spgs
30	5,973	Weld County RE-1	Gilcrest
31	5,944	Saint Vrain Valley RE-1J	Longmont
32	5,939	Valley RE-1	Sterling
33	5,918	Pueblo City 60	Pueblo
34	5,914	Montezuma-Cortez RE-1	Cortez
35	5,912	Westminster 50	Westminster
36	5,894	Keenesburg RE-3(J)	Keenesburg
37	5,861	Brush RE-2(J)	Brush
38	5,860	Thompson R-2J	Loveland
39	5,806	Florence RE-2	Florence
40	5,784	Northglenn-Thornton 12	Thornton
41	5,766	Archuleta County 50 Joint	Pagosa Springs
42	5,694	Canon City RE-1	Canon City
43	5,663	Mesa County Valley 51	Grand Junction
44	5,646	Eaton RE-2	Eaton
45	5,644	Fountain 8	Fountain
46	5,573	Mapleton 1	Denver
47	5,572	Alamosa RE-11J	Alamosa
48	5,541	Academy 20	Colorado Spgs
49	5,399	Johnstown-Milliken RE-5J	Milliken
50	5,365	Widefield 3	Colorado Spgs
51	5,306	Windsor RE-4	Windsor
52	5,239	Falcon 49	Falcon
53	5,142	Cheyenne Mountain 12	Colorado Spgs
54	5,129	Lamar RE-2	Lamar
55	5,108	Pueblo County Rural 70	Pueblo
56	5,082	Woodland Park RE-2	Woodland Park
57	5,045	Garfield RE-2	Rifle
58	4,908	Lewis-Palmer 38	Monument

Number of Diploma Recipients

Rank	Number	District Name	City
1	5,334	Jefferson County R-1	Golden
2	2,922	Cherry Creek 5	Greenwood Vlg
3	2,612	Denver County 1	Denver
4	1,898	Douglas County RE-1	Castle Rock
5	1,816	Colorado Springs 11	Colorado Spgs
6	1,810	Boulder Valley RE-2	Boulder
7	1,566	Northglenn-Thornton 12	Thornton
8	1,503	Poudre R-1	Fort Collins
9	1,223	Littleton 6	Littleton
10	1,205	Academy 20	Colorado Spgs
11	1,179	Mesa County Valley 51	Grand Junction
12	1,134	Saint Vrain Valley RE-1J	Longmont
13	1,120	Adams-Arapahoe 28J	Aurora
14	924	Thompson R-2J	Loveland
15	907	Pueblo City 60	Pueblo
16	870	Greeley 6	Greeley
17	532	Widefield 3	Colorado Spgs
18	498	Westminster 50	Westminster
19	400	Harrison 2	Colorado Spgs
20	349	Pueblo County Rural 70	Pueblo
21	348	Montrose County RE-1J	Montrose
22	327	Falcon 49	Falcon
23	319	Durango 9-R	Durango
24	316	Cheyenne Mountain 12	Colorado Spgs
25	311	Roaring Fork RE-1	Glenwood Spgs
26	306	Delta County 50(J)	Delta
27	295	Lewis-Palmer 38	Monument
28	290	Englewood 1	Englewood
29	279	Canon City RE-1	Canon City
30	271	Brighton 27J	Brighton
31	237	Eagle County RE-50	Eagle
32	236	Adams County 14	Commerce City
33	215	Elizabeth C-1	Elizabeth
34	210	Mapleton 1	Denver
34	210	Woodland Park RE-2	Woodland Park
36	184	Fountain 8	Fountain
37	168	Valley RE-1	Sterling
38	165	Moffat County RE-1	Craig
38	165	Summit RE-1	Frisco
40	164	Montezuma-Cortez RE-1	Cortez
41	158	Windsor RE-4	Windsor
42	157	Fort Morgan RE-3	Fort Morgan
43	156	Garfield RE-2	Rifle
44	143	Weld County SD RE-8	Fort Lupton
45	132	Alamosa RE-11J	Alamosa
45	132	Steamboat Springs RE-2	Steamboat Spgs
47	128	East Otero R-1	La Junta
48	109	Gunnison Watershed RE1J	Gunnison
49	105	Weld County RE-1	Gilcrest
50	100	Archuleta County 50 Joint	Pagosa Springs
51	95	Aspen 1	Aspen
52	94	Brush RE-2(J)	Brush
53	90	Lamar RE-2	Lamar
54	89	Johnstown-Milliken RE-5J	Milliken
55	87	Florence RE-2	Florence
56	85	Keenesburg RE-3(J)	Keenesburg
57	79	Eaton RE-2	Eaton
58	76	Sheridan 2	Sheridan

High School Drop-out Rate

Rank	Percent	District Name	City
1	n/a	Academy 20	Colorado Spgs
1	n/a	Adams County 14	Commerce City
1	n/a	Adams-Arapahoe 28J	Aurora
1	n/a	Alamosa RE-11J	Alamosa
1	n/a	Archuleta County 50 Joint	Pagosa Springs
1	n/a	Aspen 1	Aspen
1	n/a	Boulder Valley RE-2	Boulder
1	n/a	Brighton 27J	Brighton
1	n/a	Brush RE-2(J)	Brush
1	n/a	Canon City RE-1	Canon City
1	n/a	Cherry Creek 5	Greenwood Vlg
1	n/a	Cheyenne Mountain 12	Colorado Spgs
1	n/a	Colorado Springs 11	Colorado Spgs
1	n/a	Delta County 50(J)	Delta
1	n/a	Denver County 1	Denver
1	n/a	Douglas County RE-1	Castle Rock
1	n/a	Durango 9-R	Durango
1	n/a	Eagle County RE-50	Eagle
1	n/a	East Otero R-1	La Junta
1	n/a	Eaton RE-2	Eaton
1	n/a	Elizabeth C-1	Elizabeth
1	n/a	Englewood 1	Englewood
1	n/a	Falcon 49	Falcon
1	n/a	Florence RE-2	Florence
1	n/a	Fort Morgan RE-3	Fort Morgan
1	n/a	Fountain 8	Fountain
1	n/a	Garfield RE-2	Rifle
1	n/a	Greeley 6	Greeley
1	n/a	Gunnison Watershed RE1J	Gunnison
1	n/a	Harrison 2	Colorado Spgs
1	n/a	Jefferson County R-1	Golden
1	n/a	Johnstown-Milliken RE-5J	Milliken
1	n/a	Keenesburg RE-3(J)	Keenesburg
1	n/a	Lamar RE-2	Lamar
1	n/a	Lewis-Palmer 38	Monument
1	n/a	Littleton 6	Littleton
1	n/a	Mapleton 1	Denver
1	n/a	Mesa County Valley 51	Grand Junction
1	n/a	Moffat County RE-1	Craig
1	n/a	Montezuma-Cortez RE-1	Cortez
1	n/a	Montrose County RE-1J	Montrose
1	n/a	Northglenn-Thornton 12	Thornton
1	n/a	Poudre R-1	Fort Collins
1	n/a	Pueblo City 60	Pueblo
1	n/a	Pueblo County Rural 70	Pueblo
1	n/a	Roaring Fork RE-1	Glenwood Spgs
1	n/a	Saint Vrain Valley RE-1J	Longmont
1	n/a	Sheridan 2	Sheridan
1	n/a	Steamboat Springs RE-2	Steamboat Spgs
1	n/a	Summit RE-1	Frisco
1	n/a	Thompson R-2J	Loveland
1	n/a	Valley RE-1	Sterling
1	n/a	Weld County RE-1	Gilcrest
1	n/a	Weld County SD RE-8	Fort Lupton
1	n/a	Westminster 50	Westminster
1	n/a	Widefield 3	Colorado Spgs
1	n/a	Windsor RE-4	Windsor
1	n/a	Woodland Park RE-2	Woodland Park

Connecticut

Connecticut Public School Educational Profile

Category	Value	Category	Value
Schools *(2002-2003)*	1,248	**Diploma Recipients** *(2002-2003)*	32,322
Instructional Level		White, Non-Hispanic	24,721
Primary	698	Black, Non-Hispanic	3,617
Middle	194	Asian/Pacific Islander	1,029
High	204	American Indian/Alaskan Native	74
Other Level	152	Hispanic	2,886
Curriculum		**High School Drop-out Rate** (%) *(2000-2001)*	3.0
Regular	1,002	White, Non-Hispanic	2.0
Special Education	26	Black, Non-Hispanic	5.3
Vocational	17	Asian/Pacific Islander	1.8
Alternative	203	American Indian/Alaskan Native	3.7
Type		Hispanic	7.0
Magnet	25	**Staff** *(2002-2003)*	86,201.6
Charter	13	Teachers	42,298.6
Title I Eligible	466	Average Salary ($)	53,962
School-wide Title I	114	Librarians/Media Specialists	784.7
Students *(2002-2003)*	572,823	Guidance Counselors	1,328.2
Gender (%)		**Ratios** *(2002-2003)*	
Male	51.5	Student/Teacher Ratio	13.5 to 1
Female	48.5	Student/Librarian Ratio	730.0 to 1
Race/Ethnicity (%)		Student/Counselor Ratio	431.3 to 1
White, Non-Hispanic	69.0	**Current Spending** *($ per student in FY 2001)*	10,577
Black, Non-Hispanic	13.6	Instruction	6,772
Asian/Pacific Islander	3.0	Support Services	3,425
American Indian/Alaskan Native	0.3	**College Entrance Exam Scores** *(2003)*	
Hispanic	14.1	Scholastic Aptitude Test (SAT)	
Classification (%)		Participation Rate (%)	84
Individual Education Program (IEP)	13.0	Mean SAT I Verbal Score	512
Migrant	0.8	Mean SAT I Math Score	514
English Language Learner (ELL)	4.0	American College Testing Program (ACT)	
Eligible for Free Lunch Program	0.0	Participation Rate (%)	7
Eligible for Reduced-Price Lunch Program	0.0	Average Composite Score	22.1

***Note:** For an explanation of data, please refer to the User's Guide in the front of the book; n/a indicates data not available*

Connecticut NAEP 2003 Test Scores

Reading			Mathematics		
Grade/Category	Value	Rank	Grade/Category	Value	Rank
4th Grade			**4th Grade**		
Average Proficiency	228.3 (1.1)	1/51	Average Proficiency	240.6 (0.8)	8/51
Proficiency by Gender/Race/Ethnicity			Proficiency by Gender/Race/Ethnicity		
Male	224.4 (1.3)	2/51	Male	243.0 (0.9)	6/51
Female	232.3 (1.5)	1/51	Female	238.1 (0.9)	9/51
White, Non-Hispanic	238.3 (1.2)	2/51	White, Non-Hispanic	249.5 (0.9)	3/51
Black, Non-Hispanic	201.3 (2.2)	18/42	Black, Non-Hispanic	217.3 (1.2)	14/42
Asian, Non-Hispanic	205.6 (2.5)	17/41	Asian, Non-Hispanic	222.7 (1.7)	19/43
American Indian, Non-Hispanic	231.1 (3.9)	9/25	American Indian, Non-Hispanic	249.4 (2.6)	9/26
Hispanic	n/a	n/a	Hispanic	n/a	n/a
Proficiency by Class Size			Proficiency by Class Size		
Less than 16 Students	*209.1 (8.2)*	13/45	Less than 16 Students	225.3 (3.8)	23/47
16 to 18 Students	223.4 (3.6)	8/48	16 to 18 Students	239.2 (2.5)	9/48
19 to 20 Students	230.7 (2.8)	3/50	19 to 20 Students	243.8 (2.4)	3/50
21 to 25 Students	233.2 (2.1)	1/51	21 to 25 Students	245.0 (1.4)	1/51
Greater than 25 Students	*206.5 (4.2)*	45/49	Greater than 25 Students	*220.8 (3.0)*	47/49
Percent Attaining Achievement Levels			Percent Attaining Achievement Levels		
Below Basic	26.3 (1.2)	50/51	Below Basic	17.6 (0.9)	39/51
Basic or Above	73.7 (1.2)	2/51	Basic or Above	82.4 (0.9)	12/51
Proficient or Above	42.6 (1.6)	1/51	Proficient or Above	41.1 (1.5)	6/51
Advanced or Above	12.5 (1.1)	1/51	Advanced or Above	5.3 (0.5)	7/51
8th Grade			**8th Grade**		
Average Proficiency	267.2 (1.1)	14/51	Average Proficiency	283.7 (1.2)	11/51
Proficiency by Gender/Race/Ethnicity			Proficiency by Gender/Race/Ethnicity		
Male	261.5 (1.4)	14/51	Male	284.6 (1.5)	9/51
Female	272.9 (1.3)	12/51	Female	282.9 (1.4)	12/51
White, Non-Hispanic	275.0 (1.1)	5/50	White, Non-Hispanic	293.0 (1.0)	3/50
Black, Non-Hispanic	244.2 (2.3)	21/41	Black, Non-Hispanic	254.5 (2.2)	16/41
Asian, Non-Hispanic	243.8 (3.1)	26/37	Asian, Non-Hispanic	258.7 (2.0)	21/37
American Indian, Non-Hispanic	282.3 (4.5)	2/23	American Indian, Non-Hispanic	295.5 (7.0)	8/23
Hispanic	n/a	n/a	Hispanic	n/a	n/a
Proficiency by Parents Highest Level of Ed.			Proficiency by Parents Highest Level of Ed.		
Did Not Finish High School	244.1 (4.7)	33/50	Did Not Finish High School	259.3 (3.8)	20/50
Graduated High School	254.0 (1.9)	30/50	Graduated High School	272.8 (1.9)	13/50
Some Education After High School	267.9 (1.7)	25/50	Some Education After High School	279.7 (1.8)	30/50
Graduated College	276.3 (1.3)	8/50	Graduated College	294.8 (1.4)	4/50
Percent Attaining Achievement Levels			Percent Attaining Achievement Levels		
Below Basic	23.4 (1.4)	29/51	Below Basic	26.8 (1.3)	35/51
Basic or Above	76.6 (1.4)	23/51	Basic or Above	73.2 (1.3)	17/51
Proficient or Above	37.0 (1.5)	8/51	Proficient or Above	35.2 (1.6)	4/51
Advanced or Above	4.7 (0.8)	2/51	Advanced or Above	8.3 (0.9)	2/51

Note: *For an explanation of data, please refer to the User's Guide in the front of the book; values in italics indicate that the nature of the sample does not allow accurate determination of the variability of the statistic; n/a indicates data not available*

Fairfield County

Bethel SD

One School St • Bethel, CT 06801-0253
(203) 794-8601 • http://www.bethel.k12.ct.us/
Grade Span: PK-12; **Agency Type:** 1
Schools: 7
2 Primary; 2 Middle; 1 High; 2 Other Level
6 Regular; 0 Special Education; 0 Vocational; 1 Alternative
0 Magnet; 0 Charter; 3 Title I Eligible; 0 School-wide Title I
Students: 3,225 (51.6% male; 48.4% female)
Individual Education Program: 345 (10.7%);
English Language Learner: 104 (3.2%); Migrant: 5 (0.2%)
Eligible for Free Lunch Program: n/a
Eligible for Reduced-Price Lunch Program: n/a
Teachers: 239.8 (13.4 to 1)
Librarians/Media Specialists: 6.0 (537.5 to 1)
Guidance Counselors: 9.9 (325.8 to 1)
Current Spending: ($ per student per year):
Total: $9,306; Instruction: $5,824; Support Services: $3,161
Enrollment, Drop-out Rates and Diploma Recipients by Race/Ethnicity

Category	Total	White	Black	Asian	AIAN	Hisp.
Enrollment (%)	100.0	85.4	2.0	6.3	0.2	6.1
Drop-out Rate (%)	0.9	0.9	0.0	1.6	0.0	0.0
H.S. Diplomas (#)	186	161	2	12	0	11

Bridgeport SD

45 Lyon Terrace, Rm 303 • Bridgeport, CT 06604-4060
(203) 576-7301 • http://www.bridgeportedu.com
Grade Span: PK-12; **Agency Type:** 1
Schools: 36
28 Primary; 0 Middle; 3 High; 5 Other Level
36 Regular; 0 Special Education; 0 Vocational; 0 Alternative
0 Magnet; 0 Charter; 25 Title I Eligible; 23 School-wide Title I
Students: 22,493 (51.3% male; 48.7% female)
Individual Education Program: 3,001 (13.3%);
English Language Learner: 2,428 (10.8%); Migrant: 669 (3.0%)
Eligible for Free Lunch Program: n/a
Eligible for Reduced-Price Lunch Program: n/a
Teachers: 1,482.1 (15.2 to 1)
Librarians/Media Specialists: 18.0 (1,249.6 to 1)
Guidance Counselors: 46.0 (489.0 to 1)
Current Spending: ($ per student per year):
Total: $9,594; Instruction: $6,419; Support Services: $2,701
Enrollment, Drop-out Rates and Diploma Recipients by Race/Ethnicity

Category	Total	White	Black	Asian	AIAN	Hisp.
Enrollment (%)	100.0	10.7	42.6	3.1	0.1	43.5
Drop-out Rate (%)	11.2	14.5	10.6	1.7	20.0	11.8
H.S. Diplomas (#)	834	91	391	35	0	317

Brookfield SD

100 Pocono Rd • Brookfield, CT 06804-3331
Mailing Address: Brookfield Municipal Center 10 • Brookfield, CT 06804-3331
(203) 775-7620 • http://www.brookfield.k12.ct.us/
Grade Span: PK-12; **Agency Type:** 1
Schools: 5
2 Primary; 1 Middle; 1 High; 1 Other Level
4 Regular; 0 Special Education; 0 Vocational; 1 Alternative
0 Magnet; 0 Charter; 2 Title I Eligible; 0 School-wide Title I
Students: 3,018 (51.1% male; 48.9% female)
Individual Education Program: 217 (7.2%);
English Language Learner: 8 (0.3%); Migrant: 0 (0.0%)
Eligible for Free Lunch Program: n/a
Eligible for Reduced-Price Lunch Program: n/a
Teachers: 219.8 (13.7 to 1)
Librarians/Media Specialists: 3.0 (1,006.0 to 1)
Guidance Counselors: 7.6 (397.1 to 1)
Current Spending: ($ per student per year):
Total: $8,550; Instruction: $5,114; Support Services: $3,097
Enrollment, Drop-out Rates and Diploma Recipients by Race/Ethnicity

Category	Total	White	Black	Asian	AIAN	Hisp.
Enrollment (%)	100.0	94.1	1.0	2.8	0.2	2.0
Drop-out Rate (%)	1.0	1.1	0.0	0.0	n/a	0.0
H.S. Diplomas (#)	182	165	1	12	0	4

Danbury SD

63 Beaver Brook Rd • Danbury, CT 06810-6211
(203) 797-4701 • http://www.danbury.k12.ct.us/
Grade Span: PK-12; **Agency Type:** 1
Schools: 18
13 Primary; 2 Middle; 2 High; 1 Other Level
16 Regular; 0 Special Education; 0 Vocational; 2 Alternative
0 Magnet; 0 Charter; 9 Title I Eligible; 0 School-wide Title I
Students: 9,561 (50.9% male; 49.1% female)
Individual Education Program: 1,148 (12.0%);
English Language Learner: 1,645 (17.2%); Migrant: 294 (3.1%)
Eligible for Free Lunch Program: n/a
Eligible for Reduced-Price Lunch Program: n/a
Teachers: 641.3 (14.9 to 1)
Librarians/Media Specialists: 21.0 (455.3 to 1)
Guidance Counselors: 19.0 (503.2 to 1)
Current Spending: ($ per student per year):
Total: $9,137; Instruction: $5,997; Support Services: $2,749
Enrollment, Drop-out Rates and Diploma Recipients by Race/Ethnicity

Category	Total	White	Black	Asian	AIAN	Hisp.
Enrollment (%)	100.0	56.8	10.9	9.1	0.1	23.1
Drop-out Rate (%)	4.1	3.5	4.8	2.0	0.0	7.4
H.S. Diplomas (#)	506	351	44	47	0	64

Darien SD

2 Renshaw Rd • Darien, CT 06820-1167
Mailing Address: 2 Renshaw Road, Box 1167 • Darien, CT 06820-1167
(203) 656-7412 • http://www.darien.k12.ct.us/boe/default.php
Grade Span: PK-12; **Agency Type:** 1
Schools: 8
5 Primary; 1 Middle; 1 High; 1 Other Level
7 Regular; 0 Special Education; 0 Vocational; 1 Alternative
0 Magnet; 0 Charter; 1 Title I Eligible; 0 School-wide Title I
Students: 4,116 (51.9% male; 48.1% female)
Individual Education Program: 501 (12.2%);
English Language Learner: 33 (0.8%); Migrant: 0 (0.0%)
Eligible for Free Lunch Program: n/a
Eligible for Reduced-Price Lunch Program: n/a
Teachers: 331.9 (12.4 to 1)
Librarians/Media Specialists: 9.5 (433.3 to 1)
Guidance Counselors: 10.0 (411.6 to 1)
Current Spending: ($ per student per year):
Total: $11,203; Instruction: $7,457; Support Services: $3,175
Enrollment, Drop-out Rates and Diploma Recipients by Race/Ethnicity

Category	Total	White	Black	Asian	AIAN	Hisp.
Enrollment (%)	100.0	95.7	0.7	1.5	1.0	1.0
Drop-out Rate (%)	0.5	0.5	0.0	0.0	n/a	0.0
H.S. Diplomas (#)	190	179	2	7	0	2

Fairfield SD

785 Unquowa Rd • Fairfield, CT 06430-0222
Mailing Address: 785 Unquowa Rd, Box 222 • Fairfield, CT 06430-0222
(203) 255-8371 • http://www.fairfield.k12.ct.us/
Grade Span: PK-12; **Agency Type:** 1
Schools: 16
11 Primary; 3 Middle; 1 High; 1 Other Level
15 Regular; 1 Special Education; 0 Vocational; 0 Alternative
0 Magnet; 0 Charter; 3 Title I Eligible; 0 School-wide Title I
Students: 8,539 (50.5% male; 49.5% female)
Individual Education Program: 1,070 (12.5%);
English Language Learner: 84 (1.0%); Migrant: 0 (0.0%)
Eligible for Free Lunch Program: n/a
Eligible for Reduced-Price Lunch Program: n/a
Teachers: 683.2 (12.5 to 1)
Librarians/Media Specialists: 16.9 (505.3 to 1)
Guidance Counselors: 21.0 (406.6 to 1)
Current Spending: ($ per student per year):
Total: $11,084; Instruction: $6,552; Support Services: $4,203
Enrollment, Drop-out Rates and Diploma Recipients by Race/Ethnicity

Category	Total	White	Black	Asian	AIAN	Hisp.
Enrollment (%)	100.0	90.1	2.2	4.0	0.2	3.6
Drop-out Rate (%)	1.0	1.0	0.0	1.0	0.0	0.0
H.S. Diplomas (#)	459	422	4	21	0	12

Greenwich SD

Havemeyer Building • Greenwich, CT 06830-6521
(203) 625-7400 • http://www.greenwichschools.org/
Grade Span: PK-12; **Agency Type:** 1
Schools: 16
11 Primary; 3 Middle; 1 High; 1 Other Level
15 Regular; 0 Special Education; 0 Vocational; 1 Alternative
0 Magnet; 0 Charter; 3 Title I Eligible; 0 School-wide Title I
Students: 8,976 (52.5% male; 47.5% female)
Individual Education Program: 1,068 (11.9%);
English Language Learner: 544 (6.1%); Migrant: 0 (0.0%)
Eligible for Free Lunch Program: n/a
Eligible for Reduced-Price Lunch Program: n/a
Teachers: 740.1 (12.1 to 1)
Librarians/Media Specialists: 22.0 (408.0 to 1)
Guidance Counselors: 24.9 (360.5 to 1)
Current Spending: ($ per student per year):
Total: $13,201; Instruction: $8,525; Support Services: $4,263

Enrollment, Drop-out Rates and Diploma Recipients by Race/Ethnicity

Category	Total	White	Black	Asian	AIAN	Hisp.
Enrollment (%)	100.0	79.0	2.2	7.5	0.0	11.2
Drop-out Rate (%)	1.2	1.1	1.9	0.7	0.0	2.6
H.S. Diplomas (#)	474	390	7	28	0	49

Monroe SD

375 Monroe Turnpike • Monroe, CT 06468-2362
(203) 452-6501 • http://www.monroe.k12.ct.us/
Grade Span: PK-12; **Agency Type:** 1
Schools: 7
3 Primary; 2 Middle; 1 High; 1 Other Level
6 Regular; 0 Special Education; 0 Vocational; 1 Alternative
0 Magnet; 0 Charter; 2 Title I Eligible; 0 School-wide Title I
Students: 4,136 (51.4% male; 48.6% female)
Individual Education Program: 407 (9.8%);
English Language Learner: 14 (0.3%); Migrant: 0 (0.0%)
Eligible for Free Lunch Program: n/a
Eligible for Reduced-Price Lunch Program: n/a
Teachers: 282.1 (14.7 to 1)
Librarians/Media Specialists: 3.0 (1,378.7 to 1)
Guidance Counselors: 10.7 (386.5 to 1)
Current Spending: ($ per student per year):
Total: $8,750; Instruction: $5,498; Support Services: $2,913

Enrollment, Drop-out Rates and Diploma Recipients by Race/Ethnicity

Category	Total	White	Black	Asian	AIAN	Hisp.
Enrollment (%)	100.0	92.3	1.4	2.5	0.4	3.4
Drop-out Rate (%)	0.2	0.3	0.0	0.0	0.0	0.0
H.S. Diplomas (#)	286	270	5	6	0	5

New Canaan SD

39 Locust Ave • New Canaan, CT 06840-4723
(203) 972-4400 • http://www.newcanaan.k12.ct.us/
Grade Span: PK-12; **Agency Type:** 1
Schools: 6
3 Primary; 1 Middle; 1 High; 1 Other Level
5 Regular; 0 Special Education; 0 Vocational; 1 Alternative
0 Magnet; 0 Charter; 1 Title I Eligible; 0 School-wide Title I
Students: 3,951 (51.4% male; 48.6% female)
Individual Education Program: 390 (9.9%);
English Language Learner: 25 (0.6%); Migrant: 0 (0.0%)
Eligible for Free Lunch Program: n/a
Eligible for Reduced-Price Lunch Program: n/a
Teachers: 308.9 (12.8 to 1)
Librarians/Media Specialists: 6.8 (581.0 to 1)
Guidance Counselors: 11.0 (359.2 to 1)
Current Spending: ($ per student per year):
Total: $11,389; Instruction: $7,124; Support Services: $3,805

Enrollment, Drop-out Rates and Diploma Recipients by Race/Ethnicity

Category	Total	White	Black	Asian	AIAN	Hisp.
Enrollment (%)	100.0	95.1	0.8	2.7	0.0	1.4
Drop-out Rate (%)	0.0	0.0	0.0	0.0	n/a	0.0
H.S. Diplomas (#)	233	219	1	9	0	4

New Fairfield SD

3 Brush Hill Rd • New Fairfield, CT 06812-2618
(203) 312-5770
Grade Span: PK-12; **Agency Type:** 1
Schools: 5
2 Primary; 1 Middle; 1 High; 1 Other Level
4 Regular; 0 Special Education; 0 Vocational; 1 Alternative
0 Magnet; 0 Charter; 0 Title I Eligible; 0 School-wide Title I
Students: 3,167 (50.9% male; 49.1% female)
Individual Education Program: 310 (9.8%);
English Language Learner: 0 (0.0%); Migrant: 0 (0.0%)
Eligible for Free Lunch Program: n/a
Eligible for Reduced-Price Lunch Program: n/a
Teachers: 209.9 (15.1 to 1)
Librarians/Media Specialists: 3.0 (1,055.7 to 1)
Guidance Counselors: 6.0 (527.8 to 1)
Current Spending: ($ per student per year):
Total: $8,322; Instruction: $5,348; Support Services: $2,628

Enrollment, Drop-out Rates and Diploma Recipients by Race/Ethnicity

Category	Total	White	Black	Asian	AIAN	Hisp.
Enrollment (%)	100.0	95.9	0.4	1.4	0.1	2.2
Drop-out Rate (%)	1.7	1.8	0.0	0.0	0.0	0.0
H.S. Diplomas (#)	197	184	1	7	0	5

Newtown SD

11 Queen St • Newtown, CT 06470-2151
(203) 426-7621 • http://www.newtown.k12.ct.us/
Grade Span: PK-12; **Agency Type:** 1
Schools: 7
4 Primary; 1 Middle; 1 High; 1 Other Level
6 Regular; 0 Special Education; 0 Vocational; 1 Alternative
0 Magnet; 0 Charter; 3 Title I Eligible; 0 School-wide Title I
Students: 5,196 (51.5% male; 48.5% female)
Individual Education Program: 557 (10.7%);
English Language Learner: 8 (0.2%); Migrant: 0 (0.0%)
Eligible for Free Lunch Program: n/a
Eligible for Reduced-Price Lunch Program: n/a
Teachers: 344.5 (15.1 to 1)
Librarians/Media Specialists: 8.0 (649.5 to 1)
Guidance Counselors: 9.6 (541.3 to 1)
Current Spending: ($ per student per year):
Total: $8,715; Instruction: $5,232; Support Services: $3,121

Enrollment, Drop-out Rates and Diploma Recipients by Race/Ethnicity

Category	Total	White	Black	Asian	AIAN	Hisp.
Enrollment (%)	100.0	94.9	0.9	2.0	0.0	2.2
Drop-out Rate (%)	0.6	0.6	0.0	0.0	n/a	0.0
H.S. Diplomas (#)	286	278	1	5	0	2

Norwalk SD

125 E Ave • Norwalk, CT 06852-6001
Mailing Address: 125 E Ave, Box 6001 • Norwalk, CT 06852-6001
(203) 854-4001 • http://www.norwalkpublicschools.org/
Grade Span: PK-12; **Agency Type:** 1
Schools: 20
12 Primary; 4 Middle; 3 High; 1 Other Level
18 Regular; 0 Special Education; 0 Vocational; 2 Alternative
0 Magnet; 0 Charter; 10 Title I Eligible; 0 School-wide Title I
Students: 11,086 (52.2% male; 47.8% female)
Individual Education Program: 1,218 (11.0%);
English Language Learner: 929 (8.4%); Migrant: 0 (0.0%)
Eligible for Free Lunch Program: n/a
Eligible for Reduced-Price Lunch Program: n/a
Teachers: 820.3 (13.5 to 1)
Librarians/Media Specialists: 4.0 (2,771.5 to 1)
Guidance Counselors: 27.0 (410.6 to 1)
Current Spending: ($ per student per year):
Total: $11,099; Instruction: $7,502; Support Services: $3,268

Enrollment, Drop-out Rates and Diploma Recipients by Race/Ethnicity

Category	Total	White	Black	Asian	AIAN	Hisp.
Enrollment (%)	100.0	46.5	26.0	3.9	0.1	23.5
Drop-out Rate (%)	3.3	2.4	5.2	2.5	0.0	3.1
H.S. Diplomas (#)	613	328	149	22	3	111

Ridgefield SD

70 Prospect St • Ridgefield, CT 06877-0629
Mailing Address: 70 Prospect St, Box 629 • Ridgefield, CT 06877-0629
(203) 431-2800 • http://www.ridgefield.org/
Grade Span: PK-12; **Agency Type:** 1
Schools: 9
5 Primary; 2 Middle; 1 High; 1 Other Level
8 Regular; 0 Special Education; 0 Vocational; 1 Alternative
0 Magnet; 0 Charter; 0 Title I Eligible; 0 School-wide Title I
Students: 5,360 (50.1% male; 49.9% female)
Individual Education Program: 543 (10.1%);
English Language Learner: 31 (0.6%); Migrant: 6 (0.1%)
Eligible for Free Lunch Program: n/a
Eligible for Reduced-Price Lunch Program: n/a
Teachers: 362.6 (14.8 to 1)
Librarians/Media Specialists: 10.2 (525.5 to 1)
Guidance Counselors: 14.1 (380.1 to 1)
Current Spending: ($ per student per year):
Total: $9,891; Instruction: $6,201; Support Services: $3,259

Enrollment, Drop-out Rates and Diploma Recipients by Race/Ethnicity

Category	Total	White	Black	Asian	AIAN	Hisp.
Enrollment (%)	100.0	93.6	0.7	3.1	0.0	2.6
Drop-out Rate (%)	0.8	0.7	0.0	0.0	0.0	4.8
H.S. Diplomas (#)	280	261	2	9	1	7

Shelton SD

124 Meadow St • Shelton, CT 06484-0846
Mailing Address: PO Box 846 • Shelton, CT 06484-0846
(203) 924-1023 • http://www.sheltonpublicschools.org/
Grade Span: PK-12; **Agency Type:** 1
Schools: 10
6 Primary; 1 Middle; 1 High; 2 Other Level
8 Regular; 1 Special Education; 0 Vocational; 1 Alternative
0 Magnet; 0 Charter; 2 Title I Eligible; 0 School-wide Title I
Students: 5,610 (52.4% male; 47.6% female)
Individual Education Program: 444 (7.9%);
English Language Learner: 94 (1.7%); Migrant: 0 (0.0%)
Eligible for Free Lunch Program: n/a
Eligible for Reduced-Price Lunch Program: n/a
Teachers: 367.2 (15.3 to 1)
Librarians/Media Specialists: 5.0 (1,122.0 to 1)
Guidance Counselors: 16.6 (338.0 to 1)
Current Spending: ($ per student per year):
Total: $9,061; Instruction: $5,564; Support Services: $3,170

Enrollment, Drop-out Rates and Diploma Recipients by Race/Ethnicity

Category	Total	White	Black	Asian	AIAN	Hisp.
Enrollment (%)	100.0	90.1	2.4	2.8	0.2	4.5
Drop-out Rate (%)	2.7	2.7	0.0	2.4	0.0	3.8
H.S. Diplomas (#)	344	304	8	14	0	18

Stamford SD

888 Washington Blvd • Stamford, CT 06901-9310
(203) 977-4543 • http://stamford.k12.ct.us/
Grade Span: PK-12; **Agency Type:** 1
Schools: 21
12 Primary; 5 Middle; 2 High; 2 Other Level
19 Regular; 1 Special Education; 0 Vocational; 1 Alternative
0 Magnet; 0 Charter; 11 Title I Eligible; 0 School-wide Title I
Students: 15,231 (51.6% male; 48.4% female)
Individual Education Program: 1,938 (12.7%);
English Language Learner: 1,759 (11.5%); Migrant: 0 (0.0%)
Eligible for Free Lunch Program: n/a
Eligible for Reduced-Price Lunch Program: n/a
Teachers: 1,235.8 (12.3 to 1)
Librarians/Media Specialists: 15.0 (1,015.4 to 1)
Guidance Counselors: 35.0 (435.2 to 1)
Current Spending: ($ per student per year):
Total: $11,427; Instruction: $7,185; Support Services: $4,008

Enrollment, Drop-out Rates and Diploma Recipients by Race/Ethnicity

Category	Total	White	Black	Asian	AIAN	Hisp.
Enrollment (%)	100.0	44.6	25.6	5.2	0.0	24.7
Drop-out Rate (%)	2.9	1.7	3.1	2.0	0.0	5.0
H.S. Diplomas (#)	795	370	259	38	0	128

Stratford SD

1000 E Broadway • Stratford, CT 06615-5911
(203) 385-4210 • http://www.stratford.k12.ct.us/
Grade Span: PK-12; **Agency Type:** 1
Schools: 14
9 Primary; 2 Middle; 2 High; 1 Other Level
13 Regular; 0 Special Education; 0 Vocational; 1 Alternative
0 Magnet; 0 Charter; 3 Title I Eligible; 0 School-wide Title I
Students: 7,593 (50.4% male; 49.6% female)
Individual Education Program: 870 (11.5%);
English Language Learner: 120 (1.6%); Migrant: 6 (0.1%)
Eligible for Free Lunch Program: n/a
Eligible for Reduced-Price Lunch Program: n/a
Teachers: 527.8 (14.4 to 1)
Librarians/Media Specialists: 14.0 (542.4 to 1)
Guidance Counselors: 15.0 (506.2 to 1)
Current Spending: ($ per student per year):
Total: $9,081; Instruction: $5,517; Support Services: $3,144

Enrollment, Drop-out Rates and Diploma Recipients by Race/Ethnicity

Category	Total	White	Black	Asian	AIAN	Hisp.
Enrollment (%)	100.0	65.5	20.0	2.5	0.4	11.7
Drop-out Rate (%)	3.5	2.6	6.1	3.6	33.3	5.0
H.S. Diplomas (#)	470	320	83	11	4	52

Trumbull SD

6254 Main St • Trumbull, CT 06611-2052
(203) 452-4301 • http://www.trumbullps.org/index.asp
Grade Span: PK-12; **Agency Type:** 1
Schools: 10
6 Primary; 2 Middle; 1 High; 1 Other Level
9 Regular; 0 Special Education; 0 Vocational; 1 Alternative
0 Magnet; 0 Charter; 1 Title I Eligible; 0 School-wide Title I
Students: 6,368 (50.8% male; 49.2% female)
Individual Education Program: 585 (9.2%);
English Language Learner: 45 (0.7%); Migrant: 0 (0.0%)
Eligible for Free Lunch Program: n/a
Eligible for Reduced-Price Lunch Program: n/a
Teachers: 403.4 (15.8 to 1)
Librarians/Media Specialists: 9.0 (707.6 to 1)
Guidance Counselors: 17.0 (374.6 to 1)
Current Spending: ($ per student per year):
Total: $9,001; Instruction: $5,147; Support Services: $3,494

Enrollment, Drop-out Rates and Diploma Recipients by Race/Ethnicity

Category	Total	White	Black	Asian	AIAN	Hisp.
Enrollment (%)	100.0	89.2	3.3	3.8	0.2	3.4
Drop-out Rate (%)	0.8	0.5	1.8	4.0	0.0	5.9
H.S. Diplomas (#)	416	377	15	6	1	17

Weston SD

24 School Rd • Weston, CT 06883-1698
(203) 291-1401
Grade Span: PK-12; **Agency Type:** 1
Schools: 4
1 Primary; 1 Middle; 1 High; 1 Other Level
3 Regular; 0 Special Education; 0 Vocational; 1 Alternative
0 Magnet; 0 Charter; 0 Title I Eligible; 0 School-wide Title I
Students: 2,413 (49.6% male; 50.4% female)
Individual Education Program: 274 (11.4%);
English Language Learner: 10 (0.4%); Migrant: 0 (0.0%)
Eligible for Free Lunch Program: n/a
Eligible for Reduced-Price Lunch Program: n/a
Teachers: 198.4 (12.2 to 1)
Librarians/Media Specialists: 4.0 (603.3 to 1)
Guidance Counselors: 9.8 (246.2 to 1)
Current Spending: ($ per student per year):
Total: $12,729; Instruction: $7,581; Support Services: $4,464

Enrollment, Drop-out Rates and Diploma Recipients by Race/Ethnicity

Category	Total	White	Black	Asian	AIAN	Hisp.
Enrollment (%)	100.0	94.1	1.6	2.6	0.0	1.7
Drop-out Rate (%)	0.0	0.0	0.0	0.0	n/a	0.0
H.S. Diplomas (#)	135	125	2	3	0	5

Westport SD

110 Myrtle Ave • Westport, CT 06880-3513
(203) 341-1025 • http://teachers.westport.k12.ct.us/westportk12ctu/
Grade Span: PK-12; **Agency Type:** 1
Schools: 9
5 Primary; 2 Middle; 1 High; 1 Other Level
7 Regular; 1 Special Education; 0 Vocational; 1 Alternative
0 Magnet; 0 Charter; 2 Title I Eligible; 0 School-wide Title I
Students: 5,123 (50.9% male; 49.1% female)
Individual Education Program: 566 (11.0%);
English Language Learner: 93 (1.8%); Migrant: 0 (0.0%)
Eligible for Free Lunch Program: n/a
Eligible for Reduced-Price Lunch Program: n/a
Teachers: 434.0 (11.8 to 1)
Librarians/Media Specialists: 9.0 (569.2 to 1)
Guidance Counselors: 12.4 (413.1 to 1)
Current Spending: ($ per student per year):
Total: $12,769; Instruction: $7,533; Support Services: $4,753

Enrollment, Drop-out Rates and Diploma Recipients by Race/Ethnicity

Category	Total	White	Black	Asian	AIAN	Hisp.
Enrollment (%)	100.0	92.9	1.4	3.2	0.1	2.5
Drop-out Rate (%)	0.5	0.6	0.0	0.0	0.0	0.0
H.S. Diplomas (#)	255	231	9	8	0	7

Wilton SD

395 Danbury Rd • Wilton, CT 06897-0277
Mailing Address: 395 Danbury Rd, Box 277 • Wilton, CT 06897-0277
(203) 762-3381 • http://www.wilton.k12.ct.us/
Grade Span: PK-12; **Agency Type:** 1
Schools: 6
3 Primary; 1 Middle; 1 High; 1 Other Level
5 Regular; 0 Special Education; 0 Vocational; 1 Alternative
0 Magnet; 0 Charter; 2 Title I Eligible; 0 School-wide Title I
Students: 4,084 (53.6% male; 46.4% female)
Individual Education Program: 488 (11.9%);
English Language Learner: 2 (<0.1%); Migrant: 0 (0.0%)
Eligible for Free Lunch Program: n/a
Eligible for Reduced-Price Lunch Program: n/a
Teachers: 295.8 (13.8 to 1)
Librarians/Media Specialists: 9.0 (453.8 to 1)
Guidance Counselors: 11.2 (364.6 to 1)
Current Spending: ($ per student per year):
Total: $10,476; Instruction: $6,085; Support Services: $3,916

Enrollment, Drop-out Rates and Diploma Recipients by Race/Ethnicity

Category	Total	White	Black	Asian	AIAN	Hisp.
Enrollment (%)	100.0	95.2	0.6	2.8	0.2	1.2
Drop-out Rate (%)	0.4	0.5	0.0	0.0	n/a	0.0
H.S. Diplomas (#)	230	210	2	13	0	5

Hartford County

Avon SD

34 Simsbury Rd • Avon, CT 06001-3730
(860) 678-0482 • http://www.avon.k12.ct.us/
Grade Span: PK-12; **Agency Type:** 1
Schools: 6
2 Primary; 2 Middle; 1 High; 1 Other Level
5 Regular; 0 Special Education; 0 Vocational; 1 Alternative
0 Magnet; 0 Charter; 0 Title I Eligible; 0 School-wide Title I
Students: 3,090 (49.7% male; 50.3% female)
Individual Education Program: 290 (9.4%);
English Language Learner: 13 (0.4%); Migrant: 0 (0.0%)
Eligible for Free Lunch Program: n/a
Eligible for Reduced-Price Lunch Program: n/a
Teachers: 213.9 (14.4 to 1)
Librarians/Media Specialists: 4.1 (753.7 to 1)
Guidance Counselors: 8.6 (359.3 to 1)
Current Spending: ($ per student per year):
Total: $9,249; Instruction: $5,875; Support Services: $3,050

Enrollment, Drop-out Rates and Diploma Recipients by Race/Ethnicity

Category	Total	White	Black	Asian	AIAN	Hisp.
Enrollment (%)	100.0	90.6	2.3	5.3	0.0	1.8
Drop-out Rate (%)	0.0	0.0	0.0	0.0	n/a	0.0
H.S. Diplomas (#)	181	160	5	13	0	3

Berlin SD

240 Kensington Rd • Berlin, CT 06037-2648
(860) 828-6581 • http://www.berlinschools.org/
Grade Span: PK-12; **Agency Type:** 1
Schools: 6
3 Primary; 1 Middle; 1 High; 1 Other Level
5 Regular; 0 Special Education; 0 Vocational; 1 Alternative
0 Magnet; 0 Charter; 1 Title I Eligible; 0 School-wide Title I
Students: 3,271 (51.7% male; 48.3% female)
Individual Education Program: 407 (12.4%);
English Language Learner: 59 (1.8%); Migrant: 0 (0.0%)
Eligible for Free Lunch Program: n/a
Eligible for Reduced-Price Lunch Program: n/a
Teachers: 230.4 (14.2 to 1)
Librarians/Media Specialists: 5.0 (654.2 to 1)
Guidance Counselors: 8.3 (394.1 to 1)
Current Spending: ($ per student per year):
Total: $8,931; Instruction: $5,175; Support Services: $3,318
Enrollment, Drop-out Rates and Diploma Recipients by Race/Ethnicity

Category	Total	White	Black	Asian	AIAN	Hisp.
Enrollment (%)	100.0	95.0	0.7	3.0	0.2	1.1
Drop-out Rate (%)	1.8	1.8	0.0	0.0	0.0	11.1
H.S. Diplomas (#)	247	236	1	8	0	2

Bloomfield SD

1133 Blue Hills Ave • Bloomfield, CT 06002-2721
(860) 769-4212 • http://www.blmfld.org/
Grade Span: PK-12; **Agency Type:** 1
Schools: 6
3 Primary; 0 Middle; 1 High; 2 Other Level
5 Regular; 0 Special Education; 0 Vocational; 1 Alternative
0 Magnet; 0 Charter; 3 Title I Eligible; 0 School-wide Title I
Students: 2,512 (52.8% male; 47.2% female)
Individual Education Program: 326 (13.0%);
English Language Learner: 4 (0.2%); Migrant: 0 (0.0%)
Eligible for Free Lunch Program: n/a
Eligible for Reduced-Price Lunch Program: n/a
Teachers: 203.2 (12.4 to 1)
Librarians/Media Specialists: 2.0 (1,256.0 to 1)
Guidance Counselors: 6.0 (418.7 to 1)
Current Spending: ($ per student per year):
Total: $11,320; Instruction: $6,973; Support Services: $3,796
Enrollment, Drop-out Rates and Diploma Recipients by Race/Ethnicity

Category	Total	White	Black	Asian	AIAN	Hisp.
Enrollment (%)	100.0	5.0	88.8	1.0	0.0	5.2
Drop-out Rate (%)	2.4	0.0	2.5	0.0	n/a	4.0
H.S. Diplomas (#)	173	10	157	1	0	5

Bristol SD

129 Church St • Bristol, CT 06011-0450
(860) 584-7700 •
http://www.bristol.k12.ct.us/directory_of_services/technology_in_schools /
Grade Span: PK-12; **Agency Type:** 1
Schools: 16
10 Primary; 3 Middle; 2 High; 1 Other Level
15 Regular; 0 Special Education; 0 Vocational; 1 Alternative
0 Magnet; 0 Charter; 4 Title I Eligible; 1 School-wide Title I
Students: 8,970 (51.8% male; 48.2% female)
Individual Education Program: 1,185 (13.2%);
English Language Learner: 215 (2.4%); Migrant: 0 (0.0%)
Eligible for Free Lunch Program: n/a
Eligible for Reduced-Price Lunch Program: n/a
Teachers: 609.6 (14.7 to 1)
Librarians/Media Specialists: 5.8 (1,546.6 to 1)
Guidance Counselors: 19.3 (464.8 to 1)
Current Spending: ($ per student per year):
Total: $8,552; Instruction: $5,740; Support Services: $2,459
Enrollment, Drop-out Rates and Diploma Recipients by Race/Ethnicity

Category	Total	White	Black	Asian	AIAN	Hisp.
Enrollment (%)	100.0	80.3	6.8	2.2	0.2	10.5
Drop-out Rate (%)	2.7	2.5	2.5	0.0	0.0	6.8
H.S. Diplomas (#)	558	485	34	10	0	29

Canton SD

39 Dyer Ave • Collinsville, CT 06022-1008
(860) 693-7704 • http://www.pccs.k12.mi.us/
Grade Span: PK-12; **Agency Type:** 1
Schools: 4
1 Primary; 1 Middle; 1 High; 1 Other Level
3 Regular; 0 Special Education; 0 Vocational; 1 Alternative
0 Magnet; 0 Charter; 3 Title I Eligible; 0 School-wide Title I
Students: 1,629 (52.5% male; 47.5% female)
Individual Education Program: 180 (11.0%);
English Language Learner: 2 (0.1%); Migrant: 0 (0.0%)
Eligible for Free Lunch Program: n/a
Eligible for Reduced-Price Lunch Program: n/a
Teachers: 111.8 (14.6 to 1)
Librarians/Media Specialists: 3.0 (543.0 to 1)
Guidance Counselors: 4.5 (362.0 to 1)
Current Spending: ($ per student per year):
Total: $9,111; Instruction: $5,923; Support Services: $2,941
Enrollment, Drop-out Rates and Diploma Recipients by Race/Ethnicity

Category	Total	White	Black	Asian	AIAN	Hisp.
Enrollment (%)	100.0	96.3	2.2	0.7	0.0	0.7
Drop-out Rate (%)	0.0	0.0	0.0	0.0	n/a	0.0
H.S. Diplomas (#)	100	90	4	3	0	3

Capitol Region Education Council

111 Charter Oak Ave • Hartford, CT 06106-3567
(860) 246-3380
Grade Span: PK-12; **Agency Type:** 4
Schools: 7
3 Primary; 1 Middle; 1 High; 2 Other Level
6 Regular; 1 Special Education; 0 Vocational; 0 Alternative
6 Magnet; 0 Charter; 0 Title I Eligible; 0 School-wide Title I
Students: 2,191 (53.2% male; 46.8% female)
Individual Education Program: 0 (0.0%);
English Language Learner: 6 (0.3%); Migrant: 0 (0.0%)
Eligible for Free Lunch Program: n/a
Eligible for Reduced-Price Lunch Program: n/a
Teachers: 202.4 (10.8 to 1)
Librarians/Media Specialists: 1.6 (1,369.4 to 1)
Guidance Counselors: 5.0 (438.2 to 1)
Current Spending: ($ per student per year):
Total: n/a; Instruction: n/a; Support Services: n/a
Enrollment, Drop-out Rates and Diploma Recipients by Race/Ethnicity

Category	Total	White	Black	Asian	AIAN	Hisp.
Enrollment (%)	100.0	43.8	37.3	3.0	0.5	15.5
Drop-out Rate (%)	4.6	5.8	3.0	0.0	n/a	2.8
H.S. Diplomas (#)	18	14	2	0	0	2

East Hartford SD

31 School St • East Hartford, CT 06108-2681
(860) 282-3107 • http://www.easthartford.org/
Grade Span: PK-12; **Agency Type:** 1
Schools: 15
9 Primary; 1 Middle; 2 High; 3 Other Level
13 Regular; 1 Special Education; 0 Vocational; 1 Alternative
0 Magnet; 0 Charter; 7 Title I Eligible; 0 School-wide Title I
Students: 7,859 (51.9% male; 48.1% female)
Individual Education Program: 1,157 (14.7%);
English Language Learner: 231 (2.9%); Migrant: 4 (0.1%)
Eligible for Free Lunch Program: n/a
Eligible for Reduced-Price Lunch Program: n/a
Teachers: 552.1 (14.2 to 1)
Librarians/Media Specialists: 4.0 (1,964.8 to 1)
Guidance Counselors: 13.0 (604.5 to 1)
Current Spending: ($ per student per year):
Total: $9,519; Instruction: $6,532; Support Services: $2,602
Enrollment, Drop-out Rates and Diploma Recipients by Race/Ethnicity

Category	Total	White	Black	Asian	AIAN	Hisp.
Enrollment (%)	100.0	33.4	33.5	4.5	0.4	28.2
Drop-out Rate (%)	2.6	2.6	2.7	1.6	n/a	2.9
H.S. Diplomas (#)	475	210	137	28	0	100

East Windsor SD

70 S Main St • East Windsor, CT 06088-9704
(860) 623-3346 • http://www.eastwindsorschools.org/
Grade Span: PK-12; **Agency Type:** 1
Schools: 4
1 Primary; 1 Middle; 1 High; 1 Other Level
3 Regular; 0 Special Education; 0 Vocational; 1 Alternative
0 Magnet; 0 Charter; 1 Title I Eligible; 0 School-wide Title I
Students: 1,579 (54.1% male; 45.9% female)
Individual Education Program: 193 (12.2%);
English Language Learner: 0 (0.0%); Migrant: 0 (0.0%)
Eligible for Free Lunch Program: n/a
Eligible for Reduced-Price Lunch Program: n/a
Teachers: 100.8 (15.7 to 1)
Librarians/Media Specialists: 1.0 (1,579.0 to 1)
Guidance Counselors: 3.0 (526.3 to 1)
Current Spending: ($ per student per year):
Total: $8,544; Instruction: $5,402; Support Services: $2,902

Enrollment, Drop-out Rates and Diploma Recipients by Race/Ethnicity

Category	Total	White	Black	Asian	AIAN	Hisp.
Enrollment (%)	100.0	82.0	9.6	3.0	0.2	5.2
Drop-out Rate (%)	2.3	2.3	0.0	0.0	0.0	6.3
H.S. Diplomas (#)	78	72	2	2	0	2

Enfield SD

27 Shaker Rd • Enfield, CT 06082-3199
(860) 253-6531 • http://www.enfieldschools.org/
Grade Span: PK-12; **Agency Type:** 1
Schools: 14
10 Primary; 1 Middle; 2 High; 1 Other Level
13 Regular; 0 Special Education; 0 Vocational; 1 Alternative
0 Magnet; 0 Charter; 2 Title I Eligible; 0 School-wide Title I
Students: 6,837 (50.6% male; 49.4% female)
Individual Education Program: 918 (13.4%);
English Language Learner: 61 (0.9%); Migrant: 0 (0.0%)
Eligible for Free Lunch Program: n/a
Eligible for Reduced-Price Lunch Program: n/a
Teachers: 512.6 (13.3 to 1)
Librarians/Media Specialists: 4.0 (1,709.3 to 1)
Guidance Counselors: 21.0 (325.6 to 1)
Current Spending: ($ per student per year):
Total: $9,350; Instruction: $6,057; Support Services: $2,968
Enrollment, Drop-out Rates and Diploma Recipients by Race/Ethnicity

Category	Total	White	Black	Asian	AIAN	Hisp.
Enrollment (%)	100.0	88.7	5.3	2.2	0.3	3.5
Drop-out Rate (%)	3.8	3.9	4.7	0.0	n/a	0.0
H.S. Diplomas (#)	448	413	13	12	1	9

Farmington SD

One Monteith Dr • Farmington, CT 06032-1041
(860) 673-8268 • http://www.fpsct.org/
Grade Span: PK-12; **Agency Type:** 1
Schools: 8
4 Primary; 2 Middle; 1 High; 1 Other Level
7 Regular; 0 Special Education; 0 Vocational; 1 Alternative
0 Magnet; 0 Charter; 2 Title I Eligible; 0 School-wide Title I
Students: 4,206 (51.6% male; 48.4% female)
Individual Education Program: 372 (8.8%);
English Language Learner: 31 (0.7%); Migrant: 0 (0.0%)
Eligible for Free Lunch Program: n/a
Eligible for Reduced-Price Lunch Program: n/a
Teachers: 310.2 (13.6 to 1)
Librarians/Media Specialists: 7.4 (568.4 to 1)
Guidance Counselors: 10.9 (385.9 to 1)
Current Spending: ($ per student per year):
Total: $9,102; Instruction: $5,489; Support Services: $3,207
Enrollment, Drop-out Rates and Diploma Recipients by Race/Ethnicity

Category	Total	White	Black	Asian	AIAN	Hisp.
Enrollment (%)	100.0	86.8	4.5	5.4	0.6	2.7
Drop-out Rate (%)	1.4	1.2	2.3	0.0	0.0	14.3
H.S. Diplomas (#)	280	249	8	18	0	5

Glastonbury SD

232 Williams St • Glastonbury, CT 06033-2354
(860) 652-7961 • http://www.glastonburyus.org/
Grade Span: PK-12; **Agency Type:** 1
Schools: 9
5 Primary; 2 Middle; 1 High; 1 Other Level
8 Regular; 0 Special Education; 0 Vocational; 1 Alternative
0 Magnet; 0 Charter; 3 Title I Eligible; 0 School-wide Title I
Students: 6,413 (49.8% male; 50.2% female)
Individual Education Program: 846 (13.2%);
English Language Learner: 160 (2.5%); Migrant: 0 (0.0%)
Eligible for Free Lunch Program: n/a
Eligible for Reduced-Price Lunch Program: n/a
Teachers: 450.3 (14.2 to 1)
Librarians/Media Specialists: 9.0 (712.6 to 1)
Guidance Counselors: 16.0 (400.8 to 1)
Current Spending: ($ per student per year):
Total: $8,346; Instruction: $5,149; Support Services: $2,865
Enrollment, Drop-out Rates and Diploma Recipients by Race/Ethnicity

Category	Total	White	Black	Asian	AIAN	Hisp.
Enrollment (%)	100.0	89.1	2.6	5.0	0.1	3.2
Drop-out Rate (%)	0.5	0.5	0.0	0.0	0.0	1.6
H.S. Diplomas (#)	414	366	12	24	1	11

Granby SD

11 N Granby Rd • Granby, CT 06035-9449
(860) 844-6075 • http://www.granby.k12.ct.us/
Grade Span: KG-12; **Agency Type:** 1
Schools: 6
3 Primary; 1 Middle; 1 High; 1 Other Level
5 Regular; 0 Special Education; 0 Vocational; 1 Alternative
0 Magnet; 0 Charter; 0 Title I Eligible; 0 School-wide Title I
Students: 2,151 (51.4% male; 48.6% female)
Individual Education Program: 210 (9.8%);
English Language Learner: 6 (0.3%); Migrant: 0 (0.0%)
Eligible for Free Lunch Program: n/a
Eligible for Reduced-Price Lunch Program: n/a
Teachers: 133.5 (16.1 to 1)
Librarians/Media Specialists: 2.0 (1,075.5 to 1)
Guidance Counselors: 5.8 (370.9 to 1)
Current Spending: ($ per student per year):
Total: $8,412; Instruction: $5,254; Support Services: $2,968
Enrollment, Drop-out Rates and Diploma Recipients by Race/Ethnicity

Category	Total	White	Black	Asian	AIAN	Hisp.
Enrollment (%)	100.0	98.1	0.7	0.6	0.0	0.6
Drop-out Rate (%)	1.1	1.1	0.0	0.0	n/a	0.0
H.S. Diplomas (#)	125	121	2	1	0	1

Hartford SD

153 Market St • Hartford, CT 06103-1325
(860) 297-8401 • http://www.hartfordschools.org/
Grade Span: PK-12; **Agency Type:** 1
Schools: 38
28 Primary; 4 Middle; 4 High; 2 Other Level
36 Regular; 2 Special Education; 0 Vocational; 0 Alternative
3 Magnet; 0 Charter; 33 Title I Eligible; 33 School-wide Title I
Students: 22,734 (51.0% male; 49.0% female)
Individual Education Program: 3,855 (17.0%);
English Language Learner: 3,055 (13.4%); Migrant: 1,319 (5.8%)
Eligible for Free Lunch Program: n/a
Eligible for Reduced-Price Lunch Program: n/a
Teachers: 1,837.3 (12.4 to 1)
Librarians/Media Specialists: 37.0 (614.4 to 1)
Guidance Counselors: 46.0 (494.2 to 1)
Current Spending: ($ per student per year):
Total: $13,577; Instruction: $8,615; Support Services: $4,545
Enrollment, Drop-out Rates and Diploma Recipients by Race/Ethnicity

Category	Total	White	Black	Asian	AIAN	Hisp.
Enrollment (%)	100.0	4.7	40.2	0.8	0.1	54.2
Drop-out Rate (%)	11.5	6.7	11.1	20.5	0.0	12.7
H.S. Diplomas (#)	785	56	367	59	0	303

Manchester SD

45 N School St • Manchester, CT 06040-2022
(860) 647-3441
Grade Span: PK-12; **Agency Type:** 1
Schools: 17
11 Primary; 2 Middle; 2 High; 2 Other Level
15 Regular; 1 Special Education; 0 Vocational; 1 Alternative
1 Magnet; 0 Charter; 6 Title I Eligible; 0 School-wide Title I
Students: 7,715 (51.2% male; 48.8% female)
Individual Education Program: 1,059 (13.7%);
English Language Learner: 103 (1.3%); Migrant: 6 (0.1%)
Eligible for Free Lunch Program: n/a
Eligible for Reduced-Price Lunch Program: n/a
Teachers: 550.3 (14.0 to 1)
Librarians/Media Specialists: 8.8 (876.7 to 1)
Guidance Counselors: 17.0 (453.8 to 1)
Current Spending: ($ per student per year):
Total: $9,941; Instruction: $6,371; Support Services: $3,173
Enrollment, Drop-out Rates and Diploma Recipients by Race/Ethnicity

Category	Total	White	Black	Asian	AIAN	Hisp.
Enrollment (%)	100.0	61.7	18.9	4.6	0.3	14.5
Drop-out Rate (%)	2.1	2.0	2.5	0.0	0.0	2.2
H.S. Diplomas (#)	408	295	55	18	0	40

New Britain SD

One Liberty Square • New Britain, CT 06050-1960
(860) 827-2204
Grade Span: PK-12; **Agency Type:** 1
Schools: 16
11 Primary; 3 Middle; 1 High; 1 Other Level
15 Regular; 0 Special Education; 0 Vocational; 1 Alternative
0 Magnet; 0 Charter; 13 Title I Eligible; 0 School-wide Title I
Students: 10,658 (50.6% male; 49.4% female)
Individual Education Program: 2,067 (19.4%);
English Language Learner: 1,217 (11.4%); Migrant: 166 (1.6%)
Eligible for Free Lunch Program: n/a
Eligible for Reduced-Price Lunch Program: n/a
Teachers: 720.7 (14.8 to 1)
Librarians/Media Specialists: 11.0 (968.9 to 1)
Guidance Counselors: 19.5 (546.6 to 1)
Current Spending: ($ per student per year):
Total: $9,637; Instruction: $6,562; Support Services: $2,752

Enrollment, Drop-out Rates and Diploma Recipients by Race/Ethnicity

Category	Total	White	Black	Asian	AIAN	Hisp.
Enrollment (%)	100.0	29.8	17.5	2.3	0.2	50.2
Drop-out Rate (%)	8.8	4.1	8.5	11.0	0.0	14.0
H.S. Diplomas (#)	445	232	83	13	0	117

Newington SD

131 Cedar St • Newington, CT 06111-2698
(860) 665-8610 • http://www.newington-schools.org/
Grade Span: PK-12; **Agency Type:** 1
Schools: 8
4 Primary; 2 Middle; 1 High; 1 Other Level
7 Regular; 0 Special Education; 0 Vocational; 1 Alternative
0 Magnet; 0 Charter; 0 Title I Eligible; 0 School-wide Title I
Students: 4,616 (52.4% male; 47.6% female)
Individual Education Program: 423 (9.2%);
English Language Learner: 71 (1.5%); Migrant: 0 (0.0%)
Eligible for Free Lunch Program: n/a
Eligible for Reduced-Price Lunch Program: n/a
Teachers: 291.6 (15.8 to 1)
Librarians/Media Specialists: 8.0 (577.0 to 1)
Guidance Counselors: 10.4 (443.8 to 1)
Current Spending: ($ per student per year):
Total: $8,796; Instruction: $5,513; Support Services: $2,957
Enrollment, Drop-out Rates and Diploma Recipients by Race/Ethnicity

Category	Total	White	Black	Asian	AIAN	Hisp.
Enrollment (%)	100.0	83.7	4.3	5.5	0.2	6.3
Drop-out Rate (%)	0.4	0.4	0.0	0.0	n/a	0.0
H.S. Diplomas (#)	268	239	11	13	0	5

Plainville SD

47 Robert Holcomb Way • Plainville, CT 06062-2398
(860) 793-3202 • http://www.plainvilleschools.org/
Grade Span: PK-12; **Agency Type:** 1
Schools: 7
4 Primary; 1 Middle; 1 High; 1 Other Level
6 Regular; 0 Special Education; 0 Vocational; 1 Alternative
0 Magnet; 0 Charter; 2 Title I Eligible; 0 School-wide Title I
Students: 2,660 (50.3% male; 49.7% female)
Individual Education Program: 310 (11.7%);
English Language Learner: 36 (1.4%); Migrant: 0 (0.0%)
Eligible for Free Lunch Program: n/a
Eligible for Reduced-Price Lunch Program: n/a
Teachers: 182.7 (14.6 to 1)
Librarians/Media Specialists: 5.0 (532.0 to 1)
Guidance Counselors: 8.0 (332.5 to 1)
Current Spending: ($ per student per year):
Total: $9,560; Instruction: $5,982; Support Services: $3,204
Enrollment, Drop-out Rates and Diploma Recipients by Race/Ethnicity

Category	Total	White	Black	Asian	AIAN	Hisp.
Enrollment (%)	100.0	87.8	5.8	2.1	0.3	4.0
Drop-out Rate (%)	0.8	0.7	0.0	0.0	0.0	3.2
H.S. Diplomas (#)	188	171	7	4	0	6

Regional SD 10

24 Lyon Rd • Burlington, CT 06013-1313
(860) 673-2538 • http://users.ntplx.net/~region10/
Grade Span: PK-12; **Agency Type:** 1
Schools: 5
2 Primary; 1 Middle; 1 High; 1 Other Level
4 Regular; 0 Special Education; 0 Vocational; 1 Alternative
0 Magnet; 0 Charter; 0 Title I Eligible; 0 School-wide Title I
Students: 2,609 (50.3% male; 49.7% female)
Individual Education Program: 257 (9.9%);
English Language Learner: 0 (0.0%); Migrant: 0 (0.0%)
Eligible for Free Lunch Program: n/a
Eligible for Reduced-Price Lunch Program: n/a
Teachers: 193.6 (13.5 to 1)
Librarians/Media Specialists: 3.0 (869.7 to 1)
Guidance Counselors: 7.0 (372.7 to 1)
Current Spending: ($ per student per year):
Total: $8,986; Instruction: $5,381; Support Services: $3,429
Enrollment, Drop-out Rates and Diploma Recipients by Race/Ethnicity

Category	Total	White	Black	Asian	AIAN	Hisp.
Enrollment (%)	100.0	96.8	0.4	1.1	0.3	1.4
Drop-out Rate (%)	0.4	0.5	0.0	0.0	n/a	0.0
H.S. Diplomas (#)	162	157	0	2	0	3

Rocky Hill SD

Church St • Rocky Hill, CT 06067-0627
(860) 258-7701 • http://www.rockyhillps.us/
Grade Span: PK-12; **Agency Type:** 1
Schools: 6
3 Primary; 1 Middle; 1 High; 1 Other Level
5 Regular; 0 Special Education; 0 Vocational; 1 Alternative
0 Magnet; 0 Charter; 3 Title I Eligible; 0 School-wide Title I
Students: 2,483 (50.7% male; 49.3% female)
Individual Education Program: 266 (10.7%);
English Language Learner: 63 (2.5%); Migrant: 0 (0.0%)
Eligible for Free Lunch Program: n/a
Eligible for Reduced-Price Lunch Program: n/a
Teachers: 184.9 (13.4 to 1)
Librarians/Media Specialists: 4.0 (620.8 to 1)
Guidance Counselors: 5.0 (496.6 to 1)
Current Spending: ($ per student per year):
Total: $9,494; Instruction: $6,514; Support Services: $2,731
Enrollment, Drop-out Rates and Diploma Recipients by Race/Ethnicity

Category	Total	White	Black	Asian	AIAN	Hisp.
Enrollment (%)	100.0	85.7	4.3	5.7	0.1	4.2
Drop-out Rate (%)	1.7	1.7	0.0	0.0	n/a	4.8
H.S. Diplomas (#)	143	128	6	6	0	3

Simsbury SD

933 Hopmeadow St • Simsbury, CT 06070-1897
(860) 651-3361 • http://www.simsbury.k12.ct.us/
Grade Span: PK-12; **Agency Type:** 1
Schools: 8
5 Primary; 1 Middle; 1 High; 1 Other Level
7 Regular; 0 Special Education; 0 Vocational; 1 Alternative
0 Magnet; 0 Charter; 0 Title I Eligible; 0 School-wide Title I
Students: 5,030 (53.5% male; 46.5% female)
Individual Education Program: 716 (14.2%);
English Language Learner: 30 (0.6%); Migrant: 0 (0.0%)
Eligible for Free Lunch Program: n/a
Eligible for Reduced-Price Lunch Program: n/a
Teachers: 343.6 (14.6 to 1)
Librarians/Media Specialists: 6.6 (762.1 to 1)
Guidance Counselors: 10.5 (479.0 to 1)
Current Spending: ($ per student per year):
Total: $8,744; Instruction: $5,682; Support Services: $2,800
Enrollment, Drop-out Rates and Diploma Recipients by Race/Ethnicity

Category	Total	White	Black	Asian	AIAN	Hisp.
Enrollment (%)	100.0	93.0	2.6	2.8	0.1	1.5
Drop-out Rate (%)	0.9	0.7	4.1	5.0	n/a	0.0
H.S. Diplomas (#)	346	330	5	8	0	3

South Windsor SD

1737 Main St • South Windsor, CT 06074-1093
(860) 291-1205 • http://www.swindsor.k12.ct.us/
Grade Span: PK-12; **Agency Type:** 1
Schools: 8
5 Primary; 1 Middle; 1 High; 1 Other Level
7 Regular; 0 Special Education; 0 Vocational; 1 Alternative
0 Magnet; 0 Charter; 0 Title I Eligible; 0 School-wide Title I
Students: 5,074 (50.9% male; 49.1% female)
Individual Education Program: 617 (12.2%);
English Language Learner: 64 (1.3%); Migrant: 0 (0.0%)
Eligible for Free Lunch Program: n/a
Eligible for Reduced-Price Lunch Program: n/a
Teachers: 333.7 (15.2 to 1)
Librarians/Media Specialists: 2.0 (2,537.0 to 1)
Guidance Counselors: 12.0 (422.8 to 1)
Current Spending: ($ per student per year):
Total: $8,531; Instruction: $5,338; Support Services: $2,739
Enrollment, Drop-out Rates and Diploma Recipients by Race/Ethnicity

Category	Total	White	Black	Asian	AIAN	Hisp.
Enrollment (%)	100.0	86.2	4.8	5.5	0.4	3.1
Drop-out Rate (%)	1.6	1.4	0.0	2.1	0.0	15.0
H.S. Diplomas (#)	317	285	14	11	0	7

Southington SD

49 Beecher St • Southington, CT 06489-3097
(860) 628-3202 • http://www.southingtonschools.org/
Grade Span: PK-12; **Agency Type:** 1
Schools: 13
9 Primary; 2 Middle; 1 High; 1 Other Level
12 Regular; 0 Special Education; 0 Vocational; 1 Alternative
0 Magnet; 0 Charter; 3 Title I Eligible; 0 School-wide Title I
Students: 6,679 (51.4% male; 48.6% female)
Individual Education Program: 819 (12.3%);
English Language Learner: 42 (0.6%); Migrant: 0 (0.0%)
Eligible for Free Lunch Program: n/a
Eligible for Reduced-Price Lunch Program: n/a
Teachers: 495.2 (13.5 to 1)
Librarians/Media Specialists: 10.0 (667.9 to 1)
Guidance Counselors: 20.1 (332.3 to 1)
Current Spending: ($ per student per year):
Total: $9,172; Instruction: $5,815; Support Services: $3,074

Enrollment, Drop-out Rates and Diploma Recipients by Race/Ethnicity

Category	Total	White	Black	Asian	AIAN	Hisp.
Enrollment (%)	100.0	93.7	1.1	1.7	0.3	3.1
Drop-out Rate (%)	1.8	1.9	0.0	0.0	0.0	1.9
H.S. Diplomas (#)	479	445	8	10	2	14

Suffield SD

350 Mountain Rd • Suffield, CT 06078-2085
(860) 668-3800 • http://www.suffield.org/
Grade Span: PK-12; **Agency Type:** 1
Schools: 6
3 Primary; 1 Middle; 1 High; 1 Other Level
5 Regular; 0 Special Education; 0 Vocational; 1 Alternative
0 Magnet; 0 Charter; 2 Title I Eligible; 0 School-wide Title I
Students: 2,321 (50.2% male; 49.8% female)
Individual Education Program: 230 (9.9%);
English Language Learner: 8 (0.3%); Migrant: 0 (0.0%)
Eligible for Free Lunch Program: n/a
Eligible for Reduced-Price Lunch Program: n/a
Teachers: 163.5 (14.2 to 1)
Librarians/Media Specialists: 3.0 (773.7 to 1)
Guidance Counselors: 5.0 (464.2 to 1)
Current Spending: ($ per student per year):
Total: $7,933; Instruction: $5,492; Support Services: $2,358
Enrollment, Drop-out Rates and Diploma Recipients by Race/Ethnicity

Category	Total	White	Black	Asian	AIAN	Hisp.
Enrollment (%)	100.0	95.5	2.5	0.7	0.2	1.1
Drop-out Rate (%)	1.0	0.8	0.0	0.0	n/a	50.0
H.S. Diplomas (#)	144	139	4	1	0	0

West Hartford SD

28 S Main St • West Hartford, CT 06107-2447
(860) 523-3500 • http://www.whps.org/
Grade Span: PK-12; **Agency Type:** 1
Schools: 16
11 Primary; 2 Middle; 2 High; 1 Other Level
15 Regular; 0 Special Education; 0 Vocational; 1 Alternative
0 Magnet; 0 Charter; 7 Title I Eligible; 0 School-wide Title I
Students: 9,626 (50.4% male; 49.6% female)
Individual Education Program: 1,337 (13.9%);
English Language Learner: 462 (4.8%); Migrant: 6 (0.1%)
Eligible for Free Lunch Program: n/a
Eligible for Reduced-Price Lunch Program: n/a
Teachers: 749.6 (12.8 to 1)
Librarians/Media Specialists: 16.0 (601.6 to 1)
Guidance Counselors: 24.0 (401.1 to 1)
Current Spending: ($ per student per year):
Total: $9,373; Instruction: $5,654; Support Services: $3,317
Enrollment, Drop-out Rates and Diploma Recipients by Race/Ethnicity

Category	Total	White	Black	Asian	AIAN	Hisp.
Enrollment (%)	100.0	70.0	9.4	8.3	0.2	12.1
Drop-out Rate (%)	2.2	1.4	5.3	2.9	0.0	4.6
H.S. Diplomas (#)	668	484	61	57	1	65

Wethersfield SD

51 Willow St • Wethersfield, CT 06109-2798
(860) 571-8110 • http://www.wethersfield.k12.ct.us/
Grade Span: PK-12; **Agency Type:** 1
Schools: 8
5 Primary; 1 Middle; 1 High; 1 Other Level
7 Regular; 0 Special Education; 0 Vocational; 1 Alternative
0 Magnet; 0 Charter; 3 Title I Eligible; 0 School-wide Title I
Students: 3,595 (51.6% male; 48.4% female)
Individual Education Program: 476 (13.2%);
English Language Learner: 177 (4.9%); Migrant: 0 (0.0%)
Eligible for Free Lunch Program: n/a
Eligible for Reduced-Price Lunch Program: n/a
Teachers: 240.2 (15.0 to 1)
Librarians/Media Specialists: 2.0 (1,797.5 to 1)
Guidance Counselors: 7.0 (513.6 to 1)
Current Spending: ($ per student per year):
Total: $9,383; Instruction: $5,980; Support Services: $2,944
Enrollment, Drop-out Rates and Diploma Recipients by Race/Ethnicity

Category	Total	White	Black	Asian	AIAN	Hisp.
Enrollment (%)	100.0	84.7	3.9	2.8	0.1	8.5
Drop-out Rate (%)	2.3	2.3	0.0	0.0	n/a	4.0
H.S. Diplomas (#)	241	205	13	9	0	14

Windsor Locks SD

58 S Elm St • Windsor Locks, CT 06096-2399
(860) 292-5000
Grade Span: PK-12; **Agency Type:** 1
Schools: 5
2 Primary; 1 Middle; 1 High; 1 Other Level
4 Regular; 0 Special Education; 0 Vocational; 1 Alternative
0 Magnet; 0 Charter; 2 Title I Eligible; 0 School-wide Title I
Students: 1,963 (50.1% male; 49.9% female)
Individual Education Program: 284 (14.5%);
English Language Learner: 44 (2.2%); Migrant: 0 (0.0%)
Eligible for Free Lunch Program: n/a
Eligible for Reduced-Price Lunch Program: n/a
Teachers: 163.5 (12.0 to 1)
Librarians/Media Specialists: 4.0 (490.8 to 1)
Guidance Counselors: 5.5 (356.9 to 1)
Current Spending: ($ per student per year):
Total: $9,027; Instruction: $5,702; Support Services: $2,919
Enrollment, Drop-out Rates and Diploma Recipients by Race/Ethnicity

Category	Total	White	Black	Asian	AIAN	Hisp.
Enrollment (%)	100.0	87.1	5.0	5.2	0.1	2.6
Drop-out Rate (%)	6.1	6.4	4.5	0.0	0.0	8.7
H.S. Diplomas (#)	128	109	6	4	1	8

Windsor SD

601 Matianuk Ave • Windsor, CT 06095-0010
(860) 687-2000 • http://www.windsorct.org/
Grade Span: PK-12; **Agency Type:** 1
Schools: 8
5 Primary; 1 Middle; 1 High; 1 Other Level
7 Regular; 0 Special Education; 0 Vocational; 1 Alternative
0 Magnet; 0 Charter; 3 Title I Eligible; 0 School-wide Title I
Students: 4,432 (51.1% male; 48.9% female)
Individual Education Program: 644 (14.5%);
English Language Learner: 53 (1.2%); Migrant: 0 (0.0%)
Eligible for Free Lunch Program: n/a
Eligible for Reduced-Price Lunch Program: n/a
Teachers: 354.7 (12.5 to 1)
Librarians/Media Specialists: 7.0 (633.1 to 1)
Guidance Counselors: 10.0 (443.2 to 1)
Current Spending: ($ per student per year):
Total: $9,343; Instruction: $5,673; Support Services: $3,250
Enrollment, Drop-out Rates and Diploma Recipients by Race/Ethnicity

Category	Total	White	Black	Asian	AIAN	Hisp.
Enrollment (%)	100.0	42.7	44.8	4.1	0.5	7.9
Drop-out Rate (%)	3.0	3.4	2.5	0.0	0.0	6.1
H.S. Diplomas (#)	315	167	111	13	2	22

Litchfield County

New Milford SD

50 E St • New Milford, CT 06776-3099
(860) 355-8406 • http://www.new-milford.k12.ct.us/
Grade Span: PK-12; **Agency Type:** 1
Schools: 7
3 Primary; 2 Middle; 1 High; 1 Other Level
6 Regular; 0 Special Education; 0 Vocational; 1 Alternative
0 Magnet; 0 Charter; 3 Title I Eligible; 0 School-wide Title I
Students: 5,204 (51.5% male; 48.5% female)
Individual Education Program: 672 (12.9%);
English Language Learner: 79 (1.5%); Migrant: 0 (0.0%)
Eligible for Free Lunch Program: n/a
Eligible for Reduced-Price Lunch Program: n/a
Teachers: 343.7 (15.1 to 1)
Librarians/Media Specialists: 6.0 (867.3 to 1)
Guidance Counselors: 12.0 (433.7 to 1)
Current Spending: ($ per student per year):
Total: $8,410; Instruction: $5,329; Support Services: $2,687
Enrollment, Drop-out Rates and Diploma Recipients by Race/Ethnicity

Category	Total	White	Black	Asian	AIAN	Hisp.
Enrollment (%)	100.0	91.7	1.7	2.9	0.1	3.6
Drop-out Rate (%)	1.4	1.5	0.0	0.0	0.0	0.0
H.S. Diplomas (#)	241	233	1	3	0	4

Plymouth SD

77 E Main St • Terryville, CT 06786-1200
(860) 314-8005 • http://www.pccs.k12.mi.us/
Grade Span: PK-12; **Agency Type:** 1
Schools: 6
3 Primary; 1 Middle; 1 High; 1 Other Level
5 Regular; 0 Special Education; 0 Vocational; 1 Alternative
0 Magnet; 0 Charter; 3 Title I Eligible; 0 School-wide Title I
Students: 1,898 (51.6% male; 48.4% female)
Individual Education Program: 300 (15.8%);
English Language Learner: 23 (1.2%); Migrant: 0 (0.0%)
Eligible for Free Lunch Program: n/a
Eligible for Reduced-Price Lunch Program: n/a
Teachers: 142.8 (13.3 to 1)
Librarians/Media Specialists: 0.0 (0.0 to 1)
Guidance Counselors: 5.0 (379.6 to 1)
Current Spending: ($ per student per year):
Total: $8,626; Instruction: $5,485; Support Services: $3,067

Enrollment, Drop-out Rates and Diploma Recipients by Race/Ethnicity

Category	Total	White	Black	Asian	AIAN	Hisp.
Enrollment (%)	100.0	96.7	0.7	0.9	0.6	1.1
Drop-out Rate (%)	3.3	3.2	50.0	0.0	0.0	0.0
H.S. Diplomas (#)	120	119	1	0	0	0

Regional SD 14

129 Main Street, N • Woodbury, CT 06798-2915
(203) 263-4339 • http://www.ctreg14.com/
Grade Span: PK-12; **Agency Type:** 1
Schools: 6
3 Primary; 1 Middle; 1 High; 1 Other Level
4 Regular; 1 Special Education; 0 Vocational; 1 Alternative
0 Magnet; 0 Charter; 1 Title I Eligible; 0 School-wide Title I
Students: 2,306 (48.5% male; 51.5% female)
Individual Education Program: 261 (11.3%);
English Language Learner: 9 (0.4%); Migrant: 0 (0.0%)
Eligible for Free Lunch Program: n/a
Eligible for Reduced-Price Lunch Program: n/a
Teachers: 165.1 (14.0 to 1)
Librarians/Media Specialists: 4.0 (576.5 to 1)
Guidance Counselors: 5.5 (419.3 to 1)
Current Spending: ($ per student per year):
Total: $8,651; Instruction: $5,289; Support Services: $2,952
Enrollment, Drop-out Rates and Diploma Recipients by Race/Ethnicity

Category	Total	White	Black	Asian	AIAN	Hisp.
Enrollment (%)	100.0	95.3	0.9	1.4	0.4	2.0
Drop-out Rate (%)	0.3	0.3	0.0	0.0	0.0	0.0
H.S. Diplomas (#)	180	176	2	1	0	1

Torrington SD

355 Migeon Ave • Torrington, CT 06790-4822
(860) 489-2327 • http://www.torrington.org/
Grade Span: PK-12; **Agency Type:** 1
Schools: 9
5 Primary; 1 Middle; 2 High; 1 Other Level
7 Regular; 1 Special Education; 0 Vocational; 1 Alternative
0 Magnet; 0 Charter; 3 Title I Eligible; 0 School-wide Title I
Students: 5,026 (52.2% male; 47.8% female)
Individual Education Program: 787 (15.7%);
English Language Learner: 177 (3.5%); Migrant: 0 (0.0%)
Eligible for Free Lunch Program: n/a
Eligible for Reduced-Price Lunch Program: n/a
Teachers: 341.8 (14.7 to 1)
Librarians/Media Specialists: 6.0 (837.7 to 1)
Guidance Counselors: 11.0 (456.9 to 1)
Current Spending: ($ per student per year):
Total: $8,640; Instruction: $5,705; Support Services: $2,609
Enrollment, Drop-out Rates and Diploma Recipients by Race/Ethnicity

Category	Total	White	Black	Asian	AIAN	Hisp.
Enrollment (%)	100.0	85.4	5.1	2.6	0.2	6.6
Drop-out Rate (%)	6.5	6.2	7.3	2.4	0.0	16.3
H.S. Diplomas (#)	267	248	7	5	1	6

Watertown SD

10 Deforest St • Watertown, CT 06795-2190
(860) 945-4801 • http://watertownctschools.org/
Grade Span: PK-12; **Agency Type:** 1
Schools: 7
3 Primary; 2 Middle; 1 High; 1 Other Level
6 Regular; 0 Special Education; 0 Vocational; 1 Alternative
0 Magnet; 0 Charter; 2 Title I Eligible; 0 School-wide Title I
Students: 3,569 (49.9% male; 50.1% female)
Individual Education Program: 407 (11.4%);
English Language Learner: 11 (0.3%); Migrant: 0 (0.0%)
Eligible for Free Lunch Program: n/a
Eligible for Reduced-Price Lunch Program: n/a
Teachers: 241.2 (14.8 to 1)
Librarians/Media Specialists: 3.0 (1,189.7 to 1)
Guidance Counselors: 6.8 (524.9 to 1)
Current Spending: ($ per student per year):
Total: $8,226; Instruction: $5,330; Support Services: $2,628
Enrollment, Drop-out Rates and Diploma Recipients by Race/Ethnicity

Category	Total	White	Black	Asian	AIAN	Hisp.
Enrollment (%)	100.0	94.2	1.2	2.1	0.5	2.0
Drop-out Rate (%)	2.7	2.5	8.3	0.0	0.0	7.4
H.S. Diplomas (#)	203	194	1	4	0	4

Middlesex County

Clinton SD

137-B Glenwood Circle • Clinton, CT 06413-1493
(860) 664-6500 • http://www.clintonpublic.org/
Grade Span: PK-12; **Agency Type:** 1
Schools: 5
1 Primary; 2 Middle; 1 High; 1 Other Level
4 Regular; 0 Special Education; 0 Vocational; 1 Alternative
0 Magnet; 0 Charter; 1 Title I Eligible; 0 School-wide Title I
Students: 2,214 (51.4% male; 48.6% female)
Individual Education Program: 316 (14.3%);
English Language Learner: 20 (0.9%); Migrant: 0 (0.0%)
Eligible for Free Lunch Program: n/a
Eligible for Reduced-Price Lunch Program: n/a
Teachers: 165.7 (13.4 to 1)
Librarians/Media Specialists: 4.0 (553.5 to 1)
Guidance Counselors: 6.0 (369.0 to 1)
Current Spending: ($ per student per year):
Total: $10,172; Instruction: $7,007; Support Services: $2,862
Enrollment, Drop-out Rates and Diploma Recipients by Race/Ethnicity

Category	Total	White	Black	Asian	AIAN	Hisp.
Enrollment (%)	100.0	92.1	0.3	2.9	0.1	4.6
Drop-out Rate (%)	2.8	2.7	0.0	0.0	0.0	5.1
H.S. Diplomas (#)	157	147	0	3	0	7

Cromwell SD

9 Mann Memorial Dr • Cromwell, CT 06416-1398
(860) 632-4830
Grade Span: PK-12; **Agency Type:** 1
Schools: 4
1 Primary; 1 Middle; 1 High; 1 Other Level
3 Regular; 0 Special Education; 0 Vocational; 1 Alternative
0 Magnet; 0 Charter; 1 Title I Eligible; 0 School-wide Title I
Students: 1,849 (49.4% male; 50.6% female)
Individual Education Program: 231 (12.5%);
English Language Learner: 52 (2.8%); Migrant: 0 (0.0%)
Eligible for Free Lunch Program: n/a
Eligible for Reduced-Price Lunch Program: n/a
Teachers: 149.7 (12.4 to 1)
Librarians/Media Specialists: 2.0 (924.5 to 1)
Guidance Counselors: 4.0 (462.3 to 1)
Current Spending: ($ per student per year):
Total: $9,359; Instruction: $6,206; Support Services: $2,838
Enrollment, Drop-out Rates and Diploma Recipients by Race/Ethnicity

Category	Total	White	Black	Asian	AIAN	Hisp.
Enrollment (%)	100.0	88.2	4.9	2.3	0.3	4.2
Drop-out Rate (%)	0.2	0.2	0.0	0.0	0.0	0.0
H.S. Diplomas (#)	101	90	4	2	1	4

East Hampton SD

94 Main St • East Hampton, CT 06424-1119
(860) 365-4000
Grade Span: PK-12; **Agency Type:** 1
Schools: 5
1 Primary; 2 Middle; 1 High; 1 Other Level
4 Regular; 0 Special Education; 0 Vocational; 1 Alternative
0 Magnet; 0 Charter; 2 Title I Eligible; 2 School-wide Title I
Students: 2,027 (51.1% male; 48.9% female)
Individual Education Program: 254 (12.5%);
English Language Learner: 0 (0.0%); Migrant: 0 (0.0%)
Eligible for Free Lunch Program: n/a
Eligible for Reduced-Price Lunch Program: n/a
Teachers: 143.1 (14.2 to 1)
Librarians/Media Specialists: 1.0 (2,027.0 to 1)
Guidance Counselors: 3.0 (675.7 to 1)
Current Spending: ($ per student per year):
Total: $9,088; Instruction: $5,732; Support Services: $3,117
Enrollment, Drop-out Rates and Diploma Recipients by Race/Ethnicity

Category	Total	White	Black	Asian	AIAN	Hisp.
Enrollment (%)	100.0	97.0	0.7	1.0	0.1	1.0
Drop-out Rate (%)	0.4	0.4	0.0	0.0	n/a	0.0
H.S. Diplomas (#)	125	120	1	3	0	1

Middletown SD

311 Hunting Hill Ave • Middletown, CT 06457-4356
(860) 638-1401 • http://www.middletownschools.org/
Grade Span: PK-12; **Agency Type:** 1
Schools: 12
8 Primary; 2 Middle; 1 High; 1 Other Level
12 Regular; 0 Special Education; 0 Vocational; 0 Alternative
0 Magnet; 0 Charter; 7 Title I Eligible; 0 School-wide Title I
Students: 5,149 (50.1% male; 49.9% female)
Individual Education Program: 707 (13.7%);
English Language Learner: 107 (2.1%); Migrant: 0 (0.0%)
Eligible for Free Lunch Program: n/a
Eligible for Reduced-Price Lunch Program: n/a
Teachers: 403.0 (12.8 to 1)
Librarians/Media Specialists: 6.0 (858.2 to 1)
Guidance Counselors: 9.0 (572.1 to 1)
Current Spending: ($ per student per year):
Total: $10,102; Instruction: $7,027; Support Services: $2,645

Enrollment, Drop-out Rates and Diploma Recipients by Race/Ethnicity

Category	Total	White	Black	Asian	AIAN	Hisp.
Enrollment (%)	100.0	59.9	27.5	3.3	0.6	8.7
Drop-out Rate (%)	1.7	1.6	2.2	0.0	0.0	1.3
H.S. Diplomas (#)	246	168	59	9	0	10

Old Saybrook SD

50 Sheffield St • Old Saybrook, CT 06475-2399
(860) 395-3157
Grade Span: PK-12; **Agency Type:** 1
Schools: 4
1 Primary; 1 Middle; 1 High; 1 Other Level
3 Regular; 0 Special Education; 0 Vocational; 1 Alternative
0 Magnet; 0 Charter; 2 Title I Eligible; 0 School-wide Title I
Students: 1,598 (50.6% male; 49.4% female)
Individual Education Program: 200 (12.5%);
English Language Learner: 27 (1.7%); Migrant: 0 (0.0%)
Eligible for Free Lunch Program: n/a
Eligible for Reduced-Price Lunch Program: n/a
Teachers: 134.0 (11.9 to 1)
Librarians/Media Specialists: 3.7 (431.9 to 1)
Guidance Counselors: 4.0 (399.5 to 1)
Current Spending: ($ per student per year):
Total: $9,125; Instruction: $5,309; Support Services: $3,363

Enrollment, Drop-out Rates and Diploma Recipients by Race/Ethnicity

Category	Total	White	Black	Asian	AIAN	Hisp.
Enrollment (%)	100.0	90.5	2.1	4.6	0.0	2.9
Drop-out Rate (%)	0.2	0.3	0.0	0.0	n/a	0.0
H.S. Diplomas (#)	95	85	3	3	0	4

Regional SD 13

135-A Pickett Ln • Durham, CT 06422-2001
(860) 349-7200 • http://www.reg13.k12.ct.us
Grade Span: PK-12; **Agency Type:** 1
Schools: 7
3 Primary; 2 Middle; 1 High; 1 Other Level
6 Regular; 0 Special Education; 0 Vocational; 1 Alternative
0 Magnet; 0 Charter; 3 Title I Eligible; 0 School-wide Title I
Students: 2,114 (51.4% male; 48.6% female)
Individual Education Program: 218 (10.3%);
English Language Learner: 0 (0.0%); Migrant: 0 (0.0%)
Eligible for Free Lunch Program: n/a
Eligible for Reduced-Price Lunch Program: n/a
Teachers: 168.8 (12.5 to 1)
Librarians/Media Specialists: 1.6 (1,321.3 to 1)
Guidance Counselors: 3.0 (704.7 to 1)
Current Spending: ($ per student per year):
Total: $10,042; Instruction: $6,030; Support Services: $3,713

Enrollment, Drop-out Rates and Diploma Recipients by Race/Ethnicity

Category	Total	White	Black	Asian	AIAN	Hisp.
Enrollment (%)	100.0	97.2	0.3	1.1	0.1	1.3
Drop-out Rate (%)	0.6	0.6	0.0	0.0	n/a	0.0
H.S. Diplomas (#)	110	105	1	3	0	1

Regional SD 17

91 Little City Rd • Higganum, CT 06441-0568
Mailing Address: 91 Little City Rd, Box 568 • Higganum, CT 06441-0568
(860) 345-4534 • http://www.rsd17.k12.ct.us/
Grade Span: PK-12; **Agency Type:** 1
Schools: 6
3 Primary; 1 Middle; 1 High; 1 Other Level
5 Regular; 0 Special Education; 0 Vocational; 1 Alternative
0 Magnet; 0 Charter; 1 Title I Eligible; 0 School-wide Title I
Students: 2,383 (53.3% male; 46.7% female)
Individual Education Program: 283 (11.9%);
English Language Learner: 0 (0.0%); Migrant: 0 (0.0%)
Eligible for Free Lunch Program: n/a
Eligible for Reduced-Price Lunch Program: n/a
Teachers: 199.1 (12.0 to 1)
Librarians/Media Specialists: 1.0 (2,383.0 to 1)
Guidance Counselors: 5.5 (433.3 to 1)
Current Spending: ($ per student per year):
Total: $9,960; Instruction: $5,798; Support Services: $3,840

Enrollment, Drop-out Rates and Diploma Recipients by Race/Ethnicity

Category	Total	White	Black	Asian	AIAN	Hisp.
Enrollment (%)	100.0	96.2	1.2	1.5	0.2	0.9
Drop-out Rate (%)	0.3	0.3	0.0	0.0	0.0	0.0
H.S. Diplomas (#)	146	138	3	3	0	2

State Voc-Tech Schools

25 Industrial Park Rd • Middletown, CT 06457-1543
(860) 807-2200
Grade Span: 09-12; **Agency Type:** 5
Schools: 17
0 Primary; 0 Middle; 17 High; 0 Other Level
0 Regular; 0 Special Education; 17 Vocational; 0 Alternative
0 Magnet; 0 Charter; 6 Title I Eligible; 0 School-wide Title I
Students: 11,130 (63.7% male; 36.3% female)
Individual Education Program: 1,573 (14.1%);
English Language Learner: 494 (4.4%); Migrant: 54 (0.5%)
Eligible for Free Lunch Program: n/a
Eligible for Reduced-Price Lunch Program: n/a
Teachers: 1,098.3 (10.1 to 1)
Librarians/Media Specialists: 17.0 (654.7 to 1)
Guidance Counselors: 62.0 (179.5 to 1)
Current Spending: ($ per student per year):
Total: n/a; Instruction: n/a; Support Services: n/a

Enrollment, Drop-out Rates and Diploma Recipients by Race/Ethnicity

Category	Total	White	Black	Asian	AIAN	Hisp.
Enrollment (%)	100.0	59.1	15.8	0.6	0.8	23.7
Drop-out Rate (%)	0.9	1.1	0.2	0.0	0.0	0.8
H.S. Diplomas (#)	2,013	1,270	317	13	4	409

New Haven County

Ansonia SD

42 Grove St • Ansonia, CT 06401-1798
(203) 736-5095 • http://electronicvalley.org/ansonia/k12/
Grade Span: PK-12; **Agency Type:** 1
Schools: 5
2 Primary; 1 Middle; 1 High; 1 Other Level
4 Regular; 0 Special Education; 0 Vocational; 1 Alternative
0 Magnet; 0 Charter; 3 Title I Eligible; 0 School-wide Title I
Students: 2,631 (50.6% male; 49.4% female)
Individual Education Program: 404 (15.4%);
English Language Learner: 77 (2.9%); Migrant: 0 (0.0%)
Eligible for Free Lunch Program: n/a
Eligible for Reduced-Price Lunch Program: n/a
Teachers: 156.8 (16.8 to 1)
Librarians/Media Specialists: 1.0 (2,631.0 to 1)
Guidance Counselors: 5.0 (526.2 to 1)
Current Spending: ($ per student per year):
Total: $7,826; Instruction: $4,989; Support Services: $2,456

Enrollment, Drop-out Rates and Diploma Recipients by Race/Ethnicity

Category	Total	White	Black	Asian	AIAN	Hisp.
Enrollment (%)	100.0	65.3	18.3	1.0	0.4	15.0
Drop-out Rate (%)	2.7	2.2	2.7	0.0	n/a	7.1
H.S. Diplomas (#)	118	86	15	2	0	15

Area Coop Educational Services

350 State St • North Haven, CT 06473-3108
(203) 407-4590
Grade Span: PK-12; **Agency Type:** 4
Schools: 4
1 Primary; 1 Middle; 1 High; 1 Other Level
2 Regular; 2 Special Education; 0 Vocational; 0 Alternative
3 Magnet; 0 Charter; 0 Title I Eligible; 0 School-wide Title I
Students: 2,160 (61.6% male; 38.4% female)
Individual Education Program: 0 (0.0%);
English Language Learner: 35 (1.6%); Migrant: 1 (<0.1%)
Eligible for Free Lunch Program: n/a
Eligible for Reduced-Price Lunch Program: n/a
Teachers: 230.2 (9.4 to 1)
Librarians/Media Specialists: 2.0 (1,080.0 to 1)
Guidance Counselors: 5.0 (432.0 to 1)
Current Spending: ($ per student per year):
Total: n/a; Instruction: n/a; Support Services: n/a

Enrollment, Drop-out Rates and Diploma Recipients by Race/Ethnicity

Category	Total	White	Black	Asian	AIAN	Hisp.
Enrollment (%)	100.0	55.7	24.7	2.4	0.0	17.2
Drop-out Rate (%)	0.3	0.5	0.0	0.0	n/a	0.0
H.S. Diplomas (#)	24	16	6	0	0	2

Branford SD

1111 Main St • Branford, CT 06405-3717
(203) 488-7276 • http://www.branford.k12.ct.us/prod/index.jsp
Grade Span: PK-12; **Agency Type:** 1
Schools: 7
4 Primary; 1 Middle; 1 High; 1 Other Level
6 Regular; 0 Special Education; 0 Vocational; 1 Alternative
0 Magnet; 0 Charter; 3 Title I Eligible; 0 School-wide Title I
Students: 3,705 (50.8% male; 49.2% female)
Individual Education Program: 574 (15.5%);
English Language Learner: 77 (2.1%); Migrant: 0 (0.0%)
Eligible for Free Lunch Program: n/a
Eligible for Reduced-Price Lunch Program: n/a
Teachers: 277.6 (13.3 to 1)
Librarians/Media Specialists: 7.0 (529.3 to 1)
Guidance Counselors: 10.0 (370.5 to 1)
Current Spending: ($ per student per year):
Total: $8,960; Instruction: $5,654; Support Services: $2,890

Enrollment, Drop-out Rates and Diploma Recipients by Race/Ethnicity

Category	Total	White	Black	Asian	AIAN	Hisp.
Enrollment (%)	100.0	89.7	2.4	5.2	0.1	2.6
Drop-out Rate (%)	1.3	1.4	0.0	0.0	0.0	0.0
H.S. Diplomas (#)	238	219	4	13	0	2

Cheshire SD

29 Main St • Cheshire, CT 06410-2495
(203) 250-2430 • http://www.cheshirect.org/
Grade Span: PK-12; **Agency Type:** 1
Schools: 9
5 Primary; 1 Middle; 1 High; 2 Other Level
7 Regular; 1 Special Education; 0 Vocational; 1 Alternative
0 Magnet; 0 Charter; 0 Title I Eligible; 0 School-wide Title I
Students: 5,088 (50.9% male; 49.1% female)
Individual Education Program: 514 (10.1%);
English Language Learner: 21 (0.4%); Migrant: 0 (0.0%)
Eligible for Free Lunch Program: n/a
Eligible for Reduced-Price Lunch Program: n/a
Teachers: 336.4 (15.1 to 1)
Librarians/Media Specialists: 8.0 (636.0 to 1)
Guidance Counselors: 14.5 (350.9 to 1)
Current Spending: ($ per student per year):
Total: $9,407; Instruction: $5,815; Support Services: $3,272

Enrollment, Drop-out Rates and Diploma Recipients by Race/Ethnicity

Category	Total	White	Black	Asian	AIAN	Hisp.
Enrollment (%)	100.0	92.4	1.6	4.6	0.1	1.3
Drop-out Rate (%)	0.9	0.9	0.0	0.0	0.0	0.0
H.S. Diplomas (#)	348	333	2	9	1	3

Derby SD

8 Nutmeg Ave • Derby, CT 06418-0373
Mailing Address: 8 Nutmeg Avenue, Box 373 • Derby, CT 06418-0373
(203) 736-5027 • http://www.derbyps.org/
Grade Span: PK-12; **Agency Type:** 1
Schools: 4
2 Primary; 0 Middle; 1 High; 1 Other Level
3 Regular; 0 Special Education; 0 Vocational; 1 Alternative
0 Magnet; 0 Charter; 1 Title I Eligible; 0 School-wide Title I
Students: 1,606 (51.3% male; 48.7% female)
Individual Education Program: 171 (10.6%);
English Language Learner: 88 (5.5%); Migrant: 1 (0.1%)
Eligible for Free Lunch Program: n/a
Eligible for Reduced-Price Lunch Program: n/a
Teachers: 98.0 (16.4 to 1)
Librarians/Media Specialists: 3.0 (535.3 to 1)
Guidance Counselors: 3.0 (535.3 to 1)
Current Spending: ($ per student per year):
Total: $8,286; Instruction: $5,649; Support Services: $2,244

Enrollment, Drop-out Rates and Diploma Recipients by Race/Ethnicity

Category	Total	White	Black	Asian	AIAN	Hisp.
Enrollment (%)	100.0	74.8	7.6	1.2	0.1	16.3
Drop-out Rate (%)	2.8	1.2	13.6	0.0	n/a	9.8
H.S. Diplomas (#)	80	59	4	4	1	12

East Haven SD

35 Wheelbarrow Ln • East Haven, CT 06513-1597
(203) 468-3261 • http://www.east-haven.k12.ct.us/
Grade Span: PK-12; **Agency Type:** 1
Schools: 13
9 Primary; 1 Middle; 1 High; 2 Other Level
11 Regular; 1 Special Education; 0 Vocational; 1 Alternative
0 Magnet; 0 Charter; 5 Title I Eligible; 0 School-wide Title I
Students: 4,031 (51.9% male; 48.1% female)
Individual Education Program: 484 (12.0%);
English Language Learner: 61 (1.5%); Migrant: 3 (0.1%)
Eligible for Free Lunch Program: n/a
Eligible for Reduced-Price Lunch Program: n/a
Teachers: 247.9 (16.3 to 1)
Librarians/Media Specialists: 6.4 (629.8 to 1)
Guidance Counselors: 8.0 (503.9 to 1)
Current Spending: ($ per student per year):
Total: $8,223; Instruction: $5,021; Support Services: $2,793

Enrollment, Drop-out Rates and Diploma Recipients by Race/Ethnicity

Category	Total	White	Black	Asian	AIAN	Hisp.
Enrollment (%)	100.0	87.8	1.7	3.2	0.0	7.3
Drop-out Rate (%)	1.5	1.6	0.0	0.0	0.0	1.6
H.S. Diplomas (#)	215	197	1	3	0	14

Guilford SD

701 New England Rd • Guilford, CT 06437-0367
Mailing Address: 701 New England Rd, Box 367 • Guilford, CT 06437-0367
(203) 453-8200 • http://www.guilford.k12.ct.us/
Grade Span: PK-12; **Agency Type:** 1
Schools: 8
4 Primary; 2 Middle; 1 High; 1 Other Level
7 Regular; 0 Special Education; 0 Vocational; 1 Alternative
0 Magnet; 0 Charter; 4 Title I Eligible; 0 School-wide Title I
Students: 3,904 (49.9% male; 50.1% female)
Individual Education Program: 419 (10.7%);
English Language Learner: 18 (0.5%); Migrant: 0 (0.0%)
Eligible for Free Lunch Program: n/a
Eligible for Reduced-Price Lunch Program: n/a
Teachers: 255.3 (15.3 to 1)
Librarians/Media Specialists: 8.0 (488.0 to 1)
Guidance Counselors: 10.2 (382.7 to 1)
Current Spending: ($ per student per year):
Total: $8,840; Instruction: $5,576; Support Services: $3,006

Enrollment, Drop-out Rates and Diploma Recipients by Race/Ethnicity

Category	Total	White	Black	Asian	AIAN	Hisp.
Enrollment (%)	100.0	93.0	1.1	2.8	0.2	2.9
Drop-out Rate (%)	0.7	0.6	0.0	0.0	0.0	3.6
H.S. Diplomas (#)	287	274	1	4	0	8

Hamden SD

60 Putnam Ave • Hamden, CT 06517-2825
(203) 407-2000 • http://www.hamden.k12.ct.us/
Grade Span: PK-12; **Agency Type:** 1
Schools: 12
9 Primary; 1 Middle; 1 High; 1 Other Level
11 Regular; 0 Special Education; 0 Vocational; 1 Alternative
0 Magnet; 0 Charter; 5 Title I Eligible; 0 School-wide Title I
Students: 6,315 (52.4% male; 47.6% female)
Individual Education Program: 1,078 (17.1%);
English Language Learner: 63 (1.0%); Migrant: 7 (0.1%)
Eligible for Free Lunch Program: n/a
Eligible for Reduced-Price Lunch Program: n/a
Teachers: 409.7 (15.4 to 1)
Librarians/Media Specialists: 13.0 (485.8 to 1)
Guidance Counselors: 10.0 (631.5 to 1)
Current Spending: ($ per student per year):
Total: $11,305; Instruction: $7,596; Support Services: $3,398

Enrollment, Drop-out Rates and Diploma Recipients by Race/Ethnicity

Category	Total	White	Black	Asian	AIAN	Hisp.
Enrollment (%)	100.0	57.4	29.2	5.0	0.0	8.3
Drop-out Rate (%)	8.5	5.9	14.8	6.7	0.0	16.0
H.S. Diplomas (#)	401	286	88	11	0	16

Madison SD

10 Campus Dr • Madison, CT 06443-2562
Mailing Address: 10 Campus Dr, Drawer 71 • Madison, CT 06443-2562
(203) 245-6300 • http://www.madisonps.org/
Grade Span: PK-12; **Agency Type:** 1
Schools: 8
4 Primary; 2 Middle; 1 High; 1 Other Level
7 Regular; 0 Special Education; 0 Vocational; 1 Alternative
0 Magnet; 0 Charter; 0 Title I Eligible; 0 School-wide Title I
Students: 3,675 (50.6% male; 49.4% female)
Individual Education Program: 534 (14.5%);
English Language Learner: 6 (0.2%); Migrant: 0 (0.0%)
Eligible for Free Lunch Program: n/a
Eligible for Reduced-Price Lunch Program: n/a
Teachers: 256.7 (14.3 to 1)
Librarians/Media Specialists: 5.8 (633.6 to 1)
Guidance Counselors: 7.1 (517.6 to 1)
Current Spending: ($ per student per year):
Total: $8,590; Instruction: $5,099; Support Services: $3,087

Enrollment, Drop-out Rates and Diploma Recipients by Race/Ethnicity

Category	Total	White	Black	Asian	AIAN	Hisp.
Enrollment (%)	100.0	94.9	1.1	3.0	0.1	1.0
Drop-out Rate (%)	0.8	0.9	0.0	0.0	0.0	0.0
H.S. Diplomas (#)	210	196	1	5	0	8

Meriden SD

22 Liberty St • Meriden, CT 06450-0848
Mailing Address: 22 Liberty St, Box 848 • Meriden, CT 06450-0848
(203) 630-4171 • http://www.meriden.k12.ct.us/
Grade Span: PK-12; **Agency Type:** 1
Schools: 13
8 Primary; 2 Middle; 2 High; 1 Other Level
12 Regular; 0 Special Education; 0 Vocational; 1 Alternative
0 Magnet; 0 Charter; 6 Title I Eligible; 0 School-wide Title I
Students: 8,780 (51.4% male; 48.6% female)
Individual Education Program: 1,381 (15.7%);
English Language Learner: 568 (6.5%); Migrant: 288 (3.3%)
Eligible for Free Lunch Program: n/a
Eligible for Reduced-Price Lunch Program: n/a
Teachers: 624.4 (14.1 to 1)
Librarians/Media Specialists: 11.0 (798.2 to 1)
Guidance Counselors: 22.7 (386.8 to 1)

Current Spending: ($ per student per year):
Total: $9,343; Instruction: $6,090; Support Services: $2,914
Enrollment, Drop-out Rates and Diploma Recipients by Race/Ethnicity

Category	Total	White	Black	Asian	AIAN	Hisp.
Enrollment (%)	100.0	49.4	12.0	1.8	0.2	36.6
Drop-out Rate (%)	2.9	1.4	1.0	1.9	50.0	7.1
H.S. Diplomas (#)	433	301	32	9	0	91

Milford SD

70 W River St • Milford, CT 06460-3364
(203) 783-3402 • http://www.milforded.org/
Grade Span: PK-12; **Agency Type:** 1
Schools: 16
9 Primary; 3 Middle; 3 High; 1 Other Level
14 Regular; 0 Special Education; 0 Vocational; 2 Alternative
0 Magnet; 0 Charter; 6 Title I Eligible; 5 School-wide Title I
Students: 7,459 (50.9% male; 49.1% female)
Individual Education Program: 1,051 (14.1%);
English Language Learner: 119 (1.6%); Migrant: 0 (0.0%)
Eligible for Free Lunch Program: n/a
Eligible for Reduced-Price Lunch Program: n/a
Teachers: 570.2 (13.1 to 1)
Librarians/Media Specialists: 14.0 (532.8 to 1)
Guidance Counselors: 12.0 (621.6 to 1)
Current Spending: ($ per student per year):
Total: $9,609; Instruction: $6,553; Support Services: $2,681
Enrollment, Drop-out Rates and Diploma Recipients by Race/Ethnicity

Category	Total	White	Black	Asian	AIAN	Hisp.
Enrollment (%)	100.0	88.9	3.2	3.8	0.1	4.0
Drop-out Rate (%)	2.3	2.2	2.2	0.0	0.0	5.5
H.S. Diplomas (#)	464	424	9	15	0	16

Naugatuck SD

380 Church St • Naugatuck, CT 06770-2887
(203) 720-5265
Grade Span: PK-12; **Agency Type:** 1
Schools: 12
8 Primary; 2 Middle; 1 High; 1 Other Level
11 Regular; 0 Special Education; 0 Vocational; 1 Alternative
0 Magnet; 0 Charter; 4 Title I Eligible; 0 School-wide Title I
Students: 5,572 (51.1% male; 48.9% female)
Individual Education Program: 667 (12.0%);
English Language Learner: 238 (4.3%); Migrant: 5 (0.1%)
Eligible for Free Lunch Program: n/a
Eligible for Reduced-Price Lunch Program: n/a
Teachers: 361.5 (15.4 to 1)
Librarians/Media Specialists: 3.0 (1,857.3 to 1)
Guidance Counselors: 12.4 (449.4 to 1)
Current Spending: ($ per student per year):
Total: $8,099; Instruction: $5,346; Support Services: $2,417
Enrollment, Drop-out Rates and Diploma Recipients by Race/Ethnicity

Category	Total	White	Black	Asian	AIAN	Hisp.
Enrollment (%)	100.0	85.4	5.8	2.0	0.2	6.7
Drop-out Rate (%)	3.4	2.9	0.0	0.0	16.7	13.3
H.S. Diplomas (#)	326	287	16	3	1	19

New Haven SD

54 Meadow St • New Haven, CT 06519-1743
(203) 946-8888 • http://www.nhps.net/
Grade Span: PK-12; **Agency Type:** 1
Schools: 48
30 Primary; 7 Middle; 9 High; 2 Other Level
39 Regular; 1 Special Education; 0 Vocational; 8 Alternative
8 Magnet; 0 Charter; 25 Title I Eligible; 24 School-wide Title I
Students: 20,329 (50.9% male; 49.1% female)
Individual Education Program: 2,265 (11.1%);
English Language Learner: 1,824 (9.0%); Migrant: 444 (2.2%)
Eligible for Free Lunch Program: n/a
Eligible for Reduced-Price Lunch Program: n/a
Teachers: 1,415.0 (14.4 to 1)
Librarians/Media Specialists: 41.0 (495.8 to 1)
Guidance Counselors: 38.0 (535.0 to 1)
Current Spending: ($ per student per year):
Total: $12,251; Instruction: $7,781; Support Services: $3,894
Enrollment, Drop-out Rates and Diploma Recipients by Race/Ethnicity

Category	Total	White	Black	Asian	AIAN	Hisp.
Enrollment (%)	100.0	11.4	55.8	1.3	0.1	31.5
Drop-out Rate (%)	6.4	3.0	5.8	8.2	100.0	10.2
H.S. Diplomas (#)	788	149	451	18	2	168

North Branford SD

Middletown Ave • Northford, CT 06472-0129
Mailing Address: Middletown Ave, Box 129 • Northford, CT 06472-0129
(203) 484-1440 • http://www.northbranfordschools.org/
Grade Span: PK-12; **Agency Type:** 1
Schools: 6
3 Primary; 1 Middle; 1 High; 1 Other Level
5 Regular; 0 Special Education; 0 Vocational; 1 Alternative
0 Magnet; 0 Charter; 3 Title I Eligible; 0 School-wide Title I
Students: 2,481 (51.5% male; 48.5% female)
Individual Education Program: 277 (11.2%);
English Language Learner: 17 (0.7%); Migrant: 1 (<0.1%)
Eligible for Free Lunch Program: n/a
Eligible for Reduced-Price Lunch Program: n/a
Teachers: 152.0 (16.3 to 1)
Librarians/Media Specialists: 3.0 (827.0 to 1)
Guidance Counselors: 5.8 (427.8 to 1)
Current Spending: ($ per student per year):
Total: $8,520; Instruction: $4,993; Support Services: $3,068
Enrollment, Drop-out Rates and Diploma Recipients by Race/Ethnicity

Category	Total	White	Black	Asian	AIAN	Hisp.
Enrollment (%)	100.0	95.3	1.6	0.9	0.2	2.1
Drop-out Rate (%)	1.6	1.5	10.0	0.0	0.0	0.0
H.S. Diplomas (#)	148	137	3	1	2	5

North Haven SD

5 Linsley St • North Haven, CT 06473-2586
(203) 239-2581 • http://www.north-haven.k12.ct.us/
Grade Span: PK-12; **Agency Type:** 1
Schools: 7
4 Primary; 1 Middle; 1 High; 1 Other Level
6 Regular; 0 Special Education; 0 Vocational; 1 Alternative
0 Magnet; 0 Charter; 3 Title I Eligible; 0 School-wide Title I
Students: 3,773 (50.3% male; 49.7% female)
Individual Education Program: 382 (10.1%);
English Language Learner: 40 (1.1%); Migrant: 0 (0.0%)
Eligible for Free Lunch Program: n/a
Eligible for Reduced-Price Lunch Program: n/a
Teachers: 240.8 (15.7 to 1)
Librarians/Media Specialists: 7.6 (496.4 to 1)
Guidance Counselors: 7.6 (496.4 to 1)
Current Spending: ($ per student per year):
Total: $8,971; Instruction: $5,466; Support Services: $3,162
Enrollment, Drop-out Rates and Diploma Recipients by Race/Ethnicity

Category	Total	White	Black	Asian	AIAN	Hisp.
Enrollment (%)	100.0	90.0	2.5	5.0	0.2	2.3
Drop-out Rate (%)	1.0	1.1	0.0	0.0	0.0	0.0
H.S. Diplomas (#)	214	197	4	9	0	4

Regional SD 05

25 Newton Rd • Woodbridge, CT 06525-1598
(203) 392-2106 • http://www.amityregion5.org/District_Page/
Grade Span: 07-12; **Agency Type:** 1
Schools: 4
0 Primary; 2 Middle; 2 High; 0 Other Level
3 Regular; 0 Special Education; 0 Vocational; 1 Alternative
0 Magnet; 0 Charter; 1 Title I Eligible; 0 School-wide Title I
Students: 2,397 (49.5% male; 50.5% female)
Individual Education Program: 298 (12.4%);
English Language Learner: 9 (0.4%); Migrant: 0 (0.0%)
Eligible for Free Lunch Program: n/a
Eligible for Reduced-Price Lunch Program: n/a
Teachers: 174.5 (13.7 to 1)
Librarians/Media Specialists: 4.4 (544.8 to 1)
Guidance Counselors: 14.8 (162.0 to 1)
Current Spending: ($ per student per year):
Total: $11,076; Instruction: $6,025; Support Services: $4,546
Enrollment, Drop-out Rates and Diploma Recipients by Race/Ethnicity

Category	Total	White	Black	Asian	AIAN	Hisp.
Enrollment (%)	100.0	90.1	1.6	6.6	0.3	1.5
Drop-out Rate (%)	0.6	0.5	5.6	0.0	0.0	5.9
H.S. Diplomas (#)	323	294	6	21	0	2

Regional SD 15

286 Whittemore Rd • Middlebury, CT 06762-0395
Mailing Address: 286 Whittemore Rd, Box 395 • Middlebury, CT 06762-0395
(203) 758-8258 • http://www.region15.org/default.shtml
Grade Span: PK-12; **Agency Type:** 1
Schools: 8
4 Primary; 2 Middle; 1 High; 1 Other Level
7 Regular; 0 Special Education; 0 Vocational; 1 Alternative
0 Magnet; 0 Charter; 4 Title I Eligible; 0 School-wide Title I
Students: 4,391 (51.1% male; 48.9% female)
Individual Education Program: 627 (14.3%);

English Language Learner: 29 (0.7%); Migrant: 0 (0.0%)
Eligible for Free Lunch Program: n/a
Eligible for Reduced-Price Lunch Program: n/a
Teachers: 291.6 (15.1 to 1)
Librarians/Media Specialists: 7.0 (627.3 to 1)
Guidance Counselors: 13.2 (332.7 to 1)
Current Spending: ($ per student per year):
Total: $8,834; Instruction: $5,122; Support Services: $3,352
Enrollment, Drop-out Rates and Diploma Recipients by Race/Ethnicity

Category	Total	White	Black	Asian	AIAN	Hisp.
Enrollment (%)	100.0	93.8	1.1	3.0	0.2	1.9
Drop-out Rate (%)	1.8	1.9	0.0	0.0	0.0	0.0
H.S. Diplomas (#)	243	231	2	3	2	5

Regional SD 16

207 New Haven Rd • Prospect, CT 06712-1629
(203) 758-6671
Grade Span: PK-11; **Agency Type:** 1
Schools: 6
2 Primary; 2 Middle; 0 High; 2 Other Level
5 Regular; 0 Special Education; 0 Vocational; 1 Alternative
0 Magnet; 0 Charter; 5 Title I Eligible; 0 School-wide Title I
Students: 2,416 (51.7% male; 48.3% female)
Individual Education Program: 250 (10.3%);
English Language Learner: 3 (0.1%); Migrant: 0 (0.0%)
Eligible for Free Lunch Program: n/a
Eligible for Reduced-Price Lunch Program: n/a
Teachers: 175.8 (13.7 to 1)
Librarians/Media Specialists: 1.0 (2,416.0 to 1)
Guidance Counselors: 7.6 (317.9 to 1)
Current Spending: ($ per student per year):
Total: $8,682; Instruction: $5,245; Support Services: $3,147
Enrollment, Drop-out Rates and Diploma Recipients by Race/Ethnicity

Category	Total	White	Black	Asian	AIAN	Hisp.
Enrollment (%)	100.0	95.8	1.7	0.7	0.0	1.8
Drop-out Rate (%)	n/a	n/a	n/a	n/a	n/a	n/a
H.S. Diplomas (#)	n/a	n/a	n/a	n/a	n/a	n/a

Seymour SD

98 Bank Street, Annex Building • Seymour, CT 06483-2892
(203) 888-4565 • http://www.seymourschools.org/
Grade Span: PK-12; **Agency Type:** 1
Schools: 6
3 Primary; 1 Middle; 1 High; 1 Other Level
5 Regular; 0 Special Education; 0 Vocational; 1 Alternative
0 Magnet; 0 Charter; 4 Title I Eligible; 0 School-wide Title I
Students: 2,855 (50.0% male; 50.0% female)
Individual Education Program: 223 (7.8%);
English Language Learner: 0 (0.0%); Migrant: 0 (0.0%)
Eligible for Free Lunch Program: n/a
Eligible for Reduced-Price Lunch Program: n/a
Teachers: 184.1 (15.5 to 1)
Librarians/Media Specialists: 3.0 (951.7 to 1)
Guidance Counselors: 9.0 (317.2 to 1)
Current Spending: ($ per student per year):
Total: $7,725; Instruction: $4,853; Support Services: $2,481
Enrollment, Drop-out Rates and Diploma Recipients by Race/Ethnicity

Category	Total	White	Black	Asian	AIAN	Hisp.
Enrollment (%)	100.0	90.6	1.7	3.1	0.3	4.3
Drop-out Rate (%)	1.2	1.2	0.0	0.0	n/a	2.4
H.S. Diplomas (#)	240	220	3	6	0	11

Wallingford SD

142 Hope Hill Rd • Wallingford, CT 06492-2254
(203) 949-6500 • http://www.wallingford.k12.ct.us/index2.html
Grade Span: PK-12; **Agency Type:** 1
Schools: 14
8 Primary; 2 Middle; 2 High; 2 Other Level
12 Regular; 0 Special Education; 0 Vocational; 2 Alternative
0 Magnet; 0 Charter; 4 Title I Eligible; 0 School-wide Title I
Students: 7,196 (50.3% male; 49.7% female)
Individual Education Program: 740 (10.3%);
English Language Learner: 186 (2.6%); Migrant: 2 (<0.1%)
Eligible for Free Lunch Program: n/a
Eligible for Reduced-Price Lunch Program: n/a
Teachers: 528.6 (13.6 to 1)
Librarians/Media Specialists: 12.0 (599.7 to 1)
Guidance Counselors: 16.4 (438.8 to 1)
Current Spending: ($ per student per year):
Total: $8,529; Instruction: $5,172; Support Services: $3,024
Enrollment, Drop-out Rates and Diploma Recipients by Race/Ethnicity

Category	Total	White	Black	Asian	AIAN	Hisp.
Enrollment (%)	100.0	87.3	2.5	2.9	0.3	7.1
Drop-out Rate (%)	0.8	0.8	0.0	1.6	0.0	0.9
H.S. Diplomas (#)	462	410	10	17	0	25

Waterbury SD

236 Grand St • Waterbury, CT 06702-1972
(203) 574-8004 • http://www.waterbury.k12.ct.us/
Grade Span: PK-12; **Agency Type:** 1
Schools: 28
20 Primary; 3 Middle; 3 High; 2 Other Level
25 Regular; 2 Special Education; 0 Vocational; 1 Alternative
2 Magnet; 0 Charter; 10 Title I Eligible; 0 School-wide Title I
Students: 17,413 (51.2% male; 48.8% female)
Individual Education Program: 3,346 (19.2%);
English Language Learner: 1,914 (11.0%); Migrant: 864 (5.0%)
Eligible for Free Lunch Program: n/a
Eligible for Reduced-Price Lunch Program: n/a
Teachers: 1,220.2 (14.3 to 1)
Librarians/Media Specialists: 17.8 (978.3 to 1)
Guidance Counselors: 17.8 (978.3 to 1)
Current Spending: ($ per student per year):
Total: $10,680; Instruction: $6,104; Support Services: $4,005
Enrollment, Drop-out Rates and Diploma Recipients by Race/Ethnicity

Category	Total	White	Black	Asian	AIAN	Hisp.
Enrollment (%)	100.0	32.2	26.2	2.0	0.4	39.3
Drop-out Rate (%)	3.9	2.9	4.4	0.0	18.2	4.7
H.S. Diplomas (#)	578	236	158	11	3	170

West Haven SD

25 Ogden St • West Haven, CT 06516-1800
(203) 937-4310 • http://www.whschools.org/
Grade Span: PK-12; **Agency Type:** 1
Schools: 14
9 Primary; 2 Middle; 1 High; 2 Other Level
12 Regular; 0 Special Education; 0 Vocational; 2 Alternative
0 Magnet; 0 Charter; 7 Title I Eligible; 0 School-wide Title I
Students: 7,307 (50.6% male; 49.4% female)
Individual Education Program: 886 (12.1%);
English Language Learner: 316 (4.3%); Migrant: 1 (<0.1%)
Eligible for Free Lunch Program: n/a
Eligible for Reduced-Price Lunch Program: n/a
Teachers: 478.3 (15.3 to 1)
Librarians/Media Specialists: 9.0 (811.9 to 1)
Guidance Counselors: 11.0 (664.3 to 1)
Current Spending: ($ per student per year):
Total: $9,663; Instruction: $5,685; Support Services: $3,572
Enrollment, Drop-out Rates and Diploma Recipients by Race/Ethnicity

Category	Total	White	Black	Asian	AIAN	Hisp.
Enrollment (%)	100.0	55.1	25.7	2.9	0.5	15.7
Drop-out Rate (%)	1.6	1.2	1.9	3.6	0.0	2.1
H.S. Diplomas (#)	340	213	70	15	2	40

Wolcott SD

154 Center St • Wolcott, CT 06716-2035
(203) 879-8180
Grade Span: PK-12; **Agency Type:** 1
Schools: 6
3 Primary; 1 Middle; 1 High; 1 Other Level
5 Regular; 0 Special Education; 0 Vocational; 1 Alternative
0 Magnet; 0 Charter; 1 Title I Eligible; 0 School-wide Title I
Students: 2,938 (50.2% male; 49.8% female)
Individual Education Program: 368 (12.5%);
English Language Learner: 6 (0.2%); Migrant: 0 (0.0%)
Eligible for Free Lunch Program: n/a
Eligible for Reduced-Price Lunch Program: n/a
Teachers: 208.9 (14.1 to 1)
Librarians/Media Specialists: 2.0 (1,469.0 to 1)
Guidance Counselors: 7.0 (419.7 to 1)
Current Spending: ($ per student per year):
Total: $8,296; Instruction: $5,709; Support Services: $2,202
Enrollment, Drop-out Rates and Diploma Recipients by Race/Ethnicity

Category	Total	White	Black	Asian	AIAN	Hisp.
Enrollment (%)	100.0	95.5	1.2	1.0	0.1	2.1
Drop-out Rate (%)	0.9	0.8	5.9	0.0	0.0	0.0
H.S. Diplomas (#)	202	198	1	1	1	1

New London County

Colchester SD

127 Norwich Avenue, Ste 202 • Colchester, CT 06415-1260
(860) 537-7260 • http://www.colchesterct.org/
Grade Span: PK-12; **Agency Type:** 1
Schools: 6
2 Primary; 2 Middle; 1 High; 1 Other Level
5 Regular; 0 Special Education; 0 Vocational; 1 Alternative
0 Magnet; 0 Charter; 3 Title I Eligible; 0 School-wide Title I
Students: 3,161 (50.6% male; 49.4% female)
Individual Education Program: 388 (12.3%);
English Language Learner: 0 (0.0%); Migrant: 0 (0.0%)

Eligible for Free Lunch Program: n/a
Eligible for Reduced-Price Lunch Program: n/a
Teachers: 228.7 (13.8 to 1)
Librarians/Media Specialists: 4.0 (790.3 to 1)
Guidance Counselors: 6.0 (526.8 to 1)
Current Spending: ($ per student per year):
Total: $7,554; Instruction: $4,844; Support Services: $2,426
Enrollment, Drop-out Rates and Diploma Recipients by Race/Ethnicity

Category	Total	White	Black	Asian	AIAN	Hisp.
Enrollment (%)	100.0	93.0	2.9	1.1	0.5	2.5
Drop-out Rate (%)	2.5	2.6	0.0	0.0	0.0	0.0
H.S. Diplomas (#)	135	128	1	1	2	3

East Lyme SD

Boston Post Rd • East Lyme, CT 06333-0176
Mailing Address: Boston Post Rd, Box 176 • East Lyme, CT 06333-0176
(860) 739-3966 • http://www.eastlymeschools.org/
Grade Span: PK-12; **Agency Type:** 1
Schools: 6
3 Primary; 1 Middle; 1 High; 1 Other Level
5 Regular; 0 Special Education; 0 Vocational; 1 Alternative
0 Magnet; 0 Charter; 0 Title I Eligible; 0 School-wide Title I
Students: 3,270 (50.5% male; 49.5% female)
Individual Education Program: 381 (11.7%);
English Language Learner: 25 (0.8%); Migrant: 0 (0.0%)
Eligible for Free Lunch Program: n/a
Eligible for Reduced-Price Lunch Program: n/a
Teachers: 238.9 (13.7 to 1)
Librarians/Media Specialists: 4.8 (681.3 to 1)
Guidance Counselors: 8.5 (384.7 to 1)
Current Spending: ($ per student per year):
Total: $8,613; Instruction: $5,576; Support Services: $2,673
Enrollment, Drop-out Rates and Diploma Recipients by Race/Ethnicity

Category	Total	White	Black	Asian	AIAN	Hisp.
Enrollment (%)	100.0	88.5	2.0	6.2	0.9	2.5
Drop-out Rate (%)	1.9	2.0	0.0	0.0	0.0	0.0
H.S. Diplomas (#)	235	213	5	14	1	2

Griswold SD

305 Slater Ave • Jewett City, CT 06351-2540
(860) 376-7760 • http://www.griswold.k12.ct.us/
Grade Span: PK-12; **Agency Type:** 1
Schools: 5
1 Primary; 2 Middle; 1 High; 1 Other Level
4 Regular; 0 Special Education; 0 Vocational; 1 Alternative
0 Magnet; 0 Charter; 2 Title I Eligible; 0 School-wide Title I
Students: 2,162 (50.7% male; 49.3% female)
Individual Education Program: 243 (11.2%);
English Language Learner: 14 (0.6%); Migrant: 0 (0.0%)
Eligible for Free Lunch Program: n/a
Eligible for Reduced-Price Lunch Program: n/a
Teachers: 170.9 (12.7 to 1)
Librarians/Media Specialists: 3.0 (720.7 to 1)
Guidance Counselors: 8.0 (270.3 to 1)
Current Spending: ($ per student per year):
Total: $9,028; Instruction: $5,882; Support Services: $2,679
Enrollment, Drop-out Rates and Diploma Recipients by Race/Ethnicity

Category	Total	White	Black	Asian	AIAN	Hisp.
Enrollment (%)	100.0	93.0	1.8	1.6	1.6	2.0
Drop-out Rate (%)	3.1	3.2	0.0	0.0	0.0	0.0
H.S. Diplomas (#)	126	119	3	1	1	2

Groton SD

1300 Flanders Rd • Mystic, CT 06355-1042
Mailing Address: PO Box K • Groton, CT 06340-1411
(860) 572-2100
Grade Span: PK-12; **Agency Type:** 1
Schools: 15
10 Primary; 2 Middle; 1 High; 2 Other Level
14 Regular; 0 Special Education; 0 Vocational; 1 Alternative
0 Magnet; 0 Charter; 5 Title I Eligible; 0 School-wide Title I
Students: 5,777 (50.1% male; 49.9% female)
Individual Education Program: 846 (14.6%);
English Language Learner: 125 (2.2%); Migrant: 0 (0.0%)
Eligible for Free Lunch Program: n/a
Eligible for Reduced-Price Lunch Program: n/a
Teachers: 455.4 (12.7 to 1)
Librarians/Media Specialists: 15.0 (385.1 to 1)
Guidance Counselors: 11.5 (502.3 to 1)
Current Spending: ($ per student per year):
Total: $10,401; Instruction: $6,574; Support Services: $3,585

Enrollment, Drop-out Rates and Diploma Recipients by Race/Ethnicity

Category	Total	White	Black	Asian	AIAN	Hisp.
Enrollment (%)	100.0	73.2	13.5	5.3	1.2	6.9
Drop-out Rate (%)	0.8	0.8	1.4	0.0	0.0	1.5
H.S. Diplomas (#)	239	195	23	11	2	8

Ledyard SD

4 Blonder Blvd • Ledyard, CT 06339-1504
(860) 464-9255 • http://www.ledyardschools.org/
Grade Span: PK-12; **Agency Type:** 1
Schools: 7
4 Primary; 1 Middle; 1 High; 1 Other Level
6 Regular; 0 Special Education; 0 Vocational; 1 Alternative
0 Magnet; 0 Charter; 0 Title I Eligible; 0 School-wide Title I
Students: 3,060 (49.1% male; 50.9% female)
Individual Education Program: 343 (11.2%);
English Language Learner: 19 (0.6%); Migrant: 0 (0.0%)
Eligible for Free Lunch Program: n/a
Eligible for Reduced-Price Lunch Program: n/a
Teachers: 211.1 (14.5 to 1)
Librarians/Media Specialists: 4.0 (765.0 to 1)
Guidance Counselors: 7.8 (392.3 to 1)
Current Spending: ($ per student per year):
Total: $8,280; Instruction: $5,432; Support Services: $2,718
Enrollment, Drop-out Rates and Diploma Recipients by Race/Ethnicity

Category	Total	White	Black	Asian	AIAN	Hisp.
Enrollment (%)	100.0	83.9	4.1	3.1	4.0	4.9
Drop-out Rate (%)	3.1	3.1	0.0	0.0	12.8	0.0
H.S. Diplomas (#)	230	205	6	5	2	12

Montville SD

Old Colchester Rd • Oakdale, CT 06370-0078
(860) 848-1228 • http://www.montvilleschools.org/
Grade Span: PK-12; **Agency Type:** 1
Schools: 7
3 Primary; 1 Middle; 2 High; 1 Other Level
5 Regular; 0 Special Education; 0 Vocational; 2 Alternative
0 Magnet; 0 Charter; 3 Title I Eligible; 3 School-wide Title I
Students: 2,933 (52.5% male; 47.5% female)
Individual Education Program: 436 (14.9%);
English Language Learner: 38 (1.3%); Migrant: 0 (0.0%)
Eligible for Free Lunch Program: n/a
Eligible for Reduced-Price Lunch Program: n/a
Teachers: 231.3 (12.7 to 1)
Librarians/Media Specialists: 5.0 (586.6 to 1)
Guidance Counselors: 7.3 (401.8 to 1)
Current Spending: ($ per student per year):
Total: $9,435; Instruction: $6,014; Support Services: $3,044
Enrollment, Drop-out Rates and Diploma Recipients by Race/Ethnicity

Category	Total	White	Black	Asian	AIAN	Hisp.
Enrollment (%)	100.0	85.8	5.0	3.1	1.9	4.3
Drop-out Rate (%)	2.6	2.2	0.0	0.0	6.3	20.0
H.S. Diplomas (#)	159	141	5	4	6	3

New London SD

134 Williams St • New London, CT 06320-5296
(860) 447-6000 • http://www.newlondon.org/
Grade Span: PK-12; **Agency Type:** 1
Schools: 10
6 Primary; 1 Middle; 1 High; 2 Other Level
9 Regular; 0 Special Education; 0 Vocational; 1 Alternative
0 Magnet; 0 Charter; 4 Title I Eligible; 4 School-wide Title I
Students: 3,222 (51.1% male; 48.9% female)
Individual Education Program: 653 (20.3%);
English Language Learner: 416 (12.9%); Migrant: 134 (4.2%)
Eligible for Free Lunch Program: n/a
Eligible for Reduced-Price Lunch Program: n/a
Teachers: 268.7 (12.0 to 1)
Librarians/Media Specialists: 3.0 (1,074.0 to 1)
Guidance Counselors: 8.0 (402.8 to 1)
Current Spending: ($ per student per year):
Total: $12,617; Instruction: $7,902; Support Services: $4,206
Enrollment, Drop-out Rates and Diploma Recipients by Race/Ethnicity

Category	Total	White	Black	Asian	AIAN	Hisp.
Enrollment (%)	100.0	20.8	34.2	1.8	1.2	42.0
Drop-out Rate (%)	26.1	20.9	27.8	8.7	0.0	30.5
H.S. Diplomas (#)	121	34	47	3	3	34

Norwich Free Academy

305 Broadway • Norwich, CT 06360-3563
(860) 887-2505 • http://WWW.norwichfreeacademy.com/
Grade Span: 09-12; **Agency Type:** 7
Schools: 1
0 Primary; 0 Middle; 1 High; 0 Other Level
1 Regular; 0 Special Education; 0 Vocational; 0 Alternative

0 Magnet; 0 Charter; 0 Title I Eligible; 0 School-wide Title I
Students: 2,284 (46.5% male; 53.5% female)
Individual Education Program: 0 (0.0%);
English Language Learner: 56 (2.5%); Migrant: 2 (0.1%)
Eligible for Free Lunch Program: n/a
Eligible for Reduced-Price Lunch Program: n/a
Teachers: 151.6 (15.1 to 1)
Librarians/Media Specialists: 2.0 (1,142.0 to 1)
Guidance Counselors: 11.0 (207.6 to 1)
Current Spending: ($ per student per year):
Total: n/a; Instruction: n/a; Support Services: n/a
Enrollment, Drop-out Rates and Diploma Recipients by Race/Ethnicity

Category	Total	White	Black	Asian	AIAN	Hisp.
Enrollment (%)	100.0	78.2	10.2	3.5	2.0	6.1
Drop-out Rate (%)	4.1	3.7	5.3	3.4	7.1	6.8
H.S. Diplomas (#)	497	414	44	18	6	15

Norwich SD
90 Town St • Norwich, CT 06360-2324
(860) 823-4245 • http://www.norwichschools.org
Grade Span: PK-12; **Agency Type:** 1
Schools: 15
10 Primary; 2 Middle; 1 High; 2 Other Level
12 Regular; 1 Special Education; 0 Vocational; 2 Alternative
0 Magnet; 0 Charter; 10 Title I Eligible; 7 School-wide Title I
Students: 4,048 (51.0% male; 49.0% female)
Individual Education Program: 867 (21.4%);
English Language Learner: 107 (2.6%); Migrant: 7 (0.2%)
Eligible for Free Lunch Program: n/a
Eligible for Reduced-Price Lunch Program: n/a
Teachers: 261.4 (15.5 to 1)
Librarians/Media Specialists: 2.0 (2,024.0 to 1)
Guidance Counselors: 9.0 (449.8 to 1)
Current Spending: ($ per student per year):
Total: $10,553; Instruction: $6,765; Support Services: $3,412
Enrollment, Drop-out Rates and Diploma Recipients by Race/Ethnicity

Category	Total	White	Black	Asian	AIAN	Hisp.
Enrollment (%)	100.0	62.5	18.6	3.6	2.4	13.0
Drop-out Rate (%)	53.5	56.1	54.5	0.0	0.0	66.7
H.S. Diplomas (#)	11	8	2	0	0	1

Regional SD 18
53 Lyme St • Old Lyme, CT 06371-2334
(860) 434-7238
Grade Span: PK-12; **Agency Type:** 1
Schools: 6
3 Primary; 1 Middle; 1 High; 1 Other Level
5 Regular; 0 Special Education; 0 Vocational; 1 Alternative
0 Magnet; 0 Charter; 0 Title I Eligible; 0 School-wide Title I
Students: 1,584 (49.8% male; 50.2% female)
Individual Education Program: 195 (12.3%);
English Language Learner: 3 (0.2%); Migrant: 0 (0.0%)
Eligible for Free Lunch Program: n/a
Eligible for Reduced-Price Lunch Program: n/a
Teachers: 127.9 (12.4 to 1)
Librarians/Media Specialists: 5.0 (316.8 to 1)
Guidance Counselors: 3.5 (452.6 to 1)
Current Spending: ($ per student per year):
Total: $10,722; Instruction: $6,170; Support Services: $4,154
Enrollment, Drop-out Rates and Diploma Recipients by Race/Ethnicity

Category	Total	White	Black	Asian	AIAN	Hisp.
Enrollment (%)	100.0	95.1	0.8	2.8	0.0	1.3
Drop-out Rate (%)	1.7	1.5	33.3	0.0	n/a	0.0
H.S. Diplomas (#)	94	92	0	0	0	2

Stonington SD
49 N Stonington Rd • Old Mystic, CT 06372-0479
(860) 572-0506 • http://stamford.k12.ct.us/
Grade Span: PK-12; **Agency Type:** 1
Schools: 8
4 Primary; 2 Middle; 1 High; 1 Other Level
6 Regular; 1 Special Education; 0 Vocational; 1 Alternative
0 Magnet; 0 Charter; 3 Title I Eligible; 0 School-wide Title I
Students: 2,432 (52.1% male; 47.9% female)
Individual Education Program: 317 (13.0%);
English Language Learner: 10 (0.4%); Migrant: 0 (0.0%)
Eligible for Free Lunch Program: n/a
Eligible for Reduced-Price Lunch Program: n/a
Teachers: 178.2 (13.6 to 1)
Librarians/Media Specialists: 4.3 (565.6 to 1)
Guidance Counselors: 4.0 (608.0 to 1)
Current Spending: ($ per student per year):
Total: $10,230; Instruction: $6,363; Support Services: $3,466
Enrollment, Drop-out Rates and Diploma Recipients by Race/Ethnicity

Category	Total	White	Black	Asian	AIAN	Hisp.
Enrollment (%)	100.0	95.8	0.3	0.2	0.0	3.8
Drop-out Rate (%)	2.7	2.6	0.0	0.0	0.0	25.0
H.S. Diplomas (#)	141	136	2	1	0	2

Waterford SD
15 Rope Ferry Rd • Waterford, CT 06385-2886
(860) 444-5801 • http://www.waterfordschools.org/
Grade Span: PK-12; **Agency Type:** 1
Schools: 9
6 Primary; 1 Middle; 1 High; 1 Other Level
8 Regular; 0 Special Education; 0 Vocational; 1 Alternative
0 Magnet; 0 Charter; 3 Title I Eligible; 0 School-wide Title I
Students: 3,087 (50.3% male; 49.7% female)
Individual Education Program: 379 (12.3%);
English Language Learner: 13 (0.4%); Migrant: 0 (0.0%)
Eligible for Free Lunch Program: n/a
Eligible for Reduced-Price Lunch Program: n/a
Teachers: 236.6 (13.0 to 1)
Librarians/Media Specialists: 2.0 (1,543.5 to 1)
Guidance Counselors: 8.0 (385.9 to 1)
Current Spending: ($ per student per year):
Total: $10,733; Instruction: $6,937; Support Services: $3,447
Enrollment, Drop-out Rates and Diploma Recipients by Race/Ethnicity

Category	Total	White	Black	Asian	AIAN	Hisp.
Enrollment (%)	100.0	88.1	4.2	4.4	0.3	3.0
Drop-out Rate (%)	0.5	0.5	0.0	0.0	0.0	0.0
H.S. Diplomas (#)	191	171	9	7	2	2

Tolland County

Coventry SD
1700 Main St • Coventry, CT 06238-1654
(860) 742-7317 • http://www.CoventryPS.org/
Grade Span: PK-12; **Agency Type:** 1
Schools: 5
2 Primary; 1 Middle; 1 High; 1 Other Level
4 Regular; 0 Special Education; 0 Vocational; 1 Alternative
0 Magnet; 0 Charter; 2 Title I Eligible; 0 School-wide Title I
Students: 2,083 (51.4% male; 48.6% female)
Individual Education Program: 259 (12.4%);
English Language Learner: 0 (0.0%); Migrant: 0 (0.0%)
Eligible for Free Lunch Program: n/a
Eligible for Reduced-Price Lunch Program: n/a
Teachers: 150.5 (13.8 to 1)
Librarians/Media Specialists: 2.0 (1,041.5 to 1)
Guidance Counselors: 4.0 (520.8 to 1)
Current Spending: ($ per student per year):
Total: $7,986; Instruction: $5,009; Support Services: $2,615
Enrollment, Drop-out Rates and Diploma Recipients by Race/Ethnicity

Category	Total	White	Black	Asian	AIAN	Hisp.
Enrollment (%)	100.0	96.4	1.0	0.4	0.4	1.8
Drop-out Rate (%)	3.4	3.2	0.0	33.3	0.0	14.3
H.S. Diplomas (#)	101	98	1	1	0	1

Ellington SD
47 Main St • Ellington, CT 06029-0179
Mailing Address: 47 Main St, Box 157 • Ellington, CT 06029-0179
(860) 872-8381 • http://www.ellingtonschools.org/
Grade Span: PK-12; **Agency Type:** 1
Schools: 6
3 Primary; 1 Middle; 1 High; 1 Other Level
5 Regular; 0 Special Education; 0 Vocational; 1 Alternative
0 Magnet; 0 Charter; 1 Title I Eligible; 0 School-wide Title I
Students: 2,344 (51.4% male; 48.6% female)
Individual Education Program: 198 (8.4%);
English Language Learner: 24 (1.0%); Migrant: 0 (0.0%)
Eligible for Free Lunch Program: n/a
Eligible for Reduced-Price Lunch Program: n/a
Teachers: 169.1 (13.9 to 1)
Librarians/Media Specialists: 3.0 (781.3 to 1)
Guidance Counselors: 5.0 (468.8 to 1)
Current Spending: ($ per student per year):
Total: $8,648; Instruction: $5,600; Support Services: $2,680
Enrollment, Drop-out Rates and Diploma Recipients by Race/Ethnicity

Category	Total	White	Black	Asian	AIAN	Hisp.
Enrollment (%)	100.0	96.0	1.4	1.5	0.1	1.0
Drop-out Rate (%)	2.4	2.5	0.0	0.0	0.0	0.0
H.S. Diplomas (#)	113	110	0	1	2	0

Regional SD 08

33 Pendleton Dr • Hebron, CT 06248-1525
(860) 228-9417
Grade Span: 07-12; **Agency Type:** 1
Schools: 3
0 Primary; 1 Middle; 2 High; 0 Other Level
2 Regular; 0 Special Education; 0 Vocational; 1 Alternative
0 Magnet; 0 Charter; 2 Title I Eligible; 0 School-wide Title I
Students: 1,529 (50.9% male; 49.1% female)
Individual Education Program: 152 (9.9%);
English Language Learner: 0 (0.0%); Migrant: 0 (0.0%)
Eligible for Free Lunch Program: n/a
Eligible for Reduced-Price Lunch Program: n/a
Teachers: 127.0 (12.0 to 1)
Librarians/Media Specialists: 2.0 (764.5 to 1)
Guidance Counselors: 6.6 (231.7 to 1)
Current Spending: ($ per student per year):
Total: $9,250; Instruction: $5,977; Support Services: $2,848
Enrollment, Drop-out Rates and Diploma Recipients by Race/Ethnicity

Category	Total	White	Black	Asian	AIAN	Hisp.
Enrollment (%)	100.0	95.7	1.1	0.8	0.4	2.0
Drop-out Rate (%)	0.9	0.9	0.0	0.0	0.0	0.0
H.S. Diplomas (#)	205	201	2	1	0	1

Somers SD

Ninth District Rd • Somers, CT 06071-9609
(860) 749-2279 • http://www.somers.k12.ct.us/
Grade Span: PK-12; **Agency Type:** 1
Schools: 4
1 Primary; 1 Middle; 1 High; 1 Other Level
3 Regular; 0 Special Education; 0 Vocational; 1 Alternative
0 Magnet; 0 Charter; 0 Title I Eligible; 0 School-wide Title I
Students: 1,703 (51.3% male; 48.7% female)
Individual Education Program: 171 (10.0%);
English Language Learner: 1 (0.1%); Migrant: 0 (0.0%)
Eligible for Free Lunch Program: n/a
Eligible for Reduced-Price Lunch Program: n/a
Teachers: 122.6 (13.9 to 1)
Librarians/Media Specialists: 4.0 (425.8 to 1)
Guidance Counselors: 3.0 (567.7 to 1)
Current Spending: ($ per student per year):
Total: $8,593; Instruction: $5,827; Support Services: $2,674
Enrollment, Drop-out Rates and Diploma Recipients by Race/Ethnicity

Category	Total	White	Black	Asian	AIAN	Hisp.
Enrollment (%)	100.0	97.3	0.8	1.1	0.1	0.7
Drop-out Rate (%)	3.2	2.9	16.7	0.0	n/a	12.5
H.S. Diplomas (#)	95	93	0	2	0	0

Stafford SD

263 E Street/Rte 19 • Stafford Springs, CT 06076-0147
Mailing Address: 263 E Street/Rte 19, Box 1 • Stafford Spring, CT 06076-0147
(860) 684-4211 • http://www.stafford.ctschool.net/
Grade Span: PK-12; **Agency Type:** 1
Schools: 7
3 Primary; 2 Middle; 1 High; 1 Other Level
6 Regular; 0 Special Education; 0 Vocational; 1 Alternative
0 Magnet; 0 Charter; 2 Title I Eligible; 0 School-wide Title I
Students: 2,010 (48.8% male; 51.2% female)
Individual Education Program: 232 (11.5%);
English Language Learner: 10 (0.5%); Migrant: 0 (0.0%)
Eligible for Free Lunch Program: n/a
Eligible for Reduced-Price Lunch Program: n/a
Teachers: 161.7 (12.4 to 1)
Librarians/Media Specialists: 2.0 (1,005.0 to 1)
Guidance Counselors: 3.0 (670.0 to 1)
Current Spending: ($ per student per year):
Total: $9,431; Instruction: $6,088; Support Services: $3,045
Enrollment, Drop-out Rates and Diploma Recipients by Race/Ethnicity

Category	Total	White	Black	Asian	AIAN	Hisp.
Enrollment (%)	100.0	95.4	0.9	1.1	0.3	2.2
Drop-out Rate (%)	4.0	4.0	0.0	14.3	0.0	0.0
H.S. Diplomas (#)	92	85	1	3	0	3

Tolland SD

51 Tolland Green • Tolland, CT 06084-3099
(860) 870-6850 • http://www.tolland.k12.ct.us/
Grade Span: PK-12; **Agency Type:** 1
Schools: 5
2 Primary; 1 Middle; 1 High; 1 Other Level
4 Regular; 0 Special Education; 0 Vocational; 1 Alternative
0 Magnet; 0 Charter; 2 Title I Eligible; 0 School-wide Title I
Students: 2,963 (51.9% male; 48.1% female)
Individual Education Program: 331 (11.2%);
English Language Learner: 15 (0.5%); Migrant: 0 (0.0%)
Eligible for Free Lunch Program: n/a
Eligible for Reduced-Price Lunch Program: n/a
Teachers: 222.5 (13.3 to 1)
Librarians/Media Specialists: 3.5 (846.6 to 1)
Guidance Counselors: 8.0 (370.4 to 1)
Current Spending: ($ per student per year):
Total: $8,296; Instruction: $5,293; Support Services: $2,646
Enrollment, Drop-out Rates and Diploma Recipients by Race/Ethnicity

Category	Total	White	Black	Asian	AIAN	Hisp.
Enrollment (%)	100.0	96.2	0.9	1.8	0.3	0.8
Drop-out Rate (%)	1.4	1.4	0.0	0.0	n/a	0.0
H.S. Diplomas (#)	169	163	0	4	1	1

Vernon SD

30 Park St • Vernon, CT 06066-3244
Mailing Address: 30 Park St, Box 600 • Vernon, CT 06066-3244
(860) 870-6002 • http://www.vernonct.com/
Grade Span: PK-12; **Agency Type:** 1
Schools: 8
5 Primary; 1 Middle; 1 High; 1 Other Level
7 Regular; 0 Special Education; 0 Vocational; 1 Alternative
0 Magnet; 0 Charter; 4 Title I Eligible; 0 School-wide Title I
Students: 4,021 (50.0% male; 50.0% female)
Individual Education Program: 493 (12.3%);
English Language Learner: 95 (2.4%); Migrant: 0 (0.0%)
Eligible for Free Lunch Program: n/a
Eligible for Reduced-Price Lunch Program: n/a
Teachers: 310.2 (13.0 to 1)
Librarians/Media Specialists: 0.8 (5,026.3 to 1)
Guidance Counselors: 8.0 (502.6 to 1)
Current Spending: ($ per student per year):
Total: $9,752; Instruction: $6,260; Support Services: $3,193
Enrollment, Drop-out Rates and Diploma Recipients by Race/Ethnicity

Category	Total	White	Black	Asian	AIAN	Hisp.
Enrollment (%)	100.0	79.1	9.2	5.1	0.3	6.3
Drop-out Rate (%)	1.9	1.7	4.5	2.0	0.0	1.8
H.S. Diplomas (#)	235	225	3	6	0	1

Windham County

Killingly SD

369 Main St • Danielson, CT 06239-0210
Mailing Address: PO Box 210 • Danielson, CT 06239-0210
(860) 779-6600 • http://killingly.k12.ct.us/
Grade Span: PK-12; **Agency Type:** 1
Schools: 6
3 Primary; 1 Middle; 1 High; 1 Other Level
5 Regular; 0 Special Education; 0 Vocational; 1 Alternative
0 Magnet; 0 Charter; 2 Title I Eligible; 0 School-wide Title I
Students: 2,987 (50.9% male; 49.1% female)
Individual Education Program: 443 (14.8%);
English Language Learner: 31 (1.0%); Migrant: 5 (0.2%)
Eligible for Free Lunch Program: n/a
Eligible for Reduced-Price Lunch Program: n/a
Teachers: 213.3 (14.0 to 1)
Librarians/Media Specialists: 4.0 (746.8 to 1)
Guidance Counselors: 6.5 (459.5 to 1)
Current Spending: ($ per student per year):
Total: $8,374; Instruction: $5,233; Support Services: $2,844
Enrollment, Drop-out Rates and Diploma Recipients by Race/Ethnicity

Category	Total	White	Black	Asian	AIAN	Hisp.
Enrollment (%)	100.0	89.6	3.7	2.2	0.9	3.6
Drop-out Rate (%)	6.8	6.2	8.8	18.2	0.0	19.0
H.S. Diplomas (#)	203	187	5	9	0	2

Plainfield SD

99 Putnam Rd • Central Village, CT 06332-0705
Mailing Address: 99 Putnam Road, Box 705 • Central Village, CT 06332-0705
(860) 564-6403 • http://www.plainfieldschools.org/
Grade Span: PK-12; **Agency Type:** 1
Schools: 7
3 Primary; 2 Middle; 1 High; 1 Other Level
5 Regular; 0 Special Education; 0 Vocational; 2 Alternative
0 Magnet; 0 Charter; 3 Title I Eligible; 0 School-wide Title I
Students: 2,733 (51.9% male; 48.1% female)
Individual Education Program: 339 (12.4%);
English Language Learner: 1 (<0.1%); Migrant: 0 (0.0%)
Eligible for Free Lunch Program: n/a
Eligible for Reduced-Price Lunch Program: n/a
Teachers: 181.0 (15.1 to 1)
Librarians/Media Specialists: 1.0 (2,733.0 to 1)
Guidance Counselors: 9.0 (303.7 to 1)
Current Spending: ($ per student per year):
Total: $8,870; Instruction: $5,262; Support Services: $3,316

Enrollment, Drop-out Rates and Diploma Recipients by Race/Ethnicity

Category	Total	White	Black	Asian	AIAN	Hisp.
Enrollment (%)	100.0	92.3	2.0	1.1	1.2	3.4
Drop-out Rate (%)	6.4	5.9	0.0	66.7	0.0	25.0
H.S. Diplomas (#)	164	153	1	2	2	6

Windham SD

322 Prospect St • Willimantic, CT 06226-2202
(860) 465-2310 • http://www.windham.k12.ct.us/
Grade Span: PK-12; **Agency Type:** 1
Schools: 11
7 Primary; 1 Middle; 1 High; 2 Other Level
9 Regular; 1 Special Education; 0 Vocational; 1 Alternative
0 Magnet; 0 Charter; 6 Title I Eligible; 5 School-wide Title I
Students: 3,560 (51.7% male; 48.3% female)
Individual Education Program: 579 (16.3%);
English Language Learner: 452 (12.7%); Migrant: 238 (6.7%)
Eligible for Free Lunch Program: n/a
Eligible for Reduced-Price Lunch Program: n/a
Teachers: 275.7 (12.9 to 1)
Librarians/Media Specialists: 4.0 (890.0 to 1)
Guidance Counselors: 9.6 (370.8 to 1)
Current Spending: ($ per student per year):
Total: $11,364; Instruction: $6,927; Support Services: $3,975

Enrollment, Drop-out Rates and Diploma Recipients by Race/Ethnicity

Category	Total	White	Black	Asian	AIAN	Hisp.
Enrollment (%)	100.0	40.1	5.6	1.0	0.5	52.8
Drop-out Rate (%)	6.5	5.9	6.8	0.0	0.0	7.6
H.S. Diplomas (#)	196	135	9	7	0	45

Number of Schools

Rank	Number	District Name	City
1	48	New Haven SD	New Haven
2	38	Hartford SD	Hartford
3	36	Bridgeport SD	Bridgeport
4	28	Waterbury SD	Waterbury
5	21	Stamford SD	Stamford
6	20	Norwalk SD	Norwalk
7	18	Danbury SD	Danbury
8	17	Manchester SD	Manchester
8	17	State Voc-Tech Schools	Middletown
10	16	Bristol SD	Bristol
10	16	Fairfield SD	Fairfield
10	16	Greenwich SD	Greenwich
10	16	Milford SD	Milford
10	16	New Britain SD	New Britain
10	16	West Hartford SD	West Hartford
16	15	East Hartford SD	East Hartford
16	15	Groton SD	Mystic
16	15	Norwich SD	Norwich
19	14	Enfield SD	Enfield
19	14	Stratford SD	Stratford
19	14	Wallingford SD	Wallingford
19	14	West Haven SD	West Haven
23	13	East Haven SD	East Haven
23	13	Meriden SD	Meriden
23	13	Southington SD	Southington
26	12	Hamden SD	Hamden
26	12	Middletown SD	Middletown
26	12	Naugatuck SD	Naugatuck
29	11	Windham SD	Willimantic
30	10	New London SD	New London
30	10	Shelton SD	Shelton
30	10	Trumbull SD	Trumbull
33	9	Cheshire SD	Cheshire
33	9	Glastonbury SD	Glastonbury
33	9	Ridgefield SD	Ridgefield
33	9	Torrington SD	Torrington
33	9	Waterford SD	Waterford
33	9	Westport SD	Westport
39	8	Darien SD	Darien
39	8	Farmington SD	Farmington
39	8	Guilford SD	Guilford
39	8	Madison SD	Madison
39	8	Newington SD	Newington
39	8	Regional SD 15	Middlebury
39	8	Simsbury SD	Simsbury
39	8	South Windsor SD	South Windsor
39	8	Stonington SD	Old Mystic
39	8	Vernon SD	Vernon
39	8	Wethersfield SD	Wethersfield
39	8	Windsor SD	Windsor
51	7	Bethel SD	Bethel
51	7	Branford SD	Branford
51	7	Capitol Region Education Council	Hartford
51	7	Ledyard SD	Ledyard
51	7	Monroe SD	Monroe
51	7	Montville SD	Oakdale
51	7	New Milford SD	New Milford
51	7	Newtown SD	Newtown
51	7	North Haven SD	North Haven
51	7	Plainfield SD	Central Village
51	7	Plainville SD	Plainville
51	7	Regional SD 13	Durham
51	7	Stafford SD	Stafford Spgs
51	7	Watertown SD	Watertown
65	6	Avon SD	Avon
65	6	Berlin SD	Berlin
65	6	Bloomfield SD	Bloomfield
65	6	Colchester SD	Colchester
65	6	East Lyme SD	East Lyme
65	6	Ellington SD	Ellington
65	6	Granby SD	Granby
65	6	Killingly SD	Danielson
65	6	New Canaan SD	New Canaan
65	6	North Branford SD	Northford
65	6	Plymouth SD	Terryville
65	6	Regional SD 14	Woodbury
65	6	Regional SD 16	Prospect
65	6	Regional SD 17	Higganum
65	6	Regional SD 18	Old Lyme
65	6	Rocky Hill SD	Rocky Hill
65	6	Seymour SD	Seymour
65	6	Suffield SD	Suffield
65	6	Wilton SD	Wilton
65	6	Wolcott SD	Wolcott
85	5	Ansonia SD	Ansonia
85	5	Brookfield SD	Brookfield
85	5	Clinton SD	Clinton
85	5	Coventry SD	Coventry
85	5	East Hampton SD	East Hampton
85	5	Griswold SD	Jewett City
85	5	New Fairfield SD	New Fairfield
85	5	Regional SD 10	Burlington
85	5	Tolland SD	Tolland
85	5	Windsor Locks SD	Windsor Locks
95	4	Area Coop Educational Services	North Haven
95	4	Canton SD	Collinsville
95	4	Cromwell SD	Cromwell
95	4	Derby SD	Derby
95	4	East Windsor SD	East Windsor
95	4	Old Saybrook SD	Old Saybrook
95	4	Regional SD 05	Woodbridge
95	4	Somers SD	Somers
95	4	Weston SD	Weston
104	3	Regional SD 08	Hebron
105	1	Norwich Free Academy	Norwich

Number of Teachers

Rank	Number	District Name	City
1	1,837	Hartford SD	Hartford
2	1,482	Bridgeport SD	Bridgeport
3	1,415	New Haven SD	New Haven
4	1,235	Stamford SD	Stamford
5	1,220	Waterbury SD	Waterbury
6	1,098	State Voc-Tech Schools	Middletown
7	820	Norwalk SD	Norwalk
8	749	West Hartford SD	West Hartford
9	740	Greenwich SD	Greenwich
10	720	New Britain SD	New Britain
11	683	Fairfield SD	Fairfield
12	641	Danbury SD	Danbury
13	624	Meriden SD	Meriden
14	609	Bristol SD	Bristol
15	570	Milford SD	Milford
16	552	East Hartford SD	East Hartford
17	550	Manchester SD	Manchester
18	528	Wallingford SD	Wallingford
19	527	Stratford SD	Stratford
20	512	Enfield SD	Enfield
21	495	Southington SD	Southington
22	478	West Haven SD	West Haven
23	455	Groton SD	Mystic
24	450	Glastonbury SD	Glastonbury
25	434	Westport SD	Westport
26	409	Hamden SD	Hamden
27	403	Trumbull SD	Trumbull
28	403	Middletown SD	Middletown
29	367	Shelton SD	Shelton
30	362	Ridgefield SD	Ridgefield
31	361	Naugatuck SD	Naugatuck
32	354	Windsor SD	Windsor
33	344	Newtown SD	Newtown
34	343	New Milford SD	New Milford
35	343	Simsbury SD	Simsbury
36	341	Torrington SD	Torrington
37	336	Cheshire SD	Cheshire
38	333	South Windsor SD	South Windsor
39	331	Darien SD	Darien
40	310	Farmington SD	Farmington
40	310	Vernon SD	Vernon
42	308	New Canaan SD	New Canaan
43	295	Wilton SD	Wilton
44	291	Newington SD	Newington
44	291	Regional SD 15	Middlebury
46	282	Monroe SD	Monroe
47	277	Branford SD	Branford
48	275	Windham SD	Willimantic
49	268	New London SD	New London
50	261	Norwich SD	Norwich
51	256	Madison SD	Madison
52	255	Guilford SD	Guilford
53	247	East Haven SD	East Haven
54	241	Watertown SD	Watertown
55	240	North Haven SD	North Haven
56	240	Wethersfield SD	Wethersfield
57	239	Bethel SD	Bethel
58	238	East Lyme SD	East Lyme
59	236	Waterford SD	Waterford
60	231	Montville SD	Oakdale
61	230	Berlin SD	Berlin
62	230	Area Coop Educational Services	North Haven
63	228	Colchester SD	Colchester
64	222	Tolland SD	Tolland
65	219	Brookfield SD	Brookfield
66	213	Avon SD	Avon
67	213	Killingly SD	Danielson
68	211	Ledyard SD	Ledyard
69	209	New Fairfield SD	New Fairfield
70	208	Wolcott SD	Wolcott
71	203	Bloomfield SD	Bloomfield
72	202	Capitol Region Education Council	Hartford
73	199	Regional SD 17	Higganum
74	198	Weston SD	Weston
75	193	Regional SD 10	Burlington
76	184	Rocky Hill SD	Rocky Hill
77	184	Seymour SD	Seymour
78	182	Plainville SD	Plainville
79	181	Plainfield SD	Central Village
80	178	Stonington SD	Old Mystic
81	175	Regional SD 16	Prospect
82	174	Regional SD 05	Woodbridge
83	170	Griswold SD	Jewett City
84	169	Ellington SD	Ellington
85	168	Regional SD 13	Durham
86	165	Clinton SD	Clinton
87	165	Regional SD 14	Woodbury
88	163	Suffield SD	Suffield
88	163	Windsor Locks SD	Windsor Locks
90	161	Stafford SD	Stafford Spgs
91	156	Ansonia SD	Ansonia
92	152	North Branford SD	Northford
93	151	Norwich Free Academy	Norwich
94	150	Coventry SD	Coventry
95	149	Cromwell SD	Cromwell
96	143	East Hampton SD	East Hampton
97	142	Plymouth SD	Terryville
98	134	Old Saybrook SD	Old Saybrook
99	133	Granby SD	Granby
100	127	Regional SD 18	Old Lyme
101	127	Regional SD 08	Hebron
102	122	Somers SD	Somers
103	111	Canton SD	Collinsville
104	100	East Windsor SD	East Windsor
105	98	Derby SD	Derby

Number of Students

Rank	Number	District Name	City
1	22,734	Hartford SD	Hartford
2	22,493	Bridgeport SD	Bridgeport
3	20,329	New Haven SD	New Haven
4	17,413	Waterbury SD	Waterbury
5	15,231	Stamford SD	Stamford
6	11,130	State Voc-Tech Schools	Middletown
7	11,086	Norwalk SD	Norwalk
8	10,658	New Britain SD	New Britain
9	9,626	West Hartford SD	West Hartford
10	9,561	Danbury SD	Danbury
11	8,976	Greenwich SD	Greenwich
12	8,970	Bristol SD	Bristol
13	8,780	Meriden SD	Meriden
14	8,539	Fairfield SD	Fairfield
15	7,859	East Hartford SD	East Hartford
16	7,715	Manchester SD	Manchester
17	7,593	Stratford SD	Stratford
18	7,459	Milford SD	Milford
19	7,307	West Haven SD	West Haven
20	7,196	Wallingford SD	Wallingford
21	6,837	Enfield SD	Enfield
22	6,679	Southington SD	Southington
23	6,413	Glastonbury SD	Glastonbury
24	6,368	Trumbull SD	Trumbull
25	6,315	Hamden SD	Hamden
26	5,777	Groton SD	Mystic
27	5,610	Shelton SD	Shelton
28	5,572	Naugatuck SD	Naugatuck
29	5,360	Ridgefield SD	Ridgefield
30	5,204	New Milford SD	New Milford
31	5,196	Newtown SD	Newtown
32	5,149	Middletown SD	Middletown
33	5,123	Westport SD	Westport
34	5,088	Cheshire SD	Cheshire
35	5,074	South Windsor SD	South Windsor
36	5,030	Simsbury SD	Simsbury
37	5,026	Torrington SD	Torrington
38	4,616	Newington SD	Newington
39	4,432	Windsor SD	Windsor
40	4,391	Regional SD 15	Middlebury
41	4,206	Farmington SD	Farmington
42	4,136	Monroe SD	Monroe
43	4,116	Darien SD	Darien
44	4,084	Wilton SD	Wilton
45	4,048	Norwich SD	Norwich
46	4,031	East Haven SD	East Haven
47	4,021	Vernon SD	Vernon
48	3,951	New Canaan SD	New Canaan
49	3,904	Guilford SD	Guilford
50	3,773	North Haven SD	North Haven
51	3,705	Branford SD	Branford
52	3,675	Madison SD	Madison
53	3,595	Wethersfield SD	Wethersfield
54	3,569	Watertown SD	Watertown
55	3,560	Windham SD	Willimantic
56	3,271	Berlin SD	Berlin
57	3,270	East Lyme SD	East Lyme
58	3,225	Bethel SD	Bethel

59	3,222	New London SD	New London
60	3,167	New Fairfield SD	New Fairfield
61	3,161	Colchester SD	Colchester
62	3,090	Avon SD	Avon
63	3,087	Waterford SD	Waterford
64	3,060	Ledyard SD	Ledyard
65	3,018	Brookfield SD	Brookfield
66	2,987	Killingly SD	Danielson
67	2,963	Tolland SD	Tolland
68	2,938	Wolcott SD	Wolcott
69	2,933	Montville SD	Oakdale
70	2,855	Seymour SD	Seymour
71	2,733	Plainfield SD	Central Village
72	2,660	Plainville SD	Plainville
73	2,631	Ansonia SD	Ansonia
74	2,609	Regional SD 10	Burlington
75	2,512	Bloomfield SD	Bloomfield
76	2,483	Rocky Hill SD	Rocky Hill
77	2,481	North Branford SD	Northford
78	2,432	Stonington SD	Old Mystic
79	2,416	Regional SD 16	Prospect
80	2,413	Weston SD	Weston
81	2,397	Regional SD 05	Woodbridge
82	2,383	Regional SD 17	Higganum
83	2,344	Ellington SD	Ellington
84	2,321	Suffield SD	Suffield
85	2,306	Regional SD 14	Woodbury
86	2,284	Norwich Free Academy	Norwich
87	2,214	Clinton SD	Clinton
88	2,191	Capitol Region Education Council	Hartford
89	2,162	Griswold SD	Jewett City
90	2,160	Area Coop Educational Services	North Haven
91	2,151	Granby SD	Granby
92	2,114	Regional SD 13	Durham
93	2,083	Coventry SD	Coventry
94	2,027	East Hampton SD	East Hampton
95	2,010	Stafford SD	Stafford Spgs
96	1,963	Windsor Locks SD	Windsor Locks
97	1,898	Plymouth SD	Terryville
98	1,849	Cromwell SD	Cromwell
99	1,703	Somers SD	Somers
100	1,629	Canton SD	Collinsville
101	1,606	Derby SD	Derby
102	1,598	Old Saybrook SD	Old Saybrook
103	1,584	Regional SD 18	Old Lyme
104	1,579	East Windsor SD	East Windsor
105	1,529	Regional SD 08	Hebron

Male Students

Rank	Percent	District Name	City
1	63.7	State Voc-Tech Schools	Middletown
2	61.6	Area Coop Educational Services	North Haven
3	54.1	East Windsor SD	East Windsor
4	53.6	Wilton SD	Wilton
5	53.5	Simsbury SD	Simsbury
6	53.3	Regional SD 17	Higganum
7	53.2	Capitol Region Education Council	Hartford
8	52.8	Bloomfield SD	Bloomfield
9	52.5	Canton SD	Collinsville
9	52.5	Greenwich SD	Greenwich
9	52.5	Montville SD	Oakdale
12	52.4	Hamden SD	Hamden
12	52.4	Newington SD	Newington
12	52.4	Shelton SD	Shelton
15	52.2	Norwalk SD	Norwalk
15	52.2	Torrington SD	Torrington
17	52.1	Stonington SD	Old Mystic
18	51.9	Darien SD	Darien
18	51.9	East Hartford SD	East Hartford
18	51.9	East Haven SD	East Haven
18	51.9	Plainfield SD	Central Village
18	51.9	Tolland SD	Tolland
23	51.8	Bristol SD	Bristol
24	51.7	Berlin SD	Berlin
24	51.7	Regional SD 16	Prospect
24	51.7	Windham SD	Willimantic
27	51.6	Bethel SD	Bethel
27	51.6	Farmington SD	Farmington
27	51.6	Plymouth SD	Terryville
27	51.6	Stamford SD	Stamford
27	51.6	Wethersfield SD	Wethersfield
32	51.5	New Milford SD	New Milford
32	51.5	Newtown SD	Newtown
32	51.5	North Branford SD	Northford
35	51.4	Clinton SD	Clinton
35	51.4	Coventry SD	Coventry
35	51.4	Ellington SD	Ellington
35	51.4	Granby SD	Granby
35	51.4	Meriden SD	Meriden
35	51.4	Monroe SD	Monroe
35	51.4	New Canaan SD	New Canaan
35	51.4	Regional SD 13	Durham
35	51.4	Southington SD	Southington
44	51.3	Bridgeport SD	Bridgeport
44	51.3	Derby SD	Derby
44	51.3	Somers SD	Somers
47	51.2	Manchester SD	Manchester
47	51.2	Waterbury SD	Waterbury
49	51.1	Brookfield SD	Brookfield
49	51.1	East Hampton SD	East Hampton
49	51.1	Naugatuck SD	Naugatuck
49	51.1	New London SD	New London
49	51.1	Regional SD 15	Middlebury
49	51.1	Windsor SD	Windsor
55	51.0	Hartford SD	Hartford
55	51.0	Norwich SD	Norwich
57	50.9	Cheshire SD	Cheshire
57	50.9	Danbury SD	Danbury
57	50.9	Killingly SD	Danielson
57	50.9	Milford SD	Milford
57	50.9	New Fairfield SD	New Fairfield
57	50.9	New Haven SD	New Haven
57	50.9	Regional SD 08	Hebron
57	50.9	South Windsor SD	South Windsor
57	50.9	Westport SD	Westport
66	50.8	Branford SD	Branford
66	50.8	Trumbull SD	Trumbull
68	50.7	Griswold SD	Jewett City
68	50.7	Rocky Hill SD	Rocky Hill
70	50.6	Ansonia SD	Ansonia
70	50.6	Colchester SD	Colchester
70	50.6	Enfield SD	Enfield
70	50.6	Madison SD	Madison
70	50.6	New Britain SD	New Britain
70	50.6	Old Saybrook SD	Old Saybrook
70	50.6	West Haven SD	West Haven
77	50.5	East Lyme SD	East Lyme
77	50.5	Fairfield SD	Fairfield
79	50.4	Stratford SD	Stratford
79	50.4	West Hartford SD	West Hartford
81	50.3	North Haven SD	North Haven
81	50.3	Plainville SD	Plainville
81	50.3	Regional SD 10	Burlington
81	50.3	Wallingford SD	Wallingford
81	50.3	Waterford SD	Waterford
86	50.2	Suffield SD	Suffield
86	50.2	Wolcott SD	Wolcott
88	50.1	Groton SD	Mystic
88	50.1	Middletown SD	Middletown
88	50.1	Ridgefield SD	Ridgefield
88	50.1	Windsor Locks SD	Windsor Locks
92	50.0	Seymour SD	Seymour
92	50.0	Vernon SD	Vernon
94	49.9	Guilford SD	Guilford
94	49.9	Watertown SD	Watertown
96	49.8	Glastonbury SD	Glastonbury
96	49.8	Regional SD 18	Old Lyme
98	49.7	Avon SD	Avon
99	49.6	Weston SD	Weston
100	49.5	Regional SD 05	Woodbridge
101	49.4	Cromwell SD	Cromwell
102	49.1	Ledyard SD	Ledyard
103	48.8	Stafford SD	Stafford Spgs
104	48.5	Regional SD 14	Woodbury
105	46.5	Norwich Free Academy	Norwich

Female Students

Rank	Percent	District Name	City
1	53.5	Norwich Free Academy	Norwich
2	51.5	Regional SD 14	Woodbury
3	51.2	Stafford SD	Stafford Spgs
4	50.9	Ledyard SD	Ledyard
5	50.6	Cromwell SD	Cromwell
6	50.5	Regional SD 05	Woodbridge
7	50.4	Weston SD	Weston
8	50.3	Avon SD	Avon
9	50.2	Glastonbury SD	Glastonbury
9	50.2	Regional SD 18	Old Lyme
11	50.1	Guilford SD	Guilford
11	50.1	Watertown SD	Watertown
13	50.0	Seymour SD	Seymour
13	50.0	Vernon SD	Vernon
15	49.9	Groton SD	Mystic
15	49.9	Middletown SD	Middletown
15	49.9	Ridgefield SD	Ridgefield
15	49.9	Windsor Locks SD	Windsor Locks
19	49.8	Suffield SD	Suffield
19	49.8	Wolcott SD	Wolcott
21	49.7	North Haven SD	North Haven
21	49.7	Plainville SD	Plainville
21	49.7	Regional SD 10	Burlington
21	49.7	Wallingford SD	Wallingford
21	49.7	Waterford SD	Waterford
26	49.6	Stratford SD	Stratford
26	49.6	West Hartford SD	West Hartford
28	49.5	East Lyme SD	East Lyme
28	49.5	Fairfield SD	Fairfield
30	49.4	Ansonia SD	Ansonia
30	49.4	Colchester SD	Colchester
30	49.4	Enfield SD	Enfield
30	49.4	Madison SD	Madison
30	49.4	New Britain SD	New Britain
30	49.4	Old Saybrook SD	Old Saybrook
30	49.4	West Haven SD	West Haven
37	49.3	Griswold SD	Jewett City
37	49.3	Rocky Hill SD	Rocky Hill
39	49.2	Branford SD	Branford
39	49.2	Trumbull SD	Trumbull
41	49.1	Cheshire SD	Cheshire
41	49.1	Danbury SD	Danbury
41	49.1	Killingly SD	Danielson
41	49.1	Milford SD	Milford
41	49.1	New Fairfield SD	New Fairfield
41	49.1	New Haven SD	New Haven
41	49.1	Regional SD 08	Hebron
41	49.1	South Windsor SD	South Windsor
41	49.1	Westport SD	Westport
50	49.0	Hartford SD	Hartford
50	49.0	Norwich SD	Norwich
52	48.9	Brookfield SD	Brookfield
52	48.9	East Hampton SD	East Hampton
52	48.9	Naugatuck SD	Naugatuck
52	48.9	New London SD	New London
52	48.9	Regional SD 15	Middlebury
52	48.9	Windsor SD	Windsor
58	48.8	Manchester SD	Manchester
58	48.8	Waterbury SD	Waterbury
60	48.7	Bridgeport SD	Bridgeport
60	48.7	Derby SD	Derby
60	48.7	Somers SD	Somers
63	48.6	Clinton SD	Clinton
63	48.6	Coventry SD	Coventry
63	48.6	Ellington SD	Ellington
63	48.6	Granby SD	Granby
63	48.6	Meriden SD	Meriden
63	48.6	Monroe SD	Monroe
63	48.6	New Canaan SD	New Canaan
63	48.6	Regional SD 13	Durham
63	48.6	Southington SD	Southington
72	48.5	New Milford SD	New Milford
72	48.5	Newtown SD	Newtown
72	48.5	North Branford SD	Northford
75	48.4	Bethel SD	Bethel
75	48.4	Farmington SD	Farmington
75	48.4	Plymouth SD	Terryville
75	48.4	Stamford SD	Stamford
75	48.4	Wethersfield SD	Wethersfield
80	48.3	Berlin SD	Berlin
80	48.3	Regional SD 16	Prospect
80	48.3	Windham SD	Willimantic
83	48.2	Bristol SD	Bristol
84	48.1	Darien SD	Darien
84	48.1	East Hartford SD	East Hartford
84	48.1	East Haven SD	East Haven
84	48.1	Plainfield SD	Central Village
84	48.1	Tolland SD	Tolland
89	47.9	Stonington SD	Old Mystic
90	47.8	Norwalk SD	Norwalk
90	47.8	Torrington SD	Torrington
92	47.6	Hamden SD	Hamden
92	47.6	Newington SD	Newington
92	47.6	Shelton SD	Shelton
95	47.5	Canton SD	Collinsville
95	47.5	Greenwich SD	Greenwich
95	47.5	Montville SD	Oakdale
98	47.2	Bloomfield SD	Bloomfield
99	46.8	Capitol Region Education Council	Hartford
100	46.7	Regional SD 17	Higganum
101	46.5	Simsbury SD	Simsbury
102	46.4	Wilton SD	Wilton
103	45.9	East Windsor SD	East Windsor
104	38.4	Area Coop Educational Services	North Haven
105	36.3	State Voc-Tech Schools	Middletown

Individual Education Program Students

Rank	Percent	District Name	City
1	21.4	Norwich SD	Norwich
2	20.3	New London SD	New London
3	19.4	New Britain SD	New Britain
4	19.2	Waterbury SD	Waterbury
5	17.1	Hamden SD	Hamden
6	17.0	Hartford SD	Hartford
7	16.3	Windham SD	Willimantic
8	15.8	Plymouth SD	Terryville
9	15.7	Meriden SD	Meriden
9	15.7	Torrington SD	Torrington

11	15.5	Branford SD	Branford
12	15.4	Ansonia SD	Ansonia
13	14.9	Montville SD	Oakdale
14	14.8	Killingly SD	Danielson
15	14.7	East Hartford SD	East Hartford
16	14.6	Groton SD	Mystic
17	14.5	Madison SD	Madison
17	14.5	Windsor Locks SD	Windsor Locks
17	14.5	Windsor SD	Windsor
20	14.3	Clinton SD	Clinton
20	14.3	Regional SD 15	Middlebury
22	14.2	Simsbury SD	Simsbury
23	14.1	Milford SD	Milford
23	14.1	State Voc-Tech Schools	Middletown
25	13.9	West Hartford SD	West Hartford
26	13.7	Manchester SD	Manchester
26	13.7	Middletown SD	Middletown
28	13.4	Enfield SD	Enfield
29	13.3	Bridgeport SD	Bridgeport
30	13.2	Bristol SD	Bristol
30	13.2	Glastonbury SD	Glastonbury
30	13.2	Wethersfield SD	Wethersfield
33	13.0	Bloomfield SD	Bloomfield
33	13.0	Stonington SD	Old Mystic
35	12.9	New Milford SD	New Milford
36	12.7	Stamford SD	Stamford
37	12.5	Cromwell SD	Cromwell
37	12.5	East Hampton SD	East Hampton
37	12.5	Fairfield SD	Fairfield
37	12.5	Old Saybrook SD	Old Saybrook
37	12.5	Wolcott SD	Wolcott
42	12.4	Berlin SD	Berlin
42	12.4	Coventry SD	Coventry
42	12.4	Plainfield SD	Central Village
42	12.4	Regional SD 05	Woodbridge
46	12.3	Colchester SD	Colchester
46	12.3	Regional SD 18	Old Lyme
46	12.3	Southington SD	Southington
46	12.3	Vernon SD	Vernon
46	12.3	Waterford SD	Waterford
51	12.2	Darien SD	Darien
51	12.2	East Windsor SD	East Windsor
51	12.2	South Windsor SD	South Windsor
54	12.1	West Haven SD	West Haven
55	12.0	Danbury SD	Danbury
55	12.0	East Haven SD	East Haven
55	12.0	Naugatuck SD	Naugatuck
58	11.9	Greenwich SD	Greenwich
58	11.9	Regional SD 17	Higganum
58	11.9	Wilton SD	Wilton
61	11.7	East Lyme SD	East Lyme
61	11.7	Plainville SD	Plainville
63	11.5	Stafford SD	Stafford Spgs
63	11.5	Stratford SD	Stratford
65	11.4	Watertown SD	Watertown
65	11.4	Weston SD	Weston
67	11.3	Regional SD 14	Woodbury
68	11.2	Griswold SD	Jewett City
68	11.2	Ledyard SD	Ledyard
68	11.2	North Branford SD	Northford
68	11.2	Tolland SD	Tolland
72	11.1	New Haven SD	New Haven
73	11.0	Canton SD	Collinsville
73	11.0	Norwalk SD	Norwalk
73	11.0	Westport SD	Westport
76	10.7	Bethel SD	Bethel
76	10.7	Guilford SD	Guilford
76	10.7	Newtown SD	Newtown
76	10.7	Rocky Hill SD	Rocky Hill
80	10.6	Derby SD	Derby
81	10.3	Regional SD 13	Durham
81	10.3	Regional SD 16	Prospect
81	10.3	Wallingford SD	Wallingford
84	10.1	Cheshire SD	Cheshire
84	10.1	North Haven SD	North Haven
84	10.1	Ridgefield SD	Ridgefield
87	10.0	Somers SD	Somers
88	9.9	New Canaan SD	New Canaan
88	9.9	Regional SD 08	Hebron
88	9.9	Regional SD 10	Burlington
88	9.9	Suffield SD	Suffield
92	9.8	Granby SD	Granby
92	9.8	Monroe SD	Monroe
92	9.8	New Fairfield SD	New Fairfield
95	9.4	Avon SD	Avon
96	9.2	Newington SD	Newington
96	9.2	Trumbull SD	Trumbull
98	8.8	Farmington SD	Farmington
99	8.4	Ellington SD	Ellington
100	7.9	Shelton SD	Shelton
101	7.8	Seymour SD	Seymour
102	7.2	Brookfield SD	Brookfield
103	0.0	Area Coop Educational Services	North Haven
103	0.0	Capitol Region Education Council	Hartford
103	0.0	Norwich Free Academy	Norwich

English Language Learner Students

Rank	Percent	District Name	City
1	17.2	Danbury SD	Danbury
2	13.4	Hartford SD	Hartford
3	12.9	New London SD	New London
4	12.7	Windham SD	Willimantic
5	11.5	Stamford SD	Stamford
6	11.4	New Britain SD	New Britain
7	11.0	Waterbury SD	Waterbury
8	10.8	Bridgeport SD	Bridgeport
9	9.0	New Haven SD	New Haven
10	8.4	Norwalk SD	Norwalk
11	6.5	Meriden SD	Meriden
12	6.1	Greenwich SD	Greenwich
13	5.5	Derby SD	Derby
14	4.9	Wethersfield SD	Wethersfield
15	4.8	West Hartford SD	West Hartford
16	4.4	State Voc-Tech Schools	Middletown
17	4.3	Naugatuck SD	Naugatuck
17	4.3	West Haven SD	West Haven
19	3.5	Torrington SD	Torrington
20	3.2	Bethel SD	Bethel
21	2.9	Ansonia SD	Ansonia
21	2.9	East Hartford SD	East Hartford
23	2.8	Cromwell SD	Cromwell
24	2.6	Norwich SD	Norwich
24	2.6	Wallingford SD	Wallingford
26	2.5	Glastonbury SD	Glastonbury
26	2.5	Norwich Free Academy	Norwich
26	2.5	Rocky Hill SD	Rocky Hill
29	2.4	Bristol SD	Bristol
29	2.4	Vernon SD	Vernon
31	2.2	Groton SD	Mystic
31	2.2	Windsor Locks SD	Windsor Locks
33	2.1	Branford SD	Branford
33	2.1	Middletown SD	Middletown
35	1.8	Berlin SD	Berlin
35	1.8	Westport SD	Westport
37	1.7	Old Saybrook SD	Old Saybrook
37	1.7	Shelton SD	Shelton
39	1.6	Area Coop Educational Services	North Haven
39	1.6	Milford SD	Milford
39	1.6	Stratford SD	Stratford
42	1.5	East Haven SD	East Haven
42	1.5	New Milford SD	New Milford
42	1.5	Newington SD	Newington
45	1.4	Plainville SD	Plainville
46	1.3	Manchester SD	Manchester
46	1.3	Montville SD	Oakdale
46	1.3	South Windsor SD	South Windsor
49	1.2	Plymouth SD	Terryville
49	1.2	Windsor SD	Windsor
51	1.1	North Haven SD	North Haven
52	1.0	Ellington SD	Ellington
52	1.0	Fairfield SD	Fairfield
52	1.0	Hamden SD	Hamden
52	1.0	Killingly SD	Danielson
56	0.9	Clinton SD	Clinton
56	0.9	Enfield SD	Enfield
58	0.8	Darien SD	Darien
58	0.8	East Lyme SD	East Lyme
60	0.7	Farmington SD	Farmington
60	0.7	North Branford SD	Northford
60	0.7	Regional SD 15	Middlebury
60	0.7	Trumbull SD	Trumbull
64	0.6	Griswold SD	Jewett City
64	0.6	Ledyard SD	Ledyard
64	0.6	New Canaan SD	New Canaan
64	0.6	Ridgefield SD	Ridgefield
64	0.6	Simsbury SD	Simsbury
64	0.6	Southington SD	Southington
70	0.5	Guilford SD	Guilford
70	0.5	Stafford SD	Stafford Spgs
70	0.5	Tolland SD	Tolland
73	0.4	Avon SD	Avon
73	0.4	Cheshire SD	Cheshire
73	0.4	Regional SD 05	Woodbridge
73	0.4	Regional SD 14	Woodbury
73	0.4	Stonington SD	Old Mystic
73	0.4	Waterford SD	Waterford
73	0.4	Weston SD	Weston
80	0.3	Brookfield SD	Brookfield
80	0.3	Capitol Region Education Council	Hartford
80	0.3	Granby SD	Granby
80	0.3	Monroe SD	Monroe
80	0.3	Suffield SD	Suffield
80	0.3	Watertown SD	Watertown
86	0.2	Bloomfield SD	Bloomfield
86	0.2	Madison SD	Madison
86	0.2	Newtown SD	Newtown
86	0.2	Regional SD 18	Old Lyme
86	0.2	Wolcott SD	Wolcott
91	0.1	Canton SD	Collinsville
91	0.1	Regional SD 16	Prospect
91	0.1	Somers SD	Somers
94	0.0	Plainfield SD	Central Village
94	0.0	Wilton SD	Wilton
96	0.0	Colchester SD	Colchester
96	0.0	Coventry SD	Coventry
96	0.0	East Hampton SD	East Hampton
96	0.0	East Windsor SD	East Windsor
96	0.0	New Fairfield SD	New Fairfield
96	0.0	Regional SD 08	Hebron
96	0.0	Regional SD 10	Burlington
96	0.0	Regional SD 13	Durham
96	0.0	Regional SD 17	Higganum
96	0.0	Seymour SD	Seymour

Migrant Students

Rank	Percent	District Name	City
1	6.7	Windham SD	Willimantic
2	5.8	Hartford SD	Hartford
3	5.0	Waterbury SD	Waterbury
4	4.2	New London SD	New London
5	3.3	Meriden SD	Meriden
6	3.1	Danbury SD	Danbury
7	3.0	Bridgeport SD	Bridgeport
8	2.2	New Haven SD	New Haven
9	1.6	New Britain SD	New Britain
10	0.5	State Voc-Tech Schools	Middletown
11	0.2	Bethel SD	Bethel
11	0.2	Killingly SD	Danielson
11	0.2	Norwich SD	Norwich
14	0.1	Derby SD	Derby
14	0.1	East Hartford SD	East Hartford
14	0.1	East Haven SD	East Haven
14	0.1	Hamden SD	Hamden
14	0.1	Manchester SD	Manchester
14	0.1	Naugatuck SD	Naugatuck
14	0.1	Norwich Free Academy	Norwich
14	0.1	Ridgefield SD	Ridgefield
14	0.1	Stratford SD	Stratford
14	0.1	West Hartford SD	West Hartford
24	0.0	Area Coop Educational Services	North Haven
24	0.0	North Branford SD	Northford
24	0.0	Wallingford SD	Wallingford
24	0.0	West Haven SD	West Haven
28	0.0	Ansonia SD	Ansonia
28	0.0	Avon SD	Avon
28	0.0	Berlin SD	Berlin
28	0.0	Bloomfield SD	Bloomfield
28	0.0	Branford SD	Branford
28	0.0	Bristol SD	Bristol
28	0.0	Brookfield SD	Brookfield
28	0.0	Canton SD	Collinsville
28	0.0	Capitol Region Education Council	Hartford
28	0.0	Cheshire SD	Cheshire
28	0.0	Clinton SD	Clinton
28	0.0	Colchester SD	Colchester
28	0.0	Coventry SD	Coventry
28	0.0	Cromwell SD	Cromwell
28	0.0	Darien SD	Darien
28	0.0	East Hampton SD	East Hampton
28	0.0	East Lyme SD	East Lyme
28	0.0	East Windsor SD	East Windsor
28	0.0	Ellington SD	Ellington
28	0.0	Enfield SD	Enfield
28	0.0	Fairfield SD	Fairfield
28	0.0	Farmington SD	Farmington
28	0.0	Glastonbury SD	Glastonbury
28	0.0	Granby SD	Granby
28	0.0	Greenwich SD	Greenwich
28	0.0	Griswold SD	Jewett City
28	0.0	Groton SD	Mystic
28	0.0	Guilford SD	Guilford
28	0.0	Ledyard SD	Ledyard
28	0.0	Madison SD	Madison
28	0.0	Middletown SD	Middletown
28	0.0	Milford SD	Milford
28	0.0	Monroe SD	Monroe
28	0.0	Montville SD	Oakdale
28	0.0	New Canaan SD	New Canaan
28	0.0	New Fairfield SD	New Fairfield
28	0.0	New Milford SD	New Milford
28	0.0	Newington SD	Newington
28	0.0	Newtown SD	Newtown
28	0.0	North Haven SD	North Haven
28	0.0	Norwalk SD	Norwalk
28	0.0	Old Saybrook SD	Old Saybrook
28	0.0	Plainfield SD	Central Village

Rank	Percent	District Name	City
28	0.0	Plainville SD	Plainville
28	0.0	Plymouth SD	Terryville
28	0.0	Regional SD 05	Woodbridge
28	0.0	Regional SD 08	Hebron
28	0.0	Regional SD 10	Burlington
28	0.0	Regional SD 13	Durham
28	0.0	Regional SD 14	Woodbury
28	0.0	Regional SD 15	Middlebury
28	0.0	Regional SD 16	Prospect
28	0.0	Regional SD 17	Higganum
28	0.0	Regional SD 18	Old Lyme
28	0.0	Rocky Hill SD	Rocky Hill
28	0.0	Seymour SD	Seymour
28	0.0	Shelton SD	Shelton
28	0.0	Simsbury SD	Simsbury
28	0.0	Somers SD	Somers
28	0.0	South Windsor SD	South Windsor
28	0.0	Southington SD	Southington
28	0.0	Stafford SD	Stafford Spgs
28	0.0	Stamford SD	Stamford
28	0.0	Stonington SD	Old Mystic
28	0.0	Suffield SD	Suffield
28	0.0	Tolland SD	Tolland
28	0.0	Torrington SD	Torrington
28	0.0	Trumbull SD	Trumbull
28	0.0	Vernon SD	Vernon
28	0.0	Waterford SD	Waterford
28	0.0	Watertown SD	Watertown
28	0.0	Weston SD	Weston
28	0.0	Westport SD	Westport
28	0.0	Wethersfield SD	Wethersfield
28	0.0	Wilton SD	Wilton
28	0.0	Windsor Locks SD	Windsor Locks
28	0.0	Windsor SD	Windsor
28	0.0	Wolcott SD	Wolcott

Students Eligible for Free Lunch

Rank	Percent	District Name	City
1	n/a	Ansonia SD	Ansonia
1	n/a	Area Coop Educational Services	North Haven
1	n/a	Avon SD	Avon
1	n/a	Berlin SD	Berlin
1	n/a	Bethel SD	Bethel
1	n/a	Bloomfield SD	Bloomfield
1	n/a	Branford SD	Branford
1	n/a	Bridgeport SD	Bridgeport
1	n/a	Bristol SD	Bristol
1	n/a	Brookfield SD	Brookfield
1	n/a	Canton SD	Collinsville
1	n/a	Capitol Region Education Council	Hartford
1	n/a	Cheshire SD	Cheshire
1	n/a	Clinton SD	Clinton
1	n/a	Colchester SD	Colchester
1	n/a	Coventry SD	Coventry
1	n/a	Cromwell SD	Cromwell
1	n/a	Danbury SD	Danbury
1	n/a	Darien SD	Darien
1	n/a	Derby SD	Derby
1	n/a	East Hampton SD	East Hampton
1	n/a	East Hartford SD	East Hartford
1	n/a	East Haven SD	East Haven
1	n/a	East Lyme SD	East Lyme
1	n/a	East Windsor SD	East Windsor
1	n/a	Ellington SD	Ellington
1	n/a	Enfield SD	Enfield
1	n/a	Fairfield SD	Fairfield
1	n/a	Farmington SD	Farmington
1	n/a	Glastonbury SD	Glastonbury
1	n/a	Granby SD	Granby
1	n/a	Greenwich SD	Greenwich
1	n/a	Griswold SD	Jewett City
1	n/a	Groton SD	Mystic
1	n/a	Guilford SD	Guilford
1	n/a	Hamden SD	Hamden
1	n/a	Hartford SD	Hartford
1	n/a	Killingly SD	Danielson
1	n/a	Ledyard SD	Ledyard
1	n/a	Madison SD	Madison
1	n/a	Manchester SD	Manchester
1	n/a	Meriden SD	Meriden
1	n/a	Middletown SD	Middletown
1	n/a	Milford SD	Milford
1	n/a	Monroe SD	Monroe
1	n/a	Montville SD	Oakdale
1	n/a	Naugatuck SD	Naugatuck
1	n/a	New Britain SD	New Britain
1	n/a	New Canaan SD	New Canaan
1	n/a	New Fairfield SD	New Fairfield
1	n/a	New Haven SD	New Haven
1	n/a	New London SD	New London
1	n/a	New Milford SD	New Milford
1	n/a	Newington SD	Newington
1	n/a	Newtown SD	Newtown
1	n/a	North Branford SD	Northford
1	n/a	North Haven SD	North Haven
1	n/a	Norwalk SD	Norwalk
1	n/a	Norwich Free Academy	Norwich
1	n/a	Norwich SD	Norwich
1	n/a	Old Saybrook SD	Old Saybrook
1	n/a	Plainfield SD	Central Village
1	n/a	Plainville SD	Plainville
1	n/a	Plymouth SD	Terryville
1	n/a	Regional SD 05	Woodbridge
1	n/a	Regional SD 08	Hebron
1	n/a	Regional SD 10	Burlington
1	n/a	Regional SD 13	Durham
1	n/a	Regional SD 14	Woodbury
1	n/a	Regional SD 15	Middlebury
1	n/a	Regional SD 16	Prospect
1	n/a	Regional SD 17	Higganum
1	n/a	Regional SD 18	Old Lyme
1	n/a	Ridgefield SD	Ridgefield
1	n/a	Rocky Hill SD	Rocky Hill
1	n/a	Seymour SD	Seymour
1	n/a	Shelton SD	Shelton
1	n/a	Simsbury SD	Simsbury
1	n/a	Somers SD	Somers
1	n/a	South Windsor SD	South Windsor
1	n/a	Southington SD	Southington
1	n/a	Stafford SD	Stafford Spgs
1	n/a	Stamford SD	Stamford
1	n/a	State Voc-Tech Schools	Middletown
1	n/a	Stonington SD	Old Mystic
1	n/a	Stratford SD	Stratford
1	n/a	Suffield SD	Suffield
1	n/a	Tolland SD	Tolland
1	n/a	Torrington SD	Torrington
1	n/a	Trumbull SD	Trumbull
1	n/a	Vernon SD	Vernon
1	n/a	Wallingford SD	Wallingford
1	n/a	Waterbury SD	Waterbury
1	n/a	Waterford SD	Waterford
1	n/a	Watertown SD	Watertown
1	n/a	West Hartford SD	West Hartford
1	n/a	West Haven SD	West Haven
1	n/a	Weston SD	Weston
1	n/a	Westport SD	Westport
1	n/a	Wethersfield SD	Wethersfield
1	n/a	Wilton SD	Wilton
1	n/a	Windham SD	Willimantic
1	n/a	Windsor Locks SD	Windsor Locks
1	n/a	Windsor SD	Windsor
1	n/a	Wolcott SD	Wolcott

Students Eligible for Reduced-Price Lunch

Rank	Percent	District Name	City
1	n/a	Ansonia SD	Ansonia
1	n/a	Area Coop Educational Services	North Haven
1	n/a	Avon SD	Avon
1	n/a	Berlin SD	Berlin
1	n/a	Bethel SD	Bethel
1	n/a	Bloomfield SD	Bloomfield
1	n/a	Branford SD	Branford
1	n/a	Bridgeport SD	Bridgeport
1	n/a	Bristol SD	Bristol
1	n/a	Brookfield SD	Brookfield
1	n/a	Canton SD	Collinsville
1	n/a	Capitol Region Education Council	Hartford
1	n/a	Cheshire SD	Cheshire
1	n/a	Clinton SD	Clinton
1	n/a	Colchester SD	Colchester
1	n/a	Coventry SD	Coventry
1	n/a	Cromwell SD	Cromwell
1	n/a	Danbury SD	Danbury
1	n/a	Darien SD	Darien
1	n/a	Derby SD	Derby
1	n/a	East Hampton SD	East Hampton
1	n/a	East Hartford SD	East Hartford
1	n/a	East Haven SD	East Haven
1	n/a	East Lyme SD	East Lyme
1	n/a	East Windsor SD	East Windsor
1	n/a	Ellington SD	Ellington
1	n/a	Enfield SD	Enfield
1	n/a	Fairfield SD	Fairfield
1	n/a	Farmington SD	Farmington
1	n/a	Glastonbury SD	Glastonbury
1	n/a	Granby SD	Granby
1	n/a	Greenwich SD	Greenwich
1	n/a	Griswold SD	Jewett City
1	n/a	Groton SD	Mystic
1	n/a	Guilford SD	Guilford
1	n/a	Hamden SD	Hamden
1	n/a	Hartford SD	Hartford
1	n/a	Killingly SD	Danielson
1	n/a	Ledyard SD	Ledyard
1	n/a	Madison SD	Madison
1	n/a	Manchester SD	Manchester
1	n/a	Meriden SD	Meriden
1	n/a	Middletown SD	Middletown
1	n/a	Milford SD	Milford
1	n/a	Monroe SD	Monroe
1	n/a	Montville SD	Oakdale
1	n/a	Naugatuck SD	Naugatuck
1	n/a	New Britain SD	New Britain
1	n/a	New Canaan SD	New Canaan
1	n/a	New Fairfield SD	New Fairfield
1	n/a	New Haven SD	New Haven
1	n/a	New London SD	New London
1	n/a	New Milford SD	New Milford
1	n/a	Newington SD	Newington
1	n/a	Newtown SD	Newtown
1	n/a	North Branford SD	Northford
1	n/a	North Haven SD	North Haven
1	n/a	Norwalk SD	Norwalk
1	n/a	Norwich Free Academy	Norwich
1	n/a	Norwich SD	Norwich
1	n/a	Old Saybrook SD	Old Saybrook
1	n/a	Plainfield SD	Central Village
1	n/a	Plainville SD	Plainville
1	n/a	Plymouth SD	Terryville
1	n/a	Regional SD 05	Woodbridge
1	n/a	Regional SD 08	Hebron
1	n/a	Regional SD 10	Burlington
1	n/a	Regional SD 13	Durham
1	n/a	Regional SD 14	Woodbury
1	n/a	Regional SD 15	Middlebury
1	n/a	Regional SD 16	Prospect
1	n/a	Regional SD 17	Higganum
1	n/a	Regional SD 18	Old Lyme
1	n/a	Ridgefield SD	Ridgefield
1	n/a	Rocky Hill SD	Rocky Hill
1	n/a	Seymour SD	Seymour
1	n/a	Shelton SD	Shelton
1	n/a	Simsbury SD	Simsbury
1	n/a	Somers SD	Somers
1	n/a	South Windsor SD	South Windsor
1	n/a	Southington SD	Southington
1	n/a	Stafford SD	Stafford Spgs
1	n/a	Stamford SD	Stamford
1	n/a	State Voc-Tech Schools	Middletown
1	n/a	Stonington SD	Old Mystic
1	n/a	Stratford SD	Stratford
1	n/a	Suffield SD	Suffield
1	n/a	Tolland SD	Tolland
1	n/a	Torrington SD	Torrington
1	n/a	Trumbull SD	Trumbull
1	n/a	Vernon SD	Vernon
1	n/a	Wallingford SD	Wallingford
1	n/a	Waterbury SD	Waterbury
1	n/a	Waterford SD	Waterford
1	n/a	Watertown SD	Watertown
1	n/a	West Hartford SD	West Hartford
1	n/a	West Haven SD	West Haven
1	n/a	Weston SD	Weston
1	n/a	Westport SD	Westport
1	n/a	Wethersfield SD	Wethersfield
1	n/a	Wilton SD	Wilton
1	n/a	Windham SD	Willimantic
1	n/a	Windsor Locks SD	Windsor Locks
1	n/a	Windsor SD	Windsor
1	n/a	Wolcott SD	Wolcott

Student/Teacher Ratio

Rank	Ratio	District Name	City
1	16.8	Ansonia SD	Ansonia
2	16.4	Derby SD	Derby
3	16.3	East Haven SD	East Haven
3	16.3	North Branford SD	Northford
5	16.1	Granby SD	Granby
6	15.8	Newington SD	Newington
6	15.8	Trumbull SD	Trumbull
8	15.7	East Windsor SD	East Windsor
8	15.7	North Haven SD	North Haven
10	15.5	Norwich SD	Norwich
10	15.5	Seymour SD	Seymour
12	15.4	Hamden SD	Hamden
12	15.4	Naugatuck SD	Naugatuck
14	15.3	Guilford SD	Guilford
14	15.3	Shelton SD	Shelton
14	15.3	West Haven SD	West Haven
17	15.2	Bridgeport SD	Bridgeport
17	15.2	South Windsor SD	South Windsor
19	15.1	Cheshire SD	Cheshire
19	15.1	New Fairfield SD	New Fairfield

Rank	Ratio	District Name	City
19	15.1	New Milford SD	New Milford
19	15.1	Newtown SD	Newtown
19	15.1	Norwich Free Academy	Norwich
19	15.1	Plainfield SD	Central Village
19	15.1	Regional SD 15	Middlebury
26	15.0	Wethersfield SD	Wethersfield
27	14.9	Danbury SD	Danbury
28	14.8	New Britain SD	New Britain
28	14.8	Ridgefield SD	Ridgefield
28	14.8	Watertown SD	Watertown
31	14.7	Bristol SD	Bristol
31	14.7	Monroe SD	Monroe
31	14.7	Torrington SD	Torrington
34	14.6	Canton SD	Collinsville
34	14.6	Plainville SD	Plainville
34	14.6	Simsbury SD	Simsbury
37	14.5	Ledyard SD	Ledyard
38	14.4	Avon SD	Avon
38	14.4	New Haven SD	New Haven
38	14.4	Stratford SD	Stratford
41	14.3	Madison SD	Madison
41	14.3	Waterbury SD	Waterbury
43	14.2	Berlin SD	Berlin
43	14.2	East Hampton SD	East Hampton
43	14.2	East Hartford SD	East Hartford
43	14.2	Glastonbury SD	Glastonbury
43	14.2	Suffield SD	Suffield
48	14.1	Meriden SD	Meriden
48	14.1	Wolcott SD	Wolcott
50	14.0	Killingly SD	Danielson
50	14.0	Manchester SD	Manchester
50	14.0	Regional SD 14	Woodbury
53	13.9	Ellington SD	Ellington
53	13.9	Somers SD	Somers
55	13.8	Colchester SD	Colchester
55	13.8	Coventry SD	Coventry
55	13.8	Wilton SD	Wilton
58	13.7	Brookfield SD	Brookfield
58	13.7	East Lyme SD	East Lyme
58	13.7	Regional SD 05	Woodbridge
58	13.7	Regional SD 16	Prospect
62	13.6	Farmington SD	Farmington
62	13.6	Stonington SD	Old Mystic
62	13.6	Wallingford SD	Wallingford
65	13.5	Norwalk SD	Norwalk
65	13.5	Regional SD 10	Burlington
65	13.5	Southington SD	Southington
68	13.4	Bethel SD	Bethel
68	13.4	Clinton SD	Clinton
68	13.4	Rocky Hill SD	Rocky Hill
71	13.3	Branford SD	Branford
71	13.3	Enfield SD	Enfield
71	13.3	Plymouth SD	Terryville
71	13.3	Tolland SD	Tolland
75	13.1	Milford SD	Milford
76	13.0	Vernon SD	Vernon
76	13.0	Waterford SD	Waterford
78	12.9	Windham SD	Willimantic
79	12.8	Middletown SD	Middletown
79	12.8	New Canaan SD	New Canaan
79	12.8	West Hartford SD	West Hartford
82	12.7	Griswold SD	Jewett City
82	12.7	Groton SD	Mystic
82	12.7	Montville SD	Oakdale
85	12.5	Fairfield SD	Fairfield
85	12.5	Regional SD 13	Durham
85	12.5	Windsor SD	Windsor
88	12.4	Bloomfield SD	Bloomfield
88	12.4	Cromwell SD	Cromwell
88	12.4	Darien SD	Darien
88	12.4	Hartford SD	Hartford
88	12.4	Regional SD 18	Old Lyme
88	12.4	Stafford SD	Stafford Spgs
94	12.3	Stamford SD	Stamford
95	12.2	Weston SD	Weston
96	12.1	Greenwich SD	Greenwich
97	12.0	New London SD	New London
97	12.0	Regional SD 08	Hebron
97	12.0	Regional SD 17	Higganum
97	12.0	Windsor Locks SD	Windsor Locks
101	11.9	Old Saybrook SD	Old Saybrook
102	11.8	Westport SD	Westport
103	10.8	Capitol Region Education Council	Hartford
104	10.1	State Voc-Tech Schools	Middletown
105	9.4	Area Coop Educational Services	North Haven

Student/Librarian Ratio

Rank	Ratio	District Name	City
1	5,026.3	Vernon SD	Vernon
2	2,771.5	Norwalk SD	Norwalk
3	2,733.0	Plainfield SD	Central Village
4	2,631.0	Ansonia SD	Ansonia
5	2,537.0	South Windsor SD	South Windsor
6	2,416.0	Regional SD 16	Prospect
7	2,383.0	Regional SD 17	Higganum
8	2,027.0	East Hampton SD	East Hampton
9	2,024.0	Norwich SD	Norwich
10	1,964.8	East Hartford SD	East Hartford
11	1,857.3	Naugatuck SD	Naugatuck
12	1,797.5	Wethersfield SD	Wethersfield
13	1,709.3	Enfield SD	Enfield
14	1,579.0	East Windsor SD	East Windsor
15	1,546.6	Bristol SD	Bristol
16	1,543.5	Waterford SD	Waterford
17	1,469.0	Wolcott SD	Wolcott
18	1,378.7	Monroe SD	Monroe
19	1,369.4	Capitol Region Education Council	Hartford
20	1,321.3	Regional SD 13	Durham
21	1,256.0	Bloomfield SD	Bloomfield
22	1,249.6	Bridgeport SD	Bridgeport
23	1,189.7	Watertown SD	Watertown
24	1,142.0	Norwich Free Academy	Norwich
25	1,122.0	Shelton SD	Shelton
26	1,080.0	Area Coop Educational Services	North Haven
27	1,075.5	Granby SD	Granby
28	1,074.0	New London SD	New London
29	1,055.7	New Fairfield SD	New Fairfield
30	1,041.5	Coventry SD	Coventry
31	1,015.4	Stamford SD	Stamford
32	1,006.0	Brookfield SD	Brookfield
33	1,005.0	Stafford SD	Stafford Spgs
34	978.3	Waterbury SD	Waterbury
35	968.9	New Britain SD	New Britain
36	951.7	Seymour SD	Seymour
37	924.5	Cromwell SD	Cromwell
38	890.0	Windham SD	Willimantic
39	876.7	Manchester SD	Manchester
40	869.7	Regional SD 10	Burlington
41	867.3	New Milford SD	New Milford
42	858.2	Middletown SD	Middletown
43	846.6	Tolland SD	Tolland
44	837.7	Torrington SD	Torrington
45	827.0	North Branford SD	Northford
46	811.9	West Haven SD	West Haven
47	798.2	Meriden SD	Meriden
48	790.3	Colchester SD	Colchester
49	781.3	Ellington SD	Ellington
50	773.7	Suffield SD	Suffield
51	765.0	Ledyard SD	Ledyard
52	764.5	Regional SD 08	Hebron
53	762.1	Simsbury SD	Simsbury
54	753.7	Avon SD	Avon
55	746.8	Killingly SD	Danielson
56	720.7	Griswold SD	Jewett City
57	712.6	Glastonbury SD	Glastonbury
58	707.6	Trumbull SD	Trumbull
59	681.3	East Lyme SD	East Lyme
60	667.9	Southington SD	Southington
61	654.7	State Voc-Tech Schools	Middletown
62	654.2	Berlin SD	Berlin
63	649.5	Newtown SD	Newtown
64	636.0	Cheshire SD	Cheshire
65	633.6	Madison SD	Madison
66	633.1	Windsor SD	Windsor
67	629.8	East Haven SD	East Haven
68	627.3	Regional SD 15	Middlebury
69	620.8	Rocky Hill SD	Rocky Hill
70	614.4	Hartford SD	Hartford
71	603.3	Weston SD	Weston
72	601.6	West Hartford SD	West Hartford
73	599.7	Wallingford SD	Wallingford
74	586.6	Montville SD	Oakdale
75	581.0	New Canaan SD	New Canaan
76	577.0	Newington SD	Newington
77	576.5	Regional SD 14	Woodbury
78	569.2	Westport SD	Westport
79	568.4	Farmington SD	Farmington
80	565.6	Stonington SD	Old Mystic
81	553.5	Clinton SD	Clinton
82	544.8	Regional SD 05	Woodbridge
83	543.0	Canton SD	Collinsville
84	542.4	Stratford SD	Stratford
85	537.5	Bethel SD	Bethel
86	535.3	Derby SD	Derby
87	532.8	Milford SD	Milford
88	532.0	Plainville SD	Plainville
89	529.3	Branford SD	Branford
90	525.5	Ridgefield SD	Ridgefield
91	505.3	Fairfield SD	Fairfield
92	496.4	North Haven SD	North Haven
93	495.8	New Haven SD	New Haven
94	490.8	Windsor Locks SD	Windsor Locks
95	488.0	Guilford SD	Guilford
96	485.8	Hamden SD	Hamden
97	455.3	Danbury SD	Danbury
98	453.8	Wilton SD	Wilton
99	433.3	Darien SD	Darien
100	431.9	Old Saybrook SD	Old Saybrook
101	425.8	Somers SD	Somers
102	408.0	Greenwich SD	Greenwich
103	385.1	Groton SD	Mystic
104	316.8	Regional SD 18	Old Lyme
105	0.0	Plymouth SD	Terryville

Student/Counselor Ratio

Rank	Ratio	District Name	City
1	978.3	Waterbury SD	Waterbury
2	704.7	Regional SD 13	Durham
3	675.7	East Hampton SD	East Hampton
4	670.0	Stafford SD	Stafford Spgs
5	664.3	West Haven SD	West Haven
6	631.5	Hamden SD	Hamden
7	621.6	Milford SD	Milford
8	608.0	Stonington SD	Old Mystic
9	604.5	East Hartford SD	East Hartford
10	572.1	Middletown SD	Middletown
11	567.7	Somers SD	Somers
12	546.6	New Britain SD	New Britain
13	541.3	Newtown SD	Newtown
14	535.3	Derby SD	Derby
15	535.0	New Haven SD	New Haven
16	527.8	New Fairfield SD	New Fairfield
17	526.8	Colchester SD	Colchester
18	526.3	East Windsor SD	East Windsor
19	526.2	Ansonia SD	Ansonia
20	524.9	Watertown SD	Watertown
21	520.8	Coventry SD	Coventry
22	517.6	Madison SD	Madison
23	513.6	Wethersfield SD	Wethersfield
24	506.2	Stratford SD	Stratford
25	503.9	East Haven SD	East Haven
26	503.2	Danbury SD	Danbury
27	502.6	Vernon SD	Vernon
28	502.3	Groton SD	Mystic
29	496.6	Rocky Hill SD	Rocky Hill
30	496.4	North Haven SD	North Haven
31	494.2	Hartford SD	Hartford
32	489.0	Bridgeport SD	Bridgeport
33	479.0	Simsbury SD	Simsbury
34	468.8	Ellington SD	Ellington
35	464.8	Bristol SD	Bristol
36	464.2	Suffield SD	Suffield
37	462.3	Cromwell SD	Cromwell
38	459.5	Killingly SD	Danielson
39	456.9	Torrington SD	Torrington
40	453.8	Manchester SD	Manchester
41	452.6	Regional SD 18	Old Lyme
42	449.8	Norwich SD	Norwich
43	449.4	Naugatuck SD	Naugatuck
44	443.8	Newington SD	Newington
45	443.2	Windsor SD	Windsor
46	438.8	Wallingford SD	Wallingford
47	438.2	Capitol Region Education Council	Hartford
48	435.2	Stamford SD	Stamford
49	433.7	New Milford SD	New Milford
50	433.3	Regional SD 17	Higganum
51	432.0	Area Coop Educational Services	North Haven
52	427.8	North Branford SD	Northford
53	422.8	South Windsor SD	South Windsor
54	419.7	Wolcott SD	Wolcott
55	419.3	Regional SD 14	Woodbury
56	418.7	Bloomfield SD	Bloomfield
57	413.1	Westport SD	Westport
58	411.6	Darien SD	Darien
59	410.6	Norwalk SD	Norwalk
60	406.6	Fairfield SD	Fairfield
61	402.8	New London SD	New London
62	401.8	Montville SD	Oakdale
63	401.1	West Hartford SD	West Hartford
64	400.8	Glastonbury SD	Glastonbury
65	399.5	Old Saybrook SD	Old Saybrook
66	397.1	Brookfield SD	Brookfield
67	394.1	Berlin SD	Berlin
68	392.3	Ledyard SD	Ledyard
69	386.8	Meriden SD	Meriden
70	386.5	Monroe SD	Monroe
71	385.9	Farmington SD	Farmington
71	385.9	Waterford SD	Waterford
73	384.7	East Lyme SD	East Lyme
74	382.7	Guilford SD	Guilford
75	380.1	Ridgefield SD	Ridgefield
76	379.6	Plymouth SD	Terryville
77	374.6	Trumbull SD	Trumbull
78	372.7	Regional SD 10	Burlington
79	370.9	Granby SD	Granby
80	370.8	Windham SD	Willimantic

81	370.5	Branford SD	Branford
82	370.4	Tolland SD	Tolland
83	369.0	Clinton SD	Clinton
84	364.6	Wilton SD	Wilton
85	362.0	Canton SD	Collinsville
86	360.5	Greenwich SD	Greenwich
87	359.3	Avon SD	Avon
88	359.2	New Canaan SD	New Canaan
89	356.9	Windsor Locks SD	Windsor Locks
90	350.9	Cheshire SD	Cheshire
91	338.0	Shelton SD	Shelton
92	332.7	Regional SD 15	Middlebury
93	332.5	Plainville SD	Plainville
94	332.3	Southington SD	Southington
95	325.8	Bethel SD	Bethel
96	325.6	Enfield SD	Enfield
97	317.9	Regional SD 16	Prospect
98	317.2	Seymour SD	Seymour
99	303.7	Plainfield SD	Central Village
100	270.3	Griswold SD	Jewett City
101	246.2	Weston SD	Weston
102	231.7	Regional SD 08	Hebron
103	207.6	Norwich Free Academy	Norwich
104	179.5	State Voc-Tech Schools	Middletown
105	162.0	Regional SD 05	Woodbridge

Current Spending per Student in FY2001

Rank	Dollars	District Name	City
1	13,577	Hartford SD	Hartford
2	13,201	Greenwich SD	Greenwich
3	12,769	Westport SD	Westport
4	12,729	Weston SD	Weston
5	12,617	New London SD	New London
6	12,251	New Haven SD	New Haven
7	11,427	Stamford SD	Stamford
8	11,389	New Canaan SD	New Canaan
9	11,364	Windham SD	Willimantic
10	11,320	Bloomfield SD	Bloomfield
11	11,305	Hamden SD	Hamden
12	11,203	Darien SD	Darien
13	11,099	Norwalk SD	Norwalk
14	11,084	Fairfield SD	Fairfield
15	11,076	Regional SD 05	Woodbridge
16	10,733	Waterford SD	Waterford
17	10,722	Regional SD 18	Old Lyme
18	10,680	Waterbury SD	Waterbury
19	10,553	Norwich SD	Norwich
20	10,476	Wilton SD	Wilton
21	10,401	Groton SD	Mystic
22	10,230	Stonington SD	Old Mystic
23	10,172	Clinton SD	Clinton
24	10,102	Middletown SD	Middletown
25	10,042	Regional SD 13	Durham
26	9,960	Regional SD 17	Higganum
27	9,941	Manchester SD	Manchester
28	9,891	Ridgefield SD	Ridgefield
29	9,752	Vernon SD	Vernon
30	9,663	West Haven SD	West Haven
31	9,637	New Britain SD	New Britain
32	9,609	Milford SD	Milford
33	9,594	Bridgeport SD	Bridgeport
34	9,560	Plainville SD	Plainville
35	9,519	East Hartford SD	East Hartford
36	9,494	Rocky Hill SD	Rocky Hill
37	9,435	Montville SD	Oakdale
38	9,431	Stafford SD	Stafford Spgs
39	9,407	Cheshire SD	Cheshire
40	9,383	Wethersfield SD	Wethersfield
41	9,373	West Hartford SD	West Hartford
42	9,359	Cromwell SD	Cromwell
43	9,350	Enfield SD	Enfield
44	9,343	Meriden SD	Meriden
44	9,343	Windsor SD	Windsor
46	9,306	Bethel SD	Bethel
47	9,250	Regional SD 08	Hebron
48	9,249	Avon SD	Avon
49	9,172	Southington SD	Southington
50	9,137	Danbury SD	Danbury
51	9,125	Old Saybrook SD	Old Saybrook
52	9,111	Canton SD	Collinsville
53	9,102	Farmington SD	Farmington
54	9,088	East Hampton SD	East Hampton
55	9,081	Stratford SD	Stratford
56	9,061	Shelton SD	Shelton
57	9,028	Griswold SD	Jewett City
58	9,027	Windsor Locks SD	Windsor Locks
59	9,001	Trumbull SD	Trumbull
60	8,986	Regional SD 10	Burlington
61	8,971	North Haven SD	North Haven
62	8,960	Branford SD	Branford
63	8,931	Berlin SD	Berlin
64	8,870	Plainfield SD	Central Village
65	8,840	Guilford SD	Guilford
66	8,834	Regional SD 15	Middlebury
67	8,796	Newington SD	Newington
68	8,750	Monroe SD	Monroe
69	8,744	Simsbury SD	Simsbury
70	8,715	Newtown SD	Newtown
71	8,682	Regional SD 16	Prospect
72	8,651	Regional SD 14	Woodbury
73	8,648	Ellington SD	Ellington
74	8,640	Torrington SD	Torrington
75	8,626	Plymouth SD	Terryville
76	8,613	East Lyme SD	East Lyme
77	8,593	Somers SD	Somers
78	8,590	Madison SD	Madison
79	8,552	Bristol SD	Bristol
80	8,550	Brookfield SD	Brookfield
81	8,544	East Windsor SD	East Windsor
82	8,531	South Windsor SD	South Windsor
83	8,529	Wallingford SD	Wallingford
84	8,520	North Branford SD	Northford
85	8,412	Granby SD	Granby
86	8,410	New Milford SD	New Milford
87	8,374	Killingly SD	Danielson
88	8,346	Glastonbury SD	Glastonbury
89	8,322	New Fairfield SD	New Fairfield
90	8,296	Tolland SD	Tolland
90	8,296	Wolcott SD	Wolcott
92	8,286	Derby SD	Derby
93	8,280	Ledyard SD	Ledyard
94	8,226	Watertown SD	Watertown
95	8,223	East Haven SD	East Haven
96	8,099	Naugatuck SD	Naugatuck
97	7,986	Coventry SD	Coventry
98	7,933	Suffield SD	Suffield
99	7,826	Ansonia SD	Ansonia
100	7,725	Seymour SD	Seymour
101	7,554	Colchester SD	Colchester
102	n/a	Area Coop Educational Services	North Haven
102	n/a	Capitol Region Education Council	Hartford
102	n/a	Norwich Free Academy	Norwich
102	n/a	State Voc-Tech Schools	Middletown

Number of Diploma Recipients

Rank	Number	District Name	City
1	2,013	State Voc-Tech Schools	Middletown
2	834	Bridgeport SD	Bridgeport
3	795	Stamford SD	Stamford
4	788	New Haven SD	New Haven
5	785	Hartford SD	Hartford
6	668	West Hartford SD	West Hartford
7	613	Norwalk SD	Norwalk
8	578	Waterbury SD	Waterbury
9	558	Bristol SD	Bristol
10	506	Danbury SD	Danbury
11	497	Norwich Free Academy	Norwich
12	479	Southington SD	Southington
13	475	East Hartford SD	East Hartford
14	474	Greenwich SD	Greenwich
15	470	Stratford SD	Stratford
16	464	Milford SD	Milford
17	462	Wallingford SD	Wallingford
18	459	Fairfield SD	Fairfield
19	448	Enfield SD	Enfield
20	445	New Britain SD	New Britain
21	433	Meriden SD	Meriden
22	416	Trumbull SD	Trumbull
23	414	Glastonbury SD	Glastonbury
24	408	Manchester SD	Manchester
25	401	Hamden SD	Hamden
26	348	Cheshire SD	Cheshire
27	346	Simsbury SD	Simsbury
28	344	Shelton SD	Shelton
29	340	West Haven SD	West Haven
30	326	Naugatuck SD	Naugatuck
31	323	Regional SD 05	Woodbridge
32	317	South Windsor SD	South Windsor
33	315	Windsor SD	Windsor
34	287	Guilford SD	Guilford
35	286	Monroe SD	Monroe
35	286	Newtown SD	Newtown
37	280	Farmington SD	Farmington
37	280	Ridgefield SD	Ridgefield
39	268	Newington SD	Newington
40	267	Torrington SD	Torrington
41	255	Westport SD	Westport
42	247	Berlin SD	Berlin
43	246	Middletown SD	Middletown
44	243	Regional SD 15	Middlebury
45	241	New Milford SD	New Milford
45	241	Wethersfield SD	Wethersfield
47	240	Seymour SD	Seymour
48	239	Groton SD	Mystic
49	238	Branford SD	Branford
50	235	East Lyme SD	East Lyme
50	235	Vernon SD	Vernon
52	233	New Canaan SD	New Canaan
53	230	Ledyard SD	Ledyard
53	230	Wilton SD	Wilton
55	215	East Haven SD	East Haven
56	214	North Haven SD	North Haven
57	210	Madison SD	Madison
58	205	Regional SD 08	Hebron
59	203	Killingly SD	Danielson
59	203	Watertown SD	Watertown
61	202	Wolcott SD	Wolcott
62	197	New Fairfield SD	New Fairfield
63	196	Windham SD	Willimantic
64	191	Waterford SD	Waterford
65	190	Darien SD	Darien
66	188	Plainville SD	Plainville
67	186	Bethel SD	Bethel
68	182	Brookfield SD	Brookfield
69	181	Avon SD	Avon
70	180	Regional SD 14	Woodbury
71	173	Bloomfield SD	Bloomfield
72	169	Tolland SD	Tolland
73	164	Plainfield SD	Central Village
74	162	Regional SD 10	Burlington
75	159	Montville SD	Oakdale
76	157	Clinton SD	Clinton
77	148	North Branford SD	Northford
78	146	Regional SD 17	Higganum
79	144	Suffield SD	Suffield
80	143	Rocky Hill SD	Rocky Hill
81	141	Stonington SD	Old Mystic
82	135	Colchester SD	Colchester
82	135	Weston SD	Weston
84	128	Windsor Locks SD	Windsor Locks
85	126	Griswold SD	Jewett City
86	125	East Hampton SD	East Hampton
86	125	Granby SD	Granby
88	121	New London SD	New London
89	120	Plymouth SD	Terryville
90	118	Ansonia SD	Ansonia
91	113	Ellington SD	Ellington
92	110	Regional SD 13	Durham
93	101	Coventry SD	Coventry
93	101	Cromwell SD	Cromwell
95	100	Canton SD	Collinsville
96	95	Old Saybrook SD	Old Saybrook
96	95	Somers SD	Somers
98	94	Regional SD 18	Old Lyme
99	92	Stafford SD	Stafford Spgs
100	80	Derby SD	Derby
101	78	East Windsor SD	East Windsor
102	24	Area Coop Educational Services	North Haven
103	18	Capitol Region Education Council	Hartford
104	11	Norwich SD	Norwich
105	n/a	Regional SD 16	Prospect

High School Drop-out Rate

Rank	Percent	District Name	City
1	53.5	Norwich SD	Norwich
2	26.1	New London SD	New London
3	11.5	Hartford SD	Hartford
4	11.2	Bridgeport SD	Bridgeport
5	8.8	New Britain SD	New Britain
6	8.5	Hamden SD	Hamden
7	6.8	Killingly SD	Danielson
8	6.5	Torrington SD	Torrington
8	6.5	Windham SD	Willimantic
10	6.4	New Haven SD	New Haven
10	6.4	Plainfield SD	Central Village
12	6.1	Windsor Locks SD	Windsor Locks
13	4.6	Capitol Region Education Council	Hartford
14	4.1	Danbury SD	Danbury
14	4.1	Norwich Free Academy	Norwich
16	4.0	Stafford SD	Stafford Spgs
17	3.9	Waterbury SD	Waterbury
18	3.8	Enfield SD	Enfield
19	3.5	Stratford SD	Stratford
20	3.4	Coventry SD	Coventry
20	3.4	Naugatuck SD	Naugatuck
22	3.3	Norwalk SD	Norwalk
22	3.3	Plymouth SD	Terryville
24	3.2	Somers SD	Somers
25	3.1	Griswold SD	Jewett City
25	3.1	Ledyard SD	Ledyard
27	3.0	Windsor SD	Windsor
28	2.9	Meriden SD	Meriden
28	2.9	Stamford SD	Stamford
30	2.8	Clinton SD	Clinton
30	2.8	Derby SD	Derby
32	2.7	Ansonia SD	Ansonia

32	2.7	Bristol SD	Bristol
32	2.7	Shelton SD	Shelton
32	2.7	Stonington SD	Old Mystic
32	2.7	Watertown SD	Watertown
37	2.6	East Hartford SD	East Hartford
37	2.6	Montville SD	Oakdale
39	2.5	Colchester SD	Colchester
40	2.4	Bloomfield SD	Bloomfield
40	2.4	Ellington SD	Ellington
42	2.3	East Windsor SD	East Windsor
42	2.3	Milford SD	Milford
42	2.3	Wethersfield SD	Wethersfield
45	2.2	West Hartford SD	West Hartford
46	2.1	Manchester SD	Manchester
47	1.9	East Lyme SD	East Lyme
47	1.9	Vernon SD	Vernon
49	1.8	Berlin SD	Berlin
49	1.8	Regional SD 15	Middlebury
49	1.8	Southington SD	Southington
52	1.7	Middletown SD	Middletown
52	1.7	New Fairfield SD	New Fairfield
52	1.7	Regional SD 18	Old Lyme
52	1.7	Rocky Hill SD	Rocky Hill
56	1.6	North Branford SD	Northford
56	1.6	South Windsor SD	South Windsor
56	1.6	West Haven SD	West Haven
59	1.5	East Haven SD	East Haven
60	1.4	Farmington SD	Farmington
60	1.4	New Milford SD	New Milford
60	1.4	Tolland SD	Tolland
63	1.3	Branford SD	Branford
64	1.2	Greenwich SD	Greenwich
64	1.2	Seymour SD	Seymour
66	1.1	Granby SD	Granby
67	1.0	Brookfield SD	Brookfield
67	1.0	Fairfield SD	Fairfield
67	1.0	North Haven SD	North Haven
67	1.0	Suffield SD	Suffield
71	0.9	Bethel SD	Bethel
71	0.9	Cheshire SD	Cheshire
71	0.9	Regional SD 08	Hebron
71	0.9	Simsbury SD	Simsbury
71	0.9	State Voc-Tech Schools	Middletown
71	0.9	Wolcott SD	Wolcott
77	0.8	Groton SD	Mystic
77	0.8	Madison SD	Madison
77	0.8	Plainville SD	Plainville
77	0.8	Ridgefield SD	Ridgefield
77	0.8	Trumbull SD	Trumbull
77	0.8	Wallingford SD	Wallingford
83	0.7	Guilford SD	Guilford
84	0.6	Newtown SD	Newtown
84	0.6	Regional SD 05	Woodbridge
84	0.6	Regional SD 13	Durham
87	0.5	Darien SD	Darien
87	0.5	Glastonbury SD	Glastonbury
87	0.5	Waterford SD	Waterford
87	0.5	Westport SD	Westport
91	0.4	East Hampton SD	East Hampton
91	0.4	Newington SD	Newington
91	0.4	Regional SD 10	Burlington
91	0.4	Wilton SD	Wilton
95	0.3	Area Coop Educational Services	North Haven
95	0.3	Regional SD 14	Woodbury
95	0.3	Regional SD 17	Higganum
98	0.2	Cromwell SD	Cromwell
98	0.2	Monroe SD	Monroe
98	0.2	Old Saybrook SD	Old Saybrook
101	0.0	Avon SD	Avon
101	0.0	Canton SD	Collinsville
101	0.0	New Canaan SD	New Canaan
101	0.0	Weston SD	Weston
105	n/a	Regional SD 16	Prospect

Delaware

Delaware Public School Educational Profile

Category	Value	Category	Value
Schools *(2002-2003)*	201	**Diploma Recipients** *(2002-2003)*	6,482
Instructional Level		White, Non-Hispanic	4,358
Primary	104	Black, Non-Hispanic	1,683
Middle	44	Asian/Pacific Islander	185
High	32	American Indian/Alaskan Native	15
Other Level	21	Hispanic	241
Curriculum		**High School Drop-out Rate** (%) *(2000-2001)*	4.2
Regular	172	White, Non-Hispanic	3.6
Special Education	15	Black, Non-Hispanic	5.3
Vocational	5	Asian/Pacific Islander	2.2
Alternative	9	American Indian/Alaskan Native	2.4
Type		Hispanic	7.5
Magnet	2	**Staff** *(2002-2003)*	14,445.5
Charter	11	Teachers	7,696.7
Title I Eligible	105	Average Salary ($)	49,821
School-wide Title I	51	Librarians/Media Specialists	125.5
Students *(2002-2003)*	116,342	Guidance Counselors	237.7
Gender (%)		**Ratios** *(2002-2003)*	
Male	51.6	Student/Teacher Ratio	15.1 to 1
Female	48.4	Student/Librarian Ratio	927.0 to 1
Race/Ethnicity (%)		Student/Counselor Ratio	489.4 to 1
White, Non-Hispanic	58.4	**Current Spending** *($ per student in FY 2001)*	9,285
Black, Non-Hispanic	31.4	Instruction	5,719
Asian/Pacific Islander	2.6	Support Services	3,133
American Indian/Alaskan Native	0.3	**College Entrance Exam Scores** *(2003)*	
Hispanic	7.2	Scholastic Aptitude Test (SAT)	
Classification (%)		Participation Rate (%)	73
Individual Education Program (IEP)	14.4	Mean SAT I Verbal Score	501
Migrant	0.3	Mean SAT I Math Score	501
English Language Learner (ELL)	3.0	American College Testing Program (ACT)	
Eligible for Free Lunch Program	28.8	Participation Rate (%)	5
Eligible for Reduced-Price Lunch Program	6.7	Average Composite Score	20.8

Note: *For an explanation of data, please refer to the User's Guide in the front of the book; n/a indicates data not available*

Delaware NAEP 2003 Test Scores

Reading Grade/Category	Value	Rank	Mathematics Grade/Category	Value	Rank
4th Grade			**4th Grade**		
Average Proficiency	223.9 (0.7)	6/51	Average Proficiency	235.9 (0.5)	22/51
Proficiency by Gender/Race/Ethnicity			Proficiency by Gender/Race/Ethnicity		
Male	221.7 (1.2)	6/51	Male	236.9 (0.8)	27/51
Female	226.1 (0.8)	14/51	Female	234.8 (0.7)	23/51
White, Non-Hispanic	233.1 (0.7)	6/51	White, Non-Hispanic	244.4 (0.6)	12/51
Black, Non-Hispanic	210.8 (1.1)	3/42	Black, Non-Hispanic	222.6 (0.8)	5/42
Asian, Non-Hispanic	209.2 (3.0)	9/41	Asian, Non-Hispanic	225.8 (1.8)	12/43
American Indian, Non-Hispanic	237.6 (3.5)	1/25	American Indian, Non-Hispanic	249.6 (3.5)	7/26
Hispanic	n/a	n/a	Hispanic	n/a	n/a
Proficiency by Class Size			Proficiency by Class Size		
Less than 16 Students	203.2 (5.4)	24/45	Less than 16 Students	212.4 (2.8)	41/47
16 to 18 Students	213.2 (3.9)	27/48	16 to 18 Students	227.7 (4.3)	34/48
19 to 20 Students	218.5 (3.1)	29/50	19 to 20 Students	235.4 (1.6)	23/50
21 to 25 Students	226.9 (1.0)	6/51	21 to 25 Students	239.0 (0.7)	19/51
Greater than 25 Students	223.8 (1.1)	12/49	Greater than 25 Students	235.3 (0.7)	26/49
Percent Attaining Achievement Levels			Percent Attaining Achievement Levels		
Below Basic	29.1 (1.4)	47/51	Below Basic	19.3 (1.1)	33/51
Basic or Above	70.9 (1.4)	5/51	Basic or Above	80.7 (1.1)	19/51
Proficient or Above	32.8 (1.0)	18/51	Proficient or Above	31.1 (0.9)	30/51
Advanced or Above	6.5 (0.6)	30/51	Advanced or Above	2.9 (0.4)	31/51
8th Grade			**8th Grade**		
Average Proficiency	264.5 (0.7)	24/51	Average Proficiency	277.2 (0.7)	31/51
Proficiency by Gender/Race/Ethnicity			Proficiency by Gender/Race/Ethnicity		
Male	259.8 (0.9)	20/51	Male	278.4 (1.0)	31/51
Female	269.6 (1.0)	27/51	Female	275.9 (1.0)	33/51
White, Non-Hispanic	272.6 (0.9)	9/50	White, Non-Hispanic	286.7 (0.8)	22/50
Black, Non-Hispanic	248.4 (1.7)	8/41	Black, Non-Hispanic	260.3 (0.9)	5/41
Asian, Non-Hispanic	246.0 (3.2)	21/37	Asian, Non-Hispanic	257.2 (3.8)	25/37
American Indian, Non-Hispanic	280.7 (5.0)	5/23	American Indian, Non-Hispanic	n/a	n/a
Hispanic	n/a	n/a	Hispanic	n/a	n/a
Proficiency by Parents Highest Level of Ed.			Proficiency by Parents Highest Level of Ed.		
Did Not Finish High School	245.5 (3.6)	29/50	Did Not Finish High School	257.6 (3.5)	24/50
Graduated High School	259.4 (1.3)	13/50	Graduated High School	270.6 (1.6)	21/50
Some Education After High School	267.4 (1.2)	28/50	Some Education After High School	277.9 (1.5)	33/50
Graduated College	271.5 (1.3)	29/50	Graduated College	285.5 (1.2)	32/50
Percent Attaining Achievement Levels			Percent Attaining Achievement Levels		
Below Basic	23.2 (0.9)	30/51	Below Basic	31.5 (1.1)	22/51
Basic or Above	76.8 (0.9)	20/51	Basic or Above	68.5 (1.1)	30/51
Proficient or Above	31.0 (1.4)	30/51	Proficient or Above	25.7 (0.9)	33/51
Advanced or Above	2.4 (0.4)	30/51	Advanced or Above	4.4 (0.5)	30/51

***Note:** For an explanation of data, please refer to the User's Guide in the front of the book; values in italics indicate that the nature of the sample does not allow accurate determination of the variability of the statistic; n/a indicates data not available*

Kent County

Caesar Rodney SD

219 Old N Rd • Wyoming, DE 19934-1252
Mailing Address: PO Box 188 • Wyoming, DE 19934-1252
(302) 697-2173
Grade Span: PK-12; **Agency Type:** 1
Schools: 15
9 Primary; 3 Middle; 1 High; 1 Other Level
13 Regular; 1 Special Education; 0 Vocational; 0 Alternative
0 Magnet; 0 Charter; 7 Title I Eligible; 0 School-wide Title I
Students: 6,665 (51.6% male; 48.4% female)
Individual Education Program: 971 (14.6%);
English Language Learner: 76 (1.1%); Migrant: 42 (0.6%)
Eligible for Free Lunch Program: 1,475 (22.1%)
Eligible for Reduced-Price Lunch Program: 606 (9.1%)
Teachers: 440.7 (15.1 to 1)
Librarians/Media Specialists: 10.5 (634.8 to 1)
Guidance Counselors: 17.0 (392.1 to 1)
Current Spending: ($ per student per year):
Total: $8,206; Instruction: $5,140; Support Services: $2,751
Enrollment, Drop-out Rates and Diploma Recipients by Race/Ethnicity

Category	Total	White	Black	Asian	AIAN	Hisp.
Enrollment (%)	100.0	66.5	25.7	2.8	0.4	4.6
Drop-out Rate (%)	0.7	0.5	1.3	0.0	0.0	0.0
H.S. Diplomas (#)	310	221	67	8	1	13

Capital SD

945 Forest St • Dover, DE 19904-3498
(302) 672-1556 • http://www.k12.de.us/capital
Grade Span: PK-12; **Agency Type:** 1
Schools: 12
7 Primary; 2 Middle; 2 High; 1 Other Level
10 Regular; 2 Special Education; 0 Vocational; 0 Alternative
0 Magnet; 0 Charter; 7 Title I Eligible; 7 School-wide Title I
Students: 6,115 (51.3% male; 48.7% female)
Individual Education Program: 985 (16.1%);
English Language Learner: 146 (2.4%); Migrant: 3 (<0.1%)
Eligible for Free Lunch Program: 2,239 (36.6%)
Eligible for Reduced-Price Lunch Program: 327 (5.3%)
Teachers: 419.9 (14.6 to 1)
Librarians/Media Specialists: 6.0 (1,019.2 to 1)
Guidance Counselors: 10.0 (611.5 to 1)
Current Spending: ($ per student per year):
Total: $8,122; Instruction: $5,221; Support Services: $2,608
Enrollment, Drop-out Rates and Diploma Recipients by Race/Ethnicity

Category	Total	White	Black	Asian	AIAN	Hisp.
Enrollment (%)	100.0	44.4	47.7	2.6	0.8	4.6
Drop-out Rate (%)	4.6	3.2	6.1	4.7	0.0	7.7
H.S. Diplomas (#)	267	144	105	10	1	7

Lake Forest SD

5423 Killens Pond Rd • Felton, DE 19943-9801
(302) 284-3020 • http://www.k12.de.us/lakeforest
Grade Span: PK-12; **Agency Type:** 1
Schools: 6
3 Primary; 2 Middle; 1 High; 0 Other Level
6 Regular; 0 Special Education; 0 Vocational; 0 Alternative
0 Magnet; 0 Charter; 3 Title I Eligible; 3 School-wide Title I
Students: 3,429 (50.4% male; 49.6% female)
Individual Education Program: 498 (14.5%);
English Language Learner: 41 (1.2%); Migrant: 3 (0.1%)
Eligible for Free Lunch Program: 972 (28.3%)
Eligible for Reduced-Price Lunch Program: 313 (9.1%)
Teachers: 234.7 (14.6 to 1)
Librarians/Media Specialists: 2.0 (1,714.5 to 1)
Guidance Counselors: 10.0 (342.9 to 1)
Current Spending: ($ per student per year):
Total: $7,689; Instruction: $4,552; Support Services: $2,774
Enrollment, Drop-out Rates and Diploma Recipients by Race/Ethnicity

Category	Total	White	Black	Asian	AIAN	Hisp.
Enrollment (%)	100.0	75.6	20.0	1.2	0.4	2.7
Drop-out Rate (%)	7.3	7.1	7.0	23.1	0.0	5.6
H.S. Diplomas (#)	154	117	31	2	0	4

Milford SD

906 Lakeview Ave • Milford, DE 19963-1799
(302) 422-1600 • http://www.milford.k12.de.us
Grade Span: PK-12; **Agency Type:** 1
Schools: 6
3 Primary; 1 Middle; 1 High; 1 Other Level
5 Regular; 1 Special Education; 0 Vocational; 0 Alternative
0 Magnet; 0 Charter; 4 Title I Eligible; 4 School-wide Title I
Students: 3,742 (51.0% male; 49.0% female)
Individual Education Program: 632 (16.9%);
English Language Learner: 228 (6.1%); Migrant: 24 (0.6%)
Eligible for Free Lunch Program: 1,176 (31.4%)
Eligible for Reduced-Price Lunch Program: 207 (5.5%)
Teachers: 252.5 (14.8 to 1)
Librarians/Media Specialists: 4.0 (935.5 to 1)
Guidance Counselors: 6.7 (558.5 to 1)
Current Spending: ($ per student per year):
Total: $7,497; Instruction: $4,850; Support Services: $2,313
Enrollment, Drop-out Rates and Diploma Recipients by Race/Ethnicity

Category	Total	White	Black	Asian	AIAN	Hisp.
Enrollment (%)	100.0	64.1	27.7	0.9	0.1	7.3
Drop-out Rate (%)	3.9	2.9	5.6	0.0	0.0	11.8
H.S. Diplomas (#)	198	142	51	0	0	5

Smyrna SD

22 S Main St • Smyrna, DE 19977-1493
(302) 653-8585 • http://www.smyrna.k12.de.us
Grade Span: PK-12; **Agency Type:** 1
Schools: 6
3 Primary; 2 Middle; 1 High; 0 Other Level
6 Regular; 0 Special Education; 0 Vocational; 0 Alternative
0 Magnet; 0 Charter; 3 Title I Eligible; 0 School-wide Title I
Students: 3,246 (50.4% male; 49.6% female)
Individual Education Program: 583 (18.0%);
English Language Learner: 34 (1.0%); Migrant: 7 (0.2%)
Eligible for Free Lunch Program: 478 (14.7%)
Eligible for Reduced-Price Lunch Program: 172 (5.3%)
Teachers: 201.0 (16.1 to 1)
Librarians/Media Specialists: 3.0 (1,082.0 to 1)
Guidance Counselors: 7.0 (463.7 to 1)
Current Spending: ($ per student per year):
Total: $7,448; Instruction: $4,572; Support Services: $2,488
Enrollment, Drop-out Rates and Diploma Recipients by Race/Ethnicity

Category	Total	White	Black	Asian	AIAN	Hisp.
Enrollment (%)	100.0	81.0	15.4	1.2	0.2	2.2
Drop-out Rate (%)	4.9	5.3	1.8	0.0	0.0	12.5
H.S. Diplomas (#)	202	172	25	1	0	4

New Castle County

Appoquinimink SD

118 S Sixth St • Odessa, DE 19730-4010
Mailing Address: Box 4010 • Odessa, DE 19730-4010
(302) 378-5010 • http://www.k12.de.us/appoquinimink
Grade Span: PK-12; **Agency Type:** 1
Schools: 8
5 Primary; 2 Middle; 1 High; 0 Other Level
8 Regular; 0 Special Education; 0 Vocational; 0 Alternative
0 Magnet; 0 Charter; 4 Title I Eligible; 0 School-wide Title I
Students: 5,813 (51.9% male; 48.1% female)
Individual Education Program: 712 (12.2%);
English Language Learner: 48 (0.8%); Migrant: 1 (<0.1%)
Eligible for Free Lunch Program: 531 (9.1%)
Eligible for Reduced-Price Lunch Program: 188 (3.2%)
Teachers: 350.0 (16.6 to 1)
Librarians/Media Specialists: 6.0 (968.8 to 1)
Guidance Counselors: 9.0 (645.9 to 1)
Current Spending: ($ per student per year):
Total: $7,739; Instruction: $4,159; Support Services: $3,354
Enrollment, Drop-out Rates and Diploma Recipients by Race/Ethnicity

Category	Total	White	Black	Asian	AIAN	Hisp.
Enrollment (%)	100.0	79.3	15.5	2.0	0.2	3.1
Drop-out Rate (%)	1.7	1.5	1.7	10.0	n/a	11.1
H.S. Diplomas (#)	284	241	38	3	0	2

Brandywine SD

1000 Pennsylvania Ave • Claymont, DE 19703-1237
(302) 792-3800 • http://www.bsd.k12.de.us
Grade Span: PK-12; **Agency Type:** 1
Schools: 22
11 Primary; 6 Middle; 3 High; 2 Other Level
19 Regular; 3 Special Education; 0 Vocational; 0 Alternative
0 Magnet; 0 Charter; 8 Title I Eligible; 7 School-wide Title I
Students: 10,701 (51.6% male; 48.4% female)
Individual Education Program: 1,410 (13.2%);
English Language Learner: 306 (2.9%); Migrant: 0 (0.0%)
Eligible for Free Lunch Program: 2,905 (27.1%)
Eligible for Reduced-Price Lunch Program: 542 (5.1%)
Teachers: 677.1 (15.8 to 1)
Librarians/Media Specialists: 14.0 (764.4 to 1)
Guidance Counselors: 33.0 (324.3 to 1)
Current Spending: ($ per student per year):
Total: $9,207; Instruction: $5,628; Support Services: $3,258

Enrollment, Drop-out Rates and Diploma Recipients by Race/Ethnicity

Category	Total	White	Black	Asian	AIAN	Hisp.
Enrollment (%)	100.0	56.0	37.2	3.7	0.2	3.0
Drop-out Rate (%)	4.0	3.4	5.3	3.1	0.0	3.4
H.S. Diplomas (#)	694	494	164	23	1	12

Christina SD

83 E Main St • Newark, DE 19711-4671
(302) 454-2000 • http://www.christina.k12.de.us
Grade Span: PK-12; **Agency Type:** 1
Schools: 28
15 Primary; 7 Middle; 3 High; 3 Other Level
26 Regular; 2 Special Education; 0 Vocational; 0 Alternative
0 Magnet; 0 Charter; 15 Title I Eligible; 2 School-wide Title I
Students: 19,605 (53.1% male; 46.9% female)
Individual Education Program: 2,979 (15.2%);
English Language Learner: 458 (2.3%); Migrant: 8 (<0.1%)
Eligible for Free Lunch Program: 6,741 (34.4%)
Eligible for Reduced-Price Lunch Program: 1,536 (7.8%)
Teachers: 1,369.0 (14.3 to 1)
Librarians/Media Specialists: 27.0 (726.1 to 1)
Guidance Counselors: 12.0 (1,633.8 to 1)
Current Spending: ($ per student per year):
Total: $9,373; Instruction: $5,939; Support Services: $3,181
Enrollment, Drop-out Rates and Diploma Recipients by Race/Ethnicity

Category	Total	White	Black	Asian	AIAN	Hisp.
Enrollment (%)	100.0	49.9	37.3	3.8	0.2	8.9
Drop-out Rate (%)	5.9	4.7	7.9	1.8	0.0	7.8
H.S. Diplomas (#)	857	492	272	50	3	40

Colonial SD

318 E Basin Rd • New Castle, DE 19720-4214
(302) 323-2700 • http://www.dataservice.org/colonial
Grade Span: PK-12; **Agency Type:** 1
Schools: 15
9 Primary; 3 Middle; 1 High; 2 Other Level
13 Regular; 1 Special Education; 0 Vocational; 1 Alternative
0 Magnet; 0 Charter; 8 Title I Eligible; 0 School-wide Title I
Students: 10,353 (52.3% male; 47.7% female)
Individual Education Program: 1,557 (15.0%);
English Language Learner: 452 (4.4%); Migrant: 0 (0.0%)
Eligible for Free Lunch Program: 3,734 (36.1%)
Eligible for Reduced-Price Lunch Program: 915 (8.8%)
Teachers: 637.7 (16.2 to 1)
Librarians/Media Specialists: 11.0 (941.2 to 1)
Guidance Counselors: 26.0 (398.2 to 1)
Current Spending: ($ per student per year):
Total: $8,179; Instruction: $5,322; Support Services: $2,526
Enrollment, Drop-out Rates and Diploma Recipients by Race/Ethnicity

Category	Total	White	Black	Asian	AIAN	Hisp.
Enrollment (%)	100.0	46.0	41.1	2.4	0.3	10.2
Drop-out Rate (%)	7.4	7.1	7.9	1.8	0.0	8.8
H.S. Diplomas (#)	406	201	176	10	0	19

New Castle County Votech SD

1417 Newport Rd • Wilmington, DE 19804-3499
(302) 995-8000 • http://www.nccvotech.org
Grade Span: 08-12; **Agency Type:** 1
Schools: 3
0 Primary; 0 Middle; 3 High; 0 Other Level
0 Regular; 0 Special Education; 3 Vocational; 0 Alternative
0 Magnet; 0 Charter; 2 Title I Eligible; 0 School-wide Title I
Students: 3,285 (51.7% male; 48.3% female)
Individual Education Program: 448 (13.6%);
English Language Learner: 19 (0.6%); Migrant: 0 (0.0%)
Eligible for Free Lunch Program: 529 (16.1%)
Eligible for Reduced-Price Lunch Program: 183 (5.6%)
Teachers: 280.1 (11.7 to 1)
Librarians/Media Specialists: 3.0 (1,095.0 to 1)
Guidance Counselors: 9.3 (353.2 to 1)
Current Spending: ($ per student per year):
Total: $12,911; Instruction: $7,419; Support Services: $5,205
Enrollment, Drop-out Rates and Diploma Recipients by Race/Ethnicity

Category	Total	White	Black	Asian	AIAN	Hisp.
Enrollment (%)	100.0	61.2	33.4	0.5	0.1	4.9
Drop-out Rate (%)	0.8	1.0	0.4	0.0	0.0	0.0
H.S. Diplomas (#)	691	440	211	4	0	36

Red Clay Consolidated SD

2916 Duncan Rd • Wilmington, DE 19808
(302) 651-2600 • http://www.redclay.k12.de.us
Grade Span: PK-12; **Agency Type:** 1
Schools: 28
14 Primary; 5 Middle; 3 High; 6 Other Level
22 Regular; 2 Special Education; 0 Vocational; 4 Alternative
1 Magnet; 0 Charter; 10 Title I Eligible; 6 School-wide Title I
Students: 15,622 (50.6% male; 49.4% female)
Individual Education Program: 2,059 (13.2%);
English Language Learner: 902 (5.8%); Migrant: 7 (<0.1%)
Eligible for Free Lunch Program: 4,769 (30.5%)
Eligible for Reduced-Price Lunch Program: 878 (5.6%)
Teachers: 960.5 (16.3 to 1)
Librarians/Media Specialists: 19.0 (822.2 to 1)
Guidance Counselors: 29.0 (538.7 to 1)
Current Spending: ($ per student per year):
Total: $9,981; Instruction: $5,967; Support Services: $3,725
Enrollment, Drop-out Rates and Diploma Recipients by Race/Ethnicity

Category	Total	White	Black	Asian	AIAN	Hisp.
Enrollment (%)	100.0	51.5	29.2	3.8	0.2	15.3
Drop-out Rate (%)	5.3	4.4	5.8	0.0	0.0	11.1
H.S. Diplomas (#)	758	484	177	38	1	58

Sussex County

Cape Henlopen SD

1270 Kings Hwy • Lewes, DE 19958-1798
(302) 645-6686 • http://www.k12.de.us/capehenlopen/
Grade Span: PK-12; **Agency Type:** 1
Schools: 7
3 Primary; 2 Middle; 1 High; 1 Other Level
6 Regular; 1 Special Education; 0 Vocational; 0 Alternative
0 Magnet; 0 Charter; 5 Title I Eligible; 3 School-wide Title I
Students: 4,256 (51.5% male; 48.5% female)
Individual Education Program: 766 (18.0%);
English Language Learner: 68 (1.6%); Migrant: 19 (0.4%)
Eligible for Free Lunch Program: 1,138 (26.7%)
Eligible for Reduced-Price Lunch Program: 285 (6.7%)
Teachers: 289.5 (14.7 to 1)
Librarians/Media Specialists: 3.0 (1,418.7 to 1)
Guidance Counselors: 7.0 (608.0 to 1)
Current Spending: ($ per student per year):
Total: $9,320; Instruction: $5,883; Support Services: $3,088
Enrollment, Drop-out Rates and Diploma Recipients by Race/Ethnicity

Category	Total	White	Black	Asian	AIAN	Hisp.
Enrollment (%)	100.0	73.9	19.8	1.3	0.5	4.5
Drop-out Rate (%)	3.5	3.0	5.7	0.0	0.0	0.0
H.S. Diplomas (#)	237	188	39	4	0	6

Indian River SD

31 Hoosier St • Selbyville, DE 19975
Mailing Address: Route 2 Box 156 • Selbyville, DE 19975
(302) 436-1000 • http://www.k12.de.us/indianriver
Grade Span: PK-12; **Agency Type:** 1
Schools: 14
8 Primary; 2 Middle; 2 High; 2 Other Level
11 Regular; 1 Special Education; 0 Vocational; 2 Alternative
1 Magnet; 0 Charter; 8 Title I Eligible; 7 School-wide Title I
Students: 7,746 (50.3% male; 49.7% female)
Individual Education Program: 1,396 (18.0%);
English Language Learner: 390 (5.0%); Migrant: 141 (1.8%)
Eligible for Free Lunch Program: 2,433 (31.4%)
Eligible for Reduced-Price Lunch Program: 603 (7.8%)
Teachers: 564.5 (13.7 to 1)
Librarians/Media Specialists: 8.0 (968.3 to 1)
Guidance Counselors: 20.0 (387.3 to 1)
Current Spending: ($ per student per year):
Total: $8,511; Instruction: $5,196; Support Services: $2,981
Enrollment, Drop-out Rates and Diploma Recipients by Race/Ethnicity

Category	Total	White	Black	Asian	AIAN	Hisp.
Enrollment (%)	100.0	66.3	20.9	1.1	0.5	11.2
Drop-out Rate (%)	5.2	4.2	6.7	8.7	0.0	13.6
H.S. Diplomas (#)	379	279	76	4	3	17

Laurel SD

1160 S Central Ave • Laurel, DE 19956-1413
(302) 875-6100 • http://www.k12.de.us/laurel
Grade Span: PK-12; **Agency Type:** 1
Schools: 6
2 Primary; 2 Middle; 2 High; 0 Other Level
5 Regular; 0 Special Education; 0 Vocational; 1 Alternative
0 Magnet; 0 Charter; 2 Title I Eligible; 2 School-wide Title I
Students: 2,001 (50.7% male; 49.3% female)
Individual Education Program: 264 (13.2%);
English Language Learner: 40 (2.0%); Migrant: 0 (0.0%)
Eligible for Free Lunch Program: 790 (39.5%)
Eligible for Reduced-Price Lunch Program: 141 (7.0%)
Teachers: 136.0 (14.7 to 1)
Librarians/Media Specialists: 2.0 (1,000.5 to 1)
Guidance Counselors: 4.0 (500.3 to 1)
Current Spending: ($ per student per year):
Total: $8,012; Instruction: $4,733; Support Services: $2,776

Enrollment, Drop-out Rates and Diploma Recipients by Race/Ethnicity

Category	Total	White	Black	Asian	AIAN	Hisp.
Enrollment (%)	100.0	66.8	29.2	1.7	0.3	2.0
Drop-out Rate (%)	3.0	2.4	4.2	12.5	0.0	0.0
H.S. Diplomas (#)	102	71	30	1	0	0

Seaford SD

390 N Market St Extend • Seaford, DE 19973-1433
(302) 629-4587 • http://www.seaford.k12.de.us
Grade Span: PK-12; **Agency Type:** 1
Schools: 7
4 Primary; 1 Middle; 1 High; 1 Other Level
6 Regular; 1 Special Education; 0 Vocational; 0 Alternative
0 Magnet; 0 Charter; 5 Title I Eligible; 5 School-wide Title I
Students: 3,440 (51.2% male; 48.8% female)
Individual Education Program: 516 (15.0%);
English Language Learner: 175 (5.1%); Migrant: 7 (0.2%)
Eligible for Free Lunch Program: 1,419 (41.3%)
Eligible for Reduced-Price Lunch Program: 305 (8.9%)
Teachers: 230.2 (14.9 to 1)
Librarians/Media Specialists: 2.0 (1,720.0 to 1)
Guidance Counselors: 9.0 (382.2 to 1)
Current Spending: ($ per student per year):
Total: $8,230; Instruction: $5,350; Support Services: $2,487

Enrollment, Drop-out Rates and Diploma Recipients by Race/Ethnicity

Category	Total	White	Black	Asian	AIAN	Hisp.
Enrollment (%)	100.0	55.1	38.8	1.3	0.1	4.7
Drop-out Rate (%)	8.8	9.9	7.9	0.0	0.0	0.0
H.S. Diplomas (#)	186	111	69	4	0	2

Woodbridge SD

Governors Ave • Greenwood, DE 19950
Mailing Address: PO Box 869 • Greenwood, DE 19950
(302) 337-8296
Grade Span: PK-12; **Agency Type:** 1
Schools: 4
2 Primary; 1 Middle; 1 High; 0 Other Level
4 Regular; 0 Special Education; 0 Vocational; 0 Alternative
0 Magnet; 0 Charter; 3 Title I Eligible; 3 School-wide Title I
Students: 1,904 (49.8% male; 50.2% female)
Individual Education Program: 194 (10.2%);
English Language Learner: 54 (2.8%); Migrant: 29 (1.5%)
Eligible for Free Lunch Program: 837 (44.0%)
Eligible for Reduced-Price Lunch Program: 186 (9.8%)
Teachers: 135.0 (14.1 to 1)
Librarians/Media Specialists: 1.0 (1,904.0 to 1)
Guidance Counselors: 8.0 (238.0 to 1)
Current Spending: ($ per student per year):
Total: $7,731; Instruction: $4,412; Support Services: $2,813

Enrollment, Drop-out Rates and Diploma Recipients by Race/Ethnicity

Category	Total	White	Black	Asian	AIAN	Hisp.
Enrollment (%)	100.0	58.2	34.7	0.2	0.2	6.7
Drop-out Rate (%)	7.4	7.1	6.9	0.0	n/a	16.7
H.S. Diplomas (#)	65	51	13	0	0	1

Number of Schools

Rank	Number	District Name	City
1	28	Christina SD	Newark
1	28	Red Clay Consolidated SD	Wilmington
3	22	Brandywine SD	Claymont
4	15	Caesar Rodney SD	Wyoming
4	15	Colonial SD	New Castle
6	14	Indian River SD	Selbyville
7	12	Capital SD	Dover
8	8	Appoquinimink SD	Odessa
9	7	Cape Henlopen SD	Lewes
9	7	Seaford SD	Seaford
11	6	Lake Forest SD	Felton
11	6	Laurel SD	Laurel
11	6	Milford SD	Milford
11	6	Smyrna SD	Smyrna
15	4	Woodbridge SD	Greenwood
16	3	New Castle County Votech SD	Wilmington

Number of Teachers

Rank	Number	District Name	City
1	1,369	Christina SD	Newark
2	960	Red Clay Consolidated SD	Wilmington
3	677	Brandywine SD	Claymont
4	637	Colonial SD	New Castle
5	564	Indian River SD	Selbyville
6	440	Caesar Rodney SD	Wyoming
7	419	Capital SD	Dover
8	350	Appoquinimink SD	Odessa
9	289	Cape Henlopen SD	Lewes
10	280	New Castle County Votech SD	Wilmington
11	252	Milford SD	Milford
12	234	Lake Forest SD	Felton
13	230	Seaford SD	Seaford
14	201	Smyrna SD	Smyrna
15	136	Laurel SD	Laurel
16	135	Woodbridge SD	Greenwood

Number of Students

Rank	Number	District Name	City
1	19,605	Christina SD	Newark
2	15,622	Red Clay Consolidated SD	Wilmington
3	10,701	Brandywine SD	Claymont
4	10,353	Colonial SD	New Castle
5	7,746	Indian River SD	Selbyville
6	6,665	Caesar Rodney SD	Wyoming
7	6,115	Capital SD	Dover
8	5,813	Appoquinimink SD	Odessa
9	4,256	Cape Henlopen SD	Lewes
10	3,742	Milford SD	Milford
11	3,440	Seaford SD	Seaford
12	3,429	Lake Forest SD	Felton
13	3,285	New Castle County Votech SD	Wilmington
14	3,246	Smyrna SD	Smyrna
15	2,001	Laurel SD	Laurel
16	1,904	Woodbridge SD	Greenwood

Male Students

Rank	Percent	District Name	City
1	53.1	Christina SD	Newark
2	52.3	Colonial SD	New Castle
3	51.9	Appoquinimink SD	Odessa
4	51.7	New Castle County Votech SD	Wilmington
5	51.6	Brandywine SD	Claymont
5	51.6	Caesar Rodney SD	Wyoming
7	51.5	Cape Henlopen SD	Lewes
8	51.3	Capital SD	Dover
9	51.2	Seaford SD	Seaford
10	51.0	Milford SD	Milford
11	50.7	Laurel SD	Laurel
12	50.6	Red Clay Consolidated SD	Wilmington
13	50.4	Lake Forest SD	Felton
13	50.4	Smyrna SD	Smyrna
15	50.3	Indian River SD	Selbyville
16	49.8	Woodbridge SD	Greenwood

Female Students

Rank	Percent	District Name	City
1	50.2	Woodbridge SD	Greenwood
2	49.7	Indian River SD	Selbyville
3	49.6	Lake Forest SD	Felton
3	49.6	Smyrna SD	Smyrna
5	49.4	Red Clay Consolidated SD	Wilmington
6	49.3	Laurel SD	Laurel
7	49.0	Milford SD	Milford
8	48.8	Seaford SD	Seaford
9	48.7	Capital SD	Dover
10	48.5	Cape Henlopen SD	Lewes
11	48.4	Brandywine SD	Claymont
11	48.4	Caesar Rodney SD	Wyoming
13	48.3	New Castle County Votech SD	Wilmington
14	48.1	Appoquinimink SD	Odessa
15	47.7	Colonial SD	New Castle
16	46.9	Christina SD	Newark

Individual Education Program Students

Rank	Percent	District Name	City
1	18.0	Cape Henlopen SD	Lewes
1	18.0	Indian River SD	Selbyville
1	18.0	Smyrna SD	Smyrna
4	16.9	Milford SD	Milford
5	16.1	Capital SD	Dover
6	15.2	Christina SD	Newark
7	15.0	Colonial SD	New Castle
7	15.0	Seaford SD	Seaford
9	14.6	Caesar Rodney SD	Wyoming
10	14.5	Lake Forest SD	Felton
11	13.6	New Castle County Votech SD	Wilmington
12	13.2	Brandywine SD	Claymont
12	13.2	Laurel SD	Laurel
12	13.2	Red Clay Consolidated SD	Wilmington
15	12.2	Appoquinimink SD	Odessa
16	10.2	Woodbridge SD	Greenwood

English Language Learner Students

Rank	Percent	District Name	City
1	6.1	Milford SD	Milford
2	5.8	Red Clay Consolidated SD	Wilmington
3	5.1	Seaford SD	Seaford
4	5.0	Indian River SD	Selbyville
5	4.4	Colonial SD	New Castle
6	2.9	Brandywine SD	Claymont
7	2.8	Woodbridge SD	Greenwood
8	2.4	Capital SD	Dover
9	2.3	Christina SD	Newark
10	2.0	Laurel SD	Laurel
11	1.6	Cape Henlopen SD	Lewes
12	1.2	Lake Forest SD	Felton
13	1.1	Caesar Rodney SD	Wyoming
14	1.0	Smyrna SD	Smyrna
15	0.8	Appoquinimink SD	Odessa
16	0.6	New Castle County Votech SD	Wilmington

Migrant Students

Rank	Percent	District Name	City
1	1.8	Indian River SD	Selbyville
2	1.5	Woodbridge SD	Greenwood
3	0.6	Caesar Rodney SD	Wyoming
3	0.6	Milford SD	Milford
5	0.4	Cape Henlopen SD	Lewes
6	0.2	Seaford SD	Seaford
6	0.2	Smyrna SD	Smyrna
8	0.1	Lake Forest SD	Felton
9	0.0	Appoquinimink SD	Odessa
9	0.0	Capital SD	Dover
9	0.0	Christina SD	Newark
9	0.0	Red Clay Consolidated SD	Wilmington
13	0.0	Brandywine SD	Claymont
13	0.0	Colonial SD	New Castle
13	0.0	Laurel SD	Laurel
13	0.0	New Castle County Votech SD	Wilmington

Students Eligible for Free Lunch

Rank	Percent	District Name	City
1	44.0	Woodbridge SD	Greenwood
2	41.3	Seaford SD	Seaford
3	39.5	Laurel SD	Laurel
4	36.6	Capital SD	Dover
5	36.1	Colonial SD	New Castle
6	34.4	Christina SD	Newark
7	31.4	Indian River SD	Selbyville
7	31.4	Milford SD	Milford
9	30.5	Red Clay Consolidated SD	Wilmington
10	28.3	Lake Forest SD	Felton
11	27.1	Brandywine SD	Claymont
12	26.7	Cape Henlopen SD	Lewes
13	22.1	Caesar Rodney SD	Wyoming
14	16.1	New Castle County Votech SD	Wilmington
15	14.7	Smyrna SD	Smyrna
16	9.1	Appoquinimink SD	Odessa

Students Eligible for Reduced-Price Lunch

Rank	Percent	District Name	City
1	9.8	Woodbridge SD	Greenwood
2	9.1	Caesar Rodney SD	Wyoming
2	9.1	Lake Forest SD	Felton
4	8.9	Seaford SD	Seaford
5	8.8	Colonial SD	New Castle
6	7.8	Christina SD	Newark
6	7.8	Indian River SD	Selbyville
8	7.0	Laurel SD	Laurel
9	6.7	Cape Henlopen SD	Lewes
10	5.6	New Castle County Votech SD	Wilmington
10	5.6	Red Clay Consolidated SD	Wilmington
12	5.5	Milford SD	Milford
13	5.3	Capital SD	Dover
13	5.3	Smyrna SD	Smyrna
15	5.1	Brandywine SD	Claymont
16	3.2	Appoquinimink SD	Odessa

Student/Teacher Ratio

Rank	Ratio	District Name	City
1	16.6	Appoquinimink SD	Odessa
2	16.3	Red Clay Consolidated SD	Wilmington
3	16.2	Colonial SD	New Castle
4	16.1	Smyrna SD	Smyrna
5	15.8	Brandywine SD	Claymont
6	15.1	Caesar Rodney SD	Wyoming
7	14.9	Seaford SD	Seaford
8	14.8	Milford SD	Milford
9	14.7	Cape Henlopen SD	Lewes
9	14.7	Laurel SD	Laurel
11	14.6	Capital SD	Dover
11	14.6	Lake Forest SD	Felton
13	14.3	Christina SD	Newark
14	14.1	Woodbridge SD	Greenwood
15	13.7	Indian River SD	Selbyville
16	11.7	New Castle County Votech SD	Wilmington

Student/Librarian Ratio

Rank	Ratio	District Name	City
1	1,904.0	Woodbridge SD	Greenwood
2	1,720.0	Seaford SD	Seaford
3	1,714.5	Lake Forest SD	Felton
4	1,418.7	Cape Henlopen SD	Lewes
5	1,095.0	New Castle County Votech SD	Wilmington
6	1,082.0	Smyrna SD	Smyrna
7	1,019.2	Capital SD	Dover
8	1,000.5	Laurel SD	Laurel
9	968.8	Appoquinimink SD	Odessa
10	968.3	Indian River SD	Selbyville
11	941.2	Colonial SD	New Castle
12	935.5	Milford SD	Milford
13	822.2	Red Clay Consolidated SD	Wilmington
14	764.4	Brandywine SD	Claymont
15	726.1	Christina SD	Newark
16	634.8	Caesar Rodney SD	Wyoming

Student/Counselor Ratio

Rank	Ratio	District Name	City
1	1,633.8	Christina SD	Newark
2	645.9	Appoquinimink SD	Odessa
3	611.5	Capital SD	Dover
4	608.0	Cape Henlopen SD	Lewes
5	558.5	Milford SD	Milford
6	538.7	Red Clay Consolidated SD	Wilmington
7	500.3	Laurel SD	Laurel
8	463.7	Smyrna SD	Smyrna
9	398.2	Colonial SD	New Castle
10	392.1	Caesar Rodney SD	Wyoming
11	387.3	Indian River SD	Selbyville
12	382.2	Seaford SD	Seaford
13	353.2	New Castle County Votech SD	Wilmington
14	342.9	Lake Forest SD	Felton
15	324.3	Brandywine SD	Claymont
16	238.0	Woodbridge SD	Greenwood

Current Spending per Student in FY2001

Rank	Dollars	District Name	City
1	12,911	New Castle County Votech SD	Wilmington
2	9,981	Red Clay Consolidated SD	Wilmington
3	9,373	Christina SD	Newark
4	9,320	Cape Henlopen SD	Lewes
5	9,207	Brandywine SD	Claymont
6	8,511	Indian River SD	Selbyville
7	8,230	Seaford SD	Seaford
8	8,206	Caesar Rodney SD	Wyoming
9	8,179	Colonial SD	New Castle
10	8,122	Capital SD	Dover
11	8,012	Laurel SD	Laurel
12	7,739	Appoquinimink SD	Odessa
13	7,731	Woodbridge SD	Greenwood
14	7,689	Lake Forest SD	Felton
15	7,497	Milford SD	Milford

16	7,448	Smyrna SD	Smyrna

Number of Diploma Recipients

Rank	Number	District Name	City
1	857	Christina SD	Newark
2	758	Red Clay Consolidated SD	Wilmington
3	694	Brandywine SD	Claymont
4	691	New Castle County Votech SD	Wilmington
5	406	Colonial SD	New Castle
6	379	Indian River SD	Selbyville
7	310	Caesar Rodney SD	Wyoming
8	284	Appoquinimink SD	Odessa
9	267	Capital SD	Dover
10	237	Cape Henlopen SD	Lewes
11	202	Smyrna SD	Smyrna
12	198	Milford SD	Milford
13	186	Seaford SD	Seaford
14	154	Lake Forest SD	Felton
15	102	Laurel SD	Laurel
16	65	Woodbridge SD	Greenwood

High School Drop-out Rate

Rank	Percent	District Name	City
1	8.8	Seaford SD	Seaford
2	7.4	Colonial SD	New Castle
2	7.4	Woodbridge SD	Greenwood
4	7.3	Lake Forest SD	Felton
5	5.9	Christina SD	Newark
6	5.3	Red Clay Consolidated SD	Wilmington
7	5.2	Indian River SD	Selbyville
8	4.9	Smyrna SD	Smyrna
9	4.6	Capital SD	Dover
10	4.0	Brandywine SD	Claymont
11	3.9	Milford SD	Milford
12	3.5	Cape Henlopen SD	Lewes
13	3.0	Laurel SD	Laurel
14	1.7	Appoquinimink SD	Odessa
15	0.8	New Castle County Votech SD	Wilmington
16	0.7	Caesar Rodney SD	Wyoming

District of Columbia

District of Columbia Public School Educational Profile

Category	Value	Category	Value
Schools *(2002-2003)*	204	**Diploma Recipients** *(2002-2003)*	3,090
Instructional Level		White, Non-Hispanic	128
Primary	119	Black, Non-Hispanic	2,684
Middle	28	Asian/Pacific Islander	66
High	30	American Indian/Alaskan Native	3
Other Level	27	Hispanic	209
Curriculum		**High School Drop-out Rate** (%) *(2000-2001)*	n/a
Regular	182	White, Non-Hispanic	n/a
Special Education	13	Black, Non-Hispanic	n/a
Vocational	2	Asian/Pacific Islander	n/a
Alternative	7	American Indian/Alaskan Native	n/a
Type		Hispanic	n/a
Magnet	0	**Staff** *(2002-2003)*	11,549.0
Charter	35	Teachers	5,005.0
Title I Eligible	166	Average Salary ($)	53,194
School-wide Title I	163	Librarians/Media Specialists	119.0
Students *(2002-2003)*	76,166	Guidance Counselors	243.0
Gender (%)		**Ratios** *(2002-2003)*	
Male	50.2	Student/Teacher Ratio	15.2 to 1
Female	49.8	Student/Librarian Ratio	640.1 to 1
Race/Ethnicity (%)		Student/Counselor Ratio	313.4 to 1
White, Non-Hispanic	4.3	**Current Spending** *($ per student in FY 2001)*	12,102
Black, Non-Hispanic	83.7	Instruction	6,007
Asian/Pacific Islander	1.6	Support Services	5,726
American Indian/Alaskan Native	0.1	**College Entrance Exam Scores** *(2003)*	
Hispanic	10.4	Scholastic Aptitude Test (SAT)	
Classification (%)		Participation Rate (%)	77
Individual Education Program (IEP)	16.3	Mean SAT I Verbal Score	484
Migrant	1.1	Mean SAT I Math Score	474
English Language Learner (ELL)	7.6	American College Testing Program (ACT)	
Eligible for Free Lunch Program	55.8	Participation Rate (%)	30
Eligible for Reduced-Price Lunch Program	6.2	Average Composite Score	17.5

Note: *For an explanation of data, please refer to the User's Guide in the front of the book; n/a indicates data not available*

District of Columbia NAEP 2003 Test Scores

Reading			Mathematics		
Grade/Category	Value	Rank	Grade/Category	Value	Rank
4th Grade			**4th Grade**		
Average Proficiency	188.4 (0.9)	51/51	Average Proficiency	204.9 (0.7)	51/51
Proficiency by Gender/Race/Ethnicity			Proficiency by Gender/Race/Ethnicity		
Male	181.5 (1.2)	51/51	Male	204.0 (1.0)	51/51
Female	194.8 (1.0)	51/51	Female	205.8 (1.0)	51/51
White, Non-Hispanic	254.3 (2.6)	1/51	White, Non-Hispanic	261.9 (2.2)	1/51
Black, Non-Hispanic	184.4 (0.8)	42/42	Black, Non-Hispanic	202.2 (0.7)	42/42
Asian, Non-Hispanic	187.3 (2.8)	41/41	Asian, Non-Hispanic	205.3 (2.0)	43/43
American Indian, Non-Hispanic	n/a	n/a	American Indian, Non-Hispanic	n/a	n/a
Hispanic	n/a	n/a	Hispanic	n/a	n/a
Proficiency by Class Size			Proficiency by Class Size		
Less than 16 Students	180.3 (2.7)	43/45	Less than 16 Students	198.3 (3.0)	46/47
16 to 18 Students	183.1 (2.1)	48/48	16 to 18 Students	201.3 (1.6)	48/48
19 to 20 Students	187.7 (2.0)	50/50	19 to 20 Students	203.0 (1.3)	50/50
21 to 25 Students	193.0 (1.3)	51/51	21 to 25 Students	208.6 (1.0)	51/51
Greater than 25 Students	185.1 (2.3)	49/49	Greater than 25 Students	202.3 (1.4)	49/49
Percent Attaining Achievement Levels			Percent Attaining Achievement Levels		
Below Basic	69.0 (1.1)	1/51	Below Basic	63.6 (1.1)	1/51
Basic or Above	31.0 (1.1)	51/51	Basic or Above	36.4 (1.1)	51/51
Proficient or Above	10.4 (0.6)	51/51	Proficient or Above	7.1 (0.6)	51/51
Advanced or Above	2.8 (0.4)	51/51	Advanced or Above	1.1 (0.2)	50/51
8th Grade			**8th Grade**		
Average Proficiency	238.7 (0.8)	51/51	Average Proficiency	243.1 (0.8)	51/51
Proficiency by Gender/Race/Ethnicity			Proficiency by Gender/Race/Ethnicity		
Male	231.5 (1.2)	51/51	Male	241.5 (1.3)	51/51
Female	245.4 (1.2)	51/51	Female	244.4 (1.2)	51/51
White, Non-Hispanic	n/a	n/a	White, Non-Hispanic	n/a	n/a
Black, Non-Hispanic	236.1 (0.7)	38/41	Black, Non-Hispanic	239.6 (0.8)	40/41
Asian, Non-Hispanic	239.7 (2.7)	34/37	Asian, Non-Hispanic	245.9 (3.2)	36/37
American Indian, Non-Hispanic	n/a	n/a	American Indian, Non-Hispanic	n/a	n/a
Hispanic	n/a	n/a	Hispanic	n/a	n/a
Proficiency by Parents Highest Level of Ed.			Proficiency by Parents Highest Level of Ed.		
Did Not Finish High School	232.7 (3.5)	50/50	Did Not Finish High School	235.8 (3.1)	50/50
Graduated High School	233.3 (1.7)	50/50	Graduated High School	234.6 (1.3)	50/50
Some Education After High School	247.5 (2.1)	50/50	Some Education After High School	251.7 (2.0)	50/50
Graduated College	244.8 (1.5)	50/50	Graduated College	250.0 (1.6)	50/50
Percent Attaining Achievement Levels			Percent Attaining Achievement Levels		
Below Basic	52.9 (1.3)	1/51	Below Basic	70.6 (1.1)	1/51
Basic or Above	47.1 (1.3)	51/51	Basic or Above	29.4 (1.1)	51/51
Proficient or Above	10.4 (0.8)	51/51	Proficient or Above	5.9 (0.6)	51/51
Advanced or Above	1.2 (0.4)	49/51	Advanced or Above	1.2 (0.3)	50/51

***Note:** For an explanation of data, please refer to the User's Guide in the front of the book; values in italics indicate that the nature of the sample does not allow accurate determination of the variability of the statistic; n/a indicates data not available*

District Of Columbia County

District of Columbia Pub Schls

825 N Capitol St, NE • Washington, DC 20002-4232
(202) 442-5885 • http://www.k12.dc.us/dcps/home.html
Grade Span: PK-12; **Agency Type:** 1
Schools: 170
106 Primary; 23 Middle; 20 High; 20 Other Level
147 Regular; 13 Special Education; 2 Vocational; 7 Alternative
0 Magnet; 0 Charter; 131 Title I Eligible; 128 School-wide Title I
Students: 67,522 (50.4% male; 49.6% female)
Individual Education Program: 11,315 (16.8%);
English Language Learner: 5,363 (7.9%); Migrant: 786 (1.2%)
Eligible for Free Lunch Program: 37,385 (55.4%)
Eligible for Reduced-Price Lunch Program: 3,662 (5.4%)
Teachers: 5,005.0 (13.5 to 1)
Librarians/Media Specialists: 119.0 (567.4 to 1)
Guidance Counselors: 243.0 (277.9 to 1)
Current Spending: ($ per student per year):
Total: $12,046; Instruction: $5,982; Support Services: $5,726

Enrollment, Drop-out Rates and Diploma Recipients by Race/Ethnicity

Category	Total	White	Black	Asian	AIAN	Hisp.
Enrollment (%)	100.0	4.7	84.0	1.7	0.1	9.6
Drop-out Rate (%)	n/a	n/a	n/a	n/a	n/a	n/a
H.S. Diplomas (#)	2,894	128	2,507	63	1	195

Number of Schools

Rank	Number	District Name	City
1	170	District of Columbia Pub Schls	Washington

Number of Teachers

Rank	Number	District Name	City
1	5,005	District of Columbia Pub Schls	Washington

Number of Students

Rank	Number	District Name	City
1	67,522	District of Columbia Pub Schls	Washington

Male Students

Rank	Percent	District Name	City
1	50.4	District of Columbia Pub Schls	Washington

Female Students

Rank	Percent	District Name	City
1	49.6	District of Columbia Pub Schls	Washington

Individual Education Program Students

Rank	Percent	District Name	City
1	16.8	District of Columbia Pub Schls	Washington

English Language Learner Students

Rank	Percent	District Name	City
1	7.9	District of Columbia Pub Schls	Washington

Migrant Students

Rank	Percent	District Name	City
1	1.2	District of Columbia Pub Schls	Washington

Students Eligible for Free Lunch

Rank	Percent	District Name	City
1	55.4	District of Columbia Pub Schls	Washington

Students Eligible for Reduced-Price Lunch

Rank	Percent	District Name	City
1	5.4	District of Columbia Pub Schls	Washington

Student/Teacher Ratio

Rank	Ratio	District Name	City
1	13.5	District of Columbia Pub Schls	Washington

Student/Librarian Ratio

Rank	Ratio	District Name	City
1	567.4	District of Columbia Pub Schls	Washington

Student/Counselor Ratio

Rank	Ratio	District Name	City
1	277.9	District of Columbia Pub Schls	Washington

Current Spending per Student in FY2001

Rank	Dollars	District Name	City
1	12,046	District of Columbia Pub Schls	Washington

Number of Diploma Recipients

Rank	Number	District Name	City
1	2,894	District of Columbia Pub Schls	Washington

High School Drop-out Rate

Rank	Percent	District Name	City
1	n/a	District of Columbia Pub Schls	Washington

Florida

Florida Public School Educational Profile

Category	Value	Category	Value
Schools *(2002-2003)*	3,464	**Diploma Recipients** *(2002-2003)*	119,537
Instructional Level		White, Non-Hispanic	70,862
Primary	1,826	Black, Non-Hispanic	24,960
Middle	512	Asian/Pacific Islander	3,345
High	454	American Indian/Alaskan Native	303
Other Level	672	Hispanic	20,067
Curriculum		**High School Drop-out Rate** (%) *(2000-2001)*	4.4
Regular	3,114	White, Non-Hispanic	3.5
Special Education	127	Black, Non-Hispanic	5.9
Vocational	33	Asian/Pacific Islander	2.4
Alternative	190	American Indian/Alaskan Native	3.9
Type		Hispanic	5.6
Magnet	0	**Staff** *(2002-2003)*	287,091.0
Charter	226	Teachers	138,226.0
Title I Eligible	1,411	Average Salary ($)	40,281
School-wide Title I	1,335	Librarians/Media Specialists	2,666.0
Students *(2002-2003)*	2,541,478	Guidance Counselors	5,640.0
Gender (%)		**Ratios** *(2002-2003)*	
Male	51.5	Student/Teacher Ratio	18.4 to 1
Female	48.5	Student/Librarian Ratio	953.3 to 1
Race/Ethnicity (%)		Student/Counselor Ratio	450.6 to 1
White, Non-Hispanic	52.0	**Current Spending** *($ per student in FY 2001)*	6,213
Black, Non-Hispanic	24.5	Instruction	3,664
Asian/Pacific Islander	2.0	Support Services	2,240
American Indian/Alaskan Native	0.3	**College Entrance Exam Scores** *(2003)*	
Hispanic	21.2	Scholastic Aptitude Test (SAT)	
Classification (%)		Participation Rate (%)	61
Individual Education Program (IEP)	15.4	Mean SAT I Verbal Score	498
Migrant	1.9	Mean SAT I Math Score	498
English Language Learner (ELL)	8.0	American College Testing Program (ACT)	
Eligible for Free Lunch Program	36.6	Participation Rate (%)	41
Eligible for Reduced-Price Lunch Program	8.8	Average Composite Score	20.5

Note: *For an explanation of data, please refer to the User's Guide in the front of the book; n/a indicates data not available*

Florida NAEP 2003 Test Scores

Reading			Mathematics		
Grade/Category	**Value**	**Rank**	**Grade/Category**	**Value**	**Rank**
4th Grade			**4th Grade**		
Average Proficiency	218.0 (1.1)	32/51	Average Proficiency	233.7 (1.1)	32/51
Proficiency by Gender/Race/Ethnicity			Proficiency by Gender/Race/Ethnicity		
Male	213.8 (1.4)	32/51	Male	234.6 (1.2)	32/51
Female	222.3 (1.4)	29/51	Female	232.7 (1.1)	32/51
White, Non-Hispanic	229.1 (1.3)	11/51	White, Non-Hispanic	242.8 (1.2)	22/51
Black, Non-Hispanic	197.7 (1.9)	24/42	Black, Non-Hispanic	214.7 (1.5)	25/42
Asian, Non-Hispanic	210.8 (2.2)	6/41	Asian, Non-Hispanic	231.8 (1.3)	4/43
American Indian, Non-Hispanic	232.6 (6.2)	7/25	American Indian, Non-Hispanic	249.3 (3.9)	10/26
Hispanic	n/a	n/a	Hispanic	n/a	n/a
Proficiency by Class Size			Proficiency by Class Size		
Less than 16 Students	184.9 (7.3)	42/45	Less than 16 Students	212.2 (5.6)	42/47
16 to 18 Students	*193.1 (8.3)*	46/48	16 to 18 Students	*211.2 (4.0)*	47/48
19 to 20 Students	*210.7 (5.9)*	40/50	19 to 20 Students	*222.3 (3.1)*	47/50
21 to 25 Students	219.2 (2.2)	33/51	21 to 25 Students	234.0 (2.3)	34/51
Greater than 25 Students	221.9 (1.5)	17/49	Greater than 25 Students	237.7 (1.2)	16/49
Percent Attaining Achievement Levels			Percent Attaining Achievement Levels		
Below Basic	37.2 (1.4)	20/51	Below Basic	24.4 (1.4)	20/51
Basic or Above	62.8 (1.4)	32/51	Basic or Above	75.6 (1.4)	32/51
Proficient or Above	31.6 (1.4)	29/51	Proficient or Above	31.0 (1.3)	32/51
Advanced or Above	7.9 (0.8)	15/51	Advanced or Above	3.8 (0.5)	20/51
8th Grade			**8th Grade**		
Average Proficiency	257.3 (1.3)	41/51	Average Proficiency	271.4 (1.5)	38/51
Proficiency by Gender/Race/Ethnicity			Proficiency by Gender/Race/Ethnicity		
Male	251.0 (1.5)	41/51	Male	273.3 (1.9)	36/51
Female	263.4 (1.6)	38/51	Female	269.4 (1.5)	40/51
White, Non-Hispanic	268.4 (1.4)	31/50	White, Non-Hispanic	285.6 (1.5)	28/50
Black, Non-Hispanic	239.2 (2.1)	32/41	Black, Non-Hispanic	248.6 (1.9)	29/41
Asian, Non-Hispanic	251.1 (2.3)	7/37	Asian, Non-Hispanic	263.9 (2.6)	6/37
American Indian, Non-Hispanic	n/a	n/a	American Indian, Non-Hispanic	287.1 (4.4)	12/23
Hispanic	n/a	n/a	Hispanic	n/a	n/a
Proficiency by Parents Highest Level of Ed.			Proficiency by Parents Highest Level of Ed.		
Did Not Finish High School	250.5 (2.7)	9/50	Did Not Finish High School	255.0 (2.8)	31/50
Graduated High School	249.6 (2.1)	39/50	Graduated High School	264.2 (2.0)	37/50
Some Education After High School	265.6 (1.9)	31/50	Some Education After High School	280.4 (1.8)	28/50
Graduated College	265.3 (1.6)	40/50	Graduated College	279.8 (1.7)	39/50
Percent Attaining Achievement Levels			Percent Attaining Achievement Levels		
Below Basic	32.5 (1.5)	11/51	Below Basic	38.3 (1.8)	13/51
Basic or Above	67.5 (1.5)	41/51	Basic or Above	61.7 (1.8)	39/51
Proficient or Above	26.7 (1.3)	37/51	Proficient or Above	23.3 (1.5)	37/51
Advanced or Above	2.4 (0.6)	30/51	Advanced or Above	4.2 (0.6)	34/51

Note: *For an explanation of data, please refer to the User's Guide in the front of the book; values in italics indicate that the nature of the sample does not allow accurate determination of the variability of the statistic; n/a indicates data not available*

Alachua County

Alachua County SD

620 E University Ave • Gainesville, FL 32601-5498
(352) 955-7527 • http://www.sbac.edu/
Grade Span: PK-12; **Agency Type:** 1
Schools: 62
36 Primary; 10 Middle; 6 High; 10 Other Level
57 Regular; 3 Special Education; 0 Vocational; 2 Alternative
0 Magnet; 10 Charter; 31 Title I Eligible; 27 School-wide Title I
Students: 29,345 (50.5% male; 49.5% female)
Individual Education Program: 5,630 (19.2%);
English Language Learner: 439 (1.5%); Migrant: 54 (0.2%)
Eligible for Free Lunch Program: 12,195 (41.6%)
Eligible for Reduced-Price Lunch Program: 2,609 (8.9%)
Teachers: 1,657.0 (17.7 to 1)
Librarians/Media Specialists: 52.0 (564.3 to 1)
Guidance Counselors: 76.0 (386.1 to 1)
Current Spending: ($ per student per year):
Total: $6,038; Instruction: $3,230; Support Services: $2,487
Enrollment, Drop-out Rates and Diploma Recipients by Race/Ethnicity

Category	Total	White	Black	Asian	AIAN	Hisp.
Enrollment (%)	100.0	54.3	38.1	3.0	0.2	4.4
Drop-out Rate (%)	7.2	5.6	10.8	1.0	13.3	6.7
H.S. Diplomas (#)	1,651	1,126	404	49	4	68

Baker County

Baker County SD

392 S Blvd E • Macclenny, FL 32063-2799
(904) 259-0401 • http://prod.schoolcruiser.com/bcsd/
Grade Span: PK-12; **Agency Type:** 1
Schools: 8
4 Primary; 0 Middle; 0 High; 4 Other Level
6 Regular; 1 Special Education; 0 Vocational; 1 Alternative
0 Magnet; 0 Charter; 4 Title I Eligible; 4 School-wide Title I
Students: 4,525 (52.3% male; 47.7% female)
Individual Education Program: 580 (12.8%);
English Language Learner: 1 (<0.1%); Migrant: 13 (0.3%)
Eligible for Free Lunch Program: 1,446 (32.0%)
Eligible for Reduced-Price Lunch Program: 386 (8.5%)
Teachers: 240.0 (18.9 to 1)
Librarians/Media Specialists: 6.0 (754.2 to 1)
Guidance Counselors: 9.0 (502.8 to 1)
Current Spending: ($ per student per year):
Total: $5,543; Instruction: $2,855; Support Services: $2,367
Enrollment, Drop-out Rates and Diploma Recipients by Race/Ethnicity

Category	Total	White	Black	Asian	AIAN	Hisp.
Enrollment (%)	100.0	84.1	15.1	0.3	0.0	0.5
Drop-out Rate (%)	4.9	4.8	5.6	20.0	0.0	0.0
H.S. Diplomas (#)	223	194	26	2	1	0

Bay County

Bay County SD

1311 Balboa Ave • Panama City, FL 32401-2080
(850) 872-7700 • http://www.bay.k12.fl.us/district_schools.asp
Grade Span: PK-12; **Agency Type:** 1
Schools: 44
22 Primary; 6 Middle; 7 High; 9 Other Level
40 Regular; 3 Special Education; 1 Vocational; 0 Alternative
0 Magnet; 1 Charter; 21 Title I Eligible; 21 School-wide Title I
Students: 26,440 (51.5% male; 48.5% female)
Individual Education Program: 5,102 (19.3%);
English Language Learner: 218 (0.8%); Migrant: 122 (0.5%)
Eligible for Free Lunch Program: 9,384 (35.5%)
Eligible for Reduced-Price Lunch Program: 2,958 (11.2%)
Teachers: 1,526.0 (17.3 to 1)
Librarians/Media Specialists: 40.0 (661.0 to 1)
Guidance Counselors: 68.0 (388.8 to 1)
Current Spending: ($ per student per year):
Total: $5,992; Instruction: $3,472; Support Services: $2,164
Enrollment, Drop-out Rates and Diploma Recipients by Race/Ethnicity

Category	Total	White	Black	Asian	AIAN	Hisp.
Enrollment (%)	100.0	79.9	16.1	1.9	0.4	1.8
Drop-out Rate (%)	1.9	1.8	2.8	1.7	0.0	0.0
H.S. Diplomas (#)	1,230	1,043	141	29	4	13

Bradford County

Bradford County SD

501 W Washington St • Starke, FL 32091-2525
(904) 966-6018 • http://www.bradford.k12.fl.us/
Grade Span: PK-12; **Agency Type:** 1
Schools: 12
7 Primary; 1 Middle; 2 High; 2 Other Level
10 Regular; 1 Special Education; 1 Vocational; 0 Alternative
0 Magnet; 0 Charter; 5 Title I Eligible; 5 School-wide Title I
Students: 4,034 (52.0% male; 48.0% female)
Individual Education Program: 943 (23.4%);
English Language Learner: 23 (0.6%); Migrant: 9 (0.2%)
Eligible for Free Lunch Program: 1,806 (44.8%)
Eligible for Reduced-Price Lunch Program: 483 (12.0%)
Teachers: 241.0 (16.7 to 1)
Librarians/Media Specialists: 6.0 (672.3 to 1)
Guidance Counselors: 8.0 (504.3 to 1)
Current Spending: ($ per student per year):
Total: $6,078; Instruction: $3,356; Support Services: $2,408
Enrollment, Drop-out Rates and Diploma Recipients by Race/Ethnicity

Category	Total	White	Black	Asian	AIAN	Hisp.
Enrollment (%)	100.0	73.2	24.7	0.6	0.1	1.4
Drop-out Rate (%)	4.9	5.2	3.6	0.0	0.0	9.1
H.S. Diplomas (#)	214	167	45	1	0	1

Brevard County

Brevard County SD

2700 Judge Fran • Viera, FL 32940-6699
(321) 631-1911 • http://plx.brevard.k12.fl.us/bre/schools.pl
Grade Span: PK-12; **Agency Type:** 1
Schools: 110
64 Primary; 15 Middle; 12 High; 16 Other Level
96 Regular; 6 Special Education; 0 Vocational; 5 Alternative
0 Magnet; 10 Charter; 35 Title I Eligible; 34 School-wide Title I
Students: 72,601 (51.6% male; 48.4% female)
Individual Education Program: 12,196 (16.8%);
English Language Learner: 978 (1.3%); Migrant: 70 (0.1%)
Eligible for Free Lunch Program: 15,719 (21.7%)
Eligible for Reduced-Price Lunch Program: 4,471 (6.2%)
Teachers: 4,079.0 (17.8 to 1)
Librarians/Media Specialists: 115.0 (631.3 to 1)
Guidance Counselors: 145.0 (500.7 to 1)
Current Spending: ($ per student per year):
Total: $5,570; Instruction: $3,332; Support Services: $1,971
Enrollment, Drop-out Rates and Diploma Recipients by Race/Ethnicity

Category	Total	White	Black	Asian	AIAN	Hisp.
Enrollment (%)	100.0	78.9	13.9	1.6	0.3	5.3
Drop-out Rate (%)	2.6	2.2	5.9	0.5	3.7	3.0
H.S. Diplomas (#)	3,578	2,927	385	87	8	171

Broward County

Broward County SD

600 SE 3rd Ave • Fort Lauderdale, FL 33301-3125
(954) 765-6271 • http://www.browardschools.com/
Grade Span: PK-12; **Agency Type:** 1
Schools: 259
154 Primary; 43 Middle; 32 High; 27 Other Level
238 Regular; 9 Special Education; 2 Vocational; 7 Alternative
0 Magnet; 19 Charter; 100 Title I Eligible; 100 School-wide Title I
Students: 267,925 (51.7% male; 48.3% female)
Individual Education Program: 30,459 (11.4%);
English Language Learner: 30,139 (11.2%); Migrant: 1,026 (0.4%)
Eligible for Free Lunch Program: 83,267 (31.1%)
Eligible for Reduced-Price Lunch Program: 21,590 (8.1%)
Teachers: 13,264.0 (20.2 to 1)
Librarians/Media Specialists: 220.0 (1,217.8 to 1)
Guidance Counselors: 490.0 (546.8 to 1)
Current Spending: ($ per student per year):
Total: $5,853; Instruction: $3,262; Support Services: $2,358
Enrollment, Drop-out Rates and Diploma Recipients by Race/Ethnicity

Category	Total	White	Black	Asian	AIAN	Hisp.
Enrollment (%)	100.0	38.0	36.5	2.9	0.3	22.3
Drop-out Rate (%)	2.0	1.9	1.9	1.3	3.0	2.3
H.S. Diplomas (#)	11,654	5,119	3,864	464	38	2,169

Calhoun County

Calhoun County SD

20859 E Central Ave, G-20 • Blountstown, FL 32424-2264
(850) 674-5927 • http://www.paec.org/calhoun/district/
Grade Span: PK-12; **Agency Type:** 1
Schools: 7
2 Primary; 1 Middle; 1 High; 3 Other Level
7 Regular; 0 Special Education; 0 Vocational; 0 Alternative
0 Magnet; 0 Charter; 4 Title I Eligible; 4 School-wide Title I
Students: 2,174 (51.1% male; 48.9% female)
Individual Education Program: 451 (20.7%);
English Language Learner: 2 (0.1%); Migrant: 15 (0.7%)
Eligible for Free Lunch Program: 837 (38.5%)

Eligible for Reduced-Price Lunch Program: 245 (11.3%)
Teachers: 147.0 (14.8 to 1)
Librarians/Media Specialists: 6.0 (362.3 to 1)
Guidance Counselors: 8.0 (271.8 to 1)
Current Spending: ($ per student per year):
Total: $5,711; Instruction: $3,332; Support Services: $2,069
Enrollment, Drop-out Rates and Diploma Recipients by Race/Ethnicity

Category	Total	White	Black	Asian	AIAN	Hisp.
Enrollment (%)	100.0	83.5	14.1	0.7	0.2	1.4
Drop-out Rate (%)	3.3	3.1	4.1	0.0	33.3	0.0
H.S. Diplomas (#)	106	83	17	0	1	5

Charlotte County

Charlotte County SD

1445 Education Way • Port Charlotte, FL 33948-1053
(941) 255-0808 • http://www.ccps.k12.fl.us/
Grade Span: PK-12; **Agency Type:** 1
Schools: 24
11 Primary; 4 Middle; 5 High; 3 Other Level
21 Regular; 1 Special Education; 1 Vocational; 0 Alternative
0 Magnet; 0 Charter; 8 Title I Eligible; 8 School-wide Title I
Students: 17,714 (51.0% male; 49.0% female)
Individual Education Program: 3,443 (19.4%);
English Language Learner: 163 (0.9%); Migrant: 0 (0.0%)
Eligible for Free Lunch Program: 5,435 (30.7%)
Eligible for Reduced-Price Lunch Program: 2,434 (13.7%)
Teachers: 925.0 (19.2 to 1)
Librarians/Media Specialists: 21.0 (843.5 to 1)
Guidance Counselors: 38.0 (466.2 to 1)
Current Spending: ($ per student per year):
Total: $5,968; Instruction: $3,257; Support Services: $2,359
Enrollment, Drop-out Rates and Diploma Recipients by Race/Ethnicity

Category	Total	White	Black	Asian	AIAN	Hisp.
Enrollment (%)	100.0	84.9	8.6	1.5	0.3	4.8
Drop-out Rate (%)	4.0	4.1	3.2	1.1	0.0	4.0
H.S. Diplomas (#)	1,076	915	101	14	4	42

Citrus County

Citrus County SD

1007 W Main St • Inverness, FL 34450-4625
(352) 726-1931 • http://www.citrus.k12.fl.us/
Grade Span: PK-12; **Agency Type:** 1
Schools: 26
10 Primary; 4 Middle; 6 High; 6 Other Level
22 Regular; 1 Special Education; 2 Vocational; 1 Alternative
0 Magnet; 1 Charter; 8 Title I Eligible; 8 School-wide Title I
Students: 15,355 (51.9% male; 48.1% female)
Individual Education Program: 2,931 (19.1%);
English Language Learner: 85 (0.6%); Migrant: 65 (0.4%)
Eligible for Free Lunch Program: 4,992 (32.5%)
Eligible for Reduced-Price Lunch Program: 1,598 (10.4%)
Teachers: 926.0 (16.6 to 1)
Librarians/Media Specialists: 21.0 (731.2 to 1)
Guidance Counselors: 36.0 (426.5 to 1)
Current Spending: ($ per student per year):
Total: $5,791; Instruction: $3,230; Support Services: $2,323
Enrollment, Drop-out Rates and Diploma Recipients by Race/Ethnicity

Category	Total	White	Black	Asian	AIAN	Hisp.
Enrollment (%)	100.0	90.9	4.3	1.2	0.4	3.2
Drop-out Rate (%)	3.5	3.5	5.7	0.0	5.9	2.0
H.S. Diplomas (#)	830	750	41	15	1	23

Clay County

Clay County SD

900 Walnut St • Green Cove Springs, FL 32043-3129
(904) 284-6510 • http://www.clay.k12.fl.us/school_sites.htm
Grade Span: PK-12; **Agency Type:** 1
Schools: 32
20 Primary; 4 Middle; 6 High; 2 Other Level
31 Regular; 0 Special Education; 0 Vocational; 1 Alternative
0 Magnet; 0 Charter; 7 Title I Eligible; 5 School-wide Title I
Students: 29,861 (51.4% male; 48.6% female)
Individual Education Program: 5,829 (19.5%);
English Language Learner: 195 (0.7%); Migrant: 139 (0.5%)
Eligible for Free Lunch Program: 5,021 (16.8%)
Eligible for Reduced-Price Lunch Program: 2,198 (7.4%)
Teachers: 1,657.0 (18.0 to 1)
Librarians/Media Specialists: 36.0 (829.5 to 1)
Guidance Counselors: 74.0 (403.5 to 1)
Current Spending: ($ per student per year):
Total: $5,468; Instruction: $3,223; Support Services: $2,006

Enrollment, Drop-out Rates and Diploma Recipients by Race/Ethnicity

Category	Total	White	Black	Asian	AIAN	Hisp.
Enrollment (%)	100.0	83.3	10.1	2.1	0.2	4.3
Drop-out Rate (%)	3.0	2.8	6.1	2.7	0.0	0.7
H.S. Diplomas (#)	1,627	1,385	140	42	5	55

Collier County

Collier County SD

5775 Osceola Tr • Naples, FL 34109-0919
(239) 254-4100 • http://www.collier.k12.fl.us/
Grade Span: PK-12; **Agency Type:** 1
Schools: 53
26 Primary; 10 Middle; 6 High; 10 Other Level
46 Regular; 2 Special Education; 0 Vocational; 4 Alternative
0 Magnet; 2 Charter; 15 Title I Eligible; 12 School-wide Title I
Students: 38,110 (51.5% male; 48.5% female)
Individual Education Program: 5,922 (15.5%);
English Language Learner: 5,618 (14.7%); Migrant: 8,943 (23.5%)
Eligible for Free Lunch Program: 6,422 (16.9%)
Eligible for Reduced-Price Lunch Program: 2,210 (5.8%)
Teachers: 2,167.0 (17.6 to 1)
Librarians/Media Specialists: 42.0 (907.4 to 1)
Guidance Counselors: 119.0 (320.3 to 1)
Current Spending: ($ per student per year):
Total: $6,690; Instruction: $3,927; Support Services: $2,441
Enrollment, Drop-out Rates and Diploma Recipients by Race/Ethnicity

Category	Total	White	Black	Asian	AIAN	Hisp.
Enrollment (%)	100.0	52.3	11.5	0.9	0.4	34.9
Drop-out Rate (%)	4.9	3.3	4.7	6.7	12.1	8.8
H.S. Diplomas (#)	1,711	1,097	198	17	5	394

Columbia County

Columbia County SD

372 W Duval St • Lake City, FL 32055-3990
(386) 755-8000 • http://www.columbia.k12.fl.us/schools.html
Grade Span: PK-12; **Agency Type:** 1
Schools: 15
8 Primary; 1 Middle; 1 High; 5 Other Level
15 Regular; 0 Special Education; 0 Vocational; 0 Alternative
0 Magnet; 0 Charter; 8 Title I Eligible; 8 School-wide Title I
Students: 9,707 (51.2% male; 48.8% female)
Individual Education Program: 1,767 (18.2%);
English Language Learner: 32 (0.3%); Migrant: 29 (0.3%)
Eligible for Free Lunch Program: 4,271 (44.0%)
Eligible for Reduced-Price Lunch Program: 1,179 (12.1%)
Teachers: 569.0 (17.1 to 1)
Librarians/Media Specialists: 12.0 (808.9 to 1)
Guidance Counselors: 20.0 (485.4 to 1)
Current Spending: ($ per student per year):
Total: $5,869; Instruction: $3,395; Support Services: $2,153
Enrollment, Drop-out Rates and Diploma Recipients by Race/Ethnicity

Category	Total	White	Black	Asian	AIAN	Hisp.
Enrollment (%)	100.0	72.7	23.2	0.9	0.4	2.8
Drop-out Rate (%)	1.9	1.2	4.0	0.0	0.0	3.5
H.S. Diplomas (#)	441	327	97	6	1	10

De Soto County

Desoto County SD

PO Drawer 2000 • Arcadia, FL 34265-2000
(863) 494-4222 • http://www.desotoschools.com/web_site_links.htm
Grade Span: PK-12; **Agency Type:** 1
Schools: 13
4 Primary; 1 Middle; 1 High; 7 Other Level
11 Regular; 1 Special Education; 0 Vocational; 1 Alternative
0 Magnet; 0 Charter; 3 Title I Eligible; 3 School-wide Title I
Students: 4,916 (53.4% male; 46.6% female)
Individual Education Program: 1,024 (20.8%);
English Language Learner: 362 (7.4%); Migrant: 683 (13.9%)
Eligible for Free Lunch Program: 2,523 (51.3%)
Eligible for Reduced-Price Lunch Program: 471 (9.6%)
Teachers: 284.0 (17.3 to 1)
Librarians/Media Specialists: 6.0 (819.3 to 1)
Guidance Counselors: 9.0 (546.2 to 1)
Current Spending: ($ per student per year):
Total: $6,285; Instruction: $3,585; Support Services: $2,311
Enrollment, Drop-out Rates and Diploma Recipients by Race/Ethnicity

Category	Total	White	Black	Asian	AIAN	Hisp.
Enrollment (%)	100.0	54.3	19.7	0.4	0.1	25.5
Drop-out Rate (%)	4.3	4.2	4.2	0.0	0.0	4.9
H.S. Diplomas (#)	204	130	35	4	1	34

Dixie County

Dixie County SD

PO Box 890 • Cross City, FL 32628-0890
(352) 498-6131 • http://dixieschools.dixie.k12.fl.us/
Grade Span: PK-12; **Agency Type:** 1
Schools: 5
1 Primary; 0 Middle; 1 High; 3 Other Level
5 Regular; 0 Special Education; 0 Vocational; 0 Alternative
0 Magnet; 0 Charter; 3 Title I Eligible; 3 School-wide Title I
Students: 2,229 (51.7% male; 48.3% female)
Individual Education Program: 520 (23.3%);
English Language Learner: 0 (0.0%); Migrant: 85 (3.8%)
Eligible for Free Lunch Program: 1,231 (55.2%)
Eligible for Reduced-Price Lunch Program: 215 (9.6%)
Teachers: 128.0 (17.4 to 1)
Librarians/Media Specialists: 1.0 (2,229.0 to 1)
Guidance Counselors: 5.0 (445.8 to 1)
Current Spending: ($ per student per year):
Total: $6,216; Instruction: $3,319; Support Services: $2,512
Enrollment, Drop-out Rates and Diploma Recipients by Race/Ethnicity

Category	Total	White	Black	Asian	AIAN	Hisp.
Enrollment (%)	100.0	89.1	9.8	0.1	0.1	0.9
Drop-out Rate (%)	3.0	3.2	1.5	0.0	n/a	0.0
H.S. Diplomas (#)	150	138	11	0	0	1

Duval County

Duval County SD

1701 Prudential Dr • Jacksonville, FL 32207-8182
(904) 390-2115 • http://www.educationcentral.org/
Grade Span: PK-12; **Agency Type:** 1
Schools: 181
109 Primary; 28 Middle; 19 High; 23 Other Level
172 Regular; 3 Special Education; 0 Vocational; 4 Alternative
0 Magnet; 7 Charter; 73 Title I Eligible; 73 School-wide Title I
Students: 128,126 (50.8% male; 49.2% female)
Individual Education Program: 20,233 (15.8%);
English Language Learner: 2,557 (2.0%); Migrant: 194 (0.2%)
Eligible for Free Lunch Program: 41,797 (32.6%)
Eligible for Reduced-Price Lunch Program: 11,725 (9.2%)
Teachers: 6,620.0 (19.4 to 1)
Librarians/Media Specialists: 141.0 (908.7 to 1)
Guidance Counselors: 237.0 (540.6 to 1)
Current Spending: ($ per student per year):
Total: $5,665; Instruction: $3,227; Support Services: $2,159
Enrollment, Drop-out Rates and Diploma Recipients by Race/Ethnicity

Category	Total	White	Black	Asian	AIAN	Hisp.
Enrollment (%)	100.0	48.8	43.7	3.0	0.2	4.3
Drop-out Rate (%)	9.7	8.6	11.4	7.0	7.0	10.2
H.S. Diplomas (#)	5,260	2,922	1,871	237	10	220

Escambia County

Escambia County SD

215 W Garden St • Pensacola, FL 32501
(850) 469-6130 • http://www.escambia.k12.fl.us/schools.htm
Grade Span: PK-12; **Agency Type:** 1
Schools: 86
40 Primary; 13 Middle; 12 High; 16 Other Level
68 Regular; 6 Special Education; 1 Vocational; 6 Alternative
0 Magnet; 7 Charter; 51 Title I Eligible; 51 School-wide Title I
Students: 44,019 (51.2% male; 48.8% female)
Individual Education Program: 7,441 (16.9%);
English Language Learner: 314 (0.7%); Migrant: 392 (0.9%)
Eligible for Free Lunch Program: 20,272 (46.1%)
Eligible for Reduced-Price Lunch Program: 4,993 (11.3%)
Teachers: 2,393.0 (18.4 to 1)
Librarians/Media Specialists: 61.0 (721.6 to 1)
Guidance Counselors: 95.0 (463.4 to 1)
Current Spending: ($ per student per year):
Total: $5,757; Instruction: $3,139; Support Services: $2,247
Enrollment, Drop-out Rates and Diploma Recipients by Race/Ethnicity

Category	Total	White	Black	Asian	AIAN	Hisp.
Enrollment (%)	100.0	57.6	37.2	2.7	0.7	1.8
Drop-out Rate (%)	2.9	2.5	3.8	1.0	3.1	3.3
H.S. Diplomas (#)	2,320	1,473	699	101	15	32

Flagler County

Flagler County SD

PO Box 755 • Bunnell, FL 32110-0755
(386) 437-7526 • http://www.flagler.k12.fl.us/
Grade Span: PK-12; **Agency Type:** 1
Schools: 10
4 Primary; 1 Middle; 2 High; 3 Other Level
7 Regular; 0 Special Education; 0 Vocational; 3 Alternative
0 Magnet; 0 Charter; 3 Title I Eligible; 1 School-wide Title I
Students: 7,601 (51.4% male; 48.6% female)
Individual Education Program: 1,308 (17.2%);
English Language Learner: 201 (2.6%); Migrant: 21 (0.3%)
Eligible for Free Lunch Program: 2,102 (27.7%)
Eligible for Reduced-Price Lunch Program: 771 (10.1%)
Teachers: 453.0 (16.8 to 1)
Librarians/Media Specialists: 6.0 (1,266.8 to 1)
Guidance Counselors: 18.0 (422.3 to 1)
Current Spending: ($ per student per year):
Total: $6,073; Instruction: $3,215; Support Services: $2,591
Enrollment, Drop-out Rates and Diploma Recipients by Race/Ethnicity

Category	Total	White	Black	Asian	AIAN	Hisp.
Enrollment (%)	100.0	78.9	12.8	1.8	0.2	6.3
Drop-out Rate (%)	2.2	1.8	4.6	0.0	0.0	1.9
H.S. Diplomas (#)	385	301	59	2	0	23

Gadsden County

Gadsden County SD

35 Martin Luther King Blv • Quincy, FL 32351-4400
(850) 627-9651 • http://www.gcps.k12.fl.us/schs.html
Grade Span: PK-12; **Agency Type:** 1
Schools: 25
10 Primary; 2 Middle; 4 High; 7 Other Level
19 Regular; 2 Special Education; 1 Vocational; 1 Alternative
0 Magnet; 1 Charter; 15 Title I Eligible; 15 School-wide Title I
Students: 7,196 (50.8% male; 49.2% female)
Individual Education Program: 1,302 (18.1%);
English Language Learner: 386 (5.4%); Migrant: 530 (7.4%)
Eligible for Free Lunch Program: 4,739 (65.9%)
Eligible for Reduced-Price Lunch Program: 692 (9.6%)
Teachers: 421.0 (17.1 to 1)
Librarians/Media Specialists: 12.0 (599.7 to 1)
Guidance Counselors: 18.0 (399.8 to 1)
Current Spending: ($ per student per year):
Total: $6,689; Instruction: $3,637; Support Services: $2,615
Enrollment, Drop-out Rates and Diploma Recipients by Race/Ethnicity

Category	Total	White	Black	Asian	AIAN	Hisp.
Enrollment (%)	100.0	5.2	83.8	0.2	0.0	10.8
Drop-out Rate (%)	8.4	14.8	7.8	0.0	0.0	12.0
H.S. Diplomas (#)	346	21	312	0	0	13

Gilchrist County

Gilchrist County SD

310 NW 11th Ave • Trenton, FL 32693-3804
(352) 463-3200 • http://www.gilchristschools.org/
Grade Span: PK-12; **Agency Type:** 1
Schools: 4
1 Primary; 0 Middle; 0 High; 3 Other Level
4 Regular; 0 Special Education; 0 Vocational; 0 Alternative
0 Magnet; 0 Charter; 2 Title I Eligible; 2 School-wide Title I
Students: 2,734 (51.2% male; 48.8% female)
Individual Education Program: 647 (23.7%);
English Language Learner: 12 (0.4%); Migrant: 104 (3.8%)
Eligible for Free Lunch Program: 1,138 (41.6%)
Eligible for Reduced-Price Lunch Program: 356 (13.0%)
Teachers: 154.0 (17.8 to 1)
Librarians/Media Specialists: 4.0 (683.5 to 1)
Guidance Counselors: 7.0 (390.6 to 1)
Current Spending: ($ per student per year):
Total: $6,243; Instruction: $3,426; Support Services: $2,431
Enrollment, Drop-out Rates and Diploma Recipients by Race/Ethnicity

Category	Total	White	Black	Asian	AIAN	Hisp.
Enrollment (%)	100.0	93.0	4.8	0.1	0.3	1.9
Drop-out Rate (%)	3.9	3.7	5.7	n/a	n/a	10.0
H.S. Diplomas (#)	141	133	8	0	0	0

Gulf County

Gulf County SD

150 Middle School Rd • Port Saint Joe, FL 32456-2261
(850) 229-8256
Grade Span: PK-12; **Agency Type:** 1
Schools: 8
2 Primary; 2 Middle; 2 High; 2 Other Level
8 Regular; 0 Special Education; 0 Vocational; 0 Alternative
0 Magnet; 0 Charter; 2 Title I Eligible; 2 School-wide Title I
Students: 2,164 (51.9% male; 48.1% female)
Individual Education Program: 364 (16.8%);
English Language Learner: 3 (0.1%); Migrant: 0 (0.0%)
Eligible for Free Lunch Program: 761 (35.2%)

Eligible for Reduced-Price Lunch Program: 251 (11.6%)
Teachers: 130.0 (16.6 to 1)
Librarians/Media Specialists: 4.0 (541.0 to 1)
Guidance Counselors: 7.0 (309.1 to 1)
Current Spending: ($ per student per year):
Total: $6,645; Instruction: $3,665; Support Services: $2,670

Enrollment, Drop-out Rates and Diploma Recipients by Race/Ethnicity

Category	Total	White	Black	Asian	AIAN	Hisp.
Enrollment (%)	100.0	81.7	17.0	0.6	0.2	0.5
Drop-out Rate (%)	1.6	1.0	4.2	0.0	0.0	0.0
H.S. Diplomas (#)	117	91	23	1	0	2

Hamilton County

Hamilton County SD

4280 SW County Rd #152 • Jasper, FL 32052-3774
(386) 792-6501 •
http://www.firn.edu/schools/hamilton/hamilton/schools.htm
Grade Span: PK-12; **Agency Type:** 1
Schools: 7
3 Primary; 0 Middle; 1 High; 3 Other Level
6 Regular; 1 Special Education; 0 Vocational; 0 Alternative
0 Magnet; 0 Charter; 4 Title I Eligible; 4 School-wide Title I
Students: 2,065 (50.8% male; 49.2% female)
Individual Education Program: 369 (17.9%);
English Language Learner: 58 (2.8%); Migrant: 70 (3.4%)
Eligible for Free Lunch Program: 1,297 (62.8%)
Eligible for Reduced-Price Lunch Program: 200 (9.7%)
Teachers: 128.0 (16.1 to 1)
Librarians/Media Specialists: 4.0 (516.3 to 1)
Guidance Counselors: 6.0 (344.2 to 1)
Current Spending: ($ per student per year):
Total: $6,931; Instruction: $3,547; Support Services: $2,972

Enrollment, Drop-out Rates and Diploma Recipients by Race/Ethnicity

Category	Total	White	Black	Asian	AIAN	Hisp.
Enrollment (%)	100.0	43.3	48.0	0.4	0.1	8.2
Drop-out Rate (%)	2.5	2.4	2.8	0.0	0.0	0.0
H.S. Diplomas (#)	119	61	56	1	0	1

Hardee County

Hardee County SD

PO Drawer 1678 • Wauchula, FL 33873-1678
(863) 773-9058 • http://www.hardee.k12.fl.us/schools.htm
Grade Span: PK-12; **Agency Type:** 1
Schools: 9
4 Primary; 0 Middle; 1 High; 4 Other Level
8 Regular; 0 Special Education; 0 Vocational; 1 Alternative
0 Magnet; 0 Charter; 5 Title I Eligible; 5 School-wide Title I
Students: 5,175 (52.9% male; 47.1% female)
Individual Education Program: 1,088 (21.0%);
English Language Learner: 504 (9.7%); Migrant: 2,069 (40.0%)
Eligible for Free Lunch Program: 3,124 (60.4%)
Eligible for Reduced-Price Lunch Program: 379 (7.3%)
Teachers: 300.0 (17.3 to 1)
Librarians/Media Specialists: 7.0 (739.3 to 1)
Guidance Counselors: 9.0 (575.0 to 1)
Current Spending: ($ per student per year):
Total: $6,186; Instruction: $3,477; Support Services: $2,302

Enrollment, Drop-out Rates and Diploma Recipients by Race/Ethnicity

Category	Total	White	Black	Asian	AIAN	Hisp.
Enrollment (%)	100.0	41.4	8.3	0.9	0.0	49.4
Drop-out Rate (%)	7.9	4.5	4.6	0.0	0.0	14.1
H.S. Diplomas (#)	213	125	19	2	1	66

Hendry County

Hendry County SD

PO Box 1980 • La Belle, FL 33975-1980
(863) 674-4642 • http://www.hendry-schools.org/
Grade Span: PK-12; **Agency Type:** 1
Schools: 16
6 Primary; 0 Middle; 2 High; 8 Other Level
15 Regular; 1 Special Education; 0 Vocational; 0 Alternative
0 Magnet; 0 Charter; 8 Title I Eligible; 6 School-wide Title I
Students: 7,673 (52.0% male; 48.0% female)
Individual Education Program: 1,359 (17.7%);
English Language Learner: 597 (7.8%); Migrant: 2,746 (35.8%)
Eligible for Free Lunch Program: 4,706 (61.3%)
Eligible for Reduced-Price Lunch Program: 843 (11.0%)
Teachers: 373.0 (20.6 to 1)
Librarians/Media Specialists: 9.0 (852.6 to 1)
Guidance Counselors: 16.0 (479.6 to 1)
Current Spending: ($ per student per year):
Total: $6,135; Instruction: $3,269; Support Services: $2,464

Enrollment, Drop-out Rates and Diploma Recipients by Race/Ethnicity

Category	Total	White	Black	Asian	AIAN	Hisp.
Enrollment (%)	100.0	36.9	17.3	0.5	0.6	44.7
Drop-out Rate (%)	6.8	5.5	6.6	7.7	0.0	8.7
H.S. Diplomas (#)	290	155	39	5	0	91

Hernando County

Hernando County SD

919 N Broad St • Brooksville, FL 34601-2397
(352) 797-7001 • http://www.hcsb.k12.fl.us/
Grade Span: PK-12; **Agency Type:** 1
Schools: 23
11 Primary; 3 Middle; 3 High; 3 Other Level
19 Regular; 0 Special Education; 0 Vocational; 1 Alternative
0 Magnet; 0 Charter; 8 Title I Eligible; 8 School-wide Title I
Students: 18,605 (51.0% male; 49.0% female)
Individual Education Program: 3,204 (17.2%);
English Language Learner: 238 (1.3%); Migrant: 0 (0.0%)
Eligible for Free Lunch Program: 6,139 (33.0%)
Eligible for Reduced-Price Lunch Program: 2,046 (11.0%)
Teachers: 1,016.0 (18.3 to 1)
Librarians/Media Specialists: 20.0 (930.3 to 1)
Guidance Counselors: 54.0 (344.5 to 1)
Current Spending: ($ per student per year):
Total: $5,474; Instruction: $3,033; Support Services: $2,161

Enrollment, Drop-out Rates and Diploma Recipients by Race/Ethnicity

Category	Total	White	Black	Asian	AIAN	Hisp.
Enrollment (%)	100.0	84.1	7.4	0.9	0.3	7.5
Drop-out Rate (%)	2.2	2.2	2.8	0.0	20.0	0.7
H.S. Diplomas (#)	923	799	54	17	2	51

Highlands County

Highlands County SD

426 School St • Sebring, FL 33870-4048
(863) 471-5564 • http://www.highlands.k12.fl.us/
Grade Span: PK-12; **Agency Type:** 1
Schools: 18
7 Primary; 4 Middle; 3 High; 3 Other Level
16 Regular; 0 Special Education; 0 Vocational; 1 Alternative
0 Magnet; 0 Charter; 8 Title I Eligible; 8 School-wide Title I
Students: 11,428 (51.9% male; 48.1% female)
Individual Education Program: 2,077 (18.2%);
English Language Learner: 447 (3.9%); Migrant: 1,295 (11.3%)
Eligible for Free Lunch Program: 5,409 (47.3%)
Eligible for Reduced-Price Lunch Program: 1,216 (10.6%)
Teachers: 671.0 (17.0 to 1)
Librarians/Media Specialists: 14.0 (816.3 to 1)
Guidance Counselors: 26.0 (439.5 to 1)
Current Spending: ($ per student per year):
Total: $6,001; Instruction: $3,227; Support Services: $2,399

Enrollment, Drop-out Rates and Diploma Recipients by Race/Ethnicity

Category	Total	White	Black	Asian	AIAN	Hisp.
Enrollment (%)	100.0	59.2	20.0	1.0	0.6	19.3
Drop-out Rate (%)	6.3	5.5	8.5	7.7	10.0	7.1
H.S. Diplomas (#)	561	360	111	8	1	81

Hillsborough County

Hillsborough County SD

PO Box 3408 • Tampa, FL 33601-3408
(813) 272-4050 • http://apps.sdhc.k12.fl.us/sdhc2/schoolsite/
Grade Span: PK-12; **Agency Type:** 1
Schools: 229
129 Primary; 40 Middle; 26 High; 29 Other Level
209 Regular; 9 Special Education; 0 Vocational; 6 Alternative
0 Magnet; 16 Charter; 104 Title I Eligible; 104 School-wide Title I
Students: 175,454 (51.3% male; 48.7% female)
Individual Education Program: 27,127 (15.5%);
English Language Learner: 18,002 (10.3%); Migrant: 5,049 (2.9%)
Eligible for Free Lunch Program: 69,397 (39.6%)
Eligible for Reduced-Price Lunch Program: 16,394 (9.3%)
Teachers: 10,499.0 (16.7 to 1)
Librarians/Media Specialists: 214.0 (819.9 to 1)
Guidance Counselors: 435.0 (403.3 to 1)
Current Spending: ($ per student per year):
Total: $6,055; Instruction: $3,494; Support Services: $2,196

Enrollment, Drop-out Rates and Diploma Recipients by Race/Ethnicity

Category	Total	White	Black	Asian	AIAN	Hisp.
Enrollment (%)	100.0	49.6	23.8	2.3	0.3	23.9
Drop-out Rate (%)	3.1	2.5	4.9	1.5	6.1	3.3
H.S. Diplomas (#)	7,968	4,567	1,539	280	32	1,550

Holmes County

Holmes County SD

701 E Pennsylvania Ave • Bonifay, FL 32425-2349
(850) 547-9341 • http://www.firn.edu/schools/holmes/holmessb/
Grade Span: PK-12; **Agency Type:** 1
Schools: 9
2 Primary; 1 Middle; 2 High; 4 Other Level
9 Regular; 0 Special Education; 0 Vocational; 0 Alternative
0 Magnet; 0 Charter; 5 Title I Eligible; 5 School-wide Title I
Students: 3,414 (52.5% male; 47.5% female)
Individual Education Program: 546 (16.0%);
English Language Learner: 0 (0.0%); Migrant: 35 (1.0%)
Eligible for Free Lunch Program: 1,436 (42.1%)
Eligible for Reduced-Price Lunch Program: 466 (13.6%)
Teachers: 204.0 (16.7 to 1)
Librarians/Media Specialists: 7.0 (487.7 to 1)
Guidance Counselors: 9.0 (379.3 to 1)
Current Spending: ($ per student per year):
Total: $6,030; Instruction: $3,615; Support Services: $2,058
Enrollment, Drop-out Rates and Diploma Recipients by Race/Ethnicity

Category	Total	White	Black	Asian	AIAN	Hisp.
Enrollment (%)	100.0	95.0	2.8	1.0	0.1	1.2
Drop-out Rate (%)	3.0	3.0	0.0	0.0	0.0	10.0
H.S. Diplomas (#)	203	196	5	1	0	1

Indian River County

Indian River County SD

1990 25th St • Vero Beach, FL 32960-3395
(772) 564-3150 • http://www.indian-river.k12.fl.us/
Grade Span: PK-12; **Agency Type:** 1
Schools: 28
16 Primary; 4 Middle; 3 High; 5 Other Level
26 Regular; 2 Special Education; 0 Vocational; 0 Alternative
0 Magnet; 5 Charter; 12 Title I Eligible; 12 School-wide Title I
Students: 15,986 (51.2% male; 48.8% female)
Individual Education Program: 2,356 (14.7%);
English Language Learner: 662 (4.1%); Migrant: 904 (5.7%)
Eligible for Free Lunch Program: 4,815 (30.1%)
Eligible for Reduced-Price Lunch Program: 1,156 (7.2%)
Teachers: 393.0 (40.7 to 1)
Librarians/Media Specialists: 6.0 (2,664.3 to 1)
Guidance Counselors: 11.0 (1,453.3 to 1)
Current Spending: ($ per student per year):
Total: $6,161; Instruction: $3,430; Support Services: $2,379
Enrollment, Drop-out Rates and Diploma Recipients by Race/Ethnicity

Category	Total	White	Black	Asian	AIAN	Hisp.
Enrollment (%)	100.0	70.3	16.4	1.1	0.3	12.0
Drop-out Rate (%)	2.7	2.1	4.1	2.2	0.0	5.2
H.S. Diplomas (#)	821	620	129	8	2	62

Jackson County

Jackson County SD

PO Box 5958 • Marianna, FL 32447-5958
(850) 482-1200 • http://www.firn.edu/schools/jackson/jacksonsb/schools/
Grade Span: PK-12; **Agency Type:** 1
Schools: 21
5 Primary; 1 Middle; 3 High; 12 Other Level
17 Regular; 4 Special Education; 0 Vocational; 0 Alternative
0 Magnet; 1 Charter; 12 Title I Eligible; 12 School-wide Title I
Students: 7,245 (51.3% male; 48.7% female)
Individual Education Program: 1,468 (20.3%);
English Language Learner: 43 (0.6%); Migrant: 20 (0.3%)
Eligible for Free Lunch Program: 3,121 (43.1%)
Eligible for Reduced-Price Lunch Program: 878 (12.1%)
Teachers: 437.0 (16.6 to 1)
Librarians/Media Specialists: 12.0 (603.8 to 1)
Guidance Counselors: 24.0 (301.9 to 1)
Current Spending: ($ per student per year):
Total: $6,086; Instruction: $3,254; Support Services: $2,430
Enrollment, Drop-out Rates and Diploma Recipients by Race/Ethnicity

Category	Total	White	Black	Asian	AIAN	Hisp.
Enrollment (%)	100.0	65.2	31.9	0.4	0.5	1.9
Drop-out Rate (%)	1.8	1.9	1.6	0.0	0.0	3.4
H.S. Diplomas (#)	409	261	140	0	2	6

Jefferson County

Jefferson County SD

1490 W Washington St • Monticello, FL 32344-1100
(850) 342-0100 • http://www.paec.org/jefferson/Schools/schools.htm
Grade Span: PK-12; **Agency Type:** 1
Schools: 7
2 Primary; 1 Middle; 1 High; 2 Other Level
5 Regular; 1 Special Education; 0 Vocational; 0 Alternative
0 Magnet; 0 Charter; 1 Title I Eligible; 1 School-wide Title I
Students: 1,575 (51.2% male; 48.8% female)
Individual Education Program: 410 (26.0%);
English Language Learner: 2 (0.1%); Migrant: 4 (0.3%)
Eligible for Free Lunch Program: 989 (62.8%)
Eligible for Reduced-Price Lunch Program: 152 (9.7%)
Teachers: 103.0 (15.3 to 1)
Librarians/Media Specialists: 3.0 (525.0 to 1)
Guidance Counselors: 3.0 (525.0 to 1)
Current Spending: ($ per student per year):
Total: $7,130; Instruction: $3,755; Support Services: $2,977
Enrollment, Drop-out Rates and Diploma Recipients by Race/Ethnicity

Category	Total	White	Black	Asian	AIAN	Hisp.
Enrollment (%)	100.0	28.3	69.7	0.3	0.2	1.6
Drop-out Rate (%)	3.5	1.0	5.1	n/a	0.0	0.0
H.S. Diplomas (#)	65	27	38	0	0	0

Lake County

Lake County SD

201 W Burleigh Blvd • Tavares, FL 32778-2496
(352) 253-6510 • http://www.lake.k12.fl.us/
Grade Span: PK-12; **Agency Type:** 1
Schools: 53
23 Primary; 10 Middle; 8 High; 9 Other Level
45 Regular; 2 Special Education; 1 Vocational; 2 Alternative
0 Magnet; 7 Charter; 25 Title I Eligible; 14 School-wide Title I
Students: 31,782 (51.2% male; 48.8% female)
Individual Education Program: 5,402 (17.0%);
English Language Learner: 1,091 (3.4%); Migrant: 406 (1.3%)
Eligible for Free Lunch Program: 10,063 (31.7%)
Eligible for Reduced-Price Lunch Program: 2,704 (8.5%)
Teachers: 2,209.0 (14.4 to 1)
Librarians/Media Specialists: 42.0 (756.7 to 1)
Guidance Counselors: 76.0 (418.2 to 1)
Current Spending: ($ per student per year):
Total: $5,423; Instruction: $3,125; Support Services: $2,005
Enrollment, Drop-out Rates and Diploma Recipients by Race/Ethnicity

Category	Total	White	Black	Asian	AIAN	Hisp.
Enrollment (%)	100.0	72.4	16.2	1.1	0.3	10.0
Drop-out Rate (%)	5.2	5.1	5.2	3.5	14.3	7.0
H.S. Diplomas (#)	1,531	1,210	182	25	1	113

Lee County

Lee County SD

2055 Central Ave • Fort Myers, FL 33901-3916
(239) 337-8301 • http://www.lee.k12.fl.us/
Grade Span: PK-12; **Agency Type:** 1
Schools: 79
39 Primary; 12 Middle; 14 High; 14 Other Level
69 Regular; 4 Special Education; 3 Vocational; 3 Alternative
0 Magnet; 3 Charter; 25 Title I Eligible; 25 School-wide Title I
Students: 63,172 (51.4% male; 48.6% female)
Individual Education Program: 9,813 (15.5%);
English Language Learner: 6,707 (10.6%); Migrant: 1,443 (2.3%)
Eligible for Free Lunch Program: 23,006 (36.4%)
Eligible for Reduced-Price Lunch Program: 6,928 (11.0%)
Teachers: 3,200.0 (19.7 to 1)
Librarians/Media Specialists: 47.0 (1,344.1 to 1)
Guidance Counselors: 115.0 (549.3 to 1)
Current Spending: ($ per student per year):
Total: $6,070; Instruction: $3,289; Support Services: $2,501
Enrollment, Drop-out Rates and Diploma Recipients by Race/Ethnicity

Category	Total	White	Black	Asian	AIAN	Hisp.
Enrollment (%)	100.0	63.6	15.4	1.2	0.4	19.4
Drop-out Rate (%)	7.1	5.7	12.2	4.5	2.5	9.8
H.S. Diplomas (#)	2,846	2,105	352	56	10	323

Leon County

Leon County SD

2757 W Pensacola St • Tallahassee, FL 32304-2907
(850) 487-7147 •
http://www.leon.k12.fl.us/districtserver/Schools/Index.html
Grade Span: PK-12; **Agency Type:** 1
Schools: 58
27 Primary; 9 Middle; 6 High; 14 Other Level
49 Regular; 5 Special Education; 1 Vocational; 1 Alternative
0 Magnet; 2 Charter; 19 Title I Eligible; 19 School-wide Title I
Students: 31,857 (51.2% male; 48.8% female)
Individual Education Program: 6,455 (20.3%);
English Language Learner: 276 (0.9%); Migrant: 12 (<0.1%)

Eligible for Free Lunch Program: 8,735 (27.4%)
Eligible for Reduced-Price Lunch Program: 1,874 (5.9%)
Teachers: 1,711.0 (18.6 to 1)
Librarians/Media Specialists: 42.0 (758.5 to 1)
Guidance Counselors: 71.0 (448.7 to 1)
Current Spending: ($ per student per year):
Total: $6,326; Instruction: $3,485; Support Services: $2,572
Enrollment, Drop-out Rates and Diploma Recipients by Race/Ethnicity

Category	Total	White	Black	Asian	AIAN	Hisp.
Enrollment (%)	100.0	55.3	40.4	2.0	0.1	2.2
Drop-out Rate (%)	3.5	2.8	4.8	1.9	0.0	3.7
H.S. Diplomas (#)	1,788	1,173	543	32	3	37

Levy County

Levy County SD
PO Drawer 129 • Bronson, FL 32621-0129
(352) 486-5231 • http://www.levy.k12.fl.us/
Grade Span: PK-12; **Agency Type:** 1
Schools: 16
4 Primary; 2 Middle; 3 High; 7 Other Level
14 Regular; 0 Special Education; 0 Vocational; 2 Alternative
0 Magnet; 2 Charter; 11 Title I Eligible; 11 School-wide Title I
Students: 6,113 (51.9% male; 48.1% female)
Individual Education Program: 1,420 (23.2%);
English Language Learner: 140 (2.3%); Migrant: 252 (4.1%)
Eligible for Free Lunch Program: 2,836 (46.4%)
Eligible for Reduced-Price Lunch Program: 634 (10.4%)
Teachers: 366.0 (16.7 to 1)
Librarians/Media Specialists: 11.0 (555.7 to 1)
Guidance Counselors: 13.0 (470.2 to 1)
Current Spending: ($ per student per year):
Total: $6,103; Instruction: $3,447; Support Services: $2,308
Enrollment, Drop-out Rates and Diploma Recipients by Race/Ethnicity

Category	Total	White	Black	Asian	AIAN	Hisp.
Enrollment (%)	100.0	78.3	16.8	0.5	0.1	4.3
Drop-out Rate (%)	4.3	4.3	4.5	0.0	0.0	2.1
H.S. Diplomas (#)	301	237	53	3	0	8

Madison County

Madison County SD
312 NE Duval St • Madison, FL 32340-2552
(850) 973-5022 • http://janusgroup.com/madison/
Grade Span: PK-12; **Agency Type:** 1
Schools: 9
5 Primary; 0 Middle; 1 High; 3 Other Level
8 Regular; 0 Special Education; 0 Vocational; 1 Alternative
0 Magnet; 0 Charter; 4 Title I Eligible; 4 School-wide Title I
Students: 3,311 (54.8% male; 45.2% female)
Individual Education Program: 840 (25.4%);
English Language Learner: 8 (0.2%); Migrant: 19 (0.6%)
Eligible for Free Lunch Program: 1,819 (54.9%)
Eligible for Reduced-Price Lunch Program: 306 (9.2%)
Teachers: 173.0 (19.1 to 1)
Librarians/Media Specialists: 3.0 (1,103.7 to 1)
Guidance Counselors: 4.0 (827.8 to 1)
Current Spending: ($ per student per year):
Total: $6,147; Instruction: $3,444; Support Services: $2,307
Enrollment, Drop-out Rates and Diploma Recipients by Race/Ethnicity

Category	Total	White	Black	Asian	AIAN	Hisp.
Enrollment (%)	100.0	39.8	58.1	0.1	0.2	1.8
Drop-out Rate (%)	6.6	4.4	8.6	0.0	0.0	10.0
H.S. Diplomas (#)	180	100	75	3	0	2

Manatee County

Manatee County SD
PO Box 9069 • Bradenton, FL 34206-9069
(941) 741-7235 • http://www.manatee.k12.fl.us/school_sites.htm
Grade Span: PK-12; **Agency Type:** 1
Schools: 73
35 Primary; 9 Middle; 9 High; 19 Other Level
55 Regular; 8 Special Education; 1 Vocational; 8 Alternative
0 Magnet; 7 Charter; 15 Title I Eligible; 9 School-wide Title I
Students: 39,132 (51.7% male; 48.3% female)
Individual Education Program: 7,618 (19.5%);
English Language Learner: 2,552 (6.5%); Migrant: 1,607 (4.1%)
Eligible for Free Lunch Program: 13,024 (33.3%)
Eligible for Reduced-Price Lunch Program: 3,003 (7.7%)
Teachers: 2,159.0 (18.1 to 1)
Librarians/Media Specialists: 45.0 (869.6 to 1)
Guidance Counselors: 87.0 (449.8 to 1)
Current Spending: ($ per student per year):
Total: $6,193; Instruction: $3,629; Support Services: $2,265

Enrollment, Drop-out Rates and Diploma Recipients by Race/Ethnicity

Category	Total	White	Black	Asian	AIAN	Hisp.
Enrollment (%)	100.0	64.9	17.1	1.0	0.1	16.8
Drop-out Rate (%)	5.5	4.3	9.9	1.8	16.7	7.9
H.S. Diplomas (#)	1,709	1,309	258	23	2	117

Marion County

Marion County SD
PO Box 670 • Ocala, FL 34478-0670
(352) 671-7702 • http://www.marionschoolsk12.org/schooldir.htm
Grade Span: PK-12; **Agency Type:** 1
Schools: 65
32 Primary; 9 Middle; 8 High; 15 Other Level
53 Regular; 5 Special Education; 0 Vocational; 6 Alternative
0 Magnet; 2 Charter; 32 Title I Eligible; 32 School-wide Title I
Students: 39,710 (51.7% male; 48.3% female)
Individual Education Program: 6,957 (17.5%);
English Language Learner: 915 (2.3%); Migrant: 65 (0.2%)
Eligible for Free Lunch Program: 16,646 (41.9%)
Eligible for Reduced-Price Lunch Program: 4,528 (11.4%)
Teachers: 2,190.0 (18.1 to 1)
Librarians/Media Specialists: 46.0 (863.3 to 1)
Guidance Counselors: 78.0 (509.1 to 1)
Current Spending: ($ per student per year):
Total: $5,813; Instruction: $3,354; Support Services: $2,132
Enrollment, Drop-out Rates and Diploma Recipients by Race/Ethnicity

Category	Total	White	Black	Asian	AIAN	Hisp.
Enrollment (%)	100.0	68.1	21.2	0.9	0.3	9.4
Drop-out Rate (%)	4.4	3.9	5.7	1.7	3.4	5.8
H.S. Diplomas (#)	1,960	1,457	338	25	3	137

Martin County

Martin County SD
500 E Ocean Blvd • Stuart, FL 34994-2578
(772) 219-1200 • http://www.sbmc.org/
Grade Span: PK-12; **Agency Type:** 1
Schools: 29
14 Primary; 4 Middle; 2 High; 8 Other Level
21 Regular; 4 Special Education; 0 Vocational; 3 Alternative
0 Magnet; 0 Charter; 5 Title I Eligible; 4 School-wide Title I
Students: 17,259 (51.4% male; 48.6% female)
Individual Education Program: 2,942 (17.0%);
English Language Learner: 1,525 (8.8%); Migrant: 310 (1.8%)
Eligible for Free Lunch Program: 4,573 (26.5%)
Eligible for Reduced-Price Lunch Program: 1,034 (6.0%)
Teachers: 928.0 (18.6 to 1)
Librarians/Media Specialists: 18.0 (958.8 to 1)
Guidance Counselors: 40.0 (431.5 to 1)
Current Spending: ($ per student per year):
Total: $6,411; Instruction: $3,707; Support Services: $2,421
Enrollment, Drop-out Rates and Diploma Recipients by Race/Ethnicity

Category	Total	White	Black	Asian	AIAN	Hisp.
Enrollment (%)	100.0	73.5	10.5	1.1	0.2	14.7
Drop-out Rate (%)	0.6	0.4	1.2	0.0	0.0	2.4
H.S. Diplomas (#)	842	711	63	15	2	51

Miami-Dade County

Dade County SD
1450 NE 2nd Ave, #912 • Miami, FL 33132-1394
(305) 995-1428 • http://www.dade.k12.fl.us/schools/
Grade Span: PK-12; **Agency Type:** 1
Schools: 370
226 Primary; 54 Middle; 48 High; 38 Other Level
348 Regular; 5 Special Education; 2 Vocational; 11 Alternative
0 Magnet; 25 Charter; 174 Title I Eligible; 174 School-wide Title I
Students: 373,395 (51.3% male; 48.7% female)
Individual Education Program: 43,467 (11.6%);
English Language Learner: 66,084 (17.7%); Migrant: 2,612 (0.7%)
Eligible for Free Lunch Program: 200,001 (53.6%)
Eligible for Reduced-Price Lunch Program: 30,738 (8.2%)
Teachers: 18,656.0 (20.0 to 1)
Librarians/Media Specialists: 352.0 (1,060.8 to 1)
Guidance Counselors: 991.0 (376.8 to 1)
Current Spending: ($ per student per year):
Total: $6,552; Instruction: $3,872; Support Services: $2,372
Enrollment, Drop-out Rates and Diploma Recipients by Race/Ethnicity

Category	Total	White	Black	Asian	AIAN	Hisp.
Enrollment (%)	100.0	10.5	29.5	1.2	0.1	58.7
Drop-out Rate (%)	6.3	4.7	7.2	2.2	5.6	6.2
H.S. Diplomas (#)	16,638	2,424	4,864	321	13	9,016

Monroe County

Monroe County SD

PO Box 1788 • Key West, FL 33041-1788
(305) 293-1400 • http://www.monroe.k12.fl.us/district/schools.htm
Grade Span: PK-12; **Agency Type:** 1
Schools: 21
11 Primary; 1 Middle; 5 High; 2 Other Level
18 Regular; 0 Special Education; 0 Vocational; 1 Alternative
0 Magnet; 3 Charter; 7 Title I Eligible; 0 School-wide Title I
Students: 9,218 (52.8% male; 47.2% female)
Individual Education Program: 1,606 (17.4%);
English Language Learner: 581 (6.3%); Migrant: 26 (0.3%)
Eligible for Free Lunch Program: 2,622 (28.4%)
Eligible for Reduced-Price Lunch Program: 825 (8.9%)
Teachers: 688.0 (13.4 to 1)
Librarians/Media Specialists: 5.0 (1,843.6 to 1)
Guidance Counselors: 15.0 (614.5 to 1)
Current Spending: ($ per student per year):
Total: $7,151; Instruction: $3,890; Support Services: $2,931
Enrollment, Drop-out Rates and Diploma Recipients by Race/Ethnicity

Category	Total	White	Black	Asian	AIAN	Hisp.
Enrollment (%)	100.0	67.4	9.0	1.2	0.4	22.0
Drop-out Rate (%)	3.4	3.0	5.0	3.2	0.0	4.2
H.S. Diplomas (#)	486	346	46	6	0	88

Nassau County

Nassau County SD

1201 Atlantic Ave • Fernandina Beach, FL 32034-3499
(904) 321-5801 • http://www.nassau.k12.fl.us/
Grade Span: PK-12; **Agency Type:** 1
Schools: 19
7 Primary; 2 Middle; 2 High; 8 Other Level
18 Regular; 0 Special Education; 0 Vocational; 1 Alternative
0 Magnet; 0 Charter; 10 Title I Eligible; 0 School-wide Title I
Students: 10,533 (51.9% male; 48.1% female)
Individual Education Program: 1,680 (15.9%);
English Language Learner: 19 (0.2%); Migrant: 31 (0.3%)
Eligible for Free Lunch Program: 2,619 (24.9%)
Eligible for Reduced-Price Lunch Program: 957 (9.1%)
Teachers: 549.0 (19.2 to 1)
Librarians/Media Specialists: 16.0 (658.3 to 1)
Guidance Counselors: 22.0 (478.8 to 1)
Current Spending: ($ per student per year):
Total: $5,391; Instruction: $2,987; Support Services: $2,099
Enrollment, Drop-out Rates and Diploma Recipients by Race/Ethnicity

Category	Total	White	Black	Asian	AIAN	Hisp.
Enrollment (%)	100.0	88.8	9.3	0.5	0.3	1.2
Drop-out Rate (%)	5.5	5.0	7.4	33.3	0.0	20.0
H.S. Diplomas (#)	577	513	53	5	0	6

Okaloosa County

Okaloosa County SD

120 Lowery Place, SE • Fort Walton Beach, FL 32548-5595
(850) 833-3109 • http://www.okaloosa.k12.fl.us/schools/
Grade Span: PK-12; **Agency Type:** 1
Schools: 56
24 Primary; 8 Middle; 9 High; 14 Other Level
50 Regular; 1 Special Education; 2 Vocational; 2 Alternative
0 Magnet; 3 Charter; 15 Title I Eligible; 10 School-wide Title I
Students: 31,291 (52.1% male; 47.9% female)
Individual Education Program: 4,991 (16.0%);
English Language Learner: 169 (0.5%); Migrant: 13 (<0.1%)
Eligible for Free Lunch Program: 6,244 (20.0%)
Eligible for Reduced-Price Lunch Program: 2,580 (8.2%)
Teachers: 1,595.0 (19.6 to 1)
Librarians/Media Specialists: 36.0 (869.2 to 1)
Guidance Counselors: 56.0 (558.8 to 1)
Current Spending: ($ per student per year):
Total: $5,644; Instruction: $3,366; Support Services: $2,043
Enrollment, Drop-out Rates and Diploma Recipients by Race/Ethnicity

Category	Total	White	Black	Asian	AIAN	Hisp.
Enrollment (%)	100.0	80.3	12.8	2.7	0.5	3.6
Drop-out Rate (%)	4.3	3.8	8.1	3.8	0.0	2.5
H.S. Diplomas (#)	1,978	1,615	218	72	7	66

Okeechobee County

Okeechobee County SD

700 SW 2nd Ave • Okeechobee, FL 34974-5117
(863) 462-5000 • http://www.okee.k12.fl.us/web.nsf
Grade Span: PK-12; **Agency Type:** 1
Schools: 18
7 Primary; 1 Middle; 1 High; 9 Other Level
11 Regular; 2 Special Education; 0 Vocational; 5 Alternative
0 Magnet; 0 Charter; 5 Title I Eligible; 5 School-wide Title I
Students: 7,085 (52.0% male; 48.0% female)
Individual Education Program: 1,487 (21.0%);
English Language Learner: 429 (6.1%); Migrant: 1,230 (17.4%)
Eligible for Free Lunch Program: 3,186 (45.0%)
Eligible for Reduced-Price Lunch Program: 687 (9.7%)
Teachers: 415.0 (17.1 to 1)
Librarians/Media Specialists: 7.0 (1,012.1 to 1)
Guidance Counselors: 15.0 (472.3 to 1)
Current Spending: ($ per student per year):
Total: $5,801; Instruction: $3,219; Support Services: $2,232
Enrollment, Drop-out Rates and Diploma Recipients by Race/Ethnicity

Category	Total	White	Black	Asian	AIAN	Hisp.
Enrollment (%)	100.0	64.7	9.3	0.5	1.9	23.6
Drop-out Rate (%)	6.0	6.3	4.1	0.0	31.6	4.9
H.S. Diplomas (#)	339	248	28	2	3	58

Orange County

Orange County SD

PO Box 271 • Orlando, FL 32802-0271
(407) 317-3202 • http://www.ocps.k12.fl.us/schools/
Grade Span: PK-12; **Agency Type:** 1
Schools: 188
114 Primary; 27 Middle; 21 High; 24 Other Level
168 Regular; 5 Special Education; 4 Vocational; 9 Alternative
0 Magnet; 13 Charter; 79 Title I Eligible; 79 School-wide Title I
Students: 158,718 (51.6% male; 48.4% female)
Individual Education Program: 25,700 (16.2%);
English Language Learner: 19,613 (12.4%); Migrant: 1,510 (1.0%)
Eligible for Free Lunch Program: 53,942 (34.0%)
Eligible for Reduced-Price Lunch Program: 14,151 (8.9%)
Teachers: 9,128.0 (17.4 to 1)
Librarians/Media Specialists: 99.0 (1,603.2 to 1)
Guidance Counselors: 303.0 (523.8 to 1)
Current Spending: ($ per student per year):
Total: $5,721; Instruction: $3,143; Support Services: $2,271
Enrollment, Drop-out Rates and Diploma Recipients by Race/Ethnicity

Category	Total	White	Black	Asian	AIAN	Hisp.
Enrollment (%)	100.0	41.7	28.5	3.8	0.4	25.6
Drop-out Rate (%)	5.9	4.6	7.3	2.6	1.5	7.9
H.S. Diplomas (#)	7,361	3,737	1,713	401	34	1,476

Osceola County

Osceola County SD

817 Bill Beck Blvd • Kissimmee, FL 34744-4495
(407) 870-4008 • http://www.osceola.k12.fl.us/
Grade Span: PK-12; **Agency Type:** 1
Schools: 55
24 Primary; 8 Middle; 6 High; 17 Other Level
46 Regular; 1 Special Education; 0 Vocational; 8 Alternative
0 Magnet; 9 Charter; 21 Title I Eligible; 17 School-wide Title I
Students: 40,485 (51.5% male; 48.5% female)
Individual Education Program: 6,181 (15.3%);
English Language Learner: 6,527 (16.1%); Migrant: 127 (0.3%)
Eligible for Free Lunch Program: 15,941 (39.4%)
Eligible for Reduced-Price Lunch Program: 5,242 (12.9%)
Teachers: 1,853.0 (21.8 to 1)
Librarians/Media Specialists: 32.0 (1,265.2 to 1)
Guidance Counselors: 78.0 (519.0 to 1)
Current Spending: ($ per student per year):
Total: $5,543; Instruction: $2,993; Support Services: $2,280
Enrollment, Drop-out Rates and Diploma Recipients by Race/Ethnicity

Category	Total	White	Black	Asian	AIAN	Hisp.
Enrollment (%)	100.0	44.7	9.5	2.4	0.2	43.2
Drop-out Rate (%)	5.2	5.1	6.4	2.9	0.0	5.3
H.S. Diplomas (#)	1,853	979	172	71	1	630

Palm Beach County

Palm Beach County SD

3340 Forest Hill Blvd • West Palm Beach, FL 33406-5869
(561) 434-8200 • http://www.palmbeach.k12.fl.us/schools/
Grade Span: PK-12; **Agency Type:** 1
Schools: 208
114 Primary; 33 Middle; 27 High; 31 Other Level
186 Regular; 3 Special Education; 0 Vocational; 16 Alternative
0 Magnet; 23 Charter; 82 Title I Eligible; 82 School-wide Title I
Students: 164,896 (51.5% male; 48.5% female)
Individual Education Program: 23,875 (14.5%);
English Language Learner: 18,116 (11.0%); Migrant: 5,661 (3.4%)
Eligible for Free Lunch Program: 57,265 (34.7%)

Eligible for Reduced-Price Lunch Program: 10,851 (6.6%)
Teachers: 8,826.0 (18.7 to 1)
Librarians/Media Specialists: 153.0 (1,077.8 to 1)
Guidance Counselors: 382.0 (431.7 to 1)
Current Spending: ($ per student per year):
Total: $6,266; Instruction: $3,789; Support Services: $2,199
Enrollment, Drop-out Rates and Diploma Recipients by Race/Ethnicity

Category	Total	White	Black	Asian	AIAN	Hisp.
Enrollment (%)	100.0	47.5	29.7	2.2	0.5	20.0
Drop-out Rate (%)	3.0	2.1	4.2	1.2	0.7	4.2
H.S. Diplomas (#)	7,687	4,387	1,904	243	21	1,132

Pasco County

Pasco County SD
7227 Land O'lakes Blvd • Land O' Lakes, FL 34639-2899
(813) 794-2648 • http://www.pasco.k12.fl.us/schoollist.html
Grade Span: PK-12; **Agency Type:** 1
Schools: 72
35 Primary; 11 Middle; 8 High; 18 Other Level
70 Regular; 0 Special Education; 1 Vocational; 1 Alternative
0 Magnet; 6 Charter; 19 Title I Eligible; 19 School-wide Title I
Students: 54,957 (51.6% male; 48.4% female)
Individual Education Program: 10,639 (19.4%);
English Language Learner: 1,674 (3.0%); Migrant: 546 (1.0%)
Eligible for Free Lunch Program: 19,145 (34.8%)
Eligible for Reduced-Price Lunch Program: 6,240 (11.4%)
Teachers: 3,052.0 (18.0 to 1)
Librarians/Media Specialists: 73.0 (752.8 to 1)
Guidance Counselors: 133.0 (413.2 to 1)
Current Spending: ($ per student per year):
Total: $5,789; Instruction: $3,246; Support Services: $2,220
Enrollment, Drop-out Rates and Diploma Recipients by Race/Ethnicity

Category	Total	White	Black	Asian	AIAN	Hisp.
Enrollment (%)	100.0	85.8	4.0	1.2	0.3	8.7
Drop-out Rate (%)	5.4	5.1	8.7	1.7	0.0	8.7
H.S. Diplomas (#)	2,453	2,159	81	46	7	160

Pinellas County

Pinellas County SD
301 4th St SW • Largo, FL 33770-3536
(727) 588-6011 • http://www.pinellas.k12.fl.us/
Grade Span: PK-12; **Agency Type:** 1
Schools: 172
85 Primary; 25 Middle; 20 High; 39 Other Level
150 Regular; 8 Special Education; 2 Vocational; 9 Alternative
0 Magnet; 4 Charter; 52 Title I Eligible; 52 School-wide Title I
Students: 114,772 (51.5% male; 48.5% female)
Individual Education Program: 20,290 (17.7%);
English Language Learner: 2,871 (2.5%); Migrant: 0 (0.0%)
Eligible for Free Lunch Program: 33,946 (29.6%)
Eligible for Reduced-Price Lunch Program: 10,110 (8.8%)
Teachers: 6,516.0 (17.6 to 1)
Librarians/Media Specialists: 118.0 (972.6 to 1)
Guidance Counselors: 234.0 (490.5 to 1)
Current Spending: ($ per student per year):
Total: $6,150; Instruction: $3,591; Support Services: $2,279
Enrollment, Drop-out Rates and Diploma Recipients by Race/Ethnicity

Category	Total	White	Black	Asian	AIAN	Hisp.
Enrollment (%)	100.0	71.2	19.3	3.2	0.3	6.1
Drop-out Rate (%)	5.0	4.3	7.9	4.0	1.6	6.3
H.S. Diplomas (#)	5,413	4,332	672	207	12	190

Polk County

Polk County SD
PO Box 391 • Bartow, FL 33831-0391
(863) 534-0521 • http://www.pinellas.k12.fl.us/
Grade Span: PK-12; **Agency Type:** 1
Schools: 148
73 Primary; 21 Middle; 17 High; 33 Other Level
120 Regular; 3 Special Education; 2 Vocational; 19 Alternative
0 Magnet; 12 Charter; 61 Title I Eligible; 61 School-wide Title I
Students: 82,179 (52.1% male; 47.9% female)
Individual Education Program: 12,726 (15.5%);
English Language Learner: 3,756 (4.6%); Migrant: 1,989 (2.4%)
Eligible for Free Lunch Program: 36,545 (44.5%)
Eligible for Reduced-Price Lunch Program: 8,293 (10.1%)
Teachers: 4,801.0 (17.1 to 1)
Librarians/Media Specialists: 115.0 (714.6 to 1)
Guidance Counselors: 181.0 (454.0 to 1)
Current Spending: ($ per student per year):
Total: $5,882; Instruction: $3,418; Support Services: $2,090
Enrollment, Drop-out Rates and Diploma Recipients by Race/Ethnicity

Category	Total	White	Black	Asian	AIAN	Hisp.
Enrollment (%)	100.0	61.6	22.8	1.1	0.2	14.3
Drop-out Rate (%)	6.9	6.6	6.7	0.4	6.5	10.2
H.S. Diplomas (#)	3,815	2,594	832	67	5	317

Putnam County

Putnam County SD
200 S 7th St • Palatka, FL 32177-4615
(386) 329-0510 • http://www.putnamschools.org/
Grade Span: PK-12; **Agency Type:** 1
Schools: 21
10 Primary; 4 Middle; 3 High; 4 Other Level
18 Regular; 2 Special Education; 0 Vocational; 1 Alternative
0 Magnet; 0 Charter; 15 Title I Eligible; 15 School-wide Title I
Students: 12,483 (52.9% male; 47.1% female)
Individual Education Program: 2,266 (18.2%);
English Language Learner: 454 (3.6%); Migrant: 375 (3.0%)
Eligible for Free Lunch Program: 6,869 (55.0%)
Eligible for Reduced-Price Lunch Program: 1,210 (9.7%)
Teachers: 728.0 (17.1 to 1)
Librarians/Media Specialists: 17.0 (734.3 to 1)
Guidance Counselors: 35.0 (356.7 to 1)
Current Spending: ($ per student per year):
Total: $5,867; Instruction: $3,128; Support Services: $2,360
Enrollment, Drop-out Rates and Diploma Recipients by Race/Ethnicity

Category	Total	White	Black	Asian	AIAN	Hisp.
Enrollment (%)	100.0	63.3	26.8	0.5	0.1	9.3
Drop-out Rate (%)	2.8	2.4	2.9	0.0	0.0	6.7
H.S. Diplomas (#)	447	318	107	2	1	19

Santa Rosa County

Santa Rosa County SD
603 Canal St • Milton, FL 32570-6726
(850) 983-5010 • http://www.santarosa.k12.fl.us/
Grade Span: PK-12; **Agency Type:** 1
Schools: 37
15 Primary; 6 Middle; 9 High; 7 Other Level
35 Regular; 1 Special Education; 1 Vocational; 0 Alternative
0 Magnet; 1 Charter; 13 Title I Eligible; 10 School-wide Title I
Students: 23,645 (52.0% male; 48.0% female)
Individual Education Program: 3,863 (16.3%);
English Language Learner: 40 (0.2%); Migrant: 5 (<0.1%)
Eligible for Free Lunch Program: 5,395 (22.8%)
Eligible for Reduced-Price Lunch Program: 2,225 (9.4%)
Teachers: 1,230.0 (19.2 to 1)
Librarians/Media Specialists: 29.0 (815.3 to 1)
Guidance Counselors: 50.0 (472.9 to 1)
Current Spending: ($ per student per year):
Total: $5,771; Instruction: $3,257; Support Services: $2,215
Enrollment, Drop-out Rates and Diploma Recipients by Race/Ethnicity

Category	Total	White	Black	Asian	AIAN	Hisp.
Enrollment (%)	100.0	90.6	5.4	1.5	0.6	1.9
Drop-out Rate (%)	2.4	2.2	5.0	2.7	2.3	4.6
H.S. Diplomas (#)	1,333	1,221	45	22	12	33

Sarasota County

Sarasota County SD
1960 Landings Blvd • Sarasota, FL 34231-3331
(941) 927-9000 • http://www.sarasota.k12.fl.us/
Grade Span: PK-12; **Agency Type:** 1
Schools: 51
22 Primary; 7 Middle; 7 High; 12 Other Level
41 Regular; 3 Special Education; 1 Vocational; 3 Alternative
0 Magnet; 6 Charter; 11 Title I Eligible; 11 School-wide Title I
Students: 38,057 (51.2% male; 48.8% female)
Individual Education Program: 6,521 (17.1%);
English Language Learner: 1,545 (4.1%); Migrant: 115 (0.3%)
Eligible for Free Lunch Program: 9,362 (24.6%)
Eligible for Reduced-Price Lunch Program: 3,550 (9.3%)
Teachers: 2,139.0 (17.8 to 1)
Librarians/Media Specialists: 15.0 (2,537.1 to 1)
Guidance Counselors: 55.0 (691.9 to 1)
Current Spending: ($ per student per year):
Total: $6,606; Instruction: $3,831; Support Services: $2,467
Enrollment, Drop-out Rates and Diploma Recipients by Race/Ethnicity

Category	Total	White	Black	Asian	AIAN	Hisp.
Enrollment (%)	100.0	80.3	9.6	1.5	0.2	8.4
Drop-out Rate (%)	3.5	3.1	6.7	1.9	5.3	5.2
H.S. Diplomas (#)	1,895	1,634	118	47	1	95

Seminole County

Seminole County SD

400 E Lake Mary Blvd • Sanford, FL 32773-7127
(407) 320-0006 • http://www.scps.k12.fl.us/
Grade Span: PK-12; **Agency Type:** 1
Schools: 75
38 Primary; 12 Middle; 8 High; 14 Other Level
61 Regular; 3 Special Education; 0 Vocational; 8 Alternative
0 Magnet; 3 Charter; 20 Title I Eligible; 20 School-wide Title I
Students: 63,446 (51.3% male; 48.7% female)
Individual Education Program: 8,133 (12.8%);
English Language Learner: 1,953 (3.1%); Migrant: 0 (0.0%)
Eligible for Free Lunch Program: 13,512 (21.3%)
Eligible for Reduced-Price Lunch Program: 4,826 (7.6%)
Teachers: 3,411.0 (18.6 to 1)
Librarians/Media Specialists: 43.0 (1,475.5 to 1)
Guidance Counselors: 109.0 (582.1 to 1)
Current Spending: ($ per student per year):
Total: $5,511; Instruction: $3,340; Support Services: $1,914
Enrollment, Drop-out Rates and Diploma Recipients by Race/Ethnicity

Category	Total	White	Black	Asian	AIAN	Hisp.
Enrollment (%)	100.0	68.5	13.6	3.1	0.2	14.6
Drop-out Rate (%)	1.0	0.9	1.7	0.8	2.4	1.1
H.S. Diplomas (#)	3,420	2,516	355	138	9	402

St. Johns County

Saint Johns County SD

40 Orange St • Saint Augustine, FL 32084-3693
(904) 826-2101 • http://macserver.stjohns.k12.fl.us/
Grade Span: PK-12; **Agency Type:** 1
Schools: 36
15 Primary; 5 Middle; 7 High; 8 Other Level
34 Regular; 0 Special Education; 0 Vocational; 1 Alternative
0 Magnet; 5 Charter; 8 Title I Eligible; 5 School-wide Title I
Students: 21,975 (51.8% male; 48.2% female)
Individual Education Program: 3,490 (15.9%);
English Language Learner: 143 (0.7%); Migrant: 32 (0.1%)
Eligible for Free Lunch Program: 3,357 (15.3%)
Eligible for Reduced-Price Lunch Program: 1,081 (4.9%)
Teachers: 1,215.0 (18.1 to 1)
Librarians/Media Specialists: 27.0 (813.9 to 1)
Guidance Counselors: 51.0 (430.9 to 1)
Current Spending: ($ per student per year):
Total: $6,154; Instruction: $3,600; Support Services: $2,299
Enrollment, Drop-out Rates and Diploma Recipients by Race/Ethnicity

Category	Total	White	Black	Asian	AIAN	Hisp.
Enrollment (%)	100.0	86.8	9.5	1.2	0.1	2.3
Drop-out Rate (%)	2.8	2.6	5.4	0.0	0.0	0.7
H.S. Diplomas (#)	1,097	965	82	11	1	38

St. Lucie County

Saint Lucie County SD

2909 Delaware Ave • Fort Pierce, FL 34947-7299
(561) 468-5021 • http://plato.stlucie.k12.fl.us/
Grade Span: PK-12; **Agency Type:** 1
Schools: 43
22 Primary; 6 Middle; 5 High; 10 Other Level
35 Regular; 2 Special Education; 0 Vocational; 6 Alternative
0 Magnet; 0 Charter; 26 Title I Eligible; 26 School-wide Title I
Students: 31,554 (51.0% male; 49.0% female)
Individual Education Program: 4,528 (14.4%);
English Language Learner: 1,766 (5.6%); Migrant: 4,142 (13.1%)
Eligible for Free Lunch Program: 13,885 (44.0%)
Eligible for Reduced-Price Lunch Program: 3,190 (10.1%)
Teachers: 2,000.0 (15.8 to 1)
Librarians/Media Specialists: 37.0 (852.8 to 1)
Guidance Counselors: 81.0 (389.6 to 1)
Current Spending: ($ per student per year):
Total: $6,064; Instruction: $3,334; Support Services: $2,373
Enrollment, Drop-out Rates and Diploma Recipients by Race/Ethnicity

Category	Total	White	Black	Asian	AIAN	Hisp.
Enrollment (%)	100.0	56.5	29.1	1.3	0.3	12.7
Drop-out Rate (%)	2.1	1.7	3.2	0.9	0.0	1.2
H.S. Diplomas (#)	1,258	758	368	24	3	105

Sumter County

Sumter County SD

2680 Wc 476 • Bushnell, FL 33513-3574
(352) 793-2315 • http://www.sumter.k12.fl.us/
Grade Span: PK-12; **Agency Type:** 1
Schools: 13
6 Primary; 3 Middle; 2 High; 2 Other Level
11 Regular; 1 Special Education; 0 Vocational; 1 Alternative
0 Magnet; 2 Charter; 5 Title I Eligible; 5 School-wide Title I
Students: 6,558 (51.2% male; 48.8% female)
Individual Education Program: 1,197 (18.3%);
English Language Learner: 241 (3.7%); Migrant: 297 (4.5%)
Eligible for Free Lunch Program: 3,075 (46.9%)
Eligible for Reduced-Price Lunch Program: 676 (10.3%)
Teachers: 357.0 (18.4 to 1)
Librarians/Media Specialists: 12.0 (546.5 to 1)
Guidance Counselors: 13.0 (504.5 to 1)
Current Spending: ($ per student per year):
Total: $6,221; Instruction: $3,421; Support Services: $2,428
Enrollment, Drop-out Rates and Diploma Recipients by Race/Ethnicity

Category	Total	White	Black	Asian	AIAN	Hisp.
Enrollment (%)	100.0	70.2	21.8	0.6	0.2	7.2
Drop-out Rate (%)	3.3	2.7	4.9	0.0	0.0	5.7
H.S. Diplomas (#)	261	187	54	1	3	16

Suwannee County

Suwannee County SD

702 Second Street, NW • Live Oak, FL 32060-1608
(386) 364-2604 • http://www.suwannee.k12.fl.us/
Grade Span: PK-12; **Agency Type:** 1
Schools: 10
3 Primary; 1 Middle; 2 High; 4 Other Level
9 Regular; 0 Special Education; 1 Vocational; 0 Alternative
0 Magnet; 0 Charter; 3 Title I Eligible; 3 School-wide Title I
Students: 5,802 (53.0% male; 47.0% female)
Individual Education Program: 815 (14.0%);
English Language Learner: 101 (1.7%); Migrant: 142 (2.4%)
Eligible for Free Lunch Program: 2,382 (41.1%)
Eligible for Reduced-Price Lunch Program: 553 (9.5%)
Teachers: 309.0 (18.8 to 1)
Librarians/Media Specialists: 7.0 (828.9 to 1)
Guidance Counselors: 14.0 (414.4 to 1)
Current Spending: ($ per student per year):
Total: $5,865; Instruction: $3,418; Support Services: $2,125
Enrollment, Drop-out Rates and Diploma Recipients by Race/Ethnicity

Category	Total	White	Black	Asian	AIAN	Hisp.
Enrollment (%)	100.0	76.5	17.5	0.7	0.4	4.8
Drop-out Rate (%)	6.0	5.7	6.9	14.3	14.3	5.1
H.S. Diplomas (#)	284	228	46	2	1	7

Taylor County

Taylor County SD

318 N Clark St • Perry, FL 32347-2930
(850) 838-2500 • http://www.taylor.k12.fl.us/
Grade Span: PK-12; **Agency Type:** 1
Schools: 9
4 Primary; 1 Middle; 2 High; 2 Other Level
7 Regular; 0 Special Education; 1 Vocational; 1 Alternative
0 Magnet; 0 Charter; 4 Title I Eligible; 4 School-wide Title I
Students: 3,593 (51.3% male; 48.7% female)
Individual Education Program: 678 (18.9%);
English Language Learner: 2 (0.1%); Migrant: 1 (<0.1%)
Eligible for Free Lunch Program: 1,644 (45.8%)
Eligible for Reduced-Price Lunch Program: 286 (8.0%)
Teachers: 212.0 (16.9 to 1)
Librarians/Media Specialists: 4.0 (898.3 to 1)
Guidance Counselors: 5.0 (718.6 to 1)
Current Spending: ($ per student per year):
Total: $6,012; Instruction: $3,387; Support Services: $2,299
Enrollment, Drop-out Rates and Diploma Recipients by Race/Ethnicity

Category	Total	White	Black	Asian	AIAN	Hisp.
Enrollment (%)	100.0	74.8	23.0	0.5	0.6	1.1
Drop-out Rate (%)	2.1	1.8	3.3	0.0	0.0	0.0
H.S. Diplomas (#)	203	160	39	2	1	1

Union County

Union County SD

55 SW 6th St • Lake Butler, FL 32054-2599
(386) 496-2045 • http://www.union.k12.fl.us/
Grade Span: PK-12; **Agency Type:** 1
Schools: 6
1 Primary; 1 Middle; 1 High; 3 Other Level
5 Regular; 0 Special Education; 0 Vocational; 1 Alternative
0 Magnet; 0 Charter; 2 Title I Eligible; 2 School-wide Title I
Students: 2,174 (53.0% male; 47.0% female)
Individual Education Program: 374 (17.2%);
English Language Learner: 2 (0.1%); Migrant: 17 (0.8%)
Eligible for Free Lunch Program: 797 (36.7%)

Eligible for Reduced-Price Lunch Program: 167 (7.7%)
Teachers: 153.0 (14.2 to 1)
Librarians/Media Specialists: 2.0 (1,087.0 to 1)
Guidance Counselors: 3.0 (724.7 to 1)
Current Spending: ($ per student per year):
Total: $5,348; Instruction: $2,921; Support Services: $2,113
Enrollment, Drop-out Rates and Diploma Recipients by Race/Ethnicity

Category	Total	White	Black	Asian	AIAN	Hisp.
Enrollment (%)	100.0	79.9	17.8	0.3	0.0	1.9
Drop-out Rate (%)	4.0	4.0	4.5	0.0	n/a	0.0
H.S. Diplomas (#)	129	105	22	0	1	1

Volusia County

Volusia County SD
PO Box 2118 • Deland, FL 32721-2118
(386) 734-7190 • http://www.volusia.k12.fl.us/
Grade Span: PK-12; **Agency Type:** 1
Schools: 92
46 Primary; 11 Middle; 10 High; 24 Other Level
82 Regular; 2 Special Education; 0 Vocational; 7 Alternative
0 Magnet; 3 Charter; 47 Title I Eligible; 42 School-wide Title I
Students: 63,000 (51.6% male; 48.4% female)
Individual Education Program: 10,952 (17.4%);
English Language Learner: 1,907 (3.0%); Migrant: 1,109 (1.8%)
Eligible for Free Lunch Program: 19,089 (30.3%)
Eligible for Reduced-Price Lunch Program: 5,183 (8.2%)
Teachers: 3,824.0 (16.5 to 1)
Librarians/Media Specialists: 70.0 (900.0 to 1)
Guidance Counselors: 194.0 (324.7 to 1)
Current Spending: ($ per student per year):
Total: $5,810; Instruction: $3,426; Support Services: $2,112
Enrollment, Drop-out Rates and Diploma Recipients by Race/Ethnicity

Category	Total	White	Black	Asian	AIAN	Hisp.
Enrollment (%)	100.0	72.5	15.5	1.1	0.2	10.6
Drop-out Rate (%)	1.7	1.3	3.2	0.8	6.1	2.5
H.S. Diplomas (#)	3,386	2,675	396	59	3	253

Wakulla County

Wakulla County SD
PO Box 100 • Crawfordville, FL 32326-0100
(850) 926-7131 • http://www.firn.edu/schools/wakulla/wakulla/
Grade Span: PK-12; **Agency Type:** 1
Schools: 11
5 Primary; 2 Middle; 1 High; 3 Other Level
9 Regular; 0 Special Education; 0 Vocational; 2 Alternative
0 Magnet; 1 Charter; 5 Title I Eligible; 1 School-wide Title I
Students: 4,663 (52.1% male; 47.9% female)
Individual Education Program: 884 (19.0%);
English Language Learner: 9 (0.2%); Migrant: 0 (0.0%)
Eligible for Free Lunch Program: 1,202 (25.8%)
Eligible for Reduced-Price Lunch Program: 408 (8.7%)
Teachers: 251.0 (18.6 to 1)
Librarians/Media Specialists: 6.0 (777.2 to 1)
Guidance Counselors: 8.0 (582.9 to 1)
Current Spending: ($ per student per year):
Total: $5,777; Instruction: $3,169; Support Services: $2,322
Enrollment, Drop-out Rates and Diploma Recipients by Race/Ethnicity

Category	Total	White	Black	Asian	AIAN	Hisp.
Enrollment (%)	100.0	86.6	11.7	0.4	0.2	1.1
Drop-out Rate (%)	2.7	2.7	3.8	0.0	0.0	0.0
H.S. Diplomas (#)	233	198	30	1	2	2

Walton County

Walton County SD
145 Park Street, Ste #3 • Defuniak Springs, FL 32433-3344
(850) 892-8331 • http://www.walton.k12.fl.us/
Grade Span: PK-12; **Agency Type:** 1
Schools: 17
4 Primary; 2 Middle; 3 High; 7 Other Level
15 Regular; 0 Special Education; 1 Vocational; 0 Alternative
0 Magnet; 2 Charter; 7 Title I Eligible; 7 School-wide Title I
Students: 6,303 (52.3% male; 47.7% female)
Individual Education Program: 1,005 (15.9%);
English Language Learner: 74 (1.2%); Migrant: 23 (0.4%)
Eligible for Free Lunch Program: 2,425 (38.5%)
Eligible for Reduced-Price Lunch Program: 723 (11.5%)
Teachers: 354.0 (17.8 to 1)
Librarians/Media Specialists: 9.0 (700.3 to 1)
Guidance Counselors: 12.0 (525.3 to 1)
Current Spending: ($ per student per year):
Total: $6,108; Instruction: $3,511; Support Services: $2,263

Enrollment, Drop-out Rates and Diploma Recipients by Race/Ethnicity

Category	Total	White	Black	Asian	AIAN	Hisp.
Enrollment (%)	100.0	87.9	9.0	0.5	0.5	2.1
Drop-out Rate (%)	5.2	5.0	5.3	14.3	0.0	12.9
H.S. Diplomas (#)	246	221	20	0	1	4

Washington County

Washington County SD
652 Third St • Chipley, FL 32428-1442
(850) 638-6222 • http://www.firn.edu/schools/washington/wash/index.htm
Grade Span: PK-12; **Agency Type:** 1
Schools: 8
2 Primary; 2 Middle; 2 High; 2 Other Level
7 Regular; 0 Special Education; 0 Vocational; 1 Alternative
0 Magnet; 0 Charter; 6 Title I Eligible; 6 School-wide Title I
Students: 3,410 (51.7% male; 48.3% female)
Individual Education Program: 541 (15.9%);
English Language Learner: 0 (0.0%); Migrant: 1 (<0.1%)
Eligible for Free Lunch Program: 1,654 (48.5%)
Eligible for Reduced-Price Lunch Program: 359 (10.5%)
Teachers: 225.0 (15.2 to 1)
Librarians/Media Specialists: 5.0 (682.0 to 1)
Guidance Counselors: 10.0 (341.0 to 1)
Current Spending: ($ per student per year):
Total: $7,570; Instruction: $4,290; Support Services: $2,907
Enrollment, Drop-out Rates and Diploma Recipients by Race/Ethnicity

Category	Total	White	Black	Asian	AIAN	Hisp.
Enrollment (%)	100.0	79.1	19.0	0.4	0.7	0.8
Drop-out Rate (%)	2.9	3.4	0.6	0.0	16.7	0.0
H.S. Diplomas (#)	191	153	36	1	0	1

Number of Schools

Rank	Number	District Name	City
1	370	Dade County SD	Miami
2	259	Broward County SD	Fort Lauderdale
3	229	Hillsborough County SD	Tampa
4	208	Palm Beach County SD	West Palm Beach
5	188	Orange County SD	Orlando
6	181	Duval County SD	Jacksonville
7	172	Pinellas County SD	Largo
8	148	Polk County SD	Bartow
9	110	Brevard County SD	Viera
10	92	Volusia County SD	Deland
11	86	Escambia County SD	Pensacola
12	79	Lee County SD	Fort Myers
13	75	Seminole County SD	Sanford
14	73	Manatee County SD	Bradenton
15	72	Pasco County SD	Land O' Lakes
16	65	Marion County SD	Ocala
17	62	Alachua County SD	Gainesville
18	58	Leon County SD	Tallahassee
19	56	Okaloosa County SD	Ft Walton Beach
20	55	Osceola County SD	Kissimmee
21	53	Collier County SD	Naples
21	53	Lake County SD	Tavares
23	51	Sarasota County SD	Sarasota
24	44	Bay County SD	Panama City
25	43	Saint Lucie County SD	Fort Pierce
26	37	Santa Rosa County SD	Milton
27	36	Saint Johns County SD	Saint Augustine
28	32	Clay County SD	Green Cove Spgs
29	29	Martin County SD	Stuart
30	28	Indian River County SD	Vero Beach
31	26	Citrus County SD	Inverness
32	25	Gadsden County SD	Quincy
33	24	Charlotte County SD	Port Charlotte
34	23	Hernando County SD	Brooksville
35	21	Jackson County SD	Marianna
35	21	Monroe County SD	Key West
35	21	Putnam County SD	Palatka
38	19	Nassau County SD	Fernandina Bch
39	18	Highlands County SD	Sebring
39	18	Okeechobee County SD	Okeechobee
41	17	Walton County SD	Defuniak Spgs
42	16	Hendry County SD	La Belle
42	16	Levy County SD	Bronson
44	15	Columbia County SD	Lake City
45	13	Desoto County SD	Arcadia
45	13	Sumter County SD	Bushnell
47	12	Bradford County SD	Starke
48	11	Wakulla County SD	Crawfordville
49	10	Flagler County SD	Bunnell
49	10	Suwannee County SD	Live Oak
51	9	Hardee County SD	Wauchula
51	9	Holmes County SD	Bonifay
51	9	Madison County SD	Madison
51	9	Taylor County SD	Perry
55	8	Baker County SD	Macclenny
55	8	Gulf County SD	Port Saint Joe
55	8	Washington County SD	Chipley
58	7	Calhoun County SD	Blountstown
58	7	Hamilton County SD	Jasper
58	7	Jefferson County SD	Monticello
61	6	Union County SD	Lake Butler
62	5	Dixie County SD	Cross City
63	4	Gilchrist County SD	Trenton

Number of Teachers

Rank	Number	District Name	City
1	18,656	Dade County SD	Miami
2	13,264	Broward County SD	Fort Lauderdale
3	10,499	Hillsborough County SD	Tampa
4	9,128	Orange County SD	Orlando
5	8,826	Palm Beach County SD	West Palm Beach
6	6,620	Duval County SD	Jacksonville
7	6,516	Pinellas County SD	Largo
8	4,801	Polk County SD	Bartow
9	4,079	Brevard County SD	Viera
10	3,824	Volusia County SD	Deland
11	3,411	Seminole County SD	Sanford
12	3,200	Lee County SD	Fort Myers
13	3,052	Pasco County SD	Land O' Lakes
14	2,393	Escambia County SD	Pensacola
15	2,209	Lake County SD	Tavares
16	2,190	Marion County SD	Ocala
17	2,167	Collier County SD	Naples
18	2,159	Manatee County SD	Bradenton
19	2,139	Sarasota County SD	Sarasota
20	2,000	Saint Lucie County SD	Fort Pierce
21	1,853	Osceola County SD	Kissimmee
22	1,711	Leon County SD	Tallahassee
23	1,657	Alachua County SD	Gainesville
23	1,657	Clay County SD	Green Cove Spgs
25	1,595	Okaloosa County SD	Ft Walton Beach
26	1,526	Bay County SD	Panama City
27	1,230	Santa Rosa County SD	Milton
28	1,215	Saint Johns County SD	Saint Augustine
29	1,016	Hernando County SD	Brooksville
30	928	Martin County SD	Stuart
31	926	Citrus County SD	Inverness
32	925	Charlotte County SD	Port Charlotte
33	728	Putnam County SD	Palatka
34	688	Monroe County SD	Key West
35	671	Highlands County SD	Sebring
36	569	Columbia County SD	Lake City
37	549	Nassau County SD	Fernandina Bch
38	453	Flagler County SD	Bunnell
39	437	Jackson County SD	Marianna
40	421	Gadsden County SD	Quincy
41	415	Okeechobee County SD	Okeechobee
42	393	Indian River County SD	Vero Beach
43	373	Hendry County SD	La Belle
44	366	Levy County SD	Bronson
45	357	Sumter County SD	Bushnell
46	354	Walton County SD	Defuniak Spgs
47	309	Suwannee County SD	Live Oak
48	300	Hardee County SD	Wauchula
49	284	Desoto County SD	Arcadia
50	251	Wakulla County SD	Crawfordville
51	241	Bradford County SD	Starke
52	240	Baker County SD	Macclenny
53	225	Washington County SD	Chipley
54	212	Taylor County SD	Perry
55	204	Holmes County SD	Bonifay
56	173	Madison County SD	Madison
57	154	Gilchrist County SD	Trenton
58	153	Union County SD	Lake Butler
59	147	Calhoun County SD	Blountstown
60	130	Gulf County SD	Port Saint Joe
61	128	Dixie County SD	Cross City
61	128	Hamilton County SD	Jasper
63	103	Jefferson County SD	Monticello

Number of Students

Rank	Number	District Name	City
1	373,395	Dade County SD	Miami
2	267,925	Broward County SD	Fort Lauderdale
3	175,454	Hillsborough County SD	Tampa
4	164,896	Palm Beach County SD	West Palm Beach
5	158,718	Orange County SD	Orlando
6	128,126	Duval County SD	Jacksonville
7	114,772	Pinellas County SD	Largo
8	82,179	Polk County SD	Bartow
9	72,601	Brevard County SD	Viera
10	63,446	Seminole County SD	Sanford
11	63,172	Lee County SD	Fort Myers
12	63,000	Volusia County SD	Deland
13	54,957	Pasco County SD	Land O' Lakes
14	44,019	Escambia County SD	Pensacola
15	40,485	Osceola County SD	Kissimmee
16	39,710	Marion County SD	Ocala
17	39,132	Manatee County SD	Bradenton
18	38,110	Collier County SD	Naples
19	38,057	Sarasota County SD	Sarasota
20	31,857	Leon County SD	Tallahassee
21	31,782	Lake County SD	Tavares
22	31,554	Saint Lucie County SD	Fort Pierce
23	31,291	Okaloosa County SD	Ft Walton Beach
24	29,861	Clay County SD	Green Cove Spgs
25	29,345	Alachua County SD	Gainesville
26	26,440	Bay County SD	Panama City
27	23,645	Santa Rosa County SD	Milton
28	21,975	Saint Johns County SD	Saint Augustine
29	18,605	Hernando County SD	Brooksville
30	17,714	Charlotte County SD	Port Charlotte
31	17,259	Martin County SD	Stuart
32	15,986	Indian River County SD	Vero Beach
33	15,355	Citrus County SD	Inverness
34	12,483	Putnam County SD	Palatka
35	11,428	Highlands County SD	Sebring
36	10,533	Nassau County SD	Fernandina Bch
37	9,707	Columbia County SD	Lake City
38	9,218	Monroe County SD	Key West
39	7,673	Hendry County SD	La Belle
40	7,601	Flagler County SD	Bunnell
41	7,245	Jackson County SD	Marianna
42	7,196	Gadsden County SD	Quincy
43	7,085	Okeechobee County SD	Okeechobee
44	6,558	Sumter County SD	Bushnell
45	6,303	Walton County SD	Defuniak Spgs
46	6,113	Levy County SD	Bronson
47	5,802	Suwannee County SD	Live Oak
48	5,175	Hardee County SD	Wauchula
49	4,916	Desoto County SD	Arcadia
50	4,663	Wakulla County SD	Crawfordville
51	4,525	Baker County SD	Macclenny
52	4,034	Bradford County SD	Starke
53	3,593	Taylor County SD	Perry
54	3,414	Holmes County SD	Bonifay
55	3,410	Washington County SD	Chipley
56	3,311	Madison County SD	Madison
57	2,734	Gilchrist County SD	Trenton
58	2,229	Dixie County SD	Cross City
59	2,174	Calhoun County SD	Blountstown
59	2,174	Union County SD	Lake Butler
61	2,164	Gulf County SD	Port Saint Joe
62	2,065	Hamilton County SD	Jasper
63	1,575	Jefferson County SD	Monticello

Male Students

Rank	Percent	District Name	City
1	54.8	Madison County SD	Madison
2	53.4	Desoto County SD	Arcadia
3	53.0	Suwannee County SD	Live Oak
3	53.0	Union County SD	Lake Butler
5	52.9	Hardee County SD	Wauchula
5	52.9	Putnam County SD	Palatka
7	52.8	Monroe County SD	Key West
8	52.5	Holmes County SD	Bonifay
9	52.3	Baker County SD	Macclenny
9	52.3	Walton County SD	Defuniak Spgs
11	52.1	Okaloosa County SD	Ft Walton Beach
11	52.1	Polk County SD	Bartow
11	52.1	Wakulla County SD	Crawfordville
14	52.0	Bradford County SD	Starke
14	52.0	Hendry County SD	La Belle
14	52.0	Okeechobee County SD	Okeechobee
14	52.0	Santa Rosa County SD	Milton
18	51.9	Citrus County SD	Inverness
18	51.9	Gulf County SD	Port Saint Joe
18	51.9	Highlands County SD	Sebring
18	51.9	Levy County SD	Bronson
18	51.9	Nassau County SD	Fernandina Bch
23	51.8	Saint Johns County SD	Saint Augustine
24	51.7	Broward County SD	Fort Lauderdale
24	51.7	Dixie County SD	Cross City
24	51.7	Manatee County SD	Bradenton
24	51.7	Marion County SD	Ocala
24	51.7	Washington County SD	Chipley
29	51.6	Brevard County SD	Viera
29	51.6	Orange County SD	Orlando
29	51.6	Pasco County SD	Land O' Lakes
29	51.6	Volusia County SD	Deland
33	51.5	Bay County SD	Panama City
33	51.5	Collier County SD	Naples
33	51.5	Osceola County SD	Kissimmee
33	51.5	Palm Beach County SD	West Palm Beach
33	51.5	Pinellas County SD	Largo
38	51.4	Clay County SD	Green Cove Spgs
38	51.4	Flagler County SD	Bunnell
38	51.4	Lee County SD	Fort Myers
38	51.4	Martin County SD	Stuart
42	51.3	Dade County SD	Miami
42	51.3	Hillsborough County SD	Tampa
42	51.3	Jackson County SD	Marianna
42	51.3	Seminole County SD	Sanford
42	51.3	Taylor County SD	Perry
47	51.2	Columbia County SD	Lake City
47	51.2	Escambia County SD	Pensacola
47	51.2	Gilchrist County SD	Trenton
47	51.2	Indian River County SD	Vero Beach
47	51.2	Jefferson County SD	Monticello
47	51.2	Lake County SD	Tavares
47	51.2	Leon County SD	Tallahassee
47	51.2	Sarasota County SD	Sarasota
47	51.2	Sumter County SD	Bushnell
56	51.1	Calhoun County SD	Blountstown
57	51.0	Charlotte County SD	Port Charlotte
57	51.0	Hernando County SD	Brooksville
57	51.0	Saint Lucie County SD	Fort Pierce
60	50.8	Duval County SD	Jacksonville
60	50.8	Gadsden County SD	Quincy
60	50.8	Hamilton County SD	Jasper
63	50.5	Alachua County SD	Gainesville

Female Students

Rank	Percent	District Name	City
1	49.5	Alachua County SD	Gainesville
2	49.2	Duval County SD	Jacksonville
2	49.2	Gadsden County SD	Quincy
2	49.2	Hamilton County SD	Jasper
5	49.0	Charlotte County SD	Port Charlotte
5	49.0	Hernando County SD	Brooksville
5	49.0	Saint Lucie County SD	Fort Pierce
8	48.9	Calhoun County SD	Blountstown

9	48.8	Columbia County SD	Lake City
9	48.8	Escambia County SD	Pensacola
9	48.8	Gilchrist County SD	Trenton
9	48.8	Indian River County SD	Vero Beach
9	48.8	Jefferson County SD	Monticello
9	48.8	Lake County SD	Tavares
9	48.8	Leon County SD	Tallahassee
9	48.8	Sarasota County SD	Sarasota
9	48.8	Sumter County SD	Bushnell
18	48.7	Dade County SD	Miami
18	48.7	Hillsborough County SD	Tampa
18	48.7	Jackson County SD	Marianna
18	48.7	Seminole County SD	Sanford
18	48.7	Taylor County SD	Perry
23	48.6	Clay County SD	Green Cove Spgs
23	48.6	Flagler County SD	Bunnell
23	48.6	Lee County SD	Fort Myers
23	48.6	Martin County SD	Stuart
27	48.5	Bay County SD	Panama City
27	48.5	Collier County SD	Naples
27	48.5	Osceola County SD	Kissimmee
27	48.5	Palm Beach County SD	West Palm Beach
27	48.5	Pinellas County SD	Largo
32	48.4	Brevard County SD	Viera
32	48.4	Orange County SD	Orlando
32	48.4	Pasco County SD	Land O' Lakes
32	48.4	Volusia County SD	Deland
36	48.3	Broward County SD	Fort Lauderdale
36	48.3	Dixie County SD	Cross City
36	48.3	Manatee County SD	Bradenton
36	48.3	Marion County SD	Ocala
36	48.3	Washington County SD	Chipley
41	48.2	Saint Johns County SD	Saint Augustine
42	48.1	Citrus County SD	Inverness
42	48.1	Gulf County SD	Port Saint Joe
42	48.1	Highlands County SD	Sebring
42	48.1	Levy County SD	Bronson
42	48.1	Nassau County SD	Fernandina Bch
47	48.0	Bradford County SD	Starke
47	48.0	Hendry County SD	La Belle
47	48.0	Okeechobee County SD	Okeechobee
47	48.0	Santa Rosa County SD	Milton
51	47.9	Okaloosa County SD	Ft Walton Beach
51	47.9	Polk County SD	Bartow
51	47.9	Wakulla County SD	Crawfordville
54	47.7	Baker County SD	Macclenny
54	47.7	Walton County SD	Defuniak Spgs
56	47.5	Holmes County SD	Bonifay
57	47.2	Monroe County SD	Key West
58	47.1	Hardee County SD	Wauchula
58	47.1	Putnam County SD	Palatka
60	47.0	Suwannee County SD	Live Oak
60	47.0	Union County SD	Lake Butler
62	46.6	Desoto County SD	Arcadia
63	45.2	Madison County SD	Madison

Individual Education Program Students

Rank	Percent	District Name	City
1	26.0	Jefferson County SD	Monticello
2	25.4	Madison County SD	Madison
3	23.7	Gilchrist County SD	Trenton
4	23.4	Bradford County SD	Starke
5	23.3	Dixie County SD	Cross City
6	23.2	Levy County SD	Bronson
7	21.0	Hardee County SD	Wauchula
7	21.0	Okeechobee County SD	Okeechobee
9	20.8	Desoto County SD	Arcadia
10	20.7	Calhoun County SD	Blountstown
11	20.3	Jackson County SD	Marianna
11	20.3	Leon County SD	Tallahassee
13	19.5	Clay County SD	Green Cove Spgs
13	19.5	Manatee County SD	Bradenton
15	19.4	Charlotte County SD	Port Charlotte
15	19.4	Pasco County SD	Land O' Lakes
17	19.3	Bay County SD	Panama City
18	19.2	Alachua County SD	Gainesville
19	19.1	Citrus County SD	Inverness
20	19.0	Wakulla County SD	Crawfordville
21	18.9	Taylor County SD	Perry
22	18.3	Sumter County SD	Bushnell
23	18.2	Columbia County SD	Lake City
23	18.2	Highlands County SD	Sebring
23	18.2	Putnam County SD	Palatka
26	18.1	Gadsden County SD	Quincy
27	17.9	Hamilton County SD	Jasper
28	17.7	Hendry County SD	La Belle
28	17.7	Pinellas County SD	Largo
30	17.5	Marion County SD	Ocala
31	17.4	Monroe County SD	Key West
31	17.4	Volusia County SD	Deland
33	17.2	Flagler County SD	Bunnell
33	17.2	Hernando County SD	Brooksville
33	17.2	Union County SD	Lake Butler
36	17.1	Sarasota County SD	Sarasota
37	17.0	Lake County SD	Tavares
37	17.0	Martin County SD	Stuart
39	16.9	Escambia County SD	Pensacola
40	16.8	Brevard County SD	Viera
40	16.8	Gulf County SD	Port Saint Joe
42	16.3	Santa Rosa County SD	Milton
43	16.2	Orange County SD	Orlando
44	16.0	Holmes County SD	Bonifay
44	16.0	Okaloosa County SD	Ft Walton Beach
46	15.9	Nassau County SD	Fernandina Bch
46	15.9	Saint Johns County SD	Saint Augustine
46	15.9	Walton County SD	Defuniak Spgs
46	15.9	Washington County SD	Chipley
50	15.8	Duval County SD	Jacksonville
51	15.5	Collier County SD	Naples
51	15.5	Hillsborough County SD	Tampa
51	15.5	Lee County SD	Fort Myers
51	15.5	Polk County SD	Bartow
55	15.3	Osceola County SD	Kissimmee
56	14.7	Indian River County SD	Vero Beach
57	14.5	Palm Beach County SD	West Palm Beach
58	14.4	Saint Lucie County SD	Fort Pierce
59	14.0	Suwannee County SD	Live Oak
60	12.8	Baker County SD	Macclenny
60	12.8	Seminole County SD	Sanford
62	11.6	Dade County SD	Miami
63	11.4	Broward County SD	Fort Lauderdale

English Language Learner Students

Rank	Percent	District Name	City
1	17.7	Dade County SD	Miami
2	16.1	Osceola County SD	Kissimmee
3	14.7	Collier County SD	Naples
4	12.4	Orange County SD	Orlando
5	11.2	Broward County SD	Fort Lauderdale
6	11.0	Palm Beach County SD	West Palm Beach
7	10.6	Lee County SD	Fort Myers
8	10.3	Hillsborough County SD	Tampa
9	9.7	Hardee County SD	Wauchula
10	8.8	Martin County SD	Stuart
11	7.8	Hendry County SD	La Belle
12	7.4	Desoto County SD	Arcadia
13	6.5	Manatee County SD	Bradenton
14	6.3	Monroe County SD	Key West
15	6.1	Okeechobee County SD	Okeechobee
16	5.6	Saint Lucie County SD	Fort Pierce
17	5.4	Gadsden County SD	Quincy
18	4.6	Polk County SD	Bartow
19	4.1	Indian River County SD	Vero Beach
19	4.1	Sarasota County SD	Sarasota
21	3.9	Highlands County SD	Sebring
22	3.7	Sumter County SD	Bushnell
23	3.6	Putnam County SD	Palatka
24	3.4	Lake County SD	Tavares
25	3.1	Seminole County SD	Sanford
26	3.0	Pasco County SD	Land O' Lakes
26	3.0	Volusia County SD	Deland
28	2.8	Hamilton County SD	Jasper
29	2.6	Flagler County SD	Bunnell
30	2.5	Pinellas County SD	Largo
31	2.3	Levy County SD	Bronson
31	2.3	Marion County SD	Ocala
33	2.0	Duval County SD	Jacksonville
34	1.7	Suwannee County SD	Live Oak
35	1.5	Alachua County SD	Gainesville
36	1.3	Brevard County SD	Viera
36	1.3	Hernando County SD	Brooksville
38	1.2	Walton County SD	Defuniak Spgs
39	0.9	Charlotte County SD	Port Charlotte
39	0.9	Leon County SD	Tallahassee
41	0.8	Bay County SD	Panama City
42	0.7	Clay County SD	Green Cove Spgs
42	0.7	Escambia County SD	Pensacola
42	0.7	Saint Johns County SD	Saint Augustine
45	0.6	Bradford County SD	Starke
45	0.6	Citrus County SD	Inverness
45	0.6	Jackson County SD	Marianna
48	0.5	Okaloosa County SD	Ft Walton Beach
49	0.4	Gilchrist County SD	Trenton
50	0.3	Columbia County SD	Lake City
51	0.2	Madison County SD	Madison
51	0.2	Nassau County SD	Fernandina Bch
51	0.2	Santa Rosa County SD	Milton
51	0.2	Wakulla County SD	Crawfordville
55	0.1	Calhoun County SD	Blountstown
55	0.1	Gulf County SD	Port Saint Joe
55	0.1	Jefferson County SD	Monticello
55	0.1	Taylor County SD	Perry
55	0.1	Union County SD	Lake Butler
60	0.0	Baker County SD	Macclenny
61	0.0	Dixie County SD	Cross City
61	0.0	Holmes County SD	Bonifay
61	0.0	Washington County SD	Chipley

Migrant Students

Rank	Percent	District Name	City
1	40.0	Hardee County SD	Wauchula
2	35.8	Hendry County SD	La Belle
3	23.5	Collier County SD	Naples
4	17.4	Okeechobee County SD	Okeechobee
5	13.9	Desoto County SD	Arcadia
6	13.1	Saint Lucie County SD	Fort Pierce
7	11.3	Highlands County SD	Sebring
8	7.4	Gadsden County SD	Quincy
9	5.7	Indian River County SD	Vero Beach
10	4.5	Sumter County SD	Bushnell
11	4.1	Levy County SD	Bronson
11	4.1	Manatee County SD	Bradenton
13	3.8	Dixie County SD	Cross City
13	3.8	Gilchrist County SD	Trenton
15	3.4	Hamilton County SD	Jasper
15	3.4	Palm Beach County SD	West Palm Beach
17	3.0	Putnam County SD	Palatka
18	2.9	Hillsborough County SD	Tampa
19	2.4	Polk County SD	Bartow
19	2.4	Suwannee County SD	Live Oak
21	2.3	Lee County SD	Fort Myers
22	1.8	Martin County SD	Stuart
22	1.8	Volusia County SD	Deland
24	1.3	Lake County SD	Tavares
25	1.0	Holmes County SD	Bonifay
25	1.0	Orange County SD	Orlando
25	1.0	Pasco County SD	Land O' Lakes
28	0.9	Escambia County SD	Pensacola
29	0.8	Union County SD	Lake Butler
30	0.7	Calhoun County SD	Blountstown
30	0.7	Dade County SD	Miami
32	0.6	Madison County SD	Madison
33	0.5	Bay County SD	Panama City
33	0.5	Clay County SD	Green Cove Spgs
35	0.4	Broward County SD	Fort Lauderdale
35	0.4	Citrus County SD	Inverness
35	0.4	Walton County SD	Defuniak Spgs
38	0.3	Baker County SD	Macclenny
38	0.3	Columbia County SD	Lake City
38	0.3	Flagler County SD	Bunnell
38	0.3	Jackson County SD	Marianna
38	0.3	Jefferson County SD	Monticello
38	0.3	Monroe County SD	Key West
38	0.3	Nassau County SD	Fernandina Bch
38	0.3	Osceola County SD	Kissimmee
38	0.3	Sarasota County SD	Sarasota
47	0.2	Alachua County SD	Gainesville
47	0.2	Bradford County SD	Starke
47	0.2	Duval County SD	Jacksonville
47	0.2	Marion County SD	Ocala
51	0.1	Brevard County SD	Viera
51	0.1	Saint Johns County SD	Saint Augustine
53	0.0	Leon County SD	Tallahassee
53	0.0	Okaloosa County SD	Ft Walton Beach
53	0.0	Santa Rosa County SD	Milton
53	0.0	Taylor County SD	Perry
53	0.0	Washington County SD	Chipley
58	0.0	Charlotte County SD	Port Charlotte
58	0.0	Gulf County SD	Port Saint Joe
58	0.0	Hernando County SD	Brooksville
58	0.0	Pinellas County SD	Largo
58	0.0	Seminole County SD	Sanford
58	0.0	Wakulla County SD	Crawfordville

Students Eligible for Free Lunch

Rank	Percent	District Name	City
1	65.9	Gadsden County SD	Quincy
2	62.8	Hamilton County SD	Jasper
2	62.8	Jefferson County SD	Monticello
4	61.3	Hendry County SD	La Belle
5	60.4	Hardee County SD	Wauchula
6	55.2	Dixie County SD	Cross City
7	55.0	Putnam County SD	Palatka
8	54.9	Madison County SD	Madison
9	53.6	Dade County SD	Miami
10	51.3	Desoto County SD	Arcadia
11	48.5	Washington County SD	Chipley
12	47.3	Highlands County SD	Sebring
13	46.9	Sumter County SD	Bushnell
14	46.4	Levy County SD	Bronson
15	46.1	Escambia County SD	Pensacola
16	45.8	Taylor County SD	Perry
17	45.0	Okeechobee County SD	Okeechobee
18	44.8	Bradford County SD	Starke
19	44.5	Polk County SD	Bartow

20	44.0	Columbia County SD	Lake City
20	44.0	Saint Lucie County SD	Fort Pierce
22	43.1	Jackson County SD	Marianna
23	42.1	Holmes County SD	Bonifay
24	41.9	Marion County SD	Ocala
25	41.6	Alachua County SD	Gainesville
25	41.6	Gilchrist County SD	Trenton
27	41.1	Suwannee County SD	Live Oak
28	39.6	Hillsborough County SD	Tampa
29	39.4	Osceola County SD	Kissimmee
30	38.5	Calhoun County SD	Blountstown
30	38.5	Walton County SD	Defuniak Spgs
32	36.7	Union County SD	Lake Butler
33	36.4	Lee County SD	Fort Myers
34	35.5	Bay County SD	Panama City
35	35.2	Gulf County SD	Port Saint Joe
36	34.8	Pasco County SD	Land O' Lakes
37	34.7	Palm Beach County SD	West Palm Beach
38	34.0	Orange County SD	Orlando
39	33.3	Manatee County SD	Bradenton
40	33.0	Hernando County SD	Brooksville
41	32.6	Duval County SD	Jacksonville
42	32.5	Citrus County SD	Inverness
43	32.0	Baker County SD	Macclenny
44	31.7	Lake County SD	Tavares
45	31.1	Broward County SD	Fort Lauderdale
46	30.7	Charlotte County SD	Port Charlotte
47	30.3	Volusia County SD	Deland
48	30.1	Indian River County SD	Vero Beach
49	29.6	Pinellas County SD	Largo
50	28.4	Monroe County SD	Key West
51	27.7	Flagler County SD	Bunnell
52	27.4	Leon County SD	Tallahassee
53	26.5	Martin County SD	Stuart
54	25.8	Wakulla County SD	Crawfordville
55	24.9	Nassau County SD	Fernandina Bch
56	24.6	Sarasota County SD	Sarasota
57	22.8	Santa Rosa County SD	Milton
58	21.7	Brevard County SD	Viera
59	21.3	Seminole County SD	Sanford
60	20.0	Okaloosa County SD	Ft Walton Beach
61	16.9	Collier County SD	Naples
62	16.8	Clay County SD	Green Cove Spgs
63	15.3	Saint Johns County SD	Saint Augustine

Students Eligible for Reduced-Price Lunch

Rank	Percent	District Name	City
1	13.7	Charlotte County SD	Port Charlotte
2	13.6	Holmes County SD	Bonifay
3	13.0	Gilchrist County SD	Trenton
4	12.9	Osceola County SD	Kissimmee
5	12.1	Columbia County SD	Lake City
5	12.1	Jackson County SD	Marianna
7	12.0	Bradford County SD	Starke
8	11.6	Gulf County SD	Port Saint Joe
9	11.5	Walton County SD	Defuniak Spgs
10	11.4	Marion County SD	Ocala
10	11.4	Pasco County SD	Land O' Lakes
12	11.3	Calhoun County SD	Blountstown
12	11.3	Escambia County SD	Pensacola
14	11.2	Bay County SD	Panama City
15	11.0	Hendry County SD	La Belle
15	11.0	Hernando County SD	Brooksville
15	11.0	Lee County SD	Fort Myers
18	10.6	Highlands County SD	Sebring
19	10.5	Washington County SD	Chipley
20	10.4	Citrus County SD	Inverness
20	10.4	Levy County SD	Bronson
22	10.3	Sumter County SD	Bushnell
23	10.1	Flagler County SD	Bunnell
23	10.1	Polk County SD	Bartow
23	10.1	Saint Lucie County SD	Fort Pierce
26	9.7	Hamilton County SD	Jasper
26	9.7	Jefferson County SD	Monticello
26	9.7	Okeechobee County SD	Okeechobee
26	9.7	Putnam County SD	Palatka
30	9.6	Desoto County SD	Arcadia
30	9.6	Dixie County SD	Cross City
30	9.6	Gadsden County SD	Quincy
33	9.5	Suwannee County SD	Live Oak
34	9.4	Santa Rosa County SD	Milton
35	9.3	Hillsborough County SD	Tampa
35	9.3	Sarasota County SD	Sarasota
37	9.2	Duval County SD	Jacksonville
37	9.2	Madison County SD	Madison
39	9.1	Nassau County SD	Fernandina Bch
40	8.9	Alachua County SD	Gainesville
40	8.9	Monroe County SD	Key West
40	8.9	Orange County SD	Orlando
43	8.8	Pinellas County SD	Largo
44	8.7	Wakulla County SD	Crawfordville
45	8.5	Baker County SD	Macclenny
45	8.5	Lake County SD	Tavares
47	8.2	Dade County SD	Miami
47	8.2	Okaloosa County SD	Ft Walton Beach
47	8.2	Volusia County SD	Deland
50	8.1	Broward County SD	Fort Lauderdale
51	8.0	Taylor County SD	Perry
52	7.7	Manatee County SD	Bradenton
52	7.7	Union County SD	Lake Butler
54	7.6	Seminole County SD	Sanford
55	7.4	Clay County SD	Green Cove Spgs
56	7.3	Hardee County SD	Wauchula
57	7.2	Indian River County SD	Vero Beach
58	6.6	Palm Beach County SD	West Palm Beach
59	6.2	Brevard County SD	Viera
60	6.0	Martin County SD	Stuart
61	5.9	Leon County SD	Tallahassee
62	5.8	Collier County SD	Naples
63	4.9	Saint Johns County SD	Saint Augustine

Student/Teacher Ratio

Rank	Ratio	District Name	City
1	40.7	Indian River County SD	Vero Beach
2	21.8	Osceola County SD	Kissimmee
3	20.6	Hendry County SD	La Belle
4	20.2	Broward County SD	Fort Lauderdale
5	20.0	Dade County SD	Miami
6	19.7	Lee County SD	Fort Myers
7	19.6	Okaloosa County SD	Ft Walton Beach
8	19.4	Duval County SD	Jacksonville
9	19.2	Charlotte County SD	Port Charlotte
9	19.2	Nassau County SD	Fernandina Bch
9	19.2	Santa Rosa County SD	Milton
12	19.1	Madison County SD	Madison
13	18.9	Baker County SD	Macclenny
14	18.8	Suwannee County SD	Live Oak
15	18.7	Palm Beach County SD	West Palm Beach
16	18.6	Leon County SD	Tallahassee
16	18.6	Martin County SD	Stuart
16	18.6	Seminole County SD	Sanford
16	18.6	Wakulla County SD	Crawfordville
20	18.4	Escambia County SD	Pensacola
20	18.4	Sumter County SD	Bushnell
22	18.3	Hernando County SD	Brooksville
23	18.1	Manatee County SD	Bradenton
23	18.1	Marion County SD	Ocala
23	18.1	Saint Johns County SD	Saint Augustine
26	18.0	Clay County SD	Green Cove Spgs
26	18.0	Pasco County SD	Land O' Lakes
28	17.8	Brevard County SD	Viera
28	17.8	Gilchrist County SD	Trenton
28	17.8	Sarasota County SD	Sarasota
28	17.8	Walton County SD	Defuniak Spgs
32	17.7	Alachua County SD	Gainesville
33	17.6	Collier County SD	Naples
33	17.6	Pinellas County SD	Largo
35	17.4	Dixie County SD	Cross City
35	17.4	Orange County SD	Orlando
37	17.3	Bay County SD	Panama City
37	17.3	Desoto County SD	Arcadia
37	17.3	Hardee County SD	Wauchula
40	17.1	Columbia County SD	Lake City
40	17.1	Gadsden County SD	Quincy
40	17.1	Okeechobee County SD	Okeechobee
40	17.1	Polk County SD	Bartow
40	17.1	Putnam County SD	Palatka
45	17.0	Highlands County SD	Sebring
46	16.9	Taylor County SD	Perry
47	16.8	Flagler County SD	Bunnell
48	16.7	Bradford County SD	Starke
48	16.7	Hillsborough County SD	Tampa
48	16.7	Holmes County SD	Bonifay
48	16.7	Levy County SD	Bronson
52	16.6	Citrus County SD	Inverness
52	16.6	Gulf County SD	Port Saint Joe
52	16.6	Jackson County SD	Marianna
55	16.5	Volusia County SD	Deland
56	16.1	Hamilton County SD	Jasper
57	15.8	Saint Lucie County SD	Fort Pierce
58	15.3	Jefferson County SD	Monticello
59	15.2	Washington County SD	Chipley
60	14.8	Calhoun County SD	Blountstown
61	14.4	Lake County SD	Tavares
62	14.2	Union County SD	Lake Butler
63	13.4	Monroe County SD	Key West

Student/Librarian Ratio

Rank	Ratio	District Name	City
1	2,664.3	Indian River County SD	Vero Beach
2	2,537.1	Sarasota County SD	Sarasota
3	2,229.0	Dixie County SD	Cross City
4	1,843.6	Monroe County SD	Key West
5	1,603.2	Orange County SD	Orlando
6	1,475.5	Seminole County SD	Sanford
7	1,344.1	Lee County SD	Fort Myers
8	1,266.8	Flagler County SD	Bunnell
9	1,265.2	Osceola County SD	Kissimmee
10	1,217.8	Broward County SD	Fort Lauderdale
11	1,103.7	Madison County SD	Madison
12	1,087.0	Union County SD	Lake Butler
13	1,077.8	Palm Beach County SD	West Palm Beach
14	1,060.8	Dade County SD	Miami
15	1,012.1	Okeechobee County SD	Okeechobee
16	972.6	Pinellas County SD	Largo
17	958.8	Martin County SD	Stuart
18	930.3	Hernando County SD	Brooksville
19	908.7	Duval County SD	Jacksonville
20	907.4	Collier County SD	Naples
21	900.0	Volusia County SD	Deland
22	898.3	Taylor County SD	Perry
23	869.6	Manatee County SD	Bradenton
24	869.2	Okaloosa County SD	Ft Walton Beach
25	863.3	Marion County SD	Ocala
26	852.8	Saint Lucie County SD	Fort Pierce
27	852.6	Hendry County SD	La Belle
28	843.5	Charlotte County SD	Port Charlotte
29	829.5	Clay County SD	Green Cove Spgs
30	828.9	Suwannee County SD	Live Oak
31	819.9	Hillsborough County SD	Tampa
32	819.3	Desoto County SD	Arcadia
33	816.3	Highlands County SD	Sebring
34	815.3	Santa Rosa County SD	Milton
35	813.9	Saint Johns County SD	Saint Augustine
36	808.9	Columbia County SD	Lake City
37	777.2	Wakulla County SD	Crawfordville
38	758.5	Leon County SD	Tallahassee
39	756.7	Lake County SD	Tavares
40	754.2	Baker County SD	Macclenny
41	752.8	Pasco County SD	Land O' Lakes
42	739.3	Hardee County SD	Wauchula
43	734.3	Putnam County SD	Palatka
44	731.2	Citrus County SD	Inverness
45	721.6	Escambia County SD	Pensacola
46	714.6	Polk County SD	Bartow
47	700.3	Walton County SD	Defuniak Spgs
48	683.5	Gilchrist County SD	Trenton
49	682.0	Washington County SD	Chipley
50	672.3	Bradford County SD	Starke
51	661.0	Bay County SD	Panama City
52	658.3	Nassau County SD	Fernandina Bch
53	631.3	Brevard County SD	Viera
54	603.8	Jackson County SD	Marianna
55	599.7	Gadsden County SD	Quincy
56	564.3	Alachua County SD	Gainesville
57	555.7	Levy County SD	Bronson
58	546.5	Sumter County SD	Bushnell
59	541.0	Gulf County SD	Port Saint Joe
60	525.0	Jefferson County SD	Monticello
61	516.3	Hamilton County SD	Jasper
62	487.7	Holmes County SD	Bonifay
63	362.3	Calhoun County SD	Blountstown

Student/Counselor Ratio

Rank	Ratio	District Name	City
1	1,453.3	Indian River County SD	Vero Beach
2	827.8	Madison County SD	Madison
3	724.7	Union County SD	Lake Butler
4	718.6	Taylor County SD	Perry
5	691.9	Sarasota County SD	Sarasota
6	614.5	Monroe County SD	Key West
7	582.9	Wakulla County SD	Crawfordville
8	582.1	Seminole County SD	Sanford
9	575.0	Hardee County SD	Wauchula
10	558.8	Okaloosa County SD	Ft Walton Beach
11	549.3	Lee County SD	Fort Myers
12	546.8	Broward County SD	Fort Lauderdale
13	546.2	Desoto County SD	Arcadia
14	540.6	Duval County SD	Jacksonville
15	525.3	Walton County SD	Defuniak Spgs
16	525.0	Jefferson County SD	Monticello
17	523.8	Orange County SD	Orlando
18	519.0	Osceola County SD	Kissimmee
19	509.1	Marion County SD	Ocala
20	504.5	Sumter County SD	Bushnell
21	504.3	Bradford County SD	Starke
22	502.8	Baker County SD	Macclenny
23	500.7	Brevard County SD	Viera
24	490.5	Pinellas County SD	Largo
25	485.4	Columbia County SD	Lake City
26	479.6	Hendry County SD	La Belle
27	478.8	Nassau County SD	Fernandina Bch
28	472.9	Santa Rosa County SD	Milton

29	472.3	Okeechobee County SD	Okeechobee
30	470.2	Levy County SD	Bronson
31	466.2	Charlotte County SD	Port Charlotte
32	463.4	Escambia County SD	Pensacola
33	454.0	Polk County SD	Bartow
34	449.8	Manatee County SD	Bradenton
35	448.7	Leon County SD	Tallahassee
36	445.8	Dixie County SD	Cross City
37	439.5	Highlands County SD	Sebring
38	431.7	Palm Beach County SD	West Palm Beach
39	431.5	Martin County SD	Stuart
40	430.9	Saint Johns County SD	Saint Augustine
41	426.5	Citrus County SD	Inverness
42	422.3	Flagler County SD	Bunnell
43	418.2	Lake County SD	Tavares
44	414.4	Suwannee County SD	Live Oak
45	413.2	Pasco County SD	Land O' Lakes
46	403.5	Clay County SD	Green Cove Spgs
47	403.3	Hillsborough County SD	Tampa
48	399.8	Gadsden County SD	Quincy
49	390.6	Gilchrist County SD	Trenton
50	389.6	Saint Lucie County SD	Fort Pierce
51	388.8	Bay County SD	Panama City
52	386.1	Alachua County SD	Gainesville
53	379.3	Holmes County SD	Bonifay
54	376.8	Dade County SD	Miami
55	356.7	Putnam County SD	Palatka
56	344.5	Hernando County SD	Brooksville
57	344.2	Hamilton County SD	Jasper
58	341.0	Washington County SD	Chipley
59	324.7	Volusia County SD	Deland
60	320.3	Collier County SD	Naples
61	309.1	Gulf County SD	Port Saint Joe
62	301.9	Jackson County SD	Marianna
63	271.8	Calhoun County SD	Blountstown

Current Spending per Student in FY2001

Rank	Dollars	District Name	City
1	7,570	Washington County SD	Chipley
2	7,151	Monroe County SD	Key West
3	7,130	Jefferson County SD	Monticello
4	6,931	Hamilton County SD	Jasper
5	6,690	Collier County SD	Naples
6	6,689	Gadsden County SD	Quincy
7	6,645	Gulf County SD	Port Saint Joe
8	6,606	Sarasota County SD	Sarasota
9	6,552	Dade County SD	Miami
10	6,411	Martin County SD	Stuart
11	6,326	Leon County SD	Tallahassee
12	6,285	Desoto County SD	Arcadia
13	6,266	Palm Beach County SD	West Palm Beach
14	6,243	Gilchrist County SD	Trenton
15	6,221	Sumter County SD	Bushnell
16	6,216	Dixie County SD	Cross City
17	6,193	Manatee County SD	Bradenton
18	6,186	Hardee County SD	Wauchula
19	6,161	Indian River County SD	Vero Beach
20	6,154	Saint Johns County SD	Saint Augustine
21	6,150	Pinellas County SD	Largo
22	6,147	Madison County SD	Madison
23	6,135	Hendry County SD	La Belle
24	6,108	Walton County SD	Defuniak Spgs
25	6,103	Levy County SD	Bronson
26	6,086	Jackson County SD	Marianna
27	6,078	Bradford County SD	Starke
28	6,073	Flagler County SD	Bunnell
29	6,070	Lee County SD	Fort Myers
30	6,064	Saint Lucie County SD	Fort Pierce
31	6,055	Hillsborough County SD	Tampa
32	6,038	Alachua County SD	Gainesville
33	6,030	Holmes County SD	Bonifay
34	6,012	Taylor County SD	Perry
35	6,001	Highlands County SD	Sebring
36	5,992	Bay County SD	Panama City
37	5,968	Charlotte County SD	Port Charlotte
38	5,882	Polk County SD	Bartow
39	5,869	Columbia County SD	Lake City
40	5,867	Putnam County SD	Palatka
41	5,865	Suwannee County SD	Live Oak
42	5,853	Broward County SD	Fort Lauderdale
43	5,813	Marion County SD	Ocala
44	5,810	Volusia County SD	Deland
45	5,801	Okeechobee County SD	Okeechobee
46	5,791	Citrus County SD	Inverness
47	5,789	Pasco County SD	Land O' Lakes
48	5,777	Wakulla County SD	Crawfordville
49	5,771	Santa Rosa County SD	Milton
50	5,757	Escambia County SD	Pensacola
51	5,721	Orange County SD	Orlando
52	5,711	Calhoun County SD	Blountstown
53	5,665	Duval County SD	Jacksonville
54	5,644	Okaloosa County SD	Ft Walton Beach
55	5,570	Brevard County SD	Viera
56	5,543	Baker County SD	Macclenny
56	5,543	Osceola County SD	Kissimmee
58	5,511	Seminole County SD	Sanford
59	5,474	Hernando County SD	Brooksville
60	5,468	Clay County SD	Green Cove Spgs
61	5,423	Lake County SD	Tavares
62	5,391	Nassau County SD	Fernandina Bch
63	5,348	Union County SD	Lake Butler

Number of Diploma Recipients

Rank	Number	District Name	City
1	16,638	Dade County SD	Miami
2	11,654	Broward County SD	Fort Lauderdale
3	7,968	Hillsborough County SD	Tampa
4	7,687	Palm Beach County SD	West Palm Beach
5	7,361	Orange County SD	Orlando
6	5,413	Pinellas County SD	Largo
7	5,260	Duval County SD	Jacksonville
8	3,815	Polk County SD	Bartow
9	3,578	Brevard County SD	Viera
10	3,420	Seminole County SD	Sanford
11	3,386	Volusia County SD	Deland
12	2,846	Lee County SD	Fort Myers
13	2,453	Pasco County SD	Land O' Lakes
14	2,320	Escambia County SD	Pensacola
15	1,978	Okaloosa County SD	Ft Walton Beach
16	1,960	Marion County SD	Ocala
17	1,895	Sarasota County SD	Sarasota
18	1,853	Osceola County SD	Kissimmee
19	1,788	Leon County SD	Tallahassee
20	1,711	Collier County SD	Naples
21	1,709	Manatee County SD	Bradenton
22	1,651	Alachua County SD	Gainesville
23	1,627	Clay County SD	Green Cove Spgs
24	1,531	Lake County SD	Tavares
25	1,333	Santa Rosa County SD	Milton
26	1,258	Saint Lucie County SD	Fort Pierce
27	1,230	Bay County SD	Panama City
28	1,097	Saint Johns County SD	Saint Augustine
29	1,076	Charlotte County SD	Port Charlotte
30	923	Hernando County SD	Brooksville
31	842	Martin County SD	Stuart
32	830	Citrus County SD	Inverness
33	821	Indian River County SD	Vero Beach
34	577	Nassau County SD	Fernandina Bch
35	561	Highlands County SD	Sebring
36	486	Monroe County SD	Key West
37	447	Putnam County SD	Palatka
38	441	Columbia County SD	Lake City
39	409	Jackson County SD	Marianna
40	385	Flagler County SD	Bunnell
41	346	Gadsden County SD	Quincy
42	339	Okeechobee County SD	Okeechobee
43	301	Levy County SD	Bronson
44	290	Hendry County SD	La Belle
45	284	Suwannee County SD	Live Oak
46	261	Sumter County SD	Bushnell
47	246	Walton County SD	Defuniak Spgs
48	233	Wakulla County SD	Crawfordville
49	223	Baker County SD	Macclenny
50	214	Bradford County SD	Starke
51	213	Hardee County SD	Wauchula
52	204	Desoto County SD	Arcadia
53	203	Holmes County SD	Bonifay
53	203	Taylor County SD	Perry
55	191	Washington County SD	Chipley
56	180	Madison County SD	Madison
57	150	Dixie County SD	Cross City
58	141	Gilchrist County SD	Trenton
59	129	Union County SD	Lake Butler
60	119	Hamilton County SD	Jasper
61	117	Gulf County SD	Port Saint Joe
62	106	Calhoun County SD	Blountstown
63	65	Jefferson County SD	Monticello

High School Drop-out Rate

Rank	Percent	District Name	City
1	9.7	Duval County SD	Jacksonville
2	8.4	Gadsden County SD	Quincy
3	7.9	Hardee County SD	Wauchula
4	7.2	Alachua County SD	Gainesville
5	7.1	Lee County SD	Fort Myers
6	6.9	Polk County SD	Bartow
7	6.8	Hendry County SD	La Belle
8	6.6	Madison County SD	Madison
9	6.3	Dade County SD	Miami
9	6.3	Highlands County SD	Sebring
11	6.0	Okeechobee County SD	Okeechobee
11	6.0	Suwannee County SD	Live Oak
13	5.9	Orange County SD	Orlando
14	5.5	Manatee County SD	Bradenton
14	5.5	Nassau County SD	Fernandina Bch
16	5.4	Pasco County SD	Land O' Lakes
17	5.2	Lake County SD	Tavares
17	5.2	Osceola County SD	Kissimmee
17	5.2	Walton County SD	Defuniak Spgs
20	5.0	Pinellas County SD	Largo
21	4.9	Baker County SD	Macclenny
21	4.9	Bradford County SD	Starke
21	4.9	Collier County SD	Naples
24	4.4	Marion County SD	Ocala
25	4.3	Desoto County SD	Arcadia
25	4.3	Levy County SD	Bronson
25	4.3	Okaloosa County SD	Ft Walton Beach
28	4.0	Charlotte County SD	Port Charlotte
28	4.0	Union County SD	Lake Butler
30	3.9	Gilchrist County SD	Trenton
31	3.5	Citrus County SD	Inverness
31	3.5	Jefferson County SD	Monticello
31	3.5	Leon County SD	Tallahassee
31	3.5	Sarasota County SD	Sarasota
35	3.4	Monroe County SD	Key West
36	3.3	Calhoun County SD	Blountstown
36	3.3	Sumter County SD	Bushnell
38	3.1	Hillsborough County SD	Tampa
39	3.0	Clay County SD	Green Cove Spgs
39	3.0	Dixie County SD	Cross City
39	3.0	Holmes County SD	Bonifay
39	3.0	Palm Beach County SD	West Palm Beach
43	2.9	Escambia County SD	Pensacola
43	2.9	Washington County SD	Chipley
45	2.8	Putnam County SD	Palatka
45	2.8	Saint Johns County SD	Saint Augustine
47	2.7	Indian River County SD	Vero Beach
47	2.7	Wakulla County SD	Crawfordville
49	2.6	Brevard County SD	Viera
50	2.5	Hamilton County SD	Jasper
51	2.4	Santa Rosa County SD	Milton
52	2.2	Flagler County SD	Bunnell
52	2.2	Hernando County SD	Brooksville
54	2.1	Saint Lucie County SD	Fort Pierce
54	2.1	Taylor County SD	Perry
56	2.0	Broward County SD	Fort Lauderdale
57	1.9	Bay County SD	Panama City
57	1.9	Columbia County SD	Lake City
59	1.8	Jackson County SD	Marianna
60	1.7	Volusia County SD	Deland
61	1.6	Gulf County SD	Port Saint Joe
62	1.0	Seminole County SD	Sanford
63	0.6	Martin County SD	Stuart

Georgia

Georgia Public School Educational Profile

Category	Value	Category	Value
Schools *(2002-2003)*	2,246	**Diploma Recipients** *(2002-2003)*	65,983
Instructional Level		White, Non-Hispanic	40,801
Primary	1,214	Black, Non-Hispanic	21,357
Middle	422	Asian/Pacific Islander	2,151
High	332	American Indian/Alaskan Native	81
Other Level	278	Hispanic	1,593
Curriculum		**High School Drop-out Rate** (%) *(2000-2001)*	7.2
Regular	2,041	White, Non-Hispanic	5.7
Special Education	29	Black, Non-Hispanic	9.4
Vocational	0	Asian/Pacific Islander	3.7
Alternative	176	American Indian/Alaskan Native	6.2
Type		Hispanic	9.4
Magnet	59	**Staff** *(2002-2003)*	197,944.0
Charter	48	Teachers	96,044.6
Title I Eligible	963	Average Salary ($)	45,414
School-wide Title I	736	Librarians/Media Specialists	2,141.7
Students *(2002-2003)*	1,496,012	Guidance Counselors	3,318.5
Gender (%)		**Ratios** *(2002-2003)*	
Male	51.2	Student/Teacher Ratio	15.6 to 1
Female	48.8	Student/Librarian Ratio	698.5 to 1
Race/Ethnicity (%)		Student/Counselor Ratio	450.8 to 1
White, Non-Hispanic	53.0	**Current Spending** *($ per student in FY 2001)*	7,380
Black, Non-Hispanic	38.2	Instruction	4,714
Asian/Pacific Islander	2.5	Support Services	2,287
American Indian/Alaskan Native	0.2	**College Entrance Exam Scores** *(2003)*	
Hispanic	6.2	Scholastic Aptitude Test (SAT)	
Classification (%)		Participation Rate (%)	66
Individual Education Program (IEP)	11.9	Mean SAT I Verbal Score	493
Migrant	0.6	Mean SAT I Math Score	491
English Language Learner (ELL)	4.7	American College Testing Program (ACT)	
Eligible for Free Lunch Program	36.7	Participation Rate (%)	22
Eligible for Reduced-Price Lunch Program	8.4	Average Composite Score	19.8

Note: *For an explanation of data, please refer to the User's Guide in the front of the book; n/a indicates data not available*

Georgia NAEP 2003 Test Scores

Reading			Mathematics		
Grade/Category	**Value**	**Rank**	**Grade/Category**	**Value**	**Rank**
4th Grade			**4th Grade**		
Average Proficiency	213.6 (1.3)	38/51	Average Proficiency	230.3 (1.0)	37/51
Proficiency by Gender/Race/Ethnicity			Proficiency by Gender/Race/Ethnicity		
Male	209.8 (1.4)	39/51	Male	231.3 (1.3)	38/51
Female	217.6 (1.5)	39/51	Female	229.2 (1.1)	38/51
White, Non-Hispanic	225.7 (1.4)	27/51	White, Non-Hispanic	241.1 (1.2)	30/51
Black, Non-Hispanic	198.7 (1.3)	23/42	Black, Non-Hispanic	217.1 (1.1)	15/42
Asian, Non-Hispanic	200.6 (3.5)	28/41	Asian, Non-Hispanic	219.3 (3.5)	28/43
American Indian, Non-Hispanic	232.7 (6.2)	6/25	American Indian, Non-Hispanic	247.6 (4.0)	13/26
Hispanic	n/a	n/a	Hispanic	n/a	n/a
Proficiency by Class Size			Proficiency by Class Size		
Less than 16 Students	185.7 (3.5)	41/45	Less than 16 Students	209.1 (2.7)	43/47
16 to 18 Students	*206.3 (3.9)*	38/48	16 to 18 Students	*220.9 (3.9)*	43/48
19 to 20 Students	209.6 (2.7)	41/50	19 to 20 Students	226.8 (3.3)	43/50
21 to 25 Students	219.0 (2.0)	35/51	21 to 25 Students	232.8 (1.6)	37/51
Greater than 25 Students	222.1 (3.7)	16/49	Greater than 25 Students	241.0 (3.1)	9/49
Percent Attaining Achievement Levels			Percent Attaining Achievement Levels		
Below Basic	41.1 (1.5)	12/51	Below Basic	28.4 (1.2)	13/51
Basic or Above	58.9 (1.5)	40/51	Basic or Above	71.6 (1.2)	39/51
Proficient or Above	26.6 (1.6)	38/51	Proficient or Above	26.9 (1.3)	37/51
Advanced or Above	6.4 (0.7)	33/51	Advanced or Above	3.5 (0.5)	24/51
8th Grade			**8th Grade**		
Average Proficiency	257.7 (1.1)	40/51	Average Proficiency	269.7 (1.2)	41/51
Proficiency by Gender/Race/Ethnicity			Proficiency by Gender/Race/Ethnicity		
Male	252.5 (1.2)	39/51	Male	270.4 (1.5)	41/51
Female	262.9 (1.3)	39/51	Female	269.0 (1.2)	41/51
White, Non-Hispanic	268.5 (1.3)	29/50	White, Non-Hispanic	283.8 (1.4)	35/50
Black, Non-Hispanic	243.8 (1.7)	22/41	Black, Non-Hispanic	250.1 (1.5)	25/41
Asian, Non-Hispanic	244.9 (3.9)	22/37	Asian, Non-Hispanic	262.4 (3.3)	13/37
American Indian, Non-Hispanic	264.5 (7.1)	16/23	American Indian, Non-Hispanic	285.8 (7.2)	14/23
Hispanic	n/a	n/a	Hispanic	n/a	n/a
Proficiency by Parents Highest Level of Ed.			Proficiency by Parents Highest Level of Ed.		
Did Not Finish High School	248.3 (2.8)	14/50	Did Not Finish High School	254.5 (2.2)	35/50
Graduated High School	248.0 (1.9)	45/50	Graduated High School	258.8 (1.6)	43/50
Some Education After High School	264.7 (1.4)	36/50	Some Education After High School	276.5 (1.8)	38/50
Graduated College	264.8 (1.5)	42/50	Graduated College	279.6 (1.5)	40/50
Percent Attaining Achievement Levels			Percent Attaining Achievement Levels		
Below Basic	30.6 (1.3)	13/51	Below Basic	40.6 (1.4)	11/51
Basic or Above	69.4 (1.3)	38/51	Basic or Above	59.4 (1.4)	41/51
Proficient or Above	26.1 (1.4)	38/51	Proficient or Above	21.5 (1.2)	39/51
Advanced or Above	1.5 (0.2)	47/51	Advanced or Above	4.0 (0.6)	37/51

***Note:** For an explanation of data, please refer to the User's Guide in the front of the book; values in italics indicate that the nature of the sample does not allow accurate determination of the variability of the statistic; n/a indicates data not available*

Appling County

Appling County

249 Blackshear Hwy • Baxley, GA 31513-1513
(912) 367-8600 • http://www.appling.k12.ga.us
Grade Span: PK-12; **Agency Type:** 1
Schools: 8
4 Primary; 1 Middle; 1 High; 2 Other Level
7 Regular; 0 Special Education; 0 Vocational; 1 Alternative
0 Magnet; 0 Charter; 3 Title I Eligible; 3 School-wide Title I
Students: 3,303 (51.7% male; 48.3% female)
Individual Education Program: 475 (14.4%);
English Language Learner: 80 (2.4%); Migrant: 194 (5.9%)
Eligible for Free Lunch Program: 1,595 (48.3%)
Eligible for Reduced-Price Lunch Program: 366 (11.1%)
Teachers: 210.4 (15.7 to 1)
Librarians/Media Specialists: 7.0 (471.9 to 1)
Guidance Counselors: 8.0 (412.9 to 1)
Current Spending: ($ per student per year):
Total: $7,612; Instruction: $4,693; Support Services: $2,518
Enrollment, Drop-out Rates and Diploma Recipients by Race/Ethnicity

Category	Total	White	Black	Asian	AIAN	Hisp.
Enrollment (%)	100.0	67.9	26.3	0.4	0.0	5.4
Drop-out Rate (%)	5.7	5.9	5.8	0.0	n/a	0.0
H.S. Diplomas (#)	178	128	47	1	0	2

Atkinson County

Atkinson County

506 Roberts Ave • Pearson, GA 31642-1642
(912) 422-7373 • http://www.atkinson.k12.ga.us/
Grade Span: PK-12; **Agency Type:** 1
Schools: 3
2 Primary; 0 Middle; 1 High; 0 Other Level
3 Regular; 0 Special Education; 0 Vocational; 0 Alternative
0 Magnet; 0 Charter; 2 Title I Eligible; 2 School-wide Title I
Students: 1,648 (51.6% male; 48.4% female)
Individual Education Program: 192 (11.7%);
English Language Learner: 158 (9.6%); Migrant: 272 (16.5%)
Eligible for Free Lunch Program: 1,076 (65.3%)
Eligible for Reduced-Price Lunch Program: 228 (13.8%)
Teachers: 101.8 (16.2 to 1)
Librarians/Media Specialists: 3.0 (549.3 to 1)
Guidance Counselors: 3.1 (531.6 to 1)
Current Spending: ($ per student per year):
Total: $6,545; Instruction: $4,035; Support Services: $2,052
Enrollment, Drop-out Rates and Diploma Recipients by Race/Ethnicity

Category	Total	White	Black	Asian	AIAN	Hisp.
Enrollment (%)	100.0	53.3	21.4	0.1	0.1	25.1
Drop-out Rate (%)	8.5	8.0	10.8	n/a	n/a	5.3
H.S. Diplomas (#)	53	42	6	0	0	5

Bacon County

Bacon County

601 N Pierce St • Alma, GA 31510-1510
(912) 632-7363 • http://www.bcraiders.com/
Grade Span: PK-12; **Agency Type:** 1
Schools: 4
2 Primary; 1 Middle; 1 High; 0 Other Level
4 Regular; 0 Special Education; 0 Vocational; 0 Alternative
0 Magnet; 0 Charter; 3 Title I Eligible; 3 School-wide Title I
Students: 1,900 (53.4% male; 46.6% female)
Individual Education Program: 279 (14.7%);
English Language Learner: 40 (2.1%); Migrant: 81 (4.3%)
Eligible for Free Lunch Program: 821 (43.2%)
Eligible for Reduced-Price Lunch Program: 174 (9.2%)
Teachers: 126.9 (15.0 to 1)
Librarians/Media Specialists: 3.0 (633.3 to 1)
Guidance Counselors: 3.0 (633.3 to 1)
Current Spending: ($ per student per year):
Total: $6,305; Instruction: $4,077; Support Services: $1,853
Enrollment, Drop-out Rates and Diploma Recipients by Race/Ethnicity

Category	Total	White	Black	Asian	AIAN	Hisp.
Enrollment (%)	100.0	73.8	23.4	0.2	0.0	2.6
Drop-out Rate (%)	9.8	7.7	16.2	n/a	n/a	50.0
H.S. Diplomas (#)	76	58	18	0	0	0

Baldwin County

Baldwin County

435 N Cobb St • Milledgeville, GA 31061-1061
(912) 478-4176 • http://www.baldwin-county-schools.com
Grade Span: PK-12; **Agency Type:** 1
Schools: 11
5 Primary; 1 Middle; 2 High; 3 Other Level
8 Regular; 0 Special Education; 0 Vocational; 3 Alternative
0 Magnet; 0 Charter; 6 Title I Eligible; 6 School-wide Title I
Students: 5,894 (50.3% male; 49.7% female)
Individual Education Program: 1,024 (17.4%);
English Language Learner: 33 (0.6%); Migrant: 0 (0.0%)
Eligible for Free Lunch Program: 2,916 (49.5%)
Eligible for Reduced-Price Lunch Program: 552 (9.4%)
Teachers: 425.0 (13.9 to 1)
Librarians/Media Specialists: 7.0 (842.0 to 1)
Guidance Counselors: 11.0 (535.8 to 1)
Current Spending: ($ per student per year):
Total: $6,911; Instruction: $4,427; Support Services: $2,101
Enrollment, Drop-out Rates and Diploma Recipients by Race/Ethnicity

Category	Total	White	Black	Asian	AIAN	Hisp.
Enrollment (%)	100.0	35.4	62.2	1.2	0.1	1.1
Drop-out Rate (%)	5.3	6.2	4.9	0.0	n/a	50.0
H.S. Diplomas (#)	238	98	132	8	0	0

Banks County

Banks County

102 Hwy 51 S • Homer, GA 30547-0547
(706) 677-2224 • http://www.banks.k12.ga.us
Grade Span: PK-12; **Agency Type:** 1
Schools: 5
2 Primary; 2 Middle; 1 High; 0 Other Level
5 Regular; 0 Special Education; 0 Vocational; 0 Alternative
0 Magnet; 0 Charter; 4 Title I Eligible; 0 School-wide Title I
Students: 2,428 (51.9% male; 48.1% female)
Individual Education Program: 306 (12.6%);
English Language Learner: 70 (2.9%); Migrant: 7 (0.3%)
Eligible for Free Lunch Program: 984 (40.5%)
Eligible for Reduced-Price Lunch Program: 349 (14.4%)
Teachers: 150.2 (16.2 to 1)
Librarians/Media Specialists: 4.0 (607.0 to 1)
Guidance Counselors: 6.0 (404.7 to 1)
Current Spending: ($ per student per year):
Total: $5,924; Instruction: $3,723; Support Services: $1,802
Enrollment, Drop-out Rates and Diploma Recipients by Race/Ethnicity

Category	Total	White	Black	Asian	AIAN	Hisp.
Enrollment (%)	100.0	90.0	3.1	1.3	0.0	5.6
Drop-out Rate (%)	7.7	7.6	3.8	33.3	n/a	14.3
H.S. Diplomas (#)	94	90	1	1	0	2

Barrow County

Barrow County

179 W Athens St • Winder, GA 30680-0680
Mailing Address: PO Box 767 • Winder, GA 30680-0680
(770) 867-4527 • http://www.barrow.k12.ga.us
Grade Span: PK-12; **Agency Type:** 1
Schools: 15
8 Primary; 3 Middle; 2 High; 2 Other Level
15 Regular; 0 Special Education; 0 Vocational; 0 Alternative
0 Magnet; 0 Charter; 5 Title I Eligible; 4 School-wide Title I
Students: 9,362 (52.2% male; 47.8% female)
Individual Education Program: 1,539 (16.4%);
English Language Learner: 401 (4.3%); Migrant: 21 (0.2%)
Eligible for Free Lunch Program: 2,486 (26.6%)
Eligible for Reduced-Price Lunch Program: 845 (9.0%)
Teachers: 613.1 (15.3 to 1)
Librarians/Media Specialists: 14.0 (668.7 to 1)
Guidance Counselors: 19.0 (492.7 to 1)
Current Spending: ($ per student per year):
Total: $7,214; Instruction: $4,649; Support Services: $2,237
Enrollment, Drop-out Rates and Diploma Recipients by Race/Ethnicity

Category	Total	White	Black	Asian	AIAN	Hisp.
Enrollment (%)	100.0	77.2	12.4	5.8	0.1	4.5
Drop-out Rate (%)	7.3	7.1	8.4	5.6	n/a	14.0
H.S. Diplomas (#)	350	288	45	14	0	3

Bartow County

Bartow County

65 Gilreath Road, NW • Cartersville, GA 30120-0120
(770) 606-5800 • http://www.bartow.k12.ga.us
Grade Span: PK-12; **Agency Type:** 1
Schools: 20
11 Primary; 4 Middle; 3 High; 2 Other Level
19 Regular; 0 Special Education; 0 Vocational; 1 Alternative
2 Magnet; 8 Charter; 6 Title I Eligible; 2 School-wide Title I
Students: 13,339 (51.4% male; 48.6% female)
Individual Education Program: 1,954 (14.6%);
English Language Learner: 206 (1.5%); Migrant: 0 (0.0%)

Eligible for Free Lunch Program: 3,649 (27.4%)
Eligible for Reduced-Price Lunch Program: 1,269 (9.5%)
Teachers: 867.8 (15.4 to 1)
Librarians/Media Specialists: 20.0 (667.0 to 1)
Guidance Counselors: 28.1 (474.7 to 1)
Current Spending: ($ per student per year):
Total: $6,509; Instruction: $4,175; Support Services: $1,968
Enrollment, Drop-out Rates and Diploma Recipients by Race/Ethnicity

Category	Total	White	Black	Asian	AIAN	Hisp.
Enrollment (%)	100.0	87.2	8.0	0.2	0.5	4.0
Drop-out Rate (%)	9.3	9.6	7.3	0.0	0.0	6.5
H.S. Diplomas (#)	485	422	48	3	5	7

Cartersville City

310 Old Mill Rd • Cartersville, GA 30120-0120
(770) 387-7491 • http://www.cartersville.k12.ga.us
Grade Span: PK-12; **Agency Type:** 1
Schools: 4
2 Primary; 1 Middle; 1 High; 0 Other Level
4 Regular; 0 Special Education; 0 Vocational; 0 Alternative
0 Magnet; 4 Charter; 3 Title I Eligible; 0 School-wide Title I
Students: 3,940 (51.4% male; 48.6% female)
Individual Education Program: 318 (8.1%);
English Language Learner: 392 (9.9%); Migrant: 0 (0.0%)
Eligible for Free Lunch Program: 1,124 (28.5%)
Eligible for Reduced-Price Lunch Program: 342 (8.7%)
Teachers: 226.5 (17.4 to 1)
Librarians/Media Specialists: 4.0 (985.0 to 1)
Guidance Counselors: 8.2 (480.5 to 1)
Current Spending: ($ per student per year):
Total: $6,643; Instruction: $4,199; Support Services: $2,062
Enrollment, Drop-out Rates and Diploma Recipients by Race/Ethnicity

Category	Total	White	Black	Asian	AIAN	Hisp.
Enrollment (%)	100.0	65.1	23.5	0.4	0.6	10.4
Drop-out Rate (%)	3.8	3.8	4.3	0.0	0.0	2.4
H.S. Diplomas (#)	180	142	33	0	0	5

Ben Hill County

Ben Hill County

509 W Palm St • Fitzgerald, GA 31750-1750
(229) 426-5500 • http://www.ben-hill.k12.ga.us
Grade Span: PK-12; **Agency Type:** 1
Schools: 6
2 Primary; 1 Middle; 1 High; 2 Other Level
5 Regular; 0 Special Education; 0 Vocational; 1 Alternative
0 Magnet; 0 Charter; 3 Title I Eligible; 3 School-wide Title I
Students: 3,395 (50.8% male; 49.2% female)
Individual Education Program: 494 (14.6%);
English Language Learner: 108 (3.2%); Migrant: 14 (0.4%)
Eligible for Free Lunch Program: 1,921 (56.6%)
Eligible for Reduced-Price Lunch Program: 296 (8.7%)
Teachers: 217.0 (15.6 to 1)
Librarians/Media Specialists: 3.0 (1,131.7 to 1)
Guidance Counselors: 8.0 (424.4 to 1)
Current Spending: ($ per student per year):
Total: $6,644; Instruction: $4,330; Support Services: $1,915
Enrollment, Drop-out Rates and Diploma Recipients by Race/Ethnicity

Category	Total	White	Black	Asian	AIAN	Hisp.
Enrollment (%)	100.0	50.7	44.4	0.4	0.1	4.4
Drop-out Rate (%)	9.7	7.2	12.2	0.0	0.0	21.1
H.S. Diplomas (#)	157	106	49	0	1	1

Berrien County

Berrien County

100 E Smith Ave • Nashville, GA 31639-1639
Mailing Address: PO Box 625 • Nashville, GA 31639-1639
(912) 229-2081 • http://www.berrien.k12.ga.us
Grade Span: PK-12; **Agency Type:** 1
Schools: 5
2 Primary; 1 Middle; 1 High; 1 Other Level
4 Regular; 0 Special Education; 0 Vocational; 1 Alternative
0 Magnet; 0 Charter; 2 Title I Eligible; 2 School-wide Title I
Students: 3,037 (51.5% male; 48.5% female)
Individual Education Program: 398 (13.1%);
English Language Learner: 0 (0.0%); Migrant: 59 (1.9%)
Eligible for Free Lunch Program: 1,362 (44.8%)
Eligible for Reduced-Price Lunch Program: 379 (12.5%)
Teachers: 171.7 (17.7 to 1)
Librarians/Media Specialists: 3.8 (799.2 to 1)
Guidance Counselors: 7.0 (433.9 to 1)
Current Spending: ($ per student per year):
Total: $6,097; Instruction: $3,821; Support Services: $1,889
Enrollment, Drop-out Rates and Diploma Recipients by Race/Ethnicity

Category	Total	White	Black	Asian	AIAN	Hisp.
Enrollment (%)	100.0	80.8	16.4	0.3	0.0	2.5
Drop-out Rate (%)	6.0	6.4	3.3	20.0	0.0	7.7
H.S. Diplomas (#)	127	109	16	0	0	2

Bibb County

Bibb County

484 Mulberry St • Macon, GA 31201
(478) 765-8711 • http://www.bibb.k12.ga.us
Grade Span: PK-12; **Agency Type:** 1
Schools: 45
30 Primary; 5 Middle; 5 High; 5 Other Level
42 Regular; 0 Special Education; 0 Vocational; 3 Alternative
4 Magnet; 0 Charter; 24 Title I Eligible; 19 School-wide Title I
Students: 24,938 (50.3% male; 49.7% female)
Individual Education Program: 2,610 (10.5%);
English Language Learner: 360 (1.4%); Migrant: 17 (0.1%)
Eligible for Free Lunch Program: 13,187 (52.9%)
Eligible for Reduced-Price Lunch Program: 1,774 (7.1%)
Teachers: 1,418.2 (17.6 to 1)
Librarians/Media Specialists: 43.4 (574.6 to 1)
Guidance Counselors: 54.5 (457.6 to 1)
Current Spending: ($ per student per year):
Total: $6,441; Instruction: $4,050; Support Services: $1,980
Enrollment, Drop-out Rates and Diploma Recipients by Race/Ethnicity

Category	Total	White	Black	Asian	AIAN	Hisp.
Enrollment (%)	100.0	26.3	71.6	1.1	0.1	1.0
Drop-out Rate (%)	12.6	11.4	13.3	0.0	4.2	7.3
H.S. Diplomas (#)	831	276	541	11	0	3

Bleckley County

Bleckley County

909 Northeast Dykes St • Cochran, GA 31014-1014
(478) 934-2821 • http://www.bleckley.k12.ga.us
Grade Span: PK-12; **Agency Type:** 1
Schools: 4
2 Primary; 1 Middle; 1 High; 0 Other Level
4 Regular; 0 Special Education; 0 Vocational; 0 Alternative
0 Magnet; 0 Charter; 2 Title I Eligible; 2 School-wide Title I
Students: 2,355 (50.1% male; 49.9% female)
Individual Education Program: 319 (13.5%);
English Language Learner: 3 (0.1%); Migrant: 10 (0.4%)
Eligible for Free Lunch Program: 908 (38.6%)
Eligible for Reduced-Price Lunch Program: 236 (10.0%)
Teachers: 151.2 (15.6 to 1)
Librarians/Media Specialists: 4.0 (588.8 to 1)
Guidance Counselors: 5.0 (471.0 to 1)
Current Spending: ($ per student per year):
Total: $6,275; Instruction: $4,074; Support Services: $1,752
Enrollment, Drop-out Rates and Diploma Recipients by Race/Ethnicity

Category	Total	White	Black	Asian	AIAN	Hisp.
Enrollment (%)	100.0	69.5	28.5	1.0	0.0	0.9
Drop-out Rate (%)	6.5	6.3	7.3	0.0	0.0	0.0
H.S. Diplomas (#)	101	81	18	2	0	0

Brantley County

Brantley County

Hwy 82 W • Nahunta, GA 31553-1553
Mailing Address: RR 1, Box 3 • Nahunta, GA 31553-1553
(912) 462-6176
Grade Span: PK-12; **Agency Type:** 1
Schools: 6
3 Primary; 2 Middle; 1 High; 0 Other Level
6 Regular; 0 Special Education; 0 Vocational; 0 Alternative
0 Magnet; 0 Charter; 5 Title I Eligible; 5 School-wide Title I
Students: 3,332 (51.1% male; 48.9% female)
Individual Education Program: 473 (14.2%);
English Language Learner: 0 (0.0%); Migrant: 3 (0.1%)
Eligible for Free Lunch Program: 1,450 (43.5%)
Eligible for Reduced-Price Lunch Program: 389 (11.7%)
Teachers: 195.9 (17.0 to 1)
Librarians/Media Specialists: 6.0 (555.3 to 1)
Guidance Counselors: 6.0 (555.3 to 1)
Current Spending: ($ per student per year):
Total: $6,058; Instruction: $3,803; Support Services: $1,868
Enrollment, Drop-out Rates and Diploma Recipients by Race/Ethnicity

Category	Total	White	Black	Asian	AIAN	Hisp.
Enrollment (%)	100.0	94.8	4.4	0.1	0.1	0.6
Drop-out Rate (%)	10.5	10.1	15.0	n/a	n/a	50.0
H.S. Diplomas (#)	121	118	3	0	0	0

Brooks County

Brooks County
489 Barwick Rd • Quitman, GA 31643-1643
(229) 263-7531 • http://www.brooks.k12.ga.us
Grade Span: PK-12; **Agency Type:** 1
Schools: 4
2 Primary; 1 Middle; 1 High; 0 Other Level
4 Regular; 0 Special Education; 0 Vocational; 0 Alternative
0 Magnet; 0 Charter; 4 Title I Eligible; 3 School-wide Title I
Students: 2,563 (52.7% male; 47.3% female)
Individual Education Program: 322 (12.6%);
English Language Learner: 33 (1.3%); Migrant: 57 (2.2%)
Eligible for Free Lunch Program: 1,627 (63.5%)
Eligible for Reduced-Price Lunch Program: 305 (11.9%)
Teachers: 157.0 (16.3 to 1)
Librarians/Media Specialists: 4.0 (640.8 to 1)
Guidance Counselors: 4.5 (569.6 to 1)
Current Spending: ($ per student per year):
Total: $6,594; Instruction: $3,894; Support Services: $2,176
Enrollment, Drop-out Rates and Diploma Recipients by Race/Ethnicity

Category	Total	White	Black	Asian	AIAN	Hisp.
Enrollment (%)	100.0	33.5	63.1	0.3	0.1	3.1
Drop-out Rate (%)	13.0	14.2	11.9	25.0	n/a	23.1
H.S. Diplomas (#)	95	37	55	1	0	2

Bryan County

Bryan County
66 S Industrial Blvd • Pembroke, GA 31321-1321
(912) 653-4381 • http://www.bryan.k12.ga.us
Grade Span: PK-12; **Agency Type:** 1
Schools: 12
4 Primary; 3 Middle; 2 High; 3 Other Level
11 Regular; 0 Special Education; 0 Vocational; 1 Alternative
0 Magnet; 0 Charter; 4 Title I Eligible; 0 School-wide Title I
Students: 5,552 (51.5% male; 48.5% female)
Individual Education Program: 480 (8.6%);
English Language Learner: 6 (0.1%); Migrant: 1 (<0.1%)
Eligible for Free Lunch Program: 1,409 (25.4%)
Eligible for Reduced-Price Lunch Program: 484 (8.7%)
Teachers: 328.0 (16.9 to 1)
Librarians/Media Specialists: 9.0 (616.9 to 1)
Guidance Counselors: 11.0 (504.7 to 1)
Current Spending: ($ per student per year):
Total: $5,731; Instruction: $3,573; Support Services: $1,783
Enrollment, Drop-out Rates and Diploma Recipients by Race/Ethnicity

Category	Total	White	Black	Asian	AIAN	Hisp.
Enrollment (%)	100.0	79.9	17.5	0.9	0.1	1.6
Drop-out Rate (%)	6.4	6.4	6.1	0.0	0.0	11.5
H.S. Diplomas (#)	289	244	36	3	0	6

Bulloch County

Bulloch County
150 Williams Rd, Ste A • Statesboro, GA 30458-0458
(912) 764-6201 • http://www.bulloch.k12.ga.us
Grade Span: PK-12; **Agency Type:** 1
Schools: 16
9 Primary; 3 Middle; 2 High; 2 Other Level
15 Regular; 0 Special Education; 0 Vocational; 1 Alternative
0 Magnet; 0 Charter; 13 Title I Eligible; 13 School-wide Title I
Students: 8,279 (51.5% male; 48.5% female)
Individual Education Program: 1,255 (15.2%);
English Language Learner: 80 (1.0%); Migrant: 74 (0.9%)
Eligible for Free Lunch Program: 3,738 (45.2%)
Eligible for Reduced-Price Lunch Program: 824 (10.0%)
Teachers: 604.1 (13.7 to 1)
Librarians/Media Specialists: 15.5 (534.1 to 1)
Guidance Counselors: 21.2 (390.5 to 1)
Current Spending: ($ per student per year):
Total: $7,227; Instruction: $4,570; Support Services: $2,220
Enrollment, Drop-out Rates and Diploma Recipients by Race/Ethnicity

Category	Total	White	Black	Asian	AIAN	Hisp.
Enrollment (%)	100.0	58.7	38.8	0.8	0.1	1.7
Drop-out Rate (%)	6.2	4.8	8.5	0.0	33.3	0.0
H.S. Diplomas (#)	408	284	119	4	0	1

Burke County

Burke County
789 Perimeter Rd • Waynesboro, GA 30830-0830
(706) 554-5101 • http://www.burke.k12.ga.us
Grade Span: PK-12; **Agency Type:** 1
Schools: 6
3 Primary; 1 Middle; 1 High; 1 Other Level
5 Regular; 0 Special Education; 0 Vocational; 1 Alternative
0 Magnet; 0 Charter; 4 Title I Eligible; 3 School-wide Title I
Students: 4,614 (51.2% male; 48.8% female)
Individual Education Program: 440 (9.5%);
English Language Learner: 5 (0.1%); Migrant: 8 (0.2%)
Eligible for Free Lunch Program: 3,021 (65.5%)
Eligible for Reduced-Price Lunch Program: 593 (12.9%)
Teachers: 250.0 (18.5 to 1)
Librarians/Media Specialists: 6.0 (769.0 to 1)
Guidance Counselors: 10.0 (461.4 to 1)
Current Spending: ($ per student per year):
Total: $6,510; Instruction: $3,967; Support Services: $2,174
Enrollment, Drop-out Rates and Diploma Recipients by Race/Ethnicity

Category	Total	White	Black	Asian	AIAN	Hisp.
Enrollment (%)	100.0	30.5	68.4	0.1	0.0	1.0
Drop-out Rate (%)	10.4	10.0	10.7	16.7	0.0	0.0
H.S. Diplomas (#)	213	90	120	2	0	1

Butts County

Butts County
181 N Mulberry St • Jackson, GA 30233-0233
(770) 504-2300 • http://www.butts.k12.ga.us
Grade Span: PK-12; **Agency Type:** 1
Schools: 4
2 Primary; 1 Middle; 1 High; 0 Other Level
4 Regular; 0 Special Education; 0 Vocational; 0 Alternative
0 Magnet; 0 Charter; 3 Title I Eligible; 3 School-wide Title I
Students: 3,370 (50.9% male; 49.1% female)
Individual Education Program: 403 (12.0%);
English Language Learner: 0 (0.0%); Migrant: 1 (<0.1%)
Eligible for Free Lunch Program: 1,270 (37.7%)
Eligible for Reduced-Price Lunch Program: 370 (11.0%)
Teachers: 184.3 (18.3 to 1)
Librarians/Media Specialists: 4.0 (842.5 to 1)
Guidance Counselors: 8.1 (416.0 to 1)
Current Spending: ($ per student per year):
Total: $6,431; Instruction: $3,760; Support Services: $2,310
Enrollment, Drop-out Rates and Diploma Recipients by Race/Ethnicity

Category	Total	White	Black	Asian	AIAN	Hisp.
Enrollment (%)	100.0	62.7	35.0	0.6	0.1	1.7
Drop-out Rate (%)	7.0	6.6	7.1	0.0	n/a	40.0
H.S. Diplomas (#)	130	82	47	1	0	0

Camden County

Camden County
311 SE St • Kingsland, GA 31548-1548
(912) 729-5687 • http://www.camden.k12.ga.us/
Grade Span: PK-12; **Agency Type:** 1
Schools: 13
9 Primary; 2 Middle; 1 High; 1 Other Level
12 Regular; 0 Special Education; 0 Vocational; 1 Alternative
0 Magnet; 0 Charter; 8 Title I Eligible; 2 School-wide Title I
Students: 9,563 (50.5% male; 49.5% female)
Individual Education Program: 1,082 (11.3%);
English Language Learner: 47 (0.5%); Migrant: 0 (0.0%)
Eligible for Free Lunch Program: 2,400 (25.1%)
Eligible for Reduced-Price Lunch Program: 1,105 (11.6%)
Teachers: 540.6 (17.7 to 1)
Librarians/Media Specialists: 14.0 (683.1 to 1)
Guidance Counselors: 22.0 (434.7 to 1)
Current Spending: ($ per student per year):
Total: $5,629; Instruction: $3,438; Support Services: $1,896
Enrollment, Drop-out Rates and Diploma Recipients by Race/Ethnicity

Category	Total	White	Black	Asian	AIAN	Hisp.
Enrollment (%)	100.0	69.8	25.7	1.0	0.2	3.3
Drop-out Rate (%)	7.0	7.7	4.9	0.0	0.0	12.5
H.S. Diplomas (#)	445	322	115	0	1	7

Candler County

Candler County
210 S College St • Metter, GA 30439-0439
(912) 685-5713 • http://www.metter.org/
Grade Span: PK-12; **Agency Type:** 1
Schools: 5
1 Primary; 2 Middle; 1 High; 1 Other Level
5 Regular; 0 Special Education; 0 Vocational; 0 Alternative
0 Magnet; 0 Charter; 4 Title I Eligible; 4 School-wide Title I
Students: 1,918 (52.4% male; 47.6% female)
Individual Education Program: 266 (13.9%);
English Language Learner: 101 (5.3%); Migrant: 138 (7.2%)
Eligible for Free Lunch Program: 1,042 (54.3%)

Eligible for Reduced-Price Lunch Program: 222 (11.6%)
Teachers: 116.9 (16.4 to 1)
Librarians/Media Specialists: 3.0 (639.3 to 1)
Guidance Counselors: 3.6 (532.8 to 1)
Current Spending: ($ per student per year):
Total: $6,233; Instruction: $3,888; Support Services: $1,836
Enrollment, Drop-out Rates and Diploma Recipients by Race/Ethnicity

Category	Total	White	Black	Asian	AIAN	Hisp.
Enrollment (%)	100.0	55.3	34.0	0.3	0.1	10.4
Drop-out Rate (%)	8.5	9.2	5.6	0.0	n/a	20.7
H.S. Diplomas (#)	72	42	28	1	0	1

Carroll County

Carroll County
164 Independence Dr • Carrollton, GA 30116-0116
(770) 832-3568 • http://www.carrollcountyschools.com
Grade Span: PK-12; **Agency Type:** 1
Schools: 22
10 Primary; 4 Middle; 5 High; 3 Other Level
20 Regular; 0 Special Education; 0 Vocational; 2 Alternative
0 Magnet; 0 Charter; 8 Title I Eligible; 8 School-wide Title I
Students: 13,403 (51.9% male; 48.1% female)
Individual Education Program: 1,969 (14.7%);
English Language Learner: 158 (1.2%); Migrant: 0 (0.0%)
Eligible for Free Lunch Program: 4,489 (33.5%)
Eligible for Reduced-Price Lunch Program: 1,432 (10.7%)
Teachers: 807.6 (16.6 to 1)
Librarians/Media Specialists: 21.0 (638.2 to 1)
Guidance Counselors: 28.7 (467.0 to 1)
Current Spending: ($ per student per year):
Total: $6,524; Instruction: $4,133; Support Services: $2,016
Enrollment, Drop-out Rates and Diploma Recipients by Race/Ethnicity

Category	Total	White	Black	Asian	AIAN	Hisp.
Enrollment (%)	100.0	80.2	16.9	0.6	0.3	2.1
Drop-out Rate (%)	8.9	9.3	6.5	10.0	10.0	21.4
H.S. Diplomas (#)	536	453	77	4	0	2

Carrollton City
106 Trojan Dr • Carrollton, GA 30117-0117
(770) 832-9633 • http://www.carrolltoncityschools.net
Grade Span: PK-12; **Agency Type:** 1
Schools: 3
1 Primary; 1 Middle; 1 High; 0 Other Level
3 Regular; 0 Special Education; 0 Vocational; 0 Alternative
0 Magnet; 0 Charter; 1 Title I Eligible; 0 School-wide Title I
Students: 3,682 (50.8% male; 49.2% female)
Individual Education Program: 547 (14.9%);
English Language Learner: 105 (2.9%); Migrant: 0 (0.0%)
Eligible for Free Lunch Program: 1,424 (38.7%)
Eligible for Reduced-Price Lunch Program: 281 (7.6%)
Teachers: 212.7 (17.3 to 1)
Librarians/Media Specialists: 4.3 (856.3 to 1)
Guidance Counselors: 8.0 (460.3 to 1)
Current Spending: ($ per student per year):
Total: $6,664; Instruction: $3,981; Support Services: $2,288
Enrollment, Drop-out Rates and Diploma Recipients by Race/Ethnicity

Category	Total	White	Black	Asian	AIAN	Hisp.
Enrollment (%)	100.0	52.3	40.4	1.5	0.0	5.9
Drop-out Rate (%)	3.5	1.6	6.1	0.0	n/a	21.4
H.S. Diplomas (#)	186	125	58	1	0	2

Catoosa County

Catoosa County
307 Cleveland St • Ringgold, GA 30736-0736
(706) 965-2297 • http://www.catoosa.k12.ga.us
Grade Span: PK-12; **Agency Type:** 1
Schools: 15
9 Primary; 2 Middle; 2 High; 2 Other Level
14 Regular; 0 Special Education; 0 Vocational; 1 Alternative
0 Magnet; 0 Charter; 6 Title I Eligible; 2 School-wide Title I
Students: 9,809 (51.3% male; 48.7% female)
Individual Education Program: 1,293 (13.2%);
English Language Learner: 56 (0.6%); Migrant: 0 (0.0%)
Eligible for Free Lunch Program: 2,431 (24.8%)
Eligible for Reduced-Price Lunch Program: 1,030 (10.5%)
Teachers: 606.2 (16.2 to 1)
Librarians/Media Specialists: 15.0 (653.9 to 1)
Guidance Counselors: 22.0 (445.9 to 1)
Current Spending: ($ per student per year):
Total: $5,962; Instruction: $3,880; Support Services: $1,736

Enrollment, Drop-out Rates and Diploma Recipients by Race/Ethnicity

Category	Total	White	Black	Asian	AIAN	Hisp.
Enrollment (%)	100.0	96.2	1.3	1.5	0.1	1.0
Drop-out Rate (%)	8.7	8.5	10.3	7.0	0.0	41.2
H.S. Diplomas (#)	446	429	3	8	4	2

Charlton County

Charlton County
500 S Third St • Folkston, GA 31537-1537
(912) 496-2596 • http://boe.charlton.k12.ga.us/
Grade Span: PK-12; **Agency Type:** 1
Schools: 5
3 Primary; 0 Middle; 1 High; 1 Other Level
4 Regular; 0 Special Education; 0 Vocational; 1 Alternative
0 Magnet; 0 Charter; 3 Title I Eligible; 1 School-wide Title I
Students: 2,015 (51.3% male; 48.7% female)
Individual Education Program: 275 (13.6%);
English Language Learner: 0 (0.0%); Migrant: 0 (0.0%)
Eligible for Free Lunch Program: 946 (46.9%)
Eligible for Reduced-Price Lunch Program: 243 (12.1%)
Teachers: 113.6 (17.7 to 1)
Librarians/Media Specialists: 4.0 (503.8 to 1)
Guidance Counselors: 3.5 (575.7 to 1)
Current Spending: ($ per student per year):
Total: $6,185; Instruction: $3,774; Support Services: $2,049
Enrollment, Drop-out Rates and Diploma Recipients by Race/Ethnicity

Category	Total	White	Black	Asian	AIAN	Hisp.
Enrollment (%)	100.0	66.2	32.8	0.7	0.1	0.2
Drop-out Rate (%)	6.0	7.0	4.1	n/a	0.0	n/a
H.S. Diplomas (#)	92	71	19	2	0	0

Chatham County

Chatham County
208 Bull St • Savannah, GA 31401-1401
(912) 201-5600 • http://www.savannah.chatham.k12.ga.us/
Grade Span: PK-12; **Agency Type:** 1
Schools: 55
30 Primary; 11 Middle; 4 High; 10 Other Level
49 Regular; 0 Special Education; 0 Vocational; 6 Alternative
13 Magnet; 4 Charter; 27 Title I Eligible; 21 School-wide Title I
Students: 34,554 (50.7% male; 49.3% female)
Individual Education Program: 4,013 (11.6%);
English Language Learner: 244 (0.7%); Migrant: 3 (<0.1%)
Eligible for Free Lunch Program: 15,390 (44.5%)
Eligible for Reduced-Price Lunch Program: 3,128 (9.1%)
Teachers: 2,133.8 (16.2 to 1)
Librarians/Media Specialists: 54.0 (639.9 to 1)
Guidance Counselors: 83.0 (416.3 to 1)
Current Spending: ($ per student per year):
Total: $6,615; Instruction: $4,135; Support Services: $2,142
Enrollment, Drop-out Rates and Diploma Recipients by Race/Ethnicity

Category	Total	White	Black	Asian	AIAN	Hisp.
Enrollment (%)	100.0	29.8	66.0	1.8	0.2	2.1
Drop-out Rate (%)	11.3	11.1	11.6	5.1	11.8	10.8
H.S. Diplomas (#)	1,197	430	695	43	3	26

Chattooga County

Chattooga County
33 Middle School Rd • Summerville, GA 30747-0747
(706) 857-3447 • http://www.chattooga.k12.ga.us/
Grade Span: PK-12; **Agency Type:** 1
Schools: 10
4 Primary; 2 Middle; 1 High; 3 Other Level
9 Regular; 0 Special Education; 0 Vocational; 1 Alternative
0 Magnet; 0 Charter; 5 Title I Eligible; 5 School-wide Title I
Students: 2,834 (52.6% male; 47.4% female)
Individual Education Program: 614 (21.7%);
English Language Learner: 38 (1.3%); Migrant: 0 (0.0%)
Eligible for Free Lunch Program: 1,288 (45.4%)
Eligible for Reduced-Price Lunch Program: 393 (13.9%)
Teachers: 183.7 (15.4 to 1)
Librarians/Media Specialists: 7.0 (404.9 to 1)
Guidance Counselors: 6.1 (464.6 to 1)
Current Spending: ($ per student per year):
Total: $7,184; Instruction: $4,701; Support Services: $2,085
Enrollment, Drop-out Rates and Diploma Recipients by Race/Ethnicity

Category	Total	White	Black	Asian	AIAN	Hisp.
Enrollment (%)	100.0	84.3	12.8	0.1	0.2	2.6
Drop-out Rate (%)	9.6	10.5	4.0	n/a	n/a	25.0
H.S. Diplomas (#)	92	85	7	0	0	0

Cherokee County

Cherokee County
221 W Main St • Canton, GA 30114-0114
(770) 479-1871 • http://www.cherokee.k12.ga.us
Grade Span: PK-12; **Agency Type:** 1
Schools: 33
22 Primary; 5 Middle; 5 High; 1 Other Level
31 Regular; 0 Special Education; 0 Vocational; 2 Alternative
0 Magnet; 0 Charter; 9 Title I Eligible; 3 School-wide Title I
Students: 28,434 (51.7% male; 48.3% female)
Individual Education Program: 3,556 (12.5%);
English Language Learner: 692 (2.4%); Migrant: 60 (0.2%)
Eligible for Free Lunch Program: 3,631 (12.8%)
Eligible for Reduced-Price Lunch Program: 1,452 (5.1%)
Teachers: 1,766.4 (16.1 to 1)
Librarians/Media Specialists: 34.0 (836.3 to 1)
Guidance Counselors: 54.0 (526.6 to 1)
Current Spending: ($ per student per year):
Total: $6,452; Instruction: $4,177; Support Services: $1,831
Enrollment, Drop-out Rates and Diploma Recipients by Race/Ethnicity

Category	Total	White	Black	Asian	AIAN	Hisp.
Enrollment (%)	100.0	87.6	4.1	1.2	0.3	6.9
Drop-out Rate (%)	5.0	4.9	6.4	0.0	9.1	8.2
H.S. Diplomas (#)	1,271	1,176	40	28	1	26

Clarke County

Clarke County
500 College Ave • Athens, GA 30603-0603
(706) 546-7721 • http://www.clarke.k12.ga.us
Grade Span: PK-12; **Agency Type:** 1
Schools: 21
13 Primary; 4 Middle; 2 High; 2 Other Level
19 Regular; 0 Special Education; 0 Vocational; 2 Alternative
0 Magnet; 0 Charter; 13 Title I Eligible; 12 School-wide Title I
Students: 11,457 (50.9% male; 49.1% female)
Individual Education Program: 1,777 (15.5%);
English Language Learner: 1,674 (14.6%); Migrant: 357 (3.1%)
Eligible for Free Lunch Program: 6,570 (57.3%)
Eligible for Reduced-Price Lunch Program: 774 (6.8%)
Teachers: 808.6 (14.2 to 1)
Librarians/Media Specialists: 19.5 (587.5 to 1)
Guidance Counselors: 26.3 (435.6 to 1)
Current Spending: ($ per student per year):
Total: $7,894; Instruction: $4,701; Support Services: $2,770
Enrollment, Drop-out Rates and Diploma Recipients by Race/Ethnicity

Category	Total	White	Black	Asian	AIAN	Hisp.
Enrollment (%)	100.0	27.2	56.9	3.0	0.1	12.7
Drop-out Rate (%)	13.3	6.3	17.0	13.8	n/a	21.7
H.S. Diplomas (#)	390	211	155	12	0	12

Clayton County

Clayton County
1058 Fifth Ave • Jonesboro, GA 30236-0236
(770) 473-2700 • http://www.ccps.ga.net
Grade Span: PK-12; **Agency Type:** 1
Schools: 54
31 Primary; 12 Middle; 7 High; 4 Other Level
51 Regular; 2 Special Education; 0 Vocational; 1 Alternative
0 Magnet; 0 Charter; 28 Title I Eligible; 28 School-wide Title I
Students: 49,594 (51.3% male; 48.7% female)
Individual Education Program: 4,645 (9.4%);
English Language Learner: 2,232 (4.5%); Migrant: 2 (<0.1%)
Eligible for Free Lunch Program: 22,475 (45.3%)
Eligible for Reduced-Price Lunch Program: 7,355 (14.8%)
Teachers: 2,735.6 (18.1 to 1)
Librarians/Media Specialists: 57.5 (862.5 to 1)
Guidance Counselors: 108.8 (455.8 to 1)
Current Spending: ($ per student per year):
Total: $6,314; Instruction: $3,919; Support Services: $1,968
Enrollment, Drop-out Rates and Diploma Recipients by Race/Ethnicity

Category	Total	White	Black	Asian	AIAN	Hisp.
Enrollment (%)	100.0	15.9	71.3	4.5	0.1	8.3
Drop-out Rate (%)	9.1	8.8	9.2	8.1	15.4	11.6
H.S. Diplomas (#)	1,791	473	1,112	140	3	63

Cobb County

Cobb County
514 Glover St • Marietta, GA 30061-0061
(770) 426-3300 • http://www.cobb.k12.ga.us
Grade Span: PK-12; **Agency Type:** 1
Schools: 102
62 Primary; 21 Middle; 14 High; 5 Other Level
98 Regular; 0 Special Education; 0 Vocational; 4 Alternative
4 Magnet; 7 Charter; 22 Title I Eligible; 19 School-wide Title I
Students: 100,389 (51.4% male; 48.6% female)
Individual Education Program: 12,600 (12.6%);
English Language Learner: 8,530 (8.5%); Migrant: 22 (<0.1%)
Eligible for Free Lunch Program: 18,030 (18.0%)
Eligible for Reduced-Price Lunch Program: 6,167 (6.1%)
Teachers: 6,806.6 (14.7 to 1)
Librarians/Media Specialists: 110.9 (905.2 to 1)
Guidance Counselors: 239.8 (418.6 to 1)
Current Spending: ($ per student per year):
Total: $6,572; Instruction: $4,497; Support Services: $1,783
Enrollment, Drop-out Rates and Diploma Recipients by Race/Ethnicity

Category	Total	White	Black	Asian	AIAN	Hisp.
Enrollment (%)	100.0	60.4	26.4	3.8	0.3	9.2
Drop-out Rate (%)	3.8	3.0	5.4	2.9	9.3	8.1
H.S. Diplomas (#)	5,231	3,924	927	215	7	158

Marietta City
250 Howard St • Marietta, GA 30060
(770) 422-3500 • http://www.marietta-city.k12.ga.us
Grade Span: PK-12; **Agency Type:** 1
Schools: 11
7 Primary; 2 Middle; 1 High; 1 Other Level
10 Regular; 0 Special Education; 0 Vocational; 1 Alternative
0 Magnet; 0 Charter; 6 Title I Eligible; 3 School-wide Title I
Students: 7,524 (51.0% male; 49.0% female)
Individual Education Program: 1,032 (13.7%);
English Language Learner: 1,436 (19.1%); Migrant: 3 (<0.1%)
Eligible for Free Lunch Program: 3,439 (45.7%)
Eligible for Reduced-Price Lunch Program: 763 (10.1%)
Teachers: 523.1 (14.4 to 1)
Librarians/Media Specialists: 11.0 (684.0 to 1)
Guidance Counselors: 18.5 (406.7 to 1)
Current Spending: ($ per student per year):
Total: $8,466; Instruction: $5,620; Support Services: $2,482
Enrollment, Drop-out Rates and Diploma Recipients by Race/Ethnicity

Category	Total	White	Black	Asian	AIAN	Hisp.
Enrollment (%)	100.0	28.0	47.9	2.3	0.2	21.7
Drop-out Rate (%)	11.1	6.4	13.6	10.2	n/a	17.4
H.S. Diplomas (#)	268	138	104	12	1	13

Coffee County

Coffee County
1311 S Peterson Ave • Douglas, GA 31533
(912) 384-2086 • http://coffee.k12.ga.us/
Grade Span: PK-12; **Agency Type:** 1
Schools: 12
9 Primary; 1 Middle; 1 High; 1 Other Level
11 Regular; 0 Special Education; 0 Vocational; 1 Alternative
0 Magnet; 0 Charter; 8 Title I Eligible; 8 School-wide Title I
Students: 7,841 (50.6% male; 49.4% female)
Individual Education Program: 898 (11.5%);
English Language Learner: 353 (4.5%); Migrant: 516 (6.6%)
Eligible for Free Lunch Program: 4,249 (54.2%)
Eligible for Reduced-Price Lunch Program: 962 (12.3%)
Teachers: 439.3 (17.8 to 1)
Librarians/Media Specialists: 12.0 (653.4 to 1)
Guidance Counselors: 14.0 (560.1 to 1)
Current Spending: ($ per student per year):
Total: $6,401; Instruction: $4,100; Support Services: $1,861
Enrollment, Drop-out Rates and Diploma Recipients by Race/Ethnicity

Category	Total	White	Black	Asian	AIAN	Hisp.
Enrollment (%)	100.0	57.5	33.2	0.8	0.0	8.5
Drop-out Rate (%)	9.6	9.7	9.3	0.0	n/a	13.7
H.S. Diplomas (#)	260	174	76	3	0	7

Colquitt County

Colquitt County
710 28th Avenue, SE • Moultrie, GA 31768
(229) 985-1550 • http://www.colquitt.k12.ga.us
Grade Span: PK-12; **Agency Type:** 1
Schools: 16
10 Primary; 2 Middle; 1 High; 3 Other Level
13 Regular; 2 Special Education; 0 Vocational; 1 Alternative
0 Magnet; 0 Charter; 12 Title I Eligible; 11 School-wide Title I
Students: 8,342 (51.1% male; 48.9% female)
Individual Education Program: 1,023 (12.3%);
English Language Learner: 587 (7.0%); Migrant: 611 (7.3%)
Eligible for Free Lunch Program: 4,423 (53.0%)
Eligible for Reduced-Price Lunch Program: 737 (8.8%)
Teachers: 480.5 (17.4 to 1)

Librarians/Media Specialists: 15.0 (556.1 to 1)
Guidance Counselors: 17.0 (490.7 to 1)
Current Spending: ($ per student per year):
Total: $6,472; Instruction: $4,094; Support Services: $1,939
Enrollment, Drop-out Rates and Diploma Recipients by Race/Ethnicity

Category	Total	White	Black	Asian	AIAN	Hisp.
Enrollment (%)	100.0	57.3	31.4	0.2	0.1	11.0
Drop-out Rate (%)	9.8	9.3	10.3	10.0	0.0	13.7
H.S. Diplomas (#)	308	223	75	1	1	8

Columbia County

Columbia County
6430 Pollards Pond Rd • Appling, GA 30802-0802
(706) 541-0650 • http://www.ccboe.net
Grade Span: PK-12; **Agency Type:** 1
Schools: 26
14 Primary; 7 Middle; 4 High; 1 Other Level
25 Regular; 0 Special Education; 0 Vocational; 1 Alternative
0 Magnet; 0 Charter; 10 Title I Eligible; 4 School-wide Title I
Students: 19,426 (51.5% male; 48.5% female)
Individual Education Program: 1,913 (9.8%);
English Language Learner: 75 (0.4%); Migrant: 0 (0.0%)
Eligible for Free Lunch Program: 2,676 (13.8%)
Eligible for Reduced-Price Lunch Program: 1,073 (5.5%)
Teachers: 1,133.3 (17.1 to 1)
Librarians/Media Specialists: 27.8 (698.8 to 1)
Guidance Counselors: 45.6 (426.0 to 1)
Current Spending: ($ per student per year):
Total: $5,737; Instruction: $3,824; Support Services: $1,611
Enrollment, Drop-out Rates and Diploma Recipients by Race/Ethnicity

Category	Total	White	Black	Asian	AIAN	Hisp.
Enrollment (%)	100.0	80.9	13.5	3.3	0.1	2.1
Drop-out Rate (%)	5.1	5.3	4.9	2.8	12.5	4.2
H.S. Diplomas (#)	1,051	831	136	56	2	26

Cook County

Cook County
1109 N Parrish Ave • Adel, GA 31620-1620
(229) 896-2294 • http://www.cook.k12.ga.us
Grade Span: PK-12; **Agency Type:** 1
Schools: 4
1 Primary; 1 Middle; 1 High; 1 Other Level
4 Regular; 0 Special Education; 0 Vocational; 0 Alternative
0 Magnet; 0 Charter; 1 Title I Eligible; 1 School-wide Title I
Students: 3,215 (51.2% male; 48.8% female)
Individual Education Program: 388 (12.1%);
English Language Learner: 11 (0.3%); Migrant: 57 (1.8%)
Eligible for Free Lunch Program: 1,519 (47.2%)
Eligible for Reduced-Price Lunch Program: 324 (10.1%)
Teachers: 189.4 (17.0 to 1)
Librarians/Media Specialists: 4.0 (803.8 to 1)
Guidance Counselors: 5.0 (643.0 to 1)
Current Spending: ($ per student per year):
Total: $6,223; Instruction: $3,785; Support Services: $2,076
Enrollment, Drop-out Rates and Diploma Recipients by Race/Ethnicity

Category	Total	White	Black	Asian	AIAN	Hisp.
Enrollment (%)	100.0	57.4	38.8	0.6	0.0	3.1
Drop-out Rate (%)	6.8	8.0	4.8	0.0	n/a	9.1
H.S. Diplomas (#)	131	76	55	0	0	0

Coweta County

Coweta County
237 Jackson St • Newnan, GA 30263
Mailing Address: PO Box 280 • Newnan, GA 30263
(404) 254-2801 • http://www.coweta.k12.ga.us
Grade Span: PK-12; **Agency Type:** 1
Schools: 27
16 Primary; 5 Middle; 3 High; 3 Other Level
26 Regular; 0 Special Education; 0 Vocational; 1 Alternative
0 Magnet; 1 Charter; 9 Title I Eligible; 3 School-wide Title I
Students: 18,389 (51.3% male; 48.7% female)
Individual Education Program: 2,825 (15.4%);
English Language Learner: 182 (1.0%); Migrant: 0 (0.0%)
Eligible for Free Lunch Program: 4,050 (22.0%)
Eligible for Reduced-Price Lunch Program: 1,189 (6.5%)
Teachers: 1,163.6 (15.8 to 1)
Librarians/Media Specialists: 27.0 (681.1 to 1)
Guidance Counselors: 41.5 (443.1 to 1)
Current Spending: ($ per student per year):
Total: $6,374; Instruction: $4,186; Support Services: $1,884
Enrollment, Drop-out Rates and Diploma Recipients by Race/Ethnicity

Category	Total	White	Black	Asian	AIAN	Hisp.
Enrollment (%)	100.0	73.5	22.7	0.7	0.0	3.1
Drop-out Rate (%)	3.5	3.1	4.7	3.4	0.0	2.3
H.S. Diplomas (#)	788	627	147	8	1	5

Crawford County

Crawford County
190 Crusselle St • Roberta, GA 31078-1078
(478) 836-3131 • http://www.crawford.k12.ga.us
Grade Span: PK-12; **Agency Type:** 1
Schools: 5
1 Primary; 1 Middle; 1 High; 2 Other Level
4 Regular; 0 Special Education; 0 Vocational; 1 Alternative
0 Magnet; 0 Charter; 2 Title I Eligible; 2 School-wide Title I
Students: 2,090 (53.2% male; 46.8% female)
Individual Education Program: 270 (12.9%);
English Language Learner: 1 (<0.1%); Migrant: 6 (0.3%)
Eligible for Free Lunch Program: 944 (45.2%)
Eligible for Reduced-Price Lunch Program: 260 (12.4%)
Teachers: 127.0 (16.5 to 1)
Librarians/Media Specialists: 3.0 (696.7 to 1)
Guidance Counselors: 4.0 (522.5 to 1)
Current Spending: ($ per student per year):
Total: $6,257; Instruction: $3,702; Support Services: $2,074
Enrollment, Drop-out Rates and Diploma Recipients by Race/Ethnicity

Category	Total	White	Black	Asian	AIAN	Hisp.
Enrollment (%)	100.0	70.0	28.5	0.1	0.1	1.2
Drop-out Rate (%)	9.0	10.2	5.9	0.0	n/a	33.3
H.S. Diplomas (#)	89	57	32	0	0	0

Crisp County

Crisp County
201 Seventh St S • Cordele, GA 31015
(912) 229-3400 • http://www.crisp.k12.ga.us
Grade Span: PK-12; **Agency Type:** 1
Schools: 7
4 Primary; 1 Middle; 1 High; 1 Other Level
6 Regular; 0 Special Education; 0 Vocational; 1 Alternative
0 Magnet; 0 Charter; 5 Title I Eligible; 5 School-wide Title I
Students: 4,337 (50.5% male; 49.5% female)
Individual Education Program: 414 (9.5%);
English Language Learner: 29 (0.7%); Migrant: 21 (0.5%)
Eligible for Free Lunch Program: 2,753 (63.5%)
Eligible for Reduced-Price Lunch Program: 338 (7.8%)
Teachers: 281.0 (15.4 to 1)
Librarians/Media Specialists: 6.0 (722.8 to 1)
Guidance Counselors: 9.5 (456.5 to 1)
Current Spending: ($ per student per year):
Total: $6,896; Instruction: $4,356; Support Services: $2,108
Enrollment, Drop-out Rates and Diploma Recipients by Race/Ethnicity

Category	Total	White	Black	Asian	AIAN	Hisp.
Enrollment (%)	100.0	39.2	58.8	0.6	0.0	1.3
Drop-out Rate (%)	14.2	10.0	17.2	12.5	0.0	0.0
H.S. Diplomas (#)	165	89	74	1	1	0

Dade County

Dade County
52 Tradition Ln • Trenton, GA 30752-0752
(706) 657-4361 • http://www.dade.k12.ga.us
Grade Span: PK-12; **Agency Type:** 1
Schools: 5
2 Primary; 1 Middle; 1 High; 1 Other Level
4 Regular; 0 Special Education; 0 Vocational; 1 Alternative
0 Magnet; 0 Charter; 3 Title I Eligible; 1 School-wide Title I
Students: 2,630 (53.3% male; 46.7% female)
Individual Education Program: 296 (11.3%);
English Language Learner: 0 (0.0%); Migrant: 0 (0.0%)
Eligible for Free Lunch Program: 668 (25.4%)
Eligible for Reduced-Price Lunch Program: 336 (12.8%)
Teachers: 167.2 (15.7 to 1)
Librarians/Media Specialists: 5.1 (515.7 to 1)
Guidance Counselors: 6.7 (392.5 to 1)
Current Spending: ($ per student per year):
Total: $6,504; Instruction: $4,165; Support Services: $1,931
Enrollment, Drop-out Rates and Diploma Recipients by Race/Ethnicity

Category	Total	White	Black	Asian	AIAN	Hisp.
Enrollment (%)	100.0	98.8	0.0	0.3	0.1	0.8
Drop-out Rate (%)	6.9	6.8	0.0	0.0	0.0	50.0
H.S. Diplomas (#)	134	132	0	0	2	0

Dawson County

Dawson County
517 Allen St • Dawsonville, GA 30534-0534
(706) 265-3246 • http://www.dawson.k12.ga.us
Grade Span: PK-12; **Agency Type:** 1
Schools: 6
3 Primary; 1 Middle; 1 High; 1 Other Level
5 Regular; 0 Special Education; 0 Vocational; 1 Alternative
0 Magnet; 0 Charter; 2 Title I Eligible; 1 School-wide Title I
Students: 3,036 (51.4% male; 48.6% female)
Individual Education Program: 365 (12.0%);
English Language Learner: 25 (0.8%); Migrant: 2 (0.1%)
Eligible for Free Lunch Program: 681 (22.4%)
Eligible for Reduced-Price Lunch Program: 224 (7.4%)
Teachers: 219.1 (13.9 to 1)
Librarians/Media Specialists: 5.0 (607.2 to 1)
Guidance Counselors: 6.0 (506.0 to 1)
Current Spending: ($ per student per year):
Total: $6,571; Instruction: $4,060; Support Services: $2,096
Enrollment, Drop-out Rates and Diploma Recipients by Race/Ethnicity

Category	Total	White	Black	Asian	AIAN	Hisp.
Enrollment (%)	100.0	97.8	0.1	0.4	0.0	1.7
Drop-out Rate (%)	12.1	12.1	n/a	0.0	n/a	25.0
H.S. Diplomas (#)	113	109	0	2	0	2

De Kalb County

Decatur City
320 N Mcdonough St • Decatur, GA 30030-0030
(404) 370-4400 • http://www.decatur-city.k12.ga.us
Grade Span: PK-12; **Agency Type:** 1
Schools: 8
6 Primary; 1 Middle; 1 High; 0 Other Level
8 Regular; 0 Special Education; 0 Vocational; 0 Alternative
0 Magnet; 0 Charter; 3 Title I Eligible; 1 School-wide Title I
Students: 2,519 (50.7% male; 49.3% female)
Individual Education Program: 314 (12.5%);
English Language Learner: 40 (1.6%); Migrant: 0 (0.0%)
Eligible for Free Lunch Program: 823 (32.7%)
Eligible for Reduced-Price Lunch Program: 140 (5.6%)
Teachers: 224.1 (11.2 to 1)
Librarians/Media Specialists: 6.5 (387.5 to 1)
Guidance Counselors: 7.0 (359.9 to 1)
Current Spending: ($ per student per year):
Total: $9,562; Instruction: $5,852; Support Services: $3,245
Enrollment, Drop-out Rates and Diploma Recipients by Race/Ethnicity

Category	Total	White	Black	Asian	AIAN	Hisp.
Enrollment (%)	100.0	47.4	50.7	1.1	0.0	0.8
Drop-out Rate (%)	4.6	0.0	8.9	0.0	n/a	0.0
H.S. Diplomas (#)	125	76	43	4	0	2

Dekalb County
3770 N Decatur Rd • Decatur, GA 30032-0032
(404) 297-2300 • http://www.dekalb.k12.ga.us
Grade Span: PK-12; **Agency Type:** 1
Schools: 139
86 Primary; 19 Middle; 21 High; 13 Other Level
130 Regular; 4 Special Education; 0 Vocational; 5 Alternative
14 Magnet; 7 Charter; 0 Title I Eligible; 0 School-wide Title I
Students: 97,967 (51.1% male; 48.9% female)
Individual Education Program: 8,824 (9.0%);
English Language Learner: 13,738 (14.0%); Migrant: 0 (0.0%)
Eligible for Free Lunch Program: 47,466 (48.5%)
Eligible for Reduced-Price Lunch Program: 9,921 (10.1%)
Teachers: 6,595.1 (14.9 to 1)
Librarians/Media Specialists: 158.9 (616.5 to 1)
Guidance Counselors: 266.1 (368.2 to 1)
Current Spending: ($ per student per year):
Total: $7,413; Instruction: $4,660; Support Services: $2,377
Enrollment, Drop-out Rates and Diploma Recipients by Race/Ethnicity

Category	Total	White	Black	Asian	AIAN	Hisp.
Enrollment (%)	100.0	11.9	77.6	3.6	0.1	6.8
Drop-out Rate (%)	7.4	5.4	7.8	5.0	0.0	10.4
H.S. Diplomas (#)	4,191	638	3,251	217	4	81

Decatur County

Decatur County
100 W Street • Bainbridge, GA 39818
Mailing Address: PO Drawer 129 • Bainbridge, GA 39818
(229) 248-2200 • http://www.decatur.k12.ga.us
Grade Span: PK-12; **Agency Type:** 1
Schools: 10
6 Primary; 2 Middle; 1 High; 1 Other Level
9 Regular; 0 Special Education; 0 Vocational; 1 Alternative
0 Magnet; 0 Charter; 9 Title I Eligible; 9 School-wide Title I
Students: 5,782 (51.7% male; 48.3% female)
Individual Education Program: 625 (10.8%);
English Language Learner: 80 (1.4%); Migrant: 282 (4.9%)
Eligible for Free Lunch Program: 3,390 (58.6%)
Eligible for Reduced-Price Lunch Program: 504 (8.7%)
Teachers: 383.8 (15.1 to 1)
Librarians/Media Specialists: 10.1 (572.5 to 1)
Guidance Counselors: 13.5 (428.3 to 1)
Current Spending: ($ per student per year):
Total: $6,303; Instruction: $4,020; Support Services: $1,886
Enrollment, Drop-out Rates and Diploma Recipients by Race/Ethnicity

Category	Total	White	Black	Asian	AIAN	Hisp.
Enrollment (%)	100.0	42.3	52.6	0.3	0.0	4.7
Drop-out Rate (%)	6.4	7.2	5.7	0.0	n/a	4.0
H.S. Diplomas (#)	270	154	112	3	0	1

Dodge County

Dodge County
720 College St • Eastman, GA 31023-1023
(478) 374-3783 • http://www.dodge.k12.ga.us
Grade Span: PK-12; **Agency Type:** 1
Schools: 5
2 Primary; 1 Middle; 1 High; 1 Other Level
5 Regular; 0 Special Education; 0 Vocational; 0 Alternative
0 Magnet; 0 Charter; 4 Title I Eligible; 3 School-wide Title I
Students: 3,558 (51.7% male; 48.3% female)
Individual Education Program: 452 (12.7%);
English Language Learner: 2 (0.1%); Migrant: 18 (0.5%)
Eligible for Free Lunch Program: 1,608 (45.2%)
Eligible for Reduced-Price Lunch Program: 433 (12.2%)
Teachers: 209.9 (17.0 to 1)
Librarians/Media Specialists: 4.0 (889.5 to 1)
Guidance Counselors: 6.4 (555.9 to 1)
Current Spending: ($ per student per year):
Total: $6,542; Instruction: $4,264; Support Services: $1,838
Enrollment, Drop-out Rates and Diploma Recipients by Race/Ethnicity

Category	Total	White	Black	Asian	AIAN	Hisp.
Enrollment (%)	100.0	62.2	36.0	0.4	0.1	1.3
Drop-out Rate (%)	7.0	5.9	8.8	n/a	n/a	25.0
H.S. Diplomas (#)	161	118	43	0	0	0

Dooly County

Dooly County
202 Cotton St • Vienna, GA 31092-1092
(912) 229-4761 • http://www.dooly.k12.ga.us/
Grade Span: PK-12; **Agency Type:** 1
Schools: 4
2 Primary; 1 Middle; 1 High; 0 Other Level
4 Regular; 0 Special Education; 0 Vocational; 0 Alternative
0 Magnet; 0 Charter; 3 Title I Eligible; 3 School-wide Title I
Students: 1,545 (50.7% male; 49.3% female)
Individual Education Program: 156 (10.1%);
English Language Learner: 60 (3.9%); Migrant: 75 (4.9%)
Eligible for Free Lunch Program: 1,170 (75.7%)
Eligible for Reduced-Price Lunch Program: 140 (9.1%)
Teachers: 91.7 (16.8 to 1)
Librarians/Media Specialists: 2.5 (618.0 to 1)
Guidance Counselors: 3.0 (515.0 to 1)
Current Spending: ($ per student per year):
Total: $7,879; Instruction: $4,648; Support Services: $2,654
Enrollment, Drop-out Rates and Diploma Recipients by Race/Ethnicity

Category	Total	White	Black	Asian	AIAN	Hisp.
Enrollment (%)	100.0	12.2	79.0	0.6	0.0	8.1
Drop-out Rate (%)	6.7	9.2	6.3	0.0	0.0	10.0
H.S. Diplomas (#)	57	11	43	3	0	0

Dougherty County

Dougherty County
200 Pine Ave • Albany, GA 31701
(229) 431-1285 • http://www.dougherty.k12.ga.us
Grade Span: PK-12; **Agency Type:** 1
Schools: 28
16 Primary; 6 Middle; 4 High; 2 Other Level
26 Regular; 1 Special Education; 0 Vocational; 1 Alternative
2 Magnet; 0 Charter; 20 Title I Eligible; 20 School-wide Title I
Students: 16,607 (50.7% male; 49.3% female)
Individual Education Program: 1,953 (11.8%);
English Language Learner: 24 (0.1%); Migrant: 36 (0.2%)
Eligible for Free Lunch Program: 10,916 (65.7%)
Eligible for Reduced-Price Lunch Program: 2,184 (13.2%)

Teachers: 1,078.0 (15.4 to 1)
Librarians/Media Specialists: 30.5 (544.5 to 1)
Guidance Counselors: 39.4 (421.5 to 1)
Current Spending: ($ per student per year):
Total: $7,237; Instruction: $4,310; Support Services: $2,426
Enrollment, Drop-out Rates and Diploma Recipients by Race/Ethnicity

Category	Total	White	Black	Asian	AIAN	Hisp.
Enrollment (%)	100.0	15.2	83.6	0.4	0.1	0.6
Drop-out Rate (%)	11.4	11.7	11.4	0.0	50.0	12.5
H.S. Diplomas (#)	711	122	580	6	0	3

Douglas County

Douglas County
9030 Hwy 5 • Douglasville, GA 30133-0134
Mailing Address: PO Box 1077 • Douglasville, GA 30133-0134
(770) 920-4000 • http://www.douglas.k12.ga.us
Grade Span: PK-12; **Agency Type:** 1
Schools: 30
18 Primary; 6 Middle; 4 High; 2 Other Level
28 Regular; 0 Special Education; 0 Vocational; 2 Alternative
0 Magnet; 0 Charter; 4 Title I Eligible; 3 School-wide Title I
Students: 18,790 (51.3% male; 48.7% female)
Individual Education Program: 2,250 (12.0%);
English Language Learner: 315 (1.7%); Migrant: 2 (<0.1%)
Eligible for Free Lunch Program: 4,575 (24.3%)
Eligible for Reduced-Price Lunch Program: 1,682 (9.0%)
Teachers: 1,084.0 (17.3 to 1)
Librarians/Media Specialists: 33.0 (569.4 to 1)
Guidance Counselors: 40.0 (469.8 to 1)
Current Spending: ($ per student per year):
Total: $6,525; Instruction: $4,052; Support Services: $2,089
Enrollment, Drop-out Rates and Diploma Recipients by Race/Ethnicity

Category	Total	White	Black	Asian	AIAN	Hisp.
Enrollment (%)	100.0	64.7	29.9	1.4	0.1	3.9
Drop-out Rate (%)	5.3	5.3	5.2	4.1	9.5	6.5
H.S. Diplomas (#)	899	689	171	16	3	20

Early County

Early County
503 Columbia Rd • Blakely, GA 31723-1797
(912) 229-4337 • http://www.early.k12.ga.us
Grade Span: PK-12; **Agency Type:** 1
Schools: 4
1 Primary; 1 Middle; 1 High; 1 Other Level
3 Regular; 0 Special Education; 0 Vocational; 1 Alternative
0 Magnet; 0 Charter; 2 Title I Eligible; 2 School-wide Title I
Students: 2,764 (51.0% male; 49.0% female)
Individual Education Program: 386 (14.0%);
English Language Learner: 4 (0.1%); Migrant: 21 (0.8%)
Eligible for Free Lunch Program: 1,764 (63.8%)
Eligible for Reduced-Price Lunch Program: 215 (7.8%)
Teachers: 155.8 (17.7 to 1)
Librarians/Media Specialists: 4.0 (691.0 to 1)
Guidance Counselors: 6.5 (425.2 to 1)
Current Spending: ($ per student per year):
Total: $6,266; Instruction: $3,982; Support Services: $1,840
Enrollment, Drop-out Rates and Diploma Recipients by Race/Ethnicity

Category	Total	White	Black	Asian	AIAN	Hisp.
Enrollment (%)	100.0	35.1	63.1	0.3	0.0	1.4
Drop-out Rate (%)	2.8	2.9	2.4	33.3	n/a	25.0
H.S. Diplomas (#)	131	61	70	0	0	0

Effingham County

Effingham County
405 N Ash St • Springfield, GA 31329-1329
(912) 754-6491 • http://www.effingham.k12.ga.us
Grade Span: PK-12; **Agency Type:** 1
Schools: 13
7 Primary; 3 Middle; 2 High; 1 Other Level
12 Regular; 0 Special Education; 0 Vocational; 1 Alternative
0 Magnet; 0 Charter; 5 Title I Eligible; 3 School-wide Title I
Students: 9,037 (51.6% male; 48.4% female)
Individual Education Program: 1,218 (13.5%);
English Language Learner: 31 (0.3%); Migrant: 0 (0.0%)
Eligible for Free Lunch Program: 1,879 (20.8%)
Eligible for Reduced-Price Lunch Program: 861 (9.5%)
Teachers: 510.5 (17.7 to 1)
Librarians/Media Specialists: 14.5 (623.2 to 1)
Guidance Counselors: 19.0 (475.6 to 1)
Current Spending: ($ per student per year):
Total: $5,823; Instruction: $3,733; Support Services: $1,770

Enrollment, Drop-out Rates and Diploma Recipients by Race/Ethnicity

Category	Total	White	Black	Asian	AIAN	Hisp.
Enrollment (%)	100.0	82.8	15.5	0.6	0.1	1.0
Drop-out Rate (%)	7.7	7.5	7.5	25.0	50.0	13.0
H.S. Diplomas (#)	426	374	45	1	0	6

Elbert County

Elbert County
50 Laurel Dr • Elberton, GA 30635-0635
(706) 213-4000 • http://www.elbert.k12.ga.us
Grade Span: PK-12; **Agency Type:** 1
Schools: 8
5 Primary; 1 Middle; 1 High; 1 Other Level
7 Regular; 0 Special Education; 0 Vocational; 1 Alternative
0 Magnet; 0 Charter; 5 Title I Eligible; 4 School-wide Title I
Students: 3,793 (51.3% male; 48.7% female)
Individual Education Program: 420 (11.1%);
English Language Learner: 68 (1.8%); Migrant: 18 (0.5%)
Eligible for Free Lunch Program: 1,688 (44.5%)
Eligible for Reduced-Price Lunch Program: 371 (9.8%)
Teachers: 244.2 (15.5 to 1)
Librarians/Media Specialists: 8.0 (474.1 to 1)
Guidance Counselors: 6.0 (632.2 to 1)
Current Spending: ($ per student per year):
Total: $6,759; Instruction: $4,258; Support Services: $2,041
Enrollment, Drop-out Rates and Diploma Recipients by Race/Ethnicity

Category	Total	White	Black	Asian	AIAN	Hisp.
Enrollment (%)	100.0	55.5	41.1	0.3	0.0	3.1
Drop-out Rate (%)	7.1	7.2	6.2	0.0	n/a	40.0
H.S. Diplomas (#)	176	122	54	0	0	0

Emanuel County

Emanuel County
201 N Main St • Swainsboro, GA 30401-0401
Mailing Address: PO Box 130 • Swainsboro, GA 30401-0401
(478) 237-6674 • http://www.emanuel.k12.ga.us/
Grade Span: PK-12; **Agency Type:** 1
Schools: 11
4 Primary; 1 Middle; 1 High; 5 Other Level
10 Regular; 0 Special Education; 0 Vocational; 1 Alternative
0 Magnet; 0 Charter; 6 Title I Eligible; 6 School-wide Title I
Students: 4,664 (51.6% male; 48.4% female)
Individual Education Program: 767 (16.4%);
English Language Learner: 16 (0.3%); Migrant: 50 (1.1%)
Eligible for Free Lunch Program: 2,700 (57.9%)
Eligible for Reduced-Price Lunch Program: 475 (10.2%)
Teachers: 292.7 (15.9 to 1)
Librarians/Media Specialists: 7.5 (621.9 to 1)
Guidance Counselors: 7.3 (638.9 to 1)
Current Spending: ($ per student per year):
Total: $6,444; Instruction: $4,178; Support Services: $1,792
Enrollment, Drop-out Rates and Diploma Recipients by Race/Ethnicity

Category	Total	White	Black	Asian	AIAN	Hisp.
Enrollment (%)	100.0	52.7	45.4	0.2	0.0	1.7
Drop-out Rate (%)	10.3	8.6	12.1	0.0	0.0	60.0
H.S. Diplomas (#)	214	137	77	0	0	0

Evans County

Evans County
613 W Main St • Claxton, GA 30417-0417
(912) 739-3544 • http://www.evans.k12.ga.us/
Grade Span: PK-12; **Agency Type:** 1
Schools: 4
1 Primary; 1 Middle; 1 High; 1 Other Level
3 Regular; 0 Special Education; 0 Vocational; 1 Alternative
0 Magnet; 0 Charter; 2 Title I Eligible; 2 School-wide Title I
Students: 1,944 (52.5% male; 47.5% female)
Individual Education Program: 324 (16.7%);
English Language Learner: 96 (4.9%); Migrant: 123 (6.3%)
Eligible for Free Lunch Program: 1,142 (58.7%)
Eligible for Reduced-Price Lunch Program: 267 (13.7%)
Teachers: 125.7 (15.5 to 1)
Librarians/Media Specialists: 2.5 (777.6 to 1)
Guidance Counselors: 4.0 (486.0 to 1)
Current Spending: ($ per student per year):
Total: $6,152; Instruction: $3,775; Support Services: $1,904
Enrollment, Drop-out Rates and Diploma Recipients by Race/Ethnicity

Category	Total	White	Black	Asian	AIAN	Hisp.
Enrollment (%)	100.0	45.7	45.6	0.5	0.1	8.0
Drop-out Rate (%)	5.2	3.9	6.8	0.0	n/a	8.3
H.S. Diplomas (#)	84	51	31	1	0	1

Fannin County

Fannin County
2290 E First St • Blue Ridge, GA 30513-0513
(706) 632-3771 • http://www.fannin.k12.ga.us
Grade Span: PK-12; **Agency Type:** 1
Schools: 5
3 Primary; 1 Middle; 1 High; 0 Other Level
5 Regular; 0 Special Education; 0 Vocational; 0 Alternative
0 Magnet; 0 Charter; 4 Title I Eligible; 0 School-wide Title I
Students: 3,212 (51.5% male; 48.5% female)
Individual Education Program: 442 (13.8%);
English Language Learner: 0 (0.0%); Migrant: 0 (0.0%)
Eligible for Free Lunch Program: 925 (28.8%)
Eligible for Reduced-Price Lunch Program: 382 (11.9%)
Teachers: 178.9 (18.0 to 1)
Librarians/Media Specialists: 5.0 (642.4 to 1)
Guidance Counselors: 6.0 (535.3 to 1)
Current Spending: ($ per student per year):
Total: $6,948; Instruction: $4,425; Support Services: $2,074
Enrollment, Drop-out Rates and Diploma Recipients by Race/Ethnicity

Category	Total	White	Black	Asian	AIAN	Hisp.
Enrollment (%)	100.0	98.3	0.3	0.6	0.2	0.6
Drop-out Rate (%)	5.7	5.7	0.0	0.0	0.0	0.0
H.S. Diplomas (#)	147	145	0	1	0	1

Fayette County

Fayette County
210 Stonewall Ave • Fayetteville, GA 30214-0214
(770) 460-3535 • http://www.fcboe.org
Grade Span: PK-12; **Agency Type:** 1
Schools: 27
16 Primary; 5 Middle; 5 High; 1 Other Level
25 Regular; 0 Special Education; 0 Vocational; 2 Alternative
0 Magnet; 0 Charter; 6 Title I Eligible; 0 School-wide Title I
Students: 20,756 (51.0% male; 49.0% female)
Individual Education Program: 2,422 (11.7%);
English Language Learner: 439 (2.1%); Migrant: 0 (0.0%)
Eligible for Free Lunch Program: 1,324 (6.4%)
Eligible for Reduced-Price Lunch Program: 484 (2.3%)
Teachers: 1,380.3 (15.0 to 1)
Librarians/Media Specialists: 31.0 (669.5 to 1)
Guidance Counselors: 51.3 (404.6 to 1)
Current Spending: ($ per student per year):
Total: $6,631; Instruction: $4,384; Support Services: $1,992
Enrollment, Drop-out Rates and Diploma Recipients by Race/Ethnicity

Category	Total	White	Black	Asian	AIAN	Hisp.
Enrollment (%)	100.0	77.4	16.5	3.2	0.1	2.8
Drop-out Rate (%)	2.1	2.0	2.9	1.1	12.5	2.6
H.S. Diplomas (#)	1,380	1,130	190	37	1	22

Floyd County

Floyd County
600 Riverside Parkway, NE • Rome, GA 30161-0161
(706) 234-1031 • http://www.floydboe.net
Grade Span: PK-12; **Agency Type:** 1
Schools: 22
10 Primary; 5 Middle; 5 High; 2 Other Level
20 Regular; 0 Special Education; 0 Vocational; 2 Alternative
0 Magnet; 0 Charter; 6 Title I Eligible; 3 School-wide Title I
Students: 10,272 (51.3% male; 48.7% female)
Individual Education Program: 2,343 (22.8%);
English Language Learner: 213 (2.1%); Migrant: 2 (<0.1%)
Eligible for Free Lunch Program: 3,152 (30.7%)
Eligible for Reduced-Price Lunch Program: 913 (8.9%)
Teachers: 647.0 (15.9 to 1)
Librarians/Media Specialists: 19.0 (540.6 to 1)
Guidance Counselors: 25.0 (410.9 to 1)
Current Spending: ($ per student per year):
Total: $6,391; Instruction: $4,028; Support Services: $2,031
Enrollment, Drop-out Rates and Diploma Recipients by Race/Ethnicity

Category	Total	White	Black	Asian	AIAN	Hisp.
Enrollment (%)	100.0	91.3	4.1	0.8	0.2	3.5
Drop-out Rate (%)	3.5	3.7	0.7	5.0	0.0	2.2
H.S. Diplomas (#)	454	422	21	4	0	7

Rome City
508 E Second St • Rome, GA 30161-0161
(706) 236-5050 • http://www.rcs.rome.ga.us
Grade Span: PK-12; **Agency Type:** 1
Schools: 11
8 Primary; 1 Middle; 1 High; 1 Other Level
10 Regular; 0 Special Education; 0 Vocational; 1 Alternative
0 Magnet; 0 Charter; 7 Title I Eligible; 7 School-wide Title I
Students: 5,395 (49.8% male; 50.2% female)
Individual Education Program: 631 (11.7%);
English Language Learner: 602 (11.2%); Migrant: 63 (1.2%)
Eligible for Free Lunch Program: 2,907 (53.9%)
Eligible for Reduced-Price Lunch Program: 385 (7.1%)
Teachers: 322.8 (16.7 to 1)
Librarians/Media Specialists: 11.0 (490.5 to 1)
Guidance Counselors: 11.5 (469.1 to 1)
Current Spending: ($ per student per year):
Total: $7,021; Instruction: $4,647; Support Services: $1,953
Enrollment, Drop-out Rates and Diploma Recipients by Race/Ethnicity

Category	Total	White	Black	Asian	AIAN	Hisp.
Enrollment (%)	100.0	38.6	44.1	2.7	0.1	14.6
Drop-out Rate (%)	9.2	6.9	12.6	0.0	50.0	8.0
H.S. Diplomas (#)	238	135	83	9	0	11

Forsyth County

Forsyth County
1120 Dahlonega Hwy • Cumming, GA 30040-0040
(770) 887-2461 • http://www.forsyth.k12.ga.us
Grade Span: PK-12; **Agency Type:** 1
Schools: 23
14 Primary; 5 Middle; 3 High; 1 Other Level
22 Regular; 0 Special Education; 0 Vocational; 1 Alternative
0 Magnet; 0 Charter; 7 Title I Eligible; 0 School-wide Title I
Students: 20,407 (51.8% male; 48.2% female)
Individual Education Program: 2,380 (11.7%);
English Language Learner: 831 (4.1%); Migrant: 42 (0.2%)
Eligible for Free Lunch Program: 1,746 (8.6%)
Eligible for Reduced-Price Lunch Program: 695 (3.4%)
Teachers: 1,360.0 (15.0 to 1)
Librarians/Media Specialists: 22.0 (927.6 to 1)
Guidance Counselors: 46.0 (443.6 to 1)
Current Spending: ($ per student per year):
Total: $6,759; Instruction: $4,182; Support Services: $2,261
Enrollment, Drop-out Rates and Diploma Recipients by Race/Ethnicity

Category	Total	White	Black	Asian	AIAN	Hisp.
Enrollment (%)	100.0	92.1	0.6	1.0	0.2	6.2
Drop-out Rate (%)	5.2	5.1	8.3	5.0	10.0	9.0
H.S. Diplomas (#)	765	739	4	4	1	17

Franklin County

Franklin County
919 Hull Ave • Carnesville, GA 30521-0521
(706) 384-4554 • http://www.franklin.k12.ga.us
Grade Span: PK-12; **Agency Type:** 1
Schools: 5
3 Primary; 1 Middle; 1 High; 0 Other Level
5 Regular; 0 Special Education; 0 Vocational; 0 Alternative
0 Magnet; 0 Charter; 4 Title I Eligible; 4 School-wide Title I
Students: 3,722 (51.3% male; 48.7% female)
Individual Education Program: 588 (15.8%);
English Language Learner: 6 (0.2%); Migrant: 2 (0.1%)
Eligible for Free Lunch Program: 1,163 (31.2%)
Eligible for Reduced-Price Lunch Program: 375 (10.1%)
Teachers: 232.1 (16.0 to 1)
Librarians/Media Specialists: 5.0 (744.4 to 1)
Guidance Counselors: 7.0 (531.7 to 1)
Current Spending: ($ per student per year):
Total: $6,545; Instruction: $4,441; Support Services: $1,770
Enrollment, Drop-out Rates and Diploma Recipients by Race/Ethnicity

Category	Total	White	Black	Asian	AIAN	Hisp.
Enrollment (%)	100.0	86.0	12.0	0.5	0.0	1.5
Drop-out Rate (%)	7.0	6.3	11.7	25.0	n/a	20.0
H.S. Diplomas (#)	145	134	11	0	0	0

Fulton County

Atlanta City
210 Pryor Street, SW • Atlanta, GA 30335
(404) 827-8075 • http://www.atlanta.k12.ga.us
Grade Span: PK-12; **Agency Type:** 1
Schools: 102
70 Primary; 15 Middle; 13 High; 4 Other Level
95 Regular; 0 Special Education; 0 Vocational; 7 Alternative
6 Magnet; 5 Charter; 89 Title I Eligible; 86 School-wide Title I
Students: 54,946 (50.1% male; 49.9% female)
Individual Education Program: 4,269 (7.8%);
English Language Learner: 1,467 (2.7%); Migrant: 0 (0.0%)
Eligible for Free Lunch Program: 36,891 (67.1%)
Eligible for Reduced-Price Lunch Program: 2,363 (4.3%)
Teachers: 3,874.5 (14.2 to 1)

Librarians/Media Specialists: 88.0 (624.4 to 1)
Guidance Counselors: 141.0 (389.7 to 1)
Current Spending: ($ per student per year):
Total: $10,993; Instruction: $6,531; Support Services: $4,180
Enrollment, Drop-out Rates and Diploma Recipients by Race/Ethnicity

Category	Total	White	Black	Asian	AIAN	Hisp.
Enrollment (%)	100.0	7.2	88.6	0.7	0.1	3.4
Drop-out Rate (%)	21.9	11.4	22.3	21.1	16.7	28.1
H.S. Diplomas (#)	2,270	112	2,100	38	0	20

Fulton County
786 Cleveland Avenue, SW • Atlanta, GA 30315-0315
(404) 768-3600 • http://www.fulton.k12.ga.us
Grade Span: PK-12; **Agency Type:** 1
Schools: 81
50 Primary; 16 Middle; 12 High; 3 Other Level
78 Regular; 0 Special Education; 0 Vocational; 3 Alternative
1 Magnet; 4 Charter; 25 Title I Eligible; 22 School-wide Title I
Students: 71,372 (51.1% male; 48.9% female)
Individual Education Program: 7,314 (10.2%);
English Language Learner: 4,656 (6.5%); Migrant: 0 (0.0%)
Eligible for Free Lunch Program: 20,326 (28.5%)
Eligible for Reduced-Price Lunch Program: 3,546 (5.0%)
Teachers: 4,860.5 (14.7 to 1)
Librarians/Media Specialists: 82.0 (870.4 to 1)
Guidance Counselors: 172.0 (415.0 to 1)
Current Spending: ($ per student per year):
Total: $7,869; Instruction: $5,086; Support Services: $2,502
Enrollment, Drop-out Rates and Diploma Recipients by Race/Ethnicity

Category	Total	White	Black	Asian	AIAN	Hisp.
Enrollment (%)	100.0	46.3	39.2	6.3	0.1	8.0
Drop-out Rate (%)	4.9	3.1	7.0	2.0	9.1	11.8
H.S. Diplomas (#)	3,360	1,980	1,044	236	1	99

Gilmer County

Gilmer County
497 Bobcat Tr • Ellijay, GA 30540-5212
(706) 276-5000 •
http://www.gilmerschools.com/education/district/district.php?sectionid=1
Grade Span: PK-12; **Agency Type:** 1
Schools: 6
3 Primary; 1 Middle; 1 High; 1 Other Level
6 Regular; 0 Special Education; 0 Vocational; 0 Alternative
0 Magnet; 0 Charter; 5 Title I Eligible; 5 School-wide Title I
Students: 3,929 (52.3% male; 47.7% female)
Individual Education Program: 454 (11.6%);
English Language Learner: 245 (6.2%); Migrant: 131 (3.3%)
Eligible for Free Lunch Program: 1,523 (38.8%)
Eligible for Reduced-Price Lunch Program: 437 (11.1%)
Teachers: 256.5 (15.3 to 1)
Librarians/Media Specialists: 6.0 (654.8 to 1)
Guidance Counselors: 7.0 (561.3 to 1)
Current Spending: ($ per student per year):
Total: $6,270; Instruction: $4,158; Support Services: $1,741
Enrollment, Drop-out Rates and Diploma Recipients by Race/Ethnicity

Category	Total	White	Black	Asian	AIAN	Hisp.
Enrollment (%)	100.0	89.3	0.0	0.2	0.2	10.3
Drop-out Rate (%)	7.5	7.0	0.0	0.0	0.0	17.1
H.S. Diplomas (#)	139	134	0	0	0	5

Glynn County

Glynn County
1313 Egmont St • Brunswick, GA 31520
(912) 267-4100 • http://www.glynn.k12.ga.us
Grade Span: PK-12; **Agency Type:** 1
Schools: 17
9 Primary; 4 Middle; 2 High; 2 Other Level
16 Regular; 0 Special Education; 0 Vocational; 1 Alternative
0 Magnet; 0 Charter; 7 Title I Eligible; 5 School-wide Title I
Students: 12,071 (50.7% male; 49.3% female)
Individual Education Program: 1,621 (13.4%);
English Language Learner: 129 (1.1%); Migrant: 117 (1.0%)
Eligible for Free Lunch Program: 4,615 (38.2%)
Eligible for Reduced-Price Lunch Program: 922 (7.6%)
Teachers: 749.5 (16.1 to 1)
Librarians/Media Specialists: 17.0 (710.1 to 1)
Guidance Counselors: 27.0 (447.1 to 1)
Current Spending: ($ per student per year):
Total: $6,921; Instruction: $4,531; Support Services: $2,023

Enrollment, Drop-out Rates and Diploma Recipients by Race/Ethnicity

Category	Total	White	Black	Asian	AIAN	Hisp.
Enrollment (%)	100.0	57.2	38.7	0.8	0.1	3.2
Drop-out Rate (%)	9.0	7.5	11.5	3.7	0.0	11.4
H.S. Diplomas (#)	516	350	152	8	0	6

Gordon County

Calhoun City
700 W Line St • Calhoun, GA 30701-0701
(706) 629-2900 • http://www.calhoun-city.k12.ga.us
Grade Span: PK-12; **Agency Type:** 1
Schools: 6
2 Primary; 1 Middle; 1 High; 2 Other Level
5 Regular; 0 Special Education; 0 Vocational; 1 Alternative
0 Magnet; 0 Charter; 2 Title I Eligible; 0 School-wide Title I
Students: 2,666 (51.2% male; 48.8% female)
Individual Education Program: 295 (11.1%);
English Language Learner: 395 (14.8%); Migrant: 0 (0.0%)
Eligible for Free Lunch Program: 833 (31.2%)
Eligible for Reduced-Price Lunch Program: 163 (6.1%)
Teachers: 166.0 (16.1 to 1)
Librarians/Media Specialists: 3.0 (888.7 to 1)
Guidance Counselors: 5.0 (533.2 to 1)
Current Spending: ($ per student per year):
Total: $6,664; Instruction: $4,251; Support Services: $1,962
Enrollment, Drop-out Rates and Diploma Recipients by Race/Ethnicity

Category	Total	White	Black	Asian	AIAN	Hisp.
Enrollment (%)	100.0	70.9	9.1	1.6	0.1	18.4
Drop-out Rate (%)	6.9	5.7	1.8	9.5	n/a	23.4
H.S. Diplomas (#)	124	103	10	4	0	7

Gordon County
205 Warrior Path • Calhoun, GA 30703-0127
Mailing Address: PO Box 12001 • Calhoun, GA 30703-0127
(706) 629-7366 • http://www.gcbe.org
Grade Span: PK-12; **Agency Type:** 1
Schools: 9
5 Primary; 2 Middle; 1 High; 1 Other Level
8 Regular; 0 Special Education; 0 Vocational; 1 Alternative
0 Magnet; 0 Charter; 5 Title I Eligible; 0 School-wide Title I
Students: 6,259 (50.8% male; 49.2% female)
Individual Education Program: 961 (15.4%);
English Language Learner: 224 (3.6%); Migrant: 28 (0.4%)
Eligible for Free Lunch Program: 1,939 (31.0%)
Eligible for Reduced-Price Lunch Program: 629 (10.0%)
Teachers: 365.5 (17.1 to 1)
Librarians/Media Specialists: 9.0 (695.4 to 1)
Guidance Counselors: 10.0 (625.9 to 1)
Current Spending: ($ per student per year):
Total: $6,462; Instruction: $4,129; Support Services: $1,966
Enrollment, Drop-out Rates and Diploma Recipients by Race/Ethnicity

Category	Total	White	Black	Asian	AIAN	Hisp.
Enrollment (%)	100.0	91.0	1.9	0.5	0.1	6.4
Drop-out Rate (%)	10.6	10.8	11.1	0.0	0.0	9.1
H.S. Diplomas (#)	217	209	3	2	1	2

Grady County

Grady County
122 N Broad • Cairo, GA 31728-1728
(229) 377-3701 • http://www.grady.k12.ga.us
Grade Span: PK-12; **Agency Type:** 1
Schools: 8
5 Primary; 1 Middle; 1 High; 1 Other Level
7 Regular; 0 Special Education; 0 Vocational; 1 Alternative
0 Magnet; 0 Charter; 4 Title I Eligible; 4 School-wide Title I
Students: 4,550 (49.0% male; 51.0% female)
Individual Education Program: 534 (11.7%);
English Language Learner: 104 (2.3%); Migrant: 169 (3.7%)
Eligible for Free Lunch Program: 2,095 (46.0%)
Eligible for Reduced-Price Lunch Program: 380 (8.4%)
Teachers: 284.6 (16.0 to 1)
Librarians/Media Specialists: 8.0 (568.8 to 1)
Guidance Counselors: 10.0 (455.0 to 1)
Current Spending: ($ per student per year):
Total: $6,471; Instruction: $4,131; Support Services: $1,999
Enrollment, Drop-out Rates and Diploma Recipients by Race/Ethnicity

Category	Total	White	Black	Asian	AIAN	Hisp.
Enrollment (%)	100.0	53.3	41.5	0.5	0.1	4.6
Drop-out Rate (%)	8.8	9.0	7.9	25.0	n/a	25.0
H.S. Diplomas (#)	173	105	67	0	0	1

Greene County

Greene County
201 N Main St • Greensboro, GA 31728
(706) 453-7688 • http://www.greene.k12.ga.us
Grade Span: PK-12; **Agency Type:** 1
Schools: 6
2 Primary; 1 Middle; 1 High; 2 Other Level
5 Regular; 0 Special Education; 0 Vocational; 1 Alternative
0 Magnet; 0 Charter; 4 Title I Eligible; 4 School-wide Title I
Students: 2,280 (51.4% male; 48.6% female)
Individual Education Program: 345 (15.1%);
English Language Learner: 19 (0.8%); Migrant: 2 (0.1%)
Eligible for Free Lunch Program: 1,685 (73.9%)
Eligible for Reduced-Price Lunch Program: 143 (6.3%)
Teachers: 157.5 (14.5 to 1)
Librarians/Media Specialists: 4.0 (570.0 to 1)
Guidance Counselors: 6.0 (380.0 to 1)
Current Spending: ($ per student per year):
Total: $7,944; Instruction: $4,713; Support Services: $2,759
Enrollment, Drop-out Rates and Diploma Recipients by Race/Ethnicity

Category	Total	White	Black	Asian	AIAN	Hisp.
Enrollment (%)	100.0	25.2	71.9	0.1	0.0	2.7
Drop-out Rate (%)	8.2	6.3	8.7	0.0	n/a	0.0
H.S. Diplomas (#)	82	21	59	1	0	1

Gwinnett County

Buford City
70 Wiley Drive, Ste 200 • Buford, GA 30518-0518
(770) 945-5035 • http://www.bufordcityschools.org
Grade Span: PK-12; **Agency Type:** 1
Schools: 4
2 Primary; 1 Middle; 1 High; 0 Other Level
4 Regular; 0 Special Education; 0 Vocational; 0 Alternative
0 Magnet; 0 Charter; 3 Title I Eligible; 1 School-wide Title I
Students: 2,259 (52.1% male; 47.9% female)
Individual Education Program: 262 (11.6%);
English Language Learner: 251 (11.1%); Migrant: 0 (0.0%)
Eligible for Free Lunch Program: 791 (35.0%)
Eligible for Reduced-Price Lunch Program: 115 (5.1%)
Teachers: 152.3 (14.8 to 1)
Librarians/Media Specialists: 4.0 (564.8 to 1)
Guidance Counselors: 5.0 (451.8 to 1)
Current Spending: ($ per student per year):
Total: $8,573; Instruction: $5,184; Support Services: $2,991
Enrollment, Drop-out Rates and Diploma Recipients by Race/Ethnicity

Category	Total	White	Black	Asian	AIAN	Hisp.
Enrollment (%)	100.0	64.0	15.2	1.3	0.1	19.3
Drop-out Rate (%)	4.7	4.1	5.0	14.3	n/a	7.8
H.S. Diplomas (#)	100	80	14	0	0	6

Gwinnett County
52 Gwinnett Dr • Lawrenceville, GA 30046
Mailing Address: PO Box 343 • Lawrenceville, GA 30046
(770) 963-8651 • http://www.gwinnett.k12.ga.us
Grade Span: PK-12; **Agency Type:** 1
Schools: 89
54 Primary; 16 Middle; 14 High; 5 Other Level
85 Regular; 1 Special Education; 0 Vocational; 3 Alternative
0 Magnet; 0 Charter; 22 Title I Eligible; 7 School-wide Title I
Students: 122,570 (51.3% male; 48.7% female)
Individual Education Program: 13,809 (11.3%);
English Language Learner: 11,332 (9.2%); Migrant: 21 (<0.1%)
Eligible for Free Lunch Program: 24,262 (19.8%)
Eligible for Reduced-Price Lunch Program: 7,664 (6.3%)
Teachers: 8,047.6 (15.2 to 1)
Librarians/Media Specialists: 103.5 (1,184.3 to 1)
Guidance Counselors: 256.7 (477.5 to 1)
Current Spending: ($ per student per year):
Total: $6,664; Instruction: $4,369; Support Services: $2,036
Enrollment, Drop-out Rates and Diploma Recipients by Race/Ethnicity

Category	Total	White	Black	Asian	AIAN	Hisp.
Enrollment (%)	100.0	56.4	19.8	9.6	0.1	14.2
Drop-out Rate (%)	1.5	1.1	2.5	1.3	5.6	4.0
H.S. Diplomas (#)	6,116	4,370	760	645	10	331

Habersham County

Habersham County
132 W Stanford Mill Rd • Clarkesville, GA 30523-0523
Mailing Address: PO Box 70 • Clarkesville, GA 30523-0523
(706) 754-2118 • http://www.habersham.k12.ga.us
Grade Span: KG-12; **Agency Type:** 1
Schools: 11
7 Primary; 2 Middle; 1 High; 1 Other Level
10 Regular; 0 Special Education; 0 Vocational; 1 Alternative
0 Magnet; 0 Charter; 4 Title I Eligible; 2 School-wide Title I
Students: 5,955 (52.5% male; 47.5% female)
Individual Education Program: 806 (13.5%);
English Language Learner: 485 (8.1%); Migrant: 279 (4.7%)
Eligible for Free Lunch Program: 1,705 (28.6%)
Eligible for Reduced-Price Lunch Program: 449 (7.5%)
Teachers: 368.2 (16.2 to 1)
Librarians/Media Specialists: 9.4 (633.5 to 1)
Guidance Counselors: 10.5 (567.1 to 1)
Current Spending: ($ per student per year):
Total: $6,630; Instruction: $4,169; Support Services: $2,143
Enrollment, Drop-out Rates and Diploma Recipients by Race/Ethnicity

Category	Total	White	Black	Asian	AIAN	Hisp.
Enrollment (%)	100.0	81.1	2.4	2.7	0.1	13.7
Drop-out Rate (%)	5.3	3.4	4.0	17.1	25.0	37.5
H.S. Diplomas (#)	270	254	2	6	0	8

Hall County

Gainesville City
508 Oak Street, NW • Gainesville, GA 30501-3506
(770) 536-5275 • http://www.gainesville-city.k12.ga.us
Grade Span: PK-12; **Agency Type:** 1
Schools: 5
2 Primary; 2 Middle; 1 High; 0 Other Level
5 Regular; 0 Special Education; 0 Vocational; 0 Alternative
0 Magnet; 0 Charter; 5 Title I Eligible; 4 School-wide Title I
Students: 4,438 (50.6% male; 49.4% female)
Individual Education Program: 300 (6.8%);
English Language Learner: 934 (21.0%); Migrant: 501 (11.3%)
Eligible for Free Lunch Program: 2,533 (57.1%)
Eligible for Reduced-Price Lunch Program: 312 (7.0%)
Teachers: 282.2 (15.7 to 1)
Librarians/Media Specialists: 5.0 (887.6 to 1)
Guidance Counselors: 9.0 (493.1 to 1)
Current Spending: ($ per student per year):
Total: $7,855; Instruction: $5,022; Support Services: $2,490
Enrollment, Drop-out Rates and Diploma Recipients by Race/Ethnicity

Category	Total	White	Black	Asian	AIAN	Hisp.
Enrollment (%)	100.0	25.7	24.3	2.8	0.0	47.2
Drop-out Rate (%)	6.5	2.2	6.6	10.9	n/a	12.6
H.S. Diplomas (#)	186	114	32	10	0	30

Hall County
711 Green Street, Ste 100 • Gainesville, GA 30505
(770) 534-1080 • http://www.hallco.org
Grade Span: PK-12; **Agency Type:** 1
Schools: 32
19 Primary; 6 Middle; 7 High; 0 Other Level
31 Regular; 0 Special Education; 0 Vocational; 1 Alternative
0 Magnet; 0 Charter; 7 Title I Eligible; 7 School-wide Title I
Students: 21,730 (51.7% male; 48.3% female)
Individual Education Program: 2,177 (10.0%);
English Language Learner: 5,169 (23.8%); Migrant: 820 (3.8%)
Eligible for Free Lunch Program: 6,961 (32.0%)
Eligible for Reduced-Price Lunch Program: 1,877 (8.6%)
Teachers: 1,337.0 (16.3 to 1)
Librarians/Media Specialists: 33.0 (658.5 to 1)
Guidance Counselors: 46.2 (470.3 to 1)
Current Spending: ($ per student per year):
Total: $6,147; Instruction: $4,039; Support Services: $1,753
Enrollment, Drop-out Rates and Diploma Recipients by Race/Ethnicity

Category	Total	White	Black	Asian	AIAN	Hisp.
Enrollment (%)	100.0	69.2	5.6	0.9	0.4	23.8
Drop-out Rate (%)	6.1	5.8	6.4	3.2	0.0	8.0
H.S. Diplomas (#)	869	745	37	17	4	66

Hancock County

Hancock County
Augusta Hwy • Sparta, GA 31087-1087
(706) 444-5775 • http://www.hancock.k12.ga.us/
Grade Span: PK-12; **Agency Type:** 1
Schools: 4
2 Primary; 0 Middle; 0 High; 2 Other Level
3 Regular; 0 Special Education; 0 Vocational; 1 Alternative
0 Magnet; 0 Charter; 3 Title I Eligible; 0 School-wide Title I
Students: 1,659 (51.0% male; 49.0% female)
Individual Education Program: 206 (12.4%);
English Language Learner: 0 (0.0%); Migrant: 0 (0.0%)
Eligible for Free Lunch Program: 1,328 (80.0%)
Eligible for Reduced-Price Lunch Program: 112 (6.8%)
Teachers: 104.8 (15.8 to 1)

Librarians/Media Specialists: 2.0 (829.5 to 1)
Guidance Counselors: 3.5 (474.0 to 1)
Current Spending: ($ per student per year):
Total: $6,879; Instruction: $3,805; Support Services: $2,457
Enrollment, Drop-out Rates and Diploma Recipients by Race/Ethnicity

Category	Total	White	Black	Asian	AIAN	Hisp.
Enrollment (%)	100.0	1.2	98.6	0.2	0.1	0.0
Drop-out Rate (%)	6.6	25.0	6.5	n/a	n/a	n/a
H.S. Diplomas (#)	82	0	82	0	0	0

Haralson County

Bremen City

504 Laurel St • Bremen, GA 30110-0110
(404) 537-5508
Grade Span: PK-12; **Agency Type:** 1
Schools: 3
1 Primary; 1 Middle; 1 High; 0 Other Level
3 Regular; 0 Special Education; 0 Vocational; 0 Alternative
0 Magnet; 0 Charter; 1 Title I Eligible; 0 School-wide Title I
Students: 1,575 (49.6% male; 50.4% female)
Individual Education Program: 206 (13.1%);
English Language Learner: 0 (0.0%); Migrant: 0 (0.0%)
Eligible for Free Lunch Program: 154 (9.8%)
Eligible for Reduced-Price Lunch Program: 50 (3.2%)
Teachers: 95.9 (16.4 to 1)
Librarians/Media Specialists: 2.0 (787.5 to 1)
Guidance Counselors: 2.5 (630.0 to 1)
Current Spending: ($ per student per year):
Total: $6,414; Instruction: $4,239; Support Services: $1,805
Enrollment, Drop-out Rates and Diploma Recipients by Race/Ethnicity

Category	Total	White	Black	Asian	AIAN	Hisp.
Enrollment (%)	100.0	91.6	7.5	0.6	0.0	0.3
Drop-out Rate (%)	2.8	2.7	3.0	n/a	n/a	0.0
H.S. Diplomas (#)	89	85	4	0	0	0

Haralson County

10 Van Wert St • Buchanan, GA 30113-0113
(770) 646-3882 • http://www.haralson.k12.ga.us
Grade Span: PK-12; **Agency Type:** 1
Schools: 7
4 Primary; 1 Middle; 1 High; 1 Other Level
6 Regular; 0 Special Education; 0 Vocational; 1 Alternative
0 Magnet; 0 Charter; 5 Title I Eligible; 5 School-wide Title I
Students: 3,766 (53.6% male; 46.4% female)
Individual Education Program: 666 (17.7%);
English Language Learner: 5 (0.1%); Migrant: 102 (2.7%)
Eligible for Free Lunch Program: 1,381 (36.7%)
Eligible for Reduced-Price Lunch Program: 357 (9.5%)
Teachers: 230.7 (16.3 to 1)
Librarians/Media Specialists: 6.0 (627.7 to 1)
Guidance Counselors: 8.0 (470.8 to 1)
Current Spending: ($ per student per year):
Total: $6,186; Instruction: $4,092; Support Services: $1,734
Enrollment, Drop-out Rates and Diploma Recipients by Race/Ethnicity

Category	Total	White	Black	Asian	AIAN	Hisp.
Enrollment (%)	100.0	95.1	4.2	0.3	0.1	0.4
Drop-out Rate (%)	9.5	9.6	10.6	0.0	0.0	0.0
H.S. Diplomas (#)	142	131	9	1	1	0

Harris County

Harris County

132 Barnes Mill Rd • Hamilton, GA 31811-1811
(706) 628-4206 • http://www.harris.k12.ga.us/
Grade Span: PK-12; **Agency Type:** 1
Schools: 7
4 Primary; 1 Middle; 1 High; 1 Other Level
6 Regular; 0 Special Education; 0 Vocational; 1 Alternative
0 Magnet; 0 Charter; 3 Title I Eligible; 2 School-wide Title I
Students: 4,411 (52.2% male; 47.8% female)
Individual Education Program: 385 (8.7%);
English Language Learner: 0 (0.0%); Migrant: 0 (0.0%)
Eligible for Free Lunch Program: 1,066 (24.2%)
Eligible for Reduced-Price Lunch Program: 484 (11.0%)
Teachers: 273.9 (16.1 to 1)
Librarians/Media Specialists: 7.0 (630.1 to 1)
Guidance Counselors: 11.0 (401.0 to 1)
Current Spending: ($ per student per year):
Total: $6,395; Instruction: $3,980; Support Services: $2,028
Enrollment, Drop-out Rates and Diploma Recipients by Race/Ethnicity

Category	Total	White	Black	Asian	AIAN	Hisp.
Enrollment (%)	100.0	76.0	22.8	0.5	0.0	0.6
Drop-out Rate (%)	7.5	6.7	9.6	0.0	0.0	14.3
H.S. Diplomas (#)	221	174	44	2	0	1

Hart County

Hart County

284 Campbell Dr • Hartwell, GA 30643-0643
Mailing Address: PO Box 696 • Hartwell, GA 30643-0643
(706) 376-5141 • http://www.pioneer.resa.k12.ga.us
Grade Span: PK-12; **Agency Type:** 1
Schools: 6
3 Primary; 1 Middle; 1 High; 1 Other Level
5 Regular; 0 Special Education; 0 Vocational; 1 Alternative
0 Magnet; 0 Charter; 2 Title I Eligible; 0 School-wide Title I
Students: 3,564 (53.8% male; 46.2% female)
Individual Education Program: 423 (11.9%);
English Language Learner: 32 (0.9%); Migrant: 4 (0.1%)
Eligible for Free Lunch Program: 1,221 (34.3%)
Eligible for Reduced-Price Lunch Program: 385 (10.8%)
Teachers: 229.4 (15.5 to 1)
Librarians/Media Specialists: 5.0 (712.8 to 1)
Guidance Counselors: 7.0 (509.1 to 1)
Current Spending: ($ per student per year):
Total: $7,136; Instruction: $4,596; Support Services: $2,144
Enrollment, Drop-out Rates and Diploma Recipients by Race/Ethnicity

Category	Total	White	Black	Asian	AIAN	Hisp.
Enrollment (%)	100.0	70.2	27.6	0.5	0.0	1.7
Drop-out Rate (%)	9.4	9.1	9.9	0.0	n/a	50.0
H.S. Diplomas (#)	211	155	54	2	0	0

Heard County

Heard County

131 E Court Square • Franklin, GA 30217-0217
(706) 675-3320 • http://www.heard.k12.ga.us
Grade Span: PK-12; **Agency Type:** 1
Schools: 5
3 Primary; 1 Middle; 1 High; 0 Other Level
5 Regular; 0 Special Education; 0 Vocational; 0 Alternative
0 Magnet; 0 Charter; 4 Title I Eligible; 3 School-wide Title I
Students: 2,178 (51.7% male; 48.3% female)
Individual Education Program: 267 (12.3%);
English Language Learner: 0 (0.0%); Migrant: 0 (0.0%)
Eligible for Free Lunch Program: 838 (38.5%)
Eligible for Reduced-Price Lunch Program: 245 (11.2%)
Teachers: 132.2 (16.5 to 1)
Librarians/Media Specialists: 4.0 (544.5 to 1)
Guidance Counselors: 4.0 (544.5 to 1)
Current Spending: ($ per student per year):
Total: $5,971; Instruction: $3,861; Support Services: $1,747
Enrollment, Drop-out Rates and Diploma Recipients by Race/Ethnicity

Category	Total	White	Black	Asian	AIAN	Hisp.
Enrollment (%)	100.0	86.1	12.2	0.1	0.1	1.5
Drop-out Rate (%)	7.5	7.4	5.9	0.0	100.0	0.0
H.S. Diplomas (#)	69	67	1	1	0	0

Henry County

Henry County

396 Tomlinson St • Mcdonough, GA 30253-0253
(770) 957-6601
Grade Span: PK-12; **Agency Type:** 1
Schools: 28
17 Primary; 6 Middle; 4 High; 1 Other Level
27 Regular; 0 Special Education; 0 Vocational; 1 Alternative
0 Magnet; 0 Charter; 0 Title I Eligible; 0 School-wide Title I
Students: 27,734 (51.5% male; 48.5% female)
Individual Education Program: 3,020 (10.9%);
English Language Learner: 558 (2.0%); Migrant: 0 (0.0%)
Eligible for Free Lunch Program: 3,971 (14.3%)
Eligible for Reduced-Price Lunch Program: 1,730 (6.2%)
Teachers: 1,544.7 (18.0 to 1)
Librarians/Media Specialists: 30.0 (924.5 to 1)
Guidance Counselors: 57.0 (486.6 to 1)
Current Spending: ($ per student per year):
Total: $5,861; Instruction: $3,861; Support Services: $1,731
Enrollment, Drop-out Rates and Diploma Recipients by Race/Ethnicity

Category	Total	White	Black	Asian	AIAN	Hisp.
Enrollment (%)	100.0	69.8	25.1	2.0	0.2	2.9
Drop-out Rate (%)	4.7	4.5	5.7	2.2	0.0	5.2
H.S. Diplomas (#)	1,157	878	222	38	0	19

Houston County

Houston County
1100 Main St • Perry, GA 31069-1069
Mailing Address: PO Box 1850 • Perry, GA 31069-1069
(912) 478-6200 • http://www.houston.k12.ga.us
Grade Span: PK-12; **Agency Type:** 1
Schools: 34
20 Primary; 8 Middle; 6 High; 0 Other Level
32 Regular; 0 Special Education; 0 Vocational; 2 Alternative
0 Magnet; 0 Charter; 15 Title I Eligible; 9 School-wide Title I
Students: 22,699 (52.1% male; 47.9% female)
Individual Education Program: 3,031 (13.4%);
English Language Learner: 138 (0.6%); Migrant: 41 (0.2%)
Eligible for Free Lunch Program: 6,420 (28.3%)
Eligible for Reduced-Price Lunch Program: 2,073 (9.1%)
Teachers: 1,528.1 (14.9 to 1)
Librarians/Media Specialists: 36.0 (630.5 to 1)
Guidance Counselors: 46.6 (487.1 to 1)
Current Spending: ($ per student per year):
Total: $6,571; Instruction: $4,375; Support Services: $1,827
Enrollment, Drop-out Rates and Diploma Recipients by Race/Ethnicity

Category	Total	White	Black	Asian	AIAN	Hisp.
Enrollment (%)	100.0	62.3	33.1	1.8	0.3	2.6
Drop-out Rate (%)	5.9	5.5	6.8	4.1	6.7	7.0
H.S. Diplomas (#)	1,208	760	390	34	2	22

Irwin County

Irwin County
210 Apple St • Ocilla, GA 31774-1774
(912) 229-7485 • http://www.irwin.k12.ga.us
Grade Span: PK-12; **Agency Type:** 1
Schools: 4
1 Primary; 1 Middle; 1 High; 1 Other Level
3 Regular; 0 Special Education; 0 Vocational; 1 Alternative
0 Magnet; 0 Charter; 3 Title I Eligible; 0 School-wide Title I
Students: 1,814 (50.3% male; 49.7% female)
Individual Education Program: 307 (16.9%);
English Language Learner: 0 (0.0%); Migrant: 15 (0.8%)
Eligible for Free Lunch Program: 1,012 (55.8%)
Eligible for Reduced-Price Lunch Program: 178 (9.8%)
Teachers: 122.7 (14.8 to 1)
Librarians/Media Specialists: 2.0 (907.0 to 1)
Guidance Counselors: 5.0 (362.8 to 1)
Current Spending: ($ per student per year):
Total: $7,654; Instruction: $4,867; Support Services: $2,351
Enrollment, Drop-out Rates and Diploma Recipients by Race/Ethnicity

Category	Total	White	Black	Asian	AIAN	Hisp.
Enrollment (%)	100.0	60.5	38.0	0.2	0.0	1.3
Drop-out Rate (%)	9.0	10.0	7.1	n/a	n/a	100.0
H.S. Diplomas (#)	77	42	35	0	0	0

Jackson County

Jackson County
1660 Winder Hwy • Jefferson, GA 30549-0549
(706) 367-5151 • http://www.jackson.k12.ga.us/
Grade Span: PK-12; **Agency Type:** 1
Schools: 11
6 Primary; 2 Middle; 2 High; 1 Other Level
9 Regular; 0 Special Education; 0 Vocational; 2 Alternative
0 Magnet; 0 Charter; 0 Title I Eligible; 0 School-wide Title I
Students: 5,472 (51.8% male; 48.2% female)
Individual Education Program: 802 (14.7%);
English Language Learner: 278 (5.1%); Migrant: 29 (0.5%)
Eligible for Free Lunch Program: 1,815 (33.2%)
Eligible for Reduced-Price Lunch Program: 649 (11.9%)
Teachers: 345.4 (15.8 to 1)
Librarians/Media Specialists: 10.0 (547.2 to 1)
Guidance Counselors: 11.0 (497.5 to 1)
Current Spending: ($ per student per year):
Total: $6,991; Instruction: $4,353; Support Services: $2,222
Enrollment, Drop-out Rates and Diploma Recipients by Race/Ethnicity

Category	Total	White	Black	Asian	AIAN	Hisp.
Enrollment (%)	100.0	88.5	5.0	1.7	0.5	4.3
Drop-out Rate (%)	11.5	11.9	7.2	0.0	0.0	17.6
H.S. Diplomas (#)	236	205	22	8	0	1

Jefferson City
575 Washington St • Jefferson, GA 30549-0549
Mailing Address: PO Box 507 • Jefferson, GA 30549-0549
(706) 367-2880
Grade Span: KG-12; **Agency Type:** 1
Schools: 3
1 Primary; 1 Middle; 1 High; 0 Other Level
3 Regular; 0 Special Education; 0 Vocational; 0 Alternative
0 Magnet; 0 Charter; 0 Title I Eligible; 0 School-wide Title I
Students: 1,525 (51.9% male; 48.1% female)
Individual Education Program: 199 (13.0%);
English Language Learner: 36 (2.4%); Migrant: 2 (0.1%)
Eligible for Free Lunch Program: 363 (23.8%)
Eligible for Reduced-Price Lunch Program: 73 (4.8%)
Teachers: 114.8 (13.3 to 1)
Librarians/Media Specialists: 3.0 (508.3 to 1)
Guidance Counselors: 3.5 (435.7 to 1)
Current Spending: ($ per student per year):
Total: $6,223; Instruction: $4,173; Support Services: $1,746
Enrollment, Drop-out Rates and Diploma Recipients by Race/Ethnicity

Category	Total	White	Black	Asian	AIAN	Hisp.
Enrollment (%)	100.0	81.1	13.8	1.8	0.1	3.1
Drop-out Rate (%)	3.5	1.9	5.0	0.0	n/a	44.4
H.S. Diplomas (#)	65	57	6	1	0	1

Jasper County

Jasper County
1125-A Fred Smith St • Monticello, GA 31064-1064
(706) 468-6350 • http://www.jasper.k12.ga.us
Grade Span: PK-12; **Agency Type:** 1
Schools: 5
2 Primary; 1 Middle; 1 High; 1 Other Level
4 Regular; 0 Special Education; 0 Vocational; 1 Alternative
0 Magnet; 0 Charter; 2 Title I Eligible; 2 School-wide Title I
Students: 2,181 (49.5% male; 50.5% female)
Individual Education Program: 317 (14.5%);
English Language Learner: 0 (0.0%); Migrant: 0 (0.0%)
Eligible for Free Lunch Program: 997 (45.7%)
Eligible for Reduced-Price Lunch Program: 208 (9.5%)
Teachers: 131.5 (16.6 to 1)
Librarians/Media Specialists: 3.0 (727.0 to 1)
Guidance Counselors: 4.0 (545.3 to 1)
Current Spending: ($ per student per year):
Total: $6,317; Instruction: $3,753; Support Services: $2,145
Enrollment, Drop-out Rates and Diploma Recipients by Race/Ethnicity

Category	Total	White	Black	Asian	AIAN	Hisp.
Enrollment (%)	100.0	63.4	33.1	0.3	0.1	3.1
Drop-out Rate (%)	6.5	8.4	4.3	0.0	n/a	0.0
H.S. Diplomas (#)	74	48	25	0	0	1

Jeff Davis County

Jeff Davis County
44 Charles Rogers Blvd • Hazlehurst, GA 31539-1539
Mailing Address: PO Box 1780 • Hazlehurst, GA 31539-1539
(912) 375-6700 • http://www.jeff-davis.k12.ga.us
Grade Span: PK-12; **Agency Type:** 1
Schools: 5
2 Primary; 1 Middle; 1 High; 1 Other Level
4 Regular; 0 Special Education; 0 Vocational; 1 Alternative
0 Magnet; 0 Charter; 4 Title I Eligible; 3 School-wide Title I
Students: 2,624 (50.0% male; 50.0% female)
Individual Education Program: 336 (12.8%);
English Language Learner: 81 (3.1%); Migrant: 159 (6.1%)
Eligible for Free Lunch Program: 1,244 (47.4%)
Eligible for Reduced-Price Lunch Program: 267 (10.2%)
Teachers: 149.2 (17.6 to 1)
Librarians/Media Specialists: 4.1 (640.0 to 1)
Guidance Counselors: 5.0 (524.8 to 1)
Current Spending: ($ per student per year):
Total: $6,808; Instruction: $4,291; Support Services: $2,107
Enrollment, Drop-out Rates and Diploma Recipients by Race/Ethnicity

Category	Total	White	Black	Asian	AIAN	Hisp.
Enrollment (%)	100.0	76.4	16.5	0.3	0.1	6.7
Drop-out Rate (%)	8.0	7.7	7.9	0.0	n/a	20.0
H.S. Diplomas (#)	157	118	36	0	0	3

Jefferson County

Jefferson County
431 W Ninth St • Louisville, GA 30434-0434
Mailing Address: PO Box 449 • Louisville, GA 30434-0434
(478) 625-7626 • http://www.jefferson.k12.ga.us
Grade Span: PK-12; **Agency Type:** 1
Schools: 7
3 Primary; 2 Middle; 1 High; 1 Other Level
6 Regular; 0 Special Education; 0 Vocational; 1 Alternative
0 Magnet; 0 Charter; 6 Title I Eligible; 6 School-wide Title I
Students: 3,526 (50.8% male; 49.2% female)
Individual Education Program: 464 (13.2%);

English Language Learner: 3 (0.1%); Migrant: 9 (0.3%)
Eligible for Free Lunch Program: 2,643 (75.0%)
Eligible for Reduced-Price Lunch Program: 262 (7.4%)
Teachers: 199.5 (17.7 to 1)
Librarians/Media Specialists: 6.0 (587.7 to 1)
Guidance Counselors: 6.0 (587.7 to 1)
Current Spending: ($ per student per year):
Total: $6,258; Instruction: $3,817; Support Services: $2,018
Enrollment, Drop-out Rates and Diploma Recipients by Race/Ethnicity

Category	Total	White	Black	Asian	AIAN	Hisp.
Enrollment (%)	100.0	24.6	74.5	0.2	0.0	0.7
Drop-out Rate (%)	4.9	5.2	4.8	0.0	n/a	0.0
H.S. Diplomas (#)	146	41	105	0	0	0

Jenkins County

Jenkins County
527 Barney Ave • Millen, GA 30442-0442
(912) 478-6000 • http://www.jenkins.k12.ga.us
Grade Span: PK-12; **Agency Type:** 1
Schools: 4
1 Primary; 1 Middle; 1 High; 1 Other Level
3 Regular; 0 Special Education; 0 Vocational; 1 Alternative
0 Magnet; 0 Charter; 1 Title I Eligible; 1 School-wide Title I
Students: 1,754 (52.5% male; 47.5% female)
Individual Education Program: 232 (13.2%);
English Language Learner: 44 (2.5%); Migrant: 56 (3.2%)
Eligible for Free Lunch Program: 1,141 (65.1%)
Eligible for Reduced-Price Lunch Program: 215 (12.3%)
Teachers: 119.2 (14.7 to 1)
Librarians/Media Specialists: 2.0 (877.0 to 1)
Guidance Counselors: 3.8 (461.6 to 1)
Current Spending: ($ per student per year):
Total: $6,174; Instruction: $3,893; Support Services: $1,879
Enrollment, Drop-out Rates and Diploma Recipients by Race/Ethnicity

Category	Total	White	Black	Asian	AIAN	Hisp.
Enrollment (%)	100.0	45.7	51.8	0.1	0.0	2.5
Drop-out Rate (%)	4.0	4.8	3.4	n/a	n/a	0.0
H.S. Diplomas (#)	79	35	44	0	0	0

Jones County

Jones County
125 Stewart Ave • Gray, GA 31032-1032
(478) 986-6580 • http://www.jones.k12.ga.us/
Grade Span: PK-12; **Agency Type:** 1
Schools: 9
4 Primary; 2 Middle; 1 High; 2 Other Level
8 Regular; 0 Special Education; 0 Vocational; 1 Alternative
0 Magnet; 0 Charter; 0 Title I Eligible; 0 School-wide Title I
Students: 5,014 (51.5% male; 48.5% female)
Individual Education Program: 577 (11.5%);
English Language Learner: 5 (0.1%); Migrant: 0 (0.0%)
Eligible for Free Lunch Program: 1,240 (24.7%)
Eligible for Reduced-Price Lunch Program: 407 (8.1%)
Teachers: 294.7 (17.0 to 1)
Librarians/Media Specialists: 8.0 (626.8 to 1)
Guidance Counselors: 9.5 (527.8 to 1)
Current Spending: ($ per student per year):
Total: $5,526; Instruction: $3,573; Support Services: $1,654
Enrollment, Drop-out Rates and Diploma Recipients by Race/Ethnicity

Category	Total	White	Black	Asian	AIAN	Hisp.
Enrollment (%)	100.0	74.2	24.8	0.5	0.1	0.4
Drop-out Rate (%)	8.7	8.6	8.9	12.5	n/a	0.0
H.S. Diplomas (#)	240	191	49	0	0	0

Lamar County

Lamar County
Three Trojan Way • Barnesville, GA 30204
(706) 358-1159 • http://www.lamar.k12.ga.us
Grade Span: PK-12; **Agency Type:** 1
Schools: 3
1 Primary; 1 Middle; 1 High; 0 Other Level
3 Regular; 0 Special Education; 0 Vocational; 0 Alternative
0 Magnet; 0 Charter; 3 Title I Eligible; 2 School-wide Title I
Students: 2,600 (51.8% male; 48.2% female)
Individual Education Program: 246 (9.5%);
English Language Learner: 16 (0.6%); Migrant: 0 (0.0%)
Eligible for Free Lunch Program: 1,180 (45.4%)
Eligible for Reduced-Price Lunch Program: 298 (11.5%)
Teachers: 145.2 (17.9 to 1)
Librarians/Media Specialists: 3.0 (866.7 to 1)
Guidance Counselors: 5.0 (520.0 to 1)
Current Spending: ($ per student per year):
Total: $6,093; Instruction: $3,668; Support Services: $1,972
Enrollment, Drop-out Rates and Diploma Recipients by Race/Ethnicity

Category	Total	White	Black	Asian	AIAN	Hisp.
Enrollment (%)	100.0	58.0	40.3	0.6	0.1	0.9
Drop-out Rate (%)	7.7	8.6	5.7	33.3	0.0	50.0
H.S. Diplomas (#)	106	69	37	0	0	0

Laurens County

Dublin City
207 Shamrock Dr • Dublin, GA 31021-1021
(912) 478-3440 • http://www.dublinirish.org/
Grade Span: PK-12; **Agency Type:** 1
Schools: 7
4 Primary; 1 Middle; 1 High; 1 Other Level
6 Regular; 0 Special Education; 0 Vocational; 1 Alternative
0 Magnet; 0 Charter; 5 Title I Eligible; 5 School-wide Title I
Students: 3,262 (51.7% male; 48.3% female)
Individual Education Program: 563 (17.3%);
English Language Learner: 11 (0.3%); Migrant: 6 (0.2%)
Eligible for Free Lunch Program: 2,013 (61.7%)
Eligible for Reduced-Price Lunch Program: 243 (7.4%)
Teachers: 231.7 (14.1 to 1)
Librarians/Media Specialists: 5.0 (652.4 to 1)
Guidance Counselors: 8.0 (407.8 to 1)
Current Spending: ($ per student per year):
Total: $7,590; Instruction: $4,885; Support Services: $2,268
Enrollment, Drop-out Rates and Diploma Recipients by Race/Ethnicity

Category	Total	White	Black	Asian	AIAN	Hisp.
Enrollment (%)	100.0	25.6	71.6	1.8	0.2	0.9
Drop-out Rate (%)	9.9	5.2	13.2	0.0	n/a	0.0
H.S. Diplomas (#)	148	89	57	2	0	0

Laurens County
467 Firetower Rd • Dublin, GA 31021
(478) 272-4767 • http://www.lcboe.net/
Grade Span: PK-12; **Agency Type:** 1
Schools: 8
3 Primary; 2 Middle; 2 High; 1 Other Level
7 Regular; 0 Special Education; 0 Vocational; 1 Alternative
0 Magnet; 0 Charter; 3 Title I Eligible; 3 School-wide Title I
Students: 6,034 (51.3% male; 48.7% female)
Individual Education Program: 562 (9.3%);
English Language Learner: 28 (0.5%); Migrant: 84 (1.4%)
Eligible for Free Lunch Program: 2,677 (44.4%)
Eligible for Reduced-Price Lunch Program: 541 (9.0%)
Teachers: 381.1 (15.8 to 1)
Librarians/Media Specialists: 9.5 (635.2 to 1)
Guidance Counselors: 12.1 (498.7 to 1)
Current Spending: ($ per student per year):
Total: $6,195; Instruction: $4,179; Support Services: $1,623
Enrollment, Drop-out Rates and Diploma Recipients by Race/Ethnicity

Category	Total	White	Black	Asian	AIAN	Hisp.
Enrollment (%)	100.0	65.8	32.2	0.3	0.0	1.7
Drop-out Rate (%)	6.3	6.5	5.6	0.0	n/a	16.7
H.S. Diplomas (#)	307	203	103	0	0	1

Lee County

Lee County
102-B Starksville Ave N • Leesburg, GA 31763-1763
Mailing Address: PO Box 399 • Leesburg, GA 31763-1763
(229) 759-6100 • http://www.lee.k12.ga.us
Grade Span: PK-12; **Agency Type:** 1
Schools: 7
4 Primary; 1 Middle; 1 High; 1 Other Level
6 Regular; 0 Special Education; 0 Vocational; 1 Alternative
0 Magnet; 0 Charter; 4 Title I Eligible; 0 School-wide Title I
Students: 5,350 (51.0% male; 49.0% female)
Individual Education Program: 414 (7.7%);
English Language Learner: 1 (<0.1%); Migrant: 0 (0.0%)
Eligible for Free Lunch Program: 1,178 (22.0%)
Eligible for Reduced-Price Lunch Program: 374 (7.0%)
Teachers: 330.5 (16.2 to 1)
Librarians/Media Specialists: 8.0 (668.8 to 1)
Guidance Counselors: 11.0 (486.4 to 1)
Current Spending: ($ per student per year):
Total: $5,655; Instruction: $3,722; Support Services: $1,602
Enrollment, Drop-out Rates and Diploma Recipients by Race/Ethnicity

Category	Total	White	Black	Asian	AIAN	Hisp.
Enrollment (%)	100.0	83.3	14.8	1.0	0.2	0.7
Drop-out Rate (%)	2.8	2.1	5.7	16.7	0.0	11.1
H.S. Diplomas (#)	291	254	31	4	0	2

Liberty County

Liberty County
110 S Gause St • Hinesville, GA 31313-1313
(912) 876-2161 • http://www.liberty.k12.ga.us
Grade Span: PK-12; **Agency Type:** 1
Schools: 16
8 Primary; 3 Middle; 1 High; 4 Other Level
14 Regular; 1 Special Education; 0 Vocational; 1 Alternative
0 Magnet; 0 Charter; 8 Title I Eligible; 8 School-wide Title I
Students: 11,274 (50.9% male; 49.1% female)
Individual Education Program: 1,250 (11.1%);
English Language Learner: 74 (0.7%); Migrant: 2 (<0.1%)
Eligible for Free Lunch Program: 4,271 (37.9%)
Eligible for Reduced-Price Lunch Program: 1,679 (14.9%)
Teachers: 675.2 (16.7 to 1)
Librarians/Media Specialists: 16.0 (704.6 to 1)
Guidance Counselors: 22.0 (512.5 to 1)
Current Spending: ($ per student per year):
Total: $5,922; Instruction: $3,840; Support Services: $1,725
Enrollment, Drop-out Rates and Diploma Recipients by Race/Ethnicity

Category	Total	White	Black	Asian	AIAN	Hisp.
Enrollment (%)	100.0	34.2	57.4	1.9	0.3	6.2
Drop-out Rate (%)	4.7	3.8	5.3	3.1	0.0	4.7
H.S. Diplomas (#)	505	172	275	11	0	47

Long County

Long County
50 Mcdonald St • Ludowici, GA 31316-1316
Mailing Address: PO Box 428 • Ludowici, GA 31316-1316
(912) 545-2367 • http://www.long.k12.ga.us
Grade Span: PK-12; **Agency Type:** 1
Schools: 2
1 Primary; 0 Middle; 0 High; 1 Other Level
2 Regular; 0 Special Education; 0 Vocational; 0 Alternative
0 Magnet; 0 Charter; 2 Title I Eligible; 2 School-wide Title I
Students: 1,995 (50.3% male; 49.7% female)
Individual Education Program: 209 (10.5%);
English Language Learner: 104 (5.2%); Migrant: 184 (9.2%)
Eligible for Free Lunch Program: 1,116 (55.9%)
Eligible for Reduced-Price Lunch Program: 279 (14.0%)
Teachers: 119.3 (16.7 to 1)
Librarians/Media Specialists: 2.0 (997.5 to 1)
Guidance Counselors: 3.0 (665.0 to 1)
Current Spending: ($ per student per year):
Total: $5,417; Instruction: $3,439; Support Services: $1,575
Enrollment, Drop-out Rates and Diploma Recipients by Race/Ethnicity

Category	Total	White	Black	Asian	AIAN	Hisp.
Enrollment (%)	100.0	62.1	27.2	0.9	0.2	9.6
Drop-out Rate (%)	9.5	11.8	5.1	0.0	n/a	13.6
H.S. Diplomas (#)	75	46	27	1	0	1

Lowndes County

Lowndes County
1592 Norman Dr • Valdosta, GA 31603-1227
Mailing Address: PO Box 1227 • Valdosta, GA 31603-1227
(912) 229-2250 • http://www.lowndes.k12.ga.us
Grade Span: PK-12; **Agency Type:** 1
Schools: 11
7 Primary; 2 Middle; 1 High; 1 Other Level
10 Regular; 0 Special Education; 0 Vocational; 1 Alternative
0 Magnet; 0 Charter; 5 Title I Eligible; 3 School-wide Title I
Students: 9,245 (51.2% male; 48.8% female)
Individual Education Program: 1,313 (14.2%);
English Language Learner: 0 (0.0%); Migrant: 58 (0.6%)
Eligible for Free Lunch Program: 2,713 (29.3%)
Eligible for Reduced-Price Lunch Program: 784 (8.5%)
Teachers: 611.6 (15.1 to 1)
Librarians/Media Specialists: 13.0 (711.2 to 1)
Guidance Counselors: 17.7 (522.3 to 1)
Current Spending: ($ per student per year):
Total: $6,690; Instruction: $4,376; Support Services: $1,970
Enrollment, Drop-out Rates and Diploma Recipients by Race/Ethnicity

Category	Total	White	Black	Asian	AIAN	Hisp.
Enrollment (%)	100.0	73.4	22.7	0.9	0.1	2.8
Drop-out Rate (%)	6.3	6.3	6.6	4.5	0.0	3.2
H.S. Diplomas (#)	468	341	114	5	2	6

Valdosta City
1204 Williams St • Valdosta, GA 31603-5407
Mailing Address: PO Box 5407 • Valdosta, GA 31603-5407
(229) 333-8500 • http://wildcat.gocats.org/
Grade Span: PK-12; **Agency Type:** 1
Schools: 10
4 Primary; 4 Middle; 1 High; 1 Other Level
9 Regular; 0 Special Education; 0 Vocational; 1 Alternative
0 Magnet; 0 Charter; 7 Title I Eligible; 6 School-wide Title I
Students: 7,178 (50.6% male; 49.4% female)
Individual Education Program: 1,037 (14.4%);
English Language Learner: 61 (0.8%); Migrant: 22 (0.3%)
Eligible for Free Lunch Program: 3,853 (53.7%)
Eligible for Reduced-Price Lunch Program: 540 (7.5%)
Teachers: 447.1 (16.1 to 1)
Librarians/Media Specialists: 12.0 (598.2 to 1)
Guidance Counselors: 14.8 (485.0 to 1)
Current Spending: ($ per student per year):
Total: $6,248; Instruction: $3,996; Support Services: $1,803
Enrollment, Drop-out Rates and Diploma Recipients by Race/Ethnicity

Category	Total	White	Black	Asian	AIAN	Hisp.
Enrollment (%)	100.0	22.7	74.3	1.4	0.2	1.4
Drop-out Rate (%)	11.1	7.2	12.7	3.8	0.0	33.3
H.S. Diplomas (#)	305	120	174	10	0	1

Lumpkin County

Lumpkin County
51 Mountain View Dr • Dahlonega, GA 30533-0533
(706) 864-3611 • http://www.lumpkin.k12.ga.us
Grade Span: PK-12; **Agency Type:** 1
Schools: 6
3 Primary; 1 Middle; 1 High; 1 Other Level
5 Regular; 0 Special Education; 0 Vocational; 1 Alternative
0 Magnet; 0 Charter; 3 Title I Eligible; 3 School-wide Title I
Students: 3,511 (52.8% male; 47.2% female)
Individual Education Program: 427 (12.2%);
English Language Learner: 65 (1.9%); Migrant: 25 (0.7%)
Eligible for Free Lunch Program: 1,009 (28.7%)
Eligible for Reduced-Price Lunch Program: 219 (6.2%)
Teachers: 215.4 (16.3 to 1)
Librarians/Media Specialists: 4.0 (877.8 to 1)
Guidance Counselors: 7.0 (501.6 to 1)
Current Spending: ($ per student per year):
Total: $6,527; Instruction: $4,171; Support Services: $2,066
Enrollment, Drop-out Rates and Diploma Recipients by Race/Ethnicity

Category	Total	White	Black	Asian	AIAN	Hisp.
Enrollment (%)	100.0	92.2	1.7	0.8	0.4	4.9
Drop-out Rate (%)	5.5	5.8	0.0	0.0	0.0	3.2
H.S. Diplomas (#)	141	130	3	1	1	6

Macon County

Macon County
Hwy 49 • Oglethorpe, GA 31068-1068
(478) 472-8188 • http://www.macon.k12.ga.us./
Grade Span: PK-12; **Agency Type:** 1
Schools: 4
1 Primary; 1 Middle; 1 High; 1 Other Level
3 Regular; 0 Special Education; 0 Vocational; 1 Alternative
0 Magnet; 0 Charter; 1 Title I Eligible; 1 School-wide Title I
Students: 2,200 (51.1% male; 48.9% female)
Individual Education Program: 190 (8.6%);
English Language Learner: 40 (1.8%); Migrant: 70 (3.2%)
Eligible for Free Lunch Program: 1,603 (72.9%)
Eligible for Reduced-Price Lunch Program: 197 (9.0%)
Teachers: 129.3 (17.0 to 1)
Librarians/Media Specialists: 4.0 (550.0 to 1)
Guidance Counselors: 5.0 (440.0 to 1)
Current Spending: ($ per student per year):
Total: $7,607; Instruction: $4,580; Support Services: $2,501
Enrollment, Drop-out Rates and Diploma Recipients by Race/Ethnicity

Category	Total	White	Black	Asian	AIAN	Hisp.
Enrollment (%)	100.0	12.3	83.7	1.5	0.0	2.5
Drop-out Rate (%)	14.6	18.8	13.3	16.7	n/a	71.4
H.S. Diplomas (#)	76	15	60	1	0	0

Madison County

Madison County
55 Mary Ellen Court • Danielsville, GA 30633-0633
Mailing Address: PO Box 37 • Danielsville, GA 30633-0633
(706) 795-2191 • http://www.madison.k12.ga.us
Grade Span: PK-12; **Agency Type:** 1
Schools: 8

5 Primary; 1 Middle; 1 High; 1 Other Level
7 Regular; 0 Special Education; 0 Vocational; 1 Alternative
0 Magnet; 0 Charter; 6 Title I Eligible; 2 School-wide Title I
Students: 4,621 (51.3% male; 48.7% female)
Individual Education Program: 773 (16.7%);
English Language Learner: 88 (1.9%); Migrant: 1 (<0.1%)
Eligible for Free Lunch Program: 1,472 (31.9%)
Eligible for Reduced-Price Lunch Program: 442 (9.6%)
Teachers: 289.4 (16.0 to 1)
Librarians/Media Specialists: 9.0 (513.4 to 1)
Guidance Counselors: 9.0 (513.4 to 1)
Current Spending: ($ per student per year):
Total: $6,334; Instruction: $4,160; Support Services: $1,817
Enrollment, Drop-out Rates and Diploma Recipients by Race/Ethnicity

Category	Total	White	Black	Asian	AIAN	Hisp.
Enrollment (%)	100.0	88.1	9.7	0.2	0.1	1.9
Drop-out Rate (%)	10.5	9.7	16.4	n/a	n/a	15.8
H.S. Diplomas (#)	191	168	22	0	0	1

Marion County

Marion County
Rogers St • Buena Vista, GA 31803-1803
(912) 229-2234 • http://www.marion.k12.ga.us
Grade Span: PK-12; **Agency Type:** 1
Schools: 3
1 Primary; 1 Middle; 1 High; 0 Other Level
3 Regular; 0 Special Education; 0 Vocational; 0 Alternative
0 Magnet; 0 Charter; 3 Title I Eligible; 0 School-wide Title I
Students: 1,686 (51.2% male; 48.8% female)
Individual Education Program: 181 (10.7%);
English Language Learner: 57 (3.4%); Migrant: 43 (2.6%)
Eligible for Free Lunch Program: 926 (54.9%)
Eligible for Reduced-Price Lunch Program: 197 (11.7%)
Teachers: 107.8 (15.6 to 1)
Librarians/Media Specialists: 3.0 (562.0 to 1)
Guidance Counselors: 3.8 (443.7 to 1)
Current Spending: ($ per student per year):
Total: $6,575; Instruction: $3,784; Support Services: $2,362
Enrollment, Drop-out Rates and Diploma Recipients by Race/Ethnicity

Category	Total	White	Black	Asian	AIAN	Hisp.
Enrollment (%)	100.0	54.7	40.9	0.9	0.2	3.3
Drop-out Rate (%)	9.8	9.7	9.1	n/a	0.0	33.3
H.S. Diplomas (#)	108	53	55	0	0	0

Mcduffie County

Mcduffie County
716 N Lee St • Thomson, GA 30824-0824
(706) 595-1918 • http://www.mcduffie.k12.ga.us
Grade Span: PK-12; **Agency Type:** 1
Schools: 7
3 Primary; 2 Middle; 1 High; 1 Other Level
6 Regular; 0 Special Education; 0 Vocational; 1 Alternative
0 Magnet; 0 Charter; 6 Title I Eligible; 6 School-wide Title I
Students: 4,312 (51.4% male; 48.6% female)
Individual Education Program: 511 (11.9%);
English Language Learner: 29 (0.7%); Migrant: 20 (0.5%)
Eligible for Free Lunch Program: 2,533 (58.7%)
Eligible for Reduced-Price Lunch Program: 401 (9.3%)
Teachers: 262.0 (16.5 to 1)
Librarians/Media Specialists: 7.0 (616.0 to 1)
Guidance Counselors: 10.4 (414.6 to 1)
Current Spending: ($ per student per year):
Total: $6,308; Instruction: $4,077; Support Services: $1,951
Enrollment, Drop-out Rates and Diploma Recipients by Race/Ethnicity

Category	Total	White	Black	Asian	AIAN	Hisp.
Enrollment (%)	100.0	48.8	49.6	0.3	0.0	1.3
Drop-out Rate (%)	8.6	8.0	9.1	0.0	0.0	12.5
H.S. Diplomas (#)	231	122	103	3	0	3

Mcintosh County

Mcintosh County
200 Pine St • Darien, GA 31305-1305
(912) 437-6645 • http://www.mcintosh.k12.ga.us/
Grade Span: PK-12; **Agency Type:** 1
Schools: 3
1 Primary; 1 Middle; 1 High; 0 Other Level
3 Regular; 0 Special Education; 0 Vocational; 0 Alternative
0 Magnet; 0 Charter; 2 Title I Eligible; 1 School-wide Title I
Students: 1,979 (50.5% male; 49.5% female)
Individual Education Program: 172 (8.7%);
English Language Learner: 3 (0.2%); Migrant: 0 (0.0%)
Eligible for Free Lunch Program: 1,215 (61.4%)
Eligible for Reduced-Price Lunch Program: 171 (8.6%)
Teachers: 121.3 (16.3 to 1)
Librarians/Media Specialists: 2.3 (860.4 to 1)
Guidance Counselors: 4.0 (494.8 to 1)
Current Spending: ($ per student per year):
Total: $6,205; Instruction: $3,841; Support Services: $1,957
Enrollment, Drop-out Rates and Diploma Recipients by Race/Ethnicity

Category	Total	White	Black	Asian	AIAN	Hisp.
Enrollment (%)	100.0	47.9	50.9	0.7	0.1	0.5
Drop-out Rate (%)	12.6	16.6	8.9	0.0	n/a	0.0
H.S. Diplomas (#)	69	40	28	0	0	1

Meriwether County

Meriwether County
2100 Gaston St • Greenville, GA 30222-0070
(706) 672-4297 • http://www.meriwether.k12.ga.us
Grade Span: PK-12; **Agency Type:** 1
Schools: 10
3 Primary; 2 Middle; 2 High; 3 Other Level
7 Regular; 2 Special Education; 0 Vocational; 1 Alternative
0 Magnet; 0 Charter; 4 Title I Eligible; 4 School-wide Title I
Students: 3,948 (52.2% male; 47.8% female)
Individual Education Program: 993 (25.2%);
English Language Learner: 4 (0.1%); Migrant: 0 (0.0%)
Eligible for Free Lunch Program: 2,710 (68.6%)
Eligible for Reduced-Price Lunch Program: 501 (12.7%)
Teachers: 301.3 (13.1 to 1)
Librarians/Media Specialists: 7.0 (564.0 to 1)
Guidance Counselors: 8.5 (464.5 to 1)
Current Spending: ($ per student per year):
Total: $7,589; Instruction: $4,586; Support Services: $2,552
Enrollment, Drop-out Rates and Diploma Recipients by Race/Ethnicity

Category	Total	White	Black	Asian	AIAN	Hisp.
Enrollment (%)	100.0	38.1	61.3	0.3	0.0	0.2
Drop-out Rate (%)	9.8	13.4	7.9	n/a	n/a	0.0
H.S. Diplomas (#)	138	59	79	0	0	0

Mitchell County

Mitchell County
108 S Harney St • Camilla, GA 31730-1730
(229) 336-2100 • http://www.mitchell.k12.ga.us
Grade Span: PK-12; **Agency Type:** 1
Schools: 7
2 Primary; 1 Middle; 1 High; 3 Other Level
5 Regular; 1 Special Education; 0 Vocational; 1 Alternative
0 Magnet; 1 Charter; 3 Title I Eligible; 3 School-wide Title I
Students: 2,855 (51.9% male; 48.1% female)
Individual Education Program: 409 (14.3%);
English Language Learner: 4 (0.1%); Migrant: 69 (2.4%)
Eligible for Free Lunch Program: 1,674 (58.6%)
Eligible for Reduced-Price Lunch Program: 286 (10.0%)
Teachers: 176.0 (16.2 to 1)
Librarians/Media Specialists: 4.0 (713.8 to 1)
Guidance Counselors: 5.0 (571.0 to 1)
Current Spending: ($ per student per year):
Total: $6,938; Instruction: $4,362; Support Services: $2,128
Enrollment, Drop-out Rates and Diploma Recipients by Race/Ethnicity

Category	Total	White	Black	Asian	AIAN	Hisp.
Enrollment (%)	100.0	26.0	70.8	0.1	0.1	3.0
Drop-out Rate (%)	8.0	11.7	6.7	0.0	0.0	28.6
H.S. Diplomas (#)	132	30	98	2	0	2

Pelham City
188 W Railroad St S • Pelham, GA 31779-1779
(912) 229-8715 • http://www.pelham-city.k12.ga.us/
Grade Span: PK-12; **Agency Type:** 1
Schools: 3
1 Primary; 1 Middle; 1 High; 0 Other Level
3 Regular; 0 Special Education; 0 Vocational; 0 Alternative
0 Magnet; 0 Charter; 2 Title I Eligible; 2 School-wide Title I
Students: 1,627 (50.7% male; 49.3% female)
Individual Education Program: 275 (16.9%);
English Language Learner: 20 (1.2%); Migrant: 19 (1.2%)
Eligible for Free Lunch Program: 969 (59.6%)
Eligible for Reduced-Price Lunch Program: 157 (9.6%)
Teachers: 101.5 (16.0 to 1)
Librarians/Media Specialists: 2.2 (739.5 to 1)
Guidance Counselors: 3.2 (508.4 to 1)
Current Spending: ($ per student per year):
Total: $5,874; Instruction: $3,972; Support Services: $1,499

Enrollment, Drop-out Rates and Diploma Recipients by Race/Ethnicity

Category	Total	White	Black	Asian	AIAN	Hisp.
Enrollment (%)	100.0	42.7	54.1	0.4	0.2	2.6
Drop-out Rate (%)	8.4	6.3	10.4	n/a	0.0	11.1
H.S. Diplomas (#)	73	39	31	0	0	3

Monroe County

Monroe County

25 Brooklyn Ave • Forsyth, GA 31029-1029
(912) 478-2031 • http://www.monroe.k12.ga.us/
Grade Span: PK-12; **Agency Type:** 1
Schools: 5
2 Primary; 1 Middle; 1 High; 1 Other Level
4 Regular; 0 Special Education; 0 Vocational; 1 Alternative
0 Magnet; 0 Charter; 2 Title I Eligible; 0 School-wide Title I
Students: 3,872 (52.4% male; 47.6% female)
Individual Education Program: 519 (13.4%);
English Language Learner: 0 (0.0%); Migrant: 0 (0.0%)
Eligible for Free Lunch Program: 1,314 (33.9%)
Eligible for Reduced-Price Lunch Program: 331 (8.5%)
Teachers: 227.3 (17.0 to 1)
Librarians/Media Specialists: 4.0 (968.0 to 1)
Guidance Counselors: 7.0 (553.1 to 1)
Current Spending: ($ per student per year):
Total: $6,577; Instruction: $4,154; Support Services: $2,043
Enrollment, Drop-out Rates and Diploma Recipients by Race/Ethnicity

Category	Total	White	Black	Asian	AIAN	Hisp.
Enrollment (%)	100.0	63.3	35.2	0.5	0.0	1.0
Drop-out Rate (%)	7.2	7.8	6.2	0.0	n/a	0.0
H.S. Diplomas (#)	195	133	58	0	3	1

Morgan County

Morgan County

1065 E Ave • Madison, GA 30650-0650
(706) 342-0752 • http://www.morgan.k12.ga.us
Grade Span: PK-12; **Agency Type:** 1
Schools: 5
2 Primary; 1 Middle; 1 High; 1 Other Level
4 Regular; 0 Special Education; 0 Vocational; 1 Alternative
0 Magnet; 0 Charter; 2 Title I Eligible; 2 School-wide Title I
Students: 3,171 (51.2% male; 48.8% female)
Individual Education Program: 437 (13.8%);
English Language Learner: 10 (0.3%); Migrant: 1 (<0.1%)
Eligible for Free Lunch Program: 919 (29.0%)
Eligible for Reduced-Price Lunch Program: 266 (8.4%)
Teachers: 210.4 (15.1 to 1)
Librarians/Media Specialists: 4.0 (792.8 to 1)
Guidance Counselors: 7.5 (422.8 to 1)
Current Spending: ($ per student per year):
Total: $6,768; Instruction: $4,498; Support Services: $1,904
Enrollment, Drop-out Rates and Diploma Recipients by Race/Ethnicity

Category	Total	White	Black	Asian	AIAN	Hisp.
Enrollment (%)	100.0	64.6	32.8	0.7	0.0	1.8
Drop-out Rate (%)	4.7	3.7	6.5	0.0	n/a	11.1
H.S. Diplomas (#)	147	114	33	0	0	0

Murray County

Murray County

715 Chestnut St • Chatsworth, GA 30705-0705
(706) 695-4531 • http://www.murray.k12.ga.us
Grade Span: PK-12; **Agency Type:** 1
Schools: 9
5 Primary; 2 Middle; 1 High; 1 Other Level
8 Regular; 0 Special Education; 0 Vocational; 1 Alternative
0 Magnet; 0 Charter; 8 Title I Eligible; 8 School-wide Title I
Students: 7,345 (52.0% male; 48.0% female)
Individual Education Program: 855 (11.6%);
English Language Learner: 127 (1.7%); Migrant: 3 (<0.1%)
Eligible for Free Lunch Program: 2,668 (36.3%)
Eligible for Reduced-Price Lunch Program: 1,013 (13.8%)
Teachers: 450.8 (16.3 to 1)
Librarians/Media Specialists: 9.0 (816.1 to 1)
Guidance Counselors: 11.0 (667.7 to 1)
Current Spending: ($ per student per year):
Total: $5,790; Instruction: $3,892; Support Services: $1,517
Enrollment, Drop-out Rates and Diploma Recipients by Race/Ethnicity

Category	Total	White	Black	Asian	AIAN	Hisp.
Enrollment (%)	100.0	88.5	0.4	0.5	0.1	10.5
Drop-out Rate (%)	13.3	13.4	50.0	0.0	0.0	11.7
H.S. Diplomas (#)	218	210	1	0	0	7

Muscogee County

Fort Benning District

201 Custer Rd, Building 2670 • Fort Benning, GA 31905-5000
(706) 545-2500
Grade Span: PK-08; **Agency Type:** 6
Schools: 7
6 Primary; 1 Middle; 0 High; 0 Other Level
7 Regular; 0 Special Education; 0 Vocational; 0 Alternative
0 Magnet; 0 Charter; 0 Title I Eligible; 0 School-wide Title I
Students: 3,027 (n/a% male; n/a% female)
Individual Education Program: 301 (9.9%);
English Language Learner: 70 (2.3%); Migrant: n/a
Eligible for Free Lunch Program: n/a
Eligible for Reduced-Price Lunch Program: n/a
Teachers: 211.5 (14.3 to 1)
Librarians/Media Specialists: 7.0 (432.4 to 1)
Guidance Counselors: 10.0 (302.7 to 1)
Current Spending: ($ per student per year):
Total: n/a; Instruction: n/a; Support Services: n/a
Enrollment, Drop-out Rates and Diploma Recipients by Race/Ethnicity

Category	Total	White	Black	Asian	AIAN	Hisp.
Enrollment (%)	100.0	45.9	35.3	1.6	2.8	13.6
Drop-out Rate (%)	n/a	n/a	n/a	n/a	n/a	n/a
H.S. Diplomas (#)	n/a	n/a	n/a	n/a	n/a	n/a

Muscogee County

1200 Bradley Dr • Columbus, GA 31902-2427
Mailing Address: PO Box 2427 • Columbus, GA 31902-2427
(706) 649-0500 • http://www.mindspring.com/~muscogee
Grade Span: PK-12; **Agency Type:** 1
Schools: 61
33 Primary; 11 Middle; 8 High; 9 Other Level
55 Regular; 0 Special Education; 0 Vocational; 6 Alternative
7 Magnet; 0 Charter; 0 Title I Eligible; 0 School-wide Title I
Students: 32,944 (50.5% male; 49.5% female)
Individual Education Program: 4,029 (12.2%);
English Language Learner: 319 (1.0%); Migrant: 12 (<0.1%)
Eligible for Free Lunch Program: 14,734 (44.7%)
Eligible for Reduced-Price Lunch Program: 3,132 (9.5%)
Teachers: 2,136.7 (15.4 to 1)
Librarians/Media Specialists: 59.9 (550.0 to 1)
Guidance Counselors: 91.0 (362.0 to 1)
Current Spending: ($ per student per year):
Total: $6,826; Instruction: $4,279; Support Services: $2,115
Enrollment, Drop-out Rates and Diploma Recipients by Race/Ethnicity

Category	Total	White	Black	Asian	AIAN	Hisp.
Enrollment (%)	100.0	34.9	60.7	1.2	0.2	3.0
Drop-out Rate (%)	6.8	6.7	7.0	3.4	0.0	5.7
H.S. Diplomas (#)	1,502	683	731	28	3	57

Newton County

Newton County

3187 Newton Drive, NE • Covington, GA 30014
(770) 787-1330 • http://www.newton.k12.ga.us
Grade Span: PK-12; **Agency Type:** 1
Schools: 20
11 Primary; 4 Middle; 2 High; 3 Other Level
17 Regular; 1 Special Education; 0 Vocational; 2 Alternative
0 Magnet; 0 Charter; 11 Title I Eligible; 3 School-wide Title I
Students: 13,681 (51.3% male; 48.7% female)
Individual Education Program: 1,874 (13.7%);
English Language Learner: 156 (1.1%); Migrant: 0 (0.0%)
Eligible for Free Lunch Program: 4,539 (33.2%)
Eligible for Reduced-Price Lunch Program: 1,402 (10.2%)
Teachers: 853.1 (16.0 to 1)
Librarians/Media Specialists: 19.0 (720.1 to 1)
Guidance Counselors: 25.5 (536.5 to 1)
Current Spending: ($ per student per year):
Total: $6,298; Instruction: $4,078; Support Services: $1,873
Enrollment, Drop-out Rates and Diploma Recipients by Race/Ethnicity

Category	Total	White	Black	Asian	AIAN	Hisp.
Enrollment (%)	100.0	60.6	34.9	0.9	1.0	2.7
Drop-out Rate (%)	5.9	6.0	6.2	11.1	0.0	0.0
H.S. Diplomas (#)	370	253	104	2	2	9

Oconee County

Oconee County

34 School St • Watkinsville, GA 30677-0677
Mailing Address: PO Box 146 • Watkinsville, GA 30677-0677
(706) 769-5130 • http://www.oconee.k12.ga.us
Grade Span: PK-12; **Agency Type:** 1
Schools: 9

5 Primary; 2 Middle; 1 High; 1 Other Level
8 Regular; 0 Special Education; 0 Vocational; 1 Alternative
0 Magnet; 0 Charter; 5 Title I Eligible; 0 School-wide Title I
Students: 5,615 (52.0% male; 48.0% female)
Individual Education Program: 619 (11.0%);
English Language Learner: 139 (2.5%); Migrant: 27 (0.5%)
Eligible for Free Lunch Program: 664 (11.8%)
Eligible for Reduced-Price Lunch Program: 242 (4.3%)
Teachers: 361.3 (15.5 to 1)
Librarians/Media Specialists: 8.0 (701.9 to 1)
Guidance Counselors: 11.0 (510.5 to 1)
Current Spending: ($ per student per year):
Total: $6,093; Instruction: $4,045; Support Services: $1,753
Enrollment, Drop-out Rates and Diploma Recipients by Race/Ethnicity

Category	Total	White	Black	Asian	AIAN	Hisp.
Enrollment (%)	100.0	87.6	6.3	2.1	0.2	3.8
Drop-out Rate (%)	2.6	2.3	8.3	0.0	0.0	5.9
H.S. Diplomas (#)	359	328	22	6	0	3

Oglethorpe County

Oglethorpe County
735 Athens Rd • Lexington, GA 30648-0648
(706) 743-8128 • http://www.oglethorpe.k12.ga.us
Grade Span: PK-12; **Agency Type:** 1
Schools: 5
2 Primary; 1 Middle; 1 High; 1 Other Level
4 Regular; 0 Special Education; 0 Vocational; 1 Alternative
0 Magnet; 0 Charter; 4 Title I Eligible; 4 School-wide Title I
Students: 2,281 (52.0% male; 48.0% female)
Individual Education Program: 369 (16.2%);
English Language Learner: 0 (0.0%); Migrant: 4 (0.2%)
Eligible for Free Lunch Program: 807 (35.4%)
Eligible for Reduced-Price Lunch Program: 179 (7.8%)
Teachers: 144.6 (15.8 to 1)
Librarians/Media Specialists: 4.0 (570.3 to 1)
Guidance Counselors: 5.0 (456.2 to 1)
Current Spending: ($ per student per year):
Total: $6,552; Instruction: $4,012; Support Services: $2,221
Enrollment, Drop-out Rates and Diploma Recipients by Race/Ethnicity

Category	Total	White	Black	Asian	AIAN	Hisp.
Enrollment (%)	100.0	74.4	23.1	0.3	0.0	2.1
Drop-out Rate (%)	6.4	6.5	6.4	0.0	n/a	0.0
H.S. Diplomas (#)	86	61	23	1	0	1

Paulding County

Paulding County
522 Hardee St • Dallas, GA 30132-0132
(770) 443-8000 • http://www.paulding.k12.ga.us
Grade Span: PK-12; **Agency Type:** 1
Schools: 23
14 Primary; 5 Middle; 3 High; 1 Other Level
22 Regular; 0 Special Education; 0 Vocational; 1 Alternative
0 Magnet; 0 Charter; 7 Title I Eligible; 0 School-wide Title I
Students: 19,283 (51.7% male; 48.3% female)
Individual Education Program: 2,392 (12.4%);
English Language Learner: 171 (0.9%); Migrant: 0 (0.0%)
Eligible for Free Lunch Program: 2,817 (14.6%)
Eligible for Reduced-Price Lunch Program: 1,391 (7.2%)
Teachers: 1,218.5 (15.8 to 1)
Librarians/Media Specialists: 25.0 (771.3 to 1)
Guidance Counselors: 41.0 (470.3 to 1)
Current Spending: ($ per student per year):
Total: $5,889; Instruction: $3,860; Support Services: $1,717
Enrollment, Drop-out Rates and Diploma Recipients by Race/Ethnicity

Category	Total	White	Black	Asian	AIAN	Hisp.
Enrollment (%)	100.0	84.9	12.4	0.2	0.4	2.1
Drop-out Rate (%)	7.6	7.4	9.2	0.0	0.0	11.8
H.S. Diplomas (#)	652	582	54	3	2	11

Peach County

Peach County
523 Vineville St • Fort Valley, GA 31030-1030
(912) 478-5933 • http://www.peach.k12.ga.us/
Grade Span: PK-12; **Agency Type:** 1
Schools: 7
3 Primary; 2 Middle; 1 High; 1 Other Level
6 Regular; 0 Special Education; 0 Vocational; 1 Alternative
0 Magnet; 0 Charter; 3 Title I Eligible; 3 School-wide Title I
Students: 3,927 (51.1% male; 48.9% female)
Individual Education Program: 457 (11.6%);
English Language Learner: 65 (1.7%); Migrant: 191 (4.9%)
Eligible for Free Lunch Program: 2,117 (53.9%)
Eligible for Reduced-Price Lunch Program: 371 (9.4%)
Teachers: 272.5 (14.4 to 1)
Librarians/Media Specialists: 7.0 (561.0 to 1)
Guidance Counselors: 9.0 (436.3 to 1)
Current Spending: ($ per student per year):
Total: $6,278; Instruction: $3,836; Support Services: $1,971
Enrollment, Drop-out Rates and Diploma Recipients by Race/Ethnicity

Category	Total	White	Black	Asian	AIAN	Hisp.
Enrollment (%)	100.0	40.1	53.0	0.6	0.1	6.2
Drop-out Rate (%)	10.3	10.0	9.4	66.7	0.0	25.0
H.S. Diplomas (#)	159	72	83	0	0	4

Pickens County

Pickens County
159 Stegall Dr • Jasper, GA 30143-0143
(706) 253-1700 • http://www.pickens.k12.ga.us/
Grade Span: PK-12; **Agency Type:** 1
Schools: 6
3 Primary; 2 Middle; 1 High; 0 Other Level
6 Regular; 0 Special Education; 0 Vocational; 0 Alternative
0 Magnet; 0 Charter; 1 Title I Eligible; 1 School-wide Title I
Students: 4,060 (51.5% male; 48.5% female)
Individual Education Program: 505 (12.4%);
English Language Learner: 33 (0.8%); Migrant: 7 (0.2%)
Eligible for Free Lunch Program: 1,032 (25.4%)
Eligible for Reduced-Price Lunch Program: 446 (11.0%)
Teachers: 260.9 (15.6 to 1)
Librarians/Media Specialists: 6.0 (676.7 to 1)
Guidance Counselors: 8.0 (507.5 to 1)
Current Spending: ($ per student per year):
Total: $7,008; Instruction: $4,215; Support Services: $2,420
Enrollment, Drop-out Rates and Diploma Recipients by Race/Ethnicity

Category	Total	White	Black	Asian	AIAN	Hisp.
Enrollment (%)	100.0	96.3	1.4	0.3	0.1	2.0
Drop-out Rate (%)	6.8	6.9	0.0	25.0	n/a	0.0
H.S. Diplomas (#)	123	122	0	0	0	1

Pierce County

Pierce County
114 Strickland Ave • Blackshear, GA 31516-1516
Mailing Address: PO Box 349 • Blackshear, GA 31516-1516
(912) 449-2044 • http://www.pierce.k12.ga.us
Grade Span: PK-12; **Agency Type:** 1
Schools: 4
2 Primary; 1 Middle; 1 High; 0 Other Level
4 Regular; 0 Special Education; 0 Vocational; 0 Alternative
0 Magnet; 0 Charter; 4 Title I Eligible; 4 School-wide Title I
Students: 3,240 (51.6% male; 48.4% female)
Individual Education Program: 494 (15.2%);
English Language Learner: 78 (2.4%); Migrant: 77 (2.4%)
Eligible for Free Lunch Program: 1,371 (42.3%)
Eligible for Reduced-Price Lunch Program: 431 (13.3%)
Teachers: 216.5 (15.0 to 1)
Librarians/Media Specialists: 4.0 (810.0 to 1)
Guidance Counselors: 7.0 (462.9 to 1)
Current Spending: ($ per student per year):
Total: $6,170; Instruction: $4,020; Support Services: $1,768
Enrollment, Drop-out Rates and Diploma Recipients by Race/Ethnicity

Category	Total	White	Black	Asian	AIAN	Hisp.
Enrollment (%)	100.0	83.2	13.0	0.3	0.0	3.5
Drop-out Rate (%)	10.2	11.2	5.0	0.0	100.0	10.0
H.S. Diplomas (#)	115	95	19	0	0	1

Pike County

Pike County
115 W Jackson St • Zebulon, GA 30295-0295
Mailing Address: PO Box 386 • Zebulon, GA 30295-0295
(770) 567-8489 • http://www.pike.k12.ga.us/
Grade Span: PK-12; **Agency Type:** 1
Schools: 4
2 Primary; 1 Middle; 1 High; 0 Other Level
4 Regular; 0 Special Education; 0 Vocational; 0 Alternative
0 Magnet; 0 Charter; 2 Title I Eligible; 0 School-wide Title I
Students: 2,805 (52.5% male; 47.5% female)
Individual Education Program: 320 (11.4%);
English Language Learner: 0 (0.0%); Migrant: 0 (0.0%)
Eligible for Free Lunch Program: 670 (23.9%)
Eligible for Reduced-Price Lunch Program: 192 (6.8%)
Teachers: 156.4 (17.9 to 1)
Librarians/Media Specialists: 4.0 (701.3 to 1)
Guidance Counselors: 5.0 (561.0 to 1)

Current Spending: ($ per student per year):
Total: $5,250; Instruction: $3,382; Support Services: $1,622

Enrollment, Drop-out Rates and Diploma Recipients by Race/Ethnicity

Category	Total	White	Black	Asian	AIAN	Hisp.
Enrollment (%)	100.0	82.4	15.8	0.4	0.2	1.1
Drop-out Rate (%)	8.5	8.9	6.1	0.0	n/a	100.0
H.S. Diplomas (#)	143	126	16	1	0	0

Polk County

Polk County

612 S College St • Cedartown, GA 30125-0128
Mailing Address: PO Box 128 • Cedartown, GA 30125-0128
(770) 748-3821 • http://polk.ga.net
Grade Span: PK-12; **Agency Type:** 1
Schools: 11
6 Primary; 2 Middle; 2 High; 1 Other Level
10 Regular; 0 Special Education; 0 Vocational; 1 Alternative
0 Magnet; 0 Charter; 5 Title I Eligible; 5 School-wide Title I
Students: 7,017 (52.4% male; 47.6% female)
Individual Education Program: 972 (13.9%);
English Language Learner: 373 (5.3%); Migrant: 159 (2.3%)
Eligible for Free Lunch Program: 2,359 (33.6%)
Eligible for Reduced-Price Lunch Program: 540 (7.7%)
Teachers: 450.4 (15.6 to 1)
Librarians/Media Specialists: 12.0 (584.8 to 1)
Guidance Counselors: 14.0 (501.2 to 1)
Current Spending: ($ per student per year):
Total: $6,329; Instruction: $4,288; Support Services: $1,711

Enrollment, Drop-out Rates and Diploma Recipients by Race/Ethnicity

Category	Total	White	Black	Asian	AIAN	Hisp.
Enrollment (%)	100.0	72.6	17.5	0.4	0.0	9.4
Drop-out Rate (%)	10.0	9.3	10.1	0.0	0.0	20.4
H.S. Diplomas (#)	276	223	38	2	1	12

Pulaski County

Pulaski County

206 Mccormick Ave • Hawkinsville, GA 31036-1036
(478) 783-7200 • http://www.pulaski.k12.ga.us/
Grade Span: PK-12; **Agency Type:** 1
Schools: 5
1 Primary; 1 Middle; 1 High; 2 Other Level
4 Regular; 0 Special Education; 0 Vocational; 1 Alternative
0 Magnet; 0 Charter; 1 Title I Eligible; 1 School-wide Title I
Students: 1,632 (51.7% male; 48.3% female)
Individual Education Program: 258 (15.8%);
English Language Learner: 1 (0.1%); Migrant: 9 (0.6%)
Eligible for Free Lunch Program: 765 (46.9%)
Eligible for Reduced-Price Lunch Program: 157 (9.6%)
Teachers: 122.0 (13.4 to 1)
Librarians/Media Specialists: 2.0 (816.0 to 1)
Guidance Counselors: 3.0 (544.0 to 1)
Current Spending: ($ per student per year):
Total: $7,146; Instruction: $4,524; Support Services: $2,259

Enrollment, Drop-out Rates and Diploma Recipients by Race/Ethnicity

Category	Total	White	Black	Asian	AIAN	Hisp.
Enrollment (%)	100.0	55.3	42.2	0.7	0.1	1.7
Drop-out Rate (%)	6.7	7.3	5.4	0.0	n/a	33.3
H.S. Diplomas (#)	87	58	27	1	0	1

Putnam County

Putnam County

304 W Marion St • Eatonton, GA 31024-1024
(706) 485-5381 • http://www.putnam.k12.ga.us
Grade Span: PK-12; **Agency Type:** 1
Schools: 4
1 Primary; 1 Middle; 1 High; 1 Other Level
3 Regular; 0 Special Education; 0 Vocational; 1 Alternative
0 Magnet; 0 Charter; 2 Title I Eligible; 2 School-wide Title I
Students: 2,474 (51.4% male; 48.6% female)
Individual Education Program: 380 (15.4%);
English Language Learner: 54 (2.2%); Migrant: 30 (1.2%)
Eligible for Free Lunch Program: 1,373 (55.5%)
Eligible for Reduced-Price Lunch Program: 268 (10.8%)
Teachers: 171.0 (14.5 to 1)
Librarians/Media Specialists: 4.0 (618.5 to 1)
Guidance Counselors: 5.0 (494.8 to 1)
Current Spending: ($ per student per year):
Total: $6,806; Instruction: $4,256; Support Services: $2,102

Enrollment, Drop-out Rates and Diploma Recipients by Race/Ethnicity

Category	Total	White	Black	Asian	AIAN	Hisp.
Enrollment (%)	100.0	43.1	51.5	0.9	0.1	4.4
Drop-out Rate (%)	5.1	6.3	4.4	0.0	n/a	0.0
H.S. Diplomas (#)	101	37	61	3	0	0

Rabun County

Rabun County

Hwy 441 N • Clayton, GA 30525
Mailing Address: PO Box 468 • Clayton, GA 30525
(706) 746-5376
Grade Span: PK-12; **Agency Type:** 1
Schools: 6
2 Primary; 2 Middle; 1 High; 1 Other Level
5 Regular; 0 Special Education; 0 Vocational; 1 Alternative
0 Magnet; 0 Charter; 4 Title I Eligible; 0 School-wide Title I
Students: 2,221 (51.4% male; 48.6% female)
Individual Education Program: 278 (12.5%);
English Language Learner: 115 (5.2%); Migrant: 24 (1.1%)
Eligible for Free Lunch Program: 722 (32.5%)
Eligible for Reduced-Price Lunch Program: 355 (16.0%)
Teachers: 139.9 (15.9 to 1)
Librarians/Media Specialists: 5.0 (444.2 to 1)
Guidance Counselors: 4.0 (555.3 to 1)
Current Spending: ($ per student per year):
Total: $6,916; Instruction: $4,478; Support Services: $2,052

Enrollment, Drop-out Rates and Diploma Recipients by Race/Ethnicity

Category	Total	White	Black	Asian	AIAN	Hisp.
Enrollment (%)	100.0	91.9	0.6	0.4	0.5	6.7
Drop-out Rate (%)	9.0	9.2	0.0	0.0	0.0	5.9
H.S. Diplomas (#)	115	109	0	0	0	6

Randolph County

Randolph County

1208 Andrew St • Cuthbert, GA 39840
(912) 229-2641
Grade Span: PK-12; **Agency Type:** 1
Schools: 4
1 Primary; 1 Middle; 1 High; 1 Other Level
3 Regular; 0 Special Education; 0 Vocational; 1 Alternative
0 Magnet; 0 Charter; 3 Title I Eligible; 1 School-wide Title I
Students: 1,559 (50.8% male; 49.2% female)
Individual Education Program: 163 (10.5%);
English Language Learner: 2 (0.1%); Migrant: 3 (0.2%)
Eligible for Free Lunch Program: 1,286 (82.5%)
Eligible for Reduced-Price Lunch Program: 132 (8.5%)
Teachers: 101.7 (15.3 to 1)
Librarians/Media Specialists: 3.0 (519.7 to 1)
Guidance Counselors: 3.0 (519.7 to 1)
Current Spending: ($ per student per year):
Total: $8,512; Instruction: $4,622; Support Services: $3,084

Enrollment, Drop-out Rates and Diploma Recipients by Race/Ethnicity

Category	Total	White	Black	Asian	AIAN	Hisp.
Enrollment (%)	100.0	10.6	88.4	0.1	0.5	0.4
Drop-out Rate (%)	12.0	9.7	12.3	0.0	n/a	n/a
H.S. Diplomas (#)	83	12	71	0	0	0

Richmond County

Richmond County

2083 Heckle St • Augusta, GA 30904-0904
(706) 737-7200 • http://www.richmond.k12.ga.us
Grade Span: PK-12; **Agency Type:** 1
Schools: 57
35 Primary; 10 Middle; 9 High; 3 Other Level
55 Regular; 0 Special Education; 0 Vocational; 2 Alternative
3 Magnet; 0 Charter; 38 Title I Eligible; 38 School-wide Title I
Students: 34,691 (50.5% male; 49.5% female)
Individual Education Program: 3,612 (10.4%);
English Language Learner: 163 (0.5%); Migrant: 1 (<0.1%)
Eligible for Free Lunch Program: 19,397 (55.9%)
Eligible for Reduced-Price Lunch Program: 3,503 (10.1%)
Teachers: 2,193.5 (15.8 to 1)
Librarians/Media Specialists: 60.5 (573.4 to 1)
Guidance Counselors: 73.5 (472.0 to 1)
Current Spending: ($ per student per year):
Total: $6,447; Instruction: $3,981; Support Services: $2,111

Enrollment, Drop-out Rates and Diploma Recipients by Race/Ethnicity

Category	Total	White	Black	Asian	AIAN	Hisp.
Enrollment (%)	100.0	26.4	70.5	1.0	0.1	1.9
Drop-out Rate (%)	6.1	8.4	5.1	6.1	14.3	5.4
H.S. Diplomas (#)	1,576	499	1,014	29	2	32

Rockdale County

Rockdale County
954 N Main St • Conyers, GA 30012-0012
(770) 483-4713 • http://www.rockdale.k12.ga.us
Grade Span: PK-12; **Agency Type:** 1
Schools: 18
11 Primary; 3 Middle; 3 High; 1 Other Level
17 Regular; 0 Special Education; 0 Vocational; 1 Alternative
0 Magnet; 0 Charter; 6 Title I Eligible; 3 School-wide Title I
Students: 13,801 (51.1% male; 48.9% female)
Individual Education Program: 1,485 (10.8%);
English Language Learner: 488 (3.5%); Migrant: 0 (0.0%)
Eligible for Free Lunch Program: 3,483 (25.2%)
Eligible for Reduced-Price Lunch Program: 1,134 (8.2%)
Teachers: 891.2 (15.5 to 1)
Librarians/Media Specialists: 23.0 (600.0 to 1)
Guidance Counselors: 30.0 (460.0 to 1)
Current Spending: ($ per student per year):
Total: $6,740; Instruction: $4,245; Support Services: $2,117
Enrollment, Drop-out Rates and Diploma Recipients by Race/Ethnicity

Category	Total	White	Black	Asian	AIAN	Hisp.
Enrollment (%)	100.0	59.7	31.6	2.1	0.3	6.3
Drop-out Rate (%)	3.8	3.6	4.6	2.6	0.0	6.3
H.S. Diplomas (#)	722	550	133	29	2	8

Screven County

Screven County
216 Mims Rd • Sylvania, GA 30467-0467
(912) 564-7114 • http://www.screven.k12.ga.us
Grade Span: PK-12; **Agency Type:** 1
Schools: 4
1 Primary; 1 Middle; 1 High; 1 Other Level
3 Regular; 0 Special Education; 0 Vocational; 1 Alternative
0 Magnet; 0 Charter; 3 Title I Eligible; 3 School-wide Title I
Students: 3,130 (49.6% male; 50.4% female)
Individual Education Program: 518 (16.5%);
English Language Learner: 2 (0.1%); Migrant: 75 (2.4%)
Eligible for Free Lunch Program: 2,249 (71.9%)
Eligible for Reduced-Price Lunch Program: 199 (6.4%)
Teachers: 187.7 (16.7 to 1)
Librarians/Media Specialists: 3.0 (1,043.3 to 1)
Guidance Counselors: 5.0 (626.0 to 1)
Current Spending: ($ per student per year):
Total: $6,396; Instruction: $3,822; Support Services: $2,119
Enrollment, Drop-out Rates and Diploma Recipients by Race/Ethnicity

Category	Total	White	Black	Asian	AIAN	Hisp.
Enrollment (%)	100.0	42.8	56.6	0.1	0.1	0.4
Drop-out Rate (%)	8.4	7.8	8.8	n/a	n/a	0.0
H.S. Diplomas (#)	161	78	83	0	0	0

Seminole County

Seminole County
800 S Woolfork Ave • Donalsonville, GA 31745-1745
(229) 524-2433 • http://www.seminole.k12.ga.us
Grade Span: PK-12; **Agency Type:** 1
Schools: 3
1 Primary; 0 Middle; 0 High; 2 Other Level
2 Regular; 0 Special Education; 0 Vocational; 1 Alternative
0 Magnet; 0 Charter; 2 Title I Eligible; 2 School-wide Title I
Students: 1,754 (52.3% male; 47.7% female)
Individual Education Program: 198 (11.3%);
English Language Learner: 0 (0.0%); Migrant: 68 (3.9%)
Eligible for Free Lunch Program: 1,193 (68.0%)
Eligible for Reduced-Price Lunch Program: 106 (6.0%)
Teachers: 120.0 (14.6 to 1)
Librarians/Media Specialists: 2.0 (877.0 to 1)
Guidance Counselors: 4.0 (438.5 to 1)
Current Spending: ($ per student per year):
Total: $6,565; Instruction: $4,114; Support Services: $2,023
Enrollment, Drop-out Rates and Diploma Recipients by Race/Ethnicity

Category	Total	White	Black	Asian	AIAN	Hisp.
Enrollment (%)	100.0	46.1	51.9	0.1	0.0	1.9
Drop-out Rate (%)	17.6	20.1	15.9	n/a	n/a	0.0
H.S. Diplomas (#)	87	30	57	0	0	0

Spalding County

Spalding County
216 S Sixth St • Griffin, GA 30224-0224
Mailing Address: PO Drawer N • Griffin, GA 30224-0224
(770) 229-3700 • http://web.spalding.k12.ga.us/
Grade Span: PK-12; **Agency Type:** 1
Schools: 19
10 Primary; 4 Middle; 2 High; 3 Other Level
17 Regular; 0 Special Education; 0 Vocational; 2 Alternative
0 Magnet; 2 Charter; 8 Title I Eligible; 8 School-wide Title I
Students: 10,648 (51.3% male; 48.7% female)
Individual Education Program: 1,429 (13.4%);
English Language Learner: 86 (0.8%); Migrant: 0 (0.0%)
Eligible for Free Lunch Program: 4,966 (46.6%)
Eligible for Reduced-Price Lunch Program: 945 (8.9%)
Teachers: 692.7 (15.4 to 1)
Librarians/Media Specialists: 16.5 (645.3 to 1)
Guidance Counselors: 23.7 (449.3 to 1)
Current Spending: ($ per student per year):
Total: $7,045; Instruction: $4,391; Support Services: $2,253
Enrollment, Drop-out Rates and Diploma Recipients by Race/Ethnicity

Category	Total	White	Black	Asian	AIAN	Hisp.
Enrollment (%)	100.0	52.4	44.8	0.8	0.1	1.9
Drop-out Rate (%)	18.3	16.5	20.4	10.7	33.3	41.2
H.S. Diplomas (#)	401	239	153	7	0	2

Stephens County

Stephens County
Hwy 106 S • Toccoa, GA 30577-0577
Mailing Address: PO Box 1626 • Toccoa, GA 30577-0577
(706) 886-9415 • http://www.stephenscountyschools.com/
Grade Span: PK-12; **Agency Type:** 1
Schools: 7
4 Primary; 1 Middle; 1 High; 1 Other Level
6 Regular; 0 Special Education; 0 Vocational; 1 Alternative
0 Magnet; 0 Charter; 4 Title I Eligible; 2 School-wide Title I
Students: 4,405 (52.2% male; 47.8% female)
Individual Education Program: 564 (12.8%);
English Language Learner: 18 (0.4%); Migrant: 0 (0.0%)
Eligible for Free Lunch Program: 1,579 (35.8%)
Eligible for Reduced-Price Lunch Program: 404 (9.2%)
Teachers: 303.9 (14.5 to 1)
Librarians/Media Specialists: 6.0 (734.2 to 1)
Guidance Counselors: 10.5 (419.5 to 1)
Current Spending: ($ per student per year):
Total: $6,833; Instruction: $4,392; Support Services: $2,088
Enrollment, Drop-out Rates and Diploma Recipients by Race/Ethnicity

Category	Total	White	Black	Asian	AIAN	Hisp.
Enrollment (%)	100.0	81.8	16.2	0.5	0.3	1.2
Drop-out Rate (%)	6.3	5.7	9.9	0.0	n/a	0.0
H.S. Diplomas (#)	177	157	19	1	0	0

Sumter County

Sumter County
100 Learning Ln • Americus, GA 31719
(912) 229-2613 • http://www.sumter.k12.ga.us
Grade Span: PK-12; **Agency Type:** 1
Schools: 9
4 Primary; 2 Middle; 2 High; 1 Other Level
8 Regular; 0 Special Education; 0 Vocational; 1 Alternative
0 Magnet; 0 Charter; 6 Title I Eligible; 6 School-wide Title I
Students: 5,774 (50.8% male; 49.2% female)
Individual Education Program: 544 (9.4%);
English Language Learner: 2 (<0.1%); Migrant: 145 (2.5%)
Eligible for Free Lunch Program: 3,734 (64.7%)
Eligible for Reduced-Price Lunch Program: 548 (9.5%)
Teachers: 356.2 (16.2 to 1)
Librarians/Media Specialists: 8.0 (721.8 to 1)
Guidance Counselors: 12.0 (481.2 to 1)
Current Spending: ($ per student per year):
Total: $6,501; Instruction: $4,110; Support Services: $1,919
Enrollment, Drop-out Rates and Diploma Recipients by Race/Ethnicity

Category	Total	White	Black	Asian	AIAN	Hisp.
Enrollment (%)	100.0	23.6	73.4	0.5	0.1	2.5
Drop-out Rate (%)	10.9	7.8	11.8	12.5	0.0	19.4
H.S. Diplomas (#)	185	58	122	1	0	4

Tattnall County

Tattnall County

147 Brazell St • Reidsville, GA 30453-0157
(912) 557-4726 • http://www.tattnallcountyschools.org/
Grade Span: PK-12; **Agency Type:** 1
Schools: 8
3 Primary; 3 Middle; 1 High; 1 Other Level
7 Regular; 0 Special Education; 0 Vocational; 1 Alternative
0 Magnet; 0 Charter; 6 Title I Eligible; 6 School-wide Title I
Students: 3,305 (51.2% male; 48.8% female)
Individual Education Program: 375 (11.3%);
English Language Learner: 219 (6.6%); Migrant: 359 (10.9%)
Eligible for Free Lunch Program: 1,812 (54.8%)
Eligible for Reduced-Price Lunch Program: 351 (10.6%)
Teachers: 200.9 (16.5 to 1)
Librarians/Media Specialists: 6.0 (550.8 to 1)
Guidance Counselors: 7.0 (472.1 to 1)
Current Spending: ($ per student per year):
Total: $6,301; Instruction: $3,775; Support Services: $2,025

Enrollment, Drop-out Rates and Diploma Recipients by Race/Ethnicity

Category	Total	White	Black	Asian	AIAN	Hisp.
Enrollment (%)	100.0	56.0	32.2	0.3	0.1	11.5
Drop-out Rate (%)	6.5	5.7	5.4	0.0	0.0	23.4
H.S. Diplomas (#)	112	80	27	0	0	5

Taylor County

Taylor County

229 Mulberry St • Butler, GA 31006-3106
(912) 478-5224 • http://www.taylor.k12.ga.us
Grade Span: PK-12; **Agency Type:** 1
Schools: 3
1 Primary; 1 Middle; 1 High; 0 Other Level
3 Regular; 0 Special Education; 0 Vocational; 0 Alternative
0 Magnet; 0 Charter; 2 Title I Eligible; 0 School-wide Title I
Students: 1,735 (50.7% male; 49.3% female)
Individual Education Program: 146 (8.4%);
English Language Learner: 0 (0.0%); Migrant: 9 (0.5%)
Eligible for Free Lunch Program: 1,031 (59.4%)
Eligible for Reduced-Price Lunch Program: 172 (9.9%)
Teachers: 100.5 (17.3 to 1)
Librarians/Media Specialists: 2.0 (867.5 to 1)
Guidance Counselors: 4.0 (433.8 to 1)
Current Spending: ($ per student per year):
Total: $6,287; Instruction: $4,047; Support Services: $1,717

Enrollment, Drop-out Rates and Diploma Recipients by Race/Ethnicity

Category	Total	White	Black	Asian	AIAN	Hisp.
Enrollment (%)	100.0	46.8	51.7	0.3	0.0	1.2
Drop-out Rate (%)	11.3	5.9	16.2	n/a	n/a	0.0
H.S. Diplomas (#)	79	47	32	0	0	0

Telfair County

Telfair County

210-B Parsonage St • Mcrae, GA 31055-1055
(229) 868-5661
Grade Span: PK-12; **Agency Type:** 1
Schools: 5
2 Primary; 1 Middle; 1 High; 1 Other Level
4 Regular; 0 Special Education; 0 Vocational; 1 Alternative
0 Magnet; 0 Charter; 3 Title I Eligible; 3 School-wide Title I
Students: 1,648 (52.0% male; 48.0% female)
Individual Education Program: 217 (13.2%);
English Language Learner: 8 (0.5%); Migrant: 14 (0.8%)
Eligible for Free Lunch Program: 1,056 (64.1%)
Eligible for Reduced-Price Lunch Program: 155 (9.4%)
Teachers: 113.9 (14.5 to 1)
Librarians/Media Specialists: 3.0 (549.3 to 1)
Guidance Counselors: 4.0 (412.0 to 1)
Current Spending: ($ per student per year):
Total: $6,922; Instruction: $4,554; Support Services: $1,932

Enrollment, Drop-out Rates and Diploma Recipients by Race/Ethnicity

Category	Total	White	Black	Asian	AIAN	Hisp.
Enrollment (%)	100.0	49.9	48.9	0.5	0.0	0.6
Drop-out Rate (%)	9.1	7.8	10.6	0.0	n/a	0.0
H.S. Diplomas (#)	80	38	42	0	0	0

Terrell County

Terrell County

955 Forrester Dr • Dawson, GA 31742-1742
Mailing Address: PO Box 151 • Dawson, GA 31742-1742
(912) 229-4425
Grade Span: PK-12; **Agency Type:** 1
Schools: 3
2 Primary; 0 Middle; 0 High; 1 Other Level
3 Regular; 0 Special Education; 0 Vocational; 0 Alternative
0 Magnet; 0 Charter; 3 Title I Eligible; 3 School-wide Title I
Students: 1,764 (50.1% male; 49.9% female)
Individual Education Program: 255 (14.5%);
English Language Learner: 0 (0.0%); Migrant: 2 (0.1%)
Eligible for Free Lunch Program: 1,064 (60.3%)
Eligible for Reduced-Price Lunch Program: 175 (9.9%)
Teachers: 98.5 (17.9 to 1)
Librarians/Media Specialists: 3.0 (588.0 to 1)
Guidance Counselors: 2.9 (608.3 to 1)
Current Spending: ($ per student per year):
Total: $7,077; Instruction: $4,302; Support Services: $2,289

Enrollment, Drop-out Rates and Diploma Recipients by Race/Ethnicity

Category	Total	White	Black	Asian	AIAN	Hisp.
Enrollment (%)	100.0	4.0	95.4	0.1	0.0	0.5
Drop-out Rate (%)	8.6	0.0	9.0	n/a	n/a	0.0
H.S. Diplomas (#)	54	3	50	0	0	1

Thomas County

Thomas County

11343 US Hwy 319 N • Thomasville, GA 31757
(229) 225-4380 • http://www.thomas.k12.ga.us/
Grade Span: PK-12; **Agency Type:** 1
Schools: 7
2 Primary; 1 Middle; 2 High; 2 Other Level
6 Regular; 0 Special Education; 0 Vocational; 1 Alternative
0 Magnet; 1 Charter; 3 Title I Eligible; 3 School-wide Title I
Students: 5,466 (50.5% male; 49.5% female)
Individual Education Program: 935 (17.1%);
English Language Learner: 26 (0.5%); Migrant: 103 (1.9%)
Eligible for Free Lunch Program: 2,576 (47.1%)
Eligible for Reduced-Price Lunch Program: 592 (10.8%)
Teachers: 350.8 (15.6 to 1)
Librarians/Media Specialists: 5.0 (1,093.2 to 1)
Guidance Counselors: 10.4 (525.6 to 1)
Current Spending: ($ per student per year):
Total: $6,540; Instruction: $4,228; Support Services: $1,930

Enrollment, Drop-out Rates and Diploma Recipients by Race/Ethnicity

Category	Total	White	Black	Asian	AIAN	Hisp.
Enrollment (%)	100.0	62.8	35.3	0.4	0.1	1.4
Drop-out Rate (%)	1.9	1.6	2.4	0.0	0.0	0.0
H.S. Diplomas (#)	266	192	69	2	0	3

Thomasville City

915 E Jackson St • Thomasville, GA 31792-4776
(229) 225-2600 • http://www.tcitys.org/
Grade Span: PK-12; **Agency Type:** 1
Schools: 8
4 Primary; 1 Middle; 1 High; 2 Other Level
6 Regular; 0 Special Education; 0 Vocational; 2 Alternative
0 Magnet; 0 Charter; 3 Title I Eligible; 3 School-wide Title I
Students: 3,107 (49.6% male; 50.4% female)
Individual Education Program: 369 (11.9%);
English Language Learner: 0 (0.0%); Migrant: 0 (0.0%)
Eligible for Free Lunch Program: 1,735 (55.8%)
Eligible for Reduced-Price Lunch Program: 312 (10.0%)
Teachers: 203.7 (15.3 to 1)
Librarians/Media Specialists: 5.0 (621.4 to 1)
Guidance Counselors: 8.2 (378.9 to 1)
Current Spending: ($ per student per year):
Total: $7,102; Instruction: $4,412; Support Services: $2,185

Enrollment, Drop-out Rates and Diploma Recipients by Race/Ethnicity

Category	Total	White	Black	Asian	AIAN	Hisp.
Enrollment (%)	100.0	24.8	74.7	0.2	0.0	0.4
Drop-out Rate (%)	8.2	5.1	9.1	0.0	n/a	50.0
H.S. Diplomas (#)	159	46	111	2	0	0

Tift County

Tift County

207 N Ridge Ave • Tifton, GA 31793-0389
Mailing Address: PO Box 389 • Tifton, GA 31793-0389
(229) 386-6500 • http://www.tift.k12.ga.us
Grade Span: PK-12; **Agency Type:** 1
Schools: 12

5 Primary; 4 Middle; 1 High; 2 Other Level
11 Regular; 0 Special Education; 0 Vocational; 1 Alternative
0 Magnet; 0 Charter; 5 Title I Eligible; 5 School-wide Title I
Students: 7,641 (51.2% male; 48.8% female)
Individual Education Program: 946 (12.4%);
English Language Learner: 388 (5.1%); Migrant: 299 (3.9%)
Eligible for Free Lunch Program: 3,520 (46.1%)
Eligible for Reduced-Price Lunch Program: 616 (8.1%)
Teachers: 467.3 (16.4 to 1)
Librarians/Media Specialists: 13.0 (587.8 to 1)
Guidance Counselors: 15.0 (509.4 to 1)
Current Spending: ($ per student per year):
Total: $6,273; Instruction: $4,174; Support Services: $1,769
Enrollment, Drop-out Rates and Diploma Recipients by Race/Ethnicity

Category	Total	White	Black	Asian	AIAN	Hisp.
Enrollment (%)	100.0	51.4	38.7	0.9	0.0	9.0
Drop-out Rate (%)	8.6	7.5	10.3	7.1	n/a	7.7
H.S. Diplomas (#)	342	239	91	6	0	6

Toombs County

Toombs County
117 E Wesley Ave • Lyons, GA 30436-0436
(912) 526-3141 • http://www.toombs.k12.ga.us
Grade Span: PK-12; **Agency Type:** 1
Schools: 4
2 Primary; 1 Middle; 1 High; 0 Other Level
4 Regular; 0 Special Education; 0 Vocational; 0 Alternative
0 Magnet; 0 Charter; 2 Title I Eligible; 2 School-wide Title I
Students: 2,856 (50.9% male; 49.1% female)
Individual Education Program: 410 (14.4%);
English Language Learner: 226 (7.9%); Migrant: 406 (14.2%)
Eligible for Free Lunch Program: 1,677 (58.7%)
Eligible for Reduced-Price Lunch Program: 327 (11.4%)
Teachers: 176.9 (16.1 to 1)
Librarians/Media Specialists: 4.0 (714.0 to 1)
Guidance Counselors: 5.0 (571.2 to 1)
Current Spending: ($ per student per year):
Total: $5,874; Instruction: $3,880; Support Services: $1,566
Enrollment, Drop-out Rates and Diploma Recipients by Race/Ethnicity

Category	Total	White	Black	Asian	AIAN	Hisp.
Enrollment (%)	100.0	62.6	20.1	0.2	0.0	17.0
Drop-out Rate (%)	7.9	5.3	11.9	0.0	n/a	17.2
H.S. Diplomas (#)	94	67	17	1	0	9

Vidalia City
301 Adams St • Vidalia, GA 30474-0474
(912) 537-3088 • http://www.vidalia-city.k12.ga.us/
Grade Span: PK-12; **Agency Type:** 1
Schools: 5
2 Primary; 1 Middle; 1 High; 1 Other Level
4 Regular; 0 Special Education; 0 Vocational; 1 Alternative
0 Magnet; 0 Charter; 3 Title I Eligible; 3 School-wide Title I
Students: 2,408 (50.1% male; 49.9% female)
Individual Education Program: 182 (7.6%);
English Language Learner: 6 (0.2%); Migrant: 3 (0.1%)
Eligible for Free Lunch Program: 1,142 (47.4%)
Eligible for Reduced-Price Lunch Program: 181 (7.5%)
Teachers: 144.1 (16.7 to 1)
Librarians/Media Specialists: 4.0 (602.0 to 1)
Guidance Counselors: 5.0 (481.6 to 1)
Current Spending: ($ per student per year):
Total: $6,142; Instruction: $3,959; Support Services: $1,810
Enrollment, Drop-out Rates and Diploma Recipients by Race/Ethnicity

Category	Total	White	Black	Asian	AIAN	Hisp.
Enrollment (%)	100.0	46.8	50.2	1.2	0.0	1.8
Drop-out Rate (%)	7.6	4.8	10.6	0.0	n/a	27.3
H.S. Diplomas (#)	137	77	56	2	0	2

Towns County

Towns County
67 Lakeview Circle, Ste C • Hiawassee, GA 30546-0546
(706) 896-2279
Grade Span: PK-12; **Agency Type:** 1
Schools: 2
0 Primary; 0 Middle; 1 High; 1 Other Level
1 Regular; 0 Special Education; 0 Vocational; 1 Alternative
0 Magnet; 0 Charter; 1 Title I Eligible; 0 School-wide Title I
Students: 1,529 (51.4% male; 48.6% female)
Individual Education Program: 143 (9.4%);
English Language Learner: 8 (0.5%); Migrant: 0 (0.0%)
Eligible for Free Lunch Program: 337 (22.0%)
Eligible for Reduced-Price Lunch Program: 139 (9.1%)
Teachers: 139.3 (11.0 to 1)
Librarians/Media Specialists: 1.0 (1,529.0 to 1)
Guidance Counselors: 2.0 (764.5 to 1)
Current Spending: ($ per student per year):
Total: $6,680; Instruction: $4,341; Support Services: $1,977
Enrollment, Drop-out Rates and Diploma Recipients by Race/Ethnicity

Category	Total	White	Black	Asian	AIAN	Hisp.
Enrollment (%)	100.0	98.8	0.1	0.5	0.1	0.7
Drop-out Rate (%)	6.7	6.7	n/a	n/a	n/a	n/a
H.S. Diplomas (#)	99	98	1	0	0	0

Troup County

Troup County
200 Mooty Bridge Rd • Lagrange, GA 30240
(706) 812-7900 • http://www.troup.k12.ga.us
Grade Span: PK-12; **Agency Type:** 1
Schools: 20
13 Primary; 3 Middle; 3 High; 1 Other Level
18 Regular; 0 Special Education; 0 Vocational; 2 Alternative
2 Magnet; 0 Charter; 11 Title I Eligible; 11 School-wide Title I
Students: 11,779 (51.1% male; 48.9% female)
Individual Education Program: 1,489 (12.6%);
English Language Learner: 57 (0.5%); Migrant: 1 (<0.1%)
Eligible for Free Lunch Program: 5,195 (44.1%)
Eligible for Reduced-Price Lunch Program: 996 (8.5%)
Teachers: 823.3 (14.3 to 1)
Librarians/Media Specialists: 21.0 (560.9 to 1)
Guidance Counselors: 27.5 (428.3 to 1)
Current Spending: ($ per student per year):
Total: $6,764; Instruction: $4,336; Support Services: $2,263
Enrollment, Drop-out Rates and Diploma Recipients by Race/Ethnicity

Category	Total	White	Black	Asian	AIAN	Hisp.
Enrollment (%)	100.0	56.3	42.0	0.2	0.3	1.1
Drop-out Rate (%)	6.6	6.7	6.3	0.0	0.0	10.3
H.S. Diplomas (#)	484	323	153	4	0	4

Turner County

Turner County
423 N Cleveland St • Ashburn, GA 31714-1714
Mailing Address: PO Box 609 • Ashburn, GA 31714-1714
(229) 567-3338 • http://www.turner.k12.ga.us
Grade Span: PK-12; **Agency Type:** 1
Schools: 6
1 Primary; 1 Middle; 1 High; 3 Other Level
4 Regular; 0 Special Education; 0 Vocational; 2 Alternative
0 Magnet; 0 Charter; 2 Title I Eligible; 2 School-wide Title I
Students: 1,914 (51.0% male; 49.0% female)
Individual Education Program: 248 (13.0%);
English Language Learner: 0 (0.0%); Migrant: 12 (0.6%)
Eligible for Free Lunch Program: 1,074 (56.1%)
Eligible for Reduced-Price Lunch Program: 137 (7.2%)
Teachers: 126.4 (15.1 to 1)
Librarians/Media Specialists: 2.0 (957.0 to 1)
Guidance Counselors: 4.5 (425.3 to 1)
Current Spending: ($ per student per year):
Total: $6,958; Instruction: $4,569; Support Services: $2,007
Enrollment, Drop-out Rates and Diploma Recipients by Race/Ethnicity

Category	Total	White	Black	Asian	AIAN	Hisp.
Enrollment (%)	100.0	41.6	56.7	0.2	0.3	1.2
Drop-out Rate (%)	6.9	5.1	7.4	n/a	0.0	150.0
H.S. Diplomas (#)	82	42	40	0	0	0

Union County

Union County
10 Hughes St • Blairsville, GA 30512-0512
(706) 745-2322 • http://www.union.k12.ga.us
Grade Span: KG-12; **Agency Type:** 1
Schools: 7
2 Primary; 1 Middle; 1 High; 3 Other Level
5 Regular; 0 Special Education; 0 Vocational; 2 Alternative
0 Magnet; 0 Charter; 2 Title I Eligible; 2 School-wide Title I
Students: 2,598 (50.7% male; 49.3% female)
Individual Education Program: 413 (15.9%);
English Language Learner: 1 (<0.1%); Migrant: 0 (0.0%)
Eligible for Free Lunch Program: 800 (30.8%)
Eligible for Reduced-Price Lunch Program: 408 (15.7%)
Teachers: 178.9 (14.5 to 1)
Librarians/Media Specialists: 4.8 (541.3 to 1)
Guidance Counselors: 4.9 (530.2 to 1)
Current Spending: ($ per student per year):
Total: $6,821; Instruction: $4,375; Support Services: $2,041

Enrollment, Drop-out Rates and Diploma Recipients by Race/Ethnicity

Category	Total	White	Black	Asian	AIAN	Hisp.
Enrollment (%)	100.0	98.4	0.3	0.2	0.4	0.8
Drop-out Rate (%)	2.5	2.5	0.0	0.0	0.0	0.0
H.S. Diplomas (#)	145	145	0	0	0	0

Upson County

Thomaston-Upson County

205 Civic Center Dr • Thomaston, GA 30286-4233
(706) 647-9621 • http://www.upson.k12.ga.us/
Grade Span: PK-12; **Agency Type:** 1
Schools: 7
3 Primary; 1 Middle; 1 High; 2 Other Level
6 Regular; 0 Special Education; 0 Vocational; 1 Alternative
0 Magnet; 0 Charter; 4 Title I Eligible; 4 School-wide Title I
Students: 5,009 (51.7% male; 48.3% female)
Individual Education Program: 723 (14.4%);
English Language Learner: 5 (0.1%); Migrant: 2 (<0.1%)
Eligible for Free Lunch Program: 2,102 (42.0%)
Eligible for Reduced-Price Lunch Program: 538 (10.7%)
Teachers: 278.8 (18.0 to 1)
Librarians/Media Specialists: 7.0 (715.6 to 1)
Guidance Counselors: 9.0 (556.6 to 1)
Current Spending: ($ per student per year):
Total: $6,243; Instruction: $4,069; Support Services: $1,784

Enrollment, Drop-out Rates and Diploma Recipients by Race/Ethnicity

Category	Total	White	Black	Asian	AIAN	Hisp.
Enrollment (%)	100.0	62.8	36.0	0.3	0.1	0.8
Drop-out Rate (%)	13.1	12.0	15.9	0.0	0.0	8.3
H.S. Diplomas (#)	228	160	62	4	0	2

Walker County

Walker County

201 S Duke St • Lafayette, GA 30728-0728
(706) 638-1240 • http://www.walkerschools.org/
Grade Span: PK-12; **Agency Type:** 1
Schools: 15
9 Primary; 3 Middle; 2 High; 1 Other Level
14 Regular; 0 Special Education; 0 Vocational; 1 Alternative
0 Magnet; 0 Charter; 10 Title I Eligible; 10 School-wide Title I
Students: 8,844 (52.1% male; 47.9% female)
Individual Education Program: 1,217 (13.8%);
English Language Learner: 24 (0.3%); Migrant: 52 (0.6%)
Eligible for Free Lunch Program: 3,504 (39.6%)
Eligible for Reduced-Price Lunch Program: 1,250 (14.1%)
Teachers: 577.0 (15.3 to 1)
Librarians/Media Specialists: 15.5 (570.6 to 1)
Guidance Counselors: 19.5 (453.5 to 1)
Current Spending: ($ per student per year):
Total: $6,493; Instruction: $4,074; Support Services: $2,046

Enrollment, Drop-out Rates and Diploma Recipients by Race/Ethnicity

Category	Total	White	Black	Asian	AIAN	Hisp.
Enrollment (%)	100.0	92.9	5.8	0.3	0.1	0.8
Drop-out Rate (%)	9.4	9.5	7.0	12.5	50.0	5.6
H.S. Diplomas (#)	317	301	8	2	0	6

Walton County

Walton County

115 Oak St • Monroe, GA 30655-0655
(770) 267-6544 • http://www.walton.k12.ga.us
Grade Span: PK-12; **Agency Type:** 1
Schools: 14
8 Primary; 2 Middle; 2 High; 2 Other Level
13 Regular; 0 Special Education; 0 Vocational; 1 Alternative
0 Magnet; 0 Charter; 4 Title I Eligible; 4 School-wide Title I
Students: 10,368 (50.3% male; 49.7% female)
Individual Education Program: 1,381 (13.3%);
English Language Learner: 189 (1.8%); Migrant: 15 (0.1%)
Eligible for Free Lunch Program: 2,840 (27.4%)
Eligible for Reduced-Price Lunch Program: 767 (7.4%)
Teachers: 674.8 (15.4 to 1)
Librarians/Media Specialists: 14.0 (740.6 to 1)
Guidance Counselors: 25.5 (406.6 to 1)
Current Spending: ($ per student per year):
Total: $6,439; Instruction: $4,206; Support Services: $1,901

Enrollment, Drop-out Rates and Diploma Recipients by Race/Ethnicity

Category	Total	White	Black	Asian	AIAN	Hisp.
Enrollment (%)	100.0	76.9	19.4	1.3	0.4	2.0
Drop-out Rate (%)	6.6	5.3	13.7	2.9	0.0	0.0
H.S. Diplomas (#)	344	295	42	4	0	3

Ware County

Ware County

1301 Bailey St • Waycross, GA 31503
(912) 283-8656 • http://www.warecoschools.com
Grade Span: PK-12; **Agency Type:** 1
Schools: 12
6 Primary; 2 Middle; 1 High; 3 Other Level
11 Regular; 0 Special Education; 0 Vocational; 1 Alternative
1 Magnet; 0 Charter; 9 Title I Eligible; 7 School-wide Title I
Students: 6,370 (51.8% male; 48.2% female)
Individual Education Program: 960 (15.1%);
English Language Learner: 46 (0.7%); Migrant: 76 (1.2%)
Eligible for Free Lunch Program: 3,145 (49.4%)
Eligible for Reduced-Price Lunch Program: 564 (8.9%)
Teachers: 430.3 (14.8 to 1)
Librarians/Media Specialists: 11.0 (579.1 to 1)
Guidance Counselors: 13.1 (486.3 to 1)
Current Spending: ($ per student per year):
Total: $7,078; Instruction: $4,668; Support Services: $1,993

Enrollment, Drop-out Rates and Diploma Recipients by Race/Ethnicity

Category	Total	White	Black	Asian	AIAN	Hisp.
Enrollment (%)	100.0	60.5	37.0	0.6	0.2	1.6
Drop-out Rate (%)	9.1	8.6	10.5	0.0	0.0	0.0
H.S. Diplomas (#)	270	191	76	2	0	1

Washington County

Washington County

501 Industrial Dr • Sandersville, GA 31082-1082
Mailing Address: PO Box 716 • Sandersville, GA 31082-1082
(478) 552-3981 • http://www.washington.k12.ga.us
Grade Span: PK-12; **Agency Type:** 1
Schools: 7
4 Primary; 1 Middle; 1 High; 1 Other Level
6 Regular; 0 Special Education; 0 Vocational; 1 Alternative
0 Magnet; 0 Charter; 5 Title I Eligible; 5 School-wide Title I
Students: 3,821 (51.1% male; 48.9% female)
Individual Education Program: 381 (10.0%);
English Language Learner: 0 (0.0%); Migrant: 1 (<0.1%)
Eligible for Free Lunch Program: 2,092 (54.8%)
Eligible for Reduced-Price Lunch Program: 516 (13.5%)
Teachers: 219.8 (17.4 to 1)
Librarians/Media Specialists: 6.8 (561.9 to 1)
Guidance Counselors: 8.0 (477.6 to 1)
Current Spending: ($ per student per year):
Total: $6,598; Instruction: $3,834; Support Services: $2,351

Enrollment, Drop-out Rates and Diploma Recipients by Race/Ethnicity

Category	Total	White	Black	Asian	AIAN	Hisp.
Enrollment (%)	100.0	30.7	68.7	0.2	0.1	0.4
Drop-out Rate (%)	7.9	7.2	8.2	0.0	n/a	0.0
H.S. Diplomas (#)	207	78	128	0	0	1

Wayne County

Wayne County

555 S Sunset Boulvard • Jesup, GA 31545-1545
(912) 427-1003 • http://www.wayne.k12.ga.us/
Grade Span: PK-12; **Agency Type:** 1
Schools: 10
4 Primary; 3 Middle; 2 High; 1 Other Level
9 Regular; 0 Special Education; 0 Vocational; 1 Alternative
0 Magnet; 0 Charter; 3 Title I Eligible; 3 School-wide Title I
Students: 5,256 (52.0% male; 48.0% female)
Individual Education Program: 741 (14.1%);
English Language Learner: 92 (1.8%); Migrant: 22 (0.4%)
Eligible for Free Lunch Program: 2,323 (44.2%)
Eligible for Reduced-Price Lunch Program: 411 (7.8%)
Teachers: 319.5 (16.5 to 1)
Librarians/Media Specialists: 9.0 (584.0 to 1)
Guidance Counselors: 10.0 (525.6 to 1)
Current Spending: ($ per student per year):
Total: $6,418; Instruction: $4,056; Support Services: $1,979

Enrollment, Drop-out Rates and Diploma Recipients by Race/Ethnicity

Category	Total	White	Black	Asian	AIAN	Hisp.
Enrollment (%)	100.0	72.0	23.9	0.6	0.2	3.4
Drop-out Rate (%)	10.7	9.6	13.3	25.0	0.0	9.1
H.S. Diplomas (#)	214	162	48	2	0	2

White County

White County
113 N Brooks St • Cleveland, GA 30528-0528
(404) 865-2315 • http://www.white.k12.ga.us
Grade Span: PK-12; **Agency Type:** 1
Schools: 6
2 Primary; 2 Middle; 1 High; 1 Other Level
6 Regular; 0 Special Education; 0 Vocational; 0 Alternative
0 Magnet; 0 Charter; 3 Title I Eligible; 0 School-wide Title I
Students: 3,758 (51.5% male; 48.5% female)
Individual Education Program: 466 (12.4%);
English Language Learner: 26 (0.7%); Migrant: 9 (0.2%)
Eligible for Free Lunch Program: 1,045 (27.8%)
Eligible for Reduced-Price Lunch Program: 381 (10.1%)
Teachers: 233.0 (16.1 to 1)
Librarians/Media Specialists: 6.0 (626.3 to 1)
Guidance Counselors: 7.0 (536.9 to 1)
Current Spending: ($ per student per year):
Total: $6,357; Instruction: $4,078; Support Services: $1,932
Enrollment, Drop-out Rates and Diploma Recipients by Race/Ethnicity

Category	Total	White	Black	Asian	AIAN	Hisp.
Enrollment (%)	100.0	95.4	2.2	0.5	0.5	1.3
Drop-out Rate (%)	3.1	2.9	9.5	0.0	0.0	25.0
H.S. Diplomas (#)	152	147	2	2	1	0

Whitfield County

Dalton City
100 S Hamilton St • Dalton, GA 30720
(706) 278-8766 • http://www.dalton.k12.ga.us
Grade Span: PK-12; **Agency Type:** 1
Schools: 9
4 Primary; 2 Middle; 1 High; 2 Other Level
7 Regular; 0 Special Education; 0 Vocational; 2 Alternative
0 Magnet; 0 Charter; 6 Title I Eligible; 4 School-wide Title I
Students: 5,739 (51.6% male; 48.4% female)
Individual Education Program: 573 (10.0%);
English Language Learner: 3,450 (60.1%); Migrant: 383 (6.7%)
Eligible for Free Lunch Program: 2,746 (47.8%)
Eligible for Reduced-Price Lunch Program: 786 (13.7%)
Teachers: 366.3 (15.7 to 1)
Librarians/Media Specialists: 9.0 (637.7 to 1)
Guidance Counselors: 13.0 (441.5 to 1)
Current Spending: ($ per student per year):
Total: $8,641; Instruction: $5,376; Support Services: $2,948
Enrollment, Drop-out Rates and Diploma Recipients by Race/Ethnicity

Category	Total	White	Black	Asian	AIAN	Hisp.
Enrollment (%)	100.0	30.8	7.3	2.5	0.5	58.9
Drop-out Rate (%)	4.8	2.7	4.4	n/a	4.0	7.3
H.S. Diplomas (#)	235	138	24	9	0	64

Whitfield County
1306 S Thornton Ave • Dalton, GA 30720
(706) 278-8070 • http://www.whitfield.k12.ga.us
Grade Span: PK-12; **Agency Type:** 1
Schools: 21
11 Primary; 4 Middle; 3 High; 3 Other Level
17 Regular; 1 Special Education; 0 Vocational; 3 Alternative
0 Magnet; 0 Charter; 9 Title I Eligible; 6 School-wide Title I
Students: 12,190 (51.7% male; 48.3% female)
Individual Education Program: 1,435 (11.8%);
English Language Learner: 829 (6.8%); Migrant: 193 (1.6%)
Eligible for Free Lunch Program: 4,517 (37.1%)
Eligible for Reduced-Price Lunch Program: 1,263 (10.4%)
Teachers: 776.7 (15.7 to 1)
Librarians/Media Specialists: 21.0 (580.5 to 1)
Guidance Counselors: 26.0 (468.8 to 1)
Current Spending: ($ per student per year):
Total: $6,431; Instruction: $4,277; Support Services: $1,804
Enrollment, Drop-out Rates and Diploma Recipients by Race/Ethnicity

Category	Total	White	Black	Asian	AIAN	Hisp.
Enrollment (%)	100.0	76.1	2.3	0.7	0.1	20.9
Drop-out Rate (%)	6.9	7.0	1.6	0.0	0.0	8.0
H.S. Diplomas (#)	553	499	14	1	0	39

Wilkes County

Wilkes County
313-A N Alexander Ave • Washington, GA 30673-0673
(706) 678-2718 • http://www.wilkes.k12.ga.us/
Grade Span: PK-12; **Agency Type:** 1
Schools: 5
2 Primary; 1 Middle; 1 High; 1 Other Level
4 Regular; 0 Special Education; 0 Vocational; 1 Alternative
0 Magnet; 0 Charter; 3 Title I Eligible; 3 School-wide Title I
Students: 1,858 (50.4% male; 49.6% female)
Individual Education Program: 258 (13.9%);
English Language Learner: 11 (0.6%); Migrant: 7 (0.4%)
Eligible for Free Lunch Program: 939 (50.5%)
Eligible for Reduced-Price Lunch Program: 215 (11.6%)
Teachers: 116.1 (16.0 to 1)
Librarians/Media Specialists: 3.0 (619.3 to 1)
Guidance Counselors: 3.6 (516.1 to 1)
Current Spending: ($ per student per year):
Total: $7,088; Instruction: $4,285; Support Services: $2,277
Enrollment, Drop-out Rates and Diploma Recipients by Race/Ethnicity

Category	Total	White	Black	Asian	AIAN	Hisp.
Enrollment (%)	100.0	46.4	51.5	0.2	0.2	1.8
Drop-out Rate (%)	9.9	7.8	11.3	0.0	50.0	0.0
H.S. Diplomas (#)	99	58	40	1	0	0

Wilkinson County

Wilkinson County
100 Bacon St • Irwinton, GA 31042-1042
Mailing Address: PO Box 206 • Irwinton, GA 31042-1042
(478) 946-5521
Grade Span: PK-12; **Agency Type:** 1
Schools: 4
2 Primary; 1 Middle; 1 High; 0 Other Level
4 Regular; 0 Special Education; 0 Vocational; 0 Alternative
0 Magnet; 0 Charter; 4 Title I Eligible; 4 School-wide Title I
Students: 1,737 (50.5% male; 49.5% female)
Individual Education Program: 259 (14.9%);
English Language Learner: 1 (0.1%); Migrant: 5 (0.3%)
Eligible for Free Lunch Program: 980 (56.4%)
Eligible for Reduced-Price Lunch Program: 207 (11.9%)
Teachers: 117.5 (14.8 to 1)
Librarians/Media Specialists: 3.0 (579.0 to 1)
Guidance Counselors: 2.5 (694.8 to 1)
Current Spending: ($ per student per year):
Total: $7,966; Instruction: $4,831; Support Services: $2,619
Enrollment, Drop-out Rates and Diploma Recipients by Race/Ethnicity

Category	Total	White	Black	Asian	AIAN	Hisp.
Enrollment (%)	100.0	40.3	59.0	0.1	0.0	0.6
Drop-out Rate (%)	7.3	11.7	5.1	n/a	n/a	100.0
H.S. Diplomas (#)	100	22	78	0	0	0

Worth County

Worth County
504 E Price St • Sylvester, GA 31791-1791
(912) 229-8600 • http://www.peanut.org/wcbe
Grade Span: PK-12; **Agency Type:** 1
Schools: 6
3 Primary; 1 Middle; 1 High; 1 Other Level
5 Regular; 0 Special Education; 0 Vocational; 1 Alternative
0 Magnet; 0 Charter; 4 Title I Eligible; 4 School-wide Title I
Students: 4,354 (51.2% male; 48.8% female)
Individual Education Program: 299 (6.9%);
English Language Learner: 0 (0.0%); Migrant: 9 (0.2%)
Eligible for Free Lunch Program: 2,005 (46.0%)
Eligible for Reduced-Price Lunch Program: 420 (9.6%)
Teachers: 296.0 (14.7 to 1)
Librarians/Media Specialists: 6.0 (725.7 to 1)
Guidance Counselors: 9.0 (483.8 to 1)
Current Spending: ($ per student per year):
Total: $6,481; Instruction: $3,925; Support Services: $2,051
Enrollment, Drop-out Rates and Diploma Recipients by Race/Ethnicity

Category	Total	White	Black	Asian	AIAN	Hisp.
Enrollment (%)	100.0	58.3	40.4	0.3	0.2	0.8
Drop-out Rate (%)	10.1	9.1	11.5	25.0	0.0	9.1
H.S. Diplomas (#)	188	124	64	0	0	0

Number of Schools

Rank	Number	District Name	City
1	139	Dekalb County	Decatur
2	102	Atlanta City	Atlanta
2	102	Cobb County	Marietta
4	89	Gwinnett County	Lawrenceville
5	81	Fulton County	Atlanta
6	61	Muscogee County	Columbus
7	57	Richmond County	Augusta
8	55	Chatham County	Savannah
9	54	Clayton County	Jonesboro
10	45	Bibb County	Macon
11	34	Houston County	Perry
12	33	Cherokee County	Canton
13	32	Hall County	Gainesville
14	30	Douglas County	Douglasville
15	28	Dougherty County	Albany
15	28	Henry County	Mcdonough
17	27	Coweta County	Newnan
17	27	Fayette County	Fayetteville
19	26	Columbia County	Appling
20	23	Forsyth County	Cumming
20	23	Paulding County	Dallas
22	22	Carroll County	Carrollton
22	22	Floyd County	Rome
24	21	Clarke County	Athens
24	21	Whitfield County	Dalton
26	20	Bartow County	Cartersville
26	20	Newton County	Covington
26	20	Troup County	Lagrange
29	19	Spalding County	Griffin
30	18	Rockdale County	Conyers
31	17	Glynn County	Brunswick
32	16	Bulloch County	Statesboro
32	16	Colquitt County	Moultrie
32	16	Liberty County	Hinesville
35	15	Barrow County	Winder
35	15	Catoosa County	Ringgold
35	15	Walker County	Lafayette
38	14	Walton County	Monroe
39	13	Camden County	Kingsland
39	13	Effingham County	Springfield
41	12	Bryan County	Pembroke
41	12	Coffee County	Douglas
41	12	Tift County	Tifton
41	12	Ware County	Waycross
45	11	Baldwin County	Milledgeville
45	11	Emanuel County	Swainsboro
45	11	Habersham County	Clarkesville
45	11	Jackson County	Jefferson
45	11	Lowndes County	Valdosta
45	11	Marietta City	Marietta
45	11	Polk County	Cedartown
45	11	Rome City	Rome
53	10	Chattooga County	Summerville
53	10	Decatur County	Bainbridge
53	10	Meriwether County	Greenville
53	10	Valdosta City	Valdosta
53	10	Wayne County	Jesup
58	9	Dalton City	Dalton
58	9	Gordon County	Calhoun
58	9	Jones County	Gray
58	9	Murray County	Chatsworth
58	9	Oconee County	Watkinsville
58	9	Sumter County	Americus
64	8	Appling County	Baxley
64	8	Decatur City	Decatur
64	8	Elbert County	Elberton
64	8	Grady County	Cairo
64	8	Laurens County	Dublin
64	8	Madison County	Danielsville
64	8	Tattnall County	Reidsville
64	8	Thomasville City	Thomasville
72	7	Crisp County	Cordele
72	7	Dublin City	Dublin
72	7	Fort Benning District	Fort Benning
72	7	Haralson County	Buchanan
72	7	Harris County	Hamilton
72	7	Jefferson County	Louisville
72	7	Lee County	Leesburg
72	7	Mcduffie County	Thomson
72	7	Mitchell County	Camilla
72	7	Peach County	Fort Valley
72	7	Stephens County	Toccoa
72	7	Thomas County	Thomasville
72	7	Thomaston-Upson County	Thomaston
72	7	Union County	Blairsville
72	7	Washington County	Sandersville
87	6	Ben Hill County	Fitzgerald
87	6	Brantley County	Nahunta
87	6	Burke County	Waynesboro
87	6	Calhoun City	Calhoun
87	6	Dawson County	Dawsonville
87	6	Gilmer County	Ellijay
87	6	Greene County	Greensboro
87	6	Hart County	Hartwell
87	6	Lumpkin County	Dahlonega
87	6	Pickens County	Jasper
87	6	Rabun County	Clayton
87	6	Turner County	Ashburn
87	6	White County	Cleveland
87	6	Worth County	Sylvester
101	5	Banks County	Homer
101	5	Berrien County	Nashville
101	5	Candler County	Metter
101	5	Charlton County	Folkston
101	5	Crawford County	Roberta
101	5	Dade County	Trenton
101	5	Dodge County	Eastman
101	5	Fannin County	Blue Ridge
101	5	Franklin County	Carnesville
101	5	Gainesville City	Gainesville
101	5	Heard County	Franklin
101	5	Jasper County	Monticello
101	5	Jeff Davis County	Hazlehurst
101	5	Monroe County	Forsyth
101	5	Morgan County	Madison
101	5	Oglethorpe County	Lexington
101	5	Pulaski County	Hawkinsville
101	5	Telfair County	Mcrae
101	5	Vidalia City	Vidalia
101	5	Wilkes County	Washington
121	4	Bacon County	Alma
121	4	Bleckley County	Cochran
121	4	Brooks County	Quitman
121	4	Buford City	Buford
121	4	Butts County	Jackson
121	4	Cartersville City	Cartersville
121	4	Cook County	Adel
121	4	Dooly County	Vienna
121	4	Early County	Blakely
121	4	Evans County	Claxton
121	4	Hancock County	Sparta
121	4	Irwin County	Ocilla
121	4	Jenkins County	Millen
121	4	Macon County	Oglethorpe
121	4	Pierce County	Blackshear
121	4	Pike County	Zebulon
121	4	Putnam County	Eatonton
121	4	Randolph County	Cuthbert
121	4	Screven County	Sylvania
121	4	Toombs County	Lyons
121	4	Wilkinson County	Irwinton
142	3	Atkinson County	Pearson
142	3	Bremen City	Bremen
142	3	Carrollton City	Carrollton
142	3	Jefferson City	Jefferson
142	3	Lamar County	Barnesville
142	3	Marion County	Buena Vista
142	3	Mcintosh County	Darien
142	3	Pelham City	Pelham
142	3	Seminole County	Donalsonville
142	3	Taylor County	Butler
142	3	Terrell County	Dawson
153	2	Long County	Ludowici
153	2	Towns County	Hiawassee

Number of Teachers

Rank	Number	District Name	City
1	8,047	Gwinnett County	Lawrenceville
2	6,806	Cobb County	Marietta
3	6,595	Dekalb County	Decatur
4	4,860	Fulton County	Atlanta
5	3,874	Atlanta City	Atlanta
6	2,735	Clayton County	Jonesboro
7	2,193	Richmond County	Augusta
8	2,136	Muscogee County	Columbus
9	2,133	Chatham County	Savannah
10	1,766	Cherokee County	Canton
11	1,544	Henry County	Mcdonough
12	1,528	Houston County	Perry
13	1,418	Bibb County	Macon
14	1,380	Fayette County	Fayetteville
15	1,360	Forsyth County	Cumming
16	1,337	Hall County	Gainesville
17	1,218	Paulding County	Dallas
18	1,163	Coweta County	Newnan
19	1,133	Columbia County	Appling
20	1,084	Douglas County	Douglasville
21	1,078	Dougherty County	Albany
22	891	Rockdale County	Conyers
23	867	Bartow County	Cartersville
24	853	Newton County	Covington
25	823	Troup County	Lagrange
26	808	Clarke County	Athens
27	807	Carroll County	Carrollton
28	776	Whitfield County	Dalton
29	749	Glynn County	Brunswick
30	692	Spalding County	Griffin
31	675	Liberty County	Hinesville
32	674	Walton County	Monroe
33	647	Floyd County	Rome
34	613	Barrow County	Winder
35	611	Lowndes County	Valdosta
36	606	Catoosa County	Ringgold
37	604	Bulloch County	Statesboro
38	577	Walker County	Lafayette
39	540	Camden County	Kingsland
40	523	Marietta City	Marietta
41	510	Effingham County	Springfield
42	480	Colquitt County	Moultrie
43	467	Tift County	Tifton
44	450	Murray County	Chatsworth
45	450	Polk County	Cedartown
46	447	Valdosta City	Valdosta
47	439	Coffee County	Douglas
48	430	Ware County	Waycross
49	425	Baldwin County	Milledgeville
50	383	Decatur County	Bainbridge
51	381	Laurens County	Dublin
52	368	Habersham County	Clarkesville
53	366	Dalton City	Dalton
54	365	Gordon County	Calhoun
55	361	Oconee County	Watkinsville
56	356	Sumter County	Americus
57	350	Thomas County	Thomasville
58	345	Jackson County	Jefferson
59	330	Lee County	Leesburg
60	328	Bryan County	Pembroke
61	322	Rome City	Rome
62	319	Wayne County	Jesup
63	303	Stephens County	Toccoa
64	301	Meriwether County	Greenville
65	296	Worth County	Sylvester
66	294	Jones County	Gray
67	292	Emanuel County	Swainsboro
68	289	Madison County	Danielsville
69	284	Grady County	Cairo
70	282	Gainesville City	Gainesville
71	281	Crisp County	Cordele
72	278	Thomaston-Upson County	Thomaston
73	273	Harris County	Hamilton
74	272	Peach County	Fort Valley
75	262	Mcduffie County	Thomson
76	260	Pickens County	Jasper
77	256	Gilmer County	Ellijay
78	250	Burke County	Waynesboro
79	244	Elbert County	Elberton
80	233	White County	Cleveland
81	232	Franklin County	Carnesville
82	231	Dublin City	Dublin
83	230	Haralson County	Buchanan
84	229	Hart County	Hartwell
85	227	Monroe County	Forsyth
86	226	Cartersville City	Cartersville
87	224	Decatur City	Decatur
88	219	Washington County	Sandersville
89	219	Dawson County	Dawsonville
90	217	Ben Hill County	Fitzgerald
91	216	Pierce County	Blackshear
92	215	Lumpkin County	Dahlonega
93	212	Carrollton City	Carrollton
94	211	Fort Benning District	Fort Benning
95	210	Appling County	Baxley
95	210	Morgan County	Madison
97	209	Dodge County	Eastman
98	203	Thomasville City	Thomasville
99	200	Tattnall County	Reidsville
100	199	Jefferson County	Louisville
101	195	Brantley County	Nahunta
102	189	Cook County	Adel
103	187	Screven County	Sylvania
104	184	Butts County	Jackson
105	183	Chattooga County	Summerville
106	178	Fannin County	Blue Ridge
106	178	Union County	Blairsville
108	176	Toombs County	Lyons
109	176	Mitchell County	Camilla
110	171	Berrien County	Nashville
111	171	Putnam County	Eatonton
112	167	Dade County	Trenton
113	166	Calhoun City	Calhoun
114	157	Greene County	Greensboro
115	157	Brooks County	Quitman
116	156	Pike County	Zebulon
117	155	Early County	Blakely
118	152	Buford City	Buford

119	151	Bleckley County	Cochran
120	150	Banks County	Homer
121	149	Jeff Davis County	Hazlehurst
122	145	Lamar County	Barnesville
123	144	Oglethorpe County	Lexington
124	144	Vidalia City	Vidalia
125	139	Rabun County	Clayton
126	139	Towns County	Hiawassee
127	132	Heard County	Franklin
128	131	Jasper County	Monticello
129	129	Macon County	Oglethorpe
130	127	Crawford County	Roberta
131	126	Bacon County	Alma
132	126	Turner County	Ashburn
133	125	Evans County	Claxton
134	122	Irwin County	Ocilla
135	122	Pulaski County	Hawkinsville
136	121	Mcintosh County	Darien
137	120	Seminole County	Donalsonville
138	119	Long County	Ludowici
139	119	Jenkins County	Millen
140	117	Wilkinson County	Irwinton
141	116	Candler County	Metter
142	116	Wilkes County	Washington
143	114	Jefferson City	Jefferson
144	113	Telfair County	Mcrae
145	113	Charlton County	Folkston
146	107	Marion County	Buena Vista
147	104	Hancock County	Sparta
148	101	Atkinson County	Pearson
149	101	Randolph County	Cuthbert
150	101	Pelham City	Pelham
151	100	Taylor County	Butler
152	98	Terrell County	Dawson
153	95	Bremen City	Bremen
154	91	Dooly County	Vienna

Number of Students

Rank	Number	District Name	City
1	122,570	Gwinnett County	Lawrenceville
2	100,389	Cobb County	Marietta
3	97,967	Dekalb County	Decatur
4	71,372	Fulton County	Atlanta
5	54,946	Atlanta City	Atlanta
6	49,594	Clayton County	Jonesboro
7	34,691	Richmond County	Augusta
8	34,554	Chatham County	Savannah
9	32,944	Muscogee County	Columbus
10	28,434	Cherokee County	Canton
11	27,734	Henry County	Mcdonough
12	24,938	Bibb County	Macon
13	22,699	Houston County	Perry
14	21,730	Hall County	Gainesville
15	20,756	Fayette County	Fayetteville
16	20,407	Forsyth County	Cumming
17	19,426	Columbia County	Appling
18	19,283	Paulding County	Dallas
19	18,790	Douglas County	Douglasville
20	18,389	Coweta County	Newnan
21	16,607	Dougherty County	Albany
22	13,801	Rockdale County	Conyers
23	13,681	Newton County	Covington
24	13,403	Carroll County	Carrollton
25	13,339	Bartow County	Cartersville
26	12,190	Whitfield County	Dalton
27	12,071	Glynn County	Brunswick
28	11,779	Troup County	Lagrange
29	11,457	Clarke County	Athens
30	11,274	Liberty County	Hinesville
31	10,648	Spalding County	Griffin
32	10,368	Walton County	Monroe
33	10,272	Floyd County	Rome
34	9,809	Catoosa County	Ringgold
35	9,563	Camden County	Kingsland
36	9,362	Barrow County	Winder
37	9,245	Lowndes County	Valdosta
38	9,037	Effingham County	Springfield
39	8,844	Walker County	Lafayette
40	8,342	Colquitt County	Moultrie
41	8,279	Bulloch County	Statesboro
42	7,841	Coffee County	Douglas
43	7,641	Tift County	Tifton
44	7,524	Marietta City	Marietta
45	7,345	Murray County	Chatsworth
46	7,178	Valdosta City	Valdosta
47	7,017	Polk County	Cedartown
48	6,370	Ware County	Waycross
49	6,259	Gordon County	Calhoun
50	6,034	Laurens County	Dublin
51	5,955	Habersham County	Clarkesville
52	5,894	Baldwin County	Milledgeville
53	5,782	Decatur County	Bainbridge
54	5,774	Sumter County	Americus
55	5,739	Dalton City	Dalton
56	5,615	Oconee County	Watkinsville
57	5,552	Bryan County	Pembroke
58	5,472	Jackson County	Jefferson
59	5,466	Thomas County	Thomasville
60	5,395	Rome City	Rome
61	5,350	Lee County	Leesburg
62	5,256	Wayne County	Jesup
63	5,014	Jones County	Gray
64	5,009	Thomaston-Upson County	Thomaston
65	4,664	Emanuel County	Swainsboro
66	4,621	Madison County	Danielsville
67	4,614	Burke County	Waynesboro
68	4,550	Grady County	Cairo
69	4,438	Gainesville City	Gainesville
70	4,411	Harris County	Hamilton
71	4,405	Stephens County	Toccoa
72	4,354	Worth County	Sylvester
73	4,337	Crisp County	Cordele
74	4,312	Mcduffie County	Thomson
75	4,060	Pickens County	Jasper
76	3,948	Meriwether County	Greenville
77	3,940	Cartersville City	Cartersville
78	3,929	Gilmer County	Ellijay
79	3,927	Peach County	Fort Valley
80	3,872	Monroe County	Forsyth
81	3,821	Washington County	Sandersville
82	3,793	Elbert County	Elberton
83	3,766	Haralson County	Buchanan
84	3,758	White County	Cleveland
85	3,722	Franklin County	Carnesville
86	3,682	Carrollton City	Carrollton
87	3,564	Hart County	Hartwell
88	3,558	Dodge County	Eastman
89	3,526	Jefferson County	Louisville
90	3,511	Lumpkin County	Dahlonega
91	3,395	Ben Hill County	Fitzgerald
92	3,370	Butts County	Jackson
93	3,332	Brantley County	Nahunta
94	3,305	Tattnall County	Reidsville
95	3,303	Appling County	Baxley
96	3,262	Dublin City	Dublin
97	3,240	Pierce County	Blackshear
98	3,215	Cook County	Adel
99	3,212	Fannin County	Blue Ridge
100	3,171	Morgan County	Madison
101	3,130	Screven County	Sylvania
102	3,107	Thomasville City	Thomasville
103	3,037	Berrien County	Nashville
104	3,036	Dawson County	Dawsonville
105	3,027	Fort Benning District	Fort Benning
106	2,856	Toombs County	Lyons
107	2,855	Mitchell County	Camilla
108	2,834	Chattooga County	Summerville
109	2,805	Pike County	Zebulon
110	2,764	Early County	Blakely
111	2,666	Calhoun City	Calhoun
112	2,630	Dade County	Trenton
113	2,624	Jeff Davis County	Hazlehurst
114	2,600	Lamar County	Barnesville
115	2,598	Union County	Blairsville
116	2,563	Brooks County	Quitman
117	2,519	Decatur City	Decatur
118	2,474	Putnam County	Eatonton
119	2,428	Banks County	Homer
120	2,408	Vidalia City	Vidalia
121	2,355	Bleckley County	Cochran
122	2,281	Oglethorpe County	Lexington
123	2,280	Greene County	Greensboro
124	2,259	Buford City	Buford
125	2,221	Rabun County	Clayton
126	2,200	Macon County	Oglethorpe
127	2,181	Jasper County	Monticello
128	2,178	Heard County	Franklin
129	2,090	Crawford County	Roberta
130	2,015	Charlton County	Folkston
131	1,995	Long County	Ludowici
132	1,979	Mcintosh County	Darien
133	1,944	Evans County	Claxton
134	1,918	Candler County	Metter
135	1,914	Turner County	Ashburn
136	1,900	Bacon County	Alma
137	1,858	Wilkes County	Washington
138	1,814	Irwin County	Ocilla
139	1,764	Terrell County	Dawson
140	1,754	Jenkins County	Millen
140	1,754	Seminole County	Donalsonville
142	1,737	Wilkinson County	Irwinton
143	1,735	Taylor County	Butler
144	1,686	Marion County	Buena Vista
145	1,659	Hancock County	Sparta
146	1,648	Atkinson County	Pearson
146	1,648	Telfair County	Mcrae
148	1,632	Pulaski County	Hawkinsville
149	1,627	Pelham City	Pelham
150	1,575	Bremen City	Bremen
151	1,559	Randolph County	Cuthbert
152	1,545	Dooly County	Vienna
153	1,529	Towns County	Hiawassee
154	1,525	Jefferson City	Jefferson

Male Students

Rank	Percent	District Name	City
1	53.8	Hart County	Hartwell
2	53.6	Haralson County	Buchanan
3	53.4	Bacon County	Alma
4	53.3	Dade County	Trenton
5	53.2	Crawford County	Roberta
6	52.8	Lumpkin County	Dahlonega
7	52.7	Brooks County	Quitman
8	52.6	Chattooga County	Summerville
9	52.5	Evans County	Claxton
9	52.5	Habersham County	Clarkesville
9	52.5	Jenkins County	Millen
9	52.5	Pike County	Zebulon
13	52.4	Candler County	Metter
13	52.4	Monroe County	Forsyth
13	52.4	Polk County	Cedartown
16	52.3	Gilmer County	Ellijay
16	52.3	Seminole County	Donalsonville
18	52.2	Barrow County	Winder
18	52.2	Harris County	Hamilton
18	52.2	Meriwether County	Greenville
18	52.2	Stephens County	Toccoa
22	52.1	Buford City	Buford
22	52.1	Houston County	Perry
22	52.1	Walker County	Lafayette
25	52.0	Murray County	Chatsworth
25	52.0	Oconee County	Watkinsville
25	52.0	Oglethorpe County	Lexington
25	52.0	Telfair County	Mcrae
25	52.0	Wayne County	Jesup
30	51.9	Banks County	Homer
30	51.9	Carroll County	Carrollton
30	51.9	Jefferson City	Jefferson
30	51.9	Mitchell County	Camilla
34	51.8	Forsyth County	Cumming
34	51.8	Jackson County	Jefferson
34	51.8	Lamar County	Barnesville
34	51.8	Ware County	Waycross
38	51.7	Appling County	Baxley
38	51.7	Cherokee County	Canton
38	51.7	Decatur County	Bainbridge
38	51.7	Dodge County	Eastman
38	51.7	Dublin City	Dublin
38	51.7	Hall County	Gainesville
38	51.7	Heard County	Franklin
38	51.7	Paulding County	Dallas
38	51.7	Pulaski County	Hawkinsville
38	51.7	Thomaston-Upson County	Thomaston
38	51.7	Whitfield County	Dalton
49	51.6	Atkinson County	Pearson
49	51.6	Dalton City	Dalton
49	51.6	Effingham County	Springfield
49	51.6	Emanuel County	Swainsboro
49	51.6	Pierce County	Blackshear
54	51.5	Berrien County	Nashville
54	51.5	Bryan County	Pembroke
54	51.5	Bulloch County	Statesboro
54	51.5	Columbia County	Appling
54	51.5	Fannin County	Blue Ridge
54	51.5	Henry County	Mcdonough
54	51.5	Jones County	Gray
54	51.5	Pickens County	Jasper
54	51.5	White County	Cleveland
63	51.4	Bartow County	Cartersville
63	51.4	Cartersville City	Cartersville
63	51.4	Cobb County	Marietta
63	51.4	Dawson County	Dawsonville
63	51.4	Greene County	Greensboro
63	51.4	Mcduffie County	Thomson
63	51.4	Putnam County	Eatonton
63	51.4	Rabun County	Clayton
63	51.4	Towns County	Hiawassee
72	51.3	Catoosa County	Ringgold
72	51.3	Charlton County	Folkston
72	51.3	Clayton County	Jonesboro
72	51.3	Coweta County	Newnan
72	51.3	Douglas County	Douglasville
72	51.3	Elbert County	Elberton
72	51.3	Floyd County	Rome
72	51.3	Franklin County	Carnesville
72	51.3	Gwinnett County	Lawrenceville

72	51.3	Laurens County	Dublin
72	51.3	Madison County	Danielsville
72	51.3	Newton County	Covington
72	51.3	Spalding County	Griffin
85	51.2	Burke County	Waynesboro
85	51.2	Calhoun City	Calhoun
85	51.2	Cook County	Adel
85	51.2	Lowndes County	Valdosta
85	51.2	Marion County	Buena Vista
85	51.2	Morgan County	Madison
85	51.2	Tattnall County	Reidsville
85	51.2	Tift County	Tifton
85	51.2	Worth County	Sylvester
94	51.1	Brantley County	Nahunta
94	51.1	Colquitt County	Moultrie
94	51.1	Dekalb County	Decatur
94	51.1	Fulton County	Atlanta
94	51.1	Macon County	Oglethorpe
94	51.1	Peach County	Fort Valley
94	51.1	Rockdale County	Conyers
94	51.1	Troup County	Lagrange
94	51.1	Washington County	Sandersville
103	51.0	Early County	Blakely
103	51.0	Fayette County	Fayetteville
103	51.0	Hancock County	Sparta
103	51.0	Lee County	Leesburg
103	51.0	Marietta City	Marietta
103	51.0	Turner County	Ashburn
109	50.9	Butts County	Jackson
109	50.9	Clarke County	Athens
109	50.9	Liberty County	Hinesville
109	50.9	Toombs County	Lyons
113	50.8	Ben Hill County	Fitzgerald
113	50.8	Carrollton City	Carrollton
113	50.8	Gordon County	Calhoun
113	50.8	Jefferson County	Louisville
113	50.8	Randolph County	Cuthbert
113	50.8	Sumter County	Americus
119	50.7	Chatham County	Savannah
119	50.7	Decatur City	Decatur
119	50.7	Dooly County	Vienna
119	50.7	Dougherty County	Albany
119	50.7	Glynn County	Brunswick
119	50.7	Pelham City	Pelham
119	50.7	Taylor County	Butler
119	50.7	Union County	Blairsville
127	50.6	Coffee County	Douglas
127	50.6	Gainesville City	Gainesville
127	50.6	Valdosta City	Valdosta
130	50.5	Camden County	Kingsland
130	50.5	Crisp County	Cordele
130	50.5	Mcintosh County	Darien
130	50.5	Muscogee County	Columbus
130	50.5	Richmond County	Augusta
130	50.5	Thomas County	Thomasville
130	50.5	Wilkinson County	Irwinton
137	50.4	Wilkes County	Washington
138	50.3	Baldwin County	Milledgeville
138	50.3	Bibb County	Macon
138	50.3	Irwin County	Ocilla
138	50.3	Long County	Ludowici
138	50.3	Walton County	Monroe
143	50.1	Atlanta City	Atlanta
143	50.1	Bleckley County	Cochran
143	50.1	Terrell County	Dawson
143	50.1	Vidalia City	Vidalia
147	50.0	Jeff Davis County	Hazlehurst
148	49.8	Rome City	Rome
149	49.6	Bremen City	Bremen
149	49.6	Screven County	Sylvania
149	49.6	Thomasville City	Thomasville
152	49.5	Jasper County	Monticello
153	49.0	Grady County	Cairo
154	n/a	Fort Benning District	Fort Benning

Female Students

Rank	Percent	District Name	City
1	51.0	Grady County	Cairo
2	50.5	Jasper County	Monticello
3	50.4	Bremen City	Bremen
3	50.4	Screven County	Sylvania
3	50.4	Thomasville City	Thomasville
6	50.2	Rome City	Rome
7	50.0	Jeff Davis County	Hazlehurst
8	49.9	Atlanta City	Atlanta
8	49.9	Bleckley County	Cochran
8	49.9	Terrell County	Dawson
8	49.9	Vidalia City	Vidalia
12	49.7	Baldwin County	Milledgeville
12	49.7	Bibb County	Macon
12	49.7	Irwin County	Ocilla
12	49.7	Long County	Ludowici
12	49.7	Walton County	Monroe
17	49.6	Wilkes County	Washington
18	49.5	Camden County	Kingsland
18	49.5	Crisp County	Cordele
18	49.5	Mcintosh County	Darien
18	49.5	Muscogee County	Columbus
18	49.5	Richmond County	Augusta
18	49.5	Thomas County	Thomasville
18	49.5	Wilkinson County	Irwinton
25	49.4	Coffee County	Douglas
25	49.4	Gainesville City	Gainesville
25	49.4	Valdosta City	Valdosta
28	49.3	Chatham County	Savannah
28	49.3	Decatur City	Decatur
28	49.3	Dooly County	Vienna
28	49.3	Dougherty County	Albany
28	49.3	Glynn County	Brunswick
28	49.3	Pelham City	Pelham
28	49.3	Taylor County	Butler
28	49.3	Union County	Blairsville
36	49.2	Ben Hill County	Fitzgerald
36	49.2	Carrollton City	Carrollton
36	49.2	Gordon County	Calhoun
36	49.2	Jefferson County	Louisville
36	49.2	Randolph County	Cuthbert
36	49.2	Sumter County	Americus
42	49.1	Butts County	Jackson
42	49.1	Clarke County	Athens
42	49.1	Liberty County	Hinesville
42	49.1	Toombs County	Lyons
46	49.0	Early County	Blakely
46	49.0	Fayette County	Fayetteville
46	49.0	Hancock County	Sparta
46	49.0	Lee County	Leesburg
46	49.0	Marietta City	Marietta
46	49.0	Turner County	Ashburn
52	48.9	Brantley County	Nahunta
52	48.9	Colquitt County	Moultrie
52	48.9	Dekalb County	Decatur
52	48.9	Fulton County	Atlanta
52	48.9	Macon County	Oglethorpe
52	48.9	Peach County	Fort Valley
52	48.9	Rockdale County	Conyers
52	48.9	Troup County	Lagrange
52	48.9	Washington County	Sandersville
61	48.8	Burke County	Waynesboro
61	48.8	Calhoun City	Calhoun
61	48.8	Cook County	Adel
61	48.8	Lowndes County	Valdosta
61	48.8	Marion County	Buena Vista
61	48.8	Morgan County	Madison
61	48.8	Tattnall County	Reidsville
61	48.8	Tift County	Tifton
61	48.8	Worth County	Sylvester
70	48.7	Catoosa County	Ringgold
70	48.7	Charlton County	Folkston
70	48.7	Clayton County	Jonesboro
70	48.7	Coweta County	Newnan
70	48.7	Douglas County	Douglasville
70	48.7	Elbert County	Elberton
70	48.7	Floyd County	Rome
70	48.7	Franklin County	Carnesville
70	48.7	Gwinnett County	Lawrenceville
70	48.7	Laurens County	Dublin
70	48.7	Madison County	Danielsville
70	48.7	Newton County	Covington
70	48.7	Spalding County	Griffin
83	48.6	Bartow County	Cartersville
83	48.6	Cartersville City	Cartersville
83	48.6	Cobb County	Marietta
83	48.6	Dawson County	Dawsonville
83	48.6	Greene County	Greensboro
83	48.6	Mcduffie County	Thomson
83	48.6	Putnam County	Eatonton
83	48.6	Rabun County	Clayton
83	48.6	Towns County	Hiawassee
92	48.5	Berrien County	Nashville
92	48.5	Bryan County	Pembroke
92	48.5	Bulloch County	Statesboro
92	48.5	Columbia County	Appling
92	48.5	Fannin County	Blue Ridge
92	48.5	Henry County	Mcdonough
92	48.5	Jones County	Gray
92	48.5	Pickens County	Jasper
92	48.5	White County	Cleveland
101	48.4	Atkinson County	Pearson
101	48.4	Dalton City	Dalton
101	48.4	Effingham County	Springfield
101	48.4	Emanuel County	Swainsboro
101	48.4	Pierce County	Blackshear
106	48.3	Appling County	Baxley
106	48.3	Cherokee County	Canton
106	48.3	Decatur County	Bainbridge
106	48.3	Dodge County	Eastman
106	48.3	Dublin City	Dublin
106	48.3	Hall County	Gainesville
106	48.3	Heard County	Franklin
106	48.3	Paulding County	Dallas
106	48.3	Pulaski County	Hawkinsville
106	48.3	Thomaston-Upson County	Thomaston
106	48.3	Whitfield County	Dalton
117	48.2	Forsyth County	Cumming
117	48.2	Jackson County	Jefferson
117	48.2	Lamar County	Barnesville
117	48.2	Ware County	Waycross
121	48.1	Banks County	Homer
121	48.1	Carroll County	Carrollton
121	48.1	Jefferson City	Jefferson
121	48.1	Mitchell County	Camilla
125	48.0	Murray County	Chatsworth
125	48.0	Oconee County	Watkinsville
125	48.0	Oglethorpe County	Lexington
125	48.0	Telfair County	Mcrae
125	48.0	Wayne County	Jesup
130	47.9	Buford City	Buford
130	47.9	Houston County	Perry
130	47.9	Walker County	Lafayette
133	47.8	Barrow County	Winder
133	47.8	Harris County	Hamilton
133	47.8	Meriwether County	Greenville
133	47.8	Stephens County	Toccoa
137	47.7	Gilmer County	Ellijay
137	47.7	Seminole County	Donalsonville
139	47.6	Candler County	Metter
139	47.6	Monroe County	Forsyth
139	47.6	Polk County	Cedartown
142	47.5	Evans County	Claxton
142	47.5	Habersham County	Clarkesville
142	47.5	Jenkins County	Millen
142	47.5	Pike County	Zebulon
146	47.4	Chattooga County	Summerville
147	47.3	Brooks County	Quitman
148	47.2	Lumpkin County	Dahlonega
149	46.8	Crawford County	Roberta
150	46.7	Dade County	Trenton
151	46.6	Bacon County	Alma
152	46.4	Haralson County	Buchanan
153	46.2	Hart County	Hartwell
154	n/a	Fort Benning District	Fort Benning

Individual Education Program Students

Rank	Percent	District Name	City
1	25.2	Meriwether County	Greenville
2	22.8	Floyd County	Rome
3	21.7	Chattooga County	Summerville
4	17.7	Haralson County	Buchanan
5	17.4	Baldwin County	Milledgeville
6	17.3	Dublin City	Dublin
7	17.1	Thomas County	Thomasville
8	16.9	Irwin County	Ocilla
8	16.9	Pelham City	Pelham
10	16.7	Evans County	Claxton
10	16.7	Madison County	Danielsville
12	16.5	Screven County	Sylvania
13	16.4	Barrow County	Winder
13	16.4	Emanuel County	Swainsboro
15	16.2	Oglethorpe County	Lexington
16	15.9	Union County	Blairsville
17	15.8	Franklin County	Carnesville
17	15.8	Pulaski County	Hawkinsville
19	15.5	Clarke County	Athens
20	15.4	Coweta County	Newnan
20	15.4	Gordon County	Calhoun
20	15.4	Putnam County	Eatonton
23	15.2	Bulloch County	Statesboro
23	15.2	Pierce County	Blackshear
25	15.1	Greene County	Greensboro
25	15.1	Ware County	Waycross
27	14.9	Carrollton City	Carrollton
27	14.9	Wilkinson County	Irwinton
29	14.7	Bacon County	Alma
29	14.7	Carroll County	Carrollton
29	14.7	Jackson County	Jefferson
32	14.6	Bartow County	Cartersville
32	14.6	Ben Hill County	Fitzgerald
34	14.5	Jasper County	Monticello
34	14.5	Terrell County	Dawson
36	14.4	Appling County	Baxley
36	14.4	Thomaston-Upson County	Thomaston
36	14.4	Toombs County	Lyons
36	14.4	Valdosta City	Valdosta
40	14.3	Mitchell County	Camilla
41	14.2	Brantley County	Nahunta
41	14.2	Lowndes County	Valdosta
43	14.1	Wayne County	Jesup

Rank	Percent	District Name	City
44	14.0	Early County	Blakely
45	13.9	Candler County	Metter
45	13.9	Polk County	Cedartown
45	13.9	Wilkes County	Washington
48	13.8	Fannin County	Blue Ridge
48	13.8	Morgan County	Madison
48	13.8	Walker County	Lafayette
51	13.7	Marietta City	Marietta
51	13.7	Newton County	Covington
53	13.6	Charlton County	Folkston
54	13.5	Bleckley County	Cochran
54	13.5	Effingham County	Springfield
54	13.5	Habersham County	Clarkesville
57	13.4	Glynn County	Brunswick
57	13.4	Houston County	Perry
57	13.4	Monroe County	Forsyth
57	13.4	Spalding County	Griffin
61	13.3	Walton County	Monroe
62	13.2	Catoosa County	Ringgold
62	13.2	Jefferson County	Louisville
62	13.2	Jenkins County	Millen
62	13.2	Telfair County	Mcrae
66	13.1	Berrien County	Nashville
66	13.1	Bremen City	Bremen
68	13.0	Jefferson City	Jefferson
68	13.0	Turner County	Ashburn
70	12.9	Crawford County	Roberta
71	12.8	Jeff Davis County	Hazlehurst
71	12.8	Stephens County	Toccoa
73	12.7	Dodge County	Eastman
74	12.6	Banks County	Homer
74	12.6	Brooks County	Quitman
74	12.6	Cobb County	Marietta
74	12.6	Troup County	Lagrange
78	12.5	Cherokee County	Canton
78	12.5	Decatur City	Decatur
78	12.5	Rabun County	Clayton
81	12.4	Hancock County	Sparta
81	12.4	Paulding County	Dallas
81	12.4	Pickens County	Jasper
81	12.4	Tift County	Tifton
81	12.4	White County	Cleveland
86	12.3	Colquitt County	Moultrie
86	12.3	Heard County	Franklin
88	12.2	Lumpkin County	Dahlonega
88	12.2	Muscogee County	Columbus
90	12.1	Cook County	Adel
91	12.0	Butts County	Jackson
91	12.0	Dawson County	Dawsonville
91	12.0	Douglas County	Douglasville
94	11.9	Hart County	Hartwell
94	11.9	Mcduffie County	Thomson
94	11.9	Thomasville City	Thomasville
97	11.8	Dougherty County	Albany
97	11.8	Whitfield County	Dalton
99	11.7	Atkinson County	Pearson
99	11.7	Fayette County	Fayetteville
99	11.7	Forsyth County	Cumming
99	11.7	Grady County	Cairo
99	11.7	Rome City	Rome
104	11.6	Buford City	Buford
104	11.6	Chatham County	Savannah
104	11.6	Gilmer County	Ellijay
104	11.6	Murray County	Chatsworth
104	11.6	Peach County	Fort Valley
109	11.5	Coffee County	Douglas
109	11.5	Jones County	Gray
111	11.4	Pike County	Zebulon
112	11.3	Camden County	Kingsland
112	11.3	Dade County	Trenton
112	11.3	Gwinnett County	Lawrenceville
112	11.3	Seminole County	Donalsonville
112	11.3	Tattnall County	Reidsville
117	11.1	Calhoun City	Calhoun
117	11.1	Elbert County	Elberton
117	11.1	Liberty County	Hinesville
120	11.0	Oconee County	Watkinsville
121	10.9	Henry County	Mcdonough
122	10.8	Decatur County	Bainbridge
122	10.8	Rockdale County	Conyers
124	10.7	Marion County	Buena Vista
125	10.5	Bibb County	Macon
125	10.5	Long County	Ludowici
125	10.5	Randolph County	Cuthbert
128	10.4	Richmond County	Augusta
129	10.2	Fulton County	Atlanta
130	10.1	Dooly County	Vienna
131	10.0	Dalton City	Dalton
131	10.0	Hall County	Gainesville
131	10.0	Washington County	Sandersville
134	9.9	Fort Benning District	Fort Benning
135	9.8	Columbia County	Appling
136	9.5	Burke County	Waynesboro
136	9.5	Crisp County	Cordele
136	9.5	Lamar County	Barnesville
139	9.4	Clayton County	Jonesboro
139	9.4	Sumter County	Americus
139	9.4	Towns County	Hiawassee
142	9.3	Laurens County	Dublin
143	9.0	Dekalb County	Decatur
144	8.7	Harris County	Hamilton
144	8.7	Mcintosh County	Darien
146	8.6	Bryan County	Pembroke
146	8.6	Macon County	Oglethorpe
148	8.4	Taylor County	Butler
149	8.1	Cartersville City	Cartersville
150	7.8	Atlanta City	Atlanta
151	7.7	Lee County	Leesburg
152	7.6	Vidalia City	Vidalia
153	6.9	Worth County	Sylvester
154	6.8	Gainesville City	Gainesville

English Language Learner Students

Rank	Percent	District Name	City
1	60.1	Dalton City	Dalton
2	23.8	Hall County	Gainesville
3	21.0	Gainesville City	Gainesville
4	19.1	Marietta City	Marietta
5	14.8	Calhoun City	Calhoun
6	14.6	Clarke County	Athens
7	14.0	Dekalb County	Decatur
8	11.2	Rome City	Rome
9	11.1	Buford City	Buford
10	9.9	Cartersville City	Cartersville
11	9.6	Atkinson County	Pearson
12	9.2	Gwinnett County	Lawrenceville
13	8.5	Cobb County	Marietta
14	8.1	Habersham County	Clarkesville
15	7.9	Toombs County	Lyons
16	7.0	Colquitt County	Moultrie
17	6.8	Whitfield County	Dalton
18	6.6	Tattnall County	Reidsville
19	6.5	Fulton County	Atlanta
20	6.2	Gilmer County	Ellijay
21	5.3	Candler County	Metter
21	5.3	Polk County	Cedartown
23	5.2	Long County	Ludowici
23	5.2	Rabun County	Clayton
25	5.1	Jackson County	Jefferson
25	5.1	Tift County	Tifton
27	4.9	Evans County	Claxton
28	4.5	Clayton County	Jonesboro
28	4.5	Coffee County	Douglas
30	4.3	Barrow County	Winder
31	4.1	Forsyth County	Cumming
32	3.9	Dooly County	Vienna
33	3.6	Gordon County	Calhoun
34	3.5	Rockdale County	Conyers
35	3.4	Marion County	Buena Vista
36	3.2	Ben Hill County	Fitzgerald
37	3.1	Jeff Davis County	Hazlehurst
38	2.9	Banks County	Homer
38	2.9	Carrollton City	Carrollton
40	2.7	Atlanta City	Atlanta
41	2.5	Jenkins County	Millen
41	2.5	Oconee County	Watkinsville
43	2.4	Appling County	Baxley
43	2.4	Cherokee County	Canton
43	2.4	Jefferson City	Jefferson
43	2.4	Pierce County	Blackshear
47	2.3	Fort Benning District	Fort Benning
47	2.3	Grady County	Cairo
49	2.2	Putnam County	Eatonton
50	2.1	Bacon County	Alma
50	2.1	Fayette County	Fayetteville
50	2.1	Floyd County	Rome
53	2.0	Henry County	Mcdonough
54	1.9	Lumpkin County	Dahlonega
54	1.9	Madison County	Danielsville
56	1.8	Elbert County	Elberton
56	1.8	Macon County	Oglethorpe
56	1.8	Walton County	Monroe
56	1.8	Wayne County	Jesup
60	1.7	Douglas County	Douglasville
60	1.7	Murray County	Chatsworth
60	1.7	Peach County	Fort Valley
63	1.6	Decatur City	Decatur
64	1.5	Bartow County	Cartersville
65	1.4	Bibb County	Macon
65	1.4	Decatur County	Bainbridge
67	1.3	Brooks County	Quitman
67	1.3	Chattooga County	Summerville
69	1.2	Carroll County	Carrollton
69	1.2	Pelham City	Pelham
71	1.1	Glynn County	Brunswick
71	1.1	Newton County	Covington
73	1.0	Bulloch County	Statesboro
73	1.0	Coweta County	Newnan
73	1.0	Muscogee County	Columbus
76	0.9	Hart County	Hartwell
76	0.9	Paulding County	Dallas
78	0.8	Dawson County	Dawsonville
78	0.8	Greene County	Greensboro
78	0.8	Pickens County	Jasper
78	0.8	Spalding County	Griffin
78	0.8	Valdosta City	Valdosta
83	0.7	Chatham County	Savannah
83	0.7	Crisp County	Cordele
83	0.7	Liberty County	Hinesville
83	0.7	Mcduffie County	Thomson
83	0.7	Ware County	Waycross
83	0.7	White County	Cleveland
89	0.6	Baldwin County	Milledgeville
89	0.6	Catoosa County	Ringgold
89	0.6	Houston County	Perry
89	0.6	Lamar County	Barnesville
89	0.6	Wilkes County	Washington
94	0.5	Camden County	Kingsland
94	0.5	Laurens County	Dublin
94	0.5	Richmond County	Augusta
94	0.5	Telfair County	Mcrae
94	0.5	Thomas County	Thomasville
94	0.5	Towns County	Hiawassee
94	0.5	Troup County	Lagrange
101	0.4	Columbia County	Appling
101	0.4	Stephens County	Toccoa
103	0.3	Cook County	Adel
103	0.3	Dublin City	Dublin
103	0.3	Effingham County	Springfield
103	0.3	Emanuel County	Swainsboro
103	0.3	Morgan County	Madison
103	0.3	Walker County	Lafayette
109	0.2	Franklin County	Carnesville
109	0.2	Mcintosh County	Darien
109	0.2	Vidalia City	Vidalia
112	0.1	Bleckley County	Cochran
112	0.1	Bryan County	Pembroke
112	0.1	Burke County	Waynesboro
112	0.1	Dodge County	Eastman
112	0.1	Dougherty County	Albany
112	0.1	Early County	Blakely
112	0.1	Haralson County	Buchanan
112	0.1	Jefferson County	Louisville
112	0.1	Jones County	Gray
112	0.1	Meriwether County	Greenville
112	0.1	Mitchell County	Camilla
112	0.1	Pulaski County	Hawkinsville
112	0.1	Randolph County	Cuthbert
112	0.1	Screven County	Sylvania
112	0.1	Thomaston-Upson County	Thomaston
112	0.1	Wilkinson County	Irwinton
128	0.0	Crawford County	Roberta
128	0.0	Lee County	Leesburg
128	0.0	Sumter County	Americus
128	0.0	Union County	Blairsville
132	0.0	Berrien County	Nashville
132	0.0	Brantley County	Nahunta
132	0.0	Bremen City	Bremen
132	0.0	Butts County	Jackson
132	0.0	Charlton County	Folkston
132	0.0	Dade County	Trenton
132	0.0	Fannin County	Blue Ridge
132	0.0	Hancock County	Sparta
132	0.0	Harris County	Hamilton
132	0.0	Heard County	Franklin
132	0.0	Irwin County	Ocilla
132	0.0	Jasper County	Monticello
132	0.0	Lowndes County	Valdosta
132	0.0	Monroe County	Forsyth
132	0.0	Oglethorpe County	Lexington
132	0.0	Pike County	Zebulon
132	0.0	Seminole County	Donalsonville
132	0.0	Taylor County	Butler
132	0.0	Terrell County	Dawson
132	0.0	Thomasville City	Thomasville
132	0.0	Turner County	Ashburn
132	0.0	Washington County	Sandersville
132	0.0	Worth County	Sylvester

Migrant Students

Rank	Percent	District Name	City
1	16.5	Atkinson County	Pearson
2	14.2	Toombs County	Lyons
3	11.3	Gainesville City	Gainesville
4	10.9	Tattnall County	Reidsville
5	9.2	Long County	Ludowici
6	7.3	Colquitt County	Moultrie

7	7.2	Candler County	Metter
8	6.7	Dalton City	Dalton
9	6.6	Coffee County	Douglas
10	6.3	Evans County	Claxton
11	6.1	Jeff Davis County	Hazlehurst
12	5.9	Appling County	Baxley
13	4.9	Decatur County	Bainbridge
13	4.9	Dooly County	Vienna
13	4.9	Peach County	Fort Valley
16	4.7	Habersham County	Clarkesville
17	4.3	Bacon County	Alma
18	3.9	Seminole County	Donalsonville
18	3.9	Tift County	Tifton
20	3.8	Hall County	Gainesville
21	3.7	Grady County	Cairo
22	3.3	Gilmer County	Ellijay
23	3.2	Jenkins County	Millen
23	3.2	Macon County	Oglethorpe
25	3.1	Clarke County	Athens
26	2.7	Haralson County	Buchanan
27	2.6	Marion County	Buena Vista
28	2.5	Sumter County	Americus
29	2.4	Mitchell County	Camilla
29	2.4	Pierce County	Blackshear
29	2.4	Screven County	Sylvania
32	2.3	Polk County	Cedartown
33	2.2	Brooks County	Quitman
34	1.9	Berrien County	Nashville
34	1.9	Thomas County	Thomasville
36	1.8	Cook County	Adel
37	1.6	Whitfield County	Dalton
38	1.4	Laurens County	Dublin
39	1.2	Pelham City	Pelham
39	1.2	Putnam County	Eatonton
39	1.2	Rome City	Rome
39	1.2	Ware County	Waycross
43	1.1	Emanuel County	Swainsboro
43	1.1	Rabun County	Clayton
45	1.0	Glynn County	Brunswick
46	0.9	Bulloch County	Statesboro
47	0.8	Early County	Blakely
47	0.8	Irwin County	Ocilla
47	0.8	Telfair County	Mcrae
50	0.7	Lumpkin County	Dahlonega
51	0.6	Lowndes County	Valdosta
51	0.6	Pulaski County	Hawkinsville
51	0.6	Turner County	Ashburn
51	0.6	Walker County	Lafayette
55	0.5	Crisp County	Cordele
55	0.5	Dodge County	Eastman
55	0.5	Elbert County	Elberton
55	0.5	Jackson County	Jefferson
55	0.5	Mcduffie County	Thomson
55	0.5	Oconee County	Watkinsville
55	0.5	Taylor County	Butler
62	0.4	Ben Hill County	Fitzgerald
62	0.4	Bleckley County	Cochran
62	0.4	Gordon County	Calhoun
62	0.4	Wayne County	Jesup
62	0.4	Wilkes County	Washington
67	0.3	Banks County	Homer
67	0.3	Crawford County	Roberta
67	0.3	Jefferson County	Louisville
67	0.3	Valdosta City	Valdosta
67	0.3	Wilkinson County	Irwinton
72	0.2	Barrow County	Winder
72	0.2	Burke County	Waynesboro
72	0.2	Cherokee County	Canton
72	0.2	Dougherty County	Albany
72	0.2	Dublin City	Dublin
72	0.2	Forsyth County	Cumming
72	0.2	Houston County	Perry
72	0.2	Oglethorpe County	Lexington
72	0.2	Pickens County	Jasper
72	0.2	Randolph County	Cuthbert
72	0.2	White County	Cleveland
72	0.2	Worth County	Sylvester
84	0.1	Bibb County	Macon
84	0.1	Brantley County	Nahunta
84	0.1	Dawson County	Dawsonville
84	0.1	Franklin County	Carnesville
84	0.1	Greene County	Greensboro
84	0.1	Hart County	Hartwell
84	0.1	Jefferson City	Jefferson
84	0.1	Terrell County	Dawson
84	0.1	Vidalia City	Vidalia
84	0.1	Walton County	Monroe
94	0.0	Bryan County	Pembroke
94	0.0	Butts County	Jackson
94	0.0	Chatham County	Savannah
94	0.0	Clayton County	Jonesboro
94	0.0	Cobb County	Marietta
94	0.0	Douglas County	Douglasville
94	0.0	Floyd County	Rome
94	0.0	Gwinnett County	Lawrenceville
94	0.0	Liberty County	Hinesville
94	0.0	Madison County	Danielsville
94	0.0	Marietta City	Marietta
94	0.0	Morgan County	Madison
94	0.0	Murray County	Chatsworth
94	0.0	Muscogee County	Columbus
94	0.0	Richmond County	Augusta
94	0.0	Thomaston-Upson County	Thomaston
94	0.0	Troup County	Lagrange
94	0.0	Washington County	Sandersville
112	0.0	Atlanta City	Atlanta
112	0.0	Baldwin County	Milledgeville
112	0.0	Bartow County	Cartersville
112	0.0	Bremen City	Bremen
112	0.0	Buford City	Buford
112	0.0	Calhoun City	Calhoun
112	0.0	Camden County	Kingsland
112	0.0	Carroll County	Carrollton
112	0.0	Carrollton City	Carrollton
112	0.0	Cartersville City	Cartersville
112	0.0	Catoosa County	Ringgold
112	0.0	Charlton County	Folkston
112	0.0	Chattooga County	Summerville
112	0.0	Columbia County	Appling
112	0.0	Coweta County	Newnan
112	0.0	Dade County	Trenton
112	0.0	Decatur City	Decatur
112	0.0	Dekalb County	Decatur
112	0.0	Effingham County	Springfield
112	0.0	Fannin County	Blue Ridge
112	0.0	Fayette County	Fayetteville
112	0.0	Fulton County	Atlanta
112	0.0	Hancock County	Sparta
112	0.0	Harris County	Hamilton
112	0.0	Heard County	Franklin
112	0.0	Henry County	Mcdonough
112	0.0	Jasper County	Monticello
112	0.0	Jones County	Gray
112	0.0	Lamar County	Barnesville
112	0.0	Lee County	Leesburg
112	0.0	Mcintosh County	Darien
112	0.0	Meriwether County	Greenville
112	0.0	Monroe County	Forsyth
112	0.0	Newton County	Covington
112	0.0	Paulding County	Dallas
112	0.0	Pike County	Zebulon
112	0.0	Rockdale County	Conyers
112	0.0	Spalding County	Griffin
112	0.0	Stephens County	Toccoa
112	0.0	Thomasville City	Thomasville
112	0.0	Towns County	Hiawassee
112	0.0	Union County	Blairsville
154	n/a	Fort Benning District	Fort Benning

Students Eligible for Free Lunch

Rank	Percent	District Name	City
1	82.5	Randolph County	Cuthbert
2	80.0	Hancock County	Sparta
3	75.7	Dooly County	Vienna
4	75.0	Jefferson County	Louisville
5	73.9	Greene County	Greensboro
6	72.9	Macon County	Oglethorpe
7	71.9	Screven County	Sylvania
8	68.6	Meriwether County	Greenville
9	68.0	Seminole County	Donalsonville
10	67.1	Atlanta City	Atlanta
11	65.7	Dougherty County	Albany
12	65.5	Burke County	Waynesboro
13	65.3	Atkinson County	Pearson
14	65.1	Jenkins County	Millen
15	64.7	Sumter County	Americus
16	64.1	Telfair County	Mcrae
17	63.8	Early County	Blakely
18	63.5	Brooks County	Quitman
18	63.5	Crisp County	Cordele
20	61.7	Dublin City	Dublin
21	61.4	Mcintosh County	Darien
22	60.3	Terrell County	Dawson
23	59.6	Pelham City	Pelham
24	59.4	Taylor County	Butler
25	58.7	Evans County	Claxton
25	58.7	Mcduffie County	Thomson
25	58.7	Toombs County	Lyons
28	58.6	Decatur County	Bainbridge
28	58.6	Mitchell County	Camilla
30	57.9	Emanuel County	Swainsboro
31	57.3	Clarke County	Athens
32	57.1	Gainesville City	Gainesville
33	56.6	Ben Hill County	Fitzgerald
34	56.4	Wilkinson County	Irwinton
35	56.1	Turner County	Ashburn
36	55.9	Long County	Ludowici
36	55.9	Richmond County	Augusta
38	55.8	Irwin County	Ocilla
38	55.8	Thomasville City	Thomasville
40	55.5	Putnam County	Eatonton
41	54.9	Marion County	Buena Vista
42	54.8	Tattnall County	Reidsville
42	54.8	Washington County	Sandersville
44	54.3	Candler County	Metter
45	54.2	Coffee County	Douglas
46	53.9	Peach County	Fort Valley
46	53.9	Rome City	Rome
48	53.7	Valdosta City	Valdosta
49	53.0	Colquitt County	Moultrie
50	52.9	Bibb County	Macon
51	50.5	Wilkes County	Washington
52	49.5	Baldwin County	Milledgeville
53	49.4	Ware County	Waycross
54	48.5	Dekalb County	Decatur
55	48.3	Appling County	Baxley
56	47.8	Dalton City	Dalton
57	47.4	Jeff Davis County	Hazlehurst
57	47.4	Vidalia City	Vidalia
59	47.2	Cook County	Adel
60	47.1	Thomas County	Thomasville
61	46.9	Charlton County	Folkston
61	46.9	Pulaski County	Hawkinsville
63	46.6	Spalding County	Griffin
64	46.1	Tift County	Tifton
65	46.0	Grady County	Cairo
65	46.0	Worth County	Sylvester
67	45.7	Jasper County	Monticello
67	45.7	Marietta City	Marietta
69	45.4	Chattooga County	Summerville
69	45.4	Lamar County	Barnesville
71	45.3	Clayton County	Jonesboro
72	45.2	Bulloch County	Statesboro
72	45.2	Crawford County	Roberta
72	45.2	Dodge County	Eastman
75	44.8	Berrien County	Nashville
76	44.7	Muscogee County	Columbus
77	44.5	Chatham County	Savannah
77	44.5	Elbert County	Elberton
79	44.4	Laurens County	Dublin
80	44.2	Wayne County	Jesup
81	44.1	Troup County	Lagrange
82	43.5	Brantley County	Nahunta
83	43.2	Bacon County	Alma
84	42.3	Pierce County	Blackshear
85	42.0	Thomaston-Upson County	Thomaston
86	40.5	Banks County	Homer
87	39.6	Walker County	Lafayette
88	38.8	Gilmer County	Ellijay
89	38.7	Carrollton City	Carrollton
90	38.6	Bleckley County	Cochran
91	38.5	Heard County	Franklin
92	38.2	Glynn County	Brunswick
93	37.9	Liberty County	Hinesville
94	37.7	Butts County	Jackson
95	37.1	Whitfield County	Dalton
96	36.7	Haralson County	Buchanan
97	36.3	Murray County	Chatsworth
98	35.8	Stephens County	Toccoa
99	35.4	Oglethorpe County	Lexington
100	35.0	Buford City	Buford
101	34.3	Hart County	Hartwell
102	33.9	Monroe County	Forsyth
103	33.6	Polk County	Cedartown
104	33.5	Carroll County	Carrollton
105	33.2	Jackson County	Jefferson
105	33.2	Newton County	Covington
107	32.7	Decatur City	Decatur
108	32.5	Rabun County	Clayton
109	32.0	Hall County	Gainesville
110	31.9	Madison County	Danielsville
111	31.2	Calhoun City	Calhoun
111	31.2	Franklin County	Carnesville
113	31.0	Gordon County	Calhoun
114	30.8	Union County	Blairsville
115	30.7	Floyd County	Rome
116	29.3	Lowndes County	Valdosta
117	29.0	Morgan County	Madison
118	28.8	Fannin County	Blue Ridge
119	28.7	Lumpkin County	Dahlonega
120	28.6	Habersham County	Clarkesville
121	28.5	Cartersville City	Cartersville
121	28.5	Fulton County	Atlanta
123	28.3	Houston County	Perry
124	27.8	White County	Cleveland
125	27.4	Bartow County	Cartersville
125	27.4	Walton County	Monroe

127	26.6	Barrow County	Winder
128	25.4	Bryan County	Pembroke
128	25.4	Dade County	Trenton
128	25.4	Pickens County	Jasper
131	25.2	Rockdale County	Conyers
132	25.1	Camden County	Kingsland
133	24.8	Catoosa County	Ringgold
134	24.7	Jones County	Gray
135	24.3	Douglas County	Douglasville
136	24.2	Harris County	Hamilton
137	23.9	Pike County	Zebulon
138	23.8	Jefferson City	Jefferson
139	22.4	Dawson County	Dawsonville
140	22.0	Coweta County	Newnan
140	22.0	Lee County	Leesburg
140	22.0	Towns County	Hiawassee
143	20.8	Effingham County	Springfield
144	19.8	Gwinnett County	Lawrenceville
145	18.0	Cobb County	Marietta
146	14.6	Paulding County	Dallas
147	14.3	Henry County	Mcdonough
148	13.8	Columbia County	Appling
149	12.8	Cherokee County	Canton
150	11.8	Oconee County	Watkinsville
151	9.8	Bremen City	Bremen
152	8.6	Forsyth County	Cumming
153	6.4	Fayette County	Fayetteville
154	n/a	Fort Benning District	Fort Benning

Students Eligible for Reduced-Price Lunch

Rank	Percent	District Name	City
1	16.0	Rabun County	Clayton
2	15.7	Union County	Blairsville
3	14.9	Liberty County	Hinesville
4	14.8	Clayton County	Jonesboro
5	14.4	Banks County	Homer
6	14.1	Walker County	Lafayette
7	14.0	Long County	Ludowici
8	13.9	Chattooga County	Summerville
9	13.8	Atkinson County	Pearson
9	13.8	Murray County	Chatsworth
11	13.7	Dalton City	Dalton
11	13.7	Evans County	Claxton
13	13.5	Washington County	Sandersville
14	13.3	Pierce County	Blackshear
15	13.2	Dougherty County	Albany
16	12.9	Burke County	Waynesboro
17	12.8	Dade County	Trenton
18	12.7	Meriwether County	Greenville
19	12.5	Berrien County	Nashville
20	12.4	Crawford County	Roberta
21	12.3	Coffee County	Douglas
21	12.3	Jenkins County	Millen
23	12.2	Dodge County	Eastman
24	12.1	Charlton County	Folkston
25	11.9	Brooks County	Quitman
25	11.9	Fannin County	Blue Ridge
25	11.9	Jackson County	Jefferson
25	11.9	Wilkinson County	Irwinton
29	11.7	Brantley County	Nahunta
29	11.7	Marion County	Buena Vista
31	11.6	Camden County	Kingsland
31	11.6	Candler County	Metter
31	11.6	Wilkes County	Washington
34	11.5	Lamar County	Barnesville
35	11.4	Toombs County	Lyons
36	11.2	Heard County	Franklin
37	11.1	Appling County	Baxley
37	11.1	Gilmer County	Ellijay
39	11.0	Butts County	Jackson
39	11.0	Harris County	Hamilton
39	11.0	Pickens County	Jasper
42	10.8	Hart County	Hartwell
42	10.8	Putnam County	Eatonton
42	10.8	Thomas County	Thomasville
45	10.7	Carroll County	Carrollton
45	10.7	Thomaston-Upson County	Thomaston
47	10.6	Tattnall County	Reidsville
48	10.5	Catoosa County	Ringgold
49	10.4	Whitfield County	Dalton
50	10.2	Emanuel County	Swainsboro
50	10.2	Jeff Davis County	Hazlehurst
50	10.2	Newton County	Covington
53	10.1	Cook County	Adel
53	10.1	Dekalb County	Decatur
53	10.1	Franklin County	Carnesville
53	10.1	Marietta City	Marietta
53	10.1	Richmond County	Augusta
53	10.1	White County	Cleveland
59	10.0	Bleckley County	Cochran
59	10.0	Bulloch County	Statesboro
59	10.0	Gordon County	Calhoun
59	10.0	Mitchell County	Camilla
59	10.0	Thomasville City	Thomasville
64	9.9	Taylor County	Butler
64	9.9	Terrell County	Dawson
66	9.8	Elbert County	Elberton
66	9.8	Irwin County	Ocilla
68	9.6	Madison County	Danielsville
68	9.6	Pelham City	Pelham
68	9.6	Pulaski County	Hawkinsville
68	9.6	Worth County	Sylvester
72	9.5	Bartow County	Cartersville
72	9.5	Effingham County	Springfield
72	9.5	Haralson County	Buchanan
72	9.5	Jasper County	Monticello
72	9.5	Muscogee County	Columbus
72	9.5	Sumter County	Americus
78	9.4	Baldwin County	Milledgeville
78	9.4	Peach County	Fort Valley
78	9.4	Telfair County	Mcrae
81	9.3	Mcduffie County	Thomson
82	9.2	Bacon County	Alma
82	9.2	Stephens County	Toccoa
84	9.1	Chatham County	Savannah
84	9.1	Dooly County	Vienna
84	9.1	Houston County	Perry
84	9.1	Towns County	Hiawassee
88	9.0	Barrow County	Winder
88	9.0	Douglas County	Douglasville
88	9.0	Laurens County	Dublin
88	9.0	Macon County	Oglethorpe
92	8.9	Floyd County	Rome
92	8.9	Spalding County	Griffin
92	8.9	Ware County	Waycross
95	8.8	Colquitt County	Moultrie
96	8.7	Ben Hill County	Fitzgerald
96	8.7	Bryan County	Pembroke
96	8.7	Cartersville City	Cartersville
96	8.7	Decatur County	Bainbridge
100	8.6	Hall County	Gainesville
100	8.6	Mcintosh County	Darien
102	8.5	Lowndes County	Valdosta
102	8.5	Monroe County	Forsyth
102	8.5	Randolph County	Cuthbert
102	8.5	Troup County	Lagrange
106	8.4	Grady County	Cairo
106	8.4	Morgan County	Madison
108	8.2	Rockdale County	Conyers
109	8.1	Jones County	Gray
109	8.1	Tift County	Tifton
111	7.8	Crisp County	Cordele
111	7.8	Early County	Blakely
111	7.8	Oglethorpe County	Lexington
111	7.8	Wayne County	Jesup
115	7.7	Polk County	Cedartown
116	7.6	Carrollton City	Carrollton
116	7.6	Glynn County	Brunswick
118	7.5	Habersham County	Clarkesville
118	7.5	Valdosta City	Valdosta
118	7.5	Vidalia City	Vidalia
121	7.4	Dawson County	Dawsonville
121	7.4	Dublin City	Dublin
121	7.4	Jefferson County	Louisville
121	7.4	Walton County	Monroe
125	7.2	Paulding County	Dallas
125	7.2	Turner County	Ashburn
127	7.1	Bibb County	Macon
127	7.1	Rome City	Rome
129	7.0	Gainesville City	Gainesville
129	7.0	Lee County	Leesburg
131	6.8	Clarke County	Athens
131	6.8	Hancock County	Sparta
131	6.8	Pike County	Zebulon
134	6.5	Coweta County	Newnan
135	6.4	Screven County	Sylvania
136	6.3	Greene County	Greensboro
136	6.3	Gwinnett County	Lawrenceville
138	6.2	Henry County	Mcdonough
138	6.2	Lumpkin County	Dahlonega
140	6.1	Calhoun City	Calhoun
140	6.1	Cobb County	Marietta
142	6.0	Seminole County	Donalsonville
143	5.6	Decatur City	Decatur
144	5.5	Columbia County	Appling
145	5.1	Buford City	Buford
145	5.1	Cherokee County	Canton
147	5.0	Fulton County	Atlanta
148	4.8	Jefferson City	Jefferson
149	4.3	Atlanta City	Atlanta
149	4.3	Oconee County	Watkinsville
151	3.4	Forsyth County	Cumming
152	3.2	Bremen City	Bremen
153	2.3	Fayette County	Fayetteville
154	n/a	Fort Benning District	Fort Benning

Student/Teacher Ratio

Rank	Ratio	District Name	City
1	18.5	Burke County	Waynesboro
2	18.3	Butts County	Jackson
3	18.1	Clayton County	Jonesboro
4	18.0	Fannin County	Blue Ridge
4	18.0	Henry County	Mcdonough
4	18.0	Thomaston-Upson County	Thomaston
7	17.9	Lamar County	Barnesville
7	17.9	Pike County	Zebulon
7	17.9	Terrell County	Dawson
10	17.8	Coffee County	Douglas
11	17.7	Berrien County	Nashville
11	17.7	Camden County	Kingsland
11	17.7	Charlton County	Folkston
11	17.7	Early County	Blakely
11	17.7	Effingham County	Springfield
11	17.7	Jefferson County	Louisville
17	17.6	Bibb County	Macon
17	17.6	Jeff Davis County	Hazlehurst
19	17.4	Cartersville City	Cartersville
19	17.4	Colquitt County	Moultrie
19	17.4	Washington County	Sandersville
22	17.3	Carrollton City	Carrollton
22	17.3	Douglas County	Douglasville
22	17.3	Taylor County	Butler
25	17.1	Columbia County	Appling
25	17.1	Gordon County	Calhoun
27	17.0	Brantley County	Nahunta
27	17.0	Cook County	Adel
27	17.0	Dodge County	Eastman
27	17.0	Jones County	Gray
27	17.0	Macon County	Oglethorpe
27	17.0	Monroe County	Forsyth
33	16.9	Bryan County	Pembroke
34	16.8	Dooly County	Vienna
35	16.7	Liberty County	Hinesville
35	16.7	Long County	Ludowici
35	16.7	Rome City	Rome
35	16.7	Screven County	Sylvania
35	16.7	Vidalia City	Vidalia
40	16.6	Carroll County	Carrollton
40	16.6	Jasper County	Monticello
42	16.5	Crawford County	Roberta
42	16.5	Heard County	Franklin
42	16.5	Mcduffie County	Thomson
42	16.5	Tattnall County	Reidsville
42	16.5	Wayne County	Jesup
47	16.4	Bremen City	Bremen
47	16.4	Candler County	Metter
47	16.4	Tift County	Tifton
50	16.3	Brooks County	Quitman
50	16.3	Hall County	Gainesville
50	16.3	Haralson County	Buchanan
50	16.3	Lumpkin County	Dahlonega
50	16.3	Mcintosh County	Darien
50	16.3	Murray County	Chatsworth
56	16.2	Atkinson County	Pearson
56	16.2	Banks County	Homer
56	16.2	Catoosa County	Ringgold
56	16.2	Chatham County	Savannah
56	16.2	Habersham County	Clarkesville
56	16.2	Lee County	Leesburg
56	16.2	Mitchell County	Camilla
56	16.2	Sumter County	Americus
64	16.1	Calhoun City	Calhoun
64	16.1	Cherokee County	Canton
64	16.1	Glynn County	Brunswick
64	16.1	Harris County	Hamilton
64	16.1	Toombs County	Lyons
64	16.1	Valdosta City	Valdosta
64	16.1	White County	Cleveland
71	16.0	Franklin County	Carnesville
71	16.0	Grady County	Cairo
71	16.0	Madison County	Danielsville
71	16.0	Newton County	Covington
71	16.0	Pelham City	Pelham
71	16.0	Wilkes County	Washington
77	15.9	Emanuel County	Swainsboro
77	15.9	Floyd County	Rome
77	15.9	Rabun County	Clayton
80	15.8	Coweta County	Newnan
80	15.8	Hancock County	Sparta
80	15.8	Jackson County	Jefferson
80	15.8	Laurens County	Dublin
80	15.8	Oglethorpe County	Lexington
80	15.8	Paulding County	Dallas
80	15.8	Richmond County	Augusta

87	15.7	Appling County	Baxley
87	15.7	Dade County	Trenton
87	15.7	Dalton City	Dalton
87	15.7	Gainesville City	Gainesville
87	15.7	Whitfield County	Dalton
92	15.6	Ben Hill County	Fitzgerald
92	15.6	Bleckley County	Cochran
92	15.6	Marion County	Buena Vista
92	15.6	Pickens County	Jasper
92	15.6	Polk County	Cedartown
92	15.6	Thomas County	Thomasville
98	15.5	Elbert County	Elberton
98	15.5	Evans County	Claxton
98	15.5	Hart County	Hartwell
98	15.5	Oconee County	Watkinsville
98	15.5	Rockdale County	Conyers
103	15.4	Bartow County	Cartersville
103	15.4	Chattooga County	Summerville
103	15.4	Crisp County	Cordele
103	15.4	Dougherty County	Albany
103	15.4	Muscogee County	Columbus
103	15.4	Spalding County	Griffin
103	15.4	Walton County	Monroe
110	15.3	Barrow County	Winder
110	15.3	Gilmer County	Ellijay
110	15.3	Randolph County	Cuthbert
110	15.3	Thomasville City	Thomasville
110	15.3	Walker County	Lafayette
115	15.2	Gwinnett County	Lawrenceville
116	15.1	Decatur County	Bainbridge
116	15.1	Lowndes County	Valdosta
116	15.1	Morgan County	Madison
116	15.1	Turner County	Ashburn
120	15.0	Bacon County	Alma
120	15.0	Fayette County	Fayetteville
120	15.0	Forsyth County	Cumming
120	15.0	Pierce County	Blackshear
124	14.9	Dekalb County	Decatur
124	14.9	Houston County	Perry
126	14.8	Buford City	Buford
126	14.8	Irwin County	Ocilla
126	14.8	Ware County	Waycross
126	14.8	Wilkinson County	Irwinton
130	14.7	Cobb County	Marietta
130	14.7	Fulton County	Atlanta
130	14.7	Jenkins County	Millen
130	14.7	Worth County	Sylvester
134	14.6	Seminole County	Donalsonville
135	14.5	Greene County	Greensboro
135	14.5	Putnam County	Eatonton
135	14.5	Stephens County	Toccoa
135	14.5	Telfair County	Mcrae
135	14.5	Union County	Blairsville
140	14.4	Marietta City	Marietta
140	14.4	Peach County	Fort Valley
142	14.3	Fort Benning District	Fort Benning
142	14.3	Troup County	Lagrange
144	14.2	Atlanta City	Atlanta
144	14.2	Clarke County	Athens
146	14.1	Dublin City	Dublin
147	13.9	Baldwin County	Milledgeville
147	13.9	Dawson County	Dawsonville
149	13.7	Bulloch County	Statesboro
150	13.4	Pulaski County	Hawkinsville
151	13.3	Jefferson City	Jefferson
152	13.1	Meriwether County	Greenville
153	11.2	Decatur City	Decatur
154	11.0	Towns County	Hiawassee

Student/Librarian Ratio

Rank	Ratio	District Name	City
1	1,529.0	Towns County	Hiawassee
2	1,184.3	Gwinnett County	Lawrenceville
3	1,131.7	Ben Hill County	Fitzgerald
4	1,093.2	Thomas County	Thomasville
5	1,043.3	Screven County	Sylvania
6	997.5	Long County	Ludowici
7	985.0	Cartersville City	Cartersville
8	968.0	Monroe County	Forsyth
9	957.0	Turner County	Ashburn
10	927.6	Forsyth County	Cumming
11	924.5	Henry County	Mcdonough
12	907.0	Irwin County	Ocilla
13	905.2	Cobb County	Marietta
14	889.5	Dodge County	Eastman
15	888.7	Calhoun City	Calhoun
16	887.6	Gainesville City	Gainesville
17	877.8	Lumpkin County	Dahlonega
18	877.0	Jenkins County	Millen
18	877.0	Seminole County	Donalsonville
20	870.4	Fulton County	Atlanta
21	867.5	Taylor County	Butler
22	866.7	Lamar County	Barnesville
23	862.5	Clayton County	Jonesboro
24	860.4	Mcintosh County	Darien
25	856.3	Carrollton City	Carrollton
26	842.5	Butts County	Jackson
27	842.0	Baldwin County	Milledgeville
28	836.3	Cherokee County	Canton
29	829.5	Hancock County	Sparta
30	816.1	Murray County	Chatsworth
31	816.0	Pulaski County	Hawkinsville
32	810.0	Pierce County	Blackshear
33	803.8	Cook County	Adel
34	799.2	Berrien County	Nashville
35	792.8	Morgan County	Madison
36	787.5	Bremen City	Bremen
37	777.6	Evans County	Claxton
38	771.3	Paulding County	Dallas
39	769.0	Burke County	Waynesboro
40	744.4	Franklin County	Carnesville
41	740.6	Walton County	Monroe
42	739.5	Pelham City	Pelham
43	734.2	Stephens County	Toccoa
44	727.0	Jasper County	Monticello
45	725.7	Worth County	Sylvester
46	722.8	Crisp County	Cordele
47	721.8	Sumter County	Americus
48	720.1	Newton County	Covington
49	715.6	Thomaston-Upson County	Thomaston
50	714.0	Toombs County	Lyons
51	713.8	Mitchell County	Camilla
52	712.8	Hart County	Hartwell
53	711.2	Lowndes County	Valdosta
54	710.1	Glynn County	Brunswick
55	704.6	Liberty County	Hinesville
56	701.9	Oconee County	Watkinsville
57	701.3	Pike County	Zebulon
58	698.8	Columbia County	Appling
59	696.7	Crawford County	Roberta
60	695.4	Gordon County	Calhoun
61	691.0	Early County	Blakely
62	684.0	Marietta City	Marietta
63	683.1	Camden County	Kingsland
64	681.1	Coweta County	Newnan
65	676.7	Pickens County	Jasper
66	669.5	Fayette County	Fayetteville
67	668.8	Lee County	Leesburg
68	668.7	Barrow County	Winder
69	667.0	Bartow County	Cartersville
70	658.5	Hall County	Gainesville
71	654.8	Gilmer County	Ellijay
72	653.9	Catoosa County	Ringgold
73	653.4	Coffee County	Douglas
74	652.4	Dublin City	Dublin
75	645.3	Spalding County	Griffin
76	642.4	Fannin County	Blue Ridge
77	640.8	Brooks County	Quitman
78	640.0	Jeff Davis County	Hazlehurst
79	639.9	Chatham County	Savannah
80	639.3	Candler County	Metter
81	638.2	Carroll County	Carrollton
82	637.7	Dalton City	Dalton
83	635.2	Laurens County	Dublin
84	633.5	Habersham County	Clarkesville
85	633.3	Bacon County	Alma
86	630.5	Houston County	Perry
87	630.1	Harris County	Hamilton
88	627.7	Haralson County	Buchanan
89	626.8	Jones County	Gray
90	626.3	White County	Cleveland
91	624.4	Atlanta City	Atlanta
92	623.2	Effingham County	Springfield
93	621.9	Emanuel County	Swainsboro
94	621.4	Thomasville City	Thomasville
95	619.3	Wilkes County	Washington
96	618.5	Putnam County	Eatonton
97	618.0	Dooly County	Vienna
98	616.9	Bryan County	Pembroke
99	616.5	Dekalb County	Decatur
100	616.0	Mcduffie County	Thomson
101	607.2	Dawson County	Dawsonville
102	607.0	Banks County	Homer
103	602.0	Vidalia City	Vidalia
104	600.0	Rockdale County	Conyers
105	598.2	Valdosta City	Valdosta
106	588.8	Bleckley County	Cochran
107	588.0	Terrell County	Dawson
108	587.8	Tift County	Tifton
109	587.7	Jefferson County	Louisville
110	587.5	Clarke County	Athens
111	584.8	Polk County	Cedartown
112	584.0	Wayne County	Jesup
113	580.5	Whitfield County	Dalton
114	579.1	Ware County	Waycross
115	579.0	Wilkinson County	Irwinton
116	574.6	Bibb County	Macon
117	573.4	Richmond County	Augusta
118	572.5	Decatur County	Bainbridge
119	570.6	Walker County	Lafayette
120	570.3	Oglethorpe County	Lexington
121	570.0	Greene County	Greensboro
122	569.4	Douglas County	Douglasville
123	568.8	Grady County	Cairo
124	564.8	Buford City	Buford
125	564.0	Meriwether County	Greenville
126	562.0	Marion County	Buena Vista
127	561.9	Washington County	Sandersville
128	561.0	Peach County	Fort Valley
129	560.9	Troup County	Lagrange
130	556.1	Colquitt County	Moultrie
131	555.3	Brantley County	Nahunta
132	550.8	Tattnall County	Reidsville
133	550.0	Macon County	Oglethorpe
133	550.0	Muscogee County	Columbus
135	549.3	Atkinson County	Pearson
135	549.3	Telfair County	Mcrae
137	547.2	Jackson County	Jefferson
138	544.5	Dougherty County	Albany
138	544.5	Heard County	Franklin
140	541.3	Union County	Blairsville
141	540.6	Floyd County	Rome
142	534.1	Bulloch County	Statesboro
143	519.7	Randolph County	Cuthbert
144	515.7	Dade County	Trenton
145	513.4	Madison County	Danielsville
146	508.3	Jefferson City	Jefferson
147	503.8	Charlton County	Folkston
148	490.5	Rome City	Rome
149	474.1	Elbert County	Elberton
150	471.9	Appling County	Baxley
151	444.2	Rabun County	Clayton
152	432.4	Fort Benning District	Fort Benning
153	404.9	Chattooga County	Summerville
154	387.5	Decatur City	Decatur

Student/Counselor Ratio

Rank	Ratio	District Name	City
1	764.5	Towns County	Hiawassee
2	694.8	Wilkinson County	Irwinton
3	667.7	Murray County	Chatsworth
4	665.0	Long County	Ludowici
5	643.0	Cook County	Adel
6	638.9	Emanuel County	Swainsboro
7	633.3	Bacon County	Alma
8	632.2	Elbert County	Elberton
9	630.0	Bremen City	Bremen
10	626.0	Screven County	Sylvania
11	625.9	Gordon County	Calhoun
12	608.3	Terrell County	Dawson
13	587.7	Jefferson County	Louisville
14	575.7	Charlton County	Folkston
15	571.2	Toombs County	Lyons
16	571.0	Mitchell County	Camilla
17	569.6	Brooks County	Quitman
18	567.1	Habersham County	Clarkesville
19	561.3	Gilmer County	Ellijay
20	561.0	Pike County	Zebulon
21	560.1	Coffee County	Douglas
22	556.6	Thomaston-Upson County	Thomaston
23	555.9	Dodge County	Eastman
24	555.3	Brantley County	Nahunta
24	555.3	Rabun County	Clayton
26	553.1	Monroe County	Forsyth
27	545.3	Jasper County	Monticello
28	544.5	Heard County	Franklin
29	544.0	Pulaski County	Hawkinsville
30	536.9	White County	Cleveland
31	536.5	Newton County	Covington
32	535.8	Baldwin County	Milledgeville
33	535.3	Fannin County	Blue Ridge
34	533.2	Calhoun City	Calhoun
35	532.8	Candler County	Metter
36	531.7	Franklin County	Carnesville
37	531.6	Atkinson County	Pearson
38	530.2	Union County	Blairsville
39	527.8	Jones County	Gray
40	526.6	Cherokee County	Canton
41	525.6	Thomas County	Thomasville
41	525.6	Wayne County	Jesup
43	524.8	Jeff Davis County	Hazlehurst
44	522.5	Crawford County	Roberta
45	522.3	Lowndes County	Valdosta
46	520.0	Lamar County	Barnesville
47	519.7	Randolph County	Cuthbert
48	516.1	Wilkes County	Washington
49	515.0	Dooly County	Vienna

50	513.4	Madison County	Danielsville
51	512.5	Liberty County	Hinesville
52	510.5	Oconee County	Watkinsville
53	509.4	Tift County	Tifton
54	509.1	Hart County	Hartwell
55	508.4	Pelham City	Pelham
56	507.5	Pickens County	Jasper
57	506.0	Dawson County	Dawsonville
58	504.7	Bryan County	Pembroke
59	501.6	Lumpkin County	Dahlonega
60	501.2	Polk County	Cedartown
61	498.7	Laurens County	Dublin
62	497.5	Jackson County	Jefferson
63	494.8	Mcintosh County	Darien
63	494.8	Putnam County	Eatonton
65	493.1	Gainesville City	Gainesville
66	492.7	Barrow County	Winder
67	490.7	Colquitt County	Moultrie
68	487.1	Houston County	Perry
69	486.6	Henry County	Mcdonough
70	486.4	Lee County	Leesburg
71	486.3	Ware County	Waycross
72	486.0	Evans County	Claxton
73	485.0	Valdosta City	Valdosta
74	483.8	Worth County	Sylvester
75	481.6	Vidalia City	Vidalia
76	481.2	Sumter County	Americus
77	480.5	Cartersville City	Cartersville
78	477.6	Washington County	Sandersville
79	477.5	Gwinnett County	Lawrenceville
80	475.6	Effingham County	Springfield
81	474.7	Bartow County	Cartersville
82	474.0	Hancock County	Sparta
83	472.1	Tattnall County	Reidsville
84	472.0	Richmond County	Augusta
85	471.0	Bleckley County	Cochran
86	470.8	Haralson County	Buchanan
87	470.3	Hall County	Gainesville
87	470.3	Paulding County	Dallas
89	469.8	Douglas County	Douglasville
90	469.1	Rome City	Rome
91	468.8	Whitfield County	Dalton
92	467.0	Carroll County	Carrollton
93	464.6	Chattooga County	Summerville
94	464.5	Meriwether County	Greenville
95	462.9	Pierce County	Blackshear
96	461.6	Jenkins County	Millen
97	461.4	Burke County	Waynesboro
98	460.3	Carrollton City	Carrollton
99	460.0	Rockdale County	Conyers
100	457.6	Bibb County	Macon
101	456.5	Crisp County	Cordele
102	456.2	Oglethorpe County	Lexington
103	455.8	Clayton County	Jonesboro
104	455.0	Grady County	Cairo
105	453.5	Walker County	Lafayette
106	451.8	Buford City	Buford
107	449.3	Spalding County	Griffin
108	447.1	Glynn County	Brunswick
109	445.9	Catoosa County	Ringgold
110	443.7	Marion County	Buena Vista
111	443.6	Forsyth County	Cumming
112	443.1	Coweta County	Newnan
113	441.5	Dalton City	Dalton
114	440.0	Macon County	Oglethorpe
115	438.5	Seminole County	Donalsonville
116	436.3	Peach County	Fort Valley
117	435.7	Jefferson City	Jefferson
118	435.6	Clarke County	Athens
119	434.7	Camden County	Kingsland
120	433.9	Berrien County	Nashville
121	433.8	Taylor County	Butler
122	428.3	Decatur County	Bainbridge
122	428.3	Troup County	Lagrange
124	426.0	Columbia County	Appling
125	425.3	Turner County	Ashburn
126	425.2	Early County	Blakely
127	424.4	Ben Hill County	Fitzgerald
128	422.8	Morgan County	Madison
129	421.5	Dougherty County	Albany
130	419.5	Stephens County	Toccoa
131	418.6	Cobb County	Marietta
132	416.3	Chatham County	Savannah
133	416.0	Butts County	Jackson
134	415.0	Fulton County	Atlanta
135	414.6	Mcduffie County	Thomson
136	412.9	Appling County	Baxley
137	412.0	Telfair County	Mcrae
138	410.9	Floyd County	Rome
139	407.8	Dublin City	Dublin
140	406.7	Marietta City	Marietta
141	406.6	Walton County	Monroe
142	404.7	Banks County	Homer
143	404.6	Fayette County	Fayetteville
144	401.0	Harris County	Hamilton
145	392.5	Dade County	Trenton
146	390.5	Bulloch County	Statesboro
147	389.7	Atlanta City	Atlanta
148	380.0	Greene County	Greensboro
149	378.9	Thomasville City	Thomasville
150	368.2	Dekalb County	Decatur
151	362.8	Irwin County	Ocilla
152	362.0	Muscogee County	Columbus
153	359.9	Decatur City	Decatur
154	302.7	Fort Benning District	Fort Benning

Current Spending per Student in FY2001

Rank	Dollars	District Name	City
1	10,993	Atlanta City	Atlanta
2	9,562	Decatur City	Decatur
3	8,641	Dalton City	Dalton
4	8,573	Buford City	Buford
5	8,512	Randolph County	Cuthbert
6	8,466	Marietta City	Marietta
7	7,966	Wilkinson County	Irwinton
8	7,944	Greene County	Greensboro
9	7,894	Clarke County	Athens
10	7,879	Dooly County	Vienna
11	7,869	Fulton County	Atlanta
12	7,855	Gainesville City	Gainesville
13	7,654	Irwin County	Ocilla
14	7,612	Appling County	Baxley
15	7,607	Macon County	Oglethorpe
16	7,590	Dublin City	Dublin
17	7,589	Meriwether County	Greenville
18	7,413	Dekalb County	Decatur
19	7,237	Dougherty County	Albany
20	7,227	Bulloch County	Statesboro
21	7,214	Barrow County	Winder
22	7,184	Chattooga County	Summerville
23	7,146	Pulaski County	Hawkinsville
24	7,136	Hart County	Hartwell
25	7,102	Thomasville City	Thomasville
26	7,088	Wilkes County	Washington
27	7,078	Ware County	Waycross
28	7,077	Terrell County	Dawson
29	7,045	Spalding County	Griffin
30	7,021	Rome City	Rome
31	7,008	Pickens County	Jasper
32	6,991	Jackson County	Jefferson
33	6,958	Turner County	Ashburn
34	6,948	Fannin County	Blue Ridge
35	6,938	Mitchell County	Camilla
36	6,922	Telfair County	Mcrae
37	6,921	Glynn County	Brunswick
38	6,916	Rabun County	Clayton
39	6,911	Baldwin County	Milledgeville
40	6,896	Crisp County	Cordele
41	6,879	Hancock County	Sparta
42	6,833	Stephens County	Toccoa
43	6,826	Muscogee County	Columbus
44	6,821	Union County	Blairsville
45	6,808	Jeff Davis County	Hazlehurst
46	6,806	Putnam County	Eatonton
47	6,768	Morgan County	Madison
48	6,764	Troup County	Lagrange
49	6,759	Elbert County	Elberton
49	6,759	Forsyth County	Cumming
51	6,740	Rockdale County	Conyers
52	6,690	Lowndes County	Valdosta
53	6,680	Towns County	Hiawassee
54	6,664	Calhoun City	Calhoun
54	6,664	Carrollton City	Carrollton
54	6,664	Gwinnett County	Lawrenceville
57	6,644	Ben Hill County	Fitzgerald
58	6,643	Cartersville City	Cartersville
59	6,631	Fayette County	Fayetteville
60	6,630	Habersham County	Clarkesville
61	6,615	Chatham County	Savannah
62	6,598	Washington County	Sandersville
63	6,594	Brooks County	Quitman
64	6,577	Monroe County	Forsyth
65	6,575	Marion County	Buena Vista
66	6,572	Cobb County	Marietta
67	6,571	Dawson County	Dawsonville
67	6,571	Houston County	Perry
69	6,565	Seminole County	Donalsonville
70	6,552	Oglethorpe County	Lexington
71	6,545	Atkinson County	Pearson
71	6,545	Franklin County	Carnesville
73	6,542	Dodge County	Eastman
74	6,540	Thomas County	Thomasville
75	6,527	Lumpkin County	Dahlonega
76	6,525	Douglas County	Douglasville
77	6,524	Carroll County	Carrollton
78	6,510	Burke County	Waynesboro
79	6,509	Bartow County	Cartersville
80	6,504	Dade County	Trenton
81	6,501	Sumter County	Americus
82	6,493	Walker County	Lafayette
83	6,481	Worth County	Sylvester
84	6,472	Colquitt County	Moultrie
85	6,471	Grady County	Cairo
86	6,462	Gordon County	Calhoun
87	6,452	Cherokee County	Canton
88	6,447	Richmond County	Augusta
89	6,444	Emanuel County	Swainsboro
90	6,441	Bibb County	Macon
91	6,439	Walton County	Monroe
92	6,431	Butts County	Jackson
92	6,431	Whitfield County	Dalton
94	6,418	Wayne County	Jesup
95	6,414	Bremen City	Bremen
96	6,401	Coffee County	Douglas
97	6,396	Screven County	Sylvania
98	6,395	Harris County	Hamilton
99	6,391	Floyd County	Rome
100	6,374	Coweta County	Newnan
101	6,357	White County	Cleveland
102	6,334	Madison County	Danielsville
103	6,329	Polk County	Cedartown
104	6,317	Jasper County	Monticello
105	6,314	Clayton County	Jonesboro
106	6,308	Mcduffie County	Thomson
107	6,305	Bacon County	Alma
108	6,303	Decatur County	Bainbridge
109	6,301	Tattnall County	Reidsville
110	6,298	Newton County	Covington
111	6,287	Taylor County	Butler
112	6,278	Peach County	Fort Valley
113	6,275	Bleckley County	Cochran
114	6,273	Tift County	Tifton
115	6,270	Gilmer County	Ellijay
116	6,266	Early County	Blakely
117	6,258	Jefferson County	Louisville
118	6,257	Crawford County	Roberta
119	6,248	Valdosta City	Valdosta
120	6,243	Thomaston-Upson County	Thomaston
121	6,233	Candler County	Metter
122	6,223	Cook County	Adel
122	6,223	Jefferson City	Jefferson
124	6,205	Mcintosh County	Darien
125	6,195	Laurens County	Dublin
126	6,186	Haralson County	Buchanan
127	6,185	Charlton County	Folkston
128	6,174	Jenkins County	Millen
129	6,170	Pierce County	Blackshear
130	6,152	Evans County	Claxton
131	6,147	Hall County	Gainesville
132	6,142	Vidalia City	Vidalia
133	6,097	Berrien County	Nashville
134	6,093	Lamar County	Barnesville
134	6,093	Oconee County	Watkinsville
136	6,058	Brantley County	Nahunta
137	5,971	Heard County	Franklin
138	5,962	Catoosa County	Ringgold
139	5,924	Banks County	Homer
140	5,922	Liberty County	Hinesville
141	5,889	Paulding County	Dallas
142	5,874	Pelham City	Pelham
142	5,874	Toombs County	Lyons
144	5,861	Henry County	Mcdonough
145	5,823	Effingham County	Springfield
146	5,790	Murray County	Chatsworth
147	5,737	Columbia County	Appling
148	5,731	Bryan County	Pembroke
149	5,655	Lee County	Leesburg
150	5,629	Camden County	Kingsland
151	5,526	Jones County	Gray
152	5,417	Long County	Ludowici
153	5,250	Pike County	Zebulon
154	n/a	Fort Benning District	Fort Benning

Number of Diploma Recipients

Rank	Number	District Name	City
1	6,116	Gwinnett County	Lawrenceville
2	5,231	Cobb County	Marietta
3	4,191	Dekalb County	Decatur
4	3,360	Fulton County	Atlanta
5	2,270	Atlanta City	Atlanta
6	1,791	Clayton County	Jonesboro
7	1,576	Richmond County	Augusta
8	1,502	Muscogee County	Columbus
9	1,380	Fayette County	Fayetteville
10	1,271	Cherokee County	Canton
11	1,208	Houston County	Perry
12	1,197	Chatham County	Savannah

13	1,157	Henry County	Mcdonough
14	1,051	Columbia County	Appling
15	899	Douglas County	Douglasville
16	869	Hall County	Gainesville
17	831	Bibb County	Macon
18	788	Coweta County	Newnan
19	765	Forsyth County	Cumming
20	722	Rockdale County	Conyers
21	711	Dougherty County	Albany
22	652	Paulding County	Dallas
23	553	Whitfield County	Dalton
24	536	Carroll County	Carrollton
25	516	Glynn County	Brunswick
26	505	Liberty County	Hinesville
27	485	Bartow County	Cartersville
28	484	Troup County	Lagrange
29	468	Lowndes County	Valdosta
30	454	Floyd County	Rome
31	446	Catoosa County	Ringgold
32	445	Camden County	Kingsland
33	426	Effingham County	Springfield
34	408	Bulloch County	Statesboro
35	401	Spalding County	Griffin
36	390	Clarke County	Athens
37	370	Newton County	Covington
38	359	Oconee County	Watkinsville
39	350	Barrow County	Winder
40	344	Walton County	Monroe
41	342	Tift County	Tifton
42	317	Walker County	Lafayette
43	308	Colquitt County	Moultrie
44	307	Laurens County	Dublin
45	305	Valdosta City	Valdosta
46	291	Lee County	Leesburg
47	289	Bryan County	Pembroke
48	276	Polk County	Cedartown
49	270	Decatur County	Bainbridge
49	270	Habersham County	Clarkesville
49	270	Ware County	Waycross
52	268	Marietta City	Marietta
53	266	Thomas County	Thomasville
54	260	Coffee County	Douglas
55	240	Jones County	Gray
56	238	Baldwin County	Milledgeville
56	238	Rome City	Rome
58	236	Jackson County	Jefferson
59	235	Dalton City	Dalton
60	231	Mcduffie County	Thomson
61	228	Thomaston-Upson County	Thomaston
62	221	Harris County	Hamilton
63	218	Murray County	Chatsworth
64	217	Gordon County	Calhoun
65	214	Emanuel County	Swainsboro
65	214	Wayne County	Jesup
67	213	Burke County	Waynesboro
68	211	Hart County	Hartwell
69	207	Washington County	Sandersville
70	195	Monroe County	Forsyth
71	191	Madison County	Danielsville
72	188	Worth County	Sylvester
73	186	Carrollton City	Carrollton
73	186	Gainesville City	Gainesville
75	185	Sumter County	Americus
76	180	Cartersville City	Cartersville
77	178	Appling County	Baxley
78	177	Stephens County	Toccoa
79	176	Elbert County	Elberton
80	173	Grady County	Cairo
81	165	Crisp County	Cordele
82	161	Dodge County	Eastman
82	161	Screven County	Sylvania
84	159	Peach County	Fort Valley
84	159	Thomasville City	Thomasville
86	157	Ben Hill County	Fitzgerald
86	157	Jeff Davis County	Hazlehurst
88	152	White County	Cleveland
89	148	Dublin City	Dublin
90	147	Fannin County	Blue Ridge
90	147	Morgan County	Madison
92	146	Jefferson County	Louisville
93	145	Franklin County	Carnesville
93	145	Union County	Blairsville
95	143	Pike County	Zebulon
96	142	Haralson County	Buchanan
97	141	Lumpkin County	Dahlonega
98	139	Gilmer County	Ellijay
99	138	Meriwether County	Greenville
100	137	Vidalia City	Vidalia
101	134	Dade County	Trenton
102	132	Mitchell County	Camilla
103	131	Cook County	Adel
103	131	Early County	Blakely
105	130	Butts County	Jackson
106	127	Berrien County	Nashville
107	125	Decatur City	Decatur
108	124	Calhoun City	Calhoun
109	123	Pickens County	Jasper
110	121	Brantley County	Nahunta
111	115	Pierce County	Blackshear
111	115	Rabun County	Clayton
113	113	Dawson County	Dawsonville
114	112	Tattnall County	Reidsville
115	108	Marion County	Buena Vista
116	106	Lamar County	Barnesville
117	101	Bleckley County	Cochran
117	101	Putnam County	Eatonton
119	100	Buford City	Buford
119	100	Wilkinson County	Irwinton
121	99	Towns County	Hiawassee
121	99	Wilkes County	Washington
123	95	Brooks County	Quitman
124	94	Banks County	Homer
124	94	Toombs County	Lyons
126	92	Charlton County	Folkston
126	92	Chattooga County	Summerville
128	89	Bremen City	Bremen
128	89	Crawford County	Roberta
130	87	Pulaski County	Hawkinsville
130	87	Seminole County	Donalsonville
132	86	Oglethorpe County	Lexington
133	84	Evans County	Claxton
134	83	Randolph County	Cuthbert
135	82	Greene County	Greensboro
135	82	Hancock County	Sparta
135	82	Turner County	Ashburn
138	80	Telfair County	Mcrae
139	79	Jenkins County	Millen
139	79	Taylor County	Butler
141	77	Irwin County	Ocilla
142	76	Bacon County	Alma
142	76	Macon County	Oglethorpe
144	75	Long County	Ludowici
145	74	Jasper County	Monticello
146	73	Pelham City	Pelham
147	72	Candler County	Metter
148	69	Heard County	Franklin
148	69	Mcintosh County	Darien
150	65	Jefferson City	Jefferson
151	57	Dooly County	Vienna
152	54	Terrell County	Dawson
153	53	Atkinson County	Pearson
154	n/a	Fort Benning District	Fort Benning

High School Drop-out Rate

Rank	Percent	District Name	City
1	21.9	Atlanta City	Atlanta
2	18.3	Spalding County	Griffin
3	17.6	Seminole County	Donalsonville
4	14.6	Macon County	Oglethorpe
5	14.2	Crisp County	Cordele
6	13.3	Clarke County	Athens
6	13.3	Murray County	Chatsworth
8	13.1	Thomaston-Upson County	Thomaston
9	13.0	Brooks County	Quitman
10	12.6	Bibb County	Macon
10	12.6	Mcintosh County	Darien
12	12.1	Dawson County	Dawsonville
13	12.0	Randolph County	Cuthbert
14	11.5	Jackson County	Jefferson
15	11.4	Dougherty County	Albany
16	11.3	Chatham County	Savannah
16	11.3	Taylor County	Butler
18	11.1	Marietta City	Marietta
18	11.1	Valdosta City	Valdosta
20	10.9	Sumter County	Americus
21	10.7	Wayne County	Jesup
22	10.6	Gordon County	Calhoun
23	10.5	Brantley County	Nahunta
23	10.5	Madison County	Danielsville
25	10.4	Burke County	Waynesboro
26	10.3	Emanuel County	Swainsboro
26	10.3	Peach County	Fort Valley
28	10.2	Pierce County	Blackshear
29	10.1	Worth County	Sylvester
30	10.0	Polk County	Cedartown
31	9.9	Dublin City	Dublin
31	9.9	Wilkes County	Washington
33	9.8	Bacon County	Alma
33	9.8	Colquitt County	Moultrie
33	9.8	Marion County	Buena Vista
33	9.8	Meriwether County	Greenville
37	9.7	Ben Hill County	Fitzgerald
38	9.6	Chattooga County	Summerville
38	9.6	Coffee County	Douglas
40	9.5	Haralson County	Buchanan
40	9.5	Long County	Ludowici
42	9.4	Hart County	Hartwell
42	9.4	Walker County	Lafayette
44	9.3	Bartow County	Cartersville
45	9.2	Rome City	Rome
46	9.1	Clayton County	Jonesboro
46	9.1	Telfair County	Mcrae
46	9.1	Ware County	Waycross
49	9.0	Crawford County	Roberta
49	9.0	Glynn County	Brunswick
49	9.0	Irwin County	Ocilla
49	9.0	Rabun County	Clayton
53	8.9	Carroll County	Carrollton
54	8.8	Grady County	Cairo
55	8.7	Catoosa County	Ringgold
55	8.7	Jones County	Gray
57	8.6	Mcduffie County	Thomson
57	8.6	Terrell County	Dawson
57	8.6	Tift County	Tifton
60	8.5	Atkinson County	Pearson
60	8.5	Candler County	Metter
60	8.5	Pike County	Zebulon
63	8.4	Pelham City	Pelham
63	8.4	Screven County	Sylvania
65	8.2	Greene County	Greensboro
65	8.2	Thomasville City	Thomasville
67	8.0	Jeff Davis County	Hazlehurst
67	8.0	Mitchell County	Camilla
69	7.9	Toombs County	Lyons
69	7.9	Washington County	Sandersville
71	7.7	Banks County	Homer
71	7.7	Effingham County	Springfield
71	7.7	Lamar County	Barnesville
74	7.6	Paulding County	Dallas
74	7.6	Vidalia City	Vidalia
76	7.5	Gilmer County	Ellijay
76	7.5	Harris County	Hamilton
76	7.5	Heard County	Franklin
79	7.4	Dekalb County	Decatur
80	7.3	Barrow County	Winder
80	7.3	Wilkinson County	Irwinton
82	7.2	Monroe County	Forsyth
83	7.1	Elbert County	Elberton
84	7.0	Butts County	Jackson
84	7.0	Camden County	Kingsland
84	7.0	Dodge County	Eastman
84	7.0	Franklin County	Carnesville
88	6.9	Calhoun City	Calhoun
88	6.9	Dade County	Trenton
88	6.9	Turner County	Ashburn
88	6.9	Whitfield County	Dalton
92	6.8	Cook County	Adel
92	6.8	Muscogee County	Columbus
92	6.8	Pickens County	Jasper
95	6.7	Dooly County	Vienna
95	6.7	Pulaski County	Hawkinsville
95	6.7	Towns County	Hiawassee
98	6.6	Hancock County	Sparta
98	6.6	Troup County	Lagrange
98	6.6	Walton County	Monroe
101	6.5	Bleckley County	Cochran
101	6.5	Gainesville City	Gainesville
101	6.5	Jasper County	Monticello
101	6.5	Tattnall County	Reidsville
105	6.4	Bryan County	Pembroke
105	6.4	Decatur County	Bainbridge
105	6.4	Oglethorpe County	Lexington
108	6.3	Laurens County	Dublin
108	6.3	Lowndes County	Valdosta
108	6.3	Stephens County	Toccoa
111	6.2	Bulloch County	Statesboro
112	6.1	Hall County	Gainesville
112	6.1	Richmond County	Augusta
114	6.0	Berrien County	Nashville
114	6.0	Charlton County	Folkston
116	5.9	Houston County	Perry
116	5.9	Newton County	Covington
118	5.7	Appling County	Baxley
118	5.7	Fannin County	Blue Ridge
120	5.5	Lumpkin County	Dahlonega
121	5.3	Baldwin County	Milledgeville
121	5.3	Douglas County	Douglasville
121	5.3	Habersham County	Clarkesville
124	5.2	Evans County	Claxton
124	5.2	Forsyth County	Cumming
126	5.1	Columbia County	Appling
126	5.1	Putnam County	Eatonton
128	5.0	Cherokee County	Canton
129	4.9	Fulton County	Atlanta
129	4.9	Jefferson County	Louisville
131	4.8	Dalton City	Dalton
132	4.7	Buford City	Buford

132	4.7	Henry County	Mcdonough
132	4.7	Liberty County	Hinesville
132	4.7	Morgan County	Madison
136	4.6	Decatur City	Decatur
137	4.0	Jenkins County	Millen
138	3.8	Cartersville City	Cartersville
138	3.8	Cobb County	Marietta
138	3.8	Rockdale County	Conyers
141	3.5	Carrollton City	Carrollton
141	3.5	Coweta County	Newnan
141	3.5	Floyd County	Rome
141	3.5	Jefferson City	Jefferson
145	3.1	White County	Cleveland
146	2.8	Bremen City	Bremen
146	2.8	Early County	Blakely
146	2.8	Lee County	Leesburg
149	2.6	Oconee County	Watkinsville
150	2.5	Union County	Blairsville
151	2.1	Fayette County	Fayetteville
152	1.9	Thomas County	Thomasville
153	1.5	Gwinnett County	Lawrenceville
154	n/a	Fort Benning District	Fort Benning

Hawaii

Hawaii Public School Educational Profile

Category	Value	Category	Value
Schools *(2002-2003)*	283	**Diploma Recipients** *(2002-2003)*	10,452
Instructional Level		White, Non-Hispanic	2,013
Primary	183	Black, Non-Hispanic	167
Middle	37	Asian/Pacific Islander	7,771
High	43	American Indian/Alaskan Native	34
Other Level	20	Hispanic	467
Curriculum		**High School Drop-out Rate** (%) *(2000-2001)*	5.7
Regular	279	White, Non-Hispanic	6.3
Special Education	3	Black, Non-Hispanic	7.1
Vocational	0	Asian/Pacific Islander	5.5
Alternative	1	American Indian/Alaskan Native	9.3
Type		Hispanic	6.3
Magnet	0	**Staff** *(2002-2003)*	20,054.4
Charter	25	Teachers	10,973.4
Title I Eligible	143	Average Salary ($)	42,768
School-wide Title I	135	Librarians/Media Specialists	290.5
Students *(2002-2003)*	183,829	Guidance Counselors	648.5
Gender (%)		**Ratios** *(2002-2003)*	
Male	52.0	Student/Teacher Ratio	16.8 to 1
Female	48.0	Student/Librarian Ratio	632.8 to 1
Race/Ethnicity (%)		Student/Counselor Ratio	283.5 to 1
White, Non-Hispanic	20.4	**Current Spending** *($ per student in FY 2001)*	7,306
Black, Non-Hispanic	2.4	Instruction	4,417
Asian/Pacific Islander	72.2	Support Services	2,481
American Indian/Alaskan Native	0.5	**College Entrance Exam Scores** *(2003)*	
Hispanic	4.6	Scholastic Aptitude Test (SAT)	
Classification (%)		Participation Rate (%)	54
Individual Education Program (IEP)	12.4	Mean SAT I Verbal Score	486
Migrant	0.8	Mean SAT I Math Score	516
English Language Learner (ELL)	7.0	American College Testing Program (ACT)	
Eligible for Free Lunch Program	32.5	Participation Rate (%)	16
Eligible for Reduced-Price Lunch Program	11.3	Average Composite Score	21.8

Note: *For an explanation of data, please refer to the User's Guide in the front of the book; n/a indicates data not available*

Hawaii NAEP 2003 Test Scores

Reading			Mathematics		
Grade/Category	**Value**	**Rank**	**Grade/Category**	**Value**	**Rank**
4th Grade			**4th Grade**		
Average Proficiency	208.3 (1.4)	44/51	Average Proficiency	226.8 (1.0)	46/51
Proficiency by Gender/Race/Ethnicity			Proficiency by Gender/Race/Ethnicity		
Male	201.8 (1.6)	48/51	Male	227.4 (1.1)	46/51
Female	215.1 (1.4)	43/51	Female	226.3 (1.1)	45/51
White, Non-Hispanic	221.5 (2.2)	44/51	White, Non-Hispanic	237.5 (1.3)	42/51
Black, Non-Hispanic	211.3 (3.0)	2/42	Black, Non-Hispanic	221.3 (2.9)	10/42
Asian, Non-Hispanic	203.8 (4.7)	23/41	Asian, Non-Hispanic	219.0 (3.0)	29/43
American Indian, Non-Hispanic	205.0 (1.6)	24/25	American Indian, Non-Hispanic	224.6 (1.1)	25/26
Hispanic	n/a	n/a	Hispanic	n/a	n/a
Proficiency by Class Size			Proficiency by Class Size		
Less than 16 Students	*186.4 (9.4)*	40/45	Less than 16 Students	*203.1 (8.2)*	45/47
16 to 18 Students	n/a	n/a	16 to 18 Students	n/a	n/a
19 to 20 Students	*213.1 (4.4)*	37/50	19 to 20 Students	*223.2 (4.3)*	46/50
21 to 25 Students	208.4 (2.1)	45/51	21 to 25 Students	226.7 (1.6)	46/51
Greater than 25 Students	210.5 (2.1)	39/49	Greater than 25 Students	229.3 (1.5)	37/49
Percent Attaining Achievement Levels			Percent Attaining Achievement Levels		
Below Basic	46.5 (1.5)	8/51	Below Basic	31.6 (1.4)	7/51
Basic or Above	53.5 (1.5)	44/51	Basic or Above	68.4 (1.4)	45/51
Proficient or Above	21.3 (1.3)	45/51	Proficient or Above	23.2 (1.2)	43/51
Advanced or Above	4.4 (0.5)	46/51	Advanced or Above	1.7 (0.3)	42/51
8th Grade			**8th Grade**		
Average Proficiency	251.3 (0.9)	49/51	Average Proficiency	265.7 (0.8)	47/51
Proficiency by Gender/Race/Ethnicity			Proficiency by Gender/Race/Ethnicity		
Male	244.6 (1.3)	50/51	Male	265.4 (1.2)	46/51
Female	258.3 (1.2)	46/51	Female	266.0 (1.0)	46/51
White, Non-Hispanic	259.2 (2.0)	50/50	White, Non-Hispanic	272.8 (2.1)	49/50
Black, Non-Hispanic	n/a	n/a	Black, Non-Hispanic	n/a	n/a
Asian, Non-Hispanic	248.8 (7.6)	13/37	Asian, Non-Hispanic	263.3 (4.5)	7/37
American Indian, Non-Hispanic	249.5 (0.9)	23/23	American Indian, Non-Hispanic	264.9 (0.9)	23/23
Hispanic	n/a	n/a	Hispanic	n/a	n/a
Proficiency by Parents Highest Level of Ed.			Proficiency by Parents Highest Level of Ed.		
Did Not Finish High School	236.7 (4.8)	49/50	Did Not Finish High School	254.7 (2.8)	32/50
Graduated High School	243.8 (2.0)	48/50	Graduated High School	256.0 (1.3)	45/50
Some Education After High School	255.9 (1.7)	49/50	Some Education After High School	270.1 (1.5)	46/50
Graduated College	260.8 (1.2)	47/50	Graduated College	273.0 (1.3)	46/50
Percent Attaining Achievement Levels			Percent Attaining Achievement Levels		
Below Basic	39.0 (1.2)	2/51	Below Basic	44.3 (1.0)	5/51
Basic or Above	61.0 (1.2)	50/51	Basic or Above	55.7 (1.0)	46/51
Proficient or Above	21.6 (1.0)	47/51	Proficient or Above	16.8 (1.0)	47/51
Advanced or Above	1.9 (0.4)	38/51	Advanced or Above	2.4 (0.4)	43/51

Note: *For an explanation of data, please refer to the User's Guide in the front of the book; values in italics indicate that the nature of the sample does not allow accurate determination of the variability of the statistic; n/a indicates data not available*

Honolulu County

Hawaii Department of Education

1390 Miller St • Honolulu, HI 96813
Mailing Address: PO Box 2360 • Honolulu, HI 96804-2360
(808) 837-8012 • http://www.k12.hi.us/
Grade Span: PK-12; **Agency Type:** 1
Schools: 284
183 Primary; 37 Middle; 43 High; 20 Other Level
279 Regular; 3 Special Education; 0 Vocational; 1 Alternative
0 Magnet; 25 Charter; 143 Title I Eligible; 135 School-wide Title I
Students: 183,829 (52.0% male; 48.0% female)
Individual Education Program: 22,814 (12.4%);
English Language Learner: 12,853 (7.0%); Migrant: 1,520 (0.8%)
Eligible for Free Lunch Program: 59,796 (32.5%)
Eligible for Reduced-Price Lunch Program: 20,834 (11.3%)
Teachers: 10,973.4 (16.8 to 1)
Librarians/Media Specialists: 290.5 (632.8 to 1)
Guidance Counselors: 648.5 (283.5 to 1)
Current Spending: ($ per student per year):
Total: $6,599; Instruction: $3,973; Support Services: $2,236
Enrollment, Drop-out Rates and Diploma Recipients by Race/Ethnicity

Category	Total	White	Black	Asian	AIAN	Hisp.
Enrollment (%)	100.0	20.4	2.4	72.2	0.5	4.6
Drop-out Rate (%)	5.7	6.3	7.1	5.5	9.3	6.3
H.S. Diplomas (#)	10,452	2,013	167	7,771	34	467

Number of Schools

Rank	Number	District Name	City
1	284	Hawaii Department of Education	Honolulu

Number of Teachers

Rank	Number	District Name	City
1	10,973	Hawaii Department of Education	Honolulu

Number of Students

Rank	Number	District Name	City
1	183,829	Hawaii Department of Education	Honolulu

Male Students

Rank	Percent	District Name	City
1	52.0	Hawaii Department of Education	Honolulu

Female Students

Rank	Percent	District Name	City
1	48.0	Hawaii Department of Education	Honolulu

Individual Education Program Students

Rank	Percent	District Name	City
1	12.4	Hawaii Department of Education	Honolulu

English Language Learner Students

Rank	Percent	District Name	City
1	7.0	Hawaii Department of Education	Honolulu

Migrant Students

Rank	Percent	District Name	City
1	0.8	Hawaii Department of Education	Honolulu

Students Eligible for Free Lunch

Rank	Percent	District Name	City
1	32.5	Hawaii Department of Education	Honolulu

Students Eligible for Reduced-Price Lunch

Rank	Percent	District Name	City
1	11.3	Hawaii Department of Education	Honolulu

Student/Teacher Ratio

Rank	Ratio	District Name	City
1	16.8	Hawaii Department of Education	Honolulu

Student/Librarian Ratio

Rank	Ratio	District Name	City
1	632.8	Hawaii Department of Education	Honolulu

Student/Counselor Ratio

Rank	Ratio	District Name	City
1	283.5	Hawaii Department of Education	Honolulu

Current Spending per Student in FY2001

Rank	Dollars	District Name	City
1	6,599	Hawaii Department of Education	Honolulu

Number of Diploma Recipients

Rank	Number	District Name	City
1	10,452	Hawaii Department of Education	Honolulu

High School Drop-out Rate

Rank	Percent	District Name	City
1	5.7	Hawaii Department of Education	Honolulu

Idaho

Idaho Public School Educational Profile

Category	Value	Category	Value
Schools *(2002-2003)*	690	**Diploma Recipients** *(2002-2003)*	15,874
Instructional Level		White, Non-Hispanic	14,296
Primary	356	Black, Non-Hispanic	76
Middle	107	Asian/Pacific Islander	248
High	186	American Indian/Alaskan Native	191
Other Level	41	Hispanic	1,063
Curriculum		**High School Drop-out Rate** (%) *(2000-2001)*	5.6
Regular	599	White, Non-Hispanic	n/a
Special Education	11	Black, Non-Hispanic	n/a
Vocational	10	Asian/Pacific Islander	n/a
Alternative	70	American Indian/Alaskan Native	n/a
Type		Hispanic	n/a
Magnet	0	**Staff** *(2002-2003)*	24,896.3
Charter	16	Teachers	13,894.6
Title I Eligible	481	Average Salary ($)	39,784
School-wide Title I	108	Librarians/Media Specialists	176.4
Students *(2002-2003)*	248,604	Guidance Counselors	591.2
Gender (%)		**Ratios** *(2002-2003)*	
Male	51.8	Student/Teacher Ratio	17.9 to 1
Female	48.2	Student/Librarian Ratio	1,409.3 to 1
Race/Ethnicity (%)		Student/Counselor Ratio	420.5 to 1
White, Non-Hispanic	85.8	**Current Spending** *($ per student in FY 2001)*	6,011
Black, Non-Hispanic	0.8	Instruction	3,672
Asian/Pacific Islander	1.2	Support Services	2,079
American Indian/Alaskan Native	1.2	**College Entrance Exam Scores** *(2003)*	
Hispanic	10.9	Scholastic Aptitude Test (SAT)	
Classification (%)		Participation Rate (%)	18
Individual Education Program (IEP)	11.6	Mean SAT I Verbal Score	540
Migrant	3.4	Mean SAT I Math Score	540
English Language Learner (ELL)	7.5	American College Testing Program (ACT)	
Eligible for Free Lunch Program	26.9	Participation Rate (%)	60
Eligible for Reduced-Price Lunch Program	9.5	Average Composite Score	21.2

Note: *For an explanation of data, please refer to the User's Guide in the front of the book; n/a indicates data not available*

Idaho NAEP 2003 Test Scores

Reading			Mathematics		
Grade/Category	**Value**	**Rank**	**Grade/Category**	**Value**	**Rank**
4th Grade			**4th Grade**		
Average Proficiency	218.3 (1.0)	31/51	Average Proficiency	234.9 (0.7)	29/51
Proficiency by Gender/Race/Ethnicity			Proficiency by Gender/Race/Ethnicity		
Male	215.5 (1.4)	26/51	Male	236.6 (0.8)	28/51
Female	221.1 (1.2)	33/51	Female	233.2 (0.9)	30/51
White, Non-Hispanic	221.6 (0.9)	42/51	White, Non-Hispanic	237.9 (0.6)	41/51
Black, Non-Hispanic	n/a	n/a	Black, Non-Hispanic	n/a	n/a
Asian, Non-Hispanic	198.6 (2.1)	30/41	Asian, Non-Hispanic	217.2 (1.6)	34/43
American Indian, Non-Hispanic	n/a	n/a	American Indian, Non-Hispanic	n/a	n/a
Hispanic	n/a	n/a	Hispanic	n/a	n/a
Proficiency by Class Size			Proficiency by Class Size		
Less than 16 Students	*208.0 (9.2)*	15/45	Less than 16 Students	*220.9 (6.4)*	30/47
16 to 18 Students	*213.5 (5.8)*	26/48	16 to 18 Students	*241.0 (3.6)*	6/48
19 to 20 Students	*214.9 (6.8)*	32/50	19 to 20 Students	*233.2 (2.7)*	30/50
21 to 25 Students	219.5 (1.5)	31/51	21 to 25 Students	235.9 (1.2)	32/51
Greater than 25 Students	218.2 (1.7)	29/49	Greater than 25 Students	234.8 (1.1)	28/49
Percent Attaining Achievement Levels			Percent Attaining Achievement Levels		
Below Basic	35.5 (1.4)	24/51	Below Basic	20.4 (1.0)	30/51
Basic or Above	64.5 (1.4)	28/51	Basic or Above	79.6 (1.0)	22/51
Proficient or Above	30.1 (1.2)	33/51	Proficient or Above	30.6 (1.1)	33/51
Advanced or Above	6.1 (0.5)	35/51	Advanced or Above	2.3 (0.4)	39/51
8th Grade			**8th Grade**		
Average Proficiency	264.4 (0.9)	26/51	Average Proficiency	279.9 (0.9)	24/51
Proficiency by Gender/Race/Ethnicity			Proficiency by Gender/Race/Ethnicity		
Male	258.4 (1.2)	29/51	Male	280.5 (1.1)	25/51
Female	270.6 (1.0)	22/51	Female	279.3 (1.1)	24/51
White, Non-Hispanic	267.2 (0.9)	39/50	White, Non-Hispanic	283.8 (0.8)	35/50
Black, Non-Hispanic	n/a	n/a	Black, Non-Hispanic	n/a	n/a
Asian, Non-Hispanic	242.5 (2.8)	29/37	Asian, Non-Hispanic	250.9 (2.8)	31/37
American Indian, Non-Hispanic	n/a	n/a	American Indian, Non-Hispanic	n/a	n/a
Hispanic	n/a	n/a	Hispanic	n/a	n/a
Proficiency by Parents Highest Level of Ed.			Proficiency by Parents Highest Level of Ed.		
Did Not Finish High School	245.3 (2.6)	30/50	Did Not Finish High School	260.0 (3.1)	17/50
Graduated High School	255.9 (1.9)	24/50	Graduated High School	269.1 (1.7)	27/50
Some Education After High School	271.8 (1.7)	5/50	Some Education After High School	282.6 (1.6)	16/50
Graduated College	273.5 (1.3)	24/50	Graduated College	290.6 (0.9)	23/50
Percent Attaining Achievement Levels			Percent Attaining Achievement Levels		
Below Basic	23.5 (1.3)	28/51	Below Basic	27.3 (1.2)	34/51
Basic or Above	76.5 (1.3)	24/51	Basic or Above	72.7 (1.2)	18/51
Proficient or Above	32.3 (1.4)	27/51	Proficient or Above	28.3 (1.0)	29/51
Advanced or Above	2.4 (0.5)	30/51	Advanced or Above	4.4 (0.5)	30/51

Note: *For an explanation of data, please refer to the User's Guide in the front of the book; values in italics indicate that the nature of the sample does not allow accurate determination of the variability of the statistic; n/a indicates data not available*

Ada County

Boise Independent District

1207 W Fort St • Boise, ID 83702-5399
Mailing Address: 8169 W Victory Rd • Boise, ID 83709
(208) 338-3400 • http://www.sd01.k12.id.us/
Grade Span: PK-12; **Agency Type:** 1
Schools: 55
35 Primary; 7 Middle; 9 High; 3 Other Level
48 Regular; 0 Special Education; 1 Vocational; 5 Alternative
0 Magnet; 3 Charter; 28 Title I Eligible; 15 School-wide Title I
Students: 26,266 (51.5% male; 48.5% female)
Individual Education Program: 3,008 (11.5%);
English Language Learner: 1,251 (4.8%); Migrant: 0 (0.0%)
Eligible for Free Lunch Program: 5,950 (22.7%)
Eligible for Reduced-Price Lunch Program: 1,984 (7.6%)
Teachers: 1,491.0 (17.6 to 1)
Librarians/Media Specialists: 12.0 (2,188.8 to 1)
Guidance Counselors: 80.6 (325.9 to 1)
Current Spending: ($ per student per year):
Total: $6,681; Instruction: $4,218; Support Services: $2,211
Enrollment, Drop-out Rates and Diploma Recipients by Race/Ethnicity

Category	Total	White	Black	Asian	AIAN	Hisp.
Enrollment (%)	100.0	88.7	1.7	3.0	0.5	6.2
Drop-out Rate (%)	9.0	n/a	n/a	n/a	n/a	n/a
H.S. Diplomas (#)	1,737	1,600	17	36	28	56

Kuna Joint District

610 N School Ave • Kuna, ID 83634-1807
Mailing Address: 1450 Boise St • Kuna, ID 83634-1807
(208) 922-1000 • http://www.kunaschools.org/
Grade Span: PK-12; **Agency Type:** 1
Schools: 7
4 Primary; 1 Middle; 2 High; 0 Other Level
6 Regular; 0 Special Education; 0 Vocational; 1 Alternative
0 Magnet; 0 Charter; 5 Title I Eligible; 0 School-wide Title I
Students: 3,321 (51.0% male; 49.0% female)
Individual Education Program: 335 (10.1%);
English Language Learner: 54 (1.6%); Migrant: 25 (0.8%)
Eligible for Free Lunch Program: 480 (14.5%)
Eligible for Reduced-Price Lunch Program: 305 (9.2%)
Teachers: 166.7 (19.9 to 1)
Librarians/Media Specialists: 2.0 (1,660.5 to 1)
Guidance Counselors: 6.2 (535.6 to 1)
Current Spending: ($ per student per year):
Total: $4,686; Instruction: $3,009; Support Services: $1,498
Enrollment, Drop-out Rates and Diploma Recipients by Race/Ethnicity

Category	Total	White	Black	Asian	AIAN	Hisp.
Enrollment (%)	100.0	93.7	0.6	0.6	0.2	4.9
Drop-out Rate (%)	6.4	n/a	n/a	n/a	n/a	n/a
H.S. Diplomas (#)	186	172	0	2	4	8

Meridian Joint District

911 Meridian Rd • Meridian, ID 83642-2241
(208) 888-6701 • http://www.meridianschools.org/
Grade Span: PK-12; **Agency Type:** 1
Schools: 40
24 Primary; 6 Middle; 7 High; 0 Other Level
33 Regular; 0 Special Education; 1 Vocational; 3 Alternative
0 Magnet; 2 Charter; 12 Title I Eligible; 0 School-wide Title I
Students: 26,113 (51.8% male; 48.2% female)
Individual Education Program: 2,754 (10.5%);
English Language Learner: 431 (1.7%); Migrant: 0 (0.0%)
Eligible for Free Lunch Program: 3,036 (11.6%)
Eligible for Reduced-Price Lunch Program: 1,408 (5.4%)
Teachers: 1,312.2 (19.9 to 1)
Librarians/Media Specialists: 7.8 (3,347.8 to 1)
Guidance Counselors: 64.8 (403.0 to 1)
Current Spending: ($ per student per year):
Total: $4,856; Instruction: $3,012; Support Services: $1,632
Enrollment, Drop-out Rates and Diploma Recipients by Race/Ethnicity

Category	Total	White	Black	Asian	AIAN	Hisp.
Enrollment (%)	100.0	92.4	1.4	2.2	0.2	3.8
Drop-out Rate (%)	5.0	n/a	n/a	n/a	n/a	n/a
H.S. Diplomas (#)	1,498	1,395	10	40	10	43

Bannock County

Pocatello District

3115 Pole Line Rd • Pocatello, ID 83204-6119
(208) 232-3563 • http://www.d25.k12.id.us/
Grade Span: PK-12; **Agency Type:** 1
Schools: 30
18 Primary; 4 Middle; 6 High; 2 Other Level
23 Regular; 1 Special Education; 1 Vocational; 5 Alternative
0 Magnet; 1 Charter; 17 Title I Eligible; 2 School-wide Title I
Students: 11,949 (52.2% male; 47.8% female)
Individual Education Program: 1,557 (13.0%);
English Language Learner: 59 (0.5%); Migrant: 0 (0.0%)
Eligible for Free Lunch Program: 3,080 (25.8%)
Eligible for Reduced-Price Lunch Program: 1,030 (8.6%)
Teachers: 621.6 (19.2 to 1)
Librarians/Media Specialists: 13.0 (919.2 to 1)
Guidance Counselors: 28.3 (422.2 to 1)
Current Spending: ($ per student per year):
Total: $5,451; Instruction: $3,361; Support Services: $1,831
Enrollment, Drop-out Rates and Diploma Recipients by Race/Ethnicity

Category	Total	White	Black	Asian	AIAN	Hisp.
Enrollment (%)	100.0	86.5	1.0	1.6	4.6	6.3
Drop-out Rate (%)	5.0	n/a	n/a	n/a	n/a	n/a
H.S. Diplomas (#)	843	771	6	15	17	34

Bingham County

Blackfoot District

270 E Bridge St • Blackfoot, ID 83221-2865
(208) 785-8800 • http://www.d55.k12.id.us/
Grade Span: PK-12; **Agency Type:** 1
Schools: 15
9 Primary; 3 Middle; 2 High; 1 Other Level
11 Regular; 2 Special Education; 0 Vocational; 2 Alternative
0 Magnet; 1 Charter; 12 Title I Eligible; 6 School-wide Title I
Students: 4,139 (50.6% male; 49.4% female)
Individual Education Program: 517 (12.5%);
English Language Learner: 890 (21.5%); Migrant: 317 (7.7%)
Eligible for Free Lunch Program: 1,531 (37.0%)
Eligible for Reduced-Price Lunch Program: 435 (10.5%)
Teachers: 227.2 (18.2 to 1)
Librarians/Media Specialists: 1.3 (3,183.8 to 1)
Guidance Counselors: 7.6 (544.6 to 1)
Current Spending: ($ per student per year):
Total: $5,801; Instruction: $3,474; Support Services: $2,076
Enrollment, Drop-out Rates and Diploma Recipients by Race/Ethnicity

Category	Total	White	Black	Asian	AIAN	Hisp.
Enrollment (%)	100.0	69.9	0.4	1.1	12.0	16.5
Drop-out Rate (%)	4.7	n/a	n/a	n/a	n/a	n/a
H.S. Diplomas (#)	266	218	0	4	15	29

Shelley Joint District

545 Seminary Ave • Shelley, ID 83274-1461
(208) 357-3411 • http://sd60.k12.id.us/
Grade Span: PK-12; **Agency Type:** 1
Schools: 5
2 Primary; 1 Middle; 1 High; 0 Other Level
4 Regular; 0 Special Education; 0 Vocational; 0 Alternative
0 Magnet; 0 Charter; 3 Title I Eligible; 0 School-wide Title I
Students: 1,990 (53.7% male; 46.3% female)
Individual Education Program: 257 (12.9%);
English Language Learner: 166 (8.3%); Migrant: 45 (2.3%)
Eligible for Free Lunch Program: 451 (22.7%)
Eligible for Reduced-Price Lunch Program: 181 (9.1%)
Teachers: 99.0 (20.1 to 1)
Librarians/Media Specialists: 1.0 (1,990.0 to 1)
Guidance Counselors: 4.3 (462.8 to 1)
Current Spending: ($ per student per year):
Total: $4,871; Instruction: $3,277; Support Services: $1,365
Enrollment, Drop-out Rates and Diploma Recipients by Race/Ethnicity

Category	Total	White	Black	Asian	AIAN	Hisp.
Enrollment (%)	100.0	88.9	0.3	0.2	0.2	10.5
Drop-out Rate (%)	1.3	n/a	n/a	n/a	n/a	n/a
H.S. Diplomas (#)	160	142	2	1	1	14

Snake River District

103 S 900 W • Blackfoot, ID 83221-6065
(208) 684-3001 • http://srnt.sd52.k12.id.us/
Grade Span: PK-12; **Agency Type:** 1
Schools: 7
3 Primary; 2 Middle; 2 High; 0 Other Level
7 Regular; 0 Special Education; 0 Vocational; 0 Alternative
0 Magnet; 1 Charter; 5 Title I Eligible; 0 School-wide Title I
Students: 2,079 (50.8% male; 49.2% female)
Individual Education Program: 191 (9.2%);
English Language Learner: 326 (15.7%); Migrant: 108 (5.2%)
Eligible for Free Lunch Program: 549 (26.4%)
Eligible for Reduced-Price Lunch Program: 282 (13.6%)
Teachers: 105.9 (19.6 to 1)
Librarians/Media Specialists: 1.0 (2,079.0 to 1)
Guidance Counselors: 4.6 (452.0 to 1)
Current Spending: ($ per student per year):
Total: $5,268; Instruction: $3,171; Support Services: $1,826

Enrollment, Drop-out Rates and Diploma Recipients by Race/Ethnicity

Category	Total	White	Black	Asian	AIAN	Hisp.
Enrollment (%)	100.0	84.1	0.3	0.7	0.9	13.9
Drop-out Rate (%)	1.2	n/a	n/a	n/a	n/a	n/a
H.S. Diplomas (#)	173	153	1	3	1	15

Blaine County

Blaine County District

118 W Bullion St • Hailey, ID 83333
(208) 788-2296 • http://www.bcsd.k12.id.us/
Grade Span: PK-12; **Agency Type:** 1
Schools: 8
4 Primary; 1 Middle; 2 High; 1 Other Level
6 Regular; 1 Special Education; 0 Vocational; 1 Alternative
0 Magnet; 0 Charter; 0 Title I Eligible; 0 School-wide Title I
Students: 3,103 (52.0% male; 48.0% female)
Individual Education Program: 367 (11.8%);
English Language Learner: 366 (11.8%); Migrant: 10 (0.3%)
Eligible for Free Lunch Program: 470 (15.1%)
Eligible for Reduced-Price Lunch Program: 213 (6.9%)
Teachers: 226.9 (13.7 to 1)
Librarians/Media Specialists: 2.0 (1,551.5 to 1)
Guidance Counselors: 6.5 (477.4 to 1)
Current Spending: ($ per student per year):
Total: $8,033; Instruction: $5,413; Support Services: $2,434
Enrollment, Drop-out Rates and Diploma Recipients by Race/Ethnicity

Category	Total	White	Black	Asian	AIAN	Hisp.
Enrollment (%)	100.0	82.7	0.7	0.9	0.2	15.5
Drop-out Rate (%)	4.2	n/a	n/a	n/a	n/a	n/a
H.S. Diplomas (#)	171	146	1	3	0	21

Bonner County

Lake Pend Oreille District

901 N Triangle Dr • Sandpoint, ID 83864
(208) 263-2184 • http://www.sd84.k12.id.us/production/
Grade Span: PK-12; **Agency Type:** 1
Schools: 13
7 Primary; 2 Middle; 4 High; 0 Other Level
11 Regular; 0 Special Education; 0 Vocational; 2 Alternative
0 Magnet; 1 Charter; 10 Title I Eligible; 2 School-wide Title I
Students: 4,129 (50.2% male; 49.8% female)
Individual Education Program: 505 (12.2%);
English Language Learner: 2 (<0.1%); Migrant: 0 (0.0%)
Eligible for Free Lunch Program: 1,196 (29.0%)
Eligible for Reduced-Price Lunch Program: 541 (13.1%)
Teachers: 241.1 (17.1 to 1)
Librarians/Media Specialists: 3.0 (1,376.3 to 1)
Guidance Counselors: 10.9 (378.8 to 1)
Current Spending: ($ per student per year):
Total: $5,792; Instruction: $3,343; Support Services: $2,197
Enrollment, Drop-out Rates and Diploma Recipients by Race/Ethnicity

Category	Total	White	Black	Asian	AIAN	Hisp.
Enrollment (%)	100.0	96.6	0.6	0.4	0.9	1.6
Drop-out Rate (%)	5.4	n/a	n/a	n/a	n/a	n/a
H.S. Diplomas (#)	277	268	0	3	3	3

West Bonner County District

119 S Main St • Sandpoint, ID 83856
Mailing Address: PO Box 2531 • Priest River, ID 83856
(208) 448-4629 • http://www.sd83.k12.id.us/
Grade Span: PK-12; **Agency Type:** 1
Schools: 6
3 Primary; 1 Middle; 2 High; 0 Other Level
5 Regular; 0 Special Education; 0 Vocational; 1 Alternative
0 Magnet; 0 Charter; 6 Title I Eligible; 1 School-wide Title I
Students: 1,533 (55.3% male; 44.7% female)
Individual Education Program: 201 (13.1%);
English Language Learner: 0 (0.0%); Migrant: 0 (0.0%)
Eligible for Free Lunch Program: 608 (39.7%)
Eligible for Reduced-Price Lunch Program: 227 (14.8%)
Teachers: 89.0 (17.2 to 1)
Librarians/Media Specialists: 1.0 (1,533.0 to 1)
Guidance Counselors: 3.4 (450.9 to 1)
Current Spending: ($ per student per year):
Total: $5,772; Instruction: $3,342; Support Services: $2,119
Enrollment, Drop-out Rates and Diploma Recipients by Race/Ethnicity

Category	Total	White	Black	Asian	AIAN	Hisp.
Enrollment (%)	100.0	94.8	0.1	1.3	3.0	0.8
Drop-out Rate (%)	6.1	n/a	n/a	n/a	n/a	n/a
H.S. Diplomas (#)	87	82	0	1	1	3

Bonneville County

Bonneville Joint District

3497 N Ammon Rd • Idaho Falls, ID 83401
(208) 525-4400 • http://d93.k12.id.us/
Grade Span: PK-12; **Agency Type:** 1
Schools: 16
9 Primary; 2 Middle; 3 High; 2 Other Level
14 Regular; 0 Special Education; 0 Vocational; 2 Alternative
0 Magnet; 1 Charter; 10 Title I Eligible; 0 School-wide Title I
Students: 7,650 (52.3% male; 47.7% female)
Individual Education Program: 832 (10.9%);
English Language Learner: 294 (3.8%); Migrant: 97 (1.3%)
Eligible for Free Lunch Program: 1,587 (20.7%)
Eligible for Reduced-Price Lunch Program: 677 (8.8%)
Teachers: 388.5 (19.7 to 1)
Librarians/Media Specialists: 3.7 (2,067.6 to 1)
Guidance Counselors: 16.7 (458.1 to 1)
Current Spending: ($ per student per year):
Total: $4,921; Instruction: $3,124; Support Services: $1,578
Enrollment, Drop-out Rates and Diploma Recipients by Race/Ethnicity

Category	Total	White	Black	Asian	AIAN	Hisp.
Enrollment (%)	100.0	90.8	0.7	0.7	0.3	7.5
Drop-out Rate (%)	0.8	n/a	n/a	n/a	n/a	n/a
H.S. Diplomas (#)	579	543	0	5	4	27

Idaho Falls District

690 John Adams Pkwy • Idaho Falls, ID 83401-4073
(208) 525-7500 • http://www.d91.k12.id.us/
Grade Span: PK-12; **Agency Type:** 1
Schools: 22
14 Primary; 3 Middle; 5 High; 0 Other Level
19 Regular; 0 Special Education; 1 Vocational; 2 Alternative
0 Magnet; 0 Charter; 12 Title I Eligible; 0 School-wide Title I
Students: 10,514 (51.6% male; 48.4% female)
Individual Education Program: 1,245 (11.8%);
English Language Learner: 601 (5.7%); Migrant: 390 (3.7%)
Eligible for Free Lunch Program: 2,365 (22.5%)
Eligible for Reduced-Price Lunch Program: 601 (5.7%)
Teachers: 537.1 (19.6 to 1)
Librarians/Media Specialists: 4.3 (2,445.1 to 1)
Guidance Counselors: 19.0 (553.4 to 1)
Current Spending: ($ per student per year):
Total: $5,420; Instruction: $3,315; Support Services: $1,890
Enrollment, Drop-out Rates and Diploma Recipients by Race/Ethnicity

Category	Total	White	Black	Asian	AIAN	Hisp.
Enrollment (%)	100.0	87.3	0.9	1.1	0.4	10.2
Drop-out Rate (%)	8.0	n/a	n/a	n/a	n/a	n/a
H.S. Diplomas (#)	737	670	1	17	3	46

Boundary County

Boundary County District

7188 Oak St • Bonners Ferry, ID 83805-8580
Mailing Address: PO Box 899 • Bonners Ferry, ID 83805-8580
(208) 267-3146 • http://www.bcsd101.com/
Grade Span: PK-12; **Agency Type:** 1
Schools: 7
4 Primary; 1 Middle; 2 High; 0 Other Level
6 Regular; 0 Special Education; 0 Vocational; 1 Alternative
0 Magnet; 0 Charter; 6 Title I Eligible; 0 School-wide Title I
Students: 1,648 (52.4% male; 47.6% female)
Individual Education Program: 172 (10.4%);
English Language Learner: 77 (4.7%); Migrant: 0 (0.0%)
Eligible for Free Lunch Program: 501 (30.4%)
Eligible for Reduced-Price Lunch Program: 203 (12.3%)
Teachers: 96.1 (17.1 to 1)
Librarians/Media Specialists: 1.3 (1,267.7 to 1)
Guidance Counselors: 5.1 (323.1 to 1)
Current Spending: ($ per student per year):
Total: $6,122; Instruction: $3,944; Support Services: $1,921
Enrollment, Drop-out Rates and Diploma Recipients by Race/Ethnicity

Category	Total	White	Black	Asian	AIAN	Hisp.
Enrollment (%)	100.0	93.3	0.4	0.6	1.6	4.1
Drop-out Rate (%)	7.6	n/a	n/a	n/a	n/a	n/a
H.S. Diplomas (#)	110	106	0	0	2	2

Butte County

Butte County Joint District

250 S Water • Arco, ID 83213
Mailing Address: PO Box 89 • Arco, ID 83213
(208) 527-8235
Grade Span: PK-12; **Agency Type:** 1
Schools: 6

3 Primary; 1 Middle; 2 High; 0 Other Level
5 Regular; 0 Special Education; 0 Vocational; 1 Alternative
0 Magnet; 1 Charter; 5 Title I Eligible; 4 School-wide Title I
Students: 1,510 (51.3% male; 48.7% female)
Individual Education Program: 102 (6.8%);
English Language Learner: 0 (0.0%); Migrant: 11 (0.7%)
Eligible for Free Lunch Program: 162 (10.7%)
Eligible for Reduced-Price Lunch Program: 79 (5.2%)
Teachers: 48.3 (31.3 to 1)
Librarians/Media Specialists: 1.0 (1,510.0 to 1)
Guidance Counselors: 1.3 (1,161.5 to 1)
Current Spending: ($ per student per year):
Total: $6,533; Instruction: $3,646; Support Services: $2,642
Enrollment, Drop-out Rates and Diploma Recipients by Race/Ethnicity

Category	Total	White	Black	Asian	AIAN	Hisp.
Enrollment (%)	100.0	95.0	0.4	0.2	0.8	3.6
Drop-out Rate (%)	0.0	n/a	n/a	n/a	n/a	n/a
H.S. Diplomas (#)	36	35	0	0	0	1

Canyon County

Caldwell District
1101 Cleveland Blvd • Caldwell, ID 83605-3855
(208) 455-3300 • http://www.sd132.k12.id.us/
Grade Span: PK-12; **Agency Type:** 1
Schools: 10
5 Primary; 1 Middle; 2 High; 2 Other Level
8 Regular; 0 Special Education; 0 Vocational; 2 Alternative
0 Magnet; 0 Charter; 10 Title I Eligible; 2 School-wide Title I
Students: 5,885 (50.9% male; 49.1% female)
Individual Education Program: 681 (11.6%);
English Language Learner: 1,269 (21.6%); Migrant: 457 (7.8%)
Eligible for Free Lunch Program: 2,861 (48.6%)
Eligible for Reduced-Price Lunch Program: 555 (9.4%)
Teachers: 320.3 (18.4 to 1)
Librarians/Media Specialists: 2.7 (2,179.6 to 1)
Guidance Counselors: 12.5 (470.8 to 1)
Current Spending: ($ per student per year):
Total: $5,158; Instruction: $3,138; Support Services: $1,722
Enrollment, Drop-out Rates and Diploma Recipients by Race/Ethnicity

Category	Total	White	Black	Asian	AIAN	Hisp.
Enrollment (%)	100.0	62.0	0.5	0.6	0.3	36.6
Drop-out Rate (%)	5.7	n/a	n/a	n/a	n/a	n/a
H.S. Diplomas (#)	233	157	5	4	1	66

Middleton District
5 S 3rd Ave W • Middleton, ID 83644-5563
(208) 585-3027 • http://www.sd134.k12.id.us/
Grade Span: PK-12; **Agency Type:** 1
Schools: 6
2 Primary; 1 Middle; 2 High; 0 Other Level
4 Regular; 0 Special Education; 0 Vocational; 1 Alternative
0 Magnet; 0 Charter; 3 Title I Eligible; 0 School-wide Title I
Students: 2,368 (51.9% male; 48.1% female)
Individual Education Program: 248 (10.5%);
English Language Learner: 77 (3.3%); Migrant: 21 (0.9%)
Eligible for Free Lunch Program: 639 (27.0%)
Eligible for Reduced-Price Lunch Program: 271 (11.4%)
Teachers: 119.7 (19.8 to 1)
Librarians/Media Specialists: 4.0 (592.0 to 1)
Guidance Counselors: 6.3 (375.9 to 1)
Current Spending: ($ per student per year):
Total: $5,026; Instruction: $3,231; Support Services: $1,557
Enrollment, Drop-out Rates and Diploma Recipients by Race/Ethnicity

Category	Total	White	Black	Asian	AIAN	Hisp.
Enrollment (%)	100.0	89.9	0.4	0.6	0.1	9.0
Drop-out Rate (%)	3.2	n/a	n/a	n/a	n/a	n/a
H.S. Diplomas (#)	143	134	1	0	0	8

Nampa SD
619 S Canyon St • Nampa, ID 83686-6634
(208) 465-2700 • http://www.sd131.k12.id.us/
Grade Span: PK-12; **Agency Type:** 1
Schools: 24
13 Primary; 2 Middle; 7 High; 1 Other Level
18 Regular; 0 Special Education; 1 Vocational; 4 Alternative
0 Magnet; 1 Charter; 14 Title I Eligible; 2 School-wide Title I
Students: 12,715 (50.4% male; 49.6% female)
Individual Education Program: 1,508 (11.9%);
English Language Learner: 2,264 (17.8%); Migrant: 670 (5.3%)
Eligible for Free Lunch Program: 4,293 (33.8%)
Eligible for Reduced-Price Lunch Program: 1,149 (9.0%)
Teachers: 674.8 (18.8 to 1)
Librarians/Media Specialists: 3.2 (3,973.4 to 1)
Guidance Counselors: 22.5 (565.1 to 1)
Current Spending: ($ per student per year):
Total: $4,710; Instruction: $3,026; Support Services: $1,427
Enrollment, Drop-out Rates and Diploma Recipients by Race/Ethnicity

Category	Total	White	Black	Asian	AIAN	Hisp.
Enrollment (%)	100.0	74.4	0.7	1.0	0.3	23.6
Drop-out Rate (%)	12.9	n/a	n/a	n/a	n/a	n/a
H.S. Diplomas (#)	514	400	5	12	2	95

Vallivue SD
5207 S Montana Ave • Caldwell, ID 83605-4477
(208) 454-0445 • http://sd139.k12.id.us/default.htm
Grade Span: PK-12; **Agency Type:** 1
Schools: 6
4 Primary; 1 Middle; 1 High; 0 Other Level
6 Regular; 0 Special Education; 0 Vocational; 0 Alternative
0 Magnet; 0 Charter; 5 Title I Eligible; 2 School-wide Title I
Students: 4,090 (50.8% male; 49.2% female)
Individual Education Program: 504 (12.3%);
English Language Learner: 487 (11.9%); Migrant: 373 (9.1%)
Eligible for Free Lunch Program: 1,302 (31.8%)
Eligible for Reduced-Price Lunch Program: 453 (11.1%)
Teachers: 219.6 (18.6 to 1)
Librarians/Media Specialists: 2.0 (2,045.0 to 1)
Guidance Counselors: 11.0 (371.8 to 1)
Current Spending: ($ per student per year):
Total: $5,737; Instruction: $3,451; Support Services: $2,006
Enrollment, Drop-out Rates and Diploma Recipients by Race/Ethnicity

Category	Total	White	Black	Asian	AIAN	Hisp.
Enrollment (%)	100.0	78.0	0.4	1.1	0.5	19.9
Drop-out Rate (%)	7.7	n/a	n/a	n/a	n/a	n/a
H.S. Diplomas (#)	224	193	0	2	2	27

Cassia County

Cassia County Joint District
237 E 19th St • Burley, ID 83318-2444
(208) 878-6600 • http://www.sd151.k12.id.us/
Grade Span: PK-12; **Agency Type:** 1
Schools: 17
8 Primary; 3 Middle; 6 High; 0 Other Level
15 Regular; 0 Special Education; 1 Vocational; 1 Alternative
0 Magnet; 0 Charter; 14 Title I Eligible; 9 School-wide Title I
Students: 4,996 (52.2% male; 47.8% female)
Individual Education Program: 578 (11.6%);
English Language Learner: 916 (18.3%); Migrant: 648 (13.0%)
Eligible for Free Lunch Program: 1,792 (35.9%)
Eligible for Reduced-Price Lunch Program: 587 (11.7%)
Teachers: 282.8 (17.7 to 1)
Librarians/Media Specialists: 5.5 (908.4 to 1)
Guidance Counselors: 12.3 (406.2 to 1)
Current Spending: ($ per student per year):
Total: $5,268; Instruction: $3,140; Support Services: $1,897
Enrollment, Drop-out Rates and Diploma Recipients by Race/Ethnicity

Category	Total	White	Black	Asian	AIAN	Hisp.
Enrollment (%)	100.0	76.0	0.2	0.5	0.5	22.8
Drop-out Rate (%)	4.0	n/a	n/a	n/a	n/a	n/a
H.S. Diplomas (#)	350	305	0	3	0	42

Elmore County

Mountain Home District
140 N 3rd E • Mountain Home, ID 83647-2731
Mailing Address: PO Box 1390 • Mountain Home, ID 83647-2731
(208) 587-2580 • http://www.mtnhomesd.org/
Grade Span: PK-12; **Agency Type:** 1
Schools: 12
6 Primary; 2 Middle; 3 High; 0 Other Level
10 Regular; 0 Special Education; 0 Vocational; 1 Alternative
0 Magnet; 1 Charter; 8 Title I Eligible; 0 School-wide Title I
Students: 4,487 (53.7% male; 46.3% female)
Individual Education Program: 683 (15.2%);
English Language Learner: 355 (7.9%); Migrant: 168 (3.7%)
Eligible for Free Lunch Program: 931 (20.7%)
Eligible for Reduced-Price Lunch Program: 516 (11.5%)
Teachers: 252.3 (17.8 to 1)
Librarians/Media Specialists: 2.0 (2,243.5 to 1)
Guidance Counselors: 9.0 (498.6 to 1)
Current Spending: ($ per student per year):
Total: $5,234; Instruction: $3,111; Support Services: $1,906
Enrollment, Drop-out Rates and Diploma Recipients by Race/Ethnicity

Category	Total	White	Black	Asian	AIAN	Hisp.
Enrollment (%)	100.0	82.6	3.4	2.5	0.4	11.2
Drop-out Rate (%)	8.9	n/a	n/a	n/a	n/a	n/a
H.S. Diplomas (#)	249	207	7	9	1	25

Franklin County

Preston Joint District

120 E 2nd S St • Preston, ID 83263-1527
(208) 852-0283 • http://www.preston.k12.id.us/district/index.htm
Grade Span: PK-12; **Agency Type:** 1
Schools: 5
2 Primary; 1 Middle; 2 High; 0 Other Level
5 Regular; 0 Special Education; 0 Vocational; 0 Alternative
0 Magnet; 0 Charter; 5 Title I Eligible; 0 School-wide Title I
Students: 2,449 (51.0% male; 49.0% female)
Individual Education Program: 247 (10.1%);
English Language Learner: 105 (4.3%); Migrant: 52 (2.1%)
Eligible for Free Lunch Program: 760 (31.0%)
Eligible for Reduced-Price Lunch Program: 394 (16.1%)
Teachers: 118.1 (20.7 to 1)
Librarians/Media Specialists: 1.2 (2,040.8 to 1)
Guidance Counselors: 3.5 (699.7 to 1)
Current Spending: ($ per student per year):
Total: $4,557; Instruction: $2,918; Support Services: $1,372
Enrollment, Drop-out Rates and Diploma Recipients by Race/Ethnicity

Category	Total	White	Black	Asian	AIAN	Hisp.
Enrollment (%)	100.0	93.1	0.1	0.4	0.5	5.9
Drop-out Rate (%)	1.9	n/a	n/a	n/a	n/a	n/a
H.S. Diplomas (#)	167	161	0	0	0	6

Fremont County

Fremont County Joint District

147 N 2nd W St • Saint Anthony, ID 83445-1422
(208) 624-7542 • http://www.sd215.net/
Grade Span: PK-12; **Agency Type:** 1
Schools: 12
5 Primary; 3 Middle; 4 High; 0 Other Level
8 Regular; 1 Special Education; 0 Vocational; 3 Alternative
0 Magnet; 0 Charter; 7 Title I Eligible; 0 School-wide Title I
Students: 2,369 (53.3% male; 46.7% female)
Individual Education Program: 333 (14.1%);
English Language Learner: 366 (15.4%); Migrant: 315 (13.3%)
Eligible for Free Lunch Program: 707 (29.8%)
Eligible for Reduced-Price Lunch Program: 321 (13.6%)
Teachers: 138.6 (17.1 to 1)
Librarians/Media Specialists: 2.6 (911.2 to 1)
Guidance Counselors: 4.7 (504.0 to 1)
Current Spending: ($ per student per year):
Total: $5,940; Instruction: $3,788; Support Services: $1,890
Enrollment, Drop-out Rates and Diploma Recipients by Race/Ethnicity

Category	Total	White	Black	Asian	AIAN	Hisp.
Enrollment (%)	100.0	84.4	0.6	0.8	0.2	14.1
Drop-out Rate (%)	2.1	n/a	n/a	n/a	n/a	n/a
H.S. Diplomas (#)	165	151	0	1	1	12

Gem County

Emmett Independent District

601 E Third St • Emmett, ID 83617-3111
(208) 365-6301 • http://www.sd221.k12.id.us/
Grade Span: PK-12; **Agency Type:** 1
Schools: 8
4 Primary; 2 Middle; 2 High; 0 Other Level
7 Regular; 0 Special Education; 0 Vocational; 1 Alternative
0 Magnet; 0 Charter; 6 Title I Eligible; 0 School-wide Title I
Students: 2,928 (52.8% male; 47.2% female)
Individual Education Program: 338 (11.5%);
English Language Learner: 145 (5.0%); Migrant: 49 (1.7%)
Eligible for Free Lunch Program: 974 (33.3%)
Eligible for Reduced-Price Lunch Program: 334 (11.4%)
Teachers: 156.5 (18.7 to 1)
Librarians/Media Specialists: 2.7 (1,084.4 to 1)
Guidance Counselors: 6.0 (488.0 to 1)
Current Spending: ($ per student per year):
Total: $4,948; Instruction: $3,409; Support Services: $1,366
Enrollment, Drop-out Rates and Diploma Recipients by Race/Ethnicity

Category	Total	White	Black	Asian	AIAN	Hisp.
Enrollment (%)	100.0	86.6	0.7	1.2	0.4	11.2
Drop-out Rate (%)	3.9	n/a	n/a	n/a	n/a	n/a
H.S. Diplomas (#)	178	169	0	0	0	9

Idaho County

Grangeville Joint District

714 Jefferson Ave • Grangeville, ID 83530-1545
(208) 983-0990 • http://www.jsd241.org/
Grade Span: PK-12; **Agency Type:** 1
Schools: 9
4 Primary; 0 Middle; 3 High; 1 Other Level
8 Regular; 0 Special Education; 0 Vocational; 0 Alternative
0 Magnet; 0 Charter; 7 Title I Eligible; 2 School-wide Title I
Students: 1,520 (51.4% male; 48.6% female)
Individual Education Program: 220 (14.5%);
English Language Learner: 20 (1.3%); Migrant: 0 (0.0%)
Eligible for Free Lunch Program: 549 (36.1%)
Eligible for Reduced-Price Lunch Program: 185 (12.2%)
Teachers: 100.1 (15.2 to 1)
Librarians/Media Specialists: 1.0 (1,520.0 to 1)
Guidance Counselors: 4.7 (323.4 to 1)
Current Spending: ($ per student per year):
Total: $6,535; Instruction: $4,065; Support Services: $2,205
Enrollment, Drop-out Rates and Diploma Recipients by Race/Ethnicity

Category	Total	White	Black	Asian	AIAN	Hisp.
Enrollment (%)	100.0	92.7	0.5	1.6	2.8	2.4
Drop-out Rate (%)	5.1	n/a	n/a	n/a	n/a	n/a
H.S. Diplomas (#)	123	117	0	0	4	2

Jefferson County

Jefferson County Joint District

201 Idaho Ave • Rigby, ID 83442-1413
(208) 745-6693 • http://www.d251.k12.id.us/
Grade Span: PK-12; **Agency Type:** 1
Schools: 9
4 Primary; 1 Middle; 3 High; 1 Other Level
7 Regular; 0 Special Education; 0 Vocational; 2 Alternative
0 Magnet; 0 Charter; 7 Title I Eligible; 2 School-wide Title I
Students: 3,971 (53.0% male; 47.0% female)
Individual Education Program: 381 (9.6%);
English Language Learner: 281 (7.1%); Migrant: 148 (3.7%)
Eligible for Free Lunch Program: 969 (24.4%)
Eligible for Reduced-Price Lunch Program: 387 (9.7%)
Teachers: 201.2 (19.7 to 1)
Librarians/Media Specialists: 1.8 (2,206.1 to 1)
Guidance Counselors: 10.0 (397.1 to 1)
Current Spending: ($ per student per year):
Total: $4,997; Instruction: $3,164; Support Services: $1,600
Enrollment, Drop-out Rates and Diploma Recipients by Race/Ethnicity

Category	Total	White	Black	Asian	AIAN	Hisp.
Enrollment (%)	100.0	87.1	0.4	0.4	0.3	11.8
Drop-out Rate (%)	1.9	n/a	n/a	n/a	n/a	n/a
H.S. Diplomas (#)	263	238	1	0	0	24

Jerome County

Jerome Joint District

107 W 3rd St • Jerome, ID 83338
(208) 324-2392 • http://www.d261.k12.id.us/
Grade Span: PK-12; **Agency Type:** 1
Schools: 7
2 Primary; 2 Middle; 2 High; 1 Other Level
6 Regular; 0 Special Education; 0 Vocational; 1 Alternative
0 Magnet; 0 Charter; 5 Title I Eligible; 3 School-wide Title I
Students: 3,028 (51.5% male; 48.5% female)
Individual Education Program: 326 (10.8%);
English Language Learner: 472 (15.6%); Migrant: 131 (4.3%)
Eligible for Free Lunch Program: 1,177 (38.9%)
Eligible for Reduced-Price Lunch Program: 332 (11.0%)
Teachers: 175.7 (17.2 to 1)
Librarians/Media Specialists: 3.0 (1,009.3 to 1)
Guidance Counselors: 5.3 (571.3 to 1)
Current Spending: ($ per student per year):
Total: $4,900; Instruction: $3,040; Support Services: $1,606
Enrollment, Drop-out Rates and Diploma Recipients by Race/Ethnicity

Category	Total	White	Black	Asian	AIAN	Hisp.
Enrollment (%)	100.0	73.5	0.5	0.3	0.7	25.0
Drop-out Rate (%)	9.7	n/a	n/a	n/a	n/a	n/a
H.S. Diplomas (#)	223	181	1	11	0	30

Kootenai County

Coeur D Alene District

311 N 10th St • Coeur D Alene, ID 83814-4280
(208) 664-8241 • http://www.sd271.k12.id.us/
Grade Span: PK-12; **Agency Type:** 1
Schools: 19
10 Primary; 3 Middle; 4 High; 2 Other Level
16 Regular; 0 Special Education; 1 Vocational; 2 Alternative
0 Magnet; 1 Charter; 11 Title I Eligible; 1 School-wide Title I
Students: 9,499 (52.4% male; 47.6% female)
Individual Education Program: 978 (10.3%);
English Language Learner: 23 (0.2%); Migrant: 0 (0.0%)
Eligible for Free Lunch Program: 2,299 (24.2%)

Eligible for Reduced-Price Lunch Program: 893 (9.4%)
Teachers: 506.4 (18.8 to 1)
Librarians/Media Specialists: 4.4 (2,158.9 to 1)
Guidance Counselors: 23.3 (407.7 to 1)
Current Spending: ($ per student per year):
Total: $5,311; Instruction: $3,250; Support Services: $1,782
Enrollment, Drop-out Rates and Diploma Recipients by Race/Ethnicity

Category	Total	White	Black	Asian	AIAN	Hisp.
Enrollment (%)	100.0	95.4	0.6	0.8	0.5	2.7
Drop-out Rate (%)	6.1	n/a	n/a	n/a	n/a	n/a
H.S. Diplomas (#)	552	527	1	12	2	10

Lakeland District
1564 Washington St • Rathdrum, ID 83858-9043
Mailing Address: PO Box 39 • Rathdrum, ID 83858-9043
(208) 687-0431 • http://www.sd272.k12.id.us/DistIntranet/index.htm
Grade Span: PK-12; **Agency Type:** 1
Schools: 9
5 Primary; 1 Middle; 3 High; 0 Other Level
8 Regular; 0 Special Education; 0 Vocational; 1 Alternative
0 Magnet; 0 Charter; 7 Title I Eligible; 0 School-wide Title I
Students: 4,146 (52.2% male; 47.8% female)
Individual Education Program: 417 (10.1%);
English Language Learner: 0 (0.0%); Migrant: 0 (0.0%)
Eligible for Free Lunch Program: 1,021 (24.6%)
Eligible for Reduced-Price Lunch Program: 466 (11.2%)
Teachers: 219.3 (18.9 to 1)
Librarians/Media Specialists: 4.0 (1,036.5 to 1)
Guidance Counselors: 11.0 (376.9 to 1)
Current Spending: ($ per student per year):
Total: $4,717; Instruction: $3,077; Support Services: $1,419
Enrollment, Drop-out Rates and Diploma Recipients by Race/Ethnicity

Category	Total	White	Black	Asian	AIAN	Hisp.
Enrollment (%)	100.0	96.4	0.3	0.7	0.6	2.1
Drop-out Rate (%)	6.3	n/a	n/a	n/a	n/a	n/a
H.S. Diplomas (#)	250	238	0	5	2	5

Post Falls District
206 W Mullan Ave • Post Falls, ID 83877-7255
Mailing Address: PO Box 40 • Post Falls, ID 83877-7255
(208) 773-1658 • http://www.pfsd.com/index.html
Grade Span: PK-12; **Agency Type:** 1
Schools: 8
5 Primary; 1 Middle; 2 High; 0 Other Level
7 Regular; 0 Special Education; 0 Vocational; 1 Alternative
0 Magnet; 0 Charter; 7 Title I Eligible; 0 School-wide Title I
Students: 4,841 (51.4% male; 48.6% female)
Individual Education Program: 526 (10.9%);
English Language Learner: 7 (0.1%); Migrant: 0 (0.0%)
Eligible for Free Lunch Program: 1,305 (27.0%)
Eligible for Reduced-Price Lunch Program: 731 (15.1%)
Teachers: 236.9 (20.4 to 1)
Librarians/Media Specialists: 3.0 (1,613.7 to 1)
Guidance Counselors: 10.9 (444.1 to 1)
Current Spending: ($ per student per year):
Total: $4,982; Instruction: $3,380; Support Services: $1,326
Enrollment, Drop-out Rates and Diploma Recipients by Race/Ethnicity

Category	Total	White	Black	Asian	AIAN	Hisp.
Enrollment (%)	100.0	95.2	0.6	0.8	1.0	2.3
Drop-out Rate (%)	5.0	n/a	n/a	n/a	n/a	n/a
H.S. Diplomas (#)	232	219	0	3	4	6

Latah County

Moscow District
650 N Cleveland • Moscow, ID 83843-2923
(208) 882-1120 • http://www.sd281.k12.id.us/index.html
Grade Span: PK-12; **Agency Type:** 1
Schools: 10
6 Primary; 1 Middle; 2 High; 1 Other Level
9 Regular; 0 Special Education; 0 Vocational; 1 Alternative
0 Magnet; 2 Charter; 5 Title I Eligible; 0 School-wide Title I
Students: 2,575 (52.5% male; 47.5% female)
Individual Education Program: 290 (11.3%);
English Language Learner: 36 (1.4%); Migrant: 0 (0.0%)
Eligible for Free Lunch Program: 407 (15.8%)
Eligible for Reduced-Price Lunch Program: 159 (6.2%)
Teachers: 169.2 (15.2 to 1)
Librarians/Media Specialists: 3.0 (858.3 to 1)
Guidance Counselors: 7.2 (357.6 to 1)
Current Spending: ($ per student per year):
Total: $6,976; Instruction: $4,337; Support Services: $2,408
Enrollment, Drop-out Rates and Diploma Recipients by Race/Ethnicity

Category	Total	White	Black	Asian	AIAN	Hisp.
Enrollment (%)	100.0	92.3	1.6	3.0	1.2	1.8
Drop-out Rate (%)	4.6	n/a	n/a	n/a	n/a	n/a
H.S. Diplomas (#)	192	180	1	10	1	0

Madison County

Madison District
290 N 1st E • Rexburg, ID 83440-1520
Mailing Address: PO Box 830 • Rexburg, ID 83440-1520
(208) 359-3300 • http://d321.k12.id.us/
Grade Span: PK-12; **Agency Type:** 1
Schools: 12
7 Primary; 1 Middle; 3 High; 1 Other Level
10 Regular; 0 Special Education; 0 Vocational; 2 Alternative
0 Magnet; 0 Charter; 9 Title I Eligible; 6 School-wide Title I
Students: 4,112 (53.1% male; 46.9% female)
Individual Education Program: 404 (9.8%);
English Language Learner: 312 (7.6%); Migrant: 310 (7.5%)
Eligible for Free Lunch Program: 1,040 (25.3%)
Eligible for Reduced-Price Lunch Program: 607 (14.8%)
Teachers: 208.9 (19.7 to 1)
Librarians/Media Specialists: 1.5 (2,741.3 to 1)
Guidance Counselors: 8.0 (514.0 to 1)
Current Spending: ($ per student per year):
Total: $5,189; Instruction: $3,245; Support Services: $1,715
Enrollment, Drop-out Rates and Diploma Recipients by Race/Ethnicity

Category	Total	White	Black	Asian	AIAN	Hisp.
Enrollment (%)	100.0	93.2	0.6	0.7	0.2	5.3
Drop-out Rate (%)	3.5	n/a	n/a	n/a	n/a	n/a
H.S. Diplomas (#)	348	319	1	4	4	20

Minidoka County

Minidoka County Joint District
633 Fremont Ave • Rupert, ID 83350-1610
(208) 436-4727 • http://www.sd331.k12.id.us/
Grade Span: PK-12; **Agency Type:** 1
Schools: 12
5 Primary; 2 Middle; 3 High; 2 Other Level
9 Regular; 0 Special Education; 1 Vocational; 2 Alternative
0 Magnet; 0 Charter; 10 Title I Eligible; 4 School-wide Title I
Students: 4,338 (52.3% male; 47.7% female)
Individual Education Program: 460 (10.6%);
English Language Learner: 704 (16.2%); Migrant: 532 (12.3%)
Eligible for Free Lunch Program: 1,975 (45.5%)
Eligible for Reduced-Price Lunch Program: 496 (11.4%)
Teachers: 242.2 (17.9 to 1)
Librarians/Media Specialists: 1.9 (2,283.2 to 1)
Guidance Counselors: 6.2 (699.7 to 1)
Current Spending: ($ per student per year):
Total: $5,375; Instruction: $3,471; Support Services: $1,611
Enrollment, Drop-out Rates and Diploma Recipients by Race/Ethnicity

Category	Total	White	Black	Asian	AIAN	Hisp.
Enrollment (%)	100.0	62.7	0.3	0.6	0.4	36.0
Drop-out Rate (%)	5.3	n/a	n/a	n/a	n/a	n/a
H.S. Diplomas (#)	264	201	0	1	2	60

Nez Perce County

Lewiston Independent District
3317 12th St • Lewiston, ID 83501-5308
(208) 746-2337 • http://www.lewiston.k12.id.us/
Grade Span: PK-12; **Agency Type:** 1
Schools: 13
7 Primary; 2 Middle; 3 High; 1 Other Level
10 Regular; 0 Special Education; 1 Vocational; 2 Alternative
0 Magnet; 0 Charter; 7 Title I Eligible; 0 School-wide Title I
Students: 5,089 (52.4% male; 47.6% female)
Individual Education Program: 573 (11.3%);
English Language Learner: 11 (0.2%); Migrant: 0 (0.0%)
Eligible for Free Lunch Program: 995 (19.6%)
Eligible for Reduced-Price Lunch Program: 396 (7.8%)
Teachers: 287.1 (17.7 to 1)
Librarians/Media Specialists: 4.0 (1,272.3 to 1)
Guidance Counselors: 13.0 (391.5 to 1)
Current Spending: ($ per student per year):
Total: $6,712; Instruction: $4,267; Support Services: $2,192
Enrollment, Drop-out Rates and Diploma Recipients by Race/Ethnicity

Category	Total	White	Black	Asian	AIAN	Hisp.
Enrollment (%)	100.0	93.7	0.8	1.1	2.5	1.9
Drop-out Rate (%)	8.2	n/a	n/a	n/a	n/a	n/a
H.S. Diplomas (#)	332	315	0	4	10	3

Payette County

Fruitland District
303 Southwest 3rd St • Fruitland, ID 83619
Mailing Address: PO Box A • Fruitland, ID 83619
(208) 452-3595
Grade Span: PK-12; **Agency Type:** 1
Schools: 3
1 Primary; 1 Middle; 1 High; 0 Other Level
3 Regular; 0 Special Education; 0 Vocational; 0 Alternative
0 Magnet; 0 Charter; 2 Title I Eligible; 0 School-wide Title I
Students: 1,524 (54.7% male; 45.3% female)
Individual Education Program: 171 (11.2%);
English Language Learner: 120 (7.9%); Migrant: 156 (10.2%)
Eligible for Free Lunch Program: 461 (30.2%)
Eligible for Reduced-Price Lunch Program: 150 (9.8%)
Teachers: 81.1 (18.8 to 1)
Librarians/Media Specialists: 1.9 (802.1 to 1)
Guidance Counselors: 3.0 (508.0 to 1)
Current Spending: ($ per student per year):
Total: $4,795; Instruction: $3,120; Support Services: $1,457
Enrollment, Drop-out Rates and Diploma Recipients by Race/Ethnicity

Category	Total	White	Black	Asian	AIAN	Hisp.
Enrollment (%)	100.0	80.0	0.6	1.2	0.3	17.9
Drop-out Rate (%)	1.6	n/a	n/a	n/a	n/a	n/a
H.S. Diplomas (#)	106	99	0	2	0	5

Payette Joint District
20 N 12th St • Payette, ID 83661-2603
(208) 642-9366 • http://www.payettesd.k12.id.us/
Grade Span: PK-12; **Agency Type:** 1
Schools: 5
2 Primary; 1 Middle; 2 High; 0 Other Level
4 Regular; 0 Special Education; 0 Vocational; 1 Alternative
0 Magnet; 0 Charter; 4 Title I Eligible; 0 School-wide Title I
Students: 1,883 (52.8% male; 47.2% female)
Individual Education Program: 208 (11.0%);
English Language Learner: 204 (10.8%); Migrant: 75 (4.0%)
Eligible for Free Lunch Program: 765 (40.6%)
Eligible for Reduced-Price Lunch Program: 187 (9.9%)
Teachers: 103.2 (18.2 to 1)
Librarians/Media Specialists: 2.0 (941.5 to 1)
Guidance Counselors: 5.0 (376.6 to 1)
Current Spending: ($ per student per year):
Total: $5,099; Instruction: $3,092; Support Services: $1,728
Enrollment, Drop-out Rates and Diploma Recipients by Race/Ethnicity

Category	Total	White	Black	Asian	AIAN	Hisp.
Enrollment (%)	100.0	81.5	0.6	0.7	0.4	16.9
Drop-out Rate (%)	10.5	n/a	n/a	n/a	n/a	n/a
H.S. Diplomas (#)	115	95	0	0	0	20

Power County

American Falls Joint District
827 Fort Hall Ave • American Falls, ID 83211-1463
(208) 226-5173 • http://wtms@sd381.k12.id.us/
Grade Span: PK-12; **Agency Type:** 1
Schools: 5
2 Primary; 1 Middle; 2 High; 0 Other Level
3 Regular; 0 Special Education; 0 Vocational; 2 Alternative
0 Magnet; 0 Charter; 5 Title I Eligible; 3 School-wide Title I
Students: 1,640 (50.7% male; 49.3% female)
Individual Education Program: 202 (12.3%);
English Language Learner: 540 (32.9%); Migrant: 241 (14.7%)
Eligible for Free Lunch Program: 588 (35.9%)
Eligible for Reduced-Price Lunch Program: 152 (9.3%)
Teachers: 92.9 (17.7 to 1)
Librarians/Media Specialists: 3.0 (546.7 to 1)
Guidance Counselors: 5.0 (328.0 to 1)
Current Spending: ($ per student per year):
Total: $6,434; Instruction: $3,736; Support Services: $2,427
Enrollment, Drop-out Rates and Diploma Recipients by Race/Ethnicity

Category	Total	White	Black	Asian	AIAN	Hisp.
Enrollment (%)	100.0	59.5	0.2	0.7	2.7	36.8
Drop-out Rate (%)	5.0	n/a	n/a	n/a	n/a	n/a
H.S. Diplomas (#)	108	85	0	0	3	20

Twin Falls County

Twin Falls District
201 Main Ave W • Twin Falls, ID 83301-6103
(208) 733-6900 • http://www.tfsd.k12.id.us/tfsd/
Grade Span: PK-12; **Agency Type:** 1
Schools: 13
7 Primary; 3 Middle; 2 High; 1 Other Level
10 Regular; 0 Special Education; 0 Vocational; 3 Alternative
0 Magnet; 0 Charter; 9 Title I Eligible; 3 School-wide Title I
Students: 7,033 (50.6% male; 49.4% female)
Individual Education Program: 713 (10.1%);
English Language Learner: 451 (6.4%); Migrant: 245 (3.5%)
Eligible for Free Lunch Program: 2,040 (29.0%)
Eligible for Reduced-Price Lunch Program: 714 (10.2%)
Teachers: 374.6 (18.8 to 1)
Librarians/Media Specialists: 3.6 (1,953.6 to 1)
Guidance Counselors: 15.2 (462.7 to 1)
Current Spending: ($ per student per year):
Total: $5,169; Instruction: $3,078; Support Services: $1,827
Enrollment, Drop-out Rates and Diploma Recipients by Race/Ethnicity

Category	Total	White	Black	Asian	AIAN	Hisp.
Enrollment (%)	100.0	85.6	0.6	1.5	0.4	11.9
Drop-out Rate (%)	4.5	n/a	n/a	n/a	n/a	n/a
H.S. Diplomas (#)	395	372	1	0	3	19

Washington County

Weiser District
925 Pioneer Rd • Weiser, ID 83672-1146
(208) 414-0616 • http://www.sd431.k12.id.us/index.html.htm
Grade Span: PK-12; **Agency Type:** 1
Schools: 4
1 Primary; 2 Middle; 1 High; 0 Other Level
4 Regular; 0 Special Education; 0 Vocational; 0 Alternative
0 Magnet; 0 Charter; 4 Title I Eligible; 2 School-wide Title I
Students: 1,631 (49.4% male; 50.6% female)
Individual Education Program: 161 (9.9%);
English Language Learner: 331 (20.3%); Migrant: 164 (10.1%)
Eligible for Free Lunch Program: 615 (37.7%)
Eligible for Reduced-Price Lunch Program: 172 (10.5%)
Teachers: 90.9 (17.9 to 1)
Librarians/Media Specialists: 2.0 (815.5 to 1)
Guidance Counselors: 4.4 (370.7 to 1)
Current Spending: ($ per student per year):
Total: $5,202; Instruction: $3,378; Support Services: $1,528
Enrollment, Drop-out Rates and Diploma Recipients by Race/Ethnicity

Category	Total	White	Black	Asian	AIAN	Hisp.
Enrollment (%)	100.0	75.2	0.1	0.9	0.7	23.0
Drop-out Rate (%)	3.9	n/a	n/a	n/a	n/a	n/a
H.S. Diplomas (#)	106	80	0	5	0	21

Number of Schools

Rank	Number	District Name	City
1	55	Boise Independent District	Boise
2	40	Meridian Joint District	Meridian
3	30	Pocatello District	Pocatello
4	24	Nampa SD	Nampa
5	22	Idaho Falls District	Idaho Falls
6	19	Coeur D Alene District	Coeur D Alene
7	17	Cassia County Joint District	Burley
8	16	Bonneville Joint District	Idaho Falls
9	15	Blackfoot District	Blackfoot
10	13	Lake Pend Oreille District	Sandpoint
10	13	Lewiston Independent District	Lewiston
10	13	Twin Falls District	Twin Falls
13	12	Fremont County Joint District	Saint Anthony
13	12	Madison District	Rexburg
13	12	Minidoka County Joint District	Rupert
13	12	Mountain Home District	Mountain Home
17	10	Caldwell District	Caldwell
17	10	Moscow District	Moscow
19	9	Grangeville Joint District	Grangeville
19	9	Jefferson County Joint District	Rigby
19	9	Lakeland District	Rathdrum
22	8	Blaine County District	Hailey
22	8	Emmett Independent District	Emmett
22	8	Post Falls District	Post Falls
25	7	Boundary County District	Bonners Ferry
25	7	Jerome Joint District	Jerome
25	7	Kuna Joint District	Kuna
25	7	Snake River District	Blackfoot
29	6	Butte County Joint District	Arco
29	6	Middleton District	Middleton
29	6	Vallivue SD	Caldwell
29	6	West Bonner County District	Sandpoint
33	5	American Falls Joint District	American Falls
33	5	Payette Joint District	Payette
33	5	Preston Joint District	Preston
33	5	Shelley Joint District	Shelley
37	4	Weiser District	Weiser
38	3	Fruitland District	Fruitland

Number of Teachers

Rank	Number	District Name	City
1	1,491	Boise Independent District	Boise
2	1,312	Meridian Joint District	Meridian
3	674	Nampa SD	Nampa
4	621	Pocatello District	Pocatello
5	537	Idaho Falls District	Idaho Falls
6	506	Coeur D Alene District	Coeur D Alene
7	388	Bonneville Joint District	Idaho Falls
8	374	Twin Falls District	Twin Falls
9	320	Caldwell District	Caldwell
10	287	Lewiston Independent District	Lewiston
11	282	Cassia County Joint District	Burley
12	252	Mountain Home District	Mountain Home
13	242	Minidoka County Joint District	Rupert
14	241	Lake Pend Oreille District	Sandpoint
15	236	Post Falls District	Post Falls
16	227	Blackfoot District	Blackfoot
17	226	Blaine County District	Hailey
18	219	Vallivue SD	Caldwell
19	219	Lakeland District	Rathdrum
20	208	Madison District	Rexburg
21	201	Jefferson County Joint District	Rigby
22	175	Jerome Joint District	Jerome
23	169	Moscow District	Moscow
24	166	Kuna Joint District	Kuna
25	156	Emmett Independent District	Emmett
26	138	Fremont County Joint District	Saint Anthony
27	119	Middleton District	Middleton
28	118	Preston Joint District	Preston
29	105	Snake River District	Blackfoot
30	103	Payette Joint District	Payette
31	100	Grangeville Joint District	Grangeville
32	99	Shelley Joint District	Shelley
33	96	Boundary County District	Bonners Ferry
34	92	American Falls Joint District	American Falls
35	90	Weiser District	Weiser
36	89	West Bonner County District	Sandpoint
37	81	Fruitland District	Fruitland
38	48	Butte County Joint District	Arco

Number of Students

Rank	Number	District Name	City
1	26,266	Boise Independent District	Boise
2	26,113	Meridian Joint District	Meridian
3	12,715	Nampa SD	Nampa
4	11,949	Pocatello District	Pocatello
5	10,514	Idaho Falls District	Idaho Falls
6	9,499	Coeur D Alene District	Coeur D Alene
7	7,650	Bonneville Joint District	Idaho Falls
8	7,033	Twin Falls District	Twin Falls
9	5,885	Caldwell District	Caldwell
10	5,089	Lewiston Independent District	Lewiston
11	4,996	Cassia County Joint District	Burley
12	4,841	Post Falls District	Post Falls
13	4,487	Mountain Home District	Mountain Home
14	4,338	Minidoka County Joint District	Rupert
15	4,146	Lakeland District	Rathdrum
16	4,139	Blackfoot District	Blackfoot
17	4,129	Lake Pend Oreille District	Sandpoint
18	4,112	Madison District	Rexburg
19	4,090	Vallivue SD	Caldwell
20	3,971	Jefferson County Joint District	Rigby
21	3,321	Kuna Joint District	Kuna
22	3,103	Blaine County District	Hailey
23	3,028	Jerome Joint District	Jerome
24	2,928	Emmett Independent District	Emmett
25	2,575	Moscow District	Moscow
26	2,449	Preston Joint District	Preston
27	2,369	Fremont County Joint District	Saint Anthony
28	2,368	Middleton District	Middleton
29	2,079	Snake River District	Blackfoot
30	1,990	Shelley Joint District	Shelley
31	1,883	Payette Joint District	Payette
32	1,648	Boundary County District	Bonners Ferry
33	1,640	American Falls Joint District	American Falls
34	1,631	Weiser District	Weiser
35	1,533	West Bonner County District	Sandpoint
36	1,524	Fruitland District	Fruitland
37	1,520	Grangeville Joint District	Grangeville
38	1,510	Butte County Joint District	Arco

Male Students

Rank	Percent	District Name	City
1	55.3	West Bonner County District	Sandpoint
2	54.7	Fruitland District	Fruitland
3	53.7	Mountain Home District	Mountain Home
3	53.7	Shelley Joint District	Shelley
5	53.3	Fremont County Joint District	Saint Anthony
6	53.1	Madison District	Rexburg
7	53.0	Jefferson County Joint District	Rigby
8	52.8	Emmett Independent District	Emmett
8	52.8	Payette Joint District	Payette
10	52.5	Moscow District	Moscow
11	52.4	Boundary County District	Bonners Ferry
11	52.4	Coeur D Alene District	Coeur D Alene
11	52.4	Lewiston Independent District	Lewiston
14	52.3	Bonneville Joint District	Idaho Falls
14	52.3	Minidoka County Joint District	Rupert
16	52.2	Cassia County Joint District	Burley
16	52.2	Lakeland District	Rathdrum
16	52.2	Pocatello District	Pocatello
19	52.0	Blaine County District	Hailey
20	51.9	Middleton District	Middleton
21	51.8	Meridian Joint District	Meridian
22	51.6	Idaho Falls District	Idaho Falls
23	51.5	Boise Independent District	Boise
23	51.5	Jerome Joint District	Jerome
25	51.4	Grangeville Joint District	Grangeville
25	51.4	Post Falls District	Post Falls
27	51.3	Butte County Joint District	Arco
28	51.0	Kuna Joint District	Kuna
28	51.0	Preston Joint District	Preston
30	50.9	Caldwell District	Caldwell
31	50.8	Snake River District	Blackfoot
31	50.8	Vallivue SD	Caldwell
33	50.7	American Falls Joint District	American Falls
34	50.6	Blackfoot District	Blackfoot
34	50.6	Twin Falls District	Twin Falls
36	50.4	Nampa SD	Nampa
37	50.2	Lake Pend Oreille District	Sandpoint
38	49.4	Weiser District	Weiser

Female Students

Rank	Percent	District Name	City
1	50.6	Weiser District	Weiser
2	49.8	Lake Pend Oreille District	Sandpoint
3	49.6	Nampa SD	Nampa
4	49.4	Blackfoot District	Blackfoot
4	49.4	Twin Falls District	Twin Falls
6	49.3	American Falls Joint District	American Falls
7	49.2	Snake River District	Blackfoot
7	49.2	Vallivue SD	Caldwell
9	49.1	Caldwell District	Caldwell
10	49.0	Kuna Joint District	Kuna
10	49.0	Preston Joint District	Preston
12	48.7	Butte County Joint District	Arco
13	48.6	Grangeville Joint District	Grangeville
13	48.6	Post Falls District	Post Falls
15	48.5	Boise Independent District	Boise
15	48.5	Jerome Joint District	Jerome
17	48.4	Idaho Falls District	Idaho Falls
18	48.2	Meridian Joint District	Meridian
19	48.1	Middleton District	Middleton
20	48.0	Blaine County District	Hailey
21	47.8	Cassia County Joint District	Burley
21	47.8	Lakeland District	Rathdrum
21	47.8	Pocatello District	Pocatello
24	47.7	Bonneville Joint District	Idaho Falls
24	47.7	Minidoka County Joint District	Rupert
26	47.6	Boundary County District	Bonners Ferry
26	47.6	Coeur D Alene District	Coeur D Alene
26	47.6	Lewiston Independent District	Lewiston
29	47.5	Moscow District	Moscow
30	47.2	Emmett Independent District	Emmett
30	47.2	Payette Joint District	Payette
32	47.0	Jefferson County Joint District	Rigby
33	46.9	Madison District	Rexburg
34	46.7	Fremont County Joint District	Saint Anthony
35	46.3	Mountain Home District	Mountain Home
35	46.3	Shelley Joint District	Shelley
37	45.3	Fruitland District	Fruitland
38	44.7	West Bonner County District	Sandpoint

Individual Education Program Students

Rank	Percent	District Name	City
1	15.2	Mountain Home District	Mountain Home
2	14.5	Grangeville Joint District	Grangeville
3	14.1	Fremont County Joint District	Saint Anthony
4	13.1	West Bonner County District	Sandpoint
5	13.0	Pocatello District	Pocatello
6	12.9	Shelley Joint District	Shelley
7	12.5	Blackfoot District	Blackfoot
8	12.3	American Falls Joint District	American Falls
8	12.3	Vallivue SD	Caldwell
10	12.2	Lake Pend Oreille District	Sandpoint
11	11.9	Nampa SD	Nampa
12	11.8	Blaine County District	Hailey
12	11.8	Idaho Falls District	Idaho Falls
14	11.6	Caldwell District	Caldwell
14	11.6	Cassia County Joint District	Burley
16	11.5	Boise Independent District	Boise
16	11.5	Emmett Independent District	Emmett
18	11.3	Lewiston Independent District	Lewiston
18	11.3	Moscow District	Moscow
20	11.2	Fruitland District	Fruitland
21	11.0	Payette Joint District	Payette
22	10.9	Bonneville Joint District	Idaho Falls
22	10.9	Post Falls District	Post Falls
24	10.8	Jerome Joint District	Jerome
25	10.6	Minidoka County Joint District	Rupert
26	10.5	Meridian Joint District	Meridian
26	10.5	Middleton District	Middleton
28	10.4	Boundary County District	Bonners Ferry
29	10.3	Coeur D Alene District	Coeur D Alene
30	10.1	Kuna Joint District	Kuna
30	10.1	Lakeland District	Rathdrum
30	10.1	Preston Joint District	Preston
30	10.1	Twin Falls District	Twin Falls
34	9.9	Weiser District	Weiser
35	9.8	Madison District	Rexburg
36	9.6	Jefferson County Joint District	Rigby
37	9.2	Snake River District	Blackfoot
38	6.8	Butte County Joint District	Arco

English Language Learner Students

Rank	Percent	District Name	City
1	32.9	American Falls Joint District	American Falls
2	21.6	Caldwell District	Caldwell
3	21.5	Blackfoot District	Blackfoot
4	20.3	Weiser District	Weiser
5	18.3	Cassia County Joint District	Burley
6	17.8	Nampa SD	Nampa
7	16.2	Minidoka County Joint District	Rupert
8	15.7	Snake River District	Blackfoot
9	15.6	Jerome Joint District	Jerome
10	15.4	Fremont County Joint District	Saint Anthony
11	11.9	Vallivue SD	Caldwell
12	11.8	Blaine County District	Hailey
13	10.8	Payette Joint District	Payette
14	8.3	Shelley Joint District	Shelley
15	7.9	Fruitland District	Fruitland
15	7.9	Mountain Home District	Mountain Home
17	7.6	Madison District	Rexburg
18	7.1	Jefferson County Joint District	Rigby
19	6.4	Twin Falls District	Twin Falls
20	5.7	Idaho Falls District	Idaho Falls
21	5.0	Emmett Independent District	Emmett
22	4.8	Boise Independent District	Boise
23	4.7	Boundary County District	Bonners Ferry
24	4.3	Preston Joint District	Preston

Rank	Percent	District Name	City
25	3.8	Bonneville Joint District	Idaho Falls
26	3.3	Middleton District	Middleton
27	1.7	Meridian Joint District	Meridian
28	1.6	Kuna Joint District	Kuna
29	1.4	Moscow District	Moscow
30	1.3	Grangeville Joint District	Grangeville
31	0.5	Pocatello District	Pocatello
32	0.2	Coeur D Alene District	Coeur D Alene
32	0.2	Lewiston Independent District	Lewiston
34	0.1	Post Falls District	Post Falls
35	0.0	Lake Pend Oreille District	Sandpoint
36	0.0	Butte County Joint District	Arco
36	0.0	Lakeland District	Rathdrum
36	0.0	West Bonner County District	Sandpoint

Migrant Students

Rank	Percent	District Name	City
1	14.7	American Falls Joint District	American Falls
2	13.3	Fremont County Joint District	Saint Anthony
3	13.0	Cassia County Joint District	Burley
4	12.3	Minidoka County Joint District	Rupert
5	10.2	Fruitland District	Fruitland
6	10.1	Weiser District	Weiser
7	9.1	Vallivue SD	Caldwell
8	7.8	Caldwell District	Caldwell
9	7.7	Blackfoot District	Blackfoot
10	7.5	Madison District	Rexburg
11	5.3	Nampa SD	Nampa
12	5.2	Snake River District	Blackfoot
13	4.3	Jerome Joint District	Jerome
14	4.0	Payette Joint District	Payette
15	3.7	Idaho Falls District	Idaho Falls
15	3.7	Jefferson County Joint District	Rigby
15	3.7	Mountain Home District	Mountain Home
18	3.5	Twin Falls District	Twin Falls
19	2.3	Shelley Joint District	Shelley
20	2.1	Preston Joint District	Preston
21	1.7	Emmett Independent District	Emmett
22	1.3	Bonneville Joint District	Idaho Falls
23	0.9	Middleton District	Middleton
24	0.8	Kuna Joint District	Kuna
25	0.7	Butte County Joint District	Arco
26	0.3	Blaine County District	Hailey
27	0.0	Boise Independent District	Boise
27	0.0	Boundary County District	Bonners Ferry
27	0.0	Coeur D Alene District	Coeur D Alene
27	0.0	Grangeville Joint District	Grangeville
27	0.0	Lake Pend Oreille District	Sandpoint
27	0.0	Lakeland District	Rathdrum
27	0.0	Lewiston Independent District	Lewiston
27	0.0	Meridian Joint District	Meridian
27	0.0	Moscow District	Moscow
27	0.0	Pocatello District	Pocatello
27	0.0	Post Falls District	Post Falls
27	0.0	West Bonner County District	Sandpoint

Students Eligible for Free Lunch

Rank	Percent	District Name	City
1	48.6	Caldwell District	Caldwell
2	45.5	Minidoka County Joint District	Rupert
3	40.6	Payette Joint District	Payette
4	39.7	West Bonner County District	Sandpoint
5	38.9	Jerome Joint District	Jerome
6	37.7	Weiser District	Weiser
7	37.0	Blackfoot District	Blackfoot
8	36.1	Grangeville Joint District	Grangeville
9	35.9	American Falls Joint District	American Falls
9	35.9	Cassia County Joint District	Burley
11	33.8	Nampa SD	Nampa
12	33.3	Emmett Independent District	Emmett
13	31.8	Vallivue SD	Caldwell
14	31.0	Preston Joint District	Preston
15	30.4	Boundary County District	Bonners Ferry
16	30.2	Fruitland District	Fruitland
17	29.8	Fremont County Joint District	Saint Anthony
18	29.0	Lake Pend Oreille District	Sandpoint
18	29.0	Twin Falls District	Twin Falls
20	27.0	Middleton District	Middleton
20	27.0	Post Falls District	Post Falls
22	26.4	Snake River District	Blackfoot
23	25.8	Pocatello District	Pocatello
24	25.3	Madison District	Rexburg
25	24.6	Lakeland District	Rathdrum
26	24.4	Jefferson County Joint District	Rigby
27	24.2	Coeur D Alene District	Coeur D Alene
28	22.7	Boise Independent District	Boise
28	22.7	Shelley Joint District	Shelley
30	22.5	Idaho Falls District	Idaho Falls
31	20.7	Bonneville Joint District	Idaho Falls
31	20.7	Mountain Home District	Mountain Home
33	19.6	Lewiston Independent District	Lewiston
34	15.8	Moscow District	Moscow
35	15.1	Blaine County District	Hailey
36	14.5	Kuna Joint District	Kuna
37	11.6	Meridian Joint District	Meridian
38	10.7	Butte County Joint District	Arco

Students Eligible for Reduced-Price Lunch

Rank	Percent	District Name	City
1	16.1	Preston Joint District	Preston
2	15.1	Post Falls District	Post Falls
3	14.8	Madison District	Rexburg
3	14.8	West Bonner County District	Sandpoint
5	13.6	Fremont County Joint District	Saint Anthony
5	13.6	Snake River District	Blackfoot
7	13.1	Lake Pend Oreille District	Sandpoint
8	12.3	Boundary County District	Bonners Ferry
9	12.2	Grangeville Joint District	Grangeville
10	11.7	Cassia County Joint District	Burley
11	11.5	Mountain Home District	Mountain Home
12	11.4	Emmett Independent District	Emmett
12	11.4	Middleton District	Middleton
12	11.4	Minidoka County Joint District	Rupert
15	11.2	Lakeland District	Rathdrum
16	11.1	Vallivue SD	Caldwell
17	11.0	Jerome Joint District	Jerome
18	10.5	Blackfoot District	Blackfoot
18	10.5	Weiser District	Weiser
20	10.2	Twin Falls District	Twin Falls
21	9.9	Payette Joint District	Payette
22	9.8	Fruitland District	Fruitland
23	9.7	Jefferson County Joint District	Rigby
24	9.4	Caldwell District	Caldwell
24	9.4	Coeur D Alene District	Coeur D Alene
26	9.3	American Falls Joint District	American Falls
27	9.2	Kuna Joint District	Kuna
28	9.1	Shelley Joint District	Shelley
29	9.0	Nampa SD	Nampa
30	8.8	Bonneville Joint District	Idaho Falls
31	8.6	Pocatello District	Pocatello
32	7.8	Lewiston Independent District	Lewiston
33	7.6	Boise Independent District	Boise
34	6.9	Blaine County District	Hailey
35	6.2	Moscow District	Moscow
36	5.7	Idaho Falls District	Idaho Falls
37	5.4	Meridian Joint District	Meridian
38	5.2	Butte County Joint District	Arco

Student/Teacher Ratio

Rank	Ratio	District Name	City
1	31.3	Butte County Joint District	Arco
2	20.7	Preston Joint District	Preston
3	20.4	Post Falls District	Post Falls
4	20.1	Shelley Joint District	Shelley
5	19.9	Kuna Joint District	Kuna
5	19.9	Meridian Joint District	Meridian
7	19.8	Middleton District	Middleton
8	19.7	Bonneville Joint District	Idaho Falls
8	19.7	Jefferson County Joint District	Rigby
8	19.7	Madison District	Rexburg
11	19.6	Idaho Falls District	Idaho Falls
11	19.6	Snake River District	Blackfoot
13	19.2	Pocatello District	Pocatello
14	18.9	Lakeland District	Rathdrum
15	18.8	Coeur D Alene District	Coeur D Alene
15	18.8	Fruitland District	Fruitland
15	18.8	Nampa SD	Nampa
15	18.8	Twin Falls District	Twin Falls
19	18.7	Emmett Independent District	Emmett
20	18.6	Vallivue SD	Caldwell
21	18.4	Caldwell District	Caldwell
22	18.2	Blackfoot District	Blackfoot
22	18.2	Payette Joint District	Payette
24	17.9	Minidoka County Joint District	Rupert
24	17.9	Weiser District	Weiser
26	17.8	Mountain Home District	Mountain Home
27	17.7	American Falls Joint District	American Falls
27	17.7	Cassia County Joint District	Burley
27	17.7	Lewiston Independent District	Lewiston
30	17.6	Boise Independent District	Boise
31	17.2	Jerome Joint District	Jerome
31	17.2	West Bonner County District	Sandpoint
33	17.1	Boundary County District	Bonners Ferry
33	17.1	Fremont County Joint District	Saint Anthony
33	17.1	Lake Pend Oreille District	Sandpoint
36	15.2	Grangeville Joint District	Grangeville
36	15.2	Moscow District	Moscow
38	13.7	Blaine County District	Hailey

Student/Librarian Ratio

Rank	Ratio	District Name	City
1	3,973.4	Nampa SD	Nampa
2	3,347.8	Meridian Joint District	Meridian
3	3,183.8	Blackfoot District	Blackfoot
4	2,741.3	Madison District	Rexburg
5	2,445.1	Idaho Falls District	Idaho Falls
6	2,283.2	Minidoka County Joint District	Rupert
7	2,243.5	Mountain Home District	Mountain Home
8	2,206.1	Jefferson County Joint District	Rigby
9	2,188.8	Boise Independent District	Boise
10	2,179.6	Caldwell District	Caldwell
11	2,158.9	Coeur D Alene District	Coeur D Alene
12	2,079.0	Snake River District	Blackfoot
13	2,067.6	Bonneville Joint District	Idaho Falls
14	2,045.0	Vallivue SD	Caldwell
15	2,040.8	Preston Joint District	Preston
16	1,990.0	Shelley Joint District	Shelley
17	1,953.6	Twin Falls District	Twin Falls
18	1,660.5	Kuna Joint District	Kuna
19	1,613.7	Post Falls District	Post Falls
20	1,551.5	Blaine County District	Hailey
21	1,533.0	West Bonner County District	Sandpoint
22	1,520.0	Grangeville Joint District	Grangeville
23	1,510.0	Butte County Joint District	Arco
24	1,376.3	Lake Pend Oreille District	Sandpoint
25	1,272.3	Lewiston Independent District	Lewiston
26	1,267.7	Boundary County District	Bonners Ferry
27	1,084.4	Emmett Independent District	Emmett
28	1,036.5	Lakeland District	Rathdrum
29	1,009.3	Jerome Joint District	Jerome
30	941.5	Payette Joint District	Payette
31	919.2	Pocatello District	Pocatello
32	911.2	Fremont County Joint District	Saint Anthony
33	908.4	Cassia County Joint District	Burley
34	858.3	Moscow District	Moscow
35	815.5	Weiser District	Weiser
36	802.1	Fruitland District	Fruitland
37	592.0	Middleton District	Middleton
38	546.7	American Falls Joint District	American Falls

Student/Counselor Ratio

Rank	Ratio	District Name	City
1	1,161.5	Butte County Joint District	Arco
2	699.7	Minidoka County Joint District	Rupert
2	699.7	Preston Joint District	Preston
4	571.3	Jerome Joint District	Jerome
5	565.1	Nampa SD	Nampa
6	553.4	Idaho Falls District	Idaho Falls
7	544.6	Blackfoot District	Blackfoot
8	535.6	Kuna Joint District	Kuna
9	514.0	Madison District	Rexburg
10	508.0	Fruitland District	Fruitland
11	504.0	Fremont County Joint District	Saint Anthony
12	498.6	Mountain Home District	Mountain Home
13	488.0	Emmett Independent District	Emmett
14	477.4	Blaine County District	Hailey
15	470.8	Caldwell District	Caldwell
16	462.8	Shelley Joint District	Shelley
17	462.7	Twin Falls District	Twin Falls
18	458.1	Bonneville Joint District	Idaho Falls
19	452.0	Snake River District	Blackfoot
20	450.9	West Bonner County District	Sandpoint
21	444.1	Post Falls District	Post Falls
22	422.2	Pocatello District	Pocatello
23	407.7	Coeur D Alene District	Coeur D Alene
24	406.2	Cassia County Joint District	Burley
25	403.0	Meridian Joint District	Meridian
26	397.1	Jefferson County Joint District	Rigby
27	391.5	Lewiston Independent District	Lewiston
28	378.8	Lake Pend Oreille District	Sandpoint
29	376.9	Lakeland District	Rathdrum
30	376.6	Payette Joint District	Payette
31	375.9	Middleton District	Middleton
32	371.8	Vallivue SD	Caldwell
33	370.7	Weiser District	Weiser
34	357.6	Moscow District	Moscow
35	328.0	American Falls Joint District	American Falls
36	325.9	Boise Independent District	Boise
37	323.4	Grangeville Joint District	Grangeville
38	323.1	Boundary County District	Bonners Ferry

Current Spending per Student in FY2001

Rank	Dollars	District Name	City
1	8,033	Blaine County District	Hailey
2	6,976	Moscow District	Moscow
3	6,712	Lewiston Independent District	Lewiston
4	6,681	Boise Independent District	Boise
5	6,535	Grangeville Joint District	Grangeville
6	6,533	Butte County Joint District	Arco

7	6,434	American Falls Joint District	American Falls
8	6,122	Boundary County District	Bonners Ferry
9	5,940	Fremont County Joint District	Saint Anthony
10	5,801	Blackfoot District	Blackfoot
11	5,792	Lake Pend Oreille District	Sandpoint
12	5,772	West Bonner County District	Sandpoint
13	5,737	Vallivue SD	Caldwell
14	5,451	Pocatello District	Pocatello
15	5,420	Idaho Falls District	Idaho Falls
16	5,375	Minidoka County Joint District	Rupert
17	5,311	Coeur D Alene District	Coeur D Alene
18	5,268	Cassia County Joint District	Burley
18	5,268	Snake River District	Blackfoot
20	5,234	Mountain Home District	Mountain Home
21	5,202	Weiser District	Weiser
22	5,189	Madison District	Rexburg
23	5,169	Twin Falls District	Twin Falls
24	5,158	Caldwell District	Caldwell
25	5,099	Payette Joint District	Payette
26	5,026	Middleton District	Middleton
27	4,997	Jefferson County Joint District	Rigby
28	4,982	Post Falls District	Post Falls
29	4,948	Emmett Independent District	Emmett
30	4,921	Bonneville Joint District	Idaho Falls
31	4,900	Jerome Joint District	Jerome
32	4,871	Shelley Joint District	Shelley
33	4,856	Meridian Joint District	Meridian
34	4,795	Fruitland District	Fruitland
35	4,717	Lakeland District	Rathdrum
36	4,710	Nampa SD	Nampa
37	4,686	Kuna Joint District	Kuna
38	4,557	Preston Joint District	Preston

Number of Diploma Recipients

Rank	Number	District Name	City
1	1,737	Boise Independent District	Boise
2	1,498	Meridian Joint District	Meridian
3	843	Pocatello District	Pocatello
4	737	Idaho Falls District	Idaho Falls
5	579	Bonneville Joint District	Idaho Falls
6	552	Coeur D Alene District	Coeur D Alene
7	514	Nampa SD	Nampa
8	395	Twin Falls District	Twin Falls
9	350	Cassia County Joint District	Burley
10	348	Madison District	Rexburg
11	332	Lewiston Independent District	Lewiston
12	277	Lake Pend Oreille District	Sandpoint
13	266	Blackfoot District	Blackfoot
14	264	Minidoka County Joint District	Rupert
15	263	Jefferson County Joint District	Rigby
16	250	Lakeland District	Rathdrum
17	249	Mountain Home District	Mountain Home
18	233	Caldwell District	Caldwell
19	232	Post Falls District	Post Falls
20	224	Vallivue SD	Caldwell
21	223	Jerome Joint District	Jerome
22	192	Moscow District	Moscow
23	186	Kuna Joint District	Kuna
24	178	Emmett Independent District	Emmett
25	173	Snake River District	Blackfoot
26	171	Blaine County District	Hailey
27	167	Preston Joint District	Preston
28	165	Fremont County Joint District	Saint Anthony
29	160	Shelley Joint District	Shelley
30	143	Middleton District	Middleton
31	123	Grangeville Joint District	Grangeville
32	115	Payette Joint District	Payette
33	110	Boundary County District	Bonners Ferry
34	108	American Falls Joint District	American Falls
35	106	Fruitland District	Fruitland
35	106	Weiser District	Weiser
37	87	West Bonner County District	Sandpoint
38	36	Butte County Joint District	Arco

High School Drop-out Rate

Rank	Percent	District Name	City
1	12.9	Nampa SD	Nampa
2	10.5	Payette Joint District	Payette
3	9.7	Jerome Joint District	Jerome
4	9.0	Boise Independent District	Boise
5	8.9	Mountain Home District	Mountain Home
6	8.2	Lewiston Independent District	Lewiston
7	8.0	Idaho Falls District	Idaho Falls
8	7.7	Vallivue SD	Caldwell
9	7.6	Boundary County District	Bonners Ferry
10	6.4	Kuna Joint District	Kuna
11	6.3	Lakeland District	Rathdrum
12	6.1	Coeur D Alene District	Coeur D Alene
12	6.1	West Bonner County District	Sandpoint
14	5.7	Caldwell District	Caldwell
15	5.4	Lake Pend Oreille District	Sandpoint
16	5.3	Minidoka County Joint District	Rupert
17	5.1	Grangeville Joint District	Grangeville
18	5.0	American Falls Joint District	American Falls
18	5.0	Meridian Joint District	Meridian
18	5.0	Pocatello District	Pocatello
18	5.0	Post Falls District	Post Falls
22	4.7	Blackfoot District	Blackfoot
23	4.6	Moscow District	Moscow
24	4.5	Twin Falls District	Twin Falls
25	4.2	Blaine County District	Hailey
26	4.0	Cassia County Joint District	Burley
27	3.9	Emmett Independent District	Emmett
27	3.9	Weiser District	Weiser
29	3.5	Madison District	Rexburg
30	3.2	Middleton District	Middleton
31	2.1	Fremont County Joint District	Saint Anthony
32	1.9	Jefferson County Joint District	Rigby
32	1.9	Preston Joint District	Preston
34	1.6	Fruitland District	Fruitland
35	1.3	Shelley Joint District	Shelley
36	1.2	Snake River District	Blackfoot
37	0.8	Bonneville Joint District	Idaho Falls
38	0.0	Butte County Joint District	Arco

Illinois

Illinois Public School Educational Profile

Category	Value	Category	Value
Schools *(2002-2003)*	4,402	**Diploma Recipients** *(2002-2003)*	116,657
Instructional Level		White, Non-Hispanic	82,454
Primary	2,619	Black, Non-Hispanic	16,294
Middle	740	Asian/Pacific Islander	5,234
High	753	American Indian/Alaskan Native	433
Other Level	290	Hispanic	12,242
Curriculum		**High School Drop-out Rate** (%) *(2000-2001)*	6.0
Regular	3,933	White, Non-Hispanic	3.5
Special Education	258	Black, Non-Hispanic	12.9
Vocational	52	Asian/Pacific Islander	2.7
Alternative	159	American Indian/Alaskan Native	6.4
Type		Hispanic	10.4
Magnet	386	**Staff** *(2002-2003)*	156,215.0
Charter	23	Teachers	131,055.0
Title I Eligible	2,412	Average Salary ($)	51,496
School-wide Title I	976	Librarians/Media Specialists	1,940.3
Students *(2002-2003)*	2,084,187	Guidance Counselors	2,943.4
Gender (%)		**Ratios** *(2002-2003)*	
Male	51.5	Student/Teacher Ratio	15.9 to 1
Female	48.5	Student/Librarian Ratio	1,074.2 to 1
Race/Ethnicity (%)		Student/Counselor Ratio	708.1 to 1
White, Non-Hispanic	58.3	**Current Spending** *($ per student in FY 2001)*	7,956
Black, Non-Hispanic	21.1	Instruction	4,733
Asian/Pacific Islander	3.5	Support Services	2,964
American Indian/Alaskan Native	0.2	**College Entrance Exam Scores** *(2003)*	
Hispanic	16.9	Scholastic Aptitude Test (SAT)	
Classification (%)		Participation Rate (%)	11
Individual Education Program (IEP)	14.7	Mean SAT I Verbal Score	583
Migrant	0.0	Mean SAT I Math Score	596
English Language Learner (ELL)	8.1	American College Testing Program (ACT)	
Eligible for Free Lunch Program	30.3	Participation Rate (%)	100
Eligible for Reduced-Price Lunch Program	5.3	Average Composite Score	20.2

Note: *For an explanation of data, please refer to the User's Guide in the front of the book; n/a indicates data not available*

Illinois NAEP 2003 Test Scores

Reading		
Grade/Category	**Value**	**Rank**
4th Grade		
Average Proficiency	216.3 (1.6)	35/51
Proficiency by Gender/Race/Ethnicity		
Male	213.8 (1.7)	32/51
Female	219.0 (1.7)	35/51
White, Non-Hispanic	228.4 (1.8)	14/51
Black, Non-Hispanic	194.4 (1.8)	31/42
Asian, Non-Hispanic	197.4 (3.1)	32/41
American Indian, Non-Hispanic	235.1 (4.9)	5/25
Hispanic	n/a	n/a
Proficiency by Class Size		
Less than 16 Students	*201.4 (8.9)*	29/45
16 to 18 Students	*213.0 (8.5)*	29/48
19 to 20 Students	*220.4 (4.7)*	23/50
21 to 25 Students	223.2 (2.3)	20/51
Greater than 25 Students	211.5 (3.4)	38/49
Percent Attaining Achievement Levels		
Below Basic	38.8 (1.6)	17/51
Basic or Above	61.2 (1.6)	35/51
Proficient or Above	30.8 (1.5)	30/51
Advanced or Above	7.7 (0.9)	18/51
8th Grade		
Average Proficiency	266.4 (1.0)	18/51
Proficiency by Gender/Race/Ethnicity		
Male	263.6 (1.2)	7/51
Female	269.2 (1.1)	30/51
White, Non-Hispanic	275.7 (1.1)	4/50
Black, Non-Hispanic	246.8 (1.6)	12/41
Asian, Non-Hispanic	249.8 (1.7)	10/37
American Indian, Non-Hispanic	280.7 (3.7)	5/23
Hispanic	n/a	n/a
Proficiency by Parents Highest Level of Ed.		
Did Not Finish High School	246.7 (2.7)	26/50
Graduated High School	255.9 (1.6)	24/50
Some Education After High School	270.5 (1.7)	16/50
Graduated College	275.6 (1.3)	12/50
Percent Attaining Achievement Levels		
Below Basic	23.1 (1.1)	33/51
Basic or Above	76.9 (1.1)	19/51
Proficient or Above	34.5 (1.4)	18/51
Advanced or Above	3.5 (0.7)	8/51

Mathematics		
Grade/Category	**Value**	**Rank**
4th Grade		
Average Proficiency	232.9 (1.1)	35/51
Proficiency by Gender/Race/Ethnicity		
Male	234.1 (1.3)	35/51
Female	231.5 (1.1)	33/51
White, Non-Hispanic	244.2 (1.3)	13/51
Black, Non-Hispanic	210.4 (1.4)	35/42
Asian, Non-Hispanic	217.6 (1.6)	32/43
American Indian, Non-Hispanic	252.4 (2.9)	6/26
Hispanic	n/a	n/a
Proficiency by Class Size		
Less than 16 Students	226.4 (4.4)	19/47
16 to 18 Students	*219.4 (7.6)*	45/48
19 to 20 Students	*236.9 (4.3)*	16/50
21 to 25 Students	239.6 (1.8)	16/51
Greater than 25 Students	227.2 (2.5)	41/49
Percent Attaining Achievement Levels		
Below Basic	27.0 (1.2)	16/51
Basic or Above	73.0 (1.2)	36/51
Proficient or Above	31.5 (1.6)	27/51
Advanced or Above	4.8 (0.7)	12/51
8th Grade		
Average Proficiency	277.2 (1.2)	31/51
Proficiency by Gender/Race/Ethnicity		
Male	278.0 (1.4)	33/51
Female	276.3 (1.2)	29/51
White, Non-Hispanic	289.2 (1.4)	15/50
Black, Non-Hispanic	249.3 (1.6)	27/41
Asian, Non-Hispanic	258.8 (2.0)	20/37
American Indian, Non-Hispanic	301.9 (3.7)	5/23
Hispanic	n/a	n/a
Proficiency by Parents Highest Level of Ed.		
Did Not Finish High School	255.8 (2.7)	28/50
Graduated High School	268.7 (1.4)	29/50
Some Education After High School	277.8 (1.6)	34/50
Graduated College	288.3 (1.5)	27/50
Percent Attaining Achievement Levels		
Below Basic	33.5 (1.2)	18/51
Basic or Above	66.5 (1.2)	34/51
Proficient or Above	29.2 (1.5)	28/51
Advanced or Above	5.9 (0.6)	14/51

Note: *For an explanation of data, please refer to the User's Guide in the front of the book; values in italics indicate that the nature of the sample does not allow accurate determination of the variability of the statistic; n/a indicates data not available*

Adams County

Quincy SD 172

1444 Maine St • Quincy, IL 62301-4261
(217) 223-8700 • http://www.qps.org/
Grade Span: PK-12; **Agency Type:** 1
Schools: 16
10 Primary; 1 Middle; 3 High; 2 Other Level
11 Regular; 5 Special Education; 0 Vocational; 0 Alternative
0 Magnet; 0 Charter; 5 Title I Eligible; 5 School-wide Title I
Students: 7,256 (49.8% male; 50.2% female)
Individual Education Program: 1,213 (16.7%);
English Language Learner: 24 (0.3%); Migrant: n/a
Eligible for Free Lunch Program: 2,573 (35.5%)
Eligible for Reduced-Price Lunch Program: 690 (9.5%)
Teachers: 411.3 (17.6 to 1)
Librarians/Media Specialists: 2.0 (3,628.0 to 1)
Guidance Counselors: 9.0 (806.2 to 1)
Current Spending: ($ per student per year):
Total: $6,236; Instruction: $3,516; Support Services: $2,383
Enrollment, Drop-out Rates and Diploma Recipients by Race/Ethnicity

Category	Total	White	Black	Asian	AIAN	Hisp.
Enrollment (%)	100.0	87.9	10.3	0.6	0.0	1.2
Drop-out Rate (%)	5.3	5.1	7.2	6.7	0.0	5.0
H.S. Diplomas (#)	490	462	23	2	0	3

Bond County

Bond County CUSD 2

1008 N Hena St • Greenville, IL 62246-1378
(618) 664-0170 • http://www.bccu2.k12.il.us
Grade Span: PK-12; **Agency Type:** 1
Schools: 5
3 Primary; 1 Middle; 1 High; 0 Other Level
5 Regular; 0 Special Education; 0 Vocational; 0 Alternative
0 Magnet; 0 Charter; 3 Title I Eligible; 1 School-wide Title I
Students: 1,961 (51.8% male; 48.2% female)
Individual Education Program: 318 (16.2%);
English Language Learner: 0 (0.0%); Migrant: n/a
Eligible for Free Lunch Program: 386 (19.7%)
Eligible for Reduced-Price Lunch Program: 115 (5.9%)
Teachers: 115.6 (17.0 to 1)
Librarians/Media Specialists: 2.0 (980.5 to 1)
Guidance Counselors: 3.0 (653.7 to 1)
Current Spending: ($ per student per year):
Total: $5,644; Instruction: $3,257; Support Services: $2,095
Enrollment, Drop-out Rates and Diploma Recipients by Race/Ethnicity

Category	Total	White	Black	Asian	AIAN	Hisp.
Enrollment (%)	100.0	93.5	4.6	0.5	0.1	1.3
Drop-out Rate (%)	3.7	3.5	9.5	0.0	n/a	0.0
H.S. Diplomas (#)	132	127	4	0	0	1

Boone County

Belvidere CUSD 100

1201 5th Ave • Belvidere, IL 61008-5125
(815) 544-0301 • http://www.district100.net/
Grade Span: PK-12; **Agency Type:** 1
Schools: 9
6 Primary; 2 Middle; 1 High; 0 Other Level
9 Regular; 0 Special Education; 0 Vocational; 0 Alternative
0 Magnet; 0 Charter; 3 Title I Eligible; 0 School-wide Title I
Students: 7,166 (51.2% male; 48.8% female)
Individual Education Program: 832 (11.6%);
English Language Learner: 0 (0.0%); Migrant: n/a
Eligible for Free Lunch Program: 1,264 (17.6%)
Eligible for Reduced-Price Lunch Program: 301 (4.2%)
Teachers: 353.2 (20.3 to 1)
Librarians/Media Specialists: 5.0 (1,433.2 to 1)
Guidance Counselors: 4.0 (1,791.5 to 1)
Current Spending: ($ per student per year):
Total: $4,942; Instruction: $2,941; Support Services: $1,765
Enrollment, Drop-out Rates and Diploma Recipients by Race/Ethnicity

Category	Total	White	Black	Asian	AIAN	Hisp.
Enrollment (%)	100.0	77.0	2.2	0.8	0.1	19.9
Drop-out Rate (%)	0.9	0.6	0.0	0.0	n/a	2.9
H.S. Diplomas (#)	353	305	2	0	0	46

Champaign County

Champaign Community Unit SD 4

703 S New St • Champaign, IL 61820-5818
(217) 351-3838 • http://www.cmi.k12.il.us/Champaign/
Grade Span: PK-12; **Agency Type:** 1
Schools: 18
12 Primary; 3 Middle; 2 High; 1 Other Level
16 Regular; 2 Special Education; 0 Vocational; 0 Alternative
11 Magnet; 0 Charter; 10 Title I Eligible; 3 School-wide Title I
Students: 9,273 (52.2% male; 47.8% female)
Individual Education Program: 1,600 (17.3%);
English Language Learner: 289 (3.1%); Migrant: n/a
Eligible for Free Lunch Program: 2,770 (29.9%)
Eligible for Reduced-Price Lunch Program: 419 (4.5%)
Teachers: 665.2 (13.9 to 1)
Librarians/Media Specialists: 13.5 (686.9 to 1)
Guidance Counselors: 15.0 (618.2 to 1)
Current Spending: ($ per student per year):
Total: $7,359; Instruction: $4,701; Support Services: $2,454
Enrollment, Drop-out Rates and Diploma Recipients by Race/Ethnicity

Category	Total	White	Black	Asian	AIAN	Hisp.
Enrollment (%)	100.0	58.0	32.6	5.9	0.2	3.4
Drop-out Rate (%)	4.7	3.0	10.3	1.5	0.0	2.3
H.S. Diplomas (#)	640	471	112	42	0	15

Mahomet-Seymour CUSD 3

PO Box 229 • Mahomet, IL 61853-0229
(217) 586-4995 • http://www.ms.k12.il.us/
Grade Span: PK-12; **Agency Type:** 1
Schools: 5
3 Primary; 1 Middle; 1 High; 0 Other Level
5 Regular; 0 Special Education; 0 Vocational; 0 Alternative
0 Magnet; 0 Charter; 3 Title I Eligible; 0 School-wide Title I
Students: 2,678 (51.2% male; 48.8% female)
Individual Education Program: 378 (14.1%);
English Language Learner: 0 (0.0%); Migrant: n/a
Eligible for Free Lunch Program: 201 (7.5%)
Eligible for Reduced-Price Lunch Program: 9 (0.3%)
Teachers: 163.5 (16.4 to 1)
Librarians/Media Specialists: 4.0 (669.5 to 1)
Guidance Counselors: 4.0 (669.5 to 1)
Current Spending: ($ per student per year):
Total: $6,478; Instruction: $4,204; Support Services: $2,059
Enrollment, Drop-out Rates and Diploma Recipients by Race/Ethnicity

Category	Total	White	Black	Asian	AIAN	Hisp.
Enrollment (%)	100.0	97.0	0.8	1.0	0.4	0.8
Drop-out Rate (%)	1.5	1.5	0.0	0.0	0.0	0.0
H.S. Diplomas (#)	188	187	0	0	0	1

Rantoul City SD 137

400 E Wabash Ave • Rantoul, IL 61866-3013
(217) 893-4171 • http://www.rcs.k12.il.us/
Grade Span: KG-08; **Agency Type:** 1
Schools: 5
4 Primary; 1 Middle; 0 High; 0 Other Level
5 Regular; 0 Special Education; 0 Vocational; 0 Alternative
0 Magnet; 0 Charter; 4 Title I Eligible; 1 School-wide Title I
Students: 1,612 (51.1% male; 48.9% female)
Individual Education Program: 452 (28.0%);
English Language Learner: 39 (2.4%); Migrant: n/a
Eligible for Free Lunch Program: 774 (48.0%)
Eligible for Reduced-Price Lunch Program: 164 (10.2%)
Teachers: 106.5 (15.1 to 1)
Librarians/Media Specialists: 0.0 (0.0 to 1)
Guidance Counselors: 0.0 (0.0 to 1)
Current Spending: ($ per student per year):
Total: $6,231; Instruction: $3,956; Support Services: $2,002
Enrollment, Drop-out Rates and Diploma Recipients by Race/Ethnicity

Category	Total	White	Black	Asian	AIAN	Hisp.
Enrollment (%)	100.0	57.1	36.0	1.6	0.1	5.2
Drop-out Rate (%)	n/a	n/a	n/a	n/a	n/a	n/a
H.S. Diplomas (#)	n/a	n/a	n/a	n/a	n/a	n/a

Urbana SD 116

PO Box 3039 • Urbana, IL 61803-3039
(217) 384-3636 • http://www.cmi.k12.il.us/Urbana/
Grade Span: PK-12; **Agency Type:** 1
Schools: 9
7 Primary; 1 Middle; 1 High; 0 Other Level
8 Regular; 1 Special Education; 0 Vocational; 0 Alternative
0 Magnet; 0 Charter; 8 Title I Eligible; 2 School-wide Title I
Students: 4,599 (51.4% male; 48.6% female)
Individual Education Program: 933 (20.3%);
English Language Learner: 474 (10.3%); Migrant: n/a
Eligible for Free Lunch Program: 1,691 (36.8%)
Eligible for Reduced-Price Lunch Program: 245 (5.3%)
Teachers: 344.8 (13.3 to 1)
Librarians/Media Specialists: 8.0 (574.9 to 1)
Guidance Counselors: 7.0 (657.0 to 1)
Current Spending: ($ per student per year):
Total: $8,419; Instruction: $5,098; Support Services: $3,084

Enrollment, Drop-out Rates and Diploma Recipients by Race/Ethnicity

Category	Total	White	Black	Asian	AIAN	Hisp.
Enrollment (%)	100.0	54.7	34.0	7.7	0.2	3.4
Drop-out Rate (%)	4.6	2.8	7.3	10.4	0.0	14.3
H.S. Diplomas (#)	354	227	107	15	0	5

Christian County

Taylorville CUSD 3

101 E Adams St • Taylorville, IL 62568-2288
(217) 824-4951 • http://www.taylorvilleschools.com/
Grade Span: PK-12; **Agency Type:** 1
Schools: 8
6 Primary; 1 Middle; 1 High; 0 Other Level
8 Regular; 0 Special Education; 0 Vocational; 0 Alternative
0 Magnet; 0 Charter; 5 Title I Eligible; 0 School-wide Title I
Students: 3,041 (51.4% male; 48.6% female)
Individual Education Program: 430 (14.1%);
English Language Learner: 0 (0.0%); Migrant: n/a
Eligible for Free Lunch Program: 701 (23.1%)
Eligible for Reduced-Price Lunch Program: 238 (7.8%)
Teachers: 170.3 (17.9 to 1)
Librarians/Media Specialists: 3.0 (1,013.7 to 1)
Guidance Counselors: 3.0 (1,013.7 to 1)
Current Spending: ($ per student per year):
Total: $5,250; Instruction: $3,306; Support Services: $1,614
Enrollment, Drop-out Rates and Diploma Recipients by Race/Ethnicity

Category	Total	White	Black	Asian	AIAN	Hisp.
Enrollment (%)	100.0	97.8	1.2	0.7	0.0	0.3
Drop-out Rate (%)	5.7	5.8	0.0	0.0	n/a	0.0
H.S. Diplomas (#)	212	210	1	1	0	0

Coles County

Charleston CUSD 1

410 W Polk Ave • Charleston, IL 61920-2557
(217) 345-2106 • http://www.charleston.k12.il.us/index.html
Grade Span: PK-12; **Agency Type:** 1
Schools: 7
5 Primary; 1 Middle; 1 High; 0 Other Level
7 Regular; 0 Special Education; 0 Vocational; 0 Alternative
0 Magnet; 0 Charter; 4 Title I Eligible; 0 School-wide Title I
Students: 2,993 (52.0% male; 48.0% female)
Individual Education Program: 723 (24.2%);
English Language Learner: 17 (0.6%); Migrant: n/a
Eligible for Free Lunch Program: 646 (21.6%)
Eligible for Reduced-Price Lunch Program: 143 (4.8%)
Teachers: 182.6 (16.4 to 1)
Librarians/Media Specialists: 4.0 (748.3 to 1)
Guidance Counselors: 5.0 (598.6 to 1)
Current Spending: ($ per student per year):
Total: $6,329; Instruction: $3,681; Support Services: $2,460
Enrollment, Drop-out Rates and Diploma Recipients by Race/Ethnicity

Category	Total	White	Black	Asian	AIAN	Hisp.
Enrollment (%)	100.0	94.8	2.8	1.1	0.1	1.2
Drop-out Rate (%)	3.5	3.7	0.0	0.0	0.0	0.0
H.S. Diplomas (#)	224	211	9	1	0	3

Mattoon CUSD 2

1701 Charleston Ave • Mattoon, IL 61938-3970
(217) 235-5446 • http://www.mattoon.k12.il.us/
Grade Span: PK-12; **Agency Type:** 1
Schools: 9
4 Primary; 3 Middle; 1 High; 1 Other Level
8 Regular; 1 Special Education; 0 Vocational; 0 Alternative
0 Magnet; 0 Charter; 6 Title I Eligible; 2 School-wide Title I
Students: 3,391 (51.5% male; 48.5% female)
Individual Education Program: 754 (22.2%);
English Language Learner: 10 (0.3%); Migrant: n/a
Eligible for Free Lunch Program: 915 (27.0%)
Eligible for Reduced-Price Lunch Program: 169 (5.0%)
Teachers: 238.4 (14.2 to 1)
Librarians/Media Specialists: 3.0 (1,130.3 to 1)
Guidance Counselors: 4.0 (847.8 to 1)
Current Spending: ($ per student per year):
Total: $6,582; Instruction: $3,977; Support Services: $2,309
Enrollment, Drop-out Rates and Diploma Recipients by Race/Ethnicity

Category	Total	White	Black	Asian	AIAN	Hisp.
Enrollment (%)	100.0	94.9	3.0	0.6	0.1	1.4
Drop-out Rate (%)	9.9	9.4	23.3	20.0	0.0	14.3
H.S. Diplomas (#)	204	194	4	2	1	3

Cook County

Alsip-Hazlgrn-Oaklawn SD 126

11900 S Kostner Ave • Alsip, IL 60803-2307
(708) 389-1900
Grade Span: PK-08; **Agency Type:** 1
Schools: 4
3 Primary; 1 Middle; 0 High; 0 Other Level
4 Regular; 0 Special Education; 0 Vocational; 0 Alternative
0 Magnet; 0 Charter; 1 Title I Eligible; 0 School-wide Title I
Students: 1,709 (51.6% male; 48.4% female)
Individual Education Program: 312 (18.3%);
English Language Learner: 122 (7.1%); Migrant: n/a
Eligible for Free Lunch Program: 169 (9.9%)
Eligible for Reduced-Price Lunch Program: 27 (1.6%)
Teachers: 101.6 (16.8 to 1)
Librarians/Media Specialists: 4.0 (427.3 to 1)
Guidance Counselors: 0.0 (0.0 to 1)
Current Spending: ($ per student per year):
Total: $7,159; Instruction: $4,443; Support Services: $2,633
Enrollment, Drop-out Rates and Diploma Recipients by Race/Ethnicity

Category	Total	White	Black	Asian	AIAN	Hisp.
Enrollment (%)	100.0	81.7	4.9	2.8	0.1	10.5
Drop-out Rate (%)	n/a	n/a	n/a	n/a	n/a	n/a
H.S. Diplomas (#)	n/a	n/a	n/a	n/a	n/a	n/a

Argo Community HSD 217

7329 W 63rd St • Summit, IL 60501-1829
(708) 728-3200 • http://www.argo217.k12.il.us/
Grade Span: 09-12; **Agency Type:** 1
Schools: 1
0 Primary; 0 Middle; 1 High; 0 Other Level
1 Regular; 0 Special Education; 0 Vocational; 0 Alternative
0 Magnet; 0 Charter; 1 Title I Eligible; 1 School-wide Title I
Students: 1,729 (50.8% male; 49.2% female)
Individual Education Program: 188 (10.9%);
English Language Learner: 145 (8.4%); Migrant: n/a
Eligible for Free Lunch Program: 518 (30.0%)
Eligible for Reduced-Price Lunch Program: 101 (5.8%)
Teachers: 97.8 (17.7 to 1)
Librarians/Media Specialists: 1.0 (1,729.0 to 1)
Guidance Counselors: 6.0 (288.2 to 1)
Current Spending: ($ per student per year):
Total: $10,996; Instruction: $5,985; Support Services: $4,695
Enrollment, Drop-out Rates and Diploma Recipients by Race/Ethnicity

Category	Total	White	Black	Asian	AIAN	Hisp.
Enrollment (%)	100.0	58.4	12.5	0.3	0.1	28.6
Drop-out Rate (%)	4.3	4.2	2.8	0.0	100.0	4.9
H.S. Diplomas (#)	359	222	37	3	0	97

Arlington Heights SD 25

1200 S Dunton Ave • Arlington Heights, IL 60005-3122
(847) 758-4900 • http://www.ahsd25.n-cook.k12.il.us/
Grade Span: PK-08; **Agency Type:** 1
Schools: 9
7 Primary; 2 Middle; 0 High; 0 Other Level
9 Regular; 0 Special Education; 0 Vocational; 0 Alternative
0 Magnet; 0 Charter; 5 Title I Eligible; 0 School-wide Title I
Students: 4,908 (51.1% male; 48.9% female)
Individual Education Program: 902 (18.4%);
English Language Learner: 206 (4.2%); Migrant: n/a
Eligible for Free Lunch Program: 187 (3.8%)
Eligible for Reduced-Price Lunch Program: 102 (2.1%)
Teachers: 333.3 (14.7 to 1)
Librarians/Media Specialists: 2.5 (1,963.2 to 1)
Guidance Counselors: 0.0 (0.0 to 1)
Current Spending: ($ per student per year):
Total: $8,233; Instruction: $4,677; Support Services: $3,367
Enrollment, Drop-out Rates and Diploma Recipients by Race/Ethnicity

Category	Total	White	Black	Asian	AIAN	Hisp.
Enrollment (%)	100.0	89.3	1.0	5.1	0.3	4.4
Drop-out Rate (%)	n/a	n/a	n/a	n/a	n/a	n/a
H.S. Diplomas (#)	n/a	n/a	n/a	n/a	n/a	n/a

Bellwood SD 88

640 Eastern Ave • Bellwood, IL 60104-1878
(708) 344-9344 • http://bwshome.northstarnet.org/educatio.htm
Grade Span: PK-08; **Agency Type:** 1
Schools: 8
7 Primary; 1 Middle; 0 High; 0 Other Level
7 Regular; 1 Special Education; 0 Vocational; 0 Alternative
1 Magnet; 0 Charter; 6 Title I Eligible; 0 School-wide Title I
Students: 3,317 (52.1% male; 47.9% female)
Individual Education Program: 464 (14.0%);
English Language Learner: 487 (14.7%); Migrant: n/a

Eligible for Free Lunch Program: 1,553 (46.8%)
Eligible for Reduced-Price Lunch Program: 311 (9.4%)
Teachers: 159.0 (20.9 to 1)
Librarians/Media Specialists: 1.0 (3,317.0 to 1)
Guidance Counselors: 0.0 (0.0 to 1)
Current Spending: ($ per student per year):
Total: $5,699; Instruction: $3,202; Support Services: $2,222
Enrollment, Drop-out Rates and Diploma Recipients by Race/Ethnicity

Category	Total	White	Black	Asian	AIAN	Hisp.
Enrollment (%)	100.0	1.5	64.3	0.3	0.1	33.7
Drop-out Rate (%)	n/a	n/a	n/a	n/a	n/a	n/a
H.S. Diplomas (#)	n/a	n/a	n/a	n/a	n/a	n/a

Berkeley SD 87
1200 N Wolf Rd • Berkeley, IL 60163-1219
(708) 449-3350 • http://bwshome.northstarnet.org/educatio.htm
Grade Span: PK-08; **Agency Type:** 1
Schools: 6
4 Primary; 2 Middle; 0 High; 0 Other Level
6 Regular; 0 Special Education; 0 Vocational; 0 Alternative
1 Magnet; 0 Charter; 6 Title I Eligible; 0 School-wide Title I
Students: 2,838 (51.4% male; 48.6% female)
Individual Education Program: 512 (18.0%);
English Language Learner: 526 (18.5%); Migrant: n/a
Eligible for Free Lunch Program: 1,032 (36.4%)
Eligible for Reduced-Price Lunch Program: 367 (12.9%)
Teachers: 174.6 (16.3 to 1)
Librarians/Media Specialists: 1.0 (2,838.0 to 1)
Guidance Counselors: 4.0 (709.5 to 1)
Current Spending: ($ per student per year):
Total: $6,185; Instruction: $3,367; Support Services: $2,546
Enrollment, Drop-out Rates and Diploma Recipients by Race/Ethnicity

Category	Total	White	Black	Asian	AIAN	Hisp.
Enrollment (%)	100.0	14.1	34.9	2.4	0.1	48.4
Drop-out Rate (%)	n/a	n/a	n/a	n/a	n/a	n/a
H.S. Diplomas (#)	n/a	n/a	n/a	n/a	n/a	n/a

Berwyn North SD 98
6633 W 16th St • Berwyn, IL 60402-1320
(708) 484-6200 • http://www.d98.cook.k12.il.us/web/index.htm
Grade Span: PK-08; **Agency Type:** 1
Schools: 5
3 Primary; 1 Middle; 0 High; 1 Other Level
4 Regular; 1 Special Education; 0 Vocational; 0 Alternative
0 Magnet; 0 Charter; 3 Title I Eligible; 0 School-wide Title I
Students: 2,995 (50.7% male; 49.3% female)
Individual Education Program: 375 (12.5%);
English Language Learner: 590 (19.7%); Migrant: n/a
Eligible for Free Lunch Program: 1,569 (52.4%)
Eligible for Reduced-Price Lunch Program: 403 (13.5%)
Teachers: 148.2 (20.2 to 1)
Librarians/Media Specialists: 4.0 (748.8 to 1)
Guidance Counselors: 0.0 (0.0 to 1)
Current Spending: ($ per student per year):
Total: $5,124; Instruction: $3,244; Support Services: $1,657
Enrollment, Drop-out Rates and Diploma Recipients by Race/Ethnicity

Category	Total	White	Black	Asian	AIAN	Hisp.
Enrollment (%)	100.0	26.0	3.6	3.0	0.2	67.2
Drop-out Rate (%)	n/a	n/a	n/a	n/a	n/a	n/a
H.S. Diplomas (#)	n/a	n/a	n/a	n/a	n/a	n/a

Berwyn South SD 100
3401 S Gunderson Ave • Berwyn, IL 60402-3773
(708) 795-2300 • http://www.schooldistrict100.org/
Grade Span: PK-08; **Agency Type:** 1
Schools: 7
6 Primary; 1 Middle; 0 High; 0 Other Level
7 Regular; 0 Special Education; 0 Vocational; 0 Alternative
0 Magnet; 0 Charter; 7 Title I Eligible; 0 School-wide Title I
Students: 3,366 (50.4% male; 49.6% female)
Individual Education Program: 567 (16.8%);
English Language Learner: 590 (17.5%); Migrant: n/a
Eligible for Free Lunch Program: 1,135 (33.7%)
Eligible for Reduced-Price Lunch Program: 500 (14.9%)
Teachers: 231.3 (14.6 to 1)
Librarians/Media Specialists: 0.0 (0.0 to 1)
Guidance Counselors: 0.0 (0.0 to 1)
Current Spending: ($ per student per year):
Total: $6,613; Instruction: $4,063; Support Services: $2,320
Enrollment, Drop-out Rates and Diploma Recipients by Race/Ethnicity

Category	Total	White	Black	Asian	AIAN	Hisp.
Enrollment (%)	100.0	38.4	0.8	1.2	0.2	59.5
Drop-out Rate (%)	n/a	n/a	n/a	n/a	n/a	n/a
H.S. Diplomas (#)	n/a	n/a	n/a	n/a	n/a	n/a

Bloom Twp High SD 206
100 W 10th St • Chicago Heights, IL 60411-2002
(708) 755-7010 • http://www.bloomdistrict206.org/
Grade Span: 09-12; **Agency Type:** 1
Schools: 3
0 Primary; 0 Middle; 3 High; 0 Other Level
2 Regular; 1 Special Education; 0 Vocational; 0 Alternative
0 Magnet; 0 Charter; 2 Title I Eligible; 0 School-wide Title I
Students: 2,884 (52.8% male; 47.2% female)
Individual Education Program: 467 (16.2%);
English Language Learner: 164 (5.7%); Migrant: n/a
Eligible for Free Lunch Program: 816 (28.3%)
Eligible for Reduced-Price Lunch Program: 181 (6.3%)
Teachers: 209.0 (13.8 to 1)
Librarians/Media Specialists: 2.0 (1,442.0 to 1)
Guidance Counselors: 8.0 (360.5 to 1)
Current Spending: ($ per student per year):
Total: $11,819; Instruction: $6,963; Support Services: $4,474
Enrollment, Drop-out Rates and Diploma Recipients by Race/Ethnicity

Category	Total	White	Black	Asian	AIAN	Hisp.
Enrollment (%)	100.0	29.6	48.1	0.4	0.9	21.0
Drop-out Rate (%)	9.4	9.2	9.7	0.0	11.1	8.8
H.S. Diplomas (#)	491	193	202	0	7	89

Bremen Community HS District 228
15233 Pulaski Rd • Midlothian, IL 60445-3799
(708) 389-1175 • http://www.bhsd228.s-cook.k12.il.us/
Grade Span: 09-12; **Agency Type:** 1
Schools: 4
0 Primary; 0 Middle; 4 High; 0 Other Level
4 Regular; 0 Special Education; 0 Vocational; 0 Alternative
0 Magnet; 0 Charter; 2 Title I Eligible; 0 School-wide Title I
Students: 4,692 (50.3% male; 49.7% female)
Individual Education Program: 629 (13.4%);
English Language Learner: 49 (1.0%); Migrant: n/a
Eligible for Free Lunch Program: 0 (0.0%)
Eligible for Reduced-Price Lunch Program: 0 (0.0%)
Teachers: 297.1 (15.8 to 1)
Librarians/Media Specialists: 6.0 (782.0 to 1)
Guidance Counselors: 13.6 (345.0 to 1)
Current Spending: ($ per student per year):
Total: $10,677; Instruction: $6,349; Support Services: $4,304
Enrollment, Drop-out Rates and Diploma Recipients by Race/Ethnicity

Category	Total	White	Black	Asian	AIAN	Hisp.
Enrollment (%)	100.0	55.7	35.0	2.2	0.2	6.8
Drop-out Rate (%)	3.5	2.4	4.8	1.1	0.0	6.9
H.S. Diplomas (#)	953	600	290	23	1	39

Burbank SD 111
7600 S Central Ave • Burbank, IL 60459-1397
(708) 496-0500 • http://www.burbank.k12.il.us/
Grade Span: PK-08; **Agency Type:** 1
Schools: 7
7 Primary; 0 Middle; 0 High; 0 Other Level
7 Regular; 0 Special Education; 0 Vocational; 0 Alternative
0 Magnet; 0 Charter; 4 Title I Eligible; 0 School-wide Title I
Students: 3,336 (50.7% male; 49.3% female)
Individual Education Program: 492 (14.7%);
English Language Learner: 559 (16.8%); Migrant: n/a
Eligible for Free Lunch Program: 0 (0.0%)
Eligible for Reduced-Price Lunch Program: 0 (0.0%)
Teachers: 185.5 (18.0 to 1)
Librarians/Media Specialists: 4.0 (834.0 to 1)
Guidance Counselors: 0.0 (0.0 to 1)
Current Spending: ($ per student per year):
Total: $6,112; Instruction: $3,827; Support Services: $2,251
Enrollment, Drop-out Rates and Diploma Recipients by Race/Ethnicity

Category	Total	White	Black	Asian	AIAN	Hisp.
Enrollment (%)	100.0	78.5	0.4	1.9	0.0	19.2
Drop-out Rate (%)	n/a	n/a	n/a	n/a	n/a	n/a
H.S. Diplomas (#)	n/a	n/a	n/a	n/a	n/a	n/a

Chicago Heights SD 170
30 W 16th St • Chicago Heights, IL 60411-3412
(708) 756-4165 •
http://66.99.25.40/education/district/district.php?sectionid=1
Grade Span: PK-08; **Agency Type:** 1
Schools: 12
11 Primary; 1 Middle; 0 High; 0 Other Level
11 Regular; 1 Special Education; 0 Vocational; 0 Alternative
0 Magnet; 0 Charter; 10 Title I Eligible; 10 School-wide Title I
Students: 3,423 (50.8% male; 49.2% female)
Individual Education Program: 524 (15.3%);
English Language Learner: 315 (9.2%); Migrant: n/a
Eligible for Free Lunch Program: 2,654 (77.5%)

Eligible for Reduced-Price Lunch Program: 188 (5.5%)
Teachers: 207.0 (16.5 to 1)
Librarians/Media Specialists: 0.0 (0.0 to 1)
Guidance Counselors: 2.0 (1,711.5 to 1)
Current Spending: ($ per student per year):
Total: $7,382; Instruction: $4,491; Support Services: $2,541
Enrollment, Drop-out Rates and Diploma Recipients by Race/Ethnicity

Category	Total	White	Black	Asian	AIAN	Hisp.
Enrollment (%)	100.0	9.2	48.4	0.1	0.1	42.1
Drop-out Rate (%)	n/a	n/a	n/a	n/a	n/a	n/a
H.S. Diplomas (#)	n/a	n/a	n/a	n/a	n/a	n/a

Cicero SD 99
5110 W 24th St • Cicero, IL 60804-2931
(708) 863-4856 • http://bdcweb.cicd99.edu/
Grade Span: PK-08; **Agency Type:** 1
Schools: 15
14 Primary; 1 Middle; 0 High; 0 Other Level
15 Regular; 0 Special Education; 0 Vocational; 0 Alternative
0 Magnet; 0 Charter; 15 Title I Eligible; 15 School-wide Title I
Students: 13,276 (52.0% male; 48.0% female)
Individual Education Program: 1,762 (13.3%);
English Language Learner: 6,532 (49.2%); Migrant: n/a
Eligible for Free Lunch Program: 8,065 (60.7%)
Eligible for Reduced-Price Lunch Program: 1,787 (13.5%)
Teachers: 671.0 (19.8 to 1)
Librarians/Media Specialists: 8.0 (1,659.5 to 1)
Guidance Counselors: 0.0 (0.0 to 1)
Current Spending: ($ per student per year):
Total: $5,200; Instruction: $3,197; Support Services: $1,758
Enrollment, Drop-out Rates and Diploma Recipients by Race/Ethnicity

Category	Total	White	Black	Asian	AIAN	Hisp.
Enrollment (%)	100.0	4.8	0.7	0.3	0.0	94.2
Drop-out Rate (%)	n/a	n/a	n/a	n/a	n/a	n/a
H.S. Diplomas (#)	n/a	n/a	n/a	n/a	n/a	n/a

City of Chicago SD 299
125 S Clark • Chicago, IL 60603-4016
(773) 553-1000 • http://www.cps.k12.il.us/
Grade Span: PK-12; **Agency Type:** 1
Schools: 608
477 Primary; 22 Middle; 75 High; 34 Other Level
586 Regular; 22 Special Education; 0 Vocational; 0 Alternative
314 Magnet; 15 Charter; 477 Title I Eligible; 449 School-wide Title I
Students: 436,048 (50.5% male; 49.5% female)
Individual Education Program: 55,548 (12.7%);
English Language Learner: 83,926 (19.2%); Migrant: n/a
Eligible for Free Lunch Program: 301,138 (69.1%)
Eligible for Reduced-Price Lunch Program: 37,053 (8.5%)
Teachers: 24,584.0 (17.7 to 1)
Librarians/Media Specialists: 454.0 (960.5 to 1)
Guidance Counselors: 802.0 (543.7 to 1)
Current Spending: ($ per student per year):
Total: $7,374; Instruction: $4,626; Support Services: $2,388
Enrollment, Drop-out Rates and Diploma Recipients by Race/Ethnicity

Category	Total	White	Black	Asian	AIAN	Hisp.
Enrollment (%)	100.0	9.3	50.7	3.3	0.2	36.5
Drop-out Rate (%)	16.8	16.1	18.8	7.9	14.3	15.2
H.S. Diplomas (#)	15,653	2,018	7,623	931	26	5,055

Community CSD 168
21899 S Torrence Ave • Sauk Village, IL 60411-4405
(708) 758-1610
Grade Span: PK-08; **Agency Type:** 1
Schools: 3
2 Primary; 1 Middle; 0 High; 0 Other Level
3 Regular; 0 Special Education; 0 Vocational; 0 Alternative
0 Magnet; 0 Charter; 1 Title I Eligible; 1 School-wide Title I
Students: 1,748 (51.0% male; 49.0% female)
Individual Education Program: 241 (13.8%);
English Language Learner: 0 (0.0%); Migrant: n/a
Eligible for Free Lunch Program: 646 (37.0%)
Eligible for Reduced-Price Lunch Program: 139 (8.0%)
Teachers: 99.0 (17.7 to 1)
Librarians/Media Specialists: 0.0 (0.0 to 1)
Guidance Counselors: 0.0 (0.0 to 1)
Current Spending: ($ per student per year):
Total: $4,853; Instruction: $2,897; Support Services: $1,738
Enrollment, Drop-out Rates and Diploma Recipients by Race/Ethnicity

Category	Total	White	Black	Asian	AIAN	Hisp.
Enrollment (%)	100.0	32.3	55.5	0.4	0.2	11.6
Drop-out Rate (%)	n/a	n/a	n/a	n/a	n/a	n/a
H.S. Diplomas (#)	n/a	n/a	n/a	n/a	n/a	n/a

Community CSD 59
2123 S Arlington Hts • Arlington Heights, IL 60005-4596
(847) 593-4300 • http://www.elk-grove.k12.il.us/
Grade Span: PK-08; **Agency Type:** 1
Schools: 14
11 Primary; 3 Middle; 0 High; 0 Other Level
14 Regular; 0 Special Education; 0 Vocational; 0 Alternative
0 Magnet; 0 Charter; 2 Title I Eligible; 0 School-wide Title I
Students: 6,436 (52.5% male; 47.5% female)
Individual Education Program: 682 (10.6%);
English Language Learner: 1,889 (29.4%); Migrant: n/a
Eligible for Free Lunch Program: 1,233 (19.2%)
Eligible for Reduced-Price Lunch Program: 340 (5.3%)
Teachers: 410.6 (15.7 to 1)
Librarians/Media Specialists: 7.0 (919.4 to 1)
Guidance Counselors: 0.0 (0.0 to 1)
Current Spending: ($ per student per year):
Total: $8,708; Instruction: $4,904; Support Services: $3,576
Enrollment, Drop-out Rates and Diploma Recipients by Race/Ethnicity

Category	Total	White	Black	Asian	AIAN	Hisp.
Enrollment (%)	100.0	59.1	3.3	12.3	0.2	25.2
Drop-out Rate (%)	n/a	n/a	n/a	n/a	n/a	n/a
H.S. Diplomas (#)	n/a	n/a	n/a	n/a	n/a	n/a

Community CSD 62
777 E Algonquin Rd • Des Plaines, IL 60016-6296
(847) 824-1136 • http://www.d62.org/
Grade Span: PK-08; **Agency Type:** 1
Schools: 11
9 Primary; 2 Middle; 0 High; 0 Other Level
11 Regular; 0 Special Education; 0 Vocational; 0 Alternative
0 Magnet; 0 Charter; 4 Title I Eligible; 0 School-wide Title I
Students: 4,993 (51.6% male; 48.4% female)
Individual Education Program: 915 (18.3%);
English Language Learner: 969 (19.4%); Migrant: n/a
Eligible for Free Lunch Program: 1,056 (21.1%)
Eligible for Reduced-Price Lunch Program: 406 (8.1%)
Teachers: 363.8 (13.7 to 1)
Librarians/Media Specialists: 6.0 (832.2 to 1)
Guidance Counselors: 1.8 (2,773.9 to 1)
Current Spending: ($ per student per year):
Total: $9,255; Instruction: $6,093; Support Services: $3,024
Enrollment, Drop-out Rates and Diploma Recipients by Race/Ethnicity

Category	Total	White	Black	Asian	AIAN	Hisp.
Enrollment (%)	100.0	57.1	3.4	9.4	0.0	30.1
Drop-out Rate (%)	n/a	n/a	n/a	n/a	n/a	n/a
H.S. Diplomas (#)	n/a	n/a	n/a	n/a	n/a	n/a

Community High SD 218
10701 Kilpatrick Ave • Oak Lawn, IL 60453-5464
(708) 424-2000 • http://www.chsd218.org/
Grade Span: 09-12; **Agency Type:** 1
Schools: 4
0 Primary; 0 Middle; 4 High; 0 Other Level
3 Regular; 1 Special Education; 0 Vocational; 0 Alternative
0 Magnet; 0 Charter; 2 Title I Eligible; 0 School-wide Title I
Students: 5,018 (50.2% male; 49.8% female)
Individual Education Program: 701 (14.0%);
English Language Learner: 89 (1.8%); Migrant: n/a
Eligible for Free Lunch Program: 1,361 (27.1%)
Eligible for Reduced-Price Lunch Program: 340 (6.8%)
Teachers: 293.1 (17.1 to 1)
Librarians/Media Specialists: 5.0 (1,003.6 to 1)
Guidance Counselors: 15.0 (334.5 to 1)
Current Spending: ($ per student per year):
Total: $12,202; Instruction: $7,031; Support Services: $4,917
Enrollment, Drop-out Rates and Diploma Recipients by Race/Ethnicity

Category	Total	White	Black	Asian	AIAN	Hisp.
Enrollment (%)	100.0	56.6	25.6	1.4	0.3	16.1
Drop-out Rate (%)	7.0	5.2	9.2	5.4	5.6	9.9
H.S. Diplomas (#)	894	544	190	6	2	152

Consolidated High SD 230
15100 S 94th Ave • Orland Park, IL 60462-3820
(708) 349-5750 • http://www.d230.org/
Grade Span: 09-12; **Agency Type:** 1
Schools: 4
0 Primary; 0 Middle; 3 High; 1 Other Level
4 Regular; 0 Special Education; 0 Vocational; 0 Alternative
0 Magnet; 0 Charter; 3 Title I Eligible; 0 School-wide Title I
Students: 7,990 (50.3% male; 49.7% female)
Individual Education Program: 923 (11.6%);
English Language Learner: 157 (2.0%); Migrant: n/a
Eligible for Free Lunch Program: 0 (0.0%)
Eligible for Reduced-Price Lunch Program: 0 (0.0%)

Teachers: 469.2 (17.0 to 1)
Librarians/Media Specialists: 7.0 (1,141.4 to 1)
Guidance Counselors: 24.0 (332.9 to 1)
Current Spending: ($ per student per year):
Total: $10,526; Instruction: $5,580; Support Services: $4,722
Enrollment, Drop-out Rates and Diploma Recipients by Race/Ethnicity

Category	Total	White	Black	Asian	AIAN	Hisp.
Enrollment (%)	100.0	91.1	1.5	3.0	0.1	4.3
Drop-out Rate (%)	1.9	1.9	1.0	0.0	37.5	3.6
H.S. Diplomas (#)	1,796	1,663	19	45	22	47

Cook County SD 130

12300 S Greenwood Av • Blue Island, IL 60406-1558
(708) 385-6800 • http://www.lincolnnet.net/users/lsd130/
Grade Span: PK-08; **Agency Type:** 1
Schools: 11
6 Primary; 5 Middle; 0 High; 0 Other Level
10 Regular; 1 Special Education; 0 Vocational; 0 Alternative
0 Magnet; 0 Charter; 10 Title I Eligible; 10 School-wide Title I
Students: 3,794 (51.8% male; 48.2% female)
Individual Education Program: 814 (21.5%);
English Language Learner: 560 (14.8%); Migrant: n/a
Eligible for Free Lunch Program: 2,221 (58.5%)
Eligible for Reduced-Price Lunch Program: 327 (8.6%)
Teachers: 252.9 (15.0 to 1)
Librarians/Media Specialists: 4.0 (948.5 to 1)
Guidance Counselors: 0.0 (0.0 to 1)
Current Spending: ($ per student per year):
Total: $6,911; Instruction: $4,259; Support Services: $2,368
Enrollment, Drop-out Rates and Diploma Recipients by Race/Ethnicity

Category	Total	White	Black	Asian	AIAN	Hisp.
Enrollment (%)	100.0	27.3	25.3	0.4	0.0	46.9
Drop-out Rate (%)	n/a	n/a	n/a	n/a	n/a	n/a
H.S. Diplomas (#)	n/a	n/a	n/a	n/a	n/a	n/a

Country Club Hills SD 160

4411 W 185th St • Country Club Hill, IL 60478-5219
(708) 957-6200 • http://www.d160.s-cook.k12.il.us/
Grade Span: PK-08; **Agency Type:** 1
Schools: 3
2 Primary; 1 Middle; 0 High; 0 Other Level
3 Regular; 0 Special Education; 0 Vocational; 0 Alternative
0 Magnet; 0 Charter; 2 Title I Eligible; 2 School-wide Title I
Students: 1,585 (50.5% male; 49.5% female)
Individual Education Program: 263 (16.6%);
English Language Learner: 0 (0.0%); Migrant: n/a
Eligible for Free Lunch Program: 741 (46.8%)
Eligible for Reduced-Price Lunch Program: 47 (3.0%)
Teachers: 99.0 (16.0 to 1)
Librarians/Media Specialists: 1.0 (1,585.0 to 1)
Guidance Counselors: 1.0 (1,585.0 to 1)
Current Spending: ($ per student per year):
Total: $6,444; Instruction: $3,546; Support Services: $2,718
Enrollment, Drop-out Rates and Diploma Recipients by Race/Ethnicity

Category	Total	White	Black	Asian	AIAN	Hisp.
Enrollment (%)	100.0	1.5	97.5	0.4	0.1	0.6
Drop-out Rate (%)	n/a	n/a	n/a	n/a	n/a	n/a
H.S. Diplomas (#)	n/a	n/a	n/a	n/a	n/a	n/a

Dolton SD 148

114 W 144thst • Riverdale, IL 60827-2703
(708) 841-2290
Grade Span: PK-08; **Agency Type:** 1
Schools: 11
8 Primary; 2 Middle; 0 High; 1 Other Level
10 Regular; 1 Special Education; 0 Vocational; 0 Alternative
0 Magnet; 0 Charter; 7 Title I Eligible; 7 School-wide Title I
Students: 3,426 (53.1% male; 46.9% female)
Individual Education Program: 471 (13.7%);
English Language Learner: 1 (<0.1%); Migrant: n/a
Eligible for Free Lunch Program: 1,985 (57.9%)
Eligible for Reduced-Price Lunch Program: 304 (8.9%)
Teachers: 203.4 (16.8 to 1)
Librarians/Media Specialists: 7.0 (489.4 to 1)
Guidance Counselors: 0.0 (0.0 to 1)
Current Spending: ($ per student per year):
Total: $6,014; Instruction: $3,581; Support Services: $2,230
Enrollment, Drop-out Rates and Diploma Recipients by Race/Ethnicity

Category	Total	White	Black	Asian	AIAN	Hisp.
Enrollment (%)	100.0	1.0	96.9	0.1	0.0	2.0
Drop-out Rate (%)	n/a	n/a	n/a	n/a	n/a	n/a
H.S. Diplomas (#)	n/a	n/a	n/a	n/a	n/a	n/a

Dolton SD 149

292 Torrence Ave • Calumet City, IL 60409-1941
(708) 868-7861
Grade Span: PK-08; **Agency Type:** 1
Schools: 6
5 Primary; 1 Middle; 0 High; 0 Other Level
6 Regular; 0 Special Education; 0 Vocational; 0 Alternative
0 Magnet; 0 Charter; 5 Title I Eligible; 0 School-wide Title I
Students: 4,088 (49.7% male; 50.3% female)
Individual Education Program: 493 (12.1%);
English Language Learner: 0 (0.0%); Migrant: n/a
Eligible for Free Lunch Program: 2,207 (54.0%)
Eligible for Reduced-Price Lunch Program: 385 (9.4%)
Teachers: 205.9 (19.9 to 1)
Librarians/Media Specialists: 1.0 (4,088.0 to 1)
Guidance Counselors: 1.0 (4,088.0 to 1)
Current Spending: ($ per student per year):
Total: $6,142; Instruction: $3,356; Support Services: $2,535
Enrollment, Drop-out Rates and Diploma Recipients by Race/Ethnicity

Category	Total	White	Black	Asian	AIAN	Hisp.
Enrollment (%)	100.0	0.7	97.5	0.0	0.0	1.8
Drop-out Rate (%)	n/a	n/a	n/a	n/a	n/a	n/a
H.S. Diplomas (#)	n/a	n/a	n/a	n/a	n/a	n/a

East Maine SD 63

10150 Dee Rd • Des Plaines, IL 60016-1597
(847) 299-1900 • http://www.emsd63.n-cook.k12.il.us/
Grade Span: PK-08; **Agency Type:** 1
Schools: 7
6 Primary; 1 Middle; 0 High; 0 Other Level
7 Regular; 0 Special Education; 0 Vocational; 0 Alternative
0 Magnet; 0 Charter; 3 Title I Eligible; 0 School-wide Title I
Students: 3,635 (51.2% male; 48.8% female)
Individual Education Program: 328 (9.0%);
English Language Learner: 559 (15.4%); Migrant: n/a
Eligible for Free Lunch Program: 774 (21.3%)
Eligible for Reduced-Price Lunch Program: 211 (5.8%)
Teachers: 240.7 (15.1 to 1)
Librarians/Media Specialists: 5.0 (727.0 to 1)
Guidance Counselors: 1.9 (1,913.2 to 1)
Current Spending: ($ per student per year):
Total: $8,196; Instruction: $4,610; Support Services: $3,320
Enrollment, Drop-out Rates and Diploma Recipients by Race/Ethnicity

Category	Total	White	Black	Asian	AIAN	Hisp.
Enrollment (%)	100.0	42.9	4.2	36.4	0.1	16.4
Drop-out Rate (%)	n/a	n/a	n/a	n/a	n/a	n/a
H.S. Diplomas (#)	n/a	n/a	n/a	n/a	n/a	n/a

Elem SD 159

6202 Vollmer Rd • Matteson, IL 60443-1058
(708) 720-1300 • http://www.dist159.com/
Grade Span: PK-08; **Agency Type:** 1
Schools: 4
4 Primary; 0 Middle; 0 High; 0 Other Level
4 Regular; 0 Special Education; 0 Vocational; 0 Alternative
0 Magnet; 0 Charter; 2 Title I Eligible; 0 School-wide Title I
Students: 1,733 (53.3% male; 46.7% female)
Individual Education Program: 249 (14.4%);
English Language Learner: 0 (0.0%); Migrant: n/a
Eligible for Free Lunch Program: 478 (27.6%)
Eligible for Reduced-Price Lunch Program: 120 (6.9%)
Teachers: 128.5 (13.5 to 1)
Librarians/Media Specialists: 4.5 (385.1 to 1)
Guidance Counselors: 0.0 (0.0 to 1)
Current Spending: ($ per student per year):
Total: $9,106; Instruction: $6,296; Support Services: $2,515
Enrollment, Drop-out Rates and Diploma Recipients by Race/Ethnicity

Category	Total	White	Black	Asian	AIAN	Hisp.
Enrollment (%)	100.0	10.3	85.9	0.8	0.1	2.8
Drop-out Rate (%)	n/a	n/a	n/a	n/a	n/a	n/a
H.S. Diplomas (#)	n/a	n/a	n/a	n/a	n/a	n/a

Elmwood Park CUSD 401

8201 W Fullerton Ave • Elmwood Park, IL 60707-2499
(708) 583-5830 • http://www.epcusd.w-cook.k12.il.us/
Grade Span: PK-12; **Agency Type:** 1
Schools: 5
3 Primary; 1 Middle; 1 High; 0 Other Level
5 Regular; 0 Special Education; 0 Vocational; 0 Alternative
0 Magnet; 0 Charter; 3 Title I Eligible; 0 School-wide Title I
Students: 2,939 (50.8% male; 49.2% female)
Individual Education Program: 474 (16.1%);
English Language Learner: 288 (9.8%); Migrant: n/a
Eligible for Free Lunch Program: 295 (10.0%)
Eligible for Reduced-Price Lunch Program: 74 (2.5%)

Teachers: 160.2 (18.3 to 1)
Librarians/Media Specialists: 1.0 (2,939.0 to 1)
Guidance Counselors: 3.0 (979.7 to 1)
Current Spending: ($ per student per year):
Total: $7,027; Instruction: $4,041; Support Services: $2,774
Enrollment, Drop-out Rates and Diploma Recipients by Race/Ethnicity

Category	Total	White	Black	Asian	AIAN	Hisp.
Enrollment (%)	100.0	79.1	0.4	1.6	0.0	18.9
Drop-out Rate (%)	4.5	4.3	0.0	0.0	n/a	6.7
H.S. Diplomas (#)	187	164	0	4	0	19

Evanston CCSD 65

1500 Mcdaniel • Evanston, IL 60201-3976
(847) 859-8600 • http://www.d65.k12.il.us/
Grade Span: PK-08; **Agency Type:** 1
Schools: 17
14 Primary; 3 Middle; 0 High; 0 Other Level
15 Regular; 2 Special Education; 0 Vocational; 0 Alternative
2 Magnet; 0 Charter; 7 Title I Eligible; 0 School-wide Title I
Students: 7,003 (52.0% male; 48.0% female)
Individual Education Program: 1,491 (21.3%);
English Language Learner: 246 (3.5%); Migrant: n/a
Eligible for Free Lunch Program: 1,629 (23.3%)
Eligible for Reduced-Price Lunch Program: 428 (6.1%)
Teachers: 536.8 (13.0 to 1)
Librarians/Media Specialists: 15.0 (466.9 to 1)
Guidance Counselors: 0.0 (0.0 to 1)
Current Spending: ($ per student per year):
Total: $10,081; Instruction: $5,939; Support Services: $3,902
Enrollment, Drop-out Rates and Diploma Recipients by Race/Ethnicity

Category	Total	White	Black	Asian	AIAN	Hisp.
Enrollment (%)	100.0	40.7	43.7	3.8	0.1	11.7
Drop-out Rate (%)	0.0	0.0	0.0	n/a	n/a	0.0
H.S. Diplomas (#)	n/a	n/a	n/a	n/a	n/a	n/a

Evanston Twp HSD 202

1600 Dodge Ave • Evanston, IL 60204-3450
(847) 424-7220 • http://www.eths.k12.il.us/
Grade Span: 09-12; **Agency Type:** 1
Schools: 1
0 Primary; 0 Middle; 1 High; 0 Other Level
1 Regular; 0 Special Education; 0 Vocational; 0 Alternative
0 Magnet; 0 Charter; 1 Title I Eligible; 0 School-wide Title I
Students: 3,148 (50.0% male; 50.0% female)
Individual Education Program: 541 (17.2%);
English Language Learner: 73 (2.3%); Migrant: n/a
Eligible for Free Lunch Program: 608 (19.3%)
Eligible for Reduced-Price Lunch Program: 184 (5.8%)
Teachers: 254.4 (12.4 to 1)
Librarians/Media Specialists: 5.0 (629.6 to 1)
Guidance Counselors: 15.0 (209.9 to 1)
Current Spending: ($ per student per year):
Total: $16,240; Instruction: $8,582; Support Services: $7,149
Enrollment, Drop-out Rates and Diploma Recipients by Race/Ethnicity

Category	Total	White	Black	Asian	AIAN	Hisp.
Enrollment (%)	100.0	48.9	41.4	2.2	0.1	7.5
Drop-out Rate (%)	2.5	0.3	4.6	0.0	50.0	5.8
H.S. Diplomas (#)	667	352	237	22	1	55

Evergreen Park ESD 124

9400 S Sawyer Ave • Evergreen Park, IL 60805-2384
(708) 423-0950 • http://www.d124.s-cook.k12.il.us/
Grade Span: PK-08; **Agency Type:** 1
Schools: 5
5 Primary; 0 Middle; 0 High; 0 Other Level
5 Regular; 0 Special Education; 0 Vocational; 0 Alternative
0 Magnet; 0 Charter; 3 Title I Eligible; 0 School-wide Title I
Students: 2,094 (52.1% male; 47.9% female)
Individual Education Program: 353 (16.9%);
English Language Learner: 37 (1.8%); Migrant: n/a
Eligible for Free Lunch Program: 308 (14.7%)
Eligible for Reduced-Price Lunch Program: 62 (3.0%)
Teachers: 134.0 (15.6 to 1)
Librarians/Media Specialists: 1.0 (2,094.0 to 1)
Guidance Counselors: 0.0 (0.0 to 1)
Current Spending: ($ per student per year):
Total: $6,390; Instruction: $3,662; Support Services: $2,574
Enrollment, Drop-out Rates and Diploma Recipients by Race/Ethnicity

Category	Total	White	Black	Asian	AIAN	Hisp.
Enrollment (%)	100.0	73.2	16.5	1.9	0.1	8.3
Drop-out Rate (%)	n/a	n/a	n/a	n/a	n/a	n/a
H.S. Diplomas (#)	n/a	n/a	n/a	n/a	n/a	n/a

Flossmoor SD 161

41 E Elmwood • Chicago Heights, IL 60411-1104
(708) 647-7000 • http://www.sd161.org/
Grade Span: PK-08; **Agency Type:** 1
Schools: 5
4 Primary; 1 Middle; 0 High; 0 Other Level
5 Regular; 0 Special Education; 0 Vocational; 0 Alternative
0 Magnet; 0 Charter; 2 Title I Eligible; 0 School-wide Title I
Students: 2,588 (51.2% male; 48.8% female)
Individual Education Program: 317 (12.2%);
English Language Learner: 22 (0.9%); Migrant: n/a
Eligible for Free Lunch Program: 0 (0.0%)
Eligible for Reduced-Price Lunch Program: 0 (0.0%)
Teachers: 165.2 (15.7 to 1)
Librarians/Media Specialists: 1.0 (2,588.0 to 1)
Guidance Counselors: 2.0 (1,294.0 to 1)
Current Spending: ($ per student per year):
Total: $8,006; Instruction: $4,500; Support Services: $3,467
Enrollment, Drop-out Rates and Diploma Recipients by Race/Ethnicity

Category	Total	White	Black	Asian	AIAN	Hisp.
Enrollment (%)	100.0	41.4	51.7	1.9	0.0	5.0
Drop-out Rate (%)	n/a	n/a	n/a	n/a	n/a	n/a
H.S. Diplomas (#)	n/a	n/a	n/a	n/a	n/a	n/a

Forest Ridge SD 142

15000 S Laramie Ave • Oak Forest, IL 60452-2325
(708) 687-3334 • http://www.d142.s-cook.k12.il.us/frsd142index.htm
Grade Span: PK-08; **Agency Type:** 1
Schools: 4
3 Primary; 1 Middle; 0 High; 0 Other Level
4 Regular; 0 Special Education; 0 Vocational; 0 Alternative
0 Magnet; 0 Charter; 1 Title I Eligible; 0 School-wide Title I
Students: 1,760 (53.5% male; 46.5% female)
Individual Education Program: 303 (17.2%);
English Language Learner: 37 (2.1%); Migrant: n/a
Eligible for Free Lunch Program: n/a
Eligible for Reduced-Price Lunch Program: n/a
Teachers: 113.7 (15.5 to 1)
Librarians/Media Specialists: 0.0 (0.0 to 1)
Guidance Counselors: 1.0 (1,760.0 to 1)
Current Spending: ($ per student per year):
Total: $6,433; Instruction: $3,721; Support Services: $2,569
Enrollment, Drop-out Rates and Diploma Recipients by Race/Ethnicity

Category	Total	White	Black	Asian	AIAN	Hisp.
Enrollment (%)	100.0	89.5	2.4	1.1	0.3	6.6
Drop-out Rate (%)	n/a	n/a	n/a	n/a	n/a	n/a
H.S. Diplomas (#)	n/a	n/a	n/a	n/a	n/a	n/a

Glenview CCSD 34

1401 Greenwood Rd • Glenview, IL 60025-1599
(847) 998-5000 • http://www.ncook.k12.il.us/
Grade Span: PK-08; **Agency Type:** 1
Schools: 7
3 Primary; 4 Middle; 0 High; 0 Other Level
7 Regular; 0 Special Education; 0 Vocational; 0 Alternative
0 Magnet; 0 Charter; 3 Title I Eligible; 0 School-wide Title I
Students: 3,898 (52.2% male; 47.8% female)
Individual Education Program: 694 (17.8%);
English Language Learner: 419 (10.7%); Migrant: n/a
Eligible for Free Lunch Program: 408 (10.5%)
Eligible for Reduced-Price Lunch Program: 152 (3.9%)
Teachers: 271.0 (14.4 to 1)
Librarians/Media Specialists: 1.0 (3,898.0 to 1)
Guidance Counselors: 0.0 (0.0 to 1)
Current Spending: ($ per student per year):
Total: $8,876; Instruction: $5,265; Support Services: $3,342
Enrollment, Drop-out Rates and Diploma Recipients by Race/Ethnicity

Category	Total	White	Black	Asian	AIAN	Hisp.
Enrollment (%)	100.0	75.1	3.4	11.3	0.2	10.1
Drop-out Rate (%)	n/a	n/a	n/a	n/a	n/a	n/a
H.S. Diplomas (#)	n/a	n/a	n/a	n/a	n/a	n/a

Harvey SD 152

16001 Lincoln Ave • Harvey, IL 60426-4916
(708) 333-0300 • http://www.harvey152.org/
Grade Span: PK-08; **Agency Type:** 1
Schools: 8
7 Primary; 1 Middle; 0 High; 0 Other Level
7 Regular; 1 Special Education; 0 Vocational; 0 Alternative
0 Magnet; 0 Charter; 7 Title I Eligible; 7 School-wide Title I
Students: 3,143 (52.1% male; 47.9% female)
Individual Education Program: 497 (15.8%);
English Language Learner: 108 (3.4%); Migrant: n/a
Eligible for Free Lunch Program: 2,425 (77.2%)
Eligible for Reduced-Price Lunch Program: 173 (5.5%)

Teachers: 155.0 (20.3 to 1)
Librarians/Media Specialists: 1.0 (3,143.0 to 1)
Guidance Counselors: 0.0 (0.0 to 1)
Current Spending: ($ per student per year):
Total: $6,579; Instruction: $3,388; Support Services: $2,819
Enrollment, Drop-out Rates and Diploma Recipients by Race/Ethnicity

Category	Total	White	Black	Asian	AIAN	Hisp.
Enrollment (%)	100.0	0.9	85.5	1.1	0.1	12.4
Drop-out Rate (%)	n/a	n/a	n/a	n/a	n/a	n/a
H.S. Diplomas (#)	n/a	n/a	n/a	n/a	n/a	n/a

Homewood Flossmoor CHSD 233
999 Kedzie Ave • Flossmoor, IL 60422-2299
(708) 799-3000 • http://www.hfhighschool.org/
Grade Span: 09-12; **Agency Type:** 1
Schools: 1
0 Primary; 0 Middle; 1 High; 0 Other Level
1 Regular; 0 Special Education; 0 Vocational; 0 Alternative
0 Magnet; 0 Charter; 0 Title I Eligible; 0 School-wide Title I
Students: 2,641 (50.5% male; 49.5% female)
Individual Education Program: 281 (10.6%);
English Language Learner: 0 (0.0%); Migrant: n/a
Eligible for Free Lunch Program: 171 (6.5%)
Eligible for Reduced-Price Lunch Program: 22 (0.8%)
Teachers: 166.6 (15.9 to 1)
Librarians/Media Specialists: 2.0 (1,320.5 to 1)
Guidance Counselors: 9.0 (293.4 to 1)
Current Spending: ($ per student per year):
Total: $11,422; Instruction: $6,078; Support Services: $5,114
Enrollment, Drop-out Rates and Diploma Recipients by Race/Ethnicity

Category	Total	White	Black	Asian	AIAN	Hisp.
Enrollment (%)	100.0	55.8	38.5	2.0	0.0	3.7
Drop-out Rate (%)	2.6	1.4	4.6	1.4	n/a	6.5
H.S. Diplomas (#)	563	372	163	17	0	11

Homewood SD 153
18205 Aberdeen St • Homewood, IL 60430-2400
(708) 799-5661 • http://www.homewoodsd153.org/
Grade Span: PK-08; **Agency Type:** 1
Schools: 4
2 Primary; 2 Middle; 0 High; 0 Other Level
4 Regular; 0 Special Education; 0 Vocational; 0 Alternative
0 Magnet; 0 Charter; 0 Title I Eligible; 0 School-wide Title I
Students: 2,184 (50.4% male; 49.6% female)
Individual Education Program: 315 (14.4%);
English Language Learner: 0 (0.0%); Migrant: n/a
Eligible for Free Lunch Program: 160 (7.3%)
Eligible for Reduced-Price Lunch Program: 91 (4.2%)
Teachers: 146.8 (14.9 to 1)
Librarians/Media Specialists: 0.0 (0.0 to 1)
Guidance Counselors: 0.0 (0.0 to 1)
Current Spending: ($ per student per year):
Total: $7,157; Instruction: $4,074; Support Services: $2,886
Enrollment, Drop-out Rates and Diploma Recipients by Race/Ethnicity

Category	Total	White	Black	Asian	AIAN	Hisp.
Enrollment (%)	100.0	63.6	29.0	2.3	0.0	5.2
Drop-out Rate (%)	n/a	n/a	n/a	n/a	n/a	n/a
H.S. Diplomas (#)	n/a	n/a	n/a	n/a	n/a	n/a

Indian Springs SD 109
7540 S 86th Ave • Justice, IL 60458-1168
(708) 496-8700 • http://www.indianspringsschools.org/
Grade Span: PK-08; **Agency Type:** 1
Schools: 6
5 Primary; 0 Middle; 0 High; 1 Other Level
6 Regular; 0 Special Education; 0 Vocational; 0 Alternative
0 Magnet; 0 Charter; 4 Title I Eligible; 0 School-wide Title I
Students: 2,878 (51.6% male; 48.4% female)
Individual Education Program: 337 (11.7%);
English Language Learner: 229 (8.0%); Migrant: n/a
Eligible for Free Lunch Program: 840 (29.2%)
Eligible for Reduced-Price Lunch Program: 129 (4.5%)
Teachers: 170.0 (16.9 to 1)
Librarians/Media Specialists: 0.0 (0.0 to 1)
Guidance Counselors: 0.0 (0.0 to 1)
Current Spending: ($ per student per year):
Total: $5,681; Instruction: $3,069; Support Services: $2,358
Enrollment, Drop-out Rates and Diploma Recipients by Race/Ethnicity

Category	Total	White	Black	Asian	AIAN	Hisp.
Enrollment (%)	100.0	72.2	15.7	1.3	0.3	10.6
Drop-out Rate (%)	n/a	n/a	n/a	n/a	n/a	n/a
H.S. Diplomas (#)	n/a	n/a	n/a	n/a	n/a	n/a

J S Morton HS District 201
2423 S Austin Blvd • Cicero, IL 60804-2695
(708) 222-5702 • http://www.jsmortonhs.com/
Grade Span: 09-12; **Agency Type:** 1
Schools: 3
0 Primary; 0 Middle; 3 High; 0 Other Level
2 Regular; 1 Special Education; 0 Vocational; 0 Alternative
0 Magnet; 0 Charter; 2 Title I Eligible; 0 School-wide Title I
Students: 7,240 (50.9% male; 49.1% female)
Individual Education Program: 773 (10.7%);
English Language Learner: 569 (7.9%); Migrant: n/a
Eligible for Free Lunch Program: 2,954 (40.8%)
Eligible for Reduced-Price Lunch Program: 941 (13.0%)
Teachers: 383.0 (18.9 to 1)
Librarians/Media Specialists: 2.0 (3,620.0 to 1)
Guidance Counselors: 23.0 (314.8 to 1)
Current Spending: ($ per student per year):
Total: $8,899; Instruction: $5,332; Support Services: $3,191
Enrollment, Drop-out Rates and Diploma Recipients by Race/Ethnicity

Category	Total	White	Black	Asian	AIAN	Hisp.
Enrollment (%)	100.0	22.8	1.0	0.9	0.1	75.2
Drop-out Rate (%)	5.7	6.1	10.0	0.0	0.0	5.6
H.S. Diplomas (#)	1,222	359	7	12	4	840

Kirby SD 140
16931 S Grissom Dr • Tinley Park, IL 60477-2318
(708) 532-6462 • http://www.ksd140.org/
Grade Span: PK-08; **Agency Type:** 1
Schools: 8
6 Primary; 2 Middle; 0 High; 0 Other Level
8 Regular; 0 Special Education; 0 Vocational; 0 Alternative
0 Magnet; 0 Charter; 4 Title I Eligible; 0 School-wide Title I
Students: 4,712 (51.2% male; 48.8% female)
Individual Education Program: 633 (13.4%);
English Language Learner: 221 (4.7%); Migrant: n/a
Eligible for Free Lunch Program: 0 (0.0%)
Eligible for Reduced-Price Lunch Program: 0 (0.0%)
Teachers: 288.2 (16.3 to 1)
Librarians/Media Specialists: 2.0 (2,356.0 to 1)
Guidance Counselors: 5.0 (942.4 to 1)
Current Spending: ($ per student per year):
Total: $6,347; Instruction: $3,907; Support Services: $2,428
Enrollment, Drop-out Rates and Diploma Recipients by Race/Ethnicity

Category	Total	White	Black	Asian	AIAN	Hisp.
Enrollment (%)	100.0	91.4	1.3	2.8	0.3	4.2
Drop-out Rate (%)	n/a	n/a	n/a	n/a	n/a	n/a
H.S. Diplomas (#)	n/a	n/a	n/a	n/a	n/a	n/a

La Grange SD 102
333 N Park Rd • La Grange Park, IL 60526-1898
(708) 482-2400 • http://www.dist102.k12.il.us/
Grade Span: PK-08; **Agency Type:** 1
Schools: 5
4 Primary; 1 Middle; 0 High; 0 Other Level
5 Regular; 0 Special Education; 0 Vocational; 0 Alternative
0 Magnet; 0 Charter; 3 Title I Eligible; 0 School-wide Title I
Students: 2,596 (52.1% male; 47.9% female)
Individual Education Program: 424 (16.3%);
English Language Learner: 118 (4.5%); Migrant: n/a
Eligible for Free Lunch Program: 213 (8.2%)
Eligible for Reduced-Price Lunch Program: 35 (1.3%)
Teachers: 185.0 (14.0 to 1)
Librarians/Media Specialists: 3.0 (865.3 to 1)
Guidance Counselors: 0.0 (0.0 to 1)
Current Spending: ($ per student per year):
Total: $7,412; Instruction: $4,586; Support Services: $2,694
Enrollment, Drop-out Rates and Diploma Recipients by Race/Ethnicity

Category	Total	White	Black	Asian	AIAN	Hisp.
Enrollment (%)	100.0	82.7	8.0	1.9	0.0	7.4
Drop-out Rate (%)	n/a	n/a	n/a	n/a	n/a	n/a
H.S. Diplomas (#)	n/a	n/a	n/a	n/a	n/a	n/a

Lansing SD 158
18300 Greenbay Ave • Lansing, IL 60438-3009
(708) 474-6700 • http://www.d158.s-cook.k12.il.us/
Grade Span: PK-08; **Agency Type:** 1
Schools: 5
4 Primary; 1 Middle; 0 High; 0 Other Level
4 Regular; 1 Special Education; 0 Vocational; 0 Alternative
0 Magnet; 0 Charter; 1 Title I Eligible; 0 School-wide Title I
Students: 2,074 (51.1% male; 48.9% female)
Individual Education Program: 367 (17.7%);
English Language Learner: 0 (0.0%); Migrant: n/a
Eligible for Free Lunch Program: 0 (0.0%)
Eligible for Reduced-Price Lunch Program: 0 (0.0%)

Teachers: 114.5 (18.1 to 1)
Librarians/Media Specialists: 4.0 (518.5 to 1)
Guidance Counselors: 0.0 (0.0 to 1)
Current Spending: ($ per student per year):
Total: $6,518; Instruction: $4,184; Support Services: $2,312
Enrollment, Drop-out Rates and Diploma Recipients by Race/Ethnicity

Category	Total	White	Black	Asian	AIAN	Hisp.
Enrollment (%)	100.0	62.2	27.7	0.6	0.0	9.6
Drop-out Rate (%)	n/a	n/a	n/a	n/a	n/a	n/a
H.S. Diplomas (#)	n/a	n/a	n/a	n/a	n/a	n/a

Lemont-Bromberek CSD 113a

16100 127th St • Lemont, IL 60439-7462
(630) 257-2286 • http://www.sd113a.org/
Grade Span: PK-08; **Agency Type:** 1
Schools: 4
3 Primary; 1 Middle; 0 High; 0 Other Level
4 Regular; 0 Special Education; 0 Vocational; 0 Alternative
0 Magnet; 0 Charter; 1 Title I Eligible; 0 School-wide Title I
Students: 2,456 (51.9% male; 48.1% female)
Individual Education Program: 334 (13.6%);
English Language Learner: 25 (1.0%); Migrant: n/a
Eligible for Free Lunch Program: 65 (2.6%)
Eligible for Reduced-Price Lunch Program: 24 (1.0%)
Teachers: 133.9 (18.3 to 1)
Librarians/Media Specialists: 1.0 (2,456.0 to 1)
Guidance Counselors: 2.0 (1,228.0 to 1)
Current Spending: ($ per student per year):
Total: $5,780; Instruction: $3,459; Support Services: $2,181
Enrollment, Drop-out Rates and Diploma Recipients by Race/Ethnicity

Category	Total	White	Black	Asian	AIAN	Hisp.
Enrollment (%)	100.0	94.9	0.4	1.3	0.0	3.5
Drop-out Rate (%)	n/a	n/a	n/a	n/a	n/a	n/a
H.S. Diplomas (#)	n/a	n/a	n/a	n/a	n/a	n/a

Leyden Community HSD 212

3400 Rose St • Franklin Park, IL 60131-2155
(847) 451-3000 • http://www.leyhs.w-cook.k12.il.us/Home/leyden.htm
Grade Span: 09-12; **Agency Type:** 1
Schools: 2
0 Primary; 0 Middle; 2 High; 0 Other Level
2 Regular; 0 Special Education; 0 Vocational; 0 Alternative
0 Magnet; 0 Charter; 0 Title I Eligible; 0 School-wide Title I
Students: 3,477 (51.5% male; 48.5% female)
Individual Education Program: 430 (12.4%);
English Language Learner: 287 (8.3%); Migrant: n/a
Eligible for Free Lunch Program: 317 (9.1%)
Eligible for Reduced-Price Lunch Program: 122 (3.5%)
Teachers: 206.6 (16.8 to 1)
Librarians/Media Specialists: 5.4 (643.9 to 1)
Guidance Counselors: 12.8 (271.6 to 1)
Current Spending: ($ per student per year):
Total: $11,736; Instruction: $6,152; Support Services: $5,294
Enrollment, Drop-out Rates and Diploma Recipients by Race/Ethnicity

Category	Total	White	Black	Asian	AIAN	Hisp.
Enrollment (%)	100.0	56.0	1.4	3.8	0.5	38.3
Drop-out Rate (%)	5.5	4.2	14.0	3.1	0.0	7.4
H.S. Diplomas (#)	732	471	14	31	2	214

Lyons SD 103

4100 S Joliet Ave • Lyons, IL 60534-1595
(708) 783-4100 • http://www.district103.w-cook.k12.il.us/
Grade Span: PK-08; **Agency Type:** 1
Schools: 6
5 Primary; 1 Middle; 0 High; 0 Other Level
6 Regular; 0 Special Education; 0 Vocational; 0 Alternative
0 Magnet; 0 Charter; 3 Title I Eligible; 0 School-wide Title I
Students: 2,254 (50.7% male; 49.3% female)
Individual Education Program: 317 (14.1%);
English Language Learner: 227 (10.1%); Migrant: n/a
Eligible for Free Lunch Program: 482 (21.4%)
Eligible for Reduced-Price Lunch Program: 152 (6.7%)
Teachers: 154.1 (14.6 to 1)
Librarians/Media Specialists: 1.0 (2,254.0 to 1)
Guidance Counselors: 1.0 (2,254.0 to 1)
Current Spending: ($ per student per year):
Total: $7,075; Instruction: $4,200; Support Services: $2,677
Enrollment, Drop-out Rates and Diploma Recipients by Race/Ethnicity

Category	Total	White	Black	Asian	AIAN	Hisp.
Enrollment (%)	100.0	63.7	2.6	1.0	0.4	32.3
Drop-out Rate (%)	n/a	n/a	n/a	n/a	n/a	n/a
H.S. Diplomas (#)	n/a	n/a	n/a	n/a	n/a	n/a

Lyons Twp HSD 204

100 S Brainard • La Grange, IL 60525-2100
(708) 579-6451 • http://www.lths.net/
Grade Span: 08-12; **Agency Type:** 1
Schools: 1
0 Primary; 0 Middle; 1 High; 0 Other Level
1 Regular; 0 Special Education; 0 Vocational; 0 Alternative
0 Magnet; 0 Charter; 1 Title I Eligible; 0 School-wide Title I
Students: 3,545 (49.8% male; 50.2% female)
Individual Education Program: 343 (9.7%);
English Language Learner: 47 (1.3%); Migrant: n/a
Eligible for Free Lunch Program: 0 (0.0%)
Eligible for Reduced-Price Lunch Program: 0 (0.0%)
Teachers: 209.5 (16.9 to 1)
Librarians/Media Specialists: 4.0 (886.3 to 1)
Guidance Counselors: 14.2 (249.6 to 1)
Current Spending: ($ per student per year):
Total: $13,272; Instruction: $7,050; Support Services: $5,969
Enrollment, Drop-out Rates and Diploma Recipients by Race/Ethnicity

Category	Total	White	Black	Asian	AIAN	Hisp.
Enrollment (%)	100.0	87.4	3.0	1.8	0.1	7.7
Drop-out Rate (%)	1.3	1.1	3.1	0.0	0.0	4.0
H.S. Diplomas (#)	734	656	29	8	0	41

Maine Township HSD 207

1131 S Dee Rd • Park Ridge, IL 60068-4398
(847) 696-3600 • http://www.maine207.k12.il.us/
Grade Span: 07-12; **Agency Type:** 1
Schools: 5
0 Primary; 0 Middle; 5 High; 0 Other Level
3 Regular; 2 Special Education; 0 Vocational; 0 Alternative
0 Magnet; 0 Charter; 2 Title I Eligible; 0 School-wide Title I
Students: 6,833 (52.9% male; 47.1% female)
Individual Education Program: 956 (14.0%);
English Language Learner: 369 (5.4%); Migrant: n/a
Eligible for Free Lunch Program: 0 (0.0%)
Eligible for Reduced-Price Lunch Program: 0 (0.0%)
Teachers: 480.6 (14.2 to 1)
Librarians/Media Specialists: 9.0 (759.2 to 1)
Guidance Counselors: 26.0 (262.8 to 1)
Current Spending: ($ per student per year):
Total: $13,617; Instruction: $7,287; Support Services: $6,077
Enrollment, Drop-out Rates and Diploma Recipients by Race/Ethnicity

Category	Total	White	Black	Asian	AIAN	Hisp.
Enrollment (%)	100.0	70.5	2.3	14.3	0.4	12.5
Drop-out Rate (%)	1.4	1.1	5.9	0.7	0.0	3.5
H.S. Diplomas (#)	1,523	1,106	21	238	4	154

Mannheim SD 83

10401 W Grand Ave • Franklin Park, IL 60131-2208
(847) 455-4413 • http://www.d83.org/
Grade Span: PK-12; **Agency Type:** 1
Schools: 5
3 Primary; 1 Middle; 0 High; 1 Other Level
4 Regular; 1 Special Education; 0 Vocational; 0 Alternative
0 Magnet; 0 Charter; 3 Title I Eligible; 0 School-wide Title I
Students: 2,891 (53.7% male; 46.3% female)
Individual Education Program: 436 (15.1%);
English Language Learner: 467 (16.2%); Migrant: n/a
Eligible for Free Lunch Program: 681 (23.6%)
Eligible for Reduced-Price Lunch Program: 264 (9.1%)
Teachers: 181.1 (16.0 to 1)
Librarians/Media Specialists: 4.0 (722.8 to 1)
Guidance Counselors: 0.0 (0.0 to 1)
Current Spending: ($ per student per year):
Total: $8,492; Instruction: $5,547; Support Services: $2,698
Enrollment, Drop-out Rates and Diploma Recipients by Race/Ethnicity

Category	Total	White	Black	Asian	AIAN	Hisp.
Enrollment (%)	100.0	35.5	1.8	2.9	0.1	59.7
Drop-out Rate (%)	0.0	0.0	n/a	n/a	n/a	0.0
H.S. Diplomas (#)	1	0	0	0	0	1

Matteson ESD 162

3625 W 215th St • Matteson, IL 60443-2707
(708) 748-0100 • http://www.lincolnnet.net/users/lsd162/home.htm
Grade Span: PK-08; **Agency Type:** 1
Schools: 6
5 Primary; 1 Middle; 0 High; 0 Other Level
6 Regular; 0 Special Education; 0 Vocational; 0 Alternative
1 Magnet; 0 Charter; 6 Title I Eligible; 0 School-wide Title I
Students: 2,974 (50.9% male; 49.1% female)
Individual Education Program: 453 (15.2%);
English Language Learner: 8 (0.3%); Migrant: n/a
Eligible for Free Lunch Program: 481 (16.2%)
Eligible for Reduced-Price Lunch Program: 106 (3.6%)

Teachers: 174.6 (17.0 to 1)
Librarians/Media Specialists: 6.0 (495.7 to 1)
Guidance Counselors: 3.0 (991.3 to 1)
Current Spending: ($ per student per year):
Total: $6,728; Instruction: $3,717; Support Services: $2,938
Enrollment, Drop-out Rates and Diploma Recipients by Race/Ethnicity

Category	Total	White	Black	Asian	AIAN	Hisp.
Enrollment (%)	100.0	19.7	76.6	1.0	0.0	2.7
Drop-out Rate (%)	n/a	n/a	n/a	n/a	n/a	n/a
H.S. Diplomas (#)	n/a	n/a	n/a	n/a	n/a	n/a

Maywood-Melrose Park-Broadview-89

906 Walton St • Melrose Park, IL 60160
(708) 450-2000
Grade Span: PK-08; **Agency Type:** 1
Schools: 10
10 Primary; 0 Middle; 0 High; 0 Other Level
10 Regular; 0 Special Education; 0 Vocational; 0 Alternative
0 Magnet; 0 Charter; 10 Title I Eligible; 8 School-wide Title I
Students: 5,958 (50.4% male; 49.6% female)
Individual Education Program: 665 (11.2%);
English Language Learner: 484 (8.1%); Migrant: n/a
Eligible for Free Lunch Program: 3,176 (53.3%)
Eligible for Reduced-Price Lunch Program: 305 (5.1%)
Teachers: 328.0 (18.2 to 1)
Librarians/Media Specialists: 1.0 (5,958.0 to 1)
Guidance Counselors: 0.0 (0.0 to 1)
Current Spending: ($ per student per year):
Total: $4,919; Instruction: $2,999; Support Services: $1,694
Enrollment, Drop-out Rates and Diploma Recipients by Race/Ethnicity

Category	Total	White	Black	Asian	AIAN	Hisp.
Enrollment (%)	100.0	4.4	58.2	0.8	0.0	36.6
Drop-out Rate (%)	n/a	n/a	n/a	n/a	n/a	n/a
H.S. Diplomas (#)	53	0	52	0	0	1

Midlothian SD 143

14959 S Pulaski Rd • Midlothian, IL 60445-2833
(708) 388-6450
Grade Span: PK-08; **Agency Type:** 1
Schools: 4
4 Primary; 0 Middle; 0 High; 0 Other Level
4 Regular; 0 Special Education; 0 Vocational; 0 Alternative
0 Magnet; 0 Charter; 2 Title I Eligible; 0 School-wide Title I
Students: 1,764 (51.8% male; 48.2% female)
Individual Education Program: 340 (19.3%);
English Language Learner: 0 (0.0%); Migrant: n/a
Eligible for Free Lunch Program: 224 (12.7%)
Eligible for Reduced-Price Lunch Program: 7 (0.4%)
Teachers: 109.5 (16.1 to 1)
Librarians/Media Specialists: 0.0 (0.0 to 1)
Guidance Counselors: 0.0 (0.0 to 1)
Current Spending: ($ per student per year):
Total: $6,173; Instruction: $3,595; Support Services: $2,471
Enrollment, Drop-out Rates and Diploma Recipients by Race/Ethnicity

Category	Total	White	Black	Asian	AIAN	Hisp.
Enrollment (%)	100.0	59.4	27.6	1.7	0.0	11.3
Drop-out Rate (%)	n/a	n/a	n/a	n/a	n/a	n/a
H.S. Diplomas (#)	n/a	n/a	n/a	n/a	n/a	n/a

Mount Prospect SD 57

701 W Gregory St • Mount Prospect, IL 60056-2296
(847) 394-7300 • http://www.dist57.org/
Grade Span: PK-08; **Agency Type:** 1
Schools: 3
3 Primary; 0 Middle; 0 High; 0 Other Level
3 Regular; 0 Special Education; 0 Vocational; 0 Alternative
0 Magnet; 0 Charter; 1 Title I Eligible; 0 School-wide Title I
Students: 1,995 (52.2% male; 47.8% female)
Individual Education Program: 298 (14.9%);
English Language Learner: 94 (4.7%); Migrant: n/a
Eligible for Free Lunch Program: 21 (1.1%)
Eligible for Reduced-Price Lunch Program: 24 (1.2%)
Teachers: 117.0 (17.1 to 1)
Librarians/Media Specialists: 2.0 (997.5 to 1)
Guidance Counselors: 0.0 (0.0 to 1)
Current Spending: ($ per student per year):
Total: $7,404; Instruction: $4,047; Support Services: $3,289
Enrollment, Drop-out Rates and Diploma Recipients by Race/Ethnicity

Category	Total	White	Black	Asian	AIAN	Hisp.
Enrollment (%)	100.0	87.5	1.3	6.0	0.1	5.2
Drop-out Rate (%)	n/a	n/a	n/a	n/a	n/a	n/a
H.S. Diplomas (#)	n/a	n/a	n/a	n/a	n/a	n/a

New Trier Twp HSD 203

385 Winnetka Ave • Winnetka, IL 60093-4295
(847) 446-7000 • http://www.nths.newtrier.k12.il.us/
Grade Span: 09-12; **Agency Type:** 1
Schools: 2
0 Primary; 0 Middle; 1 High; 1 Other Level
2 Regular; 0 Special Education; 0 Vocational; 0 Alternative
0 Magnet; 0 Charter; 0 Title I Eligible; 0 School-wide Title I
Students: 3,806 (51.2% male; 48.8% female)
Individual Education Program: 569 (15.0%);
English Language Learner: 48 (1.3%); Migrant: n/a
Eligible for Free Lunch Program: n/a
Eligible for Reduced-Price Lunch Program: n/a
Teachers: 318.0 (12.0 to 1)
Librarians/Media Specialists: 3.6 (1,057.2 to 1)
Guidance Counselors: 6.0 (634.3 to 1)
Current Spending: ($ per student per year):
Total: $14,450; Instruction: $7,952; Support Services: $6,237
Enrollment, Drop-out Rates and Diploma Recipients by Race/Ethnicity

Category	Total	White	Black	Asian	AIAN	Hisp.
Enrollment (%)	100.0	88.9	0.6	8.6	0.2	1.6
Drop-out Rate (%)	0.4	0.4	0.0	0.6	0.0	0.0
H.S. Diplomas (#)	948	813	9	106	0	20

Niles Twp Community High SD 219

7700 Gross Point Rd • Skokie, IL 60077-2600
(847) 626-3000 • http://www.niles-hs.k12.il.us/
Grade Span: 09-12; **Agency Type:** 1
Schools: 2
0 Primary; 0 Middle; 2 High; 0 Other Level
2 Regular; 0 Special Education; 0 Vocational; 0 Alternative
0 Magnet; 0 Charter; 2 Title I Eligible; 0 School-wide Title I
Students: 4,795 (52.5% male; 47.5% female)
Individual Education Program: 609 (12.7%);
English Language Learner: 262 (5.5%); Migrant: n/a
Eligible for Free Lunch Program: 0 (0.0%)
Eligible for Reduced-Price Lunch Program: 0 (0.0%)
Teachers: 344.5 (13.9 to 1)
Librarians/Media Specialists: 8.0 (599.4 to 1)
Guidance Counselors: 18.9 (253.7 to 1)
Current Spending: ($ per student per year):
Total: $14,310; Instruction: $7,447; Support Services: $6,607
Enrollment, Drop-out Rates and Diploma Recipients by Race/Ethnicity

Category	Total	White	Black	Asian	AIAN	Hisp.
Enrollment (%)	100.0	58.7	2.9	31.1	0.1	7.3
Drop-out Rate (%)	0.8	0.9	0.8	0.5	0.0	1.5
H.S. Diplomas (#)	1,051	598	29	356	1	67

North Palos SD 117

7825 W 103rd St • Palos Hills, IL 60465-1252
(708) 598-5500
Grade Span: PK-08; **Agency Type:** 1
Schools: 5
4 Primary; 1 Middle; 0 High; 0 Other Level
4 Regular; 1 Special Education; 0 Vocational; 0 Alternative
0 Magnet; 0 Charter; 3 Title I Eligible; 0 School-wide Title I
Students: 2,651 (51.4% male; 48.6% female)
Individual Education Program: 419 (15.8%);
English Language Learner: 164 (6.2%); Migrant: n/a
Eligible for Free Lunch Program: 397 (15.0%)
Eligible for Reduced-Price Lunch Program: 31 (1.2%)
Teachers: 145.7 (18.2 to 1)
Librarians/Media Specialists: 4.0 (662.8 to 1)
Guidance Counselors: 0.0 (0.0 to 1)
Current Spending: ($ per student per year):
Total: $6,669; Instruction: $4,121; Support Services: $2,302
Enrollment, Drop-out Rates and Diploma Recipients by Race/Ethnicity

Category	Total	White	Black	Asian	AIAN	Hisp.
Enrollment (%)	100.0	83.7	5.2	1.4	0.5	9.2
Drop-out Rate (%)	n/a	n/a	n/a	n/a	n/a	n/a
H.S. Diplomas (#)	n/a	n/a	n/a	n/a	n/a	n/a

Northbrook SD 28

1475 Maple Ave • Northbrook, IL 60062-5418
(847) 498-7900 • http://www.district28.k12.il.us/
Grade Span: PK-08; **Agency Type:** 1
Schools: 4
3 Primary; 1 Middle; 0 High; 0 Other Level
4 Regular; 0 Special Education; 0 Vocational; 0 Alternative
0 Magnet; 0 Charter; 0 Title I Eligible; 0 School-wide Title I
Students: 1,751 (52.9% male; 47.1% female)
Individual Education Program: 348 (19.9%);
English Language Learner: 95 (5.4%); Migrant: n/a
Eligible for Free Lunch Program: 0 (0.0%)
Eligible for Reduced-Price Lunch Program: 0 (0.0%)

Teachers: 152.6 (11.5 to 1)
Librarians/Media Specialists: 4.0 (437.8 to 1)
Guidance Counselors: 4.0 (437.8 to 1)
Current Spending: ($ per student per year):
Total: $11,978; Instruction: $7,946; Support Services: $3,952
Enrollment, Drop-out Rates and Diploma Recipients by Race/Ethnicity

Category	Total	White	Black	Asian	AIAN	Hisp.
Enrollment (%)	100.0	91.3	0.4	7.0	0.0	1.4
Drop-out Rate (%)	n/a	n/a	n/a	n/a	n/a	n/a
H.S. Diplomas (#)	n/a	n/a	n/a	n/a	n/a	n/a

Northfield Twp High SD 225
1835 Landwehr Rd • Glenview, IL 60025-1289
(847) 998-6100 • http://www.glenbrook.k12.il.us/
Grade Span: 09-12; **Agency Type:** 1
Schools: 3
0 Primary; 0 Middle; 3 High; 0 Other Level
2 Regular; 1 Special Education; 0 Vocational; 0 Alternative
0 Magnet; 0 Charter; 1 Title I Eligible; 0 School-wide Title I
Students: 4,636 (51.1% male; 48.9% female)
Individual Education Program: 502 (10.8%);
English Language Learner: 149 (3.2%); Migrant: n/a
Eligible for Free Lunch Program: n/a
Eligible for Reduced-Price Lunch Program: n/a
Teachers: 327.8 (14.1 to 1)
Librarians/Media Specialists: 7.5 (618.1 to 1)
Guidance Counselors: 20.0 (231.8 to 1)
Current Spending: ($ per student per year):
Total: $14,402; Instruction: $7,704; Support Services: $6,410
Enrollment, Drop-out Rates and Diploma Recipients by Race/Ethnicity

Category	Total	White	Black	Asian	AIAN	Hisp.
Enrollment (%)	100.0	80.0	1.1	14.9	0.2	3.8
Drop-out Rate (%)	0.8	0.7	2.3	0.6	0.0	3.4
H.S. Diplomas (#)	1,127	883	10	196	2	36

Oak Lawn Community HSD 229
9400 SW Hwy • Oak Lawn, IL 60453-2396
(708) 424-5200
Grade Span: 09-12; **Agency Type:** 1
Schools: 1
0 Primary; 0 Middle; 1 High; 0 Other Level
1 Regular; 0 Special Education; 0 Vocational; 0 Alternative
0 Magnet; 0 Charter; 0 Title I Eligible; 0 School-wide Title I
Students: 1,634 (49.9% male; 50.1% female)
Individual Education Program: 213 (13.0%);
English Language Learner: 40 (2.4%); Migrant: n/a
Eligible for Free Lunch Program: n/a
Eligible for Reduced-Price Lunch Program: n/a
Teachers: 90.0 (18.2 to 1)
Librarians/Media Specialists: 2.0 (817.0 to 1)
Guidance Counselors: 5.0 (326.8 to 1)
Current Spending: ($ per student per year):
Total: $10,272; Instruction: $5,408; Support Services: $4,482
Enrollment, Drop-out Rates and Diploma Recipients by Race/Ethnicity

Category	Total	White	Black	Asian	AIAN	Hisp.
Enrollment (%)	100.0	87.2	0.9	1.5	0.7	9.6
Drop-out Rate (%)	4.9	4.9	16.7	3.2	0.0	6.1
H.S. Diplomas (#)	352	311	1	12	1	27

Oak Lawn-Hometown SD 123
4201 W 93rd St • Oak Lawn, IL 60453-1907
(708) 423-0150 • http://www.d123.s-cook.k12.il.us/
Grade Span: PK-08; **Agency Type:** 1
Schools: 6
5 Primary; 1 Middle; 0 High; 0 Other Level
6 Regular; 0 Special Education; 0 Vocational; 0 Alternative
0 Magnet; 0 Charter; 3 Title I Eligible; 0 School-wide Title I
Students: 2,677 (53.0% male; 47.0% female)
Individual Education Program: 452 (16.9%);
English Language Learner: 102 (3.8%); Migrant: n/a
Eligible for Free Lunch Program: 0 (0.0%)
Eligible for Reduced-Price Lunch Program: 0 (0.0%)
Teachers: 194.6 (13.8 to 1)
Librarians/Media Specialists: 6.0 (446.2 to 1)
Guidance Counselors: 0.0 (0.0 to 1)
Current Spending: ($ per student per year):
Total: $6,624; Instruction: $3,881; Support Services: $2,687
Enrollment, Drop-out Rates and Diploma Recipients by Race/Ethnicity

Category	Total	White	Black	Asian	AIAN	Hisp.
Enrollment (%)	100.0	84.7	1.7	1.9	0.3	11.4
Drop-out Rate (%)	n/a	n/a	n/a	n/a	n/a	n/a
H.S. Diplomas (#)	n/a	n/a	n/a	n/a	n/a	n/a

Oak Park & River Forest Dist 200
201 N Scoville Ave • Oak Park, IL 60302-2296
(708) 383-0700 • http://www.oprfhs.org/
Grade Span: 09-12; **Agency Type:** 1
Schools: 1
0 Primary; 0 Middle; 1 High; 0 Other Level
1 Regular; 0 Special Education; 0 Vocational; 0 Alternative
0 Magnet; 0 Charter; 1 Title I Eligible; 0 School-wide Title I
Students: 2,962 (50.7% male; 49.3% female)
Individual Education Program: 399 (13.5%);
English Language Learner: 17 (0.6%); Migrant: n/a
Eligible for Free Lunch Program: 136 (4.6%)
Eligible for Reduced-Price Lunch Program: 48 (1.6%)
Teachers: 179.8 (16.5 to 1)
Librarians/Media Specialists: 3.0 (987.3 to 1)
Guidance Counselors: 10.0 (296.2 to 1)
Current Spending: ($ per student per year):
Total: $13,470; Instruction: $8,078; Support Services: $4,924
Enrollment, Drop-out Rates and Diploma Recipients by Race/Ethnicity

Category	Total	White	Black	Asian	AIAN	Hisp.
Enrollment (%)	100.0	65.6	26.9	2.6	0.5	4.3
Drop-out Rate (%)	2.0	1.5	3.1	0.0	0.0	3.5
H.S. Diplomas (#)	0	0	0	0	0	0

Oak Park Elem SD 97
970 Madison St • Oak Park, IL 60302-4480
(708) 524-3000 • http://www.op97.k12.il.us/
Grade Span: PK-08; **Agency Type:** 1
Schools: 10
8 Primary; 2 Middle; 0 High; 0 Other Level
10 Regular; 0 Special Education; 0 Vocational; 0 Alternative
0 Magnet; 0 Charter; 6 Title I Eligible; 0 School-wide Title I
Students: 4,923 (51.8% male; 48.2% female)
Individual Education Program: 886 (18.0%);
English Language Learner: 121 (2.5%); Migrant: n/a
Eligible for Free Lunch Program: 608 (12.4%)
Eligible for Reduced-Price Lunch Program: 207 (4.2%)
Teachers: 375.7 (13.1 to 1)
Librarians/Media Specialists: 8.0 (615.4 to 1)
Guidance Counselors: 0.0 (0.0 to 1)
Current Spending: ($ per student per year):
Total: $9,217; Instruction: $5,627; Support Services: $3,423
Enrollment, Drop-out Rates and Diploma Recipients by Race/Ethnicity

Category	Total	White	Black	Asian	AIAN	Hisp.
Enrollment (%)	100.0	60.4	31.7	3.6	0.2	4.0
Drop-out Rate (%)	n/a	n/a	n/a	n/a	n/a	n/a
H.S. Diplomas (#)	n/a	n/a	n/a	n/a	n/a	n/a

Orland SD 135
15100 S 94th Ave • Orland Park, IL 60462-3229
(708) 349-5700 • http://www.orland135.org/
Grade Span: PK-08; **Agency Type:** 1
Schools: 10
7 Primary; 3 Middle; 0 High; 0 Other Level
10 Regular; 0 Special Education; 0 Vocational; 0 Alternative
0 Magnet; 0 Charter; 7 Title I Eligible; 0 School-wide Title I
Students: 5,919 (52.4% male; 47.6% female)
Individual Education Program: 752 (12.7%);
English Language Learner: 134 (2.3%); Migrant: n/a
Eligible for Free Lunch Program: 0 (0.0%)
Eligible for Reduced-Price Lunch Program: 0 (0.0%)
Teachers: 358.6 (16.5 to 1)
Librarians/Media Specialists: 10.0 (591.9 to 1)
Guidance Counselors: 3.0 (1,973.0 to 1)
Current Spending: ($ per student per year):
Total: $7,673; Instruction: $4,410; Support Services: $3,043
Enrollment, Drop-out Rates and Diploma Recipients by Race/Ethnicity

Category	Total	White	Black	Asian	AIAN	Hisp.
Enrollment (%)	100.0	90.1	2.2	3.7	0.0	4.0
Drop-out Rate (%)	n/a	n/a	n/a	n/a	n/a	n/a
H.S. Diplomas (#)	n/a	n/a	n/a	n/a	n/a	n/a

Palatine CCSD 15
580 N First Bank Dr • Palatine, IL 60067-8108
(847) 963-3000 • http://www.ccsd15.net/Home/
Grade Span: PK-08; **Agency Type:** 1
Schools: 20
16 Primary; 4 Middle; 0 High; 0 Other Level
18 Regular; 2 Special Education; 0 Vocational; 0 Alternative
4 Magnet; 0 Charter; 12 Title I Eligible; 0 School-wide Title I
Students: 12,933 (51.8% male; 48.2% female)
Individual Education Program: 1,662 (12.9%);
English Language Learner: 2,568 (19.9%); Migrant: n/a
Eligible for Free Lunch Program: 2,040 (15.8%)
Eligible for Reduced-Price Lunch Program: 598 (4.6%)

Teachers: 776.7 (16.7 to 1)
Librarians/Media Specialists: 8.0 (1,616.6 to 1)
Guidance Counselors: 5.0 (2,586.6 to 1)
Current Spending: ($ per student per year):
Total: $8,828; Instruction: $5,015; Support Services: $3,646
Enrollment, Drop-out Rates and Diploma Recipients by Race/Ethnicity

Category	Total	White	Black	Asian	AIAN	Hisp.
Enrollment (%)	100.0	65.9	3.5	9.9	0.2	20.5
Drop-out Rate (%)	n/a	n/a	n/a	n/a	n/a	n/a
H.S. Diplomas (#)	n/a	n/a	n/a	n/a	n/a	n/a

Palos Community CSD 118
8800 W 119th St • Palos Park, IL 60464-1099
(708) 448-4800 • http://www.palos118.org/
Grade Span: PK-08; **Agency Type:** 1
Schools: 3
2 Primary; 1 Middle; 0 High; 0 Other Level
3 Regular; 0 Special Education; 0 Vocational; 0 Alternative
0 Magnet; 0 Charter; 0 Title I Eligible; 0 School-wide Title I
Students: 2,025 (50.1% male; 49.9% female)
Individual Education Program: 331 (16.3%);
English Language Learner: 46 (2.3%); Migrant: n/a
Eligible for Free Lunch Program: 97 (4.8%)
Eligible for Reduced-Price Lunch Program: 7 (0.3%)
Teachers: 122.0 (16.6 to 1)
Librarians/Media Specialists: 2.0 (1,012.5 to 1)
Guidance Counselors: 2.0 (1,012.5 to 1)
Current Spending: ($ per student per year):
Total: $8,170; Instruction: $4,601; Support Services: $3,444
Enrollment, Drop-out Rates and Diploma Recipients by Race/Ethnicity

Category	Total	White	Black	Asian	AIAN	Hisp.
Enrollment (%)	100.0	96.7	0.2	0.8	0.2	2.0
Drop-out Rate (%)	n/a	n/a	n/a	n/a	n/a	n/a
H.S. Diplomas (#)	n/a	n/a	n/a	n/a	n/a	n/a

Park Forest SD 163
242 S Orchard Dr • Park Forest, IL 60466-2045
(708) 748-7050 • http://www.sd163.com/
Grade Span: PK-08; **Agency Type:** 1
Schools: 6
5 Primary; 1 Middle; 0 High; 0 Other Level
6 Regular; 0 Special Education; 0 Vocational; 0 Alternative
0 Magnet; 0 Charter; 6 Title I Eligible; 6 School-wide Title I
Students: 2,109 (51.8% male; 48.2% female)
Individual Education Program: 334 (15.8%);
English Language Learner: 4 (0.2%); Migrant: n/a
Eligible for Free Lunch Program: 1,392 (66.0%)
Eligible for Reduced-Price Lunch Program: 232 (11.0%)
Teachers: 141.5 (14.9 to 1)
Librarians/Media Specialists: 1.0 (2,109.0 to 1)
Guidance Counselors: 1.0 (2,109.0 to 1)
Current Spending: ($ per student per year):
Total: $8,359; Instruction: $4,704; Support Services: $3,405
Enrollment, Drop-out Rates and Diploma Recipients by Race/Ethnicity

Category	Total	White	Black	Asian	AIAN	Hisp.
Enrollment (%)	100.0	14.8	79.9	0.2	0.2	4.8
Drop-out Rate (%)	n/a	n/a	n/a	n/a	n/a	n/a
H.S. Diplomas (#)	n/a	n/a	n/a	n/a	n/a	n/a

Park Ridge CCSD 64
164 S Prospect Ave • Park Ridge, IL 60068-4079
(847) 318-4300 • http://www.d64.k12.il.us/
Grade Span: PK-08; **Agency Type:** 1
Schools: 8
6 Primary; 2 Middle; 0 High; 0 Other Level
7 Regular; 1 Special Education; 0 Vocational; 0 Alternative
0 Magnet; 0 Charter; 0 Title I Eligible; 0 School-wide Title I
Students: 4,354 (53.0% male; 47.0% female)
Individual Education Program: 895 (20.6%);
English Language Learner: 70 (1.6%); Migrant: n/a
Eligible for Free Lunch Program: 0 (0.0%)
Eligible for Reduced-Price Lunch Program: 0 (0.0%)
Teachers: 311.8 (14.0 to 1)
Librarians/Media Specialists: 0.0 (0.0 to 1)
Guidance Counselors: 2.0 (2,177.0 to 1)
Current Spending: ($ per student per year):
Total: $9,626; Instruction: $6,338; Support Services: $3,200
Enrollment, Drop-out Rates and Diploma Recipients by Race/Ethnicity

Category	Total	White	Black	Asian	AIAN	Hisp.
Enrollment (%)	100.0	93.1	0.5	3.3	0.1	3.0
Drop-out Rate (%)	n/a	n/a	n/a	n/a	n/a	n/a
H.S. Diplomas (#)	n/a	n/a	n/a	n/a	n/a	n/a

Posen-Robbins El SD 143-5
14025 Harrison Ave • Posen, IL 60469-1055
(708) 388-7200
Grade Span: PK-08; **Agency Type:** 1
Schools: 6
4 Primary; 2 Middle; 0 High; 0 Other Level
6 Regular; 0 Special Education; 0 Vocational; 0 Alternative
0 Magnet; 0 Charter; 6 Title I Eligible; 6 School-wide Title I
Students: 1,548 (52.7% male; 47.3% female)
Individual Education Program: 198 (12.8%);
English Language Learner: 208 (13.4%); Migrant: n/a
Eligible for Free Lunch Program: 1,108 (71.6%)
Eligible for Reduced-Price Lunch Program: 68 (4.4%)
Teachers: 80.0 (19.4 to 1)
Librarians/Media Specialists: 1.0 (1,548.0 to 1)
Guidance Counselors: 0.0 (0.0 to 1)
Current Spending: ($ per student per year):
Total: $6,403; Instruction: $3,321; Support Services: $2,801
Enrollment, Drop-out Rates and Diploma Recipients by Race/Ethnicity

Category	Total	White	Black	Asian	AIAN	Hisp.
Enrollment (%)	100.0	9.2	58.0	0.0	0.0	32.8
Drop-out Rate (%)	n/a	n/a	n/a	n/a	n/a	n/a
H.S. Diplomas (#)	n/a	n/a	n/a	n/a	n/a	n/a

Prairie-Hills Elem SD 144
3015 W 163rd St • Markham, IL 60426-5685
(708) 210-2888
Grade Span: PK-08; **Agency Type:** 1
Schools: 8
7 Primary; 1 Middle; 0 High; 0 Other Level
8 Regular; 0 Special Education; 0 Vocational; 0 Alternative
0 Magnet; 0 Charter; 8 Title I Eligible; 8 School-wide Title I
Students: 3,010 (52.0% male; 48.0% female)
Individual Education Program: 501 (16.6%);
English Language Learner: 72 (2.4%); Migrant: n/a
Eligible for Free Lunch Program: 2,366 (78.6%)
Eligible for Reduced-Price Lunch Program: 263 (8.7%)
Teachers: 159.0 (18.9 to 1)
Librarians/Media Specialists: 0.0 (0.0 to 1)
Guidance Counselors: 0.0 (0.0 to 1)
Current Spending: ($ per student per year):
Total: $6,965; Instruction: $3,798; Support Services: $2,923
Enrollment, Drop-out Rates and Diploma Recipients by Race/Ethnicity

Category	Total	White	Black	Asian	AIAN	Hisp.
Enrollment (%)	100.0	6.8	88.8	0.5	0.0	3.9
Drop-out Rate (%)	n/a	n/a	n/a	n/a	n/a	n/a
H.S. Diplomas (#)	n/a	n/a	n/a	n/a	n/a	n/a

Prospect Heights SD 23
700 N Schoenbeck Rd • Prospect Heights, IL 60070-1299
(847) 870-3850 • http://www.d23.org/
Grade Span: PK-08; **Agency Type:** 1
Schools: 4
3 Primary; 1 Middle; 0 High; 0 Other Level
4 Regular; 0 Special Education; 0 Vocational; 0 Alternative
0 Magnet; 0 Charter; 2 Title I Eligible; 0 School-wide Title I
Students: 1,559 (51.6% male; 48.4% female)
Individual Education Program: 257 (16.5%);
English Language Learner: 142 (9.1%); Migrant: n/a
Eligible for Free Lunch Program: 0 (0.0%)
Eligible for Reduced-Price Lunch Program: 0 (0.0%)
Teachers: 117.8 (13.2 to 1)
Librarians/Media Specialists: 0.0 (0.0 to 1)
Guidance Counselors: 0.0 (0.0 to 1)
Current Spending: ($ per student per year):
Total: $8,370; Instruction: $5,234; Support Services: $2,967
Enrollment, Drop-out Rates and Diploma Recipients by Race/Ethnicity

Category	Total	White	Black	Asian	AIAN	Hisp.
Enrollment (%)	100.0	84.3	1.9	8.8	0.1	5.0
Drop-out Rate (%)	n/a	n/a	n/a	n/a	n/a	n/a
H.S. Diplomas (#)	n/a	n/a	n/a	n/a	n/a	n/a

Proviso Twp HSD 209
807 S 1st Ave • Maywood, IL 60153-2307
(708) 344-7000 • http://www.proviso.w-cook.k12.il.us/
Grade Span: 09-12; **Agency Type:** 1
Schools: 2
0 Primary; 0 Middle; 2 High; 0 Other Level
2 Regular; 0 Special Education; 0 Vocational; 0 Alternative
0 Magnet; 0 Charter; 1 Title I Eligible; 0 School-wide Title I
Students: 4,648 (49.8% male; 50.2% female)
Individual Education Program: 916 (19.7%);
English Language Learner: 265 (5.7%); Migrant: n/a
Eligible for Free Lunch Program: 860 (18.5%)
Eligible for Reduced-Price Lunch Program: 116 (2.5%)

Teachers: 300.8 (15.5 to 1)
Librarians/Media Specialists: 4.0 (1,162.0 to 1)
Guidance Counselors: 13.0 (357.5 to 1)
Current Spending: ($ per student per year):
Total: $10,807; Instruction: $5,806; Support Services: $4,822
Enrollment, Drop-out Rates and Diploma Recipients by Race/Ethnicity

Category	Total	White	Black	Asian	AIAN	Hisp.
Enrollment (%)	100.0	4.8	68.5	1.3	0.3	25.1
Drop-out Rate (%)	9.5	9.1	9.2	6.3	0.0	10.6
H.S. Diplomas (#)	772	37	542	13	0	180

Reavis Twp HSD 220
6034 W 77th St • Burbank, IL 60459-3199
(708) 599-7200 • http://www.rhsd.s-cook.k12.il.us/
Grade Span: 09-12; **Agency Type:** 1
Schools: 1
0 Primary; 0 Middle; 1 High; 0 Other Level
1 Regular; 0 Special Education; 0 Vocational; 0 Alternative
0 Magnet; 0 Charter; 1 Title I Eligible; 0 School-wide Title I
Students: 1,607 (49.1% male; 50.9% female)
Individual Education Program: 207 (12.9%);
English Language Learner: 78 (4.9%); Migrant: n/a
Eligible for Free Lunch Program: n/a
Eligible for Reduced-Price Lunch Program: n/a
Teachers: 95.8 (16.8 to 1)
Librarians/Media Specialists: 1.0 (1,607.0 to 1)
Guidance Counselors: 4.0 (401.8 to 1)
Current Spending: ($ per student per year):
Total: $10,596; Instruction: $5,699; Support Services: $4,873
Enrollment, Drop-out Rates and Diploma Recipients by Race/Ethnicity

Category	Total	White	Black	Asian	AIAN	Hisp.
Enrollment (%)	100.0	82.6	0.0	2.2	0.4	14.9
Drop-out Rate (%)	5.5	4.6	66.7	11.6	0.0	8.9
H.S. Diplomas (#)	310	265	0	9	1	35

Rich Twp HS District 227
20290 Governors Hiwy • Olympia Fields, IL 60461-1053
(708) 679-5800 • http://www.rich227.org/
Grade Span: 09-12; **Agency Type:** 1
Schools: 4
0 Primary; 0 Middle; 4 High; 0 Other Level
3 Regular; 1 Special Education; 0 Vocational; 0 Alternative
0 Magnet; 0 Charter; 2 Title I Eligible; 0 School-wide Title I
Students: 3,426 (50.7% male; 49.3% female)
Individual Education Program: 500 (14.6%);
English Language Learner: 0 (0.0%); Migrant: n/a
Eligible for Free Lunch Program: 1,049 (30.6%)
Eligible for Reduced-Price Lunch Program: 279 (8.1%)
Teachers: 225.4 (15.2 to 1)
Librarians/Media Specialists: 3.0 (1,142.0 to 1)
Guidance Counselors: 14.5 (236.3 to 1)
Current Spending: ($ per student per year):
Total: $11,971; Instruction: $6,711; Support Services: $4,820
Enrollment, Drop-out Rates and Diploma Recipients by Race/Ethnicity

Category	Total	White	Black	Asian	AIAN	Hisp.
Enrollment (%)	100.0	17.4	78.5	1.0	0.3	2.9
Drop-out Rate (%)	1.3	2.3	1.1	0.0	0.0	1.1
H.S. Diplomas (#)	734	184	521	12	0	17

Ridgeland SD 122
6500 W 95th St • Oak Lawn, IL 60453-2195
(708) 599-5550 • http://www.ridgeland122.com/
Grade Span: PK-08; **Agency Type:** 1
Schools: 5
4 Primary; 1 Middle; 0 High; 0 Other Level
5 Regular; 0 Special Education; 0 Vocational; 0 Alternative
0 Magnet; 0 Charter; 2 Title I Eligible; 0 School-wide Title I
Students: 2,271 (51.9% male; 48.1% female)
Individual Education Program: 379 (16.7%);
English Language Learner: 227 (10.0%); Migrant: n/a
Eligible for Free Lunch Program: n/a
Eligible for Reduced-Price Lunch Program: n/a
Teachers: 121.5 (18.7 to 1)
Librarians/Media Specialists: 5.0 (454.2 to 1)
Guidance Counselors: 0.0 (0.0 to 1)
Current Spending: ($ per student per year):
Total: $6,220; Instruction: $3,337; Support Services: $2,825
Enrollment, Drop-out Rates and Diploma Recipients by Race/Ethnicity

Category	Total	White	Black	Asian	AIAN	Hisp.
Enrollment (%)	100.0	85.5	1.3	1.8	0.3	11.1
Drop-out Rate (%)	n/a	n/a	n/a	n/a	n/a	n/a
H.S. Diplomas (#)	n/a	n/a	n/a	n/a	n/a	n/a

River Trails SD 26
1900 E Kensington Rd • Mount Prospect, IL 60056-1999
(847) 297-4120 • http://www.rtsd26.org/
Grade Span: PK-08; **Agency Type:** 1
Schools: 3
2 Primary; 1 Middle; 0 High; 0 Other Level
3 Regular; 0 Special Education; 0 Vocational; 0 Alternative
0 Magnet; 0 Charter; 1 Title I Eligible; 0 School-wide Title I
Students: 1,668 (53.7% male; 46.3% female)
Individual Education Program: 338 (20.3%);
English Language Learner: 234 (14.0%); Migrant: n/a
Eligible for Free Lunch Program: 280 (16.8%)
Eligible for Reduced-Price Lunch Program: 44 (2.6%)
Teachers: 125.0 (13.3 to 1)
Librarians/Media Specialists: 3.0 (556.0 to 1)
Guidance Counselors: 0.0 (0.0 to 1)
Current Spending: ($ per student per year):
Total: $9,267; Instruction: $5,397; Support Services: $3,654
Enrollment, Drop-out Rates and Diploma Recipients by Race/Ethnicity

Category	Total	White	Black	Asian	AIAN	Hisp.
Enrollment (%)	100.0	63.8	2.1	13.1	0.1	21.0
Drop-out Rate (%)	n/a	n/a	n/a	n/a	n/a	n/a
H.S. Diplomas (#)	n/a	n/a	n/a	n/a	n/a	n/a

Schaumburg CCSD 54
524 E Schaumburg Rd • Schaumburg, IL 60194-3510
(847) 885-6716 • http://web54.sd54.k12.il.us/
Grade Span: PK-08; **Agency Type:** 1
Schools: 27
22 Primary; 5 Middle; 0 High; 0 Other Level
27 Regular; 0 Special Education; 0 Vocational; 0 Alternative
0 Magnet; 0 Charter; 27 Title I Eligible; 0 School-wide Title I
Students: 15,079 (51.8% male; 48.2% female)
Individual Education Program: 2,225 (14.8%);
English Language Learner: 1,466 (9.7%); Migrant: n/a
Eligible for Free Lunch Program: 0 (0.0%)
Eligible for Reduced-Price Lunch Program: 0 (0.0%)
Teachers: 943.0 (16.0 to 1)
Librarians/Media Specialists: 0.0 (0.0 to 1)
Guidance Counselors: 5.0 (3,015.8 to 1)
Current Spending: ($ per student per year):
Total: $8,600; Instruction: $5,377; Support Services: $3,092
Enrollment, Drop-out Rates and Diploma Recipients by Race/Ethnicity

Category	Total	White	Black	Asian	AIAN	Hisp.
Enrollment (%)	100.0	63.0	7.4	16.8	0.1	12.8
Drop-out Rate (%)	n/a	n/a	n/a	n/a	n/a	n/a
H.S. Diplomas (#)	n/a	n/a	n/a	n/a	n/a	n/a

Skokie SD 68
9440 N Kenton Ave • Skokie, IL 60076-1337
(847) 676-9000 • http://www.sd68.k12.il.us/
Grade Span: KG-08; **Agency Type:** 1
Schools: 4
3 Primary; 1 Middle; 0 High; 0 Other Level
4 Regular; 0 Special Education; 0 Vocational; 0 Alternative
0 Magnet; 0 Charter; 3 Title I Eligible; 0 School-wide Title I
Students: 1,769 (51.7% male; 48.3% female)
Individual Education Program: 323 (18.3%);
English Language Learner: 169 (9.6%); Migrant: n/a
Eligible for Free Lunch Program: 229 (12.9%)
Eligible for Reduced-Price Lunch Program: 88 (5.0%)
Teachers: 123.1 (14.4 to 1)
Librarians/Media Specialists: 4.0 (442.3 to 1)
Guidance Counselors: 0.0 (0.0 to 1)
Current Spending: ($ per student per year):
Total: $10,028; Instruction: $5,910; Support Services: $3,893
Enrollment, Drop-out Rates and Diploma Recipients by Race/Ethnicity

Category	Total	White	Black	Asian	AIAN	Hisp.
Enrollment (%)	100.0	54.4	5.8	31.7	0.1	8.1
Drop-out Rate (%)	n/a	n/a	n/a	n/a	n/a	n/a
H.S. Diplomas (#)	n/a	n/a	n/a	n/a	n/a	n/a

Steger SD 194
3753 Park Ave • Steger, IL 60475-1864
(708) 755-0022 • http://www.sd194.org/
Grade Span: PK-08; **Agency Type:** 1
Schools: 4
3 Primary; 1 Middle; 0 High; 0 Other Level
4 Regular; 0 Special Education; 0 Vocational; 0 Alternative
0 Magnet; 0 Charter; 4 Title I Eligible; 0 School-wide Title I
Students: 1,632 (52.8% male; 47.2% female)
Individual Education Program: 258 (15.8%);
English Language Learner: 44 (2.7%); Migrant: n/a
Eligible for Free Lunch Program: 480 (29.4%)
Eligible for Reduced-Price Lunch Program: 139 (8.5%)

Teachers: 104.4 (15.6 to 1)
Librarians/Media Specialists: 0.5 (3,264.0 to 1)
Guidance Counselors: 0.0 (0.0 to 1)
Current Spending: ($ per student per year):
Total: $5,281; Instruction: $3,193; Support Services: $1,895
Enrollment, Drop-out Rates and Diploma Recipients by Race/Ethnicity

Category	Total	White	Black	Asian	AIAN	Hisp.
Enrollment (%)	100.0	71.0	15.0	1.8	0.3	11.8
Drop-out Rate (%)	n/a	n/a	n/a	n/a	n/a	n/a
H.S. Diplomas (#)	n/a	n/a	n/a	n/a	n/a	n/a

Summit SD 104

6021 S 74th Ave • Summit, IL 60501-1500
(708) 458-0505 • http://www.sd104.s-cook.k12.il.us/
Grade Span: PK-08; **Agency Type:** 1
Schools: 5
4 Primary; 1 Middle; 0 High; 0 Other Level
5 Regular; 0 Special Education; 0 Vocational; 0 Alternative
0 Magnet; 0 Charter; 5 Title I Eligible; 0 School-wide Title I
Students: 1,676 (52.3% male; 47.7% female)
Individual Education Program: 240 (14.3%);
English Language Learner: 402 (24.0%); Migrant: n/a
Eligible for Free Lunch Program: 773 (46.1%)
Eligible for Reduced-Price Lunch Program: 206 (12.3%)
Teachers: 113.1 (14.8 to 1)
Librarians/Media Specialists: 0.0 (0.0 to 1)
Guidance Counselors: 0.0 (0.0 to 1)
Current Spending: ($ per student per year):
Total: $6,670; Instruction: $4,291; Support Services: $2,163
Enrollment, Drop-out Rates and Diploma Recipients by Race/Ethnicity

Category	Total	White	Black	Asian	AIAN	Hisp.
Enrollment (%)	100.0	25.4	11.7	0.4	0.1	62.5
Drop-out Rate (%)	n/a	n/a	n/a	n/a	n/a	n/a
H.S. Diplomas (#)	n/a	n/a	n/a	n/a	n/a	n/a

Thornton Fractional T HS D 215

1601 Wentworth Ave • Calumet City, IL 60409-6399
(708) 585-2309 • http://www.tfd215.s-cook.k12.il.us/
Grade Span: 09-12; **Agency Type:** 1
Schools: 3
0 Primary; 0 Middle; 2 High; 1 Other Level
2 Regular; 1 Special Education; 0 Vocational; 0 Alternative
0 Magnet; 0 Charter; 1 Title I Eligible; 1 School-wide Title I
Students: 2,867 (50.8% male; 49.2% female)
Individual Education Program: 318 (11.1%);
English Language Learner: 0 (0.0%); Migrant: n/a
Eligible for Free Lunch Program: 812 (28.3%)
Eligible for Reduced-Price Lunch Program: 240 (8.4%)
Teachers: 182.0 (15.8 to 1)
Librarians/Media Specialists: 2.0 (1,433.5 to 1)
Guidance Counselors: 8.0 (358.4 to 1)
Current Spending: ($ per student per year):
Total: $10,872; Instruction: $6,142; Support Services: $4,486
Enrollment, Drop-out Rates and Diploma Recipients by Race/Ethnicity

Category	Total	White	Black	Asian	AIAN	Hisp.
Enrollment (%)	100.0	43.0	41.9	1.2	0.8	13.1
Drop-out Rate (%)	4.0	4.3	3.3	0.0	6.3	5.1
H.S. Diplomas (#)	576	305	203	1	4	63

Thornton Twp HSD 205

465 E 170th St • South Holland, IL 60473-3481
(708) 225-4000 • http://www.district205.net/
Grade Span: 09-12; **Agency Type:** 1
Schools: 3
0 Primary; 0 Middle; 3 High; 0 Other Level
3 Regular; 0 Special Education; 0 Vocational; 0 Alternative
0 Magnet; 0 Charter; 3 Title I Eligible; 0 School-wide Title I
Students: 6,527 (50.2% male; 49.8% female)
Individual Education Program: 937 (14.4%);
English Language Learner: 57 (0.9%); Migrant: n/a
Eligible for Free Lunch Program: 2,364 (36.2%)
Eligible for Reduced-Price Lunch Program: 378 (5.8%)
Teachers: 401.1 (16.3 to 1)
Librarians/Media Specialists: 2.0 (3,263.5 to 1)
Guidance Counselors: 15.0 (435.1 to 1)
Current Spending: ($ per student per year):
Total: $11,956; Instruction: $7,469; Support Services: $4,291
Enrollment, Drop-out Rates and Diploma Recipients by Race/Ethnicity

Category	Total	White	Black	Asian	AIAN	Hisp.
Enrollment (%)	100.0	3.4	92.3	0.2	0.0	4.1
Drop-out Rate (%)	5.3	2.7	5.5	6.3	0.0	5.3
H.S. Diplomas (#)	1,136	51	827	5	207	46

Tinley Park Community Cons SD 146

6611 W 171st St • Tinley Park, IL 60477-3514
(708) 614-4500 • http://www.ccsd146.k12.il.us/
Grade Span: PK-08; **Agency Type:** 1
Schools: 6
5 Primary; 1 Middle; 0 High; 0 Other Level
6 Regular; 0 Special Education; 0 Vocational; 0 Alternative
0 Magnet; 0 Charter; 0 Title I Eligible; 0 School-wide Title I
Students: 2,393 (51.6% male; 48.4% female)
Individual Education Program: 357 (14.9%);
English Language Learner: 99 (4.1%); Migrant: n/a
Eligible for Free Lunch Program: 202 (8.4%)
Eligible for Reduced-Price Lunch Program: 62 (2.6%)
Teachers: 174.8 (13.7 to 1)
Librarians/Media Specialists: 4.0 (598.3 to 1)
Guidance Counselors: 0.0 (0.0 to 1)
Current Spending: ($ per student per year):
Total: $8,014; Instruction: $4,902; Support Services: $2,924
Enrollment, Drop-out Rates and Diploma Recipients by Race/Ethnicity

Category	Total	White	Black	Asian	AIAN	Hisp.
Enrollment (%)	100.0	89.7	2.2	2.3	0.3	5.4
Drop-out Rate (%)	n/a	n/a	n/a	n/a	n/a	n/a
H.S. Diplomas (#)	n/a	n/a	n/a	n/a	n/a	n/a

Township HSD 211

1750 S Roselle Rd • Palatine, IL 60067-7336
(847) 755-6600 • http://www.d211.org/
Grade Span: 09-12; **Agency Type:** 1
Schools: 6
0 Primary; 0 Middle; 6 High; 0 Other Level
5 Regular; 1 Special Education; 0 Vocational; 0 Alternative
0 Magnet; 0 Charter; 0 Title I Eligible; 0 School-wide Title I
Students: 12,852 (51.4% male; 48.6% female)
Individual Education Program: 1,350 (10.5%);
English Language Learner: 689 (5.4%); Migrant: n/a
Eligible for Free Lunch Program: 857 (6.7%)
Eligible for Reduced-Price Lunch Program: 301 (2.3%)
Teachers: 789.2 (16.3 to 1)
Librarians/Media Specialists: 14.0 (918.0 to 1)
Guidance Counselors: 42.5 (302.4 to 1)
Current Spending: ($ per student per year):
Total: $12,183; Instruction: $7,051; Support Services: $4,832
Enrollment, Drop-out Rates and Diploma Recipients by Race/Ethnicity

Category	Total	White	Black	Asian	AIAN	Hisp.
Enrollment (%)	100.0	71.6	4.6	13.3	0.2	10.3
Drop-out Rate (%)	1.5	1.2	2.6	0.6	0.0	4.6
H.S. Diplomas (#)	2,725	2,040	93	401	5	186

Township High SD 214

2121 S Goebbert Rd • Arlington Heights, IL 60005-4297
(847) 718-7600 • http://www.dist214.k12.il.us/
Grade Span: 09-12; **Agency Type:** 1
Schools: 12
0 Primary; 0 Middle; 11 High; 1 Other Level
7 Regular; 5 Special Education; 0 Vocational; 0 Alternative
0 Magnet; 0 Charter; 4 Title I Eligible; 0 School-wide Title I
Students: 12,145 (52.0% male; 48.0% female)
Individual Education Program: 1,511 (12.4%);
English Language Learner: 967 (8.0%); Migrant: n/a
Eligible for Free Lunch Program: 1,090 (9.0%)
Eligible for Reduced-Price Lunch Program: 274 (2.3%)
Teachers: 746.1 (16.3 to 1)
Librarians/Media Specialists: 7.0 (1,735.0 to 1)
Guidance Counselors: 60.5 (200.7 to 1)
Current Spending: ($ per student per year):
Total: $13,071; Instruction: $6,787; Support Services: $5,989
Enrollment, Drop-out Rates and Diploma Recipients by Race/Ethnicity

Category	Total	White	Black	Asian	AIAN	Hisp.
Enrollment (%)	100.0	74.4	3.0	8.1	0.4	14.1
Drop-out Rate (%)	4.2	3.0	14.5	2.9	5.1	9.7
H.S. Diplomas (#)	2,815	2,152	80	252	5	326

West Harvey-Dixmoor PSD 147

191 W 155th Place • Harvey, IL 60426-3413
(708) 339-9500 • http://www.whd147.org/
Grade Span: PK-08; **Agency Type:** 1
Schools: 6
5 Primary; 1 Middle; 0 High; 0 Other Level
6 Regular; 0 Special Education; 0 Vocational; 0 Alternative
0 Magnet; 0 Charter; 6 Title I Eligible; 6 School-wide Title I
Students: 1,729 (51.4% male; 48.6% female)
Individual Education Program: 218 (12.6%);
English Language Learner: 147 (8.5%); Migrant: n/a
Eligible for Free Lunch Program: 1,612 (93.2%)
Eligible for Reduced-Price Lunch Program: 68 (3.9%)

Teachers: 97.0 (17.8 to 1)
Librarians/Media Specialists: 5.0 (345.8 to 1)
Guidance Counselors: 4.0 (432.3 to 1)
Current Spending: ($ per student per year):
Total: $9,924; Instruction: $4,292; Support Services: $5,186
Enrollment, Drop-out Rates and Diploma Recipients by Race/Ethnicity

Category	Total	White	Black	Asian	AIAN	Hisp.
Enrollment (%)	100.0	2.4	85.4	0.0	0.0	12.2
Drop-out Rate (%)	n/a	n/a	n/a	n/a	n/a	n/a
H.S. Diplomas (#)	n/a	n/a	n/a	n/a	n/a	n/a

Wheeling CCSD 21

999 W Dundee Rd • Wheeling, IL 60090-3777
(847) 537-8270 • http://www.d21.k12.il.us/
Grade Span: PK-08; **Agency Type:** 1
Schools: 12
9 Primary; 3 Middle; 0 High; 0 Other Level
12 Regular; 0 Special Education; 0 Vocational; 0 Alternative
0 Magnet; 0 Charter; 9 Title I Eligible; 0 School-wide Title I
Students: 7,106 (50.2% male; 49.8% female)
Individual Education Program: 1,158 (16.3%);
English Language Learner: 1,544 (21.7%); Migrant: n/a
Eligible for Free Lunch Program: 1,580 (22.2%)
Eligible for Reduced-Price Lunch Program: 582 (8.2%)
Teachers: 462.7 (15.4 to 1)
Librarians/Media Specialists: 12.0 (592.2 to 1)
Guidance Counselors: 1.0 (7,106.0 to 1)
Current Spending: ($ per student per year):
Total: $7,754; Instruction: $4,735; Support Services: $2,843
Enrollment, Drop-out Rates and Diploma Recipients by Race/Ethnicity

Category	Total	White	Black	Asian	AIAN	Hisp.
Enrollment (%)	100.0	55.6	2.4	7.2	0.0	34.8
Drop-out Rate (%)	n/a	n/a	n/a	n/a	n/a	n/a
H.S. Diplomas (#)	n/a	n/a	n/a	n/a	n/a	n/a

Wilmette SD 39

615 Locust Rd • Wilmette, IL 60091-2299
(847) 256-2450 • http://wilmette.nttc.org/
Grade Span: PK-08; **Agency Type:** 1
Schools: 6
4 Primary; 2 Middle; 0 High; 0 Other Level
6 Regular; 0 Special Education; 0 Vocational; 0 Alternative
0 Magnet; 0 Charter; 0 Title I Eligible; 0 School-wide Title I
Students: 3,541 (52.7% male; 47.3% female)
Individual Education Program: 468 (13.2%);
English Language Learner: 121 (3.4%); Migrant: n/a
Eligible for Free Lunch Program: 0 (0.0%)
Eligible for Reduced-Price Lunch Program: 0 (0.0%)
Teachers: 263.0 (13.5 to 1)
Librarians/Media Specialists: 3.7 (957.0 to 1)
Guidance Counselors: 0.0 (0.0 to 1)
Current Spending: ($ per student per year):
Total: $7,972; Instruction: $4,689; Support Services: $2,997
Enrollment, Drop-out Rates and Diploma Recipients by Race/Ethnicity

Category	Total	White	Black	Asian	AIAN	Hisp.
Enrollment (%)	100.0	89.2	0.5	8.4	0.2	1.7
Drop-out Rate (%)	n/a	n/a	n/a	n/a	n/a	n/a
H.S. Diplomas (#)	n/a	n/a	n/a	n/a	n/a	n/a

Winnetka SD 36

1235 Oak St • Winnetka, IL 60093-2168
(847) 446-9400 • http://www.winnetka.k12.il.us/
Grade Span: PK-08; **Agency Type:** 1
Schools: 5
3 Primary; 2 Middle; 0 High; 0 Other Level
5 Regular; 0 Special Education; 0 Vocational; 0 Alternative
0 Magnet; 0 Charter; 0 Title I Eligible; 0 School-wide Title I
Students: 2,004 (52.1% male; 47.9% female)
Individual Education Program: 371 (18.5%);
English Language Learner: 11 (0.5%); Migrant: n/a
Eligible for Free Lunch Program: 0 (0.0%)
Eligible for Reduced-Price Lunch Program: 0 (0.0%)
Teachers: 170.0 (11.8 to 1)
Librarians/Media Specialists: 0.0 (0.0 to 1)
Guidance Counselors: 0.0 (0.0 to 1)
Current Spending: ($ per student per year):
Total: $9,646; Instruction: $5,851; Support Services: $3,664
Enrollment, Drop-out Rates and Diploma Recipients by Race/Ethnicity

Category	Total	White	Black	Asian	AIAN	Hisp.
Enrollment (%)	100.0	95.7	0.2	3.3	0.0	0.7
Drop-out Rate (%)	n/a	n/a	n/a	n/a	n/a	n/a
H.S. Diplomas (#)	n/a	n/a	n/a	n/a	n/a	n/a

Crawford County

Robinson CUSD 2

PO Box 190 • Robinson, IL 62454-0190
(618) 544-7511 •
http://nuttall.rob.crwfrd.k12.il.us/education/district/district.php
Grade Span: PK-12; **Agency Type:** 1
Schools: 4
2 Primary; 1 Middle; 1 High; 0 Other Level
4 Regular; 0 Special Education; 0 Vocational; 0 Alternative
0 Magnet; 0 Charter; 2 Title I Eligible; 0 School-wide Title I
Students: 1,813 (52.0% male; 48.0% female)
Individual Education Program: 370 (20.4%);
English Language Learner: 3 (0.2%); Migrant: n/a
Eligible for Free Lunch Program: 507 (28.0%)
Eligible for Reduced-Price Lunch Program: 152 (8.4%)
Teachers: 119.5 (15.2 to 1)
Librarians/Media Specialists: 3.0 (604.3 to 1)
Guidance Counselors: 5.0 (362.6 to 1)
Current Spending: ($ per student per year):
Total: $6,277; Instruction: $3,449; Support Services: $2,560
Enrollment, Drop-out Rates and Diploma Recipients by Race/Ethnicity

Category	Total	White	Black	Asian	AIAN	Hisp.
Enrollment (%)	100.0	94.2	2.6	1.0	0.2	2.0
Drop-out Rate (%)	3.1	3.1	0.0	0.0	0.0	8.3
H.S. Diplomas (#)	123	116	2	1	0	4

De Kalb County

Dekalb Community Unit SD 428

901 S Fourth St • De Kalb, IL 60115-4411
(815) 754-2350 • http://www.dist428.dekalb.k12.il.us/
Grade Span: PK-12; **Agency Type:** 1
Schools: 11
8 Primary; 2 Middle; 1 High; 0 Other Level
11 Regular; 0 Special Education; 0 Vocational; 0 Alternative
0 Magnet; 0 Charter; 6 Title I Eligible; 0 School-wide Title I
Students: 5,372 (50.6% male; 49.4% female)
Individual Education Program: 565 (10.5%);
English Language Learner: 400 (7.4%); Migrant: n/a
Eligible for Free Lunch Program: 1,189 (22.1%)
Eligible for Reduced-Price Lunch Program: 269 (5.0%)
Teachers: 335.8 (16.0 to 1)
Librarians/Media Specialists: 1.0 (5,372.0 to 1)
Guidance Counselors: 7.0 (767.4 to 1)
Current Spending: ($ per student per year):
Total: $6,918; Instruction: $4,247; Support Services: $2,493
Enrollment, Drop-out Rates and Diploma Recipients by Race/Ethnicity

Category	Total	White	Black	Asian	AIAN	Hisp.
Enrollment (%)	100.0	73.2	10.2	2.6	0.3	13.7
Drop-out Rate (%)	2.1	1.1	4.8	0.0	0.0	8.1
H.S. Diplomas (#)	308	257	17	8	0	26

Genoa Kingston CUSD 424

941 W Main St • Genoa, IL 60135-1098
(815) 784-6222
Grade Span: PK-12; **Agency Type:** 1
Schools: 4
2 Primary; 1 Middle; 1 High; 0 Other Level
4 Regular; 0 Special Education; 0 Vocational; 0 Alternative
0 Magnet; 0 Charter; 1 Title I Eligible; 0 School-wide Title I
Students: 1,728 (50.9% male; 49.1% female)
Individual Education Program: 210 (12.2%);
English Language Learner: 52 (3.0%); Migrant: n/a
Eligible for Free Lunch Program: 213 (12.3%)
Eligible for Reduced-Price Lunch Program: 54 (3.1%)
Teachers: 93.9 (18.4 to 1)
Librarians/Media Specialists: 1.0 (1,728.0 to 1)
Guidance Counselors: 3.0 (576.0 to 1)
Current Spending: ($ per student per year):
Total: $4,971; Instruction: $3,007; Support Services: $1,781
Enrollment, Drop-out Rates and Diploma Recipients by Race/Ethnicity

Category	Total	White	Black	Asian	AIAN	Hisp.
Enrollment (%)	100.0	89.9	0.6	0.2	0.2	9.1
Drop-out Rate (%)	1.2	1.3	n/a	0.0	n/a	0.0
H.S. Diplomas (#)	91	83	0	0	0	8

Sandwich CUSD 430

720 S Wells St • Sandwich, IL 60548-2493
(815) 786-2187 • http://www.sandwich430.org
Grade Span: PK-12; **Agency Type:** 1
Schools: 6
3 Primary; 2 Middle; 1 High; 0 Other Level
6 Regular; 0 Special Education; 0 Vocational; 0 Alternative
0 Magnet; 0 Charter; 2 Title I Eligible; 0 School-wide Title I

Students: 2,501 (53.1% male; 46.9% female)
Individual Education Program: 378 (15.1%);
English Language Learner: 88 (3.5%); Migrant: n/a
Eligible for Free Lunch Program: 211 (8.4%)
Eligible for Reduced-Price Lunch Program: 90 (3.6%)
Teachers: 149.4 (16.7 to 1)
Librarians/Media Specialists: 1.0 (2,501.0 to 1)
Guidance Counselors: 3.0 (833.7 to 1)
Current Spending: ($ per student per year):
Total: $5,135; Instruction: $3,349; Support Services: $1,614
Enrollment, Drop-out Rates and Diploma Recipients by Race/Ethnicity

Category	Total	White	Black	Asian	AIAN	Hisp.
Enrollment (%)	100.0	89.2	0.3	2.2	0.1	8.2
Drop-out Rate (%)	3.7	3.5	0.0	0.0	n/a	6.5
H.S. Diplomas (#)	151	141	0	2	3	5

Sycamore CUSD 427

245 W Exchange St • Sycamore, IL 60178-1406
(815) 899-8103 • http://www.syc.dekalb.k12.il.us/
Grade Span: KG-12; **Agency Type:** 1
Schools: 6
4 Primary; 1 Middle; 1 High; 0 Other Level
6 Regular; 0 Special Education; 0 Vocational; 0 Alternative
0 Magnet; 0 Charter; 3 Title I Eligible; 0 School-wide Title I
Students: 3,045 (51.4% male; 48.6% female)
Individual Education Program: 339 (11.1%);
English Language Learner: 32 (1.1%); Migrant: n/a
Eligible for Free Lunch Program: 222 (7.3%)
Eligible for Reduced-Price Lunch Program: 51 (1.7%)
Teachers: 193.9 (15.7 to 1)
Librarians/Media Specialists: 2.0 (1,522.5 to 1)
Guidance Counselors: 5.0 (609.0 to 1)
Current Spending: ($ per student per year):
Total: $6,767; Instruction: $3,953; Support Services: $2,626
Enrollment, Drop-out Rates and Diploma Recipients by Race/Ethnicity

Category	Total	White	Black	Asian	AIAN	Hisp.
Enrollment (%)	100.0	91.3	3.5	1.1	0.3	3.8
Drop-out Rate (%)	2.1	1.9	8.3	0.0	0.0	3.6
H.S. Diplomas (#)	216	197	8	5	0	6

De Witt County

Clinton CUSD 15

220 N Monroe • Clinton, IL 61727-1399
(217) 935-8321 • http://www.cusd15.k12.il.us/
Grade Span: PK-12; **Agency Type:** 1
Schools: 6
4 Primary; 1 Middle; 0 High; 1 Other Level
6 Regular; 0 Special Education; 0 Vocational; 0 Alternative
0 Magnet; 0 Charter; 2 Title I Eligible; 0 School-wide Title I
Students: 2,142 (50.8% male; 49.2% female)
Individual Education Program: 349 (16.3%);
English Language Learner: 0 (0.0%); Migrant: n/a
Eligible for Free Lunch Program: 454 (21.2%)
Eligible for Reduced-Price Lunch Program: 101 (4.7%)
Teachers: 162.8 (13.2 to 1)
Librarians/Media Specialists: 4.0 (535.5 to 1)
Guidance Counselors: 5.0 (428.4 to 1)
Current Spending: ($ per student per year):
Total: $7,954; Instruction: $5,160; Support Services: $2,530
Enrollment, Drop-out Rates and Diploma Recipients by Race/Ethnicity

Category	Total	White	Black	Asian	AIAN	Hisp.
Enrollment (%)	100.0	94.9	1.2	1.1	0.3	2.5
Drop-out Rate (%)	4.3	4.5	0.0	0.0	0.0	0.0
H.S. Diplomas (#)	144	140	0	0	0	4

Du Page County

Addison SD 4

222 N Kennedy Dr • Addison, IL 60101-2497
(630) 458-2425 • http://www.asd4.org/
Grade Span: PK-08; **Agency Type:** 1
Schools: 8
7 Primary; 1 Middle; 0 High; 0 Other Level
8 Regular; 0 Special Education; 0 Vocational; 0 Alternative
0 Magnet; 0 Charter; 3 Title I Eligible; 0 School-wide Title I
Students: 3,831 (51.1% male; 48.9% female)
Individual Education Program: 583 (15.2%);
English Language Learner: 971 (25.3%); Migrant: n/a
Eligible for Free Lunch Program: 792 (20.7%)
Eligible for Reduced-Price Lunch Program: 174 (4.5%)
Teachers: 216.8 (17.7 to 1)
Librarians/Media Specialists: 0.0 (0.0 to 1)
Guidance Counselors: 1.0 (3,831.0 to 1)
Current Spending: ($ per student per year):
Total: $6,363; Instruction: $4,010; Support Services: $2,169
Enrollment, Drop-out Rates and Diploma Recipients by Race/Ethnicity

Category	Total	White	Black	Asian	AIAN	Hisp.
Enrollment (%)	100.0	45.7	2.2	5.9	0.0	46.2
Drop-out Rate (%)	n/a	n/a	n/a	n/a	n/a	n/a
H.S. Diplomas (#)	n/a	n/a	n/a	n/a	n/a	n/a

Bensenville SD 2

210 S Church Rd • Bensenville, IL 60106-2303
(630) 766-5940 • http://www.bensenville2.k12.il.us/
Grade Span: PK-08; **Agency Type:** 1
Schools: 5
4 Primary; 1 Middle; 0 High; 0 Other Level
5 Regular; 0 Special Education; 0 Vocational; 0 Alternative
0 Magnet; 0 Charter; 3 Title I Eligible; 0 School-wide Title I
Students: 2,296 (53.1% male; 46.9% female)
Individual Education Program: 320 (13.9%);
English Language Learner: 785 (34.2%); Migrant: n/a
Eligible for Free Lunch Program: 94 (4.1%)
Eligible for Reduced-Price Lunch Program: 21 (0.9%)
Teachers: 132.4 (17.3 to 1)
Librarians/Media Specialists: 5.0 (459.2 to 1)
Guidance Counselors: 1.0 (2,296.0 to 1)
Current Spending: ($ per student per year):
Total: $6,200; Instruction: $3,778; Support Services: $2,322
Enrollment, Drop-out Rates and Diploma Recipients by Race/Ethnicity

Category	Total	White	Black	Asian	AIAN	Hisp.
Enrollment (%)	100.0	34.0	3.7	7.2	0.0	55.1
Drop-out Rate (%)	n/a	n/a	n/a	n/a	n/a	n/a
H.S. Diplomas (#)	n/a	n/a	n/a	n/a	n/a	n/a

CCSD 181

5905 S County Rd • Hinsdale, IL 60521-4870
(630) 887-1070 • http://www.schooldistrict181.org/
Grade Span: PK-08; **Agency Type:** 1
Schools: 9
7 Primary; 2 Middle; 0 High; 0 Other Level
9 Regular; 0 Special Education; 0 Vocational; 0 Alternative
0 Magnet; 0 Charter; 2 Title I Eligible; 0 School-wide Title I
Students: 3,909 (51.1% male; 48.9% female)
Individual Education Program: 437 (11.2%);
English Language Learner: 103 (2.6%); Migrant: n/a
Eligible for Free Lunch Program: n/a
Eligible for Reduced-Price Lunch Program: n/a
Teachers: 239.1 (16.3 to 1)
Librarians/Media Specialists: 8.0 (488.6 to 1)
Guidance Counselors: 1.0 (3,909.0 to 1)
Current Spending: ($ per student per year):
Total: $8,212; Instruction: $5,161; Support Services: $2,911
Enrollment, Drop-out Rates and Diploma Recipients by Race/Ethnicity

Category	Total	White	Black	Asian	AIAN	Hisp.
Enrollment (%)	100.0	94.4	0.6	3.5	0.0	1.6
Drop-out Rate (%)	n/a	n/a	n/a	n/a	n/a	n/a
H.S. Diplomas (#)	n/a	n/a	n/a	n/a	n/a	n/a

Community CSD 93

PO Box 88093 • Carol Stream, IL 60188-0093
(630) 462-8900 • http://www.d93.dupage.k12.il.us/
Grade Span: PK-08; **Agency Type:** 1
Schools: 8
6 Primary; 2 Middle; 0 High; 0 Other Level
8 Regular; 0 Special Education; 0 Vocational; 0 Alternative
1 Magnet; 0 Charter; 3 Title I Eligible; 0 School-wide Title I
Students: 4,973 (51.8% male; 48.2% female)
Individual Education Program: 574 (11.5%);
English Language Learner: 336 (6.8%); Migrant: n/a
Eligible for Free Lunch Program: 0 (0.0%)
Eligible for Reduced-Price Lunch Program: 0 (0.0%)
Teachers: 298.3 (16.7 to 1)
Librarians/Media Specialists: 8.0 (621.6 to 1)
Guidance Counselors: 0.0 (0.0 to 1)
Current Spending: ($ per student per year):
Total: $6,270; Instruction: $3,644; Support Services: $2,562
Enrollment, Drop-out Rates and Diploma Recipients by Race/Ethnicity

Category	Total	White	Black	Asian	AIAN	Hisp.
Enrollment (%)	100.0	68.5	4.8	14.9	0.4	11.5
Drop-out Rate (%)	n/a	n/a	n/a	n/a	n/a	n/a
H.S. Diplomas (#)	n/a	n/a	n/a	n/a	n/a	n/a

Community High SD 94

326 Joliet St • West Chicago, IL 60185-3142
(630) 876-6200 • http://www.district94.dupage.k12.il.us/
Grade Span: 09-12; **Agency Type:** 1
Schools: 1

0 Primary; 0 Middle; 1 High; 0 Other Level
1 Regular; 0 Special Education; 0 Vocational; 0 Alternative
0 Magnet; 0 Charter; 1 Title I Eligible; 0 School-wide Title I
Students: 2,122 (50.4% male; 49.6% female)
Individual Education Program: 178 (8.4%);
English Language Learner: 285 (13.4%); Migrant: n/a
Eligible for Free Lunch Program: 0 (0.0%)
Eligible for Reduced-Price Lunch Program: 0 (0.0%)
Teachers: 131.0 (16.2 to 1)
Librarians/Media Specialists: 1.0 (2,122.0 to 1)
Guidance Counselors: 8.8 (241.1 to 1)
Current Spending: ($ per student per year):
Total: $9,463; Instruction: $5,804; Support Services: $3,419
Enrollment, Drop-out Rates and Diploma Recipients by Race/Ethnicity

Category	Total	White	Black	Asian	AIAN	Hisp.
Enrollment (%)	100.0	61.5	1.0	1.5	0.5	35.4
Drop-out Rate (%)	4.8	2.8	12.5	3.3	11.1	8.4
H.S. Diplomas (#)	438	305	6	13	1	113

Community High SD 99

6301 Springside • Downers Grove, IL 60516-2489
(630) 795-7100 • http://www.csd99.k12.il.us/
Grade Span: 08-12; **Agency Type:** 1
Schools: 2
0 Primary; 0 Middle; 2 High; 0 Other Level
2 Regular; 0 Special Education; 0 Vocational; 0 Alternative
0 Magnet; 0 Charter; 1 Title I Eligible; 0 School-wide Title I
Students: 5,248 (51.7% male; 48.3% female)
Individual Education Program: 691 (13.2%);
English Language Learner: 132 (2.5%); Migrant: n/a
Eligible for Free Lunch Program: 263 (5.0%)
Eligible for Reduced-Price Lunch Program: 45 (0.9%)
Teachers: 321.3 (16.3 to 1)
Librarians/Media Specialists: 7.0 (749.7 to 1)
Guidance Counselors: 20.0 (262.4 to 1)
Current Spending: ($ per student per year):
Total: $10,636; Instruction: $6,795; Support Services: $3,576
Enrollment, Drop-out Rates and Diploma Recipients by Race/Ethnicity

Category	Total	White	Black	Asian	AIAN	Hisp.
Enrollment (%)	100.0	78.0	6.3	9.3	0.2	6.1
Drop-out Rate (%)	2.3	2.0	3.7	1.8	0.0	5.8
H.S. Diplomas (#)	1,207	964	62	123	3	55

Community Unit SD 200

130 W Park Ave • Wheaton, IL 60187-6460
(630) 682-2000 • http://www.cusd200.org/
Grade Span: PK-12; **Agency Type:** 1
Schools: 20
14 Primary; 4 Middle; 2 High; 0 Other Level
19 Regular; 1 Special Education; 0 Vocational; 0 Alternative
0 Magnet; 0 Charter; 9 Title I Eligible; 0 School-wide Title I
Students: 14,294 (52.4% male; 47.6% female)
Individual Education Program: 2,047 (14.3%);
English Language Learner: 668 (4.7%); Migrant: n/a
Eligible for Free Lunch Program: 1,228 (8.6%)
Eligible for Reduced-Price Lunch Program: 248 (1.7%)
Teachers: 893.1 (16.0 to 1)
Librarians/Media Specialists: 20.0 (714.7 to 1)
Guidance Counselors: 26.8 (533.4 to 1)
Current Spending: ($ per student per year):
Total: $7,538; Instruction: $4,602; Support Services: $2,817
Enrollment, Drop-out Rates and Diploma Recipients by Race/Ethnicity

Category	Total	White	Black	Asian	AIAN	Hisp.
Enrollment (%)	100.0	82.7	5.8	4.5	0.1	7.0
Drop-out Rate (%)	3.2	2.9	5.3	1.6	0.0	9.6
H.S. Diplomas (#)	1,018	879	36	60	0	43

Darien SD 61

7414 S Cass Ave • Darien, IL 60561-3697
(630) 968-7505 • http://www.darien61.com/
Grade Span: PK-08; **Agency Type:** 1
Schools: 4
3 Primary; 1 Middle; 0 High; 0 Other Level
4 Regular; 0 Special Education; 0 Vocational; 0 Alternative
0 Magnet; 0 Charter; 3 Title I Eligible; 0 School-wide Title I
Students: 1,778 (52.1% male; 47.9% female)
Individual Education Program: 224 (12.6%);
English Language Learner: 117 (6.6%); Migrant: n/a
Eligible for Free Lunch Program: 134 (7.5%)
Eligible for Reduced-Price Lunch Program: 29 (1.6%)
Teachers: 124.2 (14.3 to 1)
Librarians/Media Specialists: 1.0 (1,778.0 to 1)
Guidance Counselors: 0.0 (0.0 to 1)
Current Spending: ($ per student per year):
Total: $6,854; Instruction: $4,339; Support Services: $2,334
Enrollment, Drop-out Rates and Diploma Recipients by Race/Ethnicity

Category	Total	White	Black	Asian	AIAN	Hisp.
Enrollment (%)	100.0	69.2	9.3	12.4	0.0	9.0
Drop-out Rate (%)	n/a	n/a	n/a	n/a	n/a	n/a
H.S. Diplomas (#)	n/a	n/a	n/a	n/a	n/a	n/a

Downers Grove Grade SD 58

1860 63rd St • Downers Grove, IL 60516-1995
(630) 719-5800 • http://www.dg58.dupage.k12.il.us/
Grade Span: PK-08; **Agency Type:** 1
Schools: 12
10 Primary; 2 Middle; 0 High; 0 Other Level
12 Regular; 0 Special Education; 0 Vocational; 0 Alternative
0 Magnet; 0 Charter; 5 Title I Eligible; 0 School-wide Title I
Students: 4,860 (50.2% male; 49.8% female)
Individual Education Program: 733 (15.1%);
English Language Learner: 162 (3.3%); Migrant: n/a
Eligible for Free Lunch Program: 30 (0.6%)
Eligible for Reduced-Price Lunch Program: 11 (0.2%)
Teachers: 273.0 (17.8 to 1)
Librarians/Media Specialists: 11.0 (441.8 to 1)
Guidance Counselors: 4.0 (1,215.0 to 1)
Current Spending: ($ per student per year):
Total: $7,298; Instruction: $4,229; Support Services: $2,986
Enrollment, Drop-out Rates and Diploma Recipients by Race/Ethnicity

Category	Total	White	Black	Asian	AIAN	Hisp.
Enrollment (%)	100.0	85.3	3.7	6.6	0.2	4.1
Drop-out Rate (%)	n/a	n/a	n/a	n/a	n/a	n/a
H.S. Diplomas (#)	n/a	n/a	n/a	n/a	n/a	n/a

Du Page High SD 88

101 W High Ridge Rd • Villa Park, IL 60181-3205
(630) 530-3980 • http://www.hsdist88.dupage.k12.il.us/
Grade Span: 09-12; **Agency Type:** 1
Schools: 2
0 Primary; 0 Middle; 2 High; 0 Other Level
2 Regular; 0 Special Education; 0 Vocational; 0 Alternative
0 Magnet; 0 Charter; 2 Title I Eligible; 0 School-wide Title I
Students: 3,909 (50.8% male; 49.2% female)
Individual Education Program: 474 (12.1%);
English Language Learner: 256 (6.5%); Migrant: n/a
Eligible for Free Lunch Program: 559 (14.3%)
Eligible for Reduced-Price Lunch Program: 112 (2.9%)
Teachers: 242.4 (16.1 to 1)
Librarians/Media Specialists: 2.0 (1,954.5 to 1)
Guidance Counselors: 11.0 (355.4 to 1)
Current Spending: ($ per student per year):
Total: $10,805; Instruction: $5,604; Support Services: $4,955
Enrollment, Drop-out Rates and Diploma Recipients by Race/Ethnicity

Category	Total	White	Black	Asian	AIAN	Hisp.
Enrollment (%)	100.0	71.8	2.6	6.0	0.0	19.6
Drop-out Rate (%)	5.6	4.1	7.4	4.9	20.0	11.1
H.S. Diplomas (#)	780	588	24	47	1	120

Elmhurst SD 205

130 W Madison St • Elmhurst, IL 60126-3320
(630) 834-4530 • http://www.elmhurst.k12.il.us/
Grade Span: PK-12; **Agency Type:** 1
Schools: 13
9 Primary; 3 Middle; 1 High; 0 Other Level
12 Regular; 1 Special Education; 0 Vocational; 0 Alternative
0 Magnet; 0 Charter; 1 Title I Eligible; 0 School-wide Title I
Students: 7,303 (52.3% male; 47.7% female)
Individual Education Program: 947 (13.0%);
English Language Learner: 314 (4.3%); Migrant: n/a
Eligible for Free Lunch Program: 60 (0.8%)
Eligible for Reduced-Price Lunch Program: 12 (0.2%)
Teachers: 465.2 (15.7 to 1)
Librarians/Media Specialists: 10.0 (730.3 to 1)
Guidance Counselors: 18.0 (405.7 to 1)
Current Spending: ($ per student per year):
Total: $8,711; Instruction: $5,527; Support Services: $3,011
Enrollment, Drop-out Rates and Diploma Recipients by Race/Ethnicity

Category	Total	White	Black	Asian	AIAN	Hisp.
Enrollment (%)	100.0	86.4	1.6	5.4	0.1	6.6
Drop-out Rate (%)	1.1	1.2	0.0	0.0	0.0	0.9
H.S. Diplomas (#)	504	432	3	41	3	25

Fenton Community HSD 100

1000 W Green St • Bensenville, IL 60106-2099
(630) 860-6257
Grade Span: 09-12; **Agency Type:** 1
Schools: 1
0 Primary; 0 Middle; 1 High; 0 Other Level
1 Regular; 0 Special Education; 0 Vocational; 0 Alternative

0 Magnet; 0 Charter; 1 Title I Eligible; 0 School-wide Title I
Students: 1,523 (53.6% male; 46.4% female)
Individual Education Program: 254 (16.7%);
English Language Learner: 87 (5.7%); Migrant: n/a
Eligible for Free Lunch Program: 0 (0.0%)
Eligible for Reduced-Price Lunch Program: 0 (0.0%)
Teachers: 95.2 (16.0 to 1)
Librarians/Media Specialists: 1.0 (1,523.0 to 1)
Guidance Counselors: 5.0 (304.6 to 1)
Current Spending: ($ per student per year):
Total: $12,367; Instruction: $6,884; Support Services: $5,123
Enrollment, Drop-out Rates and Diploma Recipients by Race/Ethnicity

Category	Total	White	Black	Asian	AIAN	Hisp.
Enrollment (%)	100.0	57.5	1.2	6.8	0.1	34.3
Drop-out Rate (%)	5.4	3.4	5.0	1.9	0.0	10.0
H.S. Diplomas (#)	329	195	1	28	0	105

Glen Ellyn CCSD 89
22w600 Butterfield • Glen Ellyn, IL 60137-2848
(630) 469-8900 • http://www.d89.dupage.k12.il.us/
Grade Span: PK-08; **Agency Type:** 1
Schools: 5
4 Primary; 1 Middle; 0 High; 0 Other Level
5 Regular; 0 Special Education; 0 Vocational; 0 Alternative
0 Magnet; 0 Charter; 3 Title I Eligible; 0 School-wide Title I
Students: 2,451 (50.6% male; 49.4% female)
Individual Education Program: 325 (13.3%);
English Language Learner: 119 (4.9%); Migrant: n/a
Eligible for Free Lunch Program: 0 (0.0%)
Eligible for Reduced-Price Lunch Program: 0 (0.0%)
Teachers: 156.9 (15.6 to 1)
Librarians/Media Specialists: 2.0 (1,225.5 to 1)
Guidance Counselors: 2.0 (1,225.5 to 1)
Current Spending: ($ per student per year):
Total: $7,450; Instruction: $4,766; Support Services: $2,631
Enrollment, Drop-out Rates and Diploma Recipients by Race/Ethnicity

Category	Total	White	Black	Asian	AIAN	Hisp.
Enrollment (%)	100.0	79.7	6.7	9.4	0.0	4.2
Drop-out Rate (%)	n/a	n/a	n/a	n/a	n/a	n/a
H.S. Diplomas (#)	n/a	n/a	n/a	n/a	n/a	n/a

Glen Ellyn SD 41
793 N Main St • Glen Ellyn, IL 60137-3999
(630) 790-6400 • http://www.d41.dupage.k12.il.us/
Grade Span: PK-08; **Agency Type:** 1
Schools: 5
4 Primary; 1 Middle; 0 High; 0 Other Level
5 Regular; 0 Special Education; 0 Vocational; 0 Alternative
0 Magnet; 0 Charter; 3 Title I Eligible; 0 School-wide Title I
Students: 3,434 (52.0% male; 48.0% female)
Individual Education Program: 439 (12.8%);
English Language Learner: 236 (6.9%); Migrant: n/a
Eligible for Free Lunch Program: 0 (0.0%)
Eligible for Reduced-Price Lunch Program: 0 (0.0%)
Teachers: 209.2 (16.4 to 1)
Librarians/Media Specialists: 5.0 (686.8 to 1)
Guidance Counselors: 3.0 (1,144.7 to 1)
Current Spending: ($ per student per year):
Total: $6,276; Instruction: $3,910; Support Services: $2,268
Enrollment, Drop-out Rates and Diploma Recipients by Race/Ethnicity

Category	Total	White	Black	Asian	AIAN	Hisp.
Enrollment (%)	100.0	84.0	4.3	6.1	0.1	5.5
Drop-out Rate (%)	n/a	n/a	n/a	n/a	n/a	n/a
H.S. Diplomas (#)	n/a	n/a	n/a	n/a	n/a	n/a

Glenbard Twp HSD 87
596 Crescent Blvd • Glen Ellyn, IL 60137-4297
(630) 469-9100 • http://www.glenbard.org/
Grade Span: 09-12; **Agency Type:** 1
Schools: 4
0 Primary; 0 Middle; 4 High; 0 Other Level
4 Regular; 0 Special Education; 0 Vocational; 0 Alternative
0 Magnet; 0 Charter; 1 Title I Eligible; 0 School-wide Title I
Students: 8,880 (51.9% male; 48.1% female)
Individual Education Program: 902 (10.2%);
English Language Learner: 127 (1.4%); Migrant: n/a
Eligible for Free Lunch Program: 441 (5.0%)
Eligible for Reduced-Price Lunch Program: 111 (1.3%)
Teachers: 532.6 (16.7 to 1)
Librarians/Media Specialists: 13.6 (652.9 to 1)
Guidance Counselors: 35.9 (247.4 to 1)
Current Spending: ($ per student per year):
Total: $10,263; Instruction: $6,134; Support Services: $3,988
Enrollment, Drop-out Rates and Diploma Recipients by Race/Ethnicity

Category	Total	White	Black	Asian	AIAN	Hisp.
Enrollment (%)	100.0	71.4	4.9	14.1	0.2	9.3
Drop-out Rate (%)	2.1	1.7	5.7	1.2	0.0	5.8
H.S. Diplomas (#)	1,946	1,457	64	264	6	155

Hinsdale Twp HSD 86
55th And Grant St • Hinsdale, IL 60521-4578
(630) 655-6100 • http://www.district86.k12.il.us/
Grade Span: 09-12; **Agency Type:** 1
Schools: 2
0 Primary; 0 Middle; 2 High; 0 Other Level
2 Regular; 0 Special Education; 0 Vocational; 0 Alternative
0 Magnet; 0 Charter; 1 Title I Eligible; 0 School-wide Title I
Students: 4,221 (51.1% male; 48.9% female)
Individual Education Program: 391 (9.3%);
English Language Learner: 146 (3.5%); Migrant: n/a
Eligible for Free Lunch Program: 0 (0.0%)
Eligible for Reduced-Price Lunch Program: 0 (0.0%)
Teachers: 276.0 (15.3 to 1)
Librarians/Media Specialists: 5.0 (844.2 to 1)
Guidance Counselors: 19.0 (222.2 to 1)
Current Spending: ($ per student per year):
Total: $12,245; Instruction: $7,503; Support Services: $4,735
Enrollment, Drop-out Rates and Diploma Recipients by Race/Ethnicity

Category	Total	White	Black	Asian	AIAN	Hisp.
Enrollment (%)	100.0	78.6	3.6	13.5	0.3	4.0
Drop-out Rate (%)	1.3	1.3	5.9	0.4	0.0	0.7
H.S. Diplomas (#)	993	785	36	136	1	35

Indian Prairie CUSD 204
780 Shoreline Dr • Aurora, IL 60504-6192
(630) 375-3000
Grade Span: PK-12; **Agency Type:** 1
Schools: 30
21 Primary; 6 Middle; 3 High; 0 Other Level
28 Regular; 2 Special Education; 0 Vocational; 0 Alternative
0 Magnet; 0 Charter; 6 Title I Eligible; 0 School-wide Title I
Students: 25,795 (51.0% male; 49.0% female)
Individual Education Program: 2,697 (10.5%);
English Language Learner: 1,200 (4.7%); Migrant: n/a
Eligible for Free Lunch Program: 0 (0.0%)
Eligible for Reduced-Price Lunch Program: 0 (0.0%)
Teachers: 1,601.0 (16.1 to 1)
Librarians/Media Specialists: 4.0 (6,448.8 to 1)
Guidance Counselors: 42.0 (614.2 to 1)
Current Spending: ($ per student per year):
Total: $6,404; Instruction: $4,180; Support Services: $2,186
Enrollment, Drop-out Rates and Diploma Recipients by Race/Ethnicity

Category	Total	White	Black	Asian	AIAN	Hisp.
Enrollment (%)	100.0	75.8	7.6	11.1	0.2	5.3
Drop-out Rate (%)	0.9	0.8	1.2	0.2	0.0	1.8
H.S. Diplomas (#)	1,282	1,000	105	124	0	53

Keeneyville SD 20
5540 Arlington Dr E • Hanover Park, IL 60133-5569
(630) 894-2250 • http://www.esd20.dupage.k12.il.us/
Grade Span: PK-08; **Agency Type:** 1
Schools: 3
2 Primary; 1 Middle; 0 High; 0 Other Level
3 Regular; 0 Special Education; 0 Vocational; 0 Alternative
0 Magnet; 0 Charter; 2 Title I Eligible; 0 School-wide Title I
Students: 1,619 (51.5% male; 48.5% female)
Individual Education Program: 281 (17.4%);
English Language Learner: 136 (8.4%); Migrant: n/a
Eligible for Free Lunch Program: 0 (0.0%)
Eligible for Reduced-Price Lunch Program: 0 (0.0%)
Teachers: 110.0 (14.7 to 1)
Librarians/Media Specialists: 2.0 (809.5 to 1)
Guidance Counselors: 0.0 (0.0 to 1)
Current Spending: ($ per student per year):
Total: $7,683; Instruction: $4,525; Support Services: $3,072
Enrollment, Drop-out Rates and Diploma Recipients by Race/Ethnicity

Category	Total	White	Black	Asian	AIAN	Hisp.
Enrollment (%)	100.0	56.2	10.6	13.8	0.4	19.0
Drop-out Rate (%)	n/a	n/a	n/a	n/a	n/a	n/a
H.S. Diplomas (#)	n/a	n/a	n/a	n/a	n/a	n/a

Lake Park Community HSD 108
450 Spring Court • Roselle, IL 60172-1978
(630) 529-4500 • http://www.lphs.dupage.k12.il.us/
Grade Span: 09-12; **Agency Type:** 1
Schools: 1
0 Primary; 0 Middle; 1 High; 0 Other Level
1 Regular; 0 Special Education; 0 Vocational; 0 Alternative

0 Magnet; 0 Charter; 1 Title I Eligible; 0 School-wide Title I
Students: 2,839 (50.7% male; 49.3% female)
Individual Education Program: 350 (12.3%);
English Language Learner: 46 (1.6%); Migrant: n/a
Eligible for Free Lunch Program: 0 (0.0%)
Eligible for Reduced-Price Lunch Program: 0 (0.0%)
Teachers: 152.0 (18.7 to 1)
Librarians/Media Specialists: 3.0 (946.3 to 1)
Guidance Counselors: 10.0 (283.9 to 1)
Current Spending: ($ per student per year):
Total: $10,820; Instruction: $6,086; Support Services: $4,501
Enrollment, Drop-out Rates and Diploma Recipients by Race/Ethnicity

Category	Total	White	Black	Asian	AIAN	Hisp.
Enrollment (%)	100.0	81.7	2.7	7.4	0.4	7.8
Drop-out Rate (%)	1.7	1.4	4.3	0.9	0.0	5.3
H.S. Diplomas (#)	636	529	15	51	1	40

Lisle CUSD 202
5211 Center Ave • Lisle, IL 60532-2399
(630) 493-8000 • http://www.lisle.dupage.k12.il.us/
Grade Span: PK-12; **Agency Type:** 1
Schools: 4
2 Primary; 1 Middle; 1 High; 0 Other Level
4 Regular; 0 Special Education; 0 Vocational; 0 Alternative
0 Magnet; 0 Charter; 2 Title I Eligible; 0 School-wide Title I
Students: 1,807 (51.7% male; 48.3% female)
Individual Education Program: 254 (14.1%);
English Language Learner: 65 (3.6%); Migrant: n/a
Eligible for Free Lunch Program: 103 (5.7%)
Eligible for Reduced-Price Lunch Program: 33 (1.8%)
Teachers: 118.9 (15.2 to 1)
Librarians/Media Specialists: 4.0 (451.8 to 1)
Guidance Counselors: 3.0 (602.3 to 1)
Current Spending: ($ per student per year):
Total: $9,449; Instruction: $5,375; Support Services: $3,879
Enrollment, Drop-out Rates and Diploma Recipients by Race/Ethnicity

Category	Total	White	Black	Asian	AIAN	Hisp.
Enrollment (%)	100.0	81.1	7.2	6.2	0.1	5.4
Drop-out Rate (%)	0.3	0.4	0.0	0.0	0.0	0.0
H.S. Diplomas (#)	153	127	10	11	0	5

Lombard SD 44
150 W Madison St • Lombard, IL 60148-5199
(630) 827-4400 • http://www.district44.dupage.k12.il.us/
Grade Span: PK-08; **Agency Type:** 1
Schools: 7
6 Primary; 1 Middle; 0 High; 0 Other Level
7 Regular; 0 Special Education; 0 Vocational; 0 Alternative
0 Magnet; 0 Charter; 3 Title I Eligible; 0 School-wide Title I
Students: 3,325 (51.9% male; 48.1% female)
Individual Education Program: 528 (15.9%);
English Language Learner: 210 (6.3%); Migrant: n/a
Eligible for Free Lunch Program: 309 (9.3%)
Eligible for Reduced-Price Lunch Program: 104 (3.1%)
Teachers: 212.0 (15.7 to 1)
Librarians/Media Specialists: 2.0 (1,662.5 to 1)
Guidance Counselors: 3.0 (1,108.3 to 1)
Current Spending: ($ per student per year):
Total: $7,771; Instruction: $4,744; Support Services: $2,800
Enrollment, Drop-out Rates and Diploma Recipients by Race/Ethnicity

Category	Total	White	Black	Asian	AIAN	Hisp.
Enrollment (%)	100.0	76.5	5.5	9.1	0.2	8.6
Drop-out Rate (%)	n/a	n/a	n/a	n/a	n/a	n/a
H.S. Diplomas (#)	n/a	n/a	n/a	n/a	n/a	n/a

Marquardt SD 15
2174 Gladstone Ste C • Glendale Heights, IL 60139-1653
(630) 295-5450 • http://www.d15.dupage.k12.il.us/
Grade Span: PK-08; **Agency Type:** 1
Schools: 5
4 Primary; 1 Middle; 0 High; 0 Other Level
5 Regular; 0 Special Education; 0 Vocational; 0 Alternative
0 Magnet; 0 Charter; 3 Title I Eligible; 0 School-wide Title I
Students: 2,706 (50.5% male; 49.5% female)
Individual Education Program: 353 (13.0%);
English Language Learner: 401 (14.8%); Migrant: n/a
Eligible for Free Lunch Program: 589 (21.8%)
Eligible for Reduced-Price Lunch Program: 125 (4.6%)
Teachers: 152.5 (17.7 to 1)
Librarians/Media Specialists: 2.0 (1,353.0 to 1)
Guidance Counselors: 0.0 (0.0 to 1)
Current Spending: ($ per student per year):
Total: $6,753; Instruction: $4,262; Support Services: $2,318

Enrollment, Drop-out Rates and Diploma Recipients by Race/Ethnicity

Category	Total	White	Black	Asian	AIAN	Hisp.
Enrollment (%)	100.0	39.7	11.5	17.1	0.1	31.7
Drop-out Rate (%)	n/a	n/a	n/a	n/a	n/a	n/a
H.S. Diplomas (#)	n/a	n/a	n/a	n/a	n/a	n/a

Naperville C U Dist 203
203 W Hillside • Naperville, IL 60540-6589
(630) 420-6300 • http://www.ncusd203.org/
Grade Span: PK-12; **Agency Type:** 1
Schools: 21
14 Primary; 5 Middle; 2 High; 0 Other Level
21 Regular; 0 Special Education; 0 Vocational; 0 Alternative
1 Magnet; 0 Charter; 6 Title I Eligible; 0 School-wide Title I
Students: 19,020 (52.3% male; 47.7% female)
Individual Education Program: 2,184 (11.5%);
English Language Learner: 386 (2.0%); Migrant: n/a
Eligible for Free Lunch Program: 133 (0.7%)
Eligible for Reduced-Price Lunch Program: 20 (0.1%)
Teachers: 1,078.2 (17.6 to 1)
Librarians/Media Specialists: 11.0 (1,729.1 to 1)
Guidance Counselors: 33.0 (576.4 to 1)
Current Spending: ($ per student per year):
Total: $7,558; Instruction: $4,861; Support Services: $2,562
Enrollment, Drop-out Rates and Diploma Recipients by Race/Ethnicity

Category	Total	White	Black	Asian	AIAN	Hisp.
Enrollment (%)	100.0	80.7	2.9	13.0	0.2	3.3
Drop-out Rate (%)	1.0	1.1	2.3	0.0	0.0	3.7
H.S. Diplomas (#)	1,348	1,117	35	167	7	22

Queen Bee SD 16
1560 Bloomingdale Rd • Glendale Heights, IL 60139-2796
(630) 260-6100 • http://www.d16.dupage.k12.il.us/
Grade Span: PK-08; **Agency Type:** 1
Schools: 3
1 Primary; 2 Middle; 0 High; 0 Other Level
3 Regular; 0 Special Education; 0 Vocational; 0 Alternative
0 Magnet; 0 Charter; 2 Title I Eligible; 0 School-wide Title I
Students: 2,215 (51.5% male; 48.5% female)
Individual Education Program: 322 (14.5%);
English Language Learner: 364 (16.4%); Migrant: n/a
Eligible for Free Lunch Program: 0 (0.0%)
Eligible for Reduced-Price Lunch Program: 0 (0.0%)
Teachers: 143.0 (15.5 to 1)
Librarians/Media Specialists: 5.0 (443.0 to 1)
Guidance Counselors: 1.0 (2,215.0 to 1)
Current Spending: ($ per student per year):
Total: $6,626; Instruction: $4,135; Support Services: $2,414
Enrollment, Drop-out Rates and Diploma Recipients by Race/Ethnicity

Category	Total	White	Black	Asian	AIAN	Hisp.
Enrollment (%)	100.0	42.6	5.1	21.8	0.0	30.5
Drop-out Rate (%)	n/a	n/a	n/a	n/a	n/a	n/a
H.S. Diplomas (#)	n/a	n/a	n/a	n/a	n/a	n/a

SD 45 Dupage County
255 W Vermont St • Villa Park, IL 60181-1943
(630) 530-6200 • http://www.d45.dupage.k12.il.us/
Grade Span: PK-08; **Agency Type:** 1
Schools: 8
6 Primary; 2 Middle; 0 High; 0 Other Level
8 Regular; 0 Special Education; 0 Vocational; 0 Alternative
0 Magnet; 0 Charter; 4 Title I Eligible; 1 School-wide Title I
Students: 3,838 (51.7% male; 48.3% female)
Individual Education Program: 573 (14.9%);
English Language Learner: 648 (16.9%); Migrant: n/a
Eligible for Free Lunch Program: 775 (20.2%)
Eligible for Reduced-Price Lunch Program: 191 (5.0%)
Teachers: 245.0 (15.7 to 1)
Librarians/Media Specialists: 0.0 (0.0 to 1)
Guidance Counselors: 1.0 (3,838.0 to 1)
Current Spending: ($ per student per year):
Total: $7,268; Instruction: $4,791; Support Services: $2,306
Enrollment, Drop-out Rates and Diploma Recipients by Race/Ethnicity

Category	Total	White	Black	Asian	AIAN	Hisp.
Enrollment (%)	100.0	65.5	5.7	6.8	0.2	21.8
Drop-out Rate (%)	n/a	n/a	n/a	n/a	n/a	n/a
H.S. Diplomas (#)	n/a	n/a	n/a	n/a	n/a	n/a

West Chicago ESD 33
312 E Forest Ave • West Chicago, IL 60185-3599
(630) 293-6000 • http://www.wegoed33.k12.il.us/
Grade Span: PK-08; **Agency Type:** 1
Schools: 7
6 Primary; 1 Middle; 0 High; 0 Other Level
7 Regular; 0 Special Education; 0 Vocational; 0 Alternative

1 Magnet; 0 Charter; 4 Title I Eligible; 2 School-wide Title I
Students: 3,856 (51.6% male; 48.4% female)
Individual Education Program: 586 (15.2%);
English Language Learner: 1,585 (41.1%); Migrant: n/a
Eligible for Free Lunch Program: 1,140 (29.6%)
Eligible for Reduced-Price Lunch Program: 351 (9.1%)
Teachers: 250.0 (15.4 to 1)
Librarians/Media Specialists: 0.0 (0.0 to 1)
Guidance Counselors: 2.0 (1,928.0 to 1)
Current Spending: ($ per student per year):
Total: $7,227; Instruction: $4,742; Support Services: $2,315
Enrollment, Drop-out Rates and Diploma Recipients by Race/Ethnicity

Category	Total	White	Black	Asian	AIAN	Hisp.
Enrollment (%)	100.0	36.6	2.1	1.5	0.0	59.8
Drop-out Rate (%)	n/a	n/a	n/a	n/a	n/a	n/a
H.S. Diplomas (#)	n/a	n/a	n/a	n/a	n/a	n/a

Westmont CUSD 201
200 N Linden Ave • Westmont, IL 60559-1776
(630) 969-7741 • http://www.westmont.dupage.k12.il.us/
Grade Span: PK-12; **Agency Type:** 1
Schools: 5
3 Primary; 1 Middle; 1 High; 0 Other Level
5 Regular; 0 Special Education; 0 Vocational; 0 Alternative
0 Magnet; 0 Charter; 1 Title I Eligible; 0 School-wide Title I
Students: 1,712 (50.3% male; 49.7% female)
Individual Education Program: 243 (14.2%);
English Language Learner: 89 (5.2%); Migrant: n/a
Eligible for Free Lunch Program: 296 (17.3%)
Eligible for Reduced-Price Lunch Program: 62 (3.6%)
Teachers: 115.6 (14.8 to 1)
Librarians/Media Specialists: 2.0 (856.0 to 1)
Guidance Counselors: 1.0 (1,712.0 to 1)
Current Spending: ($ per student per year):
Total: $8,954; Instruction: $5,435; Support Services: $3,195
Enrollment, Drop-out Rates and Diploma Recipients by Race/Ethnicity

Category	Total	White	Black	Asian	AIAN	Hisp.
Enrollment (%)	100.0	76.5	8.6	6.0	0.0	8.9
Drop-out Rate (%)	0.7	0.8	0.0	0.0	n/a	0.0
H.S. Diplomas (#)	91	74	6	6	0	5

Woodridge SD 68
7925 Janes Ave • Woodridge, IL 60517-3821
(630) 985-7925 • http://wdgdst68.dupage.k12.il.us/
Grade Span: PK-08; **Agency Type:** 1
Schools: 7
6 Primary; 1 Middle; 0 High; 0 Other Level
7 Regular; 0 Special Education; 0 Vocational; 0 Alternative
0 Magnet; 0 Charter; 4 Title I Eligible; 0 School-wide Title I
Students: 3,198 (52.5% male; 47.5% female)
Individual Education Program: 459 (14.4%);
English Language Learner: 329 (10.3%); Migrant: n/a
Eligible for Free Lunch Program: 529 (16.5%)
Eligible for Reduced-Price Lunch Program: 154 (4.8%)
Teachers: 191.0 (16.7 to 1)
Librarians/Media Specialists: 5.0 (639.6 to 1)
Guidance Counselors: 2.0 (1,599.0 to 1)
Current Spending: ($ per student per year):
Total: $7,283; Instruction: $4,530; Support Services: $2,591
Enrollment, Drop-out Rates and Diploma Recipients by Race/Ethnicity

Category	Total	White	Black	Asian	AIAN	Hisp.
Enrollment (%)	100.0	60.2	15.1	10.7	0.0	14.1
Drop-out Rate (%)	n/a	n/a	n/a	n/a	n/a	n/a
H.S. Diplomas (#)	n/a	n/a	n/a	n/a	n/a	n/a

Edgar County

Paris-Union SD 95
414 S Main St • Paris, IL 61944-2399
(217) 465-8448 • http://www.paris95.k12.il.us/
Grade Span: PK-12; **Agency Type:** 1
Schools: 6
3 Primary; 2 Middle; 1 High; 0 Other Level
4 Regular; 2 Special Education; 0 Vocational; 0 Alternative
0 Magnet; 0 Charter; 3 Title I Eligible; 0 School-wide Title I
Students: 1,730 (50.1% male; 49.9% female)
Individual Education Program: 375 (21.7%);
English Language Learner: 2 (0.1%); Migrant: n/a
Eligible for Free Lunch Program: 520 (30.1%)
Eligible for Reduced-Price Lunch Program: 83 (4.8%)
Teachers: 115.5 (15.0 to 1)
Librarians/Media Specialists: 1.0 (1,730.0 to 1)
Guidance Counselors: 3.0 (576.7 to 1)
Current Spending: ($ per student per year):
Total: $6,855; Instruction: $4,368; Support Services: $2,235
Enrollment, Drop-out Rates and Diploma Recipients by Race/Ethnicity

Category	Total	White	Black	Asian	AIAN	Hisp.
Enrollment (%)	100.0	97.5	1.2	0.2	0.0	1.1
Drop-out Rate (%)	4.8	4.9	0.0	0.0	n/a	0.0
H.S. Diplomas (#)	99	98	0	0	0	1

Effingham County

Effingham Community Unit SD 40
PO Box 130 • Effingham, IL 62401-0130
(217) 540-1501 • http://www.effingham.k12.il.us/
Grade Span: PK-12; **Agency Type:** 1
Schools: 8
6 Primary; 1 Middle; 1 High; 0 Other Level
7 Regular; 1 Special Education; 0 Vocational; 0 Alternative
0 Magnet; 0 Charter; 5 Title I Eligible; 0 School-wide Title I
Students: 2,989 (52.5% male; 47.5% female)
Individual Education Program: 501 (16.8%);
English Language Learner: 17 (0.6%); Migrant: n/a
Eligible for Free Lunch Program: 557 (18.6%)
Eligible for Reduced-Price Lunch Program: 164 (5.5%)
Teachers: 177.9 (16.8 to 1)
Librarians/Media Specialists: 1.0 (2,989.0 to 1)
Guidance Counselors: 7.0 (427.0 to 1)
Current Spending: ($ per student per year):
Total: $5,819; Instruction: $3,383; Support Services: $2,091
Enrollment, Drop-out Rates and Diploma Recipients by Race/Ethnicity

Category	Total	White	Black	Asian	AIAN	Hisp.
Enrollment (%)	100.0	97.3	0.7	0.6	0.0	1.5
Drop-out Rate (%)	1.5	1.5	0.0	0.0	n/a	0.0
H.S. Diplomas (#)	189	187	0	1	0	1

Fayette County

Vandalia CUSD 203
1109 N 8th St • Vandalia, IL 62471-1240
(618) 283-4525 • http://www.fayette.k12.il.us/washington/district.htm
Grade Span: PK-12; **Agency Type:** 1
Schools: 4
2 Primary; 1 Middle; 1 High; 0 Other Level
4 Regular; 0 Special Education; 0 Vocational; 0 Alternative
0 Magnet; 0 Charter; 3 Title I Eligible; 0 School-wide Title I
Students: 1,753 (51.6% male; 48.4% female)
Individual Education Program: 265 (15.1%);
English Language Learner: 0 (0.0%); Migrant: n/a
Eligible for Free Lunch Program: 408 (23.3%)
Eligible for Reduced-Price Lunch Program: 125 (7.1%)
Teachers: 96.9 (18.1 to 1)
Librarians/Media Specialists: 2.0 (876.5 to 1)
Guidance Counselors: 4.5 (389.6 to 1)
Current Spending: ($ per student per year):
Total: $5,533; Instruction: $3,279; Support Services: $1,944
Enrollment, Drop-out Rates and Diploma Recipients by Race/Ethnicity

Category	Total	White	Black	Asian	AIAN	Hisp.
Enrollment (%)	100.0	97.9	1.4	0.3	0.1	0.3
Drop-out Rate (%)	3.8	3.8	0.0	n/a	n/a	n/a
H.S. Diplomas (#)	108	108	0	0	0	0

Franklin County

Frankfort Community Unit SD 168
PO Box 425 • West Frankfort, IL 62896-2326
(618) 937-2421 • http://www.wf168.frnkln.k12.il.us/Index.htm
Grade Span: PK-12; **Agency Type:** 1
Schools: 4
2 Primary; 1 Middle; 1 High; 0 Other Level
4 Regular; 0 Special Education; 0 Vocational; 0 Alternative
0 Magnet; 0 Charter; 2 Title I Eligible; 2 School-wide Title I
Students: 1,863 (50.6% male; 49.4% female)
Individual Education Program: 414 (22.2%);
English Language Learner: 0 (0.0%); Migrant: n/a
Eligible for Free Lunch Program: 636 (34.1%)
Eligible for Reduced-Price Lunch Program: 110 (5.9%)
Teachers: 111.1 (16.8 to 1)
Librarians/Media Specialists: 1.0 (1,863.0 to 1)
Guidance Counselors: 1.0 (1,863.0 to 1)
Current Spending: ($ per student per year):
Total: $6,814; Instruction: $4,811; Support Services: $1,750
Enrollment, Drop-out Rates and Diploma Recipients by Race/Ethnicity

Category	Total	White	Black	Asian	AIAN	Hisp.
Enrollment (%)	100.0	98.8	0.5	0.2	0.4	0.2
Drop-out Rate (%)	3.5	3.5	n/a	0.0	0.0	0.0
H.S. Diplomas (#)	120	120	0	0	0	0

Fulton County

Canton Union SD 66

20 W Walnut St • Canton, IL 61520-2591
(309) 647-9411 • http://www.cantonusd.org/
Grade Span: PK-12; **Agency Type:** 1
Schools: 5
3 Primary; 1 Middle; 1 High; 0 Other Level
5 Regular; 0 Special Education; 0 Vocational; 0 Alternative
0 Magnet; 0 Charter; 4 Title I Eligible; 2 School-wide Title I
Students: 2,745 (53.2% male; 46.8% female)
Individual Education Program: 419 (15.3%);
English Language Learner: 0 (0.0%); Migrant: n/a
Eligible for Free Lunch Program: 895 (32.6%)
Eligible for Reduced-Price Lunch Program: 196 (7.1%)
Teachers: 181.8 (15.1 to 1)
Librarians/Media Specialists: 1.0 (2,745.0 to 1)
Guidance Counselors: 4.0 (686.3 to 1)
Current Spending: ($ per student per year):
Total: $6,593; Instruction: $4,206; Support Services: $2,115
Enrollment, Drop-out Rates and Diploma Recipients by Race/Ethnicity

Category	Total	White	Black	Asian	AIAN	Hisp.
Enrollment (%)	100.0	97.2	1.2	0.8	0.1	0.8
Drop-out Rate (%)	7.3	7.2	16.7	0.0	20.0	25.0
H.S. Diplomas (#)	179	171	1	3	1	3

Grundy County

Coal City CUSD 1

100 S Baima St • Coal City, IL 60416-1663
(815) 634-2287 • http://www.coalcity.k12.il.us/
Grade Span: PK-12; **Agency Type:** 1
Schools: 4
2 Primary; 1 Middle; 1 High; 0 Other Level
4 Regular; 0 Special Education; 0 Vocational; 0 Alternative
0 Magnet; 0 Charter; 1 Title I Eligible; 0 School-wide Title I
Students: 1,910 (49.6% male; 50.4% female)
Individual Education Program: 250 (13.1%);
English Language Learner: 2 (0.1%); Migrant: n/a
Eligible for Free Lunch Program: 188 (9.8%)
Eligible for Reduced-Price Lunch Program: 58 (3.0%)
Teachers: 114.0 (16.8 to 1)
Librarians/Media Specialists: 1.0 (1,910.0 to 1)
Guidance Counselors: 3.0 (636.7 to 1)
Current Spending: ($ per student per year):
Total: $7,013; Instruction: $4,027; Support Services: $2,689
Enrollment, Drop-out Rates and Diploma Recipients by Race/Ethnicity

Category	Total	White	Black	Asian	AIAN	Hisp.
Enrollment (%)	100.0	94.7	0.7	0.3	0.3	4.0
Drop-out Rate (%)	1.7	1.7	n/a	n/a	n/a	0.0
H.S. Diplomas (#)	120	115	0	0	0	5

Minooka Community CSD 201

400 Coady Dr • Minooka, IL 60447-9118
(815) 467-6121
Grade Span: PK-08; **Agency Type:** 1
Schools: 3
2 Primary; 1 Middle; 0 High; 0 Other Level
3 Regular; 0 Special Education; 0 Vocational; 0 Alternative
0 Magnet; 0 Charter; 2 Title I Eligible; 0 School-wide Title I
Students: 1,536 (52.6% male; 47.4% female)
Individual Education Program: 214 (13.9%);
English Language Learner: 0 (0.0%); Migrant: n/a
Eligible for Free Lunch Program: 93 (6.1%)
Eligible for Reduced-Price Lunch Program: 29 (1.9%)
Teachers: 81.0 (19.0 to 1)
Librarians/Media Specialists: 2.0 (768.0 to 1)
Guidance Counselors: 1.0 (1,536.0 to 1)
Current Spending: ($ per student per year):
Total: $6,938; Instruction: $4,427; Support Services: $2,333
Enrollment, Drop-out Rates and Diploma Recipients by Race/Ethnicity

Category	Total	White	Black	Asian	AIAN	Hisp.
Enrollment (%)	100.0	94.6	1.0	0.7	0.1	3.6
Drop-out Rate (%)	n/a	n/a	n/a	n/a	n/a	n/a
H.S. Diplomas (#)	n/a	n/a	n/a	n/a	n/a	n/a

Henry County

Geneseo Community Unit SD 228

209 S College Ave • Geneseo, IL 61254-1405
(309) 945-0450
Grade Span: PK-12; **Agency Type:** 1
Schools: 7
4 Primary; 1 Middle; 2 High; 0 Other Level
6 Regular; 1 Special Education; 0 Vocational; 0 Alternative
0 Magnet; 0 Charter; 4 Title I Eligible; 0 School-wide Title I
Students: 2,921 (53.1% male; 46.9% female)
Individual Education Program: 393 (13.5%);
English Language Learner: 0 (0.0%); Migrant: n/a
Eligible for Free Lunch Program: 273 (9.3%)
Eligible for Reduced-Price Lunch Program: 109 (3.7%)
Teachers: 176.3 (16.6 to 1)
Librarians/Media Specialists: 3.0 (973.7 to 1)
Guidance Counselors: 4.0 (730.3 to 1)
Current Spending: ($ per student per year):
Total: $5,945; Instruction: $3,607; Support Services: $2,059
Enrollment, Drop-out Rates and Diploma Recipients by Race/Ethnicity

Category	Total	White	Black	Asian	AIAN	Hisp.
Enrollment (%)	100.0	96.7	0.8	0.5	0.0	1.9
Drop-out Rate (%)	2.8	2.8	0.0	0.0	100.0	0.0
H.S. Diplomas (#)	213	210	0	1	0	2

Kewanee Community Unit SD 229

210 Lyle St • Kewanee, IL 61443-2999
(309) 853-3341 • http://www.kewaneecommunityschools.org/
Grade Span: PK-12; **Agency Type:** 1
Schools: 6
5 Primary; 0 Middle; 1 High; 0 Other Level
5 Regular; 1 Special Education; 0 Vocational; 0 Alternative
0 Magnet; 0 Charter; 4 Title I Eligible; 4 School-wide Title I
Students: 1,877 (52.6% male; 47.4% female)
Individual Education Program: 370 (19.7%);
English Language Learner: 130 (6.9%); Migrant: n/a
Eligible for Free Lunch Program: 845 (45.0%)
Eligible for Reduced-Price Lunch Program: 128 (6.8%)
Teachers: 97.4 (19.3 to 1)
Librarians/Media Specialists: 1.0 (1,877.0 to 1)
Guidance Counselors: 1.0 (1,877.0 to 1)
Current Spending: ($ per student per year):
Total: $5,823; Instruction: $3,564; Support Services: $1,914
Enrollment, Drop-out Rates and Diploma Recipients by Race/Ethnicity

Category	Total	White	Black	Asian	AIAN	Hisp.
Enrollment (%)	100.0	77.7	8.3	0.1	0.0	14.0
Drop-out Rate (%)	6.8	6.2	21.9	0.0	n/a	2.1
H.S. Diplomas (#)	100	87	5	0	0	8

Jackson County

Murphysboro CUSD 186

819 Walnut St • Murphysboro, IL 62966-2196
(618) 684-3781 • http://www.mboro.jacksn.k12.il.us/
Grade Span: PK-12; **Agency Type:** 1
Schools: 5
3 Primary; 1 Middle; 1 High; 0 Other Level
5 Regular; 0 Special Education; 0 Vocational; 0 Alternative
0 Magnet; 0 Charter; 5 Title I Eligible; 4 School-wide Title I
Students: 2,282 (50.9% male; 49.1% female)
Individual Education Program: 478 (20.9%);
English Language Learner: 22 (1.0%); Migrant: n/a
Eligible for Free Lunch Program: 964 (42.2%)
Eligible for Reduced-Price Lunch Program: 166 (7.3%)
Teachers: 141.0 (16.2 to 1)
Librarians/Media Specialists: 2.0 (1,141.0 to 1)
Guidance Counselors: 3.0 (760.7 to 1)
Current Spending: ($ per student per year):
Total: $6,768; Instruction: $4,083; Support Services: $2,343
Enrollment, Drop-out Rates and Diploma Recipients by Race/Ethnicity

Category	Total	White	Black	Asian	AIAN	Hisp.
Enrollment (%)	100.0	81.8	15.5	0.4	0.0	2.3
Drop-out Rate (%)	3.2	2.3	8.6	0.0	0.0	10.0
H.S. Diplomas (#)	172	156	15	0	0	1

Jasper County

Jasper County Community Unit Dist 1

609 S Lafayette • Newton, IL 62448-1317
(618) 783-8459 • http://www.cusd1.jasper.k12.il.us/
Grade Span: PK-12; **Agency Type:** 1
Schools: 9
5 Primary; 3 Middle; 0 High; 1 Other Level
9 Regular; 0 Special Education; 0 Vocational; 0 Alternative
0 Magnet; 0 Charter; 5 Title I Eligible; 3 School-wide Title I
Students: 1,671 (50.9% male; 49.1% female)
Individual Education Program: 283 (16.9%);
English Language Learner: 0 (0.0%); Migrant: n/a
Eligible for Free Lunch Program: 445 (26.6%)
Eligible for Reduced-Price Lunch Program: 126 (7.5%)
Teachers: 119.0 (14.0 to 1)
Librarians/Media Specialists: 1.0 (1,671.0 to 1)
Guidance Counselors: 5.0 (334.2 to 1)

Current Spending: ($ per student per year):
Total: $7,498; Instruction: $4,430; Support Services: $2,812

Enrollment, Drop-out Rates and Diploma Recipients by Race/Ethnicity

Category	Total	White	Black	Asian	AIAN	Hisp.
Enrollment (%)	100.0	98.1	1.0	0.3	0.1	0.5
Drop-out Rate (%)	3.1	3.1	n/a	n/a	n/a	n/a
H.S. Diplomas (#)	124	124	0	0	0	0

Jefferson County

Mount Vernon SD 80

1722 Oakland • Mount Vernon, IL 62864-6304
(618) 244-8080 • http://www.district.mtv80.org/education/district/
Grade Span: PK-08; **Agency Type:** 1
Schools: 4
2 Primary; 2 Middle; 0 High; 0 Other Level
3 Regular; 1 Special Education; 0 Vocational; 0 Alternative
0 Magnet; 0 Charter; 3 Title I Eligible; 3 School-wide Title I
Students: 1,934 (49.3% male; 50.7% female)
Individual Education Program: 486 (25.1%);
English Language Learner: 6 (0.3%); Migrant: n/a
Eligible for Free Lunch Program: 1,058 (54.7%)
Eligible for Reduced-Price Lunch Program: 109 (5.6%)
Teachers: 122.0 (15.9 to 1)
Librarians/Media Specialists: 2.0 (967.0 to 1)
Guidance Counselors: 2.0 (967.0 to 1)
Current Spending: ($ per student per year):
Total: $6,956; Instruction: $4,240; Support Services: $2,278

Enrollment, Drop-out Rates and Diploma Recipients by Race/Ethnicity

Category	Total	White	Black	Asian	AIAN	Hisp.
Enrollment (%)	100.0	64.5	32.0	1.1	0.0	2.3
Drop-out Rate (%)	n/a	n/a	n/a	n/a	n/a	n/a
H.S. Diplomas (#)	n/a	n/a	n/a	n/a	n/a	n/a

Jersey County

Jersey CUSD 100

100 Lincoln St • Jerseyville, IL 62052-1425
(618) 498-5561 • http://www.jersey100.k12.il.us/
Grade Span: PK-12; **Agency Type:** 1
Schools: 8
6 Primary; 1 Middle; 1 High; 0 Other Level
8 Regular; 0 Special Education; 0 Vocational; 0 Alternative
0 Magnet; 0 Charter; 5 Title I Eligible; 0 School-wide Title I
Students: 3,117 (51.0% male; 49.0% female)
Individual Education Program: 434 (13.9%);
English Language Learner: 6 (0.2%); Migrant: n/a
Eligible for Free Lunch Program: 741 (23.8%)
Eligible for Reduced-Price Lunch Program: 181 (5.8%)
Teachers: 187.0 (16.7 to 1)
Librarians/Media Specialists: 3.0 (1,039.0 to 1)
Guidance Counselors: 3.0 (1,039.0 to 1)
Current Spending: ($ per student per year):
Total: $6,431; Instruction: $3,903; Support Services: $2,268

Enrollment, Drop-out Rates and Diploma Recipients by Race/Ethnicity

Category	Total	White	Black	Asian	AIAN	Hisp.
Enrollment (%)	100.0	98.7	0.8	0.2	0.0	0.4
Drop-out Rate (%)	3.3	3.3	0.0	0.0	n/a	0.0
H.S. Diplomas (#)	238	237	0	1	0	0

Kane County

Aurora East Unit SD 131

417 Fifth St • Aurora, IL 60505-4744
(630) 299-5554 • http://www.d131.kane.k12.il.us/home.htm
Grade Span: KG-12; **Agency Type:** 1
Schools: 16
12 Primary; 3 Middle; 1 High; 0 Other Level
16 Regular; 0 Special Education; 0 Vocational; 0 Alternative
0 Magnet; 0 Charter; 16 Title I Eligible; 13 School-wide Title I
Students: 11,213 (50.5% male; 49.5% female)
Individual Education Program: 1,456 (13.0%);
English Language Learner: 6,856 (61.1%); Migrant: n/a
Eligible for Free Lunch Program: 5,829 (52.0%)
Eligible for Reduced-Price Lunch Program: 1,206 (10.8%)
Teachers: 567.6 (19.8 to 1)
Librarians/Media Specialists: 3.0 (3,737.7 to 1)
Guidance Counselors: 11.0 (1,019.4 to 1)
Current Spending: ($ per student per year):
Total: $6,290; Instruction: $3,452; Support Services: $2,611

Enrollment, Drop-out Rates and Diploma Recipients by Race/Ethnicity

Category	Total	White	Black	Asian	AIAN	Hisp.
Enrollment (%)	100.0	10.1	12.2	0.6	0.2	76.8
Drop-out Rate (%)	7.4	4.8	7.7	5.9	0.0	8.0
H.S. Diplomas (#)	424	95	64	3	0	262

Aurora West Unit SD 129

80 So River St • Aurora, IL 60506-4108
(630) 844-4400 • http://www.sd129.org/
Grade Span: PK-12; **Agency Type:** 1
Schools: 17
12 Primary; 3 Middle; 1 High; 1 Other Level
16 Regular; 1 Special Education; 0 Vocational; 0 Alternative
0 Magnet; 0 Charter; 8 Title I Eligible; 6 School-wide Title I
Students: 11,469 (51.6% male; 48.4% female)
Individual Education Program: 1,591 (13.9%);
English Language Learner: 877 (7.6%); Migrant: n/a
Eligible for Free Lunch Program: 2,932 (25.6%)
Eligible for Reduced-Price Lunch Program: 572 (5.0%)
Teachers: 651.3 (17.6 to 1)
Librarians/Media Specialists: 8.0 (1,433.6 to 1)
Guidance Counselors: 7.0 (1,638.4 to 1)
Current Spending: ($ per student per year):
Total: $6,180; Instruction: $3,646; Support Services: $2,336

Enrollment, Drop-out Rates and Diploma Recipients by Race/Ethnicity

Category	Total	White	Black	Asian	AIAN	Hisp.
Enrollment (%)	100.0	44.1	18.8	2.0	0.1	35.0
Drop-out Rate (%)	6.3	5.4	8.6	4.0	n/a	6.7
H.S. Diplomas (#)	573	338	83	9	0	143

Batavia Unit SD 101

335 W Wilson • Batavia, IL 60510-1998
(630) 879-4600 • http://dist.bps101.net/
Grade Span: PK-12; **Agency Type:** 1
Schools: 8
6 Primary; 1 Middle; 1 High; 0 Other Level
8 Regular; 0 Special Education; 0 Vocational; 0 Alternative
1 Magnet; 0 Charter; 5 Title I Eligible; 0 School-wide Title I
Students: 5,858 (51.4% male; 48.6% female)
Individual Education Program: 657 (11.2%);
English Language Learner: 113 (1.9%); Migrant: n/a
Eligible for Free Lunch Program: 92 (1.6%)
Eligible for Reduced-Price Lunch Program: 44 (0.8%)
Teachers: 345.5 (17.0 to 1)
Librarians/Media Specialists: 8.0 (732.3 to 1)
Guidance Counselors: 7.0 (836.9 to 1)
Current Spending: ($ per student per year):
Total: $6,035; Instruction: $4,213; Support Services: $1,669

Enrollment, Drop-out Rates and Diploma Recipients by Race/Ethnicity

Category	Total	White	Black	Asian	AIAN	Hisp.
Enrollment (%)	100.0	88.8	2.8	2.2	0.1	6.1
Drop-out Rate (%)	1.5	1.2	10.5	0.0	n/a	3.0
H.S. Diplomas (#)	370	342	9	4	0	15

Central Community Unit SD 301

PO Box 396 • Burlington, IL 60109-0396
(847) 464-6005 • http://www.burlington.k12.il.us/
Grade Span: PK-12; **Agency Type:** 1
Schools: 5
3 Primary; 1 Middle; 1 High; 0 Other Level
5 Regular; 0 Special Education; 0 Vocational; 0 Alternative
0 Magnet; 0 Charter; 0 Title I Eligible; 0 School-wide Title I
Students: 2,333 (49.3% male; 50.7% female)
Individual Education Program: 317 (13.6%);
English Language Learner: 1 (<0.1%); Migrant: n/a
Eligible for Free Lunch Program: 16 (0.7%)
Eligible for Reduced-Price Lunch Program: 7 (0.3%)
Teachers: 147.4 (15.8 to 1)
Librarians/Media Specialists: 2.0 (1,166.5 to 1)
Guidance Counselors: 3.0 (777.7 to 1)
Current Spending: ($ per student per year):
Total: $7,614; Instruction: $4,211; Support Services: $3,187

Enrollment, Drop-out Rates and Diploma Recipients by Race/Ethnicity

Category	Total	White	Black	Asian	AIAN	Hisp.
Enrollment (%)	100.0	93.2	1.5	1.9	0.3	3.1
Drop-out Rate (%)	1.2	1.3	0.0	0.0	0.0	0.0
H.S. Diplomas (#)	153	145	2	3	0	3

Community Unit SD 300

300 Cleveland Ave • Carpentersville, IL 60110-1943
(847) 426-1300 • http://www.d300.kane.k12.il.us/
Grade Span: PK-12; **Agency Type:** 1
Schools: 24
15 Primary; 5 Middle; 3 High; 1 Other Level
22 Regular; 2 Special Education; 0 Vocational; 0 Alternative

1 Magnet; 0 Charter; 7 Title I Eligible; 5 School-wide Title I
Students: 18,040 (51.1% male; 48.9% female)
Individual Education Program: 2,705 (15.0%);
English Language Learner: 2,455 (13.6%); Migrant: n/a
Eligible for Free Lunch Program: 3,293 (18.3%)
Eligible for Reduced-Price Lunch Program: 818 (4.5%)
Teachers: 982.8 (18.4 to 1)
Librarians/Media Specialists: 7.0 (2,577.1 to 1)
Guidance Counselors: 19.5 (925.1 to 1)
Current Spending: ($ per student per year):
Total: $6,627; Instruction: $4,113; Support Services: $2,300
Enrollment, Drop-out Rates and Diploma Recipients by Race/Ethnicity

Category	Total	White	Black	Asian	AIAN	Hisp.
Enrollment (%)	100.0	68.5	4.1	3.0	0.4	24.0
Drop-out Rate (%)	3.5	2.7	12.9	2.5	4.3	6.5
H.S. Diplomas (#)	1,037	844	23	21	4	145

Geneva Community Unit SD 304
227 N Fourth St • Geneva, IL 60134-1307
(630) 463-3000
Grade Span: PK-12; **Agency Type:** 1
Schools: 8
6 Primary; 1 Middle; 1 High; 0 Other Level
7 Regular; 1 Special Education; 0 Vocational; 0 Alternative
0 Magnet; 0 Charter; 0 Title I Eligible; 0 School-wide Title I
Students: 5,391 (51.6% male; 48.4% female)
Individual Education Program: 614 (11.4%);
English Language Learner: 72 (1.3%); Migrant: n/a
Eligible for Free Lunch Program: 0 (0.0%)
Eligible for Reduced-Price Lunch Program: 0 (0.0%)
Teachers: 309.8 (17.4 to 1)
Librarians/Media Specialists: 6.2 (869.5 to 1)
Guidance Counselors: 8.0 (673.9 to 1)
Current Spending: ($ per student per year):
Total: $7,170; Instruction: $4,425; Support Services: $2,558
Enrollment, Drop-out Rates and Diploma Recipients by Race/Ethnicity

Category	Total	White	Black	Asian	AIAN	Hisp.
Enrollment (%)	100.0	94.4	0.7	2.2	0.2	2.6
Drop-out Rate (%)	1.6	1.6	0.0	0.0	n/a	6.3
H.S. Diplomas (#)	321	311	0	8	0	2

Kaneland CUSD 302
47w326 Keslinger Rd • Maple Park, IL 60151-9720
(630) 365-5100 • http://www.kaneland.org/
Grade Span: PK-12; **Agency Type:** 1
Schools: 4
2 Primary; 1 Middle; 1 High; 0 Other Level
4 Regular; 0 Special Education; 0 Vocational; 0 Alternative
0 Magnet; 0 Charter; 1 Title I Eligible; 0 School-wide Title I
Students: 3,049 (50.9% male; 49.1% female)
Individual Education Program: 394 (12.9%);
English Language Learner: 61 (2.0%); Migrant: n/a
Eligible for Free Lunch Program: 47 (1.5%)
Eligible for Reduced-Price Lunch Program: 16 (0.5%)
Teachers: 189.3 (16.1 to 1)
Librarians/Media Specialists: 4.0 (762.3 to 1)
Guidance Counselors: 4.0 (762.3 to 1)
Current Spending: ($ per student per year):
Total: $6,988; Instruction: $4,185; Support Services: $2,636
Enrollment, Drop-out Rates and Diploma Recipients by Race/Ethnicity

Category	Total	White	Black	Asian	AIAN	Hisp.
Enrollment (%)	100.0	94.4	0.9	1.2	0.1	3.3
Drop-out Rate (%)	1.0	1.1	0.0	0.0	0.0	0.0
H.S. Diplomas (#)	190	180	2	1	1	6

SD 46
355 E Chicago St • Elgin, IL 60120-6543
(847) 888-5000 • http://www.u46.k12.il.us/
Grade Span: PK-12; **Agency Type:** 1
Schools: 54
41 Primary; 7 Middle; 6 High; 0 Other Level
51 Regular; 3 Special Education; 0 Vocational; 0 Alternative
0 Magnet; 0 Charter; 15 Title I Eligible; 2 School-wide Title I
Students: 39,153 (50.9% male; 49.1% female)
Individual Education Program: 4,083 (10.4%);
English Language Learner: 6,179 (15.8%); Migrant: n/a
Eligible for Free Lunch Program: 9,954 (25.4%)
Eligible for Reduced-Price Lunch Program: 2,912 (7.4%)
Teachers: 2,318.4 (16.9 to 1)
Librarians/Media Specialists: 14.9 (2,627.7 to 1)
Guidance Counselors: 28.6 (1,369.0 to 1)
Current Spending: ($ per student per year):
Total: $7,544; Instruction: $4,829; Support Services: $2,512

Enrollment, Drop-out Rates and Diploma Recipients by Race/Ethnicity

Category	Total	White	Black	Asian	AIAN	Hisp.
Enrollment (%)	100.0	50.7	7.7	6.8	0.2	34.6
Drop-out Rate (%)	3.7	2.8	7.6	3.0	0.0	5.0
H.S. Diplomas (#)	1,914	1,178	113	166	1	456

Saint Charles CUSD 303
201 S 7th St • Saint Charles, IL 60174-1489
(630) 513-3030 • http://www.st-charles.k12.il.us/
Grade Span: PK-12; **Agency Type:** 1
Schools: 15
10 Primary; 3 Middle; 2 High; 0 Other Level
15 Regular; 0 Special Education; 0 Vocational; 0 Alternative
0 Magnet; 0 Charter; 9 Title I Eligible; 0 School-wide Title I
Students: 12,300 (51.2% male; 48.8% female)
Individual Education Program: 1,189 (9.7%);
English Language Learner: 190 (1.5%); Migrant: n/a
Eligible for Free Lunch Program: 280 (2.3%)
Eligible for Reduced-Price Lunch Program: 83 (0.7%)
Teachers: 671.9 (18.3 to 1)
Librarians/Media Specialists: 15.0 (820.0 to 1)
Guidance Counselors: 18.0 (683.3 to 1)
Current Spending: ($ per student per year):
Total: $6,835; Instruction: $3,987; Support Services: $2,655
Enrollment, Drop-out Rates and Diploma Recipients by Race/Ethnicity

Category	Total	White	Black	Asian	AIAN	Hisp.
Enrollment (%)	100.0	89.7	1.2	3.7	0.1	5.2
Drop-out Rate (%)	1.4	1.2	4.3	0.0	4.3	5.5
H.S. Diplomas (#)	763	697	5	17	3	41

Kankakee County

Bourbonnais SD 53
281 W John Casey Rd • Bourbonnais, IL 60914-1368
(815) 939-2574 • http://www.besd53.k12.il.us/
Grade Span: PK-08; **Agency Type:** 1
Schools: 5
3 Primary; 2 Middle; 0 High; 0 Other Level
5 Regular; 0 Special Education; 0 Vocational; 0 Alternative
0 Magnet; 0 Charter; 3 Title I Eligible; 0 School-wide Title I
Students: 2,444 (52.4% male; 47.6% female)
Individual Education Program: 359 (14.7%);
English Language Learner: 7 (0.3%); Migrant: n/a
Eligible for Free Lunch Program: 318 (13.0%)
Eligible for Reduced-Price Lunch Program: 76 (3.1%)
Teachers: 133.8 (18.3 to 1)
Librarians/Media Specialists: 1.0 (2,444.0 to 1)
Guidance Counselors: 0.0 (0.0 to 1)
Current Spending: ($ per student per year):
Total: $5,636; Instruction: $3,540; Support Services: $1,893
Enrollment, Drop-out Rates and Diploma Recipients by Race/Ethnicity

Category	Total	White	Black	Asian	AIAN	Hisp.
Enrollment (%)	100.0	84.7	7.7	2.3	0.4	5.0
Drop-out Rate (%)	n/a	n/a	n/a	n/a	n/a	n/a
H.S. Diplomas (#)	n/a	n/a	n/a	n/a	n/a	n/a

Bradley Bourbonnais CHSD 307
700 W N St • Bradley, IL 60915-1099
(815) 937-3707 • http://www.bbchs.k12.il.us/
Grade Span: 09-12; **Agency Type:** 1
Schools: 1
0 Primary; 0 Middle; 1 High; 0 Other Level
1 Regular; 0 Special Education; 0 Vocational; 0 Alternative
0 Magnet; 0 Charter; 1 Title I Eligible; 0 School-wide Title I
Students: 1,734 (52.5% male; 47.5% female)
Individual Education Program: 273 (15.7%);
English Language Learner: 0 (0.0%); Migrant: n/a
Eligible for Free Lunch Program: 104 (6.0%)
Eligible for Reduced-Price Lunch Program: 43 (2.5%)
Teachers: 86.7 (20.0 to 1)
Librarians/Media Specialists: 1.0 (1,734.0 to 1)
Guidance Counselors: 5.7 (304.2 to 1)
Current Spending: ($ per student per year):
Total: $7,174; Instruction: $4,323; Support Services: $2,639
Enrollment, Drop-out Rates and Diploma Recipients by Race/Ethnicity

Category	Total	White	Black	Asian	AIAN	Hisp.
Enrollment (%)	100.0	89.0	4.0	2.5	0.3	4.1
Drop-out Rate (%)	2.4	2.5	0.0	0.0	0.0	2.4
H.S. Diplomas (#)	376	349	12	5	2	8

Bradley SD 61
200 W State St • Bradley, IL 60915-2064
(815) 933-3371
Grade Span: PK-08; **Agency Type:** 1
Schools: 3

2 Primary; 1 Middle; 0 High; 0 Other Level
3 Regular; 0 Special Education; 0 Vocational; 0 Alternative
0 Magnet; 0 Charter; 2 Title I Eligible; 0 School-wide Title I
Students: 1,532 (50.4% male; 49.6% female)
Individual Education Program: 356 (23.2%);
English Language Learner: 11 (0.7%); Migrant: n/a
Eligible for Free Lunch Program: 265 (17.3%)
Eligible for Reduced-Price Lunch Program: 122 (8.0%)
Teachers: 86.8 (17.6 to 1)
Librarians/Media Specialists: 1.0 (1,532.0 to 1)
Guidance Counselors: 0.0 (0.0 to 1)
Current Spending: ($ per student per year):
Total: $6,178; Instruction: $4,019; Support Services: $1,956
Enrollment, Drop-out Rates and Diploma Recipients by Race/Ethnicity

Category	Total	White	Black	Asian	AIAN	Hisp.
Enrollment (%)	100.0	89.9	3.5	0.5	0.0	6.1
Drop-out Rate (%)	n/a	n/a	n/a	n/a	n/a	n/a
H.S. Diplomas (#)	n/a	n/a	n/a	n/a	n/a	n/a

Herscher Community Unit SD 2
PO Box 504 • Herscher, IL 60941-0504
(815) 426-2162 • http://www.hsd2.k12.il.us/
Grade Span: PK-12; **Agency Type:** 1
Schools: 5
4 Primary; 0 Middle; 1 High; 0 Other Level
5 Regular; 0 Special Education; 0 Vocational; 0 Alternative
0 Magnet; 0 Charter; 3 Title I Eligible; 0 School-wide Title I
Students: 2,225 (52.4% male; 47.6% female)
Individual Education Program: 319 (14.3%);
English Language Learner: 0 (0.0%); Migrant: n/a
Eligible for Free Lunch Program: 267 (12.0%)
Eligible for Reduced-Price Lunch Program: 79 (3.6%)
Teachers: 146.5 (15.2 to 1)
Librarians/Media Specialists: 3.0 (741.7 to 1)
Guidance Counselors: 3.0 (741.7 to 1)
Current Spending: ($ per student per year):
Total: $6,532; Instruction: $4,109; Support Services: $2,178
Enrollment, Drop-out Rates and Diploma Recipients by Race/Ethnicity

Category	Total	White	Black	Asian	AIAN	Hisp.
Enrollment (%)	100.0	97.8	1.0	0.2	0.1	0.9
Drop-out Rate (%)	3.2	3.3	0.0	0.0	0.0	0.0
H.S. Diplomas (#)	150	147	0	1	1	1

Kankakee SD 111
240 Warren Ave • Kankakee, IL 60901-4319
(815) 933-0700 • http://www.k111.k12.il.us/
Grade Span: PK-12; **Agency Type:** 1
Schools: 14
9 Primary; 2 Middle; 1 High; 2 Other Level
11 Regular; 3 Special Education; 0 Vocational; 0 Alternative
6 Magnet; 0 Charter; 10 Title I Eligible; 10 School-wide Title I
Students: 5,864 (51.3% male; 48.7% female)
Individual Education Program: 1,229 (21.0%);
English Language Learner: 163 (2.8%); Migrant: n/a
Eligible for Free Lunch Program: 3,799 (64.8%)
Eligible for Reduced-Price Lunch Program: 388 (6.6%)
Teachers: 342.1 (17.1 to 1)
Librarians/Media Specialists: 2.0 (2,932.0 to 1)
Guidance Counselors: 5.7 (1,028.8 to 1)
Current Spending: ($ per student per year):
Total: $7,544; Instruction: $4,103; Support Services: $3,090
Enrollment, Drop-out Rates and Diploma Recipients by Race/Ethnicity

Category	Total	White	Black	Asian	AIAN	Hisp.
Enrollment (%)	100.0	23.7	63.4	0.2	0.0	12.7
Drop-out Rate (%)	4.8	2.2	5.5	0.0	n/a	8.9
H.S. Diplomas (#)	246	88	137	1	0	20

Manteno Community Unit SD 5
250 N Poplar St • Manteno, IL 60950-1098
(815) 928-7000 • http://www.manteno.k12.il.us/
Grade Span: KG-12; **Agency Type:** 1
Schools: 5
2 Primary; 1 Middle; 2 High; 0 Other Level
4 Regular; 1 Special Education; 0 Vocational; 0 Alternative
0 Magnet; 0 Charter; 4 Title I Eligible; 0 School-wide Title I
Students: 1,790 (51.4% male; 48.6% female)
Individual Education Program: 236 (13.2%);
English Language Learner: 7 (0.4%); Migrant: n/a
Eligible for Free Lunch Program: 96 (5.4%)
Eligible for Reduced-Price Lunch Program: 28 (1.6%)
Teachers: 122.4 (14.6 to 1)
Librarians/Media Specialists: 1.0 (1,790.0 to 1)
Guidance Counselors: 1.5 (1,193.3 to 1)
Current Spending: ($ per student per year):
Total: $6,047; Instruction: $3,851; Support Services: $2,044
Enrollment, Drop-out Rates and Diploma Recipients by Race/Ethnicity

Category	Total	White	Black	Asian	AIAN	Hisp.
Enrollment (%)	100.0	92.7	4.1	0.4	0.2	2.6
Drop-out Rate (%)	1.1	1.2	0.0	0.0	n/a	0.0
H.S. Diplomas (#)	117	109	4	0	0	4

Kendall County

Oswego Community Unit SD 308
4175 Rte 71 • Oswego, IL 60543-9781
(630) 554-3447 •
http://www.oswego.kendall.k12.il.us/oswego308/default.htm
Grade Span: PK-12; **Agency Type:** 1
Schools: 11
7 Primary; 3 Middle; 1 High; 0 Other Level
11 Regular; 0 Special Education; 0 Vocational; 0 Alternative
0 Magnet; 0 Charter; 9 Title I Eligible; 0 School-wide Title I
Students: 8,679 (52.2% male; 47.8% female)
Individual Education Program: 1,029 (11.9%);
English Language Learner: 177 (2.0%); Migrant: n/a
Eligible for Free Lunch Program: 380 (4.4%)
Eligible for Reduced-Price Lunch Program: 249 (2.9%)
Teachers: 465.5 (18.6 to 1)
Librarians/Media Specialists: 8.0 (1,084.9 to 1)
Guidance Counselors: 11.0 (789.0 to 1)
Current Spending: ($ per student per year):
Total: $5,585; Instruction: $3,434; Support Services: $1,959
Enrollment, Drop-out Rates and Diploma Recipients by Race/Ethnicity

Category	Total	White	Black	Asian	AIAN	Hisp.
Enrollment (%)	100.0	77.8	5.7	3.4	0.5	12.6
Drop-out Rate (%)	3.0	2.4	7.3	0.0	0.0	8.4
H.S. Diplomas (#)	421	361	10	14	3	33

Yorkville Community Unit SD 115
PO Box 579 • Yorkville, IL 60560-0579
(630) 553-4382 • http://www.yorkville.k12.il.us/
Grade Span: PK-12; **Agency Type:** 1
Schools: 5
3 Primary; 1 Middle; 1 High; 0 Other Level
5 Regular; 0 Special Education; 0 Vocational; 0 Alternative
0 Magnet; 0 Charter; 3 Title I Eligible; 0 School-wide Title I
Students: 2,598 (51.5% male; 48.5% female)
Individual Education Program: 298 (11.5%);
English Language Learner: 9 (0.3%); Migrant: n/a
Eligible for Free Lunch Program: 0 (0.0%)
Eligible for Reduced-Price Lunch Program: 0 (0.0%)
Teachers: 135.6 (19.2 to 1)
Librarians/Media Specialists: 2.0 (1,299.0 to 1)
Guidance Counselors: 3.0 (866.0 to 1)
Current Spending: ($ per student per year):
Total: $6,900; Instruction: $3,782; Support Services: $3,088
Enrollment, Drop-out Rates and Diploma Recipients by Race/Ethnicity

Category	Total	White	Black	Asian	AIAN	Hisp.
Enrollment (%)	100.0	94.6	0.9	0.5	0.1	4.0
Drop-out Rate (%)	1.5	1.6	0.0	0.0	0.0	0.0
H.S. Diplomas (#)	175	169	0	1	1	4

Knox County

Galesburg CUSD 205
PO Box 1206 • Galesburg, IL 61402-1206
(309) 343-1151 • http://www.galesburg205.org/
Grade Span: PK-12; **Agency Type:** 1
Schools: 12
9 Primary; 2 Middle; 1 High; 0 Other Level
10 Regular; 2 Special Education; 0 Vocational; 0 Alternative
1 Magnet; 0 Charter; 5 Title I Eligible; 5 School-wide Title I
Students: 5,072 (52.9% male; 47.1% female)
Individual Education Program: 731 (14.4%);
English Language Learner: 20 (0.4%); Migrant: n/a
Eligible for Free Lunch Program: 1,919 (37.8%)
Eligible for Reduced-Price Lunch Program: 381 (7.5%)
Teachers: 315.6 (16.1 to 1)
Librarians/Media Specialists: 1.0 (5,072.0 to 1)
Guidance Counselors: 4.0 (1,268.0 to 1)
Current Spending: ($ per student per year):
Total: $6,000; Instruction: $3,691; Support Services: $2,038
Enrollment, Drop-out Rates and Diploma Recipients by Race/Ethnicity

Category	Total	White	Black	Asian	AIAN	Hisp.
Enrollment (%)	100.0	76.0	17.1	0.8	0.2	5.9
Drop-out Rate (%)	8.3	8.1	9.9	0.0	0.0	10.5
H.S. Diplomas (#)	275	229	32	5	0	9

La Salle County

Ottawa Elem SD 141
320 W Main • Ottawa, IL 61350-2848
(815) 433-1133 • http://www.ottawaelem.lasall.k12.il.us/
Grade Span: PK-08; **Agency Type:** 1
Schools: 5
4 Primary; 1 Middle; 0 High; 0 Other Level
5 Regular; 0 Special Education; 0 Vocational; 0 Alternative
0 Magnet; 0 Charter; 3 Title I Eligible; 0 School-wide Title I
Students: 2,111 (50.9% male; 49.1% female)
Individual Education Program: 425 (20.1%);
English Language Learner: 22 (1.0%); Migrant: n/a
Eligible for Free Lunch Program: 516 (24.4%)
Eligible for Reduced-Price Lunch Program: 140 (6.6%)
Teachers: 146.5 (14.4 to 1)
Librarians/Media Specialists: 2.0 (1,055.5 to 1)
Guidance Counselors: 4.0 (527.8 to 1)
Current Spending: ($ per student per year):
Total: $7,522; Instruction: $4,727; Support Services: $2,545
Enrollment, Drop-out Rates and Diploma Recipients by Race/Ethnicity

Category	Total	White	Black	Asian	AIAN	Hisp.
Enrollment (%)	100.0	91.2	2.8	0.6	0.3	5.1
Drop-out Rate (%)	n/a	n/a	n/a	n/a	n/a	n/a
H.S. Diplomas (#)	n/a	n/a	n/a	n/a	n/a	n/a

Ottawa Twp HSD 140
211 E Main St • Ottawa, IL 61350-3199
(815) 433-1323 • http://www.ottawahigh.com/
Grade Span: 09-12; **Agency Type:** 1
Schools: 1
0 Primary; 0 Middle; 1 High; 0 Other Level
1 Regular; 0 Special Education; 0 Vocational; 0 Alternative
0 Magnet; 0 Charter; 1 Title I Eligible; 0 School-wide Title I
Students: 1,580 (52.0% male; 48.0% female)
Individual Education Program: 257 (16.3%);
English Language Learner: 8 (0.5%); Migrant: n/a
Eligible for Free Lunch Program: 0 (0.0%)
Eligible for Reduced-Price Lunch Program: 0 (0.0%)
Teachers: 96.0 (16.5 to 1)
Librarians/Media Specialists: 1.0 (1,580.0 to 1)
Guidance Counselors: 4.5 (351.1 to 1)
Current Spending: ($ per student per year):
Total: $7,533; Instruction: $4,637; Support Services: $2,550
Enrollment, Drop-out Rates and Diploma Recipients by Race/Ethnicity

Category	Total	White	Black	Asian	AIAN	Hisp.
Enrollment (%)	100.0	94.2	1.6	0.7	0.1	3.4
Drop-out Rate (%)	5.5	5.1	31.6	0.0	50.0	5.8
H.S. Diplomas (#)	330	313	4	2	0	11

Streator Elem SD 44
1520 N Bloomington • Streator, IL 61364-1312
(815) 672-2926 • http://www.streatoril.com/education/
Grade Span: PK-08; **Agency Type:** 1
Schools: 5
4 Primary; 1 Middle; 0 High; 0 Other Level
5 Regular; 0 Special Education; 0 Vocational; 0 Alternative
0 Magnet; 0 Charter; 4 Title I Eligible; 1 School-wide Title I
Students: 1,842 (52.4% male; 47.6% female)
Individual Education Program: 418 (22.7%);
English Language Learner: 54 (2.9%); Migrant: n/a
Eligible for Free Lunch Program: 736 (40.0%)
Eligible for Reduced-Price Lunch Program: 182 (9.9%)
Teachers: 122.9 (15.0 to 1)
Librarians/Media Specialists: 1.0 (1,842.0 to 1)
Guidance Counselors: 0.0 (0.0 to 1)
Current Spending: ($ per student per year):
Total: $6,651; Instruction: $4,095; Support Services: $2,305
Enrollment, Drop-out Rates and Diploma Recipients by Race/Ethnicity

Category	Total	White	Black	Asian	AIAN	Hisp.
Enrollment (%)	100.0	83.1	7.0	0.7	0.0	9.3
Drop-out Rate (%)	n/a	n/a	n/a	n/a	n/a	n/a
H.S. Diplomas (#)	n/a	n/a	n/a	n/a	n/a	n/a

Lake County

Adlai E Stevenson Dist 125
Two Stevenson Dr • Lincolnshire, IL 60069-2815
(847) 634-4000 • http://www.district125.k12.il.us/
Grade Span: 09-12; **Agency Type:** 1
Schools: 1
0 Primary; 0 Middle; 1 High; 0 Other Level
1 Regular; 0 Special Education; 0 Vocational; 0 Alternative
0 Magnet; 0 Charter; 0 Title I Eligible; 0 School-wide Title I
Students: 4,319 (52.6% male; 47.4% female)
Individual Education Program: 451 (10.4%);
English Language Learner: 215 (5.0%); Migrant: n/a
Eligible for Free Lunch Program: n/a
Eligible for Reduced-Price Lunch Program: n/a
Teachers: 268.2 (16.1 to 1)
Librarians/Media Specialists: 1.0 (4,319.0 to 1)
Guidance Counselors: 16.0 (269.9 to 1)
Current Spending: ($ per student per year):
Total: $10,788; Instruction: $6,743; Support Services: $3,769
Enrollment, Drop-out Rates and Diploma Recipients by Race/Ethnicity

Category	Total	White	Black	Asian	AIAN	Hisp.
Enrollment (%)	100.0	84.2	0.9	12.0	0.1	2.9
Drop-out Rate (%)	0.4	0.5	0.0	0.4	0.0	0.0
H.S. Diplomas (#)	931	799	5	104	4	19

Antioch CCSD 34
800 N Main St • Antioch, IL 60002-1542
(847) 838-8400 • http://www.dist34.lake.k12.il.us/
Grade Span: PK-08; **Agency Type:** 1
Schools: 5
4 Primary; 1 Middle; 0 High; 0 Other Level
5 Regular; 0 Special Education; 0 Vocational; 0 Alternative
0 Magnet; 0 Charter; 3 Title I Eligible; 0 School-wide Title I
Students: 2,452 (51.6% male; 48.4% female)
Individual Education Program: 401 (16.4%);
English Language Learner: 30 (1.2%); Migrant: n/a
Eligible for Free Lunch Program: 248 (10.1%)
Eligible for Reduced-Price Lunch Program: 51 (2.1%)
Teachers: 146.9 (16.7 to 1)
Librarians/Media Specialists: 1.0 (2,452.0 to 1)
Guidance Counselors: 0.0 (0.0 to 1)
Current Spending: ($ per student per year):
Total: $5,652; Instruction: $3,234; Support Services: $2,229
Enrollment, Drop-out Rates and Diploma Recipients by Race/Ethnicity

Category	Total	White	Black	Asian	AIAN	Hisp.
Enrollment (%)	100.0	90.5	2.5	1.9	0.4	4.6
Drop-out Rate (%)	n/a	n/a	n/a	n/a	n/a	n/a
H.S. Diplomas (#)	n/a	n/a	n/a	n/a	n/a	n/a

Antioch Community High SD 117
1625 Deep Lake Rd • Lake Villa, IL 60046
(847) 395-1421
Grade Span: 02-12; **Agency Type:** 1
Schools: 3
0 Primary; 0 Middle; 2 High; 1 Other Level
1 Regular; 2 Special Education; 0 Vocational; 0 Alternative
0 Magnet; 0 Charter; 1 Title I Eligible; 0 School-wide Title I
Students: 2,325 (53.9% male; 46.1% female)
Individual Education Program: 290 (12.5%);
English Language Learner: 0 (0.0%); Migrant: n/a
Eligible for Free Lunch Program: 0 (0.0%)
Eligible for Reduced-Price Lunch Program: 0 (0.0%)
Teachers: 129.2 (18.0 to 1)
Librarians/Media Specialists: 1.0 (2,325.0 to 1)
Guidance Counselors: 6.0 (387.5 to 1)
Current Spending: ($ per student per year):
Total: $8,768; Instruction: $5,029; Support Services: $3,526
Enrollment, Drop-out Rates and Diploma Recipients by Race/Ethnicity

Category	Total	White	Black	Asian	AIAN	Hisp.
Enrollment (%)	100.0	91.2	3.7	1.0	0.4	3.6
Drop-out Rate (%)	4.2	4.2	1.4	0.0	22.2	5.2
H.S. Diplomas (#)	466	430	8	7	6	15

Aptakisic-Tripp CCSD 102
1231 Weiland Rd • Buffalo Grove, IL 60089-7040
(847) 353-5650
Grade Span: PK-08; **Agency Type:** 1
Schools: 4
2 Primary; 2 Middle; 0 High; 0 Other Level
4 Regular; 0 Special Education; 0 Vocational; 0 Alternative
0 Magnet; 0 Charter; 0 Title I Eligible; 0 School-wide Title I
Students: 2,475 (51.5% male; 48.5% female)
Individual Education Program: 412 (16.6%);
English Language Learner: 168 (6.8%); Migrant: n/a
Eligible for Free Lunch Program: 46 (1.9%)
Eligible for Reduced-Price Lunch Program: 40 (1.6%)
Teachers: 161.5 (15.3 to 1)
Librarians/Media Specialists: 3.0 (825.0 to 1)
Guidance Counselors: 0.0 (0.0 to 1)
Current Spending: ($ per student per year):
Total: $7,547; Instruction: $4,310; Support Services: $3,072

Enrollment, Drop-out Rates and Diploma Recipients by Race/Ethnicity

Category	Total	White	Black	Asian	AIAN	Hisp.
Enrollment (%)	100.0	80.6	0.9	15.1	0.2	3.2
Drop-out Rate (%)	n/a	n/a	n/a	n/a	n/a	n/a
H.S. Diplomas (#)	n/a	n/a	n/a	n/a	n/a	n/a

Barrington CUSD 220

310 James St • Barrington, IL 60010-1799
(847) 381-6300 • http://www.cusd220.lake.k12.il.us/
Grade Span: PK-12; **Agency Type:** 1
Schools: 12
9 Primary; 2 Middle; 1 High; 0 Other Level
11 Regular; 1 Special Education; 0 Vocational; 0 Alternative
0 Magnet; 0 Charter; 0 Title I Eligible; 0 School-wide Title I
Students: 8,564 (50.7% male; 49.3% female)
Individual Education Program: 1,237 (14.4%);
English Language Learner: 504 (5.9%); Migrant: n/a
Eligible for Free Lunch Program: 472 (5.5%)
Eligible for Reduced-Price Lunch Program: 137 (1.6%)
Teachers: 497.3 (17.2 to 1)
Librarians/Media Specialists: 12.0 (713.7 to 1)
Guidance Counselors: 14.0 (611.7 to 1)
Current Spending: ($ per student per year):
Total: $8,579; Instruction: $5,402; Support Services: $3,015
Enrollment, Drop-out Rates and Diploma Recipients by Race/Ethnicity

Category	Total	White	Black	Asian	AIAN	Hisp.
Enrollment (%)	100.0	82.2	1.5	5.2	0.0	11.0
Drop-out Rate (%)	0.9	0.7	3.2	0.0	0.0	3.7
H.S. Diplomas (#)	577	501	3	46	1	26

Beach Park CCSD 3

11315 W Wadsworth • Beach Park, IL 60099-3399
(847) 599-5070
Grade Span: PK-08; **Agency Type:** 1
Schools: 6
4 Primary; 1 Middle; 0 High; 1 Other Level
5 Regular; 1 Special Education; 0 Vocational; 0 Alternative
0 Magnet; 0 Charter; 4 Title I Eligible; 0 School-wide Title I
Students: 2,298 (52.1% male; 47.9% female)
Individual Education Program: 408 (17.8%);
English Language Learner: 93 (4.0%); Migrant: n/a
Eligible for Free Lunch Program: 460 (20.0%)
Eligible for Reduced-Price Lunch Program: 134 (5.8%)
Teachers: 127.9 (18.0 to 1)
Librarians/Media Specialists: 2.0 (1,149.0 to 1)
Guidance Counselors: 0.0 (0.0 to 1)
Current Spending: ($ per student per year):
Total: $6,282; Instruction: $3,597; Support Services: $2,534
Enrollment, Drop-out Rates and Diploma Recipients by Race/Ethnicity

Category	Total	White	Black	Asian	AIAN	Hisp.
Enrollment (%)	100.0	58.7	18.9	2.4	1.1	18.9
Drop-out Rate (%)	n/a	n/a	n/a	n/a	n/a	n/a
H.S. Diplomas (#)	n/a	n/a	n/a	n/a	n/a	n/a

Community CSD 46

565 Frederick Rd • Grayslake, IL 60030-3909
(847) 543-5319 • http://www.d46.k12.il.us/
Grade Span: PK-08; **Agency Type:** 1
Schools: 6
4 Primary; 2 Middle; 0 High; 0 Other Level
6 Regular; 0 Special Education; 0 Vocational; 0 Alternative
0 Magnet; 0 Charter; 1 Title I Eligible; 0 School-wide Title I
Students: 3,725 (52.5% male; 47.5% female)
Individual Education Program: 490 (13.2%);
English Language Learner: 173 (4.6%); Migrant: n/a
Eligible for Free Lunch Program: 218 (5.9%)
Eligible for Reduced-Price Lunch Program: 97 (2.6%)
Teachers: 243.0 (15.3 to 1)
Librarians/Media Specialists: 6.0 (620.8 to 1)
Guidance Counselors: 0.0 (0.0 to 1)
Current Spending: ($ per student per year):
Total: $6,414; Instruction: $3,023; Support Services: $3,243
Enrollment, Drop-out Rates and Diploma Recipients by Race/Ethnicity

Category	Total	White	Black	Asian	AIAN	Hisp.
Enrollment (%)	100.0	82.1	2.6	5.1	0.3	9.9
Drop-out Rate (%)	n/a	n/a	n/a	n/a	n/a	n/a
H.S. Diplomas (#)	n/a	n/a	n/a	n/a	n/a	n/a

Community High SD 128

940 W Park Ave • Libertyville, IL 60048-2699
(847) 367-3159 • http://www.lchs.lake.k12.il.us/
Grade Span: 09-12; **Agency Type:** 1
Schools: 2
0 Primary; 0 Middle; 2 High; 0 Other Level
2 Regular; 0 Special Education; 0 Vocational; 0 Alternative
0 Magnet; 0 Charter; 0 Title I Eligible; 0 School-wide Title I
Students: 2,926 (53.0% male; 47.0% female)
Individual Education Program: 405 (13.8%);
English Language Learner: 61 (2.1%); Migrant: n/a
Eligible for Free Lunch Program: n/a
Eligible for Reduced-Price Lunch Program: n/a
Teachers: 184.4 (15.9 to 1)
Librarians/Media Specialists: 3.0 (975.3 to 1)
Guidance Counselors: 12.0 (243.8 to 1)
Current Spending: ($ per student per year):
Total: $13,105; Instruction: $7,171; Support Services: $5,734
Enrollment, Drop-out Rates and Diploma Recipients by Race/Ethnicity

Category	Total	White	Black	Asian	AIAN	Hisp.
Enrollment (%)	100.0	84.2	1.8	8.8	0.2	4.9
Drop-out Rate (%)	1.5	1.2	2.0	1.8	50.0	6.9
H.S. Diplomas (#)	631	529	18	60	0	24

Deerfield SD 109

517 Deerfield Rd • Deerfield, IL 60015-4419
(847) 945-1844 • http://www.dps109.lake.k12.il.us/
Grade Span: PK-08; **Agency Type:** 1
Schools: 6
4 Primary; 2 Middle; 0 High; 0 Other Level
6 Regular; 0 Special Education; 0 Vocational; 0 Alternative
0 Magnet; 0 Charter; 6 Title I Eligible; 0 School-wide Title I
Students: 3,207 (52.3% male; 47.7% female)
Individual Education Program: 569 (17.7%);
English Language Learner: 35 (1.1%); Migrant: n/a
Eligible for Free Lunch Program: 0 (0.0%)
Eligible for Reduced-Price Lunch Program: 0 (0.0%)
Teachers: 223.9 (14.3 to 1)
Librarians/Media Specialists: 6.0 (534.5 to 1)
Guidance Counselors: 1.0 (3,207.0 to 1)
Current Spending: ($ per student per year):
Total: $7,616; Instruction: $4,706; Support Services: $2,839
Enrollment, Drop-out Rates and Diploma Recipients by Race/Ethnicity

Category	Total	White	Black	Asian	AIAN	Hisp.
Enrollment (%)	100.0	95.8	0.6	2.5	0.0	1.1
Drop-out Rate (%)	n/a	n/a	n/a	n/a	n/a	n/a
H.S. Diplomas (#)	n/a	n/a	n/a	n/a	n/a	n/a

Fremont SD 79

28855 N Fremont Ctr • Mundelein, IL 60060-9470
(847) 566-0169
Grade Span: PK-08; **Agency Type:** 1
Schools: 2
2 Primary; 0 Middle; 0 High; 0 Other Level
2 Regular; 0 Special Education; 0 Vocational; 0 Alternative
0 Magnet; 0 Charter; 2 Title I Eligible; 0 School-wide Title I
Students: 1,517 (50.2% male; 49.8% female)
Individual Education Program: 242 (16.0%);
English Language Learner: 51 (3.4%); Migrant: n/a
Eligible for Free Lunch Program: 0 (0.0%)
Eligible for Reduced-Price Lunch Program: 0 (0.0%)
Teachers: 81.1 (18.7 to 1)
Librarians/Media Specialists: 2.0 (758.5 to 1)
Guidance Counselors: 0.0 (0.0 to 1)
Current Spending: ($ per student per year):
Total: $6,489; Instruction: $3,369; Support Services: $2,945
Enrollment, Drop-out Rates and Diploma Recipients by Race/Ethnicity

Category	Total	White	Black	Asian	AIAN	Hisp.
Enrollment (%)	100.0	88.3	0.8	5.3	0.3	5.3
Drop-out Rate (%)	n/a	n/a	n/a	n/a	n/a	n/a
H.S. Diplomas (#)	n/a	n/a	n/a	n/a	n/a	n/a

Grayslake Community High SD 127

400 N Lake St • Grayslake, IL 60030-1499
(847) 223-8621 • http://www.gchs.lake.k12.il.us/
Grade Span: 09-12; **Agency Type:** 1
Schools: 1
0 Primary; 0 Middle; 1 High; 0 Other Level
1 Regular; 0 Special Education; 0 Vocational; 0 Alternative
0 Magnet; 0 Charter; 1 Title I Eligible; 0 School-wide Title I
Students: 1,940 (50.4% male; 49.6% female)
Individual Education Program: 229 (11.8%);
English Language Learner: 29 (1.5%); Migrant: n/a
Eligible for Free Lunch Program: 0 (0.0%)
Eligible for Reduced-Price Lunch Program: 0 (0.0%)
Teachers: 103.3 (18.8 to 1)
Librarians/Media Specialists: 1.0 (1,940.0 to 1)
Guidance Counselors: 6.0 (323.3 to 1)
Current Spending: ($ per student per year):
Total: $7,685; Instruction: $3,902; Support Services: $3,777

Enrollment, Drop-out Rates and Diploma Recipients by Race/Ethnicity

Category	Total	White	Black	Asian	AIAN	Hisp.
Enrollment (%)	100.0	83.5	2.9	4.4	0.5	8.7
Drop-out Rate (%)	3.7	3.1	7.7	6.6	0.0	9.3
H.S. Diplomas (#)	342	299	8	13	1	21

Gurnee SD 56

900 Kilbourne Rd • Gurnee, IL 60031-1998
(847) 336-0800 • http://www.d56.lake.k12.il.us/district/
Grade Span: PK-08; **Agency Type:** 1
Schools: 3
2 Primary; 1 Middle; 0 High; 0 Other Level
3 Regular; 0 Special Education; 0 Vocational; 0 Alternative
0 Magnet; 0 Charter; 1 Title I Eligible; 0 School-wide Title I
Students: 2,028 (51.5% male; 48.5% female)
Individual Education Program: 360 (17.8%);
English Language Learner: 183 (9.0%); Migrant: n/a
Eligible for Free Lunch Program: 0 (0.0%)
Eligible for Reduced-Price Lunch Program: 0 (0.0%)
Teachers: 126.2 (16.1 to 1)
Librarians/Media Specialists: 3.0 (676.0 to 1)
Guidance Counselors: 0.0 (0.0 to 1)
Current Spending: ($ per student per year):
Total: $7,844; Instruction: $4,269; Support Services: $3,536
Enrollment, Drop-out Rates and Diploma Recipients by Race/Ethnicity

Category	Total	White	Black	Asian	AIAN	Hisp.
Enrollment (%)	100.0	63.9	13.9	4.8	0.5	16.9
Drop-out Rate (%)	n/a	n/a	n/a	n/a	n/a	n/a
H.S. Diplomas (#)	n/a	n/a	n/a	n/a	n/a	n/a

Hawthorn CCSD 73

201 Hawthorn Pkwy • Vernon Hills, IL 60061-1498
(847) 990-4210 • http://www.hawthorn.k12.il.us/
Grade Span: PK-08; **Agency Type:** 1
Schools: 6
4 Primary; 2 Middle; 0 High; 0 Other Level
6 Regular; 0 Special Education; 0 Vocational; 0 Alternative
1 Magnet; 0 Charter; 2 Title I Eligible; 0 School-wide Title I
Students: 3,671 (51.6% male; 48.4% female)
Individual Education Program: 435 (11.8%);
English Language Learner: 478 (13.0%); Migrant: n/a
Eligible for Free Lunch Program: 433 (11.8%)
Eligible for Reduced-Price Lunch Program: 108 (2.9%)
Teachers: 228.5 (16.1 to 1)
Librarians/Media Specialists: 4.6 (798.0 to 1)
Guidance Counselors: 0.0 (0.0 to 1)
Current Spending: ($ per student per year):
Total: $7,270; Instruction: $4,391; Support Services: $2,668
Enrollment, Drop-out Rates and Diploma Recipients by Race/Ethnicity

Category	Total	White	Black	Asian	AIAN	Hisp.
Enrollment (%)	100.0	65.6	2.8	11.8	0.3	19.5
Drop-out Rate (%)	n/a	n/a	n/a	n/a	n/a	n/a
H.S. Diplomas (#)	n/a	n/a	n/a	n/a	n/a	n/a

Kildeer Countryside CCSD 96

1050 Ivy Hall Ln • Buffalo Grove, IL 60089-1700
(847) 459-4260 • http://www.district96.k12.il.us/
Grade Span: PK-08; **Agency Type:** 1
Schools: 7
5 Primary; 2 Middle; 0 High; 0 Other Level
7 Regular; 0 Special Education; 0 Vocational; 0 Alternative
0 Magnet; 0 Charter; 2 Title I Eligible; 0 School-wide Title I
Students: 3,516 (50.9% male; 49.1% female)
Individual Education Program: 681 (19.4%);
English Language Learner: 86 (2.4%); Migrant: n/a
Eligible for Free Lunch Program: 49 (1.4%)
Eligible for Reduced-Price Lunch Program: 25 (0.7%)
Teachers: 235.7 (14.9 to 1)
Librarians/Media Specialists: 1.0 (3,516.0 to 1)
Guidance Counselors: 1.0 (3,516.0 to 1)
Current Spending: ($ per student per year):
Total: $7,627; Instruction: $4,734; Support Services: $2,749
Enrollment, Drop-out Rates and Diploma Recipients by Race/Ethnicity

Category	Total	White	Black	Asian	AIAN	Hisp.
Enrollment (%)	100.0	86.9	0.9	9.8	0.1	2.2
Drop-out Rate (%)	n/a	n/a	n/a	n/a	n/a	n/a
H.S. Diplomas (#)	n/a	n/a	n/a	n/a	n/a	n/a

Lake Forest Community HSD 115

1285 N Mckinley Rd • Lake Forest, IL 60045-1371
(847) 234-3600 • http://www.lfhs.org/
Grade Span: 09-12; **Agency Type:** 1
Schools: 1
0 Primary; 0 Middle; 1 High; 0 Other Level
1 Regular; 0 Special Education; 0 Vocational; 0 Alternative
0 Magnet; 0 Charter; 1 Title I Eligible; 0 School-wide Title I
Students: 1,729 (51.4% male; 48.6% female)
Individual Education Program: 262 (15.2%);
English Language Learner: 0 (0.0%); Migrant: n/a
Eligible for Free Lunch Program: 0 (0.0%)
Eligible for Reduced-Price Lunch Program: 0 (0.0%)
Teachers: 117.9 (14.7 to 1)
Librarians/Media Specialists: 2.0 (864.5 to 1)
Guidance Counselors: 8.0 (216.1 to 1)
Current Spending: ($ per student per year):
Total: $14,068; Instruction: $7,736; Support Services: $6,049
Enrollment, Drop-out Rates and Diploma Recipients by Race/Ethnicity

Category	Total	White	Black	Asian	AIAN	Hisp.
Enrollment (%)	100.0	94.6	0.5	4.0	0.0	0.9
Drop-out Rate (%)	0.5	0.4	0.0	2.6	n/a	0.0
H.S. Diplomas (#)	397	362	5	23	0	7

Lake Forest SD 67

67 W Deerpath • Lake Forest, IL 60045-2198
(847) 234-6010 • http://www.lfelem.lfc.edu/
Grade Span: PK-08; **Agency Type:** 1
Schools: 4
3 Primary; 1 Middle; 0 High; 0 Other Level
4 Regular; 0 Special Education; 0 Vocational; 0 Alternative
0 Magnet; 0 Charter; 2 Title I Eligible; 0 School-wide Title I
Students: 2,172 (52.6% male; 47.4% female)
Individual Education Program: 378 (17.4%);
English Language Learner: 12 (0.6%); Migrant: n/a
Eligible for Free Lunch Program: 0 (0.0%)
Eligible for Reduced-Price Lunch Program: 0 (0.0%)
Teachers: 179.7 (12.1 to 1)
Librarians/Media Specialists: 1.0 (2,172.0 to 1)
Guidance Counselors: 1.7 (1,277.6 to 1)
Current Spending: ($ per student per year):
Total: $10,290; Instruction: $5,581; Support Services: $4,502
Enrollment, Drop-out Rates and Diploma Recipients by Race/Ethnicity

Category	Total	White	Black	Asian	AIAN	Hisp.
Enrollment (%)	100.0	94.8	0.7	2.9	0.0	1.5
Drop-out Rate (%)	n/a	n/a	n/a	n/a	n/a	n/a
H.S. Diplomas (#)	n/a	n/a	n/a	n/a	n/a	n/a

Lake Villa CCSD 41

131 Mckinley Ave • Lake Villa, IL 60046-8986
(847) 356-2385 • http://www.district41.org/
Grade Span: PK-08; **Agency Type:** 1
Schools: 5
4 Primary; 1 Middle; 0 High; 0 Other Level
5 Regular; 0 Special Education; 0 Vocational; 0 Alternative
0 Magnet; 0 Charter; 4 Title I Eligible; 0 School-wide Title I
Students: 3,188 (53.0% male; 47.0% female)
Individual Education Program: 616 (19.3%);
English Language Learner: 146 (4.6%); Migrant: n/a
Eligible for Free Lunch Program: 195 (6.1%)
Eligible for Reduced-Price Lunch Program: 88 (2.8%)
Teachers: 209.1 (15.2 to 1)
Librarians/Media Specialists: 4.5 (708.4 to 1)
Guidance Counselors: 0.0 (0.0 to 1)
Current Spending: ($ per student per year):
Total: $5,817; Instruction: $3,582; Support Services: $2,052
Enrollment, Drop-out Rates and Diploma Recipients by Race/Ethnicity

Category	Total	White	Black	Asian	AIAN	Hisp.
Enrollment (%)	100.0	81.7	3.6	3.7	0.3	10.6
Drop-out Rate (%)	n/a	n/a	n/a	n/a	n/a	n/a
H.S. Diplomas (#)	n/a	n/a	n/a	n/a	n/a	n/a

Lake Zurich CUSD 95

400 S Old Rand Rd • Lake Zurich, IL 60047-2459
(847) 438-2831 • http://www.lz95.lake.k12.il.us/
Grade Span: KG-12; **Agency Type:** 1
Schools: 8
5 Primary; 2 Middle; 1 High; 0 Other Level
8 Regular; 0 Special Education; 0 Vocational; 0 Alternative
0 Magnet; 0 Charter; 0 Title I Eligible; 0 School-wide Title I
Students: 6,439 (50.7% male; 49.3% female)
Individual Education Program: 823 (12.8%);
English Language Learner: 101 (1.6%); Migrant: n/a
Eligible for Free Lunch Program: 181 (2.8%)
Eligible for Reduced-Price Lunch Program: 42 (0.7%)
Teachers: 412.0 (15.6 to 1)
Librarians/Media Specialists: 8.5 (757.5 to 1)
Guidance Counselors: 8.0 (804.9 to 1)
Current Spending: ($ per student per year):
Total: $7,005; Instruction: $4,248; Support Services: $2,606

Enrollment, Drop-out Rates and Diploma Recipients by Race/Ethnicity

Category	Total	White	Black	Asian	AIAN	Hisp.
Enrollment (%)	100.0	91.0	0.8	3.9	0.1	4.2
Drop-out Rate (%)	0.8	0.8	0.0	0.0	0.0	1.9
H.S. Diplomas (#)	427	395	3	13	0	16

Libertyville SD 70

1381 Lake St • Libertyville, IL 60048-1731
(847) 362-8393 • http://www.d70.k12.il.us/
Grade Span: KG-08; **Agency Type:** 1
Schools: 5
4 Primary; 1 Middle; 0 High; 0 Other Level
5 Regular; 0 Special Education; 0 Vocational; 0 Alternative
0 Magnet; 0 Charter; 2 Title I Eligible; 0 School-wide Title I
Students: 2,594 (52.2% male; 47.8% female)
Individual Education Program: 420 (16.2%);
English Language Learner: 47 (1.8%); Migrant: n/a
Eligible for Free Lunch Program: 43 (1.7%)
Eligible for Reduced-Price Lunch Program: 7 (0.3%)
Teachers: 164.9 (15.7 to 1)
Librarians/Media Specialists: 5.0 (518.8 to 1)
Guidance Counselors: 2.0 (1,297.0 to 1)
Current Spending: ($ per student per year):
Total: $7,665; Instruction: $4,758; Support Services: $2,852
Enrollment, Drop-out Rates and Diploma Recipients by Race/Ethnicity

Category	Total	White	Black	Asian	AIAN	Hisp.
Enrollment (%)	100.0	90.4	2.4	4.8	0.1	2.4
Drop-out Rate (%)	n/a	n/a	n/a	n/a	n/a	n/a
H.S. Diplomas (#)	n/a	n/a	n/a	n/a	n/a	n/a

Lincolnshire-Prairieview SD 103

1370 Riverwoods Rd • Lincolnshire, IL 60069-2402
(847) 295-4030 • http://www.district103.k12.il.us/
Grade Span: KG-08; **Agency Type:** 1
Schools: 3
2 Primary; 1 Middle; 0 High; 0 Other Level
3 Regular; 0 Special Education; 0 Vocational; 0 Alternative
0 Magnet; 0 Charter; 3 Title I Eligible; 0 School-wide Title I
Students: 1,733 (49.5% male; 50.5% female)
Individual Education Program: 317 (18.3%);
English Language Learner: 44 (2.5%); Migrant: n/a
Eligible for Free Lunch Program: 0 (0.0%)
Eligible for Reduced-Price Lunch Program: 0 (0.0%)
Teachers: 128.0 (13.5 to 1)
Librarians/Media Specialists: 2.0 (866.5 to 1)
Guidance Counselors: 0.0 (0.0 to 1)
Current Spending: ($ per student per year):
Total: $8,973; Instruction: $5,417; Support Services: $3,516
Enrollment, Drop-out Rates and Diploma Recipients by Race/Ethnicity

Category	Total	White	Black	Asian	AIAN	Hisp.
Enrollment (%)	100.0	88.3	0.8	9.1	0.0	1.8
Drop-out Rate (%)	n/a	n/a	n/a	n/a	n/a	n/a
H.S. Diplomas (#)	n/a	n/a	n/a	n/a	n/a	n/a

Mundelein Cons High SD 120

1350 W Hawley St • Mundelein, IL 60060-1519
(847) 949-2200 • http://www.mundelein.lake.k12.il.us/
Grade Span: 09-12; **Agency Type:** 1
Schools: 1
0 Primary; 0 Middle; 1 High; 0 Other Level
1 Regular; 0 Special Education; 0 Vocational; 0 Alternative
0 Magnet; 0 Charter; 1 Title I Eligible; 0 School-wide Title I
Students: 1,972 (52.3% male; 47.7% female)
Individual Education Program: 293 (14.9%);
English Language Learner: 135 (6.8%); Migrant: n/a
Eligible for Free Lunch Program: 257 (13.0%)
Eligible for Reduced-Price Lunch Program: 97 (4.9%)
Teachers: 117.7 (16.8 to 1)
Librarians/Media Specialists: 2.0 (986.0 to 1)
Guidance Counselors: 7.0 (281.7 to 1)
Current Spending: ($ per student per year):
Total: $9,954; Instruction: $6,094; Support Services: $3,622
Enrollment, Drop-out Rates and Diploma Recipients by Race/Ethnicity

Category	Total	White	Black	Asian	AIAN	Hisp.
Enrollment (%)	100.0	67.8	1.8	5.1	0.1	25.2
Drop-out Rate (%)	3.6	1.8	0.0	1.1	0.0	9.4
H.S. Diplomas (#)	468	325	16	96	0	31

Mundelein Elem SD 75

470 N Lake St • Mundelein, IL 60060-1884
(847) 949-2700 • http://www.d75.lake.k12.il.us/
Grade Span: PK-08; **Agency Type:** 1
Schools: 5
4 Primary; 0 Middle; 0 High; 1 Other Level
4 Regular; 1 Special Education; 0 Vocational; 0 Alternative
0 Magnet; 0 Charter; 4 Title I Eligible; 0 School-wide Title I
Students: 2,281 (51.1% male; 48.9% female)
Individual Education Program: 370 (16.2%);
English Language Learner: 335 (14.7%); Migrant: n/a
Eligible for Free Lunch Program: 293 (12.8%)
Eligible for Reduced-Price Lunch Program: 136 (6.0%)
Teachers: 141.9 (16.1 to 1)
Librarians/Media Specialists: 4.0 (570.3 to 1)
Guidance Counselors: 1.0 (2,281.0 to 1)
Current Spending: ($ per student per year):
Total: $5,306; Instruction: $3,026; Support Services: $2,137
Enrollment, Drop-out Rates and Diploma Recipients by Race/Ethnicity

Category	Total	White	Black	Asian	AIAN	Hisp.
Enrollment (%)	100.0	64.0	2.1	6.3	0.3	27.3
Drop-out Rate (%)	n/a	n/a	n/a	n/a	n/a	n/a
H.S. Diplomas (#)	n/a	n/a	n/a	n/a	n/a	n/a

North Chicago SD 187

2000 Lewis Ave • North Chicago, IL 60064-2532
(847) 689-8150 • http://www.nchi.lfc.edu/
Grade Span: PK-12; **Agency Type:** 1
Schools: 10
7 Primary; 2 Middle; 1 High; 0 Other Level
10 Regular; 0 Special Education; 0 Vocational; 0 Alternative
0 Magnet; 0 Charter; 6 Title I Eligible; 6 School-wide Title I
Students: 4,652 (50.7% male; 49.3% female)
Individual Education Program: 787 (16.9%);
English Language Learner: 853 (18.3%); Migrant: n/a
Eligible for Free Lunch Program: 1,768 (38.0%)
Eligible for Reduced-Price Lunch Program: 389 (8.4%)
Teachers: 282.0 (16.5 to 1)
Librarians/Media Specialists: 1.0 (4,652.0 to 1)
Guidance Counselors: 9.0 (516.9 to 1)
Current Spending: ($ per student per year):
Total: $8,672; Instruction: $4,848; Support Services: $3,547
Enrollment, Drop-out Rates and Diploma Recipients by Race/Ethnicity

Category	Total	White	Black	Asian	AIAN	Hisp.
Enrollment (%)	100.0	17.3	52.6	2.8	0.3	26.9
Drop-out Rate (%)	0.0	0.0	0.0	0.0	0.0	0.0
H.S. Diplomas (#)	138	13	94	0	1	30

North Shore SD 112

1936 Green Bay Rd • Highland Park, IL 60035-3112
(847) 681-6700 • http://www.nsn.org/hpkhome/dist112/
Grade Span: PK-08; **Agency Type:** 1
Schools: 11
8 Primary; 3 Middle; 0 High; 0 Other Level
11 Regular; 0 Special Education; 0 Vocational; 0 Alternative
2 Magnet; 0 Charter; 2 Title I Eligible; 0 School-wide Title I
Students: 4,511 (51.2% male; 48.8% female)
Individual Education Program: 689 (15.3%);
English Language Learner: 501 (11.1%); Migrant: n/a
Eligible for Free Lunch Program: 270 (6.0%)
Eligible for Reduced-Price Lunch Program: 42 (0.9%)
Teachers: 336.7 (13.4 to 1)
Librarians/Media Specialists: 10.0 (451.1 to 1)
Guidance Counselors: 3.0 (1,503.7 to 1)
Current Spending: ($ per student per year):
Total: $9,842; Instruction: $6,205; Support Services: $3,579
Enrollment, Drop-out Rates and Diploma Recipients by Race/Ethnicity

Category	Total	White	Black	Asian	AIAN	Hisp.
Enrollment (%)	100.0	81.3	2.3	1.7	0.0	14.7
Drop-out Rate (%)	n/a	n/a	n/a	n/a	n/a	n/a
H.S. Diplomas (#)	n/a	n/a	n/a	n/a	n/a	n/a

Round Lake Area Schs - Dist 116

316 S Rosedale Ct • Round Lake, IL 60073-2999
(847) 270-9000 • http://www.rlas-116.org/
Grade Span: PK-12; **Agency Type:** 1
Schools: 8
6 Primary; 1 Middle; 1 High; 0 Other Level
8 Regular; 0 Special Education; 0 Vocational; 0 Alternative
0 Magnet; 0 Charter; 7 Title I Eligible; 0 School-wide Title I
Students: 6,047 (51.3% male; 48.7% female)
Individual Education Program: 974 (16.1%);
English Language Learner: 236 (3.9%); Migrant: n/a
Eligible for Free Lunch Program: 2,095 (34.6%)
Eligible for Reduced-Price Lunch Program: 514 (8.5%)
Teachers: 288.8 (20.9 to 1)
Librarians/Media Specialists: 1.0 (6,047.0 to 1)
Guidance Counselors: 3.0 (2,015.7 to 1)
Current Spending: ($ per student per year):
Total: $5,992; Instruction: $3,793; Support Services: $1,978

Enrollment, Drop-out Rates and Diploma Recipients by Race/Ethnicity

Category	Total	White	Black	Asian	AIAN	Hisp.
Enrollment (%)	100.0	38.8	5.9	1.2	0.3	53.9
Drop-out Rate (%)	9.8	9.2	12.3	0.0	0.0	10.8
H.S. Diplomas (#)	254	155	8	3	0	88

Township High SD 113

1040 Park Ave W • Highland Park, IL 60035-2283
(847) 926-9301 • http://www.d113.lake.k12.il.us/
Grade Span: 09-12; **Agency Type:** 1
Schools: 2
0 Primary; 0 Middle; 2 High; 0 Other Level
2 Regular; 0 Special Education; 0 Vocational; 0 Alternative
0 Magnet; 0 Charter; 1 Title I Eligible; 0 School-wide Title I
Students: 3,373 (50.2% male; 49.8% female)
Individual Education Program: 500 (14.8%);
English Language Learner: 163 (4.8%); Migrant: n/a
Eligible for Free Lunch Program: n/a
Eligible for Reduced-Price Lunch Program: n/a
Teachers: 228.6 (14.8 to 1)
Librarians/Media Specialists: 7.0 (481.9 to 1)
Guidance Counselors: 14.8 (227.9 to 1)
Current Spending: ($ per student per year):
Total: $17,004; Instruction: $8,973; Support Services: $7,999
Enrollment, Drop-out Rates and Diploma Recipients by Race/Ethnicity

Category	Total	White	Black	Asian	AIAN	Hisp.
Enrollment (%)	100.0	87.2	1.3	2.9	0.1	8.6
Drop-out Rate (%)	1.1	0.3	8.9	0.0	0.0	8.1
H.S. Diplomas (#)	750	656	16	19	1	58

Warren Twp High SD 121

500 N Oplaine Rd • Gurnee, IL 60031-2686
(847) 662-1400 • http://www.wths.net/
Grade Span: 09-12; **Agency Type:** 1
Schools: 1
0 Primary; 0 Middle; 1 High; 0 Other Level
1 Regular; 0 Special Education; 0 Vocational; 0 Alternative
0 Magnet; 0 Charter; 0 Title I Eligible; 0 School-wide Title I
Students: 3,570 (50.9% male; 49.1% female)
Individual Education Program: 397 (11.1%);
English Language Learner: 67 (1.9%); Migrant: n/a
Eligible for Free Lunch Program: 0 (0.0%)
Eligible for Reduced-Price Lunch Program: 0 (0.0%)
Teachers: 205.0 (17.4 to 1)
Librarians/Media Specialists: 3.0 (1,190.0 to 1)
Guidance Counselors: 8.0 (446.3 to 1)
Current Spending: ($ per student per year):
Total: $8,935; Instruction: $5,031; Support Services: $3,540
Enrollment, Drop-out Rates and Diploma Recipients by Race/Ethnicity

Category	Total	White	Black	Asian	AIAN	Hisp.
Enrollment (%)	100.0	68.7	7.9	9.2	0.6	13.6
Drop-out Rate (%)	3.2	2.7	7.5	2.0	0.0	4.5
H.S. Diplomas (#)	674	506	44	57	2	65

Wauconda Community Unit SD 118

555 N Main St • Wauconda, IL 60084-1299
(847) 526-7690 • http://www.wauconda118.org/
Grade Span: PK-12; **Agency Type:** 1
Schools: 5
2 Primary; 2 Middle; 1 High; 0 Other Level
5 Regular; 0 Special Education; 0 Vocational; 0 Alternative
0 Magnet; 0 Charter; 2 Title I Eligible; 0 School-wide Title I
Students: 3,909 (51.4% male; 48.6% female)
Individual Education Program: 595 (15.2%);
English Language Learner: 240 (6.1%); Migrant: n/a
Eligible for Free Lunch Program: 355 (9.1%)
Eligible for Reduced-Price Lunch Program: 47 (1.2%)
Teachers: 230.1 (17.0 to 1)
Librarians/Media Specialists: 4.0 (977.3 to 1)
Guidance Counselors: 5.7 (685.8 to 1)
Current Spending: ($ per student per year):
Total: $6,447; Instruction: $3,508; Support Services: $2,735
Enrollment, Drop-out Rates and Diploma Recipients by Race/Ethnicity

Category	Total	White	Black	Asian	AIAN	Hisp.
Enrollment (%)	100.0	84.2	0.8	1.8	0.2	13.0
Drop-out Rate (%)	1.6	1.8	0.0	0.0	0.0	0.0
H.S. Diplomas (#)	218	201	1	1	1	14

Waukegan CUSD 60

1201 N Sheridan Rd • Waukegan, IL 60085-2099
(847) 336-3100 • http://www.waukeganschools.org/
Grade Span: PK-12; **Agency Type:** 1
Schools: 24
15 Primary; 5 Middle; 2 High; 2 Other Level
21 Regular; 3 Special Education; 0 Vocational; 0 Alternative
2 Magnet; 0 Charter; 19 Title I Eligible; 19 School-wide Title I
Students: 15,980 (51.4% male; 48.6% female)
Individual Education Program: 2,661 (16.7%);
English Language Learner: 4,412 (27.6%); Migrant: n/a
Eligible for Free Lunch Program: 6,755 (42.3%)
Eligible for Reduced-Price Lunch Program: 1,590 (9.9%)
Teachers: 856.1 (18.7 to 1)
Librarians/Media Specialists: 6.0 (2,663.3 to 1)
Guidance Counselors: 25.0 (639.2 to 1)
Current Spending: ($ per student per year):
Total: $7,036; Instruction: $4,095; Support Services: $2,703
Enrollment, Drop-out Rates and Diploma Recipients by Race/Ethnicity

Category	Total	White	Black	Asian	AIAN	Hisp.
Enrollment (%)	100.0	10.6	21.8	2.3	0.1	65.4
Drop-out Rate (%)	2.5	1.4	4.4	0.8	66.7	2.0
H.S. Diplomas (#)	648	137	163	27	2	319

Woodland CCSD 50

1105 N Hunt Club Rd • Gurnee, IL 60031
(847) 856-3590
Grade Span: PK-08; **Agency Type:** 1
Schools: 4
2 Primary; 2 Middle; 0 High; 0 Other Level
4 Regular; 0 Special Education; 0 Vocational; 0 Alternative
0 Magnet; 0 Charter; 4 Title I Eligible; 0 School-wide Title I
Students: 6,877 (51.6% male; 48.4% female)
Individual Education Program: 1,123 (16.3%);
English Language Learner: 552 (8.0%); Migrant: n/a
Eligible for Free Lunch Program: 452 (6.6%)
Eligible for Reduced-Price Lunch Program: 196 (2.9%)
Teachers: 472.4 (14.6 to 1)
Librarians/Media Specialists: 5.0 (1,375.4 to 1)
Guidance Counselors: 0.0 (0.0 to 1)
Current Spending: ($ per student per year):
Total: $5,898; Instruction: $3,261; Support Services: $2,472
Enrollment, Drop-out Rates and Diploma Recipients by Race/Ethnicity

Category	Total	White	Black	Asian	AIAN	Hisp.
Enrollment (%)	100.0	71.2	6.5	9.4	0.2	12.7
Drop-out Rate (%)	n/a	n/a	n/a	n/a	n/a	n/a
H.S. Diplomas (#)	n/a	n/a	n/a	n/a	n/a	n/a

Zion Elementary SD 6

2200 Bethesda Blvd • Zion, IL 60099-2589
(847) 872-5455 • http://www.zion.k12.il.us/
Grade Span: PK-08; **Agency Type:** 1
Schools: 7
6 Primary; 1 Middle; 0 High; 0 Other Level
6 Regular; 1 Special Education; 0 Vocational; 0 Alternative
0 Magnet; 0 Charter; 6 Title I Eligible; 6 School-wide Title I
Students: 2,979 (50.2% male; 49.8% female)
Individual Education Program: 610 (20.5%);
English Language Learner: 250 (8.4%); Migrant: n/a
Eligible for Free Lunch Program: 1,479 (49.6%)
Eligible for Reduced-Price Lunch Program: 311 (10.4%)
Teachers: 173.5 (17.2 to 1)
Librarians/Media Specialists: 1.0 (2,979.0 to 1)
Guidance Counselors: 0.0 (0.0 to 1)
Current Spending: ($ per student per year):
Total: $6,442; Instruction: $3,896; Support Services: $2,321
Enrollment, Drop-out Rates and Diploma Recipients by Race/Ethnicity

Category	Total	White	Black	Asian	AIAN	Hisp.
Enrollment (%)	100.0	25.5	46.1	1.5	0.1	26.8
Drop-out Rate (%)	n/a	n/a	n/a	n/a	n/a	n/a
H.S. Diplomas (#)	n/a	n/a	n/a	n/a	n/a	n/a

Zion-Benton Twp HSD 126

One Z-B Way • Zion, IL 60099-2387
(847) 746-1202 • http://www.zbths.k12.il.us/
Grade Span: 09-12; **Agency Type:** 1
Schools: 1
0 Primary; 0 Middle; 1 High; 0 Other Level
1 Regular; 0 Special Education; 0 Vocational; 0 Alternative
0 Magnet; 0 Charter; 1 Title I Eligible; 0 School-wide Title I
Students: 2,258 (51.0% male; 49.0% female)
Individual Education Program: 346 (15.3%);
English Language Learner: 64 (2.8%); Migrant: n/a
Eligible for Free Lunch Program: 380 (16.8%)
Eligible for Reduced-Price Lunch Program: 49 (2.2%)
Teachers: 116.3 (19.4 to 1)
Librarians/Media Specialists: 1.0 (2,258.0 to 1)
Guidance Counselors: 6.0 (376.3 to 1)
Current Spending: ($ per student per year):
Total: $8,556; Instruction: $4,476; Support Services: $3,781

Enrollment, Drop-out Rates and Diploma Recipients by Race/Ethnicity

Category	Total	White	Black	Asian	AIAN	Hisp.
Enrollment (%)	100.0	59.3	23.6	1.8	0.8	14.5
Drop-out Rate (%)	8.6	6.7	13.1	9.8	7.4	10.7
H.S. Diplomas (#)	378	247	77	12	8	34

Lee County

Dixon Unit SD 170

1335 Franklin Gr Rd • Dixon, IL 61021-9149
(815) 284-7722 • http://www.leeogle.lth2.k12.il.us/directory/dixon.html
Grade Span: PK-12; **Agency Type:** 1
Schools: 6
3 Primary; 1 Middle; 2 High; 0 Other Level
5 Regular; 1 Special Education; 0 Vocational; 0 Alternative
0 Magnet; 0 Charter; 2 Title I Eligible; 0 School-wide Title I
Students: 3,010 (50.4% male; 49.6% female)
Individual Education Program: 429 (14.3%);
English Language Learner: 4 (0.1%); Migrant: n/a
Eligible for Free Lunch Program: 632 (21.0%)
Eligible for Reduced-Price Lunch Program: 170 (5.6%)
Teachers: 185.2 (16.3 to 1)
Librarians/Media Specialists: 1.0 (3,010.0 to 1)
Guidance Counselors: 5.0 (602.0 to 1)
Current Spending: ($ per student per year):
Total: $7,090; Instruction: $4,395; Support Services: $2,464
Enrollment, Drop-out Rates and Diploma Recipients by Race/Ethnicity

Category	Total	White	Black	Asian	AIAN	Hisp.
Enrollment (%)	100.0	89.9	3.9	2.3	0.0	4.0
Drop-out Rate (%)	6.3	6.1	7.7	0.0	n/a	14.3
H.S. Diplomas (#)	221	205	3	6	0	7

Livingston County

Prairie Central CUSD 8

PO Box 496 • Forrest, IL 61741-0496
(815) 657-8237
Grade Span: PK-12; **Agency Type:** 1
Schools: 6
3 Primary; 2 Middle; 1 High; 0 Other Level
6 Regular; 0 Special Education; 0 Vocational; 0 Alternative
0 Magnet; 0 Charter; 4 Title I Eligible; 0 School-wide Title I
Students: 1,960 (51.0% male; 49.0% female)
Individual Education Program: 345 (17.6%);
English Language Learner: 15 (0.8%); Migrant: n/a
Eligible for Free Lunch Program: 435 (22.2%)
Eligible for Reduced-Price Lunch Program: 105 (5.4%)
Teachers: 136.6 (14.3 to 1)
Librarians/Media Specialists: 4.0 (490.0 to 1)
Guidance Counselors: 2.8 (700.0 to 1)
Current Spending: ($ per student per year):
Total: $6,479; Instruction: $4,090; Support Services: $2,070
Enrollment, Drop-out Rates and Diploma Recipients by Race/Ethnicity

Category	Total	White	Black	Asian	AIAN	Hisp.
Enrollment (%)	100.0	94.2	1.6	0.8	0.1	3.3
Drop-out Rate (%)	3.6	3.4	0.0	0.0	0.0	13.3
H.S. Diplomas (#)	154	149	1	1	0	3

Macon County

Decatur SD 61

101 W Cerro Gordo St • Decatur, IL 62523-1001
(217) 424-3011 • http://www.dps61.org/
Grade Span: PK-12; **Agency Type:** 1
Schools: 25
19 Primary; 3 Middle; 2 High; 1 Other Level
23 Regular; 2 Special Education; 0 Vocational; 0 Alternative
5 Magnet; 1 Charter; 20 Title I Eligible; 20 School-wide Title I
Students: 10,137 (51.0% male; 49.0% female)
Individual Education Program: 1,679 (16.6%);
English Language Learner: 58 (0.6%); Migrant: n/a
Eligible for Free Lunch Program: 4,695 (46.3%)
Eligible for Reduced-Price Lunch Program: 785 (7.7%)
Teachers: 459.5 (22.1 to 1)
Librarians/Media Specialists: 12.0 (844.8 to 1)
Guidance Counselors: 11.5 (881.5 to 1)
Current Spending: ($ per student per year):
Total: $6,205; Instruction: $3,311; Support Services: $2,658
Enrollment, Drop-out Rates and Diploma Recipients by Race/Ethnicity

Category	Total	White	Black	Asian	AIAN	Hisp.
Enrollment (%)	100.0	52.9	45.0	0.9	0.1	1.2
Drop-out Rate (%)	11.3	10.3	13.7	0.0	14.3	0.0
H.S. Diplomas (#)	521	352	161	3	1	4

Mount Zion Community Unit SD 3

455 Elm St • Mount Zion, IL 62549-1314
(217) 864-2366 • http://www.mtzion.k12.il.us/
Grade Span: PK-12; **Agency Type:** 1
Schools: 6
3 Primary; 2 Middle; 1 High; 0 Other Level
6 Regular; 0 Special Education; 0 Vocational; 0 Alternative
0 Magnet; 0 Charter; 3 Title I Eligible; 0 School-wide Title I
Students: 2,404 (50.5% male; 49.5% female)
Individual Education Program: 210 (8.7%);
English Language Learner: 4 (0.2%); Migrant: n/a
Eligible for Free Lunch Program: 143 (5.9%)
Eligible for Reduced-Price Lunch Program: 76 (3.2%)
Teachers: 128.0 (18.8 to 1)
Librarians/Media Specialists: 4.0 (601.0 to 1)
Guidance Counselors: 3.0 (801.3 to 1)
Current Spending: ($ per student per year):
Total: $5,286; Instruction: $2,949; Support Services: $2,040
Enrollment, Drop-out Rates and Diploma Recipients by Race/Ethnicity

Category	Total	White	Black	Asian	AIAN	Hisp.
Enrollment (%)	100.0	97.8	0.8	0.7	0.2	0.5
Drop-out Rate (%)	1.8	1.8	0.0	0.0	n/a	0.0
H.S. Diplomas (#)	195	192	0	3	0	0

Macoupin County

Carlinville CUSD 1

18456 Shipman Rd • Carlinville, IL 62626-1731
(217) 854-9823 • http://www.carlinville.macoupin.k12.il.us/
Grade Span: PK-12; **Agency Type:** 1
Schools: 5
2 Primary; 2 Middle; 1 High; 0 Other Level
5 Regular; 0 Special Education; 0 Vocational; 0 Alternative
0 Magnet; 0 Charter; 3 Title I Eligible; 0 School-wide Title I
Students: 1,657 (52.7% male; 47.3% female)
Individual Education Program: 249 (15.0%);
English Language Learner: 1 (0.1%); Migrant: n/a
Eligible for Free Lunch Program: 288 (17.4%)
Eligible for Reduced-Price Lunch Program: 92 (5.6%)
Teachers: 95.9 (17.3 to 1)
Librarians/Media Specialists: 2.0 (828.5 to 1)
Guidance Counselors: 3.0 (552.3 to 1)
Current Spending: ($ per student per year):
Total: $5,807; Instruction: $3,479; Support Services: $2,046
Enrollment, Drop-out Rates and Diploma Recipients by Race/Ethnicity

Category	Total	White	Black	Asian	AIAN	Hisp.
Enrollment (%)	100.0	96.4	2.5	0.4	0.0	0.7
Drop-out Rate (%)	3.8	3.4	40.0	0.0	n/a	0.0
H.S. Diplomas (#)	134	133	1	0	0	0

Southwestern CUSD 9

PO Box 99 • Piasa, IL 62079-0099
(618) 729-3221 • http://www.sw.macoupin.k12.il.us/
Grade Span: PK-12; **Agency Type:** 1
Schools: 6
4 Primary; 1 Middle; 1 High; 0 Other Level
6 Regular; 0 Special Education; 0 Vocational; 0 Alternative
0 Magnet; 0 Charter; 3 Title I Eligible; 0 School-wide Title I
Students: 1,834 (51.0% male; 49.0% female)
Individual Education Program: 290 (15.8%);
English Language Learner: 0 (0.0%); Migrant: n/a
Eligible for Free Lunch Program: 242 (13.2%)
Eligible for Reduced-Price Lunch Program: 112 (6.1%)
Teachers: 121.2 (15.1 to 1)
Librarians/Media Specialists: 3.0 (611.3 to 1)
Guidance Counselors: 2.0 (917.0 to 1)
Current Spending: ($ per student per year):
Total: $6,126; Instruction: $3,795; Support Services: $2,012
Enrollment, Drop-out Rates and Diploma Recipients by Race/Ethnicity

Category	Total	White	Black	Asian	AIAN	Hisp.
Enrollment (%)	100.0	98.0	1.7	0.3	0.0	0.0
Drop-out Rate (%)	4.2	3.8	30.0	0.0	n/a	n/a
H.S. Diplomas (#)	150	148	2	0	0	0

Madison County

Alton Community Unit SD 11

PO Box 9028 • Alton, IL 62002-9028
(618) 474-2600 • http://www.alton.madison.k12.il.us/
Grade Span: PK-12; **Agency Type:** 1
Schools: 13
10 Primary; 2 Middle; 1 High; 0 Other Level
11 Regular; 2 Special Education; 0 Vocational; 0 Alternative
0 Magnet; 0 Charter; 11 Title I Eligible; 10 School-wide Title I
Students: 6,988 (50.8% male; 49.2% female)

Individual Education Program: 1,518 (21.7%);
English Language Learner: 13 (0.2%); Migrant: n/a
Eligible for Free Lunch Program: 2,749 (39.3%)
Eligible for Reduced-Price Lunch Program: 436 (6.2%)
Teachers: 438.8 (15.9 to 1)
Librarians/Media Specialists: 5.0 (1,397.6 to 1)
Guidance Counselors: 6.0 (1,164.7 to 1)
Current Spending: ($ per student per year):
Total: $6,953; Instruction: $3,949; Support Services: $2,748
Enrollment, Drop-out Rates and Diploma Recipients by Race/Ethnicity

Category	Total	White	Black	Asian	AIAN	Hisp.
Enrollment (%)	100.0	62.5	35.9	0.7	0.2	0.7
Drop-out Rate (%)	6.7	5.0	10.8	0.0	0.0	14.3
H.S. Diplomas (#)	432	323	102	2	1	4

Bethalto CUSD 8
322 E Central St • Bethalto, IL 62010-1399
(618) 377-7200 • http://www.bethalto.org/education/district/
Grade Span: PK-12; **Agency Type:** 1
Schools: 7
3 Primary; 3 Middle; 1 High; 0 Other Level
6 Regular; 1 Special Education; 0 Vocational; 0 Alternative
0 Magnet; 0 Charter; 5 Title I Eligible; 2 School-wide Title I
Students: 2,832 (51.9% male; 48.1% female)
Individual Education Program: 516 (18.2%);
English Language Learner: 0 (0.0%); Migrant: n/a
Eligible for Free Lunch Program: 612 (21.6%)
Eligible for Reduced-Price Lunch Program: 164 (5.8%)
Teachers: 175.5 (16.1 to 1)
Librarians/Media Specialists: 2.0 (1,416.0 to 1)
Guidance Counselors: 2.0 (1,416.0 to 1)
Current Spending: ($ per student per year):
Total: $6,161; Instruction: $3,742; Support Services: $2,152
Enrollment, Drop-out Rates and Diploma Recipients by Race/Ethnicity

Category	Total	White	Black	Asian	AIAN	Hisp.
Enrollment (%)	100.0	96.4	2.6	0.4	0.0	0.7
Drop-out Rate (%)	4.7	4.8	0.0	0.0	n/a	0.0
H.S. Diplomas (#)	217	214	3	0	0	0

Collinsville CUSD 10
201 W Clay St • Collinsville, IL 62234-3219
(618) 346-6350 • http://isd.cusd10.madison.k12.il.us/CUSD/
Grade Span: PK-12; **Agency Type:** 1
Schools: 11
9 Primary; 1 Middle; 1 High; 0 Other Level
11 Regular; 0 Special Education; 0 Vocational; 0 Alternative
0 Magnet; 0 Charter; 6 Title I Eligible; 4 School-wide Title I
Students: 6,038 (52.4% male; 47.6% female)
Individual Education Program: 1,035 (17.1%);
English Language Learner: 110 (1.8%); Migrant: n/a
Eligible for Free Lunch Program: 1,702 (28.2%)
Eligible for Reduced-Price Lunch Program: 456 (7.6%)
Teachers: 339.8 (17.8 to 1)
Librarians/Media Specialists: 2.0 (3,019.0 to 1)
Guidance Counselors: 5.0 (1,207.6 to 1)
Current Spending: ($ per student per year):
Total: $6,629; Instruction: $3,799; Support Services: $2,571
Enrollment, Drop-out Rates and Diploma Recipients by Race/Ethnicity

Category	Total	White	Black	Asian	AIAN	Hisp.
Enrollment (%)	100.0	83.4	8.3	1.0	0.2	7.1
Drop-out Rate (%)	6.5	6.4	7.6	0.0	0.0	13.5
H.S. Diplomas (#)	360	319	20	5	0	16

Edwardsville CUSD 7
708 St Louis St • Edwardsville, IL 62025-1427
(618) 656-1182 • http://www.ecusd7.org/
Grade Span: PK-12; **Agency Type:** 1
Schools: 12
7 Primary; 3 Middle; 2 High; 0 Other Level
11 Regular; 1 Special Education; 0 Vocational; 0 Alternative
0 Magnet; 1 Charter; 4 Title I Eligible; 0 School-wide Title I
Students: 6,747 (51.3% male; 48.7% female)
Individual Education Program: 1,015 (15.0%);
English Language Learner: 18 (0.3%); Migrant: n/a
Eligible for Free Lunch Program: 734 (10.9%)
Eligible for Reduced-Price Lunch Program: 248 (3.7%)
Teachers: 403.6 (16.7 to 1)
Librarians/Media Specialists: 5.0 (1,349.4 to 1)
Guidance Counselors: 4.2 (1,606.4 to 1)
Current Spending: ($ per student per year):
Total: $6,540; Instruction: $3,788; Support Services: $2,514
Enrollment, Drop-out Rates and Diploma Recipients by Race/Ethnicity

Category	Total	White	Black	Asian	AIAN	Hisp.
Enrollment (%)	100.0	88.0	9.3	1.7	0.2	0.8
Drop-out Rate (%)	3.3	3.2	5.5	0.0	0.0	0.0
H.S. Diplomas (#)	491	439	39	8	0	5

Granite City CUSD 9
1947 Adams St • Granite City, IL 62040-3397
(618) 451-5800 • http://www.granitecityschools.org/
Grade Span: PK-12; **Agency Type:** 1
Schools: 10
7 Primary; 2 Middle; 1 High; 0 Other Level
10 Regular; 0 Special Education; 0 Vocational; 0 Alternative
0 Magnet; 0 Charter; 5 Title I Eligible; 2 School-wide Title I
Students: 7,671 (51.5% male; 48.5% female)
Individual Education Program: 1,306 (17.0%);
English Language Learner: 38 (0.5%); Migrant: n/a
Eligible for Free Lunch Program: 2,308 (30.1%)
Eligible for Reduced-Price Lunch Program: 508 (6.6%)
Teachers: 355.0 (21.6 to 1)
Librarians/Media Specialists: 3.0 (2,557.0 to 1)
Guidance Counselors: 7.0 (1,095.9 to 1)
Current Spending: ($ per student per year):
Total: $6,627; Instruction: $3,962; Support Services: $2,311
Enrollment, Drop-out Rates and Diploma Recipients by Race/Ethnicity

Category	Total	White	Black	Asian	AIAN	Hisp.
Enrollment (%)	100.0	91.2	5.7	0.8	0.1	2.2
Drop-out Rate (%)	5.7	4.9	25.0	0.0	0.0	17.6
H.S. Diplomas (#)	462	448	10	2	0	2

Highland Community Unit SD 5
PO Box 149 • Highland, IL 62249-0149
(618) 654-2106 • http://www.highland.madison.k12.il.us/
Grade Span: PK-12; **Agency Type:** 1
Schools: 8
5 Primary; 2 Middle; 1 High; 0 Other Level
8 Regular; 0 Special Education; 0 Vocational; 0 Alternative
0 Magnet; 0 Charter; 3 Title I Eligible; 0 School-wide Title I
Students: 2,992 (50.1% male; 49.9% female)
Individual Education Program: 406 (13.6%);
English Language Learner: 0 (0.0%); Migrant: n/a
Eligible for Free Lunch Program: 319 (10.7%)
Eligible for Reduced-Price Lunch Program: 155 (5.2%)
Teachers: 190.7 (15.7 to 1)
Librarians/Media Specialists: 3.0 (997.3 to 1)
Guidance Counselors: 4.0 (748.0 to 1)
Current Spending: ($ per student per year):
Total: $6,530; Instruction: $3,958; Support Services: $2,317
Enrollment, Drop-out Rates and Diploma Recipients by Race/Ethnicity

Category	Total	White	Black	Asian	AIAN	Hisp.
Enrollment (%)	100.0	98.2	0.3	0.9	0.1	0.5
Drop-out Rate (%)	2.4	2.5	0.0	0.0	n/a	0.0
H.S. Diplomas (#)	234	230	2	1	0	1

Roxana Community Unit SD 1
401 Chaffer Ave • Roxana, IL 62084-1199
(618) 254-7544
Grade Span: PK-12; **Agency Type:** 1
Schools: 4
2 Primary; 1 Middle; 1 High; 0 Other Level
4 Regular; 0 Special Education; 0 Vocational; 0 Alternative
0 Magnet; 0 Charter; 2 Title I Eligible; 0 School-wide Title I
Students: 1,835 (50.1% male; 49.9% female)
Individual Education Program: 370 (20.2%);
English Language Learner: 17 (0.9%); Migrant: n/a
Eligible for Free Lunch Program: 440 (24.0%)
Eligible for Reduced-Price Lunch Program: 153 (8.3%)
Teachers: 117.7 (15.6 to 1)
Librarians/Media Specialists: 2.0 (917.5 to 1)
Guidance Counselors: 3.0 (611.7 to 1)
Current Spending: ($ per student per year):
Total: $6,991; Instruction: $4,043; Support Services: $2,443
Enrollment, Drop-out Rates and Diploma Recipients by Race/Ethnicity

Category	Total	White	Black	Asian	AIAN	Hisp.
Enrollment (%)	100.0	97.3	0.8	0.7	0.1	1.1
Drop-out Rate (%)	10.4	10.6	0.0	0.0	n/a	0.0
H.S. Diplomas (#)	129	129	0	0	0	0

Triad Community Unit SD 2
PO Box 360 • Troy, IL 62294-0360
(618) 667-8851 • http://www.triad.madison.k12.il.us/
Grade Span: PK-12; **Agency Type:** 1
Schools: 8
5 Primary; 2 Middle; 1 High; 0 Other Level
8 Regular; 0 Special Education; 0 Vocational; 0 Alternative

0 Magnet; 0 Charter; 6 Title I Eligible; 0 School-wide Title I
Students: 3,743 (51.7% male; 48.3% female)
Individual Education Program: 555 (14.8%);
English Language Learner: 0 (0.0%); Migrant: n/a
Eligible for Free Lunch Program: 349 (9.3%)
Eligible for Reduced-Price Lunch Program: 179 (4.8%)
Teachers: 229.1 (16.3 to 1)
Librarians/Media Specialists: 1.0 (3,743.0 to 1)
Guidance Counselors: 4.0 (935.8 to 1)
Current Spending: ($ per student per year):
Total: $5,897; Instruction: $3,764; Support Services: $1,874
Enrollment, Drop-out Rates and Diploma Recipients by Race/Ethnicity

Category	Total	White	Black	Asian	AIAN	Hisp.
Enrollment (%)	100.0	95.8	2.1	1.3	0.1	0.7
Drop-out Rate (%)	1.8	1.6	0.0	0.0	n/a	12.5
H.S. Diplomas (#)	273	266	3	2	0	2

Massac County

Massac Unit District #1
PO Box 530 • Metropolis, IL 62960-0530
(618) 524-9376 • http://www.unit1.massac.k12.il.us/
Grade Span: PK-12; **Agency Type:** 1
Schools: 11
8 Primary; 2 Middle; 1 High; 0 Other Level
9 Regular; 2 Special Education; 0 Vocational; 0 Alternative
1 Magnet; 0 Charter; 5 Title I Eligible; 5 School-wide Title I
Students: 2,362 (50.8% male; 49.2% female)
Individual Education Program: 403 (17.1%);
English Language Learner: 0 (0.0%); Migrant: n/a
Eligible for Free Lunch Program: 678 (28.7%)
Eligible for Reduced-Price Lunch Program: 105 (4.4%)
Teachers: 131.5 (18.0 to 1)
Librarians/Media Specialists: 1.0 (2,362.0 to 1)
Guidance Counselors: 4.0 (590.5 to 1)
Current Spending: ($ per student per year):
Total: $5,697; Instruction: $3,407; Support Services: $2,025
Enrollment, Drop-out Rates and Diploma Recipients by Race/Ethnicity

Category	Total	White	Black	Asian	AIAN	Hisp.
Enrollment (%)	100.0	89.1	9.3	0.4	0.4	0.8
Drop-out Rate (%)	5.5	5.7	2.5	0.0	0.0	0.0
H.S. Diplomas (#)	139	130	8	0	0	1

Mcdonough County

Macomb Community Unit SD 185
323 W Washington • Macomb, IL 61455-2197
(309) 833-4161 • http://www.macomb.com/~dist185/
Grade Span: PK-12; **Agency Type:** 1
Schools: 5
2 Primary; 2 Middle; 1 High; 0 Other Level
4 Regular; 1 Special Education; 0 Vocational; 0 Alternative
0 Magnet; 0 Charter; 4 Title I Eligible; 1 School-wide Title I
Students: 1,979 (51.6% male; 48.4% female)
Individual Education Program: 437 (22.1%);
English Language Learner: 16 (0.8%); Migrant: n/a
Eligible for Free Lunch Program: 610 (30.8%)
Eligible for Reduced-Price Lunch Program: 102 (5.2%)
Teachers: 135.5 (14.6 to 1)
Librarians/Media Specialists: 2.0 (989.5 to 1)
Guidance Counselors: 4.0 (494.8 to 1)
Current Spending: ($ per student per year):
Total: $7,358; Instruction: $4,332; Support Services: $2,656
Enrollment, Drop-out Rates and Diploma Recipients by Race/Ethnicity

Category	Total	White	Black	Asian	AIAN	Hisp.
Enrollment (%)	100.0	85.6	10.1	3.0	0.1	1.2
Drop-out Rate (%)	3.2	3.0	6.7	0.0	100.0	0.0
H.S. Diplomas (#)	128	115	8	3	0	2

Mchenry County

Cary CCSD 26
400 Haber Dr • Cary, IL 60013-2445
(847) 639-7788 •
http://www.northstarnet.org/cpqhome/schools/distwelcome.html
Grade Span: PK-08; **Agency Type:** 1
Schools: 7
5 Primary; 2 Middle; 0 High; 0 Other Level
7 Regular; 0 Special Education; 0 Vocational; 0 Alternative
0 Magnet; 0 Charter; 0 Title I Eligible; 0 School-wide Title I
Students: 3,577 (51.8% male; 48.2% female)
Individual Education Program: 603 (16.9%);
English Language Learner: 134 (3.7%); Migrant: n/a
Eligible for Free Lunch Program: 172 (4.8%)
Eligible for Reduced-Price Lunch Program: 51 (1.4%)
Teachers: 216.5 (16.5 to 1)
Librarians/Media Specialists: 7.0 (511.0 to 1)
Guidance Counselors: 1.0 (3,577.0 to 1)
Current Spending: ($ per student per year):
Total: $5,725; Instruction: $3,430; Support Services: $2,153
Enrollment, Drop-out Rates and Diploma Recipients by Race/Ethnicity

Category	Total	White	Black	Asian	AIAN	Hisp.
Enrollment (%)	100.0	91.2	0.5	1.4	0.0	6.8
Drop-out Rate (%)	n/a	n/a	n/a	n/a	n/a	n/a
H.S. Diplomas (#)	n/a	n/a	n/a	n/a	n/a	n/a

Community High SD 155
1 S Virginia Rd • Crystal Lake, IL 60014-6195
(815) 455-8500 • http://www.d155.org/
Grade Span: 09-12; **Agency Type:** 1
Schools: 4
0 Primary; 0 Middle; 4 High; 0 Other Level
4 Regular; 0 Special Education; 0 Vocational; 0 Alternative
0 Magnet; 0 Charter; 0 Title I Eligible; 0 School-wide Title I
Students: 6,007 (51.8% male; 48.2% female)
Individual Education Program: 732 (12.2%);
English Language Learner: 68 (1.1%); Migrant: n/a
Eligible for Free Lunch Program: 164 (2.7%)
Eligible for Reduced-Price Lunch Program: 31 (0.5%)
Teachers: 337.6 (17.8 to 1)
Librarians/Media Specialists: 4.0 (1,501.8 to 1)
Guidance Counselors: 18.0 (333.7 to 1)
Current Spending: ($ per student per year):
Total: $8,966; Instruction: $6,184; Support Services: $2,522
Enrollment, Drop-out Rates and Diploma Recipients by Race/Ethnicity

Category	Total	White	Black	Asian	AIAN	Hisp.
Enrollment (%)	100.0	93.9	0.5	1.5	0.1	4.0
Drop-out Rate (%)	2.0	1.8	4.5	0.0	12.5	5.8
H.S. Diplomas (#)	1,226	1,158	7	14	0	47

Consolidated SD 158
11302 Lincoln St • Huntley, IL 60142-9792
(847) 659-6158 • http://www.d158.k12.il.us/
Grade Span: PK-12; **Agency Type:** 1
Schools: 7
4 Primary; 1 Middle; 1 High; 1 Other Level
6 Regular; 1 Special Education; 0 Vocational; 0 Alternative
0 Magnet; 0 Charter; 1 Title I Eligible; 0 School-wide Title I
Students: 4,680 (51.0% male; 49.0% female)
Individual Education Program: 396 (8.5%);
English Language Learner: 79 (1.7%); Migrant: n/a
Eligible for Free Lunch Program: 100 (2.1%)
Eligible for Reduced-Price Lunch Program: 59 (1.3%)
Teachers: 288.0 (16.3 to 1)
Librarians/Media Specialists: 5.5 (850.9 to 1)
Guidance Counselors: 7.0 (668.6 to 1)
Current Spending: ($ per student per year):
Total: $6,852; Instruction: $3,663; Support Services: $2,987
Enrollment, Drop-out Rates and Diploma Recipients by Race/Ethnicity

Category	Total	White	Black	Asian	AIAN	Hisp.
Enrollment (%)	100.0	84.0	2.3	4.6	0.2	8.8
Drop-out Rate (%)	1.9	1.3	12.5	0.0	n/a	7.4
H.S. Diplomas (#)	130	106	2	4	0	18

Crystal Lake CCSD 47
221 Liberty Rd • Crystal Lake, IL 60014-8041
(815) 459-6070 • http://www.d47schools.org/
Grade Span: PK-08; **Agency Type:** 1
Schools: 12
9 Primary; 3 Middle; 0 High; 0 Other Level
12 Regular; 0 Special Education; 0 Vocational; 0 Alternative
0 Magnet; 0 Charter; 5 Title I Eligible; 0 School-wide Title I
Students: 8,898 (51.8% male; 48.2% female)
Individual Education Program: 1,264 (14.2%);
English Language Learner: 386 (4.3%); Migrant: n/a
Eligible for Free Lunch Program: 469 (5.3%)
Eligible for Reduced-Price Lunch Program: 198 (2.2%)
Teachers: 525.2 (16.9 to 1)
Librarians/Media Specialists: 7.0 (1,271.1 to 1)
Guidance Counselors: 0.0 (0.0 to 1)
Current Spending: ($ per student per year):
Total: $5,800; Instruction: $3,622; Support Services: $1,995
Enrollment, Drop-out Rates and Diploma Recipients by Race/Ethnicity

Category	Total	White	Black	Asian	AIAN	Hisp.
Enrollment (%)	100.0	90.1	1.1	2.4	0.0	6.3
Drop-out Rate (%)	n/a	n/a	n/a	n/a	n/a	n/a
H.S. Diplomas (#)	n/a	n/a	n/a	n/a	n/a	n/a

Harvard CUSD 50

1101 N Jefferson St • Harvard, IL 60033-1798
(815) 943-4022 • http://www.d50.mchenry.k12.il.us/
Grade Span: PK-12; **Agency Type:** 1
Schools: 5
3 Primary; 1 Middle; 1 High; 0 Other Level
5 Regular; 0 Special Education; 0 Vocational; 0 Alternative
0 Magnet; 0 Charter; 2 Title I Eligible; 0 School-wide Title I
Students: 2,368 (53.7% male; 46.3% female)
Individual Education Program: 383 (16.2%);
English Language Learner: 527 (22.3%); Migrant: n/a
Eligible for Free Lunch Program: 721 (30.4%)
Eligible for Reduced-Price Lunch Program: 183 (7.7%)
Teachers: 140.3 (16.9 to 1)
Librarians/Media Specialists: 3.0 (789.3 to 1)
Guidance Counselors: 3.0 (789.3 to 1)
Current Spending: ($ per student per year):
Total: $5,936; Instruction: $3,765; Support Services: $1,931
Enrollment, Drop-out Rates and Diploma Recipients by Race/Ethnicity

Category	Total	White	Black	Asian	AIAN	Hisp.
Enrollment (%)	100.0	56.3	1.2	0.5	0.0	42.0
Drop-out Rate (%)	7.6	4.4	0.0	0.0	n/a	20.0
H.S. Diplomas (#)	121	109	2	0	0	10

Johnsburg CUSD 12

2222 W Church St • Johnsburg, IL 60050-1910
(815) 385-6916 • http://www.jburgd12.k12.il.us/
Grade Span: PK-12; **Agency Type:** 1
Schools: 4
2 Primary; 1 Middle; 1 High; 0 Other Level
4 Regular; 0 Special Education; 0 Vocational; 0 Alternative
0 Magnet; 0 Charter; 3 Title I Eligible; 0 School-wide Title I
Students: 2,597 (52.3% male; 47.7% female)
Individual Education Program: 355 (13.7%);
English Language Learner: 6 (0.2%); Migrant: n/a
Eligible for Free Lunch Program: 96 (3.7%)
Eligible for Reduced-Price Lunch Program: 54 (2.1%)
Teachers: 145.5 (17.8 to 1)
Librarians/Media Specialists: 4.0 (649.3 to 1)
Guidance Counselors: 2.0 (1,298.5 to 1)
Current Spending: ($ per student per year):
Total: $6,815; Instruction: $4,521; Support Services: $2,112
Enrollment, Drop-out Rates and Diploma Recipients by Race/Ethnicity

Category	Total	White	Black	Asian	AIAN	Hisp.
Enrollment (%)	100.0	96.8	0.3	0.3	0.1	2.5
Drop-out Rate (%)	1.1	1.2	0.0	0.0	n/a	0.0
H.S. Diplomas (#)	181	175	1	2	0	3

Mchenry CCSD 15

1011 N Green St • Mc Henry, IL 60050-5434
(815) 385-7210
Grade Span: PK-08; **Agency Type:** 1
Schools: 8
5 Primary; 3 Middle; 0 High; 0 Other Level
8 Regular; 0 Special Education; 0 Vocational; 0 Alternative
0 Magnet; 0 Charter; 4 Title I Eligible; 0 School-wide Title I
Students: 4,698 (51.9% male; 48.1% female)
Individual Education Program: 964 (20.5%);
English Language Learner: 190 (4.0%); Migrant: n/a
Eligible for Free Lunch Program: 440 (9.4%)
Eligible for Reduced-Price Lunch Program: 88 (1.9%)
Teachers: 262.0 (17.9 to 1)
Librarians/Media Specialists: 2.0 (2,349.0 to 1)
Guidance Counselors: 0.0 (0.0 to 1)
Current Spending: ($ per student per year):
Total: $5,479; Instruction: $3,578; Support Services: $1,712
Enrollment, Drop-out Rates and Diploma Recipients by Race/Ethnicity

Category	Total	White	Black	Asian	AIAN	Hisp.
Enrollment (%)	100.0	88.8	0.9	1.0	0.4	8.8
Drop-out Rate (%)	n/a	n/a	n/a	n/a	n/a	n/a
H.S. Diplomas (#)	n/a	n/a	n/a	n/a	n/a	n/a

Mchenry Community HSD 156

4716 Crystal Lake Rd • Mc Henry, IL 60050-5427
(815) 385-7900
Grade Span: 09-12; **Agency Type:** 1
Schools: 2
0 Primary; 0 Middle; 2 High; 0 Other Level
2 Regular; 0 Special Education; 0 Vocational; 0 Alternative
0 Magnet; 0 Charter; 1 Title I Eligible; 0 School-wide Title I
Students: 2,103 (48.8% male; 51.2% female)
Individual Education Program: 364 (17.3%);
English Language Learner: 53 (2.5%); Migrant: n/a
Eligible for Free Lunch Program: n/a
Eligible for Reduced-Price Lunch Program: n/a
Teachers: 123.0 (17.1 to 1)
Librarians/Media Specialists: 2.0 (1,051.5 to 1)
Guidance Counselors: 6.0 (350.5 to 1)
Current Spending: ($ per student per year):
Total: $7,217; Instruction: $4,626; Support Services: $2,384
Enrollment, Drop-out Rates and Diploma Recipients by Race/Ethnicity

Category	Total	White	Black	Asian	AIAN	Hisp.
Enrollment (%)	100.0	93.2	0.3	1.2	0.2	5.1
Drop-out Rate (%)	4.0	3.6	0.0	5.0	0.0	12.8
H.S. Diplomas (#)	453	433	0	3	1	16

Nippersink SD 2

10006 Main St • Richmond, IL 60071-9503
(815) 678-4242
Grade Span: KG-08; **Agency Type:** 1
Schools: 3
2 Primary; 1 Middle; 0 High; 0 Other Level
3 Regular; 0 Special Education; 0 Vocational; 0 Alternative
0 Magnet; 0 Charter; 1 Title I Eligible; 0 School-wide Title I
Students: 1,571 (51.9% male; 48.1% female)
Individual Education Program: 213 (13.6%);
English Language Learner: 0 (0.0%); Migrant: n/a
Eligible for Free Lunch Program: 37 (2.4%)
Eligible for Reduced-Price Lunch Program: 18 (1.1%)
Teachers: 106.1 (14.8 to 1)
Librarians/Media Specialists: 2.0 (785.5 to 1)
Guidance Counselors: 0.6 (2,618.3 to 1)
Current Spending: ($ per student per year):
Total: $6,294; Instruction: $3,350; Support Services: $2,755
Enrollment, Drop-out Rates and Diploma Recipients by Race/Ethnicity

Category	Total	White	Black	Asian	AIAN	Hisp.
Enrollment (%)	100.0	96.2	0.6	0.7	0.0	2.4
Drop-out Rate (%)	n/a	n/a	n/a	n/a	n/a	n/a
H.S. Diplomas (#)	n/a	n/a	n/a	n/a	n/a	n/a

Woodstock CUSD 200

227 W Judd St • Woodstock, IL 60098-3799
(815) 337-5406 • http://www.d200.mchenry.k12.il.us/
Grade Span: PK-12; **Agency Type:** 1
Schools: 9
6 Primary; 2 Middle; 1 High; 0 Other Level
9 Regular; 0 Special Education; 0 Vocational; 0 Alternative
0 Magnet; 0 Charter; 4 Title I Eligible; 0 School-wide Title I
Students: 5,703 (52.1% male; 47.9% female)
Individual Education Program: 925 (16.2%);
English Language Learner: 665 (11.7%); Migrant: n/a
Eligible for Free Lunch Program: 1,199 (21.0%)
Eligible for Reduced-Price Lunch Program: 470 (8.2%)
Teachers: 325.5 (17.5 to 1)
Librarians/Media Specialists: 9.0 (633.7 to 1)
Guidance Counselors: 8.0 (712.9 to 1)
Current Spending: ($ per student per year):
Total: $7,254; Instruction: $4,280; Support Services: $2,751
Enrollment, Drop-out Rates and Diploma Recipients by Race/Ethnicity

Category	Total	White	Black	Asian	AIAN	Hisp.
Enrollment (%)	100.0	75.7	1.0	1.3	0.4	21.5
Drop-out Rate (%)	5.9	4.6	43.8	0.0	0.0	11.5
H.S. Diplomas (#)	303	259	2	4	0	38

Mclean County

Bloomington SD 87

300 E Monroe St • Bloomington, IL 61701-4083
(309) 827-6031 • http://www.district87.org/
Grade Span: PK-12; **Agency Type:** 1
Schools: 9
7 Primary; 1 Middle; 1 High; 0 Other Level
8 Regular; 1 Special Education; 0 Vocational; 0 Alternative
0 Magnet; 0 Charter; 4 Title I Eligible; 2 School-wide Title I
Students: 5,832 (51.6% male; 48.4% female)
Individual Education Program: 919 (15.8%);
English Language Learner: 155 (2.7%); Migrant: n/a
Eligible for Free Lunch Program: 1,787 (30.6%)
Eligible for Reduced-Price Lunch Program: 406 (7.0%)
Teachers: 374.5 (15.6 to 1)
Librarians/Media Specialists: 6.0 (972.0 to 1)
Guidance Counselors: 11.6 (502.8 to 1)
Current Spending: ($ per student per year):
Total: $7,239; Instruction: $4,312; Support Services: $2,564
Enrollment, Drop-out Rates and Diploma Recipients by Race/Ethnicity

Category	Total	White	Black	Asian	AIAN	Hisp.
Enrollment (%)	100.0	67.0	23.2	3.6	0.1	6.2
Drop-out Rate (%)	3.9	3.7	4.2	0.0	0.0	7.3
H.S. Diplomas (#)	264	215	37	4	0	8

Mclean County Unit Dist 5

1809 W Hovey Ave • Normal, IL 61761-4339
(309) 452-4476 • http://www.unit5.org/
Grade Span: PK-12; **Agency Type:** 1
Schools: 20
16 Primary; 2 Middle; 2 High; 0 Other Level
20 Regular; 0 Special Education; 0 Vocational; 0 Alternative
0 Magnet; 0 Charter; 6 Title I Eligible; 0 School-wide Title I
Students: 10,564 (51.6% male; 48.4% female)
Individual Education Program: 1,470 (13.9%);
English Language Learner: 171 (1.6%); Migrant: n/a
Eligible for Free Lunch Program: 1,301 (12.3%)
Eligible for Reduced-Price Lunch Program: 292 (2.8%)
Teachers: 737.2 (14.3 to 1)
Librarians/Media Specialists: 8.0 (1,320.5 to 1)
Guidance Counselors: 10.0 (1,056.4 to 1)
Current Spending: ($ per student per year):
Total: $6,682; Instruction: $4,073; Support Services: $2,365
Enrollment, Drop-out Rates and Diploma Recipients by Race/Ethnicity

Category	Total	White	Black	Asian	AIAN	Hisp.
Enrollment (%)	100.0	79.8	12.8	3.3	0.1	4.0
Drop-out Rate (%)	4.8	4.1	11.7	0.0	66.7	9.4
H.S. Diplomas (#)	615	552	37	15	0	11

Olympia CUSD 16

903 E 800 N Rd • Stanford, IL 61774-9612
(309) 379-6011 • http://www.olympia.org/
Grade Span: PK-12; **Agency Type:** 1
Schools: 8
6 Primary; 1 Middle; 1 High; 0 Other Level
8 Regular; 0 Special Education; 0 Vocational; 0 Alternative
0 Magnet; 0 Charter; 4 Title I Eligible; 0 School-wide Title I
Students: 2,289 (51.6% male; 48.4% female)
Individual Education Program: 443 (19.4%);
English Language Learner: 18 (0.8%); Migrant: n/a
Eligible for Free Lunch Program: 278 (12.1%)
Eligible for Reduced-Price Lunch Program: 132 (5.8%)
Teachers: 167.3 (13.7 to 1)
Librarians/Media Specialists: 2.0 (1,144.5 to 1)
Guidance Counselors: 3.0 (763.0 to 1)
Current Spending: ($ per student per year):
Total: $6,577; Instruction: $3,825; Support Services: $2,473
Enrollment, Drop-out Rates and Diploma Recipients by Race/Ethnicity

Category	Total	White	Black	Asian	AIAN	Hisp.
Enrollment (%)	100.0	98.4	0.6	0.3	0.0	0.7
Drop-out Rate (%)	4.9	5.0	0.0	n/a	n/a	n/a
H.S. Diplomas (#)	143	142	1	0	0	0

Monroe County

Columbia Community Unit SD 4

100 Parkview Dr • Columbia, IL 62236-2398
(618) 281-4772 • http://admin.chseagles.com/
Grade Span: PK-12; **Agency Type:** 1
Schools: 3
1 Primary; 1 Middle; 1 High; 0 Other Level
3 Regular; 0 Special Education; 0 Vocational; 0 Alternative
0 Magnet; 0 Charter; 3 Title I Eligible; 0 School-wide Title I
Students: 1,670 (52.6% male; 47.4% female)
Individual Education Program: 194 (11.6%);
English Language Learner: 2 (0.1%); Migrant: n/a
Eligible for Free Lunch Program: 47 (2.8%)
Eligible for Reduced-Price Lunch Program: 19 (1.1%)
Teachers: 104.5 (16.0 to 1)
Librarians/Media Specialists: 1.0 (1,670.0 to 1)
Guidance Counselors: 3.0 (556.7 to 1)
Current Spending: ($ per student per year):
Total: $5,916; Instruction: $3,606; Support Services: $2,094
Enrollment, Drop-out Rates and Diploma Recipients by Race/Ethnicity

Category	Total	White	Black	Asian	AIAN	Hisp.
Enrollment (%)	100.0	97.7	0.5	0.8	0.1	0.8
Drop-out Rate (%)	0.6	0.6	0.0	0.0	0.0	0.0
H.S. Diplomas (#)	121	119	0	1	0	1

Waterloo Community Unit SD 5

200 N Rogers St • Waterloo, IL 62298-1575
(618) 939-3453 • http://www.wcusd5.net/
Grade Span: PK-12; **Agency Type:** 1
Schools: 4
2 Primary; 1 Middle; 1 High; 0 Other Level
4 Regular; 0 Special Education; 0 Vocational; 0 Alternative
0 Magnet; 0 Charter; 2 Title I Eligible; 0 School-wide Title I
Students: 2,542 (50.8% male; 49.2% female)
Individual Education Program: 364 (14.3%);
English Language Learner: 0 (0.0%); Migrant: n/a
Eligible for Free Lunch Program: 136 (5.4%)
Eligible for Reduced-Price Lunch Program: 83 (3.3%)
Teachers: 150.8 (16.9 to 1)
Librarians/Media Specialists: 0.0 (0.0 to 1)
Guidance Counselors: 2.0 (1,271.0 to 1)
Current Spending: ($ per student per year):
Total: $5,763; Instruction: $3,377; Support Services: $2,126
Enrollment, Drop-out Rates and Diploma Recipients by Race/Ethnicity

Category	Total	White	Black	Asian	AIAN	Hisp.
Enrollment (%)	100.0	98.8	0.1	0.6	0.1	0.4
Drop-out Rate (%)	1.1	1.1	0.0	0.0	n/a	0.0
H.S. Diplomas (#)	179	179	0	0	0	0

Montgomery County

Hillsboro Community Unit SD 3

1311 Vandalia Rd • Hillsboro, IL 62049-2034
(217) 532-2942 • http://www.montgomery.k12.il.us/hillsboro/
Grade Span: PK-12; **Agency Type:** 1
Schools: 5
3 Primary; 1 Middle; 1 High; 0 Other Level
5 Regular; 0 Special Education; 0 Vocational; 0 Alternative
0 Magnet; 0 Charter; 0 Title I Eligible; 0 School-wide Title I
Students: 2,114 (51.5% male; 48.5% female)
Individual Education Program: 343 (16.2%);
English Language Learner: 0 (0.0%); Migrant: n/a
Eligible for Free Lunch Program: 578 (27.3%)
Eligible for Reduced-Price Lunch Program: 140 (6.6%)
Teachers: 129.7 (16.3 to 1)
Librarians/Media Specialists: 3.0 (704.7 to 1)
Guidance Counselors: 3.0 (704.7 to 1)
Current Spending: ($ per student per year):
Total: $5,945; Instruction: $3,571; Support Services: $2,026
Enrollment, Drop-out Rates and Diploma Recipients by Race/Ethnicity

Category	Total	White	Black	Asian	AIAN	Hisp.
Enrollment (%)	100.0	97.8	1.2	0.1	0.2	0.7
Drop-out Rate (%)	3.8	3.8	0.0	0.0	n/a	0.0
H.S. Diplomas (#)	129	127	1	0	0	1

Litchfield CUSD 12

1702 N State St • Litchfield, IL 62056-1196
(217) 324-2157 • http://www.litchfield.k12.il.us/
Grade Span: PK-12; **Agency Type:** 1
Schools: 7
3 Primary; 3 Middle; 1 High; 0 Other Level
6 Regular; 1 Special Education; 0 Vocational; 0 Alternative
0 Magnet; 0 Charter; 0 Title I Eligible; 0 School-wide Title I
Students: 1,719 (51.2% male; 48.8% female)
Individual Education Program: 297 (17.3%);
English Language Learner: 3 (0.2%); Migrant: n/a
Eligible for Free Lunch Program: 448 (26.1%)
Eligible for Reduced-Price Lunch Program: 87 (5.1%)
Teachers: 92.4 (18.6 to 1)
Librarians/Media Specialists: 1.0 (1,719.0 to 1)
Guidance Counselors: 1.0 (1,719.0 to 1)
Current Spending: ($ per student per year):
Total: $5,650; Instruction: $3,456; Support Services: $1,911
Enrollment, Drop-out Rates and Diploma Recipients by Race/Ethnicity

Category	Total	White	Black	Asian	AIAN	Hisp.
Enrollment (%)	100.0	97.1	1.4	0.8	0.1	0.6
Drop-out Rate (%)	1.0	0.8	0.0	0.0	n/a	50.0
H.S. Diplomas (#)	113	110	2	0	0	1

Morgan County

Jacksonville SD 117

516 Jordan St • Jacksonville, IL 62650-1941
(217) 243-9411 • http://www.morgan.k12.il.us/jvsd117/
Grade Span: PK-12; **Agency Type:** 1
Schools: 12
10 Primary; 1 Middle; 1 High; 0 Other Level
10 Regular; 2 Special Education; 0 Vocational; 0 Alternative
0 Magnet; 0 Charter; 5 Title I Eligible; 3 School-wide Title I
Students: 3,760 (51.3% male; 48.7% female)
Individual Education Program: 739 (19.7%);
English Language Learner: 11 (0.3%); Migrant: n/a
Eligible for Free Lunch Program: 1,288 (34.3%)
Eligible for Reduced-Price Lunch Program: 226 (6.0%)
Teachers: 256.2 (14.7 to 1)
Librarians/Media Specialists: 2.0 (1,880.0 to 1)
Guidance Counselors: 6.0 (626.7 to 1)
Current Spending: ($ per student per year):
Total: $6,937; Instruction: $4,077; Support Services: $2,578

Enrollment, Drop-out Rates and Diploma Recipients by Race/Ethnicity

Category	Total	White	Black	Asian	AIAN	Hisp.
Enrollment (%)	100.0	86.4	11.4	0.8	0.1	1.4
Drop-out Rate (%)	3.1	2.5	14.3	0.0	n/a	0.0
H.S. Diplomas (#)	249	237	8	2	0	2

Ogle County

Byron Community Unit SD 226

PO Box 911 • Byron, IL 61010-0911
(815) 234-5491
Grade Span: PK-12; **Agency Type:** 1
Schools: 4
2 Primary; 1 Middle; 1 High; 0 Other Level
4 Regular; 0 Special Education; 0 Vocational; 0 Alternative
0 Magnet; 0 Charter; 2 Title I Eligible; 0 School-wide Title I
Students: 1,799 (50.4% male; 49.6% female)
Individual Education Program: 278 (15.5%);
English Language Learner: 1 (0.1%); Migrant: n/a
Eligible for Free Lunch Program: 121 (6.7%)
Eligible for Reduced-Price Lunch Program: 33 (1.8%)
Teachers: 125.6 (14.3 to 1)
Librarians/Media Specialists: 1.0 (1,799.0 to 1)
Guidance Counselors: 4.2 (428.3 to 1)
Current Spending: ($ per student per year):
Total: $9,468; Instruction: $6,072; Support Services: $3,149
Enrollment, Drop-out Rates and Diploma Recipients by Race/Ethnicity

Category	Total	White	Black	Asian	AIAN	Hisp.
Enrollment (%)	100.0	96.8	0.8	1.2	0.1	1.1
Drop-out Rate (%)	0.5	0.5	0.0	0.0	n/a	0.0
H.S. Diplomas (#)	146	146	0	0	0	0

Meridian CUSD 223

207 W Main St • Stillman Valley, IL 61084-8943
(815) 645-2606 • http://www.roe47.k12.il.us/cusd223/
Grade Span: PK-12; **Agency Type:** 1
Schools: 4
2 Primary; 1 Middle; 1 High; 0 Other Level
4 Regular; 0 Special Education; 0 Vocational; 0 Alternative
0 Magnet; 0 Charter; 3 Title I Eligible; 0 School-wide Title I
Students: 1,686 (49.0% male; 51.0% female)
Individual Education Program: 193 (11.4%);
English Language Learner: 13 (0.8%); Migrant: n/a
Eligible for Free Lunch Program: 121 (7.2%)
Eligible for Reduced-Price Lunch Program: 9 (0.5%)
Teachers: 87.5 (19.3 to 1)
Librarians/Media Specialists: 2.0 (843.0 to 1)
Guidance Counselors: 2.0 (843.0 to 1)
Current Spending: ($ per student per year):
Total: $5,290; Instruction: $3,178; Support Services: $1,912
Enrollment, Drop-out Rates and Diploma Recipients by Race/Ethnicity

Category	Total	White	Black	Asian	AIAN	Hisp.
Enrollment (%)	100.0	95.8	1.0	0.7	0.1	2.4
Drop-out Rate (%)	1.2	1.2	0.0	n/a	n/a	0.0
H.S. Diplomas (#)	94	89	1	1	0	3

Oregon C U School Dist-220

206 S 10th St • Oregon, IL 61061-1711
(815) 732-2186 • http://www.ohs.ogle.k12.il.us/
Grade Span: PK-12; **Agency Type:** 1
Schools: 5
2 Primary; 2 Middle; 1 High; 0 Other Level
5 Regular; 0 Special Education; 0 Vocational; 0 Alternative
0 Magnet; 0 Charter; 4 Title I Eligible; 0 School-wide Title I
Students: 1,884 (52.4% male; 47.6% female)
Individual Education Program: 287 (15.2%);
English Language Learner: 28 (1.5%); Migrant: n/a
Eligible for Free Lunch Program: 290 (15.4%)
Eligible for Reduced-Price Lunch Program: 71 (3.8%)
Teachers: 126.2 (14.9 to 1)
Librarians/Media Specialists: 1.5 (1,256.0 to 1)
Guidance Counselors: 4.0 (471.0 to 1)
Current Spending: ($ per student per year):
Total: $6,839; Instruction: $4,670; Support Services: $2,008
Enrollment, Drop-out Rates and Diploma Recipients by Race/Ethnicity

Category	Total	White	Black	Asian	AIAN	Hisp.
Enrollment (%)	100.0	95.5	0.7	1.2	0.0	2.7
Drop-out Rate (%)	1.7	1.6	n/a	0.0	n/a	10.0
H.S. Diplomas (#)	146	143	0	1	0	2

Rochelle Community CD 231

444 N Eighth St • Rochelle, IL 61068-1460
(815) 562-6363 • http://www.leeogle.lth2.k12.il.us/directory/rochelem.html
Grade Span: PK-08; **Agency Type:** 1
Schools: 5
4 Primary; 1 Middle; 0 High; 0 Other Level
5 Regular; 0 Special Education; 0 Vocational; 0 Alternative
0 Magnet; 0 Charter; 2 Title I Eligible; 0 School-wide Title I
Students: 1,834 (51.5% male; 48.5% female)
Individual Education Program: 339 (18.5%);
English Language Learner: 140 (7.6%); Migrant: n/a
Eligible for Free Lunch Program: 476 (26.0%)
Eligible for Reduced-Price Lunch Program: 70 (3.8%)
Teachers: 121.5 (15.1 to 1)
Librarians/Media Specialists: 1.0 (1,834.0 to 1)
Guidance Counselors: 2.0 (917.0 to 1)
Current Spending: ($ per student per year):
Total: $5,341; Instruction: $3,629; Support Services: $1,548
Enrollment, Drop-out Rates and Diploma Recipients by Race/Ethnicity

Category	Total	White	Black	Asian	AIAN	Hisp.
Enrollment (%)	100.0	68.7	2.6	0.2	0.0	28.5
Drop-out Rate (%)	n/a	n/a	n/a	n/a	n/a	n/a
H.S. Diplomas (#)	n/a	n/a	n/a	n/a	n/a	n/a

Peoria County

Dunlap CUSD 323

PO Box 395 • Dunlap, IL 61525-0395
(309) 243-7716 • http://www.dunlapcusd.net/
Grade Span: PK-12; **Agency Type:** 1
Schools: 6
4 Primary; 1 Middle; 1 High; 0 Other Level
6 Regular; 0 Special Education; 0 Vocational; 0 Alternative
0 Magnet; 0 Charter; 6 Title I Eligible; 0 School-wide Title I
Students: 2,411 (51.5% male; 48.5% female)
Individual Education Program: 273 (11.3%);
English Language Learner: 16 (0.7%); Migrant: n/a
Eligible for Free Lunch Program: 130 (5.4%)
Eligible for Reduced-Price Lunch Program: 18 (0.7%)
Teachers: 131.8 (18.3 to 1)
Librarians/Media Specialists: 2.0 (1,205.5 to 1)
Guidance Counselors: 5.0 (482.2 to 1)
Current Spending: ($ per student per year):
Total: $5,081; Instruction: $3,079; Support Services: $1,768
Enrollment, Drop-out Rates and Diploma Recipients by Race/Ethnicity

Category	Total	White	Black	Asian	AIAN	Hisp.
Enrollment (%)	100.0	86.6	4.4	5.6	0.4	2.9
Drop-out Rate (%)	1.2	1.1	0.0	4.0	n/a	0.0
H.S. Diplomas (#)	180	162	5	9	0	4

Illinois Valley Central UD 321

1300 W Sycamore • Chillicothe, IL 61523-1373
(309) 274-5418 • http://www.ivc.k12.il.us/
Grade Span: PK-12; **Agency Type:** 1
Schools: 4
3 Primary; 0 Middle; 1 High; 0 Other Level
4 Regular; 0 Special Education; 0 Vocational; 0 Alternative
0 Magnet; 0 Charter; 3 Title I Eligible; 0 School-wide Title I
Students: 2,165 (51.4% male; 48.6% female)
Individual Education Program: 347 (16.0%);
English Language Learner: 0 (0.0%); Migrant: n/a
Eligible for Free Lunch Program: 264 (12.2%)
Eligible for Reduced-Price Lunch Program: 119 (5.5%)
Teachers: 138.7 (15.6 to 1)
Librarians/Media Specialists: 1.0 (2,165.0 to 1)
Guidance Counselors: 4.9 (441.8 to 1)
Current Spending: ($ per student per year):
Total: $5,594; Instruction: $3,649; Support Services: $1,738
Enrollment, Drop-out Rates and Diploma Recipients by Race/Ethnicity

Category	Total	White	Black	Asian	AIAN	Hisp.
Enrollment (%)	100.0	94.1	1.6	1.3	0.7	2.3
Drop-out Rate (%)	2.5	2.6	0.0	0.0	0.0	4.2
H.S. Diplomas (#)	146	137	1	1	3	4

Peoria SD 150

3202 N Wisconsin Ave • Peoria, IL 61603-1260
(309) 672-6768 • http://www.peoria.psd150.org/
Grade Span: PK-12; **Agency Type:** 1
Schools: 45
19 Primary; 12 Middle; 5 High; 9 Other Level
32 Regular; 13 Special Education; 0 Vocational; 0 Alternative
0 Magnet; 0 Charter; 17 Title I Eligible; 16 School-wide Title I
Students: 15,736 (51.0% male; 49.0% female)
Individual Education Program: 3,532 (22.4%);
English Language Learner: 0 (0.0%); Migrant: n/a
Eligible for Free Lunch Program: 8,535 (54.2%)
Eligible for Reduced-Price Lunch Program: 1,004 (6.4%)
Teachers: 1,089.6 (14.4 to 1)
Librarians/Media Specialists: 6.0 (2,622.7 to 1)
Guidance Counselors: 12.3 (1,279.3 to 1)

Current Spending: ($ per student per year):
Total: $8,067; Instruction: $4,736; Support Services: $3,047

Enrollment, Drop-out Rates and Diploma Recipients by Race/Ethnicity

Category	Total	White	Black	Asian	AIAN	Hisp.
Enrollment (%)	100.0	36.5	58.0	2.2	0.1	3.3
Drop-out Rate (%)	11.9	8.7	15.0	2.8	0.0	21.0
H.S. Diplomas (#)	775	431	312	13	0	19

Perry County

Du Quoin CUSD 300

845 E Jackson St • Du Quoin, IL 62832-3871
(618) 542-3856 • http://www.dqud300.perry.k12.il.us/
Grade Span: PK-12; **Agency Type:** 1
Schools: 3
1 Primary; 1 Middle; 1 High; 0 Other Level
3 Regular; 0 Special Education; 0 Vocational; 0 Alternative
0 Magnet; 0 Charter; 2 Title I Eligible; 2 School-wide Title I
Students: 1,559 (51.8% male; 48.2% female)
Individual Education Program: 291 (18.7%);
English Language Learner: 0 (0.0%); Migrant: n/a
Eligible for Free Lunch Program: 500 (32.1%)
Eligible for Reduced-Price Lunch Program: 93 (6.0%)
Teachers: 102.2 (15.3 to 1)
Librarians/Media Specialists: 0.0 (0.0 to 1)
Guidance Counselors: 3.0 (519.7 to 1)
Current Spending: ($ per student per year):
Total: $6,680; Instruction: $4,247; Support Services: $2,188

Enrollment, Drop-out Rates and Diploma Recipients by Race/Ethnicity

Category	Total	White	Black	Asian	AIAN	Hisp.
Enrollment (%)	100.0	87.9	10.8	0.4	0.0	0.8
Drop-out Rate (%)	5.0	5.0	5.7	0.0	n/a	0.0
H.S. Diplomas (#)	94	86	7	0	0	1

Piatt County

Monticello CUSD 25

2 Sage Dr • Monticello, IL 61856-1996
(217) 762-8511 • http://www.monticello.k12.il.us/
Grade Span: PK-12; **Agency Type:** 1
Schools: 4
2 Primary; 1 Middle; 1 High; 0 Other Level
4 Regular; 0 Special Education; 0 Vocational; 0 Alternative
0 Magnet; 0 Charter; 4 Title I Eligible; 0 School-wide Title I
Students: 1,603 (52.6% male; 47.4% female)
Individual Education Program: 191 (11.9%);
English Language Learner: 0 (0.0%); Migrant: n/a
Eligible for Free Lunch Program: 96 (6.0%)
Eligible for Reduced-Price Lunch Program: 52 (3.2%)
Teachers: 102.7 (15.6 to 1)
Librarians/Media Specialists: 3.0 (534.3 to 1)
Guidance Counselors: 3.0 (534.3 to 1)
Current Spending: ($ per student per year):
Total: $5,798; Instruction: $3,399; Support Services: $2,128

Enrollment, Drop-out Rates and Diploma Recipients by Race/Ethnicity

Category	Total	White	Black	Asian	AIAN	Hisp.
Enrollment (%)	100.0	98.1	0.5	0.8	0.0	0.6
Drop-out Rate (%)	1.4	1.2	100.0	n/a	n/a	0.0
H.S. Diplomas (#)	114	113	0	1	0	0

Randolph County

Sparta CUSD 140

203b Dean Ave • Sparta, IL 62286-2099
(618) 443-5331 • http://www.sparta.k12.il.us/
Grade Span: PK-12; **Agency Type:** 1
Schools: 5
3 Primary; 1 Middle; 1 High; 0 Other Level
5 Regular; 0 Special Education; 0 Vocational; 0 Alternative
0 Magnet; 0 Charter; 4 Title I Eligible; 3 School-wide Title I
Students: 1,600 (49.8% male; 50.2% female)
Individual Education Program: 283 (17.7%);
English Language Learner: 2 (0.1%); Migrant: n/a
Eligible for Free Lunch Program: 576 (36.0%)
Eligible for Reduced-Price Lunch Program: 107 (6.7%)
Teachers: 98.0 (16.3 to 1)
Librarians/Media Specialists: 1.0 (1,600.0 to 1)
Guidance Counselors: 2.0 (800.0 to 1)
Current Spending: ($ per student per year):
Total: $7,303; Instruction: $4,441; Support Services: $2,561

Enrollment, Drop-out Rates and Diploma Recipients by Race/Ethnicity

Category	Total	White	Black	Asian	AIAN	Hisp.
Enrollment (%)	100.0	80.9	17.6	0.4	0.2	0.8
Drop-out Rate (%)	4.0	3.9	5.1	0.0	n/a	0.0
H.S. Diplomas (#)	115	103	11	0	0	1

Richland County

East Richland CUSD 1

1100 E Laurel • Olney, IL 62450-2599
(618) 395-2324 • http://www.east.rchlnd.k12.il.us/
Grade Span: PK-12; **Agency Type:** 1
Schools: 3
1 Primary; 1 Middle; 1 High; 0 Other Level
3 Regular; 0 Special Education; 0 Vocational; 0 Alternative
0 Magnet; 0 Charter; 1 Title I Eligible; 1 School-wide Title I
Students: 2,134 (51.4% male; 48.6% female)
Individual Education Program: 338 (15.8%);
English Language Learner: 5 (0.2%); Migrant: n/a
Eligible for Free Lunch Program: 745 (34.9%)
Eligible for Reduced-Price Lunch Program: 101 (4.7%)
Teachers: 141.8 (15.0 to 1)
Librarians/Media Specialists: 2.0 (1,067.0 to 1)
Guidance Counselors: 4.0 (533.5 to 1)
Current Spending: ($ per student per year):
Total: $6,170; Instruction: $3,625; Support Services: $2,224

Enrollment, Drop-out Rates and Diploma Recipients by Race/Ethnicity

Category	Total	White	Black	Asian	AIAN	Hisp.
Enrollment (%)	100.0	97.6	0.9	0.6	0.0	0.8
Drop-out Rate (%)	3.8	3.9	0.0	0.0	0.0	0.0
H.S. Diplomas (#)	146	145	0	1	0	0

Rock Island County

East Moline SD 37

836 17th Ave • East Moline, IL 61244-2199
(309) 755-4533 • http://www.emsd37.org/
Grade Span: PK-08; **Agency Type:** 1
Schools: 5
4 Primary; 1 Middle; 0 High; 0 Other Level
5 Regular; 0 Special Education; 0 Vocational; 0 Alternative
0 Magnet; 0 Charter; 5 Title I Eligible; 2 School-wide Title I
Students: 2,510 (50.9% male; 49.1% female)
Individual Education Program: 461 (18.4%);
English Language Learner: 263 (10.5%); Migrant: n/a
Eligible for Free Lunch Program: 1,120 (44.6%)
Eligible for Reduced-Price Lunch Program: 142 (5.7%)
Teachers: 175.1 (14.3 to 1)
Librarians/Media Specialists: 5.0 (502.0 to 1)
Guidance Counselors: 7.0 (358.6 to 1)
Current Spending: ($ per student per year):
Total: $7,750; Instruction: $4,656; Support Services: $2,860

Enrollment, Drop-out Rates and Diploma Recipients by Race/Ethnicity

Category	Total	White	Black	Asian	AIAN	Hisp.
Enrollment (%)	100.0	57.6	15.5	1.8	0.4	24.7
Drop-out Rate (%)	n/a	n/a	n/a	n/a	n/a	n/a
H.S. Diplomas (#)	n/a	n/a	n/a	n/a	n/a	n/a

Moline Unit SD 40

1619 11th Ave • Moline, IL 61265-3198
(309) 743-1600 • http://www.moline.lth2.k12.il.us/
Grade Span: PK-12; **Agency Type:** 1
Schools: 20
14 Primary; 2 Middle; 1 High; 3 Other Level
16 Regular; 4 Special Education; 0 Vocational; 0 Alternative
2 Magnet; 0 Charter; 5 Title I Eligible; 3 School-wide Title I
Students: 7,722 (51.4% male; 48.6% female)
Individual Education Program: 1,231 (15.9%);
English Language Learner: 484 (6.3%); Migrant: n/a
Eligible for Free Lunch Program: 2,123 (27.5%)
Eligible for Reduced-Price Lunch Program: 495 (6.4%)
Teachers: 473.1 (16.3 to 1)
Librarians/Media Specialists: 12.0 (643.5 to 1)
Guidance Counselors: 12.0 (643.5 to 1)
Current Spending: ($ per student per year):
Total: $6,897; Instruction: $4,558; Support Services: $2,132

Enrollment, Drop-out Rates and Diploma Recipients by Race/Ethnicity

Category	Total	White	Black	Asian	AIAN	Hisp.
Enrollment (%)	100.0	75.6	6.2	1.9	0.2	16.2
Drop-out Rate (%)	4.5	3.7	6.9	3.0	0.0	9.2
H.S. Diplomas (#)	541	452	23	11	0	55

Rock Island SD 41

2101 6th Ave • Rock Island, IL 61201-8116
(309) 793-5900 • http://www.rockis.k12.il.us/
Grade Span: PK-12; **Agency Type:** 1
Schools: 18
13 Primary; 3 Middle; 1 High; 1 Other Level
15 Regular; 3 Special Education; 0 Vocational; 0 Alternative
0 Magnet; 0 Charter; 12 Title I Eligible; 8 School-wide Title I
Students: 6,720 (50.8% male; 49.2% female)
Individual Education Program: 1,207 (18.0%);
English Language Learner: 74 (1.1%); Migrant: n/a
Eligible for Free Lunch Program: 3,116 (46.4%)
Eligible for Reduced-Price Lunch Program: 395 (5.9%)
Teachers: 426.9 (15.7 to 1)
Librarians/Media Specialists: 2.0 (3,360.0 to 1)
Guidance Counselors: 6.0 (1,120.0 to 1)
Current Spending: ($ per student per year):
Total: $7,044; Instruction: $4,585; Support Services: $2,149
Enrollment, Drop-out Rates and Diploma Recipients by Race/Ethnicity

Category	Total	White	Black	Asian	AIAN	Hisp.
Enrollment (%)	100.0	54.8	36.2	0.5	0.2	8.3
Drop-out Rate (%)	5.1	4.0	7.8	0.0	0.0	3.4
H.S. Diplomas (#)	300	227	63	0	0	10

Sherrard Community Unit SD 200

PO Box 369 • Sherrard, IL 61281-0369
(309) 593-4075
Grade Span: PK-12; **Agency Type:** 1
Schools: 6
3 Primary; 2 Middle; 1 High; 0 Other Level
6 Regular; 0 Special Education; 0 Vocational; 0 Alternative
0 Magnet; 0 Charter; 2 Title I Eligible; 0 School-wide Title I
Students: 1,793 (50.1% male; 49.9% female)
Individual Education Program: 245 (13.7%);
English Language Learner: 8 (0.4%); Migrant: n/a
Eligible for Free Lunch Program: 273 (15.2%)
Eligible for Reduced-Price Lunch Program: 107 (6.0%)
Teachers: 124.8 (14.4 to 1)
Librarians/Media Specialists: 1.0 (1,793.0 to 1)
Guidance Counselors: 2.6 (689.6 to 1)
Current Spending: ($ per student per year):
Total: $6,193; Instruction: $3,708; Support Services: $2,167
Enrollment, Drop-out Rates and Diploma Recipients by Race/Ethnicity

Category	Total	White	Black	Asian	AIAN	Hisp.
Enrollment (%)	100.0	96.8	0.9	0.7	0.0	1.6
Drop-out Rate (%)	5.2	5.1	n/a	0.0	n/a	12.5
H.S. Diplomas (#)	106	103	0	0	0	3

United Twp HS District 30

1275 Ave The Cities • East Moline, IL 61244-4100
(309) 752-1633 • http://uths.revealed.net/
Grade Span: 09-12; **Agency Type:** 1
Schools: 1
0 Primary; 0 Middle; 1 High; 0 Other Level
1 Regular; 0 Special Education; 0 Vocational; 0 Alternative
0 Magnet; 0 Charter; 1 Title I Eligible; 0 School-wide Title I
Students: 1,850 (52.3% male; 47.7% female)
Individual Education Program: 323 (17.5%);
English Language Learner: 31 (1.7%); Migrant: n/a
Eligible for Free Lunch Program: 453 (24.5%)
Eligible for Reduced-Price Lunch Program: 116 (6.3%)
Teachers: 96.2 (19.2 to 1)
Librarians/Media Specialists: 1.0 (1,850.0 to 1)
Guidance Counselors: 6.0 (308.3 to 1)
Current Spending: ($ per student per year):
Total: $6,491; Instruction: $3,798; Support Services: $2,397
Enrollment, Drop-out Rates and Diploma Recipients by Race/Ethnicity

Category	Total	White	Black	Asian	AIAN	Hisp.
Enrollment (%)	100.0	73.5	8.0	1.6	0.6	16.3
Drop-out Rate (%)	7.2	6.8	8.8	3.6	16.7	8.9
H.S. Diplomas (#)	347	280	22	8	2	35

Saline County

Harrisburg CUSD 3

40 S Main St • Harrisburg, IL 62946-1638
(618) 253-7637 • http://www.hbg.saline.k12.il.us/
Grade Span: PK-12; **Agency Type:** 1
Schools: 4
2 Primary; 1 Middle; 1 High; 0 Other Level
4 Regular; 0 Special Education; 0 Vocational; 0 Alternative
0 Magnet; 0 Charter; 2 Title I Eligible; 2 School-wide Title I
Students: 2,167 (50.2% male; 49.8% female)
Individual Education Program: 323 (14.9%);
English Language Learner: 0 (0.0%); Migrant: n/a
Eligible for Free Lunch Program: 643 (29.7%)
Eligible for Reduced-Price Lunch Program: 112 (5.2%)
Teachers: 135.0 (16.1 to 1)
Librarians/Media Specialists: 4.0 (541.8 to 1)
Guidance Counselors: 2.0 (1,083.5 to 1)
Current Spending: ($ per student per year):
Total: $6,338; Instruction: $4,096; Support Services: $2,029
Enrollment, Drop-out Rates and Diploma Recipients by Race/Ethnicity

Category	Total	White	Black	Asian	AIAN	Hisp.
Enrollment (%)	100.0	93.1	5.4	0.8	0.0	0.7
Drop-out Rate (%)	3.9	4.0	3.1	0.0	n/a	0.0
H.S. Diplomas (#)	119	113	6	0	0	0

Sangamon County

Ball Chatham CUSD 5

201 W Mulberry • Chatham, IL 62629-1615
(217) 483-2416 • http://dist5.bcsd.k12.il.us/default.htm
Grade Span: PK-12; **Agency Type:** 1
Schools: 5
2 Primary; 2 Middle; 1 High; 0 Other Level
5 Regular; 0 Special Education; 0 Vocational; 0 Alternative
0 Magnet; 0 Charter; 0 Title I Eligible; 0 School-wide Title I
Students: 3,978 (52.0% male; 48.0% female)
Individual Education Program: 508 (12.8%);
English Language Learner: 0 (0.0%); Migrant: n/a
Eligible for Free Lunch Program: 187 (4.7%)
Eligible for Reduced-Price Lunch Program: 46 (1.2%)
Teachers: 217.9 (18.3 to 1)
Librarians/Media Specialists: 5.0 (795.6 to 1)
Guidance Counselors: 7.0 (568.3 to 1)
Current Spending: ($ per student per year):
Total: $5,098; Instruction: $2,877; Support Services: $1,921
Enrollment, Drop-out Rates and Diploma Recipients by Race/Ethnicity

Category	Total	White	Black	Asian	AIAN	Hisp.
Enrollment (%)	100.0	94.5	2.4	2.2	0.3	0.7
Drop-out Rate (%)	1.2	1.3	0.0	0.0	0.0	0.0
H.S. Diplomas (#)	305	291	5	5	0	4

Department of Corrections SD 428

925 E Ridgely • Springfield, IL 62702-2737
(217) 558-6098 • http://www.idoc.state.il.us/
Grade Span: 06-12; **Agency Type:** 5
Schools: 41
0 Primary; 0 Middle; 37 High; 4 Other Level
0 Regular; 0 Special Education; 0 Vocational; 41 Alternative
0 Magnet; 0 Charter; 0 Title I Eligible; 0 School-wide Title I
Students: 9,976 (89.9% male; 10.1% female)
Individual Education Program: 819 (8.2%);
English Language Learner: 0 (0.0%); Migrant: n/a
Eligible for Free Lunch Program: 2,158 (21.6%)
Eligible for Reduced-Price Lunch Program: 0 (0.0%)
Teachers: 307.6 (32.4 to 1)
Librarians/Media Specialists: 0.0 (0.0 to 1)
Guidance Counselors: 0.0 (0.0 to 1)
Current Spending: ($ per student per year):
Total: n/a; Instruction: n/a; Support Services: n/a
Enrollment, Drop-out Rates and Diploma Recipients by Race/Ethnicity

Category	Total	White	Black	Asian	AIAN	Hisp.
Enrollment (%)	100.0	24.5	60.5	0.2	0.1	14.6
Drop-out Rate (%)	n/a	n/a	n/a	n/a	n/a	n/a
H.S. Diplomas (#)	0	0	0	0	0	0

Rochester Community Unit SD 3A

4 Rocket Dr • Rochester, IL 62563-9282
(217) 498-6210 • http://209.7.254.7/rocket1/pform.htm
Grade Span: PK-12; **Agency Type:** 1
Schools: 4
1 Primary; 2 Middle; 1 High; 0 Other Level
4 Regular; 0 Special Education; 0 Vocational; 0 Alternative
0 Magnet; 0 Charter; 0 Title I Eligible; 0 School-wide Title I
Students: 1,883 (52.6% male; 47.4% female)
Individual Education Program: 300 (15.9%);
English Language Learner: 2 (0.1%); Migrant: n/a
Eligible for Free Lunch Program: 52 (2.8%)
Eligible for Reduced-Price Lunch Program: 13 (0.7%)
Teachers: 108.3 (17.4 to 1)
Librarians/Media Specialists: 3.0 (627.7 to 1)
Guidance Counselors: 2.0 (941.5 to 1)
Current Spending: ($ per student per year):
Total: $5,177; Instruction: $2,813; Support Services: $2,146

Enrollment, Drop-out Rates and Diploma Recipients by Race/Ethnicity

Category	Total	White	Black	Asian	AIAN	Hisp.
Enrollment (%)	100.0	97.1	0.8	1.1	0.1	0.9
Drop-out Rate (%)	0.3	0.3	0.0	0.0	0.0	n/a
H.S. Diplomas (#)	154	150	2	1	0	1

Springfield SD 186

1900 W Monroe St • Springfield, IL 62704-1599
(217) 525-3002 • http://www.springfield.k12.il.us/
Grade Span: PK-12; **Agency Type:** 1
Schools: 36
25 Primary; 5 Middle; 3 High; 3 Other Level
32 Regular; 4 Special Education; 0 Vocational; 0 Alternative
5 Magnet; 1 Charter; 20 Title I Eligible; 15 School-wide Title I
Students: 15,330 (51.5% male; 48.5% female)
Individual Education Program: 2,926 (19.1%);
English Language Learner: 31 (0.2%); Migrant: n/a
Eligible for Free Lunch Program: 7,226 (47.1%)
Eligible for Reduced-Price Lunch Program: 993 (6.5%)
Teachers: 953.8 (16.1 to 1)
Librarians/Media Specialists: 12.0 (1,277.5 to 1)
Guidance Counselors: 0.0 (0.0 to 1)
Current Spending: ($ per student per year):
Total: $7,714; Instruction: $4,149; Support Services: $3,196
Enrollment, Drop-out Rates and Diploma Recipients by Race/Ethnicity

Category	Total	White	Black	Asian	AIAN	Hisp.
Enrollment (%)	100.0	60.5	36.1	1.8	0.2	1.4
Drop-out Rate (%)	1.5	1.3	2.1	0.0	0.0	5.4
H.S. Diplomas (#)	803	593	181	21	0	8

St. Clair County

Belleville SD 118

105 W A St • Belleville, IL 62220-1326
(618) 233-2830 • http://www.belleville118.stclair.k12.il.us/
Grade Span: PK-08; **Agency Type:** 1
Schools: 11
9 Primary; 2 Middle; 0 High; 0 Other Level
11 Regular; 0 Special Education; 0 Vocational; 0 Alternative
0 Magnet; 0 Charter; 6 Title I Eligible; 1 School-wide Title I
Students: 3,695 (52.7% male; 47.3% female)
Individual Education Program: 813 (22.0%);
English Language Learner: 9 (0.2%); Migrant: n/a
Eligible for Free Lunch Program: 1,283 (34.7%)
Eligible for Reduced-Price Lunch Program: 349 (9.4%)
Teachers: 207.5 (17.8 to 1)
Librarians/Media Specialists: 0.0 (0.0 to 1)
Guidance Counselors: 0.0 (0.0 to 1)
Current Spending: ($ per student per year):
Total: $7,201; Instruction: $4,149; Support Services: $2,565
Enrollment, Drop-out Rates and Diploma Recipients by Race/Ethnicity

Category	Total	White	Black	Asian	AIAN	Hisp.
Enrollment (%)	100.0	64.4	32.0	1.4	0.5	1.7
Drop-out Rate (%)	n/a	n/a	n/a	n/a	n/a	n/a
H.S. Diplomas (#)	n/a	n/a	n/a	n/a	n/a	n/a

Belleville Twp HSD 201

2600 W Main St • Belleville, IL 62226-6651
(618) 222-8200 • http://www.bths201.stclair.k12.il.us/
Grade Span: 09-12; **Agency Type:** 1
Schools: 3
0 Primary; 0 Middle; 3 High; 0 Other Level
2 Regular; 1 Special Education; 0 Vocational; 0 Alternative
0 Magnet; 0 Charter; 2 Title I Eligible; 0 School-wide Title I
Students: 4,859 (51.6% male; 48.4% female)
Individual Education Program: 707 (14.6%);
English Language Learner: 11 (0.2%); Migrant: n/a
Eligible for Free Lunch Program: 692 (14.2%)
Eligible for Reduced-Price Lunch Program: 231 (4.8%)
Teachers: 238.6 (20.4 to 1)
Librarians/Media Specialists: 4.0 (1,214.8 to 1)
Guidance Counselors: 10.0 (485.9 to 1)
Current Spending: ($ per student per year):
Total: $6,775; Instruction: $4,252; Support Services: $2,295
Enrollment, Drop-out Rates and Diploma Recipients by Race/Ethnicity

Category	Total	White	Black	Asian	AIAN	Hisp.
Enrollment (%)	100.0	74.2	21.8	1.8	0.6	1.6
Drop-out Rate (%)	3.8	3.5	5.0	4.2	6.7	7.6
H.S. Diplomas (#)	1,009	800	176	18	5	10

Cahokia Community Unit SD 187

1700 Jerome Ln • Cahokia, IL 62206-2329
(618) 332-3700 • http://www.cahokia.stclair.k12.il.us/
Grade Span: PK-12; **Agency Type:** 1
Schools: 10
7 Primary; 1 Middle; 1 High; 1 Other Level
9 Regular; 1 Special Education; 0 Vocational; 0 Alternative
0 Magnet; 1 Charter; 8 Title I Eligible; 6 School-wide Title I
Students: 5,136 (50.1% male; 49.9% female)
Individual Education Program: 972 (18.9%);
English Language Learner: 10 (0.2%); Migrant: n/a
Eligible for Free Lunch Program: 3,170 (61.7%)
Eligible for Reduced-Price Lunch Program: 341 (6.6%)
Teachers: 258.9 (19.8 to 1)
Librarians/Media Specialists: 1.0 (5,136.0 to 1)
Guidance Counselors: 5.0 (1,027.2 to 1)
Current Spending: ($ per student per year):
Total: $7,617; Instruction: $4,310; Support Services: $2,757
Enrollment, Drop-out Rates and Diploma Recipients by Race/Ethnicity

Category	Total	White	Black	Asian	AIAN	Hisp.
Enrollment (%)	100.0	20.4	78.0	0.1	0.0	1.5
Drop-out Rate (%)	6.3	8.6	5.5	0.0	n/a	0.0
H.S. Diplomas (#)	189	57	129	0	0	3

East Saint Louis SD 189

1005 State St • East Saint Louis, IL 62201-1907
(618) 646-3009 • http://www.estlouis.stclair.k12.il.us/
Grade Span: PK-12; **Agency Type:** 1
Schools: 29
20 Primary; 3 Middle; 4 High; 2 Other Level
25 Regular; 4 Special Education; 0 Vocational; 0 Alternative
0 Magnet; 2 Charter; 25 Title I Eligible; 25 School-wide Title I
Students: 10,637 (49.4% male; 50.6% female)
Individual Education Program: 2,208 (20.8%);
English Language Learner: 55 (0.5%); Migrant: n/a
Eligible for Free Lunch Program: 7,492 (70.4%)
Eligible for Reduced-Price Lunch Program: 511 (4.8%)
Teachers: 637.0 (16.7 to 1)
Librarians/Media Specialists: 6.0 (1,772.8 to 1)
Guidance Counselors: 15.0 (709.1 to 1)
Current Spending: ($ per student per year):
Total: $7,446; Instruction: $4,390; Support Services: $2,677
Enrollment, Drop-out Rates and Diploma Recipients by Race/Ethnicity

Category	Total	White	Black	Asian	AIAN	Hisp.
Enrollment (%)	100.0	0.3	98.6	0.0	0.0	1.1
Drop-out Rate (%)	10.2	0.0	10.2	n/a	n/a	n/a
H.S. Diplomas (#)	328	1	327	0	0	0

Mascoutah C U District 19

720 W Harnett St • Mascoutah, IL 62258-1121
(618) 566-7414 • http://www.mascoutah19.k12.il.us/
Grade Span: PK-12; **Agency Type:** 1
Schools: 4
2 Primary; 1 Middle; 1 High; 0 Other Level
4 Regular; 0 Special Education; 0 Vocational; 0 Alternative
0 Magnet; 0 Charter; 1 Title I Eligible; 1 School-wide Title I
Students: 2,967 (50.5% male; 49.5% female)
Individual Education Program: 428 (14.4%);
English Language Learner: 0 (0.0%); Migrant: n/a
Eligible for Free Lunch Program: 233 (7.9%)
Eligible for Reduced-Price Lunch Program: 331 (11.2%)
Teachers: 185.5 (16.0 to 1)
Librarians/Media Specialists: 3.0 (989.0 to 1)
Guidance Counselors: 4.0 (741.8 to 1)
Current Spending: ($ per student per year):
Total: $7,073; Instruction: $4,251; Support Services: $2,528
Enrollment, Drop-out Rates and Diploma Recipients by Race/Ethnicity

Category	Total	White	Black	Asian	AIAN	Hisp.
Enrollment (%)	100.0	79.1	14.4	3.0	0.6	3.0
Drop-out Rate (%)	0.7	0.6	1.0	0.0	0.0	0.0
H.S. Diplomas (#)	172	143	21	5	0	3

O'Fallon CCSD 90

707 N Smiley St • Ofallon, IL 62269-1353
(618) 632-3666 • http://www.ofallon90.stclair.k12.il.us/
Grade Span: PK-08; **Agency Type:** 1
Schools: 5
3 Primary; 2 Middle; 0 High; 0 Other Level
5 Regular; 0 Special Education; 0 Vocational; 0 Alternative
0 Magnet; 0 Charter; 3 Title I Eligible; 0 School-wide Title I
Students: 3,095 (51.1% male; 48.9% female)
Individual Education Program: 548 (17.7%);
English Language Learner: 7 (0.2%); Migrant: n/a
Eligible for Free Lunch Program: 455 (14.7%)
Eligible for Reduced-Price Lunch Program: 77 (2.5%)
Teachers: 166.1 (18.6 to 1)
Librarians/Media Specialists: 1.0 (3,095.0 to 1)
Guidance Counselors: 0.0 (0.0 to 1)
Current Spending: ($ per student per year):
Total: $5,788; Instruction: $3,809; Support Services: $1,789

Enrollment, Drop-out Rates and Diploma Recipients by Race/Ethnicity

Category	Total	White	Black	Asian	AIAN	Hisp.
Enrollment (%)	100.0	78.5	16.8	2.7	0.3	1.7
Drop-out Rate (%)	n/a	n/a	n/a	n/a	n/a	n/a
H.S. Diplomas (#)	n/a	n/a	n/a	n/a	n/a	n/a

O'Fallon Twp High SD 203

600 S Smiley St • Ofallon, IL 62269-2399
(618) 632-3507 • http://www.oths.k12.il.us/
Grade Span: 09-12; **Agency Type:** 1
Schools: 1
0 Primary; 0 Middle; 1 High; 0 Other Level
1 Regular; 0 Special Education; 0 Vocational; 0 Alternative
0 Magnet; 0 Charter; 1 Title I Eligible; 0 School-wide Title I
Students: 2,124 (48.8% male; 51.2% female)
Individual Education Program: 205 (9.7%);
English Language Learner: 0 (0.0%); Migrant: n/a
Eligible for Free Lunch Program: 145 (6.8%)
Eligible for Reduced-Price Lunch Program: 41 (1.9%)
Teachers: 109.3 (19.4 to 1)
Librarians/Media Specialists: 1.0 (2,124.0 to 1)
Guidance Counselors: 5.0 (424.8 to 1)
Current Spending: ($ per student per year):
Total: $6,378; Instruction: $3,696; Support Services: $2,152

Enrollment, Drop-out Rates and Diploma Recipients by Race/Ethnicity

Category	Total	White	Black	Asian	AIAN	Hisp.
Enrollment (%)	100.0	78.7	15.5	3.4	0.0	2.3
Drop-out Rate (%)	1.8	1.9	2.0	0.0	n/a	3.1
H.S. Diplomas (#)	471	390	60	15	0	6

Stephenson County

Freeport SD 145

501 E S St • Freeport, IL 61032-9676
(815) 232-0300 • http://www.freeportschooldistrict.com/index.cfm
Grade Span: PK-12; **Agency Type:** 1
Schools: 10
6 Primary; 2 Middle; 1 High; 1 Other Level
9 Regular; 1 Special Education; 0 Vocational; 0 Alternative
0 Magnet; 0 Charter; 5 Title I Eligible; 2 School-wide Title I
Students: 4,497 (50.1% male; 49.9% female)
Individual Education Program: 616 (13.7%);
English Language Learner: 45 (1.0%); Migrant: n/a
Eligible for Free Lunch Program: 1,715 (38.1%)
Eligible for Reduced-Price Lunch Program: 370 (8.2%)
Teachers: 302.9 (14.8 to 1)
Librarians/Media Specialists: 3.0 (1,499.0 to 1)
Guidance Counselors: 6.0 (749.5 to 1)
Current Spending: ($ per student per year):
Total: $6,641; Instruction: $3,720; Support Services: $2,649

Enrollment, Drop-out Rates and Diploma Recipients by Race/Ethnicity

Category	Total	White	Black	Asian	AIAN	Hisp.
Enrollment (%)	100.0	69.0	25.8	1.6	0.1	3.4
Drop-out Rate (%)	6.0	5.1	10.1	3.8	0.0	4.2
H.S. Diplomas (#)	307	255	42	5	0	5

Tazewell County

East Peoria SD 86

601 Taylor St • East Peoria, IL 61611-2643
(309) 427-5100 • http://www.epd86.org/
Grade Span: PK-08; **Agency Type:** 1
Schools: 7
6 Primary; 1 Middle; 0 High; 0 Other Level
7 Regular; 0 Special Education; 0 Vocational; 0 Alternative
0 Magnet; 0 Charter; 5 Title I Eligible; 0 School-wide Title I
Students: 1,931 (52.6% male; 47.4% female)
Individual Education Program: 377 (19.5%);
English Language Learner: 22 (1.1%); Migrant: n/a
Eligible for Free Lunch Program: 514 (26.6%)
Eligible for Reduced-Price Lunch Program: 81 (4.2%)
Teachers: 120.4 (16.0 to 1)
Librarians/Media Specialists: 1.0 (1,931.0 to 1)
Guidance Counselors: 1.0 (1,931.0 to 1)
Current Spending: ($ per student per year):
Total: $7,069; Instruction: $4,388; Support Services: $2,416

Enrollment, Drop-out Rates and Diploma Recipients by Race/Ethnicity

Category	Total	White	Black	Asian	AIAN	Hisp.
Enrollment (%)	100.0	94.8	1.5	1.1	0.2	2.5
Drop-out Rate (%)	n/a	n/a	n/a	n/a	n/a	n/a
H.S. Diplomas (#)	n/a	n/a	n/a	n/a	n/a	n/a

Morton CUSD 709

235 E Jackson St • Morton, IL 61550-1600
(309) 263-2581 • http://www.morton709.org/
Grade Span: PK-12; **Agency Type:** 1
Schools: 6
4 Primary; 1 Middle; 1 High; 0 Other Level
6 Regular; 0 Special Education; 0 Vocational; 0 Alternative
0 Magnet; 0 Charter; 2 Title I Eligible; 0 School-wide Title I
Students: 2,737 (51.7% male; 48.3% female)
Individual Education Program: 361 (13.2%);
English Language Learner: 0 (0.0%); Migrant: n/a
Eligible for Free Lunch Program: 147 (5.4%)
Eligible for Reduced-Price Lunch Program: 24 (0.9%)
Teachers: 174.1 (15.7 to 1)
Librarians/Media Specialists: 3.7 (739.7 to 1)
Guidance Counselors: 4.0 (684.3 to 1)
Current Spending: ($ per student per year):
Total: $7,177; Instruction: $4,444; Support Services: $2,535

Enrollment, Drop-out Rates and Diploma Recipients by Race/Ethnicity

Category	Total	White	Black	Asian	AIAN	Hisp.
Enrollment (%)	100.0	96.2	0.5	1.7	0.3	1.3
Drop-out Rate (%)	1.9	1.9	0.0	6.3	0.0	0.0
H.S. Diplomas (#)	230	224	0	2	1	3

Pekin Community HSD 303

320 Stadium Dr • Pekin, IL 61554-5295
(309) 477-4222 • http://www.pekinhigh.net/
Grade Span: 09-12; **Agency Type:** 1
Schools: 1
0 Primary; 0 Middle; 1 High; 0 Other Level
1 Regular; 0 Special Education; 0 Vocational; 0 Alternative
0 Magnet; 0 Charter; 1 Title I Eligible; 0 School-wide Title I
Students: 2,134 (51.6% male; 48.4% female)
Individual Education Program: 254 (11.9%);
English Language Learner: 6 (0.3%); Migrant: n/a
Eligible for Free Lunch Program: 471 (22.1%)
Eligible for Reduced-Price Lunch Program: 103 (4.8%)
Teachers: 119.5 (17.9 to 1)
Librarians/Media Specialists: 1.0 (2,134.0 to 1)
Guidance Counselors: 7.0 (304.9 to 1)
Current Spending: ($ per student per year):
Total: $6,709; Instruction: $3,920; Support Services: $2,580

Enrollment, Drop-out Rates and Diploma Recipients by Race/Ethnicity

Category	Total	White	Black	Asian	AIAN	Hisp.
Enrollment (%)	100.0	99.2	0.1	0.2	0.1	0.3
Drop-out Rate (%)	2.5	2.5	0.0	0.0	0.0	0.0
H.S. Diplomas (#)	413	411	1	1	0	0

Pekin Public SD 108

501 Washington St • Pekin, IL 61554-4239
(309) 477-4740 • http://www.pekin.net/pekin108/
Grade Span: PK-12; **Agency Type:** 1
Schools: 11
6 Primary; 4 Middle; 0 High; 1 Other Level
10 Regular; 1 Special Education; 0 Vocational; 0 Alternative
0 Magnet; 0 Charter; 10 Title I Eligible; 0 School-wide Title I
Students: 3,816 (50.6% male; 49.4% female)
Individual Education Program: 802 (21.0%);
English Language Learner: 12 (0.3%); Migrant: n/a
Eligible for Free Lunch Program: 1,345 (35.2%)
Eligible for Reduced-Price Lunch Program: 345 (9.0%)
Teachers: 239.8 (15.9 to 1)
Librarians/Media Specialists: 10.0 (381.6 to 1)
Guidance Counselors: 5.0 (763.2 to 1)
Current Spending: ($ per student per year):
Total: $6,484; Instruction: $3,995; Support Services: $2,259

Enrollment, Drop-out Rates and Diploma Recipients by Race/Ethnicity

Category	Total	White	Black	Asian	AIAN	Hisp.
Enrollment (%)	100.0	97.7	0.6	0.6	0.3	0.8
Drop-out Rate (%)	0.0	0.0	n/a	n/a	n/a	n/a
H.S. Diplomas (#)	0	0	0	0	0	0

Vermilion County

Danville CCSD 118

516 N Jackson St • Danville, IL 61832-4684
(217) 444-1004 • http://www.danville.k12.il.us/Home.asp
Grade Span: PK-12; **Agency Type:** 1
Schools: 11
8 Primary; 2 Middle; 1 High; 0 Other Level
11 Regular; 0 Special Education; 0 Vocational; 0 Alternative
1 Magnet; 0 Charter; 10 Title I Eligible; 10 School-wide Title I
Students: 6,217 (50.3% male; 49.7% female)
Individual Education Program: 1,126 (18.1%);
English Language Learner: 0 (0.0%); Migrant: n/a

Eligible for Free Lunch Program: 3,304 (53.1%)
Eligible for Reduced-Price Lunch Program: 397 (6.4%)
Teachers: 409.1 (15.2 to 1)
Librarians/Media Specialists: 1.0 (6,217.0 to 1)
Guidance Counselors: 7.0 (888.1 to 1)
Current Spending: ($ per student per year):
Total: $8,025; Instruction: $4,701; Support Services: $3,014
Enrollment, Drop-out Rates and Diploma Recipients by Race/Ethnicity

Category	Total	White	Black	Asian	AIAN	Hisp.
Enrollment (%)	100.0	56.1	36.9	1.3	0.2	5.5
Drop-out Rate (%)	9.7	7.9	14.4	0.0	0.0	12.5
H.S. Diplomas (#)	272	205	52	6	0	9

Wabash County

Wabash CUSD 348

218 W 13th St • Mount Carmel, IL 62863-1297
(618) 262-4181 • http://www.d348.wabash.k12.il.us/
Grade Span: PK-12; **Agency Type:** 1
Schools: 4
2 Primary; 1 Middle; 1 High; 0 Other Level
4 Regular; 0 Special Education; 0 Vocational; 0 Alternative
0 Magnet; 0 Charter; 2 Title I Eligible; 0 School-wide Title I
Students: 1,901 (51.1% male; 48.9% female)
Individual Education Program: 274 (14.4%);
English Language Learner: 1 (0.1%); Migrant: n/a
Eligible for Free Lunch Program: 408 (21.5%)
Eligible for Reduced-Price Lunch Program: 83 (4.4%)
Teachers: 127.4 (14.9 to 1)
Librarians/Media Specialists: 1.0 (1,901.0 to 1)
Guidance Counselors: 3.0 (633.7 to 1)
Current Spending: ($ per student per year):
Total: $5,952; Instruction: $3,840; Support Services: $1,923
Enrollment, Drop-out Rates and Diploma Recipients by Race/Ethnicity

Category	Total	White	Black	Asian	AIAN	Hisp.
Enrollment (%)	100.0	98.2	0.8	0.6	0.1	0.3
Drop-out Rate (%)	5.2	5.2	n/a	n/a	n/a	n/a
H.S. Diplomas (#)	158	158	0	0	0	0

Warren County

Monmouth Unit SD 38

321 E Euclid Ave • Monmouth, IL 61462-2473
(309) 734-4712 • http://zippers.warren.k12.il.us/district/welcome.htm
Grade Span: PK-12; **Agency Type:** 1
Schools: 6
3 Primary; 2 Middle; 1 High; 0 Other Level
5 Regular; 1 Special Education; 0 Vocational; 0 Alternative
0 Magnet; 0 Charter; 4 Title I Eligible; 2 School-wide Title I
Students: 1,511 (50.1% male; 49.9% female)
Individual Education Program: 278 (18.4%);
English Language Learner: 64 (4.2%); Migrant: n/a
Eligible for Free Lunch Program: 511 (33.8%)
Eligible for Reduced-Price Lunch Program: 106 (7.0%)
Teachers: 105.0 (14.4 to 1)
Librarians/Media Specialists: 5.0 (302.2 to 1)
Guidance Counselors: 4.0 (377.8 to 1)
Current Spending: ($ per student per year):
Total: $5,499; Instruction: $3,495; Support Services: $1,765
Enrollment, Drop-out Rates and Diploma Recipients by Race/Ethnicity

Category	Total	White	Black	Asian	AIAN	Hisp.
Enrollment (%)	100.0	84.2	5.8	0.8	0.5	8.8
Drop-out Rate (%)	4.1	4.5	0.0	0.0	0.0	0.0
H.S. Diplomas (#)	93	83	4	0	0	6

White County

Carmi-White County CUSD 5

301 W Main St • Carmi, IL 62821-1499
(618) 382-2341 • http://www.carmi.white.k12.il.us/
Grade Span: PK-12; **Agency Type:** 1
Schools: 7
3 Primary; 2 Middle; 1 High; 1 Other Level
5 Regular; 2 Special Education; 0 Vocational; 0 Alternative
0 Magnet; 0 Charter; 4 Title I Eligible; 3 School-wide Title I
Students: 1,556 (51.2% male; 48.8% female)
Individual Education Program: 312 (20.1%);
English Language Learner: 0 (0.0%); Migrant: n/a
Eligible for Free Lunch Program: 483 (31.0%)
Eligible for Reduced-Price Lunch Program: 77 (4.9%)
Teachers: 104.4 (14.9 to 1)
Librarians/Media Specialists: 1.0 (1,556.0 to 1)
Guidance Counselors: 2.5 (622.4 to 1)
Current Spending: ($ per student per year):
Total: $7,135; Instruction: $4,265; Support Services: $2,578

Enrollment, Drop-out Rates and Diploma Recipients by Race/Ethnicity

Category	Total	White	Black	Asian	AIAN	Hisp.
Enrollment (%)	100.0	97.9	1.2	0.3	0.1	0.5
Drop-out Rate (%)	7.6	7.7	0.0	0.0	n/a	0.0
H.S. Diplomas (#)	107	107	0	0	0	0

Sterling C U Dist 5

410 E Le Fevre Rd • Sterling, IL 61081-1399
(815) 626-5050 • http://www.sterlingschools.org/
Grade Span: PK-12; **Agency Type:** 1
Schools: 7
4 Primary; 1 Middle; 1 High; 1 Other Level
6 Regular; 1 Special Education; 0 Vocational; 0 Alternative
0 Magnet; 0 Charter; 3 Title I Eligible; 1 School-wide Title I
Students: 3,662 (52.6% male; 47.4% female)
Individual Education Program: 582 (15.9%);
English Language Learner: 105 (2.9%); Migrant: n/a
Eligible for Free Lunch Program: 967 (26.4%)
Eligible for Reduced-Price Lunch Program: 287 (7.8%)
Teachers: 238.5 (15.4 to 1)
Librarians/Media Specialists: 1.0 (3,662.0 to 1)
Guidance Counselors: 4.0 (915.5 to 1)
Current Spending: ($ per student per year):
Total: $6,875; Instruction: $4,506; Support Services: $2,129
Enrollment, Drop-out Rates and Diploma Recipients by Race/Ethnicity

Category	Total	White	Black	Asian	AIAN	Hisp.
Enrollment (%)	100.0	72.5	4.3	0.8	0.4	22.0
Drop-out Rate (%)	8.0	6.6	13.9	0.0	0.0	13.8
H.S. Diplomas (#)	231	186	9	7	0	29

Will County

Channahon SD 17

24920 S Sage St • Channahon, IL 60410-9680
(815) 467-4315
Grade Span: PK-08; **Agency Type:** 1
Schools: 3
2 Primary; 1 Middle; 0 High; 0 Other Level
3 Regular; 0 Special Education; 0 Vocational; 0 Alternative
0 Magnet; 0 Charter; 0 Title I Eligible; 0 School-wide Title I
Students: 1,510 (52.5% male; 47.5% female)
Individual Education Program: 241 (16.0%);
English Language Learner: 0 (0.0%); Migrant: n/a
Eligible for Free Lunch Program: 71 (4.7%)
Eligible for Reduced-Price Lunch Program: 16 (1.1%)
Teachers: 72.9 (20.7 to 1)
Librarians/Media Specialists: 0.0 (0.0 to 1)
Guidance Counselors: 1.0 (1,510.0 to 1)
Current Spending: ($ per student per year):
Total: $5,339; Instruction: $2,971; Support Services: $2,164
Enrollment, Drop-out Rates and Diploma Recipients by Race/Ethnicity

Category	Total	White	Black	Asian	AIAN	Hisp.
Enrollment (%)	100.0	93.6	0.9	0.2	0.1	5.2
Drop-out Rate (%)	n/a	n/a	n/a	n/a	n/a	n/a
H.S. Diplomas (#)	n/a	n/a	n/a	n/a	n/a	n/a

Crete Monee CUSD 201U

1500 Sangamon St • Crete, IL 60417-2899
(708) 672-2680 • http://www.cm201u.org/
Grade Span: PK-12; **Agency Type:** 1
Schools: 8
5 Primary; 2 Middle; 1 High; 0 Other Level
8 Regular; 0 Special Education; 0 Vocational; 0 Alternative
0 Magnet; 0 Charter; 2 Title I Eligible; 1 School-wide Title I
Students: 4,841 (51.0% male; 49.0% female)
Individual Education Program: 978 (20.2%);
English Language Learner: 23 (0.5%); Migrant: n/a
Eligible for Free Lunch Program: 1,783 (36.8%)
Eligible for Reduced-Price Lunch Program: 321 (6.6%)
Teachers: 255.1 (19.0 to 1)
Librarians/Media Specialists: 1.0 (4,841.0 to 1)
Guidance Counselors: 5.0 (968.2 to 1)
Current Spending: ($ per student per year):
Total: $7,026; Instruction: $3,631; Support Services: $3,079
Enrollment, Drop-out Rates and Diploma Recipients by Race/Ethnicity

Category	Total	White	Black	Asian	AIAN	Hisp.
Enrollment (%)	100.0	43.2	51.4	0.8	0.0	4.6
Drop-out Rate (%)	1.4	0.9	1.8	0.0	n/a	3.3
H.S. Diplomas (#)	266	133	118	3	0	12

Frankfort CCSD 157c

10482 W Nebraska St • Frankfort, IL 60423-2235
(815) 469-5922 • http://www.fsd157c.org/
Grade Span: PK-08; **Agency Type:** 1
Schools: 3

1 Primary; 2 Middle; 0 High; 0 Other Level
3 Regular; 0 Special Education; 0 Vocational; 0 Alternative
0 Magnet; 0 Charter; 0 Title I Eligible; 0 School-wide Title I
Students: 1,788 (50.6% male; 49.4% female)
Individual Education Program: 206 (11.5%);
English Language Learner: 0 (0.0%); Migrant: n/a
Eligible for Free Lunch Program: 0 (0.0%)
Eligible for Reduced-Price Lunch Program: 0 (0.0%)
Teachers: 110.5 (16.2 to 1)
Librarians/Media Specialists: 0.0 (0.0 to 1)
Guidance Counselors: 0.0 (0.0 to 1)
Current Spending: ($ per student per year):
Total: $5,581; Instruction: $3,014; Support Services: $2,550
Enrollment, Drop-out Rates and Diploma Recipients by Race/Ethnicity

Category	Total	White	Black	Asian	AIAN	Hisp.
Enrollment (%)	100.0	94.0	1.6	1.7	0.0	2.7
Drop-out Rate (%)	n/a	n/a	n/a	n/a	n/a	n/a
H.S. Diplomas (#)	n/a	n/a	n/a	n/a	n/a	n/a

Homer Community CSD 33C
15733 Bell Rd • Lockport, IL 60441-8404
(708) 301-3034 • http://www.homerschools.org/
Grade Span: KG-08; **Agency Type:** 1
Schools: 6
4 Primary; 2 Middle; 0 High; 0 Other Level
6 Regular; 0 Special Education; 0 Vocational; 0 Alternative
0 Magnet; 0 Charter; 0 Title I Eligible; 0 School-wide Title I
Students: 3,035 (52.4% male; 47.6% female)
Individual Education Program: 428 (14.1%);
English Language Learner: 52 (1.7%); Migrant: n/a
Eligible for Free Lunch Program: 0 (0.0%)
Eligible for Reduced-Price Lunch Program: 0 (0.0%)
Teachers: 165.6 (18.3 to 1)
Librarians/Media Specialists: 1.0 (3,035.0 to 1)
Guidance Counselors: 5.0 (607.0 to 1)
Current Spending: ($ per student per year):
Total: $4,982; Instruction: $2,912; Support Services: $2,044
Enrollment, Drop-out Rates and Diploma Recipients by Race/Ethnicity

Category	Total	White	Black	Asian	AIAN	Hisp.
Enrollment (%)	100.0	92.8	0.8	1.6	0.1	4.7
Drop-out Rate (%)	n/a	n/a	n/a	n/a	n/a	n/a
H.S. Diplomas (#)	n/a	n/a	n/a	n/a	n/a	n/a

Joliet Public SD 86
420 N Raynor Ave • Joliet, IL 60435-6097
(815) 740-3196 • http://www.joliet86.will.k12.il.us/
Grade Span: PK-08; **Agency Type:** 1
Schools: 24
21 Primary; 3 Middle; 0 High; 0 Other Level
22 Regular; 2 Special Education; 0 Vocational; 0 Alternative
3 Magnet; 0 Charter; 17 Title I Eligible; 15 School-wide Title I
Students: 9,572 (50.5% male; 49.5% female)
Individual Education Program: 1,562 (16.3%);
English Language Learner: 814 (8.5%); Migrant: n/a
Eligible for Free Lunch Program: 4,905 (51.2%)
Eligible for Reduced-Price Lunch Program: 863 (9.0%)
Teachers: 518.0 (18.5 to 1)
Librarians/Media Specialists: 2.0 (4,786.0 to 1)
Guidance Counselors: 1.0 (9,572.0 to 1)
Current Spending: ($ per student per year):
Total: $6,086; Instruction: $3,511; Support Services: $2,285
Enrollment, Drop-out Rates and Diploma Recipients by Race/Ethnicity

Category	Total	White	Black	Asian	AIAN	Hisp.
Enrollment (%)	100.0	23.9	38.7	0.8	0.2	36.4
Drop-out Rate (%)	n/a	n/a	n/a	n/a	n/a	n/a
H.S. Diplomas (#)	n/a	n/a	n/a	n/a	n/a	n/a

Joliet Twp HSD 204
201 E Jefferson St • Joliet, IL 60432-2848
(815) 727-6970 • http://www.jths.org/
Grade Span: 09-12; **Agency Type:** 1
Schools: 3
0 Primary; 0 Middle; 3 High; 0 Other Level
2 Regular; 1 Special Education; 0 Vocational; 0 Alternative
0 Magnet; 0 Charter; 2 Title I Eligible; 2 School-wide Title I
Students: 4,874 (50.6% male; 49.4% female)
Individual Education Program: 872 (17.9%);
English Language Learner: 221 (4.5%); Migrant: n/a
Eligible for Free Lunch Program: 1,995 (40.9%)
Eligible for Reduced-Price Lunch Program: 565 (11.6%)
Teachers: 312.5 (15.6 to 1)
Librarians/Media Specialists: 4.0 (1,218.5 to 1)
Guidance Counselors: 15.0 (324.9 to 1)
Current Spending: ($ per student per year):
Total: $10,456; Instruction: $5,951; Support Services: $4,247
Enrollment, Drop-out Rates and Diploma Recipients by Race/Ethnicity

Category	Total	White	Black	Asian	AIAN	Hisp.
Enrollment (%)	100.0	41.7	30.9	1.4	0.2	25.8
Drop-out Rate (%)	3.7	3.2	4.1	5.3	0.0	3.9
H.S. Diplomas (#)	811	378	243	17	3	170

Lincoln Way Community HSD 210
1801 E Lincoln Hwy • New Lenox, IL 60451-2098
(815) 462-2100 • http://lwhs.will.k12.il.us/
Grade Span: 09-12; **Agency Type:** 1
Schools: 2
0 Primary; 0 Middle; 2 High; 0 Other Level
2 Regular; 0 Special Education; 0 Vocational; 0 Alternative
0 Magnet; 0 Charter; 2 Title I Eligible; 0 School-wide Title I
Students: 5,551 (50.9% male; 49.1% female)
Individual Education Program: 483 (8.7%);
English Language Learner: 12 (0.2%); Migrant: n/a
Eligible for Free Lunch Program: 96 (1.7%)
Eligible for Reduced-Price Lunch Program: 40 (0.7%)
Teachers: 288.5 (19.2 to 1)
Librarians/Media Specialists: 1.0 (5,551.0 to 1)
Guidance Counselors: 17.0 (326.5 to 1)
Current Spending: ($ per student per year):
Total: $7,387; Instruction: $4,292; Support Services: $2,830
Enrollment, Drop-out Rates and Diploma Recipients by Race/Ethnicity

Category	Total	White	Black	Asian	AIAN	Hisp.
Enrollment (%)	100.0	93.5	0.9	1.7	0.1	3.7
Drop-out Rate (%)	2.1	2.1	0.0	2.8	0.0	3.1
H.S. Diplomas (#)	1,070	1,011	11	14	7	27

Lockport Twp HSD 205
1323 E 7th St • Lockport, IL 60441-3899
(815) 588-8100 • http://www.lths.org/
Grade Span: 09-12; **Agency Type:** 1
Schools: 1
0 Primary; 0 Middle; 1 High; 0 Other Level
1 Regular; 0 Special Education; 0 Vocational; 0 Alternative
0 Magnet; 0 Charter; 1 Title I Eligible; 0 School-wide Title I
Students: 3,180 (51.8% male; 48.2% female)
Individual Education Program: 336 (10.6%);
English Language Learner: 7 (0.2%); Migrant: n/a
Eligible for Free Lunch Program: n/a
Eligible for Reduced-Price Lunch Program: n/a
Teachers: 166.9 (19.1 to 1)
Librarians/Media Specialists: 2.0 (1,590.0 to 1)
Guidance Counselors: 10.0 (318.0 to 1)
Current Spending: ($ per student per year):
Total: $8,515; Instruction: $4,854; Support Services: $3,617
Enrollment, Drop-out Rates and Diploma Recipients by Race/Ethnicity

Category	Total	White	Black	Asian	AIAN	Hisp.
Enrollment (%)	100.0	87.3	5.0	1.2	0.4	6.1
Drop-out Rate (%)	4.3	4.0	6.8	4.5	0.0	6.4
H.S. Diplomas (#)	643	564	28	14	1	36

Mokena SD 159
11244 W Willowcrest • Mokena, IL 60448-1398
(708) 342-4900 • http://207.63.182.252/
Grade Span: PK-08; **Agency Type:** 1
Schools: 3
1 Primary; 2 Middle; 0 High; 0 Other Level
3 Regular; 0 Special Education; 0 Vocational; 0 Alternative
0 Magnet; 0 Charter; 2 Title I Eligible; 0 School-wide Title I
Students: 2,396 (52.7% male; 47.3% female)
Individual Education Program: 350 (14.6%);
English Language Learner: 7 (0.3%); Migrant: n/a
Eligible for Free Lunch Program: 80 (3.3%)
Eligible for Reduced-Price Lunch Program: 16 (0.7%)
Teachers: 117.4 (20.4 to 1)
Librarians/Media Specialists: 0.0 (0.0 to 1)
Guidance Counselors: 0.0 (0.0 to 1)
Current Spending: ($ per student per year):
Total: $4,420; Instruction: $2,491; Support Services: $1,779
Enrollment, Drop-out Rates and Diploma Recipients by Race/Ethnicity

Category	Total	White	Black	Asian	AIAN	Hisp.
Enrollment (%)	100.0	95.0	1.3	1.1	0.0	2.6
Drop-out Rate (%)	n/a	n/a	n/a	n/a	n/a	n/a
H.S. Diplomas (#)	n/a	n/a	n/a	n/a	n/a	n/a

New Lenox SD 122
102 S Cedar Rd • New Lenox, IL 60451-1499
(815) 485-2169 • http://www.myschoolonline.com/
Grade Span: PK-08; **Agency Type:** 1
Schools: 9
4 Primary; 5 Middle; 0 High; 0 Other Level
9 Regular; 0 Special Education; 0 Vocational; 0 Alternative

0 Magnet; 0 Charter; 3 Title I Eligible; 0 School-wide Title I
Students: 4,994 (51.3% male; 48.7% female)
Individual Education Program: 657 (13.2%);
English Language Learner: 8 (0.2%); Migrant: n/a
Eligible for Free Lunch Program: 99 (2.0%)
Eligible for Reduced-Price Lunch Program: 30 (0.6%)
Teachers: 258.0 (19.4 to 1)
Librarians/Media Specialists: 8.0 (624.3 to 1)
Guidance Counselors: 6.0 (832.3 to 1)
Current Spending: ($ per student per year):
Total: $4,313; Instruction: $2,120; Support Services: $2,076
Enrollment, Drop-out Rates and Diploma Recipients by Race/Ethnicity

Category	Total	White	Black	Asian	AIAN	Hisp.
Enrollment (%)	100.0	95.9	0.6	0.6	0.2	2.8
Drop-out Rate (%)	n/a	n/a	n/a	n/a	n/a	n/a
H.S. Diplomas (#)	n/a	n/a	n/a	n/a	n/a	n/a

Peotone CUSD 207U

212 W Wilson St • Peotone, IL 60468-9205
(708) 258-0991 • http://www.peotone.will.k12.il.us/
Grade Span: PK-12; **Agency Type:** 1
Schools: 6
3 Primary; 2 Middle; 1 High; 0 Other Level
6 Regular; 0 Special Education; 0 Vocational; 0 Alternative
0 Magnet; 0 Charter; 1 Title I Eligible; 0 School-wide Title I
Students: 1,775 (51.4% male; 48.6% female)
Individual Education Program: 241 (13.6%);
English Language Learner: 3 (0.2%); Migrant: n/a
Eligible for Free Lunch Program: 77 (4.3%)
Eligible for Reduced-Price Lunch Program: 21 (1.2%)
Teachers: 109.6 (16.2 to 1)
Librarians/Media Specialists: 2.0 (887.5 to 1)
Guidance Counselors: 1.0 (1,775.0 to 1)
Current Spending: ($ per student per year):
Total: $5,186; Instruction: $3,581; Support Services: $1,469
Enrollment, Drop-out Rates and Diploma Recipients by Race/Ethnicity

Category	Total	White	Black	Asian	AIAN	Hisp.
Enrollment (%)	100.0	96.8	0.5	0.7	0.1	2.0
Drop-out Rate (%)	1.4	1.5	0.0	0.0	0.0	0.0
H.S. Diplomas (#)	122	117	0	2	0	3

Plainfield SD 202

15732 Howard St • Plainfield, IL 60544-2399
(815) 577-4000 • http://www.plainfield.will.k12.il.us/
Grade Span: PK-12; **Agency Type:** 1
Schools: 19
12 Primary; 4 Middle; 3 High; 0 Other Level
17 Regular; 2 Special Education; 0 Vocational; 0 Alternative
0 Magnet; 0 Charter; 9 Title I Eligible; 0 School-wide Title I
Students: 16,778 (51.6% male; 48.4% female)
Individual Education Program: 1,895 (11.3%);
English Language Learner: 557 (3.3%); Migrant: n/a
Eligible for Free Lunch Program: 264 (1.6%)
Eligible for Reduced-Price Lunch Program: 146 (0.9%)
Teachers: 976.4 (17.2 to 1)
Librarians/Media Specialists: 17.0 (986.9 to 1)
Guidance Counselors: 14.0 (1,198.4 to 1)
Current Spending: ($ per student per year):
Total: $5,552; Instruction: $3,486; Support Services: $1,885
Enrollment, Drop-out Rates and Diploma Recipients by Race/Ethnicity

Category	Total	White	Black	Asian	AIAN	Hisp.
Enrollment (%)	100.0	79.7	6.2	3.0	0.2	11.0
Drop-out Rate (%)	3.2	2.9	4.4	2.0	0.0	6.5
H.S. Diplomas (#)	748	661	26	12	2	47

Reed Custer CUSD 255U

255 Comet Dr • Braidwood, IL 60408-2098
(815) 458-2307 • http://www.rc255.will.k12.il.us/255/rc255.html
Grade Span: PK-12; **Agency Type:** 1
Schools: 4
2 Primary; 1 Middle; 1 High; 0 Other Level
4 Regular; 0 Special Education; 0 Vocational; 0 Alternative
0 Magnet; 0 Charter; 1 Title I Eligible; 0 School-wide Title I
Students: 1,771 (49.9% male; 50.1% female)
Individual Education Program: 286 (16.1%);
English Language Learner: 0 (0.0%); Migrant: n/a
Eligible for Free Lunch Program: 287 (16.2%)
Eligible for Reduced-Price Lunch Program: 122 (6.9%)
Teachers: 122.9 (14.4 to 1)
Librarians/Media Specialists: 3.0 (590.3 to 1)
Guidance Counselors: 3.0 (590.3 to 1)
Current Spending: ($ per student per year):
Total: $10,516; Instruction: $6,477; Support Services: $3,755
Enrollment, Drop-out Rates and Diploma Recipients by Race/Ethnicity

Category	Total	White	Black	Asian	AIAN	Hisp.
Enrollment (%)	100.0	95.8	1.0	0.2	0.1	3.0
Drop-out Rate (%)	2.1	2.1	n/a	0.0	0.0	0.0
H.S. Diplomas (#)	113	108	0	0	2	3

Summit Hill SD 161

21133 S 80th Ave • Frankfort, IL 60423-9326
(815) 469-9103 •
http://www.myschoolonline.com/site/0,1876,17809-27273-21-23795,00.html
Grade Span: PK-08; **Agency Type:** 1
Schools: 6
4 Primary; 2 Middle; 0 High; 0 Other Level
6 Regular; 0 Special Education; 0 Vocational; 0 Alternative
0 Magnet; 0 Charter; 1 Title I Eligible; 0 School-wide Title I
Students: 3,187 (50.0% male; 50.0% female)
Individual Education Program: 421 (13.2%);
English Language Learner: 5 (0.2%); Migrant: n/a
Eligible for Free Lunch Program: 44 (1.4%)
Eligible for Reduced-Price Lunch Program: 5 (0.2%)
Teachers: 169.1 (18.8 to 1)
Librarians/Media Specialists: 1.0 (3,187.0 to 1)
Guidance Counselors: 0.0 (0.0 to 1)
Current Spending: ($ per student per year):
Total: $4,551; Instruction: $2,734; Support Services: $1,802
Enrollment, Drop-out Rates and Diploma Recipients by Race/Ethnicity

Category	Total	White	Black	Asian	AIAN	Hisp.
Enrollment (%)	100.0	90.9	2.2	2.4	0.1	4.4
Drop-out Rate (%)	n/a	n/a	n/a	n/a	n/a	n/a
H.S. Diplomas (#)	n/a	n/a	n/a	n/a	n/a	n/a

Troy Community CSD 30C

5800 W Theodore St • Plainfield, IL 60544-5269
(815) 577-6760
Grade Span: PK-08; **Agency Type:** 1
Schools: 5
4 Primary; 1 Middle; 0 High; 0 Other Level
5 Regular; 0 Special Education; 0 Vocational; 0 Alternative
0 Magnet; 0 Charter; 4 Title I Eligible; 0 School-wide Title I
Students: 3,243 (50.9% male; 49.1% female)
Individual Education Program: 398 (12.3%);
English Language Learner: 82 (2.5%); Migrant: n/a
Eligible for Free Lunch Program: 230 (7.1%)
Eligible for Reduced-Price Lunch Program: 92 (2.8%)
Teachers: 188.0 (17.3 to 1)
Librarians/Media Specialists: 1.0 (3,243.0 to 1)
Guidance Counselors: 6.0 (540.5 to 1)
Current Spending: ($ per student per year):
Total: $5,662; Instruction: $2,905; Support Services: $2,550
Enrollment, Drop-out Rates and Diploma Recipients by Race/Ethnicity

Category	Total	White	Black	Asian	AIAN	Hisp.
Enrollment (%)	100.0	74.6	10.8	2.2	0.3	12.1
Drop-out Rate (%)	n/a	n/a	n/a	n/a	n/a	n/a
H.S. Diplomas (#)	n/a	n/a	n/a	n/a	n/a	n/a

Valley View CUSD 365U

755 Luther Dr • Romeoville, IL 60446-1157
(815) 886-2700 • http://www.vvsd.org/
Grade Span: PK-12; **Agency Type:** 1
Schools: 17
11 Primary; 4 Middle; 2 High; 0 Other Level
17 Regular; 0 Special Education; 0 Vocational; 0 Alternative
0 Magnet; 0 Charter; 4 Title I Eligible; 0 School-wide Title I
Students: 14,875 (51.6% male; 48.4% female)
Individual Education Program: 1,686 (11.3%);
English Language Learner: 645 (4.3%); Migrant: n/a
Eligible for Free Lunch Program: 2,993 (20.1%)
Eligible for Reduced-Price Lunch Program: 993 (6.7%)
Teachers: 710.6 (20.9 to 1)
Librarians/Media Specialists: 14.0 (1,062.5 to 1)
Guidance Counselors: 11.0 (1,352.3 to 1)
Current Spending: ($ per student per year):
Total: $6,172; Instruction: $3,812; Support Services: $2,092
Enrollment, Drop-out Rates and Diploma Recipients by Race/Ethnicity

Category	Total	White	Black	Asian	AIAN	Hisp.
Enrollment (%)	100.0	49.7	25.1	5.1	0.0	20.1
Drop-out Rate (%)	5.6	5.0	6.7	4.3	n/a	6.5
H.S. Diplomas (#)	753	438	183	46	0	86

Will County SD 92

708 N State St • Lockport, IL 60441-2291
(815) 838-8031 • http://www.d92.will.k12.il.us/
Grade Span: PK-08; **Agency Type:** 1
Schools: 4
2 Primary; 2 Middle; 0 High; 0 Other Level

4 Regular; 0 Special Education; 0 Vocational; 0 Alternative
0 Magnet; 0 Charter; 3 Title I Eligible; 0 School-wide Title I
Students: 1,923 (51.9% male; 48.1% female)
Individual Education Program: 277 (14.4%);
English Language Learner: 40 (2.1%); Migrant: n/a
Eligible for Free Lunch Program: 67 (3.5%)
Eligible for Reduced-Price Lunch Program: 27 (1.4%)
Teachers: 99.3 (19.4 to 1)
Librarians/Media Specialists: 0.0 (0.0 to 1)
Guidance Counselors: 0.0 (0.0 to 1)
Current Spending: ($ per student per year):
Total: $4,198; Instruction: $2,573; Support Services: $1,479

Enrollment, Drop-out Rates and Diploma Recipients by Race/Ethnicity

Category	Total	White	Black	Asian	AIAN	Hisp.
Enrollment (%)	100.0	94.9	0.3	0.6	0.6	3.6
Drop-out Rate (%)	n/a	n/a	n/a	n/a	n/a	n/a
H.S. Diplomas (#)	n/a	n/a	n/a	n/a	n/a	n/a

Wilmington CUSD 209U

715 S Joliet St • Wilmington, IL 60481-1494
(815) 476-2594 • http://www.wilmington.will.k12.il.us/
Grade Span: PK-12; **Agency Type:** 1
Schools: 4
2 Primary; 1 Middle; 1 High; 0 Other Level
4 Regular; 0 Special Education; 0 Vocational; 0 Alternative
0 Magnet; 0 Charter; 3 Title I Eligible; 0 School-wide Title I
Students: 1,528 (51.8% male; 48.2% female)
Individual Education Program: 269 (17.6%);
English Language Learner: 0 (0.0%); Migrant: n/a
Eligible for Free Lunch Program: 207 (13.5%)
Eligible for Reduced-Price Lunch Program: 77 (5.0%)
Teachers: 90.0 (17.0 to 1)
Librarians/Media Specialists: 1.0 (1,528.0 to 1)
Guidance Counselors: 2.0 (764.0 to 1)
Current Spending: ($ per student per year):
Total: $5,641; Instruction: $3,019; Support Services: $2,398

Enrollment, Drop-out Rates and Diploma Recipients by Race/Ethnicity

Category	Total	White	Black	Asian	AIAN	Hisp.
Enrollment (%)	100.0	95.2	0.6	0.2	0.1	3.9
Drop-out Rate (%)	4.7	4.8	0.0	n/a	0.0	0.0
H.S. Diplomas (#)	122	117	0	0	1	4

Carterville CUSD 5

306 Virginia Ave • Carterville, IL 62918-1239
(618) 985-4826
Grade Span: PK-12; **Agency Type:** 1
Schools: 3
1 Primary; 1 Middle; 1 High; 0 Other Level
3 Regular; 0 Special Education; 0 Vocational; 0 Alternative
0 Magnet; 0 Charter; 3 Title I Eligible; 0 School-wide Title I
Students: 1,690 (49.2% male; 50.8% female)
Individual Education Program: 312 (18.5%);
English Language Learner: 0 (0.0%); Migrant: n/a
Eligible for Free Lunch Program: 212 (12.5%)
Eligible for Reduced-Price Lunch Program: 45 (2.7%)
Teachers: 82.0 (20.6 to 1)
Librarians/Media Specialists: 1.0 (1,690.0 to 1)
Guidance Counselors: 2.0 (845.0 to 1)
Current Spending: ($ per student per year):
Total: $4,881; Instruction: $3,008; Support Services: $1,593

Enrollment, Drop-out Rates and Diploma Recipients by Race/Ethnicity

Category	Total	White	Black	Asian	AIAN	Hisp.
Enrollment (%)	100.0	94.0	2.2	1.1	1.0	1.7
Drop-out Rate (%)	1.5	1.5	0.0	0.0	0.0	0.0
H.S. Diplomas (#)	104	97	4	0	1	2

Herrin CUSD 4

500 N 10th St • Herrin, IL 62948-3399
(618) 988-8024 • http://www.neola.com/herrin-IL/
Grade Span: PK-12; **Agency Type:** 1
Schools: 4
2 Primary; 1 Middle; 1 High; 0 Other Level
4 Regular; 0 Special Education; 0 Vocational; 0 Alternative
0 Magnet; 0 Charter; 3 Title I Eligible; 3 School-wide Title I
Students: 2,209 (49.9% male; 50.1% female)
Individual Education Program: 510 (23.1%);
English Language Learner: 0 (0.0%); Migrant: n/a
Eligible for Free Lunch Program: 853 (38.6%)
Eligible for Reduced-Price Lunch Program: 151 (6.8%)
Teachers: 123.7 (17.9 to 1)
Librarians/Media Specialists: 3.0 (736.3 to 1)
Guidance Counselors: 2.0 (1,104.5 to 1)
Current Spending: ($ per student per year):
Total: $5,865; Instruction: $3,492; Support Services: $2,088

Enrollment, Drop-out Rates and Diploma Recipients by Race/Ethnicity

Category	Total	White	Black	Asian	AIAN	Hisp.
Enrollment (%)	100.0	91.9	5.7	0.9	0.3	1.3
Drop-out Rate (%)	3.1	3.0	10.0	0.0	0.0	0.0
H.S. Diplomas (#)	129	124	3	2	0	0

Marion Community Unit SD 2

1700 W Cherry St • Marion, IL 62959-1212
(618) 993-2321 • http://www.marion.wilmsn.k12.il.us/
Grade Span: PK-12; **Agency Type:** 1
Schools: 7
5 Primary; 1 Middle; 1 High; 0 Other Level
7 Regular; 0 Special Education; 0 Vocational; 0 Alternative
0 Magnet; 0 Charter; 6 Title I Eligible; 6 School-wide Title I
Students: 3,911 (51.6% male; 48.4% female)
Individual Education Program: 776 (19.8%);
English Language Learner: 20 (0.5%); Migrant: n/a
Eligible for Free Lunch Program: 1,097 (28.0%)
Eligible for Reduced-Price Lunch Program: 181 (4.6%)
Teachers: 195.3 (20.0 to 1)
Librarians/Media Specialists: 3.0 (1,303.7 to 1)
Guidance Counselors: 8.0 (488.9 to 1)
Current Spending: ($ per student per year):
Total: $4,955; Instruction: $3,106; Support Services: $1,545

Enrollment, Drop-out Rates and Diploma Recipients by Race/Ethnicity

Category	Total	White	Black	Asian	AIAN	Hisp.
Enrollment (%)	100.0	89.8	8.0	0.8	0.4	1.0
Drop-out Rate (%)	3.6	3.4	4.9	0.0	33.3	9.1
H.S. Diplomas (#)	232	211	9	3	3	6

Winnebago County

Harlem Unit Dist 122

PO Box 2021 • Loves Park, IL 61130-2021
(815) 654-4500 • http://www.harlem.winbgo.k12.il.us/
Grade Span: PK-12; **Agency Type:** 1
Schools: 11
8 Primary; 2 Middle; 1 High; 0 Other Level
11 Regular; 0 Special Education; 0 Vocational; 0 Alternative
2 Magnet; 0 Charter; 5 Title I Eligible; 0 School-wide Title I
Students: 7,664 (51.4% male; 48.6% female)
Individual Education Program: 1,121 (14.6%);
English Language Learner: 124 (1.6%); Migrant: n/a
Eligible for Free Lunch Program: 1,018 (13.3%)
Eligible for Reduced-Price Lunch Program: 393 (5.1%)
Teachers: 459.1 (16.7 to 1)
Librarians/Media Specialists: 11.0 (696.7 to 1)
Guidance Counselors: 8.0 (958.0 to 1)
Current Spending: ($ per student per year):
Total: $7,071; Instruction: $4,360; Support Services: $2,479

Enrollment, Drop-out Rates and Diploma Recipients by Race/Ethnicity

Category	Total	White	Black	Asian	AIAN	Hisp.
Enrollment (%)	100.0	90.2	3.3	1.8	0.3	4.4
Drop-out Rate (%)	2.2	2.0	5.7	0.0	20.0	3.0
H.S. Diplomas (#)	372	346	8	5	0	13

Hononegah Community HSD 207

307 Salem St • Rockton, IL 61072-2630
(815) 624-5010 • http://www.hononegah.org/
Grade Span: 08-12; **Agency Type:** 1
Schools: 1
0 Primary; 0 Middle; 1 High; 0 Other Level
1 Regular; 0 Special Education; 0 Vocational; 0 Alternative
0 Magnet; 0 Charter; 0 Title I Eligible; 0 School-wide Title I
Students: 1,785 (53.6% male; 46.4% female)
Individual Education Program: 173 (9.7%);
English Language Learner: 0 (0.0%); Migrant: n/a
Eligible for Free Lunch Program: 93 (5.2%)
Eligible for Reduced-Price Lunch Program: 23 (1.3%)
Teachers: 106.4 (16.8 to 1)
Librarians/Media Specialists: 1.0 (1,785.0 to 1)
Guidance Counselors: 5.0 (357.0 to 1)
Current Spending: ($ per student per year):
Total: $8,047; Instruction: $4,798; Support Services: $2,887

Enrollment, Drop-out Rates and Diploma Recipients by Race/Ethnicity

Category	Total	White	Black	Asian	AIAN	Hisp.
Enrollment (%)	100.0	97.4	0.9	0.6	0.3	0.8
Drop-out Rate (%)	0.7	0.7	0.0	0.0	0.0	0.0
H.S. Diplomas (#)	378	354	4	7	2	11

Kinnikinnick CCSD 131

5410 Pine Ln • Roscoe, IL 61073-9220
(815) 623-2837 • http://www.stateline-il.com/kms/
Grade Span: PK-08; **Agency Type:** 1
Schools: 4

2 Primary; 2 Middle; 0 High; 0 Other Level
4 Regular; 0 Special Education; 0 Vocational; 0 Alternative
0 Magnet; 0 Charter; 1 Title I Eligible; 0 School-wide Title I
Students: 1,757 (52.4% male; 47.6% female)
Individual Education Program: 189 (10.8%);
English Language Learner: 2 (0.1%); Migrant: n/a
Eligible for Free Lunch Program: 72 (4.1%)
Eligible for Reduced-Price Lunch Program: 57 (3.2%)
Teachers: 95.4 (18.4 to 1)
Librarians/Media Specialists: 0.0 (0.0 to 1)
Guidance Counselors: 1.0 (1,757.0 to 1)
Current Spending: ($ per student per year):
Total: $4,820; Instruction: $3,001; Support Services: $1,638
Enrollment, Drop-out Rates and Diploma Recipients by Race/Ethnicity

Category	Total	White	Black	Asian	AIAN	Hisp.
Enrollment (%)	100.0	96.0	1.3	1.3	0.0	1.5
Drop-out Rate (%)	n/a	n/a	n/a	n/a	n/a	n/a
H.S. Diplomas (#)	n/a	n/a	n/a	n/a	n/a	n/a

Rockford SD 205

201 S Madison St • Rockford, IL 61104-2092
(815) 966-3101 • http://www.rps205.com/
Grade Span: PK-12; **Agency Type:** 1
Schools: 53
40 Primary; 6 Middle; 4 High; 3 Other Level
49 Regular; 4 Special Education; 0 Vocational; 0 Alternative
11 Magnet; 0 Charter; 23 Title I Eligible; 23 School-wide Title I
Students: 28,361 (51.3% male; 48.7% female)
Individual Education Program: 4,232 (14.9%);
English Language Learner: 2,032 (7.2%); Migrant: n/a
Eligible for Free Lunch Program: 14,420 (50.8%)
Eligible for Reduced-Price Lunch Program: 2,779 (9.8%)
Teachers: 1,707.4 (16.6 to 1)
Librarians/Media Specialists: 16.5 (1,718.8 to 1)
Guidance Counselors: 42.8 (662.6 to 1)
Current Spending: ($ per student per year):
Total: $8,339; Instruction: $4,994; Support Services: $3,103
Enrollment, Drop-out Rates and Diploma Recipients by Race/Ethnicity

Category	Total	White	Black	Asian	AIAN	Hisp.
Enrollment (%)	100.0	47.8	31.7	3.2	0.2	17.2
Drop-out Rate (%)	7.6	5.1	11.2	9.6	0.0	10.7
H.S. Diplomas (#)	1,187	775	249	47	4	112

Winnebago CUSD 323

304 E Mcnair Rd • Winnebago, IL 61088-9074
(815) 335-2456 • http://www.winnebagoschools.org/
Grade Span: PK-12; **Agency Type:** 1
Schools: 5
2 Primary; 2 Middle; 1 High; 0 Other Level
5 Regular; 0 Special Education; 0 Vocational; 0 Alternative
0 Magnet; 0 Charter; 2 Title I Eligible; 0 School-wide Title I
Students: 1,679 (52.2% male; 47.8% female)
Individual Education Program: 238 (14.2%);
English Language Learner: 0 (0.0%); Migrant: n/a
Eligible for Free Lunch Program: 97 (5.8%)
Eligible for Reduced-Price Lunch Program: 38 (2.3%)
Teachers: 107.5 (15.6 to 1)
Librarians/Media Specialists: 1.0 (1,679.0 to 1)
Guidance Counselors: 1.0 (1,679.0 to 1)
Current Spending: ($ per student per year):
Total: $5,900; Instruction: $3,404; Support Services: $2,269
Enrollment, Drop-out Rates and Diploma Recipients by Race/Ethnicity

Category	Total	White	Black	Asian	AIAN	Hisp.
Enrollment (%)	100.0	96.1	2.3	0.6	0.1	0.9
Drop-out Rate (%)	2.3	2.2	0.0	0.0	n/a	25.0
H.S. Diplomas (#)	107	103	1	2	0	1

Woodford County

Eureka CU Dist 140

109 W Cruger Ave • Eureka, IL 61530-1345
(309) 467-3737 • http://www.eureka.wodfrd.k12.il.us/
Grade Span: PK-12; **Agency Type:** 1
Schools: 5
3 Primary; 1 Middle; 1 High; 0 Other Level
5 Regular; 0 Special Education; 0 Vocational; 0 Alternative
0 Magnet; 0 Charter; 2 Title I Eligible; 0 School-wide Title I
Students: 1,598 (51.3% male; 48.7% female)
Individual Education Program: 222 (13.9%);
English Language Learner: 0 (0.0%); Migrant: n/a
Eligible for Free Lunch Program: 171 (10.7%)
Eligible for Reduced-Price Lunch Program: 38 (2.4%)
Teachers: 102.5 (15.6 to 1)
Librarians/Media Specialists: 1.0 (1,598.0 to 1)
Guidance Counselors: 3.0 (532.7 to 1)
Current Spending: ($ per student per year):
Total: $5,882; Instruction: $3,754; Support Services: $1,919
Enrollment, Drop-out Rates and Diploma Recipients by Race/Ethnicity

Category	Total	White	Black	Asian	AIAN	Hisp.
Enrollment (%)	100.0	96.9	1.5	0.5	0.1	1.0
Drop-out Rate (%)	2.1	2.2	n/a	0.0	0.0	0.0
H.S. Diplomas (#)	107	103	0	1	0	3

Number of Schools

Rank	Number	District Name	City
1	608	City of Chicago SD 299	Chicago
2	54	SD 46	Elgin
3	53	Rockford SD 205	Rockford
4	45	Peoria SD 150	Peoria
5	41	Department of Corrections SD 428	Springfield
6	36	Springfield SD 186	Springfield
7	30	Indian Prairie CUSD 204	Aurora
8	29	East Saint Louis SD 189	E Saint Louis
9	27	Schaumburg CCSD 54	Schaumburg
10	25	Decatur SD 61	Decatur
11	24	Community Unit SD 300	Carpentersville
11	24	Joliet Public SD 86	Joliet
11	24	Waukegan CUSD 60	Waukegan
14	21	Naperville C U Dist 203	Naperville
15	20	Community Unit SD 200	Wheaton
15	20	Mclean County Unit Dist 5	Normal
15	20	Moline Unit SD 40	Moline
15	20	Palatine CCSD 15	Palatine
19	19	Plainfield SD 202	Plainfield
20	18	Champaign Community Unit SD 4	Champaign
20	18	Rock Island SD 41	Rock Island
22	17	Aurora West Unit SD 129	Aurora
22	17	Evanston CCSD 65	Evanston
22	17	Valley View CUSD 365U	Romeoville
25	16	Aurora East Unit SD 131	Aurora
25	16	Quincy SD 172	Quincy
27	15	Cicero SD 99	Cicero
27	15	Saint Charles CUSD 303	Saint Charles
29	14	Community CSD 59	Arlington Hgts
29	14	Kankakee SD 111	Kankakee
31	13	Alton Community Unit SD 11	Alton
31	13	Elmhurst SD 205	Elmhurst
33	12	Barrington CUSD 220	Barrington
33	12	Chicago Heights SD 170	Chicago Heights
33	12	Crystal Lake CCSD 47	Crystal Lake
33	12	Downers Grove Grade SD 58	Downers Grove
33	12	Edwardsville CUSD 7	Edwardsville
33	12	Galesburg CUSD 205	Galesburg
33	12	Jacksonville SD 117	Jacksonville
33	12	Township High SD 214	Arlington Hgts
33	12	Wheeling CCSD 21	Wheeling
42	11	Belleville SD 118	Belleville
42	11	Collinsville CUSD 10	Collinsville
42	11	Community CSD 62	Des Plaines
42	11	Cook County SD 130	Blue Island
42	11	Danville CCSD 118	Danville
42	11	Dekalb Community Unit SD 428	De Kalb
42	11	Dolton SD 148	Riverdale
42	11	Harlem Unit Dist 122	Loves Park
42	11	Massac Unit District #1	Metropolis
42	11	North Shore SD 112	Highland Park
42	11	Oswego Community Unit SD 308	Oswego
42	11	Pekin Public SD 108	Pekin
54	10	Cahokia Community Unit SD 187	Cahokia
54	10	Freeport SD 145	Freeport
54	10	Granite City CUSD 9	Granite City
54	10	Maywood-Melrose Park-Broadview-89	Melrose Park
54	10	North Chicago SD 187	North Chicago
54	10	Oak Park Elem SD 97	Oak Park
54	10	Orland SD 135	Orland Park
61	9	Arlington Heights SD 25	Arlington Hgts
61	9	Belvidere CUSD 100	Belvidere
61	9	Bloomington SD 87	Bloomington
61	9	CCSD 181	Hinsdale
61	9	Jasper County Comm Unit Dist 1	Newton
61	9	Mattoon CUSD 2	Mattoon
61	9	New Lenox SD 122	New Lenox
61	9	Urbana SD 116	Urbana
61	9	Woodstock CUSD 200	Woodstock
70	8	Addison SD 4	Addison
70	8	Batavia Unit SD 101	Batavia
70	8	Bellwood SD 88	Bellwood
70	8	Community CSD 93	Carol Stream
70	8	Crete Monee CUSD 201U	Crete
70	8	Effingham Community Unit SD 40	Effingham
70	8	Geneva Community Unit SD 304	Geneva
70	8	Harvey SD 152	Harvey
70	8	Highland Community Unit SD 5	Highland
70	8	Jersey CUSD 100	Jerseyville
70	8	Kirby SD 140	Tinley Park
70	8	Lake Zurich CUSD 95	Lake Zurich
70	8	Mchenry CCSD 15	Mc Henry
70	8	Olympia CUSD 16	Stanford
70	8	Park Ridge CCSD 64	Park Ridge
70	8	Prairie-Hills Elem SD 144	Markham
70	8	Round Lake Area Schs - Dist 116	Round Lake
70	8	SD 45 Dupage County	Villa Park
70	8	Taylorville CUSD 3	Taylorville
70	8	Triad Community Unit SD 2	Troy
90	7	Berwyn South SD 100	Berwyn
90	7	Bethalto CUSD 8	Bethalto
90	7	Burbank SD 111	Burbank
90	7	Carmi-White County CUSD 5	Carmi
90	7	Cary CCSD 26	Cary
90	7	Charleston CUSD 1	Charleston
90	7	Consolidated SD 158	Huntley
90	7	East Maine SD 63	Des Plaines
90	7	East Peoria SD 86	East Peoria
90	7	Geneseo Community Unit SD 228	Geneseo
90	7	Glenview CCSD 34	Glenview
90	7	Kildeer Countryside CCSD 96	Buffalo Grove
90	7	Litchfield CUSD 12	Litchfield
90	7	Lombard SD 44	Lombard
90	7	Marion Community Unit SD 2	Marion
90	7	Sterling C U Dist 5	Sterling
90	7	West Chicago ESD 33	West Chicago
90	7	Woodridge SD 68	Woodridge
90	7	Zion Elementary SD 6	Zion
109	6	Beach Park CCSD 3	Beach Park
109	6	Berkeley SD 87	Berkeley
109	6	Clinton CUSD 15	Clinton
109	6	Community CSD 46	Grayslake
109	6	Deerfield SD 109	Deerfield
109	6	Dixon Unit SD 170	Dixon
109	6	Dolton SD 149	Calumet City
109	6	Dunlap CUSD 323	Dunlap
109	6	Hawthorn CCSD 73	Vernon Hills
109	6	Homer Community CSD 33C	Lockport
109	6	Indian Springs SD 109	Justice
109	6	Kewanee Community Unit SD 229	Kewanee
109	6	Lyons SD 103	Lyons
109	6	Matteson ESD 162	Matteson
109	6	Monmouth Unit SD 38	Monmouth
109	6	Morton CUSD 709	Morton
109	6	Mount Zion Community Unit SD 3	Mount Zion
109	6	Oak Lawn-Hometown SD 123	Oak Lawn
109	6	Paris-Union SD 95	Paris
109	6	Park Forest SD 163	Park Forest
109	6	Peotone CUSD 207U	Peotone
109	6	Posen-Robbins El SD 143-5	Posen
109	6	Prairie Central CUSD 8	Forrest
109	6	Sandwich CUSD 430	Sandwich
109	6	Sherrard Community Unit SD 200	Sherrard
109	6	Southwestern CUSD 9	Piasa
109	6	Summit Hill SD 161	Frankfort
109	6	Sycamore CUSD 427	Sycamore
109	6	Tinley Park Community Cons SD 146	Tinley Park
109	6	Township HSD 211	Palatine
109	6	West Harvey-Dixmoor PSD 147	Harvey
109	6	Wilmette SD 39	Wilmette
141	5	Antioch CCSD 34	Antioch
141	5	Ball Chatham CUSD 5	Chatham
141	5	Bensenville SD 2	Bensenville
141	5	Berwyn North SD 98	Berwyn
141	5	Bond County CUSD 2	Greenville
141	5	Bourbonnais SD 53	Bourbonnais
141	5	Canton Union SD 66	Canton
141	5	Carlinville CUSD 1	Carlinville
141	5	Central Community Unit SD 301	Burlington
141	5	East Moline SD 37	East Moline
141	5	Elmwood Park CUSD 401	Elmwood Park
141	5	Eureka CU Dist 140	Eureka
141	5	Evergreen Park ESD 124	Evergreen Park
141	5	Flossmoor SD 161	Chicago Heights
141	5	Glen Ellyn CCSD 89	Glen Ellyn
141	5	Glen Ellyn SD 41	Glen Ellyn
141	5	Harvard CUSD 50	Harvard
141	5	Herscher Community Unit SD 2	Herscher
141	5	Hillsboro Community Unit SD 3	Hillsboro
141	5	La Grange SD 102	La Grange Park
141	5	Lake Villa CCSD 41	Lake Villa
141	5	Lansing SD 158	Lansing
141	5	Libertyville SD 70	Libertyville
141	5	Macomb Community Unit SD 185	Macomb
141	5	Mahomet-Seymour CUSD 3	Mahomet
141	5	Maine Township HSD 207	Park Ridge
141	5	Mannheim SD 83	Franklin Park
141	5	Manteno Community Unit SD 5	Manteno
141	5	Marquardt SD 15	Glendale Hgts
141	5	Mundelein Elem SD 75	Mundelein
141	5	Murphysboro CUSD 186	Murphysboro
141	5	North Palos SD 117	Palos Hills
141	5	O'Fallon CCSD 90	Ofallon
141	5	Oregon C U School Dist-220	Oregon
141	5	Ottawa Elem SD 141	Ottawa
141	5	Rantoul City SD 137	Rantoul
141	5	Ridgeland SD 122	Oak Lawn
141	5	Rochelle Community CD 231	Rochelle
141	5	Sparta CUSD 140	Sparta
141	5	Streator Elem SD 44	Streator
141	5	Summit SD 104	Summit
141	5	Troy Community CSD 30C	Plainfield
141	5	Wauconda Community Unit SD 118	Wauconda
141	5	Westmont CUSD 201	Westmont
141	5	Winnebago CUSD 323	Winnebago
141	5	Winnetka SD 36	Winnetka
141	5	Yorkville Community Unit SD 115	Yorkville
188	4	Alsip-Hazlgrn-Oaklawn SD 126	Alsip
188	4	Aptakisic-Tripp CCSD 102	Buffalo Grove
188	4	Bremen Community HS District 228	Midlothian
188	4	Byron Community Unit SD 226	Byron
188	4	Coal City CUSD 1	Coal City
188	4	Community High SD 155	Crystal Lake
188	4	Community High SD 218	Oak Lawn
188	4	Consolidated High SD 230	Orland Park
188	4	Darien SD 61	Darien
188	4	Elem SD 159	Matteson
188	4	Forest Ridge SD 142	Oak Forest
188	4	Frankfort Community Unit SD 168	West Frankfort
188	4	Genoa Kingston CUSD 424	Genoa
188	4	Glenbard Twp HSD 87	Glen Ellyn
188	4	Harrisburg CUSD 3	Harrisburg
188	4	Herrin CUSD 4	Herrin
188	4	Homewood SD 153	Homewood
188	4	Illinois Valley Central UD 321	Chillicothe
188	4	Johnsburg CUSD 12	Johnsburg
188	4	Kaneland CUSD 302	Maple Park
188	4	Kinnikinnick CCSD 131	Roscoe
188	4	Lake Forest SD 67	Lake Forest
188	4	Lemont-Bromberek CSD 113a	Lemont
188	4	Lisle CUSD 202	Lisle
188	4	Mascoutah C U District 19	Mascoutah
188	4	Meridian CUSD 223	Stillman Valley
188	4	Midlothian SD 143	Midlothian
188	4	Monticello CUSD 25	Monticello
188	4	Mount Vernon SD 80	Mount Vernon
188	4	Northbrook SD 28	Northbrook
188	4	Prospect Heights SD 23	Prospect Hgts
188	4	Reed Custer CUSD 255U	Braidwood
188	4	Rich Twp HS District 227	Olympia Fields
188	4	Robinson CUSD 2	Robinson
188	4	Rochester Community Unit SD 3A	Rochester
188	4	Roxana Community Unit SD 1	Roxana
188	4	Skokie SD 68	Skokie
188	4	Steger SD 194	Steger
188	4	Vandalia CUSD 203	Vandalia
188	4	Wabash CUSD 348	Mount Carmel
188	4	Waterloo Community Unit SD 5	Waterloo
188	4	Will County SD 92	Lockport
188	4	Wilmington CUSD 209U	Wilmington
188	4	Woodland CCSD 50	Gurnee
232	3	Antioch Community High SD 117	Lake Villa
232	3	Belleville Twp HSD 201	Belleville
232	3	Bloom Twp High SD 206	Chicago Heights
232	3	Bradley SD 61	Bradley
232	3	Carterville CUSD 5	Carterville
232	3	Channahon SD 17	Channahon
232	3	Columbia Community Unit SD 4	Columbia
232	3	Community CSD 168	Sauk Village
232	3	Country Club Hills SD 160	Ctry Club Hill
232	3	Du Quoin CUSD 300	Du Quoin
232	3	East Richland CUSD 1	Olney
232	3	Frankfort CCSD 157c	Frankfort
232	3	Gurnee SD 56	Gurnee
232	3	J S Morton HS District 201	Cicero
232	3	Joliet Twp HSD 204	Joliet
232	3	Keeneyville SD 20	Hanover Park
232	3	Lincolnshire-Prairieview SD 103	Lincolnshire
232	3	Minooka Community CSD 201	Minooka
232	3	Mokena SD 159	Mokena
232	3	Mount Prospect SD 57	Mount Prospect
232	3	Nippersink SD 2	Richmond
232	3	Northfield Twp High SD 225	Glenview
232	3	Palos Community CSD 118	Palos Park
232	3	Queen Bee SD 16	Glendale Hgts
232	3	River Trails SD 26	Mount Prospect
232	3	Thornton Fractional T HS D 215	Calumet City
232	3	Thornton Twp HSD 205	South Holland
259	2	Community High SD 128	Libertyville
259	2	Community High SD 99	Downers Grove
259	2	Du Page High SD 88	Villa Park
259	2	Fremont SD 79	Mundelein
259	2	Hinsdale Twp HSD 86	Hinsdale
259	2	Leyden Community HSD 212	Franklin Park
259	2	Lincoln Way Community HSD 210	New Lenox
259	2	Mchenry Community HSD 156	Mc Henry
259	2	New Trier Twp HSD 203	Winnetka
259	2	Niles Twp Community High SD 219	Skokie
259	2	Proviso Twp HSD 209	Maywood
259	2	Township High SD 113	Highland Park
271	1	Adlai E Stevenson Dist 125	Lincolnshire
271	1	Argo Community HSD 217	Summit
271	1	Bradley Bourbonnais CHSD 307	Bradley
271	1	Community High SD 94	West Chicago
271	1	Evanston Twp HSD 202	Evanston

Rank	Number	District Name	City
271	1	Fenton Community HSD 100	Bensenville
271	1	Grayslake Community High SD 127	Grayslake
271	1	Homewood Flossmoor CHSD 233	Flossmoor
271	1	Hononegah Community HSD 207	Rockton
271	1	Lake Forest Community HSD 115	Lake Forest
271	1	Lake Park Community HSD 108	Roselle
271	1	Lockport Twp HSD 205	Lockport
271	1	Lyons Twp HSD 204	La Grange
271	1	Mundelein Cons High SD 120	Mundelein
271	1	O'Fallon Twp High SD 203	Ofallon
271	1	Oak Lawn Community HSD 229	Oak Lawn
271	1	Oak Park & River Forest Dist 200	Oak Park
271	1	Ottawa Twp HSD 140	Ottawa
271	1	Pekin Community HSD 303	Pekin
271	1	Reavis Twp HSD 220	Burbank
271	1	United Twp HS District 30	East Moline
271	1	Warren Twp High SD 121	Gurnee
271	1	Zion-Benton Twp HSD 126	Zion

Number of Teachers

Rank	Number	District Name	City
1	24,584	City of Chicago SD 299	Chicago
2	2,318	SD 46	Elgin
3	1,707	Rockford SD 205	Rockford
4	1,601	Indian Prairie CUSD 204	Aurora
5	1,089	Peoria SD 150	Peoria
6	1,078	Naperville C U Dist 203	Naperville
7	982	Community Unit SD 300	Carpentersville
8	976	Plainfield SD 202	Plainfield
9	953	Springfield SD 186	Springfield
10	943	Schaumburg CCSD 54	Schaumburg
11	893	Community Unit SD 200	Wheaton
12	856	Waukegan CUSD 60	Waukegan
13	789	Township HSD 211	Palatine
14	776	Palatine CCSD 15	Palatine
15	746	Township High SD 214	Arlington Hgts
16	737	Mclean County Unit Dist 5	Normal
17	710	Valley View CUSD 365U	Romeoville
18	671	Saint Charles CUSD 303	Saint Charles
19	671	Cicero SD 99	Cicero
20	665	Champaign Community Unit SD 4	Champaign
21	651	Aurora West Unit SD 129	Aurora
22	637	East Saint Louis SD 189	E Saint Louis
23	567	Aurora East Unit SD 131	Aurora
24	536	Evanston CCSD 65	Evanston
25	532	Glenbard Twp HSD 87	Glen Ellyn
26	525	Crystal Lake CCSD 47	Crystal Lake
27	518	Joliet Public SD 86	Joliet
28	497	Barrington CUSD 220	Barrington
29	480	Maine Township HSD 207	Park Ridge
30	473	Moline Unit SD 40	Moline
31	472	Woodland CCSD 50	Gurnee
32	469	Consolidated High SD 230	Orland Park
33	465	Oswego Community Unit SD 308	Oswego
34	465	Elmhurst SD 205	Elmhurst
35	462	Wheeling CCSD 21	Wheeling
36	459	Decatur SD 61	Decatur
37	459	Harlem Unit Dist 122	Loves Park
38	438	Alton Community Unit SD 11	Alton
39	426	Rock Island SD 41	Rock Island
40	412	Lake Zurich CUSD 95	Lake Zurich
41	411	Quincy SD 172	Quincy
42	410	Community CSD 59	Arlington Hgts
43	409	Danville CCSD 118	Danville
44	403	Edwardsville CUSD 7	Edwardsville
45	401	Thornton Twp HSD 205	South Holland
46	383	J S Morton HS District 201	Cicero
47	375	Oak Park Elem SD 97	Oak Park
48	374	Bloomington SD 87	Bloomington
49	363	Community CSD 62	Des Plaines
50	358	Orland SD 135	Orland Park
51	355	Granite City CUSD 9	Granite City
52	353	Belvidere CUSD 100	Belvidere
53	345	Batavia Unit SD 101	Batavia
54	344	Urbana SD 116	Urbana
55	344	Niles Twp Community High SD 219	Skokie
56	342	Kankakee SD 111	Kankakee
57	339	Collinsville CUSD 10	Collinsville
58	337	Community High SD 155	Crystal Lake
59	336	North Shore SD 112	Highland Park
60	335	Dekalb Community Unit SD 428	De Kalb
61	333	Arlington Heights SD 25	Arlington Hgts
62	328	Maywood-Melrose Park-Broadview-89	Melrose Park
63	327	Northfield Twp High SD 225	Glenview
64	325	Woodstock CUSD 200	Woodstock
65	321	Community High SD 99	Downers Grove
66	318	New Trier Twp HSD 203	Winnetka
67	315	Galesburg CUSD 205	Galesburg
68	312	Joliet Twp HSD 204	Joliet
69	311	Park Ridge CCSD 64	Park Ridge
70	309	Geneva Community Unit SD 304	Geneva
71	307	Department of Corrections SD 428	Springfield
72	302	Freeport SD 145	Freeport
73	300	Proviso Twp HSD 209	Maywood
74	298	Community CSD 93	Carol Stream
75	297	Bremen Community HS District 228	Midlothian
76	293	Community High SD 218	Oak Lawn
77	288	Round Lake Area Schs - Dist 116	Round Lake
78	288	Lincoln Way Community HSD 210	New Lenox
79	288	Kirby SD 140	Tinley Park
80	288	Consolidated SD 158	Huntley
81	282	North Chicago SD 187	North Chicago
82	276	Hinsdale Twp HSD 86	Hinsdale
83	273	Downers Grove Grade SD 58	Downers Grove
84	271	Glenview CCSD 34	Glenview
85	268	Adlai E Stevenson Dist 125	Lincolnshire
86	263	Wilmette SD 39	Wilmette
87	262	Mchenry CCSD 15	Mc Henry
88	258	Cahokia Community Unit SD 187	Cahokia
89	258	New Lenox SD 122	New Lenox
90	256	Jacksonville SD 117	Jacksonville
91	255	Crete Monee CUSD 201U	Crete
92	254	Evanston Twp HSD 202	Evanston
93	252	Cook County SD 130	Blue Island
94	250	West Chicago ESD 33	West Chicago
95	245	SD 45 Dupage County	Villa Park
96	243	Community CSD 46	Grayslake
97	242	Du Page High SD 88	Villa Park
98	240	East Maine SD 63	Des Plaines
99	239	Pekin Public SD 108	Pekin
100	239	CCSD 181	Hinsdale
101	238	Belleville Twp HSD 201	Belleville
102	238	Sterling C U Dist 5	Sterling
103	238	Mattoon CUSD 2	Mattoon
104	235	Kildeer Countryside CCSD 96	Buffalo Grove
105	231	Berwyn South SD 100	Berwyn
106	230	Wauconda Community Unit SD 118	Wauconda
107	229	Triad Community Unit SD 2	Troy
108	228	Township High SD 113	Highland Park
109	228	Hawthorn CCSD 73	Vernon Hills
110	225	Rich Twp HS District 227	Olympia Fields
111	223	Deerfield SD 109	Deerfield
112	217	Ball Chatham CUSD 5	Chatham
113	216	Addison SD 4	Addison
114	216	Cary CCSD 26	Cary
115	212	Lombard SD 44	Lombard
116	209	Lyons Twp HSD 204	La Grange
117	209	Glen Ellyn SD 41	Glen Ellyn
118	209	Lake Villa CCSD 41	Lake Villa
119	209	Bloom Twp High SD 206	Chicago Heights
120	207	Belleville SD 118	Belleville
121	207	Chicago Heights SD 170	Chicago Heights
122	206	Leyden Community HSD 212	Franklin Park
123	205	Dolton SD 149	Calumet City
124	205	Warren Twp High SD 121	Gurnee
125	203	Dolton SD 148	Riverdale
126	195	Marion Community Unit SD 2	Marion
127	194	Oak Lawn-Hometown SD 123	Oak Lawn
128	193	Sycamore CUSD 427	Sycamore
129	191	Woodridge SD 68	Woodridge
130	190	Highland Community Unit SD 5	Highland
131	189	Kaneland CUSD 302	Maple Park
132	188	Troy Community CSD 30C	Plainfield
133	187	Jersey CUSD 100	Jerseyville
134	185	Burbank SD 111	Burbank
134	185	Mascoutah C U District 19	Mascoutah
136	185	Dixon Unit SD 170	Dixon
137	185	La Grange SD 102	La Grange Park
138	184	Community High SD 128	Libertyville
139	182	Charleston CUSD 1	Charleston
140	182	Thornton Fractional T HS D 215	Calumet City
141	181	Canton Union SD 66	Canton
142	181	Mannheim SD 83	Franklin Park
143	179	Oak Park & River Forest Dist 200	Oak Park
144	179	Lake Forest SD 67	Lake Forest
145	177	Effingham Community Unit SD 40	Effingham
146	176	Geneseo Community Unit SD 228	Geneseo
147	175	Bethalto CUSD 8	Bethalto
148	175	East Moline SD 37	East Moline
149	174	Tinley Park Community Cons SD 146	Tinley Park
150	174	Berkeley SD 87	Berkeley
150	174	Matteson ESD 162	Matteson
152	174	Morton CUSD 709	Morton
153	173	Zion Elementary SD 6	Zion
154	170	Taylorville CUSD 3	Taylorville
155	170	Indian Springs SD 109	Justice
155	170	Winnetka SD 36	Winnetka
157	169	Summit Hill SD 161	Frankfort
158	167	Olympia CUSD 16	Stanford
159	166	Lockport Twp HSD 205	Lockport
160	166	Homewood Flossmoor CHSD 233	Flossmoor
161	166	O'Fallon CCSD 90	Ofallon
162	165	Homer Community CSD 33C	Lockport
163	165	Flossmoor SD 161	Chicago Heights
164	164	Libertyville SD 70	Libertyville
165	163	Mahomet-Seymour CUSD 3	Mahomet
166	162	Clinton CUSD 15	Clinton
167	161	Aptakisic-Tripp CCSD 102	Buffalo Grove
168	160	Elmwood Park CUSD 401	Elmwood Park
169	159	Bellwood SD 88	Bellwood
169	159	Prairie-Hills Elem SD 144	Markham
171	156	Glen Ellyn CCSD 89	Glen Ellyn
172	155	Harvey SD 152	Harvey
173	154	Lyons SD 103	Lyons
174	152	Northbrook SD 28	Northbrook
175	152	Marquardt SD 15	Glendale Hgts
176	152	Lake Park Community HSD 108	Roselle
177	150	Waterloo Community Unit SD 5	Waterloo
178	149	Sandwich CUSD 430	Sandwich
179	148	Berwyn North SD 98	Berwyn
180	147	Central Community Unit SD 301	Burlington
181	146	Antioch CCSD 34	Antioch
182	146	Homewood SD 153	Homewood
183	146	Herscher Community Unit SD 2	Herscher
183	146	Ottawa Elem SD 141	Ottawa
185	145	North Palos SD 117	Palos Hills
186	145	Johnsburg CUSD 12	Johnsburg
187	143	Queen Bee SD 16	Glendale Hgts
188	141	Mundelein Elem SD 75	Mundelein
189	141	East Richland CUSD 1	Olney
190	141	Park Forest SD 163	Park Forest
191	141	Murphysboro CUSD 186	Murphysboro
192	140	Harvard CUSD 50	Harvard
193	138	Illinois Valley Central UD 321	Chillicothe
194	136	Prairie Central CUSD 8	Forrest
195	135	Yorkville Community Unit SD 115	Yorkville
196	135	Macomb Community Unit SD 185	Macomb
197	135	Harrisburg CUSD 3	Harrisburg
198	134	Evergreen Park ESD 124	Evergreen Park
199	133	Lemont-Bromberek CSD 113a	Lemont
200	133	Bourbonnais SD 53	Bourbonnais
201	132	Bensenville SD 2	Bensenville
202	131	Dunlap CUSD 323	Dunlap
203	131	Massac Unit District #1	Metropolis
204	131	Community High SD 94	West Chicago
205	129	Hillsboro Community Unit SD 3	Hillsboro
206	129	Antioch Community High SD 117	Lake Villa
207	128	Elem SD 159	Matteson
208	128	Lincolnshire-Prairieview SD 103	Lincolnshire
208	128	Mount Zion Community Unit SD 3	Mount Zion
210	127	Beach Park CCSD 3	Beach Park
211	127	Wabash CUSD 348	Mount Carmel
212	126	Gurnee SD 56	Gurnee
212	126	Oregon C U School Dist-220	Oregon
214	125	Byron Community Unit SD 226	Byron
215	125	River Trails SD 26	Mount Prospect
216	124	Sherrard Community Unit SD 200	Sherrard
217	124	Darien SD 61	Darien
218	123	Herrin CUSD 4	Herrin
219	123	Skokie SD 68	Skokie
220	123	Mchenry Community HSD 156	Mc Henry
221	122	Reed Custer CUSD 255U	Braidwood
221	122	Streator Elem SD 44	Streator
223	122	Manteno Community Unit SD 5	Manteno
224	122	Mount Vernon SD 80	Mount Vernon
224	122	Palos Community CSD 118	Palos Park
226	121	Ridgeland SD 122	Oak Lawn
226	121	Rochelle Community CD 231	Rochelle
228	121	Southwestern CUSD 9	Piasa
229	120	East Peoria SD 86	East Peoria
230	119	Pekin Community HSD 303	Pekin
230	119	Robinson CUSD 2	Robinson
232	119	Jasper County Comm Unit Dist 1	Newton
233	118	Lisle CUSD 202	Lisle
234	117	Lake Forest Community HSD 115	Lake Forest
235	117	Prospect Heights SD 23	Prospect Hgts
236	117	Mundelein Cons High SD 120	Mundelein
236	117	Roxana Community Unit SD 1	Roxana
238	117	Mokena SD 159	Mokena
239	117	Mount Prospect SD 57	Mount Prospect
240	116	Zion-Benton Twp HSD 126	Zion
241	115	Bond County CUSD 2	Greenville
241	115	Westmont CUSD 201	Westmont
243	115	Paris-Union SD 95	Paris
244	114	Lansing SD 158	Lansing
245	114	Coal City CUSD 1	Coal City
246	113	Forest Ridge SD 142	Oak Forest
247	113	Summit SD 104	Summit
248	111	Frankfort Community Unit SD 168	West Frankfort
249	110	Frankfort CCSD 157c	Frankfort
250	110	Keeneyville SD 20	Hanover Park
251	109	Peotone CUSD 207U	Peotone
252	109	Midlothian SD 143	Midlothian
253	109	O'Fallon Twp High SD 203	Ofallon
254	108	Rochester Community Unit SD 3A	Rochester
255	107	Winnebago CUSD 323	Winnebago
256	106	Rantoul City SD 137	Rantoul

257	106	Hononegah Community HSD 207	Rockton
258	106	Nippersink SD 2	Richmond
259	105	Monmouth Unit SD 38	Monmouth
260	104	Columbia Community Unit SD 4	Columbia
261	104	Carmi-White County CUSD 5	Carmi
261	104	Steger SD 194	Steger
263	103	Grayslake Community High SD 127	Grayslake
264	102	Monticello CUSD 25	Monticello
265	102	Eureka CU Dist 140	Eureka
266	102	Du Quoin CUSD 300	Du Quoin
267	101	Alsip-Hazlgrn-Oaklawn SD 126	Alsip
268	99	Will County SD 92	Lockport
269	99	Community CSD 168	Sauk Village
269	99	Country Club Hills SD 160	Ctry Club Hill
271	98	Sparta CUSD 140	Sparta
272	97	Argo Community HSD 217	Summit
273	97	Kewanee Community Unit SD 229	Kewanee
274	97	West Harvey-Dixmoor PSD 147	Harvey
275	96	Vandalia CUSD 203	Vandalia
276	96	United Twp HS District 30	East Moline
277	96	Ottawa Twp HSD 140	Ottawa
278	95	Carlinville CUSD 1	Carlinville
279	95	Reavis Twp HSD 220	Burbank
280	95	Kinnikinnick CCSD 131	Roscoe
281	95	Fenton Community HSD 100	Bensenville
282	93	Genoa Kingston CUSD 424	Genoa
283	92	Litchfield CUSD 12	Litchfield
284	90	Oak Lawn Community HSD 229	Oak Lawn
284	90	Wilmington CUSD 209U	Wilmington
286	87	Meridian CUSD 223	Stillman Valley
287	86	Bradley SD 61	Bradley
288	86	Bradley Bourbonnais CHSD 307	Bradley
289	82	Carterville CUSD 5	Carterville
290	81	Fremont SD 79	Mundelein
291	81	Minooka Community CSD 201	Minooka
292	80	Posen-Robbins El SD 143-5	Posen
293	72	Channahon SD 17	Channahon

Number of Students

Rank	Number	District Name	City
1	436,048	City of Chicago SD 299	Chicago
2	39,153	SD 46	Elgin
3	28,361	Rockford SD 205	Rockford
4	25,795	Indian Prairie CUSD 204	Aurora
5	19,020	Naperville C U Dist 203	Naperville
6	18,040	Community Unit SD 300	Carpentersville
7	16,778	Plainfield SD 202	Plainfield
8	15,980	Waukegan CUSD 60	Waukegan
9	15,736	Peoria SD 150	Peoria
10	15,330	Springfield SD 186	Springfield
11	15,079	Schaumburg CCSD 54	Schaumburg
12	14,875	Valley View CUSD 365U	Romeoville
13	14,294	Community Unit SD 200	Wheaton
14	13,276	Cicero SD 99	Cicero
15	12,933	Palatine CCSD 15	Palatine
16	12,852	Township HSD 211	Palatine
17	12,300	Saint Charles CUSD 303	Saint Charles
18	12,145	Township High SD 214	Arlington Hgts
19	11,469	Aurora West Unit SD 129	Aurora
20	11,213	Aurora East Unit SD 131	Aurora
21	10,637	East Saint Louis SD 189	E Saint Louis
22	10,564	Mclean County Unit Dist 5	Normal
23	10,137	Decatur SD 61	Decatur
24	9,976	Department of Corrections SD 428	Springfield
25	9,572	Joliet Public SD 86	Joliet
26	9,273	Champaign Community Unit SD 4	Champaign
27	8,898	Crystal Lake CCSD 47	Crystal Lake
28	8,880	Glenbard Twp HSD 87	Glen Ellyn
29	8,679	Oswego Community Unit SD 308	Oswego
30	8,564	Barrington CUSD 220	Barrington
31	7,990	Consolidated High SD 230	Orland Park
32	7,722	Moline Unit SD 40	Moline
33	7,671	Granite City CUSD 9	Granite City
34	7,664	Harlem Unit Dist 122	Loves Park
35	7,303	Elmhurst SD 205	Elmhurst
36	7,256	Quincy SD 172	Quincy
37	7,240	J S Morton HS District 201	Cicero
38	7,166	Belvidere CUSD 100	Belvidere
39	7,106	Wheeling CCSD 21	Wheeling
40	7,003	Evanston CCSD 65	Evanston
41	6,988	Alton Community Unit SD 11	Alton
42	6,877	Woodland CCSD 50	Gurnee
43	6,833	Maine Township HSD 207	Park Ridge
44	6,747	Edwardsville CUSD 7	Edwardsville
45	6,720	Rock Island SD 41	Rock Island
46	6,527	Thornton Twp HSD 205	South Holland
47	6,439	Lake Zurich CUSD 95	Lake Zurich
48	6,436	Community CSD 59	Arlington Hgts
49	6,217	Danville CCSD 118	Danville
50	6,047	Round Lake Area Schs - Dist 116	Round Lake
51	6,038	Collinsville CUSD 10	Collinsville
52	6,007	Community High SD 155	Crystal Lake
53	5,958	Maywood-Melrose Park-Broadview-89	Melrose Park
54	5,919	Orland SD 135	Orland Park
55	5,864	Kankakee SD 111	Kankakee
56	5,858	Batavia Unit SD 101	Batavia
57	5,832	Bloomington SD 87	Bloomington
58	5,703	Woodstock CUSD 200	Woodstock
59	5,551	Lincoln Way Community HSD 210	New Lenox
60	5,391	Geneva Community Unit SD 304	Geneva
61	5,372	Dekalb Community Unit SD 428	De Kalb
62	5,248	Community High SD 99	Downers Grove
63	5,136	Cahokia Community Unit SD 187	Cahokia
64	5,072	Galesburg CUSD 205	Galesburg
65	5,018	Community High SD 218	Oak Lawn
66	4,994	New Lenox SD 122	New Lenox
67	4,993	Community CSD 62	Des Plaines
68	4,973	Community CSD 93	Carol Stream
69	4,923	Oak Park Elem SD 97	Oak Park
70	4,908	Arlington Heights SD 25	Arlington Hgts
71	4,874	Joliet Twp HSD 204	Joliet
72	4,860	Downers Grove Grade SD 58	Downers Grove
73	4,859	Belleville Twp HSD 201	Belleville
74	4,841	Crete Monee CUSD 201U	Crete
75	4,795	Niles Twp Community High SD 219	Skokie
76	4,712	Kirby SD 140	Tinley Park
77	4,698	Mchenry CCSD 15	Mc Henry
78	4,692	Bremen Community HS District 228	Midlothian
79	4,680	Consolidated SD 158	Huntley
80	4,652	North Chicago SD 187	North Chicago
81	4,648	Proviso Twp HSD 209	Maywood
82	4,636	Northfield Twp High SD 225	Glenview
83	4,599	Urbana SD 116	Urbana
84	4,511	North Shore SD 112	Highland Park
85	4,497	Freeport SD 145	Freeport
86	4,354	Park Ridge CCSD 64	Park Ridge
87	4,319	Adlai E Stevenson Dist 125	Lincolnshire
88	4,221	Hinsdale Twp HSD 86	Hinsdale
89	4,088	Dolton SD 149	Calumet City
90	3,978	Ball Chatham CUSD 5	Chatham
91	3,911	Marion Community Unit SD 2	Marion
92	3,909	CCSD 181	Hinsdale
92	3,909	Du Page High SD 88	Villa Park
92	3,909	Wauconda Community Unit SD 118	Wauconda
95	3,898	Glenview CCSD 34	Glenview
96	3,856	West Chicago ESD 33	West Chicago
97	3,838	SD 45 Dupage County	Villa Park
98	3,831	Addison SD 4	Addison
99	3,816	Pekin Public SD 108	Pekin
100	3,806	New Trier Twp HSD 203	Winnetka
101	3,794	Cook County SD 130	Blue Island
102	3,760	Jacksonville SD 117	Jacksonville
103	3,743	Triad Community Unit SD 2	Troy
104	3,725	Community CSD 46	Grayslake
105	3,695	Belleville SD 118	Belleville
106	3,671	Hawthorn CCSD 73	Vernon Hills
107	3,662	Sterling C U Dist 5	Sterling
108	3,635	East Maine SD 63	Des Plaines
109	3,577	Cary CCSD 26	Cary
110	3,570	Warren Twp High SD 121	Gurnee
111	3,545	Lyons Twp HSD 204	La Grange
112	3,541	Wilmette SD 39	Wilmette
113	3,516	Kildeer Countryside CCSD 96	Buffalo Grove
114	3,477	Leyden Community HSD 212	Franklin Park
115	3,434	Glen Ellyn SD 41	Glen Ellyn
116	3,426	Dolton SD 148	Riverdale
116	3,426	Rich Twp HS District 227	Olympia Fields
118	3,423	Chicago Heights SD 170	Chicago Heights
119	3,391	Mattoon CUSD 2	Mattoon
120	3,373	Township High SD 113	Highland Park
121	3,366	Berwyn South SD 100	Berwyn
122	3,336	Burbank SD 111	Burbank
123	3,325	Lombard SD 44	Lombard
124	3,317	Bellwood SD 88	Bellwood
125	3,243	Troy Community CSD 30C	Plainfield
126	3,207	Deerfield SD 109	Deerfield
127	3,198	Woodridge SD 68	Woodridge
128	3,188	Lake Villa CCSD 41	Lake Villa
129	3,187	Summit Hill SD 161	Frankfort
130	3,180	Lockport Twp HSD 205	Lockport
131	3,148	Evanston Twp HSD 202	Evanston
132	3,143	Harvey SD 152	Harvey
133	3,117	Jersey CUSD 100	Jerseyville
134	3,095	O'Fallon CCSD 90	Ofallon
135	3,049	Kaneland CUSD 302	Maple Park
136	3,045	Sycamore CUSD 427	Sycamore
137	3,041	Taylorville CUSD 3	Taylorville
138	3,035	Homer Community CSD 33C	Lockport
139	3,010	Dixon Unit SD 170	Dixon
139	3,010	Prairie-Hills Elem SD 144	Markham
141	2,995	Berwyn North SD 98	Berwyn
142	2,993	Charleston CUSD 1	Charleston
143	2,992	Highland Community Unit SD 5	Highland
144	2,989	Effingham Community Unit SD 40	Effingham
145	2,979	Zion Elementary SD 6	Zion
146	2,974	Matteson ESD 162	Matteson
147	2,967	Mascoutah C U District 19	Mascoutah
148	2,962	Oak Park & River Forest Dist 200	Oak Park
149	2,939	Elmwood Park CUSD 401	Elmwood Park
150	2,926	Community High SD 128	Libertyville
151	2,921	Geneseo Community Unit SD 228	Geneseo
152	2,891	Mannheim SD 83	Franklin Park
153	2,884	Bloom Twp High SD 206	Chicago Heights
154	2,878	Indian Springs SD 109	Justice
155	2,867	Thornton Fractional T HS D 215	Calumet City
156	2,839	Lake Park Community HSD 108	Roselle
157	2,838	Berkeley SD 87	Berkeley
158	2,832	Bethalto CUSD 8	Bethalto
159	2,745	Canton Union SD 66	Canton
160	2,737	Morton CUSD 709	Morton
161	2,706	Marquardt SD 15	Glendale Hgts
162	2,678	Mahomet-Seymour CUSD 3	Mahomet
163	2,677	Oak Lawn-Hometown SD 123	Oak Lawn
164	2,651	North Palos SD 117	Palos Hills
165	2,641	Homewood Flossmoor CHSD 233	Flossmoor
166	2,598	Yorkville Community Unit SD 115	Yorkville
167	2,597	Johnsburg CUSD 12	Johnsburg
168	2,596	La Grange SD 102	La Grange Park
169	2,594	Libertyville SD 70	Libertyville
170	2,588	Flossmoor SD 161	Chicago Heights
171	2,542	Waterloo Community Unit SD 5	Waterloo
172	2,510	East Moline SD 37	East Moline
173	2,501	Sandwich CUSD 430	Sandwich
174	2,475	Aptakisic-Tripp CCSD 102	Buffalo Grove
175	2,456	Lemont-Bromberek CSD 113a	Lemont
176	2,452	Antioch CCSD 34	Antioch
177	2,451	Glen Ellyn CCSD 89	Glen Ellyn
178	2,444	Bourbonnais SD 53	Bourbonnais
179	2,411	Dunlap CUSD 323	Dunlap
180	2,404	Mount Zion Community Unit SD 3	Mount Zion
181	2,396	Mokena SD 159	Mokena
182	2,393	Tinley Park Community Cons SD 146	Tinley Park
183	2,368	Harvard CUSD 50	Harvard
184	2,362	Massac Unit District #1	Metropolis
185	2,333	Central Community Unit SD 301	Burlington
186	2,325	Antioch Community High SD 117	Lake Villa
187	2,298	Beach Park CCSD 3	Beach Park
188	2,296	Bensenville SD 2	Bensenville
189	2,289	Olympia CUSD 16	Stanford
190	2,282	Murphysboro CUSD 186	Murphysboro
191	2,281	Mundelein Elem SD 75	Mundelein
192	2,271	Ridgeland SD 122	Oak Lawn
193	2,258	Zion-Benton Twp HSD 126	Zion
194	2,254	Lyons SD 103	Lyons
195	2,225	Herscher Community Unit SD 2	Herscher
196	2,215	Queen Bee SD 16	Glendale Hgts
197	2,209	Herrin CUSD 4	Herrin
198	2,184	Homewood SD 153	Homewood
199	2,172	Lake Forest SD 67	Lake Forest
200	2,167	Harrisburg CUSD 3	Harrisburg
201	2,165	Illinois Valley Central UD 321	Chillicothe
202	2,142	Clinton CUSD 15	Clinton
203	2,134	East Richland CUSD 1	Olney
203	2,134	Pekin Community HSD 303	Pekin
205	2,124	O'Fallon Twp High SD 203	Ofallon
206	2,122	Community High SD 94	West Chicago
207	2,114	Hillsboro Community Unit SD 3	Hillsboro
208	2,111	Ottawa Elem SD 141	Ottawa
209	2,109	Park Forest SD 163	Park Forest
210	2,103	Mchenry Community HSD 156	Mc Henry
211	2,094	Evergreen Park ESD 124	Evergreen Park
212	2,074	Lansing SD 158	Lansing
213	2,028	Gurnee SD 56	Gurnee
214	2,025	Palos Community CSD 118	Palos Park
215	2,004	Winnetka SD 36	Winnetka
216	1,995	Mount Prospect SD 57	Mount Prospect
217	1,979	Macomb Community Unit SD 185	Macomb
218	1,972	Mundelein Cons High SD 120	Mundelein
219	1,961	Bond County CUSD 2	Greenville
220	1,960	Prairie Central CUSD 8	Forrest
221	1,940	Grayslake Community High SD 127	Grayslake
222	1,934	Mount Vernon SD 80	Mount Vernon
223	1,931	East Peoria SD 86	East Peoria
224	1,923	Will County SD 92	Lockport
225	1,910	Coal City CUSD 1	Coal City
226	1,901	Wabash CUSD 348	Mount Carmel
227	1,884	Oregon C U School Dist-220	Oregon
228	1,883	Rochester Community Unit SD 3A	Rochester
229	1,877	Kewanee Community Unit SD 229	Kewanee
230	1,863	Frankfort Community Unit SD 168	West Frankfort
231	1,850	United Twp HS District 30	East Moline
232	1,842	Streator Elem SD 44	Streator
233	1,835	Roxana Community Unit SD 1	Roxana
234	1,834	Rochelle Community CD 231	Rochelle
234	1,834	Southwestern CUSD 9	Piasa
236	1,813	Robinson CUSD 2	Robinson

237	1,807	Lisle CUSD 202	Lisle
238	1,799	Byron Community Unit SD 226	Byron
239	1,793	Sherrard Community Unit SD 200	Sherrard
240	1,790	Manteno Community Unit SD 5	Manteno
241	1,788	Frankfort CCSD 157c	Frankfort
242	1,785	Hononegah Community HSD 207	Rockton
243	1,778	Darien SD 61	Darien
244	1,775	Peotone CUSD 207U	Peotone
245	1,771	Reed Custer CUSD 255U	Braidwood
246	1,769	Skokie SD 68	Skokie
247	1,764	Midlothian SD 143	Midlothian
248	1,760	Forest Ridge SD 142	Oak Forest
249	1,757	Kinnikinnick CCSD 131	Roscoe
250	1,753	Vandalia CUSD 203	Vandalia
251	1,751	Northbrook SD 28	Northbrook
252	1,748	Community CSD 168	Sauk Village
253	1,734	Bradley Bourbonnais CHSD 307	Bradley
254	1,733	Elem SD 159	Matteson
254	1,733	Lincolnshire-Prairieview SD 103	Lincolnshire
256	1,730	Paris-Union SD 95	Paris
257	1,729	Argo Community HSD 217	Summit
257	1,729	Lake Forest Community HSD 115	Lake Forest
257	1,729	West Harvey-Dixmoor PSD 147	Harvey
260	1,728	Genoa Kingston CUSD 424	Genoa
261	1,719	Litchfield CUSD 12	Litchfield
262	1,712	Westmont CUSD 201	Westmont
263	1,709	Alsip-Hazlgrn-Oaklawn SD 126	Alsip
264	1,690	Carterville CUSD 5	Carterville
265	1,686	Meridian CUSD 223	Stillman Valley
266	1,679	Winnebago CUSD 323	Winnebago
267	1,676	Summit SD 104	Summit
268	1,671	Jasper County Comm Unit Dist 1	Newton
269	1,670	Columbia Community Unit SD 4	Columbia
270	1,668	River Trails SD 26	Mount Prospect
271	1,657	Carlinville CUSD 1	Carlinville
272	1,634	Oak Lawn Community HSD 229	Oak Lawn
273	1,632	Steger SD 194	Steger
274	1,619	Keeneyville SD 20	Hanover Park
275	1,612	Rantoul City SD 137	Rantoul
276	1,607	Reavis Twp HSD 220	Burbank
277	1,603	Monticello CUSD 25	Monticello
278	1,600	Sparta CUSD 140	Sparta
279	1,598	Eureka CU Dist 140	Eureka
280	1,585	Country Club Hills SD 160	Ctry Club Hill
281	1,580	Ottawa Twp HSD 140	Ottawa
282	1,571	Nippersink SD 2	Richmond
283	1,559	Du Quoin CUSD 300	Du Quoin
283	1,559	Prospect Heights SD 23	Prospect Hgts
285	1,556	Carmi-White County CUSD 5	Carmi
286	1,548	Posen-Robbins El SD 143-5	Posen
287	1,536	Minooka Community CSD 201	Minooka
288	1,532	Bradley SD 61	Bradley
289	1,528	Wilmington CUSD 209U	Wilmington
290	1,523	Fenton Community HSD 100	Bensenville
291	1,517	Fremont SD 79	Mundelein
292	1,511	Monmouth Unit SD 38	Monmouth
293	1,510	Channahon SD 17	Channahon

Male Students

Rank	Percent	District Name	City
1	89.9	Department of Corrections SD 428	Springfield
2	53.9	Antioch Community High SD 117	Lake Villa
3	53.7	Harvard CUSD 50	Harvard
3	53.7	Mannheim SD 83	Franklin Park
3	53.7	River Trails SD 26	Mount Prospect
6	53.6	Fenton Community HSD 100	Bensenville
6	53.6	Hononegah Community HSD 207	Rockton
8	53.5	Forest Ridge SD 142	Oak Forest
9	53.3	Elem SD 159	Matteson
10	53.2	Canton Union SD 66	Canton
11	53.1	Bensenville SD 2	Bensenville
11	53.1	Dolton SD 148	Riverdale
11	53.1	Geneseo Community Unit SD 228	Geneseo
11	53.1	Sandwich CUSD 430	Sandwich
15	53.0	Community High SD 128	Libertyville
15	53.0	Lake Villa CCSD 41	Lake Villa
15	53.0	Oak Lawn-Hometown SD 123	Oak Lawn
15	53.0	Park Ridge CCSD 64	Park Ridge
19	52.9	Galesburg CUSD 205	Galesburg
19	52.9	Maine Township HSD 207	Park Ridge
19	52.9	Northbrook SD 28	Northbrook
22	52.8	Bloom Twp High SD 206	Chicago Heights
22	52.8	Steger SD 194	Steger
24	52.7	Belleville SD 118	Belleville
24	52.7	Carlinville CUSD 1	Carlinville
24	52.7	Mokena SD 159	Mokena
24	52.7	Posen-Robbins El SD 143-5	Posen
24	52.7	Wilmette SD 39	Wilmette
29	52.6	Adlai E Stevenson Dist 125	Lincolnshire
29	52.6	Columbia Community Unit SD 4	Columbia
29	52.6	East Peoria SD 86	East Peoria
29	52.6	Kewanee Community Unit SD 229	Kewanee
29	52.6	Lake Forest SD 67	Lake Forest
29	52.6	Minooka Community CSD 201	Minooka
29	52.6	Monticello CUSD 25	Monticello
29	52.6	Rochester Community Unit SD 3A	Rochester
29	52.6	Sterling C U Dist 5	Sterling
38	52.5	Bradley Bourbonnais CHSD 307	Bradley
38	52.5	Channahon SD 17	Channahon
38	52.5	Community CSD 46	Grayslake
38	52.5	Community CSD 59	Arlington Hgts
38	52.5	Effingham Community Unit SD 40	Effingham
38	52.5	Niles Twp Community High SD 219	Skokie
38	52.5	Woodridge SD 68	Woodridge
45	52.4	Bourbonnais SD 53	Bourbonnais
45	52.4	Collinsville CUSD 10	Collinsville
45	52.4	Community Unit SD 200	Wheaton
45	52.4	Herscher Community Unit SD 2	Herscher
45	52.4	Homer Community CSD 33C	Lockport
45	52.4	Kinnikinnick CCSD 131	Roscoe
45	52.4	Oregon C U School Dist-220	Oregon
45	52.4	Orland SD 135	Orland Park
45	52.4	Streator Elem SD 44	Streator
54	52.3	Deerfield SD 109	Deerfield
54	52.3	Elmhurst SD 205	Elmhurst
54	52.3	Johnsburg CUSD 12	Johnsburg
54	52.3	Mundelein Cons High SD 120	Mundelein
54	52.3	Naperville C U Dist 203	Naperville
54	52.3	Summit SD 104	Summit
54	52.3	United Twp HS District 30	East Moline
61	52.2	Champaign Community Unit SD 4	Champaign
61	52.2	Glenview CCSD 34	Glenview
61	52.2	Libertyville SD 70	Libertyville
61	52.2	Mount Prospect SD 57	Mount Prospect
61	52.2	Oswego Community Unit SD 308	Oswego
61	52.2	Winnebago CUSD 323	Winnebago
67	52.1	Beach Park CCSD 3	Beach Park
67	52.1	Bellwood SD 88	Bellwood
67	52.1	Darien SD 61	Darien
67	52.1	Evergreen Park ESD 124	Evergreen Park
67	52.1	Harvey SD 152	Harvey
67	52.1	La Grange SD 102	La Grange Park
67	52.1	Winnetka SD 36	Winnetka
67	52.1	Woodstock CUSD 200	Woodstock
75	52.0	Ball Chatham CUSD 5	Chatham
75	52.0	Charleston CUSD 1	Charleston
75	52.0	Cicero SD 99	Cicero
75	52.0	Evanston CCSD 65	Evanston
75	52.0	Glen Ellyn SD 41	Glen Ellyn
75	52.0	Ottawa Twp HSD 140	Ottawa
75	52.0	Prairie-Hills Elem SD 144	Markham
75	52.0	Robinson CUSD 2	Robinson
75	52.0	Township High SD 214	Arlington Hgts
84	51.9	Bethalto CUSD 8	Bethalto
84	51.9	Glenbard Twp HSD 87	Glen Ellyn
84	51.9	Lemont-Bromberek CSD 113a	Lemont
84	51.9	Lombard SD 44	Lombard
84	51.9	Mchenry CCSD 15	Mc Henry
84	51.9	Nippersink SD 2	Richmond
84	51.9	Ridgeland SD 122	Oak Lawn
84	51.9	Will County SD 92	Lockport
92	51.8	Bond County CUSD 2	Greenville
92	51.8	Cary CCSD 26	Cary
92	51.8	Community CSD 93	Carol Stream
92	51.8	Community High SD 155	Crystal Lake
92	51.8	Cook County SD 130	Blue Island
92	51.8	Crystal Lake CCSD 47	Crystal Lake
92	51.8	Du Quoin CUSD 300	Du Quoin
92	51.8	Lockport Twp HSD 205	Lockport
92	51.8	Midlothian SD 143	Midlothian
92	51.8	Oak Park Elem SD 97	Oak Park
92	51.8	Palatine CCSD 15	Palatine
92	51.8	Park Forest SD 163	Park Forest
92	51.8	Schaumburg CCSD 54	Schaumburg
92	51.8	Wilmington CUSD 209U	Wilmington
106	51.7	Community High SD 99	Downers Grove
106	51.7	Lisle CUSD 202	Lisle
106	51.7	Morton CUSD 709	Morton
106	51.7	SD 45 Dupage County	Villa Park
106	51.7	Skokie SD 68	Skokie
106	51.7	Triad Community Unit SD 2	Troy
112	51.6	Alsip-Hazlgrn-Oaklawn SD 126	Alsip
112	51.6	Antioch CCSD 34	Antioch
112	51.6	Aurora West Unit SD 129	Aurora
112	51.6	Belleville Twp HSD 201	Belleville
112	51.6	Bloomington SD 87	Bloomington
112	51.6	Community CSD 62	Des Plaines
112	51.6	Geneva Community Unit SD 304	Geneva
112	51.6	Hawthorn CCSD 73	Vernon Hills
112	51.6	Indian Springs SD 109	Justice
112	51.6	Macomb Community Unit SD 185	Macomb
112	51.6	Marion Community Unit SD 2	Marion
112	51.6	Mclean County Unit Dist 5	Normal
112	51.6	Olympia CUSD 16	Stanford
112	51.6	Pekin Community HSD 303	Pekin
112	51.6	Plainfield SD 202	Plainfield
112	51.6	Prospect Heights SD 23	Prospect Hgts
112	51.6	Tinley Park Community Cons SD 146	Tinley Park
112	51.6	Valley View CUSD 365U	Romeoville
112	51.6	Vandalia CUSD 203	Vandalia
112	51.6	West Chicago ESD 33	West Chicago
112	51.6	Woodland CCSD 50	Gurnee
133	51.5	Aptakisic-Tripp CCSD 102	Buffalo Grove
133	51.5	Dunlap CUSD 323	Dunlap
133	51.5	Granite City CUSD 9	Granite City
133	51.5	Gurnee SD 56	Gurnee
133	51.5	Hillsboro Community Unit SD 3	Hillsboro
133	51.5	Keeneyville SD 20	Hanover Park
133	51.5	Leyden Community HSD 212	Franklin Park
133	51.5	Mattoon CUSD 2	Mattoon
133	51.5	Queen Bee SD 16	Glendale Hgts
133	51.5	Rochelle Community CD 231	Rochelle
133	51.5	Springfield SD 186	Springfield
133	51.5	Yorkville Community Unit SD 115	Yorkville
145	51.4	Batavia Unit SD 101	Batavia
145	51.4	Berkeley SD 87	Berkeley
145	51.4	East Richland CUSD 1	Olney
145	51.4	Harlem Unit Dist 122	Loves Park
145	51.4	Illinois Valley Central UD 321	Chillicothe
145	51.4	Lake Forest Community HSD 115	Lake Forest
145	51.4	Manteno Community Unit SD 5	Manteno
145	51.4	Moline Unit SD 40	Moline
145	51.4	North Palos SD 117	Palos Hills
145	51.4	Peotone CUSD 207U	Peotone
145	51.4	Sycamore CUSD 427	Sycamore
145	51.4	Taylorville CUSD 3	Taylorville
145	51.4	Township HSD 211	Palatine
145	51.4	Urbana SD 116	Urbana
145	51.4	Wauconda Community Unit SD 118	Wauconda
145	51.4	Waukegan CUSD 60	Waukegan
145	51.4	West Harvey-Dixmoor PSD 147	Harvey
162	51.3	Edwardsville CUSD 7	Edwardsville
162	51.3	Eureka CU Dist 140	Eureka
162	51.3	Jacksonville SD 117	Jacksonville
162	51.3	Kankakee SD 111	Kankakee
162	51.3	New Lenox SD 122	New Lenox
162	51.3	Rockford SD 205	Rockford
162	51.3	Round Lake Area Schs - Dist 116	Round Lake
169	51.2	Belvidere CUSD 100	Belvidere
169	51.2	Carmi-White County CUSD 5	Carmi
169	51.2	East Maine SD 63	Des Plaines
169	51.2	Flossmoor SD 161	Chicago Heights
169	51.2	Kirby SD 140	Tinley Park
169	51.2	Litchfield CUSD 12	Litchfield
169	51.2	Mahomet-Seymour CUSD 3	Mahomet
169	51.2	New Trier Twp HSD 203	Winnetka
169	51.2	North Shore SD 112	Highland Park
169	51.2	Saint Charles CUSD 303	Saint Charles
179	51.1	Addison SD 4	Addison
179	51.1	Arlington Heights SD 25	Arlington Hgts
179	51.1	CCSD 181	Hinsdale
179	51.1	Community Unit SD 300	Carpentersville
179	51.1	Hinsdale Twp HSD 86	Hinsdale
179	51.1	Lansing SD 158	Lansing
179	51.1	Mundelein Elem SD 75	Mundelein
179	51.1	Northfield Twp High SD 225	Glenview
179	51.1	O'Fallon CCSD 90	Ofallon
179	51.1	Rantoul City SD 137	Rantoul
179	51.1	Wabash CUSD 348	Mount Carmel
190	51.0	Community CSD 168	Sauk Village
190	51.0	Consolidated SD 158	Huntley
190	51.0	Crete Monee CUSD 201U	Crete
190	51.0	Decatur SD 61	Decatur
190	51.0	Indian Prairie CUSD 204	Aurora
190	51.0	Jersey CUSD 100	Jerseyville
190	51.0	Peoria SD 150	Peoria
190	51.0	Prairie Central CUSD 8	Forrest
190	51.0	Southwestern CUSD 9	Piasa
190	51.0	Zion-Benton Twp HSD 126	Zion
200	50.9	East Moline SD 37	East Moline
200	50.9	Genoa Kingston CUSD 424	Genoa
200	50.9	J S Morton HS District 201	Cicero
200	50.9	Jasper County Comm Unit Dist 1	Newton
200	50.9	Kaneland CUSD 302	Maple Park
200	50.9	Kildeer Countryside CCSD 96	Buffalo Grove
200	50.9	Lincoln Way Community HSD 210	New Lenox
200	50.9	Matteson ESD 162	Matteson
200	50.9	Murphysboro CUSD 186	Murphysboro
200	50.9	Ottawa Elem SD 141	Ottawa
200	50.9	SD 46	Elgin
200	50.9	Troy Community CSD 30C	Plainfield
200	50.9	Warren Twp High SD 121	Gurnee
213	50.8	Alton Community Unit SD 11	Alton
213	50.8	Argo Community HSD 217	Summit
213	50.8	Chicago Heights SD 170	Chicago Heights
213	50.8	Clinton CUSD 15	Clinton
213	50.8	Du Page High SD 88	Villa Park

213	50.8	Elmwood Park CUSD 401	Elmwood Park
213	50.8	Massac Unit District #1	Metropolis
213	50.8	Rock Island SD 41	Rock Island
213	50.8	Thornton Fractional T HS D 215	Calumet City
213	50.8	Waterloo Community Unit SD 5	Waterloo
223	50.7	Barrington CUSD 220	Barrington
223	50.7	Berwyn North SD 98	Berwyn
223	50.7	Burbank SD 111	Burbank
223	50.7	Lake Park Community HSD 108	Roselle
223	50.7	Lake Zurich CUSD 95	Lake Zurich
223	50.7	Lyons SD 103	Lyons
223	50.7	North Chicago SD 187	North Chicago
223	50.7	Oak Park & River Forest Dist 200	Oak Park
223	50.7	Rich Twp HS District 227	Olympia Fields
232	50.6	Dekalb Community Unit SD 428	De Kalb
232	50.6	Frankfort CCSD 157c	Frankfort
232	50.6	Frankfort Community Unit SD 168	West Frankfort
232	50.6	Glen Ellyn CCSD 89	Glen Ellyn
232	50.6	Joliet Twp HSD 204	Joliet
232	50.6	Pekin Public SD 108	Pekin
238	50.5	Aurora East Unit SD 131	Aurora
238	50.5	City of Chicago SD 299	Chicago
238	50.5	Country Club Hills SD 160	Ctry Club Hill
238	50.5	Homewood Flossmoor CHSD 233	Flossmoor
238	50.5	Joliet Public SD 86	Joliet
238	50.5	Marquardt SD 15	Glendale Hgts
238	50.5	Mascoutah C U District 19	Mascoutah
238	50.5	Mount Zion Community Unit SD 3	Mount Zion
246	50.4	Berwyn South SD 100	Berwyn
246	50.4	Bradley SD 61	Bradley
246	50.4	Byron Community Unit SD 226	Byron
246	50.4	Community High SD 94	West Chicago
246	50.4	Dixon Unit SD 170	Dixon
246	50.4	Grayslake Community High SD 127	Grayslake
246	50.4	Homewood SD 153	Homewood
246	50.4	Maywood-Melrose Park-Broadview-89	Melrose Park
254	50.3	Bremen Community HS District 228	Midlothian
254	50.3	Consolidated High SD 230	Orland Park
254	50.3	Danville CCSD 118	Danville
254	50.3	Westmont CUSD 201	Westmont
258	50.2	Community High SD 218	Oak Lawn
258	50.2	Downers Grove Grade SD 58	Downers Grove
258	50.2	Fremont SD 79	Mundelein
258	50.2	Harrisburg CUSD 3	Harrisburg
258	50.2	Thornton Twp HSD 205	South Holland
258	50.2	Township High SD 113	Highland Park
258	50.2	Wheeling CCSD 21	Wheeling
258	50.2	Zion Elementary SD 6	Zion
266	50.1	Cahokia Community Unit SD 187	Cahokia
266	50.1	Freeport SD 145	Freeport
266	50.1	Highland Community Unit SD 5	Highland
266	50.1	Monmouth Unit SD 38	Monmouth
266	50.1	Palos Community CSD 118	Palos Park
266	50.1	Paris-Union SD 95	Paris
266	50.1	Roxana Community Unit SD 1	Roxana
266	50.1	Sherrard Community Unit SD 200	Sherrard
274	50.0	Evanston Twp HSD 202	Evanston
274	50.0	Summit Hill SD 161	Frankfort
276	49.9	Herrin CUSD 4	Herrin
276	49.9	Oak Lawn Community HSD 229	Oak Lawn
276	49.9	Reed Custer CUSD 255U	Braidwood
279	49.8	Lyons Twp HSD 204	La Grange
279	49.8	Proviso Twp HSD 209	Maywood
279	49.8	Quincy SD 172	Quincy
279	49.8	Sparta CUSD 140	Sparta
283	49.7	Dolton SD 149	Calumet City
284	49.6	Coal City CUSD 1	Coal City
285	49.5	Lincolnshire-Prairieview SD 103	Lincolnshire
286	49.4	East Saint Louis SD 189	E Saint Louis
287	49.3	Central Community Unit SD 301	Burlington
287	49.3	Mount Vernon SD 80	Mount Vernon
289	49.2	Carterville CUSD 5	Carterville
290	49.1	Reavis Twp HSD 220	Burbank
291	49.0	Meridian CUSD 223	Stillman Valley
292	48.8	Mchenry Community HSD 156	Mc Henry
292	48.8	O'Fallon Twp High SD 203	Ofallon

Female Students

Rank	Percent	District Name	City
1	51.2	Mchenry Community HSD 156	Mc Henry
1	51.2	O'Fallon Twp High SD 203	Ofallon
3	51.0	Meridian CUSD 223	Stillman Valley
4	50.9	Reavis Twp HSD 220	Burbank
5	50.8	Carterville CUSD 5	Carterville
6	50.7	Central Community Unit SD 301	Burlington
6	50.7	Mount Vernon SD 80	Mount Vernon
8	50.6	East Saint Louis SD 189	E Saint Louis
9	50.5	Lincolnshire-Prairieview SD 103	Lincolnshire
10	50.4	Coal City CUSD 1	Coal City
11	50.3	Dolton SD 149	Calumet City
12	50.2	Lyons Twp HSD 204	La Grange
12	50.2	Proviso Twp HSD 209	Maywood
12	50.2	Quincy SD 172	Quincy
12	50.2	Sparta CUSD 140	Sparta
16	50.1	Herrin CUSD 4	Herrin
16	50.1	Oak Lawn Community HSD 229	Oak Lawn
16	50.1	Reed Custer CUSD 255U	Braidwood
19	50.0	Evanston Twp HSD 202	Evanston
19	50.0	Summit Hill SD 161	Frankfort
21	49.9	Cahokia Community Unit SD 187	Cahokia
21	49.9	Freeport SD 145	Freeport
21	49.9	Highland Community Unit SD 5	Highland
21	49.9	Monmouth Unit SD 38	Monmouth
21	49.9	Palos Community CSD 118	Palos Park
21	49.9	Paris-Union SD 95	Paris
21	49.9	Roxana Community Unit SD 1	Roxana
21	49.9	Sherrard Community Unit SD 200	Sherrard
29	49.8	Community High SD 218	Oak Lawn
29	49.8	Downers Grove Grade SD 58	Downers Grove
29	49.8	Fremont SD 79	Mundelein
29	49.8	Harrisburg CUSD 3	Harrisburg
29	49.8	Thornton Twp HSD 205	South Holland
29	49.8	Township High SD 113	Highland Park
29	49.8	Wheeling CCSD 21	Wheeling
29	49.8	Zion Elementary SD 6	Zion
37	49.7	Bremen Community HS District 228	Midlothian
37	49.7	Consolidated High SD 230	Orland Park
37	49.7	Danville CCSD 118	Danville
37	49.7	Westmont CUSD 201	Westmont
41	49.6	Berwyn South SD 100	Berwyn
41	49.6	Bradley SD 61	Bradley
41	49.6	Byron Community Unit SD 226	Byron
41	49.6	Community High SD 94	West Chicago
41	49.6	Dixon Unit SD 170	Dixon
41	49.6	Grayslake Community High SD 127	Grayslake
41	49.6	Homewood SD 153	Homewood
41	49.6	Maywood-Melrose Park-Broadview-89	Melrose Park
49	49.5	Aurora East Unit SD 131	Aurora
49	49.5	City of Chicago SD 299	Chicago
49	49.5	Country Club Hills SD 160	Ctry Club Hill
49	49.5	Homewood Flossmoor CHSD 233	Flossmoor
49	49.5	Joliet Public SD 86	Joliet
49	49.5	Marquardt SD 15	Glendale Hgts
49	49.5	Mascoutah C U District 19	Mascoutah
49	49.5	Mount Zion Community Unit SD 3	Mount Zion
57	49.4	Dekalb Community Unit SD 428	De Kalb
57	49.4	Frankfort CCSD 157c	Frankfort
57	49.4	Frankfort Community Unit SD 168	West Frankfort
57	49.4	Glen Ellyn CCSD 89	Glen Ellyn
57	49.4	Joliet Twp HSD 204	Joliet
57	49.4	Pekin Public SD 108	Pekin
63	49.3	Barrington CUSD 220	Barrington
63	49.3	Berwyn North SD 98	Berwyn
63	49.3	Burbank SD 111	Burbank
63	49.3	Lake Park Community HSD 108	Roselle
63	49.3	Lake Zurich CUSD 95	Lake Zurich
63	49.3	Lyons SD 103	Lyons
63	49.3	North Chicago SD 187	North Chicago
63	49.3	Oak Park & River Forest Dist 200	Oak Park
63	49.3	Rich Twp HS District 227	Olympia Fields
72	49.2	Alton Community Unit SD 11	Alton
72	49.2	Argo Community HSD 217	Summit
72	49.2	Chicago Heights SD 170	Chicago Heights
72	49.2	Clinton CUSD 15	Clinton
72	49.2	Du Page High SD 88	Villa Park
72	49.2	Elmwood Park CUSD 401	Elmwood Park
72	49.2	Massac Unit District #1	Metropolis
72	49.2	Rock Island SD 41	Rock Island
72	49.2	Thornton Fractional T HS D 215	Calumet City
72	49.2	Waterloo Community Unit SD 5	Waterloo
82	49.1	East Moline SD 37	East Moline
82	49.1	Genoa Kingston CUSD 424	Genoa
82	49.1	J S Morton HS District 201	Cicero
82	49.1	Jasper County Comm Unit Dist 1	Newton
82	49.1	Kaneland CUSD 302	Maple Park
82	49.1	Kildeer Countryside CCSD 96	Buffalo Grove
82	49.1	Lincoln Way Community HSD 210	New Lenox
82	49.1	Matteson ESD 162	Matteson
82	49.1	Murphysboro CUSD 186	Murphysboro
82	49.1	Ottawa Elem SD 141	Ottawa
82	49.1	SD 46	Elgin
82	49.1	Troy Community CSD 30C	Plainfield
82	49.1	Warren Twp High SD 121	Gurnee
95	49.0	Community CSD 168	Sauk Village
95	49.0	Consolidated SD 158	Huntley
95	49.0	Crete Monee CUSD 201U	Crete
95	49.0	Decatur SD 61	Decatur
95	49.0	Indian Prairie CUSD 204	Aurora
95	49.0	Jersey CUSD 100	Jerseyville
95	49.0	Peoria SD 150	Peoria
95	49.0	Prairie Central CUSD 8	Forrest
95	49.0	Southwestern CUSD 9	Piasa
95	49.0	Zion-Benton Twp HSD 126	Zion
105	48.9	Addison SD 4	Addison
105	48.9	Arlington Heights SD 25	Arlington Hgts
105	48.9	CCSD 181	Hinsdale
105	48.9	Community Unit SD 300	Carpentersville
105	48.9	Hinsdale Twp HSD 86	Hinsdale
105	48.9	Lansing SD 158	Lansing
105	48.9	Mundelein Elem SD 75	Mundelein
105	48.9	Northfield Twp High SD 225	Glenview
105	48.9	O'Fallon CCSD 90	Ofallon
105	48.9	Rantoul City SD 137	Rantoul
105	48.9	Wabash CUSD 348	Mount Carmel
116	48.8	Belvidere CUSD 100	Belvidere
116	48.8	Carmi-White County CUSD 5	Carmi
116	48.8	East Maine SD 63	Des Plaines
116	48.8	Flossmoor SD 161	Chicago Heights
116	48.8	Kirby SD 140	Tinley Park
116	48.8	Litchfield CUSD 12	Litchfield
116	48.8	Mahomet-Seymour CUSD 3	Mahomet
116	48.8	New Trier Twp HSD 203	Winnetka
116	48.8	North Shore SD 112	Highland Park
116	48.8	Saint Charles CUSD 303	Saint Charles
126	48.7	Edwardsville CUSD 7	Edwardsville
126	48.7	Eureka CU Dist 140	Eureka
126	48.7	Jacksonville SD 117	Jacksonville
126	48.7	Kankakee SD 111	Kankakee
126	48.7	New Lenox SD 122	New Lenox
126	48.7	Rockford SD 205	Rockford
126	48.7	Round Lake Area Schs - Dist 116	Round Lake
133	48.6	Batavia Unit SD 101	Batavia
133	48.6	Berkeley SD 87	Berkeley
133	48.6	East Richland CUSD 1	Olney
133	48.6	Harlem Unit Dist 122	Loves Park
133	48.6	Illinois Valley Central UD 321	Chillicothe
133	48.6	Lake Forest Community HSD 115	Lake Forest
133	48.6	Manteno Community Unit SD 5	Manteno
133	48.6	Moline Unit SD 40	Moline
133	48.6	North Palos SD 117	Palos Hills
133	48.6	Peotone CUSD 207U	Peotone
133	48.6	Sycamore CUSD 427	Sycamore
133	48.6	Taylorville CUSD 3	Taylorville
133	48.6	Township HSD 211	Palatine
133	48.6	Urbana SD 116	Urbana
133	48.6	Wauconda Community Unit SD 118	Wauconda
133	48.6	Waukegan CUSD 60	Waukegan
133	48.6	West Harvey-Dixmoor PSD 147	Harvey
150	48.5	Aptakisic-Tripp CCSD 102	Buffalo Grove
150	48.5	Dunlap CUSD 323	Dunlap
150	48.5	Granite City CUSD 9	Granite City
150	48.5	Gurnee SD 56	Gurnee
150	48.5	Hillsboro Community Unit SD 3	Hillsboro
150	48.5	Keeneyville SD 20	Hanover Park
150	48.5	Leyden Community HSD 212	Franklin Park
150	48.5	Mattoon CUSD 2	Mattoon
150	48.5	Queen Bee SD 16	Glendale Hgts
150	48.5	Rochelle Community CD 231	Rochelle
150	48.5	Springfield SD 186	Springfield
150	48.5	Yorkville Community Unit SD 115	Yorkville
162	48.4	Alsip-Hazlgrn-Oaklawn SD 126	Alsip
162	48.4	Antioch CCSD 34	Antioch
162	48.4	Aurora West Unit SD 129	Aurora
162	48.4	Belleville Twp HSD 201	Belleville
162	48.4	Bloomington SD 87	Bloomington
162	48.4	Community CSD 62	Des Plaines
162	48.4	Geneva Community Unit SD 304	Geneva
162	48.4	Hawthorn CCSD 73	Vernon Hills
162	48.4	Indian Springs SD 109	Justice
162	48.4	Macomb Community Unit SD 185	Macomb
162	48.4	Marion Community Unit SD 2	Marion
162	48.4	Mclean County Unit Dist 5	Normal
162	48.4	Olympia CUSD 16	Stanford
162	48.4	Pekin Community HSD 303	Pekin
162	48.4	Plainfield SD 202	Plainfield
162	48.4	Prospect Heights SD 23	Prospect Hgts
162	48.4	Tinley Park Community Cons SD 146	Tinley Park
162	48.4	Valley View CUSD 365U	Romeoville
162	48.4	Vandalia CUSD 203	Vandalia
162	48.4	West Chicago ESD 33	West Chicago
162	48.4	Woodland CCSD 50	Gurnee
183	48.3	Community High SD 99	Downers Grove
183	48.3	Lisle CUSD 202	Lisle
183	48.3	Morton CUSD 709	Morton
183	48.3	SD 45 Dupage County	Villa Park
183	48.3	Skokie SD 68	Skokie
183	48.3	Triad Community Unit SD 2	Troy
189	48.2	Bond County CUSD 2	Greenville
189	48.2	Cary CCSD 26	Cary
189	48.2	Community CSD 93	Carol Stream
189	48.2	Community High SD 155	Crystal Lake
189	48.2	Cook County SD 130	Blue Island
189	48.2	Crystal Lake CCSD 47	Crystal Lake
189	48.2	Du Quoin CUSD 300	Du Quoin
189	48.2	Lockport Twp HSD 205	Lockport
189	48.2	Midlothian SD 143	Midlothian
189	48.2	Oak Park Elem SD 97	Oak Park

189	48.2	Palatine CCSD 15	Palatine
189	48.2	Park Forest SD 163	Park Forest
189	48.2	Schaumburg CCSD 54	Schaumburg
189	48.2	Wilmington CUSD 209U	Wilmington
203	48.1	Bethalto CUSD 8	Bethalto
203	48.1	Glenbard Twp HSD 87	Glen Ellyn
203	48.1	Lemont-Bromberek CSD 113a	Lemont
203	48.1	Lombard SD 44	Lombard
203	48.1	Mchenry CCSD 15	Mc Henry
203	48.1	Nippersink SD 2	Richmond
203	48.1	Ridgeland SD 122	Oak Lawn
203	48.1	Will County SD 92	Lockport
211	48.0	Ball Chatham CUSD 5	Chatham
211	48.0	Charleston CUSD 1	Charleston
211	48.0	Cicero SD 99	Cicero
211	48.0	Evanston CCSD 65	Evanston
211	48.0	Glen Ellyn SD 41	Glen Ellyn
211	48.0	Ottawa Twp HSD 140	Ottawa
211	48.0	Prairie-Hills Elem SD 144	Markham
211	48.0	Robinson CUSD 2	Robinson
211	48.0	Township High SD 214	Arlington Hgts
220	47.9	Beach Park CCSD 3	Beach Park
220	47.9	Bellwood SD 88	Bellwood
220	47.9	Darien SD 61	Darien
220	47.9	Evergreen Park ESD 124	Evergreen Park
220	47.9	Harvey SD 152	Harvey
220	47.9	La Grange SD 102	La Grange Park
220	47.9	Winnetka SD 36	Winnetka
220	47.9	Woodstock CUSD 200	Woodstock
228	47.8	Champaign Community Unit SD 4	Champaign
228	47.8	Glenview CCSD 34	Glenview
228	47.8	Libertyville SD 70	Libertyville
228	47.8	Mount Prospect SD 57	Mount Prospect
228	47.8	Oswego Community Unit SD 308	Oswego
228	47.8	Winnebago CUSD 323	Winnebago
234	47.7	Deerfield SD 109	Deerfield
234	47.7	Elmhurst SD 205	Elmhurst
234	47.7	Johnsburg CUSD 12	Johnsburg
234	47.7	Mundelein Cons High SD 120	Mundelein
234	47.7	Naperville C U Dist 203	Naperville
234	47.7	Summit SD 104	Summit
234	47.7	United Twp HS District 30	East Moline
241	47.6	Bourbonnais SD 53	Bourbonnais
241	47.6	Collinsville CUSD 10	Collinsville
241	47.6	Community Unit SD 200	Wheaton
241	47.6	Herscher Community Unit SD 2	Herscher
241	47.6	Homer Community CSD 33C	Lockport
241	47.6	Kinnikinnick CCSD 131	Roscoe
241	47.6	Oregon C U School Dist-220	Oregon
241	47.6	Orland SD 135	Orland Park
241	47.6	Streator Elem SD 44	Streator
250	47.5	Bradley Bourbonnais CHSD 307	Bradley
250	47.5	Channahon SD 17	Channahon
250	47.5	Community SD 46	Grayslake
250	47.5	Community CSD 59	Arlington Hgts
250	47.5	Effingham Community Unit SD 40	Effingham
250	47.5	Niles Twp Community High SD 219	Skokie
250	47.5	Woodridge SD 68	Woodridge
257	47.4	Adlai E Stevenson Dist 125	Lincolnshire
257	47.4	Columbia Community Unit SD 4	Columbia
257	47.4	East Peoria SD 86	East Peoria
257	47.4	Kewanee Community Unit SD 229	Kewanee
257	47.4	Lake Forest SD 67	Lake Forest
257	47.4	Minooka Community CSD 201	Minooka
257	47.4	Monticello CUSD 25	Monticello
257	47.4	Rochester Community Unit SD 3A	Rochester
257	47.4	Sterling C U Dist 5	Sterling
266	47.3	Belleville SD 118	Belleville
266	47.3	Carlinville CUSD 1	Carlinville
266	47.3	Mokena SD 159	Mokena
266	47.3	Posen-Robbins El SD 143-5	Posen
266	47.3	Wilmette SD 39	Wilmette
271	47.2	Bloom Twp High SD 206	Chicago Heights
271	47.2	Steger SD 194	Steger
273	47.1	Galesburg CUSD 205	Galesburg
273	47.1	Maine Township HSD 207	Park Ridge
273	47.1	Northbrook SD 28	Northbrook
276	47.0	Community High SD 128	Libertyville
276	47.0	Lake Villa CCSD 41	Lake Villa
276	47.0	Oak Lawn-Hometown SD 123	Oak Lawn
276	47.0	Park Ridge CCSD 64	Park Ridge
280	46.9	Bensenville SD 2	Bensenville
280	46.9	Dolton SD 148	Riverdale
280	46.9	Geneseo Community Unit SD 228	Geneseo
280	46.9	Sandwich CUSD 430	Sandwich
284	46.8	Canton Union SD 66	Canton
285	46.7	Elem SD 159	Matteson
286	46.5	Forest Ridge SD 142	Oak Forest
287	46.4	Fenton Community HSD 100	Bensenville
287	46.4	Hononegah Community HSD 207	Rockton
289	46.3	Harvard CUSD 50	Harvard
289	46.3	Mannheim SD 83	Franklin Park
289	46.3	River Trails SD 26	Mount Prospect
292	46.1	Antioch Community High SD 117	Lake Villa
293	10.1	Department of Corrections SD 428	Springfield

Individual Education Program Students

Rank	Percent	District Name	City
1	28.0	Rantoul City SD 137	Rantoul
2	25.1	Mount Vernon SD 80	Mount Vernon
3	24.2	Charleston CUSD 1	Charleston
4	23.2	Bradley SD 61	Bradley
5	23.1	Herrin CUSD 4	Herrin
6	22.7	Streator Elem SD 44	Streator
7	22.4	Peoria SD 150	Peoria
8	22.2	Frankfort Community Unit SD 168	West Frankfort
8	22.2	Mattoon CUSD 2	Mattoon
10	22.1	Macomb Community Unit SD 185	Macomb
11	22.0	Belleville SD 118	Belleville
12	21.7	Alton Community Unit SD 11	Alton
12	21.7	Paris-Union SD 95	Paris
14	21.5	Cook County SD 130	Blue Island
15	21.3	Evanston CCSD 65	Evanston
16	21.0	Kankakee SD 111	Kankakee
16	21.0	Pekin Public SD 108	Pekin
18	20.9	Murphysboro CUSD 186	Murphysboro
19	20.8	East Saint Louis SD 189	E Saint Louis
20	20.6	Park Ridge CCSD 64	Park Ridge
21	20.5	Mchenry CCSD 15	Mc Henry
21	20.5	Zion Elementary SD 6	Zion
23	20.4	Robinson CUSD 2	Robinson
24	20.3	River Trails SD 26	Mount Prospect
24	20.3	Urbana SD 116	Urbana
26	20.2	Crete Monee CUSD 201U	Crete
26	20.2	Roxana Community Unit SD 1	Roxana
28	20.1	Carmi-White County CUSD 5	Carmi
28	20.1	Ottawa Elem SD 141	Ottawa
30	19.9	Northbrook SD 28	Northbrook
31	19.8	Marion Community Unit SD 2	Marion
32	19.7	Jacksonville SD 117	Jacksonville
32	19.7	Kewanee Community Unit SD 229	Kewanee
32	19.7	Proviso Twp HSD 209	Maywood
35	19.5	East Peoria SD 86	East Peoria
36	19.4	Kildeer Countryside CCSD 96	Buffalo Grove
36	19.4	Olympia CUSD 16	Stanford
38	19.3	Lake Villa CCSD 41	Lake Villa
38	19.3	Midlothian SD 143	Midlothian
40	19.1	Springfield SD 186	Springfield
41	18.9	Cahokia Community Unit SD 187	Cahokia
42	18.7	Du Quoin CUSD 300	Du Quoin
43	18.5	Carterville CUSD 5	Carterville
43	18.5	Rochelle Community CD 231	Rochelle
43	18.5	Winnetka SD 36	Winnetka
46	18.4	Arlington Heights SD 25	Arlington Hgts
46	18.4	East Moline SD 37	East Moline
46	18.4	Monmouth Unit SD 38	Monmouth
49	18.3	Alsip-Hazlgrn-Oaklawn SD 126	Alsip
49	18.3	Community CSD 62	Des Plaines
49	18.3	Lincolnshire-Prairieview SD 103	Lincolnshire
49	18.3	Skokie SD 68	Skokie
53	18.2	Bethalto CUSD 8	Bethalto
54	18.1	Danville CCSD 118	Danville
55	18.0	Berkeley SD 87	Berkeley
55	18.0	Oak Park Elem SD 97	Oak Park
55	18.0	Rock Island SD 41	Rock Island
58	17.9	Joliet Twp HSD 204	Joliet
59	17.8	Beach Park CCSD 3	Beach Park
59	17.8	Glenview CCSD 34	Glenview
59	17.8	Gurnee SD 56	Gurnee
62	17.7	Deerfield SD 109	Deerfield
62	17.7	Lansing SD 158	Lansing
62	17.7	O'Fallon CCSD 90	Ofallon
62	17.7	Sparta CUSD 140	Sparta
66	17.6	Prairie Central CUSD 8	Forrest
66	17.6	Wilmington CUSD 209U	Wilmington
68	17.5	United Twp HS District 30	East Moline
69	17.4	Keeneyville SD 20	Hanover Park
69	17.4	Lake Forest SD 67	Lake Forest
71	17.3	Champaign Community Unit SD 4	Champaign
71	17.3	Litchfield CUSD 12	Litchfield
71	17.3	Mchenry Community HSD 156	Mc Henry
74	17.2	Evanston Twp HSD 202	Evanston
74	17.2	Forest Ridge SD 142	Oak Forest
76	17.1	Collinsville CUSD 10	Collinsville
76	17.1	Massac Unit District #1	Metropolis
78	17.0	Granite City CUSD 9	Granite City
79	16.9	Cary CCSD 26	Cary
79	16.9	Evergreen Park ESD 124	Evergreen Park
79	16.9	Jasper County Comm Unit Dist 1	Newton
79	16.9	North Chicago SD 187	North Chicago
79	16.9	Oak Lawn-Hometown SD 123	Oak Lawn
84	16.8	Berwyn South SD 100	Berwyn
84	16.8	Effingham Community Unit SD 40	Effingham
86	16.7	Fenton Community HSD 100	Bensenville
86	16.7	Quincy SD 172	Quincy
86	16.7	Ridgeland SD 122	Oak Lawn
86	16.7	Waukegan CUSD 60	Waukegan
90	16.6	Aptakisic-Tripp CCSD 102	Buffalo Grove
90	16.6	Country Club Hills SD 160	Ctry Club Hill
90	16.6	Decatur SD 61	Decatur
90	16.6	Prairie-Hills Elem SD 144	Markham
94	16.5	Prospect Heights SD 23	Prospect Hgts
95	16.4	Antioch CCSD 34	Antioch
96	16.3	Clinton CUSD 15	Clinton
96	16.3	Joliet Public SD 86	Joliet
96	16.3	La Grange SD 102	La Grange Park
96	16.3	Ottawa Twp HSD 140	Ottawa
96	16.3	Palos Community CSD 118	Palos Park
96	16.3	Wheeling CCSD 21	Wheeling
96	16.3	Woodland CCSD 50	Gurnee
103	16.2	Bloom Twp High SD 206	Chicago Heights
103	16.2	Bond County CUSD 2	Greenville
103	16.2	Harvard CUSD 50	Harvard
103	16.2	Hillsboro Community Unit SD 3	Hillsboro
103	16.2	Libertyville SD 70	Libertyville
103	16.2	Mundelein Elem SD 75	Mundelein
103	16.2	Woodstock CUSD 200	Woodstock
110	16.1	Elmwood Park CUSD 401	Elmwood Park
110	16.1	Reed Custer CUSD 255U	Braidwood
110	16.1	Round Lake Area Schs - Dist 116	Round Lake
113	16.0	Channahon SD 17	Channahon
113	16.0	Fremont SD 79	Mundelein
113	16.0	Illinois Valley Central UD 321	Chillicothe
116	15.9	Lombard SD 44	Lombard
116	15.9	Moline Unit SD 40	Moline
116	15.9	Rochester Community Unit SD 3A	Rochester
116	15.9	Sterling C U Dist 5	Sterling
120	15.8	Bloomington SD 87	Bloomington
120	15.8	East Richland CUSD 1	Olney
120	15.8	Harvey SD 152	Harvey
120	15.8	North Palos SD 117	Palos Hills
120	15.8	Park Forest SD 163	Park Forest
120	15.8	Southwestern CUSD 9	Piasa
120	15.8	Steger SD 194	Steger
127	15.7	Bradley Bourbonnais CHSD 307	Bradley
128	15.5	Byron Community Unit SD 226	Byron
129	15.3	Canton Union SD 66	Canton
129	15.3	Chicago Heights SD 170	Chicago Heights
129	15.3	North Shore SD 112	Highland Park
129	15.3	Zion-Benton Twp HSD 126	Zion
133	15.2	Addison SD 4	Addison
133	15.2	Lake Forest Community HSD 115	Lake Forest
133	15.2	Matteson ESD 162	Matteson
133	15.2	Oregon C U School Dist-220	Oregon
133	15.2	Wauconda Community Unit SD 118	Wauconda
133	15.2	West Chicago ESD 33	West Chicago
139	15.1	Downers Grove Grade SD 58	Downers Grove
139	15.1	Mannheim SD 83	Franklin Park
139	15.1	Sandwich CUSD 430	Sandwich
139	15.1	Vandalia CUSD 203	Vandalia
143	15.0	Carlinville CUSD 1	Carlinville
143	15.0	Community Unit SD 300	Carpentersville
143	15.0	Edwardsville CUSD 7	Edwardsville
143	15.0	New Trier Twp HSD 203	Winnetka
147	14.9	Harrisburg CUSD 3	Harrisburg
147	14.9	Mount Prospect SD 57	Mount Prospect
147	14.9	Mundelein Cons High SD 120	Mundelein
147	14.9	Rockford SD 205	Rockford
147	14.9	SD 45 Dupage County	Villa Park
147	14.9	Tinley Park Community Cons SD 146	Tinley Park
153	14.8	Schaumburg CCSD 54	Schaumburg
153	14.8	Township High SD 113	Highland Park
153	14.8	Triad Community Unit SD 2	Troy
156	14.7	Bourbonnais SD 53	Bourbonnais
156	14.7	Burbank SD 111	Burbank
158	14.6	Belleville Twp HSD 201	Belleville
158	14.6	Harlem Unit Dist 122	Loves Park
158	14.6	Mokena SD 159	Mokena
158	14.6	Rich Twp HS District 227	Olympia Fields
162	14.5	Queen Bee SD 16	Glendale Hgts
163	14.4	Barrington CUSD 220	Barrington
163	14.4	Elem SD 159	Matteson
163	14.4	Galesburg CUSD 205	Galesburg
163	14.4	Homewood SD 153	Homewood
163	14.4	Mascoutah C U District 19	Mascoutah
163	14.4	Thornton Twp HSD 205	South Holland
163	14.4	Wabash CUSD 348	Mount Carmel
163	14.4	Will County SD 92	Lockport
163	14.4	Woodridge SD 68	Woodridge
172	14.3	Community Unit SD 200	Wheaton
172	14.3	Dixon Unit SD 170	Dixon
172	14.3	Herscher Community Unit SD 2	Herscher
172	14.3	Summit SD 104	Summit
172	14.3	Waterloo Community Unit SD 5	Waterloo
177	14.2	Crystal Lake CCSD 47	Crystal Lake
177	14.2	Westmont CUSD 201	Westmont
177	14.2	Winnebago CUSD 323	Winnebago

180	14.1	Homer Community CSD 33C	Lockport
180	14.1	Lisle CUSD 202	Lisle
180	14.1	Lyons SD 103	Lyons
180	14.1	Mahomet-Seymour CUSD 3	Mahomet
180	14.1	Taylorville CUSD 3	Taylorville
185	14.0	Bellwood SD 88	Bellwood
185	14.0	Community High SD 218	Oak Lawn
185	14.0	Maine Township HSD 207	Park Ridge
188	13.9	Aurora West Unit SD 129	Aurora
188	13.9	Bensenville SD 2	Bensenville
188	13.9	Eureka CU Dist 140	Eureka
188	13.9	Jersey CUSD 100	Jerseyville
188	13.9	Mclean County Unit Dist 5	Normal
188	13.9	Minooka Community CSD 201	Minooka
194	13.8	Community CSD 168	Sauk Village
194	13.8	Community High SD 128	Libertyville
196	13.7	Dolton SD 148	Riverdale
196	13.7	Freeport SD 145	Freeport
196	13.7	Johnsburg CUSD 12	Johnsburg
196	13.7	Sherrard Community Unit SD 200	Sherrard
200	13.6	Central Community Unit SD 301	Burlington
200	13.6	Highland Community Unit SD 5	Highland
200	13.6	Lemont-Bromberek CSD 113a	Lemont
200	13.6	Nippersink SD 2	Richmond
200	13.6	Peotone CUSD 207U	Peotone
205	13.5	Geneseo Community Unit SD 228	Geneseo
205	13.5	Oak Park & River Forest Dist 200	Oak Park
207	13.4	Bremen Community HS District 228	Midlothian
207	13.4	Kirby SD 140	Tinley Park
209	13.3	Cicero SD 99	Cicero
209	13.3	Glen Ellyn CCSD 89	Glen Ellyn
211	13.2	Community CSD 46	Grayslake
211	13.2	Community High SD 99	Downers Grove
211	13.2	Manteno Community Unit SD 5	Manteno
211	13.2	Morton CUSD 709	Morton
211	13.2	New Lenox SD 122	New Lenox
211	13.2	Summit Hill SD 161	Frankfort
211	13.2	Wilmette SD 39	Wilmette
218	13.1	Coal City CUSD 1	Coal City
219	13.0	Aurora East Unit SD 131	Aurora
219	13.0	Elmhurst SD 205	Elmhurst
219	13.0	Marquardt SD 15	Glendale Hgts
219	13.0	Oak Lawn Community HSD 229	Oak Lawn
223	12.9	Kaneland CUSD 302	Maple Park
223	12.9	Palatine CCSD 15	Palatine
223	12.9	Reavis Twp HSD 220	Burbank
226	12.8	Ball Chatham CUSD 5	Chatham
226	12.8	Glen Ellyn SD 41	Glen Ellyn
226	12.8	Lake Zurich CUSD 95	Lake Zurich
226	12.8	Posen-Robbins El SD 143-5	Posen
230	12.7	City of Chicago SD 299	Chicago
230	12.7	Niles Twp Community High SD 219	Skokie
230	12.7	Orland SD 135	Orland Park
233	12.6	Darien SD 61	Darien
233	12.6	West Harvey-Dixmoor PSD 147	Harvey
235	12.5	Antioch Community High SD 117	Lake Villa
235	12.5	Berwyn North SD 98	Berwyn
237	12.4	Leyden Community HSD 212	Franklin Park
237	12.4	Township High SD 214	Arlington Hgts
239	12.3	Lake Park Community HSD 108	Roselle
239	12.3	Troy Community CSD 30C	Plainfield
241	12.2	Community High SD 155	Crystal Lake
241	12.2	Flossmoor SD 161	Chicago Heights
241	12.2	Genoa Kingston CUSD 424	Genoa
244	12.1	Dolton SD 149	Calumet City
244	12.1	Du Page High SD 88	Villa Park
246	11.9	Monticello CUSD 25	Monticello
246	11.9	Oswego Community Unit SD 308	Oswego
246	11.9	Pekin Community HSD 303	Pekin
249	11.8	Grayslake Community High SD 127	Grayslake
249	11.8	Hawthorn CCSD 73	Vernon Hills
251	11.7	Indian Springs SD 109	Justice
252	11.6	Belvidere CUSD 100	Belvidere
252	11.6	Columbia Community Unit SD 4	Columbia
252	11.6	Consolidated High SD 230	Orland Park
255	11.5	Community CSD 93	Carol Stream
255	11.5	Frankfort CCSD 157c	Frankfort
255	11.5	Naperville C U Dist 203	Naperville
255	11.5	Yorkville Community Unit SD 115	Yorkville
259	11.4	Geneva Community Unit SD 304	Geneva
259	11.4	Meridian CUSD 223	Stillman Valley
261	11.3	Dunlap CUSD 323	Dunlap
261	11.3	Plainfield SD 202	Plainfield
261	11.3	Valley View CUSD 365U	Romeoville
264	11.2	Batavia Unit SD 101	Batavia
264	11.2	CCSD 181	Hinsdale
264	11.2	Maywood-Melrose Park-Broadview-89	Melrose Park
267	11.1	Sycamore CUSD 427	Sycamore
267	11.1	Thornton Fractional T HS D 215	Calumet City
267	11.1	Warren Twp High SD 121	Gurnee
270	10.9	Argo Community HSD 217	Summit
271	10.8	Kinnikinnick CCSD 131	Roscoe
271	10.8	Northfield Twp High SD 225	Glenview
273	10.7	J S Morton HS District 201	Cicero
274	10.6	Community CSD 59	Arlington Hgts
274	10.6	Homewood Flossmoor CHSD 233	Flossmoor
274	10.6	Lockport Twp HSD 205	Lockport
277	10.5	Dekalb Community Unit SD 428	De Kalb
277	10.5	Indian Prairie CUSD 204	Aurora
277	10.5	Township HSD 211	Palatine
280	10.4	Adlai E Stevenson Dist 125	Lincolnshire
280	10.4	SD 46	Elgin
282	10.2	Glenbard Twp HSD 87	Glen Ellyn
283	9.7	Hononegah Community HSD 207	Rockton
283	9.7	Lyons Twp HSD 204	La Grange
283	9.7	O'Fallon Twp High SD 203	Ofallon
283	9.7	Saint Charles CUSD 303	Saint Charles
287	9.3	Hinsdale Twp HSD 86	Hinsdale
288	9.0	East Maine SD 63	Des Plaines
289	8.7	Lincoln Way Community HSD 210	New Lenox
289	8.7	Mount Zion Community Unit SD 3	Mount Zion
291	8.5	Consolidated SD 158	Huntley
292	8.4	Community High SD 94	West Chicago
293	8.2	Department of Corrections SD 428	Springfield

English Language Learner Students

Rank	Percent	District Name	City
1	61.1	Aurora East Unit SD 131	Aurora
2	49.2	Cicero SD 99	Cicero
3	41.1	West Chicago ESD 33	West Chicago
4	34.2	Bensenville SD 2	Bensenville
5	29.4	Community CSD 59	Arlington Hgts
6	27.6	Waukegan CUSD 60	Waukegan
7	25.3	Addison SD 4	Addison
8	24.0	Summit SD 104	Summit
9	22.3	Harvard CUSD 50	Harvard
10	21.7	Wheeling CCSD 21	Wheeling
11	19.9	Palatine CCSD 15	Palatine
12	19.7	Berwyn North SD 98	Berwyn
13	19.4	Community CSD 62	Des Plaines
14	19.2	City of Chicago SD 299	Chicago
15	18.5	Berkeley SD 87	Berkeley
16	18.3	North Chicago SD 187	North Chicago
17	17.5	Berwyn South SD 100	Berwyn
18	16.9	SD 45 Dupage County	Villa Park
19	16.8	Burbank SD 111	Burbank
20	16.4	Queen Bee SD 16	Glendale Hgts
21	16.2	Mannheim SD 83	Franklin Park
22	15.8	SD 46	Elgin
23	15.4	East Maine SD 63	Des Plaines
24	14.8	Cook County SD 130	Blue Island
24	14.8	Marquardt SD 15	Glendale Hgts
26	14.7	Bellwood SD 88	Bellwood
26	14.7	Mundelein Elem SD 75	Mundelein
28	14.0	River Trails SD 26	Mount Prospect
29	13.6	Community Unit SD 300	Carpentersville
30	13.4	Community High SD 94	West Chicago
30	13.4	Posen-Robbins El SD 143-5	Posen
32	13.0	Hawthorn CCSD 73	Vernon Hills
33	11.7	Woodstock CUSD 200	Woodstock
34	11.1	North Shore SD 112	Highland Park
35	10.7	Glenview CCSD 34	Glenview
36	10.5	East Moline SD 37	East Moline
37	10.3	Urbana SD 116	Urbana
37	10.3	Woodridge SD 68	Woodridge
39	10.1	Lyons SD 103	Lyons
40	10.0	Ridgeland SD 122	Oak Lawn
41	9.8	Elmwood Park CUSD 401	Elmwood Park
42	9.7	Schaumburg CCSD 54	Schaumburg
43	9.6	Skokie SD 68	Skokie
44	9.2	Chicago Heights SD 170	Chicago Heights
45	9.1	Prospect Heights SD 23	Prospect Hgts
46	9.0	Gurnee SD 56	Gurnee
47	8.5	Joliet Public SD 86	Joliet
47	8.5	West Harvey-Dixmoor PSD 147	Harvey
49	8.4	Argo Community HSD 217	Summit
49	8.4	Keeneyville SD 20	Hanover Park
49	8.4	Zion Elementary SD 6	Zion
52	8.3	Leyden Community HSD 212	Franklin Park
53	8.1	Maywood-Melrose Park-Broadview-89	Melrose Park
54	8.0	Indian Springs SD 109	Justice
54	8.0	Township High SD 214	Arlington Hgts
54	8.0	Woodland CCSD 50	Gurnee
57	7.9	J S Morton HS District 201	Cicero
58	7.6	Aurora West Unit SD 129	Aurora
58	7.6	Rochelle Community CD 231	Rochelle
60	7.4	Dekalb Community Unit SD 428	De Kalb
61	7.2	Rockford SD 205	Rockford
62	7.1	Alsip-Hazlgrn-Oaklawn SD 126	Alsip
63	6.9	Glen Ellyn SD 41	Glen Ellyn
63	6.9	Kewanee Community Unit SD 229	Kewanee
65	6.8	Aptakisic-Tripp CCSD 102	Buffalo Grove
65	6.8	Community CSD 93	Carol Stream
65	6.8	Mundelein Cons High SD 120	Mundelein
68	6.6	Darien SD 61	Darien
69	6.5	Du Page High SD 88	Villa Park
70	6.3	Lombard SD 44	Lombard
70	6.3	Moline Unit SD 40	Moline
72	6.2	North Palos SD 117	Palos Hills
73	6.1	Wauconda Community Unit SD 118	Wauconda
74	5.9	Barrington CUSD 220	Barrington
75	5.7	Bloom Twp High SD 206	Chicago Heights
75	5.7	Fenton Community HSD 100	Bensenville
75	5.7	Proviso Twp HSD 209	Maywood
78	5.5	Niles Twp Community High SD 219	Skokie
79	5.4	Maine Township HSD 207	Park Ridge
79	5.4	Northbrook SD 28	Northbrook
79	5.4	Township HSD 211	Palatine
82	5.2	Westmont CUSD 201	Westmont
83	5.0	Adlai E Stevenson Dist 125	Lincolnshire
84	4.9	Glen Ellyn CCSD 89	Glen Ellyn
84	4.9	Reavis Twp HSD 220	Burbank
86	4.8	Township High SD 113	Highland Park
87	4.7	Community Unit SD 200	Wheaton
87	4.7	Indian Prairie CUSD 204	Aurora
87	4.7	Kirby SD 140	Tinley Park
87	4.7	Mount Prospect SD 57	Mount Prospect
91	4.6	Community CSD 46	Grayslake
91	4.6	Lake Villa CCSD 41	Lake Villa
93	4.5	Joliet Twp HSD 204	Joliet
93	4.5	La Grange SD 102	La Grange Park
95	4.3	Crystal Lake CCSD 47	Crystal Lake
95	4.3	Elmhurst SD 205	Elmhurst
95	4.3	Valley View CUSD 365U	Romeoville
98	4.2	Arlington Heights SD 25	Arlington Hgts
98	4.2	Monmouth Unit SD 38	Monmouth
100	4.1	Tinley Park Community Cons SD 146	Tinley Park
101	4.0	Beach Park CCSD 3	Beach Park
101	4.0	Mchenry CCSD 15	Mc Henry
103	3.9	Round Lake Area Schs - Dist 116	Round Lake
104	3.8	Oak Lawn-Hometown SD 123	Oak Lawn
105	3.7	Cary CCSD 26	Cary
106	3.6	Lisle CUSD 202	Lisle
107	3.5	Evanston CCSD 65	Evanston
107	3.5	Hinsdale Twp HSD 86	Hinsdale
107	3.5	Sandwich CUSD 430	Sandwich
110	3.4	Fremont SD 79	Mundelein
110	3.4	Harvey SD 152	Harvey
110	3.4	Wilmette SD 39	Wilmette
113	3.3	Downers Grove Grade SD 58	Downers Grove
113	3.3	Plainfield SD 202	Plainfield
115	3.2	Northfield Twp High SD 225	Glenview
116	3.1	Champaign Community Unit SD 4	Champaign
117	3.0	Genoa Kingston CUSD 424	Genoa
118	2.9	Sterling C U Dist 5	Sterling
118	2.9	Streator Elem SD 44	Streator
120	2.8	Kankakee SD 111	Kankakee
120	2.8	Zion-Benton Twp HSD 126	Zion
122	2.7	Bloomington SD 87	Bloomington
122	2.7	Steger SD 194	Steger
124	2.6	CCSD 181	Hinsdale
125	2.5	Community High SD 99	Downers Grove
125	2.5	Lincolnshire-Prairieview SD 103	Lincolnshire
125	2.5	Mchenry Community HSD 156	Mc Henry
125	2.5	Oak Park Elem SD 97	Oak Park
125	2.5	Troy Community CSD 30C	Plainfield
130	2.4	Kildeer Countryside CCSD 96	Buffalo Grove
130	2.4	Oak Lawn Community HSD 229	Oak Lawn
130	2.4	Prairie-Hills Elem SD 144	Markham
130	2.4	Rantoul City SD 137	Rantoul
134	2.3	Evanston Twp HSD 202	Evanston
134	2.3	Orland SD 135	Orland Park
134	2.3	Palos Community CSD 118	Palos Park
137	2.1	Community High SD 128	Libertyville
137	2.1	Forest Ridge SD 142	Oak Forest
137	2.1	Will County SD 92	Lockport
140	2.0	Consolidated High SD 230	Orland Park
140	2.0	Kaneland CUSD 302	Maple Park
140	2.0	Naperville C U Dist 203	Naperville
140	2.0	Oswego Community Unit SD 308	Oswego
144	1.9	Batavia Unit SD 101	Batavia
144	1.9	Warren Twp High SD 121	Gurnee
146	1.8	Collinsville CUSD 10	Collinsville
146	1.8	Community High SD 218	Oak Lawn
146	1.8	Evergreen Park ESD 124	Evergreen Park
146	1.8	Libertyville SD 70	Libertyville
150	1.7	Consolidated SD 158	Huntley
150	1.7	Homer Community CSD 33C	Lockport
150	1.7	United Twp HS District 30	East Moline
153	1.6	Harlem Unit Dist 122	Loves Park
153	1.6	Lake Park Community HSD 108	Roselle
153	1.6	Lake Zurich CUSD 95	Lake Zurich
153	1.6	Mclean County Unit Dist 5	Normal
153	1.6	Park Ridge CCSD 64	Park Ridge
158	1.5	Grayslake Community High SD 127	Grayslake
158	1.5	Oregon C U School Dist-220	Oregon
158	1.5	Saint Charles CUSD 303	Saint Charles

161	1.4	Glenbard Twp HSD 87	Glen Ellyn
162	1.3	Geneva Community Unit SD 304	Geneva
162	1.3	Lyons Twp HSD 204	La Grange
162	1.3	New Trier Twp HSD 203	Winnetka
165	1.2	Antioch CCSD 34	Antioch
166	1.1	Community High SD 155	Crystal Lake
166	1.1	Deerfield SD 109	Deerfield
166	1.1	East Peoria SD 86	East Peoria
166	1.1	Rock Island SD 41	Rock Island
166	1.1	Sycamore CUSD 427	Sycamore
171	1.0	Bremen Community HS District 228	Midlothian
171	1.0	Freeport SD 145	Freeport
171	1.0	Lemont-Bromberek CSD 113a	Lemont
171	1.0	Murphysboro CUSD 186	Murphysboro
171	1.0	Ottawa Elem SD 141	Ottawa
176	0.9	Flossmoor SD 161	Chicago Heights
176	0.9	Roxana Community Unit SD 1	Roxana
176	0.9	Thornton Twp HSD 205	South Holland
179	0.8	Macomb Community Unit SD 185	Macomb
179	0.8	Meridian CUSD 223	Stillman Valley
179	0.8	Olympia CUSD 16	Stanford
179	0.8	Prairie Central CUSD 8	Forrest
183	0.7	Bradley SD 61	Bradley
183	0.7	Dunlap CUSD 323	Dunlap
185	0.6	Charleston CUSD 1	Charleston
185	0.6	Decatur SD 61	Decatur
185	0.6	Effingham Community Unit SD 40	Effingham
185	0.6	Lake Forest SD 67	Lake Forest
185	0.6	Oak Park & River Forest Dist 200	Oak Park
190	0.5	Crete Monee CUSD 201U	Crete
190	0.5	East Saint Louis SD 189	E Saint Louis
190	0.5	Granite City CUSD 9	Granite City
190	0.5	Marion Community Unit SD 2	Marion
190	0.5	Ottawa Twp HSD 140	Ottawa
190	0.5	Winnetka SD 36	Winnetka
196	0.4	Galesburg CUSD 205	Galesburg
196	0.4	Manteno Community Unit SD 5	Manteno
196	0.4	Sherrard Community Unit SD 200	Sherrard
199	0.3	Bourbonnais SD 53	Bourbonnais
199	0.3	Edwardsville CUSD 7	Edwardsville
199	0.3	Jacksonville SD 117	Jacksonville
199	0.3	Matteson ESD 162	Matteson
199	0.3	Mattoon CUSD 2	Mattoon
199	0.3	Mokena SD 159	Mokena
199	0.3	Mount Vernon SD 80	Mount Vernon
199	0.3	Pekin Community HSD 303	Pekin
199	0.3	Pekin Public SD 108	Pekin
199	0.3	Quincy SD 172	Quincy
199	0.3	Yorkville Community Unit SD 115	Yorkville
210	0.2	Alton Community Unit SD 11	Alton
210	0.2	Belleville SD 118	Belleville
210	0.2	Belleville Twp HSD 201	Belleville
210	0.2	Cahokia Community Unit SD 187	Cahokia
210	0.2	East Richland CUSD 1	Olney
210	0.2	Jersey CUSD 100	Jerseyville
210	0.2	Johnsburg CUSD 12	Johnsburg
210	0.2	Lincoln Way Community HSD 210	New Lenox
210	0.2	Litchfield CUSD 12	Litchfield
210	0.2	Lockport Twp HSD 205	Lockport
210	0.2	Mount Zion Community Unit SD 3	Mount Zion
210	0.2	New Lenox SD 122	New Lenox
210	0.2	O'Fallon CCSD 90	Ofallon
210	0.2	Park Forest SD 163	Park Forest
210	0.2	Peotone CUSD 207U	Peotone
210	0.2	Robinson CUSD 2	Robinson
210	0.2	Springfield SD 186	Springfield
210	0.2	Summit Hill SD 161	Frankfort
228	0.1	Byron Community Unit SD 226	Byron
228	0.1	Carlinville CUSD 1	Carlinville
228	0.1	Coal City CUSD 1	Coal City
228	0.1	Columbia Community Unit SD 4	Columbia
228	0.1	Dixon Unit SD 170	Dixon
228	0.1	Kinnikinnick CCSD 131	Roscoe
228	0.1	Paris-Union SD 95	Paris
228	0.1	Rochester Community Unit SD 3A	Rochester
228	0.1	Sparta CUSD 140	Sparta
228	0.1	Wabash CUSD 348	Mount Carmel
238	0.0	Central Community Unit SD 301	Burlington
238	0.0	Dolton SD 148	Riverdale
240	0.0	Antioch Community High SD 117	Lake Villa
240	0.0	Ball Chatham CUSD 5	Chatham
240	0.0	Belvidere CUSD 100	Belvidere
240	0.0	Bethalto CUSD 8	Bethalto
240	0.0	Bond County CUSD 2	Greenville
240	0.0	Bradley Bourbonnais CHSD 307	Bradley
240	0.0	Canton Union SD 66	Canton
240	0.0	Carmi-White County CUSD 5	Carmi
240	0.0	Carterville CUSD 5	Carterville
240	0.0	Channahon SD 17	Channahon
240	0.0	Clinton CUSD 15	Clinton
240	0.0	Community CSD 168	Sauk Village
240	0.0	Country Club Hills SD 160	Ctry Club Hill
240	0.0	Danville CCSD 118	Danville
240	0.0	Department of Corrections SD 428	Springfield
240	0.0	Dolton SD 149	Calumet City
240	0.0	Du Quoin CUSD 300	Du Quoin
240	0.0	Elem SD 159	Matteson
240	0.0	Eureka CU Dist 140	Eureka
240	0.0	Frankfort CCSD 157c	Frankfort
240	0.0	Frankfort Community Unit SD 168	West Frankfort
240	0.0	Geneseo Community Unit SD 228	Geneseo
240	0.0	Harrisburg CUSD 3	Harrisburg
240	0.0	Herrin CUSD 4	Herrin
240	0.0	Herscher Community Unit SD 2	Herscher
240	0.0	Highland Community Unit SD 5	Highland
240	0.0	Hillsboro Community Unit SD 3	Hillsboro
240	0.0	Homewood Flossmoor CHSD 233	Flossmoor
240	0.0	Homewood SD 153	Homewood
240	0.0	Hononegah Community HSD 207	Rockton
240	0.0	Illinois Valley Central UD 321	Chillicothe
240	0.0	Jasper County Comm Unit Dist 1	Newton
240	0.0	Lake Forest Community HSD 115	Lake Forest
240	0.0	Lansing SD 158	Lansing
240	0.0	Mahomet-Seymour CUSD 3	Mahomet
240	0.0	Mascoutah C U District 19	Mascoutah
240	0.0	Massac Unit District #1	Metropolis
240	0.0	Midlothian SD 143	Midlothian
240	0.0	Minooka Community CSD 201	Minooka
240	0.0	Monticello CUSD 25	Monticello
240	0.0	Morton CUSD 709	Morton
240	0.0	Nippersink SD 2	Richmond
240	0.0	O'Fallon Twp High SD 203	Ofallon
240	0.0	Peoria SD 150	Peoria
240	0.0	Reed Custer CUSD 255U	Braidwood
240	0.0	Rich Twp HS District 227	Olympia Fields
240	0.0	Southwestern CUSD 9	Piasa
240	0.0	Taylorville CUSD 3	Taylorville
240	0.0	Thornton Fractional T HS D 215	Calumet City
240	0.0	Triad Community Unit SD 2	Troy
240	0.0	Vandalia CUSD 203	Vandalia
240	0.0	Waterloo Community Unit SD 5	Waterloo
240	0.0	Wilmington CUSD 209U	Wilmington
240	0.0	Winnebago CUSD 323	Winnebago

Migrant Students

Rank	Percent	District Name	City
1	n/a	Addison SD 4	Addison
1	n/a	Adlai E Stevenson Dist 125	Lincolnshire
1	n/a	Alsip-Hazlgrn-Oaklawn SD 126	Alsip
1	n/a	Alton Community Unit SD 11	Alton
1	n/a	Antioch CCSD 34	Antioch
1	n/a	Antioch Community High SD 117	Lake Villa
1	n/a	Aptakisic-Tripp CCSD 102	Buffalo Grove
1	n/a	Argo Community HSD 217	Summit
1	n/a	Arlington Heights SD 25	Arlington Hgts
1	n/a	Aurora East Unit SD 131	Aurora
1	n/a	Aurora West Unit SD 129	Aurora
1	n/a	Ball Chatham CUSD 5	Chatham
1	n/a	Barrington CUSD 220	Barrington
1	n/a	Batavia Unit SD 101	Batavia
1	n/a	Beach Park CCSD 3	Beach Park
1	n/a	Belleville SD 118	Belleville
1	n/a	Belleville Twp HSD 201	Belleville
1	n/a	Bellwood SD 88	Bellwood
1	n/a	Belvidere CUSD 100	Belvidere
1	n/a	Bensenville SD 2	Bensenville
1	n/a	Berkeley SD 87	Berkeley
1	n/a	Berwyn North SD 98	Berwyn
1	n/a	Berwyn South SD 100	Berwyn
1	n/a	Bethalto CUSD 8	Bethalto
1	n/a	Bloom Twp High SD 206	Chicago Heights
1	n/a	Bloomington SD 87	Bloomington
1	n/a	Bond County CUSD 2	Greenville
1	n/a	Bourbonnais SD 53	Bourbonnais
1	n/a	Bradley Bourbonnais CHSD 307	Bradley
1	n/a	Bradley SD 61	Bradley
1	n/a	Bremen Community HS District 228	Midlothian
1	n/a	Burbank SD 111	Burbank
1	n/a	Byron Community Unit SD 226	Byron
1	n/a	CCSD 181	Hinsdale
1	n/a	Cahokia Community Unit SD 187	Cahokia
1	n/a	Canton Union SD 66	Canton
1	n/a	Carlinville CUSD 1	Carlinville
1	n/a	Carmi-White County CUSD 5	Carmi
1	n/a	Carterville CUSD 5	Carterville
1	n/a	Cary CCSD 26	Cary
1	n/a	Central Community Unit SD 301	Burlington
1	n/a	Champaign Community Unit SD 4	Champaign
1	n/a	Channahon SD 17	Channahon
1	n/a	Charleston CUSD 1	Charleston
1	n/a	Chicago Heights SD 170	Chicago Heights
1	n/a	Cicero SD 99	Cicero
1	n/a	City of Chicago SD 299	Chicago
1	n/a	Clinton CUSD 15	Clinton
1	n/a	Coal City CUSD 1	Coal City
1	n/a	Collinsville CUSD 10	Collinsville
1	n/a	Columbia Community Unit SD 4	Columbia
1	n/a	Community CSD 168	Sauk Village
1	n/a	Community CSD 46	Grayslake
1	n/a	Community CSD 59	Arlington Hgts
1	n/a	Community CSD 62	Des Plaines
1	n/a	Community CSD 93	Carol Stream
1	n/a	Community High SD 128	Libertyville
1	n/a	Community High SD 155	Crystal Lake
1	n/a	Community High SD 218	Oak Lawn
1	n/a	Community High SD 94	West Chicago
1	n/a	Community High SD 99	Downers Grove
1	n/a	Community Unit SD 200	Wheaton
1	n/a	Community Unit SD 300	Carpentersville
1	n/a	Consolidated High SD 230	Orland Park
1	n/a	Consolidated SD 158	Huntley
1	n/a	Cook County SD 130	Blue Island
1	n/a	Country Club Hills SD 160	Ctry Club Hill
1	n/a	Crete Monee CUSD 201U	Crete
1	n/a	Crystal Lake CCSD 47	Crystal Lake
1	n/a	Danville CCSD 118	Danville
1	n/a	Darien SD 61	Darien
1	n/a	Decatur SD 61	Decatur
1	n/a	Deerfield SD 109	Deerfield
1	n/a	Dekalb Community Unit SD 428	De Kalb
1	n/a	Department of Corrections SD 428	Springfield
1	n/a	Dixon Unit SD 170	Dixon
1	n/a	Dolton SD 148	Riverdale
1	n/a	Dolton SD 149	Calumet City
1	n/a	Downers Grove Grade SD 58	Downers Grove
1	n/a	Du Page High SD 88	Villa Park
1	n/a	Du Quoin CUSD 300	Du Quoin
1	n/a	Dunlap CUSD 323	Dunlap
1	n/a	East Maine SD 63	Des Plaines
1	n/a	East Moline SD 37	East Moline
1	n/a	East Peoria SD 86	East Peoria
1	n/a	East Richland CUSD 1	Olney
1	n/a	East Saint Louis SD 189	E Saint Louis
1	n/a	Edwardsville CUSD 7	Edwardsville
1	n/a	Effingham Community Unit SD 40	Effingham
1	n/a	Elem SD 159	Matteson
1	n/a	Elmhurst SD 205	Elmhurst
1	n/a	Elmwood Park CUSD 401	Elmwood Park
1	n/a	Eureka CU Dist 140	Eureka
1	n/a	Evanston CCSD 65	Evanston
1	n/a	Evanston Twp HSD 202	Evanston
1	n/a	Evergreen Park ESD 124	Evergreen Park
1	n/a	Fenton Community HSD 100	Bensenville
1	n/a	Flossmoor SD 161	Chicago Heights
1	n/a	Forest Ridge SD 142	Oak Forest
1	n/a	Frankfort CCSD 157c	Frankfort
1	n/a	Frankfort Community Unit SD 168	West Frankfort
1	n/a	Freeport SD 145	Freeport
1	n/a	Fremont SD 79	Mundelein
1	n/a	Galesburg CUSD 205	Galesburg
1	n/a	Geneseo Community Unit SD 228	Geneseo
1	n/a	Geneva Community Unit SD 304	Geneva
1	n/a	Genoa Kingston CUSD 424	Genoa
1	n/a	Glen Ellyn CCSD 89	Glen Ellyn
1	n/a	Glen Ellyn SD 41	Glen Ellyn
1	n/a	Glenbard Twp HSD 87	Glen Ellyn
1	n/a	Glenview CCSD 34	Glenview
1	n/a	Granite City CUSD 9	Granite City
1	n/a	Grayslake Community High SD 127	Grayslake
1	n/a	Gurnee SD 56	Gurnee
1	n/a	Harlem Unit Dist 122	Loves Park
1	n/a	Harrisburg CUSD 3	Harrisburg
1	n/a	Harvard CUSD 50	Harvard
1	n/a	Harvey SD 152	Harvey
1	n/a	Hawthorn CCSD 73	Vernon Hills
1	n/a	Herrin CUSD 4	Herrin
1	n/a	Herscher Community Unit SD 2	Herscher
1	n/a	Highland Community Unit SD 5	Highland
1	n/a	Hillsboro Community Unit SD 3	Hillsboro
1	n/a	Hinsdale Twp HSD 86	Hinsdale
1	n/a	Homer Community CSD 33C	Lockport
1	n/a	Homewood Flossmoor CHSD 233	Flossmoor
1	n/a	Homewood SD 153	Homewood
1	n/a	Hononegah Community HSD 207	Rockton
1	n/a	Illinois Valley Central UD 321	Chillicothe
1	n/a	Indian Prairie CUSD 204	Aurora
1	n/a	Indian Springs SD 109	Justice
1	n/a	J S Morton HS District 201	Cicero
1	n/a	Jacksonville SD 117	Jacksonville
1	n/a	Jasper County Comm Unit Dist 1	Newton
1	n/a	Jersey CUSD 100	Jerseyville
1	n/a	Johnsburg CUSD 12	Johnsburg
1	n/a	Joliet Public SD 86	Joliet
1	n/a	Joliet Twp HSD 204	Joliet
1	n/a	Kaneland CUSD 302	Maple Park
1	n/a	Kankakee SD 111	Kankakee

1	n/a	Keeneyville SD 20	Hanover Park
1	n/a	Kewanee Community Unit SD 229	Kewanee
1	n/a	Kildeer Countryside CCSD 96	Buffalo Grove
1	n/a	Kinnikinnick CCSD 131	Roscoe
1	n/a	Kirby SD 140	Tinley Park
1	n/a	La Grange SD 102	La Grange Park
1	n/a	Lake Forest Community HSD 115	Lake Forest
1	n/a	Lake Forest SD 67	Lake Forest
1	n/a	Lake Park Community HSD 108	Roselle
1	n/a	Lake Villa CCSD 41	Lake Villa
1	n/a	Lake Zurich CUSD 95	Lake Zurich
1	n/a	Lansing SD 158	Lansing
1	n/a	Lemont-Bromberek CSD 113a	Lemont
1	n/a	Leyden Community HSD 212	Franklin Park
1	n/a	Libertyville SD 70	Libertyville
1	n/a	Lincoln Way Community HSD 210	New Lenox
1	n/a	Lincolnshire-Prairieview SD 103	Lincolnshire
1	n/a	Lisle CUSD 202	Lisle
1	n/a	Litchfield CUSD 12	Litchfield
1	n/a	Lockport Twp HSD 205	Lockport
1	n/a	Lombard SD 44	Lombard
1	n/a	Lyons SD 103	Lyons
1	n/a	Lyons Twp HSD 204	La Grange
1	n/a	Macomb Community Unit SD 185	Macomb
1	n/a	Mahomet-Seymour CUSD 3	Mahomet
1	n/a	Maine Township HSD 207	Park Ridge
1	n/a	Mannheim SD 83	Franklin Park
1	n/a	Manteno Community Unit SD 5	Manteno
1	n/a	Marion Community Unit SD 2	Marion
1	n/a	Marquardt SD 15	Glendale Hgts
1	n/a	Mascoutah C U District 19	Mascoutah
1	n/a	Massac Unit District #1	Metropolis
1	n/a	Matteson ESD 162	Matteson
1	n/a	Mattoon CUSD 2	Mattoon
1	n/a	Maywood-Melrose Park-Broadview-89	Melrose Park
1	n/a	Mchenry CCSD 15	Mc Henry
1	n/a	Mchenry Community HSD 156	Mc Henry
1	n/a	Mclean County Unit Dist 5	Normal
1	n/a	Meridian CUSD 223	Stillman Valley
1	n/a	Midlothian SD 143	Midlothian
1	n/a	Minooka Community CSD 201	Minooka
1	n/a	Mokena SD 159	Mokena
1	n/a	Moline Unit SD 40	Moline
1	n/a	Monmouth Unit SD 38	Monmouth
1	n/a	Monticello CUSD 25	Monticello
1	n/a	Morton CUSD 709	Morton
1	n/a	Mount Prospect SD 57	Mount Prospect
1	n/a	Mount Vernon SD 80	Mount Vernon
1	n/a	Mount Zion Community Unit SD 3	Mount Zion
1	n/a	Mundelein Cons High SD 120	Mundelein
1	n/a	Mundelein Elem SD 75	Mundelein
1	n/a	Murphysboro CUSD 186	Murphysboro
1	n/a	Naperville C U Dist 203	Naperville
1	n/a	New Lenox SD 122	New Lenox
1	n/a	New Trier Twp HSD 203	Winnetka
1	n/a	Niles Twp Community High SD 219	Skokie
1	n/a	Nippersink SD 2	Richmond
1	n/a	North Chicago SD 187	North Chicago
1	n/a	North Palos SD 117	Palos Hills
1	n/a	North Shore SD 112	Highland Park
1	n/a	Northbrook SD 28	Northbrook
1	n/a	Northfield Twp High SD 225	Glenview
1	n/a	O'Fallon CCSD 90	Ofallon
1	n/a	O'Fallon Twp High SD 203	Ofallon
1	n/a	Oak Lawn Community HSD 229	Oak Lawn
1	n/a	Oak Lawn-Hometown SD 123	Oak Lawn
1	n/a	Oak Park & River Forest Dist 200	Oak Park
1	n/a	Oak Park Elem SD 97	Oak Park
1	n/a	Olympia CUSD 16	Stanford
1	n/a	Oregon C U School Dist-220	Oregon
1	n/a	Orland SD 135	Orland Park
1	n/a	Oswego Community Unit SD 308	Oswego
1	n/a	Ottawa Elem SD 141	Ottawa
1	n/a	Ottawa Twp HSD 140	Ottawa
1	n/a	Palatine CCSD 15	Palatine
1	n/a	Palos Community CSD 118	Palos Park
1	n/a	Paris-Union SD 95	Paris
1	n/a	Park Forest SD 163	Park Forest
1	n/a	Park Ridge CCSD 64	Park Ridge
1	n/a	Pekin Community HSD 303	Pekin
1	n/a	Pekin Public SD 108	Pekin
1	n/a	Peoria SD 150	Peoria
1	n/a	Peotone CUSD 207U	Peotone
1	n/a	Plainfield SD 202	Plainfield
1	n/a	Posen-Robbins El SD 143-5	Posen
1	n/a	Prairie Central CUSD 8	Forrest
1	n/a	Prairie-Hills Elem SD 144	Markham
1	n/a	Prospect Heights SD 23	Prospect Hgts
1	n/a	Proviso Twp HSD 209	Maywood
1	n/a	Queen Bee SD 16	Glendale Hgts
1	n/a	Quincy SD 172	Quincy
1	n/a	Rantoul City SD 137	Rantoul
1	n/a	Reavis Twp HSD 220	Burbank
1	n/a	Reed Custer CUSD 255U	Braidwood
1	n/a	Rich Twp HS District 227	Olympia Fields
1	n/a	Ridgeland SD 122	Oak Lawn
1	n/a	River Trails SD 26	Mount Prospect
1	n/a	Robinson CUSD 2	Robinson
1	n/a	Rochelle Community CD 231	Rochelle
1	n/a	Rochester Community Unit SD 3A	Rochester
1	n/a	Rock Island SD 41	Rock Island
1	n/a	Rockford SD 205	Rockford
1	n/a	Round Lake Area Schs - Dist 116	Round Lake
1	n/a	Roxana Community Unit SD 1	Roxana
1	n/a	SD 45 Dupage County	Villa Park
1	n/a	SD 46	Elgin
1	n/a	Saint Charles CUSD 303	Saint Charles
1	n/a	Sandwich CUSD 430	Sandwich
1	n/a	Schaumburg CCSD 54	Schaumburg
1	n/a	Sherrard Community Unit SD 200	Sherrard
1	n/a	Skokie SD 68	Skokie
1	n/a	Southwestern CUSD 9	Piasa
1	n/a	Sparta CUSD 140	Sparta
1	n/a	Springfield SD 186	Springfield
1	n/a	Steger SD 194	Steger
1	n/a	Sterling C U Dist 5	Sterling
1	n/a	Streator Elem SD 44	Streator
1	n/a	Summit Hill SD 161	Frankfort
1	n/a	Summit SD 104	Summit
1	n/a	Sycamore CUSD 427	Sycamore
1	n/a	Taylorville CUSD 3	Taylorville
1	n/a	Thornton Fractional T HS D 215	Calumet City
1	n/a	Thornton Twp HSD 205	South Holland
1	n/a	Tinley Park Community Cons SD 146	Tinley Park
1	n/a	Township HSD 211	Palatine
1	n/a	Township High SD 113	Highland Park
1	n/a	Township High SD 214	Arlington Hgts
1	n/a	Triad Community Unit SD 2	Troy
1	n/a	Troy Community CSD 30C	Plainfield
1	n/a	United Twp HS District 30	East Moline
1	n/a	Urbana SD 116	Urbana
1	n/a	Valley View CUSD 365U	Romeoville
1	n/a	Vandalia CUSD 203	Vandalia
1	n/a	Wabash CUSD 348	Mount Carmel
1	n/a	Warren Twp High SD 121	Gurnee
1	n/a	Waterloo Community Unit SD 5	Waterloo
1	n/a	Wauconda Community Unit SD 118	Wauconda
1	n/a	Waukegan CUSD 60	Waukegan
1	n/a	West Chicago ESD 33	West Chicago
1	n/a	West Harvey-Dixmoor PSD 147	Harvey
1	n/a	Westmont CUSD 201	Westmont
1	n/a	Wheeling CCSD 21	Wheeling
1	n/a	Will County SD 92	Lockport
1	n/a	Wilmette SD 39	Wilmette
1	n/a	Wilmington CUSD 209U	Wilmington
1	n/a	Winnebago CUSD 323	Winnebago
1	n/a	Winnetka SD 36	Winnetka
1	n/a	Woodland CCSD 50	Gurnee
1	n/a	Woodridge SD 68	Woodridge
1	n/a	Woodstock CUSD 200	Woodstock
1	n/a	Yorkville Community Unit SD 115	Yorkville
1	n/a	Zion Elementary SD 6	Zion
1	n/a	Zion-Benton Twp HSD 126	Zion

Students Eligible for Free Lunch

Rank	Percent	District Name	City
1	93.2	West Harvey-Dixmoor PSD 147	Harvey
2	78.6	Prairie-Hills Elem SD 144	Markham
3	77.5	Chicago Heights SD 170	Chicago Heights
4	77.2	Harvey SD 152	Harvey
5	71.6	Posen-Robbins El SD 143-5	Posen
6	70.4	East Saint Louis SD 189	E Saint Louis
7	69.1	City of Chicago SD 299	Chicago
8	66.0	Park Forest SD 163	Park Forest
9	64.8	Kankakee SD 111	Kankakee
10	61.7	Cahokia Community Unit SD 187	Cahokia
11	60.7	Cicero SD 99	Cicero
12	58.5	Cook County SD 130	Blue Island
13	57.9	Dolton SD 148	Riverdale
14	54.7	Mount Vernon SD 80	Mount Vernon
15	54.2	Peoria SD 150	Peoria
16	54.0	Dolton SD 149	Calumet City
17	53.3	Maywood-Melrose Park-Broadview-89	Melrose Park
18	53.1	Danville CCSD 118	Danville
19	52.4	Berwyn North SD 98	Berwyn
20	52.0	Aurora East Unit SD 131	Aurora
21	51.2	Joliet Public SD 86	Joliet
22	50.8	Rockford SD 205	Rockford
23	49.6	Zion Elementary SD 6	Zion
24	48.0	Rantoul City SD 137	Rantoul
25	47.1	Springfield SD 186	Springfield
26	46.8	Bellwood SD 88	Bellwood
26	46.8	Country Club Hills SD 160	Ctry Club Hill
28	46.4	Rock Island SD 41	Rock Island
29	46.3	Decatur SD 61	Decatur
30	46.1	Summit SD 104	Summit
31	45.0	Kewanee Community Unit SD 229	Kewanee
32	44.6	East Moline SD 37	East Moline
33	42.3	Waukegan CUSD 60	Waukegan
34	42.2	Murphysboro CUSD 186	Murphysboro
35	40.9	Joliet Twp HSD 204	Joliet
36	40.8	J S Morton HS District 201	Cicero
37	40.0	Streator Elem SD 44	Streator
38	39.3	Alton Community Unit SD 11	Alton
39	38.6	Herrin CUSD 4	Herrin
40	38.1	Freeport SD 145	Freeport
41	38.0	North Chicago SD 187	North Chicago
42	37.8	Galesburg CUSD 205	Galesburg
43	37.0	Community CSD 168	Sauk Village
44	36.8	Crete Monee CUSD 201U	Crete
44	36.8	Urbana SD 116	Urbana
46	36.4	Berkeley SD 87	Berkeley
47	36.2	Thornton Twp HSD 205	South Holland
48	36.0	Sparta CUSD 140	Sparta
49	35.5	Quincy SD 172	Quincy
50	35.2	Pekin Public SD 108	Pekin
51	34.9	East Richland CUSD 1	Olney
52	34.7	Belleville SD 118	Belleville
53	34.6	Round Lake Area Schs - Dist 116	Round Lake
54	34.3	Jacksonville SD 117	Jacksonville
55	34.1	Frankfort Community Unit SD 168	West Frankfort
56	33.8	Monmouth Unit SD 38	Monmouth
57	33.7	Berwyn South SD 100	Berwyn
58	32.6	Canton Union SD 66	Canton
59	32.1	Du Quoin CUSD 300	Du Quoin
60	31.0	Carmi-White County CUSD 5	Carmi
61	30.8	Macomb Community Unit SD 185	Macomb
62	30.6	Bloomington SD 87	Bloomington
62	30.6	Rich Twp HS District 227	Olympia Fields
64	30.4	Harvard CUSD 50	Harvard
65	30.1	Granite City CUSD 9	Granite City
65	30.1	Paris-Union SD 95	Paris
67	30.0	Argo Community HSD 217	Summit
68	29.9	Champaign Community Unit SD 4	Champaign
69	29.7	Harrisburg CUSD 3	Harrisburg
70	29.6	West Chicago ESD 33	West Chicago
71	29.4	Steger SD 194	Steger
72	29.2	Indian Springs SD 109	Justice
73	28.7	Massac Unit District #1	Metropolis
74	28.3	Bloom Twp High SD 206	Chicago Heights
74	28.3	Thornton Fractional T HS D 215	Calumet City
76	28.2	Collinsville CUSD 10	Collinsville
77	28.0	Marion Community Unit SD 2	Marion
77	28.0	Robinson CUSD 2	Robinson
79	27.6	Elem SD 159	Matteson
80	27.5	Moline Unit SD 40	Moline
81	27.3	Hillsboro Community Unit SD 3	Hillsboro
82	27.1	Community High SD 218	Oak Lawn
83	27.0	Mattoon CUSD 2	Mattoon
84	26.6	East Peoria SD 86	East Peoria
84	26.6	Jasper County Comm Unit Dist 1	Newton
86	26.4	Sterling C U Dist 5	Sterling
87	26.1	Litchfield CUSD 12	Litchfield
88	26.0	Rochelle Community CD 231	Rochelle
89	25.6	Aurora West Unit SD 129	Aurora
90	25.4	SD 46	Elgin
91	24.5	United Twp HS District 30	East Moline
92	24.4	Ottawa Elem SD 141	Ottawa
93	24.0	Roxana Community Unit SD 1	Roxana
94	23.8	Jersey CUSD 100	Jerseyville
95	23.6	Mannheim SD 83	Franklin Park
96	23.3	Evanston CCSD 65	Evanston
96	23.3	Vandalia CUSD 203	Vandalia
98	23.1	Taylorville CUSD 3	Taylorville
99	22.2	Prairie Central CUSD 8	Forrest
99	22.2	Wheeling CCSD 21	Wheeling
101	22.1	Dekalb Community Unit SD 428	De Kalb
101	22.1	Pekin Community HSD 303	Pekin
103	21.8	Marquardt SD 15	Glendale Hgts
104	21.6	Bethalto CUSD 8	Bethalto
104	21.6	Charleston CUSD 1	Charleston
104	21.6	Department of Corrections SD 428	Springfield
107	21.5	Wabash CUSD 348	Mount Carmel
108	21.4	Lyons SD 103	Lyons
109	21.3	East Maine SD 63	Des Plaines
110	21.2	Clinton CUSD 15	Clinton
111	21.1	Community CSD 62	Des Plaines
112	21.0	Dixon Unit SD 170	Dixon
112	21.0	Woodstock CUSD 200	Woodstock
114	20.7	Addison SD 4	Addison
115	20.2	SD 45 Dupage County	Villa Park
116	20.1	Valley View CUSD 365U	Romeoville
117	20.0	Beach Park CCSD 3	Beach Park
118	19.7	Bond County CUSD 2	Greenville
119	19.3	Evanston Twp HSD 202	Evanston
120	19.2	Community CSD 59	Arlington Hgts
121	18.6	Effingham Community Unit SD 40	Effingham

122	18.5	Proviso Twp HSD 209	Maywood
123	18.3	Community Unit SD 300	Carpentersville
124	17.6	Belvidere CUSD 100	Belvidere
125	17.4	Carlinville CUSD 1	Carlinville
126	17.3	Bradley SD 61	Bradley
126	17.3	Westmont CUSD 201	Westmont
128	16.8	River Trails SD 26	Mount Prospect
128	16.8	Zion-Benton Twp HSD 126	Zion
130	16.5	Woodridge SD 68	Woodridge
131	16.2	Matteson ESD 162	Matteson
131	16.2	Reed Custer CUSD 255U	Braidwood
133	15.8	Palatine CCSD 15	Palatine
134	15.4	Oregon C U School Dist-220	Oregon
135	15.2	Sherrard Community Unit SD 200	Sherrard
136	15.0	North Palos SD 117	Palos Hills
137	14.7	Evergreen Park ESD 124	Evergreen Park
137	14.7	O'Fallon CCSD 90	Ofallon
139	14.3	Du Page High SD 88	Villa Park
140	14.2	Belleville Twp HSD 201	Belleville
141	13.5	Wilmington CUSD 209U	Wilmington
142	13.3	Harlem Unit Dist 122	Loves Park
143	13.2	Southwestern CUSD 9	Piasa
144	13.0	Bourbonnais SD 53	Bourbonnais
144	13.0	Mundelein Cons High SD 120	Mundelein
146	12.9	Skokie SD 68	Skokie
147	12.8	Mundelein Elem SD 75	Mundelein
148	12.7	Midlothian SD 143	Midlothian
149	12.5	Carterville CUSD 5	Carterville
150	12.4	Oak Park Elem SD 97	Oak Park
151	12.3	Genoa Kingston CUSD 424	Genoa
151	12.3	Mclean County Unit Dist 5	Normal
153	12.2	Illinois Valley Central UD 321	Chillicothe
154	12.1	Olympia CUSD 16	Stanford
155	12.0	Herscher Community Unit SD 2	Herscher
156	11.8	Hawthorn CCSD 73	Vernon Hills
157	10.9	Edwardsville CUSD 7	Edwardsville
158	10.7	Eureka CU Dist 140	Eureka
158	10.7	Highland Community Unit SD 5	Highland
160	10.5	Glenview CCSD 34	Glenview
161	10.1	Antioch CCSD 34	Antioch
162	10.0	Elmwood Park CUSD 401	Elmwood Park
163	9.9	Alsip-Hazlgrn-Oaklawn SD 126	Alsip
164	9.8	Coal City CUSD 1	Coal City
165	9.4	Mchenry CCSD 15	Mc Henry
166	9.3	Geneseo Community Unit SD 228	Geneseo
166	9.3	Lombard SD 44	Lombard
166	9.3	Triad Community Unit SD 2	Troy
169	9.1	Leyden Community HSD 212	Franklin Park
169	9.1	Wauconda Community Unit SD 118	Wauconda
171	9.0	Township High SD 214	Arlington Hgts
172	8.6	Community Unit SD 200	Wheaton
173	8.4	Sandwich CUSD 430	Sandwich
173	8.4	Tinley Park Community Cons SD 146	Tinley Park
175	8.2	La Grange SD 102	La Grange Park
176	7.9	Mascoutah C U District 19	Mascoutah
177	7.5	Darien SD 61	Darien
177	7.5	Mahomet-Seymour CUSD 3	Mahomet
179	7.3	Homewood SD 153	Homewood
179	7.3	Sycamore CUSD 427	Sycamore
181	7.2	Meridian CUSD 223	Stillman Valley
182	7.1	Troy Community CSD 30C	Plainfield
183	6.8	O'Fallon Twp High SD 203	Ofallon
184	6.7	Byron Community Unit SD 226	Byron
184	6.7	Township HSD 211	Palatine
186	6.6	Woodland CCSD 50	Gurnee
187	6.5	Homewood Flossmoor CHSD 233	Flossmoor
188	6.1	Lake Villa CCSD 41	Lake Villa
188	6.1	Minooka Community CSD 201	Minooka
190	6.0	Bradley Bourbonnais CHSD 307	Bradley
190	6.0	Monticello CUSD 25	Monticello
190	6.0	North Shore SD 112	Highland Park
193	5.9	Community CSD 46	Grayslake
193	5.9	Mount Zion Community Unit SD 3	Mount Zion
195	5.8	Winnebago CUSD 323	Winnebago
196	5.7	Lisle CUSD 202	Lisle
197	5.5	Barrington CUSD 220	Barrington
198	5.4	Dunlap CUSD 323	Dunlap
198	5.4	Manteno Community Unit SD 5	Manteno
198	5.4	Morton CUSD 709	Morton
198	5.4	Waterloo Community Unit SD 5	Waterloo
202	5.3	Crystal Lake CCSD 47	Crystal Lake
203	5.2	Hononegah Community HSD 207	Rockton
204	5.0	Community High SD 99	Downers Grove
204	5.0	Glenbard Twp HSD 87	Glen Ellyn
206	4.8	Cary CCSD 26	Cary
206	4.8	Palos Community CSD 118	Palos Park
208	4.7	Ball Chatham CUSD 5	Chatham
208	4.7	Channahon SD 17	Channahon
210	4.6	Oak Park & River Forest Dist 200	Oak Park
211	4.4	Oswego Community Unit SD 308	Oswego
212	4.3	Peotone CUSD 207U	Peotone
213	4.1	Bensenville SD 2	Bensenville
213	4.1	Kinnikinnick CCSD 131	Roscoe
215	3.8	Arlington Heights SD 25	Arlington Hgts
216	3.7	Johnsburg CUSD 12	Johnsburg
217	3.5	Will County SD 92	Lockport
218	3.3	Mokena SD 159	Mokena
219	2.8	Columbia Community Unit SD 4	Columbia
219	2.8	Lake Zurich CUSD 95	Lake Zurich
219	2.8	Rochester Community Unit SD 3A	Rochester
222	2.7	Community High SD 155	Crystal Lake
223	2.6	Lemont-Bromberek CSD 113a	Lemont
224	2.4	Nippersink SD 2	Richmond
225	2.3	Saint Charles CUSD 303	Saint Charles
226	2.1	Consolidated SD 158	Huntley
227	2.0	New Lenox SD 122	New Lenox
228	1.9	Aptakisic-Tripp CCSD 102	Buffalo Grove
229	1.7	Libertyville SD 70	Libertyville
229	1.7	Lincoln Way Community HSD 210	New Lenox
231	1.6	Batavia Unit SD 101	Batavia
231	1.6	Plainfield SD 202	Plainfield
233	1.5	Kaneland CUSD 302	Maple Park
234	1.4	Kildeer Countryside CCSD 96	Buffalo Grove
234	1.4	Summit Hill SD 161	Frankfort
236	1.1	Mount Prospect SD 57	Mount Prospect
237	0.8	Elmhurst SD 205	Elmhurst
238	0.7	Central Community Unit SD 301	Burlington
238	0.7	Naperville C U Dist 203	Naperville
240	0.6	Downers Grove Grade SD 58	Downers Grove
241	0.0	Antioch Community High SD 117	Lake Villa
241	0.0	Bremen Community HS District 228	Midlothian
241	0.0	Burbank SD 111	Burbank
241	0.0	Community CSD 93	Carol Stream
241	0.0	Community High SD 94	West Chicago
241	0.0	Consolidated High SD 230	Orland Park
241	0.0	Deerfield SD 109	Deerfield
241	0.0	Fenton Community HSD 100	Bensenville
241	0.0	Flossmoor SD 161	Chicago Heights
241	0.0	Frankfort CCSD 157c	Frankfort
241	0.0	Fremont SD 79	Mundelein
241	0.0	Geneva Community Unit SD 304	Geneva
241	0.0	Glen Ellyn CCSD 89	Glen Ellyn
241	0.0	Glen Ellyn SD 41	Glen Ellyn
241	0.0	Grayslake Community High SD 127	Grayslake
241	0.0	Gurnee SD 56	Gurnee
241	0.0	Hinsdale Twp HSD 86	Hinsdale
241	0.0	Homer Community CSD 33C	Lockport
241	0.0	Indian Prairie CUSD 204	Aurora
241	0.0	Keeneyville SD 20	Hanover Park
241	0.0	Kirby SD 140	Tinley Park
241	0.0	Lake Forest Community HSD 115	Lake Forest
241	0.0	Lake Forest SD 67	Lake Forest
241	0.0	Lake Park Community HSD 108	Roselle
241	0.0	Lansing SD 158	Lansing
241	0.0	Lincolnshire-Prairieview SD 103	Lincolnshire
241	0.0	Lyons Twp HSD 204	La Grange
241	0.0	Maine Township HSD 207	Park Ridge
241	0.0	Niles Twp Community High SD 219	Skokie
241	0.0	Northbrook SD 28	Northbrook
241	0.0	Oak Lawn-Hometown SD 123	Oak Lawn
241	0.0	Orland SD 135	Orland Park
241	0.0	Ottawa Twp HSD 140	Ottawa
241	0.0	Park Ridge CCSD 64	Park Ridge
241	0.0	Prospect Heights SD 23	Prospect Hgts
241	0.0	Queen Bee SD 16	Glendale Hgts
241	0.0	Schaumburg CCSD 54	Schaumburg
241	0.0	Warren Twp High SD 121	Gurnee
241	0.0	Wilmette SD 39	Wilmette
241	0.0	Winnetka SD 36	Winnetka
241	0.0	Yorkville Community Unit SD 115	Yorkville
282	n/a	Adlai E Stevenson Dist 125	Lincolnshire
282	n/a	CCSD 181	Hinsdale
282	n/a	Community High SD 128	Libertyville
282	n/a	Forest Ridge SD 142	Oak Forest
282	n/a	Lockport Twp HSD 205	Lockport
282	n/a	Mchenry Community HSD 156	Mc Henry
282	n/a	New Trier Twp HSD 203	Winnetka
282	n/a	Northfield Twp High SD 225	Glenview
282	n/a	Oak Lawn Community HSD 229	Oak Lawn
282	n/a	Reavis Twp HSD 220	Burbank
282	n/a	Ridgeland SD 122	Oak Lawn
282	n/a	Township High SD 113	Highland Park

Students Eligible for Reduced-Price Lunch

Rank	Percent	District Name	City
1	14.9	Berwyn South SD 100	Berwyn
2	13.5	Berwyn North SD 98	Berwyn
2	13.5	Cicero SD 99	Cicero
4	13.0	J S Morton HS District 201	Cicero
5	12.9	Berkeley SD 87	Berkeley
6	12.3	Summit SD 104	Summit
7	11.6	Joliet Twp HSD 204	Joliet
8	11.2	Mascoutah C U District 19	Mascoutah
9	11.0	Park Forest SD 163	Park Forest
10	10.8	Aurora East Unit SD 131	Aurora
11	10.4	Zion Elementary SD 6	Zion
12	10.2	Rantoul City SD 137	Rantoul
13	9.9	Streator Elem SD 44	Streator
13	9.9	Waukegan CUSD 60	Waukegan
15	9.8	Rockford SD 205	Rockford
16	9.5	Quincy SD 172	Quincy
17	9.4	Belleville SD 118	Belleville
17	9.4	Bellwood SD 88	Bellwood
17	9.4	Dolton SD 149	Calumet City
20	9.1	Mannheim SD 83	Franklin Park
20	9.1	West Chicago ESD 33	West Chicago
22	9.0	Joliet Public SD 86	Joliet
22	9.0	Pekin Public SD 108	Pekin
24	8.9	Dolton SD 148	Riverdale
25	8.7	Prairie-Hills Elem SD 144	Markham
26	8.6	Cook County SD 130	Blue Island
27	8.5	City of Chicago SD 299	Chicago
27	8.5	Round Lake Area Schs - Dist 116	Round Lake
27	8.5	Steger SD 194	Steger
30	8.4	North Chicago SD 187	North Chicago
30	8.4	Robinson CUSD 2	Robinson
30	8.4	Thornton Fractional T HS D 215	Calumet City
33	8.3	Roxana Community Unit SD 1	Roxana
34	8.2	Freeport SD 145	Freeport
34	8.2	Wheeling CCSD 21	Wheeling
34	8.2	Woodstock CUSD 200	Woodstock
37	8.1	Community CSD 62	Des Plaines
37	8.1	Rich Twp HS District 227	Olympia Fields
39	8.0	Bradley SD 61	Bradley
39	8.0	Community CSD 168	Sauk Village
41	7.8	Sterling C U Dist 5	Sterling
41	7.8	Taylorville CUSD 3	Taylorville
43	7.7	Decatur SD 61	Decatur
43	7.7	Harvard CUSD 50	Harvard
45	7.6	Collinsville CUSD 10	Collinsville
46	7.5	Galesburg CUSD 205	Galesburg
46	7.5	Jasper County Comm Unit Dist 1	Newton
48	7.4	SD 46	Elgin
49	7.3	Murphysboro CUSD 186	Murphysboro
50	7.1	Canton Union SD 66	Canton
50	7.1	Vandalia CUSD 203	Vandalia
52	7.0	Bloomington SD 87	Bloomington
52	7.0	Monmouth Unit SD 38	Monmouth
54	6.9	Elem SD 159	Matteson
54	6.9	Reed Custer CUSD 255U	Braidwood
56	6.8	Community High SD 218	Oak Lawn
56	6.8	Herrin CUSD 4	Herrin
56	6.8	Kewanee Community Unit SD 229	Kewanee
59	6.7	Lyons SD 103	Lyons
59	6.7	Sparta CUSD 140	Sparta
59	6.7	Valley View CUSD 365U	Romeoville
62	6.6	Cahokia Community Unit SD 187	Cahokia
62	6.6	Crete Monee CUSD 201U	Crete
62	6.6	Granite City CUSD 9	Granite City
62	6.6	Hillsboro Community Unit SD 3	Hillsboro
62	6.6	Kankakee SD 111	Kankakee
62	6.6	Ottawa Elem SD 141	Ottawa
68	6.5	Springfield SD 186	Springfield
69	6.4	Danville CCSD 118	Danville
69	6.4	Moline Unit SD 40	Moline
69	6.4	Peoria SD 150	Peoria
72	6.3	Bloom Twp High SD 206	Chicago Heights
72	6.3	United Twp HS District 30	East Moline
74	6.2	Alton Community Unit SD 11	Alton
75	6.1	Evanston CCSD 65	Evanston
75	6.1	Southwestern CUSD 9	Piasa
77	6.0	Du Quoin CUSD 300	Du Quoin
77	6.0	Jacksonville SD 117	Jacksonville
77	6.0	Mundelein Elem SD 75	Mundelein
77	6.0	Sherrard Community Unit SD 200	Sherrard
81	5.9	Bond County CUSD 2	Greenville
81	5.9	Frankfort Community Unit SD 168	West Frankfort
81	5.9	Rock Island SD 41	Rock Island
84	5.8	Argo Community HSD 217	Summit
84	5.8	Beach Park CCSD 3	Beach Park
84	5.8	Bethalto CUSD 8	Bethalto
84	5.8	East Maine SD 63	Des Plaines
84	5.8	Evanston Twp HSD 202	Evanston
84	5.8	Jersey CUSD 100	Jerseyville
84	5.8	Olympia CUSD 16	Stanford
84	5.8	Thornton Twp HSD 205	South Holland
92	5.7	East Moline SD 37	East Moline
93	5.6	Carlinville CUSD 1	Carlinville
93	5.6	Dixon Unit SD 170	Dixon
93	5.6	Mount Vernon SD 80	Mount Vernon
96	5.5	Chicago Heights SD 170	Chicago Heights
96	5.5	Effingham Community Unit SD 40	Effingham
96	5.5	Harvey SD 152	Harvey
96	5.5	Illinois Valley Central UD 321	Chillicothe
100	5.4	Prairie Central CUSD 8	Forrest
101	5.3	Community CSD 59	Arlington Hgts

101	5.3	Urbana SD 116	Urbana
103	5.2	Harrisburg CUSD 3	Harrisburg
103	5.2	Highland Community Unit SD 5	Highland
103	5.2	Macomb Community Unit SD 185	Macomb
106	5.1	Harlem Unit Dist 122	Loves Park
106	5.1	Litchfield CUSD 12	Litchfield
106	5.1	Maywood-Melrose Park-Broadview-89	Melrose Park
109	5.0	Aurora West Unit SD 129	Aurora
109	5.0	Dekalb Community Unit SD 428	De Kalb
109	5.0	Mattoon CUSD 2	Mattoon
109	5.0	SD 45 Dupage County	Villa Park
109	5.0	Skokie SD 68	Skokie
109	5.0	Wilmington CUSD 209U	Wilmington
115	4.9	Carmi-White County CUSD 5	Carmi
115	4.9	Mundelein Cons High SD 120	Mundelein
117	4.8	Belleville Twp HSD 201	Belleville
117	4.8	Charleston CUSD 1	Charleston
117	4.8	East Saint Louis SD 189	E Saint Louis
117	4.8	Paris-Union SD 95	Paris
117	4.8	Pekin Community HSD 303	Pekin
117	4.8	Triad Community Unit SD 2	Troy
117	4.8	Woodridge SD 68	Woodridge
124	4.7	Clinton CUSD 15	Clinton
124	4.7	East Richland CUSD 1	Olney
126	4.6	Marion Community Unit SD 2	Marion
126	4.6	Marquardt SD 15	Glendale Hgts
126	4.6	Palatine CCSD 15	Palatine
129	4.5	Addison SD 4	Addison
129	4.5	Champaign Community Unit SD 4	Champaign
129	4.5	Community Unit SD 300	Carpentersville
129	4.5	Indian Springs SD 109	Justice
133	4.4	Massac Unit District #1	Metropolis
133	4.4	Posen-Robbins El SD 143-5	Posen
133	4.4	Wabash CUSD 348	Mount Carmel
136	4.2	Belvidere CUSD 100	Belvidere
136	4.2	East Peoria SD 86	East Peoria
136	4.2	Homewood SD 153	Homewood
136	4.2	Oak Park Elem SD 97	Oak Park
140	3.9	Glenview CCSD 34	Glenview
140	3.9	West Harvey-Dixmoor PSD 147	Harvey
142	3.8	Oregon C U School Dist-220	Oregon
142	3.8	Rochelle Community CD 231	Rochelle
144	3.7	Edwardsville CUSD 7	Edwardsville
144	3.7	Geneseo Community Unit SD 228	Geneseo
146	3.6	Herscher Community Unit SD 2	Herscher
146	3.6	Matteson ESD 162	Matteson
146	3.6	Sandwich CUSD 430	Sandwich
146	3.6	Westmont CUSD 201	Westmont
150	3.5	Leyden Community HSD 212	Franklin Park
151	3.3	Waterloo Community Unit SD 5	Waterloo
152	3.2	Kinnikinnick CCSD 131	Roscoe
152	3.2	Monticello CUSD 25	Monticello
152	3.2	Mount Zion Community Unit SD 3	Mount Zion
155	3.1	Bourbonnais SD 53	Bourbonnais
155	3.1	Genoa Kingston CUSD 424	Genoa
155	3.1	Lombard SD 44	Lombard
158	3.0	Coal City CUSD 1	Coal City
158	3.0	Country Club Hills SD 160	Ctry Club Hill
158	3.0	Evergreen Park ESD 124	Evergreen Park
161	2.9	Du Page High SD 88	Villa Park
161	2.9	Hawthorn CCSD 73	Vernon Hills
161	2.9	Oswego Community Unit SD 308	Oswego
161	2.9	Woodland CCSD 50	Gurnee
165	2.8	Lake Villa CCSD 41	Lake Villa
165	2.8	Mclean County Unit Dist 5	Normal
165	2.8	Troy Community CSD 30C	Plainfield
168	2.7	Carterville CUSD 5	Carterville
169	2.6	Community CSD 46	Grayslake
169	2.6	River Trails SD 26	Mount Prospect
169	2.6	Tinley Park Community Cons SD 146	Tinley Park
172	2.5	Bradley Bourbonnais CHSD 307	Bradley
172	2.5	Elmwood Park CUSD 401	Elmwood Park
172	2.5	O'Fallon CCSD 90	Ofallon
172	2.5	Proviso Twp HSD 209	Maywood
176	2.4	Eureka CU Dist 140	Eureka
177	2.3	Township HSD 211	Palatine
177	2.3	Township High SD 214	Arlington Hgts
177	2.3	Winnebago CUSD 323	Winnebago
180	2.2	Crystal Lake CCSD 47	Crystal Lake
180	2.2	Zion-Benton Twp HSD 126	Zion
182	2.1	Antioch CCSD 34	Antioch
182	2.1	Arlington Heights SD 25	Arlington Hgts
182	2.1	Johnsburg CUSD 12	Johnsburg
185	1.9	Mchenry CCSD 15	Mc Henry
185	1.9	Minooka Community CSD 201	Minooka
185	1.9	O'Fallon Twp High SD 203	Ofallon
188	1.8	Byron Community Unit SD 226	Byron
188	1.8	Lisle CUSD 202	Lisle
190	1.7	Community Unit SD 200	Wheaton
190	1.7	Sycamore CUSD 427	Sycamore
192	1.6	Alsip-Hazlgrn-Oaklawn SD 126	Alsip
192	1.6	Aptakisic-Tripp CCSD 102	Buffalo Grove
192	1.6	Barrington CUSD 220	Barrington
192	1.6	Darien SD 61	Darien
192	1.6	Manteno Community Unit SD 5	Manteno
192	1.6	Oak Park & River Forest Dist 200	Oak Park
198	1.4	Cary CCSD 26	Cary
198	1.4	Will County SD 92	Lockport
200	1.3	Consolidated SD 158	Huntley
200	1.3	Glenbard Twp HSD 87	Glen Ellyn
200	1.3	Hononegah Community HSD 207	Rockton
200	1.3	La Grange SD 102	La Grange Park
204	1.2	Ball Chatham CUSD 5	Chatham
204	1.2	Mount Prospect SD 57	Mount Prospect
204	1.2	North Palos SD 117	Palos Hills
204	1.2	Peotone CUSD 207U	Peotone
204	1.2	Wauconda Community Unit SD 118	Wauconda
209	1.1	Channahon SD 17	Channahon
209	1.1	Columbia Community Unit SD 4	Columbia
209	1.1	Nippersink SD 2	Richmond
212	1.0	Lemont-Bromberek CSD 113a	Lemont
213	0.9	Bensenville SD 2	Bensenville
213	0.9	Community High SD 99	Downers Grove
213	0.9	Morton CUSD 709	Morton
213	0.9	North Shore SD 112	Highland Park
213	0.9	Plainfield SD 202	Plainfield
218	0.8	Batavia Unit SD 101	Batavia
218	0.8	Homewood Flossmoor CHSD 233	Flossmoor
220	0.7	Dunlap CUSD 323	Dunlap
220	0.7	Kildeer Countryside CCSD 96	Buffalo Grove
220	0.7	Lake Zurich CUSD 95	Lake Zurich
220	0.7	Lincoln Way Community HSD 210	New Lenox
220	0.7	Mokena SD 159	Mokena
220	0.7	Rochester Community Unit SD 3A	Rochester
220	0.7	Saint Charles CUSD 303	Saint Charles
227	0.6	New Lenox SD 122	New Lenox
228	0.5	Community High SD 155	Crystal Lake
228	0.5	Kaneland CUSD 302	Maple Park
228	0.5	Meridian CUSD 223	Stillman Valley
231	0.4	Midlothian SD 143	Midlothian
232	0.3	Central Community Unit SD 301	Burlington
232	0.3	Libertyville SD 70	Libertyville
232	0.3	Mahomet-Seymour CUSD 3	Mahomet
232	0.3	Palos Community CSD 118	Palos Park
236	0.2	Downers Grove Grade SD 58	Downers Grove
236	0.2	Elmhurst SD 205	Elmhurst
236	0.2	Summit Hill SD 161	Frankfort
239	0.1	Naperville C U Dist 203	Naperville
240	0.0	Antioch Community High SD 117	Lake Villa
240	0.0	Bremen Community HS District 228	Midlothian
240	0.0	Burbank SD 111	Burbank
240	0.0	Community CSD 93	Carol Stream
240	0.0	Community High SD 94	West Chicago
240	0.0	Consolidated High SD 230	Orland Park
240	0.0	Deerfield SD 109	Deerfield
240	0.0	Department of Corrections SD 428	Springfield
240	0.0	Fenton Community HSD 100	Bensenville
240	0.0	Flossmoor SD 161	Chicago Heights
240	0.0	Frankfort CCSD 157c	Frankfort
240	0.0	Fremont SD 79	Mundelein
240	0.0	Geneva Community Unit SD 304	Geneva
240	0.0	Glen Ellyn CCSD 89	Glen Ellyn
240	0.0	Glen Ellyn SD 41	Glen Ellyn
240	0.0	Grayslake Community High SD 127	Grayslake
240	0.0	Gurnee SD 56	Gurnee
240	0.0	Hinsdale Twp HSD 86	Hinsdale
240	0.0	Homer Community CSD 33C	Lockport
240	0.0	Indian Prairie CUSD 204	Aurora
240	0.0	Keeneyville SD 20	Hanover Park
240	0.0	Kirby SD 140	Tinley Park
240	0.0	Lake Forest Community HSD 115	Lake Forest
240	0.0	Lake Forest SD 67	Lake Forest
240	0.0	Lake Park Community HSD 108	Roselle
240	0.0	Lansing SD 158	Lansing
240	0.0	Lincolnshire-Prairieview SD 103	Lincolnshire
240	0.0	Lyons Twp HSD 204	La Grange
240	0.0	Maine Township HSD 207	Park Ridge
240	0.0	Niles Twp Community High SD 219	Skokie
240	0.0	Northbrook SD 28	Northbrook
240	0.0	Oak Lawn-Hometown SD 123	Oak Lawn
240	0.0	Orland SD 135	Orland Park
240	0.0	Ottawa Twp HSD 140	Ottawa
240	0.0	Park Ridge CCSD 64	Park Ridge
240	0.0	Prospect Heights SD 23	Prospect Hgts
240	0.0	Queen Bee SD 16	Glendale Hgts
240	0.0	Schaumburg CCSD 54	Schaumburg
240	0.0	Warren Twp High SD 121	Gurnee
240	0.0	Wilmette SD 39	Wilmette
240	0.0	Winnetka SD 36	Winnetka
240	0.0	Yorkville Community Unit SD 115	Yorkville
282	n/a	Adlai E Stevenson Dist 125	Lincolnshire
282	n/a	CCSD 181	Hinsdale
282	n/a	Community High SD 128	Libertyville
282	n/a	Forest Ridge SD 142	Oak Forest
282	n/a	Lockport Twp HSD 205	Lockport
282	n/a	Mchenry Community HSD 156	Mc Henry
282	n/a	New Trier Twp HSD 203	Winnetka
282	n/a	Northfield Twp High SD 225	Glenview
282	n/a	Oak Lawn Community HSD 229	Oak Lawn
282	n/a	Reavis Twp HSD 220	Burbank
282	n/a	Ridgeland SD 122	Oak Lawn
282	n/a	Township High SD 113	Highland Park

Student/Teacher Ratio

Rank	Ratio	District Name	City
1	32.4	Department of Corrections SD 428	Springfield
2	22.1	Decatur SD 61	Decatur
3	21.6	Granite City CUSD 9	Granite City
4	20.9	Bellwood SD 88	Bellwood
4	20.9	Round Lake Area Schs - Dist 116	Round Lake
4	20.9	Valley View CUSD 365U	Romeoville
7	20.7	Channahon SD 17	Channahon
8	20.6	Carterville CUSD 5	Carterville
9	20.4	Belleville Twp HSD 201	Belleville
9	20.4	Mokena SD 159	Mokena
11	20.3	Belvidere CUSD 100	Belvidere
11	20.3	Harvey SD 152	Harvey
13	20.2	Berwyn North SD 98	Berwyn
14	20.0	Bradley Bourbonnais CHSD 307	Bradley
14	20.0	Marion Community Unit SD 2	Marion
16	19.9	Dolton SD 149	Calumet City
17	19.8	Aurora East Unit SD 131	Aurora
17	19.8	Cahokia Community Unit SD 187	Cahokia
17	19.8	Cicero SD 99	Cicero
20	19.4	New Lenox SD 122	New Lenox
20	19.4	O'Fallon Twp High SD 203	Ofallon
20	19.4	Posen-Robbins El SD 143-5	Posen
20	19.4	Will County SD 92	Lockport
20	19.4	Zion-Benton Twp HSD 126	Zion
25	19.3	Kewanee Community Unit SD 229	Kewanee
25	19.3	Meridian CUSD 223	Stillman Valley
27	19.2	Lincoln Way Community HSD 210	New Lenox
27	19.2	United Twp HS District 30	East Moline
27	19.2	Yorkville Community Unit SD 115	Yorkville
30	19.1	Lockport Twp HSD 205	Lockport
31	19.0	Crete Monee CUSD 201U	Crete
31	19.0	Minooka Community CSD 201	Minooka
33	18.9	J S Morton HS District 201	Cicero
33	18.9	Prairie-Hills Elem SD 144	Markham
35	18.8	Grayslake Community High SD 127	Grayslake
35	18.8	Mount Zion Community Unit SD 3	Mount Zion
35	18.8	Summit Hill SD 161	Frankfort
38	18.7	Fremont SD 79	Mundelein
38	18.7	Lake Park Community HSD 108	Roselle
38	18.7	Ridgeland SD 122	Oak Lawn
38	18.7	Waukegan CUSD 60	Waukegan
42	18.6	Litchfield CUSD 12	Litchfield
42	18.6	O'Fallon CCSD 90	Ofallon
42	18.6	Oswego Community Unit SD 308	Oswego
45	18.5	Joliet Public SD 86	Joliet
46	18.4	Community Unit SD 300	Carpentersville
46	18.4	Genoa Kingston CUSD 424	Genoa
46	18.4	Kinnikinnick CCSD 131	Roscoe
49	18.3	Ball Chatham CUSD 5	Chatham
49	18.3	Bourbonnais SD 53	Bourbonnais
49	18.3	Dunlap CUSD 323	Dunlap
49	18.3	Elmwood Park CUSD 401	Elmwood Park
49	18.3	Homer Community CSD 33C	Lockport
49	18.3	Lemont-Bromberek CSD 113a	Lemont
49	18.3	Saint Charles CUSD 303	Saint Charles
56	18.2	Maywood-Melrose Park-Broadview-89	Melrose Park
56	18.2	North Palos SD 117	Palos Hills
56	18.2	Oak Lawn Community HSD 229	Oak Lawn
59	18.1	Lansing SD 158	Lansing
59	18.1	Vandalia CUSD 203	Vandalia
61	18.0	Antioch Community High SD 117	Lake Villa
61	18.0	Beach Park CCSD 3	Beach Park
61	18.0	Burbank SD 111	Burbank
61	18.0	Massac Unit District #1	Metropolis
65	17.9	Herrin CUSD 4	Herrin
65	17.9	Mchenry CCSD 15	Mc Henry
65	17.9	Pekin Community HSD 303	Pekin
65	17.9	Taylorville CUSD 3	Taylorville
69	17.8	Belleville SD 118	Belleville
69	17.8	Collinsville CUSD 10	Collinsville
69	17.8	Community High SD 155	Crystal Lake
69	17.8	Downers Grove Grade SD 58	Downers Grove
69	17.8	Johnsburg CUSD 12	Johnsburg
69	17.8	West Harvey-Dixmoor PSD 147	Harvey
75	17.7	Addison SD 4	Addison
75	17.7	Argo Community HSD 217	Summit
75	17.7	City of Chicago SD 299	Chicago
75	17.7	Community CSD 168	Sauk Village
75	17.7	Marquardt SD 15	Glendale Hgts
80	17.6	Aurora West Unit SD 129	Aurora
80	17.6	Bradley SD 61	Bradley
80	17.6	Naperville C U Dist 203	Naperville

80	17.6	Quincy SD 172	Quincy
84	17.5	Woodstock CUSD 200	Woodstock
85	17.4	Geneva Community Unit SD 304	Geneva
85	17.4	Rochester Community Unit SD 3A	Rochester
85	17.4	Warren Twp High SD 121	Gurnee
88	17.3	Bensenville SD 2	Bensenville
88	17.3	Carlinville CUSD 1	Carlinville
88	17.3	Troy Community CSD 30C	Plainfield
91	17.2	Barrington CUSD 220	Barrington
91	17.2	Plainfield SD 202	Plainfield
91	17.2	Zion Elementary SD 6	Zion
94	17.1	Community High SD 218	Oak Lawn
94	17.1	Kankakee SD 111	Kankakee
94	17.1	Mchenry Community HSD 156	Mc Henry
94	17.1	Mount Prospect SD 57	Mount Prospect
98	17.0	Batavia Unit SD 101	Batavia
98	17.0	Bond County CUSD 2	Greenville
98	17.0	Consolidated High SD 230	Orland Park
98	17.0	Matteson ESD 162	Matteson
98	17.0	Wauconda Community Unit SD 118	Wauconda
98	17.0	Wilmington CUSD 209U	Wilmington
104	16.9	Crystal Lake CCSD 47	Crystal Lake
104	16.9	Harvard CUSD 50	Harvard
104	16.9	Indian Springs SD 109	Justice
104	16.9	Lyons Twp HSD 204	La Grange
104	16.9	SD 46	Elgin
104	16.9	Waterloo Community Unit SD 5	Waterloo
110	16.8	Alsip-Hazlgrn-Oaklawn SD 126	Alsip
110	16.8	Coal City CUSD 1	Coal City
110	16.8	Dolton SD 148	Riverdale
110	16.8	Effingham Community Unit SD 40	Effingham
110	16.8	Frankfort Community Unit SD 168	West Frankfort
110	16.8	Hononegah Community HSD 207	Rockton
110	16.8	Leyden Community HSD 212	Franklin Park
110	16.8	Mundelein Cons High SD 120	Mundelein
110	16.8	Reavis Twp HSD 220	Burbank
119	16.7	Antioch CCSD 34	Antioch
119	16.7	Community CSD 93	Carol Stream
119	16.7	East Saint Louis SD 189	E Saint Louis
119	16.7	Edwardsville CUSD 7	Edwardsville
119	16.7	Glenbard Twp HSD 87	Glen Ellyn
119	16.7	Harlem Unit Dist 122	Loves Park
119	16.7	Jersey CUSD 100	Jerseyville
119	16.7	Palatine CCSD 15	Palatine
119	16.7	Sandwich CUSD 430	Sandwich
119	16.7	Woodridge SD 68	Woodridge
129	16.6	Geneseo Community Unit SD 228	Geneseo
129	16.6	Palos Community CSD 118	Palos Park
129	16.6	Rockford SD 205	Rockford
132	16.5	Cary CCSD 26	Cary
132	16.5	Chicago Heights SD 170	Chicago Heights
132	16.5	North Chicago SD 187	North Chicago
132	16.5	Oak Park & River Forest Dist 200	Oak Park
132	16.5	Orland SD 135	Orland Park
132	16.5	Ottawa Twp HSD 140	Ottawa
138	16.4	Charleston CUSD 1	Charleston
138	16.4	Glen Ellyn SD 41	Glen Ellyn
138	16.4	Mahomet-Seymour CUSD 3	Mahomet
141	16.3	Berkeley SD 87	Berkeley
141	16.3	CCSD 181	Hinsdale
141	16.3	Community High SD 99	Downers Grove
141	16.3	Consolidated SD 158	Huntley
141	16.3	Dixon Unit SD 170	Dixon
141	16.3	Hillsboro Community Unit SD 3	Hillsboro
141	16.3	Kirby SD 140	Tinley Park
141	16.3	Moline Unit SD 40	Moline
141	16.3	Sparta CUSD 140	Sparta
141	16.3	Thornton Twp HSD 205	South Holland
141	16.3	Township HSD 211	Palatine
141	16.3	Township High SD 214	Arlington Hgts
141	16.3	Triad Community Unit SD 2	Troy
154	16.2	Community High SD 94	West Chicago
154	16.2	Frankfort CCSD 157c	Frankfort
154	16.2	Murphysboro CUSD 186	Murphysboro
154	16.2	Peotone CUSD 207U	Peotone
158	16.1	Adlai E Stevenson Dist 125	Lincolnshire
158	16.1	Bethalto CUSD 8	Bethalto
158	16.1	Du Page High SD 88	Villa Park
158	16.1	Galesburg CUSD 205	Galesburg
158	16.1	Gurnee SD 56	Gurnee
158	16.1	Harrisburg CUSD 3	Harrisburg
158	16.1	Hawthorn CCSD 73	Vernon Hills
158	16.1	Indian Prairie CUSD 204	Aurora
158	16.1	Kaneland CUSD 302	Maple Park
158	16.1	Midlothian SD 143	Midlothian
158	16.1	Mundelein Elem SD 75	Mundelein
158	16.1	Springfield SD 186	Springfield
170	16.0	Columbia Community Unit SD 4	Columbia
170	16.0	Community Unit SD 200	Wheaton
170	16.0	Country Club Hills SD 160	Ctry Club Hill
170	16.0	Dekalb Community Unit SD 428	De Kalb
170	16.0	East Peoria SD 86	East Peoria
170	16.0	Fenton Community HSD 100	Bensenville
170	16.0	Mannheim SD 83	Franklin Park
170	16.0	Mascoutah C U District 19	Mascoutah
170	16.0	Schaumburg CCSD 54	Schaumburg
179	15.9	Alton Community Unit SD 11	Alton
179	15.9	Community High SD 128	Libertyville
179	15.9	Homewood Flossmoor CHSD 233	Flossmoor
179	15.9	Mount Vernon SD 80	Mount Vernon
179	15.9	Pekin Public SD 108	Pekin
184	15.8	Bremen Community HS District 228	Midlothian
184	15.8	Central Community Unit SD 301	Burlington
184	15.8	Thornton Fractional T HS D 215	Calumet City
187	15.7	Community CSD 59	Arlington Hgts
187	15.7	Elmhurst SD 205	Elmhurst
187	15.7	Flossmoor SD 161	Chicago Heights
187	15.7	Highland Community Unit SD 5	Highland
187	15.7	Libertyville SD 70	Libertyville
187	15.7	Lombard SD 44	Lombard
187	15.7	Morton CUSD 709	Morton
187	15.7	Rock Island SD 41	Rock Island
187	15.7	SD 45 Dupage County	Villa Park
187	15.7	Sycamore CUSD 427	Sycamore
197	15.6	Bloomington SD 87	Bloomington
197	15.6	Eureka CU Dist 140	Eureka
197	15.6	Evergreen Park ESD 124	Evergreen Park
197	15.6	Glen Ellyn CCSD 89	Glen Ellyn
197	15.6	Illinois Valley Central UD 321	Chillicothe
197	15.6	Joliet Twp HSD 204	Joliet
197	15.6	Lake Zurich CUSD 95	Lake Zurich
197	15.6	Monticello CUSD 25	Monticello
197	15.6	Roxana Community Unit SD 1	Roxana
197	15.6	Steger SD 194	Steger
197	15.6	Winnebago CUSD 323	Winnebago
208	15.5	Forest Ridge SD 142	Oak Forest
208	15.5	Proviso Twp HSD 209	Maywood
208	15.5	Queen Bee SD 16	Glendale Hgts
211	15.4	Sterling C U Dist 5	Sterling
211	15.4	West Chicago ESD 33	West Chicago
211	15.4	Wheeling CCSD 21	Wheeling
214	15.3	Aptakisic-Tripp CCSD 102	Buffalo Grove
214	15.3	Community CSD 46	Grayslake
214	15.3	Du Quoin CUSD 300	Du Quoin
214	15.3	Hinsdale Twp HSD 86	Hinsdale
218	15.2	Danville CCSD 118	Danville
218	15.2	Herscher Community Unit SD 2	Herscher
218	15.2	Lake Villa CCSD 41	Lake Villa
218	15.2	Lisle CUSD 202	Lisle
218	15.2	Rich Twp HS District 227	Olympia Fields
218	15.2	Robinson CUSD 2	Robinson
224	15.1	Canton Union SD 66	Canton
224	15.1	East Maine SD 63	Des Plaines
224	15.1	Rantoul City SD 137	Rantoul
224	15.1	Rochelle Community CD 231	Rochelle
224	15.1	Southwestern CUSD 9	Piasa
229	15.0	Cook County SD 130	Blue Island
229	15.0	East Richland CUSD 1	Olney
229	15.0	Paris-Union SD 95	Paris
229	15.0	Streator Elem SD 44	Streator
233	14.9	Carmi-White County CUSD 5	Carmi
233	14.9	Homewood SD 153	Homewood
233	14.9	Kildeer Countryside CCSD 96	Buffalo Grove
233	14.9	Oregon C U School Dist-220	Oregon
233	14.9	Park Forest SD 163	Park Forest
233	14.9	Wabash CUSD 348	Mount Carmel
239	14.8	Freeport SD 145	Freeport
239	14.8	Nippersink SD 2	Richmond
239	14.8	Summit SD 104	Summit
239	14.8	Township High SD 113	Highland Park
239	14.8	Westmont CUSD 201	Westmont
244	14.7	Arlington Heights SD 25	Arlington Hgts
244	14.7	Jacksonville SD 117	Jacksonville
244	14.7	Keeneyville SD 20	Hanover Park
244	14.7	Lake Forest Community HSD 115	Lake Forest
248	14.6	Berwyn South SD 100	Berwyn
248	14.6	Lyons SD 103	Lyons
248	14.6	Macomb Community Unit SD 185	Macomb
248	14.6	Manteno Community Unit SD 5	Manteno
248	14.6	Woodland CCSD 50	Gurnee
253	14.4	Glenview CCSD 34	Glenview
253	14.4	Monmouth Unit SD 38	Monmouth
253	14.4	Ottawa Elem SD 141	Ottawa
253	14.4	Peoria SD 150	Peoria
253	14.4	Reed Custer CUSD 255U	Braidwood
253	14.4	Sherrard Community Unit SD 200	Sherrard
253	14.4	Skokie SD 68	Skokie
260	14.3	Byron Community Unit SD 226	Byron
260	14.3	Darien SD 61	Darien
260	14.3	Deerfield SD 109	Deerfield
260	14.3	East Moline SD 37	East Moline
260	14.3	Mclean County Unit Dist 5	Normal
260	14.3	Prairie Central CUSD 8	Forrest
266	14.2	Maine Township HSD 207	Park Ridge
266	14.2	Mattoon CUSD 2	Mattoon
268	14.1	Northfield Twp High SD 225	Glenview
269	14.0	Jasper County Comm Unit Dist 1	Newton
269	14.0	La Grange SD 102	La Grange Park
269	14.0	Park Ridge CCSD 64	Park Ridge
272	13.9	Champaign Community Unit SD 4	Champaign
272	13.9	Niles Twp Community High SD 219	Skokie
274	13.8	Bloom Twp High SD 206	Chicago Heights
274	13.8	Oak Lawn-Hometown SD 123	Oak Lawn
276	13.7	Community CSD 62	Des Plaines
276	13.7	Olympia CUSD 16	Stanford
276	13.7	Tinley Park Community Cons SD 146	Tinley Park
279	13.5	Elem SD 159	Matteson
279	13.5	Lincolnshire-Prairieview SD 103	Lincolnshire
279	13.5	Wilmette SD 39	Wilmette
282	13.4	North Shore SD 112	Highland Park
283	13.3	River Trails SD 26	Mount Prospect
283	13.3	Urbana SD 116	Urbana
285	13.2	Clinton CUSD 15	Clinton
285	13.2	Prospect Heights SD 23	Prospect Hgts
287	13.1	Oak Park Elem SD 97	Oak Park
288	13.0	Evanston CCSD 65	Evanston
289	12.4	Evanston Twp HSD 202	Evanston
290	12.1	Lake Forest SD 67	Lake Forest
291	12.0	New Trier Twp HSD 203	Winnetka
292	11.8	Winnetka SD 36	Winnetka
293	11.5	Northbrook SD 28	Northbrook

Student/Librarian Ratio

Rank	Ratio	District Name	City
1	6,448.8	Indian Prairie CUSD 204	Aurora
2	6,217.0	Danville CCSD 118	Danville
3	6,047.0	Round Lake Area Schs - Dist 116	Round Lake
4	5,958.0	Maywood-Melrose Park-Broadview-89	Melrose Park
5	5,551.0	Lincoln Way Community HSD 210	New Lenox
6	5,372.0	Dekalb Community Unit SD 428	De Kalb
7	5,136.0	Cahokia Community Unit SD 187	Cahokia
8	5,072.0	Galesburg CUSD 205	Galesburg
9	4,841.0	Crete Monee CUSD 201U	Crete
10	4,786.0	Joliet Public SD 86	Joliet
11	4,652.0	North Chicago SD 187	North Chicago
12	4,319.0	Adlai E Stevenson Dist 125	Lincolnshire
13	4,088.0	Dolton SD 149	Calumet City
14	3,898.0	Glenview CCSD 34	Glenview
15	3,743.0	Triad Community Unit SD 2	Troy
16	3,737.7	Aurora East Unit SD 131	Aurora
17	3,662.0	Sterling C U Dist 5	Sterling
18	3,628.0	Quincy SD 172	Quincy
19	3,620.0	J S Morton HS District 201	Cicero
20	3,516.0	Kildeer Countryside CCSD 96	Buffalo Grove
21	3,360.0	Rock Island SD 41	Rock Island
22	3,317.0	Bellwood SD 88	Bellwood
23	3,264.0	Steger SD 194	Steger
24	3,263.5	Thornton Twp HSD 205	South Holland
25	3,243.0	Troy Community CSD 30C	Plainfield
26	3,187.0	Summit Hill SD 161	Frankfort
27	3,143.0	Harvey SD 152	Harvey
28	3,095.0	O'Fallon CCSD 90	Ofallon
29	3,035.0	Homer Community CSD 33C	Lockport
30	3,019.0	Collinsville CUSD 10	Collinsville
31	3,010.0	Dixon Unit SD 170	Dixon
32	2,989.0	Effingham Community Unit SD 40	Effingham
33	2,979.0	Zion Elementary SD 6	Zion
34	2,939.0	Elmwood Park CUSD 401	Elmwood Park
35	2,932.0	Kankakee SD 111	Kankakee
36	2,838.0	Berkeley SD 87	Berkeley
37	2,745.0	Canton Union SD 66	Canton
38	2,663.3	Waukegan CUSD 60	Waukegan
39	2,627.7	SD 46	Elgin
40	2,622.7	Peoria SD 150	Peoria
41	2,588.0	Flossmoor SD 161	Chicago Heights
42	2,577.1	Community Unit SD 300	Carpentersville
43	2,557.0	Granite City CUSD 9	Granite City
44	2,501.0	Sandwich CUSD 430	Sandwich
45	2,456.0	Lemont-Bromberek CSD 113a	Lemont
46	2,452.0	Antioch CCSD 34	Antioch
47	2,444.0	Bourbonnais SD 53	Bourbonnais
48	2,362.0	Massac Unit District #1	Metropolis
49	2,356.0	Kirby SD 140	Tinley Park
50	2,349.0	Mchenry CCSD 15	Mc Henry
51	2,325.0	Antioch Community High SD 117	Lake Villa
52	2,258.0	Zion-Benton Twp HSD 126	Zion
53	2,254.0	Lyons SD 103	Lyons
54	2,172.0	Lake Forest SD 67	Lake Forest
55	2,165.0	Illinois Valley Central UD 321	Chillicothe
56	2,134.0	Pekin Community HSD 303	Pekin
57	2,124.0	O'Fallon Twp High SD 203	Ofallon
58	2,122.0	Community High SD 94	West Chicago
59	2,109.0	Park Forest SD 163	Park Forest
60	2,094.0	Evergreen Park ESD 124	Evergreen Park
61	1,963.2	Arlington Heights SD 25	Arlington Hgts
62	1,954.5	Du Page High SD 88	Villa Park

63	1,940.0	Grayslake Community High SD 127	Grayslake
64	1,931.0	East Peoria SD 86	East Peoria
65	1,910.0	Coal City CUSD 1	Coal City
66	1,901.0	Wabash CUSD 348	Mount Carmel
67	1,880.0	Jacksonville SD 117	Jacksonville
68	1,877.0	Kewanee Community Unit SD 229	Kewanee
69	1,863.0	Frankfort Community Unit SD 168	West Frankfort
70	1,850.0	United Twp HS District 30	East Moline
71	1,842.0	Streator Elem SD 44	Streator
72	1,834.0	Rochelle Community CD 231	Rochelle
73	1,799.0	Byron Community Unit SD 226	Byron
74	1,793.0	Sherrard Community Unit SD 200	Sherrard
75	1,790.0	Manteno Community Unit SD 5	Manteno
76	1,785.0	Hononegah Community HSD 207	Rockton
77	1,778.0	Darien SD 61	Darien
78	1,772.8	East Saint Louis SD 189	E Saint Louis
79	1,735.0	Township High SD 214	Arlington Hgts
80	1,734.0	Bradley Bourbonnais CHSD 307	Bradley
81	1,730.0	Paris-Union SD 95	Paris
82	1,729.1	Naperville C U Dist 203	Naperville
83	1,729.0	Argo Community HSD 217	Summit
84	1,728.0	Genoa Kingston CUSD 424	Genoa
85	1,719.0	Litchfield CUSD 12	Litchfield
86	1,718.8	Rockford SD 205	Rockford
87	1,690.0	Carterville CUSD 5	Carterville
88	1,679.0	Winnebago CUSD 323	Winnebago
89	1,671.0	Jasper County Comm Unit Dist 1	Newton
90	1,670.0	Columbia Community Unit SD 4	Columbia
91	1,662.5	Lombard SD 44	Lombard
92	1,659.5	Cicero SD 99	Cicero
93	1,616.6	Palatine CCSD 15	Palatine
94	1,607.0	Reavis Twp HSD 220	Burbank
95	1,600.0	Sparta CUSD 140	Sparta
96	1,598.0	Eureka CU Dist 140	Eureka
97	1,590.0	Lockport Twp HSD 205	Lockport
98	1,585.0	Country Club Hills SD 160	Ctry Club Hill
99	1,580.0	Ottawa Twp HSD 140	Ottawa
100	1,556.0	Carmi-White County CUSD 5	Carmi
101	1,548.0	Posen-Robbins El SD 143-5	Posen
102	1,532.0	Bradley SD 61	Bradley
103	1,528.0	Wilmington CUSD 209U	Wilmington
104	1,523.0	Fenton Community HSD 100	Bensenville
105	1,522.5	Sycamore CUSD 427	Sycamore
106	1,501.8	Community High SD 155	Crystal Lake
107	1,499.0	Freeport SD 145	Freeport
108	1,442.0	Bloom Twp High SD 206	Chicago Heights
109	1,433.6	Aurora West Unit SD 129	Aurora
110	1,433.5	Thornton Fractional T HS D 215	Calumet City
111	1,433.2	Belvidere CUSD 100	Belvidere
112	1,416.0	Bethalto CUSD 8	Bethalto
113	1,397.6	Alton Community Unit SD 11	Alton
114	1,375.4	Woodland CCSD 50	Gurnee
115	1,353.0	Marquardt SD 15	Glendale Hgts
116	1,349.4	Edwardsville CUSD 7	Edwardsville
117	1,320.5	Homewood Flossmoor CHSD 233	Flossmoor
117	1,320.5	Mclean County Unit Dist 5	Normal
119	1,303.7	Marion Community Unit SD 2	Marion
120	1,299.0	Yorkville Community Unit SD 115	Yorkville
121	1,277.5	Springfield SD 186	Springfield
122	1,271.1	Crystal Lake CCSD 47	Crystal Lake
123	1,256.0	Oregon C U School Dist-220	Oregon
124	1,225.5	Glen Ellyn CCSD 89	Glen Ellyn
125	1,218.5	Joliet Twp HSD 204	Joliet
126	1,214.8	Belleville Twp HSD 201	Belleville
127	1,205.5	Dunlap CUSD 323	Dunlap
128	1,190.0	Warren Twp High SD 121	Gurnee
129	1,166.5	Central Community Unit SD 301	Burlington
130	1,162.0	Proviso Twp HSD 209	Maywood
131	1,149.0	Beach Park CCSD 3	Beach Park
132	1,144.5	Olympia CUSD 16	Stanford
133	1,142.0	Rich Twp HS District 227	Olympia Fields
134	1,141.4	Consolidated High SD 230	Orland Park
135	1,141.0	Murphysboro CUSD 186	Murphysboro
136	1,130.3	Mattoon CUSD 2	Mattoon
137	1,084.9	Oswego Community Unit SD 308	Oswego
138	1,067.0	East Richland CUSD 1	Olney
139	1,062.5	Valley View CUSD 365U	Romeoville
140	1,057.2	New Trier Twp HSD 203	Winnetka
141	1,055.5	Ottawa Elem SD 141	Ottawa
142	1,051.5	Mchenry Community HSD 156	Mc Henry
143	1,039.0	Jersey CUSD 100	Jerseyville
144	1,013.7	Taylorville CUSD 3	Taylorville
145	1,012.5	Palos Community CSD 118	Palos Park
146	1,003.6	Community High SD 218	Oak Lawn
147	997.5	Mount Prospect SD 57	Mount Prospect
148	997.3	Highland Community Unit SD 5	Highland
149	989.5	Macomb Community Unit SD 185	Macomb
150	989.0	Mascoutah C U District 19	Mascoutah
151	987.3	Oak Park & River Forest Dist 200	Oak Park
152	986.9	Plainfield SD 202	Plainfield
153	986.0	Mundelein Cons High SD 120	Mundelein
154	980.5	Bond County CUSD 2	Greenville
155	977.3	Wauconda Community Unit SD 118	Wauconda
156	975.3	Community High SD 128	Libertyville
157	973.7	Geneseo Community Unit SD 228	Geneseo
158	972.0	Bloomington SD 87	Bloomington
159	967.0	Mount Vernon SD 80	Mount Vernon
160	960.5	City of Chicago SD 299	Chicago
161	957.0	Wilmette SD 39	Wilmette
162	948.5	Cook County SD 130	Blue Island
163	946.3	Lake Park Community HSD 108	Roselle
164	919.4	Community CSD 59	Arlington Hgts
165	918.0	Township HSD 211	Palatine
166	917.5	Roxana Community Unit SD 1	Roxana
167	887.5	Peotone CUSD 207U	Peotone
168	886.3	Lyons Twp HSD 204	La Grange
169	876.5	Vandalia CUSD 203	Vandalia
170	869.5	Geneva Community Unit SD 304	Geneva
171	866.5	Lincolnshire-Prairieview SD 103	Lincolnshire
172	865.3	La Grange SD 102	La Grange Park
173	864.5	Lake Forest Community HSD 115	Lake Forest
174	856.0	Westmont CUSD 201	Westmont
175	850.9	Consolidated SD 158	Huntley
176	844.8	Decatur SD 61	Decatur
177	844.2	Hinsdale Twp HSD 86	Hinsdale
178	843.0	Meridian CUSD 223	Stillman Valley
179	834.0	Burbank SD 111	Burbank
180	832.2	Community CSD 62	Des Plaines
181	828.5	Carlinville CUSD 1	Carlinville
182	825.0	Aptakisic-Tripp CCSD 102	Buffalo Grove
183	820.0	Saint Charles CUSD 303	Saint Charles
184	817.0	Oak Lawn Community HSD 229	Oak Lawn
185	809.5	Keeneyville SD 20	Hanover Park
186	798.0	Hawthorn CCSD 73	Vernon Hills
187	795.6	Ball Chatham CUSD 5	Chatham
188	789.3	Harvard CUSD 50	Harvard
189	785.5	Nippersink SD 2	Richmond
190	782.0	Bremen Community HS District 228	Midlothian
191	768.0	Minooka Community CSD 201	Minooka
192	762.3	Kaneland CUSD 302	Maple Park
193	759.2	Maine Township HSD 207	Park Ridge
194	758.5	Fremont SD 79	Mundelein
195	757.5	Lake Zurich CUSD 95	Lake Zurich
196	749.7	Community High SD 99	Downers Grove
197	748.8	Berwyn North SD 98	Berwyn
198	748.3	Charleston CUSD 1	Charleston
199	741.7	Herscher Community Unit SD 2	Herscher
200	739.7	Morton CUSD 709	Morton
201	736.3	Herrin CUSD 4	Herrin
202	732.3	Batavia Unit SD 101	Batavia
203	730.3	Elmhurst SD 205	Elmhurst
204	727.0	East Maine SD 63	Des Plaines
205	722.8	Mannheim SD 83	Franklin Park
206	714.7	Community Unit SD 200	Wheaton
207	713.7	Barrington CUSD 220	Barrington
208	708.4	Lake Villa CCSD 41	Lake Villa
209	704.7	Hillsboro Community Unit SD 3	Hillsboro
210	696.7	Harlem Unit Dist 122	Loves Park
211	686.9	Champaign Community Unit SD 4	Champaign
212	686.8	Glen Ellyn SD 41	Glen Ellyn
213	676.0	Gurnee SD 56	Gurnee
214	669.5	Mahomet-Seymour CUSD 3	Mahomet
215	662.8	North Palos SD 117	Palos Hills
216	652.9	Glenbard Twp HSD 87	Glen Ellyn
217	649.3	Johnsburg CUSD 12	Johnsburg
218	643.9	Leyden Community HSD 212	Franklin Park
219	643.5	Moline Unit SD 40	Moline
220	639.6	Woodridge SD 68	Woodridge
221	633.7	Woodstock CUSD 200	Woodstock
222	629.6	Evanston Twp HSD 202	Evanston
223	627.7	Rochester Community Unit SD 3A	Rochester
224	624.3	New Lenox SD 122	New Lenox
225	621.6	Community CSD 93	Carol Stream
226	620.8	Community CSD 46	Grayslake
227	618.1	Northfield Twp High SD 225	Glenview
228	615.4	Oak Park Elem SD 97	Oak Park
229	611.3	Southwestern CUSD 9	Piasa
230	604.3	Robinson CUSD 2	Robinson
231	601.0	Mount Zion Community Unit SD 3	Mount Zion
232	599.4	Niles Twp Community High SD 219	Skokie
233	598.3	Tinley Park Community Cons SD 146	Tinley Park
234	592.2	Wheeling CCSD 21	Wheeling
235	591.9	Orland SD 135	Orland Park
236	590.3	Reed Custer CUSD 255U	Braidwood
237	574.9	Urbana SD 116	Urbana
238	570.3	Mundelein Elem SD 75	Mundelein
239	556.0	River Trails SD 26	Mount Prospect
240	541.8	Harrisburg CUSD 3	Harrisburg
241	535.5	Clinton CUSD 15	Clinton
242	534.5	Deerfield SD 109	Deerfield
243	534.3	Monticello CUSD 25	Monticello
244	518.8	Libertyville SD 70	Libertyville
245	518.5	Lansing SD 158	Lansing
246	511.0	Cary CCSD 26	Cary
247	502.0	East Moline SD 37	East Moline
248	495.7	Matteson ESD 162	Matteson
249	490.0	Prairie Central CUSD 8	Forrest
250	489.4	Dolton SD 148	Riverdale
251	488.6	CCSD 181	Hinsdale
252	481.9	Township High SD 113	Highland Park
253	466.9	Evanston CCSD 65	Evanston
254	459.2	Bensenville SD 2	Bensenville
255	454.2	Ridgeland SD 122	Oak Lawn
256	451.8	Lisle CUSD 202	Lisle
257	451.1	North Shore SD 112	Highland Park
258	446.2	Oak Lawn-Hometown SD 123	Oak Lawn
259	443.0	Queen Bee SD 16	Glendale Hgts
260	442.3	Skokie SD 68	Skokie
261	441.8	Downers Grove Grade SD 58	Downers Grove
262	437.8	Northbrook SD 28	Northbrook
263	427.3	Alsip-Hazlgrn-Oaklawn SD 126	Alsip
264	385.1	Elem SD 159	Matteson
265	381.6	Pekin Public SD 108	Pekin
266	345.8	West Harvey-Dixmoor PSD 147	Harvey
267	302.2	Monmouth Unit SD 38	Monmouth
268	0.0	Addison SD 4	Addison
268	0.0	Belleville SD 118	Belleville
268	0.0	Berwyn South SD 100	Berwyn
268	0.0	Channahon SD 17	Channahon
268	0.0	Chicago Heights SD 170	Chicago Heights
268	0.0	Community CSD 168	Sauk Village
268	0.0	Department of Corrections SD 428	Springfield
268	0.0	Du Quoin CUSD 300	Du Quoin
268	0.0	Forest Ridge SD 142	Oak Forest
268	0.0	Frankfort CCSD 157c	Frankfort
268	0.0	Homewood SD 153	Homewood
268	0.0	Indian Springs SD 109	Justice
268	0.0	Kinnikinnick CCSD 131	Roscoe
268	0.0	Midlothian SD 143	Midlothian
268	0.0	Mokena SD 159	Mokena
268	0.0	Park Ridge CCSD 64	Park Ridge
268	0.0	Prairie-Hills Elem SD 144	Markham
268	0.0	Prospect Heights SD 23	Prospect Hgts
268	0.0	Rantoul City SD 137	Rantoul
268	0.0	SD 45 Dupage County	Villa Park
268	0.0	Schaumburg CCSD 54	Schaumburg
268	0.0	Summit SD 104	Summit
268	0.0	Waterloo Community Unit SD 5	Waterloo
268	0.0	West Chicago ESD 33	West Chicago
268	0.0	Will County SD 92	Lockport
268	0.0	Winnetka SD 36	Winnetka

Student/Counselor Ratio

Rank	Ratio	District Name	City
1	9,572.0	Joliet Public SD 86	Joliet
2	7,106.0	Wheeling CCSD 21	Wheeling
3	4,088.0	Dolton SD 149	Calumet City
4	3,909.0	CCSD 181	Hinsdale
5	3,838.0	SD 45 Dupage County	Villa Park
6	3,831.0	Addison SD 4	Addison
7	3,577.0	Cary CCSD 26	Cary
8	3,516.0	Kildeer Countryside CCSD 96	Buffalo Grove
9	3,207.0	Deerfield SD 109	Deerfield
10	3,015.8	Schaumburg CCSD 54	Schaumburg
11	2,773.9	Community CSD 62	Des Plaines
12	2,618.3	Nippersink SD 2	Richmond
13	2,586.6	Palatine CCSD 15	Palatine
14	2,296.0	Bensenville SD 2	Bensenville
15	2,281.0	Mundelein Elem SD 75	Mundelein
16	2,254.0	Lyons SD 103	Lyons
17	2,215.0	Queen Bee SD 16	Glendale Hgts
18	2,177.0	Park Ridge CCSD 64	Park Ridge
19	2,109.0	Park Forest SD 163	Park Forest
20	2,015.7	Round Lake Area Schs - Dist 116	Round Lake
21	1,973.0	Orland SD 135	Orland Park
22	1,931.0	East Peoria SD 86	East Peoria
23	1,928.0	West Chicago ESD 33	West Chicago
24	1,913.2	East Maine SD 63	Des Plaines
25	1,877.0	Kewanee Community Unit SD 229	Kewanee
26	1,863.0	Frankfort Community Unit SD 168	West Frankfort
27	1,791.5	Belvidere CUSD 100	Belvidere
28	1,775.0	Peotone CUSD 207U	Peotone
29	1,760.0	Forest Ridge SD 142	Oak Forest
30	1,757.0	Kinnikinnick CCSD 131	Roscoe
31	1,719.0	Litchfield CUSD 12	Litchfield
32	1,712.0	Westmont CUSD 201	Westmont
33	1,711.5	Chicago Heights SD 170	Chicago Heights
34	1,679.0	Winnebago CUSD 323	Winnebago
35	1,638.4	Aurora West Unit SD 129	Aurora
36	1,606.4	Edwardsville CUSD 7	Edwardsville
37	1,599.0	Woodridge SD 68	Woodridge
38	1,585.0	Country Club Hills SD 160	Ctry Club Hill
39	1,536.0	Minooka Community CSD 201	Minooka
40	1,510.0	Channahon SD 17	Channahon
41	1,503.7	North Shore SD 112	Highland Park
42	1,416.0	Bethalto CUSD 8	Bethalto
43	1,369.0	SD 46	Elgin

44	1,352.3	Valley View CUSD 365U	Romeoville
45	1,298.5	Johnsburg CUSD 12	Johnsburg
46	1,297.0	Libertyville SD 70	Libertyville
47	1,294.0	Flossmoor SD 161	Chicago Heights
48	1,279.3	Peoria SD 150	Peoria
49	1,277.6	Lake Forest SD 67	Lake Forest
50	1,271.0	Waterloo Community Unit SD 5	Waterloo
51	1,268.0	Galesburg CUSD 205	Galesburg
52	1,228.0	Lemont-Bromberek CSD 113a	Lemont
53	1,225.5	Glen Ellyn CCSD 89	Glen Ellyn
54	1,215.0	Downers Grove Grade SD 58	Downers Grove
55	1,207.6	Collinsville CUSD 10	Collinsville
56	1,198.4	Plainfield SD 202	Plainfield
57	1,193.3	Manteno Community Unit SD 5	Manteno
58	1,164.7	Alton Community Unit SD 11	Alton
59	1,144.7	Glen Ellyn SD 41	Glen Ellyn
60	1,120.0	Rock Island SD 41	Rock Island
61	1,108.3	Lombard SD 44	Lombard
62	1,104.5	Herrin CUSD 4	Herrin
63	1,095.9	Granite City CUSD 9	Granite City
64	1,083.5	Harrisburg CUSD 3	Harrisburg
65	1,056.4	Mclean County Unit Dist 5	Normal
66	1,039.0	Jersey CUSD 100	Jerseyville
67	1,028.8	Kankakee SD 111	Kankakee
68	1,027.2	Cahokia Community Unit SD 187	Cahokia
69	1,019.4	Aurora East Unit SD 131	Aurora
70	1,013.7	Taylorville CUSD 3	Taylorville
71	1,012.5	Palos Community CSD 118	Palos Park
72	991.3	Matteson ESD 162	Matteson
73	979.7	Elmwood Park CUSD 401	Elmwood Park
74	968.2	Crete Monee CUSD 201U	Crete
75	967.0	Mount Vernon SD 80	Mount Vernon
76	958.0	Harlem Unit Dist 122	Loves Park
77	942.4	Kirby SD 140	Tinley Park
78	941.5	Rochester Community Unit SD 3A	Rochester
79	935.8	Triad Community Unit SD 2	Troy
80	925.1	Community Unit SD 300	Carpentersville
81	917.0	Rochelle Community CD 231	Rochelle
81	917.0	Southwestern CUSD 9	Piasa
83	915.5	Sterling C U Dist 5	Sterling
84	888.1	Danville CCSD 118	Danville
85	881.5	Decatur SD 61	Decatur
86	866.0	Yorkville Community Unit SD 115	Yorkville
87	847.8	Mattoon CUSD 2	Mattoon
88	845.0	Carterville CUSD 5	Carterville
89	843.0	Meridian CUSD 223	Stillman Valley
90	836.9	Batavia Unit SD 101	Batavia
91	833.7	Sandwich CUSD 430	Sandwich
92	832.3	New Lenox SD 122	New Lenox
93	806.2	Quincy SD 172	Quincy
94	804.9	Lake Zurich CUSD 95	Lake Zurich
95	801.3	Mount Zion Community Unit SD 3	Mount Zion
96	800.0	Sparta CUSD 140	Sparta
97	789.3	Harvard CUSD 50	Harvard
98	789.0	Oswego Community Unit SD 308	Oswego
99	777.7	Central Community Unit SD 301	Burlington
100	767.4	Dekalb Community Unit SD 428	De Kalb
101	764.0	Wilmington CUSD 209U	Wilmington
102	763.2	Pekin Public SD 108	Pekin
103	763.0	Olympia CUSD 16	Stanford
104	762.3	Kaneland CUSD 302	Maple Park
105	760.7	Murphysboro CUSD 186	Murphysboro
106	749.5	Freeport SD 145	Freeport
107	748.0	Highland Community Unit SD 5	Highland
108	741.8	Mascoutah C U District 19	Mascoutah
109	741.7	Herscher Community Unit SD 2	Herscher
110	730.3	Geneseo Community Unit SD 228	Geneseo
111	712.9	Woodstock CUSD 200	Woodstock
112	709.5	Berkeley SD 87	Berkeley
113	709.1	East Saint Louis SD 189	E Saint Louis
114	704.7	Hillsboro Community Unit SD 3	Hillsboro
115	700.0	Prairie Central CUSD 8	Forrest
116	689.6	Sherrard Community Unit SD 200	Sherrard
117	686.3	Canton Union SD 66	Canton
118	685.8	Wauconda Community Unit SD 118	Wauconda
119	684.3	Morton CUSD 709	Morton
120	683.3	Saint Charles CUSD 303	Saint Charles
121	673.9	Geneva Community Unit SD 304	Geneva
122	669.5	Mahomet-Seymour CUSD 3	Mahomet
123	668.6	Consolidated SD 158	Huntley
124	662.6	Rockford SD 205	Rockford
125	657.0	Urbana SD 116	Urbana
126	653.7	Bond County CUSD 2	Greenville
127	643.5	Moline Unit SD 40	Moline
128	639.2	Waukegan CUSD 60	Waukegan
129	636.7	Coal City CUSD 1	Coal City
130	634.3	New Trier Twp HSD 203	Winnetka
131	633.7	Wabash CUSD 348	Mount Carmel
132	626.7	Jacksonville SD 117	Jacksonville
133	622.4	Carmi-White County CUSD 5	Carmi
134	618.2	Champaign Community Unit SD 4	Champaign
135	614.2	Indian Prairie CUSD 204	Aurora
136	611.7	Barrington CUSD 220	Barrington
136	611.7	Roxana Community Unit SD 1	Roxana
138	609.0	Sycamore CUSD 427	Sycamore
139	607.0	Homer Community CSD 33C	Lockport
140	602.3	Lisle CUSD 202	Lisle
141	602.0	Dixon Unit SD 170	Dixon
142	598.6	Charleston CUSD 1	Charleston
143	590.5	Massac Unit District #1	Metropolis
144	590.3	Reed Custer CUSD 255U	Braidwood
145	576.7	Paris-Union SD 95	Paris
146	576.4	Naperville C U Dist 203	Naperville
147	576.0	Genoa Kingston CUSD 424	Genoa
148	568.3	Ball Chatham CUSD 5	Chatham
149	556.7	Columbia Community Unit SD 4	Columbia
150	552.3	Carlinville CUSD 1	Carlinville
151	543.7	City of Chicago SD 299	Chicago
152	540.5	Troy Community CSD 30C	Plainfield
153	534.3	Monticello CUSD 25	Monticello
154	533.5	East Richland CUSD 1	Olney
155	533.4	Community Unit SD 200	Wheaton
156	532.7	Eureka CU Dist 140	Eureka
157	527.8	Ottawa Elem SD 141	Ottawa
158	519.7	Du Quoin CUSD 300	Du Quoin
159	516.9	North Chicago SD 187	North Chicago
160	502.8	Bloomington SD 87	Bloomington
161	494.8	Macomb Community Unit SD 185	Macomb
162	488.9	Marion Community Unit SD 2	Marion
163	485.9	Belleville Twp HSD 201	Belleville
164	482.2	Dunlap CUSD 323	Dunlap
165	471.0	Oregon C U School Dist-220	Oregon
166	446.3	Warren Twp High SD 121	Gurnee
167	441.8	Illinois Valley Central UD 321	Chillicothe
168	437.8	Northbrook SD 28	Northbrook
169	435.1	Thornton Twp HSD 205	South Holland
170	432.3	West Harvey-Dixmoor PSD 147	Harvey
171	428.4	Clinton CUSD 15	Clinton
172	428.3	Byron Community Unit SD 226	Byron
173	427.0	Effingham Community Unit SD 40	Effingham
174	424.8	O'Fallon Twp High SD 203	Ofallon
175	405.7	Elmhurst SD 205	Elmhurst
176	401.8	Reavis Twp HSD 220	Burbank
177	389.6	Vandalia CUSD 203	Vandalia
178	387.5	Antioch Community High SD 117	Lake Villa
179	377.8	Monmouth Unit SD 38	Monmouth
180	376.3	Zion-Benton Twp HSD 126	Zion
181	362.6	Robinson CUSD 2	Robinson
182	360.5	Bloom Twp High SD 206	Chicago Heights
183	358.6	East Moline SD 37	East Moline
184	358.4	Thornton Fractional T HS D 215	Calumet City
185	357.5	Proviso Twp HSD 209	Maywood
186	357.0	Hononegah Community HSD 207	Rockton
187	355.4	Du Page High SD 88	Villa Park
188	351.1	Ottawa Twp HSD 140	Ottawa
189	350.5	Mchenry Community HSD 156	Mc Henry
190	345.0	Bremen Community HS District 228	Midlothian
191	334.5	Community High SD 218	Oak Lawn
192	334.2	Jasper County Comm Unit Dist 1	Newton
193	333.7	Community High SD 155	Crystal Lake
194	332.9	Consolidated High SD 230	Orland Park
195	326.8	Oak Lawn Community HSD 229	Oak Lawn
196	326.5	Lincoln Way Community HSD 210	New Lenox
197	324.9	Joliet Twp HSD 204	Joliet
198	323.3	Grayslake Community High SD 127	Grayslake
199	318.0	Lockport Twp HSD 205	Lockport
200	314.8	J S Morton HS District 201	Cicero
201	308.3	United Twp HS District 30	East Moline
202	304.9	Pekin Community HSD 303	Pekin
203	304.6	Fenton Community HSD 100	Bensenville
204	304.2	Bradley Bourbonnais CHSD 307	Bradley
205	302.4	Township HSD 211	Palatine
206	296.2	Oak Park & River Forest Dist 200	Oak Park
207	293.4	Homewood Flossmoor CHSD 233	Flossmoor
208	288.2	Argo Community HSD 217	Summit
209	283.9	Lake Park Community HSD 108	Roselle
210	281.7	Mundelein Cons High SD 120	Mundelein
211	271.6	Leyden Community HSD 212	Franklin Park
212	269.9	Adlai E Stevenson Dist 125	Lincolnshire
213	262.8	Maine Township HSD 207	Park Ridge
214	262.4	Community High SD 99	Downers Grove
215	253.7	Niles Twp Community High SD 219	Skokie
216	249.6	Lyons Twp HSD 204	La Grange
217	247.4	Glenbard Twp HSD 87	Glen Ellyn
218	243.8	Community High SD 128	Libertyville
219	241.1	Community High SD 94	West Chicago
220	236.3	Rich Twp HS District 227	Olympia Fields
221	231.8	Northfield Twp High SD 225	Glenview
222	227.9	Township High SD 113	Highland Park
223	222.2	Hinsdale Twp HSD 86	Hinsdale
224	216.1	Lake Forest Community HSD 115	Lake Forest
225	209.9	Evanston Twp HSD 202	Evanston
226	200.7	Township High SD 214	Arlington Hgts
227	0.0	Alsip-Hazlgrn-Oaklawn SD 126	Alsip
227	0.0	Antioch CCSD 34	Antioch
227	0.0	Aptakisic-Tripp CCSD 102	Buffalo Grove
227	0.0	Arlington Heights SD 25	Arlington Hgts
227	0.0	Beach Park CCSD 3	Beach Park
227	0.0	Belleville SD 118	Belleville
227	0.0	Bellwood SD 88	Bellwood
227	0.0	Berwyn North SD 98	Berwyn
227	0.0	Berwyn South SD 100	Berwyn
227	0.0	Bourbonnais SD 53	Bourbonnais
227	0.0	Bradley SD 61	Bradley
227	0.0	Burbank SD 111	Burbank
227	0.0	Cicero SD 99	Cicero
227	0.0	Community CSD 168	Sauk Village
227	0.0	Community CSD 46	Grayslake
227	0.0	Community CSD 59	Arlington Hgts
227	0.0	Community CSD 93	Carol Stream
227	0.0	Cook County SD 130	Blue Island
227	0.0	Crystal Lake CCSD 47	Crystal Lake
227	0.0	Darien SD 61	Darien
227	0.0	Department of Corrections SD 428	Springfield
227	0.0	Dolton SD 148	Riverdale
227	0.0	Elem SD 159	Matteson
227	0.0	Evanston CCSD 65	Evanston
227	0.0	Evergreen Park ESD 124	Evergreen Park
227	0.0	Frankfort CCSD 157c	Frankfort
227	0.0	Fremont SD 79	Mundelein
227	0.0	Glenview CCSD 34	Glenview
227	0.0	Gurnee SD 56	Gurnee
227	0.0	Harvey SD 152	Harvey
227	0.0	Hawthorn CCSD 73	Vernon Hills
227	0.0	Homewood SD 153	Homewood
227	0.0	Indian Springs SD 109	Justice
227	0.0	Keeneyville SD 20	Hanover Park
227	0.0	La Grange SD 102	La Grange Park
227	0.0	Lake Villa CCSD 41	Lake Villa
227	0.0	Lansing SD 158	Lansing
227	0.0	Lincolnshire-Prairieview SD 103	Lincolnshire
227	0.0	Mannheim SD 83	Franklin Park
227	0.0	Marquardt SD 15	Glendale Hgts
227	0.0	Maywood-Melrose Park-Broadview-89	Melrose Park
227	0.0	Mchenry CCSD 15	Mc Henry
227	0.0	Midlothian SD 143	Midlothian
227	0.0	Mokena SD 159	Mokena
227	0.0	Mount Prospect SD 57	Mount Prospect
227	0.0	North Palos SD 117	Palos Hills
227	0.0	O'Fallon CCSD 90	Ofallon
227	0.0	Oak Lawn-Hometown SD 123	Oak Lawn
227	0.0	Oak Park Elem SD 97	Oak Park
227	0.0	Posen-Robbins El SD 143-5	Posen
227	0.0	Prairie-Hills Elem SD 144	Markham
227	0.0	Prospect Heights SD 23	Prospect Hgts
227	0.0	Rantoul City SD 137	Rantoul
227	0.0	Ridgeland SD 122	Oak Lawn
227	0.0	River Trails SD 26	Mount Prospect
227	0.0	Skokie SD 68	Skokie
227	0.0	Springfield SD 186	Springfield
227	0.0	Steger SD 194	Steger
227	0.0	Streator Elem SD 44	Streator
227	0.0	Summit Hill SD 161	Frankfort
227	0.0	Summit SD 104	Summit
227	0.0	Tinley Park Community Cons SD 146	Tinley Park
227	0.0	Will County SD 92	Lockport
227	0.0	Wilmette SD 39	Wilmette
227	0.0	Winnetka SD 36	Winnetka
227	0.0	Woodland CCSD 50	Gurnee
227	0.0	Zion Elementary SD 6	Zion

Current Spending per Student in FY2001

Rank	Dollars	District Name	City
1	17,004	Township High SD 113	Highland Park
2	16,240	Evanston Twp HSD 202	Evanston
3	14,450	New Trier Twp HSD 203	Winnetka
4	14,402	Northfield Twp High SD 225	Glenview
5	14,310	Niles Twp Community High SD 219	Skokie
6	14,068	Lake Forest Community HSD 115	Lake Forest
7	13,617	Maine Township HSD 207	Park Ridge
8	13,470	Oak Park & River Forest Dist 200	Oak Park
9	13,272	Lyons Twp HSD 204	La Grange
10	13,105	Community High SD 128	Libertyville
11	13,071	Township High SD 214	Arlington Hgts
12	12,367	Fenton Community HSD 100	Bensenville
13	12,245	Hinsdale Twp HSD 86	Hinsdale
14	12,202	Community High SD 218	Oak Lawn
15	12,183	Township HSD 211	Palatine
16	11,978	Northbrook SD 28	Northbrook
17	11,971	Rich Twp HS District 227	Olympia Fields
18	11,956	Thornton Twp HSD 205	South Holland
19	11,819	Bloom Twp High SD 206	Chicago Heights
20	11,736	Leyden Community HSD 212	Franklin Park
21	11,422	Homewood Flossmoor CHSD 233	Flossmoor
22	10,996	Argo Community HSD 217	Summit
23	10,872	Thornton Fractional T HS D 215	Calumet City
24	10,820	Lake Park Community HSD 108	Roselle

25	10,807	Proviso Twp HSD 209	Maywood
26	10,805	Du Page High SD 88	Villa Park
27	10,788	Adlai E Stevenson Dist 125	Lincolnshire
28	10,677	Bremen Community HS District 228	Midlothian
29	10,636	Community High SD 99	Downers Grove
30	10,596	Reavis Twp HSD 220	Burbank
31	10,526	Consolidated High SD 230	Orland Park
32	10,516	Reed Custer CUSD 255U	Braidwood
33	10,456	Joliet Twp HSD 204	Joliet
34	10,290	Lake Forest SD 67	Lake Forest
35	10,272	Oak Lawn Community HSD 229	Oak Lawn
36	10,263	Glenbard Twp HSD 87	Glen Ellyn
37	10,081	Evanston CCSD 65	Evanston
38	10,028	Skokie SD 68	Skokie
39	9,954	Mundelein Cons High SD 120	Mundelein
40	9,924	West Harvey-Dixmoor PSD 147	Harvey
41	9,842	North Shore SD 112	Highland Park
42	9,646	Winnetka SD 36	Winnetka
43	9,626	Park Ridge CCSD 64	Park Ridge
44	9,468	Byron Community Unit SD 226	Byron
45	9,463	Community High SD 94	West Chicago
46	9,449	Lisle CUSD 202	Lisle
47	9,267	River Trails SD 26	Mount Prospect
48	9,255	Community CSD 62	Des Plaines
49	9,217	Oak Park Elem SD 97	Oak Park
50	9,106	Elem SD 159	Matteson
51	8,973	Lincolnshire-Prairieview SD 103	Lincolnshire
52	8,966	Community High SD 155	Crystal Lake
53	8,954	Westmont CUSD 201	Westmont
54	8,935	Warren Twp High SD 121	Gurnee
55	8,899	J S Morton HS District 201	Cicero
56	8,876	Glenview CCSD 34	Glenview
57	8,828	Palatine CCSD 15	Palatine
58	8,768	Antioch Community High SD 117	Lake Villa
59	8,711	Elmhurst SD 205	Elmhurst
60	8,708	Community CSD 59	Arlington Hgts
61	8,672	North Chicago SD 187	North Chicago
62	8,600	Schaumburg CCSD 54	Schaumburg
63	8,579	Barrington CUSD 220	Barrington
64	8,556	Zion-Benton Twp HSD 126	Zion
65	8,515	Lockport Twp HSD 205	Lockport
66	8,492	Mannheim SD 83	Franklin Park
67	8,419	Urbana SD 116	Urbana
68	8,370	Prospect Heights SD 23	Prospect Hgts
69	8,359	Park Forest SD 163	Park Forest
70	8,339	Rockford SD 205	Rockford
71	8,233	Arlington Heights SD 25	Arlington Hgts
72	8,212	CCSD 181	Hinsdale
73	8,196	East Maine SD 63	Des Plaines
74	8,170	Palos Community CSD 118	Palos Park
75	8,067	Peoria SD 150	Peoria
76	8,047	Hononegah Community HSD 207	Rockton
77	8,025	Danville CCSD 118	Danville
78	8,014	Tinley Park Community Cons SD 146	Tinley Park
79	8,006	Flossmoor SD 161	Chicago Heights
80	7,972	Wilmette SD 39	Wilmette
81	7,954	Clinton CUSD 15	Clinton
82	7,844	Gurnee SD 56	Gurnee
83	7,771	Lombard SD 44	Lombard
84	7,754	Wheeling CCSD 21	Wheeling
85	7,750	East Moline SD 37	East Moline
86	7,714	Springfield SD 186	Springfield
87	7,685	Grayslake Community High SD 127	Grayslake
88	7,683	Keeneyville SD 20	Hanover Park
89	7,673	Orland SD 135	Orland Park
90	7,665	Libertyville SD 70	Libertyville
91	7,627	Kildeer Countryside CCSD 96	Buffalo Grove
92	7,617	Cahokia Community Unit SD 187	Cahokia
93	7,616	Deerfield SD 109	Deerfield
94	7,614	Central Community Unit SD 301	Burlington
95	7,558	Naperville C U Dist 203	Naperville
96	7,547	Aptakisic-Tripp CCSD 102	Buffalo Grove
97	7,544	Kankakee SD 111	Kankakee
97	7,544	SD 46	Elgin
99	7,538	Community Unit SD 200	Wheaton
100	7,533	Ottawa Twp HSD 140	Ottawa
101	7,522	Ottawa Elem SD 141	Ottawa
102	7,498	Jasper County Comm Unit Dist 1	Newton
103	7,450	Glen Ellyn CCSD 89	Glen Ellyn
104	7,446	East Saint Louis SD 189	E Saint Louis
105	7,412	La Grange SD 102	La Grange Park
106	7,404	Mount Prospect SD 57	Mount Prospect
107	7,387	Lincoln Way Community HSD 210	New Lenox
108	7,382	Chicago Heights SD 170	Chicago Heights
109	7,374	City of Chicago SD 299	Chicago
110	7,359	Champaign Community Unit SD 4	Champaign
111	7,358	Macomb Community Unit SD 185	Macomb
112	7,303	Sparta CUSD 140	Sparta
113	7,298	Downers Grove Grade SD 58	Downers Grove
114	7,283	Woodridge SD 68	Woodridge
115	7,270	Hawthorn CCSD 73	Vernon Hills
116	7,268	SD 45 Dupage County	Villa Park
117	7,254	Woodstock CUSD 200	Woodstock
118	7,239	Bloomington SD 87	Bloomington
119	7,227	West Chicago ESD 33	West Chicago
120	7,217	Mchenry Community HSD 156	Mc Henry
121	7,201	Belleville SD 118	Belleville
122	7,177	Morton CUSD 709	Morton
123	7,174	Bradley Bourbonnais CHSD 307	Bradley
124	7,170	Geneva Community Unit SD 304	Geneva
125	7,159	Alsip-Hazlgrn-Oaklawn SD 126	Alsip
126	7,157	Homewood SD 153	Homewood
127	7,135	Carmi-White County CUSD 5	Carmi
128	7,090	Dixon Unit SD 170	Dixon
129	7,075	Lyons SD 103	Lyons
130	7,073	Mascoutah C U District 19	Mascoutah
131	7,071	Harlem Unit Dist 122	Loves Park
132	7,069	East Peoria SD 86	East Peoria
133	7,044	Rock Island SD 41	Rock Island
134	7,036	Waukegan CUSD 60	Waukegan
135	7,027	Elmwood Park CUSD 401	Elmwood Park
136	7,026	Crete Monee CUSD 201U	Crete
137	7,013	Coal City CUSD 1	Coal City
138	7,005	Lake Zurich CUSD 95	Lake Zurich
139	6,991	Roxana Community Unit SD 1	Roxana
140	6,988	Kaneland CUSD 302	Maple Park
141	6,965	Prairie-Hills Elem SD 144	Markham
142	6,956	Mount Vernon SD 80	Mount Vernon
143	6,953	Alton Community Unit SD 11	Alton
144	6,938	Minooka Community CSD 201	Minooka
145	6,937	Jacksonville SD 117	Jacksonville
146	6,918	Dekalb Community Unit SD 428	De Kalb
147	6,911	Cook County SD 130	Blue Island
148	6,900	Yorkville Community Unit SD 115	Yorkville
149	6,897	Moline Unit SD 40	Moline
150	6,875	Sterling C U Dist 5	Sterling
151	6,855	Paris-Union SD 95	Paris
152	6,854	Darien SD 61	Darien
153	6,852	Consolidated SD 158	Huntley
154	6,839	Oregon C U School Dist-220	Oregon
155	6,835	Saint Charles CUSD 303	Saint Charles
156	6,815	Johnsburg CUSD 12	Johnsburg
157	6,814	Frankfort Community Unit SD 168	West Frankfort
158	6,775	Belleville Twp HSD 201	Belleville
159	6,768	Murphysboro CUSD 186	Murphysboro
160	6,767	Sycamore CUSD 427	Sycamore
161	6,753	Marquardt SD 15	Glendale Hgts
162	6,728	Matteson ESD 162	Matteson
163	6,709	Pekin Community HSD 303	Pekin
164	6,682	Mclean County Unit Dist 5	Normal
165	6,680	Du Quoin CUSD 300	Du Quoin
166	6,670	Summit SD 104	Summit
167	6,669	North Palos SD 117	Palos Hills
168	6,651	Streator Elem SD 44	Streator
169	6,641	Freeport SD 145	Freeport
170	6,629	Collinsville CUSD 10	Collinsville
171	6,627	Community Unit SD 300	Carpentersville
171	6,627	Granite City CUSD 9	Granite City
173	6,626	Queen Bee SD 16	Glendale Hgts
174	6,624	Oak Lawn-Hometown SD 123	Oak Lawn
175	6,613	Berwyn South SD 100	Berwyn
176	6,593	Canton Union SD 66	Canton
177	6,582	Mattoon CUSD 2	Mattoon
178	6,579	Harvey SD 152	Harvey
179	6,577	Olympia CUSD 16	Stanford
180	6,540	Edwardsville CUSD 7	Edwardsville
181	6,532	Herscher Community Unit SD 2	Herscher
182	6,530	Highland Community Unit SD 5	Highland
183	6,518	Lansing SD 158	Lansing
184	6,491	United Twp HS District 30	East Moline
185	6,489	Fremont SD 79	Mundelein
186	6,484	Pekin Public SD 108	Pekin
187	6,479	Prairie Central CUSD 8	Forrest
188	6,478	Mahomet-Seymour CUSD 3	Mahomet
189	6,447	Wauconda Community Unit SD 118	Wauconda
190	6,444	Country Club Hills SD 160	Ctry Club Hill
191	6,442	Zion Elementary SD 6	Zion
192	6,433	Forest Ridge SD 142	Oak Forest
193	6,431	Jersey CUSD 100	Jerseyville
194	6,414	Community CSD 46	Grayslake
195	6,404	Indian Prairie CUSD 204	Aurora
196	6,403	Posen-Robbins El SD 143-5	Posen
197	6,390	Evergreen Park ESD 124	Evergreen Park
198	6,378	O'Fallon Twp High SD 203	Ofallon
199	6,363	Addison SD 4	Addison
200	6,347	Kirby SD 140	Tinley Park
201	6,338	Harrisburg CUSD 3	Harrisburg
202	6,329	Charleston CUSD 1	Charleston
203	6,294	Nippersink SD 2	Richmond
204	6,290	Aurora East Unit SD 131	Aurora
205	6,282	Beach Park CCSD 3	Beach Park
206	6,277	Robinson CUSD 2	Robinson
207	6,276	Glen Ellyn SD 41	Glen Ellyn
208	6,270	Community CSD 93	Carol Stream
209	6,236	Quincy SD 172	Quincy
210	6,231	Rantoul City SD 137	Rantoul
211	6,220	Ridgeland SD 122	Oak Lawn
212	6,205	Decatur SD 61	Decatur
213	6,200	Bensenville SD 2	Bensenville
214	6,193	Sherrard Community Unit SD 200	Sherrard
215	6,185	Berkeley SD 87	Berkeley
216	6,180	Aurora West Unit SD 129	Aurora
217	6,178	Bradley SD 61	Bradley
218	6,173	Midlothian SD 143	Midlothian
219	6,172	Valley View CUSD 365U	Romeoville
220	6,170	East Richland CUSD 1	Olney
221	6,161	Bethalto CUSD 8	Bethalto
222	6,142	Dolton SD 149	Calumet City
223	6,126	Southwestern CUSD 9	Piasa
224	6,112	Burbank SD 111	Burbank
225	6,086	Joliet Public SD 86	Joliet
226	6,047	Manteno Community Unit SD 5	Manteno
227	6,035	Batavia Unit SD 101	Batavia
228	6,014	Dolton SD 148	Riverdale
229	6,000	Galesburg CUSD 205	Galesburg
230	5,992	Round Lake Area Schs - Dist 116	Round Lake
231	5,952	Wabash CUSD 348	Mount Carmel
232	5,945	Geneseo Community Unit SD 228	Geneseo
232	5,945	Hillsboro Community Unit SD 3	Hillsboro
234	5,936	Harvard CUSD 50	Harvard
235	5,916	Columbia Community Unit SD 4	Columbia
236	5,900	Winnebago CUSD 323	Winnebago
237	5,898	Woodland CCSD 50	Gurnee
238	5,897	Triad Community Unit SD 2	Troy
239	5,882	Eureka CU Dist 140	Eureka
240	5,865	Herrin CUSD 4	Herrin
241	5,823	Kewanee Community Unit SD 229	Kewanee
242	5,819	Effingham Community Unit SD 40	Effingham
243	5,817	Lake Villa CCSD 41	Lake Villa
244	5,807	Carlinville CUSD 1	Carlinville
245	5,800	Crystal Lake CCSD 47	Crystal Lake
246	5,798	Monticello CUSD 25	Monticello
247	5,788	O'Fallon CCSD 90	Ofallon
248	5,780	Lemont-Bromberek CSD 113a	Lemont
249	5,763	Waterloo Community Unit SD 5	Waterloo
250	5,725	Cary CCSD 26	Cary
251	5,699	Bellwood SD 88	Bellwood
252	5,697	Massac Unit District #1	Metropolis
253	5,681	Indian Springs SD 109	Justice
254	5,662	Troy Community CSD 30C	Plainfield
255	5,652	Antioch CCSD 34	Antioch
256	5,650	Litchfield CUSD 12	Litchfield
257	5,644	Bond County CUSD 2	Greenville
258	5,641	Wilmington CUSD 209U	Wilmington
259	5,636	Bourbonnais SD 53	Bourbonnais
260	5,594	Illinois Valley Central UD 321	Chillicothe
261	5,585	Oswego Community Unit SD 308	Oswego
262	5,581	Frankfort CCSD 157c	Frankfort
263	5,552	Plainfield SD 202	Plainfield
264	5,533	Vandalia CUSD 203	Vandalia
265	5,499	Monmouth Unit SD 38	Monmouth
266	5,479	Mchenry CCSD 15	Mc Henry
267	5,341	Rochelle Community CD 231	Rochelle
268	5,339	Channahon SD 17	Channahon
269	5,306	Mundelein Elem SD 75	Mundelein
270	5,290	Meridian CUSD 223	Stillman Valley
271	5,286	Mount Zion Community Unit SD 3	Mount Zion
272	5,281	Steger SD 194	Steger
273	5,250	Taylorville CUSD 3	Taylorville
274	5,200	Cicero SD 99	Cicero
275	5,186	Peotone CUSD 207U	Peotone
276	5,177	Rochester Community Unit SD 3A	Rochester
277	5,135	Sandwich CUSD 430	Sandwich
278	5,124	Berwyn North SD 98	Berwyn
279	5,098	Ball Chatham CUSD 5	Chatham
280	5,081	Dunlap CUSD 323	Dunlap
281	4,982	Homer Community CSD 33C	Lockport
282	4,971	Genoa Kingston CUSD 424	Genoa
283	4,955	Marion Community Unit SD 2	Marion
284	4,942	Belvidere CUSD 100	Belvidere
285	4,919	Maywood-Melrose Park-Broadview-89	Melrose Park
286	4,881	Carterville CUSD 5	Carterville
287	4,853	Community CSD 168	Sauk Village
288	4,820	Kinnikinnick CCSD 131	Roscoe
289	4,551	Summit Hill SD 161	Frankfort
290	4,420	Mokena SD 159	Mokena
291	4,313	New Lenox SD 122	New Lenox
292	4,198	Will County SD 92	Lockport
293	n/a	Department of Corrections SD 428	Springfield

Number of Diploma Recipients

Rank	Number	District Name	City
1	15,653	City of Chicago SD 299	Chicago
2	2,815	Township High SD 214	Arlington Hgts
3	2,725	Township HSD 211	Palatine
4	1,946	Glenbard Twp HSD 87	Glen Ellyn
5	1,914	SD 46	Elgin

6	1,796	Consolidated High SD 230	Orland Park
7	1,523	Maine Township HSD 207	Park Ridge
8	1,348	Naperville C U Dist 203	Naperville
9	1,282	Indian Prairie CUSD 204	Aurora
10	1,226	Community High SD 155	Crystal Lake
11	1,222	J S Morton HS District 201	Cicero
12	1,207	Community High SD 99	Downers Grove
13	1,187	Rockford SD 205	Rockford
14	1,136	Thornton Twp HSD 205	South Holland
15	1,127	Northfield Twp High SD 225	Glenview
16	1,070	Lincoln Way Community HSD 210	New Lenox
17	1,051	Niles Twp Community High SD 219	Skokie
18	1,037	Community Unit SD 300	Carpentersville
19	1,018	Community Unit SD 200	Wheaton
20	1,009	Belleville Twp HSD 201	Belleville
21	993	Hinsdale Twp HSD 86	Hinsdale
22	953	Bremen Community HS District 228	Midlothian
23	948	New Trier Twp HSD 203	Winnetka
24	931	Adlai E Stevenson Dist 125	Lincolnshire
25	894	Community High SD 218	Oak Lawn
26	811	Joliet Twp HSD 204	Joliet
27	803	Springfield SD 186	Springfield
28	780	Du Page High SD 88	Villa Park
29	775	Peoria SD 150	Peoria
30	772	Proviso Twp HSD 209	Maywood
31	763	Saint Charles CUSD 303	Saint Charles
32	753	Valley View CUSD 365U	Romeoville
33	750	Township High SD 113	Highland Park
34	748	Plainfield SD 202	Plainfield
35	734	Lyons Twp HSD 204	La Grange
35	734	Rich Twp HS District 227	Olympia Fields
37	732	Leyden Community HSD 212	Franklin Park
38	674	Warren Twp High SD 121	Gurnee
39	667	Evanston Twp HSD 202	Evanston
40	648	Waukegan CUSD 60	Waukegan
41	643	Lockport Twp HSD 205	Lockport
42	640	Champaign Community Unit SD 4	Champaign
43	636	Lake Park Community HSD 108	Roselle
44	631	Community High SD 128	Libertyville
45	615	Mclean County Unit Dist 5	Normal
46	577	Barrington CUSD 220	Barrington
47	576	Thornton Fractional T H S D 215	Calumet City
48	573	Aurora West Unit SD 129	Aurora
49	563	Homewood Flossmoor CHSD 233	Flossmoor
50	541	Moline Unit SD 40	Moline
51	521	Decatur SD 61	Decatur
52	504	Elmhurst SD 205	Elmhurst
53	491	Bloom Twp High SD 206	Chicago Heights
53	491	Edwardsville CUSD 7	Edwardsville
55	490	Quincy SD 172	Quincy
56	471	O'Fallon Twp High SD 203	Ofallon
57	468	Mundelein Cons High SD 120	Mundelein
58	466	Antioch Community High SD 117	Lake Villa
59	462	Granite City CUSD 9	Granite City
60	453	Mchenry Community HSD 156	Mc Henry
61	438	Community High SD 94	West Chicago
62	432	Alton Community Unit SD 11	Alton
63	427	Lake Zurich CUSD 95	Lake Zurich
64	424	Aurora East Unit SD 131	Aurora
65	421	Oswego Community Unit SD 308	Oswego
66	413	Pekin Community HSD 303	Pekin
67	397	Lake Forest Community HSD 115	Lake Forest
68	378	Hononegah Community HSD 207	Rockton
68	378	Zion-Benton Twp HSD 126	Zion
70	376	Bradley Bourbonnais CHSD 307	Bradley
71	372	Harlem Unit Dist 122	Loves Park
72	370	Batavia Unit SD 101	Batavia
73	360	Collinsville CUSD 10	Collinsville
74	359	Argo Community HSD 217	Summit
75	354	Urbana SD 116	Urbana
76	353	Belvidere CUSD 100	Belvidere
77	352	Oak Lawn Community HSD 229	Oak Lawn
78	347	United Twp HS District 30	East Moline
79	342	Grayslake Community High SD 127	Grayslake
80	330	Ottawa Twp HSD 140	Ottawa
81	329	Fenton Community HSD 100	Bensenville
82	328	East Saint Louis SD 189	E Saint Louis
83	321	Geneva Community Unit SD 304	Geneva
84	310	Reavis Twp HSD 220	Burbank
85	308	Dekalb Community Unit SD 428	De Kalb
86	307	Freeport SD 145	Freeport
87	305	Ball Chatham CUSD 5	Chatham
88	303	Woodstock CUSD 200	Woodstock
89	300	Rock Island SD 41	Rock Island
90	275	Galesburg CUSD 205	Galesburg
91	273	Triad Community Unit SD 2	Troy
92	272	Danville CCSD 118	Danville
93	266	Crete Monee CUSD 201U	Crete
94	264	Bloomington SD 87	Bloomington
95	254	Round Lake Area Schs - Dist 116	Round Lake
96	249	Jacksonville SD 117	Jacksonville
97	246	Kankakee SD 111	Kankakee
98	238	Jersey CUSD 100	Jerseyville
99	234	Highland Community Unit SD 5	Highland
100	232	Marion Community Unit SD 2	Marion
101	231	Sterling C U Dist 5	Sterling
102	230	Morton CUSD 709	Morton
103	224	Charleston CUSD 1	Charleston
104	221	Dixon Unit SD 170	Dixon
105	218	Wauconda Community Unit SD 118	Wauconda
106	217	Bethalto CUSD 8	Bethalto
107	216	Sycamore CUSD 427	Sycamore
108	213	Geneseo Community Unit SD 228	Geneseo
109	212	Taylorville CUSD 3	Taylorville
110	204	Mattoon CUSD 2	Mattoon
111	195	Mount Zion Community Unit SD 3	Mount Zion
112	190	Kaneland CUSD 302	Maple Park
113	189	Cahokia Community Unit SD 187	Cahokia
113	189	Effingham Community Unit SD 40	Effingham
115	188	Mahomet-Seymour CUSD 3	Mahomet
116	187	Elmwood Park CUSD 401	Elmwood Park
117	181	Johnsburg CUSD 12	Johnsburg
118	180	Dunlap CUSD 323	Dunlap
119	179	Canton Union SD 66	Canton
119	179	Waterloo Community Unit SD 5	Waterloo
121	175	Yorkville Community Unit SD 115	Yorkville
122	172	Mascoutah C U District 19	Mascoutah
122	172	Murphysboro CUSD 186	Murphysboro
124	158	Wabash CUSD 348	Mount Carmel
125	154	Prairie Central CUSD 8	Forrest
125	154	Rochester Community Unit SD 3A	Rochester
127	153	Central Community Unit SD 301	Burlington
127	153	Lisle CUSD 202	Lisle
129	151	Sandwich CUSD 430	Sandwich
130	150	Herscher Community Unit SD 2	Herscher
130	150	Southwestern CUSD 9	Piasa
132	146	Byron Community Unit SD 226	Byron
132	146	East Richland CUSD 1	Olney
132	146	Illinois Valley Central UD 321	Chillicothe
132	146	Oregon C U School Dist-220	Oregon
136	144	Clinton CUSD 15	Clinton
137	143	Olympia CUSD 16	Stanford
138	139	Massac Unit District #1	Metropolis
139	138	North Chicago SD 187	North Chicago
140	134	Carlinville CUSD 1	Carlinville
141	132	Bond County CUSD 2	Greenville
142	130	Consolidated SD 158	Huntley
143	129	Herrin CUSD 4	Herrin
143	129	Hillsboro Community Unit SD 3	Hillsboro
143	129	Roxana Community Unit SD 1	Roxana
146	128	Macomb Community Unit SD 185	Macomb
147	124	Jasper County Comm Unit Dist 1	Newton
148	123	Robinson CUSD 2	Robinson
149	122	Peotone CUSD 207U	Peotone
149	122	Wilmington CUSD 209U	Wilmington
151	121	Columbia Community Unit SD 4	Columbia
151	121	Harvard CUSD 50	Harvard
153	120	Coal City CUSD 1	Coal City
153	120	Frankfort Community Unit SD 168	West Frankfort
155	119	Harrisburg CUSD 3	Harrisburg
156	117	Manteno Community Unit SD 5	Manteno
157	115	Sparta CUSD 140	Sparta
158	114	Monticello CUSD 25	Monticello
159	113	Litchfield CUSD 12	Litchfield
159	113	Reed Custer CUSD 255U	Braidwood
161	108	Vandalia CUSD 203	Vandalia
162	107	Carmi-White County CUSD 5	Carmi
162	107	Eureka CU Dist 140	Eureka
162	107	Winnebago CUSD 323	Winnebago
165	106	Sherrard Community Unit SD 200	Sherrard
166	104	Carterville CUSD 5	Carterville
167	100	Kewanee Community Unit SD 229	Kewanee
168	99	Paris-Union SD 95	Paris
169	94	Du Quoin CUSD 300	Du Quoin
169	94	Meridian CUSD 223	Stillman Valley
171	93	Monmouth Unit SD 38	Monmouth
172	91	Genoa Kingston CUSD 424	Genoa
172	91	Westmont CUSD 201	Westmont
174	53	Maywood-Melrose Park-Broadview-89	Melrose Park
175	1	Mannheim SD 83	Franklin Park
176	0	Department of Corrections SD 428	Springfield
176	0	Oak Park & River Forest Dist 200	Oak Park
176	0	Pekin Public SD 108	Pekin
179	n/a	Addison SD 4	Addison
179	n/a	Alsip-Hazlgrn-Oaklawn SD 126	Alsip
179	n/a	Antioch CCSD 34	Antioch
179	n/a	Aptakisic-Tripp CCSD 102	Buffalo Grove
179	n/a	Arlington Heights SD 25	Arlington Hgts
179	n/a	Beach Park CCSD 3	Beach Park
179	n/a	Belleville SD 118	Belleville
179	n/a	Bellwood SD 88	Bellwood
179	n/a	Bensenville SD 2	Bensenville
179	n/a	Berkeley SD 87	Berkeley
179	n/a	Berwyn North SD 98	Berwyn
179	n/a	Berwyn South SD 100	Berwyn
179	n/a	Bourbonnais SD 53	Bourbonnais
179	n/a	Bradley SD 61	Bradley
179	n/a	Burbank SD 111	Burbank
179	n/a	CCSD 181	Hinsdale
179	n/a	Cary CCSD 26	Cary
179	n/a	Channahon SD 17	Channahon
179	n/a	Chicago Heights SD 170	Chicago Heights
179	n/a	Cicero SD 99	Cicero
179	n/a	Community CSD 168	Sauk Village
179	n/a	Community CSD 46	Grayslake
179	n/a	Community CSD 59	Arlington Hgts
179	n/a	Community CSD 62	Des Plaines
179	n/a	Community CSD 93	Carol Stream
179	n/a	Cook County SD 130	Blue Island
179	n/a	Country Club Hills SD 160	Ctry Club Hill
179	n/a	Crystal Lake CCSD 47	Crystal Lake
179	n/a	Darien SD 61	Darien
179	n/a	Deerfield SD 109	Deerfield
179	n/a	Dolton SD 148	Riverdale
179	n/a	Dolton SD 149	Calumet City
179	n/a	Downers Grove Grade SD 58	Downers Grove
179	n/a	East Maine SD 63	Des Plaines
179	n/a	East Moline SD 37	East Moline
179	n/a	East Peoria SD 86	East Peoria
179	n/a	Elem SD 159	Matteson
179	n/a	Evanston CCSD 65	Evanston
179	n/a	Evergreen Park ESD 124	Evergreen Park
179	n/a	Flossmoor SD 161	Chicago Heights
179	n/a	Forest Ridge SD 142	Oak Forest
179	n/a	Frankfort CCSD 157c	Frankfort
179	n/a	Fremont SD 79	Mundelein
179	n/a	Glen Ellyn CCSD 89	Glen Ellyn
179	n/a	Glen Ellyn SD 41	Glen Ellyn
179	n/a	Glenview CCSD 34	Glenview
179	n/a	Gurnee SD 56	Gurnee
179	n/a	Harvey SD 152	Harvey
179	n/a	Hawthorn CCSD 73	Vernon Hills
179	n/a	Homer Community CSD 33C	Lockport
179	n/a	Homewood SD 153	Homewood
179	n/a	Indian Springs SD 109	Justice
179	n/a	Joliet Public SD 86	Joliet
179	n/a	Keeneyville SD 20	Hanover Park
179	n/a	Kildeer Countryside CCSD 96	Buffalo Grove
179	n/a	Kinnikinnick CCSD 131	Roscoe
179	n/a	Kirby SD 140	Tinley Park
179	n/a	La Grange SD 102	La Grange Park
179	n/a	Lake Forest SD 67	Lake Forest
179	n/a	Lake Villa CCSD 41	Lake Villa
179	n/a	Lansing SD 158	Lansing
179	n/a	Lemont-Bromberek CSD 113a	Lemont
179	n/a	Libertyville SD 70	Libertyville
179	n/a	Lincolnshire-Prairieview SD 103	Lincolnshire
179	n/a	Lombard SD 44	Lombard
179	n/a	Lyons SD 103	Lyons
179	n/a	Marquardt SD 15	Glendale Hgts
179	n/a	Matteson ESD 162	Matteson
179	n/a	Mchenry CCSD 15	Mc Henry
179	n/a	Midlothian SD 143	Midlothian
179	n/a	Minooka Community CSD 201	Minooka
179	n/a	Mokena SD 159	Mokena
179	n/a	Mount Prospect SD 57	Mount Prospect
179	n/a	Mount Vernon SD 80	Mount Vernon
179	n/a	Mundelein Elem SD 75	Mundelein
179	n/a	New Lenox SD 122	New Lenox
179	n/a	Nippersink SD 2	Richmond
179	n/a	North Palos SD 117	Palos Hills
179	n/a	North Shore SD 112	Highland Park
179	n/a	Northbrook SD 28	Northbrook
179	n/a	O'Fallon CCSD 90	Ofallon
179	n/a	Oak Lawn-Hometown SD 123	Oak Lawn
179	n/a	Oak Park Elem SD 97	Oak Park
179	n/a	Orland SD 135	Orland Park
179	n/a	Ottawa Elem SD 141	Ottawa
179	n/a	Palatine CCSD 15	Palatine
179	n/a	Palos Community CSD 118	Palos Park
179	n/a	Park Forest SD 163	Park Forest
179	n/a	Park Ridge CCSD 64	Park Ridge
179	n/a	Posen-Robbins El SD 143-5	Posen
179	n/a	Prairie-Hills Elem SD 144	Markham
179	n/a	Prospect Heights SD 23	Prospect Hgts
179	n/a	Queen Bee SD 16	Glendale Hgts
179	n/a	Rantoul City SD 137	Rantoul
179	n/a	Ridgeland SD 122	Oak Lawn
179	n/a	River Trails SD 26	Mount Prospect
179	n/a	Rochelle Community CD 231	Rochelle
179	n/a	SD 45 Dupage County	Villa Park
179	n/a	Schaumburg CCSD 54	Schaumburg
179	n/a	Skokie SD 68	Skokie
179	n/a	Steger SD 194	Steger
179	n/a	Streator Elem SD 44	Streator
179	n/a	Summit Hill SD 161	Frankfort
179	n/a	Summit SD 104	Summit

Rank	Percent	District Name	City
179	n/a	Tinley Park Community Cons SD 146	Tinley Park
179	n/a	Troy Community CSD 30C	Plainfield
179	n/a	West Chicago ESD 33	West Chicago
179	n/a	West Harvey-Dixmoor PSD 147	Harvey
179	n/a	Wheeling CCSD 21	Wheeling
179	n/a	Will County SD 92	Lockport
179	n/a	Wilmette SD 39	Wilmette
179	n/a	Winnetka SD 36	Winnetka
179	n/a	Woodland CCSD 50	Gurnee
179	n/a	Woodridge SD 68	Woodridge
179	n/a	Zion Elementary SD 6	Zion

High School Drop-out Rate

Rank	Percent	District Name	City
1	16.8	City of Chicago SD 299	Chicago
2	11.9	Peoria SD 150	Peoria
3	11.3	Decatur SD 61	Decatur
4	10.4	Roxana Community Unit SD 1	Roxana
5	10.2	East Saint Louis SD 189	E Saint Louis
6	9.9	Mattoon CUSD 2	Mattoon
7	9.8	Round Lake Area Schs - Dist 116	Round Lake
8	9.7	Danville CCSD 118	Danville
9	9.5	Proviso Twp HSD 209	Maywood
10	9.4	Bloom Twp High SD 206	Chicago Heights
11	8.6	Zion-Benton Twp HSD 126	Zion
12	8.3	Galesburg CUSD 205	Galesburg
13	8.0	Sterling C U Dist 5	Sterling
14	7.6	Carmi-White County CUSD 5	Carmi
14	7.6	Harvard CUSD 50	Harvard
14	7.6	Rockford SD 205	Rockford
17	7.4	Aurora East Unit SD 131	Aurora
18	7.3	Canton Union SD 66	Canton
19	7.2	United Twp HS District 30	East Moline
20	7.0	Community High SD 218	Oak Lawn
21	6.8	Kewanee Community Unit SD 229	Kewanee
22	6.7	Alton Community Unit SD 11	Alton
23	6.5	Collinsville CUSD 10	Collinsville
24	6.3	Aurora West Unit SD 129	Aurora
24	6.3	Cahokia Community Unit SD 187	Cahokia
24	6.3	Dixon Unit SD 170	Dixon
27	6.0	Freeport SD 145	Freeport
28	5.9	Woodstock CUSD 200	Woodstock
29	5.7	Granite City CUSD 9	Granite City
29	5.7	J S Morton HS District 201	Cicero
29	5.7	Taylorville CUSD 3	Taylorville
32	5.6	Du Page High SD 88	Villa Park
32	5.6	Valley View CUSD 365U	Romeoville
34	5.5	Leyden Community HSD 212	Franklin Park
34	5.5	Massac Unit District #1	Metropolis
34	5.5	Ottawa Twp HSD 140	Ottawa
34	5.5	Reavis Twp HSD 220	Burbank
38	5.4	Fenton Community HSD 100	Bensenville
39	5.3	Quincy SD 172	Quincy
39	5.3	Thornton Twp HSD 205	South Holland
41	5.2	Sherrard Community Unit SD 200	Sherrard
41	5.2	Wabash CUSD 348	Mount Carmel
43	5.1	Rock Island SD 41	Rock Island
44	5.0	Du Quoin CUSD 300	Du Quoin
45	4.9	Oak Lawn Community HSD 229	Oak Lawn
45	4.9	Olympia CUSD 16	Stanford
47	4.8	Community High SD 94	West Chicago
47	4.8	Kankakee SD 111	Kankakee
47	4.8	Mclean County Unit Dist 5	Normal
47	4.8	Paris-Union SD 95	Paris
51	4.7	Bethalto CUSD 8	Bethalto
51	4.7	Champaign Community Unit SD 4	Champaign
51	4.7	Wilmington CUSD 209U	Wilmington
54	4.6	Urbana SD 116	Urbana
55	4.5	Elmwood Park CUSD 401	Elmwood Park
55	4.5	Moline Unit SD 40	Moline
57	4.3	Argo Community HSD 217	Summit
57	4.3	Clinton CUSD 15	Clinton
57	4.3	Lockport Twp HSD 205	Lockport
60	4.2	Antioch Community High SD 117	Lake Villa
60	4.2	Southwestern CUSD 9	Piasa
60	4.2	Township High SD 214	Arlington Hgts
63	4.1	Monmouth Unit SD 38	Monmouth
64	4.0	Mchenry Community HSD 156	Mc Henry
64	4.0	Sparta CUSD 140	Sparta
64	4.0	Thornton Fractional T HS D 215	Calumet City
67	3.9	Bloomington SD 87	Bloomington
67	3.9	Harrisburg CUSD 3	Harrisburg
69	3.8	Belleville Twp HSD 201	Belleville
69	3.8	Carlinville CUSD 1	Carlinville
69	3.8	East Richland CUSD 1	Olney
69	3.8	Hillsboro Community Unit SD 3	Hillsboro
69	3.8	Vandalia CUSD 203	Vandalia
74	3.7	Bond County CUSD 2	Greenville
74	3.7	Grayslake Community High SD 127	Grayslake
74	3.7	Joliet Twp HSD 204	Joliet
74	3.7	SD 46	Elgin
74	3.7	Sandwich CUSD 430	Sandwich
79	3.6	Marion Community Unit SD 2	Marion
79	3.6	Mundelein Cons High SD 120	Mundelein
79	3.6	Prairie Central CUSD 8	Forrest
82	3.5	Bremen Community HS District 228	Midlothian
82	3.5	Charleston CUSD 1	Charleston
82	3.5	Community Unit SD 300	Carpentersville
82	3.5	Frankfort Community Unit SD 168	West Frankfort
86	3.3	Edwardsville CUSD 7	Edwardsville
86	3.3	Jersey CUSD 100	Jerseyville
88	3.2	Community Unit SD 200	Wheaton
88	3.2	Herscher Community Unit SD 2	Herscher
88	3.2	Macomb Community Unit SD 185	Macomb
88	3.2	Murphysboro CUSD 186	Murphysboro
88	3.2	Plainfield SD 202	Plainfield
88	3.2	Warren Twp High SD 121	Gurnee
94	3.1	Herrin CUSD 4	Herrin
94	3.1	Jacksonville SD 117	Jacksonville
94	3.1	Jasper County Comm Unit Dist 1	Newton
94	3.1	Robinson CUSD 2	Robinson
98	3.0	Oswego Community Unit SD 308	Oswego
99	2.8	Geneseo Community Unit SD 228	Geneseo
100	2.6	Homewood Flossmoor CHSD 233	Flossmoor
101	2.5	Evanston Twp HSD 202	Evanston
101	2.5	Illinois Valley Central UD 321	Chillicothe
101	2.5	Pekin Community HSD 303	Pekin
101	2.5	Waukegan CUSD 60	Waukegan
105	2.4	Bradley Bourbonnais CHSD 307	Bradley
105	2.4	Highland Community Unit SD 5	Highland
107	2.3	Community High SD 99	Downers Grove
107	2.3	Winnebago CUSD 323	Winnebago
109	2.2	Harlem Unit Dist 122	Loves Park
110	2.1	Dekalb Community Unit SD 428	De Kalb
110	2.1	Eureka CU Dist 140	Eureka
110	2.1	Glenbard Twp HSD 87	Glen Ellyn
110	2.1	Lincoln Way Community HSD 210	New Lenox
110	2.1	Reed Custer CUSD 255U	Braidwood
110	2.1	Sycamore CUSD 427	Sycamore
116	2.0	Community High SD 155	Crystal Lake
116	2.0	Oak Park & River Forest Dist 200	Oak Park
118	1.9	Consolidated High SD 230	Orland Park
118	1.9	Consolidated SD 158	Huntley
118	1.9	Morton CUSD 709	Morton
121	1.8	Mount Zion Community Unit SD 3	Mount Zion
121	1.8	O'Fallon Twp High SD 203	Ofallon
121	1.8	Triad Community Unit SD 2	Troy
124	1.7	Coal City CUSD 1	Coal City
124	1.7	Lake Park Community HSD 108	Roselle
124	1.7	Oregon C U School Dist-220	Oregon
127	1.6	Geneva Community Unit SD 304	Geneva
127	1.6	Wauconda Community Unit SD 118	Wauconda
129	1.5	Batavia Unit SD 101	Batavia
129	1.5	Carterville CUSD 5	Carterville
129	1.5	Community High SD 128	Libertyville
129	1.5	Effingham Community Unit SD 40	Effingham
129	1.5	Mahomet-Seymour CUSD 3	Mahomet
129	1.5	Springfield SD 186	Springfield
129	1.5	Township HSD 211	Palatine
129	1.5	Yorkville Community Unit SD 115	Yorkville
137	1.4	Crete Monee CUSD 201U	Crete
137	1.4	Maine Township HSD 207	Park Ridge
137	1.4	Monticello CUSD 25	Monticello
137	1.4	Peotone CUSD 207U	Peotone
137	1.4	Saint Charles CUSD 303	Saint Charles
142	1.3	Hinsdale Twp HSD 86	Hinsdale
142	1.3	Lyons Twp HSD 204	La Grange
142	1.3	Rich Twp HS District 227	Olympia Fields
145	1.2	Ball Chatham CUSD 5	Chatham
145	1.2	Central Community Unit SD 301	Burlington
145	1.2	Dunlap CUSD 323	Dunlap
145	1.2	Genoa Kingston CUSD 424	Genoa
145	1.2	Meridian CUSD 223	Stillman Valley
150	1.1	Elmhurst SD 205	Elmhurst
150	1.1	Johnsburg CUSD 12	Johnsburg
150	1.1	Manteno Community Unit SD 5	Manteno
150	1.1	Township High SD 113	Highland Park
150	1.1	Waterloo Community Unit SD 5	Waterloo
155	1.0	Kaneland CUSD 302	Maple Park
155	1.0	Litchfield CUSD 12	Litchfield
155	1.0	Naperville C U Dist 203	Naperville
158	0.9	Barrington CUSD 220	Barrington
158	0.9	Belvidere CUSD 100	Belvidere
158	0.9	Indian Prairie CUSD 204	Aurora
161	0.8	Lake Zurich CUSD 95	Lake Zurich
161	0.8	Niles Twp Community High SD 219	Skokie
161	0.8	Northfield Twp High SD 225	Glenview
164	0.7	Hononegah Community HSD 207	Rockton
164	0.7	Mascoutah C U District 19	Mascoutah
164	0.7	Westmont CUSD 201	Westmont
167	0.6	Columbia Community Unit SD 4	Columbia
168	0.5	Byron Community Unit SD 226	Byron
168	0.5	Lake Forest Community HSD 115	Lake Forest
170	0.4	Adlai E Stevenson Dist 125	Lincolnshire
170	0.4	New Trier Twp HSD 203	Winnetka
172	0.3	Lisle CUSD 202	Lisle
172	0.3	Rochester Community Unit SD 3A	Rochester
174	0.0	Evanston CCSD 65	Evanston
174	0.0	Mannheim SD 83	Franklin Park
174	0.0	North Chicago SD 187	North Chicago
174	0.0	Pekin Public SD 108	Pekin
178	n/a	Addison SD 4	Addison
178	n/a	Alsip-Hazlgrn-Oaklawn SD 126	Alsip
178	n/a	Antioch CCSD 34	Antioch
178	n/a	Aptakisic-Tripp CCSD 102	Buffalo Grove
178	n/a	Arlington Heights SD 25	Arlington Hgts
178	n/a	Beach Park CCSD 3	Beach Park
178	n/a	Belleville SD 118	Belleville
178	n/a	Bellwood SD 88	Bellwood
178	n/a	Bensenville SD 2	Bensenville
178	n/a	Berkeley SD 87	Berkeley
178	n/a	Berwyn North SD 98	Berwyn
178	n/a	Berwyn South SD 100	Berwyn
178	n/a	Bourbonnais SD 53	Bourbonnais
178	n/a	Bradley SD 61	Bradley
178	n/a	Burbank SD 111	Burbank
178	n/a	CCSD 181	Hinsdale
178	n/a	Cary CCSD 26	Cary
178	n/a	Channahon SD 17	Channahon
178	n/a	Chicago Heights SD 170	Chicago Heights
178	n/a	Cicero SD 99	Cicero
178	n/a	Community CSD 168	Sauk Village
178	n/a	Community CSD 46	Grayslake
178	n/a	Community CSD 59	Arlington Hgts
178	n/a	Community CSD 62	Des Plaines
178	n/a	Community CSD 93	Carol Stream
178	n/a	Cook County SD 130	Blue Island
178	n/a	Country Club Hills SD 160	Ctry Club Hill
178	n/a	Crystal Lake CCSD 47	Crystal Lake
178	n/a	Darien SD 61	Darien
178	n/a	Deerfield SD 109	Deerfield
178	n/a	Department of Corrections SD 428	Springfield
178	n/a	Dolton SD 148	Riverdale
178	n/a	Dolton SD 149	Calumet City
178	n/a	Downers Grove Grade SD 58	Downers Grove
178	n/a	East Maine SD 63	Des Plaines
178	n/a	East Moline SD 37	East Moline
178	n/a	East Peoria SD 86	East Peoria
178	n/a	Elem SD 159	Matteson
178	n/a	Evergreen Park ESD 124	Evergreen Park
178	n/a	Flossmoor SD 161	Chicago Heights
178	n/a	Forest Ridge SD 142	Oak Forest
178	n/a	Frankfort CCSD 157c	Frankfort
178	n/a	Fremont SD 79	Mundelein
178	n/a	Glen Ellyn CCSD 89	Glen Ellyn
178	n/a	Glen Ellyn SD 41	Glen Ellyn
178	n/a	Glenview CCSD 34	Glenview
178	n/a	Gurnee SD 56	Gurnee
178	n/a	Harvey SD 152	Harvey
178	n/a	Hawthorn CCSD 73	Vernon Hills
178	n/a	Homer Community CSD 33C	Lockport
178	n/a	Homewood SD 153	Homewood
178	n/a	Indian Springs SD 109	Justice
178	n/a	Joliet Public SD 86	Joliet
178	n/a	Keeneyville SD 20	Hanover Park
178	n/a	Kildeer Countryside CCSD 96	Buffalo Grove
178	n/a	Kinnikinnick CCSD 131	Roscoe
178	n/a	Kirby SD 140	Tinley Park
178	n/a	La Grange SD 102	La Grange Park
178	n/a	Lake Forest SD 67	Lake Forest
178	n/a	Lake Villa CCSD 41	Lake Villa
178	n/a	Lansing SD 158	Lansing
178	n/a	Lemont-Bromberek CSD 113a	Lemont
178	n/a	Libertyville SD 70	Libertyville
178	n/a	Lincolnshire-Prairieview SD 103	Lincolnshire
178	n/a	Lombard SD 44	Lombard
178	n/a	Lyons SD 103	Lyons
178	n/a	Marquardt SD 15	Glendale Hgts
178	n/a	Matteson ESD 162	Matteson
178	n/a	Maywood-Melrose Park-Broadview-89	Melrose Park
178	n/a	Mchenry CCSD 15	Mc Henry
178	n/a	Midlothian SD 143	Midlothian
178	n/a	Minooka Community CSD 201	Minooka
178	n/a	Mokena SD 159	Mokena
178	n/a	Mount Prospect SD 57	Mount Prospect
178	n/a	Mount Vernon SD 80	Mount Vernon
178	n/a	Mundelein Elem SD 75	Mundelein
178	n/a	New Lenox SD 122	New Lenox
178	n/a	Nippersink SD 2	Richmond
178	n/a	North Palos SD 117	Palos Hills
178	n/a	North Shore SD 112	Highland Park
178	n/a	Northbrook SD 28	Northbrook
178	n/a	O'Fallon CCSD 90	Ofallon
178	n/a	Oak Lawn-Hometown SD 123	Oak Lawn
178	n/a	Oak Park Elem SD 97	Oak Park
178	n/a	Orland SD 135	Orland Park
178	n/a	Ottawa Elem SD 141	Ottawa

178	n/a	Palatine CCSD 15	Palatine
178	n/a	Palos Community CSD 118	Palos Park
178	n/a	Park Forest SD 163	Park Forest
178	n/a	Park Ridge CCSD 64	Park Ridge
178	n/a	Posen-Robbins El SD 143-5	Posen
178	n/a	Prairie-Hills Elem SD 144	Markham
178	n/a	Prospect Heights SD 23	Prospect Hgts
178	n/a	Queen Bee SD 16	Glendale Hgts
178	n/a	Rantoul City SD 137	Rantoul
178	n/a	Ridgeland SD 122	Oak Lawn
178	n/a	River Trails SD 26	Mount Prospect
178	n/a	Rochelle Community CD 231	Rochelle
178	n/a	SD 45 Dupage County	Villa Park
178	n/a	Schaumburg CCSD 54	Schaumburg
178	n/a	Skokie SD 68	Skokie
178	n/a	Steger SD 194	Steger
178	n/a	Streator Elem SD 44	Streator
178	n/a	Summit Hill SD 161	Frankfort
178	n/a	Summit SD 104	Summit
178	n/a	Tinley Park Community Cons SD 146	Tinley Park
178	n/a	Troy Community CSD 30C	Plainfield
178	n/a	West Chicago ESD 33	West Chicago
178	n/a	West Harvey-Dixmoor PSD 147	Harvey
178	n/a	Wheeling CCSD 21	Wheeling
178	n/a	Will County SD 92	Lockport
178	n/a	Wilmette SD 39	Wilmette
178	n/a	Winnetka SD 36	Winnetka
178	n/a	Woodland CCSD 50	Gurnee
178	n/a	Woodridge SD 68	Woodridge
178	n/a	Zion Elementary SD 6	Zion

Indiana

Indiana Public School Educational Profile

Category	Value	Category	Value
Schools *(2002-2003)*	1,987	**Diploma Recipients** *(2002-2003)*	56,722
Instructional Level		White, Non-Hispanic	49,846
Primary	1,169	Black, Non-Hispanic	4,650
Middle	321	Asian/Pacific Islander	657
High	351	American Indian/Alaskan Native	141
Other Level	146	Hispanic	1,428
Curriculum		**High School Drop-out Rate** (%) *(2000-2001)*	n/a
Regular	1,850	White, Non-Hispanic	n/a
Special Education	49	Black, Non-Hispanic	n/a
Vocational	29	Asian/Pacific Islander	n/a
Alternative	59	American Indian/Alaskan Native	n/a
Type		Hispanic	n/a
Magnet	26	**Staff** *(2002-2003)*	126,995.0
Charter	11	Teachers	59,967.6
Title I Eligible	1,044	Average Salary ($)	44,966
School-wide Title I	181	Librarians/Media Specialists	1,028.9
Students *(2002-2003)*	1,003,874	Guidance Counselors	1,812.7
Gender (%)		**Ratios** *(2002-2003)*	
Male	51.4	Student/Teacher Ratio	16.7 to 1
Female	48.6	Student/Librarian Ratio	975.7 to 1
Race/Ethnicity (%)		Student/Counselor Ratio	553.8 to 1
White, Non-Hispanic	82.1	**Current Spending** *($ per student in FY 2001)*	7,734
Black, Non-Hispanic	12.2	Instruction	4,707
Asian/Pacific Islander	1.0	Support Services	2,710
American Indian/Alaskan Native	0.3	**College Entrance Exam Scores** *(2003)*	
Hispanic	4.3	Scholastic Aptitude Test (SAT)	
Classification (%)		Participation Rate (%)	63
Individual Education Program (IEP)	16.6	Mean SAT I Verbal Score	500
Migrant	0.0	Mean SAT I Math Score	504
English Language Learner (ELL)	4.2	American College Testing Program (ACT)	
Eligible for Free Lunch Program	25.0	Participation Rate (%)	21
Eligible for Reduced-Price Lunch Program	7.5	Average Composite Score	21.6

Note: *For an explanation of data, please refer to the User's Guide in the front of the book; n/a indicates data not available*

Indiana NAEP 2003 Test Scores

Reading			Mathematics		
Grade/Category	Value	Rank	Grade/Category	Value	Rank
4th Grade			**4th Grade**		
Average Proficiency	220.4 (1.0)	23/51	Average Proficiency	238.0 (0.9)	13/51
Proficiency by Gender/Race/Ethnicity			Proficiency by Gender/Race/Ethnicity		
Male	216.2 (1.2)	22/51	Male	238.8 (1.0)	16/51
Female	224.5 (1.1)	22/51	Female	237.1 (1.0)	11/51
White, Non-Hispanic	224.3 (1.0)	32/51	White, Non-Hispanic	242.1 (0.9)	25/51
Black, Non-Hispanic	196.6 (3.9)	26/42	Black, Non-Hispanic	215.3 (1.7)	23/42
Asian, Non-Hispanic	*212.5 (3.1)*	3/41	Asian, Non-Hispanic	*226.0 (3.1)*	11/43
American Indian, Non-Hispanic	n/a	n/a	American Indian, Non-Hispanic	n/a	n/a
Hispanic	n/a	n/a	Hispanic	n/a	n/a
Proficiency by Class Size			Proficiency by Class Size		
Less than 16 Students	n/a	n/a	Less than 16 Students	n/a	n/a
16 to 18 Students	*214.8 (5.8)*	24/48	16 to 18 Students	*247.4 (3.8)*	1/48
19 to 20 Students	*214.8 (7.2)*	33/50	19 to 20 Students	*232.3 (4.9)*	34/50
21 to 25 Students	221.8 (1.5)	23/51	21 to 25 Students	238.0 (1.2)	24/51
Greater than 25 Students	221.5 (2.5)	19/49	Greater than 25 Students	240.3 (2.0)	10/49
Percent Attaining Achievement Levels			Percent Attaining Achievement Levels		
Below Basic	34.0 (1.2)	28/51	Below Basic	17.6 (1.0)	39/51
Basic or Above	66.0 (1.2)	23/51	Basic or Above	82.4 (1.0)	12/51
Proficient or Above	32.7 (1.2)	20/51	Proficient or Above	35.1 (1.4)	16/51
Advanced or Above	7.9 (0.6)	15/51	Advanced or Above	3.6 (0.5)	22/51
8th Grade			**8th Grade**		
Average Proficiency	264.8 (1.0)	23/51	Average Proficiency	281.2 (1.1)	19/51
Proficiency by Gender/Race/Ethnicity			Proficiency by Gender/Race/Ethnicity		
Male	259.2 (1.6)	23/51	Male	282.4 (1.4)	18/51
Female	270.2 (1.2)	23/51	Female	280.0 (1.2)	21/51
White, Non-Hispanic	268.6 (1.1)	28/50	White, Non-Hispanic	286.4 (0.9)	24/50
Black, Non-Hispanic	244.4 (3.3)	20/41	Black, Non-Hispanic	251.0 (3.1)	22/41
Asian, Non-Hispanic	246.6 (5.1)	17/37	Asian, Non-Hispanic	260.6 (4.1)	18/37
American Indian, Non-Hispanic	n/a	n/a	American Indian, Non-Hispanic	n/a	n/a
Hispanic	n/a	n/a	Hispanic	n/a	n/a
Proficiency by Parents Highest Level of Ed.			Proficiency by Parents Highest Level of Ed.		
Did Not Finish High School	252.0 (3.5)	4/50	Did Not Finish High School	264.6 (2.2)	5/50
Graduated High School	256.0 (1.6)	23/50	Graduated High School	274.4 (1.9)	11/50
Some Education After High School	267.7 (2.0)	26/50	Some Education After High School	284.0 (1.6)	11/50
Graduated College	274.3 (1.1)	18/50	Graduated College	290.1 (1.4)	24/50
Percent Attaining Achievement Levels			Percent Attaining Achievement Levels		
Below Basic	23.2 (1.2)	30/51	Below Basic	26.5 (1.4)	36/51
Basic or Above	76.8 (1.2)	20/51	Basic or Above	73.5 (1.4)	16/51
Proficient or Above	32.7 (1.4)	25/51	Proficient or Above	30.7 (1.2)	22/51
Advanced or Above	2.5 (0.5)	26/51	Advanced or Above	5.2 (0.4)	21/51

Note: *For an explanation of data, please refer to the User's Guide in the front of the book; values in italics indicate that the nature of the sample does not allow accurate determination of the variability of the statistic; n/a indicates data not available*

Adams County

North Adams Community Schools

625 Stadium Dr • Decatur, IN 46733-0670
Mailing Address: PO Box 670 • Decatur, IN 46733-0670
(260) 724-7146 • http://www.nadams.k12.in.us/
Grade Span: KG-12; **Agency Type:** 1
Schools: 5
3 Primary; 1 Middle; 1 High; 0 Other Level
5 Regular; 0 Special Education; 0 Vocational; 0 Alternative
0 Magnet; 0 Charter; 4 Title I Eligible; 0 School-wide Title I
Students: 2,339 (51.2% male; 48.8% female)
Individual Education Program: 346 (14.8%);
English Language Learner: 38 (1.6%); Migrant: n/a
Eligible for Free Lunch Program: 460 (19.7%)
Eligible for Reduced-Price Lunch Program: 133 (5.7%)
Teachers: 139.8 (16.7 to 1)
Librarians/Media Specialists: 2.8 (835.4 to 1)
Guidance Counselors: 10.0 (233.9 to 1)
Current Spending: ($ per student per year):
Total: $7,605; Instruction: $4,446; Support Services: $2,791
Enrollment, Drop-out Rates and Diploma Recipients by Race/Ethnicity

Category	Total	White	Black	Asian	AIAN	Hisp.
Enrollment (%)	100.0	92.8	0.3	0.4	0.2	6.4
Drop-out Rate (%)	n/a	n/a	n/a	n/a	n/a	n/a
H.S. Diplomas (#)	205	192	1	0	0	12

Allen County

East Allen County Schools

1240 Sr 930 E • New Haven, IN 46774-1732
(260) 446-0100 • http://www.eacs.k12.in.us/
Grade Span: PK-12; **Agency Type:** 1
Schools: 20
10 Primary; 4 Middle; 5 High; 1 Other Level
18 Regular; 1 Special Education; 0 Vocational; 1 Alternative
0 Magnet; 0 Charter; 7 Title I Eligible; 2 School-wide Title I
Students: 9,731 (51.7% male; 48.3% female)
Individual Education Program: 1,460 (15.0%);
English Language Learner: 328 (3.4%); Migrant: n/a
Eligible for Free Lunch Program: 2,061 (21.2%)
Eligible for Reduced-Price Lunch Program: 751 (7.7%)
Teachers: 573.7 (17.0 to 1)
Librarians/Media Specialists: 7.0 (1,390.1 to 1)
Guidance Counselors: 23.0 (423.1 to 1)
Current Spending: ($ per student per year):
Total: $7,583; Instruction: $4,725; Support Services: $2,538
Enrollment, Drop-out Rates and Diploma Recipients by Race/Ethnicity

Category	Total	White	Black	Asian	AIAN	Hisp.
Enrollment (%)	100.0	77.8	18.4	0.7	0.3	2.8
Drop-out Rate (%)	n/a	n/a	n/a	n/a	n/a	n/a
H.S. Diplomas (#)	609	529	70	3	2	5

Fort Wayne Community Schools

1200 S Clinton St • Fort Wayne, IN 46802-3594
(260) 425-7272 • http://www.fwcs.k12.in.us/
Grade Span: PK-12; **Agency Type:** 1
Schools: 55
34 Primary; 11 Middle; 7 High; 3 Other Level
51 Regular; 1 Special Education; 1 Vocational; 2 Alternative
6 Magnet; 0 Charter; 28 Title I Eligible; 10 School-wide Title I
Students: 32,114 (51.2% male; 48.8% female)
Individual Education Program: 5,606 (17.5%);
English Language Learner: 2,496 (7.8%); Migrant: n/a
Eligible for Free Lunch Program: 12,476 (38.8%)
Eligible for Reduced-Price Lunch Program: 2,868 (8.9%)
Teachers: 1,833.2 (17.5 to 1)
Librarians/Media Specialists: 16.3 (1,970.2 to 1)
Guidance Counselors: 31.6 (1,016.3 to 1)
Current Spending: ($ per student per year):
Total: $7,859; Instruction: $4,679; Support Services: $2,876
Enrollment, Drop-out Rates and Diploma Recipients by Race/Ethnicity

Category	Total	White	Black	Asian	AIAN	Hisp.
Enrollment (%)	100.0	62.9	26.4	2.2	0.6	7.9
Drop-out Rate (%)	n/a	n/a	n/a	n/a	n/a	n/a
H.S. Diplomas (#)	1,596	1,183	312	36	10	55

MSD Southwest Allen County

4824 Homestead Rd • Fort Wayne, IN 46814-5455
(260) 431-2010 • http://www.sacs.k12.in.us/
Grade Span: PK-12; **Agency Type:** 1
Schools: 9
6 Primary; 2 Middle; 1 High; 0 Other Level
9 Regular; 0 Special Education; 0 Vocational; 0 Alternative
0 Magnet; 0 Charter; 0 Title I Eligible; 0 School-wide Title I
Students: 6,011 (52.2% male; 47.8% female)
Individual Education Program: 871 (14.5%);
English Language Learner: 281 (4.7%); Migrant: n/a
Eligible for Free Lunch Program: 152 (2.5%)
Eligible for Reduced-Price Lunch Program: 80 (1.3%)
Teachers: 333.8 (18.0 to 1)
Librarians/Media Specialists: 4.0 (1,502.8 to 1)
Guidance Counselors: 15.0 (400.7 to 1)
Current Spending: ($ per student per year):
Total: $6,979; Instruction: $4,627; Support Services: $2,096
Enrollment, Drop-out Rates and Diploma Recipients by Race/Ethnicity

Category	Total	White	Black	Asian	AIAN	Hisp.
Enrollment (%)	100.0	91.0	2.9	3.3	0.4	2.4
Drop-out Rate (%)	n/a	n/a	n/a	n/a	n/a	n/a
H.S. Diplomas (#)	371	345	9	11	2	4

Northwest Allen County Schools

13119 Coldwater Rd • Fort Wayne, IN 46845-9632
(260) 637-3155 • http://www.nacs.k12.in.us/
Grade Span: PK-12; **Agency Type:** 1
Schools: 10
5 Primary; 2 Middle; 2 High; 1 Other Level
8 Regular; 0 Special Education; 0 Vocational; 2 Alternative
0 Magnet; 0 Charter; 3 Title I Eligible; 0 School-wide Title I
Students: 4,992 (49.9% male; 50.1% female)
Individual Education Program: 556 (11.1%);
English Language Learner: 55 (1.1%); Migrant: n/a
Eligible for Free Lunch Program: 234 (4.7%)
Eligible for Reduced-Price Lunch Program: 172 (3.4%)
Teachers: 259.1 (19.3 to 1)
Librarians/Media Specialists: 3.0 (1,664.0 to 1)
Guidance Counselors: 12.0 (416.0 to 1)
Current Spending: ($ per student per year):
Total: $6,264; Instruction: $3,857; Support Services: $2,120
Enrollment, Drop-out Rates and Diploma Recipients by Race/Ethnicity

Category	Total	White	Black	Asian	AIAN	Hisp.
Enrollment (%)	100.0	94.8	1.6	1.8	0.4	1.3
Drop-out Rate (%)	n/a	n/a	n/a	n/a	n/a	n/a
H.S. Diplomas (#)	290	279	5	2	0	4

Bartholomew County

Bartholomew Con School Corp

2650 Home Ave • Columbus, IN 47201-3152
(812) 376-4220 • http://www.bcsc.k12.in.us/
Grade Span: PK-12; **Agency Type:** 1
Schools: 17
11 Primary; 2 Middle; 3 High; 1 Other Level
15 Regular; 0 Special Education; 1 Vocational; 1 Alternative
0 Magnet; 0 Charter; 7 Title I Eligible; 2 School-wide Title I
Students: 10,580 (52.2% male; 47.8% female)
Individual Education Program: 1,649 (15.6%);
English Language Learner: 401 (3.8%); Migrant: n/a
Eligible for Free Lunch Program: 2,414 (22.8%)
Eligible for Reduced-Price Lunch Program: 854 (8.1%)
Teachers: 604.7 (17.5 to 1)
Librarians/Media Specialists: 8.0 (1,322.5 to 1)
Guidance Counselors: 20.8 (508.7 to 1)
Current Spending: ($ per student per year):
Total: $7,586; Instruction: $4,805; Support Services: $2,520
Enrollment, Drop-out Rates and Diploma Recipients by Race/Ethnicity

Category	Total	White	Black	Asian	AIAN	Hisp.
Enrollment (%)	100.0	93.0	2.3	1.6	0.2	3.0
Drop-out Rate (%)	n/a	n/a	n/a	n/a	n/a	n/a
H.S. Diplomas (#)	620	590	20	7	1	2

Benton County

Benton Community School Corp

405 S Grant Ave • Fowler, IN 47944-1635
Mailing Address: PO Box 512 • Fowler, IN 47944-0512
(765) 884-0850 • http://www.benton.k12.in.us/
Grade Span: KG-12; **Agency Type:** 1
Schools: 5
4 Primary; 0 Middle; 1 High; 0 Other Level
5 Regular; 0 Special Education; 0 Vocational; 0 Alternative
0 Magnet; 0 Charter; 3 Title I Eligible; 0 School-wide Title I
Students: 2,029 (52.2% male; 47.8% female)
Individual Education Program: 513 (25.3%);
English Language Learner: 73 (3.6%); Migrant: n/a
Eligible for Free Lunch Program: 411 (20.3%)
Eligible for Reduced-Price Lunch Program: 189 (9.3%)
Teachers: 135.7 (15.0 to 1)
Librarians/Media Specialists: 1.0 (2,029.0 to 1)
Guidance Counselors: 5.0 (405.8 to 1)

Current Spending: ($ per student per year):
Total: $7,585; Instruction: $4,539; Support Services: $2,771
Enrollment, Drop-out Rates and Diploma Recipients by Race/Ethnicity

Category	Total	White	Black	Asian	AIAN	Hisp.
Enrollment (%)	100.0	96.0	0.5	0.0	0.0	3.4
Drop-out Rate (%)	n/a	n/a	n/a	n/a	n/a	n/a
H.S. Diplomas (#)	158	155	0	0	0	3

Blackford County

Blackford County Schools
0668 W 200 S • Hartford City, IN 47348-3018
(765) 348-7550 • http://www.bcs.k12.in.us/
Grade Span: PK-12; **Agency Type:** 1
Schools: 5
3 Primary; 1 Middle; 1 High; 0 Other Level
5 Regular; 0 Special Education; 0 Vocational; 0 Alternative
0 Magnet; 0 Charter; 4 Title I Eligible; 0 School-wide Title I
Students: 2,296 (51.7% male; 48.3% female)
Individual Education Program: 445 (19.4%);
English Language Learner: n/a; Migrant: n/a
Eligible for Free Lunch Program: 550 (24.0%)
Eligible for Reduced-Price Lunch Program: 204 (8.9%)
Teachers: 147.5 (15.6 to 1)
Librarians/Media Specialists: 3.0 (765.3 to 1)
Guidance Counselors: 4.0 (574.0 to 1)
Current Spending: ($ per student per year):
Total: $7,646; Instruction: $4,645; Support Services: $2,712
Enrollment, Drop-out Rates and Diploma Recipients by Race/Ethnicity

Category	Total	White	Black	Asian	AIAN	Hisp.
Enrollment (%)	100.0	98.9	0.0	0.2	0.3	0.6
Drop-out Rate (%)	n/a	n/a	n/a	n/a	n/a	n/a
H.S. Diplomas (#)	133	131	0	0	0	2

Boone County

Lebanon Community School Corp
1810 N Grant St • Lebanon, IN 46052-2241
(765) 482-0380 • http://www.bccn.boone.in.us/lcsc/index.html
Grade Span: PK-12; **Agency Type:** 1
Schools: 6
4 Primary; 1 Middle; 1 High; 0 Other Level
6 Regular; 0 Special Education; 0 Vocational; 0 Alternative
0 Magnet; 0 Charter; 4 Title I Eligible; 0 School-wide Title I
Students: 3,335 (50.5% male; 49.5% female)
Individual Education Program: 579 (17.4%);
English Language Learner: 34 (1.0%); Migrant: n/a
Eligible for Free Lunch Program: 601 (18.0%)
Eligible for Reduced-Price Lunch Program: 242 (7.3%)
Teachers: 195.0 (17.1 to 1)
Librarians/Media Specialists: 6.0 (555.8 to 1)
Guidance Counselors: 9.0 (370.6 to 1)
Current Spending: ($ per student per year):
Total: $6,640; Instruction: $3,883; Support Services: $2,472
Enrollment, Drop-out Rates and Diploma Recipients by Race/Ethnicity

Category	Total	White	Black	Asian	AIAN	Hisp.
Enrollment (%)	100.0	98.4	0.2	0.3	0.1	1.1
Drop-out Rate (%)	n/a	n/a	n/a	n/a	n/a	n/a
H.S. Diplomas (#)	183	179	1	1	0	2

Western Boone County Com SD
1201 N Sr 75 • Thorntown, IN 46071-9229
(765) 482-6333 • http://www.bccn.boone.in.us/wbsc/index.html
Grade Span: PK-12; **Agency Type:** 1
Schools: 3
2 Primary; 0 Middle; 1 High; 0 Other Level
3 Regular; 0 Special Education; 0 Vocational; 0 Alternative
0 Magnet; 0 Charter; 1 Title I Eligible; 0 School-wide Title I
Students: 1,901 (51.8% male; 48.2% female)
Individual Education Program: 249 (13.1%);
English Language Learner: 3 (0.2%); Migrant: n/a
Eligible for Free Lunch Program: 284 (14.9%)
Eligible for Reduced-Price Lunch Program: 82 (4.3%)
Teachers: 107.5 (17.7 to 1)
Librarians/Media Specialists: 3.0 (633.7 to 1)
Guidance Counselors: 5.0 (380.2 to 1)
Current Spending: ($ per student per year):
Total: $6,300; Instruction: $3,842; Support Services: $2,162
Enrollment, Drop-out Rates and Diploma Recipients by Race/Ethnicity

Category	Total	White	Black	Asian	AIAN	Hisp.
Enrollment (%)	100.0	99.5	0.1	0.2	0.2	0.1
Drop-out Rate (%)	n/a	n/a	n/a	n/a	n/a	n/a
H.S. Diplomas (#)	128	128	0	0	0	0

Zionsville Community Schools
900 Mulberry St • Zionsville, IN 46077
(317) 873-2858
Grade Span: PK-12; **Agency Type:** 1
Schools: 6
5 Primary; 0 Middle; 1 High; 0 Other Level
6 Regular; 0 Special Education; 0 Vocational; 0 Alternative
0 Magnet; 0 Charter; 0 Title I Eligible; 0 School-wide Title I
Students: 4,012 (51.6% male; 48.4% female)
Individual Education Program: 545 (13.6%);
English Language Learner: 32 (0.8%); Migrant: n/a
Eligible for Free Lunch Program: 77 (1.9%)
Eligible for Reduced-Price Lunch Program: 66 (1.6%)
Teachers: 228.2 (17.6 to 1)
Librarians/Media Specialists: 3.0 (1,337.3 to 1)
Guidance Counselors: 9.5 (422.3 to 1)
Current Spending: ($ per student per year):
Total: $6,160; Instruction: $3,807; Support Services: $2,103
Enrollment, Drop-out Rates and Diploma Recipients by Race/Ethnicity

Category	Total	White	Black	Asian	AIAN	Hisp.
Enrollment (%)	100.0	97.0	0.2	1.0	0.4	1.3
Drop-out Rate (%)	n/a	n/a	n/a	n/a	n/a	n/a
H.S. Diplomas (#)	230	220	2	1	3	4

Brown County

Brown County School Corporation
357 E Main St • Nashville, IN 47448-0038
Mailing Address: PO Box 38 • Nashville, IN 47448-0038
(812) 988-6601 • http://www.brownco.k12.in.us/
Grade Span: PK-12; **Agency Type:** 1
Schools: 6
4 Primary; 1 Middle; 1 High; 0 Other Level
6 Regular; 0 Special Education; 0 Vocational; 0 Alternative
0 Magnet; 0 Charter; 4 Title I Eligible; 0 School-wide Title I
Students: 2,260 (53.1% male; 46.9% female)
Individual Education Program: 359 (15.9%);
English Language Learner: 9 (0.4%); Migrant: n/a
Eligible for Free Lunch Program: 442 (19.6%)
Eligible for Reduced-Price Lunch Program: 154 (6.8%)
Teachers: 152.2 (14.8 to 1)
Librarians/Media Specialists: 3.3 (684.8 to 1)
Guidance Counselors: 3.0 (753.3 to 1)
Current Spending: ($ per student per year):
Total: $7,017; Instruction: $4,244; Support Services: $2,475
Enrollment, Drop-out Rates and Diploma Recipients by Race/Ethnicity

Category	Total	White	Black	Asian	AIAN	Hisp.
Enrollment (%)	100.0	98.1	0.2	0.4	0.6	0.7
Drop-out Rate (%)	n/a	n/a	n/a	n/a	n/a	n/a
H.S. Diplomas (#)	131	130	0	0	0	1

Carroll County

Delphi Community School Corp
501 Armory Rd • Delphi, IN 46923-1999
(765) 564-2100 • http://www.delphi.k12.in.us/
Grade Span: PK-12; **Agency Type:** 1
Schools: 4
2 Primary; 1 Middle; 1 High; 0 Other Level
4 Regular; 0 Special Education; 0 Vocational; 0 Alternative
0 Magnet; 0 Charter; 1 Title I Eligible; 0 School-wide Title I
Students: 1,742 (51.6% male; 48.4% female)
Individual Education Program: 220 (12.6%);
English Language Learner: 107 (6.1%); Migrant: n/a
Eligible for Free Lunch Program: 346 (19.9%)
Eligible for Reduced-Price Lunch Program: 157 (9.0%)
Teachers: 94.0 (18.5 to 1)
Librarians/Media Specialists: 3.0 (580.7 to 1)
Guidance Counselors: 3.0 (580.7 to 1)
Current Spending: ($ per student per year):
Total: $7,246; Instruction: $3,661; Support Services: $3,335
Enrollment, Drop-out Rates and Diploma Recipients by Race/Ethnicity

Category	Total	White	Black	Asian	AIAN	Hisp.
Enrollment (%)	100.0	93.1	0.2	0.2	0.3	6.3
Drop-out Rate (%)	n/a	n/a	n/a	n/a	n/a	n/a
H.S. Diplomas (#)	91	90	0	0	0	1

Cass County

Logansport Community Sch Corp
2829 George St • Logansport, IN 46947-3997
(574) 722-2911 • http://www.lcsc.k12.in.us/
Grade Span: PK-12; **Agency Type:** 1
Schools: 9
4 Primary; 2 Middle; 1 High; 2 Other Level

7 Regular; 1 Special Education; 1 Vocational; 0 Alternative
0 Magnet; 0 Charter; 4 Title I Eligible; 0 School-wide Title I
Students: 4,116 (51.8% male; 48.2% female)
Individual Education Program: 616 (15.0%);
English Language Learner: 619 (15.0%); Migrant: n/a
Eligible for Free Lunch Program: 1,280 (31.1%)
Eligible for Reduced-Price Lunch Program: 538 (13.1%)
Teachers: 328.3 (12.5 to 1)
Librarians/Media Specialists: 6.5 (633.2 to 1)
Guidance Counselors: 4.0 (1,029.0 to 1)
Current Spending: ($ per student per year):
Total: $6,759; Instruction: $4,223; Support Services: $2,280
Enrollment, Drop-out Rates and Diploma Recipients by Race/Ethnicity

Category	Total	White	Black	Asian	AIAN	Hisp.
Enrollment (%)	100.0	81.6	1.3	1.2	0.0	16.0
Drop-out Rate (%)	n/a	n/a	n/a	n/a	n/a	n/a
H.S. Diplomas (#)	255	229	2	2	1	21

Southeastern School Corp
6422 E Sr 218 • Walton, IN 46994-0320
(574) 626-2525 • http://www.sesc.k12.in.us/
Grade Span: KG-12; **Agency Type:** 1
Schools: 3
2 Primary; 0 Middle; 1 High; 0 Other Level
3 Regular; 0 Special Education; 0 Vocational; 0 Alternative
0 Magnet; 0 Charter; 1 Title I Eligible; 0 School-wide Title I
Students: 1,636 (51.0% male; 49.0% female)
Individual Education Program: 234 (14.3%);
English Language Learner: 100 (6.1%); Migrant: n/a
Eligible for Free Lunch Program: 239 (14.6%)
Eligible for Reduced-Price Lunch Program: 120 (7.3%)
Teachers: 97.0 (16.9 to 1)
Librarians/Media Specialists: 2.0 (818.0 to 1)
Guidance Counselors: 2.0 (818.0 to 1)
Current Spending: ($ per student per year):
Total: $6,198; Instruction: $3,985; Support Services: $2,077
Enrollment, Drop-out Rates and Diploma Recipients by Race/Ethnicity

Category	Total	White	Black	Asian	AIAN	Hisp.
Enrollment (%)	100.0	93.5	0.7	0.4	0.4	5.1
Drop-out Rate (%)	n/a	n/a	n/a	n/a	n/a	n/a
H.S. Diplomas (#)	119	111	1	1	0	6

Clark County

Greater Clark County Schools
2112 Utica-Sellersburg Rd • Jeffersonville, IN 47130-8506
(812) 283-0701 • http://www.gcs.k12.in.us/
Grade Span: PK-12; **Agency Type:** 1
Schools: 20
12 Primary; 3 Middle; 2 High; 3 Other Level
18 Regular; 1 Special Education; 0 Vocational; 1 Alternative
0 Magnet; 0 Charter; 10 Title I Eligible; 4 School-wide Title I
Students: 9,903 (51.0% male; 49.0% female)
Individual Education Program: 2,189 (22.1%);
English Language Learner: 198 (2.0%); Migrant: n/a
Eligible for Free Lunch Program: 2,419 (24.4%)
Eligible for Reduced-Price Lunch Program: 684 (6.9%)
Teachers: 612.7 (16.2 to 1)
Librarians/Media Specialists: 12.0 (825.3 to 1)
Guidance Counselors: 18.0 (550.2 to 1)
Current Spending: ($ per student per year):
Total: $7,611; Instruction: $4,961; Support Services: $2,397
Enrollment, Drop-out Rates and Diploma Recipients by Race/Ethnicity

Category	Total	White	Black	Asian	AIAN	Hisp.
Enrollment (%)	100.0	83.2	12.9	0.8	0.7	2.3
Drop-out Rate (%)	n/a	n/a	n/a	n/a	n/a	n/a
H.S. Diplomas (#)	425	356	56	6	2	5

West Clark Community Schools
601 Renz Ave • Sellersburg, IN 47172-1398
(812) 246-3375 • http://www.wclark.k12.in.us/
Grade Span: KG-12; **Agency Type:** 1
Schools: 8
4 Primary; 1 Middle; 3 High; 0 Other Level
8 Regular; 0 Special Education; 0 Vocational; 0 Alternative
0 Magnet; 0 Charter; 4 Title I Eligible; 0 School-wide Title I
Students: 3,279 (50.4% male; 49.6% female)
Individual Education Program: 541 (16.5%);
English Language Learner: 10 (0.3%); Migrant: n/a
Eligible for Free Lunch Program: 454 (13.8%)
Eligible for Reduced-Price Lunch Program: 229 (7.0%)
Teachers: 177.3 (18.5 to 1)
Librarians/Media Specialists: 3.0 (1,093.0 to 1)
Guidance Counselors: 4.0 (819.8 to 1)
Current Spending: ($ per student per year):
Total: $6,192; Instruction: $3,960; Support Services: $2,008

Enrollment, Drop-out Rates and Diploma Recipients by Race/Ethnicity

Category	Total	White	Black	Asian	AIAN	Hisp.
Enrollment (%)	100.0	98.6	0.1	0.3	0.2	0.7
Drop-out Rate (%)	n/a	n/a	n/a	n/a	n/a	n/a
H.S. Diplomas (#)	175	172	0	0	0	3

Clay County

Clay Community Schools
9750 N Crawford St • Knightsville, IN 47857-0169
Mailing Address: PO Box 169 • Knightsville, IN 47857-0169
(812) 443-4461 • http://www.clay.k12.in.us/
Grade Span: PK-12; **Agency Type:** 1
Schools: 10
7 Primary; 1 Middle; 2 High; 0 Other Level
10 Regular; 0 Special Education; 0 Vocational; 0 Alternative
0 Magnet; 0 Charter; 4 Title I Eligible; 3 School-wide Title I
Students: 4,619 (51.5% male; 48.5% female)
Individual Education Program: 968 (21.0%);
English Language Learner: 7 (0.2%); Migrant: n/a
Eligible for Free Lunch Program: 1,159 (25.1%)
Eligible for Reduced-Price Lunch Program: 416 (9.0%)
Teachers: 299.1 (15.4 to 1)
Librarians/Media Specialists: 7.0 (659.9 to 1)
Guidance Counselors: 9.0 (513.2 to 1)
Current Spending: ($ per student per year):
Total: $6,713; Instruction: $4,355; Support Services: $2,053
Enrollment, Drop-out Rates and Diploma Recipients by Race/Ethnicity

Category	Total	White	Black	Asian	AIAN	Hisp.
Enrollment (%)	100.0	98.2	1.3	0.1	0.1	0.3
Drop-out Rate (%)	n/a	n/a	n/a	n/a	n/a	n/a
H.S. Diplomas (#)	301	299	1	0	1	0

Clinton County

Community Schools of Frankfort
50 S Maish Rd • Frankfort, IN 46041-2824
(765) 654-5585 • http://fhs.frankfort.k12.in.us/
Grade Span: PK-12; **Agency Type:** 1
Schools: 6
4 Primary; 1 Middle; 1 High; 0 Other Level
6 Regular; 0 Special Education; 0 Vocational; 0 Alternative
0 Magnet; 0 Charter; 3 Title I Eligible; 2 School-wide Title I
Students: 3,232 (50.0% male; 50.0% female)
Individual Education Program: 425 (13.1%);
English Language Learner: 538 (16.6%); Migrant: n/a
Eligible for Free Lunch Program: 1,242 (38.4%)
Eligible for Reduced-Price Lunch Program: 360 (11.1%)
Teachers: 193.4 (16.7 to 1)
Librarians/Media Specialists: 4.0 (808.0 to 1)
Guidance Counselors: 5.7 (567.0 to 1)
Current Spending: ($ per student per year):
Total: $6,569; Instruction: $4,007; Support Services: $2,249
Enrollment, Drop-out Rates and Diploma Recipients by Race/Ethnicity

Category	Total	White	Black	Asian	AIAN	Hisp.
Enrollment (%)	100.0	78.5	0.5	0.3	0.0	20.7
Drop-out Rate (%)	n/a	n/a	n/a	n/a	n/a	n/a
H.S. Diplomas (#)	144	129	0	1	0	14

Crawford County

Crawford County Com School Corp
5805 E Administration Rd • Marengo, IN 47140-8415
(812) 365-2135 • http://www.cccs.k12.in.us/
Grade Span: PK-12; **Agency Type:** 1
Schools: 6
5 Primary; 0 Middle; 1 High; 0 Other Level
6 Regular; 0 Special Education; 0 Vocational; 0 Alternative
0 Magnet; 0 Charter; 5 Title I Eligible; 0 School-wide Title I
Students: 1,820 (51.3% male; 48.7% female)
Individual Education Program: 342 (18.8%);
English Language Learner: 17 (0.9%); Migrant: n/a
Eligible for Free Lunch Program: 661 (36.3%)
Eligible for Reduced-Price Lunch Program: 249 (13.7%)
Teachers: 101.0 (18.0 to 1)
Librarians/Media Specialists: 1.0 (1,820.0 to 1)
Guidance Counselors: 3.0 (606.7 to 1)
Current Spending: ($ per student per year):
Total: $7,359; Instruction: $4,894; Support Services: $2,109
Enrollment, Drop-out Rates and Diploma Recipients by Race/Ethnicity

Category	Total	White	Black	Asian	AIAN	Hisp.
Enrollment (%)	100.0	99.8	0.0	0.0	0.0	0.2
Drop-out Rate (%)	n/a	n/a	n/a	n/a	n/a	n/a
H.S. Diplomas (#)	91	91	0	0	0	0

Daviess County

Washington Com Schools Inc
301 E S St • Washington, IN 47501-3294
(812) 254-5536
Grade Span: KG-12; **Agency Type:** 1
Schools: 6
4 Primary; 1 Middle; 1 High; 0 Other Level
6 Regular; 0 Special Education; 0 Vocational; 0 Alternative
0 Magnet; 0 Charter; 3 Title I Eligible; 0 School-wide Title I
Students: 2,479 (53.1% male; 46.9% female)
Individual Education Program: 527 (21.3%);
English Language Learner: 130 (5.2%); Migrant: n/a
Eligible for Free Lunch Program: 713 (28.8%)
Eligible for Reduced-Price Lunch Program: 192 (7.7%)
Teachers: 139.0 (17.8 to 1)
Librarians/Media Specialists: 2.0 (1,239.5 to 1)
Guidance Counselors: 4.0 (619.8 to 1)
Current Spending: ($ per student per year):
Total: $5,949; Instruction: $3,806; Support Services: $1,941
Enrollment, Drop-out Rates and Diploma Recipients by Race/Ethnicity

Category	Total	White	Black	Asian	AIAN	Hisp.
Enrollment (%)	100.0	94.1	0.3	0.7	0.1	4.8
Drop-out Rate (%)	n/a	n/a	n/a	n/a	n/a	n/a
H.S. Diplomas (#)	175	170	1	1	0	3

De Kalb County

Dekalb County Ctl United SD
3326 Cr 427 • Waterloo, IN 46793
(260) 925-3914 • http://www.dekalb.k12.in.us/
Grade Span: PK-12; **Agency Type:** 1
Schools: 6
4 Primary; 1 Middle; 1 High; 0 Other Level
6 Regular; 0 Special Education; 0 Vocational; 0 Alternative
0 Magnet; 0 Charter; 5 Title I Eligible; 0 School-wide Title I
Students: 4,090 (50.3% male; 49.7% female)
Individual Education Program: 576 (14.1%);
English Language Learner: 55 (1.3%); Migrant: n/a
Eligible for Free Lunch Program: 513 (12.5%)
Eligible for Reduced-Price Lunch Program: 311 (7.6%)
Teachers: 209.2 (19.6 to 1)
Librarians/Media Specialists: 3.0 (1,363.3 to 1)
Guidance Counselors: 9.0 (454.4 to 1)
Current Spending: ($ per student per year):
Total: $6,724; Instruction: $4,141; Support Services: $2,324
Enrollment, Drop-out Rates and Diploma Recipients by Race/Ethnicity

Category	Total	White	Black	Asian	AIAN	Hisp.
Enrollment (%)	100.0	97.6	0.2	0.5	0.1	1.5
Drop-out Rate (%)	n/a	n/a	n/a	n/a	n/a	n/a
H.S. Diplomas (#)	220	216	1	0	0	3

Garrett-Keyser-Butler Com
900 E Warfield • Garrett, IN 46738-1699
Mailing Address: 801 E Houston St • Garrett, IN 46738-1699
(260) 357-3185
Grade Span: KG-12; **Agency Type:** 1
Schools: 4
1 Primary; 1 Middle; 1 High; 1 Other Level
3 Regular; 0 Special Education; 1 Vocational; 0 Alternative
0 Magnet; 0 Charter; 2 Title I Eligible; 0 School-wide Title I
Students: 1,623 (50.1% male; 49.9% female)
Individual Education Program: 299 (18.4%);
English Language Learner: 12 (0.7%); Migrant: n/a
Eligible for Free Lunch Program: 328 (20.2%)
Eligible for Reduced-Price Lunch Program: 159 (9.8%)
Teachers: 106.6 (15.2 to 1)
Librarians/Media Specialists: 2.0 (811.5 to 1)
Guidance Counselors: 5.0 (324.6 to 1)
Current Spending: ($ per student per year):
Total: $8,318; Instruction: $5,011; Support Services: $2,955
Enrollment, Drop-out Rates and Diploma Recipients by Race/Ethnicity

Category	Total	White	Black	Asian	AIAN	Hisp.
Enrollment (%)	100.0	98.6	0.3	0.7	0.1	0.4
Drop-out Rate (%)	n/a	n/a	n/a	n/a	n/a	n/a
H.S. Diplomas (#)	109	102	1	4	0	2

Dearborn County

South Dearborn Com School Corp
6109 Squire Pl • Aurora, IN 47001-1499
(812) 926-2090 • http://www.venus.net/~sdearad1/
Grade Span: PK-12; **Agency Type:** 1
Schools: 6
4 Primary; 1 Middle; 1 High; 0 Other Level
6 Regular; 0 Special Education; 0 Vocational; 0 Alternative
0 Magnet; 0 Charter; 3 Title I Eligible; 0 School-wide Title I
Students: 2,955 (50.8% male; 49.2% female)
Individual Education Program: 598 (20.2%);
English Language Learner: 4 (0.1%); Migrant: n/a
Eligible for Free Lunch Program: 489 (16.5%)
Eligible for Reduced-Price Lunch Program: 143 (4.8%)
Teachers: 178.4 (16.6 to 1)
Librarians/Media Specialists: 3.0 (985.0 to 1)
Guidance Counselors: 2.0 (1,477.5 to 1)
Current Spending: ($ per student per year):
Total: $6,609; Instruction: $4,257; Support Services: $2,071
Enrollment, Drop-out Rates and Diploma Recipients by Race/Ethnicity

Category	Total	White	Black	Asian	AIAN	Hisp.
Enrollment (%)	100.0	99.8	0.0	0.1	0.0	0.1
Drop-out Rate (%)	n/a	n/a	n/a	n/a	n/a	n/a
H.S. Diplomas (#)	199	198	0	1	0	0

Sunman-Dearborn Com Sch Corp
PO Box 210 • Sunman, IN 47041-0210
(812) 623-2291 • http://sunmandearborn.k12.in.us/
Grade Span: KG-12; **Agency Type:** 1
Schools: 6
3 Primary; 1 Middle; 1 High; 1 Other Level
5 Regular; 1 Special Education; 0 Vocational; 0 Alternative
0 Magnet; 0 Charter; 2 Title I Eligible; 0 School-wide Title I
Students: 4,220 (52.4% male; 47.6% female)
Individual Education Program: 727 (17.2%);
English Language Learner: 25 (0.6%); Migrant: n/a
Eligible for Free Lunch Program: 313 (7.4%)
Eligible for Reduced-Price Lunch Program: 149 (3.5%)
Teachers: 224.9 (18.8 to 1)
Librarians/Media Specialists: 5.0 (844.0 to 1)
Guidance Counselors: 9.0 (468.9 to 1)
Current Spending: ($ per student per year):
Total: $6,521; Instruction: $3,970; Support Services: $2,265
Enrollment, Drop-out Rates and Diploma Recipients by Race/Ethnicity

Category	Total	White	Black	Asian	AIAN	Hisp.
Enrollment (%)	100.0	98.9	0.3	0.4	0.0	0.4
Drop-out Rate (%)	n/a	n/a	n/a	n/a	n/a	n/a
H.S. Diplomas (#)	312	312	0	0	0	0

Decatur County

Decatur County Com Schools
1645 W Sr 46 • Greensburg, IN 47240-9054
(812) 663-4595 • http://www.decaturco.k12.in.us/
Grade Span: PK-12; **Agency Type:** 1
Schools: 4
2 Primary; 0 Middle; 2 High; 0 Other Level
4 Regular; 0 Special Education; 0 Vocational; 0 Alternative
0 Magnet; 0 Charter; 2 Title I Eligible; 0 School-wide Title I
Students: 2,195 (53.1% male; 46.9% female)
Individual Education Program: 353 (16.1%);
English Language Learner: 2 (0.1%); Migrant: n/a
Eligible for Free Lunch Program: 314 (14.3%)
Eligible for Reduced-Price Lunch Program: 163 (7.4%)
Teachers: 132.9 (16.5 to 1)
Librarians/Media Specialists: 4.0 (548.8 to 1)
Guidance Counselors: 4.0 (548.8 to 1)
Current Spending: ($ per student per year):
Total: $6,500; Instruction: $4,090; Support Services: $2,129
Enrollment, Drop-out Rates and Diploma Recipients by Race/Ethnicity

Category	Total	White	Black	Asian	AIAN	Hisp.
Enrollment (%)	100.0	99.5	0.0	0.1	0.1	0.2
Drop-out Rate (%)	n/a	n/a	n/a	n/a	n/a	n/a
H.S. Diplomas (#)	146	144	0	0	0	2

Greensburg Community Schools
504 E Central Ave • Greensburg, IN 47240-1898
(812) 663-4774 • http://www.treecity.com/community/gschools/grbg.html
Grade Span: KG-12; **Agency Type:** 1
Schools: 5
2 Primary; 2 Middle; 1 High; 0 Other Level
5 Regular; 0 Special Education; 0 Vocational; 0 Alternative
0 Magnet; 0 Charter; 3 Title I Eligible; 0 School-wide Title I
Students: 2,021 (52.2% male; 47.8% female)
Individual Education Program: 312 (15.4%);
English Language Learner: 33 (1.6%); Migrant: n/a
Eligible for Free Lunch Program: 402 (19.9%)
Eligible for Reduced-Price Lunch Program: 131 (6.5%)
Teachers: 116.6 (17.3 to 1)
Librarians/Media Specialists: 1.5 (1,347.3 to 1)
Guidance Counselors: 2.0 (1,010.5 to 1)
Current Spending: ($ per student per year):
Total: $6,592; Instruction: $3,912; Support Services: $2,325

Enrollment, Drop-out Rates and Diploma Recipients by Race/Ethnicity

Category	Total	White	Black	Asian	AIAN	Hisp.
Enrollment (%)	100.0	98.0	0.1	1.1	0.0	0.7
Drop-out Rate (%)	n/a	n/a	n/a	n/a	n/a	n/a
H.S. Diplomas (#)	106	105	0	1	0	0

Delaware County

Delaware Community School Corp

7821 Sr 3 N • Muncie, IN 47303-9803
(765) 284-5074 • http://www.delcomschools.org/
Grade Span: KG-12; **Agency Type:** 1
Schools: 6
4 Primary; 1 Middle; 1 High; 0 Other Level
6 Regular; 0 Special Education; 0 Vocational; 0 Alternative
0 Magnet; 0 Charter; 2 Title I Eligible; 0 School-wide Title I
Students: 2,899 (52.0% male; 48.0% female)
Individual Education Program: 445 (15.4%);
English Language Learner: 10 (0.3%); Migrant: n/a
Eligible for Free Lunch Program: 453 (15.6%)
Eligible for Reduced-Price Lunch Program: 237 (8.2%)
Teachers: 166.8 (17.4 to 1)
Librarians/Media Specialists: 3.0 (966.3 to 1)
Guidance Counselors: 7.0 (414.1 to 1)
Current Spending: ($ per student per year):
Total: $5,898; Instruction: $3,541; Support Services: $2,101

Enrollment, Drop-out Rates and Diploma Recipients by Race/Ethnicity

Category	Total	White	Black	Asian	AIAN	Hisp.
Enrollment (%)	100.0	98.0	1.3	0.2	0.1	0.4
Drop-out Rate (%)	n/a	n/a	n/a	n/a	n/a	n/a
H.S. Diplomas (#)	199	193	2	2	0	2

Mount Pleasant Twp Com Sch Corp

8800 W Smith St • Yorktown, IN 47396-1399
(765) 759-2720 • http://www.yorktown.k12.in.us/
Grade Span: KG-12; **Agency Type:** 1
Schools: 4
2 Primary; 1 Middle; 1 High; 0 Other Level
4 Regular; 0 Special Education; 0 Vocational; 0 Alternative
0 Magnet; 0 Charter; 0 Title I Eligible; 0 School-wide Title I
Students: 2,225 (53.0% male; 47.0% female)
Individual Education Program: 428 (19.2%);
English Language Learner: 31 (1.4%); Migrant: n/a
Eligible for Free Lunch Program: 196 (8.8%)
Eligible for Reduced-Price Lunch Program: 124 (5.6%)
Teachers: 123.0 (18.1 to 1)
Librarians/Media Specialists: 4.0 (556.3 to 1)
Guidance Counselors: 4.0 (556.3 to 1)
Current Spending: ($ per student per year):
Total: $6,012; Instruction: $3,766; Support Services: $2,116

Enrollment, Drop-out Rates and Diploma Recipients by Race/Ethnicity

Category	Total	White	Black	Asian	AIAN	Hisp.
Enrollment (%)	100.0	97.4	1.0	1.1	0.0	0.4
Drop-out Rate (%)	n/a	n/a	n/a	n/a	n/a	n/a
H.S. Diplomas (#)	141	136	2	1	0	2

Muncie Community Schools

2501 N Oakwood Ave • Muncie, IN 47304-2399
(765) 747-5205 • http://www.muncie.k12.in.us/
Grade Span: PK-12; **Agency Type:** 1
Schools: 18
12 Primary; 2 Middle; 2 High; 2 Other Level
16 Regular; 0 Special Education; 1 Vocational; 1 Alternative
0 Magnet; 0 Charter; 8 Title I Eligible; 7 School-wide Title I
Students: 8,166 (50.6% male; 49.4% female)
Individual Education Program: 1,867 (22.9%);
English Language Learner: 135 (1.7%); Migrant: n/a
Eligible for Free Lunch Program: 3,857 (47.2%)
Eligible for Reduced-Price Lunch Program: 971 (11.9%)
Teachers: 579.8 (14.1 to 1)
Librarians/Media Specialists: 10.0 (816.6 to 1)
Guidance Counselors: 21.0 (388.9 to 1)
Current Spending: ($ per student per year):
Total: $9,570; Instruction: $5,665; Support Services: $3,598

Enrollment, Drop-out Rates and Diploma Recipients by Race/Ethnicity

Category	Total	White	Black	Asian	AIAN	Hisp.
Enrollment (%)	100.0	78.2	18.9	1.1	0.6	1.2
Drop-out Rate (%)	n/a	n/a	n/a	n/a	n/a	n/a
H.S. Diplomas (#)	408	305	93	4	0	6

Dubois County

Greater Jasper Con Schs

1520 St Charles St Ste 1 • Jasper, IN 47546-8228
(812) 482-1801
Grade Span: PK-12; **Agency Type:** 1
Schools: 6
3 Primary; 1 Middle; 1 High; 1 Other Level
5 Regular; 1 Special Education; 0 Vocational; 0 Alternative
0 Magnet; 0 Charter; 2 Title I Eligible; 0 School-wide Title I
Students: 3,102 (51.8% male; 48.2% female)
Individual Education Program: 382 (12.3%);
English Language Learner: 147 (4.7%); Migrant: n/a
Eligible for Free Lunch Program: 269 (8.7%)
Eligible for Reduced-Price Lunch Program: 137 (4.4%)
Teachers: 191.7 (16.2 to 1)
Librarians/Media Specialists: 4.0 (775.5 to 1)
Guidance Counselors: 2.0 (1,551.0 to 1)
Current Spending: ($ per student per year):
Total: $7,330; Instruction: $4,776; Support Services: $2,286

Enrollment, Drop-out Rates and Diploma Recipients by Race/Ethnicity

Category	Total	White	Black	Asian	AIAN	Hisp.
Enrollment (%)	100.0	94.3	0.1	0.7	0.4	4.5
Drop-out Rate (%)	n/a	n/a	n/a	n/a	n/a	n/a
H.S. Diplomas (#)	240	230	1	3	0	6

Southeast Dubois County Sch Corp

432 E 15th St • Ferdinand, IN 47532-9199
(812) 367-1653 • http://www.sedubois.k12.in.us/
Grade Span: KG-12; **Agency Type:** 1
Schools: 4
3 Primary; 0 Middle; 1 High; 0 Other Level
4 Regular; 0 Special Education; 0 Vocational; 0 Alternative
0 Magnet; 0 Charter; 3 Title I Eligible; 0 School-wide Title I
Students: 1,542 (48.6% male; 51.4% female)
Individual Education Program: 187 (12.1%);
English Language Learner: 11 (0.7%); Migrant: n/a
Eligible for Free Lunch Program: 109 (7.1%)
Eligible for Reduced-Price Lunch Program: 90 (5.8%)
Teachers: 83.0 (18.6 to 1)
Librarians/Media Specialists: 1.0 (1,542.0 to 1)
Guidance Counselors: 0.8 (1,927.5 to 1)
Current Spending: ($ per student per year):
Total: $6,053; Instruction: $3,871; Support Services: $1,907

Enrollment, Drop-out Rates and Diploma Recipients by Race/Ethnicity

Category	Total	White	Black	Asian	AIAN	Hisp.
Enrollment (%)	100.0	99.0	0.3	0.6	0.0	0.1
Drop-out Rate (%)	n/a	n/a	n/a	n/a	n/a	n/a
H.S. Diplomas (#)	89	88	0	1	0	0

Southwest Dubois County Sch Corp

113 N Jackson St • Huntingburg, IN 47542-0398
Mailing Address: PO Box 398 • Huntingburg, IN 47542-0398
(812) 683-3971 • http://www.swdubois.k12.in.us/
Grade Span: PK-12; **Agency Type:** 1
Schools: 4
2 Primary; 1 Middle; 1 High; 0 Other Level
4 Regular; 0 Special Education; 0 Vocational; 0 Alternative
0 Magnet; 0 Charter; 1 Title I Eligible; 0 School-wide Title I
Students: 1,839 (49.9% male; 50.1% female)
Individual Education Program: 280 (15.2%);
English Language Learner: 108 (5.9%); Migrant: n/a
Eligible for Free Lunch Program: 262 (14.2%)
Eligible for Reduced-Price Lunch Program: 135 (7.3%)
Teachers: 97.3 (18.9 to 1)
Librarians/Media Specialists: 3.0 (613.0 to 1)
Guidance Counselors: 2.7 (681.1 to 1)
Current Spending: ($ per student per year):
Total: $8,030; Instruction: $4,643; Support Services: $3,090

Enrollment, Drop-out Rates and Diploma Recipients by Race/Ethnicity

Category	Total	White	Black	Asian	AIAN	Hisp.
Enrollment (%)	100.0	93.2	0.2	0.3	0.0	6.4
Drop-out Rate (%)	n/a	n/a	n/a	n/a	n/a	n/a
H.S. Diplomas (#)	122	120	0	0	0	2

Elkhart County

Baugo Community Schools

29125 Cr 22 W • Elkhart, IN 46517-9510
(574) 293-8583 • http://www.baugo.k12.in.us/
Grade Span: KG-12; **Agency Type:** 1
Schools: 4
2 Primary; 1 Middle; 1 High; 0 Other Level
4 Regular; 0 Special Education; 0 Vocational; 0 Alternative
0 Magnet; 0 Charter; 2 Title I Eligible; 0 School-wide Title I

Students: 1,734 (52.9% male; 47.1% female)
Individual Education Program: 298 (17.2%);
English Language Learner: 24 (1.4%); Migrant: n/a
Eligible for Free Lunch Program: 280 (16.1%)
Eligible for Reduced-Price Lunch Program: 139 (8.0%)
Teachers: 95.5 (18.2 to 1)
Librarians/Media Specialists: 1.0 (1,734.0 to 1)
Guidance Counselors: 5.0 (346.8 to 1)
Current Spending: ($ per student per year):
Total: $6,049; Instruction: $3,720; Support Services: $2,111
Enrollment, Drop-out Rates and Diploma Recipients by Race/Ethnicity

Category	Total	White	Black	Asian	AIAN	Hisp.
Enrollment (%)	100.0	93.4	2.9	0.7	0.2	2.7
Drop-out Rate (%)	n/a	n/a	n/a	n/a	n/a	n/a
H.S. Diplomas (#)	118	111	3	0	0	4

Concord Community Schools
59040 Minuteman Way • Elkhart, IN 46517-3499
(574) 875-5161 • http://www.concord.k12.in.us/
Grade Span: KG-12; **Agency Type:** 1
Schools: 6
4 Primary; 1 Middle; 1 High; 0 Other Level
6 Regular; 0 Special Education; 0 Vocational; 0 Alternative
0 Magnet; 0 Charter; 4 Title I Eligible; 0 School-wide Title I
Students: 4,383 (50.2% male; 49.8% female)
Individual Education Program: 671 (15.3%);
English Language Learner: 478 (10.9%); Migrant: n/a
Eligible for Free Lunch Program: 902 (20.6%)
Eligible for Reduced-Price Lunch Program: 368 (8.4%)
Teachers: 238.4 (18.4 to 1)
Librarians/Media Specialists: 1.0 (4,383.0 to 1)
Guidance Counselors: 9.0 (487.0 to 1)
Current Spending: ($ per student per year):
Total: $6,502; Instruction: $3,885; Support Services: $2,359
Enrollment, Drop-out Rates and Diploma Recipients by Race/Ethnicity

Category	Total	White	Black	Asian	AIAN	Hisp.
Enrollment (%)	100.0	82.3	7.0	1.1	0.3	9.2
Drop-out Rate (%)	n/a	n/a	n/a	n/a	n/a	n/a
H.S. Diplomas (#)	244	215	11	4	1	13

Elkhart Community Schools
2720 California Rd • Elkhart, IN 46514-1297
(574) 262-5516 • http://www.elkhart.k12.in.us/
Grade Span: PK-12; **Agency Type:** 1
Schools: 20
14 Primary; 3 Middle; 2 High; 1 Other Level
19 Regular; 0 Special Education; 1 Vocational; 0 Alternative
1 Magnet; 0 Charter; 10 Title I Eligible; 4 School-wide Title I
Students: 12,736 (51.6% male; 48.4% female)
Individual Education Program: 2,110 (16.6%);
English Language Learner: 1,958 (15.4%); Migrant: n/a
Eligible for Free Lunch Program: 4,743 (37.2%)
Eligible for Reduced-Price Lunch Program: 1,269 (10.0%)
Teachers: 797.0 (16.0 to 1)
Librarians/Media Specialists: 5.0 (2,547.2 to 1)
Guidance Counselors: 19.0 (670.3 to 1)
Current Spending: ($ per student per year):
Total: $7,489; Instruction: $4,471; Support Services: $2,713
Enrollment, Drop-out Rates and Diploma Recipients by Race/Ethnicity

Category	Total	White	Black	Asian	AIAN	Hisp.
Enrollment (%)	100.0	66.1	17.0	1.6	0.3	15.1
Drop-out Rate (%)	n/a	n/a	n/a	n/a	n/a	n/a
H.S. Diplomas (#)	544	423	82	9	2	28

Fairfield Community Schools
67240 Cr 31 • Goshen, IN 46528-9300
(574) 831-2188 • http://www.fairfield.k12.in.us/
Grade Span: KG-12; **Agency Type:** 1
Schools: 4
3 Primary; 0 Middle; 1 High; 0 Other Level
4 Regular; 0 Special Education; 0 Vocational; 0 Alternative
0 Magnet; 0 Charter; 3 Title I Eligible; 0 School-wide Title I
Students: 2,054 (50.8% male; 49.2% female)
Individual Education Program: 280 (13.6%);
English Language Learner: 327 (15.9%); Migrant: n/a
Eligible for Free Lunch Program: 143 (7.0%)
Eligible for Reduced-Price Lunch Program: 158 (7.7%)
Teachers: 113.6 (18.1 to 1)
Librarians/Media Specialists: 2.0 (1,027.0 to 1)
Guidance Counselors: 3.0 (684.7 to 1)
Current Spending: ($ per student per year):
Total: $5,671; Instruction: $3,578; Support Services: $1,846
Enrollment, Drop-out Rates and Diploma Recipients by Race/Ethnicity

Category	Total	White	Black	Asian	AIAN	Hisp.
Enrollment (%)	100.0	98.9	0.0	0.3	0.0	0.7
Drop-out Rate (%)	n/a	n/a	n/a	n/a	n/a	n/a
H.S. Diplomas (#)	120	120	0	0	0	0

Goshen Community Schools
721 E Madison St • Goshen, IN 46528-3521
(574) 533-8631 • http://www.goshenschools.org/
Grade Span: KG-12; **Agency Type:** 1
Schools: 9
6 Primary; 1 Middle; 1 High; 1 Other Level
8 Regular; 1 Special Education; 0 Vocational; 0 Alternative
0 Magnet; 0 Charter; 5 Title I Eligible; 0 School-wide Title I
Students: 5,640 (51.6% male; 48.4% female)
Individual Education Program: 1,018 (18.0%);
English Language Learner: 1,526 (27.1%); Migrant: n/a
Eligible for Free Lunch Program: 1,830 (32.4%)
Eligible for Reduced-Price Lunch Program: 618 (11.0%)
Teachers: 370.6 (15.2 to 1)
Librarians/Media Specialists: 2.0 (2,820.0 to 1)
Guidance Counselors: 13.0 (433.8 to 1)
Current Spending: ($ per student per year):
Total: $6,613; Instruction: $4,110; Support Services: $2,244
Enrollment, Drop-out Rates and Diploma Recipients by Race/Ethnicity

Category	Total	White	Black	Asian	AIAN	Hisp.
Enrollment (%)	100.0	72.0	1.3	1.3	0.3	25.1
Drop-out Rate (%)	n/a	n/a	n/a	n/a	n/a	n/a
H.S. Diplomas (#)	271	237	1	0	0	33

Middlebury Community Schools
57853 Northridge Dr • Middlebury, IN 46540-9408
(574) 825-9425 • http://www.mcsin-k12.org/
Grade Span: KG-12; **Agency Type:** 1
Schools: 6
4 Primary; 1 Middle; 1 High; 0 Other Level
6 Regular; 0 Special Education; 0 Vocational; 0 Alternative
0 Magnet; 0 Charter; 4 Title I Eligible; 0 School-wide Title I
Students: 3,640 (52.2% male; 47.8% female)
Individual Education Program: 448 (12.3%);
English Language Learner: 227 (6.2%); Migrant: n/a
Eligible for Free Lunch Program: 323 (8.9%)
Eligible for Reduced-Price Lunch Program: 252 (6.9%)
Teachers: 203.7 (17.9 to 1)
Librarians/Media Specialists: 2.5 (1,456.0 to 1)
Guidance Counselors: 8.0 (455.0 to 1)
Current Spending: ($ per student per year):
Total: $6,766; Instruction: $3,787; Support Services: $2,746
Enrollment, Drop-out Rates and Diploma Recipients by Race/Ethnicity

Category	Total	White	Black	Asian	AIAN	Hisp.
Enrollment (%)	100.0	96.9	0.1	0.9	0.4	1.6
Drop-out Rate (%)	n/a	n/a	n/a	n/a	n/a	n/a
H.S. Diplomas (#)	221	210	1	5	1	4

Wa-Nee Community Schools
1300 N Main St • Nappanee, IN 46550-1015
(574) 773-3131 • http://www.wanee.k12.in.us/
Grade Span: KG-12; **Agency Type:** 1
Schools: 5
3 Primary; 1 Middle; 1 High; 0 Other Level
5 Regular; 0 Special Education; 0 Vocational; 0 Alternative
0 Magnet; 0 Charter; 2 Title I Eligible; 0 School-wide Title I
Students: 3,007 (51.0% male; 49.0% female)
Individual Education Program: 459 (15.3%);
English Language Learner: 298 (9.9%); Migrant: n/a
Eligible for Free Lunch Program: 356 (11.8%)
Eligible for Reduced-Price Lunch Program: 184 (6.1%)
Teachers: 165.1 (18.2 to 1)
Librarians/Media Specialists: 3.0 (1,002.3 to 1)
Guidance Counselors: 6.0 (501.2 to 1)
Current Spending: ($ per student per year):
Total: $6,724; Instruction: $4,211; Support Services: $2,244
Enrollment, Drop-out Rates and Diploma Recipients by Race/Ethnicity

Category	Total	White	Black	Asian	AIAN	Hisp.
Enrollment (%)	100.0	95.8	0.6	0.2	0.0	3.5
Drop-out Rate (%)	n/a	n/a	n/a	n/a	n/a	n/a
H.S. Diplomas (#)	169	167	0	1	0	1

Fayette County

Fayette County School Corp
1401 Spartan Dr • Connersville, IN 47331-1053
(765) 825-2178 • http://fayette.k12.in.us/admin/
Grade Span: PK-12; **Agency Type:** 1
Schools: 13

8 Primary; 1 Middle; 2 High; 2 Other Level
10 Regular; 1 Special Education; 1 Vocational; 1 Alternative
0 Magnet; 0 Charter; 6 Title I Eligible; 0 School-wide Title I
Students: 4,129 (51.7% male; 48.3% female)
Individual Education Program: 870 (21.1%);
English Language Learner: 15 (0.4%); Migrant: n/a
Eligible for Free Lunch Program: 1,447 (35.0%)
Eligible for Reduced-Price Lunch Program: 279 (6.8%)
Teachers: 310.3 (13.3 to 1)
Librarians/Media Specialists: 2.0 (2,064.5 to 1)
Guidance Counselors: 9.0 (458.8 to 1)
Current Spending: ($ per student per year):
Total: $7,134; Instruction: $4,578; Support Services: $2,258
Enrollment, Drop-out Rates and Diploma Recipients by Race/Ethnicity

Category	Total	White	Black	Asian	AIAN	Hisp.
Enrollment (%)	100.0	97.3	2.1	0.3	0.1	0.2
Drop-out Rate (%)	n/a	n/a	n/a	n/a	n/a	n/a
H.S. Diplomas (#)	197	194	2	0	0	1

Floyd County

New Albany-Floyd County Con Sch
2813 Grant Line • New Albany, IN 47150-1087
Mailing Address: PO Box 1087 • New Albany, IN 47150-1087
(812) 949-4200 • http://www.nafcs.k12.in.us/
Grade Span: PK-12; **Agency Type:** 1
Schools: 18
13 Primary; 2 Middle; 2 High; 1 Other Level
17 Regular; 0 Special Education; 1 Vocational; 0 Alternative
0 Magnet; 0 Charter; 10 Title I Eligible; 4 School-wide Title I
Students: 11,092 (51.1% male; 48.9% female)
Individual Education Program: 2,136 (19.3%);
English Language Learner: 152 (1.4%); Migrant: n/a
Eligible for Free Lunch Program: 2,740 (24.7%)
Eligible for Reduced-Price Lunch Program: 710 (6.4%)
Teachers: 619.2 (17.9 to 1)
Librarians/Media Specialists: 6.0 (1,848.7 to 1)
Guidance Counselors: 31.5 (352.1 to 1)
Current Spending: ($ per student per year):
Total: $7,710; Instruction: $4,862; Support Services: $2,526
Enrollment, Drop-out Rates and Diploma Recipients by Race/Ethnicity

Category	Total	White	Black	Asian	AIAN	Hisp.
Enrollment (%)	100.0	91.2	6.9	0.9	0.3	0.8
Drop-out Rate (%)	n/a	n/a	n/a	n/a	n/a	n/a
H.S. Diplomas (#)	660	611	42	2	0	5

Franklin County

Franklin County Com Sch Corp
1020 Franklin Ave • Brookville, IN 47012-0309
(765) 647-4128 • http://fcsc.k12.in.us/
Grade Span: PK-12; **Agency Type:** 1
Schools: 5
3 Primary; 1 Middle; 1 High; 0 Other Level
5 Regular; 0 Special Education; 0 Vocational; 0 Alternative
0 Magnet; 0 Charter; 2 Title I Eligible; 1 School-wide Title I
Students: 3,001 (51.5% male; 48.5% female)
Individual Education Program: 509 (17.0%);
English Language Learner: n/a; Migrant: n/a
Eligible for Free Lunch Program: 680 (22.7%)
Eligible for Reduced-Price Lunch Program: 242 (8.1%)
Teachers: 162.7 (18.4 to 1)
Librarians/Media Specialists: 3.0 (1,000.3 to 1)
Guidance Counselors: 4.6 (652.4 to 1)
Current Spending: ($ per student per year):
Total: $6,315; Instruction: $3,730; Support Services: $2,316
Enrollment, Drop-out Rates and Diploma Recipients by Race/Ethnicity

Category	Total	White	Black	Asian	AIAN	Hisp.
Enrollment (%)	100.0	99.7	0.0	0.2	0.0	0.0
Drop-out Rate (%)	n/a	n/a	n/a	n/a	n/a	n/a
H.S. Diplomas (#)	207	207	0	0	0	0

Fulton County

Rochester Community Sch Corp
690 Zebra Ln • Rochester, IN 46975-0108
Mailing Address: 690 Zebra Ln, Box 108 • Rochester, IN 46975-0108
(574) 223-2159 • http://www.rochester.k12.in.us/
Grade Span: PK-12; **Agency Type:** 1
Schools: 4
2 Primary; 1 Middle; 1 High; 0 Other Level
4 Regular; 0 Special Education; 0 Vocational; 0 Alternative
0 Magnet; 0 Charter; 3 Title I Eligible; 0 School-wide Title I
Students: 1,994 (53.0% male; 47.0% female)
Individual Education Program: 263 (13.2%);
English Language Learner: 31 (1.6%); Migrant: n/a
Eligible for Free Lunch Program: 413 (20.7%)
Eligible for Reduced-Price Lunch Program: 141 (7.1%)
Teachers: 106.0 (18.8 to 1)
Librarians/Media Specialists: 3.0 (664.7 to 1)
Guidance Counselors: 3.0 (664.7 to 1)
Current Spending: ($ per student per year):
Total: $6,176; Instruction: $3,891; Support Services: $1,978
Enrollment, Drop-out Rates and Diploma Recipients by Race/Ethnicity

Category	Total	White	Black	Asian	AIAN	Hisp.
Enrollment (%)	100.0	97.2	0.7	1.1	0.3	0.8
Drop-out Rate (%)	n/a	n/a	n/a	n/a	n/a	n/a
H.S. Diplomas (#)	135	132	0	1	0	2

Gibson County

North Gibson School Corp
RR 4 Box 49 • Princeton, IN 47670-9405
(812) 385-4851 • http://www.ngsc.k12.in.us/
Grade Span: KG-12; **Agency Type:** 1
Schools: 4
2 Primary; 1 Middle; 1 High; 0 Other Level
4 Regular; 0 Special Education; 0 Vocational; 0 Alternative
0 Magnet; 0 Charter; 2 Title I Eligible; 0 School-wide Title I
Students: 2,034 (49.9% male; 50.1% female)
Individual Education Program: 393 (19.3%);
English Language Learner: 12 (0.6%); Migrant: n/a
Eligible for Free Lunch Program: 463 (22.8%)
Eligible for Reduced-Price Lunch Program: 187 (9.2%)
Teachers: 116.3 (17.5 to 1)
Librarians/Media Specialists: 1.5 (1,356.0 to 1)
Guidance Counselors: 4.0 (508.5 to 1)
Current Spending: ($ per student per year):
Total: $6,722; Instruction: $4,063; Support Services: $2,300
Enrollment, Drop-out Rates and Diploma Recipients by Race/Ethnicity

Category	Total	White	Black	Asian	AIAN	Hisp.
Enrollment (%)	100.0	94.1	4.9	0.2	0.0	0.8
Drop-out Rate (%)	n/a	n/a	n/a	n/a	n/a	n/a
H.S. Diplomas (#)	140	129	8	1	0	2

South Gibson School Corp
204 W Vine St • Fort Branch, IN 47648-1099
(812) 753-4230 • http://www.sgibson.k12.in.us/
Grade Span: KG-12; **Agency Type:** 1
Schools: 4
3 Primary; 0 Middle; 1 High; 0 Other Level
4 Regular; 0 Special Education; 0 Vocational; 0 Alternative
0 Magnet; 0 Charter; 2 Title I Eligible; 0 School-wide Title I
Students: 1,868 (50.2% male; 49.8% female)
Individual Education Program: 298 (16.0%);
English Language Learner: 2 (0.1%); Migrant: n/a
Eligible for Free Lunch Program: 171 (9.2%)
Eligible for Reduced-Price Lunch Program: 97 (5.2%)
Teachers: 99.3 (18.8 to 1)
Librarians/Media Specialists: 0.6 (3,113.3 to 1)
Guidance Counselors: 2.0 (934.0 to 1)
Current Spending: ($ per student per year):
Total: $6,263; Instruction: $4,073; Support Services: $1,868
Enrollment, Drop-out Rates and Diploma Recipients by Race/Ethnicity

Category	Total	White	Black	Asian	AIAN	Hisp.
Enrollment (%)	100.0	99.4	0.4	0.2	0.0	0.1
Drop-out Rate (%)	n/a	n/a	n/a	n/a	n/a	n/a
H.S. Diplomas (#)	145	144	0	0	0	1

Grant County

Eastbrook Community Sch Corp
Cr 560 S 900 E • Marion, IN 46953-9699
(765) 664-0624 • http://www.eastbrook.k12.in.us/
Grade Span: KG-12; **Agency Type:** 1
Schools: 6
4 Primary; 1 Middle; 1 High; 0 Other Level
6 Regular; 0 Special Education; 0 Vocational; 0 Alternative
0 Magnet; 0 Charter; 3 Title I Eligible; 0 School-wide Title I
Students: 1,761 (49.8% male; 50.2% female)
Individual Education Program: 282 (16.0%);
English Language Learner: 7 (0.4%); Migrant: n/a
Eligible for Free Lunch Program: 256 (14.5%)
Eligible for Reduced-Price Lunch Program: 140 (8.0%)
Teachers: 101.5 (17.3 to 1)
Librarians/Media Specialists: 2.0 (880.5 to 1)
Guidance Counselors: 4.0 (440.3 to 1)
Current Spending: ($ per student per year):
Total: $6,116; Instruction: $3,682; Support Services: $2,176

Enrollment, Drop-out Rates and Diploma Recipients by Race/Ethnicity

Category	Total	White	Black	Asian	AIAN	Hisp.
Enrollment (%)	100.0	98.9	0.1	0.1	0.2	0.7
Drop-out Rate (%)	n/a	n/a	n/a	n/a	n/a	n/a
H.S. Diplomas (#)	94	91	0	1	0	2

Madison-Grant United Sch Corp

11580 SE 00 W • Fairmount, IN 46928-9318
(765) 948-4143 • http://www.mgusc.k12.in.us/
Grade Span: PK-12; **Agency Type:** 1
Schools: 5
3 Primary; 1 Middle; 1 High; 0 Other Level
5 Regular; 0 Special Education; 0 Vocational; 0 Alternative
0 Magnet; 0 Charter; 3 Title I Eligible; 0 School-wide Title I
Students: 1,632 (51.8% male; 48.2% female)
Individual Education Program: 210 (12.9%);
English Language Learner: 14 (0.9%); Migrant: n/a
Eligible for Free Lunch Program: 332 (20.3%)
Eligible for Reduced-Price Lunch Program: 134 (8.2%)
Teachers: 103.2 (15.8 to 1)
Librarians/Media Specialists: 1.7 (960.0 to 1)
Guidance Counselors: 3.0 (544.0 to 1)
Current Spending: ($ per student per year):
Total: $7,014; Instruction: $4,418; Support Services: $2,277
Enrollment, Drop-out Rates and Diploma Recipients by Race/Ethnicity

Category	Total	White	Black	Asian	AIAN	Hisp.
Enrollment (%)	100.0	98.3	0.1	0.0	0.2	1.3
Drop-out Rate (%)	n/a	n/a	n/a	n/a	n/a	n/a
H.S. Diplomas (#)	81	80	0	0	1	0

Marion Community Schools

1240 S Adams St • Marion, IN 46952-8420
Mailing Address: PO Box 2020 • Marion, IN 46952-8420
(765) 662-2546 • http://www.mcslink.net/
Grade Span: PK-12; **Agency Type:** 1
Schools: 15
7 Primary; 3 Middle; 1 High; 4 Other Level
11 Regular; 1 Special Education; 1 Vocational; 2 Alternative
0 Magnet; 0 Charter; 8 Title I Eligible; 5 School-wide Title I
Students: 5,912 (50.5% male; 49.5% female)
Individual Education Program: 902 (15.3%);
English Language Learner: 167 (2.8%); Migrant: n/a
Eligible for Free Lunch Program: 2,419 (40.9%)
Eligible for Reduced-Price Lunch Program: 495 (8.4%)
Teachers: 388.0 (15.2 to 1)
Librarians/Media Specialists: 4.0 (1,478.0 to 1)
Guidance Counselors: 9.0 (656.9 to 1)
Current Spending: ($ per student per year):
Total: $8,789; Instruction: $5,279; Support Services: $3,218
Enrollment, Drop-out Rates and Diploma Recipients by Race/Ethnicity

Category	Total	White	Black	Asian	AIAN	Hisp.
Enrollment (%)	100.0	70.5	23.8	0.9	0.1	4.8
Drop-out Rate (%)	n/a	n/a	n/a	n/a	n/a	n/a
H.S. Diplomas (#)	271	198	62	4	0	7

Mississinewa Community School Corp

424 E S 'a' St • Gas City, IN 46933
(765) 674-8528 • http://www.olemiss.k12.in.us/
Grade Span: PK-12; **Agency Type:** 1
Schools: 4
2 Primary; 1 Middle; 1 High; 0 Other Level
4 Regular; 0 Special Education; 0 Vocational; 0 Alternative
0 Magnet; 0 Charter; 3 Title I Eligible; 0 School-wide Title I
Students: 2,131 (52.7% male; 47.3% female)
Individual Education Program: 327 (15.3%);
English Language Learner: 11 (0.5%); Migrant: n/a
Eligible for Free Lunch Program: 587 (27.5%)
Eligible for Reduced-Price Lunch Program: 173 (8.1%)
Teachers: 135.5 (15.7 to 1)
Librarians/Media Specialists: 2.0 (1,065.5 to 1)
Guidance Counselors: 4.0 (532.8 to 1)
Current Spending: ($ per student per year):
Total: $6,687; Instruction: $4,244; Support Services: $2,162
Enrollment, Drop-out Rates and Diploma Recipients by Race/Ethnicity

Category	Total	White	Black	Asian	AIAN	Hisp.
Enrollment (%)	100.0	97.7	0.1	0.2	0.4	1.5
Drop-out Rate (%)	n/a	n/a	n/a	n/a	n/a	n/a
H.S. Diplomas (#)	123	122	0	0	0	1

Hamilton County

Carmel Clay Schools

5201 E 131st St • Carmel, IN 46033-9311
(317) 844-9961 • http://www.ccs.k12.in.us/
Grade Span: PK-12; **Agency Type:** 1
Schools: 15
10 Primary; 2 Middle; 1 High; 2 Other Level
13 Regular; 2 Special Education; 0 Vocational; 0 Alternative
0 Magnet; 0 Charter; 0 Title I Eligible; 0 School-wide Title I
Students: 12,905 (51.0% male; 49.0% female)
Individual Education Program: 1,576 (12.2%);
English Language Learner: 850 (6.6%); Migrant: n/a
Eligible for Free Lunch Program: 332 (2.6%)
Eligible for Reduced-Price Lunch Program: 171 (1.3%)
Teachers: 766.9 (16.8 to 1)
Librarians/Media Specialists: 15.5 (832.6 to 1)
Guidance Counselors: 25.0 (516.2 to 1)
Current Spending: ($ per student per year):
Total: $6,989; Instruction: $4,373; Support Services: $2,341
Enrollment, Drop-out Rates and Diploma Recipients by Race/Ethnicity

Category	Total	White	Black	Asian	AIAN	Hisp.
Enrollment (%)	100.0	89.6	1.9	6.9	0.0	1.6
Drop-out Rate (%)	n/a	n/a	n/a	n/a	n/a	n/a
H.S. Diplomas (#)	765	699	8	46	2	10

Hamilton Heights School Corp

410 W Main St • Arcadia, IN 46030-0469
Mailing Address: PO Box 469 • Arcadia, IN 46030-0469
(317) 984-3538 • http://www.hhsc.k12.in.us/
Grade Span: PK-12; **Agency Type:** 1
Schools: 4
2 Primary; 1 Middle; 1 High; 0 Other Level
4 Regular; 0 Special Education; 0 Vocational; 0 Alternative
0 Magnet; 0 Charter; 3 Title I Eligible; 0 School-wide Title I
Students: 2,273 (51.2% male; 48.8% female)
Individual Education Program: 425 (18.7%);
English Language Learner: 22 (1.0%); Migrant: n/a
Eligible for Free Lunch Program: 279 (12.3%)
Eligible for Reduced-Price Lunch Program: 108 (4.8%)
Teachers: 124.8 (18.2 to 1)
Librarians/Media Specialists: 3.0 (757.7 to 1)
Guidance Counselors: 4.7 (483.6 to 1)
Current Spending: ($ per student per year):
Total: $6,190; Instruction: $3,808; Support Services: $2,124
Enrollment, Drop-out Rates and Diploma Recipients by Race/Ethnicity

Category	Total	White	Black	Asian	AIAN	Hisp.
Enrollment (%)	100.0	98.5	0.4	0.1	0.1	0.9
Drop-out Rate (%)	n/a	n/a	n/a	n/a	n/a	n/a
H.S. Diplomas (#)	145	145	0	0	0	0

Hamilton Southeastern Schools

13485 Cumberland Rd • Fishers, IN 46038-3602
(317) 594-4100 • http://www.hse.k12.in.us/
Grade Span: PK-12; **Agency Type:** 1
Schools: 13
8 Primary; 4 Middle; 1 High; 0 Other Level
13 Regular; 0 Special Education; 0 Vocational; 0 Alternative
0 Magnet; 0 Charter; 8 Title I Eligible; 0 School-wide Title I
Students: 10,717 (51.8% male; 48.2% female)
Individual Education Program: 1,508 (14.1%);
English Language Learner: 469 (4.4%); Migrant: n/a
Eligible for Free Lunch Program: 349 (3.3%)
Eligible for Reduced-Price Lunch Program: 185 (1.7%)
Teachers: 583.9 (18.4 to 1)
Librarians/Media Specialists: 13.8 (776.6 to 1)
Guidance Counselors: 24.0 (446.5 to 1)
Current Spending: ($ per student per year):
Total: $6,665; Instruction: $3,856; Support Services: $2,530
Enrollment, Drop-out Rates and Diploma Recipients by Race/Ethnicity

Category	Total	White	Black	Asian	AIAN	Hisp.
Enrollment (%)	100.0	90.6	4.0	3.3	0.1	1.9
Drop-out Rate (%)	n/a	n/a	n/a	n/a	n/a	n/a
H.S. Diplomas (#)	434	401	13	11	0	9

Noblesville Schools

1775 Field Dr • Noblesville, IN 46060-1797
(317) 773-3171 • http://www.nobl.k12.in.us/
Grade Span: PK-12; **Agency Type:** 1
Schools: 9
6 Primary; 2 Middle; 1 High; 0 Other Level
9 Regular; 0 Special Education; 0 Vocational; 0 Alternative
0 Magnet; 0 Charter; 5 Title I Eligible; 0 School-wide Title I
Students: 6,854 (51.5% male; 48.5% female)
Individual Education Program: 1,184 (17.3%);

English Language Learner: 109 (1.6%); Migrant: n/a
Eligible for Free Lunch Program: 640 (9.3%)
Eligible for Reduced-Price Lunch Program: 275 (4.0%)
Teachers: 397.3 (17.3 to 1)
Librarians/Media Specialists: 10.0 (685.4 to 1)
Guidance Counselors: 13.5 (507.7 to 1)
Current Spending: ($ per student per year):
Total: $6,371; Instruction: $3,850; Support Services: $2,229
Enrollment, Drop-out Rates and Diploma Recipients by Race/Ethnicity

Category	Total	White	Black	Asian	AIAN	Hisp.
Enrollment (%)	100.0	96.2	1.1	1.2	0.1	1.5
Drop-out Rate (%)	n/a	n/a	n/a	n/a	n/a	n/a
H.S. Diplomas (#)	401	389	1	10	0	1

Westfield-Washington Schools

322 W Main St • Westfield, IN 46074-9384
(317) 867-8000 • http://www.wws.k12.in.us/
Grade Span: PK-12; **Agency Type:** 1
Schools: 7
4 Primary; 2 Middle; 1 High; 0 Other Level
7 Regular; 0 Special Education; 0 Vocational; 0 Alternative
0 Magnet; 0 Charter; 3 Title I Eligible; 0 School-wide Title I
Students: 4,356 (52.0% male; 48.0% female)
Individual Education Program: 688 (15.8%);
English Language Learner: 92 (2.1%); Migrant: n/a
Eligible for Free Lunch Program: 321 (7.4%)
Eligible for Reduced-Price Lunch Program: 217 (5.0%)
Teachers: 251.5 (17.3 to 1)
Librarians/Media Specialists: 7.0 (622.3 to 1)
Guidance Counselors: 9.0 (484.0 to 1)
Current Spending: ($ per student per year):
Total: $7,300; Instruction: $3,663; Support Services: $3,399
Enrollment, Drop-out Rates and Diploma Recipients by Race/Ethnicity

Category	Total	White	Black	Asian	AIAN	Hisp.
Enrollment (%)	100.0	94.7	1.3	1.5	0.1	2.5
Drop-out Rate (%)	n/a	n/a	n/a	n/a	n/a	n/a
H.S. Diplomas (#)	233	221	1	9	0	2

Hancock County

Greenfield-Central Com Schools

110 W N St • Greenfield, IN 46140-2172
(317) 462-4434 • http://gcsc.k12.in.us/
Grade Span: PK-12; **Agency Type:** 1
Schools: 8
4 Primary; 2 Middle; 1 High; 1 Other Level
7 Regular; 1 Special Education; 0 Vocational; 0 Alternative
0 Magnet; 0 Charter; 3 Title I Eligible; 0 School-wide Title I
Students: 4,016 (50.7% male; 49.3% female)
Individual Education Program: 849 (21.1%);
English Language Learner: 7 (0.2%); Migrant: n/a
Eligible for Free Lunch Program: 447 (11.1%)
Eligible for Reduced-Price Lunch Program: 217 (5.4%)
Teachers: 309.1 (13.0 to 1)
Librarians/Media Specialists: 2.0 (2,008.0 to 1)
Guidance Counselors: 6.0 (669.3 to 1)
Current Spending: ($ per student per year):
Total: $6,477; Instruction: $4,067; Support Services: $2,111
Enrollment, Drop-out Rates and Diploma Recipients by Race/Ethnicity

Category	Total	White	Black	Asian	AIAN	Hisp.
Enrollment (%)	100.0	98.9	0.1	0.3	0.2	0.4
Drop-out Rate (%)	n/a	n/a	n/a	n/a	n/a	n/a
H.S. Diplomas (#)	238	238	0	0	0	0

Mount Vernon Community Sch Corp

One Shoppell Blvd • Fortville, IN 46040-9707
(317) 485-3100 • http://www.mvcsc.k12.in.us/
Grade Span: PK-12; **Agency Type:** 1
Schools: 4
2 Primary; 1 Middle; 1 High; 0 Other Level
4 Regular; 0 Special Education; 0 Vocational; 0 Alternative
0 Magnet; 0 Charter; 1 Title I Eligible; 0 School-wide Title I
Students: 2,858 (53.1% male; 46.9% female)
Individual Education Program: 489 (17.1%);
English Language Learner: 15 (0.5%); Migrant: n/a
Eligible for Free Lunch Program: 120 (4.2%)
Eligible for Reduced-Price Lunch Program: 104 (3.6%)
Teachers: 139.8 (20.4 to 1)
Librarians/Media Specialists: 3.0 (952.7 to 1)
Guidance Counselors: 6.0 (476.3 to 1)
Current Spending: ($ per student per year):
Total: $5,766; Instruction: $3,509; Support Services: $1,968
Enrollment, Drop-out Rates and Diploma Recipients by Race/Ethnicity

Category	Total	White	Black	Asian	AIAN	Hisp.
Enrollment (%)	100.0	95.6	2.5	0.5	0.3	1.1
Drop-out Rate (%)	n/a	n/a	n/a	n/a	n/a	n/a
H.S. Diplomas (#)	183	179	2	0	0	2

Southern Hancock Co Com Sch Corp

4711 S 500 W • New Palestine, IN 46163-0508
Mailing Address: PO Box 508 • New Palestine, IN 46163-0508
(317) 861-4463 • http://www.kiva.net/~shancock/
Grade Span: PK-12; **Agency Type:** 1
Schools: 5
3 Primary; 1 Middle; 1 High; 0 Other Level
5 Regular; 0 Special Education; 0 Vocational; 0 Alternative
0 Magnet; 0 Charter; 2 Title I Eligible; 0 School-wide Title I
Students: 2,860 (50.0% male; 50.0% female)
Individual Education Program: 504 (17.6%);
English Language Learner: 1 (<0.1%); Migrant: n/a
Eligible for Free Lunch Program: 141 (4.9%)
Eligible for Reduced-Price Lunch Program: 57 (2.0%)
Teachers: 142.0 (20.1 to 1)
Librarians/Media Specialists: 4.7 (608.5 to 1)
Guidance Counselors: 4.0 (715.0 to 1)
Current Spending: ($ per student per year):
Total: $6,322; Instruction: $3,589; Support Services: $2,352
Enrollment, Drop-out Rates and Diploma Recipients by Race/Ethnicity

Category	Total	White	Black	Asian	AIAN	Hisp.
Enrollment (%)	100.0	99.2	0.1	0.4	0.1	0.2
Drop-out Rate (%)	n/a	n/a	n/a	n/a	n/a	n/a
H.S. Diplomas (#)	182	179	0	2	0	1

Harrison County

North Harrison Com School Corp

1260 Hwy 64 NW • Ramsey, IN 47166-0008
Mailing Address: PO Box 8 • Ramsey, IN 47166-0008
(812) 347-2407 • http://nhcs.k12.in.us/
Grade Span: KG-12; **Agency Type:** 1
Schools: 5
2 Primary; 2 Middle; 1 High; 0 Other Level
5 Regular; 0 Special Education; 0 Vocational; 0 Alternative
0 Magnet; 0 Charter; 3 Title I Eligible; 0 School-wide Title I
Students: 2,348 (51.0% male; 49.0% female)
Individual Education Program: 421 (17.9%);
English Language Learner: 6 (0.3%); Migrant: n/a
Eligible for Free Lunch Program: 410 (17.5%)
Eligible for Reduced-Price Lunch Program: 222 (9.5%)
Teachers: 130.0 (18.1 to 1)
Librarians/Media Specialists: 5.0 (469.6 to 1)
Guidance Counselors: 6.0 (391.3 to 1)
Current Spending: ($ per student per year):
Total: $6,858; Instruction: $4,270; Support Services: $2,297
Enrollment, Drop-out Rates and Diploma Recipients by Race/Ethnicity

Category	Total	White	Black	Asian	AIAN	Hisp.
Enrollment (%)	100.0	99.6	0.2	0.1	0.0	0.1
Drop-out Rate (%)	n/a	n/a	n/a	n/a	n/a	n/a
H.S. Diplomas (#)	169	169	0	0	0	0

South Harrison Com Schools

315 S Harrison Dr • Corydon, IN 47112-8417
(812) 738-2168 • http://www.shcsc.k12.in.us/
Grade Span: KG-12; **Agency Type:** 1
Schools: 9
4 Primary; 2 Middle; 2 High; 1 Other Level
8 Regular; 1 Special Education; 0 Vocational; 0 Alternative
0 Magnet; 0 Charter; 6 Title I Eligible; 0 School-wide Title I
Students: 3,154 (51.9% male; 48.1% female)
Individual Education Program: 592 (18.8%);
English Language Learner: 22 (0.7%); Migrant: n/a
Eligible for Free Lunch Program: 599 (19.0%)
Eligible for Reduced-Price Lunch Program: 267 (8.5%)
Teachers: 177.5 (17.8 to 1)
Librarians/Media Specialists: 0.0 (0.0 to 1)
Guidance Counselors: 4.0 (788.5 to 1)
Current Spending: ($ per student per year):
Total: $7,039; Instruction: $4,282; Support Services: $2,455
Enrollment, Drop-out Rates and Diploma Recipients by Race/Ethnicity

Category	Total	White	Black	Asian	AIAN	Hisp.
Enrollment (%)	100.0	98.5	0.3	0.4	0.1	0.7
Drop-out Rate (%)	n/a	n/a	n/a	n/a	n/a	n/a
H.S. Diplomas (#)	193	192	0	0	0	1

Hendricks County

Avon Community School Corp

7203 E US Hwy 36 • Avon, IN 46123
(317) 272-2920 • http://www.avon.k12.in.us/
Grade Span: KG-12; **Agency Type:** 1
Schools: 8
5 Primary; 2 Middle; 1 High; 0 Other Level
8 Regular; 0 Special Education; 0 Vocational; 0 Alternative
0 Magnet; 0 Charter; 3 Title I Eligible; 0 School-wide Title I
Students: 5,946 (51.3% male; 48.7% female)
Individual Education Program: 975 (16.4%);
English Language Learner: 92 (1.5%); Migrant: n/a
Eligible for Free Lunch Program: 656 (11.0%)
Eligible for Reduced-Price Lunch Program: 57 (1.0%)
Teachers: 317.0 (18.8 to 1)
Librarians/Media Specialists: 8.0 (743.3 to 1)
Guidance Counselors: 14.0 (424.7 to 1)
Current Spending: ($ per student per year):
Total: $6,691; Instruction: $3,579; Support Services: $2,857
Enrollment, Drop-out Rates and Diploma Recipients by Race/Ethnicity

Category	Total	White	Black	Asian	AIAN	Hisp.
Enrollment (%)	100.0	94.0	1.9	1.7	0.3	2.0
Drop-out Rate (%)	n/a	n/a	n/a	n/a	n/a	n/a
H.S. Diplomas (#)	298	274	4	13	0	7

Brownsburg Community Sch Corp

444 E Tilden Dr • Brownsburg, IN 46112-1498
(317) 852-5726 • http://www.brownsburg.k12.in.us/
Grade Span: PK-12; **Agency Type:** 1
Schools: 8
5 Primary; 1 Middle; 2 High; 0 Other Level
7 Regular; 0 Special Education; 0 Vocational; 1 Alternative
0 Magnet; 0 Charter; 3 Title I Eligible; 0 School-wide Title I
Students: 5,656 (51.6% male; 48.4% female)
Individual Education Program: 617 (10.9%);
English Language Learner: 119 (2.1%); Migrant: n/a
Eligible for Free Lunch Program: 321 (5.7%)
Eligible for Reduced-Price Lunch Program: 147 (2.6%)
Teachers: 302.7 (18.7 to 1)
Librarians/Media Specialists: 7.0 (808.0 to 1)
Guidance Counselors: 11.0 (514.2 to 1)
Current Spending: ($ per student per year):
Total: $6,415; Instruction: $3,894; Support Services: $2,202
Enrollment, Drop-out Rates and Diploma Recipients by Race/Ethnicity

Category	Total	White	Black	Asian	AIAN	Hisp.
Enrollment (%)	100.0	95.6	1.9	1.3	0.2	1.1
Drop-out Rate (%)	n/a	n/a	n/a	n/a	n/a	n/a
H.S. Diplomas (#)	378	354	20	3	0	1

Danville Community School Corp

200 Westview Dr • Danville, IN 46122-0469
Mailing Address: PO Box 469 • Danville, IN 46122-0469
(317) 745-2212 • http://www.danville.k12.in.us/
Grade Span: PK-12; **Agency Type:** 1
Schools: 4
1 Primary; 2 Middle; 1 High; 0 Other Level
4 Regular; 0 Special Education; 0 Vocational; 0 Alternative
0 Magnet; 0 Charter; 2 Title I Eligible; 0 School-wide Title I
Students: 2,271 (50.1% male; 49.9% female)
Individual Education Program: 314 (13.8%);
English Language Learner: 13 (0.6%); Migrant: n/a
Eligible for Free Lunch Program: 150 (6.6%)
Eligible for Reduced-Price Lunch Program: 119 (5.2%)
Teachers: 123.7 (18.4 to 1)
Librarians/Media Specialists: 2.0 (1,135.5 to 1)
Guidance Counselors: 3.0 (757.0 to 1)
Current Spending: ($ per student per year):
Total: $6,320; Instruction: $3,506; Support Services: $2,490
Enrollment, Drop-out Rates and Diploma Recipients by Race/Ethnicity

Category	Total	White	Black	Asian	AIAN	Hisp.
Enrollment (%)	100.0	98.7	0.4	0.0	0.0	0.8
Drop-out Rate (%)	n/a	n/a	n/a	n/a	n/a	n/a
H.S. Diplomas (#)	151	151	0	0	0	0

Mill Creek Community Sch Corp

6631 S Cr 200 W • Clayton, IN 46118-4906
(317) 539-9200
Grade Span: PK-12; **Agency Type:** 1
Schools: 4
2 Primary; 1 Middle; 1 High; 0 Other Level
4 Regular; 0 Special Education; 0 Vocational; 0 Alternative
0 Magnet; 0 Charter; 3 Title I Eligible; 0 School-wide Title I
Students: 1,569 (51.1% male; 48.9% female)
Individual Education Program: 281 (17.9%);
English Language Learner: 3 (0.2%); Migrant: n/a
Eligible for Free Lunch Program: 186 (11.9%)
Eligible for Reduced-Price Lunch Program: 96 (6.1%)
Teachers: 94.0 (16.7 to 1)
Librarians/Media Specialists: 1.0 (1,569.0 to 1)
Guidance Counselors: 3.5 (448.3 to 1)
Current Spending: ($ per student per year):
Total: $6,645; Instruction: $3,668; Support Services: $2,831
Enrollment, Drop-out Rates and Diploma Recipients by Race/Ethnicity

Category	Total	White	Black	Asian	AIAN	Hisp.
Enrollment (%)	100.0	99.6	0.0	0.3	0.0	0.1
Drop-out Rate (%)	n/a	n/a	n/a	n/a	n/a	n/a
H.S. Diplomas (#)	77	77	0	0	0	0

North West Hendricks Schools

104 N Church St • Lizton, IN 46149
Mailing Address: Box 70 • Lizton, IN 46149-0070
(317) 994-4100
Grade Span: PK-12; **Agency Type:** 1
Schools: 4
2 Primary; 1 Middle; 1 High; 0 Other Level
4 Regular; 0 Special Education; 0 Vocational; 0 Alternative
0 Magnet; 0 Charter; 1 Title I Eligible; 0 School-wide Title I
Students: 1,559 (50.0% male; 50.0% female)
Individual Education Program: 248 (15.9%);
English Language Learner: n/a; Migrant: n/a
Eligible for Free Lunch Program: 87 (5.6%)
Eligible for Reduced-Price Lunch Program: 68 (4.4%)
Teachers: 84.5 (18.4 to 1)
Librarians/Media Specialists: 1.0 (1,559.0 to 1)
Guidance Counselors: 3.0 (519.7 to 1)
Current Spending: ($ per student per year):
Total: $6,491; Instruction: $3,624; Support Services: $2,534
Enrollment, Drop-out Rates and Diploma Recipients by Race/Ethnicity

Category	Total	White	Black	Asian	AIAN	Hisp.
Enrollment (%)	100.0	99.2	0.2	0.3	0.2	0.2
Drop-out Rate (%)	n/a	n/a	n/a	n/a	n/a	n/a
H.S. Diplomas (#)	88	86	1	0	0	1

Plainfield Community Sch Corp

985 S Longfellow Dr • Plainfield, IN 46168-1443
(317) 839-2578 • http://www.plainfield.k12.in.us/
Grade Span: PK-12; **Agency Type:** 1
Schools: 6
4 Primary; 1 Middle; 1 High; 0 Other Level
6 Regular; 0 Special Education; 0 Vocational; 0 Alternative
0 Magnet; 0 Charter; 3 Title I Eligible; 0 School-wide Title I
Students: 3,971 (50.8% male; 49.2% female)
Individual Education Program: 572 (14.4%);
English Language Learner: 55 (1.4%); Migrant: n/a
Eligible for Free Lunch Program: 457 (11.5%)
Eligible for Reduced-Price Lunch Program: 253 (6.4%)
Teachers: 203.5 (19.5 to 1)
Librarians/Media Specialists: 5.0 (794.2 to 1)
Guidance Counselors: 6.0 (661.8 to 1)
Current Spending: ($ per student per year):
Total: $6,133; Instruction: $3,829; Support Services: $2,018
Enrollment, Drop-out Rates and Diploma Recipients by Race/Ethnicity

Category	Total	White	Black	Asian	AIAN	Hisp.
Enrollment (%)	100.0	96.8	0.8	1.2	0.1	1.1
Drop-out Rate (%)	n/a	n/a	n/a	n/a	n/a	n/a
H.S. Diplomas (#)	272	267	0	3	0	2

Henry County

New Castle Community Sch Corp

322 Elliott Ave • New Castle, IN 47362-4878
(765) 521-7201 • http://nccsc.k12.in.us/
Grade Span: PK-12; **Agency Type:** 1
Schools: 11
7 Primary; 1 Middle; 1 High; 2 Other Level
9 Regular; 0 Special Education; 1 Vocational; 1 Alternative
0 Magnet; 0 Charter; 4 Title I Eligible; 3 School-wide Title I
Students: 3,855 (51.4% male; 48.6% female)
Individual Education Program: 1,011 (26.2%);
English Language Learner: 5 (0.1%); Migrant: n/a
Eligible for Free Lunch Program: 1,300 (33.7%)
Eligible for Reduced-Price Lunch Program: 289 (7.5%)
Teachers: 286.9 (13.4 to 1)
Librarians/Media Specialists: 3.0 (1,285.0 to 1)
Guidance Counselors: 6.0 (642.5 to 1)
Current Spending: ($ per student per year):
Total: $7,519; Instruction: $4,637; Support Services: $2,543

Enrollment, Drop-out Rates and Diploma Recipients by Race/Ethnicity

Category	Total	White	Black	Asian	AIAN	Hisp.
Enrollment (%)	100.0	96.8	1.6	0.5	0.1	0.9
Drop-out Rate (%)	n/a	n/a	n/a	n/a	n/a	n/a
H.S. Diplomas (#)	235	230	5	0	0	0

Howard County

Kokomo-Center Twp Con Sch Corp

100 W Lincoln • Kokomo, IN 46904-2188
Mailing Address: PO Box 2188 • Kokomo, IN 46904-2188
(765) 455-8000 • http://www.kokomo.k12.in.us/
Grade Span: PK-12; **Agency Type:** 1
Schools: 17
10 Primary; 4 Middle; 1 High; 2 Other Level
16 Regular; 0 Special Education; 1 Vocational; 0 Alternative
0 Magnet; 0 Charter; 9 Title I Eligible; 7 School-wide Title I
Students: 7,013 (50.9% male; 49.1% female)
Individual Education Program: 1,601 (22.8%);
English Language Learner: 121 (1.7%); Migrant: n/a
Eligible for Free Lunch Program: 2,570 (36.6%)
Eligible for Reduced-Price Lunch Program: 590 (8.4%)
Teachers: 499.8 (14.0 to 1)
Librarians/Media Specialists: 6.0 (1,168.8 to 1)
Guidance Counselors: 9.0 (779.2 to 1)
Current Spending: ($ per student per year):
Total: $8,938; Instruction: $5,381; Support Services: $3,264

Enrollment, Drop-out Rates and Diploma Recipients by Race/Ethnicity

Category	Total	White	Black	Asian	AIAN	Hisp.
Enrollment (%)	100.0	79.7	16.9	0.9	0.4	2.1
Drop-out Rate (%)	n/a	n/a	n/a	n/a	n/a	n/a
H.S. Diplomas (#)	367	297	55	3	1	11

Northwestern School Corp

4154 W Rd 350 N • Kokomo, IN 46901-9121
(765) 454-2321 • http://www.nwsc.k12.in.us/
Grade Span: KG-12; **Agency Type:** 1
Schools: 4
2 Primary; 1 Middle; 1 High; 0 Other Level
4 Regular; 0 Special Education; 0 Vocational; 0 Alternative
0 Magnet; 0 Charter; 2 Title I Eligible; 0 School-wide Title I
Students: 1,694 (53.5% male; 46.5% female)
Individual Education Program: 278 (16.4%);
English Language Learner: 23 (1.4%); Migrant: n/a
Eligible for Free Lunch Program: 150 (8.9%)
Eligible for Reduced-Price Lunch Program: 57 (3.4%)
Teachers: 104.9 (16.1 to 1)
Librarians/Media Specialists: 2.0 (847.0 to 1)
Guidance Counselors: 3.0 (564.7 to 1)
Current Spending: ($ per student per year):
Total: $7,212; Instruction: $4,593; Support Services: $2,352

Enrollment, Drop-out Rates and Diploma Recipients by Race/Ethnicity

Category	Total	White	Black	Asian	AIAN	Hisp.
Enrollment (%)	100.0	96.6	0.9	0.7	0.4	1.4
Drop-out Rate (%)	n/a	n/a	n/a	n/a	n/a	n/a
H.S. Diplomas (#)	127	126	1	0	0	0

Taylor Community School Corp

3750 E Cr 300 S • Kokomo, IN 46902-9509
(765) 453-3035 • http://taylor.in.schoolwebpages.com
Grade Span: KG-12; **Agency Type:** 1
Schools: 4
2 Primary; 1 Middle; 1 High; 0 Other Level
4 Regular; 0 Special Education; 0 Vocational; 0 Alternative
0 Magnet; 0 Charter; 2 Title I Eligible; 0 School-wide Title I
Students: 1,523 (52.6% male; 47.4% female)
Individual Education Program: 296 (19.4%);
English Language Learner: 22 (1.4%); Migrant: n/a
Eligible for Free Lunch Program: 345 (22.7%)
Eligible for Reduced-Price Lunch Program: 125 (8.2%)
Teachers: 100.4 (15.2 to 1)
Librarians/Media Specialists: 1.0 (1,523.0 to 1)
Guidance Counselors: 4.0 (380.8 to 1)
Current Spending: ($ per student per year):
Total: $7,305; Instruction: $4,578; Support Services: $2,473

Enrollment, Drop-out Rates and Diploma Recipients by Race/Ethnicity

Category	Total	White	Black	Asian	AIAN	Hisp.
Enrollment (%)	100.0	91.5	4.7	1.8	0.5	1.5
Drop-out Rate (%)	n/a	n/a	n/a	n/a	n/a	n/a
H.S. Diplomas (#)	82	79	1	2	0	0

Western School Corp

600 W 2600 S • Russiaville, IN 46979-0247
(765) 883-5576 • http://www.western.k12.in.us/
Grade Span: KG-12; **Agency Type:** 1
Schools: 4
2 Primary; 1 Middle; 1 High; 0 Other Level
4 Regular; 0 Special Education; 0 Vocational; 0 Alternative
0 Magnet; 0 Charter; 3 Title I Eligible; 0 School-wide Title I
Students: 2,285 (50.8% male; 49.2% female)
Individual Education Program: 323 (14.1%);
English Language Learner: 47 (2.1%); Migrant: n/a
Eligible for Free Lunch Program: 236 (10.3%)
Eligible for Reduced-Price Lunch Program: 90 (3.9%)
Teachers: 122.5 (18.7 to 1)
Librarians/Media Specialists: 1.0 (2,285.0 to 1)
Guidance Counselors: 4.0 (571.3 to 1)
Current Spending: ($ per student per year):
Total: $6,042; Instruction: $3,667; Support Services: $2,135

Enrollment, Drop-out Rates and Diploma Recipients by Race/Ethnicity

Category	Total	White	Black	Asian	AIAN	Hisp.
Enrollment (%)	100.0	93.2	3.9	1.7	0.2	1.0
Drop-out Rate (%)	n/a	n/a	n/a	n/a	n/a	n/a
H.S. Diplomas (#)	162	147	10	2	0	3

Huntington County

Huntington County Com Sch Corp

1360 Warren Rd • Huntington, IN 46750-2192
(260) 356-7812 • http://www.hccsc.k12.in.us/
Grade Span: KG-12; **Agency Type:** 1
Schools: 11
8 Primary; 2 Middle; 1 High; 0 Other Level
11 Regular; 0 Special Education; 0 Vocational; 0 Alternative
0 Magnet; 0 Charter; 6 Title I Eligible; 2 School-wide Title I
Students: 6,410 (50.6% male; 49.4% female)
Individual Education Program: 986 (15.4%);
English Language Learner: 25 (0.4%); Migrant: n/a
Eligible for Free Lunch Program: 1,057 (16.5%)
Eligible for Reduced-Price Lunch Program: 562 (8.8%)
Teachers: 388.6 (16.5 to 1)
Librarians/Media Specialists: 4.0 (1,602.5 to 1)
Guidance Counselors: 18.2 (352.2 to 1)
Current Spending: ($ per student per year):
Total: $6,232; Instruction: $3,970; Support Services: $1,934

Enrollment, Drop-out Rates and Diploma Recipients by Race/Ethnicity

Category	Total	White	Black	Asian	AIAN	Hisp.
Enrollment (%)	100.0	98.6	0.1	0.3	0.3	0.7
Drop-out Rate (%)	n/a	n/a	n/a	n/a	n/a	n/a
H.S. Diplomas (#)	453	452	0	1	0	0

Jackson County

Brownstown Cnt Com Sch Corp

608 W Commerce St • Brownstown, IN 47220
(812) 358-4271 • http://www.btownccs.k12.in.us/
Grade Span: PK-12; **Agency Type:** 1
Schools: 5
2 Primary; 1 Middle; 1 High; 1 Other Level
4 Regular; 0 Special Education; 0 Vocational; 1 Alternative
0 Magnet; 0 Charter; 2 Title I Eligible; 0 School-wide Title I
Students: 1,732 (51.3% male; 48.7% female)
Individual Education Program: 257 (14.8%);
English Language Learner: 9 (0.5%); Migrant: n/a
Eligible for Free Lunch Program: 335 (19.3%)
Eligible for Reduced-Price Lunch Program: 125 (7.2%)
Teachers: 93.8 (18.5 to 1)
Librarians/Media Specialists: 2.0 (866.0 to 1)
Guidance Counselors: 4.0 (433.0 to 1)
Current Spending: ($ per student per year):
Total: $6,915; Instruction: $4,471; Support Services: $2,184

Enrollment, Drop-out Rates and Diploma Recipients by Race/Ethnicity

Category	Total	White	Black	Asian	AIAN	Hisp.
Enrollment (%)	100.0	99.6	0.1	0.1	0.0	0.2
Drop-out Rate (%)	n/a	n/a	n/a	n/a	n/a	n/a
H.S. Diplomas (#)	115	115	0	0	0	0

Seymour Community Schools

1638 S Walnut St • Seymour, IN 47274-0366
(812) 522-3340 • http://scsc.k12.in.us/
Grade Span: PK-12; **Agency Type:** 1
Schools: 8
6 Primary; 1 Middle; 1 High; 0 Other Level
7 Regular; 0 Special Education; 0 Vocational; 1 Alternative
0 Magnet; 0 Charter; 4 Title I Eligible; 0 School-wide Title I
Students: 3,780 (50.1% male; 49.9% female)

Individual Education Program: 744 (19.7%);
English Language Learner: 164 (4.3%); Migrant: n/a
Eligible for Free Lunch Program: 819 (21.7%)
Eligible for Reduced-Price Lunch Program: 356 (9.4%)
Teachers: 212.8 (17.8 to 1)
Librarians/Media Specialists: 1.5 (2,520.0 to 1)
Guidance Counselors: 7.0 (540.0 to 1)
Current Spending: ($ per student per year):
Total: $6,464; Instruction: $4,123; Support Services: $2,043
Enrollment, Drop-out Rates and Diploma Recipients by Race/Ethnicity

Category	Total	White	Black	Asian	AIAN	Hisp.
Enrollment (%)	100.0	93.2	0.9	1.9	0.2	3.7
Drop-out Rate (%)	n/a	n/a	n/a	n/a	n/a	n/a
H.S. Diplomas (#)	242	230	1	9	0	2

Jasper County

Kankakee Valley School Corp
PO Box 278 • Wheatfield, IN 46392-0278
(219) 987-4711 • http://www.kv.k12.in.us/qguide.htm
Grade Span: KG-12; **Agency Type:** 1
Schools: 5
2 Primary; 2 Middle; 1 High; 0 Other Level
5 Regular; 0 Special Education; 0 Vocational; 0 Alternative
0 Magnet; 0 Charter; 4 Title I Eligible; 0 School-wide Title I
Students: 3,143 (52.4% male; 47.6% female)
Individual Education Program: 564 (17.9%);
English Language Learner: 119 (3.8%); Migrant: n/a
Eligible for Free Lunch Program: 500 (15.9%)
Eligible for Reduced-Price Lunch Program: 294 (9.4%)
Teachers: 173.0 (18.2 to 1)
Librarians/Media Specialists: 4.0 (785.8 to 1)
Guidance Counselors: 6.5 (483.5 to 1)
Current Spending: ($ per student per year):
Total: $6,266; Instruction: $3,969; Support Services: $2,015
Enrollment, Drop-out Rates and Diploma Recipients by Race/Ethnicity

Category	Total	White	Black	Asian	AIAN	Hisp.
Enrollment (%)	100.0	93.8	0.3	0.4	0.6	4.9
Drop-out Rate (%)	n/a	n/a	n/a	n/a	n/a	n/a
H.S. Diplomas (#)	212	204	1	2	0	5

Rensselaer Central School Corp
605 Grove St • Rensselaer, IN 47978-0069
(219) 866-7822 • http://www.rcsc.k12.in.us/
Grade Span: PK-12; **Agency Type:** 1
Schools: 4
2 Primary; 1 Middle; 1 High; 0 Other Level
4 Regular; 0 Special Education; 0 Vocational; 0 Alternative
0 Magnet; 0 Charter; 3 Title I Eligible; 0 School-wide Title I
Students: 1,776 (53.3% male; 46.7% female)
Individual Education Program: 354 (19.9%);
English Language Learner: 38 (2.1%); Migrant: n/a
Eligible for Free Lunch Program: 365 (20.6%)
Eligible for Reduced-Price Lunch Program: 161 (9.1%)
Teachers: 107.3 (16.6 to 1)
Librarians/Media Specialists: 2.2 (807.3 to 1)
Guidance Counselors: 4.0 (444.0 to 1)
Current Spending: ($ per student per year):
Total: $6,612; Instruction: $3,808; Support Services: $2,480
Enrollment, Drop-out Rates and Diploma Recipients by Race/Ethnicity

Category	Total	White	Black	Asian	AIAN	Hisp.
Enrollment (%)	100.0	96.6	0.1	0.1	0.1	3.1
Drop-out Rate (%)	n/a	n/a	n/a	n/a	n/a	n/a
H.S. Diplomas (#)	98	90	0	3	1	4

Jay County

Jay School Corp
404 E Arch • Portland, IN 47371-3239
Mailing Address: PO Box 1239 • Portland, IN 47371
(260) 726-9341 • http://www.jayschools.k12.in.us/
Grade Span: PK-12; **Agency Type:** 1
Schools: 10
7 Primary; 2 Middle; 1 High; 0 Other Level
10 Regular; 0 Special Education; 0 Vocational; 0 Alternative
0 Magnet; 0 Charter; 6 Title I Eligible; 0 School-wide Title I
Students: 3,867 (52.9% male; 47.1% female)
Individual Education Program: 657 (17.0%);
English Language Learner: 98 (2.5%); Migrant: n/a
Eligible for Free Lunch Program: 971 (25.1%)
Eligible for Reduced-Price Lunch Program: 426 (11.0%)
Teachers: 228.0 (17.0 to 1)
Librarians/Media Specialists: 7.0 (552.4 to 1)
Guidance Counselors: 3.0 (1,289.0 to 1)
Current Spending: ($ per student per year):
Total: $7,729; Instruction: $4,855; Support Services: $2,565
Enrollment, Drop-out Rates and Diploma Recipients by Race/Ethnicity

Category	Total	White	Black	Asian	AIAN	Hisp.
Enrollment (%)	100.0	97.6	0.0	0.4	0.0	2.0
Drop-out Rate (%)	n/a	n/a	n/a	n/a	n/a	n/a
H.S. Diplomas (#)	211	204	0	0	0	7

Jefferson County

Madison Consolidated Schools
2421 Wilson Ave • Madison, IN 47250-2134
(812) 273-8511 • http://www.madisonconsolidatedschools.com/
Grade Span: PK-12; **Agency Type:** 1
Schools: 10
7 Primary; 2 Middle; 1 High; 0 Other Level
10 Regular; 0 Special Education; 0 Vocational; 0 Alternative
0 Magnet; 0 Charter; 7 Title I Eligible; 0 School-wide Title I
Students: 3,490 (52.4% male; 47.6% female)
Individual Education Program: 895 (25.6%);
English Language Learner: 37 (1.1%); Migrant: n/a
Eligible for Free Lunch Program: 867 (24.8%)
Eligible for Reduced-Price Lunch Program: 369 (10.6%)
Teachers: 199.0 (17.5 to 1)
Librarians/Media Specialists: 4.0 (872.5 to 1)
Guidance Counselors: 5.0 (698.0 to 1)
Current Spending: ($ per student per year):
Total: $7,559; Instruction: $4,744; Support Services: $2,474
Enrollment, Drop-out Rates and Diploma Recipients by Race/Ethnicity

Category	Total	White	Black	Asian	AIAN	Hisp.
Enrollment (%)	100.0	97.2	1.4	0.8	0.0	0.5
Drop-out Rate (%)	n/a	n/a	n/a	n/a	n/a	n/a
H.S. Diplomas (#)	176	174	1	1	0	0

Southwestern-Jefferson County
239 S Main Cross St • Hanover, IN 47243-9309
(812) 866-6250
Grade Span: PK-12; **Agency Type:** 1
Schools: 2
1 Primary; 0 Middle; 0 High; 1 Other Level
2 Regular; 0 Special Education; 0 Vocational; 0 Alternative
0 Magnet; 0 Charter; 1 Title I Eligible; 0 School-wide Title I
Students: 1,500 (49.3% male; 50.7% female)
Individual Education Program: 352 (23.5%);
English Language Learner: 6 (0.4%); Migrant: n/a
Eligible for Free Lunch Program: 426 (28.4%)
Eligible for Reduced-Price Lunch Program: 151 (10.1%)
Teachers: 89.0 (16.9 to 1)
Librarians/Media Specialists: 2.0 (750.0 to 1)
Guidance Counselors: 3.0 (500.0 to 1)
Current Spending: ($ per student per year):
Total: $6,443; Instruction: $4,000; Support Services: $2,131
Enrollment, Drop-out Rates and Diploma Recipients by Race/Ethnicity

Category	Total	White	Black	Asian	AIAN	Hisp.
Enrollment (%)	100.0	98.6	0.9	0.2	0.1	0.3
Drop-out Rate (%)	n/a	n/a	n/a	n/a	n/a	n/a
H.S. Diplomas (#)	80	75	5	0	0	0

Jennings County

Jennings County Schools
34 Main St • North Vernon, IN 47265-1706
(812) 346-4483 • http://www.jcsc.org/
Grade Span: PK-12; **Agency Type:** 1
Schools: 10
7 Primary; 1 Middle; 2 High; 0 Other Level
9 Regular; 0 Special Education; 0 Vocational; 1 Alternative
0 Magnet; 0 Charter; 5 Title I Eligible; 0 School-wide Title I
Students: 5,185 (51.7% male; 48.3% female)
Individual Education Program: 1,127 (21.7%);
English Language Learner: 32 (0.6%); Migrant: n/a
Eligible for Free Lunch Program: 1,169 (22.5%)
Eligible for Reduced-Price Lunch Program: 499 (9.6%)
Teachers: 289.3 (17.9 to 1)
Librarians/Media Specialists: 2.0 (2,592.5 to 1)
Guidance Counselors: 14.0 (370.4 to 1)
Current Spending: ($ per student per year):
Total: $6,341; Instruction: $3,685; Support Services: $2,377
Enrollment, Drop-out Rates and Diploma Recipients by Race/Ethnicity

Category	Total	White	Black	Asian	AIAN	Hisp.
Enrollment (%)	100.0	97.6	0.7	0.3	0.8	0.8
Drop-out Rate (%)	n/a	n/a	n/a	n/a	n/a	n/a
H.S. Diplomas (#)	234	230	2	1	0	1

Johnson County

Center Grove Com Sch Corp

2929 S Morgantown Rd • Greenwood, IN 46143-9100
(317) 881-9326 • http://www.centergrove.k12.in.us/
Grade Span: KG-12; **Agency Type:** 1
Schools: 8
6 Primary; 1 Middle; 1 High; 0 Other Level
8 Regular; 0 Special Education; 0 Vocational; 0 Alternative
0 Magnet; 0 Charter; 5 Title I Eligible; 0 School-wide Title I
Students: 6,986 (51.3% male; 48.7% female)
Individual Education Program: 876 (12.5%);
English Language Learner: 98 (1.4%); Migrant: n/a
Eligible for Free Lunch Program: 447 (6.4%)
Eligible for Reduced-Price Lunch Program: 242 (3.5%)
Teachers: 363.8 (19.2 to 1)
Librarians/Media Specialists: 6.0 (1,164.3 to 1)
Guidance Counselors: 14.0 (499.0 to 1)
Current Spending: ($ per student per year):
Total: $5,560; Instruction: $3,336; Support Services: $1,954
Enrollment, Drop-out Rates and Diploma Recipients by Race/Ethnicity

Category	Total	White	Black	Asian	AIAN	Hisp.
Enrollment (%)	100.0	97.0	0.3	1.6	0.1	1.0
Drop-out Rate (%)	n/a	n/a	n/a	n/a	n/a	n/a
H.S. Diplomas (#)	445	436	1	4	1	3

Clark-Pleasant Com School Corp

50 Center St • Whiteland, IN 46184-1698
(317) 535-7579 • http://www.cpcsc.k12.in.us/
Grade Span: KG-12; **Agency Type:** 1
Schools: 6
4 Primary; 1 Middle; 1 High; 0 Other Level
6 Regular; 0 Special Education; 0 Vocational; 0 Alternative
0 Magnet; 0 Charter; 4 Title I Eligible; 0 School-wide Title I
Students: 3,776 (50.5% male; 49.5% female)
Individual Education Program: 502 (13.3%);
English Language Learner: 21 (0.6%); Migrant: n/a
Eligible for Free Lunch Program: 386 (10.2%)
Eligible for Reduced-Price Lunch Program: 320 (8.5%)
Teachers: 176.0 (21.5 to 1)
Librarians/Media Specialists: 2.0 (1,888.0 to 1)
Guidance Counselors: 8.0 (472.0 to 1)
Current Spending: ($ per student per year):
Total: $5,944; Instruction: $3,459; Support Services: $2,207
Enrollment, Drop-out Rates and Diploma Recipients by Race/Ethnicity

Category	Total	White	Black	Asian	AIAN	Hisp.
Enrollment (%)	100.0	97.7	0.2	0.5	0.2	1.4
Drop-out Rate (%)	n/a	n/a	n/a	n/a	n/a	n/a
H.S. Diplomas (#)	178	176	0	0	1	1

Franklin Community School Corp

998 Grizzly Cub Dr • Franklin, IN 46131-1398
(317) 738-5800 • http://fcsc.k12.in.us/
Grade Span: KG-12; **Agency Type:** 1
Schools: 7
5 Primary; 1 Middle; 1 High; 0 Other Level
7 Regular; 0 Special Education; 0 Vocational; 0 Alternative
0 Magnet; 0 Charter; 3 Title I Eligible; 0 School-wide Title I
Students: 4,370 (50.8% male; 49.2% female)
Individual Education Program: 800 (18.3%);
English Language Learner: 45 (1.0%); Migrant: n/a
Eligible for Free Lunch Program: 913 (20.9%)
Eligible for Reduced-Price Lunch Program: 291 (6.7%)
Teachers: 255.5 (17.1 to 1)
Librarians/Media Specialists: 3.5 (1,248.6 to 1)
Guidance Counselors: 12.0 (364.2 to 1)
Current Spending: ($ per student per year):
Total: $6,253; Instruction: $3,687; Support Services: $2,235
Enrollment, Drop-out Rates and Diploma Recipients by Race/Ethnicity

Category	Total	White	Black	Asian	AIAN	Hisp.
Enrollment (%)	100.0	96.7	1.4	0.4	0.3	1.2
Drop-out Rate (%)	n/a	n/a	n/a	n/a	n/a	n/a
H.S. Diplomas (#)	208	204	0	1	0	3

Greenwood Community Sch Corp

605 W Smith Valley Rd • Greenwood, IN 46142-0218
(317) 889-4060
Grade Span: KG-12; **Agency Type:** 1
Schools: 6
4 Primary; 1 Middle; 1 High; 0 Other Level
6 Regular; 0 Special Education; 0 Vocational; 0 Alternative
0 Magnet; 0 Charter; 3 Title I Eligible; 0 School-wide Title I
Students: 3,856 (50.6% male; 49.4% female)
Individual Education Program: 520 (13.5%);
English Language Learner: 92 (2.4%); Migrant: n/a
Eligible for Free Lunch Program: 536 (13.9%)
Eligible for Reduced-Price Lunch Program: 207 (5.4%)
Teachers: 187.5 (20.6 to 1)
Librarians/Media Specialists: 2.0 (1,928.0 to 1)
Guidance Counselors: 5.0 (771.2 to 1)
Current Spending: ($ per student per year):
Total: $6,098; Instruction: $3,990; Support Services: $1,847
Enrollment, Drop-out Rates and Diploma Recipients by Race/Ethnicity

Category	Total	White	Black	Asian	AIAN	Hisp.
Enrollment (%)	100.0	95.8	1.0	1.2	0.2	1.8
Drop-out Rate (%)	n/a	n/a	n/a	n/a	n/a	n/a
H.S. Diplomas (#)	210	202	0	4	3	1

Nineveh-Hensley-Jackson United

802 S Indian Creek Dr • Trafalgar, IN 46181
(317) 878-2100 • http://www.nhj.k12.in.us/
Grade Span: KG-12; **Agency Type:** 1
Schools: 4
2 Primary; 1 Middle; 1 High; 0 Other Level
4 Regular; 0 Special Education; 0 Vocational; 0 Alternative
0 Magnet; 0 Charter; 2 Title I Eligible; 0 School-wide Title I
Students: 1,821 (50.5% male; 49.5% female)
Individual Education Program: 240 (13.2%);
English Language Learner: 3 (0.2%); Migrant: n/a
Eligible for Free Lunch Program: 170 (9.3%)
Eligible for Reduced-Price Lunch Program: 78 (4.3%)
Teachers: 103.5 (17.6 to 1)
Librarians/Media Specialists: 3.0 (607.0 to 1)
Guidance Counselors: 4.7 (387.4 to 1)
Current Spending: ($ per student per year):
Total: $6,197; Instruction: $3,556; Support Services: $2,380
Enrollment, Drop-out Rates and Diploma Recipients by Race/Ethnicity

Category	Total	White	Black	Asian	AIAN	Hisp.
Enrollment (%)	100.0	99.4	0.2	0.3	0.1	0.1
Drop-out Rate (%)	n/a	n/a	n/a	n/a	n/a	n/a
H.S. Diplomas (#)	110	110	0	0	0	0

Knox County

North Knox School Corp

11110 N Sr 159 • Bicknell, IN 47512-9801
Mailing Address: PO Box 187 • Bicknell, IN 47512-9801
(812) 735-4434 • http://www.nknox.k12.in.us/local.htm
Grade Span: KG-12; **Agency Type:** 1
Schools: 5
3 Primary; 0 Middle; 1 High; 1 Other Level
4 Regular; 0 Special Education; 0 Vocational; 1 Alternative
0 Magnet; 0 Charter; 2 Title I Eligible; 1 School-wide Title I
Students: 1,576 (51.1% male; 48.9% female)
Individual Education Program: 233 (14.8%);
English Language Learner: n/a; Migrant: n/a
Eligible for Free Lunch Program: 482 (30.6%)
Eligible for Reduced-Price Lunch Program: 175 (11.1%)
Teachers: 95.0 (16.6 to 1)
Librarians/Media Specialists: 2.0 (788.0 to 1)
Guidance Counselors: 2.5 (630.4 to 1)
Current Spending: ($ per student per year):
Total: $7,094; Instruction: $4,667; Support Services: $2,156
Enrollment, Drop-out Rates and Diploma Recipients by Race/Ethnicity

Category	Total	White	Black	Asian	AIAN	Hisp.
Enrollment (%)	100.0	99.4	0.2	0.1	0.0	0.3
Drop-out Rate (%)	n/a	n/a	n/a	n/a	n/a	n/a
H.S. Diplomas (#)	103	103	0	0	0	0

Vincennes Community Sch Corp

PO Box 1267 • Vincennes, IN 47591-1267
(812) 882-4844 • http://www.vcsc.k12.in.us/
Grade Span: KG-12; **Agency Type:** 1
Schools: 7
5 Primary; 1 Middle; 1 High; 0 Other Level
7 Regular; 0 Special Education; 0 Vocational; 0 Alternative
0 Magnet; 0 Charter; 5 Title I Eligible; 2 School-wide Title I
Students: 3,072 (53.0% male; 47.0% female)
Individual Education Program: 538 (17.5%);
English Language Learner: 24 (0.8%); Migrant: n/a
Eligible for Free Lunch Program: 911 (29.7%)
Eligible for Reduced-Price Lunch Program: 269 (8.8%)
Teachers: 202.9 (15.1 to 1)
Librarians/Media Specialists: 2.0 (1,536.0 to 1)
Guidance Counselors: 4.0 (768.0 to 1)
Current Spending: ($ per student per year):
Total: $7,298; Instruction: $4,499; Support Services: $2,422

Enrollment, Drop-out Rates and Diploma Recipients by Race/Ethnicity

Category	Total	White	Black	Asian	AIAN	Hisp.
Enrollment (%)	100.0	97.3	1.6	0.6	0.1	0.5
Drop-out Rate (%)	n/a	n/a	n/a	n/a	n/a	n/a
H.S. Diplomas (#)	197	192	2	2	0	1

Kosciusko County

Tippecanoe Valley School Corp

8343 S Sr 19 • Akron, IN 46910
(574) 353-7741 • http://www.tvsc.k12.in.us/
Grade Span: KG-12; **Agency Type:** 1
Schools: 5
4 Primary; 0 Middle; 1 High; 0 Other Level
5 Regular; 0 Special Education; 0 Vocational; 0 Alternative
0 Magnet; 0 Charter; 4 Title I Eligible; 0 School-wide Title I
Students: 2,130 (53.7% male; 46.3% female)
Individual Education Program: 302 (14.2%);
English Language Learner: 69 (3.2%); Migrant: n/a
Eligible for Free Lunch Program: 402 (18.9%)
Eligible for Reduced-Price Lunch Program: 165 (7.7%)
Teachers: 118.1 (18.0 to 1)
Librarians/Media Specialists: 2.0 (1,065.0 to 1)
Guidance Counselors: 5.0 (426.0 to 1)
Current Spending: ($ per student per year):
Total: $6,909; Instruction: $4,097; Support Services: $2,463

Enrollment, Drop-out Rates and Diploma Recipients by Race/Ethnicity

Category	Total	White	Black	Asian	AIAN	Hisp.
Enrollment (%)	100.0	95.9	0.1	0.0	0.2	3.8
Drop-out Rate (%)	n/a	n/a	n/a	n/a	n/a	n/a
H.S. Diplomas (#)	135	134	0	0	0	1

Warsaw Community Schools

1 Administration Dr • Warsaw, IN 46581-0288
(574) 267-3238 • http://www.warsaw.k12.in.us/
Grade Span: KG-12; **Agency Type:** 1
Schools: 15
10 Primary; 2 Middle; 2 High; 1 Other Level
13 Regular; 1 Special Education; 0 Vocational; 1 Alternative
0 Magnet; 0 Charter; 7 Title I Eligible; 0 School-wide Title I
Students: 6,419 (51.7% male; 48.3% female)
Individual Education Program: 875 (13.6%);
English Language Learner: 574 (8.9%); Migrant: n/a
Eligible for Free Lunch Program: 1,195 (18.6%)
Eligible for Reduced-Price Lunch Program: 632 (9.8%)
Teachers: 363.6 (17.7 to 1)
Librarians/Media Specialists: 5.0 (1,283.8 to 1)
Guidance Counselors: 8.8 (729.4 to 1)
Current Spending: ($ per student per year):
Total: $7,071; Instruction: $4,393; Support Services: $2,404

Enrollment, Drop-out Rates and Diploma Recipients by Race/Ethnicity

Category	Total	White	Black	Asian	AIAN	Hisp.
Enrollment (%)	100.0	88.1	1.0	1.0	0.0	9.9
Drop-out Rate (%)	n/a	n/a	n/a	n/a	n/a	n/a
H.S. Diplomas (#)	388	362	3	7	2	14

Wawasee Community School Corp

12659 N Syracuse Webster Rd • Syracuse, IN 46567-9131
(574) 457-3188 • http://www.wawasee.k12.in.us/
Grade Span: KG-12; **Agency Type:** 1
Schools: 5
3 Primary; 1 Middle; 1 High; 0 Other Level
5 Regular; 0 Special Education; 0 Vocational; 0 Alternative
0 Magnet; 0 Charter; 3 Title I Eligible; 0 School-wide Title I
Students: 3,515 (51.0% male; 49.0% female)
Individual Education Program: 360 (10.2%);
English Language Learner: 191 (5.4%); Migrant: n/a
Eligible for Free Lunch Program: 720 (20.5%)
Eligible for Reduced-Price Lunch Program: 222 (6.3%)
Teachers: 195.3 (18.0 to 1)
Librarians/Media Specialists: 2.0 (1,757.5 to 1)
Guidance Counselors: 7.7 (456.5 to 1)
Current Spending: ($ per student per year):
Total: $7,152; Instruction: $4,374; Support Services: $2,491

Enrollment, Drop-out Rates and Diploma Recipients by Race/Ethnicity

Category	Total	White	Black	Asian	AIAN	Hisp.
Enrollment (%)	100.0	93.9	0.2	0.4	0.2	5.4
Drop-out Rate (%)	n/a	n/a	n/a	n/a	n/a	n/a
H.S. Diplomas (#)	206	200	0	1	0	5

Whitko Community School Corp

432 S First St • Pierceton, IN 46562-0114
Mailing Address: PO Box 114 • Pierceton, IN 46562-0114
(574) 594-2658 • http://www.whitko.k12.in.us/
Grade Span: PK-12; **Agency Type:** 1
Schools: 4
2 Primary; 1 Middle; 1 High; 0 Other Level
4 Regular; 0 Special Education; 0 Vocational; 0 Alternative
0 Magnet; 0 Charter; 2 Title I Eligible; 0 School-wide Title I
Students: 2,037 (51.6% male; 48.4% female)
Individual Education Program: 282 (13.8%);
English Language Learner: 24 (1.2%); Migrant: n/a
Eligible for Free Lunch Program: 345 (16.9%)
Eligible for Reduced-Price Lunch Program: 212 (10.4%)
Teachers: 115.5 (17.6 to 1)
Librarians/Media Specialists: 1.0 (2,037.0 to 1)
Guidance Counselors: 6.0 (339.5 to 1)
Current Spending: ($ per student per year):
Total: $7,115; Instruction: $4,221; Support Services: $2,580

Enrollment, Drop-out Rates and Diploma Recipients by Race/Ethnicity

Category	Total	White	Black	Asian	AIAN	Hisp.
Enrollment (%)	100.0	97.8	0.2	0.2	0.1	1.6
Drop-out Rate (%)	n/a	n/a	n/a	n/a	n/a	n/a
H.S. Diplomas (#)	91	91	0	0	0	0

La Porte County

Laporte Community School Corp

1921 'a' St • Laporte, IN 46350-6697
(219) 362-7056
Grade Span: PK-12; **Agency Type:** 1
Schools: 12
9 Primary; 2 Middle; 1 High; 0 Other Level
12 Regular; 0 Special Education; 0 Vocational; 0 Alternative
0 Magnet; 0 Charter; 7 Title I Eligible; 0 School-wide Title I
Students: 6,229 (51.4% male; 48.6% female)
Individual Education Program: 828 (13.3%);
English Language Learner: 271 (4.4%); Migrant: n/a
Eligible for Free Lunch Program: 1,408 (22.6%)
Eligible for Reduced-Price Lunch Program: 438 (7.0%)
Teachers: 388.8 (16.0 to 1)
Librarians/Media Specialists: 5.0 (1,245.8 to 1)
Guidance Counselors: 12.5 (498.3 to 1)
Current Spending: ($ per student per year):
Total: $6,377; Instruction: $3,832; Support Services: $2,218

Enrollment, Drop-out Rates and Diploma Recipients by Race/Ethnicity

Category	Total	White	Black	Asian	AIAN	Hisp.
Enrollment (%)	100.0	92.8	1.8	0.4	0.2	4.7
Drop-out Rate (%)	n/a	n/a	n/a	n/a	n/a	n/a
H.S. Diplomas (#)	401	385	5	1	2	8

Michigan City Area Schools

408 S Carroll Ave • Michigan City, IN 46360-5345
(219) 873-2000 • http://www.mcas.k12.in.us/homepage/
Grade Span: PK-12; **Agency Type:** 1
Schools: 16
10 Primary; 3 Middle; 2 High; 1 Other Level
14 Regular; 0 Special Education; 1 Vocational; 1 Alternative
0 Magnet; 0 Charter; 11 Title I Eligible; 4 School-wide Title I
Students: 6,846 (52.1% male; 47.9% female)
Individual Education Program: 1,321 (19.3%);
English Language Learner: 128 (1.9%); Migrant: n/a
Eligible for Free Lunch Program: 2,808 (41.0%)
Eligible for Reduced-Price Lunch Program: 607 (8.9%)
Teachers: 452.7 (15.1 to 1)
Librarians/Media Specialists: 6.0 (1,141.0 to 1)
Guidance Counselors: 21.0 (326.0 to 1)
Current Spending: ($ per student per year):
Total: $8,348; Instruction: $5,050; Support Services: $2,968

Enrollment, Drop-out Rates and Diploma Recipients by Race/Ethnicity

Category	Total	White	Black	Asian	AIAN	Hisp.
Enrollment (%)	100.0	64.1	31.2	0.8	0.7	3.2
Drop-out Rate (%)	n/a	n/a	n/a	n/a	n/a	n/a
H.S. Diplomas (#)	350	266	67	8	0	9

New Prairie United School Corp

511 W Michigan St • New Carlisle, IN 46552-9505
Mailing Address: PO Box 831 • New Carlisle, IN 46552-9505
(574) 654-7273
Grade Span: KG-12; **Agency Type:** 1
Schools: 5
3 Primary; 1 Middle; 1 High; 0 Other Level
5 Regular; 0 Special Education; 0 Vocational; 0 Alternative
0 Magnet; 0 Charter; 3 Title I Eligible; 0 School-wide Title I
Students: 2,592 (51.4% male; 48.6% female)

Individual Education Program: 324 (12.5%);
English Language Learner: 51 (2.0%); Migrant: n/a
Eligible for Free Lunch Program: 300 (11.6%)
Eligible for Reduced-Price Lunch Program: 121 (4.7%)
Teachers: 139.0 (18.6 to 1)
Librarians/Media Specialists: 1.0 (2,592.0 to 1)
Guidance Counselors: 3.0 (864.0 to 1)
Current Spending: ($ per student per year):
Total: $5,681; Instruction: $3,441; Support Services: $2,137
Enrollment, Drop-out Rates and Diploma Recipients by Race/Ethnicity

Category	Total	White	Black	Asian	AIAN	Hisp.
Enrollment (%)	100.0	94.6	0.3	0.2	2.8	2.2
Drop-out Rate (%)	n/a	n/a	n/a	n/a	n/a	n/a
H.S. Diplomas (#)	150	149	0	0	0	1

Lagrange County

Lakeland School Corporation
200 S Cherry St • Lagrange, IN 46761-2099
(260) 463-7101 • http://www.lakeland.k12.in.us/
Grade Span: KG-12; **Agency Type:** 1
Schools: 5
3 Primary; 1 Middle; 1 High; 0 Other Level
5 Regular; 0 Special Education; 0 Vocational; 0 Alternative
0 Magnet; 0 Charter; 4 Title I Eligible; 0 School-wide Title I
Students: 2,295 (53.0% male; 47.0% female)
Individual Education Program: 332 (14.5%);
English Language Learner: 238 (10.4%); Migrant: n/a
Eligible for Free Lunch Program: 484 (21.1%)
Eligible for Reduced-Price Lunch Program: 230 (10.0%)
Teachers: 137.5 (16.7 to 1)
Librarians/Media Specialists: 1.5 (1,530.0 to 1)
Guidance Counselors: 4.0 (573.8 to 1)
Current Spending: ($ per student per year):
Total: $6,660; Instruction: $4,156; Support Services: $2,166
Enrollment, Drop-out Rates and Diploma Recipients by Race/Ethnicity

Category	Total	White	Black	Asian	AIAN	Hisp.
Enrollment (%)	100.0	89.5	0.3	0.5	0.3	9.5
Drop-out Rate (%)	n/a	n/a	n/a	n/a	n/a	n/a
H.S. Diplomas (#)	103	94	0	0	2	7

Prairie Heights Com Sch Corp
0305 S 1150 E • Lagrange, IN 46761-9653
(260) 351-3214
Grade Span: KG-12; **Agency Type:** 1
Schools: 4
2 Primary; 1 Middle; 1 High; 0 Other Level
4 Regular; 0 Special Education; 0 Vocational; 0 Alternative
0 Magnet; 0 Charter; 3 Title I Eligible; 0 School-wide Title I
Students: 1,789 (48.4% male; 51.6% female)
Individual Education Program: 246 (13.8%);
English Language Learner: 71 (4.0%); Migrant: n/a
Eligible for Free Lunch Program: 289 (16.2%)
Eligible for Reduced-Price Lunch Program: 146 (8.2%)
Teachers: 102.4 (17.5 to 1)
Librarians/Media Specialists: 2.0 (894.5 to 1)
Guidance Counselors: 4.7 (380.6 to 1)
Current Spending: ($ per student per year):
Total: $6,902; Instruction: $4,150; Support Services: $2,446
Enrollment, Drop-out Rates and Diploma Recipients by Race/Ethnicity

Category	Total	White	Black	Asian	AIAN	Hisp.
Enrollment (%)	100.0	97.4	0.1	0.2	0.2	2.1
Drop-out Rate (%)	n/a	n/a	n/a	n/a	n/a	n/a
H.S. Diplomas (#)	110	110	0	0	0	0

Westview School Corporation
1545 S 600 W • Topeka, IN 46571-9741
(260) 768-4404 • http://www.westview.k12.in.us/
Grade Span: KG-12; **Agency Type:** 1
Schools: 5
3 Primary; 1 Middle; 1 High; 0 Other Level
5 Regular; 0 Special Education; 0 Vocational; 0 Alternative
0 Magnet; 0 Charter; 4 Title I Eligible; 0 School-wide Title I
Students: 2,217 (51.8% male; 48.2% female)
Individual Education Program: 238 (10.7%);
English Language Learner: 925 (41.7%); Migrant: n/a
Eligible for Free Lunch Program: 190 (8.6%)
Eligible for Reduced-Price Lunch Program: 117 (5.3%)
Teachers: 134.9 (16.4 to 1)
Librarians/Media Specialists: 2.0 (1,108.5 to 1)
Guidance Counselors: 2.0 (1,108.5 to 1)
Current Spending: ($ per student per year):
Total: $7,261; Instruction: $4,464; Support Services: $2,543
Enrollment, Drop-out Rates and Diploma Recipients by Race/Ethnicity

Category	Total	White	Black	Asian	AIAN	Hisp.
Enrollment (%)	100.0	98.9	0.1	0.1	0.0	0.8
Drop-out Rate (%)	n/a	n/a	n/a	n/a	n/a	n/a
H.S. Diplomas (#)	91	90	1	0	0	0

Lake County

Crown Point Community Sch Corp
200 E N St • Crown Point, IN 46307-4078
(219) 663-3371 • http://www.cps.k12.in.us/index.html
Grade Span: PK-12; **Agency Type:** 1
Schools: 8
6 Primary; 1 Middle; 1 High; 0 Other Level
8 Regular; 0 Special Education; 0 Vocational; 0 Alternative
0 Magnet; 0 Charter; 4 Title I Eligible; 0 School-wide Title I
Students: 5,796 (50.7% male; 49.3% female)
Individual Education Program: 587 (10.1%);
English Language Learner: 200 (3.5%); Migrant: n/a
Eligible for Free Lunch Program: 520 (9.0%)
Eligible for Reduced-Price Lunch Program: 165 (2.8%)
Teachers: 268.7 (21.6 to 1)
Librarians/Media Specialists: 3.0 (1,932.0 to 1)
Guidance Counselors: 6.0 (966.0 to 1)
Current Spending: ($ per student per year):
Total: $6,050; Instruction: $3,612; Support Services: $2,140
Enrollment, Drop-out Rates and Diploma Recipients by Race/Ethnicity

Category	Total	White	Black	Asian	AIAN	Hisp.
Enrollment (%)	100.0	95.0	0.4	0.8	0.3	3.4
Drop-out Rate (%)	n/a	n/a	n/a	n/a	n/a	n/a
H.S. Diplomas (#)	427	412	2	2	4	7

Gary Community School Corp
620 E 10th Pl • Gary, IN 46402-2731
(219) 881-5401 • http://www.garycsc.k12.in.us/
Grade Span: PK-12; **Agency Type:** 1
Schools: 38
22 Primary; 7 Middle; 6 High; 3 Other Level
34 Regular; 1 Special Education; 1 Vocational; 2 Alternative
0 Magnet; 0 Charter; 31 Title I Eligible; 27 School-wide Title I
Students: 19,035 (50.8% male; 49.2% female)
Individual Education Program: 2,636 (13.8%);
English Language Learner: 129 (0.7%); Migrant: n/a
Eligible for Free Lunch Program: 10,762 (56.5%)
Eligible for Reduced-Price Lunch Program: 432 (2.3%)
Teachers: 1,016.8 (18.7 to 1)
Librarians/Media Specialists: 35.0 (543.9 to 1)
Guidance Counselors: 60.5 (314.6 to 1)
Current Spending: ($ per student per year):
Total: $9,349; Instruction: $4,929; Support Services: $4,178
Enrollment, Drop-out Rates and Diploma Recipients by Race/Ethnicity

Category	Total	White	Black	Asian	AIAN	Hisp.
Enrollment (%)	100.0	0.7	97.7	0.2	0.1	1.2
Drop-out Rate (%)	n/a	n/a	n/a	n/a	n/a	n/a
H.S. Diplomas (#)	706	0	695	1	0	10

Griffith Public Schools
132 N Broad St • Griffith, IN 46319-2289
(219) 924-4250 • http://165.138.244.1/
Grade Span: KG-12; **Agency Type:** 1
Schools: 6
4 Primary; 1 Middle; 1 High; 0 Other Level
6 Regular; 0 Special Education; 0 Vocational; 0 Alternative
0 Magnet; 0 Charter; 2 Title I Eligible; 0 School-wide Title I
Students: 2,703 (50.5% male; 49.5% female)
Individual Education Program: 341 (12.6%);
English Language Learner: 146 (5.4%); Migrant: n/a
Eligible for Free Lunch Program: 304 (11.2%)
Eligible for Reduced-Price Lunch Program: 133 (4.9%)
Teachers: 136.0 (19.9 to 1)
Librarians/Media Specialists: 1.0 (2,703.0 to 1)
Guidance Counselors: 4.0 (675.8 to 1)
Current Spending: ($ per student per year):
Total: $6,251; Instruction: $3,827; Support Services: $2,210
Enrollment, Drop-out Rates and Diploma Recipients by Race/Ethnicity

Category	Total	White	Black	Asian	AIAN	Hisp.
Enrollment (%)	100.0	77.0	12.9	0.0	0.4	9.7
Drop-out Rate (%)	n/a	n/a	n/a	n/a	n/a	n/a
H.S. Diplomas (#)	188	159	6	0	2	21

Hanover Community School Corp

9520 W 133rd Ave • Cedar Lake, IN 46303-0645
Mailing Address: PO Box 645 • Cedar Lake, IN 46303-0645
(219) 374-3500 • http://www.hanover.k12.in.us/
Grade Span: KG-12; **Agency Type:** 1
Schools: 3
2 Primary; 0 Middle; 1 High; 0 Other Level
3 Regular; 0 Special Education; 0 Vocational; 0 Alternative
0 Magnet; 0 Charter; 1 Title I Eligible; 0 School-wide Title I
Students: 1,567 (51.9% male; 48.1% female)
Individual Education Program: 206 (13.1%);
English Language Learner: 26 (1.7%); Migrant: n/a
Eligible for Free Lunch Program: 209 (13.3%)
Eligible for Reduced-Price Lunch Program: 115 (7.3%)
Teachers: 77.1 (20.3 to 1)
Librarians/Media Specialists: 1.0 (1,567.0 to 1)
Guidance Counselors: 2.0 (783.5 to 1)
Current Spending: ($ per student per year):
Total: $5,889; Instruction: $3,574; Support Services: $2,082
Enrollment, Drop-out Rates and Diploma Recipients by Race/Ethnicity

Category	Total	White	Black	Asian	AIAN	Hisp.
Enrollment (%)	100.0	96.0	0.1	0.3	0.2	3.4
Drop-out Rate (%)	n/a	n/a	n/a	n/a	n/a	n/a
H.S. Diplomas (#)	102	99	0	0	0	3

Lake Central School Corp

8260 Wicker Ave • Saint John, IN 46373-9711
(219) 365-8507 • http://www.lakecentral.k12.in.us/
Grade Span: PK-12; **Agency Type:** 1
Schools: 10
6 Primary; 2 Middle; 1 High; 1 Other Level
9 Regular; 1 Special Education; 0 Vocational; 0 Alternative
0 Magnet; 0 Charter; 3 Title I Eligible; 0 School-wide Title I
Students: 8,461 (52.8% male; 47.2% female)
Individual Education Program: 1,420 (16.8%);
English Language Learner: 534 (6.3%); Migrant: n/a
Eligible for Free Lunch Program: 535 (6.3%)
Eligible for Reduced-Price Lunch Program: 273 (3.2%)
Teachers: 450.4 (18.8 to 1)
Librarians/Media Specialists: 3.5 (2,417.4 to 1)
Guidance Counselors: 8.5 (995.4 to 1)
Current Spending: ($ per student per year):
Total: $6,463; Instruction: $3,967; Support Services: $2,216
Enrollment, Drop-out Rates and Diploma Recipients by Race/Ethnicity

Category	Total	White	Black	Asian	AIAN	Hisp.
Enrollment (%)	100.0	89.9	1.4	1.8	0.4	6.4
Drop-out Rate (%)	n/a	n/a	n/a	n/a	n/a	n/a
H.S. Diplomas (#)	452	418	4	5	2	23

Lake Ridge Schools

6111 W Ridge Rd • Gary, IN 46408-1797
(219) 838-1819 • http://lakeridgeschools.homestead.com/
Grade Span: KG-12; **Agency Type:** 1
Schools: 6
3 Primary; 1 Middle; 1 High; 1 Other Level
5 Regular; 0 Special Education; 0 Vocational; 1 Alternative
0 Magnet; 0 Charter; 3 Title I Eligible; 0 School-wide Title I
Students: 2,399 (51.1% male; 48.9% female)
Individual Education Program: 357 (14.9%);
English Language Learner: 32 (1.3%); Migrant: n/a
Eligible for Free Lunch Program: 1,180 (49.2%)
Eligible for Reduced-Price Lunch Program: 224 (9.3%)
Teachers: 126.0 (19.0 to 1)
Librarians/Media Specialists: 1.0 (2,399.0 to 1)
Guidance Counselors: 4.7 (510.4 to 1)
Current Spending: ($ per student per year):
Total: $9,172; Instruction: $5,337; Support Services: $3,380
Enrollment, Drop-out Rates and Diploma Recipients by Race/Ethnicity

Category	Total	White	Black	Asian	AIAN	Hisp.
Enrollment (%)	100.0	67.5	18.5	0.3	1.0	12.7
Drop-out Rate (%)	n/a	n/a	n/a	n/a	n/a	n/a
H.S. Diplomas (#)	133	89	31	0	0	13

Merrillville Community School

6701 Delaware St • Merrillville, IN 46410-3586
(219) 650-5300 • http://www.mvsc.k12.in.us/index.htm
Grade Span: KG-12; **Agency Type:** 1
Schools: 8
5 Primary; 2 Middle; 1 High; 0 Other Level
8 Regular; 0 Special Education; 0 Vocational; 0 Alternative
0 Magnet; 0 Charter; 6 Title I Eligible; 0 School-wide Title I
Students: 6,360 (51.1% male; 48.9% female)
Individual Education Program: 658 (10.3%);
English Language Learner: 400 (6.3%); Migrant: n/a
Eligible for Free Lunch Program: 1,036 (16.3%)
Eligible for Reduced-Price Lunch Program: 485 (7.6%)
Teachers: 314.6 (20.2 to 1)
Librarians/Media Specialists: 2.0 (3,180.0 to 1)
Guidance Counselors: 8.0 (795.0 to 1)
Current Spending: ($ per student per year):
Total: $6,279; Instruction: $3,644; Support Services: $2,374
Enrollment, Drop-out Rates and Diploma Recipients by Race/Ethnicity

Category	Total	White	Black	Asian	AIAN	Hisp.
Enrollment (%)	100.0	51.6	36.6	1.4	0.3	10.1
Drop-out Rate (%)	n/a	n/a	n/a	n/a	n/a	n/a
H.S. Diplomas (#)	468	264	141	8	0	55

School City of East Chicago

210 E Columbus Dr • East Chicago, IN 46312-2799
(219) 391-4100 • http://www.ecps.org/
Grade Span: PK-12; **Agency Type:** 1
Schools: 10
7 Primary; 2 Middle; 1 High; 0 Other Level
10 Regular; 0 Special Education; 0 Vocational; 0 Alternative
0 Magnet; 0 Charter; 7 Title I Eligible; 7 School-wide Title I
Students: 6,410 (51.3% male; 48.7% female)
Individual Education Program: 848 (13.2%);
English Language Learner: 1,396 (21.8%); Migrant: n/a
Eligible for Free Lunch Program: 4,898 (76.4%)
Eligible for Reduced-Price Lunch Program: 480 (7.5%)
Teachers: 365.0 (17.6 to 1)
Librarians/Media Specialists: 4.0 (1,602.5 to 1)
Guidance Counselors: 7.0 (915.7 to 1)
Current Spending: ($ per student per year):
Total: $9,682; Instruction: $5,229; Support Services: $4,023
Enrollment, Drop-out Rates and Diploma Recipients by Race/Ethnicity

Category	Total	White	Black	Asian	AIAN	Hisp.
Enrollment (%)	100.0	3.4	45.4	0.4	0.0	50.8
Drop-out Rate (%)	n/a	n/a	n/a	n/a	n/a	n/a
H.S. Diplomas (#)	256	11	112	2	0	131

School City of Hammond

41 Williams St • Hammond, IN 46320-1948
(219) 933-2400 • http://hammond.k12.in.us/
Grade Span: PK-12; **Agency Type:** 1
Schools: 23
16 Primary; 2 Middle; 2 High; 3 Other Level
22 Regular; 0 Special Education; 1 Vocational; 0 Alternative
0 Magnet; 0 Charter; 10 Title I Eligible; 8 School-wide Title I
Students: 13,251 (52.2% male; 47.8% female)
Individual Education Program: 2,007 (15.1%);
English Language Learner: 2,811 (21.2%); Migrant: n/a
Eligible for Free Lunch Program: 7,156 (54.0%)
Eligible for Reduced-Price Lunch Program: 1,538 (11.6%)
Teachers: 754.2 (17.6 to 1)
Librarians/Media Specialists: 17.7 (748.6 to 1)
Guidance Counselors: 16.7 (793.5 to 1)
Current Spending: ($ per student per year):
Total: $8,391; Instruction: $4,829; Support Services: $3,246
Enrollment, Drop-out Rates and Diploma Recipients by Race/Ethnicity

Category	Total	White	Black	Asian	AIAN	Hisp.
Enrollment (%)	100.0	43.8	25.6	0.4	0.3	29.9
Drop-out Rate (%)	n/a	n/a	n/a	n/a	n/a	n/a
H.S. Diplomas (#)	545	314	102	4	0	125

School City of Hobart

32 E 7th St • Hobart, IN 46342-5197
(219) 942-8885 • http://www.hobart.k12.in.us/
Grade Span: KG-12; **Agency Type:** 1
Schools: 6
4 Primary; 1 Middle; 1 High; 0 Other Level
6 Regular; 0 Special Education; 0 Vocational; 0 Alternative
0 Magnet; 0 Charter; 4 Title I Eligible; 0 School-wide Title I
Students: 3,430 (51.5% male; 48.5% female)
Individual Education Program: 366 (10.7%);
English Language Learner: 301 (8.8%); Migrant: n/a
Eligible for Free Lunch Program: 676 (19.7%)
Eligible for Reduced-Price Lunch Program: 218 (6.4%)
Teachers: 181.0 (19.0 to 1)
Librarians/Media Specialists: 2.0 (1,715.0 to 1)
Guidance Counselors: 4.0 (857.5 to 1)
Current Spending: ($ per student per year):
Total: $6,069; Instruction: $3,412; Support Services: $2,402
Enrollment, Drop-out Rates and Diploma Recipients by Race/Ethnicity

Category	Total	White	Black	Asian	AIAN	Hisp.
Enrollment (%)	100.0	84.3	1.9	0.7	0.8	12.4
Drop-out Rate (%)	n/a	n/a	n/a	n/a	n/a	n/a
H.S. Diplomas (#)	241	213	3	0	1	24

School Town of Highland

9145 Kennedy Ave • Highland, IN 46322-2796
(219) 922-5615 • http://stoh.highland.k12.in.us/
Grade Span: KG-12; **Agency Type:** 1
Schools: 6
4 Primary; 1 Middle; 1 High; 0 Other Level
6 Regular; 0 Special Education; 0 Vocational; 0 Alternative
0 Magnet; 0 Charter; 4 Title I Eligible; 0 School-wide Title I
Students: 3,333 (51.6% male; 48.4% female)
Individual Education Program: 408 (12.2%);
English Language Learner: 170 (5.1%); Migrant: n/a
Eligible for Free Lunch Program: 220 (6.6%)
Eligible for Reduced-Price Lunch Program: 114 (3.4%)
Teachers: 151.5 (22.0 to 1)
Librarians/Media Specialists: 2.0 (1,666.5 to 1)
Guidance Counselors: 7.0 (476.1 to 1)
Current Spending: ($ per student per year):
Total: $6,799; Instruction: $3,710; Support Services: $2,732
Enrollment, Drop-out Rates and Diploma Recipients by Race/Ethnicity

Category	Total	White	Black	Asian	AIAN	Hisp.
Enrollment (%)	100.0	90.7	1.5	1.8	0.1	6.0
Drop-out Rate (%)	n/a	n/a	n/a	n/a	n/a	n/a
H.S. Diplomas (#)	251	248	0	0	0	3

School Town of Munster

8616 Columbia Ave • Munster, IN 46321-2597
(219) 836-9111 • http://www.munster.k12.in.us/
Grade Span: KG-12; **Agency Type:** 1
Schools: 5
3 Primary; 1 Middle; 1 High; 0 Other Level
5 Regular; 0 Special Education; 0 Vocational; 0 Alternative
0 Magnet; 0 Charter; 0 Title I Eligible; 0 School-wide Title I
Students: 3,799 (52.1% male; 47.9% female)
Individual Education Program: 639 (16.8%);
English Language Learner: 413 (10.9%); Migrant: n/a
Eligible for Free Lunch Program: 145 (3.8%)
Eligible for Reduced-Price Lunch Program: 123 (3.2%)
Teachers: 216.0 (17.6 to 1)
Librarians/Media Specialists: 4.0 (949.8 to 1)
Guidance Counselors: 6.0 (633.2 to 1)
Current Spending: ($ per student per year):
Total: $7,041; Instruction: $4,139; Support Services: $2,643
Enrollment, Drop-out Rates and Diploma Recipients by Race/Ethnicity

Category	Total	White	Black	Asian	AIAN	Hisp.
Enrollment (%)	100.0	86.9	1.8	6.2	0.1	5.0
Drop-out Rate (%)	n/a	n/a	n/a	n/a	n/a	n/a
H.S. Diplomas (#)	281	250	1	14	1	15

Tri-Creek School Corp

195 W Oakley Ave • Lowell, IN 46356-2293
(219) 696-6661 • http://www.tricreek.k12.in.us/
Grade Span: KG-12; **Agency Type:** 1
Schools: 5
3 Primary; 1 Middle; 1 High; 0 Other Level
5 Regular; 0 Special Education; 0 Vocational; 0 Alternative
0 Magnet; 0 Charter; 3 Title I Eligible; 0 School-wide Title I
Students: 3,367 (51.8% male; 48.2% female)
Individual Education Program: 454 (13.5%);
English Language Learner: 40 (1.2%); Migrant: n/a
Eligible for Free Lunch Program: 394 (11.7%)
Eligible for Reduced-Price Lunch Program: 133 (4.0%)
Teachers: 148.3 (22.7 to 1)
Librarians/Media Specialists: 0.0 (0.0 to 1)
Guidance Counselors: 4.0 (841.8 to 1)
Current Spending: ($ per student per year):
Total: $6,217; Instruction: $3,552; Support Services: $2,301
Enrollment, Drop-out Rates and Diploma Recipients by Race/Ethnicity

Category	Total	White	Black	Asian	AIAN	Hisp.
Enrollment (%)	100.0	97.3	0.0	0.1	0.7	1.9
Drop-out Rate (%)	n/a	n/a	n/a	n/a	n/a	n/a
H.S. Diplomas (#)	224	212	1	1	3	7

Lawrence County

Mitchell Community Schools

441 N 8th St • Mitchell, IN 47446-1020
(812) 849-4481 • http://www.mitchell.k12.in.us/
Grade Span: PK-12; **Agency Type:** 1
Schools: 4
2 Primary; 1 Middle; 1 High; 0 Other Level
4 Regular; 0 Special Education; 0 Vocational; 0 Alternative
0 Magnet; 0 Charter; 2 Title I Eligible; 0 School-wide Title I
Students: 2,008 (50.8% male; 49.2% female)
Individual Education Program: 346 (17.2%);
English Language Learner: 17 (0.8%); Migrant: n/a
Eligible for Free Lunch Program: 616 (30.7%)
Eligible for Reduced-Price Lunch Program: 133 (6.6%)
Teachers: 110.8 (18.1 to 1)
Librarians/Media Specialists: 3.0 (669.3 to 1)
Guidance Counselors: 4.0 (502.0 to 1)
Current Spending: ($ per student per year):
Total: $6,103; Instruction: $3,717; Support Services: $2,136
Enrollment, Drop-out Rates and Diploma Recipients by Race/Ethnicity

Category	Total	White	Black	Asian	AIAN	Hisp.
Enrollment (%)	100.0	98.9	0.4	0.1	0.0	0.5
Drop-out Rate (%)	n/a	n/a	n/a	n/a	n/a	n/a
H.S. Diplomas (#)	118	118	0	0	0	0

North Lawrence Com Schools

460 'W' St • Bedford, IN 47421-0729
Mailing Address: PO Box 729 • Bedford, IN 47421-0729
(812) 279-3521 • http://www.nlcs.k12.in.us/
Grade Span: PK-12; **Agency Type:** 1
Schools: 16
10 Primary; 3 Middle; 1 High; 2 Other Level
14 Regular; 1 Special Education; 1 Vocational; 0 Alternative
0 Magnet; 0 Charter; 8 Title I Eligible; 0 School-wide Title I
Students: 5,323 (53.0% male; 47.0% female)
Individual Education Program: 939 (17.6%);
English Language Learner: 52 (1.0%); Migrant: n/a
Eligible for Free Lunch Program: 1,283 (24.1%)
Eligible for Reduced-Price Lunch Program: 439 (8.2%)
Teachers: 326.9 (16.3 to 1)
Librarians/Media Specialists: 2.0 (2,661.5 to 1)
Guidance Counselors: 8.0 (665.4 to 1)
Current Spending: ($ per student per year):
Total: $7,068; Instruction: $4,286; Support Services: $2,505
Enrollment, Drop-out Rates and Diploma Recipients by Race/Ethnicity

Category	Total	White	Black	Asian	AIAN	Hisp.
Enrollment (%)	100.0	97.4	0.8	0.6	0.3	0.8
Drop-out Rate (%)	n/a	n/a	n/a	n/a	n/a	n/a
H.S. Diplomas (#)	352	332	2	8	4	6

Madison County

Alexandria Com School Corp

202 E Washington St • Alexandria, IN 46001-2005
(765) 724-4496 • http://www.alex.k12.in.us/centraloffice/centraloffice.html
Grade Span: PK-12; **Agency Type:** 1
Schools: 5
3 Primary; 1 Middle; 1 High; 0 Other Level
5 Regular; 0 Special Education; 0 Vocational; 0 Alternative
0 Magnet; 0 Charter; 4 Title I Eligible; 0 School-wide Title I
Students: 1,779 (53.0% male; 47.0% female)
Individual Education Program: 248 (13.9%);
English Language Learner: 70 (3.9%); Migrant: n/a
Eligible for Free Lunch Program: 420 (23.6%)
Eligible for Reduced-Price Lunch Program: 134 (7.5%)
Teachers: 106.8 (16.7 to 1)
Librarians/Media Specialists: 2.0 (889.5 to 1)
Guidance Counselors: 1.0 (1,779.0 to 1)
Current Spending: ($ per student per year):
Total: $5,935; Instruction: $3,797; Support Services: $1,895
Enrollment, Drop-out Rates and Diploma Recipients by Race/Ethnicity

Category	Total	White	Black	Asian	AIAN	Hisp.
Enrollment (%)	100.0	95.6	0.3	0.2	0.1	3.9
Drop-out Rate (%)	n/a	n/a	n/a	n/a	n/a	n/a
H.S. Diplomas (#)	119	117	2	0	0	0

Anderson Community School Corp

1229 Lincoln St • Anderson, IN 46016-1479
(765) 641-2028 • http://www.acsc.net/
Grade Span: PK-12; **Agency Type:** 1
Schools: 22
15 Primary; 3 Middle; 3 High; 1 Other Level
19 Regular; 1 Special Education; 1 Vocational; 1 Alternative
0 Magnet; 0 Charter; 10 Title I Eligible; 3 School-wide Title I
Students: 10,316 (51.2% male; 48.8% female)
Individual Education Program: 1,993 (19.3%);
English Language Learner: 165 (1.6%); Migrant: n/a
Eligible for Free Lunch Program: 4,308 (41.8%)
Eligible for Reduced-Price Lunch Program: 812 (7.9%)
Teachers: 681.3 (15.1 to 1)
Librarians/Media Specialists: 13.0 (793.5 to 1)
Guidance Counselors: 13.5 (764.1 to 1)
Current Spending: ($ per student per year):
Total: $8,764; Instruction: $5,936; Support Services: $2,421

Enrollment, Drop-out Rates and Diploma Recipients by Race/Ethnicity

Category	Total	White	Black	Asian	AIAN	Hisp.
Enrollment (%)	100.0	76.4	21.2	0.4	0.0	2.0
Drop-out Rate (%)	n/a	n/a	n/a	n/a	n/a	n/a
H.S. Diplomas (#)	504	421	63	7	2	11

Elwood Community School Corp

1306 N Anderson St • Elwood, IN 46036-9460
(765) 552-9861 • http://www.elwood.k12.in.us/
Grade Span: PK-12; **Agency Type:** 1
Schools: 6
3 Primary; 1 Middle; 1 High; 1 Other Level
5 Regular; 0 Special Education; 1 Vocational; 0 Alternative
0 Magnet; 0 Charter; 4 Title I Eligible; 1 School-wide Title I
Students: 1,965 (51.2% male; 48.8% female)
Individual Education Program: 369 (18.8%);
English Language Learner: 43 (2.2%); Migrant: n/a
Eligible for Free Lunch Program: 651 (33.1%)
Eligible for Reduced-Price Lunch Program: 173 (8.8%)
Teachers: 130.5 (15.1 to 1)
Librarians/Media Specialists: 3.0 (655.0 to 1)
Guidance Counselors: 3.0 (655.0 to 1)
Current Spending: ($ per student per year):
Total: $7,258; Instruction: $4,655; Support Services: $2,261
Enrollment, Drop-out Rates and Diploma Recipients by Race/Ethnicity

Category	Total	White	Black	Asian	AIAN	Hisp.
Enrollment (%)	100.0	96.9	0.1	0.5	0.2	2.4
Drop-out Rate (%)	n/a	n/a	n/a	n/a	n/a	n/a
H.S. Diplomas (#)	119	115	0	2	0	2

Frankton-Lapel Community Schs

7916 W 300 N • Anderson, IN 46011-9129
(765) 734-1261 • http://www.flcs.k12.in.us/
Grade Span: PK-12; **Agency Type:** 1
Schools: 4
2 Primary; 0 Middle; 2 High; 0 Other Level
4 Regular; 0 Special Education; 0 Vocational; 0 Alternative
0 Magnet; 0 Charter; 1 Title I Eligible; 0 School-wide Title I
Students: 2,432 (51.4% male; 48.6% female)
Individual Education Program: 388 (16.0%);
English Language Learner: 12 (0.5%); Migrant: n/a
Eligible for Free Lunch Program: 332 (13.7%)
Eligible for Reduced-Price Lunch Program: 168 (6.9%)
Teachers: 124.1 (19.6 to 1)
Librarians/Media Specialists: 2.0 (1,216.0 to 1)
Guidance Counselors: 2.5 (972.8 to 1)
Current Spending: ($ per student per year):
Total: $6,475; Instruction: $3,853; Support Services: $2,341
Enrollment, Drop-out Rates and Diploma Recipients by Race/Ethnicity

Category	Total	White	Black	Asian	AIAN	Hisp.
Enrollment (%)	100.0	98.9	0.3	0.3	0.0	0.4
Drop-out Rate (%)	n/a	n/a	n/a	n/a	n/a	n/a
H.S. Diplomas (#)	137	137	0	0	0	0

South Madison Com Sch Corp

201 SE St • Pendleton, IN 46064-1211
(765) 778-2152 • http://www.smadison.k12.in.us/
Grade Span: PK-12; **Agency Type:** 1
Schools: 5
3 Primary; 1 Middle; 1 High; 0 Other Level
5 Regular; 0 Special Education; 0 Vocational; 0 Alternative
0 Magnet; 0 Charter; 3 Title I Eligible; 0 School-wide Title I
Students: 3,478 (50.7% male; 49.3% female)
Individual Education Program: 796 (22.9%);
English Language Learner: 9 (0.3%); Migrant: n/a
Eligible for Free Lunch Program: 318 (9.1%)
Eligible for Reduced-Price Lunch Program: 106 (3.0%)
Teachers: 175.9 (19.8 to 1)
Librarians/Media Specialists: 5.0 (695.6 to 1)
Guidance Counselors: 5.0 (695.6 to 1)
Current Spending: ($ per student per year):
Total: $6,291; Instruction: $3,761; Support Services: $2,221
Enrollment, Drop-out Rates and Diploma Recipients by Race/Ethnicity

Category	Total	White	Black	Asian	AIAN	Hisp.
Enrollment (%)	100.0	99.1	0.2	0.4	0.1	0.2
Drop-out Rate (%)	n/a	n/a	n/a	n/a	n/a	n/a
H.S. Diplomas (#)	232	229	0	1	1	1

Marion County

Beech Grove City Schools

5334 Hornet Ave • Beech Grove, IN 46107-2306
(317) 788-4481 • http://www.bgcs.k12.in.us/01default.html
Grade Span: PK-12; **Agency Type:** 1
Schools: 5
2 Primary; 2 Middle; 1 High; 0 Other Level
5 Regular; 0 Special Education; 0 Vocational; 0 Alternative
0 Magnet; 0 Charter; 3 Title I Eligible; 0 School-wide Title I
Students: 2,445 (52.0% male; 48.0% female)
Individual Education Program: 362 (14.8%);
English Language Learner: 35 (1.4%); Migrant: n/a
Eligible for Free Lunch Program: 512 (20.9%)
Eligible for Reduced-Price Lunch Program: 193 (7.9%)
Teachers: 133.3 (18.3 to 1)
Librarians/Media Specialists: 2.0 (1,222.5 to 1)
Guidance Counselors: 3.0 (815.0 to 1)
Current Spending: ($ per student per year):
Total: $6,467; Instruction: $3,996; Support Services: $2,172
Enrollment, Drop-out Rates and Diploma Recipients by Race/Ethnicity

Category	Total	White	Black	Asian	AIAN	Hisp.
Enrollment (%)	100.0	94.8	2.2	0.8	0.2	2.1
Drop-out Rate (%)	n/a	n/a	n/a	n/a	n/a	n/a
H.S. Diplomas (#)	145	141	0	3	0	1

Franklin Township Com Sch Corp

6141 S Franklin Rd • Indianapolis, IN 46259-1399
(317) 862-2411 • http://www.ftcsc.k12.in.us/
Grade Span: PK-12; **Agency Type:** 1
Schools: 8
5 Primary; 2 Middle; 1 High; 0 Other Level
8 Regular; 0 Special Education; 0 Vocational; 0 Alternative
0 Magnet; 0 Charter; 4 Title I Eligible; 0 School-wide Title I
Students: 6,454 (51.2% male; 48.8% female)
Individual Education Program: 926 (14.3%);
English Language Learner: 126 (2.0%); Migrant: n/a
Eligible for Free Lunch Program: 825 (12.8%)
Eligible for Reduced-Price Lunch Program: 307 (4.8%)
Teachers: 317.6 (20.3 to 1)
Librarians/Media Specialists: 5.5 (1,173.5 to 1)
Guidance Counselors: 14.0 (461.0 to 1)
Current Spending: ($ per student per year):
Total: $6,298; Instruction: $3,739; Support Services: $2,246
Enrollment, Drop-out Rates and Diploma Recipients by Race/Ethnicity

Category	Total	White	Black	Asian	AIAN	Hisp.
Enrollment (%)	100.0	90.8	6.5	1.2	0.3	1.2
Drop-out Rate (%)	n/a	n/a	n/a	n/a	n/a	n/a
H.S. Diplomas (#)	305	285	13	4	0	3

Indianapolis Public Schools

120 E Walnut St • Indianapolis, IN 46204-1389
(317) 226-4411 • http://www.ips.k12.in.us/
Grade Span: PK-12; **Agency Type:** 1
Schools: 93
57 Primary; 12 Middle; 2 High; 22 Other Level
78 Regular; 5 Special Education; 0 Vocational; 10 Alternative
17 Magnet; 0 Charter; 55 Title I Eligible; 18 School-wide Title I
Students: 40,731 (51.5% male; 48.5% female)
Individual Education Program: 7,457 (18.3%);
English Language Learner: 2,758 (6.8%); Migrant: n/a
Eligible for Free Lunch Program: 26,899 (66.0%)
Eligible for Reduced-Price Lunch Program: 5,164 (12.7%)
Teachers: 2,789.7 (14.6 to 1)
Librarians/Media Specialists: 35.9 (1,134.6 to 1)
Guidance Counselors: 71.1 (572.9 to 1)
Current Spending: ($ per student per year):
Total: $9,214; Instruction: $5,188; Support Services: $3,734
Enrollment, Drop-out Rates and Diploma Recipients by Race/Ethnicity

Category	Total	White	Black	Asian	AIAN	Hisp.
Enrollment (%)	100.0	32.1	59.6	0.5	0.2	7.7
Drop-out Rate (%)	n/a	n/a	n/a	n/a	n/a	n/a
H.S. Diplomas (#)	1,203	341	816	0	2	44

MSD Decatur Township

5275 Kentucky Ave • Indianapolis, IN 46221-9616
(317) 856-5265 • http://www.msddecatur.k12.in.us/
Grade Span: KG-12; **Agency Type:** 1
Schools: 7
5 Primary; 1 Middle; 1 High; 0 Other Level
7 Regular; 0 Special Education; 0 Vocational; 0 Alternative
0 Magnet; 0 Charter; 3 Title I Eligible; 3 School-wide Title I
Students: 5,370 (50.9% male; 49.1% female)
Individual Education Program: 938 (17.5%);
English Language Learner: 81 (1.5%); Migrant: n/a
Eligible for Free Lunch Program: 1,574 (29.3%)
Eligible for Reduced-Price Lunch Program: 464 (8.6%)
Teachers: 292.5 (18.4 to 1)
Librarians/Media Specialists: 4.0 (1,342.5 to 1)
Guidance Counselors: 5.0 (1,074.0 to 1)
Current Spending: ($ per student per year):
Total: $7,349; Instruction: $4,609; Support Services: $2,411

Enrollment, Drop-out Rates and Diploma Recipients by Race/Ethnicity

Category	Total	White	Black	Asian	AIAN	Hisp.
Enrollment (%)	100.0	88.0	9.8	0.4	0.1	1.7
Drop-out Rate (%)	n/a	n/a	n/a	n/a	n/a	n/a
H.S. Diplomas (#)	246	216	20	1	0	9

MSD Lawrence Township

7601 E 56th St • Indianapolis, IN 46226-1306
(317) 423-8357 • http://www.msdlt.k12.in.us/
Grade Span: PK-12; **Agency Type:** 1
Schools: 19
12 Primary; 3 Middle; 3 High; 1 Other Level
17 Regular; 0 Special Education; 1 Vocational; 1 Alternative
2 Magnet; 0 Charter; 8 Title I Eligible; 0 School-wide Title I
Students: 16,118 (51.4% male; 48.6% female)
Individual Education Program: 2,436 (15.1%);
English Language Learner: 891 (5.5%); Migrant: n/a
Eligible for Free Lunch Program: 3,353 (20.8%)
Eligible for Reduced-Price Lunch Program: 1,109 (6.9%)
Teachers: 923.9 (17.4 to 1)
Librarians/Media Specialists: 16.0 (1,007.4 to 1)
Guidance Counselors: 25.5 (632.1 to 1)
Current Spending: ($ per student per year):
Total: $7,720; Instruction: $5,415; Support Services: $2,029

Enrollment, Drop-out Rates and Diploma Recipients by Race/Ethnicity

Category	Total	White	Black	Asian	AIAN	Hisp.
Enrollment (%)	100.0	61.4	31.7	1.9	0.2	4.8
Drop-out Rate (%)	n/a	n/a	n/a	n/a	n/a	n/a
H.S. Diplomas (#)	871	609	221	25	0	16

MSD Perry Township

6548 Orinoco Ave • Indianapolis, IN 46227-4820
(317) 789-3700 • http://www.msdpt.k12.in.us/
Grade Span: PK-12; **Agency Type:** 1
Schools: 16
10 Primary; 2 Middle; 2 High; 2 Other Level
14 Regular; 1 Special Education; 0 Vocational; 1 Alternative
0 Magnet; 0 Charter; 7 Title I Eligible; 0 School-wide Title I
Students: 12,971 (51.6% male; 48.4% female)
Individual Education Program: 1,792 (13.8%);
English Language Learner: 562 (4.3%); Migrant: n/a
Eligible for Free Lunch Program: 3,590 (27.7%)
Eligible for Reduced-Price Lunch Program: 1,102 (8.5%)
Teachers: 743.3 (17.5 to 1)
Librarians/Media Specialists: 13.0 (997.8 to 1)
Guidance Counselors: 17.0 (763.0 to 1)
Current Spending: ($ per student per year):
Total: $6,846; Instruction: $4,114; Support Services: $2,377

Enrollment, Drop-out Rates and Diploma Recipients by Race/Ethnicity

Category	Total	White	Black	Asian	AIAN	Hisp.
Enrollment (%)	100.0	81.9	13.0	1.2	0.2	3.7
Drop-out Rate (%)	n/a	n/a	n/a	n/a	n/a	n/a
H.S. Diplomas (#)	611	554	35	10	3	9

MSD Pike Township

6901 Zionsville Rd • Indianapolis, IN 46268-2467
(317) 293-0393 • http://www.pike.k12.in.us/
Grade Span: PK-12; **Agency Type:** 1
Schools: 13
10 Primary; 2 Middle; 1 High; 0 Other Level
13 Regular; 0 Special Education; 0 Vocational; 0 Alternative
0 Magnet; 0 Charter; 8 Title I Eligible; 0 School-wide Title I
Students: 10,092 (51.0% male; 49.0% female)
Individual Education Program: 1,739 (17.2%);
English Language Learner: 730 (7.2%); Migrant: n/a
Eligible for Free Lunch Program: 2,225 (22.0%)
Eligible for Reduced-Price Lunch Program: 839 (8.3%)
Teachers: 604.3 (16.7 to 1)
Librarians/Media Specialists: 12.0 (841.0 to 1)
Guidance Counselors: 18.0 (560.7 to 1)
Current Spending: ($ per student per year):
Total: $6,898; Instruction: $4,213; Support Services: $2,437

Enrollment, Drop-out Rates and Diploma Recipients by Race/Ethnicity

Category	Total	White	Black	Asian	AIAN	Hisp.
Enrollment (%)	100.0	31.1	58.6	3.7	0.1	6.4
Drop-out Rate (%)	n/a	n/a	n/a	n/a	n/a	n/a
H.S. Diplomas (#)	480	224	217	27	1	11

MSD Warren Township

975 N Post Rd • Indianapolis, IN 46219
(317) 869-4300 • http://www.warren.k12.in.us/
Grade Span: PK-12; **Agency Type:** 1
Schools: 19
12 Primary; 3 Middle; 1 High; 3 Other Level
16 Regular; 1 Special Education; 1 Vocational; 1 Alternative
0 Magnet; 0 Charter; 9 Title I Eligible; 1 School-wide Title I
Students: 11,288 (51.2% male; 48.8% female)
Individual Education Program: 1,981 (17.5%);
English Language Learner: 423 (3.7%); Migrant: n/a
Eligible for Free Lunch Program: 3,382 (30.0%)
Eligible for Reduced-Price Lunch Program: 1,038 (9.2%)
Teachers: 657.9 (17.2 to 1)
Librarians/Media Specialists: 10.5 (1,075.0 to 1)
Guidance Counselors: 22.5 (501.7 to 1)
Current Spending: ($ per student per year):
Total: $8,626; Instruction: $4,953; Support Services: $3,354

Enrollment, Drop-out Rates and Diploma Recipients by Race/Ethnicity

Category	Total	White	Black	Asian	AIAN	Hisp.
Enrollment (%)	100.0	59.6	35.9	1.0	0.2	3.2
Drop-out Rate (%)	n/a	n/a	n/a	n/a	n/a	n/a
H.S. Diplomas (#)	550	392	136	7	0	15

MSD Washington Township

8550 Woodfield Crossing Blvd • Indianapolis, IN 46240-2478
(317) 845-9400 • http://www.msdwt.k12.in.us/
Grade Span: PK-12; **Agency Type:** 1
Schools: 15
10 Primary; 3 Middle; 1 High; 1 Other Level
14 Regular; 0 Special Education; 1 Vocational; 0 Alternative
0 Magnet; 0 Charter; 9 Title I Eligible; 0 School-wide Title I
Students: 10,146 (51.1% male; 48.9% female)
Individual Education Program: 1,478 (14.6%);
English Language Learner: 999 (9.8%); Migrant: n/a
Eligible for Free Lunch Program: 2,462 (24.3%)
Eligible for Reduced-Price Lunch Program: 963 (9.5%)
Teachers: 594.2 (17.1 to 1)
Librarians/Media Specialists: 13.0 (780.5 to 1)
Guidance Counselors: 16.5 (614.9 to 1)
Current Spending: ($ per student per year):
Total: $7,510; Instruction: $4,536; Support Services: $2,697

Enrollment, Drop-out Rates and Diploma Recipients by Race/Ethnicity

Category	Total	White	Black	Asian	AIAN	Hisp.
Enrollment (%)	100.0	50.8	40.5	1.8	0.1	6.7
Drop-out Rate (%)	n/a	n/a	n/a	n/a	n/a	n/a
H.S. Diplomas (#)	662	432	202	18	2	8

MSD Wayne Township

1220 S High Sch Rd • Indianapolis, IN 46241-3199
(317) 243-8251 • http://www.wayne.k12.in.us/
Grade Span: PK-12; **Agency Type:** 1
Schools: 15
10 Primary; 3 Middle; 1 High; 1 Other Level
14 Regular; 1 Special Education; 0 Vocational; 0 Alternative
0 Magnet; 0 Charter; 7 Title I Eligible; 0 School-wide Title I
Students: 14,245 (51.0% male; 49.0% female)
Individual Education Program: 2,212 (15.5%);
English Language Learner: 828 (5.8%); Migrant: n/a
Eligible for Free Lunch Program: 5,136 (36.1%)
Eligible for Reduced-Price Lunch Program: 1,171 (8.2%)
Teachers: 810.4 (17.6 to 1)
Librarians/Media Specialists: 14.5 (982.4 to 1)
Guidance Counselors: 21.5 (662.6 to 1)
Current Spending: ($ per student per year):
Total: $7,615; Instruction: $5,045; Support Services: $2,260

Enrollment, Drop-out Rates and Diploma Recipients by Race/Ethnicity

Category	Total	White	Black	Asian	AIAN	Hisp.
Enrollment (%)	100.0	65.1	27.8	1.6	0.3	5.2
Drop-out Rate (%)	n/a	n/a	n/a	n/a	n/a	n/a
H.S. Diplomas (#)	585	425	138	11	0	11

School Town of Speedway

5335 W 25th St • Speedway, IN 46224-3905
(317) 244-0236 • http://www.speedway.k12.in.us/
Grade Span: KG-12; **Agency Type:** 1
Schools: 6
4 Primary; 1 Middle; 1 High; 0 Other Level
6 Regular; 0 Special Education; 0 Vocational; 0 Alternative
0 Magnet; 0 Charter; 0 Title I Eligible; 0 School-wide Title I
Students: 1,647 (53.2% male; 46.8% female)
Individual Education Program: 258 (15.7%);
English Language Learner: 94 (5.7%); Migrant: n/a
Eligible for Free Lunch Program: 459 (27.9%)
Eligible for Reduced-Price Lunch Program: 120 (7.3%)
Teachers: 99.0 (16.6 to 1)
Librarians/Media Specialists: 2.0 (823.5 to 1)
Guidance Counselors: 3.0 (549.0 to 1)
Current Spending: ($ per student per year):
Total: $6,387; Instruction: $4,051; Support Services: $1,975

Enrollment, Drop-out Rates and Diploma Recipients by Race/Ethnicity

Category	Total	White	Black	Asian	AIAN	Hisp.
Enrollment (%)	100.0	73.3	21.3	1.2	0.2	4.1
Drop-out Rate (%)	n/a	n/a	n/a	n/a	n/a	n/a
H.S. Diplomas (#)	84	74	4	5	0	1

Marshall County

Plymouth Community School Corp

611 Berkley St • Plymouth, IN 46563-1817
(574) 936-3115 • http://www.epcsc.k12.in.us/index.htm
Grade Span: PK-12; **Agency Type:** 1
Schools: 6
4 Primary; 1 Middle; 1 High; 0 Other Level
6 Regular; 0 Special Education; 0 Vocational; 0 Alternative
0 Magnet; 0 Charter; 4 Title I Eligible; 0 School-wide Title I
Students: 3,292 (52.2% male; 47.8% female)
Individual Education Program: 412 (12.5%);
English Language Learner: 264 (8.0%); Migrant: n/a
Eligible for Free Lunch Program: 799 (24.3%)
Eligible for Reduced-Price Lunch Program: 324 (9.8%)
Teachers: 164.3 (20.0 to 1)
Librarians/Media Specialists: 3.0 (1,097.3 to 1)
Guidance Counselors: 5.0 (658.4 to 1)
Current Spending: ($ per student per year):
Total: $6,265; Instruction: $3,731; Support Services: $2,269

Enrollment, Drop-out Rates and Diploma Recipients by Race/Ethnicity

Category	Total	White	Black	Asian	AIAN	Hisp.
Enrollment (%)	100.0	87.5	0.4	0.7	0.3	11.1
Drop-out Rate (%)	n/a	n/a	n/a	n/a	n/a	n/a
H.S. Diplomas (#)	266	241	0	1	0	24

Miami County

Maconaquah School Corp

7932 S Strawtown Pk • Bunker Hill, IN 46914-9667
(765) 689-9131 • http://www.maconaquah.k12.in.us/
Grade Span: PK-12; **Agency Type:** 1
Schools: 4
2 Primary; 1 Middle; 1 High; 0 Other Level
4 Regular; 0 Special Education; 0 Vocational; 0 Alternative
0 Magnet; 0 Charter; 2 Title I Eligible; 0 School-wide Title I
Students: 2,363 (50.5% male; 49.5% female)
Individual Education Program: 358 (15.2%);
English Language Learner: 32 (1.4%); Migrant: n/a
Eligible for Free Lunch Program: 495 (20.9%)
Eligible for Reduced-Price Lunch Program: 198 (8.4%)
Teachers: 144.3 (16.4 to 1)
Librarians/Media Specialists: 4.0 (590.8 to 1)
Guidance Counselors: 3.0 (787.7 to 1)
Current Spending: ($ per student per year):
Total: $7,123; Instruction: $4,251; Support Services: $2,566

Enrollment, Drop-out Rates and Diploma Recipients by Race/Ethnicity

Category	Total	White	Black	Asian	AIAN	Hisp.
Enrollment (%)	100.0	94.5	2.3	0.4	0.9	1.9
Drop-out Rate (%)	n/a	n/a	n/a	n/a	n/a	n/a
H.S. Diplomas (#)	124	120	1	0	2	1

Peru Community Schools

35 W 3rd St • Peru, IN 46970
(765) 473-3081 • http://www.peru.k12.in.us/
Grade Span: PK-12; **Agency Type:** 1
Schools: 7
5 Primary; 1 Middle; 1 High; 0 Other Level
7 Regular; 0 Special Education; 0 Vocational; 0 Alternative
0 Magnet; 0 Charter; 6 Title I Eligible; 0 School-wide Title I
Students: 2,493 (50.3% male; 49.7% female)
Individual Education Program: 442 (17.7%);
English Language Learner: 21 (0.8%); Migrant: n/a
Eligible for Free Lunch Program: 750 (30.1%)
Eligible for Reduced-Price Lunch Program: 240 (9.6%)
Teachers: 155.0 (16.1 to 1)
Librarians/Media Specialists: 2.0 (1,246.5 to 1)
Guidance Counselors: 4.0 (623.3 to 1)
Current Spending: ($ per student per year):
Total: $7,023; Instruction: $4,502; Support Services: $2,180

Enrollment, Drop-out Rates and Diploma Recipients by Race/Ethnicity

Category	Total	White	Black	Asian	AIAN	Hisp.
Enrollment (%)	100.0	93.3	2.9	0.7	1.9	1.2
Drop-out Rate (%)	n/a	n/a	n/a	n/a	n/a	n/a
H.S. Diplomas (#)	152	143	4	0	4	1

Monroe County

Monroe County Com Sch Corp

315 N Dr • Bloomington, IN 47401-6595
(812) 330-7700 • http://www.mccsc.edu/
Grade Span: PK-12; **Agency Type:** 1
Schools: 21
14 Primary; 3 Middle; 3 High; 1 Other Level
19 Regular; 0 Special Education; 1 Vocational; 1 Alternative
0 Magnet; 0 Charter; 11 Title I Eligible; 1 School-wide Title I
Students: 10,503 (50.8% male; 49.2% female)
Individual Education Program: 1,669 (15.9%);
English Language Learner: 582 (5.5%); Migrant: n/a
Eligible for Free Lunch Program: 2,239 (21.3%)
Eligible for Reduced-Price Lunch Program: 804 (7.7%)
Teachers: 646.3 (16.3 to 1)
Librarians/Media Specialists: 16.0 (656.4 to 1)
Guidance Counselors: 16.5 (636.5 to 1)
Current Spending: ($ per student per year):
Total: $7,407; Instruction: $4,291; Support Services: $2,862

Enrollment, Drop-out Rates and Diploma Recipients by Race/Ethnicity

Category	Total	White	Black	Asian	AIAN	Hisp.
Enrollment (%)	100.0	88.9	4.1	4.3	0.7	2.0
Drop-out Rate (%)	n/a	n/a	n/a	n/a	n/a	n/a
H.S. Diplomas (#)	647	596	20	12	5	14

Richland-Bean Blossom C S C

600 S Edgewood Dr • Ellettsville, IN 47429-1134
(812) 876-7100 • http://www.rbbcsc.k12.in.us/
Grade Span: PK-12; **Agency Type:** 1
Schools: 7
4 Primary; 0 Middle; 1 High; 2 Other Level
6 Regular; 1 Special Education; 0 Vocational; 0 Alternative
0 Magnet; 0 Charter; 4 Title I Eligible; 0 School-wide Title I
Students: 2,693 (51.8% male; 48.2% female)
Individual Education Program: 476 (17.7%);
English Language Learner: 9 (0.3%); Migrant: n/a
Eligible for Free Lunch Program: 366 (13.6%)
Eligible for Reduced-Price Lunch Program: 191 (7.1%)
Teachers: 169.8 (15.9 to 1)
Librarians/Media Specialists: 3.0 (897.7 to 1)
Guidance Counselors: 7.0 (384.7 to 1)
Current Spending: ($ per student per year):
Total: $6,600; Instruction: $4,232; Support Services: $2,166

Enrollment, Drop-out Rates and Diploma Recipients by Race/Ethnicity

Category	Total	White	Black	Asian	AIAN	Hisp.
Enrollment (%)	100.0	98.0	0.6	0.7	0.0	0.7
Drop-out Rate (%)	n/a	n/a	n/a	n/a	n/a	n/a
H.S. Diplomas (#)	154	151	1	1	0	1

Montgomery County

Crawfordsville Com Schools

1000 Fairview Ave • Crawfordsville, IN 47933-1511
(765) 362-2342 • http://www.cville.k12.in.us/Cville/Webpages/Start.aspx
Grade Span: PK-12; **Agency Type:** 1
Schools: 8
5 Primary; 1 Middle; 1 High; 1 Other Level
6 Regular; 1 Special Education; 0 Vocational; 1 Alternative
0 Magnet; 0 Charter; 4 Title I Eligible; 1 School-wide Title I
Students: 2,606 (50.2% male; 49.8% female)
Individual Education Program: 437 (16.8%);
English Language Learner: 96 (3.7%); Migrant: n/a
Eligible for Free Lunch Program: 780 (29.9%)
Eligible for Reduced-Price Lunch Program: 180 (6.9%)
Teachers: 155.1 (16.8 to 1)
Librarians/Media Specialists: 5.0 (521.2 to 1)
Guidance Counselors: 4.0 (651.5 to 1)
Current Spending: ($ per student per year):
Total: $7,482; Instruction: $4,195; Support Services: $2,975

Enrollment, Drop-out Rates and Diploma Recipients by Race/Ethnicity

Category	Total	White	Black	Asian	AIAN	Hisp.
Enrollment (%)	100.0	93.2	1.3	0.8	0.5	4.2
Drop-out Rate (%)	n/a	n/a	n/a	n/a	n/a	n/a
H.S. Diplomas (#)	127	120	3	1	0	3

North Montgomery Com Sch Corp

220 S Main • Linden, IN 47955-0070
Mailing Address: PO Box 70 • Linden, IN 47955-0070
(765) 339-7262 • http://www.nm.k12.in.us/
Grade Span: KG-12; **Agency Type:** 1
Schools: 5
3 Primary; 1 Middle; 1 High; 0 Other Level
5 Regular; 0 Special Education; 0 Vocational; 0 Alternative
0 Magnet; 0 Charter; 4 Title I Eligible; 0 School-wide Title I

Students: 2,059 (52.0% male; 48.0% female)
Individual Education Program: 320 (15.5%);
English Language Learner: 4 (0.2%); Migrant: n/a
Eligible for Free Lunch Program: 346 (16.8%)
Eligible for Reduced-Price Lunch Program: 128 (6.2%)
Teachers: 119.0 (17.3 to 1)
Librarians/Media Specialists: 1.5 (1,372.7 to 1)
Guidance Counselors: 4.3 (478.8 to 1)
Current Spending: ($ per student per year):
Total: $6,814; Instruction: $3,921; Support Services: $2,585
Enrollment, Drop-out Rates and Diploma Recipients by Race/Ethnicity

Category	Total	White	Black	Asian	AIAN	Hisp.
Enrollment (%)	100.0	99.1	0.2	0.2	0.1	0.3
Drop-out Rate (%)	n/a	n/a	n/a	n/a	n/a	n/a
H.S. Diplomas (#)	108	107	0	1	0	0

South Montgomery Com Sch Corp

200 N 3rd St • New Market, IN 47965
Mailing Address: PO Box 8 • New Market, IN 47965-0008
(765) 866-0203 • http://www.southmont.k12.in.us/
Grade Span: KG-12; **Agency Type:** 1
Schools: 6
4 Primary; 1 Middle; 1 High; 0 Other Level
6 Regular; 0 Special Education; 0 Vocational; 0 Alternative
0 Magnet; 0 Charter; 4 Title I Eligible; 0 School-wide Title I
Students: 2,063 (51.5% male; 48.5% female)
Individual Education Program: 336 (16.3%);
English Language Learner: n/a; Migrant: n/a
Eligible for Free Lunch Program: 301 (14.6%)
Eligible for Reduced-Price Lunch Program: 128 (6.2%)
Teachers: 125.5 (16.4 to 1)
Librarians/Media Specialists: 1.0 (2,063.0 to 1)
Guidance Counselors: 5.0 (412.6 to 1)
Current Spending: ($ per student per year):
Total: $6,272; Instruction: $4,034; Support Services: $1,944
Enrollment, Drop-out Rates and Diploma Recipients by Race/Ethnicity

Category	Total	White	Black	Asian	AIAN	Hisp.
Enrollment (%)	100.0	99.0	0.1	0.2	0.0	0.6
Drop-out Rate (%)	n/a	n/a	n/a	n/a	n/a	n/a
H.S. Diplomas (#)	117	116	0	0	0	1

Morgan County

MSD Martinsville Schools

460 S Main St • Martinsville, IN 46151-1416
Mailing Address: PO Box 1416 • Martinsville, IN 46151-1416
(765) 342-6641 • http://msdadmin.scican.net/
Grade Span: PK-12; **Agency Type:** 1
Schools: 12
8 Primary; 2 Middle; 2 High; 0 Other Level
11 Regular; 0 Special Education; 0 Vocational; 1 Alternative
0 Magnet; 0 Charter; 7 Title I Eligible; 0 School-wide Title I
Students: 5,412 (52.3% male; 47.7% female)
Individual Education Program: 967 (17.9%);
English Language Learner: 20 (0.4%); Migrant: n/a
Eligible for Free Lunch Program: 929 (17.2%)
Eligible for Reduced-Price Lunch Program: 465 (8.6%)
Teachers: 304.2 (17.8 to 1)
Librarians/Media Specialists: 4.0 (1,353.0 to 1)
Guidance Counselors: 9.0 (601.3 to 1)
Current Spending: ($ per student per year):
Total: $6,511; Instruction: $4,048; Support Services: $2,185
Enrollment, Drop-out Rates and Diploma Recipients by Race/Ethnicity

Category	Total	White	Black	Asian	AIAN	Hisp.
Enrollment (%)	100.0	99.5	0.0	0.1	0.1	0.3
Drop-out Rate (%)	n/a	n/a	n/a	n/a	n/a	n/a
H.S. Diplomas (#)	312	312	0	0	0	0

Mooresville Con School Corp

11 W Carlisle St • Mooresville, IN 46158-1509
(317) 831-0950 • http://mcsc.k12.in.us/
Grade Span: PK-12; **Agency Type:** 1
Schools: 7
5 Primary; 1 Middle; 1 High; 0 Other Level
7 Regular; 0 Special Education; 0 Vocational; 0 Alternative
0 Magnet; 0 Charter; 3 Title I Eligible; 0 School-wide Title I
Students: 4,300 (50.7% male; 49.3% female)
Individual Education Program: 526 (12.2%);
English Language Learner: 17 (0.4%); Migrant: n/a
Eligible for Free Lunch Program: 610 (14.2%)
Eligible for Reduced-Price Lunch Program: 187 (4.3%)
Teachers: 246.9 (17.4 to 1)
Librarians/Media Specialists: 3.0 (1,433.3 to 1)
Guidance Counselors: 8.0 (537.5 to 1)
Current Spending: ($ per student per year):
Total: $6,573; Instruction: $4,037; Support Services: $2,242
Enrollment, Drop-out Rates and Diploma Recipients by Race/Ethnicity

Category	Total	White	Black	Asian	AIAN	Hisp.
Enrollment (%)	100.0	98.9	0.2	0.3	0.1	0.3
Drop-out Rate (%)	n/a	n/a	n/a	n/a	n/a	n/a
H.S. Diplomas (#)	262	262	0	0	0	0

Newton County

North Newton School Corp

108 E State St • Morocco, IN 47963-0008
Mailing Address: PO Box 8 • Morocco, IN 47963-0008
(219) 285-2228 • http://www.nn.k12.in.us/
Grade Span: KG-12; **Agency Type:** 1
Schools: 4
3 Primary; 0 Middle; 1 High; 0 Other Level
4 Regular; 0 Special Education; 0 Vocational; 0 Alternative
0 Magnet; 0 Charter; 3 Title I Eligible; 0 School-wide Title I
Students: 1,698 (50.4% male; 49.6% female)
Individual Education Program: 298 (17.6%);
English Language Learner: 31 (1.8%); Migrant: n/a
Eligible for Free Lunch Program: 306 (18.0%)
Eligible for Reduced-Price Lunch Program: 146 (8.6%)
Teachers: 103.0 (16.5 to 1)
Librarians/Media Specialists: 1.0 (1,698.0 to 1)
Guidance Counselors: 2.5 (679.2 to 1)
Current Spending: ($ per student per year):
Total: $6,438; Instruction: $3,782; Support Services: $2,391
Enrollment, Drop-out Rates and Diploma Recipients by Race/Ethnicity

Category	Total	White	Black	Asian	AIAN	Hisp.
Enrollment (%)	100.0	96.6	0.1	0.3	0.1	2.9
Drop-out Rate (%)	n/a	n/a	n/a	n/a	n/a	n/a
H.S. Diplomas (#)	75	75	0	0	0	0

Noble County

East Noble School Corp

702 E Dowling St • Kendallville, IN 46755-1298
(260) 347-2502 • http://www.enoble.k12.in.us/
Grade Span: PK-12; **Agency Type:** 1
Schools: 8
6 Primary; 1 Middle; 1 High; 0 Other Level
8 Regular; 0 Special Education; 0 Vocational; 0 Alternative
0 Magnet; 0 Charter; 5 Title I Eligible; 0 School-wide Title I
Students: 3,709 (49.4% male; 50.6% female)
Individual Education Program: 591 (15.9%);
English Language Learner: 71 (1.9%); Migrant: n/a
Eligible for Free Lunch Program: 605 (16.3%)
Eligible for Reduced-Price Lunch Program: 377 (10.2%)
Teachers: 226.6 (16.4 to 1)
Librarians/Media Specialists: 4.0 (927.3 to 1)
Guidance Counselors: 8.0 (463.6 to 1)
Current Spending: ($ per student per year):
Total: $6,563; Instruction: $3,971; Support Services: $2,266
Enrollment, Drop-out Rates and Diploma Recipients by Race/Ethnicity

Category	Total	White	Black	Asian	AIAN	Hisp.
Enrollment (%)	100.0	96.5	0.3	0.4	0.2	2.5
Drop-out Rate (%)	n/a	n/a	n/a	n/a	n/a	n/a
H.S. Diplomas (#)	224	213	0	4	0	7

West Noble School Corporation

5050 N US 33 • Ligonier, IN 46767-9606
(260) 894-3191 • http://westnoble.k12.in.us/
Grade Span: KG-12; **Agency Type:** 1
Schools: 4
2 Primary; 1 Middle; 1 High; 0 Other Level
4 Regular; 0 Special Education; 0 Vocational; 0 Alternative
0 Magnet; 0 Charter; 3 Title I Eligible; 0 School-wide Title I
Students: 2,497 (51.6% male; 48.4% female)
Individual Education Program: 275 (11.0%);
English Language Learner: 795 (31.8%); Migrant: n/a
Eligible for Free Lunch Program: 902 (36.1%)
Eligible for Reduced-Price Lunch Program: 295 (11.8%)
Teachers: 142.2 (17.6 to 1)
Librarians/Media Specialists: 2.0 (1,248.5 to 1)
Guidance Counselors: 3.3 (756.7 to 1)
Current Spending: ($ per student per year):
Total: $6,952; Instruction: $4,314; Support Services: $2,316
Enrollment, Drop-out Rates and Diploma Recipients by Race/Ethnicity

Category	Total	White	Black	Asian	AIAN	Hisp.
Enrollment (%)	100.0	67.8	0.3	0.2	0.1	31.6
Drop-out Rate (%)	n/a	n/a	n/a	n/a	n/a	n/a
H.S. Diplomas (#)	119	95	0	2	0	22

Orange County

Paoli Community School Corp

501 Elm St - Ofc Supt • Paoli, IN 47454-1197
(812) 723-4717
Grade Span: KG-12; **Agency Type:** 1
Schools: 2
1 Primary; 0 Middle; 1 High; 0 Other Level
2 Regular; 0 Special Education; 0 Vocational; 0 Alternative
0 Magnet; 0 Charter; 1 Title I Eligible; 0 School-wide Title I
Students: 1,726 (51.9% male; 48.1% female)
Individual Education Program: 308 (17.8%);
English Language Learner: 5 (0.3%); Migrant: n/a
Eligible for Free Lunch Program: 513 (29.7%)
Eligible for Reduced-Price Lunch Program: 200 (11.6%)
Teachers: 91.2 (18.9 to 1)
Librarians/Media Specialists: 1.0 (1,726.0 to 1)
Guidance Counselors: 3.0 (575.3 to 1)
Current Spending: ($ per student per year):
Total: $5,989; Instruction: $3,963; Support Services: $1,708
Enrollment, Drop-out Rates and Diploma Recipients by Race/Ethnicity

Category	Total	White	Black	Asian	AIAN	Hisp.
Enrollment (%)	100.0	99.2	0.3	0.1	0.1	0.2
Drop-out Rate (%)	n/a	n/a	n/a	n/a	n/a	n/a
H.S. Diplomas (#)	108	108	0	0	0	0

Owen County

Spencer-Owen Community Schools

205 E Hillside • Spencer, IN 47460-1099
(812) 829-2233 • http://www.socs.k12.in.us/
Grade Span: PK-12; **Agency Type:** 1
Schools: 6
4 Primary; 1 Middle; 1 High; 0 Other Level
6 Regular; 0 Special Education; 0 Vocational; 0 Alternative
0 Magnet; 0 Charter; 5 Title I Eligible; 2 School-wide Title I
Students: 3,118 (51.1% male; 48.9% female)
Individual Education Program: 662 (21.2%);
English Language Learner: 2 (0.1%); Migrant: n/a
Eligible for Free Lunch Program: 782 (25.1%)
Eligible for Reduced-Price Lunch Program: 303 (9.7%)
Teachers: 197.4 (15.8 to 1)
Librarians/Media Specialists: 4.0 (779.5 to 1)
Guidance Counselors: 6.0 (519.7 to 1)
Current Spending: ($ per student per year):
Total: $7,191; Instruction: $4,493; Support Services: $2,445
Enrollment, Drop-out Rates and Diploma Recipients by Race/Ethnicity

Category	Total	White	Black	Asian	AIAN	Hisp.
Enrollment (%)	100.0	98.8	0.2	0.2	0.4	0.4
Drop-out Rate (%)	n/a	n/a	n/a	n/a	n/a	n/a
H.S. Diplomas (#)	187	187	0	0	0	0

Perry County

Tell City-Troy Twp School Corp

837 17th St • Tell City, IN 47586-1698
(812) 547-3300 • http://www.tellcity.k12.in.us/
Grade Span: PK-12; **Agency Type:** 1
Schools: 3
1 Primary; 1 Middle; 1 High; 0 Other Level
3 Regular; 0 Special Education; 0 Vocational; 0 Alternative
0 Magnet; 0 Charter; 2 Title I Eligible; 0 School-wide Title I
Students: 1,708 (52.5% male; 47.5% female)
Individual Education Program: 237 (13.9%);
English Language Learner: 6 (0.4%); Migrant: n/a
Eligible for Free Lunch Program: 353 (20.7%)
Eligible for Reduced-Price Lunch Program: 140 (8.2%)
Teachers: 94.5 (18.1 to 1)
Librarians/Media Specialists: 3.0 (569.3 to 1)
Guidance Counselors: 4.5 (379.6 to 1)
Current Spending: ($ per student per year):
Total: $6,307; Instruction: $4,111; Support Services: $1,948
Enrollment, Drop-out Rates and Diploma Recipients by Race/Ethnicity

Category	Total	White	Black	Asian	AIAN	Hisp.
Enrollment (%)	100.0	98.8	0.0	0.6	0.1	0.5
Drop-out Rate (%)	n/a	n/a	n/a	n/a	n/a	n/a
H.S. Diplomas (#)	108	108	0	0	0	0

Pike County

Pike County School Corp

907 Walnut St • Petersburg, IN 47567-1561
(812) 354-8731 • http://www.pcsc.k12.in.us/
Grade Span: PK-12; **Agency Type:** 1
Schools: 5
3 Primary; 1 Middle; 1 High; 0 Other Level
5 Regular; 0 Special Education; 0 Vocational; 0 Alternative
0 Magnet; 0 Charter; 3 Title I Eligible; 0 School-wide Title I
Students: 2,161 (51.0% male; 49.0% female)
Individual Education Program: 391 (18.1%);
English Language Learner: 2 (0.1%); Migrant: n/a
Eligible for Free Lunch Program: 537 (24.8%)
Eligible for Reduced-Price Lunch Program: 244 (11.3%)
Teachers: 122.3 (17.7 to 1)
Librarians/Media Specialists: 1.0 (2,161.0 to 1)
Guidance Counselors: 3.0 (720.3 to 1)
Current Spending: ($ per student per year):
Total: $6,563; Instruction: $4,020; Support Services: $2,266
Enrollment, Drop-out Rates and Diploma Recipients by Race/Ethnicity

Category	Total	White	Black	Asian	AIAN	Hisp.
Enrollment (%)	100.0	99.5	0.0	0.2	0.0	0.2
Drop-out Rate (%)	n/a	n/a	n/a	n/a	n/a	n/a
H.S. Diplomas (#)	124	124	0	0	0	0

Porter County

Duneland School Corporation

700 W Porter Ave • Chesterton, IN 46304-2205
(219) 983-3605 • http://www.duneland.k12.in.us/
Grade Span: KG-12; **Agency Type:** 1
Schools: 9
5 Primary; 3 Middle; 1 High; 0 Other Level
9 Regular; 0 Special Education; 0 Vocational; 0 Alternative
0 Magnet; 0 Charter; 5 Title I Eligible; 0 School-wide Title I
Students: 5,369 (52.2% male; 47.8% female)
Individual Education Program: 938 (17.5%);
English Language Learner: 72 (1.3%); Migrant: n/a
Eligible for Free Lunch Program: 699 (13.0%)
Eligible for Reduced-Price Lunch Program: 281 (5.2%)
Teachers: 266.6 (20.1 to 1)
Librarians/Media Specialists: 10.0 (536.9 to 1)
Guidance Counselors: 11.0 (488.1 to 1)
Current Spending: ($ per student per year):
Total: $7,839; Instruction: $4,437; Support Services: $3,083
Enrollment, Drop-out Rates and Diploma Recipients by Race/Ethnicity

Category	Total	White	Black	Asian	AIAN	Hisp.
Enrollment (%)	100.0	95.5	0.5	1.1	0.3	2.6
Drop-out Rate (%)	n/a	n/a	n/a	n/a	n/a	n/a
H.S. Diplomas (#)	390	365	1	5	2	17

East Porter County School Corp

502 E College • Kouts, IN 46347
Mailing Address: PO Box 370 • Kouts, IN 46347
(219) 766-2214
Grade Span: KG-12; **Agency Type:** 1
Schools: 6
3 Primary; 0 Middle; 0 High; 3 Other Level
6 Regular; 0 Special Education; 0 Vocational; 0 Alternative
0 Magnet; 0 Charter; 3 Title I Eligible; 0 School-wide Title I
Students: 1,963 (50.1% male; 49.9% female)
Individual Education Program: 319 (16.3%);
English Language Learner: 6 (0.3%); Migrant: n/a
Eligible for Free Lunch Program: 142 (7.2%)
Eligible for Reduced-Price Lunch Program: 74 (3.8%)
Teachers: 114.5 (17.1 to 1)
Librarians/Media Specialists: 2.0 (981.5 to 1)
Guidance Counselors: 3.0 (654.3 to 1)
Current Spending: ($ per student per year):
Total: $6,813; Instruction: $3,929; Support Services: $2,610
Enrollment, Drop-out Rates and Diploma Recipients by Race/Ethnicity

Category	Total	White	Black	Asian	AIAN	Hisp.
Enrollment (%)	100.0	98.9	0.1	0.2	0.2	0.7
Drop-out Rate (%)	n/a	n/a	n/a	n/a	n/a	n/a
H.S. Diplomas (#)	138	138	0	0	0	0

Portage Township Schools

6240 US Hwy 6 • Portage, IN 46368-5057
(219) 762-6511 • http://www.portage.k12.in.us/
Grade Span: PK-12; **Agency Type:** 1
Schools: 11
9 Primary; 1 Middle; 1 High; 0 Other Level
11 Regular; 0 Special Education; 0 Vocational; 0 Alternative
0 Magnet; 0 Charter; 8 Title I Eligible; 0 School-wide Title I
Students: 8,010 (51.6% male; 48.4% female)
Individual Education Program: 1,238 (15.5%);
English Language Learner: 234 (2.9%); Migrant: n/a
Eligible for Free Lunch Program: 1,757 (21.9%)
Eligible for Reduced-Price Lunch Program: 580 (7.2%)
Teachers: 404.0 (19.8 to 1)
Librarians/Media Specialists: 6.0 (1,335.0 to 1)
Guidance Counselors: 9.0 (890.0 to 1)

Current Spending: ($ per student per year):
Total: $6,727; Instruction: $3,862; Support Services: $2,614
Enrollment, Drop-out Rates and Diploma Recipients by Race/Ethnicity

Category	Total	White	Black	Asian	AIAN	Hisp.
Enrollment (%)	100.0	87.9	1.6	0.8	0.6	9.0
Drop-out Rate (%)	n/a	n/a	n/a	n/a	n/a	n/a
H.S. Diplomas (#)	521	459	8	6	3	45

Porter Township School Corp
248 S 500 W • Valparaiso, IN 46383-9642
(219) 477-4933 • http://www.ptsc.k12.in.us/
Grade Span: KG-12; **Agency Type:** 1
Schools: 4
2 Primary; 1 Middle; 1 High; 0 Other Level
4 Regular; 0 Special Education; 0 Vocational; 0 Alternative
0 Magnet; 0 Charter; 2 Title I Eligible; 0 School-wide Title I
Students: 1,552 (51.0% male; 49.0% female)
Individual Education Program: 174 (11.2%);
English Language Learner: 10 (0.6%); Migrant: n/a
Eligible for Free Lunch Program: 95 (6.1%)
Eligible for Reduced-Price Lunch Program: 56 (3.6%)
Teachers: 78.5 (19.8 to 1)
Librarians/Media Specialists: 2.0 (776.0 to 1)
Guidance Counselors: 2.0 (776.0 to 1)
Current Spending: ($ per student per year):
Total: $6,631; Instruction: $3,538; Support Services: $2,820
Enrollment, Drop-out Rates and Diploma Recipients by Race/Ethnicity

Category	Total	White	Black	Asian	AIAN	Hisp.
Enrollment (%)	100.0	94.0	0.5	0.8	0.5	4.3
Drop-out Rate (%)	n/a	n/a	n/a	n/a	n/a	n/a
H.S. Diplomas (#)	137	130	0	3	0	4

Union Township School Corp
599 W 300 N Ste A • Valparaiso, IN 46385-9212
(219) 759-2531
Grade Span: KG-12; **Agency Type:** 1
Schools: 4
2 Primary; 1 Middle; 1 High; 0 Other Level
4 Regular; 0 Special Education; 0 Vocational; 0 Alternative
0 Magnet; 0 Charter; 0 Title I Eligible; 0 School-wide Title I
Students: 1,518 (50.6% male; 49.4% female)
Individual Education Program: 256 (16.9%);
English Language Learner: 34 (2.2%); Migrant: n/a
Eligible for Free Lunch Program: 99 (6.5%)
Eligible for Reduced-Price Lunch Program: 47 (3.1%)
Teachers: 89.9 (16.9 to 1)
Librarians/Media Specialists: 0.0 (0.0 to 1)
Guidance Counselors: 1.0 (1,518.0 to 1)
Current Spending: ($ per student per year):
Total: $7,025; Instruction: $4,012; Support Services: $2,722
Enrollment, Drop-out Rates and Diploma Recipients by Race/Ethnicity

Category	Total	White	Black	Asian	AIAN	Hisp.
Enrollment (%)	100.0	91.7	0.5	1.5	1.3	5.0
Drop-out Rate (%)	n/a	n/a	n/a	n/a	n/a	n/a
H.S. Diplomas (#)	109	100	0	1	3	5

Valparaiso Community Schools
3801 N Campbell St • Valparaiso, IN 46385
(219) 531-3000 • http://www.valpo.k12.in.us/
Grade Span: KG-12; **Agency Type:** 1
Schools: 12
8 Primary; 2 Middle; 1 High; 1 Other Level
11 Regular; 0 Special Education; 1 Vocational; 0 Alternative
0 Magnet; 0 Charter; 6 Title I Eligible; 0 School-wide Title I
Students: 6,010 (50.4% male; 49.6% female)
Individual Education Program: 799 (13.3%);
English Language Learner: 181 (3.0%); Migrant: n/a
Eligible for Free Lunch Program: 665 (11.1%)
Eligible for Reduced-Price Lunch Program: 251 (4.2%)
Teachers: 314.2 (19.1 to 1)
Librarians/Media Specialists: 4.0 (1,502.5 to 1)
Guidance Counselors: 10.0 (601.0 to 1)
Current Spending: ($ per student per year):
Total: $7,290; Instruction: $4,702; Support Services: $2,237
Enrollment, Drop-out Rates and Diploma Recipients by Race/Ethnicity

Category	Total	White	Black	Asian	AIAN	Hisp.
Enrollment (%)	100.0	92.9	2.0	2.1	0.1	2.8
Drop-out Rate (%)	n/a	n/a	n/a	n/a	n/a	n/a
H.S. Diplomas (#)	494	468	5	13	1	7

Posey County

MSD Mount Vernon
1000 W 4th St • Mount Vernon, IN 47620-1696
(812) 838-4471
Grade Span: PK-12; **Agency Type:** 1
Schools: 6
4 Primary; 1 Middle; 1 High; 0 Other Level
6 Regular; 0 Special Education; 0 Vocational; 0 Alternative
0 Magnet; 0 Charter; 2 Title I Eligible; 0 School-wide Title I
Students: 2,799 (51.8% male; 48.2% female)
Individual Education Program: 584 (20.9%);
English Language Learner: 8 (0.3%); Migrant: n/a
Eligible for Free Lunch Program: 508 (18.1%)
Eligible for Reduced-Price Lunch Program: 99 (3.5%)
Teachers: 169.6 (16.5 to 1)
Librarians/Media Specialists: 3.5 (799.7 to 1)
Guidance Counselors: 5.0 (559.8 to 1)
Current Spending: ($ per student per year):
Total: $8,550; Instruction: $5,178; Support Services: $3,035
Enrollment, Drop-out Rates and Diploma Recipients by Race/Ethnicity

Category	Total	White	Black	Asian	AIAN	Hisp.
Enrollment (%)	100.0	97.3	1.8	0.3	0.4	0.3
Drop-out Rate (%)	n/a	n/a	n/a	n/a	n/a	n/a
H.S. Diplomas (#)	192	188	4	0	0	0

MSD North Posey County Schools
101 N Church St • Poseyville, IN 47633
(812) 874-2243 • http://www.northposey.k12.in.us/
Grade Span: PK-12; **Agency Type:** 1
Schools: 4
2 Primary; 1 Middle; 1 High; 0 Other Level
4 Regular; 0 Special Education; 0 Vocational; 0 Alternative
0 Magnet; 0 Charter; 2 Title I Eligible; 0 School-wide Title I
Students: 1,571 (52.8% male; 47.2% female)
Individual Education Program: 284 (18.1%);
English Language Learner: 2 (0.1%); Migrant: n/a
Eligible for Free Lunch Program: 149 (9.5%)
Eligible for Reduced-Price Lunch Program: 132 (8.4%)
Teachers: 99.5 (15.8 to 1)
Librarians/Media Specialists: 2.0 (785.5 to 1)
Guidance Counselors: 2.0 (785.5 to 1)
Current Spending: ($ per student per year):
Total: $6,657; Instruction: $4,419; Support Services: $1,980
Enrollment, Drop-out Rates and Diploma Recipients by Race/Ethnicity

Category	Total	White	Black	Asian	AIAN	Hisp.
Enrollment (%)	100.0	99.6	0.1	0.3	0.0	0.1
Drop-out Rate (%)	n/a	n/a	n/a	n/a	n/a	n/a
H.S. Diplomas (#)	116	116	0	0	0	0

Putnam County

Cloverdale Community Schools
310 E Logan • Cloverdale, IN 46120-9803
(765) 795-4664 • http://www.cloverdale.k12.in.us/
Grade Span: PK-12; **Agency Type:** 1
Schools: 4
1 Primary; 1 Middle; 1 High; 1 Other Level
3 Regular; 0 Special Education; 1 Vocational; 0 Alternative
0 Magnet; 0 Charter; 2 Title I Eligible; 0 School-wide Title I
Students: 1,526 (51.2% male; 48.8% female)
Individual Education Program: 341 (22.3%);
English Language Learner: n/a; Migrant: n/a
Eligible for Free Lunch Program: 446 (29.2%)
Eligible for Reduced-Price Lunch Program: 127 (8.3%)
Teachers: 95.5 (16.0 to 1)
Librarians/Media Specialists: 3.0 (508.7 to 1)
Guidance Counselors: 3.0 (508.7 to 1)
Current Spending: ($ per student per year):
Total: $6,577; Instruction: $3,607; Support Services: $2,640
Enrollment, Drop-out Rates and Diploma Recipients by Race/Ethnicity

Category	Total	White	Black	Asian	AIAN	Hisp.
Enrollment (%)	100.0	97.8	1.6	0.1	0.3	0.2
Drop-out Rate (%)	n/a	n/a	n/a	n/a	n/a	n/a
H.S. Diplomas (#)	101	101	0	0	0	0

Greencastle Community Sch Corp
PO Box 480 • Greencastle, IN 46135-0480
(765) 653-9771 • http://www.greencastle.k12.in.us/
Grade Span: KG-12; **Agency Type:** 1
Schools: 5
3 Primary; 1 Middle; 1 High; 0 Other Level
5 Regular; 0 Special Education; 0 Vocational; 0 Alternative
0 Magnet; 0 Charter; 4 Title I Eligible; 0 School-wide Title I
Students: 1,940 (53.0% male; 47.0% female)

Individual Education Program: 404 (20.8%);
English Language Learner: 18 (0.9%); Migrant: n/a
Eligible for Free Lunch Program: 440 (22.7%)
Eligible for Reduced-Price Lunch Program: 141 (7.3%)
Teachers: 103.5 (18.7 to 1)
Librarians/Media Specialists: 3.0 (646.7 to 1)
Guidance Counselors: 5.5 (352.7 to 1)
Current Spending: ($ per student per year):
Total: $6,327; Instruction: $3,397; Support Services: $2,605
Enrollment, Drop-out Rates and Diploma Recipients by Race/Ethnicity

Category	Total	White	Black	Asian	AIAN	Hisp.
Enrollment (%)	100.0	97.1	1.4	0.8	0.3	0.4
Drop-out Rate (%)	n/a	n/a	n/a	n/a	n/a	n/a
H.S. Diplomas (#)	136	136	0	0	0	0

North Putnam Community Schools

300 N Washington • Bainbridge, IN 46105-0169
Mailing Address: PO Box 169 • Bainbridge, IN 46105-0169
(765) 522-6218 • http://www.nputnam.k12.in.us/
Grade Span: PK-12; **Agency Type:** 1
Schools: 5
2 Primary; 1 Middle; 1 High; 1 Other Level
4 Regular; 1 Special Education; 0 Vocational; 0 Alternative
0 Magnet; 0 Charter; 3 Title I Eligible; 0 School-wide Title I
Students: 1,909 (52.5% male; 47.5% female)
Individual Education Program: 489 (25.6%);
English Language Learner: n/a; Migrant: n/a
Eligible for Free Lunch Program: 341 (17.9%)
Eligible for Reduced-Price Lunch Program: 171 (9.0%)
Teachers: 150.0 (12.7 to 1)
Librarians/Media Specialists: 3.0 (636.3 to 1)
Guidance Counselors: 5.0 (381.8 to 1)
Current Spending: ($ per student per year):
Total: $6,381; Instruction: $3,589; Support Services: $2,445
Enrollment, Drop-out Rates and Diploma Recipients by Race/Ethnicity

Category	Total	White	Black	Asian	AIAN	Hisp.
Enrollment (%)	100.0	99.2	0.4	0.2	0.0	0.2
Drop-out Rate (%)	n/a	n/a	n/a	n/a	n/a	n/a
H.S. Diplomas (#)	109	109	0	0	0	0

Randolph County

Randolph Central School Corp

103 NE St • Winchester, IN 47394-1604
(765) 584-1401 • http://www.rc.k12.in.us/
Grade Span: KG-12; **Agency Type:** 1
Schools: 5
3 Primary; 1 Middle; 1 High; 0 Other Level
5 Regular; 0 Special Education; 0 Vocational; 0 Alternative
0 Magnet; 0 Charter; 3 Title I Eligible; 0 School-wide Title I
Students: 1,721 (51.3% male; 48.7% female)
Individual Education Program: 396 (23.0%);
English Language Learner: 14 (0.8%); Migrant: n/a
Eligible for Free Lunch Program: 432 (25.1%)
Eligible for Reduced-Price Lunch Program: 138 (8.0%)
Teachers: 108.0 (15.9 to 1)
Librarians/Media Specialists: 1.5 (1,147.3 to 1)
Guidance Counselors: 3.5 (491.7 to 1)
Current Spending: ($ per student per year):
Total: $7,032; Instruction: $4,404; Support Services: $2,382
Enrollment, Drop-out Rates and Diploma Recipients by Race/Ethnicity

Category	Total	White	Black	Asian	AIAN	Hisp.
Enrollment (%)	100.0	98.6	0.2	0.4	0.1	0.8
Drop-out Rate (%)	n/a	n/a	n/a	n/a	n/a	n/a
H.S. Diplomas (#)	98	95	1	2	0	0

Ripley County

Batesville Community School Corp

626 N Huntersville Rd • Batesville, IN 47006-0121
Mailing Address: PO Box 121 • Batesville, IN 47006-0121
(812) 934-2194 • http://www.batesville.k12.in.us/bcsc/default.html
Grade Span: PK-12; **Agency Type:** 1
Schools: 4
1 Primary; 2 Middle; 1 High; 0 Other Level
4 Regular; 0 Special Education; 0 Vocational; 0 Alternative
0 Magnet; 0 Charter; 3 Title I Eligible; 0 School-wide Title I
Students: 1,911 (50.5% male; 49.5% female)
Individual Education Program: 298 (15.6%);
English Language Learner: 35 (1.8%); Migrant: n/a
Eligible for Free Lunch Program: 148 (7.7%)
Eligible for Reduced-Price Lunch Program: 89 (4.7%)
Teachers: 111.6 (17.1 to 1)
Librarians/Media Specialists: 4.0 (477.8 to 1)
Guidance Counselors: 5.0 (382.2 to 1)
Current Spending: ($ per student per year):
Total: $7,036; Instruction: $4,118; Support Services: $2,682
Enrollment, Drop-out Rates and Diploma Recipients by Race/Ethnicity

Category	Total	White	Black	Asian	AIAN	Hisp.
Enrollment (%)	100.0	98.1	0.0	0.4	0.0	1.5
Drop-out Rate (%)	n/a	n/a	n/a	n/a	n/a	n/a
H.S. Diplomas (#)	125	122	0	0	1	2

Rush County

Rush County Schools

330 W 8th St • Rushville, IN 46173-1217
(765) 932-4186 • http://rcs.rushville.k12.in.us/
Grade Span: PK-12; **Agency Type:** 1
Schools: 6
4 Primary; 1 Middle; 1 High; 0 Other Level
6 Regular; 0 Special Education; 0 Vocational; 0 Alternative
0 Magnet; 0 Charter; 2 Title I Eligible; 0 School-wide Title I
Students: 2,675 (51.1% male; 48.9% female)
Individual Education Program: 400 (15.0%);
English Language Learner: 19 (0.7%); Migrant: n/a
Eligible for Free Lunch Program: 474 (17.7%)
Eligible for Reduced-Price Lunch Program: 239 (8.9%)
Teachers: 165.3 (16.2 to 1)
Librarians/Media Specialists: 4.0 (668.8 to 1)
Guidance Counselors: 4.0 (668.8 to 1)
Current Spending: ($ per student per year):
Total: $6,627; Instruction: $4,063; Support Services: $2,163
Enrollment, Drop-out Rates and Diploma Recipients by Race/Ethnicity

Category	Total	White	Black	Asian	AIAN	Hisp.
Enrollment (%)	100.0	98.1	0.7	0.4	0.0	0.7
Drop-out Rate (%)	n/a	n/a	n/a	n/a	n/a	n/a
H.S. Diplomas (#)	146	145	0	0	0	1

Scott County

Scott County SD 2

375 E Mcclain Ave • Scottsburg, IN 47170-1798
(812) 752-8946 • http://www.scott1.k12.in.us/
Grade Span: KG-12; **Agency Type:** 1
Schools: 6
4 Primary; 1 Middle; 1 High; 0 Other Level
6 Regular; 0 Special Education; 0 Vocational; 0 Alternative
0 Magnet; 0 Charter; 4 Title I Eligible; 0 School-wide Title I
Students: 2,794 (53.6% male; 46.4% female)
Individual Education Program: 390 (14.0%);
English Language Learner: 12 (0.4%); Migrant: n/a
Eligible for Free Lunch Program: 710 (25.4%)
Eligible for Reduced-Price Lunch Program: 254 (9.1%)
Teachers: 152.4 (18.3 to 1)
Librarians/Media Specialists: 3.0 (931.3 to 1)
Guidance Counselors: 7.7 (362.9 to 1)
Current Spending: ($ per student per year):
Total: $6,526; Instruction: $4,057; Support Services: $2,179
Enrollment, Drop-out Rates and Diploma Recipients by Race/Ethnicity

Category	Total	White	Black	Asian	AIAN	Hisp.
Enrollment (%)	100.0	99.1	0.0	0.3	0.2	0.5
Drop-out Rate (%)	n/a	n/a	n/a	n/a	n/a	n/a
H.S. Diplomas (#)	139	139	0	0	0	0

Shelby County

Shelby Eastern Schools

2451 N 600 E • Shelbyville, IN 46176-9113
(765) 544-2246 • http://www.ses.k12.in.us/
Grade Span: KG-12; **Agency Type:** 1
Schools: 4
2 Primary; 0 Middle; 0 High; 2 Other Level
4 Regular; 0 Special Education; 0 Vocational; 0 Alternative
0 Magnet; 0 Charter; 3 Title I Eligible; 0 School-wide Title I
Students: 1,682 (51.3% male; 48.7% female)
Individual Education Program: 254 (15.1%);
English Language Learner: n/a; Migrant: n/a
Eligible for Free Lunch Program: 161 (9.6%)
Eligible for Reduced-Price Lunch Program: 69 (4.1%)
Teachers: 100.0 (16.8 to 1)
Librarians/Media Specialists: 3.5 (480.6 to 1)
Guidance Counselors: 5.0 (336.4 to 1)
Current Spending: ($ per student per year):
Total: $6,559; Instruction: $3,858; Support Services: $2,444

Enrollment, Drop-out Rates and Diploma Recipients by Race/Ethnicity

Category	Total	White	Black	Asian	AIAN	Hisp.
Enrollment (%)	100.0	99.1	0.1	0.2	0.1	0.5
Drop-out Rate (%)	n/a	n/a	n/a	n/a	n/a	n/a
H.S. Diplomas (#)	131	127	1	2	0	1

Shelbyville Central Schools

803 St Joseph St • Shelbyville, IN 46176-1295
(317) 392-2505 • http://www.shelbycs.org/
Grade Span: KG-12; **Agency Type:** 1
Schools: 5
3 Primary; 1 Middle; 1 High; 0 Other Level
5 Regular; 0 Special Education; 0 Vocational; 0 Alternative
0 Magnet; 0 Charter; 3 Title I Eligible; 0 School-wide Title I
Students: 3,589 (51.7% male; 48.3% female)
Individual Education Program: 799 (22.3%);
English Language Learner: 168 (4.7%); Migrant: n/a
Eligible for Free Lunch Program: 867 (24.2%)
Eligible for Reduced-Price Lunch Program: 289 (8.1%)
Teachers: 188.0 (19.1 to 1)
Librarians/Media Specialists: 2.0 (1,794.5 to 1)
Guidance Counselors: 8.0 (448.6 to 1)
Current Spending: ($ per student per year):
Total: $5,596; Instruction: $3,485; Support Services: $1,799
Enrollment, Drop-out Rates and Diploma Recipients by Race/Ethnicity

Category	Total	White	Black	Asian	AIAN	Hisp.
Enrollment (%)	100.0	93.4	1.5	1.0	1.0	3.1
Drop-out Rate (%)	n/a	n/a	n/a	n/a	n/a	n/a
H.S. Diplomas (#)	170	164	3	2	0	1

Spencer County

North Spencer County Sch Corp

3720 E Sr 162 • Lincoln City, IN 47552
Mailing Address: PO Box 316 • Lincoln City, IN 47552-0316
(812) 937-2400 • http://www.nspencer.k12.in.us/
Grade Span: PK-12; **Agency Type:** 1
Schools: 5
4 Primary; 0 Middle; 1 High; 0 Other Level
5 Regular; 0 Special Education; 0 Vocational; 0 Alternative
0 Magnet; 0 Charter; 2 Title I Eligible; 0 School-wide Title I
Students: 2,372 (48.8% male; 51.2% female)
Individual Education Program: 307 (12.9%);
English Language Learner: 66 (2.8%); Migrant: n/a
Eligible for Free Lunch Program: 269 (11.3%)
Eligible for Reduced-Price Lunch Program: 146 (6.2%)
Teachers: 132.2 (17.9 to 1)
Librarians/Media Specialists: 3.0 (790.7 to 1)
Guidance Counselors: 3.0 (790.7 to 1)
Current Spending: ($ per student per year):
Total: $6,287; Instruction: $4,069; Support Services: $1,898
Enrollment, Drop-out Rates and Diploma Recipients by Race/Ethnicity

Category	Total	White	Black	Asian	AIAN	Hisp.
Enrollment (%)	100.0	96.6	0.2	0.5	0.0	2.7
Drop-out Rate (%)	n/a	n/a	n/a	n/a	n/a	n/a
H.S. Diplomas (#)	160	157	1	0	0	2

South Spencer County Sch Corp

321 S 5th St • Rockport, IN 47635-0026
Mailing Address: PO Box 26 • Rockport, IN 47635-0026
(812) 649-2591 • http://www.sspencer.k12.in.us/
Grade Span: PK-12; **Agency Type:** 1
Schools: 4
2 Primary; 1 Middle; 1 High; 0 Other Level
4 Regular; 0 Special Education; 0 Vocational; 0 Alternative
0 Magnet; 0 Charter; 3 Title I Eligible; 0 School-wide Title I
Students: 1,511 (50.8% male; 49.2% female)
Individual Education Program: 190 (12.6%);
English Language Learner: 4 (0.3%); Migrant: n/a
Eligible for Free Lunch Program: 310 (20.5%)
Eligible for Reduced-Price Lunch Program: 93 (6.2%)
Teachers: 83.6 (18.1 to 1)
Librarians/Media Specialists: 1.0 (1,511.0 to 1)
Guidance Counselors: 3.0 (503.7 to 1)
Current Spending: ($ per student per year):
Total: $7,212; Instruction: $4,543; Support Services: $2,248
Enrollment, Drop-out Rates and Diploma Recipients by Race/Ethnicity

Category	Total	White	Black	Asian	AIAN	Hisp.
Enrollment (%)	100.0	98.1	0.7	0.8	0.1	0.3
Drop-out Rate (%)	n/a	n/a	n/a	n/a	n/a	n/a
H.S. Diplomas (#)	111	111	0	0	0	0

St. Joseph County

John Glenn School Corporation

101 John Glenn Dr • Walkerton, IN 46574-1288
(574) 586-3129 • http://www.jgsc.k12.in.us/
Grade Span: PK-12; **Agency Type:** 1
Schools: 4
2 Primary; 1 Middle; 1 High; 0 Other Level
4 Regular; 0 Special Education; 0 Vocational; 0 Alternative
0 Magnet; 0 Charter; 1 Title I Eligible; 0 School-wide Title I
Students: 1,693 (52.3% male; 47.7% female)
Individual Education Program: 226 (13.3%);
English Language Learner: 23 (1.4%); Migrant: n/a
Eligible for Free Lunch Program: 297 (17.5%)
Eligible for Reduced-Price Lunch Program: 130 (7.7%)
Teachers: 90.5 (18.7 to 1)
Librarians/Media Specialists: 3.0 (564.3 to 1)
Guidance Counselors: 4.0 (423.3 to 1)
Current Spending: ($ per student per year):
Total: $6,396; Instruction: $4,025; Support Services: $2,092
Enrollment, Drop-out Rates and Diploma Recipients by Race/Ethnicity

Category	Total	White	Black	Asian	AIAN	Hisp.
Enrollment (%)	100.0	97.3	0.2	0.4	0.1	2.0
Drop-out Rate (%)	n/a	n/a	n/a	n/a	n/a	n/a
H.S. Diplomas (#)	113	112	0	0	0	1

Penn-Harris-Madison Sch Corp

55900 Bittersweet Rd • Mishawaka, IN 46545-7717
(574) 259-7941 • http://www.phm.k12.in.us/
Grade Span: KG-12; **Agency Type:** 1
Schools: 16
11 Primary; 3 Middle; 2 High; 0 Other Level
15 Regular; 0 Special Education; 0 Vocational; 1 Alternative
0 Magnet; 0 Charter; 7 Title I Eligible; 0 School-wide Title I
Students: 9,958 (50.6% male; 49.4% female)
Individual Education Program: 1,305 (13.1%);
English Language Learner: 361 (3.6%); Migrant: n/a
Eligible for Free Lunch Program: 851 (8.5%)
Eligible for Reduced-Price Lunch Program: 394 (4.0%)
Teachers: 476.5 (20.9 to 1)
Librarians/Media Specialists: 1.0 (9,958.0 to 1)
Guidance Counselors: 14.0 (711.3 to 1)
Current Spending: ($ per student per year):
Total: $7,132; Instruction: $4,205; Support Services: $2,663
Enrollment, Drop-out Rates and Diploma Recipients by Race/Ethnicity

Category	Total	White	Black	Asian	AIAN	Hisp.
Enrollment (%)	100.0	93.2	2.2	2.4	0.7	1.6
Drop-out Rate (%)	n/a	n/a	n/a	n/a	n/a	n/a
H.S. Diplomas (#)	619	587	9	15	1	7

School City of Mishawaka

1402 S Main St • Mishawaka, IN 46544-5297
(574) 254-4537
Grade Span: PK-12; **Agency Type:** 1
Schools: 11
7 Primary; 1 Middle; 1 High; 2 Other Level
9 Regular; 2 Special Education; 0 Vocational; 0 Alternative
0 Magnet; 0 Charter; 5 Title I Eligible; 2 School-wide Title I
Students: 5,528 (52.3% male; 47.7% female)
Individual Education Program: 985 (17.8%);
English Language Learner: 98 (1.8%); Migrant: n/a
Eligible for Free Lunch Program: 1,571 (28.4%)
Eligible for Reduced-Price Lunch Program: 584 (10.6%)
Teachers: 377.5 (14.6 to 1)
Librarians/Media Specialists: 2.0 (2,764.0 to 1)
Guidance Counselors: 7.0 (789.7 to 1)
Current Spending: ($ per student per year):
Total: $7,240; Instruction: $4,599; Support Services: $2,339
Enrollment, Drop-out Rates and Diploma Recipients by Race/Ethnicity

Category	Total	White	Black	Asian	AIAN	Hisp.
Enrollment (%)	100.0	92.7	3.4	0.8	0.4	2.7
Drop-out Rate (%)	n/a	n/a	n/a	n/a	n/a	n/a
H.S. Diplomas (#)	261	248	6	2	1	4

South Bend Community Sch Corp

635 S Main St • South Bend, IN 46601-2295
(574) 283-8000 • http://www.sbcsc.k12.in.us/
Grade Span: PK-12; **Agency Type:** 1
Schools: 37
24 Primary; 5 Middle; 5 High; 3 Other Level
34 Regular; 1 Special Education; 0 Vocational; 2 Alternative
0 Magnet; 0 Charter; 19 Title I Eligible; 10 School-wide Title I
Students: 21,662 (51.4% male; 48.6% female)
Individual Education Program: 5,172 (23.9%);
English Language Learner: 2,884 (13.3%); Migrant: n/a

Eligible for Free Lunch Program: 10,071 (46.5%)
Eligible for Reduced-Price Lunch Program: 1,946 (9.0%)
Teachers: 1,309.9 (16.5 to 1)
Librarians/Media Specialists: 16.0 (1,353.9 to 1)
Guidance Counselors: 25.5 (849.5 to 1)
Current Spending: ($ per student per year):
Total: $9,105; Instruction: $5,702; Support Services: $3,051
Enrollment, Drop-out Rates and Diploma Recipients by Race/Ethnicity

Category	Total	White	Black	Asian	AIAN	Hisp.
Enrollment (%)	100.0	49.5	36.9	1.3	0.5	11.8
Drop-out Rate (%)	n/a	n/a	n/a	n/a	n/a	n/a
H.S. Diplomas (#)	1,206	773	305	31	2	95

Starke County

Knox Community School Corp
2 Redskin Trl • Knox, IN 46534-2238
(574) 772-1600 • http://www.niesc.k12.in.us/knox/index.html
Grade Span: KG-12; **Agency Type:** 1
Schools: 3
1 Primary; 1 Middle; 1 High; 0 Other Level
3 Regular; 0 Special Education; 0 Vocational; 0 Alternative
0 Magnet; 0 Charter; 2 Title I Eligible; 0 School-wide Title I
Students: 2,032 (51.0% male; 49.0% female)
Individual Education Program: 301 (14.8%);
English Language Learner: 67 (3.3%); Migrant: n/a
Eligible for Free Lunch Program: 750 (36.9%)
Eligible for Reduced-Price Lunch Program: 193 (9.5%)
Teachers: 113.0 (18.0 to 1)
Librarians/Media Specialists: 3.0 (677.3 to 1)
Guidance Counselors: 4.0 (508.0 to 1)
Current Spending: ($ per student per year):
Total: $7,222; Instruction: $4,333; Support Services: $2,531
Enrollment, Drop-out Rates and Diploma Recipients by Race/Ethnicity

Category	Total	White	Black	Asian	AIAN	Hisp.
Enrollment (%)	100.0	96.9	0.3	0.2	0.1	2.5
Drop-out Rate (%)	n/a	n/a	n/a	n/a	n/a	n/a
H.S. Diplomas (#)	101	96	0	0	0	5

North Judson-San Pierre Sch Corp
801 Campbell Dr • North Judson, IN 46366-1220
(574) 896-2155 • http://www.njsp.k12.in.us/
Grade Span: KG-12; **Agency Type:** 1
Schools: 4
2 Primary; 1 Middle; 1 High; 0 Other Level
4 Regular; 0 Special Education; 0 Vocational; 0 Alternative
0 Magnet; 0 Charter; 3 Title I Eligible; 0 School-wide Title I
Students: 1,522 (52.0% male; 48.0% female)
Individual Education Program: 228 (15.0%);
English Language Learner: 30 (2.0%); Migrant: n/a
Eligible for Free Lunch Program: 504 (33.1%)
Eligible for Reduced-Price Lunch Program: 203 (13.3%)
Teachers: 88.5 (17.2 to 1)
Librarians/Media Specialists: 2.0 (761.0 to 1)
Guidance Counselors: 5.0 (304.4 to 1)
Current Spending: ($ per student per year):
Total: $6,085; Instruction: $3,846; Support Services: $2,124
Enrollment, Drop-out Rates and Diploma Recipients by Race/Ethnicity

Category	Total	White	Black	Asian	AIAN	Hisp.
Enrollment (%)	100.0	96.4	0.1	0.2	0.1	3.2
Drop-out Rate (%)	n/a	n/a	n/a	n/a	n/a	n/a
H.S. Diplomas (#)	109	94	0	0	11	4

Steuben County

MSD Steuben County
400 S Martha St • Angola, IN 46703-1953
(260) 665-2854 • http://www.msdsteuben.k12.in.us/
Grade Span: KG-12; **Agency Type:** 1
Schools: 6
4 Primary; 1 Middle; 1 High; 0 Other Level
6 Regular; 0 Special Education; 0 Vocational; 0 Alternative
0 Magnet; 0 Charter; 4 Title I Eligible; 0 School-wide Title I
Students: 3,067 (51.3% male; 48.7% female)
Individual Education Program: 351 (11.4%);
English Language Learner: 93 (3.0%); Migrant: n/a
Eligible for Free Lunch Program: 573 (18.7%)
Eligible for Reduced-Price Lunch Program: 274 (8.9%)
Teachers: 158.0 (19.4 to 1)
Librarians/Media Specialists: 2.5 (1,226.8 to 1)
Guidance Counselors: 6.0 (511.2 to 1)
Current Spending: ($ per student per year):
Total: $6,454; Instruction: $3,687; Support Services: $2,474

Enrollment, Drop-out Rates and Diploma Recipients by Race/Ethnicity

Category	Total	White	Black	Asian	AIAN	Hisp.
Enrollment (%)	100.0	95.4	0.6	0.4	0.7	2.8
Drop-out Rate (%)	n/a	n/a	n/a	n/a	n/a	n/a
H.S. Diplomas (#)	178	171	2	0	1	4

Sullivan County

Northeast School Corp
406 N Vine St • Hymera, IN 47855-0493
Mailing Address: PO Box 493 • Hymera, IN 47855-0493
(812) 383-5761 • http://www.nesc.k12.in.us/
Grade Span: PK-12; **Agency Type:** 1
Schools: 6
4 Primary; 0 Middle; 2 High; 0 Other Level
6 Regular; 0 Special Education; 0 Vocational; 0 Alternative
0 Magnet; 0 Charter; 3 Title I Eligible; 0 School-wide Title I
Students: 1,522 (53.4% male; 46.6% female)
Individual Education Program: 337 (22.1%);
English Language Learner: n/a; Migrant: n/a
Eligible for Free Lunch Program: 475 (31.2%)
Eligible for Reduced-Price Lunch Program: 176 (11.6%)
Teachers: 104.5 (14.6 to 1)
Librarians/Media Specialists: 2.0 (761.0 to 1)
Guidance Counselors: 1.5 (1,014.7 to 1)
Current Spending: ($ per student per year):
Total: $6,926; Instruction: $4,485; Support Services: $2,161
Enrollment, Drop-out Rates and Diploma Recipients by Race/Ethnicity

Category	Total	White	Black	Asian	AIAN	Hisp.
Enrollment (%)	100.0	99.5	0.0	0.1	0.2	0.1
Drop-out Rate (%)	n/a	n/a	n/a	n/a	n/a	n/a
H.S. Diplomas (#)	96	96	0	0	0	0

Southwest School Corp
31 N Court St • Sullivan, IN 47882-1509
(812) 268-6311 • http://www.swest.k12.in.us/
Grade Span: PK-12; **Agency Type:** 1
Schools: 5
3 Primary; 0 Middle; 1 High; 1 Other Level
5 Regular; 0 Special Education; 0 Vocational; 0 Alternative
0 Magnet; 0 Charter; 4 Title I Eligible; 0 School-wide Title I
Students: 1,983 (51.9% male; 48.1% female)
Individual Education Program: 455 (22.9%);
English Language Learner: 6 (0.3%); Migrant: n/a
Eligible for Free Lunch Program: 458 (23.1%)
Eligible for Reduced-Price Lunch Program: 170 (8.6%)
Teachers: 116.0 (17.1 to 1)
Librarians/Media Specialists: 1.0 (1,983.0 to 1)
Guidance Counselors: 3.0 (661.0 to 1)
Current Spending: ($ per student per year):
Total: $7,762; Instruction: $5,012; Support Services: $2,450
Enrollment, Drop-out Rates and Diploma Recipients by Race/Ethnicity

Category	Total	White	Black	Asian	AIAN	Hisp.
Enrollment (%)	100.0	99.2	0.2	0.2	0.1	0.3
Drop-out Rate (%)	n/a	n/a	n/a	n/a	n/a	n/a
H.S. Diplomas (#)	136	136	0	0	0	0

Switzerland County

Switzerland County School Corp
305 W Seminary St • Vevay, IN 47043-1141
(812) 427-2611 • http://www.switzerland.k12.in.us/
Grade Span: PK-12; **Agency Type:** 1
Schools: 4
2 Primary; 1 Middle; 1 High; 0 Other Level
4 Regular; 0 Special Education; 0 Vocational; 0 Alternative
0 Magnet; 0 Charter; 2 Title I Eligible; 0 School-wide Title I
Students: 1,599 (51.2% male; 48.8% female)
Individual Education Program: 294 (18.4%);
English Language Learner: 3 (0.2%); Migrant: n/a
Eligible for Free Lunch Program: 456 (28.5%)
Eligible for Reduced-Price Lunch Program: 146 (9.1%)
Teachers: 81.5 (19.6 to 1)
Librarians/Media Specialists: 1.0 (1,599.0 to 1)
Guidance Counselors: 4.0 (399.8 to 1)
Current Spending: ($ per student per year):
Total: $6,381; Instruction: $3,526; Support Services: $2,574
Enrollment, Drop-out Rates and Diploma Recipients by Race/Ethnicity

Category	Total	White	Black	Asian	AIAN	Hisp.
Enrollment (%)	100.0	98.7	0.5	0.4	0.0	0.4
Drop-out Rate (%)	n/a	n/a	n/a	n/a	n/a	n/a
H.S. Diplomas (#)	89	88	1	0	0	0

Tippecanoe County

Lafayette School Corporation

2300 Cason St • Lafayette, IN 47904-2692
(765) 771-6000 • http://www.lsc.k12.in.us/
Grade Span: KG-12; **Agency Type:** 1
Schools: 15
11 Primary; 2 Middle; 1 High; 1 Other Level
14 Regular; 1 Special Education; 0 Vocational; 0 Alternative
0 Magnet; 0 Charter; 9 Title I Eligible; 4 School-wide Title I
Students: 7,349 (50.7% male; 49.3% female)
Individual Education Program: 1,633 (22.2%);
English Language Learner: 1,028 (14.0%); Migrant: n/a
Eligible for Free Lunch Program: 2,144 (29.2%)
Eligible for Reduced-Price Lunch Program: 749 (10.2%)
Teachers: 518.8 (14.2 to 1)
Librarians/Media Specialists: 13.0 (565.3 to 1)
Guidance Counselors: 15.2 (483.5 to 1)
Current Spending: ($ per student per year):
Total: $6,991; Instruction: $4,285; Support Services: $2,454
Enrollment, Drop-out Rates and Diploma Recipients by Race/Ethnicity

Category	Total	White	Black	Asian	AIAN	Hisp.
Enrollment (%)	100.0	78.5	6.5	0.5	0.2	14.2
Drop-out Rate (%)	n/a	n/a	n/a	n/a	n/a	n/a
H.S. Diplomas (#)	357	312	16	0	0	29

Tippecanoe School Corp

21 Elston Rd • Lafayette, IN 47909-2899
(765) 474-2481 • http://tsc.k12.in.us/
Grade Span: KG-12; **Agency Type:** 1
Schools: 16
9 Primary; 5 Middle; 2 High; 0 Other Level
16 Regular; 0 Special Education; 0 Vocational; 0 Alternative
0 Magnet; 0 Charter; 10 Title I Eligible; 0 School-wide Title I
Students: 9,995 (52.4% male; 47.6% female)
Individual Education Program: 1,429 (14.3%);
English Language Learner: 547 (5.5%); Migrant: n/a
Eligible for Free Lunch Program: 1,530 (15.3%)
Eligible for Reduced-Price Lunch Program: 481 (4.8%)
Teachers: 542.5 (18.4 to 1)
Librarians/Media Specialists: 20.3 (492.4 to 1)
Guidance Counselors: 21.0 (476.0 to 1)
Current Spending: ($ per student per year):
Total: $6,559; Instruction: $4,027; Support Services: $2,290
Enrollment, Drop-out Rates and Diploma Recipients by Race/Ethnicity

Category	Total	White	Black	Asian	AIAN	Hisp.
Enrollment (%)	100.0	91.2	1.6	2.3	0.9	4.0
Drop-out Rate (%)	n/a	n/a	n/a	n/a	n/a	n/a
H.S. Diplomas (#)	599	576	3	4	9	7

West Lafayette Com School Corp

1130 N Salisbury • West Lafayette, IN 47906-2497
(765) 746-1641 • http://www.wl.k12.in.us/
Grade Span: KG-12; **Agency Type:** 1
Schools: 3
1 Primary; 1 Middle; 1 High; 0 Other Level
3 Regular; 0 Special Education; 0 Vocational; 0 Alternative
0 Magnet; 0 Charter; 2 Title I Eligible; 0 School-wide Title I
Students: 2,044 (50.6% male; 49.4% female)
Individual Education Program: 231 (11.3%);
English Language Learner: 326 (15.9%); Migrant: n/a
Eligible for Free Lunch Program: 119 (5.8%)
Eligible for Reduced-Price Lunch Program: 49 (2.4%)
Teachers: 108.8 (18.8 to 1)
Librarians/Media Specialists: 3.0 (681.3 to 1)
Guidance Counselors: 3.0 (681.3 to 1)
Current Spending: ($ per student per year):
Total: $7,486; Instruction: $4,622; Support Services: $2,686
Enrollment, Drop-out Rates and Diploma Recipients by Race/Ethnicity

Category	Total	White	Black	Asian	AIAN	Hisp.
Enrollment (%)	100.0	77.6	3.1	16.9	0.3	2.1
Drop-out Rate (%)	n/a	n/a	n/a	n/a	n/a	n/a
H.S. Diplomas (#)	148	126	3	14	1	4

Tipton County

Tipton Community School Corp

221 N Main St Ste A • Tipton, IN 46072-1698
(765) 675-2147 • http://www.tcsc.k12.in.us/
Grade Span: KG-12; **Agency Type:** 1
Schools: 3
1 Primary; 1 Middle; 1 High; 0 Other Level
3 Regular; 0 Special Education; 0 Vocational; 0 Alternative
0 Magnet; 0 Charter; 2 Title I Eligible; 0 School-wide Title I
Students: 1,875 (52.2% male; 47.8% female)
Individual Education Program: 296 (15.8%);
English Language Learner: 43 (2.3%); Migrant: n/a
Eligible for Free Lunch Program: 249 (13.3%)
Eligible for Reduced-Price Lunch Program: 119 (6.3%)
Teachers: 112.0 (16.7 to 1)
Librarians/Media Specialists: 3.0 (625.0 to 1)
Guidance Counselors: 4.0 (468.8 to 1)
Current Spending: ($ per student per year):
Total: $6,672; Instruction: $3,881; Support Services: $2,603
Enrollment, Drop-out Rates and Diploma Recipients by Race/Ethnicity

Category	Total	White	Black	Asian	AIAN	Hisp.
Enrollment (%)	100.0	97.7	0.3	0.6	0.5	0.9
Drop-out Rate (%)	n/a	n/a	n/a	n/a	n/a	n/a
H.S. Diplomas (#)	131	127	0	3	1	0

Union County

Union Co-Clg Corner Joint SD

107 Layman St • Liberty, IN 47353-1203
(765) 458-7471 • http://www.uc.k12.in.us/
Grade Span: KG-12; **Agency Type:** 1
Schools: 4
2 Primary; 1 Middle; 1 High; 0 Other Level
4 Regular; 0 Special Education; 0 Vocational; 0 Alternative
0 Magnet; 0 Charter; 3 Title I Eligible; 0 School-wide Title I
Students: 1,606 (52.4% male; 47.6% female)
Individual Education Program: 281 (17.5%);
English Language Learner: 1 (0.1%); Migrant: n/a
Eligible for Free Lunch Program: 465 (29.0%)
Eligible for Reduced-Price Lunch Program: 64 (4.0%)
Teachers: 99.5 (16.1 to 1)
Librarians/Media Specialists: 1.0 (1,606.0 to 1)
Guidance Counselors: 1.0 (1,606.0 to 1)
Current Spending: ($ per student per year):
Total: $6,279; Instruction: $3,712; Support Services: $2,247
Enrollment, Drop-out Rates and Diploma Recipients by Race/Ethnicity

Category	Total	White	Black	Asian	AIAN	Hisp.
Enrollment (%)	100.0	99.5	0.2	0.1	0.2	0.1
Drop-out Rate (%)	n/a	n/a	n/a	n/a	n/a	n/a
H.S. Diplomas (#)	109	106	0	3	0	0

Vanderburgh County

Evansville-Vanderburgh Sch Corp

1 SE 9th St • Evansville, IN 47708-1821
(812) 435-8477 • http://www.evsc.k12.in.us/
Grade Span: PK-12; **Agency Type:** 1
Schools: 42
20 Primary; 10 Middle; 9 High; 3 Other Level
35 Regular; 3 Special Education; 0 Vocational; 4 Alternative
0 Magnet; 0 Charter; 20 Title I Eligible; 11 School-wide Title I
Students: 22,825 (51.0% male; 49.0% female)
Individual Education Program: 4,516 (19.8%);
English Language Learner: 348 (1.5%); Migrant: n/a
Eligible for Free Lunch Program: 7,980 (35.0%)
Eligible for Reduced-Price Lunch Program: 2,162 (9.5%)
Teachers: 1,436.9 (15.9 to 1)
Librarians/Media Specialists: 31.8 (717.8 to 1)
Guidance Counselors: 51.0 (447.5 to 1)
Current Spending: ($ per student per year):
Total: $7,704; Instruction: $4,846; Support Services: $2,522
Enrollment, Drop-out Rates and Diploma Recipients by Race/Ethnicity

Category	Total	White	Black	Asian	AIAN	Hisp.
Enrollment (%)	100.0	82.5	15.4	0.9	0.2	0.9
Drop-out Rate (%)	n/a	n/a	n/a	n/a	n/a	n/a
H.S. Diplomas (#)	1,344	1,186	140	8	2	8

Vermillion County

South Vermillion Com Sch Corp

PO Box 387 • Clinton, IN 47842-0387
(765) 832-2426 • http://www.svcs.k12.in.us/
Grade Span: KG-12; **Agency Type:** 1
Schools: 5
3 Primary; 1 Middle; 1 High; 0 Other Level
5 Regular; 0 Special Education; 0 Vocational; 0 Alternative
0 Magnet; 0 Charter; 3 Title I Eligible; 0 School-wide Title I
Students: 1,951 (50.9% male; 49.1% female)
Individual Education Program: 359 (18.4%);
English Language Learner: 12 (0.6%); Migrant: n/a
Eligible for Free Lunch Program: 549 (28.1%)
Eligible for Reduced-Price Lunch Program: 181 (9.3%)
Teachers: 123.8 (15.8 to 1)
Librarians/Media Specialists: 3.0 (650.3 to 1)
Guidance Counselors: 4.0 (487.8 to 1)

Current Spending: ($ per student per year):
Total: $6,944; Instruction: $4,277; Support Services: $2,266
Enrollment, Drop-out Rates and Diploma Recipients by Race/Ethnicity

Category	Total	White	Black	Asian	AIAN	Hisp.
Enrollment (%)	100.0	99.6	0.0	0.3	0.1	0.1
Drop-out Rate (%)	n/a	n/a	n/a	n/a	n/a	n/a
H.S. Diplomas (#)	119	118	0	0	0	1

Vigo County

Vigo County School Corp
686 Wabash Ave • Terre Haute, IN 47807-0703
Mailing Address: PO Box 3703 • Terre Haute, IN 47803-0703
(812) 462-4216 • http://www.vigoco.k12.in.us/
Grade Span: PK-12; **Agency Type:** 1
Schools: 29
18 Primary; 6 Middle; 4 High; 1 Other Level
27 Regular; 0 Special Education; 0 Vocational; 2 Alternative
0 Magnet; 0 Charter; 17 Title I Eligible; 10 School-wide Title I
Students: 16,433 (51.7% male; 48.3% female)
Individual Education Program: 3,062 (18.6%);
English Language Learner: 55 (0.3%); Migrant: n/a
Eligible for Free Lunch Program: 5,370 (32.7%)
Eligible for Reduced-Price Lunch Program: 1,718 (10.5%)
Teachers: 1,014.2 (16.2 to 1)
Librarians/Media Specialists: 29.0 (566.7 to 1)
Guidance Counselors: 28.0 (586.9 to 1)
Current Spending: ($ per student per year):
Total: $6,537; Instruction: $4,053; Support Services: $2,209
Enrollment, Drop-out Rates and Diploma Recipients by Race/Ethnicity

Category	Total	White	Black	Asian	AIAN	Hisp.
Enrollment (%)	100.0	91.7	6.6	1.1	0.0	0.5
Drop-out Rate (%)	n/a	n/a	n/a	n/a	n/a	n/a
H.S. Diplomas (#)	997	895	74	20	1	7

Wabash County

MSD Wabash County Schools
204 N 300 W • Wabash, IN 46992-8689
(260) 563-8050 • http://www.msdwc.k12.in.us/
Grade Span: KG-12; **Agency Type:** 1
Schools: 8
4 Primary; 0 Middle; 2 High; 2 Other Level
6 Regular; 1 Special Education; 0 Vocational; 1 Alternative
0 Magnet; 0 Charter; 4 Title I Eligible; 0 School-wide Title I
Students: 2,701 (52.8% male; 47.2% female)
Individual Education Program: 476 (17.6%);
English Language Learner: 17 (0.6%); Migrant: n/a
Eligible for Free Lunch Program: 308 (11.4%)
Eligible for Reduced-Price Lunch Program: 151 (5.6%)
Teachers: 188.2 (14.4 to 1)
Librarians/Media Specialists: 2.0 (1,350.5 to 1)
Guidance Counselors: 6.2 (435.6 to 1)
Current Spending: ($ per student per year):
Total: $7,118; Instruction: $4,677; Support Services: $2,152
Enrollment, Drop-out Rates and Diploma Recipients by Race/Ethnicity

Category	Total	White	Black	Asian	AIAN	Hisp.
Enrollment (%)	100.0	97.8	0.7	0.6	0.3	0.5
Drop-out Rate (%)	n/a	n/a	n/a	n/a	n/a	n/a
H.S. Diplomas (#)	137	133	0	3	0	1

Manchester Community Schools
107 S Buffalo • N Manchester, IN 46962-0308
(260) 982-7518 • http://mcs.k12.in.us/welcome.htm
Grade Span: KG-12; **Agency Type:** 1
Schools: 4
2 Primary; 1 Middle; 1 High; 0 Other Level
4 Regular; 0 Special Education; 0 Vocational; 0 Alternative
0 Magnet; 0 Charter; 2 Title I Eligible; 0 School-wide Title I
Students: 1,609 (51.3% male; 48.7% female)
Individual Education Program: 242 (15.0%);
English Language Learner: 18 (1.1%); Migrant: n/a
Eligible for Free Lunch Program: 335 (20.8%)
Eligible for Reduced-Price Lunch Program: 155 (9.6%)
Teachers: 90.2 (17.8 to 1)
Librarians/Media Specialists: 2.8 (574.6 to 1)
Guidance Counselors: 3.0 (536.3 to 1)
Current Spending: ($ per student per year):
Total: $6,694; Instruction: $3,978; Support Services: $2,355
Enrollment, Drop-out Rates and Diploma Recipients by Race/Ethnicity

Category	Total	White	Black	Asian	AIAN	Hisp.
Enrollment (%)	100.0	98.3	0.6	0.7	0.0	0.4
Drop-out Rate (%)	n/a	n/a	n/a	n/a	n/a	n/a
H.S. Diplomas (#)	102	100	0	1	0	1

Wabash City Schools
1101 Colerain St Box 744 • Wabash, IN 46992-0744
(260) 563-2151 • http://apaches.k12.in.us/
Grade Span: PK-12; **Agency Type:** 1
Schools: 4
1 Primary; 2 Middle; 1 High; 0 Other Level
4 Regular; 0 Special Education; 0 Vocational; 0 Alternative
0 Magnet; 0 Charter; 3 Title I Eligible; 0 School-wide Title I
Students: 1,512 (54.0% male; 46.0% female)
Individual Education Program: 302 (20.0%);
English Language Learner: 10 (0.7%); Migrant: n/a
Eligible for Free Lunch Program: 406 (26.9%)
Eligible for Reduced-Price Lunch Program: 163 (10.8%)
Teachers: 95.6 (15.8 to 1)
Librarians/Media Specialists: 2.0 (756.0 to 1)
Guidance Counselors: 2.5 (604.8 to 1)
Current Spending: ($ per student per year):
Total: $6,610; Instruction: $4,261; Support Services: $2,084
Enrollment, Drop-out Rates and Diploma Recipients by Race/Ethnicity

Category	Total	White	Black	Asian	AIAN	Hisp.
Enrollment (%)	100.0	96.4	0.4	0.1	1.9	1.3
Drop-out Rate (%)	n/a	n/a	n/a	n/a	n/a	n/a
H.S. Diplomas (#)	98	98	0	0	0	0

Warrick County

Warrick County School Corp
300 E Gum • Boonville, IN 47601-0809
Mailing Address: PO Box 809 • Boonville, IN 47601-0809
(812) 897-0400 • http://www.warrick.k12.in.us/
Grade Span: KG-12; **Agency Type:** 1
Schools: 16
10 Primary; 2 Middle; 4 High; 0 Other Level
15 Regular; 0 Special Education; 0 Vocational; 1 Alternative
0 Magnet; 0 Charter; 9 Title I Eligible; 0 School-wide Title I
Students: 9,145 (51.6% male; 48.4% female)
Individual Education Program: 1,652 (18.1%);
English Language Learner: 85 (0.9%); Migrant: n/a
Eligible for Free Lunch Program: 1,122 (12.3%)
Eligible for Reduced-Price Lunch Program: 542 (5.9%)
Teachers: 478.0 (19.1 to 1)
Librarians/Media Specialists: 6.0 (1,524.2 to 1)
Guidance Counselors: 11.5 (795.2 to 1)
Current Spending: ($ per student per year):
Total: $6,119; Instruction: $3,859; Support Services: $1,968
Enrollment, Drop-out Rates and Diploma Recipients by Race/Ethnicity

Category	Total	White	Black	Asian	AIAN	Hisp.
Enrollment (%)	100.0	97.1	1.1	1.1	0.2	0.5
Drop-out Rate (%)	n/a	n/a	n/a	n/a	n/a	n/a
H.S. Diplomas (#)	596	580	5	9	0	2

Washington County

East Washington School Corp
1050 N Eastern School Rd • Pekin, IN 47165-7901
(812) 967-3926 • http://ewsc.k12.in.us/
Grade Span: KG-12; **Agency Type:** 1
Schools: 3
1 Primary; 1 Middle; 1 High; 0 Other Level
3 Regular; 0 Special Education; 0 Vocational; 0 Alternative
0 Magnet; 0 Charter; 2 Title I Eligible; 0 School-wide Title I
Students: 1,766 (51.4% male; 48.6% female)
Individual Education Program: 306 (17.3%);
English Language Learner: 5 (0.3%); Migrant: n/a
Eligible for Free Lunch Program: 392 (22.2%)
Eligible for Reduced-Price Lunch Program: 199 (11.3%)
Teachers: 90.0 (19.6 to 1)
Librarians/Media Specialists: 2.0 (883.0 to 1)
Guidance Counselors: 4.5 (392.4 to 1)
Current Spending: ($ per student per year):
Total: $6,512; Instruction: $4,196; Support Services: $2,027
Enrollment, Drop-out Rates and Diploma Recipients by Race/Ethnicity

Category	Total	White	Black	Asian	AIAN	Hisp.
Enrollment (%)	100.0	99.0	0.1	0.1	0.1	0.8
Drop-out Rate (%)	n/a	n/a	n/a	n/a	n/a	n/a
H.S. Diplomas (#)	85	85	0	0	0	0

Salem Community Schools
500 N Harrison St • Salem, IN 47167-1671
(812) 883-4437 • http://www.salemschools.com/
Grade Span: KG-12; **Agency Type:** 1
Schools: 4
2 Primary; 1 Middle; 1 High; 0 Other Level
4 Regular; 0 Special Education; 0 Vocational; 0 Alternative
0 Magnet; 0 Charter; 2 Title I Eligible; 0 School-wide Title I

Students: 2,081 (51.5% male; 48.5% female)
Individual Education Program: 305 (14.7%);
English Language Learner: 13 (0.6%); Migrant: n/a
Eligible for Free Lunch Program: 476 (22.9%)
Eligible for Reduced-Price Lunch Program: 132 (6.3%)
Teachers: 108.0 (19.3 to 1)
Librarians/Media Specialists: 3.0 (693.7 to 1)
Guidance Counselors: 2.6 (800.4 to 1)
Current Spending: ($ per student per year):
Total: $6,253; Instruction: $3,772; Support Services: $2,206
Enrollment, Drop-out Rates and Diploma Recipients by Race/Ethnicity

Category	Total	White	Black	Asian	AIAN	Hisp.
Enrollment (%)	100.0	99.6	0.0	0.1	0.0	0.3
Drop-out Rate (%)	n/a	n/a	n/a	n/a	n/a	n/a
H.S. Diplomas (#)	115	115	0	0	0	0

Wayne County

Centerville-Abington Com Schs
115 W S St • Centerville, IN 47330-1499
(765) 855-3475 • http://www.centerville.k12.in.us/
Grade Span: PK-12; **Agency Type:** 1
Schools: 4
2 Primary; 1 Middle; 1 High; 0 Other Level
4 Regular; 0 Special Education; 0 Vocational; 0 Alternative
0 Magnet; 0 Charter; 3 Title I Eligible; 0 School-wide Title I
Students: 1,585 (53.6% male; 46.4% female)
Individual Education Program: 231 (14.6%);
English Language Learner: 8 (0.5%); Migrant: n/a
Eligible for Free Lunch Program: 196 (12.4%)
Eligible for Reduced-Price Lunch Program: 98 (6.2%)
Teachers: 98.4 (16.1 to 1)
Librarians/Media Specialists: 2.0 (792.5 to 1)
Guidance Counselors: 4.5 (352.2 to 1)
Current Spending: ($ per student per year):
Total: $6,940; Instruction: $4,213; Support Services: $2,430
Enrollment, Drop-out Rates and Diploma Recipients by Race/Ethnicity

Category	Total	White	Black	Asian	AIAN	Hisp.
Enrollment (%)	100.0	99.1	0.0	0.3	0.1	0.4
Drop-out Rate (%)	n/a	n/a	n/a	n/a	n/a	n/a
H.S. Diplomas (#)	97	96	0	1	0	0

Richmond Community School Corp
300 Hub Etchison Pky • Richmond, IN 47374-5399
(765) 973-3300 • http://www.rcs.k12.in.us/
Grade Span: PK-12; **Agency Type:** 1
Schools: 15
10 Primary; 1 Middle; 2 High; 2 Other Level
13 Regular; 1 Special Education; 0 Vocational; 1 Alternative
0 Magnet; 0 Charter; 8 Title I Eligible; 6 School-wide Title I
Students: 6,148 (51.9% male; 48.1% female)
Individual Education Program: 1,457 (23.7%);
English Language Learner: 101 (1.6%); Migrant: n/a
Eligible for Free Lunch Program: 2,419 (39.3%)
Eligible for Reduced-Price Lunch Program: 693 (11.3%)
Teachers: 403.5 (15.2 to 1)
Librarians/Media Specialists: 14.0 (439.1 to 1)
Guidance Counselors: 8.0 (768.5 to 1)
Current Spending: ($ per student per year):
Total: $7,905; Instruction: $4,895; Support Services: $2,740
Enrollment, Drop-out Rates and Diploma Recipients by Race/Ethnicity

Category	Total	White	Black	Asian	AIAN	Hisp.
Enrollment (%)	100.0	86.0	11.4	0.7	0.3	1.7
Drop-out Rate (%)	n/a	n/a	n/a	n/a	n/a	n/a
H.S. Diplomas (#)	306	250	36	12	1	7

Wells County

MSD Bluffton-Harrison
628 S Bennett St • Bluffton, IN 46714-3399
(260) 824-2620
Grade Span: KG-12; **Agency Type:** 1
Schools: 3
1 Primary; 1 Middle; 1 High; 0 Other Level
3 Regular; 0 Special Education; 0 Vocational; 0 Alternative
0 Magnet; 0 Charter; 1 Title I Eligible; 0 School-wide Title I
Students: 1,527 (50.3% male; 49.7% female)
Individual Education Program: 192 (12.6%);
English Language Learner: 71 (4.6%); Migrant: n/a
Eligible for Free Lunch Program: 204 (13.4%)
Eligible for Reduced-Price Lunch Program: 130 (8.5%)
Teachers: 88.0 (17.4 to 1)
Librarians/Media Specialists: 3.0 (509.0 to 1)
Guidance Counselors: 2.5 (610.8 to 1)
Current Spending: ($ per student per year):
Total: $5,951; Instruction: $3,664; Support Services: $2,128
Enrollment, Drop-out Rates and Diploma Recipients by Race/Ethnicity

Category	Total	White	Black	Asian	AIAN	Hisp.
Enrollment (%)	100.0	95.7	0.6	1.3	0.3	2.1
Drop-out Rate (%)	n/a	n/a	n/a	n/a	n/a	n/a
H.S. Diplomas (#)	112	107	0	1	0	4

Northern Wells Com Schools
PO Box 386 • Ossian, IN 46777-0386
(260) 622-4125 • http://www.nwcs.k12.in.us/
Grade Span: PK-12; **Agency Type:** 1
Schools: 4
2 Primary; 1 Middle; 1 High; 0 Other Level
4 Regular; 0 Special Education; 0 Vocational; 0 Alternative
0 Magnet; 0 Charter; 3 Title I Eligible; 0 School-wide Title I
Students: 2,617 (52.5% male; 47.5% female)
Individual Education Program: 409 (15.6%);
English Language Learner: 4 (0.2%); Migrant: n/a
Eligible for Free Lunch Program: 300 (11.5%)
Eligible for Reduced-Price Lunch Program: 174 (6.6%)
Teachers: 148.2 (17.7 to 1)
Librarians/Media Specialists: 2.0 (1,308.5 to 1)
Guidance Counselors: 7.0 (373.9 to 1)
Current Spending: ($ per student per year):
Total: $6,046; Instruction: $3,410; Support Services: $2,337
Enrollment, Drop-out Rates and Diploma Recipients by Race/Ethnicity

Category	Total	White	Black	Asian	AIAN	Hisp.
Enrollment (%)	100.0	98.2	0.2	0.5	0.0	1.0
Drop-out Rate (%)	n/a	n/a	n/a	n/a	n/a	n/a
H.S. Diplomas (#)	203	195	1	5	0	2

White County

Twin Lakes School Corp
565 S Main St • Monticello, IN 47960-2446
(574) 583-7211 • http://www.twinlakes.k12.in.us/
Grade Span: PK-12; **Agency Type:** 1
Schools: 6
4 Primary; 1 Middle; 1 High; 0 Other Level
6 Regular; 0 Special Education; 0 Vocational; 0 Alternative
0 Magnet; 0 Charter; 5 Title I Eligible; 0 School-wide Title I
Students: 2,695 (51.9% male; 48.1% female)
Individual Education Program: 438 (16.3%);
English Language Learner: 213 (7.9%); Migrant: n/a
Eligible for Free Lunch Program: 640 (23.7%)
Eligible for Reduced-Price Lunch Program: 256 (9.5%)
Teachers: 144.5 (18.7 to 1)
Librarians/Media Specialists: 2.0 (1,347.5 to 1)
Guidance Counselors: 7.0 (385.0 to 1)
Current Spending: ($ per student per year):
Total: $5,837; Instruction: $3,401; Support Services: $2,127
Enrollment, Drop-out Rates and Diploma Recipients by Race/Ethnicity

Category	Total	White	Black	Asian	AIAN	Hisp.
Enrollment (%)	100.0	91.3	0.3	0.5	0.0	7.9
Drop-out Rate (%)	n/a	n/a	n/a	n/a	n/a	n/a
H.S. Diplomas (#)	180	173	0	0	0	7

Whitley County

Whitley County Cons Schools
107 N Walnut St Ste A • Columbia City, IN 46725
(260) 244-5772 • http://www.wccs.k12.in.us/
Grade Span: PK-12; **Agency Type:** 1
Schools: 8
5 Primary; 1 Middle; 2 High; 0 Other Level
7 Regular; 0 Special Education; 0 Vocational; 1 Alternative
0 Magnet; 0 Charter; 3 Title I Eligible; 0 School-wide Title I
Students: 3,549 (51.5% male; 48.5% female)
Individual Education Program: 443 (12.5%);
English Language Learner: 22 (0.6%); Migrant: n/a
Eligible for Free Lunch Program: 373 (10.5%)
Eligible for Reduced-Price Lunch Program: 211 (5.9%)
Teachers: 208.6 (17.0 to 1)
Librarians/Media Specialists: 4.0 (887.3 to 1)
Guidance Counselors: 8.5 (417.5 to 1)
Current Spending: ($ per student per year):
Total: $7,161; Instruction: $4,079; Support Services: $2,725
Enrollment, Drop-out Rates and Diploma Recipients by Race/Ethnicity

Category	Total	White	Black	Asian	AIAN	Hisp.
Enrollment (%)	100.0	98.5	0.1	0.3	0.3	0.8
Drop-out Rate (%)	n/a	n/a	n/a	n/a	n/a	n/a
H.S. Diplomas (#)	244	239	0	2	3	0

Number of Schools

Rank	Number	District Name	City
1	93	Indianapolis Public Schools	Indianapolis
2	55	Fort Wayne Community Schools	Fort Wayne
3	42	Evansville-Vanderburgh Sch Corp	Evansville
4	38	Gary Community School Corp	Gary
5	37	South Bend Community Sch Corp	South Bend
6	29	Vigo County School Corp	Terre Haute
7	23	School City of Hammond	Hammond
8	22	Anderson Community School Corp	Anderson
9	21	Monroe County Com Sch Corp	Bloomington
10	20	East Allen County Schools	New Haven
10	20	Elkhart Community Schools	Elkhart
10	20	Greater Clark County Schools	Jeffersonville
13	19	MSD Lawrence Township	Indianapolis
13	19	MSD Warren Township	Indianapolis
15	18	Muncie Community Schools	Muncie
15	18	New Albany-Floyd County Con Sch	New Albany
17	17	Bartholomew Con School Corp	Columbus
17	17	Kokomo-Center Twp Con Sch Corp	Kokomo
19	16	MSD Perry Township	Indianapolis
19	16	Michigan City Area Schools	Michigan City
19	16	North Lawrence Com Schools	Bedford
19	16	Penn-Harris-Madison Sch Corp	Mishawaka
19	16	Tippecanoe School Corp	Lafayette
19	16	Warrick County School Corp	Boonville
25	15	Carmel Clay Schools	Carmel
25	15	Lafayette School Corporation	Lafayette
25	15	MSD Washington Township	Indianapolis
25	15	MSD Wayne Township	Indianapolis
25	15	Marion Community Schools	Marion
25	15	Richmond Community School Corp	Richmond
25	15	Warsaw Community Schools	Warsaw
32	13	Fayette County School Corp	Connersville
32	13	Hamilton Southeastern Schools	Fishers
32	13	MSD Pike Township	Indianapolis
35	12	Laporte Community School Corp	Laporte
35	12	MSD Martinsville Schools	Martinsville
35	12	Valparaiso Community Schools	Valparaiso
38	11	Huntington County Com Sch Corp	Huntington
38	11	New Castle Community Sch Corp	New Castle
38	11	Portage Township Schools	Portage
38	11	School City of Mishawaka	Mishawaka
42	10	Clay Community Schools	Knightsville
42	10	Jay School Corp	Portland
42	10	Jennings County Schools	North Vernon
42	10	Lake Central School Corp	Saint John
42	10	Madison Consolidated Schools	Madison
42	10	Northwest Allen County Schools	Fort Wayne
42	10	School City of East Chicago	East Chicago
49	9	Duneland School Corporation	Chesterton
49	9	Goshen Community Schools	Goshen
49	9	Logansport Community Sch Corp	Logansport
49	9	MSD Southwest Allen County	Fort Wayne
49	9	Noblesville Schools	Noblesville
49	9	South Harrison Com Schools	Corydon
55	8	Avon Community School Corp	Avon
55	8	Brownsburg Community Sch Corp	Brownsburg
55	8	Center Grove Com Sch Corp	Greenwood
55	8	Crawfordsville Com Schools	Crawfordsville
55	8	Crown Point Community Sch Corp	Crown Point
55	8	East Noble School Corp	Kendallville
55	8	Franklin Township Com Sch Corp	Indianapolis
55	8	Greenfield-Central Com Schools	Greenfield
55	8	MSD Wabash County Schools	Wabash
55	8	Merrillville Community School	Merrillville
55	8	Seymour Community Schools	Seymour
55	8	West Clark Community Schools	Sellersburg
55	8	Whitley County Cons Schools	Columbia City
68	7	Franklin Community School Corp	Franklin
68	7	MSD Decatur Township	Indianapolis
68	7	Mooresville Con School Corp	Mooresville
68	7	Peru Community Schools	Peru
68	7	Richland-Bean Blossom C S C	Ellettsville
68	7	Vincennes Community Sch Corp	Vincennes
68	7	Westfield-Washington Schools	Westfield
75	6	Brown County School Corporation	Nashville
75	6	Clark-Pleasant Com School Corp	Whiteland
75	6	Community Schools of Frankfort	Frankfort
75	6	Concord Community Schools	Elkhart
75	6	Crawford County Com School Corp	Marengo
75	6	Dekalb County Ctl United SD	Waterloo
75	6	Delaware Community School Corp	Muncie
75	6	East Porter County School Corp	Kouts
75	6	Eastbrook Community Sch Corp	Marion
75	6	Elwood Community School Corp	Elwood
75	6	Greater Jasper Con Schs	Jasper
75	6	Greenwood Community Sch Corp	Greenwood
75	6	Griffith Public Schools	Griffith
75	6	Lake Ridge Schools	Gary
75	6	Lebanon Community School Corp	Lebanon
75	6	MSD Mount Vernon	Mount Vernon
75	6	MSD Steuben County	Angola
75	6	Middlebury Community Schools	Middlebury
75	6	Northeast School Corp	Hymera
75	6	Plainfield Community Sch Corp	Plainfield
75	6	Plymouth Community School Corp	Plymouth
75	6	Rush County Schools	Rushville
75	6	School City of Hobart	Hobart
75	6	School Town of Highland	Highland
75	6	School Town of Speedway	Speedway
75	6	Scott County SD 2	Scottsburg
75	6	South Dearborn Com School Corp	Aurora
75	6	South Montgomery Com Sch Corp	New Market
75	6	Spencer-Owen Community Schools	Spencer
75	6	Sunman-Dearborn Com Sch Corp	Sunman
75	6	Twin Lakes School Corp	Monticello
75	6	Washington Com Schools Inc	Washington
75	6	Zionsville Community Schools	Zionsville
108	5	Alexandria Com School Corp	Alexandria
108	5	Beech Grove City Schools	Beech Grove
108	5	Benton Community School Corp	Fowler
108	5	Blackford County Schools	Hartford City
108	5	Brownstown Cnt Com Sch Corp	Brownstown
108	5	Franklin County Com Sch Corp	Brookville
108	5	Greencastle Community Sch Corp	Greencastle
108	5	Greensburg Community Schools	Greensburg
108	5	Kankakee Valley School Corp	Wheatfield
108	5	Lakeland School Corporation	Lagrange
108	5	Madison-Grant United Sch Corp	Fairmount
108	5	New Prairie United School Corp	New Carlisle
108	5	North Adams Community Schools	Decatur
108	5	North Harrison Com School Corp	Ramsey
108	5	North Knox School Corp	Bicknell
108	5	North Montgomery Com Sch Corp	Linden
108	5	North Putnam Community Schools	Bainbridge
108	5	North Spencer County Sch Corp	Lincoln City
108	5	Pike County School Corp	Petersburg
108	5	Randolph Central School Corp	Winchester
108	5	School Town of Munster	Munster
108	5	Shelbyville Central Schools	Shelbyville
108	5	South Madison Com Sch Corp	Pendleton
108	5	South Vermillion Com Sch Corp	Clinton
108	5	Southern Hancock Co Com Sch Corp	New Palestine
108	5	Southwest School Corp	Sullivan
108	5	Tippecanoe Valley School Corp	Akron
108	5	Tri-Creek School Corp	Lowell
108	5	Wa-Nee Community Schools	Nappanee
108	5	Wawasee Community School Corp	Syracuse
108	5	Westview School Corporation	Topeka
139	4	Batesville Community School Corp	Batesville
139	4	Baugo Community Schools	Elkhart
139	4	Centerville-Abington Com Schs	Centerville
139	4	Cloverdale Community Schools	Cloverdale
139	4	Danville Community School Corp	Danville
139	4	Decatur County Com Schools	Greensburg
139	4	Delphi Community School Corp	Delphi
139	4	Fairfield Community Schools	Goshen
139	4	Frankton-Lapel Community Schs	Anderson
139	4	Garrett-Keyser-Butler Com	Garrett
139	4	Hamilton Heights School Corp	Arcadia
139	4	John Glenn School Corporation	Walkerton
139	4	MSD North Posey County Schools	Poseyville
139	4	Maconaquah School Corp	Bunker Hill
139	4	Manchester Community Schools	N Manchester
139	4	Mill Creek Community Sch Corp	Clayton
139	4	Mississinewa Community School Corp	Gas City
139	4	Mitchell Community Schools	Mitchell
139	4	Mount Pleasant Twp Com Sch Corp	Yorktown
139	4	Mount Vernon Community Sch Corp	Fortville
139	4	Nineveh-Hensley-Jackson United	Trafalgar
139	4	North Gibson School Corp	Princeton
139	4	North Judson-San Pierre Sch Corp	North Judson
139	4	North Newton School Corp	Morocco
139	4	North West Hendricks Schools	Lizton
139	4	Northern Wells Com Schools	Ossian
139	4	Northwestern School Corp	Kokomo
139	4	Porter Township School Corp	Valparaiso
139	4	Prairie Heights Com Sch Corp	Lagrange
139	4	Rensselaer Central School Corp	Rensselaer
139	4	Rochester Community Sch Corp	Rochester
139	4	Salem Community Schools	Salem
139	4	Shelby Eastern Schools	Shelbyville
139	4	South Gibson School Corp	Fort Branch
139	4	South Spencer County Sch Corp	Rockport
139	4	Southeast Dubois County Sch Corp	Ferdinand
139	4	Southwest Dubois County Sch Corp	Huntingburg
139	4	Switzerland County School Corp	Vevay
139	4	Taylor Community School Corp	Kokomo
139	4	Union Co-Clg Corner Joint SD	Liberty
139	4	Union Township School Corp	Valparaiso
139	4	Wabash City Schools	Wabash
139	4	West Noble School Corporation	Ligonier
139	4	Western School Corp	Russiaville
139	4	Whitko Community School Corp	Pierceton
184	3	East Washington School Corp	Pekin
184	3	Hanover Community School Corp	Cedar Lake
184	3	Knox Community School Corp	Knox
184	3	MSD Bluffton-Harrison	Bluffton
184	3	Southeastern School Corp	Walton
184	3	Tell City-Troy Twp School Corp	Tell City
184	3	Tipton Community School Corp	Tipton
184	3	West Lafayette Com School Corp	West Lafayette
184	3	Western Boone County Com SD	Thorntown
193	2	Paoli Community School Corp	Paoli
193	2	Southwestern-Jefferson County	Hanover

Number of Teachers

Rank	Number	District Name	City
1	2,789	Indianapolis Public Schools	Indianapolis
2	1,833	Fort Wayne Community Schools	Fort Wayne
3	1,436	Evansville-Vanderburgh Sch Corp	Evansville
4	1,309	South Bend Community Sch Corp	South Bend
5	1,016	Gary Community School Corp	Gary
6	1,014	Vigo County School Corp	Terre Haute
7	923	MSD Lawrence Township	Indianapolis
8	810	MSD Wayne Township	Indianapolis
9	797	Elkhart Community Schools	Elkhart
10	766	Carmel Clay Schools	Carmel
11	754	School City of Hammond	Hammond
12	743	MSD Perry Township	Indianapolis
13	681	Anderson Community School Corp	Anderson
14	657	MSD Warren Township	Indianapolis
15	646	Monroe County Com Sch Corp	Bloomington
16	619	New Albany-Floyd County Con Sch	New Albany
17	612	Greater Clark County Schools	Jeffersonville
18	604	Bartholomew Con School Corp	Columbus
19	604	MSD Pike Township	Indianapolis
20	594	MSD Washington Township	Indianapolis
21	583	Hamilton Southeastern Schools	Fishers
22	579	Muncie Community Schools	Muncie
23	573	East Allen County Schools	New Haven
24	542	Tippecanoe School Corp	Lafayette
25	518	Lafayette School Corporation	Lafayette
26	499	Kokomo-Center Twp Con Sch Corp	Kokomo
27	478	Warrick County School Corp	Boonville
28	476	Penn-Harris-Madison Sch Corp	Mishawaka
29	452	Michigan City Area Schools	Michigan City
30	450	Lake Central School Corp	Saint John
31	404	Portage Township Schools	Portage
32	403	Richmond Community School Corp	Richmond
33	397	Noblesville Schools	Noblesville
34	388	Laporte Community School Corp	Laporte
35	388	Huntington County Com Sch Corp	Huntington
36	388	Marion Community Schools	Marion
37	377	School City of Mishawaka	Mishawaka
38	370	Goshen Community Schools	Goshen
39	365	School City of East Chicago	East Chicago
40	363	Center Grove Com Sch Corp	Greenwood
41	363	Warsaw Community Schools	Warsaw
42	333	MSD Southwest Allen County	Fort Wayne
43	328	Logansport Community Sch Corp	Logansport
44	326	North Lawrence Com Schools	Bedford
45	317	Franklin Township Com Sch Corp	Indianapolis
46	317	Avon Community School Corp	Avon
47	314	Merrillville Community School	Merrillville
48	314	Valparaiso Community Schools	Valparaiso
49	310	Fayette County School Corp	Connersville
50	309	Greenfield-Central Com Schools	Greenfield
51	304	MSD Martinsville Schools	Martinsville
52	302	Brownsburg Community Sch Corp	Brownsburg
53	299	Clay Community Schools	Knightsville
54	292	MSD Decatur Township	Indianapolis
55	289	Jennings County Schools	North Vernon
56	286	New Castle Community Sch Corp	New Castle
57	268	Crown Point Community Sch Corp	Crown Point
58	266	Duneland School Corporation	Chesterton
59	259	Northwest Allen County Schools	Fort Wayne
60	255	Franklin Community School Corp	Franklin
61	251	Westfield-Washington Schools	Westfield
62	246	Mooresville Con School Corp	Mooresville
63	238	Concord Community Schools	Elkhart
64	228	Zionsville Community Schools	Zionsville
65	228	Jay School Corp	Portland
66	226	East Noble School Corp	Kendallville
67	224	Sunman-Dearborn Com Sch Corp	Sunman
68	216	School Town of Munster	Munster
69	212	Seymour Community Schools	Seymour
70	209	Dekalb County Ctl United SD	Waterloo
71	208	Whitley County Cons Schools	Columbia City
72	203	Middlebury Community Schools	Middlebury
73	203	Plainfield Community Sch Corp	Plainfield
74	202	Vincennes Community Sch Corp	Vincennes
75	199	Madison Consolidated Schools	Madison
76	197	Spencer-Owen Community Schools	Spencer
77	195	Wawasee Community School Corp	Syracuse

Rank	Number	District Name	City
78	195	Lebanon Community School Corp	Lebanon
79	193	Community Schools of Frankfort	Frankfort
80	191	Greater Jasper Con Schs	Jasper
81	188	MSD Wabash County Schools	Wabash
82	188	Shelbyville Central Schools	Shelbyville
83	187	Greenwood Community Sch Corp	Greenwood
84	181	School City of Hobart	Hobart
85	178	South Dearborn Com School Corp	Aurora
86	177	South Harrison Com Schools	Corydon
87	177	West Clark Community Schools	Sellersburg
88	176	Clark-Pleasant Com School Corp	Whiteland
89	175	South Madison Com Sch Corp	Pendleton
90	173	Kankakee Valley School Corp	Wheatfield
91	169	Richland-Bean Blossom C S C	Ellettsville
92	169	MSD Mount Vernon	Mount Vernon
93	166	Delaware Community School Corp	Muncie
94	165	Rush County Schools	Rushville
95	165	Wa-Nee Community Schools	Nappanee
96	164	Plymouth Community School Corp	Plymouth
97	162	Franklin County Com Sch Corp	Brookville
98	158	MSD Steuben County	Angola
99	155	Crawfordsville Com Schools	Crawfordsville
100	155	Peru Community Schools	Peru
101	152	Scott County SD 2	Scottsburg
102	152	Brown County School Corporation	Nashville
103	151	School Town of Highland	Highland
104	150	North Putnam Community Schools	Bainbridge
105	148	Tri-Creek School Corp	Lowell
106	148	Northern Wells Com Schools	Ossian
107	147	Blackford County Schools	Hartford City
108	144	Twin Lakes School Corp	Monticello
109	144	Maconaquah School Corp	Bunker Hill
110	142	West Noble School Corporation	Ligonier
111	142	Southern Hancock Co Com Sch Corp	New Palestine
112	139	Mount Vernon Community Sch Corp	Fortville
112	139	North Adams Community Schools	Decatur
114	139	New Prairie United School Corp	New Carlisle
114	139	Washington Com Schools Inc	Washington
116	137	Lakeland School Corporation	Lagrange
117	136	Griffith Public Schools	Griffith
118	135	Benton Community School Corp	Fowler
119	135	Mississinewa Community School Corp	Gas City
120	134	Westview School Corporation	Topeka
121	133	Beech Grove City Schools	Beech Grove
122	132	Decatur County Com Schools	Greensburg
123	132	North Spencer County Sch Corp	Lincoln City
124	130	Elwood Community School Corp	Elwood
125	130	North Harrison Com School Corp	Ramsey
126	126	Lake Ridge Schools	Gary
127	125	South Montgomery Com Sch Corp	New Market
128	124	Hamilton Heights School Corp	Arcadia
129	124	Frankton-Lapel Community Schs	Anderson
130	123	South Vermillion Com Sch Corp	Clinton
131	123	Danville Community School Corp	Danville
132	123	Mount Pleasant Twp Com Sch Corp	Yorktown
133	122	Western School Corp	Russiaville
134	122	Pike County School Corp	Petersburg
135	119	North Montgomery Com Sch Corp	Linden
136	118	Tippecanoe Valley School Corp	Akron
137	116	Greensburg Community Schools	Greensburg
138	116	North Gibson School Corp	Princeton
139	116	Southwest School Corp	Sullivan
140	115	Whitko Community School Corp	Pierceton
141	114	East Porter County School Corp	Kouts
142	113	Fairfield Community Schools	Goshen
143	113	Knox Community School Corp	Knox
144	112	Tipton Community School Corp	Tipton
145	111	Batesville Community School Corp	Batesville
146	110	Mitchell Community Schools	Mitchell
147	108	West Lafayette Com School Corp	West Lafayette
148	108	Randolph Central School Corp	Winchester
148	108	Salem Community Schools	Salem
150	107	Western Boone County Com SD	Thorntown
151	107	Rensselaer Central School Corp	Rensselaer
152	106	Alexandria Com School Corp	Alexandria
153	106	Garrett-Keyser-Butler Com	Garrett
154	106	Rochester Community Sch Corp	Rochester
155	104	Northwestern School Corp	Kokomo
156	104	Northeast School Corp	Hymera
157	103	Greencastle Community Sch Corp	Greencastle
157	103	Nineveh-Hensley-Jackson United	Trafalgar
159	103	Madison-Grant United Sch Corp	Fairmount
160	103	North Newton School Corp	Morocco
161	102	Prairie Heights Com Sch Corp	Lagrange
162	101	Eastbrook Community Sch Corp	Marion
163	101	Crawford County Com School Corp	Marengo
164	100	Taylor Community School Corp	Kokomo
165	100	Shelby Eastern Schools	Shelbyville
166	99	MSD North Posey County Schools	Poseyville
166	99	Union Co-Clg Corner Joint SD	Liberty
168	99	South Gibson School Corp	Fort Branch
169	99	School Town of Speedway	Speedway
170	98	Centerville-Abington Com Schs	Centerville
171	97	Southwest Dubois County Sch Corp	Huntingburg
172	97	Southeastern School Corp	Walton
173	95	Wabash City Schools	Wabash
174	95	Baugo Community Schools	Elkhart
174	95	Cloverdale Community Schools	Cloverdale
176	95	North Knox School Corp	Bicknell
177	94	Tell City-Troy Twp School Corp	Tell City
178	94	Delphi Community School Corp	Delphi
178	94	Mill Creek Community Sch Corp	Clayton
180	93	Brownstown Cnt Com Sch Corp	Brownstown
181	91	Paoli Community School Corp	Paoli
182	90	John Glenn School Corporation	Walkerton
183	90	Manchester Community Schools	N Manchester
184	90	East Washington School Corp	Pekin
185	89	Union Township School Corp	Valparaiso
186	89	Southwestern-Jefferson County	Hanover
187	88	North Judson-San Pierre Sch Corp	North Judson
188	88	MSD Bluffton-Harrison	Bluffton
189	84	North West Hendricks Schools	Lizton
190	83	South Spencer County Sch Corp	Rockport
191	83	Southeast Dubois County Sch Corp	Ferdinand
192	81	Switzerland County School Corp	Vevay
193	78	Porter Township School Corp	Valparaiso
194	77	Hanover Community School Corp	Cedar Lake

Number of Students

Rank	Number	District Name	City
1	40,731	Indianapolis Public Schools	Indianapolis
2	32,114	Fort Wayne Community Schools	Fort Wayne
3	22,825	Evansville-Vanderburgh Sch Corp	Evansville
4	21,662	South Bend Community Sch Corp	South Bend
5	19,035	Gary Community School Corp	Gary
6	16,433	Vigo County School Corp	Terre Haute
7	16,118	MSD Lawrence Township	Indianapolis
8	14,245	MSD Wayne Township	Indianapolis
9	13,251	School City of Hammond	Hammond
10	12,971	MSD Perry Township	Indianapolis
11	12,905	Carmel Clay Schools	Carmel
12	12,736	Elkhart Community Schools	Elkhart
13	11,288	MSD Warren Township	Indianapolis
14	11,092	New Albany-Floyd County Con Sch	New Albany
15	10,717	Hamilton Southeastern Schools	Fishers
16	10,580	Bartholomew Con School Corp	Columbus
17	10,503	Monroe County Com Sch Corp	Bloomington
18	10,316	Anderson Community School Corp	Anderson
19	10,146	MSD Washington Township	Indianapolis
20	10,092	MSD Pike Township	Indianapolis
21	9,995	Tippecanoe School Corp	Lafayette
22	9,958	Penn-Harris-Madison Sch Corp	Mishawaka
23	9,903	Greater Clark County Schools	Jeffersonville
24	9,731	East Allen County Schools	New Haven
25	9,145	Warrick County School Corp	Boonville
26	8,461	Lake Central School Corp	Saint John
27	8,166	Muncie Community Schools	Muncie
28	8,010	Portage Township Schools	Portage
29	7,349	Lafayette School Corporation	Lafayette
30	7,013	Kokomo-Center Twp Con Sch Corp	Kokomo
31	6,986	Center Grove Com Sch Corp	Greenwood
32	6,854	Noblesville Schools	Noblesville
33	6,846	Michigan City Area Schools	Michigan City
34	6,454	Franklin Township Com Sch Corp	Indianapolis
35	6,419	Warsaw Community Schools	Warsaw
36	6,410	Huntington County Com Sch Corp	Huntington
36	6,410	School City of East Chicago	East Chicago
38	6,360	Merrillville Community School	Merrillville
39	6,229	Laporte Community School Corp	Laporte
40	6,148	Richmond Community School Corp	Richmond
41	6,011	MSD Southwest Allen County	Fort Wayne
42	6,010	Valparaiso Community Schools	Valparaiso
43	5,946	Avon Community School Corp	Avon
44	5,912	Marion Community Schools	Marion
45	5,796	Crown Point Community Sch Corp	Crown Point
46	5,656	Brownsburg Community Sch Corp	Brownsburg
47	5,640	Goshen Community Schools	Goshen
48	5,528	School City of Mishawaka	Mishawaka
49	5,412	MSD Martinsville Schools	Martinsville
50	5,370	MSD Decatur Township	Indianapolis
51	5,369	Duneland School Corporation	Chesterton
52	5,323	North Lawrence Com Schools	Bedford
53	5,185	Jennings County Schools	North Vernon
54	4,992	Northwest Allen County Schools	Fort Wayne
55	4,619	Clay Community Schools	Knightsville
56	4,383	Concord Community Schools	Elkhart
57	4,370	Franklin Community School Corp	Franklin
58	4,356	Westfield-Washington Schools	Westfield
59	4,300	Mooresville Con School Corp	Mooresville
60	4,220	Sunman-Dearborn Com Sch Corp	Sunman
61	4,129	Fayette County School Corp	Connersville
62	4,116	Logansport Community Sch Corp	Logansport
63	4,090	Dekalb County Ctl United SD	Waterloo
64	4,016	Greenfield-Central Com Schools	Greenfield
65	4,012	Zionsville Community Schools	Zionsville
66	3,971	Plainfield Community Sch Corp	Plainfield
67	3,867	Jay School Corp	Portland
68	3,856	Greenwood Community Sch Corp	Greenwood
69	3,855	New Castle Community Sch Corp	New Castle
70	3,799	School Town of Munster	Munster
71	3,780	Seymour Community Schools	Seymour
72	3,776	Clark-Pleasant Com School Corp	Whiteland
73	3,709	East Noble School Corp	Kendallville
74	3,640	Middlebury Community Schools	Middlebury
75	3,589	Shelbyville Central Schools	Shelbyville
76	3,549	Whitley County Cons Schools	Columbia City
77	3,515	Wawasee Community School Corp	Syracuse
78	3,490	Madison Consolidated Schools	Madison
79	3,478	South Madison Com Sch Corp	Pendleton
80	3,430	School City of Hobart	Hobart
81	3,367	Tri-Creek School Corp	Lowell
82	3,335	Lebanon Community School Corp	Lebanon
83	3,333	School Town of Highland	Highland
84	3,292	Plymouth Community School Corp	Plymouth
85	3,279	West Clark Community Schools	Sellersburg
86	3,232	Community Schools of Frankfort	Frankfort
87	3,154	South Harrison Com Schools	Corydon
88	3,143	Kankakee Valley School Corp	Wheatfield
89	3,118	Spencer-Owen Community Schools	Spencer
90	3,102	Greater Jasper Con Schs	Jasper
91	3,072	Vincennes Community Sch Corp	Vincennes
92	3,067	MSD Steuben County	Angola
93	3,007	Wa-Nee Community Schools	Nappanee
94	3,001	Franklin County Com Sch Corp	Brookville
95	2,955	South Dearborn Com School Corp	Aurora
96	2,899	Delaware Community School Corp	Muncie
97	2,860	Southern Hancock Co Com Sch Corp	New Palestine
98	2,858	Mount Vernon Community Sch Corp	Fortville
99	2,799	MSD Mount Vernon	Mount Vernon
100	2,794	Scott County SD 2	Scottsburg
101	2,703	Griffith Public Schools	Griffith
102	2,701	MSD Wabash County Schools	Wabash
103	2,695	Twin Lakes School Corp	Monticello
104	2,693	Richland-Bean Blossom C S C	Ellettsville
105	2,675	Rush County Schools	Rushville
106	2,617	Northern Wells Com Schools	Ossian
107	2,606	Crawfordsville Com Schools	Crawfordsville
108	2,592	New Prairie United School Corp	New Carlisle
109	2,497	West Noble School Corporation	Ligonier
110	2,493	Peru Community Schools	Peru
111	2,479	Washington Com Schools Inc	Washington
112	2,445	Beech Grove City Schools	Beech Grove
113	2,432	Frankton-Lapel Community Schs	Anderson
114	2,399	Lake Ridge Schools	Gary
115	2,372	North Spencer County Sch Corp	Lincoln City
116	2,363	Maconaquah School Corp	Bunker Hill
117	2,348	North Harrison Com School Corp	Ramsey
118	2,339	North Adams Community Schools	Decatur
119	2,296	Blackford County Schools	Hartford City
120	2,295	Lakeland School Corporation	Lagrange
121	2,285	Western School Corp	Russiaville
122	2,273	Hamilton Heights School Corp	Arcadia
123	2,271	Danville Community School Corp	Danville
124	2,260	Brown County School Corporation	Nashville
125	2,225	Mount Pleasant Twp Com Sch Corp	Yorktown
126	2,217	Westview School Corporation	Topeka
127	2,195	Decatur County Com Schools	Greensburg
128	2,161	Pike County School Corp	Petersburg
129	2,131	Mississinewa Community School Corp	Gas City
130	2,130	Tippecanoe Valley School Corp	Akron
131	2,081	Salem Community Schools	Salem
132	2,063	South Montgomery Com Sch Corp	New Market
133	2,059	North Montgomery Com Sch Corp	Linden
134	2,054	Fairfield Community Schools	Goshen
135	2,044	West Lafayette Com School Corp	West Lafayette
136	2,037	Whitko Community School Corp	Pierceton
137	2,034	North Gibson School Corp	Princeton
138	2,032	Knox Community School Corp	Knox
139	2,029	Benton Community School Corp	Fowler
140	2,021	Greensburg Community Schools	Greensburg
141	2,008	Mitchell Community Schools	Mitchell
142	1,994	Rochester Community Sch Corp	Rochester
143	1,983	Southwest School Corp	Sullivan
144	1,965	Elwood Community School Corp	Elwood
145	1,963	East Porter County School Corp	Kouts
146	1,951	South Vermillion Com Sch Corp	Clinton
147	1,940	Greencastle Community Sch Corp	Greencastle
148	1,911	Batesville Community School Corp	Batesville
149	1,909	North Putnam Community Schools	Bainbridge
150	1,901	Western Boone County Com SD	Thorntown
151	1,875	Tipton Community School Corp	Tipton
152	1,868	South Gibson School Corp	Fort Branch
153	1,839	Southwest Dubois County Sch Corp	Huntingburg
154	1,821	Nineveh-Hensley-Jackson United	Trafalgar
155	1,820	Crawford County Com School Corp	Marengo
156	1,789	Prairie Heights Com Sch Corp	Lagrange

157	1,779	Alexandria Com School Corp	Alexandria
158	1,776	Rensselaer Central School Corp	Rensselaer
159	1,766	East Washington School Corp	Pekin
160	1,761	Eastbrook Community Sch Corp	Marion
161	1,742	Delphi Community School Corp	Delphi
162	1,734	Baugo Community Schools	Elkhart
163	1,732	Brownstown Cnt Com Sch Corp	Brownstown
164	1,726	Paoli Community School Corp	Paoli
165	1,721	Randolph Central School Corp	Winchester
166	1,708	Tell City-Troy Twp School Corp	Tell City
167	1,698	North Newton School Corp	Morocco
168	1,694	Northwestern School Corp	Kokomo
169	1,693	John Glenn School Corporation	Walkerton
170	1,682	Shelby Eastern Schools	Shelbyville
171	1,647	School Town of Speedway	Speedway
172	1,636	Southeastern School Corp	Walton
173	1,632	Madison-Grant United Sch Corp	Fairmount
174	1,623	Garrett-Keyser-Butler Com	Garrett
175	1,609	Manchester Community Schools	N Manchester
176	1,606	Union Co-Clg Corner Joint SD	Liberty
177	1,599	Switzerland County School Corp	Vevay
178	1,585	Centerville-Abington Com Schs	Centerville
179	1,576	North Knox School Corp	Bicknell
180	1,571	MSD North Posey County Schools	Poseyville
181	1,569	Mill Creek Community Sch Corp	Clayton
182	1,567	Hanover Community School Corp	Cedar Lake
183	1,559	North West Hendricks Schools	Lizton
184	1,552	Porter Township School Corp	Valparaiso
185	1,542	Southeast Dubois County Sch Corp	Ferdinand
186	1,527	MSD Bluffton-Harrison	Bluffton
187	1,526	Cloverdale Community Schools	Cloverdale
188	1,523	Taylor Community School Corp	Kokomo
189	1,522	North Judson-San Pierre Sch Corp	North Judson
189	1,522	Northeast School Corp	Hymera
191	1,518	Union Township School Corp	Valparaiso
192	1,512	Wabash City Schools	Wabash
193	1,511	South Spencer County Sch Corp	Rockport
194	1,500	Southwestern-Jefferson County	Hanover

Male Students

Rank	Percent	District Name	City
1	54.0	Wabash City Schools	Wabash
2	53.7	Tippecanoe Valley School Corp	Akron
3	53.6	Centerville-Abington Com Schs	Centerville
3	53.6	Scott County SD 2	Scottsburg
5	53.5	Northwestern School Corp	Kokomo
6	53.4	Northeast School Corp	Hymera
7	53.3	Rensselaer Central School Corp	Rensselaer
8	53.2	School Town of Speedway	Speedway
9	53.1	Brown County School Corporation	Nashville
9	53.1	Decatur County Com Schools	Greensburg
9	53.1	Mount Vernon Community Sch Corp	Fortville
9	53.1	Washington Com Schools Inc	Washington
13	53.0	Alexandria Com School Corp	Alexandria
13	53.0	Greencastle Community Sch Corp	Greencastle
13	53.0	Lakeland School Corporation	Lagrange
13	53.0	Mount Pleasant Twp Com Sch Corp	Yorktown
13	53.0	North Lawrence Com Schools	Bedford
13	53.0	Rochester Community Sch Corp	Rochester
13	53.0	Vincennes Community Sch Corp	Vincennes
20	52.9	Baugo Community Schools	Elkhart
20	52.9	Jay School Corp	Portland
22	52.8	Lake Central School Corp	Saint John
22	52.8	MSD North Posey County Schools	Poseyville
22	52.8	MSD Wabash County Schools	Wabash
25	52.7	Mississinewa Community School Corp	Gas City
26	52.6	Taylor Community School Corp	Kokomo
27	52.5	North Putnam Community Schools	Bainbridge
27	52.5	Northern Wells Com Schools	Ossian
27	52.5	Tell City-Troy Twp School Corp	Tell City
30	52.4	Kankakee Valley School Corp	Wheatfield
30	52.4	Madison Consolidated Schools	Madison
30	52.4	Sunman-Dearborn Com Sch Corp	Sunman
30	52.4	Tippecanoe School Corp	Lafayette
30	52.4	Union Co-Clg Corner Joint SD	Liberty
35	52.3	John Glenn School Corporation	Walkerton
35	52.3	MSD Martinsville Schools	Martinsville
35	52.3	School City of Mishawaka	Mishawaka
38	52.2	Bartholomew Con School Corp	Columbus
38	52.2	Benton Community School Corp	Fowler
38	52.2	Duneland School Corporation	Chesterton
38	52.2	Greensburg Community Schools	Greensburg
38	52.2	MSD Southwest Allen County	Fort Wayne
38	52.2	Middlebury Community Schools	Middlebury
38	52.2	Plymouth Community School Corp	Plymouth
38	52.2	School City of Hammond	Hammond
38	52.2	Tipton Community School Corp	Tipton
47	52.1	Michigan City Area Schools	Michigan City
47	52.1	School Town of Munster	Munster
49	52.0	Beech Grove City Schools	Beech Grove
49	52.0	Delaware Community School Corp	Muncie
49	52.0	North Judson-San Pierre Sch Corp	North Judson
49	52.0	North Montgomery Com Sch Corp	Linden
49	52.0	Westfield-Washington Schools	Westfield
54	51.9	Hanover Community School Corp	Cedar Lake
54	51.9	Paoli Community School Corp	Paoli
54	51.9	Richmond Community School Corp	Richmond
54	51.9	South Harrison Com Schools	Corydon
54	51.9	Southwest School Corp	Sullivan
54	51.9	Twin Lakes School Corp	Monticello
60	51.8	Greater Jasper Con Schs	Jasper
60	51.8	Hamilton Southeastern Schools	Fishers
60	51.8	Logansport Community Sch Corp	Logansport
60	51.8	MSD Mount Vernon	Mount Vernon
60	51.8	Madison-Grant United Sch Corp	Fairmount
60	51.8	Richland-Bean Blossom C S C	Ellettsville
60	51.8	Tri-Creek School Corp	Lowell
60	51.8	Western Boone County Com SD	Thorntown
60	51.8	Westview School Corporation	Topeka
69	51.7	Blackford County Schools	Hartford City
69	51.7	East Allen County Schools	New Haven
69	51.7	Fayette County School Corp	Connersville
69	51.7	Jennings County Schools	North Vernon
69	51.7	Shelbyville Central Schools	Shelbyville
69	51.7	Vigo County School Corp	Terre Haute
69	51.7	Warsaw Community Schools	Warsaw
76	51.6	Brownsburg Community Sch Corp	Brownsburg
76	51.6	Delphi Community School Corp	Delphi
76	51.6	Elkhart Community Schools	Elkhart
76	51.6	Goshen Community Schools	Goshen
76	51.6	MSD Perry Township	Indianapolis
76	51.6	Portage Township Schools	Portage
76	51.6	School Town of Highland	Highland
76	51.6	Warrick County School Corp	Boonville
76	51.6	West Noble School Corporation	Ligonier
76	51.6	Whitko Community School Corp	Pierceton
76	51.6	Zionsville Community Schools	Zionsville
87	51.5	Clay Community Schools	Knightsville
87	51.5	Franklin County Com Sch Corp	Brookville
87	51.5	Indianapolis Public Schools	Indianapolis
87	51.5	Noblesville Schools	Noblesville
87	51.5	Salem Community Schools	Salem
87	51.5	School City of Hobart	Hobart
87	51.5	South Montgomery Com Sch Corp	New Market
87	51.5	Whitley County Cons Schools	Columbia City
95	51.4	East Washington School Corp	Pekin
95	51.4	Frankton-Lapel Community Schs	Anderson
95	51.4	Laporte Community School Corp	Laporte
95	51.4	MSD Lawrence Township	Indianapolis
95	51.4	New Castle Community Sch Corp	New Castle
95	51.4	New Prairie United School Corp	New Carlisle
95	51.4	South Bend Community Sch Corp	South Bend
102	51.3	Avon Community School Corp	Avon
102	51.3	Brownstown Cnt Com Sch Corp	Brownstown
102	51.3	Center Grove Com Sch Corp	Greenwood
102	51.3	Crawford County Com School Corp	Marengo
102	51.3	MSD Steuben County	Angola
102	51.3	Manchester Community Schools	N Manchester
102	51.3	Randolph Central School Corp	Winchester
102	51.3	School City of East Chicago	East Chicago
102	51.3	Shelby Eastern Schools	Shelbyville
111	51.2	Anderson Community School Corp	Anderson
111	51.2	Cloverdale Community Schools	Cloverdale
111	51.2	Elwood Community School Corp	Elwood
111	51.2	Fort Wayne Community Schools	Fort Wayne
111	51.2	Franklin Township Com Sch Corp	Indianapolis
111	51.2	Hamilton Heights School Corp	Arcadia
111	51.2	MSD Warren Township	Indianapolis
111	51.2	North Adams Community Schools	Decatur
111	51.2	Switzerland County School Corp	Vevay
120	51.1	Lake Ridge Schools	Gary
120	51.1	MSD Washington Township	Indianapolis
120	51.1	Merrillville Community School	Merrillville
120	51.1	Mill Creek Community Sch Corp	Clayton
120	51.1	New Albany-Floyd County Con Sch	New Albany
120	51.1	North Knox School Corp	Bicknell
120	51.1	Rush County Schools	Rushville
120	51.1	Spencer-Owen Community Schools	Spencer
128	51.0	Carmel Clay Schools	Carmel
128	51.0	Evansville-Vanderburgh Sch Corp	Evansville
128	51.0	Greater Clark County Schools	Jeffersonville
128	51.0	Knox Community School Corp	Knox
128	51.0	MSD Pike Township	Indianapolis
128	51.0	MSD Wayne Township	Indianapolis
128	51.0	North Harrison Com School Corp	Ramsey
128	51.0	Pike County School Corp	Petersburg
128	51.0	Porter Township School Corp	Valparaiso
128	51.0	Southeastern School Corp	Walton
128	51.0	Wa-Nee Community Schools	Nappanee
128	51.0	Wawasee Community School Corp	Syracuse
140	50.9	Kokomo-Center Twp Con Sch Corp	Kokomo
140	50.9	MSD Decatur Township	Indianapolis
140	50.9	South Vermillion Com Sch Corp	Clinton
143	50.8	Fairfield Community Schools	Goshen
143	50.8	Franklin Community School Corp	Franklin
143	50.8	Gary Community School Corp	Gary
143	50.8	Mitchell Community Schools	Mitchell
143	50.8	Monroe County Com Sch Corp	Bloomington
143	50.8	Plainfield Community Sch Corp	Plainfield
143	50.8	South Dearborn Com School Corp	Aurora
143	50.8	South Spencer County Sch Corp	Rockport
143	50.8	Western School Corp	Russiaville
152	50.7	Crown Point Community Sch Corp	Crown Point
152	50.7	Greenfield-Central Com Schools	Greenfield
152	50.7	Lafayette School Corporation	Lafayette
152	50.7	Mooresville Con School Corp	Mooresville
152	50.7	South Madison Com Sch Corp	Pendleton
157	50.6	Greenwood Community Sch Corp	Greenwood
157	50.6	Huntington County Com Sch Corp	Huntington
157	50.6	Muncie Community Schools	Muncie
157	50.6	Penn-Harris-Madison Sch Corp	Mishawaka
157	50.6	Union Township School Corp	Valparaiso
157	50.6	West Lafayette Com School Corp	West Lafayette
163	50.5	Batesville Community School Corp	Batesville
163	50.5	Clark-Pleasant Com School Corp	Whiteland
163	50.5	Griffith Public Schools	Griffith
163	50.5	Lebanon Community School Corp	Lebanon
163	50.5	Maconaquah School Corp	Bunker Hill
163	50.5	Marion Community Schools	Marion
163	50.5	Nineveh-Hensley-Jackson United	Trafalgar
170	50.4	North Newton School Corp	Morocco
170	50.4	Valparaiso Community Schools	Valparaiso
170	50.4	West Clark Community Schools	Sellersburg
173	50.3	Dekalb County Ctl United SD	Waterloo
173	50.3	MSD Bluffton-Harrison	Bluffton
173	50.3	Peru Community Schools	Peru
176	50.2	Concord Community Schools	Elkhart
176	50.2	Crawfordsville Com Schools	Crawfordsville
176	50.2	South Gibson School Corp	Fort Branch
179	50.1	Danville Community School Corp	Danville
179	50.1	East Porter County School Corp	Kouts
179	50.1	Garrett-Keyser-Butler Com	Garrett
179	50.1	Seymour Community Schools	Seymour
183	50.0	Community Schools of Frankfort	Frankfort
183	50.0	North West Hendricks Schools	Lizton
183	50.0	Southern Hancock Co Com Sch Corp	New Palestine
186	49.9	North Gibson School Corp	Princeton
186	49.9	Northwest Allen County Schools	Fort Wayne
186	49.9	Southwest Dubois County Sch Corp	Huntingburg
189	49.8	Eastbrook Community Sch Corp	Marion
190	49.4	East Noble School Corp	Kendallville
191	49.3	Southwestern-Jefferson County	Hanover
192	48.8	North Spencer County Sch Corp	Lincoln City
193	48.6	Southeast Dubois County Sch Corp	Ferdinand
194	48.4	Prairie Heights Com Sch Corp	Lagrange

Female Students

Rank	Percent	District Name	City
1	51.6	Prairie Heights Com Sch Corp	Lagrange
2	51.4	Southeast Dubois County Sch Corp	Ferdinand
3	51.2	North Spencer County Sch Corp	Lincoln City
4	50.7	Southwestern-Jefferson County	Hanover
5	50.6	East Noble School Corp	Kendallville
6	50.2	Eastbrook Community Sch Corp	Marion
7	50.1	North Gibson School Corp	Princeton
7	50.1	Northwest Allen County Schools	Fort Wayne
7	50.1	Southwest Dubois County Sch Corp	Huntingburg
10	50.0	Community Schools of Frankfort	Frankfort
10	50.0	North West Hendricks Schools	Lizton
10	50.0	Southern Hancock Co Com Sch Corp	New Palestine
13	49.9	Danville Community School Corp	Danville
13	49.9	East Porter County School Corp	Kouts
13	49.9	Garrett-Keyser-Butler Com	Garrett
13	49.9	Seymour Community Schools	Seymour
17	49.8	Concord Community Schools	Elkhart
17	49.8	Crawfordsville Com Schools	Crawfordsville
17	49.8	South Gibson School Corp	Fort Branch
20	49.7	Dekalb County Ctl United SD	Waterloo
20	49.7	MSD Bluffton-Harrison	Bluffton
20	49.7	Peru Community Schools	Peru
23	49.6	North Newton School Corp	Morocco
23	49.6	Valparaiso Community Schools	Valparaiso
23	49.6	West Clark Community Schools	Sellersburg
26	49.5	Batesville Community School Corp	Batesville
26	49.5	Clark-Pleasant Com School Corp	Whiteland
26	49.5	Griffith Public Schools	Griffith
26	49.5	Lebanon Community School Corp	Lebanon
26	49.5	Maconaquah School Corp	Bunker Hill
26	49.5	Marion Community Schools	Marion
26	49.5	Nineveh-Hensley-Jackson United	Trafalgar
33	49.4	Greenwood Community Sch Corp	Greenwood
33	49.4	Huntington County Com Sch Corp	Huntington
33	49.4	Muncie Community Schools	Muncie
33	49.4	Penn-Harris-Madison Sch Corp	Mishawaka
33	49.4	Union Township School Corp	Valparaiso
33	49.4	West Lafayette Com School Corp	West Lafayette
39	49.3	Crown Point Community Sch Corp	Crown Point

39	49.3	Greenfield-Central Com Schools	Greenfield
39	49.3	Lafayette School Corporation	Lafayette
39	49.3	Mooresville Con School Corp	Mooresville
39	49.3	South Madison Com Sch Corp	Pendleton
44	49.2	Fairfield Community Schools	Goshen
44	49.2	Franklin Community School Corp	Franklin
44	49.2	Gary Community School Corp	Gary
44	49.2	Mitchell Community Schools	Mitchell
44	49.2	Monroe County Com Sch Corp	Bloomington
44	49.2	Plainfield Community Sch Corp	Plainfield
44	49.2	South Dearborn Com School Corp	Aurora
44	49.2	South Spencer County Sch Corp	Rockport
44	49.2	Western School Corp	Russiaville
53	49.1	Kokomo-Center Twp Con Sch Corp	Kokomo
53	49.1	MSD Decatur Township	Indianapolis
53	49.1	South Vermillion Com Sch Corp	Clinton
56	49.0	Carmel Clay Schools	Carmel
56	49.0	Evansville-Vanderburgh Sch Corp	Evansville
56	49.0	Greater Clark County Schools	Jeffersonville
56	49.0	Knox Community School Corp	Knox
56	49.0	MSD Pike Township	Indianapolis
56	49.0	MSD Wayne Township	Indianapolis
56	49.0	North Harrison Com School Corp	Ramsey
56	49.0	Pike County School Corp	Petersburg
56	49.0	Porter Township School Corp	Valparaiso
56	49.0	Southeastern School Corp	Walton
56	49.0	Wa-Nee Community Schools	Nappanee
56	49.0	Wawasee Community School Corp	Syracuse
68	48.9	Lake Ridge Schools	Gary
68	48.9	MSD Washington Township	Indianapolis
68	48.9	Merrillville Community School	Merrillville
68	48.9	Mill Creek Community Sch Corp	Clayton
68	48.9	New Albany-Floyd County Con Sch	New Albany
68	48.9	North Knox School Corp	Bicknell
68	48.9	Rush County Schools	Rushville
68	48.9	Spencer-Owen Community Schools	Spencer
76	48.8	Anderson Community School Corp	Anderson
76	48.8	Cloverdale Community Schools	Cloverdale
76	48.8	Elwood Community School Corp	Elwood
76	48.8	Fort Wayne Community Schools	Fort Wayne
76	48.8	Franklin Township Com Sch Corp	Indianapolis
76	48.8	Hamilton Heights School Corp	Arcadia
76	48.8	MSD Warren Township	Indianapolis
76	48.8	North Adams Community Schools	Decatur
76	48.8	Switzerland County School Corp	Vevay
85	48.7	Avon Community School Corp	Avon
85	48.7	Brownstown Cnt Com Sch Corp	Brownstown
85	48.7	Center Grove Com Sch Corp	Greenwood
85	48.7	Crawford County Com School Corp	Marengo
85	48.7	MSD Steuben County	Angola
85	48.7	Manchester Community Schools	N Manchester
85	48.7	Randolph Central School Corp	Winchester
85	48.7	School City of East Chicago	East Chicago
85	48.7	Shelby Eastern Schools	Shelbyville
94	48.6	East Washington School Corp	Pekin
94	48.6	Frankton-Lapel Community Schs	Anderson
94	48.6	Laporte Community School Corp	Laporte
94	48.6	MSD Lawrence Township	Indianapolis
94	48.6	New Castle Community Sch Corp	New Castle
94	48.6	New Prairie United School Corp	New Carlisle
94	48.6	South Bend Community Sch Corp	South Bend
101	48.5	Clay Community Schools	Knightsville
101	48.5	Franklin County Com Sch Corp	Brookville
101	48.5	Indianapolis Public Schools	Indianapolis
101	48.5	Noblesville Schools	Noblesville
101	48.5	Salem Community Schools	Salem
101	48.5	School City of Hobart	Hobart
101	48.5	South Montgomery Com Sch Corp	New Market
101	48.5	Whitley County Cons Schools	Columbia City
109	48.4	Brownsburg Community Sch Corp	Brownsburg
109	48.4	Delphi Community School Corp	Delphi
109	48.4	Elkhart Community Schools	Elkhart
109	48.4	Goshen Community Schools	Goshen
109	48.4	MSD Perry Township	Indianapolis
109	48.4	Portage Township Schools	Portage
109	48.4	School Town of Highland	Highland
109	48.4	Warrick County School Corp	Boonville
109	48.4	West Noble School Corporation	Ligonier
109	48.4	Whitko Community School Corp	Pierceton
109	48.4	Zionsville Community Schools	Zionsville
120	48.3	Blackford County Schools	Hartford City
120	48.3	East Allen County Schools	New Haven
120	48.3	Fayette County School Corp	Connersville
120	48.3	Jennings County Schools	North Vernon
120	48.3	Shelbyville Central Schools	Shelbyville
120	48.3	Vigo County School Corp	Terre Haute
120	48.3	Warsaw Community Schools	Warsaw
127	48.2	Greater Jasper Con Schs	Jasper
127	48.2	Hamilton Southeastern Schools	Fishers
127	48.2	Logansport Community Sch Corp	Logansport
127	48.2	MSD Mount Vernon	Mount Vernon
127	48.2	Madison-Grant United Sch Corp	Fairmount
127	48.2	Richland-Bean Blossom C S C	Ellettsville
127	48.2	Tri-Creek School Corp	Lowell
127	48.2	Western Boone County Com SD	Thorntown
127	48.2	Westview School Corporation	Topeka
136	48.1	Hanover Community School Corp	Cedar Lake
136	48.1	Paoli Community School Corp	Paoli
136	48.1	Richmond Community School Corp	Richmond
136	48.1	South Harrison Com Schools	Corydon
136	48.1	Southwest School Corp	Sullivan
136	48.1	Twin Lakes School Corp	Monticello
142	48.0	Beech Grove City Schools	Beech Grove
142	48.0	Delaware Community School Corp	Muncie
142	48.0	North Judson-San Pierre Sch Corp	North Judson
142	48.0	North Montgomery Com Sch Corp	Linden
142	48.0	Westfield-Washington Schools	Westfield
147	47.9	Michigan City Area Schools	Michigan City
147	47.9	School Town of Munster	Munster
149	47.8	Bartholomew Con School Corp	Columbus
149	47.8	Benton Community School Corp	Fowler
149	47.8	Duneland School Corporation	Chesterton
149	47.8	Greensburg Community Schools	Greensburg
149	47.8	MSD Southwest Allen County	Fort Wayne
149	47.8	Middlebury Community Schools	Middlebury
149	47.8	Plymouth Community School Corp	Plymouth
149	47.8	School City of Hammond	Hammond
149	47.8	Tipton Community School Corp	Tipton
158	47.7	John Glenn School Corporation	Walkerton
158	47.7	MSD Martinsville Schools	Martinsville
158	47.7	School City of Mishawaka	Mishawaka
161	47.6	Kankakee Valley School Corp	Wheatfield
161	47.6	Madison Consolidated Schools	Madison
161	47.6	Sunman-Dearborn Com Sch Corp	Sunman
161	47.6	Tippecanoe School Corp	Lafayette
161	47.6	Union Co-Clg Corner Joint SD	Liberty
166	47.5	North Putnam Community Schools	Bainbridge
166	47.5	Northern Wells Com Schools	Ossian
166	47.5	Tell City-Troy Twp School Corp	Tell City
169	47.4	Taylor Community School Corp	Kokomo
170	47.3	Mississinewa Community School Corp	Gas City
171	47.2	Lake Central School Corp	Saint John
171	47.2	MSD North Posey County Schools	Poseyville
171	47.2	MSD Wabash County Schools	Wabash
174	47.1	Baugo Community Schools	Elkhart
174	47.1	Jay School Corp	Portland
176	47.0	Alexandria Com School Corp	Alexandria
176	47.0	Greencastle Community Sch Corp	Greencastle
176	47.0	Lakeland School Corporation	Lagrange
176	47.0	Mount Pleasant Twp Com Sch Corp	Yorktown
176	47.0	North Lawrence Com Schools	Bedford
176	47.0	Rochester Community Sch Corp	Rochester
176	47.0	Vincennes Community Sch Corp	Vincennes
183	46.9	Brown County School Corporation	Nashville
183	46.9	Decatur County Com Schools	Greensburg
183	46.9	Mount Vernon Community Sch Corp	Fortville
183	46.9	Washington Com Schools Inc	Washington
187	46.8	School Town of Speedway	Speedway
188	46.7	Rensselaer Central School Corp	Rensselaer
189	46.6	Northeast School Corp	Hymera
190	46.5	Northwestern School Corp	Kokomo
191	46.4	Centerville-Abington Com Schs	Centerville
191	46.4	Scott County SD 2	Scottsburg
193	46.3	Tippecanoe Valley School Corp	Akron
194	46.0	Wabash City Schools	Wabash

Individual Education Program Students

Rank	Percent	District Name	City
1	26.2	New Castle Community Sch Corp	New Castle
2	25.6	Madison Consolidated Schools	Madison
2	25.6	North Putnam Community Schools	Bainbridge
4	25.3	Benton Community School Corp	Fowler
5	23.9	South Bend Community Sch Corp	South Bend
6	23.7	Richmond Community School Corp	Richmond
7	23.5	Southwestern-Jefferson County	Hanover
8	23.0	Randolph Central School Corp	Winchester
9	22.9	Muncie Community Schools	Muncie
9	22.9	South Madison Com Sch Corp	Pendleton
9	22.9	Southwest School Corp	Sullivan
12	22.8	Kokomo-Center Twp Con Sch Corp	Kokomo
13	22.3	Cloverdale Community Schools	Cloverdale
13	22.3	Shelbyville Central Schools	Shelbyville
15	22.2	Lafayette School Corporation	Lafayette
16	22.1	Greater Clark County Schools	Jeffersonville
16	22.1	Northeast School Corp	Hymera
18	21.7	Jennings County Schools	North Vernon
19	21.3	Washington Com Schools Inc	Washington
20	21.2	Spencer-Owen Community Schools	Spencer
21	21.1	Fayette County School Corp	Connersville
21	21.1	Greenfield-Central Com Schools	Greenfield
23	21.0	Clay Community Schools	Knightsville
24	20.9	MSD Mount Vernon	Mount Vernon
25	20.8	Greencastle Community Sch Corp	Greencastle
26	20.2	South Dearborn Com School Corp	Aurora
27	20.0	Wabash City Schools	Wabash
28	19.9	Rensselaer Central School Corp	Rensselaer
29	19.8	Evansville-Vanderburgh Sch Corp	Evansville
30	19.7	Seymour Community Schools	Seymour
31	19.4	Blackford County Schools	Hartford City
31	19.4	Taylor Community School Corp	Kokomo
33	19.3	Anderson Community School Corp	Anderson
33	19.3	Michigan City Area Schools	Michigan City
33	19.3	New Albany-Floyd County Con Sch	New Albany
33	19.3	North Gibson School Corp	Princeton
37	19.2	Mount Pleasant Twp Com Sch Corp	Yorktown
38	18.8	Crawford County Com School Corp	Marengo
38	18.8	Elwood Community School Corp	Elwood
38	18.8	South Harrison Com Schools	Corydon
41	18.7	Hamilton Heights School Corp	Arcadia
42	18.6	Vigo County School Corp	Terre Haute
43	18.4	Garrett-Keyser-Butler Com	Garrett
43	18.4	South Vermillion Com Sch Corp	Clinton
43	18.4	Switzerland County School Corp	Vevay
46	18.3	Franklin Community School Corp	Franklin
46	18.3	Indianapolis Public Schools	Indianapolis
48	18.1	MSD North Posey County Schools	Poseyville
48	18.1	Pike County School Corp	Petersburg
48	18.1	Warrick County School Corp	Boonville
51	18.0	Goshen Community Schools	Goshen
52	17.9	Kankakee Valley School Corp	Wheatfield
52	17.9	MSD Martinsville Schools	Martinsville
52	17.9	Mill Creek Community Sch Corp	Clayton
52	17.9	North Harrison Com School Corp	Ramsey
56	17.8	Paoli Community School Corp	Paoli
56	17.8	School City of Mishawaka	Mishawaka
58	17.7	Peru Community Schools	Peru
58	17.7	Richland-Bean Blossom C S C	Ellettsville
60	17.6	MSD Wabash County Schools	Wabash
60	17.6	North Lawrence Com Schools	Bedford
60	17.6	North Newton School Corp	Morocco
60	17.6	Southern Hancock Co Com Sch Corp	New Palestine
64	17.5	Duneland School Corporation	Chesterton
64	17.5	Fort Wayne Community Schools	Fort Wayne
64	17.5	MSD Decatur Township	Indianapolis
64	17.5	MSD Warren Township	Indianapolis
64	17.5	Union Co-Clg Corner Joint SD	Liberty
64	17.5	Vincennes Community Sch Corp	Vincennes
70	17.4	Lebanon Community School Corp	Lebanon
71	17.3	East Washington School Corp	Pekin
71	17.3	Noblesville Schools	Noblesville
73	17.2	Baugo Community Schools	Elkhart
73	17.2	MSD Pike Township	Indianapolis
73	17.2	Mitchell Community Schools	Mitchell
73	17.2	Sunman-Dearborn Com Sch Corp	Sunman
77	17.1	Mount Vernon Community Sch Corp	Fortville
78	17.0	Franklin County Com Sch Corp	Brookville
78	17.0	Jay School Corp	Portland
80	16.9	Union Township School Corp	Valparaiso
81	16.8	Crawfordsville Com Schools	Crawfordsville
81	16.8	Lake Central School Corp	Saint John
81	16.8	School Town of Munster	Munster
84	16.6	Elkhart Community Schools	Elkhart
85	16.5	West Clark Community Schools	Sellersburg
86	16.4	Avon Community School Corp	Avon
86	16.4	Northwestern School Corp	Kokomo
88	16.3	East Porter County School Corp	Kouts
88	16.3	South Montgomery Com Sch Corp	New Market
88	16.3	Twin Lakes School Corp	Monticello
91	16.1	Decatur County Com Schools	Greensburg
92	16.0	Eastbrook Community Sch Corp	Marion
92	16.0	Frankton-Lapel Community Schs	Anderson
92	16.0	South Gibson School Corp	Fort Branch
95	15.9	Brown County School Corporation	Nashville
95	15.9	East Noble School Corp	Kendallville
95	15.9	Monroe County Com Sch Corp	Bloomington
95	15.9	North West Hendricks Schools	Lizton
99	15.8	Tipton Community School Corp	Tipton
99	15.8	Westfield-Washington Schools	Westfield
101	15.7	School Town of Speedway	Speedway
102	15.6	Bartholomew Con School Corp	Columbus
102	15.6	Batesville Community School Corp	Batesville
102	15.6	Northern Wells Com Schools	Ossian
105	15.5	MSD Wayne Township	Indianapolis
105	15.5	North Montgomery Com Sch Corp	Linden
105	15.5	Portage Township Schools	Portage
108	15.4	Delaware Community School Corp	Muncie
108	15.4	Greensburg Community Schools	Greensburg
108	15.4	Huntington County Com Sch Corp	Huntington
111	15.3	Concord Community Schools	Elkhart
111	15.3	Marion Community Schools	Marion
111	15.3	Mississinewa Community School Corp	Gas City
111	15.3	Wa-Nee Community Schools	Nappanee
115	15.2	Maconaquah School Corp	Bunker Hill
115	15.2	Southwest Dubois County Sch Corp	Huntingburg
117	15.1	MSD Lawrence Township	Indianapolis
117	15.1	School City of Hammond	Hammond
117	15.1	Shelby Eastern Schools	Shelbyville
120	15.0	East Allen County Schools	New Haven

120	15.0	Logansport Community Sch Corp	Logansport
120	15.0	Manchester Community Schools	N Manchester
120	15.0	North Judson-San Pierre Sch Corp	North Judson
120	15.0	Rush County Schools	Rushville
125	14.9	Lake Ridge Schools	Gary
126	14.8	Beech Grove City Schools	Beech Grove
126	14.8	Brownstown Cnt Com Sch Corp	Brownstown
126	14.8	Knox Community School Corp	Knox
126	14.8	North Adams Community Schools	Decatur
126	14.8	North Knox School Corp	Bicknell
131	14.7	Salem Community Schools	Salem
132	14.6	Centerville-Abington Com Schs	Centerville
132	14.6	MSD Washington Township	Indianapolis
134	14.5	Lakeland School Corporation	Lagrange
134	14.5	MSD Southwest Allen County	Fort Wayne
136	14.4	Plainfield Community Sch Corp	Plainfield
137	14.3	Franklin Township Com Sch Corp	Indianapolis
137	14.3	Southeastern School Corp	Walton
137	14.3	Tippecanoe School Corp	Lafayette
140	14.2	Tippecanoe Valley School Corp	Akron
141	14.1	Dekalb County Ctl United SD	Waterloo
141	14.1	Hamilton Southeastern Schools	Fishers
141	14.1	Western School Corp	Russiaville
144	14.0	Scott County SD 2	Scottsburg
145	13.9	Alexandria Com School Corp	Alexandria
145	13.9	Tell City-Troy Twp School Corp	Tell City
147	13.8	Danville Community School Corp	Danville
147	13.8	Gary Community School Corp	Gary
147	13.8	MSD Perry Township	Indianapolis
147	13.8	Prairie Heights Com Sch Corp	Lagrange
147	13.8	Whitko Community School Corp	Pierceton
152	13.6	Fairfield Community Schools	Goshen
152	13.6	Warsaw Community Schools	Warsaw
152	13.6	Zionsville Community Schools	Zionsville
155	13.5	Greenwood Community Sch Corp	Greenwood
155	13.5	Tri-Creek School Corp	Lowell
157	13.3	Clark-Pleasant Com School Corp	Whiteland
157	13.3	John Glenn School Corporation	Walkerton
157	13.3	Laporte Community School Corp	Laporte
157	13.3	Valparaiso Community Schools	Valparaiso
161	13.2	Nineveh-Hensley-Jackson United	Trafalgar
161	13.2	Rochester Community Sch Corp	Rochester
161	13.2	School City of East Chicago	East Chicago
164	13.1	Community Schools of Frankfort	Frankfort
164	13.1	Hanover Community School Corp	Cedar Lake
164	13.1	Penn-Harris-Madison Sch Corp	Mishawaka
164	13.1	Western Boone County Com SD	Thorntown
168	12.9	Madison-Grant United Sch Corp	Fairmount
168	12.9	North Spencer County Sch Corp	Lincoln City
170	12.6	Delphi Community School Corp	Delphi
170	12.6	Griffith Public Schools	Griffith
170	12.6	MSD Bluffton-Harrison	Bluffton
170	12.6	South Spencer County Sch Corp	Rockport
174	12.5	Center Grove Com Sch Corp	Greenwood
174	12.5	New Prairie United School Corp	New Carlisle
174	12.5	Plymouth Community School Corp	Plymouth
174	12.5	Whitley County Cons Schools	Columbia City
178	12.3	Greater Jasper Con Schs	Jasper
178	12.3	Middlebury Community Schools	Middlebury
180	12.2	Carmel Clay Schools	Carmel
180	12.2	Mooresville Con School Corp	Mooresville
180	12.2	School Town of Highland	Highland
183	12.1	Southeast Dubois County Sch Corp	Ferdinand
184	11.4	MSD Steuben County	Angola
185	11.3	West Lafayette Com School Corp	West Lafayette
186	11.2	Porter Township School Corp	Valparaiso
187	11.1	Northwest Allen County Schools	Fort Wayne
188	11.0	West Noble School Corporation	Ligonier
189	10.9	Brownsburg Community Sch Corp	Brownsburg
190	10.7	School City of Hobart	Hobart
190	10.7	Westview School Corporation	Topeka
192	10.3	Merrillville Community School	Merrillville
193	10.2	Wawasee Community School Corp	Syracuse
194	10.1	Crown Point Community Sch Corp	Crown Point

English Language Learner Students

Rank	Percent	District Name	City
1	41.7	Westview School Corporation	Topeka
2	31.8	West Noble School Corporation	Ligonier
3	27.1	Goshen Community Schools	Goshen
4	21.8	School City of East Chicago	East Chicago
5	21.2	School City of Hammond	Hammond
6	16.6	Community Schools of Frankfort	Frankfort
7	15.9	Fairfield Community Schools	Goshen
7	15.9	West Lafayette Com School Corp	West Lafayette
9	15.4	Elkhart Community Schools	Elkhart
10	15.0	Logansport Community Sch Corp	Logansport
11	14.0	Lafayette School Corporation	Lafayette
12	13.3	South Bend Community Sch Corp	South Bend
13	10.9	Concord Community Schools	Elkhart
13	10.9	School Town of Munster	Munster
15	10.4	Lakeland School Corporation	Lagrange
16	9.9	Wa-Nee Community Schools	Nappanee
17	9.8	MSD Washington Township	Indianapolis
18	8.9	Warsaw Community Schools	Warsaw
19	8.8	School City of Hobart	Hobart
20	8.0	Plymouth Community School Corp	Plymouth
21	7.9	Twin Lakes School Corp	Monticello
22	7.8	Fort Wayne Community Schools	Fort Wayne
23	7.2	MSD Pike Township	Indianapolis
24	6.8	Indianapolis Public Schools	Indianapolis
25	6.6	Carmel Clay Schools	Carmel
26	6.3	Lake Central School Corp	Saint John
26	6.3	Merrillville Community School	Merrillville
28	6.2	Middlebury Community Schools	Middlebury
29	6.1	Delphi Community School Corp	Delphi
29	6.1	Southeastern School Corp	Walton
31	5.9	Southwest Dubois County Sch Corp	Huntingburg
32	5.8	MSD Wayne Township	Indianapolis
33	5.7	School Town of Speedway	Speedway
34	5.5	MSD Lawrence Township	Indianapolis
34	5.5	Monroe County Com Sch Corp	Bloomington
34	5.5	Tippecanoe School Corp	Lafayette
37	5.4	Griffith Public Schools	Griffith
37	5.4	Wawasee Community School Corp	Syracuse
39	5.2	Washington Com Schools Inc	Washington
40	5.1	School Town of Highland	Highland
41	4.7	Greater Jasper Con Schs	Jasper
41	4.7	MSD Southwest Allen County	Fort Wayne
41	4.7	Shelbyville Central Schools	Shelbyville
44	4.6	MSD Bluffton-Harrison	Bluffton
45	4.4	Hamilton Southeastern Schools	Fishers
45	4.4	Laporte Community School Corp	Laporte
47	4.3	MSD Perry Township	Indianapolis
47	4.3	Seymour Community Schools	Seymour
49	4.0	Prairie Heights Com Sch Corp	Lagrange
50	3.9	Alexandria Com School Corp	Alexandria
51	3.8	Bartholomew Con School Corp	Columbus
51	3.8	Kankakee Valley School Corp	Wheatfield
53	3.7	Crawfordsville Com Schools	Crawfordsville
53	3.7	MSD Warren Township	Indianapolis
55	3.6	Benton Community School Corp	Fowler
55	3.6	Penn-Harris-Madison Sch Corp	Mishawaka
57	3.5	Crown Point Community Sch Corp	Crown Point
58	3.4	East Allen County Schools	New Haven
59	3.3	Knox Community School Corp	Knox
60	3.2	Tippecanoe Valley School Corp	Akron
61	3.0	MSD Steuben County	Angola
61	3.0	Valparaiso Community Schools	Valparaiso
63	2.9	Portage Township Schools	Portage
64	2.8	Marion Community Schools	Marion
64	2.8	North Spencer County Sch Corp	Lincoln City
66	2.5	Jay School Corp	Portland
67	2.4	Greenwood Community Sch Corp	Greenwood
68	2.3	Tipton Community School Corp	Tipton
69	2.2	Elwood Community School Corp	Elwood
69	2.2	Union Township School Corp	Valparaiso
71	2.1	Brownsburg Community Sch Corp	Brownsburg
71	2.1	Rensselaer Central School Corp	Rensselaer
71	2.1	Western School Corp	Russiaville
71	2.1	Westfield-Washington Schools	Westfield
75	2.0	Franklin Township Com Sch Corp	Indianapolis
75	2.0	Greater Clark County Schools	Jeffersonville
75	2.0	New Prairie United School Corp	New Carlisle
75	2.0	North Judson-San Pierre Sch Corp	North Judson
79	1.9	East Noble School Corp	Kendallville
79	1.9	Michigan City Area Schools	Michigan City
81	1.8	Batesville Community School Corp	Batesville
81	1.8	North Newton School Corp	Morocco
81	1.8	School City of Mishawaka	Mishawaka
84	1.7	Hanover Community School Corp	Cedar Lake
84	1.7	Kokomo-Center Twp Con Sch Corp	Kokomo
84	1.7	Muncie Community Schools	Muncie
87	1.6	Anderson Community School Corp	Anderson
87	1.6	Greensburg Community Schools	Greensburg
87	1.6	Noblesville Schools	Noblesville
87	1.6	North Adams Community Schools	Decatur
87	1.6	Richmond Community School Corp	Richmond
87	1.6	Rochester Community Sch Corp	Rochester
93	1.5	Avon Community School Corp	Avon
93	1.5	Evansville-Vanderburgh Sch Corp	Evansville
93	1.5	MSD Decatur Township	Indianapolis
96	1.4	Baugo Community Schools	Elkhart
96	1.4	Beech Grove City Schools	Beech Grove
96	1.4	Center Grove Com Sch Corp	Greenwood
96	1.4	John Glenn School Corporation	Walkerton
96	1.4	Maconaquah School Corp	Bunker Hill
96	1.4	Mount Pleasant Twp Com Sch Corp	Yorktown
96	1.4	New Albany-Floyd County Con Sch	New Albany
96	1.4	Northwestern School Corp	Kokomo
96	1.4	Plainfield Community Sch Corp	Plainfield
96	1.4	Taylor Community School Corp	Kokomo
106	1.3	Dekalb County Ctl United SD	Waterloo
106	1.3	Duneland School Corporation	Chesterton
106	1.3	Lake Ridge Schools	Gary
109	1.2	Tri-Creek School Corp	Lowell
109	1.2	Whitko Community School Corp	Pierceton
111	1.1	Madison Consolidated Schools	Madison
111	1.1	Manchester Community Schools	N Manchester
111	1.1	Northwest Allen County Schools	Fort Wayne
114	1.0	Franklin Community School Corp	Franklin
114	1.0	Hamilton Heights School Corp	Arcadia
114	1.0	Lebanon Community School Corp	Lebanon
114	1.0	North Lawrence Com Schools	Bedford
118	0.9	Crawford County Com School Corp	Marengo
118	0.9	Greencastle Community Sch Corp	Greencastle
118	0.9	Madison-Grant United Sch Corp	Fairmount
118	0.9	Warrick County School Corp	Boonville
122	0.8	Mitchell Community Schools	Mitchell
122	0.8	Peru Community Schools	Peru
122	0.8	Randolph Central School Corp	Winchester
122	0.8	Vincennes Community Sch Corp	Vincennes
122	0.8	Zionsville Community Schools	Zionsville
127	0.7	Garrett-Keyser-Butler Com	Garrett
127	0.7	Gary Community School Corp	Gary
127	0.7	Rush County Schools	Rushville
127	0.7	South Harrison Com Schools	Corydon
127	0.7	Southeast Dubois County Sch Corp	Ferdinand
127	0.7	Wabash City Schools	Wabash
133	0.6	Clark-Pleasant Com School Corp	Whiteland
133	0.6	Danville Community School Corp	Danville
133	0.6	Jennings County Schools	North Vernon
133	0.6	MSD Wabash County Schools	Wabash
133	0.6	North Gibson School Corp	Princeton
133	0.6	Porter Township School Corp	Valparaiso
133	0.6	Salem Community Schools	Salem
133	0.6	South Vermillion Com Sch Corp	Clinton
133	0.6	Sunman-Dearborn Com Sch Corp	Sunman
133	0.6	Whitley County Cons Schools	Columbia City
143	0.5	Brownstown Cnt Com Sch Corp	Brownstown
143	0.5	Centerville-Abington Com Schs	Centerville
143	0.5	Frankton-Lapel Community Schs	Anderson
143	0.5	Mississinewa Community School Corp	Gas City
143	0.5	Mount Vernon Community Sch Corp	Fortville
148	0.4	Brown County School Corporation	Nashville
148	0.4	Eastbrook Community Sch Corp	Marion
148	0.4	Fayette County School Corp	Connersville
148	0.4	Huntington County Com Sch Corp	Huntington
148	0.4	MSD Martinsville Schools	Martinsville
148	0.4	Mooresville Con School Corp	Mooresville
148	0.4	Scott County SD 2	Scottsburg
148	0.4	Southwestern-Jefferson County	Hanover
148	0.4	Tell City-Troy Twp School Corp	Tell City
157	0.3	Delaware Community School Corp	Muncie
157	0.3	East Porter County School Corp	Kouts
157	0.3	East Washington School Corp	Pekin
157	0.3	MSD Mount Vernon	Mount Vernon
157	0.3	North Harrison Com School Corp	Ramsey
157	0.3	Paoli Community School Corp	Paoli
157	0.3	Richland-Bean Blossom C S C	Ellettsville
157	0.3	South Madison Com Sch Corp	Pendleton
157	0.3	South Spencer County Sch Corp	Rockport
157	0.3	Southwest School Corp	Sullivan
157	0.3	Vigo County School Corp	Terre Haute
157	0.3	West Clark Community Schools	Sellersburg
169	0.2	Clay Community Schools	Knightsville
169	0.2	Greenfield-Central Com Schools	Greenfield
169	0.2	Mill Creek Community Sch Corp	Clayton
169	0.2	Nineveh-Hensley-Jackson United	Trafalgar
169	0.2	North Montgomery Com Sch Corp	Linden
169	0.2	Northern Wells Com Schools	Ossian
169	0.2	Switzerland County School Corp	Vevay
169	0.2	Western Boone County Com SD	Thorntown
177	0.1	Decatur County Com Schools	Greensburg
177	0.1	MSD North Posey County Schools	Poseyville
177	0.1	New Castle Community Sch Corp	New Castle
177	0.1	Pike County School Corp	Petersburg
177	0.1	South Dearborn Com School Corp	Aurora
177	0.1	South Gibson School Corp	Fort Branch
177	0.1	Spencer-Owen Community Schools	Spencer
177	0.1	Union Co-Clg Corner Joint SD	Liberty
185	0.0	Southern Hancock Co Com Sch Corp	New Palestine
186	n/a	Blackford County Schools	Hartford City
186	n/a	Cloverdale Community Schools	Cloverdale
186	n/a	Franklin County Com Sch Corp	Brookville
186	n/a	North Knox School Corp	Bicknell
186	n/a	North Putnam Community Schools	Bainbridge
186	n/a	North West Hendricks Schools	Lizton
186	n/a	Northeast School Corp	Hymera
186	n/a	Shelby Eastern Schools	Shelbyville
186	n/a	South Montgomery Com Sch Corp	New Market

Migrant Students

Rank	Percent	District Name	City
1	n/a	Alexandria Com School Corp	Alexandria
1	n/a	Anderson Community School Corp	Anderson
1	n/a	Avon Community School Corp	Avon

Rank	Percent	District Name	City
1	n/a	Bartholomew Con School Corp	Columbus
1	n/a	Batesville Community School Corp	Batesville
1	n/a	Baugo Community Schools	Elkhart
1	n/a	Beech Grove City Schools	Beech Grove
1	n/a	Benton Community School Corp	Fowler
1	n/a	Blackford County Schools	Hartford City
1	n/a	Brown County School Corporation	Nashville
1	n/a	Brownsburg Community Sch Corp	Brownsburg
1	n/a	Brownstown Cnt Com Sch Corp	Brownstown
1	n/a	Carmel Clay Schools	Carmel
1	n/a	Center Grove Com Sch Corp	Greenwood
1	n/a	Centerville-Abington Com Schs	Centerville
1	n/a	Clark-Pleasant Com School Corp	Whiteland
1	n/a	Clay Community Schools	Knightsville
1	n/a	Cloverdale Community Schools	Cloverdale
1	n/a	Community Schools of Frankfort	Frankfort
1	n/a	Concord Community Schools	Elkhart
1	n/a	Crawford County Com School Corp	Marengo
1	n/a	Crawfordsville Com Schools	Crawfordsville
1	n/a	Crown Point Community Sch Corp	Crown Point
1	n/a	Danville Community School Corp	Danville
1	n/a	Decatur County Com Schools	Greensburg
1	n/a	Dekalb County Ctl United SD	Waterloo
1	n/a	Delaware Community School Corp	Muncie
1	n/a	Delphi Community School Corp	Delphi
1	n/a	Duneland School Corporation	Chesterton
1	n/a	East Allen County Schools	New Haven
1	n/a	East Noble School Corp	Kendallville
1	n/a	East Porter County School Corp	Kouts
1	n/a	East Washington School Corp	Pekin
1	n/a	Eastbrook Community Sch Corp	Marion
1	n/a	Elkhart Community Schools	Elkhart
1	n/a	Elwood Community School Corp	Elwood
1	n/a	Evansville-Vanderburgh Sch Corp	Evansville
1	n/a	Fairfield Community Schools	Goshen
1	n/a	Fayette County School Corp	Connersville
1	n/a	Fort Wayne Community Schools	Fort Wayne
1	n/a	Franklin Community School Corp	Franklin
1	n/a	Franklin County Com Sch Corp	Brookville
1	n/a	Franklin Township Com Sch Corp	Indianapolis
1	n/a	Frankton-Lapel Community Schs	Anderson
1	n/a	Garrett-Keyser-Butler Com	Garrett
1	n/a	Gary Community School Corp	Gary
1	n/a	Goshen Community Schools	Goshen
1	n/a	Greater Clark County Schools	Jeffersonville
1	n/a	Greater Jasper Con Schs	Jasper
1	n/a	Greencastle Community Sch Corp	Greencastle
1	n/a	Greenfield-Central Com Schools	Greenfield
1	n/a	Greensburg Community Schools	Greensburg
1	n/a	Greenwood Community Sch Corp	Greenwood
1	n/a	Griffith Public Schools	Griffith
1	n/a	Hamilton Heights School Corp	Arcadia
1	n/a	Hamilton Southeastern Schools	Fishers
1	n/a	Hanover Community School Corp	Cedar Lake
1	n/a	Huntington County Com Sch Corp	Huntington
1	n/a	Indianapolis Public Schools	Indianapolis
1	n/a	Jay School Corp	Portland
1	n/a	Jennings County Schools	North Vernon
1	n/a	John Glenn School Corporation	Walkerton
1	n/a	Kankakee Valley School Corp	Wheatfield
1	n/a	Knox Community School Corp	Knox
1	n/a	Kokomo-Center Twp Con Sch Corp	Kokomo
1	n/a	Lafayette School Corporation	Lafayette
1	n/a	Lake Central School Corp	Saint John
1	n/a	Lake Ridge Schools	Gary
1	n/a	Lakeland School Corporation	Lagrange
1	n/a	Laporte Community School Corp	Laporte
1	n/a	Lebanon Community School Corp	Lebanon
1	n/a	Logansport Community Sch Corp	Logansport
1	n/a	MSD Bluffton-Harrison	Bluffton
1	n/a	MSD Decatur Township	Indianapolis
1	n/a	MSD Lawrence Township	Indianapolis
1	n/a	MSD Martinsville Schools	Martinsville
1	n/a	MSD Mount Vernon	Mount Vernon
1	n/a	MSD North Posey County Schools	Poseyville
1	n/a	MSD Perry Township	Indianapolis
1	n/a	MSD Pike Township	Indianapolis
1	n/a	MSD Southwest Allen County	Fort Wayne
1	n/a	MSD Steuben County	Angola
1	n/a	MSD Wabash County Schools	Wabash
1	n/a	MSD Warren Township	Indianapolis
1	n/a	MSD Washington Township	Indianapolis
1	n/a	MSD Wayne Township	Indianapolis
1	n/a	Maconaquah School Corp	Bunker Hill
1	n/a	Madison Consolidated Schools	Madison
1	n/a	Madison-Grant United Sch Corp	Fairmount
1	n/a	Manchester Community Schools	N Manchester
1	n/a	Marion Community Schools	Marion
1	n/a	Merrillville Community School	Merrillville
1	n/a	Michigan City Area Schools	Michigan City
1	n/a	Middlebury Community Schools	Middlebury
1	n/a	Mill Creek Community Sch Corp	Clayton
1	n/a	Mississinewa Community School Corp	Gas City
1	n/a	Mitchell Community Schools	Mitchell
1	n/a	Monroe County Com Sch Corp	Bloomington
1	n/a	Mooresville Con School Corp	Mooresville
1	n/a	Mount Pleasant Twp Com Sch Corp	Yorktown
1	n/a	Mount Vernon Community Sch Corp	Fortville
1	n/a	Muncie Community Schools	Muncie
1	n/a	New Albany-Floyd County Con Sch	New Albany
1	n/a	New Castle Community Sch Corp	New Castle
1	n/a	New Prairie United School Corp	New Carlisle
1	n/a	Nineveh-Hensley-Jackson United	Trafalgar
1	n/a	Noblesville Schools	Noblesville
1	n/a	North Adams Community Schools	Decatur
1	n/a	North Gibson School Corp	Princeton
1	n/a	North Harrison Com School Corp	Ramsey
1	n/a	North Judson-San Pierre Sch Corp	North Judson
1	n/a	North Knox School Corp	Bicknell
1	n/a	North Lawrence Com Schools	Bedford
1	n/a	North Montgomery Com Sch Corp	Linden
1	n/a	North Newton School Corp	Morocco
1	n/a	North Putnam Community Schools	Bainbridge
1	n/a	North Spencer County Sch Corp	Lincoln City
1	n/a	North West Hendricks Schools	Lizton
1	n/a	Northeast School Corp	Hymera
1	n/a	Northern Wells Com Schools	Ossian
1	n/a	Northwest Allen County Schools	Fort Wayne
1	n/a	Northwestern School Corp	Kokomo
1	n/a	Paoli Community School Corp	Paoli
1	n/a	Penn-Harris-Madison Sch Corp	Mishawaka
1	n/a	Peru Community Schools	Peru
1	n/a	Pike County School Corp	Petersburg
1	n/a	Plainfield Community Sch Corp	Plainfield
1	n/a	Plymouth Community School Corp	Plymouth
1	n/a	Portage Township Schools	Portage
1	n/a	Porter Township School Corp	Valparaiso
1	n/a	Prairie Heights Com Sch Corp	Lagrange
1	n/a	Randolph Central School Corp	Winchester
1	n/a	Rensselaer Central School Corp	Rensselaer
1	n/a	Richland-Bean Blossom C S C	Ellettsville
1	n/a	Richmond Community School Corp	Richmond
1	n/a	Rochester Community Sch Corp	Rochester
1	n/a	Rush County Schools	Rushville
1	n/a	Salem Community Schools	Salem
1	n/a	School City of East Chicago	East Chicago
1	n/a	School City of Hammond	Hammond
1	n/a	School City of Hobart	Hobart
1	n/a	School City of Mishawaka	Mishawaka
1	n/a	School Town of Highland	Highland
1	n/a	School Town of Munster	Munster
1	n/a	School Town of Speedway	Speedway
1	n/a	Scott County SD 2	Scottsburg
1	n/a	Seymour Community Schools	Seymour
1	n/a	Shelby Eastern Schools	Shelbyville
1	n/a	Shelbyville Central Schools	Shelbyville
1	n/a	South Bend Community Sch Corp	South Bend
1	n/a	South Dearborn Com School Corp	Aurora
1	n/a	South Gibson School Corp	Fort Branch
1	n/a	South Harrison Com Schools	Corydon
1	n/a	South Madison Com Sch Corp	Pendleton
1	n/a	South Montgomery Com Sch Corp	New Market
1	n/a	South Spencer County Sch Corp	Rockport
1	n/a	South Vermillion Com Sch Corp	Clinton
1	n/a	Southeast Dubois County Sch Corp	Ferdinand
1	n/a	Southeastern School Corp	Walton
1	n/a	Southern Hancock Co Com Sch Corp	New Palestine
1	n/a	Southwest Dubois County Sch Corp	Huntingburg
1	n/a	Southwest School Corp	Sullivan
1	n/a	Southwestern-Jefferson County	Hanover
1	n/a	Spencer-Owen Community Schools	Spencer
1	n/a	Sunman-Dearborn Com Sch Corp	Sunman
1	n/a	Switzerland County School Corp	Vevay
1	n/a	Taylor Community School Corp	Kokomo
1	n/a	Tell City-Troy Twp School Corp	Tell City
1	n/a	Tippecanoe School Corp	Lafayette
1	n/a	Tippecanoe Valley School Corp	Akron
1	n/a	Tipton Community School Corp	Tipton
1	n/a	Tri-Creek School Corp	Lowell
1	n/a	Twin Lakes School Corp	Monticello
1	n/a	Union Co-Clg Corner Joint SD	Liberty
1	n/a	Union Township School Corp	Valparaiso
1	n/a	Valparaiso Community Schools	Valparaiso
1	n/a	Vigo County School Corp	Terre Haute
1	n/a	Vincennes Community Sch Corp	Vincennes
1	n/a	Wa-Nee Community Schools	Nappanee
1	n/a	Wabash City Schools	Wabash
1	n/a	Warrick County School Corp	Boonville
1	n/a	Warsaw Community Schools	Warsaw
1	n/a	Washington Com Schools Inc	Washington
1	n/a	Wawasee Community School Corp	Syracuse
1	n/a	West Clark Community Schools	Sellersburg
1	n/a	West Lafayette Com School Corp	West Lafayette
1	n/a	West Noble School Corporation	Ligonier
1	n/a	Western Boone County Com SD	Thorntown
1	n/a	Western School Corp	Russiaville
1	n/a	Westfield-Washington Schools	Westfield
1	n/a	Westview School Corporation	Topeka
1	n/a	Whitko Community School Corp	Pierceton
1	n/a	Whitley County Cons Schools	Columbia City
1	n/a	Zionsville Community Schools	Zionsville

Students Eligible for Free Lunch

Rank	Percent	District Name	City
1	76.4	School City of East Chicago	East Chicago
2	66.0	Indianapolis Public Schools	Indianapolis
3	56.5	Gary Community School Corp	Gary
4	54.0	School City of Hammond	Hammond
5	49.2	Lake Ridge Schools	Gary
6	47.2	Muncie Community Schools	Muncie
7	46.5	South Bend Community Sch Corp	South Bend
8	41.8	Anderson Community School Corp	Anderson
9	41.0	Michigan City Area Schools	Michigan City
10	40.9	Marion Community Schools	Marion
11	39.3	Richmond Community School Corp	Richmond
12	38.8	Fort Wayne Community Schools	Fort Wayne
13	38.4	Community Schools of Frankfort	Frankfort
14	37.2	Elkhart Community Schools	Elkhart
15	36.9	Knox Community School Corp	Knox
16	36.6	Kokomo-Center Twp Con Sch Corp	Kokomo
17	36.3	Crawford County Com School Corp	Marengo
18	36.1	MSD Wayne Township	Indianapolis
18	36.1	West Noble School Corporation	Ligonier
20	35.0	Evansville-Vanderburgh Sch Corp	Evansville
20	35.0	Fayette County School Corp	Connersville
22	33.7	New Castle Community Sch Corp	New Castle
23	33.1	Elwood Community School Corp	Elwood
23	33.1	North Judson-San Pierre Sch Corp	North Judson
25	32.7	Vigo County School Corp	Terre Haute
26	32.4	Goshen Community Schools	Goshen
27	31.2	Northeast School Corp	Hymera
28	31.1	Logansport Community Sch Corp	Logansport
29	30.7	Mitchell Community Schools	Mitchell
30	30.6	North Knox School Corp	Bicknell
31	30.1	Peru Community Schools	Peru
32	30.0	MSD Warren Township	Indianapolis
33	29.9	Crawfordsville Com Schools	Crawfordsville
34	29.7	Paoli Community School Corp	Paoli
34	29.7	Vincennes Community Sch Corp	Vincennes
36	29.3	MSD Decatur Township	Indianapolis
37	29.2	Cloverdale Community Schools	Cloverdale
37	29.2	Lafayette School Corporation	Lafayette
39	29.0	Union Co-Clg Corner Joint SD	Liberty
40	28.8	Washington Com Schools Inc	Washington
41	28.5	Switzerland County School Corp	Vevay
42	28.4	School City of Mishawaka	Mishawaka
42	28.4	Southwestern-Jefferson County	Hanover
44	28.1	South Vermillion Com Sch Corp	Clinton
45	27.9	School Town of Speedway	Speedway
46	27.7	MSD Perry Township	Indianapolis
47	27.5	Mississinewa Community School Corp	Gas City
48	26.9	Wabash City Schools	Wabash
49	25.4	Scott County SD 2	Scottsburg
50	25.1	Clay Community Schools	Knightsville
50	25.1	Jay School Corp	Portland
50	25.1	Randolph Central School Corp	Winchester
50	25.1	Spencer-Owen Community Schools	Spencer
54	24.8	Madison Consolidated Schools	Madison
54	24.8	Pike County School Corp	Petersburg
56	24.7	New Albany-Floyd County Con Sch	New Albany
57	24.4	Greater Clark County Schools	Jeffersonville
58	24.3	MSD Washington Township	Indianapolis
58	24.3	Plymouth Community School Corp	Plymouth
60	24.2	Shelbyville Central Schools	Shelbyville
61	24.1	North Lawrence Com Schools	Bedford
62	24.0	Blackford County Schools	Hartford City
63	23.7	Twin Lakes School Corp	Monticello
64	23.6	Alexandria Com School Corp	Alexandria
65	23.1	Southwest School Corp	Sullivan
66	22.9	Salem Community Schools	Salem
67	22.8	Bartholomew Con School Corp	Columbus
67	22.8	North Gibson School Corp	Princeton
69	22.7	Franklin County Com Sch Corp	Brookville
69	22.7	Greencastle Community Sch Corp	Greencastle
69	22.7	Taylor Community School Corp	Kokomo
72	22.6	Laporte Community School Corp	Laporte
73	22.5	Jennings County Schools	North Vernon
74	22.2	East Washington School Corp	Pekin
75	22.0	MSD Pike Township	Indianapolis
76	21.9	Portage Township Schools	Portage
77	21.7	Seymour Community Schools	Seymour
78	21.3	Monroe County Com Sch Corp	Bloomington
79	21.2	East Allen County Schools	New Haven
80	21.1	Lakeland School Corporation	Lagrange
81	20.9	Beech Grove City Schools	Beech Grove
81	20.9	Franklin Community School Corp	Franklin
81	20.9	Maconaquah School Corp	Bunker Hill

84	20.8	MSD Lawrence Township	Indianapolis
84	20.8	Manchester Community Schools	N Manchester
86	20.7	Rochester Community Sch Corp	Rochester
86	20.7	Tell City-Troy Twp School Corp	Tell City
88	20.6	Concord Community Schools	Elkhart
88	20.6	Rensselaer Central School Corp	Rensselaer
90	20.5	South Spencer County Sch Corp	Rockport
90	20.5	Wawasee Community School Corp	Syracuse
92	20.3	Benton Community School Corp	Fowler
92	20.3	Madison-Grant United Sch Corp	Fairmount
94	20.2	Garrett-Keyser-Butler Com	Garrett
95	19.9	Delphi Community School Corp	Delphi
95	19.9	Greensburg Community Schools	Greensburg
97	19.7	North Adams Community Schools	Decatur
97	19.7	School City of Hobart	Hobart
99	19.6	Brown County School Corporation	Nashville
100	19.3	Brownstown Cnt Com Sch Corp	Brownstown
101	19.0	South Harrison Com Schools	Corydon
102	18.9	Tippecanoe Valley School Corp	Akron
103	18.7	MSD Steuben County	Angola
104	18.6	Warsaw Community Schools	Warsaw
105	18.1	MSD Mount Vernon	Mount Vernon
106	18.0	Lebanon Community School Corp	Lebanon
106	18.0	North Newton School Corp	Morocco
108	17.9	North Putnam Community Schools	Bainbridge
109	17.7	Rush County Schools	Rushville
110	17.5	John Glenn School Corporation	Walkerton
110	17.5	North Harrison Com School Corp	Ramsey
112	17.2	MSD Martinsville Schools	Martinsville
113	16.9	Whitko Community School Corp	Pierceton
114	16.8	North Montgomery Com Sch Corp	Linden
115	16.5	Huntington County Com Sch Corp	Huntington
115	16.5	South Dearborn Com School Corp	Aurora
117	16.3	East Noble School Corp	Kendallville
117	16.3	Merrillville Community School	Merrillville
119	16.2	Prairie Heights Com Sch Corp	Lagrange
120	16.1	Baugo Community Schools	Elkhart
121	15.9	Kankakee Valley School Corp	Wheatfield
122	15.6	Delaware Community School Corp	Muncie
123	15.3	Tippecanoe School Corp	Lafayette
124	14.9	Western Boone County Com SD	Thorntown
125	14.6	South Montgomery Com Sch Corp	New Market
125	14.6	Southeastern School Corp	Walton
127	14.5	Eastbrook Community Sch Corp	Marion
128	14.3	Decatur County Com Schools	Greensburg
129	14.2	Mooresville Con School Corp	Mooresville
129	14.2	Southwest Dubois County Sch Corp	Huntingburg
131	13.9	Greenwood Community Sch Corp	Greenwood
132	13.8	West Clark Community Schools	Sellersburg
133	13.7	Frankton-Lapel Community Schs	Anderson
134	13.6	Richland-Bean Blossom C S C	Ellettsville
135	13.4	MSD Bluffton-Harrison	Bluffton
136	13.3	Hanover Community School Corp	Cedar Lake
136	13.3	Tipton Community School Corp	Tipton
138	13.0	Duneland School Corporation	Chesterton
139	12.8	Franklin Township Com Sch Corp	Indianapolis
140	12.5	Dekalb County Ctl United SD	Waterloo
141	12.4	Centerville-Abington Com Schs	Centerville
142	12.3	Hamilton Heights School Corp	Arcadia
142	12.3	Warrick County School Corp	Boonville
144	11.9	Mill Creek Community Sch Corp	Clayton
145	11.8	Wa-Nee Community Schools	Nappanee
146	11.7	Tri-Creek School Corp	Lowell
147	11.6	New Prairie United School Corp	New Carlisle
148	11.5	Northern Wells Com Schools	Ossian
148	11.5	Plainfield Community Sch Corp	Plainfield
150	11.4	MSD Wabash County Schools	Wabash
151	11.3	North Spencer County Sch Corp	Lincoln City
152	11.2	Griffith Public Schools	Griffith
153	11.1	Greenfield-Central Com Schools	Greenfield
153	11.1	Valparaiso Community Schools	Valparaiso
155	11.0	Avon Community School Corp	Avon
156	10.5	Whitley County Cons Schools	Columbia City
157	10.3	Western School Corp	Russiaville
158	10.2	Clark-Pleasant Com School Corp	Whiteland
159	9.6	Shelby Eastern Schools	Shelbyville
160	9.5	MSD North Posey County Schools	Poseyville
161	9.3	Nineveh-Hensley-Jackson United	Trafalgar
161	9.3	Noblesville Schools	Noblesville
163	9.2	South Gibson School Corp	Fort Branch
164	9.1	South Madison Com Sch Corp	Pendleton
165	9.0	Crown Point Community Sch Corp	Crown Point
166	8.9	Middlebury Community Schools	Middlebury
166	8.9	Northwestern School Corp	Kokomo
168	8.8	Mount Pleasant Twp Com Sch Corp	Yorktown
169	8.7	Greater Jasper Con Schs	Jasper
170	8.6	Westview School Corporation	Topeka
171	8.5	Penn-Harris-Madison Sch Corp	Mishawaka
172	7.7	Batesville Community School Corp	Batesville
173	7.4	Sunman-Dearborn Com Sch Corp	Sunman
173	7.4	Westfield-Washington Schools	Westfield
175	7.2	East Porter County School Corp	Kouts
176	7.1	Southeast Dubois County Sch Corp	Ferdinand
177	7.0	Fairfield Community Schools	Goshen
178	6.6	Danville Community School Corp	Danville
178	6.6	School Town of Highland	Highland
180	6.5	Union Township School Corp	Valparaiso
181	6.4	Center Grove Com Sch Corp	Greenwood
182	6.3	Lake Central School Corp	Saint John
183	6.1	Porter Township School Corp	Valparaiso
184	5.8	West Lafayette Com School Corp	West Lafayette
185	5.7	Brownsburg Community Sch Corp	Brownsburg
186	5.6	North West Hendricks Schools	Lizton
187	4.9	Southern Hancock Co Com Sch Corp	New Palestine
188	4.7	Northwest Allen County Schools	Fort Wayne
189	4.2	Mount Vernon Community Sch Corp	Fortville
190	3.8	School Town of Munster	Munster
191	3.3	Hamilton Southeastern Schools	Fishers
192	2.6	Carmel Clay Schools	Carmel
193	2.5	MSD Southwest Allen County	Fort Wayne
194	1.9	Zionsville Community Schools	Zionsville

Students Eligible for Reduced-Price Lunch

Rank	Percent	District Name	City
1	13.7	Crawford County Com School Corp	Marengo
2	13.3	North Judson-San Pierre Sch Corp	North Judson
3	13.1	Logansport Community Sch Corp	Logansport
4	12.7	Indianapolis Public Schools	Indianapolis
5	11.9	Muncie Community Schools	Muncie
6	11.8	West Noble School Corporation	Ligonier
7	11.6	Northeast School Corp	Hymera
7	11.6	Paoli Community School Corp	Paoli
7	11.6	School City of Hammond	Hammond
10	11.3	East Washington School Corp	Pekin
10	11.3	Pike County School Corp	Petersburg
10	11.3	Richmond Community School Corp	Richmond
13	11.1	Community Schools of Frankfort	Frankfort
13	11.1	North Knox School Corp	Bicknell
15	11.0	Goshen Community Schools	Goshen
15	11.0	Jay School Corp	Portland
17	10.8	Wabash City Schools	Wabash
18	10.6	Madison Consolidated Schools	Madison
18	10.6	School City of Mishawaka	Mishawaka
20	10.5	Vigo County School Corp	Terre Haute
21	10.4	Whitko Community School Corp	Pierceton
22	10.2	East Noble School Corp	Kendallville
22	10.2	Lafayette School Corporation	Lafayette
24	10.1	Southwestern-Jefferson County	Hanover
25	10.0	Elkhart Community Schools	Elkhart
25	10.0	Lakeland School Corporation	Lagrange
27	9.8	Garrett-Keyser-Butler Com	Garrett
27	9.8	Plymouth Community School Corp	Plymouth
27	9.8	Warsaw Community Schools	Warsaw
30	9.7	Spencer-Owen Community Schools	Spencer
31	9.6	Jennings County Schools	North Vernon
31	9.6	Manchester Community Schools	N Manchester
31	9.6	Peru Community Schools	Peru
34	9.5	Evansville-Vanderburgh Sch Corp	Evansville
34	9.5	Knox Community School Corp	Knox
34	9.5	MSD Washington Township	Indianapolis
34	9.5	North Harrison Com School Corp	Ramsey
34	9.5	Twin Lakes School Corp	Monticello
39	9.4	Kankakee Valley School Corp	Wheatfield
39	9.4	Seymour Community Schools	Seymour
41	9.3	Benton Community School Corp	Fowler
41	9.3	Lake Ridge Schools	Gary
41	9.3	South Vermillion Com Sch Corp	Clinton
44	9.2	MSD Warren Township	Indianapolis
44	9.2	North Gibson School Corp	Princeton
46	9.1	Rensselaer Central School Corp	Rensselaer
46	9.1	Scott County SD 2	Scottsburg
46	9.1	Switzerland County School Corp	Vevay
49	9.0	Clay Community Schools	Knightsville
49	9.0	Delphi Community School Corp	Delphi
49	9.0	North Putnam Community Schools	Bainbridge
49	9.0	South Bend Community Sch Corp	South Bend
53	8.9	Blackford County Schools	Hartford City
53	8.9	Fort Wayne Community Schools	Fort Wayne
53	8.9	MSD Steuben County	Angola
53	8.9	Michigan City Area Schools	Michigan City
53	8.9	Rush County Schools	Rushville
58	8.8	Elwood Community School Corp	Elwood
58	8.8	Huntington County Com Sch Corp	Huntington
58	8.8	Vincennes Community Sch Corp	Vincennes
61	8.6	MSD Decatur Township	Indianapolis
61	8.6	MSD Martinsville Schools	Martinsville
61	8.6	North Newton School Corp	Morocco
61	8.6	Southwest School Corp	Sullivan
65	8.5	Clark-Pleasant Com School Corp	Whiteland
65	8.5	MSD Bluffton-Harrison	Bluffton
65	8.5	MSD Perry Township	Indianapolis
65	8.5	South Harrison Com Schools	Corydon
69	8.4	Concord Community Schools	Elkhart
69	8.4	Kokomo-Center Twp Con Sch Corp	Kokomo
69	8.4	MSD North Posey County Schools	Poseyville
69	8.4	Maconaquah School Corp	Bunker Hill
69	8.4	Marion Community Schools	Marion
74	8.3	Cloverdale Community Schools	Cloverdale
74	8.3	MSD Pike Township	Indianapolis
76	8.2	Delaware Community School Corp	Muncie
76	8.2	MSD Wayne Township	Indianapolis
76	8.2	Madison-Grant United Sch Corp	Fairmount
76	8.2	North Lawrence Com Schools	Bedford
76	8.2	Prairie Heights Com Sch Corp	Lagrange
76	8.2	Taylor Community School Corp	Kokomo
76	8.2	Tell City-Troy Twp School Corp	Tell City
83	8.1	Bartholomew Con School Corp	Columbus
83	8.1	Franklin County Com Sch Corp	Brookville
83	8.1	Mississinewa Community School Corp	Gas City
83	8.1	Shelbyville Central Schools	Shelbyville
87	8.0	Baugo Community Schools	Elkhart
87	8.0	Eastbrook Community Sch Corp	Marion
87	8.0	Randolph Central School Corp	Winchester
90	7.9	Anderson Community School Corp	Anderson
90	7.9	Beech Grove City Schools	Beech Grove
92	7.7	East Allen County Schools	New Haven
92	7.7	Fairfield Community Schools	Goshen
92	7.7	John Glenn School Corporation	Walkerton
92	7.7	Monroe County Com Sch Corp	Bloomington
92	7.7	Tippecanoe Valley School Corp	Akron
92	7.7	Washington Com Schools Inc	Washington
98	7.6	Dekalb County Ctl United SD	Waterloo
98	7.6	Merrillville Community School	Merrillville
100	7.5	Alexandria Com School Corp	Alexandria
100	7.5	New Castle Community Sch Corp	New Castle
100	7.5	School City of East Chicago	East Chicago
103	7.4	Decatur County Com Schools	Greensburg
104	7.3	Greencastle Community Sch Corp	Greencastle
104	7.3	Hanover Community School Corp	Cedar Lake
104	7.3	Lebanon Community School Corp	Lebanon
104	7.3	School Town of Speedway	Speedway
104	7.3	Southeastern School Corp	Walton
104	7.3	Southwest Dubois County Sch Corp	Huntingburg
110	7.2	Brownstown Cnt Com Sch Corp	Brownstown
110	7.2	Portage Township Schools	Portage
112	7.1	Richland-Bean Blossom C S C	Ellettsville
112	7.1	Rochester Community Sch Corp	Rochester
114	7.0	Laporte Community School Corp	Laporte
114	7.0	West Clark Community Schools	Sellersburg
116	6.9	Crawfordsville Com Schools	Crawfordsville
116	6.9	Frankton-Lapel Community Schs	Anderson
116	6.9	Greater Clark County Schools	Jeffersonville
116	6.9	MSD Lawrence Township	Indianapolis
116	6.9	Middlebury Community Schools	Middlebury
121	6.8	Brown County School Corporation	Nashville
121	6.8	Fayette County School Corp	Connersville
123	6.7	Franklin Community School Corp	Franklin
124	6.6	Mitchell Community Schools	Mitchell
124	6.6	Northern Wells Com Schools	Ossian
126	6.5	Greensburg Community Schools	Greensburg
127	6.4	New Albany-Floyd County Con Sch	New Albany
127	6.4	Plainfield Community Sch Corp	Plainfield
127	6.4	School City of Hobart	Hobart
130	6.3	Salem Community Schools	Salem
130	6.3	Tipton Community School Corp	Tipton
130	6.3	Wawasee Community School Corp	Syracuse
133	6.2	Centerville-Abington Com Schs	Centerville
133	6.2	North Montgomery Com Sch Corp	Linden
133	6.2	North Spencer County Sch Corp	Lincoln City
133	6.2	South Montgomery Com Sch Corp	New Market
133	6.2	South Spencer County Sch Corp	Rockport
138	6.1	Mill Creek Community Sch Corp	Clayton
138	6.1	Wa-Nee Community Schools	Nappanee
140	5.9	Warrick County School Corp	Boonville
140	5.9	Whitley County Cons Schools	Columbia City
142	5.8	Southeast Dubois County Sch Corp	Ferdinand
143	5.7	North Adams Community Schools	Decatur
144	5.6	MSD Wabash County Schools	Wabash
144	5.6	Mount Pleasant Twp Com Sch Corp	Yorktown
146	5.4	Greenfield-Central Com Schools	Greenfield
146	5.4	Greenwood Community Sch Corp	Greenwood
148	5.3	Westview School Corporation	Topeka
149	5.2	Danville Community School Corp	Danville
149	5.2	Duneland School Corporation	Chesterton
149	5.2	South Gibson School Corp	Fort Branch
152	5.0	Westfield-Washington Schools	Westfield
153	4.9	Griffith Public Schools	Griffith
154	4.8	Franklin Township Com Sch Corp	Indianapolis
154	4.8	Hamilton Heights School Corp	Arcadia
154	4.8	South Dearborn Com School Corp	Aurora
154	4.8	Tippecanoe School Corp	Lafayette
158	4.7	Batesville Community School Corp	Batesville
158	4.7	New Prairie United School Corp	New Carlisle
160	4.4	Greater Jasper Con Schs	Jasper
160	4.4	North West Hendricks Schools	Lizton

162	4.3	Mooresville Con School Corp	Mooresville
162	4.3	Nineveh-Hensley-Jackson United	Trafalgar
162	4.3	Western Boone County Com SD	Thorntown
165	4.2	Valparaiso Community Schools	Valparaiso
166	4.1	Shelby Eastern Schools	Shelbyville
167	4.0	Noblesville Schools	Noblesville
167	4.0	Penn-Harris-Madison Sch Corp	Mishawaka
167	4.0	Tri-Creek School Corp	Lowell
167	4.0	Union Co-Clg Corner Joint SD	Liberty
171	3.9	Western School Corp	Russiaville
172	3.8	East Porter County School Corp	Kouts
173	3.6	Mount Vernon Community Sch Corp	Fortville
173	3.6	Porter Township School Corp	Valparaiso
175	3.5	Center Grove Com Sch Corp	Greenwood
175	3.5	MSD Mount Vernon	Mount Vernon
175	3.5	Sunman-Dearborn Com Sch Corp	Sunman
178	3.4	Northwest Allen County Schools	Fort Wayne
178	3.4	Northwestern School Corp	Kokomo
178	3.4	School Town of Highland	Highland
181	3.2	Lake Central School Corp	Saint John
181	3.2	School Town of Munster	Munster
183	3.1	Union Township School Corp	Valparaiso
184	3.0	South Madison Com Sch Corp	Pendleton
185	2.8	Crown Point Community Sch Corp	Crown Point
186	2.6	Brownsburg Community Sch Corp	Brownsburg
187	2.4	West Lafayette Com School Corp	West Lafayette
188	2.3	Gary Community School Corp	Gary
189	2.0	Southern Hancock Co Com Sch Corp	New Palestine
190	1.7	Hamilton Southeastern Schools	Fishers
191	1.6	Zionsville Community Schools	Zionsville
192	1.3	Carmel Clay Schools	Carmel
192	1.3	MSD Southwest Allen County	Fort Wayne
194	1.0	Avon Community School Corp	Avon

Student/Teacher Ratio

Rank	Ratio	District Name	City
1	22.7	Tri-Creek School Corp	Lowell
2	22.0	School Town of Highland	Highland
3	21.6	Crown Point Community Sch Corp	Crown Point
4	21.5	Clark-Pleasant Com School Corp	Whiteland
5	20.9	Penn-Harris-Madison Sch Corp	Mishawaka
6	20.6	Greenwood Community Sch Corp	Greenwood
7	20.4	Mount Vernon Community Sch Corp	Fortville
8	20.3	Franklin Township Com Sch Corp	Indianapolis
8	20.3	Hanover Community School Corp	Cedar Lake
10	20.2	Merrillville Community School	Merrillville
11	20.1	Duneland School Corporation	Chesterton
11	20.1	Southern Hancock Co Com Sch Corp	New Palestine
13	20.0	Plymouth Community School Corp	Plymouth
14	19.9	Griffith Public Schools	Griffith
15	19.8	Portage Township Schools	Portage
15	19.8	Porter Township School Corp	Valparaiso
15	19.8	South Madison Com Sch Corp	Pendleton
18	19.6	Dekalb County Ctl United SD	Waterloo
18	19.6	East Washington School Corp	Pekin
18	19.6	Frankton-Lapel Community Schs	Anderson
18	19.6	Switzerland County School Corp	Vevay
22	19.5	Plainfield Community Sch Corp	Plainfield
23	19.4	MSD Steuben County	Angola
24	19.3	Northwest Allen County Schools	Fort Wayne
24	19.3	Salem Community Schools	Salem
26	19.2	Center Grove Com Sch Corp	Greenwood
27	19.1	Shelbyville Central Schools	Shelbyville
27	19.1	Valparaiso Community Schools	Valparaiso
27	19.1	Warrick County School Corp	Boonville
30	19.0	Lake Ridge Schools	Gary
30	19.0	School City of Hobart	Hobart
32	18.9	Paoli Community School Corp	Paoli
32	18.9	Southwest Dubois County Sch Corp	Huntingburg
34	18.8	Avon Community School Corp	Avon
34	18.8	Lake Central School Corp	Saint John
34	18.8	Rochester Community Sch Corp	Rochester
34	18.8	South Gibson School Corp	Fort Branch
34	18.8	Sunman-Dearborn Com Sch Corp	Sunman
34	18.8	West Lafayette Com School Corp	West Lafayette
40	18.7	Brownsburg Community Sch Corp	Brownsburg
40	18.7	Gary Community School Corp	Gary
40	18.7	Greencastle Community Sch Corp	Greencastle
40	18.7	John Glenn School Corporation	Walkerton
40	18.7	Twin Lakes School Corp	Monticello
40	18.7	Western School Corp	Russiaville
46	18.6	New Prairie United School Corp	New Carlisle
46	18.6	Southeast Dubois County Sch Corp	Ferdinand
48	18.5	Brownstown Cnt Com Sch Corp	Brownstown
48	18.5	Delphi Community School Corp	Delphi
48	18.5	West Clark Community Schools	Sellersburg
51	18.4	Concord Community Schools	Elkhart
51	18.4	Danville Community School Corp	Danville
51	18.4	Franklin County Com Sch Corp	Brookville
51	18.4	Hamilton Southeastern Schools	Fishers
51	18.4	MSD Decatur Township	Indianapolis
51	18.4	North West Hendricks Schools	Lizton
51	18.4	Tippecanoe School Corp	Lafayette
58	18.3	Beech Grove City Schools	Beech Grove
58	18.3	Scott County SD 2	Scottsburg
60	18.2	Baugo Community Schools	Elkhart
60	18.2	Hamilton Heights School Corp	Arcadia
60	18.2	Kankakee Valley School Corp	Wheatfield
60	18.2	Wa-Nee Community Schools	Nappanee
64	18.1	Fairfield Community Schools	Goshen
64	18.1	Mitchell Community Schools	Mitchell
64	18.1	Mount Pleasant Twp Com Sch Corp	Yorktown
64	18.1	North Harrison Com School Corp	Ramsey
64	18.1	South Spencer County Sch Corp	Rockport
64	18.1	Tell City-Troy Twp School Corp	Tell City
70	18.0	Crawford County Com School Corp	Marengo
70	18.0	Knox Community School Corp	Knox
70	18.0	MSD Southwest Allen County	Fort Wayne
70	18.0	Tippecanoe Valley School Corp	Akron
70	18.0	Wawasee Community School Corp	Syracuse
75	17.9	Jennings County Schools	North Vernon
75	17.9	Middlebury Community Schools	Middlebury
75	17.9	New Albany-Floyd County Con Sch	New Albany
75	17.9	North Spencer County Sch Corp	Lincoln City
79	17.8	MSD Martinsville Schools	Martinsville
79	17.8	Manchester Community Schools	N Manchester
79	17.8	Seymour Community Schools	Seymour
79	17.8	South Harrison Com Schools	Corydon
79	17.8	Washington Com Schools Inc	Washington
84	17.7	Northern Wells Com Schools	Ossian
84	17.7	Pike County School Corp	Petersburg
84	17.7	Warsaw Community Schools	Warsaw
84	17.7	Western Boone County Com SD	Thorntown
88	17.6	MSD Wayne Township	Indianapolis
88	17.6	Nineveh-Hensley-Jackson United	Trafalgar
88	17.6	School City of East Chicago	East Chicago
88	17.6	School City of Hammond	Hammond
88	17.6	School Town of Munster	Munster
88	17.6	West Noble School Corporation	Ligonier
88	17.6	Whitko Community School Corp	Pierceton
88	17.6	Zionsville Community Schools	Zionsville
96	17.5	Bartholomew Con School Corp	Columbus
96	17.5	Fort Wayne Community Schools	Fort Wayne
96	17.5	MSD Perry Township	Indianapolis
96	17.5	Madison Consolidated Schools	Madison
96	17.5	North Gibson School Corp	Princeton
96	17.5	Prairie Heights Com Sch Corp	Lagrange
102	17.4	Delaware Community School Corp	Muncie
102	17.4	MSD Bluffton-Harrison	Bluffton
102	17.4	MSD Lawrence Township	Indianapolis
102	17.4	Mooresville Con School Corp	Mooresville
106	17.3	Eastbrook Community Sch Corp	Marion
106	17.3	Greensburg Community Schools	Greensburg
106	17.3	Noblesville Schools	Noblesville
106	17.3	North Montgomery Com Sch Corp	Linden
106	17.3	Westfield-Washington Schools	Westfield
111	17.2	MSD Warren Township	Indianapolis
111	17.2	North Judson-San Pierre Sch Corp	North Judson
113	17.1	Batesville Community School Corp	Batesville
113	17.1	East Porter County School Corp	Kouts
113	17.1	Franklin Community School Corp	Franklin
113	17.1	Lebanon Community School Corp	Lebanon
113	17.1	MSD Washington Township	Indianapolis
113	17.1	Southwest School Corp	Sullivan
119	17.0	East Allen County Schools	New Haven
119	17.0	Jay School Corp	Portland
119	17.0	Whitley County Cons Schools	Columbia City
122	16.9	Southeastern School Corp	Walton
122	16.9	Southwestern-Jefferson County	Hanover
122	16.9	Union Township School Corp	Valparaiso
125	16.8	Carmel Clay Schools	Carmel
125	16.8	Crawfordsville Com Schools	Crawfordsville
125	16.8	Shelby Eastern Schools	Shelbyville
128	16.7	Alexandria Com School Corp	Alexandria
128	16.7	Community Schools of Frankfort	Frankfort
128	16.7	Lakeland School Corporation	Lagrange
128	16.7	MSD Pike Township	Indianapolis
128	16.7	Mill Creek Community Sch Corp	Clayton
128	16.7	North Adams Community Schools	Decatur
128	16.7	Tipton Community School Corp	Tipton
135	16.6	North Knox School Corp	Bicknell
135	16.6	Rensselaer Central School Corp	Rensselaer
135	16.6	School Town of Speedway	Speedway
135	16.6	South Dearborn Com School Corp	Aurora
139	16.5	Decatur County Com Schools	Greensburg
139	16.5	Huntington County Com Sch Corp	Huntington
139	16.5	MSD Mount Vernon	Mount Vernon
139	16.5	North Newton School Corp	Morocco
139	16.5	South Bend Community Sch Corp	South Bend
144	16.4	East Noble School Corp	Kendallville
144	16.4	Maconaquah School Corp	Bunker Hill
144	16.4	South Montgomery Com Sch Corp	New Market
144	16.4	Westview School Corporation	Topeka
148	16.3	Monroe County Com Sch Corp	Bloomington
148	16.3	North Lawrence Com Schools	Bedford
150	16.2	Greater Clark County Schools	Jeffersonville
150	16.2	Greater Jasper Con Schs	Jasper
150	16.2	Rush County Schools	Rushville
150	16.2	Vigo County School Corp	Terre Haute
154	16.1	Centerville-Abington Com Schs	Centerville
154	16.1	Northwestern School Corp	Kokomo
154	16.1	Peru Community Schools	Peru
154	16.1	Union Co-Clg Corner Joint SD	Liberty
158	16.0	Cloverdale Community Schools	Cloverdale
158	16.0	Elkhart Community Schools	Elkhart
158	16.0	Laporte Community School Corp	Laporte
161	15.9	Evansville-Vanderburgh Sch Corp	Evansville
161	15.9	Randolph Central School Corp	Winchester
161	15.9	Richland-Bean Blossom C S C	Ellettsville
164	15.8	MSD North Posey County Schools	Poseyville
164	15.8	Madison-Grant United Sch Corp	Fairmount
164	15.8	South Vermillion Com Sch Corp	Clinton
164	15.8	Spencer-Owen Community Schools	Spencer
164	15.8	Wabash City Schools	Wabash
169	15.7	Mississinewa Community School Corp	Gas City
170	15.6	Blackford County Schools	Hartford City
171	15.4	Clay Community Schools	Knightsville
172	15.2	Garrett-Keyser-Butler Com	Garrett
172	15.2	Goshen Community Schools	Goshen
172	15.2	Marion Community Schools	Marion
172	15.2	Richmond Community School Corp	Richmond
172	15.2	Taylor Community School Corp	Kokomo
177	15.1	Anderson Community School Corp	Anderson
177	15.1	Elwood Community School Corp	Elwood
177	15.1	Michigan City Area Schools	Michigan City
177	15.1	Vincennes Community Sch Corp	Vincennes
181	15.0	Benton Community School Corp	Fowler
182	14.8	Brown County School Corporation	Nashville
183	14.6	Indianapolis Public Schools	Indianapolis
183	14.6	Northeast School Corp	Hymera
183	14.6	School City of Mishawaka	Mishawaka
186	14.4	MSD Wabash County Schools	Wabash
187	14.2	Lafayette School Corporation	Lafayette
188	14.1	Muncie Community Schools	Muncie
189	14.0	Kokomo-Center Twp Con Sch Corp	Kokomo
190	13.4	New Castle Community Sch Corp	New Castle
191	13.3	Fayette County School Corp	Connersville
192	13.0	Greenfield-Central Com Schools	Greenfield
193	12.7	North Putnam Community Schools	Bainbridge
194	12.5	Logansport Community Sch Corp	Logansport

Student/Librarian Ratio

Rank	Ratio	District Name	City
1	9,958.0	Penn-Harris-Madison Sch Corp	Mishawaka
2	4,383.0	Concord Community Schools	Elkhart
3	3,180.0	Merrillville Community School	Merrillville
4	3,113.3	South Gibson School Corp	Fort Branch
5	2,820.0	Goshen Community Schools	Goshen
6	2,764.0	School City of Mishawaka	Mishawaka
7	2,703.0	Griffith Public Schools	Griffith
8	2,661.5	North Lawrence Com Schools	Bedford
9	2,592.5	Jennings County Schools	North Vernon
10	2,592.0	New Prairie United School Corp	New Carlisle
11	2,547.2	Elkhart Community Schools	Elkhart
12	2,520.0	Seymour Community Schools	Seymour
13	2,417.4	Lake Central School Corp	Saint John
14	2,399.0	Lake Ridge Schools	Gary
15	2,285.0	Western School Corp	Russiaville
16	2,161.0	Pike County School Corp	Petersburg
17	2,064.5	Fayette County School Corp	Connersville
18	2,063.0	South Montgomery Com Sch Corp	New Market
19	2,037.0	Whitko Community School Corp	Pierceton
20	2,029.0	Benton Community School Corp	Fowler
21	2,008.0	Greenfield-Central Com Schools	Greenfield
22	1,983.0	Southwest School Corp	Sullivan
23	1,970.2	Fort Wayne Community Schools	Fort Wayne
24	1,932.0	Crown Point Community Sch Corp	Crown Point
25	1,928.0	Greenwood Community Sch Corp	Greenwood
26	1,888.0	Clark-Pleasant Com School Corp	Whiteland
27	1,848.7	New Albany-Floyd County Con Sch	New Albany
28	1,820.0	Crawford County Com School Corp	Marengo
29	1,794.5	Shelbyville Central Schools	Shelbyville
30	1,757.5	Wawasee Community School Corp	Syracuse
31	1,734.0	Baugo Community Schools	Elkhart
32	1,726.0	Paoli Community School Corp	Paoli
33	1,715.0	School City of Hobart	Hobart
34	1,698.0	North Newton School Corp	Morocco
35	1,666.5	School Town of Highland	Highland
36	1,664.0	Northwest Allen County Schools	Fort Wayne
37	1,606.0	Union Co-Clg Corner Joint SD	Liberty
38	1,602.5	Huntington County Com Sch Corp	Huntington
38	1,602.5	School City of East Chicago	East Chicago
40	1,599.0	Switzerland County School Corp	Vevay
41	1,569.0	Mill Creek Community Sch Corp	Clayton
42	1,567.0	Hanover Community School Corp	Cedar Lake
43	1,559.0	North West Hendricks Schools	Lizton
44	1,542.0	Southeast Dubois County Sch Corp	Ferdinand

45	1,536.0	Vincennes Community Sch Corp	Vincennes
46	1,530.0	Lakeland School Corporation	Lagrange
47	1,524.2	Warrick County School Corp	Boonville
48	1,523.0	Taylor Community School Corp	Kokomo
49	1,511.0	South Spencer County Sch Corp	Rockport
50	1,502.8	MSD Southwest Allen County	Fort Wayne
51	1,502.5	Valparaiso Community Schools	Valparaiso
52	1,478.0	Marion Community Schools	Marion
53	1,456.0	Middlebury Community Schools	Middlebury
54	1,433.3	Mooresville Con School Corp	Mooresville
55	1,390.1	East Allen County Schools	New Haven
56	1,372.7	North Montgomery Com Sch Corp	Linden
57	1,363.3	Dekalb County Ctl United SD	Waterloo
58	1,356.0	North Gibson School Corp	Princeton
59	1,353.9	South Bend Community Sch Corp	South Bend
60	1,353.0	MSD Martinsville Schools	Martinsville
61	1,350.5	MSD Wabash County Schools	Wabash
62	1,347.5	Twin Lakes School Corp	Monticello
63	1,347.3	Greensburg Community Schools	Greensburg
64	1,342.5	MSD Decatur Township	Indianapolis
65	1,337.3	Zionsville Community Schools	Zionsville
66	1,335.0	Portage Township Schools	Portage
67	1,322.5	Bartholomew Con School Corp	Columbus
68	1,308.5	Northern Wells Com Schools	Ossian
69	1,285.0	New Castle Community Sch Corp	New Castle
70	1,283.8	Warsaw Community Schools	Warsaw
71	1,248.6	Franklin Community School Corp	Franklin
72	1,248.5	West Noble School Corporation	Ligonier
73	1,246.5	Peru Community Schools	Peru
74	1,245.8	Laporte Community School Corp	Laporte
75	1,239.5	Washington Com Schools Inc	Washington
76	1,226.8	MSD Steuben County	Angola
77	1,222.5	Beech Grove City Schools	Beech Grove
78	1,216.0	Frankton-Lapel Community Schs	Anderson
79	1,173.5	Franklin Township Com Sch Corp	Indianapolis
80	1,168.8	Kokomo-Center Twp Con Sch Corp	Kokomo
81	1,164.3	Center Grove Com Sch Corp	Greenwood
82	1,147.3	Randolph Central School Corp	Winchester
83	1,141.0	Michigan City Area Schools	Michigan City
84	1,135.5	Danville Community School Corp	Danville
85	1,134.6	Indianapolis Public Schools	Indianapolis
86	1,108.5	Westview School Corporation	Topeka
87	1,097.3	Plymouth Community School Corp	Plymouth
88	1,093.0	West Clark Community Schools	Sellersburg
89	1,075.0	MSD Warren Township	Indianapolis
90	1,065.5	Mississinewa Community School Corp	Gas City
91	1,065.0	Tippecanoe Valley School Corp	Akron
92	1,027.0	Fairfield Community Schools	Goshen
93	1,007.4	MSD Lawrence Township	Indianapolis
94	1,002.3	Wa-Nee Community Schools	Nappanee
95	1,000.3	Franklin County Com Sch Corp	Brookville
96	997.8	MSD Perry Township	Indianapolis
97	985.0	South Dearborn Com School Corp	Aurora
98	982.4	MSD Wayne Township	Indianapolis
99	981.5	East Porter County School Corp	Kouts
100	966.3	Delaware Community School Corp	Muncie
101	960.0	Madison-Grant United Sch Corp	Fairmount
102	952.7	Mount Vernon Community Sch Corp	Fortville
103	949.8	School Town of Munster	Munster
104	931.3	Scott County SD 2	Scottsburg
105	927.3	East Noble School Corp	Kendallville
106	897.7	Richland-Bean Blossom C S C	Ellettsville
107	894.5	Prairie Heights Com Sch Corp	Lagrange
108	889.5	Alexandria Com School Corp	Alexandria
109	887.3	Whitley County Cons Schools	Columbia City
110	883.0	East Washington School Corp	Pekin
111	880.5	Eastbrook Community Sch Corp	Marion
112	872.5	Madison Consolidated Schools	Madison
113	866.0	Brownstown Cnt Com Sch Corp	Brownstown
114	847.0	Northwestern School Corp	Kokomo
115	844.0	Sunman-Dearborn Com Sch Corp	Sunman
116	841.0	MSD Pike Township	Indianapolis
117	835.4	North Adams Community Schools	Decatur
118	832.6	Carmel Clay Schools	Carmel
119	825.3	Greater Clark County Schools	Jeffersonville
120	823.5	School Town of Speedway	Speedway
121	818.0	Southeastern School Corp	Walton
122	816.6	Muncie Community Schools	Muncie
123	811.5	Garrett-Keyser-Butler Com	Garrett
124	808.0	Brownsburg Community Sch Corp	Brownsburg
124	808.0	Community Schools of Frankfort	Frankfort
126	807.3	Rensselaer Central School Corp	Rensselaer
127	799.7	MSD Mount Vernon	Mount Vernon
128	794.2	Plainfield Community Sch Corp	Plainfield
129	793.5	Anderson Community School Corp	Anderson
130	792.5	Centerville-Abington Com Schs	Centerville
131	790.7	North Spencer County Sch Corp	Lincoln City
132	788.0	North Knox School Corp	Bicknell
133	785.8	Kankakee Valley School Corp	Wheatfield
134	785.5	MSD North Posey County Schools	Poseyville
135	780.5	MSD Washington Township	Indianapolis
136	779.5	Spencer-Owen Community Schools	Spencer
137	776.6	Hamilton Southeastern Schools	Fishers
138	776.0	Porter Township School Corp	Valparaiso
139	775.5	Greater Jasper Con Schs	Jasper
140	765.3	Blackford County Schools	Hartford City
141	761.0	North Judson-San Pierre Sch Corp	North Judson
141	761.0	Northeast School Corp	Hymera
143	757.7	Hamilton Heights School Corp	Arcadia
144	756.0	Wabash City Schools	Wabash
145	750.0	Southwestern-Jefferson County	Hanover
146	748.6	School City of Hammond	Hammond
147	743.3	Avon Community School Corp	Avon
148	717.8	Evansville-Vanderburgh Sch Corp	Evansville
149	695.6	South Madison Com Sch Corp	Pendleton
150	693.7	Salem Community Schools	Salem
151	685.4	Noblesville Schools	Noblesville
152	684.8	Brown County School Corporation	Nashville
153	681.3	West Lafayette Com School Corp	West Lafayette
154	677.3	Knox Community School Corp	Knox
155	669.3	Mitchell Community Schools	Mitchell
156	668.8	Rush County Schools	Rushville
157	664.7	Rochester Community Sch Corp	Rochester
158	659.9	Clay Community Schools	Knightsville
159	656.4	Monroe County Com Sch Corp	Bloomington
160	655.0	Elwood Community School Corp	Elwood
161	650.3	South Vermillion Com Sch Corp	Clinton
162	646.7	Greencastle Community Sch Corp	Greencastle
163	636.3	North Putnam Community Schools	Bainbridge
164	633.7	Western Boone County Com SD	Thorntown
165	633.2	Logansport Community Sch Corp	Logansport
166	625.0	Tipton Community School Corp	Tipton
167	622.3	Westfield-Washington Schools	Westfield
168	613.0	Southwest Dubois County Sch Corp	Huntingburg
169	608.5	Southern Hancock Co Com Sch Corp	New Palestine
170	607.0	Nineveh-Hensley-Jackson United	Trafalgar
171	590.8	Maconaquah School Corp	Bunker Hill
172	580.7	Delphi Community School Corp	Delphi
173	574.6	Manchester Community Schools	N Manchester
174	569.3	Tell City-Troy Twp School Corp	Tell City
175	566.7	Vigo County School Corp	Terre Haute
176	565.3	Lafayette School Corporation	Lafayette
177	564.3	John Glenn School Corporation	Walkerton
178	556.3	Mount Pleasant Twp Com Sch Corp	Yorktown
179	555.8	Lebanon Community School Corp	Lebanon
180	552.4	Jay School Corp	Portland
181	548.8	Decatur County Com Schools	Greensburg
182	543.9	Gary Community School Corp	Gary
183	536.9	Duneland School Corporation	Chesterton
184	521.2	Crawfordsville Com Schools	Crawfordsville
185	509.0	MSD Bluffton-Harrison	Bluffton
186	508.7	Cloverdale Community Schools	Cloverdale
187	492.4	Tippecanoe School Corp	Lafayette
188	480.6	Shelby Eastern Schools	Shelbyville
189	477.8	Batesville Community School Corp	Batesville
190	469.6	North Harrison Com School Corp	Ramsey
191	439.1	Richmond Community School Corp	Richmond
192	0.0	South Harrison Com Schools	Corydon
192	0.0	Tri-Creek School Corp	Lowell
192	0.0	Union Township School Corp	Valparaiso

Student/Counselor Ratio

Rank	Ratio	District Name	City
1	1,927.5	Southeast Dubois County Sch Corp	Ferdinand
2	1,779.0	Alexandria Com School Corp	Alexandria
3	1,606.0	Union Co-Clg Corner Joint SD	Liberty
4	1,551.0	Greater Jasper Con Schs	Jasper
5	1,518.0	Union Township School Corp	Valparaiso
6	1,477.5	South Dearborn Com School Corp	Aurora
7	1,289.0	Jay School Corp	Portland
8	1,108.5	Westview School Corporation	Topeka
9	1,074.0	MSD Decatur Township	Indianapolis
10	1,029.0	Logansport Community Sch Corp	Logansport
11	1,016.3	Fort Wayne Community Schools	Fort Wayne
12	1,014.7	Northeast School Corp	Hymera
13	1,010.5	Greensburg Community Schools	Greensburg
14	995.4	Lake Central School Corp	Saint John
15	972.8	Frankton-Lapel Community Schs	Anderson
16	966.0	Crown Point Community Sch Corp	Crown Point
17	934.0	South Gibson School Corp	Fort Branch
18	915.7	School City of East Chicago	East Chicago
19	890.0	Portage Township Schools	Portage
20	864.0	New Prairie United School Corp	New Carlisle
21	857.5	School City of Hobart	Hobart
22	849.5	South Bend Community Sch Corp	South Bend
23	841.8	Tri-Creek School Corp	Lowell
24	819.8	West Clark Community Schools	Sellersburg
25	818.0	Southeastern School Corp	Walton
26	815.0	Beech Grove City Schools	Beech Grove
27	800.4	Salem Community Schools	Salem
28	795.2	Warrick County School Corp	Boonville
29	795.0	Merrillville Community School	Merrillville
30	793.5	School City of Hammond	Hammond
31	790.7	North Spencer County Sch Corp	Lincoln City
32	789.7	School City of Mishawaka	Mishawaka
33	788.5	South Harrison Com Schools	Corydon
34	787.7	Maconaquah School Corp	Bunker Hill
35	785.5	MSD North Posey County Schools	Poseyville
36	783.5	Hanover Community School Corp	Cedar Lake
37	779.2	Kokomo-Center Twp Con Sch Corp	Kokomo
38	776.0	Porter Township School Corp	Valparaiso
39	771.2	Greenwood Community Sch Corp	Greenwood
40	768.5	Richmond Community School Corp	Richmond
41	768.0	Vincennes Community Sch Corp	Vincennes
42	764.1	Anderson Community School Corp	Anderson
43	763.0	MSD Perry Township	Indianapolis
44	757.0	Danville Community School Corp	Danville
45	756.7	West Noble School Corporation	Ligonier
46	753.3	Brown County School Corporation	Nashville
47	729.4	Warsaw Community Schools	Warsaw
48	720.3	Pike County School Corp	Petersburg
49	715.0	Southern Hancock Co Com Sch Corp	New Palestine
50	711.3	Penn-Harris-Madison Sch Corp	Mishawaka
51	698.0	Madison Consolidated Schools	Madison
52	695.6	South Madison Com Sch Corp	Pendleton
53	684.7	Fairfield Community Schools	Goshen
54	681.3	West Lafayette Com School Corp	West Lafayette
55	681.1	Southwest Dubois County Sch Corp	Huntingburg
56	679.2	North Newton School Corp	Morocco
57	675.8	Griffith Public Schools	Griffith
58	670.3	Elkhart Community Schools	Elkhart
59	669.3	Greenfield-Central Com Schools	Greenfield
60	668.8	Rush County Schools	Rushville
61	665.4	North Lawrence Com Schools	Bedford
62	664.7	Rochester Community Sch Corp	Rochester
63	662.6	MSD Wayne Township	Indianapolis
64	661.8	Plainfield Community Sch Corp	Plainfield
65	661.0	Southwest School Corp	Sullivan
66	658.4	Plymouth Community School Corp	Plymouth
67	656.9	Marion Community Schools	Marion
68	655.0	Elwood Community School Corp	Elwood
69	654.3	East Porter County School Corp	Kouts
70	652.4	Franklin County Com Sch Corp	Brookville
71	651.5	Crawfordsville Com Schools	Crawfordsville
72	642.5	New Castle Community Sch Corp	New Castle
73	636.5	Monroe County Com Sch Corp	Bloomington
74	633.2	School Town of Munster	Munster
75	632.1	MSD Lawrence Township	Indianapolis
76	630.4	North Knox School Corp	Bicknell
77	623.3	Peru Community Schools	Peru
78	619.8	Washington Com Schools Inc	Washington
79	614.9	MSD Washington Township	Indianapolis
80	610.8	MSD Bluffton-Harrison	Bluffton
81	606.7	Crawford County Com School Corp	Marengo
82	604.8	Wabash City Schools	Wabash
83	601.3	MSD Martinsville Schools	Martinsville
84	601.0	Valparaiso Community Schools	Valparaiso
85	586.9	Vigo County School Corp	Terre Haute
86	580.7	Delphi Community School Corp	Delphi
87	575.3	Paoli Community School Corp	Paoli
88	574.0	Blackford County Schools	Hartford City
89	573.8	Lakeland School Corporation	Lagrange
90	572.9	Indianapolis Public Schools	Indianapolis
91	571.3	Western School Corp	Russiaville
92	567.0	Community Schools of Frankfort	Frankfort
93	564.7	Northwestern School Corp	Kokomo
94	560.7	MSD Pike Township	Indianapolis
95	559.8	MSD Mount Vernon	Mount Vernon
96	556.3	Mount Pleasant Twp Com Sch Corp	Yorktown
97	550.2	Greater Clark County Schools	Jeffersonville
98	549.0	School Town of Speedway	Speedway
99	548.8	Decatur County Com Schools	Greensburg
100	544.0	Madison-Grant United Sch Corp	Fairmount
101	540.0	Seymour Community Schools	Seymour
102	537.5	Mooresville Con School Corp	Mooresville
103	536.3	Manchester Community Schools	N Manchester
104	532.8	Mississinewa Community School Corp	Gas City
105	519.7	North West Hendricks Schools	Lizton
105	519.7	Spencer-Owen Community Schools	Spencer
107	516.2	Carmel Clay Schools	Carmel
108	514.2	Brownsburg Community Sch Corp	Brownsburg
109	513.2	Clay Community Schools	Knightsville
110	511.2	MSD Steuben County	Angola
111	510.4	Lake Ridge Schools	Gary
112	508.7	Bartholomew Con School Corp	Columbus
112	508.7	Cloverdale Community Schools	Cloverdale
114	508.5	North Gibson School Corp	Princeton
115	508.0	Knox Community School Corp	Knox
116	507.7	Noblesville Schools	Noblesville
117	503.7	South Spencer County Sch Corp	Rockport
118	502.0	Mitchell Community Schools	Mitchell
119	501.7	MSD Warren Township	Indianapolis
120	501.2	Wa-Nee Community Schools	Nappanee
121	500.0	Southwestern-Jefferson County	Hanover
122	499.0	Center Grove Com Sch Corp	Greenwood
123	498.3	Laporte Community School Corp	Laporte
124	491.7	Randolph Central School Corp	Winchester
125	488.1	Duneland School Corporation	Chesterton

126	487.8	South Vermillion Com Sch Corp	Clinton
127	487.0	Concord Community Schools	Elkhart
128	484.0	Westfield-Washington Schools	Westfield
129	483.6	Hamilton Heights School Corp	Arcadia
130	483.5	Kankakee Valley School Corp	Wheatfield
130	483.5	Lafayette School Corporation	Lafayette
132	478.8	North Montgomery Com Sch Corp	Linden
133	476.3	Mount Vernon Community Sch Corp	Fortville
134	476.1	School Town of Highland	Highland
135	476.0	Tippecanoe School Corp	Lafayette
136	472.0	Clark-Pleasant Com School Corp	Whiteland
137	468.9	Sunman-Dearborn Com Sch Corp	Sunman
138	468.8	Tipton Community School Corp	Tipton
139	463.6	East Noble School Corp	Kendallville
140	461.0	Franklin Township Com Sch Corp	Indianapolis
141	458.8	Fayette County School Corp	Connersville
142	456.5	Wawasee Community School Corp	Syracuse
143	455.0	Middlebury Community Schools	Middlebury
144	454.4	Dekalb County Ctl United SD	Waterloo
145	448.6	Shelbyville Central Schools	Shelbyville
146	448.3	Mill Creek Community Sch Corp	Clayton
147	447.5	Evansville-Vanderburgh Sch Corp	Evansville
148	446.5	Hamilton Southeastern Schools	Fishers
149	444.0	Rensselaer Central School Corp	Rensselaer
150	440.3	Eastbrook Community Sch Corp	Marion
151	435.6	MSD Wabash County Schools	Wabash
152	433.8	Goshen Community Schools	Goshen
153	433.0	Brownstown Cnt Com Sch Corp	Brownstown
154	426.0	Tippecanoe Valley School Corp	Akron
155	424.7	Avon Community School Corp	Avon
156	423.3	John Glenn School Corporation	Walkerton
157	423.1	East Allen County Schools	New Haven
158	422.3	Zionsville Community Schools	Zionsville
159	417.5	Whitley County Cons Schools	Columbia City
160	416.0	Northwest Allen County Schools	Fort Wayne
161	414.1	Delaware Community School Corp	Muncie
162	412.6	South Montgomery Com Sch Corp	New Market
163	405.8	Benton Community School Corp	Fowler
164	400.7	MSD Southwest Allen County	Fort Wayne
165	399.8	Switzerland County School Corp	Vevay
166	392.4	East Washington School Corp	Pekin
167	391.3	North Harrison Com School Corp	Ramsey
168	388.9	Muncie Community Schools	Muncie
169	387.4	Nineveh-Hensley-Jackson United	Trafalgar
170	385.0	Twin Lakes School Corp	Monticello
171	384.7	Richland-Bean Blossom C S C	Ellettsville
172	382.2	Batesville Community School Corp	Batesville
173	381.8	North Putnam Community Schools	Bainbridge
174	380.8	Taylor Community School Corp	Kokomo
175	380.6	Prairie Heights Com Sch Corp	Lagrange
176	380.2	Western Boone County Com SD	Thorntown
177	379.6	Tell City-Troy Twp School Corp	Tell City
178	373.9	Northern Wells Com Schools	Ossian
179	370.6	Lebanon Community School Corp	Lebanon
180	370.4	Jennings County Schools	North Vernon
181	364.2	Franklin Community School Corp	Franklin
182	362.9	Scott County SD 2	Scottsburg
183	352.7	Greencastle Community Sch Corp	Greencastle
184	352.2	Centerville-Abington Com Schs	Centerville
184	352.2	Huntington County Com Sch Corp	Huntington
186	352.1	New Albany-Floyd County Con Sch	New Albany
187	346.8	Baugo Community Schools	Elkhart
188	339.5	Whitko Community School Corp	Pierceton
189	336.4	Shelby Eastern Schools	Shelbyville
190	326.0	Michigan City Area Schools	Michigan City
191	324.6	Garrett-Keyser-Butler Com	Garrett
192	314.6	Gary Community School Corp	Gary
193	304.4	North Judson-San Pierre Sch Corp	North Judson
194	233.9	North Adams Community Schools	Decatur

Current Spending per Student in FY2001

Rank	Dollars	District Name	City
1	9,682	School City of East Chicago	East Chicago
2	9,570	Muncie Community Schools	Muncie
3	9,349	Gary Community School Corp	Gary
4	9,214	Indianapolis Public Schools	Indianapolis
5	9,172	Lake Ridge Schools	Gary
6	9,105	South Bend Community Sch Corp	South Bend
7	8,938	Kokomo-Center Twp Con Sch Corp	Kokomo
8	8,789	Marion Community Schools	Marion
9	8,764	Anderson Community School Corp	Anderson
10	8,626	MSD Warren Township	Indianapolis
11	8,550	MSD Mount Vernon	Mount Vernon
12	8,391	School City of Hammond	Hammond
13	8,348	Michigan City Area Schools	Michigan City
14	8,318	Garrett-Keyser-Butler Com	Garrett
15	8,030	Southwest Dubois County Sch Corp	Huntingburg
16	7,905	Richmond Community School Corp	Richmond
17	7,859	Fort Wayne Community Schools	Fort Wayne
18	7,839	Duneland School Corporation	Chesterton
19	7,762	Southwest School Corp	Sullivan
20	7,729	Jay School Corp	Portland
21	7,720	MSD Lawrence Township	Indianapolis
22	7,710	New Albany-Floyd County Con Sch	New Albany
23	7,704	Evansville-Vanderburgh Sch Corp	Evansville
24	7,646	Blackford County Schools	Hartford City
25	7,615	MSD Wayne Township	Indianapolis
26	7,611	Greater Clark County Schools	Jeffersonville
27	7,605	North Adams Community Schools	Decatur
28	7,586	Bartholomew Con School Corp	Columbus
29	7,585	Benton Community School Corp	Fowler
30	7,583	East Allen County Schools	New Haven
31	7,559	Madison Consolidated Schools	Madison
32	7,519	New Castle Community Sch Corp	New Castle
33	7,510	MSD Washington Township	Indianapolis
34	7,489	Elkhart Community Schools	Elkhart
35	7,486	West Lafayette Com School Corp	West Lafayette
36	7,482	Crawfordsville Com Schools	Crawfordsville
37	7,407	Monroe County Com Sch Corp	Bloomington
38	7,359	Crawford County Com School Corp	Marengo
39	7,349	MSD Decatur Township	Indianapolis
40	7,330	Greater Jasper Con Schs	Jasper
41	7,305	Taylor Community School Corp	Kokomo
42	7,300	Westfield-Washington Schools	Westfield
43	7,298	Vincennes Community Sch Corp	Vincennes
44	7,290	Valparaiso Community Schools	Valparaiso
45	7,261	Westview School Corporation	Topeka
46	7,258	Elwood Community School Corp	Elwood
47	7,246	Delphi Community School Corp	Delphi
48	7,240	School City of Mishawaka	Mishawaka
49	7,222	Knox Community School Corp	Knox
50	7,212	Northwestern School Corp	Kokomo
50	7,212	South Spencer County Sch Corp	Rockport
52	7,191	Spencer-Owen Community Schools	Spencer
53	7,161	Whitley County Cons Schools	Columbia City
54	7,152	Wawasee Community School Corp	Syracuse
55	7,134	Fayette County School Corp	Connersville
56	7,132	Penn-Harris-Madison Sch Corp	Mishawaka
57	7,123	Maconaquah School Corp	Bunker Hill
58	7,118	MSD Wabash County Schools	Wabash
59	7,115	Whitko Community School Corp	Pierceton
60	7,094	North Knox School Corp	Bicknell
61	7,071	Warsaw Community Schools	Warsaw
62	7,068	North Lawrence Com Schools	Bedford
63	7,041	School Town of Munster	Munster
64	7,039	South Harrison Com Schools	Corydon
65	7,036	Batesville Community School Corp	Batesville
66	7,032	Randolph Central School Corp	Winchester
67	7,025	Union Township School Corp	Valparaiso
68	7,023	Peru Community Schools	Peru
69	7,017	Brown County School Corporation	Nashville
70	7,014	Madison-Grant United Sch Corp	Fairmount
71	6,991	Lafayette School Corporation	Lafayette
72	6,989	Carmel Clay Schools	Carmel
73	6,979	MSD Southwest Allen County	Fort Wayne
74	6,952	West Noble School Corporation	Ligonier
75	6,944	South Vermillion Com Sch Corp	Clinton
76	6,940	Centerville-Abington Com Schs	Centerville
77	6,926	Northeast School Corp	Hymera
78	6,915	Brownstown Cnt Com Sch Corp	Brownstown
79	6,909	Tippecanoe Valley School Corp	Akron
80	6,902	Prairie Heights Com Sch Corp	Lagrange
81	6,898	MSD Pike Township	Indianapolis
82	6,858	North Harrison Com School Corp	Ramsey
83	6,846	MSD Perry Township	Indianapolis
84	6,814	North Montgomery Com Sch Corp	Linden
85	6,813	East Porter County School Corp	Kouts
86	6,799	School Town of Highland	Highland
87	6,766	Middlebury Community Schools	Middlebury
88	6,759	Logansport Community Sch Corp	Logansport
89	6,727	Portage Township Schools	Portage
90	6,724	Dekalb County Ctl United SD	Waterloo
90	6,724	Wa-Nee Community Schools	Nappanee
92	6,722	North Gibson School Corp	Princeton
93	6,713	Clay Community Schools	Knightsville
94	6,694	Manchester Community Schools	N Manchester
95	6,691	Avon Community School Corp	Avon
96	6,687	Mississinewa Community School Corp	Gas City
97	6,672	Tipton Community School Corp	Tipton
98	6,665	Hamilton Southeastern Schools	Fishers
99	6,660	Lakeland School Corporation	Lagrange
100	6,657	MSD North Posey County Schools	Poseyville
101	6,645	Mill Creek Community Sch Corp	Clayton
102	6,640	Lebanon Community School Corp	Lebanon
103	6,631	Porter Township School Corp	Valparaiso
104	6,627	Rush County Schools	Rushville
105	6,613	Goshen Community Schools	Goshen
106	6,612	Rensselaer Central School Corp	Rensselaer
107	6,610	Wabash City Schools	Wabash
108	6,609	South Dearborn Com School Corp	Aurora
109	6,600	Richland-Bean Blossom C S C	Ellettsville
110	6,592	Greensburg Community Schools	Greensburg
111	6,577	Cloverdale Community Schools	Cloverdale
112	6,573	Mooresville Con School Corp	Mooresville
113	6,569	Community Schools of Frankfort	Frankfort
114	6,563	East Noble School Corp	Kendallville
114	6,563	Pike County School Corp	Petersburg
116	6,559	Shelby Eastern Schools	Shelbyville
116	6,559	Tippecanoe School Corp	Lafayette
118	6,537	Vigo County School Corp	Terre Haute
119	6,526	Scott County SD 2	Scottsburg
120	6,521	Sunman-Dearborn Com Sch Corp	Sunman
121	6,512	East Washington School Corp	Pekin
122	6,511	MSD Martinsville Schools	Martinsville
123	6,502	Concord Community Schools	Elkhart
124	6,500	Decatur County Com Schools	Greensburg
125	6,491	North West Hendricks Schools	Lizton
126	6,477	Greenfield-Central Com Schools	Greenfield
127	6,475	Frankton-Lapel Community Schs	Anderson
128	6,467	Beech Grove City Schools	Beech Grove
129	6,464	Seymour Community Schools	Seymour
130	6,463	Lake Central School Corp	Saint John
131	6,454	MSD Steuben County	Angola
132	6,443	Southwestern-Jefferson County	Hanover
133	6,438	North Newton School Corp	Morocco
134	6,415	Brownsburg Community Sch Corp	Brownsburg
135	6,396	John Glenn School Corporation	Walkerton
136	6,387	School Town of Speedway	Speedway
137	6,381	North Putnam Community Schools	Bainbridge
137	6,381	Switzerland County School Corp	Vevay
139	6,377	Laporte Community School Corp	Laporte
140	6,371	Noblesville Schools	Noblesville
141	6,341	Jennings County Schools	North Vernon
142	6,327	Greencastle Community Sch Corp	Greencastle
143	6,322	Southern Hancock Co Com Sch Corp	New Palestine
144	6,320	Danville Community School Corp	Danville
145	6,315	Franklin County Com Sch Corp	Brookville
146	6,307	Tell City-Troy Twp School Corp	Tell City
147	6,300	Western Boone County Com SD	Thorntown
148	6,298	Franklin Township Com Sch Corp	Indianapolis
149	6,291	South Madison Com Sch Corp	Pendleton
150	6,287	North Spencer County Sch Corp	Lincoln City
151	6,279	Merrillville Community School	Merrillville
151	6,279	Union Co-Clg Corner Joint SD	Liberty
153	6,272	South Montgomery Com Sch Corp	New Market
154	6,266	Kankakee Valley School Corp	Wheatfield
155	6,265	Plymouth Community School Corp	Plymouth
156	6,264	Northwest Allen County Schools	Fort Wayne
157	6,263	South Gibson School Corp	Fort Branch
158	6,253	Franklin Community School Corp	Franklin
158	6,253	Salem Community Schools	Salem
160	6,251	Griffith Public Schools	Griffith
161	6,232	Huntington County Com Sch Corp	Huntington
162	6,217	Tri-Creek School Corp	Lowell
163	6,198	Southeastern School Corp	Walton
164	6,197	Nineveh-Hensley-Jackson United	Trafalgar
165	6,192	West Clark Community Schools	Sellersburg
166	6,190	Hamilton Heights School Corp	Arcadia
167	6,176	Rochester Community Sch Corp	Rochester
168	6,160	Zionsville Community Schools	Zionsville
169	6,133	Plainfield Community Sch Corp	Plainfield
170	6,119	Warrick County School Corp	Boonville
171	6,116	Eastbrook Community Sch Corp	Marion
172	6,103	Mitchell Community Schools	Mitchell
173	6,098	Greenwood Community Sch Corp	Greenwood
174	6,085	North Judson-San Pierre Sch Corp	North Judson
175	6,069	School City of Hobart	Hobart
176	6,053	Southeast Dubois County Sch Corp	Ferdinand
177	6,050	Crown Point Community Sch Corp	Crown Point
178	6,049	Baugo Community Schools	Elkhart
179	6,046	Northern Wells Com Schools	Ossian
180	6,042	Western School Corp	Russiaville
181	6,012	Mount Pleasant Twp Com Sch Corp	Yorktown
182	5,989	Paoli Community School Corp	Paoli
183	5,951	MSD Bluffton-Harrison	Bluffton
184	5,949	Washington Com Schools Inc	Washington
185	5,944	Clark-Pleasant Com School Corp	Whiteland
186	5,935	Alexandria Com School Corp	Alexandria
187	5,898	Delaware Community School Corp	Muncie
188	5,889	Hanover Community School Corp	Cedar Lake
189	5,837	Twin Lakes School Corp	Monticello
190	5,766	Mount Vernon Community Sch Corp	Fortville
191	5,681	New Prairie United School Corp	New Carlisle
192	5,671	Fairfield Community Schools	Goshen
193	5,596	Shelbyville Central Schools	Shelbyville
194	5,560	Center Grove Com Sch Corp	Greenwood

Number of Diploma Recipients

Rank	Number	District Name	City
1	1,596	Fort Wayne Community Schools	Fort Wayne
2	1,344	Evansville-Vanderburgh Sch Corp	Evansville
3	1,206	South Bend Community Sch Corp	South Bend
4	1,203	Indianapolis Public Schools	Indianapolis
5	997	Vigo County School Corp	Terre Haute
6	871	MSD Lawrence Township	Indianapolis
7	765	Carmel Clay Schools	Carmel
8	706	Gary Community School Corp	Gary

9	662	MSD Washington Township	Indianapolis
10	660	New Albany-Floyd County Con Sch	New Albany
11	647	Monroe County Com Sch Corp	Bloomington
12	620	Bartholomew Con School Corp	Columbus
13	619	Penn-Harris-Madison Sch Corp	Mishawaka
14	611	MSD Perry Township	Indianapolis
15	609	East Allen County Schools	New Haven
16	599	Tippecanoe School Corp	Lafayette
17	596	Warrick County School Corp	Boonville
18	585	MSD Wayne Township	Indianapolis
19	550	MSD Warren Township	Indianapolis
20	545	School City of Hammond	Hammond
21	544	Elkhart Community Schools	Elkhart
22	521	Portage Township Schools	Portage
23	504	Anderson Community School Corp	Anderson
24	494	Valparaiso Community Schools	Valparaiso
25	480	MSD Pike Township	Indianapolis
26	468	Merrillville Community School	Merrillville
27	453	Huntington County Com Sch Corp	Huntington
28	452	Lake Central School Corp	Saint John
29	445	Center Grove Com Sch Corp	Greenwood
30	434	Hamilton Southeastern Schools	Fishers
31	427	Crown Point Community Sch Corp	Crown Point
32	425	Greater Clark County Schools	Jeffersonville
33	408	Muncie Community Schools	Muncie
34	401	Laporte Community School Corp	Laporte
34	401	Noblesville Schools	Noblesville
36	390	Duneland School Corporation	Chesterton
37	388	Warsaw Community Schools	Warsaw
38	378	Brownsburg Community Sch Corp	Brownsburg
39	371	MSD Southwest Allen County	Fort Wayne
40	367	Kokomo-Center Twp Con Sch Corp	Kokomo
41	357	Lafayette School Corporation	Lafayette
42	352	North Lawrence Com Schools	Bedford
43	350	Michigan City Area Schools	Michigan City
44	312	MSD Martinsville Schools	Martinsville
44	312	Sunman-Dearborn Com Sch Corp	Sunman
46	306	Richmond Community School Corp	Richmond
47	305	Franklin Township Com Sch Corp	Indianapolis
48	301	Clay Community Schools	Knightsville
49	298	Avon Community School Corp	Avon
50	290	Northwest Allen County Schools	Fort Wayne
51	281	School Town of Munster	Munster
52	272	Plainfield Community Sch Corp	Plainfield
53	271	Goshen Community Schools	Goshen
53	271	Marion Community Schools	Marion
55	266	Plymouth Community School Corp	Plymouth
56	262	Mooresville Con School Corp	Mooresville
57	261	School City of Mishawaka	Mishawaka
58	256	School City of East Chicago	East Chicago
59	255	Logansport Community Sch Corp	Logansport
60	251	School Town of Highland	Highland
61	246	MSD Decatur Township	Indianapolis
62	244	Concord Community Schools	Elkhart
62	244	Whitley County Cons Schools	Columbia City
64	242	Seymour Community Schools	Seymour
65	241	School City of Hobart	Hobart
66	240	Greater Jasper Con Schs	Jasper
67	238	Greenfield-Central Com Schools	Greenfield
68	235	New Castle Community Sch Corp	New Castle
69	234	Jennings County Schools	North Vernon
70	233	Westfield-Washington Schools	Westfield
71	232	South Madison Com Sch Corp	Pendleton
72	230	Zionsville Community Schools	Zionsville
73	224	East Noble School Corp	Kendallville
73	224	Tri-Creek School Corp	Lowell
75	221	Middlebury Community Schools	Middlebury
76	220	Dekalb County Ctl United SD	Waterloo
77	212	Kankakee Valley School Corp	Wheatfield
78	211	Jay School Corp	Portland
79	210	Greenwood Community Sch Corp	Greenwood
80	208	Franklin Community School Corp	Franklin
81	207	Franklin County Com Sch Corp	Brookville
82	206	Wawasee Community School Corp	Syracuse
83	205	North Adams Community Schools	Decatur
84	203	Northern Wells Com Schools	Ossian
85	199	Delaware Community School Corp	Muncie
85	199	South Dearborn Com School Corp	Aurora
87	197	Fayette County School Corp	Connersville
87	197	Vincennes Community Sch Corp	Vincennes
89	193	South Harrison Com Schools	Corydon
90	192	MSD Mount Vernon	Mount Vernon
91	188	Griffith Public Schools	Griffith
92	187	Spencer-Owen Community Schools	Spencer
93	183	Lebanon Community School Corp	Lebanon
93	183	Mount Vernon Community Sch Corp	Fortville
95	182	Southern Hancock Co Com Sch Corp	New Palestine
96	180	Twin Lakes School Corp	Monticello
97	178	Clark-Pleasant Com School Corp	Whiteland
97	178	MSD Steuben County	Angola
99	176	Madison Consolidated Schools	Madison
100	175	Washington Com Schools Inc	Washington
100	175	West Clark Community Schools	Sellersburg
102	170	Shelbyville Central Schools	Shelbyville
103	169	North Harrison Com School Corp	Ramsey
103	169	Wa-Nee Community Schools	Nappanee
105	162	Western School Corp	Russiaville
106	160	North Spencer County Sch Corp	Lincoln City
107	158	Benton Community School Corp	Fowler
108	154	Richland-Bean Blossom C S C	Ellettsville
109	152	Peru Community Schools	Peru
110	151	Danville Community School Corp	Danville
111	150	New Prairie United School Corp	New Carlisle
112	148	West Lafayette Com School Corp	West Lafayette
113	146	Decatur County Com Schools	Greensburg
113	146	Rush County Schools	Rushville
115	145	Beech Grove City Schools	Beech Grove
115	145	Hamilton Heights School Corp	Arcadia
115	145	South Gibson School Corp	Fort Branch
118	144	Community Schools of Frankfort	Frankfort
119	141	Mount Pleasant Twp Com Sch Corp	Yorktown
120	140	North Gibson School Corp	Princeton
121	139	Scott County SD 2	Scottsburg
122	138	East Porter County School Corp	Kouts
123	137	Frankton-Lapel Community Schs	Anderson
123	137	MSD Wabash County Schools	Wabash
123	137	Porter Township School Corp	Valparaiso
126	136	Greencastle Community Sch Corp	Greencastle
126	136	Southwest School Corp	Sullivan
128	135	Rochester Community Sch Corp	Rochester
128	135	Tippecanoe Valley School Corp	Akron
130	133	Blackford County Schools	Hartford City
130	133	Lake Ridge Schools	Gary
132	131	Brown County School Corporation	Nashville
132	131	Shelby Eastern Schools	Shelbyville
132	131	Tipton Community School Corp	Tipton
135	128	Western Boone County Com SD	Thorntown
136	127	Crawfordsville Com Schools	Crawfordsville
136	127	Northwestern School Corp	Kokomo
138	125	Batesville Community School Corp	Batesville
139	124	Maconaquah School Corp	Bunker Hill
139	124	Pike County School Corp	Petersburg
141	123	Mississinewa Community School Corp	Gas City
142	122	Southwest Dubois County Sch Corp	Huntingburg
143	120	Fairfield Community Schools	Goshen
144	119	Alexandria Com School Corp	Alexandria
144	119	Elwood Community School Corp	Elwood
144	119	South Vermillion Com Sch Corp	Clinton
144	119	Southeastern School Corp	Walton
144	119	West Noble School Corporation	Ligonier
149	118	Baugo Community Schools	Elkhart
149	118	Mitchell Community Schools	Mitchell
151	117	South Montgomery Com Sch Corp	New Market
152	116	MSD North Posey County Schools	Poseyville
153	115	Brownstown Cnt Com Sch Corp	Brownstown
153	115	Salem Community Schools	Salem
155	113	John Glenn School Corporation	Walkerton
156	112	MSD Bluffton-Harrison	Bluffton
157	111	South Spencer County Sch Corp	Rockport
158	110	Nineveh-Hensley-Jackson United	Trafalgar
158	110	Prairie Heights Com Sch Corp	Lagrange
160	109	Garrett-Keyser-Butler Com	Garrett
160	109	North Judson-San Pierre Sch Corp	North Judson
160	109	North Putnam Community Schools	Bainbridge
160	109	Union Co-Clg Corner Joint SD	Liberty
160	109	Union Township School Corp	Valparaiso
165	108	North Montgomery Com Sch Corp	Linden
165	108	Paoli Community School Corp	Paoli
165	108	Tell City-Troy Twp School Corp	Tell City
168	106	Greensburg Community Schools	Greensburg
169	103	Lakeland School Corporation	Lagrange
169	103	North Knox School Corp	Bicknell
171	102	Hanover Community School Corp	Cedar Lake
171	102	Manchester Community Schools	N Manchester
173	101	Cloverdale Community Schools	Cloverdale
173	101	Knox Community School Corp	Knox
175	98	Randolph Central School Corp	Winchester
175	98	Rensselaer Central School Corp	Rensselaer
175	98	Wabash City Schools	Wabash
178	97	Centerville-Abington Com Schs	Centerville
179	96	Northeast School Corp	Hymera
180	94	Eastbrook Community Sch Corp	Marion
181	91	Crawford County Com School Corp	Marengo
181	91	Delphi Community School Corp	Delphi
181	91	Westview School Corporation	Topeka
181	91	Whitko Community School Corp	Pierceton
185	89	Southeast Dubois County Sch Corp	Ferdinand
185	89	Switzerland County School Corp	Vevay
187	88	North West Hendricks Schools	Lizton
188	85	East Washington School Corp	Pekin
189	84	School Town of Speedway	Speedway
190	82	Taylor Community School Corp	Kokomo
191	81	Madison-Grant United Sch Corp	Fairmount
192	80	Southwestern-Jefferson County	Hanover
193	77	Mill Creek Community Sch Corp	Clayton
194	75	North Newton School Corp	Morocco

High School Drop-out Rate

Rank	Percent	District Name	City
1	n/a	Alexandria Com School Corp	Alexandria
1	n/a	Anderson Community School Corp	Anderson
1	n/a	Avon Community School Corp	Avon
1	n/a	Bartholomew Con School Corp	Columbus
1	n/a	Batesville Community School Corp	Batesville
1	n/a	Baugo Community Schools	Elkhart
1	n/a	Beech Grove City Schools	Beech Grove
1	n/a	Benton Community School Corp	Fowler
1	n/a	Blackford County Schools	Hartford City
1	n/a	Brown County School Corporation	Nashville
1	n/a	Brownsburg Community Sch Corp	Brownsburg
1	n/a	Brownstown Cnt Com Sch Corp	Brownstown
1	n/a	Carmel Clay Schools	Carmel
1	n/a	Center Grove Com Sch Corp	Greenwood
1	n/a	Centerville-Abington Com Schs	Centerville
1	n/a	Clark-Pleasant Com School Corp	Whiteland
1	n/a	Clay Community Schools	Knightsville
1	n/a	Cloverdale Community Schools	Cloverdale
1	n/a	Community Schools of Frankfort	Frankfort
1	n/a	Concord Community Schools	Elkhart
1	n/a	Crawford County Com School Corp	Marengo
1	n/a	Crawfordsville Com Schools	Crawfordsville
1	n/a	Crown Point Community Sch Corp	Crown Point
1	n/a	Danville Community School Corp	Danville
1	n/a	Decatur County Com Schools	Greensburg
1	n/a	Dekalb County Ctl United SD	Waterloo
1	n/a	Delaware Community School Corp	Muncie
1	n/a	Delphi Community School Corp	Delphi
1	n/a	Duneland School Corporation	Chesterton
1	n/a	East Allen County Schools	New Haven
1	n/a	East Noble School Corp	Kendallville
1	n/a	East Porter County School Corp	Kouts
1	n/a	East Washington School Corp	Pekin
1	n/a	Eastbrook Community Sch Corp	Marion
1	n/a	Elkhart Community Schools	Elkhart
1	n/a	Elwood Community School Corp	Elwood
1	n/a	Evansville-Vanderburgh Sch Corp	Evansville
1	n/a	Fairfield Community Schools	Goshen
1	n/a	Fayette County School Corp	Connersville
1	n/a	Fort Wayne Community Schools	Fort Wayne
1	n/a	Franklin Community School Corp	Franklin
1	n/a	Franklin County Com Sch Corp	Brookville
1	n/a	Franklin Township Com Sch Corp	Indianapolis
1	n/a	Frankton-Lapel Community Schs	Anderson
1	n/a	Garrett-Keyser-Butler Com	Garrett
1	n/a	Gary Community School Corp	Gary
1	n/a	Goshen Community Schools	Goshen
1	n/a	Greater Clark County Schools	Jeffersonville
1	n/a	Greater Jasper Con Schs	Jasper
1	n/a	Greencastle Community Sch Corp	Greencastle
1	n/a	Greenfield-Central Com Schools	Greenfield
1	n/a	Greensburg Community Schools	Greensburg
1	n/a	Greenwood Community Sch Corp	Greenwood
1	n/a	Griffith Public Schools	Griffith
1	n/a	Hamilton Heights School Corp	Arcadia
1	n/a	Hamilton Southeastern Schools	Fishers
1	n/a	Hanover Community School Corp	Cedar Lake
1	n/a	Huntington County Com Sch Corp	Huntington
1	n/a	Indianapolis Public Schools	Indianapolis
1	n/a	Jay School Corp	Portland
1	n/a	Jennings County Schools	North Vernon
1	n/a	John Glenn School Corporation	Walkerton
1	n/a	Kankakee Valley School Corp	Wheatfield
1	n/a	Knox Community School Corp	Knox
1	n/a	Kokomo-Center Twp Con Sch Corp	Kokomo
1	n/a	Lafayette School Corporation	Lafayette
1	n/a	Lake Central School Corp	Saint John
1	n/a	Lake Ridge Schools	Gary
1	n/a	Lakeland School Corporation	Lagrange
1	n/a	Laporte Community School Corp	Laporte
1	n/a	Lebanon Community School Corp	Lebanon
1	n/a	Logansport Community Sch Corp	Logansport
1	n/a	MSD Bluffton-Harrison	Bluffton
1	n/a	MSD Decatur Township	Indianapolis
1	n/a	MSD Lawrence Township	Indianapolis
1	n/a	MSD Martinsville Schools	Martinsville
1	n/a	MSD Mount Vernon	Mount Vernon
1	n/a	MSD North Posey County Schools	Poseyville
1	n/a	MSD Perry Township	Indianapolis
1	n/a	MSD Pike Township	Indianapolis
1	n/a	MSD Southwest Allen County	Fort Wayne
1	n/a	MSD Steuben County	Angola
1	n/a	MSD Wabash County Schools	Wabash
1	n/a	MSD Warren Township	Indianapolis
1	n/a	MSD Washington Township	Indianapolis
1	n/a	MSD Wayne Township	Indianapolis
1	n/a	Maconaquah School Corp	Bunker Hill
1	n/a	Madison Consolidated Schools	Madison

1	n/a	Madison-Grant United Sch Corp	Fairmount
1	n/a	Manchester Community Schools	N Manchester
1	n/a	Marion Community Schools	Marion
1	n/a	Merrillville Community School	Merrillville
1	n/a	Michigan City Area Schools	Michigan City
1	n/a	Middlebury Community Schools	Middlebury
1	n/a	Mill Creek Community Sch Corp	Clayton
1	n/a	Mississinewa Community School Corp	Gas City
1	n/a	Mitchell Community Schools	Mitchell
1	n/a	Monroe County Com Sch Corp	Bloomington
1	n/a	Mooresville Con School Corp	Mooresville
1	n/a	Mount Pleasant Twp Com Sch Corp	Yorktown
1	n/a	Mount Vernon Community Sch Corp	Fortville
1	n/a	Muncie Community Schools	Muncie
1	n/a	New Albany-Floyd County Con Sch	New Albany
1	n/a	New Castle Community Sch Corp	New Castle
1	n/a	New Prairie United School Corp	New Carlisle
1	n/a	Nineveh-Hensley-Jackson United	Trafalgar
1	n/a	Noblesville Schools	Noblesville
1	n/a	North Adams Community Schools	Decatur
1	n/a	North Gibson School Corp	Princeton
1	n/a	North Harrison Com School Corp	Ramsey
1	n/a	North Judson-San Pierre Sch Corp	North Judson
1	n/a	North Knox School Corp	Bicknell
1	n/a	North Lawrence Com Schools	Bedford
1	n/a	North Montgomery Com Sch Corp	Linden
1	n/a	North Newton School Corp	Morocco
1	n/a	North Putnam Community Schools	Bainbridge
1	n/a	North Spencer County Sch Corp	Lincoln City
1	n/a	North West Hendricks Schools	Lizton
1	n/a	Northeast School Corp	Hymera
1	n/a	Northern Wells Com Schools	Ossian
1	n/a	Northwest Allen County Schools	Fort Wayne
1	n/a	Northwestern School Corp	Kokomo
1	n/a	Paoli Community School Corp	Paoli
1	n/a	Penn-Harris-Madison Sch Corp	Mishawaka
1	n/a	Peru Community Schools	Peru
1	n/a	Pike County School Corp	Petersburg
1	n/a	Plainfield Community Sch Corp	Plainfield
1	n/a	Plymouth Community School Corp	Plymouth
1	n/a	Portage Township Schools	Portage
1	n/a	Porter Township School Corp	Valparaiso
1	n/a	Prairie Heights Com Sch Corp	Lagrange
1	n/a	Randolph Central School Corp	Winchester
1	n/a	Rensselaer Central School Corp	Rensselaer
1	n/a	Richland-Bean Blossom C S C	Ellettsville
1	n/a	Richmond Community School Corp	Richmond
1	n/a	Rochester Community Sch Corp	Rochester
1	n/a	Rush County Schools	Rushville
1	n/a	Salem Community Schools	Salem
1	n/a	School City of East Chicago	East Chicago
1	n/a	School City of Hammond	Hammond
1	n/a	School City of Hobart	Hobart
1	n/a	School City of Mishawaka	Mishawaka
1	n/a	School Town of Highland	Highland
1	n/a	School Town of Munster	Munster
1	n/a	School Town of Speedway	Speedway
1	n/a	Scott County SD 2	Scottsburg
1	n/a	Seymour Community Schools	Seymour
1	n/a	Shelby Eastern Schools	Shelbyville
1	n/a	Shelbyville Central Schools	Shelbyville
1	n/a	South Bend Community Sch Corp	South Bend
1	n/a	South Dearborn Com School Corp	Aurora
1	n/a	South Gibson School Corp	Fort Branch
1	n/a	South Harrison Com Schools	Corydon
1	n/a	South Madison Com Sch Corp	Pendleton
1	n/a	South Montgomery Com Sch Corp	New Market
1	n/a	South Spencer County Sch Corp	Rockport
1	n/a	South Vermillion Com Sch Corp	Clinton
1	n/a	Southeast Dubois County Sch Corp	Ferdinand
1	n/a	Southeastern School Corp	Walton
1	n/a	Southern Hancock Co Com Sch Corp	New Palestine
1	n/a	Southwest Dubois County Sch Corp	Huntingburg
1	n/a	Southwest School Corp	Sullivan
1	n/a	Southwestern-Jefferson County	Hanover
1	n/a	Spencer-Owen Community Schools	Spencer
1	n/a	Sunman-Dearborn Com Sch Corp	Sunman
1	n/a	Switzerland County School Corp	Vevay
1	n/a	Taylor Community School Corp	Kokomo
1	n/a	Tell City-Troy Twp School Corp	Tell City
1	n/a	Tippecanoe School Corp	Lafayette
1	n/a	Tippecanoe Valley School Corp	Akron
1	n/a	Tipton Community School Corp	Tipton
1	n/a	Tri-Creek School Corp	Lowell
1	n/a	Twin Lakes School Corp	Monticello
1	n/a	Union Co-Clg Corner Joint SD	Liberty
1	n/a	Union Township School Corp	Valparaiso
1	n/a	Valparaiso Community Schools	Valparaiso
1	n/a	Vigo County School Corp	Terre Haute
1	n/a	Vincennes Community Sch Corp	Vincennes
1	n/a	Wa-Nee Community Schools	Nappanee
1	n/a	Wabash City Schools	Wabash
1	n/a	Warrick County School Corp	Boonville
1	n/a	Warsaw Community Schools	Warsaw
1	n/a	Washington Com Schools Inc	Washington
1	n/a	Wawasee Community School Corp	Syracuse
1	n/a	West Clark Community Schools	Sellersburg
1	n/a	West Lafayette Com School Corp	West Lafayette
1	n/a	West Noble School Corporation	Ligonier
1	n/a	Western Boone County Com SD	Thorntown
1	n/a	Western School Corp	Russiaville
1	n/a	Westfield-Washington Schools	Westfield
1	n/a	Westview School Corporation	Topeka
1	n/a	Whitko Community School Corp	Pierceton
1	n/a	Whitley County Cons Schools	Columbia City
1	n/a	Zionsville Community Schools	Zionsville

Iowa

Iowa Public School Educational Profile

Category	Value	Category	Value
Schools *(2002-2003)*	1,503	**Diploma Recipients** *(2002-2003)*	33,789
Instructional Level		White, Non-Hispanic	31,608
Primary	797	Black, Non-Hispanic	756
Middle	293	Asian/Pacific Islander	657
High	368	American Indian/Alaskan Native	108
Other Level	45	Hispanic	660
Curriculum		**High School Drop-out Rate** (%) *(2000-2001)*	2.7
Regular	1,454	White, Non-Hispanic	2.3
Special Education	11	Black, Non-Hispanic	7.3
Vocational	0	Asian/Pacific Islander	2.3
Alternative	38	American Indian/Alaskan Native	10.4
Type		Hispanic	9.1
Magnet	0	**Staff** *(2002-2003)*	67,424.7
Charter	0	Teachers	34,565.1
Title I Eligible	710	Average Salary ($)	38,000
School-wide Title I	121	Librarians/Media Specialists	612.0
Students *(2002-2003)*	482,210	Guidance Counselors	1,197.0
Gender (%)		**Ratios** *(2002-2003)*	
Male	51.5	Student/Teacher Ratio	14.0 to 1
Female	48.5	Student/Librarian Ratio	787.9 to 1
Race/Ethnicity (%)		Student/Counselor Ratio	402.8 to 1
White, Non-Hispanic	89.0	**Current Spending** *($ per student in FY 2001)*	7,338
Black, Non-Hispanic	4.3	Instruction	4,373
Asian/Pacific Islander	1.8	Support Services	2,432
American Indian/Alaskan Native	0.5	**College Entrance Exam Scores** *(2003)*	
Hispanic	4.4	Scholastic Aptitude Test (SAT)	
Classification (%)		Participation Rate (%)	5
Individual Education Program (IEP)	15.2	Mean SAT I Verbal Score	586
Migrant	0.9	Mean SAT I Math Score	597
English Language Learner (ELL)	2.9	American College Testing Program (ACT)	
Eligible for Free Lunch Program	20.8	Participation Rate (%)	66
Eligible for Reduced-Price Lunch Program	7.6	Average Composite Score	22.0

Note: *For an explanation of data, please refer to the User's Guide in the front of the book; n/a indicates data not available*

Iowa NAEP 2003 Test Scores

Reading		
Grade/Category	Value	Rank
4th Grade		
Average Proficiency	223.3 (1.1)	9/51
Proficiency by Gender/Race/Ethnicity		
Male	220.0 (1.3)	9/51
Female	226.6 (1.2)	11/51
White, Non-Hispanic	225.9 (1.1)	26/51
Black, Non-Hispanic	196.1 (2.7)	27/42
Asian, Non-Hispanic	205.1 (3.6)	19/41
American Indian, Non-Hispanic	n/a	n/a
Hispanic	n/a	n/a
Proficiency by Class Size		
Less than 16 Students	*211.8 (6.4)*	11/45
16 to 18 Students	224.9 (2.8)	6/48
19 to 20 Students	*219.0 (3.0)*	26/50
21 to 25 Students	225.9 (1.7)	11/51
Greater than 25 Students	*222.8 (2.5)*	14/49
Percent Attaining Achievement Levels		
Below Basic	29.8 (1.3)	45/51
Basic or Above	70.2 (1.3)	7/51
Proficient or Above	34.7 (1.5)	11/51
Advanced or Above	7.1 (0.6)	25/51
8th Grade		
Average Proficiency	267.5 (0.8)	12/51
Proficiency by Gender/Race/Ethnicity		
Male	261.3 (1.3)	16/51
Female	273.4 (1.0)	11/51
White, Non-Hispanic	269.5 (0.8)	24/50
Black, Non-Hispanic	245.0 (3.3)	16/41
Asian, Non-Hispanic	244.2 (4.1)	24/37
American Indian, Non-Hispanic	n/a	n/a
Hispanic	n/a	n/a
Proficiency by Parents Highest Level of Ed.		
Did Not Finish High School	244.1 (3.6)	33/50
Graduated High School	259.9 (1.5)	9/50
Some Education After High School	269.1 (2.0)	20/50
Graduated College	275.1 (0.7)	15/50
Percent Attaining Achievement Levels		
Below Basic	20.5 (0.9)	44/51
Basic or Above	79.5 (0.9)	7/51
Proficient or Above	35.6 (1.4)	14/51
Advanced or Above	2.7 (0.4)	21/51

Mathematics		
Grade/Category	Value	Rank
4th Grade		
Average Proficiency	238.5 (0.7)	11/51
Proficiency by Gender/Race/Ethnicity		
Male	240.5 (0.9)	9/51
Female	236.3 (0.8)	14/51
White, Non-Hispanic	240.9 (0.7)	31/51
Black, Non-Hispanic	214.7 (2.2)	25/42
Asian, Non-Hispanic	222.4 (2.8)	20/43
American Indian, Non-Hispanic	n/a	n/a
Hispanic	n/a	n/a
Proficiency by Class Size		
Less than 16 Students	*230.8 (3.4)*	10/47
16 to 18 Students	241.5 (1.6)	5/48
19 to 20 Students	233.3 (2.8)	29/50
21 to 25 Students	241.2 (1.0)	11/51
Greater than 25 Students	*235.8 (1.9)*	24/49
Percent Attaining Achievement Levels		
Below Basic	16.8 (1.0)	43/51
Basic or Above	83.2 (1.0)	8/51
Proficient or Above	35.5 (1.2)	14/51
Advanced or Above	3.3 (0.5)	27/51
8th Grade		
Average Proficiency	284.0 (0.8)	9/51
Proficiency by Gender/Race/Ethnicity		
Male	285.3 (1.0)	8/51
Female	282.5 (1.1)	13/51
White, Non-Hispanic	286.6 (0.8)	23/50
Black, Non-Hispanic	256.7 (3.9)	11/41
Asian, Non-Hispanic	255.0 (4.6)	27/37
American Indian, Non-Hispanic	n/a	n/a
Hispanic	n/a	n/a
Proficiency by Parents Highest Level of Ed.		
Did Not Finish High School	254.6 (2.9)	34/50
Graduated High School	271.9 (1.5)	15/50
Some Education After High School	287.7 (1.4)	4/50
Graduated College	293.7 (0.9)	8/50
Percent Attaining Achievement Levels		
Below Basic	23.6 (1.1)	44/51
Basic or Above	76.4 (1.1)	8/51
Proficient or Above	33.4 (1.2)	12/51
Advanced or Above	5.5 (0.5)	20/51

***Note:** For an explanation of data, please refer to the User's Guide in the front of the book; values in italics indicate that the nature of the sample does not allow accurate determination of the variability of the statistic; n/a indicates data not available*

Allamakee County

Allamakee Community SD
1059 3rd Ave NW • Waukon, IA 52172
(563) 568-3409 • http://www.allamakee.k12.ia.us
Grade Span: PK-12; **Agency Type:** 1
Schools: 5
3 Primary; 1 Middle; 1 High; 0 Other Level
5 Regular; 0 Special Education; 0 Vocational; 0 Alternative
0 Magnet; 0 Charter; 3 Title I Eligible; 0 School-wide Title I
Students: 1,535 (48.7% male; 51.3% female)
Individual Education Program: 237 (15.4%);
English Language Learner: 2 (0.1%); Migrant: 0 (0.0%)
Eligible for Free Lunch Program: 339 (22.1%)
Eligible for Reduced-Price Lunch Program: 159 (10.4%)
Teachers: 94.0 (16.3 to 1)
Librarians/Media Specialists: 2.5 (614.0 to 1)
Guidance Counselors: 2.0 (767.5 to 1)
Current Spending: ($ per student per year):
Total: $6,162; Instruction: $3,874; Support Services: $1,822
Enrollment, Drop-out Rates and Diploma Recipients by Race/Ethnicity

Category	Total	White	Black	Asian	AIAN	Hisp.
Enrollment (%)	100.0	98.8	0.3	0.5	0.1	0.5
Drop-out Rate (%)	0.6	0.6	n/a	0.0	n/a	n/a
H.S. Diplomas (#)	124	122	0	2	0	0

Appanoose County

Centerville Community SD
634 N Main • Centerville, IA 52544-0370
Mailing Address: Box 370 • Centerville, IA 52544-0370
(641) 856-0601
Grade Span: PK-12; **Agency Type:** 1
Schools: 10
6 Primary; 2 Middle; 2 High; 0 Other Level
8 Regular; 1 Special Education; 0 Vocational; 1 Alternative
0 Magnet; 0 Charter; 6 Title I Eligible; 4 School-wide Title I
Students: 1,573 (49.3% male; 50.7% female)
Individual Education Program: 352 (22.4%);
English Language Learner: 0 (0.0%); Migrant: 0 (0.0%)
Eligible for Free Lunch Program: 543 (34.5%)
Eligible for Reduced-Price Lunch Program: 142 (9.0%)
Teachers: 134.0 (11.7 to 1)
Librarians/Media Specialists: 3.0 (524.3 to 1)
Guidance Counselors: 2.0 (786.5 to 1)
Current Spending: ($ per student per year):
Total: $6,680; Instruction: $4,484; Support Services: $1,748
Enrollment, Drop-out Rates and Diploma Recipients by Race/Ethnicity

Category	Total	White	Black	Asian	AIAN	Hisp.
Enrollment (%)	100.0	98.5	1.0	0.3	0.0	0.2
Drop-out Rate (%)	1.5	1.6	0.0	0.0	0.0	0.0
H.S. Diplomas (#)	118	113	2	1	1	1

Benton County

Benton Community SD
304 1st St • Van Horne, IA 52346
Mailing Address: Box 70 • Van Horne, IA 52346
(319) 228-8701
Grade Span: PK-12; **Agency Type:** 1
Schools: 6
4 Primary; 1 Middle; 1 High; 0 Other Level
6 Regular; 0 Special Education; 0 Vocational; 0 Alternative
0 Magnet; 0 Charter; 4 Title I Eligible; 0 School-wide Title I
Students: 1,590 (51.4% male; 48.6% female)
Individual Education Program: 271 (17.0%);
English Language Learner: 3 (0.2%); Migrant: 0 (0.0%)
Eligible for Free Lunch Program: 135 (8.5%)
Eligible for Reduced-Price Lunch Program: 79 (5.0%)
Teachers: 110.0 (14.5 to 1)
Librarians/Media Specialists: 2.0 (795.0 to 1)
Guidance Counselors: 4.0 (397.5 to 1)
Current Spending: ($ per student per year):
Total: $6,049; Instruction: $3,779; Support Services: $1,704
Enrollment, Drop-out Rates and Diploma Recipients by Race/Ethnicity

Category	Total	White	Black	Asian	AIAN	Hisp.
Enrollment (%)	100.0	98.2	0.5	0.1	0.3	0.8
Drop-out Rate (%)	1.1	1.1	n/a	0.0	0.0	0.0
H.S. Diplomas (#)	135	134	0	1	0	0

Vinton-Shellsburg Community SD
810 W 9th St • Vinton, IA 52349
(319) 436-4728 • http://www.vinton-shellsburg.k12.ia.us
Grade Span: PK-12; **Agency Type:** 1
Schools: 5
3 Primary; 1 Middle; 1 High; 0 Other Level
5 Regular; 0 Special Education; 0 Vocational; 0 Alternative
0 Magnet; 0 Charter; 3 Title I Eligible; 0 School-wide Title I
Students: 1,796 (51.6% male; 48.4% female)
Individual Education Program: 283 (15.8%);
English Language Learner: 2 (0.1%); Migrant: 0 (0.0%)
Eligible for Free Lunch Program: 427 (23.8%)
Eligible for Reduced-Price Lunch Program: 108 (6.0%)
Teachers: 136.0 (13.2 to 1)
Librarians/Media Specialists: 4.0 (449.0 to 1)
Guidance Counselors: 5.0 (359.2 to 1)
Current Spending: ($ per student per year):
Total: $6,359; Instruction: $4,080; Support Services: $1,793
Enrollment, Drop-out Rates and Diploma Recipients by Race/Ethnicity

Category	Total	White	Black	Asian	AIAN	Hisp.
Enrollment (%)	100.0	98.5	0.6	0.4	0.0	0.4
Drop-out Rate (%)	0.7	0.7	0.0	0.0	n/a	0.0
H.S. Diplomas (#)	123	121	1	0	1	0

Black Hawk County

Cedar Falls Community SD
1002 W 1st St • Cedar Falls, IA 50613
(319) 277-8800 • http://www.cedar-falls.k12.ia.us
Grade Span: KG-12; **Agency Type:** 1
Schools: 9
6 Primary; 2 Middle; 1 High; 0 Other Level
9 Regular; 0 Special Education; 0 Vocational; 0 Alternative
0 Magnet; 0 Charter; 3 Title I Eligible; 1 School-wide Title I
Students: 4,303 (52.1% male; 47.9% female)
Individual Education Program: 728 (16.9%);
English Language Learner: 29 (0.7%); Migrant: 0 (0.0%)
Eligible for Free Lunch Program: 578 (13.4%)
Eligible for Reduced-Price Lunch Program: 138 (3.2%)
Teachers: 300.5 (14.3 to 1)
Librarians/Media Specialists: 7.0 (614.7 to 1)
Guidance Counselors: 14.0 (307.4 to 1)
Current Spending: ($ per student per year):
Total: $6,383; Instruction: $4,066; Support Services: $1,825
Enrollment, Drop-out Rates and Diploma Recipients by Race/Ethnicity

Category	Total	White	Black	Asian	AIAN	Hisp.
Enrollment (%)	100.0	92.7	3.9	2.1	0.2	1.1
Drop-out Rate (%)	1.0	1.0	5.3	0.0	0.0	0.0
H.S. Diplomas (#)	369	343	4	17	3	2

Waterloo Community SD
1516 Washington St • Waterloo, IA 50702
(319) 291-4800 • http://www.waterloo.k12.ia.us/home.html
Grade Span: PK-12; **Agency Type:** 1
Schools: 22
15 Primary; 4 Middle; 3 High; 0 Other Level
21 Regular; 0 Special Education; 0 Vocational; 1 Alternative
0 Magnet; 0 Charter; 14 Title I Eligible; 12 School-wide Title I
Students: 10,402 (51.6% male; 48.4% female)
Individual Education Program: 1,952 (18.8%);
English Language Learner: 1,036 (10.0%); Migrant: 367 (3.5%)
Eligible for Free Lunch Program: 4,348 (41.8%)
Eligible for Reduced-Price Lunch Program: 1,222 (11.7%)
Teachers: 697.5 (14.9 to 1)
Librarians/Media Specialists: 17.5 (594.4 to 1)
Guidance Counselors: 23.0 (452.3 to 1)
Current Spending: ($ per student per year):
Total: $6,657; Instruction: $4,265; Support Services: $1,975
Enrollment, Drop-out Rates and Diploma Recipients by Race/Ethnicity

Category	Total	White	Black	Asian	AIAN	Hisp.
Enrollment (%)	100.0	67.6	26.5	1.0	0.4	4.5
Drop-out Rate (%)	6.8	5.1	11.4	6.5	14.3	12.9
H.S. Diplomas (#)	596	479	101	8	2	6

Boone County

Boone Community SD
500 7th St • Boone, IA 50036
(515) 433-0750 • http://www.boone.k12.ia.us
Grade Span: PK-12; **Agency Type:** 1
Schools: 9
6 Primary; 1 Middle; 2 High; 0 Other Level
8 Regular; 0 Special Education; 0 Vocational; 1 Alternative
0 Magnet; 0 Charter; 6 Title I Eligible; 0 School-wide Title I
Students: 2,320 (50.5% male; 49.5% female)
Individual Education Program: 350 (15.1%);
English Language Learner: 5 (0.2%); Migrant: 0 (0.0%)
Eligible for Free Lunch Program: 429 (18.5%)
Eligible for Reduced-Price Lunch Program: 166 (7.2%)
Teachers: 156.5 (14.8 to 1)

Librarians/Media Specialists: 2.5 (928.0 to 1)
Guidance Counselors: 6.0 (386.7 to 1)
Current Spending: ($ per student per year):
Total: $6,802; Instruction: $4,667; Support Services: $1,741
Enrollment, Drop-out Rates and Diploma Recipients by Race/Ethnicity

Category	Total	White	Black	Asian	AIAN	Hisp.
Enrollment (%)	100.0	96.9	1.0	0.6	0.6	0.9
Drop-out Rate (%)	1.6	1.4	0.0	28.6	0.0	0.0
H.S. Diplomas (#)	191	188	0	2	1	0

Bremer County

Waverly-Shell Rock Community SD

1415 4th Ave SW • Waverly, IA 50677
(319) 352-3630 • http://www.waverly-shellrock.k12.ia.us
Grade Span: PK-12; **Agency Type:** 1
Schools: 7
4 Primary; 2 Middle; 1 High; 0 Other Level
7 Regular; 0 Special Education; 0 Vocational; 0 Alternative
0 Magnet; 0 Charter; 3 Title I Eligible; 0 School-wide Title I
Students: 2,011 (51.8% male; 48.2% female)
Individual Education Program: 250 (12.4%);
English Language Learner: 0 (0.0%); Migrant: 0 (0.0%)
Eligible for Free Lunch Program: 245 (12.2%)
Eligible for Reduced-Price Lunch Program: 67 (3.3%)
Teachers: 117.5 (17.1 to 1)
Librarians/Media Specialists: 2.0 (1,005.5 to 1)
Guidance Counselors: 3.5 (574.6 to 1)
Current Spending: ($ per student per year):
Total: $5,578; Instruction: $3,260; Support Services: $1,725
Enrollment, Drop-out Rates and Diploma Recipients by Race/Ethnicity

Category	Total	White	Black	Asian	AIAN	Hisp.
Enrollment (%)	100.0	96.8	1.4	1.1	0.1	0.5
Drop-out Rate (%)	3.4	3.5	0.0	0.0	n/a	0.0
H.S. Diplomas (#)	177	176	1	0	0	0

Buchanan County

Independence Community SD

1207 1st St W • Independence, IA 50644
Mailing Address: PO Box 900 • Independence, IA 50644
(319) 334-7400 • http://www.indee.k12.ia.us
Grade Span: PK-12; **Agency Type:** 1
Schools: 5
3 Primary; 1 Middle; 1 High; 0 Other Level
5 Regular; 0 Special Education; 0 Vocational; 0 Alternative
0 Magnet; 0 Charter; 3 Title I Eligible; 0 School-wide Title I
Students: 1,530 (49.0% male; 51.0% female)
Individual Education Program: 258 (16.9%);
English Language Learner: 0 (0.0%); Migrant: 0 (0.0%)
Eligible for Free Lunch Program: 324 (21.2%)
Eligible for Reduced-Price Lunch Program: 137 (9.0%)
Teachers: 114.5 (13.4 to 1)
Librarians/Media Specialists: 3.0 (510.0 to 1)
Guidance Counselors: 3.0 (510.0 to 1)
Current Spending: ($ per student per year):
Total: $6,824; Instruction: $4,424; Support Services: $1,753
Enrollment, Drop-out Rates and Diploma Recipients by Race/Ethnicity

Category	Total	White	Black	Asian	AIAN	Hisp.
Enrollment (%)	100.0	97.1	0.5	1.5	0.3	0.7
Drop-out Rate (%)	2.6	2.7	0.0	0.0	n/a	0.0
H.S. Diplomas (#)	122	121	0	1	0	0

Buena Vista County

Storm Lake Community SD

419 Lake Ave • Storm Lake, IA 50588-0638
Mailing Address: PO Box 638 • Storm Lake, IA 50588-0638
(712) 732-8060 • http://www.storm-lake.k12.ia.us
Grade Span: PK-12; **Agency Type:** 1
Schools: 6
4 Primary; 1 Middle; 1 High; 0 Other Level
6 Regular; 0 Special Education; 0 Vocational; 0 Alternative
0 Magnet; 0 Charter; 5 Title I Eligible; 5 School-wide Title I
Students: 2,001 (51.4% male; 48.6% female)
Individual Education Program: 258 (12.9%);
English Language Learner: 899 (44.9%); Migrant: 847 (42.3%)
Eligible for Free Lunch Program: 675 (33.7%)
Eligible for Reduced-Price Lunch Program: 231 (11.5%)
Teachers: 138.5 (14.4 to 1)
Librarians/Media Specialists: 1.0 (2,001.0 to 1)
Guidance Counselors: 4.0 (500.3 to 1)
Current Spending: ($ per student per year):
Total: $6,879; Instruction: $4,325; Support Services: $1,898
Enrollment, Drop-out Rates and Diploma Recipients by Race/Ethnicity

Category	Total	White	Black	Asian	AIAN	Hisp.
Enrollment (%)	100.0	48.5	0.6	12.1	0.1	38.7
Drop-out Rate (%)	3.0	0.5	20.0	4.9	0.0	9.8
H.S. Diplomas (#)	122	82	0	19	0	21

Carroll County

Carroll Community SD

1026 N Adams • Carroll, IA 51401
(712) 792-8001 • http://www.carroll.k12.ia.us
Grade Span: PK-12; **Agency Type:** 1
Schools: 5
1 Primary; 2 Middle; 2 High; 0 Other Level
4 Regular; 0 Special Education; 0 Vocational; 1 Alternative
0 Magnet; 0 Charter; 1 Title I Eligible; 0 School-wide Title I
Students: 1,765 (48.8% male; 51.2% female)
Individual Education Program: 241 (13.7%);
English Language Learner: 17 (1.0%); Migrant: 0 (0.0%)
Eligible for Free Lunch Program: 270 (15.3%)
Eligible for Reduced-Price Lunch Program: 143 (8.1%)
Teachers: 115.5 (15.3 to 1)
Librarians/Media Specialists: 3.0 (588.3 to 1)
Guidance Counselors: 5.0 (353.0 to 1)
Current Spending: ($ per student per year):
Total: $6,319; Instruction: $3,798; Support Services: $2,021
Enrollment, Drop-out Rates and Diploma Recipients by Race/Ethnicity

Category	Total	White	Black	Asian	AIAN	Hisp.
Enrollment (%)	100.0	96.9	1.2	0.4	0.1	1.4
Drop-out Rate (%)	1.0	1.0	n/a	n/a	n/a	0.0
H.S. Diplomas (#)	147	144	0	0	0	3

Cass County

Atlantic Community SD

1100 Linn St • Atlantic, IA 50022
(712) 243-4252 • http://www.atlantic.k12.ia.us
Grade Span: PK-12; **Agency Type:** 1
Schools: 4
1 Primary; 2 Middle; 1 High; 0 Other Level
4 Regular; 0 Special Education; 0 Vocational; 0 Alternative
0 Magnet; 0 Charter; 1 Title I Eligible; 0 School-wide Title I
Students: 1,579 (53.3% male; 46.7% female)
Individual Education Program: 230 (14.6%);
English Language Learner: 0 (0.0%); Migrant: 0 (0.0%)
Eligible for Free Lunch Program: 364 (23.1%)
Eligible for Reduced-Price Lunch Program: 152 (9.6%)
Teachers: 108.5 (14.6 to 1)
Librarians/Media Specialists: 2.0 (789.5 to 1)
Guidance Counselors: 3.0 (526.3 to 1)
Current Spending: ($ per student per year):
Total: $5,963; Instruction: $3,754; Support Services: $1,733
Enrollment, Drop-out Rates and Diploma Recipients by Race/Ethnicity

Category	Total	White	Black	Asian	AIAN	Hisp.
Enrollment (%)	100.0	97.8	0.8	0.6	0.3	0.6
Drop-out Rate (%)	1.1	1.1	0.0	0.0	0.0	0.0
H.S. Diplomas (#)	122	115	1	3	2	1

Cerro Gordo County

Mason City Community SD

1515 S Pennsylvania • Mason City, IA 50401
(641) 421-4400 • http://www.mason-city.k12.ia.us
Grade Span: PK-12; **Agency Type:** 1
Schools: 10
6 Primary; 2 Middle; 2 High; 0 Other Level
9 Regular; 0 Special Education; 0 Vocational; 1 Alternative
0 Magnet; 0 Charter; 4 Title I Eligible; 0 School-wide Title I
Students: 4,412 (50.3% male; 49.7% female)
Individual Education Program: 909 (20.6%);
English Language Learner: 8 (0.2%); Migrant: 0 (0.0%)
Eligible for Free Lunch Program: 1,026 (23.3%)
Eligible for Reduced-Price Lunch Program: 352 (8.0%)
Teachers: 287.0 (15.4 to 1)
Librarians/Media Specialists: 5.0 (882.4 to 1)
Guidance Counselors: 10.0 (441.2 to 1)
Current Spending: ($ per student per year):
Total: $6,275; Instruction: $4,081; Support Services: $1,713
Enrollment, Drop-out Rates and Diploma Recipients by Race/Ethnicity

Category	Total	White	Black	Asian	AIAN	Hisp.
Enrollment (%)	100.0	87.7	3.6	2.0	0.3	6.5
Drop-out Rate (%)	2.5	2.6	4.3	0.0	0.0	0.0
H.S. Diplomas (#)	315	282	7	9	0	17

Clay County

Spencer Community SD
23 E 7th St • Spencer, IA 51301
Mailing Address: Ste A-Box 200 • Spencer, IA 51301
(712) 262-8950 • http://www.spencer.k12.ia.us
Grade Span: PK-12; **Agency Type:** 1
Schools: 6
4 Primary; 1 Middle; 1 High; 0 Other Level
6 Regular; 0 Special Education; 0 Vocational; 0 Alternative
0 Magnet; 0 Charter; 3 Title I Eligible; 0 School-wide Title I
Students: 2,097 (50.2% male; 49.8% female)
Individual Education Program: 292 (13.9%);
English Language Learner: 17 (0.8%); Migrant: 0 (0.0%)
Eligible for Free Lunch Program: 395 (18.8%)
Eligible for Reduced-Price Lunch Program: 184 (8.8%)
Teachers: 141.5 (14.8 to 1)
Librarians/Media Specialists: 2.0 (1,048.5 to 1)
Guidance Counselors: 5.0 (419.4 to 1)
Current Spending: ($ per student per year):
Total: $6,103; Instruction: $4,032; Support Services: $1,569
Enrollment, Drop-out Rates and Diploma Recipients by Race/Ethnicity

Category	Total	White	Black	Asian	AIAN	Hisp.
Enrollment (%)	100.0	95.3	0.6	2.1	0.2	1.8
Drop-out Rate (%)	1.6	1.5	0.0	6.3	n/a	0.0
H.S. Diplomas (#)	174	172	0	2	0	0

Clinton County

Central Clinton Community SD
923 4th Ave E • De Witt, IA 52742-0240
Mailing Address: PO Box 110 • De Witt, IA 52742-0240
(563) 659-0700 • http://www.central-clinton.k12.ia.us
Grade Span: PK-12; **Agency Type:** 1
Schools: 4
2 Primary; 1 Middle; 1 High; 0 Other Level
4 Regular; 0 Special Education; 0 Vocational; 0 Alternative
0 Magnet; 0 Charter; 2 Title I Eligible; 0 School-wide Title I
Students: 1,642 (52.8% male; 47.2% female)
Individual Education Program: 252 (15.3%);
English Language Learner: 0 (0.0%); Migrant: 0 (0.0%)
Eligible for Free Lunch Program: 225 (13.7%)
Eligible for Reduced-Price Lunch Program: 104 (6.3%)
Teachers: 123.5 (13.3 to 1)
Librarians/Media Specialists: 2.5 (656.8 to 1)
Guidance Counselors: 4.0 (410.5 to 1)
Current Spending: ($ per student per year):
Total: $6,369; Instruction: $3,827; Support Services: $2,046
Enrollment, Drop-out Rates and Diploma Recipients by Race/Ethnicity

Category	Total	White	Black	Asian	AIAN	Hisp.
Enrollment (%)	100.0	97.0	1.2	0.7	0.2	0.9
Drop-out Rate (%)	1.8	1.8	0.0	0.0	n/a	0.0
H.S. Diplomas (#)	138	135	1	1	0	1

Clinton Community SD
600 S 4th St • Clinton, IA 52732
(563) 243-9600 • http://www.clinton.k12.ia.us
Grade Span: PK-12; **Agency Type:** 1
Schools: 10
6 Primary; 2 Middle; 2 High; 0 Other Level
9 Regular; 0 Special Education; 0 Vocational; 1 Alternative
0 Magnet; 0 Charter; 5 Title I Eligible; 2 School-wide Title I
Students: 4,409 (51.5% male; 48.5% female)
Individual Education Program: 841 (19.1%);
English Language Learner: 3 (0.1%); Migrant: 0 (0.0%)
Eligible for Free Lunch Program: 1,377 (31.2%)
Eligible for Reduced-Price Lunch Program: 359 (8.1%)
Teachers: 313.0 (14.1 to 1)
Librarians/Media Specialists: 7.0 (629.9 to 1)
Guidance Counselors: 10.5 (419.9 to 1)
Current Spending: ($ per student per year):
Total: $6,607; Instruction: $4,168; Support Services: $1,958
Enrollment, Drop-out Rates and Diploma Recipients by Race/Ethnicity

Category	Total	White	Black	Asian	AIAN	Hisp.
Enrollment (%)	100.0	88.8	7.2	1.6	0.5	1.9
Drop-out Rate (%)	6.3	6.4	7.2	0.0	0.0	0.0
H.S. Diplomas (#)	326	295	15	4	2	10

Crawford County

Denison Community SD
819 N 16th St • Denison, IA 51442
(712) 263-2176 • http://www.denison.k12.ia.us
Grade Span: PK-12; **Agency Type:** 1
Schools: 3
1 Primary; 1 Middle; 1 High; 0 Other Level
3 Regular; 0 Special Education; 0 Vocational; 0 Alternative
0 Magnet; 0 Charter; 1 Title I Eligible; 1 School-wide Title I
Students: 1,777 (52.3% male; 47.7% female)
Individual Education Program: 229 (12.9%);
English Language Learner: 285 (16.0%); Migrant: 560 (31.5%)
Eligible for Free Lunch Program: 624 (35.1%)
Eligible for Reduced-Price Lunch Program: 189 (10.6%)
Teachers: 113.5 (15.7 to 1)
Librarians/Media Specialists: 3.0 (592.3 to 1)
Guidance Counselors: 4.0 (444.3 to 1)
Current Spending: ($ per student per year):
Total: $6,331; Instruction: $3,959; Support Services: $1,788
Enrollment, Drop-out Rates and Diploma Recipients by Race/Ethnicity

Category	Total	White	Black	Asian	AIAN	Hisp.
Enrollment (%)	100.0	71.8	0.9	1.7	0.6	25.0
Drop-out Rate (%)	3.1	2.0	n/a	0.0	n/a	27.6
H.S. Diplomas (#)	127	120	0	3	0	4

Dallas County

Dallas Center-Grimes Community SD
1500 Linden Ave • Dallas Center, IA 50063
Mailing Address: PO Box 512 • Dallas Center, IA 50063
(515) 992-3866
Grade Span: PK-12; **Agency Type:** 1
Schools: 4
2 Primary; 1 Middle; 1 High; 0 Other Level
4 Regular; 0 Special Education; 0 Vocational; 0 Alternative
0 Magnet; 0 Charter; 1 Title I Eligible; 0 School-wide Title I
Students: 1,589 (52.6% male; 47.4% female)
Individual Education Program: 148 (9.3%);
English Language Learner: 0 (0.0%); Migrant: 0 (0.0%)
Eligible for Free Lunch Program: 98 (6.2%)
Eligible for Reduced-Price Lunch Program: 44 (2.8%)
Teachers: 108.0 (14.7 to 1)
Librarians/Media Specialists: 3.0 (529.7 to 1)
Guidance Counselors: 3.0 (529.7 to 1)
Current Spending: ($ per student per year):
Total: $5,669; Instruction: $3,292; Support Services: $1,859
Enrollment, Drop-out Rates and Diploma Recipients by Race/Ethnicity

Category	Total	White	Black	Asian	AIAN	Hisp.
Enrollment (%)	100.0	98.2	0.5	0.6	0.1	0.6
Drop-out Rate (%)	0.4	0.4	0.0	0.0	0.0	0.0
H.S. Diplomas (#)	90	87	0	1	1	1

Perry Community SD
1219 Warford St • Perry, IA 50220
(515) 465-4656 • http://www.perry.k12.ia.us
Grade Span: PK-12; **Agency Type:** 1
Schools: 3
1 Primary; 1 Middle; 1 High; 0 Other Level
3 Regular; 0 Special Education; 0 Vocational; 0 Alternative
0 Magnet; 0 Charter; 1 Title I Eligible; 0 School-wide Title I
Students: 1,771 (53.2% male; 46.8% female)
Individual Education Program: 275 (15.5%);
English Language Learner: 262 (14.8%); Migrant: 327 (18.5%)
Eligible for Free Lunch Program: 623 (35.2%)
Eligible for Reduced-Price Lunch Program: 226 (12.8%)
Teachers: 136.5 (13.0 to 1)
Librarians/Media Specialists: 2.0 (885.5 to 1)
Guidance Counselors: 2.0 (885.5 to 1)
Current Spending: ($ per student per year):
Total: $6,534; Instruction: $4,082; Support Services: $2,005
Enrollment, Drop-out Rates and Diploma Recipients by Race/Ethnicity

Category	Total	White	Black	Asian	AIAN	Hisp.
Enrollment (%)	100.0	65.8	1.2	1.1	0.1	31.7
Drop-out Rate (%)	5.1	1.1	0.0	0.0	n/a	22.0
H.S. Diplomas (#)	124	97	4	4	0	19

Waukee Community SD
445 5th St • Waukee, IA 50263
(515) 987-5161 • http://www.waukee.k12.ia.us
Grade Span: PK-12; **Agency Type:** 1
Schools: 5
3 Primary; 1 Middle; 1 High; 0 Other Level
5 Regular; 0 Special Education; 0 Vocational; 0 Alternative
0 Magnet; 0 Charter; 1 Title I Eligible; 0 School-wide Title I
Students: 3,095 (51.7% male; 48.3% female)
Individual Education Program: 309 (10.0%);
English Language Learner: 38 (1.2%); Migrant: 0 (0.0%)
Eligible for Free Lunch Program: 182 (5.9%)
Eligible for Reduced-Price Lunch Program: 80 (2.6%)
Teachers: 206.5 (15.0 to 1)
Librarians/Media Specialists: 5.0 (619.0 to 1)
Guidance Counselors: 3.0 (1,031.7 to 1)

Current Spending: ($ per student per year):
Total: $5,752; Instruction: $3,493; Support Services: $1,797
Enrollment, Drop-out Rates and Diploma Recipients by Race/Ethnicity

Category	Total	White	Black	Asian	AIAN	Hisp.
Enrollment (%)	100.0	94.2	1.9	2.5	0.1	1.3
Drop-out Rate (%)	0.3	0.3	0.0	0.0	n/a	0.0
H.S. Diplomas (#)	130	128	0	2	0	0

Delaware County

West Delaware County Community SD

601 New St • Manchester, IA 52057
(563) 927-3515 • http://www.w-delaware.k12.ia.us
Grade Span: PK-12; **Agency Type:** 1
Schools: 4
1 Primary; 1 Middle; 1 High; 1 Other Level
4 Regular; 0 Special Education; 0 Vocational; 0 Alternative
0 Magnet; 0 Charter; 1 Title I Eligible; 0 School-wide Title I
Students: 1,761 (49.6% male; 50.4% female)
Individual Education Program: 207 (11.8%);
English Language Learner: 0 (0.0%); Migrant: 0 (0.0%)
Eligible for Free Lunch Program: 246 (14.0%)
Eligible for Reduced-Price Lunch Program: 119 (6.8%)
Teachers: 119.5 (14.7 to 1)
Librarians/Media Specialists: 3.0 (587.0 to 1)
Guidance Counselors: 5.0 (352.2 to 1)
Current Spending: ($ per student per year):
Total: $5,943; Instruction: $3,585; Support Services: $1,849
Enrollment, Drop-out Rates and Diploma Recipients by Race/Ethnicity

Category	Total	White	Black	Asian	AIAN	Hisp.
Enrollment (%)	100.0	98.4	0.3	0.6	0.3	0.5
Drop-out Rate (%)	3.4	3.3	n/a	0.0	n/a	25.0
H.S. Diplomas (#)	168	162	0	4	0	2

Des Moines County

Burlington Community SD

1429 W Ave • Burlington, IA 52601
(319) 753-6791 • http://www.burlington.k12.ia.us
Grade Span: PK-12; **Agency Type:** 1
Schools: 12
7 Primary; 3 Middle; 2 High; 0 Other Level
11 Regular; 0 Special Education; 0 Vocational; 1 Alternative
0 Magnet; 0 Charter; 5 Title I Eligible; 4 School-wide Title I
Students: 4,535 (51.2% male; 48.8% female)
Individual Education Program: 1,008 (22.2%);
English Language Learner: 15 (0.3%); Migrant: 0 (0.0%)
Eligible for Free Lunch Program: 1,370 (30.2%)
Eligible for Reduced-Price Lunch Program: 296 (6.5%)
Teachers: 341.0 (13.3 to 1)
Librarians/Media Specialists: 7.0 (647.9 to 1)
Guidance Counselors: 13.0 (348.8 to 1)
Current Spending: ($ per student per year):
Total: $6,676; Instruction: $4,668; Support Services: $1,613
Enrollment, Drop-out Rates and Diploma Recipients by Race/Ethnicity

Category	Total	White	Black	Asian	AIAN	Hisp.
Enrollment (%)	100.0	84.2	11.5	1.4	0.2	2.7
Drop-out Rate (%)	7.2	6.8	15.2	3.7	0.0	0.0
H.S. Diplomas (#)	289	266	10	9	0	4

Dubuque County

Dubuque Community SD

2300 Chaney • Dubuque, IA 52001
(563) 588-5100 • http://www.dubuque.k12.ia.us
Grade Span: PK-12; **Agency Type:** 1
Schools: 18
12 Primary; 3 Middle; 3 High; 0 Other Level
17 Regular; 0 Special Education; 0 Vocational; 1 Alternative
0 Magnet; 0 Charter; 9 Title I Eligible; 0 School-wide Title I
Students: 9,949 (51.5% male; 48.5% female)
Individual Education Program: 1,938 (19.5%);
English Language Learner: 42 (0.4%); Migrant: 0 (0.0%)
Eligible for Free Lunch Program: 2,125 (21.4%)
Eligible for Reduced-Price Lunch Program: 889 (8.9%)
Teachers: 636.5 (15.6 to 1)
Librarians/Media Specialists: 10.0 (994.9 to 1)
Guidance Counselors: 25.5 (390.2 to 1)
Current Spending: ($ per student per year):
Total: $6,327; Instruction: $3,796; Support Services: $2,102
Enrollment, Drop-out Rates and Diploma Recipients by Race/Ethnicity

Category	Total	White	Black	Asian	AIAN	Hisp.
Enrollment (%)	100.0	93.1	4.3	1.4	0.3	0.9
Drop-out Rate (%)	4.4	4.3	5.6	0.0	7.1	10.3
H.S. Diplomas (#)	702	683	6	8	0	5

Western Dubuque Community SD

405 3rd Ave NE • Farley, IA 52046
(563) 744-3885
Grade Span: PK-12; **Agency Type:** 1
Schools: 9
6 Primary; 1 Middle; 2 High; 0 Other Level
8 Regular; 1 Special Education; 0 Vocational; 0 Alternative
0 Magnet; 0 Charter; 5 Title I Eligible; 0 School-wide Title I
Students: 2,639 (52.3% male; 47.7% female)
Individual Education Program: 491 (18.6%);
English Language Learner: 4 (0.2%); Migrant: 0 (0.0%)
Eligible for Free Lunch Program: 359 (13.6%)
Eligible for Reduced-Price Lunch Program: 211 (8.0%)
Teachers: 186.0 (14.2 to 1)
Librarians/Media Specialists: 3.5 (754.0 to 1)
Guidance Counselors: 6.0 (439.8 to 1)
Current Spending: ($ per student per year):
Total: $6,603; Instruction: $4,218; Support Services: $1,826
Enrollment, Drop-out Rates and Diploma Recipients by Race/Ethnicity

Category	Total	White	Black	Asian	AIAN	Hisp.
Enrollment (%)	100.0	98.6	0.7	0.2	0.0	0.5
Drop-out Rate (%)	0.4	0.4	0.0	0.0	n/a	0.0
H.S. Diplomas (#)	270	268	0	1	0	1

Floyd County

Charles City Community SD

500 N Grand Ave • Charles City, IA 50616
(641) 257-6500 • http://comet.charles-city.k12.ia.us
Grade Span: PK-12; **Agency Type:** 1
Schools: 5
3 Primary; 1 Middle; 1 High; 0 Other Level
5 Regular; 0 Special Education; 0 Vocational; 0 Alternative
0 Magnet; 0 Charter; 4 Title I Eligible; 4 School-wide Title I
Students: 1,726 (52.1% male; 47.9% female)
Individual Education Program: 321 (18.6%);
English Language Learner: 16 (0.9%); Migrant: 0 (0.0%)
Eligible for Free Lunch Program: 506 (29.3%)
Eligible for Reduced-Price Lunch Program: 143 (8.3%)
Teachers: 125.5 (13.8 to 1)
Librarians/Media Specialists: 3.0 (575.3 to 1)
Guidance Counselors: 5.0 (345.2 to 1)
Current Spending: ($ per student per year):
Total: $6,861; Instruction: $4,389; Support Services: $1,940
Enrollment, Drop-out Rates and Diploma Recipients by Race/Ethnicity

Category	Total	White	Black	Asian	AIAN	Hisp.
Enrollment (%)	100.0	94.7	1.2	1.3	0.1	2.7
Drop-out Rate (%)	2.3	1.8	n/a	0.0	n/a	26.7
H.S. Diplomas (#)	121	117	2	2	0	0

Hamilton County

Webster City Community SD

825 Beach St • Webster City, IA 50595-1948
(515) 832-9200 • http://www.webster-city.k12.ia.us
Grade Span: PK-12; **Agency Type:** 1
Schools: 5
3 Primary; 1 Middle; 1 High; 0 Other Level
5 Regular; 0 Special Education; 0 Vocational; 0 Alternative
0 Magnet; 0 Charter; 2 Title I Eligible; 0 School-wide Title I
Students: 1,777 (50.1% male; 49.9% female)
Individual Education Program: 238 (13.4%);
English Language Learner: 73 (4.1%); Migrant: 0 (0.0%)
Eligible for Free Lunch Program: 287 (16.2%)
Eligible for Reduced-Price Lunch Program: 158 (8.9%)
Teachers: 116.5 (15.3 to 1)
Librarians/Media Specialists: 2.0 (888.5 to 1)
Guidance Counselors: 6.0 (296.2 to 1)
Current Spending: ($ per student per year):
Total: $6,408; Instruction: $3,766; Support Services: $1,902
Enrollment, Drop-out Rates and Diploma Recipients by Race/Ethnicity

Category	Total	White	Black	Asian	AIAN	Hisp.
Enrollment (%)	100.0	93.1	0.6	3.5	0.0	2.8
Drop-out Rate (%)	0.0	0.0	0.0	0.0	n/a	0.0
H.S. Diplomas (#)	138	132	0	1	0	5

Henry County

Mount Pleasant Community SD

202 N Main • Mount Pleasant, IA 52641
(319) 385-7750 • http://www.mtpleasantschools.com
Grade Span: PK-12; **Agency Type:** 1
Schools: 6
4 Primary; 1 Middle; 1 High; 0 Other Level
6 Regular; 0 Special Education; 0 Vocational; 0 Alternative
0 Magnet; 0 Charter; 4 Title I Eligible; 0 School-wide Title I
Students: 2,154 (49.2% male; 50.8% female)
Individual Education Program: 264 (12.3%);
English Language Learner: 63 (2.9%); Migrant: 0 (0.0%)
Eligible for Free Lunch Program: 353 (16.4%)
Eligible for Reduced-Price Lunch Program: 151 (7.0%)
Teachers: 144.5 (14.9 to 1)
Librarians/Media Specialists: 2.0 (1,077.0 to 1)
Guidance Counselors: 3.0 (718.0 to 1)
Current Spending: ($ per student per year):
Total: $6,117; Instruction: $3,792; Support Services: $1,886
Enrollment, Drop-out Rates and Diploma Recipients by Race/Ethnicity

Category	Total	White	Black	Asian	AIAN	Hisp.
Enrollment (%)	100.0	90.5	1.7	5.2	0.3	2.3
Drop-out Rate (%)	0.7	0.8	0.0	0.0	n/a	0.0
H.S. Diplomas (#)	163	154	1	6	0	2

Jackson County

Maquoketa Community SD

612 So Vermont • Maquoketa, IA 52060
(563) 652-4984 • http://www.maquoketa.k12.ia.us
Grade Span: PK-12; **Agency Type:** 1
Schools: 4
2 Primary; 1 Middle; 1 High; 0 Other Level
4 Regular; 0 Special Education; 0 Vocational; 0 Alternative
0 Magnet; 0 Charter; 2 Title I Eligible; 1 School-wide Title I
Students: 1,669 (51.8% male; 48.2% female)
Individual Education Program: 289 (17.3%);
English Language Learner: 4 (0.2%); Migrant: 0 (0.0%)
Eligible for Free Lunch Program: 468 (28.0%)
Eligible for Reduced-Price Lunch Program: 156 (9.3%)
Teachers: 133.0 (12.5 to 1)
Librarians/Media Specialists: 2.0 (834.5 to 1)
Guidance Counselors: 5.0 (333.8 to 1)
Current Spending: ($ per student per year):
Total: $7,106; Instruction: $4,698; Support Services: $1,911
Enrollment, Drop-out Rates and Diploma Recipients by Race/Ethnicity

Category	Total	White	Black	Asian	AIAN	Hisp.
Enrollment (%)	100.0	97.2	1.4	0.9	0.4	0.1
Drop-out Rate (%)	3.3	3.4	0.0	0.0	0.0	0.0
H.S. Diplomas (#)	115	115	0	0	0	0

Jasper County

Newton Community SD

807 S 6th Ave W • Newton, IA 50208
(641) 792-5809 • http://www.newton.k12.ia.us
Grade Span: PK-12; **Agency Type:** 1
Schools: 8
5 Primary; 1 Middle; 2 High; 0 Other Level
7 Regular; 0 Special Education; 0 Vocational; 1 Alternative
0 Magnet; 0 Charter; 3 Title I Eligible; 0 School-wide Title I
Students: 3,405 (51.2% male; 48.8% female)
Individual Education Program: 532 (15.6%);
English Language Learner: 6 (0.2%); Migrant: 0 (0.0%)
Eligible for Free Lunch Program: 589 (17.3%)
Eligible for Reduced-Price Lunch Program: 176 (5.2%)
Teachers: 231.0 (14.7 to 1)
Librarians/Media Specialists: 5.0 (681.0 to 1)
Guidance Counselors: 12.0 (283.8 to 1)
Current Spending: ($ per student per year):
Total: $6,260; Instruction: $3,883; Support Services: $1,932
Enrollment, Drop-out Rates and Diploma Recipients by Race/Ethnicity

Category	Total	White	Black	Asian	AIAN	Hisp.
Enrollment (%)	100.0	96.7	1.1	0.9	0.4	0.9
Drop-out Rate (%)	3.3	3.3	0.0	0.0	0.0	0.0
H.S. Diplomas (#)	261	255	0	3	0	3

Jefferson County

Fairfield Community SD

607 E Broadway • Fairfield, IA 52556
(641) 472-2655 • http://www.aea15.k12.ia.us./fairfld.htm
Grade Span: PK-12; **Agency Type:** 1
Schools: 6
4 Primary; 1 Middle; 1 High; 0 Other Level
6 Regular; 0 Special Education; 0 Vocational; 0 Alternative
0 Magnet; 0 Charter; 5 Title I Eligible; 0 School-wide Title I
Students: 1,963 (50.1% male; 49.9% female)
Individual Education Program: 264 (13.4%);
English Language Learner: 23 (1.2%); Migrant: 0 (0.0%)
Eligible for Free Lunch Program: 354 (18.0%)
Eligible for Reduced-Price Lunch Program: 128 (6.5%)
Teachers: 137.5 (14.3 to 1)
Librarians/Media Specialists: 2.0 (981.5 to 1)
Guidance Counselors: 6.0 (327.2 to 1)
Current Spending: ($ per student per year):
Total: $6,492; Instruction: $3,857; Support Services: $2,151
Enrollment, Drop-out Rates and Diploma Recipients by Race/Ethnicity

Category	Total	White	Black	Asian	AIAN	Hisp.
Enrollment (%)	100.0	93.2	1.7	2.1	0.3	2.8
Drop-out Rate (%)	2.7	2.8	0.0	0.0	0.0	0.0
H.S. Diplomas (#)	133	127	2	2	1	1

Johnson County

Iowa City Community SD

509 S Dubuque St • Iowa City, IA 52240
(319) 688-1000 • http://www.iowa-city.k12.ia.us
Grade Span: PK-12; **Agency Type:** 1
Schools: 21
17 Primary; 2 Middle; 2 High; 0 Other Level
21 Regular; 0 Special Education; 0 Vocational; 0 Alternative
0 Magnet; 0 Charter; 10 Title I Eligible; 0 School-wide Title I
Students: 10,740 (52.5% male; 47.5% female)
Individual Education Program: 1,548 (14.4%);
English Language Learner: 205 (1.9%); Migrant: 0 (0.0%)
Eligible for Free Lunch Program: 1,528 (14.2%)
Eligible for Reduced-Price Lunch Program: 452 (4.2%)
Teachers: 699.7 (15.3 to 1)
Librarians/Media Specialists: 19.5 (550.8 to 1)
Guidance Counselors: 22.5 (477.3 to 1)
Current Spending: ($ per student per year):
Total: $6,437; Instruction: $4,009; Support Services: $2,026
Enrollment, Drop-out Rates and Diploma Recipients by Race/Ethnicity

Category	Total	White	Black	Asian	AIAN	Hisp.
Enrollment (%)	100.0	77.4	10.5	6.4	0.6	5.2
Drop-out Rate (%)	1.8	1.9	2.3	0.0	9.1	2.1
H.S. Diplomas (#)	721	599	45	48	5	24

Lee County

Fort Madison Community SD

1930 Ave M • Fort Madison, IA 52627
Mailing Address: PO Box 1423 • Fort Madison, IA 52627
(319) 372-7252 • http://www.ft-madison.k12.ia.us
Grade Span: PK-12; **Agency Type:** 1
Schools: 6
3 Primary; 1 Middle; 2 High; 0 Other Level
5 Regular; 0 Special Education; 0 Vocational; 1 Alternative
0 Magnet; 0 Charter; 2 Title I Eligible; 0 School-wide Title I
Students: 2,475 (51.7% male; 48.3% female)
Individual Education Program: 460 (18.6%);
English Language Learner: 1 (<0.1%); Migrant: 0 (0.0%)
Eligible for Free Lunch Program: 646 (26.1%)
Eligible for Reduced-Price Lunch Program: 179 (7.2%)
Teachers: 159.5 (15.5 to 1)
Librarians/Media Specialists: 1.0 (2,475.0 to 1)
Guidance Counselors: 4.0 (618.8 to 1)
Current Spending: ($ per student per year):
Total: $6,214; Instruction: $4,224; Support Services: $1,562
Enrollment, Drop-out Rates and Diploma Recipients by Race/Ethnicity

Category	Total	White	Black	Asian	AIAN	Hisp.
Enrollment (%)	100.0	89.1	4.5	1.1	0.2	5.2
Drop-out Rate (%)	4.1	4.3	3.8	0.0	0.0	2.8
H.S. Diplomas (#)	186	175	1	0	0	10

Keokuk Community SD

727 Washington St • Keokuk, IA 52632
(319) 524-1402 • http://www.keokuk.k12.ia.us
Grade Span: PK-12; **Agency Type:** 1
Schools: 7
5 Primary; 1 Middle; 1 High; 0 Other Level
7 Regular; 0 Special Education; 0 Vocational; 0 Alternative
0 Magnet; 0 Charter; 4 Title I Eligible; 0 School-wide Title I
Students: 2,237 (51.6% male; 48.4% female)
Individual Education Program: 380 (17.0%);
English Language Learner: 0 (0.0%); Migrant: 0 (0.0%)
Eligible for Free Lunch Program: 981 (43.9%)
Eligible for Reduced-Price Lunch Program: 246 (11.0%)

Teachers: 149.5 (15.0 to 1)
Librarians/Media Specialists: 2.0 (1,118.5 to 1)
Guidance Counselors: 5.0 (447.4 to 1)
Current Spending: ($ per student per year):
Total: $6,686; Instruction: $4,314; Support Services: $1,974
Enrollment, Drop-out Rates and Diploma Recipients by Race/Ethnicity

Category	Total	White	Black	Asian	AIAN	Hisp.
Enrollment (%)	100.0	87.4	9.3	1.2	0.6	1.5
Drop-out Rate (%)	3.2	3.2	3.8	0.0	0.0	0.0
H.S. Diplomas (#)	161	150	9	2	0	0

Linn County

Cedar Rapids Community SD
346 2nd Ave SW • Cedar Rapids, IA 52404
(319) 398-2000 • http://www.cr.k12.ia.us
Grade Span: PK-12; **Agency Type:** 1
Schools: 34
24 Primary; 6 Middle; 4 High; 0 Other Level
32 Regular; 0 Special Education; 0 Vocational; 2 Alternative
0 Magnet; 0 Charter; 9 Title I Eligible; 9 School-wide Title I
Students: 17,528 (51.1% male; 48.9% female)
Individual Education Program: 3,415 (19.5%);
English Language Learner: 158 (0.9%); Migrant: 0 (0.0%)
Eligible for Free Lunch Program: 4,173 (23.8%)
Eligible for Reduced-Price Lunch Program: 1,314 (7.5%)
Teachers: 1,080.5 (16.2 to 1)
Librarians/Media Specialists: 29.0 (604.4 to 1)
Guidance Counselors: 43.0 (407.6 to 1)
Current Spending: ($ per student per year):
Total: $6,936; Instruction: $4,312; Support Services: $2,113
Enrollment, Drop-out Rates and Diploma Recipients by Race/Ethnicity

Category	Total	White	Black	Asian	AIAN	Hisp.
Enrollment (%)	100.0	84.2	10.9	2.2	0.5	2.2
Drop-out Rate (%)	2.5	2.4	5.0	0.7	4.2	4.9
H.S. Diplomas (#)	1,013	925	48	25	6	9

College Community SD
401 76th Ave SW • Cedar Rapids, IA 52404
(319) 848-5201 • http://www.prairiepride.org
Grade Span: PK-12; **Agency Type:** 1
Schools: 6
4 Primary; 1 Middle; 1 High; 0 Other Level
5 Regular; 1 Special Education; 0 Vocational; 0 Alternative
0 Magnet; 0 Charter; 4 Title I Eligible; 0 School-wide Title I
Students: 3,624 (52.1% male; 47.9% female)
Individual Education Program: 451 (12.4%);
English Language Learner: 0 (0.0%); Migrant: 0 (0.0%)
Eligible for Free Lunch Program: 568 (15.7%)
Eligible for Reduced-Price Lunch Program: 207 (5.7%)
Teachers: 229.0 (15.8 to 1)
Librarians/Media Specialists: 5.0 (724.8 to 1)
Guidance Counselors: 8.0 (453.0 to 1)
Current Spending: ($ per student per year):
Total: $6,197; Instruction: $3,786; Support Services: $1,832
Enrollment, Drop-out Rates and Diploma Recipients by Race/Ethnicity

Category	Total	White	Black	Asian	AIAN	Hisp.
Enrollment (%)	100.0	92.6	3.8	1.7	0.5	1.5
Drop-out Rate (%)	0.7	0.7	0.0	0.0	0.0	0.0
H.S. Diplomas (#)	228	223	2	1	0	2

Linn-Mar Community SD
3333 N 10th St • Marion, IA 52302
(319) 377-7373 • http://www.linnmar.k12.ia.us
Grade Span: PK-12; **Agency Type:** 1
Schools: 7
5 Primary; 1 Middle; 1 High; 0 Other Level
7 Regular; 0 Special Education; 0 Vocational; 0 Alternative
0 Magnet; 0 Charter; 3 Title I Eligible; 0 School-wide Title I
Students: 4,716 (51.0% male; 49.0% female)
Individual Education Program: 578 (12.3%);
English Language Learner: 0 (0.0%); Migrant: 0 (0.0%)
Eligible for Free Lunch Program: 282 (6.0%)
Eligible for Reduced-Price Lunch Program: 142 (3.0%)
Teachers: 302.0 (15.6 to 1)
Librarians/Media Specialists: 7.0 (673.7 to 1)
Guidance Counselors: 10.0 (471.6 to 1)
Current Spending: ($ per student per year):
Total: $5,902; Instruction: $3,606; Support Services: $1,897
Enrollment, Drop-out Rates and Diploma Recipients by Race/Ethnicity

Category	Total	White	Black	Asian	AIAN	Hisp.
Enrollment (%)	100.0	93.5	2.0	2.9	0.1	1.5
Drop-out Rate (%)	0.2	0.0	27.3	0.0	n/a	0.0
H.S. Diplomas (#)	291	280	1	8	0	2

Marion Independent SD
777 S 15th St • Marion, IA 52302
Mailing Address: PO Box 606 • Marion, IA 52302
(319) 377-4691 • http://www.marion.k12.ia.us
Grade Span: PK-12; **Agency Type:** 1
Schools: 5
2 Primary; 2 Middle; 1 High; 0 Other Level
5 Regular; 0 Special Education; 0 Vocational; 0 Alternative
0 Magnet; 0 Charter; 1 Title I Eligible; 0 School-wide Title I
Students: 1,929 (51.7% male; 48.3% female)
Individual Education Program: 289 (15.0%);
English Language Learner: 0 (0.0%); Migrant: 0 (0.0%)
Eligible for Free Lunch Program: 215 (11.1%)
Eligible for Reduced-Price Lunch Program: 118 (6.1%)
Teachers: 141.0 (13.7 to 1)
Librarians/Media Specialists: 3.5 (551.1 to 1)
Guidance Counselors: 4.5 (428.7 to 1)
Current Spending: ($ per student per year):
Total: $6,394; Instruction: $3,758; Support Services: $2,157
Enrollment, Drop-out Rates and Diploma Recipients by Race/Ethnicity

Category	Total	White	Black	Asian	AIAN	Hisp.
Enrollment (%)	100.0	94.9	1.9	1.2	0.3	1.8
Drop-out Rate (%)	0.9	0.9	0.0	0.0	0.0	0.0
H.S. Diplomas (#)	141	135	3	1	1	1

Madison County

Winterset Community SD
302 W S St • Winterset, IA 50273
Mailing Address: PO Box 30 • Winterset, IA 50273
(515) 462-2718
Grade Span: PK-12; **Agency Type:** 1
Schools: 4
1 Primary; 2 Middle; 1 High; 0 Other Level
4 Regular; 0 Special Education; 0 Vocational; 0 Alternative
0 Magnet; 0 Charter; 1 Title I Eligible; 0 School-wide Title I
Students: 1,603 (51.1% male; 48.9% female)
Individual Education Program: 221 (13.8%);
English Language Learner: 0 (0.0%); Migrant: 0 (0.0%)
Eligible for Free Lunch Program: 227 (14.2%)
Eligible for Reduced-Price Lunch Program: 103 (6.4%)
Teachers: 108.5 (14.8 to 1)
Librarians/Media Specialists: 1.0 (1,603.0 to 1)
Guidance Counselors: 4.0 (400.8 to 1)
Current Spending: ($ per student per year):
Total: $6,248; Instruction: $3,718; Support Services: $2,061
Enrollment, Drop-out Rates and Diploma Recipients by Race/Ethnicity

Category	Total	White	Black	Asian	AIAN	Hisp.
Enrollment (%)	100.0	98.2	0.3	0.4	0.4	0.7
Drop-out Rate (%)	2.9	3.0	0.0	0.0	n/a	0.0
H.S. Diplomas (#)	143	142	0	1	0	0

Mahaska County

Oskaloosa Community SD
1800 N 3rd • Oskaloosa, IA 52577
Mailing Address: PO Box 710 • Oskaloosa, IA 52577
(641) 673-8345
Grade Span: KG-12; **Agency Type:** 1
Schools: 8
5 Primary; 2 Middle; 1 High; 0 Other Level
8 Regular; 0 Special Education; 0 Vocational; 0 Alternative
0 Magnet; 0 Charter; 4 Title I Eligible; 0 School-wide Title I
Students: 2,540 (52.0% male; 48.0% female)
Individual Education Program: 345 (13.6%);
English Language Learner: 10 (0.4%); Migrant: 0 (0.0%)
Eligible for Free Lunch Program: 594 (23.4%)
Eligible for Reduced-Price Lunch Program: 179 (7.0%)
Teachers: 152.5 (16.7 to 1)
Librarians/Media Specialists: 2.0 (1,270.0 to 1)
Guidance Counselors: 10.0 (254.0 to 1)
Current Spending: ($ per student per year):
Total: $6,116; Instruction: $3,763; Support Services: $1,848
Enrollment, Drop-out Rates and Diploma Recipients by Race/Ethnicity

Category	Total	White	Black	Asian	AIAN	Hisp.
Enrollment (%)	100.0	95.9	0.8	1.7	0.4	1.1
Drop-out Rate (%)	3.0	2.9	0.0	7.7	0.0	0.0
H.S. Diplomas (#)	171	164	1	6	0	0

Marion County

Knoxville Community SD

309 W Main • Knoxville, IA 50138
(641) 842-6552 • http://www.knoxville.k12.ia.us
Grade Span: PK-12; **Agency Type:** 1
Schools: 6
3 Primary; 1 Middle; 2 High; 0 Other Level
5 Regular; 0 Special Education; 0 Vocational; 1 Alternative
0 Magnet; 0 Charter; 3 Title I Eligible; 0 School-wide Title I
Students: 2,050 (52.7% male; 47.3% female)
Individual Education Program: 303 (14.8%);
English Language Learner: 6 (0.3%); Migrant: 0 (0.0%)
Eligible for Free Lunch Program: 394 (19.2%)
Eligible for Reduced-Price Lunch Program: 141 (6.9%)
Teachers: 135.0 (15.2 to 1)
Librarians/Media Specialists: 1.0 (2,050.0 to 1)
Guidance Counselors: 7.0 (292.9 to 1)
Current Spending: ($ per student per year):
Total: $5,873; Instruction: $3,332; Support Services: $2,030
Enrollment, Drop-out Rates and Diploma Recipients by Race/Ethnicity

Category	Total	White	Black	Asian	AIAN	Hisp.
Enrollment (%)	100.0	95.9	1.4	1.1	0.2	1.3
Drop-out Rate (%)	2.5	2.5	0.0	0.0	0.0	0.0
H.S. Diplomas (#)	158	157	0	0	0	1

Pella Community SD

210 E University St • Pella, IA 50219-0989
Mailing Address: PO Box 468 • Pella, IA 50219-0989
(641) 628-1111 • http://www.pella.k12.ia.us
Grade Span: PK-12; **Agency Type:** 1
Schools: 5
3 Primary; 1 Middle; 1 High; 0 Other Level
5 Regular; 0 Special Education; 0 Vocational; 0 Alternative
0 Magnet; 0 Charter; 3 Title I Eligible; 0 School-wide Title I
Students: 2,140 (49.7% male; 50.3% female)
Individual Education Program: 208 (9.7%);
English Language Learner: 29 (1.4%); Migrant: 0 (0.0%)
Eligible for Free Lunch Program: 210 (9.8%)
Eligible for Reduced-Price Lunch Program: 87 (4.1%)
Teachers: 129.5 (16.5 to 1)
Librarians/Media Specialists: 3.0 (713.3 to 1)
Guidance Counselors: 4.0 (535.0 to 1)
Current Spending: ($ per student per year):
Total: $5,776; Instruction: $3,604; Support Services: $1,723
Enrollment, Drop-out Rates and Diploma Recipients by Race/Ethnicity

Category	Total	White	Black	Asian	AIAN	Hisp.
Enrollment (%)	100.0	94.8	0.6	3.6	0.0	1.0
Drop-out Rate (%)	2.9	2.9	0.0	0.0	100.0	0.0
H.S. Diplomas (#)	137	127	0	7	0	3

Marshall County

Marshalltown Community SD

317 Columbus Dr • Marshalltown, IA 50158
(641) 754-1000 • http://www.marshalltown.k12.ia.us
Grade Span: PK-12; **Agency Type:** 1
Schools: 9
6 Primary; 2 Middle; 1 High; 0 Other Level
9 Regular; 0 Special Education; 0 Vocational; 0 Alternative
0 Magnet; 0 Charter; 4 Title I Eligible; 3 School-wide Title I
Students: 4,939 (52.2% male; 47.8% female)
Individual Education Program: 823 (16.7%);
English Language Learner: 899 (18.2%); Migrant: 219 (4.4%)
Eligible for Free Lunch Program: 1,627 (32.9%)
Eligible for Reduced-Price Lunch Program: 426 (8.6%)
Teachers: 317.0 (15.6 to 1)
Librarians/Media Specialists: 8.0 (617.4 to 1)
Guidance Counselors: 12.5 (395.1 to 1)
Current Spending: ($ per student per year):
Total: $6,633; Instruction: $4,074; Support Services: $2,034
Enrollment, Drop-out Rates and Diploma Recipients by Race/Ethnicity

Category	Total	White	Black	Asian	AIAN	Hisp.
Enrollment (%)	100.0	68.7	3.6	2.0	0.7	25.1
Drop-out Rate (%)	2.4	1.4	0.0	0.0	0.0	9.0
H.S. Diplomas (#)	310	273	6	10	0	21

Mills County

Glenwood Community SD

103 Central • Glenwood, IA 51534
(712) 527-9034
Grade Span: PK-12; **Agency Type:** 1
Schools: 6
1 Primary; 2 Middle; 1 High; 2 Other Level
4 Regular; 1 Special Education; 0 Vocational; 1 Alternative
0 Magnet; 0 Charter; 1 Title I Eligible; 0 School-wide Title I
Students: 2,032 (54.1% male; 45.9% female)
Individual Education Program: 300 (14.8%);
English Language Learner: 0 (0.0%); Migrant: 0 (0.0%)
Eligible for Free Lunch Program: 395 (19.4%)
Eligible for Reduced-Price Lunch Program: 138 (6.8%)
Teachers: 140.0 (14.5 to 1)
Librarians/Media Specialists: 2.0 (1,016.0 to 1)
Guidance Counselors: 4.0 (508.0 to 1)
Current Spending: ($ per student per year):
Total: $6,461; Instruction: $3,931; Support Services: $2,064
Enrollment, Drop-out Rates and Diploma Recipients by Race/Ethnicity

Category	Total	White	Black	Asian	AIAN	Hisp.
Enrollment (%)	100.0	95.7	1.1	1.0	0.2	1.9
Drop-out Rate (%)	0.8	0.7	0.0	14.3	0.0	0.0
H.S. Diplomas (#)	147	142	1	1	1	2

Muscatine County

Muscatine Community SD

1403 Park Ave • Muscatine, IA 52761
(563) 263-7223 • http://www.muscatine.k12.ia.us/index2.htm
Grade Span: PK-12; **Agency Type:** 1
Schools: 12
9 Primary; 2 Middle; 1 High; 0 Other Level
12 Regular; 0 Special Education; 0 Vocational; 0 Alternative
0 Magnet; 0 Charter; 6 Title I Eligible; 3 School-wide Title I
Students: 5,453 (53.0% male; 47.0% female)
Individual Education Program: 930 (17.1%);
English Language Learner: 269 (4.9%); Migrant: 114 (2.1%)
Eligible for Free Lunch Program: 1,281 (23.5%)
Eligible for Reduced-Price Lunch Program: 355 (6.5%)
Teachers: 377.0 (14.5 to 1)
Librarians/Media Specialists: 7.0 (779.0 to 1)
Guidance Counselors: 14.0 (389.5 to 1)
Current Spending: ($ per student per year):
Total: $6,450; Instruction: $4,473; Support Services: $1,528
Enrollment, Drop-out Rates and Diploma Recipients by Race/Ethnicity

Category	Total	White	Black	Asian	AIAN	Hisp.
Enrollment (%)	100.0	77.2	1.7	1.5	0.3	19.3
Drop-out Rate (%)	12.3	10.1	15.8	14.3	33.3	23.5
H.S. Diplomas (#)	336	287	2	6	0	41

Plymouth County

Le Mars Community SD

921 3rd Ave NW • Le Mars, IA 51031
(712) 546-4155 • http://www.lemars.k12.ia.us
Grade Span: PK-12; **Agency Type:** 1
Schools: 6
4 Primary; 1 Middle; 1 High; 0 Other Level
6 Regular; 0 Special Education; 0 Vocational; 0 Alternative
0 Magnet; 0 Charter; 4 Title I Eligible; 0 School-wide Title I
Students: 2,252 (51.6% male; 48.4% female)
Individual Education Program: 217 (9.6%);
English Language Learner: 20 (0.9%); Migrant: 0 (0.0%)
Eligible for Free Lunch Program: 241 (10.7%)
Eligible for Reduced-Price Lunch Program: 133 (5.9%)
Teachers: 148.0 (15.2 to 1)
Librarians/Media Specialists: 2.0 (1,126.0 to 1)
Guidance Counselors: 6.0 (375.3 to 1)
Current Spending: ($ per student per year):
Total: $5,506; Instruction: $3,452; Support Services: $1,642
Enrollment, Drop-out Rates and Diploma Recipients by Race/Ethnicity

Category	Total	White	Black	Asian	AIAN	Hisp.
Enrollment (%)	100.0	94.3	1.2	1.1	0.2	3.2
Drop-out Rate (%)	1.1	1.1	n/a	0.0	0.0	0.0
H.S. Diplomas (#)	181	178	1	1	0	1

Polk County

Ankeny Community SD

306 SW School St • Ankeny, IA 50021
Mailing Address: PO Box 189 • Ankeny, IA 50021
(515) 965-9600 • http://www.ankeny.k12.ia.us
Grade Span: PK-12; **Agency Type:** 1
Schools: 9
6 Primary; 1 Middle; 1 High; 1 Other Level
9 Regular; 0 Special Education; 0 Vocational; 0 Alternative
0 Magnet; 0 Charter; 4 Title I Eligible; 0 School-wide Title I
Students: 6,056 (50.7% male; 49.3% female)
Individual Education Program: 589 (9.7%);
English Language Learner: 52 (0.9%); Migrant: 0 (0.0%)
Eligible for Free Lunch Program: 218 (3.6%)

Eligible for Reduced-Price Lunch Program: 132 (2.2%)
Teachers: 345.5 (17.5 to 1)
Librarians/Media Specialists: 9.0 (672.9 to 1)
Guidance Counselors: 14.0 (432.6 to 1)
Current Spending: ($ per student per year):
Total: $5,723; Instruction: $3,496; Support Services: $1,763
Enrollment, Drop-out Rates and Diploma Recipients by Race/Ethnicity

Category	Total	White	Black	Asian	AIAN	Hisp.
Enrollment (%)	100.0	95.9	1.5	1.3	0.0	1.3
Drop-out Rate (%)	0.9	0.8	5.3	5.0	0.0	0.0
H.S. Diplomas (#)	386	374	6	2	2	2

Des Moines Independent Community SD

1801 16th St • Des Moines, IA 50314-1992
(515) 242-7911 • http://www.des-moines.k12.ia.us/
Grade Span: PK-12; **Agency Type:** 1
Schools: 62
42 Primary; 10 Middle; 6 High; 3 Other Level
57 Regular; 3 Special Education; 0 Vocational; 1 Alternative
0 Magnet; 0 Charter; 20 Title I Eligible; 17 School-wide Title I
Students: 31,553 (51.7% male; 48.3% female)
Individual Education Program: 5,627 (17.8%);
English Language Learner: 3,165 (10.0%); Migrant: 1 (<0.1%)
Eligible for Free Lunch Program: 11,769 (37.3%)
Eligible for Reduced-Price Lunch Program: 3,451 (10.9%)
Teachers: 2,341.5 (13.5 to 1)
Librarians/Media Specialists: 23.0 (1,371.9 to 1)
Guidance Counselors: 90.0 (350.6 to 1)
Current Spending: ($ per student per year):
Total: $7,407; Instruction: $4,608; Support Services: $2,294
Enrollment, Drop-out Rates and Diploma Recipients by Race/Ethnicity

Category	Total	White	Black	Asian	AIAN	Hisp.
Enrollment (%)	100.0	68.4	15.3	4.7	0.7	11.0
Drop-out Rate (%)	6.4	5.7	7.1	6.2	11.9	13.1
H.S. Diplomas (#)	1,659	1,280	201	96	3	79

Johnston Community SD

5608 Merle Hay Rd • Johnston, IA 50131
Mailing Address: PO Box 10 • Johnston, IA 50131
(515) 278-0470 • http://www.johnston.k12.ia.us
Grade Span: PK-12; **Agency Type:** 1
Schools: 7
4 Primary; 1 Middle; 1 High; 1 Other Level
6 Regular; 0 Special Education; 0 Vocational; 1 Alternative
0 Magnet; 0 Charter; 1 Title I Eligible; 0 School-wide Title I
Students: 4,517 (52.6% male; 47.4% female)
Individual Education Program: 432 (9.6%);
English Language Learner: 69 (1.5%); Migrant: 0 (0.0%)
Eligible for Free Lunch Program: 176 (3.9%)
Eligible for Reduced-Price Lunch Program: 51 (1.1%)
Teachers: 283.5 (15.9 to 1)
Librarians/Media Specialists: 6.0 (752.8 to 1)
Guidance Counselors: 7.0 (645.3 to 1)
Current Spending: ($ per student per year):
Total: $5,888; Instruction: $3,347; Support Services: $2,083
Enrollment, Drop-out Rates and Diploma Recipients by Race/Ethnicity

Category	Total	White	Black	Asian	AIAN	Hisp.
Enrollment (%)	100.0	92.6	2.2	3.3	0.1	1.9
Drop-out Rate (%)	0.6	0.5	4.2	0.0	n/a	0.0
H.S. Diplomas (#)	262	243	4	10	0	5

Southeast Polk Community SD

8379 NE University • Runnells, IA 50237
Mailing Address: RR 2 • Runnells, IA 50237
(515) 967-4294 • http://www.se-polk.k12.ia.us
Grade Span: PK-12; **Agency Type:** 1
Schools: 10
7 Primary; 1 Middle; 2 High; 0 Other Level
9 Regular; 0 Special Education; 0 Vocational; 1 Alternative
0 Magnet; 0 Charter; 4 Title I Eligible; 0 School-wide Title I
Students: 4,700 (50.9% male; 49.1% female)
Individual Education Program: 626 (13.3%);
English Language Learner: 23 (0.5%); Migrant: 0 (0.0%)
Eligible for Free Lunch Program: 488 (10.4%)
Eligible for Reduced-Price Lunch Program: 188 (4.0%)
Teachers: 301.5 (15.6 to 1)
Librarians/Media Specialists: 4.0 (1,175.0 to 1)
Guidance Counselors: 16.0 (293.8 to 1)
Current Spending: ($ per student per year):
Total: $6,153; Instruction: $3,679; Support Services: $2,020
Enrollment, Drop-out Rates and Diploma Recipients by Race/Ethnicity

Category	Total	White	Black	Asian	AIAN	Hisp.
Enrollment (%)	100.0	95.1	1.5	1.3	0.3	1.8
Drop-out Rate (%)	0.8	0.9	0.0	0.0	0.0	0.0
H.S. Diplomas (#)	322	313	0	3	2	4

Urbandale Community SD

6200 Aurora Ave • Urbandale, IA 50322
Mailing Address: Merle Hay Ctr, 500 W • Urbandale, IA 50322
(515) 457-5000 • http://www.urbandale.k12.ia.us
Grade Span: PK-12; **Agency Type:** 1
Schools: 8
5 Primary; 1 Middle; 2 High; 0 Other Level
7 Regular; 0 Special Education; 0 Vocational; 1 Alternative
0 Magnet; 0 Charter; 1 Title I Eligible; 0 School-wide Title I
Students: 3,345 (51.5% male; 48.5% female)
Individual Education Program: 328 (9.8%);
English Language Learner: 208 (6.2%); Migrant: 0 (0.0%)
Eligible for Free Lunch Program: 191 (5.7%)
Eligible for Reduced-Price Lunch Program: 138 (4.1%)
Teachers: 203.5 (16.4 to 1)
Librarians/Media Specialists: 3.0 (1,115.0 to 1)
Guidance Counselors: 8.0 (418.1 to 1)
Current Spending: ($ per student per year):
Total: $6,163; Instruction: $3,552; Support Services: $2,102
Enrollment, Drop-out Rates and Diploma Recipients by Race/Ethnicity

Category	Total	White	Black	Asian	AIAN	Hisp.
Enrollment (%)	100.0	93.5	2.9	1.8	0.0	1.8
Drop-out Rate (%)	1.3	1.3	0.0	0.0	0.0	0.0
H.S. Diplomas (#)	332	320	3	4	1	4

West Des Moines Community SD

Civic Pkwy • West Des Moines, IA 50265
Mailing Address: 3550 George M Mills • West Des Moines, IA 50265
(515) 226-2700 • http://www.wdm.k12.ia.us
Grade Span: PK-12; **Agency Type:** 1
Schools: 15
10 Primary; 2 Middle; 2 High; 1 Other Level
14 Regular; 0 Special Education; 0 Vocational; 1 Alternative
0 Magnet; 0 Charter; 3 Title I Eligible; 1 School-wide Title I
Students: 8,749 (52.2% male; 47.8% female)
Individual Education Program: 938 (10.7%);
English Language Learner: 213 (2.4%); Migrant: 0 (0.0%)
Eligible for Free Lunch Program: 667 (7.6%)
Eligible for Reduced-Price Lunch Program: 311 (3.6%)
Teachers: 545.5 (16.0 to 1)
Librarians/Media Specialists: 8.0 (1,093.6 to 1)
Guidance Counselors: 18.5 (472.9 to 1)
Current Spending: ($ per student per year):
Total: $6,386; Instruction: $3,730; Support Services: $1,993
Enrollment, Drop-out Rates and Diploma Recipients by Race/Ethnicity

Category	Total	White	Black	Asian	AIAN	Hisp.
Enrollment (%)	100.0	87.5	3.7	4.1	0.2	4.5
Drop-out Rate (%)	2.9	2.6	9.4	0.0	50.0	12.2
H.S. Diplomas (#)	554	509	8	24	2	11

Pottawattamie County

Council Bluffs Community SD

12 Scott St • Council Bluffs, IA 51503
(712) 328-6418 • http://www.council-bluffs.k12.ia.us
Grade Span: PK-12; **Agency Type:** 1
Schools: 22
14 Primary; 2 Middle; 4 High; 2 Other Level
20 Regular; 0 Special Education; 0 Vocational; 2 Alternative
0 Magnet; 0 Charter; 8 Title I Eligible; 8 School-wide Title I
Students: 9,364 (50.9% male; 49.1% female)
Individual Education Program: 1,779 (19.0%);
English Language Learner: 93 (1.0%); Migrant: 0 (0.0%)
Eligible for Free Lunch Program: 3,022 (32.3%)
Eligible for Reduced-Price Lunch Program: 794 (8.5%)
Teachers: 660.0 (14.2 to 1)
Librarians/Media Specialists: 8.0 (1,170.5 to 1)
Guidance Counselors: 28.5 (328.6 to 1)
Current Spending: ($ per student per year):
Total: $5,807; Instruction: $3,635; Support Services: $1,803
Enrollment, Drop-out Rates and Diploma Recipients by Race/Ethnicity

Category	Total	White	Black	Asian	AIAN	Hisp.
Enrollment (%)	100.0	90.3	2.2	0.9	0.9	5.7
Drop-out Rate (%)	5.9	5.7	9.1	0.0	9.5	10.3
H.S. Diplomas (#)	545	505	15	8	4	13

Lewis Central Community SD

1600 E S Omaha Brdg Rd • Council Bluffs, IA 51503
(712) 366-8202 • http://www.lewiscentral.k12.ia.us
Grade Span: PK-12; **Agency Type:** 1
Schools: 5
3 Primary; 1 Middle; 1 High; 0 Other Level
5 Regular; 0 Special Education; 0 Vocational; 0 Alternative
0 Magnet; 0 Charter; 3 Title I Eligible; 0 School-wide Title I
Students: 2,698 (50.8% male; 49.2% female)

Individual Education Program: 353 (13.1%);
English Language Learner: 31 (1.1%); Migrant: 0 (0.0%)
Eligible for Free Lunch Program: 568 (21.1%)
Eligible for Reduced-Price Lunch Program: 199 (7.4%)
Teachers: 172.0 (15.7 to 1)
Librarians/Media Specialists: 3.5 (770.9 to 1)
Guidance Counselors: 5.0 (539.6 to 1)
Current Spending: ($ per student per year):
Total: $6,179; Instruction: $3,988; Support Services: $1,615
Enrollment, Drop-out Rates and Diploma Recipients by Race/Ethnicity

Category	Total	White	Black	Asian	AIAN	Hisp.
Enrollment (%)	100.0	92.6	1.0	0.8	0.2	5.4
Drop-out Rate (%)	4.3	4.4	0.0	0.0	n/a	4.2
H.S. Diplomas (#)	176	167	4	0	0	5

Poweshiek County

Grinnell-Newburg Community SD
927 4th Ave • Grinnell, IA 50112-2055
(641) 236-2700 • http://www.grinnell.k12.ia.us
Grade Span: PK-12; **Agency Type:** 1
Schools: 5
3 Primary; 1 Middle; 1 High; 0 Other Level
5 Regular; 0 Special Education; 0 Vocational; 0 Alternative
0 Magnet; 0 Charter; 4 Title I Eligible; 0 School-wide Title I
Students: 1,737 (52.0% male; 48.0% female)
Individual Education Program: 269 (15.5%);
English Language Learner: 8 (0.5%); Migrant: 0 (0.0%)
Eligible for Free Lunch Program: 354 (20.4%)
Eligible for Reduced-Price Lunch Program: 87 (5.0%)
Teachers: 131.5 (13.2 to 1)
Librarians/Media Specialists: 3.0 (579.0 to 1)
Guidance Counselors: 6.0 (289.5 to 1)
Current Spending: ($ per student per year):
Total: $6,904; Instruction: $4,312; Support Services: $1,990
Enrollment, Drop-out Rates and Diploma Recipients by Race/Ethnicity

Category	Total	White	Black	Asian	AIAN	Hisp.
Enrollment (%)	100.0	94.8	1.4	1.4	1.4	1.0
Drop-out Rate (%)	1.8	1.7	0.0	7.1	0.0	0.0
H.S. Diplomas (#)	123	115	3	3	0	2

Scott County

Bettendorf Community SD
3311 Central Ave • Bettendorf, IA 52722
(563) 359-3681 • http://www.bettendorf.k12.ia.us
Grade Span: PK-12; **Agency Type:** 1
Schools: 8
6 Primary; 1 Middle; 1 High; 0 Other Level
8 Regular; 0 Special Education; 0 Vocational; 0 Alternative
0 Magnet; 0 Charter; 4 Title I Eligible; 0 School-wide Title I
Students: 4,371 (51.2% male; 48.8% female)
Individual Education Program: 405 (9.3%);
English Language Learner: 40 (0.9%); Migrant: 0 (0.0%)
Eligible for Free Lunch Program: 436 (10.0%)
Eligible for Reduced-Price Lunch Program: 214 (4.9%)
Teachers: 262.5 (16.7 to 1)
Librarians/Media Specialists: 9.0 (485.7 to 1)
Guidance Counselors: 12.0 (364.3 to 1)
Current Spending: ($ per student per year):
Total: $6,501; Instruction: $4,039; Support Services: $2,022
Enrollment, Drop-out Rates and Diploma Recipients by Race/Ethnicity

Category	Total	White	Black	Asian	AIAN	Hisp.
Enrollment (%)	100.0	91.4	3.8	2.0	0.3	2.4
Drop-out Rate (%)	2.5	2.5	3.7	3.3	0.0	2.3
H.S. Diplomas (#)	295	276	8	6	0	5

Davenport Community SD
1606 Brady St • Davenport, IA 52803
(563) 336-5000 • http://www.davenport.k12.ia.us
Grade Span: PK-12; **Agency Type:** 1
Schools: 31
20 Primary; 6 Middle; 4 High; 1 Other Level
29 Regular; 1 Special Education; 0 Vocational; 1 Alternative
0 Magnet; 0 Charter; 7 Title I Eligible; 7 School-wide Title I
Students: 16,544 (51.5% male; 48.5% female)
Individual Education Program: 2,243 (13.6%);
English Language Learner: 368 (2.2%); Migrant: 0 (0.0%)
Eligible for Free Lunch Program: 5,957 (36.0%)
Eligible for Reduced-Price Lunch Program: 1,384 (8.4%)
Teachers: 1,097.0 (15.1 to 1)
Librarians/Media Specialists: 4.0 (4,136.0 to 1)
Guidance Counselors: 31.0 (533.7 to 1)
Current Spending: ($ per student per year):
Total: $6,998; Instruction: $4,590; Support Services: $1,961
Enrollment, Drop-out Rates and Diploma Recipients by Race/Ethnicity

Category	Total	White	Black	Asian	AIAN	Hisp.
Enrollment (%)	100.0	73.3	16.6	2.4	1.1	6.5
Drop-out Rate (%)	3.4	2.8	5.9	1.5	6.1	5.8
H.S. Diplomas (#)	956	768	111	28	9	40

North Scott Community SD
251 E Iowa St • Eldridge, IA 52748
(563) 285-9081 • http://www.north-scott.k12.ia.us
Grade Span: PK-12; **Agency Type:** 1
Schools: 7
5 Primary; 1 Middle; 1 High; 0 Other Level
7 Regular; 0 Special Education; 0 Vocational; 0 Alternative
0 Magnet; 0 Charter; 5 Title I Eligible; 0 School-wide Title I
Students: 2,957 (52.1% male; 47.9% female)
Individual Education Program: 355 (12.0%);
English Language Learner: 0 (0.0%); Migrant: 0 (0.0%)
Eligible for Free Lunch Program: 337 (11.4%)
Eligible for Reduced-Price Lunch Program: 139 (4.7%)
Teachers: 194.0 (15.2 to 1)
Librarians/Media Specialists: 6.0 (492.8 to 1)
Guidance Counselors: 10.0 (295.7 to 1)
Current Spending: ($ per student per year):
Total: $6,573; Instruction: $3,866; Support Services: $2,220
Enrollment, Drop-out Rates and Diploma Recipients by Race/Ethnicity

Category	Total	White	Black	Asian	AIAN	Hisp.
Enrollment (%)	100.0	96.8	1.0	0.6	0.3	1.3
Drop-out Rate (%)	1.6	1.7	0.0	0.0	n/a	0.0
H.S. Diplomas (#)	194	185	1	2	0	6

Pleasant Valley Community SD
525 Belmont Rd • Pleasant Valley, IA 52767
Mailing Address: PO Box 332 • Pleasant Valley, IA 52767
(563) 332-5550 • http://www.pleasval.k12.ia.us/
Grade Span: PK-12; **Agency Type:** 1
Schools: 6
4 Primary; 1 Middle; 1 High; 0 Other Level
6 Regular; 0 Special Education; 0 Vocational; 0 Alternative
0 Magnet; 0 Charter; 2 Title I Eligible; 0 School-wide Title I
Students: 3,158 (51.1% male; 48.9% female)
Individual Education Program: 270 (8.5%);
English Language Learner: 4 (0.1%); Migrant: 0 (0.0%)
Eligible for Free Lunch Program: 192 (6.1%)
Eligible for Reduced-Price Lunch Program: 63 (2.0%)
Teachers: 197.5 (16.0 to 1)
Librarians/Media Specialists: 5.0 (631.6 to 1)
Guidance Counselors: 8.0 (394.8 to 1)
Current Spending: ($ per student per year):
Total: $5,991; Instruction: $3,798; Support Services: $1,704
Enrollment, Drop-out Rates and Diploma Recipients by Race/Ethnicity

Category	Total	White	Black	Asian	AIAN	Hisp.
Enrollment (%)	100.0	93.9	0.7	2.1	1.1	2.1
Drop-out Rate (%)	3.1	3.2	0.0	0.0	0.0	5.6
H.S. Diplomas (#)	241	222	0	8	3	8

Shelby County

Harlan Community SD
2102 Durant • Harlan, IA 51537-1299
(712) 755-2152 • http://www.harlan.k12.ia.us
Grade Span: PK-12; **Agency Type:** 1
Schools: 5
2 Primary; 1 Middle; 2 High; 0 Other Level
4 Regular; 0 Special Education; 0 Vocational; 1 Alternative
0 Magnet; 0 Charter; 2 Title I Eligible; 0 School-wide Title I
Students: 1,639 (51.0% male; 49.0% female)
Individual Education Program: 237 (14.5%);
English Language Learner: 6 (0.4%); Migrant: 0 (0.0%)
Eligible for Free Lunch Program: 316 (19.3%)
Eligible for Reduced-Price Lunch Program: 143 (8.7%)
Teachers: 100.5 (16.3 to 1)
Librarians/Media Specialists: 3.0 (546.3 to 1)
Guidance Counselors: 4.0 (409.8 to 1)
Current Spending: ($ per student per year):
Total: $6,044; Instruction: $3,666; Support Services: $1,849
Enrollment, Drop-out Rates and Diploma Recipients by Race/Ethnicity

Category	Total	White	Black	Asian	AIAN	Hisp.
Enrollment (%)	100.0	96.6	0.9	0.5	0.4	1.6
Drop-out Rate (%)	1.5	1.5	n/a	0.0	0.0	0.0
H.S. Diplomas (#)	153	150	0	3	0	0

Story County

Ames Community SD
424 Main St • Ames, IA 50010
Mailing Address: PO Box 3011 • Ames, IA 50010
(515) 268-6600 • http://www.ames.k12.ia.us
Grade Span: PK-12; **Agency Type:** 1
Schools: 10
8 Primary; 1 Middle; 1 High; 0 Other Level
9 Regular; 1 Special Education; 0 Vocational; 0 Alternative
0 Magnet; 0 Charter; 7 Title I Eligible; 0 School-wide Title I
Students: 4,658 (52.9% male; 47.1% female)
Individual Education Program: 602 (12.9%);
English Language Learner: 178 (3.8%); Migrant: 0 (0.0%)
Eligible for Free Lunch Program: 491 (10.5%)
Eligible for Reduced-Price Lunch Program: 154 (3.3%)
Teachers: 308.5 (15.1 to 1)
Librarians/Media Specialists: 6.0 (776.3 to 1)
Guidance Counselors: 14.5 (321.2 to 1)
Current Spending: ($ per student per year):
Total: $7,443; Instruction: $4,849; Support Services: $2,025
Enrollment, Drop-out Rates and Diploma Recipients by Race/Ethnicity

Category	Total	White	Black	Asian	AIAN	Hisp.
Enrollment (%)	100.0	80.5	6.8	9.5	0.2	2.9
Drop-out Rate (%)	1.2	0.9	8.2	0.9	0.0	0.0
H.S. Diplomas (#)	397	343	16	31	1	6

Tama County

South Tama County Community SD
1702 Harding St • Tama, IA 52339-1028
(641) 484-4811 • http://www.aea6.k12.ia.us/schools/tama.html
Grade Span: PK-12; **Agency Type:** 1
Schools: 5
3 Primary; 1 Middle; 1 High; 0 Other Level
5 Regular; 0 Special Education; 0 Vocational; 0 Alternative
0 Magnet; 0 Charter; 3 Title I Eligible; 1 School-wide Title I
Students: 1,663 (53.0% male; 47.0% female)
Individual Education Program: 275 (16.5%);
English Language Learner: 102 (6.1%); Migrant: 0 (0.0%)
Eligible for Free Lunch Program: 450 (27.1%)
Eligible for Reduced-Price Lunch Program: 176 (10.6%)
Teachers: 116.0 (14.3 to 1)
Librarians/Media Specialists: 2.0 (831.5 to 1)
Guidance Counselors: 4.0 (415.8 to 1)
Current Spending: ($ per student per year):
Total: $6,021; Instruction: $3,792; Support Services: $1,644
Enrollment, Drop-out Rates and Diploma Recipients by Race/Ethnicity

Category	Total	White	Black	Asian	AIAN	Hisp.
Enrollment (%)	100.0	67.3	1.6	0.5	16.7	13.9
Drop-out Rate (%)	6.7	5.9	0.0	0.0	10.3	9.4
H.S. Diplomas (#)	116	96	0	2	8	10

Wapello County

Ottumwa Community SD
422 Mccarroll Dr • Ottumwa, IA 52501
(641) 684-6596
Grade Span: PK-12; **Agency Type:** 1
Schools: 12
9 Primary; 1 Middle; 2 High; 0 Other Level
10 Regular; 1 Special Education; 0 Vocational; 1 Alternative
0 Magnet; 0 Charter; 5 Title I Eligible; 4 School-wide Title I
Students: 4,895 (50.9% male; 49.1% female)
Individual Education Program: 879 (18.0%);
English Language Learner: 234 (4.8%); Migrant: 333 (6.8%)
Eligible for Free Lunch Program: 1,897 (38.8%)
Eligible for Reduced-Price Lunch Program: 354 (7.2%)
Teachers: 322.5 (15.2 to 1)
Librarians/Media Specialists: 5.0 (979.0 to 1)
Guidance Counselors: 8.0 (611.9 to 1)
Current Spending: ($ per student per year):
Total: $5,910; Instruction: $3,611; Support Services: $1,854
Enrollment, Drop-out Rates and Diploma Recipients by Race/Ethnicity

Category	Total	White	Black	Asian	AIAN	Hisp.
Enrollment (%)	100.0	86.6	2.2	1.7	0.5	9.0
Drop-out Rate (%)	6.7	6.3	19.0	2.2	50.0	14.6
H.S. Diplomas (#)	291	273	1	10	0	7

Warren County

Indianola Community SD
1304 E 2nd Ave • Indianola, IA 50125
(515) 961-9500 • http://www.indianola.ia.us/k12/
Grade Span: PK-12; **Agency Type:** 1
Schools: 6
3 Primary; 1 Middle; 2 High; 0 Other Level
5 Regular; 0 Special Education; 0 Vocational; 1 Alternative
0 Magnet; 0 Charter; 3 Title I Eligible; 0 School-wide Title I
Students: 3,172 (50.3% male; 49.7% female)
Individual Education Program: 400 (12.6%);
English Language Learner: 5 (0.2%); Migrant: 0 (0.0%)
Eligible for Free Lunch Program: 367 (11.6%)
Eligible for Reduced-Price Lunch Program: 177 (5.6%)
Teachers: 203.0 (15.6 to 1)
Librarians/Media Specialists: 3.0 (1,057.3 to 1)
Guidance Counselors: 10.0 (317.2 to 1)
Current Spending: ($ per student per year):
Total: $6,213; Instruction: $3,797; Support Services: $1,867
Enrollment, Drop-out Rates and Diploma Recipients by Race/Ethnicity

Category	Total	White	Black	Asian	AIAN	Hisp.
Enrollment (%)	100.0	97.1	0.8	1.0	0.3	0.9
Drop-out Rate (%)	2.2	2.3	0.0	0.0	0.0	0.0
H.S. Diplomas (#)	218	216	1	1	0	0

Norwalk Community SD
906 School Ave • Norwalk, IA 50211
(515) 981-0676 • http://www.norwalk.k12.ia.us/
Grade Span: PK-12; **Agency Type:** 1
Schools: 5
2 Primary; 2 Middle; 1 High; 0 Other Level
5 Regular; 0 Special Education; 0 Vocational; 0 Alternative
0 Magnet; 0 Charter; 2 Title I Eligible; 0 School-wide Title I
Students: 2,173 (51.9% male; 48.1% female)
Individual Education Program: 336 (15.5%);
English Language Learner: 11 (0.5%); Migrant: 0 (0.0%)
Eligible for Free Lunch Program: 130 (6.0%)
Eligible for Reduced-Price Lunch Program: 82 (3.8%)
Teachers: 153.5 (14.2 to 1)
Librarians/Media Specialists: 3.0 (724.3 to 1)
Guidance Counselors: 7.0 (310.4 to 1)
Current Spending: ($ per student per year):
Total: $5,951; Instruction: $3,489; Support Services: $1,998
Enrollment, Drop-out Rates and Diploma Recipients by Race/Ethnicity

Category	Total	White	Black	Asian	AIAN	Hisp.
Enrollment (%)	100.0	97.0	0.7	1.1	0.1	1.2
Drop-out Rate (%)	1.2	1.2	0.0	0.0	0.0	0.0
H.S. Diplomas (#)	129	129	0	0	0	0

Washington County

Washington Community SD
404 W Main • Washington, IA 52353
Mailing Address: PO Box 926 • Washington, IA 52353
(319) 653-6543 • http://www.washington.k12.ia.us
Grade Span: PK-12; **Agency Type:** 1
Schools: 5
1 Primary; 2 Middle; 2 High; 0 Other Level
4 Regular; 0 Special Education; 0 Vocational; 1 Alternative
0 Magnet; 0 Charter; 2 Title I Eligible; 0 School-wide Title I
Students: 1,730 (50.9% male; 49.1% female)
Individual Education Program: 294 (17.0%);
English Language Learner: 141 (8.2%); Migrant: 0 (0.0%)
Eligible for Free Lunch Program: 343 (19.8%)
Eligible for Reduced-Price Lunch Program: 127 (7.3%)
Teachers: 126.0 (13.7 to 1)
Librarians/Media Specialists: 3.0 (576.7 to 1)
Guidance Counselors: 5.0 (346.0 to 1)
Current Spending: ($ per student per year):
Total: $6,544; Instruction: $3,885; Support Services: $2,176
Enrollment, Drop-out Rates and Diploma Recipients by Race/Ethnicity

Category	Total	White	Black	Asian	AIAN	Hisp.
Enrollment (%)	100.0	88.0	2.3	0.8	0.0	9.0
Drop-out Rate (%)	2.4	2.2	12.5	0.0	n/a	3.3
H.S. Diplomas (#)	90	82	1	1	0	6

Webster County

Fort Dodge Community SD
104 S 17th St • Fort Dodge, IA 50501
(515) 576-1161 • http://www.fort-dodge.k12.ia.us
Grade Span: PK-12; **Agency Type:** 1
Schools: 10
6 Primary; 2 Middle; 2 High; 0 Other Level

9 Regular; 0 Special Education; 0 Vocational; 1 Alternative
0 Magnet; 0 Charter; 5 Title I Eligible; 0 School-wide Title I
Students: 4,192 (51.2% male; 48.8% female)
Individual Education Program: 797 (19.0%);
English Language Learner: 33 (0.8%); Migrant: 0 (0.0%)
Eligible for Free Lunch Program: 1,193 (28.5%)
Eligible for Reduced-Price Lunch Program: 350 (8.3%)
Teachers: 311.0 (13.5 to 1)
Librarians/Media Specialists: 5.0 (838.4 to 1)
Guidance Counselors: 13.0 (322.5 to 1)
Current Spending: ($ per student per year):
Total: $6,943; Instruction: $4,457; Support Services: $1,986
Enrollment, Drop-out Rates and Diploma Recipients by Race/Ethnicity

Category	Total	White	Black	Asian	AIAN	Hisp.
Enrollment (%)	100.0	87.5	7.3	2.1	0.2	2.9
Drop-out Rate (%)	4.1	3.5	12.6	0.0	100.0	0.0
H.S. Diplomas (#)	293	265	15	7	2	4

Winneshiek County

Decorah Community SD

510 Winnebago St • Decorah, IA 52101
(563) 382-4208 • http://www.decorah.k12.ia.us
Grade Span: PK-12; **Agency Type:** 1
Schools: 4
2 Primary; 1 Middle; 1 High; 0 Other Level
4 Regular; 0 Special Education; 0 Vocational; 0 Alternative
0 Magnet; 0 Charter; 1 Title I Eligible; 0 School-wide Title I
Students: 1,724 (50.2% male; 49.8% female)
Individual Education Program: 292 (16.9%);
English Language Learner: 0 (0.0%); Migrant: 0 (0.0%)
Eligible for Free Lunch Program: 181 (10.5%)
Eligible for Reduced-Price Lunch Program: 99 (5.7%)
Teachers: 117.0 (14.7 to 1)
Librarians/Media Specialists: 3.0 (574.7 to 1)
Guidance Counselors: 3.0 (574.7 to 1)
Current Spending: ($ per student per year):
Total: $6,399; Instruction: $3,898; Support Services: $1,910
Enrollment, Drop-out Rates and Diploma Recipients by Race/Ethnicity

Category	Total	White	Black	Asian	AIAN	Hisp.
Enrollment (%)	100.0	97.2	0.5	1.7	0.1	0.5
Drop-out Rate (%)	0.4	0.3	0.0	25.0	n/a	n/a
H.S. Diplomas (#)	139	134	1	4	0	0

Woodbury County

Sioux City Community SD

1221 Pierce St • Sioux City, IA 51105
(712) 279-6667 • http://www.sioux-city.k12.ia.us
Grade Span: PK-12; **Agency Type:** 1
Schools: 30
22 Primary; 4 Middle; 4 High; 0 Other Level
29 Regular; 0 Special Education; 0 Vocational; 1 Alternative
0 Magnet; 0 Charter; 13 Title I Eligible; 13 School-wide Title I
Students: 13,846 (51.6% male; 48.4% female)
Individual Education Program: 2,245 (16.2%);
English Language Learner: 2,405 (17.4%); Migrant: 747 (5.4%)
Eligible for Free Lunch Program: 3,978 (28.7%)
Eligible for Reduced-Price Lunch Program: 1,090 (7.9%)
Teachers: 945.0 (14.7 to 1)
Librarians/Media Specialists: 7.5 (1,846.1 to 1)
Guidance Counselors: 26.0 (532.5 to 1)
Current Spending: ($ per student per year):
Total: $6,460; Instruction: $4,487; Support Services: $1,600
Enrollment, Drop-out Rates and Diploma Recipients by Race/Ethnicity

Category	Total	White	Black	Asian	AIAN	Hisp.
Enrollment (%)	100.0	67.7	5.7	3.8	4.6	18.2
Drop-out Rate (%)	6.6	5.5	10.3	1.6	15.0	10.4
H.S. Diplomas (#)	834	678	31	40	15	70

Number of Schools

Rank	Number	District Name	City
1	62	Des Moines ICSD	Des Moines
2	34	Cedar Rapids Community SD	Cedar Rapids
3	31	Davenport Community SD	Davenport
4	30	Sioux City Community SD	Sioux City
5	22	Council Bluffs Community SD	Council Bluffs
5	22	Waterloo Community SD	Waterloo
7	21	Iowa City Community SD	Iowa City
8	18	Dubuque Community SD	Dubuque
9	15	West Des Moines Community SD	West Des Moines
10	12	Burlington Community SD	Burlington
10	12	Muscatine Community SD	Muscatine
10	12	Ottumwa Community SD	Ottumwa
13	10	Ames Community SD	Ames
13	10	Centerville Community SD	Centerville
13	10	Clinton Community SD	Clinton
13	10	Fort Dodge Community SD	Fort Dodge
13	10	Mason City Community SD	Mason City
13	10	Southeast Polk Community SD	Runnells
19	9	Ankeny Community SD	Ankeny
19	9	Boone Community SD	Boone
19	9	Cedar Falls Community SD	Cedar Falls
19	9	Marshalltown Community SD	Marshalltown
19	9	Western Dubuque Community SD	Farley
24	8	Bettendorf Community SD	Bettendorf
24	8	Newton Community SD	Newton
24	8	Oskaloosa Community SD	Oskaloosa
24	8	Urbandale Community SD	Urbandale
28	7	Johnston Community SD	Johnston
28	7	Keokuk Community SD	Keokuk
28	7	Linn-Mar Community SD	Marion
28	7	North Scott Community SD	Eldridge
28	7	Waverly-Shell Rock Community SD	Waverly
33	6	Benton Community SD	Van Horne
33	6	College Community SD	Cedar Rapids
33	6	Fairfield Community SD	Fairfield
33	6	Fort Madison Community SD	Fort Madison
33	6	Glenwood Community SD	Glenwood
33	6	Indianola Community SD	Indianola
33	6	Knoxville Community SD	Knoxville
33	6	Le Mars Community SD	Le Mars
33	6	Mount Pleasant Community SD	Mount Pleasant
33	6	Pleasant Valley Community SD	Pleasant Valley
33	6	Spencer Community SD	Spencer
33	6	Storm Lake Community SD	Storm Lake
45	5	Allamakee Community SD	Waukon
45	5	Carroll Community SD	Carroll
45	5	Charles City Community SD	Charles City
45	5	Grinnell-Newburg Community SD	Grinnell
45	5	Harlan Community SD	Harlan
45	5	Independence Community SD	Independence
45	5	Lewis Central Community SD	Council Bluffs
45	5	Marion Independent SD	Marion
45	5	Norwalk Community SD	Norwalk
45	5	Pella Community SD	Pella
45	5	South Tama County Community SD	Tama
45	5	Vinton-Shellsburg Community SD	Vinton
45	5	Washington Community SD	Washington
45	5	Waukee Community SD	Waukee
45	5	Webster City Community SD	Webster City
60	4	Atlantic Community SD	Atlantic
60	4	Central Clinton Community SD	De Witt
60	4	Dallas Center-Grimes Community SD	Dallas Center
60	4	Decorah Community SD	Decorah
60	4	Maquoketa Community SD	Maquoketa
60	4	West Delaware County Community SD	Manchester
60	4	Winterset Community SD	Winterset
67	3	Denison Community SD	Denison
67	3	Perry Community SD	Perry

Number of Teachers

Rank	Number	District Name	City
1	2,341	Des Moines ICSD	Des Moines
2	1,097	Davenport Community SD	Davenport
3	1,080	Cedar Rapids Community SD	Cedar Rapids
4	945	Sioux City Community SD	Sioux City
5	699	Iowa City Community SD	Iowa City
6	697	Waterloo Community SD	Waterloo
7	660	Council Bluffs Community SD	Council Bluffs
8	636	Dubuque Community SD	Dubuque
9	545	West Des Moines Community SD	West Des Moines
10	377	Muscatine Community SD	Muscatine
11	345	Ankeny Community SD	Ankeny
12	341	Burlington Community SD	Burlington
13	322	Ottumwa Community SD	Ottumwa
14	317	Marshalltown Community SD	Marshalltown
15	313	Clinton Community SD	Clinton
16	311	Fort Dodge Community SD	Fort Dodge
17	308	Ames Community SD	Ames
18	302	Linn-Mar Community SD	Marion
19	301	Southeast Polk Community SD	Runnells
20	300	Cedar Falls Community SD	Cedar Falls
21	287	Mason City Community SD	Mason City
22	283	Johnston Community SD	Johnston
23	262	Bettendorf Community SD	Bettendorf
24	231	Newton Community SD	Newton
25	229	College Community SD	Cedar Rapids
26	206	Waukee Community SD	Waukee
27	203	Urbandale Community SD	Urbandale
28	203	Indianola Community SD	Indianola
29	197	Pleasant Valley Community SD	Pleasant Valley
30	194	North Scott Community SD	Eldridge
31	186	Western Dubuque Community SD	Farley
32	172	Lewis Central Community SD	Council Bluffs
33	159	Fort Madison Community SD	Fort Madison
34	156	Boone Community SD	Boone
35	153	Norwalk Community SD	Norwalk
36	152	Oskaloosa Community SD	Oskaloosa
37	149	Keokuk Community SD	Keokuk
38	148	Le Mars Community SD	Le Mars
39	144	Mount Pleasant Community SD	Mount Pleasant
40	141	Spencer Community SD	Spencer
41	141	Marion Independent SD	Marion
42	140	Glenwood Community SD	Glenwood
43	138	Storm Lake Community SD	Storm Lake
44	137	Fairfield Community SD	Fairfield
45	136	Perry Community SD	Perry
46	136	Vinton-Shellsburg Community SD	Vinton
47	135	Knoxville Community SD	Knoxville
48	134	Centerville Community SD	Centerville
49	133	Maquoketa Community SD	Maquoketa
50	131	Grinnell-Newburg Community SD	Grinnell
51	129	Pella Community SD	Pella
52	126	Washington Community SD	Washington
53	125	Charles City Community SD	Charles City
54	123	Central Clinton Community SD	De Witt
55	119	West Delaware County Community SD	Manchester
56	117	Waverly-Shell Rock Community SD	Waverly
57	117	Decorah Community SD	Decorah
58	116	Webster City Community SD	Webster City
59	116	South Tama County Community SD	Tama
60	115	Carroll Community SD	Carroll
61	114	Independence Community SD	Independence
62	113	Denison Community SD	Denison
63	110	Benton Community SD	Van Horne
64	108	Atlantic Community SD	Atlantic
64	108	Winterset Community SD	Winterset
66	108	Dallas Center-Grimes Community SD	Dallas Center
67	100	Harlan Community SD	Harlan
68	94	Allamakee Community SD	Waukon

Number of Students

Rank	Number	District Name	City
1	31,553	Des Moines ICSD	Des Moines
2	17,528	Cedar Rapids Community SD	Cedar Rapids
3	16,544	Davenport Community SD	Davenport
4	13,846	Sioux City Community SD	Sioux City
5	10,740	Iowa City Community SD	Iowa City
6	10,402	Waterloo Community SD	Waterloo
7	9,949	Dubuque Community SD	Dubuque
8	9,364	Council Bluffs Community SD	Council Bluffs
9	8,749	West Des Moines Community SD	West Des Moines
10	6,056	Ankeny Community SD	Ankeny
11	5,453	Muscatine Community SD	Muscatine
12	4,939	Marshalltown Community SD	Marshalltown
13	4,895	Ottumwa Community SD	Ottumwa
14	4,716	Linn-Mar Community SD	Marion
15	4,700	Southeast Polk Community SD	Runnells
16	4,658	Ames Community SD	Ames
17	4,535	Burlington Community SD	Burlington
18	4,517	Johnston Community SD	Johnston
19	4,412	Mason City Community SD	Mason City
20	4,409	Clinton Community SD	Clinton
21	4,371	Bettendorf Community SD	Bettendorf
22	4,303	Cedar Falls Community SD	Cedar Falls
23	4,192	Fort Dodge Community SD	Fort Dodge
24	3,624	College Community SD	Cedar Rapids
25	3,405	Newton Community SD	Newton
26	3,345	Urbandale Community SD	Urbandale
27	3,172	Indianola Community SD	Indianola
28	3,158	Pleasant Valley Community SD	Pleasant Valley
29	3,095	Waukee Community SD	Waukee
30	2,957	North Scott Community SD	Eldridge
31	2,698	Lewis Central Community SD	Council Bluffs
32	2,639	Western Dubuque Community SD	Farley
33	2,540	Oskaloosa Community SD	Oskaloosa
34	2,475	Fort Madison Community SD	Fort Madison
35	2,320	Boone Community SD	Boone
36	2,252	Le Mars Community SD	Le Mars
37	2,237	Keokuk Community SD	Keokuk
38	2,173	Norwalk Community SD	Norwalk
39	2,154	Mount Pleasant Community SD	Mount Pleasant
40	2,140	Pella Community SD	Pella
41	2,097	Spencer Community SD	Spencer
42	2,050	Knoxville Community SD	Knoxville
43	2,032	Glenwood Community SD	Glenwood
44	2,011	Waverly-Shell Rock Community SD	Waverly
45	2,001	Storm Lake Community SD	Storm Lake
46	1,963	Fairfield Community SD	Fairfield
47	1,929	Marion Independent SD	Marion
48	1,796	Vinton-Shellsburg Community SD	Vinton
49	1,777	Denison Community SD	Denison
49	1,777	Webster City Community SD	Webster City
51	1,771	Perry Community SD	Perry
52	1,765	Carroll Community SD	Carroll
53	1,761	West Delaware County Community SD	Manchester
54	1,737	Grinnell-Newburg Community SD	Grinnell
55	1,730	Washington Community SD	Washington
56	1,726	Charles City Community SD	Charles City
57	1,724	Decorah Community SD	Decorah
58	1,669	Maquoketa Community SD	Maquoketa
59	1,663	South Tama County Community SD	Tama
60	1,642	Central Clinton Community SD	De Witt
61	1,639	Harlan Community SD	Harlan
62	1,603	Winterset Community SD	Winterset
63	1,590	Benton Community SD	Van Horne
64	1,589	Dallas Center-Grimes Community SD	Dallas Center
65	1,579	Atlantic Community SD	Atlantic
66	1,573	Centerville Community SD	Centerville
67	1,535	Allamakee Community SD	Waukon
68	1,530	Independence Community SD	Independence

Male Students

Rank	Percent	District Name	City
1	54.1	Glenwood Community SD	Glenwood
2	53.3	Atlantic Community SD	Atlantic
3	53.2	Perry Community SD	Perry
4	53.0	Muscatine Community SD	Muscatine
4	53.0	South Tama County Community SD	Tama
6	52.9	Ames Community SD	Ames
7	52.8	Central Clinton Community SD	De Witt
8	52.7	Knoxville Community SD	Knoxville
9	52.6	Dallas Center-Grimes Community SD	Dallas Center
9	52.6	Johnston Community SD	Johnston
11	52.5	Iowa City Community SD	Iowa City
12	52.3	Denison Community SD	Denison
12	52.3	Western Dubuque Community SD	Farley
14	52.2	Marshalltown Community SD	Marshalltown
14	52.2	West Des Moines Community SD	West Des Moines
16	52.1	Cedar Falls Community SD	Cedar Falls
16	52.1	Charles City Community SD	Charles City
16	52.1	College Community SD	Cedar Rapids
16	52.1	North Scott Community SD	Eldridge
20	52.0	Grinnell-Newburg Community SD	Grinnell
20	52.0	Oskaloosa Community SD	Oskaloosa
22	51.9	Norwalk Community SD	Norwalk
23	51.8	Maquoketa Community SD	Maquoketa
23	51.8	Waverly-Shell Rock Community SD	Waverly
25	51.7	Des Moines ICSD	Des Moines
25	51.7	Fort Madison Community SD	Fort Madison
25	51.7	Marion Independent SD	Marion
25	51.7	Waukee Community SD	Waukee
29	51.6	Keokuk Community SD	Keokuk
29	51.6	Le Mars Community SD	Le Mars
29	51.6	Sioux City Community SD	Sioux City
29	51.6	Vinton-Shellsburg Community SD	Vinton
29	51.6	Waterloo Community SD	Waterloo
34	51.5	Clinton Community SD	Clinton
34	51.5	Davenport Community SD	Davenport
34	51.5	Dubuque Community SD	Dubuque
34	51.5	Urbandale Community SD	Urbandale
38	51.4	Benton Community SD	Van Horne
38	51.4	Storm Lake Community SD	Storm Lake
40	51.2	Bettendorf Community SD	Bettendorf
40	51.2	Burlington Community SD	Burlington
40	51.2	Fort Dodge Community SD	Fort Dodge
40	51.2	Newton Community SD	Newton
44	51.1	Cedar Rapids Community SD	Cedar Rapids
44	51.1	Pleasant Valley Community SD	Pleasant Valley
44	51.1	Winterset Community SD	Winterset
47	51.0	Harlan Community SD	Harlan
47	51.0	Linn-Mar Community SD	Marion
49	50.9	Council Bluffs Community SD	Council Bluffs
49	50.9	Ottumwa Community SD	Ottumwa
49	50.9	Southeast Polk Community SD	Runnells
49	50.9	Washington Community SD	Washington
53	50.8	Lewis Central Community SD	Council Bluffs
54	50.7	Ankeny Community SD	Ankeny
55	50.5	Boone Community SD	Boone
56	50.3	Indianola Community SD	Indianola
56	50.3	Mason City Community SD	Mason City

Rank	Percent	District Name	City
58	50.2	Decorah Community SD	Decorah
58	50.2	Spencer Community SD	Spencer
60	50.1	Fairfield Community SD	Fairfield
60	50.1	Webster City Community SD	Webster City
62	49.7	Pella Community SD	Pella
63	49.6	West Delaware County Community SD	Manchester
64	49.3	Centerville Community SD	Centerville
65	49.2	Mount Pleasant Community SD	Mount Pleasant
66	49.0	Independence Community SD	Independence
67	48.8	Carroll Community SD	Carroll
68	48.7	Allamakee Community SD	Waukon

Female Students

Rank	Percent	District Name	City
1	51.3	Allamakee Community SD	Waukon
2	51.2	Carroll Community SD	Carroll
3	51.0	Independence Community SD	Independence
4	50.8	Mount Pleasant Community SD	Mount Pleasant
5	50.7	Centerville Community SD	Centerville
6	50.4	West Delaware County Community SD	Manchester
7	50.3	Pella Community SD	Pella
8	49.9	Fairfield Community SD	Fairfield
8	49.9	Webster City Community SD	Webster City
10	49.8	Decorah Community SD	Decorah
10	49.8	Spencer Community SD	Spencer
12	49.7	Indianola Community SD	Indianola
12	49.7	Mason City Community SD	Mason City
14	49.5	Boone Community SD	Boone
15	49.3	Ankeny Community SD	Ankeny
16	49.2	Lewis Central Community SD	Council Bluffs
17	49.1	Council Bluffs Community SD	Council Bluffs
17	49.1	Ottumwa Community SD	Ottumwa
17	49.1	Southeast Polk Community SD	Runnells
17	49.1	Washington Community SD	Washington
21	49.0	Harlan Community SD	Harlan
21	49.0	Linn-Mar Community SD	Marion
23	48.9	Cedar Rapids Community SD	Cedar Rapids
23	48.9	Pleasant Valley Community SD	Pleasant Valley
23	48.9	Winterset Community SD	Winterset
26	48.8	Bettendorf Community SD	Bettendorf
26	48.8	Burlington Community SD	Burlington
26	48.8	Fort Dodge Community SD	Fort Dodge
26	48.8	Newton Community SD	Newton
30	48.6	Benton Community SD	Van Horne
30	48.6	Storm Lake Community SD	Storm Lake
32	48.5	Clinton Community SD	Clinton
32	48.5	Davenport Community SD	Davenport
32	48.5	Dubuque Community SD	Dubuque
32	48.5	Urbandale Community SD	Urbandale
36	48.4	Keokuk Community SD	Keokuk
36	48.4	Le Mars Community SD	Le Mars
36	48.4	Sioux City Community SD	Sioux City
36	48.4	Vinton-Shellsburg Community SD	Vinton
36	48.4	Waterloo Community SD	Waterloo
41	48.3	Des Moines ICSD	Des Moines
41	48.3	Fort Madison Community SD	Fort Madison
41	48.3	Marion Independent SD	Marion
41	48.3	Waukee Community SD	Waukee
45	48.2	Maquoketa Community SD	Maquoketa
45	48.2	Waverly-Shell Rock Community SD	Waverly
47	48.1	Norwalk Community SD	Norwalk
48	48.0	Grinnell-Newburg Community SD	Grinnell
48	48.0	Oskaloosa Community SD	Oskaloosa
50	47.9	Cedar Falls Community SD	Cedar Falls
50	47.9	Charles City Community SD	Charles City
50	47.9	College Community SD	Cedar Rapids
50	47.9	North Scott Community SD	Eldridge
54	47.8	Marshalltown Community SD	Marshalltown
54	47.8	West Des Moines Community SD	West Des Moines
56	47.7	Denison Community SD	Denison
56	47.7	Western Dubuque Community SD	Farley
58	47.5	Iowa City Community SD	Iowa City
59	47.4	Dallas Center-Grimes Community SD	Dallas Center
59	47.4	Johnston Community SD	Johnston
61	47.3	Knoxville Community SD	Knoxville
62	47.2	Central Clinton Community SD	De Witt
63	47.1	Ames Community SD	Ames
64	47.0	Muscatine Community SD	Muscatine
64	47.0	South Tama County Community SD	Tama
66	46.8	Perry Community SD	Perry
67	46.7	Atlantic Community SD	Atlantic
68	45.9	Glenwood Community SD	Glenwood

Individual Education Program Students

Rank	Percent	District Name	City
1	22.4	Centerville Community SD	Centerville
2	22.2	Burlington Community SD	Burlington
3	20.6	Mason City Community SD	Mason City
4	19.5	Cedar Rapids Community SD	Cedar Rapids
4	19.5	Dubuque Community SD	Dubuque
6	19.1	Clinton Community SD	Clinton
7	19.0	Council Bluffs Community SD	Council Bluffs
7	19.0	Fort Dodge Community SD	Fort Dodge
9	18.8	Waterloo Community SD	Waterloo
10	18.6	Charles City Community SD	Charles City
10	18.6	Fort Madison Community SD	Fort Madison
10	18.6	Western Dubuque Community SD	Farley
13	18.0	Ottumwa Community SD	Ottumwa
14	17.8	Des Moines ICSD	Des Moines
15	17.3	Maquoketa Community SD	Maquoketa
16	17.1	Muscatine Community SD	Muscatine
17	17.0	Benton Community SD	Van Horne
17	17.0	Keokuk Community SD	Keokuk
17	17.0	Washington Community SD	Washington
20	16.9	Cedar Falls Community SD	Cedar Falls
20	16.9	Decorah Community SD	Decorah
20	16.9	Independence Community SD	Independence
23	16.7	Marshalltown Community SD	Marshalltown
24	16.5	South Tama County Community SD	Tama
25	16.2	Sioux City Community SD	Sioux City
26	15.8	Vinton-Shellsburg Community SD	Vinton
27	15.6	Newton Community SD	Newton
28	15.5	Grinnell-Newburg Community SD	Grinnell
28	15.5	Norwalk Community SD	Norwalk
28	15.5	Perry Community SD	Perry
31	15.4	Allamakee Community SD	Waukon
32	15.3	Central Clinton Community SD	De Witt
33	15.1	Boone Community SD	Boone
34	15.0	Marion Independent SD	Marion
35	14.8	Glenwood Community SD	Glenwood
35	14.8	Knoxville Community SD	Knoxville
37	14.6	Atlantic Community SD	Atlantic
38	14.5	Harlan Community SD	Harlan
39	14.4	Iowa City Community SD	Iowa City
40	13.9	Spencer Community SD	Spencer
41	13.8	Winterset Community SD	Winterset
42	13.7	Carroll Community SD	Carroll
43	13.6	Davenport Community SD	Davenport
43	13.6	Oskaloosa Community SD	Oskaloosa
45	13.4	Fairfield Community SD	Fairfield
45	13.4	Webster City Community SD	Webster City
47	13.3	Southeast Polk Community SD	Runnells
48	13.1	Lewis Central Community SD	Council Bluffs
49	12.9	Ames Community SD	Ames
49	12.9	Denison Community SD	Denison
49	12.9	Storm Lake Community SD	Storm Lake
52	12.6	Indianola Community SD	Indianola
53	12.4	College Community SD	Cedar Rapids
53	12.4	Waverly-Shell Rock Community SD	Waverly
55	12.3	Linn-Mar Community SD	Marion
55	12.3	Mount Pleasant Community SD	Mount Pleasant
57	12.0	North Scott Community SD	Eldridge
58	11.8	West Delaware County Community SD	Manchester
59	10.7	West Des Moines Community SD	West Des Moines
60	10.0	Waukee Community SD	Waukee
61	9.8	Urbandale Community SD	Urbandale
62	9.7	Ankeny Community SD	Ankeny
62	9.7	Pella Community SD	Pella
64	9.6	Johnston Community SD	Johnston
64	9.6	Le Mars Community SD	Le Mars
66	9.3	Bettendorf Community SD	Bettendorf
66	9.3	Dallas Center-Grimes Community SD	Dallas Center
68	8.5	Pleasant Valley Community SD	Pleasant Valley

English Language Learner Students

Rank	Percent	District Name	City
1	44.9	Storm Lake Community SD	Storm Lake
2	18.2	Marshalltown Community SD	Marshalltown
3	17.4	Sioux City Community SD	Sioux City
4	16.0	Denison Community SD	Denison
5	14.8	Perry Community SD	Perry
6	10.0	Des Moines ICSD	Des Moines
6	10.0	Waterloo Community SD	Waterloo
8	8.2	Washington Community SD	Washington
9	6.2	Urbandale Community SD	Urbandale
10	6.1	South Tama County Community SD	Tama
11	4.9	Muscatine Community SD	Muscatine
12	4.8	Ottumwa Community SD	Ottumwa
13	4.1	Webster City Community SD	Webster City
14	3.8	Ames Community SD	Ames
15	2.9	Mount Pleasant Community SD	Mount Pleasant
16	2.4	West Des Moines Community SD	West Des Moines
17	2.2	Davenport Community SD	Davenport
18	1.9	Iowa City Community SD	Iowa City
19	1.5	Johnston Community SD	Johnston
20	1.4	Pella Community SD	Pella
21	1.2	Fairfield Community SD	Fairfield
21	1.2	Waukee Community SD	Waukee
23	1.1	Lewis Central Community SD	Council Bluffs
24	1.0	Carroll Community SD	Carroll
24	1.0	Council Bluffs Community SD	Council Bluffs
26	0.9	Ankeny Community SD	Ankeny
26	0.9	Bettendorf Community SD	Bettendorf
26	0.9	Cedar Rapids Community SD	Cedar Rapids
26	0.9	Charles City Community SD	Charles City
26	0.9	Le Mars Community SD	Le Mars
31	0.8	Fort Dodge Community SD	Fort Dodge
31	0.8	Spencer Community SD	Spencer
33	0.7	Cedar Falls Community SD	Cedar Falls
34	0.5	Grinnell-Newburg Community SD	Grinnell
34	0.5	Norwalk Community SD	Norwalk
34	0.5	Southeast Polk Community SD	Runnells
37	0.4	Dubuque Community SD	Dubuque
37	0.4	Harlan Community SD	Harlan
37	0.4	Oskaloosa Community SD	Oskaloosa
40	0.3	Burlington Community SD	Burlington
40	0.3	Knoxville Community SD	Knoxville
42	0.2	Benton Community SD	Van Horne
42	0.2	Boone Community SD	Boone
42	0.2	Indianola Community SD	Indianola
42	0.2	Maquoketa Community SD	Maquoketa
42	0.2	Mason City Community SD	Mason City
42	0.2	Newton Community SD	Newton
42	0.2	Western Dubuque Community SD	Farley
49	0.1	Allamakee Community SD	Waukon
49	0.1	Clinton Community SD	Clinton
49	0.1	Pleasant Valley Community SD	Pleasant Valley
49	0.1	Vinton-Shellsburg Community SD	Vinton
53	0.0	Fort Madison Community SD	Fort Madison
54	0.0	Atlantic Community SD	Atlantic
54	0.0	Centerville Community SD	Centerville
54	0.0	Central Clinton Community SD	De Witt
54	0.0	College Community SD	Cedar Rapids
54	0.0	Dallas Center-Grimes Community SD	Dallas Center
54	0.0	Decorah Community SD	Decorah
54	0.0	Glenwood Community SD	Glenwood
54	0.0	Independence Community SD	Independence
54	0.0	Keokuk Community SD	Keokuk
54	0.0	Linn-Mar Community SD	Marion
54	0.0	Marion Independent SD	Marion
54	0.0	North Scott Community SD	Eldridge
54	0.0	Waverly-Shell Rock Community SD	Waverly
54	0.0	West Delaware County Community SD	Manchester
54	0.0	Winterset Community SD	Winterset

Migrant Students

Rank	Percent	District Name	City
1	42.3	Storm Lake Community SD	Storm Lake
2	31.5	Denison Community SD	Denison
3	18.5	Perry Community SD	Perry
4	6.8	Ottumwa Community SD	Ottumwa
5	5.4	Sioux City Community SD	Sioux City
6	4.4	Marshalltown Community SD	Marshalltown
7	3.5	Waterloo Community SD	Waterloo
8	2.1	Muscatine Community SD	Muscatine
9	0.0	Des Moines ICSD	Des Moines
10	0.0	Allamakee Community SD	Waukon
10	0.0	Ames Community SD	Ames
10	0.0	Ankeny Community SD	Ankeny
10	0.0	Atlantic Community SD	Atlantic
10	0.0	Benton Community SD	Van Horne
10	0.0	Bettendorf Community SD	Bettendorf
10	0.0	Boone Community SD	Boone
10	0.0	Burlington Community SD	Burlington
10	0.0	Carroll Community SD	Carroll
10	0.0	Cedar Falls Community SD	Cedar Falls
10	0.0	Cedar Rapids Community SD	Cedar Rapids
10	0.0	Centerville Community SD	Centerville
10	0.0	Central Clinton Community SD	De Witt
10	0.0	Charles City Community SD	Charles City
10	0.0	Clinton Community SD	Clinton
10	0.0	College Community SD	Cedar Rapids
10	0.0	Council Bluffs Community SD	Council Bluffs
10	0.0	Dallas Center-Grimes Community SD	Dallas Center
10	0.0	Davenport Community SD	Davenport
10	0.0	Decorah Community SD	Decorah
10	0.0	Dubuque Community SD	Dubuque
10	0.0	Fairfield Community SD	Fairfield
10	0.0	Fort Dodge Community SD	Fort Dodge
10	0.0	Fort Madison Community SD	Fort Madison
10	0.0	Glenwood Community SD	Glenwood
10	0.0	Grinnell-Newburg Community SD	Grinnell
10	0.0	Harlan Community SD	Harlan
10	0.0	Independence Community SD	Independence
10	0.0	Indianola Community SD	Indianola
10	0.0	Iowa City Community SD	Iowa City
10	0.0	Johnston Community SD	Johnston
10	0.0	Keokuk Community SD	Keokuk
10	0.0	Knoxville Community SD	Knoxville
10	0.0	Le Mars Community SD	Le Mars
10	0.0	Lewis Central Community SD	Council Bluffs

Rank	Percent	District Name	City
10	0.0	Linn-Mar Community SD	Marion
10	0.0	Maquoketa Community SD	Maquoketa
10	0.0	Marion Independent SD	Marion
10	0.0	Mason City Community SD	Mason City
10	0.0	Mount Pleasant Community SD	Mount Pleasant
10	0.0	Newton Community SD	Newton
10	0.0	North Scott Community SD	Eldridge
10	0.0	Norwalk Community SD	Norwalk
10	0.0	Oskaloosa Community SD	Oskaloosa
10	0.0	Pella Community SD	Pella
10	0.0	Pleasant Valley Community SD	Pleasant Valley
10	0.0	South Tama County Community SD	Tama
10	0.0	Southeast Polk Community SD	Runnells
10	0.0	Spencer Community SD	Spencer
10	0.0	Urbandale Community SD	Urbandale
10	0.0	Vinton-Shellsburg Community SD	Vinton
10	0.0	Washington Community SD	Washington
10	0.0	Waukee Community SD	Waukee
10	0.0	Waverly-Shell Rock Community SD	Waverly
10	0.0	Webster City Community SD	Webster City
10	0.0	West Delaware County Community SD	Manchester
10	0.0	West Des Moines Community SD	West Des Moines
10	0.0	Western Dubuque Community SD	Farley
10	0.0	Winterset Community SD	Winterset

Students Eligible for Free Lunch

Rank	Percent	District Name	City
1	43.9	Keokuk Community SD	Keokuk
2	41.8	Waterloo Community SD	Waterloo
3	38.8	Ottumwa Community SD	Ottumwa
4	37.3	Des Moines ICSD	Des Moines
5	36.0	Davenport Community SD	Davenport
6	35.2	Perry Community SD	Perry
7	35.1	Denison Community SD	Denison
8	34.5	Centerville Community SD	Centerville
9	33.7	Storm Lake Community SD	Storm Lake
10	32.9	Marshalltown Community SD	Marshalltown
11	32.3	Council Bluffs Community SD	Council Bluffs
12	31.2	Clinton Community SD	Clinton
13	30.2	Burlington Community SD	Burlington
14	29.3	Charles City Community SD	Charles City
15	28.7	Sioux City Community SD	Sioux City
16	28.5	Fort Dodge Community SD	Fort Dodge
17	28.0	Maquoketa Community SD	Maquoketa
18	27.1	South Tama County Community SD	Tama
19	26.1	Fort Madison Community SD	Fort Madison
20	23.8	Cedar Rapids Community SD	Cedar Rapids
20	23.8	Vinton-Shellsburg Community SD	Vinton
22	23.5	Muscatine Community SD	Muscatine
23	23.4	Oskaloosa Community SD	Oskaloosa
24	23.3	Mason City Community SD	Mason City
25	23.1	Atlantic Community SD	Atlantic
26	22.1	Allamakee Community SD	Waukon
27	21.4	Dubuque Community SD	Dubuque
28	21.2	Independence Community SD	Independence
29	21.1	Lewis Central Community SD	Council Bluffs
30	20.4	Grinnell-Newburg Community SD	Grinnell
31	19.8	Washington Community SD	Washington
32	19.4	Glenwood Community SD	Glenwood
33	19.3	Harlan Community SD	Harlan
34	19.2	Knoxville Community SD	Knoxville
35	18.8	Spencer Community SD	Spencer
36	18.5	Boone Community SD	Boone
37	18.0	Fairfield Community SD	Fairfield
38	17.3	Newton Community SD	Newton
39	16.4	Mount Pleasant Community SD	Mount Pleasant
40	16.2	Webster City Community SD	Webster City
41	15.7	College Community SD	Cedar Rapids
42	15.3	Carroll Community SD	Carroll
43	14.2	Iowa City Community SD	Iowa City
43	14.2	Winterset Community SD	Winterset
45	14.0	West Delaware County Community SD	Manchester
46	13.7	Central Clinton Community SD	De Witt
47	13.6	Western Dubuque Community SD	Farley
48	13.4	Cedar Falls Community SD	Cedar Falls
49	12.2	Waverly-Shell Rock Community SD	Waverly
50	11.6	Indianola Community SD	Indianola
51	11.4	North Scott Community SD	Eldridge
52	11.1	Marion Independent SD	Marion
53	10.7	Le Mars Community SD	Le Mars
54	10.5	Ames Community SD	Ames
54	10.5	Decorah Community SD	Decorah
56	10.4	Southeast Polk Community SD	Runnells
57	10.0	Bettendorf Community SD	Bettendorf
58	9.8	Pella Community SD	Pella
59	8.5	Benton Community SD	Van Horne
60	7.6	West Des Moines Community SD	West Des Moines
61	6.2	Dallas Center-Grimes Community SD	Dallas Center
62	6.1	Pleasant Valley Community SD	Pleasant Valley
63	6.0	Linn-Mar Community SD	Marion
63	6.0	Norwalk Community SD	Norwalk
65	5.9	Waukee Community SD	Waukee
66	5.7	Urbandale Community SD	Urbandale
67	3.9	Johnston Community SD	Johnston
68	3.6	Ankeny Community SD	Ankeny

Students Eligible for Reduced-Price Lunch

Rank	Percent	District Name	City
1	12.8	Perry Community SD	Perry
2	11.7	Waterloo Community SD	Waterloo
3	11.5	Storm Lake Community SD	Storm Lake
4	11.0	Keokuk Community SD	Keokuk
5	10.9	Des Moines ICSD	Des Moines
6	10.6	Denison Community SD	Denison
6	10.6	South Tama County Community SD	Tama
8	10.4	Allamakee Community SD	Waukon
9	9.6	Atlantic Community SD	Atlantic
10	9.3	Maquoketa Community SD	Maquoketa
11	9.0	Centerville Community SD	Centerville
11	9.0	Independence Community SD	Independence
13	8.9	Dubuque Community SD	Dubuque
13	8.9	Webster City Community SD	Webster City
15	8.8	Spencer Community SD	Spencer
16	8.7	Harlan Community SD	Harlan
17	8.6	Marshalltown Community SD	Marshalltown
18	8.5	Council Bluffs Community SD	Council Bluffs
19	8.4	Davenport Community SD	Davenport
20	8.3	Charles City Community SD	Charles City
20	8.3	Fort Dodge Community SD	Fort Dodge
22	8.1	Carroll Community SD	Carroll
22	8.1	Clinton Community SD	Clinton
24	8.0	Mason City Community SD	Mason City
24	8.0	Western Dubuque Community SD	Farley
26	7.9	Sioux City Community SD	Sioux City
27	7.5	Cedar Rapids Community SD	Cedar Rapids
28	7.4	Lewis Central Community SD	Council Bluffs
29	7.3	Washington Community SD	Washington
30	7.2	Boone Community SD	Boone
30	7.2	Fort Madison Community SD	Fort Madison
30	7.2	Ottumwa Community SD	Ottumwa
33	7.0	Mount Pleasant Community SD	Mount Pleasant
33	7.0	Oskaloosa Community SD	Oskaloosa
35	6.9	Knoxville Community SD	Knoxville
36	6.8	Glenwood Community SD	Glenwood
36	6.8	West Delaware County Community SD	Manchester
38	6.5	Burlington Community SD	Burlington
38	6.5	Fairfield Community SD	Fairfield
38	6.5	Muscatine Community SD	Muscatine
41	6.4	Winterset Community SD	Winterset
42	6.3	Central Clinton Community SD	De Witt
43	6.1	Marion Independent SD	Marion
44	6.0	Vinton-Shellsburg Community SD	Vinton
45	5.9	Le Mars Community SD	Le Mars
46	5.7	College Community SD	Cedar Rapids
46	5.7	Decorah Community SD	Decorah
48	5.6	Indianola Community SD	Indianola
49	5.2	Newton Community SD	Newton
50	5.0	Benton Community SD	Van Horne
50	5.0	Grinnell-Newburg Community SD	Grinnell
52	4.9	Bettendorf Community SD	Bettendorf
53	4.7	North Scott Community SD	Eldridge
54	4.2	Iowa City Community SD	Iowa City
55	4.1	Pella Community SD	Pella
55	4.1	Urbandale Community SD	Urbandale
57	4.0	Southeast Polk Community SD	Runnells
58	3.8	Norwalk Community SD	Norwalk
59	3.6	West Des Moines Community SD	West Des Moines
60	3.3	Ames Community SD	Ames
60	3.3	Waverly-Shell Rock Community SD	Waverly
62	3.2	Cedar Falls Community SD	Cedar Falls
63	3.0	Linn-Mar Community SD	Marion
64	2.8	Dallas Center-Grimes Community SD	Dallas Center
65	2.6	Waukee Community SD	Waukee
66	2.2	Ankeny Community SD	Ankeny
67	2.0	Pleasant Valley Community SD	Pleasant Valley
68	1.1	Johnston Community SD	Johnston

Student/Teacher Ratio

Rank	Ratio	District Name	City
1	17.5	Ankeny Community SD	Ankeny
2	17.1	Waverly-Shell Rock Community SD	Waverly
3	16.7	Bettendorf Community SD	Bettendorf
3	16.7	Oskaloosa Community SD	Oskaloosa
5	16.5	Pella Community SD	Pella
6	16.4	Urbandale Community SD	Urbandale
7	16.3	Allamakee Community SD	Waukon
7	16.3	Harlan Community SD	Harlan
9	16.2	Cedar Rapids Community SD	Cedar Rapids
10	16.0	Pleasant Valley Community SD	Pleasant Valley
10	16.0	West Des Moines Community SD	West Des Moines
12	15.9	Johnston Community SD	Johnston
13	15.8	College Community SD	Cedar Rapids
14	15.7	Denison Community SD	Denison
14	15.7	Lewis Central Community SD	Council Bluffs
16	15.6	Dubuque Community SD	Dubuque
16	15.6	Indianola Community SD	Indianola
16	15.6	Linn-Mar Community SD	Marion
16	15.6	Marshalltown Community SD	Marshalltown
16	15.6	Southeast Polk Community SD	Runnells
21	15.5	Fort Madison Community SD	Fort Madison
22	15.4	Mason City Community SD	Mason City
23	15.3	Carroll Community SD	Carroll
23	15.3	Iowa City Community SD	Iowa City
23	15.3	Webster City Community SD	Webster City
26	15.2	Knoxville Community SD	Knoxville
26	15.2	Le Mars Community SD	Le Mars
26	15.2	North Scott Community SD	Eldridge
26	15.2	Ottumwa Community SD	Ottumwa
30	15.1	Ames Community SD	Ames
30	15.1	Davenport Community SD	Davenport
32	15.0	Keokuk Community SD	Keokuk
32	15.0	Waukee Community SD	Waukee
34	14.9	Mount Pleasant Community SD	Mount Pleasant
34	14.9	Waterloo Community SD	Waterloo
36	14.8	Boone Community SD	Boone
36	14.8	Spencer Community SD	Spencer
36	14.8	Winterset Community SD	Winterset
39	14.7	Dallas Center-Grimes Community SD	Dallas Center
39	14.7	Decorah Community SD	Decorah
39	14.7	Newton Community SD	Newton
39	14.7	Sioux City Community SD	Sioux City
39	14.7	West Delaware County Community SD	Manchester
44	14.6	Atlantic Community SD	Atlantic
45	14.5	Benton Community SD	Van Horne
45	14.5	Glenwood Community SD	Glenwood
45	14.5	Muscatine Community SD	Muscatine
48	14.4	Storm Lake Community SD	Storm Lake
49	14.3	Cedar Falls Community SD	Cedar Falls
49	14.3	Fairfield Community SD	Fairfield
49	14.3	South Tama County Community SD	Tama
52	14.2	Council Bluffs Community SD	Council Bluffs
52	14.2	Norwalk Community SD	Norwalk
52	14.2	Western Dubuque Community SD	Farley
55	14.1	Clinton Community SD	Clinton
56	13.8	Charles City Community SD	Charles City
57	13.7	Marion Independent SD	Marion
57	13.7	Washington Community SD	Washington
59	13.5	Des Moines ICSD	Des Moines
59	13.5	Fort Dodge Community SD	Fort Dodge
61	13.4	Independence Community SD	Independence
62	13.3	Burlington Community SD	Burlington
62	13.3	Central Clinton Community SD	De Witt
64	13.2	Grinnell-Newburg Community SD	Grinnell
64	13.2	Vinton-Shellsburg Community SD	Vinton
66	13.0	Perry Community SD	Perry
67	12.5	Maquoketa Community SD	Maquoketa
68	11.7	Centerville Community SD	Centerville

Student/Librarian Ratio

Rank	Ratio	District Name	City
1	4,136.0	Davenport Community SD	Davenport
2	2,475.0	Fort Madison Community SD	Fort Madison
3	2,050.0	Knoxville Community SD	Knoxville
4	2,001.0	Storm Lake Community SD	Storm Lake
5	1,846.1	Sioux City Community SD	Sioux City
6	1,603.0	Winterset Community SD	Winterset
7	1,371.9	Des Moines ICSD	Des Moines
8	1,270.0	Oskaloosa Community SD	Oskaloosa
9	1,175.0	Southeast Polk Community SD	Runnells
10	1,170.5	Council Bluffs Community SD	Council Bluffs
11	1,126.0	Le Mars Community SD	Le Mars
12	1,118.5	Keokuk Community SD	Keokuk
13	1,115.0	Urbandale Community SD	Urbandale
14	1,093.6	West Des Moines Community SD	West Des Moines
15	1,077.0	Mount Pleasant Community SD	Mount Pleasant
16	1,057.3	Indianola Community SD	Indianola
17	1,048.5	Spencer Community SD	Spencer
18	1,016.0	Glenwood Community SD	Glenwood
19	1,005.5	Waverly-Shell Rock Community SD	Waverly
20	994.9	Dubuque Community SD	Dubuque
21	981.5	Fairfield Community SD	Fairfield
22	979.0	Ottumwa Community SD	Ottumwa
23	928.0	Boone Community SD	Boone
24	888.5	Webster City Community SD	Webster City
25	885.5	Perry Community SD	Perry
26	882.4	Mason City Community SD	Mason City
27	838.4	Fort Dodge Community SD	Fort Dodge
28	834.5	Maquoketa Community SD	Maquoketa
29	831.5	South Tama County Community SD	Tama
30	795.0	Benton Community SD	Van Horne

31	789.5	Atlantic Community SD	Atlantic
32	779.0	Muscatine Community SD	Muscatine
33	776.3	Ames Community SD	Ames
34	770.9	Lewis Central Community SD	Council Bluffs
35	754.0	Western Dubuque Community SD	Farley
36	752.8	Johnston Community SD	Johnston
37	724.8	College Community SD	Cedar Rapids
38	724.3	Norwalk Community SD	Norwalk
39	713.3	Pella Community SD	Pella
40	681.0	Newton Community SD	Newton
41	673.7	Linn-Mar Community SD	Marion
42	672.9	Ankeny Community SD	Ankeny
43	656.8	Central Clinton Community SD	De Witt
44	647.9	Burlington Community SD	Burlington
45	631.6	Pleasant Valley Community SD	Pleasant Valley
46	629.9	Clinton Community SD	Clinton
47	619.0	Waukee Community SD	Waukee
48	617.4	Marshalltown Community SD	Marshalltown
49	614.7	Cedar Falls Community SD	Cedar Falls
50	614.0	Allamakee Community SD	Waukon
51	604.4	Cedar Rapids Community SD	Cedar Rapids
52	594.4	Waterloo Community SD	Waterloo
53	592.3	Denison Community SD	Denison
54	588.3	Carroll Community SD	Carroll
55	587.0	West Delaware County Community SD	Manchester
56	579.0	Grinnell-Newburg Community SD	Grinnell
57	576.7	Washington Community SD	Washington
58	575.3	Charles City Community SD	Charles City
59	574.7	Decorah Community SD	Decorah
60	551.1	Marion Independent SD	Marion
61	550.8	Iowa City Community SD	Iowa City
62	546.3	Harlan Community SD	Harlan
63	529.7	Dallas Center-Grimes Community SD	Dallas Center
64	524.3	Centerville Community SD	Centerville
65	510.0	Independence Community SD	Independence
66	492.8	North Scott Community SD	Eldridge
67	485.7	Bettendorf Community SD	Bettendorf
68	449.0	Vinton-Shellsburg Community SD	Vinton

Student/Counselor Ratio

Rank	Ratio	District Name	City
1	1,031.7	Waukee Community SD	Waukee
2	885.5	Perry Community SD	Perry
3	786.5	Centerville Community SD	Centerville
4	767.5	Allamakee Community SD	Waukon
5	718.0	Mount Pleasant Community SD	Mount Pleasant
6	645.3	Johnston Community SD	Johnston
7	618.8	Fort Madison Community SD	Fort Madison
8	611.9	Ottumwa Community SD	Ottumwa
9	574.7	Decorah Community SD	Decorah
10	574.6	Waverly-Shell Rock Community SD	Waverly
11	539.6	Lewis Central Community SD	Council Bluffs
12	535.0	Pella Community SD	Pella
13	533.7	Davenport Community SD	Davenport
14	532.5	Sioux City Community SD	Sioux City
15	529.7	Dallas Center-Grimes Community SD	Dallas Center
16	526.3	Atlantic Community SD	Atlantic
17	510.0	Independence Community SD	Independence
18	508.0	Glenwood Community SD	Glenwood
19	500.3	Storm Lake Community SD	Storm Lake
20	477.3	Iowa City Community SD	Iowa City
21	472.9	West Des Moines Community SD	West Des Moines
22	471.6	Linn-Mar Community SD	Marion
23	453.0	College Community SD	Cedar Rapids
24	452.3	Waterloo Community SD	Waterloo
25	447.4	Keokuk Community SD	Keokuk
26	444.3	Denison Community SD	Denison
27	441.2	Mason City Community SD	Mason City
28	439.8	Western Dubuque Community SD	Farley
29	432.6	Ankeny Community SD	Ankeny
30	428.7	Marion Independent SD	Marion
31	419.9	Clinton Community SD	Clinton
32	419.4	Spencer Community SD	Spencer
33	418.1	Urbandale Community SD	Urbandale
34	415.8	South Tama County Community SD	Tama
35	410.5	Central Clinton Community SD	De Witt
36	409.8	Harlan Community SD	Harlan
37	407.6	Cedar Rapids Community SD	Cedar Rapids
38	400.8	Winterset Community SD	Winterset
39	397.5	Benton Community SD	Van Horne
40	395.1	Marshalltown Community SD	Marshalltown
41	394.8	Pleasant Valley Community SD	Pleasant Valley
42	390.2	Dubuque Community SD	Dubuque
43	389.5	Muscatine Community SD	Muscatine
44	386.7	Boone Community SD	Boone
45	375.3	Le Mars Community SD	Le Mars
46	364.3	Bettendorf Community SD	Bettendorf
47	359.2	Vinton-Shellsburg Community SD	Vinton
48	353.0	Carroll Community SD	Carroll
49	352.2	West Delaware County Community SD	Manchester
50	350.6	Des Moines ICSD	Des Moines
51	348.8	Burlington Community SD	Burlington
52	346.0	Washington Community SD	Washington
53	345.2	Charles City Community SD	Charles City
54	333.8	Maquoketa Community SD	Maquoketa
55	328.6	Council Bluffs Community SD	Council Bluffs
56	327.2	Fairfield Community SD	Fairfield
57	322.5	Fort Dodge Community SD	Fort Dodge
58	321.2	Ames Community SD	Ames
59	317.2	Indianola Community SD	Indianola
60	310.4	Norwalk Community SD	Norwalk
61	307.4	Cedar Falls Community SD	Cedar Falls
62	296.2	Webster City Community SD	Webster City
63	295.7	North Scott Community SD	Eldridge
64	293.8	Southeast Polk Community SD	Runnells
65	292.9	Knoxville Community SD	Knoxville
66	289.5	Grinnell-Newburg Community SD	Grinnell
67	283.8	Newton Community SD	Newton
68	254.0	Oskaloosa Community SD	Oskaloosa

Current Spending per Student in FY2001

Rank	Dollars	District Name	City
1	7,443	Ames Community SD	Ames
2	7,407	Des Moines ICSD	Des Moines
3	7,106	Maquoketa Community SD	Maquoketa
4	6,998	Davenport Community SD	Davenport
5	6,943	Fort Dodge Community SD	Fort Dodge
6	6,936	Cedar Rapids Community SD	Cedar Rapids
7	6,904	Grinnell-Newburg Community SD	Grinnell
8	6,879	Storm Lake Community SD	Storm Lake
9	6,861	Charles City Community SD	Charles City
10	6,824	Independence Community SD	Independence
11	6,802	Boone Community SD	Boone
12	6,686	Keokuk Community SD	Keokuk
13	6,680	Centerville Community SD	Centerville
14	6,676	Burlington Community SD	Burlington
15	6,657	Waterloo Community SD	Waterloo
16	6,633	Marshalltown Community SD	Marshalltown
17	6,607	Clinton Community SD	Clinton
18	6,603	Western Dubuque Community SD	Farley
19	6,573	North Scott Community SD	Eldridge
20	6,544	Washington Community SD	Washington
21	6,534	Perry Community SD	Perry
22	6,501	Bettendorf Community SD	Bettendorf
23	6,492	Fairfield Community SD	Fairfield
24	6,461	Glenwood Community SD	Glenwood
25	6,460	Sioux City Community SD	Sioux City
26	6,450	Muscatine Community SD	Muscatine
27	6,437	Iowa City Community SD	Iowa City
28	6,408	Webster City Community SD	Webster City
29	6,399	Decorah Community SD	Decorah
30	6,394	Marion Independent SD	Marion
31	6,386	West Des Moines Community SD	West Des Moines
32	6,383	Cedar Falls Community SD	Cedar Falls
33	6,369	Central Clinton Community SD	De Witt
34	6,359	Vinton-Shellsburg Community SD	Vinton
35	6,331	Denison Community SD	Denison
36	6,327	Dubuque Community SD	Dubuque
37	6,319	Carroll Community SD	Carroll
38	6,275	Mason City Community SD	Mason City
39	6,260	Newton Community SD	Newton
40	6,248	Winterset Community SD	Winterset
41	6,214	Fort Madison Community SD	Fort Madison
42	6,213	Indianola Community SD	Indianola
43	6,197	College Community SD	Cedar Rapids
44	6,179	Lewis Central Community SD	Council Bluffs
45	6,163	Urbandale Community SD	Urbandale
46	6,162	Allamakee Community SD	Waukon
47	6,153	Southeast Polk Community SD	Runnells
48	6,117	Mount Pleasant Community SD	Mount Pleasant
49	6,116	Oskaloosa Community SD	Oskaloosa
50	6,103	Spencer Community SD	Spencer
51	6,049	Benton Community SD	Van Horne
52	6,044	Harlan Community SD	Harlan
53	6,021	South Tama County Community SD	Tama
54	5,991	Pleasant Valley Community SD	Pleasant Valley
55	5,963	Atlantic Community SD	Atlantic
56	5,951	Norwalk Community SD	Norwalk
57	5,943	West Delaware County Community SD	Manchester
58	5,910	Ottumwa Community SD	Ottumwa
59	5,902	Linn-Mar Community SD	Marion
60	5,888	Johnston Community SD	Johnston
61	5,873	Knoxville Community SD	Knoxville
62	5,807	Council Bluffs Community SD	Council Bluffs
63	5,776	Pella Community SD	Pella
64	5,752	Waukee Community SD	Waukee
65	5,723	Ankeny Community SD	Ankeny
66	5,669	Dallas Center-Grimes Community SD	Dallas Center
67	5,578	Waverly-Shell Rock Community SD	Waverly
68	5,506	Le Mars Community SD	Le Mars

Number of Diploma Recipients

Rank	Number	District Name	City
1	1,659	Des Moines ICSD	Des Moines
2	1,013	Cedar Rapids Community SD	Cedar Rapids
3	956	Davenport Community SD	Davenport
4	834	Sioux City Community SD	Sioux City
5	721	Iowa City Community SD	Iowa City
6	702	Dubuque Community SD	Dubuque
7	596	Waterloo Community SD	Waterloo
8	554	West Des Moines Community SD	West Des Moines
9	545	Council Bluffs Community SD	Council Bluffs
10	397	Ames Community SD	Ames
11	386	Ankeny Community SD	Ankeny
12	369	Cedar Falls Community SD	Cedar Falls
13	336	Muscatine Community SD	Muscatine
14	332	Urbandale Community SD	Urbandale
15	326	Clinton Community SD	Clinton
16	322	Southeast Polk Community SD	Runnells
17	315	Mason City Community SD	Mason City
18	310	Marshalltown Community SD	Marshalltown
19	295	Bettendorf Community SD	Bettendorf
20	293	Fort Dodge Community SD	Fort Dodge
21	291	Linn-Mar Community SD	Marion
21	291	Ottumwa Community SD	Ottumwa
23	289	Burlington Community SD	Burlington
24	270	Western Dubuque Community SD	Farley
25	262	Johnston Community SD	Johnston
26	261	Newton Community SD	Newton
27	241	Pleasant Valley Community SD	Pleasant Valley
28	228	College Community SD	Cedar Rapids
29	218	Indianola Community SD	Indianola
30	194	North Scott Community SD	Eldridge
31	191	Boone Community SD	Boone
32	186	Fort Madison Community SD	Fort Madison
33	181	Le Mars Community SD	Le Mars
34	177	Waverly-Shell Rock Community SD	Waverly
35	176	Lewis Central Community SD	Council Bluffs
36	174	Spencer Community SD	Spencer
37	171	Oskaloosa Community SD	Oskaloosa
38	168	West Delaware County Community SD	Manchester
39	163	Mount Pleasant Community SD	Mount Pleasant
40	161	Keokuk Community SD	Keokuk
41	158	Knoxville Community SD	Knoxville
42	153	Harlan Community SD	Harlan
43	147	Carroll Community SD	Carroll
43	147	Glenwood Community SD	Glenwood
45	143	Winterset Community SD	Winterset
46	141	Marion Independent SD	Marion
47	139	Decorah Community SD	Decorah
48	138	Central Clinton Community SD	De Witt
48	138	Webster City Community SD	Webster City
50	137	Pella Community SD	Pella
51	135	Benton Community SD	Van Horne
52	133	Fairfield Community SD	Fairfield
53	130	Waukee Community SD	Waukee
54	129	Norwalk Community SD	Norwalk
55	127	Denison Community SD	Denison
56	124	Allamakee Community SD	Waukon
56	124	Perry Community SD	Perry
58	123	Grinnell-Newburg Community SD	Grinnell
58	123	Vinton-Shellsburg Community SD	Vinton
60	122	Atlantic Community SD	Atlantic
60	122	Independence Community SD	Independence
60	122	Storm Lake Community SD	Storm Lake
63	121	Charles City Community SD	Charles City
64	118	Centerville Community SD	Centerville
65	116	South Tama County Community SD	Tama
66	115	Maquoketa Community SD	Maquoketa
67	90	Dallas Center-Grimes Community SD	Dallas Center
67	90	Washington Community SD	Washington

High School Drop-out Rate

Rank	Percent	District Name	City
1	12.3	Muscatine Community SD	Muscatine
2	7.2	Burlington Community SD	Burlington
3	6.8	Waterloo Community SD	Waterloo
4	6.7	Ottumwa Community SD	Ottumwa
4	6.7	South Tama County Community SD	Tama
6	6.6	Sioux City Community SD	Sioux City
7	6.4	Des Moines ICSD	Des Moines
8	6.3	Clinton Community SD	Clinton
9	5.9	Council Bluffs Community SD	Council Bluffs
10	5.1	Perry Community SD	Perry
11	4.4	Dubuque Community SD	Dubuque
12	4.3	Lewis Central Community SD	Council Bluffs
13	4.1	Fort Dodge Community SD	Fort Dodge
13	4.1	Fort Madison Community SD	Fort Madison
15	3.4	Davenport Community SD	Davenport
15	3.4	Waverly-Shell Rock Community SD	Waverly

15	3.4	West Delaware County Community SD	Manchester
18	3.3	Maquoketa Community SD	Maquoketa
18	3.3	Newton Community SD	Newton
20	3.2	Keokuk Community SD	Keokuk
21	3.1	Denison Community SD	Denison
21	3.1	Pleasant Valley Community SD	Pleasant Valley
23	3.0	Oskaloosa Community SD	Oskaloosa
23	3.0	Storm Lake Community SD	Storm Lake
25	2.9	Pella Community SD	Pella
25	2.9	West Des Moines Community SD	West Des Moines
25	2.9	Winterset Community SD	Winterset
28	2.7	Fairfield Community SD	Fairfield
29	2.6	Independence Community SD	Independence
30	2.5	Bettendorf Community SD	Bettendorf
30	2.5	Cedar Rapids Community SD	Cedar Rapids
30	2.5	Knoxville Community SD	Knoxville
30	2.5	Mason City Community SD	Mason City
34	2.4	Marshalltown Community SD	Marshalltown
34	2.4	Washington Community SD	Washington
36	2.3	Charles City Community SD	Charles City
37	2.2	Indianola Community SD	Indianola
38	1.8	Central Clinton Community SD	De Witt
38	1.8	Grinnell-Newburg Community SD	Grinnell
38	1.8	Iowa City Community SD	Iowa City
41	1.6	Boone Community SD	Boone
41	1.6	North Scott Community SD	Eldridge
41	1.6	Spencer Community SD	Spencer
44	1.5	Centerville Community SD	Centerville
44	1.5	Harlan Community SD	Harlan
46	1.3	Urbandale Community SD	Urbandale
47	1.2	Ames Community SD	Ames
47	1.2	Norwalk Community SD	Norwalk
49	1.1	Atlantic Community SD	Atlantic
49	1.1	Benton Community SD	Van Horne
49	1.1	Le Mars Community SD	Le Mars
52	1.0	Carroll Community SD	Carroll
52	1.0	Cedar Falls Community SD	Cedar Falls
54	0.9	Ankeny Community SD	Ankeny
54	0.9	Marion Independent SD	Marion
56	0.8	Glenwood Community SD	Glenwood
56	0.8	Southeast Polk Community SD	Runnells
58	0.7	College Community SD	Cedar Rapids
58	0.7	Mount Pleasant Community SD	Mount Pleasant
58	0.7	Vinton-Shellsburg Community SD	Vinton
61	0.6	Allamakee Community SD	Waukon
61	0.6	Johnston Community SD	Johnston
63	0.4	Dallas Center-Grimes Community SD	Dallas Center
63	0.4	Decorah Community SD	Decorah
63	0.4	Western Dubuque Community SD	Farley
66	0.3	Waukee Community SD	Waukee
67	0.2	Linn-Mar Community SD	Marion
68	0.0	Webster City Community SD	Webster City

Kansas

Kansas Public School Educational Profile

Category	Value	Category	Value
Schools *(2002-2003)*	1,432	**Diploma Recipients** *(2002-2003)*	29,541
Instructional Level		White, Non-Hispanic	25,219
Primary	804	Black, Non-Hispanic	1,856
Middle	258	Asian/Pacific Islander	685
High	364	American Indian/Alaskan Native	283
Other Level	6	Hispanic	1,498
Curriculum		**High School Drop-out Rate** (%) *(2000-2001)*	3.2
Regular	1,422	White, Non-Hispanic	2.6
Special Education	5	Black, Non-Hispanic	5.4
Vocational	0	Asian/Pacific Islander	2.1
Alternative	5	American Indian/Alaskan Native	5.6
Type		Hispanic	7.6
Magnet	33	**Staff** *(2002-2003)*	63,909.2
Charter	18	Teachers	32,639.7
Title I Eligible	648	Average Salary ($)	38,030
School-wide Title I	183	Librarians/Media Specialists	950.1
Students *(2002-2003)*	470,987	Guidance Counselors	1,141.2
Gender (%)		**Ratios** *(2002-2003)*	
Male	51.7	Student/Teacher Ratio	14.4 to 1
Female	48.3	Student/Librarian Ratio	495.7 to 1
Race/Ethnicity (%)		Student/Counselor Ratio	412.7 to 1
White, Non-Hispanic	76.7	**Current Spending** *($ per student in FY 2001)*	7,339
Black, Non-Hispanic	9.1	Instruction	4,290
Asian/Pacific Islander	2.3	Support Services	2,707
American Indian/Alaskan Native	1.4	**College Entrance Exam Scores** *(2003)*	
Hispanic	10.4	Scholastic Aptitude Test (SAT)	
Classification (%)		Participation Rate (%)	9
Individual Education Program (IEP)	13.6	Mean SAT I Verbal Score	578
Migrant	2.7	Mean SAT I Math Score	582
English Language Learner (ELL)	3.8	American College Testing Program (ACT)	
Eligible for Free Lunch Program	26.4	Participation Rate (%)	76
Eligible for Reduced-Price Lunch Program	9.6	Average Composite Score	21.5

Note: *For an explanation of data, please refer to the User's Guide in the front of the book; n/a indicates data not available*

Kansas NAEP 2003 Test Scores

Reading			Mathematics		
Grade/Category	**Value**	**Rank**	**Grade/Category**	**Value**	**Rank**
4th Grade			**4th Grade**		
Average Proficiency	220.1 (1.2)	24/51	Average Proficiency	241.7 (1.0)	5/51
Proficiency by Gender/Race/Ethnicity			Proficiency by Gender/Race/Ethnicity		
Male	216.3 (1.5)	20/51	Male	243.5 (1.2)	4/51
Female	224.2 (1.3)	23/51	Female	239.8 (1.1)	5/51
White, Non-Hispanic	224.9 (1.3)	29/51	White, Non-Hispanic	246.2 (1.0)	8/51
Black, Non-Hispanic	196.7 (2.9)	25/42	Black, Non-Hispanic	217.0 (1.5)	17/42
Asian, Non-Hispanic	206.8 (2.5)	14/41	Asian, Non-Hispanic	230.4 (1.8)	5/43
American Indian, Non-Hispanic	n/a	n/a	American Indian, Non-Hispanic	n/a	n/a
Hispanic	n/a	n/a	Hispanic	n/a	n/a
Proficiency by Class Size			Proficiency by Class Size		
Less than 16 Students	208.6 (3.7)	14/45	Less than 16 Students	237.5 (3.0)	3/47
16 to 18 Students	218.5 (3.0)	18/48	16 to 18 Students	240.4 (3.0)	7/48
19 to 20 Students	221.5 (3.0)	18/50	19 to 20 Students	240.6 (2.2)	8/50
21 to 25 Students	220.4 (2.0)	29/51	21 to 25 Students	242.5 (1.7)	8/51
Greater than 25 Students	*224.7 (4.3)*	9/49	Greater than 25 Students	*244.3 (2.5)*	3/49
Percent Attaining Achievement Levels			Percent Attaining Achievement Levels		
Below Basic	34.0 (1.4)	28/51	Below Basic	15.1 (1.2)	49/51
Basic or Above	66.0 (1.4)	23/51	Basic or Above	84.9 (1.2)	3/51
Proficient or Above	32.5 (1.5)	23/51	Proficient or Above	41.3 (1.6)	4/51
Advanced or Above	7.4 (0.8)	21/51	Advanced or Above	5.7 (0.8)	4/51
8th Grade			**8th Grade**		
Average Proficiency	266.0 (1.5)	21/51	Average Proficiency	284.2 (1.3)	8/51
Proficiency by Gender/Race/Ethnicity			Proficiency by Gender/Race/Ethnicity		
Male	259.7 (1.9)	21/51	Male	284.2 (1.5)	10/51
Female	272.3 (1.3)	14/51	Female	284.1 (1.4)	6/51
White, Non-Hispanic	270.6 (1.4)	22/50	White, Non-Hispanic	290.0 (1.2)	11/50
Black, Non-Hispanic	243.2 (3.1)	26/41	Black, Non-Hispanic	251.6 (3.5)	20/41
Asian, Non-Hispanic	244.8 (3.8)	23/37	Asian, Non-Hispanic	263.3 (2.6)	7/37
American Indian, Non-Hispanic	266.3 (3.9)	14/23	American Indian, Non-Hispanic	283.8 (4.9)	17/23
Hispanic	n/a	n/a	Hispanic	n/a	n/a
Proficiency by Parents Highest Level of Ed.			Proficiency by Parents Highest Level of Ed.		
Did Not Finish High School	246.8 (3.5)	24/50	Did Not Finish High School	260.1 (2.5)	16/50
Graduated High School	255.1 (3.0)	27/50	Graduated High School	275.4 (2.0)	10/50
Some Education After High School	270.2 (1.9)	17/50	Some Education After High School	286.9 (1.5)	6/50
Graduated College	274.0 (1.3)	21/50	Graduated College	293.9 (1.3)	7/50
Percent Attaining Achievement Levels			Percent Attaining Achievement Levels		
Below Basic	23.2 (1.6)	30/51	Below Basic	24.4 (1.5)	42/51
Basic or Above	76.8 (1.6)	20/51	Basic or Above	75.6 (1.5)	10/51
Proficient or Above	35.0 (1.8)	16/51	Proficient or Above	34.0 (1.5)	11/51
Advanced or Above	3.3 (0.5)	12/51	Advanced or Above	6.4 (0.6)	10/51

Note: *For an explanation of data, please refer to the User's Guide in the front of the book; values in italics indicate that the nature of the sample does not allow accurate determination of the variability of the statistic; n/a indicates data not available*

Allen County

Iola

408 N Cottonwood • Iola, KS 66749-2997
(620) 365-4700 • http://www.iola.com/usd256.htm
Grade Span: KG-12; **Agency Type:** 1
Schools: 6
4 Primary; 1 Middle; 1 High; 0 Other Level
6 Regular; 0 Special Education; 0 Vocational; 0 Alternative
0 Magnet; 0 Charter; 4 Title I Eligible; 2 School-wide Title I
Students: 1,536 (52.8% male; 47.2% female)
Individual Education Program: 323 (21.0%);
English Language Learner: 0 (0.0%); Migrant: 5 (0.3%)
Eligible for Free Lunch Program: 529 (34.4%)
Eligible for Reduced-Price Lunch Program: 163 (10.6%)
Teachers: 108.5 (14.2 to 1)
Librarians/Media Specialists: 4.0 (384.0 to 1)
Guidance Counselors: 5.0 (307.2 to 1)
Current Spending: ($ per student per year):
Total: $5,565; Instruction: $2,909; Support Services: $2,161
Enrollment, Drop-out Rates and Diploma Recipients by Race/Ethnicity

Category	Total	White	Black	Asian	AIAN	Hisp.
Enrollment (%)	100.0	90.5	3.9	1.1	2.0	2.4
Drop-out Rate (%)	6.2	5.6	22.2	0.0	0.0	25.0
H.S. Diplomas (#)	117	109	3	1	3	1

Atchison County

Atchison Public Schools

215 N 8th St • Atchison, KS 66002
(913) 367-4384 • http://www.atchison.k12.ks.us
Grade Span: KG-12; **Agency Type:** 1
Schools: 3
1 Primary; 1 Middle; 1 High; 0 Other Level
3 Regular; 0 Special Education; 0 Vocational; 0 Alternative
0 Magnet; 0 Charter; 1 Title I Eligible; 0 School-wide Title I
Students: 1,738 (52.1% male; 47.9% female)
Individual Education Program: 383 (22.0%);
English Language Learner: 0 (0.0%); Migrant: 0 (0.0%)
Eligible for Free Lunch Program: 698 (40.2%)
Eligible for Reduced-Price Lunch Program: 248 (14.3%)
Teachers: 127.9 (13.6 to 1)
Librarians/Media Specialists: 3.0 (579.3 to 1)
Guidance Counselors: 3.0 (579.3 to 1)
Current Spending: ($ per student per year):
Total: $7,469; Instruction: $4,189; Support Services: $2,827
Enrollment, Drop-out Rates and Diploma Recipients by Race/Ethnicity

Category	Total	White	Black	Asian	AIAN	Hisp.
Enrollment (%)	100.0	81.4	15.7	0.5	0.6	1.7
Drop-out Rate (%)	5.0	5.3	4.1	0.0	n/a	0.0
H.S. Diplomas (#)	107	90	14	2	0	1

Barton County

Great Bend

201 Patton Rd • Great Bend, KS 67530-4613
(620) 793-1500 • http://www.usd428.org/
Grade Span: PK-12; **Agency Type:** 1
Schools: 7
5 Primary; 1 Middle; 1 High; 0 Other Level
7 Regular; 0 Special Education; 0 Vocational; 0 Alternative
0 Magnet; 0 Charter; 2 Title I Eligible; 2 School-wide Title I
Students: 3,209 (51.9% male; 48.1% female)
Individual Education Program: 418 (13.0%);
English Language Learner: 234 (7.3%); Migrant: 554 (17.3%)
Eligible for Free Lunch Program: 1,212 (37.8%)
Eligible for Reduced-Price Lunch Program: 251 (7.8%)
Teachers: 239.0 (13.4 to 1)
Librarians/Media Specialists: 5.0 (641.8 to 1)
Guidance Counselors: 7.5 (427.9 to 1)
Current Spending: ($ per student per year):
Total: $6,229; Instruction: $3,328; Support Services: $2,483
Enrollment, Drop-out Rates and Diploma Recipients by Race/Ethnicity

Category	Total	White	Black	Asian	AIAN	Hisp.
Enrollment (%)	100.0	72.3	3.4	0.4	0.6	23.3
Drop-out Rate (%)	5.0	5.1	0.0	0.0	0.0	5.8
H.S. Diplomas (#)	217	188	6	1	0	22

Bourbon County

Fort Scott

424 S Main • Fort Scott, KS 66701-2097
(620) 223-0800 • http://www.usd234.org/
Grade Span: KG-12; **Agency Type:** 1
Schools: 4
2 Primary; 1 Middle; 1 High; 0 Other Level
4 Regular; 0 Special Education; 0 Vocational; 0 Alternative
0 Magnet; 0 Charter; 3 Title I Eligible; 1 School-wide Title I
Students: 2,056 (51.0% male; 49.0% female)
Individual Education Program: 223 (10.8%);
English Language Learner: 11 (0.5%); Migrant: 7 (0.3%)
Eligible for Free Lunch Program: 723 (35.2%)
Eligible for Reduced-Price Lunch Program: 253 (12.3%)
Teachers: 144.4 (14.2 to 1)
Librarians/Media Specialists: 4.0 (514.0 to 1)
Guidance Counselors: 4.6 (447.0 to 1)
Current Spending: ($ per student per year):
Total: $5,211; Instruction: $3,240; Support Services: $1,664
Enrollment, Drop-out Rates and Diploma Recipients by Race/Ethnicity

Category	Total	White	Black	Asian	AIAN	Hisp.
Enrollment (%)	100.0	91.7	5.5	0.4	0.4	1.9
Drop-out Rate (%)	5.1	4.3	17.2	0.0	0.0	21.4
H.S. Diplomas (#)	150	143	1	1	1	4

Butler County

Andover

1432 N Andover Rd • Andover, KS 67002-0248
(316) 733-5017 • http://www.usd385.org
Grade Span: KG-12; **Agency Type:** 1
Schools: 8
4 Primary; 2 Middle; 2 High; 0 Other Level
8 Regular; 0 Special Education; 0 Vocational; 0 Alternative
0 Magnet; 0 Charter; 2 Title I Eligible; 0 School-wide Title I
Students: 3,313 (52.0% male; 48.0% female)
Individual Education Program: 321 (9.7%);
English Language Learner: 4 (0.1%); Migrant: 0 (0.0%)
Eligible for Free Lunch Program: 240 (7.2%)
Eligible for Reduced-Price Lunch Program: 117 (3.5%)
Teachers: 199.0 (16.6 to 1)
Librarians/Media Specialists: 7.0 (473.3 to 1)
Guidance Counselors: 10.0 (331.3 to 1)
Current Spending: ($ per student per year):
Total: $5,705; Instruction: $3,293; Support Services: $2,060
Enrollment, Drop-out Rates and Diploma Recipients by Race/Ethnicity

Category	Total	White	Black	Asian	AIAN	Hisp.
Enrollment (%)	100.0	92.3	1.8	1.8	1.2	2.9
Drop-out Rate (%)	0.9	0.9	0.0	0.0	0.0	0.0
H.S. Diplomas (#)	216	209	0	1	0	6

Augusta

2345 Greyhound Dr • Augusta, KS 67010-1699
(316) 775-5484 • http://www.usd402.com/
Grade Span: KG-12; **Agency Type:** 1
Schools: 6
4 Primary; 1 Middle; 1 High; 0 Other Level
6 Regular; 0 Special Education; 0 Vocational; 0 Alternative
0 Magnet; 0 Charter; 2 Title I Eligible; 0 School-wide Title I
Students: 2,237 (52.0% male; 48.0% female)
Individual Education Program: 284 (12.7%);
English Language Learner: 0 (0.0%); Migrant: 0 (0.0%)
Eligible for Free Lunch Program: 421 (18.8%)
Eligible for Reduced-Price Lunch Program: 175 (7.8%)
Teachers: 131.0 (17.1 to 1)
Librarians/Media Specialists: 6.0 (372.8 to 1)
Guidance Counselors: 6.0 (372.8 to 1)
Current Spending: ($ per student per year):
Total: $4,734; Instruction: $2,865; Support Services: $1,612
Enrollment, Drop-out Rates and Diploma Recipients by Race/Ethnicity

Category	Total	White	Black	Asian	AIAN	Hisp.
Enrollment (%)	100.0	93.6	0.8	1.0	1.5	3.1
Drop-out Rate (%)	0.9	0.9	0.0	0.0	0.0	0.0
H.S. Diplomas (#)	142	135	1	1	1	4

Circle

901 Main • Towanda, KS 67144-0009
Mailing Address: PO Box 9 • Towanda, KS 67144-0009
(316) 541-2577
Grade Span: KG-12; **Agency Type:** 1
Schools: 5
3 Primary; 1 Middle; 1 High; 0 Other Level
5 Regular; 0 Special Education; 0 Vocational; 0 Alternative
0 Magnet; 0 Charter; 2 Title I Eligible; 0 School-wide Title I
Students: 1,519 (50.7% male; 49.3% female)
Individual Education Program: 196 (12.9%);
English Language Learner: 0 (0.0%); Migrant: 0 (0.0%)
Eligible for Free Lunch Program: 228 (15.0%)
Eligible for Reduced-Price Lunch Program: 135 (8.9%)
Teachers: 86.0 (17.7 to 1)
Librarians/Media Specialists: 5.0 (303.8 to 1)
Guidance Counselors: 5.0 (303.8 to 1)

Current Spending: ($ per student per year):
Total: $5,601; Instruction: $3,049; Support Services: $2,199

Enrollment, Drop-out Rates and Diploma Recipients by Race/Ethnicity

Category	Total	White	Black	Asian	AIAN	Hisp.
Enrollment (%)	100.0	93.3	1.8	0.7	2.0	2.2
Drop-out Rate (%)	5.5	5.2	0.0	0.0	28.6	0.0
H.S. Diplomas (#)	99	94	2	1	0	2

El Dorado

124 W Central Ave • El Dorado, KS 67042-2138
(316) 322-4800 • http://http://www.eldoradoschools.org
Grade Span: KG-12; **Agency Type:** 1
Schools: 7
5 Primary; 1 Middle; 1 High; 0 Other Level
7 Regular; 0 Special Education; 0 Vocational; 0 Alternative
0 Magnet; 0 Charter; 5 Title I Eligible; 0 School-wide Title I
Students: 2,258 (54.8% male; 45.2% female)
Individual Education Program: 331 (14.7%);
English Language Learner: 0 (0.0%); Migrant: 0 (0.0%)
Eligible for Free Lunch Program: 649 (28.7%)
Eligible for Reduced-Price Lunch Program: 164 (7.3%)
Teachers: 226.8 (10.0 to 1)
Librarians/Media Specialists: 4.5 (501.8 to 1)
Guidance Counselors: 7.0 (322.6 to 1)
Current Spending: ($ per student per year):
Total: $9,407; Instruction: $6,119; Support Services: $2,904

Enrollment, Drop-out Rates and Diploma Recipients by Race/Ethnicity

Category	Total	White	Black	Asian	AIAN	Hisp.
Enrollment (%)	100.0	91.1	3.4	0.6	1.0	3.9
Drop-out Rate (%)	3.8	3.7	4.3	0.0	0.0	5.6
H.S. Diplomas (#)	114	103	4	1	1	5

Rose Hill Public Schools

104 N Rose Hill Rd • Rose Hill, KS 67133-9785
(316) 776-3300
Grade Span: KG-12; **Agency Type:** 1
Schools: 4
2 Primary; 1 Middle; 1 High; 0 Other Level
4 Regular; 0 Special Education; 0 Vocational; 0 Alternative
0 Magnet; 0 Charter; 2 Title I Eligible; 0 School-wide Title I
Students: 1,799 (52.6% male; 47.4% female)
Individual Education Program: 159 (8.8%);
English Language Learner: 0 (0.0%); Migrant: 0 (0.0%)
Eligible for Free Lunch Program: 165 (9.2%)
Eligible for Reduced-Price Lunch Program: 109 (6.1%)
Teachers: 103.0 (17.5 to 1)
Librarians/Media Specialists: 2.0 (899.5 to 1)
Guidance Counselors: 4.0 (449.8 to 1)
Current Spending: ($ per student per year):
Total: $5,057; Instruction: $2,851; Support Services: $1,928

Enrollment, Drop-out Rates and Diploma Recipients by Race/Ethnicity

Category	Total	White	Black	Asian	AIAN	Hisp.
Enrollment (%)	100.0	96.1	0.9	0.7	0.7	1.6
Drop-out Rate (%)	1.4	1.3	0.0	0.0	0.0	7.7
H.S. Diplomas (#)	127	125	0	0	1	1

Clay County

Clay Center

807 Dexter • Clay Center, KS 67432-0097
Mailing Address: Box 97 • Clay Center, KS 67432-0097
(785) 632-3176 • http://www.usd379.org/
Grade Span: PK-12; **Agency Type:** 1
Schools: 9
5 Primary; 2 Middle; 2 High; 0 Other Level
9 Regular; 0 Special Education; 0 Vocational; 0 Alternative
0 Magnet; 0 Charter; 5 Title I Eligible; 3 School-wide Title I
Students: 1,565 (52.7% male; 47.3% female)
Individual Education Program: 233 (14.9%);
English Language Learner: 0 (0.0%); Migrant: 0 (0.0%)
Eligible for Free Lunch Program: 369 (23.6%)
Eligible for Reduced-Price Lunch Program: 185 (11.8%)
Teachers: 141.8 (11.0 to 1)
Librarians/Media Specialists: 3.8 (411.8 to 1)
Guidance Counselors: 6.0 (260.8 to 1)
Current Spending: ($ per student per year):
Total: $7,072; Instruction: $4,216; Support Services: $2,466

Enrollment, Drop-out Rates and Diploma Recipients by Race/Ethnicity

Category	Total	White	Black	Asian	AIAN	Hisp.
Enrollment (%)	100.0	95.5	2.0	0.6	0.6	1.3
Drop-out Rate (%)	3.4	3.5	0.0	0.0	0.0	0.0
H.S. Diplomas (#)	108	106	1	0	0	1

Cowley County

Arkansas City

119 W Washington • Arkansas City, KS 67005-1028
Mailing Address: PO Box 1028 • Arkansas City, KS 67005-1028
(620) 441-2000 • http://www.arkcity.com
Grade Span: PK-12; **Agency Type:** 1
Schools: 8
6 Primary; 1 Middle; 1 High; 0 Other Level
8 Regular; 0 Special Education; 0 Vocational; 0 Alternative
0 Magnet; 0 Charter; 4 Title I Eligible; 0 School-wide Title I
Students: 3,062 (50.7% male; 49.3% female)
Individual Education Program: 588 (19.2%);
English Language Learner: 0 (0.0%); Migrant: 115 (3.8%)
Eligible for Free Lunch Program: 1,343 (43.9%)
Eligible for Reduced-Price Lunch Program: 295 (9.6%)
Teachers: 182.2 (16.8 to 1)
Librarians/Media Specialists: 5.0 (612.4 to 1)
Guidance Counselors: 7.0 (437.4 to 1)
Current Spending: ($ per student per year):
Total: $5,072; Instruction: $2,736; Support Services: $1,804

Enrollment, Drop-out Rates and Diploma Recipients by Race/Ethnicity

Category	Total	White	Black	Asian	AIAN	Hisp.
Enrollment (%)	100.0	75.9	5.5	1.1	5.7	11.8
Drop-out Rate (%)	4.7	4.0	14.3	0.0	8.8	3.0
H.S. Diplomas (#)	169	147	5	2	9	6

Winfield

920 Millington • Winfield, KS 67156-3691
(620) 221-5100 • http://www.usd465.com/
Grade Span: PK-12; **Agency Type:** 1
Schools: 8
6 Primary; 1 Middle; 1 High; 0 Other Level
8 Regular; 0 Special Education; 0 Vocational; 0 Alternative
0 Magnet; 0 Charter; 4 Title I Eligible; 1 School-wide Title I
Students: 2,775 (51.8% male; 48.2% female)
Individual Education Program: 463 (16.7%);
English Language Learner: 181 (6.5%); Migrant: 0 (0.0%)
Eligible for Free Lunch Program: 708 (25.5%)
Eligible for Reduced-Price Lunch Program: 346 (12.5%)
Teachers: 244.6 (11.3 to 1)
Librarians/Media Specialists: 4.5 (616.7 to 1)
Guidance Counselors: 4.0 (693.8 to 1)
Current Spending: ($ per student per year):
Total: $7,636; Instruction: $4,616; Support Services: $2,491

Enrollment, Drop-out Rates and Diploma Recipients by Race/Ethnicity

Category	Total	White	Black	Asian	AIAN	Hisp.
Enrollment (%)	100.0	85.5	3.0	4.9	1.2	5.4
Drop-out Rate (%)	1.2	1.4	0.0	0.0	0.0	0.0
H.S. Diplomas (#)	217	195	6	10	0	6

Crawford County

Pittsburg

510 Deill St • Pittsburg, KS 66762-0075
Mailing Address: Drawer 75 • Pittsburg, KS 66762-0075
(620) 235-3100 • http://www.usd250.k12.ks.us/
Grade Span: KG-12; **Agency Type:** 1
Schools: 5
3 Primary; 1 Middle; 1 High; 0 Other Level
5 Regular; 0 Special Education; 0 Vocational; 0 Alternative
0 Magnet; 0 Charter; 3 Title I Eligible; 1 School-wide Title I
Students: 2,562 (51.8% male; 48.2% female)
Individual Education Program: 335 (13.1%);
English Language Learner: 87 (3.4%); Migrant: 85 (3.3%)
Eligible for Free Lunch Program: 1,069 (41.7%)
Eligible for Reduced-Price Lunch Program: 246 (9.6%)
Teachers: 147.4 (17.4 to 1)
Librarians/Media Specialists: 6.1 (420.0 to 1)
Guidance Counselors: 9.0 (284.7 to 1)
Current Spending: ($ per student per year):
Total: $8,697; Instruction: $5,846; Support Services: $2,504

Enrollment, Drop-out Rates and Diploma Recipients by Race/Ethnicity

Category	Total	White	Black	Asian	AIAN	Hisp.
Enrollment (%)	100.0	84.9	6.6	2.3	0.6	5.6
Drop-out Rate (%)	5.4	5.4	0.0	0.0	16.7	14.3
H.S. Diplomas (#)	144	132	4	7	0	1

Douglas County

Lawrence

110 Mcdonald Dr • Lawrence, KS 66044-1063
(785) 832-5000 • http://www.usd497.org/
Grade Span: KG-12; **Agency Type:** 1
Schools: 24

18 Primary; 4 Middle; 2 High; 0 Other Level
24 Regular; 0 Special Education; 0 Vocational; 0 Alternative
0 Magnet; 0 Charter; 9 Title I Eligible; 3 School-wide Title I
Students: 10,182 (50.7% male; 49.3% female)
Individual Education Program: 1,590 (15.6%);
English Language Learner: 158 (1.6%); Migrant: 37 (0.4%)
Eligible for Free Lunch Program: 2,047 (20.1%)
Eligible for Reduced-Price Lunch Program: 892 (8.8%)
Teachers: 761.2 (13.4 to 1)
Librarians/Media Specialists: 23.5 (433.3 to 1)
Guidance Counselors: 26.0 (391.6 to 1)
Current Spending: ($ per student per year):
Total: $6,771; Instruction: $3,897; Support Services: $2,459
Enrollment, Drop-out Rates and Diploma Recipients by Race/Ethnicity

Category	Total	White	Black	Asian	AIAN	Hisp.
Enrollment (%)	100.0	75.8	11.4	3.8	4.9	4.2
Drop-out Rate (%)	2.2	1.9	2.9	1.7	7.7	2.2
H.S. Diplomas (#)	772	639	68	27	20	18

Ellis County

Hays
323 W 12th St • Hays, KS 67601-3893
(785) 623-2400 • http://www.hays489.k12.ks.us/
Grade Span: PK-12; **Agency Type:** 1
Schools: 9
6 Primary; 2 Middle; 1 High; 0 Other Level
9 Regular; 0 Special Education; 0 Vocational; 0 Alternative
0 Magnet; 0 Charter; 5 Title I Eligible; 0 School-wide Title I
Students: 3,399 (52.4% male; 47.6% female)
Individual Education Program: 539 (15.9%);
English Language Learner: 70 (2.1%); Migrant: 43 (1.3%)
Eligible for Free Lunch Program: 713 (21.0%)
Eligible for Reduced-Price Lunch Program: 319 (9.4%)
Teachers: 275.9 (12.3 to 1)
Librarians/Media Specialists: 5.9 (576.1 to 1)
Guidance Counselors: 8.0 (424.9 to 1)
Current Spending: ($ per student per year):
Total: $7,082; Instruction: $4,354; Support Services: $2,363
Enrollment, Drop-out Rates and Diploma Recipients by Race/Ethnicity

Category	Total	White	Black	Asian	AIAN	Hisp.
Enrollment (%)	100.0	91.3	2.5	0.8	0.3	5.1
Drop-out Rate (%)	3.4	3.3	0.0	0.0	100.0	5.9
H.S. Diplomas (#)	229	221	1	2	0	5

Finney County

Garden City
1205 Fleming St • Garden City, KS 67846-4751
(620) 276-5100 • http://www.gckschools.com/
Grade Span: PK-12; **Agency Type:** 1
Schools: 16
11 Primary; 4 Middle; 1 High; 0 Other Level
16 Regular; 0 Special Education; 0 Vocational; 0 Alternative
0 Magnet; 0 Charter; 6 Title I Eligible; 4 School-wide Title I
Students: 7,839 (50.6% male; 49.4% female)
Individual Education Program: 968 (12.3%);
English Language Learner: 1,688 (21.5%); Migrant: 688 (8.8%)
Eligible for Free Lunch Program: 3,243 (41.4%)
Eligible for Reduced-Price Lunch Program: 856 (10.9%)
Teachers: 497.4 (15.8 to 1)
Librarians/Media Specialists: 16.0 (489.9 to 1)
Guidance Counselors: 21.0 (373.3 to 1)
Current Spending: ($ per student per year):
Total: $5,907; Instruction: $2,916; Support Services: $2,642
Enrollment, Drop-out Rates and Diploma Recipients by Race/Ethnicity

Category	Total	White	Black	Asian	AIAN	Hisp.
Enrollment (%)	100.0	34.9	1.4	2.8	0.3	60.5
Drop-out Rate (%)	4.4	2.5	5.7	2.2	0.0	6.7
H.S. Diplomas (#)	279	180	6	11	2	80

Ford County

Dodge City
1000 Second Ave • Dodge City, KS 67801-0460
Mailing Address: Box 460 • Dodge City, KS 67801-0460
(620) 227-1620 • http://www.usd443.org/
Grade Span: KG-12; **Agency Type:** 1
Schools: 11
7 Primary; 3 Middle; 1 High; 0 Other Level
11 Regular; 0 Special Education; 0 Vocational; 0 Alternative
1 Magnet; 0 Charter; 7 Title I Eligible; 7 School-wide Title I
Students: 5,814 (52.3% male; 47.7% female)
Individual Education Program: 688 (11.8%);
English Language Learner: 2,165 (37.2%); Migrant: 2,245 (38.6%)
Eligible for Free Lunch Program: 2,952 (50.8%)
Eligible for Reduced-Price Lunch Program: 811 (13.9%)
Teachers: 333.9 (17.4 to 1)
Librarians/Media Specialists: 10.0 (581.4 to 1)
Guidance Counselors: 13.4 (433.9 to 1)
Current Spending: ($ per student per year):
Total: $5,112; Instruction: $2,845; Support Services: $1,864
Enrollment, Drop-out Rates and Diploma Recipients by Race/Ethnicity

Category	Total	White	Black	Asian	AIAN	Hisp.
Enrollment (%)	100.0	35.6	2.5	2.4	0.6	58.8
Drop-out Rate (%)	2.8	0.6	3.0	4.3	0.0	6.0
H.S. Diplomas (#)	303	197	3	17	1	85

Franklin County

Ottawa
123 W 4th St • Ottawa, KS 66067-2223
(785) 229-8010 • http://www.ottawa.k12.ks.us/
Grade Span: KG-12; **Agency Type:** 1
Schools: 7
5 Primary; 1 Middle; 1 High; 0 Other Level
7 Regular; 0 Special Education; 0 Vocational; 0 Alternative
0 Magnet; 0 Charter; 5 Title I Eligible; 5 School-wide Title I
Students: 2,517 (52.5% male; 47.5% female)
Individual Education Program: 353 (14.0%);
English Language Learner: 0 (0.0%); Migrant: 0 (0.0%)
Eligible for Free Lunch Program: 664 (26.4%)
Eligible for Reduced-Price Lunch Program: 177 (7.0%)
Teachers: 167.7 (15.0 to 1)
Librarians/Media Specialists: 4.5 (559.3 to 1)
Guidance Counselors: 9.5 (264.9 to 1)
Current Spending: ($ per student per year):
Total: $5,514; Instruction: $3,469; Support Services: $1,785
Enrollment, Drop-out Rates and Diploma Recipients by Race/Ethnicity

Category	Total	White	Black	Asian	AIAN	Hisp.
Enrollment (%)	100.0	91.2	3.0	0.5	1.2	4.0
Drop-out Rate (%)	0.9	1.0	0.0	0.0	0.0	0.0
H.S. Diplomas (#)	121	115	3	2	0	1

Geary County

Geary County Schools
123 N Eisenhower • Junction City, KS 66441
(785) 238-6184 • http://www.usd475.org/
Grade Span: PK-12; **Agency Type:** 1
Schools: 16
13 Primary; 2 Middle; 1 High; 0 Other Level
16 Regular; 0 Special Education; 0 Vocational; 0 Alternative
0 Magnet; 0 Charter; 10 Title I Eligible; 10 School-wide Title I
Students: 6,490 (51.4% male; 48.6% female)
Individual Education Program: 948 (14.6%);
English Language Learner: 0 (0.0%); Migrant: 0 (0.0%)
Eligible for Free Lunch Program: 2,195 (33.8%)
Eligible for Reduced-Price Lunch Program: 1,366 (21.0%)
Teachers: 430.5 (15.1 to 1)
Librarians/Media Specialists: 16.0 (405.6 to 1)
Guidance Counselors: 8.0 (811.3 to 1)
Current Spending: ($ per student per year):
Total: $6,127; Instruction: $3,197; Support Services: $2,499
Enrollment, Drop-out Rates and Diploma Recipients by Race/Ethnicity

Category	Total	White	Black	Asian	AIAN	Hisp.
Enrollment (%)	100.0	54.1	32.6	3.3	1.0	9.1
Drop-out Rate (%)	2.4	3.2	1.2	1.2	6.3	3.3
H.S. Diplomas (#)	226	116	81	12	1	16

Grant County

Ulysses
111 S Baughman • Ulysses, KS 67880-2402
(620) 356-3655 • http://www.ulysses.org
Grade Span: PK-12; **Agency Type:** 1
Schools: 4
2 Primary; 1 Middle; 1 High; 0 Other Level
4 Regular; 0 Special Education; 0 Vocational; 0 Alternative
0 Magnet; 0 Charter; 3 Title I Eligible; 0 School-wide Title I
Students: 1,795 (52.6% male; 47.4% female)
Individual Education Program: 193 (10.8%);
English Language Learner: 172 (9.6%); Migrant: 286 (15.9%)
Eligible for Free Lunch Program: 558 (31.1%)
Eligible for Reduced-Price Lunch Program: 239 (13.3%)
Teachers: 113.0 (15.9 to 1)
Librarians/Media Specialists: 4.0 (448.8 to 1)
Guidance Counselors: 4.0 (448.8 to 1)
Current Spending: ($ per student per year):
Total: $5,487; Instruction: $3,127; Support Services: $1,913

Enrollment, Drop-out Rates and Diploma Recipients by Race/Ethnicity

Category	Total	White	Black	Asian	AIAN	Hisp.
Enrollment (%)	100.0	49.4	0.0	0.4	0.1	50.1
Drop-out Rate (%)	2.0	1.0	n/a	0.0	0.0	3.8
H.S. Diplomas (#)	121	90	0	2	0	29

Harvey County

Newton

308 E First • Newton, KS 67114-3846
(316) 284-6200 • http://www.newton.k12.ks.us/home/
Grade Span: PK-12; **Agency Type:** 1
Schools: 10
5 Primary; 3 Middle; 2 High; 0 Other Level
10 Regular; 0 Special Education; 0 Vocational; 0 Alternative
0 Magnet; 0 Charter; 5 Title I Eligible; 0 School-wide Title I
Students: 3,696 (52.3% male; 47.7% female)
Individual Education Program: 547 (14.8%);
English Language Learner: 141 (3.8%); Migrant: 0 (0.0%)
Eligible for Free Lunch Program: 1,042 (28.2%)
Eligible for Reduced-Price Lunch Program: 441 (11.9%)
Teachers: 248.6 (14.9 to 1)
Librarians/Media Specialists: 7.0 (528.0 to 1)
Guidance Counselors: 7.0 (528.0 to 1)
Current Spending: ($ per student per year):
Total: $6,624; Instruction: $3,659; Support Services: $2,537

Enrollment, Drop-out Rates and Diploma Recipients by Race/Ethnicity

Category	Total	White	Black	Asian	AIAN	Hisp.
Enrollment (%)	100.0	77.4	3.8	0.8	0.8	17.2
Drop-out Rate (%)	3.2	2.5	2.2	0.0	14.3	7.7
H.S. Diplomas (#)	199	166	4	5	2	22

Johnson County

Blue Valley

15020 Metcalf • Overland Park, KS 66223-2200
Mailing Address: Box 23901 • Overland Park, KS 66283-0901
(913) 239-4000 • http://www.bluevalleyk12.org/
Grade Span: PK-12; **Agency Type:** 1
Schools: 29
17 Primary; 8 Middle; 4 High; 0 Other Level
29 Regular; 0 Special Education; 0 Vocational; 0 Alternative
0 Magnet; 0 Charter; 0 Title I Eligible; 0 School-wide Title I
Students: 18,641 (52.0% male; 48.0% female)
Individual Education Program: 1,536 (8.2%);
English Language Learner: 182 (1.0%); Migrant: 0 (0.0%)
Eligible for Free Lunch Program: 254 (1.4%)
Eligible for Reduced-Price Lunch Program: 141 (0.8%)
Teachers: 1,231.3 (15.1 to 1)
Librarians/Media Specialists: 34.0 (548.3 to 1)
Guidance Counselors: 52.8 (353.0 to 1)
Current Spending: ($ per student per year):
Total: $7,109; Instruction: $3,745; Support Services: $2,905

Enrollment, Drop-out Rates and Diploma Recipients by Race/Ethnicity

Category	Total	White	Black	Asian	AIAN	Hisp.
Enrollment (%)	100.0	89.5	3.0	5.5	0.2	1.8
Drop-out Rate (%)	0.7	0.7	0.8	0.5	0.0	2.5
H.S. Diplomas (#)	1,190	1,099	27	44	4	16

De Soto

35200 W 91st St • De Soto, KS 66018-0449
(913) 583-8300 •
http://www.usd232.org/education/district/district.php?sectionid=1
Grade Span: PK-12; **Agency Type:** 1
Schools: 8
4 Primary; 2 Middle; 2 High; 0 Other Level
8 Regular; 0 Special Education; 0 Vocational; 0 Alternative
0 Magnet; 0 Charter; 1 Title I Eligible; 0 School-wide Title I
Students: 4,130 (50.7% male; 49.3% female)
Individual Education Program: 390 (9.4%);
English Language Learner: 106 (2.6%); Migrant: 0 (0.0%)
Eligible for Free Lunch Program: 342 (8.3%)
Eligible for Reduced-Price Lunch Program: 140 (3.4%)
Teachers: 291.8 (14.2 to 1)
Librarians/Media Specialists: 8.0 (516.3 to 1)
Guidance Counselors: 8.4 (491.7 to 1)
Current Spending: ($ per student per year):
Total: $6,807; Instruction: $3,289; Support Services: $3,043

Enrollment, Drop-out Rates and Diploma Recipients by Race/Ethnicity

Category	Total	White	Black	Asian	AIAN	Hisp.
Enrollment (%)	100.0	89.7	2.4	2.1	0.6	5.1
Drop-out Rate (%)	1.9	2.0	0.0	0.0	0.0	2.1
H.S. Diplomas (#)	203	180	7	3	2	11

Gardner Edgerton

231 E Madison • Gardner, KS 66030
Mailing Address: Box 97 • Gardner, KS 66030
(913) 856-2000 • http://usd231.com/
Grade Span: KG-12; **Agency Type:** 1
Schools: 7
4 Primary; 2 Middle; 1 High; 0 Other Level
7 Regular; 0 Special Education; 0 Vocational; 0 Alternative
0 Magnet; 0 Charter; 2 Title I Eligible; 0 School-wide Title I
Students: 3,215 (51.4% male; 48.6% female)
Individual Education Program: 421 (13.1%);
English Language Learner: 14 (0.4%); Migrant: 27 (0.8%)
Eligible for Free Lunch Program: 373 (11.6%)
Eligible for Reduced-Price Lunch Program: 240 (7.5%)
Teachers: 226.5 (14.2 to 1)
Librarians/Media Specialists: 6.0 (535.8 to 1)
Guidance Counselors: 15.0 (214.3 to 1)
Current Spending: ($ per student per year):
Total: $6,803; Instruction: $4,015; Support Services: $2,477

Enrollment, Drop-out Rates and Diploma Recipients by Race/Ethnicity

Category	Total	White	Black	Asian	AIAN	Hisp.
Enrollment (%)	100.0	91.8	2.8	1.9	0.5	3.0
Drop-out Rate (%)	1.9	1.9	6.3	0.0	n/a	0.0
H.S. Diplomas (#)	138	133	2	0	0	3

Olathe

14160 Black Bob Rd • Olathe, KS 66063-2000
Mailing Address: PO Box 2000 • Olathe, KS 66063-2000
(913) 780-7000 • http://www.olathe.k12.ks.us/
Grade Span: PK-12; **Agency Type:** 1
Schools: 38
28 Primary; 7 Middle; 3 High; 0 Other Level
38 Regular; 0 Special Education; 0 Vocational; 0 Alternative
0 Magnet; 0 Charter; 10 Title I Eligible; 3 School-wide Title I
Students: 22,174 (51.5% male; 48.5% female)
Individual Education Program: 3,020 (13.6%);
English Language Learner: 472 (2.1%); Migrant: 431 (1.9%)
Eligible for Free Lunch Program: 1,780 (8.0%)
Eligible for Reduced-Price Lunch Program: 805 (3.6%)
Teachers: 1,484.4 (14.9 to 1)
Librarians/Media Specialists: 39.5 (561.4 to 1)
Guidance Counselors: 55.0 (403.2 to 1)
Current Spending: ($ per student per year):
Total: $6,796; Instruction: $3,648; Support Services: $2,712

Enrollment, Drop-out Rates and Diploma Recipients by Race/Ethnicity

Category	Total	White	Black	Asian	AIAN	Hisp.
Enrollment (%)	100.0	84.9	6.0	3.4	0.5	5.2
Drop-out Rate (%)	2.0	1.9	3.0	1.0	0.0	3.2
H.S. Diplomas (#)	1,319	1,165	65	46	4	39

Shawnee Mission Public Schools

7235 Antioch • Shawnee Mission, KS 66204-1798
(913) 993-6200 • http://www.smsd.org/
Grade Span: KG-12; **Agency Type:** 1
Schools: 53
41 Primary; 7 Middle; 5 High; 0 Other Level
53 Regular; 0 Special Education; 0 Vocational; 0 Alternative
0 Magnet; 0 Charter; 7 Title I Eligible; 0 School-wide Title I
Students: 29,824 (51.9% male; 48.1% female)
Individual Education Program: 3,394 (11.4%);
English Language Learner: 774 (2.6%); Migrant: 0 (0.0%)
Eligible for Free Lunch Program: 2,459 (8.2%)
Eligible for Reduced-Price Lunch Program: 1,202 (4.0%)
Teachers: 1,884.6 (15.8 to 1)
Librarians/Media Specialists: 55.6 (536.4 to 1)
Guidance Counselors: 50.0 (596.5 to 1)
Current Spending: ($ per student per year):
Total: $6,494; Instruction: $3,928; Support Services: $2,223

Enrollment, Drop-out Rates and Diploma Recipients by Race/Ethnicity

Category	Total	White	Black	Asian	AIAN	Hisp.
Enrollment (%)	100.0	84.8	6.1	2.9	0.5	5.7
Drop-out Rate (%)	2.1	2.0	2.7	1.3	0.0	4.2
H.S. Diplomas (#)	2,226	1,964	89	74	10	89

Spring Hill

101 E S St • Spring Hill, KS 66083
(913) 592-7200
Grade Span: PK-12; **Agency Type:** 1
Schools: 4
2 Primary; 1 Middle; 1 High; 0 Other Level
4 Regular; 0 Special Education; 0 Vocational; 0 Alternative
0 Magnet; 1 Charter; 1 Title I Eligible; 0 School-wide Title I
Students: 1,562 (50.0% male; 50.0% female)
Individual Education Program: 188 (12.0%);
English Language Learner: 0 (0.0%); Migrant: 0 (0.0%)

Eligible for Free Lunch Program: 111 (7.1%)
Eligible for Reduced-Price Lunch Program: 43 (2.8%)
Teachers: 100.4 (15.6 to 1)
Librarians/Media Specialists: 3.5 (446.3 to 1)
Guidance Counselors: 3.0 (520.7 to 1)
Current Spending: ($ per student per year):
Total: $6,721; Instruction: $3,765; Support Services: $2,668
Enrollment, Drop-out Rates and Diploma Recipients by Race/Ethnicity

Category	Total	White	Black	Asian	AIAN	Hisp.
Enrollment (%)	100.0	95.0	1.1	0.5	0.8	2.6
Drop-out Rate (%)	1.8	1.8	0.0	0.0	0.0	0.0
H.S. Diplomas (#)	93	90	0	0	2	1

Labette County

Labette County
521 S Huston Ave • Altamont, KS 67330-0188
Mailing Address: Box 188 • Altamont, KS 67330-0188
(620) 784-5326 • http://www.usd506.k12.ks.us/
Grade Span: KG-12; **Agency Type:** 1
Schools: 6
5 Primary; 0 Middle; 1 High; 0 Other Level
6 Regular; 0 Special Education; 0 Vocational; 0 Alternative
0 Magnet; 0 Charter; 4 Title I Eligible; 0 School-wide Title I
Students: 1,707 (51.3% male; 48.7% female)
Individual Education Program: 163 (9.5%);
English Language Learner: 0 (0.0%); Migrant: 112 (6.6%)
Eligible for Free Lunch Program: 340 (19.9%)
Eligible for Reduced-Price Lunch Program: 217 (12.7%)
Teachers: 107.4 (15.9 to 1)
Librarians/Media Specialists: 3.0 (569.0 to 1)
Guidance Counselors: 1.0 (1,707.0 to 1)
Current Spending: ($ per student per year):
Total: $5,399; Instruction: $2,955; Support Services: $2,033
Enrollment, Drop-out Rates and Diploma Recipients by Race/Ethnicity

Category	Total	White	Black	Asian	AIAN	Hisp.
Enrollment (%)	100.0	90.2	0.9	0.5	6.0	2.5
Drop-out Rate (%)	0.5	0.5	n/a	0.0	0.0	0.0
H.S. Diplomas (#)	152	146	0	1	2	3

Parsons
2900 Southern • Parsons, KS 67357-1056
Mailing Address: Box 1056 • Parsons, KS 67357-1056
(620) 421-5950 • http://www.vikingnet.net/
Grade Span: PK-12; **Agency Type:** 1
Schools: 5
3 Primary; 1 Middle; 1 High; 0 Other Level
5 Regular; 0 Special Education; 0 Vocational; 0 Alternative
0 Magnet; 0 Charter; 3 Title I Eligible; 3 School-wide Title I
Students: 1,658 (52.2% male; 47.8% female)
Individual Education Program: 212 (12.8%);
English Language Learner: 0 (0.0%); Migrant: 35 (2.1%)
Eligible for Free Lunch Program: 696 (42.0%)
Eligible for Reduced-Price Lunch Program: 202 (12.2%)
Teachers: 103.0 (16.1 to 1)
Librarians/Media Specialists: 3.0 (552.7 to 1)
Guidance Counselors: 5.0 (331.6 to 1)
Current Spending: ($ per student per year):
Total: $5,097; Instruction: $2,794; Support Services: $1,875
Enrollment, Drop-out Rates and Diploma Recipients by Race/Ethnicity

Category	Total	White	Black	Asian	AIAN	Hisp.
Enrollment (%)	100.0	75.1	18.6	0.5	1.2	4.6
Drop-out Rate (%)	1.3	1.6	0.0	0.0	0.0	0.0
H.S. Diplomas (#)	106	86	13	2	0	5

Leavenworth County

Basehor-Linwood
2008 N 155th St • Basehor, KS 66007-0282
Mailing Address: PO Box 282 • Basehor, KS 66007-0282
(913) 724-1396 • http://www.usd458.k12.ks.us
Grade Span: KG-12; **Agency Type:** 1
Schools: 6
3 Primary; 1 Middle; 2 High; 0 Other Level
6 Regular; 0 Special Education; 0 Vocational; 0 Alternative
0 Magnet; 1 Charter; 2 Title I Eligible; 0 School-wide Title I
Students: 2,075 (50.2% male; 49.8% female)
Individual Education Program: 195 (9.4%);
English Language Learner: 0 (0.0%); Migrant: 0 (0.0%)
Eligible for Free Lunch Program: 86 (4.1%)
Eligible for Reduced-Price Lunch Program: 68 (3.3%)
Teachers: 97.0 (21.4 to 1)
Librarians/Media Specialists: 3.0 (691.7 to 1)
Guidance Counselors: 6.0 (345.8 to 1)
Current Spending: ($ per student per year):
Total: $4,796; Instruction: $2,279; Support Services: $2,259
Enrollment, Drop-out Rates and Diploma Recipients by Race/Ethnicity

Category	Total	White	Black	Asian	AIAN	Hisp.
Enrollment (%)	100.0	92.7	2.5	0.7	0.6	3.4
Drop-out Rate (%)	3.8	4.0	0.0	0.0	0.0	0.0
H.S. Diplomas (#)	127	125	1	0	1	0

Fort Leavenworth
5 Grant Ave • Fort Leavenworth, KS 66027-2701
(913) 651-7373 • http://www.ftlvn.com/district/index.htm
Grade Span: KG-09; **Agency Type:** 1
Schools: 4
3 Primary; 1 Middle; 0 High; 0 Other Level
4 Regular; 0 Special Education; 0 Vocational; 0 Alternative
0 Magnet; 0 Charter; 1 Title I Eligible; 0 School-wide Title I
Students: 1,989 (50.6% male; 49.4% female)
Individual Education Program: 261 (13.1%);
English Language Learner: 0 (0.0%); Migrant: 0 (0.0%)
Eligible for Free Lunch Program: 34 (1.7%)
Eligible for Reduced-Price Lunch Program: 112 (5.6%)
Teachers: 109.5 (18.2 to 1)
Librarians/Media Specialists: 4.0 (497.3 to 1)
Guidance Counselors: 4.0 (497.3 to 1)
Current Spending: ($ per student per year):
Total: $4,642; Instruction: $2,818; Support Services: $1,534
Enrollment, Drop-out Rates and Diploma Recipients by Race/Ethnicity

Category	Total	White	Black	Asian	AIAN	Hisp.
Enrollment (%)	100.0	74.7	15.6	3.0	0.8	6.0
Drop-out Rate (%)	0.0	0.0	0.0	n/a	0.0	0.0
H.S. Diplomas (#)	n/a	n/a	n/a	n/a	n/a	n/a

Lansing
613 Holiday Plaza • Lansing, KS 66043
(913) 727-1100 • http://usd469.net/
Grade Span: PK-12; **Agency Type:** 1
Schools: 4
1 Primary; 2 Middle; 1 High; 0 Other Level
4 Regular; 0 Special Education; 0 Vocational; 0 Alternative
0 Magnet; 0 Charter; 1 Title I Eligible; 0 School-wide Title I
Students: 2,086 (51.2% male; 48.8% female)
Individual Education Program: 217 (10.4%);
English Language Learner: 0 (0.0%); Migrant: 0 (0.0%)
Eligible for Free Lunch Program: 113 (5.4%)
Eligible for Reduced-Price Lunch Program: 61 (2.9%)
Teachers: 109.1 (19.1 to 1)
Librarians/Media Specialists: 4.0 (521.5 to 1)
Guidance Counselors: 4.0 (521.5 to 1)
Current Spending: ($ per student per year):
Total: $4,968; Instruction: $2,635; Support Services: $1,904
Enrollment, Drop-out Rates and Diploma Recipients by Race/Ethnicity

Category	Total	White	Black	Asian	AIAN	Hisp.
Enrollment (%)	100.0	88.3	6.9	1.5	0.4	3.0
Drop-out Rate (%)	1.6	1.8	0.0	0.0	0.0	0.0
H.S. Diplomas (#)	147	134	5	1	1	6

Leavenworth
200 N 4th • Leavenworth, KS 66048
Mailing Address: PO Box 186 • Leavenworth, KS 66048
(913) 684-1400 • http://www.lvksch.org/
Grade Span: KG-12; **Agency Type:** 1
Schools: 9
6 Primary; 2 Middle; 1 High; 0 Other Level
9 Regular; 0 Special Education; 0 Vocational; 0 Alternative
0 Magnet; 0 Charter; 4 Title I Eligible; 4 School-wide Title I
Students: 4,385 (52.7% male; 47.3% female)
Individual Education Program: 765 (17.4%);
English Language Learner: 96 (2.2%); Migrant: 0 (0.0%)
Eligible for Free Lunch Program: 1,511 (34.5%)
Eligible for Reduced-Price Lunch Program: 490 (11.2%)
Teachers: 413.8 (10.6 to 1)
Librarians/Media Specialists: 9.0 (487.2 to 1)
Guidance Counselors: 12.0 (365.4 to 1)
Current Spending: ($ per student per year):
Total: $7,738; Instruction: $4,488; Support Services: $2,855
Enrollment, Drop-out Rates and Diploma Recipients by Race/Ethnicity

Category	Total	White	Black	Asian	AIAN	Hisp.
Enrollment (%)	100.0	65.7	26.0	3.0	0.6	4.6
Drop-out Rate (%)	6.9	6.5	7.6	0.0	0.0	13.2
H.S. Diplomas (#)	282	196	64	6	3	13

Tonganoxie

330 E 24/40 Hwy • Tonganoxie, KS 66086-0199
Mailing Address: Box 199 • Tonganoxie, KS 66086-0199
(913) 845-2153
Grade Span: KG-12; **Agency Type:** 1
Schools: 3
1 Primary; 1 Middle; 1 High; 0 Other Level
3 Regular; 0 Special Education; 0 Vocational; 0 Alternative
0 Magnet; 0 Charter; 1 Title I Eligible; 0 School-wide Title I
Students: 1,546 (51.0% male; 49.0% female)
Individual Education Program: 200 (12.9%);
English Language Learner: 0 (0.0%); Migrant: 0 (0.0%)
Eligible for Free Lunch Program: 169 (10.9%)
Eligible for Reduced-Price Lunch Program: 147 (9.5%)
Teachers: 92.0 (16.8 to 1)
Librarians/Media Specialists: 2.0 (773.0 to 1)
Guidance Counselors: 4.0 (386.5 to 1)
Current Spending: ($ per student per year):
Total: $5,435; Instruction: $3,203; Support Services: $1,830
Enrollment, Drop-out Rates and Diploma Recipients by Race/Ethnicity

Category	Total	White	Black	Asian	AIAN	Hisp.
Enrollment (%)	100.0	93.1	1.6	1.0	0.6	3.7
Drop-out Rate (%)	2.7	2.6	25.0	0.0	0.0	0.0
H.S. Diplomas (#)	112	110	0	1	1	0

Lyon County

Emporia

501 Merchant • Emporia, KS 66801-7201
Mailing Address: Box 1008 • Emporia, KS 66801-1008
(620) 341-2200 • http://www.usd253.org/
Grade Span: PK-12; **Agency Type:** 1
Schools: 11
7 Primary; 3 Middle; 1 High; 0 Other Level
11 Regular; 0 Special Education; 0 Vocational; 0 Alternative
0 Magnet; 0 Charter; 5 Title I Eligible; 5 School-wide Title I
Students: 5,068 (51.0% male; 49.0% female)
Individual Education Program: 561 (11.1%);
English Language Learner: 1,152 (22.7%); Migrant: 467 (9.2%)
Eligible for Free Lunch Program: 2,102 (41.5%)
Eligible for Reduced-Price Lunch Program: 581 (11.5%)
Teachers: 386.8 (13.1 to 1)
Librarians/Media Specialists: 7.2 (703.9 to 1)
Guidance Counselors: 10.6 (478.1 to 1)
Current Spending: ($ per student per year):
Total: $7,178; Instruction: $4,475; Support Services: $2,399
Enrollment, Drop-out Rates and Diploma Recipients by Race/Ethnicity

Category	Total	White	Black	Asian	AIAN	Hisp.
Enrollment (%)	100.0	55.1	4.4	2.9	0.4	37.2
Drop-out Rate (%)	2.0	1.6	1.4	0.0	0.0	3.1
H.S. Diplomas (#)	296	221	12	9	2	52

Mcpherson County

Mcpherson

514 N Main • Mcpherson, KS 67460-3499
(620) 241-9400
Grade Span: KG-12; **Agency Type:** 1
Schools: 6
4 Primary; 1 Middle; 1 High; 0 Other Level
6 Regular; 0 Special Education; 0 Vocational; 0 Alternative
0 Magnet; 0 Charter; 0 Title I Eligible; 0 School-wide Title I
Students: 2,567 (51.4% male; 48.6% female)
Individual Education Program: 414 (16.1%);
English Language Learner: 11 (0.4%); Migrant: 0 (0.0%)
Eligible for Free Lunch Program: 364 (14.2%)
Eligible for Reduced-Price Lunch Program: 159 (6.2%)
Teachers: 211.8 (12.1 to 1)
Librarians/Media Specialists: 5.0 (513.4 to 1)
Guidance Counselors: 8.0 (320.9 to 1)
Current Spending: ($ per student per year):
Total: $6,868; Instruction: $3,813; Support Services: $2,617
Enrollment, Drop-out Rates and Diploma Recipients by Race/Ethnicity

Category	Total	White	Black	Asian	AIAN	Hisp.
Enrollment (%)	100.0	92.6	3.0	1.2	0.5	2.7
Drop-out Rate (%)	1.9	1.7	7.7	11.1	0.0	4.8
H.S. Diplomas (#)	234	227	3	2	0	2

Miami County

Paola

202 E Wea • Paola, KS 66071-0268
Mailing Address: Box 268 • Paola, KS 66071-0268
(913) 294-3646 • http://usd368.k12.ks.us/
Grade Span: KG-12; **Agency Type:** 1
Schools: 5
3 Primary; 1 Middle; 1 High; 0 Other Level
5 Regular; 0 Special Education; 0 Vocational; 0 Alternative
0 Magnet; 0 Charter; 1 Title I Eligible; 0 School-wide Title I
Students: 2,116 (50.8% male; 49.2% female)
Individual Education Program: 297 (14.0%);
English Language Learner: 0 (0.0%); Migrant: 0 (0.0%)
Eligible for Free Lunch Program: 360 (17.0%)
Eligible for Reduced-Price Lunch Program: 154 (7.3%)
Teachers: 181.2 (11.7 to 1)
Librarians/Media Specialists: 4.0 (529.0 to 1)
Guidance Counselors: 6.0 (352.7 to 1)
Current Spending: ($ per student per year):
Total: $8,430; Instruction: $5,553; Support Services: $2,522
Enrollment, Drop-out Rates and Diploma Recipients by Race/Ethnicity

Category	Total	White	Black	Asian	AIAN	Hisp.
Enrollment (%)	100.0	93.3	4.1	0.5	0.4	1.7
Drop-out Rate (%)	3.9	4.1	0.0	0.0	0.0	0.0
H.S. Diplomas (#)	147	141	4	0	0	2

Montgomery County

Coffeyville

615 Ellis • Coffeyville, KS 67337-3427
(620) 252-6800 • http://cvilleschools.com/
Grade Span: KG-12; **Agency Type:** 1
Schools: 5
3 Primary; 1 Middle; 1 High; 0 Other Level
5 Regular; 0 Special Education; 0 Vocational; 0 Alternative
0 Magnet; 0 Charter; 3 Title I Eligible; 2 School-wide Title I
Students: 2,000 (52.2% male; 47.8% female)
Individual Education Program: 300 (15.0%);
English Language Learner: 0 (0.0%); Migrant: 75 (3.8%)
Eligible for Free Lunch Program: 876 (43.8%)
Eligible for Reduced-Price Lunch Program: 232 (11.6%)
Teachers: 124.0 (16.1 to 1)
Librarians/Media Specialists: 2.0 (1,000.0 to 1)
Guidance Counselors: 6.0 (333.3 to 1)
Current Spending: ($ per student per year):
Total: $5,267; Instruction: $3,045; Support Services: $1,848
Enrollment, Drop-out Rates and Diploma Recipients by Race/Ethnicity

Category	Total	White	Black	Asian	AIAN	Hisp.
Enrollment (%)	100.0	60.8	19.0	1.3	15.1	3.8
Drop-out Rate (%)	3.5	3.0	7.8	0.0	2.1	0.0
H.S. Diplomas (#)	168	106	24	5	31	2

Independence

517 N Tenth • Independence, KS 67301-0487
Mailing Address: PO Drawer 487 • Independence, KS 67301-0487
(620) 332-1800 • http://www.indyschools.com/
Grade Span: KG-12; **Agency Type:** 1
Schools: 5
2 Primary; 2 Middle; 1 High; 0 Other Level
5 Regular; 0 Special Education; 0 Vocational; 0 Alternative
0 Magnet; 0 Charter; 3 Title I Eligible; 3 School-wide Title I
Students: 2,062 (53.5% male; 46.5% female)
Individual Education Program: 247 (12.0%);
English Language Learner: 0 (0.0%); Migrant: 51 (2.5%)
Eligible for Free Lunch Program: 654 (31.7%)
Eligible for Reduced-Price Lunch Program: 227 (11.0%)
Teachers: 125.5 (16.4 to 1)
Librarians/Media Specialists: 5.0 (412.4 to 1)
Guidance Counselors: 5.5 (374.9 to 1)
Current Spending: ($ per student per year):
Total: $4,990; Instruction: $2,890; Support Services: $1,727
Enrollment, Drop-out Rates and Diploma Recipients by Race/Ethnicity

Category	Total	White	Black	Asian	AIAN	Hisp.
Enrollment (%)	100.0	84.3	9.9	0.6	1.5	3.7
Drop-out Rate (%)	3.3	3.5	1.6	0.0	0.0	4.2
H.S. Diplomas (#)	162	146	7	2	1	6

Neosho County

Chanute Public Schools

410 S Evergreen • Chanute, KS 66720-2394
(620) 432-2500 • http://www.usd413.k12.ks.us/
Grade Span: KG-12; **Agency Type:** 1
Schools: 7

4 Primary; 1 Middle; 2 High; 0 Other Level
7 Regular; 0 Special Education; 0 Vocational; 0 Alternative
0 Magnet; 2 Charter; 4 Title I Eligible; 1 School-wide Title I
Students: 1,919 (50.1% male; 49.9% female)
Individual Education Program: 354 (18.4%);
English Language Learner: 0 (0.0%); Migrant: 72 (3.8%)
Eligible for Free Lunch Program: 619 (32.3%)
Eligible for Reduced-Price Lunch Program: 214 (11.2%)
Teachers: 120.0 (16.0 to 1)
Librarians/Media Specialists: 5.0 (383.8 to 1)
Guidance Counselors: 5.0 (383.8 to 1)
Current Spending: ($ per student per year):
Total: $5,139; Instruction: $3,225; Support Services: $1,569
Enrollment, Drop-out Rates and Diploma Recipients by Race/Ethnicity

Category	Total	White	Black	Asian	AIAN	Hisp.
Enrollment (%)	100.0	91.4	2.4	1.0	1.8	3.4
Drop-out Rate (%)	3.2	2.9	0.0	0.0	0.0	22.2
H.S. Diplomas (#)	117	111	3	1	1	1

Reno County

Buhler
406 W 7th • Buhler, KS 67522-0320
Mailing Address: Box 320 • Buhler, KS 67522-0320
(620) 543-2258 • http://buhler.usd313.k12.ks.us/
Grade Span: PK-12; **Agency Type:** 1
Schools: 6
3 Primary; 2 Middle; 1 High; 0 Other Level
6 Regular; 0 Special Education; 0 Vocational; 0 Alternative
0 Magnet; 0 Charter; 2 Title I Eligible; 0 School-wide Title I
Students: 2,279 (51.2% male; 48.8% female)
Individual Education Program: 270 (11.8%);
English Language Learner: 4 (0.2%); Migrant: 0 (0.0%)
Eligible for Free Lunch Program: 394 (17.3%)
Eligible for Reduced-Price Lunch Program: 204 (9.0%)
Teachers: 135.0 (16.9 to 1)
Librarians/Media Specialists: 5.8 (392.9 to 1)
Guidance Counselors: 3.8 (599.7 to 1)
Current Spending: ($ per student per year):
Total: $5,604; Instruction: $2,919; Support Services: $2,290
Enrollment, Drop-out Rates and Diploma Recipients by Race/Ethnicity

Category	Total	White	Black	Asian	AIAN	Hisp.
Enrollment (%)	100.0	91.1	2.3	1.0	0.7	4.9
Drop-out Rate (%)	2.8	2.5	9.1	0.0	0.0	11.1
H.S. Diplomas (#)	167	159	1	4	0	3

Hutchinson Public Schools
1520 N Plum • Hutchinson, KS 67501
Mailing Address: Box 1908 • Hutchinson, KS 67504-1908
(620) 665-4400 • http://www.usd308.com/
Grade Span: PK-12; **Agency Type:** 1
Schools: 11
8 Primary; 2 Middle; 1 High; 0 Other Level
11 Regular; 0 Special Education; 0 Vocational; 0 Alternative
0 Magnet; 0 Charter; 4 Title I Eligible; 3 School-wide Title I
Students: 5,049 (51.2% male; 48.8% female)
Individual Education Program: 806 (16.0%);
English Language Learner: 36 (0.7%); Migrant: 0 (0.0%)
Eligible for Free Lunch Program: 1,902 (37.7%)
Eligible for Reduced-Price Lunch Program: 533 (10.6%)
Teachers: 333.8 (15.1 to 1)
Librarians/Media Specialists: 9.0 (561.0 to 1)
Guidance Counselors: 9.0 (561.0 to 1)
Current Spending: ($ per student per year):
Total: $6,382; Instruction: $3,210; Support Services: $2,766
Enrollment, Drop-out Rates and Diploma Recipients by Race/Ethnicity

Category	Total	White	Black	Asian	AIAN	Hisp.
Enrollment (%)	100.0	79.7	6.6	0.7	0.6	12.3
Drop-out Rate (%)	4.5	3.9	8.1	0.0	14.3	8.5
H.S. Diplomas (#)	294	243	19	4	2	26

Riley County

Manhattan
2031 Poyntz • Manhattan, KS 66502
(785) 587-2000 • http://www.usd383.org/
Grade Span: KG-12; **Agency Type:** 1
Schools: 11
8 Primary; 2 Middle; 1 High; 0 Other Level
11 Regular; 0 Special Education; 0 Vocational; 0 Alternative
0 Magnet; 0 Charter; 6 Title I Eligible; 1 School-wide Title I
Students: 5,445 (52.2% male; 47.8% female)
Individual Education Program: 787 (14.5%);
English Language Learner: 121 (2.2%); Migrant: 0 (0.0%)
Eligible for Free Lunch Program: 1,027 (18.9%)
Eligible for Reduced-Price Lunch Program: 523 (9.6%)
Teachers: 378.0 (14.4 to 1)
Librarians/Media Specialists: 13.0 (418.8 to 1)
Guidance Counselors: 8.5 (640.6 to 1)
Current Spending: ($ per student per year):
Total: $6,982; Instruction: $3,974; Support Services: $2,546
Enrollment, Drop-out Rates and Diploma Recipients by Race/Ethnicity

Category	Total	White	Black	Asian	AIAN	Hisp.
Enrollment (%)	100.0	81.6	8.9	4.9	0.5	4.2
Drop-out Rate (%)	1.1	1.0	2.4	0.0	0.0	0.0
H.S. Diplomas (#)	417	358	33	11	1	14

Saline County

Salina
1511 Gypsum • Salina, KS 67402-0797
Mailing Address: Box 797 • Salina, KS 67402-0797
(785) 309-4700 • http://www.usd305.com/
Grade Span: KG-12; **Agency Type:** 1
Schools: 14
10 Primary; 2 Middle; 2 High; 0 Other Level
14 Regular; 0 Special Education; 0 Vocational; 0 Alternative
0 Magnet; 0 Charter; 6 Title I Eligible; 6 School-wide Title I
Students: 7,715 (51.5% male; 48.5% female)
Individual Education Program: 1,105 (14.3%);
English Language Learner: 239 (3.1%); Migrant: 29 (0.4%)
Eligible for Free Lunch Program: 2,292 (29.7%)
Eligible for Reduced-Price Lunch Program: 923 (12.0%)
Teachers: 575.0 (13.4 to 1)
Librarians/Media Specialists: 14.0 (551.1 to 1)
Guidance Counselors: 21.3 (362.2 to 1)
Current Spending: ($ per student per year):
Total: $7,276; Instruction: $4,439; Support Services: $2,438
Enrollment, Drop-out Rates and Diploma Recipients by Race/Ethnicity

Category	Total	White	Black	Asian	AIAN	Hisp.
Enrollment (%)	100.0	79.0	6.9	2.7	0.8	10.5
Drop-out Rate (%)	2.5	2.4	4.1	0.0	0.0	4.0
H.S. Diplomas (#)	462	409	19	13	1	20

Sedgwick County

Derby
120 E Washington • Derby, KS 67037-1489
(316) 788-8400 • http://www.derbyschools.com/
Grade Span: PK-12; **Agency Type:** 1
Schools: 12
9 Primary; 2 Middle; 1 High; 0 Other Level
12 Regular; 0 Special Education; 0 Vocational; 0 Alternative
0 Magnet; 0 Charter; 4 Title I Eligible; 2 School-wide Title I
Students: 6,752 (51.1% male; 48.9% female)
Individual Education Program: 908 (13.4%);
English Language Learner: 0 (0.0%); Migrant: 0 (0.0%)
Eligible for Free Lunch Program: 1,262 (18.7%)
Eligible for Reduced-Price Lunch Program: 590 (8.7%)
Teachers: 425.8 (15.9 to 1)
Librarians/Media Specialists: 13.0 (519.4 to 1)
Guidance Counselors: 7.0 (964.6 to 1)
Current Spending: ($ per student per year):
Total: $5,722; Instruction: $3,375; Support Services: $1,989
Enrollment, Drop-out Rates and Diploma Recipients by Race/Ethnicity

Category	Total	White	Black	Asian	AIAN	Hisp.
Enrollment (%)	100.0	81.9	6.0	5.0	1.7	5.4
Drop-out Rate (%)	0.9	0.9	0.9	0.0	0.0	1.2
H.S. Diplomas (#)	420	365	17	16	5	17

Goddard
201 S Main • Goddard, KS 67052-0249
Mailing Address: Box 249 • Goddard, KS 67052-0249
(316) 794-4000 • http://www.goddardusd.com/
Grade Span: KG-12; **Agency Type:** 1
Schools: 8
3 Primary; 4 Middle; 1 High; 0 Other Level
8 Regular; 0 Special Education; 0 Vocational; 0 Alternative
0 Magnet; 0 Charter; 3 Title I Eligible; 0 School-wide Title I
Students: 3,939 (52.3% male; 47.7% female)
Individual Education Program: 494 (12.5%);
English Language Learner: 0 (0.0%); Migrant: 0 (0.0%)
Eligible for Free Lunch Program: 325 (8.3%)
Eligible for Reduced-Price Lunch Program: 251 (6.4%)
Teachers: 203.5 (19.4 to 1)
Librarians/Media Specialists: 7.0 (562.7 to 1)
Guidance Counselors: 10.0 (393.9 to 1)
Current Spending: ($ per student per year):
Total: $5,235; Instruction: $2,827; Support Services: $2,062

Enrollment, Drop-out Rates and Diploma Recipients by Race/Ethnicity

Category	Total	White	Black	Asian	AIAN	Hisp.
Enrollment (%)	100.0	90.0	2.1	2.3	1.3	4.4
Drop-out Rate (%)	1.7	1.8	0.0	4.2	0.0	0.0
H.S. Diplomas (#)	247	217	3	12	5	10

Haysville

1745 W Grand Ave • Haysville, KS 67060-1234
(316) 554-2200 • http://www.usd261.com/
Grade Span: PK-12; **Agency Type:** 1
Schools: 7
5 Primary; 1 Middle; 1 High; 0 Other Level
7 Regular; 0 Special Education; 0 Vocational; 0 Alternative
0 Magnet; 0 Charter; 3 Title I Eligible; 1 School-wide Title I
Students: 4,588 (51.9% male; 48.1% female)
Individual Education Program: 701 (15.3%);
English Language Learner: 79 (1.7%); Migrant: 323 (7.0%)
Eligible for Free Lunch Program: 991 (21.6%)
Eligible for Reduced-Price Lunch Program: 444 (9.7%)
Teachers: 285.7 (16.1 to 1)
Librarians/Media Specialists: 8.0 (573.5 to 1)
Guidance Counselors: 11.5 (399.0 to 1)
Current Spending: ($ per student per year):
Total: $5,898; Instruction: $3,300; Support Services: $2,226

Enrollment, Drop-out Rates and Diploma Recipients by Race/Ethnicity

Category	Total	White	Black	Asian	AIAN	Hisp.
Enrollment (%)	100.0	87.2	1.6	3.5	2.5	5.2
Drop-out Rate (%)	3.2	2.8	0.0	2.7	36.8	5.2
H.S. Diplomas (#)	250	231	4	7	4	4

Maize

201 S Park • Maize, KS 67101-0580
(316) 722-0614 • http://www.usd266.com/
Grade Span: KG-12; **Agency Type:** 1
Schools: 6
3 Primary; 2 Middle; 1 High; 0 Other Level
6 Regular; 0 Special Education; 0 Vocational; 0 Alternative
0 Magnet; 0 Charter; 1 Title I Eligible; 0 School-wide Title I
Students: 5,585 (50.5% male; 49.5% female)
Individual Education Program: 523 (9.4%);
English Language Learner: 47 (0.8%); Migrant: 0 (0.0%)
Eligible for Free Lunch Program: 254 (4.5%)
Eligible for Reduced-Price Lunch Program: 123 (2.2%)
Teachers: 296.5 (18.8 to 1)
Librarians/Media Specialists: 6.0 (930.8 to 1)
Guidance Counselors: 15.0 (372.3 to 1)
Current Spending: ($ per student per year):
Total: $5,258; Instruction: $3,381; Support Services: $1,588

Enrollment, Drop-out Rates and Diploma Recipients by Race/Ethnicity

Category	Total	White	Black	Asian	AIAN	Hisp.
Enrollment (%)	100.0	89.9	2.0	2.8	0.9	4.3
Drop-out Rate (%)	1.8	1.6	0.0	0.0	0.0	8.0
H.S. Diplomas (#)	308	285	4	11	1	7

Mulvane

430 E Main • Mulvane, KS 67110
Mailing Address: Box 129 • Mulvane, KS 67110
(316) 777-1102 • http://www.usd263.k12.ks.us/
Grade Span: KG-12; **Agency Type:** 1
Schools: 5
2 Primary; 2 Middle; 1 High; 0 Other Level
5 Regular; 0 Special Education; 0 Vocational; 0 Alternative
0 Magnet; 0 Charter; 2 Title I Eligible; 0 School-wide Title I
Students: 1,961 (50.9% male; 49.1% female)
Individual Education Program: 159 (8.1%);
English Language Learner: 0 (0.0%); Migrant: 0 (0.0%)
Eligible for Free Lunch Program: 262 (13.4%)
Eligible for Reduced-Price Lunch Program: 170 (8.7%)
Teachers: 119.7 (16.4 to 1)
Librarians/Media Specialists: 4.0 (490.3 to 1)
Guidance Counselors: 6.0 (326.8 to 1)
Current Spending: ($ per student per year):
Total: $5,280; Instruction: $2,972; Support Services: $1,918

Enrollment, Drop-out Rates and Diploma Recipients by Race/Ethnicity

Category	Total	White	Black	Asian	AIAN	Hisp.
Enrollment (%)	100.0	92.8	1.1	0.4	2.4	3.3
Drop-out Rate (%)	0.6	0.6	n/a	0.0	0.0	0.0
H.S. Diplomas (#)	157	152	0	1	3	1

Renwick

326 N Main • Andale, KS 67001-0068
Mailing Address: Box 68 • Andale, KS 67001-0068
(316) 444-2165 • http://www.usd267.com/
Grade Span: KG-12; **Agency Type:** 1
Schools: 7
5 Primary; 0 Middle; 2 High; 0 Other Level
7 Regular; 0 Special Education; 0 Vocational; 0 Alternative
0 Magnet; 1 Charter; 4 Title I Eligible; 0 School-wide Title I
Students: 2,021 (53.6% male; 46.4% female)
Individual Education Program: 178 (8.8%);
English Language Learner: 0 (0.0%); Migrant: 0 (0.0%)
Eligible for Free Lunch Program: 190 (9.4%)
Eligible for Reduced-Price Lunch Program: 192 (9.5%)
Teachers: 125.8 (16.1 to 1)
Librarians/Media Specialists: 3.6 (561.4 to 1)
Guidance Counselors: 3.0 (673.7 to 1)
Current Spending: ($ per student per year):
Total: $5,495; Instruction: $3,139; Support Services: $1,974

Enrollment, Drop-out Rates and Diploma Recipients by Race/Ethnicity

Category	Total	White	Black	Asian	AIAN	Hisp.
Enrollment (%)	100.0	98.0	0.1	0.1	0.8	0.9
Drop-out Rate (%)	0.2	0.2	n/a	0.0	0.0	0.0
H.S. Diplomas (#)	124	123	0	1	0	0

Valley Center Public Schools

132 S Park • Valley Center, KS 67147-0157
Mailing Address: Box 157 • Valley Center, KS 67147-0157
(316) 755-7100 • http://www.usd262.net/
Grade Span: KG-12; **Agency Type:** 1
Schools: 6
2 Primary; 2 Middle; 2 High; 0 Other Level
6 Regular; 0 Special Education; 0 Vocational; 0 Alternative
0 Magnet; 1 Charter; 3 Title I Eligible; 0 School-wide Title I
Students: 2,374 (51.7% male; 48.3% female)
Individual Education Program: 323 (13.6%);
English Language Learner: 0 (0.0%); Migrant: 0 (0.0%)
Eligible for Free Lunch Program: 275 (11.6%)
Eligible for Reduced-Price Lunch Program: 141 (5.9%)
Teachers: 127.5 (18.6 to 1)
Librarians/Media Specialists: 4.7 (505.1 to 1)
Guidance Counselors: 5.0 (474.8 to 1)
Current Spending: ($ per student per year):
Total: $5,123; Instruction: $2,919; Support Services: $1,810

Enrollment, Drop-out Rates and Diploma Recipients by Race/Ethnicity

Category	Total	White	Black	Asian	AIAN	Hisp.
Enrollment (%)	100.0	92.2	1.4	0.6	2.1	3.6
Drop-out Rate (%)	1.6	1.3	0.0	0.0	4.5	10.0
H.S. Diplomas (#)	177	171	1	0	3	2

Wichita

201 N Water • Wichita, KS 67202-1292
(316) 973-4000 • http://www.usd259.com/
Grade Span: PK-12; **Agency Type:** 1
Schools: 90
61 Primary; 16 Middle; 12 High; 1 Other Level
90 Regular; 0 Special Education; 0 Vocational; 0 Alternative
29 Magnet; 0 Charter; 23 Title I Eligible; 23 School-wide Title I
Students: 48,913 (51.0% male; 49.0% female)
Individual Education Program: 7,007 (14.3%);
English Language Learner: 4,902 (10.0%); Migrant: 2,252 (4.6%)
Eligible for Free Lunch Program: 23,532 (48.1%)
Eligible for Reduced-Price Lunch Program: 5,944 (12.2%)
Teachers: 3,041.4 (16.1 to 1)
Librarians/Media Specialists: 67.4 (725.7 to 1)
Guidance Counselors: 90.6 (539.9 to 1)
Current Spending: ($ per student per year):
Total: $6,533; Instruction: $3,767; Support Services: $2,503

Enrollment, Drop-out Rates and Diploma Recipients by Race/Ethnicity

Category	Total	White	Black	Asian	AIAN	Hisp.
Enrollment (%)	100.0	49.8	23.6	5.5	2.7	18.4
Drop-out Rate (%)	8.0	7.5	8.2	2.9	9.6	13.2
H.S. Diplomas (#)	2,147	1,325	401	162	36	223

Seward County

Liberal

401 N Kansas • Liberal, KS 67901
Mailing Address: Box 949 • Liberal, KS 67905-0949
(620) 626-3800 • http://www.usd480.net/
Grade Span: PK-12; **Agency Type:** 1
Schools: 12
7 Primary; 4 Middle; 1 High; 0 Other Level
12 Regular; 0 Special Education; 0 Vocational; 0 Alternative
0 Magnet; 0 Charter; 4 Title I Eligible; 4 School-wide Title I
Students: 4,603 (52.7% male; 47.3% female)
Individual Education Program: 412 (9.0%);
English Language Learner: 0 (0.0%); Migrant: 1,255 (27.3%)
Eligible for Free Lunch Program: 2,291 (49.8%)
Eligible for Reduced-Price Lunch Program: 443 (9.6%)
Teachers: 277.5 (16.6 to 1)
Librarians/Media Specialists: 4.0 (1,150.8 to 1)

Guidance Counselors: 9.0 (511.4 to 1)
Current Spending: ($ per student per year):
Total: $5,861; Instruction: $3,228; Support Services: $2,194
Enrollment, Drop-out Rates and Diploma Recipients by Race/Ethnicity

Category	Total	White	Black	Asian	AIAN	Hisp.
Enrollment (%)	100.0	30.2	5.2	3.4	0.2	61.0
Drop-out Rate (%)	9.4	5.4	7.6	0.0	16.7	14.6
H.S. Diplomas (#)	178	92	14	11	1	60

Shawnee County

Auburn Washburn
5928 SW 53rd • Topeka, KS 66610-9451
(785) 339-4000 • http://www.usd437.net
Grade Span: PK-12; **Agency Type:** 1
Schools: 8
5 Primary; 2 Middle; 1 High; 0 Other Level
8 Regular; 0 Special Education; 0 Vocational; 0 Alternative
0 Magnet; 0 Charter; 3 Title I Eligible; 0 School-wide Title I
Students: 5,132 (50.1% male; 49.9% female)
Individual Education Program: 674 (13.1%);
English Language Learner: 43 (0.8%); Migrant: 0 (0.0%)
Eligible for Free Lunch Program: 588 (11.5%)
Eligible for Reduced-Price Lunch Program: 305 (5.9%)
Teachers: 373.7 (13.7 to 1)
Librarians/Media Specialists: 9.0 (570.2 to 1)
Guidance Counselors: 14.0 (366.6 to 1)
Current Spending: ($ per student per year):
Total: $5,878; Instruction: $3,385; Support Services: $2,118
Enrollment, Drop-out Rates and Diploma Recipients by Race/Ethnicity

Category	Total	White	Black	Asian	AIAN	Hisp.
Enrollment (%)	100.0	86.1	5.2	2.5	1.5	4.7
Drop-out Rate (%)	3.0	3.1	3.0	3.1	0.0	0.0
H.S. Diplomas (#)	325	295	10	10	2	8

Seaman
901 NW Lyman Rd • Topeka, KS 66608-1900
(785) 575-8600 • http://www.usd345.com/
Grade Span: PK-12; **Agency Type:** 1
Schools: 11
8 Primary; 2 Middle; 1 High; 0 Other Level
11 Regular; 0 Special Education; 0 Vocational; 0 Alternative
0 Magnet; 0 Charter; 3 Title I Eligible; 0 School-wide Title I
Students: 3,506 (52.3% male; 47.7% female)
Individual Education Program: 473 (13.5%);
English Language Learner: 0 (0.0%); Migrant: 0 (0.0%)
Eligible for Free Lunch Program: 428 (12.2%)
Eligible for Reduced-Price Lunch Program: 225 (6.4%)
Teachers: 255.0 (13.7 to 1)
Librarians/Media Specialists: 7.0 (500.9 to 1)
Guidance Counselors: 9.0 (389.6 to 1)
Current Spending: ($ per student per year):
Total: $6,078; Instruction: $3,277; Support Services: $2,352
Enrollment, Drop-out Rates and Diploma Recipients by Race/Ethnicity

Category	Total	White	Black	Asian	AIAN	Hisp.
Enrollment (%)	100.0	91.4	1.5	0.9	2.1	4.1
Drop-out Rate (%)	2.0	2.1	0.0	0.0	2.1	0.0
H.S. Diplomas (#)	235	224	1	1	0	9

Shawnee Heights
4401 SE Shawnee Heights Rd • Tecumseh, KS 66542-9799
(785) 379-5800 • http://www.snh450.k12.ks.us/district/index.htm
Grade Span: PK-12; **Agency Type:** 1
Schools: 6
4 Primary; 1 Middle; 1 High; 0 Other Level
6 Regular; 0 Special Education; 0 Vocational; 0 Alternative
0 Magnet; 0 Charter; 1 Title I Eligible; 0 School-wide Title I
Students: 3,392 (52.5% male; 47.5% female)
Individual Education Program: 509 (15.0%);
English Language Learner: 0 (0.0%); Migrant: 0 (0.0%)
Eligible for Free Lunch Program: 455 (13.4%)
Eligible for Reduced-Price Lunch Program: 214 (6.3%)
Teachers: 222.3 (15.3 to 1)
Librarians/Media Specialists: 7.0 (484.6 to 1)
Guidance Counselors: 10.0 (339.2 to 1)
Current Spending: ($ per student per year):
Total: $6,174; Instruction: $3,463; Support Services: $2,376
Enrollment, Drop-out Rates and Diploma Recipients by Race/Ethnicity

Category	Total	White	Black	Asian	AIAN	Hisp.
Enrollment (%)	100.0	84.6	7.4	0.5	0.9	6.6
Drop-out Rate (%)	0.7	0.7	1.5	0.0	0.0	0.0
H.S. Diplomas (#)	255	222	10	4	4	15

Topeka Public Schools
624 SW 24th • Topeka, KS 66611-1294
(785) 575-6100 • http://www.topeka.k12.ks.us/
Grade Span: PK-12; **Agency Type:** 1
Schools: 32
21 Primary; 6 Middle; 4 High; 1 Other Level
32 Regular; 0 Special Education; 0 Vocational; 0 Alternative
0 Magnet; 1 Charter; 20 Title I Eligible; 12 School-wide Title I
Students: 14,025 (51.4% male; 48.6% female)
Individual Education Program: 2,397 (17.1%);
English Language Learner: 352 (2.5%); Migrant: 319 (2.3%)
Eligible for Free Lunch Program: 6,988 (49.8%)
Eligible for Reduced-Price Lunch Program: 1,754 (12.5%)
Teachers: 1,071.4 (13.1 to 1)
Librarians/Media Specialists: 31.5 (445.2 to 1)
Guidance Counselors: 35.5 (395.1 to 1)
Current Spending: ($ per student per year):
Total: $6,758; Instruction: $3,443; Support Services: $3,040
Enrollment, Drop-out Rates and Diploma Recipients by Race/Ethnicity

Category	Total	White	Black	Asian	AIAN	Hisp.
Enrollment (%)	100.0	53.6	25.8	1.1	3.4	16.0
Drop-out Rate (%)	6.3	5.0	8.1	0.0	10.0	8.7
H.S. Diplomas (#)	769	496	148	17	28	80

Sumner County

Wellington
221 S Washington • Wellington, KS 67152-0648
Mailing Address: Box 648 • Wellington, KS 67152-0648
(620) 326-4300 • http://www.usd353.com/
Grade Span: KG-12; **Agency Type:** 1
Schools: 7
4 Primary; 2 Middle; 1 High; 0 Other Level
7 Regular; 0 Special Education; 0 Vocational; 0 Alternative
0 Magnet; 0 Charter; 3 Title I Eligible; 0 School-wide Title I
Students: 1,765 (51.4% male; 48.6% female)
Individual Education Program: 283 (16.0%);
English Language Learner: 0 (0.0%); Migrant: 0 (0.0%)
Eligible for Free Lunch Program: 551 (31.2%)
Eligible for Reduced-Price Lunch Program: 218 (12.4%)
Teachers: 128.8 (13.7 to 1)
Librarians/Media Specialists: 2.0 (882.5 to 1)
Guidance Counselors: 3.8 (464.5 to 1)
Current Spending: ($ per student per year):
Total: $6,203; Instruction: $3,871; Support Services: $2,041
Enrollment, Drop-out Rates and Diploma Recipients by Race/Ethnicity

Category	Total	White	Black	Asian	AIAN	Hisp.
Enrollment (%)	100.0	86.8	3.1	0.3	0.6	9.2
Drop-out Rate (%)	1.9	2.0	12.5	0.0	0.0	0.0
H.S. Diplomas (#)	140	127	2	0	0	11

Wyandotte County

Bonner Springs
2200 S 138th St • Bonner Springs, KS 66012-0435
Mailing Address: PO Box 435 • Bonner Springs, KS 66012-0435
(913) 422-5600 • http://www.usd204.k12.ks.us/
Grade Span: KG-12; **Agency Type:** 1
Schools: 4
2 Primary; 1 Middle; 1 High; 0 Other Level
4 Regular; 0 Special Education; 0 Vocational; 0 Alternative
0 Magnet; 0 Charter; 2 Title I Eligible; 0 School-wide Title I
Students: 2,225 (52.5% male; 47.5% female)
Individual Education Program: 287 (12.9%);
English Language Learner: 0 (0.0%); Migrant: 181 (8.1%)
Eligible for Free Lunch Program: 442 (19.9%)
Eligible for Reduced-Price Lunch Program: 194 (8.7%)
Teachers: 138.1 (16.1 to 1)
Librarians/Media Specialists: 4.0 (556.3 to 1)
Guidance Counselors: 5.0 (445.0 to 1)
Current Spending: ($ per student per year):
Total: $5,303; Instruction: $3,011; Support Services: $1,981
Enrollment, Drop-out Rates and Diploma Recipients by Race/Ethnicity

Category	Total	White	Black	Asian	AIAN	Hisp.
Enrollment (%)	100.0	82.5	8.1	0.5	0.8	8.0
Drop-out Rate (%)	4.4	4.4	0.0	14.3	0.0	6.9
H.S. Diplomas (#)	150	126	12	2	1	9

Kansas City
625 Minnesota Ave • Kansas City, KS 66101-2805
(913) 551-3200 • http://www.kckps.k12.ks.us/
Grade Span: KG-12; **Agency Type:** 1
Schools: 42
28 Primary; 8 Middle; 6 High; 0 Other Level
42 Regular; 0 Special Education; 0 Vocational; 0 Alternative

3 Magnet; 0 Charter; 31 Title I Eligible; 31 School-wide Title I
Students: 20,810 (51.9% male; 48.1% female)
Individual Education Program: 2,754 (13.2%);
English Language Learner: 2,376 (11.4%); Migrant: 599 (2.9%)
Eligible for Free Lunch Program: 12,635 (60.7%)
Eligible for Reduced-Price Lunch Program: 2,646 (12.7%)
Teachers: 1,583.1 (13.1 to 1)
Librarians/Media Specialists: 30.0 (693.7 to 1)
Guidance Counselors: 33.0 (630.6 to 1)
Current Spending: ($ per student per year):
Total: $7,082; Instruction: $3,858; Support Services: $2,786
Enrollment, Drop-out Rates and Diploma Recipients by Race/Ethnicity

Category	Total	White	Black	Asian	AIAN	Hisp.
Enrollment (%)	100.0	21.5	49.7	3.5	0.5	24.8
Drop-out Rate (%)	6.7	7.6	4.4	8.2	15.0	13.4
H.S. Diplomas (#)	938	227	548	34	2	127

Turner-Kansas City

800 S 55th St • Kansas City, KS 66106-1566
(913) 288-4100 • http://www.turnerusd202.org/
Grade Span: KG-12; **Agency Type:** 1
Schools: 9
6 Primary; 1 Middle; 2 High; 0 Other Level
9 Regular; 0 Special Education; 0 Vocational; 0 Alternative
0 Magnet; 0 Charter; 5 Title I Eligible; 5 School-wide Title I
Students: 3,856 (50.5% male; 49.5% female)
Individual Education Program: 550 (14.3%);
English Language Learner: 142 (3.7%); Migrant: 0 (0.0%)
Eligible for Free Lunch Program: 1,324 (34.3%)
Eligible for Reduced-Price Lunch Program: 569 (14.8%)
Teachers: 227.9 (16.9 to 1)
Librarians/Media Specialists: 7.0 (550.9 to 1)
Guidance Counselors: 8.0 (482.0 to 1)
Current Spending: ($ per student per year):
Total: $6,144; Instruction: $3,549; Support Services: $2,286
Enrollment, Drop-out Rates and Diploma Recipients by Race/Ethnicity

Category	Total	White	Black	Asian	AIAN	Hisp.
Enrollment (%)	100.0	70.7	10.8	2.4	1.0	15.1
Drop-out Rate (%)	8.7	9.0	1.7	4.0	0.0	12.5
H.S. Diplomas (#)	161	128	11	7	1	14

Number of Schools

Rank	Number	District Name	City
1	90	Wichita	Wichita
2	53	Shawnee Mission Public Schools	Shawnee Mission
3	42	Kansas City	Kansas City
4	38	Olathe	Olathe
5	32	Topeka Public Schools	Topeka
6	29	Blue Valley	Overland Park
7	24	Lawrence	Lawrence
8	16	Garden City	Garden City
8	16	Geary County Schools	Junction City
10	14	Salina	Salina
11	12	Derby	Derby
11	12	Liberal	Liberal
13	11	Dodge City	Dodge City
13	11	Emporia	Emporia
13	11	Hutchinson Public Schools	Hutchinson
13	11	Manhattan	Manhattan
13	11	Seaman	Topeka
18	10	Newton	Newton
19	9	Clay Center	Clay Center
19	9	Hays	Hays
19	9	Leavenworth	Leavenworth
19	9	Turner-Kansas City	Kansas City
23	8	Andover	Andover
23	8	Arkansas City	Arkansas City
23	8	Auburn Washburn	Topeka
23	8	De Soto	De Soto
23	8	Goddard	Goddard
23	8	Winfield	Winfield
29	7	Chanute Public Schools	Chanute
29	7	El Dorado	El Dorado
29	7	Gardner Edgerton	Gardner
29	7	Great Bend	Great Bend
29	7	Haysville	Haysville
29	7	Ottawa	Ottawa
29	7	Renwick	Andale
29	7	Wellington	Wellington
37	6	Augusta	Augusta
37	6	Basehor-Linwood	Basehor
37	6	Buhler	Buhler
37	6	Iola	Iola
37	6	Labette County	Altamont
37	6	Maize	Maize
37	6	Mcpherson	Mcpherson
37	6	Shawnee Heights	Tecumseh
37	6	Valley Center Public Schools	Valley Center
46	5	Circle	Towanda
46	5	Coffeyville	Coffeyville
46	5	Independence	Independence
46	5	Mulvane	Mulvane
46	5	Paola	Paola
46	5	Parsons	Parsons
46	5	Pittsburg	Pittsburg
53	4	Bonner Springs	Bonner Springs
53	4	Fort Leavenworth	Ft Leavenworth
53	4	Fort Scott	Fort Scott
53	4	Lansing	Lansing
53	4	Rose Hill Public Schools	Rose Hill
53	4	Spring Hill	Spring Hill
53	4	Ulysses	Ulysses
60	3	Atchison Public Schools	Atchison
60	3	Tonganoxie	Tonganoxie

Number of Teachers

Rank	Number	District Name	City
1	3,041	Wichita	Wichita
2	1,884	Shawnee Mission Public Schools	Shawnee Mission
3	1,583	Kansas City	Kansas City
4	1,484	Olathe	Olathe
5	1,231	Blue Valley	Overland Park
6	1,071	Topeka Public Schools	Topeka
7	761	Lawrence	Lawrence
8	575	Salina	Salina
9	497	Garden City	Garden City
10	430	Geary County Schools	Junction City
11	425	Derby	Derby
12	413	Leavenworth	Leavenworth
13	386	Emporia	Emporia
14	378	Manhattan	Manhattan
15	373	Auburn Washburn	Topeka
16	333	Dodge City	Dodge City
17	333	Hutchinson Public Schools	Hutchinson
18	296	Maize	Maize
19	291	De Soto	De Soto
20	285	Haysville	Haysville
21	277	Liberal	Liberal
22	275	Hays	Hays
23	255	Seaman	Topeka
24	248	Newton	Newton
25	244	Winfield	Winfield
26	239	Great Bend	Great Bend
27	227	Turner-Kansas City	Kansas City
28	226	El Dorado	El Dorado
29	226	Gardner Edgerton	Gardner
30	222	Shawnee Heights	Tecumseh
31	211	Mcpherson	Mcpherson
32	203	Goddard	Goddard
33	199	Andover	Andover
34	182	Arkansas City	Arkansas City
35	181	Paola	Paola
36	167	Ottawa	Ottawa
37	147	Pittsburg	Pittsburg
38	144	Fort Scott	Fort Scott
39	141	Clay Center	Clay Center
40	138	Bonner Springs	Bonner Springs
41	135	Buhler	Buhler
42	131	Augusta	Augusta
43	128	Wellington	Wellington
44	127	Atchison Public Schools	Atchison
45	127	Valley Center Public Schools	Valley Center
46	125	Renwick	Andale
47	125	Independence	Independence
48	124	Coffeyville	Coffeyville
49	120	Chanute Public Schools	Chanute
50	119	Mulvane	Mulvane
51	113	Ulysses	Ulysses
52	109	Fort Leavenworth	Ft Leavenworth
53	109	Lansing	Lansing
54	108	Iola	Iola
55	107	Labette County	Altamont
56	103	Parsons	Parsons
56	103	Rose Hill Public Schools	Rose Hill
58	100	Spring Hill	Spring Hill
59	97	Basehor-Linwood	Basehor
60	92	Tonganoxie	Tonganoxie
61	86	Circle	Towanda

Number of Students

Rank	Number	District Name	City
1	48,913	Wichita	Wichita
2	29,824	Shawnee Mission Public Schools	Shawnee Mission
3	22,174	Olathe	Olathe
4	20,810	Kansas City	Kansas City
5	18,641	Blue Valley	Overland Park
6	14,025	Topeka Public Schools	Topeka
7	10,182	Lawrence	Lawrence
8	7,839	Garden City	Garden City
9	7,715	Salina	Salina
10	6,752	Derby	Derby
11	6,490	Geary County Schools	Junction City
12	5,814	Dodge City	Dodge City
13	5,585	Maize	Maize
14	5,445	Manhattan	Manhattan
15	5,132	Auburn Washburn	Topeka
16	5,068	Emporia	Emporia
17	5,049	Hutchinson Public Schools	Hutchinson
18	4,603	Liberal	Liberal
19	4,588	Haysville	Haysville
20	4,385	Leavenworth	Leavenworth
21	4,130	De Soto	De Soto
22	3,939	Goddard	Goddard
23	3,856	Turner-Kansas City	Kansas City
24	3,696	Newton	Newton
25	3,506	Seaman	Topeka
26	3,399	Hays	Hays
27	3,392	Shawnee Heights	Tecumseh
28	3,313	Andover	Andover
29	3,215	Gardner Edgerton	Gardner
30	3,209	Great Bend	Great Bend
31	3,062	Arkansas City	Arkansas City
32	2,775	Winfield	Winfield
33	2,567	Mcpherson	Mcpherson
34	2,562	Pittsburg	Pittsburg
35	2,517	Ottawa	Ottawa
36	2,374	Valley Center Public Schools	Valley Center
37	2,279	Buhler	Buhler
38	2,258	El Dorado	El Dorado
39	2,237	Augusta	Augusta
40	2,225	Bonner Springs	Bonner Springs
41	2,116	Paola	Paola
42	2,086	Lansing	Lansing
43	2,075	Basehor-Linwood	Basehor
44	2,062	Independence	Independence
45	2,056	Fort Scott	Fort Scott
46	2,021	Renwick	Andale
47	2,000	Coffeyville	Coffeyville
48	1,989	Fort Leavenworth	Ft Leavenworth
49	1,961	Mulvane	Mulvane
50	1,919	Chanute Public Schools	Chanute
51	1,799	Rose Hill Public Schools	Rose Hill
52	1,795	Ulysses	Ulysses
53	1,765	Wellington	Wellington
54	1,738	Atchison Public Schools	Atchison
55	1,707	Labette County	Altamont
56	1,658	Parsons	Parsons
57	1,565	Clay Center	Clay Center
58	1,562	Spring Hill	Spring Hill
59	1,546	Tonganoxie	Tonganoxie
60	1,536	Iola	Iola
61	1,519	Circle	Towanda

Male Students

Rank	Percent	District Name	City
1	54.8	El Dorado	El Dorado
2	53.6	Renwick	Andale
3	53.5	Independence	Independence
4	52.8	Iola	Iola
5	52.7	Clay Center	Clay Center
5	52.7	Leavenworth	Leavenworth
5	52.7	Liberal	Liberal
8	52.6	Rose Hill Public Schools	Rose Hill
8	52.6	Ulysses	Ulysses
10	52.5	Bonner Springs	Bonner Springs
10	52.5	Ottawa	Ottawa
10	52.5	Shawnee Heights	Tecumseh
13	52.4	Hays	Hays
14	52.3	Dodge City	Dodge City
14	52.3	Goddard	Goddard
14	52.3	Newton	Newton
14	52.3	Seaman	Topeka
18	52.2	Coffeyville	Coffeyville
18	52.2	Manhattan	Manhattan
18	52.2	Parsons	Parsons
21	52.1	Atchison Public Schools	Atchison
22	52.0	Andover	Andover
22	52.0	Augusta	Augusta
22	52.0	Blue Valley	Overland Park
25	51.9	Great Bend	Great Bend
25	51.9	Haysville	Haysville
25	51.9	Kansas City	Kansas City
25	51.9	Shawnee Mission Public Schools	Shawnee Mission
29	51.8	Pittsburg	Pittsburg
29	51.8	Winfield	Winfield
31	51.7	Valley Center Public Schools	Valley Center
32	51.5	Olathe	Olathe
32	51.5	Salina	Salina
34	51.4	Gardner Edgerton	Gardner
34	51.4	Geary County Schools	Junction City
34	51.4	Mcpherson	Mcpherson
34	51.4	Topeka Public Schools	Topeka
34	51.4	Wellington	Wellington
39	51.3	Labette County	Altamont
40	51.2	Buhler	Buhler
40	51.2	Hutchinson Public Schools	Hutchinson
40	51.2	Lansing	Lansing
43	51.1	Derby	Derby
44	51.0	Emporia	Emporia
44	51.0	Fort Scott	Fort Scott
44	51.0	Tonganoxie	Tonganoxie
44	51.0	Wichita	Wichita
48	50.9	Mulvane	Mulvane
49	50.8	Paola	Paola
50	50.7	Arkansas City	Arkansas City
50	50.7	Circle	Towanda
50	50.7	De Soto	De Soto
50	50.7	Lawrence	Lawrence
54	50.6	Fort Leavenworth	Ft Leavenworth
54	50.6	Garden City	Garden City
56	50.5	Maize	Maize
56	50.5	Turner-Kansas City	Kansas City
58	50.2	Basehor-Linwood	Basehor
59	50.1	Auburn Washburn	Topeka
59	50.1	Chanute Public Schools	Chanute
61	50.0	Spring Hill	Spring Hill

Female Students

Rank	Percent	District Name	City
1	50.0	Spring Hill	Spring Hill
2	49.9	Auburn Washburn	Topeka
2	49.9	Chanute Public Schools	Chanute
4	49.8	Basehor-Linwood	Basehor
5	49.5	Maize	Maize
5	49.5	Turner-Kansas City	Kansas City
7	49.4	Fort Leavenworth	Ft Leavenworth
7	49.4	Garden City	Garden City
9	49.3	Arkansas City	Arkansas City
9	49.3	Circle	Towanda
9	49.3	De Soto	De Soto
9	49.3	Lawrence	Lawrence
13	49.2	Paola	Paola
14	49.1	Mulvane	Mulvane
15	49.0	Emporia	Emporia
15	49.0	Fort Scott	Fort Scott

Rank	Percent	District Name	City
15	49.0	Tonganoxie	Tonganoxie
15	49.0	Wichita	Wichita
19	48.9	Derby	Derby
20	48.8	Buhler	Buhler
20	48.8	Hutchinson Public Schools	Hutchinson
20	48.8	Lansing	Lansing
23	48.7	Labette County	Altamont
24	48.6	Gardner Edgerton	Gardner
24	48.6	Geary County Schools	Junction City
24	48.6	Mcpherson	Mcpherson
24	48.6	Topeka Public Schools	Topeka
24	48.6	Wellington	Wellington
29	48.5	Olathe	Olathe
29	48.5	Salina	Salina
31	48.3	Valley Center Public Schools	Valley Center
32	48.2	Pittsburg	Pittsburg
32	48.2	Winfield	Winfield
34	48.1	Great Bend	Great Bend
34	48.1	Haysville	Haysville
34	48.1	Kansas City	Kansas City
34	48.1	Shawnee Mission Public Schools	Shawnee Mission
38	48.0	Andover	Andover
38	48.0	Augusta	Augusta
38	48.0	Blue Valley	Overland Park
41	47.9	Atchison Public Schools	Atchison
42	47.8	Coffeyville	Coffeyville
42	47.8	Manhattan	Manhattan
42	47.8	Parsons	Parsons
45	47.7	Dodge City	Dodge City
45	47.7	Goddard	Goddard
45	47.7	Newton	Newton
45	47.7	Seaman	Topeka
49	47.6	Hays	Hays
50	47.5	Bonner Springs	Bonner Springs
50	47.5	Ottawa	Ottawa
50	47.5	Shawnee Heights	Tecumseh
53	47.4	Rose Hill Public Schools	Rose Hill
53	47.4	Ulysses	Ulysses
55	47.3	Clay Center	Clay Center
55	47.3	Leavenworth	Leavenworth
55	47.3	Liberal	Liberal
58	47.2	Iola	Iola
59	46.5	Independence	Independence
60	46.4	Renwick	Andale
61	45.2	El Dorado	El Dorado

Individual Education Program Students

Rank	Percent	District Name	City
1	22.0	Atchison Public Schools	Atchison
2	21.0	Iola	Iola
3	19.2	Arkansas City	Arkansas City
4	18.4	Chanute Public Schools	Chanute
5	17.4	Leavenworth	Leavenworth
6	17.1	Topeka Public Schools	Topeka
7	16.7	Winfield	Winfield
8	16.1	Mcpherson	Mcpherson
9	16.0	Hutchinson Public Schools	Hutchinson
9	16.0	Wellington	Wellington
11	15.9	Hays	Hays
12	15.6	Lawrence	Lawrence
13	15.3	Haysville	Haysville
14	15.0	Coffeyville	Coffeyville
14	15.0	Shawnee Heights	Tecumseh
16	14.9	Clay Center	Clay Center
17	14.8	Newton	Newton
18	14.7	El Dorado	El Dorado
19	14.6	Geary County Schools	Junction City
20	14.5	Manhattan	Manhattan
21	14.3	Salina	Salina
21	14.3	Turner-Kansas City	Kansas City
21	14.3	Wichita	Wichita
24	14.0	Ottawa	Ottawa
24	14.0	Paola	Paola
26	13.6	Olathe	Olathe
26	13.6	Valley Center Public Schools	Valley Center
28	13.5	Seaman	Topeka
29	13.4	Derby	Derby
30	13.2	Kansas City	Kansas City
31	13.1	Auburn Washburn	Topeka
31	13.1	Fort Leavenworth	Ft Leavenworth
31	13.1	Gardner Edgerton	Gardner
31	13.1	Pittsburg	Pittsburg
35	13.0	Great Bend	Great Bend
36	12.9	Bonner Springs	Bonner Springs
36	12.9	Circle	Towanda
36	12.9	Tonganoxie	Tonganoxie
39	12.8	Parsons	Parsons
40	12.7	Augusta	Augusta
41	12.5	Goddard	Goddard
42	12.3	Garden City	Garden City
43	12.0	Independence	Independence
43	12.0	Spring Hill	Spring Hill
45	11.8	Buhler	Buhler
45	11.8	Dodge City	Dodge City
47	11.4	Shawnee Mission Public Schools	Shawnee Mission
48	11.1	Emporia	Emporia
49	10.8	Fort Scott	Fort Scott
49	10.8	Ulysses	Ulysses
51	10.4	Lansing	Lansing
52	9.7	Andover	Andover
53	9.5	Labette County	Altamont
54	9.4	Basehor-Linwood	Basehor
54	9.4	De Soto	De Soto
54	9.4	Maize	Maize
57	9.0	Liberal	Liberal
58	8.8	Renwick	Andale
58	8.8	Rose Hill Public Schools	Rose Hill
60	8.2	Blue Valley	Overland Park
61	8.1	Mulvane	Mulvane

English Language Learner Students

Rank	Percent	District Name	City
1	37.2	Dodge City	Dodge City
2	22.7	Emporia	Emporia
3	21.5	Garden City	Garden City
4	11.4	Kansas City	Kansas City
5	10.0	Wichita	Wichita
6	9.6	Ulysses	Ulysses
7	7.3	Great Bend	Great Bend
8	6.5	Winfield	Winfield
9	3.8	Newton	Newton
10	3.7	Turner-Kansas City	Kansas City
11	3.4	Pittsburg	Pittsburg
12	3.1	Salina	Salina
13	2.6	De Soto	De Soto
13	2.6	Shawnee Mission Public Schools	Shawnee Mission
15	2.5	Topeka Public Schools	Topeka
16	2.2	Leavenworth	Leavenworth
16	2.2	Manhattan	Manhattan
18	2.1	Hays	Hays
18	2.1	Olathe	Olathe
20	1.7	Haysville	Haysville
21	1.6	Lawrence	Lawrence
22	1.0	Blue Valley	Overland Park
23	0.8	Auburn Washburn	Topeka
23	0.8	Maize	Maize
25	0.7	Hutchinson Public Schools	Hutchinson
26	0.5	Fort Scott	Fort Scott
27	0.4	Gardner Edgerton	Gardner
27	0.4	Mcpherson	Mcpherson
29	0.2	Buhler	Buhler
30	0.1	Andover	Andover
31	0.0	Arkansas City	Arkansas City
31	0.0	Atchison Public Schools	Atchison
31	0.0	Augusta	Augusta
31	0.0	Basehor-Linwood	Basehor
31	0.0	Bonner Springs	Bonner Springs
31	0.0	Chanute Public Schools	Chanute
31	0.0	Circle	Towanda
31	0.0	Clay Center	Clay Center
31	0.0	Coffeyville	Coffeyville
31	0.0	Derby	Derby
31	0.0	El Dorado	El Dorado
31	0.0	Fort Leavenworth	Ft Leavenworth
31	0.0	Geary County Schools	Junction City
31	0.0	Goddard	Goddard
31	0.0	Independence	Independence
31	0.0	Iola	Iola
31	0.0	Labette County	Altamont
31	0.0	Lansing	Lansing
31	0.0	Liberal	Liberal
31	0.0	Mulvane	Mulvane
31	0.0	Ottawa	Ottawa
31	0.0	Paola	Paola
31	0.0	Parsons	Parsons
31	0.0	Renwick	Andale
31	0.0	Rose Hill Public Schools	Rose Hill
31	0.0	Seaman	Topeka
31	0.0	Shawnee Heights	Tecumseh
31	0.0	Spring Hill	Spring Hill
31	0.0	Tonganoxie	Tonganoxie
31	0.0	Valley Center Public Schools	Valley Center
31	0.0	Wellington	Wellington

Migrant Students

Rank	Percent	District Name	City
1	38.6	Dodge City	Dodge City
2	27.3	Liberal	Liberal
3	17.3	Great Bend	Great Bend
4	15.9	Ulysses	Ulysses
5	9.2	Emporia	Emporia
6	8.8	Garden City	Garden City
7	8.1	Bonner Springs	Bonner Springs
8	7.0	Haysville	Haysville
9	6.6	Labette County	Altamont
10	4.6	Wichita	Wichita
11	3.8	Arkansas City	Arkansas City
11	3.8	Chanute Public Schools	Chanute
11	3.8	Coffeyville	Coffeyville
14	3.3	Pittsburg	Pittsburg
15	2.9	Kansas City	Kansas City
16	2.5	Independence	Independence
17	2.3	Topeka Public Schools	Topeka
18	2.1	Parsons	Parsons
19	1.9	Olathe	Olathe
20	1.3	Hays	Hays
21	0.8	Gardner Edgerton	Gardner
22	0.4	Lawrence	Lawrence
22	0.4	Salina	Salina
24	0.3	Fort Scott	Fort Scott
24	0.3	Iola	Iola
26	0.0	Andover	Andover
26	0.0	Atchison Public Schools	Atchison
26	0.0	Auburn Washburn	Topeka
26	0.0	Augusta	Augusta
26	0.0	Basehor-Linwood	Basehor
26	0.0	Blue Valley	Overland Park
26	0.0	Buhler	Buhler
26	0.0	Circle	Towanda
26	0.0	Clay Center	Clay Center
26	0.0	De Soto	De Soto
26	0.0	Derby	Derby
26	0.0	El Dorado	El Dorado
26	0.0	Fort Leavenworth	Ft Leavenworth
26	0.0	Geary County Schools	Junction City
26	0.0	Goddard	Goddard
26	0.0	Hutchinson Public Schools	Hutchinson
26	0.0	Lansing	Lansing
26	0.0	Leavenworth	Leavenworth
26	0.0	Maize	Maize
26	0.0	Manhattan	Manhattan
26	0.0	Mcpherson	Mcpherson
26	0.0	Mulvane	Mulvane
26	0.0	Newton	Newton
26	0.0	Ottawa	Ottawa
26	0.0	Paola	Paola
26	0.0	Renwick	Andale
26	0.0	Rose Hill Public Schools	Rose Hill
26	0.0	Seaman	Topeka
26	0.0	Shawnee Heights	Tecumseh
26	0.0	Shawnee Mission Public Schools	Shawnee Mission
26	0.0	Spring Hill	Spring Hill
26	0.0	Tonganoxie	Tonganoxie
26	0.0	Turner-Kansas City	Kansas City
26	0.0	Valley Center Public Schools	Valley Center
26	0.0	Wellington	Wellington
26	0.0	Winfield	Winfield

Students Eligible for Free Lunch

Rank	Percent	District Name	City
1	60.7	Kansas City	Kansas City
2	50.8	Dodge City	Dodge City
3	49.8	Liberal	Liberal
3	49.8	Topeka Public Schools	Topeka
5	48.1	Wichita	Wichita
6	43.9	Arkansas City	Arkansas City
7	43.8	Coffeyville	Coffeyville
8	42.0	Parsons	Parsons
9	41.7	Pittsburg	Pittsburg
10	41.5	Emporia	Emporia
11	41.4	Garden City	Garden City
12	40.2	Atchison Public Schools	Atchison
13	37.8	Great Bend	Great Bend
14	37.7	Hutchinson Public Schools	Hutchinson
15	35.2	Fort Scott	Fort Scott
16	34.5	Leavenworth	Leavenworth
17	34.4	Iola	Iola
18	34.3	Turner-Kansas City	Kansas City
19	33.8	Geary County Schools	Junction City
20	32.3	Chanute Public Schools	Chanute
21	31.7	Independence	Independence
22	31.2	Wellington	Wellington
23	31.1	Ulysses	Ulysses
24	29.7	Salina	Salina
25	28.7	El Dorado	El Dorado
26	28.2	Newton	Newton
27	26.4	Ottawa	Ottawa
28	25.5	Winfield	Winfield
29	23.6	Clay Center	Clay Center
30	21.6	Haysville	Haysville
31	21.0	Hays	Hays
32	20.1	Lawrence	Lawrence
33	19.9	Bonner Springs	Bonner Springs
33	19.9	Labette County	Altamont
35	18.9	Manhattan	Manhattan

36	18.8	Augusta	Augusta
37	18.7	Derby	Derby
38	17.3	Buhler	Buhler
39	17.0	Paola	Paola
40	15.0	Circle	Towanda
41	14.2	Mcpherson	Mcpherson
42	13.4	Mulvane	Mulvane
42	13.4	Shawnee Heights	Tecumseh
44	12.2	Seaman	Topeka
45	11.6	Gardner Edgerton	Gardner
45	11.6	Valley Center Public Schools	Valley Center
47	11.5	Auburn Washburn	Topeka
48	10.9	Tonganoxie	Tonganoxie
49	9.4	Renwick	Andale
50	9.2	Rose Hill Public Schools	Rose Hill
51	8.3	De Soto	De Soto
51	8.3	Goddard	Goddard
53	8.2	Shawnee Mission Public Schools	Shawnee Mission
54	8.0	Olathe	Olathe
55	7.2	Andover	Andover
56	7.1	Spring Hill	Spring Hill
57	5.4	Lansing	Lansing
58	4.5	Maize	Maize
59	4.1	Basehor-Linwood	Basehor
60	1.7	Fort Leavenworth	Ft Leavenworth
61	1.4	Blue Valley	Overland Park

Students Eligible for Reduced-Price Lunch

Rank	Percent	District Name	City
1	21.0	Geary County Schools	Junction City
2	14.8	Turner-Kansas City	Kansas City
3	14.3	Atchison Public Schools	Atchison
4	13.9	Dodge City	Dodge City
5	13.3	Ulysses	Ulysses
6	12.7	Kansas City	Kansas City
6	12.7	Labette County	Altamont
8	12.5	Topeka Public Schools	Topeka
8	12.5	Winfield	Winfield
10	12.4	Wellington	Wellington
11	12.3	Fort Scott	Fort Scott
12	12.2	Parsons	Parsons
12	12.2	Wichita	Wichita
14	12.0	Salina	Salina
15	11.9	Newton	Newton
16	11.8	Clay Center	Clay Center
17	11.6	Coffeyville	Coffeyville
18	11.5	Emporia	Emporia
19	11.2	Chanute Public Schools	Chanute
19	11.2	Leavenworth	Leavenworth
21	11.0	Independence	Independence
22	10.9	Garden City	Garden City
23	10.6	Hutchinson Public Schools	Hutchinson
23	10.6	Iola	Iola
25	9.7	Haysville	Haysville
26	9.6	Arkansas City	Arkansas City
26	9.6	Liberal	Liberal
26	9.6	Manhattan	Manhattan
26	9.6	Pittsburg	Pittsburg
30	9.5	Renwick	Andale
30	9.5	Tonganoxie	Tonganoxie
32	9.4	Hays	Hays
33	9.0	Buhler	Buhler
34	8.9	Circle	Towanda
35	8.8	Lawrence	Lawrence
36	8.7	Bonner Springs	Bonner Springs
36	8.7	Derby	Derby
36	8.7	Mulvane	Mulvane
39	7.8	Augusta	Augusta
39	7.8	Great Bend	Great Bend
41	7.5	Gardner Edgerton	Gardner
42	7.3	El Dorado	El Dorado
42	7.3	Paola	Paola
44	7.0	Ottawa	Ottawa
45	6.4	Goddard	Goddard
45	6.4	Seaman	Topeka
47	6.3	Shawnee Heights	Tecumseh
48	6.2	Mcpherson	Mcpherson
49	6.1	Rose Hill Public Schools	Rose Hill
50	5.9	Auburn Washburn	Topeka
50	5.9	Valley Center Public Schools	Valley Center
52	5.6	Fort Leavenworth	Ft Leavenworth
53	4.0	Shawnee Mission Public Schools	Shawnee Mission
54	3.6	Olathe	Olathe
55	3.5	Andover	Andover
56	3.4	De Soto	De Soto
57	3.3	Basehor-Linwood	Basehor
58	2.9	Lansing	Lansing
59	2.8	Spring Hill	Spring Hill
60	2.2	Maize	Maize
61	0.8	Blue Valley	Overland Park

Student/Teacher Ratio

Rank	Ratio	District Name	City
1	21.4	Basehor-Linwood	Basehor
2	19.4	Goddard	Goddard
3	19.1	Lansing	Lansing
4	18.8	Maize	Maize
5	18.6	Valley Center Public Schools	Valley Center
6	18.2	Fort Leavenworth	Ft Leavenworth
7	17.7	Circle	Towanda
8	17.5	Rose Hill Public Schools	Rose Hill
9	17.4	Dodge City	Dodge City
9	17.4	Pittsburg	Pittsburg
11	17.1	Augusta	Augusta
12	16.9	Buhler	Buhler
12	16.9	Turner-Kansas City	Kansas City
14	16.8	Arkansas City	Arkansas City
14	16.8	Tonganoxie	Tonganoxie
16	16.6	Andover	Andover
16	16.6	Liberal	Liberal
18	16.4	Independence	Independence
18	16.4	Mulvane	Mulvane
20	16.1	Bonner Springs	Bonner Springs
20	16.1	Coffeyville	Coffeyville
20	16.1	Haysville	Haysville
20	16.1	Parsons	Parsons
20	16.1	Renwick	Andale
20	16.1	Wichita	Wichita
26	16.0	Chanute Public Schools	Chanute
27	15.9	Derby	Derby
27	15.9	Labette County	Altamont
27	15.9	Ulysses	Ulysses
30	15.8	Garden City	Garden City
30	15.8	Shawnee Mission Public Schools	Shawnee Mission
32	15.6	Spring Hill	Spring Hill
33	15.3	Shawnee Heights	Tecumseh
34	15.1	Blue Valley	Overland Park
34	15.1	Geary County Schools	Junction City
34	15.1	Hutchinson Public Schools	Hutchinson
37	15.0	Ottawa	Ottawa
38	14.9	Newton	Newton
38	14.9	Olathe	Olathe
40	14.4	Manhattan	Manhattan
41	14.2	De Soto	De Soto
41	14.2	Fort Scott	Fort Scott
41	14.2	Gardner Edgerton	Gardner
41	14.2	Iola	Iola
45	13.7	Auburn Washburn	Topeka
45	13.7	Seaman	Topeka
45	13.7	Wellington	Wellington
48	13.6	Atchison Public Schools	Atchison
49	13.4	Great Bend	Great Bend
49	13.4	Lawrence	Lawrence
49	13.4	Salina	Salina
52	13.1	Emporia	Emporia
52	13.1	Kansas City	Kansas City
52	13.1	Topeka Public Schools	Topeka
55	12.3	Hays	Hays
56	12.1	Mcpherson	Mcpherson
57	11.7	Paola	Paola
58	11.3	Winfield	Winfield
59	11.0	Clay Center	Clay Center
60	10.6	Leavenworth	Leavenworth
61	10.0	El Dorado	El Dorado

Student/Librarian Ratio

Rank	Ratio	District Name	City
1	1,150.8	Liberal	Liberal
2	1,000.0	Coffeyville	Coffeyville
3	930.8	Maize	Maize
4	899.5	Rose Hill Public Schools	Rose Hill
5	882.5	Wellington	Wellington
6	773.0	Tonganoxie	Tonganoxie
7	725.7	Wichita	Wichita
8	703.9	Emporia	Emporia
9	693.7	Kansas City	Kansas City
10	691.7	Basehor-Linwood	Basehor
11	641.8	Great Bend	Great Bend
12	616.7	Winfield	Winfield
13	612.4	Arkansas City	Arkansas City
14	581.4	Dodge City	Dodge City
15	579.3	Atchison Public Schools	Atchison
16	576.1	Hays	Hays
17	573.5	Haysville	Haysville
18	570.2	Auburn Washburn	Topeka
19	569.0	Labette County	Altamont
20	562.7	Goddard	Goddard
21	561.4	Olathe	Olathe
21	561.4	Renwick	Andale
23	561.0	Hutchinson Public Schools	Hutchinson
24	559.3	Ottawa	Ottawa
25	556.3	Bonner Springs	Bonner Springs
26	552.7	Parsons	Parsons
27	551.1	Salina	Salina
28	550.9	Turner-Kansas City	Kansas City
29	548.3	Blue Valley	Overland Park
30	536.4	Shawnee Mission Public Schools	Shawnee Mission
31	535.8	Gardner Edgerton	Gardner
32	529.0	Paola	Paola
33	528.0	Newton	Newton
34	521.5	Lansing	Lansing
35	519.4	Derby	Derby
36	516.3	De Soto	De Soto
37	514.0	Fort Scott	Fort Scott
38	513.4	Mcpherson	Mcpherson
39	505.1	Valley Center Public Schools	Valley Center
40	501.8	El Dorado	El Dorado
41	500.9	Seaman	Topeka
42	497.3	Fort Leavenworth	Ft Leavenworth
43	490.3	Mulvane	Mulvane
44	489.9	Garden City	Garden City
45	487.2	Leavenworth	Leavenworth
46	484.6	Shawnee Heights	Tecumseh
47	473.3	Andover	Andover
48	448.8	Ulysses	Ulysses
49	446.3	Spring Hill	Spring Hill
50	445.2	Topeka Public Schools	Topeka
51	433.3	Lawrence	Lawrence
52	420.0	Pittsburg	Pittsburg
53	418.8	Manhattan	Manhattan
54	412.4	Independence	Independence
55	411.8	Clay Center	Clay Center
56	405.6	Geary County Schools	Junction City
57	392.9	Buhler	Buhler
58	384.0	Iola	Iola
59	383.8	Chanute Public Schools	Chanute
60	372.8	Augusta	Augusta
61	303.8	Circle	Towanda

Student/Counselor Ratio

Rank	Ratio	District Name	City
1	1,707.0	Labette County	Altamont
2	964.6	Derby	Derby
3	811.3	Geary County Schools	Junction City
4	693.8	Winfield	Winfield
5	673.7	Renwick	Andale
6	640.6	Manhattan	Manhattan
7	630.6	Kansas City	Kansas City
8	599.7	Buhler	Buhler
9	596.5	Shawnee Mission Public Schools	Shawnee Mission
10	579.3	Atchison Public Schools	Atchison
11	561.0	Hutchinson Public Schools	Hutchinson
12	539.9	Wichita	Wichita
13	528.0	Newton	Newton
14	521.5	Lansing	Lansing
15	520.7	Spring Hill	Spring Hill
16	511.4	Liberal	Liberal
17	497.3	Fort Leavenworth	Ft Leavenworth
18	491.7	De Soto	De Soto
19	482.0	Turner-Kansas City	Kansas City
20	478.1	Emporia	Emporia
21	474.8	Valley Center Public Schools	Valley Center
22	464.5	Wellington	Wellington
23	449.8	Rose Hill Public Schools	Rose Hill
24	448.8	Ulysses	Ulysses
25	447.0	Fort Scott	Fort Scott
26	445.0	Bonner Springs	Bonner Springs
27	437.4	Arkansas City	Arkansas City
28	433.9	Dodge City	Dodge City
29	427.9	Great Bend	Great Bend
30	424.9	Hays	Hays
31	403.2	Olathe	Olathe
32	399.0	Haysville	Haysville
33	395.1	Topeka Public Schools	Topeka
34	393.9	Goddard	Goddard
35	391.6	Lawrence	Lawrence
36	389.6	Seaman	Topeka
37	386.5	Tonganoxie	Tonganoxie
38	383.8	Chanute Public Schools	Chanute
39	374.9	Independence	Independence
40	373.3	Garden City	Garden City
41	372.8	Augusta	Augusta
42	372.3	Maize	Maize
43	366.6	Auburn Washburn	Topeka
44	365.4	Leavenworth	Leavenworth
45	362.2	Salina	Salina
46	353.0	Blue Valley	Overland Park
47	352.7	Paola	Paola
48	345.8	Basehor-Linwood	Basehor
49	339.2	Shawnee Heights	Tecumseh
50	333.3	Coffeyville	Coffeyville
51	331.6	Parsons	Parsons
52	331.3	Andover	Andover
53	326.8	Mulvane	Mulvane

54	322.6	El Dorado	El Dorado
55	320.9	Mcpherson	Mcpherson
56	307.2	Iola	Iola
57	303.8	Circle	Towanda
58	284.7	Pittsburg	Pittsburg
59	264.9	Ottawa	Ottawa
60	260.8	Clay Center	Clay Center
61	214.3	Gardner Edgerton	Gardner

Current Spending per Student in FY2001

Rank	Dollars	District Name	City
1	9,407	El Dorado	El Dorado
2	8,697	Pittsburg	Pittsburg
3	8,430	Paola	Paola
4	7,738	Leavenworth	Leavenworth
5	7,636	Winfield	Winfield
6	7,469	Atchison Public Schools	Atchison
7	7,276	Salina	Salina
8	7,178	Emporia	Emporia
9	7,109	Blue Valley	Overland Park
10	7,082	Hays	Hays
10	7,082	Kansas City	Kansas City
12	7,072	Clay Center	Clay Center
13	6,982	Manhattan	Manhattan
14	6,868	Mcpherson	Mcpherson
15	6,807	De Soto	De Soto
16	6,803	Gardner Edgerton	Gardner
17	6,796	Olathe	Olathe
18	6,771	Lawrence	Lawrence
19	6,758	Topeka Public Schools	Topeka
20	6,721	Spring Hill	Spring Hill
21	6,624	Newton	Newton
22	6,533	Wichita	Wichita
23	6,494	Shawnee Mission Public Schools	Shawnee Mission
24	6,382	Hutchinson Public Schools	Hutchinson
25	6,229	Great Bend	Great Bend
26	6,203	Wellington	Wellington
27	6,174	Shawnee Heights	Tecumseh
28	6,144	Turner-Kansas City	Kansas City
29	6,127	Geary County Schools	Junction City
30	6,078	Seaman	Topeka
31	5,907	Garden City	Garden City
32	5,898	Haysville	Haysville
33	5,878	Auburn Washburn	Topeka
34	5,861	Liberal	Liberal
35	5,722	Derby	Derby
36	5,705	Andover	Andover
37	5,604	Buhler	Buhler
38	5,601	Circle	Towanda
39	5,565	Iola	Iola
40	5,514	Ottawa	Ottawa
41	5,495	Renwick	Andale
42	5,487	Ulysses	Ulysses
43	5,435	Tonganoxie	Tonganoxie
44	5,399	Labette County	Altamont
45	5,303	Bonner Springs	Bonner Springs
46	5,280	Mulvane	Mulvane
47	5,267	Coffeyville	Coffeyville
48	5,258	Maize	Maize
49	5,235	Goddard	Goddard
50	5,211	Fort Scott	Fort Scott
51	5,139	Chanute Public Schools	Chanute
52	5,123	Valley Center Public Schools	Valley Center
53	5,112	Dodge City	Dodge City
54	5,097	Parsons	Parsons
55	5,072	Arkansas City	Arkansas City
56	5,057	Rose Hill Public Schools	Rose Hill
57	4,990	Independence	Independence
58	4,968	Lansing	Lansing
59	4,796	Basehor-Linwood	Basehor
60	4,734	Augusta	Augusta
61	4,642	Fort Leavenworth	Ft Leavenworth

Number of Diploma Recipients

Rank	Number	District Name	City
1	2,226	Shawnee Mission Public Schools	Shawnee Mission
2	2,147	Wichita	Wichita
3	1,319	Olathe	Olathe
4	1,190	Blue Valley	Overland Park
5	938	Kansas City	Kansas City
6	772	Lawrence	Lawrence
7	769	Topeka Public Schools	Topeka
8	462	Salina	Salina
9	420	Derby	Derby
10	417	Manhattan	Manhattan
11	325	Auburn Washburn	Topeka
12	308	Maize	Maize
13	303	Dodge City	Dodge City
14	296	Emporia	Emporia
15	294	Hutchinson Public Schools	Hutchinson
16	282	Leavenworth	Leavenworth
17	279	Garden City	Garden City
18	255	Shawnee Heights	Tecumseh
19	250	Haysville	Haysville
20	247	Goddard	Goddard
21	235	Seaman	Topeka
22	234	Mcpherson	Mcpherson
23	229	Hays	Hays
24	226	Geary County Schools	Junction City
25	217	Great Bend	Great Bend
25	217	Winfield	Winfield
27	216	Andover	Andover
28	203	De Soto	De Soto
29	199	Newton	Newton
30	178	Liberal	Liberal
31	177	Valley Center Public Schools	Valley Center
32	169	Arkansas City	Arkansas City
33	168	Coffeyville	Coffeyville
34	167	Buhler	Buhler
35	162	Independence	Independence
36	161	Turner-Kansas City	Kansas City
37	157	Mulvane	Mulvane
38	152	Labette County	Altamont
39	150	Bonner Springs	Bonner Springs
39	150	Fort Scott	Fort Scott
41	147	Lansing	Lansing
41	147	Paola	Paola
43	144	Pittsburg	Pittsburg
44	142	Augusta	Augusta
45	140	Wellington	Wellington
46	138	Gardner Edgerton	Gardner
47	127	Basehor-Linwood	Basehor
47	127	Rose Hill Public Schools	Rose Hill
49	124	Renwick	Andale
50	121	Ottawa	Ottawa
50	121	Ulysses	Ulysses
52	117	Chanute Public Schools	Chanute
52	117	Iola	Iola
54	114	El Dorado	El Dorado
55	112	Tonganoxie	Tonganoxie
56	108	Clay Center	Clay Center
57	107	Atchison Public Schools	Atchison
58	106	Parsons	Parsons
59	99	Circle	Towanda
60	93	Spring Hill	Spring Hill
61	n/a	Fort Leavenworth	Ft Leavenworth

High School Drop-out Rate

Rank	Percent	District Name	City
1	9.4	Liberal	Liberal
2	8.7	Turner-Kansas City	Kansas City
3	8.0	Wichita	Wichita
4	6.9	Leavenworth	Leavenworth
5	6.7	Kansas City	Kansas City
6	6.3	Topeka Public Schools	Topeka
7	6.2	Iola	Iola
8	5.5	Circle	Towanda
9	5.4	Pittsburg	Pittsburg
10	5.1	Fort Scott	Fort Scott
11	5.0	Atchison Public Schools	Atchison
11	5.0	Great Bend	Great Bend
13	4.7	Arkansas City	Arkansas City
14	4.5	Hutchinson Public Schools	Hutchinson
15	4.4	Bonner Springs	Bonner Springs
15	4.4	Garden City	Garden City
17	3.9	Paola	Paola
18	3.8	Basehor-Linwood	Basehor
18	3.8	El Dorado	El Dorado
20	3.5	Coffeyville	Coffeyville
21	3.4	Clay Center	Clay Center
21	3.4	Hays	Hays
23	3.3	Independence	Independence
24	3.2	Chanute Public Schools	Chanute
24	3.2	Haysville	Haysville
24	3.2	Newton	Newton
27	3.0	Auburn Washburn	Topeka
28	2.8	Buhler	Buhler
28	2.8	Dodge City	Dodge City
30	2.7	Tonganoxie	Tonganoxie
31	2.5	Salina	Salina
32	2.4	Geary County Schools	Junction City
33	2.2	Lawrence	Lawrence
34	2.1	Shawnee Mission Public Schools	Shawnee Mission
35	2.0	Emporia	Emporia
35	2.0	Olathe	Olathe
35	2.0	Seaman	Topeka
35	2.0	Ulysses	Ulysses
39	1.9	De Soto	De Soto
39	1.9	Gardner Edgerton	Gardner
39	1.9	Mcpherson	Mcpherson
39	1.9	Wellington	Wellington
43	1.8	Maize	Maize
43	1.8	Spring Hill	Spring Hill
45	1.7	Goddard	Goddard
46	1.6	Lansing	Lansing
46	1.6	Valley Center Public Schools	Valley Center
48	1.4	Rose Hill Public Schools	Rose Hill
49	1.3	Parsons	Parsons
50	1.2	Winfield	Winfield
51	1.1	Manhattan	Manhattan
52	0.9	Andover	Andover
52	0.9	Augusta	Augusta
52	0.9	Derby	Derby
52	0.9	Ottawa	Ottawa
56	0.7	Blue Valley	Overland Park
56	0.7	Shawnee Heights	Tecumseh
58	0.6	Mulvane	Mulvane
59	0.5	Labette County	Altamont
60	0.2	Renwick	Andale
61	0.0	Fort Leavenworth	Ft Leavenworth

Kentucky

Kentucky Public School Educational Profile

Category	Value	Category	Value
Schools *(2002-2003)*	1,473	**Diploma Recipients** *(2002-2003)*	36,337
Instructional Level		White, Non-Hispanic	32,556
Primary	817	Black, Non-Hispanic	3,151
Middle	241	Asian/Pacific Islander	350
High	320	American Indian/Alaskan Native	31
Other Level	95	Hispanic	249
Curriculum		**High School Drop-out Rate** (%) *(2000-2001)*	4.6
Regular	1,279	White, Non-Hispanic	4.5
Special Education	11	Black, Non-Hispanic	6.5
Vocational	11	Asian/Pacific Islander	2.7
Alternative	172	American Indian/Alaskan Native	n/a
Type		Hispanic	4.6
Magnet	36	**Staff** *(2002-2003)*	95,844.2
Charter	0	Teachers	40,662.8
Title I Eligible	1,037	Average Salary ($)	38,486
School-wide Title I	748	Librarians/Media Specialists	1,159.7
Students *(2002-2003)*	661,003	Guidance Counselors	1,460.1
Gender (%)		**Ratios** *(2002-2003)*	
Male	52.0	Student/Teacher Ratio	16.3 to 1
Female	48.0	Student/Librarian Ratio	570.0 to 1
Race/Ethnicity (%)		Student/Counselor Ratio	452.7 to 1
White, Non-Hispanic	87.3	**Current Spending** *($ per student in FY 2001)*	6,523
Black, Non-Hispanic	10.4	Instruction	4,003
Asian/Pacific Islander	0.8	Support Services	2,160
American Indian/Alaskan Native	0.2	**College Entrance Exam Scores** *(2003)*	
Hispanic	1.3	Scholastic Aptitude Test (SAT)	
Classification (%)		Participation Rate (%)	13
Individual Education Program (IEP)	15.9	Mean SAT I Verbal Score	554
Migrant	2.4	Mean SAT I Math Score	552
English Language Learner (ELL)	1.0	American College Testing Program (ACT)	
Eligible for Free Lunch Program	55.3	Participation Rate (%)	73
Eligible for Reduced-Price Lunch Program	13.7	Average Composite Score	20.2

Note: *For an explanation of data, please refer to the User's Guide in the front of the book; n/a indicates data not available*

Kentucky NAEP 2003 Test Scores

Reading			Mathematics		
Grade/Category	**Value**	**Rank**	**Grade/Category**	**Value**	**Rank**
4th Grade			**4th Grade**		
Average Proficiency	219.0 (1.3)	27/51	Average Proficiency	228.7 (1.1)	42/51
Proficiency by Gender/Race/Ethnicity			Proficiency by Gender/Race/Ethnicity		
Male	215.2 (1.5)	28/51	Male	230.3 (1.2)	40/51
Female	222.8 (1.5)	27/51	Female	227.1 (1.2)	43/51
White, Non-Hispanic	221.4 (1.2)	45/51	White, Non-Hispanic	230.8 (1.0)	51/51
Black, Non-Hispanic	201.6 (3.3)	17/42	Black, Non-Hispanic	214.5 (2.4)	28/42
Asian, Non-Hispanic	n/a	n/a	Asian, Non-Hispanic	n/a	n/a
American Indian, Non-Hispanic	n/a	n/a	American Indian, Non-Hispanic	n/a	n/a
Hispanic	n/a	n/a	Hispanic	n/a	n/a
Proficiency by Class Size			Proficiency by Class Size		
Less than 16 Students	*206.4 (4.2)*	20/45	Less than 16 Students	*214.1 (3.0)*	40/47
16 to 18 Students	*221.8 (7.0)*	11/48	16 to 18 Students	*232.9 (6.9)*	25/48
19 to 20 Students	*217.5 (2.6)*	30/50	19 to 20 Students	*228.5 (2.9)*	38/50
21 to 25 Students	220.2 (1.8)	30/51	21 to 25 Students	229.4 (1.2)	43/51
Greater than 25 Students	220.6 (2.9)	20/49	Greater than 25 Students	231.1 (2.5)	34/49
Percent Attaining Achievement Levels			Percent Attaining Achievement Levels		
Below Basic	35.9 (1.6)	22/51	Below Basic	27.8 (1.6)	14/51
Basic or Above	64.1 (1.6)	29/51	Basic or Above	72.2 (1.6)	38/51
Proficient or Above	30.6 (1.3)	31/51	Proficient or Above	22.1 (1.4)	46/51
Advanced or Above	6.5 (0.9)	30/51	Advanced or Above	1.6 (0.3)	43/51
8th Grade			**8th Grade**		
Average Proficiency	266.2 (1.3)	20/51	Average Proficiency	274.3 (1.2)	35/51
Proficiency by Gender/Race/Ethnicity			Proficiency by Gender/Race/Ethnicity		
Male	260.7 (1.6)	19/51	Male	274.5 (1.4)	35/51
Female	271.8 (1.5)	17/51	Female	274.0 (1.4)	35/51
White, Non-Hispanic	268.8 (1.2)	27/50	White, Non-Hispanic	276.7 (1.3)	45/50
Black, Non-Hispanic	244.6 (2.7)	19/41	Black, Non-Hispanic	250.2 (2.7)	24/41
Asian, Non-Hispanic	n/a	n/a	Asian, Non-Hispanic	n/a	n/a
American Indian, Non-Hispanic	n/a	n/a	American Indian, Non-Hispanic	n/a	n/a
Hispanic	n/a	n/a	Hispanic	n/a	n/a
Proficiency by Parents Highest Level of Ed.			Proficiency by Parents Highest Level of Ed.		
Did Not Finish High School	251.6 (2.9)	7/50	Did Not Finish High School	258.0 (2.3)	23/50
Graduated High School	261.5 (1.4)	3/50	Graduated High School	266.1 (1.8)	32/50
Some Education After High School	271.7 (1.5)	6/50	Some Education After High School	277.7 (1.6)	35/50
Graduated College	274.4 (1.7)	17/50	Graduated College	285.7 (1.7)	31/50
Percent Attaining Achievement Levels			Percent Attaining Achievement Levels		
Below Basic	22.1 (1.2)	37/51	Below Basic	34.7 (1.5)	17/51
Basic or Above	77.9 (1.2)	15/51	Basic or Above	65.3 (1.5)	35/51
Proficient or Above	33.6 (1.9)	22/51	Proficient or Above	23.7 (1.3)	36/51
Advanced or Above	3.0 (0.6)	15/51	Advanced or Above	3.7 (0.5)	38/51

***Note:** For an explanation of data, please refer to the User's Guide in the front of the book; values in italics indicate that the nature of the sample does not allow accurate determination of the variability of the statistic; n/a indicates data not available*

Adair County

Adair County

1204 Greensburg St • Columbia, KY 42728-1811
(270) 384-2476 • http://www.adair.k12.ky.us/
Grade Span: PK-12; **Agency Type:** 1
Schools: 8
4 Primary; 2 Middle; 1 High; 1 Other Level
7 Regular; 0 Special Education; 0 Vocational; 1 Alternative
0 Magnet; 0 Charter; 7 Title I Eligible; 6 School-wide Title I
Students: 2,752 (50.7% male; 49.3% female)
Individual Education Program: 466 (16.9%);
English Language Learner: 5 (0.2%); Migrant: 177 (6.4%)
Eligible for Free Lunch Program: 1,822 (66.2%)
Eligible for Reduced-Price Lunch Program: 633 (23.0%)
Teachers: 190.5 (14.4 to 1)
Librarians/Media Specialists: 7.0 (393.1 to 1)
Guidance Counselors: 6.0 (458.7 to 1)
Current Spending: ($ per student per year):
Total: $6,184; Instruction: $4,021; Support Services: $1,791
Enrollment, Drop-out Rates and Diploma Recipients by Race/Ethnicity

Category	Total	White	Black	Asian	AIAN	Hisp.
Enrollment (%)	100.0	95.4	3.4	0.4	0.2	0.6
Drop-out Rate (%)	5.9	6.1	0.0	0.0	0.0	0.0
H.S. Diplomas (#)	127	123	4	0	0	0

Allen County

Allen County

238 Blgn Rd • Scottsville, KY 42164-9650
(270) 237-3181 • http://www.allen.k12.ky.us/
Grade Span: PK-12; **Agency Type:** 1
Schools: 4
1 Primary; 2 Middle; 1 High; 0 Other Level
4 Regular; 0 Special Education; 0 Vocational; 0 Alternative
0 Magnet; 0 Charter; 4 Title I Eligible; 0 School-wide Title I
Students: 3,085 (50.7% male; 49.3% female)
Individual Education Program: 374 (12.1%);
English Language Learner: 0 (0.0%); Migrant: 54 (1.8%)
Eligible for Free Lunch Program: 1,621 (52.5%)
Eligible for Reduced-Price Lunch Program: 438 (14.2%)
Teachers: 167.6 (18.4 to 1)
Librarians/Media Specialists: 5.0 (617.0 to 1)
Guidance Counselors: 3.0 (1,028.3 to 1)
Current Spending: ($ per student per year):
Total: $5,394; Instruction: $3,357; Support Services: $1,702
Enrollment, Drop-out Rates and Diploma Recipients by Race/Ethnicity

Category	Total	White	Black	Asian	AIAN	Hisp.
Enrollment (%)	100.0	98.6	0.7	0.3	0.0	0.4
Drop-out Rate (%)	6.2	6.3	0.0	0.0	n/a	0.0
H.S. Diplomas (#)	184	180	2	1	0	1

Anderson County

Anderson County

103 N Main • Lawrenceburg, KY 40342-1013
(502) 839-3406 • http://www.anderson.k12.ky.us/
Grade Span: PK-12; **Agency Type:** 1
Schools: 6
4 Primary; 1 Middle; 1 High; 0 Other Level
6 Regular; 0 Special Education; 0 Vocational; 0 Alternative
0 Magnet; 0 Charter; 2 Title I Eligible; 0 School-wide Title I
Students: 3,938 (51.2% male; 48.8% female)
Individual Education Program: 718 (18.2%);
English Language Learner: 1 (<0.1%); Migrant: 4 (0.1%)
Eligible for Free Lunch Program: 1,042 (26.5%)
Eligible for Reduced-Price Lunch Program: 402 (10.2%)
Teachers: 205.9 (19.1 to 1)
Librarians/Media Specialists: 5.0 (787.6 to 1)
Guidance Counselors: 7.0 (562.6 to 1)
Current Spending: ($ per student per year):
Total: $4,925; Instruction: $3,176; Support Services: $1,482
Enrollment, Drop-out Rates and Diploma Recipients by Race/Ethnicity

Category	Total	White	Black	Asian	AIAN	Hisp.
Enrollment (%)	100.0	96.4	2.8	0.1	0.0	0.6
Drop-out Rate (%)	3.2	3.3	0.0	0.0	n/a	0.0
H.S. Diplomas (#)	189	184	3	0	0	2

Ballard County

Ballard County

Rt 1 3465 Paducah Rd • Barlow, KY 42024-9529
(270) 665-8400
Grade Span: PK-12; **Agency Type:** 1
Schools: 4
2 Primary; 1 Middle; 1 High; 0 Other Level
4 Regular; 0 Special Education; 0 Vocational; 0 Alternative
0 Magnet; 0 Charter; 2 Title I Eligible; 2 School-wide Title I
Students: 1,509 (52.6% male; 47.4% female)
Individual Education Program: 309 (20.5%);
English Language Learner: 0 (0.0%); Migrant: 147 (9.7%)
Eligible for Free Lunch Program: 603 (40.0%)
Eligible for Reduced-Price Lunch Program: 192 (12.7%)
Teachers: 87.7 (17.2 to 1)
Librarians/Media Specialists: 2.0 (754.5 to 1)
Guidance Counselors: 3.0 (503.0 to 1)
Current Spending: ($ per student per year):
Total: $5,917; Instruction: $3,516; Support Services: $2,048
Enrollment, Drop-out Rates and Diploma Recipients by Race/Ethnicity

Category	Total	White	Black	Asian	AIAN	Hisp.
Enrollment (%)	100.0	95.7	3.7	0.1	0.1	0.4
Drop-out Rate (%)	1.7	1.8	0.0	0.0	n/a	0.0
H.S. Diplomas (#)	101	96	3	2	0	0

Barren County

Barren County

202 W Washington St • Glasgow, KY 42141
Mailing Address: PO Box 879 • Glasgow, KY 42141
(270) 651-3787 • http://www.bchs.barren.k12.ky.us/
Grade Span: PK-12; **Agency Type:** 1
Schools: 9
6 Primary; 1 Middle; 2 High; 0 Other Level
8 Regular; 0 Special Education; 0 Vocational; 1 Alternative
0 Magnet; 0 Charter; 8 Title I Eligible; 5 School-wide Title I
Students: 4,144 (50.5% male; 49.5% female)
Individual Education Program: 631 (15.2%);
English Language Learner: 0 (0.0%); Migrant: 391 (9.4%)
Eligible for Free Lunch Program: 2,240 (54.1%)
Eligible for Reduced-Price Lunch Program: 512 (12.4%)
Teachers: 269.6 (15.4 to 1)
Librarians/Media Specialists: 8.4 (493.3 to 1)
Guidance Counselors: 10.0 (414.4 to 1)
Current Spending: ($ per student per year):
Total: $6,087; Instruction: $3,848; Support Services: $1,843
Enrollment, Drop-out Rates and Diploma Recipients by Race/Ethnicity

Category	Total	White	Black	Asian	AIAN	Hisp.
Enrollment (%)	100.0	98.5	0.6	0.1	0.1	0.5
Drop-out Rate (%)	4.0	4.1	0.0	0.0	0.0	0.0
H.S. Diplomas (#)	208	205	2	0	0	1

Glasgow Independent

1108 Cleveland Ave • Glasgow, KY 42142-1239
(270) 651-6757 •
http://www.glasgowbarren.com/commun/edu/glas_sch/index.htm
Grade Span: PK-12; **Agency Type:** 1
Schools: 6
4 Primary; 1 Middle; 1 High; 0 Other Level
6 Regular; 0 Special Education; 0 Vocational; 0 Alternative
0 Magnet; 0 Charter; 5 Title I Eligible; 4 School-wide Title I
Students: 2,029 (52.4% male; 47.6% female)
Individual Education Program: 305 (15.0%);
English Language Learner: 30 (1.5%); Migrant: 229 (11.3%)
Eligible for Free Lunch Program: 975 (48.1%)
Eligible for Reduced-Price Lunch Program: 185 (9.1%)
Teachers: 135.2 (15.0 to 1)
Librarians/Media Specialists: 4.5 (450.9 to 1)
Guidance Counselors: 5.0 (405.8 to 1)
Current Spending: ($ per student per year):
Total: $6,115; Instruction: $3,875; Support Services: $1,851
Enrollment, Drop-out Rates and Diploma Recipients by Race/Ethnicity

Category	Total	White	Black	Asian	AIAN	Hisp.
Enrollment (%)	100.0	84.9	12.6	0.8	0.1	1.6
Drop-out Rate (%)	4.2	4.2	4.6	0.0	n/a	0.0
H.S. Diplomas (#)	118	99	18	1	0	0

Bath County

Bath County

405 W Main St • Owingsv, KY 40360-0409
(606) 674-6314 • http://www.bath.k12.ky.us/
Grade Span: PK-12; **Agency Type:** 1
Schools: 5
3 Primary; 1 Middle; 1 High; 0 Other Level
5 Regular; 0 Special Education; 0 Vocational; 0 Alternative
0 Magnet; 0 Charter; 5 Title I Eligible; 4 School-wide Title I
Students: 2,059 (52.8% male; 47.2% female)
Individual Education Program: 269 (13.1%);
English Language Learner: 0 (0.0%); Migrant: 201 (9.8%)
Eligible for Free Lunch Program: 1,502 (72.9%)

Eligible for Reduced-Price Lunch Program: 318 (15.4%)
Teachers: 126.0 (16.3 to 1)
Librarians/Media Specialists: 4.0 (514.8 to 1)
Guidance Counselors: 3.5 (588.3 to 1)
Current Spending: ($ per student per year):
Total: $6,336; Instruction: $3,851; Support Services: $2,060
Enrollment, Drop-out Rates and Diploma Recipients by Race/Ethnicity

Category	Total	White	Black	Asian	AIAN	Hisp.
Enrollment (%)	100.0	98.1	1.6	0.1	0.1	0.2
Drop-out Rate (%)	5.9	6.0	0.0	0.0	n/a	0.0
H.S. Diplomas (#)	107	105	0	1	0	1

Bell County

Bell County
211 Virginia Ave • Pineville, KY 40977-0340
(606) 337-7051 •
http://www.bellcountyschools.bell.k12.ky.us/education/district/district.php?sectionid=1
Grade Span: PK-12; **Agency Type:** 1
Schools: 8
6 Primary; 0 Middle; 1 High; 1 Other Level
7 Regular; 0 Special Education; 0 Vocational; 1 Alternative
0 Magnet; 0 Charter; 7 Title I Eligible; 6 School-wide Title I
Students: 3,311 (51.9% male; 48.1% female)
Individual Education Program: 514 (15.5%);
English Language Learner: 0 (0.0%); Migrant: 0 (0.0%)
Eligible for Free Lunch Program: 2,547 (76.9%)
Eligible for Reduced-Price Lunch Program: 494 (14.9%)
Teachers: 226.0 (14.7 to 1)
Librarians/Media Specialists: 7.0 (473.0 to 1)
Guidance Counselors: 8.0 (413.9 to 1)
Current Spending: ($ per student per year):
Total: $6,424; Instruction: $3,706; Support Services: $2,322
Enrollment, Drop-out Rates and Diploma Recipients by Race/Ethnicity

Category	Total	White	Black	Asian	AIAN	Hisp.
Enrollment (%)	100.0	99.6	0.3	0.0	0.0	0.1
Drop-out Rate (%)	7.3	7.3	0.0	n/a	n/a	n/a
H.S. Diplomas (#)	195	194	1	0	0	0

Middlesboro Independent
220 N 20th St • Middlesboro, KY 40965-0959
(606) 242-8800 • http://www.mboro.k12.ky.us/
Grade Span: PK-12; **Agency Type:** 1
Schools: 5
1 Primary; 2 Middle; 2 High; 0 Other Level
4 Regular; 0 Special Education; 0 Vocational; 1 Alternative
0 Magnet; 0 Charter; 4 Title I Eligible; 4 School-wide Title I
Students: 1,868 (51.9% male; 48.1% female)
Individual Education Program: 313 (16.8%);
English Language Learner: 0 (0.0%); Migrant: 0 (0.0%)
Eligible for Free Lunch Program: 1,454 (77.8%)
Eligible for Reduced-Price Lunch Program: 200 (10.7%)
Teachers: 117.0 (16.0 to 1)
Librarians/Media Specialists: 4.0 (467.0 to 1)
Guidance Counselors: 4.0 (467.0 to 1)
Current Spending: ($ per student per year):
Total: $6,007; Instruction: $3,813; Support Services: $1,780
Enrollment, Drop-out Rates and Diploma Recipients by Race/Ethnicity

Category	Total	White	Black	Asian	AIAN	Hisp.
Enrollment (%)	100.0	92.3	6.6	0.2	0.7	0.2
Drop-out Rate (%)	5.0	5.3	0.0	0.0	0.0	0.0
H.S. Diplomas (#)	97	91	5	1	0	0

Boone County

Boone County
8330 US 42 • Florence, KY 41042-9286
(859) 283-1003 • http://www.boone.k12.ky.us/
Grade Span: PK-12; **Agency Type:** 1
Schools: 21
13 Primary; 4 Middle; 4 High; 0 Other Level
18 Regular; 0 Special Education; 0 Vocational; 3 Alternative
0 Magnet; 0 Charter; 7 Title I Eligible; 3 School-wide Title I
Students: 14,650 (52.0% male; 48.0% female)
Individual Education Program: 1,940 (13.2%);
English Language Learner: 328 (2.2%); Migrant: 0 (0.0%)
Eligible for Free Lunch Program: 3,402 (23.2%)
Eligible for Reduced-Price Lunch Program: 1,665 (11.4%)
Teachers: 856.7 (17.1 to 1)
Librarians/Media Specialists: 19.0 (771.1 to 1)
Guidance Counselors: 22.5 (651.1 to 1)
Current Spending: ($ per student per year):
Total: $5,627; Instruction: $3,491; Support Services: $1,892
Enrollment, Drop-out Rates and Diploma Recipients by Race/Ethnicity

Category	Total	White	Black	Asian	AIAN	Hisp.
Enrollment (%)	100.0	94.3	2.2	1.4	0.2	1.9
Drop-out Rate (%)	2.3	2.4	3.1	0.0	0.0	0.0
H.S. Diplomas (#)	722	702	8	6	0	6

Bourbon County

Bourbon County
3343 Lexington Rd • Paris, KY 40361-1000
(859) 987-2180 • http://www.bourbon.k12.ky.us/boco/
Grade Span: PK-12; **Agency Type:** 1
Schools: 6
4 Primary; 1 Middle; 1 High; 0 Other Level
6 Regular; 0 Special Education; 0 Vocational; 0 Alternative
0 Magnet; 0 Charter; 5 Title I Eligible; 2 School-wide Title I
Students: 2,919 (51.1% male; 48.9% female)
Individual Education Program: 451 (15.5%);
English Language Learner: 12 (0.4%); Migrant: 146 (5.0%)
Eligible for Free Lunch Program: 1,370 (46.9%)
Eligible for Reduced-Price Lunch Program: 382 (13.1%)
Teachers: 178.9 (16.3 to 1)
Librarians/Media Specialists: 5.0 (583.8 to 1)
Guidance Counselors: 4.0 (729.8 to 1)
Current Spending: ($ per student per year):
Total: $6,164; Instruction: $4,036; Support Services: $1,786
Enrollment, Drop-out Rates and Diploma Recipients by Race/Ethnicity

Category	Total	White	Black	Asian	AIAN	Hisp.
Enrollment (%)	100.0	92.7	4.2	0.3	0.2	2.7
Drop-out Rate (%)	3.4	3.5	0.0	0.0	0.0	0.0
H.S. Diplomas (#)	182	174	6	0	0	2

Boyd County

Ashland Ind
1420 Central Ave • Ashland, KY 41101-7552
(606) 327-2706 • http://www.ashland.k12.ky.us/
Grade Span: PK-12; **Agency Type:** 1
Schools: 9
6 Primary; 1 Middle; 2 High; 0 Other Level
8 Regular; 0 Special Education; 0 Vocational; 1 Alternative
0 Magnet; 0 Charter; 5 Title I Eligible; 5 School-wide Title I
Students: 3,354 (51.4% male; 48.6% female)
Individual Education Program: 523 (15.6%);
English Language Learner: 1 (<0.1%); Migrant: 110 (3.3%)
Eligible for Free Lunch Program: 1,763 (52.6%)
Eligible for Reduced-Price Lunch Program: 259 (7.7%)
Teachers: 211.1 (15.9 to 1)
Librarians/Media Specialists: 8.5 (394.6 to 1)
Guidance Counselors: 7.0 (479.1 to 1)
Current Spending: ($ per student per year):
Total: $6,524; Instruction: $4,385; Support Services: $1,823
Enrollment, Drop-out Rates and Diploma Recipients by Race/Ethnicity

Category	Total	White	Black	Asian	AIAN	Hisp.
Enrollment (%)	100.0	94.6	4.1	0.7	0.3	0.4
Drop-out Rate (%)	3.9	4.2	0.0	0.0	0.0	0.0
H.S. Diplomas (#)	205	193	8	3	1	0

Boyd County
1104 Bob Mccullough • Ashland, KY 41102-9275
(606) 928-4141 • http://www.boyd.k12.ky.us/
Grade Span: PK-12; **Agency Type:** 1
Schools: 9
5 Primary; 1 Middle; 3 High; 0 Other Level
7 Regular; 0 Special Education; 1 Vocational; 1 Alternative
0 Magnet; 0 Charter; 6 Title I Eligible; 5 School-wide Title I
Students: 3,749 (51.9% male; 48.1% female)
Individual Education Program: 659 (17.6%);
English Language Learner: 0 (0.0%); Migrant: 63 (1.7%)
Eligible for Free Lunch Program: 1,924 (51.3%)
Eligible for Reduced-Price Lunch Program: 385 (10.3%)
Teachers: 246.1 (15.2 to 1)
Librarians/Media Specialists: 6.5 (576.8 to 1)
Guidance Counselors: 9.0 (416.6 to 1)
Current Spending: ($ per student per year):
Total: $6,969; Instruction: $4,445; Support Services: $2,183
Enrollment, Drop-out Rates and Diploma Recipients by Race/Ethnicity

Category	Total	White	Black	Asian	AIAN	Hisp.
Enrollment (%)	100.0	97.2	1.8	0.2	0.4	0.4
Drop-out Rate (%)	3.2	3.4	0.0	0.0	n/a	0.0
H.S. Diplomas (#)	198	194	1	1	1	1

Boyle County

Boyle County

352 N Danville By-pass • Danville, KY 40422
Mailing Address: PO Box 520 • Danville, KY 40422
(859) 236-6634 • http://www.boyle.k12.ky.us/
Grade Span: PK-12; **Agency Type:** 1
Schools: 7
3 Primary; 1 Middle; 2 High; 1 Other Level
5 Regular; 0 Special Education; 0 Vocational; 2 Alternative
0 Magnet; 0 Charter; 2 Title I Eligible; 1 School-wide Title I
Students: 2,886 (51.5% male; 48.5% female)
Individual Education Program: 580 (20.1%);
English Language Learner: 0 (0.0%); Migrant: 56 (1.9%)
Eligible for Free Lunch Program: 1,015 (35.2%)
Eligible for Reduced-Price Lunch Program: 257 (8.9%)
Teachers: 186.4 (15.5 to 1)
Librarians/Media Specialists: 5.0 (577.2 to 1)
Guidance Counselors: 7.0 (412.3 to 1)
Current Spending: ($ per student per year):
Total: $5,993; Instruction: $4,034; Support Services: $1,685
Enrollment, Drop-out Rates and Diploma Recipients by Race/Ethnicity

Category	Total	White	Black	Asian	AIAN	Hisp.
Enrollment (%)	100.0	97.3	0.9	0.8	0.2	0.8
Drop-out Rate (%)	4.0	4.2	0.0	0.0	0.0	0.0
H.S. Diplomas (#)	182	178	1	1	1	1

Danville Independent

359 Proctor St • Danville, KY 40422-1577
(859) 936-8500 • http://www.danville.k12.ky.us/
Grade Span: PK-12; **Agency Type:** 1
Schools: 6
4 Primary; 1 Middle; 1 High; 0 Other Level
5 Regular; 0 Special Education; 0 Vocational; 1 Alternative
0 Magnet; 0 Charter; 5 Title I Eligible; 3 School-wide Title I
Students: 1,876 (55.0% male; 45.0% female)
Individual Education Program: 318 (17.0%);
English Language Learner: 17 (0.9%); Migrant: 33 (1.8%)
Eligible for Free Lunch Program: 1,097 (58.5%)
Eligible for Reduced-Price Lunch Program: 226 (12.0%)
Teachers: 128.0 (14.7 to 1)
Librarians/Media Specialists: 6.0 (312.7 to 1)
Guidance Counselors: 6.0 (312.7 to 1)
Current Spending: ($ per student per year):
Total: $6,840; Instruction: $4,209; Support Services: $2,241
Enrollment, Drop-out Rates and Diploma Recipients by Race/Ethnicity

Category	Total	White	Black	Asian	AIAN	Hisp.
Enrollment (%)	100.0	70.9	24.7	1.2	0.3	2.9
Drop-out Rate (%)	3.9	2.8	8.1	0.0	0.0	0.0
H.S. Diplomas (#)	108	82	23	1	0	2

Breathitt County

Breathitt County

420 Court St • Jackson, KY 41339-0750
Mailing Address: PO Box 750 • Jackson, KY 41339-0750
(606) 666-2491 • http://www.breathitt.k12.ky.us/
Grade Span: PK-12; **Agency Type:** 1
Schools: 9
4 Primary; 1 Middle; 3 High; 1 Other Level
6 Regular; 0 Special Education; 0 Vocational; 3 Alternative
0 Magnet; 0 Charter; 6 Title I Eligible; 6 School-wide Title I
Students: 2,386 (54.3% male; 45.7% female)
Individual Education Program: 513 (21.5%);
English Language Learner: 0 (0.0%); Migrant: 120 (5.0%)
Eligible for Free Lunch Program: 1,787 (74.9%)
Eligible for Reduced-Price Lunch Program: 319 (13.4%)
Teachers: 159.9 (14.9 to 1)
Librarians/Media Specialists: 5.0 (477.2 to 1)
Guidance Counselors: 5.0 (477.2 to 1)
Current Spending: ($ per student per year):
Total: $7,377; Instruction: $4,400; Support Services: $2,529
Enrollment, Drop-out Rates and Diploma Recipients by Race/Ethnicity

Category	Total	White	Black	Asian	AIAN	Hisp.
Enrollment (%)	100.0	98.8	1.0	0.1	0.0	0.1
Drop-out Rate (%)	13.5	13.6	0.0	n/a	n/a	0.0
H.S. Diplomas (#)	117	117	0	0	0	0

Breckinridge County

Breckinridge County

#1 Airport Rd • Hardinsburg, KY 40143-0148
Mailing Address: PO Box 148 • Hardinsburg, KY 40143-0148
(270) 756-3000 • http://www.breck.k12.ky.us/
Grade Span: PK-12; **Agency Type:** 1
Schools: 6
4 Primary; 1 Middle; 1 High; 0 Other Level
6 Regular; 0 Special Education; 0 Vocational; 0 Alternative
0 Magnet; 0 Charter; 6 Title I Eligible; 5 School-wide Title I
Students: 2,816 (51.7% male; 48.3% female)
Individual Education Program: 430 (15.3%);
English Language Learner: 0 (0.0%); Migrant: 70 (2.5%)
Eligible for Free Lunch Program: 1,757 (62.4%)
Eligible for Reduced-Price Lunch Program: 481 (17.1%)
Teachers: 152.3 (18.5 to 1)
Librarians/Media Specialists: 5.0 (563.2 to 1)
Guidance Counselors: 5.4 (521.5 to 1)
Current Spending: ($ per student per year):
Total: $6,433; Instruction: $3,784; Support Services: $2,194
Enrollment, Drop-out Rates and Diploma Recipients by Race/Ethnicity

Category	Total	White	Black	Asian	AIAN	Hisp.
Enrollment (%)	100.0	96.2	2.9	0.2	0.1	0.6
Drop-out Rate (%)	3.2	3.2	3.6	n/a	0.0	0.0
H.S. Diplomas (#)	175	167	7	0	0	1

Bullitt County

Bullitt County

1040 Hwy 44E • Shepherdsville, KY 40165-6168
(502) 543-2271 • http://www.bullitt.k12.ky.us/
Grade Span: PK-12; **Agency Type:** 1
Schools: 20
11 Primary; 4 Middle; 4 High; 1 Other Level
18 Regular; 0 Special Education; 0 Vocational; 2 Alternative
0 Magnet; 0 Charter; 10 Title I Eligible; 7 School-wide Title I
Students: 11,451 (51.8% male; 48.2% female)
Individual Education Program: 1,591 (13.9%);
English Language Learner: 4 (<0.1%); Migrant: 78 (0.7%)
Eligible for Free Lunch Program: 3,900 (34.1%)
Eligible for Reduced-Price Lunch Program: 1,568 (13.7%)
Teachers: 644.5 (17.8 to 1)
Librarians/Media Specialists: 18.5 (619.0 to 1)
Guidance Counselors: 21.5 (532.6 to 1)
Current Spending: ($ per student per year):
Total: $5,505; Instruction: $3,469; Support Services: $1,759
Enrollment, Drop-out Rates and Diploma Recipients by Race/Ethnicity

Category	Total	White	Black	Asian	AIAN	Hisp.
Enrollment (%)	100.0	98.6	0.5	0.3	0.3	0.4
Drop-out Rate (%)	3.8	3.9	0.0	0.0	0.0	0.0
H.S. Diplomas (#)	630	620	6	1	0	3

Butler County

Butler County

203 N Tyler St • Morgantown, KY 42261-0339
Mailing Address: PO Box 339 • Morgantown, KY 42261-0339
(270) 526-5624 • http://www.butler.k12.ky.us/
Grade Span: PK-12; **Agency Type:** 1
Schools: 7
4 Primary; 1 Middle; 2 High; 0 Other Level
6 Regular; 0 Special Education; 0 Vocational; 1 Alternative
0 Magnet; 0 Charter; 6 Title I Eligible; 5 School-wide Title I
Students: 2,263 (51.0% male; 49.0% female)
Individual Education Program: 359 (15.9%);
English Language Learner: 1 (<0.1%); Migrant: 22 (1.0%)
Eligible for Free Lunch Program: 1,138 (50.3%)
Eligible for Reduced-Price Lunch Program: 344 (15.2%)
Teachers: 149.5 (15.1 to 1)
Librarians/Media Specialists: 5.0 (452.6 to 1)
Guidance Counselors: 5.0 (452.6 to 1)
Current Spending: ($ per student per year):
Total: $6,171; Instruction: $3,753; Support Services: $2,013
Enrollment, Drop-out Rates and Diploma Recipients by Race/Ethnicity

Category	Total	White	Black	Asian	AIAN	Hisp.
Enrollment (%)	100.0	98.8	0.7	0.2	0.0	0.2
Drop-out Rate (%)	3.6	3.7	0.0	n/a	n/a	0.0
H.S. Diplomas (#)	138	136	1	0	0	1

Caldwell County

Caldwell County
611 Washington St • Princeton, KY 42445-0229
Mailing Address: PO Box 229 • Princeton, KY 42445-0229
(270) 365-8000 • http://www.caldwell.k12.ky.us/
Grade Span: PK-12; **Agency Type:** 1
Schools: 4
2 Primary; 1 Middle; 1 High; 0 Other Level
4 Regular; 0 Special Education; 0 Vocational; 0 Alternative
0 Magnet; 0 Charter; 4 Title I Eligible; 3 School-wide Title I
Students: 2,120 (52.1% male; 47.9% female)
Individual Education Program: 307 (14.5%);
English Language Learner: 0 (0.0%); Migrant: 258 (12.2%)
Eligible for Free Lunch Program: 1,218 (57.5%)
Eligible for Reduced-Price Lunch Program: 222 (10.5%)
Teachers: 137.0 (15.5 to 1)
Librarians/Media Specialists: 4.0 (530.0 to 1)
Guidance Counselors: 4.0 (530.0 to 1)
Current Spending: ($ per student per year):
Total: $5,888; Instruction: $3,317; Support Services: $2,240
Enrollment, Drop-out Rates and Diploma Recipients by Race/Ethnicity

Category	Total	White	Black	Asian	AIAN	Hisp.
Enrollment (%)	100.0	91.7	7.5	0.3	0.5	0.1
Drop-out Rate (%)	2.7	2.7	3.0	0.0	0.0	n/a
H.S. Diplomas (#)	132	121	10	1	0	0

Calloway County

Calloway County
2110 College Farm Rd • Murray, KY 42071-0800
Mailing Address: PO Box 800 • Murray, KY 42071-0800
(270) 762-7300 • http://www.calloway.k12.ky.us/
Grade Span: PK-12; **Agency Type:** 1
Schools: 6
4 Primary; 1 Middle; 1 High; 0 Other Level
6 Regular; 0 Special Education; 0 Vocational; 0 Alternative
0 Magnet; 0 Charter; 5 Title I Eligible; 5 School-wide Title I
Students: 3,146 (51.5% male; 48.5% female)
Individual Education Program: 563 (17.9%);
English Language Learner: 23 (0.7%); Migrant: 142 (4.5%)
Eligible for Free Lunch Program: 1,524 (48.4%)
Eligible for Reduced-Price Lunch Program: 570 (18.1%)
Teachers: 203.5 (15.5 to 1)
Librarians/Media Specialists: 5.0 (629.2 to 1)
Guidance Counselors: 9.4 (334.7 to 1)
Current Spending: ($ per student per year):
Total: $6,110; Instruction: $4,085; Support Services: $1,612
Enrollment, Drop-out Rates and Diploma Recipients by Race/Ethnicity

Category	Total	White	Black	Asian	AIAN	Hisp.
Enrollment (%)	100.0	97.4	0.9	0.3	0.2	1.1
Drop-out Rate (%)	2.4	2.5	0.0	0.0	0.0	0.0
H.S. Diplomas (#)	218	213	3	0	0	2

Murray Independent
208 S 13th St • Murray, KY 42071-2302
(270) 753-4363
Grade Span: PK-12; **Agency Type:** 1
Schools: 4
2 Primary; 1 Middle; 1 High; 0 Other Level
4 Regular; 0 Special Education; 0 Vocational; 0 Alternative
0 Magnet; 0 Charter; 3 Title I Eligible; 0 School-wide Title I
Students: 1,721 (50.9% male; 49.1% female)
Individual Education Program: 248 (14.4%);
English Language Learner: 20 (1.2%); Migrant: 58 (3.4%)
Eligible for Free Lunch Program: 558 (32.4%)
Eligible for Reduced-Price Lunch Program: 158 (9.2%)
Teachers: 99.6 (17.3 to 1)
Librarians/Media Specialists: 3.0 (573.7 to 1)
Guidance Counselors: 3.0 (573.7 to 1)
Current Spending: ($ per student per year):
Total: $5,408; Instruction: $3,434; Support Services: $1,655
Enrollment, Drop-out Rates and Diploma Recipients by Race/Ethnicity

Category	Total	White	Black	Asian	AIAN	Hisp.
Enrollment (%)	100.0	86.4	9.1	1.7	0.3	2.4
Drop-out Rate (%)	0.9	0.8	2.9	0.0	0.0	0.0
H.S. Diplomas (#)	127	111	13	2	0	1

Campbell County

Campbell County
101 Orchard • Alexandria, KY 41001-1223
(859) 635-2173 • http://www.campbell.k12.ky.us/
Grade Span: PK-12; **Agency Type:** 1
Schools: 10
6 Primary; 1 Middle; 2 High; 1 Other Level
8 Regular; 0 Special Education; 0 Vocational; 2 Alternative
0 Magnet; 0 Charter; 4 Title I Eligible; 1 School-wide Title I
Students: 4,741 (52.9% male; 47.1% female)
Individual Education Program: 821 (17.3%);
English Language Learner: 10 (0.2%); Migrant: 3 (0.1%)
Eligible for Free Lunch Program: 1,185 (25.0%)
Eligible for Reduced-Price Lunch Program: 555 (11.7%)
Teachers: 285.4 (16.6 to 1)
Librarians/Media Specialists: 5.0 (948.2 to 1)
Guidance Counselors: 12.5 (379.3 to 1)
Current Spending: ($ per student per year):
Total: $5,815; Instruction: $3,376; Support Services: $2,158
Enrollment, Drop-out Rates and Diploma Recipients by Race/Ethnicity

Category	Total	White	Black	Asian	AIAN	Hisp.
Enrollment (%)	100.0	98.3	0.9	0.6	0.0	0.2
Drop-out Rate (%)	3.0	3.0	0.0	0.0	n/a	0.0
H.S. Diplomas (#)	322	321	0	0	0	1

Fort Thomas Independent
28 N Ft Thomas Ave • Fort Thomas, KY 41075-1527
(859) 781-3333 • http://www.ft-thomas.k12.ky.us/
Grade Span: PK-12; **Agency Type:** 1
Schools: 5
3 Primary; 1 Middle; 1 High; 0 Other Level
5 Regular; 0 Special Education; 0 Vocational; 0 Alternative
0 Magnet; 0 Charter; 2 Title I Eligible; 2 School-wide Title I
Students: 2,301 (52.1% male; 47.9% female)
Individual Education Program: 206 (9.0%);
English Language Learner: 0 (0.0%); Migrant: 0 (0.0%)
Eligible for Free Lunch Program: 117 (5.1%)
Eligible for Reduced-Price Lunch Program: 49 (2.1%)
Teachers: 144.9 (15.9 to 1)
Librarians/Media Specialists: 5.0 (460.2 to 1)
Guidance Counselors: 5.5 (418.4 to 1)
Current Spending: ($ per student per year):
Total: $5,735; Instruction: $3,480; Support Services: $2,019
Enrollment, Drop-out Rates and Diploma Recipients by Race/Ethnicity

Category	Total	White	Black	Asian	AIAN	Hisp.
Enrollment (%)	100.0	99.0	0.5	0.3	0.1	0.1
Drop-out Rate (%)	0.7	0.7	0.0	0.0	0.0	n/a
H.S. Diplomas (#)	193	191	1	1	0	0

Newport Independent
301 E 8th St • Newport, KY 41071-1963
(859) 292-3004 • http://www.newportwildcats.org/
Grade Span: PK-12; **Agency Type:** 1
Schools: 7
3 Primary; 1 Middle; 1 High; 2 Other Level
5 Regular; 0 Special Education; 0 Vocational; 2 Alternative
0 Magnet; 0 Charter; 5 Title I Eligible; 4 School-wide Title I
Students: 2,554 (50.9% male; 49.1% female)
Individual Education Program: 443 (17.3%);
English Language Learner: 2 (0.1%); Migrant: 0 (0.0%)
Eligible for Free Lunch Program: 1,851 (72.5%)
Eligible for Reduced-Price Lunch Program: 335 (13.1%)
Teachers: 186.8 (13.7 to 1)
Librarians/Media Specialists: 5.0 (510.8 to 1)
Guidance Counselors: 5.0 (510.8 to 1)
Current Spending: ($ per student per year):
Total: $7,044; Instruction: $4,699; Support Services: $1,969
Enrollment, Drop-out Rates and Diploma Recipients by Race/Ethnicity

Category	Total	White	Black	Asian	AIAN	Hisp.
Enrollment (%)	100.0	88.6	10.2	0.2	0.2	0.8
Drop-out Rate (%)	3.0	3.1	2.7	0.0	n/a	0.0
H.S. Diplomas (#)	106	98	6	2	0	0

Carroll County

Carroll County
813 Hawkins St • Carrollton, KY 41008-0090
(502) 732-7070 • http://www.carroll.k12.ky.us/
Grade Span: PK-12; **Agency Type:** 1
Schools: 5
1 Primary; 2 Middle; 1 High; 1 Other Level
4 Regular; 0 Special Education; 0 Vocational; 1 Alternative
0 Magnet; 0 Charter; 4 Title I Eligible; 3 School-wide Title I
Students: 1,911 (52.0% male; 48.0% female)
Individual Education Program: 238 (12.5%);
English Language Learner: 54 (2.8%); Migrant: 92 (4.8%)
Eligible for Free Lunch Program: 1,157 (60.5%)
Eligible for Reduced-Price Lunch Program: 201 (10.5%)
Teachers: 111.5 (17.1 to 1)
Librarians/Media Specialists: 5.0 (382.2 to 1)
Guidance Counselors: 7.9 (241.9 to 1)

Current Spending: ($ per student per year):
Total: $7,508; Instruction: $4,382; Support Services: $2,749
Enrollment, Drop-out Rates and Diploma Recipients by Race/Ethnicity

Category	Total	White	Black	Asian	AIAN	Hisp.
Enrollment (%)	100.0	94.1	2.0	0.1	0.4	3.5
Drop-out Rate (%)	7.4	7.7	0.0	n/a	n/a	0.0
H.S. Diplomas (#)	116	108	6	0	2	0

Carter County

Carter County
228 S Carol Malone Blvd • Grayson, KY 41143-1345
(606) 474-6696 • http://www.carter.k12.ky.us/
Grade Span: PK-12; **Agency Type:** 1
Schools: 11
6 Primary; 2 Middle; 3 High; 0 Other Level
10 Regular; 0 Special Education; 1 Vocational; 0 Alternative
0 Magnet; 0 Charter; 10 Title I Eligible; 10 School-wide Title I
Students: 5,177 (50.8% male; 49.2% female)
Individual Education Program: 905 (17.5%);
English Language Learner: 0 (0.0%); Migrant: 185 (3.6%)
Eligible for Free Lunch Program: 3,637 (70.3%)
Eligible for Reduced-Price Lunch Program: 703 (13.6%)
Teachers: 333.5 (15.5 to 1)
Librarians/Media Specialists: 8.0 (647.1 to 1)
Guidance Counselors: 16.0 (323.6 to 1)
Current Spending: ($ per student per year):
Total: $6,198; Instruction: $3,821; Support Services: $2,068
Enrollment, Drop-out Rates and Diploma Recipients by Race/Ethnicity

Category	Total	White	Black	Asian	AIAN	Hisp.
Enrollment (%)	100.0	99.6	0.1	0.0	0.1	0.2
Drop-out Rate (%)	4.0	4.0	n/a	0.0	n/a	0.0
H.S. Diplomas (#)	227	226	0	0	1	0

Casey County

Casey County
1922 N US 127 • Liberty, KY 42539-9705
(606) 787-6941 • http://www.casey.k12.ky.us/
Grade Span: PK-12; **Agency Type:** 1
Schools: 8
6 Primary; 1 Middle; 1 High; 0 Other Level
8 Regular; 0 Special Education; 0 Vocational; 0 Alternative
0 Magnet; 0 Charter; 8 Title I Eligible; 7 School-wide Title I
Students: 2,515 (50.8% male; 49.2% female)
Individual Education Program: 414 (16.5%);
English Language Learner: 0 (0.0%); Migrant: 110 (4.4%)
Eligible for Free Lunch Program: 1,657 (65.9%)
Eligible for Reduced-Price Lunch Program: 456 (18.1%)
Teachers: 159.1 (15.8 to 1)
Librarians/Media Specialists: 4.5 (558.9 to 1)
Guidance Counselors: 5.0 (503.0 to 1)
Current Spending: ($ per student per year):
Total: $6,175; Instruction: $3,898; Support Services: $1,869
Enrollment, Drop-out Rates and Diploma Recipients by Race/Ethnicity

Category	Total	White	Black	Asian	AIAN	Hisp.
Enrollment (%)	100.0	98.0	0.2	0.2	0.3	1.4
Drop-out Rate (%)	4.6	4.7	0.0	n/a	0.0	0.0
H.S. Diplomas (#)	119	119	0	0	0	0

Christian County

Christian County
200 Glass St • Hopkinsville, KY 42240-0609
(270) 887-1300 • http://www.christian.k12.ky.us/
Grade Span: PK-12; **Agency Type:** 1
Schools: 20
11 Primary; 3 Middle; 4 High; 2 Other Level
16 Regular; 0 Special Education; 1 Vocational; 3 Alternative
0 Magnet; 0 Charter; 16 Title I Eligible; 14 School-wide Title I
Students: 9,609 (52.0% male; 48.0% female)
Individual Education Program: 1,658 (17.3%);
English Language Learner: 62 (0.6%); Migrant: 292 (3.0%)
Eligible for Free Lunch Program: 6,070 (63.2%)
Eligible for Reduced-Price Lunch Program: 1,995 (20.8%)
Teachers: 546.0 (17.6 to 1)
Librarians/Media Specialists: 16.0 (600.6 to 1)
Guidance Counselors: 26.0 (369.6 to 1)
Current Spending: ($ per student per year):
Total: $6,407; Instruction: $3,839; Support Services: $2,179
Enrollment, Drop-out Rates and Diploma Recipients by Race/Ethnicity

Category	Total	White	Black	Asian	AIAN	Hisp.
Enrollment (%)	100.0	61.6	35.0	0.8	0.5	2.1
Drop-out Rate (%)	6.2	5.2	8.3	0.0	0.0	6.5
H.S. Diplomas (#)	416	264	141	4	1	6

Fort Campbell District
77 Texas Ave • Fort Campbell, KY 42223-5127
(502) 439-1927
Grade Span: PK-12; **Agency Type:** 6
Schools: 8
5 Primary; 2 Middle; 1 High; 0 Other Level
8 Regular; 0 Special Education; 0 Vocational; 0 Alternative
0 Magnet; 0 Charter; 0 Title I Eligible; 0 School-wide Title I
Students: 4,376 (n/a% male; n/a% female)
Individual Education Program: 519 (11.9%);
English Language Learner: 65 (1.5%); Migrant: n/a
Eligible for Free Lunch Program: n/a
Eligible for Reduced-Price Lunch Program: n/a
Teachers: 310.0 (14.1 to 1)
Librarians/Media Specialists: 8.0 (547.0 to 1)
Guidance Counselors: 12.5 (350.1 to 1)
Current Spending: ($ per student per year):
Total: n/a; Instruction: n/a; Support Services: n/a
Enrollment, Drop-out Rates and Diploma Recipients by Race/Ethnicity

Category	Total	White	Black	Asian	AIAN	Hisp.
Enrollment (%)	100.0	43.6	21.3	1.8	0.7	9.7
Drop-out Rate (%)	n/a	n/a	n/a	n/a	n/a	n/a
H.S. Diplomas (#)	114	45	36	0	0	33

Clark County

Clark County
1600 W Lexington Ave • Winchester, KY 40391-1145
(859) 744-4545 • http://www.clark.k12.ky.us/
Grade Span: KG-12; **Agency Type:** 1
Schools: 13
8 Primary; 2 Middle; 2 High; 1 Other Level
11 Regular; 0 Special Education; 0 Vocational; 2 Alternative
1 Magnet; 0 Charter; 9 Title I Eligible; 7 School-wide Title I
Students: 5,457 (51.6% male; 48.4% female)
Individual Education Program: 801 (14.7%);
English Language Learner: 37 (0.7%); Migrant: 154 (2.8%)
Eligible for Free Lunch Program: 2,656 (48.7%)
Eligible for Reduced-Price Lunch Program: 683 (12.5%)
Teachers: 332.1 (16.4 to 1)
Librarians/Media Specialists: 10.0 (545.7 to 1)
Guidance Counselors: 16.0 (341.1 to 1)
Current Spending: ($ per student per year):
Total: $5,824; Instruction: $3,641; Support Services: $1,872
Enrollment, Drop-out Rates and Diploma Recipients by Race/Ethnicity

Category	Total	White	Black	Asian	AIAN	Hisp.
Enrollment (%)	100.0	92.1	6.1	0.2	0.3	1.2
Drop-out Rate (%)	5.0	5.2	2.4	n/a	n/a	0.0
H.S. Diplomas (#)	299	284	15	0	0	0

Clay County

Clay County
128 Richmond Rd • Manchester, KY 40962-1207
(606) 598-2168 • http://www.clay.k12.ky.us/
Grade Span: PK-12; **Agency Type:** 1
Schools: 12
9 Primary; 1 Middle; 1 High; 1 Other Level
11 Regular; 0 Special Education; 0 Vocational; 1 Alternative
0 Magnet; 0 Charter; 11 Title I Eligible; 10 School-wide Title I
Students: 4,247 (52.5% male; 47.5% female)
Individual Education Program: 964 (22.7%);
English Language Learner: 0 (0.0%); Migrant: 0 (0.0%)
Eligible for Free Lunch Program: 3,325 (78.3%)
Eligible for Reduced-Price Lunch Program: 467 (11.0%)
Teachers: 313.0 (13.6 to 1)
Librarians/Media Specialists: 12.0 (353.9 to 1)
Guidance Counselors: 4.0 (1,061.8 to 1)
Current Spending: ($ per student per year):
Total: $6,991; Instruction: $4,083; Support Services: $2,482
Enrollment, Drop-out Rates and Diploma Recipients by Race/Ethnicity

Category	Total	White	Black	Asian	AIAN	Hisp.
Enrollment (%)	100.0	99.0	0.6	0.2	0.2	0.1
Drop-out Rate (%)	8.7	8.8	0.0	0.0	0.0	n/a
H.S. Diplomas (#)	161	159	2	0	0	0

Clinton County

Clinton County
Hwy 127 • Albany, KY 42602-9304
Mailing Address: Rt 4 Box 100 Hwy 127 • Albany, KY 42602-9304
(606) 387-6480 • http://www.clinton.k12.ky.us/
Grade Span: PK-12; **Agency Type:** 1
Schools: 3
1 Primary; 1 Middle; 1 High; 0 Other Level
3 Regular; 0 Special Education; 0 Vocational; 0 Alternative
0 Magnet; 0 Charter; 3 Title I Eligible; 3 School-wide Title I
Students: 1,653 (50.4% male; 49.6% female)
Individual Education Program: 315 (19.1%);
English Language Learner: 17 (1.0%); Migrant: 89 (5.4%)
Eligible for Free Lunch Program: 1,156 (69.9%)
Eligible for Reduced-Price Lunch Program: 332 (20.1%)
Teachers: 103.9 (15.9 to 1)
Librarians/Media Specialists: 1.2 (1,377.5 to 1)
Guidance Counselors: 7.0 (236.1 to 1)
Current Spending: ($ per student per year):
Total: $7,709; Instruction: $4,699; Support Services: $2,515
Enrollment, Drop-out Rates and Diploma Recipients by Race/Ethnicity

Category	Total	White	Black	Asian	AIAN	Hisp.
Enrollment (%)	100.0	97.8	0.3	0.1	0.0	1.7
Drop-out Rate (%)	5.4	5.5	n/a	0.0	n/a	0.0
H.S. Diplomas (#)	79	79	0	0	0	0

Daviess County

Daviess County
1622 Southeastern Pkwy • Owensboro, KY 42304-1510
(270) 852-7000 • http://www.daviess.k12.ky.us/
Grade Span: PK-12; **Agency Type:** 1
Schools: 22
13 Primary; 3 Middle; 4 High; 1 Other Level
17 Regular; 0 Special Education; 0 Vocational; 4 Alternative
0 Magnet; 0 Charter; 11 Title I Eligible; 8 School-wide Title I
Students: 10,786 (52.1% male; 47.9% female)
Individual Education Program: 1,656 (15.4%);
English Language Learner: 57 (0.5%); Migrant: 202 (1.9%)
Eligible for Free Lunch Program: 4,057 (37.6%)
Eligible for Reduced-Price Lunch Program: 1,427 (13.2%)
Teachers: 649.9 (16.6 to 1)
Librarians/Media Specialists: 17.0 (634.5 to 1)
Guidance Counselors: 27.8 (388.0 to 1)
Current Spending: ($ per student per year):
Total: $5,869; Instruction: $3,653; Support Services: $1,842
Enrollment, Drop-out Rates and Diploma Recipients by Race/Ethnicity

Category	Total	White	Black	Asian	AIAN	Hisp.
Enrollment (%)	100.0	95.4	3.1	0.6	0.2	0.8
Drop-out Rate (%)	2.6	2.4	8.0	0.0	0.0	0.0
H.S. Diplomas (#)	720	702	11	1	1	5

Owensboro Independent
1335 W 11th St • Owensboro, KY 42302-0249
(270) 686-1000 • http://www.owensboro.k12.ky.us/
Grade Span: PK-12; **Agency Type:** 1
Schools: 14
7 Primary; 3 Middle; 3 High; 1 Other Level
10 Regular; 0 Special Education; 0 Vocational; 4 Alternative
0 Magnet; 0 Charter; 8 Title I Eligible; 8 School-wide Title I
Students: 4,292 (52.0% male; 48.0% female)
Individual Education Program: 768 (17.9%);
English Language Learner: 0 (0.0%); Migrant: 157 (3.7%)
Eligible for Free Lunch Program: 2,864 (66.7%)
Eligible for Reduced-Price Lunch Program: 598 (13.9%)
Teachers: 323.2 (13.3 to 1)
Librarians/Media Specialists: 8.5 (504.9 to 1)
Guidance Counselors: 15.0 (286.1 to 1)
Current Spending: ($ per student per year):
Total: $7,766; Instruction: $4,508; Support Services: $2,838
Enrollment, Drop-out Rates and Diploma Recipients by Race/Ethnicity

Category	Total	White	Black	Asian	AIAN	Hisp.
Enrollment (%)	100.0	81.8	16.4	0.3	0.3	1.1
Drop-out Rate (%)	3.2	3.9	1.0	0.0	0.0	0.0
H.S. Diplomas (#)	215	180	33	0	0	2

Edmonson County

Edmonson County
100 Wildcat Way • Brownsville, KY 42210-0129
Mailing Address: 100 High School Rd • Brownsville, KY 42210-0129
(270) 597-2101 • http://www.edmonson.k12.ky.us/
Grade Span: PK-12; **Agency Type:** 1
Schools: 5
3 Primary; 1 Middle; 1 High; 0 Other Level
5 Regular; 0 Special Education; 0 Vocational; 0 Alternative
0 Magnet; 0 Charter; 4 Title I Eligible; 3 School-wide Title I
Students: 2,103 (52.5% male; 47.5% female)
Individual Education Program: 394 (18.7%);
English Language Learner: 1 (<0.1%); Migrant: 21 (1.0%)
Eligible for Free Lunch Program: 1,221 (58.1%)
Eligible for Reduced-Price Lunch Program: 322 (15.3%)
Teachers: 132.0 (15.9 to 1)
Librarians/Media Specialists: 4.0 (525.8 to 1)
Guidance Counselors: 5.0 (420.6 to 1)
Current Spending: ($ per student per year):
Total: $5,993; Instruction: $3,655; Support Services: $1,930
Enrollment, Drop-out Rates and Diploma Recipients by Race/Ethnicity

Category	Total	White	Black	Asian	AIAN	Hisp.
Enrollment (%)	100.0	99.0	0.5	0.1	0.3	0.2
Drop-out Rate (%)	5.0	5.1	n/a	0.0	0.0	0.0
H.S. Diplomas (#)	99	98	0	0	1	0

Estill County

Estill County
253 Main St • Irvine, KY 40336-0391
(606) 723-2181 • http://www.estill.k12.ky.us/
Grade Span: PK-12; **Agency Type:** 1
Schools: 7
3 Primary; 1 Middle; 1 High; 2 Other Level
5 Regular; 0 Special Education; 0 Vocational; 2 Alternative
0 Magnet; 0 Charter; 5 Title I Eligible; 4 School-wide Title I
Students: 2,703 (51.5% male; 48.5% female)
Individual Education Program: 502 (18.6%);
English Language Learner: 0 (0.0%); Migrant: 43 (1.6%)
Eligible for Free Lunch Program: 1,788 (66.1%)
Eligible for Reduced-Price Lunch Program: 348 (12.9%)
Teachers: 184.2 (14.7 to 1)
Librarians/Media Specialists: 5.0 (540.6 to 1)
Guidance Counselors: 6.0 (450.5 to 1)
Current Spending: ($ per student per year):
Total: $5,911; Instruction: $3,828; Support Services: $1,760
Enrollment, Drop-out Rates and Diploma Recipients by Race/Ethnicity

Category	Total	White	Black	Asian	AIAN	Hisp.
Enrollment (%)	100.0	98.9	0.5	0.3	0.1	0.2
Drop-out Rate (%)	6.2	6.3	0.0	0.0	0.0	0.0
H.S. Diplomas (#)	154	154	0	0	0	0

Fayette County

Fayette County
701 E Main St • Lexington, KY 40502-1601
(859) 381-4000 • http://www.fayette.k12.ky.us/
Grade Span: PK-12; **Agency Type:** 1
Schools: 64
37 Primary; 11 Middle; 9 High; 6 Other Level
52 Regular; 0 Special Education; 2 Vocational; 9 Alternative
21 Magnet; 0 Charter; 28 Title I Eligible; 23 School-wide Title I
Students: 34,296 (51.5% male; 48.5% female)
Individual Education Program: 3,568 (10.4%);
English Language Learner: 997 (2.9%); Migrant: 344 (1.0%)
Eligible for Free Lunch Program: 14,756 (43.0%)
Eligible for Reduced-Price Lunch Program: 3,278 (9.6%)
Teachers: 2,491.2 (13.8 to 1)
Librarians/Media Specialists: 61.5 (557.7 to 1)
Guidance Counselors: 78.5 (436.9 to 1)
Current Spending: ($ per student per year):
Total: $6,883; Instruction: $4,228; Support Services: $2,352
Enrollment, Drop-out Rates and Diploma Recipients by Race/Ethnicity

Category	Total	White	Black	Asian	AIAN	Hisp.
Enrollment (%)	100.0	69.3	23.2	2.9	0.1	4.4
Drop-out Rate (%)	6.2	6.2	6.3	7.0	0.0	9.1
H.S. Diplomas (#)	1,643	1,244	313	53	3	30

Fleming County

Fleming County
211 W Water St • Flemingsburg, KY 41041-1022
(606) 845-5851 • http://www.fleming.k12.ky.us/
Grade Span: KG-12; **Agency Type:** 1
Schools: 6
4 Primary; 1 Middle; 1 High; 0 Other Level
6 Regular; 0 Special Education; 0 Vocational; 0 Alternative
0 Magnet; 0 Charter; 6 Title I Eligible; 6 School-wide Title I
Students: 2,473 (51.6% male; 48.4% female)
Individual Education Program: 329 (13.3%);
English Language Learner: 3 (0.1%); Migrant: 49 (2.0%)
Eligible for Free Lunch Program: 1,515 (61.3%)

Eligible for Reduced-Price Lunch Program: 509 (20.6%)
Teachers: 155.7 (15.9 to 1)
Librarians/Media Specialists: 5.0 (494.6 to 1)
Guidance Counselors: 5.0 (494.6 to 1)
Current Spending: ($ per student per year):
Total: $6,430; Instruction: $4,044; Support Services: $2,053

Enrollment, Drop-out Rates and Diploma Recipients by Race/Ethnicity

Category	Total	White	Black	Asian	AIAN	Hisp.
Enrollment (%)	100.0	96.8	2.2	0.2	0.1	0.7
Drop-out Rate (%)	4.0	4.1	0.0	0.0	n/a	0.0
H.S. Diplomas (#)	131	129	1	1	0	0

Floyd County

Floyd County
106 N Front Ave • Prestons, KY 41653-1209
(606) 886-2354
Grade Span: PK-12; **Agency Type:** 1
Schools: 18
9 Primary; 3 Middle; 4 High; 2 Other Level
16 Regular; 0 Special Education; 0 Vocational; 2 Alternative
0 Magnet; 0 Charter; 16 Title I Eligible; 16 School-wide Title I
Students: 7,149 (52.0% male; 48.0% female)
Individual Education Program: 1,101 (15.4%);
English Language Learner: 0 (0.0%); Migrant: 0 (0.0%)
Eligible for Free Lunch Program: 4,993 (69.8%)
Eligible for Reduced-Price Lunch Program: 849 (11.9%)
Teachers: 440.0 (16.2 to 1)
Librarians/Media Specialists: 12.0 (595.8 to 1)
Guidance Counselors: 16.0 (446.8 to 1)
Current Spending: ($ per student per year):
Total: $6,309; Instruction: $3,789; Support Services: $2,153

Enrollment, Drop-out Rates and Diploma Recipients by Race/Ethnicity

Category	Total	White	Black	Asian	AIAN	Hisp.
Enrollment (%)	100.0	98.9	0.3	0.1	0.7	0.1
Drop-out Rate (%)	6.4	6.4	0.0	n/a	0.0	n/a
H.S. Diplomas (#)	407	405	1	1	0	0

Franklin County

Franklin County
916 E Main St • Frankfort, KY 40601-2521
(502) 695-6700 • http://www.franklin.k12.ky.us/
Grade Span: PK-12; **Agency Type:** 1
Schools: 12
6 Primary; 2 Middle; 3 High; 1 Other Level
10 Regular; 0 Special Education; 1 Vocational; 1 Alternative
0 Magnet; 0 Charter; 6 Title I Eligible; 0 School-wide Title I
Students: 6,025 (52.6% male; 47.4% female)
Individual Education Program: 791 (13.1%);
English Language Learner: 9 (0.1%); Migrant: 0 (0.0%)
Eligible for Free Lunch Program: 2,536 (42.1%)
Eligible for Reduced-Price Lunch Program: 663 (11.0%)
Teachers: 366.2 (16.5 to 1)
Librarians/Media Specialists: 9.5 (634.2 to 1)
Guidance Counselors: 11.5 (523.9 to 1)
Current Spending: ($ per student per year):
Total: $5,692; Instruction: $3,381; Support Services: $2,034

Enrollment, Drop-out Rates and Diploma Recipients by Race/Ethnicity

Category	Total	White	Black	Asian	AIAN	Hisp.
Enrollment (%)	100.0	89.4	8.7	0.5	0.2	1.2
Drop-out Rate (%)	5.1	5.3	3.2	0.0	0.0	0.0
H.S. Diplomas (#)	361	324	30	5	0	2

Garrard County

Garrard County
322 W Maple St • Lancaster, KY 40444-1064
(859) 792-3018 • http://www.garrard.k12.ky.us/
Grade Span: PK-12; **Agency Type:** 1
Schools: 6
3 Primary; 1 Middle; 1 High; 1 Other Level
5 Regular; 0 Special Education; 0 Vocational; 1 Alternative
0 Magnet; 0 Charter; 4 Title I Eligible; 2 School-wide Title I
Students: 2,634 (52.9% male; 47.1% female)
Individual Education Program: 393 (14.9%);
English Language Learner: 13 (0.5%); Migrant: 213 (8.1%)
Eligible for Free Lunch Program: 1,590 (60.4%)
Eligible for Reduced-Price Lunch Program: 518 (19.7%)
Teachers: 169.0 (15.6 to 1)
Librarians/Media Specialists: 5.0 (526.8 to 1)
Guidance Counselors: 5.5 (478.9 to 1)
Current Spending: ($ per student per year):
Total: $5,678; Instruction: $3,537; Support Services: $1,792

Enrollment, Drop-out Rates and Diploma Recipients by Race/Ethnicity

Category	Total	White	Black	Asian	AIAN	Hisp.
Enrollment (%)	100.0	95.7	3.0	0.0	0.1	1.2
Drop-out Rate (%)	5.9	6.1	0.0	n/a	0.0	0.0
H.S. Diplomas (#)	136	132	1	0	1	2

Grant County

Grant County
505 S Main St • Williamsto, KY 41097-0369
(859) 824-3323
Grade Span: KG-12; **Agency Type:** 1
Schools: 6
3 Primary; 1 Middle; 2 High; 0 Other Level
5 Regular; 0 Special Education; 0 Vocational; 1 Alternative
0 Magnet; 0 Charter; 4 Title I Eligible; 0 School-wide Title I
Students: 3,887 (52.0% male; 48.0% female)
Individual Education Program: 527 (13.6%);
English Language Learner: 80 (2.1%); Migrant: 108 (2.8%)
Eligible for Free Lunch Program: 2,196 (56.5%)
Eligible for Reduced-Price Lunch Program: 599 (15.4%)
Teachers: 210.7 (18.4 to 1)
Librarians/Media Specialists: 5.0 (777.4 to 1)
Guidance Counselors: 8.0 (485.9 to 1)
Current Spending: ($ per student per year):
Total: $5,157; Instruction: $3,136; Support Services: $1,690

Enrollment, Drop-out Rates and Diploma Recipients by Race/Ethnicity

Category	Total	White	Black	Asian	AIAN	Hisp.
Enrollment (%)	100.0	98.3	0.2	0.2	0.4	0.8
Drop-out Rate (%)	3.1	3.2	0.0	0.0	0.0	0.0
H.S. Diplomas (#)	169	168	0	1	0	0

Graves County

Graves County
2290 State Rt 121 N • Mayfield, KY 42066-3267
(270) 247-2656 • http://www.graves.k12.ky.us/
Grade Span: KG-12; **Agency Type:** 1
Schools: 12
7 Primary; 1 Middle; 4 High; 0 Other Level
9 Regular; 0 Special Education; 0 Vocational; 3 Alternative
0 Magnet; 0 Charter; 8 Title I Eligible; 0 School-wide Title I
Students: 4,704 (51.9% male; 48.1% female)
Individual Education Program: 652 (13.9%);
English Language Learner: 0 (0.0%); Migrant: 328 (7.0%)
Eligible for Free Lunch Program: 2,403 (51.1%)
Eligible for Reduced-Price Lunch Program: 649 (13.8%)
Teachers: 269.3 (17.5 to 1)
Librarians/Media Specialists: 6.0 (784.0 to 1)
Guidance Counselors: 8.8 (534.5 to 1)
Current Spending: ($ per student per year):
Total: $5,276; Instruction: $3,327; Support Services: $1,578

Enrollment, Drop-out Rates and Diploma Recipients by Race/Ethnicity

Category	Total	White	Black	Asian	AIAN	Hisp.
Enrollment (%)	100.0	95.7	1.8	0.3	1.8	0.4
Drop-out Rate (%)	4.0	4.0	0.0	n/a	n/a	0.0
H.S. Diplomas (#)	271	267	3	1	0	0

Mayfield Independent
709 S Eighth St • Mayfiel, KY 42066-3037
(270) 247-3868
Grade Span: PK-12; **Agency Type:** 1
Schools: 5
2 Primary; 2 Middle; 1 High; 0 Other Level
5 Regular; 0 Special Education; 0 Vocational; 0 Alternative
0 Magnet; 0 Charter; 5 Title I Eligible; 3 School-wide Title I
Students: 1,556 (53.1% male; 46.9% female)
Individual Education Program: 238 (15.3%);
English Language Learner: 66 (4.2%); Migrant: 194 (12.5%)
Eligible for Free Lunch Program: 1,145 (73.6%)
Eligible for Reduced-Price Lunch Program: 146 (9.4%)
Teachers: 102.5 (15.2 to 1)
Librarians/Media Specialists: 4.0 (389.0 to 1)
Guidance Counselors: 3.5 (444.6 to 1)
Current Spending: ($ per student per year):
Total: $6,773; Instruction: $4,105; Support Services: $2,209

Enrollment, Drop-out Rates and Diploma Recipients by Race/Ethnicity

Category	Total	White	Black	Asian	AIAN	Hisp.
Enrollment (%)	100.0	62.4	24.3	0.8	0.1	12.3
Drop-out Rate (%)	4.7	4.6	4.0	0.0	n/a	10.5
H.S. Diplomas (#)	83	64	17	0	0	2

Grayson County

Grayson County
909 Brandenburg Rd • Leitchfield, KY 42754-4009
(270) 259-4011 • http://www.grayson.k12.ky.us/
Grade Span: PK-12; **Agency Type:** 1
Schools: 7
4 Primary; 1 Middle; 1 High; 1 Other Level
6 Regular; 0 Special Education; 0 Vocational; 1 Alternative
0 Magnet; 0 Charter; 5 Title I Eligible; 5 School-wide Title I
Students: 4,317 (52.3% male; 47.7% female)
Individual Education Program: 611 (14.2%);
English Language Learner: 1 (<0.1%); Migrant: 126 (2.9%)
Eligible for Free Lunch Program: 2,258 (52.3%)
Eligible for Reduced-Price Lunch Program: 743 (17.2%)
Teachers: 272.5 (15.8 to 1)
Librarians/Media Specialists: 6.0 (719.5 to 1)
Guidance Counselors: 11.2 (385.4 to 1)
Current Spending: ($ per student per year):
Total: $5,491; Instruction: $3,547; Support Services: $1,616
Enrollment, Drop-out Rates and Diploma Recipients by Race/Ethnicity

Category	Total	White	Black	Asian	AIAN	Hisp.
Enrollment (%)	100.0	99.1	0.4	0.0	0.0	0.4
Drop-out Rate (%)	3.4	3.4	0.0	0.0	n/a	0.0
H.S. Diplomas (#)	252	252	0	0	0	0

Green County

Green County
206 W Court St • Greensburg, KY 42743-0369
(270) 932-5231 • http://www.green.k12.ky.us/
Grade Span: KG-12; **Agency Type:** 1
Schools: 5
3 Primary; 1 Middle; 1 High; 0 Other Level
5 Regular; 0 Special Education; 0 Vocational; 0 Alternative
0 Magnet; 0 Charter; 5 Title I Eligible; 4 School-wide Title I
Students: 1,702 (52.1% male; 47.9% female)
Individual Education Program: 256 (15.0%);
English Language Learner: 0 (0.0%); Migrant: 75 (4.4%)
Eligible for Free Lunch Program: 967 (56.8%)
Eligible for Reduced-Price Lunch Program: 258 (15.2%)
Teachers: 114.5 (14.9 to 1)
Librarians/Media Specialists: 4.0 (425.5 to 1)
Guidance Counselors: 3.0 (567.3 to 1)
Current Spending: ($ per student per year):
Total: $5,994; Instruction: $3,611; Support Services: $2,036
Enrollment, Drop-out Rates and Diploma Recipients by Race/Ethnicity

Category	Total	White	Black	Asian	AIAN	Hisp.
Enrollment (%)	100.0	96.1	2.8	0.2	0.1	0.7
Drop-out Rate (%)	2.7	2.8	0.0	0.0	0.0	0.0
H.S. Diplomas (#)	119	115	3	0	0	1

Greenup County
8000 US 23 N • Greenup, KY 41144-9618
(606) 473-9819 • http://www.greenup.k12.ky.us/
Grade Span: PK-12; **Agency Type:** 1
Schools: 8
4 Primary; 3 Middle; 1 High; 0 Other Level
8 Regular; 0 Special Education; 0 Vocational; 0 Alternative
0 Magnet; 0 Charter; 8 Title I Eligible; 7 School-wide Title I
Students: 3,236 (51.3% male; 48.7% female)
Individual Education Program: 555 (17.2%);
English Language Learner: 0 (0.0%); Migrant: 102 (3.2%)
Eligible for Free Lunch Program: 2,113 (65.3%)
Eligible for Reduced-Price Lunch Program: 473 (14.6%)
Teachers: 197.5 (16.4 to 1)
Librarians/Media Specialists: 8.0 (404.5 to 1)
Guidance Counselors: 9.0 (359.6 to 1)
Current Spending: ($ per student per year):
Total: $6,093; Instruction: $3,582; Support Services: $2,085
Enrollment, Drop-out Rates and Diploma Recipients by Race/Ethnicity

Category	Total	White	Black	Asian	AIAN	Hisp.
Enrollment (%)	100.0	98.1	1.0	0.1	0.6	0.1
Drop-out Rate (%)	5.5	5.6	0.0	0.0	0.0	0.0
H.S. Diplomas (#)	182	180	1	1	0	0

Russell Independent
409 Belfont St • Russell, KY 41169-1320
(606) 836-9679 • http://www.russell.k12.ky.us/
Grade Span: PK-12; **Agency Type:** 1
Schools: 4
1 Primary; 2 Middle; 1 High; 0 Other Level
4 Regular; 0 Special Education; 0 Vocational; 0 Alternative
0 Magnet; 0 Charter; 4 Title I Eligible; 0 School-wide Title I
Students: 2,152 (51.7% male; 48.3% female)
Individual Education Program: 239 (11.1%);
English Language Learner: 0 (0.0%); Migrant: 21 (1.0%)
Eligible for Free Lunch Program: 725 (33.7%)
Eligible for Reduced-Price Lunch Program: 158 (7.3%)
Teachers: 117.8 (18.3 to 1)
Librarians/Media Specialists: 4.0 (538.0 to 1)
Guidance Counselors: 6.0 (358.7 to 1)
Current Spending: ($ per student per year):
Total: $5,519; Instruction: $3,353; Support Services: $1,930
Enrollment, Drop-out Rates and Diploma Recipients by Race/Ethnicity

Category	Total	White	Black	Asian	AIAN	Hisp.
Enrollment (%)	100.0	97.9	1.0	0.9	0.0	0.2
Drop-out Rate (%)	0.9	0.9	0.0	0.0	0.0	0.0
H.S. Diplomas (#)	152	151	0	1	0	0

Hancock County

Hancock County
83 State Rt 271 N • Hawesville, KY 42348-6809
(270) 927-6914 • http://www.hancock.k12.ky.us/hcboe/
Grade Span: KG-12; **Agency Type:** 1
Schools: 5
3 Primary; 1 Middle; 1 High; 0 Other Level
5 Regular; 0 Special Education; 0 Vocational; 0 Alternative
0 Magnet; 0 Charter; 3 Title I Eligible; 1 School-wide Title I
Students: 1,605 (51.3% male; 48.7% female)
Individual Education Program: 225 (14.0%);
English Language Learner: 4 (0.2%); Migrant: 0 (0.0%)
Eligible for Free Lunch Program: 620 (38.6%)
Eligible for Reduced-Price Lunch Program: 239 (14.9%)
Teachers: 95.4 (16.8 to 1)
Librarians/Media Specialists: 3.0 (535.0 to 1)
Guidance Counselors: 3.0 (535.0 to 1)
Current Spending: ($ per student per year):
Total: $6,361; Instruction: $3,738; Support Services: $2,276
Enrollment, Drop-out Rates and Diploma Recipients by Race/Ethnicity

Category	Total	White	Black	Asian	AIAN	Hisp.
Enrollment (%)	100.0	98.4	0.8	0.1	0.1	0.7
Drop-out Rate (%)	0.5	0.5	0.0	n/a	n/a	n/a
H.S. Diplomas (#)	109	107	1	1	0	0

Hardin County

Elizabethtown Independent
219 Helm St • Elizabethtow, KY 42701-0605
(270) 765-6146 • http://www.etown.k12.ky.us/
Grade Span: KG-12; **Agency Type:** 1
Schools: 4
2 Primary; 1 Middle; 1 High; 0 Other Level
4 Regular; 0 Special Education; 0 Vocational; 0 Alternative
0 Magnet; 0 Charter; 3 Title I Eligible; 2 School-wide Title I
Students: 2,345 (50.7% male; 49.3% female)
Individual Education Program: 258 (11.0%);
English Language Learner: 13 (0.6%); Migrant: 5 (0.2%)
Eligible for Free Lunch Program: 1,085 (46.3%)
Eligible for Reduced-Price Lunch Program: 293 (12.5%)
Teachers: 137.6 (17.0 to 1)
Librarians/Media Specialists: 4.0 (586.3 to 1)
Guidance Counselors: 4.5 (521.1 to 1)
Current Spending: ($ per student per year):
Total: $5,586; Instruction: $3,607; Support Services: $1,721
Enrollment, Drop-out Rates and Diploma Recipients by Race/Ethnicity

Category	Total	White	Black	Asian	AIAN	Hisp.
Enrollment (%)	100.0	81.0	13.3	3.3	0.8	1.6
Drop-out Rate (%)	2.3	2.7	1.2	0.0	0.0	0.0
H.S. Diplomas (#)	146	120	19	3	0	4

Fort Knox District
Sch Bldg 4553, Dixie Hwy • Fort Knox, KY 40121-2707
(502) 624-3606
Grade Span: PK-12; **Agency Type:** 6
Schools: 8
4 Primary; 3 Middle; 1 High; 0 Other Level
8 Regular; 0 Special Education; 0 Vocational; 0 Alternative
0 Magnet; 0 Charter; 0 Title I Eligible; 0 School-wide Title I
Students: 2,988 (n/a% male; n/a% female)
Individual Education Program: 301 (10.1%);
English Language Learner: 20 (0.7%); Migrant: n/a
Eligible for Free Lunch Program: n/a
Eligible for Reduced-Price Lunch Program: n/a
Teachers: 228.5 (13.1 to 1)
Librarians/Media Specialists: 8.0 (373.5 to 1)
Guidance Counselors: 11.0 (271.6 to 1)
Current Spending: ($ per student per year):
Total: n/a; Instruction: n/a; Support Services: n/a

Enrollment, Drop-out Rates and Diploma Recipients by Race/Ethnicity

Category	Total	White	Black	Asian	AIAN	Hisp.
Enrollment (%)	100.0	56.6	26.3	2.2	1.0	11.1
Drop-out Rate (%)	n/a	n/a	n/a	n/a	n/a	n/a
H.S. Diplomas (#)	110	47	41	1	0	14

Hardin County

65 W A Jenkins Rd • Elizabe, KY 42701-1419
(270) 769-8800 • http://www.hardin.k12.ky.us/
Grade Span: PK-12; **Agency Type:** 1
Schools: 25
12 Primary; 5 Middle; 3 High; 4 Other Level
20 Regular; 0 Special Education; 0 Vocational; 4 Alternative
0 Magnet; 0 Charter; 19 Title I Eligible; 13 School-wide Title I
Students: 13,391 (52.5% male; 47.5% female)
Individual Education Program: 2,013 (15.0%);
English Language Learner: 103 (0.8%); Migrant: 72 (0.5%)
Eligible for Free Lunch Program: 6,144 (45.9%)
Eligible for Reduced-Price Lunch Program: 2,529 (18.9%)
Teachers: 810.9 (16.5 to 1)
Librarians/Media Specialists: 24.0 (558.0 to 1)
Guidance Counselors: 32.0 (418.5 to 1)
Current Spending: ($ per student per year):
Total: $5,796; Instruction: $3,542; Support Services: $1,880

Enrollment, Drop-out Rates and Diploma Recipients by Race/Ethnicity

Category	Total	White	Black	Asian	AIAN	Hisp.
Enrollment (%)	100.0	80.0	14.4	2.3	0.6	2.7
Drop-out Rate (%)	4.0	4.1	4.0	1.9	0.0	4.3
H.S. Diplomas (#)	817	632	130	29	3	23

Harlan County

Harlan County

251 Ball Park Rd • Harlan, KY 40831-1756
(606) 573-4330 • http://www.harlan.k12.ky.us/
Grade Span: PK-12; **Agency Type:** 1
Schools: 11
8 Primary; 0 Middle; 3 High; 0 Other Level
11 Regular; 0 Special Education; 0 Vocational; 0 Alternative
0 Magnet; 0 Charter; 11 Title I Eligible; 11 School-wide Title I
Students: 5,284 (52.0% male; 48.0% female)
Individual Education Program: 842 (15.9%);
English Language Learner: 0 (0.0%); Migrant: 0 (0.0%)
Eligible for Free Lunch Program: 3,831 (72.5%)
Eligible for Reduced-Price Lunch Program: 979 (18.5%)
Teachers: 342.0 (15.5 to 1)
Librarians/Media Specialists: 12.0 (440.3 to 1)
Guidance Counselors: 12.0 (440.3 to 1)
Current Spending: ($ per student per year):
Total: $6,251; Instruction: $3,782; Support Services: $2,034

Enrollment, Drop-out Rates and Diploma Recipients by Race/Ethnicity

Category	Total	White	Black	Asian	AIAN	Hisp.
Enrollment (%)	100.0	97.4	2.4	0.0	0.1	0.1
Drop-out Rate (%)	6.9	7.2	0.0	0.0	n/a	0.0
H.S. Diplomas (#)	265	258	6	0	0	1

Harrison County

Harrison County

308 Webster Ave • Cynthiana, KY 41031-8803
Mailing Address: 324 Webster Ave • Cynthiana, KY 41031-8834
(859) 234-7110 • http://www.harrison.k12.ky.us/
Grade Span: KG-12; **Agency Type:** 1
Schools: 8
4 Primary; 1 Middle; 2 High; 1 Other Level
6 Regular; 0 Special Education; 0 Vocational; 2 Alternative
0 Magnet; 0 Charter; 6 Title I Eligible; 2 School-wide Title I
Students: 3,316 (52.5% male; 47.5% female)
Individual Education Program: 518 (15.6%);
English Language Learner: 2 (0.1%); Migrant: 125 (3.8%)
Eligible for Free Lunch Program: 1,691 (51.0%)
Eligible for Reduced-Price Lunch Program: 408 (12.3%)
Teachers: 191.2 (17.3 to 1)
Librarians/Media Specialists: 7.0 (473.7 to 1)
Guidance Counselors: 6.0 (552.7 to 1)
Current Spending: ($ per student per year):
Total: $5,929; Instruction: $3,737; Support Services: $1,801

Enrollment, Drop-out Rates and Diploma Recipients by Race/Ethnicity

Category	Total	White	Black	Asian	AIAN	Hisp.
Enrollment (%)	100.0	94.7	3.6	0.2	0.4	1.0
Drop-out Rate (%)	4.3	4.6	0.0	0.0	0.0	0.0
H.S. Diplomas (#)	192	187	4	0	0	1

Hart County

Hart County

511 W Union St • Munfordville, KY 42765-0068
(270) 524-2631 • http://www.hart.k12.ky.us/
Grade Span: PK-12; **Agency Type:** 1
Schools: 6
5 Primary; 0 Middle; 1 High; 0 Other Level
6 Regular; 0 Special Education; 0 Vocational; 0 Alternative
0 Magnet; 0 Charter; 5 Title I Eligible; 4 School-wide Title I
Students: 2,507 (53.4% male; 46.6% female)
Individual Education Program: 459 (18.3%);
English Language Learner: 10 (0.4%); Migrant: 119 (4.7%)
Eligible for Free Lunch Program: 1,642 (65.5%)
Eligible for Reduced-Price Lunch Program: 437 (17.4%)
Teachers: 155.8 (16.1 to 1)
Librarians/Media Specialists: 5.0 (501.4 to 1)
Guidance Counselors: 7.0 (358.1 to 1)
Current Spending: ($ per student per year):
Total: $6,334; Instruction: $3,728; Support Services: $2,232

Enrollment, Drop-out Rates and Diploma Recipients by Race/Ethnicity

Category	Total	White	Black	Asian	AIAN	Hisp.
Enrollment (%)	100.0	95.0	4.3	0.0	0.1	0.6
Drop-out Rate (%)	4.3	4.5	0.0	n/a	n/a	0.0
H.S. Diplomas (#)	133	122	10	0	0	1

Henderson County

Henderson County

1805 Second St • Henderson, KY 42420-3367
(270) 831-5000 • http://www.henderson.k12.ky.us/
Grade Span: PK-12; **Agency Type:** 1
Schools: 13
8 Primary; 2 Middle; 2 High; 1 Other Level
11 Regular; 0 Special Education; 1 Vocational; 1 Alternative
0 Magnet; 0 Charter; 9 Title I Eligible; 4 School-wide Title I
Students: 7,122 (51.7% male; 48.3% female)
Individual Education Program: 1,161 (16.3%);
English Language Learner: 34 (0.5%); Migrant: 152 (2.1%)
Eligible for Free Lunch Program: 3,247 (45.6%)
Eligible for Reduced-Price Lunch Program: 678 (9.5%)
Teachers: 435.4 (16.4 to 1)
Librarians/Media Specialists: 12.0 (593.5 to 1)
Guidance Counselors: 22.9 (311.0 to 1)
Current Spending: ($ per student per year):
Total: $5,942; Instruction: $3,568; Support Services: $2,028

Enrollment, Drop-out Rates and Diploma Recipients by Race/Ethnicity

Category	Total	White	Black	Asian	AIAN	Hisp.
Enrollment (%)	100.0	89.2	9.9	0.1	0.7	0.1
Drop-out Rate (%)	6.0	5.9	7.8	0.0	0.0	0.0
H.S. Diplomas (#)	455	411	42	2	0	0

Henry County

Henry County

326 S Main St • New Castle, KY 40050-0299
(502) 845-8600 • http://www.henry.k12.ky.us/
Grade Span: PK-12; **Agency Type:** 1
Schools: 5
3 Primary; 1 Middle; 1 High; 0 Other Level
5 Regular; 0 Special Education; 0 Vocational; 0 Alternative
0 Magnet; 0 Charter; 4 Title I Eligible; 3 School-wide Title I
Students: 2,213 (52.7% male; 47.3% female)
Individual Education Program: 254 (11.5%);
English Language Learner: 0 (0.0%); Migrant: 53 (2.4%)
Eligible for Free Lunch Program: 1,081 (48.8%)
Eligible for Reduced-Price Lunch Program: 367 (16.6%)
Teachers: 128.5 (17.2 to 1)
Librarians/Media Specialists: 3.5 (632.3 to 1)
Guidance Counselors: 4.5 (491.8 to 1)
Current Spending: ($ per student per year):
Total: $5,889; Instruction: $3,408; Support Services: $2,027

Enrollment, Drop-out Rates and Diploma Recipients by Race/Ethnicity

Category	Total	White	Black	Asian	AIAN	Hisp.
Enrollment (%)	100.0	96.8	1.4	0.2	0.1	1.5
Drop-out Rate (%)	6.4	6.6	0.0	0.0	0.0	0.0
H.S. Diplomas (#)	107	103	3	0	0	1

Hopkins County

Hopkins County

320 S Seminary St • Madisonvi, KY 42431-0509
(270) 825-6000 • http://www.hopkins.k12.ky.us/
Grade Span: PK-12; **Agency Type:** 1
Schools: 14

8 Primary; 3 Middle; 2 High; 1 Other Level
13 Regular; 0 Special Education; 0 Vocational; 1 Alternative
0 Magnet; 0 Charter; 10 Title I Eligible; 8 School-wide Title I
Students: 7,455 (50.9% male; 49.1% female)
Individual Education Program: 1,366 (18.3%);
English Language Learner: 13 (0.2%); Migrant: 304 (4.1%)
Eligible for Free Lunch Program: 4,082 (54.8%)
Eligible for Reduced-Price Lunch Program: 995 (13.3%)
Teachers: 454.9 (16.4 to 1)
Librarians/Media Specialists: 15.0 (497.0 to 1)
Guidance Counselors: 19.0 (392.4 to 1)
Current Spending: ($ per student per year):
Total: $6,000; Instruction: $3,664; Support Services: $2,007
Enrollment, Drop-out Rates and Diploma Recipients by Race/Ethnicity

Category	Total	White	Black	Asian	AIAN	Hisp.
Enrollment (%)	100.0	88.0	10.7	0.7	0.0	0.6
Drop-out Rate (%)	3.1	3.0	4.6	0.0	n/a	0.0
H.S. Diplomas (#)	375	338	34	2	0	1

Jackson County

Jackson County
Hwy 421 • Mckee, KY 40447-0217
(606) 287-7181
Grade Span: PK-12; **Agency Type:** 1
Schools: 6
3 Primary; 1 Middle; 1 High; 1 Other Level
5 Regular; 0 Special Education; 0 Vocational; 1 Alternative
0 Magnet; 0 Charter; 5 Title I Eligible; 4 School-wide Title I
Students: 2,435 (52.5% male; 47.5% female)
Individual Education Program: 422 (17.3%);
English Language Learner: 0 (0.0%); Migrant: 25 (1.0%)
Eligible for Free Lunch Program: 1,775 (72.9%)
Eligible for Reduced-Price Lunch Program: 485 (19.9%)
Teachers: 164.8 (14.8 to 1)
Librarians/Media Specialists: 7.0 (347.9 to 1)
Guidance Counselors: 6.0 (405.8 to 1)
Current Spending: ($ per student per year):
Total: $6,986; Instruction: $4,003; Support Services: $2,506
Enrollment, Drop-out Rates and Diploma Recipients by Race/Ethnicity

Category	Total	White	Black	Asian	AIAN	Hisp.
Enrollment (%)	100.0	99.1	0.2	0.0	0.6	0.1
Drop-out Rate (%)	4.7	4.7	0.0	0.0	n/a	0.0
H.S. Diplomas (#)	122	122	0	0	0	0

Jefferson County

Jefferson County
3332 Newburg Rd • Louisville, KY 40232-4020
(502) 485-3011 • http://www.jefferson.k12.ky.us/
Grade Span: PK-12; **Agency Type:** 1
Schools: 175
99 Primary; 25 Middle; 39 High; 12 Other Level
139 Regular; 7 Special Education; 1 Vocational; 28 Alternative
14 Magnet; 0 Charter; 99 Title I Eligible; 80 School-wide Title I
Students: 95,651 (51.4% male; 48.6% female)
Individual Education Program: 13,326 (13.9%);
English Language Learner: 2,452 (2.6%); Migrant: 151 (0.2%)
Eligible for Free Lunch Program: 52,869 (55.3%)
Eligible for Reduced-Price Lunch Program: 11,315 (11.8%)
Teachers: 5,328.8 (17.9 to 1)
Librarians/Media Specialists: 150.3 (636.4 to 1)
Guidance Counselors: 240.1 (398.4 to 1)
Current Spending: ($ per student per year):
Total: $7,067; Instruction: $4,066; Support Services: $2,823
Enrollment, Drop-out Rates and Diploma Recipients by Race/Ethnicity

Category	Total	White	Black	Asian	AIAN	Hisp.
Enrollment (%)	100.0	60.9	34.9	1.8	0.1	2.4
Drop-out Rate (%)	6.7	6.1	8.3	4.3	0.0	10.1
H.S. Diplomas (#)	4,932	3,347	1,400	126	0	59

Jessamine County

Jessamine County
501 E Maple • Nicholasville, KY 40356-1642
(859) 885-4179 • http://www.jessamine.k12.ky.us/
Grade Span: PK-12; **Agency Type:** 1
Schools: 11
6 Primary; 2 Middle; 2 High; 1 Other Level
10 Regular; 0 Special Education; 0 Vocational; 1 Alternative
0 Magnet; 0 Charter; 8 Title I Eligible; 8 School-wide Title I
Students: 7,056 (52.7% male; 47.3% female)
Individual Education Program: 1,124 (15.9%);
English Language Learner: 71 (1.0%); Migrant: 129 (1.8%)
Eligible for Free Lunch Program: 3,625 (51.4%)
Eligible for Reduced-Price Lunch Program: 889 (12.6%)
Teachers: 446.7 (15.8 to 1)
Librarians/Media Specialists: 8.5 (830.1 to 1)
Guidance Counselors: 14.0 (504.0 to 1)
Current Spending: ($ per student per year):
Total: $5,759; Instruction: $3,565; Support Services: $1,936
Enrollment, Drop-out Rates and Diploma Recipients by Race/Ethnicity

Category	Total	White	Black	Asian	AIAN	Hisp.
Enrollment (%)	100.0	94.9	3.6	0.5	0.2	0.9
Drop-out Rate (%)	5.6	5.9	1.4	0.0	0.0	0.0
H.S. Diplomas (#)	322	294	22	3	1	2

Johnson County

Johnson County
253 N Mayo Tr • Paintsville, KY 41240-1803
(606) 789-2530 • http://www.johnson.k12.ky.us/
Grade Span: PK-12; **Agency Type:** 1
Schools: 9
6 Primary; 1 Middle; 2 High; 0 Other Level
8 Regular; 0 Special Education; 0 Vocational; 1 Alternative
0 Magnet; 0 Charter; 8 Title I Eligible; 8 School-wide Title I
Students: 3,786 (51.8% male; 48.2% female)
Individual Education Program: 550 (14.5%);
English Language Learner: 0 (0.0%); Migrant: 0 (0.0%)
Eligible for Free Lunch Program: 2,576 (68.0%)
Eligible for Reduced-Price Lunch Program: 560 (14.8%)
Teachers: 242.1 (15.6 to 1)
Librarians/Media Specialists: 5.0 (757.2 to 1)
Guidance Counselors: 7.0 (540.9 to 1)
Current Spending: ($ per student per year):
Total: $6,237; Instruction: $4,133; Support Services: $1,716
Enrollment, Drop-out Rates and Diploma Recipients by Race/Ethnicity

Category	Total	White	Black	Asian	AIAN	Hisp.
Enrollment (%)	100.0	99.7	0.1	0.1	0.0	0.1
Drop-out Rate (%)	3.7	3.7	0.0	n/a	n/a	n/a
H.S. Diplomas (#)	213	213	0	0	0	0

Kenton County

Covington Independent
25 E 7th St • Covington, KY 41011-2401
(859) 392-1000 • http://www.covington.k12.ky.us/
Grade Span: PK-12; **Agency Type:** 1
Schools: 13
7 Primary; 2 Middle; 3 High; 1 Other Level
11 Regular; 0 Special Education; 0 Vocational; 2 Alternative
0 Magnet; 0 Charter; 9 Title I Eligible; 7 School-wide Title I
Students: 4,733 (53.6% male; 46.4% female)
Individual Education Program: 814 (17.2%);
English Language Learner: 0 (0.0%); Migrant: 0 (0.0%)
Eligible for Free Lunch Program: 3,024 (63.9%)
Eligible for Reduced-Price Lunch Program: 548 (11.6%)
Teachers: 344.2 (13.8 to 1)
Librarians/Media Specialists: 9.0 (525.9 to 1)
Guidance Counselors: 8.3 (570.2 to 1)
Current Spending: ($ per student per year):
Total: $8,070; Instruction: $4,760; Support Services: $2,914
Enrollment, Drop-out Rates and Diploma Recipients by Race/Ethnicity

Category	Total	White	Black	Asian	AIAN	Hisp.
Enrollment (%)	100.0	73.7	25.5	0.1	0.7	0.0
Drop-out Rate (%)	2.0	2.0	2.2	0.0	0.0	0.0
H.S. Diplomas (#)	200	153	45	2	0	0

Erlanger-Elsmere Independent
500 Graves Ave • Erlanger, KY 41018-1620
(859) 727-2009 • http://www.erlanger.k12.ky.us/
Grade Span: PK-12; **Agency Type:** 1
Schools: 6
4 Primary; 1 Middle; 1 High; 0 Other Level
6 Regular; 0 Special Education; 0 Vocational; 0 Alternative
0 Magnet; 0 Charter; 3 Title I Eligible; 1 School-wide Title I
Students: 2,239 (53.5% male; 46.5% female)
Individual Education Program: 370 (16.5%);
English Language Learner: 15 (0.7%); Migrant: 0 (0.0%)
Eligible for Free Lunch Program: 894 (39.9%)
Eligible for Reduced-Price Lunch Program: 281 (12.6%)
Teachers: 133.0 (16.8 to 1)
Librarians/Media Specialists: 4.0 (559.8 to 1)
Guidance Counselors: 5.5 (407.1 to 1)
Current Spending: ($ per student per year):
Total: $6,025; Instruction: $3,750; Support Services: $1,983

Enrollment, Drop-out Rates and Diploma Recipients by Race/Ethnicity

Category	Total	White	Black	Asian	AIAN	Hisp.
Enrollment (%)	100.0	86.8	9.5	0.6	0.2	2.9
Drop-out Rate (%)	2.7	3.0	0.0	0.0	n/a	0.0
H.S. Diplomas (#)	123	113	8	0	0	2

Kenton County

20 Kenton Lands Rd • Erlanger, KY 41018-1878
(859) 344-8888 • http://www.kenton.k12.ky.us/
Grade Span: PK-12; **Agency Type:** 1
Schools: 22
12 Primary; 4 Middle; 5 High; 1 Other Level
19 Regular; 1 Special Education; 0 Vocational; 2 Alternative
0 Magnet; 0 Charter; 10 Title I Eligible; 3 School-wide Title I
Students: 12,668 (53.3% male; 46.7% female)
Individual Education Program: 1,624 (12.8%);
English Language Learner: 95 (0.7%); Migrant: 0 (0.0%)
Eligible for Free Lunch Program: 3,237 (25.6%)
Eligible for Reduced-Price Lunch Program: 1,287 (10.2%)
Teachers: 705.9 (17.9 to 1)
Librarians/Media Specialists: 19.0 (666.7 to 1)
Guidance Counselors: 27.1 (467.5 to 1)
Current Spending: ($ per student per year):
Total: $5,617; Instruction: $3,398; Support Services: $1,965
Enrollment, Drop-out Rates and Diploma Recipients by Race/Ethnicity

Category	Total	White	Black	Asian	AIAN	Hisp.
Enrollment (%)	100.0	97.3	1.2	0.7	0.1	0.8
Drop-out Rate (%)	1.8	1.8	2.7	0.0	0.0	0.0
H.S. Diplomas (#)	758	741	5	3	0	9

Knott County

Knott County

Route 160 • Hindman, KY 41822-0869
(606) 785-3153 • http://www.knott.k12.ky.us/
Grade Span: PK-12; **Agency Type:** 1
Schools: 11
8 Primary; 0 Middle; 3 High; 0 Other Level
10 Regular; 0 Special Education; 0 Vocational; 1 Alternative
0 Magnet; 0 Charter; 10 Title I Eligible; 10 School-wide Title I
Students: 2,928 (52.5% male; 47.5% female)
Individual Education Program: 563 (19.2%);
English Language Learner: 0 (0.0%); Migrant: 0 (0.0%)
Eligible for Free Lunch Program: 2,305 (78.7%)
Eligible for Reduced-Price Lunch Program: 436 (14.9%)
Teachers: 192.3 (15.2 to 1)
Librarians/Media Specialists: 7.2 (406.7 to 1)
Guidance Counselors: 5.0 (585.6 to 1)
Current Spending: ($ per student per year):
Total: $6,522; Instruction: $4,135; Support Services: $1,995
Enrollment, Drop-out Rates and Diploma Recipients by Race/Ethnicity

Category	Total	White	Black	Asian	AIAN	Hisp.
Enrollment (%)	100.0	99.1	0.9	0.0	0.1	0.0
Drop-out Rate (%)	4.8	4.9	0.0	n/a	n/a	n/a
H.S. Diplomas (#)	178	173	5	0	0	0

Knox County

Knox County

200 Daniel Boone Dr • Barbourvill, KY 40906-1104
(606) 546-3157 • http://www.knox.k12.ky.us/
Grade Span: PK-12; **Agency Type:** 1
Schools: 11
8 Primary; 0 Middle; 2 High; 1 Other Level
10 Regular; 0 Special Education; 0 Vocational; 1 Alternative
0 Magnet; 0 Charter; 10 Title I Eligible; 8 School-wide Title I
Students: 5,198 (52.4% male; 47.6% female)
Individual Education Program: 809 (15.6%);
English Language Learner: 6 (0.1%); Migrant: 0 (0.0%)
Eligible for Free Lunch Program: 4,034 (77.6%)
Eligible for Reduced-Price Lunch Program: 681 (13.1%)
Teachers: 310.5 (16.7 to 1)
Librarians/Media Specialists: 10.0 (519.8 to 1)
Guidance Counselors: 8.0 (649.8 to 1)
Current Spending: ($ per student per year):
Total: $6,124; Instruction: $3,782; Support Services: $1,934
Enrollment, Drop-out Rates and Diploma Recipients by Race/Ethnicity

Category	Total	White	Black	Asian	AIAN	Hisp.
Enrollment (%)	100.0	99.3	0.5	0.0	0.1	0.0
Drop-out Rate (%)	8.0	8.1	0.0	n/a	n/a	n/a
H.S. Diplomas (#)	224	222	2	0	0	0

Larue County

Larue County

2375 Lincoln Farm Rd • Hodgenville, KY 42748-0039
(270) 358-4111 • http://www.larue.k12.ky.us/
Grade Span: KG-12; **Agency Type:** 1
Schools: 6
3 Primary; 2 Middle; 1 High; 0 Other Level
6 Regular; 0 Special Education; 0 Vocational; 0 Alternative
0 Magnet; 0 Charter; 5 Title I Eligible; 4 School-wide Title I
Students: 2,411 (52.5% male; 47.5% female)
Individual Education Program: 425 (17.6%);
English Language Learner: 0 (0.0%); Migrant: 58 (2.4%)
Eligible for Free Lunch Program: 1,416 (58.7%)
Eligible for Reduced-Price Lunch Program: 419 (17.4%)
Teachers: 148.0 (16.3 to 1)
Librarians/Media Specialists: 5.0 (482.2 to 1)
Guidance Counselors: 8.0 (301.4 to 1)
Current Spending: ($ per student per year):
Total: $6,142; Instruction: $3,769; Support Services: $1,984
Enrollment, Drop-out Rates and Diploma Recipients by Race/Ethnicity

Category	Total	White	Black	Asian	AIAN	Hisp.
Enrollment (%)	100.0	94.5	4.2	0.1	0.6	0.6
Drop-out Rate (%)	3.3	3.5	0.0	0.0	0.0	0.0
H.S. Diplomas (#)	168	164	4	0	0	0

Laurel County

Laurel County

275 S Laurel Rd • London, KY 40744-7914
(606) 862-4600 • http://www.laurel.k12.ky.us/
Grade Span: PK-12; **Agency Type:** 1
Schools: 18
11 Primary; 2 Middle; 3 High; 2 Other Level
15 Regular; 0 Special Education; 0 Vocational; 3 Alternative
0 Magnet; 0 Charter; 13 Title I Eligible; 12 School-wide Title I
Students: 8,884 (52.0% male; 48.0% female)
Individual Education Program: 1,406 (15.8%);
English Language Learner: 0 (0.0%); Migrant: 0 (0.0%)
Eligible for Free Lunch Program: 5,690 (64.0%)
Eligible for Reduced-Price Lunch Program: 1,127 (12.7%)
Teachers: 494.5 (18.0 to 1)
Librarians/Media Specialists: 17.0 (522.6 to 1)
Guidance Counselors: 16.2 (548.4 to 1)
Current Spending: ($ per student per year):
Total: $5,875; Instruction: $3,573; Support Services: $1,963
Enrollment, Drop-out Rates and Diploma Recipients by Race/Ethnicity

Category	Total	White	Black	Asian	AIAN	Hisp.
Enrollment (%)	100.0	98.1	1.0	0.5	0.1	0.2
Drop-out Rate (%)	5.9	6.1	0.0	0.0	0.0	0.0
H.S. Diplomas (#)	458	454	2	0	1	1

Lawrence County

Lawrence County

Hwy 644 • Louisa, KY 41230-0607
(606) 638-9671 • http://www.lawrence.k12.ky.us/
Grade Span: PK-12; **Agency Type:** 1
Schools: 5
3 Primary; 1 Middle; 1 High; 0 Other Level
5 Regular; 0 Special Education; 0 Vocational; 0 Alternative
0 Magnet; 0 Charter; 5 Title I Eligible; 4 School-wide Title I
Students: 2,744 (53.2% male; 46.8% female)
Individual Education Program: 428 (15.6%);
English Language Learner: 0 (0.0%); Migrant: 146 (5.3%)
Eligible for Free Lunch Program: 2,057 (75.0%)
Eligible for Reduced-Price Lunch Program: 365 (13.3%)
Teachers: 183.6 (14.9 to 1)
Librarians/Media Specialists: 4.0 (686.0 to 1)
Guidance Counselors: 5.5 (498.9 to 1)
Current Spending: ($ per student per year):
Total: $6,067; Instruction: $3,895; Support Services: $1,822
Enrollment, Drop-out Rates and Diploma Recipients by Race/Ethnicity

Category	Total	White	Black	Asian	AIAN	Hisp.
Enrollment (%)	100.0	99.7	0.2	0.0	0.0	0.1
Drop-out Rate (%)	6.3	6.3	0.0	n/a	n/a	n/a
H.S. Diplomas (#)	168	166	1	1	0	0

Leslie County

Leslie County

108 Maple St • Hyden, KY 41749-0949
(606) 672-2397 • http://leslie.k12.ky.us/
Grade Span: PK-12; **Agency Type:** 1
Schools: 8

6 Primary; 1 Middle; 1 High; 0 Other Level
8 Regular; 0 Special Education; 0 Vocational; 0 Alternative
0 Magnet; 0 Charter; 8 Title I Eligible; 7 School-wide Title I
Students: 2,260 (53.3% male; 46.7% female)
Individual Education Program: 412 (18.2%);
English Language Learner: 0 (0.0%); Migrant: 0 (0.0%)
Eligible for Free Lunch Program: 1,806 (79.9%)
Eligible for Reduced-Price Lunch Program: 341 (15.1%)
Teachers: 143.0 (15.8 to 1)
Librarians/Media Specialists: 5.0 (452.0 to 1)
Guidance Counselors: 3.0 (753.3 to 1)
Current Spending: ($ per student per year):
Total: $6,569; Instruction: $3,780; Support Services: $2,415
Enrollment, Drop-out Rates and Diploma Recipients by Race/Ethnicity

Category	Total	White	Black	Asian	AIAN	Hisp.
Enrollment (%)	100.0	99.9	0.1	0.0	0.0	0.0
Drop-out Rate (%)	4.7	4.7	n/a	n/a	n/a	n/a
H.S. Diplomas (#)	139	138	0	1	0	0

Letcher County

Letcher County
224 Park St • Whitesburg, KY 41858-0788
(606) 633-4455 • http://www.letcher.k12.ky.us/
Grade Span: PK-12; **Agency Type:** 1
Schools: 13
8 Primary; 1 Middle; 4 High; 0 Other Level
12 Regular; 0 Special Education; 0 Vocational; 1 Alternative
0 Magnet; 0 Charter; 12 Title I Eligible; 9 School-wide Title I
Students: 3,512 (53.6% male; 46.4% female)
Individual Education Program: 720 (20.5%);
English Language Learner: 0 (0.0%); Migrant: 175 (5.0%)
Eligible for Free Lunch Program: 2,588 (73.7%)
Eligible for Reduced-Price Lunch Program: 635 (18.1%)
Teachers: 246.3 (14.3 to 1)
Librarians/Media Specialists: 10.0 (351.2 to 1)
Guidance Counselors: 11.0 (319.3 to 1)
Current Spending: ($ per student per year):
Total: $6,859; Instruction: $4,080; Support Services: $2,471
Enrollment, Drop-out Rates and Diploma Recipients by Race/Ethnicity

Category	Total	White	Black	Asian	AIAN	Hisp.
Enrollment (%)	100.0	98.7	0.2	0.1	0.9	0.1
Drop-out Rate (%)	4.4	4.4	0.0	n/a	0.0	0.0
H.S. Diplomas (#)	196	196	0	0	0	0

Lewis County

Lewis County
520 Plummer Ln • Vanceburg, KY 41179-0159
(606) 796-2811 • http://www.lewis.k12.ky.us/
Grade Span: PK-12; **Agency Type:** 1
Schools: 7
4 Primary; 1 Middle; 2 High; 0 Other Level
6 Regular; 0 Special Education; 1 Vocational; 0 Alternative
0 Magnet; 0 Charter; 6 Title I Eligible; 5 School-wide Title I
Students: 2,517 (53.6% male; 46.4% female)
Individual Education Program: 417 (16.6%);
English Language Learner: 0 (0.0%); Migrant: 170 (6.8%)
Eligible for Free Lunch Program: 1,921 (76.3%)
Eligible for Reduced-Price Lunch Program: 345 (13.7%)
Teachers: 167.4 (15.0 to 1)
Librarians/Media Specialists: 3.5 (719.1 to 1)
Guidance Counselors: 4.0 (629.3 to 1)
Current Spending: ($ per student per year):
Total: $6,172; Instruction: $3,747; Support Services: $2,018
Enrollment, Drop-out Rates and Diploma Recipients by Race/Ethnicity

Category	Total	White	Black	Asian	AIAN	Hisp.
Enrollment (%)	100.0	99.5	0.2	0.0	0.2	0.0
Drop-out Rate (%)	5.6	5.6	n/a	n/a	n/a	n/a
H.S. Diplomas (#)	142	142	0	0	0	0

Lincoln County

Lincoln County
305 Danville Ave • Stanford, KY 40484-0265
(606) 365-2124 • http://www.lincoln.k12.ky.us/
Grade Span: PK-12; **Agency Type:** 1
Schools: 10
7 Primary; 1 Middle; 2 High; 0 Other Level
9 Regular; 0 Special Education; 0 Vocational; 1 Alternative
0 Magnet; 0 Charter; 9 Title I Eligible; 7 School-wide Title I
Students: 4,419 (52.4% male; 47.6% female)
Individual Education Program: 887 (20.1%);
English Language Learner: 0 (0.0%); Migrant: 101 (2.3%)
Eligible for Free Lunch Program: 2,810 (63.6%)
Eligible for Reduced-Price Lunch Program: 833 (18.9%)
Teachers: 264.8 (16.7 to 1)
Librarians/Media Specialists: 8.0 (552.4 to 1)
Guidance Counselors: 7.0 (631.3 to 1)
Current Spending: ($ per student per year):
Total: $6,301; Instruction: $4,286; Support Services: $1,673
Enrollment, Drop-out Rates and Diploma Recipients by Race/Ethnicity

Category	Total	White	Black	Asian	AIAN	Hisp.
Enrollment (%)	100.0	96.1	2.9	0.0	0.1	0.8
Drop-out Rate (%)	8.3	8.7	0.0	0.0	0.0	0.0
H.S. Diplomas (#)	214	205	8	0	0	1

Logan County

Logan County
2222 Bowling Green Rd • Russellville, KY 42276-0417
(270) 726-2436 • http://www.logan.k12.ky.us/
Grade Span: PK-12; **Agency Type:** 1
Schools: 6
5 Primary; 0 Middle; 1 High; 0 Other Level
6 Regular; 0 Special Education; 0 Vocational; 0 Alternative
0 Magnet; 0 Charter; 5 Title I Eligible; 5 School-wide Title I
Students: 3,467 (51.8% male; 48.2% female)
Individual Education Program: 633 (18.3%);
English Language Learner: 0 (0.0%); Migrant: 80 (2.3%)
Eligible for Free Lunch Program: 1,869 (53.9%)
Eligible for Reduced-Price Lunch Program: 646 (18.6%)
Teachers: 209.8 (16.5 to 1)
Librarians/Media Specialists: 6.0 (577.8 to 1)
Guidance Counselors: 6.0 (577.8 to 1)
Current Spending: ($ per student per year):
Total: $5,606; Instruction: $3,468; Support Services: $1,779
Enrollment, Drop-out Rates and Diploma Recipients by Race/Ethnicity

Category	Total	White	Black	Asian	AIAN	Hisp.
Enrollment (%)	100.0	96.5	3.2	0.0	0.0	0.2
Drop-out Rate (%)	3.2	3.1	5.0	0.0	0.0	0.0
H.S. Diplomas (#)	225	212	11	0	0	2

Madison County

Madison County
550 S Keeneland Dr • Richmond, KY 40475-0768
(859) 624-4500 • http://www.madison.k12.ky.us/
Grade Span: PK-12; **Agency Type:** 1
Schools: 18
10 Primary; 4 Middle; 4 High; 0 Other Level
17 Regular; 0 Special Education; 0 Vocational; 1 Alternative
0 Magnet; 0 Charter; 12 Title I Eligible; 11 School-wide Title I
Students: 9,744 (51.3% male; 48.7% female)
Individual Education Program: 1,867 (19.2%);
English Language Learner: 27 (0.3%); Migrant: 490 (5.0%)
Eligible for Free Lunch Program: 4,720 (48.4%)
Eligible for Reduced-Price Lunch Program: 1,377 (14.1%)
Teachers: 567.2 (17.2 to 1)
Librarians/Media Specialists: 15.0 (649.6 to 1)
Guidance Counselors: 17.0 (573.2 to 1)
Current Spending: ($ per student per year):
Total: $5,651; Instruction: $3,668; Support Services: $1,706
Enrollment, Drop-out Rates and Diploma Recipients by Race/Ethnicity

Category	Total	White	Black	Asian	AIAN	Hisp.
Enrollment (%)	100.0	92.5	5.7	0.6	0.2	1.0
Drop-out Rate (%)	3.2	3.3	1.6	0.0	0.0	0.0
H.S. Diplomas (#)	442	412	25	1	0	4

Magoffin County

Magoffin County
109 Gardner Tr • Salyersville, KY 41465-0109
(606) 349-6117 • http://www.magoffin.k12.ky.us/
Grade Span: PK-12; **Agency Type:** 1
Schools: 8
6 Primary; 1 Middle; 1 High; 0 Other Level
8 Regular; 0 Special Education; 0 Vocational; 0 Alternative
0 Magnet; 0 Charter; 8 Title I Eligible; 7 School-wide Title I
Students: 2,557 (51.5% male; 48.5% female)
Individual Education Program: 392 (15.3%);
English Language Learner: 0 (0.0%); Migrant: 0 (0.0%)
Eligible for Free Lunch Program: 1,994 (78.0%)
Eligible for Reduced-Price Lunch Program: 328 (12.8%)
Teachers: 169.0 (15.1 to 1)
Librarians/Media Specialists: 7.0 (365.3 to 1)
Guidance Counselors: 4.0 (639.3 to 1)
Current Spending: ($ per student per year):
Total: $6,704; Instruction: $3,959; Support Services: $2,272

Enrollment, Drop-out Rates and Diploma Recipients by Race/Ethnicity

Category	Total	White	Black	Asian	AIAN	Hisp.
Enrollment (%)	100.0	100.0	0.0	0.0	0.0	0.0
Drop-out Rate (%)	6.7	6.7	n/a	n/a	n/a	n/a
H.S. Diplomas (#)	160	160	0	0	0	0

Marion County

Marion County

755 E Main St • Lebanon, KY 40033-1518
(270) 692-3721 • http://www.marion.k12.ky.us/
Grade Span: PK-12; **Agency Type:** 1
Schools: 7
4 Primary; 2 Middle; 1 High; 0 Other Level
7 Regular; 0 Special Education; 0 Vocational; 0 Alternative
0 Magnet; 0 Charter; 7 Title I Eligible; 6 School-wide Title I
Students: 3,032 (51.6% male; 48.4% female)
Individual Education Program: 519 (17.1%);
English Language Learner: 0 (0.0%); Migrant: 91 (3.0%)
Eligible for Free Lunch Program: 1,680 (55.4%)
Eligible for Reduced-Price Lunch Program: 675 (22.3%)
Teachers: 195.0 (15.5 to 1)
Librarians/Media Specialists: 6.0 (505.3 to 1)
Guidance Counselors: 8.0 (379.0 to 1)
Current Spending: ($ per student per year):
Total: $6,137; Instruction: $3,932; Support Services: $1,786

Enrollment, Drop-out Rates and Diploma Recipients by Race/Ethnicity

Category	Total	White	Black	Asian	AIAN	Hisp.
Enrollment (%)	100.0	89.7	8.1	0.9	0.0	1.2
Drop-out Rate (%)	4.3	4.1	6.9	0.0	n/a	0.0
H.S. Diplomas (#)	202	181	19	2	0	0

Marshall County

Marshall County

86 High School Rd • Benton, KY 42025-7017
(270) 527-8628 • http://www.marshall.k12.ky.us/
Grade Span: PK-12; **Agency Type:** 1
Schools: 11
6 Primary; 3 Middle; 2 High; 0 Other Level
10 Regular; 0 Special Education; 1 Vocational; 0 Alternative
0 Magnet; 0 Charter; 6 Title I Eligible; 5 School-wide Title I
Students: 4,823 (52.1% male; 47.9% female)
Individual Education Program: 612 (12.7%);
English Language Learner: 0 (0.0%); Migrant: 122 (2.5%)
Eligible for Free Lunch Program: 2,335 (48.4%)
Eligible for Reduced-Price Lunch Program: 535 (11.1%)
Teachers: 306.2 (15.8 to 1)
Librarians/Media Specialists: 9.0 (535.9 to 1)
Guidance Counselors: 13.5 (357.3 to 1)
Current Spending: ($ per student per year):
Total: $5,455; Instruction: $3,546; Support Services: $1,586

Enrollment, Drop-out Rates and Diploma Recipients by Race/Ethnicity

Category	Total	White	Black	Asian	AIAN	Hisp.
Enrollment (%)	100.0	99.4	0.1	0.1	0.2	0.2
Drop-out Rate (%)	2.8	2.8	n/a	0.0	n/a	0.0
H.S. Diplomas (#)	272	271	0	1	0	0

Martin County

Martin County

Rt 40 • Inez, KY 41224-0366
(606) 298-3572 • http://www.martin.k12.ky.us/
Grade Span: PK-12; **Agency Type:** 1
Schools: 9
6 Primary; 2 Middle; 1 High; 0 Other Level
9 Regular; 0 Special Education; 0 Vocational; 0 Alternative
0 Magnet; 0 Charter; 7 Title I Eligible; 5 School-wide Title I
Students: 2,535 (55.8% male; 44.2% female)
Individual Education Program: 532 (21.0%);
English Language Learner: 0 (0.0%); Migrant: 64 (2.5%)
Eligible for Free Lunch Program: 1,595 (62.9%)
Eligible for Reduced-Price Lunch Program: 246 (9.7%)
Teachers: 172.6 (14.7 to 1)
Librarians/Media Specialists: 4.0 (633.8 to 1)
Guidance Counselors: 6.5 (390.0 to 1)
Current Spending: ($ per student per year):
Total: $8,064; Instruction: $4,569; Support Services: $3,000

Enrollment, Drop-out Rates and Diploma Recipients by Race/Ethnicity

Category	Total	White	Black	Asian	AIAN	Hisp.
Enrollment (%)	100.0	99.6	0.3	0.0	0.0	0.1
Drop-out Rate (%)	3.2	3.2	0.0	n/a	n/a	n/a
H.S. Diplomas (#)	154	153	0	1	0	0

Mason County

Mason County

2nd And Limestone • Maysville, KY 41056-0099
(606) 564-5563 • http://www.mason.k12.ky.us/
Grade Span: PK-12; **Agency Type:** 1
Schools: 4
1 Primary; 2 Middle; 1 High; 0 Other Level
4 Regular; 0 Special Education; 0 Vocational; 0 Alternative
0 Magnet; 0 Charter; 4 Title I Eligible; 3 School-wide Title I
Students: 2,806 (52.5% male; 47.5% female)
Individual Education Program: 419 (14.9%);
English Language Learner: 8 (0.3%); Migrant: 100 (3.6%)
Eligible for Free Lunch Program: 1,728 (61.6%)
Eligible for Reduced-Price Lunch Program: 317 (11.3%)
Teachers: 175.9 (16.0 to 1)
Librarians/Media Specialists: 4.0 (701.5 to 1)
Guidance Counselors: 6.0 (467.7 to 1)
Current Spending: ($ per student per year):
Total: $6,105; Instruction: $4,050; Support Services: $1,766

Enrollment, Drop-out Rates and Diploma Recipients by Race/Ethnicity

Category	Total	White	Black	Asian	AIAN	Hisp.
Enrollment (%)	100.0	89.5	9.1	0.6	0.1	0.7
Drop-out Rate (%)	3.4	3.8	1.2	0.0	0.0	0.0
H.S. Diplomas (#)	171	148	22	0	0	1

Mccracken County

Mccracken County

260 Bleich Rd • Paducah, KY 42003-5573
(270) 744-4000 • http://www.mccracken.k12.ky.us/
Grade Span: PK-12; **Agency Type:** 1
Schools: 15
6 Primary; 3 Middle; 3 High; 3 Other Level
12 Regular; 0 Special Education; 0 Vocational; 3 Alternative
0 Magnet; 0 Charter; 6 Title I Eligible; 4 School-wide Title I
Students: 6,930 (52.3% male; 47.7% female)
Individual Education Program: 1,014 (14.6%);
English Language Learner: 38 (0.5%); Migrant: 261 (3.8%)
Eligible for Free Lunch Program: 3,091 (44.6%)
Eligible for Reduced-Price Lunch Program: 765 (11.0%)
Teachers: 389.0 (17.8 to 1)
Librarians/Media Specialists: 12.0 (577.5 to 1)
Guidance Counselors: 15.0 (462.0 to 1)
Current Spending: ($ per student per year):
Total: $6,344; Instruction: $3,983; Support Services: $1,979

Enrollment, Drop-out Rates and Diploma Recipients by Race/Ethnicity

Category	Total	White	Black	Asian	AIAN	Hisp.
Enrollment (%)	100.0	95.2	3.1	0.4	0.3	0.9
Drop-out Rate (%)	1.7	1.8	0.0	0.0	0.0	0.0
H.S. Diplomas (#)	436	426	5	2	1	2

Paducah Independent

800 Caldwell St • Paducah, KY 42003-2550
(270) 444-5600 • http://www.paducah.k12.ky.us/
Grade Span: PK-12; **Agency Type:** 1
Schools: 9
5 Primary; 1 Middle; 2 High; 1 Other Level
7 Regular; 0 Special Education; 0 Vocational; 2 Alternative
0 Magnet; 0 Charter; 6 Title I Eligible; 6 School-wide Title I
Students: 3,289 (49.6% male; 50.4% female)
Individual Education Program: 430 (13.1%);
English Language Learner: 32 (1.0%); Migrant: 23 (0.7%)
Eligible for Free Lunch Program: 1,918 (58.3%)
Eligible for Reduced-Price Lunch Program: 169 (5.1%)
Teachers: 221.2 (14.9 to 1)
Librarians/Media Specialists: 6.0 (548.2 to 1)
Guidance Counselors: 7.0 (469.9 to 1)
Current Spending: ($ per student per year):
Total: $7,954; Instruction: $4,745; Support Services: $2,761

Enrollment, Drop-out Rates and Diploma Recipients by Race/Ethnicity

Category	Total	White	Black	Asian	AIAN	Hisp.
Enrollment (%)	100.0	47.6	49.8	0.7	1.5	0.4
Drop-out Rate (%)	6.2	5.6	7.3	0.0	n/a	0.0
H.S. Diplomas (#)	153	96	52	3	0	2

Mccreary County

Mccreary County

120 Raider Way • Stearns, KY 42647-9715
(606) 376-2591 • http://www.mccreary.k12.ky.us/
Grade Span: PK-12; **Agency Type:** 1
Schools: 11
6 Primary; 2 Middle; 2 High; 1 Other Level
9 Regular; 0 Special Education; 0 Vocational; 2 Alternative

0 Magnet; 0 Charter; 8 Title I Eligible; 7 School-wide Title I
Students: 3,446 (51.7% male; 48.3% female)
Individual Education Program: 566 (16.4%);
English Language Learner: 0 (0.0%); Migrant: 0 (0.0%)
Eligible for Free Lunch Program: 2,711 (78.7%)
Eligible for Reduced-Price Lunch Program: 416 (12.1%)
Teachers: 233.5 (14.8 to 1)
Librarians/Media Specialists: 6.0 (574.3 to 1)
Guidance Counselors: 7.0 (492.3 to 1)
Current Spending: ($ per student per year):
Total: $6,246; Instruction: $3,703; Support Services: $2,144
Enrollment, Drop-out Rates and Diploma Recipients by Race/Ethnicity

Category	Total	White	Black	Asian	AIAN	Hisp.
Enrollment (%)	100.0	97.8	1.6	0.0	0.1	0.5
Drop-out Rate (%)	4.5	4.5	6.4	0.0	0.0	0.0
H.S. Diplomas (#)	170	170	0	0	0	0

Mclean County

Mclean County
283 Main St • Calhoun, KY 42327-0245
(270) 273-5257 • http://www.mclean.k12.ky.us/
Grade Span: KG-12; **Agency Type:** 1
Schools: 6
3 Primary; 1 Middle; 1 High; 1 Other Level
5 Regular; 0 Special Education; 0 Vocational; 1 Alternative
0 Magnet; 0 Charter; 5 Title I Eligible; 3 School-wide Title I
Students: 1,697 (51.0% male; 49.0% female)
Individual Education Program: 249 (14.7%);
English Language Learner: 0 (0.0%); Migrant: 111 (6.5%)
Eligible for Free Lunch Program: 786 (46.3%)
Eligible for Reduced-Price Lunch Program: 288 (17.0%)
Teachers: 106.0 (16.0 to 1)
Librarians/Media Specialists: 3.0 (565.7 to 1)
Guidance Counselors: 2.5 (678.8 to 1)
Current Spending: ($ per student per year):
Total: $5,995; Instruction: $3,319; Support Services: $2,291
Enrollment, Drop-out Rates and Diploma Recipients by Race/Ethnicity

Category	Total	White	Black	Asian	AIAN	Hisp.
Enrollment (%)	100.0	99.3	0.3	0.0	0.1	0.4
Drop-out Rate (%)	5.3	5.3	0.0	n/a	0.0	n/a
H.S. Diplomas (#)	93	93	0	0	0	0

Meade County

Meade County
1155 Old Ekron Rd • Brandenburg, KY 40108-0337
(270) 422-7500 • http://www.meade.k12.ky.us/
Grade Span: PK-12; **Agency Type:** 1
Schools: 10
6 Primary; 2 Middle; 2 High; 0 Other Level
9 Regular; 0 Special Education; 0 Vocational; 1 Alternative
0 Magnet; 0 Charter; 8 Title I Eligible; 5 School-wide Title I
Students: 4,674 (51.4% male; 48.6% female)
Individual Education Program: 715 (15.3%);
English Language Learner: 0 (0.0%); Migrant: 38 (0.8%)
Eligible for Free Lunch Program: 1,922 (41.1%)
Eligible for Reduced-Price Lunch Program: 815 (17.4%)
Teachers: 265.3 (17.6 to 1)
Librarians/Media Specialists: 7.0 (667.7 to 1)
Guidance Counselors: 10.6 (440.9 to 1)
Current Spending: ($ per student per year):
Total: $5,281; Instruction: $3,418; Support Services: $1,548
Enrollment, Drop-out Rates and Diploma Recipients by Race/Ethnicity

Category	Total	White	Black	Asian	AIAN	Hisp.
Enrollment (%)	100.0	95.8	2.4	0.7	0.5	0.7
Drop-out Rate (%)	4.2	4.2	4.4	0.0	0.0	0.0
H.S. Diplomas (#)	336	319	11	3	2	1

Mercer County

Mercer County
961 Moberly Rd • Harrodsburg, KY 40330-9104
(859) 734-4364 • http://www.mercer.k12.ky.us/
Grade Span: PK-12; **Agency Type:** 1
Schools: 4
1 Primary; 1 Middle; 1 High; 1 Other Level
3 Regular; 0 Special Education; 0 Vocational; 1 Alternative
0 Magnet; 0 Charter; 3 Title I Eligible; 0 School-wide Title I
Students: 2,274 (53.5% male; 46.5% female)
Individual Education Program: 369 (16.2%);
English Language Learner: 5 (0.2%); Migrant: 7 (0.3%)
Eligible for Free Lunch Program: 642 (28.2%)
Eligible for Reduced-Price Lunch Program: 260 (11.4%)
Teachers: 136.5 (16.7 to 1)
Librarians/Media Specialists: 3.0 (758.0 to 1)
Guidance Counselors: 4.0 (568.5 to 1)
Current Spending: ($ per student per year):
Total: $5,292; Instruction: $3,271; Support Services: $1,757
Enrollment, Drop-out Rates and Diploma Recipients by Race/Ethnicity

Category	Total	White	Black	Asian	AIAN	Hisp.
Enrollment (%)	100.0	98.4	0.6	0.7	0.0	0.3
Drop-out Rate (%)	2.2	2.3	0.0	0.0	n/a	0.0
H.S. Diplomas (#)	149	149	0	0	0	0

Metcalfe County

Metcalfe County
1007 W Stockton • Edmonton, KY 42129-8127
(270) 432-3171 • http://www.metcalfe.k12.ky.us/
Grade Span: PK-12; **Agency Type:** 1
Schools: 5
3 Primary; 1 Middle; 1 High; 0 Other Level
5 Regular; 0 Special Education; 0 Vocational; 0 Alternative
0 Magnet; 0 Charter; 5 Title I Eligible; 3 School-wide Title I
Students: 1,673 (52.7% male; 47.3% female)
Individual Education Program: 248 (14.8%);
English Language Learner: 2 (0.1%); Migrant: 214 (12.8%)
Eligible for Free Lunch Program: 1,185 (70.8%)
Eligible for Reduced-Price Lunch Program: 280 (16.7%)
Teachers: 112.8 (14.8 to 1)
Librarians/Media Specialists: 2.8 (597.5 to 1)
Guidance Counselors: 4.0 (418.3 to 1)
Current Spending: ($ per student per year):
Total: $6,877; Instruction: $3,803; Support Services: $2,642
Enrollment, Drop-out Rates and Diploma Recipients by Race/Ethnicity

Category	Total	White	Black	Asian	AIAN	Hisp.
Enrollment (%)	100.0	98.3	1.5	0.1	0.1	0.1
Drop-out Rate (%)	4.1	4.3	0.0	n/a	0.0	0.0
H.S. Diplomas (#)	87	83	4	0	0	0

Monroe County

Monroe County
1209 N Main St • Tompkinsville, KY 42167-0518
(270) 487-5456 • http://www.monroe.k12.ky.us/
Grade Span: PK-12; **Agency Type:** 1
Schools: 5
3 Primary; 1 Middle; 1 High; 0 Other Level
5 Regular; 0 Special Education; 0 Vocational; 0 Alternative
0 Magnet; 0 Charter; 5 Title I Eligible; 2 School-wide Title I
Students: 2,088 (54.5% male; 45.5% female)
Individual Education Program: 317 (15.2%);
English Language Learner: 17 (0.8%); Migrant: 219 (10.5%)
Eligible for Free Lunch Program: 1,496 (71.6%)
Eligible for Reduced-Price Lunch Program: 334 (16.0%)
Teachers: 141.5 (14.8 to 1)
Librarians/Media Specialists: 4.7 (444.3 to 1)
Guidance Counselors: 4.8 (435.0 to 1)
Current Spending: ($ per student per year):
Total: $6,075; Instruction: $3,599; Support Services: $2,053
Enrollment, Drop-out Rates and Diploma Recipients by Race/Ethnicity

Category	Total	White	Black	Asian	AIAN	Hisp.
Enrollment (%)	100.0	94.3	4.4	0.0	0.0	1.3
Drop-out Rate (%)	2.6	2.7	0.0	n/a	n/a	0.0
H.S. Diplomas (#)	128	120	7	0	0	1

Montgomery County

Montgomery County
212 N Maysville St • Mount Sterling, KY 40353-9504
(859) 497-8760 • http://www.montgomery.k12.ky.us/
Grade Span: PK-12; **Agency Type:** 1
Schools: 9
3 Primary; 1 Middle; 2 High; 3 Other Level
5 Regular; 0 Special Education; 0 Vocational; 4 Alternative
0 Magnet; 0 Charter; 5 Title I Eligible; 4 School-wide Title I
Students: 4,355 (51.3% male; 48.7% female)
Individual Education Program: 562 (12.9%);
English Language Learner: 29 (0.7%); Migrant: 389 (8.9%)
Eligible for Free Lunch Program: 2,243 (51.5%)
Eligible for Reduced-Price Lunch Program: 614 (14.1%)
Teachers: 259.0 (16.8 to 1)
Librarians/Media Specialists: 5.0 (871.0 to 1)
Guidance Counselors: 10.0 (435.5 to 1)
Current Spending: ($ per student per year):
Total: $5,860; Instruction: $3,697; Support Services: $1,834

Enrollment, Drop-out Rates and Diploma Recipients by Race/Ethnicity

Category	Total	White	Black	Asian	AIAN	Hisp.
Enrollment (%)	100.0	95.3	2.8	0.3	0.1	1.5
Drop-out Rate (%)	6.0	6.3	0.0	n/a	n/a	0.0
H.S. Diplomas (#)	221	211	8	0	0	2

Morgan County

Morgan County

496 Prestonsburg St • West Liberty, KY 41472-0489
(606) 743-8002 • http://www.morgan.k12.ky.us/
Grade Span: KG-12; **Agency Type:** 1
Schools: 8
5 Primary; 1 Middle; 1 High; 1 Other Level
7 Regular; 0 Special Education; 0 Vocational; 1 Alternative
0 Magnet; 0 Charter; 7 Title I Eligible; 7 School-wide Title I
Students: 2,489 (53.7% male; 46.3% female)
Individual Education Program: 441 (17.7%);
English Language Learner: 0 (0.0%); Migrant: 76 (3.1%)
Eligible for Free Lunch Program: 1,821 (73.2%)
Eligible for Reduced-Price Lunch Program: 305 (12.3%)
Teachers: 171.5 (14.5 to 1)
Librarians/Media Specialists: 4.0 (622.3 to 1)
Guidance Counselors: 2.0 (1,244.5 to 1)
Current Spending: ($ per student per year):
Total: $6,652; Instruction: $4,027; Support Services: $2,185

Enrollment, Drop-out Rates and Diploma Recipients by Race/Ethnicity

Category	Total	White	Black	Asian	AIAN	Hisp.
Enrollment (%)	100.0	99.4	0.6	0.0	0.0	0.0
Drop-out Rate (%)	5.7	5.7	0.0	n/a	n/a	n/a
H.S. Diplomas (#)	126	126	0	0	0	0

Muhlenberg County

Muhlenberg County

510 W Main St • Greenville, KY 42345-0167
(270) 338-2871 • http://www.mberg.k12.ky.us/
Grade Span: PK-12; **Agency Type:** 1
Schools: 14
8 Primary; 2 Middle; 4 High; 0 Other Level
12 Regular; 0 Special Education; 0 Vocational; 2 Alternative
0 Magnet; 0 Charter; 11 Title I Eligible; 8 School-wide Title I
Students: 5,316 (51.9% male; 48.1% female)
Individual Education Program: 886 (16.7%);
English Language Learner: 0 (0.0%); Migrant: 205 (3.9%)
Eligible for Free Lunch Program: 2,739 (51.5%)
Eligible for Reduced-Price Lunch Program: 662 (12.5%)
Teachers: 358.0 (14.8 to 1)
Librarians/Media Specialists: 12.0 (443.0 to 1)
Guidance Counselors: 13.0 (408.9 to 1)
Current Spending: ($ per student per year):
Total: $6,497; Instruction: $4,173; Support Services: $1,943

Enrollment, Drop-out Rates and Diploma Recipients by Race/Ethnicity

Category	Total	White	Black	Asian	AIAN	Hisp.
Enrollment (%)	100.0	95.2	4.3	0.2	0.1	0.2
Drop-out Rate (%)	2.9	3.0	1.4	0.0	n/a	0.0
H.S. Diplomas (#)	321	307	12	1	0	1

Nelson County

Bardstown Independent

308 N 5th • Bardstown, KY 40004-1406
(502) 331-8800 • http://www.btown.k12.ky.us/
Grade Span: PK-12; **Agency Type:** 1
Schools: 5
3 Primary; 1 Middle; 1 High; 0 Other Level
5 Regular; 0 Special Education; 0 Vocational; 0 Alternative
0 Magnet; 0 Charter; 3 Title I Eligible; 1 School-wide Title I
Students: 2,094 (51.6% male; 48.4% female)
Individual Education Program: 303 (14.5%);
English Language Learner: 8 (0.4%); Migrant: 0 (0.0%)
Eligible for Free Lunch Program: 1,056 (50.4%)
Eligible for Reduced-Price Lunch Program: 312 (14.9%)
Teachers: 126.0 (16.6 to 1)
Librarians/Media Specialists: 3.0 (698.0 to 1)
Guidance Counselors: 5.0 (418.8 to 1)
Current Spending: ($ per student per year):
Total: $6,305; Instruction: $3,774; Support Services: $2,147

Enrollment, Drop-out Rates and Diploma Recipients by Race/Ethnicity

Category	Total	White	Black	Asian	AIAN	Hisp.
Enrollment (%)	100.0	74.6	22.9	1.5	0.2	0.8
Drop-out Rate (%)	5.1	5.3	4.7	0.0	n/a	0.0
H.S. Diplomas (#)	111	70	40	1	0	0

Nelson County

1200 Cardinal Dr • Bardstown, KY 40004-1740
(502) 349-7000 • http://www.nelson.k12.ky.us/
Grade Span: PK-12; **Agency Type:** 1
Schools: 10
6 Primary; 2 Middle; 2 High; 0 Other Level
9 Regular; 0 Special Education; 0 Vocational; 1 Alternative
0 Magnet; 0 Charter; 7 Title I Eligible; 4 School-wide Title I
Students: 4,850 (51.1% male; 48.9% female)
Individual Education Program: 772 (15.9%);
English Language Learner: 4 (0.1%); Migrant: 0 (0.0%)
Eligible for Free Lunch Program: 2,171 (44.8%)
Eligible for Reduced-Price Lunch Program: 669 (13.8%)
Teachers: 284.5 (17.0 to 1)
Librarians/Media Specialists: 9.2 (527.2 to 1)
Guidance Counselors: 10.5 (461.9 to 1)
Current Spending: ($ per student per year):
Total: $6,088; Instruction: $3,712; Support Services: $2,016

Enrollment, Drop-out Rates and Diploma Recipients by Race/Ethnicity

Category	Total	White	Black	Asian	AIAN	Hisp.
Enrollment (%)	100.0	97.2	2.0	0.4	0.0	0.4
Drop-out Rate (%)	3.2	3.4	0.0	0.0	n/a	0.0
H.S. Diplomas (#)	312	304	6	2	0	0

Ohio County

Ohio County

315 E Union St • Hartford, KY 42347-0070
(270) 298-3249 • http://www.ohio.k12.ky.us/
Grade Span: PK-12; **Agency Type:** 1
Schools: 10
6 Primary; 1 Middle; 3 High; 0 Other Level
8 Regular; 0 Special Education; 0 Vocational; 2 Alternative
0 Magnet; 0 Charter; 7 Title I Eligible; 7 School-wide Title I
Students: 4,136 (51.3% male; 48.7% female)
Individual Education Program: 667 (16.1%);
English Language Learner: 20 (0.5%); Migrant: 171 (4.1%)
Eligible for Free Lunch Program: 2,361 (57.1%)
Eligible for Reduced-Price Lunch Program: 743 (18.0%)
Teachers: 259.1 (16.0 to 1)
Librarians/Media Specialists: 6.0 (689.3 to 1)
Guidance Counselors: 4.5 (919.1 to 1)
Current Spending: ($ per student per year):
Total: $5,757; Instruction: $3,418; Support Services: $2,028

Enrollment, Drop-out Rates and Diploma Recipients by Race/Ethnicity

Category	Total	White	Black	Asian	AIAN	Hisp.
Enrollment (%)	100.0	98.5	0.6	0.0	0.1	0.8
Drop-out Rate (%)	1.8	1.9	0.0	0.0	0.0	0.0
H.S. Diplomas (#)	254	248	1	1	1	3

Oldham County

Oldham County

1350 N Hwy 393 • Buckner, KY 40010-0218
(502) 222-8880 • http://www.oldham.k12.ky.us/
Grade Span: PK-12; **Agency Type:** 1
Schools: 17
9 Primary; 3 Middle; 4 High; 0 Other Level
13 Regular; 0 Special Education; 1 Vocational; 2 Alternative
0 Magnet; 0 Charter; 7 Title I Eligible; 1 School-wide Title I
Students: 9,689 (51.3% male; 48.7% female)
Individual Education Program: 1,452 (15.0%);
English Language Learner: 63 (0.7%); Migrant: 68 (0.7%)
Eligible for Free Lunch Program: 1,428 (14.7%)
Eligible for Reduced-Price Lunch Program: 487 (5.0%)
Teachers: 561.0 (17.3 to 1)
Librarians/Media Specialists: 15.5 (625.1 to 1)
Guidance Counselors: 26.4 (367.0 to 1)
Current Spending: ($ per student per year):
Total: $5,606; Instruction: $3,484; Support Services: $1,886

Enrollment, Drop-out Rates and Diploma Recipients by Race/Ethnicity

Category	Total	White	Black	Asian	AIAN	Hisp.
Enrollment (%)	100.0	94.7	3.2	0.5	0.2	1.4
Drop-out Rate (%)	1.1	1.1	2.5	0.0	0.0	0.0
H.S. Diplomas (#)	606	584	17	2	0	3

Owen County

Owen County

1600 Hwy 22 E • Owenton, KY 40359-9042
(502) 484-3934 • http://www.owen.k12.ky.us/
Grade Span: PK-12; **Agency Type:** 1
Schools: 4
2 Primary; 1 Middle; 1 High; 0 Other Level
4 Regular; 0 Special Education; 0 Vocational; 0 Alternative

0 Magnet; 0 Charter; 4 Title I Eligible; 3 School-wide Title I
Students: 1,976 (53.7% male; 46.3% female)
Individual Education Program: 274 (13.9%);
English Language Learner: 16 (0.8%); Migrant: 121 (6.1%)
Eligible for Free Lunch Program: 1,071 (54.2%)
Eligible for Reduced-Price Lunch Program: 226 (11.4%)
Teachers: 108.0 (18.3 to 1)
Librarians/Media Specialists: 4.0 (494.0 to 1)
Guidance Counselors: 4.0 (494.0 to 1)
Current Spending: ($ per student per year):
Total: $5,505; Instruction: $3,292; Support Services: $1,872
Enrollment, Drop-out Rates and Diploma Recipients by Race/Ethnicity

Category	Total	White	Black	Asian	AIAN	Hisp.
Enrollment (%)	100.0	97.4	0.8	0.2	0.5	1.1
Drop-out Rate (%)	6.4	6.7	0.0	0.0	n/a	n/a
H.S. Diplomas (#)	104	100	2	0	0	2

Pendleton County

Pendleton County
2525 Hwy 27 N • Falmouth, KY 41040-9805
(859) 654-6911
Grade Span: PK-12; **Agency Type:** 1
Schools: 4
2 Primary; 1 Middle; 1 High; 0 Other Level
4 Regular; 0 Special Education; 0 Vocational; 0 Alternative
0 Magnet; 0 Charter; 4 Title I Eligible; 2 School-wide Title I
Students: 2,988 (51.6% male; 48.4% female)
Individual Education Program: 402 (13.5%);
English Language Learner: 5 (0.2%); Migrant: 453 (15.2%)
Eligible for Free Lunch Program: 1,758 (58.8%)
Eligible for Reduced-Price Lunch Program: 429 (14.4%)
Teachers: 178.6 (16.7 to 1)
Librarians/Media Specialists: 4.0 (747.0 to 1)
Guidance Counselors: 5.0 (597.6 to 1)
Current Spending: ($ per student per year):
Total: $5,415; Instruction: $3,329; Support Services: $1,795
Enrollment, Drop-out Rates and Diploma Recipients by Race/Ethnicity

Category	Total	White	Black	Asian	AIAN	Hisp.
Enrollment (%)	100.0	98.1	1.0	0.0	0.3	0.6
Drop-out Rate (%)	2.8	2.8	0.0	n/a	n/a	0.0
H.S. Diplomas (#)	155	155	0	0	0	0

Perry County

Perry County
315 Park Ave • Hazard, KY 41701-9548
(606) 439-5814 • http://www.perry.k12.ky.us/
Grade Span: PK-12; **Agency Type:** 1
Schools: 14
11 Primary; 0 Middle; 2 High; 1 Other Level
13 Regular; 0 Special Education; 0 Vocational; 1 Alternative
0 Magnet; 0 Charter; 13 Title I Eligible; 11 School-wide Title I
Students: 4,851 (52.5% male; 47.5% female)
Individual Education Program: 887 (18.3%);
English Language Learner: 0 (0.0%); Migrant: 0 (0.0%)
Eligible for Free Lunch Program: 3,416 (70.4%)
Eligible for Reduced-Price Lunch Program: 618 (12.7%)
Teachers: 333.7 (14.5 to 1)
Librarians/Media Specialists: 11.0 (441.0 to 1)
Guidance Counselors: 8.0 (606.4 to 1)
Current Spending: ($ per student per year):
Total: $6,545; Instruction: $4,148; Support Services: $2,029
Enrollment, Drop-out Rates and Diploma Recipients by Race/Ethnicity

Category	Total	White	Black	Asian	AIAN	Hisp.
Enrollment (%)	100.0	99.1	0.7	0.1	0.0	0.2
Drop-out Rate (%)	7.6	7.7	0.0	0.0	n/a	0.0
H.S. Diplomas (#)	242	237	1	0	1	3

Pike County

Pike County
314 S Mayo Tr • Pikeville, KY 41501-3097
(606) 432-7724 • http://lvillage.pike.k12.ky.us/lt/district.nsf
Grade Span: PK-12; **Agency Type:** 1
Schools: 26
16 Primary; 3 Middle; 6 High; 1 Other Level
24 Regular; 0 Special Education; 0 Vocational; 2 Alternative
0 Magnet; 0 Charter; 23 Title I Eligible; 16 School-wide Title I
Students: 10,625 (53.2% male; 46.8% female)
Individual Education Program: 1,398 (13.2%);
English Language Learner: 0 (0.0%); Migrant: 364 (3.4%)
Eligible for Free Lunch Program: 6,459 (60.8%)
Eligible for Reduced-Price Lunch Program: 1,557 (14.7%)
Teachers: 688.0 (15.4 to 1)
Librarians/Media Specialists: 23.0 (462.0 to 1)
Guidance Counselors: 12.0 (885.4 to 1)
Current Spending: ($ per student per year):
Total: $6,514; Instruction: $4,005; Support Services: $2,162
Enrollment, Drop-out Rates and Diploma Recipients by Race/Ethnicity

Category	Total	White	Black	Asian	AIAN	Hisp.
Enrollment (%)	100.0	99.2	0.3	0.2	0.2	0.1
Drop-out Rate (%)	4.0	4.0	0.0	0.0	0.0	0.0
H.S. Diplomas (#)	602	599	2	0	0	1

Powell County

Powell County
691 Breckinridge St • Stanton, KY 40380-0430
(606) 663-3300 • http://www.powell.k12.ky.us/
Grade Span: PK-12; **Agency Type:** 1
Schools: 5
3 Primary; 1 Middle; 1 High; 0 Other Level
5 Regular; 0 Special Education; 0 Vocational; 0 Alternative
0 Magnet; 0 Charter; 5 Title I Eligible; 4 School-wide Title I
Students: 2,662 (52.4% male; 47.6% female)
Individual Education Program: 470 (17.7%);
English Language Learner: 2 (0.1%); Migrant: 329 (12.4%)
Eligible for Free Lunch Program: 1,793 (67.4%)
Eligible for Reduced-Price Lunch Program: 367 (13.8%)
Teachers: 179.0 (14.9 to 1)
Librarians/Media Specialists: 5.0 (532.4 to 1)
Guidance Counselors: 6.0 (443.7 to 1)
Current Spending: ($ per student per year):
Total: $6,268; Instruction: $3,946; Support Services: $1,971
Enrollment, Drop-out Rates and Diploma Recipients by Race/Ethnicity

Category	Total	White	Black	Asian	AIAN	Hisp.
Enrollment (%)	100.0	98.8	0.6	0.1	0.1	0.5
Drop-out Rate (%)	6.5	6.6	0.0	0.0	0.0	0.0
H.S. Diplomas (#)	136	135	0	0	0	1

Pulaski County

Pulaski County
501 University Dr • Somerset, KY 42502-1055
(606) 679-1123 • http://www.pulaski.net/
Grade Span: PK-12; **Agency Type:** 1
Schools: 14
8 Primary; 2 Middle; 2 High; 2 Other Level
12 Regular; 0 Special Education; 0 Vocational; 2 Alternative
0 Magnet; 0 Charter; 12 Title I Eligible; 8 School-wide Title I
Students: 7,923 (52.1% male; 47.9% female)
Individual Education Program: 1,123 (14.2%);
English Language Learner: 12 (0.2%); Migrant: 226 (2.9%)
Eligible for Free Lunch Program: 4,765 (60.1%)
Eligible for Reduced-Price Lunch Program: 1,241 (15.7%)
Teachers: 479.0 (16.5 to 1)
Librarians/Media Specialists: 12.0 (660.3 to 1)
Guidance Counselors: 18.0 (440.2 to 1)
Current Spending: ($ per student per year):
Total: $6,008; Instruction: $3,772; Support Services: $1,890
Enrollment, Drop-out Rates and Diploma Recipients by Race/Ethnicity

Category	Total	White	Black	Asian	AIAN	Hisp.
Enrollment (%)	100.0	98.3	0.7	0.3	0.2	0.5
Drop-out Rate (%)	6.0	6.1	0.0	0.0	0.0	0.0
H.S. Diplomas (#)	462	456	2	1	0	3

Somerset Independent
305 N College St • Somerset, KY 42502-1311
(606) 679-4451 • http://www.somerset.k12.ky.us/
Grade Span: PK-12; **Agency Type:** 1
Schools: 3
1 Primary; 1 Middle; 1 High; 0 Other Level
3 Regular; 0 Special Education; 0 Vocational; 0 Alternative
0 Magnet; 0 Charter; 3 Title I Eligible; 1 School-wide Title I
Students: 1,568 (52.4% male; 47.6% female)
Individual Education Program: 202 (12.9%);
English Language Learner: 0 (0.0%); Migrant: 25 (1.6%)
Eligible for Free Lunch Program: 986 (62.9%)
Eligible for Reduced-Price Lunch Program: 249 (15.9%)
Teachers: 99.4 (15.8 to 1)
Librarians/Media Specialists: 3.0 (522.7 to 1)
Guidance Counselors: 4.0 (392.0 to 1)
Current Spending: ($ per student per year):
Total: $5,649; Instruction: $3,718; Support Services: $1,632
Enrollment, Drop-out Rates and Diploma Recipients by Race/Ethnicity

Category	Total	White	Black	Asian	AIAN	Hisp.
Enrollment (%)	100.0	88.9	7.3	2.1	0.1	1.6
Drop-out Rate (%)	4.2	4.7	0.0	0.0	0.0	0.0
H.S. Diplomas (#)	98	86	10	2	0	0

Rockcastle County

Rockcastle County
245 Richmond St • Mount Verno, KY 40456-2705
(606) 256-2125 • http://www.rockcastle.k12.ky.us/
Grade Span: PK-12; **Agency Type:** 1
Schools: 6
3 Primary; 1 Middle; 1 High; 1 Other Level
5 Regular; 0 Special Education; 0 Vocational; 1 Alternative
0 Magnet; 0 Charter; 5 Title I Eligible; 3 School-wide Title I
Students: 3,038 (52.1% male; 47.9% female)
Individual Education Program: 476 (15.7%);
English Language Learner: 0 (0.0%); Migrant: 413 (13.6%)
Eligible for Free Lunch Program: 2,062 (67.9%)
Eligible for Reduced-Price Lunch Program: 593 (19.5%)
Teachers: 199.5 (15.2 to 1)
Librarians/Media Specialists: 5.0 (607.6 to 1)
Guidance Counselors: 6.0 (506.3 to 1)
Current Spending: ($ per student per year):
Total: $6,209; Instruction: $3,974; Support Services: $1,897
Enrollment, Drop-out Rates and Diploma Recipients by Race/Ethnicity

Category	Total	White	Black	Asian	AIAN	Hisp.
Enrollment (%)	100.0	99.9	0.0	0.0	0.0	0.1
Drop-out Rate (%)	5.2	5.2	n/a	0.0	0.0	0.0
H.S. Diplomas (#)	184	183	1	0	0	0

Rowan County

Rowan County
121 E Second St • Morehead, KY 40351-1669
(606) 784-8928 • http://www.rowan.k12.ky.us/
Grade Span: PK-12; **Agency Type:** 1
Schools: 7
4 Primary; 1 Middle; 2 High; 0 Other Level
6 Regular; 0 Special Education; 0 Vocational; 1 Alternative
0 Magnet; 0 Charter; 6 Title I Eligible; 6 School-wide Title I
Students: 3,148 (49.8% male; 50.2% female)
Individual Education Program: 599 (19.0%);
English Language Learner: 13 (0.4%); Migrant: 64 (2.0%)
Eligible for Free Lunch Program: 1,800 (57.2%)
Eligible for Reduced-Price Lunch Program: 481 (15.3%)
Teachers: 206.0 (15.3 to 1)
Librarians/Media Specialists: 5.0 (629.6 to 1)
Guidance Counselors: 8.0 (393.5 to 1)
Current Spending: ($ per student per year):
Total: $6,412; Instruction: $4,124; Support Services: $1,931
Enrollment, Drop-out Rates and Diploma Recipients by Race/Ethnicity

Category	Total	White	Black	Asian	AIAN	Hisp.
Enrollment (%)	100.0	97.8	1.0	0.6	0.2	0.5
Drop-out Rate (%)	3.1	3.2	0.0	0.0	n/a	n/a
H.S. Diplomas (#)	183	181	1	1	0	0

Russell County

Russell County
404 S Main St • Jamestown, KY 42629-2148
(270) 343-3191 • http://russell-ind.k12.ky.us/
Grade Span: PK-12; **Agency Type:** 1
Schools: 6
4 Primary; 1 Middle; 1 High; 0 Other Level
6 Regular; 0 Special Education; 0 Vocational; 0 Alternative
0 Magnet; 0 Charter; 6 Title I Eligible; 5 School-wide Title I
Students: 2,867 (50.8% male; 49.2% female)
Individual Education Program: 490 (17.1%);
English Language Learner: 0 (0.0%); Migrant: 145 (5.1%)
Eligible for Free Lunch Program: 1,888 (65.9%)
Eligible for Reduced-Price Lunch Program: 610 (21.3%)
Teachers: 204.7 (14.0 to 1)
Librarians/Media Specialists: 6.0 (477.8 to 1)
Guidance Counselors: 6.0 (477.8 to 1)
Current Spending: ($ per student per year):
Total: $6,085; Instruction: $3,760; Support Services: $1,965
Enrollment, Drop-out Rates and Diploma Recipients by Race/Ethnicity

Category	Total	White	Black	Asian	AIAN	Hisp.
Enrollment (%)	100.0	98.8	0.7	0.2	0.0	0.4
Drop-out Rate (%)	7.0	7.2	0.0	0.0	0.0	n/a
H.S. Diplomas (#)	140	137	1	2	0	0

Scott County

Scott County
2168 Frankfort Pk • Georgetown, KY 40324-0561
(502) 863-3663 • http://www.scott.k12.ky.us/
Grade Span: PK-12; **Agency Type:** 1
Schools: 14
9 Primary; 2 Middle; 1 High; 1 Other Level
13 Regular; 0 Special Education; 0 Vocational; 0 Alternative
0 Magnet; 0 Charter; 7 Title I Eligible; 0 School-wide Title I
Students: 6,344 (54.1% male; 45.9% female)
Individual Education Program: 902 (14.2%);
English Language Learner: 19 (0.3%); Migrant: 150 (2.4%)
Eligible for Free Lunch Program: 2,467 (38.9%)
Eligible for Reduced-Price Lunch Program: 469 (7.4%)
Teachers: 401.3 (15.8 to 1)
Librarians/Media Specialists: 11.0 (576.7 to 1)
Guidance Counselors: 14.5 (437.5 to 1)
Current Spending: ($ per student per year):
Total: $6,020; Instruction: $3,824; Support Services: $1,918
Enrollment, Drop-out Rates and Diploma Recipients by Race/Ethnicity

Category	Total	White	Black	Asian	AIAN	Hisp.
Enrollment (%)	100.0	92.1	5.8	0.5	0.1	1.6
Drop-out Rate (%)	5.8	5.9	6.0	0.0	n/a	0.0
H.S. Diplomas (#)	334	307	23	0	1	3

Shelby County

Shelby County
403 Washington St • Shelbyville, KY 40066-0159
(502) 633-2375 • http://www.shelby.k12.ky.us/
Grade Span: PK-12; **Agency Type:** 1
Schools: 10
6 Primary; 2 Middle; 1 High; 1 Other Level
9 Regular; 0 Special Education; 0 Vocational; 1 Alternative
0 Magnet; 0 Charter; 6 Title I Eligible; 0 School-wide Title I
Students: 5,509 (52.0% male; 48.0% female)
Individual Education Program: 729 (13.2%);
English Language Learner: 194 (3.5%); Migrant: 196 (3.6%)
Eligible for Free Lunch Program: 2,074 (37.6%)
Eligible for Reduced-Price Lunch Program: 496 (9.0%)
Teachers: 324.8 (17.0 to 1)
Librarians/Media Specialists: 8.5 (648.1 to 1)
Guidance Counselors: 9.0 (612.1 to 1)
Current Spending: ($ per student per year):
Total: $5,600; Instruction: $3,349; Support Services: $1,837
Enrollment, Drop-out Rates and Diploma Recipients by Race/Ethnicity

Category	Total	White	Black	Asian	AIAN	Hisp.
Enrollment (%)	100.0	81.9	10.1	0.5	0.2	7.3
Drop-out Rate (%)	4.8	4.8	7.1	0.0	0.0	0.0
H.S. Diplomas (#)	306	267	28	5	1	5

Simpson County

Simpson County
430 S College St • Franklin, KY 42135-0467
(270) 586-8877 • http://www.simpson.k12.ky.us/
Grade Span: PK-12; **Agency Type:** 1
Schools: 6
2 Primary; 2 Middle; 2 High; 0 Other Level
5 Regular; 0 Special Education; 0 Vocational; 1 Alternative
0 Magnet; 0 Charter; 4 Title I Eligible; 0 School-wide Title I
Students: 3,070 (52.2% male; 47.8% female)
Individual Education Program: 358 (11.7%);
English Language Learner: 16 (0.5%); Migrant: 26 (0.8%)
Eligible for Free Lunch Program: 1,370 (44.6%)
Eligible for Reduced-Price Lunch Program: 406 (13.2%)
Teachers: 183.0 (16.8 to 1)
Librarians/Media Specialists: 5.0 (614.0 to 1)
Guidance Counselors: 6.0 (511.7 to 1)
Current Spending: ($ per student per year):
Total: $5,560; Instruction: $3,651; Support Services: $1,612
Enrollment, Drop-out Rates and Diploma Recipients by Race/Ethnicity

Category	Total	White	Black	Asian	AIAN	Hisp.
Enrollment (%)	100.0	86.4	12.3	0.3	0.1	0.8
Drop-out Rate (%)	2.9	2.8	3.9	0.0	0.0	0.0
H.S. Diplomas (#)	201	166	30	5	0	0

Spencer County

Spencer County
207 W Main St • Taylorsvil, KY 40071-0339
(502) 477-3250 • http://www.spencer.k12.ky.us/
Grade Span: PK-12; **Agency Type:** 1
Schools: 3
1 Primary; 1 Middle; 1 High; 0 Other Level
3 Regular; 0 Special Education; 0 Vocational; 0 Alternative
0 Magnet; 0 Charter; 3 Title I Eligible; 1 School-wide Title I
Students: 2,401 (52.4% male; 47.6% female)
Individual Education Program: 409 (17.0%);
English Language Learner: 6 (0.2%); Migrant: 10 (0.4%)
Eligible for Free Lunch Program: 1,009 (42.0%)

Eligible for Reduced-Price Lunch Program: 317 (13.2%)
Teachers: 130.3 (18.4 to 1)
Librarians/Media Specialists: 3.0 (800.3 to 1)
Guidance Counselors: 4.0 (600.3 to 1)
Current Spending: ($ per student per year):
Total: $5,923; Instruction: $3,731; Support Services: $1,817
Enrollment, Drop-out Rates and Diploma Recipients by Race/Ethnicity

Category	Total	White	Black	Asian	AIAN	Hisp.
Enrollment (%)	100.0	97.2	2.1	0.3	0.0	0.5
Drop-out Rate (%)	3.5	3.5	0.0	0.0	n/a	n/a
H.S. Diplomas (#)	113	112	1	0	0	0

Taylor County

Taylor County
1209 E Broadway • Campbellsville, KY 42718-1500
(270) 465-5371 • http://www.taylor.k12.ky.us/
Grade Span: PK-12; **Agency Type:** 1
Schools: 4
2 Primary; 1 Middle; 1 High; 0 Other Level
4 Regular; 0 Special Education; 0 Vocational; 0 Alternative
0 Magnet; 0 Charter; 3 Title I Eligible; 2 School-wide Title I
Students: 2,701 (50.7% male; 49.3% female)
Individual Education Program: 362 (13.4%);
English Language Learner: 0 (0.0%); Migrant: 54 (2.0%)
Eligible for Free Lunch Program: 1,371 (50.8%)
Eligible for Reduced-Price Lunch Program: 361 (13.4%)
Teachers: 158.5 (17.0 to 1)
Librarians/Media Specialists: 3.5 (771.7 to 1)
Guidance Counselors: 5.0 (540.2 to 1)
Current Spending: ($ per student per year):
Total: $5,844; Instruction: $3,659; Support Services: $1,880
Enrollment, Drop-out Rates and Diploma Recipients by Race/Ethnicity

Category	Total	White	Black	Asian	AIAN	Hisp.
Enrollment (%)	100.0	97.8	1.0	0.2	0.2	0.8
Drop-out Rate (%)	2.8	2.9	0.0	0.0	n/a	n/a
H.S. Diplomas (#)	162	157	5	0	0	0

Todd County

Todd County
804 S Main • Elkton, KY 42220-8812
(270) 265-2436 • http://www.todd.k12.ky.us/
Grade Span: PK-12; **Agency Type:** 1
Schools: 4
2 Primary; 1 Middle; 1 High; 0 Other Level
4 Regular; 0 Special Education; 0 Vocational; 0 Alternative
0 Magnet; 0 Charter; 4 Title I Eligible; 2 School-wide Title I
Students: 2,168 (50.6% male; 49.4% female)
Individual Education Program: 419 (19.3%);
English Language Learner: 14 (0.6%); Migrant: 132 (6.1%)
Eligible for Free Lunch Program: 1,324 (61.1%)
Eligible for Reduced-Price Lunch Program: 377 (17.4%)
Teachers: 121.0 (17.9 to 1)
Librarians/Media Specialists: 4.0 (542.0 to 1)
Guidance Counselors: 4.0 (542.0 to 1)
Current Spending: ($ per student per year):
Total: $5,880; Instruction: $3,342; Support Services: $2,120
Enrollment, Drop-out Rates and Diploma Recipients by Race/Ethnicity

Category	Total	White	Black	Asian	AIAN	Hisp.
Enrollment (%)	100.0	86.8	11.3	0.2	0.3	1.5
Drop-out Rate (%)	2.6	2.4	4.0	n/a	0.0	0.0
H.S. Diplomas (#)	115	102	13	0	0	0

Trigg County

Trigg County
202 Main St • Cadiz, KY 42211-6124
(270) 522-6075 • http://www.rowan.k12.ky.us/
Grade Span: PK-12; **Agency Type:** 1
Schools: 3
1 Primary; 1 Middle; 1 High; 0 Other Level
3 Regular; 0 Special Education; 0 Vocational; 0 Alternative
0 Magnet; 0 Charter; 3 Title I Eligible; 2 School-wide Title I
Students: 2,129 (53.5% male; 46.5% female)
Individual Education Program: 339 (15.9%);
English Language Learner: 1 (<0.1%); Migrant: 62 (2.9%)
Eligible for Free Lunch Program: 953 (44.8%)
Eligible for Reduced-Price Lunch Program: 346 (16.3%)
Teachers: 128.1 (16.6 to 1)
Librarians/Media Specialists: 3.0 (709.7 to 1)
Guidance Counselors: 4.0 (532.3 to 1)
Current Spending: ($ per student per year):
Total: $5,749; Instruction: $3,525; Support Services: $1,921

Enrollment, Drop-out Rates and Diploma Recipients by Race/Ethnicity

Category	Total	White	Black	Asian	AIAN	Hisp.
Enrollment (%)	100.0	84.8	14.1	0.3	0.2	0.6
Drop-out Rate (%)	2.4	1.9	5.1	n/a	n/a	0.0
H.S. Diplomas (#)	111	94	17	0	0	0

Trimble County

Trimble County
68 Wentworth Ave • Bedford, KY 40006-0275
(502) 255-3201
Grade Span: KG-12; **Agency Type:** 1
Schools: 4
2 Primary; 1 Middle; 1 High; 0 Other Level
4 Regular; 0 Special Education; 0 Vocational; 0 Alternative
0 Magnet; 0 Charter; 3 Title I Eligible; 2 School-wide Title I
Students: 1,611 (52.1% male; 47.9% female)
Individual Education Program: 211 (13.1%);
English Language Learner: 22 (1.4%); Migrant: 77 (4.8%)
Eligible for Free Lunch Program: 827 (51.3%)
Eligible for Reduced-Price Lunch Program: 281 (17.4%)
Teachers: 86.5 (18.6 to 1)
Librarians/Media Specialists: 3.0 (537.0 to 1)
Guidance Counselors: 3.0 (537.0 to 1)
Current Spending: ($ per student per year):
Total: $5,577; Instruction: $3,468; Support Services: $1,755
Enrollment, Drop-out Rates and Diploma Recipients by Race/Ethnicity

Category	Total	White	Black	Asian	AIAN	Hisp.
Enrollment (%)	100.0	97.3	0.8	0.1	0.3	1.6
Drop-out Rate (%)	2.4	2.5	0.0	n/a	n/a	0.0
H.S. Diplomas (#)	102	102	0	0	0	0

Union County

Union County
510 S Mart St • Morganfiel, KY 42437-1724
(270) 389-1694 • http://www.union.k12.ky.us/
Grade Span: PK-12; **Agency Type:** 1
Schools: 9
4 Primary; 1 Middle; 3 High; 1 Other Level
6 Regular; 0 Special Education; 0 Vocational; 3 Alternative
0 Magnet; 0 Charter; 4 Title I Eligible; 4 School-wide Title I
Students: 2,556 (51.4% male; 48.6% female)
Individual Education Program: 593 (23.2%);
English Language Learner: 1 (<0.1%); Migrant: 66 (2.6%)
Eligible for Free Lunch Program: 1,344 (52.6%)
Eligible for Reduced-Price Lunch Program: 359 (14.0%)
Teachers: 166.7 (15.3 to 1)
Librarians/Media Specialists: 5.0 (511.2 to 1)
Guidance Counselors: 7.2 (355.0 to 1)
Current Spending: ($ per student per year):
Total: $6,830; Instruction: $4,291; Support Services: $2,214
Enrollment, Drop-out Rates and Diploma Recipients by Race/Ethnicity

Category	Total	White	Black	Asian	AIAN	Hisp.
Enrollment (%)	100.0	85.9	13.6	0.2	0.0	0.4
Drop-out Rate (%)	7.0	4.2	30.6	0.0	0.0	0.0
H.S. Diplomas (#)	156	138	17	0	0	1

Warren County

Bowling Green Independent
1211 Center St • Bowling Green, KY 42101-6801
(270) 746-2200 • http://www.b-g.k12.ky.us/
Grade Span: PK-12; **Agency Type:** 1
Schools: 11
6 Primary; 1 Middle; 3 High; 1 Other Level
8 Regular; 0 Special Education; 0 Vocational; 3 Alternative
0 Magnet; 0 Charter; 7 Title I Eligible; 5 School-wide Title I
Students: 3,633 (51.4% male; 48.6% female)
Individual Education Program: 429 (11.8%);
English Language Learner: 324 (8.9%); Migrant: 61 (1.7%)
Eligible for Free Lunch Program: 2,160 (59.5%)
Eligible for Reduced-Price Lunch Program: 299 (8.2%)
Teachers: 231.0 (15.7 to 1)
Librarians/Media Specialists: 8.0 (454.1 to 1)
Guidance Counselors: 12.0 (302.8 to 1)
Current Spending: ($ per student per year):
Total: $6,660; Instruction: $4,100; Support Services: $2,138
Enrollment, Drop-out Rates and Diploma Recipients by Race/Ethnicity

Category	Total	White	Black	Asian	AIAN	Hisp.
Enrollment (%)	100.0	68.7	22.0	2.7	0.2	6.3
Drop-out Rate (%)	2.9	3.1	3.5	0.0	0.0	0.0
H.S. Diplomas (#)	222	173	33	10	0	6

Warren County

303 Lover's Ln • Bowling Gre, KY 42101-2310
(270) 781-5150 • http://www.warren.k12.ky.us/
Grade Span: PK-12; **Agency Type:** 1
Schools: 24
13 Primary; 4 Middle; 7 High; 0 Other Level
18 Regular; 0 Special Education; 0 Vocational; 6 Alternative
0 Magnet; 0 Charter; 12 Title I Eligible; 9 School-wide Title I
Students: 11,592 (52.6% male; 47.4% female)
Individual Education Program: 1,379 (11.9%);
English Language Learner: 459 (4.0%); Migrant: 73 (0.6%)
Eligible for Free Lunch Program: 5,547 (47.9%)
Eligible for Reduced-Price Lunch Program: 1,290 (11.1%)
Teachers: 693.0 (16.7 to 1)
Librarians/Media Specialists: 20.1 (576.7 to 1)
Guidance Counselors: 22.0 (526.9 to 1)
Current Spending: ($ per student per year):
Total: $5,391; Instruction: $3,429; Support Services: $1,610
Enrollment, Drop-out Rates and Diploma Recipients by Race/Ethnicity

Category	Total	White	Black	Asian	AIAN	Hisp.
Enrollment (%)	100.0	86.9	9.5	1.3	0.2	2.1
Drop-out Rate (%)	2.7	2.7	2.8	2.2	0.0	3.0
H.S. Diplomas (#)	706	631	54	12	2	7

Washington County

Washington County

120 Mackville Hill • Springfie, KY 40069-0192
(859) 336-5470
Grade Span: PK-12; **Agency Type:** 1
Schools: 5
3 Primary; 0 Middle; 2 High; 0 Other Level
4 Regular; 0 Special Education; 0 Vocational; 1 Alternative
0 Magnet; 0 Charter; 4 Title I Eligible; 3 School-wide Title I
Students: 1,922 (51.5% male; 48.5% female)
Individual Education Program: 360 (18.7%);
English Language Learner: 0 (0.0%); Migrant: 43 (2.2%)
Eligible for Free Lunch Program: 1,012 (52.7%)
Eligible for Reduced-Price Lunch Program: 389 (20.2%)
Teachers: 117.7 (16.3 to 1)
Librarians/Media Specialists: 3.0 (640.7 to 1)
Guidance Counselors: 2.0 (961.0 to 1)
Current Spending: ($ per student per year):
Total: $5,740; Instruction: $3,625; Support Services: $1,768
Enrollment, Drop-out Rates and Diploma Recipients by Race/Ethnicity

Category	Total	White	Black	Asian	AIAN	Hisp.
Enrollment (%)	100.0	87.1	9.6	0.4	0.1	2.9
Drop-out Rate (%)	4.9	5.1	3.3	0.0	n/a	0.0
H.S. Diplomas (#)	108	97	10	1	0	0

Wayne County

Wayne County

534 Albany Rd • Monticello, KY 42633-0437
(606) 348-8484 • http://www.wayne.k12.ky.us/
Grade Span: PK-12; **Agency Type:** 1
Schools: 8
3 Primary; 2 Middle; 1 High; 2 Other Level
6 Regular; 0 Special Education; 0 Vocational; 2 Alternative
0 Magnet; 0 Charter; 5 Title I Eligible; 4 School-wide Title I
Students: 2,837 (53.4% male; 46.6% female)
Individual Education Program: 421 (14.8%);
English Language Learner: 0 (0.0%); Migrant: 215 (7.6%)
Eligible for Free Lunch Program: 1,935 (68.2%)
Eligible for Reduced-Price Lunch Program: 550 (19.4%)
Teachers: 165.8 (17.1 to 1)
Librarians/Media Specialists: 5.0 (567.4 to 1)
Guidance Counselors: 7.0 (405.3 to 1)
Current Spending: ($ per student per year):
Total: $6,757; Instruction: $4,095; Support Services: $2,292
Enrollment, Drop-out Rates and Diploma Recipients by Race/Ethnicity

Category	Total	White	Black	Asian	AIAN	Hisp.
Enrollment (%)	100.0	97.2	2.2	0.0	0.2	0.4
Drop-out Rate (%)	5.6	5.8	0.0	n/a	n/a	0.0
H.S. Diplomas (#)	140	134	4	0	0	2

Webster County

Webster County

US Hwy 41A • Dixon, KY 42409-0420
(270) 639-5083 • http://proxy.atc.webster.k12.ky.us/
Grade Span: PK-12; **Agency Type:** 1
Schools: 6
4 Primary; 0 Middle; 1 High; 1 Other Level
5 Regular; 0 Special Education; 0 Vocational; 1 Alternative
0 Magnet; 0 Charter; 4 Title I Eligible; 0 School-wide Title I
Students: 2,051 (49.5% male; 50.5% female)
Individual Education Program: 295 (14.4%);
English Language Learner: 69 (3.4%); Migrant: 76 (3.7%)
Eligible for Free Lunch Program: 913 (44.5%)
Eligible for Reduced-Price Lunch Program: 273 (13.3%)
Teachers: 108.9 (18.8 to 1)
Librarians/Media Specialists: 3.0 (683.7 to 1)
Guidance Counselors: 4.5 (455.8 to 1)
Current Spending: ($ per student per year):
Total: $5,814; Instruction: $3,304; Support Services: $2,133
Enrollment, Drop-out Rates and Diploma Recipients by Race/Ethnicity

Category	Total	White	Black	Asian	AIAN	Hisp.
Enrollment (%)	100.0	96.6	1.4	0.2	0.0	1.8
Drop-out Rate (%)	4.5	4.6	0.0	0.0	n/a	0.0
H.S. Diplomas (#)	137	135	2	0	0	0

Whitley County

Corbin Independent

108 E Center St • Corbin, KY 40701-1302
Mailing Address: 108 Roy Kidd Ave • Corbin, KY 40701-1302
(606) 528-1303 • http://www.corbinschools.org/
Grade Span: PK-12; **Agency Type:** 1
Schools: 9
2 Primary; 2 Middle; 4 High; 1 Other Level
4 Regular; 0 Special Education; 0 Vocational; 5 Alternative
0 Magnet; 0 Charter; 4 Title I Eligible; 3 School-wide Title I
Students: 2,174 (51.2% male; 48.8% female)
Individual Education Program: 281 (12.9%);
English Language Learner: 0 (0.0%); Migrant: 0 (0.0%)
Eligible for Free Lunch Program: 1,046 (48.1%)
Eligible for Reduced-Price Lunch Program: 337 (15.5%)
Teachers: 136.8 (15.9 to 1)
Librarians/Media Specialists: 4.0 (543.5 to 1)
Guidance Counselors: 6.0 (362.3 to 1)
Current Spending: ($ per student per year):
Total: $6,345; Instruction: $4,319; Support Services: $1,533
Enrollment, Drop-out Rates and Diploma Recipients by Race/Ethnicity

Category	Total	White	Black	Asian	AIAN	Hisp.
Enrollment (%)	100.0	99.2	0.1	0.5	0.0	0.1
Drop-out Rate (%)	3.5	3.5	n/a	0.0	n/a	0.0
H.S. Diplomas (#)	150	148	0	1	0	1

Whitley County

116 N 4th St • Williamsburg, KY 40769-1115
(606) 549-7000 • http://whitley.k12.ky.us/
Grade Span: PK-12; **Agency Type:** 1
Schools: 11
8 Primary; 1 Middle; 2 High; 0 Other Level
10 Regular; 0 Special Education; 0 Vocational; 1 Alternative
0 Magnet; 0 Charter; 9 Title I Eligible; 9 School-wide Title I
Students: 4,706 (51.7% male; 48.3% female)
Individual Education Program: 784 (16.7%);
English Language Learner: 0 (0.0%); Migrant: 0 (0.0%)
Eligible for Free Lunch Program: 3,593 (76.3%)
Eligible for Reduced-Price Lunch Program: 870 (18.5%)
Teachers: 292.0 (16.1 to 1)
Librarians/Media Specialists: 9.0 (522.9 to 1)
Guidance Counselors: 5.0 (941.2 to 1)
Current Spending: ($ per student per year):
Total: $6,197; Instruction: $3,653; Support Services: $2,176
Enrollment, Drop-out Rates and Diploma Recipients by Race/Ethnicity

Category	Total	White	Black	Asian	AIAN	Hisp.
Enrollment (%)	100.0	99.8	0.1	0.0	0.0	0.0
Drop-out Rate (%)	5.2	5.3	n/a	n/a	n/a	0.0
H.S. Diplomas (#)	225	225	0	0	0	0

Woodford County

Woodford County

330 Pisgah Pike • Versailles, KY 40383-1418
(859) 873-4701 • http://www.woodford.k12.ky.us/
Grade Span: PK-12; **Agency Type:** 1
Schools: 8
5 Primary; 1 Middle; 1 High; 1 Other Level
7 Regular; 0 Special Education; 0 Vocational; 1 Alternative
0 Magnet; 0 Charter; 3 Title I Eligible; 0 School-wide Title I
Students: 3,829 (50.3% male; 49.7% female)
Individual Education Program: 442 (11.5%);
English Language Learner: 119 (3.1%); Migrant: 64 (1.7%)
Eligible for Free Lunch Program: 963 (25.2%)
Eligible for Reduced-Price Lunch Program: 273 (7.1%)
Teachers: 233.9 (16.4 to 1)
Librarians/Media Specialists: 8.0 (478.6 to 1)

Guidance Counselors: 6.9 (554.9 to 1)
Current Spending: ($ per student per year):
Total: $5,476; Instruction: $3,548; Support Services: $1,635

Enrollment, Drop-out Rates and Diploma Recipients by Race/Ethnicity

Category	Total	White	Black	Asian	AIAN	Hisp.
Enrollment (%)	100.0	89.9	6.5	0.2	0.2	3.3
Drop-out Rate (%)	3.6	3.6	5.6	0.0	0.0	0.0
H.S. Diplomas (#)	222	205	11	2	0	4

Number of Schools

Rank	Number	District Name	City
1	175	Jefferson County	Louisville
2	64	Fayette County	Lexington
3	26	Pike County	Pikeville
4	25	Hardin County	Elizabe
5	24	Warren County	Bowling Gre
6	22	Daviess County	Owensboro
6	22	Kenton County	Erlanger
8	21	Boone County	Florence
9	20	Bullitt County	Shepherdsville
9	20	Christian County	Hopkinsville
11	18	Floyd County	Prestons
11	18	Laurel County	London
11	18	Madison County	Richmond
14	17	Oldham County	Buckner
15	15	Mccracken County	Paducah
16	14	Hopkins County	Madisonvi
16	14	Muhlenberg County	Greenville
16	14	Owensboro Independent	Owensboro
16	14	Perry County	Hazard
16	14	Pulaski County	Somerset
16	14	Scott County	Georgetown
22	13	Clark County	Winchester
22	13	Covington Independent	Covington
22	13	Henderson County	Henderson
22	13	Letcher County	Whitesburg
26	12	Clay County	Manchester
26	12	Franklin County	Frankfort
26	12	Graves County	Mayfield
29	11	Bowling Green Independent	Bowling Green
29	11	Carter County	Grayson
29	11	Harlan County	Harlan
29	11	Jessamine County	Nicholasville
29	11	Knott County	Hindman
29	11	Knox County	Barbourvill
29	11	Marshall County	Benton
29	11	Mccreary County	Stearns
29	11	Whitley County	Williamsburg
38	10	Campbell County	Alexandria
38	10	Lincoln County	Stanford
38	10	Meade County	Brandenburg
38	10	Nelson County	Bardstown
38	10	Ohio County	Hartford
38	10	Shelby County	Shelbyville
44	9	Ashland Ind	Ashland
44	9	Barren County	Glasgow
44	9	Boyd County	Ashland
44	9	Breathitt County	Jackson
44	9	Corbin Independent	Corbin
44	9	Johnson County	Paintsville
44	9	Martin County	Inez
44	9	Montgomery County	Mount Sterling
44	9	Paducah Independent	Paducah
44	9	Union County	Morganfiel
54	8	Adair County	Columbia
54	8	Bell County	Pineville
54	8	Casey County	Liberty
54	8	Fort Campbell District	Fort Campbell
54	8	Fort Knox District	Fort Knox
54	8	Greenup County	Greenup
54	8	Harrison County	Cynthiana
54	8	Leslie County	Hyden
54	8	Magoffin County	Salyersville
54	8	Morgan County	West Liberty
54	8	Wayne County	Monticello
54	8	Woodford County	Versailles
66	7	Boyle County	Danville
66	7	Butler County	Morgantown
66	7	Estill County	Irvine
66	7	Grayson County	Leitchfield
66	7	Lewis County	Vanceburg
66	7	Marion County	Lebanon
66	7	Newport Independent	Newport
66	7	Rowan County	Morehead
74	6	Anderson County	Lawrenceburg
74	6	Bourbon County	Paris
74	6	Breckinridge County	Hardinsburg
74	6	Calloway County	Murray
74	6	Danville Independent	Danville
74	6	Erlanger-Elsmere Independent	Erlanger
74	6	Fleming County	Flemingsburg
74	6	Garrard County	Lancaster
74	6	Glasgow Independent	Glasgow
74	6	Grant County	Williamsto
74	6	Hart County	Munfordville
74	6	Jackson County	Mckee
74	6	Larue County	Hodgenville
74	6	Logan County	Russellville
74	6	Mclean County	Calhoun
74	6	Rockcastle County	Mount Verno
74	6	Russell County	Jamestown
74	6	Simpson County	Franklin
74	6	Webster County	Dixon
93	5	Bardstown Independent	Bardstown
93	5	Bath County	Owingsv
93	5	Carroll County	Carrollton
93	5	Edmonson County	Brownsville
93	5	Fort Thomas Independent	Fort Thomas
93	5	Green County	Greensburg
93	5	Hancock County	Hawesville
93	5	Henry County	New Castle
93	5	Lawrence County	Louisa
93	5	Mayfield Independent	Mayfiel
93	5	Metcalfe County	Edmonton
93	5	Middlesboro Independent	Middlesboro
93	5	Monroe County	Tompkinsville
93	5	Powell County	Stanton
93	5	Washington County	Springfie
108	4	Allen County	Scottsville
108	4	Ballard County	Barlow
108	4	Caldwell County	Princeton
108	4	Elizabethtown Independent	Elizabethtow
108	4	Mason County	Maysville
108	4	Mercer County	Harrodsburg
108	4	Murray Independent	Murray
108	4	Owen County	Owenton
108	4	Pendleton County	Falmouth
108	4	Russell Independent	Russell
108	4	Taylor County	Campbellsville
108	4	Todd County	Elkton
108	4	Trimble County	Bedford
121	3	Clinton County	Albany
121	3	Somerset Independent	Somerset
121	3	Spencer County	Taylorsvil
121	3	Trigg County	Cadiz

Number of Teachers

Rank	Number	District Name	City
1	5,328	Jefferson County	Louisville
2	2,491	Fayette County	Lexington
3	856	Boone County	Florence
4	810	Hardin County	Elizabe
5	705	Kenton County	Erlanger
6	693	Warren County	Bowling Gre
7	688	Pike County	Pikeville
8	649	Daviess County	Owensboro
9	644	Bullitt County	Shepherdsville
10	567	Madison County	Richmond
11	561	Oldham County	Buckner
12	546	Christian County	Hopkinsville
13	494	Laurel County	London
14	479	Pulaski County	Somerset
15	454	Hopkins County	Madisonvi
16	446	Jessamine County	Nicholasville
17	440	Floyd County	Prestons
18	435	Henderson County	Henderson
19	401	Scott County	Georgetown
20	389	Mccracken County	Paducah
21	366	Franklin County	Frankfort
22	358	Muhlenberg County	Greenville
23	344	Covington Independent	Covington
24	342	Harlan County	Harlan
25	333	Perry County	Hazard
26	333	Carter County	Grayson
27	332	Clark County	Winchester
28	324	Shelby County	Shelbyville
29	323	Owensboro Independent	Owensboro
30	313	Clay County	Manchester
31	310	Knox County	Barbourvill
32	310	Fort Campbell District	Fort Campbell
33	306	Marshall County	Benton
34	292	Whitley County	Williamsburg
35	285	Campbell County	Alexandria
36	284	Nelson County	Bardstown
37	272	Grayson County	Leitchfield
38	269	Barren County	Glasgow
39	269	Graves County	Mayfield
40	265	Meade County	Brandenburg
41	264	Lincoln County	Stanford
42	259	Ohio County	Hartford
43	259	Montgomery County	Mount Sterling
44	246	Letcher County	Whitesburg
45	246	Boyd County	Ashland
46	242	Johnson County	Paintsville
47	233	Woodford County	Versailles
48	233	Mccreary County	Stearns
49	231	Bowling Green Independent	Bowling Green
50	228	Fort Knox District	Fort Knox
51	226	Bell County	Pineville
52	221	Paducah Independent	Paducah
53	211	Ashland Ind	Ashland
54	210	Grant County	Williamsto
55	209	Logan County	Russellville
56	206	Rowan County	Morehead
57	205	Anderson County	Lawrenceburg
58	204	Russell County	Jamestown
59	203	Calloway County	Murray
60	199	Rockcastle County	Mount Verno
61	197	Greenup County	Greenup
62	195	Marion County	Lebanon
63	192	Knott County	Hindman
64	191	Harrison County	Cynthiana
65	190	Adair County	Columbia
66	186	Newport Independent	Newport
67	186	Boyle County	Danville
68	184	Estill County	Irvine
69	183	Lawrence County	Louisa
70	183	Simpson County	Franklin
71	179	Powell County	Stanton
72	178	Bourbon County	Paris
73	178	Pendleton County	Falmouth
74	175	Mason County	Maysville
75	172	Martin County	Inez
76	171	Morgan County	West Liberty
77	169	Garrard County	Lancaster
77	169	Magoffin County	Salyersville
79	167	Allen County	Scottsville
80	167	Lewis County	Vanceburg
81	166	Union County	Morganfiel
82	165	Wayne County	Monticello
83	164	Jackson County	Mckee
84	159	Breathitt County	Jackson
85	159	Casey County	Liberty
86	158	Taylor County	Campbellsville
87	155	Hart County	Munfordville
88	155	Fleming County	Flemingsburg
89	152	Breckinridge County	Hardinsburg
90	149	Butler County	Morgantown
91	148	Larue County	Hodgenville
92	144	Fort Thomas Independent	Fort Thomas
93	143	Leslie County	Hyden
94	141	Monroe County	Tompkinsville
95	137	Elizabethtown Independent	Elizabethtow
96	137	Caldwell County	Princeton
97	136	Corbin Independent	Corbin
98	136	Mercer County	Harrodsburg
99	135	Glasgow Independent	Glasgow
100	133	Erlanger-Elsmere Independent	Erlanger
101	132	Edmonson County	Brownsville
102	130	Spencer County	Taylorsvil
103	128	Henry County	New Castle
104	128	Trigg County	Cadiz
105	128	Danville Independent	Danville
106	126	Bardstown Independent	Bardstown
106	126	Bath County	Owingsv
108	121	Todd County	Elkton
109	117	Russell Independent	Russell
110	117	Washington County	Springfie
111	117	Middlesboro Independent	Middlesboro
112	114	Green County	Greensburg
113	112	Metcalfe County	Edmonton
114	111	Carroll County	Carrollton
115	108	Webster County	Dixon
116	108	Owen County	Owenton
117	106	Mclean County	Calhoun
118	103	Clinton County	Albany
119	102	Mayfield Independent	Mayfiel
120	99	Murray Independent	Murray
121	99	Somerset Independent	Somerset
122	95	Hancock County	Hawesville
123	87	Ballard County	Barlow
124	86	Trimble County	Bedford

Number of Students

Rank	Number	District Name	City
1	95,651	Jefferson County	Louisville
2	34,296	Fayette County	Lexington
3	14,650	Boone County	Florence
4	13,391	Hardin County	Elizabe
5	12,668	Kenton County	Erlanger
6	11,592	Warren County	Bowling Gre
7	11,451	Bullitt County	Shepherdsville
8	10,786	Daviess County	Owensboro
9	10,625	Pike County	Pikeville
10	9,744	Madison County	Richmond
11	9,689	Oldham County	Buckner
12	9,609	Christian County	Hopkinsville
13	8,884	Laurel County	London
14	7,923	Pulaski County	Somerset
15	7,455	Hopkins County	Madisonvi
16	7,149	Floyd County	Prestons
17	7,122	Henderson County	Henderson
18	7,056	Jessamine County	Nicholasville
19	6,930	Mccracken County	Paducah
20	6,344	Scott County	Georgetown

21	6,025	Franklin County	Frankfort
22	5,509	Shelby County	Shelbyville
23	5,457	Clark County	Winchester
24	5,316	Muhlenberg County	Greenville
25	5,284	Harlan County	Harlan
26	5,198	Knox County	Barbourvill
27	5,177	Carter County	Grayson
28	4,851	Perry County	Hazard
29	4,850	Nelson County	Bardstown
30	4,823	Marshall County	Benton
31	4,741	Campbell County	Alexandria
32	4,733	Covington Independent	Covington
33	4,706	Whitley County	Williamsburg
34	4,704	Graves County	Mayfield
35	4,674	Meade County	Brandenburg
36	4,419	Lincoln County	Stanford
37	4,376	Fort Campbell District	Fort Campbell
38	4,355	Montgomery County	Mount Sterling
39	4,317	Grayson County	Leitchfield
40	4,292	Owensboro Independent	Owensboro
41	4,247	Clay County	Manchester
42	4,144	Barren County	Glasgow
43	4,136	Ohio County	Hartford
44	3,938	Anderson County	Lawrenceburg
45	3,887	Grant County	Williamsto
46	3,829	Woodford County	Versailles
47	3,786	Johnson County	Paintsville
48	3,749	Boyd County	Ashland
49	3,633	Bowling Green Independent	Bowling Green
50	3,512	Letcher County	Whitesburg
51	3,467	Logan County	Russellville
52	3,446	Mccreary County	Stearns
53	3,354	Ashland Ind	Ashland
54	3,316	Harrison County	Cynthiana
55	3,311	Bell County	Pineville
56	3,289	Paducah Independent	Paducah
57	3,236	Greenup County	Greenup
58	3,148	Rowan County	Morehead
59	3,146	Calloway County	Murray
60	3,085	Allen County	Scottsville
61	3,070	Simpson County	Franklin
62	3,038	Rockcastle County	Mount Verno
63	3,032	Marion County	Lebanon
64	2,988	Fort Knox District	Fort Knox
64	2,988	Pendleton County	Falmouth
66	2,928	Knott County	Hindman
67	2,919	Bourbon County	Paris
68	2,886	Boyle County	Danville
69	2,867	Russell County	Jamestown
70	2,837	Wayne County	Monticello
71	2,816	Breckinridge County	Hardinsburg
72	2,806	Mason County	Maysville
73	2,752	Adair County	Columbia
74	2,744	Lawrence County	Louisa
75	2,703	Estill County	Irvine
76	2,701	Taylor County	Campbellsville
77	2,662	Powell County	Stanton
78	2,634	Garrard County	Lancaster
79	2,557	Magoffin County	Salyersville
80	2,556	Union County	Morganfiel
81	2,554	Newport Independent	Newport
82	2,535	Martin County	Inez
83	2,517	Lewis County	Vanceburg
84	2,515	Casey County	Liberty
85	2,507	Hart County	Munfordville
86	2,489	Morgan County	West Liberty
87	2,473	Fleming County	Flemingsburg
88	2,435	Jackson County	Mckee
89	2,411	Larue County	Hodgenville
90	2,401	Spencer County	Taylorsvil
91	2,386	Breathitt County	Jackson
92	2,345	Elizabethtown Independent	Elizabethtow
93	2,301	Fort Thomas Independent	Fort Thomas
94	2,274	Mercer County	Harrodsburg
95	2,263	Butler County	Morgantown
96	2,260	Leslie County	Hyden
97	2,239	Erlanger-Elsmere Independent	Erlanger
98	2,213	Henry County	New Castle
99	2,174	Corbin Independent	Corbin
100	2,168	Todd County	Elkton
101	2,152	Russell Independent	Russell
102	2,129	Trigg County	Cadiz
103	2,120	Caldwell County	Princeton
104	2,103	Edmonson County	Brownsville
105	2,094	Bardstown Independent	Bardstown
106	2,088	Monroe County	Tompkinsville
107	2,059	Bath County	Owingsv
108	2,051	Webster County	Dixon
109	2,029	Glasgow Independent	Glasgow
110	1,976	Owen County	Owenton
111	1,922	Washington County	Springfie
112	1,911	Carroll County	Carrollton
113	1,876	Danville Independent	Danville
114	1,868	Middlesboro Independent	Middlesboro
115	1,721	Murray Independent	Murray
116	1,702	Green County	Greensburg
117	1,697	Mclean County	Calhoun
118	1,673	Metcalfe County	Edmonton
119	1,653	Clinton County	Albany
120	1,611	Trimble County	Bedford
121	1,605	Hancock County	Hawesville
122	1,568	Somerset Independent	Somerset
123	1,556	Mayfield Independent	Mayfiel
124	1,509	Ballard County	Barlow

Male Students

Rank	Percent	District Name	City
1	55.8	Martin County	Inez
2	55.0	Danville Independent	Danville
3	54.5	Monroe County	Tompkinsville
4	54.3	Breathitt County	Jackson
5	54.1	Scott County	Georgetown
6	53.7	Morgan County	West Liberty
6	53.7	Owen County	Owenton
8	53.6	Covington Independent	Covington
8	53.6	Letcher County	Whitesburg
8	53.6	Lewis County	Vanceburg
11	53.5	Erlanger-Elsmere Independent	Erlanger
11	53.5	Mercer County	Harrodsburg
11	53.5	Trigg County	Cadiz
14	53.4	Hart County	Munfordville
14	53.4	Wayne County	Monticello
16	53.3	Kenton County	Erlanger
16	53.3	Leslie County	Hyden
18	53.2	Lawrence County	Louisa
18	53.2	Pike County	Pikeville
20	53.1	Mayfield Independent	Mayfiel
21	52.9	Campbell County	Alexandria
21	52.9	Garrard County	Lancaster
23	52.8	Bath County	Owingsv
24	52.7	Henry County	New Castle
24	52.7	Jessamine County	Nicholasville
24	52.7	Metcalfe County	Edmonton
27	52.6	Ballard County	Barlow
27	52.6	Franklin County	Frankfort
27	52.6	Warren County	Bowling Gre
30	52.5	Clay County	Manchester
30	52.5	Edmonson County	Brownsville
30	52.5	Hardin County	Elizabe
30	52.5	Harrison County	Cynthiana
30	52.5	Jackson County	Mckee
30	52.5	Knott County	Hindman
30	52.5	Larue County	Hodgenville
30	52.5	Mason County	Maysville
30	52.5	Perry County	Hazard
39	52.4	Glasgow Independent	Glasgow
39	52.4	Knox County	Barbourvill
39	52.4	Lincoln County	Stanford
39	52.4	Powell County	Stanton
39	52.4	Somerset Independent	Somerset
39	52.4	Spencer County	Taylorsvil
45	52.3	Grayson County	Leitchfield
45	52.3	Mccracken County	Paducah
47	52.2	Simpson County	Franklin
48	52.1	Caldwell County	Princeton
48	52.1	Daviess County	Owensboro
48	52.1	Fort Thomas Independent	Fort Thomas
48	52.1	Green County	Greensburg
48	52.1	Marshall County	Benton
48	52.1	Pulaski County	Somerset
48	52.1	Rockcastle County	Mount Verno
48	52.1	Trimble County	Bedford
56	52.0	Boone County	Florence
56	52.0	Carroll County	Carrollton
56	52.0	Christian County	Hopkinsville
56	52.0	Floyd County	Prestons
56	52.0	Grant County	Williamsto
56	52.0	Harlan County	Harlan
56	52.0	Laurel County	London
56	52.0	Owensboro Independent	Owensboro
56	52.0	Shelby County	Shelbyville
65	51.9	Bell County	Pineville
65	51.9	Boyd County	Ashland
65	51.9	Graves County	Mayfield
65	51.9	Middlesboro Independent	Middlesboro
65	51.9	Muhlenberg County	Greenville
70	51.8	Bullitt County	Shepherdsville
70	51.8	Johnson County	Paintsville
70	51.8	Logan County	Russellville
73	51.7	Breckinridge County	Hardinsburg
73	51.7	Henderson County	Henderson
73	51.7	Mccreary County	Stearns
73	51.7	Russell Independent	Russell
73	51.7	Whitley County	Williamsburg
78	51.6	Bardstown Independent	Bardstown
78	51.6	Clark County	Winchester
78	51.6	Fleming County	Flemingsburg
78	51.6	Marion County	Lebanon
78	51.6	Pendleton County	Falmouth
83	51.5	Boyle County	Danville
83	51.5	Calloway County	Murray
83	51.5	Estill County	Irvine
83	51.5	Fayette County	Lexington
83	51.5	Magoffin County	Salyersville
83	51.5	Washington County	Springfie
89	51.4	Ashland Ind	Ashland
89	51.4	Bowling Green Independent	Bowling Green
89	51.4	Jefferson County	Louisville
89	51.4	Meade County	Brandenburg
89	51.4	Union County	Morganfiel
94	51.3	Greenup County	Greenup
94	51.3	Hancock County	Hawesville
94	51.3	Madison County	Richmond
94	51.3	Montgomery County	Mount Sterling
94	51.3	Ohio County	Hartford
94	51.3	Oldham County	Buckner
100	51.2	Anderson County	Lawrenceburg
100	51.2	Corbin Independent	Corbin
102	51.1	Bourbon County	Paris
102	51.1	Nelson County	Bardstown
104	51.0	Butler County	Morgantown
104	51.0	Mclean County	Calhoun
106	50.9	Hopkins County	Madisonvi
106	50.9	Murray Independent	Murray
106	50.9	Newport Independent	Newport
109	50.8	Carter County	Grayson
109	50.8	Casey County	Liberty
109	50.8	Russell County	Jamestown
112	50.7	Adair County	Columbia
112	50.7	Allen County	Scottsville
112	50.7	Elizabethtown Independent	Elizabethtow
112	50.7	Taylor County	Campbellsville
116	50.6	Todd County	Elkton
117	50.5	Barren County	Glasgow
118	50.4	Clinton County	Albany
119	50.3	Woodford County	Versailles
120	49.8	Rowan County	Morehead
121	49.6	Paducah Independent	Paducah
122	49.5	Webster County	Dixon
123	n/a	Fort Campbell District	Fort Campbell
123	n/a	Fort Knox District	Fort Knox

Female Students

Rank	Percent	District Name	City
1	50.5	Webster County	Dixon
2	50.4	Paducah Independent	Paducah
3	50.2	Rowan County	Morehead
4	49.7	Woodford County	Versailles
5	49.6	Clinton County	Albany
6	49.5	Barren County	Glasgow
7	49.4	Todd County	Elkton
8	49.3	Adair County	Columbia
8	49.3	Allen County	Scottsville
8	49.3	Elizabethtown Independent	Elizabethtow
8	49.3	Taylor County	Campbellsville
12	49.2	Carter County	Grayson
12	49.2	Casey County	Liberty
12	49.2	Russell County	Jamestown
15	49.1	Hopkins County	Madisonvi
15	49.1	Murray Independent	Murray
15	49.1	Newport Independent	Newport
18	49.0	Butler County	Morgantown
18	49.0	Mclean County	Calhoun
20	48.9	Bourbon County	Paris
20	48.9	Nelson County	Bardstown
22	48.8	Anderson County	Lawrenceburg
22	48.8	Corbin Independent	Corbin
24	48.7	Greenup County	Greenup
24	48.7	Hancock County	Hawesville
24	48.7	Madison County	Richmond
24	48.7	Montgomery County	Mount Sterling
24	48.7	Ohio County	Hartford
24	48.7	Oldham County	Buckner
30	48.6	Ashland Ind	Ashland
30	48.6	Bowling Green Independent	Bowling Green
30	48.6	Jefferson County	Louisville
30	48.6	Meade County	Brandenburg
30	48.6	Union County	Morganfiel
35	48.5	Boyle County	Danville
35	48.5	Calloway County	Murray
35	48.5	Estill County	Irvine
35	48.5	Fayette County	Lexington
35	48.5	Magoffin County	Salyersville
35	48.5	Washington County	Springfie
41	48.4	Bardstown Independent	Bardstown
41	48.4	Clark County	Winchester
41	48.4	Fleming County	Flemingsburg

41	48.4	Marion County	Lebanon
41	48.4	Pendleton County	Falmouth
46	48.3	Breckinridge County	Hardinsburg
46	48.3	Henderson County	Henderson
46	48.3	Mccreary County	Stearns
46	48.3	Russell Independent	Russell
46	48.3	Whitley County	Williamsburg
51	48.2	Bullitt County	Shepherdsville
51	48.2	Johnson County	Paintsville
51	48.2	Logan County	Russellville
54	48.1	Bell County	Pineville
54	48.1	Boyd County	Ashland
54	48.1	Graves County	Mayfield
54	48.1	Middlesboro Independent	Middlesboro
54	48.1	Muhlenberg County	Greenville
59	48.0	Boone County	Florence
59	48.0	Carroll County	Carrollton
59	48.0	Christian County	Hopkinsville
59	48.0	Floyd County	Prestons
59	48.0	Grant County	Williamsto
59	48.0	Harlan County	Harlan
59	48.0	Laurel County	London
59	48.0	Owensboro Independent	Owensboro
59	48.0	Shelby County	Shelbyville
68	47.9	Caldwell County	Princeton
68	47.9	Daviess County	Owensboro
68	47.9	Fort Thomas Independent	Fort Thomas
68	47.9	Green County	Greensburg
68	47.9	Marshall County	Benton
68	47.9	Pulaski County	Somerset
68	47.9	Rockcastle County	Mount Verno
68	47.9	Trimble County	Bedford
76	47.8	Simpson County	Franklin
77	47.7	Grayson County	Leitchfield
77	47.7	Mccracken County	Paducah
79	47.6	Glasgow Independent	Glasgow
79	47.6	Knox County	Barbourvill
79	47.6	Lincoln County	Stanford
79	47.6	Powell County	Stanton
79	47.6	Somerset Independent	Somerset
79	47.6	Spencer County	Taylorsvil
85	47.5	Clay County	Manchester
85	47.5	Edmonson County	Brownsville
85	47.5	Hardin County	Elizabe
85	47.5	Harrison County	Cynthiana
85	47.5	Jackson County	Mckee
85	47.5	Knott County	Hindman
85	47.5	Larue County	Hodgenville
85	47.5	Mason County	Maysville
85	47.5	Perry County	Hazard
94	47.4	Ballard County	Barlow
94	47.4	Franklin County	Frankfort
94	47.4	Warren County	Bowling Gre
97	47.3	Henry County	New Castle
97	47.3	Jessamine County	Nicholasville
97	47.3	Metcalfe County	Edmonton
100	47.2	Bath County	Owingsv
101	47.1	Campbell County	Alexandria
101	47.1	Garrard County	Lancaster
103	46.9	Mayfield Independent	Mayfiel
104	46.8	Lawrence County	Louisa
104	46.8	Pike County	Pikeville
106	46.7	Kenton County	Erlanger
106	46.7	Leslie County	Hyden
108	46.6	Hart County	Munfordville
108	46.6	Wayne County	Monticello
110	46.5	Erlanger-Elsmere Independent	Erlanger
110	46.5	Mercer County	Harrodsburg
110	46.5	Trigg County	Cadiz
113	46.4	Covington Independent	Covington
113	46.4	Letcher County	Whitesburg
113	46.4	Lewis County	Vanceburg
116	46.3	Morgan County	West Liberty
116	46.3	Owen County	Owenton
118	45.9	Scott County	Georgetown
119	45.7	Breathitt County	Jackson
120	45.5	Monroe County	Tompkinsville
121	45.0	Danville Independent	Danville
122	44.2	Martin County	Inez
123	n/a	Fort Campbell District	Fort Campbell
123	n/a	Fort Knox District	Fort Knox

Individual Education Program Students

Rank	Percent	District Name	City
1	23.2	Union County	Morganfiel
2	22.7	Clay County	Manchester
3	21.5	Breathitt County	Jackson
4	21.0	Martin County	Inez
5	20.5	Ballard County	Barlow
5	20.5	Letcher County	Whitesburg
7	20.1	Boyle County	Danville
7	20.1	Lincoln County	Stanford
9	19.3	Todd County	Elkton
10	19.2	Knott County	Hindman
10	19.2	Madison County	Richmond
12	19.1	Clinton County	Albany
13	19.0	Rowan County	Morehead
14	18.7	Edmonson County	Brownsville
14	18.7	Washington County	Springfie
16	18.6	Estill County	Irvine
17	18.3	Hart County	Munfordville
17	18.3	Hopkins County	Madisonvi
17	18.3	Logan County	Russellville
17	18.3	Perry County	Hazard
21	18.2	Anderson County	Lawrenceburg
21	18.2	Leslie County	Hyden
23	17.9	Calloway County	Murray
23	17.9	Owensboro Independent	Owensboro
25	17.7	Morgan County	West Liberty
25	17.7	Powell County	Stanton
27	17.6	Boyd County	Ashland
27	17.6	Larue County	Hodgenville
29	17.5	Carter County	Grayson
30	17.3	Campbell County	Alexandria
30	17.3	Christian County	Hopkinsville
30	17.3	Jackson County	Mckee
30	17.3	Newport Independent	Newport
34	17.2	Covington Independent	Covington
34	17.2	Greenup County	Greenup
36	17.1	Marion County	Lebanon
36	17.1	Russell County	Jamestown
38	17.0	Danville Independent	Danville
38	17.0	Spencer County	Taylorsvil
40	16.9	Adair County	Columbia
41	16.8	Middlesboro Independent	Middlesboro
42	16.7	Muhlenberg County	Greenville
42	16.7	Whitley County	Williamsburg
44	16.6	Lewis County	Vanceburg
45	16.5	Casey County	Liberty
45	16.5	Erlanger-Elsmere Independent	Erlanger
47	16.4	Mccreary County	Stearns
48	16.3	Henderson County	Henderson
49	16.2	Mercer County	Harrodsburg
50	16.1	Ohio County	Hartford
51	15.9	Butler County	Morgantown
51	15.9	Harlan County	Harlan
51	15.9	Jessamine County	Nicholasville
51	15.9	Nelson County	Bardstown
51	15.9	Trigg County	Cadiz
56	15.8	Laurel County	London
57	15.7	Rockcastle County	Mount Verno
58	15.6	Ashland Ind	Ashland
58	15.6	Harrison County	Cynthiana
58	15.6	Knox County	Barbourvill
58	15.6	Lawrence County	Louisa
62	15.5	Bell County	Pineville
62	15.5	Bourbon County	Paris
64	15.4	Daviess County	Owensboro
64	15.4	Floyd County	Prestons
66	15.3	Breckinridge County	Hardinsburg
66	15.3	Magoffin County	Salyersville
66	15.3	Mayfield Independent	Mayfiel
66	15.3	Meade County	Brandenburg
70	15.2	Barren County	Glasgow
70	15.2	Monroe County	Tompkinsville
72	15.0	Glasgow Independent	Glasgow
72	15.0	Green County	Greensburg
72	15.0	Hardin County	Elizabe
72	15.0	Oldham County	Buckner
76	14.9	Garrard County	Lancaster
76	14.9	Mason County	Maysville
78	14.8	Metcalfe County	Edmonton
78	14.8	Wayne County	Monticello
80	14.7	Clark County	Winchester
80	14.7	Mclean County	Calhoun
82	14.6	Mccracken County	Paducah
83	14.5	Bardstown Independent	Bardstown
83	14.5	Caldwell County	Princeton
83	14.5	Johnson County	Paintsville
86	14.4	Murray Independent	Murray
86	14.4	Webster County	Dixon
88	14.2	Grayson County	Leitchfield
88	14.2	Pulaski County	Somerset
88	14.2	Scott County	Georgetown
91	14.0	Hancock County	Hawesville
92	13.9	Bullitt County	Shepherdsville
92	13.9	Graves County	Mayfield
92	13.9	Jefferson County	Louisville
92	13.9	Owen County	Owenton
96	13.6	Grant County	Williamsto
97	13.5	Pendleton County	Falmouth
98	13.4	Taylor County	Campbellsville
99	13.3	Fleming County	Flemingsburg
100	13.2	Boone County	Florence
100	13.2	Pike County	Pikeville
100	13.2	Shelby County	Shelbyville
103	13.1	Bath County	Owingsv
103	13.1	Franklin County	Frankfort
103	13.1	Paducah Independent	Paducah
103	13.1	Trimble County	Bedford
107	12.9	Corbin Independent	Corbin
107	12.9	Montgomery County	Mount Sterling
107	12.9	Somerset Independent	Somerset
110	12.8	Kenton County	Erlanger
111	12.7	Marshall County	Benton
112	12.5	Carroll County	Carrollton
113	12.1	Allen County	Scottsville
114	11.9	Fort Campbell District	Fort Campbell
114	11.9	Warren County	Bowling Gre
116	11.8	Bowling Green Independent	Bowling Green
117	11.7	Simpson County	Franklin
118	11.5	Henry County	New Castle
118	11.5	Woodford County	Versailles
120	11.1	Russell Independent	Russell
121	11.0	Elizabethtown Independent	Elizabethtow
122	10.4	Fayette County	Lexington
123	10.1	Fort Knox District	Fort Knox
124	9.0	Fort Thomas Independent	Fort Thomas

English Language Learner Students

Rank	Percent	District Name	City
1	8.9	Bowling Green Independent	Bowling Green
2	4.2	Mayfield Independent	Mayfiel
3	4.0	Warren County	Bowling Gre
4	3.5	Shelby County	Shelbyville
5	3.4	Webster County	Dixon
6	3.1	Woodford County	Versailles
7	2.9	Fayette County	Lexington
8	2.8	Carroll County	Carrollton
9	2.6	Jefferson County	Louisville
10	2.2	Boone County	Florence
11	2.1	Grant County	Williamsto
12	1.5	Fort Campbell District	Fort Campbell
12	1.5	Glasgow Independent	Glasgow
14	1.4	Trimble County	Bedford
15	1.2	Murray Independent	Murray
16	1.0	Clinton County	Albany
16	1.0	Jessamine County	Nicholasville
16	1.0	Paducah Independent	Paducah
19	0.9	Danville Independent	Danville
20	0.8	Hardin County	Elizabe
20	0.8	Monroe County	Tompkinsville
20	0.8	Owen County	Owenton
23	0.7	Calloway County	Murray
23	0.7	Clark County	Winchester
23	0.7	Erlanger-Elsmere Independent	Erlanger
23	0.7	Fort Knox District	Fort Knox
23	0.7	Kenton County	Erlanger
23	0.7	Montgomery County	Mount Sterling
23	0.7	Oldham County	Buckner
30	0.6	Christian County	Hopkinsville
30	0.6	Elizabethtown Independent	Elizabethtow
30	0.6	Todd County	Elkton
33	0.5	Daviess County	Owensboro
33	0.5	Garrard County	Lancaster
33	0.5	Henderson County	Henderson
33	0.5	Mccracken County	Paducah
33	0.5	Ohio County	Hartford
33	0.5	Simpson County	Franklin
39	0.4	Bardstown Independent	Bardstown
39	0.4	Bourbon County	Paris
39	0.4	Hart County	Munfordville
39	0.4	Rowan County	Morehead
43	0.3	Madison County	Richmond
43	0.3	Mason County	Maysville
43	0.3	Scott County	Georgetown
46	0.2	Adair County	Columbia
46	0.2	Campbell County	Alexandria
46	0.2	Hancock County	Hawesville
46	0.2	Hopkins County	Madisonvi
46	0.2	Mercer County	Harrodsburg
46	0.2	Pendleton County	Falmouth
46	0.2	Pulaski County	Somerset
46	0.2	Spencer County	Taylorsvil
54	0.1	Fleming County	Flemingsburg
54	0.1	Franklin County	Frankfort
54	0.1	Harrison County	Cynthiana
54	0.1	Knox County	Barbourvill
54	0.1	Metcalfe County	Edmonton
54	0.1	Nelson County	Bardstown
54	0.1	Newport Independent	Newport
54	0.1	Powell County	Stanton
62	0.0	Anderson County	Lawrenceburg
62	0.0	Ashland Ind	Ashland
62	0.0	Bullitt County	Shepherdsville
62	0.0	Butler County	Morgantown
62	0.0	Edmonson County	Brownsville

62	0.0	Grayson County	Leitchfield
62	0.0	Trigg County	Cadiz
62	0.0	Union County	Morganfiel
70	0.0	Allen County	Scottsville
70	0.0	Ballard County	Barlow
70	0.0	Barren County	Glasgow
70	0.0	Bath County	Owingsv
70	0.0	Bell County	Pineville
70	0.0	Boyd County	Ashland
70	0.0	Boyle County	Danville
70	0.0	Breathitt County	Jackson
70	0.0	Breckinridge County	Hardinsburg
70	0.0	Caldwell County	Princeton
70	0.0	Carter County	Grayson
70	0.0	Casey County	Liberty
70	0.0	Clay County	Manchester
70	0.0	Corbin Independent	Corbin
70	0.0	Covington Independent	Covington
70	0.0	Estill County	Irvine
70	0.0	Floyd County	Prestons
70	0.0	Fort Thomas Independent	Fort Thomas
70	0.0	Graves County	Mayfield
70	0.0	Green County	Greensburg
70	0.0	Greenup County	Greenup
70	0.0	Harlan County	Harlan
70	0.0	Henry County	New Castle
70	0.0	Jackson County	Mckee
70	0.0	Johnson County	Paintsville
70	0.0	Knott County	Hindman
70	0.0	Larue County	Hodgenville
70	0.0	Laurel County	London
70	0.0	Lawrence County	Louisa
70	0.0	Leslie County	Hyden
70	0.0	Letcher County	Whitesburg
70	0.0	Lewis County	Vanceburg
70	0.0	Lincoln County	Stanford
70	0.0	Logan County	Russellville
70	0.0	Magoffin County	Salyersville
70	0.0	Marion County	Lebanon
70	0.0	Marshall County	Benton
70	0.0	Martin County	Inez
70	0.0	Mccreary County	Stearns
70	0.0	Mclean County	Calhoun
70	0.0	Meade County	Brandenburg
70	0.0	Middlesboro Independent	Middlesboro
70	0.0	Morgan County	West Liberty
70	0.0	Muhlenberg County	Greenville
70	0.0	Owensboro Independent	Owensboro
70	0.0	Perry County	Hazard
70	0.0	Pike County	Pikeville
70	0.0	Rockcastle County	Mount Verno
70	0.0	Russell County	Jamestown
70	0.0	Russell Independent	Russell
70	0.0	Somerset Independent	Somerset
70	0.0	Taylor County	Campbellsville
70	0.0	Washington County	Springfie
70	0.0	Wayne County	Monticello
70	0.0	Whitley County	Williamsburg

Migrant Students

Rank	Percent	District Name	City
1	15.2	Pendleton County	Falmouth
2	13.6	Rockcastle County	Mount Verno
3	12.8	Metcalfe County	Edmonton
4	12.5	Mayfield Independent	Mayfiel
5	12.4	Powell County	Stanton
6	12.2	Caldwell County	Princeton
7	11.3	Glasgow Independent	Glasgow
8	10.5	Monroe County	Tompkinsville
9	9.8	Bath County	Owingsv
10	9.7	Ballard County	Barlow
11	9.4	Barren County	Glasgow
12	8.9	Montgomery County	Mount Sterling
13	8.1	Garrard County	Lancaster
14	7.6	Wayne County	Monticello
15	7.0	Graves County	Mayfield
16	6.8	Lewis County	Vanceburg
17	6.5	Mclean County	Calhoun
18	6.4	Adair County	Columbia
19	6.1	Owen County	Owenton
19	6.1	Todd County	Elkton
21	5.4	Clinton County	Albany
22	5.3	Lawrence County	Louisa
23	5.1	Russell County	Jamestown
24	5.0	Bourbon County	Paris
24	5.0	Breathitt County	Jackson
24	5.0	Letcher County	Whitesburg
24	5.0	Madison County	Richmond
28	4.8	Carroll County	Carrollton
28	4.8	Trimble County	Bedford
30	4.7	Hart County	Munfordville
31	4.5	Calloway County	Murray
32	4.4	Casey County	Liberty
32	4.4	Green County	Greensburg
34	4.1	Hopkins County	Madisonvi
34	4.1	Ohio County	Hartford
36	3.9	Muhlenberg County	Greenville
37	3.8	Harrison County	Cynthiana
37	3.8	Mccracken County	Paducah
39	3.7	Owensboro Independent	Owensboro
39	3.7	Webster County	Dixon
41	3.6	Carter County	Grayson
41	3.6	Mason County	Maysville
41	3.6	Shelby County	Shelbyville
44	3.4	Murray Independent	Murray
44	3.4	Pike County	Pikeville
46	3.3	Ashland Ind	Ashland
47	3.2	Greenup County	Greenup
48	3.1	Morgan County	West Liberty
49	3.0	Christian County	Hopkinsville
49	3.0	Marion County	Lebanon
51	2.9	Grayson County	Leitchfield
51	2.9	Pulaski County	Somerset
51	2.9	Trigg County	Cadiz
54	2.8	Clark County	Winchester
54	2.8	Grant County	Williamsto
56	2.6	Union County	Morganfiel
57	2.5	Breckinridge County	Hardinsburg
57	2.5	Marshall County	Benton
57	2.5	Martin County	Inez
60	2.4	Henry County	New Castle
60	2.4	Larue County	Hodgenville
60	2.4	Scott County	Georgetown
63	2.3	Lincoln County	Stanford
63	2.3	Logan County	Russellville
65	2.2	Washington County	Springfie
66	2.1	Henderson County	Henderson
67	2.0	Fleming County	Flemingsburg
67	2.0	Rowan County	Morehead
67	2.0	Taylor County	Campbellsville
70	1.9	Boyle County	Danville
70	1.9	Daviess County	Owensboro
72	1.8	Allen County	Scottsville
72	1.8	Danville Independent	Danville
72	1.8	Jessamine County	Nicholasville
75	1.7	Bowling Green Independent	Bowling Green
75	1.7	Boyd County	Ashland
75	1.7	Woodford County	Versailles
78	1.6	Estill County	Irvine
78	1.6	Somerset Independent	Somerset
80	1.0	Butler County	Morgantown
80	1.0	Edmonson County	Brownsville
80	1.0	Fayette County	Lexington
80	1.0	Jackson County	Mckee
80	1.0	Russell Independent	Russell
85	0.8	Meade County	Brandenburg
85	0.8	Simpson County	Franklin
87	0.7	Bullitt County	Shepherdsville
87	0.7	Oldham County	Buckner
87	0.7	Paducah Independent	Paducah
90	0.6	Warren County	Bowling Gre
91	0.5	Hardin County	Elizabe
92	0.4	Spencer County	Taylorsvil
93	0.3	Mercer County	Harrodsburg
94	0.2	Elizabethtown Independent	Elizabethtow
94	0.2	Jefferson County	Louisville
96	0.1	Anderson County	Lawrenceburg
96	0.1	Campbell County	Alexandria
98	0.0	Bardstown Independent	Bardstown
98	0.0	Bell County	Pineville
98	0.0	Boone County	Florence
98	0.0	Clay County	Manchester
98	0.0	Corbin Independent	Corbin
98	0.0	Covington Independent	Covington
98	0.0	Erlanger-Elsmere Independent	Erlanger
98	0.0	Floyd County	Prestons
98	0.0	Fort Thomas Independent	Fort Thomas
98	0.0	Franklin County	Frankfort
98	0.0	Hancock County	Hawesville
98	0.0	Harlan County	Harlan
98	0.0	Johnson County	Paintsville
98	0.0	Kenton County	Erlanger
98	0.0	Knott County	Hindman
98	0.0	Knox County	Barbourvill
98	0.0	Laurel County	London
98	0.0	Leslie County	Hyden
98	0.0	Magoffin County	Salyersville
98	0.0	Mccreary County	Stearns
98	0.0	Middlesboro Independent	Middlesboro
98	0.0	Nelson County	Bardstown
98	0.0	Newport Independent	Newport
98	0.0	Perry County	Hazard
98	0.0	Whitley County	Williamsburg
123	n/a	Fort Campbell District	Fort Campbell
123	n/a	Fort Knox District	Fort Knox

Students Eligible for Free Lunch

Rank	Percent	District Name	City
1	79.9	Leslie County	Hyden
2	78.7	Knott County	Hindman
2	78.7	Mccreary County	Stearns
4	78.3	Clay County	Manchester
5	78.0	Magoffin County	Salyersville
6	77.8	Middlesboro Independent	Middlesboro
7	77.6	Knox County	Barbourvill
8	76.9	Bell County	Pineville
9	76.3	Lewis County	Vanceburg
9	76.3	Whitley County	Williamsburg
11	75.0	Lawrence County	Louisa
12	74.9	Breathitt County	Jackson
13	73.7	Letcher County	Whitesburg
14	73.6	Mayfield Independent	Mayfiel
15	73.2	Morgan County	West Liberty
16	72.9	Bath County	Owingsv
16	72.9	Jackson County	Mckee
18	72.5	Harlan County	Harlan
18	72.5	Newport Independent	Newport
20	71.6	Monroe County	Tompkinsville
21	70.8	Metcalfe County	Edmonton
22	70.4	Perry County	Hazard
23	70.3	Carter County	Grayson
24	69.9	Clinton County	Albany
25	69.8	Floyd County	Prestons
26	68.2	Wayne County	Monticello
27	68.0	Johnson County	Paintsville
28	67.9	Rockcastle County	Mount Verno
29	67.4	Powell County	Stanton
30	66.7	Owensboro Independent	Owensboro
31	66.2	Adair County	Columbia
32	66.1	Estill County	Irvine
33	65.9	Casey County	Liberty
33	65.9	Russell County	Jamestown
35	65.5	Hart County	Munfordville
36	65.3	Greenup County	Greenup
37	64.0	Laurel County	London
38	63.9	Covington Independent	Covington
39	63.6	Lincoln County	Stanford
40	63.2	Christian County	Hopkinsville
41	62.9	Martin County	Inez
41	62.9	Somerset Independent	Somerset
43	62.4	Breckinridge County	Hardinsburg
44	61.6	Mason County	Maysville
45	61.3	Fleming County	Flemingsburg
46	61.1	Todd County	Elkton
47	60.8	Pike County	Pikeville
48	60.5	Carroll County	Carrollton
49	60.4	Garrard County	Lancaster
50	60.1	Pulaski County	Somerset
51	59.5	Bowling Green Independent	Bowling Green
52	58.8	Pendleton County	Falmouth
53	58.7	Larue County	Hodgenville
54	58.5	Danville Independent	Danville
55	58.3	Paducah Independent	Paducah
56	58.1	Edmonson County	Brownsville
57	57.5	Caldwell County	Princeton
58	57.2	Rowan County	Morehead
59	57.1	Ohio County	Hartford
60	56.8	Green County	Greensburg
61	56.5	Grant County	Williamsto
62	55.4	Marion County	Lebanon
63	55.3	Jefferson County	Louisville
64	54.8	Hopkins County	Madisonvi
65	54.2	Owen County	Owenton
66	54.1	Barren County	Glasgow
67	53.9	Logan County	Russellville
68	52.7	Washington County	Springfie
69	52.6	Ashland Ind	Ashland
69	52.6	Union County	Morganfiel
71	52.5	Allen County	Scottsville
72	52.3	Grayson County	Leitchfield
73	51.5	Montgomery County	Mount Sterling
73	51.5	Muhlenberg County	Greenville
75	51.4	Jessamine County	Nicholasville
76	51.3	Boyd County	Ashland
76	51.3	Trimble County	Bedford
78	51.1	Graves County	Mayfield
79	51.0	Harrison County	Cynthiana
80	50.8	Taylor County	Campbellsville
81	50.4	Bardstown Independent	Bardstown
82	50.3	Butler County	Morgantown
83	48.8	Henry County	New Castle
84	48.7	Clark County	Winchester
85	48.4	Calloway County	Murray
85	48.4	Madison County	Richmond
85	48.4	Marshall County	Benton
88	48.1	Corbin Independent	Corbin
88	48.1	Glasgow Independent	Glasgow
90	47.9	Warren County	Bowling Gre

91	46.9	Bourbon County	Paris
92	46.3	Elizabethtown Independent	Elizabethtow
92	46.3	Mclean County	Calhoun
94	45.9	Hardin County	Elizabe
95	45.6	Henderson County	Henderson
96	44.8	Nelson County	Bardstown
96	44.8	Trigg County	Cadiz
98	44.6	Mccracken County	Paducah
98	44.6	Simpson County	Franklin
100	44.5	Webster County	Dixon
101	43.0	Fayette County	Lexington
102	42.1	Franklin County	Frankfort
103	42.0	Spencer County	Taylorsvil
104	41.1	Meade County	Brandenburg
105	40.0	Ballard County	Barlow
106	39.9	Erlanger-Elsmere Independent	Erlanger
107	38.9	Scott County	Georgetown
108	38.6	Hancock County	Hawesville
109	37.6	Daviess County	Owensboro
109	37.6	Shelby County	Shelbyville
111	35.2	Boyle County	Danville
112	34.1	Bullitt County	Shepherdsville
113	33.7	Russell Independent	Russell
114	32.4	Murray Independent	Murray
115	28.2	Mercer County	Harrodsburg
116	26.5	Anderson County	Lawrenceburg
117	25.6	Kenton County	Erlanger
118	25.2	Woodford County	Versailles
119	25.0	Campbell County	Alexandria
120	23.2	Boone County	Florence
121	14.7	Oldham County	Buckner
122	5.1	Fort Thomas Independent	Fort Thomas
123	n/a	Fort Campbell District	Fort Campbell
123	n/a	Fort Knox District	Fort Knox

Students Eligible for Reduced-Price Lunch

Rank	Percent	District Name	City
1	23.0	Adair County	Columbia
2	22.3	Marion County	Lebanon
3	21.3	Russell County	Jamestown
4	20.8	Christian County	Hopkinsville
5	20.6	Fleming County	Flemingsburg
6	20.2	Washington County	Springfie
7	20.1	Clinton County	Albany
8	19.9	Jackson County	Mckee
9	19.7	Garrard County	Lancaster
10	19.5	Rockcastle County	Mount Verno
11	19.4	Wayne County	Monticello
12	18.9	Hardin County	Elizabe
12	18.9	Lincoln County	Stanford
14	18.6	Logan County	Russellville
15	18.5	Harlan County	Harlan
15	18.5	Whitley County	Williamsburg
17	18.1	Calloway County	Murray
17	18.1	Casey County	Liberty
17	18.1	Letcher County	Whitesburg
20	18.0	Ohio County	Hartford
21	17.4	Hart County	Munfordville
21	17.4	Larue County	Hodgenville
21	17.4	Meade County	Brandenburg
21	17.4	Todd County	Elkton
21	17.4	Trimble County	Bedford
26	17.2	Grayson County	Leitchfield
27	17.1	Breckinridge County	Hardinsburg
28	17.0	Mclean County	Calhoun
29	16.7	Metcalfe County	Edmonton
30	16.6	Henry County	New Castle
31	16.3	Trigg County	Cadiz
32	16.0	Monroe County	Tompkinsville
33	15.9	Somerset Independent	Somerset
34	15.7	Pulaski County	Somerset
35	15.5	Corbin Independent	Corbin
36	15.4	Bath County	Owingsv
36	15.4	Grant County	Williamsto
38	15.3	Edmonson County	Brownsville
38	15.3	Rowan County	Morehead
40	15.2	Butler County	Morgantown
40	15.2	Green County	Greensburg
42	15.1	Leslie County	Hyden
43	14.9	Bardstown Independent	Bardstown
43	14.9	Bell County	Pineville
43	14.9	Hancock County	Hawesville
43	14.9	Knott County	Hindman
47	14.8	Johnson County	Paintsville
48	14.7	Pike County	Pikeville
49	14.6	Greenup County	Greenup
50	14.4	Pendleton County	Falmouth
51	14.2	Allen County	Scottsville
52	14.1	Madison County	Richmond
52	14.1	Montgomery County	Mount Sterling
54	14.0	Union County	Morganfiel
55	13.9	Owensboro Independent	Owensboro
56	13.8	Graves County	Mayfield
56	13.8	Nelson County	Bardstown
56	13.8	Powell County	Stanton
59	13.7	Bullitt County	Shepherdsville
59	13.7	Lewis County	Vanceburg
61	13.6	Carter County	Grayson
62	13.4	Breathitt County	Jackson
62	13.4	Taylor County	Campbellsville
64	13.3	Hopkins County	Madisonvi
64	13.3	Lawrence County	Louisa
64	13.3	Webster County	Dixon
67	13.2	Daviess County	Owensboro
67	13.2	Simpson County	Franklin
67	13.2	Spencer County	Taylorsvil
70	13.1	Bourbon County	Paris
70	13.1	Knox County	Barbourvill
70	13.1	Newport Independent	Newport
73	12.9	Estill County	Irvine
74	12.8	Magoffin County	Salyersville
75	12.7	Ballard County	Barlow
75	12.7	Laurel County	London
75	12.7	Perry County	Hazard
78	12.6	Erlanger-Elsmere Independent	Erlanger
78	12.6	Jessamine County	Nicholasville
80	12.5	Clark County	Winchester
80	12.5	Elizabethtown Independent	Elizabethtow
80	12.5	Muhlenberg County	Greenville
83	12.4	Barren County	Glasgow
84	12.3	Harrison County	Cynthiana
84	12.3	Morgan County	West Liberty
86	12.1	Mccreary County	Stearns
87	12.0	Danville Independent	Danville
88	11.9	Floyd County	Prestons
89	11.8	Jefferson County	Louisville
90	11.7	Campbell County	Alexandria
91	11.6	Covington Independent	Covington
92	11.4	Boone County	Florence
92	11.4	Mercer County	Harrodsburg
92	11.4	Owen County	Owenton
95	11.3	Mason County	Maysville
96	11.1	Marshall County	Benton
96	11.1	Warren County	Bowling Gre
98	11.0	Clay County	Manchester
98	11.0	Franklin County	Frankfort
98	11.0	Mccracken County	Paducah
101	10.7	Middlesboro Independent	Middlesboro
102	10.5	Caldwell County	Princeton
102	10.5	Carroll County	Carrollton
104	10.3	Boyd County	Ashland
105	10.2	Anderson County	Lawrenceburg
105	10.2	Kenton County	Erlanger
107	9.7	Martin County	Inez
108	9.6	Fayette County	Lexington
109	9.5	Henderson County	Henderson
110	9.4	Mayfield Independent	Mayfiel
111	9.2	Murray Independent	Murray
112	9.1	Glasgow Independent	Glasgow
113	9.0	Shelby County	Shelbyville
114	8.9	Boyle County	Danville
115	8.2	Bowling Green Independent	Bowling Green
116	7.7	Ashland Ind	Ashland
117	7.4	Scott County	Georgetown
118	7.3	Russell Independent	Russell
119	7.1	Woodford County	Versailles
120	5.1	Paducah Independent	Paducah
121	5.0	Oldham County	Buckner
122	2.1	Fort Thomas Independent	Fort Thomas
123	n/a	Fort Campbell District	Fort Campbell
123	n/a	Fort Knox District	Fort Knox

Student/Teacher Ratio

Rank	Ratio	District Name	City
1	19.1	Anderson County	Lawrenceburg
2	18.8	Webster County	Dixon
3	18.6	Trimble County	Bedford
4	18.5	Breckinridge County	Hardinsburg
5	18.4	Allen County	Scottsville
5	18.4	Grant County	Williamsto
5	18.4	Spencer County	Taylorsvil
8	18.3	Owen County	Owenton
8	18.3	Russell Independent	Russell
10	18.0	Laurel County	London
11	17.9	Jefferson County	Louisville
11	17.9	Kenton County	Erlanger
11	17.9	Todd County	Elkton
14	17.8	Bullitt County	Shepherdsville
14	17.8	Mccracken County	Paducah
16	17.6	Christian County	Hopkinsville
16	17.6	Meade County	Brandenburg
18	17.5	Graves County	Mayfield
19	17.3	Harrison County	Cynthiana
19	17.3	Murray Independent	Murray
19	17.3	Oldham County	Buckner
22	17.2	Ballard County	Barlow
22	17.2	Henry County	New Castle
22	17.2	Madison County	Richmond
25	17.1	Boone County	Florence
25	17.1	Carroll County	Carrollton
25	17.1	Wayne County	Monticello
28	17.0	Elizabethtown Independent	Elizabethtow
28	17.0	Nelson County	Bardstown
28	17.0	Shelby County	Shelbyville
28	17.0	Taylor County	Campbellsville
32	16.8	Erlanger-Elsmere Independent	Erlanger
32	16.8	Hancock County	Hawesville
32	16.8	Montgomery County	Mount Sterling
32	16.8	Simpson County	Franklin
36	16.7	Knox County	Barbourvill
36	16.7	Lincoln County	Stanford
36	16.7	Mercer County	Harrodsburg
36	16.7	Pendleton County	Falmouth
36	16.7	Warren County	Bowling Gre
41	16.6	Bardstown Independent	Bardstown
41	16.6	Campbell County	Alexandria
41	16.6	Daviess County	Owensboro
41	16.6	Trigg County	Cadiz
45	16.5	Franklin County	Frankfort
45	16.5	Hardin County	Elizabe
45	16.5	Logan County	Russellville
45	16.5	Pulaski County	Somerset
49	16.4	Clark County	Winchester
49	16.4	Greenup County	Greenup
49	16.4	Henderson County	Henderson
49	16.4	Hopkins County	Madisonvi
49	16.4	Woodford County	Versailles
54	16.3	Bath County	Owingsv
54	16.3	Bourbon County	Paris
54	16.3	Larue County	Hodgenville
54	16.3	Washington County	Springfie
58	16.2	Floyd County	Prestons
59	16.1	Hart County	Munfordville
59	16.1	Whitley County	Williamsburg
61	16.0	Mason County	Maysville
61	16.0	Mclean County	Calhoun
61	16.0	Middlesboro Independent	Middlesboro
61	16.0	Ohio County	Hartford
65	15.9	Ashland Ind	Ashland
65	15.9	Clinton County	Albany
65	15.9	Corbin Independent	Corbin
65	15.9	Edmonson County	Brownsville
65	15.9	Fleming County	Flemingsburg
65	15.9	Fort Thomas Independent	Fort Thomas
71	15.8	Casey County	Liberty
71	15.8	Grayson County	Leitchfield
71	15.8	Jessamine County	Nicholasville
71	15.8	Leslie County	Hyden
71	15.8	Marshall County	Benton
71	15.8	Scott County	Georgetown
71	15.8	Somerset Independent	Somerset
78	15.7	Bowling Green Independent	Bowling Green
79	15.6	Garrard County	Lancaster
79	15.6	Johnson County	Paintsville
81	15.5	Boyle County	Danville
81	15.5	Caldwell County	Princeton
81	15.5	Calloway County	Murray
81	15.5	Carter County	Grayson
81	15.5	Harlan County	Harlan
81	15.5	Marion County	Lebanon
87	15.4	Barren County	Glasgow
87	15.4	Pike County	Pikeville
89	15.3	Rowan County	Morehead
89	15.3	Union County	Morganfiel
91	15.2	Boyd County	Ashland
91	15.2	Knott County	Hindman
91	15.2	Mayfield Independent	Mayfiel
91	15.2	Rockcastle County	Mount Verno
95	15.1	Butler County	Morgantown
95	15.1	Magoffin County	Salyersville
97	15.0	Glasgow Independent	Glasgow
97	15.0	Lewis County	Vanceburg
99	14.9	Breathitt County	Jackson
99	14.9	Green County	Greensburg
99	14.9	Lawrence County	Louisa
99	14.9	Paducah Independent	Paducah
99	14.9	Powell County	Stanton
104	14.8	Jackson County	Mckee
104	14.8	Mccreary County	Stearns
104	14.8	Metcalfe County	Edmonton
104	14.8	Monroe County	Tompkinsville
104	14.8	Muhlenberg County	Greenville
109	14.7	Bell County	Pineville
109	14.7	Danville Independent	Danville

109	14.7	Estill County	Irvine
109	14.7	Martin County	Inez
113	14.5	Morgan County	West Liberty
113	14.5	Perry County	Hazard
115	14.4	Adair County	Columbia
116	14.3	Letcher County	Whitesburg
117	14.1	Fort Campbell District	Fort Campbell
118	14.0	Russell County	Jamestown
119	13.8	Covington Independent	Covington
119	13.8	Fayette County	Lexington
121	13.7	Newport Independent	Newport
122	13.6	Clay County	Manchester
123	13.3	Owensboro Independent	Owensboro
124	13.1	Fort Knox District	Fort Knox

Student/Librarian Ratio

Rank	Ratio	District Name	City
1	1,377.5	Clinton County	Albany
2	948.2	Campbell County	Alexandria
3	871.0	Montgomery County	Mount Sterling
4	830.1	Jessamine County	Nicholasville
5	800.3	Spencer County	Taylorsvil
6	787.6	Anderson County	Lawrenceburg
7	784.0	Graves County	Mayfield
8	777.4	Grant County	Williamsto
9	771.7	Taylor County	Campbellsville
10	771.1	Boone County	Florence
11	758.0	Mercer County	Harrodsburg
12	757.2	Johnson County	Paintsville
13	754.5	Ballard County	Barlow
14	747.0	Pendleton County	Falmouth
15	719.5	Grayson County	Leitchfield
16	719.1	Lewis County	Vanceburg
17	709.7	Trigg County	Cadiz
18	701.5	Mason County	Maysville
19	698.0	Bardstown Independent	Bardstown
20	689.3	Ohio County	Hartford
21	686.0	Lawrence County	Louisa
22	683.7	Webster County	Dixon
23	667.7	Meade County	Brandenburg
24	666.7	Kenton County	Erlanger
25	660.3	Pulaski County	Somerset
26	649.6	Madison County	Richmond
27	648.1	Shelby County	Shelbyville
28	647.1	Carter County	Grayson
29	640.7	Washington County	Springfie
30	636.4	Jefferson County	Louisville
31	634.5	Daviess County	Owensboro
32	634.2	Franklin County	Frankfort
33	633.8	Martin County	Inez
34	632.3	Henry County	New Castle
35	629.6	Rowan County	Morehead
36	629.2	Calloway County	Murray
37	625.1	Oldham County	Buckner
38	622.3	Morgan County	West Liberty
39	619.0	Bullitt County	Shepherdsville
40	617.0	Allen County	Scottsville
41	614.0	Simpson County	Franklin
42	607.6	Rockcastle County	Mount Verno
43	600.6	Christian County	Hopkinsville
44	597.5	Metcalfe County	Edmonton
45	595.8	Floyd County	Prestons
46	593.5	Henderson County	Henderson
47	586.3	Elizabethtown Independent	Elizabethtow
48	583.8	Bourbon County	Paris
49	577.8	Logan County	Russellville
50	577.5	Mccracken County	Paducah
51	577.2	Boyle County	Danville
52	576.8	Boyd County	Ashland
53	576.7	Scott County	Georgetown
53	576.7	Warren County	Bowling Gre
55	574.3	Mccreary County	Stearns
56	573.7	Murray Independent	Murray
57	567.4	Wayne County	Monticello
58	565.7	Mclean County	Calhoun
59	563.2	Breckinridge County	Hardinsburg
60	559.8	Erlanger-Elsmere Independent	Erlanger
61	558.9	Casey County	Liberty
62	558.0	Hardin County	Elizabe
63	557.7	Fayette County	Lexington
64	552.4	Lincoln County	Stanford
65	548.2	Paducah Independent	Paducah
66	547.0	Fort Campbell District	Fort Campbell
67	545.7	Clark County	Winchester
68	543.5	Corbin Independent	Corbin
69	542.0	Todd County	Elkton
70	540.6	Estill County	Irvine
71	538.0	Russell Independent	Russell
72	537.0	Trimble County	Bedford
73	535.9	Marshall County	Benton
74	535.0	Hancock County	Hawesville
75	532.4	Powell County	Stanton
76	530.0	Caldwell County	Princeton
77	527.2	Nelson County	Bardstown
78	526.8	Garrard County	Lancaster
79	525.9	Covington Independent	Covington
80	525.8	Edmonson County	Brownsville
81	522.9	Whitley County	Williamsburg
82	522.7	Somerset Independent	Somerset
83	522.6	Laurel County	London
84	519.8	Knox County	Barbourvill
85	514.8	Bath County	Owingsv
86	511.2	Union County	Morganfiel
87	510.8	Newport Independent	Newport
88	505.3	Marion County	Lebanon
89	504.9	Owensboro Independent	Owensboro
90	501.4	Hart County	Munfordville
91	497.0	Hopkins County	Madisonvi
92	494.6	Fleming County	Flemingsburg
93	494.0	Owen County	Owenton
94	493.3	Barren County	Glasgow
95	482.2	Larue County	Hodgenville
96	478.6	Woodford County	Versailles
97	477.8	Russell County	Jamestown
98	477.2	Breathitt County	Jackson
99	473.7	Harrison County	Cynthiana
100	473.0	Bell County	Pineville
101	467.0	Middlesboro Independent	Middlesboro
102	462.0	Pike County	Pikeville
103	460.2	Fort Thomas Independent	Fort Thomas
104	454.1	Bowling Green Independent	Bowling Green
105	452.6	Butler County	Morgantown
106	452.0	Leslie County	Hyden
107	450.9	Glasgow Independent	Glasgow
108	444.3	Monroe County	Tompkinsville
109	443.0	Muhlenberg County	Greenville
110	441.0	Perry County	Hazard
111	440.3	Harlan County	Harlan
112	425.5	Green County	Greensburg
113	406.7	Knott County	Hindman
114	404.5	Greenup County	Greenup
115	394.6	Ashland Ind	Ashland
116	393.1	Adair County	Columbia
117	389.0	Mayfield Independent	Mayfiel
118	382.2	Carroll County	Carrollton
119	373.5	Fort Knox District	Fort Knox
120	365.3	Magoffin County	Salyersville
121	353.9	Clay County	Manchester
122	351.2	Letcher County	Whitesburg
123	347.9	Jackson County	Mckee
124	312.7	Danville Independent	Danville

Student/Counselor Ratio

Rank	Ratio	District Name	City
1	1,244.5	Morgan County	West Liberty
2	1,061.8	Clay County	Manchester
3	1,028.3	Allen County	Scottsville
4	961.0	Washington County	Springfie
5	941.2	Whitley County	Williamsburg
6	919.1	Ohio County	Hartford
7	885.4	Pike County	Pikeville
8	753.3	Leslie County	Hyden
9	729.8	Bourbon County	Paris
10	678.8	Mclean County	Calhoun
11	651.1	Boone County	Florence
12	649.8	Knox County	Barbourvill
13	639.3	Magoffin County	Salyersville
14	631.3	Lincoln County	Stanford
15	629.3	Lewis County	Vanceburg
16	612.1	Shelby County	Shelbyville
17	606.4	Perry County	Hazard
18	600.3	Spencer County	Taylorsvil
19	597.6	Pendleton County	Falmouth
20	588.3	Bath County	Owingsv
21	585.6	Knott County	Hindman
22	577.8	Logan County	Russellville
23	573.7	Murray Independent	Murray
24	573.2	Madison County	Richmond
25	570.2	Covington Independent	Covington
26	568.5	Mercer County	Harrodsburg
27	567.3	Green County	Greensburg
28	562.6	Anderson County	Lawrenceburg
29	554.9	Woodford County	Versailles
30	552.7	Harrison County	Cynthiana
31	548.4	Laurel County	London
32	542.0	Todd County	Elkton
33	540.9	Johnson County	Paintsville
34	540.2	Taylor County	Campbellsville
35	537.0	Trimble County	Bedford
36	535.0	Hancock County	Hawesville
37	534.5	Graves County	Mayfield
38	532.6	Bullitt County	Shepherdsville
39	532.3	Trigg County	Cadiz
40	530.0	Caldwell County	Princeton
41	526.9	Warren County	Bowling Gre
42	523.9	Franklin County	Frankfort
43	521.5	Breckinridge County	Hardinsburg
44	521.1	Elizabethtown Independent	Elizabethtow
45	511.7	Simpson County	Franklin
46	510.8	Newport Independent	Newport
47	506.3	Rockcastle County	Mount Verno
48	504.0	Jessamine County	Nicholasville
49	503.0	Ballard County	Barlow
49	503.0	Casey County	Liberty
51	498.9	Lawrence County	Louisa
52	494.6	Fleming County	Flemingsburg
53	494.0	Owen County	Owenton
54	492.3	Mccreary County	Stearns
55	491.8	Henry County	New Castle
56	485.9	Grant County	Williamsto
57	479.1	Ashland Ind	Ashland
58	478.9	Garrard County	Lancaster
59	477.8	Russell County	Jamestown
60	477.2	Breathitt County	Jackson
61	469.9	Paducah Independent	Paducah
62	467.7	Mason County	Maysville
63	467.5	Kenton County	Erlanger
64	467.0	Middlesboro Independent	Middlesboro
65	462.0	Mccracken County	Paducah
66	461.9	Nelson County	Bardstown
67	458.7	Adair County	Columbia
68	455.8	Webster County	Dixon
69	452.6	Butler County	Morgantown
70	450.5	Estill County	Irvine
71	446.8	Floyd County	Prestons
72	444.6	Mayfield Independent	Mayfiel
73	443.7	Powell County	Stanton
74	440.9	Meade County	Brandenburg
75	440.3	Harlan County	Harlan
76	440.2	Pulaski County	Somerset
77	437.5	Scott County	Georgetown
78	436.9	Fayette County	Lexington
79	435.5	Montgomery County	Mount Sterling
80	435.0	Monroe County	Tompkinsville
81	420.6	Edmonson County	Brownsville
82	418.8	Bardstown Independent	Bardstown
83	418.5	Hardin County	Elizabe
84	418.4	Fort Thomas Independent	Fort Thomas
85	418.3	Metcalfe County	Edmonton
86	416.6	Boyd County	Ashland
87	414.4	Barren County	Glasgow
88	413.9	Bell County	Pineville
89	412.3	Boyle County	Danville
90	408.9	Muhlenberg County	Greenville
91	407.1	Erlanger-Elsmere Independent	Erlanger
92	405.8	Glasgow Independent	Glasgow
92	405.8	Jackson County	Mckee
94	405.3	Wayne County	Monticello
95	398.4	Jefferson County	Louisville
96	393.5	Rowan County	Morehead
97	392.4	Hopkins County	Madisonvi
98	392.0	Somerset Independent	Somerset
99	390.0	Martin County	Inez
100	388.0	Daviess County	Owensboro
101	385.4	Grayson County	Leitchfield
102	379.3	Campbell County	Alexandria
103	379.0	Marion County	Lebanon
104	369.6	Christian County	Hopkinsville
105	367.0	Oldham County	Buckner
106	362.3	Corbin Independent	Corbin
107	359.6	Greenup County	Greenup
108	358.7	Russell Independent	Russell
109	358.1	Hart County	Munfordville
110	357.3	Marshall County	Benton
111	355.0	Union County	Morganfiel
112	350.1	Fort Campbell District	Fort Campbell
113	341.1	Clark County	Winchester
114	334.7	Calloway County	Murray
115	323.6	Carter County	Grayson
116	319.3	Letcher County	Whitesburg
117	312.7	Danville Independent	Danville
118	311.0	Henderson County	Henderson
119	302.8	Bowling Green Independent	Bowling Green
120	301.4	Larue County	Hodgenville
121	286.1	Owensboro Independent	Owensboro
122	271.6	Fort Knox District	Fort Knox
123	241.9	Carroll County	Carrollton
124	236.1	Clinton County	Albany

Current Spending per Student in FY2001

Rank	Dollars	District Name	City
1	8,070	Covington Independent	Covington
2	8,064	Martin County	Inez
3	7,954	Paducah Independent	Paducah
4	7,766	Owensboro Independent	Owensboro
5	7,709	Clinton County	Albany

6	7,508	Carroll County	Carrollton
7	7,377	Breathitt County	Jackson
8	7,067	Jefferson County	Louisville
9	7,044	Newport Independent	Newport
10	6,991	Clay County	Manchester
11	6,986	Jackson County	Mckee
12	6,969	Boyd County	Ashland
13	6,883	Fayette County	Lexington
14	6,877	Metcalfe County	Edmonton
15	6,859	Letcher County	Whitesburg
16	6,840	Danville Independent	Danville
17	6,830	Union County	Morganfiel
18	6,773	Mayfield Independent	Mayfiel
19	6,757	Wayne County	Monticello
20	6,704	Magoffin County	Salyersville
21	6,660	Bowling Green Independent	Bowling Green
22	6,652	Morgan County	West Liberty
23	6,569	Leslie County	Hyden
24	6,545	Perry County	Hazard
25	6,524	Ashland Ind	Ashland
26	6,522	Knott County	Hindman
27	6,514	Pike County	Pikeville
28	6,497	Muhlenberg County	Greenville
29	6,433	Breckinridge County	Hardinsburg
30	6,430	Fleming County	Flemingsburg
31	6,424	Bell County	Pineville
32	6,412	Rowan County	Morehead
33	6,407	Christian County	Hopkinsville
34	6,361	Hancock County	Hawesville
35	6,345	Corbin Independent	Corbin
36	6,344	Mccracken County	Paducah
37	6,336	Bath County	Owingsv
38	6,334	Hart County	Munfordville
39	6,309	Floyd County	Prestons
40	6,305	Bardstown Independent	Bardstown
41	6,301	Lincoln County	Stanford
42	6,268	Powell County	Stanton
43	6,251	Harlan County	Harlan
44	6,246	Mccreary County	Stearns
45	6,237	Johnson County	Paintsville
46	6,209	Rockcastle County	Mount Verno
47	6,198	Carter County	Grayson
48	6,197	Whitley County	Williamsburg
49	6,184	Adair County	Columbia
50	6,175	Casey County	Liberty
51	6,172	Lewis County	Vanceburg
52	6,171	Butler County	Morgantown
53	6,164	Bourbon County	Paris
54	6,142	Larue County	Hodgenville
55	6,137	Marion County	Lebanon
56	6,124	Knox County	Barbourvill
57	6,115	Glasgow Independent	Glasgow
58	6,110	Calloway County	Murray
59	6,105	Mason County	Maysville
60	6,093	Greenup County	Greenup
61	6,088	Nelson County	Bardstown
62	6,087	Barren County	Glasgow
63	6,085	Russell County	Jamestown
64	6,075	Monroe County	Tompkinsville
65	6,067	Lawrence County	Louisa
66	6,025	Erlanger-Elsmere Independent	Erlanger
67	6,020	Scott County	Georgetown
68	6,008	Pulaski County	Somerset
69	6,007	Middlesboro Independent	Middlesboro
70	6,000	Hopkins County	Madisonvi
71	5,995	Mclean County	Calhoun
72	5,994	Green County	Greensburg
73	5,993	Boyle County	Danville
73	5,993	Edmonson County	Brownsville
75	5,942	Henderson County	Henderson
76	5,929	Harrison County	Cynthiana
77	5,923	Spencer County	Taylorsvil
78	5,917	Ballard County	Barlow
79	5,911	Estill County	Irvine
80	5,889	Henry County	New Castle
81	5,888	Caldwell County	Princeton
82	5,880	Todd County	Elkton
83	5,875	Laurel County	London
84	5,869	Daviess County	Owensboro
85	5,860	Montgomery County	Mount Sterling
86	5,844	Taylor County	Campbellsville
87	5,824	Clark County	Winchester
88	5,815	Campbell County	Alexandria
89	5,814	Webster County	Dixon
90	5,796	Hardin County	Elizabe
91	5,759	Jessamine County	Nicholasville
92	5,757	Ohio County	Hartford
93	5,749	Trigg County	Cadiz
94	5,740	Washington County	Springfie
95	5,735	Fort Thomas Independent	Fort Thomas
96	5,692	Franklin County	Frankfort
97	5,678	Garrard County	Lancaster
98	5,651	Madison County	Richmond
99	5,649	Somerset Independent	Somerset
100	5,627	Boone County	Florence
101	5,617	Kenton County	Erlanger
102	5,606	Logan County	Russellville
102	5,606	Oldham County	Buckner
104	5,600	Shelby County	Shelbyville
105	5,586	Elizabethtown Independent	Elizabethtow
106	5,577	Trimble County	Bedford
107	5,560	Simpson County	Franklin
108	5,519	Russell Independent	Russell
109	5,505	Bullitt County	Shepherdsville
109	5,505	Owen County	Owenton
111	5,491	Grayson County	Leitchfield
112	5,476	Woodford County	Versailles
113	5,455	Marshall County	Benton
114	5,415	Pendleton County	Falmouth
115	5,408	Murray Independent	Murray
116	5,394	Allen County	Scottsville
117	5,391	Warren County	Bowling Gre
118	5,292	Mercer County	Harrodsburg
119	5,281	Meade County	Brandenburg
120	5,276	Graves County	Mayfield
121	5,157	Grant County	Williamsto
122	4,925	Anderson County	Lawrenceburg
123	n/a	Fort Campbell District	Fort Campbell
123	n/a	Fort Knox District	Fort Knox

Number of Diploma Recipients

Rank	Number	District Name	City
1	4,932	Jefferson County	Louisville
2	1,643	Fayette County	Lexington
3	817	Hardin County	Elizabe
4	758	Kenton County	Erlanger
5	722	Boone County	Florence
6	720	Daviess County	Owensboro
7	706	Warren County	Bowling Gre
8	630	Bullitt County	Shepherdsville
9	606	Oldham County	Buckner
10	602	Pike County	Pikeville
11	462	Pulaski County	Somerset
12	458	Laurel County	London
13	455	Henderson County	Henderson
14	442	Madison County	Richmond
15	436	Mccracken County	Paducah
16	416	Christian County	Hopkinsville
17	407	Floyd County	Prestons
18	375	Hopkins County	Madisonvi
19	361	Franklin County	Frankfort
20	336	Meade County	Brandenburg
21	334	Scott County	Georgetown
22	322	Campbell County	Alexandria
22	322	Jessamine County	Nicholasville
24	321	Muhlenberg County	Greenville
25	312	Nelson County	Bardstown
26	306	Shelby County	Shelbyville
27	299	Clark County	Winchester
28	272	Marshall County	Benton
29	271	Graves County	Mayfield
30	265	Harlan County	Harlan
31	254	Ohio County	Hartford
32	252	Grayson County	Leitchfield
33	242	Perry County	Hazard
34	227	Carter County	Grayson
35	225	Logan County	Russellville
35	225	Whitley County	Williamsburg
37	224	Knox County	Barbourvill
38	222	Bowling Green Independent	Bowling Green
38	222	Woodford County	Versailles
40	221	Montgomery County	Mount Sterling
41	218	Calloway County	Murray
42	215	Owensboro Independent	Owensboro
43	214	Lincoln County	Stanford
44	213	Johnson County	Paintsville
45	208	Barren County	Glasgow
46	205	Ashland Ind	Ashland
47	202	Marion County	Lebanon
48	201	Simpson County	Franklin
49	200	Covington Independent	Covington
50	198	Boyd County	Ashland
51	196	Letcher County	Whitesburg
52	195	Bell County	Pineville
53	193	Fort Thomas Independent	Fort Thomas
54	192	Harrison County	Cynthiana
55	189	Anderson County	Lawrenceburg
56	184	Allen County	Scottsville
56	184	Rockcastle County	Mount Verno
58	183	Rowan County	Morehead
59	182	Bourbon County	Paris
59	182	Boyle County	Danville
59	182	Greenup County	Greenup
62	178	Knott County	Hindman
63	175	Breckinridge County	Hardinsburg
64	171	Mason County	Maysville
65	170	Mccreary County	Stearns
66	169	Grant County	Williamsto
67	168	Larue County	Hodgenville
67	168	Lawrence County	Louisa
69	162	Taylor County	Campbellsville
70	161	Clay County	Manchester
71	160	Magoffin County	Salyersville
72	156	Union County	Morganfiel
73	155	Pendleton County	Falmouth
74	154	Estill County	Irvine
74	154	Martin County	Inez
76	153	Paducah Independent	Paducah
77	152	Russell Independent	Russell
78	150	Corbin Independent	Corbin
79	149	Mercer County	Harrodsburg
80	146	Elizabethtown Independent	Elizabethtow
81	142	Lewis County	Vanceburg
82	140	Russell County	Jamestown
82	140	Wayne County	Monticello
84	139	Leslie County	Hyden
85	138	Butler County	Morgantown
86	137	Webster County	Dixon
87	136	Garrard County	Lancaster
87	136	Powell County	Stanton
89	133	Hart County	Munfordville
90	132	Caldwell County	Princeton
91	131	Fleming County	Flemingsburg
92	128	Monroe County	Tompkinsville
93	127	Adair County	Columbia
93	127	Murray Independent	Murray
95	126	Morgan County	West Liberty
96	123	Erlanger-Elsmere Independent	Erlanger
97	122	Jackson County	Mckee
98	119	Casey County	Liberty
98	119	Green County	Greensburg
100	118	Glasgow Independent	Glasgow
101	117	Breathitt County	Jackson
102	116	Carroll County	Carrollton
103	115	Todd County	Elkton
104	114	Fort Campbell District	Fort Campbell
105	113	Spencer County	Taylorsvil
106	111	Bardstown Independent	Bardstown
106	111	Trigg County	Cadiz
108	110	Fort Knox District	Fort Knox
109	109	Hancock County	Hawesville
110	108	Danville Independent	Danville
110	108	Washington County	Springfie
112	107	Bath County	Owingsv
112	107	Henry County	New Castle
114	106	Newport Independent	Newport
115	104	Owen County	Owenton
116	102	Trimble County	Bedford
117	101	Ballard County	Barlow
118	99	Edmonson County	Brownsville
119	98	Somerset Independent	Somerset
120	97	Middlesboro Independent	Middlesboro
121	93	Mclean County	Calhoun
122	87	Metcalfe County	Edmonton
123	83	Mayfield Independent	Mayfiel
124	79	Clinton County	Albany

High School Drop-out Rate

Rank	Percent	District Name	City
1	13.5	Breathitt County	Jackson
2	8.7	Clay County	Manchester
3	8.3	Lincoln County	Stanford
4	8.0	Knox County	Barbourvill
5	7.6	Perry County	Hazard
6	7.4	Carroll County	Carrollton
7	7.3	Bell County	Pineville
8	7.0	Russell County	Jamestown
8	7.0	Union County	Morganfiel
10	6.9	Harlan County	Harlan
11	6.7	Jefferson County	Louisville
11	6.7	Magoffin County	Salyersville
13	6.5	Powell County	Stanton
14	6.4	Floyd County	Prestons
14	6.4	Henry County	New Castle
14	6.4	Owen County	Owenton
17	6.3	Lawrence County	Louisa
18	6.2	Allen County	Scottsville
18	6.2	Christian County	Hopkinsville
18	6.2	Estill County	Irvine
18	6.2	Fayette County	Lexington
18	6.2	Paducah Independent	Paducah
23	6.0	Henderson County	Henderson
23	6.0	Montgomery County	Mount Sterling
23	6.0	Pulaski County	Somerset
26	5.9	Adair County	Columbia
26	5.9	Bath County	Owingsv

26	5.9	Garrard County	Lancaster
26	5.9	Laurel County	London
30	5.8	Scott County	Georgetown
31	5.7	Morgan County	West Liberty
32	5.6	Jessamine County	Nicholasville
32	5.6	Lewis County	Vanceburg
32	5.6	Wayne County	Monticello
35	5.5	Greenup County	Greenup
36	5.4	Clinton County	Albany
37	5.3	Mclean County	Calhoun
38	5.2	Rockcastle County	Mount Verno
38	5.2	Whitley County	Williamsburg
40	5.1	Bardstown Independent	Bardstown
40	5.1	Franklin County	Frankfort
42	5.0	Clark County	Winchester
42	5.0	Edmonson County	Brownsville
42	5.0	Middlesboro Independent	Middlesboro
45	4.9	Washington County	Springfie
46	4.8	Knott County	Hindman
46	4.8	Shelby County	Shelbyville
48	4.7	Jackson County	Mckee
48	4.7	Leslie County	Hyden
48	4.7	Mayfield Independent	Mayfiel
51	4.6	Casey County	Liberty
52	4.5	Mccreary County	Stearns
52	4.5	Webster County	Dixon
54	4.4	Letcher County	Whitesburg
55	4.3	Harrison County	Cynthiana
55	4.3	Hart County	Munfordville
55	4.3	Marion County	Lebanon
58	4.2	Glasgow Independent	Glasgow
58	4.2	Meade County	Brandenburg
58	4.2	Somerset Independent	Somerset
61	4.1	Metcalfe County	Edmonton
62	4.0	Barren County	Glasgow
62	4.0	Boyle County	Danville
62	4.0	Carter County	Grayson
62	4.0	Fleming County	Flemingsburg
62	4.0	Graves County	Mayfield
62	4.0	Hardin County	Elizabe
62	4.0	Pike County	Pikeville
69	3.9	Ashland Ind	Ashland
69	3.9	Danville Independent	Danville
71	3.8	Bullitt County	Shepherdsville
72	3.7	Johnson County	Paintsville
73	3.6	Butler County	Morgantown
73	3.6	Woodford County	Versailles
75	3.5	Corbin Independent	Corbin
75	3.5	Spencer County	Taylorsvil
77	3.4	Bourbon County	Paris
77	3.4	Grayson County	Leitchfield
77	3.4	Mason County	Maysville
80	3.3	Larue County	Hodgenville
81	3.2	Anderson County	Lawrenceburg
81	3.2	Boyd County	Ashland
81	3.2	Breckinridge County	Hardinsburg
81	3.2	Logan County	Russellville
81	3.2	Madison County	Richmond
81	3.2	Martin County	Inez
81	3.2	Nelson County	Bardstown
81	3.2	Owensboro Independent	Owensboro
89	3.1	Grant County	Williamsto
89	3.1	Hopkins County	Madisonvi
89	3.1	Rowan County	Morehead
92	3.0	Campbell County	Alexandria
92	3.0	Newport Independent	Newport
94	2.9	Bowling Green Independent	Bowling Green
94	2.9	Muhlenberg County	Greenville
94	2.9	Simpson County	Franklin
97	2.8	Marshall County	Benton
97	2.8	Pendleton County	Falmouth
97	2.8	Taylor County	Campbellsville
100	2.7	Caldwell County	Princeton
100	2.7	Erlanger-Elsmere Independent	Erlanger
100	2.7	Green County	Greensburg
100	2.7	Warren County	Bowling Gre
104	2.6	Daviess County	Owensboro
104	2.6	Monroe County	Tompkinsville
104	2.6	Todd County	Elkton
107	2.4	Calloway County	Murray
107	2.4	Trigg County	Cadiz
107	2.4	Trimble County	Bedford
110	2.3	Boone County	Florence
110	2.3	Elizabethtown Independent	Elizabethtow
112	2.2	Mercer County	Harrodsburg
113	2.0	Covington Independent	Covington
114	1.8	Kenton County	Erlanger
114	1.8	Ohio County	Hartford
116	1.7	Ballard County	Barlow
116	1.7	Mccracken County	Paducah
118	1.1	Oldham County	Buckner
119	0.9	Murray Independent	Murray
119	0.9	Russell Independent	Russell
121	0.7	Fort Thomas Independent	Fort Thomas
122	0.5	Hancock County	Hawesville
123	n/a	Fort Campbell District	Fort Campbell
123	n/a	Fort Knox District	Fort Knox

Louisiana

Louisiana Public School Educational Profile

Category	Value	Category	Value
Schools *(2002-2003)*	1,550	**Diploma Recipients** *(2002-2003)*	37,905
Instructional Level		White, Non-Hispanic	21,252
Primary	805	Black, Non-Hispanic	15,322
Middle	287	Asian/Pacific Islander	622
High	260	American Indian/Alaskan Native	225
Other Level	198	Hispanic	484
Curriculum		**High School Drop-out Rate** (%) *(2000-2001)*	8.3
Regular	1,389	White, Non-Hispanic	6.5
Special Education	36	Black, Non-Hispanic	10.8
Vocational	9	Asian/Pacific Islander	4.8
Alternative	116	American Indian/Alaskan Native	9.7
Type		Hispanic	8.8
Magnet	67	**Staff** *(2002-2003)*	102,334.0
Charter	20	Teachers	50,062.1
Title I Eligible	932	Average Salary ($)	37,116
School-wide Title I	783	Librarians/Media Specialists	1,244.8
Students *(2002-2003)*	730,464	Guidance Counselors	3,094.6
Gender (%)		**Ratios** *(2002-2003)*	
Male	51.2	Student/Teacher Ratio	14.6 to 1
Female	48.8	Student/Librarian Ratio	586.8 to 1
Race/Ethnicity (%)		Student/Counselor Ratio	236.0 to 1
White, Non-Hispanic	48.5	**Current Spending** *($ per student in FY 2001)*	6,567
Black, Non-Hispanic	47.8	Instruction	4,014
Asian/Pacific Islander	1.3	Support Services	2,136
American Indian/Alaskan Native	0.7	**College Entrance Exam Scores** *(2003)*	
Hispanic	1.7	Scholastic Aptitude Test (SAT)	
Classification (%)		Participation Rate (%)	8
Individual Education Program (IEP)	13.7	Mean SAT I Verbal Score	563
Migrant	0.6	Mean SAT I Math Score	559
English Language Learner (ELL)	1.5	American College Testing Program (ACT)	
Eligible for Free Lunch Program	52.1	Participation Rate (%)	80
Eligible for Reduced-Price Lunch Program	8.5	Average Composite Score	19.6

Note: *For an explanation of data, please refer to the User's Guide in the front of the book; n/a indicates data not available*

Louisiana NAEP 2003 Test Scores

Reading			Mathematics		
Grade/Category	**Value**	**Rank**	**Grade/Category**	**Value**	**Rank**
4th Grade			**4th Grade**		
Average Proficiency	204.7 (1.4)	49/51	Average Proficiency	226.2 (1.0)	47/51
Proficiency by Gender/Race/Ethnicity			Proficiency by Gender/Race/Ethnicity		
Male	200.2 (1.6)	50/51	Male	226.6 (1.1)	47/51
Female	209.7 (1.8)	47/51	Female	225.9 (1.3)	46/51
White, Non-Hispanic	223.2 (1.4)	38/51	White, Non-Hispanic	241.6 (1.1)	28/51
Black, Non-Hispanic	188.7 (1.6)	39/42	Black, Non-Hispanic	213.2 (1.2)	29/42
Asian, Non-Hispanic	n/a	n/a	Asian, Non-Hispanic	n/a	n/a
American Indian, Non-Hispanic	n/a	n/a	American Indian, Non-Hispanic	n/a	n/a
Hispanic	n/a	n/a	Hispanic	n/a	n/a
Proficiency by Class Size			Proficiency by Class Size		
Less than 16 Students	189.2 (5.0)	37/45	Less than 16 Students	216.7 (3.1)	36/47
16 to 18 Students	202.3 (3.5)	41/48	16 to 18 Students	225.6 (2.9)	36/48
19 to 20 Students	204.5 (4.0)	45/50	19 to 20 Students	231.2 (2.3)	36/50
21 to 25 Students	209.9 (2.9)	43/51	21 to 25 Students	229.9 (2.4)	42/51
Greater than 25 Students	208.8 (4.6)	40/49	Greater than 25 Students	*225.2 (3.1)*	42/49
Percent Attaining Achievement Levels			Percent Attaining Achievement Levels		
Below Basic	51.2 (1.7)	4/51	Below Basic	33.2 (1.8)	5/51
Basic or Above	48.8 (1.7)	48/51	Basic or Above	66.8 (1.8)	47/51
Proficient or Above	19.9 (1.1)	48/51	Proficient or Above	21.3 (1.2)	47/51
Advanced or Above	3.7 (0.5)	47/51	Advanced or Above	1.6 (0.4)	43/51
8th Grade			**8th Grade**		
Average Proficiency	253.4 (1.6)	45/51	Average Proficiency	266.3 (1.5)	45/51
Proficiency by Gender/Race/Ethnicity			Proficiency by Gender/Race/Ethnicity		
Male	248.2 (1.9)	45/51	Male	267.1 (1.6)	45/51
Female	258.3 (1.6)	46/51	Female	265.6 (1.7)	47/51
White, Non-Hispanic	266.8 (1.7)	41/50	White, Non-Hispanic	280.9 (1.5)	40/50
Black, Non-Hispanic	238.4 (2.0)	36/41	Black, Non-Hispanic	249.6 (1.8)	26/41
Asian, Non-Hispanic	n/a	n/a	Asian, Non-Hispanic	n/a	n/a
American Indian, Non-Hispanic	n/a	n/a	American Indian, Non-Hispanic	n/a	n/a
Hispanic	n/a	n/a	Hispanic	n/a	n/a
Proficiency by Parents Highest Level of Ed.			Proficiency by Parents Highest Level of Ed.		
Did Not Finish High School	247.1 (3.8)	21/50	Did Not Finish High School	256.0 (3.2)	27/50
Graduated High School	250.8 (2.1)	35/50	Graduated High School	261.5 (1.9)	41/50
Some Education After High School	262.7 (1.9)	42/50	Some Education After High School	273.7 (1.9)	44/50
Graduated College	256.2 (2.1)	49/50	Graduated College	271.4 (2.1)	47/50
Percent Attaining Achievement Levels			Percent Attaining Achievement Levels		
Below Basic	36.1 (1.9)	6/51	Below Basic	43.0 (1.8)	7/51
Basic or Above	63.9 (1.9)	46/51	Basic or Above	57.0 (1.8)	45/51
Proficient or Above	21.7 (1.4)	46/51	Proficient or Above	17.2 (1.3)	46/51
Advanced or Above	1.6 (0.3)	44/51	Advanced or Above	1.8 (0.5)	47/51

Note: *For an explanation of data, please refer to the User's Guide in the front of the book; values in italics indicate that the nature of the sample does not allow accurate determination of the variability of the statistic; n/a indicates data not available*

Acadia Parish

Acadia Parish School Board

2402 N Parkerson Ave • Crowley, LA 70526
Mailing Address: PO Drawer 309 • Crowley, LA 70527-0309
(337) 783-3664 • http://www.acadia.k12.la.us/
Grade Span: PK-12; **Agency Type:** 1
Schools: 27
17 Primary; 4 Middle; 5 High; 1 Other Level
26 Regular; 0 Special Education; 0 Vocational; 1 Alternative
0 Magnet; 0 Charter; 21 Title I Eligible; 21 School-wide Title I
Students: 9,666 (51.1% male; 48.9% female)
Individual Education Program: 1,771 (18.3%);
English Language Learner: 34 (0.4%); Migrant: 61 (0.6%)
Eligible for Free Lunch Program: 5,163 (53.4%)
Eligible for Reduced-Price Lunch Program: 1,171 (12.1%)
Teachers: 668.4 (14.5 to 1)
Librarians/Media Specialists: 17.0 (568.6 to 1)
Guidance Counselors: 51.0 (189.5 to 1)
Current Spending: ($ per student per year):
Total: $5,302; Instruction: $3,183; Support Services: $1,702
Enrollment, Drop-out Rates and Diploma Recipients by Race/Ethnicity

Category	Total	White	Black	Asian	AIAN	Hisp.
Enrollment (%)	100.0	70.9	28.3	0.1	0.2	0.4
Drop-out Rate (%)	7.5	6.5	11.1	0.0	0.0	0.0
H.S. Diplomas (#)	444	356	83	2	0	3

Allen Parish

Allen Parish School Board

417 W Court St • Oberlin, LA 70655
Mailing Address: PO Drawer C • Oberlin, LA 70655
(337) 639-4311 • http://www.allen.k12.la.us/
Grade Span: PK-12; **Agency Type:** 1
Schools: 12
3 Primary; 2 Middle; 3 High; 4 Other Level
11 Regular; 0 Special Education; 0 Vocational; 1 Alternative
0 Magnet; 0 Charter; 8 Title I Eligible; 0 School-wide Title I
Students: 4,340 (52.2% male; 47.8% female)
Individual Education Program: 519 (12.0%);
English Language Learner: 1 (<0.1%); Migrant: 15 (0.3%)
Eligible for Free Lunch Program: 1,914 (44.1%)
Eligible for Reduced-Price Lunch Program: 541 (12.5%)
Teachers: 333.0 (13.0 to 1)
Librarians/Media Specialists: 10.0 (434.0 to 1)
Guidance Counselors: 18.0 (241.1 to 1)
Current Spending: ($ per student per year):
Total: $5,996; Instruction: $3,323; Support Services: $2,245
Enrollment, Drop-out Rates and Diploma Recipients by Race/Ethnicity

Category	Total	White	Black	Asian	AIAN	Hisp.
Enrollment (%)	100.0	73.6	24.5	0.2	0.7	1.0
Drop-out Rate (%)	3.7	3.2	5.0	0.0	16.7	0.0
H.S. Diplomas (#)	218	161	52	1	1	3

Ascension Parish

Ascension Parish School Board

1100 Webster St • Donaldsonville, LA 70346-0189
Mailing Address: PO Box 189 • Donaldsonville, LA 70346-0189
(225) 473-7981
Grade Span: PK-12; **Agency Type:** 1
Schools: 23
13 Primary; 5 Middle; 4 High; 1 Other Level
22 Regular; 0 Special Education; 0 Vocational; 1 Alternative
0 Magnet; 0 Charter; 13 Title I Eligible; 6 School-wide Title I
Students: 15,469 (51.6% male; 48.4% female)
Individual Education Program: 2,405 (15.5%);
English Language Learner: 276 (1.8%); Migrant: 0 (0.0%)
Eligible for Free Lunch Program: 5,337 (34.5%)
Eligible for Reduced-Price Lunch Program: 1,314 (8.5%)
Teachers: 1,088.0 (14.2 to 1)
Librarians/Media Specialists: 23.0 (672.6 to 1)
Guidance Counselors: 94.0 (164.6 to 1)
Current Spending: ($ per student per year):
Total: $6,088; Instruction: $3,820; Support Services: $1,915
Enrollment, Drop-out Rates and Diploma Recipients by Race/Ethnicity

Category	Total	White	Black	Asian	AIAN	Hisp.
Enrollment (%)	100.0	67.3	29.2	0.5	0.3	2.7
Drop-out Rate (%)	6.2	5.7	7.0	0.0	23.5	22.2
H.S. Diplomas (#)	772	580	178	4	1	9

Assumption Parish

Assumption Parish School Board

4901 Hwy 308 • Napoleonville, LA 70390
(985) 369-7251 • http://www.assumption.k12.la.us/home.htm
Grade Span: PK-12; **Agency Type:** 1
Schools: 10
5 Primary; 4 Middle; 1 High; 0 Other Level
10 Regular; 0 Special Education; 0 Vocational; 0 Alternative
0 Magnet; 0 Charter; 9 Title I Eligible; 8 School-wide Title I
Students: 4,516 (50.8% male; 49.2% female)
Individual Education Program: 591 (13.1%);
English Language Learner: 28 (0.6%); Migrant: 97 (2.1%)
Eligible for Free Lunch Program: 2,357 (52.2%)
Eligible for Reduced-Price Lunch Program: 391 (8.7%)
Teachers: 313.2 (14.4 to 1)
Librarians/Media Specialists: 2.0 (2,258.0 to 1)
Guidance Counselors: 6.0 (752.7 to 1)
Current Spending: ($ per student per year):
Total: $6,408; Instruction: $3,853; Support Services: $2,119
Enrollment, Drop-out Rates and Diploma Recipients by Race/Ethnicity

Category	Total	White	Black	Asian	AIAN	Hisp.
Enrollment (%)	100.0	56.5	42.2	0.5	0.0	0.8
Drop-out Rate (%)	11.0	7.7	15.9	33.3	0.0	20.0
H.S. Diplomas (#)	201	128	71	2	0	0

Avoyelles Parish

Avoyelles Parish School Board

221 Tunica Dr W • Marksville, LA 71351
(318) 240-0201 • http://www.avoyellespsb.com/
Grade Span: PK-12; **Agency Type:** 1
Schools: 14
6 Primary; 3 Middle; 3 High; 2 Other Level
12 Regular; 0 Special Education; 0 Vocational; 2 Alternative
1 Magnet; 1 Charter; 10 Title I Eligible; 9 School-wide Title I
Students: 6,740 (51.4% male; 48.6% female)
Individual Education Program: 735 (10.9%);
English Language Learner: 14 (0.2%); Migrant: 65 (1.0%)
Eligible for Free Lunch Program: 4,467 (66.3%)
Eligible for Reduced-Price Lunch Program: 669 (9.9%)
Teachers: 387.0 (17.4 to 1)
Librarians/Media Specialists: 10.0 (674.0 to 1)
Guidance Counselors: 11.0 (612.7 to 1)
Current Spending: ($ per student per year):
Total: $5,330; Instruction: $3,201; Support Services: $1,633
Enrollment, Drop-out Rates and Diploma Recipients by Race/Ethnicity

Category	Total	White	Black	Asian	AIAN	Hisp.
Enrollment (%)	100.0	55.5	42.8	0.1	0.9	0.6
Drop-out Rate (%)	8.8	6.8	12.4	0.0	23.1	11.1
H.S. Diplomas (#)	399	281	116	0	2	0

Beauregard Parish

Beauregard Parish School Board

202 W Third St • Deridder, LA 70634-0938
Mailing Address: PO Drawer 938 • Deridder, LA 70634-0938
(337) 463-5551 • http://www.beau.k12.la.us/
Grade Span: PK-12; **Agency Type:** 1
Schools: 14
4 Primary; 2 Middle; 1 High; 7 Other Level
12 Regular; 0 Special Education; 0 Vocational; 2 Alternative
0 Magnet; 0 Charter; 8 Title I Eligible; 2 School-wide Title I
Students: 6,058 (52.0% male; 48.0% female)
Individual Education Program: 769 (12.7%);
English Language Learner: 25 (0.4%); Migrant: 27 (0.4%)
Eligible for Free Lunch Program: 2,139 (35.3%)
Eligible for Reduced-Price Lunch Program: 540 (8.9%)
Teachers: 411.5 (14.7 to 1)
Librarians/Media Specialists: 13.0 (466.0 to 1)
Guidance Counselors: 25.4 (238.5 to 1)
Current Spending: ($ per student per year):
Total: $5,664; Instruction: $3,235; Support Services: $2,068
Enrollment, Drop-out Rates and Diploma Recipients by Race/Ethnicity

Category	Total	White	Black	Asian	AIAN	Hisp.
Enrollment (%)	100.0	81.6	16.3	0.5	0.4	1.1
Drop-out Rate (%)	3.9	4.1	3.1	10.0	0.0	0.0
H.S. Diplomas (#)	371	299	64	2	1	5

Bienville Parish

Bienville Parish School Board

1956 First St • Arcadia, LA 71001-0418
Mailing Address: PO Box 418 • Arcadia, LA 71001-0418
(318) 263-9416 • http://bienville.nls.k12.la.us/
Grade Span: PK-12; **Agency Type:** 1
Schools: 8
2 Primary; 0 Middle; 2 High; 4 Other Level
8 Regular; 0 Special Education; 0 Vocational; 0 Alternative
0 Magnet; 0 Charter; 8 Title I Eligible; 8 School-wide Title I
Students: 2,528 (51.1% male; 48.9% female)
Individual Education Program: 367 (14.5%);
English Language Learner: 1 (<0.1%); Migrant: 28 (1.1%)
Eligible for Free Lunch Program: 1,459 (57.7%)
Eligible for Reduced-Price Lunch Program: 196 (7.8%)
Teachers: 189.9 (13.3 to 1)
Librarians/Media Specialists: 4.0 (632.0 to 1)
Guidance Counselors: 4.0 (632.0 to 1)
Current Spending: ($ per student per year):
Total: $7,103; Instruction: $3,899; Support Services: $2,609
Enrollment, Drop-out Rates and Diploma Recipients by Race/Ethnicity

Category	Total	White	Black	Asian	AIAN	Hisp.
Enrollment (%)	100.0	40.3	59.3	0.1	0.1	0.3
Drop-out Rate (%)	7.3	7.7	6.9	n/a	n/a	0.0
H.S. Diplomas (#)	138	57	81	0	0	0

Bossier Parish

Bossier Parish School Board

316 Sibley St • Benton, LA 71006-2000
Mailing Address: PO Box 2000 • Benton, LA 71006-2000
(318) 549-5000 • http://www.bossier.k12.la.us/
Grade Span: PK-12; **Agency Type:** 1
Schools: 36
15 Primary; 9 Middle; 8 High; 4 Other Level
30 Regular; 1 Special Education; 1 Vocational; 4 Alternative
0 Magnet; 0 Charter; 9 Title I Eligible; 7 School-wide Title I
Students: 18,686 (50.7% male; 49.3% female)
Individual Education Program: 2,212 (11.8%);
English Language Learner: 534 (2.9%); Migrant: 33 (0.2%)
Eligible for Free Lunch Program: 6,265 (33.5%)
Eligible for Reduced-Price Lunch Program: 1,354 (7.2%)
Teachers: 1,144.1 (16.3 to 1)
Librarians/Media Specialists: 31.0 (602.8 to 1)
Guidance Counselors: 78.0 (239.6 to 1)
Current Spending: ($ per student per year):
Total: $5,439; Instruction: $3,171; Support Services: $1,906
Enrollment, Drop-out Rates and Diploma Recipients by Race/Ethnicity

Category	Total	White	Black	Asian	AIAN	Hisp.
Enrollment (%)	100.0	65.4	30.3	1.3	0.3	2.7
Drop-out Rate (%)	6.7	5.5	10.2	1.3	22.2	5.8
H.S. Diplomas (#)	983	704	230	25	1	23

Caddo Parish

Caddo Parish School Board

1961 Midway St • Shreveport, LA 71108
Mailing Address: PO Box 32000 • Shreveport, LA 71130-2000
(318) 603-6509 • http://www.caddo.k12.la.us/
Grade Span: PK-12; **Agency Type:** 1
Schools: 75
46 Primary; 10 Middle; 12 High; 6 Other Level
67 Regular; 1 Special Education; 1 Vocational; 5 Alternative
19 Magnet; 0 Charter; 37 Title I Eligible; 31 School-wide Title I
Students: 44,556 (50.7% male; 49.3% female)
Individual Education Program: 6,212 (13.9%);
English Language Learner: 512 (1.1%); Migrant: 24 (0.1%)
Eligible for Free Lunch Program: 22,400 (50.3%)
Eligible for Reduced-Price Lunch Program: 2,156 (4.8%)
Teachers: 2,991.8 (14.9 to 1)
Librarians/Media Specialists: 84.0 (530.4 to 1)
Guidance Counselors: 261.0 (170.7 to 1)
Current Spending: ($ per student per year):
Total: $6,467; Instruction: $3,957; Support Services: $2,124
Enrollment, Drop-out Rates and Diploma Recipients by Race/Ethnicity

Category	Total	White	Black	Asian	AIAN	Hisp.
Enrollment (%)	100.0	35.3	62.9	0.7	0.2	0.9
Drop-out Rate (%)	10.6	5.1	14.8	1.3	7.1	5.8
H.S. Diplomas (#)	2,223	996	1,183	18	3	23

Calcasieu Parish

Calcasieu Parish School Board

1724 Kirkman St • Lake Charles, LA 70601-6299
Mailing Address: PO Box 800 • Lake Charles, LA 70602-0800
(337) 491-1600 • http://www.cpsb.org/
Grade Span: PK-12; **Agency Type:** 1
Schools: 60
35 Primary; 11 Middle; 11 High; 3 Other Level
58 Regular; 1 Special Education; 0 Vocational; 1 Alternative
1 Magnet; 0 Charter; 28 Title I Eligible; 24 School-wide Title I
Students: 31,909 (51.1% male; 48.9% female)
Individual Education Program: 4,745 (14.9%);
English Language Learner: 12 (<0.1%); Migrant: 15 (<0.1%)
Eligible for Free Lunch Program: 12,137 (38.0%)
Eligible for Reduced-Price Lunch Program: 2,463 (7.7%)
Teachers: 2,181.4 (14.6 to 1)
Librarians/Media Specialists: 64.0 (498.6 to 1)
Guidance Counselors: 154.1 (207.1 to 1)
Current Spending: ($ per student per year):
Total: $5,637; Instruction: $3,394; Support Services: $1,884
Enrollment, Drop-out Rates and Diploma Recipients by Race/Ethnicity

Category	Total	White	Black	Asian	AIAN	Hisp.
Enrollment (%)	100.0	64.5	33.9	0.6	0.2	0.7
Drop-out Rate (%)	5.9	4.6	8.9	3.4	0.0	9.4
H.S. Diplomas (#)	1,747	1,238	493	9	0	7

Caldwell Parish

Caldwell Parish School Board

219 Main St - Courthouse Sq • Columbia, LA 71418-1019
Mailing Address: PO Box 1019 • Columbia, LA 71418-1019
(318) 649-2689 • http://caldwell.nls.k12.la.us/
Grade Span: PK-12; **Agency Type:** 1
Schools: 6
4 Primary; 1 Middle; 0 High; 1 Other Level
6 Regular; 0 Special Education; 0 Vocational; 0 Alternative
0 Magnet; 0 Charter; 4 Title I Eligible; 4 School-wide Title I
Students: 1,888 (54.7% male; 45.3% female)
Individual Education Program: 242 (12.8%);
English Language Learner: 3 (0.2%); Migrant: 16 (0.8%)
Eligible for Free Lunch Program: 871 (46.1%)
Eligible for Reduced-Price Lunch Program: 202 (10.7%)
Teachers: 139.0 (13.6 to 1)
Librarians/Media Specialists: 0.0 (0.0 to 1)
Guidance Counselors: 5.0 (377.6 to 1)
Current Spending: ($ per student per year):
Total: $5,943; Instruction: $3,541; Support Services: $1,883
Enrollment, Drop-out Rates and Diploma Recipients by Race/Ethnicity

Category	Total	White	Black	Asian	AIAN	Hisp.
Enrollment (%)	100.0	79.9	19.0	0.3	0.1	0.8
Drop-out Rate (%)	7.6	6.1	14.1	0.0	n/a	16.7
H.S. Diplomas (#)	66	60	5	0	0	1

Cameron Parish

Cameron Parish School Board

246 Dewey St • Cameron, LA 70631
Mailing Address: PO Box 1548 • Cameron, LA 70631
(337) 775-5784 • http://www.cameron.k12.la.us/
Grade Span: PK-12; **Agency Type:** 1
Schools: 6
2 Primary; 0 Middle; 1 High; 3 Other Level
6 Regular; 0 Special Education; 0 Vocational; 0 Alternative
0 Magnet; 0 Charter; 6 Title I Eligible; 0 School-wide Title I
Students: 1,847 (51.6% male; 48.4% female)
Individual Education Program: 309 (16.7%);
English Language Learner: 1 (0.1%); Migrant: 58 (3.1%)
Eligible for Free Lunch Program: 509 (27.6%)
Eligible for Reduced-Price Lunch Program: 223 (12.1%)
Teachers: 152.0 (12.2 to 1)
Librarians/Media Specialists: 6.0 (307.8 to 1)
Guidance Counselors: 7.0 (263.9 to 1)
Current Spending: ($ per student per year):
Total: $7,043; Instruction: $3,845; Support Services: $2,747
Enrollment, Drop-out Rates and Diploma Recipients by Race/Ethnicity

Category	Total	White	Black	Asian	AIAN	Hisp.
Enrollment (%)	100.0	93.0	4.7	0.3	0.1	1.9
Drop-out Rate (%)	2.7	2.8	0.0	0.0	0.0	0.0
H.S. Diplomas (#)	109	104	4	1	0	0

Catahoula Parish

Catahoula Parish School Board

200 Bushley St • Harrisonburg, LA 71340-0290
Mailing Address: PO Box 290 • Harrisonburg, LA 71340-0290
(318) 744-5727 • http://catahoula.nls.k12.la.us/
Grade Span: PK-12; **Agency Type:** 1
Schools: 10
4 Primary; 1 Middle; 3 High; 2 Other Level
9 Regular; 0 Special Education; 0 Vocational; 1 Alternative
0 Magnet; 0 Charter; 5 Title I Eligible; 5 School-wide Title I
Students: 1,811 (51.5% male; 48.5% female)
Individual Education Program: 195 (10.8%);
English Language Learner: 0 (0.0%); Migrant: 36 (2.0%)
Eligible for Free Lunch Program: 933 (51.5%)
Eligible for Reduced-Price Lunch Program: 218 (12.0%)
Teachers: 137.4 (13.2 to 1)
Librarians/Media Specialists: 2.6 (696.5 to 1)
Guidance Counselors: 4.5 (402.4 to 1)
Current Spending: ($ per student per year):
Total: $6,316; Instruction: $3,368; Support Services: $2,480
Enrollment, Drop-out Rates and Diploma Recipients by Race/Ethnicity

Category	Total	White	Black	Asian	AIAN	Hisp.
Enrollment (%)	100.0	62.5	36.9	0.0	0.0	0.6
Drop-out Rate (%)	8.8	7.8	11.1	n/a	n/a	0.0
H.S. Diplomas (#)	94	63	29	0	0	2

Claiborne Parish

Claiborne Parish School Board

415 E Main St • Homer, LA 71040-0600
Mailing Address: PO Box 600 • Homer, LA 71040-0600
(318) 927-3502
Grade Span: PK-12; **Agency Type:** 1
Schools: 9
2 Primary; 1 Middle; 1 High; 5 Other Level
8 Regular; 0 Special Education; 0 Vocational; 1 Alternative
0 Magnet; 0 Charter; 5 Title I Eligible; 5 School-wide Title I
Students: 2,803 (51.2% male; 48.8% female)
Individual Education Program: 463 (16.5%);
English Language Learner: 1 (<0.1%); Migrant: 19 (0.7%)
Eligible for Free Lunch Program: 1,687 (60.2%)
Eligible for Reduced-Price Lunch Program: 288 (10.3%)
Teachers: 199.4 (14.1 to 1)
Librarians/Media Specialists: 1.0 (2,803.0 to 1)
Guidance Counselors: 8.0 (350.4 to 1)
Current Spending: ($ per student per year):
Total: $6,077; Instruction: $3,624; Support Services: $1,927
Enrollment, Drop-out Rates and Diploma Recipients by Race/Ethnicity

Category	Total	White	Black	Asian	AIAN	Hisp.
Enrollment (%)	100.0	31.4	68.1	0.2	0.1	0.3
Drop-out Rate (%)	3.5	3.1	3.7	0.0	0.0	0.0
H.S. Diplomas (#)	149	57	92	0	0	0

Concordia Parish

Concordia Parish School Board

4358 Hwy 84 W • Vidalia, LA 71373-0950
Mailing Address: PO Box 950 • Vidalia, LA 71373-0950
(318) 336-4226 • http://nls.k12.la.us/~ccps/
Grade Span: PK-12; **Agency Type:** 1
Schools: 11
5 Primary; 2 Middle; 3 High; 1 Other Level
10 Regular; 0 Special Education; 0 Vocational; 1 Alternative
0 Magnet; 0 Charter; 10 Title I Eligible; 6 School-wide Title I
Students: 3,845 (50.8% male; 49.2% female)
Individual Education Program: 413 (10.7%);
English Language Learner: 4 (0.1%); Migrant: 58 (1.5%)
Eligible for Free Lunch Program: 2,565 (66.7%)
Eligible for Reduced-Price Lunch Program: 267 (6.9%)
Teachers: 264.4 (14.5 to 1)
Librarians/Media Specialists: 9.5 (404.7 to 1)
Guidance Counselors: 9.0 (427.2 to 1)
Current Spending: ($ per student per year):
Total: $5,811; Instruction: $3,508; Support Services: $1,857
Enrollment, Drop-out Rates and Diploma Recipients by Race/Ethnicity

Category	Total	White	Black	Asian	AIAN	Hisp.
Enrollment (%)	100.0	48.8	51.0	0.1	0.0	0.2
Drop-out Rate (%)	7.5	6.4	8.5	0.0	n/a	n/a
H.S. Diplomas (#)	205	102	103	0	0	0

De Soto Parish

Desoto Parish School Board

201 Crosby St • Mansfield, LA 71052
(318) 872-2836 • http://www.desoto.k12.la.us/
Grade Span: PK-12; **Agency Type:** 1
Schools: 13
4 Primary; 2 Middle; 2 High; 5 Other Level
11 Regular; 0 Special Education; 0 Vocational; 2 Alternative
0 Magnet; 0 Charter; 8 Title I Eligible; 7 School-wide Title I
Students: 5,042 (50.8% male; 49.2% female)
Individual Education Program: 761 (15.1%);
English Language Learner: 21 (0.4%); Migrant: 38 (0.8%)
Eligible for Free Lunch Program: 2,955 (58.6%)
Eligible for Reduced-Price Lunch Program: 345 (6.8%)
Teachers: 361.7 (13.9 to 1)
Librarians/Media Specialists: 11.0 (458.4 to 1)
Guidance Counselors: 13.0 (387.8 to 1)
Current Spending: ($ per student per year):
Total: $6,464; Instruction: $3,637; Support Services: $2,346
Enrollment, Drop-out Rates and Diploma Recipients by Race/Ethnicity

Category	Total	White	Black	Asian	AIAN	Hisp.
Enrollment (%)	100.0	42.3	56.4	0.2	0.2	1.0
Drop-out Rate (%)	9.2	8.8	9.5	100.0	0.0	0.0
H.S. Diplomas (#)	248	128	117	0	0	3

East Baton Rouge Parish

East Baton Rouge Parish School Bd

1050 S Foster Dr • Baton Rouge, LA 70806
Mailing Address: PO Box 2950 • Baton Rouge, LA 70821-2950
(225) 922-5618
Grade Span: PK-12; **Agency Type:** 1
Schools: 107
64 Primary; 20 Middle; 18 High; 4 Other Level
96 Regular; 2 Special Education; 0 Vocational; 8 Alternative
26 Magnet; 3 Charter; 63 Title I Eligible; 63 School-wide Title I
Students: 52,434 (50.9% male; 49.1% female)
Individual Education Program: 5,227 (10.0%);
English Language Learner: 1,462 (2.8%); Migrant: 11 (<0.1%)
Eligible for Free Lunch Program: 31,584 (60.2%)
Eligible for Reduced-Price Lunch Program: 4,186 (8.0%)
Teachers: 3,554.7 (14.8 to 1)
Librarians/Media Specialists: 109.0 (481.0 to 1)
Guidance Counselors: 338.0 (155.1 to 1)
Current Spending: ($ per student per year):
Total: $6,861; Instruction: $3,849; Support Services: $2,565
Enrollment, Drop-out Rates and Diploma Recipients by Race/Ethnicity

Category	Total	White	Black	Asian	AIAN	Hisp.
Enrollment (%)	100.0	24.2	72.7	2.0	0.1	1.0
Drop-out Rate (%)	9.6	7.9	10.7	5.9	0.0	13.5
H.S. Diplomas (#)	2,815	1,199	1,527	65	2	22

East Carroll Parish

East Carroll Parish School Board

504 Third St • Lake Providence, LA 71254-0792
Mailing Address: PO Box 792 • Lake Providence, LA 71254-0792
(318) 559-2222 • http://www.e-carrollschools.org/
Grade Span: PK-12; **Agency Type:** 1
Schools: 6
3 Primary; 1 Middle; 1 High; 1 Other Level
6 Regular; 0 Special Education; 0 Vocational; 0 Alternative
0 Magnet; 0 Charter; 6 Title I Eligible; 6 School-wide Title I
Students: 1,746 (48.8% male; 51.2% female)
Individual Education Program: 234 (13.4%);
English Language Learner: 6 (0.3%); Migrant: 13 (0.7%)
Eligible for Free Lunch Program: 1,494 (85.6%)
Eligible for Reduced-Price Lunch Program: 69 (4.0%)
Teachers: 137.9 (12.7 to 1)
Librarians/Media Specialists: 2.0 (873.0 to 1)
Guidance Counselors: 4.0 (436.5 to 1)
Current Spending: ($ per student per year):
Total: $6,295; Instruction: $3,541; Support Services: $2,051
Enrollment, Drop-out Rates and Diploma Recipients by Race/Ethnicity

Category	Total	White	Black	Asian	AIAN	Hisp.
Enrollment (%)	100.0	7.8	91.5	0.3	0.0	0.4
Drop-out Rate (%)	9.3	11.1	9.2	n/a	n/a	n/a
H.S. Diplomas (#)	83	4	79	0	0	0

East Feliciana Parish

East Feliciana Parish School Board

12732 Silliman St • Clinton, LA 70722-0397
Mailing Address: PO Box 397 • Clinton, LA 70722-0397
(225) 683-3040
Grade Span: PK-12; **Agency Type:** 1
Schools: 8
3 Primary; 2 Middle; 2 High; 1 Other Level
7 Regular; 0 Special Education; 0 Vocational; 1 Alternative
0 Magnet; 0 Charter; 7 Title I Eligible; 0 School-wide Title I
Students: 2,504 (52.8% male; 47.2% female)
Individual Education Program: 392 (15.7%);
English Language Learner: 7 (0.3%); Migrant: 0 (0.0%)
Eligible for Free Lunch Program: 1,835 (73.3%)
Eligible for Reduced-Price Lunch Program: 242 (9.7%)
Teachers: 169.0 (14.8 to 1)
Librarians/Media Specialists: 6.0 (417.3 to 1)
Guidance Counselors: 13.0 (192.6 to 1)
Current Spending: ($ per student per year):
Total: $6,069; Instruction: $3,463; Support Services: $2,110
Enrollment, Drop-out Rates and Diploma Recipients by Race/Ethnicity

Category	Total	White	Black	Asian	AIAN	Hisp.
Enrollment (%)	100.0	19.6	80.1	0.3	0.0	0.0
Drop-out Rate (%)	7.0	10.6	6.5	n/a	n/a	n/a
H.S. Diplomas (#)	142	13	129	0	0	0

Evangeline Parish

Evangeline Parish School Board

1123 Te Mamou Rd • Ville Platte, LA 70586
(337) 363-6651
Grade Span: PK-12; **Agency Type:** 1
Schools: 14
6 Primary; 1 Middle; 2 High; 5 Other Level
14 Regular; 0 Special Education; 0 Vocational; 0 Alternative
0 Magnet; 0 Charter; 14 Title I Eligible; 14 School-wide Title I
Students: 6,337 (52.0% male; 48.0% female)
Individual Education Program: 1,054 (16.6%);
English Language Learner: 11 (0.2%); Migrant: 56 (0.9%)
Eligible for Free Lunch Program: 4,081 (64.4%)
Eligible for Reduced-Price Lunch Program: 667 (10.5%)
Teachers: 424.6 (14.9 to 1)
Librarians/Media Specialists: 10.0 (633.7 to 1)
Guidance Counselors: 20.7 (306.1 to 1)
Current Spending: ($ per student per year):
Total: $5,276; Instruction: $3,114; Support Services: $1,766
Enrollment, Drop-out Rates and Diploma Recipients by Race/Ethnicity

Category	Total	White	Black	Asian	AIAN	Hisp.
Enrollment (%)	100.0	59.8	39.7	0.2	0.1	0.3
Drop-out Rate (%)	7.7	6.9	9.0	100.0	n/a	25.0
H.S. Diplomas (#)	286	175	110	0	0	1

Franklin Parish

Franklin Parish School Board

7293 Prairie Rd • Winnsboro, LA 71295
(318) 435-9046 • http://www.franklin.k12.la.us/
Grade Span: PK-12; **Agency Type:** 1
Schools: 12
7 Primary; 2 Middle; 2 High; 1 Other Level
11 Regular; 0 Special Education; 0 Vocational; 1 Alternative
0 Magnet; 0 Charter; 8 Title I Eligible; 5 School-wide Title I
Students: 3,913 (51.0% male; 49.0% female)
Individual Education Program: 417 (10.7%);
English Language Learner: 1 (<0.1%); Migrant: 98 (2.5%)
Eligible for Free Lunch Program: 2,475 (63.3%)
Eligible for Reduced-Price Lunch Program: 293 (7.5%)
Teachers: 321.9 (12.2 to 1)
Librarians/Media Specialists: 1.0 (3,913.0 to 1)
Guidance Counselors: 7.0 (559.0 to 1)
Current Spending: ($ per student per year):
Total: $5,606; Instruction: $3,466; Support Services: $1,658
Enrollment, Drop-out Rates and Diploma Recipients by Race/Ethnicity

Category	Total	White	Black	Asian	AIAN	Hisp.
Enrollment (%)	100.0	50.8	48.6	0.3	0.0	0.4
Drop-out Rate (%)	11.7	10.9	12.9	0.0	0.0	0.0
H.S. Diplomas (#)	199	108	88	3	0	0

Grant Parish

Grant Parish School Board

512 Main St • Colfax, LA 71417-0208
Mailing Address: PO Box 208 • Colfax, LA 71417-0208
(318) 627-3274
Grade Span: PK-12; **Agency Type:** 1
Schools: 8
4 Primary; 1 Middle; 2 High; 1 Other Level
8 Regular; 0 Special Education; 0 Vocational; 0 Alternative
0 Magnet; 0 Charter; 7 Title I Eligible; 7 School-wide Title I
Students: 3,572 (51.6% male; 48.4% female)
Individual Education Program: 529 (14.8%);
English Language Learner: 0 (0.0%); Migrant: 43 (1.2%)
Eligible for Free Lunch Program: 1,720 (48.2%)
Eligible for Reduced-Price Lunch Program: 459 (12.8%)
Teachers: 242.1 (14.8 to 1)
Librarians/Media Specialists: 7.0 (510.3 to 1)
Guidance Counselors: 8.5 (420.2 to 1)
Current Spending: ($ per student per year):
Total: $5,471; Instruction: $3,030; Support Services: $1,976
Enrollment, Drop-out Rates and Diploma Recipients by Race/Ethnicity

Category	Total	White	Black	Asian	AIAN	Hisp.
Enrollment (%)	100.0	83.8	15.0	0.2	0.2	0.8
Drop-out Rate (%)	20.3	21.2	16.4	100.0	0.0	0.0
H.S. Diplomas (#)	184	152	29	0	2	1

Iberia Parish

Iberia Parish School Board

1500 Jane St • New Iberia, LA 70560
Mailing Address: PO Box 200 • New Iberia, LA 70562-0200
(337) 365-2341 • http://www.iberia.k12.la.us/
Grade Span: PK-12; **Agency Type:** 1
Schools: 33
22 Primary; 5 Middle; 4 High; 2 Other Level
32 Regular; 0 Special Education; 0 Vocational; 1 Alternative
0 Magnet; 0 Charter; 22 Title I Eligible; 21 School-wide Title I
Students: 14,227 (50.6% male; 49.4% female)
Individual Education Program: 2,373 (16.7%);
English Language Learner: 212 (1.5%); Migrant: 124 (0.9%)
Eligible for Free Lunch Program: 7,353 (51.7%)
Eligible for Reduced-Price Lunch Program: 1,185 (8.3%)
Teachers: 1,052.0 (13.5 to 1)
Librarians/Media Specialists: 29.0 (490.6 to 1)
Guidance Counselors: 62.5 (227.6 to 1)
Current Spending: ($ per student per year):
Total: $6,209; Instruction: $3,714; Support Services: $2,089
Enrollment, Drop-out Rates and Diploma Recipients by Race/Ethnicity

Category	Total	White	Black	Asian	AIAN	Hisp.
Enrollment (%)	100.0	53.3	42.9	2.8	0.2	0.7
Drop-out Rate (%)	5.5	5.1	6.0	7.1	0.0	11.8
H.S. Diplomas (#)	637	395	218	22	1	1

Iberville Parish

Iberville Parish School Board

58030 Plaquemine St • Plaquemine, LA 70764
Mailing Address: PO Box 151 • Plaquemine, LA 70765-0151
(225) 687-4341 • http://www.ipsb.net/
Grade Span: PK-12; **Agency Type:** 1
Schools: 9
3 Primary; 1 Middle; 2 High; 3 Other Level
8 Regular; 0 Special Education; 0 Vocational; 1 Alternative
0 Magnet; 0 Charter; 8 Title I Eligible; 4 School-wide Title I
Students: 4,622 (50.6% male; 49.4% female)
Individual Education Program: 688 (14.9%);
English Language Learner: 12 (0.3%); Migrant: 10 (0.2%)
Eligible for Free Lunch Program: 3,424 (74.1%)
Eligible for Reduced-Price Lunch Program: 357 (7.7%)
Teachers: 327.0 (14.1 to 1)
Librarians/Media Specialists: 8.0 (577.8 to 1)
Guidance Counselors: 19.0 (243.3 to 1)
Current Spending: ($ per student per year):
Total: $6,819; Instruction: $3,670; Support Services: $2,567
Enrollment, Drop-out Rates and Diploma Recipients by Race/Ethnicity

Category	Total	White	Black	Asian	AIAN	Hisp.
Enrollment (%)	100.0	23.2	76.0	0.1	0.1	0.7
Drop-out Rate (%)	10.0	9.9	10.1	0.0	n/a	n/a
H.S. Diplomas (#)	253	67	185	1	0	0

Jackson Parish

Jackson Parish School Board
315 Pershing Hwy • Jonesboro, LA 71251-0705
Mailing Address: PO Box 705 • Jonesboro, LA 71251-0705
(318) 259-4456
Grade Span: PK-12; **Agency Type:** 1
Schools: 7
2 Primary; 1 Middle; 1 High; 3 Other Level
7 Regular; 0 Special Education; 0 Vocational; 0 Alternative
0 Magnet; 0 Charter; 4 Title I Eligible; 4 School-wide Title I
Students: 2,442 (51.6% male; 48.4% female)
Individual Education Program: 277 (11.3%);
English Language Learner: 0 (0.0%); Migrant: 30 (1.2%)
Eligible for Free Lunch Program: 1,109 (45.4%)
Eligible for Reduced-Price Lunch Program: 207 (8.5%)
Teachers: 178.2 (13.7 to 1)
Librarians/Media Specialists: 5.9 (413.9 to 1)
Guidance Counselors: 8.0 (305.3 to 1)
Current Spending: ($ per student per year):
Total: $6,769; Instruction: $3,719; Support Services: $2,523
Enrollment, Drop-out Rates and Diploma Recipients by Race/Ethnicity

Category	Total	White	Black	Asian	AIAN	Hisp.
Enrollment (%)	100.0	62.9	36.2	0.5	0.0	0.5
Drop-out Rate (%)	6.0	6.4	5.5	0.0	n/a	n/a
H.S. Diplomas (#)	169	83	83	2	0	1

Jefferson Parish

Jefferson Parish School Board
501 Manhattan Blvd • Harvey, LA 70058
(504) 349-7802 • http://www.jppss.k12.la.us/
Grade Span: PK-12; **Agency Type:** 1
Schools: 85
57 Primary; 17 Middle; 9 High; 2 Other Level
79 Regular; 2 Special Education; 1 Vocational; 3 Alternative
0 Magnet; 1 Charter; 43 Title I Eligible; 43 School-wide Title I
Students: 51,501 (51.5% male; 48.5% female)
Individual Education Program: 7,759 (15.1%);
English Language Learner: 2,996 (5.8%); Migrant: 217 (0.4%)
Eligible for Free Lunch Program: 31,500 (61.2%)
Eligible for Reduced-Price Lunch Program: 6,198 (12.0%)
Teachers: 3,372.8 (15.3 to 1)
Librarians/Media Specialists: 49.0 (1,051.0 to 1)
Guidance Counselors: 236.8 (217.5 to 1)
Current Spending: ($ per student per year):
Total: $6,195; Instruction: $3,803; Support Services: $2,071
Enrollment, Drop-out Rates and Diploma Recipients by Race/Ethnicity

Category	Total	White	Black	Asian	AIAN	Hisp.
Enrollment (%)	100.0	37.1	49.6	4.3	0.5	8.5
Drop-out Rate (%)	10.9	11.7	11.1	4.7	8.9	9.5
H.S. Diplomas (#)	2,261	976	973	132	11	169

Jefferson Davis Parish School Board
203 E Plaquemine St • Jennings, LA 70546-0640
Mailing Address: PO Box 640 • Jennings, LA 70546-0640
(337) 824-1834
Grade Span: PK-12; **Agency Type:** 1
Schools: 14
6 Primary; 2 Middle; 3 High; 3 Other Level
14 Regular; 0 Special Education; 0 Vocational; 0 Alternative
0 Magnet; 0 Charter; 8 Title I Eligible; 8 School-wide Title I
Students: 5,811 (52.0% male; 48.0% female)
Individual Education Program: 960 (16.5%);
English Language Learner: 21 (0.4%); Migrant: 45 (0.8%)
Eligible for Free Lunch Program: 2,416 (41.6%)
Eligible for Reduced-Price Lunch Program: 840 (14.5%)
Teachers: 370.0 (15.7 to 1)
Librarians/Media Specialists: 12.0 (484.3 to 1)
Guidance Counselors: 26.0 (223.5 to 1)
Current Spending: ($ per student per year):
Total: $5,924; Instruction: $3,330; Support Services: $2,083
Enrollment, Drop-out Rates and Diploma Recipients by Race/Ethnicity

Category	Total	White	Black	Asian	AIAN	Hisp.
Enrollment (%)	100.0	73.5	24.7	0.2	1.5	0.1
Drop-out Rate (%)	5.4	4.9	7.6	0.0	0.0	0.0
H.S. Diplomas (#)	318	266	45	0	4	3

La Salle Parish

Lasalle Parish School Board
3012 N First St • Jena, LA 71342-0090
Mailing Address: PO Drawer 90 • Jena, LA 71342-0090
(318) 992-2161 • http://www.lpsb.org/
Grade Span: PK-12; **Agency Type:** 1
Schools: 10
4 Primary; 3 Middle; 2 High; 1 Other Level
9 Regular; 0 Special Education; 0 Vocational; 1 Alternative
0 Magnet; 0 Charter; 4 Title I Eligible; 4 School-wide Title I
Students: 2,693 (50.0% male; 50.0% female)
Individual Education Program: 236 (8.8%);
English Language Learner: 0 (0.0%); Migrant: 30 (1.1%)
Eligible for Free Lunch Program: 1,139 (42.3%)
Eligible for Reduced-Price Lunch Program: 321 (11.9%)
Teachers: 189.3 (14.2 to 1)
Librarians/Media Specialists: 7.0 (384.7 to 1)
Guidance Counselors: 5.0 (538.6 to 1)
Current Spending: ($ per student per year):
Total: $5,825; Instruction: $3,348; Support Services: $1,978
Enrollment, Drop-out Rates and Diploma Recipients by Race/Ethnicity

Category	Total	White	Black	Asian	AIAN	Hisp.
Enrollment (%)	100.0	85.7	12.6	0.1	1.1	0.5
Drop-out Rate (%)	4.0	3.9	5.2	0.0	0.0	0.0
H.S. Diplomas (#)	163	150	13	0	0	0

Lafayette Parish

Lafayette Parish School Board
113 Chaplin Dr • Lafayette, LA 70508
Mailing Address: PO Drawer 2158 • Lafayette, LA 70502-2158
(337) 236-6825 • http://www.lft.k12.la.us/
Grade Span: PK-12; **Agency Type:** 1
Schools: 45
24 Primary; 11 Middle; 5 High; 5 Other Level
41 Regular; 0 Special Education; 0 Vocational; 4 Alternative
0 Magnet; 1 Charter; 21 Title I Eligible; 21 School-wide Title I
Students: 29,554 (51.1% male; 48.9% female)
Individual Education Program: 3,407 (11.5%);
English Language Learner: 506 (1.7%); Migrant: 86 (0.3%)
Eligible for Free Lunch Program: 12,350 (41.8%)
Eligible for Reduced-Price Lunch Program: 2,317 (7.8%)
Teachers: 2,036.6 (14.5 to 1)
Librarians/Media Specialists: 46.0 (642.5 to 1)
Guidance Counselors: 140.3 (210.6 to 1)
Current Spending: ($ per student per year):
Total: $5,560; Instruction: $3,666; Support Services: $1,609
Enrollment, Drop-out Rates and Diploma Recipients by Race/Ethnicity

Category	Total	White	Black	Asian	AIAN	Hisp.
Enrollment (%)	100.0	57.4	39.7	1.3	0.2	1.3
Drop-out Rate (%)	8.6	7.4	11.2	10.2	10.0	14.3
H.S. Diplomas (#)	1,624	1,153	438	21	1	11

Lafourche Parish

Lafourche Parish School Board
805 E Seventh St • Thibodaux, LA 70301
Mailing Address: PO Box 879 • Thibodaux, LA 70302-0879
(985) 446-5631 • http://lafourche.k12.la.us/
Grade Span: PK-12; **Agency Type:** 1
Schools: 29
14 Primary; 10 Middle; 3 High; 1 Other Level
27 Regular; 0 Special Education; 0 Vocational; 1 Alternative
0 Magnet; 0 Charter; 17 Title I Eligible; 17 School-wide Title I
Students: 15,023 (51.8% male; 48.2% female)
Individual Education Program: 1,989 (13.2%);
English Language Learner: 374 (2.5%); Migrant: 252 (1.7%)
Eligible for Free Lunch Program: 6,448 (42.9%)
Eligible for Reduced-Price Lunch Program: 1,677 (11.2%)
Teachers: 1,156.6 (13.0 to 1)
Librarians/Media Specialists: 33.0 (455.2 to 1)
Guidance Counselors: 88.0 (170.7 to 1)
Current Spending: ($ per student per year):
Total: $5,968; Instruction: $3,669; Support Services: $1,911
Enrollment, Drop-out Rates and Diploma Recipients by Race/Ethnicity

Category	Total	White	Black	Asian	AIAN	Hisp.
Enrollment (%)	100.0	71.4	22.1	0.9	3.9	1.6
Drop-out Rate (%)	5.5	4.6	8.6	1.9	11.6	6.7
H.S. Diplomas (#)	810	656	110	13	24	7

Lincoln Parish

Lincoln Parish School Board

410 S Farmerville St • Ruston, LA 71270-4699
(318) 255-1430 • http://www.lincolnschools.org/
Grade Span: PK-12; **Agency Type:** 1
Schools: 19
9 Primary; 3 Middle; 5 High; 2 Other Level
16 Regular; 0 Special Education; 0 Vocational; 3 Alternative
0 Magnet; 0 Charter; 10 Title I Eligible; 10 School-wide Title I
Students: 6,650 (50.9% male; 49.1% female)
Individual Education Program: 828 (12.5%);
English Language Learner: 18 (0.3%); Migrant: 25 (0.4%)
Eligible for Free Lunch Program: 3,066 (46.1%)
Eligible for Reduced-Price Lunch Program: 522 (7.8%)
Teachers: 475.2 (14.0 to 1)
Librarians/Media Specialists: 17.0 (391.2 to 1)
Guidance Counselors: 28.8 (230.9 to 1)
Current Spending: ($ per student per year):
Total: $5,713; Instruction: $3,485; Support Services: $1,805
Enrollment, Drop-out Rates and Diploma Recipients by Race/Ethnicity

Category	Total	White	Black	Asian	AIAN	Hisp.
Enrollment (%)	100.0	49.7	48.5	0.8	0.0	0.9
Drop-out Rate (%)	6.6	5.1	8.8	5.3	n/a	0.0
H.S. Diplomas (#)	418	236	172	6	0	4

Livingston Parish

Livingston Parish School Board

13909 Florida Blvd • Livingston, LA 70754-1130
Mailing Address: PO Box 1130 • Livingston, LA 70754-1130
(225) 686-7044 • http://www.nls.k12.la.us/~mpsb/
Grade Span: PK-12; **Agency Type:** 1
Schools: 37
19 Primary; 7 Middle; 7 High; 4 Other Level
36 Regular; 1 Special Education; 0 Vocational; 0 Alternative
0 Magnet; 0 Charter; 19 Title I Eligible; 19 School-wide Title I
Students: 20,334 (51.3% male; 48.7% female)
Individual Education Program: 2,275 (11.2%);
English Language Learner: 69 (0.3%); Migrant: 11 (0.1%)
Eligible for Free Lunch Program: 5,933 (29.2%)
Eligible for Reduced-Price Lunch Program: 2,427 (11.9%)
Teachers: 1,314.0 (15.5 to 1)
Librarians/Media Specialists: 22.0 (924.3 to 1)
Guidance Counselors: 59.0 (344.6 to 1)
Current Spending: ($ per student per year):
Total: $4,949; Instruction: $3,120; Support Services: $1,412
Enrollment, Drop-out Rates and Diploma Recipients by Race/Ethnicity

Category	Total	White	Black	Asian	AIAN	Hisp.
Enrollment (%)	100.0	93.6	5.3	0.2	0.2	0.6
Drop-out Rate (%)	1.0	1.0	1.1	0.0	0.0	0.0
H.S. Diplomas (#)	1,056	997	50	4	0	5

Madison Parish

Madison Parish School Board

301 S Chestnut St • Tallulah, LA 71282
Mailing Address: PO Box 1620 • Tallulah, LA 71284-1620
(318) 574-3616 • http://nls.k12.la.us/~mpsb/
Grade Span: PK-12; **Agency Type:** 1
Schools: 7
2 Primary; 2 Middle; 2 High; 1 Other Level
6 Regular; 0 Special Education; 0 Vocational; 1 Alternative
0 Magnet; 0 Charter; 7 Title I Eligible; 7 School-wide Title I
Students: 2,387 (51.9% male; 48.1% female)
Individual Education Program: 274 (11.5%);
English Language Learner: 1 (<0.1%); Migrant: 58 (2.4%)
Eligible for Free Lunch Program: 1,892 (79.3%)
Eligible for Reduced-Price Lunch Program: 93 (3.9%)
Teachers: 155.0 (15.4 to 1)
Librarians/Media Specialists: 5.0 (477.4 to 1)
Guidance Counselors: 6.0 (397.8 to 1)
Current Spending: ($ per student per year):
Total: $5,516; Instruction: $2,940; Support Services: $2,035
Enrollment, Drop-out Rates and Diploma Recipients by Race/Ethnicity

Category	Total	White	Black	Asian	AIAN	Hisp.
Enrollment (%)	100.0	10.2	88.5	0.2	0.0	1.0
Drop-out Rate (%)	11.9	17.1	11.3	0.0	n/a	0.0
H.S. Diplomas (#)	111	11	97	1	0	2

Morehouse Parish

Morehouse Parish School Board

714 S Washington St • Bastrop, LA 71220
Mailing Address: PO Box 872 • Bastrop, LA 71221-0872
(318) 281-5784
Grade Span: PK-12; **Agency Type:** 1
Schools: 16
11 Primary; 2 Middle; 1 High; 2 Other Level
14 Regular; 0 Special Education; 0 Vocational; 2 Alternative
1 Magnet; 0 Charter; 9 Title I Eligible; 9 School-wide Title I
Students: 5,209 (51.8% male; 48.2% female)
Individual Education Program: 792 (15.2%);
English Language Learner: 13 (0.2%); Migrant: 21 (0.4%)
Eligible for Free Lunch Program: 3,237 (62.1%)
Eligible for Reduced-Price Lunch Program: 412 (7.9%)
Teachers: 375.9 (13.9 to 1)
Librarians/Media Specialists: 6.0 (868.2 to 1)
Guidance Counselors: 16.0 (325.6 to 1)
Current Spending: ($ per student per year):
Total: $5,585; Instruction: $3,326; Support Services: $1,807
Enrollment, Drop-out Rates and Diploma Recipients by Race/Ethnicity

Category	Total	White	Black	Asian	AIAN	Hisp.
Enrollment (%)	100.0	35.5	63.9	0.1	0.1	0.4
Drop-out Rate (%)	12.0	9.8	13.3	0.0	0.0	0.0
H.S. Diplomas (#)	230	93	137	0	0	0

Natchitoches Parish

Natchitoches Parish School Board

310 Royal St • Natchitoches, LA 71457-5709
Mailing Address: PO Box 16 • Natchitoches, LA 71458-0016
(318) 352-2358 • http://www.nat.k12.la.us/
Grade Span: PK-12; **Agency Type:** 1
Schools: 15
9 Primary; 3 Middle; 0 High; 3 Other Level
14 Regular; 0 Special Education; 0 Vocational; 1 Alternative
0 Magnet; 0 Charter; 11 Title I Eligible; 11 School-wide Title I
Students: 6,978 (51.3% male; 48.7% female)
Individual Education Program: 822 (11.8%);
English Language Learner: 20 (0.3%); Migrant: 201 (2.9%)
Eligible for Free Lunch Program: 4,062 (58.2%)
Eligible for Reduced-Price Lunch Program: 694 (9.9%)
Teachers: 472.3 (14.8 to 1)
Librarians/Media Specialists: 14.0 (498.4 to 1)
Guidance Counselors: 13.0 (536.8 to 1)
Current Spending: ($ per student per year):
Total: $5,771; Instruction: $3,435; Support Services: $1,919
Enrollment, Drop-out Rates and Diploma Recipients by Race/Ethnicity

Category	Total	White	Black	Asian	AIAN	Hisp.
Enrollment (%)	100.0	42.2	55.9	0.4	0.7	0.8
Drop-out Rate (%)	13.4	9.1	17.4	14.3	16.7	0.0
H.S. Diplomas (#)	353	185	159	1	3	5

Orleans Parish

Orleans Parish School Board

3510 General Degaulle Dr • New Orleans, LA 70114
(504) 365-8730 • http://www.nops.k12.la.us/
Grade Span: PK-12; **Agency Type:** 1
Schools: 128
78 Primary; 24 Middle; 24 High; 2 Other Level
116 Regular; 0 Special Education; 1 Vocational; 11 Alternative
6 Magnet; 2 Charter; 91 Title I Eligible; 91 School-wide Title I
Students: 70,246 (50.3% male; 49.7% female)
Individual Education Program: 7,553 (10.8%);
English Language Learner: 1,335 (1.9%); Migrant: 134 (0.2%)
Eligible for Free Lunch Program: 51,771 (73.7%)
Eligible for Reduced-Price Lunch Program: 3,179 (4.5%)
Teachers: 4,236.4 (16.6 to 1)
Librarians/Media Specialists: 81.0 (867.2 to 1)
Guidance Counselors: 140.0 (501.8 to 1)
Current Spending: ($ per student per year):
Total: $5,789; Instruction: $3,574; Support Services: $1,883
Enrollment, Drop-out Rates and Diploma Recipients by Race/Ethnicity

Category	Total	White	Black	Asian	AIAN	Hisp.
Enrollment (%)	100.0	3.5	93.4	1.9	0.1	1.2
Drop-out Rate (%)	11.4	2.3	12.1	3.6	0.0	9.0
H.S. Diplomas (#)	3,471	162	3,131	136	2	40

Ouachita Parish

City of Monroe School Board

2101 Roselawn Ave • Monroe, LA 71201
Mailing Address: PO Box 4180 • Monroe, LA 71211-4180
(318) 325-0601
Grade Span: PK-12; **Agency Type:** 1
Schools: 20
12 Primary; 3 Middle; 4 High; 1 Other Level
18 Regular; 0 Special Education; 0 Vocational; 2 Alternative
3 Magnet; 0 Charter; 15 Title I Eligible; 12 School-wide Title I
Students: 9,678 (50.0% male; 50.0% female)
Individual Education Program: 1,321 (13.6%);
English Language Learner: 23 (0.2%); Migrant: 8 (0.1%)
Eligible for Free Lunch Program: 6,916 (71.5%)
Eligible for Reduced-Price Lunch Program: 526 (5.4%)
Teachers: 659.7 (14.7 to 1)
Librarians/Media Specialists: 18.0 (537.7 to 1)
Guidance Counselors: 40.9 (236.6 to 1)
Current Spending: ($ per student per year):
Total: $5,295; Instruction: $3,369; Support Services: $1,512
Enrollment, Drop-out Rates and Diploma Recipients by Race/Ethnicity

Category	Total	White	Black	Asian	AIAN	Hisp.
Enrollment (%)	100.0	10.5	88.8	0.3	0.1	0.3
Drop-out Rate (%)	10.2	5.9	10.9	0.0	n/a	25.0
H.S. Diplomas (#)	469	83	384	0	0	2

Ouachita Parish School Board

100 Bry St • Monroe, LA 71201
Mailing Address: PO Box 1642 • Monroe, LA 71210-1642
(318) 338-5300 • http://www.opsb.net/
Grade Span: PK-12; **Agency Type:** 1
Schools: 35
21 Primary; 7 Middle; 6 High; 0 Other Level
32 Regular; 0 Special Education; 0 Vocational; 2 Alternative
0 Magnet; 0 Charter; 10 Title I Eligible; 8 School-wide Title I
Students: 17,793 (50.3% male; 49.7% female)
Individual Education Program: 2,208 (12.4%);
English Language Learner: 52 (0.3%); Migrant: 42 (0.2%)
Eligible for Free Lunch Program: 6,461 (36.3%)
Eligible for Reduced-Price Lunch Program: 1,295 (7.3%)
Teachers: 1,313.4 (13.5 to 1)
Librarians/Media Specialists: 37.0 (480.9 to 1)
Guidance Counselors: 70.5 (252.4 to 1)
Current Spending: ($ per student per year):
Total: $5,706; Instruction: $3,569; Support Services: $1,742
Enrollment, Drop-out Rates and Diploma Recipients by Race/Ethnicity

Category	Total	White	Black	Asian	AIAN	Hisp.
Enrollment (%)	100.0	71.4	27.3	0.6	0.1	0.7
Drop-out Rate (%)	8.4	7.8	10.6	0.0	0.0	0.0
H.S. Diplomas (#)	923	720	188	7	1	7

Plaquemines Parish

Plaquemines Parish School Board

26138 Hwy 23 S • Port Sulphur, LA 70083-0070
Mailing Address: PO Box 70 • Port Sulphur, LA 70083-0070
(985) 564-2743 • http://www.ppsb.org/
Grade Span: PK-12; **Agency Type:** 1
Schools: 9
1 Primary; 2 Middle; 2 High; 4 Other Level
8 Regular; 0 Special Education; 0 Vocational; 1 Alternative
0 Magnet; 0 Charter; 5 Title I Eligible; 4 School-wide Title I
Students: 4,811 (52.4% male; 47.6% female)
Individual Education Program: 600 (12.5%);
English Language Learner: 99 (2.1%); Migrant: 196 (4.1%)
Eligible for Free Lunch Program: 2,647 (55.0%)
Eligible for Reduced-Price Lunch Program: 535 (11.1%)
Teachers: 328.2 (14.7 to 1)
Librarians/Media Specialists: 9.0 (534.6 to 1)
Guidance Counselors: 21.0 (229.1 to 1)
Current Spending: ($ per student per year):
Total: $5,927; Instruction: $3,257; Support Services: $2,241
Enrollment, Drop-out Rates and Diploma Recipients by Race/Ethnicity

Category	Total	White	Black	Asian	AIAN	Hisp.
Enrollment (%)	100.0	59.0	33.2	5.3	1.5	1.0
Drop-out Rate (%)	3.5	3.8	3.4	0.0	0.0	0.0
H.S. Diplomas (#)	278	166	95	9	3	5

Pointe Coupee Parish

Pointe Coupee Parish School Board

1662 Morganza Hwy • New Roads, LA 70760-0579
Mailing Address: PO Drawer 579 • New Roads, LA 70760-0579
(225) 638-8674
Grade Span: PK-12; **Agency Type:** 1
Schools: 9
6 Primary; 0 Middle; 2 High; 1 Other Level
8 Regular; 0 Special Education; 0 Vocational; 1 Alternative
1 Magnet; 0 Charter; 6 Title I Eligible; 6 School-wide Title I
Students: 3,185 (49.8% male; 50.2% female)
Individual Education Program: 663 (20.8%);
English Language Learner: 2 (0.1%); Migrant: 30 (0.9%)
Eligible for Free Lunch Program: 2,172 (68.2%)
Eligible for Reduced-Price Lunch Program: 276 (8.7%)
Teachers: 233.0 (13.7 to 1)
Librarians/Media Specialists: 3.0 (1,061.7 to 1)
Guidance Counselors: 14.0 (227.5 to 1)
Current Spending: ($ per student per year):
Total: $5,972; Instruction: $3,469; Support Services: $2,029
Enrollment, Drop-out Rates and Diploma Recipients by Race/Ethnicity

Category	Total	White	Black	Asian	AIAN	Hisp.
Enrollment (%)	100.0	34.6	64.6	0.1	0.0	0.7
Drop-out Rate (%)	16.4	16.8	16.2	n/a	0.0	0.0
H.S. Diplomas (#)	167	46	120	0	1	0

Rapides Parish

Rapides Parish School Board

619 Sixth St • Alexandria, LA 71301
Mailing Address: PO Box 1230 • Alexandria, LA 71309-1230
(318) 487-0888 • http://www.rapides.k12.la.us/
Grade Span: PK-12; **Agency Type:** 1
Schools: 53
29 Primary; 8 Middle; 9 High; 7 Other Level
48 Regular; 2 Special Education; 0 Vocational; 3 Alternative
4 Magnet; 0 Charter; 29 Title I Eligible; 26 School-wide Title I
Students: 22,872 (51.4% male; 48.6% female)
Individual Education Program: 3,202 (14.0%);
English Language Learner: 333 (1.5%); Migrant: 133 (0.6%)
Eligible for Free Lunch Program: 12,168 (53.2%)
Eligible for Reduced-Price Lunch Program: 2,344 (10.2%)
Teachers: 1,619.9 (14.1 to 1)
Librarians/Media Specialists: 50.0 (457.4 to 1)
Guidance Counselors: 120.0 (190.6 to 1)
Current Spending: ($ per student per year):
Total: $5,971; Instruction: $3,425; Support Services: $1,988
Enrollment, Drop-out Rates and Diploma Recipients by Race/Ethnicity

Category	Total	White	Black	Asian	AIAN	Hisp.
Enrollment (%)	100.0	53.8	43.1	1.1	1.0	0.9
Drop-out Rate (%)	6.9	5.2	9.7	5.8	10.0	2.6
H.S. Diplomas (#)	1,294	799	450	14	29	2

Red River Parish

Red River Parish School Board

1922 Alonzo St • Coushatta, LA 71019-1369
Mailing Address: PO Box 1369 • Coushatta, LA 71019-1369
(318) 932-4081
Grade Span: PK-12; **Agency Type:** 1
Schools: 5
1 Primary; 1 Middle; 1 High; 2 Other Level
3 Regular; 0 Special Education; 0 Vocational; 2 Alternative
0 Magnet; 0 Charter; 3 Title I Eligible; 3 School-wide Title I
Students: 1,604 (50.2% male; 49.8% female)
Individual Education Program: 227 (14.2%);
English Language Learner: 1 (0.1%); Migrant: 1 (0.1%)
Eligible for Free Lunch Program: 1,138 (70.9%)
Eligible for Reduced-Price Lunch Program: 132 (8.2%)
Teachers: 135.8 (11.8 to 1)
Librarians/Media Specialists: 0.0 (0.0 to 1)
Guidance Counselors: 6.0 (267.3 to 1)
Current Spending: ($ per student per year):
Total: $6,448; Instruction: $3,734; Support Services: $2,212
Enrollment, Drop-out Rates and Diploma Recipients by Race/Ethnicity

Category	Total	White	Black	Asian	AIAN	Hisp.
Enrollment (%)	100.0	31.3	68.3	0.1	0.4	0.0
Drop-out Rate (%)	12.0	15.0	9.6	n/a	n/a	100.0
H.S. Diplomas (#)	75	26	49	0	0	0

Richland Parish

Richland Parish School Board

411 Foster St • Rayville, LA 71269-0599
Mailing Address: PO Box 599 • Rayville, LA 71269-0599
(318) 728-5964 • http://www.nls.k12.la.us/~richland/
Grade Span: PK-12; **Agency Type:** 1
Schools: 12
6 Primary; 2 Middle; 3 High; 1 Other Level
11 Regular; 0 Special Education; 0 Vocational; 1 Alternative
0 Magnet; 0 Charter; 9 Title I Eligible; 8 School-wide Title I
Students: 3,527 (52.0% male; 48.0% female)
Individual Education Program: 495 (14.0%);
English Language Learner: 0 (0.0%); Migrant: 29 (0.8%)
Eligible for Free Lunch Program: 2,266 (64.2%)
Eligible for Reduced-Price Lunch Program: 224 (6.4%)
Teachers: 269.3 (13.1 to 1)
Librarians/Media Specialists: 0.0 (0.0 to 1)
Guidance Counselors: 10.0 (352.7 to 1)
Current Spending: ($ per student per year):
Total: $5,849; Instruction: $3,570; Support Services: $1,785
Enrollment, Drop-out Rates and Diploma Recipients by Race/Ethnicity

Category	Total	White	Black	Asian	AIAN	Hisp.
Enrollment (%)	100.0	42.1	57.2	0.2	0.0	0.5
Drop-out Rate (%)	7.5	8.6	6.8	n/a	n/a	0.0
H.S. Diplomas (#)	175	70	105	0	0	0

Sabine Parish

Sabine Parish School Board

695 Peterson St • Many, LA 71449-1079
Mailing Address: PO Box 1079 • Many, LA 71449-1079
(318) 256-9228 • http://www.sabine.k12.la.us/
Grade Span: PK-12; **Agency Type:** 1
Schools: 14
5 Primary; 1 Middle; 3 High; 5 Other Level
13 Regular; 0 Special Education; 0 Vocational; 1 Alternative
0 Magnet; 0 Charter; 10 Title I Eligible; 10 School-wide Title I
Students: 4,299 (52.7% male; 47.3% female)
Individual Education Program: 644 (15.0%);
English Language Learner: 11 (0.3%); Migrant: 11 (0.3%)
Eligible for Free Lunch Program: 2,253 (52.4%)
Eligible for Reduced-Price Lunch Program: 466 (10.8%)
Teachers: 291.6 (14.7 to 1)
Librarians/Media Specialists: 11.0 (390.8 to 1)
Guidance Counselors: 10.0 (429.9 to 1)
Current Spending: ($ per student per year):
Total: $5,653; Instruction: $3,237; Support Services: $1,979
Enrollment, Drop-out Rates and Diploma Recipients by Race/Ethnicity

Category	Total	White	Black	Asian	AIAN	Hisp.
Enrollment (%)	100.0	50.5	26.3	0.1	19.0	4.1
Drop-out Rate (%)	7.2	5.3	13.1	0.0	5.1	5.8
H.S. Diplomas (#)	257	148	62	1	35	11

St. Bernard Parish

Saint Bernard Parish School Board

200 E Saint Bernard Hwy • Chalmette, LA 70043
(504) 301-2000 • http://www.gnofn.org/~sbpsb/
Grade Span: PK-12; **Agency Type:** 1
Schools: 14
7 Primary; 3 Middle; 3 High; 1 Other Level
13 Regular; 0 Special Education; 0 Vocational; 1 Alternative
1 Magnet; 0 Charter; 8 Title I Eligible; 0 School-wide Title I
Students: 8,734 (50.4% male; 49.6% female)
Individual Education Program: 1,269 (14.5%);
English Language Learner: 45 (0.5%); Migrant: 2 (<0.1%)
Eligible for Free Lunch Program: 4,125 (47.2%)
Eligible for Reduced-Price Lunch Program: 939 (10.8%)
Teachers: 625.2 (14.0 to 1)
Librarians/Media Specialists: 14.0 (623.9 to 1)
Guidance Counselors: 22.0 (397.0 to 1)
Current Spending: ($ per student per year):
Total: $6,067; Instruction: $3,673; Support Services: $2,037
Enrollment, Drop-out Rates and Diploma Recipients by Race/Ethnicity

Category	Total	White	Black	Asian	AIAN	Hisp.
Enrollment (%)	100.0	77.2	15.2	2.3	1.2	4.1
Drop-out Rate (%)	6.6	6.1	12.1	1.9	4.5	6.2
H.S. Diplomas (#)	382	325	38	5	3	11

St. Charles Parish

Saint Charles Parish School Board

13855 River Rd • Luling, LA 70070-0046
Mailing Address: PO Box 46 • Luling, LA 70070-0046
(985) 785-6289 • http://www.stcharles.k12.la.us/
Grade Span: PK-12; **Agency Type:** 1
Schools: 20
12 Primary; 6 Middle; 2 High; 0 Other Level
20 Regular; 0 Special Education; 0 Vocational; 0 Alternative
0 Magnet; 0 Charter; 4 Title I Eligible; 0 School-wide Title I
Students: 9,717 (50.8% male; 49.2% female)
Individual Education Program: 1,093 (11.2%);
English Language Learner: 125 (1.3%); Migrant: 18 (0.2%)
Eligible for Free Lunch Program: 3,532 (36.3%)
Eligible for Reduced-Price Lunch Program: 771 (7.9%)
Teachers: 778.2 (12.5 to 1)
Librarians/Media Specialists: 19.0 (511.4 to 1)
Guidance Counselors: 31.0 (313.5 to 1)
Current Spending: ($ per student per year):
Total: $7,502; Instruction: $4,348; Support Services: $2,807
Enrollment, Drop-out Rates and Diploma Recipients by Race/Ethnicity

Category	Total	White	Black	Asian	AIAN	Hisp.
Enrollment (%)	100.0	60.3	36.1	0.9	0.3	2.4
Drop-out Rate (%)	5.2	4.3	7.7	0.0	0.0	3.3
H.S. Diplomas (#)	628	438	172	5	0	13

St. James Parish

Saint James Parish School Board

1876 W Main St • Lutcher, LA 70071-0338
Mailing Address: PO Box 338 • Lutcher, LA 70071-0338
(225) 869-5375
Grade Span: PK-12; **Agency Type:** 1
Schools: 12
7 Primary; 2 Middle; 2 High; 1 Other Level
11 Regular; 0 Special Education; 0 Vocational; 1 Alternative
0 Magnet; 0 Charter; 11 Title I Eligible; 0 School-wide Title I
Students: 4,076 (51.0% male; 49.0% female)
Individual Education Program: 520 (12.8%);
English Language Learner: 3 (0.1%); Migrant: 12 (0.3%)
Eligible for Free Lunch Program: 2,550 (62.6%)
Eligible for Reduced-Price Lunch Program: 279 (6.8%)
Teachers: 276.1 (14.8 to 1)
Librarians/Media Specialists: 5.0 (815.2 to 1)
Guidance Counselors: 14.9 (273.6 to 1)
Current Spending: ($ per student per year):
Total: $6,767; Instruction: $3,508; Support Services: $2,754
Enrollment, Drop-out Rates and Diploma Recipients by Race/Ethnicity

Category	Total	White	Black	Asian	AIAN	Hisp.
Enrollment (%)	100.0	30.4	69.3	0.0	0.0	0.3
Drop-out Rate (%)	6.0	2.1	8.3	n/a	n/a	0.0
H.S. Diplomas (#)	230	95	135	0	0	0

St. John The Baptist Parish

Saint John the Baptist Parish SB

118 W Tenth St • Reserve, LA 70084
Mailing Address: PO Drawer AI • Reserve, LA 70084
(985) 536-3797 • http://www.stjohn.k12.la.us/
Grade Span: PK-12; **Agency Type:** 1
Schools: 12
8 Primary; 1 Middle; 2 High; 1 Other Level
11 Regular; 0 Special Education; 0 Vocational; 1 Alternative
2 Magnet; 0 Charter; 10 Title I Eligible; 10 School-wide Title I
Students: 6,282 (51.7% male; 48.3% female)
Individual Education Program: 1,253 (19.9%);
English Language Learner: 65 (1.0%); Migrant: 1 (<0.1%)
Eligible for Free Lunch Program: 4,567 (72.7%)
Eligible for Reduced-Price Lunch Program: 485 (7.7%)
Teachers: 487.9 (12.9 to 1)
Librarians/Media Specialists: 3.0 (2,094.0 to 1)
Guidance Counselors: 37.5 (167.5 to 1)
Current Spending: ($ per student per year):
Total: $6,634; Instruction: $4,156; Support Services: $2,124
Enrollment, Drop-out Rates and Diploma Recipients by Race/Ethnicity

Category	Total	White	Black	Asian	AIAN	Hisp.
Enrollment (%)	100.0	21.4	75.7	0.6	0.1	2.2
Drop-out Rate (%)	8.6	11.6	7.9	0.0	0.0	3.1
H.S. Diplomas (#)	276	61	207	2	2	4

St. Landry Parish

Saint Landry Parish School Board

1013 E Creswell Ln • Opelousas, LA 70570
Mailing Address: PO Box 310 • Opelousas, LA 70571-0310
(337) 948-3657
Grade Span: PK-12; **Agency Type:** 1
Schools: 38
25 Primary; 5 Middle; 8 High; 0 Other Level
36 Regular; 0 Special Education; 2 Vocational; 0 Alternative
0 Magnet; 0 Charter; 29 Title I Eligible; 10 School-wide Title I
Students: 15,331 (51.2% male; 48.8% female)
Individual Education Program: 2,380 (15.5%);
English Language Learner: 64 (0.4%); Migrant: 219 (1.4%)
Eligible for Free Lunch Program: 10,176 (66.4%)
Eligible for Reduced-Price Lunch Program: 1,738 (11.3%)
Teachers: 1,048.5 (14.6 to 1)
Librarians/Media Specialists: 21.0 (730.0 to 1)
Guidance Counselors: 31.0 (494.5 to 1)
Current Spending: ($ per student per year):
Total: $5,879; Instruction: $3,636; Support Services: $1,634
Enrollment, Drop-out Rates and Diploma Recipients by Race/Ethnicity

Category	Total	White	Black	Asian	AIAN	Hisp.
Enrollment (%)	100.0	43.6	55.6	0.3	0.1	0.4
Drop-out Rate (%)	6.1	5.3	6.7	0.0	12.5	17.6
H.S. Diplomas (#)	805	417	383	3	0	2

St. Martin Parish

Saint Martin Parish School Board

305 Washington St • Saint Martinville, LA 70582-0859
Mailing Address: PO Box 859 • Saint Martinville, LA 70582-0859
(337) 394-6261 • http://www.stmartin.k12.la.us/
Grade Span: PK-12; **Agency Type:** 1
Schools: 18
7 Primary; 7 Middle; 3 High; 1 Other Level
17 Regular; 0 Special Education; 0 Vocational; 1 Alternative
0 Magnet; 0 Charter; 11 Title I Eligible; 11 School-wide Title I
Students: 8,614 (51.6% male; 48.4% female)
Individual Education Program: 1,265 (14.7%);
English Language Learner: 86 (1.0%); Migrant: 73 (0.8%)
Eligible for Free Lunch Program: 5,144 (59.7%)
Eligible for Reduced-Price Lunch Program: 849 (9.9%)
Teachers: 600.5 (14.3 to 1)
Librarians/Media Specialists: 13.0 (662.6 to 1)
Guidance Counselors: 28.0 (307.6 to 1)
Current Spending: ($ per student per year):
Total: $5,640; Instruction: $3,443; Support Services: $1,769
Enrollment, Drop-out Rates and Diploma Recipients by Race/Ethnicity

Category	Total	White	Black	Asian	AIAN	Hisp.
Enrollment (%)	100.0	50.7	47.7	1.3	0.1	0.2
Drop-out Rate (%)	8.8	7.9	10.0	4.3	0.0	16.7
H.S. Diplomas (#)	460	274	181	3	0	2

St. Mary Parish

Saint Mary Parish School Board

474 Hwy 317 • Centerville, LA 70522-0170
Mailing Address: PO Box 170 • Centerville, LA 70522-0170
(337) 836-9661 • http://www.stmary.k12.la.us/
Grade Span: PK-12; **Agency Type:** 1
Schools: 27
14 Primary; 6 Middle; 5 High; 2 Other Level
26 Regular; 0 Special Education; 0 Vocational; 1 Alternative
0 Magnet; 0 Charter; 12 Title I Eligible; 12 School-wide Title I
Students: 10,363 (50.7% male; 49.3% female)
Individual Education Program: 1,623 (15.7%);
English Language Learner: 289 (2.8%); Migrant: 89 (0.9%)
Eligible for Free Lunch Program: 5,948 (57.4%)
Eligible for Reduced-Price Lunch Program: 995 (9.6%)
Teachers: 725.9 (14.3 to 1)
Librarians/Media Specialists: 23.0 (450.6 to 1)
Guidance Counselors: 23.0 (450.6 to 1)
Current Spending: ($ per student per year):
Total: $5,966; Instruction: $3,469; Support Services: $2,044
Enrollment, Drop-out Rates and Diploma Recipients by Race/Ethnicity

Category	Total	White	Black	Asian	AIAN	Hisp.
Enrollment (%)	100.0	47.8	47.2	2.5	0.8	1.7
Drop-out Rate (%)	7.3	6.8	7.5	5.6	23.7	5.6
H.S. Diplomas (#)	614	332	249	15	7	11

St. Tammany Parish

Saint Tammany Parish School Board

212 W Seventeenth Ave • Covington, LA 70433
Mailing Address: PO Box 940 • Covington, LA 70434-0940
(985) 892-3216 • http://www.stpsb.org.
Grade Span: PK-12; **Agency Type:** 1
Schools: 51
23 Primary; 18 Middle; 7 High; 3 Other Level
48 Regular; 2 Special Education; 0 Vocational; 1 Alternative
0 Magnet; 0 Charter; 26 Title I Eligible; 13 School-wide Title I
Students: 34,081 (51.6% male; 48.4% female)
Individual Education Program: 5,809 (17.0%);
English Language Learner: 441 (1.3%); Migrant: 8 (<0.1%)
Eligible for Free Lunch Program: 8,406 (24.7%)
Eligible for Reduced-Price Lunch Program: 2,009 (5.9%)
Teachers: 2,395.6 (14.2 to 1)
Librarians/Media Specialists: 54.0 (631.1 to 1)
Guidance Counselors: 204.8 (166.4 to 1)
Current Spending: ($ per student per year):
Total: $6,408; Instruction: $4,043; Support Services: $2,002
Enrollment, Drop-out Rates and Diploma Recipients by Race/Ethnicity

Category	Total	White	Black	Asian	AIAN	Hisp.
Enrollment (%)	100.0	80.6	16.5	1.0	0.2	1.6
Drop-out Rate (%)	8.0	7.8	9.9	2.7	7.1	6.4
H.S. Diplomas (#)	1,834	1,595	195	19	5	20

Tangipahoa Parish

Tangipahoa Parish School Board

313 E Oak St • Amite, LA 70422-0457
Mailing Address: PO Box 457 • Amite, LA 70422-0457
(985) 748-7153 • http://www.tangischools.org/
Grade Span: PK-12; **Agency Type:** 1
Schools: 36
17 Primary; 10 Middle; 8 High; 1 Other Level
33 Regular; 0 Special Education; 0 Vocational; 3 Alternative
0 Magnet; 0 Charter; 26 Title I Eligible; 26 School-wide Title I
Students: 17,926 (50.8% male; 49.2% female)
Individual Education Program: 2,609 (14.6%);
English Language Learner: 207 (1.2%); Migrant: 107 (0.6%)
Eligible for Free Lunch Program: 10,664 (59.5%)
Eligible for Reduced-Price Lunch Program: 1,477 (8.2%)
Teachers: 1,059.2 (16.9 to 1)
Librarians/Media Specialists: 24.9 (719.9 to 1)
Guidance Counselors: 57.7 (310.7 to 1)
Current Spending: ($ per student per year):
Total: $5,311; Instruction: $3,334; Support Services: $1,582
Enrollment, Drop-out Rates and Diploma Recipients by Race/Ethnicity

Category	Total	White	Black	Asian	AIAN	Hisp.
Enrollment (%)	100.0	53.7	44.6	0.5	0.0	1.2
Drop-out Rate (%)	8.6	7.1	11.1	7.1	0.0	0.0
H.S. Diplomas (#)	1,030	611	404	6	3	6

Terrebonne Parish

Terrebonne Parish School Board

201 Stadium Dr • Houma, LA 70360
Mailing Address: PO Box 5097 • Houma, LA 70361-5097
(985) 876-7400
Grade Span: PK-12; **Agency Type:** 1
Schools: 41
21 Primary; 11 Middle; 5 High; 4 Other Level
36 Regular; 1 Special Education; 1 Vocational; 3 Alternative
0 Magnet; 0 Charter; 25 Title I Eligible; 25 School-wide Title I
Students: 19,345 (51.0% male; 49.0% female)
Individual Education Program: 3,020 (15.6%);
English Language Learner: 327 (1.7%); Migrant: 604 (3.1%)
Eligible for Free Lunch Program: 9,325 (48.2%)
Eligible for Reduced-Price Lunch Program: 2,156 (11.1%)
Teachers: 1,410.2 (13.7 to 1)
Librarians/Media Specialists: 41.8 (462.8 to 1)
Guidance Counselors: 89.6 (215.9 to 1)
Current Spending: ($ per student per year):
Total: $5,730; Instruction: $3,568; Support Services: $1,777
Enrollment, Drop-out Rates and Diploma Recipients by Race/Ethnicity

Category	Total	White	Black	Asian	AIAN	Hisp.
Enrollment (%)	100.0	61.6	27.8	1.2	8.3	1.0
Drop-out Rate (%)	9.9	8.5	13.0	5.6	12.0	11.1
H.S. Diplomas (#)	1,007	691	232	14	64	6

Union Parish

Union Parish School Board

1206 Marion Hwy • Farmerville, LA 71241-0308
Mailing Address: PO Box 308 • Farmerville, LA 71241-0308
(318) 368-9715 • http://www.unionparishschools.org/
Grade Span: PK-12; **Agency Type:** 1
Schools: 10
2 Primary; 2 Middle; 1 High; 5 Other Level
10 Regular; 0 Special Education; 0 Vocational; 0 Alternative
0 Magnet; 0 Charter; 9 Title I Eligible; 7 School-wide Title I
Students: 3,479 (50.5% male; 49.5% female)
Individual Education Program: 456 (13.1%);
English Language Learner: 78 (2.2%); Migrant: 88 (2.5%)
Eligible for Free Lunch Program: 1,946 (55.9%)
Eligible for Reduced-Price Lunch Program: 321 (9.2%)
Teachers: 224.0 (15.5 to 1)
Librarians/Media Specialists: 8.0 (434.9 to 1)
Guidance Counselors: 6.0 (579.8 to 1)
Current Spending: ($ per student per year):
Total: $5,059; Instruction: $2,906; Support Services: $1,657
Enrollment, Drop-out Rates and Diploma Recipients by Race/Ethnicity

Category	Total	White	Black	Asian	AIAN	Hisp.
Enrollment (%)	100.0	55.4	41.6	0.3	0.0	2.7
Drop-out Rate (%)	4.4	4.0	4.6	0.0	0.0	33.3
H.S. Diplomas (#)	217	131	81	1	1	3

Vermilion Parish

Vermilion Parish School Board

220 S Jefferson St • Abbeville, LA 70510
Mailing Address: PO Drawer 520 • Abbeville, LA 70511-0520
(337) 898-5770 • http://www.vrml.k12.la.us/
Grade Span: PK-12; **Agency Type:** 1
Schools: 20
11 Primary; 3 Middle; 4 High; 2 Other Level
20 Regular; 0 Special Education; 0 Vocational; 0 Alternative
0 Magnet; 0 Charter; 13 Title I Eligible; 9 School-wide Title I
Students: 8,905 (51.3% male; 48.7% female)
Individual Education Program: 1,412 (15.9%);
English Language Learner: 115 (1.3%); Migrant: 108 (1.2%)
Eligible for Free Lunch Program: 3,878 (43.5%)
Eligible for Reduced-Price Lunch Program: 837 (9.4%)
Teachers: 594.8 (15.0 to 1)
Librarians/Media Specialists: 19.0 (468.7 to 1)
Guidance Counselors: 47.0 (189.5 to 1)
Current Spending: ($ per student per year):
Total: $5,491; Instruction: $3,301; Support Services: $1,849
Enrollment, Drop-out Rates and Diploma Recipients by Race/Ethnicity

Category	Total	White	Black	Asian	AIAN	Hisp.
Enrollment (%)	100.0	74.7	21.8	3.0	0.1	0.5
Drop-out Rate (%)	5.7	5.3	6.8	8.5	0.0	33.3
H.S. Diplomas (#)	480	395	75	10	0	0

Vernon Parish

Vernon Parish School Board

201 Belview Rd • Leesville, LA 71446
(337) 239-3401
Grade Span: PK-12; **Agency Type:** 1
Schools: 20
8 Primary; 2 Middle; 5 High; 5 Other Level
19 Regular; 0 Special Education; 0 Vocational; 1 Alternative
0 Magnet; 0 Charter; 13 Title I Eligible; 11 School-wide Title I
Students: 9,841 (51.3% male; 48.7% female)
Individual Education Program: 1,276 (13.0%);
English Language Learner: 97 (1.0%); Migrant: 4 (<0.1%)
Eligible for Free Lunch Program: 3,513 (35.7%)
Eligible for Reduced-Price Lunch Program: 1,657 (16.8%)
Teachers: 687.0 (14.3 to 1)
Librarians/Media Specialists: 18.0 (546.7 to 1)
Guidance Counselors: 31.0 (317.5 to 1)
Current Spending: ($ per student per year):
Total: $5,908; Instruction: $3,547; Support Services: $1,968
Enrollment, Drop-out Rates and Diploma Recipients by Race/Ethnicity

Category	Total	White	Black	Asian	AIAN	Hisp.
Enrollment (%)	100.0	71.0	21.3	1.9	1.4	4.4
Drop-out Rate (%)	7.5	6.2	9.9	10.9	8.6	17.4
H.S. Diplomas (#)	455	327	94	10	9	15

Washington Parish

City of Bogalusa School Board

1705 Sullivan Dr • Bogalusa, LA 70427
Mailing Address: PO Box 310 • Bogalusa, LA 70429-0310
(985) 735-1392
Grade Span: PK-12; **Agency Type:** 1
Schools: 9
5 Primary; 2 Middle; 2 High; 0 Other Level
8 Regular; 0 Special Education; 0 Vocational; 1 Alternative
0 Magnet; 0 Charter; 6 Title I Eligible; 5 School-wide Title I
Students: 3,018 (50.7% male; 49.3% female)
Individual Education Program: 660 (21.9%);
English Language Learner: 19 (0.6%); Migrant: 0 (0.0%)
Eligible for Free Lunch Program: 2,116 (70.1%)
Eligible for Reduced-Price Lunch Program: 270 (8.9%)
Teachers: 226.7 (13.3 to 1)
Librarians/Media Specialists: 2.0 (1,509.0 to 1)
Guidance Counselors: 18.0 (167.7 to 1)
Current Spending: ($ per student per year):
Total: $6,281; Instruction: $3,762; Support Services: $2,068
Enrollment, Drop-out Rates and Diploma Recipients by Race/Ethnicity

Category	Total	White	Black	Asian	AIAN	Hisp.
Enrollment (%)	100.0	46.7	52.1	0.5	0.1	0.6
Drop-out Rate (%)	6.2	5.8	6.5	0.0	0.0	20.0
H.S. Diplomas (#)	164	90	73	0	0	1

Washington Parish School Board

800 Main St • Franklinton, LA 70438-0587
Mailing Address: PO Box 587 • Franklinton, LA 70438-0587
(985) 839-3436 • http://www.wpsb.org/
Grade Span: PK-12; **Agency Type:** 1
Schools: 13
6 Primary; 2 Middle; 3 High; 2 Other Level
12 Regular; 0 Special Education; 1 Vocational; 0 Alternative
0 Magnet; 0 Charter; 12 Title I Eligible; 12 School-wide Title I
Students: 4,739 (51.8% male; 48.2% female)
Individual Education Program: 745 (15.7%);
English Language Learner: 7 (0.1%); Migrant: 14 (0.3%)
Eligible for Free Lunch Program: 3,396 (71.7%)
Eligible for Reduced-Price Lunch Program: 413 (8.7%)
Teachers: 357.0 (13.3 to 1)
Librarians/Media Specialists: 12.0 (394.9 to 1)
Guidance Counselors: 25.0 (189.6 to 1)
Current Spending: ($ per student per year):
Total: $6,012; Instruction: $3,705; Support Services: $1,810
Enrollment, Drop-out Rates and Diploma Recipients by Race/Ethnicity

Category	Total	White	Black	Asian	AIAN	Hisp.
Enrollment (%)	100.0	62.4	37.0	0.1	0.1	0.4
Drop-out Rate (%)	4.0	4.3	3.6	n/a	n/a	0.0
H.S. Diplomas (#)	270	170	98	0	0	2

Webster Parish

Webster Parish School Board

1422 Sheppard St • Minden, LA 71055
Mailing Address: PO Box 520 • Minden, LA 71058-0520
(318) 377-7052 • http://www.webster.k12.la.us/
Grade Span: PK-12; **Agency Type:** 1
Schools: 23
12 Primary; 1 Middle; 3 High; 7 Other Level
20 Regular; 0 Special Education; 0 Vocational; 3 Alternative
0 Magnet; 0 Charter; 12 Title I Eligible; 8 School-wide Title I
Students: 7,728 (51.2% male; 48.8% female)
Individual Education Program: 1,037 (13.4%);
English Language Learner: 2 (<0.1%); Migrant: 29 (0.4%)
Eligible for Free Lunch Program: 3,509 (45.4%)
Eligible for Reduced-Price Lunch Program: 717 (9.3%)
Teachers: 504.7 (15.3 to 1)
Librarians/Media Specialists: 19.0 (406.7 to 1)
Guidance Counselors: 40.7 (189.9 to 1)
Current Spending: ($ per student per year):
Total: $5,501; Instruction: $3,274; Support Services: $1,746
Enrollment, Drop-out Rates and Diploma Recipients by Race/Ethnicity

Category	Total	White	Black	Asian	AIAN	Hisp.
Enrollment (%)	100.0	56.2	43.0	0.3	0.0	0.5
Drop-out Rate (%)	6.3	5.4	7.5	0.0	0.0	33.3
H.S. Diplomas (#)	369	219	146	2	2	0

West Baton Rouge Parish

West Baton Rouge Parish School Bd

3761 Rosedale Rd • Port Allen, LA 70767
(225) 343-8309
Grade Span: PK-12; **Agency Type:** 1
Schools: 11
5 Primary; 3 Middle; 3 High; 0 Other Level
10 Regular; 0 Special Education; 1 Vocational; 0 Alternative
0 Magnet; 0 Charter; 6 Title I Eligible; 0 School-wide Title I
Students: 3,529 (52.5% male; 47.5% female)
Individual Education Program: 455 (12.9%);
English Language Learner: 1 (<0.1%); Migrant: 30 (0.9%)
Eligible for Free Lunch Program: 1,897 (53.8%)
Eligible for Reduced-Price Lunch Program: 316 (9.0%)
Teachers: 254.6 (13.9 to 1)
Librarians/Media Specialists: 10.0 (352.9 to 1)
Guidance Counselors: 12.0 (294.1 to 1)
Current Spending: ($ per student per year):
Total: $6,166; Instruction: $3,574; Support Services: $2,054

Enrollment, Drop-out Rates and Diploma Recipients by Race/Ethnicity

Category	Total	White	Black	Asian	AIAN	Hisp.
Enrollment (%)	100.0	50.4	48.7	0.3	0.0	0.7
Drop-out Rate (%)	8.2	6.1	11.1	0.0	0.0	0.0
H.S. Diplomas (#)	243	147	93	1	0	2

West Carroll Parish

West Carroll Parish School Board

314 E Main St • Oak Grove, LA 71263-1318
Mailing Address: PO Box 1318 • Oak Grove, LA 71263-1318
(318) 428-2378
Grade Span: PK-12; **Agency Type:** 1
Schools: 8
4 Primary; 0 Middle; 1 High; 3 Other Level
8 Regular; 0 Special Education; 0 Vocational; 0 Alternative
0 Magnet; 0 Charter; 8 Title I Eligible; 7 School-wide Title I
Students: 2,376 (52.4% male; 47.6% female)
Individual Education Program: 278 (11.7%);
English Language Learner: 14 (0.6%); Migrant: 37 (1.6%)
Eligible for Free Lunch Program: 1,322 (55.6%)
Eligible for Reduced-Price Lunch Program: 282 (11.9%)
Teachers: 177.0 (13.4 to 1)
Librarians/Media Specialists: 4.0 (594.0 to 1)
Guidance Counselors: 5.8 (409.7 to 1)
Current Spending: ($ per student per year):
Total: $5,152; Instruction: $3,090; Support Services: $1,590

Enrollment, Drop-out Rates and Diploma Recipients by Race/Ethnicity

Category	Total	White	Black	Asian	AIAN	Hisp.
Enrollment (%)	100.0	77.2	21.0	0.1	0.2	1.4
Drop-out Rate (%)	10.8	10.6	10.7	n/a	100.0	0.0
H.S. Diplomas (#)	131	113	18	0	0	0

West Feliciana Parish

West Feliciana Parish School Board

4727 Fidelity St • Saint Francisville, LA 70775-1910
Mailing Address: PO Box 1910 • Saint Francisville, LA 70775-1910
(225) 635-3891
Grade Span: PK-12; **Agency Type:** 1
Schools: 5
3 Primary; 1 Middle; 1 High; 0 Other Level
5 Regular; 0 Special Education; 0 Vocational; 0 Alternative
0 Magnet; 0 Charter; 3 Title I Eligible; 3 School-wide Title I
Students: 2,409 (51.3% male; 48.7% female)
Individual Education Program: 363 (15.1%);
English Language Learner: 4 (0.2%); Migrant: 0 (0.0%)
Eligible for Free Lunch Program: 875 (36.3%)
Eligible for Reduced-Price Lunch Program: 244 (10.1%)
Teachers: 201.0 (12.0 to 1)
Librarians/Media Specialists: 5.0 (481.8 to 1)
Guidance Counselors: 10.0 (240.9 to 1)
Current Spending: ($ per student per year):
Total: $7,727; Instruction: $4,233; Support Services: $3,086

Enrollment, Drop-out Rates and Diploma Recipients by Race/Ethnicity

Category	Total	White	Black	Asian	AIAN	Hisp.
Enrollment (%)	100.0	55.8	43.7	0.2	0.2	0.1
Drop-out Rate (%)	4.1	2.0	6.6	0.0	n/a	n/a
H.S. Diplomas (#)	122	65	56	1	0	0

Winn Parish

Winn Parish School Board

304 E Court St • Winnfield, LA 71483-0430
Mailing Address: PO Box 430 • Winnfield, LA 71483-0430
(318) 628-6936 • http://www.winnpsb.org/
Grade Span: PK-12; **Agency Type:** 1
Schools: 8
2 Primary; 2 Middle; 1 High; 3 Other Level
8 Regular; 0 Special Education; 0 Vocational; 0 Alternative
0 Magnet; 0 Charter; 6 Title I Eligible; 5 School-wide Title I
Students: 2,815 (50.5% male; 49.5% female)
Individual Education Program: 330 (11.7%);
English Language Learner: 1 (<0.1%); Migrant: 65 (2.3%)
Eligible for Free Lunch Program: 1,518 (53.9%)
Eligible for Reduced-Price Lunch Program: 284 (10.1%)
Teachers: 204.4 (13.8 to 1)
Librarians/Media Specialists: 7.0 (402.1 to 1)
Guidance Counselors: 10.0 (281.5 to 1)
Current Spending: ($ per student per year):
Total: $6,166; Instruction: $3,473; Support Services: $2,157

Enrollment, Drop-out Rates and Diploma Recipients by Race/Ethnicity

Category	Total	White	Black	Asian	AIAN	Hisp.
Enrollment (%)	100.0	61.7	37.3	0.4	0.1	0.5
Drop-out Rate (%)	5.9	4.9	7.9	n/a	n/a	0.0
H.S. Diplomas (#)	150	102	46	0	0	2

Number of Schools

Rank	Number	District Name	City
1	128	Orleans Parish School Board	New Orleans
2	107	East Baton Rouge Parish School Bd	Baton Rouge
3	85	Jefferson Parish School Board	Harvey
4	75	Caddo Parish School Board	Shreveport
5	60	Calcasieu Parish School Board	Lake Charles
6	53	Rapides Parish School Board	Alexandria
7	51	Saint Tammany Parish School Board	Covington
8	45	Lafayette Parish School Board	Lafayette
9	41	Terrebonne Parish School Board	Houma
10	38	Saint Landry Parish School Board	Opelousas
11	37	Livingston Parish School Board	Livingston
12	36	Bossier Parish School Board	Benton
12	36	Tangipahoa Parish School Board	Amite
14	35	Ouachita Parish School Board	Monroe
15	33	Iberia Parish School Board	New Iberia
16	29	Lafourche Parish School Board	Thibodaux
17	27	Acadia Parish School Board	Crowley
17	27	Saint Mary Parish School Board	Centerville
19	23	Ascension Parish School Board	Donaldsonville
19	23	Webster Parish School Board	Minden
21	20	City of Monroe School Board	Monroe
21	20	Saint Charles Parish School Board	Luling
21	20	Vermilion Parish School Board	Abbeville
21	20	Vernon Parish School Board	Leesville
25	19	Lincoln Parish School Board	Ruston
26	18	Saint Martin Parish School Board	St Martinville
27	16	Morehouse Parish School Board	Bastrop
28	15	Natchitoches Parish School Board	Natchitoches
29	14	Avoyelles Parish School Board	Marksville
29	14	Beauregard Parish School Board	Deridder
29	14	Evangeline Parish School Board	Ville Platte
29	14	Jefferson Davis Parish SB	Jennings
29	14	Sabine Parish School Board	Many
29	14	Saint Bernard Parish School Board	Chalmette
35	13	Desoto Parish School Board	Mansfield
35	13	Washington Parish School Board	Franklinton
37	12	Allen Parish School Board	Oberlin
37	12	Franklin Parish School Board	Winnsboro
37	12	Richland Parish School Board	Rayville
37	12	Saint James Parish School Board	Lutcher
37	12	Saint John the Baptist Parish SB	Reserve
42	11	Concordia Parish School Board	Vidalia
42	11	West Baton Rouge Parish School Bd	Port Allen
44	10	Assumption Parish School Board	Napoleonville
44	10	Catahoula Parish School Board	Harrisonburg
44	10	Lasalle Parish School Board	Jena
44	10	Union Parish School Board	Farmerville
48	9	City of Bogalusa School Board	Bogalusa
48	9	Claiborne Parish School Board	Homer
48	9	Iberville Parish School Board	Plaquemine
48	9	Plaquemines Parish School Board	Port Sulphur
48	9	Pointe Coupee Parish School Board	New Roads
53	8	Bienville Parish School Board	Arcadia
53	8	East Feliciana Parish School Board	Clinton
53	8	Grant Parish School Board	Colfax
53	8	West Carroll Parish School Board	Oak Grove
53	8	Winn Parish School Board	Winnfield
58	7	Jackson Parish School Board	Jonesboro
58	7	Madison Parish School Board	Tallulah
60	6	Caldwell Parish School Board	Columbia
60	6	Cameron Parish School Board	Cameron
60	6	East Carroll Parish School Board	Lake Providence
63	5	Red River Parish School Board	Coushatta
63	5	West Feliciana Parish School Board	St Francisville

Number of Teachers

Rank	Number	District Name	City
1	4,236	Orleans Parish School Board	New Orleans
2	3,554	East Baton Rouge Parish School Bd	Baton Rouge
3	3,372	Jefferson Parish School Board	Harvey
4	2,991	Caddo Parish School Board	Shreveport
5	2,395	Saint Tammany Parish School Board	Covington
6	2,181	Calcasieu Parish School Board	Lake Charles
7	2,036	Lafayette Parish School Board	Lafayette
8	1,619	Rapides Parish School Board	Alexandria
9	1,410	Terrebonne Parish School Board	Houma
10	1,314	Livingston Parish School Board	Livingston
11	1,313	Ouachita Parish School Board	Monroe
12	1,156	Lafourche Parish School Board	Thibodaux
13	1,144	Bossier Parish School Board	Benton
14	1,088	Ascension Parish School Board	Donaldsonville
15	1,059	Tangipahoa Parish School Board	Amite
16	1,052	Iberia Parish School Board	New Iberia
17	1,048	Saint Landry Parish School Board	Opelousas
18	778	Saint Charles Parish School Board	Luling
19	725	Saint Mary Parish School Board	Centerville
20	687	Vernon Parish School Board	Leesville
21	668	Acadia Parish School Board	Crowley
22	659	City of Monroe School Board	Monroe
23	625	Saint Bernard Parish School Board	Chalmette
24	600	Saint Martin Parish School Board	St Martinville
25	594	Vermilion Parish School Board	Abbeville
26	504	Webster Parish School Board	Minden
27	487	Saint John the Baptist Parish SB	Reserve
28	475	Lincoln Parish School Board	Ruston
29	472	Natchitoches Parish School Board	Natchitoches
30	424	Evangeline Parish School Board	Ville Platte
31	411	Beauregard Parish School Board	Deridder
32	387	Avoyelles Parish School Board	Marksville
33	375	Morehouse Parish School Board	Bastrop
34	370	Jefferson Davis Parish SB	Jennings
35	361	Desoto Parish School Board	Mansfield
36	357	Washington Parish School Board	Franklinton
37	333	Allen Parish School Board	Oberlin
38	328	Plaquemines Parish School Board	Port Sulphur
39	327	Iberville Parish School Board	Plaquemine
40	321	Franklin Parish School Board	Winnsboro
41	313	Assumption Parish School Board	Napoleonville
42	291	Sabine Parish School Board	Many
43	276	Saint James Parish School Board	Lutcher
44	269	Richland Parish School Board	Rayville
45	264	Concordia Parish School Board	Vidalia
46	254	West Baton Rouge Parish School Bd	Port Allen
47	242	Grant Parish School Board	Colfax
48	233	Pointe Coupee Parish School Board	New Roads
49	226	City of Bogalusa School Board	Bogalusa
50	224	Union Parish School Board	Farmerville
51	204	Winn Parish School Board	Winnfield
52	201	West Feliciana Parish School Board	St Francisville
53	199	Claiborne Parish School Board	Homer
54	189	Bienville Parish School Board	Arcadia
55	189	Lasalle Parish School Board	Jena
56	178	Jackson Parish School Board	Jonesboro
57	177	West Carroll Parish School Board	Oak Grove
58	169	East Feliciana Parish School Board	Clinton
59	155	Madison Parish School Board	Tallulah
60	152	Cameron Parish School Board	Cameron
61	139	Caldwell Parish School Board	Columbia
62	137	East Carroll Parish School Board	Lake Providence
63	137	Catahoula Parish School Board	Harrisonburg
64	135	Red River Parish School Board	Coushatta

Number of Students

Rank	Number	District Name	City
1	70,246	Orleans Parish School Board	New Orleans
2	52,434	East Baton Rouge Parish School Bd	Baton Rouge
3	51,501	Jefferson Parish School Board	Harvey
4	44,556	Caddo Parish School Board	Shreveport
5	34,081	Saint Tammany Parish School Board	Covington
6	31,909	Calcasieu Parish School Board	Lake Charles
7	29,554	Lafayette Parish School Board	Lafayette
8	22,872	Rapides Parish School Board	Alexandria
9	20,334	Livingston Parish School Board	Livingston
10	19,345	Terrebonne Parish School Board	Houma
11	18,686	Bossier Parish School Board	Benton
12	17,926	Tangipahoa Parish School Board	Amite
13	17,793	Ouachita Parish School Board	Monroe
14	15,469	Ascension Parish School Board	Donaldsonville
15	15,331	Saint Landry Parish School Board	Opelousas
16	15,023	Lafourche Parish School Board	Thibodaux
17	14,227	Iberia Parish School Board	New Iberia
18	10,363	Saint Mary Parish School Board	Centerville
19	9,841	Vernon Parish School Board	Leesville
20	9,717	Saint Charles Parish School Board	Luling
21	9,678	City of Monroe School Board	Monroe
22	9,666	Acadia Parish School Board	Crowley
23	8,905	Vermilion Parish School Board	Abbeville
24	8,734	Saint Bernard Parish School Board	Chalmette
25	8,614	Saint Martin Parish School Board	St Martinville
26	7,728	Webster Parish School Board	Minden
27	6,978	Natchitoches Parish School Board	Natchitoches
28	6,740	Avoyelles Parish School Board	Marksville
29	6,650	Lincoln Parish School Board	Ruston
30	6,337	Evangeline Parish School Board	Ville Platte
31	6,282	Saint John the Baptist Parish SB	Reserve
32	6,058	Beauregard Parish School Board	Deridder
33	5,811	Jefferson Davis Parish SB	Jennings
34	5,209	Morehouse Parish School Board	Bastrop
35	5,042	Desoto Parish School Board	Mansfield
36	4,811	Plaquemines Parish School Board	Port Sulphur
37	4,739	Washington Parish School Board	Franklinton
38	4,622	Iberville Parish School Board	Plaquemine
39	4,516	Assumption Parish School Board	Napoleonville
40	4,340	Allen Parish School Board	Oberlin
41	4,299	Sabine Parish School Board	Many
42	4,076	Saint James Parish School Board	Lutcher
43	3,913	Franklin Parish School Board	Winnsboro
44	3,845	Concordia Parish School Board	Vidalia
45	3,572	Grant Parish School Board	Colfax
46	3,529	West Baton Rouge Parish School Bd	Port Allen
47	3,527	Richland Parish School Board	Rayville
48	3,479	Union Parish School Board	Farmerville
49	3,185	Pointe Coupee Parish School Board	New Roads
50	3,018	City of Bogalusa School Board	Bogalusa
51	2,815	Winn Parish School Board	Winnfield
52	2,803	Claiborne Parish School Board	Homer
53	2,693	Lasalle Parish School Board	Jena
54	2,528	Bienville Parish School Board	Arcadia
55	2,504	East Feliciana Parish School Board	Clinton
56	2,442	Jackson Parish School Board	Jonesboro
57	2,409	West Feliciana Parish School Board	St Francisville
58	2,387	Madison Parish School Board	Tallulah
59	2,376	West Carroll Parish School Board	Oak Grove
60	1,888	Caldwell Parish School Board	Columbia
61	1,847	Cameron Parish School Board	Cameron
62	1,811	Catahoula Parish School Board	Harrisonburg
63	1,746	East Carroll Parish School Board	Lake Providence
64	1,604	Red River Parish School Board	Coushatta

Male Students

Rank	Percent	District Name	City
1	54.7	Caldwell Parish School Board	Columbia
2	52.8	East Feliciana Parish School Board	Clinton
3	52.7	Sabine Parish School Board	Many
4	52.5	West Baton Rouge Parish School Bd	Port Allen
5	52.4	Plaquemines Parish School Board	Port Sulphur
5	52.4	West Carroll Parish School Board	Oak Grove
7	52.2	Allen Parish School Board	Oberlin
8	52.0	Beauregard Parish School Board	Deridder
8	52.0	Evangeline Parish School Board	Ville Platte
8	52.0	Jefferson Davis Parish SB	Jennings
8	52.0	Richland Parish School Board	Rayville
12	51.9	Madison Parish School Board	Tallulah
13	51.8	Lafourche Parish School Board	Thibodaux
13	51.8	Morehouse Parish School Board	Bastrop
13	51.8	Washington Parish School Board	Franklinton
16	51.7	Saint John the Baptist Parish SB	Reserve
17	51.6	Ascension Parish School Board	Donaldsonville
17	51.6	Cameron Parish School Board	Cameron
17	51.6	Grant Parish School Board	Colfax
17	51.6	Jackson Parish School Board	Jonesboro
17	51.6	Saint Martin Parish School Board	St Martinville
17	51.6	Saint Tammany Parish School Board	Covington
23	51.5	Catahoula Parish School Board	Harrisonburg
23	51.5	Jefferson Parish School Board	Harvey
25	51.4	Avoyelles Parish School Board	Marksville
25	51.4	Rapides Parish School Board	Alexandria
27	51.3	Livingston Parish School Board	Livingston
27	51.3	Natchitoches Parish School Board	Natchitoches
27	51.3	Vermilion Parish School Board	Abbeville
27	51.3	Vernon Parish School Board	Leesville
27	51.3	West Feliciana Parish School Board	St Francisville
32	51.2	Claiborne Parish School Board	Homer
32	51.2	Saint Landry Parish School Board	Opelousas
32	51.2	Webster Parish School Board	Minden
35	51.1	Acadia Parish School Board	Crowley
35	51.1	Bienville Parish School Board	Arcadia
35	51.1	Calcasieu Parish School Board	Lake Charles
35	51.1	Lafayette Parish School Board	Lafayette
39	51.0	Franklin Parish School Board	Winnsboro
39	51.0	Saint James Parish School Board	Lutcher
39	51.0	Terrebonne Parish School Board	Houma
42	50.9	East Baton Rouge Parish School Bd	Baton Rouge
42	50.9	Lincoln Parish School Board	Ruston
44	50.8	Assumption Parish School Board	Napoleonville
44	50.8	Concordia Parish School Board	Vidalia
44	50.8	Desoto Parish School Board	Mansfield
44	50.8	Saint Charles Parish School Board	Luling
44	50.8	Tangipahoa Parish School Board	Amite
49	50.7	Bossier Parish School Board	Benton
49	50.7	Caddo Parish School Board	Shreveport
49	50.7	City of Bogalusa School Board	Bogalusa
49	50.7	Saint Mary Parish School Board	Centerville
53	50.6	Iberia Parish School Board	New Iberia
53	50.6	Iberville Parish School Board	Plaquemine
55	50.5	Union Parish School Board	Farmerville
55	50.5	Winn Parish School Board	Winnfield
57	50.4	Saint Bernard Parish School Board	Chalmette
58	50.3	Orleans Parish School Board	New Orleans
58	50.3	Ouachita Parish School Board	Monroe
60	50.2	Red River Parish School Board	Coushatta
61	50.0	City of Monroe School Board	Monroe
61	50.0	Lasalle Parish School Board	Jena
63	49.8	Pointe Coupee Parish School Board	New Roads
64	48.8	East Carroll Parish School Board	Lake Providence

Female Students

Rank	Percent	District Name	City
1	51.2	East Carroll Parish School Board	Lake Providence
2	50.2	Pointe Coupee Parish School Board	New Roads
3	50.0	City of Monroe School Board	Monroe
3	50.0	Lasalle Parish School Board	Jena

Rank	Percent	District Name	City
5	49.8	Red River Parish School Board	Coushatta
6	49.7	Orleans Parish School Board	New Orleans
6	49.7	Ouachita Parish School Board	Monroe
8	49.6	Saint Bernard Parish School Board	Chalmette
9	49.5	Union Parish School Board	Farmerville
9	49.5	Winn Parish School Board	Winnfield
11	49.4	Iberia Parish School Board	New Iberia
11	49.4	Iberville Parish School Board	Plaquemine
13	49.3	Bossier Parish School Board	Benton
13	49.3	Caddo Parish School Board	Shreveport
13	49.3	City of Bogalusa School Board	Bogalusa
13	49.3	Saint Mary Parish School Board	Centerville
17	49.2	Assumption Parish School Board	Napoleonville
17	49.2	Concordia Parish School Board	Vidalia
17	49.2	Desoto Parish School Board	Mansfield
17	49.2	Saint Charles Parish School Board	Luling
17	49.2	Tangipahoa Parish School Board	Amite
22	49.1	East Baton Rouge Parish School Bd	Baton Rouge
22	49.1	Lincoln Parish School Board	Ruston
24	49.0	Franklin Parish School Board	Winnsboro
24	49.0	Saint James Parish School Board	Lutcher
24	49.0	Terrebonne Parish School Board	Houma
27	48.9	Acadia Parish School Board	Crowley
27	48.9	Bienville Parish School Board	Arcadia
27	48.9	Calcasieu Parish School Board	Lake Charles
27	48.9	Lafayette Parish School Board	Lafayette
31	48.8	Claiborne Parish School Board	Homer
31	48.8	Saint Landry Parish School Board	Opelousas
31	48.8	Webster Parish School Board	Minden
34	48.7	Livingston Parish School Board	Livingston
34	48.7	Natchitoches Parish School Board	Natchitoches
34	48.7	Vermilion Parish School Board	Abbeville
34	48.7	Vernon Parish School Board	Leesville
34	48.7	West Feliciana Parish School Board	St Francisville
39	48.6	Avoyelles Parish School Board	Marksville
39	48.6	Rapides Parish School Board	Alexandria
41	48.5	Catahoula Parish School Board	Harrisonburg
41	48.5	Jefferson Parish School Board	Harvey
43	48.4	Ascension Parish School Board	Donaldsonville
43	48.4	Cameron Parish School Board	Cameron
43	48.4	Grant Parish School Board	Colfax
43	48.4	Jackson Parish School Board	Jonesboro
43	48.4	Saint Martin Parish School Board	St Martinville
43	48.4	Saint Tammany Parish School Board	Covington
49	48.3	Saint John the Baptist Parish SB	Reserve
50	48.2	Lafourche Parish School Board	Thibodaux
50	48.2	Morehouse Parish School Board	Bastrop
50	48.2	Washington Parish School Board	Franklinton
53	48.1	Madison Parish School Board	Tallulah
54	48.0	Beauregard Parish School Board	Deridder
54	48.0	Evangeline Parish School Board	Ville Platte
54	48.0	Jefferson Davis Parish SB	Jennings
54	48.0	Richland Parish School Board	Rayville
58	47.8	Allen Parish School Board	Oberlin
59	47.6	Plaquemines Parish School Board	Port Sulphur
59	47.6	West Carroll Parish School Board	Oak Grove
61	47.5	West Baton Rouge Parish School Bd	Port Allen
62	47.3	Sabine Parish School Board	Many
63	47.2	East Feliciana Parish School Board	Clinton
64	45.3	Caldwell Parish School Board	Columbia

Individual Education Program Students

Rank	Percent	District Name	City
1	21.9	City of Bogalusa School Board	Bogalusa
2	20.8	Pointe Coupee Parish School Board	New Roads
3	19.9	Saint John the Baptist Parish SB	Reserve
4	18.3	Acadia Parish School Board	Crowley
5	17.0	Saint Tammany Parish School Board	Covington
6	16.7	Cameron Parish School Board	Cameron
6	16.7	Iberia Parish School Board	New Iberia
8	16.6	Evangeline Parish School Board	Ville Platte
9	16.5	Claiborne Parish School Board	Homer
9	16.5	Jefferson Davis Parish SB	Jennings
11	15.9	Vermilion Parish School Board	Abbeville
12	15.7	East Feliciana Parish School Board	Clinton
12	15.7	Saint Mary Parish School Board	Centerville
12	15.7	Washington Parish School Board	Franklinton
15	15.6	Terrebonne Parish School Board	Houma
16	15.5	Ascension Parish School Board	Donaldsonville
16	15.5	Saint Landry Parish School Board	Opelousas
18	15.2	Morehouse Parish School Board	Bastrop
19	15.1	Desoto Parish School Board	Mansfield
19	15.1	Jefferson Parish School Board	Harvey
19	15.1	West Feliciana Parish School Board	St Francisville
22	15.0	Sabine Parish School Board	Many
23	14.9	Calcasieu Parish School Board	Lake Charles
23	14.9	Iberville Parish School Board	Plaquemine
25	14.8	Grant Parish School Board	Colfax
26	14.7	Saint Martin Parish School Board	St Martinville
27	14.6	Tangipahoa Parish School Board	Amite
28	14.5	Bienville Parish School Board	Arcadia
28	14.5	Saint Bernard Parish School Board	Chalmette
30	14.2	Red River Parish School Board	Coushatta
31	14.0	Rapides Parish School Board	Alexandria
31	14.0	Richland Parish School Board	Rayville
33	13.9	Caddo Parish School Board	Shreveport
34	13.6	City of Monroe School Board	Monroe
35	13.4	East Carroll Parish School Board	Lake Providence
35	13.4	Webster Parish School Board	Minden
37	13.2	Lafourche Parish School Board	Thibodaux
38	13.1	Assumption Parish School Board	Napoleonville
38	13.1	Union Parish School Board	Farmerville
40	13.0	Vernon Parish School Board	Leesville
41	12.9	West Baton Rouge Parish School Bd	Port Allen
42	12.8	Caldwell Parish School Board	Columbia
42	12.8	Saint James Parish School Board	Lutcher
44	12.7	Beauregard Parish School Board	Deridder
45	12.5	Lincoln Parish School Board	Ruston
45	12.5	Plaquemines Parish School Board	Port Sulphur
47	12.4	Ouachita Parish School Board	Monroe
48	12.0	Allen Parish School Board	Oberlin
49	11.8	Bossier Parish School Board	Benton
49	11.8	Natchitoches Parish School Board	Natchitoches
51	11.7	West Carroll Parish School Board	Oak Grove
51	11.7	Winn Parish School Board	Winnfield
53	11.5	Lafayette Parish School Board	Lafayette
53	11.5	Madison Parish School Board	Tallulah
55	11.3	Jackson Parish School Board	Jonesboro
56	11.2	Livingston Parish School Board	Livingston
56	11.2	Saint Charles Parish School Board	Luling
58	10.9	Avoyelles Parish School Board	Marksville
59	10.8	Catahoula Parish School Board	Harrisonburg
59	10.8	Orleans Parish School Board	New Orleans
61	10.7	Concordia Parish School Board	Vidalia
61	10.7	Franklin Parish School Board	Winnsboro
63	10.0	East Baton Rouge Parish School Bd	Baton Rouge
64	8.8	Lasalle Parish School Board	Jena

English Language Learner Students

Rank	Percent	District Name	City
1	5.8	Jefferson Parish School Board	Harvey
2	2.9	Bossier Parish School Board	Benton
3	2.8	East Baton Rouge Parish School Bd	Baton Rouge
3	2.8	Saint Mary Parish School Board	Centerville
5	2.5	Lafourche Parish School Board	Thibodaux
6	2.2	Union Parish School Board	Farmerville
7	2.1	Plaquemines Parish School Board	Port Sulphur
8	1.9	Orleans Parish School Board	New Orleans
9	1.8	Ascension Parish School Board	Donaldsonville
10	1.7	Lafayette Parish School Board	Lafayette
10	1.7	Terrebonne Parish School Board	Houma
12	1.5	Iberia Parish School Board	New Iberia
12	1.5	Rapides Parish School Board	Alexandria
14	1.3	Saint Charles Parish School Board	Luling
14	1.3	Saint Tammany Parish School Board	Covington
14	1.3	Vermilion Parish School Board	Abbeville
17	1.2	Tangipahoa Parish School Board	Amite
18	1.1	Caddo Parish School Board	Shreveport
19	1.0	Saint John the Baptist Parish SB	Reserve
19	1.0	Saint Martin Parish School Board	St Martinville
19	1.0	Vernon Parish School Board	Leesville
22	0.6	Assumption Parish School Board	Napoleonville
22	0.6	City of Bogalusa School Board	Bogalusa
22	0.6	West Carroll Parish School Board	Oak Grove
25	0.5	Saint Bernard Parish School Board	Chalmette
26	0.4	Acadia Parish School Board	Crowley
26	0.4	Beauregard Parish School Board	Deridder
26	0.4	Desoto Parish School Board	Mansfield
26	0.4	Jefferson Davis Parish SB	Jennings
26	0.4	Saint Landry Parish School Board	Opelousas
31	0.3	East Carroll Parish School Board	Lake Providence
31	0.3	East Feliciana Parish School Board	Clinton
31	0.3	Iberville Parish School Board	Plaquemine
31	0.3	Lincoln Parish School Board	Ruston
31	0.3	Livingston Parish School Board	Livingston
31	0.3	Natchitoches Parish School Board	Natchitoches
31	0.3	Ouachita Parish School Board	Monroe
31	0.3	Sabine Parish School Board	Many
39	0.2	Avoyelles Parish School Board	Marksville
39	0.2	Caldwell Parish School Board	Columbia
39	0.2	City of Monroe School Board	Monroe
39	0.2	Evangeline Parish School Board	Ville Platte
39	0.2	Morehouse Parish School Board	Bastrop
39	0.2	West Feliciana Parish School Board	St Francisville
45	0.1	Cameron Parish School Board	Cameron
45	0.1	Concordia Parish School Board	Vidalia
45	0.1	Pointe Coupee Parish School Board	New Roads
45	0.1	Red River Parish School Board	Coushatta
45	0.1	Saint James Parish School Board	Lutcher
45	0.1	Washington Parish School Board	Franklinton
51	0.0	Allen Parish School Board	Oberlin
51	0.0	Bienville Parish School Board	Arcadia
51	0.0	Calcasieu Parish School Board	Lake Charles
51	0.0	Claiborne Parish School Board	Homer
51	0.0	Franklin Parish School Board	Winnsboro
51	0.0	Madison Parish School Board	Tallulah
51	0.0	Webster Parish School Board	Minden
51	0.0	West Baton Rouge Parish School Bd	Port Allen
51	0.0	Winn Parish School Board	Winnfield
60	0.0	Catahoula Parish School Board	Harrisonburg
60	0.0	Grant Parish School Board	Colfax
60	0.0	Jackson Parish School Board	Jonesboro
60	0.0	Lasalle Parish School Board	Jena
60	0.0	Richland Parish School Board	Rayville

Migrant Students

Rank	Percent	District Name	City
1	4.1	Plaquemines Parish School Board	Port Sulphur
2	3.1	Cameron Parish School Board	Cameron
2	3.1	Terrebonne Parish School Board	Houma
4	2.9	Natchitoches Parish School Board	Natchitoches
5	2.5	Franklin Parish School Board	Winnsboro
5	2.5	Union Parish School Board	Farmerville
7	2.4	Madison Parish School Board	Tallulah
8	2.3	Winn Parish School Board	Winnfield
9	2.1	Assumption Parish School Board	Napoleonville
10	2.0	Catahoula Parish School Board	Harrisonburg
11	1.7	Lafourche Parish School Board	Thibodaux
12	1.6	West Carroll Parish School Board	Oak Grove
13	1.5	Concordia Parish School Board	Vidalia
14	1.4	Saint Landry Parish School Board	Opelousas
15	1.2	Grant Parish School Board	Colfax
15	1.2	Jackson Parish School Board	Jonesboro
15	1.2	Vermilion Parish School Board	Abbeville
18	1.1	Bienville Parish School Board	Arcadia
18	1.1	Lasalle Parish School Board	Jena
20	1.0	Avoyelles Parish School Board	Marksville
21	0.9	Evangeline Parish School Board	Ville Platte
21	0.9	Iberia Parish School Board	New Iberia
21	0.9	Pointe Coupee Parish School Board	New Roads
21	0.9	Saint Mary Parish School Board	Centerville
21	0.9	West Baton Rouge Parish School Bd	Port Allen
26	0.8	Caldwell Parish School Board	Columbia
26	0.8	Desoto Parish School Board	Mansfield
26	0.8	Jefferson Davis Parish SB	Jennings
26	0.8	Richland Parish School Board	Rayville
26	0.8	Saint Martin Parish School Board	St Martinville
31	0.7	Claiborne Parish School Board	Homer
31	0.7	East Carroll Parish School Board	Lake Providence
33	0.6	Acadia Parish School Board	Crowley
33	0.6	Rapides Parish School Board	Alexandria
33	0.6	Tangipahoa Parish School Board	Amite
36	0.4	Beauregard Parish School Board	Deridder
36	0.4	Jefferson Parish School Board	Harvey
36	0.4	Lincoln Parish School Board	Ruston
36	0.4	Morehouse Parish School Board	Bastrop
36	0.4	Webster Parish School Board	Minden
41	0.3	Allen Parish School Board	Oberlin
41	0.3	Lafayette Parish School Board	Lafayette
41	0.3	Sabine Parish School Board	Many
41	0.3	Saint James Parish School Board	Lutcher
41	0.3	Washington Parish School Board	Franklinton
46	0.2	Bossier Parish School Board	Benton
46	0.2	Iberville Parish School Board	Plaquemine
46	0.2	Orleans Parish School Board	New Orleans
46	0.2	Ouachita Parish School Board	Monroe
46	0.2	Saint Charles Parish School Board	Luling
51	0.1	Caddo Parish School Board	Shreveport
51	0.1	City of Monroe School Board	Monroe
51	0.1	Livingston Parish School Board	Livingston
51	0.1	Red River Parish School Board	Coushatta
55	0.0	Calcasieu Parish School Board	Lake Charles
55	0.0	East Baton Rouge Parish School Bd	Baton Rouge
55	0.0	Saint Bernard Parish School Board	Chalmette
55	0.0	Saint John the Baptist Parish SB	Reserve
55	0.0	Saint Tammany Parish School Board	Covington
55	0.0	Vernon Parish School Board	Leesville
61	0.0	Ascension Parish School Board	Donaldsonville
61	0.0	City of Bogalusa School Board	Bogalusa
61	0.0	East Feliciana Parish School Board	Clinton
61	0.0	West Feliciana Parish School Board	St Francisville

Students Eligible for Free Lunch

Rank	Percent	District Name	City
1	85.6	East Carroll Parish School Board	Lake Providence
2	79.3	Madison Parish School Board	Tallulah
3	74.1	Iberville Parish School Board	Plaquemine
4	73.7	Orleans Parish School Board	New Orleans
5	73.3	East Feliciana Parish School Board	Clinton
6	72.7	Saint John the Baptist Parish SB	Reserve
7	71.7	Washington Parish School Board	Franklinton
8	71.5	City of Monroe School Board	Monroe
9	70.9	Red River Parish School Board	Coushatta
10	70.1	City of Bogalusa School Board	Bogalusa
11	68.2	Pointe Coupee Parish School Board	New Roads

12	66.7	Concordia Parish School Board	Vidalia
13	66.4	Saint Landry Parish School Board	Opelousas
14	66.3	Avoyelles Parish School Board	Marksville
15	64.4	Evangeline Parish School Board	Ville Platte
16	64.2	Richland Parish School Board	Rayville
17	63.3	Franklin Parish School Board	Winnsboro
18	62.6	Saint James Parish School Board	Lutcher
19	62.1	Morehouse Parish School Board	Bastrop
20	61.2	Jefferson Parish School Board	Harvey
21	60.2	Claiborne Parish School Board	Homer
21	60.2	East Baton Rouge Parish School Bd	Baton Rouge
23	59.7	Saint Martin Parish School Board	St Martinville
24	59.5	Tangipahoa Parish School Board	Amite
25	58.6	Desoto Parish School Board	Mansfield
26	58.2	Natchitoches Parish School Board	Natchitoches
27	57.7	Bienville Parish School Board	Arcadia
28	57.4	Saint Mary Parish School Board	Centerville
29	55.9	Union Parish School Board	Farmerville
30	55.6	West Carroll Parish School Board	Oak Grove
31	55.0	Plaquemines Parish School Board	Port Sulphur
32	53.9	Winn Parish School Board	Winnfield
33	53.8	West Baton Rouge Parish School Bd	Port Allen
34	53.4	Acadia Parish School Board	Crowley
35	53.2	Rapides Parish School Board	Alexandria
36	52.4	Sabine Parish School Board	Many
37	52.2	Assumption Parish School Board	Napoleonville
38	51.7	Iberia Parish School Board	New Iberia
39	51.5	Catahoula Parish School Board	Harrisonburg
40	50.3	Caddo Parish School Board	Shreveport
41	48.2	Grant Parish School Board	Colfax
41	48.2	Terrebonne Parish School Board	Houma
43	47.2	Saint Bernard Parish School Board	Chalmette
44	46.1	Caldwell Parish School Board	Columbia
44	46.1	Lincoln Parish School Board	Ruston
46	45.4	Jackson Parish School Board	Jonesboro
46	45.4	Webster Parish School Board	Minden
48	44.1	Allen Parish School Board	Oberlin
49	43.5	Vermilion Parish School Board	Abbeville
50	42.9	Lafourche Parish School Board	Thibodaux
51	42.3	Lasalle Parish School Board	Jena
52	41.8	Lafayette Parish School Board	Lafayette
53	41.6	Jefferson Davis Parish SB	Jennings
54	38.0	Calcasieu Parish School Board	Lake Charles
55	36.3	Ouachita Parish School Board	Monroe
55	36.3	Saint Charles Parish School Board	Luling
55	36.3	West Feliciana Parish School Board	St Francisville
58	35.7	Vernon Parish School Board	Leesville
59	35.3	Beauregard Parish School Board	Deridder
60	34.5	Ascension Parish School Board	Donaldsonville
61	33.5	Bossier Parish School Board	Benton
62	29.2	Livingston Parish School Board	Livingston
63	27.6	Cameron Parish School Board	Cameron
64	24.7	Saint Tammany Parish School Board	Covington

Students Eligible for Reduced-Price Lunch

Rank	Percent	District Name	City
1	16.8	Vernon Parish School Board	Leesville
2	14.5	Jefferson Davis Parish SB	Jennings
3	12.8	Grant Parish School Board	Colfax
4	12.5	Allen Parish School Board	Oberlin
5	12.1	Acadia Parish School Board	Crowley
5	12.1	Cameron Parish School Board	Cameron
7	12.0	Catahoula Parish School Board	Harrisonburg
7	12.0	Jefferson Parish School Board	Harvey
9	11.9	Lasalle Parish School Board	Jena
9	11.9	Livingston Parish School Board	Livingston
9	11.9	West Carroll Parish School Board	Oak Grove
12	11.3	Saint Landry Parish School Board	Opelousas
13	11.2	Lafourche Parish School Board	Thibodaux
14	11.1	Plaquemines Parish School Board	Port Sulphur
14	11.1	Terrebonne Parish School Board	Houma
16	10.8	Sabine Parish School Board	Many
16	10.8	Saint Bernard Parish School Board	Chalmette
18	10.7	Caldwell Parish School Board	Columbia
19	10.5	Evangeline Parish School Board	Ville Platte
20	10.3	Claiborne Parish School Board	Homer
21	10.2	Rapides Parish School Board	Alexandria
22	10.1	West Feliciana Parish School Board	St Francisville
22	10.1	Winn Parish School Board	Winnfield
24	9.9	Avoyelles Parish School Board	Marksville
24	9.9	Natchitoches Parish School Board	Natchitoches
24	9.9	Saint Martin Parish School Board	St Martinville
27	9.7	East Feliciana Parish School Board	Clinton
28	9.6	Saint Mary Parish School Board	Centerville
29	9.4	Vermilion Parish School Board	Abbeville
30	9.3	Webster Parish School Board	Minden
31	9.2	Union Parish School Board	Farmerville
32	9.0	West Baton Rouge Parish School Bd	Port Allen
33	8.9	Beauregard Parish School Board	Deridder
33	8.9	City of Bogalusa School Board	Bogalusa
35	8.7	Assumption Parish School Board	Napoleonville
35	8.7	Pointe Coupee Parish School Board	New Roads
35	8.7	Washington Parish School Board	Franklinton
38	8.5	Ascension Parish School Board	Donaldsonville
38	8.5	Jackson Parish School Board	Jonesboro
40	8.3	Iberia Parish School Board	New Iberia
41	8.2	Red River Parish School Board	Coushatta
41	8.2	Tangipahoa Parish School Board	Amite
43	8.0	East Baton Rouge Parish School Bd	Baton Rouge
44	7.9	Morehouse Parish School Board	Bastrop
44	7.9	Saint Charles Parish School Board	Luling
46	7.8	Bienville Parish School Board	Arcadia
46	7.8	Lafayette Parish School Board	Lafayette
46	7.8	Lincoln Parish School Board	Ruston
49	7.7	Calcasieu Parish School Board	Lake Charles
49	7.7	Iberville Parish School Board	Plaquemine
49	7.7	Saint John the Baptist Parish SB	Reserve
52	7.5	Franklin Parish School Board	Winnsboro
53	7.3	Ouachita Parish School Board	Monroe
54	7.2	Bossier Parish School Board	Benton
55	6.9	Concordia Parish School Board	Vidalia
56	6.8	Desoto Parish School Board	Mansfield
56	6.8	Saint James Parish School Board	Lutcher
58	6.4	Richland Parish School Board	Rayville
59	5.9	Saint Tammany Parish School Board	Covington
60	5.4	City of Monroe School Board	Monroe
61	4.8	Caddo Parish School Board	Shreveport
62	4.5	Orleans Parish School Board	New Orleans
63	4.0	East Carroll Parish School Board	Lake Providence
64	3.9	Madison Parish School Board	Tallulah

Student/Teacher Ratio

Rank	Ratio	District Name	City
1	17.4	Avoyelles Parish School Board	Marksville
2	16.9	Tangipahoa Parish School Board	Amite
3	16.6	Orleans Parish School Board	New Orleans
4	16.3	Bossier Parish School Board	Benton
5	15.7	Jefferson Davis Parish SB	Jennings
6	15.5	Livingston Parish School Board	Livingston
6	15.5	Union Parish School Board	Farmerville
8	15.4	Madison Parish School Board	Tallulah
9	15.3	Jefferson Parish School Board	Harvey
9	15.3	Webster Parish School Board	Minden
11	15.0	Vermilion Parish School Board	Abbeville
12	14.9	Caddo Parish School Board	Shreveport
12	14.9	Evangeline Parish School Board	Ville Platte
14	14.8	East Baton Rouge Parish School Bd	Baton Rouge
14	14.8	East Feliciana Parish School Board	Clinton
14	14.8	Grant Parish School Board	Colfax
14	14.8	Natchitoches Parish School Board	Natchitoches
14	14.8	Saint James Parish School Board	Lutcher
19	14.7	Beauregard Parish School Board	Deridder
19	14.7	City of Monroe School Board	Monroe
19	14.7	Plaquemines Parish School Board	Port Sulphur
19	14.7	Sabine Parish School Board	Many
23	14.6	Calcasieu Parish School Board	Lake Charles
23	14.6	Saint Landry Parish School Board	Opelousas
25	14.5	Acadia Parish School Board	Crowley
25	14.5	Concordia Parish School Board	Vidalia
25	14.5	Lafayette Parish School Board	Lafayette
28	14.4	Assumption Parish School Board	Napoleonville
29	14.3	Saint Martin Parish School Board	St Martinville
29	14.3	Saint Mary Parish School Board	Centerville
29	14.3	Vernon Parish School Board	Leesville
32	14.2	Ascension Parish School Board	Donaldsonville
32	14.2	Lasalle Parish School Board	Jena
32	14.2	Saint Tammany Parish School Board	Covington
35	14.1	Claiborne Parish School Board	Homer
35	14.1	Iberville Parish School Board	Plaquemine
35	14.1	Rapides Parish School Board	Alexandria
38	14.0	Lincoln Parish School Board	Ruston
38	14.0	Saint Bernard Parish School Board	Chalmette
40	13.9	Desoto Parish School Board	Mansfield
40	13.9	Morehouse Parish School Board	Bastrop
40	13.9	West Baton Rouge Parish School Bd	Port Allen
43	13.8	Winn Parish School Board	Winnfield
44	13.7	Jackson Parish School Board	Jonesboro
44	13.7	Pointe Coupee Parish School Board	New Roads
44	13.7	Terrebonne Parish School Board	Houma
47	13.6	Caldwell Parish School Board	Columbia
48	13.5	Iberia Parish School Board	New Iberia
48	13.5	Ouachita Parish School Board	Monroe
50	13.4	West Carroll Parish School Board	Oak Grove
51	13.3	Bienville Parish School Board	Arcadia
51	13.3	City of Bogalusa School Board	Bogalusa
51	13.3	Washington Parish School Board	Franklinton
54	13.2	Catahoula Parish School Board	Harrisonburg
55	13.1	Richland Parish School Board	Rayville
56	13.0	Allen Parish School Board	Oberlin
56	13.0	Lafourche Parish School Board	Thibodaux
58	12.9	Saint John the Baptist Parish SB	Reserve
59	12.7	East Carroll Parish School Board	Lake Providence
60	12.5	Saint Charles Parish School Board	Luling
61	12.2	Cameron Parish School Board	Cameron
61	12.2	Franklin Parish School Board	Winnsboro
63	12.0	West Feliciana Parish School Board	St Francisville
64	11.8	Red River Parish School Board	Coushatta

Student/Librarian Ratio

Rank	Ratio	District Name	City
1	3,913.0	Franklin Parish School Board	Winnsboro
2	2,803.0	Claiborne Parish School Board	Homer
3	2,258.0	Assumption Parish School Board	Napoleonville
4	2,094.0	Saint John the Baptist Parish SB	Reserve
5	1,509.0	City of Bogalusa School Board	Bogalusa
6	1,061.7	Pointe Coupee Parish School Board	New Roads
7	1,051.0	Jefferson Parish School Board	Harvey
8	924.3	Livingston Parish School Board	Livingston
9	873.0	East Carroll Parish School Board	Lake Providence
10	868.2	Morehouse Parish School Board	Bastrop
11	867.2	Orleans Parish School Board	New Orleans
12	815.2	Saint James Parish School Board	Lutcher
13	730.0	Saint Landry Parish School Board	Opelousas
14	719.9	Tangipahoa Parish School Board	Amite
15	696.5	Catahoula Parish School Board	Harrisonburg
16	674.0	Avoyelles Parish School Board	Marksville
17	672.6	Ascension Parish School Board	Donaldsonville
18	662.6	Saint Martin Parish School Board	St Martinville
19	642.5	Lafayette Parish School Board	Lafayette
20	633.7	Evangeline Parish School Board	Ville Platte
21	632.0	Bienville Parish School Board	Arcadia
22	631.1	Saint Tammany Parish School Board	Covington
23	623.9	Saint Bernard Parish School Board	Chalmette
24	602.8	Bossier Parish School Board	Benton
25	594.0	West Carroll Parish School Board	Oak Grove
26	577.8	Iberville Parish School Board	Plaquemine
27	568.6	Acadia Parish School Board	Crowley
28	546.7	Vernon Parish School Board	Leesville
29	537.7	City of Monroe School Board	Monroe
30	534.6	Plaquemines Parish School Board	Port Sulphur
31	530.4	Caddo Parish School Board	Shreveport
32	511.4	Saint Charles Parish School Board	Luling
33	510.3	Grant Parish School Board	Colfax
34	498.6	Calcasieu Parish School Board	Lake Charles
35	498.4	Natchitoches Parish School Board	Natchitoches
36	490.6	Iberia Parish School Board	New Iberia
37	484.3	Jefferson Davis Parish SB	Jennings
38	481.8	West Feliciana Parish School Board	St Francisville
39	481.0	East Baton Rouge Parish School Bd	Baton Rouge
40	480.9	Ouachita Parish School Board	Monroe
41	477.4	Madison Parish School Board	Tallulah
42	468.7	Vermilion Parish School Board	Abbeville
43	466.0	Beauregard Parish School Board	Deridder
44	462.8	Terrebonne Parish School Board	Houma
45	458.4	Desoto Parish School Board	Mansfield
46	457.4	Rapides Parish School Board	Alexandria
47	455.2	Lafourche Parish School Board	Thibodaux
48	450.6	Saint Mary Parish School Board	Centerville
49	434.9	Union Parish School Board	Farmerville
50	434.0	Allen Parish School Board	Oberlin
51	417.3	East Feliciana Parish School Board	Clinton
52	413.9	Jackson Parish School Board	Jonesboro
53	406.7	Webster Parish School Board	Minden
54	404.7	Concordia Parish School Board	Vidalia
55	402.1	Winn Parish School Board	Winnfield
56	394.9	Washington Parish School Board	Franklinton
57	391.2	Lincoln Parish School Board	Ruston
58	390.8	Sabine Parish School Board	Many
59	384.7	Lasalle Parish School Board	Jena
60	352.9	West Baton Rouge Parish School Bd	Port Allen
61	307.8	Cameron Parish School Board	Cameron
62	0.0	Caldwell Parish School Board	Columbia
62	0.0	Red River Parish School Board	Coushatta
62	0.0	Richland Parish School Board	Rayville

Student/Counselor Ratio

Rank	Ratio	District Name	City
1	752.7	Assumption Parish School Board	Napoleonville
2	632.0	Bienville Parish School Board	Arcadia
3	612.7	Avoyelles Parish School Board	Marksville
4	579.8	Union Parish School Board	Farmerville
5	559.0	Franklin Parish School Board	Winnsboro
6	538.6	Lasalle Parish School Board	Jena
7	536.8	Natchitoches Parish School Board	Natchitoches
8	501.8	Orleans Parish School Board	New Orleans
9	494.5	Saint Landry Parish School Board	Opelousas
10	450.6	Saint Mary Parish School Board	Centerville
11	436.5	East Carroll Parish School Board	Lake Providence
12	429.9	Sabine Parish School Board	Many
13	427.2	Concordia Parish School Board	Vidalia
14	420.2	Grant Parish School Board	Colfax
15	409.7	West Carroll Parish School Board	Oak Grove
16	402.4	Catahoula Parish School Board	Harrisonburg

17	397.8	Madison Parish School Board	Tallulah
18	397.0	Saint Bernard Parish School Board	Chalmette
19	387.8	Desoto Parish School Board	Mansfield
20	377.6	Caldwell Parish School Board	Columbia
21	352.7	Richland Parish School Board	Rayville
22	350.4	Claiborne Parish School Board	Homer
23	344.6	Livingston Parish School Board	Livingston
24	325.6	Morehouse Parish School Board	Bastrop
25	317.5	Vernon Parish School Board	Leesville
26	313.5	Saint Charles Parish School Board	Luling
27	310.7	Tangipahoa Parish School Board	Amite
28	307.6	Saint Martin Parish School Board	St Martinville
29	306.1	Evangeline Parish School Board	Ville Platte
30	305.3	Jackson Parish School Board	Jonesboro
31	294.1	West Baton Rouge Parish School Bd	Port Allen
32	281.5	Winn Parish School Board	Winnfield
33	273.6	Saint James Parish School Board	Lutcher
34	267.3	Red River Parish School Board	Coushatta
35	263.9	Cameron Parish School Board	Cameron
36	252.4	Ouachita Parish School Board	Monroe
37	243.3	Iberville Parish School Board	Plaquemine
38	241.1	Allen Parish School Board	Oberlin
39	240.9	West Feliciana Parish School Board	St Francisville
40	239.6	Bossier Parish School Board	Benton
41	238.5	Beauregard Parish School Board	Deridder
42	236.6	City of Monroe School Board	Monroe
43	230.9	Lincoln Parish School Board	Ruston
44	229.1	Plaquemines Parish School Board	Port Sulphur
45	227.6	Iberia Parish School Board	New Iberia
46	227.5	Pointe Coupee Parish School Board	New Roads
47	223.5	Jefferson Davis Parish SB	Jennings
48	217.5	Jefferson Parish School Board	Harvey
49	215.9	Terrebonne Parish School Board	Houma
50	210.6	Lafayette Parish School Board	Lafayette
51	207.1	Calcasieu Parish School Board	Lake Charles
52	192.6	East Feliciana Parish School Board	Clinton
53	190.6	Rapides Parish School Board	Alexandria
54	189.9	Webster Parish School Board	Minden
55	189.6	Washington Parish School Board	Franklinton
56	189.5	Acadia Parish School Board	Crowley
56	189.5	Vermilion Parish School Board	Abbeville
58	170.7	Caddo Parish School Board	Shreveport
58	170.7	Lafourche Parish School Board	Thibodaux
60	167.7	City of Bogalusa School Board	Bogalusa
61	167.5	Saint John the Baptist Parish SB	Reserve
62	166.4	Saint Tammany Parish School Board	Covington
63	164.6	Ascension Parish School Board	Donaldsonville
64	155.1	East Baton Rouge Parish School Bd	Baton Rouge

Current Spending per Student in FY2001

Rank	Dollars	District Name	City
1	7,727	West Feliciana Parish School Board	St Francisville
2	7,502	Saint Charles Parish School Board	Luling
3	7,103	Bienville Parish School Board	Arcadia
4	7,043	Cameron Parish School Board	Cameron
5	6,861	East Baton Rouge Parish School Bd	Baton Rouge
6	6,819	Iberville Parish School Board	Plaquemine
7	6,769	Jackson Parish School Board	Jonesboro
8	6,767	Saint James Parish School Board	Lutcher
9	6,634	Saint John the Baptist Parish SB	Reserve
10	6,467	Caddo Parish School Board	Shreveport
11	6,464	Desoto Parish School Board	Mansfield
12	6,448	Red River Parish School Board	Coushatta
13	6,408	Assumption Parish School Board	Napoleonville
13	6,408	Saint Tammany Parish School Board	Covington
15	6,316	Catahoula Parish School Board	Harrisonburg
16	6,295	East Carroll Parish School Board	Lake Providence
17	6,281	City of Bogalusa School Board	Bogalusa
18	6,209	Iberia Parish School Board	New Iberia
19	6,195	Jefferson Parish School Board	Harvey
20	6,166	West Baton Rouge Parish School Bd	Port Allen
20	6,166	Winn Parish School Board	Winnfield
22	6,088	Ascension Parish School Board	Donaldsonville
23	6,077	Claiborne Parish School Board	Homer
24	6,069	East Feliciana Parish School Board	Clinton
25	6,067	Saint Bernard Parish School Board	Chalmette
26	6,012	Washington Parish School Board	Franklinton
27	5,996	Allen Parish School Board	Oberlin
28	5,972	Pointe Coupee Parish School Board	New Roads
29	5,971	Rapides Parish School Board	Alexandria
30	5,968	Lafourche Parish School Board	Thibodaux
31	5,966	Saint Mary Parish School Board	Centerville
32	5,943	Caldwell Parish School Board	Columbia
33	5,927	Plaquemines Parish School Board	Port Sulphur
34	5,924	Jefferson Davis Parish SB	Jennings
35	5,908	Vernon Parish School Board	Leesville
36	5,879	Saint Landry Parish School Board	Opelousas
37	5,849	Richland Parish School Board	Rayville
38	5,825	Lasalle Parish School Board	Jena
39	5,811	Concordia Parish School Board	Vidalia
40	5,789	Orleans Parish School Board	New Orleans
41	5,771	Natchitoches Parish School Board	Natchitoches
42	5,730	Terrebonne Parish School Board	Houma
43	5,713	Lincoln Parish School Board	Ruston
44	5,706	Ouachita Parish School Board	Monroe
45	5,664	Beauregard Parish School Board	Deridder
46	5,653	Sabine Parish School Board	Many
47	5,640	Saint Martin Parish School Board	St Martinville
48	5,637	Calcasieu Parish School Board	Lake Charles
49	5,606	Franklin Parish School Board	Winnsboro
50	5,585	Morehouse Parish School Board	Bastrop
51	5,560	Lafayette Parish School Board	Lafayette
52	5,516	Madison Parish School Board	Tallulah
53	5,501	Webster Parish School Board	Minden
54	5,491	Vermilion Parish School Board	Abbeville
55	5,471	Grant Parish School Board	Colfax
56	5,439	Bossier Parish School Board	Benton
57	5,330	Avoyelles Parish School Board	Marksville
58	5,311	Tangipahoa Parish School Board	Amite
59	5,302	Acadia Parish School Board	Crowley
60	5,295	City of Monroe School Board	Monroe
61	5,276	Evangeline Parish School Board	Ville Platte
62	5,152	West Carroll Parish School Board	Oak Grove
63	5,059	Union Parish School Board	Farmerville
64	4,949	Livingston Parish School Board	Livingston

Number of Diploma Recipients

Rank	Number	District Name	City
1	3,471	Orleans Parish School Board	New Orleans
2	2,815	East Baton Rouge Parish School Bd	Baton Rouge
3	2,261	Jefferson Parish School Board	Harvey
4	2,223	Caddo Parish School Board	Shreveport
5	1,834	Saint Tammany Parish School Board	Covington
6	1,747	Calcasieu Parish School Board	Lake Charles
7	1,624	Lafayette Parish School Board	Lafayette
8	1,294	Rapides Parish School Board	Alexandria
9	1,056	Livingston Parish School Board	Livingston
10	1,030	Tangipahoa Parish School Board	Amite
11	1,007	Terrebonne Parish School Board	Houma
12	983	Bossier Parish School Board	Benton
13	923	Ouachita Parish School Board	Monroe
14	810	Lafourche Parish School Board	Thibodaux
15	805	Saint Landry Parish School Board	Opelousas
16	772	Ascension Parish School Board	Donaldsonville
17	637	Iberia Parish School Board	New Iberia
18	628	Saint Charles Parish School Board	Luling
19	614	Saint Mary Parish School Board	Centerville
20	480	Vermilion Parish School Board	Abbeville
21	469	City of Monroe School Board	Monroe
22	460	Saint Martin Parish School Board	St Martinville
23	455	Vernon Parish School Board	Leesville
24	444	Acadia Parish School Board	Crowley
25	418	Lincoln Parish School Board	Ruston
26	399	Avoyelles Parish School Board	Marksville
27	382	Saint Bernard Parish School Board	Chalmette
28	371	Beauregard Parish School Board	Deridder
29	369	Webster Parish School Board	Minden
30	353	Natchitoches Parish School Board	Natchitoches
31	318	Jefferson Davis Parish SB	Jennings
32	286	Evangeline Parish School Board	Ville Platte
33	278	Plaquemines Parish School Board	Port Sulphur
34	276	Saint John the Baptist Parish SB	Reserve
35	270	Washington Parish School Board	Franklinton
36	257	Sabine Parish School Board	Many
37	253	Iberville Parish School Board	Plaquemine
38	248	Desoto Parish School Board	Mansfield
39	243	West Baton Rouge Parish School Bd	Port Allen
40	230	Morehouse Parish School Board	Bastrop
40	230	Saint James Parish School Board	Lutcher
42	218	Allen Parish School Board	Oberlin
43	217	Union Parish School Board	Farmerville
44	205	Concordia Parish School Board	Vidalia
45	201	Assumption Parish School Board	Napoleonville
46	199	Franklin Parish School Board	Winnsboro
47	184	Grant Parish School Board	Colfax
48	175	Richland Parish School Board	Rayville
49	169	Jackson Parish School Board	Jonesboro
50	167	Pointe Coupee Parish School Board	New Roads
51	164	City of Bogalusa School Board	Bogalusa
52	163	Lasalle Parish School Board	Jena
53	150	Winn Parish School Board	Winnfield
54	149	Claiborne Parish School Board	Homer
55	142	East Feliciana Parish School Board	Clinton
56	138	Bienville Parish School Board	Arcadia
57	131	West Carroll Parish School Board	Oak Grove
58	122	West Feliciana Parish School Board	St Francisville
59	111	Madison Parish School Board	Tallulah
60	109	Cameron Parish School Board	Cameron
61	94	Catahoula Parish School Board	Harrisonburg
62	83	East Carroll Parish School Board	Lake Providence
63	75	Red River Parish School Board	Coushatta
64	66	Caldwell Parish School Board	Columbia

High School Drop-out Rate

Rank	Percent	District Name	City
1	20.3	Grant Parish School Board	Colfax
2	16.4	Pointe Coupee Parish School Board	New Roads
3	13.4	Natchitoches Parish School Board	Natchitoches
4	12.0	Morehouse Parish School Board	Bastrop
4	12.0	Red River Parish School Board	Coushatta
6	11.9	Madison Parish School Board	Tallulah
7	11.7	Franklin Parish School Board	Winnsboro
8	11.4	Orleans Parish School Board	New Orleans
9	11.0	Assumption Parish School Board	Napoleonville
10	10.9	Jefferson Parish School Board	Harvey
11	10.8	West Carroll Parish School Board	Oak Grove
12	10.6	Caddo Parish School Board	Shreveport
13	10.2	City of Monroe School Board	Monroe
14	10.0	Iberville Parish School Board	Plaquemine
15	9.9	Terrebonne Parish School Board	Houma
16	9.6	East Baton Rouge Parish School Bd	Baton Rouge
17	9.3	East Carroll Parish School Board	Lake Providence
18	9.2	Desoto Parish School Board	Mansfield
19	8.8	Avoyelles Parish School Board	Marksville
19	8.8	Catahoula Parish School Board	Harrisonburg
19	8.8	Saint Martin Parish School Board	St Martinville
22	8.6	Lafayette Parish School Board	Lafayette
22	8.6	Saint John the Baptist Parish SB	Reserve
22	8.6	Tangipahoa Parish School Board	Amite
25	8.4	Ouachita Parish School Board	Monroe
26	8.2	West Baton Rouge Parish School Bd	Port Allen
27	8.0	Saint Tammany Parish School Board	Covington
28	7.7	Evangeline Parish School Board	Ville Platte
29	7.6	Caldwell Parish School Board	Columbia
30	7.5	Acadia Parish School Board	Crowley
30	7.5	Concordia Parish School Board	Vidalia
30	7.5	Richland Parish School Board	Rayville
30	7.5	Vernon Parish School Board	Leesville
34	7.3	Bienville Parish School Board	Arcadia
34	7.3	Saint Mary Parish School Board	Centerville
36	7.2	Sabine Parish School Board	Many
37	7.0	East Feliciana Parish School Board	Clinton
38	6.9	Rapides Parish School Board	Alexandria
39	6.7	Bossier Parish School Board	Benton
40	6.6	Lincoln Parish School Board	Ruston
40	6.6	Saint Bernard Parish School Board	Chalmette
42	6.3	Webster Parish School Board	Minden
43	6.2	Ascension Parish School Board	Donaldsonville
43	6.2	City of Bogalusa School Board	Bogalusa
45	6.1	Saint Landry Parish School Board	Opelousas
46	6.0	Jackson Parish School Board	Jonesboro
46	6.0	Saint James Parish School Board	Lutcher
48	5.9	Calcasieu Parish School Board	Lake Charles
48	5.9	Winn Parish School Board	Winnfield
50	5.7	Vermilion Parish School Board	Abbeville
51	5.5	Iberia Parish School Board	New Iberia
51	5.5	Lafourche Parish School Board	Thibodaux
53	5.4	Jefferson Davis Parish SB	Jennings
54	5.2	Saint Charles Parish School Board	Luling
55	4.4	Union Parish School Board	Farmerville
56	4.1	West Feliciana Parish School Board	St Francisville
57	4.0	Lasalle Parish School Board	Jena
57	4.0	Washington Parish School Board	Franklinton
59	3.9	Beauregard Parish School Board	Deridder
60	3.7	Allen Parish School Board	Oberlin
61	3.5	Claiborne Parish School Board	Homer
61	3.5	Plaquemines Parish School Board	Port Sulphur
63	2.7	Cameron Parish School Board	Cameron
64	1.0	Livingston Parish School Board	Livingston

Maine

Maine Public School Educational Profile

Category	Value	Category	Value
Schools *(2002-2003)*	704	**Diploma Recipients** *(2002-2003)*	12,596
Instructional Level		White, Non-Hispanic	12,201
Primary	422	Black, Non-Hispanic	110
Middle	126	Asian/Pacific Islander	144
High	139	American Indian/Alaskan Native	80
Other Level	17	Hispanic	61
Curriculum		**High School Drop-out Rate** (%) *(2000-2001)*	3.1
Regular	675	White, Non-Hispanic	3.1
Special Education	2	Black, Non-Hispanic	3.6
Vocational	27	Asian/Pacific Islander	4.5
Alternative	0	American Indian/Alaskan Native	5.9
Type		Hispanic	2.6
Magnet	1	**Staff** *(2002-2003)*	34,586.1
Charter	0	Teachers	16,837.2
Title I Eligible	533	Average Salary ($)	38,518
School-wide Title I	53	Librarians/Media Specialists	241.7
Students *(2002-2003)*	209,225	Guidance Counselors	655.5
Gender (%)		**Ratios** *(2002-2003)*	
Male	51.5	Student/Teacher Ratio	12.4 to 1
Female	48.5	Student/Librarian Ratio	865.6 to 1
Race/Ethnicity (%)		Student/Counselor Ratio	319.2 to 1
White, Non-Hispanic	96.1	**Current Spending** *($ per student in FY 2001)*	8,818
Black, Non-Hispanic	1.6	Instruction	5,877
Asian/Pacific Islander	1.1	Support Services	2,646
American Indian/Alaskan Native	0.5	**College Entrance Exam Scores** *(2003)*	
Hispanic	0.7	Scholastic Aptitude Test (SAT)	
Classification (%)		Participation Rate (%)	70
Individual Education Program (IEP)	16.6	Mean SAT I Verbal Score	503
Migrant	0.0	Mean SAT I Math Score	501
English Language Learner (ELL)	1.3	American College Testing Program (ACT)	
Eligible for Free Lunch Program	22.8	Participation Rate (%)	7
Eligible for Reduced-Price Lunch Program	7.6	Average Composite Score	22.5

Note: *For an explanation of data, please refer to the User's Guide in the front of the book; n/a indicates data not available*

Maine NAEP 2003 Test Scores

Reading			Mathematics		
Grade/Category	**Value**	**Rank**	**Grade/Category**	**Value**	**Rank**
4th Grade			**4th Grade**		
Average Proficiency	223.9 (0.9)	6/51	Average Proficiency	237.6 (0.7)	15/51
Proficiency by Gender/Race/Ethnicity			Proficiency by Gender/Race/Ethnicity		
Male	221.3 (1.4)	7/51	Male	239.2 (0.9)	14/51
Female	226.5 (1.0)	12/51	Female	235.9 (0.9)	15/51
White, Non-Hispanic	224.2 (0.9)	34/51	White, Non-Hispanic	238.0 (0.7)	39/51
Black, Non-Hispanic	n/a	n/a	Black, Non-Hispanic	n/a	n/a
Asian, Non-Hispanic	n/a	n/a	Asian, Non-Hispanic	n/a	n/a
American Indian, Non-Hispanic	n/a	n/a	American Indian, Non-Hispanic	n/a	n/a
Hispanic	n/a	n/a	Hispanic	n/a	n/a
Proficiency by Class Size			Proficiency by Class Size		
Less than 16 Students	219.7 (1.7)	4/45	Less than 16 Students	232.6 (1.3)	7/47
16 to 18 Students	223.1 (1.6)	9/48	16 to 18 Students	236.9 (1.6)	15/48
19 to 20 Students	225.6 (2.0)	6/50	19 to 20 Students	240.3 (1.2)	10/50
21 to 25 Students	225.7 (1.9)	12/51	21 to 25 Students	239.5 (1.3)	17/51
Greater than 25 Students	n/a	n/a	Greater than 25 Students	n/a	n/a
Percent Attaining Achievement Levels			Percent Attaining Achievement Levels		
Below Basic	29.7 (1.3)	46/51	Below Basic	17.5 (1.3)	41/51
Basic or Above	70.3 (1.3)	6/51	Basic or Above	82.5 (1.3)	11/51
Proficient or Above	35.5 (1.3)	8/51	Proficient or Above	33.9 (1.3)	19/51
Advanced or Above	7.7 (0.5)	18/51	Advanced or Above	3.1 (0.5)	29/51
8th Grade			**8th Grade**		
Average Proficiency	268.3 (1.0)	7/51	Average Proficiency	281.9 (0.9)	15/51
Proficiency by Gender/Race/Ethnicity			Proficiency by Gender/Race/Ethnicity		
Male	261.7 (1.4)	13/51	Male	283.0 (1.0)	16/51
Female	275.2 (1.2)	5/51	Female	280.8 (1.1)	15/51
White, Non-Hispanic	268.5 (1.0)	29/50	White, Non-Hispanic	282.3 (0.9)	38/50
Black, Non-Hispanic	n/a	n/a	Black, Non-Hispanic	n/a	n/a
Asian, Non-Hispanic	n/a	n/a	Asian, Non-Hispanic	n/a	n/a
American Indian, Non-Hispanic	n/a	n/a	American Indian, Non-Hispanic	n/a	n/a
Hispanic	n/a	n/a	Hispanic	n/a	n/a
Proficiency by Parents Highest Level of Ed.			Proficiency by Parents Highest Level of Ed.		
Did Not Finish High School	240.2 (3.3)	40/50	Did Not Finish High School	255.4 (3.0)	29/50
Graduated High School	259.7 (1.9)	11/50	Graduated High School	272.3 (1.5)	14/50
Some Education After High School	268.7 (1.5)	21/50	Some Education After High School	281.1 (1.4)	25/50
Graduated College	276.8 (1.3)	5/50	Graduated College	290.9 (1.0)	20/50
Percent Attaining Achievement Levels			Percent Attaining Achievement Levels		
Below Basic	20.7 (1.0)	43/51	Below Basic	25.2 (1.1)	40/51
Basic or Above	79.3 (1.0)	9/51	Basic or Above	74.8 (1.1)	12/51
Proficient or Above	36.8 (1.3)	10/51	Proficient or Above	29.4 (1.2)	27/51
Advanced or Above	3.4 (0.6)	10/51	Advanced or Above	5.0 (0.6)	24/51

Note: *For an explanation of data, please refer to the User's Guide in the front of the book; values in italics indicate that the nature of the sample does not allow accurate determination of the variability of the statistic; n/a indicates data not available*

Androscoggin County

Auburn School Department

23 High St • Auburn, ME 04212-0800
Mailing Address: PO Box 800 • Auburn, ME 04212-0800
(207) 784-6431 • http://www.auburnschl.edu/default.html
Grade Span: KG-12; **Agency Type:** 1
Schools: 12
6 Primary; 2 Middle; 2 High; 2 Other Level
11 Regular; 1 Special Education; 0 Vocational; 0 Alternative
0 Magnet; 0 Charter; 5 Title I Eligible; 0 School-wide Title I
Students: 3,691 (51.5% male; 48.5% female)
Individual Education Program: 716 (19.4%);
English Language Learner: 92 (2.5%); Migrant: n/a
Eligible for Free Lunch Program: 796 (21.6%)
Eligible for Reduced-Price Lunch Program: 207 (5.6%)
Teachers: 338.2 (10.9 to 1)
Librarians/Media Specialists: 2.9 (1,272.8 to 1)
Guidance Counselors: 16.8 (219.7 to 1)
Current Spending: ($ per student per year):
Total: $7,708; Instruction: $5,379; Support Services: $2,173
Enrollment, Drop-out Rates and Diploma Recipients by Race/Ethnicity

Category	Total	White	Black	Asian	AIAN	Hisp.
Enrollment (%)	100.0	93.6	3.2	1.2	0.9	1.2
Drop-out Rate (%)	7.2	7.4	0.0	5.9	0.0	0.0
H.S. Diplomas (#)	228	223	1	3	1	0

Lewiston School Department

Dingley Bldg 36 Oak St • Lewiston, ME 04240-7190
(207) 795-4100 • http://www.lewiston.k12.me.us/
Grade Span: KG-12; **Agency Type:** 1
Schools: 9
6 Primary; 1 Middle; 2 High; 0 Other Level
8 Regular; 0 Special Education; 1 Vocational; 0 Alternative
0 Magnet; 0 Charter; 6 Title I Eligible; 1 School-wide Title I
Students: 4,689 (50.7% male; 49.3% female)
Individual Education Program: 842 (18.0%);
English Language Learner: 274 (5.8%); Migrant: n/a
Eligible for Free Lunch Program: 1,850 (39.5%)
Eligible for Reduced-Price Lunch Program: 349 (7.4%)
Teachers: 336.0 (14.0 to 1)
Librarians/Media Specialists: 3.0 (1,563.0 to 1)
Guidance Counselors: 17.0 (275.8 to 1)
Current Spending: ($ per student per year):
Total: $8,215; Instruction: $5,469; Support Services: $2,423
Enrollment, Drop-out Rates and Diploma Recipients by Race/Ethnicity

Category	Total	White	Black	Asian	AIAN	Hisp.
Enrollment (%)	100.0	87.1	9.7	1.1	0.8	1.3
Drop-out Rate (%)	5.0	4.6	11.4	12.5	25.0	15.4
H.S. Diplomas (#)	270	255	9	5	1	0

MSAD 52 - Turner

98 Matthews Way • Turner, ME 04282-9778
(207) 225-3795 • http://www.yarmouth.k12.me.us/
Grade Span: PK-12; **Agency Type:** 1
Schools: 6
3 Primary; 2 Middle; 1 High; 0 Other Level
6 Regular; 0 Special Education; 0 Vocational; 0 Alternative
0 Magnet; 0 Charter; 4 Title I Eligible; 0 School-wide Title I
Students: 2,331 (52.3% male; 47.7% female)
Individual Education Program: 321 (13.8%);
English Language Learner: 71 (3.0%); Migrant: n/a
Eligible for Free Lunch Program: 337 (14.5%)
Eligible for Reduced-Price Lunch Program: 167 (7.2%)
Teachers: 189.2 (12.3 to 1)
Librarians/Media Specialists: 2.9 (803.8 to 1)
Guidance Counselors: 10.0 (233.1 to 1)
Current Spending: ($ per student per year):
Total: $7,621; Instruction: $4,936; Support Services: $2,425
Enrollment, Drop-out Rates and Diploma Recipients by Race/Ethnicity

Category	Total	White	Black	Asian	AIAN	Hisp.
Enrollment (%)	100.0	96.7	0.6	0.5	0.3	1.9
Drop-out Rate (%)	0.5	0.4	0.0	0.0	n/a	7.7
H.S. Diplomas (#)	150	148	0	1	0	1

Aroostook County

MSAD 01 - Presque Isle

79 Blake St Ste 1 PO Box 1118 • Presque Isle, ME 04769-2484
(207) 764-4101 • http://www.sad1.k12.me.us/
Grade Span: PK-12; **Agency Type:** 1
Schools: 9
4 Primary; 2 Middle; 3 High; 0 Other Level
8 Regular; 0 Special Education; 1 Vocational; 0 Alternative
0 Magnet; 0 Charter; 4 Title I Eligible; 0 School-wide Title I
Students: 2,164 (52.9% male; 47.1% female)
Individual Education Program: 266 (12.3%);
English Language Learner: 4 (0.2%); Migrant: n/a
Eligible for Free Lunch Program: 525 (24.3%)
Eligible for Reduced-Price Lunch Program: 182 (8.4%)
Teachers: 167.2 (12.9 to 1)
Librarians/Media Specialists: 1.0 (2,164.0 to 1)
Guidance Counselors: 3.9 (554.9 to 1)
Current Spending: ($ per student per year):
Total: $7,674; Instruction: $4,662; Support Services: $2,628
Enrollment, Drop-out Rates and Diploma Recipients by Race/Ethnicity

Category	Total	White	Black	Asian	AIAN	Hisp.
Enrollment (%)	100.0	95.0	0.8	0.9	2.9	0.5
Drop-out Rate (%)	2.3	2.2	0.0	0.0	8.7	0.0
H.S. Diplomas (#)	128	120	0	1	5	2

Cumberland County

Brunswick School Department

35 Union St • Brunswick, ME 04011-1922
(207) 729-4148 • http://www.brunswick.k12.me.us/
Grade Span: KG-12; **Agency Type:** 1
Schools: 6
4 Primary; 1 Middle; 1 High; 0 Other Level
6 Regular; 0 Special Education; 0 Vocational; 0 Alternative
0 Magnet; 0 Charter; 4 Title I Eligible; 0 School-wide Title I
Students: 3,192 (52.3% male; 47.7% female)
Individual Education Program: 476 (14.9%);
English Language Learner: 32 (1.0%); Migrant: n/a
Eligible for Free Lunch Program: 280 (8.8%)
Eligible for Reduced-Price Lunch Program: 131 (4.1%)
Teachers: 235.7 (13.5 to 1)
Librarians/Media Specialists: 5.5 (580.4 to 1)
Guidance Counselors: 11.9 (268.2 to 1)
Current Spending: ($ per student per year):
Total: $7,199; Instruction: $4,642; Support Services: $2,319
Enrollment, Drop-out Rates and Diploma Recipients by Race/Ethnicity

Category	Total	White	Black	Asian	AIAN	Hisp.
Enrollment (%)	100.0	93.7	2.3	2.0	0.3	1.7
Drop-out Rate (%)	2.3	2.2	5.9	11.1	0.0	0.0
H.S. Diplomas (#)	230	223	3	2	1	1

Cape Elizabeth School Department

PO Box 6267 • Cape Elizabeth, ME 04107-0067
(207) 799-2217 • http://www.cape.k12.me.us/
Grade Span: KG-12; **Agency Type:** 1
Schools: 3
1 Primary; 1 Middle; 1 High; 0 Other Level
3 Regular; 0 Special Education; 0 Vocational; 0 Alternative
0 Magnet; 0 Charter; 1 Title I Eligible; 0 School-wide Title I
Students: 1,779 (53.0% male; 47.0% female)
Individual Education Program: 222 (12.5%);
English Language Learner: 3 (0.2%); Migrant: n/a
Eligible for Free Lunch Program: 79 (4.4%)
Eligible for Reduced-Price Lunch Program: 18 (1.0%)
Teachers: 133.3 (13.3 to 1)
Librarians/Media Specialists: 3.0 (593.0 to 1)
Guidance Counselors: 5.7 (312.1 to 1)
Current Spending: ($ per student per year):
Total: $8,148; Instruction: $5,545; Support Services: $2,313
Enrollment, Drop-out Rates and Diploma Recipients by Race/Ethnicity

Category	Total	White	Black	Asian	AIAN	Hisp.
Enrollment (%)	100.0	97.2	0.5	1.6	0.0	0.7
Drop-out Rate (%)	0.0	0.0	n/a	0.0	n/a	0.0
H.S. Diplomas (#)	107	107	0	0	0	0

Falmouth School Department

51 Woodville Rd • Falmouth, ME 04105-1105
(207) 781-3200 • http://www.falmouthschools.org/
Grade Span: KG-12; **Agency Type:** 1
Schools: 4
2 Primary; 1 Middle; 1 High; 0 Other Level
4 Regular; 0 Special Education; 0 Vocational; 0 Alternative
0 Magnet; 0 Charter; 1 Title I Eligible; 0 School-wide Title I
Students: 2,119 (52.0% male; 48.0% female)
Individual Education Program: 254 (12.0%);
English Language Learner: 1 (<0.1%); Migrant: n/a
Eligible for Free Lunch Program: 30 (1.4%)
Eligible for Reduced-Price Lunch Program: 11 (0.5%)
Teachers: 168.1 (12.6 to 1)
Librarians/Media Specialists: 3.0 (706.3 to 1)
Guidance Counselors: 8.0 (264.9 to 1)
Current Spending: ($ per student per year):
Total: $7,978; Instruction: $5,155; Support Services: $2,619

Enrollment, Drop-out Rates and Diploma Recipients by Race/Ethnicity

Category	Total	White	Black	Asian	AIAN	Hisp.
Enrollment (%)	100.0	95.9	0.6	2.3	0.1	1.0
Drop-out Rate (%)	0.0	0.0	0.0	0.0	n/a	0.0
H.S. Diplomas (#)	113	107	1	1	1	3

Gorham School Department

381 Main St • Gorham, ME 04038-1309
(207) 839-5000 • http://www.gorhamschools.org/
Grade Span: KG-12; **Agency Type:** 1
Schools: 6
3 Primary; 2 Middle; 1 High; 0 Other Level
6 Regular; 0 Special Education; 0 Vocational; 0 Alternative
0 Magnet; 0 Charter; 3 Title I Eligible; 0 School-wide Title I
Students: 2,716 (50.6% male; 49.4% female)
Individual Education Program: 387 (14.2%);
English Language Learner: 10 (0.4%); Migrant: n/a
Eligible for Free Lunch Program: 271 (10.0%)
Eligible for Reduced-Price Lunch Program: 104 (3.8%)
Teachers: 184.6 (14.7 to 1)
Librarians/Media Specialists: 4.0 (679.0 to 1)
Guidance Counselors: 6.0 (452.7 to 1)
Current Spending: ($ per student per year):
Total: $7,103; Instruction: $4,699; Support Services: $2,170

Enrollment, Drop-out Rates and Diploma Recipients by Race/Ethnicity

Category	Total	White	Black	Asian	AIAN	Hisp.
Enrollment (%)	100.0	97.1	1.1	0.9	0.4	0.6
Drop-out Rate (%)	2.5	2.6	0.0	0.0	0.0	0.0
H.S. Diplomas (#)	149	146	0	3	0	0

MSAD 15 - Gray

14 Shaker Rd • Gray, ME 04039-1080
(207) 657-3335 • http://www.msad15.org
Grade Span: KG-12; **Agency Type:** 1
Schools: 5
3 Primary; 1 Middle; 1 High; 0 Other Level
5 Regular; 0 Special Education; 0 Vocational; 0 Alternative
0 Magnet; 0 Charter; 4 Title I Eligible; 0 School-wide Title I
Students: 2,063 (52.2% male; 47.8% female)
Individual Education Program: 314 (15.2%);
English Language Learner: 1 (<0.1%); Migrant: n/a
Eligible for Free Lunch Program: 283 (13.7%)
Eligible for Reduced-Price Lunch Program: 131 (6.4%)
Teachers: 153.1 (13.5 to 1)
Librarians/Media Specialists: 1.0 (2,063.0 to 1)
Guidance Counselors: 8.0 (257.9 to 1)
Current Spending: ($ per student per year):
Total: $7,379; Instruction: $4,507; Support Services: $2,611

Enrollment, Drop-out Rates and Diploma Recipients by Race/Ethnicity

Category	Total	White	Black	Asian	AIAN	Hisp.
Enrollment (%)	100.0	98.2	1.2	0.3	0.2	0.1
Drop-out Rate (%)	0.6	0.6	0.0	0.0	n/a	0.0
H.S. Diplomas (#)	117	116	1	0	0	0

MSAD 51 - Cumberland

357 Tuttle Rd PO Box 6a • Cumberland Center, ME 04021-0606
(207) 829-4800
Grade Span: KG-12; **Agency Type:** 1
Schools: 6
2 Primary; 3 Middle; 1 High; 0 Other Level
6 Regular; 0 Special Education; 0 Vocational; 0 Alternative
0 Magnet; 0 Charter; 5 Title I Eligible; 0 School-wide Title I
Students: 2,342 (49.5% male; 50.5% female)
Individual Education Program: 151 (6.4%);
English Language Learner: 6 (0.3%); Migrant: n/a
Eligible for Free Lunch Program: 35 (1.5%)
Eligible for Reduced-Price Lunch Program: 16 (0.7%)
Teachers: 181.7 (12.9 to 1)
Librarians/Media Specialists: 1.0 (2,342.0 to 1)
Guidance Counselors: 6.7 (349.6 to 1)
Current Spending: ($ per student per year):
Total: $7,587; Instruction: $4,958; Support Services: $2,374

Enrollment, Drop-out Rates and Diploma Recipients by Race/Ethnicity

Category	Total	White	Black	Asian	AIAN	Hisp.
Enrollment (%)	100.0	98.7	0.5	0.5	0.0	0.3
Drop-out Rate (%)	0.5	0.5	0.0	0.0	n/a	0.0
H.S. Diplomas (#)	148	147	0	1	0	0

MSAD 61 - Bridgton

RR 2 Box 554 • Bridgton, ME 04009-9802
(207) 647-3048 • http://www.yorkschools.org/
Grade Span: KG-12; **Agency Type:** 1
Schools: 7
3 Primary; 2 Middle; 2 High; 0 Other Level
6 Regular; 0 Special Education; 1 Vocational; 0 Alternative
0 Magnet; 0 Charter; 5 Title I Eligible; 0 School-wide Title I
Students: 2,206 (53.7% male; 46.3% female)
Individual Education Program: 481 (21.8%);
English Language Learner: 1 (<0.1%); Migrant: n/a
Eligible for Free Lunch Program: 547 (24.8%)
Eligible for Reduced-Price Lunch Program: 162 (7.3%)
Teachers: 211.6 (10.4 to 1)
Librarians/Media Specialists: 1.8 (1,225.6 to 1)
Guidance Counselors: 7.0 (315.1 to 1)
Current Spending: ($ per student per year):
Total: $8,461; Instruction: $5,479; Support Services: $2,784

Enrollment, Drop-out Rates and Diploma Recipients by Race/Ethnicity

Category	Total	White	Black	Asian	AIAN	Hisp.
Enrollment (%)	100.0	97.2	1.0	0.3	0.7	0.8
Drop-out Rate (%)	0.3	0.3	0.0	n/a	0.0	n/a
H.S. Diplomas (#)	128	123	1	2	2	0

Portland Public Schools

331 Veranda St • Portland, ME 04103-5535
(207) 874-8100 • http://www.portlandschools.org/
Grade Span: KG-12; **Agency Type:** 1
Schools: 18
11 Primary; 3 Middle; 3 High; 1 Other Level
17 Regular; 0 Special Education; 1 Vocational; 0 Alternative
0 Magnet; 0 Charter; 8 Title I Eligible; 2 School-wide Title I
Students: 7,555 (51.4% male; 48.6% female)
Individual Education Program: 1,135 (15.0%);
English Language Learner: 974 (12.9%); Migrant: n/a
Eligible for Free Lunch Program: 2,546 (33.7%)
Eligible for Reduced-Price Lunch Program: 375 (5.0%)
Teachers: 673.8 (11.2 to 1)
Librarians/Media Specialists: 9.7 (778.9 to 1)
Guidance Counselors: 19.0 (397.6 to 1)
Current Spending: ($ per student per year):
Total: $9,987; Instruction: $6,597; Support Services: $3,123

Enrollment, Drop-out Rates and Diploma Recipients by Race/Ethnicity

Category	Total	White	Black	Asian	AIAN	Hisp.
Enrollment (%)	100.0	79.3	10.1	7.6	0.5	2.5
Drop-out Rate (%)	6.3	6.0	3.9	12.1	8.3	5.4
H.S. Diplomas (#)	288	275	6	3	1	3

Scarborough School Department

PO Box 370 • Scarborough, ME 04070-0370
(207) 883-4315 • http://www.scarborough.k12.me.us/
Grade Span: KG-12; **Agency Type:** 1
Schools: 6
4 Primary; 1 Middle; 1 High; 0 Other Level
6 Regular; 0 Special Education; 0 Vocational; 0 Alternative
0 Magnet; 0 Charter; 3 Title I Eligible; 0 School-wide Title I
Students: 3,213 (51.3% male; 48.7% female)
Individual Education Program: 424 (13.2%);
English Language Learner: 48 (1.5%); Migrant: n/a
Eligible for Free Lunch Program: 186 (5.8%)
Eligible for Reduced-Price Lunch Program: 102 (3.2%)
Teachers: 238.9 (13.4 to 1)
Librarians/Media Specialists: 3.0 (1,071.0 to 1)
Guidance Counselors: 7.3 (440.1 to 1)
Current Spending: ($ per student per year):
Total: $7,005; Instruction: $4,716; Support Services: $2,002

Enrollment, Drop-out Rates and Diploma Recipients by Race/Ethnicity

Category	Total	White	Black	Asian	AIAN	Hisp.
Enrollment (%)	100.0	97.4	0.6	1.0	0.2	0.8
Drop-out Rate (%)	1.6	1.4	16.7	0.0	n/a	0.0
H.S. Diplomas (#)	178	176	0	1	0	1

South Portland School Department

130 Wescott Rd • South Portland, ME 04106-3420
(207) 871-0555 • http://www.spsd.org/
Grade Span: KG-12; **Agency Type:** 1
Schools: 9
6 Primary; 2 Middle; 1 High; 0 Other Level
9 Regular; 0 Special Education; 0 Vocational; 0 Alternative
0 Magnet; 0 Charter; 5 Title I Eligible; 0 School-wide Title I
Students: 3,247 (52.2% male; 47.8% female)
Individual Education Program: 593 (18.3%);
English Language Learner: 51 (1.6%); Migrant: n/a
Eligible for Free Lunch Program: 463 (14.3%)
Eligible for Reduced-Price Lunch Program: 171 (5.3%)
Teachers: 265.6 (12.2 to 1)
Librarians/Media Specialists: 3.0 (1,082.3 to 1)
Guidance Counselors: 18.9 (171.8 to 1)
Current Spending: ($ per student per year):
Total: $9,624; Instruction: $7,044; Support Services: $2,286

Enrollment, Drop-out Rates and Diploma Recipients by Race/Ethnicity

Category	Total	White	Black	Asian	AIAN	Hisp.
Enrollment (%)	100.0	93.5	2.2	3.1	0.1	1.1
Drop-out Rate (%)	3.3	3.4	0.0	4.5	0.0	0.0
H.S. Diplomas (#)	228	220	1	3	0	4

Westbrook School Department

117 Stroudwater St • Westbrook, ME 04092-4130
(207) 854-0800 • http://www.westbrookschools.org/
Grade Span: KG-12; **Agency Type:** 1
Schools: 7
4 Primary; 1 Middle; 2 High; 0 Other Level
6 Regular; 0 Special Education; 1 Vocational; 0 Alternative
0 Magnet; 0 Charter; 4 Title I Eligible; 0 School-wide Title I
Students: 2,687 (52.7% male; 47.3% female)
Individual Education Program: 324 (12.1%);
English Language Learner: 36 (1.3%); Migrant: n/a
Eligible for Free Lunch Program: 709 (26.4%)
Eligible for Reduced-Price Lunch Program: 190 (7.1%)
Teachers: 234.8 (11.4 to 1)
Librarians/Media Specialists: 2.0 (1,343.5 to 1)
Guidance Counselors: 8.0 (335.9 to 1)
Current Spending: ($ per student per year):
Total: $8,718; Instruction: $5,645; Support Services: $2,760

Enrollment, Drop-out Rates and Diploma Recipients by Race/Ethnicity

Category	Total	White	Black	Asian	AIAN	Hisp.
Enrollment (%)	100.0	94.7	2.8	1.4	0.2	0.9
Drop-out Rate (%)	2.2	2.2	0.0	0.0	33.3	0.0
H.S. Diplomas (#)	153	147	2	3	0	1

Windham School Department

228 Windham Center Rd • Windham, ME 04062-4862
(207) 892-1800 • http://www.windham.k12.me.us/
Grade Span: KG-12; **Agency Type:** 1
Schools: 5
1 Primary; 2 Middle; 2 High; 0 Other Level
5 Regular; 0 Special Education; 0 Vocational; 0 Alternative
0 Magnet; 0 Charter; 2 Title I Eligible; 0 School-wide Title I
Students: 2,620 (52.0% male; 48.0% female)
Individual Education Program: 299 (11.4%);
English Language Learner: 14 (0.5%); Migrant: n/a
Eligible for Free Lunch Program: 299 (11.4%)
Eligible for Reduced-Price Lunch Program: 91 (3.5%)
Teachers: 196.1 (13.4 to 1)
Librarians/Media Specialists: 2.0 (1,310.0 to 1)
Guidance Counselors: 8.4 (311.9 to 1)
Current Spending: ($ per student per year):
Total: $7,250; Instruction: $4,827; Support Services: $2,194

Enrollment, Drop-out Rates and Diploma Recipients by Race/Ethnicity

Category	Total	White	Black	Asian	AIAN	Hisp.
Enrollment (%)	100.0	97.4	0.9	0.7	0.4	0.5
Drop-out Rate (%)	2.4	2.2	0.0	0.0	8.3	33.3
H.S. Diplomas (#)	4	1	0	1	2	0

Franklin County

MSAD 09 - Farmington

11 School Ln • New Sharon, ME 04955-9739
(207) 778-6571 • http://www.route2.com/msad9.htm
Grade Span: KG-12; **Agency Type:** 1
Schools: 9
5 Primary; 2 Middle; 2 High; 0 Other Level
8 Regular; 0 Special Education; 1 Vocational; 0 Alternative
0 Magnet; 0 Charter; 6 Title I Eligible; 0 School-wide Title I
Students: 2,692 (51.6% male; 48.4% female)
Individual Education Program: 343 (12.7%);
English Language Learner: 4 (0.1%); Migrant: n/a
Eligible for Free Lunch Program: 713 (26.5%)
Eligible for Reduced-Price Lunch Program: 335 (12.4%)
Teachers: 232.4 (11.6 to 1)
Librarians/Media Specialists: 4.9 (549.4 to 1)
Guidance Counselors: 7.4 (363.8 to 1)
Current Spending: ($ per student per year):
Total: $7,444; Instruction: $4,528; Support Services: $2,669

Enrollment, Drop-out Rates and Diploma Recipients by Race/Ethnicity

Category	Total	White	Black	Asian	AIAN	Hisp.
Enrollment (%)	100.0	97.5	0.6	1.0	0.2	0.7
Drop-out Rate (%)	1.2	1.3	0.0	0.0	0.0	0.0
H.S. Diplomas (#)	197	193	0	2	1	1

Kennebec County

Augusta Dept of Public Schools

RR 7 Box 2525 • Augusta, ME 04330-9105
(207) 626-2468 • http://www.cony-hs.augusta.k12.me.us/
Grade Span: PK-12; **Agency Type:** 1
Schools: 8
4 Primary; 2 Middle; 2 High; 0 Other Level
7 Regular; 0 Special Education; 1 Vocational; 0 Alternative
0 Magnet; 0 Charter; 5 Title I Eligible; 0 School-wide Title I
Students: 2,506 (51.4% male; 48.6% female)
Individual Education Program: 569 (22.7%);
English Language Learner: 65 (2.6%); Migrant: n/a
Eligible for Free Lunch Program: 840 (33.5%)
Eligible for Reduced-Price Lunch Program: 209 (8.3%)
Teachers: 242.7 (10.3 to 1)
Librarians/Media Specialists: 2.0 (1,253.0 to 1)
Guidance Counselors: 10.9 (229.9 to 1)
Current Spending: ($ per student per year):
Total: $9,194; Instruction: $5,938; Support Services: $2,888

Enrollment, Drop-out Rates and Diploma Recipients by Race/Ethnicity

Category	Total	White	Black	Asian	AIAN	Hisp.
Enrollment (%)	100.0	96.6	0.9	1.8	0.2	0.5
Drop-out Rate (%)	0.4	0.4	0.0	0.0	n/a	0.0
H.S. Diplomas (#)	183	173	2	3	1	4

MSAD 11 - Gardiner

150 Highland Ave • Gardiner, ME 04345-1812
(207) 582-5346 • http://www.sad11.k12.me.us/
Grade Span: KG-12; **Agency Type:** 1
Schools: 8
6 Primary; 1 Middle; 1 High; 0 Other Level
8 Regular; 0 Special Education; 0 Vocational; 0 Alternative
0 Magnet; 0 Charter; 8 Title I Eligible; 0 School-wide Title I
Students: 2,330 (53.1% male; 46.9% female)
Individual Education Program: 373 (16.0%);
English Language Learner: 1 (<0.1%); Migrant: n/a
Eligible for Free Lunch Program: 528 (22.7%)
Eligible for Reduced-Price Lunch Program: 222 (9.5%)
Teachers: 172.1 (13.5 to 1)
Librarians/Media Specialists: 1.9 (1,226.3 to 1)
Guidance Counselors: 6.8 (342.6 to 1)
Current Spending: ($ per student per year):
Total: $7,150; Instruction: $4,395; Support Services: $2,447

Enrollment, Drop-out Rates and Diploma Recipients by Race/Ethnicity

Category	Total	White	Black	Asian	AIAN	Hisp.
Enrollment (%)	100.0	96.3	0.9	0.9	1.3	0.6
Drop-out Rate (%)	2.1	2.1	0.0	0.0	3.4	0.0
H.S. Diplomas (#)	169	159	1	2	4	3

MSAD 47 - Oakland

47 Heath St • Oakland, ME 04963-1102
(207) 465-7384 • http://www.sad47.me.us/
Grade Span: KG-12; **Agency Type:** 1
Schools: 6
3 Primary; 2 Middle; 1 High; 0 Other Level
6 Regular; 0 Special Education; 0 Vocational; 0 Alternative
0 Magnet; 0 Charter; 4 Title I Eligible; 0 School-wide Title I
Students: 2,516 (49.7% male; 50.3% female)
Individual Education Program: 336 (13.4%);
English Language Learner: 2 (0.1%); Migrant: n/a
Eligible for Free Lunch Program: 495 (19.7%)
Eligible for Reduced-Price Lunch Program: 200 (7.9%)
Teachers: 203.3 (12.4 to 1)
Librarians/Media Specialists: 3.0 (838.7 to 1)
Guidance Counselors: 10.1 (249.1 to 1)
Current Spending: ($ per student per year):
Total: $6,988; Instruction: $4,459; Support Services: $2,284

Enrollment, Drop-out Rates and Diploma Recipients by Race/Ethnicity

Category	Total	White	Black	Asian	AIAN	Hisp.
Enrollment (%)	100.0	98.7	0.4	0.6	0.2	0.1
Drop-out Rate (%)	0.8	0.8	0.0	0.0	0.0	0.0
H.S. Diplomas (#)	197	194	0	3	0	0

Waterville Public Schools

21 Gilman St • Waterville, ME 04901-5437
(207) 873-4281 • http://web.wtvl.k12.me.us/
Grade Span: KG-12; **Agency Type:** 1
Schools: 5
1 Primary; 2 Middle; 2 High; 0 Other Level
4 Regular; 0 Special Education; 1 Vocational; 0 Alternative
0 Magnet; 0 Charter; 4 Title I Eligible; 2 School-wide Title I
Students: 1,892 (52.4% male; 47.6% female)
Individual Education Program: 406 (21.5%);
English Language Learner: 13 (0.7%); Migrant: n/a

Eligible for Free Lunch Program: 723 (38.2%)
Eligible for Reduced-Price Lunch Program: 140 (7.4%)
Teachers: 173.6 (10.9 to 1)
Librarians/Media Specialists: 2.0 (946.0 to 1)
Guidance Counselors: 7.9 (239.5 to 1)
Current Spending: ($ per student per year):
Total: $8,332; Instruction: $5,488; Support Services: $2,563

Enrollment, Drop-out Rates and Diploma Recipients by Race/Ethnicity

Category	Total	White	Black	Asian	AIAN	Hisp.
Enrollment (%)	100.0	95.0	2.4	1.3	0.2	1.1
Drop-out Rate (%)	5.1	5.3	0.0	0.0	0.0	0.0
H.S. Diplomas (#)	141	136	1	2	0	2

Knox County

MSAD 05 - Rockland

28 Lincoln St • Rockland, ME 04841-2881
(207) 596-6620 • http://www.msad5.org/
Grade Span: KG-12; **Agency Type:** 1
Schools: 6
4 Primary; 1 Middle; 1 High; 0 Other Level
6 Regular; 0 Special Education; 0 Vocational; 0 Alternative
0 Magnet; 0 Charter; 3 Title I Eligible; 0 School-wide Title I
Students: 1,516 (48.9% male; 51.1% female)
Individual Education Program: 205 (13.5%);
English Language Learner: 9 (0.6%); Migrant: n/a
Eligible for Free Lunch Program: 409 (27.0%)
Eligible for Reduced-Price Lunch Program: 148 (9.8%)
Teachers: 116.2 (13.0 to 1)
Librarians/Media Specialists: 2.0 (758.0 to 1)
Guidance Counselors: 6.0 (252.7 to 1)
Current Spending: ($ per student per year):
Total: $7,626; Instruction: $4,875; Support Services: $2,559

Enrollment, Drop-out Rates and Diploma Recipients by Race/Ethnicity

Category	Total	White	Black	Asian	AIAN	Hisp.
Enrollment (%)	100.0	97.7	0.7	0.9	0.2	0.6
Drop-out Rate (%)	3.2	3.3	0.0	0.0	n/a	0.0
H.S. Diplomas (#)	103	99	1	3	0	0

MSAD 40 - Waldoboro

44 School St • Warren, ME 04864-0913
(207) 273-4070
Grade Span: KG-12; **Agency Type:** 1
Schools: 7
5 Primary; 1 Middle; 1 High; 0 Other Level
7 Regular; 0 Special Education; 0 Vocational; 0 Alternative
0 Magnet; 0 Charter; 5 Title I Eligible; 0 School-wide Title I
Students: 2,130 (50.5% male; 49.5% female)
Individual Education Program: 367 (17.2%);
English Language Learner: 4 (0.2%); Migrant: n/a
Eligible for Free Lunch Program: 743 (34.9%)
Eligible for Reduced-Price Lunch Program: 224 (10.5%)
Teachers: 186.7 (11.4 to 1)
Librarians/Media Specialists: 3.0 (710.0 to 1)
Guidance Counselors: 9.5 (224.2 to 1)
Current Spending: ($ per student per year):
Total: $7,328; Instruction: $5,072; Support Services: $2,048

Enrollment, Drop-out Rates and Diploma Recipients by Race/Ethnicity

Category	Total	White	Black	Asian	AIAN	Hisp.
Enrollment (%)	100.0	98.2	0.6	0.3	0.1	0.8
Drop-out Rate (%)	5.4	5.4	100.0	0.0	n/a	0.0
H.S. Diplomas (#)	158	157	0	1	0	0

Oxford County

MSAD 17 - Oxford

1570 Main St Ste 11 • Oxford, ME 04270-3390
(207) 743-8972
Grade Span: KG-12; **Agency Type:** 1
Schools: 12
9 Primary; 2 Middle; 1 High; 0 Other Level
12 Regular; 0 Special Education; 0 Vocational; 0 Alternative
0 Magnet; 0 Charter; 10 Title I Eligible; 0 School-wide Title I
Students: 3,657 (51.3% male; 48.7% female)
Individual Education Program: 414 (11.3%);
English Language Learner: 1 (<0.1%); Migrant: n/a
Eligible for Free Lunch Program: 1,071 (29.3%)
Eligible for Reduced-Price Lunch Program: 344 (9.4%)
Teachers: 282.2 (13.0 to 1)
Librarians/Media Specialists: 2.0 (1,828.5 to 1)
Guidance Counselors: 14.3 (255.7 to 1)
Current Spending: ($ per student per year):
Total: $6,664; Instruction: $4,163; Support Services: $2,250

Enrollment, Drop-out Rates and Diploma Recipients by Race/Ethnicity

Category	Total	White	Black	Asian	AIAN	Hisp.
Enrollment (%)	100.0	97.8	0.7	0.9	0.1	0.5
Drop-out Rate (%)	4.8	4.8	0.0	0.0	n/a	0.0
H.S. Diplomas (#)	245	238	3	4	0	0

MSAD 43 - Mexico

3 Recreation Dr • Mexico, ME 04257-1531
(207) 364-7896 • http://valnet.mtvalleyhs.sad43.k12.me.us/
Grade Span: PK-12; **Agency Type:** 1
Schools: 5
3 Primary; 1 Middle; 1 High; 0 Other Level
5 Regular; 0 Special Education; 0 Vocational; 0 Alternative
0 Magnet; 0 Charter; 4 Title I Eligible; 2 School-wide Title I
Students: 1,605 (52.5% male; 47.5% female)
Individual Education Program: 325 (20.2%);
English Language Learner: 0 (0.0%); Migrant: n/a
Eligible for Free Lunch Program: 645 (40.2%)
Eligible for Reduced-Price Lunch Program: 146 (9.1%)
Teachers: 145.8 (11.0 to 1)
Librarians/Media Specialists: 4.0 (401.3 to 1)
Guidance Counselors: 7.0 (229.3 to 1)
Current Spending: ($ per student per year):
Total: $8,075; Instruction: $5,054; Support Services: $2,650

Enrollment, Drop-out Rates and Diploma Recipients by Race/Ethnicity

Category	Total	White	Black	Asian	AIAN	Hisp.
Enrollment (%)	100.0	98.1	0.5	0.9	0.4	0.2
Drop-out Rate (%)	3.4	3.5	0.0	0.0	0.0	0.0
H.S. Diplomas (#)	108	106	1	0	0	1

Penobscot County

Bangor School Department

73 Harlow St • Bangor, ME 04401-5118
(207) 945-4400 • http://www.bangorschools.net/
Grade Span: KG-12; **Agency Type:** 1
Schools: 10
5 Primary; 4 Middle; 1 High; 0 Other Level
10 Regular; 0 Special Education; 0 Vocational; 0 Alternative
0 Magnet; 0 Charter; 5 Title I Eligible; 0 School-wide Title I
Students: 4,079 (51.7% male; 48.3% female)
Individual Education Program: 556 (13.6%);
English Language Learner: 43 (1.1%); Migrant: n/a
Eligible for Free Lunch Program: 1,062 (26.0%)
Eligible for Reduced-Price Lunch Program: 210 (5.1%)
Teachers: 343.6 (11.9 to 1)
Librarians/Media Specialists: 3.0 (1,359.7 to 1)
Guidance Counselors: 12.1 (337.1 to 1)
Current Spending: ($ per student per year):
Total: $7,706; Instruction: $5,400; Support Services: $2,076

Enrollment, Drop-out Rates and Diploma Recipients by Race/Ethnicity

Category	Total	White	Black	Asian	AIAN	Hisp.
Enrollment (%)	100.0	93.9	2.2	2.0	0.9	1.1
Drop-out Rate (%)	4.9	5.0	5.9	0.0	0.0	0.0
H.S. Diplomas (#)	298	289	3	4	1	1

MSAD 22 - Hampden

24 Main Rd N • Hampden, ME 04444-0279
(207) 862-3255 • http://www.sad22.us/
Grade Span: KG-12; **Agency Type:** 1
Schools: 7
4 Primary; 2 Middle; 1 High; 0 Other Level
7 Regular; 0 Special Education; 0 Vocational; 0 Alternative
0 Magnet; 0 Charter; 3 Title I Eligible; 0 School-wide Title I
Students: 2,272 (53.3% male; 46.7% female)
Individual Education Program: 361 (15.9%);
English Language Learner: 10 (0.4%); Migrant: n/a
Eligible for Free Lunch Program: 266 (11.7%)
Eligible for Reduced-Price Lunch Program: 104 (4.6%)
Teachers: 178.4 (12.7 to 1)
Librarians/Media Specialists: 4.0 (568.0 to 1)
Guidance Counselors: 8.3 (273.7 to 1)
Current Spending: ($ per student per year):
Total: $7,854; Instruction: $5,132; Support Services: $2,438

Enrollment, Drop-out Rates and Diploma Recipients by Race/Ethnicity

Category	Total	White	Black	Asian	AIAN	Hisp.
Enrollment (%)	100.0	97.5	0.8	0.8	0.2	0.6
Drop-out Rate (%)	1.9	2.0	0.0	0.0	0.0	0.0
H.S. Diplomas (#)	174	169	0	0	4	1

MSAD 48 - Newport

PO Box 40 • Newport, ME 04953-0040
(207) 368-5091 • http://www.msad48.org/mainfrm.cfm
Grade Span: PK-12; **Agency Type:** 1
Schools: 8

5 Primary; 2 Middle; 1 High; 0 Other Level
8 Regular; 0 Special Education; 0 Vocational; 0 Alternative
0 Magnet; 0 Charter; 7 Title I Eligible; 0 School-wide Title I
Students: 2,124 (50.9% male; 49.1% female)
Individual Education Program: 393 (18.5%);
English Language Learner: 0 (0.0%); Migrant: n/a
Eligible for Free Lunch Program: 707 (33.3%)
Eligible for Reduced-Price Lunch Program: 289 (13.6%)
Teachers: 165.2 (12.9 to 1)
Librarians/Media Specialists: 2.0 (1,062.0 to 1)
Guidance Counselors: 8.0 (265.5 to 1)
Current Spending: ($ per student per year):
Total: $7,163; Instruction: $4,396; Support Services: $2,506
Enrollment, Drop-out Rates and Diploma Recipients by Race/Ethnicity

Category	Total	White	Black	Asian	AIAN	Hisp.
Enrollment (%)	100.0	98.5	0.9	0.5	0.1	0.0
Drop-out Rate (%)	2.1	2.1	0.0	0.0	0.0	0.0
H.S. Diplomas (#)	154	153	0	1	0	0

Sagadahoc County

MSAD 75 - Topsham
50 Republic Ave • Topsham, ME 04086-0475
(207) 729-9961
Grade Span: KG-12; **Agency Type:** 1
Schools: 8
6 Primary; 1 Middle; 1 High; 0 Other Level
8 Regular; 0 Special Education; 0 Vocational; 0 Alternative
0 Magnet; 0 Charter; 6 Title I Eligible; 0 School-wide Title I
Students: 3,418 (53.2% male; 46.8% female)
Individual Education Program: 682 (20.0%);
English Language Learner: 29 (0.8%); Migrant: n/a
Eligible for Free Lunch Program: 494 (14.5%)
Eligible for Reduced-Price Lunch Program: 224 (6.6%)
Teachers: 275.0 (12.4 to 1)
Librarians/Media Specialists: 6.0 (569.7 to 1)
Guidance Counselors: 9.8 (348.8 to 1)
Current Spending: ($ per student per year):
Total: $7,993; Instruction: $5,129; Support Services: $2,601
Enrollment, Drop-out Rates and Diploma Recipients by Race/Ethnicity

Category	Total	White	Black	Asian	AIAN	Hisp.
Enrollment (%)	100.0	95.9	1.4	1.2	0.3	1.2
Drop-out Rate (%)	3.9	4.0	0.0	0.0	0.0	6.3
H.S. Diplomas (#)	252	231	3	7	1	10

Somerset County

MSAD 49 - Fairfield
8 School St • Fairfield, ME 04937-1370
(207) 453-4200 • http://www.lhs.sad49.k12.me.us/
Grade Span: PK-12; **Agency Type:** 1
Schools: 6
4 Primary; 1 Middle; 1 High; 0 Other Level
6 Regular; 0 Special Education; 0 Vocational; 0 Alternative
0 Magnet; 0 Charter; 6 Title I Eligible; 0 School-wide Title I
Students: 2,694 (50.9% male; 49.1% female)
Individual Education Program: 497 (18.4%);
English Language Learner: 0 (0.0%); Migrant: n/a
Eligible for Free Lunch Program: 723 (26.8%)
Eligible for Reduced-Price Lunch Program: 280 (10.4%)
Teachers: 214.5 (12.6 to 1)
Librarians/Media Specialists: 3.0 (898.0 to 1)
Guidance Counselors: 10.4 (259.0 to 1)
Current Spending: ($ per student per year):
Total: $7,795; Instruction: $5,018; Support Services: $2,533
Enrollment, Drop-out Rates and Diploma Recipients by Race/Ethnicity

Category	Total	White	Black	Asian	AIAN	Hisp.
Enrollment (%)	100.0	97.9	1.3	0.4	0.1	0.3
Drop-out Rate (%)	2.6	2.6	0.0	0.0	n/a	n/a
H.S. Diplomas (#)	174	173	1	0	0	0

MSAD 54 - Skowhegan
196 W Front St • Skowhegan, ME 04976-9739
(207) 474-9508 • http://www.msad54.k12.me.us/
Grade Span: KG-12; **Agency Type:** 1
Schools: 11
6 Primary; 3 Middle; 2 High; 0 Other Level
10 Regular; 0 Special Education; 1 Vocational; 0 Alternative
0 Magnet; 0 Charter; 8 Title I Eligible; 3 School-wide Title I
Students: 2,977 (51.7% male; 48.3% female)
Individual Education Program: 522 (17.5%);
English Language Learner: 11 (0.4%); Migrant: n/a
Eligible for Free Lunch Program: 897 (30.1%)
Eligible for Reduced-Price Lunch Program: 260 (8.7%)
Teachers: 241.4 (12.3 to 1)
Librarians/Media Specialists: 2.0 (1,488.5 to 1)
Guidance Counselors: 5.8 (513.3 to 1)
Current Spending: ($ per student per year):
Total: $8,155; Instruction: $5,453; Support Services: $2,445
Enrollment, Drop-out Rates and Diploma Recipients by Race/Ethnicity

Category	Total	White	Black	Asian	AIAN	Hisp.
Enrollment (%)	100.0	97.4	0.9	1.0	0.1	0.6
Drop-out Rate (%)	3.9	4.0	0.0	0.0	0.0	0.0
H.S. Diplomas (#)	213	206	2	5	0	0

Waldo County

MSAD 03 - Unity
74 School St • Unity, ME 04988-9734
(207) 948-6136
Grade Span: KG-12; **Agency Type:** 1
Schools: 8
6 Primary; 1 Middle; 1 High; 0 Other Level
8 Regular; 0 Special Education; 0 Vocational; 0 Alternative
0 Magnet; 0 Charter; 7 Title I Eligible; 0 School-wide Title I
Students: 1,623 (50.9% male; 49.1% female)
Individual Education Program: 292 (18.0%);
English Language Learner: 0 (0.0%); Migrant: n/a
Eligible for Free Lunch Program: 623 (38.4%)
Eligible for Reduced-Price Lunch Program: 224 (13.8%)
Teachers: 134.9 (12.0 to 1)
Librarians/Media Specialists: 0.9 (1,803.3 to 1)
Guidance Counselors: 7.1 (228.6 to 1)
Current Spending: ($ per student per year):
Total: $7,624; Instruction: $4,664; Support Services: $2,610
Enrollment, Drop-out Rates and Diploma Recipients by Race/Ethnicity

Category	Total	White	Black	Asian	AIAN	Hisp.
Enrollment (%)	100.0	98.5	0.4	0.2	0.1	0.7
Drop-out Rate (%)	4.2	4.2	0.0	0.0	n/a	0.0
H.S. Diplomas (#)	115	115	0	0	0	0

MSAD 34 - Belfast
PO Box 363 • Belfast, ME 04915-0363
(207) 338-1960 • http://www.sad34.net/
Grade Span: PK-12; **Agency Type:** 1
Schools: 10
8 Primary; 1 Middle; 1 High; 0 Other Level
10 Regular; 0 Special Education; 0 Vocational; 0 Alternative
0 Magnet; 0 Charter; 6 Title I Eligible; 0 School-wide Title I
Students: 2,019 (51.8% male; 48.2% female)
Individual Education Program: 435 (21.5%);
English Language Learner: 5 (0.2%); Migrant: n/a
Eligible for Free Lunch Program: 609 (30.2%)
Eligible for Reduced-Price Lunch Program: 148 (7.3%)
Teachers: 170.9 (11.8 to 1)
Librarians/Media Specialists: 2.0 (1,009.5 to 1)
Guidance Counselors: 9.1 (221.9 to 1)
Current Spending: ($ per student per year):
Total: $8,339; Instruction: $5,760; Support Services: $2,278
Enrollment, Drop-out Rates and Diploma Recipients by Race/Ethnicity

Category	Total	White	Black	Asian	AIAN	Hisp.
Enrollment (%)	100.0	98.6	0.7	0.2	0.0	0.4
Drop-out Rate (%)	1.2	1.2	n/a	0.0	n/a	0.0
H.S. Diplomas (#)	136	135	0	1	0	0

York County

Biddeford School Department
205 Main St • Biddeford, ME 04005-1865
Mailing Address: PO Box 1865 • Biddeford, ME 04005-1865
(207) 282-8280 • http://www.biddschools.org/
Grade Span: PK-12; **Agency Type:** 1
Schools: 5
2 Primary; 1 Middle; 2 High; 0 Other Level
4 Regular; 0 Special Education; 1 Vocational; 0 Alternative
0 Magnet; 0 Charter; 3 Title I Eligible; 0 School-wide Title I
Students: 2,975 (51.6% male; 48.4% female)
Individual Education Program: 466 (15.7%);
English Language Learner: 26 (0.9%); Migrant: n/a
Eligible for Free Lunch Program: 871 (29.3%)
Eligible for Reduced-Price Lunch Program: 171 (5.7%)
Teachers: 223.2 (13.3 to 1)
Librarians/Media Specialists: 3.9 (762.8 to 1)
Guidance Counselors: 7.8 (381.4 to 1)
Current Spending: ($ per student per year):
Total: $7,298; Instruction: $5,307; Support Services: $1,776

Enrollment, Drop-out Rates and Diploma Recipients by Race/Ethnicity

Category	Total	White	Black	Asian	AIAN	Hisp.
Enrollment (%)	100.0	96.3	1.7	1.4	0.1	0.6
Drop-out Rate (%)	3.4	3.5	0.0	0.0	n/a	0.0
H.S. Diplomas (#)	163	157	0	5	0	1

MSAD 06 - Buxton

100 Main St • Bar Mills, ME 04004-0038
Mailing Address: PO Box 38 • Bar Mills, ME 04004-0038
(207) 929-3831 • http://www.sad6.k12.me.us/
Grade Span: KG-12; **Agency Type:** 1
Schools: 11
7 Primary; 3 Middle; 1 High; 0 Other Level
11 Regular; 0 Special Education; 0 Vocational; 0 Alternative
0 Magnet; 0 Charter; 9 Title I Eligible; 1 School-wide Title I
Students: 4,132 (53.2% male; 46.8% female)
Individual Education Program: 642 (15.5%);
English Language Learner: 2 (<0.1%); Migrant: n/a
Eligible for Free Lunch Program: 728 (17.6%)
Eligible for Reduced-Price Lunch Program: 439 (10.6%)
Teachers: 313.9 (13.2 to 1)
Librarians/Media Specialists: 7.0 (590.3 to 1)
Guidance Counselors: 12.8 (322.8 to 1)
Current Spending: ($ per student per year):
Total: $7,624; Instruction: $4,942; Support Services: $2,337
Enrollment, Drop-out Rates and Diploma Recipients by Race/Ethnicity

Category	Total	White	Black	Asian	AIAN	Hisp.
Enrollment (%)	100.0	98.0	0.8	0.7	0.2	0.4
Drop-out Rate (%)	4.5	4.6	0.0	n/a	n/a	n/a
H.S. Diplomas (#)	282	281	1	0	0	0

MSAD 35 - South Berwick

64 Depot Rd • Eliot, ME 03903
(207) 439-2438 • http://web.mhs.sad35.k12.me.us/msad35/current.htm
Grade Span: PK-12; **Agency Type:** 1
Schools: 5
2 Primary; 2 Middle; 1 High; 0 Other Level
5 Regular; 0 Special Education; 0 Vocational; 0 Alternative
0 Magnet; 0 Charter; 4 Title I Eligible; 0 School-wide Title I
Students: 2,763 (50.7% male; 49.3% female)
Individual Education Program: 351 (12.7%);
English Language Learner: 5 (0.2%); Migrant: n/a
Eligible for Free Lunch Program: 145 (5.2%)
Eligible for Reduced-Price Lunch Program: 56 (2.0%)
Teachers: 184.7 (15.0 to 1)
Librarians/Media Specialists: 1.0 (2,763.0 to 1)
Guidance Counselors: 8.7 (317.6 to 1)
Current Spending: ($ per student per year):
Total: $6,089; Instruction: $3,897; Support Services: $1,995
Enrollment, Drop-out Rates and Diploma Recipients by Race/Ethnicity

Category	Total	White	Black	Asian	AIAN	Hisp.
Enrollment (%)	100.0	98.8	0.6	0.3	0.0	0.2
Drop-out Rate (%)	1.7	1.8	0.0	0.0	0.0	0.0
H.S. Diplomas (#)	204	202	1	0	1	0

MSAD 57 - Waterboro

PO Box 499 • Waterboro, ME 04087-0499
(207) 247-3221 • http://www.sad57.k12.me.us/
Grade Span: KG-12; **Agency Type:** 1
Schools: 7
5 Primary; 1 Middle; 1 High; 0 Other Level
7 Regular; 0 Special Education; 0 Vocational; 0 Alternative
0 Magnet; 0 Charter; 5 Title I Eligible; 0 School-wide Title I
Students: 3,760 (52.2% male; 47.8% female)
Individual Education Program: 570 (15.2%);
English Language Learner: 2 (0.1%); Migrant: n/a
Eligible for Free Lunch Program: 524 (13.9%)
Eligible for Reduced-Price Lunch Program: 331 (8.8%)
Teachers: 247.6 (15.2 to 1)
Librarians/Media Specialists: 3.0 (1,253.3 to 1)
Guidance Counselors: 9.5 (395.8 to 1)
Current Spending: ($ per student per year):
Total: $6,307; Instruction: $3,966; Support Services: $2,066
Enrollment, Drop-out Rates and Diploma Recipients by Race/Ethnicity

Category	Total	White	Black	Asian	AIAN	Hisp.
Enrollment (%)	100.0	97.7	0.6	0.6	0.5	0.6
Drop-out Rate (%)	0.7	0.7	0.0	0.0	0.0	0.0
H.S. Diplomas (#)	206	199	2	2	2	1

MSAD 60 - North Berwick

PO Box 819 • North Berwick, ME 03906-0819
(207) 676-2234 • http://www.sad60.k12.me.us/
Grade Span: KG-12; **Agency Type:** 1
Schools: 7
3 Primary; 3 Middle; 1 High; 0 Other Level
7 Regular; 0 Special Education; 0 Vocational; 0 Alternative
0 Magnet; 0 Charter; 4 Title I Eligible; 0 School-wide Title I
Students: 3,257 (49.3% male; 50.7% female)
Individual Education Program: 645 (19.8%);
English Language Learner: 26 (0.8%); Migrant: n/a
Eligible for Free Lunch Program: 471 (14.5%)
Eligible for Reduced-Price Lunch Program: 219 (6.7%)
Teachers: 263.6 (12.4 to 1)
Librarians/Media Specialists: 3.0 (1,085.7 to 1)
Guidance Counselors: 14.8 (220.1 to 1)
Current Spending: ($ per student per year):
Total: $7,459; Instruction: $5,047; Support Services: $2,092
Enrollment, Drop-out Rates and Diploma Recipients by Race/Ethnicity

Category	Total	White	Black	Asian	AIAN	Hisp.
Enrollment (%)	100.0	98.0	0.8	1.0	0.0	0.2
Drop-out Rate (%)	3.5	3.5	n/a	0.0	n/a	n/a
H.S. Diplomas (#)	191	188	1	2	0	0

MSAD 71 - Kennebunk

1 Storer St • Kennebunk, ME 04043-6830
(207) 985-1100 • http://www.msad71.net/
Grade Span: PK-12; **Agency Type:** 1
Schools: 6
3 Primary; 2 Middle; 1 High; 0 Other Level
6 Regular; 0 Special Education; 0 Vocational; 0 Alternative
0 Magnet; 0 Charter; 2 Title I Eligible; 0 School-wide Title I
Students: 2,535 (51.1% male; 48.9% female)
Individual Education Program: 406 (16.0%);
English Language Learner: 27 (1.1%); Migrant: n/a
Eligible for Free Lunch Program: 123 (4.9%)
Eligible for Reduced-Price Lunch Program: 70 (2.8%)
Teachers: 195.7 (13.0 to 1)
Librarians/Media Specialists: 3.0 (845.0 to 1)
Guidance Counselors: 10.1 (251.0 to 1)
Current Spending: ($ per student per year):
Total: $8,493; Instruction: $5,610; Support Services: $2,621
Enrollment, Drop-out Rates and Diploma Recipients by Race/Ethnicity

Category	Total	White	Black	Asian	AIAN	Hisp.
Enrollment (%)	100.0	97.6	0.6	1.3	0.2	0.3
Drop-out Rate (%)	1.2	1.1	0.0	11.1	0.0	0.0
H.S. Diplomas (#)	162	162	0	0	0	0

Saco School Department

56 Industrial Park Rd Ste 2 • Saco, ME 04072-1878
(207) 284-4505 • http://www.saco.org/admin/index.html
Grade Span: KG-08; **Agency Type:** 2
Schools: 4
3 Primary; 1 Middle; 0 High; 0 Other Level
4 Regular; 0 Special Education; 0 Vocational; 0 Alternative
0 Magnet; 0 Charter; 2 Title I Eligible; 0 School-wide Title I
Students: 2,866 (50.2% male; 49.8% female)
Individual Education Program: 470 (16.4%);
English Language Learner: 16 (0.6%); Migrant: n/a
Eligible for Free Lunch Program: 286 (10.0%)
Eligible for Reduced-Price Lunch Program: 107 (3.7%)
Teachers: 130.9 (21.9 to 1)
Librarians/Media Specialists: 0.0 (0.0 to 1)
Guidance Counselors: 4.8 (597.1 to 1)
Current Spending: ($ per student per year):
Total: $9,626; Instruction: $7,604; Support Services: $1,790
Enrollment, Drop-out Rates and Diploma Recipients by Race/Ethnicity

Category	Total	White	Black	Asian	AIAN	Hisp.
Enrollment (%)	100.0	95.3	1.6	1.6	0.6	0.9
Drop-out Rate (%)	n/a	n/a	n/a	n/a	n/a	n/a
H.S. Diplomas (#)	n/a	n/a	n/a	n/a	n/a	n/a

Sanford School Department

917 Main St Ste 200 • Sanford, ME 04073-3545
(207) 324-2810 • http://www.sanford.org/
Grade Span: KG-12; **Agency Type:** 1
Schools: 9
5 Primary; 2 Middle; 2 High; 0 Other Level
8 Regular; 0 Special Education; 1 Vocational; 0 Alternative
0 Magnet; 0 Charter; 4 Title I Eligible; 0 School-wide Title I
Students: 3,834 (51.2% male; 48.8% female)
Individual Education Program: 676 (17.6%);
English Language Learner: 91 (2.4%); Migrant: n/a
Eligible for Free Lunch Program: 1,146 (29.9%)
Eligible for Reduced-Price Lunch Program: 301 (7.9%)
Teachers: 279.0 (13.7 to 1)
Librarians/Media Specialists: 4.9 (782.4 to 1)
Guidance Counselors: 14.8 (259.1 to 1)
Current Spending: ($ per student per year):
Total: $7,021; Instruction: $4,742; Support Services: $1,990

Enrollment, Drop-out Rates and Diploma Recipients by Race/Ethnicity

Category	Total	White	Black	Asian	AIAN	Hisp.
Enrollment (%)	100.0	96.4	0.8	2.2	0.1	0.5
Drop-out Rate (%)	6.9	7.2	0.0	0.0	n/a	0.0
H.S. Diplomas (#)	219	212	0	6	0	1

Wells-Ogunquit CSD

PO Box 578 • Wells, ME 04090-0578
(207) 646-8331 • http://wocsd.maine.org/
Grade Span: KG-12; **Agency Type:** 1
Schools: 4
2 Primary; 1 Middle; 1 High; 0 Other Level
4 Regular; 0 Special Education; 0 Vocational; 0 Alternative
0 Magnet; 0 Charter; 2 Title I Eligible; 0 School-wide Title I
Students: 1,510 (51.0% male; 49.0% female)
Individual Education Program: 220 (14.6%);
English Language Learner: 13 (0.9%); Migrant: n/a
Eligible for Free Lunch Program: 159 (10.5%)
Eligible for Reduced-Price Lunch Program: 38 (2.5%)
Teachers: 133.1 (11.3 to 1)
Librarians/Media Specialists: 2.5 (604.0 to 1)
Guidance Counselors: 5.0 (302.0 to 1)
Current Spending: ($ per student per year):
Total: $9,748; Instruction: $6,536; Support Services: $2,877

Enrollment, Drop-out Rates and Diploma Recipients by Race/Ethnicity

Category	Total	White	Black	Asian	AIAN	Hisp.
Enrollment (%)	100.0	97.2	0.5	0.8	0.1	1.3
Drop-out Rate (%)	1.7	1.7	0.0	0.0	0.0	0.0
H.S. Diplomas (#)	126	126	0	0	0	0

York School Department

469 US Route 1 • York, ME 03909-1006
(207) 363-3403 • http://www.yorkschools.org/
Grade Span: KG-12; **Agency Type:** 1
Schools: 4
2 Primary; 1 Middle; 1 High; 0 Other Level
4 Regular; 0 Special Education; 0 Vocational; 0 Alternative
0 Magnet; 0 Charter; 2 Title I Eligible; 0 School-wide Title I
Students: 2,118 (51.4% male; 48.6% female)
Individual Education Program: 308 (14.5%);
English Language Learner: 2 (0.1%); Migrant: n/a
Eligible for Free Lunch Program: 107 (5.1%)
Eligible for Reduced-Price Lunch Program: 65 (3.1%)
Teachers: 153.0 (13.8 to 1)
Librarians/Media Specialists: 1.0 (2,118.0 to 1)
Guidance Counselors: 7.2 (294.2 to 1)
Current Spending: ($ per student per year):
Total: $8,737; Instruction: $5,901; Support Services: $2,588

Enrollment, Drop-out Rates and Diploma Recipients by Race/Ethnicity

Category	Total	White	Black	Asian	AIAN	Hisp.
Enrollment (%)	100.0	97.8	0.7	0.7	0.0	0.8
Drop-out Rate (%)	3.6	3.6	0.0	0.0	n/a	0.0
H.S. Diplomas (#)	137	133	4	0	0	0

Number of Schools

Rank	Number	District Name	City
1	18	Portland Public Schools	Portland
2	12	Auburn School Department	Auburn
2	12	MSAD 17 - Oxford	Oxford
4	11	MSAD 06 - Buxton	Bar Mills
4	11	MSAD 54 - Skowhegan	Skowhegan
6	10	Bangor School Department	Bangor
6	10	MSAD 34 - Belfast	Belfast
8	9	Lewiston School Department	Lewiston
8	9	MSAD 01 - Presque Isle	Presque Isle
8	9	MSAD 09 - Farmington	New Sharon
8	9	Sanford School Department	Sanford
8	9	South Portland School Department	South Portland
13	8	Augusta Dept of Public Schools	Augusta
13	8	MSAD 03 - Unity	Unity
13	8	MSAD 11 - Gardiner	Gardiner
13	8	MSAD 48 - Newport	Newport
13	8	MSAD 75 - Topsham	Topsham
18	7	MSAD 22 - Hampden	Hampden
18	7	MSAD 40 - Waldoboro	Warren
18	7	MSAD 57 - Waterboro	Waterboro
18	7	MSAD 60 - North Berwick	North Berwick
18	7	MSAD 61 - Bridgton	Bridgton
18	7	Westbrook School Department	Westbrook
24	6	Brunswick School Department	Brunswick
24	6	Gorham School Department	Gorham
24	6	MSAD 05 - Rockland	Rockland
24	6	MSAD 47 - Oakland	Oakland
24	6	MSAD 49 - Fairfield	Fairfield
24	6	MSAD 51 - Cumberland	Cumberland Ctr
24	6	MSAD 52 - Turner	Turner
24	6	MSAD 71 - Kennebunk	Kennebunk
24	6	Scarborough School Department	Scarborough
33	5	Biddeford School Department	Biddeford
33	5	MSAD 15 - Gray	Gray
33	5	MSAD 35 - South Berwick	Eliot
33	5	MSAD 43 - Mexico	Mexico
33	5	Waterville Public Schools	Waterville
33	5	Windham School Department	Windham
39	4	Falmouth School Department	Falmouth
39	4	Saco School Department	Saco
39	4	Wells-Ogunquit CSD	Wells
39	4	York School Department	York
43	3	Cape Elizabeth School Department	Cape Elizabeth

Number of Teachers

Rank	Number	District Name	City
1	673	Portland Public Schools	Portland
2	343	Bangor School Department	Bangor
3	338	Auburn School Department	Auburn
4	336	Lewiston School Department	Lewiston
5	313	MSAD 06 - Buxton	Bar Mills
6	282	MSAD 17 - Oxford	Oxford
7	279	Sanford School Department	Sanford
8	275	MSAD 75 - Topsham	Topsham
9	265	South Portland School Department	South Portland
10	263	MSAD 60 - North Berwick	North Berwick
11	247	MSAD 57 - Waterboro	Waterboro
12	242	Augusta Dept of Public Schools	Augusta
13	241	MSAD 54 - Skowhegan	Skowhegan
14	238	Scarborough School Department	Scarborough
15	235	Brunswick School Department	Brunswick
16	234	Westbrook School Department	Westbrook
17	232	MSAD 09 - Farmington	New Sharon
18	223	Biddeford School Department	Biddeford
19	214	MSAD 49 - Fairfield	Fairfield
20	211	MSAD 61 - Bridgton	Bridgton
21	203	MSAD 47 - Oakland	Oakland
22	196	Windham School Department	Windham
23	195	MSAD 71 - Kennebunk	Kennebunk
24	189	MSAD 52 - Turner	Turner
25	186	MSAD 40 - Waldoboro	Warren
26	184	MSAD 35 - South Berwick	Eliot
27	184	Gorham School Department	Gorham
28	181	MSAD 51 - Cumberland	Cumberland Ctr
29	178	MSAD 22 - Hampden	Hampden
30	173	Waterville Public Schools	Waterville
31	172	MSAD 11 - Gardiner	Gardiner
32	170	MSAD 34 - Belfast	Belfast
33	168	Falmouth School Department	Falmouth
34	167	MSAD 01 - Presque Isle	Presque Isle
35	165	MSAD 48 - Newport	Newport
36	153	MSAD 15 - Gray	Gray
37	153	York School Department	York
38	145	MSAD 43 - Mexico	Mexico
39	134	MSAD 03 - Unity	Unity
40	133	Cape Elizabeth School Department	Cape Elizabeth
41	133	Wells-Ogunquit CSD	Wells
42	130	Saco School Department	Saco
43	116	MSAD 05 - Rockland	Rockland

Number of Students

Rank	Number	District Name	City
1	7,555	Portland Public Schools	Portland
2	4,689	Lewiston School Department	Lewiston
3	4,132	MSAD 06 - Buxton	Bar Mills
4	4,079	Bangor School Department	Bangor
5	3,834	Sanford School Department	Sanford
6	3,760	MSAD 57 - Waterboro	Waterboro
7	3,691	Auburn School Department	Auburn
8	3,657	MSAD 17 - Oxford	Oxford
9	3,418	MSAD 75 - Topsham	Topsham
10	3,257	MSAD 60 - North Berwick	North Berwick
11	3,247	South Portland School Department	South Portland
12	3,213	Scarborough School Department	Scarborough
13	3,192	Brunswick School Department	Brunswick
14	2,977	MSAD 54 - Skowhegan	Skowhegan
15	2,975	Biddeford School Department	Biddeford
16	2,866	Saco School Department	Saco
17	2,763	MSAD 35 - South Berwick	Eliot
18	2,716	Gorham School Department	Gorham
19	2,694	MSAD 49 - Fairfield	Fairfield
20	2,692	MSAD 09 - Farmington	New Sharon
21	2,687	Westbrook School Department	Westbrook
22	2,620	Windham School Department	Windham
23	2,535	MSAD 71 - Kennebunk	Kennebunk
24	2,516	MSAD 47 - Oakland	Oakland
25	2,506	Augusta Dept of Public Schools	Augusta
26	2,342	MSAD 51 - Cumberland	Cumberland Ctr
27	2,331	MSAD 52 - Turner	Turner
28	2,330	MSAD 11 - Gardiner	Gardiner
29	2,272	MSAD 22 - Hampden	Hampden
30	2,206	MSAD 61 - Bridgton	Bridgton
31	2,164	MSAD 01 - Presque Isle	Presque Isle
32	2,130	MSAD 40 - Waldoboro	Warren
33	2,124	MSAD 48 - Newport	Newport
34	2,119	Falmouth School Department	Falmouth
35	2,118	York School Department	York
36	2,063	MSAD 15 - Gray	Gray
37	2,019	MSAD 34 - Belfast	Belfast
38	1,892	Waterville Public Schools	Waterville
39	1,779	Cape Elizabeth School Department	Cape Elizabeth
40	1,623	MSAD 03 - Unity	Unity
41	1,605	MSAD 43 - Mexico	Mexico
42	1,516	MSAD 05 - Rockland	Rockland
43	1,510	Wells-Ogunquit CSD	Wells

Male Students

Rank	Percent	District Name	City
1	53.7	MSAD 61 - Bridgton	Bridgton
2	53.3	MSAD 22 - Hampden	Hampden
3	53.2	MSAD 06 - Buxton	Bar Mills
3	53.2	MSAD 75 - Topsham	Topsham
5	53.1	MSAD 11 - Gardiner	Gardiner
6	53.0	Cape Elizabeth School Department	Cape Elizabeth
7	52.9	MSAD 01 - Presque Isle	Presque Isle
8	52.7	Westbrook School Department	Westbrook
9	52.5	MSAD 43 - Mexico	Mexico
10	52.4	Waterville Public Schools	Waterville
11	52.3	Brunswick School Department	Brunswick
11	52.3	MSAD 52 - Turner	Turner
13	52.2	MSAD 15 - Gray	Gray
13	52.2	MSAD 57 - Waterboro	Waterboro
13	52.2	South Portland School Department	South Portland
16	52.0	Falmouth School Department	Falmouth
16	52.0	Windham School Department	Windham
18	51.8	MSAD 34 - Belfast	Belfast
19	51.7	Bangor School Department	Bangor
19	51.7	MSAD 54 - Skowhegan	Skowhegan
21	51.6	Biddeford School Department	Biddeford
21	51.6	MSAD 09 - Farmington	New Sharon
23	51.5	Auburn School Department	Auburn
24	51.4	Augusta Dept of Public Schools	Augusta
24	51.4	Portland Public Schools	Portland
24	51.4	York School Department	York
27	51.3	MSAD 17 - Oxford	Oxford
27	51.3	Scarborough School Department	Scarborough
29	51.2	Sanford School Department	Sanford
30	51.1	MSAD 71 - Kennebunk	Kennebunk
31	51.0	Wells-Ogunquit CSD	Wells
32	50.9	MSAD 03 - Unity	Unity
32	50.9	MSAD 48 - Newport	Newport
32	50.9	MSAD 49 - Fairfield	Fairfield
35	50.7	Lewiston School Department	Lewiston
35	50.7	MSAD 35 - South Berwick	Eliot
37	50.6	Gorham School Department	Gorham
38	50.5	MSAD 40 - Waldoboro	Warren
39	50.2	Saco School Department	Saco
40	49.7	MSAD 47 - Oakland	Oakland
41	49.5	MSAD 51 - Cumberland	Cumberland Ctr
42	49.3	MSAD 60 - North Berwick	North Berwick
43	48.9	MSAD 05 - Rockland	Rockland

Female Students

Rank	Percent	District Name	City
1	51.1	MSAD 05 - Rockland	Rockland
2	50.7	MSAD 60 - North Berwick	North Berwick
3	50.5	MSAD 51 - Cumberland	Cumberland Ctr
4	50.3	MSAD 47 - Oakland	Oakland
5	49.8	Saco School Department	Saco
6	49.5	MSAD 40 - Waldoboro	Warren
7	49.4	Gorham School Department	Gorham
8	49.3	Lewiston School Department	Lewiston
8	49.3	MSAD 35 - South Berwick	Eliot
10	49.1	MSAD 03 - Unity	Unity
10	49.1	MSAD 48 - Newport	Newport
10	49.1	MSAD 49 - Fairfield	Fairfield
13	49.0	Wells-Ogunquit CSD	Wells
14	48.9	MSAD 71 - Kennebunk	Kennebunk
15	48.8	Sanford School Department	Sanford
16	48.7	MSAD 17 - Oxford	Oxford
16	48.7	Scarborough School Department	Scarborough
18	48.6	Augusta Dept of Public Schools	Augusta
18	48.6	Portland Public Schools	Portland
18	48.6	York School Department	York
21	48.5	Auburn School Department	Auburn
22	48.4	Biddeford School Department	Biddeford
22	48.4	MSAD 09 - Farmington	New Sharon
24	48.3	Bangor School Department	Bangor
24	48.3	MSAD 54 - Skowhegan	Skowhegan
26	48.2	MSAD 34 - Belfast	Belfast
27	48.0	Falmouth School Department	Falmouth
27	48.0	Windham School Department	Windham
29	47.8	MSAD 15 - Gray	Gray
29	47.8	MSAD 57 - Waterboro	Waterboro
29	47.8	South Portland School Department	South Portland
32	47.7	Brunswick School Department	Brunswick
32	47.7	MSAD 52 - Turner	Turner
34	47.6	Waterville Public Schools	Waterville
35	47.5	MSAD 43 - Mexico	Mexico
36	47.3	Westbrook School Department	Westbrook
37	47.1	MSAD 01 - Presque Isle	Presque Isle
38	47.0	Cape Elizabeth School Department	Cape Elizabeth
39	46.9	MSAD 11 - Gardiner	Gardiner
40	46.8	MSAD 06 - Buxton	Bar Mills
40	46.8	MSAD 75 - Topsham	Topsham
42	46.7	MSAD 22 - Hampden	Hampden
43	46.3	MSAD 61 - Bridgton	Bridgton

Individual Education Program Students

Rank	Percent	District Name	City
1	22.7	Augusta Dept of Public Schools	Augusta
2	21.8	MSAD 61 - Bridgton	Bridgton
3	21.5	MSAD 34 - Belfast	Belfast
3	21.5	Waterville Public Schools	Waterville
5	20.2	MSAD 43 - Mexico	Mexico
6	20.0	MSAD 75 - Topsham	Topsham
7	19.8	MSAD 60 - North Berwick	North Berwick
8	19.4	Auburn School Department	Auburn
9	18.5	MSAD 48 - Newport	Newport
10	18.4	MSAD 49 - Fairfield	Fairfield
11	18.3	South Portland School Department	South Portland
12	18.0	Lewiston School Department	Lewiston
12	18.0	MSAD 03 - Unity	Unity
14	17.6	Sanford School Department	Sanford
15	17.5	MSAD 54 - Skowhegan	Skowhegan
16	17.2	MSAD 40 - Waldoboro	Warren
17	16.4	Saco School Department	Saco
18	16.0	MSAD 11 - Gardiner	Gardiner
18	16.0	MSAD 71 - Kennebunk	Kennebunk
20	15.9	MSAD 22 - Hampden	Hampden
21	15.7	Biddeford School Department	Biddeford
22	15.5	MSAD 06 - Buxton	Bar Mills
23	15.2	MSAD 15 - Gray	Gray
23	15.2	MSAD 57 - Waterboro	Waterboro
25	15.0	Portland Public Schools	Portland
26	14.9	Brunswick School Department	Brunswick
27	14.6	Wells-Ogunquit CSD	Wells
28	14.5	York School Department	York
29	14.2	Gorham School Department	Gorham
30	13.8	MSAD 52 - Turner	Turner
31	13.6	Bangor School Department	Bangor
32	13.5	MSAD 05 - Rockland	Rockland
33	13.4	MSAD 47 - Oakland	Oakland
34	13.2	Scarborough School Department	Scarborough
35	12.7	MSAD 09 - Farmington	New Sharon
35	12.7	MSAD 35 - South Berwick	Eliot
37	12.5	Cape Elizabeth School Department	Cape Elizabeth
38	12.3	MSAD 01 - Presque Isle	Presque Isle
39	12.1	Westbrook School Department	Westbrook
40	12.0	Falmouth School Department	Falmouth
41	11.4	Windham School Department	Windham
42	11.3	MSAD 17 - Oxford	Oxford
43	6.4	MSAD 51 - Cumberland	Cumberland Ctr

English Language Learner Students

Rank	Percent	District Name	City
1	12.9	Portland Public Schools	Portland
2	5.8	Lewiston School Department	Lewiston
3	3.0	MSAD 52 - Turner	Turner
4	2.6	Augusta Dept of Public Schools	Augusta
5	2.5	Auburn School Department	Auburn
6	2.4	Sanford School Department	Sanford
7	1.6	South Portland School Department	South Portland
8	1.5	Scarborough School Department	Scarborough
9	1.3	Westbrook School Department	Westbrook
10	1.1	Bangor School Department	Bangor
10	1.1	MSAD 71 - Kennebunk	Kennebunk
12	1.0	Brunswick School Department	Brunswick
13	0.9	Biddeford School Department	Biddeford
13	0.9	Wells-Ogunquit CSD	Wells
15	0.8	MSAD 60 - North Berwick	North Berwick
15	0.8	MSAD 75 - Topsham	Topsham
17	0.7	Waterville Public Schools	Waterville
18	0.6	MSAD 05 - Rockland	Rockland
18	0.6	Saco School Department	Saco
20	0.5	Windham School Department	Windham
21	0.4	Gorham School Department	Gorham
21	0.4	MSAD 22 - Hampden	Hampden
21	0.4	MSAD 54 - Skowhegan	Skowhegan
24	0.3	MSAD 51 - Cumberland	Cumberland Ctr
25	0.2	Cape Elizabeth School Department	Cape Elizabeth
25	0.2	MSAD 01 - Presque Isle	Presque Isle
25	0.2	MSAD 34 - Belfast	Belfast
25	0.2	MSAD 35 - South Berwick	Eliot
25	0.2	MSAD 40 - Waldoboro	Warren
30	0.1	MSAD 09 - Farmington	New Sharon
30	0.1	MSAD 47 - Oakland	Oakland
30	0.1	MSAD 57 - Waterboro	Waterboro
30	0.1	York School Department	York
34	0.0	Falmouth School Department	Falmouth
34	0.0	MSAD 06 - Buxton	Bar Mills
34	0.0	MSAD 11 - Gardiner	Gardiner
34	0.0	MSAD 15 - Gray	Gray
34	0.0	MSAD 17 - Oxford	Oxford
34	0.0	MSAD 61 - Bridgton	Bridgton
40	0.0	MSAD 03 - Unity	Unity
40	0.0	MSAD 43 - Mexico	Mexico
40	0.0	MSAD 48 - Newport	Newport
40	0.0	MSAD 49 - Fairfield	Fairfield

Migrant Students

Rank	Percent	District Name	City
1	n/a	Auburn School Department	Auburn
1	n/a	Augusta Dept of Public Schools	Augusta
1	n/a	Bangor School Department	Bangor
1	n/a	Biddeford School Department	Biddeford
1	n/a	Brunswick School Department	Brunswick
1	n/a	Cape Elizabeth School Department	Cape Elizabeth
1	n/a	Falmouth School Department	Falmouth
1	n/a	Gorham School Department	Gorham
1	n/a	Lewiston School Department	Lewiston
1	n/a	MSAD 01 - Presque Isle	Presque Isle
1	n/a	MSAD 03 - Unity	Unity
1	n/a	MSAD 05 - Rockland	Rockland
1	n/a	MSAD 06 - Buxton	Bar Mills
1	n/a	MSAD 09 - Farmington	New Sharon
1	n/a	MSAD 11 - Gardiner	Gardiner
1	n/a	MSAD 15 - Gray	Gray
1	n/a	MSAD 17 - Oxford	Oxford
1	n/a	MSAD 22 - Hampden	Hampden
1	n/a	MSAD 34 - Belfast	Belfast
1	n/a	MSAD 35 - South Berwick	Eliot
1	n/a	MSAD 40 - Waldoboro	Warren
1	n/a	MSAD 43 - Mexico	Mexico
1	n/a	MSAD 47 - Oakland	Oakland
1	n/a	MSAD 48 - Newport	Newport
1	n/a	MSAD 49 - Fairfield	Fairfield
1	n/a	MSAD 51 - Cumberland	Cumberland Ctr
1	n/a	MSAD 52 - Turner	Turner
1	n/a	MSAD 54 - Skowhegan	Skowhegan
1	n/a	MSAD 57 - Waterboro	Waterboro
1	n/a	MSAD 60 - North Berwick	North Berwick
1	n/a	MSAD 61 - Bridgton	Bridgton
1	n/a	MSAD 71 - Kennebunk	Kennebunk
1	n/a	MSAD 75 - Topsham	Topsham
1	n/a	Portland Public Schools	Portland
1	n/a	Saco School Department	Saco
1	n/a	Sanford School Department	Sanford
1	n/a	Scarborough School Department	Scarborough
1	n/a	South Portland School Department	South Portland
1	n/a	Waterville Public Schools	Waterville
1	n/a	Wells-Ogunquit CSD	Wells
1	n/a	Westbrook School Department	Westbrook
1	n/a	Windham School Department	Windham
1	n/a	York School Department	York

Students Eligible for Free Lunch

Rank	Percent	District Name	City
1	40.2	MSAD 43 - Mexico	Mexico
2	39.5	Lewiston School Department	Lewiston
3	38.4	MSAD 03 - Unity	Unity
4	38.2	Waterville Public Schools	Waterville
5	34.9	MSAD 40 - Waldoboro	Warren
6	33.7	Portland Public Schools	Portland
7	33.5	Augusta Dept of Public Schools	Augusta
8	33.3	MSAD 48 - Newport	Newport
9	30.2	MSAD 34 - Belfast	Belfast
10	30.1	MSAD 54 - Skowhegan	Skowhegan
11	29.9	Sanford School Department	Sanford
12	29.3	Biddeford School Department	Biddeford
12	29.3	MSAD 17 - Oxford	Oxford
14	27.0	MSAD 05 - Rockland	Rockland
15	26.8	MSAD 49 - Fairfield	Fairfield
16	26.5	MSAD 09 - Farmington	New Sharon
17	26.4	Westbrook School Department	Westbrook
18	26.0	Bangor School Department	Bangor
19	24.8	MSAD 61 - Bridgton	Bridgton
20	24.3	MSAD 01 - Presque Isle	Presque Isle
21	22.7	MSAD 11 - Gardiner	Gardiner
22	21.6	Auburn School Department	Auburn
23	19.7	MSAD 47 - Oakland	Oakland
24	17.6	MSAD 06 - Buxton	Bar Mills
25	14.5	MSAD 52 - Turner	Turner
25	14.5	MSAD 60 - North Berwick	North Berwick
25	14.5	MSAD 75 - Topsham	Topsham
28	14.3	South Portland School Department	South Portland
29	13.9	MSAD 57 - Waterboro	Waterboro
30	13.7	MSAD 15 - Gray	Gray
31	11.7	MSAD 22 - Hampden	Hampden
32	11.4	Windham School Department	Windham
33	10.5	Wells-Ogunquit CSD	Wells
34	10.0	Gorham School Department	Gorham
34	10.0	Saco School Department	Saco
36	8.8	Brunswick School Department	Brunswick
37	5.8	Scarborough School Department	Scarborough
38	5.2	MSAD 35 - South Berwick	Eliot
39	5.1	York School Department	York
40	4.9	MSAD 71 - Kennebunk	Kennebunk
41	4.4	Cape Elizabeth School Department	Cape Elizabeth
42	1.5	MSAD 51 - Cumberland	Cumberland Ctr
43	1.4	Falmouth School Department	Falmouth

Students Eligible for Reduced-Price Lunch

Rank	Percent	District Name	City
1	13.8	MSAD 03 - Unity	Unity
2	13.6	MSAD 48 - Newport	Newport
3	12.4	MSAD 09 - Farmington	New Sharon
4	10.6	MSAD 06 - Buxton	Bar Mills
5	10.5	MSAD 40 - Waldoboro	Warren
6	10.4	MSAD 49 - Fairfield	Fairfield
7	9.8	MSAD 05 - Rockland	Rockland
8	9.5	MSAD 11 - Gardiner	Gardiner
9	9.4	MSAD 17 - Oxford	Oxford
10	9.1	MSAD 43 - Mexico	Mexico
11	8.8	MSAD 57 - Waterboro	Waterboro
12	8.7	MSAD 54 - Skowhegan	Skowhegan
13	8.4	MSAD 01 - Presque Isle	Presque Isle
14	8.3	Augusta Dept of Public Schools	Augusta
15	7.9	MSAD 47 - Oakland	Oakland
15	7.9	Sanford School Department	Sanford
17	7.4	Lewiston School Department	Lewiston
17	7.4	Waterville Public Schools	Waterville
19	7.3	MSAD 34 - Belfast	Belfast
19	7.3	MSAD 61 - Bridgton	Bridgton
21	7.2	MSAD 52 - Turner	Turner
22	7.1	Westbrook School Department	Westbrook
23	6.7	MSAD 60 - North Berwick	North Berwick
24	6.6	MSAD 75 - Topsham	Topsham
25	6.4	MSAD 15 - Gray	Gray
26	5.7	Biddeford School Department	Biddeford
27	5.6	Auburn School Department	Auburn
28	5.3	South Portland School Department	South Portland
29	5.1	Bangor School Department	Bangor
30	5.0	Portland Public Schools	Portland
31	4.6	MSAD 22 - Hampden	Hampden
32	4.1	Brunswick School Department	Brunswick
33	3.8	Gorham School Department	Gorham
34	3.7	Saco School Department	Saco
35	3.5	Windham School Department	Windham
36	3.2	Scarborough School Department	Scarborough
37	3.1	York School Department	York
38	2.8	MSAD 71 - Kennebunk	Kennebunk
39	2.5	Wells-Ogunquit CSD	Wells
40	2.0	MSAD 35 - South Berwick	Eliot
41	1.0	Cape Elizabeth School Department	Cape Elizabeth
42	0.7	MSAD 51 - Cumberland	Cumberland Ctr
43	0.5	Falmouth School Department	Falmouth

Student/Teacher Ratio

Rank	Ratio	District Name	City
1	21.9	Saco School Department	Saco
2	15.2	MSAD 57 - Waterboro	Waterboro
3	15.0	MSAD 35 - South Berwick	Eliot
4	14.7	Gorham School Department	Gorham
5	14.0	Lewiston School Department	Lewiston
6	13.8	York School Department	York
7	13.7	Sanford School Department	Sanford
8	13.5	Brunswick School Department	Brunswick
8	13.5	MSAD 11 - Gardiner	Gardiner
8	13.5	MSAD 15 - Gray	Gray
11	13.4	Scarborough School Department	Scarborough
11	13.4	Windham School Department	Windham
13	13.3	Biddeford School Department	Biddeford
13	13.3	Cape Elizabeth School Department	Cape Elizabeth
15	13.2	MSAD 06 - Buxton	Bar Mills
16	13.0	MSAD 05 - Rockland	Rockland
16	13.0	MSAD 17 - Oxford	Oxford
16	13.0	MSAD 71 - Kennebunk	Kennebunk
19	12.9	MSAD 01 - Presque Isle	Presque Isle
19	12.9	MSAD 48 - Newport	Newport
19	12.9	MSAD 51 - Cumberland	Cumberland Ctr
22	12.7	MSAD 22 - Hampden	Hampden
23	12.6	Falmouth School Department	Falmouth
23	12.6	MSAD 49 - Fairfield	Fairfield
25	12.4	MSAD 47 - Oakland	Oakland
25	12.4	MSAD 60 - North Berwick	North Berwick
25	12.4	MSAD 75 - Topsham	Topsham
28	12.3	MSAD 52 - Turner	Turner
28	12.3	MSAD 54 - Skowhegan	Skowhegan
30	12.2	South Portland School Department	South Portland
31	12.0	MSAD 03 - Unity	Unity
32	11.9	Bangor School Department	Bangor
33	11.8	MSAD 34 - Belfast	Belfast
34	11.6	MSAD 09 - Farmington	New Sharon
35	11.4	MSAD 40 - Waldoboro	Warren
35	11.4	Westbrook School Department	Westbrook
37	11.3	Wells-Ogunquit CSD	Wells
38	11.2	Portland Public Schools	Portland
39	11.0	MSAD 43 - Mexico	Mexico
40	10.9	Auburn School Department	Auburn
40	10.9	Waterville Public Schools	Waterville
42	10.4	MSAD 61 - Bridgton	Bridgton
43	10.3	Augusta Dept of Public Schools	Augusta

Student/Librarian Ratio

Rank	Ratio	District Name	City
1	2,763.0	MSAD 35 - South Berwick	Eliot
2	2,342.0	MSAD 51 - Cumberland	Cumberland Ctr
3	2,164.0	MSAD 01 - Presque Isle	Presque Isle
4	2,118.0	York School Department	York
5	2,063.0	MSAD 15 - Gray	Gray
6	1,828.5	MSAD 17 - Oxford	Oxford
7	1,803.3	MSAD 03 - Unity	Unity
8	1,563.0	Lewiston School Department	Lewiston
9	1,488.5	MSAD 54 - Skowhegan	Skowhegan
10	1,359.7	Bangor School Department	Bangor
11	1,343.5	Westbrook School Department	Westbrook
12	1,310.0	Windham School Department	Windham
13	1,272.8	Auburn School Department	Auburn
14	1,253.3	MSAD 57 - Waterboro	Waterboro
15	1,253.0	Augusta Dept of Public Schools	Augusta
16	1,226.3	MSAD 11 - Gardiner	Gardiner
17	1,225.6	MSAD 61 - Bridgton	Bridgton
18	1,085.7	MSAD 60 - North Berwick	North Berwick
19	1,082.3	South Portland School Department	South Portland
20	1,071.0	Scarborough School Department	Scarborough
21	1,062.0	MSAD 48 - Newport	Newport
22	1,009.5	MSAD 34 - Belfast	Belfast
23	946.0	Waterville Public Schools	Waterville
24	898.0	MSAD 49 - Fairfield	Fairfield
25	845.0	MSAD 71 - Kennebunk	Kennebunk
26	838.7	MSAD 47 - Oakland	Oakland
27	803.8	MSAD 52 - Turner	Turner
28	782.4	Sanford School Department	Sanford
29	778.9	Portland Public Schools	Portland
30	762.8	Biddeford School Department	Biddeford
31	758.0	MSAD 05 - Rockland	Rockland
32	710.0	MSAD 40 - Waldoboro	Warren
33	706.3	Falmouth School Department	Falmouth
34	679.0	Gorham School Department	Gorham
35	604.0	Wells-Ogunquit CSD	Wells
36	593.0	Cape Elizabeth School Department	Cape Elizabeth
37	590.3	MSAD 06 - Buxton	Bar Mills
38	580.4	Brunswick School Department	Brunswick
39	569.7	MSAD 75 - Topsham	Topsham
40	568.0	MSAD 22 - Hampden	Hampden
41	549.4	MSAD 09 - Farmington	New Sharon

Rank	Ratio	District Name	City
42	401.3	MSAD 43 - Mexico	Mexico
43	0.0	Saco School Department	Saco

Student/Counselor Ratio

Rank	Ratio	District Name	City
1	597.1	Saco School Department	Saco
2	554.9	MSAD 01 - Presque Isle	Presque Isle
3	513.3	MSAD 54 - Skowhegan	Skowhegan
4	452.7	Gorham School Department	Gorham
5	440.1	Scarborough School Department	Scarborough
6	397.6	Portland Public Schools	Portland
7	395.8	MSAD 57 - Waterboro	Waterboro
8	381.4	Biddeford School Department	Biddeford
9	363.8	MSAD 09 - Farmington	New Sharon
10	349.6	MSAD 51 - Cumberland	Cumberland Ctr
11	348.8	MSAD 75 - Topsham	Topsham
12	342.6	MSAD 11 - Gardiner	Gardiner
13	337.1	Bangor School Department	Bangor
14	335.9	Westbrook School Department	Westbrook
15	322.8	MSAD 06 - Buxton	Bar Mills
16	317.6	MSAD 35 - South Berwick	Eliot
17	315.1	MSAD 61 - Bridgton	Bridgton
18	312.1	Cape Elizabeth School Department	Cape Elizabeth
19	311.9	Windham School Department	Windham
20	302.0	Wells-Ogunquit CSD	Wells
21	294.2	York School Department	York
22	275.8	Lewiston School Department	Lewiston
23	273.7	MSAD 22 - Hampden	Hampden
24	268.2	Brunswick School Department	Brunswick
25	265.5	MSAD 48 - Newport	Newport
26	264.9	Falmouth School Department	Falmouth
27	259.1	Sanford School Department	Sanford
28	259.0	MSAD 49 - Fairfield	Fairfield
29	257.9	MSAD 15 - Gray	Gray
30	255.7	MSAD 17 - Oxford	Oxford
31	252.7	MSAD 05 - Rockland	Rockland
32	251.0	MSAD 71 - Kennebunk	Kennebunk
33	249.1	MSAD 47 - Oakland	Oakland
34	239.5	Waterville Public Schools	Waterville
35	233.1	MSAD 52 - Turner	Turner
36	229.9	Augusta Dept of Public Schools	Augusta
37	229.3	MSAD 43 - Mexico	Mexico
38	228.6	MSAD 03 - Unity	Unity
39	224.2	MSAD 40 - Waldoboro	Warren
40	221.9	MSAD 34 - Belfast	Belfast
41	220.1	MSAD 60 - North Berwick	North Berwick
42	219.7	Auburn School Department	Auburn
43	171.8	South Portland School Department	South Portland

Current Spending per Student in FY2001

Rank	Dollars	District Name	City
1	9,987	Portland Public Schools	Portland
2	9,748	Wells-Ogunquit CSD	Wells
3	9,626	Saco School Department	Saco
4	9,624	South Portland School Department	South Portland
5	9,194	Augusta Dept of Public Schools	Augusta
6	8,737	York School Department	York
7	8,718	Westbrook School Department	Westbrook
8	8,493	MSAD 71 - Kennebunk	Kennebunk
9	8,461	MSAD 61 - Bridgton	Bridgton
10	8,339	MSAD 34 - Belfast	Belfast
11	8,332	Waterville Public Schools	Waterville
12	8,215	Lewiston School Department	Lewiston
13	8,155	MSAD 54 - Skowhegan	Skowhegan
14	8,148	Cape Elizabeth School Department	Cape Elizabeth
15	8,075	MSAD 43 - Mexico	Mexico
16	7,993	MSAD 75 - Topsham	Topsham
17	7,978	Falmouth School Department	Falmouth
18	7,854	MSAD 22 - Hampden	Hampden
19	7,795	MSAD 49 - Fairfield	Fairfield
20	7,708	Auburn School Department	Auburn
21	7,706	Bangor School Department	Bangor
22	7,674	MSAD 01 - Presque Isle	Presque Isle
23	7,626	MSAD 05 - Rockland	Rockland
24	7,624	MSAD 03 - Unity	Unity
24	7,624	MSAD 06 - Buxton	Bar Mills
26	7,621	MSAD 52 - Turner	Turner
27	7,587	MSAD 51 - Cumberland	Cumberland Ctr
28	7,459	MSAD 60 - North Berwick	North Berwick
29	7,444	MSAD 09 - Farmington	New Sharon
30	7,379	MSAD 15 - Gray	Gray
31	7,328	MSAD 40 - Waldoboro	Warren
32	7,298	Biddeford School Department	Biddeford
33	7,250	Windham School Department	Windham
34	7,199	Brunswick School Department	Brunswick
35	7,163	MSAD 48 - Newport	Newport
36	7,150	MSAD 11 - Gardiner	Gardiner
37	7,103	Gorham School Department	Gorham
38	7,021	Sanford School Department	Sanford
39	7,005	Scarborough School Department	Scarborough
40	6,988	MSAD 47 - Oakland	Oakland
41	6,664	MSAD 17 - Oxford	Oxford
42	6,307	MSAD 57 - Waterboro	Waterboro
43	6,089	MSAD 35 - South Berwick	Eliot

Number of Diploma Recipients

Rank	Number	District Name	City
1	298	Bangor School Department	Bangor
2	288	Portland Public Schools	Portland
3	282	MSAD 06 - Buxton	Bar Mills
4	270	Lewiston School Department	Lewiston
5	252	MSAD 75 - Topsham	Topsham
6	245	MSAD 17 - Oxford	Oxford
7	230	Brunswick School Department	Brunswick
8	228	Auburn School Department	Auburn
8	228	South Portland School Department	South Portland
10	219	Sanford School Department	Sanford
11	213	MSAD 54 - Skowhegan	Skowhegan
12	206	MSAD 57 - Waterboro	Waterboro
13	204	MSAD 35 - South Berwick	Eliot
14	197	MSAD 09 - Farmington	New Sharon
14	197	MSAD 47 - Oakland	Oakland
16	191	MSAD 60 - North Berwick	North Berwick
17	183	Augusta Dept of Public Schools	Augusta
18	178	Scarborough School Department	Scarborough
19	174	MSAD 22 - Hampden	Hampden
19	174	MSAD 49 - Fairfield	Fairfield
21	169	MSAD 11 - Gardiner	Gardiner
22	163	Biddeford School Department	Biddeford
23	162	MSAD 71 - Kennebunk	Kennebunk
24	158	MSAD 40 - Waldoboro	Warren
25	154	MSAD 48 - Newport	Newport
26	153	Westbrook School Department	Westbrook
27	150	MSAD 52 - Turner	Turner
28	149	Gorham School Department	Gorham
29	148	MSAD 51 - Cumberland	Cumberland Ctr
30	141	Waterville Public Schools	Waterville
31	137	York School Department	York
32	136	MSAD 34 - Belfast	Belfast
33	128	MSAD 01 - Presque Isle	Presque Isle
33	128	MSAD 61 - Bridgton	Bridgton
35	126	Wells-Ogunquit CSD	Wells
36	117	MSAD 15 - Gray	Gray
37	115	MSAD 03 - Unity	Unity
38	113	Falmouth School Department	Falmouth
39	108	MSAD 43 - Mexico	Mexico
40	107	Cape Elizabeth School Department	Cape Elizabeth
41	103	MSAD 05 - Rockland	Rockland
42	4	Windham School Department	Windham
43	n/a	Saco School Department	Saco

High School Drop-out Rate

Rank	Percent	District Name	City
1	7.2	Auburn School Department	Auburn
2	6.9	Sanford School Department	Sanford
3	6.3	Portland Public Schools	Portland
4	5.4	MSAD 40 - Waldoboro	Warren
5	5.1	Waterville Public Schools	Waterville
6	5.0	Lewiston School Department	Lewiston
7	4.9	Bangor School Department	Bangor
8	4.8	MSAD 17 - Oxford	Oxford
9	4.5	MSAD 06 - Buxton	Bar Mills
10	4.2	MSAD 03 - Unity	Unity
11	3.9	MSAD 54 - Skowhegan	Skowhegan
11	3.9	MSAD 75 - Topsham	Topsham
13	3.6	York School Department	York
14	3.5	MSAD 60 - North Berwick	North Berwick
15	3.4	Biddeford School Department	Biddeford
15	3.4	MSAD 43 - Mexico	Mexico
17	3.3	South Portland School Department	South Portland
18	3.2	MSAD 05 - Rockland	Rockland
19	2.6	MSAD 49 - Fairfield	Fairfield
20	2.5	Gorham School Department	Gorham
21	2.4	Windham School Department	Windham
22	2.3	Brunswick School Department	Brunswick
22	2.3	MSAD 01 - Presque Isle	Presque Isle
24	2.2	Westbrook School Department	Westbrook
25	2.1	MSAD 11 - Gardiner	Gardiner
25	2.1	MSAD 48 - Newport	Newport
27	1.9	MSAD 22 - Hampden	Hampden
28	1.7	MSAD 35 - South Berwick	Eliot
28	1.7	Wells-Ogunquit CSD	Wells
30	1.6	Scarborough School Department	Scarborough
31	1.2	MSAD 09 - Farmington	New Sharon
31	1.2	MSAD 34 - Belfast	Belfast
31	1.2	MSAD 71 - Kennebunk	Kennebunk
34	0.8	MSAD 47 - Oakland	Oakland
35	0.7	MSAD 57 - Waterboro	Waterboro
36	0.6	MSAD 15 - Gray	Gray
37	0.5	MSAD 51 - Cumberland	Cumberland Ctr
37	0.5	MSAD 52 - Turner	Turner
39	0.4	Augusta Dept of Public Schools	Augusta
40	0.3	MSAD 61 - Bridgton	Bridgton
41	0.0	Cape Elizabeth School Department	Cape Elizabeth
41	0.0	Falmouth School Department	Falmouth
43	n/a	Saco School Department	Saco

Maryland

Maryland Public School Educational Profile

Category	Value	Category	Value
Schools *(2002-2003)*	1,404	**Diploma Recipients** *(2002-2003)*	50,881
Instructional Level		White, Non-Hispanic	29,363
Primary	867	Black, Non-Hispanic	16,745
Middle	241	Asian/Pacific Islander	2,725
High	234	American Indian/Alaskan Native	158
Other Level	62	Hispanic	1,890
Curriculum		**High School Drop-out Rate** (%) *(2000-2001)*	4.1
Regular	1,252	White, Non-Hispanic	3.2
Special Education	50	Black, Non-Hispanic	5.9
Vocational	25	Asian/Pacific Islander	1.6
Alternative	77	American Indian/Alaskan Native	4.7
Type		Hispanic	3.7
Magnet	0	**Staff** *(2002-2003)*	102,678.0
Charter	0	Teachers	55,383.0
Title I Eligible	466	Average Salary ($)	50,410
School-wide Title I	365	Librarians/Media Specialists	1,130.0
Students *(2002-2003)*	866,743	Guidance Counselors	2,230.0
Gender (%)		**Ratios** *(2002-2003)*	
Male	51.2	Student/Teacher Ratio	15.6 to 1
Female	48.8	Student/Librarian Ratio	767.0 to 1
Race/Ethnicity (%)		Student/Counselor Ratio	388.7 to 1
White, Non-Hispanic	51.5	**Current Spending** *($ per student in FY 2001)*	8,692
Black, Non-Hispanic	37.5	Instruction	5,408
Asian/Pacific Islander	4.7	Support Services	2,872
American Indian/Alaskan Native	0.4	**College Entrance Exam Scores** *(2003)*	
Hispanic	5.8	Scholastic Aptitude Test (SAT)	
Classification (%)		Participation Rate (%)	68
Individual Education Program (IEP)	12.3	Mean SAT I Verbal Score	509
Migrant	0.0	Mean SAT I Math Score	515
English Language Learner (ELL)	3.2	American College Testing Program (ACT)	
Eligible for Free Lunch Program	23.6	Participation Rate (%)	12
Eligible for Reduced-Price Lunch Program	7.1	Average Composite Score	20.7

Note: *For an explanation of data, please refer to the User's Guide in the front of the book; n/a indicates data not available*

Maryland NAEP 2003 Test Scores

Reading			Mathematics		
Grade/Category	**Value**	**Rank**	**Grade/Category**	**Value**	**Rank**
4th Grade			**4th Grade**		
Average Proficiency	218.7 (1.4)	29/51	Average Proficiency	233.1 (1.3)	33/51
Proficiency by Gender/Race/Ethnicity			Proficiency by Gender/Race/Ethnicity		
Male	215.0 (1.7)	30/51	Male	234.6 (1.4)	32/51
Female	222.3 (1.5)	29/51	Female	231.5 (1.4)	33/51
White, Non-Hispanic	231.0 (1.5)	10/51	White, Non-Hispanic	243.7 (1.4)	16/51
Black, Non-Hispanic	199.9 (2.1)	19/42	Black, Non-Hispanic	216.2 (1.2)	21/42
Asian, Non-Hispanic	209.4 (4.5)	8/41	Asian, Non-Hispanic	226.8 (2.4)	10/43
American Indian, Non-Hispanic	236.9 (4.0)	2/25	American Indian, Non-Hispanic	254.4 (3.2)	5/26
Hispanic	n/a	n/a	Hispanic	n/a	n/a
Proficiency by Class Size			Proficiency by Class Size		
Less than 16 Students	*206.8 (8.5)*	19/45	Less than 16 Students	*220.2 (7.1)*	31/47
16 to 18 Students	*196.8 (6.4)*	44/48	16 to 18 Students	*221.4 (6.4)*	42/48
19 to 20 Students	221.2 (4.3)	21/50	19 to 20 Students	234.8 (4.4)	25/50
21 to 25 Students	220.7 (2.3)	27/51	21 to 25 Students	233.7 (2.1)	35/51
Greater than 25 Students	218.5 (2.6)	27/49	Greater than 25 Students	234.2 (2.4)	29/49
Percent Attaining Achievement Levels			Percent Attaining Achievement Levels		
Below Basic	37.9 (1.5)	18/51	Below Basic	27.4 (1.4)	15/51
Basic or Above	62.1 (1.5)	34/51	Basic or Above	72.6 (1.4)	37/51
Proficient or Above	32.2 (1.5)	25/51	Proficient or Above	31.2 (1.7)	29/51
Advanced or Above	8.9 (0.9)	6/51	Advanced or Above	5.3 (0.8)	7/51
8th Grade			**8th Grade**		
Average Proficiency	261.6 (1.4)	33/51	Average Proficiency	277.7 (1.0)	29/51
Proficiency by Gender/Race/Ethnicity			Proficiency by Gender/Race/Ethnicity		
Male	254.9 (1.7)	34/51	Male	279.4 (1.4)	30/51
Female	268.6 (1.6)	31/51	Female	276.0 (1.2)	30/51
White, Non-Hispanic	270.5 (2.0)	23/50	White, Non-Hispanic	289.1 (1.2)	16/50
Black, Non-Hispanic	245.0 (1.9)	16/41	Black, Non-Hispanic	256.3 (1.2)	13/41
Asian, Non-Hispanic	250.9 (3.9)	8/37	Asian, Non-Hispanic	261.8 (4.4)	14/37
American Indian, Non-Hispanic	281.7 (3.8)	3/23	American Indian, Non-Hispanic	302.0 (3.9)	4/23
Hispanic	n/a	n/a	Hispanic	n/a	n/a
Proficiency by Parents Highest Level of Ed.			Proficiency by Parents Highest Level of Ed.		
Did Not Finish High School	243.6 (3.8)	37/50	Did Not Finish High School	258.5 (2.7)	22/50
Graduated High School	252.1 (1.9)	33/50	Graduated High School	264.7 (2.0)	36/50
Some Education After High School	267.6 (2.1)	27/50	Some Education After High School	280.6 (1.7)	27/50
Graduated College	268.2 (1.8)	35/50	Graduated College	287.9 (1.3)	28/50
Percent Attaining Achievement Levels			Percent Attaining Achievement Levels		
Below Basic	29.3 (1.5)	17/51	Below Basic	33.1 (1.2)	19/51
Basic or Above	70.7 (1.5)	35/51	Basic or Above	66.9 (1.2)	33/51
Proficient or Above	30.6 (1.7)	31/51	Proficient or Above	29.8 (1.3)	26/51
Advanced or Above	3.7 (0.7)	6/51	Advanced or Above	6.8 (0.8)	6/51

Note: *For an explanation of data, please refer to the User's Guide in the front of the book; values in italics indicate that the nature of the sample does not allow accurate determination of the variability of the statistic; n/a indicates data not available*

Allegany County

Board of Ed of Allegany County
108 Washington St • Cumberland, MD 21502-2931
Mailing Address: PO Box 1724 • Cumberland, MD 21502-1724
(301) 759-2038 • http://boe.allconet.org/
Grade Span: PK-12; **Agency Type:** 1
Schools: 26
14 Primary; 3 Middle; 5 High; 4 Other Level
21 Regular; 0 Special Education; 1 Vocational; 4 Alternative
0 Magnet; 0 Charter; 11 Title I Eligible; 10 School-wide Title I
Students: 10,128 (52.2% male; 47.8% female)
Individual Education Program: 1,726 (17.0%);
English Language Learner: 16 (0.2%); Migrant: 0 (0.0%)
Eligible for Free Lunch Program: 3,318 (32.8%)
Eligible for Reduced-Price Lunch Program: 1,167 (11.5%)
Teachers: 688.0 (14.7 to 1)
Librarians/Media Specialists: 22.0 (460.4 to 1)
Guidance Counselors: 23.0 (440.3 to 1)
Current Spending: ($ per student per year):
Total: $7,863; Instruction: $4,884; Support Services: $2,337
Enrollment, Drop-out Rates and Diploma Recipients by Race/Ethnicity

Category	Total	White	Black	Asian	AIAN	Hisp.
Enrollment (%)	100.0	94.9	4.0	0.6	0.2	0.2
Drop-out Rate (%)	3.7	3.7	5.9	0.0	12.5	0.0
H.S. Diplomas (#)	733	710	12	9	1	1

Anne Arundel County

Anne Arundel County Pub Schls
2644 Riva Rd • Annapolis, MD 21401-7305
(410) 222-5304 • http://www.aacps.org/
Grade Span: PK-12; **Agency Type:** 1
Schools: 119
77 Primary; 20 Middle; 17 High; 5 Other Level
108 Regular; 4 Special Education; 2 Vocational; 5 Alternative
0 Magnet; 0 Charter; 21 Title I Eligible; 5 School-wide Title I
Students: 74,787 (51.2% male; 48.8% female)
Individual Education Program: 9,958 (13.3%);
English Language Learner: 1,119 (1.5%); Migrant: 0 (0.0%)
Eligible for Free Lunch Program: 8,620 (11.5%)
Eligible for Reduced-Price Lunch Program: 3,417 (4.6%)
Teachers: 4,511.0 (16.6 to 1)
Librarians/Media Specialists: 109.0 (686.1 to 1)
Guidance Counselors: 199.0 (375.8 to 1)
Current Spending: ($ per student per year):
Total: $7,793; Instruction: $4,654; Support Services: $2,754
Enrollment, Drop-out Rates and Diploma Recipients by Race/Ethnicity

Category	Total	White	Black	Asian	AIAN	Hisp.
Enrollment (%)	100.0	73.5	20.3	3.0	0.2	2.9
Drop-out Rate (%)	4.5	4.1	6.2	2.7	8.6	4.6
H.S. Diplomas (#)	4,466	3,502	734	148	10	72

Baltimore County

Baltimore County Public Schls
6901 N Charles St • Towson, MD 21204-3711
(410) 887-4281 • http://www.bcps.org/
Grade Span: PK-12; **Agency Type:** 1
Schools: 170
106 Primary; 27 Middle; 32 High; 5 Other Level
147 Regular; 9 Special Education; 4 Vocational; 10 Alternative
0 Magnet; 0 Charter; 38 Title I Eligible; 35 School-wide Title I
Students: 108,297 (51.3% male; 48.7% female)
Individual Education Program: 12,775 (11.8%);
English Language Learner: 2,064 (1.9%); Migrant: 0 (0.0%)
Eligible for Free Lunch Program: 22,040 (20.4%)
Eligible for Reduced-Price Lunch Program: 8,742 (8.1%)
Teachers: 7,078.0 (15.3 to 1)
Librarians/Media Specialists: 172.0 (629.6 to 1)
Guidance Counselors: 295.0 (367.1 to 1)
Current Spending: ($ per student per year):
Total: $8,051; Instruction: $4,714; Support Services: $2,957
Enrollment, Drop-out Rates and Diploma Recipients by Race/Ethnicity

Category	Total	White	Black	Asian	AIAN	Hisp.
Enrollment (%)	100.0	57.8	35.3	4.2	0.5	2.2
Drop-out Rate (%)	2.9	2.8	3.3	1.1	4.4	3.6
H.S. Diplomas (#)	6,859	4,482	1,973	275	32	97

Baltimore City Public Schools Sys
200 E N Ave • Baltimore, MD 21202-5910
(410) 396-8803 • http://www.bcps.k12.md.us/
Grade Span: PK-12; **Agency Type:** 1
Schools: 184
120 Primary; 28 Middle; 27 High; 9 Other Level
152 Regular; 10 Special Education; 3 Vocational; 19 Alternative
0 Magnet; 0 Charter; 131 Title I Eligible; 129 School-wide Title I
Students: 96,230 (50.5% male; 49.5% female)
Individual Education Program: 14,271 (14.8%);
English Language Learner: 1,256 (1.3%); Migrant: 2 (<0.1%)
Eligible for Free Lunch Program: 58,194 (60.5%)
Eligible for Reduced-Price Lunch Program: 8,126 (8.4%)
Teachers: 6,530.0 (14.7 to 1)
Librarians/Media Specialists: 86.0 (1,119.0 to 1)
Guidance Counselors: 177.0 (543.7 to 1)
Current Spending: ($ per student per year):
Total: $8,810; Instruction: $5,411; Support Services: $3,005
Enrollment, Drop-out Rates and Diploma Recipients by Race/Ethnicity

Category	Total	White	Black	Asian	AIAN	Hisp.
Enrollment (%)	100.0	9.6	88.3	0.6	0.3	1.2
Drop-out Rate (%)	12.5	16.0	12.2	11.1	10.7	18.7
H.S. Diplomas (#)	4,524	362	4,090	35	21	16

Calvert County

Calvert County Public Schools
1305 Dares Beach Rd • Prince Frederick, MD 20678
(410) 535-7207 • http://www.calvertnet.k12.md.us/
Grade Span: PK-12; **Agency Type:** 1
Schools: 25
12 Primary; 6 Middle; 5 High; 2 Other Level
21 Regular; 1 Special Education; 1 Vocational; 2 Alternative
0 Magnet; 0 Charter; 8 Title I Eligible; 0 School-wide Title I
Students: 17,153 (51.3% male; 48.7% female)
Individual Education Program: 2,253 (13.1%);
English Language Learner: 75 (0.4%); Migrant: 0 (0.0%)
Eligible for Free Lunch Program: 1,667 (9.7%)
Eligible for Reduced-Price Lunch Program: 517 (3.0%)
Teachers: 1,013.0 (16.9 to 1)
Librarians/Media Specialists: 21.0 (816.8 to 1)
Guidance Counselors: 38.0 (451.4 to 1)
Current Spending: ($ per student per year):
Total: $7,171; Instruction: $4,424; Support Services: $2,355
Enrollment, Drop-out Rates and Diploma Recipients by Race/Ethnicity

Category	Total	White	Black	Asian	AIAN	Hisp.
Enrollment (%)	100.0	82.0	15.6	1.1	0.2	1.1
Drop-out Rate (%)	4.0	3.9	4.5	0.0	0.0	2.1
H.S. Diplomas (#)	1,043	878	146	5	1	13

Caroline County

Caroline County Board of Ed
204 Franklin St • Denton, MD 21629-1035
(410) 479-3250 • http://cl.k12.md.us/
Grade Span: PK-12; **Agency Type:** 1
Schools: 10
5 Primary; 2 Middle; 3 High; 0 Other Level
9 Regular; 0 Special Education; 1 Vocational; 0 Alternative
0 Magnet; 0 Charter; 5 Title I Eligible; 3 School-wide Title I
Students: 5,535 (51.7% male; 48.3% female)
Individual Education Program: 717 (13.0%);
English Language Learner: 134 (2.4%); Migrant: 88 (1.6%)
Eligible for Free Lunch Program: 1,708 (30.9%)
Eligible for Reduced-Price Lunch Program: 639 (11.5%)
Teachers: 344.0 (16.1 to 1)
Librarians/Media Specialists: 9.0 (615.0 to 1)
Guidance Counselors: 15.0 (369.0 to 1)
Current Spending: ($ per student per year):
Total: $6,973; Instruction: $4,146; Support Services: $2,363
Enrollment, Drop-out Rates and Diploma Recipients by Race/Ethnicity

Category	Total	White	Black	Asian	AIAN	Hisp.
Enrollment (%)	100.0	76.9	19.2	0.8	0.2	2.9
Drop-out Rate (%)	5.0	4.0	8.5	0.0	100.0	16.7
H.S. Diplomas (#)	341	276	61	3	0	1

Carroll County

Carroll County Public Schools
55 N Court St • Westminster, MD 21157-5155
(410) 751-3128 • http://www.carr.org/ccps/
Grade Span: PK-12; **Agency Type:** 1
Schools: 42
21 Primary; 9 Middle; 7 High; 5 Other Level
37 Regular; 1 Special Education; 1 Vocational; 3 Alternative
0 Magnet; 0 Charter; 9 Title I Eligible; 0 School-wide Title I
Students: 28,430 (51.3% male; 48.7% female)
Individual Education Program: 3,406 (12.0%);
English Language Learner: 105 (0.4%); Migrant: 0 (0.0%)
Eligible for Free Lunch Program: 1,825 (6.4%)
Eligible for Reduced-Price Lunch Program: 697 (2.5%)

Teachers: 1,654.0 (17.2 to 1)
Librarians/Media Specialists: 35.0 (812.3 to 1)
Guidance Counselors: 77.0 (369.2 to 1)
Current Spending: ($ per student per year):
Total: $7,112; Instruction: $4,252; Support Services: $2,545
Enrollment, Drop-out Rates and Diploma Recipients by Race/Ethnicity

Category	Total	White	Black	Asian	AIAN	Hisp.
Enrollment (%)	100.0	95.1	2.6	1.1	0.2	1.0
Drop-out Rate (%)	2.3	2.2	4.3	2.8	0.0	10.9
H.S. Diplomas (#)	1,910	1,831	42	29	0	8

Cecil County

Board of Ed of Cecil County

201 Booth St • Elkton, MD 21921-5684
(410) 996-5499 • http://www.ccps.org/
Grade Span: PK-12; **Agency Type:** 1
Schools: 31
17 Primary; 6 Middle; 6 High; 2 Other Level
28 Regular; 0 Special Education; 1 Vocational; 2 Alternative
0 Magnet; 0 Charter; 8 Title I Eligible; 4 School-wide Title I
Students: 16,203 (51.3% male; 48.7% female)
Individual Education Program: 2,519 (15.5%);
English Language Learner: 102 (0.6%); Migrant: 0 (0.0%)
Eligible for Free Lunch Program: 2,658 (16.4%)
Eligible for Reduced-Price Lunch Program: 878 (5.4%)
Teachers: 1,022.0 (15.9 to 1)
Librarians/Media Specialists: 24.0 (675.1 to 1)
Guidance Counselors: 46.0 (352.2 to 1)
Current Spending: ($ per student per year):
Total: $7,175; Instruction: $4,312; Support Services: $2,456
Enrollment, Drop-out Rates and Diploma Recipients by Race/Ethnicity

Category	Total	White	Black	Asian	AIAN	Hisp.
Enrollment (%)	100.0	90.2	6.8	0.7	0.3	2.0
Drop-out Rate (%)	3.6	3.6	4.6	2.3	0.0	4.8
H.S. Diplomas (#)	878	815	45	9	1	8

Charles County

Board of Ed of Charles County

5980 Radio Station Rd • La Plata, MD 20646-0170
Mailing Address: PO Box 2770 • La Plata, MD 20646-2770
(301) 934-7223 • http://www.ccboe.com/
Grade Span: PK-12; **Agency Type:** 1
Schools: 34
19 Primary; 7 Middle; 7 High; 1 Other Level
31 Regular; 0 Special Education; 1 Vocational; 2 Alternative
0 Magnet; 0 Charter; 16 Title I Eligible; 14 School-wide Title I
Students: 24,794 (50.9% male; 49.1% female)
Individual Education Program: 2,441 (9.8%);
English Language Learner: 173 (0.7%); Migrant: 0 (0.0%)
Eligible for Free Lunch Program: 4,094 (16.5%)
Eligible for Reduced-Price Lunch Program: 1,364 (5.5%)
Teachers: 1,393.0 (17.8 to 1)
Librarians/Media Specialists: 30.0 (826.5 to 1)
Guidance Counselors: 55.0 (450.8 to 1)
Current Spending: ($ per student per year):
Total: $7,225; Instruction: $4,162; Support Services: $2,628
Enrollment, Drop-out Rates and Diploma Recipients by Race/Ethnicity

Category	Total	White	Black	Asian	AIAN	Hisp.
Enrollment (%)	100.0	55.0	39.2	2.6	0.9	2.3
Drop-out Rate (%)	3.5	3.2	4.3	1.2	2.5	1.5
H.S. Diplomas (#)	1,481	935	453	49	12	32

Dorchester County

Dorchester County Board of Ed

700 Glasgow St • Cambridge, MD 21613-1738
Mailing Address: PO Box 619 • Cambridge, MD 21613-0619
(410) 221-5230 • http://www.dcps.k12.md.us/
Grade Span: PK-12; **Agency Type:** 1
Schools: 14
8 Primary; 2 Middle; 4 High; 0 Other Level
11 Regular; 0 Special Education; 1 Vocational; 2 Alternative
0 Magnet; 0 Charter; 4 Title I Eligible; 4 School-wide Title I
Students: 4,817 (49.9% male; 50.1% female)
Individual Education Program: 590 (12.2%);
English Language Learner: 81 (1.7%); Migrant: 90 (1.9%)
Eligible for Free Lunch Program: 1,942 (40.3%)
Eligible for Reduced-Price Lunch Program: 366 (7.6%)
Teachers: 317.0 (15.2 to 1)
Librarians/Media Specialists: 10.0 (481.7 to 1)
Guidance Counselors: 15.0 (321.1 to 1)
Current Spending: ($ per student per year):
Total: $8,261; Instruction: $4,732; Support Services: $2,991

Enrollment, Drop-out Rates and Diploma Recipients by Race/Ethnicity

Category	Total	White	Black	Asian	AIAN	Hisp.
Enrollment (%)	100.0	55.0	42.1	1.1	0.3	1.6
Drop-out Rate (%)	4.1	3.1	5.6	0.0	100.0	0.0
H.S. Diplomas (#)	283	177	98	4	0	4

Frederick County

Frederick County Board of Ed

115 E Church St • Frederick, MD 21701-5403
(301) 696-6910 • http://www.fcps.org/
Grade Span: PK-12; **Agency Type:** 1
Schools: 58
34 Primary; 12 Middle; 11 High; 1 Other Level
53 Regular; 3 Special Education; 1 Vocational; 1 Alternative
0 Magnet; 0 Charter; 12 Title I Eligible; 3 School-wide Title I
Students: 38,559 (51.1% male; 48.9% female)
Individual Education Program: 4,610 (12.0%);
English Language Learner: 447 (1.2%); Migrant: 0 (0.0%)
Eligible for Free Lunch Program: 3,491 (9.1%)
Eligible for Reduced-Price Lunch Program: 1,469 (3.8%)
Teachers: 2,414.0 (16.0 to 1)
Librarians/Media Specialists: 52.0 (741.5 to 1)
Guidance Counselors: 91.0 (423.7 to 1)
Current Spending: ($ per student per year):
Total: $7,004; Instruction: $4,236; Support Services: $2,428
Enrollment, Drop-out Rates and Diploma Recipients by Race/Ethnicity

Category	Total	White	Black	Asian	AIAN	Hisp.
Enrollment (%)	100.0	84.2	9.5	2.6	0.2	3.4
Drop-out Rate (%)	3.0	2.8	5.4	0.5	5.6	6.1
H.S. Diplomas (#)	2,465	2,201	164	48	3	49

Garrett County

Board of Ed of Garrett County

40 S 2nd St • Oakland, MD 21550-1506
(301) 334-8901 • http://www.ga.k12.md.us/
Grade Span: PK-12; **Agency Type:** 1
Schools: 18
11 Primary; 3 Middle; 4 High; 0 Other Level
15 Regular; 0 Special Education; 0 Vocational; 3 Alternative
0 Magnet; 0 Charter; 8 Title I Eligible; 8 School-wide Title I
Students: 4,833 (51.6% male; 48.4% female)
Individual Education Program: 672 (13.9%);
English Language Learner: 0 (0.0%); Migrant: 0 (0.0%)
Eligible for Free Lunch Program: 1,395 (28.9%)
Eligible for Reduced-Price Lunch Program: 639 (13.2%)
Teachers: 360.0 (13.4 to 1)
Librarians/Media Specialists: 2.0 (2,416.5 to 1)
Guidance Counselors: 12.0 (402.8 to 1)
Current Spending: ($ per student per year):
Total: $8,005; Instruction: $4,877; Support Services: $2,600
Enrollment, Drop-out Rates and Diploma Recipients by Race/Ethnicity

Category	Total	White	Black	Asian	AIAN	Hisp.
Enrollment (%)	100.0	99.5	0.2	0.1	0.0	0.1
Drop-out Rate (%)	4.9	4.9	0.0	0.0	n/a	0.0
H.S. Diplomas (#)	293	291	2	0	0	0

Harford County

Harford County Public Schools

45 E Gordon St • Bel Air, MD 21014-2915
(410) 588-5204 • http://www.co.ha.md.us/harford_schools/
Grade Span: PK-12; **Agency Type:** 1
Schools: 51
33 Primary; 8 Middle; 10 High; 0 Other Level
48 Regular; 1 Special Education; 1 Vocational; 1 Alternative
0 Magnet; 0 Charter; 9 Title I Eligible; 6 School-wide Title I
Students: 40,252 (51.2% male; 48.8% female)
Individual Education Program: 5,928 (14.7%);
English Language Learner: 280 (0.7%); Migrant: 0 (0.0%)
Eligible for Free Lunch Program: 5,165 (12.8%)
Eligible for Reduced-Price Lunch Program: 2,008 (5.0%)
Teachers: 2,524.0 (15.9 to 1)
Librarians/Media Specialists: 53.0 (759.5 to 1)
Guidance Counselors: 85.0 (473.6 to 1)
Current Spending: ($ per student per year):
Total: $6,958; Instruction: $4,192; Support Services: $2,422
Enrollment, Drop-out Rates and Diploma Recipients by Race/Ethnicity

Category	Total	White	Black	Asian	AIAN	Hisp.
Enrollment (%)	100.0	79.2	15.5	2.2	0.5	2.5
Drop-out Rate (%)	3.7	3.5	4.9	3.7	4.5	3.9
H.S. Diplomas (#)	2,425	2,028	272	53	9	63

Howard County

Howard County Pub Schls System

10910 State Route 108 • Ellicott City, MD 21042-6198
(410) 313-6674 • http://www.howard.k12.md.us/
Grade Span: PK-12; **Agency Type:** 1
Schools: 69
37 Primary; 18 Middle; 11 High; 3 Other Level
66 Regular; 1 Special Education; 0 Vocational; 2 Alternative
0 Magnet; 0 Charter; 10 Title I Eligible; 1 School-wide Title I
Students: 47,197 (52.0% male; 48.0% female)
Individual Education Program: 4,890 (10.4%);
English Language Learner: 1,460 (3.1%); Migrant: 0 (0.0%)
Eligible for Free Lunch Program: 3,236 (6.9%)
Eligible for Reduced-Price Lunch Program: 1,330 (2.8%)
Teachers: 3,205.0 (14.7 to 1)
Librarians/Media Specialists: 79.0 (597.4 to 1)
Guidance Counselors: 119.0 (396.6 to 1)
Current Spending: ($ per student per year):
Total: $8,490; Instruction: $5,387; Support Services: $2,696
Enrollment, Drop-out Rates and Diploma Recipients by Race/Ethnicity

Category	Total	White	Black	Asian	AIAN	Hisp.
Enrollment (%)	100.0	67.6	17.9	11.0	0.2	3.2
Drop-out Rate (%)	2.0	1.6	3.8	1.9	0.0	4.7
H.S. Diplomas (#)	2,990	2,098	490	337	3	62

Kent County

Board of Ed of Kent County

215 Washington Ave • Chestertown, MD 21620-1668
(410) 778-7113 • http://www.kent.k12.md.us/
Grade Span: PK-12; **Agency Type:** 1
Schools: 8
3 Primary; 3 Middle; 1 High; 1 Other Level
8 Regular; 0 Special Education; 0 Vocational; 0 Alternative
0 Magnet; 0 Charter; 4 Title I Eligible; 4 School-wide Title I
Students: 2,629 (51.8% male; 48.2% female)
Individual Education Program: 344 (13.1%);
English Language Learner: 52 (2.0%); Migrant: 49 (1.9%)
Eligible for Free Lunch Program: 752 (28.6%)
Eligible for Reduced-Price Lunch Program: 278 (10.6%)
Teachers: 174.0 (15.1 to 1)
Librarians/Media Specialists: 3.0 (876.3 to 1)
Guidance Counselors: 11.0 (239.0 to 1)
Current Spending: ($ per student per year):
Total: $8,760; Instruction: $4,989; Support Services: $3,325
Enrollment, Drop-out Rates and Diploma Recipients by Race/Ethnicity

Category	Total	White	Black	Asian	AIAN	Hisp.
Enrollment (%)	100.0	70.6	25.8	0.5	0.2	2.9
Drop-out Rate (%)	3.8	2.7	7.0	0.0	0.0	0.0
H.S. Diplomas (#)	185	128	53	0	1	3

Montgomery County

Montgomery County Public Schls

850 Hungerford Dr • Rockville, MD 20850-1718
(301) 279-3301 • http://www.mcps.k12.md.us/
Grade Span: PK-12; **Agency Type:** 1
Schools: 194
127 Primary; 36 Middle; 27 High; 4 Other Level
184 Regular; 7 Special Education; 1 Vocational; 2 Alternative
0 Magnet; 0 Charter; 31 Title I Eligible; 18 School-wide Title I
Students: 138,983 (51.5% male; 48.5% female)
Individual Education Program: 16,123 (11.6%);
English Language Learner: 11,837 (8.5%); Migrant: 0 (0.0%)
Eligible for Free Lunch Program: 21,391 (15.4%)
Eligible for Reduced-Price Lunch Program: 9,737 (7.0%)
Teachers: 9,015.0 (15.4 to 1)
Librarians/Media Specialists: 191.0 (727.7 to 1)
Guidance Counselors: 417.0 (333.3 to 1)
Current Spending: ($ per student per year):
Total: $9,543; Instruction: $6,075; Support Services: $3,015
Enrollment, Drop-out Rates and Diploma Recipients by Race/Ethnicity

Category	Total	White	Black	Asian	AIAN	Hisp.
Enrollment (%)	100.0	46.1	21.4	14.2	0.3	17.9
Drop-out Rate (%)	1.8	1.4	2.7	1.1	1.9	2.5
H.S. Diplomas (#)	8,282	4,286	1,624	1,336	21	1,015

Prince George's County

Prince Georges County Pub Schools

14201 School Ln • Upper Marlboro, MD 20772-2866
(301) 952-6008 • http://www.pgcps.pg.k12.md.us/
Grade Span: PK-12; **Agency Type:** 1
Schools: 204
140 Primary; 27 Middle; 27 High; 10 Other Level
184 Regular; 9 Special Education; 2 Vocational; 9 Alternative
0 Magnet; 0 Charter; 93 Title I Eligible; 91 School-wide Title I
Students: 135,439 (51.3% male; 48.7% female)
Individual Education Program: 13,954 (10.3%);
English Language Learner: 7,162 (5.3%); Migrant: 0 (0.0%)
Eligible for Free Lunch Program: 46,348 (34.2%)
Eligible for Reduced-Price Lunch Program: 14,998 (11.1%)
Teachers: 8,365.0 (16.2 to 1)
Librarians/Media Specialists: 124.0 (1,092.3 to 1)
Guidance Counselors: 348.0 (389.2 to 1)
Current Spending: ($ per student per year):
Total: $7,625; Instruction: $4,414; Support Services: $2,767
Enrollment, Drop-out Rates and Diploma Recipients by Race/Ethnicity

Category	Total	White	Black	Asian	AIAN	Hisp.
Enrollment (%)	100.0	9.1	77.6	3.1	0.6	9.5
Drop-out Rate (%)	3.2	4.9	2.8	2.1	1.9	5.4
H.S. Diplomas (#)	7,552	972	5,847	307	38	388

Queen Anne's County

Board of Ed of Queen Annes County

202 Chesterfield Ave • Centreville, MD 21617-0080
(410) 758-2403 • http://www.boe.qacps.k12.md.us/
Grade Span: PK-12; **Agency Type:** 1
Schools: 13
7 Primary; 3 Middle; 3 High; 0 Other Level
12 Regular; 0 Special Education; 0 Vocational; 1 Alternative
0 Magnet; 0 Charter; 6 Title I Eligible; 2 School-wide Title I
Students: 7,523 (51.5% male; 48.5% female)
Individual Education Program: 985 (13.1%);
English Language Learner: 50 (0.7%); Migrant: 34 (0.5%)
Eligible for Free Lunch Program: 785 (10.4%)
Eligible for Reduced-Price Lunch Program: 333 (4.4%)
Teachers: 455.0 (16.5 to 1)
Librarians/Media Specialists: 12.0 (626.9 to 1)
Guidance Counselors: 18.0 (417.9 to 1)
Current Spending: ($ per student per year):
Total: $7,343; Instruction: $4,321; Support Services: $2,668
Enrollment, Drop-out Rates and Diploma Recipients by Race/Ethnicity

Category	Total	White	Black	Asian	AIAN	Hisp.
Enrollment (%)	100.0	88.3	9.7	0.8	0.2	0.9
Drop-out Rate (%)	3.6	3.4	5.8	0.0	0.0	0.0
H.S. Diplomas (#)	393	348	40	3	2	0

Somerset County

Somerset County Public Schools

7982a Crisfield Hwy • Princess Anne, MD 21871
(410) 651-1616 • http://www.somerset.k12.md.us/
Grade Span: PK-12; **Agency Type:** 1
Schools: 11
6 Primary; 2 Middle; 3 High; 0 Other Level
10 Regular; 0 Special Education; 1 Vocational; 0 Alternative
0 Magnet; 0 Charter; 5 Title I Eligible; 4 School-wide Title I
Students: 2,978 (50.8% male; 49.2% female)
Individual Education Program: 354 (11.9%);
English Language Learner: 60 (2.0%); Migrant: 19 (0.6%)
Eligible for Free Lunch Program: 1,419 (47.6%)
Eligible for Reduced-Price Lunch Program: 341 (11.5%)
Teachers: 209.0 (14.2 to 1)
Librarians/Media Specialists: 3.0 (992.7 to 1)
Guidance Counselors: 9.0 (330.9 to 1)
Current Spending: ($ per student per year):
Total: $8,569; Instruction: $4,924; Support Services: $3,058
Enrollment, Drop-out Rates and Diploma Recipients by Race/Ethnicity

Category	Total	White	Black	Asian	AIAN	Hisp.
Enrollment (%)	100.0	51.5	45.6	1.0	0.0	1.8
Drop-out Rate (%)	7.5	5.5	10.1	0.0	0.0	25.0
H.S. Diplomas (#)	163	101	57	4	0	1

St. Mary's County

Saint Marys County Public Schools

23160 Moakley St • Leonardtown, MD 20650-0641
Mailing Address: PO Box 641 • Leonardtown, MD 20650-0641
(301) 475-4250 • http://www.smcps.k12.md.us/
Grade Span: PK-12; **Agency Type:** 1
Schools: 27
16 Primary; 4 Middle; 5 High; 2 Other Level
22 Regular; 1 Special Education; 1 Vocational; 3 Alternative
0 Magnet; 0 Charter; 8 Title I Eligible; 7 School-wide Title I
Students: 16,110 (51.0% male; 49.0% female)
Individual Education Program: 2,085 (12.9%);
English Language Learner: 182 (1.1%); Migrant: 0 (0.0%)

Eligible for Free Lunch Program: 2,590 (16.1%)
Eligible for Reduced-Price Lunch Program: 993 (6.2%)
Teachers: 966.0 (16.7 to 1)
Librarians/Media Specialists: 28.0 (575.4 to 1)
Guidance Counselors: 39.0 (413.1 to 1)
Current Spending: ($ per student per year):
Total: $7,385; Instruction: $4,268; Support Services: $2,691
Enrollment, Drop-out Rates and Diploma Recipients by Race/Ethnicity

Category	Total	White	Black	Asian	AIAN	Hisp.
Enrollment (%)	100.0	76.4	18.9	2.2	0.6	2.0
Drop-out Rate (%)	3.1	2.7	5.0	2.6	15.0	0.0
H.S. Diplomas (#)	845	707	108	15	2	13

Talbot County

Talbot County Public Schools
12 Magnolia St • Easton, MD 21601-1029
Mailing Address: PO Box 1029 • Easton, MD 21601-1029
(410) 822-0330 • http://www.tcps.k12.md.us/
Grade Span: PK-12; **Agency Type:** 1
Schools: 9
6 Primary; 1 Middle; 2 High; 0 Other Level
9 Regular; 0 Special Education; 0 Vocational; 0 Alternative
0 Magnet; 0 Charter; 2 Title I Eligible; 0 School-wide Title I
Students: 4,498 (51.3% male; 48.7% female)
Individual Education Program: 458 (10.2%);
English Language Learner: 122 (2.7%); Migrant: 23 (0.5%)
Eligible for Free Lunch Program: 1,022 (22.7%)
Eligible for Reduced-Price Lunch Program: 271 (6.0%)
Teachers: 307.0 (14.7 to 1)
Librarians/Media Specialists: 5.0 (899.6 to 1)
Guidance Counselors: 15.0 (299.9 to 1)
Current Spending: ($ per student per year):
Total: $7,582; Instruction: $4,726; Support Services: $2,391
Enrollment, Drop-out Rates and Diploma Recipients by Race/Ethnicity

Category	Total	White	Black	Asian	AIAN	Hisp.
Enrollment (%)	100.0	72.3	22.8	1.8	0.3	2.8
Drop-out Rate (%)	2.8	2.2	5.1	0.0	0.0	5.6
H.S. Diplomas (#)	272	216	52	1	0	3

Washington County

Board of Ed of Washington County
820 Commonwealth Ave • Hagerstown, MD 21741-0730
Mailing Address: PO Box 730 • Hagerstown, MD 21741-0730
(301) 766-2817 • http://www.wcboe.k12.md.us/
Grade Span: PK-12; **Agency Type:** 1
Schools: 46
26 Primary; 7 Middle; 8 High; 5 Other Level
40 Regular; 2 Special Education; 1 Vocational; 3 Alternative
0 Magnet; 0 Charter; 10 Title I Eligible; 10 School-wide Title I
Students: 20,102 (51.1% male; 48.9% female)
Individual Education Program: 2,721 (13.5%);
English Language Learner: 157 (0.8%); Migrant: 0 (0.0%)
Eligible for Free Lunch Program: 4,552 (22.6%)
Eligible for Reduced-Price Lunch Program: 1,562 (7.8%)
Teachers: 1,325.0 (15.2 to 1)
Librarians/Media Specialists: 40.0 (502.6 to 1)
Guidance Counselors: 50.0 (402.0 to 1)
Current Spending: ($ per student per year):
Total: $7,068; Instruction: $4,451; Support Services: $2,337
Enrollment, Drop-out Rates and Diploma Recipients by Race/Ethnicity

Category	Total	White	Black	Asian	AIAN	Hisp.
Enrollment (%)	100.0	88.0	8.9	1.2	0.2	1.7
Drop-out Rate (%)	4.0	3.9	5.8	1.1	0.0	7.5
H.S. Diplomas (#)	1,234	1,130	61	22	0	21

Wicomico County

Wicomico County Board of Ed
101 Long Ave • Salisbury, MD 21802-1538
Mailing Address: PO Box 1538 • Salisbury, MD 21802-1538
(410) 677-4596 • http://www.wcboe.org/
Grade Span: PK-12; **Agency Type:** 1
Schools: 27
17 Primary; 3 Middle; 5 High; 2 Other Level
24 Regular; 0 Special Education; 0 Vocational; 3 Alternative
0 Magnet; 0 Charter; 12 Title I Eligible; 4 School-wide Title I
Students: 14,395 (51.9% male; 48.1% female)
Individual Education Program: 1,663 (11.6%);
English Language Learner: 293 (2.0%); Migrant: 43 (0.3%)
Eligible for Free Lunch Program: 4,625 (32.1%)
Eligible for Reduced-Price Lunch Program: 971 (6.7%)
Teachers: 1,013.0 (14.2 to 1)
Librarians/Media Specialists: 8.0 (1,799.4 to 1)
Guidance Counselors: 55.0 (261.7 to 1)
Current Spending: ($ per student per year):
Total: $7,692; Instruction: $4,700; Support Services: $2,559
Enrollment, Drop-out Rates and Diploma Recipients by Race/Ethnicity

Category	Total	White	Black	Asian	AIAN	Hisp.
Enrollment (%)	100.0	58.5	36.2	2.6	0.2	2.6
Drop-out Rate (%)	5.2	4.0	8.1	2.7	0.0	3.6
H.S. Diplomas (#)	780	527	211	26	1	15

Worcester County

Board of Ed of Worcester County
6270 Worcester Hwy • Newark, MD 21841-2224
(410) 632-2582 • http://www.co.worcester.md.us/
Grade Span: PK-12; **Agency Type:** 1
Schools: 14
5 Primary; 4 Middle; 4 High; 1 Other Level
12 Regular; 1 Special Education; 1 Vocational; 0 Alternative
0 Magnet; 0 Charter; 5 Title I Eligible; 3 School-wide Title I
Students: 6,871 (51.0% male; 49.0% female)
Individual Education Program: 856 (12.5%);
English Language Learner: 84 (1.2%); Migrant: 0 (0.0%)
Eligible for Free Lunch Program: 1,823 (26.5%)
Eligible for Reduced-Price Lunch Program: 486 (7.1%)
Teachers: 501.0 (13.7 to 1)
Librarians/Media Specialists: 12.0 (572.6 to 1)
Guidance Counselors: 21.0 (327.2 to 1)
Current Spending: ($ per student per year):
Total: $8,477; Instruction: $5,210; Support Services: $2,735
Enrollment, Drop-out Rates and Diploma Recipients by Race/Ethnicity

Category	Total	White	Black	Asian	AIAN	Hisp.
Enrollment (%)	100.0	71.6	25.5	0.7	0.2	2.1
Drop-out Rate (%)	2.9	2.8	2.7	9.1	0.0	0.0
H.S. Diplomas (#)	486	363	111	7	0	5

Number of Schools

Rank	Number	District Name	City
1	204	Prince Georges County Pub Schools	Upper Marlboro
2	194	Montgomery County Public Schls	Rockville
3	184	Baltimore City Public Schools Sys	Baltimore
4	170	Baltimore County Public Schls	Towson
5	119	Anne Arundel County Pub Schls	Annapolis
6	69	Howard County Pub Schls System	Ellicott City
7	58	Frederick County Board of Ed	Frederick
8	51	Harford County Public Schools	Bel Air
9	46	Board of Ed of Washington County	Hagerstown
10	42	Carroll County Public Schools	Westminster
11	34	Board of Ed of Charles County	La Plata
12	31	Board of Ed of Cecil County	Elkton
13	27	Saint Marys County Public Schools	Leonardtown
13	27	Wicomico County Board of Ed	Salisbury
15	26	Board of Ed of Allegany County	Cumberland
16	25	Calvert County Public Schools	Prince Frederick
17	18	Board of Ed of Garrett County	Oakland
18	14	Board of Ed of Worcester County	Newark
18	14	Dorchester County Board of Ed	Cambridge
20	13	Board of Ed of Queen Annes County	Centreville
21	11	Somerset County Public Schools	Princess Anne
22	10	Caroline County Board of Ed	Denton
23	9	Talbot County Public Schools	Easton
24	8	Board of Ed of Kent County	Chestertown

Number of Teachers

Rank	Number	District Name	City
1	9,015	Montgomery County Public Schls	Rockville
2	8,365	Prince Georges County Pub Schools	Upper Marlboro
3	7,078	Baltimore County Public Schls	Towson
4	6,530	Baltimore City Public Schools Sys	Baltimore
5	4,511	Anne Arundel County Pub Schls	Annapolis
6	3,205	Howard County Pub Schls System	Ellicott City
7	2,524	Harford County Public Schools	Bel Air
8	2,414	Frederick County Board of Ed	Frederick
9	1,654	Carroll County Public Schools	Westminster
10	1,393	Board of Ed of Charles County	La Plata
11	1,325	Board of Ed of Washington County	Hagerstown
12	1,022	Board of Ed of Cecil County	Elkton
13	1,013	Calvert County Public Schools	Prince Frederick
13	1,013	Wicomico County Board of Ed	Salisbury
15	966	Saint Marys County Public Schools	Leonardtown
16	688	Board of Ed of Allegany County	Cumberland
17	501	Board of Ed of Worcester County	Newark
18	455	Board of Ed of Queen Annes County	Centreville
19	360	Board of Ed of Garrett County	Oakland
20	344	Caroline County Board of Ed	Denton
21	317	Dorchester County Board of Ed	Cambridge
22	307	Talbot County Public Schools	Easton
23	209	Somerset County Public Schools	Princess Anne
24	174	Board of Ed of Kent County	Chestertown

Number of Students

Rank	Number	District Name	City
1	138,983	Montgomery County Public Schls	Rockville
2	135,439	Prince Georges County Pub Schools	Upper Marlboro
3	108,297	Baltimore County Public Schls	Towson
4	96,230	Baltimore City Public Schools Sys	Baltimore
5	74,787	Anne Arundel County Pub Schls	Annapolis
6	47,197	Howard County Pub Schls System	Ellicott City
7	40,252	Harford County Public Schools	Bel Air
8	38,559	Frederick County Board of Ed	Frederick
9	28,430	Carroll County Public Schools	Westminster
10	24,794	Board of Ed of Charles County	La Plata
11	20,102	Board of Ed of Washington County	Hagerstown
12	17,153	Calvert County Public Schools	Prince Frederick
13	16,203	Board of Ed of Cecil County	Elkton
14	16,110	Saint Marys County Public Schools	Leonardtown
15	14,395	Wicomico County Board of Ed	Salisbury
16	10,128	Board of Ed of Allegany County	Cumberland
17	7,523	Board of Ed of Queen Annes County	Centreville
18	6,871	Board of Ed of Worcester County	Newark
19	5,535	Caroline County Board of Ed	Denton
20	4,833	Board of Ed of Garrett County	Oakland
21	4,817	Dorchester County Board of Ed	Cambridge
22	4,498	Talbot County Public Schools	Easton
23	2,978	Somerset County Public Schools	Princess Anne
24	2,629	Board of Ed of Kent County	Chestertown

Male Students

Rank	Percent	District Name	City
1	52.2	Board of Ed of Allegany County	Cumberland
2	52.0	Howard County Pub Schls System	Ellicott City
3	51.9	Wicomico County Board of Ed	Salisbury
4	51.8	Board of Ed of Kent County	Chestertown
5	51.7	Caroline County Board of Ed	Denton
6	51.6	Board of Ed of Garrett County	Oakland
7	51.5	Board of Ed of Queen Annes County	Centreville
7	51.5	Montgomery County Public Schls	Rockville
9	51.3	Baltimore County Public Schls	Towson
9	51.3	Board of Ed of Cecil County	Elkton
9	51.3	Calvert County Public Schools	Prince Frederick
9	51.3	Carroll County Public Schools	Westminster
9	51.3	Prince Georges County Pub Schools	Upper Marlboro
9	51.3	Talbot County Public Schools	Easton
15	51.2	Anne Arundel County Pub Schls	Annapolis
15	51.2	Harford County Public Schools	Bel Air
17	51.1	Board of Ed of Washington County	Hagerstown
17	51.1	Frederick County Board of Ed	Frederick
19	51.0	Board of Ed of Worcester County	Newark
19	51.0	Saint Marys County Public Schools	Leonardtown
21	50.9	Board of Ed of Charles County	La Plata
22	50.8	Somerset County Public Schools	Princess Anne
23	50.5	Baltimore City Public Schools Sys	Baltimore
24	49.9	Dorchester County Board of Ed	Cambridge

Female Students

Rank	Percent	District Name	City
1	50.1	Dorchester County Board of Ed	Cambridge
2	49.5	Baltimore City Public Schools Sys	Baltimore
3	49.2	Somerset County Public Schools	Princess Anne
4	49.1	Board of Ed of Charles County	La Plata
5	49.0	Board of Ed of Worcester County	Newark
5	49.0	Saint Marys County Public Schools	Leonardtown
7	48.9	Board of Ed of Washington County	Hagerstown
7	48.9	Frederick County Board of Ed	Frederick
9	48.8	Anne Arundel County Pub Schls	Annapolis
9	48.8	Harford County Public Schools	Bel Air
11	48.7	Baltimore County Public Schls	Towson
11	48.7	Board of Ed of Cecil County	Elkton
11	48.7	Calvert County Public Schools	Prince Frederick
11	48.7	Carroll County Public Schools	Westminster
11	48.7	Prince Georges County Pub Schools	Upper Marlboro
11	48.7	Talbot County Public Schools	Easton
17	48.5	Board of Ed of Queen Annes County	Centreville
17	48.5	Montgomery County Public Schls	Rockville
19	48.4	Board of Ed of Garrett County	Oakland
20	48.3	Caroline County Board of Ed	Denton
21	48.2	Board of Ed of Kent County	Chestertown
22	48.1	Wicomico County Board of Ed	Salisbury
23	48.0	Howard County Pub Schls System	Ellicott City
24	47.8	Board of Ed of Allegany County	Cumberland

Individual Education Program Students

Rank	Percent	District Name	City
1	17.0	Board of Ed of Allegany County	Cumberland
2	15.5	Board of Ed of Cecil County	Elkton
3	14.8	Baltimore City Public Schools Sys	Baltimore
4	14.7	Harford County Public Schools	Bel Air
5	13.9	Board of Ed of Garrett County	Oakland
6	13.5	Board of Ed of Washington County	Hagerstown
7	13.3	Anne Arundel County Pub Schls	Annapolis
8	13.1	Board of Ed of Kent County	Chestertown
8	13.1	Board of Ed of Queen Annes County	Centreville
8	13.1	Calvert County Public Schools	Prince Frederick
11	13.0	Caroline County Board of Ed	Denton
12	12.9	Saint Marys County Public Schools	Leonardtown
13	12.5	Board of Ed of Worcester County	Newark
14	12.2	Dorchester County Board of Ed	Cambridge
15	12.0	Carroll County Public Schools	Westminster
15	12.0	Frederick County Board of Ed	Frederick
17	11.9	Somerset County Public Schools	Princess Anne
18	11.8	Baltimore County Public Schls	Towson
19	11.6	Montgomery County Public Schls	Rockville
19	11.6	Wicomico County Board of Ed	Salisbury
21	10.4	Howard County Pub Schls System	Ellicott City
22	10.3	Prince Georges County Pub Schools	Upper Marlboro
23	10.2	Talbot County Public Schools	Easton
24	9.8	Board of Ed of Charles County	La Plata

English Language Learner Students

Rank	Percent	District Name	City
1	8.5	Montgomery County Public Schls	Rockville
2	5.3	Prince Georges County Pub Schools	Upper Marlboro
3	3.1	Howard County Pub Schls System	Ellicott City
4	2.7	Talbot County Public Schools	Easton
5	2.4	Caroline County Board of Ed	Denton
6	2.0	Board of Ed of Kent County	Chestertown
6	2.0	Somerset County Public Schools	Princess Anne
6	2.0	Wicomico County Board of Ed	Salisbury
9	1.9	Baltimore County Public Schls	Towson
10	1.7	Dorchester County Board of Ed	Cambridge
11	1.5	Anne Arundel County Pub Schls	Annapolis
12	1.3	Baltimore City Public Schools Sys	Baltimore
13	1.2	Board of Ed of Worcester County	Newark
13	1.2	Frederick County Board of Ed	Frederick
15	1.1	Saint Marys County Public Schools	Leonardtown
16	0.8	Board of Ed of Washington County	Hagerstown
17	0.7	Board of Ed of Charles County	La Plata
17	0.7	Board of Ed of Queen Annes County	Centreville
17	0.7	Harford County Public Schools	Bel Air
20	0.6	Board of Ed of Cecil County	Elkton
21	0.4	Calvert County Public Schools	Prince Frederick
21	0.4	Carroll County Public Schools	Westminster
23	0.2	Board of Ed of Allegany County	Cumberland
24	0.0	Board of Ed of Garrett County	Oakland

Migrant Students

Rank	Percent	District Name	City
1	1.9	Board of Ed of Kent County	Chestertown
1	1.9	Dorchester County Board of Ed	Cambridge
3	1.6	Caroline County Board of Ed	Denton
4	0.6	Somerset County Public Schools	Princess Anne
5	0.5	Board of Ed of Queen Annes County	Centreville
5	0.5	Talbot County Public Schools	Easton
7	0.3	Wicomico County Board of Ed	Salisbury
8	0.0	Baltimore City Public Schools Sys	Baltimore
9	0.0	Anne Arundel County Pub Schls	Annapolis
9	0.0	Baltimore County Public Schls	Towson
9	0.0	Board of Ed of Allegany County	Cumberland
9	0.0	Board of Ed of Cecil County	Elkton
9	0.0	Board of Ed of Charles County	La Plata
9	0.0	Board of Ed of Garrett County	Oakland
9	0.0	Board of Ed of Washington County	Hagerstown
9	0.0	Board of Ed of Worcester County	Newark
9	0.0	Calvert County Public Schools	Prince Frederick
9	0.0	Carroll County Public Schools	Westminster
9	0.0	Frederick County Board of Ed	Frederick
9	0.0	Harford County Public Schools	Bel Air
9	0.0	Howard County Pub Schls System	Ellicott City
9	0.0	Montgomery County Public Schls	Rockville
9	0.0	Prince Georges County Pub Schools	Upper Marlboro
9	0.0	Saint Marys County Public Schools	Leonardtown

Students Eligible for Free Lunch

Rank	Percent	District Name	City
1	60.5	Baltimore City Public Schools Sys	Baltimore
2	47.6	Somerset County Public Schools	Princess Anne
3	40.3	Dorchester County Board of Ed	Cambridge
4	34.2	Prince Georges County Pub Schools	Upper Marlboro
5	32.8	Board of Ed of Allegany County	Cumberland
6	32.1	Wicomico County Board of Ed	Salisbury
7	30.9	Caroline County Board of Ed	Denton
8	28.9	Board of Ed of Garrett County	Oakland
9	28.6	Board of Ed of Kent County	Chestertown
10	26.5	Board of Ed of Worcester County	Newark
11	22.7	Talbot County Public Schools	Easton
12	22.6	Board of Ed of Washington County	Hagerstown
13	20.4	Baltimore County Public Schls	Towson
14	16.5	Board of Ed of Charles County	La Plata
15	16.4	Board of Ed of Cecil County	Elkton
16	16.1	Saint Marys County Public Schools	Leonardtown
17	15.4	Montgomery County Public Schls	Rockville
18	12.8	Harford County Public Schools	Bel Air
19	11.5	Anne Arundel County Pub Schls	Annapolis
20	10.4	Board of Ed of Queen Annes County	Centreville
21	9.7	Calvert County Public Schools	Prince Frederick
22	9.1	Frederick County Board of Ed	Frederick
23	6.9	Howard County Pub Schls System	Ellicott City
24	6.4	Carroll County Public Schools	Westminster

Students Eligible for Reduced-Price Lunch

Rank	Percent	District Name	City
1	13.2	Board of Ed of Garrett County	Oakland
2	11.5	Board of Ed of Allegany County	Cumberland
2	11.5	Caroline County Board of Ed	Denton
2	11.5	Somerset County Public Schools	Princess Anne
5	11.1	Prince Georges County Pub Schools	Upper Marlboro
6	10.6	Board of Ed of Kent County	Chestertown
7	8.4	Baltimore City Public Schools Sys	Baltimore
8	8.1	Baltimore County Public Schls	Towson
9	7.8	Board of Ed of Washington County	Hagerstown
10	7.6	Dorchester County Board of Ed	Cambridge
11	7.1	Board of Ed of Worcester County	Newark
12	7.0	Montgomery County Public Schls	Rockville
13	6.7	Wicomico County Board of Ed	Salisbury
14	6.2	Saint Marys County Public Schools	Leonardtown
15	6.0	Talbot County Public Schools	Easton
16	5.5	Board of Ed of Charles County	La Plata
17	5.4	Board of Ed of Cecil County	Elkton
18	5.0	Harford County Public Schools	Bel Air
19	4.6	Anne Arundel County Pub Schls	Annapolis
20	4.4	Board of Ed of Queen Annes County	Centreville
21	3.8	Frederick County Board of Ed	Frederick
22	3.0	Calvert County Public Schools	Prince Frederick
23	2.8	Howard County Pub Schls System	Ellicott City

24	2.5	Carroll County Public Schools	Westminster

Student/Teacher Ratio

Rank	Ratio	District Name	City
1	17.8	Board of Ed of Charles County	La Plata
2	17.2	Carroll County Public Schools	Westminster
3	16.9	Calvert County Public Schools	Prince Frederick
4	16.7	Saint Marys County Public Schools	Leonardtown
5	16.6	Anne Arundel County Pub Schls	Annapolis
6	16.5	Board of Ed of Queen Annes County	Centreville
7	16.2	Prince Georges County Pub Schools	Upper Marlboro
8	16.1	Caroline County Board of Ed	Denton
9	16.0	Frederick County Board of Ed	Frederick
10	15.9	Board of Ed of Cecil County	Elkton
10	15.9	Harford County Public Schools	Bel Air
12	15.4	Montgomery County Public Schls	Rockville
13	15.3	Baltimore County Public Schls	Towson
14	15.2	Board of Ed of Washington County	Hagerstown
14	15.2	Dorchester County Board of Ed	Cambridge
16	15.1	Board of Ed of Kent County	Chestertown
17	14.7	Baltimore City Public Schools Sys	Baltimore
17	14.7	Board of Ed of Allegany County	Cumberland
17	14.7	Howard County Pub Schls System	Ellicott City
17	14.7	Talbot County Public Schools	Easton
21	14.2	Somerset County Public Schools	Princess Anne
21	14.2	Wicomico County Board of Ed	Salisbury
23	13.7	Board of Ed of Worcester County	Newark
24	13.4	Board of Ed of Garrett County	Oakland

Student/Librarian Ratio

Rank	Ratio	District Name	City
1	2,416.5	Board of Ed of Garrett County	Oakland
2	1,799.4	Wicomico County Board of Ed	Salisbury
3	1,119.0	Baltimore City Public Schools Sys	Baltimore
4	1,092.3	Prince Georges County Pub Schools	Upper Marlboro
5	992.7	Somerset County Public Schools	Princess Anne
6	899.6	Talbot County Public Schools	Easton
7	876.3	Board of Ed of Kent County	Chestertown
8	826.5	Board of Ed of Charles County	La Plata
9	816.8	Calvert County Public Schools	Prince Frederick
10	812.3	Carroll County Public Schools	Westminster
11	759.5	Harford County Public Schools	Bel Air
12	741.5	Frederick County Board of Ed	Frederick
13	727.7	Montgomery County Public Schls	Rockville
14	686.1	Anne Arundel County Pub Schls	Annapolis
15	675.1	Board of Ed of Cecil County	Elkton
16	629.6	Baltimore County Public Schls	Towson
17	626.9	Board of Ed of Queen Annes County	Centreville
18	615.0	Caroline County Board of Ed	Denton
19	597.4	Howard County Pub Schls System	Ellicott City
20	575.4	Saint Marys County Public Schools	Leonardtown
21	572.6	Board of Ed of Worcester County	Newark
22	502.6	Board of Ed of Washington County	Hagerstown
23	481.7	Dorchester County Board of Ed	Cambridge
24	460.4	Board of Ed of Allegany County	Cumberland

Student/Counselor Ratio

Rank	Ratio	District Name	City
1	543.7	Baltimore City Public Schools Sys	Baltimore
2	473.6	Harford County Public Schools	Bel Air
3	451.4	Calvert County Public Schools	Prince Frederick
4	450.8	Board of Ed of Charles County	La Plata
5	440.3	Board of Ed of Allegany County	Cumberland
6	423.7	Frederick County Board of Ed	Frederick
7	417.9	Board of Ed of Queen Annes County	Centreville
8	413.1	Saint Marys County Public Schools	Leonardtown
9	402.8	Board of Ed of Garrett County	Oakland
10	402.0	Board of Ed of Washington County	Hagerstown
11	396.6	Howard County Pub Schls System	Ellicott City
12	389.2	Prince Georges County Pub Schools	Upper Marlboro
13	375.8	Anne Arundel County Pub Schls	Annapolis
14	369.2	Carroll County Public Schools	Westminster
15	369.0	Caroline County Board of Ed	Denton
16	367.1	Baltimore County Public Schls	Towson
17	352.2	Board of Ed of Cecil County	Elkton
18	333.3	Montgomery County Public Schls	Rockville
19	330.9	Somerset County Public Schools	Princess Anne
20	327.2	Board of Ed of Worcester County	Newark
21	321.1	Dorchester County Board of Ed	Cambridge
22	299.9	Talbot County Public Schools	Easton
23	261.7	Wicomico County Board of Ed	Salisbury
24	239.0	Board of Ed of Kent County	Chestertown

Current Spending per Student in FY2001

Rank	Dollars	District Name	City
1	9,543	Montgomery County Public Schls	Rockville
2	8,810	Baltimore City Public Schools Sys	Baltimore
3	8,760	Board of Ed of Kent County	Chestertown
4	8,569	Somerset County Public Schools	Princess Anne
5	8,490	Howard County Pub Schls System	Ellicott City
6	8,477	Board of Ed of Worcester County	Newark
7	8,261	Dorchester County Board of Ed	Cambridge
8	8,051	Baltimore County Public Schls	Towson
9	8,005	Board of Ed of Garrett County	Oakland
10	7,863	Board of Ed of Allegany County	Cumberland
11	7,793	Anne Arundel County Pub Schls	Annapolis
12	7,692	Wicomico County Board of Ed	Salisbury
13	7,625	Prince Georges County Pub Schools	Upper Marlboro
14	7,582	Talbot County Public Schools	Easton
15	7,385	Saint Marys County Public Schools	Leonardtown
16	7,343	Board of Ed of Queen Annes County	Centreville
17	7,225	Board of Ed of Charles County	La Plata
18	7,175	Board of Ed of Cecil County	Elkton
19	7,171	Calvert County Public Schools	Prince Frederick
20	7,112	Carroll County Public Schools	Westminster
21	7,068	Board of Ed of Washington County	Hagerstown
22	7,004	Frederick County Board of Ed	Frederick
23	6,973	Caroline County Board of Ed	Denton
24	6,958	Harford County Public Schools	Bel Air

Number of Diploma Recipients

Rank	Number	District Name	City
1	8,282	Montgomery County Public Schls	Rockville
2	7,552	Prince Georges County Pub Schools	Upper Marlboro
3	6,859	Baltimore County Public Schls	Towson
4	4,524	Baltimore City Public Schools Sys	Baltimore
5	4,466	Anne Arundel County Pub Schls	Annapolis
6	2,990	Howard County Pub Schls System	Ellicott City
7	2,465	Frederick County Board of Ed	Frederick
8	2,425	Harford County Public Schools	Bel Air
9	1,910	Carroll County Public Schools	Westminster
10	1,481	Board of Ed of Charles County	La Plata
11	1,234	Board of Ed of Washington County	Hagerstown
12	1,043	Calvert County Public Schools	Prince Frederick
13	878	Board of Ed of Cecil County	Elkton
14	845	Saint Marys County Public Schools	Leonardtown
15	780	Wicomico County Board of Ed	Salisbury
16	733	Board of Ed of Allegany County	Cumberland
17	486	Board of Ed of Worcester County	Newark
18	393	Board of Ed of Queen Annes County	Centreville
19	341	Caroline County Board of Ed	Denton
20	293	Board of Ed of Garrett County	Oakland
21	283	Dorchester County Board of Ed	Cambridge
22	272	Talbot County Public Schools	Easton
23	185	Board of Ed of Kent County	Chestertown
24	163	Somerset County Public Schools	Princess Anne

High School Drop-out Rate

Rank	Percent	District Name	City
1	12.5	Baltimore City Public Schools Sys	Baltimore
2	7.5	Somerset County Public Schools	Princess Anne
3	5.2	Wicomico County Board of Ed	Salisbury
4	5.0	Caroline County Board of Ed	Denton
5	4.9	Board of Ed of Garrett County	Oakland
6	4.5	Anne Arundel County Pub Schls	Annapolis
7	4.1	Dorchester County Board of Ed	Cambridge
8	4.0	Board of Ed of Washington County	Hagerstown
8	4.0	Calvert County Public Schools	Prince Frederick
10	3.8	Board of Ed of Kent County	Chestertown
11	3.7	Board of Ed of Allegany County	Cumberland
11	3.7	Harford County Public Schools	Bel Air
13	3.6	Board of Ed of Cecil County	Elkton
13	3.6	Board of Ed of Queen Annes County	Centreville
15	3.5	Board of Ed of Charles County	La Plata
16	3.2	Prince Georges County Pub Schools	Upper Marlboro
17	3.1	Saint Marys County Public Schools	Leonardtown
18	3.0	Frederick County Board of Ed	Frederick
19	2.9	Baltimore County Public Schls	Towson
19	2.9	Board of Ed of Worcester County	Newark
21	2.8	Talbot County Public Schools	Easton
22	2.3	Carroll County Public Schools	Westminster
23	2.0	Howard County Pub Schls System	Ellicott City
24	1.8	Montgomery County Public Schls	Rockville

Massachusetts

Massachusetts Public School Educational Profile

Category	Value	Category	Value
Schools *(2002-2003)*	1,904	**Diploma Recipients** *(2002-2003)*	55,272
Instructional Level		White, Non-Hispanic	44,973
Primary	1,210	Black, Non-Hispanic	3,944
Middle	325	Asian/Pacific Islander	2,693
High	296	American Indian/Alaskan Native	136
Other Level	73	Hispanic	3,526
Curriculum		**High School Drop-out Rate** (%) *(2000-2001)*	3.4
Regular	1,828	White, Non-Hispanic	2.6
Special Education	6	Black, Non-Hispanic	6.0
Vocational	41	Asian/Pacific Islander	3.9
Alternative	29	American Indian/Alaskan Native	3.2
Type		Hispanic	7.9
Magnet	6	**Staff** *(2002-2003)*	140,512.0
Charter	47	Teachers	74,216.5
Title I Eligible	1,131	Average Salary ($)	51,942
School-wide Title I	451	Librarians/Media Specialists	1,007.0
Students *(2002-2003)*	982,989	Guidance Counselors	2,923.8
Gender (%)		**Ratios** *(2002-2003)*	
Male	51.4	Student/Teacher Ratio	13.2 to 1
Female	48.6	Student/Librarian Ratio	976.2 to 1
Race/Ethnicity (%)		Student/Counselor Ratio	336.2 to 1
White, Non-Hispanic	75.1	**Current Spending** *($ per student in FY 2001)*	10,232
Black, Non-Hispanic	8.8	Instruction	6,515
Asian/Pacific Islander	4.6	Support Services	3,399
American Indian/Alaskan Native	0.3	**College Entrance Exam Scores** *(2003)*	
Hispanic	11.2	Scholastic Aptitude Test (SAT)	
Classification (%)		Participation Rate (%)	82
Individual Education Program (IEP)	15.3	Mean SAT I Verbal Score	516
Migrant	0.2	Mean SAT I Math Score	522
English Language Learner (ELL)	5.3	American College Testing Program (ACT)	
Eligible for Free Lunch Program	0.0	Participation Rate (%)	10
Eligible for Reduced-Price Lunch Program	0.0	Average Composite Score	22.3

Note: *For an explanation of data, please refer to the User's Guide in the front of the book; n/a indicates data not available*

Massachusetts NAEP 2003 Test Scores

Reading			Mathematics		
Grade/Category	Value	Rank	Grade/Category	Value	Rank
4th Grade			**4th Grade**		
Average Proficiency	227.6 (1.2)	3/51	Average Proficiency	241.7 (0.8)	5/51
Proficiency by Gender/Race/Ethnicity			Proficiency by Gender/Race/Ethnicity		
Male	225.1 (1.3)	1/51	Male	243.9 (0.9)	2/51
Female	230.5 (1.3)	3/51	Female	239.3 (1.0)	7/51
White, Non-Hispanic	234.3 (1.3)	5/51	White, Non-Hispanic	247.4 (0.8)	6/51
Black, Non-Hispanic	207.2 (1.6)	6/42	Black, Non-Hispanic	221.7 (1.8)	8/42
Asian, Non-Hispanic	202.2 (2.1)	25/41	Asian, Non-Hispanic	222.0 (2.3)	21/43
American Indian, Non-Hispanic	229.4 (3.4)	11/25	American Indian, Non-Hispanic	248.4 (2.8)	11/26
Hispanic	n/a	n/a	Hispanic	n/a	n/a
Proficiency by Class Size			Proficiency by Class Size		
Less than 16 Students	201.7 (5.2)	28/45	Less than 16 Students	*223.2 (3.7)*	26/47
16 to 18 Students	228.5 (2.6)	3/48	16 to 18 Students	238.6 (2.3)	12/48
19 to 20 Students	232.8 (2.3)	1/50	19 to 20 Students	244.2 (1.8)	2/50
21 to 25 Students	227.1 (1.9)	5/51	21 to 25 Students	242.9 (1.5)	6/51
Greater than 25 Students	*228.9 (3.5)*	2/49	Greater than 25 Students	*242.1 (2.7)*	8/49
Percent Attaining Achievement Levels			Percent Attaining Achievement Levels		
Below Basic	26.8 (1.3)	48/51	Below Basic	15.5 (1.0)	46/51
Basic or Above	73.2 (1.3)	4/51	Basic or Above	84.5 (1.0)	6/51
Proficient or Above	40.4 (1.7)	2/51	Proficient or Above	41.2 (1.4)	5/51
Advanced or Above	10.5 (1.2)	3/51	Advanced or Above	5.8 (0.6)	3/51
8th Grade			**8th Grade**		
Average Proficiency	272.9 (1.0)	1/51	Average Proficiency	286.5 (0.9)	3/51
Proficiency by Gender/Race/Ethnicity			Proficiency by Gender/Race/Ethnicity		
Male	267.8 (1.3)	1/51	Male	289.3 (1.0)	1/51
Female	278.1 (1.0)	1/51	Female	283.7 (1.2)	8/51
White, Non-Hispanic	277.9 (1.0)	1/50	White, Non-Hispanic	292.5 (0.9)	5/50
Black, Non-Hispanic	251.7 (2.4)	1/41	Black, Non-Hispanic	259.7 (1.5)	8/41
Asian, Non-Hispanic	246.3 (2.8)	19/37	Asian, Non-Hispanic	255.2 (1.7)	26/37
American Indian, Non-Hispanic	281.4 (4.5)	4/23	American Indian, Non-Hispanic	303.8 (4.6)	2/23
Hispanic	n/a	n/a	Hispanic	n/a	n/a
Proficiency by Parents Highest Level of Ed.			Proficiency by Parents Highest Level of Ed.		
Did Not Finish High School	249.5 (2.7)	13/50	Did Not Finish High School	261.8 (3.3)	13/50
Graduated High School	260.4 (1.9)	7/50	Graduated High School	271.2 (1.9)	17/50
Some Education After High School	271.0 (1.8)	14/50	Some Education After High School	281.0 (1.7)	26/50
Graduated College	284.2 (1.0)	1/50	Graduated College	297.7 (1.0)	2/50
Percent Attaining Achievement Levels			Percent Attaining Achievement Levels		
Below Basic	18.6 (0.9)	48/51	Below Basic	23.7 (1.0)	43/51
Basic or Above	81.4 (0.9)	4/51	Basic or Above	76.3 (1.0)	9/51
Proficient or Above	43.3 (1.2)	1/51	Proficient or Above	38.3 (1.1)	2/51
Advanced or Above	5.4 (0.7)	1/51	Advanced or Above	8.3 (0.8)	2/51

***Note:** For an explanation of data, please refer to the User's Guide in the front of the book; values in italics indicate that the nature of the sample does not allow accurate determination of the variability of the statistic; n/a indicates data not available*

Barnstable County

Barnstable

230 S St • Hyannis, MA 02601-0955
Mailing Address: PO Box 955 • Hyannis, MA 02601-0955
(508) 790-9802 • http://www.barnstable.k12.ma.us/
Grade Span: PK-12; **Agency Type:** 1
Schools: 12
9 Primary; 2 Middle; 1 High; 0 Other Level
12 Regular; 0 Special Education; 0 Vocational; 0 Alternative
0 Magnet; 0 Charter; 7 Title I Eligible; 2 School-wide Title I
Students: 6,229 (51.6% male; 48.4% female)
Individual Education Program: 946 (15.2%);
English Language Learner: 268 (4.3%); Migrant: 4 (0.1%)
Eligible for Free Lunch Program: n/a
Eligible for Reduced-Price Lunch Program: n/a
Teachers: 444.9 (14.0 to 1)
Librarians/Media Specialists: 3.0 (2,076.3 to 1)
Guidance Counselors: 27.0 (230.7 to 1)
Current Spending: ($ per student per year):
Total: $9,283; Instruction: $6,399; Support Services: $2,587
Enrollment, Drop-out Rates and Diploma Recipients by Race/Ethnicity

Category	Total	White	Black	Asian	AIAN	Hisp.
Enrollment (%)	100.0	86.9	5.4	1.7	1.1	5.0
Drop-out Rate (%)	2.1	1.5	3.4	0.0	0.0	8.7
H.S. Diplomas (#)	393	342	22	5	2	22

Bourne

36 Sandwich Rd • Bourne, MA 02532-3609
(508) 759-0660 • http://www.bourne.k12.ma.us/
Grade Span: PK-12; **Agency Type:** 1
Schools: 5
3 Primary; 1 Middle; 1 High; 0 Other Level
5 Regular; 0 Special Education; 0 Vocational; 0 Alternative
0 Magnet; 0 Charter; 4 Title I Eligible; 0 School-wide Title I
Students: 2,611 (49.7% male; 50.3% female)
Individual Education Program: 328 (12.6%);
English Language Learner: 0 (0.0%); Migrant: 5 (0.2%)
Eligible for Free Lunch Program: n/a
Eligible for Reduced-Price Lunch Program: n/a
Teachers: 242.9 (10.7 to 1)
Librarians/Media Specialists: 2.0 (1,305.5 to 1)
Guidance Counselors: 5.0 (522.2 to 1)
Current Spending: ($ per student per year):
Total: $8,269; Instruction: $5,421; Support Services: $2,608
Enrollment, Drop-out Rates and Diploma Recipients by Race/Ethnicity

Category	Total	White	Black	Asian	AIAN	Hisp.
Enrollment (%)	100.0	92.5	4.1	0.9	0.4	2.1
Drop-out Rate (%)	3.9	3.5	11.8	0.0	33.3	11.1
H.S. Diplomas (#)	113	108	1	2	1	1

Dennis-Yarmouth

296 Station Ave • South Yarmouth, MA 02664-1898
(508) 398-7600 • http://dy-regional.k12.ma.us/
Grade Span: PK-12; **Agency Type:** 3
Schools: 8
5 Primary; 2 Middle; 1 High; 0 Other Level
8 Regular; 0 Special Education; 0 Vocational; 0 Alternative
0 Magnet; 0 Charter; 7 Title I Eligible; 0 School-wide Title I
Students: 4,325 (51.8% male; 48.2% female)
Individual Education Program: 627 (14.5%);
English Language Learner: 167 (3.9%); Migrant: 1 (<0.1%)
Eligible for Free Lunch Program: n/a
Eligible for Reduced-Price Lunch Program: n/a
Teachers: 344.2 (12.6 to 1)
Librarians/Media Specialists: 8.0 (540.6 to 1)
Guidance Counselors: 5.5 (786.4 to 1)
Current Spending: ($ per student per year):
Total: $8,884; Instruction: $6,142; Support Services: $2,480
Enrollment, Drop-out Rates and Diploma Recipients by Race/Ethnicity

Category	Total	White	Black	Asian	AIAN	Hisp.
Enrollment (%)	100.0	90.2	4.1	1.2	0.9	3.5
Drop-out Rate (%)	1.9	1.7	8.7	0.0	n/a	3.5
H.S. Diplomas (#)	269	251	5	5	0	8

Falmouth

340 Teaticket Hwy • East Falmouth, MA 02536-6527
(508) 548-0151 • http://www.falmouth.k12.ma.us/
Grade Span: PK-12; **Agency Type:** 1
Schools: 7
4 Primary; 2 Middle; 1 High; 0 Other Level
7 Regular; 0 Special Education; 0 Vocational; 0 Alternative
0 Magnet; 0 Charter; 3 Title I Eligible; 0 School-wide Title I
Students: 4,578 (50.5% male; 49.5% female)
Individual Education Program: 589 (12.9%);
English Language Learner: 43 (0.9%); Migrant: 4 (0.1%)
Eligible for Free Lunch Program: n/a
Eligible for Reduced-Price Lunch Program: n/a
Teachers: 327.3 (14.0 to 1)
Librarians/Media Specialists: 8.0 (572.3 to 1)
Guidance Counselors: 8.5 (538.6 to 1)
Current Spending: ($ per student per year):
Total: $8,463; Instruction: $5,574; Support Services: $2,663
Enrollment, Drop-out Rates and Diploma Recipients by Race/Ethnicity

Category	Total	White	Black	Asian	AIAN	Hisp.
Enrollment (%)	100.0	92.5	3.1	0.9	1.2	2.3
Drop-out Rate (%)	4.6	4.5	9.1	0.0	0.0	5.9
H.S. Diplomas (#)	238	231	1	1	2	3

Harwich

81 Oak St • Harwich, MA 02645-2701
(508) 430-7200 • http://www.harwich.edu/
Grade Span: PK-12; **Agency Type:** 1
Schools: 3
1 Primary; 1 Middle; 1 High; 0 Other Level
3 Regular; 0 Special Education; 0 Vocational; 0 Alternative
0 Magnet; 0 Charter; 2 Title I Eligible; 0 School-wide Title I
Students: 1,500 (52.1% male; 47.9% female)
Individual Education Program: 248 (16.5%);
English Language Learner: 4 (0.3%); Migrant: 0 (0.0%)
Eligible for Free Lunch Program: n/a
Eligible for Reduced-Price Lunch Program: n/a
Teachers: 122.2 (12.3 to 1)
Librarians/Media Specialists: 3.0 (500.0 to 1)
Guidance Counselors: 4.5 (333.3 to 1)
Current Spending: ($ per student per year):
Total: $9,663; Instruction: $6,501; Support Services: $2,924
Enrollment, Drop-out Rates and Diploma Recipients by Race/Ethnicity

Category	Total	White	Black	Asian	AIAN	Hisp.
Enrollment (%)	100.0	95.9	1.7	0.8	0.3	1.3
Drop-out Rate (%)	3.3	3.4	0.0	0.0	0.0	0.0
H.S. Diplomas (#)	91	88	1	0	0	2

Mashpee

150-A Old Barnstable Rd • Mashpee, MA 02649-3130
(508) 539-1500 • http://www.mashpee.k12.ma.us/
Grade Span: PK-12; **Agency Type:** 1
Schools: 3
2 Primary; 0 Middle; 0 High; 1 Other Level
3 Regular; 0 Special Education; 0 Vocational; 0 Alternative
0 Magnet; 0 Charter; 2 Title I Eligible; 0 School-wide Title I
Students: 2,218 (51.2% male; 48.8% female)
Individual Education Program: 388 (17.5%);
English Language Learner: 0 (0.0%); Migrant: 2 (0.1%)
Eligible for Free Lunch Program: n/a
Eligible for Reduced-Price Lunch Program: n/a
Teachers: 172.0 (12.9 to 1)
Librarians/Media Specialists: 3.0 (739.3 to 1)
Guidance Counselors: 15.0 (147.9 to 1)
Current Spending: ($ per student per year):
Total: $8,061; Instruction: $5,408; Support Services: $2,478
Enrollment, Drop-out Rates and Diploma Recipients by Race/Ethnicity

Category	Total	White	Black	Asian	AIAN	Hisp.
Enrollment (%)	100.0	85.1	4.9	1.0	7.0	2.0
Drop-out Rate (%)	1.7	1.5	4.2	0.0	2.6	0.0
H.S. Diplomas (#)	117	101	7	0	7	2

Nauset

78 Eldredge Pkwy • Orleans, MA 02653-3326
(508) 255-8800 • http://www.nausetschools.org
Grade Span: PK-12; **Agency Type:** 3
Schools: 2
1 Primary; 0 Middle; 1 High; 0 Other Level
2 Regular; 0 Special Education; 0 Vocational; 0 Alternative
0 Magnet; 0 Charter; 2 Title I Eligible; 0 School-wide Title I
Students: 1,847 (51.1% male; 48.9% female)
Individual Education Program: 265 (14.3%);
English Language Learner: 8 (0.4%); Migrant: 1 (0.1%)
Eligible for Free Lunch Program: n/a
Eligible for Reduced-Price Lunch Program: n/a
Teachers: 141.9 (13.0 to 1)
Librarians/Media Specialists: 2.0 (923.5 to 1)
Guidance Counselors: 6.0 (307.8 to 1)
Current Spending: ($ per student per year):
Total: $10,789; Instruction: $7,437; Support Services: $2,915
Enrollment, Drop-out Rates and Diploma Recipients by Race/Ethnicity

Category	Total	White	Black	Asian	AIAN	Hisp.
Enrollment (%)	100.0	96.3	0.9	1.2	0.4	1.2
Drop-out Rate (%)	3.3	3.3	14.3	0.0	0.0	0.0
H.S. Diplomas (#)	212	202	1	5	2	2

Sandwich

16 Dewey Ave • Sandwich, MA 02563-2096
(508) 888-1054 • http://www.sandwich.k12.ma.us/
Grade Span: PK-12; **Agency Type:** 1
Schools: 4
3 Primary; 0 Middle; 1 High; 0 Other Level
4 Regular; 0 Special Education; 0 Vocational; 0 Alternative
0 Magnet; 0 Charter; 3 Title I Eligible; 0 School-wide Title I
Students: 4,171 (51.6% male; 48.4% female)
Individual Education Program: 596 (14.3%);
English Language Learner: 4 (0.1%); Migrant: 0 (0.0%)
Eligible for Free Lunch Program: n/a
Eligible for Reduced-Price Lunch Program: n/a
Teachers: 284.0 (14.7 to 1)
Librarians/Media Specialists: 5.0 (834.2 to 1)
Guidance Counselors: 9.0 (463.4 to 1)
Current Spending: ($ per student per year):
Total: $6,700; Instruction: $4,493; Support Services: $2,007
Enrollment, Drop-out Rates and Diploma Recipients by Race/Ethnicity

Category	Total	White	Black	Asian	AIAN	Hisp.
Enrollment (%)	100.0	97.6	0.6	1.2	0.2	0.5
Drop-out Rate (%)	2.0	1.9	20.0	0.0	0.0	25.0
H.S. Diplomas (#)	237	232	2	2	0	1

Berkshire County

Adams-Cheshire

125 Savoy Rd • Cheshire, MA 01225-9522
(413) 743-2939
Grade Span: PK-12; **Agency Type:** 3
Schools: 4
2 Primary; 1 Middle; 1 High; 0 Other Level
4 Regular; 0 Special Education; 0 Vocational; 0 Alternative
0 Magnet; 0 Charter; 1 Title I Eligible; 1 School-wide Title I
Students: 1,870 (50.4% male; 49.6% female)
Individual Education Program: 304 (16.3%);
English Language Learner: 1 (0.1%); Migrant: 0 (0.0%)
Eligible for Free Lunch Program: n/a
Eligible for Reduced-Price Lunch Program: n/a
Teachers: 130.7 (14.3 to 1)
Librarians/Media Specialists: 1.0 (1,870.0 to 1)
Guidance Counselors: 7.6 (246.1 to 1)
Current Spending: ($ per student per year):
Total: $8,369; Instruction: $5,607; Support Services: $2,448
Enrollment, Drop-out Rates and Diploma Recipients by Race/Ethnicity

Category	Total	White	Black	Asian	AIAN	Hisp.
Enrollment (%)	100.0	95.3	2.3	0.7	0.7	0.9
Drop-out Rate (%)	4.2	4.3	0.0	0.0	0.0	n/a
H.S. Diplomas (#)	112	109	1	2	0	0

Berkshire Hills

Bhrsd - PO Box 956 • Stockbridge, MA 01262-0956
(413) 298-3711 • http://www.bhrsd.org/
Grade Span: PK-12; **Agency Type:** 3
Schools: 6
4 Primary; 1 Middle; 1 High; 0 Other Level
6 Regular; 0 Special Education; 0 Vocational; 0 Alternative
0 Magnet; 0 Charter; 4 Title I Eligible; 0 School-wide Title I
Students: 1,519 (52.0% male; 48.0% female)
Individual Education Program: 231 (15.2%);
English Language Learner: 21 (1.4%); Migrant: 7 (0.5%)
Eligible for Free Lunch Program: n/a
Eligible for Reduced-Price Lunch Program: n/a
Teachers: 133.7 (11.4 to 1)
Librarians/Media Specialists: 0.0 (0.0 to 1)
Guidance Counselors: 4.0 (379.8 to 1)
Current Spending: ($ per student per year):
Total: $11,949; Instruction: $8,285; Support Services: $3,370
Enrollment, Drop-out Rates and Diploma Recipients by Race/Ethnicity

Category	Total	White	Black	Asian	AIAN	Hisp.
Enrollment (%)	100.0	93.4	2.0	1.5	0.1	3.0
Drop-out Rate (%)	1.4	1.5	0.0	0.0	n/a	0.0
H.S. Diplomas (#)	148	144	1	1	0	2

Central Berkshire

20 Cleveland • Dalton, MA 01227-0299
Mailing Address: PO Box 299 • Dalton, MA 01227-0299
(413) 684-0320 • http://www.cbrsd.org/
Grade Span: PK-12; **Agency Type:** 3
Schools: 6
4 Primary; 1 Middle; 1 High; 0 Other Level
6 Regular; 0 Special Education; 0 Vocational; 0 Alternative
0 Magnet; 0 Charter; 5 Title I Eligible; 0 School-wide Title I
Students: 2,316 (53.6% male; 46.4% female)
Individual Education Program: 362 (15.6%);
English Language Learner: 0 (0.0%); Migrant: 0 (0.0%)
Eligible for Free Lunch Program: n/a
Eligible for Reduced-Price Lunch Program: n/a
Teachers: 156.6 (14.8 to 1)
Librarians/Media Specialists: 2.7 (857.8 to 1)
Guidance Counselors: 5.0 (463.2 to 1)
Current Spending: ($ per student per year):
Total: $9,120; Instruction: $5,919; Support Services: $2,909
Enrollment, Drop-out Rates and Diploma Recipients by Race/Ethnicity

Category	Total	White	Black	Asian	AIAN	Hisp.
Enrollment (%)	100.0	97.4	0.9	1.2	0.1	0.4
Drop-out Rate (%)	5.4	5.5	0.0	0.0	n/a	0.0
H.S. Diplomas (#)	171	170	0	1	0	0

North Adams

191 E Main St • North Adams, MA 01247-4434
(413) 662-3225 • http://www.northadamsschools.com
Grade Span: PK-12; **Agency Type:** 1
Schools: 5
3 Primary; 1 Middle; 1 High; 0 Other Level
5 Regular; 0 Special Education; 0 Vocational; 0 Alternative
0 Magnet; 0 Charter; 4 Title I Eligible; 4 School-wide Title I
Students: 2,117 (48.3% male; 51.7% female)
Individual Education Program: 356 (16.8%);
English Language Learner: 23 (1.1%); Migrant: 3 (0.1%)
Eligible for Free Lunch Program: n/a
Eligible for Reduced-Price Lunch Program: n/a
Teachers: 242.1 (8.7 to 1)
Librarians/Media Specialists: 1.0 (2,117.0 to 1)
Guidance Counselors: 3.0 (705.7 to 1)
Current Spending: ($ per student per year):
Total: $9,585; Instruction: $7,237; Support Services: $2,237
Enrollment, Drop-out Rates and Diploma Recipients by Race/Ethnicity

Category	Total	White	Black	Asian	AIAN	Hisp.
Enrollment (%)	100.0	91.1	4.1	1.3	0.3	3.2
Drop-out Rate (%)	7.7	6.7	35.7	0.0	100.0	16.7
H.S. Diplomas (#)	105	99	1	4	0	1

Pittsfield

269 First St • Pittsfield, MA 01201-4727
(413) 499-9512 • http://www.pittsfield.net/
Grade Span: PK-12; **Agency Type:** 1
Schools: 13
8 Primary; 2 Middle; 2 High; 1 Other Level
12 Regular; 0 Special Education; 0 Vocational; 1 Alternative
0 Magnet; 0 Charter; 3 Title I Eligible; 1 School-wide Title I
Students: 6,714 (51.5% male; 48.5% female)
Individual Education Program: 928 (13.8%);
English Language Learner: 132 (2.0%); Migrant: 0 (0.0%)
Eligible for Free Lunch Program: n/a
Eligible for Reduced-Price Lunch Program: n/a
Teachers: 668.8 (10.0 to 1)
Librarians/Media Specialists: 12.0 (559.5 to 1)
Guidance Counselors: 27.0 (248.7 to 1)
Current Spending: ($ per student per year):
Total: $9,864; Instruction: $6,801; Support Services: $2,723
Enrollment, Drop-out Rates and Diploma Recipients by Race/Ethnicity

Category	Total	White	Black	Asian	AIAN	Hisp.
Enrollment (%)	100.0	86.4	8.4	1.4	0.3	3.5
Drop-out Rate (%)	8.9	8.0	18.0	11.1	n/a	18.5
H.S. Diplomas (#)	316	291	13	6	0	6

Bristol County

Attleboro

100 Rathbun Willard Dr • Attleboro, MA 02703-2799
(508) 222-0012 • http://www.attleboroschools.com/
Grade Span: PK-12; **Agency Type:** 1
Schools: 11
6 Primary; 3 Middle; 2 High; 0 Other Level
10 Regular; 0 Special Education; 1 Vocational; 0 Alternative
0 Magnet; 0 Charter; 6 Title I Eligible; 0 School-wide Title I
Students: 6,728 (51.6% male; 48.4% female)
Individual Education Program: 1,021 (15.2%);
English Language Learner: 207 (3.1%); Migrant: 1 (<0.1%)
Eligible for Free Lunch Program: n/a
Eligible for Reduced-Price Lunch Program: n/a
Teachers: 317.5 (21.2 to 1)
Librarians/Media Specialists: 3.0 (2,242.7 to 1)
Guidance Counselors: 6.6 (1,019.4 to 1)
Current Spending: ($ per student per year):
Total: $7,554; Instruction: $5,106; Support Services: $2,163

Enrollment, Drop-out Rates and Diploma Recipients by Race/Ethnicity

Category	Total	White	Black	Asian	AIAN	Hisp.
Enrollment (%)	100.0	85.1	3.4	5.5	0.3	5.8
Drop-out Rate (%)	7.7	7.0	7.3	13.5	0.0	12.0
H.S. Diplomas (#)	342	308	5	18	0	11

Bridgewater-Raynham

687 Pleasant St • Raynham, MA 02767-1534
(508) 824-2730 • http://bridge-rayn.org/
Grade Span: PK-12; **Agency Type:** 3
Schools: 8
5 Primary; 2 Middle; 1 High; 0 Other Level
8 Regular; 0 Special Education; 0 Vocational; 0 Alternative
0 Magnet; 0 Charter; 3 Title I Eligible; 0 School-wide Title I
Students: 6,156 (51.1% male; 48.9% female)
Individual Education Program: 916 (14.9%);
English Language Learner: 3 (<0.1%); Migrant: 0 (0.0%)
Eligible for Free Lunch Program: n/a
Eligible for Reduced-Price Lunch Program: n/a
Teachers: 339.3 (18.1 to 1)
Librarians/Media Specialists: 4.0 (1,539.0 to 1)
Guidance Counselors: 6.0 (1,026.0 to 1)
Current Spending: ($ per student per year):
Total: $7,255; Instruction: $5,121; Support Services: $1,881
Enrollment, Drop-out Rates and Diploma Recipients by Race/Ethnicity

Category	Total	White	Black	Asian	AIAN	Hisp.
Enrollment (%)	100.0	95.5	2.1	1.2	0.2	0.9
Drop-out Rate (%)	0.8	0.9	0.0	0.0	0.0	0.0
H.S. Diplomas (#)	331	320	3	5	0	3

Dartmouth

8 Bush St • South Dartmouth, MA 02748-3102
(508) 997-3391 • http://dartmouth.mec.edu/
Grade Span: PK-12; **Agency Type:** 1
Schools: 6
5 Primary; 0 Middle; 1 High; 0 Other Level
6 Regular; 0 Special Education; 0 Vocational; 0 Alternative
0 Magnet; 0 Charter; 3 Title I Eligible; 0 School-wide Title I
Students: 4,250 (51.9% male; 48.1% female)
Individual Education Program: 601 (14.1%);
English Language Learner: 38 (0.9%); Migrant: 0 (0.0%)
Eligible for Free Lunch Program: n/a
Eligible for Reduced-Price Lunch Program: n/a
Teachers: 260.3 (16.3 to 1)
Librarians/Media Specialists: 2.0 (2,125.0 to 1)
Guidance Counselors: 12.0 (354.2 to 1)
Current Spending: ($ per student per year):
Total: $7,371; Instruction: $5,058; Support Services: $2,060
Enrollment, Drop-out Rates and Diploma Recipients by Race/Ethnicity

Category	Total	White	Black	Asian	AIAN	Hisp.
Enrollment (%)	100.0	95.0	1.6	2.1	0.4	1.0
Drop-out Rate (%)	2.8	2.9	0.0	0.0	0.0	0.0
H.S. Diplomas (#)	303	291	2	4	2	4

Dighton-Rehoboth

340 Anawan St • Rehoboth, MA 02769-2617
(508) 252-5000
Grade Span: PK-12; **Agency Type:** 3
Schools: 5
2 Primary; 2 Middle; 1 High; 0 Other Level
5 Regular; 0 Special Education; 0 Vocational; 0 Alternative
0 Magnet; 0 Charter; 0 Title I Eligible; 0 School-wide Title I
Students: 3,307 (52.1% male; 47.9% female)
Individual Education Program: 414 (12.5%);
English Language Learner: 1 (<0.1%); Migrant: 0 (0.0%)
Eligible for Free Lunch Program: n/a
Eligible for Reduced-Price Lunch Program: n/a
Teachers: 244.8 (13.5 to 1)
Librarians/Media Specialists: 4.0 (826.8 to 1)
Guidance Counselors: 7.0 (472.4 to 1)
Current Spending: ($ per student per year):
Total: $7,137; Instruction: $4,817; Support Services: $2,307
Enrollment, Drop-out Rates and Diploma Recipients by Race/Ethnicity

Category	Total	White	Black	Asian	AIAN	Hisp.
Enrollment (%)	100.0	97.6	0.9	1.0	0.1	0.4
Drop-out Rate (%)	2.0	2.1	0.0	0.0	n/a	0.0
H.S. Diplomas (#)	205	199	4	2	0	0

Easton

50 Oliver • North Easton, MA 02356-0359
Mailing Address: PO Box 359 • North Easton, MA 02356-0359
(508) 230-3200 • http://www.easton.k12.ma.us/
Grade Span: PK-12; **Agency Type:** 1
Schools: 7
4 Primary; 2 Middle; 1 High; 0 Other Level
7 Regular; 0 Special Education; 0 Vocational; 0 Alternative
0 Magnet; 0 Charter; 3 Title I Eligible; 0 School-wide Title I
Students: 3,843 (51.9% male; 48.1% female)
Individual Education Program: 648 (16.9%);
English Language Learner: 9 (0.2%); Migrant: 0 (0.0%)
Eligible for Free Lunch Program: n/a
Eligible for Reduced-Price Lunch Program: n/a
Teachers: 246.3 (15.6 to 1)
Librarians/Media Specialists: 0.0 (0.0 to 1)
Guidance Counselors: 7.0 (549.0 to 1)
Current Spending: ($ per student per year):
Total: $7,205; Instruction: $4,918; Support Services: $2,100
Enrollment, Drop-out Rates and Diploma Recipients by Race/Ethnicity

Category	Total	White	Black	Asian	AIAN	Hisp.
Enrollment (%)	100.0	94.0	2.2	2.3	0.2	1.4
Drop-out Rate (%)	0.3	0.3	0.0	0.0	n/a	0.0
H.S. Diplomas (#)	271	251	9	7	0	4

Fairhaven

128 Washington St • Fairhaven, MA 02719-4037
(508) 979-4000 • http://www.fairhavenps.org/
Grade Span: PK-12; **Agency Type:** 1
Schools: 6
4 Primary; 1 Middle; 1 High; 0 Other Level
6 Regular; 0 Special Education; 0 Vocational; 0 Alternative
0 Magnet; 0 Charter; 5 Title I Eligible; 0 School-wide Title I
Students: 2,343 (50.6% male; 49.4% female)
Individual Education Program: 322 (13.7%);
English Language Learner: 1 (<0.1%); Migrant: 0 (0.0%)
Eligible for Free Lunch Program: n/a
Eligible for Reduced-Price Lunch Program: n/a
Teachers: 156.2 (15.0 to 1)
Librarians/Media Specialists: 0.2 (11,715.0 to 1)
Guidance Counselors: 5.0 (468.6 to 1)
Current Spending: ($ per student per year):
Total: $8,468; Instruction: $5,179; Support Services: $2,961
Enrollment, Drop-out Rates and Diploma Recipients by Race/Ethnicity

Category	Total	White	Black	Asian	AIAN	Hisp.
Enrollment (%)	100.0	96.5	2.0	0.5	0.2	0.8
Drop-out Rate (%)	4.9	5.2	0.0	0.0	0.0	0.0
H.S. Diplomas (#)	129	125	2	1	0	1

Fall River

417 Rock St • Fall River, MA 02720-3344
(508) 675-8442 • http://www.fallriver.k12.ma.us/
Grade Span: PK-12; **Agency Type:** 1
Schools: 35
29 Primary; 5 Middle; 1 High; 0 Other Level
32 Regular; 0 Special Education; 0 Vocational; 3 Alternative
0 Magnet; 0 Charter; 24 Title I Eligible; 24 School-wide Title I
Students: 12,128 (51.1% male; 48.9% female)
Individual Education Program: 1,790 (14.8%);
English Language Learner: 664 (5.5%); Migrant: 236 (1.9%)
Eligible for Free Lunch Program: n/a
Eligible for Reduced-Price Lunch Program: n/a
Teachers: 701.2 (17.3 to 1)
Librarians/Media Specialists: 5.8 (2,091.0 to 1)
Guidance Counselors: 23.0 (527.3 to 1)
Current Spending: ($ per student per year):
Total: $9,816; Instruction: $7,090; Support Services: $2,424
Enrollment, Drop-out Rates and Diploma Recipients by Race/Ethnicity

Category	Total	White	Black	Asian	AIAN	Hisp.
Enrollment (%)	100.0	77.3	8.1	5.1	0.6	9.0
Drop-out Rate (%)	6.9	6.5	8.5	8.8	5.6	10.8
H.S. Diplomas (#)	499	422	18	38	3	18

Freetown-Lakeville

98 Howland Rd • Lakeville, MA 02347-2230
(508) 923-2000 • http://www.freelake.mec.edu/
Grade Span: 05-12; **Agency Type:** 3
Schools: 2
0 Primary; 1 Middle; 1 High; 0 Other Level
2 Regular; 0 Special Education; 0 Vocational; 0 Alternative
0 Magnet; 0 Charter; 1 Title I Eligible; 0 School-wide Title I
Students: 1,828 (49.3% male; 50.7% female)
Individual Education Program: 221 (12.1%);
English Language Learner: 0 (0.0%); Migrant: 0 (0.0%)
Eligible for Free Lunch Program: n/a
Eligible for Reduced-Price Lunch Program: n/a
Teachers: 127.6 (14.3 to 1)
Librarians/Media Specialists: 2.0 (914.0 to 1)
Guidance Counselors: 6.0 (304.7 to 1)
Current Spending: ($ per student per year):
Total: $8,112; Instruction: $5,271; Support Services: $2,564

Enrollment, Drop-out Rates and Diploma Recipients by Race/Ethnicity

Category	Total	White	Black	Asian	AIAN	Hisp.
Enrollment (%)	100.0	98.1	1.4	0.1	0.0	0.4
Drop-out Rate (%)	3.1	3.0	20.0	0.0	n/a	0.0
H.S. Diplomas (#)	148	145	2	0	0	1

Greater New Bedford

1121 Ashley Blvd • New Bedford, MA 02745-2419
(508) 998-3321 • http://www.gnbvt.edu/
Grade Span: 09-12; **Agency Type:** 4
Schools: 1
0 Primary; 0 Middle; 1 High; 0 Other Level
0 Regular; 0 Special Education; 1 Vocational; 0 Alternative
0 Magnet; 0 Charter; 1 Title I Eligible; 0 School-wide Title I
Students: 1,825 (55.5% male; 44.5% female)
Individual Education Program: 188 (10.3%);
English Language Learner: 59 (3.2%); Migrant: 0 (0.0%)
Eligible for Free Lunch Program: n/a
Eligible for Reduced-Price Lunch Program: n/a
Teachers: 88.0 (20.7 to 1)
Librarians/Media Specialists: 0.0 (0.0 to 1)
Guidance Counselors: 9.0 (202.8 to 1)
Current Spending: ($ per student per year):
Total: $12,354; Instruction: $7,596; Support Services: $4,426
Enrollment, Drop-out Rates and Diploma Recipients by Race/Ethnicity

Category	Total	White	Black	Asian	AIAN	Hisp.
Enrollment (%)	100.0	81.4	8.8	0.6	0.6	8.6
Drop-out Rate (%)	3.9	3.6	0.7	50.0	9.1	8.1
H.S. Diplomas (#)	258	228	13	3	1	13

Mansfield

2 Park Row • Mansfield, MA 02048-2433
(508) 261-7500 • http://www.mansfieldschools.com/
Grade Span: PK-12; **Agency Type:** 1
Schools: 5
3 Primary; 1 Middle; 1 High; 0 Other Level
5 Regular; 0 Special Education; 0 Vocational; 0 Alternative
0 Magnet; 0 Charter; 1 Title I Eligible; 0 School-wide Title I
Students: 4,535 (52.7% male; 47.3% female)
Individual Education Program: 628 (13.8%);
English Language Learner: 16 (0.4%); Migrant: 0 (0.0%)
Eligible for Free Lunch Program: n/a
Eligible for Reduced-Price Lunch Program: n/a
Teachers: 456.5 (9.9 to 1)
Librarians/Media Specialists: 1.0 (4,535.0 to 1)
Guidance Counselors: 6.0 (755.8 to 1)
Current Spending: ($ per student per year):
Total: $7,614; Instruction: $5,291; Support Services: $2,159
Enrollment, Drop-out Rates and Diploma Recipients by Race/Ethnicity

Category	Total	White	Black	Asian	AIAN	Hisp.
Enrollment (%)	100.0	94.0	3.0	1.5	0.7	0.9
Drop-out Rate (%)	0.3	0.4	0.0	0.0	n/a	0.0
H.S. Diplomas (#)	209	197	8	2	0	2

New Bedford

455 County St • New Bedford, MA 02740-5194
(508) 997-4511 • http://www.newbedford.k12.ma.us/
Grade Span: PK-12; **Agency Type:** 1
Schools: 28
23 Primary; 3 Middle; 2 High; 0 Other Level
28 Regular; 0 Special Education; 0 Vocational; 0 Alternative
0 Magnet; 0 Charter; 25 Title I Eligible; 23 School-wide Title I
Students: 14,580 (51.3% male; 48.7% female)
Individual Education Program: 2,619 (18.0%);
English Language Learner: 530 (3.6%); Migrant: 143 (1.0%)
Eligible for Free Lunch Program: n/a
Eligible for Reduced-Price Lunch Program: n/a
Teachers: 1,295.2 (11.3 to 1)
Librarians/Media Specialists: 6.0 (2,430.0 to 1)
Guidance Counselors: 89.5 (162.9 to 1)
Current Spending: ($ per student per year):
Total: $9,521; Instruction: $6,229; Support Services: $2,875
Enrollment, Drop-out Rates and Diploma Recipients by Race/Ethnicity

Category	Total	White	Black	Asian	AIAN	Hisp.
Enrollment (%)	100.0	65.6	15.2	0.9	0.4	17.9
Drop-out Rate (%)	7.0	6.3	8.3	10.6	0.0	9.2
H.S. Diplomas (#)	565	428	83	6	0	48

North Attleborough

6 Morse St • North Attleborough, MA 02760-2702
(508) 643-2100 • http://www.naschools.net/
Grade Span: PK-12; **Agency Type:** 1
Schools: 9
7 Primary; 1 Middle; 1 High; 0 Other Level
9 Regular; 0 Special Education; 0 Vocational; 0 Alternative
0 Magnet; 0 Charter; 2 Title I Eligible; 0 School-wide Title I
Students: 4,685 (52.3% male; 47.7% female)
Individual Education Program: 696 (14.9%);
English Language Learner: 33 (0.7%); Migrant: 0 (0.0%)
Eligible for Free Lunch Program: n/a
Eligible for Reduced-Price Lunch Program: n/a
Teachers: 301.2 (15.6 to 1)
Librarians/Media Specialists: 4.5 (1,041.1 to 1)
Guidance Counselors: 12.5 (374.8 to 1)
Current Spending: ($ per student per year):
Total: $7,562; Instruction: $5,215; Support Services: $2,099
Enrollment, Drop-out Rates and Diploma Recipients by Race/Ethnicity

Category	Total	White	Black	Asian	AIAN	Hisp.
Enrollment (%)	100.0	95.4	1.1	2.2	0.3	1.1
Drop-out Rate (%)	1.8	1.9	0.0	0.0	0.0	0.0
H.S. Diplomas (#)	263	242	4	10	0	7

Norton

64 W Main St • Norton, MA 02766-2713
(508) 285-0100 • http://www.norton.mec.edu/index.htm
Grade Span: PK-12; **Agency Type:** 1
Schools: 5
2 Primary; 2 Middle; 1 High; 0 Other Level
5 Regular; 0 Special Education; 0 Vocational; 0 Alternative
0 Magnet; 0 Charter; 3 Title I Eligible; 0 School-wide Title I
Students: 3,231 (52.6% male; 47.4% female)
Individual Education Program: 688 (21.3%);
English Language Learner: 0 (0.0%); Migrant: 0 (0.0%)
Eligible for Free Lunch Program: n/a
Eligible for Reduced-Price Lunch Program: n/a
Teachers: 204.2 (15.8 to 1)
Librarians/Media Specialists: 1.0 (3,231.0 to 1)
Guidance Counselors: 7.5 (430.8 to 1)
Current Spending: ($ per student per year):
Total: $6,887; Instruction: $4,584; Support Services: $2,077
Enrollment, Drop-out Rates and Diploma Recipients by Race/Ethnicity

Category	Total	White	Black	Asian	AIAN	Hisp.
Enrollment (%)	100.0	96.9	1.4	1.1	0.1	0.4
Drop-out Rate (%)	3.3	3.4	0.0	0.0	0.0	n/a
H.S. Diplomas (#)	128	125	2	1	0	0

Seekonk

69 School St • Seekonk, MA 02771-5992
(508) 336-7711 • http://seekonkschools.lucasproject.com/controller.action
Grade Span: PK-12; **Agency Type:** 1
Schools: 5
3 Primary; 1 Middle; 1 High; 0 Other Level
5 Regular; 0 Special Education; 0 Vocational; 0 Alternative
0 Magnet; 0 Charter; 3 Title I Eligible; 0 School-wide Title I
Students: 2,307 (50.2% male; 49.8% female)
Individual Education Program: 239 (10.4%);
English Language Learner: 0 (0.0%); Migrant: 0 (0.0%)
Eligible for Free Lunch Program: n/a
Eligible for Reduced-Price Lunch Program: n/a
Teachers: 162.7 (14.2 to 1)
Librarians/Media Specialists: 3.0 (769.0 to 1)
Guidance Counselors: 5.0 (461.4 to 1)
Current Spending: ($ per student per year):
Total: $8,063; Instruction: $5,280; Support Services: $2,573
Enrollment, Drop-out Rates and Diploma Recipients by Race/Ethnicity

Category	Total	White	Black	Asian	AIAN	Hisp.
Enrollment (%)	100.0	96.4	1.3	1.4	0.4	0.4
Drop-out Rate (%)	0.7	0.7	0.0	0.0	0.0	0.0
H.S. Diplomas (#)	128	123	3	2	0	0

Somerset

580 Whetstone Hill Rd • Somerset, MA 02726-3702
(508) 324-3100 • http://www.somerset.k12.ma.us/SchoolFrontEnd/
Grade Span: PK-12; **Agency Type:** 1
Schools: 6
4 Primary; 1 Middle; 1 High; 0 Other Level
6 Regular; 0 Special Education; 0 Vocational; 0 Alternative
0 Magnet; 0 Charter; 4 Title I Eligible; 0 School-wide Title I
Students: 2,891 (50.4% male; 49.6% female)
Individual Education Program: 242 (8.4%);
English Language Learner: 0 (0.0%); Migrant: 0 (0.0%)
Eligible for Free Lunch Program: n/a
Eligible for Reduced-Price Lunch Program: n/a
Teachers: 229.9 (12.6 to 1)
Librarians/Media Specialists: 3.0 (963.7 to 1)
Guidance Counselors: 6.0 (481.8 to 1)
Current Spending: ($ per student per year):
Total: $8,705; Instruction: $5,772; Support Services: $2,726

Enrollment, Drop-out Rates and Diploma Recipients by Race/Ethnicity

Category	Total	White	Black	Asian	AIAN	Hisp.
Enrollment (%)	100.0	97.5	1.0	0.8	0.2	0.5
Drop-out Rate (%)	2.6	2.5	50.0	0.0	n/a	n/a
H.S. Diplomas (#)	211	210	1	0	0	0

Swansea

1 Gardner's Neck Rd • Swansea, MA 02777-3201
(508) 675-1195
Grade Span: PK-12; **Agency Type:** 1
Schools: 6
2 Primary; 1 Middle; 1 High; 0 Other Level
6 Regular; 0 Special Education; 0 Vocational; 0 Alternative
0 Magnet; 0 Charter; 5 Title I Eligible; 1 School-wide Title I
Students: 2,232 (52.7% male; 47.3% female)
Individual Education Program: 326 (14.6%);
English Language Learner: 0 (0.0%); Migrant: 0 (0.0%)
Eligible for Free Lunch Program: n/a
Eligible for Reduced-Price Lunch Program: n/a
Teachers: 163.9 (13.6 to 1)
Librarians/Media Specialists: 1.0 (2,232.0 to 1)
Guidance Counselors: 5.5 (405.8 to 1)
Current Spending: ($ per student per year):
Total: $7,962; Instruction: $5,276; Support Services: $2,351

Enrollment, Drop-out Rates and Diploma Recipients by Race/Ethnicity

Category	Total	White	Black	Asian	AIAN	Hisp.
Enrollment (%)	100.0	97.7	1.1	1.0	0.0	0.2
Drop-out Rate (%)	2.6	2.6	0.0	0.0	0.0	n/a
H.S. Diplomas (#)	148	146	0	1	0	1

Taunton

50 Williams St • Taunton, MA 02780-2747
(508) 821-1201 • http://www.tauntonschools.org/
Grade Span: PK-12; **Agency Type:** 1
Schools: 16
11 Primary; 4 Middle; 1 High; 0 Other Level
16 Regular; 0 Special Education; 0 Vocational; 0 Alternative
0 Magnet; 0 Charter; 6 Title I Eligible; 6 School-wide Title I
Students: 8,381 (51.5% male; 48.5% female)
Individual Education Program: 1,392 (16.6%);
English Language Learner: 258 (3.1%); Migrant: 6 (0.1%)
Eligible for Free Lunch Program: n/a
Eligible for Reduced-Price Lunch Program: n/a
Teachers: 529.0 (15.8 to 1)
Librarians/Media Specialists: 7.0 (1,197.3 to 1)
Guidance Counselors: 21.5 (389.8 to 1)
Current Spending: ($ per student per year):
Total: $7,899; Instruction: $5,348; Support Services: $2,214

Enrollment, Drop-out Rates and Diploma Recipients by Race/Ethnicity

Category	Total	White	Black	Asian	AIAN	Hisp.
Enrollment (%)	100.0	86.5	6.2	0.9	0.1	6.3
Drop-out Rate (%)	3.7	3.3	4.9	5.0	n/a	6.3
H.S. Diplomas (#)	316	275	16	5	0	20

Westport

17 Main Rd • Westport, MA 02790-4201
(508) 636-1137 • http://www.westportschools.org/
Grade Span: PK-12; **Agency Type:** 1
Schools: 4
2 Primary; 1 Middle; 1 High; 0 Other Level
4 Regular; 0 Special Education; 0 Vocational; 0 Alternative
0 Magnet; 0 Charter; 1 Title I Eligible; 0 School-wide Title I
Students: 1,972 (51.4% male; 48.6% female)
Individual Education Program: 282 (14.3%);
English Language Learner: 0 (0.0%); Migrant: 2 (0.1%)
Eligible for Free Lunch Program: n/a
Eligible for Reduced-Price Lunch Program: n/a
Teachers: 154.1 (12.8 to 1)
Librarians/Media Specialists: 3.0 (657.3 to 1)
Guidance Counselors: 3.5 (563.4 to 1)
Current Spending: ($ per student per year):
Total: $7,457; Instruction: $4,467; Support Services: $2,704

Enrollment, Drop-out Rates and Diploma Recipients by Race/Ethnicity

Category	Total	White	Black	Asian	AIAN	Hisp.
Enrollment (%)	100.0	98.1	0.6	0.6	0.2	0.6
Drop-out Rate (%)	4.6	4.6	0.0	0.0	n/a	n/a
H.S. Diplomas (#)	81	79	1	1	0	0

Essex County

Amesbury

10 Congress St • Amesbury, MA 01913-2812
(978) 388-0507 •
http://www.ci.amesbury.ma.us/home.nfs?a=amesbury&s=1091469238:185 25&group=2
Grade Span: PK-12; **Agency Type:** 1
Schools: 4
2 Primary; 1 Middle; 1 High; 0 Other Level
4 Regular; 0 Special Education; 0 Vocational; 0 Alternative
0 Magnet; 0 Charter; 2 Title I Eligible; 0 School-wide Title I
Students: 2,773 (51.4% male; 48.6% female)
Individual Education Program: 427 (15.4%);
English Language Learner: 12 (0.4%); Migrant: 0 (0.0%)
Eligible for Free Lunch Program: n/a
Eligible for Reduced-Price Lunch Program: n/a
Teachers: 208.0 (13.3 to 1)
Librarians/Media Specialists: 4.0 (693.3 to 1)
Guidance Counselors: 4.0 (693.3 to 1)
Current Spending: ($ per student per year):
Total: $8,556; Instruction: $5,857; Support Services: $2,427

Enrollment, Drop-out Rates and Diploma Recipients by Race/Ethnicity

Category	Total	White	Black	Asian	AIAN	Hisp.
Enrollment (%)	100.0	96.1	1.1	0.8	0.3	1.6
Drop-out Rate (%)	4.3	4.2	0.0	0.0	0.0	50.0
H.S. Diplomas (#)	174	172	1	0	1	0

Andover

36 Bartlet St • Andover, MA 01810-3813
(978) 623-8501 • http://www.aps1.net/
Grade Span: PK-12; **Agency Type:** 1
Schools: 10
6 Primary; 3 Middle; 1 High; 0 Other Level
10 Regular; 0 Special Education; 0 Vocational; 0 Alternative
0 Magnet; 0 Charter; 2 Title I Eligible; 0 School-wide Title I
Students: 5,915 (51.8% male; 48.2% female)
Individual Education Program: 779 (13.2%);
English Language Learner: 21 (0.4%); Migrant: 4 (0.1%)
Eligible for Free Lunch Program: n/a
Eligible for Reduced-Price Lunch Program: n/a
Teachers: 451.2 (13.1 to 1)
Librarians/Media Specialists: 9.5 (622.6 to 1)
Guidance Counselors: 11.0 (537.7 to 1)
Current Spending: ($ per student per year):
Total: $8,986; Instruction: $5,871; Support Services: $2,929

Enrollment, Drop-out Rates and Diploma Recipients by Race/Ethnicity

Category	Total	White	Black	Asian	AIAN	Hisp.
Enrollment (%)	100.0	88.9	0.9	7.8	0.1	2.3
Drop-out Rate (%)	0.1	0.1	0.0	0.0	0.0	0.0
H.S. Diplomas (#)	383	337	5	36	0	5

Beverly

20 Colon St • Beverly, MA 01915-3444
(978) 921-6100 • http://www.beverlyschools.org/index2.shtm
Grade Span: PK-12; **Agency Type:** 1
Schools: 9
6 Primary; 2 Middle; 1 High; 0 Other Level
9 Regular; 0 Special Education; 0 Vocational; 0 Alternative
0 Magnet; 0 Charter; 4 Title I Eligible; 0 School-wide Title I
Students: 4,648 (50.4% male; 49.6% female)
Individual Education Program: 699 (15.0%);
English Language Learner: 79 (1.7%); Migrant: 3 (0.1%)
Eligible for Free Lunch Program: n/a
Eligible for Reduced-Price Lunch Program: n/a
Teachers: 349.6 (13.3 to 1)
Librarians/Media Specialists: 8.0 (581.0 to 1)
Guidance Counselors: 11.0 (422.5 to 1)
Current Spending: ($ per student per year):
Total: $8,750; Instruction: $6,011; Support Services: $2,456

Enrollment, Drop-out Rates and Diploma Recipients by Race/Ethnicity

Category	Total	White	Black	Asian	AIAN	Hisp.
Enrollment (%)	100.0	92.4	2.4	1.2	0.2	3.8
Drop-out Rate (%)	3.1	2.8	11.1	0.0	0.0	23.5
H.S. Diplomas (#)	285	276	2	2	0	5

Danvers

64 Cabot Rd • Danvers, MA 01923-2355
(978) 777-4539 • http://www.danvers.mec.edu/
Grade Span: PK-12; **Agency Type:** 1
Schools: 7
5 Primary; 1 Middle; 1 High; 0 Other Level
7 Regular; 0 Special Education; 0 Vocational; 0 Alternative
0 Magnet; 0 Charter; 5 Title I Eligible; 0 School-wide Title I
Students: 3,696 (48.5% male; 51.5% female)

Individual Education Program: 400 (10.8%);
English Language Learner: 14 (0.4%); Migrant: 0 (0.0%)
Eligible for Free Lunch Program: n/a
Eligible for Reduced-Price Lunch Program: n/a
Teachers: 280.2 (13.2 to 1)
Librarians/Media Specialists: 2.0 (1,848.0 to 1)
Guidance Counselors: 7.0 (528.0 to 1)
Current Spending: ($ per student per year):
Total: $8,299; Instruction: $5,588; Support Services: $2,520

Enrollment, Drop-out Rates and Diploma Recipients by Race/Ethnicity

Category	Total	White	Black	Asian	AIAN	Hisp.
Enrollment (%)	100.0	96.7	0.5	1.2	0.1	1.5
Drop-out Rate (%)	1.2	1.3	0.0	0.0	n/a	0.0
H.S. Diplomas (#)	238	234	0	3	0	1

Georgetown

51 N St • Georgetown, MA 01833-1699
(978) 352-5777
Grade Span: PK-12; **Agency Type:** 1
Schools: 3
2 Primary; 0 Middle; 0 High; 1 Other Level
3 Regular; 0 Special Education; 0 Vocational; 0 Alternative
0 Magnet; 0 Charter; 2 Title I Eligible; 0 School-wide Title I
Students: 1,622 (51.4% male; 48.6% female)
Individual Education Program: 199 (12.3%);
English Language Learner: 0 (0.0%); Migrant: 0 (0.0%)
Eligible for Free Lunch Program: n/a
Eligible for Reduced-Price Lunch Program: n/a
Teachers: 122.6 (13.2 to 1)
Librarians/Media Specialists: 1.0 (1,622.0 to 1)
Guidance Counselors: 4.7 (345.1 to 1)
Current Spending: ($ per student per year):
Total: $7,525; Instruction: $5,077; Support Services: $2,157

Enrollment, Drop-out Rates and Diploma Recipients by Race/Ethnicity

Category	Total	White	Black	Asian	AIAN	Hisp.
Enrollment (%)	100.0	96.7	0.4	1.3	0.2	1.3
Drop-out Rate (%)	1.5	1.5	0.0	0.0	0.0	0.0
H.S. Diplomas (#)	94	92	0	0	1	1

Gloucester

6 School House Rd • Gloucester, MA 01930-2702
(978) 281-9800 • http://www.gloucester.k12.ma.us/
Grade Span: PK-12; **Agency Type:** 1
Schools: 8
6 Primary; 1 Middle; 1 High; 0 Other Level
8 Regular; 0 Special Education; 0 Vocational; 0 Alternative
0 Magnet; 0 Charter; 2 Title I Eligible; 0 School-wide Title I
Students: 4,146 (52.1% male; 47.9% female)
Individual Education Program: 704 (17.0%);
English Language Learner: 39 (0.9%); Migrant: 93 (2.2%)
Eligible for Free Lunch Program: n/a
Eligible for Reduced-Price Lunch Program: n/a
Teachers: 323.7 (12.8 to 1)
Librarians/Media Specialists: 1.0 (4,146.0 to 1)
Guidance Counselors: 9.0 (460.7 to 1)
Current Spending: ($ per student per year):
Total: $8,344; Instruction: $5,727; Support Services: $2,320

Enrollment, Drop-out Rates and Diploma Recipients by Race/Ethnicity

Category	Total	White	Black	Asian	AIAN	Hisp.
Enrollment (%)	100.0	95.2	1.3	0.8	0.0	2.7
Drop-out Rate (%)	3.3	2.9	20.0	50.0	0.0	11.5
H.S. Diplomas (#)	290	285	2	1	0	2

Hamilton-Wenham

5 School St • Wenham, MA 01984-1053
(978) 468-5310
Grade Span: PK-12; **Agency Type:** 3
Schools: 5
3 Primary; 1 Middle; 1 High; 0 Other Level
5 Regular; 0 Special Education; 0 Vocational; 0 Alternative
0 Magnet; 0 Charter; 3 Title I Eligible; 0 School-wide Title I
Students: 2,254 (49.3% male; 50.7% female)
Individual Education Program: 300 (13.3%);
English Language Learner: 0 (0.0%); Migrant: 1 (<0.1%)
Eligible for Free Lunch Program: n/a
Eligible for Reduced-Price Lunch Program: n/a
Teachers: 167.9 (13.4 to 1)
Librarians/Media Specialists: 2.0 (1,127.0 to 1)
Guidance Counselors: 4.0 (563.5 to 1)
Current Spending: ($ per student per year):
Total: $8,946; Instruction: $6,182; Support Services: $2,504

Enrollment, Drop-out Rates and Diploma Recipients by Race/Ethnicity

Category	Total	White	Black	Asian	AIAN	Hisp.
Enrollment (%)	100.0	95.7	0.9	2.2	0.4	0.8
Drop-out Rate (%)	0.5	0.6	0.0	0.0	0.0	0.0
H.S. Diplomas (#)	158	145	1	5	5	2

Haverhill

4 Summer St • Haverhill, MA 01830-5877
(978) 374-3400 • http://www.haverhill-ma.com/
Grade Span: PK-12; **Agency Type:** 1
Schools: 20
13 Primary; 4 Middle; 1 High; 2 Other Level
20 Regular; 0 Special Education; 0 Vocational; 0 Alternative
0 Magnet; 0 Charter; 7 Title I Eligible; 1 School-wide Title I
Students: 8,303 (51.5% male; 48.5% female)
Individual Education Program: 1,395 (16.8%);
English Language Learner: 266 (3.2%); Migrant: 2 (<0.1%)
Eligible for Free Lunch Program: n/a
Eligible for Reduced-Price Lunch Program: n/a
Teachers: 585.5 (14.2 to 1)
Librarians/Media Specialists: 4.0 (2,075.8 to 1)
Guidance Counselors: 26.0 (319.3 to 1)
Current Spending: ($ per student per year):
Total: $8,583; Instruction: $5,602; Support Services: $2,660

Enrollment, Drop-out Rates and Diploma Recipients by Race/Ethnicity

Category	Total	White	Black	Asian	AIAN	Hisp.
Enrollment (%)	100.0	80.0	3.1	1.7	0.0	15.2
Drop-out Rate (%)	4.6	4.5	9.6	0.0	0.0	5.0
H.S. Diplomas (#)	377	311	12	6	0	48

Ipswich

1 Lord Square • Ipswich, MA 01938-1909
(978) 356-2935 • http://www.ipswichschools.org/
Grade Span: PK-12; **Agency Type:** 1
Schools: 4
2 Primary; 1 Middle; 1 High; 0 Other Level
4 Regular; 0 Special Education; 0 Vocational; 0 Alternative
0 Magnet; 0 Charter; 1 Title I Eligible; 0 School-wide Title I
Students: 2,068 (49.4% male; 50.6% female)
Individual Education Program: 273 (13.2%);
English Language Learner: 16 (0.8%); Migrant: 1 (<0.1%)
Eligible for Free Lunch Program: n/a
Eligible for Reduced-Price Lunch Program: n/a
Teachers: 147.9 (14.0 to 1)
Librarians/Media Specialists: 2.0 (1,034.0 to 1)
Guidance Counselors: 4.3 (480.9 to 1)
Current Spending: ($ per student per year):
Total: $8,322; Instruction: $5,837; Support Services: $2,184

Enrollment, Drop-out Rates and Diploma Recipients by Race/Ethnicity

Category	Total	White	Black	Asian	AIAN	Hisp.
Enrollment (%)	100.0	95.8	1.3	1.8	0.2	1.0
Drop-out Rate (%)	2.0	2.0	0.0	0.0	n/a	0.0
H.S. Diplomas (#)	116	113	0	1	1	1

Lawrence

255 Essex St • Lawrence, MA 01840-1492
(978) 975-5900 • http://www.lawrence.k12.ma.us/
Grade Span: PK-12; **Agency Type:** 1
Schools: 20
17 Primary; 1 Middle; 1 High; 1 Other Level
20 Regular; 0 Special Education; 0 Vocational; 0 Alternative
0 Magnet; 0 Charter; 20 Title I Eligible; 20 School-wide Title I
Students: 12,587 (50.9% male; 49.1% female)
Individual Education Program: 1,789 (14.2%);
English Language Learner: 3,358 (26.7%); Migrant: 98 (0.8%)
Eligible for Free Lunch Program: n/a
Eligible for Reduced-Price Lunch Program: n/a
Teachers: 1,026.0 (12.3 to 1)
Librarians/Media Specialists: 10.0 (1,258.7 to 1)
Guidance Counselors: 43.0 (292.7 to 1)
Current Spending: ($ per student per year):
Total: $10,440; Instruction: $7,235; Support Services: $2,782

Enrollment, Drop-out Rates and Diploma Recipients by Race/Ethnicity

Category	Total	White	Black	Asian	AIAN	Hisp.
Enrollment (%)	100.0	10.6	2.4	3.1	0.0	83.9
Drop-out Rate (%)	12.5	17.4	13.8	5.1	0.0	12.5
H.S. Diplomas (#)	270	10	11	21	0	228

Lynn

14 Central Ave • Lynn, MA 01901-1201
(781) 593-1680 • http://www.lynnschools.org/
Grade Span: PK-12; **Agency Type:** 1
Schools: 30
19 Primary; 5 Middle; 5 High; 1 Other Level
24 Regular; 0 Special Education; 1 Vocational; 5 Alternative

0 Magnet; 0 Charter; 20 Title I Eligible; 20 School-wide Title I
Students: 15,114 (51.6% male; 48.4% female)
Individual Education Program: 2,250 (14.9%);
English Language Learner: 1,790 (11.8%); Migrant: 159 (1.1%)
Eligible for Free Lunch Program: n/a
Eligible for Reduced-Price Lunch Program: n/a
Teachers: 1,094.7 (13.8 to 1)
Librarians/Media Specialists: 15.4 (981.4 to 1)
Guidance Counselors: 24.0 (629.8 to 1)
Current Spending: ($ per student per year):
Total: $9,105; Instruction: $6,442; Support Services: $2,358
Enrollment, Drop-out Rates and Diploma Recipients by Race/Ethnicity

Category	Total	White	Black	Asian	AIAN	Hisp.
Enrollment (%)	100.0	39.9	14.8	12.8	0.2	32.2
Drop-out Rate (%)	3.9	3.3	2.6	4.1	0.0	5.6
H.S. Diplomas (#)	676	333	89	98	1	155

Lynnfield
55 Summer St • Lynnfield, MA 01940-1789
(781) 334-5800 •
http://www.lynnfield.k12.ma.us/education/district/district.php?sectionid=1
Grade Span: PK-12; **Agency Type:** 1
Schools: 4
2 Primary; 1 Middle; 1 High; 0 Other Level
4 Regular; 0 Special Education; 0 Vocational; 0 Alternative
0 Magnet; 0 Charter; 1 Title I Eligible; 0 School-wide Title I
Students: 1,985 (52.1% male; 47.9% female)
Individual Education Program: 210 (10.6%);
English Language Learner: 2 (0.1%); Migrant: 0 (0.0%)
Eligible for Free Lunch Program: n/a
Eligible for Reduced-Price Lunch Program: n/a
Teachers: 135.5 (14.6 to 1)
Librarians/Media Specialists: 4.0 (496.3 to 1)
Guidance Counselors: 4.0 (496.3 to 1)
Current Spending: ($ per student per year):
Total: $8,866; Instruction: $5,870; Support Services: $2,767
Enrollment, Drop-out Rates and Diploma Recipients by Race/Ethnicity

Category	Total	White	Black	Asian	AIAN	Hisp.
Enrollment (%)	100.0	94.0	1.6	3.1	0.3	1.1
Drop-out Rate (%)	0.6	0.6	0.0	0.0	0.0	0.0
H.S. Diplomas (#)	106	102	1	0	1	2

Marblehead
9 Widger Rd • Marblehead, MA 01945-1920
(781) 639-3141 • http://www.marblehead.com/schools/
Grade Span: PK-12; **Agency Type:** 1
Schools: 7
5 Primary; 1 Middle; 1 High; 0 Other Level
7 Regular; 0 Special Education; 0 Vocational; 0 Alternative
0 Magnet; 0 Charter; 3 Title I Eligible; 0 School-wide Title I
Students: 2,960 (51.0% male; 49.0% female)
Individual Education Program: 494 (16.7%);
English Language Learner: 10 (0.3%); Migrant: 10 (0.3%)
Eligible for Free Lunch Program: n/a
Eligible for Reduced-Price Lunch Program: n/a
Teachers: 230.0 (12.9 to 1)
Librarians/Media Specialists: 5.0 (592.0 to 1)
Guidance Counselors: 10.0 (296.0 to 1)
Current Spending: ($ per student per year):
Total: $9,570; Instruction: $7,128; Support Services: $2,418
Enrollment, Drop-out Rates and Diploma Recipients by Race/Ethnicity

Category	Total	White	Black	Asian	AIAN	Hisp.
Enrollment (%)	100.0	94.1	3.4	1.3	0.1	1.1
Drop-out Rate (%)	1.0	0.9	0.0	0.0	n/a	12.5
H.S. Diplomas (#)	208	201	4	2	0	1

Masconomet
20 Endicott Rd • Topsfield, MA 01983-2009
(978) 887-2323 • http://www.masconomet.org/
Grade Span: 07-12; **Agency Type:** 4
Schools: 2
0 Primary; 1 Middle; 1 High; 0 Other Level
2 Regular; 0 Special Education; 0 Vocational; 0 Alternative
0 Magnet; 0 Charter; 2 Title I Eligible; 0 School-wide Title I
Students: 1,890 (48.5% male; 51.5% female)
Individual Education Program: 259 (13.7%);
English Language Learner: 0 (0.0%); Migrant: 0 (0.0%)
Eligible for Free Lunch Program: n/a
Eligible for Reduced-Price Lunch Program: n/a
Teachers: 130.9 (14.4 to 1)
Librarians/Media Specialists: 2.0 (945.0 to 1)
Guidance Counselors: 10.6 (178.3 to 1)
Current Spending: ($ per student per year):
Total: $9,873; Instruction: $6,519; Support Services: $2,924
Enrollment, Drop-out Rates and Diploma Recipients by Race/Ethnicity

Category	Total	White	Black	Asian	AIAN	Hisp.
Enrollment (%)	100.0	97.7	0.6	0.8	0.1	0.8
Drop-out Rate (%)	1.0	1.0	0.0	0.0	n/a	0.0
H.S. Diplomas (#)	269	260	0	6	0	3

Methuen
10 Ditson Place • Methuen, MA 01844-6117
(978) 681-1317 • http://www.methuen.k12.ma.us/
Grade Span: PK-12; **Agency Type:** 1
Schools: 6
5 Primary; 0 Middle; 1 High; 0 Other Level
6 Regular; 0 Special Education; 0 Vocational; 0 Alternative
0 Magnet; 0 Charter; 4 Title I Eligible; 0 School-wide Title I
Students: 7,057 (51.7% male; 48.3% female)
Individual Education Program: 904 (12.8%);
English Language Learner: 367 (5.2%); Migrant: 0 (0.0%)
Eligible for Free Lunch Program: n/a
Eligible for Reduced-Price Lunch Program: n/a
Teachers: 444.1 (15.9 to 1)
Librarians/Media Specialists: 9.2 (767.1 to 1)
Guidance Counselors: 20.5 (344.2 to 1)
Current Spending: ($ per student per year):
Total: $7,596; Instruction: $4,859; Support Services: $2,477
Enrollment, Drop-out Rates and Diploma Recipients by Race/Ethnicity

Category	Total	White	Black	Asian	AIAN	Hisp.
Enrollment (%)	100.0	79.5	1.5	2.9	0.4	15.8
Drop-out Rate (%)	2.0	2.0	0.0	1.5	0.0	2.6
H.S. Diplomas (#)	354	297	8	11	1	37

Newburyport
70 Low St • Newburyport, MA 01950-4049
(978) 465-4457 • http://www.newburyport.k12.ma.us
Grade Span: PK-12; **Agency Type:** 1
Schools: 5
3 Primary; 1 Middle; 1 High; 0 Other Level
5 Regular; 0 Special Education; 0 Vocational; 0 Alternative
0 Magnet; 0 Charter; 2 Title I Eligible; 0 School-wide Title I
Students: 2,375 (52.3% male; 47.7% female)
Individual Education Program: 326 (13.7%);
English Language Learner: 10 (0.4%); Migrant: 0 (0.0%)
Eligible for Free Lunch Program: n/a
Eligible for Reduced-Price Lunch Program: n/a
Teachers: 191.9 (12.4 to 1)
Librarians/Media Specialists: 7.0 (339.3 to 1)
Guidance Counselors: 9.0 (263.9 to 1)
Current Spending: ($ per student per year):
Total: $9,789; Instruction: $6,650; Support Services: $2,829
Enrollment, Drop-out Rates and Diploma Recipients by Race/Ethnicity

Category	Total	White	Black	Asian	AIAN	Hisp.
Enrollment (%)	100.0	97.1	0.9	0.8	0.3	0.8
Drop-out Rate (%)	2.7	n/a	0.0	0.0	0.0	0.0
H.S. Diplomas (#)	130	128	0	1	1	0

North Andover
43 High St • North Andover, MA 01845-1901
(978) 794-1503 • http://www.nandover.mec.edu
Grade Span: PK-12; **Agency Type:** 1
Schools: 8
6 Primary; 1 Middle; 1 High; 0 Other Level
8 Regular; 0 Special Education; 0 Vocational; 0 Alternative
0 Magnet; 0 Charter; 2 Title I Eligible; 0 School-wide Title I
Students: 4,320 (53.1% male; 46.9% female)
Individual Education Program: 471 (10.9%);
English Language Learner: 44 (1.0%); Migrant: 9 (0.2%)
Eligible for Free Lunch Program: n/a
Eligible for Reduced-Price Lunch Program: n/a
Teachers: 292.2 (14.8 to 1)
Librarians/Media Specialists: 5.0 (864.0 to 1)
Guidance Counselors: 12.4 (348.4 to 1)
Current Spending: ($ per student per year):
Total: $7,617; Instruction: $5,054; Support Services: $2,315
Enrollment, Drop-out Rates and Diploma Recipients by Race/Ethnicity

Category	Total	White	Black	Asian	AIAN	Hisp.
Enrollment (%)	100.0	90.7	0.8	5.6	0.6	2.2
Drop-out Rate (%)	1.0	0.9	14.3	0.0	n/a	0.0
H.S. Diplomas (#)	248	232	0	11	0	5

Peabody
70 Endicott St • Peabody, MA 01960-8199
(978) 531-1600 • http://www.peabody.k12.ma.us/
Grade Span: PK-12; **Agency Type:** 1
Schools: 10
8 Primary; 1 Middle; 1 High; 0 Other Level
10 Regular; 0 Special Education; 0 Vocational; 0 Alternative

0 Magnet; 0 Charter; 4 Title I Eligible; 0 School-wide Title I
Students: 6,641 (50.7% male; 49.3% female)
Individual Education Program: 887 (13.4%);
English Language Learner: 181 (2.7%); Migrant: 41 (0.6%)
Eligible for Free Lunch Program: n/a
Eligible for Reduced-Price Lunch Program: n/a
Teachers: 450.4 (14.7 to 1)
Librarians/Media Specialists: 2.0 (3,320.5 to 1)
Guidance Counselors: 42.0 (158.1 to 1)
Current Spending: ($ per student per year):
Total: $8,075; Instruction: $5,206; Support Services: $2,631
Enrollment, Drop-out Rates and Diploma Recipients by Race/Ethnicity

Category	Total	White	Black	Asian	AIAN	Hisp.
Enrollment (%)	100.0	89.8	1.6	1.9	0.1	6.7
Drop-out Rate (%)	3.7	3.5	6.7	0.0	n/a	7.0
H.S. Diplomas (#)	384	363	1	6	0	14

Pentucket

22 Main St • West Newbury, MA 01985-1897
(978) 363-2280 • http://www.prsd.org/
Grade Span: PK-12; **Agency Type:** 3
Schools: 6
4 Primary; 1 Middle; 1 High; 0 Other Level
6 Regular; 0 Special Education; 0 Vocational; 0 Alternative
0 Magnet; 0 Charter; 2 Title I Eligible; 0 School-wide Title I
Students: 3,445 (51.0% male; 49.0% female)
Individual Education Program: 421 (12.2%);
English Language Learner: 0 (0.0%); Migrant: 0 (0.0%)
Eligible for Free Lunch Program: n/a
Eligible for Reduced-Price Lunch Program: n/a
Teachers: 242.6 (14.2 to 1)
Librarians/Media Specialists: 4.4 (783.0 to 1)
Guidance Counselors: 9.0 (382.8 to 1)
Current Spending: ($ per student per year):
Total: $6,926; Instruction: $4,456; Support Services: $2,246
Enrollment, Drop-out Rates and Diploma Recipients by Race/Ethnicity

Category	Total	White	Black	Asian	AIAN	Hisp.
Enrollment (%)	100.0	97.6	0.6	1.0	0.0	0.8
Drop-out Rate (%)	2.1	2.0	20.0	0.0	0.0	0.0
H.S. Diplomas (#)	197	192	1	2	0	2

Salem

29 Highland Ave • Salem, MA 01970-2116
(978) 740-1212 • http://salem.k12.ma.us/
Grade Span: PK-12; **Agency Type:** 1
Schools: 10
8 Primary; 1 Middle; 1 High; 0 Other Level
10 Regular; 0 Special Education; 0 Vocational; 0 Alternative
0 Magnet; 0 Charter; 8 Title I Eligible; 3 School-wide Title I
Students: 5,000 (50.6% male; 49.4% female)
Individual Education Program: 865 (17.3%);
English Language Learner: 546 (10.9%); Migrant: 31 (0.6%)
Eligible for Free Lunch Program: n/a
Eligible for Reduced-Price Lunch Program: n/a
Teachers: 473.0 (10.6 to 1)
Librarians/Media Specialists: 4.0 (1,250.0 to 1)
Guidance Counselors: 5.0 (1,000.0 to 1)
Current Spending: ($ per student per year):
Total: $10,088; Instruction: $7,063; Support Services: $2,707
Enrollment, Drop-out Rates and Diploma Recipients by Race/Ethnicity

Category	Total	White	Black	Asian	AIAN	Hisp.
Enrollment (%)	100.0	64.0	4.6	2.7	0.1	28.6
Drop-out Rate (%)	2.8	1.8	11.4	0.0	0.0	4.5
H.S. Diplomas (#)	217	136	10	7	0	64

Saugus

23 Main St • Saugus, MA 01906-2347
(781) 231-5000
Grade Span: PK-12; **Agency Type:** 1
Schools: 8
6 Primary; 1 Middle; 0 High; 1 Other Level
8 Regular; 0 Special Education; 0 Vocational; 0 Alternative
0 Magnet; 0 Charter; 3 Title I Eligible; 0 School-wide Title I
Students: 3,394 (50.7% male; 49.3% female)
Individual Education Program: 309 (9.1%);
English Language Learner: 0 (0.0%); Migrant: 0 (0.0%)
Eligible for Free Lunch Program: n/a
Eligible for Reduced-Price Lunch Program: n/a
Teachers: 279.4 (12.1 to 1)
Librarians/Media Specialists: 1.0 (3,394.0 to 1)
Guidance Counselors: 9.0 (377.1 to 1)
Current Spending: ($ per student per year):
Total: $8,353; Instruction: $5,456; Support Services: $2,639
Enrollment, Drop-out Rates and Diploma Recipients by Race/Ethnicity

Category	Total	White	Black	Asian	AIAN	Hisp.
Enrollment (%)	100.0	93.2	1.4	2.7	0.3	2.4
Drop-out Rate (%)	3.8	3.3	16.7	21.4	0.0	20.0
H.S. Diplomas (#)	175	170	1	3	0	1

Swampscott

207 Forest Ave • Swampscott, MA 01907-2293
(781) 596-8800
Grade Span: PK-12; **Agency Type:** 1
Schools: 6
4 Primary; 1 Middle; 0 High; 1 Other Level
6 Regular; 0 Special Education; 0 Vocational; 0 Alternative
0 Magnet; 0 Charter; 2 Title I Eligible; 0 School-wide Title I
Students: 2,357 (50.5% male; 49.5% female)
Individual Education Program: 332 (14.1%);
English Language Learner: 11 (0.5%); Migrant: 0 (0.0%)
Eligible for Free Lunch Program: n/a
Eligible for Reduced-Price Lunch Program: n/a
Teachers: 186.6 (12.6 to 1)
Librarians/Media Specialists: 4.5 (523.8 to 1)
Guidance Counselors: 17.0 (138.6 to 1)
Current Spending: ($ per student per year):
Total: $8,848; Instruction: $5,989; Support Services: $2,566
Enrollment, Drop-out Rates and Diploma Recipients by Race/Ethnicity

Category	Total	White	Black	Asian	AIAN	Hisp.
Enrollment (%)	100.0	95.5	1.7	1.4	0.1	1.3
Drop-out Rate (%)	1.9	1.9	0.0	0.0	0.0	11.1
H.S. Diplomas (#)	171	167	2	1	0	1

Triton

112 Elm St • Byfield, MA 01922-2814
(978) 465-2397 • http://www.triton1.org/district/
Grade Span: PK-12; **Agency Type:** 3
Schools: 5
3 Primary; 1 Middle; 1 High; 0 Other Level
5 Regular; 0 Special Education; 0 Vocational; 0 Alternative
0 Magnet; 0 Charter; 1 Title I Eligible; 0 School-wide Title I
Students: 3,565 (50.7% male; 49.3% female)
Individual Education Program: 341 (9.6%);
English Language Learner: 2 (0.1%); Migrant: 5 (0.1%)
Eligible for Free Lunch Program: n/a
Eligible for Reduced-Price Lunch Program: n/a
Teachers: 233.9 (15.2 to 1)
Librarians/Media Specialists: 8.0 (445.6 to 1)
Guidance Counselors: 8.0 (445.6 to 1)
Current Spending: ($ per student per year):
Total: $7,720; Instruction: $5,329; Support Services: $2,139
Enrollment, Drop-out Rates and Diploma Recipients by Race/Ethnicity

Category	Total	White	Black	Asian	AIAN	Hisp.
Enrollment (%)	100.0	97.1	0.8	0.6	0.8	0.8
Drop-out Rate (%)	2.0	2.0	0.0	0.0	n/a	0.0
H.S. Diplomas (#)	198	195	1	1	0	1

Franklin County

Greenfield

141 Davis St • Greenfield, MA 01301-2504
(413) 772-1311 • http://gpsk12.org/
Grade Span: PK-12; **Agency Type:** 1
Schools: 7
5 Primary; 1 Middle; 1 High; 0 Other Level
7 Regular; 0 Special Education; 0 Vocational; 0 Alternative
0 Magnet; 0 Charter; 6 Title I Eligible; 3 School-wide Title I
Students: 2,244 (51.4% male; 48.6% female)
Individual Education Program: 363 (16.2%);
English Language Learner: 86 (3.8%); Migrant: 2 (0.1%)
Eligible for Free Lunch Program: n/a
Eligible for Reduced-Price Lunch Program: n/a
Teachers: 203.2 (11.0 to 1)
Librarians/Media Specialists: 2.4 (935.0 to 1)
Guidance Counselors: 12.0 (187.0 to 1)
Current Spending: ($ per student per year):
Total: $9,773; Instruction: $6,592; Support Services: $2,735
Enrollment, Drop-out Rates and Diploma Recipients by Race/Ethnicity

Category	Total	White	Black	Asian	AIAN	Hisp.
Enrollment (%)	100.0	87.9	2.5	2.2	0.4	7.0
Drop-out Rate (%)	5.3	4.5	0.0	30.0	0.0	17.4
H.S. Diplomas (#)	124	117	2	3	0	2

Mohawk Trail

24 Ashfield Rd • Shelburne Falls, MA 01370-9416
(413) 625-0192 • http://www.mohawk.k14.mass.edu/
Grade Span: PK-12; **Agency Type:** 3
Schools: 5

4 Primary; 0 Middle; 1 High; 0 Other Level
5 Regular; 0 Special Education; 0 Vocational; 0 Alternative
0 Magnet; 0 Charter; 3 Title I Eligible; 0 School-wide Title I
Students: 1,558 (51.4% male; 48.6% female)
Individual Education Program: 287 (18.4%);
English Language Learner: 0 (0.0%); Migrant: 1 (0.1%)
Eligible for Free Lunch Program: n/a
Eligible for Reduced-Price Lunch Program: n/a
Teachers: 146.8 (10.6 to 1)
Librarians/Media Specialists: 6.8 (229.1 to 1)
Guidance Counselors: 6.3 (247.3 to 1)
Current Spending: ($ per student per year):
Total: $9,773; Instruction: $6,535; Support Services: $3,051
Enrollment, Drop-out Rates and Diploma Recipients by Race/Ethnicity

Category	Total	White	Black	Asian	AIAN	Hisp.
Enrollment (%)	100.0	97.1	1.2	0.6	0.4	0.6
Drop-out Rate (%)	3.3	3.4	0.0	0.0	0.0	0.0
H.S. Diplomas (#)	96	95	0	1	0	0

Hampden County

Agawam
1305 Springfield St - Suit • Feeding Hills, MA 01030-2198
(413) 821-0548 • http://www.agawampublicschools.org/
Grade Span: PK-12; **Agency Type:** 1
Schools: 8
5 Primary; 2 Middle; 1 High; 0 Other Level
8 Regular; 0 Special Education; 0 Vocational; 0 Alternative
0 Magnet; 0 Charter; 4 Title I Eligible; 0 School-wide Title I
Students: 4,380 (51.2% male; 48.8% female)
Individual Education Program: 780 (17.8%);
English Language Learner: 70 (1.6%); Migrant: 0 (0.0%)
Eligible for Free Lunch Program: n/a
Eligible for Reduced-Price Lunch Program: n/a
Teachers: 403.0 (10.9 to 1)
Librarians/Media Specialists: 4.0 (1,095.0 to 1)
Guidance Counselors: 16.0 (273.8 to 1)
Current Spending: ($ per student per year):
Total: $7,825; Instruction: $5,194; Support Services: $2,404
Enrollment, Drop-out Rates and Diploma Recipients by Race/Ethnicity

Category	Total	White	Black	Asian	AIAN	Hisp.
Enrollment (%)	100.0	95.2	1.2	1.4	0.3	2.0
Drop-out Rate (%)	0.0	0.0	0.0	0.0	0.0	0.0
H.S. Diplomas (#)	245	236	0	6	2	1

Chicopee
180 Broadway • Chicopee, MA 01020-2638
(413) 594-3410 • http://www.chicopee.mec.edu/
Grade Span: PK-12; **Agency Type:** 1
Schools: 16
11 Primary; 1 Middle; 3 High; 1 Other Level
15 Regular; 0 Special Education; 0 Vocational; 1 Alternative
0 Magnet; 0 Charter; 9 Title I Eligible; 6 School-wide Title I
Students: 7,702 (51.5% male; 48.5% female)
Individual Education Program: 1,203 (15.6%);
English Language Learner: 494 (6.4%); Migrant: 2 (<0.1%)
Eligible for Free Lunch Program: n/a
Eligible for Reduced-Price Lunch Program: n/a
Teachers: 590.8 (13.0 to 1)
Librarians/Media Specialists: 4.0 (1,925.5 to 1)
Guidance Counselors: 28.0 (275.1 to 1)
Current Spending: ($ per student per year):
Total: $9,066; Instruction: $6,616; Support Services: $2,134
Enrollment, Drop-out Rates and Diploma Recipients by Race/Ethnicity

Category	Total	White	Black	Asian	AIAN	Hisp.
Enrollment (%)	100.0	78.7	3.0	0.7	0.2	17.4
Drop-out Rate (%)	5.9	5.7	7.7	4.3	0.0	7.7
H.S. Diplomas (#)	426	389	8	0	2	27

East Longmeadow
180 Maple St • East Longmeadow, MA 01028-2721
(413) 525-5450 • http://www.eastlongmeadow.org/Schools/Schools.htm
Grade Span: PK-12; **Agency Type:** 1
Schools: 5
3 Primary; 1 Middle; 1 High; 0 Other Level
5 Regular; 0 Special Education; 0 Vocational; 0 Alternative
0 Magnet; 0 Charter; 2 Title I Eligible; 0 School-wide Title I
Students: 2,670 (50.1% male; 49.9% female)
Individual Education Program: 666 (24.9%);
English Language Learner: 0 (0.0%); Migrant: 0 (0.0%)
Eligible for Free Lunch Program: n/a
Eligible for Reduced-Price Lunch Program: n/a
Teachers: 194.6 (13.7 to 1)
Librarians/Media Specialists: 2.6 (1,026.9 to 1)
Guidance Counselors: 10.0 (267.0 to 1)
Current Spending: ($ per student per year):
Total: $7,887; Instruction: $5,378; Support Services: $2,269
Enrollment, Drop-out Rates and Diploma Recipients by Race/Ethnicity

Category	Total	White	Black	Asian	AIAN	Hisp.
Enrollment (%)	100.0	95.4	2.4	1.2	0.1	0.9
Drop-out Rate (%)	1.2	1.3	0.0	0.0	n/a	0.0
H.S. Diplomas (#)	186	180	4	2	0	0

Hampden-Wilbraham
621 Main St • Wilbraham, MA 01095-1689
(413) 596-3884 • http://www.hwrsd.org/
Grade Span: PK-12; **Agency Type:** 3
Schools: 8
5 Primary; 2 Middle; 1 High; 0 Other Level
8 Regular; 0 Special Education; 0 Vocational; 0 Alternative
0 Magnet; 0 Charter; 7 Title I Eligible; 0 School-wide Title I
Students: 3,878 (51.2% male; 48.8% female)
Individual Education Program: 589 (15.2%);
English Language Learner: 18 (0.5%); Migrant: 1 (<0.1%)
Eligible for Free Lunch Program: n/a
Eligible for Reduced-Price Lunch Program: n/a
Teachers: 248.3 (15.6 to 1)
Librarians/Media Specialists: 2.5 (1,551.2 to 1)
Guidance Counselors: 7.0 (554.0 to 1)
Current Spending: ($ per student per year):
Total: $7,779; Instruction: $4,978; Support Services: $2,501
Enrollment, Drop-out Rates and Diploma Recipients by Race/Ethnicity

Category	Total	White	Black	Asian	AIAN	Hisp.
Enrollment (%)	100.0	95.7	1.6	1.5	0.1	1.1
Drop-out Rate (%)	1.1	1.1	0.0	0.0	25.0	0.0
H.S. Diplomas (#)	303	287	5	9	0	2

Holyoke
57 Suffolk St • Holyoke, MA 01040-5015
(413) 534-2005 • http://www.hps.holyoke.ma.us/
Grade Span: PK-12; **Agency Type:** 1
Schools: 14
8 Primary; 3 Middle; 2 High; 1 Other Level
12 Regular; 0 Special Education; 1 Vocational; 1 Alternative
1 Magnet; 0 Charter; 14 Title I Eligible; 12 School-wide Title I
Students: 7,255 (52.1% male; 47.9% female)
Individual Education Program: 1,394 (19.2%);
English Language Learner: 1,451 (20.0%); Migrant: 64 (0.9%)
Eligible for Free Lunch Program: n/a
Eligible for Reduced-Price Lunch Program: n/a
Teachers: 685.8 (10.6 to 1)
Librarians/Media Specialists: 0.0 (0.0 to 1)
Guidance Counselors: 31.0 (234.0 to 1)
Current Spending: ($ per student per year):
Total: $11,880; Instruction: $8,242; Support Services: $3,639
Enrollment, Drop-out Rates and Diploma Recipients by Race/Ethnicity

Category	Total	White	Black	Asian	AIAN	Hisp.
Enrollment (%)	100.0	23.9	3.6	0.9	0.0	71.6
Drop-out Rate (%)	8.6	4.2	5.8	6.3	0.0	11.5
H.S. Diplomas (#)	275	141	15	1	1	117

Longmeadow
127 Grassy Gutter Rd • Longmeadow, MA 01106-2238
(413) 565-4200 • http://www.longmeadow.k12.ma.us/
Grade Span: PK-12; **Agency Type:** 1
Schools: 6
3 Primary; 2 Middle; 0 High; 1 Other Level
6 Regular; 0 Special Education; 0 Vocational; 0 Alternative
0 Magnet; 0 Charter; 1 Title I Eligible; 0 School-wide Title I
Students: 3,319 (52.5% male; 47.5% female)
Individual Education Program: 292 (8.8%);
English Language Learner: 14 (0.4%); Migrant: 1 (<0.1%)
Eligible for Free Lunch Program: n/a
Eligible for Reduced-Price Lunch Program: n/a
Teachers: 229.7 (14.4 to 1)
Librarians/Media Specialists: 3.1 (1,070.6 to 1)
Guidance Counselors: 7.0 (474.1 to 1)
Current Spending: ($ per student per year):
Total: $8,450; Instruction: $5,632; Support Services: $2,503
Enrollment, Drop-out Rates and Diploma Recipients by Race/Ethnicity

Category	Total	White	Black	Asian	AIAN	Hisp.
Enrollment (%)	100.0	92.1	2.2	4.9	0.1	0.7
Drop-out Rate (%)	0.3	0.3	0.0	0.0	0.0	0.0
H.S. Diplomas (#)	246	233	1	11	0	1

Ludlow
63 Chestnut St • Ludlow, MA 01056-3468
(413) 583-5662
Grade Span: PK-12; **Agency Type:** 1
Schools: 6

4 Primary; 1 Middle; 1 High; 0 Other Level
6 Regular; 0 Special Education; 0 Vocational; 0 Alternative
0 Magnet; 0 Charter; 3 Title I Eligible; 0 School-wide Title I
Students: 3,035 (51.8% male; 48.2% female)
Individual Education Program: 536 (17.7%);
English Language Learner: 38 (1.3%); Migrant: 1 (<0.1%)
Eligible for Free Lunch Program: n/a
Eligible for Reduced-Price Lunch Program: n/a
Teachers: 217.2 (14.0 to 1)
Librarians/Media Specialists: 2.6 (1,167.3 to 1)
Guidance Counselors: 6.6 (459.8 to 1)
Current Spending: ($ per student per year):
Total: $7,880; Instruction: $5,112; Support Services: $2,437
Enrollment, Drop-out Rates and Diploma Recipients by Race/Ethnicity

Category	Total	White	Black	Asian	AIAN	Hisp.
Enrollment (%)	100.0	95.9	1.1	1.0	0.2	1.8
Drop-out Rate (%)	3.1	3.2	0.0	0.0	n/a	n/a
H.S. Diplomas (#)	195	190	1	1	1	2

Palmer
24 Converse St • Palmer, MA 01069-1770
(413) 283-2650 • http://www.palmerschools.org/main.htm
Grade Span: PK-12; **Agency Type:** 1
Schools: 3
1 Primary; 1 Middle; 1 High; 0 Other Level
3 Regular; 0 Special Education; 0 Vocational; 0 Alternative
0 Magnet; 0 Charter; 2 Title I Eligible; 0 School-wide Title I
Students: 2,114 (50.9% male; 49.1% female)
Individual Education Program: 391 (18.5%);
English Language Learner: 0 (0.0%); Migrant: 0 (0.0%)
Eligible for Free Lunch Program: n/a
Eligible for Reduced-Price Lunch Program: n/a
Teachers: 168.8 (12.5 to 1)
Librarians/Media Specialists: 1.0 (2,114.0 to 1)
Guidance Counselors: 6.0 (352.3 to 1)
Current Spending: ($ per student per year):
Total: $7,785; Instruction: $5,718; Support Services: $2,064
Enrollment, Drop-out Rates and Diploma Recipients by Race/Ethnicity

Category	Total	White	Black	Asian	AIAN	Hisp.
Enrollment (%)	100.0	98.2	0.5	0.4	0.4	0.5
Drop-out Rate (%)	3.6	3.7	0.0	0.0	n/a	0.0
H.S. Diplomas (#)	102	101	1	0	0	0

Southwick-Tolland
86 Powder Mill Rd • Southwick, MA 01077-9326
(413) 569-5391 • http://strsd.southwick.ma.us/
Grade Span: PK-12; **Agency Type:** 3
Schools: 3
1 Primary; 1 Middle; 1 High; 0 Other Level
3 Regular; 0 Special Education; 0 Vocational; 0 Alternative
0 Magnet; 0 Charter; 2 Title I Eligible; 0 School-wide Title I
Students: 1,868 (51.3% male; 48.7% female)
Individual Education Program: 262 (14.0%);
English Language Learner: 1 (0.1%); Migrant: 2 (0.1%)
Eligible for Free Lunch Program: n/a
Eligible for Reduced-Price Lunch Program: n/a
Teachers: 131.4 (14.2 to 1)
Librarians/Media Specialists: 3.0 (622.7 to 1)
Guidance Counselors: 7.0 (266.9 to 1)
Current Spending: ($ per student per year):
Total: $7,926; Instruction: $5,366; Support Services: $2,327
Enrollment, Drop-out Rates and Diploma Recipients by Race/Ethnicity

Category	Total	White	Black	Asian	AIAN	Hisp.
Enrollment (%)	100.0	97.4	1.2	0.5	0.2	0.7
Drop-out Rate (%)	2.2	1.7	10.0	100.0	0.0	25.0
H.S. Diplomas (#)	134	131	1	0	1	1

Springfield
195 State, Box 1410 • Springfield, MA 01102-1410
(413) 787-7000 • http://sps.springfield.ma.us/
Grade Span: PK-12; **Agency Type:** 1
Schools: 49
33 Primary; 6 Middle; 5 High; 5 Other Level
42 Regular; 1 Special Education; 1 Vocational; 5 Alternative
0 Magnet; 0 Charter; 48 Title I Eligible; 44 School-wide Title I
Students: 26,594 (51.7% male; 48.3% female)
Individual Education Program: 5,279 (19.9%);
English Language Learner: 2,701 (10.2%); Migrant: 267 (1.0%)
Eligible for Free Lunch Program: n/a
Eligible for Reduced-Price Lunch Program: n/a
Teachers: 2,377.6 (11.2 to 1)
Librarians/Media Specialists: 25.6 (1,038.8 to 1)
Guidance Counselors: 46.0 (578.1 to 1)
Current Spending: ($ per student per year):
Total: $10,934; Instruction: $7,524; Support Services: $2,930
Enrollment, Drop-out Rates and Diploma Recipients by Race/Ethnicity

Category	Total	White	Black	Asian	AIAN	Hisp.
Enrollment (%)	100.0	21.8	28.5	2.4	0.2	47.2
Drop-out Rate (%)	8.0	6.8	5.3	5.2	0.0	11.2
H.S. Diplomas (#)	839	268	289	36	1	245

West Springfield
26 Central St • West Springfield, MA 01089-2753
(413) 263-3290 • http://www.wsps.org/
Grade Span: PK-12; **Agency Type:** 1
Schools: 8
6 Primary; 1 Middle; 1 High; 0 Other Level
8 Regular; 0 Special Education; 0 Vocational; 0 Alternative
0 Magnet; 0 Charter; 5 Title I Eligible; 2 School-wide Title I
Students: 3,990 (52.7% male; 47.3% female)
Individual Education Program: 592 (14.8%);
English Language Learner: 288 (7.2%); Migrant: 0 (0.0%)
Eligible for Free Lunch Program: n/a
Eligible for Reduced-Price Lunch Program: n/a
Teachers: 316.7 (12.6 to 1)
Librarians/Media Specialists: 3.0 (1,330.0 to 1)
Guidance Counselors: 10.0 (399.0 to 1)
Current Spending: ($ per student per year):
Total: $8,548; Instruction: $5,299; Support Services: $2,971
Enrollment, Drop-out Rates and Diploma Recipients by Race/Ethnicity

Category	Total	White	Black	Asian	AIAN	Hisp.
Enrollment (%)	100.0	84.2	3.0	2.5	0.2	10.1
Drop-out Rate (%)	6.6	5.8	30.0	50.0	n/a	116.7
H.S. Diplomas (#)	222	196	3	9	1	13

Westfield
22 Ashley St • Westfield, MA 01085-3899
(413) 572-6403 • http://www.westfield.k12.wi.us/
Grade Span: PK-12; **Agency Type:** 1
Schools: 14
10 Primary; 2 Middle; 2 High; 0 Other Level
13 Regular; 0 Special Education; 1 Vocational; 0 Alternative
0 Magnet; 0 Charter; 7 Title I Eligible; 3 School-wide Title I
Students: 6,724 (52.5% male; 47.5% female)
Individual Education Program: 1,113 (16.6%);
English Language Learner: 348 (5.2%); Migrant: 1 (<0.1%)
Eligible for Free Lunch Program: n/a
Eligible for Reduced-Price Lunch Program: n/a
Teachers: 535.8 (12.5 to 1)
Librarians/Media Specialists: 7.0 (960.6 to 1)
Guidance Counselors: 22.0 (305.6 to 1)
Current Spending: ($ per student per year):
Total: $8,770; Instruction: $5,952; Support Services: $2,555
Enrollment, Drop-out Rates and Diploma Recipients by Race/Ethnicity

Category	Total	White	Black	Asian	AIAN	Hisp.
Enrollment (%)	100.0	90.2	1.2	1.1	0.0	7.5
Drop-out Rate (%)	3.5	3.3	12.5	0.0	0.0	5.5
H.S. Diplomas (#)	412	375	6	4	1	26

Hampshire County

Amherst
170 Chestnut St • Amherst, MA 01002-1825
(413) 362-1810 • http://www.arps.org/
Grade Span: PK-06; **Agency Type:** 2
Schools: 4
4 Primary; 0 Middle; 0 High; 0 Other Level
4 Regular; 0 Special Education; 0 Vocational; 0 Alternative
0 Magnet; 0 Charter; 3 Title I Eligible; 0 School-wide Title I
Students: 1,524 (48.5% male; 51.5% female)
Individual Education Program: 232 (15.2%);
English Language Learner: 161 (10.6%); Migrant: 3 (0.2%)
Eligible for Free Lunch Program: n/a
Eligible for Reduced-Price Lunch Program: n/a
Teachers: 152.3 (10.0 to 1)
Librarians/Media Specialists: 4.0 (381.0 to 1)
Guidance Counselors: 6.0 (254.0 to 1)
Current Spending: ($ per student per year):
Total: $10,999; Instruction: $7,552; Support Services: $3,038
Enrollment, Drop-out Rates and Diploma Recipients by Race/Ethnicity

Category	Total	White	Black	Asian	AIAN	Hisp.
Enrollment (%)	100.0	62.6	12.7	12.3	0.7	11.8
Drop-out Rate (%)	n/a	n/a	n/a	n/a	n/a	n/a
H.S. Diplomas (#)	n/a	n/a	n/a	n/a	n/a	n/a

Amherst-Pelham
170 Chestnut St • Amherst, MA 01002-1825
(413) 362-1810 • http://www.arps.org/
Grade Span: 07-12; **Agency Type:** 3
Schools: 2

0 Primary; 1 Middle; 1 High; 0 Other Level
2 Regular; 0 Special Education; 0 Vocational; 0 Alternative
0 Magnet; 0 Charter; 2 Title I Eligible; 0 School-wide Title I
Students: 2,040 (52.0% male; 48.0% female)
Individual Education Program: 353 (17.3%);
English Language Learner: 81 (4.0%); Migrant: 5 (0.2%)
Eligible for Free Lunch Program: n/a
Eligible for Reduced-Price Lunch Program: n/a
Teachers: 150.1 (13.6 to 1)
Librarians/Media Specialists: 2.0 (1,020.0 to 1)
Guidance Counselors: 9.0 (226.7 to 1)
Current Spending: ($ per student per year):
Total: $11,038; Instruction: $7,156; Support Services: $3,566
Enrollment, Drop-out Rates and Diploma Recipients by Race/Ethnicity

Category	Total	White	Black	Asian	AIAN	Hisp.
Enrollment (%)	100.0	72.3	10.1	9.3	0.8	7.5
Drop-out Rate (%)	2.6	2.0	3.7	4.5	0.0	5.1
H.S. Diplomas (#)	298	226	26	32	1	13

Belchertown

14 Maple St • Belchertown, MA 01007-0841
Mailing Address: PO Box 841 • Belchertown, MA 01007-0841
(413) 323-0456 • http://www.belchertownps.org/
Grade Span: PK-12; **Agency Type:** 1
Schools: 6
4 Primary; 0 Middle; 1 High; 1 Other Level
6 Regular; 0 Special Education; 0 Vocational; 0 Alternative
0 Magnet; 0 Charter; 3 Title I Eligible; 0 School-wide Title I
Students: 2,440 (49.9% male; 50.1% female)
Individual Education Program: 288 (11.8%);
English Language Learner: 10 (0.4%); Migrant: 0 (0.0%)
Eligible for Free Lunch Program: n/a
Eligible for Reduced-Price Lunch Program: n/a
Teachers: 133.5 (18.3 to 1)
Librarians/Media Specialists: 0.0 (0.0 to 1)
Guidance Counselors: 8.0 (305.0 to 1)
Current Spending: ($ per student per year):
Total: $7,708; Instruction: $4,784; Support Services: $2,683
Enrollment, Drop-out Rates and Diploma Recipients by Race/Ethnicity

Category	Total	White	Black	Asian	AIAN	Hisp.
Enrollment (%)	100.0	95.8	1.1	1.1	0.1	1.9
Drop-out Rate (%)	3.6	3.1	0.0	33.3	n/a	40.0
H.S. Diplomas (#)	126	122	0	1	0	3

Easthampton

50 Payson Ave • Easthampton, MA 01027-2023
(413) 529-1500 • http://www.easthampton.k12.ma.us/
Grade Span: PK-12; **Agency Type:** 1
Schools: 6
4 Primary; 1 Middle; 1 High; 0 Other Level
6 Regular; 0 Special Education; 0 Vocational; 0 Alternative
0 Magnet; 0 Charter; 4 Title I Eligible; 0 School-wide Title I
Students: 1,704 (50.2% male; 49.8% female)
Individual Education Program: 287 (16.8%);
English Language Learner: 25 (1.5%); Migrant: 3 (0.2%)
Eligible for Free Lunch Program: n/a
Eligible for Reduced-Price Lunch Program: n/a
Teachers: 179.1 (9.5 to 1)
Librarians/Media Specialists: 1.0 (1,704.0 to 1)
Guidance Counselors: 4.0 (426.0 to 1)
Current Spending: ($ per student per year):
Total: $8,859; Instruction: $5,956; Support Services: $2,577
Enrollment, Drop-out Rates and Diploma Recipients by Race/Ethnicity

Category	Total	White	Black	Asian	AIAN	Hisp.
Enrollment (%)	100.0	92.8	1.4	3.2	0.2	2.4
Drop-out Rate (%)	3.1	3.4	0.0	0.0	n/a	0.0
H.S. Diplomas (#)	130	119	1	9	0	1

Northampton

212 Main St • Northampton, MA 01060-3112
(413) 587-1328 • http://www.nps.northampton.ma.us/
Grade Span: PK-12; **Agency Type:** 1
Schools: 6
4 Primary; 1 Middle; 1 High; 0 Other Level
6 Regular; 0 Special Education; 0 Vocational; 0 Alternative
0 Magnet; 0 Charter; 4 Title I Eligible; 0 School-wide Title I
Students: 2,919 (50.7% male; 49.3% female)
Individual Education Program: 523 (17.9%);
English Language Learner: 104 (3.6%); Migrant: 2 (0.1%)
Eligible for Free Lunch Program: n/a
Eligible for Reduced-Price Lunch Program: n/a
Teachers: 225.8 (12.9 to 1)
Librarians/Media Specialists: 1.0 (2,919.0 to 1)
Guidance Counselors: 9.6 (304.1 to 1)
Current Spending: ($ per student per year):
Total: $9,829; Instruction: $6,545; Support Services: $2,811

Enrollment, Drop-out Rates and Diploma Recipients by Race/Ethnicity

Category	Total	White	Black	Asian	AIAN	Hisp.
Enrollment (%)	100.0	81.1	2.9	4.4	0.4	11.2
Drop-out Rate (%)	2.1	1.2	0.0	2.1	0.0	12.7
H.S. Diplomas (#)	181	166	3	5	1	6

South Hadley

116 Main St • South Hadley, MA 01075-2898
(413) 538-5060 • http://www.shschools.com/
Grade Span: PK-12; **Agency Type:** 1
Schools: 4
2 Primary; 1 Middle; 1 High; 0 Other Level
4 Regular; 0 Special Education; 0 Vocational; 0 Alternative
0 Magnet; 0 Charter; 2 Title I Eligible; 0 School-wide Title I
Students: 2,286 (51.0% male; 49.0% female)
Individual Education Program: 358 (15.7%);
English Language Learner: 0 (0.0%); Migrant: 0 (0.0%)
Eligible for Free Lunch Program: n/a
Eligible for Reduced-Price Lunch Program: n/a
Teachers: 163.1 (14.0 to 1)
Librarians/Media Specialists: 1.0 (2,286.0 to 1)
Guidance Counselors: 6.1 (374.8 to 1)
Current Spending: ($ per student per year):
Total: $8,119; Instruction: $5,528; Support Services: $2,350
Enrollment, Drop-out Rates and Diploma Recipients by Race/Ethnicity

Category	Total	White	Black	Asian	AIAN	Hisp.
Enrollment (%)	100.0	92.3	2.1	1.7	0.3	3.7
Drop-out Rate (%)	1.4	1.5	0.0	0.0	n/a	0.0
H.S. Diplomas (#)	160	154	2	2	0	2

Middlesex County

Acton

16 Charter Rd • Acton, MA 01720-2931
(978) 264-4700 • http://ab.mec.edu/
Grade Span: PK-06; **Agency Type:** 2
Schools: 5
5 Primary; 0 Middle; 0 High; 0 Other Level
5 Regular; 0 Special Education; 0 Vocational; 0 Alternative
0 Magnet; 0 Charter; 3 Title I Eligible; 0 School-wide Title I
Students: 2,547 (51.9% male; 48.1% female)
Individual Education Program: 326 (12.8%);
English Language Learner: 57 (2.2%); Migrant: 0 (0.0%)
Eligible for Free Lunch Program: n/a
Eligible for Reduced-Price Lunch Program: n/a
Teachers: 149.2 (17.1 to 1)
Librarians/Media Specialists: 1.0 (2,547.0 to 1)
Guidance Counselors: 5.0 (509.4 to 1)
Current Spending: ($ per student per year):
Total: $7,234; Instruction: $4,923; Support Services: $2,138
Enrollment, Drop-out Rates and Diploma Recipients by Race/Ethnicity

Category	Total	White	Black	Asian	AIAN	Hisp.
Enrollment (%)	100.0	79.8	0.7	17.5	0.0	1.9
Drop-out Rate (%)	n/a	n/a	n/a	n/a	n/a	n/a
H.S. Diplomas (#)	n/a	n/a	n/a	n/a	n/a	n/a

Acton-Boxborough

16 Charter Rd • Acton, MA 01720-2931
(978) 264-4700 • http://ab.mec.edu/
Grade Span: 07-12; **Agency Type:** 3
Schools: 2
0 Primary; 1 Middle; 1 High; 0 Other Level
2 Regular; 0 Special Education; 0 Vocational; 0 Alternative
0 Magnet; 0 Charter; 1 Title I Eligible; 0 School-wide Title I
Students: 2,497 (50.5% male; 49.5% female)
Individual Education Program: 329 (13.2%);
English Language Learner: 29 (1.2%); Migrant: 0 (0.0%)
Eligible for Free Lunch Program: n/a
Eligible for Reduced-Price Lunch Program: n/a
Teachers: 162.4 (15.4 to 1)
Librarians/Media Specialists: 3.0 (832.3 to 1)
Guidance Counselors: 11.6 (215.3 to 1)
Current Spending: ($ per student per year):
Total: $9,142; Instruction: $5,779; Support Services: $3,084
Enrollment, Drop-out Rates and Diploma Recipients by Race/Ethnicity

Category	Total	White	Black	Asian	AIAN	Hisp.
Enrollment (%)	100.0	85.6	0.9	11.8	0.2	1.5
Drop-out Rate (%)	0.0	0.0	0.0	0.0	0.0	0.0
H.S. Diplomas (#)	350	307	2	32	1	8

Arlington

869 Massachusetts Ave • Arlington, MA 02476-0002
(781) 316-3501 • http://www.arlington.k12.ma.us/
Grade Span: PK-12; **Agency Type:** 1
Schools: 10

8 Primary; 1 Middle; 1 High; 0 Other Level
10 Regular; 0 Special Education; 0 Vocational; 0 Alternative
0 Magnet; 0 Charter; 4 Title I Eligible; 0 School-wide Title I
Students: 4,481 (50.3% male; 49.7% female)
Individual Education Program: 612 (13.7%);
English Language Learner: 239 (5.3%); Migrant: 2 (<0.1%)
Eligible for Free Lunch Program: n/a
Eligible for Reduced-Price Lunch Program: n/a
Teachers: 347.0 (12.9 to 1)
Librarians/Media Specialists: 5.2 (861.7 to 1)
Guidance Counselors: 8.6 (521.0 to 1)
Current Spending: ($ per student per year):
Total: $9,710; Instruction: $6,407; Support Services: $2,951
Enrollment, Drop-out Rates and Diploma Recipients by Race/Ethnicity

Category	Total	White	Black	Asian	AIAN	Hisp.
Enrollment (%)	100.0	86.4	4.5	6.5	0.1	2.5
Drop-out Rate (%)	1.1	1.1	1.7	0.0	n/a	4.5
H.S. Diplomas (#)	260	226	14	15	0	5

Ashland
90 Concord St • Ashland, MA 01721-1699
(508) 881-0150 • http://www.ashlandhs.org/
Grade Span: PK-12; **Agency Type:** 1
Schools: 5
2 Primary; 2 Middle; 1 High; 0 Other Level
5 Regular; 0 Special Education; 0 Vocational; 0 Alternative
0 Magnet; 0 Charter; 1 Title I Eligible; 0 School-wide Title I
Students: 2,553 (50.1% male; 49.9% female)
Individual Education Program: 441 (17.3%);
English Language Learner: 11 (0.4%); Migrant: 0 (0.0%)
Eligible for Free Lunch Program: n/a
Eligible for Reduced-Price Lunch Program: n/a
Teachers: 182.1 (14.0 to 1)
Librarians/Media Specialists: 3.8 (671.8 to 1)
Guidance Counselors: 6.6 (386.8 to 1)
Current Spending: ($ per student per year):
Total: $8,811; Instruction: $6,130; Support Services: $2,404
Enrollment, Drop-out Rates and Diploma Recipients by Race/Ethnicity

Category	Total	White	Black	Asian	AIAN	Hisp.
Enrollment (%)	100.0	90.6	2.6	3.5	0.1	3.2
Drop-out Rate (%)	0.3	0.4	0.0	0.0	0.0	0.0
H.S. Diplomas (#)	135	123	4	6	0	2

Bedford
97 Mcmahon Rd • Bedford, MA 01730-2166
(781) 275-7588 • http://www.bedford.k12.ma.us/
Grade Span: PK-12; **Agency Type:** 1
Schools: 4
2 Primary; 1 Middle; 1 High; 0 Other Level
4 Regular; 0 Special Education; 0 Vocational; 0 Alternative
0 Magnet; 0 Charter; 0 Title I Eligible; 0 School-wide Title I
Students: 2,219 (49.8% male; 50.2% female)
Individual Education Program: 351 (15.8%);
English Language Learner: 38 (1.7%); Migrant: 10 (0.5%)
Eligible for Free Lunch Program: n/a
Eligible for Reduced-Price Lunch Program: n/a
Teachers: 182.2 (12.2 to 1)
Librarians/Media Specialists: 4.0 (554.8 to 1)
Guidance Counselors: 8.9 (249.3 to 1)
Current Spending: ($ per student per year):
Total: $11,364; Instruction: $6,718; Support Services: $4,375
Enrollment, Drop-out Rates and Diploma Recipients by Race/Ethnicity

Category	Total	White	Black	Asian	AIAN	Hisp.
Enrollment (%)	100.0	83.1	5.4	8.7	0.6	2.1
Drop-out Rate (%)	0.6	0.7	0.0	0.0	0.0	0.0
H.S. Diplomas (#)	154	139	9	5	1	0

Belmont
644 Pleasant St • Belmont, MA 02478-2589
(617) 484-2642 • http://www.belmont.k12.ma.us/
Grade Span: PK-12; **Agency Type:** 1
Schools: 6
4 Primary; 1 Middle; 1 High; 0 Other Level
6 Regular; 0 Special Education; 0 Vocational; 0 Alternative
0 Magnet; 0 Charter; 2 Title I Eligible; 0 School-wide Title I
Students: 3,601 (51.8% male; 48.2% female)
Individual Education Program: 504 (14.0%);
English Language Learner: 77 (2.1%); Migrant: 1 (<0.1%)
Eligible for Free Lunch Program: n/a
Eligible for Reduced-Price Lunch Program: n/a
Teachers: 349.7 (10.3 to 1)
Librarians/Media Specialists: 3.0 (1,200.3 to 1)
Guidance Counselors: 25.0 (144.0 to 1)
Current Spending: ($ per student per year):
Total: $8,521; Instruction: $5,837; Support Services: $2,470
Enrollment, Drop-out Rates and Diploma Recipients by Race/Ethnicity

Category	Total	White	Black	Asian	AIAN	Hisp.
Enrollment (%)	100.0	81.8	4.1	11.2	0.3	2.6
Drop-out Rate (%)	1.1	1.0	2.7	1.1	0.0	4.8
H.S. Diplomas (#)	203	163	10	24	1	5

Billerica
365 Boston Rd • Billerica, MA 01821-1888
(978) 436-9500 • http://www.billerica.mec.edu
Grade Span: PK-12; **Agency Type:** 1
Schools: 9
6 Primary; 2 Middle; 0 High; 1 Other Level
9 Regular; 0 Special Education; 0 Vocational; 0 Alternative
0 Magnet; 0 Charter; 2 Title I Eligible; 0 School-wide Title I
Students: 6,363 (51.3% male; 48.7% female)
Individual Education Program: 96 (1.5%);
English Language Learner: 6 (0.1%); Migrant: 2 (<0.1%)
Eligible for Free Lunch Program: n/a
Eligible for Reduced-Price Lunch Program: n/a
Teachers: 304.8 (20.9 to 1)
Librarians/Media Specialists: 7.0 (909.0 to 1)
Guidance Counselors: 18.0 (353.5 to 1)
Current Spending: ($ per student per year):
Total: $8,322; Instruction: $5,854; Support Services: $2,210
Enrollment, Drop-out Rates and Diploma Recipients by Race/Ethnicity

Category	Total	White	Black	Asian	AIAN	Hisp.
Enrollment (%)	100.0	95.1	0.7	2.3	0.4	1.5
Drop-out Rate (%)	2.6	2.7	0.0	0.0	0.0	11.1
H.S. Diplomas (#)	335	311	3	15	2	4

Burlington
123 Cambridge St • Burlington, MA 01803-3755
(781) 270-1800 • http://www.burlington.mec.edu/
Grade Span: PK-12; **Agency Type:** 1
Schools: 6
4 Primary; 1 Middle; 0 High; 1 Other Level
6 Regular; 0 Special Education; 0 Vocational; 0 Alternative
0 Magnet; 0 Charter; 4 Title I Eligible; 0 School-wide Title I
Students: 3,511 (51.3% male; 48.7% female)
Individual Education Program: 499 (14.2%);
English Language Learner: 0 (0.0%); Migrant: 0 (0.0%)
Eligible for Free Lunch Program: n/a
Eligible for Reduced-Price Lunch Program: n/a
Teachers: 288.1 (12.2 to 1)
Librarians/Media Specialists: 0.0 (0.0 to 1)
Guidance Counselors: 13.0 (270.1 to 1)
Current Spending: ($ per student per year):
Total: $9,781; Instruction: $6,719; Support Services: $2,789
Enrollment, Drop-out Rates and Diploma Recipients by Race/Ethnicity

Category	Total	White	Black	Asian	AIAN	Hisp.
Enrollment (%)	100.0	89.3	1.5	8.7	0.0	0.5
Drop-out Rate (%)	0.4	0.5	0.0	0.0	0.0	0.0
H.S. Diplomas (#)	202	170	2	29	0	1

Cambridge
159 Thorndike St • Cambridge, MA 02141-1528
(617) 349-6494 • http://www.cpsd.us/index.cfm
Grade Span: PK-12; **Agency Type:** 1
Schools: 16
11 Primary; 0 Middle; 1 High; 4 Other Level
16 Regular; 0 Special Education; 0 Vocational; 0 Alternative
0 Magnet; 0 Charter; 9 Title I Eligible; 7 School-wide Title I
Students: 6,765 (51.2% male; 48.8% female)
Individual Education Program: 1,497 (22.1%);
English Language Learner: 673 (9.9%); Migrant: 1 (<0.1%)
Eligible for Free Lunch Program: n/a
Eligible for Reduced-Price Lunch Program: n/a
Teachers: 660.6 (10.2 to 1)
Librarians/Media Specialists: 18.2 (371.7 to 1)
Guidance Counselors: 21.0 (322.1 to 1)
Current Spending: ($ per student per year):
Total: $17,286; Instruction: $11,274; Support Services: $5,491
Enrollment, Drop-out Rates and Diploma Recipients by Race/Ethnicity

Category	Total	White	Black	Asian	AIAN	Hisp.
Enrollment (%)	100.0	37.4	37.8	10.2	0.6	14.0
Drop-out Rate (%)	3.1	3.1	2.5	0.0	0.0	6.3
H.S. Diplomas (#)	338	145	122	28	0	43

Chelmsford
190 Richardson Rd • North Chelmsford, MA 01863-2323
(978) 251-5100 • http://www.chelmsford.k12.ma.us/
Grade Span: PK-12; **Agency Type:** 1
Schools: 8
5 Primary; 2 Middle; 1 High; 0 Other Level
8 Regular; 0 Special Education; 0 Vocational; 0 Alternative

0 Magnet; 0 Charter; 5 Title I Eligible; 0 School-wide Title I
Students: 5,728 (51.1% male; 48.9% female)
Individual Education Program: 721 (12.6%);
English Language Learner: 28 (0.5%); Migrant: 4 (0.1%)
Eligible for Free Lunch Program: n/a
Eligible for Reduced-Price Lunch Program: n/a
Teachers: 377.0 (15.2 to 1)
Librarians/Media Specialists: 4.0 (1,432.0 to 1)
Guidance Counselors: 18.0 (318.2 to 1)
Current Spending: ($ per student per year):
Total: $8,206; Instruction: $5,696; Support Services: $2,255
Enrollment, Drop-out Rates and Diploma Recipients by Race/Ethnicity

Category	Total	White	Black	Asian	AIAN	Hisp.
Enrollment (%)	100.0	91.2	1.1	6.8	0.1	0.9
Drop-out Rate (%)	1.2	1.1	30.0	0.0	0.0	0.0
H.S. Diplomas (#)	401	359	3	36	1	2

Concord

120 Meriam Rd • Concord, MA 01742-2699
(978) 318-1510 • http://www.colonial.net/
Grade Span: PK-08; **Agency Type:** 2
Schools: 4
3 Primary; 1 Middle; 0 High; 0 Other Level
4 Regular; 0 Special Education; 0 Vocational; 0 Alternative
0 Magnet; 0 Charter; 2 Title I Eligible; 0 School-wide Title I
Students: 1,988 (47.6% male; 52.4% female)
Individual Education Program: 337 (17.0%);
English Language Learner: 19 (1.0%); Migrant: 10 (0.5%)
Eligible for Free Lunch Program: n/a
Eligible for Reduced-Price Lunch Program: n/a
Teachers: 162.5 (12.2 to 1)
Librarians/Media Specialists: 4.0 (497.0 to 1)
Guidance Counselors: 3.0 (662.7 to 1)
Current Spending: ($ per student per year):
Total: $9,751; Instruction: $6,675; Support Services: $2,893
Enrollment, Drop-out Rates and Diploma Recipients by Race/Ethnicity

Category	Total	White	Black	Asian	AIAN	Hisp.
Enrollment (%)	100.0	86.0	5.5	6.0	0.6	2.0
Drop-out Rate (%)	n/a	n/a	n/a	n/a	n/a	n/a
H.S. Diplomas (#)	n/a	n/a	n/a	n/a	n/a	n/a

Dracut

2063 Lakeview Ave • Dracut, MA 01826-3005
(978) 957-2660 • http://www.dracut.k12.ma.us/
Grade Span: PK-12; **Agency Type:** 1
Schools: 7
4 Primary; 2 Middle; 1 High; 0 Other Level
7 Regular; 0 Special Education; 0 Vocational; 0 Alternative
0 Magnet; 0 Charter; 3 Title I Eligible; 0 School-wide Title I
Students: 4,259 (52.7% male; 47.3% female)
Individual Education Program: 444 (10.4%);
English Language Learner: 47 (1.1%); Migrant: 1 (<0.1%)
Eligible for Free Lunch Program: n/a
Eligible for Reduced-Price Lunch Program: n/a
Teachers: 270.2 (15.8 to 1)
Librarians/Media Specialists: 2.0 (2,129.5 to 1)
Guidance Counselors: 14.0 (304.2 to 1)
Current Spending: ($ per student per year):
Total: $7,184; Instruction: $4,504; Support Services: $2,371
Enrollment, Drop-out Rates and Diploma Recipients by Race/Ethnicity

Category	Total	White	Black	Asian	AIAN	Hisp.
Enrollment (%)	100.0	94.3	1.2	3.2	0.1	1.2
Drop-out Rate (%)	2.3	2.1	0.0	2.4	n/a	18.2
H.S. Diplomas (#)	246	232	0	12	0	2

Everett

121 Vine St • Everett, MA 02149-4827
(617) 389-7950 • http://www.everett.k12.ma.us/
Grade Span: PK-12; **Agency Type:** 1
Schools: 8
7 Primary; 0 Middle; 1 High; 0 Other Level
8 Regular; 0 Special Education; 0 Vocational; 0 Alternative
0 Magnet; 0 Charter; 6 Title I Eligible; 6 School-wide Title I
Students: 5,371 (50.3% male; 49.7% female)
Individual Education Program: 746 (13.9%);
English Language Learner: 558 (10.4%); Migrant: 3 (0.1%)
Eligible for Free Lunch Program: n/a
Eligible for Reduced-Price Lunch Program: n/a
Teachers: 423.0 (12.7 to 1)
Librarians/Media Specialists: 5.0 (1,074.2 to 1)
Guidance Counselors: 15.0 (358.1 to 1)
Current Spending: ($ per student per year):
Total: $8,515; Instruction: $6,174; Support Services: $2,060
Enrollment, Drop-out Rates and Diploma Recipients by Race/Ethnicity

Category	Total	White	Black	Asian	AIAN	Hisp.
Enrollment (%)	100.0	71.6	8.8	5.5	0.1	14.0
Drop-out Rate (%)	3.5	3.5	1.9	3.2	0.0	5.4
H.S. Diplomas (#)	294	231	30	11	0	22

Framingham

14 Vernon Street, Ste 201 • Framingham, MA 01701-7433
(508) 626-9117 • http://www.framingham.k12.ma.us/
Grade Span: PK-12; **Agency Type:** 1
Schools: 14
10 Primary; 3 Middle; 1 High; 0 Other Level
14 Regular; 0 Special Education; 0 Vocational; 0 Alternative
0 Magnet; 0 Charter; 7 Title I Eligible; 2 School-wide Title I
Students: 8,364 (50.7% male; 49.3% female)
Individual Education Program: 1,328 (15.9%);
English Language Learner: 1,519 (18.2%); Migrant: 0 (0.0%)
Eligible for Free Lunch Program: n/a
Eligible for Reduced-Price Lunch Program: n/a
Teachers: 671.5 (12.5 to 1)
Librarians/Media Specialists: 4.0 (2,091.0 to 1)
Guidance Counselors: 42.1 (198.7 to 1)
Current Spending: ($ per student per year):
Total: $10,702; Instruction: $7,126; Support Services: $3,304
Enrollment, Drop-out Rates and Diploma Recipients by Race/Ethnicity

Category	Total	White	Black	Asian	AIAN	Hisp.
Enrollment (%)	100.0	69.3	7.1	5.6	0.3	17.7
Drop-out Rate (%)	1.9	1.9	2.2	2.9	n/a	1.5
H.S. Diplomas (#)	395	311	27	23	0	34

Greater Lowell Voc Tec

250 Pawtucket Blvd • Tyngsborough, MA 01879-2199
(978) 441-4800 • http://www.gltech.org/
Grade Span: 09-12; **Agency Type:** 4
Schools: 1
0 Primary; 0 Middle; 1 High; 0 Other Level
0 Regular; 0 Special Education; 1 Vocational; 0 Alternative
0 Magnet; 0 Charter; 1 Title I Eligible; 1 School-wide Title I
Students: 1,858 (51.9% male; 48.1% female)
Individual Education Program: 462 (24.9%);
English Language Learner: 38 (2.0%); Migrant: 0 (0.0%)
Eligible for Free Lunch Program: n/a
Eligible for Reduced-Price Lunch Program: n/a
Teachers: 109.0 (17.0 to 1)
Librarians/Media Specialists: 0.0 (0.0 to 1)
Guidance Counselors: 15.0 (123.9 to 1)
Current Spending: ($ per student per year):
Total: $12,799; Instruction: $7,605; Support Services: $4,792
Enrollment, Drop-out Rates and Diploma Recipients by Race/Ethnicity

Category	Total	White	Black	Asian	AIAN	Hisp.
Enrollment (%)	100.0	62.5	2.7	10.5	0.4	23.8
Drop-out Rate (%)	0.2	0.2	0.0	0.0	0.0	0.6
H.S. Diplomas (#)	337	250	9	19	2	57

Groton-Dunstable

73 Pepperell St • Groton, MA 01450-0729
Mailing Address: PO Box 729 • Groton, MA 01450-0729
(978) 448-5505 • http://www.gdrsd.org/
Grade Span: PK-12; **Agency Type:** 3
Schools: 6
4 Primary; 1 Middle; 1 High; 0 Other Level
6 Regular; 0 Special Education; 0 Vocational; 0 Alternative
0 Magnet; 0 Charter; 1 Title I Eligible; 0 School-wide Title I
Students: 2,774 (52.2% male; 47.8% female)
Individual Education Program: 270 (9.7%);
English Language Learner: 0 (0.0%); Migrant: 0 (0.0%)
Eligible for Free Lunch Program: n/a
Eligible for Reduced-Price Lunch Program: n/a
Teachers: 181.1 (15.3 to 1)
Librarians/Media Specialists: 2.0 (1,387.0 to 1)
Guidance Counselors: 10.9 (254.5 to 1)
Current Spending: ($ per student per year):
Total: $7,647; Instruction: $4,745; Support Services: $2,669
Enrollment, Drop-out Rates and Diploma Recipients by Race/Ethnicity

Category	Total	White	Black	Asian	AIAN	Hisp.
Enrollment (%)	100.0	96.9	0.4	2.2	0.1	0.4
Drop-out Rate (%)	1.7	1.7	n/a	0.0	n/a	0.0
H.S. Diplomas (#)	118	115	0	1	0	2

Holliston

370 Hollis St • Holliston, MA 01746-1803
(508) 429-0654 • http://www.holliston.k12.ma.us/
Grade Span: PK-12; **Agency Type:** 1
Schools: 4
2 Primary; 1 Middle; 1 High; 0 Other Level

4 Regular; 0 Special Education; 0 Vocational; 0 Alternative
0 Magnet; 0 Charter; 0 Title I Eligible; 0 School-wide Title I
Students: 3,082 (51.1% male; 48.9% female)
Individual Education Program: 374 (12.1%);
English Language Learner: 0 (0.0%); Migrant: 0 (0.0%)
Eligible for Free Lunch Program: n/a
Eligible for Reduced-Price Lunch Program: n/a
Teachers: 234.7 (13.1 to 1)
Librarians/Media Specialists: 3.0 (1,027.3 to 1)
Guidance Counselors: 19.0 (162.2 to 1)
Current Spending: ($ per student per year):
Total: $8,295; Instruction: $5,527; Support Services: $2,588
Enrollment, Drop-out Rates and Diploma Recipients by Race/Ethnicity

Category	Total	White	Black	Asian	AIAN	Hisp.
Enrollment (%)	100.0	96.0	1.0	1.6	0.1	1.3
Drop-out Rate (%)	0.7	0.6	16.7	0.0	n/a	0.0
H.S. Diplomas (#)	187	180	2	2	0	3

Hopkinton
88-A Hayden Rowe St • Hopkinton, MA 01748-2533
(508) 497-9800 • http://www.hopkinton.k12.ma.us/
Grade Span: PK-12; **Agency Type:** 1
Schools: 5
3 Primary; 1 Middle; 1 High; 0 Other Level
5 Regular; 0 Special Education; 0 Vocational; 0 Alternative
0 Magnet; 0 Charter; 1 Title I Eligible; 0 School-wide Title I
Students: 2,924 (51.0% male; 49.0% female)
Individual Education Program: 366 (12.5%);
English Language Learner: 0 (0.0%); Migrant: 0 (0.0%)
Eligible for Free Lunch Program: n/a
Eligible for Reduced-Price Lunch Program: n/a
Teachers: 234.2 (12.5 to 1)
Librarians/Media Specialists: 5.0 (584.8 to 1)
Guidance Counselors: 10.8 (270.7 to 1)
Current Spending: ($ per student per year):
Total: $7,821; Instruction: $5,533; Support Services: $2,103
Enrollment, Drop-out Rates and Diploma Recipients by Race/Ethnicity

Category	Total	White	Black	Asian	AIAN	Hisp.
Enrollment (%)	100.0	96.2	0.7	2.4	0.1	0.6
Drop-out Rate (%)	0.8	0.8	0.0	0.0	n/a	0.0
H.S. Diplomas (#)	162	151	3	6	1	1

Hudson
155 Apsley St • Hudson, MA 01749-1645
(978) 567-6100 • http://www.hudson.k12.ma.us/
Grade Span: PK-12; **Agency Type:** 1
Schools: 6
4 Primary; 1 Middle; 0 High; 1 Other Level
6 Regular; 0 Special Education; 0 Vocational; 0 Alternative
0 Magnet; 0 Charter; 3 Title I Eligible; 0 School-wide Title I
Students: 2,769 (53.0% male; 47.0% female)
Individual Education Program: 493 (17.8%);
English Language Learner: 97 (3.5%); Migrant: 0 (0.0%)
Eligible for Free Lunch Program: n/a
Eligible for Reduced-Price Lunch Program: n/a
Teachers: 234.8 (11.8 to 1)
Librarians/Media Specialists: 3.4 (814.4 to 1)
Guidance Counselors: 7.5 (369.2 to 1)
Current Spending: ($ per student per year):
Total: $9,369; Instruction: $6,145; Support Services: $2,914
Enrollment, Drop-out Rates and Diploma Recipients by Race/Ethnicity

Category	Total	White	Black	Asian	AIAN	Hisp.
Enrollment (%)	100.0	93.8	1.4	1.4	0.4	2.9
Drop-out Rate (%)	4.2	4.2	20.0	0.0	n/a	0.0
H.S. Diplomas (#)	177	175	0	0	0	2

Lexington
1557 Mass Ave • Lexington, MA 02420-3801
(781) 861-2550 • http://lps.lexingtonma.org/
Grade Span: PK-12; **Agency Type:** 1
Schools: 9
6 Primary; 2 Middle; 1 High; 0 Other Level
9 Regular; 0 Special Education; 0 Vocational; 0 Alternative
0 Magnet; 0 Charter; 3 Title I Eligible; 0 School-wide Title I
Students: 6,051 (51.0% male; 49.0% female)
Individual Education Program: 1,027 (17.0%);
English Language Learner: 198 (3.3%); Migrant: 0 (0.0%)
Eligible for Free Lunch Program: n/a
Eligible for Reduced-Price Lunch Program: n/a
Teachers: 522.6 (11.6 to 1)
Librarians/Media Specialists: 10.0 (605.1 to 1)
Guidance Counselors: 46.8 (129.3 to 1)
Current Spending: ($ per student per year):
Total: $10,336; Instruction: $6,938; Support Services: $3,376

Enrollment, Drop-out Rates and Diploma Recipients by Race/Ethnicity

Category	Total	White	Black	Asian	AIAN	Hisp.
Enrollment (%)	100.0	76.5	4.9	16.7	0.1	1.8
Drop-out Rate (%)	0.3	0.3	0.0	0.4	0.0	0.0
H.S. Diplomas (#)	396	308	18	64	1	5

Littleton
33 Shattuck St • Littleton, MA 01460-4486
Mailing Address: PO Box 1486 • Littleton, MA 01460-4486
(978) 486-8951
Grade Span: PK-12; **Agency Type:** 1
Schools: 4
2 Primary; 1 Middle; 1 High; 0 Other Level
4 Regular; 0 Special Education; 0 Vocational; 0 Alternative
0 Magnet; 0 Charter; 3 Title I Eligible; 0 School-wide Title I
Students: 1,550 (48.3% male; 51.7% female)
Individual Education Program: 266 (17.2%);
English Language Learner: 0 (0.0%); Migrant: 0 (0.0%)
Eligible for Free Lunch Program: n/a
Eligible for Reduced-Price Lunch Program: n/a
Teachers: 109.7 (14.1 to 1)
Librarians/Media Specialists: 2.0 (775.0 to 1)
Guidance Counselors: 6.0 (258.3 to 1)
Current Spending: ($ per student per year):
Total: $8,241; Instruction: $5,465; Support Services: $2,599
Enrollment, Drop-out Rates and Diploma Recipients by Race/Ethnicity

Category	Total	White	Black	Asian	AIAN	Hisp.
Enrollment (%)	100.0	96.5	0.3	1.9	0.0	1.3
Drop-out Rate (%)	0.9	1.0	0.0	0.0	n/a	0.0
H.S. Diplomas (#)	82	78	1	2	0	1

Lowell
155 Merrimack St • Lowell, MA 01852-1723
(978) 937-7647 • http://www.lowell.k12.ma.us
Grade Span: PK-12; **Agency Type:** 1
Schools: 26
18 Primary; 7 Middle; 1 High; 0 Other Level
25 Regular; 0 Special Education; 0 Vocational; 1 Alternative
1 Magnet; 0 Charter; 25 Title I Eligible; 25 School-wide Title I
Students: 15,472 (51.6% male; 48.4% female)
Individual Education Program: 1,940 (12.5%);
English Language Learner: 2,208 (14.3%); Migrant: 269 (1.7%)
Eligible for Free Lunch Program: n/a
Eligible for Reduced-Price Lunch Program: n/a
Teachers: 1,151.0 (13.4 to 1)
Librarians/Media Specialists: 23.0 (672.7 to 1)
Guidance Counselors: 25.0 (618.9 to 1)
Current Spending: ($ per student per year):
Total: $10,622; Instruction: $7,460; Support Services: $2,876
Enrollment, Drop-out Rates and Diploma Recipients by Race/Ethnicity

Category	Total	White	Black	Asian	AIAN	Hisp.
Enrollment (%)	100.0	44.0	5.4	29.9	0.2	20.5
Drop-out Rate (%)	9.8	6.4	9.3	12.5	100.0	12.4
H.S. Diplomas (#)	732	319	38	285	0	90

Malden
77 Salem St • Malden, MA 02148-5289
(781) 397-7204 • http://www.malden.mec.edu/
Grade Span: PK-12; **Agency Type:** 1
Schools: 6
5 Primary; 0 Middle; 1 High; 0 Other Level
6 Regular; 0 Special Education; 0 Vocational; 0 Alternative
0 Magnet; 0 Charter; 5 Title I Eligible; 1 School-wide Title I
Students: 5,945 (51.7% male; 48.3% female)
Individual Education Program: 968 (16.3%);
English Language Learner: 613 (10.3%); Migrant: 0 (0.0%)
Eligible for Free Lunch Program: n/a
Eligible for Reduced-Price Lunch Program: n/a
Teachers: 463.0 (12.8 to 1)
Librarians/Media Specialists: 6.0 (990.8 to 1)
Guidance Counselors: 9.0 (660.6 to 1)
Current Spending: ($ per student per year):
Total: $10,570; Instruction: $7,542; Support Services: $2,683
Enrollment, Drop-out Rates and Diploma Recipients by Race/Ethnicity

Category	Total	White	Black	Asian	AIAN	Hisp.
Enrollment (%)	100.0	54.0	16.0	20.8	0.3	9.0
Drop-out Rate (%)	3.8	4.4	1.7	3.6	0.0	4.7
H.S. Diplomas (#)	308	131	53	91	1	32

Marlborough
District Education Center • Marlborough, MA 01752-2225
(508) 460-3509 • http://www.marlborough.k12.ma.us/
Grade Span: PK-12; **Agency Type:** 1
Schools: 7
4 Primary; 2 Middle; 1 High; 0 Other Level

7 Regular; 0 Special Education; 0 Vocational; 0 Alternative
0 Magnet; 0 Charter; 3 Title I Eligible; 0 School-wide Title I
Students: 4,729 (52.7% male; 47.3% female)
Individual Education Program: 971 (20.5%);
English Language Learner: 562 (11.9%); Migrant: 5 (0.1%)
Eligible for Free Lunch Program: n/a
Eligible for Reduced-Price Lunch Program: n/a
Teachers: 375.3 (12.6 to 1)
Librarians/Media Specialists: 2.0 (2,364.5 to 1)
Guidance Counselors: 12.8 (369.5 to 1)
Current Spending: ($ per student per year):
Total: $9,109; Instruction: $6,220; Support Services: $2,683
Enrollment, Drop-out Rates and Diploma Recipients by Race/Ethnicity

Category	Total	White	Black	Asian	AIAN	Hisp.
Enrollment (%)	100.0	70.9	2.7	3.8	0.4	22.2
Drop-out Rate (%)	4.2	2.7	0.0	0.0	n/a	14.5
H.S. Diplomas (#)	188	145	4	9	1	29

Medford

489 Winthrop St • Medford, MA 02155-2349
(781) 393-2442 • http://www.medford.k12.ma.us/
Grade Span: PK-12; **Agency Type:** 1
Schools: 13
9 Primary; 1 Middle; 2 High; 1 Other Level
12 Regular; 0 Special Education; 1 Vocational; 0 Alternative
0 Magnet; 0 Charter; 5 Title I Eligible; 0 School-wide Title I
Students: 4,722 (51.3% male; 48.7% female)
Individual Education Program: 770 (16.3%);
English Language Learner: 686 (14.5%); Migrant: 36 (0.8%)
Eligible for Free Lunch Program: n/a
Eligible for Reduced-Price Lunch Program: n/a
Teachers: 427.7 (11.0 to 1)
Librarians/Media Specialists: 5.0 (944.4 to 1)
Guidance Counselors: 12.0 (393.5 to 1)
Current Spending: ($ per student per year):
Total: $12,777; Instruction: $8,519; Support Services: $3,965
Enrollment, Drop-out Rates and Diploma Recipients by Race/Ethnicity

Category	Total	White	Black	Asian	AIAN	Hisp.
Enrollment (%)	100.0	73.8	14.1	5.5	0.8	5.9
Drop-out Rate (%)	2.6	2.3	3.1	1.5	0.0	6.2
H.S. Diplomas (#)	283	200	43	13	5	22

Melrose

360 Lynn Fells Pkwy • Melrose, MA 02176-2244
(781) 662-2000 • http://www.melroseschools.com/
Grade Span: PK-12; **Agency Type:** 1
Schools: 8
6 Primary; 1 Middle; 1 High; 0 Other Level
8 Regular; 0 Special Education; 0 Vocational; 0 Alternative
0 Magnet; 0 Charter; 0 Title I Eligible; 0 School-wide Title I
Students: 3,498 (50.4% male; 49.6% female)
Individual Education Program: 571 (16.3%);
English Language Learner: 52 (1.5%); Migrant: 0 (0.0%)
Eligible for Free Lunch Program: n/a
Eligible for Reduced-Price Lunch Program: n/a
Teachers: 246.3 (14.2 to 1)
Librarians/Media Specialists: 1.0 (3,498.0 to 1)
Guidance Counselors: 8.4 (416.4 to 1)
Current Spending: ($ per student per year):
Total: $9,187; Instruction: $6,135; Support Services: $2,769
Enrollment, Drop-out Rates and Diploma Recipients by Race/Ethnicity

Category	Total	White	Black	Asian	AIAN	Hisp.
Enrollment (%)	100.0	92.9	3.8	2.3	0.2	0.9
Drop-out Rate (%)	1.4	1.2	0.0	5.6	n/a	12.5
H.S. Diplomas (#)	213	192	15	5	0	1

Natick

13 E Central St • Natick, MA 01760-4629
(508) 647-6500 • http://www.natick.k12.ma.us/
Grade Span: PK-12; **Agency Type:** 1
Schools: 8
5 Primary; 2 Middle; 1 High; 0 Other Level
8 Regular; 0 Special Education; 0 Vocational; 0 Alternative
0 Magnet; 0 Charter; 3 Title I Eligible; 0 School-wide Title I
Students: 4,555 (52.4% male; 47.6% female)
Individual Education Program: 775 (17.0%);
English Language Learner: 61 (1.3%); Migrant: 3 (0.1%)
Eligible for Free Lunch Program: n/a
Eligible for Reduced-Price Lunch Program: n/a
Teachers: 350.0 (13.0 to 1)
Librarians/Media Specialists: 3.0 (1,518.3 to 1)
Guidance Counselors: 13.6 (334.9 to 1)
Current Spending: ($ per student per year):
Total: $9,231; Instruction: $6,269; Support Services: $2,733
Enrollment, Drop-out Rates and Diploma Recipients by Race/Ethnicity

Category	Total	White	Black	Asian	AIAN	Hisp.
Enrollment (%)	100.0	90.6	3.1	4.5	0.2	1.7
Drop-out Rate (%)	1.4	1.4	0.0	0.0	n/a	10.0
H.S. Diplomas (#)	257	237	9	7	0	4

Newton

100 Walnut St • Newtonville, MA 02460-1314
(617) 559-6100 • http://newton.mec.edu
Grade Span: PK-12; **Agency Type:** 1
Schools: 22
16 Primary; 4 Middle; 2 High; 0 Other Level
22 Regular; 0 Special Education; 0 Vocational; 0 Alternative
0 Magnet; 0 Charter; 4 Title I Eligible; 0 School-wide Title I
Students: 11,358 (51.1% male; 48.9% female)
Individual Education Program: 1,927 (17.0%);
English Language Learner: 545 (4.8%); Migrant: 0 (0.0%)
Eligible for Free Lunch Program: n/a
Eligible for Reduced-Price Lunch Program: n/a
Teachers: 981.0 (11.6 to 1)
Librarians/Media Specialists: 30.4 (373.6 to 1)
Guidance Counselors: 46.1 (246.4 to 1)
Current Spending: ($ per student per year):
Total: $11,810; Instruction: $8,277; Support Services: $3,246
Enrollment, Drop-out Rates and Diploma Recipients by Race/Ethnicity

Category	Total	White	Black	Asian	AIAN	Hisp.
Enrollment (%)	100.0	80.8	5.3	10.9	0.1	2.9
Drop-out Rate (%)	0.4	0.3	1.1	0.6	0.0	2.5
H.S. Diplomas (#)	848	716	39	74	0	19

North Middlesex

23 Main St • Townsend, MA 01469-1356
(978) 597-8713 • http://www.nmiddlesex.mec.edu/
Grade Span: PK-12; **Agency Type:** 3
Schools: 8
5 Primary; 2 Middle; 1 High; 0 Other Level
8 Regular; 0 Special Education; 0 Vocational; 0 Alternative
0 Magnet; 0 Charter; 4 Title I Eligible; 0 School-wide Title I
Students: 4,659 (50.6% male; 49.4% female)
Individual Education Program: 525 (11.3%);
English Language Learner: 0 (0.0%); Migrant: 0 (0.0%)
Eligible for Free Lunch Program: n/a
Eligible for Reduced-Price Lunch Program: n/a
Teachers: 345.7 (13.5 to 1)
Librarians/Media Specialists: 8.0 (582.4 to 1)
Guidance Counselors: 15.0 (310.6 to 1)
Current Spending: ($ per student per year):
Total: $7,509; Instruction: $5,091; Support Services: $2,256
Enrollment, Drop-out Rates and Diploma Recipients by Race/Ethnicity

Category	Total	White	Black	Asian	AIAN	Hisp.
Enrollment (%)	100.0	97.7	0.7	0.7	0.1	0.8
Drop-out Rate (%)	1.5	1.1	23.1	0.0	0.0	14.3
H.S. Diplomas (#)	241	239	0	0	2	0

North Reading

19 Sherman Rd • North Reading, MA 01864-2398
(978) 664-7810
Grade Span: PK-12; **Agency Type:** 1
Schools: 5
3 Primary; 1 Middle; 1 High; 0 Other Level
5 Regular; 0 Special Education; 0 Vocational; 0 Alternative
0 Magnet; 0 Charter; 2 Title I Eligible; 0 School-wide Title I
Students: 2,604 (50.7% male; 49.3% female)
Individual Education Program: 366 (14.1%);
English Language Learner: 5 (0.2%); Migrant: 0 (0.0%)
Eligible for Free Lunch Program: n/a
Eligible for Reduced-Price Lunch Program: n/a
Teachers: 160.1 (16.3 to 1)
Librarians/Media Specialists: 1.0 (2,604.0 to 1)
Guidance Counselors: 5.5 (473.5 to 1)
Current Spending: ($ per student per year):
Total: $6,879; Instruction: $4,597; Support Services: $2,091
Enrollment, Drop-out Rates and Diploma Recipients by Race/Ethnicity

Category	Total	White	Black	Asian	AIAN	Hisp.
Enrollment (%)	100.0	97.0	0.2	1.7	0.5	0.6
Drop-out Rate (%)	2.0	2.1	0.0	0.0	0.0	0.0
H.S. Diplomas (#)	90	88	1	1	0	0

Reading

82 Oakland Rd • Reading, MA 01867-1613
(781) 944-5800 • http://www.reading.k12.ma.us/
Grade Span: PK-12; **Agency Type:** 1
Schools: 7
5 Primary; 1 Middle; 0 High; 1 Other Level
7 Regular; 0 Special Education; 0 Vocational; 0 Alternative

0 Magnet; 0 Charter; 0 Title I Eligible; 0 School-wide Title I
Students: 4,293 (51.2% male; 48.8% female)
Individual Education Program: 608 (14.2%);
English Language Learner: 29 (0.7%); Migrant: 1 (<0.1%)
Eligible for Free Lunch Program: n/a
Eligible for Reduced-Price Lunch Program: n/a
Teachers: 280.2 (15.3 to 1)
Librarians/Media Specialists: 7.0 (613.3 to 1)
Guidance Counselors: 6.0 (715.5 to 1)
Current Spending: ($ per student per year):
Total: $7,954; Instruction: $5,612; Support Services: $2,118
Enrollment, Drop-out Rates and Diploma Recipients by Race/Ethnicity

Category	Total	White	Black	Asian	AIAN	Hisp.
Enrollment (%)	100.0	94.7	1.4	3.1	0.1	0.7
Drop-out Rate (%)	1.0	1.1	0.0	0.0	0.0	0.0
H.S. Diplomas (#)	288	269	8	9	0	2

Somerville
181 Washington St • Somerville, MA 02143-1717
(617) 625-6600 •
http://www.somerville.k12.ma.us/education/district/district.php?sectionid=1
Grade Span: PK-12; **Agency Type:** 1
Schools: 13
10 Primary; 1 Middle; 2 High; 0 Other Level
11 Regular; 0 Special Education; 0 Vocational; 2 Alternative
0 Magnet; 0 Charter; 9 Title I Eligible; 9 School-wide Title I
Students: 5,757 (50.9% male; 49.1% female)
Individual Education Program: 1,145 (19.9%);
English Language Learner: 1,039 (18.0%); Migrant: 9 (0.2%)
Eligible for Free Lunch Program: n/a
Eligible for Reduced-Price Lunch Program: n/a
Teachers: 503.1 (11.4 to 1)
Librarians/Media Specialists: 10.0 (575.7 to 1)
Guidance Counselors: 19.0 (303.0 to 1)
Current Spending: ($ per student per year):
Total: $13,001; Instruction: $8,438; Support Services: $3,921
Enrollment, Drop-out Rates and Diploma Recipients by Race/Ethnicity

Category	Total	White	Black	Asian	AIAN	Hisp.
Enrollment (%)	100.0	46.4	15.8	7.6	0.3	29.9
Drop-out Rate (%)	4.3	4.4	2.5	1.4	25.0	7.4
H.S. Diplomas (#)	334	152	76	30	0	76

Stoneham
149 Franklin St • Stoneham, MA 02180-1513
(781) 279-3800
Grade Span: PK-12; **Agency Type:** 1
Schools: 6
4 Primary; 1 Middle; 1 High; 0 Other Level
6 Regular; 0 Special Education; 0 Vocational; 0 Alternative
0 Magnet; 0 Charter; 4 Title I Eligible; 0 School-wide Title I
Students: 2,969 (51.2% male; 48.8% female)
Individual Education Program: 461 (15.5%);
English Language Learner: 61 (2.1%); Migrant: 1 (<0.1%)
Eligible for Free Lunch Program: n/a
Eligible for Reduced-Price Lunch Program: n/a
Teachers: 168.0 (17.7 to 1)
Librarians/Media Specialists: 4.0 (742.3 to 1)
Guidance Counselors: 6.6 (449.8 to 1)
Current Spending: ($ per student per year):
Total: $8,180; Instruction: $5,521; Support Services: $2,375
Enrollment, Drop-out Rates and Diploma Recipients by Race/Ethnicity

Category	Total	White	Black	Asian	AIAN	Hisp.
Enrollment (%)	100.0	93.5	1.3	3.4	0.0	1.8
Drop-out Rate (%)	0.7	0.7	0.0	0.0	n/a	0.0
H.S. Diplomas (#)	203	193	1	4	0	5

Sudbury
40 Fairbank Rd • Sudbury, MA 01776-1681
(978) 443-1058 • http://www.sudbury-k8.org/
Grade Span: PK-08; **Agency Type:** 1
Schools: 5
4 Primary; 1 Middle; 0 High; 0 Other Level
5 Regular; 0 Special Education; 0 Vocational; 0 Alternative
0 Magnet; 0 Charter; 0 Title I Eligible; 0 School-wide Title I
Students: 3,079 (50.1% male; 49.9% female)
Individual Education Program: 365 (11.9%);
English Language Learner: 4 (0.1%); Migrant: 0 (0.0%)
Eligible for Free Lunch Program: n/a
Eligible for Reduced-Price Lunch Program: n/a
Teachers: 217.7 (14.1 to 1)
Librarians/Media Specialists: 4.6 (669.3 to 1)
Guidance Counselors: 6.9 (446.2 to 1)
Current Spending: ($ per student per year):
Total: $8,101; Instruction: $5,416; Support Services: $2,493
Enrollment, Drop-out Rates and Diploma Recipients by Race/Ethnicity

Category	Total	White	Black	Asian	AIAN	Hisp.
Enrollment (%)	100.0	91.6	2.3	4.7	0.1	1.3
Drop-out Rate (%)	n/a	n/a	n/a	n/a	n/a	n/a
H.S. Diplomas (#)	n/a	n/a	n/a	n/a	n/a	n/a

Tewksbury
1469 Andover St • Tewksbury, MA 01876-2725
(978) 640-7800 • http://www.tewksbury.mec.edu/
Grade Span: PK-12; **Agency Type:** 1
Schools: 8
5 Primary; 2 Middle; 1 High; 0 Other Level
8 Regular; 0 Special Education; 0 Vocational; 0 Alternative
0 Magnet; 0 Charter; 3 Title I Eligible; 0 School-wide Title I
Students: 4,738 (50.4% male; 49.6% female)
Individual Education Program: 683 (14.4%);
English Language Learner: 0 (0.0%); Migrant: 0 (0.0%)
Eligible for Free Lunch Program: n/a
Eligible for Reduced-Price Lunch Program: n/a
Teachers: 285.0 (16.6 to 1)
Librarians/Media Specialists: 5.0 (947.6 to 1)
Guidance Counselors: 5.0 (947.6 to 1)
Current Spending: ($ per student per year):
Total: $7,688; Instruction: $5,130; Support Services: $2,325
Enrollment, Drop-out Rates and Diploma Recipients by Race/Ethnicity

Category	Total	White	Black	Asian	AIAN	Hisp.
Enrollment (%)	100.0	94.9	0.8	2.1	0.0	2.3
Drop-out Rate (%)	2.4	2.5	0.0	0.0	n/a	0.0
H.S. Diplomas (#)	181	173	1	4	0	3

Tyngsborough
50 Norris Rd • Tyngsborough, MA 01879-1228
(978) 649-7488
Grade Span: PK-12; **Agency Type:** 1
Schools: 4
2 Primary; 1 Middle; 1 High; 0 Other Level
4 Regular; 0 Special Education; 0 Vocational; 0 Alternative
0 Magnet; 0 Charter; 2 Title I Eligible; 0 School-wide Title I
Students: 2,225 (51.1% male; 48.9% female)
Individual Education Program: 257 (11.6%);
English Language Learner: 3 (0.1%); Migrant: 0 (0.0%)
Eligible for Free Lunch Program: n/a
Eligible for Reduced-Price Lunch Program: n/a
Teachers: 155.2 (14.3 to 1)
Librarians/Media Specialists: 0.0 (0.0 to 1)
Guidance Counselors: 7.0 (317.9 to 1)
Current Spending: ($ per student per year):
Total: $7,515; Instruction: $4,864; Support Services: $2,416
Enrollment, Drop-out Rates and Diploma Recipients by Race/Ethnicity

Category	Total	White	Black	Asian	AIAN	Hisp.
Enrollment (%)	100.0	95.1	0.4	3.2	0.0	1.3
Drop-out Rate (%)	0.7	0.8	0.0	0.0	0.0	0.0
H.S. Diplomas (#)	127	122	1	4	0	0

Wakefield
60 Farm St • Wakefield, MA 01880-3502
(781) 246-6400 • http://www.wakefield.k12.ma.us/
Grade Span: PK-12; **Agency Type:** 1
Schools: 8
6 Primary; 1 Middle; 1 High; 0 Other Level
8 Regular; 0 Special Education; 0 Vocational; 0 Alternative
0 Magnet; 0 Charter; 2 Title I Eligible; 0 School-wide Title I
Students: 3,445 (50.4% male; 49.6% female)
Individual Education Program: 567 (16.5%);
English Language Learner: 21 (0.6%); Migrant: 0 (0.0%)
Eligible for Free Lunch Program: n/a
Eligible for Reduced-Price Lunch Program: n/a
Teachers: 280.8 (12.3 to 1)
Librarians/Media Specialists: 5.0 (689.0 to 1)
Guidance Counselors: 6.0 (574.2 to 1)
Current Spending: ($ per student per year):
Total: $8,440; Instruction: $5,779; Support Services: $2,402
Enrollment, Drop-out Rates and Diploma Recipients by Race/Ethnicity

Category	Total	White	Black	Asian	AIAN	Hisp.
Enrollment (%)	100.0	96.5	1.2	1.3	0.0	1.0
Drop-out Rate (%)	1.0	1.0	0.0	0.0	n/a	n/a
H.S. Diplomas (#)	213	206	2	1	0	4

Waltham
617 Lexington St • Waltham, MA 02452-3099
(781) 314-5440 •
http://www.city.waltham.ma.us/SCHOOL/WebPAge/tofc.htm
Grade Span: PK-12; **Agency Type:** 1
Schools: 12
8 Primary; 3 Middle; 1 High; 0 Other Level

12 Regular; 0 Special Education; 0 Vocational; 0 Alternative
0 Magnet; 0 Charter; 6 Title I Eligible; 1 School-wide Title I
Students: 4,825 (52.0% male; 48.0% female)
Individual Education Program: 890 (18.4%);
English Language Learner: 284 (5.9%); Migrant: 0 (0.0%)
Eligible for Free Lunch Program: n/a
Eligible for Reduced-Price Lunch Program: n/a
Teachers: 464.4 (10.4 to 1)
Librarians/Media Specialists: 12.3 (392.3 to 1)
Guidance Counselors: 9.0 (536.1 to 1)
Current Spending: ($ per student per year):
Total: $12,684; Instruction: $8,376; Support Services: $3,889
Enrollment, Drop-out Rates and Diploma Recipients by Race/Ethnicity

Category	Total	White	Black	Asian	AIAN	Hisp.
Enrollment (%)	100.0	63.7	9.7	7.0	0.1	19.5
Drop-out Rate (%)	2.0	2.2	0.7	1.8	n/a	2.2
H.S. Diplomas (#)	328	244	31	19	0	34

Watertown
30 Common St • Watertown, MA 02472-3492
(617) 926-7700 • http://www.watertown.k12.ma.us/
Grade Span: PK-12; **Agency Type:** 1
Schools: 5
3 Primary; 1 Middle; 1 High; 0 Other Level
5 Regular; 0 Special Education; 0 Vocational; 0 Alternative
0 Magnet; 0 Charter; 3 Title I Eligible; 0 School-wide Title I
Students: 2,422 (50.9% male; 49.1% female)
Individual Education Program: 490 (20.2%);
English Language Learner: 127 (5.2%); Migrant: 0 (0.0%)
Eligible for Free Lunch Program: n/a
Eligible for Reduced-Price Lunch Program: n/a
Teachers: 223.2 (10.9 to 1)
Librarians/Media Specialists: 4.5 (538.2 to 1)
Guidance Counselors: 21.4 (113.2 to 1)
Current Spending: ($ per student per year):
Total: $12,673; Instruction: $8,722; Support Services: $3,548
Enrollment, Drop-out Rates and Diploma Recipients by Race/Ethnicity

Category	Total	White	Black	Asian	AIAN	Hisp.
Enrollment (%)	100.0	87.3	2.7	5.5	0.5	4.0
Drop-out Rate (%)	1.7	1.7	0.0	3.6	n/a	0.0
H.S. Diplomas (#)	200	177	7	11	0	5

Wayland
41 Cochituate Rd • Wayland, MA 01778-2018
(508) 358-3774 • http://www.wayland.k12.ma.us/index.html
Grade Span: KG-12; **Agency Type:** 1
Schools: 5
3 Primary; 1 Middle; 1 High; 0 Other Level
5 Regular; 0 Special Education; 0 Vocational; 0 Alternative
0 Magnet; 0 Charter; 2 Title I Eligible; 0 School-wide Title I
Students: 2,922 (51.8% male; 48.2% female)
Individual Education Program: 441 (15.1%);
English Language Learner: 14 (0.5%); Migrant: 0 (0.0%)
Eligible for Free Lunch Program: n/a
Eligible for Reduced-Price Lunch Program: n/a
Teachers: 219.5 (13.3 to 1)
Librarians/Media Specialists: 5.0 (584.4 to 1)
Guidance Counselors: 12.5 (233.8 to 1)
Current Spending: ($ per student per year):
Total: $9,714; Instruction: $6,719; Support Services: $2,744
Enrollment, Drop-out Rates and Diploma Recipients by Race/Ethnicity

Category	Total	White	Black	Asian	AIAN	Hisp.
Enrollment (%)	100.0	84.5	4.3	8.7	0.0	2.5
Drop-out Rate (%)	0.1	0.1	0.0	0.0	n/a	0.0
H.S. Diplomas (#)	187	163	6	14	0	4

Westford
35 Town Farm Rd • Westford, MA 01886-2338
(978) 692-5560 • http://westford.mec.edu/schools/index.html
Grade Span: PK-12; **Agency Type:** 1
Schools: 9
6 Primary; 2 Middle; 1 High; 0 Other Level
9 Regular; 0 Special Education; 0 Vocational; 0 Alternative
0 Magnet; 0 Charter; 0 Title I Eligible; 0 School-wide Title I
Students: 4,925 (52.3% male; 47.7% female)
Individual Education Program: 427 (8.7%);
English Language Learner: 15 (0.3%); Migrant: 0 (0.0%)
Eligible for Free Lunch Program: n/a
Eligible for Reduced-Price Lunch Program: n/a
Teachers: 340.7 (14.5 to 1)
Librarians/Media Specialists: 6.0 (820.8 to 1)
Guidance Counselors: 29.8 (165.3 to 1)
Current Spending: ($ per student per year):
Total: $7,700; Instruction: $5,061; Support Services: $2,395
Enrollment, Drop-out Rates and Diploma Recipients by Race/Ethnicity

Category	Total	White	Black	Asian	AIAN	Hisp.
Enrollment (%)	100.0	91.7	0.4	7.0	0.2	0.7
Drop-out Rate (%)	0.9	0.9	0.0	0.0	0.0	0.0
H.S. Diplomas (#)	312	289	2	17	2	2

Weston
89 Wellesley St • Weston, MA 02493-2509
(781) 529-8080 • http://www.westonschools.org/
Grade Span: PK-12; **Agency Type:** 1
Schools: 5
2 Primary; 2 Middle; 1 High; 0 Other Level
5 Regular; 0 Special Education; 0 Vocational; 0 Alternative
0 Magnet; 0 Charter; 3 Title I Eligible; 0 School-wide Title I
Students: 2,353 (51.1% male; 48.9% female)
Individual Education Program: 351 (14.9%);
English Language Learner: 38 (1.6%); Migrant: 0 (0.0%)
Eligible for Free Lunch Program: n/a
Eligible for Reduced-Price Lunch Program: n/a
Teachers: 188.8 (12.5 to 1)
Librarians/Media Specialists: 3.0 (784.3 to 1)
Guidance Counselors: 12.8 (183.8 to 1)
Current Spending: ($ per student per year):
Total: $12,015; Instruction: $7,561; Support Services: $4,137
Enrollment, Drop-out Rates and Diploma Recipients by Race/Ethnicity

Category	Total	White	Black	Asian	AIAN	Hisp.
Enrollment (%)	100.0	81.2	6.3	10.2	0.2	2.2
Drop-out Rate (%)	0.0	0.0	0.0	0.0	0.0	0.0
H.S. Diplomas (#)	139	107	12	17	1	2

Wilmington
161 Church St • Wilmington, MA 01887-2736
(978) 694-6000 • http://www.wilmington.k12.ma.us/
Grade Span: PK-12; **Agency Type:** 1
Schools: 8
4 Primary; 3 Middle; 1 High; 0 Other Level
8 Regular; 0 Special Education; 0 Vocational; 0 Alternative
0 Magnet; 0 Charter; 2 Title I Eligible; 0 School-wide Title I
Students: 3,811 (51.4% male; 48.6% female)
Individual Education Program: 447 (11.7%);
English Language Learner: 0 (0.0%); Migrant: 4 (0.1%)
Eligible for Free Lunch Program: n/a
Eligible for Reduced-Price Lunch Program: n/a
Teachers: 279.9 (13.6 to 1)
Librarians/Media Specialists: 4.0 (952.8 to 1)
Guidance Counselors: 9.0 (423.4 to 1)
Current Spending: ($ per student per year):
Total: $8,066; Instruction: $5,310; Support Services: $2,477
Enrollment, Drop-out Rates and Diploma Recipients by Race/Ethnicity

Category	Total	White	Black	Asian	AIAN	Hisp.
Enrollment (%)	100.0	95.7	0.5	2.3	0.7	0.8
Drop-out Rate (%)	1.1	1.2	0.0	0.0	0.0	0.0
H.S. Diplomas (#)	193	181	2	6	1	3

Winchester
154 Horn Pond Brk Rd • Winchester, MA 01890-1887
(781) 721-7004 • http://www.winchester.k12.ma.us/
Grade Span: PK-12; **Agency Type:** 1
Schools: 7
1 Primary; 0 Middle; 1 High; 5 Other Level
7 Regular; 0 Special Education; 0 Vocational; 0 Alternative
0 Magnet; 0 Charter; 2 Title I Eligible; 0 School-wide Title I
Students: 3,501 (50.7% male; 49.3% female)
Individual Education Program: 466 (13.3%);
English Language Learner: 21 (0.6%); Migrant: 0 (0.0%)
Eligible for Free Lunch Program: n/a
Eligible for Reduced-Price Lunch Program: n/a
Teachers: 256.0 (13.7 to 1)
Librarians/Media Specialists: 0.0 (0.0 to 1)
Guidance Counselors: 8.1 (432.2 to 1)
Current Spending: ($ per student per year):
Total: $9,426; Instruction: $6,274; Support Services: $2,886
Enrollment, Drop-out Rates and Diploma Recipients by Race/Ethnicity

Category	Total	White	Black	Asian	AIAN	Hisp.
Enrollment (%)	100.0	90.8	1.2	5.3	0.0	2.7
Drop-out Rate (%)	0.4	0.5	0.0	0.0	n/a	0.0
H.S. Diplomas (#)	216	196	3	14	0	3

Woburn
55 Locust St • Woburn, MA 01801-3841
(781) 937-8200 • http://www.woburnpublicschools.com/
Grade Span: PK-12; **Agency Type:** 1
Schools: 12
9 Primary; 2 Middle; 0 High; 1 Other Level
12 Regular; 0 Special Education; 0 Vocational; 0 Alternative

0 Magnet; 0 Charter; 6 Title I Eligible; 1 School-wide Title I
Students: 4,682 (50.4% male; 49.6% female)
Individual Education Program: 554 (11.8%);
English Language Learner: 83 (1.8%); Migrant: 1 (<0.1%)
Eligible for Free Lunch Program: n/a
Eligible for Reduced-Price Lunch Program: n/a
Teachers: 361.2 (13.0 to 1)
Librarians/Media Specialists: 5.0 (936.4 to 1)
Guidance Counselors: 15.0 (312.1 to 1)
Current Spending: ($ per student per year):
Total: $10,496; Instruction: $6,629; Support Services: $3,491
Enrollment, Drop-out Rates and Diploma Recipients by Race/Ethnicity

Category	Total	White	Black	Asian	AIAN	Hisp.
Enrollment (%)	100.0	86.1	3.2	4.9	0.1	5.7
Drop-out Rate (%)	3.1	2.8	6.5	3.4	n/a	7.3
H.S. Diplomas (#)	291	260	6	12	0	13

Norfolk County

Bellingham
60 Harpin St • Bellingham, MA 02019-2011
(508) 883-1706 • http://www.bellingham.k12.ma.us/
Grade Span: PK-12; **Agency Type:** 1
Schools: 7
4 Primary; 1 Middle; 2 High; 0 Other Level
7 Regular; 0 Special Education; 0 Vocational; 0 Alternative
0 Magnet; 0 Charter; 3 Title I Eligible; 0 School-wide Title I
Students: 2,834 (49.6% male; 50.4% female)
Individual Education Program: 373 (13.2%);
English Language Learner: 15 (0.5%); Migrant: 3 (0.1%)
Eligible for Free Lunch Program: n/a
Eligible for Reduced-Price Lunch Program: n/a
Teachers: 191.7 (14.8 to 1)
Librarians/Media Specialists: 1.0 (2,834.0 to 1)
Guidance Counselors: 5.0 (566.8 to 1)
Current Spending: ($ per student per year):
Total: $7,528; Instruction: $5,012; Support Services: $2,321
Enrollment, Drop-out Rates and Diploma Recipients by Race/Ethnicity

Category	Total	White	Black	Asian	AIAN	Hisp.
Enrollment (%)	100.0	95.8	1.0	1.6	0.2	1.4
Drop-out Rate (%)	3.0	3.2	0.0	0.0	0.0	0.0
H.S. Diplomas (#)	161	149	3	5	1	3

Braintree
348 Pond St • Braintree, MA 02184-5310
(781) 380-0130 • http://www.braintreeschools.org/
Grade Span: PK-12; **Agency Type:** 1
Schools: 11
8 Primary; 2 Middle; 0 High; 1 Other Level
11 Regular; 0 Special Education; 0 Vocational; 0 Alternative
0 Magnet; 0 Charter; 5 Title I Eligible; 0 School-wide Title I
Students: 4,941 (51.1% male; 48.9% female)
Individual Education Program: 878 (17.8%);
English Language Learner: 51 (1.0%); Migrant: 0 (0.0%)
Eligible for Free Lunch Program: n/a
Eligible for Reduced-Price Lunch Program: n/a
Teachers: 388.6 (12.7 to 1)
Librarians/Media Specialists: 7.3 (676.8 to 1)
Guidance Counselors: 10.7 (461.8 to 1)
Current Spending: ($ per student per year):
Total: $9,062; Instruction: $6,227; Support Services: $2,619
Enrollment, Drop-out Rates and Diploma Recipients by Race/Ethnicity

Category	Total	White	Black	Asian	AIAN	Hisp.
Enrollment (%)	100.0	89.7	3.3	4.8	0.4	1.8
Drop-out Rate (%)	1.0	1.0	2.9	0.0	0.0	0.0
H.S. Diplomas (#)	322	294	6	18	0	4

Brookline
333 Washington St • Brookline, MA 02445-6853
(617) 730-2403 • http://bec.brookline.mec.edu/publicschools/
Grade Span: PK-12; **Agency Type:** 1
Schools: 9
8 Primary; 0 Middle; 1 High; 0 Other Level
9 Regular; 0 Special Education; 0 Vocational; 0 Alternative
0 Magnet; 0 Charter; 4 Title I Eligible; 0 School-wide Title I
Students: 6,038 (50.8% male; 49.2% female)
Individual Education Program: 939 (15.6%);
English Language Learner: 523 (8.7%); Migrant: 0 (0.0%)
Eligible for Free Lunch Program: n/a
Eligible for Reduced-Price Lunch Program: n/a
Teachers: 509.0 (11.9 to 1)
Librarians/Media Specialists: 18.8 (321.2 to 1)
Guidance Counselors: 47.1 (128.2 to 1)
Current Spending: ($ per student per year):
Total: $12,193; Instruction: $8,364; Support Services: $3,561

Enrollment, Drop-out Rates and Diploma Recipients by Race/Ethnicity

Category	Total	White	Black	Asian	AIAN	Hisp.
Enrollment (%)	100.0	65.6	9.7	18.8	0.2	5.7
Drop-out Rate (%)	0.3	0.4	0.5	0.0	0.0	0.0
H.S. Diplomas (#)	390	274	39	62	0	15

Canton
960 Washington St • Canton, MA 02021-2574
(781) 821-5060 • http://www.cantonma.org/
Grade Span: PK-12; **Agency Type:** 1
Schools: 5
3 Primary; 1 Middle; 1 High; 0 Other Level
5 Regular; 0 Special Education; 0 Vocational; 0 Alternative
0 Magnet; 0 Charter; 0 Title I Eligible; 0 School-wide Title I
Students: 2,957 (49.6% male; 50.4% female)
Individual Education Program: 320 (10.8%);
English Language Learner: 6 (0.2%); Migrant: 2 (0.1%)
Eligible for Free Lunch Program: n/a
Eligible for Reduced-Price Lunch Program: n/a
Teachers: 232.8 (12.7 to 1)
Librarians/Media Specialists: 2.0 (1,478.5 to 1)
Guidance Counselors: 4.0 (739.3 to 1)
Current Spending: ($ per student per year):
Total: $8,815; Instruction: $5,902; Support Services: $2,636
Enrollment, Drop-out Rates and Diploma Recipients by Race/Ethnicity

Category	Total	White	Black	Asian	AIAN	Hisp.
Enrollment (%)	100.0	85.9	6.4	5.3	0.2	2.3
Drop-out Rate (%)	0.8	0.3	10.3	0.0	n/a	0.0
H.S. Diplomas (#)	172	153	9	9	0	1

Dedham
30 Whiting Ave • Dedham, MA 02027-0246
(781) 326-5622 • http://www.dedham.k12.ma.us/
Grade Span: PK-12; **Agency Type:** 1
Schools: 7
5 Primary; 1 Middle; 1 High; 0 Other Level
7 Regular; 0 Special Education; 0 Vocational; 0 Alternative
0 Magnet; 0 Charter; 3 Title I Eligible; 0 School-wide Title I
Students: 2,983 (49.9% male; 50.1% female)
Individual Education Program: 534 (17.9%);
English Language Learner: 93 (3.1%); Migrant: 20 (0.7%)
Eligible for Free Lunch Program: n/a
Eligible for Reduced-Price Lunch Program: n/a
Teachers: 217.9 (13.7 to 1)
Librarians/Media Specialists: 7.0 (426.1 to 1)
Guidance Counselors: 8.0 (372.9 to 1)
Current Spending: ($ per student per year):
Total: $9,632; Instruction: $6,217; Support Services: $3,294
Enrollment, Drop-out Rates and Diploma Recipients by Race/Ethnicity

Category	Total	White	Black	Asian	AIAN	Hisp.
Enrollment (%)	100.0	90.2	3.1	2.0	0.8	4.0
Drop-out Rate (%)	0.7	0.7	0.0	0.0	0.0	0.0
H.S. Diplomas (#)	144	132	2	1	2	7

Foxborough
Igo Administration Building • Foxborough, MA 02035-2317
(508) 543-1660 • http://foxborough.k12.ma.us/fpsweb/index.html
Grade Span: PK-12; **Agency Type:** 1
Schools: 5
3 Primary; 1 Middle; 1 High; 0 Other Level
5 Regular; 0 Special Education; 0 Vocational; 0 Alternative
0 Magnet; 0 Charter; 3 Title I Eligible; 0 School-wide Title I
Students: 2,850 (50.3% male; 49.7% female)
Individual Education Program: 607 (21.3%);
English Language Learner: 0 (0.0%); Migrant: 0 (0.0%)
Eligible for Free Lunch Program: n/a
Eligible for Reduced-Price Lunch Program: n/a
Teachers: 214.8 (13.3 to 1)
Librarians/Media Specialists: 2.0 (1,425.0 to 1)
Guidance Counselors: 9.0 (316.7 to 1)
Current Spending: ($ per student per year):
Total: $8,858; Instruction: $6,132; Support Services: $2,472
Enrollment, Drop-out Rates and Diploma Recipients by Race/Ethnicity

Category	Total	White	Black	Asian	AIAN	Hisp.
Enrollment (%)	100.0	94.7	2.4	1.8	0.0	1.2
Drop-out Rate (%)	1.9	2.0	0.0	0.0	0.0	7.1
H.S. Diplomas (#)	191	175	5	8	0	3

Franklin
397 E Central St • Franklin, MA 02038-1304
(508) 541-5243 • http://www.franklin.ma.us/auto/schools/FPS/
Grade Span: PK-12; **Agency Type:** 1
Schools: 10
7 Primary; 2 Middle; 1 High; 0 Other Level
10 Regular; 0 Special Education; 0 Vocational; 0 Alternative

0 Magnet; 0 Charter; 2 Title I Eligible; 0 School-wide Title I
Students: 5,711 (50.5% male; 49.5% female)
Individual Education Program: 801 (14.0%);
English Language Learner: 1 (<0.1%); Migrant: 0 (0.0%)
Eligible for Free Lunch Program: n/a
Eligible for Reduced-Price Lunch Program: n/a
Teachers: 434.5 (13.1 to 1)
Librarians/Media Specialists: 3.0 (1,903.7 to 1)
Guidance Counselors: 6.0 (951.8 to 1)
Current Spending: ($ per student per year):
Total: $8,039; Instruction: $5,705; Support Services: $2,157
Enrollment, Drop-out Rates and Diploma Recipients by Race/Ethnicity

Category	Total	White	Black	Asian	AIAN	Hisp.
Enrollment (%)	100.0	96.0	0.9	2.0	0.6	0.5
Drop-out Rate (%)	1.3	1.2	25.0	4.5	0.0	0.0
H.S. Diplomas (#)	305	295	0	7	2	1

King Philip
201 Franklin St • Wrentham, MA 02093-1292
(508) 384-3144 • http://www.kingphilip.org/homekp.html
Grade Span: 07-12; **Agency Type:** 4
Schools: 2
0 Primary; 1 Middle; 1 High; 0 Other Level
2 Regular; 0 Special Education; 0 Vocational; 0 Alternative
0 Magnet; 0 Charter; 1 Title I Eligible; 0 School-wide Title I
Students: 1,900 (48.3% male; 51.7% female)
Individual Education Program: 291 (15.3%);
English Language Learner: 0 (0.0%); Migrant: 0 (0.0%)
Eligible for Free Lunch Program: n/a
Eligible for Reduced-Price Lunch Program: n/a
Teachers: 127.6 (14.9 to 1)
Librarians/Media Specialists: 1.0 (1,900.0 to 1)
Guidance Counselors: 6.0 (316.7 to 1)
Current Spending: ($ per student per year):
Total: $8,574; Instruction: $5,632; Support Services: $2,652
Enrollment, Drop-out Rates and Diploma Recipients by Race/Ethnicity

Category	Total	White	Black	Asian	AIAN	Hisp.
Enrollment (%)	100.0	97.2	0.7	1.5	0.1	0.5
Drop-out Rate (%)	1.9	1.8	0.0	0.0	0.0	12.5
H.S. Diplomas (#)	217	205	2	5	1	4

Medfield
459 Main St, 3rd Fl • Medfield, MA 02052-1606
(508) 359-2302 • http://medfield.net/
Grade Span: PK-12; **Agency Type:** 1
Schools: 5
2 Primary; 2 Middle; 1 High; 0 Other Level
5 Regular; 0 Special Education; 0 Vocational; 0 Alternative
0 Magnet; 0 Charter; 0 Title I Eligible; 0 School-wide Title I
Students: 2,978 (51.4% male; 48.6% female)
Individual Education Program: 332 (11.1%);
English Language Learner: 2 (0.1%); Migrant: 0 (0.0%)
Eligible for Free Lunch Program: n/a
Eligible for Reduced-Price Lunch Program: n/a
Teachers: 203.0 (14.7 to 1)
Librarians/Media Specialists: 4.5 (661.8 to 1)
Guidance Counselors: 5.8 (513.4 to 1)
Current Spending: ($ per student per year):
Total: $6,914; Instruction: $4,510; Support Services: $2,170
Enrollment, Drop-out Rates and Diploma Recipients by Race/Ethnicity

Category	Total	White	Black	Asian	AIAN	Hisp.
Enrollment (%)	100.0	96.5	0.7	2.1	0.1	0.7
Drop-out Rate (%)	0.2	0.2	0.0	0.0	0.0	0.0
H.S. Diplomas (#)	155	151	0	2	0	2

Medway
45 Holliston St • Medway, MA 02053-1404
(508) 533-3222 • http://www.medway.k12.ma.us/
Grade Span: PK-12; **Agency Type:** 1
Schools: 5
3 Primary; 1 Middle; 1 High; 0 Other Level
5 Regular; 0 Special Education; 0 Vocational; 0 Alternative
0 Magnet; 0 Charter; 3 Title I Eligible; 0 School-wide Title I
Students: 2,848 (50.8% male; 49.2% female)
Individual Education Program: 411 (14.4%);
English Language Learner: 0 (0.0%); Migrant: 0 (0.0%)
Eligible for Free Lunch Program: n/a
Eligible for Reduced-Price Lunch Program: n/a
Teachers: 177.6 (16.0 to 1)
Librarians/Media Specialists: 1.0 (2,848.0 to 1)
Guidance Counselors: 5.0 (569.6 to 1)
Current Spending: ($ per student per year):
Total: $7,402; Instruction: $5,190; Support Services: $2,031
Enrollment, Drop-out Rates and Diploma Recipients by Race/Ethnicity

Category	Total	White	Black	Asian	AIAN	Hisp.
Enrollment (%)	100.0	97.0	1.1	1.3	0.1	0.5
Drop-out Rate (%)	0.9	1.0	0.0	0.0	n/a	0.0
H.S. Diplomas (#)	154	148	2	2	0	2

Milton
1372 Brush Hill Rd • Milton, MA 02186-2845
(617) 696-4809 • http://www.miltonps.org/
Grade Span: PK-12; **Agency Type:** 1
Schools: 6
4 Primary; 1 Middle; 0 High; 1 Other Level
6 Regular; 0 Special Education; 0 Vocational; 0 Alternative
0 Magnet; 0 Charter; 2 Title I Eligible; 0 School-wide Title I
Students: 3,597 (51.3% male; 48.7% female)
Individual Education Program: 520 (14.5%);
English Language Learner: 10 (0.3%); Migrant: 0 (0.0%)
Eligible for Free Lunch Program: n/a
Eligible for Reduced-Price Lunch Program: n/a
Teachers: 263.6 (13.6 to 1)
Librarians/Media Specialists: 3.0 (1,199.0 to 1)
Guidance Counselors: 12.4 (290.1 to 1)
Current Spending: ($ per student per year):
Total: $8,103; Instruction: $5,145; Support Services: $2,737
Enrollment, Drop-out Rates and Diploma Recipients by Race/Ethnicity

Category	Total	White	Black	Asian	AIAN	Hisp.
Enrollment (%)	100.0	76.6	17.4	3.6	0.1	2.3
Drop-out Rate (%)	0.9	1.1	0.5	0.0	n/a	0.0
H.S. Diplomas (#)	220	171	38	6	0	5

Needham
1330 Highland Ave • Needham, MA 02492-2613
(781) 455-0400 • http://www.needham.k12.ma.us/
Grade Span: PK-12; **Agency Type:** 1
Schools: 7
5 Primary; 1 Middle; 1 High; 0 Other Level
7 Regular; 0 Special Education; 0 Vocational; 0 Alternative
0 Magnet; 0 Charter; 2 Title I Eligible; 0 School-wide Title I
Students: 4,639 (52.5% male; 47.5% female)
Individual Education Program: 568 (12.2%);
English Language Learner: 31 (0.7%); Migrant: 2 (<0.1%)
Eligible for Free Lunch Program: n/a
Eligible for Reduced-Price Lunch Program: n/a
Teachers: 332.8 (13.9 to 1)
Librarians/Media Specialists: 12.4 (374.1 to 1)
Guidance Counselors: 19.1 (242.9 to 1)
Current Spending: ($ per student per year):
Total: $10,342; Instruction: $6,895; Support Services: $3,096
Enrollment, Drop-out Rates and Diploma Recipients by Race/Ethnicity

Category	Total	White	Black	Asian	AIAN	Hisp.
Enrollment (%)	100.0	89.0	3.7	5.1	0.1	2.0
Drop-out Rate (%)	0.2	0.2	0.0	0.0	n/a	0.0
H.S. Diplomas (#)	302	277	10	12	0	3

Norwood
100 Westover Pkwy • Norwood, MA 02062-0067
(781) 762-6804 • http://www.norwood.k12.ma.us/
Grade Span: PK-12; **Agency Type:** 1
Schools: 8
6 Primary; 1 Middle; 1 High; 0 Other Level
8 Regular; 0 Special Education; 0 Vocational; 0 Alternative
0 Magnet; 0 Charter; 3 Title I Eligible; 0 School-wide Title I
Students: 3,741 (50.8% male; 49.2% female)
Individual Education Program: 589 (15.7%);
English Language Learner: 239 (6.4%); Migrant: 0 (0.0%)
Eligible for Free Lunch Program: n/a
Eligible for Reduced-Price Lunch Program: n/a
Teachers: 295.8 (12.6 to 1)
Librarians/Media Specialists: 5.0 (748.2 to 1)
Guidance Counselors: 8.0 (467.6 to 1)
Current Spending: ($ per student per year):
Total: $9,136; Instruction: $5,709; Support Services: $3,152
Enrollment, Drop-out Rates and Diploma Recipients by Race/Ethnicity

Category	Total	White	Black	Asian	AIAN	Hisp.
Enrollment (%)	100.0	84.5	5.1	7.2	0.1	3.2
Drop-out Rate (%)	1.3	1.3	0.0	0.0	n/a	3.7
H.S. Diplomas (#)	234	217	6	7	0	4

Quincy
70 Coddington St • Quincy, MA 02169-4501
(617) 984-8700 • http://QuincyPublicSchools.com/qpshome.htm
Grade Span: PK-12; **Agency Type:** 1
Schools: 18
11 Primary; 5 Middle; 2 High; 0 Other Level
18 Regular; 0 Special Education; 0 Vocational; 0 Alternative

0 Magnet; 0 Charter; 3 Title I Eligible; 1 School-wide Title I
Students: 8,846 (51.2% male; 48.8% female)
Individual Education Program: 1,369 (15.5%);
English Language Learner: 1,081 (12.2%); Migrant: 0 (0.0%)
Eligible for Free Lunch Program: n/a
Eligible for Reduced-Price Lunch Program: n/a
Teachers: 699.0 (12.7 to 1)
Librarians/Media Specialists: 13.0 (680.5 to 1)
Guidance Counselors: 41.0 (215.8 to 1)
Current Spending: ($ per student per year):
Total: $9,691; Instruction: $6,494; Support Services: $2,915
Enrollment, Drop-out Rates and Diploma Recipients by Race/Ethnicity

Category	Total	White	Black	Asian	AIAN	Hisp.
Enrollment (%)	100.0	67.2	3.7	25.5	0.4	3.2
Drop-out Rate (%)	3.9	4.1	12.7	2.2	11.1	5.0
H.S. Diplomas (#)	591	409	19	148	2	13

Randolph

40 Highland Ave • Randolph, MA 02368-4513
(781) 961-6205 • http://www.randolph.mec.edu/
Grade Span: PK-12; **Agency Type:** 1
Schools: 8
6 Primary; 1 Middle; 1 High; 0 Other Level
8 Regular; 0 Special Education; 0 Vocational; 0 Alternative
0 Magnet; 0 Charter; 6 Title I Eligible; 0 School-wide Title I
Students: 3,987 (51.4% male; 48.6% female)
Individual Education Program: 693 (17.4%);
English Language Learner: 277 (6.9%); Migrant: 0 (0.0%)
Eligible for Free Lunch Program: n/a
Eligible for Reduced-Price Lunch Program: n/a
Teachers: 309.1 (12.9 to 1)
Librarians/Media Specialists: 2.0 (1,993.5 to 1)
Guidance Counselors: 6.0 (664.5 to 1)
Current Spending: ($ per student per year):
Total: $8,345; Instruction: $5,699; Support Services: $2,350
Enrollment, Drop-out Rates and Diploma Recipients by Race/Ethnicity

Category	Total	White	Black	Asian	AIAN	Hisp.
Enrollment (%)	100.0	40.2	38.9	13.6	0.4	7.0
Drop-out Rate (%)	3.8	4.0	3.3	3.9	0.0	5.8
H.S. Diplomas (#)	196	88	64	34	0	10

Sharon

1 School St • Sharon, MA 02067-1298
(781) 784-1570 • http://www.sharonschools.com/
Grade Span: PK-12; **Agency Type:** 1
Schools: 5
3 Primary; 1 Middle; 0 High; 1 Other Level
5 Regular; 0 Special Education; 0 Vocational; 0 Alternative
0 Magnet; 0 Charter; 3 Title I Eligible; 0 School-wide Title I
Students: 3,545 (49.6% male; 50.4% female)
Individual Education Program: 500 (14.1%);
English Language Learner: 44 (1.2%); Migrant: 1 (<0.1%)
Eligible for Free Lunch Program: n/a
Eligible for Reduced-Price Lunch Program: n/a
Teachers: 256.1 (13.8 to 1)
Librarians/Media Specialists: 3.0 (1,181.7 to 1)
Guidance Counselors: 8.6 (412.2 to 1)
Current Spending: ($ per student per year):
Total: $8,471; Instruction: $6,202; Support Services: $2,101
Enrollment, Drop-out Rates and Diploma Recipients by Race/Ethnicity

Category	Total	White	Black	Asian	AIAN	Hisp.
Enrollment (%)	100.0	87.4	4.9	6.5	0.0	1.2
Drop-out Rate (%)	0.5	0.2	6.5	0.0	n/a	0.0
H.S. Diplomas (#)	254	226	14	10	0	4

Stoughton

232 Pearl St • Stoughton, MA 02072-2397
(781) 344-4000 • http://www.stoughton.k12.ma.us/
Grade Span: PK-12; **Agency Type:** 1
Schools: 8
6 Primary; 1 Middle; 1 High; 0 Other Level
8 Regular; 0 Special Education; 0 Vocational; 0 Alternative
0 Magnet; 0 Charter; 5 Title I Eligible; 0 School-wide Title I
Students: 4,121 (52.6% male; 47.4% female)
Individual Education Program: 743 (18.0%);
English Language Learner: 68 (1.7%); Migrant: 3 (0.1%)
Eligible for Free Lunch Program: n/a
Eligible for Reduced-Price Lunch Program: n/a
Teachers: 313.6 (13.1 to 1)
Librarians/Media Specialists: 4.0 (1,030.3 to 1)
Guidance Counselors: 12.0 (343.4 to 1)
Current Spending: ($ per student per year):
Total: $8,493; Instruction: $5,667; Support Services: $2,552
Enrollment, Drop-out Rates and Diploma Recipients by Race/Ethnicity

Category	Total	White	Black	Asian	AIAN	Hisp.
Enrollment (%)	100.0	85.0	9.3	3.3	0.1	2.2
Drop-out Rate (%)	2.6	2.8	0.9	5.3	0.0	0.0
H.S. Diplomas (#)	219	189	21	8	0	1

Walpole

135 School St • Walpole, MA 02081
(508) 660-7200 • http://www.walpole.ma.us/walpoleschools.htm
Grade Span: PK-12; **Agency Type:** 1
Schools: 7
4 Primary; 2 Middle; 1 High; 0 Other Level
7 Regular; 0 Special Education; 0 Vocational; 0 Alternative
0 Magnet; 0 Charter; 3 Title I Eligible; 0 School-wide Title I
Students: 3,676 (50.4% male; 49.6% female)
Individual Education Program: 664 (18.1%);
English Language Learner: 1 (<0.1%); Migrant: 0 (0.0%)
Eligible for Free Lunch Program: n/a
Eligible for Reduced-Price Lunch Program: n/a
Teachers: 266.0 (13.8 to 1)
Librarians/Media Specialists: 6.5 (565.5 to 1)
Guidance Counselors: 9.0 (408.4 to 1)
Current Spending: ($ per student per year):
Total: $7,991; Instruction: $5,479; Support Services: $2,275
Enrollment, Drop-out Rates and Diploma Recipients by Race/Ethnicity

Category	Total	White	Black	Asian	AIAN	Hisp.
Enrollment (%)	100.0	96.7	1.6	1.0	0.1	0.7
Drop-out Rate (%)	0.6	0.6	0.0	0.0	n/a	0.0
H.S. Diplomas (#)	206	203	3	0	0	0

Wellesley

40 Kingsbury St • Wellesley, MA 02481-4827
(781) 446-6210 • http://www.wellesley.mec.edu/
Grade Span: PK-12; **Agency Type:** 1
Schools: 9
8 Primary; 0 Middle; 1 High; 0 Other Level
9 Regular; 0 Special Education; 0 Vocational; 0 Alternative
0 Magnet; 0 Charter; 3 Title I Eligible; 0 School-wide Title I
Students: 4,079 (49.7% male; 50.3% female)
Individual Education Program: 586 (14.4%);
English Language Learner: 35 (0.9%); Migrant: 0 (0.0%)
Eligible for Free Lunch Program: n/a
Eligible for Reduced-Price Lunch Program: n/a
Teachers: 319.1 (12.8 to 1)
Librarians/Media Specialists: 7.3 (558.8 to 1)
Guidance Counselors: 10.4 (392.2 to 1)
Current Spending: ($ per student per year):
Total: $11,103; Instruction: $7,541; Support Services: $3,297
Enrollment, Drop-out Rates and Diploma Recipients by Race/Ethnicity

Category	Total	White	Black	Asian	AIAN	Hisp.
Enrollment (%)	100.0	87.4	3.9	6.4	0.2	2.1
Drop-out Rate (%)	0.5	0.6	0.0	0.0	0.0	0.0
H.S. Diplomas (#)	244	210	9	16	0	9

Westwood

660 High St • Westwood, MA 02090-1687
(781) 326-7500 • http://www.westwood.k12.ma.us/
Grade Span: PK-12; **Agency Type:** 1
Schools: 7
5 Primary; 1 Middle; 1 High; 0 Other Level
7 Regular; 0 Special Education; 0 Vocational; 0 Alternative
0 Magnet; 0 Charter; 4 Title I Eligible; 0 School-wide Title I
Students: 2,697 (49.8% male; 50.2% female)
Individual Education Program: 348 (12.9%);
English Language Learner: 18 (0.7%); Migrant: 0 (0.0%)
Eligible for Free Lunch Program: n/a
Eligible for Reduced-Price Lunch Program: n/a
Teachers: 230.0 (11.7 to 1)
Librarians/Media Specialists: 8.0 (337.1 to 1)
Guidance Counselors: 11.0 (245.2 to 1)
Current Spending: ($ per student per year):
Total: $10,478; Instruction: $6,492; Support Services: $3,702
Enrollment, Drop-out Rates and Diploma Recipients by Race/Ethnicity

Category	Total	White	Black	Asian	AIAN	Hisp.
Enrollment (%)	100.0	93.4	1.6	3.7	0.3	1.0
Drop-out Rate (%)	0.0	0.0	0.0	n/a	n/a	0.0
H.S. Diplomas (#)	151	140	4	5	0	2

Weymouth

111 Middle St • Weymouth, MA 02189-1332
(781) 335-1460 • http://www.weymouth.ma.us/schools/
Grade Span: PK-12; **Agency Type:** 1
Schools: 13
10 Primary; 2 Middle; 1 High; 0 Other Level
13 Regular; 0 Special Education; 0 Vocational; 0 Alternative

0 Magnet; 0 Charter; 3 Title I Eligible; 1 School-wide Title I
Students: 7,031 (52.2% male; 47.8% female)
Individual Education Program: 1,386 (19.7%);
English Language Learner: 98 (1.4%); Migrant: 3 (<0.1%)
Eligible for Free Lunch Program: n/a
Eligible for Reduced-Price Lunch Program: n/a
Teachers: 482.1 (14.6 to 1)
Librarians/Media Specialists: 6.0 (1,171.8 to 1)
Guidance Counselors: 12.6 (558.0 to 1)
Current Spending: ($ per student per year):
Total: $7,961; Instruction: $5,611; Support Services: $2,094
Enrollment, Drop-out Rates and Diploma Recipients by Race/Ethnicity

Category	Total	White	Black	Asian	AIAN	Hisp.
Enrollment (%)	100.0	91.4	2.4	2.4	0.4	3.5
Drop-out Rate (%)	3.0	3.0	0.0	0.0	n/a	9.5
H.S. Diplomas (#)	383	366	6	5	0	6

Plymouth County

Abington
1 Ralph Hamlin Ln • Abington, MA 02351-2003
(781) 982-2150 • http://www.abington.k12.ma.us/
Grade Span: PK-12; **Agency Type:** 1
Schools: 6
4 Primary; 1 Middle; 1 High; 0 Other Level
6 Regular; 0 Special Education; 0 Vocational; 0 Alternative
0 Magnet; 0 Charter; 1 Title I Eligible; 0 School-wide Title I
Students: 2,348 (50.7% male; 49.3% female)
Individual Education Program: 324 (13.8%);
English Language Learner: 9 (0.4%); Migrant: 0 (0.0%)
Eligible for Free Lunch Program: n/a
Eligible for Reduced-Price Lunch Program: n/a
Teachers: 153.6 (15.3 to 1)
Librarians/Media Specialists: 2.0 (1,174.0 to 1)
Guidance Counselors: 5.0 (469.6 to 1)
Current Spending: ($ per student per year):
Total: $7,202; Instruction: $4,960; Support Services: $2,008
Enrollment, Drop-out Rates and Diploma Recipients by Race/Ethnicity

Category	Total	White	Black	Asian	AIAN	Hisp.
Enrollment (%)	100.0	95.7	1.7	0.7	0.8	1.2
Drop-out Rate (%)	1.6	1.6	0.0	0.0	n/a	0.0
H.S. Diplomas (#)	115	111	1	2	0	1

Brockton
43 Crescent St • Brockton, MA 02301-4376
(508) 580-7511 • http://www.brocktonpublicschools.com/
Grade Span: PK-12; **Agency Type:** 1
Schools: 25
18 Primary; 4 Middle; 1 High; 2 Other Level
24 Regular; 0 Special Education; 1 Vocational; 0 Alternative
0 Magnet; 0 Charter; 18 Title I Eligible; 11 School-wide Title I
Students: 16,681 (51.7% male; 48.3% female)
Individual Education Program: 2,090 (12.5%);
English Language Learner: 1,207 (7.2%); Migrant: 52 (0.3%)
Eligible for Free Lunch Program: n/a
Eligible for Reduced-Price Lunch Program: n/a
Teachers: 1,197.5 (13.9 to 1)
Librarians/Media Specialists: 15.0 (1,112.1 to 1)
Guidance Counselors: 30.0 (556.0 to 1)
Current Spending: ($ per student per year):
Total: $9,722; Instruction: $6,053; Support Services: $3,520
Enrollment, Drop-out Rates and Diploma Recipients by Race/Ethnicity

Category	Total	White	Black	Asian	AIAN	Hisp.
Enrollment (%)	100.0	39.5	44.7	3.0	0.9	11.9
Drop-out Rate (%)	5.7	4.1	6.2	3.4	5.0	10.9
H.S. Diplomas (#)	689	279	309	32	2	67

Carver
3 Carver Square Blvd • Carver, MA 02330-1200
(508) 866-6160 • http://www.carver.org/
Grade Span: PK-12; **Agency Type:** 1
Schools: 4
2 Primary; 1 Middle; 1 High; 0 Other Level
4 Regular; 0 Special Education; 0 Vocational; 0 Alternative
0 Magnet; 0 Charter; 2 Title I Eligible; 0 School-wide Title I
Students: 2,132 (52.1% male; 47.9% female)
Individual Education Program: 296 (13.9%);
English Language Learner: 0 (0.0%); Migrant: 0 (0.0%)
Eligible for Free Lunch Program: n/a
Eligible for Reduced-Price Lunch Program: n/a
Teachers: 160.8 (13.3 to 1)
Librarians/Media Specialists: 2.0 (1,066.0 to 1)
Guidance Counselors: 3.0 (710.7 to 1)
Current Spending: ($ per student per year):
Total: $7,897; Instruction: $5,148; Support Services: $2,475
Enrollment, Drop-out Rates and Diploma Recipients by Race/Ethnicity

Category	Total	White	Black	Asian	AIAN	Hisp.
Enrollment (%)	100.0	95.6	3.0	0.1	0.9	0.3
Drop-out Rate (%)	3.6	3.4	9.5	0.0	0.0	0.0
H.S. Diplomas (#)	108	103	5	0	0	0

Duxbury
130 St George St • Duxbury, MA 02332-3871
(781) 934-7600 • http://www.duxbury.k12.ma.us/
Grade Span: PK-12; **Agency Type:** 1
Schools: 4
2 Primary; 1 Middle; 1 High; 0 Other Level
4 Regular; 0 Special Education; 0 Vocational; 0 Alternative
0 Magnet; 0 Charter; 2 Title I Eligible; 2 School-wide Title I
Students: 3,234 (51.9% male; 48.1% female)
Individual Education Program: 394 (12.2%);
English Language Learner: 0 (0.0%); Migrant: 0 (0.0%)
Eligible for Free Lunch Program: n/a
Eligible for Reduced-Price Lunch Program: n/a
Teachers: 241.9 (13.4 to 1)
Librarians/Media Specialists: 4.0 (808.5 to 1)
Guidance Counselors: 17.0 (190.2 to 1)
Current Spending: ($ per student per year):
Total: $7,887; Instruction: $5,153; Support Services: $2,540
Enrollment, Drop-out Rates and Diploma Recipients by Race/Ethnicity

Category	Total	White	Black	Asian	AIAN	Hisp.
Enrollment (%)	100.0	97.8	0.5	0.9	0.1	0.7
Drop-out Rate (%)	0.3	0.1	50.0	0.0	n/a	0.0
H.S. Diplomas (#)	236	229	1	5	0	1

East Bridgewater
11 Plymouth St • East Bridgewater, MA 02333-1995
(508) 378-8200 • http://ebps.net/
Grade Span: PK-12; **Agency Type:** 1
Schools: 3
1 Primary; 1 Middle; 1 High; 0 Other Level
3 Regular; 0 Special Education; 0 Vocational; 0 Alternative
0 Magnet; 0 Charter; 2 Title I Eligible; 0 School-wide Title I
Students: 2,468 (50.5% male; 49.5% female)
Individual Education Program: 248 (10.0%);
English Language Learner: 0 (0.0%); Migrant: 0 (0.0%)
Eligible for Free Lunch Program: n/a
Eligible for Reduced-Price Lunch Program: n/a
Teachers: 144.9 (17.0 to 1)
Librarians/Media Specialists: 0.0 (0.0 to 1)
Guidance Counselors: 7.0 (352.6 to 1)
Current Spending: ($ per student per year):
Total: $7,474; Instruction: $5,173; Support Services: $2,110
Enrollment, Drop-out Rates and Diploma Recipients by Race/Ethnicity

Category	Total	White	Black	Asian	AIAN	Hisp.
Enrollment (%)	100.0	97.4	1.7	0.3	0.0	0.6
Drop-out Rate (%)	2.5	2.6	0.0	0.0	0.0	0.0
H.S. Diplomas (#)	156	153	2	0	0	1

Hanover
188 Broadway • Hanover, MA 02339-1572
(781) 878-0786 • http://hanoverschools.org/
Grade Span: PK-12; **Agency Type:** 1
Schools: 5
3 Primary; 1 Middle; 1 High; 0 Other Level
5 Regular; 0 Special Education; 0 Vocational; 0 Alternative
0 Magnet; 0 Charter; 3 Title I Eligible; 0 School-wide Title I
Students: 2,724 (50.6% male; 49.4% female)
Individual Education Program: 490 (18.0%);
English Language Learner: 0 (0.0%); Migrant: 0 (0.0%)
Eligible for Free Lunch Program: n/a
Eligible for Reduced-Price Lunch Program: n/a
Teachers: 186.3 (14.6 to 1)
Librarians/Media Specialists: 2.0 (1,362.0 to 1)
Guidance Counselors: 12.0 (227.0 to 1)
Current Spending: ($ per student per year):
Total: $7,852; Instruction: $5,500; Support Services: $2,122
Enrollment, Drop-out Rates and Diploma Recipients by Race/Ethnicity

Category	Total	White	Black	Asian	AIAN	Hisp.
Enrollment (%)	100.0	97.7	0.7	1.2	0.0	0.4
Drop-out Rate (%)	1.3	1.3	0.0	0.0	n/a	0.0
H.S. Diplomas (#)	150	148	2	0	0	0

Hingham
220 Central St • Hingham, MA 02043-2745
(781) 741-1500 • http://www.hinghamschools.com/
Grade Span: PK-12; **Agency Type:** 1
Schools: 5
3 Primary; 1 Middle; 1 High; 0 Other Level
5 Regular; 0 Special Education; 0 Vocational; 0 Alternative

0 Magnet; 0 Charter; 2 Title I Eligible; 0 School-wide Title I
Students: 3,550 (50.9% male; 49.1% female)
Individual Education Program: 482 (13.6%);
English Language Learner: 0 (0.0%); Migrant: 0 (0.0%)
Eligible for Free Lunch Program: n/a
Eligible for Reduced-Price Lunch Program: n/a
Teachers: 217.9 (16.3 to 1)
Librarians/Media Specialists: 6.0 (591.7 to 1)
Guidance Counselors: 8.5 (417.6 to 1)
Current Spending: ($ per student per year):
Total: $8,136; Instruction: $5,540; Support Services: $2,403
Enrollment, Drop-out Rates and Diploma Recipients by Race/Ethnicity

Category	Total	White	Black	Asian	AIAN	Hisp.
Enrollment (%)	100.0	95.7	1.1	1.9	0.1	1.2
Drop-out Rate (%)	0.9	1.0	0.0	0.0	n/a	0.0
H.S. Diplomas (#)	232	225	1	4	0	2

Marshfield

76 S River St • Marshfield, MA 02050-2499
(781) 834-5000 • http://www.mpsd.org/
Grade Span: PK-12; **Agency Type:** 1
Schools: 7
5 Primary; 1 Middle; 1 High; 0 Other Level
7 Regular; 0 Special Education; 0 Vocational; 0 Alternative
0 Magnet; 0 Charter; 4 Title I Eligible; 0 School-wide Title I
Students: 4,654 (51.4% male; 48.6% female)
Individual Education Program: 644 (13.8%);
English Language Learner: 5 (0.1%); Migrant: 0 (0.0%)
Eligible for Free Lunch Program: n/a
Eligible for Reduced-Price Lunch Program: n/a
Teachers: 330.7 (14.1 to 1)
Librarians/Media Specialists: 2.0 (2,327.0 to 1)
Guidance Counselors: 9.0 (517.1 to 1)
Current Spending: ($ per student per year):
Total: $7,548; Instruction: $5,168; Support Services: $2,122
Enrollment, Drop-out Rates and Diploma Recipients by Race/Ethnicity

Category	Total	White	Black	Asian	AIAN	Hisp.
Enrollment (%)	100.0	97.8	0.5	0.7	0.2	0.9
Drop-out Rate (%)	1.8	n/a	0.0	0.0	0.0	0.1
H.S. Diplomas (#)	277	269	3	2	0	3

Middleborough

30 Forest St • Middleborough, MA 02346-4012
(508) 946-2000 • http://www.middleboro.k12.ma.us/
Grade Span: PK-12; **Agency Type:** 1
Schools: 6
4 Primary; 1 Middle; 1 High; 0 Other Level
6 Regular; 0 Special Education; 0 Vocational; 0 Alternative
0 Magnet; 0 Charter; 2 Title I Eligible; 0 School-wide Title I
Students: 3,704 (51.9% male; 48.1% female)
Individual Education Program: 573 (15.5%);
English Language Learner: 3 (0.1%); Migrant: 0 (0.0%)
Eligible for Free Lunch Program: n/a
Eligible for Reduced-Price Lunch Program: n/a
Teachers: 236.8 (15.6 to 1)
Librarians/Media Specialists: 3.0 (1,234.7 to 1)
Guidance Counselors: 6.0 (617.3 to 1)
Current Spending: ($ per student per year):
Total: $7,454; Instruction: $4,711; Support Services: $2,475
Enrollment, Drop-out Rates and Diploma Recipients by Race/Ethnicity

Category	Total	White	Black	Asian	AIAN	Hisp.
Enrollment (%)	100.0	95.0	2.6	0.9	0.2	1.3
Drop-out Rate (%)	2.4	2.3	14.3	0.0	n/a	0.0
H.S. Diplomas (#)	189	184	2	2	0	1

Norwell

322 Main St • Norwell, MA 02061-2420
(781) 659-8800 • http://www.norwellschools.org/
Grade Span: PK-12; **Agency Type:** 1
Schools: 4
2 Primary; 1 Middle; 1 High; 0 Other Level
4 Regular; 0 Special Education; 0 Vocational; 0 Alternative
0 Magnet; 0 Charter; 1 Title I Eligible; 0 School-wide Title I
Students: 2,020 (52.3% male; 47.7% female)
Individual Education Program: 317 (15.7%);
English Language Learner: 0 (0.0%); Migrant: 0 (0.0%)
Eligible for Free Lunch Program: n/a
Eligible for Reduced-Price Lunch Program: n/a
Teachers: 144.1 (14.0 to 1)
Librarians/Media Specialists: 3.0 (673.3 to 1)
Guidance Counselors: 12.8 (157.8 to 1)
Current Spending: ($ per student per year):
Total: $8,437; Instruction: $5,550; Support Services: $2,640

Enrollment, Drop-out Rates and Diploma Recipients by Race/Ethnicity

Category	Total	White	Black	Asian	AIAN	Hisp.
Enrollment (%)	100.0	96.7	0.7	1.9	0.0	0.6
Drop-out Rate (%)	0.4	0.4	0.0	0.0	n/a	0.0
H.S. Diplomas (#)	131	128	0	2	0	1

Pembroke

Office of the Superintendent • Pembroke, MA 02359
(781) 829-1178
Grade Span: KG-06; **Agency Type:** 2
Schools: 3
3 Primary; 0 Middle; 0 High; 0 Other Level
3 Regular; 0 Special Education; 0 Vocational; 0 Alternative
0 Magnet; 0 Charter; 1 Title I Eligible; 0 School-wide Title I
Students: 1,828 (52.0% male; 48.0% female)
Individual Education Program: 255 (13.9%);
English Language Learner: 0 (0.0%); Migrant: 0 (0.0%)
Eligible for Free Lunch Program: n/a
Eligible for Reduced-Price Lunch Program: n/a
Teachers: 100.4 (18.2 to 1)
Librarians/Media Specialists: 1.0 (1,828.0 to 1)
Guidance Counselors: 0.0 (0.0 to 1)
Current Spending: ($ per student per year):
Total: $7,263; Instruction: $4,747; Support Services: $2,324
Enrollment, Drop-out Rates and Diploma Recipients by Race/Ethnicity

Category	Total	White	Black	Asian	AIAN	Hisp.
Enrollment (%)	100.0	97.7	0.6	1.4	0.0	0.3
Drop-out Rate (%)	n/a	n/a	n/a	n/a	n/a	n/a
H.S. Diplomas (#)	n/a	n/a	n/a	n/a	n/a	n/a

Plymouth

253 S Meadow Rd • Plymouth, MA 02360-4739
(508) 830-4300
Grade Span: PK-12; **Agency Type:** 1
Schools: 14
9 Primary; 2 Middle; 3 High; 0 Other Level
13 Regular; 0 Special Education; 1 Vocational; 0 Alternative
0 Magnet; 0 Charter; 6 Title I Eligible; 1 School-wide Title I
Students: 8,927 (52.1% male; 47.9% female)
Individual Education Program: 1,306 (14.6%);
English Language Learner: 16 (0.2%); Migrant: 0 (0.0%)
Eligible for Free Lunch Program: n/a
Eligible for Reduced-Price Lunch Program: n/a
Teachers: 578.9 (15.4 to 1)
Librarians/Media Specialists: 11.0 (811.5 to 1)
Guidance Counselors: 26.0 (343.3 to 1)
Current Spending: ($ per student per year):
Total: $8,600; Instruction: $5,862; Support Services: $2,473
Enrollment, Drop-out Rates and Diploma Recipients by Race/Ethnicity

Category	Total	White	Black	Asian	AIAN	Hisp.
Enrollment (%)	100.0	94.7	2.8	0.7	0.3	1.6
Drop-out Rate (%)	4.1	3.8	12.1	0.0	0.0	8.3
H.S. Diplomas (#)	534	509	14	6	2	3

Rockland

34 Mackinlay Way • Rockland, MA 02370-2374
(781) 878-3893 • http://www.rockland.mec.edu/
Grade Span: PK-12; **Agency Type:** 1
Schools: 5
3 Primary; 1 Middle; 1 High; 0 Other Level
5 Regular; 0 Special Education; 0 Vocational; 0 Alternative
0 Magnet; 0 Charter; 4 Title I Eligible; 0 School-wide Title I
Students: 2,796 (52.6% male; 47.4% female)
Individual Education Program: 331 (11.8%);
English Language Learner: 0 (0.0%); Migrant: 0 (0.0%)
Eligible for Free Lunch Program: n/a
Eligible for Reduced-Price Lunch Program: n/a
Teachers: 176.7 (15.8 to 1)
Librarians/Media Specialists: 1.0 (2,796.0 to 1)
Guidance Counselors: 4.0 (699.0 to 1)
Current Spending: ($ per student per year):
Total: $8,299; Instruction: $5,440; Support Services: $2,574
Enrollment, Drop-out Rates and Diploma Recipients by Race/Ethnicity

Category	Total	White	Black	Asian	AIAN	Hisp.
Enrollment (%)	100.0	91.5	3.5	1.9	0.6	2.5
Drop-out Rate (%)	2.9	3.0	4.2	0.0	0.0	0.0
H.S. Diplomas (#)	177	163	4	7	2	1

Scituate

606 C J Cushing Hwy • Scituate, MA 02066-3296
(781) 545-8759 • http://www.scituate.k12.ma.us/
Grade Span: PK-12; **Agency Type:** 1
Schools: 5
3 Primary; 1 Middle; 0 High; 1 Other Level
5 Regular; 0 Special Education; 0 Vocational; 0 Alternative

0 Magnet; 0 Charter; 3 Title I Eligible; 0 School-wide Title I
Students: 3,119 (50.2% male; 49.8% female)
Individual Education Program: 410 (13.1%);
English Language Learner: 41 (1.3%); Migrant: 2 (0.1%)
Eligible for Free Lunch Program: n/a
Eligible for Reduced-Price Lunch Program: n/a
Teachers: 204.1 (15.3 to 1)
Librarians/Media Specialists: 2.0 (1,559.5 to 1)
Guidance Counselors: 10.0 (311.9 to 1)
Current Spending: ($ per student per year):
Total: $7,387; Instruction: $5,069; Support Services: $2,142
Enrollment, Drop-out Rates and Diploma Recipients by Race/Ethnicity

Category	Total	White	Black	Asian	AIAN	Hisp.
Enrollment (%)	100.0	95.7	2.9	0.5	0.1	0.8
Drop-out Rate (%)	1.6	1.4	0.0	0.0	n/a	n/a
H.S. Diplomas (#)	176	169	6	0	0	1

Silver Lake
250 Pembroke St • Kingston, MA 02364-1153
(781) 585-4313 • http://www.silverlake.mec.edu/
Grade Span: 07-12; **Agency Type:** 3
Schools: 2
0 Primary; 1 Middle; 1 High; 0 Other Level
2 Regular; 0 Special Education; 0 Vocational; 0 Alternative
0 Magnet; 0 Charter; 1 Title I Eligible; 1 School-wide Title I
Students: 2,896 (50.7% male; 49.3% female)
Individual Education Program: 349 (12.1%);
English Language Learner: 0 (0.0%); Migrant: 0 (0.0%)
Eligible for Free Lunch Program: n/a
Eligible for Reduced-Price Lunch Program: n/a
Teachers: 204.4 (14.2 to 1)
Librarians/Media Specialists: 0.0 (0.0 to 1)
Guidance Counselors: 14.0 (206.9 to 1)
Current Spending: ($ per student per year):
Total: $9,504; Instruction: $5,904; Support Services: $3,561
Enrollment, Drop-out Rates and Diploma Recipients by Race/Ethnicity

Category	Total	White	Black	Asian	AIAN	Hisp.
Enrollment (%)	100.0	98.2	1.0	0.6	0.0	0.2
Drop-out Rate (%)	2.0	2.1	0.0	0.0	n/a	0.0
H.S. Diplomas (#)	352	350	1	1	0	0

Wareham
54 Marion Rd • Wareham, MA 02571-1428
(508) 291-3500 • http://www.wareham.mec.edu/
Grade Span: PK-12; **Agency Type:** 1
Schools: 7
5 Primary; 1 Middle; 1 High; 0 Other Level
7 Regular; 0 Special Education; 0 Vocational; 0 Alternative
0 Magnet; 0 Charter; 6 Title I Eligible; 6 School-wide Title I
Students: 3,489 (51.9% male; 48.1% female)
Individual Education Program: 563 (16.1%);
English Language Learner: 0 (0.0%); Migrant: 4 (0.1%)
Eligible for Free Lunch Program: n/a
Eligible for Reduced-Price Lunch Program: n/a
Teachers: 271.8 (12.8 to 1)
Librarians/Media Specialists: 3.0 (1,163.0 to 1)
Guidance Counselors: 6.6 (528.6 to 1)
Current Spending: ($ per student per year):
Total: $8,274; Instruction: $5,453; Support Services: $2,471
Enrollment, Drop-out Rates and Diploma Recipients by Race/Ethnicity

Category	Total	White	Black	Asian	AIAN	Hisp.
Enrollment (%)	100.0	84.1	12.1	0.8	1.0	2.0
Drop-out Rate (%)	0.5	0.4	1.9	0.0	0.0	0.0
H.S. Diplomas (#)	164	140	17	3	2	2

Whitman-Hanson
600 Franklin St • Whitman, MA 02382-2599
(781) 618-7412 • http://www.whrsd.k12.ma.us/
Grade Span: PK-12; **Agency Type:** 3
Schools: 8
5 Primary; 2 Middle; 1 High; 0 Other Level
8 Regular; 0 Special Education; 0 Vocational; 0 Alternative
0 Magnet; 0 Charter; 4 Title I Eligible; 0 School-wide Title I
Students: 4,521 (52.4% male; 47.6% female)
Individual Education Program: 633 (14.0%);
English Language Learner: 2 (<0.1%); Migrant: 0 (0.0%)
Eligible for Free Lunch Program: n/a
Eligible for Reduced-Price Lunch Program: n/a
Teachers: 304.0 (14.9 to 1)
Librarians/Media Specialists: 6.0 (753.5 to 1)
Guidance Counselors: 9.0 (502.3 to 1)
Current Spending: ($ per student per year):
Total: $7,584; Instruction: $5,251; Support Services: $2,077

Enrollment, Drop-out Rates and Diploma Recipients by Race/Ethnicity

Category	Total	White	Black	Asian	AIAN	Hisp.
Enrollment (%)	100.0	96.5	1.7	0.4	0.1	1.4
Drop-out Rate (%)	1.0	1.0	0.0	0.0	n/a	0.0
H.S. Diplomas (#)	258	250	3	4	0	1

Suffolk County

Boston
26 Court St • Boston, MA 02108-2581
(617) 635-9050 • http://www.boston.k12.ma.us/
Grade Span: PK-12; **Agency Type:** 1
Schools: 135
85 Primary; 22 Middle; 23 High; 5 Other Level
125 Regular; 1 Special Education; 0 Vocational; 9 Alternative
0 Magnet; 0 Charter; 127 Title I Eligible; 127 School-wide Title I
Students: 61,552 (51.8% male; 48.2% female)
Individual Education Program: 11,833 (19.2%);
English Language Learner: 14,964 (24.3%); Migrant: 427 (0.7%)
Eligible for Free Lunch Program: n/a
Eligible for Reduced-Price Lunch Program: n/a
Teachers: 4,517.8 (13.6 to 1)
Librarians/Media Specialists: 24.0 (2,564.7 to 1)
Guidance Counselors: 106.1 (580.1 to 1)
Current Spending: ($ per student per year):
Total: $12,717; Instruction: $8,378; Support Services: $3,941
Enrollment, Drop-out Rates and Diploma Recipients by Race/Ethnicity

Category	Total	White	Black	Asian	AIAN	Hisp.
Enrollment (%)	100.0	14.1	47.2	8.9	0.4	29.3
Drop-out Rate (%)	8.1	7.1	8.5	3.7	6.3	9.8
H.S. Diplomas (#)	2,816	525	1,372	345	10	564

Chelsea
City Hall Room 216 • Chelsea, MA 02150
(617) 889-8415 • http://www.chelseaschools.com/
Grade Span: PK-12; **Agency Type:** 1
Schools: 9
5 Primary; 2 Middle; 1 High; 1 Other Level
8 Regular; 0 Special Education; 0 Vocational; 1 Alternative
0 Magnet; 0 Charter; 9 Title I Eligible; 9 School-wide Title I
Students: 5,777 (51.8% male; 48.2% female)
Individual Education Program: 763 (13.2%);
English Language Learner: 891 (15.4%); Migrant: 0 (0.0%)
Eligible for Free Lunch Program: n/a
Eligible for Reduced-Price Lunch Program: n/a
Teachers: 501.3 (11.5 to 1)
Librarians/Media Specialists: 5.0 (1,155.4 to 1)
Guidance Counselors: 11.0 (525.2 to 1)
Current Spending: ($ per student per year):
Total: $9,755; Instruction: $6,170; Support Services: $3,101
Enrollment, Drop-out Rates and Diploma Recipients by Race/Ethnicity

Category	Total	White	Black	Asian	AIAN	Hisp.
Enrollment (%)	100.0	15.8	6.9	5.2	0.2	72.0
Drop-out Rate (%)	10.5	15.1	9.9	9.1	n/a	9.4
H.S. Diplomas (#)	161	28	14	21	0	98

Revere
101 School St • Revere, MA 02151-3001
(781) 286-8226 • http://www.revereps.mec.edu/
Grade Span: PK-12; **Agency Type:** 1
Schools: 8
6 Primary; 0 Middle; 2 High; 0 Other Level
8 Regular; 0 Special Education; 0 Vocational; 0 Alternative
1 Magnet; 0 Charter; 6 Title I Eligible; 0 School-wide Title I
Students: 5,936 (52.4% male; 47.6% female)
Individual Education Program: 742 (12.5%);
English Language Learner: 381 (6.4%); Migrant: 0 (0.0%)
Eligible for Free Lunch Program: n/a
Eligible for Reduced-Price Lunch Program: n/a
Teachers: 462.6 (12.8 to 1)
Librarians/Media Specialists: 3.0 (1,978.7 to 1)
Guidance Counselors: 14.0 (424.0 to 1)
Current Spending: ($ per student per year):
Total: $8,638; Instruction: $5,737; Support Services: $2,585
Enrollment, Drop-out Rates and Diploma Recipients by Race/Ethnicity

Category	Total	White	Black	Asian	AIAN	Hisp.
Enrollment (%)	100.0	65.1	5.6	9.5	0.5	19.4
Drop-out Rate (%)	6.8	5.8	8.1	5.4	0.0	17.2
H.S. Diplomas (#)	236	158	15	36	3	24

Winthrop
45 Pauline St • Winthrop, MA 02152-3011
(617) 846-5500 • http://www.winthrop.k12.ma.us/
Grade Span: PK-12; **Agency Type:** 1
Schools: 4

2 Primary; 1 Middle; 1 High; 0 Other Level
4 Regular; 0 Special Education; 0 Vocational; 0 Alternative
0 Magnet; 0 Charter; 2 Title I Eligible; 0 School-wide Title I
Students: 2,138 (49.3% male; 50.7% female)
Individual Education Program: 284 (13.3%);
English Language Learner: 0 (0.0%); Migrant: 0 (0.0%)
Eligible for Free Lunch Program: n/a
Eligible for Reduced-Price Lunch Program: n/a
Teachers: 165.5 (12.9 to 1)
Librarians/Media Specialists: 3.0 (712.7 to 1)
Guidance Counselors: 4.0 (534.5 to 1)
Current Spending: ($ per student per year):
Total: $8,279; Instruction: $6,087; Support Services: $1,993
Enrollment, Drop-out Rates and Diploma Recipients by Race/Ethnicity

Category	Total	White	Black	Asian	AIAN	Hisp.
Enrollment (%)	100.0	93.7	1.5	1.2	0.1	3.5
Drop-out Rate (%)	3.5	3.0	0.0	0.0	0.0	23.1
H.S. Diplomas (#)	90	88	0	1	0	1

Worcester County

Ashburnham-Westminster
2 Narrows Rd, Ste 101 • Westminster, MA 01473-1619
(978) 874-1501 • http://www.awrsd.org/
Grade Span: PK-12; **Agency Type:** 3
Schools: 5
3 Primary; 1 Middle; 1 High; 0 Other Level
5 Regular; 0 Special Education; 0 Vocational; 0 Alternative
0 Magnet; 0 Charter; 2 Title I Eligible; 0 School-wide Title I
Students: 2,463 (53.0% male; 47.0% female)
Individual Education Program: 440 (17.9%);
English Language Learner: 0 (0.0%); Migrant: 0 (0.0%)
Eligible for Free Lunch Program: n/a
Eligible for Reduced-Price Lunch Program: n/a
Teachers: 194.5 (12.7 to 1)
Librarians/Media Specialists: 3.0 (821.0 to 1)
Guidance Counselors: 8.0 (307.9 to 1)
Current Spending: ($ per student per year):
Total: $8,032; Instruction: $5,318; Support Services: $2,522
Enrollment, Drop-out Rates and Diploma Recipients by Race/Ethnicity

Category	Total	White	Black	Asian	AIAN	Hisp.
Enrollment (%)	100.0	96.5	0.9	1.2	0.0	1.3
Drop-out Rate (%)	0.4	0.4	0.0	0.0	n/a	0.0
H.S. Diplomas (#)	174	169	0	2	0	3

Athol-Royalston
250 S Main St • Athol, MA 01331-3526
Mailing Address: PO Box 968 • Athol, MA 01331-3526
(978) 249-2400 • http://www.athol-royalstonschools.org/
Grade Span: PK-12; **Agency Type:** 3
Schools: 9
6 Primary; 1 Middle; 1 High; 1 Other Level
9 Regular; 0 Special Education; 0 Vocational; 0 Alternative
0 Magnet; 0 Charter; 6 Title I Eligible; 0 School-wide Title I
Students: 2,209 (53.0% male; 47.0% female)
Individual Education Program: 355 (16.1%);
English Language Learner: 3 (0.1%); Migrant: 0 (0.0%)
Eligible for Free Lunch Program: n/a
Eligible for Reduced-Price Lunch Program: n/a
Teachers: 172.5 (12.8 to 1)
Librarians/Media Specialists: 2.0 (1,104.5 to 1)
Guidance Counselors: 6.0 (368.2 to 1)
Current Spending: ($ per student per year):
Total: $10,196; Instruction: $6,777; Support Services: $3,053
Enrollment, Drop-out Rates and Diploma Recipients by Race/Ethnicity

Category	Total	White	Black	Asian	AIAN	Hisp.
Enrollment (%)	100.0	93.2	1.9	0.9	0.4	3.6
Drop-out Rate (%)	3.0	3.0	0.0	0.0	0.0	8.3
H.S. Diplomas (#)	108	103	3	0	0	2

Auburn
5 W St • Auburn, MA 01501-1301
(508) 832-7755 • http://www.auburn.mec.edu/
Grade Span: PK-12; **Agency Type:** 1
Schools: 6
4 Primary; 1 Middle; 1 High; 0 Other Level
6 Regular; 0 Special Education; 0 Vocational; 0 Alternative
0 Magnet; 0 Charter; 1 Title I Eligible; 0 School-wide Title I
Students: 2,422 (51.5% male; 48.5% female)
Individual Education Program: 242 (10.0%);
English Language Learner: 0 (0.0%); Migrant: 0 (0.0%)
Eligible for Free Lunch Program: n/a
Eligible for Reduced-Price Lunch Program: n/a
Teachers: 150.4 (16.1 to 1)
Librarians/Media Specialists: 0.0 (0.0 to 1)
Guidance Counselors: 8.0 (302.8 to 1)
Current Spending: ($ per student per year):
Total: $7,897; Instruction: $5,512; Support Services: $2,126
Enrollment, Drop-out Rates and Diploma Recipients by Race/Ethnicity

Category	Total	White	Black	Asian	AIAN	Hisp.
Enrollment (%)	100.0	94.4	0.9	2.1	0.7	1.9
Drop-out Rate (%)	2.4	2.6	0.0	0.0	0.0	0.0
H.S. Diplomas (#)	151	144	3	3	0	1

Blackstone-Millville
175 Lincoln St • Blackstone, MA 01504-1202
(508) 883-4400 • http://www.bmrsd.net/
Grade Span: PK-12; **Agency Type:** 3
Schools: 5
2 Primary; 2 Middle; 1 High; 0 Other Level
5 Regular; 0 Special Education; 0 Vocational; 0 Alternative
0 Magnet; 0 Charter; 3 Title I Eligible; 0 School-wide Title I
Students: 2,314 (51.1% male; 48.9% female)
Individual Education Program: 330 (14.3%);
English Language Learner: 0 (0.0%); Migrant: 0 (0.0%)
Eligible for Free Lunch Program: n/a
Eligible for Reduced-Price Lunch Program: n/a
Teachers: 321.8 (7.2 to 1)
Librarians/Media Specialists: 1.0 (2,314.0 to 1)
Guidance Counselors: 5.4 (428.5 to 1)
Current Spending: ($ per student per year):
Total: $7,432; Instruction: $5,213; Support Services: $1,979
Enrollment, Drop-out Rates and Diploma Recipients by Race/Ethnicity

Category	Total	White	Black	Asian	AIAN	Hisp.
Enrollment (%)	100.0	96.5	1.1	1.0	0.0	1.3
Drop-out Rate (%)	3.9	4.0	0.0	0.0	n/a	0.0
H.S. Diplomas (#)	143	141	1	0	0	1

Clinton
150 School St • Clinton, MA 01510-2504
(978) 365-4200 • http://www.clinton.k12.ma.us/
Grade Span: PK-12; **Agency Type:** 1
Schools: 4
3 Primary; 0 Middle; 1 High; 0 Other Level
4 Regular; 0 Special Education; 0 Vocational; 0 Alternative
0 Magnet; 0 Charter; 1 Title I Eligible; 0 School-wide Title I
Students: 1,984 (51.6% male; 48.4% female)
Individual Education Program: 300 (15.1%);
English Language Learner: 71 (3.6%); Migrant: 4 (0.2%)
Eligible for Free Lunch Program: n/a
Eligible for Reduced-Price Lunch Program: n/a
Teachers: 151.9 (13.1 to 1)
Librarians/Media Specialists: 2.5 (793.6 to 1)
Guidance Counselors: 8.0 (248.0 to 1)
Current Spending: ($ per student per year):
Total: $8,648; Instruction: $6,166; Support Services: $2,200
Enrollment, Drop-out Rates and Diploma Recipients by Race/Ethnicity

Category	Total	White	Black	Asian	AIAN	Hisp.
Enrollment (%)	100.0	76.7	2.7	1.1	0.0	19.5
Drop-out Rate (%)	2.2	1.0	9.1	0.0	n/a	5.7
H.S. Diplomas (#)	131	111	0	1	0	19

Dudley-Charlton Regional
68 Dudley Oxford Rd • Dudley, MA 01571-6116
(508) 943-6888 • http://www.dc-regional.k12.ma.us/
Grade Span: PK-12; **Agency Type:** 3
Schools: 7
4 Primary; 2 Middle; 1 High; 0 Other Level
7 Regular; 0 Special Education; 0 Vocational; 0 Alternative
0 Magnet; 0 Charter; 6 Title I Eligible; 0 School-wide Title I
Students: 4,329 (50.2% male; 49.8% female)
Individual Education Program: 541 (12.5%);
English Language Learner: 0 (0.0%); Migrant: 0 (0.0%)
Eligible for Free Lunch Program: n/a
Eligible for Reduced-Price Lunch Program: n/a
Teachers: 226.3 (19.1 to 1)
Librarians/Media Specialists: 5.0 (865.8 to 1)
Guidance Counselors: 9.2 (470.5 to 1)
Current Spending: ($ per student per year):
Total: $7,172; Instruction: $4,813; Support Services: $2,143
Enrollment, Drop-out Rates and Diploma Recipients by Race/Ethnicity

Category	Total	White	Black	Asian	AIAN	Hisp.
Enrollment (%)	100.0	99.1	0.2	0.0	0.0	0.6
Drop-out Rate (%)	3.3	3.3	25.0	0.0	0.0	0.0
H.S. Diplomas (#)	221	219	0	0	0	2

Fitchburg
376 S St • Fitchburg, MA 01420-7942
(978) 345-3200 • http://www.fitchburg.k12.ma.us/
Grade Span: PK-12; **Agency Type:** 1
Schools: 10

6 Primary; 3 Middle; 0 High; 1 Other Level
10 Regular; 0 Special Education; 0 Vocational; 0 Alternative
0 Magnet; 0 Charter; 10 Title I Eligible; 5 School-wide Title I
Students: 5,977 (50.3% male; 49.7% female)
Individual Education Program: 887 (14.8%);
English Language Learner: 998 (16.7%); Migrant: 14 (0.2%)
Eligible for Free Lunch Program: n/a
Eligible for Reduced-Price Lunch Program: n/a
Teachers: 481.5 (12.4 to 1)
Librarians/Media Specialists: 6.5 (919.5 to 1)
Guidance Counselors: 19.0 (314.6 to 1)
Current Spending: ($ per student per year):
Total: $8,897; Instruction: $6,021; Support Services: $2,359
Enrollment, Drop-out Rates and Diploma Recipients by Race/Ethnicity

Category	Total	White	Black	Asian	AIAN	Hisp.
Enrollment (%)	100.0	52.4	7.2	10.4	0.3	29.7
Drop-out Rate (%)	5.0	3.7	0.8	3.5	0.0	11.6
H.S. Diplomas (#)	300	221	22	25	0	32

Gardner
130 Elm/ Sauter Sch • Gardner, MA 01440-2373
(978) 632-1000 • http://www.gardnerk12.org/
Grade Span: PK-12; **Agency Type:** 1
Schools: 6
4 Primary; 1 Middle; 1 High; 0 Other Level
6 Regular; 0 Special Education; 0 Vocational; 0 Alternative
0 Magnet; 0 Charter; 5 Title I Eligible; 0 School-wide Title I
Students: 3,230 (50.6% male; 49.4% female)
Individual Education Program: 625 (19.3%);
English Language Learner: 0 (0.0%); Migrant: 0 (0.0%)
Eligible for Free Lunch Program: n/a
Eligible for Reduced-Price Lunch Program: n/a
Teachers: 225.3 (14.3 to 1)
Librarians/Media Specialists: 2.0 (1,615.0 to 1)
Guidance Counselors: 22.0 (146.8 to 1)
Current Spending: ($ per student per year):
Total: $7,341; Instruction: $5,002; Support Services: $2,085
Enrollment, Drop-out Rates and Diploma Recipients by Race/Ethnicity

Category	Total	White	Black	Asian	AIAN	Hisp.
Enrollment (%)	100.0	88.3	3.4	2.3	0.4	5.7
Drop-out Rate (%)	3.2	3.3	0.0	0.0	0.0	3.6
H.S. Diplomas (#)	172	162	3	5	0	2

Grafton
30 Providence Rd • Grafton, MA 01519-1178
(508) 839-5421 • http://www.grafton.k12.ma.us/district/index.cfm
Grade Span: PK-12; **Agency Type:** 1
Schools: 5
3 Primary; 1 Middle; 1 High; 0 Other Level
5 Regular; 0 Special Education; 0 Vocational; 0 Alternative
0 Magnet; 0 Charter; 1 Title I Eligible; 0 School-wide Title I
Students: 2,293 (52.6% male; 47.4% female)
Individual Education Program: 379 (16.5%);
English Language Learner: 1 (<0.1%); Migrant: 3 (0.1%)
Eligible for Free Lunch Program: n/a
Eligible for Reduced-Price Lunch Program: n/a
Teachers: 186.9 (12.3 to 1)
Librarians/Media Specialists: 7.0 (327.6 to 1)
Guidance Counselors: 16.0 (143.3 to 1)
Current Spending: ($ per student per year):
Total: $7,424; Instruction: $4,920; Support Services: $2,298
Enrollment, Drop-out Rates and Diploma Recipients by Race/Ethnicity

Category	Total	White	Black	Asian	AIAN	Hisp.
Enrollment (%)	100.0	94.1	1.0	2.3	0.8	1.7
Drop-out Rate (%)	3.3	3.5	0.0	0.0	0.0	0.0
H.S. Diplomas (#)	119	112	2	4	0	1

Leicester
1078 Main St • Leicester, MA 01524-1349
(508) 892-7040 • http://www.leicester.k12.ma.us/
Grade Span: PK-12; **Agency Type:** 1
Schools: 4
2 Primary; 1 Middle; 1 High; 0 Other Level
4 Regular; 0 Special Education; 0 Vocational; 0 Alternative
0 Magnet; 0 Charter; 3 Title I Eligible; 0 School-wide Title I
Students: 1,944 (51.2% male; 48.8% female)
Individual Education Program: 274 (14.1%);
English Language Learner: 0 (0.0%); Migrant: 2 (0.1%)
Eligible for Free Lunch Program: n/a
Eligible for Reduced-Price Lunch Program: n/a
Teachers: 129.6 (15.0 to 1)
Librarians/Media Specialists: 3.0 (648.0 to 1)
Guidance Counselors: 8.0 (243.0 to 1)
Current Spending: ($ per student per year):
Total: $7,739; Instruction: $5,114; Support Services: $2,354

Enrollment, Drop-out Rates and Diploma Recipients by Race/Ethnicity

Category	Total	White	Black	Asian	AIAN	Hisp.
Enrollment (%)	100.0	94.3	1.4	1.6	0.4	2.3
Drop-out Rate (%)	2.2	2.1	0.0	0.0	n/a	6.7
H.S. Diplomas (#)	106	99	1	3	0	3

Leominster
24 Church St • Leominster, MA 01453-3102
(978) 534-7700 • http://www.leominster.mec.edu/
Grade Span: PK-12; **Agency Type:** 1
Schools: 9
5 Primary; 2 Middle; 2 High; 0 Other Level
8 Regular; 0 Special Education; 1 Vocational; 0 Alternative
0 Magnet; 0 Charter; 4 Title I Eligible; 0 School-wide Title I
Students: 6,141 (51.8% male; 48.2% female)
Individual Education Program: 1,007 (16.4%);
English Language Learner: 510 (8.3%); Migrant: 4 (0.1%)
Eligible for Free Lunch Program: n/a
Eligible for Reduced-Price Lunch Program: n/a
Teachers: 421.9 (14.6 to 1)
Librarians/Media Specialists: 6.0 (1,023.5 to 1)
Guidance Counselors: 15.2 (404.0 to 1)
Current Spending: ($ per student per year):
Total: $8,324; Instruction: $5,514; Support Services: $2,502
Enrollment, Drop-out Rates and Diploma Recipients by Race/Ethnicity

Category	Total	White	Black	Asian	AIAN	Hisp.
Enrollment (%)	100.0	71.2	4.5	4.1	0.4	19.8
Drop-out Rate (%)	3.8	3.5	0.0	1.4	50.0	6.8
H.S. Diplomas (#)	350	284	11	13	0	42

Lunenburg
1033 Mass Ave • Lunenburg, MA 01462-1479
(978) 582-4100
Grade Span: PK-12; **Agency Type:** 1
Schools: 3
1 Primary; 1 Middle; 1 High; 0 Other Level
3 Regular; 0 Special Education; 0 Vocational; 0 Alternative
0 Magnet; 0 Charter; 2 Title I Eligible; 0 School-wide Title I
Students: 1,887 (52.2% male; 47.8% female)
Individual Education Program: 232 (12.3%);
English Language Learner: 1 (0.1%); Migrant: 0 (0.0%)
Eligible for Free Lunch Program: n/a
Eligible for Reduced-Price Lunch Program: n/a
Teachers: 120.3 (15.7 to 1)
Librarians/Media Specialists: 1.5 (1,258.0 to 1)
Guidance Counselors: 5.0 (377.4 to 1)
Current Spending: ($ per student per year):
Total: $7,475; Instruction: $5,276; Support Services: $1,987
Enrollment, Drop-out Rates and Diploma Recipients by Race/Ethnicity

Category	Total	White	Black	Asian	AIAN	Hisp.
Enrollment (%)	100.0	95.2	1.0	1.6	0.2	2.0
Drop-out Rate (%)	2.8	2.3	0.0	9.1	n/a	18.8
H.S. Diplomas (#)	128	123	1	2	1	1

Mendon-Upton
150 N Ave, PO Box 5 • Mendon, MA 01756-0176
(508) 634-1585 • http://www.mu-regional.k12.ma.us/
Grade Span: PK-12; **Agency Type:** 3
Schools: 4
3 Primary; 0 Middle; 1 High; 0 Other Level
4 Regular; 0 Special Education; 0 Vocational; 0 Alternative
0 Magnet; 0 Charter; 3 Title I Eligible; 0 School-wide Title I
Students: 2,450 (50.5% male; 49.5% female)
Individual Education Program: 233 (9.5%);
English Language Learner: 0 (0.0%); Migrant: 0 (0.0%)
Eligible for Free Lunch Program: n/a
Eligible for Reduced-Price Lunch Program: n/a
Teachers: 151.4 (16.2 to 1)
Librarians/Media Specialists: 1.0 (2,450.0 to 1)
Guidance Counselors: 14.0 (175.0 to 1)
Current Spending: ($ per student per year):
Total: $7,307; Instruction: $4,788; Support Services: $2,259
Enrollment, Drop-out Rates and Diploma Recipients by Race/Ethnicity

Category	Total	White	Black	Asian	AIAN	Hisp.
Enrollment (%)	100.0	97.3	0.4	0.8	0.6	0.9
Drop-out Rate (%)	1.2	1.0	0.0	0.0	0.0	25.0
H.S. Diplomas (#)	111	111	0	0	0	0

Milford
31 W Fountain St • Milford, MA 01757-4098
(508) 478-1100 • http://mail.milfordma.com/schools/
Grade Span: PK-12; **Agency Type:** 1
Schools: 7
4 Primary; 1 Middle; 0 High; 2 Other Level
7 Regular; 0 Special Education; 0 Vocational; 0 Alternative

0 Magnet; 0 Charter; 3 Title I Eligible; 0 School-wide Title I
Students: 4,100 (52.0% male; 48.0% female)
Individual Education Program: 523 (12.8%);
English Language Learner: 162 (4.0%); Migrant: 24 (0.6%)
Eligible for Free Lunch Program: n/a
Eligible for Reduced-Price Lunch Program: n/a
Teachers: 324.4 (12.6 to 1)
Librarians/Media Specialists: 2.0 (2,050.0 to 1)
Guidance Counselors: 10.0 (410.0 to 1)
Current Spending: ($ per student per year):
Total: $8,137; Instruction: $5,526; Support Services: $2,337
Enrollment, Drop-out Rates and Diploma Recipients by Race/Ethnicity

Category	Total	White	Black	Asian	AIAN	Hisp.
Enrollment (%)	100.0	87.2	2.3	2.4	0.3	7.9
Drop-out Rate (%)	4.0	3.6	0.0	7.3	0.0	10.2
H.S. Diplomas (#)	227	186	6	5	0	30

Millbury
12 Martin St • Millbury, MA 01527-2014
(508) 865-9501 • http://www.millbury.k12.ma.us/
Grade Span: PK-12; **Agency Type:** 1
Schools: 3
1 Primary; 1 Middle; 1 High; 0 Other Level
3 Regular; 0 Special Education; 0 Vocational; 0 Alternative
0 Magnet; 0 Charter; 1 Title I Eligible; 0 School-wide Title I
Students: 1,928 (51.0% male; 49.0% female)
Individual Education Program: 269 (14.0%);
English Language Learner: 4 (0.2%); Migrant: 1 (0.1%)
Eligible for Free Lunch Program: n/a
Eligible for Reduced-Price Lunch Program: n/a
Teachers: 134.3 (14.4 to 1)
Librarians/Media Specialists: 2.0 (964.0 to 1)
Guidance Counselors: 5.0 (385.6 to 1)
Current Spending: ($ per student per year):
Total: $7,654; Instruction: $5,607; Support Services: $1,810
Enrollment, Drop-out Rates and Diploma Recipients by Race/Ethnicity

Category	Total	White	Black	Asian	AIAN	Hisp.
Enrollment (%)	100.0	94.7	1.7	1.4	0.4	1.9
Drop-out Rate (%)	2.7	2.9	0.0	0.0	n/a	0.0
H.S. Diplomas (#)	92	89	1	0	1	1

Narragansett
462 Baldwinville Rd • Baldwinville, MA 01436-1225
(978) 939-5661 • http://www.nrsd.org/
Grade Span: PK-12; **Agency Type:** 3
Schools: 6
4 Primary; 1 Middle; 1 High; 0 Other Level
6 Regular; 0 Special Education; 0 Vocational; 0 Alternative
0 Magnet; 0 Charter; 4 Title I Eligible; 0 School-wide Title I
Students: 1,582 (50.4% male; 49.6% female)
Individual Education Program: 236 (14.9%);
English Language Learner: 0 (0.0%); Migrant: 1 (0.1%)
Eligible for Free Lunch Program: n/a
Eligible for Reduced-Price Lunch Program: n/a
Teachers: 119.0 (13.3 to 1)
Librarians/Media Specialists: 0.0 (0.0 to 1)
Guidance Counselors: 4.0 (395.5 to 1)
Current Spending: ($ per student per year):
Total: $7,684; Instruction: $5,117; Support Services: $2,299
Enrollment, Drop-out Rates and Diploma Recipients by Race/Ethnicity

Category	Total	White	Black	Asian	AIAN	Hisp.
Enrollment (%)	100.0	97.3	1.1	0.6	0.1	0.9
Drop-out Rate (%)	4.2	4.3	0.0	n/a	n/a	0.0
H.S. Diplomas (#)	79	78	0	1	0	0

Nashoba
50 Mechanic St • Bolton, MA 01740-3300
(978) 779-0539 • http://www.nrsd.net/
Grade Span: PK-12; **Agency Type:** 3
Schools: 7
4 Primary; 2 Middle; 1 High; 0 Other Level
7 Regular; 0 Special Education; 0 Vocational; 0 Alternative
0 Magnet; 0 Charter; 2 Title I Eligible; 0 School-wide Title I
Students: 3,049 (52.0% male; 48.0% female)
Individual Education Program: 407 (13.3%);
English Language Learner: 5 (0.2%); Migrant: 0 (0.0%)
Eligible for Free Lunch Program: n/a
Eligible for Reduced-Price Lunch Program: n/a
Teachers: 243.8 (12.5 to 1)
Librarians/Media Specialists: 1.0 (3,049.0 to 1)
Guidance Counselors: 12.4 (245.9 to 1)
Current Spending: ($ per student per year):
Total: $9,763; Instruction: $6,676; Support Services: $2,840
Enrollment, Drop-out Rates and Diploma Recipients by Race/Ethnicity

Category	Total	White	Black	Asian	AIAN	Hisp.
Enrollment (%)	100.0	94.8	1.2	1.6	0.0	2.4
Drop-out Rate (%)	1.4	1.3	0.0	5.0	n/a	5.9
H.S. Diplomas (#)	190	176	4	7	0	3

Northborough
44 Bearfoot Rd • Northborough, MA 01532-1657
(508) 351-7000 • http://www.nsboro.k12.ma.us/
Grade Span: PK-08; **Agency Type:** 2
Schools: 5
4 Primary; 1 Middle; 0 High; 0 Other Level
5 Regular; 0 Special Education; 0 Vocational; 0 Alternative
0 Magnet; 0 Charter; 5 Title I Eligible; 0 School-wide Title I
Students: 2,000 (53.4% male; 46.7% female)
Individual Education Program: 259 (13.0%);
English Language Learner: 9 (0.5%); Migrant: 1 (0.1%)
Eligible for Free Lunch Program: n/a
Eligible for Reduced-Price Lunch Program: n/a
Teachers: 148.4 (13.5 to 1)
Librarians/Media Specialists: 5.0 (400.0 to 1)
Guidance Counselors: 2.0 (1,000.0 to 1)
Current Spending: ($ per student per year):
Total: $6,934; Instruction: $4,951; Support Services: $1,793
Enrollment, Drop-out Rates and Diploma Recipients by Race/Ethnicity

Category	Total	White	Black	Asian	AIAN	Hisp.
Enrollment (%)	100.0	90.7	1.2	5.5	0.3	2.3
Drop-out Rate (%)	n/a	n/a	n/a	n/a	n/a	n/a
H.S. Diplomas (#)	n/a	n/a	n/a	n/a	n/a	n/a

Northbridge
87 Linwood Ave • Whitinsville, MA 01588-2309
(508) 234-8156 • http://www.northbridge.k12.ma.us/
Grade Span: PK-12; **Agency Type:** 1
Schools: 5
3 Primary; 1 Middle; 1 High; 0 Other Level
5 Regular; 0 Special Education; 0 Vocational; 0 Alternative
0 Magnet; 0 Charter; 3 Title I Eligible; 0 School-wide Title I
Students: 2,490 (50.7% male; 49.3% female)
Individual Education Program: 330 (13.3%);
English Language Learner: 7 (0.3%); Migrant: 0 (0.0%)
Eligible for Free Lunch Program: n/a
Eligible for Reduced-Price Lunch Program: n/a
Teachers: 217.0 (11.5 to 1)
Librarians/Media Specialists: 3.0 (830.0 to 1)
Guidance Counselors: 4.0 (622.5 to 1)
Current Spending: ($ per student per year):
Total: $7,842; Instruction: $5,365; Support Services: $2,217
Enrollment, Drop-out Rates and Diploma Recipients by Race/Ethnicity

Category	Total	White	Black	Asian	AIAN	Hisp.
Enrollment (%)	100.0	94.4	2.0	0.3	0.3	3.0
Drop-out Rate (%)	2.4	2.3	16.7	0.0	n/a	0.0
H.S. Diplomas (#)	102	96	2	0	0	4

Oxford
5 Sigourney St • Oxford, MA 01540-1998
(508) 987-6050 • http://www.oxps.org/
Grade Span: PK-12; **Agency Type:** 1
Schools: 4
2 Primary; 1 Middle; 1 High; 0 Other Level
4 Regular; 0 Special Education; 0 Vocational; 0 Alternative
0 Magnet; 0 Charter; 2 Title I Eligible; 0 School-wide Title I
Students: 2,261 (51.2% male; 48.8% female)
Individual Education Program: 240 (10.6%);
English Language Learner: 1 (<0.1%); Migrant: 1 (<0.1%)
Eligible for Free Lunch Program: n/a
Eligible for Reduced-Price Lunch Program: n/a
Teachers: 144.6 (15.6 to 1)
Librarians/Media Specialists: 1.4 (1,615.0 to 1)
Guidance Counselors: 3.0 (753.7 to 1)
Current Spending: ($ per student per year):
Total: $8,095; Instruction: $5,220; Support Services: $2,646
Enrollment, Drop-out Rates and Diploma Recipients by Race/Ethnicity

Category	Total	White	Black	Asian	AIAN	Hisp.
Enrollment (%)	100.0	93.3	1.9	1.6	0.3	2.9
Drop-out Rate (%)	3.4	3.4	0.0	0.0	n/a	7.1
H.S. Diplomas (#)	151	145	2	0	0	4

Quabbin
872 S St • Barre, MA 01005
(978) 355-4668 • http://www.quabbin.k12.ma.us/
Grade Span: PK-12; **Agency Type:** 3
Schools: 6
5 Primary; 0 Middle; 1 High; 0 Other Level
6 Regular; 0 Special Education; 0 Vocational; 0 Alternative

0 Magnet; 0 Charter; 3 Title I Eligible; 0 School-wide Title I
Students: 3,214 (50.5% male; 49.5% female)
Individual Education Program: 372 (11.6%);
English Language Learner: 3 (0.1%); Migrant: 0 (0.0%)
Eligible for Free Lunch Program: n/a
Eligible for Reduced-Price Lunch Program: n/a
Teachers: 210.2 (15.3 to 1)
Librarians/Media Specialists: 3.0 (1,071.3 to 1)
Guidance Counselors: 10.0 (321.4 to 1)
Current Spending: ($ per student per year):
Total: $7,598; Instruction: $5,105; Support Services: $2,260
Enrollment, Drop-out Rates and Diploma Recipients by Race/Ethnicity

Category	Total	White	Black	Asian	AIAN	Hisp.
Enrollment (%)	100.0	96.2	1.1	0.7	0.3	1.6
Drop-out Rate (%)	2.4	2.5	0.0	0.0	0.0	0.0
H.S. Diplomas (#)	161	158	1	0	0	2

Quaboag Regional

48 High St • Warren, MA 01083-1538
Mailing Address: PO Box 1538 • Warren, MA 01083-1538
(413) 436-9256 • http://www.quaboag.org/
Grade Span: PK-12; **Agency Type:** 3
Schools: 3
2 Primary; 0 Middle; 1 High; 0 Other Level
3 Regular; 0 Special Education; 0 Vocational; 0 Alternative
0 Magnet; 0 Charter; 1 Title I Eligible; 0 School-wide Title I
Students: 1,513 (47.6% male; 52.4% female)
Individual Education Program: 279 (18.4%);
English Language Learner: 3 (0.2%); Migrant: 0 (0.0%)
Eligible for Free Lunch Program: n/a
Eligible for Reduced-Price Lunch Program: n/a
Teachers: 121.1 (12.5 to 1)
Librarians/Media Specialists: 1.0 (1,513.0 to 1)
Guidance Counselors: 3.0 (504.3 to 1)
Current Spending: ($ per student per year):
Total: $8,023; Instruction: $5,195; Support Services: $2,559
Enrollment, Drop-out Rates and Diploma Recipients by Race/Ethnicity

Category	Total	White	Black	Asian	AIAN	Hisp.
Enrollment (%)	100.0	96.3	0.8	0.9	0.3	1.7
Drop-out Rate (%)	2.6	2.7	0.0	0.0	0.0	n/a
H.S. Diplomas (#)	72	71	0	1	0	0

Shrewsbury

100 Maple Ave • Shrewsbury, MA 01545-5398
(508) 841-8400
Grade Span: PK-12; **Agency Type:** 1
Schools: 8
6 Primary; 1 Middle; 1 High; 0 Other Level
8 Regular; 0 Special Education; 0 Vocational; 0 Alternative
0 Magnet; 0 Charter; 4 Title I Eligible; 0 School-wide Title I
Students: 5,315 (48.8% male; 51.2% female)
Individual Education Program: 731 (13.8%);
English Language Learner: 65 (1.2%); Migrant: 0 (0.0%)
Eligible for Free Lunch Program: n/a
Eligible for Reduced-Price Lunch Program: n/a
Teachers: 352.2 (15.1 to 1)
Librarians/Media Specialists: 7.0 (759.3 to 1)
Guidance Counselors: 7.0 (759.3 to 1)
Current Spending: ($ per student per year):
Total: $7,595; Instruction: $5,138; Support Services: $2,178
Enrollment, Drop-out Rates and Diploma Recipients by Race/Ethnicity

Category	Total	White	Black	Asian	AIAN	Hisp.
Enrollment (%)	100.0	85.5	1.9	9.8	0.3	2.5
Drop-out Rate (%)	1.1	1.0	4.5	0.0	0.0	4.8
H.S. Diplomas (#)	259	225	5	23	2	4

Southborough

44 Bearfoot Rd • Northborough, MA 01532-1657
(508) 351-7000
Grade Span: PK-08; **Agency Type:** 2
Schools: 3
2 Primary; 1 Middle; 0 High; 0 Other Level
3 Regular; 0 Special Education; 0 Vocational; 0 Alternative
0 Magnet; 0 Charter; 0 Title I Eligible; 0 School-wide Title I
Students: 1,614 (51.5% male; 48.5% female)
Individual Education Program: 177 (11.0%);
English Language Learner: 3 (0.2%); Migrant: 0 (0.0%)
Eligible for Free Lunch Program: n/a
Eligible for Reduced-Price Lunch Program: n/a
Teachers: 109.7 (14.7 to 1)
Librarians/Media Specialists: 3.0 (538.0 to 1)
Guidance Counselors: 3.5 (461.1 to 1)
Current Spending: ($ per student per year):
Total: $7,385; Instruction: $4,925; Support Services: $2,340
Enrollment, Drop-out Rates and Diploma Recipients by Race/Ethnicity

Category	Total	White	Black	Asian	AIAN	Hisp.
Enrollment (%)	100.0	91.5	2.5	3.8	0.2	2.0
Drop-out Rate (%)	n/a	n/a	n/a	n/a	n/a	n/a
H.S. Diplomas (#)	n/a	n/a	n/a	n/a	n/a	n/a

Southbridge

41 Elm St • Southbridge, MA 01550-0665
(508) 764-5414
Grade Span: PK-12; **Agency Type:** 1
Schools: 5
3 Primary; 1 Middle; 1 High; 0 Other Level
5 Regular; 0 Special Education; 0 Vocational; 0 Alternative
0 Magnet; 0 Charter; 3 Title I Eligible; 0 School-wide Title I
Students: 2,629 (52.7% male; 47.3% female)
Individual Education Program: 479 (18.2%);
English Language Learner: 123 (4.7%); Migrant: 0 (0.0%)
Eligible for Free Lunch Program: n/a
Eligible for Reduced-Price Lunch Program: n/a
Teachers: 227.0 (11.6 to 1)
Librarians/Media Specialists: 5.0 (525.8 to 1)
Guidance Counselors: 19.0 (138.4 to 1)
Current Spending: ($ per student per year):
Total: $9,052; Instruction: $6,357; Support Services: $2,385
Enrollment, Drop-out Rates and Diploma Recipients by Race/Ethnicity

Category	Total	White	Black	Asian	AIAN	Hisp.
Enrollment (%)	100.0	61.0	2.0	1.7	0.0	35.2
Drop-out Rate (%)	4.2	4.3	0.0	6.3	n/a	4.0
H.S. Diplomas (#)	92	60	4	1	0	27

Spencer-E Brookfield

306 Main St • Spencer, MA 01562-1856
(508) 885-8500 • http://www.seb.k12.ma.us/
Grade Span: PK-12; **Agency Type:** 3
Schools: 7
3 Primary; 3 Middle; 1 High; 0 Other Level
7 Regular; 0 Special Education; 0 Vocational; 0 Alternative
0 Magnet; 0 Charter; 4 Title I Eligible; 0 School-wide Title I
Students: 2,220 (51.8% male; 48.2% female)
Individual Education Program: 442 (19.9%);
English Language Learner: 2 (0.1%); Migrant: 1 (<0.1%)
Eligible for Free Lunch Program: n/a
Eligible for Reduced-Price Lunch Program: n/a
Teachers: 158.4 (14.0 to 1)
Librarians/Media Specialists: 2.0 (1,110.0 to 1)
Guidance Counselors: 5.0 (444.0 to 1)
Current Spending: ($ per student per year):
Total: $8,641; Instruction: $5,762; Support Services: $2,586
Enrollment, Drop-out Rates and Diploma Recipients by Race/Ethnicity

Category	Total	White	Black	Asian	AIAN	Hisp.
Enrollment (%)	100.0	96.8	0.7	0.4	0.2	1.9
Drop-out Rate (%)	3.8	3.6	16.7	0.0	0.0	9.1
H.S. Diplomas (#)	128	126	1	1	0	0

Sutton

Boston Rd • Sutton, MA 01590-1804
(508) 865-9270
Grade Span: PK-12; **Agency Type:** 1
Schools: 4
2 Primary; 1 Middle; 1 High; 0 Other Level
4 Regular; 0 Special Education; 0 Vocational; 0 Alternative
0 Magnet; 0 Charter; 2 Title I Eligible; 0 School-wide Title I
Students: 1,626 (50.0% male; 50.0% female)
Individual Education Program: 197 (12.1%);
English Language Learner: 0 (0.0%); Migrant: 2 (0.1%)
Eligible for Free Lunch Program: n/a
Eligible for Reduced-Price Lunch Program: n/a
Teachers: 111.4 (14.6 to 1)
Librarians/Media Specialists: 1.0 (1,626.0 to 1)
Guidance Counselors: 8.5 (191.3 to 1)
Current Spending: ($ per student per year):
Total: $7,170; Instruction: $4,933; Support Services: $2,054
Enrollment, Drop-out Rates and Diploma Recipients by Race/Ethnicity

Category	Total	White	Black	Asian	AIAN	Hisp.
Enrollment (%)	100.0	97.8	0.7	0.7	0.1	0.7
Drop-out Rate (%)	2.1	2.1	0.0	n/a	n/a	0.0
H.S. Diplomas (#)	107	106	0	0	0	1

Tantasqua

320 Brookfield Rd • Fiskdale, MA 01518-1098
(508) 347-5977 • http://www.tantasqua.org/
Grade Span: 07-12; **Agency Type:** 3
Schools: 3
0 Primary; 1 Middle; 2 High; 0 Other Level
2 Regular; 0 Special Education; 1 Vocational; 0 Alternative

0 Magnet; 0 Charter; 2 Title I Eligible; 0 School-wide Title I
Students: 1,723 (50.7% male; 49.3% female)
Individual Education Program: 259 (15.0%);
English Language Learner: 0 (0.0%); Migrant: 2 (0.1%)
Eligible for Free Lunch Program: n/a
Eligible for Reduced-Price Lunch Program: n/a
Teachers: 128.7 (13.4 to 1)
Librarians/Media Specialists: 1.5 (1,148.7 to 1)
Guidance Counselors: 7.0 (246.1 to 1)
Current Spending: ($ per student per year):
Total: $8,717; Instruction: $6,055; Support Services: $2,477

Enrollment, Drop-out Rates and Diploma Recipients by Race/Ethnicity

Category	Total	White	Black	Asian	AIAN	Hisp.
Enrollment (%)	100.0	96.4	0.5	0.5	1.0	1.6
Drop-out Rate (%)	2.6	2.7	0.0	0.0	n/a	0.0
H.S. Diplomas (#)	212	210	0	0	1	1

Uxbridge

62 Capron St • Uxbridge, MA 01569-1530
(508) 278-8648 • http://www.uxbridge.mec.edu/
Grade Span: PK-12; **Agency Type:** 1
Schools: 4
2 Primary; 1 Middle; 1 High; 0 Other Level
4 Regular; 0 Special Education; 0 Vocational; 0 Alternative
0 Magnet; 0 Charter; 1 Title I Eligible; 0 School-wide Title I
Students: 2,357 (53.2% male; 46.8% female)
Individual Education Program: 359 (15.2%);
English Language Learner: 3 (0.1%); Migrant: 0 (0.0%)
Eligible for Free Lunch Program: n/a
Eligible for Reduced-Price Lunch Program: n/a
Teachers: 147.9 (15.9 to 1)
Librarians/Media Specialists: 1.0 (2,357.0 to 1)
Guidance Counselors: 6.0 (392.8 to 1)
Current Spending: ($ per student per year):
Total: $7,202; Instruction: $5,000; Support Services: $1,957

Enrollment, Drop-out Rates and Diploma Recipients by Race/Ethnicity

Category	Total	White	Black	Asian	AIAN	Hisp.
Enrollment (%)	100.0	96.4	0.7	0.6	0.6	1.7
Drop-out Rate (%)	3.0	3.1	n/a	0.0	n/a	0.0
H.S. Diplomas (#)	118	116	1	1	0	0

Wachusett

Jefferson School • Jefferson, MA 01522-1097
(508) 829-1670
Grade Span: PK-12; **Agency Type:** 3
Schools: 11
7 Primary; 3 Middle; 1 High; 0 Other Level
11 Regular; 0 Special Education; 0 Vocational; 0 Alternative
0 Magnet; 0 Charter; 8 Title I Eligible; 0 School-wide Title I
Students: 6,847 (51.5% male; 48.5% female)
Individual Education Program: 872 (12.7%);
English Language Learner: 7 (0.1%); Migrant: 0 (0.0%)
Eligible for Free Lunch Program: n/a
Eligible for Reduced-Price Lunch Program: n/a
Teachers: 456.5 (15.0 to 1)
Librarians/Media Specialists: 1.0 (6,847.0 to 1)
Guidance Counselors: 6.0 (1,141.2 to 1)
Current Spending: ($ per student per year):
Total: $7,522; Instruction: $5,106; Support Services: $2,199

Enrollment, Drop-out Rates and Diploma Recipients by Race/Ethnicity

Category	Total	White	Black	Asian	AIAN	Hisp.
Enrollment (%)	100.0	96.5	1.1	1.2	0.1	1.1
Drop-out Rate (%)	1.0	0.9	0.0	3.6	0.0	10.0
H.S. Diplomas (#)	363	359	1	2	1	0

Webster

Box 430 • Webster, MA 01570-0430
Mailing Address: PO Box 430 • Webster, MA 01570-0430
(508) 943-0104
Grade Span: PK-12; **Agency Type:** 1
Schools: 3
2 Primary; 0 Middle; 0 High; 1 Other Level
3 Regular; 0 Special Education; 0 Vocational; 0 Alternative
0 Magnet; 0 Charter; 2 Title I Eligible; 0 School-wide Title I
Students: 1,859 (52.5% male; 47.5% female)
Individual Education Program: 317 (17.1%);
English Language Learner: 27 (1.5%); Migrant: 0 (0.0%)
Eligible for Free Lunch Program: n/a
Eligible for Reduced-Price Lunch Program: n/a
Teachers: 136.0 (13.7 to 1)
Librarians/Media Specialists: 1.0 (1,859.0 to 1)
Guidance Counselors: 5.0 (371.8 to 1)
Current Spending: ($ per student per year):
Total: $8,857; Instruction: $6,050; Support Services: $2,494

Enrollment, Drop-out Rates and Diploma Recipients by Race/Ethnicity

Category	Total	White	Black	Asian	AIAN	Hisp.
Enrollment (%)	100.0	84.1	4.0	1.7	1.2	9.0
Drop-out Rate (%)	4.7	4.2	0.0	0.0	0.0	13.9
H.S. Diplomas (#)	99	90	3	0	0	6

Westborough

45 W Main St • Westborough, MA 01581-6152
Mailing Address: PO Box 1152 • Westborough, MA 01581-6152
(508) 836-7700 • http://www.westborough.org
Grade Span: PK-12; **Agency Type:** 1
Schools: 6
3 Primary; 2 Middle; 1 High; 0 Other Level
6 Regular; 0 Special Education; 0 Vocational; 0 Alternative
0 Magnet; 0 Charter; 3 Title I Eligible; 0 School-wide Title I
Students: 3,528 (50.1% male; 49.9% female)
Individual Education Program: 387 (11.0%);
English Language Learner: 97 (2.7%); Migrant: 0 (0.0%)
Eligible for Free Lunch Program: n/a
Eligible for Reduced-Price Lunch Program: n/a
Teachers: 267.7 (13.2 to 1)
Librarians/Media Specialists: 4.0 (882.0 to 1)
Guidance Counselors: 14.5 (243.3 to 1)
Current Spending: ($ per student per year):
Total: $9,019; Instruction: $6,219; Support Services: $2,553

Enrollment, Drop-out Rates and Diploma Recipients by Race/Ethnicity

Category	Total	White	Black	Asian	AIAN	Hisp.
Enrollment (%)	100.0	85.0	0.9	10.1	0.0	4.0
Drop-out Rate (%)	0.6	0.7	0.0	0.0	0.0	0.0
H.S. Diplomas (#)	224	195	2	23	0	4

Winchendon

175 Grove St • Winchendon, MA 01475-1198
(978) 297-0031 • http://www.winchendonk12.org
Grade Span: PK-12; **Agency Type:** 1
Schools: 3
1 Primary; 1 Middle; 1 High; 0 Other Level
3 Regular; 0 Special Education; 0 Vocational; 0 Alternative
0 Magnet; 0 Charter; 2 Title I Eligible; 0 School-wide Title I
Students: 1,896 (50.9% male; 49.1% female)
Individual Education Program: 365 (19.3%);
English Language Learner: 0 (0.0%); Migrant: 2 (0.1%)
Eligible for Free Lunch Program: n/a
Eligible for Reduced-Price Lunch Program: n/a
Teachers: 149.0 (12.7 to 1)
Librarians/Media Specialists: 3.0 (632.0 to 1)
Guidance Counselors: 6.0 (316.0 to 1)
Current Spending: ($ per student per year):
Total: $7,569; Instruction: $5,311; Support Services: $2,040

Enrollment, Drop-out Rates and Diploma Recipients by Race/Ethnicity

Category	Total	White	Black	Asian	AIAN	Hisp.
Enrollment (%)	100.0	94.6	1.5	1.3	0.0	2.6
Drop-out Rate (%)	6.0	6.3	0.0	0.0	n/a	0.0
H.S. Diplomas (#)	89	83	0	2	0	4

Worcester

20 Irving St • Worcester, MA 01609-2432
(508) 799-3116 • http://www.wpsweb.com/default2.asp
Grade Span: PK-12; **Agency Type:** 1
Schools: 50
39 Primary; 4 Middle; 6 High; 1 Other Level
49 Regular; 0 Special Education; 1 Vocational; 0 Alternative
3 Magnet; 0 Charter; 36 Title I Eligible; 36 School-wide Title I
Students: 25,680 (51.3% male; 48.7% female)
Individual Education Program: 4,432 (17.3%);
English Language Learner: 3,373 (13.1%); Migrant: 0 (0.0%)
Eligible for Free Lunch Program: n/a
Eligible for Reduced-Price Lunch Program: n/a
Teachers: 2,117.5 (12.1 to 1)
Librarians/Media Specialists: 16.0 (1,605.0 to 1)
Guidance Counselors: 63.0 (407.6 to 1)
Current Spending: ($ per student per year):
Total: $10,234; Instruction: $7,398; Support Services: $2,506

Enrollment, Drop-out Rates and Diploma Recipients by Race/Ethnicity

Category	Total	White	Black	Asian	AIAN	Hisp.
Enrollment (%)	100.0	49.7	11.8	8.1	0.6	29.8
Drop-out Rate (%)	6.3	5.4	5.5	3.8	16.7	9.1
H.S. Diplomas (#)	1,087	624	144	104	4	211

Number of Schools

Rank	Number	District Name	City
1	135	Boston	Boston
2	50	Worcester	Worcester
3	49	Springfield	Springfield
4	35	Fall River	Fall River
5	30	Lynn	Lynn
6	28	New Bedford	New Bedford
7	26	Lowell	Lowell
8	25	Brockton	Brockton
9	22	Newton	Newtonville
10	20	Haverhill	Haverhill
10	20	Lawrence	Lawrence
12	18	Quincy	Quincy
13	16	Cambridge	Cambridge
13	16	Chicopee	Chicopee
13	16	Taunton	Taunton
16	14	Framingham	Framingham
16	14	Holyoke	Holyoke
16	14	Plymouth	Plymouth
16	14	Westfield	Westfield
20	13	Medford	Medford
20	13	Pittsfield	Pittsfield
20	13	Somerville	Somerville
20	13	Weymouth	Weymouth
24	12	Barnstable	Hyannis
24	12	Waltham	Waltham
24	12	Woburn	Woburn
27	11	Attleboro	Attleboro
27	11	Braintree	Braintree
27	11	Wachusett	Jefferson
30	10	Andover	Andover
30	10	Arlington	Arlington
30	10	Fitchburg	Fitchburg
30	10	Franklin	Franklin
30	10	Peabody	Peabody
30	10	Salem	Salem
36	9	Athol-Royalston	Athol
36	9	Beverly	Beverly
36	9	Billerica	Billerica
36	9	Brookline	Brookline
36	9	Chelsea	Chelsea
36	9	Leominster	Leominster
36	9	Lexington	Lexington
36	9	North Attleborough	N Attleborough
36	9	Wellesley	Wellesley
36	9	Westford	Westford
46	8	Agawam	Feeding Hills
46	8	Bridgewater-Raynham	Raynham
46	8	Chelmsford	N Chelmsford
46	8	Dennis-Yarmouth	South Yarmouth
46	8	Everett	Everett
46	8	Gloucester	Gloucester
46	8	Hampden-Wilbraham	Wilbraham
46	8	Melrose	Melrose
46	8	Natick	Natick
46	8	North Andover	North Andover
46	8	North Middlesex	Townsend
46	8	Norwood	Norwood
46	8	Randolph	Randolph
46	8	Revere	Revere
46	8	Saugus	Saugus
46	8	Shrewsbury	Shrewsbury
46	8	Stoughton	Stoughton
46	8	Tewksbury	Tewksbury
46	8	Wakefield	Wakefield
46	8	West Springfield	W Springfield
46	8	Whitman-Hanson	Whitman
46	8	Wilmington	Wilmington
68	7	Bellingham	Bellingham
68	7	Danvers	Danvers
68	7	Dedham	Dedham
68	7	Dracut	Dracut
68	7	Dudley-Charlton Regional	Dudley
68	7	Easton	North Easton
68	7	Falmouth	East Falmouth
68	7	Greenfield	Greenfield
68	7	Marblehead	Marblehead
68	7	Marlborough	Marlborough
68	7	Marshfield	Marshfield
68	7	Milford	Milford
68	7	Nashoba	Bolton
68	7	Needham	Needham
68	7	Reading	Reading
68	7	Spencer-E Brookfield	Spencer
68	7	Walpole	Walpole
68	7	Wareham	Wareham
68	7	Westwood	Westwood
68	7	Winchester	Winchester
88	6	Abington	Abington
88	6	Auburn	Auburn
88	6	Belchertown	Belchertown
88	6	Belmont	Belmont
88	6	Berkshire Hills	Stockbridge
88	6	Burlington	Burlington
88	6	Central Berkshire	Dalton
88	6	Dartmouth	South Dartmouth
88	6	Easthampton	Easthampton
88	6	Fairhaven	Fairhaven
88	6	Gardner	Gardner
88	6	Groton-Dunstable	Groton
88	6	Hudson	Hudson
88	6	Longmeadow	Longmeadow
88	6	Ludlow	Ludlow
88	6	Malden	Malden
88	6	Methuen	Methuen
88	6	Middleborough	Middleborough
88	6	Milton	Milton
88	6	Narragansett	Baldwinville
88	6	Northampton	Northampton
88	6	Pentucket	West Newbury
88	6	Quabbin	Barre
88	6	Somerset	Somerset
88	6	Stoneham	Stoneham
88	6	Swampscott	Swampscott
88	6	Swansea	Swansea
88	6	Westborough	Westborough
116	5	Acton	Acton
116	5	Ashburnham-Westminster	Westminster
116	5	Ashland	Ashland
116	5	Blackstone-Millville	Blackstone
116	5	Bourne	Bourne
116	5	Canton	Canton
116	5	Dighton-Rehoboth	Rehoboth
116	5	East Longmeadow	East Longmeadow
116	5	Foxborough	Foxborough
116	5	Grafton	Grafton
116	5	Hamilton-Wenham	Wenham
116	5	Hanover	Hanover
116	5	Hingham	Hingham
116	5	Hopkinton	Hopkinton
116	5	Mansfield	Mansfield
116	5	Medfield	Medfield
116	5	Medway	Medway
116	5	Mohawk Trail	Shelburne Falls
116	5	Newburyport	Newburyport
116	5	North Adams	North Adams
116	5	North Reading	North Reading
116	5	Northborough	Northborough
116	5	Northbridge	Whitinsville
116	5	Norton	Norton
116	5	Rockland	Rockland
116	5	Scituate	Scituate
116	5	Seekonk	Seekonk
116	5	Sharon	Sharon
116	5	Southbridge	Southbridge
116	5	Sudbury	Sudbury
116	5	Triton	Byfield
116	5	Watertown	Watertown
116	5	Wayland	Wayland
116	5	Weston	Weston
150	4	Adams-Cheshire	Cheshire
150	4	Amesbury	Amesbury
150	4	Amherst	Amherst
150	4	Bedford	Bedford
150	4	Carver	Carver
150	4	Clinton	Clinton
150	4	Concord	Concord
150	4	Duxbury	Duxbury
150	4	Holliston	Holliston
150	4	Ipswich	Ipswich
150	4	Leicester	Leicester
150	4	Littleton	Littleton
150	4	Lynnfield	Lynnfield
150	4	Mendon-Upton	Mendon
150	4	Norwell	Norwell
150	4	Oxford	Oxford
150	4	Sandwich	Sandwich
150	4	South Hadley	South Hadley
150	4	Sutton	Sutton
150	4	Tyngsborough	Tyngsborough
150	4	Uxbridge	Uxbridge
150	4	Westport	Westport
150	4	Winthrop	Winthrop
173	3	East Bridgewater	E Bridgewater
173	3	Georgetown	Georgetown
173	3	Harwich	Harwich
173	3	Lunenburg	Lunenburg
173	3	Mashpee	Mashpee
173	3	Millbury	Millbury
173	3	Palmer	Palmer
173	3	Pembroke	Pembroke
173	3	Quaboag Regional	Warren
173	3	Southborough	Northborough
173	3	Southwick-Tolland	Southwick
173	3	Tantasqua	Fiskdale
173	3	Webster	Webster
173	3	Winchendon	Winchendon
187	2	Acton-Boxborough	Acton
187	2	Amherst-Pelham	Amherst
187	2	Freetown-Lakeville	Lakeville
187	2	King Philip	Wrentham
187	2	Masconomet	Topsfield
187	2	Nauset	Orleans
187	2	Silver Lake	Kingston
194	1	Greater Lowell Voc Tec	Tyngsborough
194	1	Greater New Bedford	New Bedford

Number of Teachers

Rank	Number	District Name	City
1	4,517	Boston	Boston
2	2,377	Springfield	Springfield
3	2,117	Worcester	Worcester
4	1,295	New Bedford	New Bedford
5	1,197	Brockton	Brockton
6	1,151	Lowell	Lowell
7	1,094	Lynn	Lynn
8	1,026	Lawrence	Lawrence
9	981	Newton	Newtonville
10	701	Fall River	Fall River
11	699	Quincy	Quincy
12	685	Holyoke	Holyoke
13	671	Framingham	Framingham
14	668	Pittsfield	Pittsfield
15	660	Cambridge	Cambridge
16	590	Chicopee	Chicopee
17	585	Haverhill	Haverhill
18	578	Plymouth	Plymouth
19	535	Westfield	Westfield
20	529	Taunton	Taunton
21	522	Lexington	Lexington
22	509	Brookline	Brookline
23	503	Somerville	Somerville
24	501	Chelsea	Chelsea
25	482	Weymouth	Weymouth
26	481	Fitchburg	Fitchburg
27	473	Salem	Salem
28	464	Waltham	Waltham
29	463	Malden	Malden
30	462	Revere	Revere
31	456	Mansfield	Mansfield
31	456	Wachusett	Jefferson
33	451	Andover	Andover
34	450	Peabody	Peabody
35	444	Barnstable	Hyannis
36	444	Methuen	Methuen
37	434	Franklin	Franklin
38	427	Medford	Medford
39	423	Everett	Everett
40	421	Leominster	Leominster
41	403	Agawam	Feeding Hills
42	388	Braintree	Braintree
43	377	Chelmsford	N Chelmsford
44	375	Marlborough	Marlborough
45	361	Woburn	Woburn
46	352	Shrewsbury	Shrewsbury
47	350	Natick	Natick
48	349	Belmont	Belmont
49	349	Beverly	Beverly
50	347	Arlington	Arlington
51	345	North Middlesex	Townsend
52	344	Dennis-Yarmouth	South Yarmouth
53	340	Westford	Westford
54	339	Bridgewater-Raynham	Raynham
55	332	Needham	Needham
56	330	Marshfield	Marshfield
57	327	Falmouth	East Falmouth
58	324	Milford	Milford
59	323	Gloucester	Gloucester
60	321	Blackstone-Millville	Blackstone
61	319	Wellesley	Wellesley
62	317	Attleboro	Attleboro
63	316	West Springfield	W Springfield
64	313	Stoughton	Stoughton
65	309	Randolph	Randolph
66	304	Billerica	Billerica
67	304	Whitman-Hanson	Whitman
68	301	North Attleborough	N Attleborough
69	295	Norwood	Norwood
70	292	North Andover	North Andover
71	288	Burlington	Burlington
72	285	Tewksbury	Tewksbury
73	284	Sandwich	Sandwich
74	280	Wakefield	Wakefield
75	280	Danvers	Danvers
75	280	Reading	Reading

77	279	Wilmington	Wilmington
78	279	Saugus	Saugus
79	271	Wareham	Wareham
80	270	Dracut	Dracut
81	267	Westborough	Westborough
82	266	Walpole	Walpole
83	263	Milton	Milton
84	260	Dartmouth	South Dartmouth
85	256	Sharon	Sharon
86	256	Winchester	Winchester
87	248	Hampden-Wilbraham	Wilbraham
88	246	Easton	North Easton
88	246	Melrose	Melrose
90	244	Dighton-Rehoboth	Rehoboth
91	243	Nashoba	Bolton
92	242	Bourne	Bourne
93	242	Pentucket	West Newbury
94	242	North Adams	North Adams
95	241	Duxbury	Duxbury
96	236	Middleborough	Middleborough
97	234	Hudson	Hudson
98	234	Holliston	Holliston
99	234	Hopkinton	Hopkinton
100	233	Triton	Byfield
101	232	Canton	Canton
102	230	Marblehead	Marblehead
102	230	Westwood	Westwood
104	229	Somerset	Somerset
105	229	Longmeadow	Longmeadow
106	227	Southbridge	Southbridge
107	226	Dudley-Charlton Regional	Dudley
108	225	Northampton	Northampton
109	225	Gardner	Gardner
110	223	Watertown	Watertown
111	219	Wayland	Wayland
112	217	Dedham	Dedham
112	217	Hingham	Hingham
114	217	Sudbury	Sudbury
115	217	Ludlow	Ludlow
116	217	Northbridge	Whitinsville
117	214	Foxborough	Foxborough
118	210	Quabbin	Barre
119	208	Amesbury	Amesbury
120	204	Silver Lake	Kingston
121	204	Norton	Norton
122	204	Scituate	Scituate
123	203	Greenfield	Greenfield
124	203	Medfield	Medfield
125	194	East Longmeadow	East Longmeadow
126	194	Ashburnham-Westminster	Westminster
127	191	Newburyport	Newburyport
128	191	Bellingham	Bellingham
129	188	Weston	Weston
130	186	Grafton	Grafton
131	186	Swampscott	Swampscott
132	186	Hanover	Hanover
133	182	Bedford	Bedford
134	182	Ashland	Ashland
135	181	Groton-Dunstable	Groton
136	179	Easthampton	Easthampton
137	177	Medway	Medway
138	176	Rockland	Rockland
139	172	Athol-Royalston	Athol
140	172	Mashpee	Mashpee
141	168	Palmer	Palmer
142	166	Stoneham	Stoneham
143	167	Hamilton-Wenham	Wenham
144	165	Winthrop	Winthrop
145	163	Swansea	Swansea
146	163	South Hadley	South Hadley
147	162	Seekonk	Seekonk
148	162	Concord	Concord
149	162	Acton-Boxborough	Acton
150	160	Carver	Carver
151	160	North Reading	North Reading
152	158	Spencer-E Brookfield	Spencer
153	156	Central Berkshire	Dalton
154	156	Fairhaven	Fairhaven
155	155	Tyngsborough	Tyngsborough
156	154	Westport	Westport
157	153	Abington	Abington
158	152	Amherst	Amherst
159	151	Clinton	Clinton
160	151	Mendon-Upton	Mendon
161	150	Auburn	Auburn
162	150	Amherst-Pelham	Amherst
163	149	Acton	Acton
164	149	Winchendon	Winchendon
165	148	Northborough	Northborough
166	147	Ipswich	Ipswich
166	147	Uxbridge	Uxbridge
168	146	Mohawk Trail	Shelburne Falls
169	144	East Bridgewater	E Bridgewater
170	144	Oxford	Oxford
171	144	Norwell	Norwell
172	141	Nauset	Orleans
173	136	Webster	Webster
174	135	Lynnfield	Lynnfield
175	134	Millbury	Millbury
176	133	Berkshire Hills	Stockbridge
177	133	Belchertown	Belchertown
178	131	Southwick-Tolland	Southwick
179	130	Masconomet	Topsfield
180	130	Adams-Cheshire	Cheshire
181	129	Leicester	Leicester
182	128	Tantasqua	Fiskdale
183	127	Freetown-Lakeville	Lakeville
183	127	King Philip	Wrentham
185	122	Georgetown	Georgetown
186	122	Harwich	Harwich
187	121	Quaboag Regional	Warren
188	120	Lunenburg	Lunenburg
189	119	Narragansett	Baldwinville
190	111	Sutton	Sutton
191	109	Littleton	Littleton
191	109	Southborough	Northborough
193	109	Greater Lowell Voc Tec	Tyngsborough
194	100	Pembroke	Pembroke
195	88	Greater New Bedford	New Bedford

Number of Students

Rank	Number	District Name	City
1	61,552	Boston	Boston
2	26,594	Springfield	Springfield
3	25,680	Worcester	Worcester
4	16,681	Brockton	Brockton
5	15,472	Lowell	Lowell
6	15,114	Lynn	Lynn
7	14,580	New Bedford	New Bedford
8	12,587	Lawrence	Lawrence
9	12,128	Fall River	Fall River
10	11,358	Newton	Newtonville
11	8,927	Plymouth	Plymouth
12	8,846	Quincy	Quincy
13	8,381	Taunton	Taunton
14	8,364	Framingham	Framingham
15	8,303	Haverhill	Haverhill
16	7,702	Chicopee	Chicopee
17	7,255	Holyoke	Holyoke
18	7,057	Methuen	Methuen
19	7,031	Weymouth	Weymouth
20	6,847	Wachusett	Jefferson
21	6,765	Cambridge	Cambridge
22	6,728	Attleboro	Attleboro
23	6,724	Westfield	Westfield
24	6,714	Pittsfield	Pittsfield
25	6,641	Peabody	Peabody
26	6,363	Billerica	Billerica
27	6,229	Barnstable	Hyannis
28	6,156	Bridgewater-Raynham	Raynham
29	6,141	Leominster	Leominster
30	6,051	Lexington	Lexington
31	6,038	Brookline	Brookline
32	5,977	Fitchburg	Fitchburg
33	5,945	Malden	Malden
34	5,936	Revere	Revere
35	5,915	Andover	Andover
36	5,777	Chelsea	Chelsea
37	5,757	Somerville	Somerville
38	5,728	Chelmsford	N Chelmsford
39	5,711	Franklin	Franklin
40	5,371	Everett	Everett
41	5,315	Shrewsbury	Shrewsbury
42	5,000	Salem	Salem
43	4,941	Braintree	Braintree
44	4,925	Westford	Westford
45	4,825	Waltham	Waltham
46	4,738	Tewksbury	Tewksbury
47	4,729	Marlborough	Marlborough
48	4,722	Medford	Medford
49	4,685	North Attleborough	N Attleborough
50	4,682	Woburn	Woburn
51	4,659	North Middlesex	Townsend
52	4,654	Marshfield	Marshfield
53	4,648	Beverly	Beverly
54	4,639	Needham	Needham
55	4,578	Falmouth	East Falmouth
56	4,555	Natick	Natick
57	4,535	Mansfield	Mansfield
58	4,521	Whitman-Hanson	Whitman
59	4,481	Arlington	Arlington
60	4,380	Agawam	Feeding Hills
61	4,329	Dudley-Charlton Regional	Dudley
62	4,325	Dennis-Yarmouth	South Yarmouth
63	4,320	North Andover	North Andover
64	4,293	Reading	Reading
65	4,259	Dracut	Dracut
66	4,250	Dartmouth	South Dartmouth
67	4,171	Sandwich	Sandwich
68	4,146	Gloucester	Gloucester
69	4,121	Stoughton	Stoughton
70	4,100	Milford	Milford
71	4,079	Wellesley	Wellesley
72	3,990	West Springfield	W Springfield
73	3,987	Randolph	Randolph
74	3,878	Hampden-Wilbraham	Wilbraham
75	3,843	Easton	North Easton
76	3,811	Wilmington	Wilmington
77	3,741	Norwood	Norwood
78	3,704	Middleborough	Middleborough
79	3,696	Danvers	Danvers
80	3,676	Walpole	Walpole
81	3,601	Belmont	Belmont
82	3,597	Milton	Milton
83	3,565	Triton	Byfield
84	3,550	Hingham	Hingham
85	3,545	Sharon	Sharon
86	3,528	Westborough	Westborough
87	3,511	Burlington	Burlington
88	3,501	Winchester	Winchester
89	3,498	Melrose	Melrose
90	3,489	Wareham	Wareham
91	3,445	Pentucket	West Newbury
91	3,445	Wakefield	Wakefield
93	3,394	Saugus	Saugus
94	3,319	Longmeadow	Longmeadow
95	3,307	Dighton-Rehoboth	Rehoboth
96	3,234	Duxbury	Duxbury
97	3,231	Norton	Norton
98	3,230	Gardner	Gardner
99	3,214	Quabbin	Barre
100	3,119	Scituate	Scituate
101	3,082	Holliston	Holliston
102	3,079	Sudbury	Sudbury
103	3,049	Nashoba	Bolton
104	3,035	Ludlow	Ludlow
105	2,983	Dedham	Dedham
106	2,978	Medfield	Medfield
107	2,969	Stoneham	Stoneham
108	2,960	Marblehead	Marblehead
109	2,957	Canton	Canton
110	2,924	Hopkinton	Hopkinton
111	2,922	Wayland	Wayland
112	2,919	Northampton	Northampton
113	2,896	Silver Lake	Kingston
114	2,891	Somerset	Somerset
115	2,850	Foxborough	Foxborough
116	2,848	Medway	Medway
117	2,834	Bellingham	Bellingham
118	2,796	Rockland	Rockland
119	2,774	Groton-Dunstable	Groton
120	2,773	Amesbury	Amesbury
121	2,769	Hudson	Hudson
122	2,724	Hanover	Hanover
123	2,697	Westwood	Westwood
124	2,670	East Longmeadow	East Longmeadow
125	2,629	Southbridge	Southbridge
126	2,611	Bourne	Bourne
127	2,604	North Reading	North Reading
128	2,553	Ashland	Ashland
129	2,547	Acton	Acton
130	2,497	Acton-Boxborough	Acton
131	2,490	Northbridge	Whitinsville
132	2,468	East Bridgewater	E Bridgewater
133	2,463	Ashburnham-Westminster	Westminster
134	2,450	Mendon-Upton	Mendon
135	2,440	Belchertown	Belchertown
136	2,422	Auburn	Auburn
136	2,422	Watertown	Watertown
138	2,375	Newburyport	Newburyport
139	2,357	Swampscott	Swampscott
139	2,357	Uxbridge	Uxbridge
141	2,353	Weston	Weston
142	2,348	Abington	Abington
143	2,343	Fairhaven	Fairhaven
144	2,316	Central Berkshire	Dalton
145	2,314	Blackstone-Millville	Blackstone
146	2,307	Seekonk	Seekonk
147	2,293	Grafton	Grafton
148	2,286	South Hadley	South Hadley
149	2,261	Oxford	Oxford
150	2,254	Hamilton-Wenham	Wenham
151	2,244	Greenfield	Greenfield
152	2,232	Swansea	Swansea
153	2,225	Tyngsborough	Tyngsborough
154	2,220	Spencer-E Brookfield	Spencer

Rank	Number	District Name	City
155	2,219	Bedford	Bedford
156	2,218	Mashpee	Mashpee
157	2,209	Athol-Royalston	Athol
158	2,138	Winthrop	Winthrop
159	2,132	Carver	Carver
160	2,117	North Adams	North Adams
161	2,114	Palmer	Palmer
162	2,068	Ipswich	Ipswich
163	2,040	Amherst-Pelham	Amherst
164	2,020	Norwell	Norwell
165	2,000	Northborough	Northborough
166	1,988	Concord	Concord
167	1,985	Lynnfield	Lynnfield
168	1,984	Clinton	Clinton
169	1,972	Westport	Westport
170	1,944	Leicester	Leicester
171	1,928	Millbury	Millbury
172	1,900	King Philip	Wrentham
173	1,896	Winchendon	Winchendon
174	1,890	Masconomet	Topsfield
175	1,887	Lunenburg	Lunenburg
176	1,870	Adams-Cheshire	Cheshire
177	1,868	Southwick-Tolland	Southwick
178	1,859	Webster	Webster
179	1,858	Greater Lowell Voc Tec	Tyngsborough
180	1,847	Nauset	Orleans
181	1,828	Freetown-Lakeville	Lakeville
181	1,828	Pembroke	Pembroke
183	1,825	Greater New Bedford	New Bedford
184	1,723	Tantasqua	Fiskdale
185	1,704	Easthampton	Easthampton
186	1,626	Sutton	Sutton
187	1,622	Georgetown	Georgetown
188	1,614	Southborough	Northborough
189	1,582	Narragansett	Baldwinville
190	1,558	Mohawk Trail	Shelburne Falls
191	1,550	Littleton	Littleton
192	1,524	Amherst	Amherst
193	1,519	Berkshire Hills	Stockbridge
194	1,513	Quaboag Regional	Warren
195	1,500	Harwich	Harwich

Male Students

Rank	Percent	District Name	City
1	55.5	Greater New Bedford	New Bedford
2	53.6	Central Berkshire	Dalton
3	53.4	Northborough	Northborough
4	53.2	Uxbridge	Uxbridge
5	53.1	North Andover	North Andover
6	53.0	Ashburnham-Westminster	Westminster
6	53.0	Athol-Royalston	Athol
6	53.0	Hudson	Hudson
9	52.7	Dracut	Dracut
9	52.7	Mansfield	Mansfield
9	52.7	Marlborough	Marlborough
9	52.7	Southbridge	Southbridge
9	52.7	Swansea	Swansea
9	52.7	West Springfield	W Springfield
15	52.6	Grafton	Grafton
15	52.6	Norton	Norton
15	52.6	Rockland	Rockland
15	52.6	Stoughton	Stoughton
19	52.5	Longmeadow	Longmeadow
19	52.5	Needham	Needham
19	52.5	Webster	Webster
19	52.5	Westfield	Westfield
23	52.4	Natick	Natick
23	52.4	Revere	Revere
23	52.4	Whitman-Hanson	Whitman
26	52.3	Newburyport	Newburyport
26	52.3	North Attleborough	N Attleborough
26	52.3	Norwell	Norwell
26	52.3	Westford	Westford
30	52.2	Groton-Dunstable	Groton
30	52.2	Lunenburg	Lunenburg
30	52.2	Weymouth	Weymouth
33	52.1	Carver	Carver
33	52.1	Dighton-Rehoboth	Rehoboth
33	52.1	Gloucester	Gloucester
33	52.1	Harwich	Harwich
33	52.1	Holyoke	Holyoke
33	52.1	Lynnfield	Lynnfield
33	52.1	Plymouth	Plymouth
40	52.0	Amherst-Pelham	Amherst
40	52.0	Berkshire Hills	Stockbridge
40	52.0	Milford	Milford
40	52.0	Nashoba	Bolton
40	52.0	Pembroke	Pembroke
40	52.0	Waltham	Waltham
46	51.9	Acton	Acton
46	51.9	Dartmouth	South Dartmouth
46	51.9	Duxbury	Duxbury
46	51.9	Easton	North Easton
46	51.9	Greater Lowell Voc Tec	Tyngsborough
46	51.9	Middleborough	Middleborough
46	51.9	Wareham	Wareham
53	51.8	Andover	Andover
53	51.8	Belmont	Belmont
53	51.8	Boston	Boston
53	51.8	Chelsea	Chelsea
53	51.8	Dennis-Yarmouth	South Yarmouth
53	51.8	Leominster	Leominster
53	51.8	Ludlow	Ludlow
53	51.8	Spencer-E Brookfield	Spencer
53	51.8	Wayland	Wayland
62	51.7	Brockton	Brockton
62	51.7	Malden	Malden
62	51.7	Methuen	Methuen
62	51.7	Springfield	Springfield
66	51.6	Attleboro	Attleboro
66	51.6	Barnstable	Hyannis
66	51.6	Clinton	Clinton
66	51.6	Lowell	Lowell
66	51.6	Lynn	Lynn
66	51.6	Sandwich	Sandwich
72	51.5	Auburn	Auburn
72	51.5	Chicopee	Chicopee
72	51.5	Haverhill	Haverhill
72	51.5	Pittsfield	Pittsfield
72	51.5	Southborough	Northborough
72	51.5	Taunton	Taunton
72	51.5	Wachusett	Jefferson
79	51.4	Amesbury	Amesbury
79	51.4	Georgetown	Georgetown
79	51.4	Greenfield	Greenfield
79	51.4	Marshfield	Marshfield
79	51.4	Medfield	Medfield
79	51.4	Mohawk Trail	Shelburne Falls
79	51.4	Randolph	Randolph
79	51.4	Westport	Westport
79	51.4	Wilmington	Wilmington
88	51.3	Billerica	Billerica
88	51.3	Burlington	Burlington
88	51.3	Medford	Medford
88	51.3	Milton	Milton
88	51.3	New Bedford	New Bedford
88	51.3	Southwick-Tolland	Southwick
88	51.3	Worcester	Worcester
95	51.2	Agawam	Feeding Hills
95	51.2	Cambridge	Cambridge
95	51.2	Hampden-Wilbraham	Wilbraham
95	51.2	Leicester	Leicester
95	51.2	Mashpee	Mashpee
95	51.2	Oxford	Oxford
95	51.2	Quincy	Quincy
95	51.2	Reading	Reading
95	51.2	Stoneham	Stoneham
104	51.1	Blackstone-Millville	Blackstone
104	51.1	Braintree	Braintree
104	51.1	Bridgewater-Raynham	Raynham
104	51.1	Chelmsford	N Chelmsford
104	51.1	Fall River	Fall River
104	51.1	Holliston	Holliston
104	51.1	Nauset	Orleans
104	51.1	Newton	Newtonville
104	51.1	Tyngsborough	Tyngsborough
104	51.1	Weston	Weston
114	51.0	Hopkinton	Hopkinton
114	51.0	Lexington	Lexington
114	51.0	Marblehead	Marblehead
114	51.0	Millbury	Millbury
114	51.0	Pentucket	West Newbury
114	51.0	South Hadley	South Hadley
120	50.9	Hingham	Hingham
120	50.9	Lawrence	Lawrence
120	50.9	Palmer	Palmer
120	50.9	Somerville	Somerville
120	50.9	Watertown	Watertown
120	50.9	Winchendon	Winchendon
126	50.8	Brookline	Brookline
126	50.8	Medway	Medway
126	50.8	Norwood	Norwood
129	50.7	Abington	Abington
129	50.7	Framingham	Framingham
129	50.7	North Reading	North Reading
129	50.7	Northampton	Northampton
129	50.7	Northbridge	Whitinsville
129	50.7	Peabody	Peabody
129	50.7	Saugus	Saugus
129	50.7	Silver Lake	Kingston
129	50.7	Tantasqua	Fiskdale
129	50.7	Triton	Byfield
129	50.7	Winchester	Winchester
140	50.6	Fairhaven	Fairhaven
140	50.6	Gardner	Gardner
140	50.6	Hanover	Hanover
140	50.6	North Middlesex	Townsend
140	50.6	Salem	Salem
145	50.5	Acton-Boxborough	Acton
145	50.5	East Bridgewater	E Bridgewater
145	50.5	Falmouth	East Falmouth
145	50.5	Franklin	Franklin
145	50.5	Mendon-Upton	Mendon
145	50.5	Quabbin	Barre
145	50.5	Swampscott	Swampscott
152	50.4	Adams-Cheshire	Cheshire
152	50.4	Beverly	Beverly
152	50.4	Melrose	Melrose
152	50.4	Narragansett	Baldwinville
152	50.4	Somerset	Somerset
152	50.4	Tewksbury	Tewksbury
152	50.4	Wakefield	Wakefield
152	50.4	Walpole	Walpole
152	50.4	Woburn	Woburn
161	50.3	Arlington	Arlington
161	50.3	Everett	Everett
161	50.3	Fitchburg	Fitchburg
161	50.3	Foxborough	Foxborough
165	50.2	Dudley-Charlton Regional	Dudley
165	50.2	Easthampton	Easthampton
165	50.2	Scituate	Scituate
165	50.2	Seekonk	Seekonk
169	50.1	Ashland	Ashland
169	50.1	East Longmeadow	East Longmeadow
169	50.1	Sudbury	Sudbury
169	50.1	Westborough	Westborough
173	50.0	Sutton	Sutton
174	49.9	Belchertown	Belchertown
174	49.9	Dedham	Dedham
176	49.8	Bedford	Bedford
176	49.8	Westwood	Westwood
178	49.7	Bourne	Bourne
178	49.7	Wellesley	Wellesley
180	49.6	Bellingham	Bellingham
180	49.6	Canton	Canton
180	49.6	Sharon	Sharon
183	49.4	Ipswich	Ipswich
184	49.3	Freetown-Lakeville	Lakeville
184	49.3	Hamilton-Wenham	Wenham
184	49.3	Winthrop	Winthrop
187	48.8	Shrewsbury	Shrewsbury
188	48.5	Amherst	Amherst
188	48.5	Danvers	Danvers
188	48.5	Masconomet	Topsfield
191	48.3	King Philip	Wrentham
191	48.3	Littleton	Littleton
191	48.3	North Adams	North Adams
194	47.6	Concord	Concord
194	47.6	Quaboag Regional	Warren

Female Students

Rank	Percent	District Name	City
1	52.4	Concord	Concord
1	52.4	Quaboag Regional	Warren
3	51.7	King Philip	Wrentham
3	51.7	Littleton	Littleton
3	51.7	North Adams	North Adams
6	51.5	Amherst	Amherst
6	51.5	Danvers	Danvers
6	51.5	Masconomet	Topsfield
9	51.2	Shrewsbury	Shrewsbury
10	50.7	Freetown-Lakeville	Lakeville
10	50.7	Hamilton-Wenham	Wenham
10	50.7	Winthrop	Winthrop
13	50.6	Ipswich	Ipswich
14	50.4	Bellingham	Bellingham
14	50.4	Canton	Canton
14	50.4	Sharon	Sharon
17	50.3	Bourne	Bourne
17	50.3	Wellesley	Wellesley
19	50.2	Bedford	Bedford
19	50.2	Westwood	Westwood
21	50.1	Belchertown	Belchertown
21	50.1	Dedham	Dedham
23	50.0	Sutton	Sutton
24	49.9	Ashland	Ashland
24	49.9	East Longmeadow	East Longmeadow
24	49.9	Sudbury	Sudbury
24	49.9	Westborough	Westborough
28	49.8	Dudley-Charlton Regional	Dudley
28	49.8	Easthampton	Easthampton
28	49.8	Scituate	Scituate
28	49.8	Seekonk	Seekonk
32	49.7	Arlington	Arlington

32	49.7	Everett	Everett
32	49.7	Fitchburg	Fitchburg
32	49.7	Foxborough	Foxborough
36	49.6	Adams-Cheshire	Cheshire
36	49.6	Beverly	Beverly
36	49.6	Melrose	Melrose
36	49.6	Narragansett	Baldwinville
36	49.6	Somerset	Somerset
36	49.6	Tewksbury	Tewksbury
36	49.6	Wakefield	Wakefield
36	49.6	Walpole	Walpole
36	49.6	Woburn	Woburn
45	49.5	Acton-Boxborough	Acton
45	49.5	East Bridgewater	E Bridgewater
45	49.5	Falmouth	East Falmouth
45	49.5	Franklin	Franklin
45	49.5	Mendon-Upton	Mendon
45	49.5	Quabbin	Barre
45	49.5	Swampscott	Swampscott
52	49.4	Fairhaven	Fairhaven
52	49.4	Gardner	Gardner
52	49.4	Hanover	Hanover
52	49.4	North Middlesex	Townsend
52	49.4	Salem	Salem
57	49.3	Abington	Abington
57	49.3	Framingham	Framingham
57	49.3	North Reading	North Reading
57	49.3	Northampton	Northampton
57	49.3	Northbridge	Whitinsville
57	49.3	Peabody	Peabody
57	49.3	Saugus	Saugus
57	49.3	Silver Lake	Kingston
57	49.3	Tantasqua	Fiskdale
57	49.3	Triton	Byfield
57	49.3	Winchester	Winchester
68	49.2	Brookline	Brookline
68	49.2	Medway	Medway
68	49.2	Norwood	Norwood
71	49.1	Hingham	Hingham
71	49.1	Lawrence	Lawrence
71	49.1	Palmer	Palmer
71	49.1	Somerville	Somerville
71	49.1	Watertown	Watertown
71	49.1	Winchendon	Winchendon
77	49.0	Hopkinton	Hopkinton
77	49.0	Lexington	Lexington
77	49.0	Marblehead	Marblehead
77	49.0	Millbury	Millbury
77	49.0	Pentucket	West Newbury
77	49.0	South Hadley	South Hadley
83	48.9	Blackstone-Millville	Blackstone
83	48.9	Braintree	Braintree
83	48.9	Bridgewater-Raynham	Raynham
83	48.9	Chelmsford	N Chelmsford
83	48.9	Fall River	Fall River
83	48.9	Holliston	Holliston
83	48.9	Nauset	Orleans
83	48.9	Newton	Newtonville
83	48.9	Tyngsborough	Tyngsborough
83	48.9	Weston	Weston
93	48.8	Agawam	Feeding Hills
93	48.8	Cambridge	Cambridge
93	48.8	Hampden-Wilbraham	Wilbraham
93	48.8	Leicester	Leicester
93	48.8	Mashpee	Mashpee
93	48.8	Oxford	Oxford
93	48.8	Quincy	Quincy
93	48.8	Reading	Reading
93	48.8	Stoneham	Stoneham
102	48.7	Billerica	Billerica
102	48.7	Burlington	Burlington
102	48.7	Medford	Medford
102	48.7	Milton	Milton
102	48.7	New Bedford	New Bedford
102	48.7	Southwick-Tolland	Southwick
102	48.7	Worcester	Worcester
109	48.6	Amesbury	Amesbury
109	48.6	Georgetown	Georgetown
109	48.6	Greenfield	Greenfield
109	48.6	Marshfield	Marshfield
109	48.6	Medfield	Medfield
109	48.6	Mohawk Trail	Shelburne Falls
109	48.6	Randolph	Randolph
109	48.6	Westport	Westport
109	48.6	Wilmington	Wilmington
118	48.5	Auburn	Auburn
118	48.5	Chicopee	Chicopee
118	48.5	Haverhill	Haverhill
118	48.5	Pittsfield	Pittsfield
118	48.5	Southborough	Northborough
118	48.5	Taunton	Taunton
118	48.5	Wachusett	Jefferson
125	48.4	Attleboro	Attleboro
125	48.4	Barnstable	Hyannis
125	48.4	Clinton	Clinton
125	48.4	Lowell	Lowell
125	48.4	Lynn	Lynn
125	48.4	Sandwich	Sandwich
131	48.3	Brockton	Brockton
131	48.3	Malden	Malden
131	48.3	Methuen	Methuen
131	48.3	Springfield	Springfield
135	48.2	Andover	Andover
135	48.2	Belmont	Belmont
135	48.2	Boston	Boston
135	48.2	Chelsea	Chelsea
135	48.2	Dennis-Yarmouth	South Yarmouth
135	48.2	Leominster	Leominster
135	48.2	Ludlow	Ludlow
135	48.2	Spencer-E Brookfield	Spencer
135	48.2	Wayland	Wayland
144	48.1	Acton	Acton
144	48.1	Dartmouth	South Dartmouth
144	48.1	Duxbury	Duxbury
144	48.1	Easton	North Easton
144	48.1	Greater Lowell Voc Tec	Tyngsborough
144	48.1	Middleborough	Middleborough
144	48.1	Wareham	Wareham
151	48.0	Amherst-Pelham	Amherst
151	48.0	Berkshire Hills	Stockbridge
151	48.0	Milford	Milford
151	48.0	Nashoba	Bolton
151	48.0	Pembroke	Pembroke
151	48.0	Waltham	Waltham
157	47.9	Carver	Carver
157	47.9	Dighton-Rehoboth	Rehoboth
157	47.9	Gloucester	Gloucester
157	47.9	Harwich	Harwich
157	47.9	Holyoke	Holyoke
157	47.9	Lynnfield	Lynnfield
157	47.9	Plymouth	Plymouth
164	47.8	Groton-Dunstable	Groton
164	47.8	Lunenburg	Lunenburg
164	47.8	Weymouth	Weymouth
167	47.7	Newburyport	Newburyport
167	47.7	North Attleborough	N Attleborough
167	47.7	Norwell	Norwell
167	47.7	Westford	Westford
171	47.6	Natick	Natick
171	47.6	Revere	Revere
171	47.6	Whitman-Hanson	Whitman
174	47.5	Longmeadow	Longmeadow
174	47.5	Needham	Needham
174	47.5	Webster	Webster
174	47.5	Westfield	Westfield
178	47.4	Grafton	Grafton
178	47.4	Norton	Norton
178	47.4	Rockland	Rockland
178	47.4	Stoughton	Stoughton
182	47.3	Dracut	Dracut
182	47.3	Mansfield	Mansfield
182	47.3	Marlborough	Marlborough
182	47.3	Southbridge	Southbridge
182	47.3	Swansea	Swansea
182	47.3	West Springfield	W Springfield
188	47.0	Ashburnham-Westminster	Westminster
188	47.0	Athol-Royalston	Athol
188	47.0	Hudson	Hudson
191	46.9	North Andover	North Andover
192	46.8	Uxbridge	Uxbridge
193	46.7	Northborough	Northborough
194	46.4	Central Berkshire	Dalton
195	44.5	Greater New Bedford	New Bedford

Individual Education Program Students

Rank	Percent	District Name	City
1	24.9	East Longmeadow	East Longmeadow
1	24.9	Greater Lowell Voc Tec	Tyngsborough
3	22.1	Cambridge	Cambridge
4	21.3	Foxborough	Foxborough
4	21.3	Norton	Norton
6	20.5	Marlborough	Marlborough
7	20.2	Watertown	Watertown
8	19.9	Somerville	Somerville
8	19.9	Spencer-E Brookfield	Spencer
8	19.9	Springfield	Springfield
11	19.7	Weymouth	Weymouth
12	19.3	Gardner	Gardner
12	19.3	Winchendon	Winchendon
14	19.2	Boston	Boston
14	19.2	Holyoke	Holyoke
16	18.5	Palmer	Palmer
17	18.4	Mohawk Trail	Shelburne Falls
17	18.4	Quaboag Regional	Warren
17	18.4	Waltham	Waltham
20	18.2	Southbridge	Southbridge
21	18.1	Walpole	Walpole
22	18.0	Hanover	Hanover
22	18.0	New Bedford	New Bedford
22	18.0	Stoughton	Stoughton
25	17.9	Ashburnham-Westminster	Westminster
25	17.9	Dedham	Dedham
25	17.9	Northampton	Northampton
28	17.8	Agawam	Feeding Hills
28	17.8	Braintree	Braintree
28	17.8	Hudson	Hudson
31	17.7	Ludlow	Ludlow
32	17.5	Mashpee	Mashpee
33	17.4	Randolph	Randolph
34	17.3	Amherst-Pelham	Amherst
34	17.3	Ashland	Ashland
34	17.3	Salem	Salem
34	17.3	Worcester	Worcester
38	17.2	Littleton	Littleton
39	17.1	Webster	Webster
40	17.0	Concord	Concord
40	17.0	Gloucester	Gloucester
40	17.0	Lexington	Lexington
40	17.0	Natick	Natick
40	17.0	Newton	Newtonville
45	16.9	Easton	North Easton
46	16.8	Easthampton	Easthampton
46	16.8	Haverhill	Haverhill
46	16.8	North Adams	North Adams
49	16.7	Marblehead	Marblehead
50	16.6	Taunton	Taunton
50	16.6	Westfield	Westfield
52	16.5	Grafton	Grafton
52	16.5	Harwich	Harwich
52	16.5	Wakefield	Wakefield
55	16.4	Leominster	Leominster
56	16.3	Adams-Cheshire	Cheshire
56	16.3	Malden	Malden
56	16.3	Medford	Medford
56	16.3	Melrose	Melrose
60	16.2	Greenfield	Greenfield
61	16.1	Athol-Royalston	Athol
61	16.1	Wareham	Wareham
63	15.9	Framingham	Framingham
64	15.8	Bedford	Bedford
65	15.7	Norwell	Norwell
65	15.7	Norwood	Norwood
65	15.7	South Hadley	South Hadley
68	15.6	Brookline	Brookline
68	15.6	Central Berkshire	Dalton
68	15.6	Chicopee	Chicopee
71	15.5	Middleborough	Middleborough
71	15.5	Quincy	Quincy
71	15.5	Stoneham	Stoneham
74	15.4	Amesbury	Amesbury
75	15.3	King Philip	Wrentham
76	15.2	Amherst	Amherst
76	15.2	Attleboro	Attleboro
76	15.2	Barnstable	Hyannis
76	15.2	Berkshire Hills	Stockbridge
76	15.2	Hampden-Wilbraham	Wilbraham
76	15.2	Uxbridge	Uxbridge
82	15.1	Clinton	Clinton
82	15.1	Wayland	Wayland
84	15.0	Beverly	Beverly
84	15.0	Tantasqua	Fiskdale
86	14.9	Bridgewater-Raynham	Raynham
86	14.9	Lynn	Lynn
86	14.9	Narragansett	Baldwinville
86	14.9	North Attleborough	N Attleborough
86	14.9	Weston	Weston
91	14.8	Fall River	Fall River
91	14.8	Fitchburg	Fitchburg
91	14.8	West Springfield	W Springfield
94	14.6	Plymouth	Plymouth
94	14.6	Swansea	Swansea
96	14.5	Dennis-Yarmouth	South Yarmouth
96	14.5	Milton	Milton
98	14.4	Medway	Medway
98	14.4	Tewksbury	Tewksbury
98	14.4	Wellesley	Wellesley
101	14.3	Blackstone-Millville	Blackstone
101	14.3	Nauset	Orleans
101	14.3	Sandwich	Sandwich
101	14.3	Westport	Westport
105	14.2	Burlington	Burlington
105	14.2	Lawrence	Lawrence
105	14.2	Reading	Reading
108	14.1	Dartmouth	South Dartmouth
108	14.1	Leicester	Leicester
108	14.1	North Reading	North Reading

Rank	Percent	District Name	City
108	14.1	Sharon	Sharon
108	14.1	Swampscott	Swampscott
113	14.0	Belmont	Belmont
113	14.0	Franklin	Franklin
113	14.0	Millbury	Millbury
113	14.0	Southwick-Tolland	Southwick
113	14.0	Whitman-Hanson	Whitman
118	13.9	Carver	Carver
118	13.9	Everett	Everett
118	13.9	Pembroke	Pembroke
121	13.8	Abington	Abington
121	13.8	Mansfield	Mansfield
121	13.8	Marshfield	Marshfield
121	13.8	Pittsfield	Pittsfield
121	13.8	Shrewsbury	Shrewsbury
126	13.7	Arlington	Arlington
126	13.7	Fairhaven	Fairhaven
126	13.7	Masconomet	Topsfield
126	13.7	Newburyport	Newburyport
130	13.6	Hingham	Hingham
131	13.4	Peabody	Peabody
132	13.3	Hamilton-Wenham	Wenham
132	13.3	Nashoba	Bolton
132	13.3	Northbridge	Whitinsville
132	13.3	Winchester	Winchester
132	13.3	Winthrop	Winthrop
137	13.2	Acton-Boxborough	Acton
137	13.2	Andover	Andover
137	13.2	Bellingham	Bellingham
137	13.2	Chelsea	Chelsea
137	13.2	Ipswich	Ipswich
142	13.1	Scituate	Scituate
143	13.0	Northborough	Northborough
144	12.9	Falmouth	East Falmouth
144	12.9	Westwood	Westwood
146	12.8	Acton	Acton
146	12.8	Methuen	Methuen
146	12.8	Milford	Milford
149	12.7	Wachusett	Jefferson
150	12.6	Bourne	Bourne
150	12.6	Chelmsford	N Chelmsford
152	12.5	Brockton	Brockton
152	12.5	Dighton-Rehoboth	Rehoboth
152	12.5	Dudley-Charlton Regional	Dudley
152	12.5	Hopkinton	Hopkinton
152	12.5	Lowell	Lowell
152	12.5	Revere	Revere
158	12.3	Georgetown	Georgetown
158	12.3	Lunenburg	Lunenburg
160	12.2	Duxbury	Duxbury
160	12.2	Needham	Needham
160	12.2	Pentucket	West Newbury
163	12.1	Freetown-Lakeville	Lakeville
163	12.1	Holliston	Holliston
163	12.1	Silver Lake	Kingston
163	12.1	Sutton	Sutton
167	11.9	Sudbury	Sudbury
168	11.8	Belchertown	Belchertown
168	11.8	Rockland	Rockland
168	11.8	Woburn	Woburn
171	11.7	Wilmington	Wilmington
172	11.6	Quabbin	Barre
172	11.6	Tyngsborough	Tyngsborough
174	11.3	North Middlesex	Townsend
175	11.1	Medfield	Medfield
176	11.0	Southborough	Northborough
176	11.0	Westborough	Westborough
178	10.9	North Andover	North Andover
179	10.8	Canton	Canton
179	10.8	Danvers	Danvers
181	10.6	Lynnfield	Lynnfield
181	10.6	Oxford	Oxford
183	10.4	Dracut	Dracut
183	10.4	Seekonk	Seekonk
185	10.3	Greater New Bedford	New Bedford
186	10.0	Auburn	Auburn
186	10.0	East Bridgewater	E Bridgewater
188	9.7	Groton-Dunstable	Groton
189	9.6	Triton	Byfield
190	9.5	Mendon-Upton	Mendon
191	9.1	Saugus	Saugus
192	8.8	Longmeadow	Longmeadow
193	8.7	Westford	Westford
194	8.4	Somerset	Somerset
195	1.5	Billerica	Billerica

English Language Learner Students

Rank	Percent	District Name	City
1	26.7	Lawrence	Lawrence
2	24.3	Boston	Boston
3	20.0	Holyoke	Holyoke
4	18.2	Framingham	Framingham
5	18.0	Somerville	Somerville
6	16.7	Fitchburg	Fitchburg
7	15.4	Chelsea	Chelsea
8	14.5	Medford	Medford
9	14.3	Lowell	Lowell
10	13.1	Worcester	Worcester
11	12.2	Quincy	Quincy
12	11.9	Marlborough	Marlborough
13	11.8	Lynn	Lynn
14	10.9	Salem	Salem
15	10.6	Amherst	Amherst
16	10.4	Everett	Everett
17	10.3	Malden	Malden
18	10.2	Springfield	Springfield
19	9.9	Cambridge	Cambridge
20	8.7	Brookline	Brookline
21	8.3	Leominster	Leominster
22	7.2	Brockton	Brockton
22	7.2	West Springfield	W Springfield
24	6.9	Randolph	Randolph
25	6.4	Chicopee	Chicopee
25	6.4	Norwood	Norwood
25	6.4	Revere	Revere
28	5.9	Waltham	Waltham
29	5.5	Fall River	Fall River
30	5.3	Arlington	Arlington
31	5.2	Methuen	Methuen
31	5.2	Watertown	Watertown
31	5.2	Westfield	Westfield
34	4.8	Newton	Newtonville
35	4.7	Southbridge	Southbridge
36	4.3	Barnstable	Hyannis
37	4.0	Amherst-Pelham	Amherst
37	4.0	Milford	Milford
39	3.9	Dennis-Yarmouth	South Yarmouth
40	3.8	Greenfield	Greenfield
41	3.6	Clinton	Clinton
41	3.6	New Bedford	New Bedford
41	3.6	Northampton	Northampton
44	3.5	Hudson	Hudson
45	3.3	Lexington	Lexington
46	3.2	Greater New Bedford	New Bedford
46	3.2	Haverhill	Haverhill
48	3.1	Attleboro	Attleboro
48	3.1	Dedham	Dedham
48	3.1	Taunton	Taunton
51	2.7	Peabody	Peabody
51	2.7	Westborough	Westborough
53	2.2	Acton	Acton
54	2.1	Belmont	Belmont
54	2.1	Stoneham	Stoneham
56	2.0	Greater Lowell Voc Tec	Tyngsborough
56	2.0	Pittsfield	Pittsfield
58	1.8	Woburn	Woburn
59	1.7	Bedford	Bedford
59	1.7	Beverly	Beverly
59	1.7	Stoughton	Stoughton
62	1.6	Agawam	Feeding Hills
62	1.6	Weston	Weston
64	1.5	Easthampton	Easthampton
64	1.5	Melrose	Melrose
64	1.5	Webster	Webster
67	1.4	Berkshire Hills	Stockbridge
67	1.4	Weymouth	Weymouth
69	1.3	Ludlow	Ludlow
69	1.3	Natick	Natick
69	1.3	Scituate	Scituate
72	1.2	Acton-Boxborough	Acton
72	1.2	Sharon	Sharon
72	1.2	Shrewsbury	Shrewsbury
75	1.1	Dracut	Dracut
75	1.1	North Adams	North Adams
77	1.0	Braintree	Braintree
77	1.0	Concord	Concord
77	1.0	North Andover	North Andover
80	0.9	Dartmouth	South Dartmouth
80	0.9	Falmouth	East Falmouth
80	0.9	Gloucester	Gloucester
80	0.9	Wellesley	Wellesley
84	0.8	Ipswich	Ipswich
85	0.7	Needham	Needham
85	0.7	North Attleborough	N Attleborough
85	0.7	Reading	Reading
85	0.7	Westwood	Westwood
89	0.6	Wakefield	Wakefield
89	0.6	Winchester	Winchester
91	0.5	Bellingham	Bellingham
91	0.5	Chelmsford	N Chelmsford
91	0.5	Hampden-Wilbraham	Wilbraham
91	0.5	Northborough	Northborough
91	0.5	Swampscott	Swampscott
91	0.5	Wayland	Wayland
97	0.4	Abington	Abington
97	0.4	Amesbury	Amesbury
97	0.4	Andover	Andover
97	0.4	Ashland	Ashland
97	0.4	Belchertown	Belchertown
97	0.4	Danvers	Danvers
97	0.4	Longmeadow	Longmeadow
97	0.4	Mansfield	Mansfield
97	0.4	Nauset	Orleans
97	0.4	Newburyport	Newburyport
107	0.3	Harwich	Harwich
107	0.3	Marblehead	Marblehead
107	0.3	Milton	Milton
107	0.3	Northbridge	Whitinsville
107	0.3	Westford	Westford
112	0.2	Canton	Canton
112	0.2	Easton	North Easton
112	0.2	Millbury	Millbury
112	0.2	Nashoba	Bolton
112	0.2	North Reading	North Reading
112	0.2	Plymouth	Plymouth
112	0.2	Quaboag Regional	Warren
112	0.2	Southborough	Northborough
120	0.1	Adams-Cheshire	Cheshire
120	0.1	Athol-Royalston	Athol
120	0.1	Billerica	Billerica
120	0.1	Lunenburg	Lunenburg
120	0.1	Lynnfield	Lynnfield
120	0.1	Marshfield	Marshfield
120	0.1	Medfield	Medfield
120	0.1	Middleborough	Middleborough
120	0.1	Quabbin	Barre
120	0.1	Sandwich	Sandwich
120	0.1	Southwick-Tolland	Southwick
120	0.1	Spencer-E Brookfield	Spencer
120	0.1	Sudbury	Sudbury
120	0.1	Triton	Byfield
120	0.1	Tyngsborough	Tyngsborough
120	0.1	Uxbridge	Uxbridge
120	0.1	Wachusett	Jefferson
137	0.0	Bridgewater-Raynham	Raynham
137	0.0	Dighton-Rehoboth	Rehoboth
137	0.0	Fairhaven	Fairhaven
137	0.0	Franklin	Franklin
137	0.0	Grafton	Grafton
137	0.0	Oxford	Oxford
137	0.0	Walpole	Walpole
137	0.0	Whitman-Hanson	Whitman
145	0.0	Ashburnham-Westminster	Westminster
145	0.0	Auburn	Auburn
145	0.0	Blackstone-Millville	Blackstone
145	0.0	Bourne	Bourne
145	0.0	Burlington	Burlington
145	0.0	Carver	Carver
145	0.0	Central Berkshire	Dalton
145	0.0	Dudley-Charlton Regional	Dudley
145	0.0	Duxbury	Duxbury
145	0.0	East Bridgewater	E Bridgewater
145	0.0	East Longmeadow	East Longmeadow
145	0.0	Foxborough	Foxborough
145	0.0	Freetown-Lakeville	Lakeville
145	0.0	Gardner	Gardner
145	0.0	Georgetown	Georgetown
145	0.0	Groton-Dunstable	Groton
145	0.0	Hamilton-Wenham	Wenham
145	0.0	Hanover	Hanover
145	0.0	Hingham	Hingham
145	0.0	Holliston	Holliston
145	0.0	Hopkinton	Hopkinton
145	0.0	King Philip	Wrentham
145	0.0	Leicester	Leicester
145	0.0	Littleton	Littleton
145	0.0	Masconomet	Topsfield
145	0.0	Mashpee	Mashpee
145	0.0	Medway	Medway
145	0.0	Mendon-Upton	Mendon
145	0.0	Mohawk Trail	Shelburne Falls
145	0.0	Narragansett	Baldwinville
145	0.0	North Middlesex	Townsend
145	0.0	Norton	Norton
145	0.0	Norwell	Norwell
145	0.0	Palmer	Palmer
145	0.0	Pembroke	Pembroke
145	0.0	Pentucket	West Newbury
145	0.0	Rockland	Rockland
145	0.0	Saugus	Saugus
145	0.0	Seekonk	Seekonk
145	0.0	Silver Lake	Kingston
145	0.0	Somerset	Somerset
145	0.0	South Hadley	South Hadley
145	0.0	Sutton	Sutton
145	0.0	Swansea	Swansea

145	0.0	Tantasqua	Fiskdale
145	0.0	Tewksbury	Tewksbury
145	0.0	Wareham	Wareham
145	0.0	Westport	Westport
145	0.0	Wilmington	Wilmington
145	0.0	Winchendon	Winchendon
145	0.0	Winthrop	Winthrop

Migrant Students

Rank	Percent	District Name	City
1	2.2	Gloucester	Gloucester
2	1.9	Fall River	Fall River
3	1.7	Lowell	Lowell
4	1.1	Lynn	Lynn
5	1.0	New Bedford	New Bedford
5	1.0	Springfield	Springfield
7	0.9	Holyoke	Holyoke
8	0.8	Lawrence	Lawrence
8	0.8	Medford	Medford
10	0.7	Boston	Boston
10	0.7	Dedham	Dedham
12	0.6	Milford	Milford
12	0.6	Peabody	Peabody
12	0.6	Salem	Salem
15	0.5	Bedford	Bedford
15	0.5	Berkshire Hills	Stockbridge
15	0.5	Concord	Concord
18	0.3	Brockton	Brockton
18	0.3	Marblehead	Marblehead
20	0.2	Amherst	Amherst
20	0.2	Amherst-Pelham	Amherst
20	0.2	Bourne	Bourne
20	0.2	Clinton	Clinton
20	0.2	Easthampton	Easthampton
20	0.2	Fitchburg	Fitchburg
20	0.2	North Andover	North Andover
20	0.2	Somerville	Somerville
28	0.1	Andover	Andover
28	0.1	Barnstable	Hyannis
28	0.1	Bellingham	Bellingham
28	0.1	Beverly	Beverly
28	0.1	Canton	Canton
28	0.1	Chelmsford	N Chelmsford
28	0.1	Everett	Everett
28	0.1	Falmouth	East Falmouth
28	0.1	Grafton	Grafton
28	0.1	Greenfield	Greenfield
28	0.1	Leicester	Leicester
28	0.1	Leominster	Leominster
28	0.1	Marlborough	Marlborough
28	0.1	Mashpee	Mashpee
28	0.1	Millbury	Millbury
28	0.1	Mohawk Trail	Shelburne Falls
28	0.1	Narragansett	Baldwinville
28	0.1	Natick	Natick
28	0.1	Nauset	Orleans
28	0.1	North Adams	North Adams
28	0.1	Northampton	Northampton
28	0.1	Northborough	Northborough
28	0.1	Scituate	Scituate
28	0.1	Southwick-Tolland	Southwick
28	0.1	Stoughton	Stoughton
28	0.1	Sutton	Sutton
28	0.1	Tantasqua	Fiskdale
28	0.1	Taunton	Taunton
28	0.1	Triton	Byfield
28	0.1	Wareham	Wareham
28	0.1	Westport	Westport
28	0.1	Wilmington	Wilmington
28	0.1	Winchendon	Winchendon
61	0.0	Arlington	Arlington
61	0.0	Attleboro	Attleboro
61	0.0	Belmont	Belmont
61	0.0	Billerica	Billerica
61	0.0	Cambridge	Cambridge
61	0.0	Chicopee	Chicopee
61	0.0	Dennis-Yarmouth	South Yarmouth
61	0.0	Dracut	Dracut
61	0.0	Hamilton-Wenham	Wenham
61	0.0	Hampden-Wilbraham	Wilbraham
61	0.0	Haverhill	Haverhill
61	0.0	Ipswich	Ipswich
61	0.0	Longmeadow	Longmeadow
61	0.0	Ludlow	Ludlow
61	0.0	Needham	Needham
61	0.0	Oxford	Oxford
61	0.0	Reading	Reading
61	0.0	Sharon	Sharon
61	0.0	Spencer-E Brookfield	Spencer
61	0.0	Stoneham	Stoneham
61	0.0	Westfield	Westfield
61	0.0	Weymouth	Weymouth
61	0.0	Woburn	Woburn
84	0.0	Abington	Abington
84	0.0	Acton	Acton
84	0.0	Acton-Boxborough	Acton
84	0.0	Adams-Cheshire	Cheshire
84	0.0	Agawam	Feeding Hills
84	0.0	Amesbury	Amesbury
84	0.0	Ashburnham-Westminster	Westminster
84	0.0	Ashland	Ashland
84	0.0	Athol-Royalston	Athol
84	0.0	Auburn	Auburn
84	0.0	Belchertown	Belchertown
84	0.0	Blackstone-Millville	Blackstone
84	0.0	Braintree	Braintree
84	0.0	Bridgewater-Raynham	Raynham
84	0.0	Brookline	Brookline
84	0.0	Burlington	Burlington
84	0.0	Carver	Carver
84	0.0	Central Berkshire	Dalton
84	0.0	Chelsea	Chelsea
84	0.0	Danvers	Danvers
84	0.0	Dartmouth	South Dartmouth
84	0.0	Dighton-Rehoboth	Rehoboth
84	0.0	Dudley-Charlton Regional	Dudley
84	0.0	Duxbury	Duxbury
84	0.0	East Bridgewater	E Bridgewater
84	0.0	East Longmeadow	East Longmeadow
84	0.0	Easton	North Easton
84	0.0	Fairhaven	Fairhaven
84	0.0	Foxborough	Foxborough
84	0.0	Framingham	Framingham
84	0.0	Franklin	Franklin
84	0.0	Freetown-Lakeville	Lakeville
84	0.0	Gardner	Gardner
84	0.0	Georgetown	Georgetown
84	0.0	Greater Lowell Voc Tec	Tyngsborough
84	0.0	Greater New Bedford	New Bedford
84	0.0	Groton-Dunstable	Groton
84	0.0	Hanover	Hanover
84	0.0	Harwich	Harwich
84	0.0	Hingham	Hingham
84	0.0	Holliston	Holliston
84	0.0	Hopkinton	Hopkinton
84	0.0	Hudson	Hudson
84	0.0	King Philip	Wrentham
84	0.0	Lexington	Lexington
84	0.0	Littleton	Littleton
84	0.0	Lunenburg	Lunenburg
84	0.0	Lynnfield	Lynnfield
84	0.0	Malden	Malden
84	0.0	Mansfield	Mansfield
84	0.0	Marshfield	Marshfield
84	0.0	Masconomet	Topsfield
84	0.0	Medfield	Medfield
84	0.0	Medway	Medway
84	0.0	Melrose	Melrose
84	0.0	Mendon-Upton	Mendon
84	0.0	Methuen	Methuen
84	0.0	Middleborough	Middleborough
84	0.0	Milton	Milton
84	0.0	Nashoba	Bolton
84	0.0	Newburyport	Newburyport
84	0.0	Newton	Newtonville
84	0.0	North Attleborough	N Attleborough
84	0.0	North Middlesex	Townsend
84	0.0	North Reading	North Reading
84	0.0	Northbridge	Whitinsville
84	0.0	Norton	Norton
84	0.0	Norwell	Norwell
84	0.0	Norwood	Norwood
84	0.0	Palmer	Palmer
84	0.0	Pembroke	Pembroke
84	0.0	Pentucket	West Newbury
84	0.0	Pittsfield	Pittsfield
84	0.0	Plymouth	Plymouth
84	0.0	Quabbin	Barre
84	0.0	Quaboag Regional	Warren
84	0.0	Quincy	Quincy
84	0.0	Randolph	Randolph
84	0.0	Revere	Revere
84	0.0	Rockland	Rockland
84	0.0	Sandwich	Sandwich
84	0.0	Saugus	Saugus
84	0.0	Seekonk	Seekonk
84	0.0	Shrewsbury	Shrewsbury
84	0.0	Silver Lake	Kingston
84	0.0	Somerset	Somerset
84	0.0	South Hadley	South Hadley
84	0.0	Southborough	Northborough
84	0.0	Southbridge	Southbridge
84	0.0	Sudbury	Sudbury
84	0.0	Swampscott	Swampscott
84	0.0	Swansea	Swansea
84	0.0	Tewksbury	Tewksbury
84	0.0	Tyngsborough	Tyngsborough
84	0.0	Uxbridge	Uxbridge
84	0.0	Wachusett	Jefferson
84	0.0	Wakefield	Wakefield
84	0.0	Walpole	Walpole
84	0.0	Waltham	Waltham
84	0.0	Watertown	Watertown
84	0.0	Wayland	Wayland
84	0.0	Webster	Webster
84	0.0	Wellesley	Wellesley
84	0.0	West Springfield	W Springfield
84	0.0	Westborough	Westborough
84	0.0	Westford	Westford
84	0.0	Weston	Weston
84	0.0	Westwood	Westwood
84	0.0	Whitman-Hanson	Whitman
84	0.0	Winchester	Winchester
84	0.0	Winthrop	Winthrop
84	0.0	Worcester	Worcester

Students Eligible for Free Lunch

Rank	Percent	District Name	City
1	n/a	Abington	Abington
1	n/a	Acton	Acton
1	n/a	Acton-Boxborough	Acton
1	n/a	Adams-Cheshire	Cheshire
1	n/a	Agawam	Feeding Hills
1	n/a	Amesbury	Amesbury
1	n/a	Amherst	Amherst
1	n/a	Amherst-Pelham	Amherst
1	n/a	Andover	Andover
1	n/a	Arlington	Arlington
1	n/a	Ashburnham-Westminster	Westminster
1	n/a	Ashland	Ashland
1	n/a	Athol-Royalston	Athol
1	n/a	Attleboro	Attleboro
1	n/a	Auburn	Auburn
1	n/a	Barnstable	Hyannis
1	n/a	Bedford	Bedford
1	n/a	Belchertown	Belchertown
1	n/a	Bellingham	Bellingham
1	n/a	Belmont	Belmont
1	n/a	Berkshire Hills	Stockbridge
1	n/a	Beverly	Beverly
1	n/a	Billerica	Billerica
1	n/a	Blackstone-Millville	Blackstone
1	n/a	Boston	Boston
1	n/a	Bourne	Bourne
1	n/a	Braintree	Braintree
1	n/a	Bridgewater-Raynham	Raynham
1	n/a	Brockton	Brockton
1	n/a	Brookline	Brookline
1	n/a	Burlington	Burlington
1	n/a	Cambridge	Cambridge
1	n/a	Canton	Canton
1	n/a	Carver	Carver
1	n/a	Central Berkshire	Dalton
1	n/a	Chelmsford	N Chelmsford
1	n/a	Chelsea	Chelsea
1	n/a	Chicopee	Chicopee
1	n/a	Clinton	Clinton
1	n/a	Concord	Concord
1	n/a	Danvers	Danvers
1	n/a	Dartmouth	South Dartmouth
1	n/a	Dedham	Dedham
1	n/a	Dennis-Yarmouth	South Yarmouth
1	n/a	Dighton-Rehoboth	Rehoboth
1	n/a	Dracut	Dracut
1	n/a	Dudley-Charlton Regional	Dudley
1	n/a	Duxbury	Duxbury
1	n/a	East Bridgewater	E Bridgewater
1	n/a	East Longmeadow	East Longmeadow
1	n/a	Easthampton	Easthampton
1	n/a	Easton	North Easton
1	n/a	Everett	Everett
1	n/a	Fairhaven	Fairhaven
1	n/a	Fall River	Fall River
1	n/a	Falmouth	East Falmouth
1	n/a	Fitchburg	Fitchburg
1	n/a	Foxborough	Foxborough
1	n/a	Framingham	Framingham
1	n/a	Franklin	Franklin
1	n/a	Freetown-Lakeville	Lakeville
1	n/a	Gardner	Gardner
1	n/a	Georgetown	Georgetown
1	n/a	Gloucester	Gloucester
1	n/a	Grafton	Grafton
1	n/a	Greater Lowell Voc Tec	Tyngsborough
1	n/a	Greater New Bedford	New Bedford

1	n/a	Greenfield	Greenfield
1	n/a	Groton-Dunstable	Groton
1	n/a	Hamilton-Wenham	Wenham
1	n/a	Hampden-Wilbraham	Wilbraham
1	n/a	Hanover	Hanover
1	n/a	Harwich	Harwich
1	n/a	Haverhill	Haverhill
1	n/a	Hingham	Hingham
1	n/a	Holliston	Holliston
1	n/a	Holyoke	Holyoke
1	n/a	Hopkinton	Hopkinton
1	n/a	Hudson	Hudson
1	n/a	Ipswich	Ipswich
1	n/a	King Philip	Wrentham
1	n/a	Lawrence	Lawrence
1	n/a	Leicester	Leicester
1	n/a	Leominster	Leominster
1	n/a	Lexington	Lexington
1	n/a	Littleton	Littleton
1	n/a	Longmeadow	Longmeadow
1	n/a	Lowell	Lowell
1	n/a	Ludlow	Ludlow
1	n/a	Lunenburg	Lunenburg
1	n/a	Lynn	Lynn
1	n/a	Lynnfield	Lynnfield
1	n/a	Malden	Malden
1	n/a	Mansfield	Mansfield
1	n/a	Marblehead	Marblehead
1	n/a	Marlborough	Marlborough
1	n/a	Marshfield	Marshfield
1	n/a	Masconomet	Topsfield
1	n/a	Mashpee	Mashpee
1	n/a	Medfield	Medfield
1	n/a	Medford	Medford
1	n/a	Medway	Medway
1	n/a	Melrose	Melrose
1	n/a	Mendon-Upton	Mendon
1	n/a	Methuen	Methuen
1	n/a	Middleborough	Middleborough
1	n/a	Milford	Milford
1	n/a	Millbury	Millbury
1	n/a	Milton	Milton
1	n/a	Mohawk Trail	Shelburne Falls
1	n/a	Narragansett	Baldwinville
1	n/a	Nashoba	Bolton
1	n/a	Natick	Natick
1	n/a	Nauset	Orleans
1	n/a	Needham	Needham
1	n/a	New Bedford	New Bedford
1	n/a	Newburyport	Newburyport
1	n/a	Newton	Newtonville
1	n/a	North Adams	North Adams
1	n/a	North Andover	North Andover
1	n/a	North Attleborough	N Attleborough
1	n/a	North Middlesex	Townsend
1	n/a	North Reading	North Reading
1	n/a	Northampton	Northampton
1	n/a	Northborough	Northborough
1	n/a	Northbridge	Whitinsville
1	n/a	Norton	Norton
1	n/a	Norwell	Norwell
1	n/a	Norwood	Norwood
1	n/a	Oxford	Oxford
1	n/a	Palmer	Palmer
1	n/a	Peabody	Peabody
1	n/a	Pembroke	Pembroke
1	n/a	Pentucket	West Newbury
1	n/a	Pittsfield	Pittsfield
1	n/a	Plymouth	Plymouth
1	n/a	Quabbin	Barre
1	n/a	Quaboag Regional	Warren
1	n/a	Quincy	Quincy
1	n/a	Randolph	Randolph
1	n/a	Reading	Reading
1	n/a	Revere	Revere
1	n/a	Rockland	Rockland
1	n/a	Salem	Salem
1	n/a	Sandwich	Sandwich
1	n/a	Saugus	Saugus
1	n/a	Scituate	Scituate
1	n/a	Seekonk	Seekonk
1	n/a	Sharon	Sharon
1	n/a	Shrewsbury	Shrewsbury
1	n/a	Silver Lake	Kingston
1	n/a	Somerset	Somerset
1	n/a	Somerville	Somerville
1	n/a	South Hadley	South Hadley
1	n/a	Southborough	Northborough
1	n/a	Southbridge	Southbridge
1	n/a	Southwick-Tolland	Southwick
1	n/a	Spencer-E Brookfield	Spencer
1	n/a	Springfield	Springfield
1	n/a	Stoneham	Stoneham
1	n/a	Stoughton	Stoughton
1	n/a	Sudbury	Sudbury
1	n/a	Sutton	Sutton
1	n/a	Swampscott	Swampscott
1	n/a	Swansea	Swansea
1	n/a	Tantasqua	Fiskdale
1	n/a	Taunton	Taunton
1	n/a	Tewksbury	Tewksbury
1	n/a	Triton	Byfield
1	n/a	Tyngsborough	Tyngsborough
1	n/a	Uxbridge	Uxbridge
1	n/a	Wachusett	Jefferson
1	n/a	Wakefield	Wakefield
1	n/a	Walpole	Walpole
1	n/a	Waltham	Waltham
1	n/a	Wareham	Wareham
1	n/a	Watertown	Watertown
1	n/a	Wayland	Wayland
1	n/a	Webster	Webster
1	n/a	Wellesley	Wellesley
1	n/a	West Springfield	W Springfield
1	n/a	Westborough	Westborough
1	n/a	Westfield	Westfield
1	n/a	Westford	Westford
1	n/a	Weston	Weston
1	n/a	Westport	Westport
1	n/a	Westwood	Westwood
1	n/a	Weymouth	Weymouth
1	n/a	Whitman-Hanson	Whitman
1	n/a	Wilmington	Wilmington
1	n/a	Winchendon	Winchendon
1	n/a	Winchester	Winchester
1	n/a	Winthrop	Winthrop
1	n/a	Woburn	Woburn
1	n/a	Worcester	Worcester

Students Eligible for Reduced-Price Lunch

Rank	Percent	District Name	City
1	n/a	Abington	Abington
1	n/a	Acton	Acton
1	n/a	Acton-Boxborough	Acton
1	n/a	Adams-Cheshire	Cheshire
1	n/a	Agawam	Feeding Hills
1	n/a	Amesbury	Amesbury
1	n/a	Amherst	Amherst
1	n/a	Amherst-Pelham	Amherst
1	n/a	Andover	Andover
1	n/a	Arlington	Arlington
1	n/a	Ashburnham-Westminster	Westminster
1	n/a	Ashland	Ashland
1	n/a	Athol-Royalston	Athol
1	n/a	Attleboro	Attleboro
1	n/a	Auburn	Auburn
1	n/a	Barnstable	Hyannis
1	n/a	Bedford	Bedford
1	n/a	Belchertown	Belchertown
1	n/a	Bellingham	Bellingham
1	n/a	Belmont	Belmont
1	n/a	Berkshire Hills	Stockbridge
1	n/a	Beverly	Beverly
1	n/a	Billerica	Billerica
1	n/a	Blackstone-Millville	Blackstone
1	n/a	Boston	Boston
1	n/a	Bourne	Bourne
1	n/a	Braintree	Braintree
1	n/a	Bridgewater-Raynham	Raynham
1	n/a	Brockton	Brockton
1	n/a	Brookline	Brookline
1	n/a	Burlington	Burlington
1	n/a	Cambridge	Cambridge
1	n/a	Canton	Canton
1	n/a	Carver	Carver
1	n/a	Central Berkshire	Dalton
1	n/a	Chelmsford	N Chelmsford
1	n/a	Chelsea	Chelsea
1	n/a	Chicopee	Chicopee
1	n/a	Clinton	Clinton
1	n/a	Concord	Concord
1	n/a	Danvers	Danvers
1	n/a	Dartmouth	South Dartmouth
1	n/a	Dedham	Dedham
1	n/a	Dennis-Yarmouth	South Yarmouth
1	n/a	Dighton-Rehoboth	Rehoboth
1	n/a	Dracut	Dracut
1	n/a	Dudley-Charlton Regional	Dudley
1	n/a	Duxbury	Duxbury
1	n/a	East Bridgewater	E Bridgewater
1	n/a	East Longmeadow	East Longmeadow
1	n/a	Easthampton	Easthampton
1	n/a	Easton	North Easton
1	n/a	Everett	Everett
1	n/a	Fairhaven	Fairhaven
1	n/a	Fall River	Fall River
1	n/a	Falmouth	East Falmouth
1	n/a	Fitchburg	Fitchburg
1	n/a	Foxborough	Foxborough
1	n/a	Framingham	Framingham
1	n/a	Franklin	Franklin
1	n/a	Freetown-Lakeville	Lakeville
1	n/a	Gardner	Gardner
1	n/a	Georgetown	Georgetown
1	n/a	Gloucester	Gloucester
1	n/a	Grafton	Grafton
1	n/a	Greater Lowell Voc Tec	Tyngsborough
1	n/a	Greater New Bedford	New Bedford
1	n/a	Greenfield	Greenfield
1	n/a	Groton-Dunstable	Groton
1	n/a	Hamilton-Wenham	Wenham
1	n/a	Hampden-Wilbraham	Wilbraham
1	n/a	Hanover	Hanover
1	n/a	Harwich	Harwich
1	n/a	Haverhill	Haverhill
1	n/a	Hingham	Hingham
1	n/a	Holliston	Holliston
1	n/a	Holyoke	Holyoke
1	n/a	Hopkinton	Hopkinton
1	n/a	Hudson	Hudson
1	n/a	Ipswich	Ipswich
1	n/a	King Philip	Wrentham
1	n/a	Lawrence	Lawrence
1	n/a	Leicester	Leicester
1	n/a	Leominster	Leominster
1	n/a	Lexington	Lexington
1	n/a	Littleton	Littleton
1	n/a	Longmeadow	Longmeadow
1	n/a	Lowell	Lowell
1	n/a	Ludlow	Ludlow
1	n/a	Lunenburg	Lunenburg
1	n/a	Lynn	Lynn
1	n/a	Lynnfield	Lynnfield
1	n/a	Malden	Malden
1	n/a	Mansfield	Mansfield
1	n/a	Marblehead	Marblehead
1	n/a	Marlborough	Marlborough
1	n/a	Marshfield	Marshfield
1	n/a	Masconomet	Topsfield
1	n/a	Mashpee	Mashpee
1	n/a	Medfield	Medfield
1	n/a	Medford	Medford
1	n/a	Medway	Medway
1	n/a	Melrose	Melrose
1	n/a	Mendon-Upton	Mendon
1	n/a	Methuen	Methuen
1	n/a	Middleborough	Middleborough
1	n/a	Milford	Milford
1	n/a	Millbury	Millbury
1	n/a	Milton	Milton
1	n/a	Mohawk Trail	Shelburne Falls
1	n/a	Narragansett	Baldwinville
1	n/a	Nashoba	Bolton
1	n/a	Natick	Natick
1	n/a	Nauset	Orleans
1	n/a	Needham	Needham
1	n/a	New Bedford	New Bedford
1	n/a	Newburyport	Newburyport
1	n/a	Newton	Newtonville
1	n/a	North Adams	North Adams
1	n/a	North Andover	North Andover
1	n/a	North Attleborough	N Attleborough
1	n/a	North Middlesex	Townsend
1	n/a	North Reading	North Reading
1	n/a	Northampton	Northampton
1	n/a	Northborough	Northborough
1	n/a	Northbridge	Whitinsville
1	n/a	Norton	Norton
1	n/a	Norwell	Norwell
1	n/a	Norwood	Norwood
1	n/a	Oxford	Oxford
1	n/a	Palmer	Palmer
1	n/a	Peabody	Peabody
1	n/a	Pembroke	Pembroke
1	n/a	Pentucket	West Newbury
1	n/a	Pittsfield	Pittsfield
1	n/a	Plymouth	Plymouth
1	n/a	Quabbin	Barre
1	n/a	Quaboag Regional	Warren
1	n/a	Quincy	Quincy
1	n/a	Randolph	Randolph
1	n/a	Reading	Reading
1	n/a	Revere	Revere
1	n/a	Rockland	Rockland
1	n/a	Salem	Salem

1	n/a	Sandwich	Sandwich
1	n/a	Saugus	Saugus
1	n/a	Scituate	Scituate
1	n/a	Seekonk	Seekonk
1	n/a	Sharon	Sharon
1	n/a	Shrewsbury	Shrewsbury
1	n/a	Silver Lake	Kingston
1	n/a	Somerset	Somerset
1	n/a	Somerville	Somerville
1	n/a	South Hadley	South Hadley
1	n/a	Southborough	Northborough
1	n/a	Southbridge	Southbridge
1	n/a	Southwick-Tolland	Southwick
1	n/a	Spencer-E Brookfield	Spencer
1	n/a	Springfield	Springfield
1	n/a	Stoneham	Stoneham
1	n/a	Stoughton	Stoughton
1	n/a	Sudbury	Sudbury
1	n/a	Sutton	Sutton
1	n/a	Swampscott	Swampscott
1	n/a	Swansea	Swansea
1	n/a	Tantasqua	Fiskdale
1	n/a	Taunton	Taunton
1	n/a	Tewksbury	Tewksbury
1	n/a	Triton	Byfield
1	n/a	Tyngsborough	Tyngsborough
1	n/a	Uxbridge	Uxbridge
1	n/a	Wachusett	Jefferson
1	n/a	Wakefield	Wakefield
1	n/a	Walpole	Walpole
1	n/a	Waltham	Waltham
1	n/a	Wareham	Wareham
1	n/a	Watertown	Watertown
1	n/a	Wayland	Wayland
1	n/a	Webster	Webster
1	n/a	Wellesley	Wellesley
1	n/a	West Springfield	W Springfield
1	n/a	Westborough	Westborough
1	n/a	Westfield	Westfield
1	n/a	Westford	Westford
1	n/a	Weston	Weston
1	n/a	Westport	Westport
1	n/a	Westwood	Westwood
1	n/a	Weymouth	Weymouth
1	n/a	Whitman-Hanson	Whitman
1	n/a	Wilmington	Wilmington
1	n/a	Winchendon	Winchendon
1	n/a	Winchester	Winchester
1	n/a	Winthrop	Winthrop
1	n/a	Woburn	Woburn
1	n/a	Worcester	Worcester

Student/Teacher Ratio

Rank	Ratio	District Name	City
1	21.2	Attleboro	Attleboro
2	20.9	Billerica	Billerica
3	20.7	Greater New Bedford	New Bedford
4	19.1	Dudley-Charlton Regional	Dudley
5	18.3	Belchertown	Belchertown
6	18.2	Pembroke	Pembroke
7	18.1	Bridgewater-Raynham	Raynham
8	17.7	Stoneham	Stoneham
9	17.3	Fall River	Fall River
10	17.1	Acton	Acton
11	17.0	East Bridgewater	E Bridgewater
11	17.0	Greater Lowell Voc Tec	Tyngsborough
13	16.6	Tewksbury	Tewksbury
14	16.3	Dartmouth	South Dartmouth
14	16.3	Hingham	Hingham
14	16.3	North Reading	North Reading
17	16.2	Mendon-Upton	Mendon
18	16.1	Auburn	Auburn
19	16.0	Medway	Medway
20	15.9	Methuen	Methuen
20	15.9	Uxbridge	Uxbridge
22	15.8	Dracut	Dracut
22	15.8	Norton	Norton
22	15.8	Rockland	Rockland
22	15.8	Taunton	Taunton
26	15.7	Lunenburg	Lunenburg
27	15.6	Easton	North Easton
27	15.6	Hampden-Wilbraham	Wilbraham
27	15.6	Middleborough	Middleborough
27	15.6	North Attleborough	N Attleborough
27	15.6	Oxford	Oxford
32	15.4	Acton-Boxborough	Acton
32	15.4	Plymouth	Plymouth
34	15.3	Abington	Abington
34	15.3	Groton-Dunstable	Groton
34	15.3	Quabbin	Barre
34	15.3	Reading	Reading
34	15.3	Scituate	Scituate
39	15.2	Chelmsford	N Chelmsford
39	15.2	Triton	Byfield
41	15.1	Shrewsbury	Shrewsbury
42	15.0	Fairhaven	Fairhaven
42	15.0	Leicester	Leicester
42	15.0	Wachusett	Jefferson
45	14.9	King Philip	Wrentham
45	14.9	Whitman-Hanson	Whitman
47	14.8	Bellingham	Bellingham
47	14.8	Central Berkshire	Dalton
47	14.8	North Andover	North Andover
50	14.7	Medfield	Medfield
50	14.7	Peabody	Peabody
50	14.7	Sandwich	Sandwich
50	14.7	Southborough	Northborough
54	14.6	Hanover	Hanover
54	14.6	Leominster	Leominster
54	14.6	Lynnfield	Lynnfield
54	14.6	Sutton	Sutton
54	14.6	Weymouth	Weymouth
59	14.5	Westford	Westford
60	14.4	Longmeadow	Longmeadow
60	14.4	Masconomet	Topsfield
60	14.4	Millbury	Millbury
63	14.3	Adams-Cheshire	Cheshire
63	14.3	Freetown-Lakeville	Lakeville
63	14.3	Gardner	Gardner
63	14.3	Tyngsborough	Tyngsborough
67	14.2	Haverhill	Haverhill
67	14.2	Melrose	Melrose
67	14.2	Pentucket	West Newbury
67	14.2	Seekonk	Seekonk
67	14.2	Silver Lake	Kingston
67	14.2	Southwick-Tolland	Southwick
73	14.1	Littleton	Littleton
73	14.1	Marshfield	Marshfield
73	14.1	Sudbury	Sudbury
76	14.0	Ashland	Ashland
76	14.0	Barnstable	Hyannis
76	14.0	Falmouth	East Falmouth
76	14.0	Ipswich	Ipswich
76	14.0	Ludlow	Ludlow
76	14.0	Norwell	Norwell
76	14.0	South Hadley	South Hadley
76	14.0	Spencer-E Brookfield	Spencer
84	13.9	Brockton	Brockton
84	13.9	Needham	Needham
86	13.8	Lynn	Lynn
86	13.8	Sharon	Sharon
86	13.8	Walpole	Walpole
89	13.7	Dedham	Dedham
89	13.7	East Longmeadow	East Longmeadow
89	13.7	Webster	Webster
89	13.7	Winchester	Winchester
93	13.6	Amherst-Pelham	Amherst
93	13.6	Boston	Boston
93	13.6	Milton	Milton
93	13.6	Swansea	Swansea
93	13.6	Wilmington	Wilmington
98	13.5	Dighton-Rehoboth	Rehoboth
98	13.5	North Middlesex	Townsend
98	13.5	Northborough	Northborough
101	13.4	Duxbury	Duxbury
101	13.4	Hamilton-Wenham	Wenham
101	13.4	Lowell	Lowell
101	13.4	Tantasqua	Fiskdale
105	13.3	Amesbury	Amesbury
105	13.3	Beverly	Beverly
105	13.3	Carver	Carver
105	13.3	Foxborough	Foxborough
105	13.3	Narragansett	Baldwinville
105	13.3	Wayland	Wayland
111	13.2	Danvers	Danvers
111	13.2	Georgetown	Georgetown
111	13.2	Westborough	Westborough
114	13.1	Andover	Andover
114	13.1	Clinton	Clinton
114	13.1	Franklin	Franklin
114	13.1	Holliston	Holliston
114	13.1	Stoughton	Stoughton
119	13.0	Chicopee	Chicopee
119	13.0	Natick	Natick
119	13.0	Nauset	Orleans
119	13.0	Woburn	Woburn
123	12.9	Arlington	Arlington
123	12.9	Marblehead	Marblehead
123	12.9	Mashpee	Mashpee
123	12.9	Northampton	Northampton
123	12.9	Randolph	Randolph
123	12.9	Winthrop	Winthrop
129	12.8	Athol-Royalston	Athol
129	12.8	Gloucester	Gloucester
129	12.8	Malden	Malden
129	12.8	Revere	Revere
129	12.8	Wareham	Wareham
129	12.8	Wellesley	Wellesley
129	12.8	Westport	Westport
136	12.7	Ashburnham-Westminster	Westminster
136	12.7	Braintree	Braintree
136	12.7	Canton	Canton
136	12.7	Everett	Everett
136	12.7	Quincy	Quincy
136	12.7	Winchendon	Winchendon
142	12.6	Dennis-Yarmouth	South Yarmouth
142	12.6	Marlborough	Marlborough
142	12.6	Milford	Milford
142	12.6	Norwood	Norwood
142	12.6	Somerset	Somerset
142	12.6	Swampscott	Swampscott
142	12.6	West Springfield	W Springfield
149	12.5	Framingham	Framingham
149	12.5	Hopkinton	Hopkinton
149	12.5	Nashoba	Bolton
149	12.5	Palmer	Palmer
149	12.5	Quaboag Regional	Warren
149	12.5	Westfield	Westfield
149	12.5	Weston	Weston
156	12.4	Fitchburg	Fitchburg
156	12.4	Newburyport	Newburyport
158	12.3	Grafton	Grafton
158	12.3	Harwich	Harwich
158	12.3	Lawrence	Lawrence
158	12.3	Wakefield	Wakefield
162	12.2	Bedford	Bedford
162	12.2	Burlington	Burlington
162	12.2	Concord	Concord
165	12.1	Saugus	Saugus
165	12.1	Worcester	Worcester
167	11.9	Brookline	Brookline
168	11.8	Hudson	Hudson
169	11.7	Westwood	Westwood
170	11.6	Lexington	Lexington
170	11.6	Newton	Newtonville
170	11.6	Southbridge	Southbridge
173	11.5	Chelsea	Chelsea
173	11.5	Northbridge	Whitinsville
175	11.4	Berkshire Hills	Stockbridge
175	11.4	Somerville	Somerville
177	11.3	New Bedford	New Bedford
178	11.2	Springfield	Springfield
179	11.0	Greenfield	Greenfield
179	11.0	Medford	Medford
181	10.9	Agawam	Feeding Hills
181	10.9	Watertown	Watertown
183	10.7	Bourne	Bourne
184	10.6	Holyoke	Holyoke
184	10.6	Mohawk Trail	Shelburne Falls
184	10.6	Salem	Salem
187	10.4	Waltham	Waltham
188	10.3	Belmont	Belmont
189	10.2	Cambridge	Cambridge
190	10.0	Amherst	Amherst
190	10.0	Pittsfield	Pittsfield
192	9.9	Mansfield	Mansfield
193	9.5	Easthampton	Easthampton
194	8.7	North Adams	North Adams
195	7.2	Blackstone-Millville	Blackstone

Student/Librarian Ratio

Rank	Ratio	District Name	City
1	11,715.0	Fairhaven	Fairhaven
2	6,847.0	Wachusett	Jefferson
3	4,535.0	Mansfield	Mansfield
4	4,146.0	Gloucester	Gloucester
5	3,498.0	Melrose	Melrose
6	3,394.0	Saugus	Saugus
7	3,320.5	Peabody	Peabody
8	3,231.0	Norton	Norton
9	3,049.0	Nashoba	Bolton
10	2,919.0	Northampton	Northampton
11	2,848.0	Medway	Medway
12	2,834.0	Bellingham	Bellingham
13	2,796.0	Rockland	Rockland
14	2,604.0	North Reading	North Reading
15	2,564.7	Boston	Boston
16	2,547.0	Acton	Acton
17	2,450.0	Mendon-Upton	Mendon
18	2,430.0	New Bedford	New Bedford
19	2,364.5	Marlborough	Marlborough
20	2,357.0	Uxbridge	Uxbridge
21	2,327.0	Marshfield	Marshfield
22	2,314.0	Blackstone-Millville	Blackstone
23	2,286.0	South Hadley	South Hadley
24	2,242.7	Attleboro	Attleboro

Rank	Value	District Name	City
25	2,232.0	Swansea	Swansea
26	2,129.5	Dracut	Dracut
27	2,125.0	Dartmouth	South Dartmouth
28	2,117.0	North Adams	North Adams
29	2,114.0	Palmer	Palmer
30	2,091.0	Fall River	Fall River
30	2,091.0	Framingham	Framingham
32	2,076.3	Barnstable	Hyannis
33	2,075.8	Haverhill	Haverhill
34	2,050.0	Milford	Milford
35	1,993.5	Randolph	Randolph
36	1,978.7	Revere	Revere
37	1,925.5	Chicopee	Chicopee
38	1,903.7	Franklin	Franklin
39	1,900.0	King Philip	Wrentham
40	1,870.0	Adams-Cheshire	Cheshire
41	1,859.0	Webster	Webster
42	1,848.0	Danvers	Danvers
43	1,828.0	Pembroke	Pembroke
44	1,704.0	Easthampton	Easthampton
45	1,626.0	Sutton	Sutton
46	1,622.0	Georgetown	Georgetown
47	1,615.0	Gardner	Gardner
47	1,615.0	Oxford	Oxford
49	1,605.0	Worcester	Worcester
50	1,559.5	Scituate	Scituate
51	1,551.2	Hampden-Wilbraham	Wilbraham
52	1,539.0	Bridgewater-Raynham	Raynham
53	1,518.3	Natick	Natick
54	1,513.0	Quaboag Regional	Warren
55	1,478.5	Canton	Canton
56	1,432.0	Chelmsford	N Chelmsford
57	1,425.0	Foxborough	Foxborough
58	1,387.0	Groton-Dunstable	Groton
59	1,362.0	Hanover	Hanover
60	1,330.0	West Springfield	W Springfield
61	1,305.5	Bourne	Bourne
62	1,258.7	Lawrence	Lawrence
63	1,258.0	Lunenburg	Lunenburg
64	1,250.0	Salem	Salem
65	1,234.7	Middleborough	Middleborough
66	1,200.3	Belmont	Belmont
67	1,199.0	Milton	Milton
68	1,197.3	Taunton	Taunton
69	1,181.7	Sharon	Sharon
70	1,174.0	Abington	Abington
71	1,171.8	Weymouth	Weymouth
72	1,167.3	Ludlow	Ludlow
73	1,163.0	Wareham	Wareham
74	1,155.4	Chelsea	Chelsea
75	1,148.7	Tantasqua	Fiskdale
76	1,127.0	Hamilton-Wenham	Wenham
77	1,112.1	Brockton	Brockton
78	1,110.0	Spencer-E Brookfield	Spencer
79	1,104.5	Athol-Royalston	Athol
80	1,095.0	Agawam	Feeding Hills
81	1,074.2	Everett	Everett
82	1,071.3	Quabbin	Barre
83	1,070.6	Longmeadow	Longmeadow
84	1,066.0	Carver	Carver
85	1,041.1	North Attleborough	N Attleborough
86	1,038.8	Springfield	Springfield
87	1,034.0	Ipswich	Ipswich
88	1,030.3	Stoughton	Stoughton
89	1,027.3	Holliston	Holliston
90	1,026.9	East Longmeadow	East Longmeadow
91	1,023.5	Leominster	Leominster
92	1,020.0	Amherst-Pelham	Amherst
93	990.8	Malden	Malden
94	981.4	Lynn	Lynn
95	964.0	Millbury	Millbury
96	963.7	Somerset	Somerset
97	960.6	Westfield	Westfield
98	952.8	Wilmington	Wilmington
99	947.6	Tewksbury	Tewksbury
100	945.0	Masconomet	Topsfield
101	944.4	Medford	Medford
102	936.4	Woburn	Woburn
103	935.0	Greenfield	Greenfield
104	923.5	Nauset	Orleans
105	919.5	Fitchburg	Fitchburg
106	914.0	Freetown-Lakeville	Lakeville
107	909.0	Billerica	Billerica
108	882.0	Westborough	Westborough
109	865.8	Dudley-Charlton Regional	Dudley
110	864.0	North Andover	North Andover
111	861.7	Arlington	Arlington
112	857.8	Central Berkshire	Dalton
113	834.2	Sandwich	Sandwich
114	832.3	Acton-Boxborough	Acton
115	830.0	Northbridge	Whitinsville
116	826.8	Dighton-Rehoboth	Rehoboth
117	821.0	Ashburnham-Westminster	Westminster
118	820.8	Westford	Westford
119	814.4	Hudson	Hudson
120	811.5	Plymouth	Plymouth
121	808.5	Duxbury	Duxbury
122	793.6	Clinton	Clinton
123	784.3	Weston	Weston
124	783.0	Pentucket	West Newbury
125	775.0	Littleton	Littleton
126	769.0	Seekonk	Seekonk
127	767.1	Methuen	Methuen
128	759.3	Shrewsbury	Shrewsbury
129	753.5	Whitman-Hanson	Whitman
130	748.2	Norwood	Norwood
131	742.3	Stoneham	Stoneham
132	739.3	Mashpee	Mashpee
133	712.7	Winthrop	Winthrop
134	693.3	Amesbury	Amesbury
135	689.0	Wakefield	Wakefield
136	680.5	Quincy	Quincy
137	676.8	Braintree	Braintree
138	673.3	Norwell	Norwell
139	672.7	Lowell	Lowell
140	671.8	Ashland	Ashland
141	669.3	Sudbury	Sudbury
142	661.8	Medfield	Medfield
143	657.3	Westport	Westport
144	648.0	Leicester	Leicester
145	632.0	Winchendon	Winchendon
146	622.7	Southwick-Tolland	Southwick
147	622.6	Andover	Andover
148	613.3	Reading	Reading
149	605.1	Lexington	Lexington
150	592.0	Marblehead	Marblehead
151	591.7	Hingham	Hingham
152	584.8	Hopkinton	Hopkinton
153	584.4	Wayland	Wayland
154	582.4	North Middlesex	Townsend
155	581.0	Beverly	Beverly
156	575.7	Somerville	Somerville
157	572.3	Falmouth	East Falmouth
158	565.5	Walpole	Walpole
159	559.5	Pittsfield	Pittsfield
160	558.8	Wellesley	Wellesley
161	554.8	Bedford	Bedford
162	540.6	Dennis-Yarmouth	South Yarmouth
163	538.2	Watertown	Watertown
164	538.0	Southborough	Northborough
165	525.8	Southbridge	Southbridge
166	523.8	Swampscott	Swampscott
167	500.0	Harwich	Harwich
168	497.0	Concord	Concord
169	496.3	Lynnfield	Lynnfield
170	445.6	Triton	Byfield
171	426.1	Dedham	Dedham
172	400.0	Northborough	Northborough
173	392.3	Waltham	Waltham
174	381.0	Amherst	Amherst
175	374.1	Needham	Needham
176	373.6	Newton	Newtonville
177	371.7	Cambridge	Cambridge
178	339.3	Newburyport	Newburyport
179	337.1	Westwood	Westwood
180	327.6	Grafton	Grafton
181	321.2	Brookline	Brookline
182	229.1	Mohawk Trail	Shelburne Falls
183	0.0	Auburn	Auburn
183	0.0	Belchertown	Belchertown
183	0.0	Berkshire Hills	Stockbridge
183	0.0	Burlington	Burlington
183	0.0	East Bridgewater	E Bridgewater
183	0.0	Easton	North Easton
183	0.0	Greater Lowell Voc Tec	Tyngsborough
183	0.0	Greater New Bedford	New Bedford
183	0.0	Holyoke	Holyoke
183	0.0	Narragansett	Baldwinville
183	0.0	Silver Lake	Kingston
183	0.0	Tyngsborough	Tyngsborough
183	0.0	Winchester	Winchester

Student/Counselor Ratio

Rank	Ratio	District Name	City
1	1,141.2	Wachusett	Jefferson
2	1,026.0	Bridgewater-Raynham	Raynham
3	1,019.4	Attleboro	Attleboro
4	1,000.0	Northborough	Northborough
4	1,000.0	Salem	Salem
6	951.8	Franklin	Franklin
7	947.6	Tewksbury	Tewksbury
8	786.4	Dennis-Yarmouth	South Yarmouth
9	759.3	Shrewsbury	Shrewsbury
10	755.8	Mansfield	Mansfield
11	753.7	Oxford	Oxford
12	739.3	Canton	Canton
13	715.5	Reading	Reading
14	710.7	Carver	Carver
15	705.7	North Adams	North Adams
16	699.0	Rockland	Rockland
17	693.3	Amesbury	Amesbury
18	664.5	Randolph	Randolph
19	662.7	Concord	Concord
20	660.6	Malden	Malden
21	629.8	Lynn	Lynn
22	622.5	Northbridge	Whitinsville
23	618.9	Lowell	Lowell
24	617.3	Middleborough	Middleborough
25	580.1	Boston	Boston
26	578.1	Springfield	Springfield
27	574.2	Wakefield	Wakefield
28	569.6	Medway	Medway
29	566.8	Bellingham	Bellingham
30	563.5	Hamilton-Wenham	Wenham
31	563.4	Westport	Westport
32	558.0	Weymouth	Weymouth
33	556.0	Brockton	Brockton
34	554.0	Hampden-Wilbraham	Wilbraham
35	549.0	Easton	North Easton
36	538.6	Falmouth	East Falmouth
37	537.7	Andover	Andover
38	536.1	Waltham	Waltham
39	534.5	Winthrop	Winthrop
40	528.6	Wareham	Wareham
41	528.0	Danvers	Danvers
42	527.3	Fall River	Fall River
43	525.2	Chelsea	Chelsea
44	522.2	Bourne	Bourne
45	521.0	Arlington	Arlington
46	517.1	Marshfield	Marshfield
47	513.4	Medfield	Medfield
48	509.4	Acton	Acton
49	504.3	Quaboag Regional	Warren
50	502.3	Whitman-Hanson	Whitman
51	496.3	Lynnfield	Lynnfield
52	481.8	Somerset	Somerset
53	480.9	Ipswich	Ipswich
54	474.1	Longmeadow	Longmeadow
55	473.5	North Reading	North Reading
56	472.4	Dighton-Rehoboth	Rehoboth
57	470.5	Dudley-Charlton Regional	Dudley
58	469.6	Abington	Abington
59	468.6	Fairhaven	Fairhaven
60	467.6	Norwood	Norwood
61	463.4	Sandwich	Sandwich
62	463.2	Central Berkshire	Dalton
63	461.8	Braintree	Braintree
64	461.4	Seekonk	Seekonk
65	461.1	Southborough	Northborough
66	460.7	Gloucester	Gloucester
67	459.8	Ludlow	Ludlow
68	449.8	Stoneham	Stoneham
69	446.2	Sudbury	Sudbury
70	445.6	Triton	Byfield
71	444.0	Spencer-E Brookfield	Spencer
72	432.2	Winchester	Winchester
73	430.8	Norton	Norton
74	428.5	Blackstone-Millville	Blackstone
75	426.0	Easthampton	Easthampton
76	424.0	Revere	Revere
77	423.4	Wilmington	Wilmington
78	422.5	Beverly	Beverly
79	417.6	Hingham	Hingham
80	416.4	Melrose	Melrose
81	412.2	Sharon	Sharon
82	410.0	Milford	Milford
83	408.4	Walpole	Walpole
84	407.6	Worcester	Worcester
85	405.8	Swansea	Swansea
86	404.0	Leominster	Leominster
87	399.0	West Springfield	W Springfield
88	395.5	Narragansett	Baldwinville
89	393.5	Medford	Medford
90	392.8	Uxbridge	Uxbridge
91	392.2	Wellesley	Wellesley
92	389.8	Taunton	Taunton
93	386.8	Ashland	Ashland
94	385.6	Millbury	Millbury
95	382.8	Pentucket	West Newbury
96	379.8	Berkshire Hills	Stockbridge
97	377.4	Lunenburg	Lunenburg
98	377.1	Saugus	Saugus
99	374.8	North Attleborough	N Attleborough
99	374.8	South Hadley	South Hadley
101	372.9	Dedham	Dedham
102	371.8	Webster	Webster

103	369.5	Marlborough	Marlborough
104	369.2	Hudson	Hudson
105	368.2	Athol-Royalston	Athol
106	358.1	Everett	Everett
107	354.2	Dartmouth	South Dartmouth
108	353.5	Billerica	Billerica
109	352.6	East Bridgewater	E Bridgewater
110	352.3	Palmer	Palmer
111	348.4	North Andover	North Andover
112	345.1	Georgetown	Georgetown
113	344.2	Methuen	Methuen
114	343.4	Stoughton	Stoughton
115	343.3	Plymouth	Plymouth
116	334.9	Natick	Natick
117	333.3	Harwich	Harwich
118	322.1	Cambridge	Cambridge
119	321.4	Quabbin	Barre
120	319.3	Haverhill	Haverhill
121	318.2	Chelmsford	N Chelmsford
122	317.9	Tyngsborough	Tyngsborough
123	316.7	Foxborough	Foxborough
123	316.7	King Philip	Wrentham
125	316.0	Winchendon	Winchendon
126	314.6	Fitchburg	Fitchburg
127	312.1	Woburn	Woburn
128	311.9	Scituate	Scituate
129	310.6	North Middlesex	Townsend
130	307.9	Ashburnham-Westminster	Westminster
131	307.8	Nauset	Orleans
132	305.6	Westfield	Westfield
133	305.0	Belchertown	Belchertown
134	304.7	Freetown-Lakeville	Lakeville
135	304.2	Dracut	Dracut
136	304.1	Northampton	Northampton
137	303.0	Somerville	Somerville
138	302.8	Auburn	Auburn
139	296.0	Marblehead	Marblehead
140	292.7	Lawrence	Lawrence
141	290.1	Milton	Milton
142	275.1	Chicopee	Chicopee
143	273.8	Agawam	Feeding Hills
144	270.7	Hopkinton	Hopkinton
145	270.1	Burlington	Burlington
146	267.0	East Longmeadow	East Longmeadow
147	266.9	Southwick-Tolland	Southwick
148	263.9	Newburyport	Newburyport
149	258.3	Littleton	Littleton
150	254.5	Groton-Dunstable	Groton
151	254.0	Amherst	Amherst
152	249.3	Bedford	Bedford
153	248.7	Pittsfield	Pittsfield
154	248.0	Clinton	Clinton
155	247.3	Mohawk Trail	Shelburne Falls
156	246.4	Newton	Newtonville
157	246.1	Adams-Cheshire	Cheshire
157	246.1	Tantasqua	Fiskdale
159	245.9	Nashoba	Bolton
160	245.2	Westwood	Westwood
161	243.3	Westborough	Westborough
162	243.0	Leicester	Leicester
163	242.9	Needham	Needham
164	234.0	Holyoke	Holyoke
165	233.8	Wayland	Wayland
166	230.7	Barnstable	Hyannis
167	227.0	Hanover	Hanover
168	226.7	Amherst-Pelham	Amherst
169	215.8	Quincy	Quincy
170	215.3	Acton-Boxborough	Acton
171	206.9	Silver Lake	Kingston
172	202.8	Greater New Bedford	New Bedford
173	198.7	Framingham	Framingham
174	191.3	Sutton	Sutton
175	190.2	Duxbury	Duxbury
176	187.0	Greenfield	Greenfield
177	183.8	Weston	Weston
178	178.3	Masconomet	Topsfield
179	175.0	Mendon-Upton	Mendon
180	165.3	Westford	Westford
181	162.9	New Bedford	New Bedford
182	162.2	Holliston	Holliston
183	158.1	Peabody	Peabody
184	157.8	Norwell	Norwell
185	147.9	Mashpee	Mashpee
186	146.8	Gardner	Gardner
187	144.0	Belmont	Belmont
188	143.3	Grafton	Grafton
189	138.6	Swampscott	Swampscott
190	138.4	Southbridge	Southbridge
191	129.3	Lexington	Lexington
192	128.2	Brookline	Brookline
193	123.9	Greater Lowell Voc Tec	Tyngsborough
194	113.2	Watertown	Watertown
195	0.0	Pembroke	Pembroke

Current Spending per Student in FY2001

Rank	Dollars	District Name	City
1	17,286	Cambridge	Cambridge
2	13,001	Somerville	Somerville
3	12,799	Greater Lowell Voc Tec	Tyngsborough
4	12,777	Medford	Medford
5	12,717	Boston	Boston
6	12,684	Waltham	Waltham
7	12,673	Watertown	Watertown
8	12,354	Greater New Bedford	New Bedford
9	12,193	Brookline	Brookline
10	12,015	Weston	Weston
11	11,949	Berkshire Hills	Stockbridge
12	11,880	Holyoke	Holyoke
13	11,810	Newton	Newtonville
14	11,364	Bedford	Bedford
15	11,103	Wellesley	Wellesley
16	11,038	Amherst-Pelham	Amherst
17	10,999	Amherst	Amherst
18	10,934	Springfield	Springfield
19	10,789	Nauset	Orleans
20	10,702	Framingham	Framingham
21	10,622	Lowell	Lowell
22	10,570	Malden	Malden
23	10,496	Woburn	Woburn
24	10,478	Westwood	Westwood
25	10,440	Lawrence	Lawrence
26	10,342	Needham	Needham
27	10,336	Lexington	Lexington
28	10,234	Worcester	Worcester
29	10,196	Athol-Royalston	Athol
30	10,088	Salem	Salem
31	9,873	Masconomet	Topsfield
32	9,864	Pittsfield	Pittsfield
33	9,829	Northampton	Northampton
34	9,816	Fall River	Fall River
35	9,789	Newburyport	Newburyport
36	9,781	Burlington	Burlington
37	9,773	Greenfield	Greenfield
37	9,773	Mohawk Trail	Shelburne Falls
39	9,763	Nashoba	Bolton
40	9,755	Chelsea	Chelsea
41	9,751	Concord	Concord
42	9,722	Brockton	Brockton
43	9,714	Wayland	Wayland
44	9,710	Arlington	Arlington
45	9,691	Quincy	Quincy
46	9,663	Harwich	Harwich
47	9,632	Dedham	Dedham
48	9,585	North Adams	North Adams
49	9,570	Marblehead	Marblehead
50	9,521	New Bedford	New Bedford
51	9,504	Silver Lake	Kingston
52	9,426	Winchester	Winchester
53	9,369	Hudson	Hudson
54	9,283	Barnstable	Hyannis
55	9,231	Natick	Natick
56	9,187	Melrose	Melrose
57	9,142	Acton-Boxborough	Acton
58	9,136	Norwood	Norwood
59	9,120	Central Berkshire	Dalton
60	9,109	Marlborough	Marlborough
61	9,105	Lynn	Lynn
62	9,066	Chicopee	Chicopee
63	9,062	Braintree	Braintree
64	9,052	Southbridge	Southbridge
65	9,019	Westborough	Westborough
66	8,986	Andover	Andover
67	8,946	Hamilton-Wenham	Wenham
68	8,897	Fitchburg	Fitchburg
69	8,884	Dennis-Yarmouth	South Yarmouth
70	8,866	Lynnfield	Lynnfield
71	8,859	Easthampton	Easthampton
72	8,858	Foxborough	Foxborough
73	8,857	Webster	Webster
74	8,848	Swampscott	Swampscott
75	8,815	Canton	Canton
76	8,811	Ashland	Ashland
77	8,770	Westfield	Westfield
78	8,750	Beverly	Beverly
79	8,717	Tantasqua	Fiskdale
80	8,705	Somerset	Somerset
81	8,648	Clinton	Clinton
82	8,641	Spencer-E Brookfield	Spencer
83	8,638	Revere	Revere
84	8,600	Plymouth	Plymouth
85	8,583	Haverhill	Haverhill
86	8,574	King Philip	Wrentham
87	8,556	Amesbury	Amesbury
88	8,548	West Springfield	W Springfield
89	8,521	Belmont	Belmont
90	8,515	Everett	Everett
91	8,493	Stoughton	Stoughton
92	8,471	Sharon	Sharon
93	8,468	Fairhaven	Fairhaven
94	8,463	Falmouth	East Falmouth
95	8,450	Longmeadow	Longmeadow
96	8,440	Wakefield	Wakefield
97	8,437	Norwell	Norwell
98	8,369	Adams-Cheshire	Cheshire
99	8,353	Saugus	Saugus
100	8,345	Randolph	Randolph
101	8,344	Gloucester	Gloucester
102	8,324	Leominster	Leominster
103	8,322	Billerica	Billerica
103	8,322	Ipswich	Ipswich
105	8,299	Danvers	Danvers
105	8,299	Rockland	Rockland
107	8,295	Holliston	Holliston
108	8,279	Winthrop	Winthrop
109	8,274	Wareham	Wareham
110	8,269	Bourne	Bourne
111	8,241	Littleton	Littleton
112	8,206	Chelmsford	N Chelmsford
113	8,180	Stoneham	Stoneham
114	8,137	Milford	Milford
115	8,136	Hingham	Hingham
116	8,119	South Hadley	South Hadley
117	8,112	Freetown-Lakeville	Lakeville
118	8,103	Milton	Milton
119	8,101	Sudbury	Sudbury
120	8,095	Oxford	Oxford
121	8,075	Peabody	Peabody
122	8,066	Wilmington	Wilmington
123	8,063	Seekonk	Seekonk
124	8,061	Mashpee	Mashpee
125	8,039	Franklin	Franklin
126	8,032	Ashburnham-Westminster	Westminster
127	8,023	Quaboag Regional	Warren
128	7,991	Walpole	Walpole
129	7,962	Swansea	Swansea
130	7,961	Weymouth	Weymouth
131	7,954	Reading	Reading
132	7,926	Southwick-Tolland	Southwick
133	7,899	Taunton	Taunton
134	7,897	Auburn	Auburn
134	7,897	Carver	Carver
136	7,887	Duxbury	Duxbury
136	7,887	East Longmeadow	East Longmeadow
138	7,880	Ludlow	Ludlow
139	7,852	Hanover	Hanover
140	7,842	Northbridge	Whitinsville
141	7,825	Agawam	Feeding Hills
142	7,821	Hopkinton	Hopkinton
143	7,785	Palmer	Palmer
144	7,779	Hampden-Wilbraham	Wilbraham
145	7,739	Leicester	Leicester
146	7,720	Triton	Byfield
147	7,708	Belchertown	Belchertown
148	7,700	Westford	Westford
149	7,688	Tewksbury	Tewksbury
150	7,684	Narragansett	Baldwinville
151	7,654	Millbury	Millbury
152	7,647	Groton-Dunstable	Groton
153	7,617	North Andover	North Andover
154	7,614	Mansfield	Mansfield
155	7,598	Quabbin	Barre
156	7,596	Methuen	Methuen
157	7,595	Shrewsbury	Shrewsbury
158	7,584	Whitman-Hanson	Whitman
159	7,569	Winchendon	Winchendon
160	7,562	North Attleborough	N Attleborough
161	7,554	Attleboro	Attleboro
162	7,548	Marshfield	Marshfield
163	7,528	Bellingham	Bellingham
164	7,525	Georgetown	Georgetown
165	7,522	Wachusett	Jefferson
166	7,515	Tyngsborough	Tyngsborough
167	7,509	North Middlesex	Townsend
168	7,475	Lunenburg	Lunenburg
169	7,474	East Bridgewater	E Bridgewater
170	7,457	Westport	Westport
171	7,454	Middleborough	Middleborough
172	7,432	Blackstone-Millville	Blackstone
173	7,424	Grafton	Grafton
174	7,402	Medway	Medway
175	7,387	Scituate	Scituate
176	7,385	Southborough	Northborough
177	7,371	Dartmouth	South Dartmouth
178	7,341	Gardner	Gardner
179	7,307	Mendon-Upton	Mendon
180	7,263	Pembroke	Pembroke

Rank	Number	District Name	City
181	7,255	Bridgewater-Raynham	Raynham
182	7,234	Acton	Acton
183	7,205	Easton	North Easton
184	7,202	Abington	Abington
184	7,202	Uxbridge	Uxbridge
186	7,184	Dracut	Dracut
187	7,172	Dudley-Charlton Regional	Dudley
188	7,170	Sutton	Sutton
189	7,137	Dighton-Rehoboth	Rehoboth
190	6,934	Northborough	Northborough
191	6,926	Pentucket	West Newbury
192	6,914	Medfield	Medfield
193	6,887	Norton	Norton
194	6,879	North Reading	North Reading
195	6,700	Sandwich	Sandwich

Number of Diploma Recipients

Rank	Number	District Name	City
1	2,816	Boston	Boston
2	1,087	Worcester	Worcester
3	848	Newton	Newtonville
4	839	Springfield	Springfield
5	732	Lowell	Lowell
6	689	Brockton	Brockton
7	676	Lynn	Lynn
8	591	Quincy	Quincy
9	565	New Bedford	New Bedford
10	534	Plymouth	Plymouth
11	499	Fall River	Fall River
12	426	Chicopee	Chicopee
13	412	Westfield	Westfield
14	401	Chelmsford	N Chelmsford
15	396	Lexington	Lexington
16	395	Framingham	Framingham
17	393	Barnstable	Hyannis
18	390	Brookline	Brookline
19	384	Peabody	Peabody
20	383	Andover	Andover
20	383	Weymouth	Weymouth
22	377	Haverhill	Haverhill
23	363	Wachusett	Jefferson
24	354	Methuen	Methuen
25	352	Silver Lake	Kingston
26	350	Acton-Boxborough	Acton
26	350	Leominster	Leominster
28	342	Attleboro	Attleboro
29	338	Cambridge	Cambridge
30	337	Greater Lowell Voc Tec	Tyngsborough
31	335	Billerica	Billerica
32	334	Somerville	Somerville
33	331	Bridgewater-Raynham	Raynham
34	328	Waltham	Waltham
35	322	Braintree	Braintree
36	316	Pittsfield	Pittsfield
36	316	Taunton	Taunton
38	312	Westford	Westford
39	308	Malden	Malden
40	305	Franklin	Franklin
41	303	Dartmouth	South Dartmouth
41	303	Hampden-Wilbraham	Wilbraham
43	302	Needham	Needham
44	300	Fitchburg	Fitchburg
45	298	Amherst-Pelham	Amherst
46	294	Everett	Everett
47	291	Woburn	Woburn
48	290	Gloucester	Gloucester
49	288	Reading	Reading
50	285	Beverly	Beverly
51	283	Medford	Medford
52	277	Marshfield	Marshfield
53	275	Holyoke	Holyoke
54	271	Easton	North Easton
55	270	Lawrence	Lawrence
56	269	Dennis-Yarmouth	South Yarmouth
56	269	Masconomet	Topsfield
58	263	North Attleborough	N Attleborough
59	260	Arlington	Arlington
60	259	Shrewsbury	Shrewsbury
61	258	Greater New Bedford	New Bedford
61	258	Whitman-Hanson	Whitman
63	257	Natick	Natick
64	254	Sharon	Sharon
65	248	North Andover	North Andover
66	246	Dracut	Dracut
66	246	Longmeadow	Longmeadow
68	245	Agawam	Feeding Hills
69	244	Wellesley	Wellesley
70	241	North Middlesex	Townsend
71	238	Danvers	Danvers
71	238	Falmouth	East Falmouth
73	237	Sandwich	Sandwich
74	236	Duxbury	Duxbury
74	236	Revere	Revere
76	234	Norwood	Norwood
77	232	Hingham	Hingham
78	227	Milford	Milford
79	224	Westborough	Westborough
80	222	West Springfield	W Springfield
81	221	Dudley-Charlton Regional	Dudley
82	220	Milton	Milton
83	219	Stoughton	Stoughton
84	217	King Philip	Wrentham
84	217	Salem	Salem
86	216	Winchester	Winchester
87	213	Melrose	Melrose
87	213	Wakefield	Wakefield
89	212	Nauset	Orleans
89	212	Tantasqua	Fiskdale
91	211	Somerset	Somerset
92	209	Mansfield	Mansfield
93	208	Marblehead	Marblehead
94	206	Walpole	Walpole
95	205	Dighton-Rehoboth	Rehoboth
96	203	Belmont	Belmont
96	203	Stoneham	Stoneham
98	202	Burlington	Burlington
99	200	Watertown	Watertown
100	198	Triton	Byfield
101	197	Pentucket	West Newbury
102	196	Randolph	Randolph
103	195	Ludlow	Ludlow
104	193	Wilmington	Wilmington
105	191	Foxborough	Foxborough
106	190	Nashoba	Bolton
107	189	Middleborough	Middleborough
108	188	Marlborough	Marlborough
109	187	Holliston	Holliston
109	187	Wayland	Wayland
111	186	East Longmeadow	East Longmeadow
112	181	Northampton	Northampton
112	181	Tewksbury	Tewksbury
114	177	Hudson	Hudson
114	177	Rockland	Rockland
116	176	Scituate	Scituate
117	175	Saugus	Saugus
118	174	Amesbury	Amesbury
118	174	Ashburnham-Westminster	Westminster
120	172	Canton	Canton
120	172	Gardner	Gardner
122	171	Central Berkshire	Dalton
122	171	Swampscott	Swampscott
124	164	Wareham	Wareham
125	162	Hopkinton	Hopkinton
126	161	Bellingham	Bellingham
126	161	Chelsea	Chelsea
126	161	Quabbin	Barre
129	160	South Hadley	South Hadley
130	158	Hamilton-Wenham	Wenham
131	156	East Bridgewater	E Bridgewater
132	155	Medfield	Medfield
133	154	Bedford	Bedford
133	154	Medway	Medway
135	151	Auburn	Auburn
135	151	Oxford	Oxford
135	151	Westwood	Westwood
138	150	Hanover	Hanover
139	148	Berkshire Hills	Stockbridge
139	148	Freetown-Lakeville	Lakeville
139	148	Swansea	Swansea
142	144	Dedham	Dedham
143	143	Blackstone-Millville	Blackstone
144	139	Weston	Weston
145	135	Ashland	Ashland
146	134	Southwick-Tolland	Southwick
147	131	Clinton	Clinton
147	131	Norwell	Norwell
149	130	Easthampton	Easthampton
149	130	Newburyport	Newburyport
151	129	Fairhaven	Fairhaven
152	128	Lunenburg	Lunenburg
152	128	Norton	Norton
152	128	Seekonk	Seekonk
152	128	Spencer-E Brookfield	Spencer
156	127	Tyngsborough	Tyngsborough
157	126	Belchertown	Belchertown
158	124	Greenfield	Greenfield
159	119	Grafton	Grafton
160	118	Groton-Dunstable	Groton
160	118	Uxbridge	Uxbridge
162	117	Mashpee	Mashpee
163	116	Ipswich	Ipswich
164	115	Abington	Abington
165	113	Bourne	Bourne
166	112	Adams-Cheshire	Cheshire
167	111	Mendon-Upton	Mendon
168	108	Athol-Royalston	Athol
168	108	Carver	Carver
170	107	Sutton	Sutton
171	106	Leicester	Leicester
171	106	Lynnfield	Lynnfield
173	105	North Adams	North Adams
174	102	Northbridge	Whitinsville
174	102	Palmer	Palmer
176	99	Webster	Webster
177	96	Mohawk Trail	Shelburne Falls
178	94	Georgetown	Georgetown
179	92	Millbury	Millbury
179	92	Southbridge	Southbridge
181	91	Harwich	Harwich
182	90	North Reading	North Reading
182	90	Winthrop	Winthrop
184	89	Winchendon	Winchendon
185	82	Littleton	Littleton
186	81	Westport	Westport
187	79	Narragansett	Baldwinville
188	72	Quaboag Regional	Warren
189	n/a	Acton	Acton
189	n/a	Amherst	Amherst
189	n/a	Concord	Concord
189	n/a	Northborough	Northborough
189	n/a	Pembroke	Pembroke
189	n/a	Southborough	Northborough
189	n/a	Sudbury	Sudbury

High School Drop-out Rate

Rank	Percent	District Name	City
1	12.5	Lawrence	Lawrence
2	10.5	Chelsea	Chelsea
3	9.8	Lowell	Lowell
4	8.9	Pittsfield	Pittsfield
5	8.6	Holyoke	Holyoke
6	8.1	Boston	Boston
7	8.0	Springfield	Springfield
8	7.7	Attleboro	Attleboro
8	7.7	North Adams	North Adams
10	7.0	New Bedford	New Bedford
11	6.9	Fall River	Fall River
12	6.8	Revere	Revere
13	6.6	West Springfield	W Springfield
14	6.3	Worcester	Worcester
15	6.0	Winchendon	Winchendon
16	5.9	Chicopee	Chicopee
17	5.7	Brockton	Brockton
18	5.4	Central Berkshire	Dalton
19	5.3	Greenfield	Greenfield
20	5.0	Fitchburg	Fitchburg
21	4.9	Fairhaven	Fairhaven
22	4.7	Webster	Webster
23	4.6	Falmouth	East Falmouth
23	4.6	Haverhill	Haverhill
23	4.6	Westport	Westport
26	4.3	Amesbury	Amesbury
26	4.3	Somerville	Somerville
28	4.2	Adams-Cheshire	Cheshire
28	4.2	Hudson	Hudson
28	4.2	Marlborough	Marlborough
28	4.2	Narragansett	Baldwinville
28	4.2	Southbridge	Southbridge
33	4.1	Plymouth	Plymouth
34	4.0	Milford	Milford
35	3.9	Blackstone-Millville	Blackstone
35	3.9	Bourne	Bourne
35	3.9	Greater New Bedford	New Bedford
35	3.9	Lynn	Lynn
35	3.9	Quincy	Quincy
40	3.8	Leominster	Leominster
40	3.8	Malden	Malden
40	3.8	Randolph	Randolph
40	3.8	Saugus	Saugus
40	3.8	Spencer-E Brookfield	Spencer
45	3.7	Peabody	Peabody
45	3.7	Taunton	Taunton
47	3.6	Belchertown	Belchertown
47	3.6	Carver	Carver
47	3.6	Palmer	Palmer
50	3.5	Everett	Everett
50	3.5	Westfield	Westfield
50	3.5	Winthrop	Winthrop
53	3.4	Oxford	Oxford
54	3.3	Dudley-Charlton Regional	Dudley
54	3.3	Gloucester	Gloucester
54	3.3	Grafton	Grafton
54	3.3	Harwich	Harwich
54	3.3	Mohawk Trail	Shelburne Falls
54	3.3	Nauset	Orleans
54	3.3	Norton	Norton

61	3.2	Gardner	Gardner
62	3.1	Beverly	Beverly
62	3.1	Cambridge	Cambridge
62	3.1	Easthampton	Easthampton
62	3.1	Freetown-Lakeville	Lakeville
62	3.1	Ludlow	Ludlow
62	3.1	Woburn	Woburn
68	3.0	Athol-Royalston	Athol
68	3.0	Bellingham	Bellingham
68	3.0	Uxbridge	Uxbridge
68	3.0	Weymouth	Weymouth
72	2.9	Rockland	Rockland
73	2.8	Dartmouth	South Dartmouth
73	2.8	Lunenburg	Lunenburg
73	2.8	Salem	Salem
76	2.7	Millbury	Millbury
76	2.7	Newburyport	Newburyport
78	2.6	Amherst-Pelham	Amherst
78	2.6	Billerica	Billerica
78	2.6	Medford	Medford
78	2.6	Quaboag Regional	Warren
78	2.6	Somerset	Somerset
78	2.6	Stoughton	Stoughton
78	2.6	Swansea	Swansea
78	2.6	Tantasqua	Fiskdale
86	2.5	East Bridgewater	E Bridgewater
87	2.4	Auburn	Auburn
87	2.4	Middleborough	Middleborough
87	2.4	Northbridge	Whitinsville
87	2.4	Quabbin	Barre
87	2.4	Tewksbury	Tewksbury
92	2.3	Dracut	Dracut
93	2.2	Clinton	Clinton
93	2.2	Leicester	Leicester
93	2.2	Southwick-Tolland	Southwick
96	2.1	Barnstable	Hyannis
96	2.1	Northampton	Northampton
96	2.1	Pentucket	West Newbury
96	2.1	Sutton	Sutton
100	2.0	Dighton-Rehoboth	Rehoboth
100	2.0	Ipswich	Ipswich
100	2.0	Methuen	Methuen
100	2.0	North Reading	North Reading
100	2.0	Sandwich	Sandwich
100	2.0	Silver Lake	Kingston
100	2.0	Triton	Byfield
100	2.0	Waltham	Waltham
108	1.9	Dennis-Yarmouth	South Yarmouth
108	1.9	Foxborough	Foxborough
108	1.9	Framingham	Framingham
108	1.9	King Philip	Wrentham
108	1.9	Swampscott	Swampscott
113	1.8	Marshfield	Marshfield
113	1.8	North Attleborough	N Attleborough
115	1.7	Groton-Dunstable	Groton
115	1.7	Mashpee	Mashpee
115	1.7	Watertown	Watertown
118	1.6	Abington	Abington
118	1.6	Scituate	Scituate
120	1.5	Georgetown	Georgetown
120	1.5	North Middlesex	Townsend
122	1.4	Berkshire Hills	Stockbridge
122	1.4	Melrose	Melrose
122	1.4	Nashoba	Bolton
122	1.4	Natick	Natick
122	1.4	South Hadley	South Hadley
127	1.3	Franklin	Franklin
127	1.3	Hanover	Hanover
127	1.3	Norwood	Norwood
130	1.2	Chelmsford	N Chelmsford
130	1.2	Danvers	Danvers
130	1.2	East Longmeadow	East Longmeadow
130	1.2	Mendon-Upton	Mendon
134	1.1	Arlington	Arlington
134	1.1	Belmont	Belmont
134	1.1	Hampden-Wilbraham	Wilbraham
134	1.1	Shrewsbury	Shrewsbury
134	1.1	Wilmington	Wilmington
139	1.0	Braintree	Braintree
139	1.0	Marblehead	Marblehead
139	1.0	Masconomet	Topsfield
139	1.0	North Andover	North Andover
139	1.0	Reading	Reading
139	1.0	Wachusett	Jefferson
139	1.0	Wakefield	Wakefield
139	1.0	Whitman-Hanson	Whitman
147	0.9	Hingham	Hingham
147	0.9	Littleton	Littleton
147	0.9	Medway	Medway
147	0.9	Milton	Milton
147	0.9	Westford	Westford
152	0.8	Bridgewater-Raynham	Raynham
152	0.8	Canton	Canton
152	0.8	Hopkinton	Hopkinton
155	0.7	Dedham	Dedham
155	0.7	Holliston	Holliston
155	0.7	Seekonk	Seekonk
155	0.7	Stoneham	Stoneham
155	0.7	Tyngsborough	Tyngsborough
160	0.6	Bedford	Bedford
160	0.6	Lynnfield	Lynnfield
160	0.6	Walpole	Walpole
160	0.6	Westborough	Westborough
164	0.5	Hamilton-Wenham	Wenham
164	0.5	Sharon	Sharon
164	0.5	Wareham	Wareham
164	0.5	Wellesley	Wellesley
168	0.4	Ashburnham-Westminster	Westminster
168	0.4	Burlington	Burlington
168	0.4	Newton	Newtonville
168	0.4	Norwell	Norwell
168	0.4	Winchester	Winchester
173	0.3	Ashland	Ashland
173	0.3	Brookline	Brookline
173	0.3	Duxbury	Duxbury
173	0.3	Easton	North Easton
173	0.3	Lexington	Lexington
173	0.3	Longmeadow	Longmeadow
173	0.3	Mansfield	Mansfield
180	0.2	Greater Lowell Voc Tec	Tyngsborough
180	0.2	Medfield	Medfield
180	0.2	Needham	Needham
183	0.1	Andover	Andover
183	0.1	Wayland	Wayland
185	0.0	Acton-Boxborough	Acton
185	0.0	Agawam	Feeding Hills
185	0.0	Weston	Weston
185	0.0	Westwood	Westwood
189	n/a	Acton	Acton
189	n/a	Amherst	Amherst
189	n/a	Concord	Concord
189	n/a	Northborough	Northborough
189	n/a	Pembroke	Pembroke
189	n/a	Southborough	Northborough
189	n/a	Sudbury	Sudbury

Michigan

Michigan Public School Educational Profile

Category	Value	Category	Value
Schools *(2002-2003)*	4,030	**Diploma Recipients** *(2002-2003)*	95,001
Instructional Level		White, Non-Hispanic	77,947
Primary	2,196	Black, Non-Hispanic	11,619
Middle	652	Asian/Pacific Islander	2,250
High	683	American Indian/Alaskan Native	901
Other Level	499	Hispanic	2,284
Curriculum		**High School Drop-out Rate** (%) *(2000-2001)*	n/a
Regular	3,571	White, Non-Hispanic	n/a
Special Education	172	Black, Non-Hispanic	n/a
Vocational	44	Asian/Pacific Islander	n/a
Alternative	243	American Indian/Alaskan Native	n/a
Type		Hispanic	n/a
Magnet	258	**Staff** *(2002-2003)*	94,832.3
Charter	198	Teachers	89,579.5
Title I Eligible	699	Average Salary ($)	54,020
School-wide Title I	699	Librarians/Media Specialists	1,367.9
Students *(2002-2003)*	1,785,160	Guidance Counselors	2,660.7
Gender (%)		**Ratios** *(2002-2003)*	
Male	51.6	Student/Teacher Ratio	19.9 to 1
Female	48.4	Student/Librarian Ratio	1,305.0 to 1
Race/Ethnicity (%)		Student/Counselor Ratio	670.9 to 1
White, Non-Hispanic	72.3	**Current Spending** *($ per student in FY 2001)*	8,653
Black, Non-Hispanic	20.2	Instruction	4,968
Asian/Pacific Islander	2.0	Support Services	3,419
American Indian/Alaskan Native	1.5	**College Entrance Exam Scores** *(2003)*	
Hispanic	3.8	Scholastic Aptitude Test (SAT)	
Classification (%)		Participation Rate (%)	11
Individual Education Program (IEP)	13.4	Mean SAT I Verbal Score	564
Migrant	0.0	Mean SAT I Math Score	576
English Language Learner (ELL)	3.4	American College Testing Program (ACT)	
Eligible for Free Lunch Program	25.3	Participation Rate (%)	69
Eligible for Reduced-Price Lunch Program	5.9	Average Composite Score	21.3

Note: *For an explanation of data, please refer to the User's Guide in the front of the book; n/a indicates data not available*

Michigan NAEP 2003 Test Scores

Reading			Mathematics		
Grade/Category	**Value**	**Rank**	**Grade/Category**	**Value**	**Rank**
4th Grade			**4th Grade**		
Average Proficiency	218.8 (1.2)	28/51	Average Proficiency	235.7 (0.9)	27/51
Proficiency by Gender/Race/Ethnicity			Proficiency by Gender/Race/Ethnicity		
Male	215.6 (1.4)	25/51	Male	238.1 (1.1)	19/51
Female	221.9 (1.3)	32/51	Female	233.1 (1.0)	31/51
White, Non-Hispanic	228.4 (0.9)	14/51	White, Non-Hispanic	244.0 (0.9)	14/51
Black, Non-Hispanic	188.8 (2.0)	38/42	Black, Non-Hispanic	209.5 (1.3)	37/42
Asian, Non-Hispanic	*204.5 (3.4)*	22/41	Asian, Non-Hispanic	*223.3 (3.4)*	16/43
American Indian, Non-Hispanic	*231.9 (8.4)*	8/25	American Indian, Non-Hispanic	247.8 (3.6)	12/26
Hispanic	n/a	n/a	Hispanic	n/a	n/a
Proficiency by Class Size			Proficiency by Class Size		
Less than 16 Students	*206.3 (11.3)*	21/45	Less than 16 Students	*222.9 (6.5)*	27/47
16 to 18 Students	*220.8 (5.9)*	14/48	16 to 18 Students	*238.9 (5.1)*	11/48
19 to 20 Students	*223.0 (6.5)*	10/50	19 to 20 Students	*240.5 (3.7)*	9/50
21 to 25 Students	220.5 (1.8)	28/51	21 to 25 Students	237.7 (1.6)	25/51
Greater than 25 Students	215.8 (2.8)	34/49	Greater than 25 Students	232.9 (1.9)	31/49
Percent Attaining Achievement Levels			Percent Attaining Achievement Levels		
Below Basic	35.9 (1.5)	22/51	Below Basic	23.0 (1.0)	21/51
Basic or Above	64.1 (1.5)	29/51	Basic or Above	77.0 (1.0)	30/51
Proficient or Above	31.9 (1.4)	26/51	Proficient or Above	34.2 (1.4)	17/51
Advanced or Above	7.3 (0.8)	23/51	Advanced or Above	4.5 (0.5)	13/51
8th Grade			**8th Grade**		
Average Proficiency	264.4 (1.8)	26/51	Average Proficiency	276.4 (2.0)	34/51
Proficiency by Gender/Race/Ethnicity			Proficiency by Gender/Race/Ethnicity		
Male	259.0 (2.1)	25/51	Male	276.9 (2.3)	34/51
Female	269.8 (2.0)	25/51	Female	276.0 (2.0)	30/51
White, Non-Hispanic	272.2 (1.1)	12/50	White, Non-Hispanic	286.2 (1.3)	25/50
Black, Non-Hispanic	241.7 (4.5)	29/41	Black, Non-Hispanic	244.9 (3.5)	35/41
Asian, Non-Hispanic	*256.5 (3.4)*	5/37	Asian, Non-Hispanic	*266.8 (4.2)*	4/37
American Indian, Non-Hispanic	n/a	n/a	American Indian, Non-Hispanic	n/a	n/a
Hispanic	n/a	n/a	Hispanic	n/a	n/a
Proficiency by Parents Highest Level of Ed.			Proficiency by Parents Highest Level of Ed.		
Did Not Finish High School	244.9 (4.4)	32/50	Did Not Finish High School	253.3 (3.2)	38/50
Graduated High School	256.8 (1.9)	22/50	Graduated High School	267.7 (2.0)	30/50
Some Education After High School	268.0 (2.1)	24/50	Some Education After High School	279.6 (2.1)	32/50
Graduated College	271.1 (2.2)	31/50	Graduated College	283.6 (2.4)	36/50
Percent Attaining Achievement Levels			Percent Attaining Achievement Levels		
Below Basic	24.7 (2.1)	24/51	Below Basic	32.2 (2.2)	20/51
Basic or Above	75.3 (2.1)	28/51	Basic or Above	67.8 (2.2)	31/51
Proficient or Above	32.3 (1.8)	27/51	Proficient or Above	27.8 (1.9)	31/51
Advanced or Above	2.7 (0.6)	21/51	Advanced or Above	4.8 (0.6)	27/51

Note: *For an explanation of data, please refer to the User's Guide in the front of the book; values in italics indicate that the nature of the sample does not allow accurate determination of the variability of the statistic; n/a indicates data not available*

Allegan County

Allegan Public Schools

550 Fifth St • Allegan, MI 49010-1698
(269) 673-5431 • http://www.accn.org/~aps/
Grade Span: KG-12; **Agency Type:** 1
Schools: 7
4 Primary; 1 Middle; 2 High; 0 Other Level
6 Regular; 0 Special Education; 0 Vocational; 1 Alternative
0 Magnet; 0 Charter; 1 Title I Eligible; 1 School-wide Title I
Students: 3,033 (50.3% male; 49.7% female)
Individual Education Program: 388 (12.8%);
English Language Learner: 5 (0.2%); Migrant: n/a
Eligible for Free Lunch Program: 649 (21.4%)
Eligible for Reduced-Price Lunch Program: 275 (9.1%)
Teachers: 178.6 (17.0 to 1)
Librarians/Media Specialists: 1.0 (3,033.0 to 1)
Guidance Counselors: 7.0 (433.3 to 1)
Current Spending: ($ per student per year):
Total: $6,621; Instruction: $4,130; Support Services: $2,248
Enrollment, Drop-out Rates and Diploma Recipients by Race/Ethnicity

Category	Total	White	Black	Asian	AIAN	Hisp.
Enrollment (%)	100.0	93.0	3.5	1.0	0.3	2.1
Drop-out Rate (%)	n/a	n/a	n/a	n/a	n/a	n/a
H.S. Diplomas (#)	150	145	2	2	0	1

Fennville Public Schools

5 Memorial Dr • Fennville, MI 49408-0001
Mailing Address: PO Box 1 • Fennville, MI 49408-0001
(269) 561-7331 • http://www.accn.org/~fps/
Grade Span: PK-12; **Agency Type:** 1
Schools: 5
2 Primary; 1 Middle; 1 High; 1 Other Level
4 Regular; 0 Special Education; 0 Vocational; 1 Alternative
0 Magnet; 0 Charter; 0 Title I Eligible; 0 School-wide Title I
Students: 1,563 (51.7% male; 48.3% female)
Individual Education Program: 157 (10.0%);
English Language Learner: 180 (11.5%); Migrant: n/a
Eligible for Free Lunch Program: 475 (30.4%)
Eligible for Reduced-Price Lunch Program: 184 (11.8%)
Teachers: 93.1 (16.8 to 1)
Librarians/Media Specialists: 2.0 (781.5 to 1)
Guidance Counselors: 2.0 (781.5 to 1)
Current Spending: ($ per student per year):
Total: $7,202; Instruction: $4,248; Support Services: $2,608
Enrollment, Drop-out Rates and Diploma Recipients by Race/Ethnicity

Category	Total	White	Black	Asian	AIAN	Hisp.
Enrollment (%)	100.0	61.9	2.8	0.3	0.1	35.1
Drop-out Rate (%)	n/a	n/a	n/a	n/a	n/a	n/a
H.S. Diplomas (#)	88	54	2	1	0	31

Hamilton Community Schools

4815 136th Ave • Hamilton, MI 49419-0300
Mailing Address: PO Box 300 • Hamilton, MI 49419-0300
(269) 751-5148 • http://www.remc7.k12.mi.us/hamilton/
Grade Span: KG-12; **Agency Type:** 1
Schools: 6
4 Primary; 1 Middle; 1 High; 0 Other Level
6 Regular; 0 Special Education; 0 Vocational; 0 Alternative
6 Magnet; 0 Charter; 0 Title I Eligible; 0 School-wide Title I
Students: 2,689 (51.2% male; 48.8% female)
Individual Education Program: 278 (10.3%);
English Language Learner: 23 (0.9%); Migrant: n/a
Eligible for Free Lunch Program: 179 (6.7%)
Eligible for Reduced-Price Lunch Program: 127 (4.7%)
Teachers: 134.4 (20.0 to 1)
Librarians/Media Specialists: 4.0 (672.3 to 1)
Guidance Counselors: 4.0 (672.3 to 1)
Current Spending: ($ per student per year):
Total: $6,006; Instruction: $3,752; Support Services: $2,071
Enrollment, Drop-out Rates and Diploma Recipients by Race/Ethnicity

Category	Total	White	Black	Asian	AIAN	Hisp.
Enrollment (%)	100.0	94.6	0.5	1.7	0.1	3.0
Drop-out Rate (%)	n/a	n/a	n/a	n/a	n/a	n/a
H.S. Diplomas (#)	131	127	0	2	1	1

Otsego Public Schools

313 W Allegan St • Otsego, MI 49078-1097
(269) 692-6066 • http://www.accn.org/~roo/
Grade Span: PK-12; **Agency Type:** 1
Schools: 5
3 Primary; 1 Middle; 1 High; 0 Other Level
5 Regular; 0 Special Education; 0 Vocational; 0 Alternative
0 Magnet; 0 Charter; 0 Title I Eligible; 0 School-wide Title I
Students: 2,330 (52.2% male; 47.8% female)
Individual Education Program: 269 (11.5%);
English Language Learner: 18 (0.8%); Migrant: n/a
Eligible for Free Lunch Program: 314 (13.5%)
Eligible for Reduced-Price Lunch Program: 193 (8.3%)
Teachers: 131.0 (17.8 to 1)
Librarians/Media Specialists: 3.0 (776.7 to 1)
Guidance Counselors: 5.0 (466.0 to 1)
Current Spending: ($ per student per year):
Total: $6,175; Instruction: $3,708; Support Services: $2,212
Enrollment, Drop-out Rates and Diploma Recipients by Race/Ethnicity

Category	Total	White	Black	Asian	AIAN	Hisp.
Enrollment (%)	100.0	97.6	1.0	0.4	0.2	0.5
Drop-out Rate (%)	n/a	n/a	n/a	n/a	n/a	n/a
H.S. Diplomas (#)	168	161	4	1	0	2

Plainwell Community Schools

600 School Dr • Plainwell, MI 49080-1582
(269) 685-5823 • http://www.plainwellschools.org
Grade Span: PK-12; **Agency Type:** 1
Schools: 6
3 Primary; 1 Middle; 1 High; 1 Other Level
5 Regular; 0 Special Education; 0 Vocational; 1 Alternative
0 Magnet; 0 Charter; 0 Title I Eligible; 0 School-wide Title I
Students: 2,897 (51.1% male; 48.9% female)
Individual Education Program: 318 (11.0%);
English Language Learner: n/a; Migrant: n/a
Eligible for Free Lunch Program: 369 (12.7%)
Eligible for Reduced-Price Lunch Program: 171 (5.9%)
Teachers: 156.9 (18.5 to 1)
Librarians/Media Specialists: 3.0 (965.7 to 1)
Guidance Counselors: 6.8 (426.0 to 1)
Current Spending: ($ per student per year):
Total: $6,399; Instruction: $4,070; Support Services: $2,135
Enrollment, Drop-out Rates and Diploma Recipients by Race/Ethnicity

Category	Total	White	Black	Asian	AIAN	Hisp.
Enrollment (%)	100.0	96.6	1.1	0.8	0.2	1.0
Drop-out Rate (%)	n/a	n/a	n/a	n/a	n/a	n/a
H.S. Diplomas (#)	187	180	2	4	0	1

Wayland Union Schools

835 E Superior St • Wayland, MI 49348-9505
(269) 792-2181 • http://wayland.k12.mi.us/
Grade Span: PK-12; **Agency Type:** 1
Schools: 7
4 Primary; 2 Middle; 1 High; 0 Other Level
7 Regular; 0 Special Education; 0 Vocational; 0 Alternative
0 Magnet; 0 Charter; 1 Title I Eligible; 1 School-wide Title I
Students: 3,335 (50.9% male; 49.1% female)
Individual Education Program: 524 (15.7%);
English Language Learner: n/a; Migrant: n/a
Eligible for Free Lunch Program: 550 (16.5%)
Eligible for Reduced-Price Lunch Program: 293 (8.8%)
Teachers: 176.6 (18.9 to 1)
Librarians/Media Specialists: 3.0 (1,111.7 to 1)
Guidance Counselors: 4.0 (833.8 to 1)
Current Spending: ($ per student per year):
Total: $6,950; Instruction: $4,192; Support Services: $2,454
Enrollment, Drop-out Rates and Diploma Recipients by Race/Ethnicity

Category	Total	White	Black	Asian	AIAN	Hisp.
Enrollment (%)	100.0	95.7	0.9	0.6	1.1	1.8
Drop-out Rate (%)	n/a	n/a	n/a	n/a	n/a	n/a
H.S. Diplomas (#)	209	206	0	1	0	2

Alpena County

Alpena Public Schools

2373 Gordon Rd • Alpena, MI 49707-4627
(989) 358-5040 • http://www.alpenaschools.com/
Grade Span: PK-12; **Agency Type:** 1
Schools: 13
10 Primary; 1 Middle; 1 High; 1 Other Level
12 Regular; 0 Special Education; 0 Vocational; 1 Alternative
0 Magnet; 0 Charter; 10 Title I Eligible; 10 School-wide Title I
Students: 5,270 (51.3% male; 48.7% female)
Individual Education Program: 560 (10.6%);
English Language Learner: n/a; Migrant: n/a
Eligible for Free Lunch Program: 1,433 (27.2%)
Eligible for Reduced-Price Lunch Program: 530 (10.1%)
Teachers: 285.7 (18.4 to 1)
Librarians/Media Specialists: 5.0 (1,054.0 to 1)
Guidance Counselors: 9.0 (585.6 to 1)
Current Spending: ($ per student per year):
Total: $7,045; Instruction: $3,973; Support Services: $2,747

Enrollment, Drop-out Rates and Diploma Recipients by Race/Ethnicity

Category	Total	White	Black	Asian	AIAN	Hisp.
Enrollment (%)	100.0	97.9	0.6	0.7	0.4	0.3
Drop-out Rate (%)	n/a	n/a	n/a	n/a	n/a	n/a
H.S. Diplomas (#)	383	372	4	4	1	2

Antrim County

Elk Rapids Schools

707 E 3rd St • Elk Rapids, MI 49629-9760
(231) 264-8692 • http://www.erschools.com/
Grade Span: PK-12; **Agency Type:** 1
Schools: 4
2 Primary; 1 Middle; 1 High; 0 Other Level
4 Regular; 0 Special Education; 0 Vocational; 0 Alternative
0 Magnet; 0 Charter; 0 Title I Eligible; 0 School-wide Title I
Students: 1,520 (51.2% male; 48.8% female)
Individual Education Program: 153 (10.1%);
English Language Learner: n/a; Migrant: n/a
Eligible for Free Lunch Program: 235 (15.5%)
Eligible for Reduced-Price Lunch Program: 104 (6.8%)
Teachers: 83.5 (18.2 to 1)
Librarians/Media Specialists: 2.6 (584.6 to 1)
Guidance Counselors: 2.0 (760.0 to 1)
Current Spending: ($ per student per year):
Total: $6,880; Instruction: $4,458; Support Services: $2,198
Enrollment, Drop-out Rates and Diploma Recipients by Race/Ethnicity

Category	Total	White	Black	Asian	AIAN	Hisp.
Enrollment (%)	100.0	92.8	0.5	0.7	1.6	4.3
Drop-out Rate (%)	n/a	n/a	n/a	n/a	n/a	n/a
H.S. Diplomas (#)	119	115	0	0	0	4

Arenac County

Standish-Sterling Community Schools

3789 W Wyatt Rd • Standish, MI 48658-9168
(989) 846-4526 • http://www.standish-sterling.org/
Grade Span: PK-12; **Agency Type:** 1
Schools: 4
2 Primary; 1 Middle; 1 High; 0 Other Level
4 Regular; 0 Special Education; 0 Vocational; 0 Alternative
0 Magnet; 0 Charter; 0 Title I Eligible; 0 School-wide Title I
Students: 1,979 (51.7% male; 48.3% female)
Individual Education Program: 235 (11.9%);
English Language Learner: 0 (0.0%); Migrant: n/a
Eligible for Free Lunch Program: 670 (33.9%)
Eligible for Reduced-Price Lunch Program: 206 (10.4%)
Teachers: 104.0 (19.0 to 1)
Librarians/Media Specialists: 1.0 (1,979.0 to 1)
Guidance Counselors: 3.0 (659.7 to 1)
Current Spending: ($ per student per year):
Total: $6,015; Instruction: $3,963; Support Services: $1,752
Enrollment, Drop-out Rates and Diploma Recipients by Race/Ethnicity

Category	Total	White	Black	Asian	AIAN	Hisp.
Enrollment (%)	100.0	97.5	0.2	0.3	1.3	0.8
Drop-out Rate (%)	n/a	n/a	n/a	n/a	n/a	n/a
H.S. Diplomas (#)	129	125	0	0	2	2

Barry County

Delton-Kellogg SD

327 N Grove St • Delton, MI 49046-9701
(616) 623-9246 • http://delton-kellogg.k12.mi.us/
Grade Span: PK-12; **Agency Type:** 1
Schools: 4
1 Primary; 1 Middle; 1 High; 1 Other Level
3 Regular; 0 Special Education; 0 Vocational; 1 Alternative
0 Magnet; 0 Charter; 0 Title I Eligible; 0 School-wide Title I
Students: 2,059 (51.3% male; 48.7% female)
Individual Education Program: 225 (10.9%);
English Language Learner: n/a; Migrant: n/a
Eligible for Free Lunch Program: 461 (22.4%)
Eligible for Reduced-Price Lunch Program: 137 (6.7%)
Teachers: 123.6 (16.7 to 1)
Librarians/Media Specialists: 1.0 (2,059.0 to 1)
Guidance Counselors: 4.0 (514.8 to 1)
Current Spending: ($ per student per year):
Total: $6,572; Instruction: $4,190; Support Services: $2,028
Enrollment, Drop-out Rates and Diploma Recipients by Race/Ethnicity

Category	Total	White	Black	Asian	AIAN	Hisp.
Enrollment (%)	100.0	96.0	0.8	0.5	0.9	1.8
Drop-out Rate (%)	n/a	n/a	n/a	n/a	n/a	n/a
H.S. Diplomas (#)	142	137	1	0	1	3

Hastings Area SD

232 W Grand St • Hastings, MI 49058-2298
(269) 948-4400 •
http://www.hassk12.org/education/district/district.php?sectionid=1
Grade Span: PK-12; **Agency Type:** 1
Schools: 7
5 Primary; 1 Middle; 1 High; 0 Other Level
7 Regular; 0 Special Education; 0 Vocational; 0 Alternative
0 Magnet; 0 Charter; 0 Title I Eligible; 0 School-wide Title I
Students: 3,370 (50.1% male; 49.9% female)
Individual Education Program: 370 (11.0%);
English Language Learner: 4 (0.1%); Migrant: n/a
Eligible for Free Lunch Program: 479 (14.2%)
Eligible for Reduced-Price Lunch Program: 247 (7.3%)
Teachers: 197.8 (17.0 to 1)
Librarians/Media Specialists: 5.0 (674.0 to 1)
Guidance Counselors: 8.0 (421.3 to 1)
Current Spending: ($ per student per year):
Total: $6,797; Instruction: $4,465; Support Services: $2,115
Enrollment, Drop-out Rates and Diploma Recipients by Race/Ethnicity

Category	Total	White	Black	Asian	AIAN	Hisp.
Enrollment (%)	100.0	97.4	0.6	0.2	0.3	1.4
Drop-out Rate (%)	n/a	n/a	n/a	n/a	n/a	n/a
H.S. Diplomas (#)	192	184	1	3	2	2

Thornapple Kellogg SD

10051 Green Lake Rd • Middleville, MI 49333-9274
(269) 795-3313 • http://www.tk.k12.mi.us/
Grade Span: PK-12; **Agency Type:** 1
Schools: 6
2 Primary; 2 Middle; 1 High; 1 Other Level
5 Regular; 0 Special Education; 0 Vocational; 1 Alternative
0 Magnet; 0 Charter; 0 Title I Eligible; 0 School-wide Title I
Students: 2,863 (52.7% male; 47.3% female)
Individual Education Program: 261 (9.1%);
English Language Learner: 32 (1.1%); Migrant: n/a
Eligible for Free Lunch Program: 282 (9.8%)
Eligible for Reduced-Price Lunch Program: 203 (7.1%)
Teachers: 153.0 (18.7 to 1)
Librarians/Media Specialists: 2.0 (1,431.5 to 1)
Guidance Counselors: 6.0 (477.2 to 1)
Current Spending: ($ per student per year):
Total: $6,458; Instruction: $4,009; Support Services: $2,192
Enrollment, Drop-out Rates and Diploma Recipients by Race/Ethnicity

Category	Total	White	Black	Asian	AIAN	Hisp.
Enrollment (%)	100.0	94.4	0.6	1.9	0.9	2.1
Drop-out Rate (%)	n/a	n/a	n/a	n/a	n/a	n/a
H.S. Diplomas (#)	209	200	1	1	1	6

Bay County

Bangor Township Schools

3520 Old Kawkawlin Rd • Bay City, MI 48706-2039
(989) 684-8121 • http://www.bangorschools.org/
Grade Span: PK-12; **Agency Type:** 1
Schools: 6
4 Primary; 1 Middle; 1 High; 0 Other Level
6 Regular; 0 Special Education; 0 Vocational; 0 Alternative
0 Magnet; 0 Charter; 0 Title I Eligible; 0 School-wide Title I
Students: 2,457 (51.1% male; 48.9% female)
Individual Education Program: 297 (12.1%);
English Language Learner: n/a; Migrant: n/a
Eligible for Free Lunch Program: 542 (22.1%)
Eligible for Reduced-Price Lunch Program: 141 (5.7%)
Teachers: 128.9 (19.1 to 1)
Librarians/Media Specialists: 1.0 (2,457.0 to 1)
Guidance Counselors: 4.0 (614.3 to 1)
Current Spending: ($ per student per year):
Total: $7,133; Instruction: $4,316; Support Services: $2,540
Enrollment, Drop-out Rates and Diploma Recipients by Race/Ethnicity

Category	Total	White	Black	Asian	AIAN	Hisp.
Enrollment (%)	100.0	88.4	4.1	4.7	0.4	2.3
Drop-out Rate (%)	n/a	n/a	n/a	n/a	n/a	n/a
H.S. Diplomas (#)	175	159	1	5	0	10

Bay City SD

910 N Walnut St • Bay City, MI 48706-3773
(989) 686-9700 • http://www.bcschools.net/
Grade Span: PK-12; **Agency Type:** 1
Schools: 18
12 Primary; 3 Middle; 2 High; 1 Other Level
16 Regular; 1 Special Education; 0 Vocational; 1 Alternative
0 Magnet; 0 Charter; 6 Title I Eligible; 6 School-wide Title I
Students: 9,937 (52.7% male; 47.3% female)
Individual Education Program: 1,262 (12.7%);

English Language Learner: 568 (5.7%); Migrant: n/a
Eligible for Free Lunch Program: 2,782 (28.0%)
Eligible for Reduced-Price Lunch Program: 709 (7.1%)
Teachers: 537.1 (18.5 to 1)
Librarians/Media Specialists: 11.8 (842.1 to 1)
Guidance Counselors: 20.2 (491.9 to 1)
Current Spending: ($ per student per year):
Total: $7,336; Instruction: $4,461; Support Services: $2,620
Enrollment, Drop-out Rates and Diploma Recipients by Race/Ethnicity

Category	Total	White	Black	Asian	AIAN	Hisp.
Enrollment (%)	100.0	87.5	4.8	0.5	1.1	6.0
Drop-out Rate (%)	n/a	n/a	n/a	n/a	n/a	n/a
H.S. Diplomas (#)	590	554	9	5	5	17

Essexville-Hampton Public Schools
303 Pine St • Essexville, MI 48732-1598
(989) 894-9700 • http://www.e-hps.net/
Grade Span: KG-12; **Agency Type:** 1
Schools: 5
3 Primary; 1 Middle; 1 High; 0 Other Level
5 Regular; 0 Special Education; 0 Vocational; 0 Alternative
0 Magnet; 0 Charter; 0 Title I Eligible; 0 School-wide Title I
Students: 1,926 (49.8% male; 50.2% female)
Individual Education Program: 182 (9.4%);
English Language Learner: n/a; Migrant: n/a
Eligible for Free Lunch Program: 325 (16.9%)
Eligible for Reduced-Price Lunch Program: 77 (4.0%)
Teachers: 103.0 (18.7 to 1)
Librarians/Media Specialists: 2.0 (963.0 to 1)
Guidance Counselors: 5.0 (385.2 to 1)
Current Spending: ($ per student per year):
Total: $6,986; Instruction: $4,432; Support Services: $2,358
Enrollment, Drop-out Rates and Diploma Recipients by Race/Ethnicity

Category	Total	White	Black	Asian	AIAN	Hisp.
Enrollment (%)	100.0	95.0	2.3	0.6	0.1	2.0
Drop-out Rate (%)	n/a	n/a	n/a	n/a	n/a	n/a
H.S. Diplomas (#)	137	125	1	1	1	9

Pinconning Area Schools
605 W 5th St • Pinconning, MI 48650-8712
(989) 879-4556 • http://www.pasd.org/
Grade Span: PK-12; **Agency Type:** 1
Schools: 6
3 Primary; 1 Middle; 1 High; 1 Other Level
5 Regular; 0 Special Education; 0 Vocational; 1 Alternative
0 Magnet; 0 Charter; 4 Title I Eligible; 4 School-wide Title I
Students: 2,066 (49.8% male; 50.2% female)
Individual Education Program: 210 (10.2%);
English Language Learner: 1 (<0.1%); Migrant: n/a
Eligible for Free Lunch Program: 550 (26.6%)
Eligible for Reduced-Price Lunch Program: 182 (8.8%)
Teachers: 110.0 (18.8 to 1)
Librarians/Media Specialists: 1.0 (2,066.0 to 1)
Guidance Counselors: 3.0 (688.7 to 1)
Current Spending: ($ per student per year):
Total: $7,201; Instruction: $4,306; Support Services: $2,603
Enrollment, Drop-out Rates and Diploma Recipients by Race/Ethnicity

Category	Total	White	Black	Asian	AIAN	Hisp.
Enrollment (%)	100.0	92.5	2.0	0.2	0.1	5.1
Drop-out Rate (%)	n/a	n/a	n/a	n/a	n/a	n/a
H.S. Diplomas (#)	163	156	0	0	3	4

Benzie County

Benzie County Central Schools
9222 Homestead Rd • Benzonia, MI 49616-0240
Mailing Address: PO Box 240 • Benzonia, MI 49616-0240
(231) 882-9654 • http://www.benzie.k12.mi.us/
Grade Span: KG-12; **Agency Type:** 1
Schools: 6
4 Primary; 1 Middle; 1 High; 0 Other Level
6 Regular; 0 Special Education; 0 Vocational; 0 Alternative
6 Magnet; 0 Charter; 0 Title I Eligible; 0 School-wide Title I
Students: 2,006 (53.2% male; 46.8% female)
Individual Education Program: 219 (10.9%);
English Language Learner: n/a; Migrant: n/a
Eligible for Free Lunch Program: 527 (26.3%)
Eligible for Reduced-Price Lunch Program: 250 (12.5%)
Teachers: 111.0 (18.1 to 1)
Librarians/Media Specialists: 1.0 (2,006.0 to 1)
Guidance Counselors: 4.0 (501.5 to 1)
Current Spending: ($ per student per year):
Total: $6,515; Instruction: $3,987; Support Services: $2,200
Enrollment, Drop-out Rates and Diploma Recipients by Race/Ethnicity

Category	Total	White	Black	Asian	AIAN	Hisp.
Enrollment (%)	100.0	92.9	0.5	0.2	3.3	3.0
Drop-out Rate (%)	n/a	n/a	n/a	n/a	n/a	n/a
H.S. Diplomas (#)	111	110	0	0	0	1

Berrien County

Benton Harbor Area Schools
777 Riverview Drive, Bldg B • Benton Harbor, MI 49023-1107
Mailing Address: PO Box 1107 • Benton Harbor, MI 49023-1107
(269) 927-0600 • http://www.remc11.k12.mi.us/bhas/
Grade Span: PK-12; **Agency Type:** 1
Schools: 16
10 Primary; 3 Middle; 2 High; 1 Other Level
14 Regular; 0 Special Education; 1 Vocational; 1 Alternative
1 Magnet; 0 Charter; 13 Title I Eligible; 13 School-wide Title I
Students: 5,324 (50.0% male; 50.0% female)
Individual Education Program: 715 (13.4%);
English Language Learner: n/a; Migrant: n/a
Eligible for Free Lunch Program: 4,030 (75.7%)
Eligible for Reduced-Price Lunch Program: 222 (4.2%)
Teachers: 304.0 (17.5 to 1)
Librarians/Media Specialists: 5.0 (1,064.8 to 1)
Guidance Counselors: 9.0 (591.6 to 1)
Current Spending: ($ per student per year):
Total: $9,536; Instruction: $5,083; Support Services: $3,935
Enrollment, Drop-out Rates and Diploma Recipients by Race/Ethnicity

Category	Total	White	Black	Asian	AIAN	Hisp.
Enrollment (%)	100.0	4.5	93.6	0.0	0.1	1.7
Drop-out Rate (%)	n/a	n/a	n/a	n/a	n/a	n/a
H.S. Diplomas (#)	201	12	187	0	0	2

Berrien Springs Public Schools
One Sylvester Ave • Berrien Springs, MI 49103-1182
(269) 471-2891 • http://www.remc11.k12.mi.us/bsps/bsp/
Grade Span: PK-12; **Agency Type:** 1
Schools: 5
2 Primary; 1 Middle; 1 High; 1 Other Level
4 Regular; 0 Special Education; 0 Vocational; 1 Alternative
3 Magnet; 0 Charter; 2 Title I Eligible; 2 School-wide Title I
Students: 1,579 (52.4% male; 47.6% female)
Individual Education Program: 229 (14.5%);
English Language Learner: 123 (7.8%); Migrant: n/a
Eligible for Free Lunch Program: 528 (33.4%)
Eligible for Reduced-Price Lunch Program: 158 (10.0%)
Teachers: 106.3 (14.9 to 1)
Librarians/Media Specialists: 1.0 (1,579.0 to 1)
Guidance Counselors: 2.0 (789.5 to 1)
Current Spending: ($ per student per year):
Total: $8,068; Instruction: $4,702; Support Services: $3,053
Enrollment, Drop-out Rates and Diploma Recipients by Race/Ethnicity

Category	Total	White	Black	Asian	AIAN	Hisp.
Enrollment (%)	100.0	63.7	20.4	4.7	0.3	11.0
Drop-out Rate (%)	n/a	n/a	n/a	n/a	n/a	n/a
H.S. Diplomas (#)	93	68	19	3	0	3

Brandywine Public SD
1830 S Third St • Niles, MI 49120-4633
(269) 684-7150 • http://www.remc11.k12.mi.us/brandy/
Grade Span: PK-12; **Agency Type:** 1
Schools: 5
2 Primary; 1 Middle; 1 High; 1 Other Level
4 Regular; 0 Special Education; 0 Vocational; 1 Alternative
0 Magnet; 0 Charter; 0 Title I Eligible; 0 School-wide Title I
Students: 1,657 (51.8% male; 48.2% female)
Individual Education Program: 230 (13.9%);
English Language Learner: n/a; Migrant: n/a
Eligible for Free Lunch Program: 380 (22.9%)
Eligible for Reduced-Price Lunch Program: 181 (10.9%)
Teachers: 97.3 (17.0 to 1)
Librarians/Media Specialists: 1.0 (1,657.0 to 1)
Guidance Counselors: 5.0 (331.4 to 1)
Current Spending: ($ per student per year):
Total: $6,091; Instruction: $3,521; Support Services: $2,299
Enrollment, Drop-out Rates and Diploma Recipients by Race/Ethnicity

Category	Total	White	Black	Asian	AIAN	Hisp.
Enrollment (%)	100.0	91.2	4.2	0.5	1.2	2.9
Drop-out Rate (%)	n/a	n/a	n/a	n/a	n/a	n/a
H.S. Diplomas (#)	97	90	3	1	0	3

Buchanan Community Schools

401 W Chicago St • Buchanan, MI 49107-1044
(269) 695-8401 • http://www.buchanan.k12.mi.us/
Grade Span: PK-12; **Agency Type:** 1
Schools: 5
3 Primary; 1 Middle; 1 High; 0 Other Level
5 Regular; 0 Special Education; 0 Vocational; 0 Alternative
0 Magnet; 0 Charter; 0 Title I Eligible; 0 School-wide Title I
Students: 1,771 (54.2% male; 45.8% female)
Individual Education Program: 299 (16.9%);
English Language Learner: n/a; Migrant: n/a
Eligible for Free Lunch Program: 486 (27.4%)
Eligible for Reduced-Price Lunch Program: 154 (8.7%)
Teachers: 100.6 (17.6 to 1)
Librarians/Media Specialists: 3.0 (590.3 to 1)
Guidance Counselors: 6.0 (295.2 to 1)
Current Spending: ($ per student per year):
Total: $6,532; Instruction: $4,080; Support Services: $2,159
Enrollment, Drop-out Rates and Diploma Recipients by Race/Ethnicity

Category	Total	White	Black	Asian	AIAN	Hisp.
Enrollment (%)	100.0	87.0	9.4	0.8	0.6	2.3
Drop-out Rate (%)	n/a	n/a	n/a	n/a	n/a	n/a
H.S. Diplomas (#)	93	85	7	0	0	1

Coloma Community Schools

2518 Boyer Rd • Coloma, MI 49038-0550
Mailing Address: PO Box 550 • Coloma, MI 49038-0550
(269) 468-2424 • http://www.remc11.k12.mi.us/coloma/
Grade Span: PK-12; **Agency Type:** 1
Schools: 6
3 Primary; 1 Middle; 1 High; 1 Other Level
6 Regular; 0 Special Education; 0 Vocational; 0 Alternative
0 Magnet; 0 Charter; 3 Title I Eligible; 3 School-wide Title I
Students: 2,120 (51.5% male; 48.5% female)
Individual Education Program: 326 (15.4%);
English Language Learner: n/a; Migrant: n/a
Eligible for Free Lunch Program: 604 (28.5%)
Eligible for Reduced-Price Lunch Program: 190 (9.0%)
Teachers: 135.9 (15.6 to 1)
Librarians/Media Specialists: 5.1 (415.7 to 1)
Guidance Counselors: 6.5 (326.2 to 1)
Current Spending: ($ per student per year):
Total: $7,208; Instruction: $4,252; Support Services: $2,673
Enrollment, Drop-out Rates and Diploma Recipients by Race/Ethnicity

Category	Total	White	Black	Asian	AIAN	Hisp.
Enrollment (%)	100.0	80.0	14.2	0.3	0.3	5.2
Drop-out Rate (%)	n/a	n/a	n/a	n/a	n/a	n/a
H.S. Diplomas (#)	132	93	34	0	0	5

Lakeshore SD (Berrien)

5771 Cleveland Ave • Stevensville, MI 49127-9497
(269) 428-1400 • http://www.remc11.k12.mi.us/bcisd/
Grade Span: PK-12; **Agency Type:** 1
Schools: 5
3 Primary; 1 Middle; 1 High; 0 Other Level
5 Regular; 0 Special Education; 0 Vocational; 0 Alternative
0 Magnet; 0 Charter; 0 Title I Eligible; 0 School-wide Title I
Students: 2,897 (51.6% male; 48.4% female)
Individual Education Program: 314 (10.8%);
English Language Learner: n/a; Migrant: n/a
Eligible for Free Lunch Program: 227 (7.8%)
Eligible for Reduced-Price Lunch Program: 98 (3.4%)
Teachers: 138.8 (20.9 to 1)
Librarians/Media Specialists: 2.0 (1,448.5 to 1)
Guidance Counselors: 8.0 (362.1 to 1)
Current Spending: ($ per student per year):
Total: $6,424; Instruction: $3,856; Support Services: $2,322
Enrollment, Drop-out Rates and Diploma Recipients by Race/Ethnicity

Category	Total	White	Black	Asian	AIAN	Hisp.
Enrollment (%)	100.0	94.6	2.1	1.2	0.1	1.9
Drop-out Rate (%)	n/a	n/a	n/a	n/a	n/a	n/a
H.S. Diplomas (#)	237	223	6	8	0	0

Niles Community SD

111 Spruce St • Niles, MI 49120-2963
(269) 683-0732
Grade Span: PK-12; **Agency Type:** 1
Schools: 10
6 Primary; 1 Middle; 1 High; 2 Other Level
8 Regular; 1 Special Education; 0 Vocational; 1 Alternative
0 Magnet; 0 Charter; 6 Title I Eligible; 6 School-wide Title I
Students: 4,220 (54.2% male; 45.8% female)
Individual Education Program: 733 (17.4%);
English Language Learner: n/a; Migrant: n/a
Eligible for Free Lunch Program: 1,307 (31.0%)
Eligible for Reduced-Price Lunch Program: 372 (8.8%)
Teachers: n/a
Librarians/Media Specialists: n/a
Guidance Counselors: n/a
Current Spending: ($ per student per year):
Total: $7,267; Instruction: $4,425; Support Services: $2,575
Enrollment, Drop-out Rates and Diploma Recipients by Race/Ethnicity

Category	Total	White	Black	Asian	AIAN	Hisp.
Enrollment (%)	100.0	79.9	15.2	0.5	0.4	3.9
Drop-out Rate (%)	n/a	n/a	n/a	n/a	n/a	n/a
H.S. Diplomas (#)	160	134	18	2	3	3

Saint Joseph Public Schools

2214 S State St • Saint Joseph, MI 49085-1910
(269) 982-4621 • http://www.remc11.k12.mi.us/stjoe/
Grade Span: PK-12; **Agency Type:** 1
Schools: 6
4 Primary; 1 Middle; 1 High; 0 Other Level
6 Regular; 0 Special Education; 0 Vocational; 0 Alternative
0 Magnet; 0 Charter; 0 Title I Eligible; 0 School-wide Title I
Students: 2,864 (51.9% male; 48.1% female)
Individual Education Program: 238 (8.3%);
English Language Learner: n/a; Migrant: n/a
Eligible for Free Lunch Program: 159 (5.6%)
Eligible for Reduced-Price Lunch Program: 96 (3.4%)
Teachers: 155.6 (18.4 to 1)
Librarians/Media Specialists: 3.0 (954.7 to 1)
Guidance Counselors: 5.0 (572.8 to 1)
Current Spending: ($ per student per year):
Total: $7,376; Instruction: $4,137; Support Services: $2,918
Enrollment, Drop-out Rates and Diploma Recipients by Race/Ethnicity

Category	Total	White	Black	Asian	AIAN	Hisp.
Enrollment (%)	100.0	91.3	3.4	3.5	0.2	1.6
Drop-out Rate (%)	n/a	n/a	n/a	n/a	n/a	n/a
H.S. Diplomas (#)	210	195	3	10	0	2

Branch County

Bronson Community SD

215 W Chicago St • Bronson, MI 49028-1320
(517) 369-3257
Grade Span: KG-12; **Agency Type:** 1
Schools: 4
2 Primary; 1 Middle; 1 High; 0 Other Level
4 Regular; 0 Special Education; 0 Vocational; 0 Alternative
0 Magnet; 0 Charter; 3 Title I Eligible; 3 School-wide Title I
Students: 1,502 (52.1% male; 47.9% female)
Individual Education Program: 189 (12.6%);
English Language Learner: n/a; Migrant: n/a
Eligible for Free Lunch Program: 433 (28.8%)
Eligible for Reduced-Price Lunch Program: 125 (8.3%)
Teachers: 69.7 (21.5 to 1)
Librarians/Media Specialists: 1.0 (1,502.0 to 1)
Guidance Counselors: 2.0 (751.0 to 1)
Current Spending: ($ per student per year):
Total: $6,467; Instruction: $3,890; Support Services: $2,232
Enrollment, Drop-out Rates and Diploma Recipients by Race/Ethnicity

Category	Total	White	Black	Asian	AIAN	Hisp.
Enrollment (%)	100.0	91.1	0.5	0.5	0.3	7.6
Drop-out Rate (%)	n/a	n/a	n/a	n/a	n/a	n/a
H.S. Diplomas (#)	114	112	0	0	0	2

Coldwater Community Schools

401 Sauk River Dr • Coldwater, MI 49036-2067
(517) 279-5910 • http://www.coldwater.k12.mi.us/
Grade Span: PK-12; **Agency Type:** 1
Schools: 8
5 Primary; 1 Middle; 1 High; 1 Other Level
7 Regular; 0 Special Education; 0 Vocational; 1 Alternative
7 Magnet; 0 Charter; 2 Title I Eligible; 2 School-wide Title I
Students: 3,805 (53.3% male; 46.7% female)
Individual Education Program: 456 (12.0%);
English Language Learner: 296 (7.8%); Migrant: n/a
Eligible for Free Lunch Program: 708 (18.6%)
Eligible for Reduced-Price Lunch Program: 183 (4.8%)
Teachers: 181.3 (21.0 to 1)
Librarians/Media Specialists: 3.5 (1,087.1 to 1)
Guidance Counselors: 6.0 (634.2 to 1)
Current Spending: ($ per student per year):
Total: $6,798; Instruction: $4,071; Support Services: $2,447
Enrollment, Drop-out Rates and Diploma Recipients by Race/Ethnicity

Category	Total	White	Black	Asian	AIAN	Hisp.
Enrollment (%)	100.0	94.3	0.6	1.2	0.3	3.6
Drop-out Rate (%)	n/a	n/a	n/a	n/a	n/a	n/a
H.S. Diplomas (#)	211	206	2	0	0	3

Quincy Community SD
1 Educational Pkwy • Quincy, MI 49082-1173
(517) 639-7141
Grade Span: KG-12; **Agency Type:** 1
Schools: 3
1 Primary; 1 Middle; 1 High; 0 Other Level
3 Regular; 0 Special Education; 0 Vocational; 0 Alternative
0 Magnet; 0 Charter; 0 Title I Eligible; 0 School-wide Title I
Students: 1,683 (53.2% male; 46.8% female)
Individual Education Program: 206 (12.2%);
English Language Learner: n/a; Migrant: n/a
Eligible for Free Lunch Program: 272 (16.2%)
Eligible for Reduced-Price Lunch Program: 112 (6.7%)
Teachers: 86.7 (19.4 to 1)
Librarians/Media Specialists: 1.9 (885.8 to 1)
Guidance Counselors: 3.0 (561.0 to 1)
Current Spending: ($ per student per year):
Total: $6,333; Instruction: $4,360; Support Services: $1,768
Enrollment, Drop-out Rates and Diploma Recipients by Race/Ethnicity

Category	Total	White	Black	Asian	AIAN	Hisp.
Enrollment (%)	100.0	98.3	0.3	0.9	0.2	0.2
Drop-out Rate (%)	n/a	n/a	n/a	n/a	n/a	n/a
H.S. Diplomas (#)	87	87	0	0	0	0

Calhoun County

Albion Public Schools
401 E Michigan Ave • Albion, MI 49224-1898
(517) 629-9166 • http://www.albion.k12.mi.us/
Grade Span: PK-12; **Agency Type:** 1
Schools: 7
4 Primary; 1 Middle; 1 High; 1 Other Level
6 Regular; 0 Special Education; 0 Vocational; 1 Alternative
0 Magnet; 0 Charter; 5 Title I Eligible; 5 School-wide Title I
Students: 1,847 (53.1% male; 46.9% female)
Individual Education Program: 244 (13.2%);
English Language Learner: n/a; Migrant: n/a
Eligible for Free Lunch Program: 937 (50.7%)
Eligible for Reduced-Price Lunch Program: 121 (6.6%)
Teachers: 107.0 (17.3 to 1)
Librarians/Media Specialists: 3.0 (615.7 to 1)
Guidance Counselors: 4.0 (461.8 to 1)
Current Spending: ($ per student per year):
Total: $7,926; Instruction: $4,753; Support Services: $2,846
Enrollment, Drop-out Rates and Diploma Recipients by Race/Ethnicity

Category	Total	White	Black	Asian	AIAN	Hisp.
Enrollment (%)	100.0	44.3	50.6	0.5	0.4	4.2
Drop-out Rate (%)	n/a	n/a	n/a	n/a	n/a	n/a
H.S. Diplomas (#)	101	53	40	0	0	8

Battle Creek Public Schools
3 W Van Buren St • Battle Creek, MI 49017-3009
(269) 965-9465 • http://www.woburn.k12.ma.us/
Grade Span: PK-12; **Agency Type:** 1
Schools: 26
16 Primary; 4 Middle; 5 High; 1 Other Level
22 Regular; 0 Special Education; 1 Vocational; 3 Alternative
1 Magnet; 0 Charter; 21 Title I Eligible; 21 School-wide Title I
Students: 8,255 (51.4% male; 48.6% female)
Individual Education Program: 1,179 (14.3%);
English Language Learner: 190 (2.3%); Migrant: n/a
Eligible for Free Lunch Program: 3,995 (48.4%)
Eligible for Reduced-Price Lunch Program: 620 (7.5%)
Teachers: 541.0 (15.3 to 1)
Librarians/Media Specialists: 3.0 (2,751.7 to 1)
Guidance Counselors: 23.0 (358.9 to 1)
Current Spending: ($ per student per year):
Total: $8,329; Instruction: $4,770; Support Services: $3,249
Enrollment, Drop-out Rates and Diploma Recipients by Race/Ethnicity

Category	Total	White	Black	Asian	AIAN	Hisp.
Enrollment (%)	100.0	56.0	35.5	0.7	1.8	6.1
Drop-out Rate (%)	n/a	n/a	n/a	n/a	n/a	n/a
H.S. Diplomas (#)	278	147	113	3	3	12

Harper Creek Community Schools
201 Crosby Dr • Battle Creek, MI 49014-9564
(269) 979-1136 • http://www.harpercreek.net/
Grade Span: PK-12; **Agency Type:** 1
Schools: 5
3 Primary; 1 Middle; 1 High; 0 Other Level
5 Regular; 0 Special Education; 0 Vocational; 0 Alternative
0 Magnet; 0 Charter; 0 Title I Eligible; 0 School-wide Title I
Students: 2,720 (51.5% male; 48.5% female)
Individual Education Program: 235 (8.6%);
English Language Learner: n/a; Migrant: n/a
Eligible for Free Lunch Program: 427 (15.7%)
Eligible for Reduced-Price Lunch Program: 115 (4.2%)
Teachers: 140.8 (19.3 to 1)
Librarians/Media Specialists: 1.0 (2,720.0 to 1)
Guidance Counselors: 4.0 (680.0 to 1)
Current Spending: ($ per student per year):
Total: $6,682; Instruction: $4,213; Support Services: $2,197
Enrollment, Drop-out Rates and Diploma Recipients by Race/Ethnicity

Category	Total	White	Black	Asian	AIAN	Hisp.
Enrollment (%)	100.0	94.5	1.3	1.4	0.6	2.1
Drop-out Rate (%)	n/a	n/a	n/a	n/a	n/a	n/a
H.S. Diplomas (#)	156	151	0	1	1	3

Lakeview SD (Calhoun)
15 Arbor St • Battle Creek, MI 49015-2903
(269) 565-2411 • http://www.lakeviewspartans.org/index.taf
Grade Span: PK-12; **Agency Type:** 1
Schools: 8
5 Primary; 2 Middle; 1 High; 0 Other Level
8 Regular; 0 Special Education; 0 Vocational; 0 Alternative
0 Magnet; 0 Charter; 1 Title I Eligible; 1 School-wide Title I
Students: 3,388 (50.6% male; 49.4% female)
Individual Education Program: 351 (10.4%);
English Language Learner: n/a; Migrant: n/a
Eligible for Free Lunch Program: 453 (13.4%)
Eligible for Reduced-Price Lunch Program: 119 (3.5%)
Teachers: 195.7 (17.3 to 1)
Librarians/Media Specialists: 3.0 (1,129.3 to 1)
Guidance Counselors: 6.0 (564.7 to 1)
Current Spending: ($ per student per year):
Total: $6,889; Instruction: $4,219; Support Services: $2,443
Enrollment, Drop-out Rates and Diploma Recipients by Race/Ethnicity

Category	Total	White	Black	Asian	AIAN	Hisp.
Enrollment (%)	100.0	84.5	5.2	6.4	1.1	2.8
Drop-out Rate (%)	n/a	n/a	n/a	n/a	n/a	n/a
H.S. Diplomas (#)	238	215	8	10	0	5

Marshall Public Schools
100 E Green St • Marshall, MI 49068-1594
(269) 781-1256 • http://www.marshallschools.com/
Grade Span: KG-12; **Agency Type:** 1
Schools: 9
3 Primary; 2 Middle; 1 High; 1 Other Level
7 Regular; 0 Special Education; 0 Vocational; 0 Alternative
0 Magnet; 0 Charter; 0 Title I Eligible; 0 School-wide Title I
Students: 2,473 (51.6% male; 48.4% female)
Individual Education Program: 284 (11.5%);
English Language Learner: n/a; Migrant: n/a
Eligible for Free Lunch Program: 303 (12.3%)
Eligible for Reduced-Price Lunch Program: 82 (3.3%)
Teachers: 140.4 (17.6 to 1)
Librarians/Media Specialists: 7.0 (353.3 to 1)
Guidance Counselors: 5.5 (449.6 to 1)
Current Spending: ($ per student per year):
Total: $7,058; Instruction: $4,562; Support Services: $2,305
Enrollment, Drop-out Rates and Diploma Recipients by Race/Ethnicity

Category	Total	White	Black	Asian	AIAN	Hisp.
Enrollment (%)	100.0	93.5	1.3	0.8	1.2	3.2
Drop-out Rate (%)	n/a	n/a	n/a	n/a	n/a	n/a
H.S. Diplomas (#)	203	186	0	4	1	12

Pennfield SD
8587 Q Dr N • Battle Creek, MI 49017-8159
(269) 961-9781 • http://www.pennfield.k12.mi.us/
Grade Span: PK-12; **Agency Type:** 1
Schools: 6
3 Primary; 2 Middle; 1 High; 0 Other Level
6 Regular; 0 Special Education; 0 Vocational; 0 Alternative
0 Magnet; 0 Charter; 4 Title I Eligible; 4 School-wide Title I
Students: 1,891 (50.8% male; 49.2% female)
Individual Education Program: 186 (9.8%);
English Language Learner: n/a; Migrant: n/a
Eligible for Free Lunch Program: 308 (16.3%)
Eligible for Reduced-Price Lunch Program: 111 (5.9%)
Teachers: 100.4 (18.8 to 1)
Librarians/Media Specialists: 2.0 (945.5 to 1)
Guidance Counselors: 4.0 (472.8 to 1)
Current Spending: ($ per student per year):
Total: $6,718; Instruction: $4,181; Support Services: $2,286
Enrollment, Drop-out Rates and Diploma Recipients by Race/Ethnicity

Category	Total	White	Black	Asian	AIAN	Hisp.
Enrollment (%)	100.0	93.0	3.8	0.9	0.6	1.7
Drop-out Rate (%)	n/a	n/a	n/a	n/a	n/a	n/a
H.S. Diplomas (#)	114	109	3	2	0	0

Cass County

Dowagiac Union SD

206 Main St • Dowagiac, MI 49047-1743
(269) 782-4402 • http://www.remc11.k12.mi.us/dowagiac/
Grade Span: PK-12; **Agency Type:** 1
Schools: 9
5 Primary; 2 Middle; 2 High; 0 Other Level
8 Regular; 0 Special Education; 0 Vocational; 1 Alternative
0 Magnet; 0 Charter; 0 Title I Eligible; 0 School-wide Title I
Students: 2,895 (52.0% male; 48.0% female)
Individual Education Program: 351 (12.1%);
English Language Learner: n/a; Migrant: n/a
Eligible for Free Lunch Program: 952 (32.9%)
Eligible for Reduced-Price Lunch Program: 260 (9.0%)
Teachers: 156.7 (18.5 to 1)
Librarians/Media Specialists: 2.0 (1,447.5 to 1)
Guidance Counselors: 7.0 (413.6 to 1)
Current Spending: ($ per student per year):
Total: $6,695; Instruction: $4,160; Support Services: $2,289
Enrollment, Drop-out Rates and Diploma Recipients by Race/Ethnicity

Category	Total	White	Black	Asian	AIAN	Hisp.
Enrollment (%)	100.0	76.2	11.4	0.4	1.3	10.5
Drop-out Rate (%)	n/a	n/a	n/a	n/a	n/a	n/a
H.S. Diplomas (#)	140	115	15	2	0	8

Edwardsburg Public Schools

69410 Section St • Edwardsburg, MI 49112-9668
(269) 663-1053 • http://www.remc11.k12.mi.us/edward/
Grade Span: PK-12; **Agency Type:** 1
Schools: 6
2 Primary; 2 Middle; 1 High; 1 Other Level
5 Regular; 0 Special Education; 0 Vocational; 1 Alternative
0 Magnet; 0 Charter; 0 Title I Eligible; 0 School-wide Title I
Students: 2,236 (52.0% male; 48.0% female)
Individual Education Program: 205 (9.2%);
English Language Learner: n/a; Migrant: n/a
Eligible for Free Lunch Program: 353 (15.8%)
Eligible for Reduced-Price Lunch Program: 155 (6.9%)
Teachers: 115.2 (19.4 to 1)
Librarians/Media Specialists: 2.0 (1,118.0 to 1)
Guidance Counselors: 3.0 (745.3 to 1)
Current Spending: ($ per student per year):
Total: $5,532; Instruction: $2,891; Support Services: $2,402
Enrollment, Drop-out Rates and Diploma Recipients by Race/Ethnicity

Category	Total	White	Black	Asian	AIAN	Hisp.
Enrollment (%)	100.0	96.6	1.0	1.0	0.5	0.9
Drop-out Rate (%)	n/a	n/a	n/a	n/a	n/a	n/a
H.S. Diplomas (#)	114	111	1	0	0	2

Cheboygan County

Cheboygan Area Schools

504 Division St • Cheboygan, MI 49721-0100
Mailing Address: PO Box 100 • Cheboygan, MI 49721-0100
(231) 627-4436
Grade Span: PK-12; **Agency Type:** 1
Schools: 6
4 Primary; 1 Middle; 1 High; 0 Other Level
6 Regular; 0 Special Education; 0 Vocational; 0 Alternative
0 Magnet; 0 Charter; 0 Title I Eligible; 0 School-wide Title I
Students: 2,367 (52.0% male; 48.0% female)
Individual Education Program: 255 (10.8%);
English Language Learner: n/a; Migrant: n/a
Eligible for Free Lunch Program: 702 (29.7%)
Eligible for Reduced-Price Lunch Program: 210 (8.9%)
Teachers: 143.3 (16.5 to 1)
Librarians/Media Specialists: 1.0 (2,367.0 to 1)
Guidance Counselors: 8.0 (295.9 to 1)
Current Spending: ($ per student per year):
Total: $6,581; Instruction: $4,173; Support Services: $2,137
Enrollment, Drop-out Rates and Diploma Recipients by Race/Ethnicity

Category	Total	White	Black	Asian	AIAN	Hisp.
Enrollment (%)	100.0	93.4	1.1	0.8	4.5	0.3
Drop-out Rate (%)	n/a	n/a	n/a	n/a	n/a	n/a
H.S. Diplomas (#)	164	161	0	2	0	1

Chippewa County

Sault Sainte Marie Area Schools

876 Marquette Ave • Sault Sainte Marie, MI 49783-1800
(906) 635-6609
Grade Span: PK-12; **Agency Type:** 1
Schools: 8
5 Primary; 1 Middle; 2 High; 0 Other Level
7 Regular; 0 Special Education; 0 Vocational; 1 Alternative
8 Magnet; 0 Charter; 5 Title I Eligible; 5 School-wide Title I
Students: 3,250 (52.2% male; 47.8% female)
Individual Education Program: 400 (12.3%);
English Language Learner: 31 (1.0%); Migrant: n/a
Eligible for Free Lunch Program: 771 (23.7%)
Eligible for Reduced-Price Lunch Program: 308 (9.5%)
Teachers: 174.8 (18.6 to 1)
Librarians/Media Specialists: 3.0 (1,083.3 to 1)
Guidance Counselors: 5.0 (650.0 to 1)
Current Spending: ($ per student per year):
Total: $6,931; Instruction: $4,135; Support Services: $2,460
Enrollment, Drop-out Rates and Diploma Recipients by Race/Ethnicity

Category	Total	White	Black	Asian	AIAN	Hisp.
Enrollment (%)	100.0	64.9	0.8	0.6	33.2	0.5
Drop-out Rate (%)	n/a	n/a	n/a	n/a	n/a	n/a
H.S. Diplomas (#)	213	138	0	0	73	2

Clare County

Clare Public Schools

201 E State St • Clare, MI 48617-1317
(989) 386-9945 • http://www.clare.k12.mi.us/district/index.php
Grade Span: KG-12; **Agency Type:** 1
Schools: 4
1 Primary; 1 Middle; 1 High; 1 Other Level
3 Regular; 0 Special Education; 0 Vocational; 1 Alternative
0 Magnet; 0 Charter; 0 Title I Eligible; 0 School-wide Title I
Students: 1,670 (48.8% male; 51.2% female)
Individual Education Program: 191 (11.4%);
English Language Learner: 2 (0.1%); Migrant: n/a
Eligible for Free Lunch Program: 479 (28.7%)
Eligible for Reduced-Price Lunch Program: 163 (9.8%)
Teachers: 87.7 (19.0 to 1)
Librarians/Media Specialists: 3.0 (556.7 to 1)
Guidance Counselors: 3.5 (477.1 to 1)
Current Spending: ($ per student per year):
Total: $6,653; Instruction: $4,330; Support Services: $2,042
Enrollment, Drop-out Rates and Diploma Recipients by Race/Ethnicity

Category	Total	White	Black	Asian	AIAN	Hisp.
Enrollment (%)	100.0	97.8	0.5	0.1	0.5	1.1
Drop-out Rate (%)	n/a	n/a	n/a	n/a	n/a	n/a
H.S. Diplomas (#)	107	106	0	0	1	0

Farwell Area Schools

371 E Main St • Farwell, MI 48622-9463
(989) 588-9917 • http://farwell.edzone.net/
Grade Span: KG-12; **Agency Type:** 1
Schools: 3
1 Primary; 0 Middle; 1 High; 1 Other Level
3 Regular; 0 Special Education; 0 Vocational; 0 Alternative
3 Magnet; 0 Charter; 0 Title I Eligible; 0 School-wide Title I
Students: 1,693 (51.0% male; 49.0% female)
Individual Education Program: 202 (11.9%);
English Language Learner: 0 (0.0%); Migrant: n/a
Eligible for Free Lunch Program: 731 (43.2%)
Eligible for Reduced-Price Lunch Program: 220 (13.0%)
Teachers: 93.0 (18.2 to 1)
Librarians/Media Specialists: 3.0 (564.3 to 1)
Guidance Counselors: 5.0 (338.6 to 1)
Current Spending: ($ per student per year):
Total: $7,039; Instruction: $4,848; Support Services: $1,904
Enrollment, Drop-out Rates and Diploma Recipients by Race/Ethnicity

Category	Total	White	Black	Asian	AIAN	Hisp.
Enrollment (%)	100.0	97.0	0.5	0.1	1.4	0.9
Drop-out Rate (%)	n/a	n/a	n/a	n/a	n/a	n/a
H.S. Diplomas (#)	87	83	2	2	0	0

Harrison Community Schools

224 S Main St • Harrison, MI 48625-0529
Mailing Address: PO Box 529 • Harrison, MI 48625-0529
(989) 539-7871 • http://www.hcs.cgresd.net/
Grade Span: KG-12; **Agency Type:** 1
Schools: 6
3 Primary; 1 Middle; 1 High; 1 Other Level
5 Regular; 0 Special Education; 0 Vocational; 1 Alternative
0 Magnet; 0 Charter; 6 Title I Eligible; 6 School-wide Title I
Students: 2,153 (51.9% male; 48.1% female)
Individual Education Program: 405 (18.8%);
English Language Learner: 4 (0.2%); Migrant: n/a
Eligible for Free Lunch Program: 1,013 (47.1%)
Eligible for Reduced-Price Lunch Program: 192 (8.9%)
Teachers: 125.6 (17.1 to 1)
Librarians/Media Specialists: 1.0 (2,153.0 to 1)
Guidance Counselors: 2.0 (1,076.5 to 1)

Current Spending: ($ per student per year):
Total: $7,016; Instruction: $4,377; Support Services: $2,318
Enrollment, Drop-out Rates and Diploma Recipients by Race/Ethnicity

Category	Total	White	Black	Asian	AIAN	Hisp.
Enrollment (%)	100.0	96.7	0.5	0.6	1.3	1.0
Drop-out Rate (%)	n/a	n/a	n/a	n/a	n/a	n/a
H.S. Diplomas (#)	108	104	0	1	1	2

Clinton County

Dewitt Public Schools

2957 W Herbison Rd • Dewitt, MI 48820-0800
Mailing Address: PO Box 800 • Dewitt, MI 48820-0800
(517) 668-3000 • http://dewitt.k12.mi.us/
Grade Span: PK-12; **Agency Type:** 1
Schools: 6
3 Primary; 2 Middle; 1 High; 0 Other Level
6 Regular; 0 Special Education; 0 Vocational; 0 Alternative
0 Magnet; 0 Charter; 0 Title I Eligible; 0 School-wide Title I
Students: 2,747 (52.5% male; 47.5% female)
Individual Education Program: 251 (9.1%);
English Language Learner: n/a; Migrant: n/a
Eligible for Free Lunch Program: 137 (5.0%)
Eligible for Reduced-Price Lunch Program: 40 (1.5%)
Teachers: 143.7 (19.1 to 1)
Librarians/Media Specialists: 3.0 (915.7 to 1)
Guidance Counselors: 5.0 (549.4 to 1)
Current Spending: ($ per student per year):
Total: $6,328; Instruction: $4,067; Support Services: $2,073
Enrollment, Drop-out Rates and Diploma Recipients by Race/Ethnicity

Category	Total	White	Black	Asian	AIAN	Hisp.
Enrollment (%)	100.0	93.9	1.2	0.7	1.2	2.7
Drop-out Rate (%)	n/a	n/a	n/a	n/a	n/a	n/a
H.S. Diplomas (#)	194	186	1	1	0	6

Ovid-Elsie Area Schools

8989 Colony Rd • Elsie, MI 48831-9724
(989) 834-2271 • http://www.oe.k12.mi.us/
Grade Span: KG-12; **Agency Type:** 1
Schools: 6
2 Primary; 2 Middle; 1 High; 1 Other Level
5 Regular; 0 Special Education; 0 Vocational; 1 Alternative
0 Magnet; 0 Charter; 1 Title I Eligible; 1 School-wide Title I
Students: 1,780 (53.2% male; 46.8% female)
Individual Education Program: 265 (14.9%);
English Language Learner: n/a; Migrant: n/a
Eligible for Free Lunch Program: 315 (17.7%)
Eligible for Reduced-Price Lunch Program: 137 (7.7%)
Teachers: 34.5 (51.6 to 1)
Librarians/Media Specialists: 1.0 (1,780.0 to 1)
Guidance Counselors: 1.0 (1,780.0 to 1)
Current Spending: ($ per student per year):
Total: $6,757; Instruction: $4,220; Support Services: $2,231
Enrollment, Drop-out Rates and Diploma Recipients by Race/Ethnicity

Category	Total	White	Black	Asian	AIAN	Hisp.
Enrollment (%)	100.0	96.2	0.5	1.0	0.3	2.0
Drop-out Rate (%)	n/a	n/a	n/a	n/a	n/a	n/a
H.S. Diplomas (#)	125	122	0	1	0	2

Saint Johns Public Schools

501 W Sickels St • Saint Johns, MI 48879-0230
Mailing Address: PO Box 230 • Saint Johns, MI 48879-0230
(989) 227-4050 • http://stjohns.edzone.net/
Grade Span: KG-12; **Agency Type:** 1
Schools: 8
6 Primary; 1 Middle; 1 High; 0 Other Level
8 Regular; 0 Special Education; 0 Vocational; 0 Alternative
0 Magnet; 0 Charter; 0 Title I Eligible; 0 School-wide Title I
Students: 3,404 (52.6% male; 47.4% female)
Individual Education Program: 430 (12.6%);
English Language Learner: n/a; Migrant: n/a
Eligible for Free Lunch Program: 298 (8.8%)
Eligible for Reduced-Price Lunch Program: 178 (5.2%)
Teachers: 266.0 (12.8 to 1)
Librarians/Media Specialists: 3.0 (1,134.7 to 1)
Guidance Counselors: 10.0 (340.4 to 1)
Current Spending: ($ per student per year):
Total: $6,690; Instruction: $3,974; Support Services: $2,449
Enrollment, Drop-out Rates and Diploma Recipients by Race/Ethnicity

Category	Total	White	Black	Asian	AIAN	Hisp.
Enrollment (%)	100.0	94.1	0.9	1.0	0.6	3.4
Drop-out Rate (%)	n/a	n/a	n/a	n/a	n/a	n/a
H.S. Diplomas (#)	238	228	0	2	0	8

Crawford County

Crawford Ausable Schools

403 E Michigan Ave • Grayling, MI 49738-1600
(989) 344-3500 • http://www.casdk12.net/
Grade Span: PK-12; **Agency Type:** 1
Schools: 5
3 Primary; 1 Middle; 1 High; 0 Other Level
5 Regular; 0 Special Education; 0 Vocational; 0 Alternative
0 Magnet; 0 Charter; 5 Title I Eligible; 5 School-wide Title I
Students: 2,146 (53.1% male; 46.9% female)
Individual Education Program: 335 (15.6%);
English Language Learner: n/a; Migrant: n/a
Eligible for Free Lunch Program: 728 (33.9%)
Eligible for Reduced-Price Lunch Program: 216 (10.1%)
Teachers: 124.1 (17.3 to 1)
Librarians/Media Specialists: 3.0 (715.3 to 1)
Guidance Counselors: 4.0 (536.5 to 1)
Current Spending: ($ per student per year):
Total: $6,871; Instruction: $3,938; Support Services: $2,586
Enrollment, Drop-out Rates and Diploma Recipients by Race/Ethnicity

Category	Total	White	Black	Asian	AIAN	Hisp.
Enrollment (%)	100.0	97.7	0.9	0.7	0.2	0.4
Drop-out Rate (%)	n/a	n/a	n/a	n/a	n/a	n/a
H.S. Diplomas (#)	122	122	0	0	0	0

Delta County

Escanaba Area Public Schools

111 N 5th St • Escanaba, MI 49829-3944
(906) 786-5411 • http://www.escanabaschools.com/
Grade Span: KG-12; **Agency Type:** 1
Schools: 8
6 Primary; 1 Middle; 1 High; 0 Other Level
8 Regular; 0 Special Education; 0 Vocational; 0 Alternative
0 Magnet; 0 Charter; 0 Title I Eligible; 0 School-wide Title I
Students: 3,205 (52.3% male; 47.7% female)
Individual Education Program: 357 (11.1%);
English Language Learner: 1 (<0.1%); Migrant: n/a
Eligible for Free Lunch Program: 1,037 (32.4%)
Eligible for Reduced-Price Lunch Program: 306 (9.5%)
Teachers: 175.1 (18.3 to 1)
Librarians/Media Specialists: 1.7 (1,885.3 to 1)
Guidance Counselors: 3.0 (1,068.3 to 1)
Current Spending: ($ per student per year):
Total: $6,797; Instruction: $4,332; Support Services: $2,234
Enrollment, Drop-out Rates and Diploma Recipients by Race/Ethnicity

Category	Total	White	Black	Asian	AIAN	Hisp.
Enrollment (%)	100.0	95.7	0.0	0.3	3.4	0.1
Drop-out Rate (%)	n/a	n/a	n/a	n/a	n/a	n/a
H.S. Diplomas (#)	263	246	1	5	11	0

Gladstone Area Schools

400 S 10th St • Gladstone, MI 49837-1598
(906) 428-2417 • http://www.gladstoneschools.com/
Grade Span: KG-12; **Agency Type:** 1
Schools: 5
3 Primary; 1 Middle; 1 High; 0 Other Level
5 Regular; 0 Special Education; 0 Vocational; 0 Alternative
5 Magnet; 0 Charter; 1 Title I Eligible; 1 School-wide Title I
Students: 1,803 (51.1% male; 48.9% female)
Individual Education Program: 193 (10.7%);
English Language Learner: n/a; Migrant: n/a
Eligible for Free Lunch Program: 417 (23.1%)
Eligible for Reduced-Price Lunch Program: 169 (9.4%)
Teachers: 102.4 (17.6 to 1)
Librarians/Media Specialists: n/a
Guidance Counselors: 1.0 (1,803.0 to 1)
Current Spending: ($ per student per year):
Total: $6,666; Instruction: $4,306; Support Services: $2,083
Enrollment, Drop-out Rates and Diploma Recipients by Race/Ethnicity

Category	Total	White	Black	Asian	AIAN	Hisp.
Enrollment (%)	100.0	95.6	0.2	0.2	3.9	0.1
Drop-out Rate (%)	n/a	n/a	n/a	n/a	n/a	n/a
H.S. Diplomas (#)	149	132	1	3	13	0

Dickinson County

Breitung Township Schools

2000 W Pyle Dr • Kingsford, MI 49802-4250
(906) 779-2650 • http://www.kingsford.org/
Grade Span: KG-12; **Agency Type:** 1
Schools: 3
1 Primary; 1 Middle; 1 High; 0 Other Level
3 Regular; 0 Special Education; 0 Vocational; 0 Alternative

0 Magnet; 0 Charter; 0 Title I Eligible; 0 School-wide Title I
Students: 2,114 (52.2% male; 47.8% female)
Individual Education Program: 222 (10.5%);
English Language Learner: n/a; Migrant: n/a
Eligible for Free Lunch Program: 341 (16.1%)
Eligible for Reduced-Price Lunch Program: 190 (9.0%)
Teachers: 116.5 (18.1 to 1)
Librarians/Media Specialists: 2.0 (1,057.0 to 1)
Guidance Counselors: 3.0 (704.7 to 1)
Current Spending: ($ per student per year):
Total: $6,474; Instruction: $4,137; Support Services: $2,044
Enrollment, Drop-out Rates and Diploma Recipients by Race/Ethnicity

Category	Total	White	Black	Asian	AIAN	Hisp.
Enrollment (%)	100.0	99.0	0.1	0.3	0.2	0.1
Drop-out Rate (%)	n/a	n/a	n/a	n/a	n/a	n/a
H.S. Diplomas (#)	171	166	0	3	2	0

Eaton County

Charlotte Public Schools
378 State St • Charlotte, MI 48813-1797
(517) 541-5100 • http://scnc.cps.k12.mi.us/
Grade Span: PK-12; **Agency Type:** 1
Schools: 7
4 Primary; 1 Middle; 1 High; 1 Other Level
6 Regular; 0 Special Education; 0 Vocational; 1 Alternative
6 Magnet; 0 Charter; 0 Title I Eligible; 0 School-wide Title I
Students: 3,370 (51.1% male; 48.9% female)
Individual Education Program: 522 (15.5%);
English Language Learner: n/a; Migrant: n/a
Eligible for Free Lunch Program: 672 (19.9%)
Eligible for Reduced-Price Lunch Program: 223 (6.6%)
Teachers: 19.0 (177.4 to 1)
Librarians/Media Specialists: n/a
Guidance Counselors: n/a
Current Spending: ($ per student per year):
Total: $6,551; Instruction: $3,872; Support Services: $2,434
Enrollment, Drop-out Rates and Diploma Recipients by Race/Ethnicity

Category	Total	White	Black	Asian	AIAN	Hisp.
Enrollment (%)	100.0	95.5	1.1	0.4	0.0	2.9
Drop-out Rate (%)	n/a	n/a	n/a	n/a	n/a	n/a
H.S. Diplomas (#)	189	183	2	1	0	3

Eaton Rapids Public Schools
501 King St • Eaton Rapids, MI 48827-1251
(517) 663-8155 • http://scnc.erps.k12.mi.us/
Grade Span: KG-12; **Agency Type:** 1
Schools: 6
3 Primary; 2 Middle; 1 High; 0 Other Level
6 Regular; 0 Special Education; 0 Vocational; 0 Alternative
0 Magnet; 0 Charter; 0 Title I Eligible; 0 School-wide Title I
Students: 3,268 (51.7% male; 48.3% female)
Individual Education Program: 525 (16.1%);
English Language Learner: n/a; Migrant: n/a
Eligible for Free Lunch Program: 445 (13.6%)
Eligible for Reduced-Price Lunch Program: 257 (7.9%)
Teachers: 186.8 (17.5 to 1)
Librarians/Media Specialists: 4.0 (817.0 to 1)
Guidance Counselors: 6.0 (544.7 to 1)
Current Spending: ($ per student per year):
Total: $6,582; Instruction: $4,004; Support Services: $2,322
Enrollment, Drop-out Rates and Diploma Recipients by Race/Ethnicity

Category	Total	White	Black	Asian	AIAN	Hisp.
Enrollment (%)	100.0	95.0	1.2	0.7	0.4	2.7
Drop-out Rate (%)	n/a	n/a	n/a	n/a	n/a	n/a
H.S. Diplomas (#)	237	222	0	1	5	9

Grand Ledge Public Schools
220 Lamson St • Grand Ledge, MI 48837-1760
(517) 627-3241 • http://scnc.glps.k12.mi.us/
Grade Span: KG-12; **Agency Type:** 1
Schools: 10
6 Primary; 2 Middle; 2 High; 0 Other Level
9 Regular; 0 Special Education; 0 Vocational; 1 Alternative
0 Magnet; 0 Charter; 0 Title I Eligible; 0 School-wide Title I
Students: 5,501 (51.5% male; 48.5% female)
Individual Education Program: 849 (15.4%);
English Language Learner: n/a; Migrant: n/a
Eligible for Free Lunch Program: 449 (8.2%)
Eligible for Reduced-Price Lunch Program: 198 (3.6%)
Teachers: 305.4 (18.0 to 1)
Librarians/Media Specialists: 3.0 (1,833.7 to 1)
Guidance Counselors: 7.0 (785.9 to 1)
Current Spending: ($ per student per year):
Total: $6,737; Instruction: $4,069; Support Services: $2,379
Enrollment, Drop-out Rates and Diploma Recipients by Race/Ethnicity

Category	Total	White	Black	Asian	AIAN	Hisp.
Enrollment (%)	100.0	93.6	2.8	2.0	0.4	1.3
Drop-out Rate (%)	n/a	n/a	n/a	n/a	n/a	n/a
H.S. Diplomas (#)	386	365	10	3	1	7

Maple Valley Schools
11090 Nashville Hwy • Vermontville, MI 49096-9503
(517) 852-9699 • http://scnc.mvs.k12.mi.us/
Grade Span: PK-12; **Agency Type:** 1
Schools: 5
1 Primary; 1 Middle; 1 High; 2 Other Level
3 Regular; 0 Special Education; 0 Vocational; 2 Alternative
4 Magnet; 0 Charter; 2 Title I Eligible; 2 School-wide Title I
Students: 1,779 (50.3% male; 49.7% female)
Individual Education Program: 228 (12.8%);
English Language Learner: n/a; Migrant: n/a
Eligible for Free Lunch Program: 466 (26.2%)
Eligible for Reduced-Price Lunch Program: 111 (6.2%)
Teachers: 99.4 (17.9 to 1)
Librarians/Media Specialists: 1.0 (1,779.0 to 1)
Guidance Counselors: 2.0 (889.5 to 1)
Current Spending: ($ per student per year):
Total: $6,470; Instruction: $4,161; Support Services: $2,084
Enrollment, Drop-out Rates and Diploma Recipients by Race/Ethnicity

Category	Total	White	Black	Asian	AIAN	Hisp.
Enrollment (%)	100.0	96.7	0.6	0.7	0.4	1.6
Drop-out Rate (%)	n/a	n/a	n/a	n/a	n/a	n/a
H.S. Diplomas (#)	93	90	0	2	0	1

Emmet County

Public Schools of Petoskey
1130 Howard St • Petoskey, MI 49770-3026
Mailing Address: PO Box 247 • Petoskey, MI 49770-3026
(231) 348-2100 • http://www.petoskeyschools.org/
Grade Span: KG-12; **Agency Type:** 1
Schools: 7
5 Primary; 1 Middle; 1 High; 0 Other Level
7 Regular; 0 Special Education; 0 Vocational; 0 Alternative
7 Magnet; 0 Charter; 0 Title I Eligible; 0 School-wide Title I
Students: 2,999 (52.6% male; 47.4% female)
Individual Education Program: 279 (9.3%);
English Language Learner: 6 (0.2%); Migrant: n/a
Eligible for Free Lunch Program: 468 (15.6%)
Eligible for Reduced-Price Lunch Program: 227 (7.6%)
Teachers: 165.3 (18.1 to 1)
Librarians/Media Specialists: 2.0 (1,499.5 to 1)
Guidance Counselors: 5.0 (599.8 to 1)
Current Spending: ($ per student per year):
Total: $6,647; Instruction: $4,343; Support Services: $2,050
Enrollment, Drop-out Rates and Diploma Recipients by Race/Ethnicity

Category	Total	White	Black	Asian	AIAN	Hisp.
Enrollment (%)	100.0	93.7	0.8	0.7	4.0	0.8
Drop-out Rate (%)	n/a	n/a	n/a	n/a	n/a	n/a
H.S. Diplomas (#)	0	0	0	0	0	0

Genesee County

Beecher Community SD
1020 W Coldwater Rd • Flint, MI 48505-4895
(810) 591-9200 • http://www.beecherschools.org/
Grade Span: PK-12; **Agency Type:** 1
Schools: 7
5 Primary; 1 Middle; 1 High; 0 Other Level
7 Regular; 0 Special Education; 0 Vocational; 0 Alternative
0 Magnet; 0 Charter; 5 Title I Eligible; 5 School-wide Title I
Students: 2,009 (49.4% male; 50.6% female)
Individual Education Program: 201 (10.0%);
English Language Learner: n/a; Migrant: n/a
Eligible for Free Lunch Program: 1,375 (68.4%)
Eligible for Reduced-Price Lunch Program: 131 (6.5%)
Teachers: 79.0 (25.4 to 1)
Librarians/Media Specialists: n/a
Guidance Counselors: 1.0 (2,009.0 to 1)
Current Spending: ($ per student per year):
Total: $10,539; Instruction: $5,377; Support Services: $4,527
Enrollment, Drop-out Rates and Diploma Recipients by Race/Ethnicity

Category	Total	White	Black	Asian	AIAN	Hisp.
Enrollment (%)	100.0	9.7	88.5	0.0	0.1	1.7
Drop-out Rate (%)	n/a	n/a	n/a	n/a	n/a	n/a
H.S. Diplomas (#)	63	8	52	0	0	3

Bendle Public Schools

2283 E Scottwood Ave • Burton, MI 48529-1721
(810) 591-2501 • http://www.bendleschools.org/
Grade Span: PK-12; **Agency Type:** 1
Schools: 5
3 Primary; 1 Middle; 1 High; 0 Other Level
5 Regular; 0 Special Education; 0 Vocational; 0 Alternative
0 Magnet; 0 Charter; 3 Title I Eligible; 3 School-wide Title I
Students: 1,701 (52.7% male; 47.3% female)
Individual Education Program: 217 (12.8%);
English Language Learner: n/a; Migrant: n/a
Eligible for Free Lunch Program: 581 (34.2%)
Eligible for Reduced-Price Lunch Program: 83 (4.9%)
Teachers: 91.7 (18.5 to 1)
Librarians/Media Specialists: 1.0 (1,701.0 to 1)
Guidance Counselors: 4.0 (425.3 to 1)
Current Spending: ($ per student per year):
Total: $6,336; Instruction: $3,956; Support Services: $2,191
Enrollment, Drop-out Rates and Diploma Recipients by Race/Ethnicity

Category	Total	White	Black	Asian	AIAN	Hisp.
Enrollment (%)	100.0	92.9	1.9	0.4	1.6	3.2
Drop-out Rate (%)	n/a	n/a	n/a	n/a	n/a	n/a
H.S. Diplomas (#)	65	61	0	0	3	1

Carman-Ainsworth Community Schools

G-3475 W Court St • Flint, MI 48532-4700
(810) 591-3205 • http://www.carman.k12.mi.us/
Grade Span: PK-12; **Agency Type:** 1
Schools: 10
7 Primary; 2 Middle; 1 High; 0 Other Level
10 Regular; 0 Special Education; 0 Vocational; 0 Alternative
0 Magnet; 0 Charter; 5 Title I Eligible; 5 School-wide Title I
Students: 5,273 (51.2% male; 48.8% female)
Individual Education Program: 711 (13.5%);
English Language Learner: 16 (0.3%); Migrant: n/a
Eligible for Free Lunch Program: 2,023 (38.4%)
Eligible for Reduced-Price Lunch Program: 401 (7.6%)
Teachers: 309.8 (17.0 to 1)
Librarians/Media Specialists: 6.0 (878.8 to 1)
Guidance Counselors: 12.3 (428.7 to 1)
Current Spending: ($ per student per year):
Total: $8,447; Instruction: $4,918; Support Services: $3,223
Enrollment, Drop-out Rates and Diploma Recipients by Race/Ethnicity

Category	Total	White	Black	Asian	AIAN	Hisp.
Enrollment (%)	100.0	64.7	22.6	2.2	7.5	2.4
Drop-out Rate (%)	n/a	n/a	n/a	n/a	n/a	n/a
H.S. Diplomas (#)	272	189	55	7	18	3

Clio Area SD

430 N Mill St • Clio, MI 48420-1282
(810) 591-0502 • http://www.hs.clio.k12.mi.us/
Grade Span: PK-12; **Agency Type:** 1
Schools: 5
3 Primary; 1 Middle; 1 High; 0 Other Level
5 Regular; 0 Special Education; 0 Vocational; 0 Alternative
0 Magnet; 0 Charter; 0 Title I Eligible; 0 School-wide Title I
Students: 3,649 (53.6% male; 46.4% female)
Individual Education Program: 392 (10.7%);
English Language Learner: 3 (0.1%); Migrant: n/a
Eligible for Free Lunch Program: 635 (17.4%)
Eligible for Reduced-Price Lunch Program: 200 (5.5%)
Teachers: 183.0 (19.9 to 1)
Librarians/Media Specialists: 1.0 (3,649.0 to 1)
Guidance Counselors: 5.0 (729.8 to 1)
Current Spending: ($ per student per year):
Total: $6,357; Instruction: $3,994; Support Services: $2,131
Enrollment, Drop-out Rates and Diploma Recipients by Race/Ethnicity

Category	Total	White	Black	Asian	AIAN	Hisp.
Enrollment (%)	100.0	95.8	1.3	0.6	0.5	1.7
Drop-out Rate (%)	n/a	n/a	n/a	n/a	n/a	n/a
H.S. Diplomas (#)	185	180	0	3	0	2

Davison Community Schools

1490 N Oak Rd • Davison, MI 48423-1865
Mailing Address: PO Box 319 • Davison, MI 48423-1865
(810) 591-0801 • http://www.davison.k12.mi.us
Grade Span: PK-12; **Agency Type:** 1
Schools: 9
5 Primary; 2 Middle; 1 High; 1 Other Level
8 Regular; 0 Special Education; 0 Vocational; 1 Alternative
0 Magnet; 0 Charter; 0 Title I Eligible; 0 School-wide Title I
Students: 5,317 (50.5% male; 49.5% female)
Individual Education Program: 578 (10.9%);
English Language Learner: n/a; Migrant: n/a
Eligible for Free Lunch Program: 835 (15.7%)
Eligible for Reduced-Price Lunch Program: 287 (5.4%)
Teachers: 266.0 (20.0 to 1)
Librarians/Media Specialists: 3.0 (1,772.3 to 1)
Guidance Counselors: 10.0 (531.7 to 1)
Current Spending: ($ per student per year):
Total: $6,350; Instruction: $3,923; Support Services: $2,220
Enrollment, Drop-out Rates and Diploma Recipients by Race/Ethnicity

Category	Total	White	Black	Asian	AIAN	Hisp.
Enrollment (%)	100.0	91.4	1.9	1.1	3.1	2.1
Drop-out Rate (%)	n/a	n/a	n/a	n/a	n/a	n/a
H.S. Diplomas (#)	296	274	5	2	13	2

Fenton Area Public Schools

3100 Owen Rd • Fenton, MI 48430-1754
(810) 591-4700 • http://www.fenton.k12.mi.us/
Grade Span: PK-12; **Agency Type:** 1
Schools: 7
3 Primary; 2 Middle; 2 High; 0 Other Level
6 Regular; 0 Special Education; 0 Vocational; 1 Alternative
0 Magnet; 0 Charter; 0 Title I Eligible; 0 School-wide Title I
Students: 3,721 (50.8% male; 49.2% female)
Individual Education Program: 466 (12.5%);
English Language Learner: 2 (0.1%); Migrant: n/a
Eligible for Free Lunch Program: 320 (8.6%)
Eligible for Reduced-Price Lunch Program: 104 (2.8%)
Teachers: 194.2 (19.2 to 1)
Librarians/Media Specialists: 2.0 (1,860.5 to 1)
Guidance Counselors: 5.0 (744.2 to 1)
Current Spending: ($ per student per year):
Total: $6,978; Instruction: $3,885; Support Services: $2,807
Enrollment, Drop-out Rates and Diploma Recipients by Race/Ethnicity

Category	Total	White	Black	Asian	AIAN	Hisp.
Enrollment (%)	100.0	97.5	0.5	1.2	0.3	0.5
Drop-out Rate (%)	n/a	n/a	n/a	n/a	n/a	n/a
H.S. Diplomas (#)	229	229	0	0	0	0

Flint City SD

923 E Kearsley St • Flint, MI 48503-6106
(810) 760-1249 • http://www.flintschools.org/
Grade Span: PK-12; **Agency Type:** 1
Schools: 43
29 Primary; 4 Middle; 4 High; 5 Other Level
40 Regular; 0 Special Education; 1 Vocational; 1 Alternative
0 Magnet; 0 Charter; 28 Title I Eligible; 28 School-wide Title I
Students: 21,443 (50.2% male; 49.8% female)
Individual Education Program: 2,678 (12.5%);
English Language Learner: 832 (3.9%); Migrant: n/a
Eligible for Free Lunch Program: 13,184 (61.5%)
Eligible for Reduced-Price Lunch Program: 717 (3.3%)
Teachers: 1,321.9 (16.2 to 1)
Librarians/Media Specialists: 9.0 (2,382.6 to 1)
Guidance Counselors: 32.0 (670.1 to 1)
Current Spending: ($ per student per year):
Total: $8,879; Instruction: $4,796; Support Services: $3,737
Enrollment, Drop-out Rates and Diploma Recipients by Race/Ethnicity

Category	Total	White	Black	Asian	AIAN	Hisp.
Enrollment (%)	100.0	19.2	77.2	0.6	0.3	2.5
Drop-out Rate (%)	n/a	n/a	n/a	n/a	n/a	n/a
H.S. Diplomas (#)	714	152	538	1	2	21

Flushing Community Schools

522 N Mckinley Rd • Flushing, MI 48433-1379
(810) 591-0600 • http://www.flushing.k12.mi.us/
Grade Span: PK-12; **Agency Type:** 1
Schools: 6
4 Primary; 1 Middle; 1 High; 0 Other Level
6 Regular; 0 Special Education; 0 Vocational; 0 Alternative
0 Magnet; 0 Charter; 0 Title I Eligible; 0 School-wide Title I
Students: 4,777 (50.0% male; 50.0% female)
Individual Education Program: 489 (10.2%);
English Language Learner: n/a; Migrant: n/a
Eligible for Free Lunch Program: 285 (6.0%)
Eligible for Reduced-Price Lunch Program: 81 (1.7%)
Teachers: 211.3 (22.6 to 1)
Librarians/Media Specialists: 3.0 (1,592.3 to 1)
Guidance Counselors: 5.0 (955.4 to 1)
Current Spending: ($ per student per year):
Total: $5,928; Instruction: $3,841; Support Services: $1,929
Enrollment, Drop-out Rates and Diploma Recipients by Race/Ethnicity

Category	Total	White	Black	Asian	AIAN	Hisp.
Enrollment (%)	100.0	93.7	2.6	1.8	0.3	1.4
Drop-out Rate (%)	n/a	n/a	n/a	n/a	n/a	n/a
H.S. Diplomas (#)	315	301	5	5	0	4

Goodrich Area Schools

8029 S Gale Rd • Goodrich, MI 48438-9203
(810) 591-2201 • http://www.goodrich.k12.mi.us/
Grade Span: KG-12; **Agency Type:** 1
Schools: 4
2 Primary; 1 Middle; 1 High; 0 Other Level
4 Regular; 0 Special Education; 0 Vocational; 0 Alternative
0 Magnet; 0 Charter; 1 Title I Eligible; 1 School-wide Title I
Students: 2,022 (52.0% male; 48.0% female)
Individual Education Program: 192 (9.5%);
English Language Learner: n/a; Migrant: n/a
Eligible for Free Lunch Program: 48 (2.4%)
Eligible for Reduced-Price Lunch Program: 26 (1.3%)
Teachers: 104.0 (19.4 to 1)
Librarians/Media Specialists: 1.0 (2,022.0 to 1)
Guidance Counselors: 3.0 (674.0 to 1)
Current Spending: ($ per student per year):
Total: $6,328; Instruction: $3,986; Support Services: $2,041
Enrollment, Drop-out Rates and Diploma Recipients by Race/Ethnicity

Category	Total	White	Black	Asian	AIAN	Hisp.
Enrollment (%)	100.0	96.9	0.7	1.1	0.5	0.7
Drop-out Rate (%)	n/a	n/a	n/a	n/a	n/a	n/a
H.S. Diplomas (#)	129	128	0	0	0	1

Grand Blanc Community Schools

G-11920 S Saginaw St • Grand Blanc, MI 48439-1402
(810) 591-6000 • http://www.grand-blanc.k12.mi.us/
Grade Span: KG-12; **Agency Type:** 1
Schools: 11
8 Primary; 1 Middle; 1 High; 0 Other Level
10 Regular; 0 Special Education; 0 Vocational; 0 Alternative
0 Magnet; 0 Charter; 0 Title I Eligible; 0 School-wide Title I
Students: 6,814 (50.7% male; 49.3% female)
Individual Education Program: 671 (9.8%);
English Language Learner: 51 (0.7%); Migrant: n/a
Eligible for Free Lunch Program: 545 (8.0%)
Eligible for Reduced-Price Lunch Program: 221 (3.2%)
Teachers: 383.0 (17.8 to 1)
Librarians/Media Specialists: 12.0 (567.8 to 1)
Guidance Counselors: 6.0 (1,135.7 to 1)
Current Spending: ($ per student per year):
Total: $6,709; Instruction: $4,091; Support Services: $2,387
Enrollment, Drop-out Rates and Diploma Recipients by Race/Ethnicity

Category	Total	White	Black	Asian	AIAN	Hisp.
Enrollment (%)	100.0	84.6	7.5	3.8	0.1	1.7
Drop-out Rate (%)	n/a	n/a	n/a	n/a	n/a	n/a
H.S. Diplomas (#)	416	351	39	19	1	6

Kearsley Community Schools

4396 Underhill Dr • Flint, MI 48506-1534
(810) 591-8000 • http://www.kearsley.k12.mi.us/
Grade Span: KG-12; **Agency Type:** 1
Schools: 7
4 Primary; 1 Middle; 1 High; 1 Other Level
6 Regular; 0 Special Education; 0 Vocational; 1 Alternative
0 Magnet; 0 Charter; 0 Title I Eligible; 0 School-wide Title I
Students: 3,940 (51.8% male; 48.2% female)
Individual Education Program: 378 (9.6%);
English Language Learner: n/a; Migrant: n/a
Eligible for Free Lunch Program: 760 (19.3%)
Eligible for Reduced-Price Lunch Program: 157 (4.0%)
Teachers: 188.5 (20.9 to 1)
Librarians/Media Specialists: 3.0 (1,313.3 to 1)
Guidance Counselors: 11.0 (358.2 to 1)
Current Spending: ($ per student per year):
Total: $6,503; Instruction: $3,719; Support Services: $2,572
Enrollment, Drop-out Rates and Diploma Recipients by Race/Ethnicity

Category	Total	White	Black	Asian	AIAN	Hisp.
Enrollment (%)	100.0	92.1	2.5	0.7	0.9	2.5
Drop-out Rate (%)	n/a	n/a	n/a	n/a	n/a	n/a
H.S. Diplomas (#)	247	233	3	5	0	6

Lakeville Community Schools

11107 Washburn Rd • Otisville, MI 48463-9731
(810) 591-3980 • http://www.lakeville.k12.mi.us/
Grade Span: KG-12; **Agency Type:** 1
Schools: 8
4 Primary; 1 Middle; 1 High; 2 Other Level
6 Regular; 0 Special Education; 0 Vocational; 2 Alternative
0 Magnet; 0 Charter; 0 Title I Eligible; 0 School-wide Title I
Students: 2,155 (51.6% male; 48.4% female)
Individual Education Program: 219 (10.2%);
English Language Learner: n/a; Migrant: n/a
Eligible for Free Lunch Program: 421 (19.5%)
Eligible for Reduced-Price Lunch Program: 166 (7.7%)
Teachers: 115.1 (18.7 to 1)
Librarians/Media Specialists: 1.0 (2,155.0 to 1)
Guidance Counselors: 3.0 (718.3 to 1)
Current Spending: ($ per student per year):
Total: $6,650; Instruction: $3,895; Support Services: $2,488
Enrollment, Drop-out Rates and Diploma Recipients by Race/Ethnicity

Category	Total	White	Black	Asian	AIAN	Hisp.
Enrollment (%)	100.0	97.2	0.8	0.6	0.1	1.3
Drop-out Rate (%)	n/a	n/a	n/a	n/a	n/a	n/a
H.S. Diplomas (#)	141	138	0	0	1	2

Linden Community Schools

7205 W Silver Lake Rd • Linden, MI 48451-8805
(810) 591-7821 • http://www.lindenschools.org/
Grade Span: PK-12; **Agency Type:** 1
Schools: 5
3 Primary; 1 Middle; 1 High; 0 Other Level
5 Regular; 0 Special Education; 0 Vocational; 0 Alternative
0 Magnet; 0 Charter; 0 Title I Eligible; 0 School-wide Title I
Students: 2,934 (50.7% male; 49.3% female)
Individual Education Program: 356 (12.1%);
English Language Learner: 1 (<0.1%); Migrant: n/a
Eligible for Free Lunch Program: 199 (6.8%)
Eligible for Reduced-Price Lunch Program: 83 (2.8%)
Teachers: 126.1 (23.3 to 1)
Librarians/Media Specialists: 2.0 (1,467.0 to 1)
Guidance Counselors: 3.0 (978.0 to 1)
Current Spending: ($ per student per year):
Total: $6,453; Instruction: $4,341; Support Services: $1,864
Enrollment, Drop-out Rates and Diploma Recipients by Race/Ethnicity

Category	Total	White	Black	Asian	AIAN	Hisp.
Enrollment (%)	100.0	98.5	0.3	0.2	0.3	0.7
Drop-out Rate (%)	n/a	n/a	n/a	n/a	n/a	n/a
H.S. Diplomas (#)	151	143	0	4	1	3

Montrose Community Schools

300 Nanita Dr • Montrose, MI 48457-0829
Mailing Address: PO Box 3129 • Montrose, MI 48457-0829
(810) 591-7267 • http://www.montrose.k12.mi.us/Default.asp?Res=746
Grade Span: PK-12; **Agency Type:** 1
Schools: 3
1 Primary; 1 Middle; 1 High; 0 Other Level
3 Regular; 0 Special Education; 0 Vocational; 0 Alternative
0 Magnet; 0 Charter; 0 Title I Eligible; 0 School-wide Title I
Students: 1,710 (53.0% male; 47.0% female)
Individual Education Program: 218 (12.7%);
English Language Learner: 0 (0.0%); Migrant: n/a
Eligible for Free Lunch Program: 448 (26.2%)
Eligible for Reduced-Price Lunch Program: 151 (8.8%)
Teachers: 63.0 (27.1 to 1)
Librarians/Media Specialists: 1.0 (1,710.0 to 1)
Guidance Counselors: 3.0 (570.0 to 1)
Current Spending: ($ per student per year):
Total: $7,133; Instruction: $4,485; Support Services: $2,342
Enrollment, Drop-out Rates and Diploma Recipients by Race/Ethnicity

Category	Total	White	Black	Asian	AIAN	Hisp.
Enrollment (%)	100.0	91.7	1.6	0.4	2.5	3.8
Drop-out Rate (%)	n/a	n/a	n/a	n/a	n/a	n/a
H.S. Diplomas (#)	98	93	1	0	0	4

Mount Morris Consolidated Schools

12356 Walter St • Mount Morris, MI 48458-1749
(810) 591-8760 • http://www.mtmorrisschools.org/
Grade Span: KG-12; **Agency Type:** 1
Schools: 7
3 Primary; 2 Middle; 1 High; 1 Other Level
6 Regular; 0 Special Education; 0 Vocational; 1 Alternative
1 Magnet; 0 Charter; 4 Title I Eligible; 4 School-wide Title I
Students: 3,480 (51.6% male; 48.4% female)
Individual Education Program: 532 (15.3%);
English Language Learner: 3 (0.1%); Migrant: n/a
Eligible for Free Lunch Program: 1,096 (31.5%)
Eligible for Reduced-Price Lunch Program: 275 (7.9%)
Teachers: 188.6 (18.5 to 1)
Librarians/Media Specialists: 3.0 (1,160.0 to 1)
Guidance Counselors: 5.0 (696.0 to 1)
Current Spending: ($ per student per year):
Total: $7,030; Instruction: $4,390; Support Services: $2,414
Enrollment, Drop-out Rates and Diploma Recipients by Race/Ethnicity

Category	Total	White	Black	Asian	AIAN	Hisp.
Enrollment (%)	100.0	77.9	12.2	0.6	6.8	2.6
Drop-out Rate (%)	n/a	n/a	n/a	n/a	n/a	n/a
H.S. Diplomas (#)	164	124	3	2	35	0

Swartz Creek Community Schools

8354 Cappy Ln • Swartz Creek, MI 48473-1242
(810) 591-2300 • http://www.swartzcreek.org/
Grade Span: PK-12; **Agency Type:** 1
Schools: 8
5 Primary; 1 Middle; 2 High; 0 Other Level
7 Regular; 0 Special Education; 0 Vocational; 1 Alternative
0 Magnet; 0 Charter; 0 Title I Eligible; 0 School-wide Title I
Students: 4,167 (52.0% male; 48.0% female)
Individual Education Program: 542 (13.0%);
English Language Learner: n/a; Migrant: n/a
Eligible for Free Lunch Program: 507 (12.2%)
Eligible for Reduced-Price Lunch Program: 137 (3.3%)
Teachers: 221.7 (18.8 to 1)
Librarians/Media Specialists: 2.0 (2,083.5 to 1)
Guidance Counselors: 7.0 (595.3 to 1)
Current Spending: ($ per student per year):
Total: $6,595; Instruction: $4,171; Support Services: $2,227
Enrollment, Drop-out Rates and Diploma Recipients by Race/Ethnicity

Category	Total	White	Black	Asian	AIAN	Hisp.
Enrollment (%)	100.0	91.8	2.3	0.8	2.8	2.3
Drop-out Rate (%)	n/a	n/a	n/a	n/a	n/a	n/a
H.S. Diplomas (#)	268	242	5	7	10	4

Gladwin County

Beaverton Rural Schools

468 S Ross St • Beaverton, MI 48612-0529
Mailing Address: PO Box 529 • Beaverton, MI 48612-0529
(989) 246-3000 • http://beaverton.k12.mi.us
Grade Span: KG-12; **Agency Type:** 1
Schools: 4
2 Primary; 1 Middle; 1 High; 0 Other Level
4 Regular; 0 Special Education; 0 Vocational; 0 Alternative
4 Magnet; 0 Charter; 1 Title I Eligible; 1 School-wide Title I
Students: 1,755 (52.1% male; 47.9% female)
Individual Education Program: 268 (15.3%);
English Language Learner: 0 (0.0%); Migrant: n/a
Eligible for Free Lunch Program: 513 (29.2%)
Eligible for Reduced-Price Lunch Program: 167 (9.5%)
Teachers: 105.0 (16.7 to 1)
Librarians/Media Specialists: 3.0 (585.0 to 1)
Guidance Counselors: 3.0 (585.0 to 1)
Current Spending: ($ per student per year):
Total: $6,748; Instruction: $4,166; Support Services: $2,306
Enrollment, Drop-out Rates and Diploma Recipients by Race/Ethnicity

Category	Total	White	Black	Asian	AIAN	Hisp.
Enrollment (%)	100.0	96.2	1.0	0.3	1.5	1.1
Drop-out Rate (%)	n/a	n/a	n/a	n/a	n/a	n/a
H.S. Diplomas (#)	118	115	0	0	1	2

Gladwin Community Schools

1206 N Spring St • Gladwin, MI 48624-1041
(989) 426-9255 • http://www.gladwin.k12.mi.us/
Grade Span: PK-12; **Agency Type:** 1
Schools: 5
1 Primary; 1 Middle; 1 High; 2 Other Level
4 Regular; 0 Special Education; 0 Vocational; 1 Alternative
0 Magnet; 0 Charter; 2 Title I Eligible; 2 School-wide Title I
Students: 2,106 (51.6% male; 48.4% female)
Individual Education Program: 339 (16.1%);
English Language Learner: n/a; Migrant: n/a
Eligible for Free Lunch Program: 583 (27.7%)
Eligible for Reduced-Price Lunch Program: 196 (9.3%)
Teachers: 118.8 (17.7 to 1)
Librarians/Media Specialists: 0.5 (4,212.0 to 1)
Guidance Counselors: 1.7 (1,238.8 to 1)
Current Spending: ($ per student per year):
Total: $6,583; Instruction: $4,205; Support Services: $2,153
Enrollment, Drop-out Rates and Diploma Recipients by Race/Ethnicity

Category	Total	White	Black	Asian	AIAN	Hisp.
Enrollment (%)	100.0	97.7	0.6	0.4	0.2	0.7
Drop-out Rate (%)	n/a	n/a	n/a	n/a	n/a	n/a
H.S. Diplomas (#)	141	138	1	1	0	1

Grand Traverse County

Traverse City Area Public Schools

412 Webster St • Traverse City, MI 49685-0032
Mailing Address: PO Box 32 • Traverse City, MI 49685-0032
(231) 933-1727 • http://www.tcaps.net/
Grade Span: PK-12; **Agency Type:** 1
Schools: 22
17 Primary; 2 Middle; 3 High; 0 Other Level
21 Regular; 0 Special Education; 0 Vocational; 1 Alternative
0 Magnet; 0 Charter; 1 Title I Eligible; 1 School-wide Title I
Students: 11,339 (51.1% male; 48.9% female)
Individual Education Program: 1,370 (12.1%);
English Language Learner: 116 (1.0%); Migrant: n/a
Eligible for Free Lunch Program: 1,876 (16.5%)
Eligible for Reduced-Price Lunch Program: 869 (7.7%)
Teachers: 610.5 (18.6 to 1)
Librarians/Media Specialists: 5.0 (2,267.8 to 1)
Guidance Counselors: 14.2 (798.5 to 1)
Current Spending: ($ per student per year):
Total: $6,627; Instruction: $3,857; Support Services: $2,404
Enrollment, Drop-out Rates and Diploma Recipients by Race/Ethnicity

Category	Total	White	Black	Asian	AIAN	Hisp.
Enrollment (%)	100.0	94.6	0.5	1.0	1.6	2.2
Drop-out Rate (%)	n/a	n/a	n/a	n/a	n/a	n/a
H.S. Diplomas (#)	760	732	0	11	9	8

Gratiot County

Alma Public Schools

1500 N Pine Ave • Alma, MI 48801-1275
(989) 463-3111 • http://www.esu11.k12.ne.us/alma/home.html
Grade Span: PK-12; **Agency Type:** 1
Schools: 5
3 Primary; 1 Middle; 1 High; 0 Other Level
5 Regular; 0 Special Education; 0 Vocational; 0 Alternative
0 Magnet; 0 Charter; 2 Title I Eligible; 2 School-wide Title I
Students: 2,601 (51.5% male; 48.5% female)
Individual Education Program: 381 (14.6%);
English Language Learner: n/a; Migrant: n/a
Eligible for Free Lunch Program: 747 (28.7%)
Eligible for Reduced-Price Lunch Program: 263 (10.1%)
Teachers: 147.0 (17.7 to 1)
Librarians/Media Specialists: 2.0 (1,300.5 to 1)
Guidance Counselors: 5.0 (520.2 to 1)
Current Spending: ($ per student per year):
Total: $6,994; Instruction: $4,146; Support Services: $2,585
Enrollment, Drop-out Rates and Diploma Recipients by Race/Ethnicity

Category	Total	White	Black	Asian	AIAN	Hisp.
Enrollment (%)	100.0	94.6	0.3	0.4	0.6	4.0
Drop-out Rate (%)	n/a	n/a	n/a	n/a	n/a	n/a
H.S. Diplomas (#)	147	131	2	1	1	12

Hillsdale County

Hillsdale Community Schools

30 S Norwood Ave • Hillsdale, MI 49242-1854
(517) 437-4401 •
http://hillsdale-isd.org/Directory/Hillsdale%20Schools.htm
Grade Span: PK-12; **Agency Type:** 1
Schools: 5
3 Primary; 1 Middle; 1 High; 0 Other Level
5 Regular; 0 Special Education; 0 Vocational; 0 Alternative
0 Magnet; 0 Charter; 3 Title I Eligible; 3 School-wide Title I
Students: 1,958 (51.9% male; 48.1% female)
Individual Education Program: 200 (10.2%);
English Language Learner: n/a; Migrant: n/a
Eligible for Free Lunch Program: 584 (29.8%)
Eligible for Reduced-Price Lunch Program: 234 (12.0%)
Teachers: 109.8 (17.8 to 1)
Librarians/Media Specialists: 1.0 (1,958.0 to 1)
Guidance Counselors: 4.0 (489.5 to 1)
Current Spending: ($ per student per year):
Total: $6,433; Instruction: $4,268; Support Services: $1,846
Enrollment, Drop-out Rates and Diploma Recipients by Race/Ethnicity

Category	Total	White	Black	Asian	AIAN	Hisp.
Enrollment (%)	100.0	97.5	0.7	0.7	0.3	0.9
Drop-out Rate (%)	n/a	n/a	n/a	n/a	n/a	n/a
H.S. Diplomas (#)	117	111	1	3	0	2

Houghton County

Public Schools of Calumet

57070 Mine St • Calumet, MI 49913-1715
(906) 337-0311 • http://www.clk.k12.mi.us/
Grade Span: KG-12; **Agency Type:** 1
Schools: 4
2 Primary; 1 Middle; 1 High; 0 Other Level
4 Regular; 0 Special Education; 0 Vocational; 0 Alternative
0 Magnet; 0 Charter; 0 Title I Eligible; 0 School-wide Title I
Students: 1,614 (52.3% male; 47.7% female)
Individual Education Program: 137 (8.5%);
English Language Learner: n/a; Migrant: n/a
Eligible for Free Lunch Program: 605 (37.5%)
Eligible for Reduced-Price Lunch Program: 226 (14.0%)

Teachers: 95.9 (16.8 to 1)
Librarians/Media Specialists: 1.0 (1,614.0 to 1)
Guidance Counselors: 2.0 (807.0 to 1)
Current Spending: ($ per student per year):
Total: $6,386; Instruction: $3,941; Support Services: $2,120
Enrollment, Drop-out Rates and Diploma Recipients by Race/Ethnicity

Category	Total	White	Black	Asian	AIAN	Hisp.
Enrollment (%)	100.0	98.6	0.4	0.3	0.4	0.3
Drop-out Rate (%)	n/a	n/a	n/a	n/a	n/a	n/a
H.S. Diplomas (#)	108	107	0	0	0	1

Ingham County

East Lansing SD
841 Timberlane, Ste A • East Lansing, MI 48823-2750
(517) 333-7424 • http://scnc.elps.k12.mi.us/
Grade Span: KG-12; **Agency Type:** 1
Schools: 9
7 Primary; 1 Middle; 1 High; 0 Other Level
9 Regular; 0 Special Education; 0 Vocational; 0 Alternative
0 Magnet; 0 Charter; 0 Title I Eligible; 0 School-wide Title I
Students: 3,632 (50.8% male; 49.2% female)
Individual Education Program: 359 (9.9%);
English Language Learner: 572 (15.7%); Migrant: n/a
Eligible for Free Lunch Program: 534 (14.7%)
Eligible for Reduced-Price Lunch Program: 154 (4.2%)
Teachers: 220.7 (16.5 to 1)
Librarians/Media Specialists: 1.6 (2,270.0 to 1)
Guidance Counselors: 6.1 (595.4 to 1)
Current Spending: ($ per student per year):
Total: $8,982; Instruction: $5,114; Support Services: $3,643
Enrollment, Drop-out Rates and Diploma Recipients by Race/Ethnicity

Category	Total	White	Black	Asian	AIAN	Hisp.
Enrollment (%)	100.0	66.1	15.7	12.5	0.5	5.3
Drop-out Rate (%)	n/a	n/a	n/a	n/a	n/a	n/a
H.S. Diplomas (#)	273	190	39	24	1	19

Haslett Public Schools
5593 Franklin St • Haslett, MI 48840-8434
(517) 339-8242 • http://scnc.haslett.k12.mi.us/
Grade Span: PK-12; **Agency Type:** 1
Schools: 6
3 Primary; 1 Middle; 2 High; 0 Other Level
5 Regular; 0 Special Education; 0 Vocational; 1 Alternative
0 Magnet; 0 Charter; 3 Title I Eligible; 3 School-wide Title I
Students: 2,968 (51.9% male; 48.1% female)
Individual Education Program: 426 (14.4%);
English Language Learner: 16 (0.5%); Migrant: n/a
Eligible for Free Lunch Program: 156 (5.3%)
Eligible for Reduced-Price Lunch Program: 67 (2.3%)
Teachers: 176.9 (16.8 to 1)
Librarians/Media Specialists: 2.0 (1,484.0 to 1)
Guidance Counselors: 6.0 (494.7 to 1)
Current Spending: ($ per student per year):
Total: $7,169; Instruction: $4,215; Support Services: $2,702
Enrollment, Drop-out Rates and Diploma Recipients by Race/Ethnicity

Category	Total	White	Black	Asian	AIAN	Hisp.
Enrollment (%)	100.0	88.3	4.4	3.7	0.4	3.2
Drop-out Rate (%)	n/a	n/a	n/a	n/a	n/a	n/a
H.S. Diplomas (#)	216	198	8	3	2	5

Holt Public Schools
4610 Spahr Ave • Holt, MI 48842-1197
(517) 694-5715 • http://www.holt.k12.mi.us/
Grade Span: PK-12; **Agency Type:** 1
Schools: 11
6 Primary; 2 Middle; 2 High; 1 Other Level
10 Regular; 0 Special Education; 0 Vocational; 1 Alternative
0 Magnet; 0 Charter; 0 Title I Eligible; 0 School-wide Title I
Students: 5,570 (51.4% male; 48.6% female)
Individual Education Program: 927 (16.6%);
English Language Learner: n/a; Migrant: n/a
Eligible for Free Lunch Program: 604 (10.8%)
Eligible for Reduced-Price Lunch Program: 258 (4.6%)
Teachers: 124.4 (44.8 to 1)
Librarians/Media Specialists: 3.0 (1,856.7 to 1)
Guidance Counselors: 2.8 (1,989.3 to 1)
Current Spending: ($ per student per year):
Total: $7,171; Instruction: $4,530; Support Services: $2,477
Enrollment, Drop-out Rates and Diploma Recipients by Race/Ethnicity

Category	Total	White	Black	Asian	AIAN	Hisp.
Enrollment (%)	100.0	85.2	5.4	1.9	1.3	6.1
Drop-out Rate (%)	n/a	n/a	n/a	n/a	n/a	n/a
H.S. Diplomas (#)	301	267	4	9	7	14

Lansing Public SD
519 W Kalamazoo St • Lansing, MI 48933-2080
(517) 325-6007 • http://scnc.lsd.k12.mi.us/
Grade Span: PK-12; **Agency Type:** 1
Schools: 43
30 Primary; 6 Middle; 4 High; 3 Other Level
39 Regular; 1 Special Education; 2 Vocational; 1 Alternative
5 Magnet; 0 Charter; 0 Title I Eligible; 0 School-wide Title I
Students: 17,616 (51.2% male; 48.8% female)
Individual Education Program: 3,260 (18.5%);
English Language Learner: 1,588 (9.0%); Migrant: n/a
Eligible for Free Lunch Program: 8,512 (48.3%)
Eligible for Reduced-Price Lunch Program: 1,476 (8.4%)
Teachers: 119.0 (148.0 to 1)
Librarians/Media Specialists: n/a
Guidance Counselors: 1.0 (17,616.0 to 1)
Current Spending: ($ per student per year):
Total: $9,406; Instruction: $5,086; Support Services: $4,026
Enrollment, Drop-out Rates and Diploma Recipients by Race/Ethnicity

Category	Total	White	Black	Asian	AIAN	Hisp.
Enrollment (%)	100.0	38.5	40.3	5.1	1.2	14.9
Drop-out Rate (%)	n/a	n/a	n/a	n/a	n/a	n/a
H.S. Diplomas (#)	778	331	301	63	7	76

Mason Public Schools (Ingham)
118 W Oak St • Mason, MI 48854-1618
(517) 676-2484 • http://www.mason.k12.mi.us/
Grade Span: PK-12; **Agency Type:** 1
Schools: 6
4 Primary; 1 Middle; 1 High; 0 Other Level
6 Regular; 0 Special Education; 0 Vocational; 0 Alternative
0 Magnet; 0 Charter; 0 Title I Eligible; 0 School-wide Title I
Students: 3,299 (50.3% male; 49.7% female)
Individual Education Program: 436 (13.2%);
English Language Learner: n/a; Migrant: n/a
Eligible for Free Lunch Program: 254 (7.7%)
Eligible for Reduced-Price Lunch Program: 150 (4.5%)
Teachers: 179.5 (18.4 to 1)
Librarians/Media Specialists: 2.0 (1,649.5 to 1)
Guidance Counselors: 4.0 (824.8 to 1)
Current Spending: ($ per student per year):
Total: $7,014; Instruction: $4,384; Support Services: $2,291
Enrollment, Drop-out Rates and Diploma Recipients by Race/Ethnicity

Category	Total	White	Black	Asian	AIAN	Hisp.
Enrollment (%)	100.0	92.1	1.5	1.8	0.8	3.7
Drop-out Rate (%)	n/a	n/a	n/a	n/a	n/a	n/a
H.S. Diplomas (#)	235	219	2	4	0	10

Okemos Public Schools
4406 N Okemos Rd • Okemos, MI 48864-1792
(517) 349-9460 • http://okemos.k12.mi.us/
Grade Span: PK-12; **Agency Type:** 1
Schools: 9
6 Primary; 2 Middle; 1 High; 0 Other Level
9 Regular; 0 Special Education; 0 Vocational; 0 Alternative
0 Magnet; 0 Charter; 0 Title I Eligible; 0 School-wide Title I
Students: 4,194 (51.2% male; 48.8% female)
Individual Education Program: 434 (10.3%);
English Language Learner: n/a; Migrant: n/a
Eligible for Free Lunch Program: 177 (4.2%)
Eligible for Reduced-Price Lunch Program: 49 (1.2%)
Teachers: 240.4 (17.4 to 1)
Librarians/Media Specialists: 4.0 (1,048.5 to 1)
Guidance Counselors: 14.0 (299.6 to 1)
Current Spending: ($ per student per year):
Total: $8,203; Instruction: $4,757; Support Services: $3,119
Enrollment, Drop-out Rates and Diploma Recipients by Race/Ethnicity

Category	Total	White	Black	Asian	AIAN	Hisp.
Enrollment (%)	100.0	77.2	4.7	12.8	0.5	1.6
Drop-out Rate (%)	n/a	n/a	n/a	n/a	n/a	n/a
H.S. Diplomas (#)	351	286	17	40	5	3

Stockbridge Community Schools
305 W Elizabeth St • Stockbridge, MI 49285-9791
(517) 851-7188 • http://scs.k12.mi.us/
Grade Span: KG-12; **Agency Type:** 1
Schools: 6
3 Primary; 1 Middle; 1 High; 0 Other Level
5 Regular; 0 Special Education; 0 Vocational; 0 Alternative
0 Magnet; 0 Charter; 0 Title I Eligible; 0 School-wide Title I
Students: 1,824 (52.2% male; 47.8% female)
Individual Education Program: 285 (15.6%);
English Language Learner: 5 (0.3%); Migrant: n/a
Eligible for Free Lunch Program: 363 (19.9%)
Eligible for Reduced-Price Lunch Program: 179 (9.8%)

Teachers: 98.8 (18.5 to 1)
Librarians/Media Specialists: 1.0 (1,824.0 to 1)
Guidance Counselors: 3.0 (608.0 to 1)
Current Spending: ($ per student per year):
Total: $6,553; Instruction: $3,936; Support Services: $2,327
Enrollment, Drop-out Rates and Diploma Recipients by Race/Ethnicity

Category	Total	White	Black	Asian	AIAN	Hisp.
Enrollment (%)	100.0	95.5	1.2	0.5	0.0	2.9
Drop-out Rate (%)	n/a	n/a	n/a	n/a	n/a	n/a
H.S. Diplomas (#)	106	102	0	1	0	3

Waverly Community Schools
515 Snow Rd • Lansing, MI 48917-4501
(517) 321-7265 • http://web.waverly.k12.mi.us/intro.cfm
Grade Span: KG-12; **Agency Type:** 1
Schools: 7
4 Primary; 2 Middle; 1 High; 0 Other Level
7 Regular; 0 Special Education; 0 Vocational; 0 Alternative
0 Magnet; 0 Charter; 0 Title I Eligible; 0 School-wide Title I
Students: 3,420 (52.2% male; 47.8% female)
Individual Education Program: 447 (13.1%);
English Language Learner: 59 (1.7%); Migrant: n/a
Eligible for Free Lunch Program: 541 (15.8%)
Eligible for Reduced-Price Lunch Program: 153 (4.5%)
Teachers: n/a
Librarians/Media Specialists: n/a
Guidance Counselors: n/a
Current Spending: ($ per student per year):
Total: $8,970; Instruction: $5,241; Support Services: $3,497
Enrollment, Drop-out Rates and Diploma Recipients by Race/Ethnicity

Category	Total	White	Black	Asian	AIAN	Hisp.
Enrollment (%)	100.0	61.4	24.4	5.2	0.9	8.1
Drop-out Rate (%)	n/a	n/a	n/a	n/a	n/a	n/a
H.S. Diplomas (#)	255	188	46	11	0	10

Williamston Community Schools
418 Highland St • Williamston, MI 48895-1133
(517) 655-4361 • http://www.wmston.k12.mi.us/
Grade Span: KG-12; **Agency Type:** 1
Schools: 4
2 Primary; 1 Middle; 1 High; 0 Other Level
4 Regular; 0 Special Education; 0 Vocational; 0 Alternative
0 Magnet; 0 Charter; 0 Title I Eligible; 0 School-wide Title I
Students: 2,056 (50.4% male; 49.6% female)
Individual Education Program: 217 (10.6%);
English Language Learner: n/a; Migrant: n/a
Eligible for Free Lunch Program: 121 (5.9%)
Eligible for Reduced-Price Lunch Program: 68 (3.3%)
Teachers: 113.3 (18.1 to 1)
Librarians/Media Specialists: 1.0 (2,056.0 to 1)
Guidance Counselors: 5.0 (411.2 to 1)
Current Spending: ($ per student per year):
Total: $6,666; Instruction: $3,959; Support Services: $2,524
Enrollment, Drop-out Rates and Diploma Recipients by Race/Ethnicity

Category	Total	White	Black	Asian	AIAN	Hisp.
Enrollment (%)	100.0	95.1	1.3	1.4	0.4	1.8
Drop-out Rate (%)	n/a	n/a	n/a	n/a	n/a	n/a
H.S. Diplomas (#)	130	125	3	2	0	0

Ionia County

Belding Area SD
321 Wilson St • Belding, MI 48809-1744
(616) 794-4444 • http://www.belding.k12.mi.us/
Grade Span: PK-12; **Agency Type:** 1
Schools: 7
4 Primary; 1 Middle; 2 High; 0 Other Level
6 Regular; 0 Special Education; 0 Vocational; 1 Alternative
0 Magnet; 0 Charter; 4 Title I Eligible; 4 School-wide Title I
Students: 2,618 (49.8% male; 50.2% female)
Individual Education Program: 392 (15.0%);
English Language Learner: 359 (13.7%); Migrant: n/a
Eligible for Free Lunch Program: 712 (27.2%)
Eligible for Reduced-Price Lunch Program: 331 (12.6%)
Teachers: 158.5 (16.5 to 1)
Librarians/Media Specialists: 1.0 (2,618.0 to 1)
Guidance Counselors: 3.0 (872.7 to 1)
Current Spending: ($ per student per year):
Total: $6,743; Instruction: $4,113; Support Services: $2,374
Enrollment, Drop-out Rates and Diploma Recipients by Race/Ethnicity

Category	Total	White	Black	Asian	AIAN	Hisp.
Enrollment (%)	100.0	93.7	0.6	0.4	0.3	5.0
Drop-out Rate (%)	n/a	n/a	n/a	n/a	n/a	n/a
H.S. Diplomas (#)	152	148	0	1	1	2

Ionia Public Schools
250 E Tuttle Rd • Ionia, MI 48846-9698
(616) 527-9280 • http://www.ionia.k12.mi.us/
Grade Span: PK-12; **Agency Type:** 1
Schools: 8
5 Primary; 1 Middle; 1 High; 1 Other Level
7 Regular; 0 Special Education; 0 Vocational; 1 Alternative
0 Magnet; 0 Charter; 6 Title I Eligible; 6 School-wide Title I
Students: 3,435 (51.2% male; 48.8% female)
Individual Education Program: 569 (16.6%);
English Language Learner: n/a; Migrant: n/a
Eligible for Free Lunch Program: 1,012 (29.5%)
Eligible for Reduced-Price Lunch Program: 356 (10.4%)
Teachers: 212.1 (16.2 to 1)
Librarians/Media Specialists: 1.0 (3,435.0 to 1)
Guidance Counselors: 6.0 (572.5 to 1)
Current Spending: ($ per student per year):
Total: $6,971; Instruction: $4,430; Support Services: $2,242
Enrollment, Drop-out Rates and Diploma Recipients by Race/Ethnicity

Category	Total	White	Black	Asian	AIAN	Hisp.
Enrollment (%)	100.0	91.6	0.8	2.0	0.2	4.4
Drop-out Rate (%)	n/a	n/a	n/a	n/a	n/a	n/a
H.S. Diplomas (#)	207	197	3	1	0	6

Lakewood Public Schools
639 Jordan Lake St • Lake Odessa, MI 48849-1299
(616) 374-8043 • http://www.lakewood.k12.mi.us/
Grade Span: PK-12; **Agency Type:** 1
Schools: 7
4 Primary; 1 Middle; 1 High; 1 Other Level
6 Regular; 0 Special Education; 0 Vocational; 1 Alternative
0 Magnet; 0 Charter; 0 Title I Eligible; 0 School-wide Title I
Students: 2,606 (50.3% male; 49.7% female)
Individual Education Program: 393 (15.1%);
English Language Learner: 8 (0.3%); Migrant: n/a
Eligible for Free Lunch Program: 524 (20.1%)
Eligible for Reduced-Price Lunch Program: 214 (8.2%)
Teachers: 140.3 (18.6 to 1)
Librarians/Media Specialists: 1.0 (2,606.0 to 1)
Guidance Counselors: 3.0 (868.7 to 1)
Current Spending: ($ per student per year):
Total: $6,599; Instruction: $4,042; Support Services: $2,273
Enrollment, Drop-out Rates and Diploma Recipients by Race/Ethnicity

Category	Total	White	Black	Asian	AIAN	Hisp.
Enrollment (%)	100.0	94.5	0.7	0.8	0.4	3.6
Drop-out Rate (%)	n/a	n/a	n/a	n/a	n/a	n/a
H.S. Diplomas (#)	182	178	0	0	2	2

Portland Public SD
1100 Ionia Rd • Portland, MI 48875-1035
(517) 647-4161 • http://www.portlandpublicschools.cc/
Grade Span: PK-12; **Agency Type:** 1
Schools: 5
2 Primary; 1 Middle; 1 High; 1 Other Level
4 Regular; 0 Special Education; 0 Vocational; 1 Alternative
0 Magnet; 0 Charter; 1 Title I Eligible; 1 School-wide Title I
Students: 2,071 (50.5% male; 49.5% female)
Individual Education Program: 329 (15.9%);
English Language Learner: n/a; Migrant: n/a
Eligible for Free Lunch Program: 133 (6.4%)
Eligible for Reduced-Price Lunch Program: 83 (4.0%)
Teachers: 110.6 (18.7 to 1)
Librarians/Media Specialists: n/a
Guidance Counselors: 4.0 (517.8 to 1)
Current Spending: ($ per student per year):
Total: $6,405; Instruction: $4,026; Support Services: $2,170
Enrollment, Drop-out Rates and Diploma Recipients by Race/Ethnicity

Category	Total	White	Black	Asian	AIAN	Hisp.
Enrollment (%)	100.0	98.0	0.5	0.4	0.1	0.9
Drop-out Rate (%)	n/a	n/a	n/a	n/a	n/a	n/a
H.S. Diplomas (#)	153	151	0	2	0	0

Iosco County

Oscoda Area Schools
3550 E River Rd • Oscoda, MI 48750-9298
(989) 739-2033 • http://www.oscodaschools.org/
Grade Span: PK-12; **Agency Type:** 1
Schools: 6
3 Primary; 1 Middle; 1 High; 1 Other Level
5 Regular; 0 Special Education; 0 Vocational; 1 Alternative
0 Magnet; 0 Charter; 3 Title I Eligible; 3 School-wide Title I
Students: 1,956 (52.0% male; 48.0% female)
Individual Education Program: 324 (16.6%);
English Language Learner: n/a; Migrant: n/a

Eligible for Free Lunch Program: 837 (42.8%)
Eligible for Reduced-Price Lunch Program: 299 (15.3%)
Teachers: 111.0 (17.6 to 1)
Librarians/Media Specialists: 2.0 (978.0 to 1)
Guidance Counselors: 5.0 (391.2 to 1)
Current Spending: ($ per student per year):
Total: $7,121; Instruction: $4,062; Support Services: $2,746

Enrollment, Drop-out Rates and Diploma Recipients by Race/Ethnicity

Category	Total	White	Black	Asian	AIAN	Hisp.
Enrollment (%)	100.0	96.3	1.1	0.2	1.1	1.3
Drop-out Rate (%)	n/a	n/a	n/a	n/a	n/a	n/a
H.S. Diplomas (#)	133	123	1	3	2	4

Tawas Area Schools

245 M-55 W • Tawas City, MI 48763-9252
(989) 984-2250 • http://www.tawas.net/
Grade Span: PK-12; **Agency Type:** 1
Schools: 4
1 Primary; 2 Middle; 1 High; 0 Other Level
4 Regular; 0 Special Education; 0 Vocational; 0 Alternative
0 Magnet; 0 Charter; 0 Title I Eligible; 0 School-wide Title I
Students: 1,629 (51.4% male; 48.6% female)
Individual Education Program: 209 (12.8%);
English Language Learner: n/a; Migrant: n/a
Eligible for Free Lunch Program: 404 (24.8%)
Eligible for Reduced-Price Lunch Program: 154 (9.5%)
Teachers: 91.7 (17.8 to 1)
Librarians/Media Specialists: 1.0 (1,629.0 to 1)
Guidance Counselors: 3.0 (543.0 to 1)
Current Spending: ($ per student per year):
Total: $6,412; Instruction: $4,231; Support Services: $1,935

Enrollment, Drop-out Rates and Diploma Recipients by Race/Ethnicity

Category	Total	White	Black	Asian	AIAN	Hisp.
Enrollment (%)	100.0	98.3	0.7	0.2	0.5	0.3
Drop-out Rate (%)	n/a	n/a	n/a	n/a	n/a	n/a
H.S. Diplomas (#)	134	127	0	4	1	2

Isabella County

Mount Pleasant City SD

201 S University St • Mount Pleasant, MI 48858-2594
(989) 775-2301 • http://www.edzone.net/mpps/
Grade Span: PK-12; **Agency Type:** 1
Schools: 11
5 Primary; 2 Middle; 2 High; 2 Other Level
9 Regular; 0 Special Education; 0 Vocational; 2 Alternative
0 Magnet; 0 Charter; 0 Title I Eligible; 0 School-wide Title I
Students: 4,068 (51.4% male; 48.6% female)
Individual Education Program: 587 (14.4%);
English Language Learner: 5 (0.1%); Migrant: n/a
Eligible for Free Lunch Program: 820 (20.2%)
Eligible for Reduced-Price Lunch Program: 223 (5.5%)
Teachers: n/a
Librarians/Media Specialists: n/a
Guidance Counselors: n/a
Current Spending: ($ per student per year):
Total: $7,151; Instruction: $4,198; Support Services: $2,704

Enrollment, Drop-out Rates and Diploma Recipients by Race/Ethnicity

Category	Total	White	Black	Asian	AIAN	Hisp.
Enrollment (%)	100.0	85.2	3.0	2.6	6.4	2.1
Drop-out Rate (%)	n/a	n/a	n/a	n/a	n/a	n/a
H.S. Diplomas (#)	270	240	8	11	6	5

Shepherd Public SD

258 W Wright • Shepherd, MI 48883-0219
Mailing Address: PO Box 219 • Shepherd, MI 48883-0219
(989) 828-5520 • http://shepherd.edzone.net/
Grade Span: KG-12; **Agency Type:** 1
Schools: 5
2 Primary; 1 Middle; 2 High; 0 Other Level
4 Regular; 0 Special Education; 0 Vocational; 1 Alternative
0 Magnet; 0 Charter; 2 Title I Eligible; 2 School-wide Title I
Students: 1,731 (51.1% male; 48.9% female)
Individual Education Program: 295 (17.0%);
English Language Learner: n/a; Migrant: n/a
Eligible for Free Lunch Program: 330 (19.1%)
Eligible for Reduced-Price Lunch Program: 147 (8.5%)
Teachers: 103.9 (16.7 to 1)
Librarians/Media Specialists: 1.0 (1,731.0 to 1)
Guidance Counselors: 3.0 (577.0 to 1)
Current Spending: ($ per student per year):
Total: $6,839; Instruction: $4,414; Support Services: $2,126

Enrollment, Drop-out Rates and Diploma Recipients by Race/Ethnicity

Category	Total	White	Black	Asian	AIAN	Hisp.
Enrollment (%)	100.0	92.7	0.9	0.6	3.4	2.5
Drop-out Rate (%)	n/a	n/a	n/a	n/a	n/a	n/a
H.S. Diplomas (#)	116	111	0	1	2	2

Jackson County

Columbia SD

11775 Hewitt Rd • Brooklyn, MI 49230-8961
(517) 592-6641 • http://scnc.csd.k12.mi.us/
Grade Span: KG-12; **Agency Type:** 1
Schools: 5
2 Primary; 1 Middle; 1 High; 1 Other Level
4 Regular; 0 Special Education; 0 Vocational; 1 Alternative
0 Magnet; 0 Charter; 0 Title I Eligible; 0 School-wide Title I
Students: 1,924 (51.8% male; 48.2% female)
Individual Education Program: 252 (13.1%);
English Language Learner: n/a; Migrant: n/a
Eligible for Free Lunch Program: 243 (12.6%)
Eligible for Reduced-Price Lunch Program: 122 (6.3%)
Teachers: 100.5 (19.1 to 1)
Librarians/Media Specialists: 3.0 (641.3 to 1)
Guidance Counselors: 3.0 (641.3 to 1)
Current Spending: ($ per student per year):
Total: $6,901; Instruction: $4,014; Support Services: $2,635

Enrollment, Drop-out Rates and Diploma Recipients by Race/Ethnicity

Category	Total	White	Black	Asian	AIAN	Hisp.
Enrollment (%)	100.0	96.0	1.1	0.4	1.1	1.4
Drop-out Rate (%)	n/a	n/a	n/a	n/a	n/a	n/a
H.S. Diplomas (#)	115	111	1	0	1	2

East Jackson Community Schools

1404 N Sutton Rd • Jackson, MI 49202-2822
(517) 764-2090 • http://scnc.ejs.k12.mi.us/MAIN%20PAGE/links_page.htm
Grade Span: KG-12; **Agency Type:** 1
Schools: 4
2 Primary; 1 Middle; 1 High; 0 Other Level
4 Regular; 0 Special Education; 0 Vocational; 0 Alternative
1 Magnet; 0 Charter; 1 Title I Eligible; 1 School-wide Title I
Students: 1,570 (50.5% male; 49.5% female)
Individual Education Program: 215 (13.7%);
English Language Learner: n/a; Migrant: n/a
Eligible for Free Lunch Program: 455 (29.0%)
Eligible for Reduced-Price Lunch Program: 107 (6.8%)
Teachers: 89.5 (17.5 to 1)
Librarians/Media Specialists: 2.8 (560.7 to 1)
Guidance Counselors: 5.0 (314.0 to 1)
Current Spending: ($ per student per year):
Total: $6,476; Instruction: $4,009; Support Services: $2,179

Enrollment, Drop-out Rates and Diploma Recipients by Race/Ethnicity

Category	Total	White	Black	Asian	AIAN	Hisp.
Enrollment (%)	100.0	94.6	2.3	0.9	1.0	1.3
Drop-out Rate (%)	n/a	n/a	n/a	n/a	n/a	n/a
H.S. Diplomas (#)	88	86	2	0	0	0

Jackson Public Schools

105 E Michigan Ave • Jackson, MI 49201
(517) 841-2200 • http://scnc.jps.k12.mi.us/
Grade Span: PK-12; **Agency Type:** 1
Schools: 15
11 Primary; 2 Middle; 1 High; 1 Other Level
13 Regular; 0 Special Education; 0 Vocational; 2 Alternative
0 Magnet; 0 Charter; 10 Title I Eligible; 10 School-wide Title I
Students: 7,515 (51.3% male; 48.7% female)
Individual Education Program: 1,143 (15.2%);
English Language Learner: 185 (2.5%); Migrant: n/a
Eligible for Free Lunch Program: 4,018 (53.5%)
Eligible for Reduced-Price Lunch Program: 578 (7.7%)
Teachers: n/a
Librarians/Media Specialists: n/a
Guidance Counselors: n/a
Current Spending: ($ per student per year):
Total: $8,680; Instruction: $4,956; Support Services: $3,381

Enrollment, Drop-out Rates and Diploma Recipients by Race/Ethnicity

Category	Total	White	Black	Asian	AIAN	Hisp.
Enrollment (%)	100.0	57.9	35.7	1.3	1.5	3.7
Drop-out Rate (%)	n/a	n/a	n/a	n/a	n/a	n/a
H.S. Diplomas (#)	333	227	85	7	1	13

Michigan Center SD

400 S State St • Michigan Center, MI 49254-1217
(517) 764-5778
Grade Span: PK-12; **Agency Type:** 1
Schools: 4

2 Primary; 0 Middle; 2 High; 0 Other Level
3 Regular; 0 Special Education; 0 Vocational; 1 Alternative
0 Magnet; 0 Charter; 0 Title I Eligible; 0 School-wide Title I
Students: 1,535 (51.1% male; 48.9% female)
Individual Education Program: 212 (13.8%);
English Language Learner: n/a; Migrant: n/a
Eligible for Free Lunch Program: 382 (24.9%)
Eligible for Reduced-Price Lunch Program: 106 (6.9%)
Teachers: 79.0 (19.4 to 1)
Librarians/Media Specialists: 2.0 (767.5 to 1)
Guidance Counselors: 3.0 (511.7 to 1)
Current Spending: ($ per student per year):
Total: $6,138; Instruction: $3,651; Support Services: $2,151
Enrollment, Drop-out Rates and Diploma Recipients by Race/Ethnicity

Category	Total	White	Black	Asian	AIAN	Hisp.
Enrollment (%)	100.0	96.4	1.2	0.7	0.5	1.1
Drop-out Rate (%)	n/a	n/a	n/a	n/a	n/a	n/a
H.S. Diplomas (#)	70	69	0	1	0	0

Napoleon Community Schools
200 W Ave • Napoleon, MI 49261-0308
Mailing Address: PO Box 308 • Napoleon, MI 49261-0308
(517) 536-8667 • http://scnc.ncs.k12.mi.us/
Grade Span: KG-12; **Agency Type:** 1
Schools: 4
1 Primary; 1 Middle; 1 High; 1 Other Level
3 Regular; 0 Special Education; 0 Vocational; 1 Alternative
0 Magnet; 0 Charter; 2 Title I Eligible; 2 School-wide Title I
Students: 1,820 (52.9% male; 47.1% female)
Individual Education Program: 174 (9.6%);
English Language Learner: n/a; Migrant: n/a
Eligible for Free Lunch Program: 240 (13.2%)
Eligible for Reduced-Price Lunch Program: 104 (5.7%)
Teachers: 96.0 (19.0 to 1)
Librarians/Media Specialists: 3.0 (606.7 to 1)
Guidance Counselors: 4.0 (455.0 to 1)
Current Spending: ($ per student per year):
Total: $6,492; Instruction: $4,098; Support Services: $2,155
Enrollment, Drop-out Rates and Diploma Recipients by Race/Ethnicity

Category	Total	White	Black	Asian	AIAN	Hisp.
Enrollment (%)	100.0	97.4	0.7	0.2	0.3	1.0
Drop-out Rate (%)	n/a	n/a	n/a	n/a	n/a	n/a
H.S. Diplomas (#)	94	91	0	2	0	1

Northwest Community Schools
4000 Van Horn Rd • Jackson, MI 49201-9404
(517) 569-2247 • http://nsd.k12.mi.us/
Grade Span: PK-12; **Agency Type:** 1
Schools: 6
2 Primary; 2 Middle; 1 High; 1 Other Level
5 Regular; 0 Special Education; 0 Vocational; 1 Alternative
0 Magnet; 0 Charter; 0 Title I Eligible; 0 School-wide Title I
Students: 3,693 (50.4% male; 49.6% female)
Individual Education Program: 468 (12.7%);
English Language Learner: n/a; Migrant: n/a
Eligible for Free Lunch Program: 824 (22.3%)
Eligible for Reduced-Price Lunch Program: 190 (5.1%)
Teachers: n/a
Librarians/Media Specialists: n/a
Guidance Counselors: n/a
Current Spending: ($ per student per year):
Total: $6,473; Instruction: $3,972; Support Services: $2,241
Enrollment, Drop-out Rates and Diploma Recipients by Race/Ethnicity

Category	Total	White	Black	Asian	AIAN	Hisp.
Enrollment (%)	100.0	93.3	2.8	1.1	0.5	2.4
Drop-out Rate (%)	n/a	n/a	n/a	n/a	n/a	n/a
H.S. Diplomas (#)	206	195	2	4	1	4

Western SD
1400 S Dearing Rd • Parma, MI 49269-9712
(517) 841-8100 • http://scnc.western.k12.mi.us/
Grade Span: KG-12; **Agency Type:** 1
Schools: 6
3 Primary; 1 Middle; 2 High; 0 Other Level
5 Regular; 0 Special Education; 0 Vocational; 1 Alternative
0 Magnet; 0 Charter; 6 Title I Eligible; 6 School-wide Title I
Students: 2,818 (50.1% male; 49.9% female)
Individual Education Program: 349 (12.4%);
English Language Learner: n/a; Migrant: n/a
Eligible for Free Lunch Program: 636 (22.6%)
Eligible for Reduced-Price Lunch Program: 217 (7.7%)
Teachers: 143.4 (19.7 to 1)
Librarians/Media Specialists: 2.1 (1,341.9 to 1)
Guidance Counselors: 4.2 (671.0 to 1)
Current Spending: ($ per student per year):
Total: $6,341; Instruction: $3,757; Support Services: $2,371
Enrollment, Drop-out Rates and Diploma Recipients by Race/Ethnicity

Category	Total	White	Black	Asian	AIAN	Hisp.
Enrollment (%)	100.0	95.0	1.8	1.0	0.6	1.5
Drop-out Rate (%)	n/a	n/a	n/a	n/a	n/a	n/a
H.S. Diplomas (#)	148	146	1	0	0	1

Kalamazoo County

Comstock Public Schools
301 N 26th St • Kalamazoo, MI 49048
(269) 388-9461 • http://www.remc12.k12.mi.us/comstock/
Grade Span: PK-12; **Agency Type:** 1
Schools: 7
4 Primary; 1 Middle; 1 High; 1 Other Level
6 Regular; 0 Special Education; 0 Vocational; 1 Alternative
0 Magnet; 0 Charter; 1 Title I Eligible; 1 School-wide Title I
Students: 2,987 (52.9% male; 47.1% female)
Individual Education Program: 406 (13.6%);
English Language Learner: n/a; Migrant: n/a
Eligible for Free Lunch Program: 962 (32.2%)
Eligible for Reduced-Price Lunch Program: 294 (9.8%)
Teachers: 192.8 (15.5 to 1)
Librarians/Media Specialists: 6.0 (497.8 to 1)
Guidance Counselors: 3.0 (995.7 to 1)
Current Spending: ($ per student per year):
Total: $7,260; Instruction: $4,126; Support Services: $2,884
Enrollment, Drop-out Rates and Diploma Recipients by Race/Ethnicity

Category	Total	White	Black	Asian	AIAN	Hisp.
Enrollment (%)	100.0	86.8	8.6	1.0	1.0	1.7
Drop-out Rate (%)	n/a	n/a	n/a	n/a	n/a	n/a
H.S. Diplomas (#)	143	125	12	3	2	1

Gull Lake Community Schools
11775 E D Ave • Richland, MI 49083-9669
(269) 629-5880 • http://www.gull-lake.k12.mi.us/
Grade Span: PK-12; **Agency Type:** 1
Schools: 6
3 Primary; 2 Middle; 1 High; 0 Other Level
6 Regular; 0 Special Education; 0 Vocational; 0 Alternative
0 Magnet; 0 Charter; 0 Title I Eligible; 0 School-wide Title I
Students: 3,091 (51.6% male; 48.4% female)
Individual Education Program: 273 (8.8%);
English Language Learner: n/a; Migrant: n/a
Eligible for Free Lunch Program: 262 (8.5%)
Eligible for Reduced-Price Lunch Program: 137 (4.4%)
Teachers: 171.6 (18.0 to 1)
Librarians/Media Specialists: 3.0 (1,030.3 to 1)
Guidance Counselors: 5.0 (618.2 to 1)
Current Spending: ($ per student per year):
Total: $6,359; Instruction: $3,835; Support Services: $2,331
Enrollment, Drop-out Rates and Diploma Recipients by Race/Ethnicity

Category	Total	White	Black	Asian	AIAN	Hisp.
Enrollment (%)	100.0	95.3	2.3	1.0	0.4	1.1
Drop-out Rate (%)	n/a	n/a	n/a	n/a	n/a	n/a
H.S. Diplomas (#)	210	203	1	2	0	4

Kalamazoo Public SD
1220 Howard St • Kalamazoo, MI 49008-1882
(269) 337-0123 • http://63.241.176.180/
Grade Span: PK-12; **Agency Type:** 1
Schools: 29
19 Primary; 3 Middle; 6 High; 1 Other Level
26 Regular; 1 Special Education; 0 Vocational; 2 Alternative
8 Magnet; 0 Charter; 20 Title I Eligible; 20 School-wide Title I
Students: 11,536 (52.0% male; 48.0% female)
Individual Education Program: 1,533 (13.3%);
English Language Learner: 830 (7.2%); Migrant: n/a
Eligible for Free Lunch Program: 5,866 (50.8%)
Eligible for Reduced-Price Lunch Program: 817 (7.1%)
Teachers: 798.3 (14.5 to 1)
Librarians/Media Specialists: 11.0 (1,048.7 to 1)
Guidance Counselors: 4.0 (2,884.0 to 1)
Current Spending: ($ per student per year):
Total: $9,330; Instruction: $5,696; Support Services: $3,289
Enrollment, Drop-out Rates and Diploma Recipients by Race/Ethnicity

Category	Total	White	Black	Asian	AIAN	Hisp.
Enrollment (%)	100.0	43.8	45.7	1.7	1.2	7.6
Drop-out Rate (%)	n/a	n/a	n/a	n/a	n/a	n/a
H.S. Diplomas (#)	434	255	90	61	4	24

Parchment SD
520 N Orient St • Parchment, MI 49004-1757
(269) 488-1050 • http://www.remc12.k12.mi.us/parchment/
Grade Span: PK-12; **Agency Type:** 1
Schools: 6

3 Primary; 1 Middle; 1 High; 1 Other Level
5 Regular; 0 Special Education; 0 Vocational; 1 Alternative
0 Magnet; 0 Charter; 0 Title I Eligible; 0 School-wide Title I
Students: 2,008 (51.8% male; 48.2% female)
Individual Education Program: 196 (9.8%);
English Language Learner: n/a; Migrant: n/a
Eligible for Free Lunch Program: 524 (26.1%)
Eligible for Reduced-Price Lunch Program: 260 (12.9%)
Teachers: 116.1 (17.3 to 1)
Librarians/Media Specialists: 3.0 (669.3 to 1)
Guidance Counselors: 5.8 (346.2 to 1)
Current Spending: ($ per student per year):
Total: $7,511; Instruction: $4,709; Support Services: $2,565
Enrollment, Drop-out Rates and Diploma Recipients by Race/Ethnicity

Category	Total	White	Black	Asian	AIAN	Hisp.
Enrollment (%)	100.0	88.0	7.1	1.1	0.3	2.9
Drop-out Rate (%)	n/a	n/a	n/a	n/a	n/a	n/a
H.S. Diplomas (#)	107	99	2	2	0	4

Portage Public Schools

8111 S Westnedge Ave • Portage, MI 49002-5433
(269) 323-5000 • http://www.portageps.org/
Grade Span: PK-12; **Agency Type:** 1
Schools: 14
8 Primary; 3 Middle; 2 High; 1 Other Level
13 Regular; 0 Special Education; 0 Vocational; 1 Alternative
0 Magnet; 0 Charter; 0 Title I Eligible; 0 School-wide Title I
Students: 9,140 (51.3% male; 48.7% female)
Individual Education Program: 798 (8.7%);
English Language Learner: n/a; Migrant: n/a
Eligible for Free Lunch Program: 866 (9.5%)
Eligible for Reduced-Price Lunch Program: 357 (3.9%)
Teachers: 468.3 (19.5 to 1)
Librarians/Media Specialists: 11.0 (830.9 to 1)
Guidance Counselors: 15.2 (601.3 to 1)
Current Spending: ($ per student per year):
Total: $6,734; Instruction: $4,050; Support Services: $2,498
Enrollment, Drop-out Rates and Diploma Recipients by Race/Ethnicity

Category	Total	White	Black	Asian	AIAN	Hisp.
Enrollment (%)	100.0	88.7	5.0	4.4	0.4	1.4
Drop-out Rate (%)	n/a	n/a	n/a	n/a	n/a	n/a
H.S. Diplomas (#)	616	576	16	22	2	0

Vicksburg Community Schools

301 S Kalamazoo Ave • Vicksburg, MI 49097-0158
Mailing Address: PO Box 158 • Vicksburg, MI 49097-0158
(269) 321-1000 • http://www.remc12.k12.mi.us/vicksburg/
Grade Span: KG-12; **Agency Type:** 1
Schools: 5
3 Primary; 1 Middle; 1 High; 0 Other Level
5 Regular; 0 Special Education; 0 Vocational; 0 Alternative
0 Magnet; 0 Charter; 0 Title I Eligible; 0 School-wide Title I
Students: 2,779 (50.4% male; 49.6% female)
Individual Education Program: 246 (8.9%);
English Language Learner: n/a; Migrant: n/a
Eligible for Free Lunch Program: 320 (11.5%)
Eligible for Reduced-Price Lunch Program: 137 (4.9%)
Teachers: 137.1 (20.3 to 1)
Librarians/Media Specialists: 2.0 (1,389.5 to 1)
Guidance Counselors: 6.5 (427.5 to 1)
Current Spending: ($ per student per year):
Total: $6,781; Instruction: $3,757; Support Services: $2,747
Enrollment, Drop-out Rates and Diploma Recipients by Race/Ethnicity

Category	Total	White	Black	Asian	AIAN	Hisp.
Enrollment (%)	100.0	95.9	1.3	1.0	0.1	1.7
Drop-out Rate (%)	n/a	n/a	n/a	n/a	n/a	n/a
H.S. Diplomas (#)	209	203	3	1	0	2

Kalkaska County

Kalkaska Public Schools

315 S Coral St • Kalkaska, MI 49646-0580
Mailing Address: PO Box 580 • Kalkaska, MI 49646-0580
(231) 258-9109 • http://tcnet.org/schools/kk/kps.htm
Grade Span: KG-12; **Agency Type:** 1
Schools: 6
2 Primary; 2 Middle; 2 High; 0 Other Level
5 Regular; 0 Special Education; 0 Vocational; 1 Alternative
0 Magnet; 0 Charter; 3 Title I Eligible; 3 School-wide Title I
Students: 1,841 (51.8% male; 48.2% female)
Individual Education Program: 284 (15.4%);
English Language Learner: n/a; Migrant: n/a
Eligible for Free Lunch Program: 622 (33.8%)
Eligible for Reduced-Price Lunch Program: 274 (14.9%)
Teachers: n/a
Librarians/Media Specialists: n/a
Guidance Counselors: n/a
Current Spending: ($ per student per year):
Total: $6,687; Instruction: $3,979; Support Services: $2,461
Enrollment, Drop-out Rates and Diploma Recipients by Race/Ethnicity

Category	Total	White	Black	Asian	AIAN	Hisp.
Enrollment (%)	100.0	97.2	0.3	0.4	1.6	0.4
Drop-out Rate (%)	n/a	n/a	n/a	n/a	n/a	n/a
H.S. Diplomas (#)	132	126	1	1	2	2

Kent County

Byron Center Public Schools

2475 84th St SW • Byron Center, MI 49315-2500
(616) 878-6100 • http://www.remc8.k12.mi.us/byroncen/
Grade Span: PK-12; **Agency Type:** 1
Schools: 8
5 Primary; 2 Middle; 1 High; 0 Other Level
7 Regular; 1 Special Education; 0 Vocational; 0 Alternative
0 Magnet; 0 Charter; 0 Title I Eligible; 0 School-wide Title I
Students: 2,810 (52.5% male; 47.5% female)
Individual Education Program: 410 (14.6%);
English Language Learner: n/a; Migrant: n/a
Eligible for Free Lunch Program: 290 (10.3%)
Eligible for Reduced-Price Lunch Program: 192 (6.8%)
Teachers: 157.6 (17.8 to 1)
Librarians/Media Specialists: 1.0 (2,810.0 to 1)
Guidance Counselors: 2.5 (1,124.0 to 1)
Current Spending: ($ per student per year):
Total: $7,004; Instruction: $4,122; Support Services: $2,606
Enrollment, Drop-out Rates and Diploma Recipients by Race/Ethnicity

Category	Total	White	Black	Asian	AIAN	Hisp.
Enrollment (%)	100.0	93.3	1.3	1.9	0.4	3.1
Drop-out Rate (%)	n/a	n/a	n/a	n/a	n/a	n/a
H.S. Diplomas (#)	165	160	1	2	0	2

Caledonia Community Schools

203 E Main St SE • Caledonia, MI 49316-9487
(616) 891-8185 • http://www.caledonia.k12.mi.us/
Grade Span: PK-12; **Agency Type:** 1
Schools: 7
4 Primary; 1 Middle; 2 High; 0 Other Level
6 Regular; 0 Special Education; 0 Vocational; 1 Alternative
0 Magnet; 0 Charter; 0 Title I Eligible; 0 School-wide Title I
Students: 3,340 (53.7% male; 46.3% female)
Individual Education Program: 410 (12.3%);
English Language Learner: n/a; Migrant: n/a
Eligible for Free Lunch Program: 175 (5.2%)
Eligible for Reduced-Price Lunch Program: 118 (3.5%)
Teachers: 189.8 (17.6 to 1)
Librarians/Media Specialists: 1.0 (3,340.0 to 1)
Guidance Counselors: 2.5 (1,336.0 to 1)
Current Spending: ($ per student per year):
Total: $7,822; Instruction: $4,855; Support Services: $2,666
Enrollment, Drop-out Rates and Diploma Recipients by Race/Ethnicity

Category	Total	White	Black	Asian	AIAN	Hisp.
Enrollment (%)	100.0	97.7	0.3	1.0	0.2	0.7
Drop-out Rate (%)	n/a	n/a	n/a	n/a	n/a	n/a
H.S. Diplomas (#)	202	197	2	1	1	1

Cedar Springs Public Schools

204 E Muskegon St • Cedar Springs, MI 49319-9599
(616) 696-1204 • http://www.cedar-springs.k12.mi.us/
Grade Span: PK-12; **Agency Type:** 1
Schools: 6
2 Primary; 2 Middle; 2 High; 0 Other Level
5 Regular; 0 Special Education; 0 Vocational; 1 Alternative
0 Magnet; 0 Charter; 2 Title I Eligible; 2 School-wide Title I
Students: 3,489 (49.9% male; 50.1% female)
Individual Education Program: 430 (12.3%);
English Language Learner: 33 (0.9%); Migrant: n/a
Eligible for Free Lunch Program: 686 (19.7%)
Eligible for Reduced-Price Lunch Program: 261 (7.5%)
Teachers: 17.7 (197.1 to 1)
Librarians/Media Specialists: n/a
Guidance Counselors: 1.0 (3,489.0 to 1)
Current Spending: ($ per student per year):
Total: $6,665; Instruction: $4,052; Support Services: $2,367
Enrollment, Drop-out Rates and Diploma Recipients by Race/Ethnicity

Category	Total	White	Black	Asian	AIAN	Hisp.
Enrollment (%)	100.0	94.6	0.8	0.7	0.9	3.1
Drop-out Rate (%)	n/a	n/a	n/a	n/a	n/a	n/a
H.S. Diplomas (#)	132	126	2	4	0	0

Comstock Park Public Schools

101 School St NE • Comstock Park, MI 49321-0800
Mailing Address: PO Box 800 • Comstock Park, MI 49321-0800
(616) 254-5001 • http://www.cppschools.com
Grade Span: PK-12; **Agency Type:** 1
Schools: 6
3 Primary; 1 Middle; 1 High; 1 Other Level
5 Regular; 0 Special Education; 0 Vocational; 1 Alternative
0 Magnet; 0 Charter; 0 Title I Eligible; 0 School-wide Title I
Students: 2,262 (52.1% male; 47.9% female)
Individual Education Program: 353 (15.6%);
English Language Learner: n/a; Migrant: n/a
Eligible for Free Lunch Program: 232 (10.3%)
Eligible for Reduced-Price Lunch Program: 73 (3.2%)
Teachers: n/a
Librarians/Media Specialists: n/a
Guidance Counselors: n/a
Current Spending: ($ per student per year):
Total: $6,871; Instruction: $4,089; Support Services: $2,615
Enrollment, Drop-out Rates and Diploma Recipients by Race/Ethnicity

Category	Total	White	Black	Asian	AIAN	Hisp.
Enrollment (%)	100.0	88.2	5.4	1.7	0.6	4.1
Drop-out Rate (%)	n/a	n/a	n/a	n/a	n/a	n/a
H.S. Diplomas (#)	104	92	1	3	1	7

East Grand Rapids Public Schools

2915 Hall St SE • East Grand Rapids, MI 49506-3111
(616) 235-3535 • http://remc8.k12.mi.us/eastgr/egrps.html
Grade Span: KG-12; **Agency Type:** 1
Schools: 5
3 Primary; 1 Middle; 1 High; 0 Other Level
5 Regular; 0 Special Education; 0 Vocational; 0 Alternative
0 Magnet; 0 Charter; 0 Title I Eligible; 0 School-wide Title I
Students: 2,883 (51.4% male; 48.6% female)
Individual Education Program: 337 (11.7%);
English Language Learner: n/a; Migrant: n/a
Eligible for Free Lunch Program: 89 (3.1%)
Eligible for Reduced-Price Lunch Program: 6 (0.2%)
Teachers: 162.6 (17.7 to 1)
Librarians/Media Specialists: 2.3 (1,253.5 to 1)
Guidance Counselors: 4.0 (720.8 to 1)
Current Spending: ($ per student per year):
Total: $7,609; Instruction: $4,496; Support Services: $2,821
Enrollment, Drop-out Rates and Diploma Recipients by Race/Ethnicity

Category	Total	White	Black	Asian	AIAN	Hisp.
Enrollment (%)	100.0	94.5	2.2	1.7	0.0	1.5
Drop-out Rate (%)	n/a	n/a	n/a	n/a	n/a	n/a
H.S. Diplomas (#)	218	202	4	8	0	4

Forest Hills Public Schools

6590 Cascade Rd SE • Grand Rapids, MI 49546-6497
(616) 493-8800 • http://www.fhps.k12.mi.us/
Grade Span: PK-12; **Agency Type:** 1
Schools: 15
7 Primary; 5 Middle; 2 High; 0 Other Level
14 Regular; 0 Special Education; 0 Vocational; 0 Alternative
0 Magnet; 0 Charter; 0 Title I Eligible; 0 School-wide Title I
Students: 8,775 (51.5% male; 48.5% female)
Individual Education Program: 1,095 (12.5%);
English Language Learner: 179 (2.0%); Migrant: n/a
Eligible for Free Lunch Program: 212 (2.4%)
Eligible for Reduced-Price Lunch Program: 134 (1.5%)
Teachers: 507.7 (17.3 to 1)
Librarians/Media Specialists: 5.0 (1,755.0 to 1)
Guidance Counselors: 20.0 (438.8 to 1)
Current Spending: ($ per student per year):
Total: $8,217; Instruction: $4,976; Support Services: $3,021
Enrollment, Drop-out Rates and Diploma Recipients by Race/Ethnicity

Category	Total	White	Black	Asian	AIAN	Hisp.
Enrollment (%)	100.0	95.8	1.3	2.0	0.2	0.6
Drop-out Rate (%)	n/a	n/a	n/a	n/a	n/a	n/a
H.S. Diplomas (#)	659	618	5	26	1	9

Godfrey-Lee Public Schools

963 Joosten SW • Wyoming, MI 49509-1464
(616) 241-4722
Grade Span: PK-12; **Agency Type:** 1
Schools: 6
2 Primary; 1 Middle; 1 High; 2 Other Level
4 Regular; 0 Special Education; 0 Vocational; 2 Alternative
0 Magnet; 0 Charter; 0 Title I Eligible; 0 School-wide Title I
Students: 1,597 (49.5% male; 50.5% female)
Individual Education Program: 248 (15.5%);
English Language Learner: 534 (33.4%); Migrant: n/a
Eligible for Free Lunch Program: 887 (55.5%)
Eligible for Reduced-Price Lunch Program: 111 (7.0%)
Teachers: n/a
Librarians/Media Specialists: n/a
Guidance Counselors: n/a
Current Spending: ($ per student per year):
Total: $7,333; Instruction: $4,871; Support Services: $2,178
Enrollment, Drop-out Rates and Diploma Recipients by Race/Ethnicity

Category	Total	White	Black	Asian	AIAN	Hisp.
Enrollment (%)	100.0	41.6	13.9	1.7	0.8	42.0
Drop-out Rate (%)	n/a	n/a	n/a	n/a	n/a	n/a
H.S. Diplomas (#)	46	24	4	3	0	15

Godwin Heights Public Schools

15 36th St SW • Wyoming, MI 49548-2101
(616) 252-2090 • http://fp.remc8.k12.mi.us/godwin/
Grade Span: PK-12; **Agency Type:** 1
Schools: 6
3 Primary; 1 Middle; 1 High; 1 Other Level
5 Regular; 0 Special Education; 0 Vocational; 1 Alternative
0 Magnet; 0 Charter; 5 Title I Eligible; 5 School-wide Title I
Students: 2,341 (53.0% male; 47.0% female)
Individual Education Program: 359 (15.3%);
English Language Learner: 284 (12.1%); Migrant: n/a
Eligible for Free Lunch Program: 1,099 (46.9%)
Eligible for Reduced-Price Lunch Program: 287 (12.3%)
Teachers: 150.3 (15.6 to 1)
Librarians/Media Specialists: 2.0 (1,170.5 to 1)
Guidance Counselors: 6.0 (390.2 to 1)
Current Spending: ($ per student per year):
Total: $8,887; Instruction: $5,452; Support Services: $3,141
Enrollment, Drop-out Rates and Diploma Recipients by Race/Ethnicity

Category	Total	White	Black	Asian	AIAN	Hisp.
Enrollment (%)	100.0	60.4	13.3	4.7	1.0	20.6
Drop-out Rate (%)	n/a	n/a	n/a	n/a	n/a	n/a
H.S. Diplomas (#)	114	74	16	6	1	17

Grand Rapids Public Schools

1331 Franklin St SE • Grand Rapids, MI 49501-0117
Mailing Address: PO Box 117 • Grand Rapids, MI 49501-0117
(616) 771-2000 • http://www.grps.k12.mi.us/
Grade Span: PK-12; **Agency Type:** 1
Schools: 94
48 Primary; 8 Middle; 6 High; 32 Other Level
60 Regular; 15 Special Education; 0 Vocational; 19 Alternative
11 Magnet; 0 Charter; 47 Title I Eligible; 47 School-wide Title I
Students: 23,418 (52.3% male; 47.7% female)
Individual Education Program: 5,978 (25.5%);
English Language Learner: 4,818 (20.6%); Migrant: n/a
Eligible for Free Lunch Program: 14,438 (61.7%)
Eligible for Reduced-Price Lunch Program: 1,943 (8.3%)
Teachers: 1,637.1 (14.3 to 1)
Librarians/Media Specialists: 10.8 (2,168.3 to 1)
Guidance Counselors: 35.0 (669.1 to 1)
Current Spending: ($ per student per year):
Total: $9,625; Instruction: $5,565; Support Services: $3,760
Enrollment, Drop-out Rates and Diploma Recipients by Race/Ethnicity

Category	Total	White	Black	Asian	AIAN	Hisp.
Enrollment (%)	100.0	30.2	42.9	1.6	1.5	23.8
Drop-out Rate (%)	n/a	n/a	n/a	n/a	n/a	n/a
H.S. Diplomas (#)	708	259	308	21	9	111

Grandville Public Schools

3131 Barrett Ave SW • Grandville, MI 49418-1688
(616) 254-6550 • http://www.grandville.k12.mi.us/home/home.asp
Grade Span: KG-12; **Agency Type:** 1
Schools: 12
8 Primary; 2 Middle; 2 High; 0 Other Level
11 Regular; 0 Special Education; 0 Vocational; 1 Alternative
0 Magnet; 0 Charter; 0 Title I Eligible; 0 School-wide Title I
Students: 6,116 (50.9% male; 49.1% female)
Individual Education Program: 753 (12.3%);
English Language Learner: n/a; Migrant: n/a
Eligible for Free Lunch Program: 519 (8.5%)
Eligible for Reduced-Price Lunch Program: 269 (4.4%)
Teachers: 321.3 (19.0 to 1)
Librarians/Media Specialists: 6.0 (1,019.3 to 1)
Guidance Counselors: 8.0 (764.5 to 1)
Current Spending: ($ per student per year):
Total: $6,618; Instruction: $4,041; Support Services: $2,401
Enrollment, Drop-out Rates and Diploma Recipients by Race/Ethnicity

Category	Total	White	Black	Asian	AIAN	Hisp.
Enrollment (%)	100.0	90.2	2.9	2.7	0.4	3.7
Drop-out Rate (%)	n/a	n/a	n/a	n/a	n/a	n/a
H.S. Diplomas (#)	371	350	1	10	1	9

Kelloggsville Public Schools

242 52nd St SE • Grand Rapids, MI 49548-5899
(616) 538-7460 • http://www.kelloggsville.k12.mi.us/
Grade Span: PK-12; **Agency Type:** 1
Schools: 7
4 Primary; 1 Middle; 1 High; 1 Other Level
6 Regular; 0 Special Education; 0 Vocational; 1 Alternative
0 Magnet; 0 Charter; 0 Title I Eligible; 0 School-wide Title I
Students: 2,236 (50.7% male; 49.3% female)
Individual Education Program: 248 (11.1%);
English Language Learner: n/a; Migrant: n/a
Eligible for Free Lunch Program: 708 (31.7%)
Eligible for Reduced-Price Lunch Program: 256 (11.4%)
Teachers: 121.4 (18.4 to 1)
Librarians/Media Specialists: 2.0 (1,118.0 to 1)
Guidance Counselors: 4.3 (520.0 to 1)
Current Spending: ($ per student per year):
Total: $7,241; Instruction: $4,712; Support Services: $2,264
Enrollment, Drop-out Rates and Diploma Recipients by Race/Ethnicity

Category	Total	White	Black	Asian	AIAN	Hisp.
Enrollment (%)	100.0	66.2	13.0	4.7	1.9	14.3
Drop-out Rate (%)	n/a	n/a	n/a	n/a	n/a	n/a
H.S. Diplomas (#)	115	87	8	5	11	4

Kenowa Hills Public Schools

2325 4 Mile Rd NW • Grand Rapids, MI 49544-9704
(616) 784-2511 • http://www.remc8.k12.mi.us/kenowa/
Grade Span: PK-12; **Agency Type:** 1
Schools: 9
6 Primary; 2 Middle; 1 High; 0 Other Level
9 Regular; 0 Special Education; 0 Vocational; 0 Alternative
0 Magnet; 0 Charter; 0 Title I Eligible; 0 School-wide Title I
Students: 3,727 (52.0% male; 48.0% female)
Individual Education Program: 478 (12.8%);
English Language Learner: 123 (3.3%); Migrant: n/a
Eligible for Free Lunch Program: 613 (16.4%)
Eligible for Reduced-Price Lunch Program: 271 (7.3%)
Teachers: 204.2 (18.3 to 1)
Librarians/Media Specialists: 5.0 (745.4 to 1)
Guidance Counselors: 5.0 (745.4 to 1)
Current Spending: ($ per student per year):
Total: $7,399; Instruction: $4,299; Support Services: $2,794
Enrollment, Drop-out Rates and Diploma Recipients by Race/Ethnicity

Category	Total	White	Black	Asian	AIAN	Hisp.
Enrollment (%)	100.0	87.9	2.6	1.2	1.2	6.9
Drop-out Rate (%)	n/a	n/a	n/a	n/a	n/a	n/a
H.S. Diplomas (#)	217	209	4	1	2	1

Kentwood Public Schools

5820 Eastern Ave SE • Kentwood, MI 49508-6200
(616) 455-4400 • http://www.kentwoodps.org/
Grade Span: PK-12; **Agency Type:** 1
Schools: 17
10 Primary; 3 Middle; 2 High; 2 Other Level
15 Regular; 1 Special Education; 0 Vocational; 1 Alternative
0 Magnet; 0 Charter; 7 Title I Eligible; 7 School-wide Title I
Students: 9,218 (51.6% male; 48.4% female)
Individual Education Program: 1,156 (12.5%);
English Language Learner: 290 (3.1%); Migrant: n/a
Eligible for Free Lunch Program: 2,188 (23.7%)
Eligible for Reduced-Price Lunch Program: 634 (6.9%)
Teachers: 519.5 (17.7 to 1)
Librarians/Media Specialists: 5.0 (1,843.6 to 1)
Guidance Counselors: 17.0 (542.2 to 1)
Current Spending: ($ per student per year):
Total: $7,374; Instruction: $4,505; Support Services: $2,638
Enrollment, Drop-out Rates and Diploma Recipients by Race/Ethnicity

Category	Total	White	Black	Asian	AIAN	Hisp.
Enrollment (%)	100.0	62.5	24.5	6.1	0.9	6.0
Drop-out Rate (%)	n/a	n/a	n/a	n/a	n/a	n/a
H.S. Diplomas (#)	570	406	85	60	3	16

Lowell Area Schools

300 High St • Lowell, MI 49331-1478
(616) 897-8415 • http://www.lowell.k12.mi.us/
Grade Span: KG-12; **Agency Type:** 1
Schools: 6
3 Primary; 1 Middle; 1 High; 1 Other Level
5 Regular; 0 Special Education; 0 Vocational; 1 Alternative
0 Magnet; 0 Charter; 0 Title I Eligible; 0 School-wide Title I
Students: 4,004 (50.9% male; 49.1% female)
Individual Education Program: 466 (11.6%);
English Language Learner: n/a; Migrant: n/a
Eligible for Free Lunch Program: 425 (10.6%)
Eligible for Reduced-Price Lunch Program: 262 (6.5%)
Teachers: 214.4 (18.7 to 1)
Librarians/Media Specialists: 3.0 (1,334.7 to 1)
Guidance Counselors: 4.0 (1,001.0 to 1)
Current Spending: ($ per student per year):
Total: $6,718; Instruction: $4,013; Support Services: $2,421
Enrollment, Drop-out Rates and Diploma Recipients by Race/Ethnicity

Category	Total	White	Black	Asian	AIAN	Hisp.
Enrollment (%)	100.0	96.2	0.9	0.9	0.2	1.8
Drop-out Rate (%)	n/a	n/a	n/a	n/a	n/a	n/a
H.S. Diplomas (#)	224	216	0	3	4	1

Northview Public SD

4365 Hunsberger Dr NE • Grand Rapids, MI 49525-6128
(616) 363-6861 • http://www.nvps.net/
Grade Span: PK-12; **Agency Type:** 1
Schools: 7
3 Primary; 2 Middle; 2 High; 0 Other Level
6 Regular; 0 Special Education; 0 Vocational; 1 Alternative
0 Magnet; 0 Charter; 0 Title I Eligible; 0 School-wide Title I
Students: 3,447 (52.7% male; 47.3% female)
Individual Education Program: 478 (13.9%);
English Language Learner: n/a; Migrant: n/a
Eligible for Free Lunch Program: 361 (10.5%)
Eligible for Reduced-Price Lunch Program: 186 (5.4%)
Teachers: 176.3 (19.6 to 1)
Librarians/Media Specialists: 1.0 (3,447.0 to 1)
Guidance Counselors: 4.4 (783.4 to 1)
Current Spending: ($ per student per year):
Total: $7,091; Instruction: $4,557; Support Services: $2,286
Enrollment, Drop-out Rates and Diploma Recipients by Race/Ethnicity

Category	Total	White	Black	Asian	AIAN	Hisp.
Enrollment (%)	100.0	93.6	3.4	1.0	0.3	1.6
Drop-out Rate (%)	n/a	n/a	n/a	n/a	n/a	n/a
H.S. Diplomas (#)	258	242	3	5	0	8

Rockford Public Schools

350 N Main St • Rockford, MI 49341-1092
(616) 866-6557 • http://www.rockfordschools.org/
Grade Span: KG-12; **Agency Type:** 1
Schools: 13
8 Primary; 2 Middle; 1 High; 2 Other Level
12 Regular; 0 Special Education; 0 Vocational; 1 Alternative
0 Magnet; 0 Charter; 0 Title I Eligible; 0 School-wide Title I
Students: 7,590 (52.1% male; 47.9% female)
Individual Education Program: 798 (10.5%);
English Language Learner: n/a; Migrant: n/a
Eligible for Free Lunch Program: 292 (3.8%)
Eligible for Reduced-Price Lunch Program: 104 (1.4%)
Teachers: 395.1 (19.2 to 1)
Librarians/Media Specialists: 3.0 (2,530.0 to 1)
Guidance Counselors: 10.0 (759.0 to 1)
Current Spending: ($ per student per year):
Total: $7,027; Instruction: $4,257; Support Services: $2,528
Enrollment, Drop-out Rates and Diploma Recipients by Race/Ethnicity

Category	Total	White	Black	Asian	AIAN	Hisp.
Enrollment (%)	100.0	96.7	0.9	0.9	0.1	1.3
Drop-out Rate (%)	n/a	n/a	n/a	n/a	n/a	n/a
H.S. Diplomas (#)	559	537	3	9	1	9

Sparta Area Schools

465 S Union St • Sparta, MI 49345-1550
(616) 887-8253 • http://www.spartaschools.org/
Grade Span: PK-12; **Agency Type:** 1
Schools: 6
3 Primary; 1 Middle; 2 High; 0 Other Level
5 Regular; 0 Special Education; 0 Vocational; 1 Alternative
0 Magnet; 0 Charter; 0 Title I Eligible; 0 School-wide Title I
Students: 2,866 (51.6% male; 48.4% female)
Individual Education Program: 499 (17.4%);
English Language Learner: 245 (8.5%); Migrant: n/a
Eligible for Free Lunch Program: 570 (19.9%)
Eligible for Reduced-Price Lunch Program: 188 (6.6%)
Teachers: 166.3 (17.2 to 1)
Librarians/Media Specialists: 1.0 (2,866.0 to 1)
Guidance Counselors: 5.5 (521.1 to 1)
Current Spending: ($ per student per year):
Total: $6,650; Instruction: $4,300; Support Services: $2,136
Enrollment, Drop-out Rates and Diploma Recipients by Race/Ethnicity

Category	Total	White	Black	Asian	AIAN	Hisp.
Enrollment (%)	100.0	89.0	1.2	0.7	0.1	8.8
Drop-out Rate (%)	n/a	n/a	n/a	n/a	n/a	n/a
H.S. Diplomas (#)	190	181	1	5	0	3

Wyoming Public Schools

3575 Gladiola St SW • Wyoming, MI 49509-6299
(616) 530-7555 • http://www.remc8.k12.mi.us/wyoming/
Grade Span: PK-12; **Agency Type:** 1
Schools: 13
8 Primary; 2 Middle; 2 High; 1 Other Level
12 Regular; 1 Special Education; 0 Vocational; 0 Alternative
0 Magnet; 0 Charter; 5 Title I Eligible; 5 School-wide Title I
Students: 5,911 (52.0% male; 48.0% female)
Individual Education Program: 825 (14.0%);
English Language Learner: 391 (6.6%); Migrant: n/a
Eligible for Free Lunch Program: 1,568 (26.5%)
Eligible for Reduced-Price Lunch Program: 547 (9.3%)
Teachers: 346.8 (17.0 to 1)
Librarians/Media Specialists: 4.0 (1,477.8 to 1)
Guidance Counselors: 9.5 (622.2 to 1)
Current Spending: ($ per student per year):
Total: $7,716; Instruction: $4,711; Support Services: $2,738
Enrollment, Drop-out Rates and Diploma Recipients by Race/Ethnicity

Category	Total	White	Black	Asian	AIAN	Hisp.
Enrollment (%)	100.0	71.2	9.4	4.4	0.6	14.4
Drop-out Rate (%)	n/a	n/a	n/a	n/a	n/a	n/a
H.S. Diplomas (#)	347	292	11	16	1	27

Lapeer County

Almont Community Schools

401 Church St • Almont, MI 48003-1030
(810) 798-8561 • http://www.almont.k12.mi.us/
Grade Span: KG-12; **Agency Type:** 1
Schools: 3
2 Primary; 0 Middle; 1 High; 0 Other Level
3 Regular; 0 Special Education; 0 Vocational; 0 Alternative
0 Magnet; 0 Charter; 0 Title I Eligible; 0 School-wide Title I
Students: 1,755 (52.0% male; 48.0% female)
Individual Education Program: 147 (8.4%);
English Language Learner: n/a; Migrant: n/a
Eligible for Free Lunch Program: 163 (9.3%)
Eligible for Reduced-Price Lunch Program: 38 (2.2%)
Teachers: 87.5 (20.1 to 1)
Librarians/Media Specialists: 1.0 (1,755.0 to 1)
Guidance Counselors: 3.0 (585.0 to 1)
Current Spending: ($ per student per year):
Total: $6,011; Instruction: $3,578; Support Services: $2,246
Enrollment, Drop-out Rates and Diploma Recipients by Race/Ethnicity

Category	Total	White	Black	Asian	AIAN	Hisp.
Enrollment (%)	100.0	94.4	0.4	0.5	0.9	3.8
Drop-out Rate (%)	n/a	n/a	n/a	n/a	n/a	n/a
H.S. Diplomas (#)	88	86	0	1	1	0

Imlay City Community Schools

634 W Borland Rd • Imlay City, MI 48444-1416
Mailing Address: PO Box 128 • Imlay City, MI 48444-1416
(810) 724-9861 • http://imlay.imlay.k12.mi.us/
Grade Span: PK-12; **Agency Type:** 1
Schools: 5
1 Primary; 1 Middle; 1 High; 2 Other Level
4 Regular; 0 Special Education; 0 Vocational; 1 Alternative
5 Magnet; 0 Charter; 0 Title I Eligible; 0 School-wide Title I
Students: 2,390 (50.5% male; 49.5% female)
Individual Education Program: 266 (11.1%);
English Language Learner: 170 (7.1%); Migrant: n/a
Eligible for Free Lunch Program: 535 (22.4%)
Eligible for Reduced-Price Lunch Program: 175 (7.3%)
Teachers: 116.6 (20.5 to 1)
Librarians/Media Specialists: 1.0 (2,390.0 to 1)
Guidance Counselors: 3.0 (796.7 to 1)
Current Spending: ($ per student per year):
Total: $6,395; Instruction: $3,722; Support Services: $2,395
Enrollment, Drop-out Rates and Diploma Recipients by Race/Ethnicity

Category	Total	White	Black	Asian	AIAN	Hisp.
Enrollment (%)	100.0	80.5	0.7	1.3	0.0	17.3
Drop-out Rate (%)	n/a	n/a	n/a	n/a	n/a	n/a
H.S. Diplomas (#)	140	130	0	1	0	9

Lapeer Community Schools

1025 W Nepessing St • Lapeer, MI 48446-1873
(810) 667-2401 • http://www.lapeerschools.net/
Grade Span: PK-12; **Agency Type:** 1
Schools: 16
11 Primary; 2 Middle; 2 High; 1 Other Level
15 Regular; 0 Special Education; 0 Vocational; 1 Alternative
0 Magnet; 0 Charter; 2 Title I Eligible; 2 School-wide Title I
Students: 7,674 (52.2% male; 47.8% female)
Individual Education Program: 927 (12.1%);
English Language Learner: 10 (0.1%); Migrant: n/a
Eligible for Free Lunch Program: 1,141 (14.9%)
Eligible for Reduced-Price Lunch Program: 485 (6.3%)
Teachers: 384.4 (20.0 to 1)
Librarians/Media Specialists: 3.0 (2,558.0 to 1)
Guidance Counselors: 10.0 (767.4 to 1)
Current Spending: ($ per student per year):
Total: $6,493; Instruction: $4,024; Support Services: $2,208
Enrollment, Drop-out Rates and Diploma Recipients by Race/Ethnicity

Category	Total	White	Black	Asian	AIAN	Hisp.
Enrollment (%)	100.0	95.9	0.5	0.7	0.7	2.1
Drop-out Rate (%)	n/a	n/a	n/a	n/a	n/a	n/a
H.S. Diplomas (#)	475	452	1	7	2	13

North Branch Area Schools

6600 Brush St • North Branch, MI 48461-0620
Mailing Address: PO Box 3620 • North Branch, MI 48461-0620
(810) 688-3570
Grade Span: KG-12; **Agency Type:** 1
Schools: 5
2 Primary; 2 Middle; 1 High; 0 Other Level
5 Regular; 0 Special Education; 0 Vocational; 0 Alternative
0 Magnet; 0 Charter; 0 Title I Eligible; 0 School-wide Title I
Students: 2,664 (51.9% male; 48.1% female)
Individual Education Program: 308 (11.6%);
English Language Learner: n/a; Migrant: n/a
Eligible for Free Lunch Program: 494 (18.5%)
Eligible for Reduced-Price Lunch Program: 259 (9.7%)
Teachers: 141.2 (18.9 to 1)
Librarians/Media Specialists: 1.2 (2,220.0 to 1)
Guidance Counselors: 4.0 (666.0 to 1)
Current Spending: ($ per student per year):
Total: $6,353; Instruction: $4,086; Support Services: $2,014
Enrollment, Drop-out Rates and Diploma Recipients by Race/Ethnicity

Category	Total	White	Black	Asian	AIAN	Hisp.
Enrollment (%)	100.0	97.9	0.2	0.3	0.3	1.4
Drop-out Rate (%)	n/a	n/a	n/a	n/a	n/a	n/a
H.S. Diplomas (#)	169	164	1	1	0	3

Lenawee County

Adrian City SD

227 N Winter St • Adrian, MI 49221-2066
(517) 263-2115 • http://www.adrian.k12.mi.us/
Grade Span: PK-12; **Agency Type:** 1
Schools: 10
7 Primary; 2 Middle; 1 High; 0 Other Level
10 Regular; 0 Special Education; 0 Vocational; 0 Alternative
0 Magnet; 0 Charter; 5 Title I Eligible; 5 School-wide Title I
Students: 4,032 (51.2% male; 48.8% female)
Individual Education Program: 742 (18.4%);
English Language Learner: 598 (14.8%); Migrant: n/a
Eligible for Free Lunch Program: 1,517 (37.6%)
Eligible for Reduced-Price Lunch Program: 309 (7.7%)
Teachers: 233.1 (17.3 to 1)
Librarians/Media Specialists: 1.0 (4,032.0 to 1)
Guidance Counselors: 5.0 (806.4 to 1)
Current Spending: ($ per student per year):
Total: $7,712; Instruction: $4,505; Support Services: $2,922
Enrollment, Drop-out Rates and Diploma Recipients by Race/Ethnicity

Category	Total	White	Black	Asian	AIAN	Hisp.
Enrollment (%)	100.0	68.9	6.0	1.0	0.3	23.3
Drop-out Rate (%)	n/a	n/a	n/a	n/a	n/a	n/a
H.S. Diplomas (#)	246	199	8	4	1	34

Onsted Community Schools

10109 Slee Rd • Onsted, MI 49265-0220
Mailing Address: PO Box 220 • Onsted, MI 49265-0220
(517) 467-2174 • http://www.onsted.k12.mi.us/
Grade Span: KG-12; **Agency Type:** 1
Schools: 5
2 Primary; 1 Middle; 2 High; 0 Other Level
4 Regular; 0 Special Education; 0 Vocational; 1 Alternative
0 Magnet; 0 Charter; 5 Title I Eligible; 5 School-wide Title I
Students: 1,841 (52.9% male; 47.1% female)
Individual Education Program: 181 (9.8%);
English Language Learner: 1 (0.1%); Migrant: n/a
Eligible for Free Lunch Program: 158 (8.6%)
Eligible for Reduced-Price Lunch Program: 52 (2.8%)
Teachers: 106.0 (17.4 to 1)
Librarians/Media Specialists: 3.0 (613.7 to 1)
Guidance Counselors: 3.5 (526.0 to 1)
Current Spending: ($ per student per year):
Total: $6,317; Instruction: $4,029; Support Services: $2,005

Enrollment, Drop-out Rates and Diploma Recipients by Race/Ethnicity

Category	Total	White	Black	Asian	AIAN	Hisp.
Enrollment (%)	100.0	94.8	0.3	0.3	0.8	1.2
Drop-out Rate (%)	n/a	n/a	n/a	n/a	n/a	n/a
H.S. Diplomas (#)	120	114	1	0	1	4

Tecumseh Public Schools

304 W Chicago Blvd • Tecumseh, MI 49286-1399
(517) 424-7318 • http://www.tps.k12.mi.us/
Grade Span: KG-12; **Agency Type:** 1
Schools: 7
4 Primary; 1 Middle; 2 High; 0 Other Level
6 Regular; 0 Special Education; 0 Vocational; 1 Alternative
0 Magnet; 0 Charter; 0 Title I Eligible; 0 School-wide Title I
Students: 3,460 (50.7% male; 49.3% female)
Individual Education Program: 439 (12.7%);
English Language Learner: n/a; Migrant: n/a
Eligible for Free Lunch Program: 307 (8.9%)
Eligible for Reduced-Price Lunch Program: 115 (3.3%)
Teachers: 86.5 (40.0 to 1)
Librarians/Media Specialists: n/a
Guidance Counselors: 6.0 (576.7 to 1)
Current Spending: ($ per student per year):
Total: $6,326; Instruction: $4,043; Support Services: $2,038
Enrollment, Drop-out Rates and Diploma Recipients by Race/Ethnicity

Category	Total	White	Black	Asian	AIAN	Hisp.
Enrollment (%)	100.0	96.1	0.7	0.3	0.4	2.2
Drop-out Rate (%)	n/a	n/a	n/a	n/a	n/a	n/a
H.S. Diplomas (#)	214	197	1	3	4	9

Livingston County

Brighton Area Schools

125 S Church St • Brighton, MI 48116-2403
(810) 299-4000 • http://bas.k12.mi.us/
Grade Span: KG-12; **Agency Type:** 1
Schools: 9
6 Primary; 2 Middle; 1 High; 0 Other Level
9 Regular; 0 Special Education; 0 Vocational; 0 Alternative
0 Magnet; 0 Charter; 0 Title I Eligible; 0 School-wide Title I
Students: 7,221 (51.9% male; 48.1% female)
Individual Education Program: 924 (12.8%);
English Language Learner: n/a; Migrant: n/a
Eligible for Free Lunch Program: 226 (3.1%)
Eligible for Reduced-Price Lunch Program: 95 (1.3%)
Teachers: 373.4 (19.3 to 1)
Librarians/Media Specialists: 5.5 (1,312.9 to 1)
Guidance Counselors: 9.5 (760.1 to 1)
Current Spending: ($ per student per year):
Total: $6,590; Instruction: $4,095; Support Services: $2,253
Enrollment, Drop-out Rates and Diploma Recipients by Race/Ethnicity

Category	Total	White	Black	Asian	AIAN	Hisp.
Enrollment (%)	100.0	95.1	0.4	1.3	1.9	1.3
Drop-out Rate (%)	n/a	n/a	n/a	n/a	n/a	n/a
H.S. Diplomas (#)	485	459	0	10	14	2

Fowlerville Community Schools

735 N Grand • Fowlerville, MI 48836-0769
Mailing Address: PO Box 769 • Fowlerville, MI 48836-0769
(517) 223-6015 • http://scnc.fvl.k12.mi.us/
Grade Span: KG-12; **Agency Type:** 1
Schools: 6
2 Primary; 2 Middle; 1 High; 1 Other Level
5 Regular; 0 Special Education; 0 Vocational; 1 Alternative
0 Magnet; 0 Charter; 0 Title I Eligible; 0 School-wide Title I
Students: 3,211 (52.8% male; 47.2% female)
Individual Education Program: 392 (12.2%);
English Language Learner: n/a; Migrant: n/a
Eligible for Free Lunch Program: 383 (11.9%)
Eligible for Reduced-Price Lunch Program: 140 (4.4%)
Teachers: 169.5 (18.9 to 1)
Librarians/Media Specialists: 5.0 (642.2 to 1)
Guidance Counselors: 7.0 (458.7 to 1)
Current Spending: ($ per student per year):
Total: $6,560; Instruction: $3,887; Support Services: $2,388
Enrollment, Drop-out Rates and Diploma Recipients by Race/Ethnicity

Category	Total	White	Black	Asian	AIAN	Hisp.
Enrollment (%)	100.0	97.8	0.1	0.3	0.7	1.0
Drop-out Rate (%)	n/a	n/a	n/a	n/a	n/a	n/a
H.S. Diplomas (#)	206	197	0	3	2	4

Hartland Consolidated Schools

3642 Washington St • Hartland, MI 48353-0900
Mailing Address: PO Box 900 • Hartland, MI 48353-0900
(810) 632-7481 • http://hartland.k12.mi.us/
Grade Span: PK-12; **Agency Type:** 1
Schools: 8
4 Primary; 2 Middle; 1 High; 1 Other Level
7 Regular; 0 Special Education; 0 Vocational; 1 Alternative
0 Magnet; 0 Charter; 0 Title I Eligible; 0 School-wide Title I
Students: 4,964 (51.5% male; 48.5% female)
Individual Education Program: 566 (11.4%);
English Language Learner: n/a; Migrant: n/a
Eligible for Free Lunch Program: 143 (2.9%)
Eligible for Reduced-Price Lunch Program: 75 (1.5%)
Teachers: 252.5 (19.7 to 1)
Librarians/Media Specialists: 7.0 (709.1 to 1)
Guidance Counselors: 5.2 (954.6 to 1)
Current Spending: ($ per student per year):
Total: $6,461; Instruction: $3,966; Support Services: $2,309
Enrollment, Drop-out Rates and Diploma Recipients by Race/Ethnicity

Category	Total	White	Black	Asian	AIAN	Hisp.
Enrollment (%)	100.0	98.5	0.4	0.6	0.1	0.5
Drop-out Rate (%)	n/a	n/a	n/a	n/a	n/a	n/a
H.S. Diplomas (#)	285	276	1	2	3	3

Howell Public Schools

411 N Highlander Way • Howell, MI 48843-1021
(517) 548-6234 • http://hps.k12.mi.us/
Grade Span: KG-12; **Agency Type:** 1
Schools: 10
7 Primary; 2 Middle; 1 High; 0 Other Level
10 Regular; 0 Special Education; 0 Vocational; 0 Alternative
0 Magnet; 0 Charter; 0 Title I Eligible; 0 School-wide Title I
Students: 8,106 (52.3% male; 47.7% female)
Individual Education Program: 1,187 (14.6%);
English Language Learner: n/a; Migrant: n/a
Eligible for Free Lunch Program: 620 (7.6%)
Eligible for Reduced-Price Lunch Program: 268 (3.3%)
Teachers: 432.1 (18.8 to 1)
Librarians/Media Specialists: 2.0 (4,053.0 to 1)
Guidance Counselors: 7.0 (1,158.0 to 1)
Current Spending: ($ per student per year):
Total: $6,252; Instruction: $3,805; Support Services: $2,253
Enrollment, Drop-out Rates and Diploma Recipients by Race/Ethnicity

Category	Total	White	Black	Asian	AIAN	Hisp.
Enrollment (%)	100.0	97.1	0.4	0.6	0.7	1.2
Drop-out Rate (%)	n/a	n/a	n/a	n/a	n/a	n/a
H.S. Diplomas (#)	437	426	0	4	5	2

Pinckney Community Schools

2130 E M-36 • Pinckney, MI 48169-0009
(810) 225-3900 • http://www.pcs.k12.mi.us/
Grade Span: PK-12; **Agency Type:** 1
Schools: 9
6 Primary; 2 Middle; 1 High; 0 Other Level
9 Regular; 0 Special Education; 0 Vocational; 0 Alternative
0 Magnet; 0 Charter; 0 Title I Eligible; 0 School-wide Title I
Students: 5,078 (51.1% male; 48.9% female)
Individual Education Program: 641 (12.6%);
English Language Learner: n/a; Migrant: n/a
Eligible for Free Lunch Program: 220 (4.3%)
Eligible for Reduced-Price Lunch Program: 73 (1.4%)
Teachers: 267.5 (19.0 to 1)
Librarians/Media Specialists: 3.0 (1,692.7 to 1)
Guidance Counselors: 7.0 (725.4 to 1)
Current Spending: ($ per student per year):
Total: $6,412; Instruction: $3,909; Support Services: $2,312
Enrollment, Drop-out Rates and Diploma Recipients by Race/Ethnicity

Category	Total	White	Black	Asian	AIAN	Hisp.
Enrollment (%)	100.0	98.5	0.5	0.6	0.1	0.4
Drop-out Rate (%)	n/a	n/a	n/a	n/a	n/a	n/a
H.S. Diplomas (#)	301	294	1	2	1	3

Macomb County

Anchor Bay SD

52801 Ashley St • New Baltimore, MI 48047-3277
(586) 725-2861 • http://www.anchorbay.misd.net
Grade Span: PK-12; **Agency Type:** 1
Schools: 13
8 Primary; 1 Middle; 1 High; 2 Other Level
11 Regular; 0 Special Education; 0 Vocational; 1 Alternative
0 Magnet; 0 Charter; 0 Title I Eligible; 0 School-wide Title I
Students: 6,429 (51.2% male; 48.8% female)
Individual Education Program: 857 (13.3%);

English Language Learner: n/a; Migrant: n/a
Eligible for Free Lunch Program: 706 (11.0%)
Eligible for Reduced-Price Lunch Program: 336 (5.2%)
Teachers: 340.2 (18.9 to 1)
Librarians/Media Specialists: 3.0 (2,143.0 to 1)
Guidance Counselors: 6.0 (1,071.5 to 1)
Current Spending: ($ per student per year):
Total: $6,699; Instruction: $4,785; Support Services: $1,685
Enrollment, Drop-out Rates and Diploma Recipients by Race/Ethnicity

Category	Total	White	Black	Asian	AIAN	Hisp.
Enrollment (%)	100.0	90.2	4.1	1.1	0.5	3.9
Drop-out Rate (%)	n/a	n/a	n/a	n/a	n/a	n/a
H.S. Diplomas (#)	276	267	5	2	1	1

Armada Area Schools
74500 Burk St • Armada, MI 48005-3314
(586) 784-4511 •
http://www.macomb.k12.mi.us/armada/armada/armada.htm
Grade Span: PK-12; **Agency Type:** 1
Schools: 5
2 Primary; 1 Middle; 2 High; 0 Other Level
5 Regular; 0 Special Education; 0 Vocational; 0 Alternative
0 Magnet; 0 Charter; 0 Title I Eligible; 0 School-wide Title I
Students: 2,161 (52.6% male; 47.4% female)
Individual Education Program: 237 (11.0%);
English Language Learner: n/a; Migrant: n/a
Eligible for Free Lunch Program: 88 (4.1%)
Eligible for Reduced-Price Lunch Program: 25 (1.2%)
Teachers: 106.4 (20.3 to 1)
Librarians/Media Specialists: 3.0 (720.3 to 1)
Guidance Counselors: 3.0 (720.3 to 1)
Current Spending: ($ per student per year):
Total: $8,522; Instruction: $4,406; Support Services: $3,949
Enrollment, Drop-out Rates and Diploma Recipients by Race/Ethnicity

Category	Total	White	Black	Asian	AIAN	Hisp.
Enrollment (%)	100.0	96.9	0.4	0.6	0.5	1.7
Drop-out Rate (%)	n/a	n/a	n/a	n/a	n/a	n/a
H.S. Diplomas (#)	131	130	0	0	0	1

Center Line Public Schools
26400 Arsenal St • Center Line, MI 48015-1600
(586) 757-7000 • http://www.clps.org/
Grade Span: PK-12; **Agency Type:** 1
Schools: 7
5 Primary; 1 Middle; 1 High; 0 Other Level
7 Regular; 0 Special Education; 0 Vocational; 0 Alternative
0 Magnet; 0 Charter; 5 Title I Eligible; 5 School-wide Title I
Students: 2,949 (51.6% male; 48.4% female)
Individual Education Program: 478 (16.2%);
English Language Learner: n/a; Migrant: n/a
Eligible for Free Lunch Program: 697 (23.6%)
Eligible for Reduced-Price Lunch Program: 215 (7.3%)
Teachers: 180.1 (16.4 to 1)
Librarians/Media Specialists: 2.0 (1,474.5 to 1)
Guidance Counselors: 8.0 (368.6 to 1)
Current Spending: ($ per student per year):
Total: $9,260; Instruction: $5,664; Support Services: $3,372
Enrollment, Drop-out Rates and Diploma Recipients by Race/Ethnicity

Category	Total	White	Black	Asian	AIAN	Hisp.
Enrollment (%)	100.0	88.9	3.2	4.9	1.5	1.6
Drop-out Rate (%)	n/a	n/a	n/a	n/a	n/a	n/a
H.S. Diplomas (#)	154	139	3	7	3	2

Chippewa Valley Schools
19120 Cass Ave • Clinton Township, MI 48038-2301
(586) 723-2000 • http://www.chippewavalleyschools.org/
Grade Span: KG-12; **Agency Type:** 1
Schools: 17
11 Primary; 4 Middle; 2 High; 0 Other Level
17 Regular; 0 Special Education; 0 Vocational; 0 Alternative
17 Magnet; 0 Charter; 0 Title I Eligible; 0 School-wide Title I
Students: 13,272 (50.7% male; 49.3% female)
Individual Education Program: 1,268 (9.6%);
English Language Learner: 325 (2.4%); Migrant: n/a
Eligible for Free Lunch Program: 714 (5.4%)
Eligible for Reduced-Price Lunch Program: 342 (2.6%)
Teachers: 644.6 (20.6 to 1)
Librarians/Media Specialists: 7.0 (1,896.0 to 1)
Guidance Counselors: 26.0 (510.5 to 1)
Current Spending: ($ per student per year):
Total: $6,863; Instruction: $4,187; Support Services: $2,501
Enrollment, Drop-out Rates and Diploma Recipients by Race/Ethnicity

Category	Total	White	Black	Asian	AIAN	Hisp.
Enrollment (%)	100.0	94.0	2.4	2.2	0.2	1.1
Drop-out Rate (%)	n/a	n/a	n/a	n/a	n/a	n/a
H.S. Diplomas (#)	762	742	2	9	2	7

Clintondale Community Schools
35100 Little Mack Ave • Clinton Township, MI 48035-2633
(586) 791-6300 • http://www.clintondale.k12.mi.us/
Grade Span: PK-12; **Agency Type:** 1
Schools: 5
4 Primary; 0 Middle; 1 High; 0 Other Level
5 Regular; 0 Special Education; 0 Vocational; 0 Alternative
0 Magnet; 0 Charter; 0 Title I Eligible; 0 School-wide Title I
Students: 4,031 (52.1% male; 47.9% female)
Individual Education Program: 507 (12.6%);
English Language Learner: n/a; Migrant: n/a
Eligible for Free Lunch Program: 833 (20.7%)
Eligible for Reduced-Price Lunch Program: 190 (4.7%)
Teachers: 153.0 (26.3 to 1)
Librarians/Media Specialists: 1.0 (4,031.0 to 1)
Guidance Counselors: 3.0 (1,343.7 to 1)
Current Spending: ($ per student per year):
Total: $6,827; Instruction: $3,853; Support Services: $2,744
Enrollment, Drop-out Rates and Diploma Recipients by Race/Ethnicity

Category	Total	White	Black	Asian	AIAN	Hisp.
Enrollment (%)	100.0	62.8	32.0	3.6	0.1	1.5
Drop-out Rate (%)	n/a	n/a	n/a	n/a	n/a	n/a
H.S. Diplomas (#)	119	84	33	2	0	0

East Detroit Public Schools
15115 Deerfield Ave • Eastpointe, MI 48021-1515
(586) 445-4410 • http://www.macomb.k12.mi.us/eastdet/scheast.htm
Grade Span: PK-12; **Agency Type:** 1
Schools: 12
8 Primary; 2 Middle; 1 High; 1 Other Level
11 Regular; 0 Special Education; 0 Vocational; 1 Alternative
0 Magnet; 0 Charter; 0 Title I Eligible; 0 School-wide Title I
Students: 6,455 (51.0% male; 49.0% female)
Individual Education Program: 877 (13.6%);
English Language Learner: 99 (1.5%); Migrant: n/a
Eligible for Free Lunch Program: 1,669 (25.9%)
Eligible for Reduced-Price Lunch Program: 810 (12.5%)
Teachers: 353.6 (18.3 to 1)
Librarians/Media Specialists: 12.5 (516.4 to 1)
Guidance Counselors: 9.0 (717.2 to 1)
Current Spending: ($ per student per year):
Total: $7,573; Instruction: $4,560; Support Services: $2,774
Enrollment, Drop-out Rates and Diploma Recipients by Race/Ethnicity

Category	Total	White	Black	Asian	AIAN	Hisp.
Enrollment (%)	100.0	82.0	11.5	2.5	2.7	1.1
Drop-out Rate (%)	n/a	n/a	n/a	n/a	n/a	n/a
H.S. Diplomas (#)	342	303	21	8	10	0

Fitzgerald Public Schools
23200 Ryan Rd • Warren, MI 48091-1999
(586) 757-1750 • http://www.fitz.k12.mi.us/
Grade Span: PK-12; **Agency Type:** 1
Schools: 7
4 Primary; 1 Middle; 2 High; 0 Other Level
6 Regular; 0 Special Education; 0 Vocational; 1 Alternative
0 Magnet; 0 Charter; 0 Title I Eligible; 0 School-wide Title I
Students: 3,343 (53.6% male; 46.4% female)
Individual Education Program: 458 (13.7%);
English Language Learner: 162 (4.8%); Migrant: n/a
Eligible for Free Lunch Program: 982 (29.4%)
Eligible for Reduced-Price Lunch Program: 305 (9.1%)
Teachers: 165.5 (20.2 to 1)
Librarians/Media Specialists: 4.0 (835.8 to 1)
Guidance Counselors: 5.0 (668.6 to 1)
Current Spending: ($ per student per year):
Total: $8,634; Instruction: $4,654; Support Services: $3,712
Enrollment, Drop-out Rates and Diploma Recipients by Race/Ethnicity

Category	Total	White	Black	Asian	AIAN	Hisp.
Enrollment (%)	100.0	80.7	9.5	8.6	1.1	0.1
Drop-out Rate (%)	n/a	n/a	n/a	n/a	n/a	n/a
H.S. Diplomas (#)	169	133	6	24	4	2

Fraser Public Schools
33466 Garfield Rd • Fraser, MI 48026-1892
(586) 293-5100 • http://www.macomb.k12.mi.us/fraser/schfras.htm
Grade Span: PK-12; **Agency Type:** 1
Schools: 10
8 Primary; 1 Middle; 1 High; 0 Other Level
10 Regular; 0 Special Education; 0 Vocational; 0 Alternative

0 Magnet; 0 Charter; 0 Title I Eligible; 0 School-wide Title I
Students: 4,917 (52.1% male; 47.9% female)
Individual Education Program: 506 (10.3%);
English Language Learner: n/a; Migrant: n/a
Eligible for Free Lunch Program: 459 (9.3%)
Eligible for Reduced-Price Lunch Program: 185 (3.8%)
Teachers: 285.8 (17.2 to 1)
Librarians/Media Specialists: 3.0 (1,639.0 to 1)
Guidance Counselors: 6.0 (819.5 to 1)
Current Spending: ($ per student per year):
Total: $8,204; Instruction: $4,930; Support Services: $2,996
Enrollment, Drop-out Rates and Diploma Recipients by Race/Ethnicity

Category	Total	White	Black	Asian	AIAN	Hisp.
Enrollment (%)	100.0	93.5	3.6	1.5	1.0	0.4
Drop-out Rate (%)	n/a	n/a	n/a	n/a	n/a	n/a
H.S. Diplomas (#)	300	283	1	9	4	3

L'anse Creuse Public Schools
36727 Jefferson Ave • Harrison Township, MI 48045-2917
(586) 783-6300 • http://www.lc-ps.org/
Grade Span: PK-12; **Agency Type:** 1
Schools: 19
11 Primary; 4 Middle; 2 High; 2 Other Level
18 Regular; 0 Special Education; 1 Vocational; 0 Alternative
15 Magnet; 0 Charter; 4 Title I Eligible; 4 School-wide Title I
Students: 12,217 (50.4% male; 49.6% female)
Individual Education Program: 1,285 (10.5%);
English Language Learner: 264 (2.2%); Migrant: n/a
Eligible for Free Lunch Program: 1,398 (11.4%)
Eligible for Reduced-Price Lunch Program: 533 (4.4%)
Teachers: 605.2 (20.2 to 1)
Librarians/Media Specialists: 11.0 (1,110.6 to 1)
Guidance Counselors: 18.0 (678.7 to 1)
Current Spending: ($ per student per year):
Total: $7,454; Instruction: $4,411; Support Services: $2,813
Enrollment, Drop-out Rates and Diploma Recipients by Race/Ethnicity

Category	Total	White	Black	Asian	AIAN	Hisp.
Enrollment (%)	100.0	91.2	5.2	1.1	0.3	2.3
Drop-out Rate (%)	n/a	n/a	n/a	n/a	n/a	n/a
H.S. Diplomas (#)	615	576	21	10	3	5

Lake Shore Public Schools (Macomb)
28850 Harper Ave • Saint Clair Shores, MI 48081-1249
(586) 285-8480 • http://www.lakeshoreschools.org/
Grade Span: KG-12; **Agency Type:** 1
Schools: 5
3 Primary; 1 Middle; 1 High; 0 Other Level
5 Regular; 0 Special Education; 0 Vocational; 0 Alternative
0 Magnet; 0 Charter; 0 Title I Eligible; 0 School-wide Title I
Students: 3,385 (51.2% male; 48.8% female)
Individual Education Program: 438 (12.9%);
English Language Learner: n/a; Migrant: n/a
Eligible for Free Lunch Program: 287 (8.5%)
Eligible for Reduced-Price Lunch Program: 154 (4.5%)
Teachers: 181.2 (18.7 to 1)
Librarians/Media Specialists: 5.0 (677.0 to 1)
Guidance Counselors: 5.0 (677.0 to 1)
Current Spending: ($ per student per year):
Total: $7,809; Instruction: $4,148; Support Services: $3,366
Enrollment, Drop-out Rates and Diploma Recipients by Race/Ethnicity

Category	Total	White	Black	Asian	AIAN	Hisp.
Enrollment (%)	100.0	91.1	2.7	0.9	4.3	1.0
Drop-out Rate (%)	n/a	n/a	n/a	n/a	n/a	n/a
H.S. Diplomas (#)	194	175	5	2	9	3

Lakeview Public Schools (Macomb)
20300 Statler St • Saint Clair Shores, MI 48081-2181
(586) 445-4015 • http://www.lakeview.misd.net/
Grade Span: PK-12; **Agency Type:** 1
Schools: 6
4 Primary; 1 Middle; 1 High; 0 Other Level
6 Regular; 0 Special Education; 0 Vocational; 0 Alternative
0 Magnet; 0 Charter; 0 Title I Eligible; 0 School-wide Title I
Students: 3,409 (50.9% male; 49.1% female)
Individual Education Program: 380 (11.1%);
English Language Learner: n/a; Migrant: n/a
Eligible for Free Lunch Program: 177 (5.2%)
Eligible for Reduced-Price Lunch Program: 78 (2.3%)
Teachers: 154.2 (22.1 to 1)
Librarians/Media Specialists: 1.5 (2,272.7 to 1)
Guidance Counselors: 3.0 (1,136.3 to 1)
Current Spending: ($ per student per year):
Total: $7,607; Instruction: $4,261; Support Services: $3,181

Enrollment, Drop-out Rates and Diploma Recipients by Race/Ethnicity

Category	Total	White	Black	Asian	AIAN	Hisp.
Enrollment (%)	100.0	95.8	0.8	0.7	2.1	0.6
Drop-out Rate (%)	n/a	n/a	n/a	n/a	n/a	n/a
H.S. Diplomas (#)	218	210	0	2	5	1

Macomb ISD
44001 Garfield Rd • Clinton Township, MI 48038-1100
(586) 228-3300
Grade Span: 06-09; **Agency Type:** 4
Schools: 9
0 Primary; 1 Middle; 0 High; 8 Other Level
0 Regular; 9 Special Education; 0 Vocational; 0 Alternative
0 Magnet; 0 Charter; 0 Title I Eligible; 0 School-wide Title I
Students: 1,652 (69.9% male; 30.1% female)
Individual Education Program: n/a;
English Language Learner: 846 (51.2%); Migrant: n/a
Eligible for Free Lunch Program: n/a
Eligible for Reduced-Price Lunch Program: n/a
Teachers: 197.0 (8.4 to 1)
Librarians/Media Specialists: n/a
Guidance Counselors: n/a
Current Spending: ($ per student per year):
Total: n/a; Instruction: n/a; Support Services: n/a
Enrollment, Drop-out Rates and Diploma Recipients by Race/Ethnicity

Category	Total	White	Black	Asian	AIAN	Hisp.
Enrollment (%)	100.0	91.0	4.9	1.8	1.0	0.6
Drop-out Rate (%)	n/a	n/a	n/a	n/a	n/a	n/a
H.S. Diplomas (#)	n/a	n/a	n/a	n/a	n/a	n/a

Mount Clemens Community SD
167 Cass Ave • Mount Clemens, MI 48043-2297
(810) 469-6100 • http://www.mtclemens.k12.mi.us
Grade Span: PK-12; **Agency Type:** 1
Schools: 8
5 Primary; 1 Middle; 2 High; 0 Other Level
8 Regular; 0 Special Education; 0 Vocational; 0 Alternative
0 Magnet; 0 Charter; 0 Title I Eligible; 0 School-wide Title I
Students: 3,200 (49.7% male; 50.3% female)
Individual Education Program: 637 (19.9%);
English Language Learner: n/a; Migrant: n/a
Eligible for Free Lunch Program: 1,643 (51.3%)
Eligible for Reduced-Price Lunch Program: 302 (9.4%)
Teachers: 220.5 (14.5 to 1)
Librarians/Media Specialists: 4.0 (800.0 to 1)
Guidance Counselors: 3.0 (1,066.7 to 1)
Current Spending: ($ per student per year):
Total: $8,177; Instruction: $5,461; Support Services: $2,368
Enrollment, Drop-out Rates and Diploma Recipients by Race/Ethnicity

Category	Total	White	Black	Asian	AIAN	Hisp.
Enrollment (%)	100.0	48.3	45.8	1.7	0.6	2.5
Drop-out Rate (%)	n/a	n/a	n/a	n/a	n/a	n/a
H.S. Diplomas (#)	89	56	30	1	1	1

Richmond Community Schools
68931 S Main St • Richmond, MI 48062-1527
(586) 727-3565 • http://www.rcs.k12.in.us/default.asp
Grade Span: PK-12; **Agency Type:** 1
Schools: 3
1 Primary; 1 Middle; 1 High; 0 Other Level
3 Regular; 0 Special Education; 0 Vocational; 0 Alternative
0 Magnet; 0 Charter; 0 Title I Eligible; 0 School-wide Title I
Students: 2,039 (51.4% male; 48.6% female)
Individual Education Program: 332 (16.3%);
English Language Learner: n/a; Migrant: n/a
Eligible for Free Lunch Program: 169 (8.3%)
Eligible for Reduced-Price Lunch Program: 105 (5.1%)
Teachers: 106.5 (19.1 to 1)
Librarians/Media Specialists: 2.0 (1,019.5 to 1)
Guidance Counselors: 3.0 (679.7 to 1)
Current Spending: ($ per student per year):
Total: $6,583; Instruction: $3,737; Support Services: $2,614
Enrollment, Drop-out Rates and Diploma Recipients by Race/Ethnicity

Category	Total	White	Black	Asian	AIAN	Hisp.
Enrollment (%)	100.0	94.7	0.9	1.1	0.4	2.8
Drop-out Rate (%)	n/a	n/a	n/a	n/a	n/a	n/a
H.S. Diplomas (#)	145	144	0	1	0	0

Romeo Community Schools
316 N Main St • Romeo, MI 48065-4621
(586) 752-0200 • http://www.romeo.k12.mi.us/
Grade Span: PK-12; **Agency Type:** 1
Schools: 11
6 Primary; 2 Middle; 1 High; 1 Other Level
9 Regular; 0 Special Education; 0 Vocational; 1 Alternative

0 Magnet; 0 Charter; 0 Title I Eligible; 0 School-wide Title I
Students: 5,492 (51.1% male; 48.9% female)
Individual Education Program: 635 (11.6%);
English Language Learner: n/a; Migrant: n/a
Eligible for Free Lunch Program: 481 (8.8%)
Eligible for Reduced-Price Lunch Program: 210 (3.8%)
Teachers: 281.9 (19.5 to 1)
Librarians/Media Specialists: 9.0 (610.2 to 1)
Guidance Counselors: 13.5 (406.8 to 1)
Current Spending: ($ per student per year):
Total: $6,830; Instruction: $4,024; Support Services: $2,622

Enrollment, Drop-out Rates and Diploma Recipients by Race/Ethnicity

Category	Total	White	Black	Asian	AIAN	Hisp.
Enrollment (%)	100.0	94.6	1.6	0.7	0.4	2.7
Drop-out Rate (%)	n/a	n/a	n/a	n/a	n/a	n/a
H.S. Diplomas (#)	343	326	5	8	2	2

Roseville Community Schools
18975 Church St • Roseville, MI 48066-3952
(586) 445-5505 • http://www.rcs.misd.net/
Grade Span: PK-12; **Agency Type:** 1
Schools: 14
10 Primary; 2 Middle; 1 High; 1 Other Level
13 Regular; 0 Special Education; 0 Vocational; 1 Alternative
0 Magnet; 0 Charter; 1 Title I Eligible; 1 School-wide Title I
Students: 6,409 (52.9% male; 47.1% female)
Individual Education Program: 959 (15.0%);
English Language Learner: n/a; Migrant: n/a
Eligible for Free Lunch Program: 1,501 (23.4%)
Eligible for Reduced-Price Lunch Program: 668 (10.4%)
Teachers: 353.1 (18.2 to 1)
Librarians/Media Specialists: 9.0 (712.1 to 1)
Guidance Counselors: 8.0 (801.1 to 1)
Current Spending: ($ per student per year):
Total: $7,910; Instruction: $4,377; Support Services: $3,273

Enrollment, Drop-out Rates and Diploma Recipients by Race/Ethnicity

Category	Total	White	Black	Asian	AIAN	Hisp.
Enrollment (%)	100.0	86.2	6.8	2.7	2.7	1.5
Drop-out Rate (%)	n/a	n/a	n/a	n/a	n/a	n/a
H.S. Diplomas (#)	308	286	5	11	4	2

South Lake Schools
23101 Stadium Blvd • Saint Clair Shores, MI 48080-1172
(586) 435-1600
Grade Span: KG-12; **Agency Type:** 1
Schools: 6
4 Primary; 1 Middle; 1 High; 0 Other Level
6 Regular; 0 Special Education; 0 Vocational; 0 Alternative
0 Magnet; 0 Charter; 0 Title I Eligible; 0 School-wide Title I
Students: 2,439 (51.1% male; 48.9% female)
Individual Education Program: 356 (14.6%);
English Language Learner: n/a; Migrant: n/a
Eligible for Free Lunch Program: 281 (11.5%)
Eligible for Reduced-Price Lunch Program: 112 (4.6%)
Teachers: 141.3 (17.3 to 1)
Librarians/Media Specialists: 5.0 (487.8 to 1)
Guidance Counselors: 7.0 (348.4 to 1)
Current Spending: ($ per student per year):
Total: $9,084; Instruction: $4,467; Support Services: $4,409

Enrollment, Drop-out Rates and Diploma Recipients by Race/Ethnicity

Category	Total	White	Black	Asian	AIAN	Hisp.
Enrollment (%)	100.0	84.1	9.2	1.8	1.6	1.4
Drop-out Rate (%)	n/a	n/a	n/a	n/a	n/a	n/a
H.S. Diplomas (#)	155	138	8	2	6	1

Utica Community Schools
11303 Greendale Dr • Sterling Heights, MI 48312-2925
(586) 797-1000 • http://www.macomb.k12.mi.us/utica/schutic.htm
Grade Span: PK-12; **Agency Type:** 1
Schools: 43
30 Primary; 7 Middle; 6 High; 0 Other Level
42 Regular; 0 Special Education; 0 Vocational; 1 Alternative
0 Magnet; 0 Charter; 0 Title I Eligible; 0 School-wide Title I
Students: 29,177 (52.2% male; 47.8% female)
Individual Education Program: 3,268 (11.2%);
English Language Learner: 608 (2.1%); Migrant: n/a
Eligible for Free Lunch Program: 2,035 (7.0%)
Eligible for Reduced-Price Lunch Program: 692 (2.4%)
Teachers: 1,524.2 (19.1 to 1)
Librarians/Media Specialists: 44.5 (655.7 to 1)
Guidance Counselors: 44.0 (663.1 to 1)
Current Spending: ($ per student per year):
Total: $7,129; Instruction: $4,389; Support Services: $2,585

Enrollment, Drop-out Rates and Diploma Recipients by Race/Ethnicity

Category	Total	White	Black	Asian	AIAN	Hisp.
Enrollment (%)	100.0	92.9	1.4	3.2	0.2	2.2
Drop-out Rate (%)	n/a	n/a	n/a	n/a	n/a	n/a
H.S. Diplomas (#)	1,867	1,763	18	61	3	22

Van Dyke Public Schools
22100 Federal Ave • Warren, MI 48089-5301
(586) 758-8333 • http://www.macomb.k12.mi.us/vandyke/vandyke.htm
Grade Span: PK-12; **Agency Type:** 1
Schools: 11
7 Primary; 2 Middle; 2 High; 0 Other Level
9 Regular; 0 Special Education; 0 Vocational; 2 Alternative
0 Magnet; 0 Charter; 8 Title I Eligible; 8 School-wide Title I
Students: 4,201 (52.4% male; 47.6% female)
Individual Education Program: 664 (15.8%);
English Language Learner: n/a; Migrant: n/a
Eligible for Free Lunch Program: 2,063 (49.1%)
Eligible for Reduced-Price Lunch Program: 652 (15.5%)
Teachers: 203.7 (20.6 to 1)
Librarians/Media Specialists: 7.0 (600.1 to 1)
Guidance Counselors: 4.0 (1,050.3 to 1)
Current Spending: ($ per student per year):
Total: $8,995; Instruction: $4,763; Support Services: $3,888

Enrollment, Drop-out Rates and Diploma Recipients by Race/Ethnicity

Category	Total	White	Black	Asian	AIAN	Hisp.
Enrollment (%)	100.0	78.5	10.4	7.1	1.7	1.5
Drop-out Rate (%)	n/a	n/a	n/a	n/a	n/a	n/a
H.S. Diplomas (#)	155	118	10	19	6	2

Warren Consolidated Schools
31300 Anita St • Warren, MI 48093-1697
(586) 825-2400 • http://www.wcs.k12.mi.us/
Grade Span: PK-12; **Agency Type:** 1
Schools: 28
16 Primary; 6 Middle; 3 High; 3 Other Level
25 Regular; 1 Special Education; 1 Vocational; 1 Alternative
0 Magnet; 0 Charter; 0 Title I Eligible; 0 School-wide Title I
Students: 15,405 (50.6% male; 49.4% female)
Individual Education Program: 1,603 (10.4%);
English Language Learner: 3,882 (25.2%); Migrant: n/a
Eligible for Free Lunch Program: 2,339 (15.2%)
Eligible for Reduced-Price Lunch Program: 631 (4.1%)
Teachers: 861.7 (17.9 to 1)
Librarians/Media Specialists: 24.0 (641.9 to 1)
Guidance Counselors: 37.6 (409.7 to 1)
Current Spending: ($ per student per year):
Total: $8,945; Instruction: $4,829; Support Services: $3,923

Enrollment, Drop-out Rates and Diploma Recipients by Race/Ethnicity

Category	Total	White	Black	Asian	AIAN	Hisp.
Enrollment (%)	100.0	90.1	4.5	4.0	0.7	0.7
Drop-out Rate (%)	n/a	n/a	n/a	n/a	n/a	n/a
H.S. Diplomas (#)	970	905	19	39	0	7

Warren Woods Public Schools
27100 Schoenherr Rd • Warren, MI 48088
(586) 439-4401 • http://www.macomb.k12.mi.us/warrenw/home/home.htm
Grade Span: PK-12; **Agency Type:** 1
Schools: 7
4 Primary; 1 Middle; 2 High; 0 Other Level
6 Regular; 0 Special Education; 0 Vocational; 1 Alternative
0 Magnet; 0 Charter; 0 Title I Eligible; 0 School-wide Title I
Students: 3,243 (50.3% male; 49.7% female)
Individual Education Program: 469 (14.5%);
English Language Learner: n/a; Migrant: n/a
Eligible for Free Lunch Program: 306 (9.4%)
Eligible for Reduced-Price Lunch Program: 124 (3.8%)
Teachers: 172.2 (18.8 to 1)
Librarians/Media Specialists: 5.0 (648.6 to 1)
Guidance Counselors: 3.0 (1,081.0 to 1)
Current Spending: ($ per student per year):
Total: $8,714; Instruction: $4,965; Support Services: $3,534

Enrollment, Drop-out Rates and Diploma Recipients by Race/Ethnicity

Category	Total	White	Black	Asian	AIAN	Hisp.
Enrollment (%)	100.0	89.4	3.1	4.8	2.2	0.3
Drop-out Rate (%)	n/a	n/a	n/a	n/a	n/a	n/a
H.S. Diplomas (#)	191	184	0	7	0	0

Manistee County

Manistee Area Schools
550 Maple St • Manistee, MI 49660-1821
(231) 723-3521 • http://www.honoredstudents.org/maps/html/
Grade Span: KG-12; **Agency Type:** 1
Schools: 6

3 Primary; 2 Middle; 1 High; 0 Other Level
6 Regular; 0 Special Education; 0 Vocational; 0 Alternative
0 Magnet; 0 Charter; 0 Title I Eligible; 0 School-wide Title I
Students: 1,744 (51.4% male; 48.6% female)
Individual Education Program: 175 (10.0%);
English Language Learner: n/a; Migrant: n/a
Eligible for Free Lunch Program: 430 (24.7%)
Eligible for Reduced-Price Lunch Program: 182 (10.4%)
Teachers: n/a
Librarians/Media Specialists: n/a
Guidance Counselors: n/a
Current Spending: ($ per student per year):
Total: $7,222; Instruction: $4,567; Support Services: $2,391
Enrollment, Drop-out Rates and Diploma Recipients by Race/Ethnicity

Category	Total	White	Black	Asian	AIAN	Hisp.
Enrollment (%)	100.0	90.8	1.4	1.7	4.1	2.0
Drop-out Rate (%)	n/a	n/a	n/a	n/a	n/a	n/a
H.S. Diplomas (#)	135	129	0	2	1	3

Marquette County

Marquette Area Public Schools
1201 W Fair Ave • Marquette, MI 49855-2668
(906) 225-4200 • http://www.wpsweb.com
Grade Span: KG-12; **Agency Type:** 1
Schools: 7
4 Primary; 2 Middle; 1 High; 0 Other Level
7 Regular; 0 Special Education; 0 Vocational; 0 Alternative
0 Magnet; 0 Charter; 0 Title I Eligible; 0 School-wide Title I
Students: 3,767 (51.8% male; 48.2% female)
Individual Education Program: 607 (16.1%);
English Language Learner: 11 (0.3%); Migrant: n/a
Eligible for Free Lunch Program: 549 (14.6%)
Eligible for Reduced-Price Lunch Program: 162 (4.3%)
Teachers: 208.6 (18.1 to 1)
Librarians/Media Specialists: 1.7 (2,215.9 to 1)
Guidance Counselors: 7.7 (489.2 to 1)
Current Spending: ($ per student per year):
Total: $6,756; Instruction: $4,270; Support Services: $2,312
Enrollment, Drop-out Rates and Diploma Recipients by Race/Ethnicity

Category	Total	White	Black	Asian	AIAN	Hisp.
Enrollment (%)	100.0	91.7	1.3	1.1	5.2	0.7
Drop-out Rate (%)	n/a	n/a	n/a	n/a	n/a	n/a
H.S. Diplomas (#)	331	311	5	2	13	0

Mason County

Ludington Area SD
809 E Tinkham Ave • Ludington, MI 49431-1594
(231) 845-7303 • http://www.lasd.net
Grade Span: PK-12; **Agency Type:** 1
Schools: 8
6 Primary; 1 Middle; 1 High; 0 Other Level
8 Regular; 0 Special Education; 0 Vocational; 0 Alternative
8 Magnet; 0 Charter; 0 Title I Eligible; 0 School-wide Title I
Students: 2,560 (51.5% male; 48.5% female)
Individual Education Program: 328 (12.8%);
English Language Learner: n/a; Migrant: n/a
Eligible for Free Lunch Program: 543 (21.2%)
Eligible for Reduced-Price Lunch Program: 201 (7.9%)
Teachers: 160.0 (16.0 to 1)
Librarians/Media Specialists: 1.0 (2,560.0 to 1)
Guidance Counselors: 4.0 (640.0 to 1)
Current Spending: ($ per student per year):
Total: $6,999; Instruction: $4,812; Support Services: $1,984
Enrollment, Drop-out Rates and Diploma Recipients by Race/Ethnicity

Category	Total	White	Black	Asian	AIAN	Hisp.
Enrollment (%)	100.0	93.9	0.0	0.1	0.0	0.2
Drop-out Rate (%)	n/a	n/a	n/a	n/a	n/a	n/a
H.S. Diplomas (#)	178	167	2	3	0	6

Mason County Central Schools
300 W Broadway St • Scottville, MI 49454-1095
(231) 757-3713 • http://www.masoncountycentral.com/main/main.asp
Grade Span: KG-12; **Agency Type:** 1
Schools: 6
3 Primary; 1 Middle; 2 High; 0 Other Level
5 Regular; 0 Special Education; 0 Vocational; 1 Alternative
0 Magnet; 0 Charter; 4 Title I Eligible; 4 School-wide Title I
Students: 1,734 (54.6% male; 45.4% female)
Individual Education Program: 210 (12.1%);
English Language Learner: n/a; Migrant: n/a
Eligible for Free Lunch Program: 530 (30.6%)
Eligible for Reduced-Price Lunch Program: 214 (12.3%)
Teachers: 98.4 (17.6 to 1)
Librarians/Media Specialists: n/a
Guidance Counselors: 3.5 (495.4 to 1)
Current Spending: ($ per student per year):
Total: $7,705; Instruction: $4,911; Support Services: $2,262
Enrollment, Drop-out Rates and Diploma Recipients by Race/Ethnicity

Category	Total	White	Black	Asian	AIAN	Hisp.
Enrollment (%)	100.0	89.5	2.2	0.3	2.0	6.0
Drop-out Rate (%)	n/a	n/a	n/a	n/a	n/a	n/a
H.S. Diplomas (#)	114	111	0	1	0	2

Mecosta County

Big Rapids Public Schools
21034 15 Mile Rd • Big Rapids, MI 49307-9225
(231) 796-2627 • http://www.brps.k12.mi.us/
Grade Span: PK-12; **Agency Type:** 1
Schools: 7
4 Primary; 1 Middle; 1 High; 1 Other Level
6 Regular; 0 Special Education; 0 Vocational; 1 Alternative
0 Magnet; 0 Charter; 0 Title I Eligible; 0 School-wide Title I
Students: 2,197 (52.9% male; 47.1% female)
Individual Education Program: 412 (18.8%);
English Language Learner: n/a; Migrant: n/a
Eligible for Free Lunch Program: 717 (32.6%)
Eligible for Reduced-Price Lunch Program: 169 (7.7%)
Teachers: 119.0 (18.5 to 1)
Librarians/Media Specialists: 3.0 (732.3 to 1)
Guidance Counselors: 3.0 (732.3 to 1)
Current Spending: ($ per student per year):
Total: $6,747; Instruction: $4,047; Support Services: $2,318
Enrollment, Drop-out Rates and Diploma Recipients by Race/Ethnicity

Category	Total	White	Black	Asian	AIAN	Hisp.
Enrollment (%)	100.0	88.6	7.6	2.2	0.5	1.0
Drop-out Rate (%)	n/a	n/a	n/a	n/a	n/a	n/a
H.S. Diplomas (#)	170	163	1	6	0	0

Chippewa Hills SD
3226 Arthur Rd • Remus, MI 49340-9541
(989) 967-2000 • http://www.chippewa-hills.k12.mi.us/
Grade Span: PK-12; **Agency Type:** 1
Schools: 7
4 Primary; 1 Middle; 2 High; 0 Other Level
6 Regular; 0 Special Education; 0 Vocational; 1 Alternative
0 Magnet; 0 Charter; 3 Title I Eligible; 3 School-wide Title I
Students: 2,601 (50.5% male; 49.5% female)
Individual Education Program: 476 (18.3%);
English Language Learner: n/a; Migrant: n/a
Eligible for Free Lunch Program: 1,081 (41.6%)
Eligible for Reduced-Price Lunch Program: 316 (12.1%)
Teachers: 149.7 (17.4 to 1)
Librarians/Media Specialists: 2.0 (1,300.5 to 1)
Guidance Counselors: 5.5 (472.9 to 1)
Current Spending: ($ per student per year):
Total: $6,688; Instruction: $4,281; Support Services: $2,114
Enrollment, Drop-out Rates and Diploma Recipients by Race/Ethnicity

Category	Total	White	Black	Asian	AIAN	Hisp.
Enrollment (%)	100.0	89.5	1.4	0.3	8.1	0.7
Drop-out Rate (%)	n/a	n/a	n/a	n/a	n/a	n/a
H.S. Diplomas (#)	143	135	2	1	3	2

Morley Stanwood Community Schools
4700 Northland Dr • Morley, MI 49336-9522
(231) 856-4392 • http://www.moisd.k12.mi.us/
Grade Span: KG-12; **Agency Type:** 1
Schools: 4
2 Primary; 1 Middle; 1 High; 0 Other Level
4 Regular; 0 Special Education; 0 Vocational; 0 Alternative
0 Magnet; 0 Charter; 4 Title I Eligible; 4 School-wide Title I
Students: 1,615 (51.0% male; 49.0% female)
Individual Education Program: 226 (14.0%);
English Language Learner: n/a; Migrant: n/a
Eligible for Free Lunch Program: 587 (36.3%)
Eligible for Reduced-Price Lunch Program: 174 (10.8%)
Teachers: 94.5 (17.1 to 1)
Librarians/Media Specialists: 1.0 (1,615.0 to 1)
Guidance Counselors: 2.0 (807.5 to 1)
Current Spending: ($ per student per year):
Total: $6,484; Instruction: $4,180; Support Services: $2,004
Enrollment, Drop-out Rates and Diploma Recipients by Race/Ethnicity

Category	Total	White	Black	Asian	AIAN	Hisp.
Enrollment (%)	100.0	95.4	1.3	0.4	1.2	1.7
Drop-out Rate (%)	n/a	n/a	n/a	n/a	n/a	n/a
H.S. Diplomas (#)	86	83	1	0	1	1

Menominee County

Menominee Area Public Schools

1230 13th St • Menominee, MI 49858-2763
(906) 863-9951 • http://www.menominee.k12.mi.us/
Grade Span: PK-12; **Agency Type:** 1
Schools: 6
3 Primary; 1 Middle; 2 High; 0 Other Level
5 Regular; 0 Special Education; 0 Vocational; 1 Alternative
0 Magnet; 0 Charter; 0 Title I Eligible; 0 School-wide Title I
Students: 2,027 (51.8% male; 48.2% female)
Individual Education Program: 248 (12.2%);
English Language Learner: n/a; Migrant: n/a
Eligible for Free Lunch Program: 407 (20.1%)
Eligible for Reduced-Price Lunch Program: 165 (8.1%)
Teachers: 108.3 (18.7 to 1)
Librarians/Media Specialists: 2.0 (1,013.5 to 1)
Guidance Counselors: 6.0 (337.8 to 1)
Current Spending: ($ per student per year):
Total: $6,572; Instruction: $4,124; Support Services: $2,156
Enrollment, Drop-out Rates and Diploma Recipients by Race/Ethnicity

Category	Total	White	Black	Asian	AIAN	Hisp.
Enrollment (%)	100.0	96.9	0.7	0.3	0.0	0.3
Drop-out Rate (%)	n/a	n/a	n/a	n/a	n/a	n/a
H.S. Diplomas (#)	144	142	0	0	0	2

Midland County

Bullock Creek SD

1420 S Badour Rd • Midland, MI 48640-9545
(989) 631-9022 • http://www.bullockcreekschools.com/
Grade Span: KG-12; **Agency Type:** 1
Schools: 5
3 Primary; 1 Middle; 1 High; 0 Other Level
5 Regular; 0 Special Education; 0 Vocational; 0 Alternative
0 Magnet; 0 Charter; 1 Title I Eligible; 1 School-wide Title I
Students: 2,202 (51.4% male; 48.6% female)
Individual Education Program: 357 (16.2%);
English Language Learner: 1 (<0.1%); Migrant: n/a
Eligible for Free Lunch Program: 494 (22.4%)
Eligible for Reduced-Price Lunch Program: 135 (6.1%)
Teachers: 124.6 (17.7 to 1)
Librarians/Media Specialists: 3.0 (734.0 to 1)
Guidance Counselors: 6.0 (367.0 to 1)
Current Spending: ($ per student per year):
Total: $6,455; Instruction: $3,846; Support Services: $2,381
Enrollment, Drop-out Rates and Diploma Recipients by Race/Ethnicity

Category	Total	White	Black	Asian	AIAN	Hisp.
Enrollment (%)	100.0	97.0	1.0	0.6	0.7	0.6
Drop-out Rate (%)	n/a	n/a	n/a	n/a	n/a	n/a
H.S. Diplomas (#)	118	115	0	0	1	2

Meridian Public Schools

3361 N M-30 • Sanford, MI 48657-9503
(989) 687-3200 • http://www.merps.k12.mi.us/
Grade Span: PK-12; **Agency Type:** 1
Schools: 5
3 Primary; 1 Middle; 1 High; 0 Other Level
5 Regular; 0 Special Education; 0 Vocational; 0 Alternative
0 Magnet; 0 Charter; 1 Title I Eligible; 1 School-wide Title I
Students: 1,571 (50.6% male; 49.4% female)
Individual Education Program: 259 (16.5%);
English Language Learner: n/a; Migrant: n/a
Eligible for Free Lunch Program: 388 (24.7%)
Eligible for Reduced-Price Lunch Program: 154 (9.8%)
Teachers: 14.8 (106.1 to 1)
Librarians/Media Specialists: n/a
Guidance Counselors: n/a
Current Spending: ($ per student per year):
Total: $6,952; Instruction: $4,318; Support Services: $2,317
Enrollment, Drop-out Rates and Diploma Recipients by Race/Ethnicity

Category	Total	White	Black	Asian	AIAN	Hisp.
Enrollment (%)	100.0	98.1	0.6	0.3	0.4	0.6
Drop-out Rate (%)	n/a	n/a	n/a	n/a	n/a	n/a
H.S. Diplomas (#)	91	91	0	0	0	0

Midland Public Schools

600 E Carpenter St • Midland, MI 48640-5417
(989) 923-5001 • http://www.mps.k12.mi.us/
Grade Span: KG-12; **Agency Type:** 1
Schools: 20
12 Primary; 3 Middle; 2 High; 3 Other Level
17 Regular; 1 Special Education; 0 Vocational; 2 Alternative
0 Magnet; 0 Charter; 0 Title I Eligible; 0 School-wide Title I
Students: 9,685 (51.9% male; 48.1% female)
Individual Education Program: 1,218 (12.6%);
English Language Learner: 46 (0.5%); Migrant: n/a
Eligible for Free Lunch Program: 1,016 (10.5%)
Eligible for Reduced-Price Lunch Program: 381 (3.9%)
Teachers: 545.2 (17.8 to 1)
Librarians/Media Specialists: 16.6 (583.4 to 1)
Guidance Counselors: 21.4 (452.6 to 1)
Current Spending: ($ per student per year):
Total: $8,282; Instruction: $5,082; Support Services: $2,995
Enrollment, Drop-out Rates and Diploma Recipients by Race/Ethnicity

Category	Total	White	Black	Asian	AIAN	Hisp.
Enrollment (%)	100.0	92.3	2.5	2.6	0.7	1.9
Drop-out Rate (%)	n/a	n/a	n/a	n/a	n/a	n/a
H.S. Diplomas (#)	678	637	8	19	2	12

Monroe County

Airport Community SD

11270 Grafton Rd • Carleton, MI 48117-9392
(734) 654-2414 • http://airport.k12.mi.us/
Grade Span: KG-12; **Agency Type:** 1
Schools: 6
4 Primary; 1 Middle; 1 High; 0 Other Level
6 Regular; 0 Special Education; 0 Vocational; 0 Alternative
0 Magnet; 0 Charter; 0 Title I Eligible; 0 School-wide Title I
Students: 3,464 (52.2% male; 47.8% female)
Individual Education Program: 411 (11.9%);
English Language Learner: n/a; Migrant: n/a
Eligible for Free Lunch Program: 626 (18.1%)
Eligible for Reduced-Price Lunch Program: 201 (5.8%)
Teachers: 180.6 (19.2 to 1)
Librarians/Media Specialists: 2.0 (1,732.0 to 1)
Guidance Counselors: 5.0 (692.8 to 1)
Current Spending: ($ per student per year):
Total: $6,898; Instruction: $3,878; Support Services: $2,718
Enrollment, Drop-out Rates and Diploma Recipients by Race/Ethnicity

Category	Total	White	Black	Asian	AIAN	Hisp.
Enrollment (%)	100.0	93.9	3.6	0.5	0.4	1.6
Drop-out Rate (%)	n/a	n/a	n/a	n/a	n/a	n/a
H.S. Diplomas (#)	171	165	3	1	0	2

Bedford Public Schools

1623 W Sterns Rd • Temperance, MI 48182-1554
(734) 850-6000 • http://www.bedford.k12.mi.us/
Grade Span: KG-12; **Agency Type:** 1
Schools: 7
5 Primary; 1 Middle; 1 High; 0 Other Level
7 Regular; 0 Special Education; 0 Vocational; 0 Alternative
0 Magnet; 0 Charter; 0 Title I Eligible; 0 School-wide Title I
Students: 5,438 (50.5% male; 49.5% female)
Individual Education Program: 697 (12.8%);
English Language Learner: n/a; Migrant: n/a
Eligible for Free Lunch Program: 339 (6.2%)
Eligible for Reduced-Price Lunch Program: 135 (2.5%)
Teachers: 298.0 (18.2 to 1)
Librarians/Media Specialists: 6.0 (906.3 to 1)
Guidance Counselors: 7.2 (755.3 to 1)
Current Spending: ($ per student per year):
Total: $6,526; Instruction: $3,778; Support Services: $2,519
Enrollment, Drop-out Rates and Diploma Recipients by Race/Ethnicity

Category	Total	White	Black	Asian	AIAN	Hisp.
Enrollment (%)	100.0	95.2	1.4	0.8	0.3	2.4
Drop-out Rate (%)	n/a	n/a	n/a	n/a	n/a	n/a
H.S. Diplomas (#)	392	388	1	0	0	3

Dundee Community Schools

420 Ypsilanti St • Dundee, MI 48131-1199
(734) 529-2350 • http://www.dundee.k12.mi.us/
Grade Span: PK-12; **Agency Type:** 1
Schools: 4
1 Primary; 1 Middle; 1 High; 1 Other Level
3 Regular; 0 Special Education; 0 Vocational; 1 Alternative
0 Magnet; 0 Charter; 0 Title I Eligible; 0 School-wide Title I
Students: 1,646 (52.9% male; 47.1% female)
Individual Education Program: 156 (9.5%);
English Language Learner: n/a; Migrant: n/a
Eligible for Free Lunch Program: 250 (15.2%)
Eligible for Reduced-Price Lunch Program: 48 (2.9%)
Teachers: 39.0 (42.2 to 1)
Librarians/Media Specialists: 2.0 (823.0 to 1)
Guidance Counselors: 2.0 (823.0 to 1)
Current Spending: ($ per student per year):
Total: $6,214; Instruction: $3,823; Support Services: $2,170

Enrollment, Drop-out Rates and Diploma Recipients by Race/Ethnicity

Category	Total	White	Black	Asian	AIAN	Hisp.
Enrollment (%)	100.0	97.8	1.5	0.2	0.1	0.4
Drop-out Rate (%)	n/a	n/a	n/a	n/a	n/a	n/a
H.S. Diplomas (#)	91	91	0	0	0	0

Ida Public SD

3145 Prairie St • Ida, MI 48140-9778
(734) 269-9003 • http://www.idaschools.org/
Grade Span: PK-12; **Agency Type:** 1
Schools: 3
1 Primary; 1 Middle; 1 High; 0 Other Level
3 Regular; 0 Special Education; 0 Vocational; 0 Alternative
0 Magnet; 0 Charter; 0 Title I Eligible; 0 School-wide Title I
Students: 1,671 (53.5% male; 46.5% female)
Individual Education Program: 288 (17.2%);
English Language Learner: n/a; Migrant: n/a
Eligible for Free Lunch Program: 97 (5.8%)
Eligible for Reduced-Price Lunch Program: 53 (3.2%)
Teachers: 93.5 (17.9 to 1)
Librarians/Media Specialists: 1.0 (1,671.0 to 1)
Guidance Counselors: 2.0 (835.5 to 1)
Current Spending: ($ per student per year):
Total: $6,880; Instruction: $4,096; Support Services: $2,491
Enrollment, Drop-out Rates and Diploma Recipients by Race/Ethnicity

Category	Total	White	Black	Asian	AIAN	Hisp.
Enrollment (%)	100.0	98.5	0.2	0.2	0.1	1.0
Drop-out Rate (%)	n/a	n/a	n/a	n/a	n/a	n/a
H.S. Diplomas (#)	128	126	1	0	0	1

Jefferson Schools (Monroe)

2400 N Dixie Hwy • Monroe, MI 48162-5291
(734) 289-5550 • http://jefferson.k12.mi.us
Grade Span: PK-12; **Agency Type:** 1
Schools: 6
3 Primary; 1 Middle; 2 High; 0 Other Level
5 Regular; 0 Special Education; 0 Vocational; 1 Alternative
0 Magnet; 0 Charter; 0 Title I Eligible; 0 School-wide Title I
Students: 2,715 (51.5% male; 48.5% female)
Individual Education Program: 405 (14.9%);
English Language Learner: n/a; Migrant: n/a
Eligible for Free Lunch Program: 401 (14.8%)
Eligible for Reduced-Price Lunch Program: 197 (7.3%)
Teachers: 151.4 (17.9 to 1)
Librarians/Media Specialists: 3.8 (714.5 to 1)
Guidance Counselors: 4.0 (678.8 to 1)
Current Spending: ($ per student per year):
Total: $8,775; Instruction: $5,216; Support Services: $3,294
Enrollment, Drop-out Rates and Diploma Recipients by Race/Ethnicity

Category	Total	White	Black	Asian	AIAN	Hisp.
Enrollment (%)	100.0	96.3	0.7	0.5	0.8	1.8
Drop-out Rate (%)	n/a	n/a	n/a	n/a	n/a	n/a
H.S. Diplomas (#)	178	168	0	0	5	5

Mason Consolidated Schools (Monroe)

2400 Lakeside Rd • Erie, MI 48133-9318
(734) 848-9303 • http://scnc.eriemason.k12.mi.us
Grade Span: KG-12; **Agency Type:** 1
Schools: 5
3 Primary; 1 Middle; 1 High; 0 Other Level
5 Regular; 0 Special Education; 0 Vocational; 0 Alternative
0 Magnet; 0 Charter; 1 Title I Eligible; 1 School-wide Title I
Students: 1,567 (51.5% male; 48.5% female)
Individual Education Program: 225 (14.4%);
English Language Learner: n/a; Migrant: n/a
Eligible for Free Lunch Program: 309 (19.7%)
Eligible for Reduced-Price Lunch Program: 91 (5.8%)
Teachers: n/a
Librarians/Media Specialists: n/a
Guidance Counselors: n/a
Current Spending: ($ per student per year):
Total: $6,682; Instruction: $3,598; Support Services: $2,821
Enrollment, Drop-out Rates and Diploma Recipients by Race/Ethnicity

Category	Total	White	Black	Asian	AIAN	Hisp.
Enrollment (%)	100.0	86.9	1.0	0.4	6.8	4.9
Drop-out Rate (%)	n/a	n/a	n/a	n/a	n/a	n/a
H.S. Diplomas (#)	113	108	1	0	0	4

Monroe Public Schools

1275 N Macomb St • Monroe, MI 48162-0733
Mailing Address: PO Box 733 • Monroe, MI 48162-0733
(734) 241-0330 • http://www.monroe.k12.mi.us/
Grade Span: KG-12; **Agency Type:** 1
Schools: 13
9 Primary; 2 Middle; 1 High; 1 Other Level
12 Regular; 0 Special Education; 0 Vocational; 1 Alternative
0 Magnet; 0 Charter; 4 Title I Eligible; 4 School-wide Title I
Students: 7,226 (51.9% male; 48.1% female)
Individual Education Program: 922 (12.8%);
English Language Learner: 94 (1.3%); Migrant: n/a
Eligible for Free Lunch Program: 1,650 (22.8%)
Eligible for Reduced-Price Lunch Program: 376 (5.2%)
Teachers: 370.2 (19.5 to 1)
Librarians/Media Specialists: 4.0 (1,806.5 to 1)
Guidance Counselors: 20.0 (361.3 to 1)
Current Spending: ($ per student per year):
Total: $7,175; Instruction: $4,111; Support Services: $2,756
Enrollment, Drop-out Rates and Diploma Recipients by Race/Ethnicity

Category	Total	White	Black	Asian	AIAN	Hisp.
Enrollment (%)	100.0	87.8	7.8	1.1	0.1	3.1
Drop-out Rate (%)	n/a	n/a	n/a	n/a	n/a	n/a
H.S. Diplomas (#)	386	364	15	0	0	7

Montcalm County

Central Montcalm Public Schools

621 New St • Stanton, MI 48888-0009
Mailing Address: PO Box 9 • Stanton, MI 48888-0009
(989) 831-5243 • http://www.maisd.com/cms/
Grade Span: PK-12; **Agency Type:** 1
Schools: 6
2 Primary; 2 Middle; 1 High; 1 Other Level
5 Regular; 0 Special Education; 0 Vocational; 1 Alternative
0 Magnet; 0 Charter; 0 Title I Eligible; 0 School-wide Title I
Students: 2,123 (49.3% male; 50.7% female)
Individual Education Program: 289 (13.6%);
English Language Learner: n/a; Migrant: n/a
Eligible for Free Lunch Program: 569 (26.8%)
Eligible for Reduced-Price Lunch Program: 198 (9.3%)
Teachers: 120.5 (17.6 to 1)
Librarians/Media Specialists: 3.0 (707.7 to 1)
Guidance Counselors: 5.0 (424.6 to 1)
Current Spending: ($ per student per year):
Total: $6,564; Instruction: $4,030; Support Services: $2,251
Enrollment, Drop-out Rates and Diploma Recipients by Race/Ethnicity

Category	Total	White	Black	Asian	AIAN	Hisp.
Enrollment (%)	100.0	95.7	0.1	0.6	0.0	3.5
Drop-out Rate (%)	n/a	n/a	n/a	n/a	n/a	n/a
H.S. Diplomas (#)	122	122	0	0	0	0

Greenville Public Schools

1414 W Chase Rd • Greenville, MI 48838-1799
(616) 754-3686 • http://www.greenville.k12.mi.us/
Grade Span: PK-12; **Agency Type:** 1
Schools: 6
4 Primary; 1 Middle; 1 High; 0 Other Level
6 Regular; 0 Special Education; 0 Vocational; 0 Alternative
0 Magnet; 0 Charter; 2 Title I Eligible; 2 School-wide Title I
Students: 3,930 (51.4% male; 48.6% female)
Individual Education Program: 622 (15.8%);
English Language Learner: 13 (0.3%); Migrant: n/a
Eligible for Free Lunch Program: 766 (19.5%)
Eligible for Reduced-Price Lunch Program: 319 (8.1%)
Teachers: 217.3 (18.1 to 1)
Librarians/Media Specialists: 3.0 (1,310.0 to 1)
Guidance Counselors: 9.0 (436.7 to 1)
Current Spending: ($ per student per year):
Total: $6,484; Instruction: $4,039; Support Services: $2,246
Enrollment, Drop-out Rates and Diploma Recipients by Race/Ethnicity

Category	Total	White	Black	Asian	AIAN	Hisp.
Enrollment (%)	100.0	96.4	0.5	0.5	0.1	2.5
Drop-out Rate (%)	n/a	n/a	n/a	n/a	n/a	n/a
H.S. Diplomas (#)	242	235	1	2	0	4

Lakeview Community Schools (Montcalm)

123 5th St • Lakeview, MI 48850-9153
(989) 352-6226
Grade Span: PK-12; **Agency Type:** 1
Schools: 5
3 Primary; 1 Middle; 1 High; 0 Other Level
5 Regular; 0 Special Education; 0 Vocational; 0 Alternative
0 Magnet; 0 Charter; 0 Title I Eligible; 0 School-wide Title I
Students: 1,948 (51.8% male; 48.2% female)
Individual Education Program: 322 (16.5%);
English Language Learner: n/a; Migrant: n/a
Eligible for Free Lunch Program: 562 (28.9%)
Eligible for Reduced-Price Lunch Program: 200 (10.3%)
Teachers: 114.7 (17.0 to 1)
Librarians/Media Specialists: 2.0 (974.0 to 1)
Guidance Counselors: 4.0 (487.0 to 1)

Current Spending: ($ per student per year):
Total: $6,612; Instruction: $3,969; Support Services: $2,377

Enrollment, Drop-out Rates and Diploma Recipients by Race/Ethnicity

Category	Total	White	Black	Asian	AIAN	Hisp.
Enrollment (%)	100.0	96.1	0.9	1.3	0.6	1.2
Drop-out Rate (%)	n/a	n/a	n/a	n/a	n/a	n/a
H.S. Diplomas (#)	115	110	0	1	2	2

Tri County Area Schools

208 E Edgerton St • Howard City, MI 49329-0189
Mailing Address: PO Box 189 • Howard City, MI 49329-0189
(231) 937-5611 • http://www.tricountyschools.com/
Grade Span: PK-12; **Agency Type:** 1
Schools: 5
2 Primary; 2 Middle; 1 High; 0 Other Level
5 Regular; 0 Special Education; 0 Vocational; 0 Alternative
0 Magnet; 0 Charter; 0 Title I Eligible; 0 School-wide Title I
Students: 2,430 (52.5% male; 47.5% female)
Individual Education Program: 335 (13.8%);
English Language Learner: n/a; Migrant: n/a
Eligible for Free Lunch Program: 464 (19.1%)
Eligible for Reduced-Price Lunch Program: 319 (13.1%)
Teachers: 133.5 (18.2 to 1)
Librarians/Media Specialists: 5.0 (486.0 to 1)
Guidance Counselors: 2.0 (1,215.0 to 1)
Current Spending: ($ per student per year):
Total: $6,099; Instruction: $3,776; Support Services: $2,067

Enrollment, Drop-out Rates and Diploma Recipients by Race/Ethnicity

Category	Total	White	Black	Asian	AIAN	Hisp.
Enrollment (%)	100.0	95.9	0.2	0.2	0.5	2.3
Drop-out Rate (%)	n/a	n/a	n/a	n/a	n/a	n/a
H.S. Diplomas (#)	69	69	0	0	0	0

Muskegon County

Fruitport Community Schools

3255 Pontaluna Rd • Fruitport, MI 49415-9600
(231) 865-3154 • http://remc4.k12.mi.us/fport/home.htm
Grade Span: PK-12; **Agency Type:** 1
Schools: 6
3 Primary; 1 Middle; 1 High; 1 Other Level
5 Regular; 0 Special Education; 0 Vocational; 1 Alternative
0 Magnet; 0 Charter; 0 Title I Eligible; 0 School-wide Title I
Students: 3,360 (51.0% male; 49.0% female)
Individual Education Program: 550 (16.4%);
English Language Learner: n/a; Migrant: n/a
Eligible for Free Lunch Program: 722 (21.5%)
Eligible for Reduced-Price Lunch Program: 323 (9.6%)
Teachers: 182.8 (18.4 to 1)
Librarians/Media Specialists: 1.0 (3,360.0 to 1)
Guidance Counselors: 7.0 (480.0 to 1)
Current Spending: ($ per student per year):
Total: $7,316; Instruction: $4,110; Support Services: $2,980

Enrollment, Drop-out Rates and Diploma Recipients by Race/Ethnicity

Category	Total	White	Black	Asian	AIAN	Hisp.
Enrollment (%)	100.0	93.4	1.8	1.3	0.6	2.9
Drop-out Rate (%)	n/a	n/a	n/a	n/a	n/a	n/a
H.S. Diplomas (#)	201	197	2	1	0	1

Mona Shores Public SD

3374 Mccracken St • Norton Shores, MI 49441-3696
(231) 780-4751 • http://www.mona-shores.k12.mi.us/
Grade Span: PK-12; **Agency Type:** 1
Schools: 6
4 Primary; 1 Middle; 1 High; 0 Other Level
6 Regular; 0 Special Education; 0 Vocational; 0 Alternative
0 Magnet; 0 Charter; 0 Title I Eligible; 0 School-wide Title I
Students: 4,295 (51.6% male; 48.4% female)
Individual Education Program: 461 (10.7%);
English Language Learner: n/a; Migrant: n/a
Eligible for Free Lunch Program: 495 (11.5%)
Eligible for Reduced-Price Lunch Program: 237 (5.5%)
Teachers: 199.0 (21.6 to 1)
Librarians/Media Specialists: 3.0 (1,431.7 to 1)
Guidance Counselors: 5.0 (859.0 to 1)
Current Spending: ($ per student per year):
Total: $6,435; Instruction: $3,590; Support Services: $2,618

Enrollment, Drop-out Rates and Diploma Recipients by Race/Ethnicity

Category	Total	White	Black	Asian	AIAN	Hisp.
Enrollment (%)	100.0	89.2	4.3	1.8	1.2	3.4
Drop-out Rate (%)	n/a	n/a	n/a	n/a	n/a	n/a
H.S. Diplomas (#)	303	282	9	4	1	7

Montague Area Public Schools

4900 Stanton Blvd • Montague, MI 49437-1040
(231) 893-1515 • http://www.montague.k12.mi.us/
Grade Span: PK-12; **Agency Type:** 1
Schools: 3
1 Primary; 1 Middle; 1 High; 0 Other Level
3 Regular; 0 Special Education; 0 Vocational; 0 Alternative
0 Magnet; 0 Charter; 0 Title I Eligible; 0 School-wide Title I
Students: 1,599 (51.2% male; 48.8% female)
Individual Education Program: 237 (14.8%);
English Language Learner: 10 (0.6%); Migrant: n/a
Eligible for Free Lunch Program: 450 (28.1%)
Eligible for Reduced-Price Lunch Program: 155 (9.7%)
Teachers: 85.6 (18.7 to 1)
Librarians/Media Specialists: 0.6 (2,665.0 to 1)
Guidance Counselors: 4.0 (399.8 to 1)
Current Spending: ($ per student per year):
Total: $6,673; Instruction: $4,363; Support Services: $2,018

Enrollment, Drop-out Rates and Diploma Recipients by Race/Ethnicity

Category	Total	White	Black	Asian	AIAN	Hisp.
Enrollment (%)	100.0	92.4	1.4	0.6	0.2	5.4
Drop-out Rate (%)	n/a	n/a	n/a	n/a	n/a	n/a
H.S. Diplomas (#)	104	99	0	1	0	4

Muskegon City SD

349 W Webster Ave • Muskegon, MI 49440-1275
(231) 720-2000 • http://www.muskegon.k12.mi.us/
Grade Span: PK-12; **Agency Type:** 1
Schools: 18
12 Primary; 2 Middle; 1 High; 3 Other Level
14 Regular; 2 Special Education; 0 Vocational; 2 Alternative
0 Magnet; 0 Charter; 0 Title I Eligible; 0 School-wide Title I
Students: 7,687 (53.0% male; 47.0% female)
Individual Education Program: 1,478 (19.2%);
English Language Learner: 322 (4.2%); Migrant: n/a
Eligible for Free Lunch Program: 4,126 (53.7%)
Eligible for Reduced-Price Lunch Program: 605 (7.9%)
Teachers: 401.4 (19.2 to 1)
Librarians/Media Specialists: 3.0 (2,562.3 to 1)
Guidance Counselors: 10.0 (768.7 to 1)
Current Spending: ($ per student per year):
Total: $9,544; Instruction: $5,211; Support Services: $4,014

Enrollment, Drop-out Rates and Diploma Recipients by Race/Ethnicity

Category	Total	White	Black	Asian	AIAN	Hisp.
Enrollment (%)	100.0	44.5	43.3	1.8	1.4	9.0
Drop-out Rate (%)	n/a	n/a	n/a	n/a	n/a	n/a
H.S. Diplomas (#)	247	102	128	2	1	14

Muskegon Heights SD

2603 Leahy St • Muskegon Heights, MI 49444-2121
(231) 830-3221 • http://www.muskegon-heights.k12.mi.us/
Grade Span: PK-12; **Agency Type:** 1
Schools: 8
6 Primary; 1 Middle; 1 High; 0 Other Level
8 Regular; 0 Special Education; 0 Vocational; 0 Alternative
0 Magnet; 0 Charter; 0 Title I Eligible; 0 School-wide Title I
Students: 2,340 (50.6% male; 49.4% female)
Individual Education Program: 441 (18.8%);
English Language Learner: n/a; Migrant: n/a
Eligible for Free Lunch Program: 1,863 (79.6%)
Eligible for Reduced-Price Lunch Program: 149 (6.4%)
Teachers: 155.0 (15.1 to 1)
Librarians/Media Specialists: 1.0 (2,340.0 to 1)
Guidance Counselors: 2.0 (1,170.0 to 1)
Current Spending: ($ per student per year):
Total: $9,691; Instruction: $5,266; Support Services: $3,809

Enrollment, Drop-out Rates and Diploma Recipients by Race/Ethnicity

Category	Total	White	Black	Asian	AIAN	Hisp.
Enrollment (%)	100.0	2.1	93.7	2.4	0.2	1.7
Drop-out Rate (%)	n/a	n/a	n/a	n/a	n/a	n/a
H.S. Diplomas (#)	73	0	72	0	0	1

Oakridge Public Schools

275 S Wolf Lake Rd • Muskegon, MI 49442-3033
(231) 788-7100 • http://www.oakridge.k12.mi.us/
Grade Span: PK-12; **Agency Type:** 1
Schools: 5
1 Primary; 2 Middle; 1 High; 1 Other Level
5 Regular; 0 Special Education; 0 Vocational; 0 Alternative
0 Magnet; 0 Charter; 4 Title I Eligible; 4 School-wide Title I
Students: 1,987 (53.2% male; 46.8% female)
Individual Education Program: 236 (11.9%);
English Language Learner: 2 (0.1%); Migrant: n/a
Eligible for Free Lunch Program: 603 (30.3%)
Eligible for Reduced-Price Lunch Program: 282 (14.2%)

Teachers: 119.8 (16.6 to 1)
Librarians/Media Specialists: 2.0 (993.5 to 1)
Guidance Counselors: 3.0 (662.3 to 1)
Current Spending: ($ per student per year):
Total: $6,885; Instruction: $4,325; Support Services: $2,271
Enrollment, Drop-out Rates and Diploma Recipients by Race/Ethnicity

Category	Total	White	Black	Asian	AIAN	Hisp.
Enrollment (%)	100.0	93.9	0.8	0.7	0.4	4.4
Drop-out Rate (%)	n/a	n/a	n/a	n/a	n/a	n/a
H.S. Diplomas (#)	106	99	2	0	1	4

Orchard View Schools
2310 Marquette Ave • Muskegon, MI 49442-1498
(231) 760-1309 • http://www.orchardview.k12.mi.us/
Grade Span: PK-12; **Agency Type:** 1
Schools: 6
3 Primary; 1 Middle; 2 High; 0 Other Level
5 Regular; 0 Special Education; 0 Vocational; 1 Alternative
0 Magnet; 0 Charter; 0 Title I Eligible; 0 School-wide Title I
Students: 2,894 (50.7% male; 49.3% female)
Individual Education Program: 327 (11.3%);
English Language Learner: n/a; Migrant: n/a
Eligible for Free Lunch Program: 1,158 (40.0%)
Eligible for Reduced-Price Lunch Program: 386 (13.3%)
Teachers: 165.2 (17.5 to 1)
Librarians/Media Specialists: 4.0 (723.5 to 1)
Guidance Counselors: 4.0 (723.5 to 1)
Current Spending: ($ per student per year):
Total: $7,115; Instruction: $4,333; Support Services: $2,500
Enrollment, Drop-out Rates and Diploma Recipients by Race/Ethnicity

Category	Total	White	Black	Asian	AIAN	Hisp.
Enrollment (%)	100.0	85.2	7.9	0.5	1.6	4.8
Drop-out Rate (%)	n/a	n/a	n/a	n/a	n/a	n/a
H.S. Diplomas (#)	126	106	12	3	0	5

Reeths-Puffer Schools
991 W Giles Rd • Muskegon, MI 49445-1329
(231) 744-4736 • http://www.reeths-puffer.k12.mi.us/
Grade Span: PK-12; **Agency Type:** 1
Schools: 9
5 Primary; 1 Middle; 2 High; 1 Other Level
8 Regular; 0 Special Education; 0 Vocational; 1 Alternative
0 Magnet; 0 Charter; 0 Title I Eligible; 0 School-wide Title I
Students: 4,546 (52.0% male; 48.0% female)
Individual Education Program: 685 (15.1%);
English Language Learner: n/a; Migrant: n/a
Eligible for Free Lunch Program: 891 (19.6%)
Eligible for Reduced-Price Lunch Program: 290 (6.4%)
Teachers: 257.9 (17.6 to 1)
Librarians/Media Specialists: 2.0 (2,273.0 to 1)
Guidance Counselors: 5.0 (909.2 to 1)
Current Spending: ($ per student per year):
Total: $7,018; Instruction: $4,233; Support Services: $2,541
Enrollment, Drop-out Rates and Diploma Recipients by Race/Ethnicity

Category	Total	White	Black	Asian	AIAN	Hisp.
Enrollment (%)	100.0	91.1	5.6	0.6	0.6	2.2
Drop-out Rate (%)	n/a	n/a	n/a	n/a	n/a	n/a
H.S. Diplomas (#)	279	257	13	2	5	2

Whitehall District Schools
541 E Slocum St • Whitehall, MI 49461-1199
(231) 893-1005 • http://www.whitehallsd.k12.wi.us/
Grade Span: PK-12; **Agency Type:** 1
Schools: 4
1 Primary; 2 Middle; 1 High; 0 Other Level
4 Regular; 0 Special Education; 0 Vocational; 0 Alternative
3 Magnet; 0 Charter; 0 Title I Eligible; 0 School-wide Title I
Students: 2,273 (53.1% male; 46.9% female)
Individual Education Program: 276 (12.1%);
English Language Learner: 4 (0.2%); Migrant: n/a
Eligible for Free Lunch Program: 520 (22.9%)
Eligible for Reduced-Price Lunch Program: 118 (5.2%)
Teachers: 129.9 (17.5 to 1)
Librarians/Media Specialists: 2.0 (1,136.5 to 1)
Guidance Counselors: 5.0 (454.6 to 1)
Current Spending: ($ per student per year):
Total: $6,735; Instruction: $4,311; Support Services: $2,202
Enrollment, Drop-out Rates and Diploma Recipients by Race/Ethnicity

Category	Total	White	Black	Asian	AIAN	Hisp.
Enrollment (%)	100.0	91.0	6.1	0.6	0.7	1.5
Drop-out Rate (%)	n/a	n/a	n/a	n/a	n/a	n/a
H.S. Diplomas (#)	132	118	7	0	4	3

Newaygo County

Fremont Public SD
220 W Pine St • Fremont, MI 49412-1595
(231) 924-2350 • http://www.fpsweb.org/
Grade Span: KG-12; **Agency Type:** 1
Schools: 6
2 Primary; 2 Middle; 1 High; 1 Other Level
5 Regular; 0 Special Education; 0 Vocational; 1 Alternative
0 Magnet; 0 Charter; 0 Title I Eligible; 0 School-wide Title I
Students: 2,659 (49.9% male; 50.1% female)
Individual Education Program: 454 (17.1%);
English Language Learner: n/a; Migrant: n/a
Eligible for Free Lunch Program: 704 (26.5%)
Eligible for Reduced-Price Lunch Program: 188 (7.1%)
Teachers: 148.2 (17.9 to 1)
Librarians/Media Specialists: 2.7 (984.8 to 1)
Guidance Counselors: 4.5 (590.9 to 1)
Current Spending: ($ per student per year):
Total: $6,744; Instruction: $4,648; Support Services: $1,867
Enrollment, Drop-out Rates and Diploma Recipients by Race/Ethnicity

Category	Total	White	Black	Asian	AIAN	Hisp.
Enrollment (%)	100.0	92.7	1.1	1.0	0.3	4.9
Drop-out Rate (%)	n/a	n/a	n/a	n/a	n/a	n/a
H.S. Diplomas (#)	193	179	1	0	8	5

Grant Public SD
12192 S Elder Ave • Grant, MI 49327-9359
(231) 834-5621 • http://www.grantps.net/
Grade Span: KG-12; **Agency Type:** 1
Schools: 4
2 Primary; 1 Middle; 1 High; 0 Other Level
4 Regular; 0 Special Education; 0 Vocational; 0 Alternative
0 Magnet; 0 Charter; 0 Title I Eligible; 0 School-wide Title I
Students: 2,418 (52.7% male; 47.3% female)
Individual Education Program: 324 (13.4%);
English Language Learner: 252 (10.4%); Migrant: n/a
Eligible for Free Lunch Program: 690 (28.5%)
Eligible for Reduced-Price Lunch Program: 198 (8.2%)
Teachers: 134.3 (18.0 to 1)
Librarians/Media Specialists: 2.0 (1,209.0 to 1)
Guidance Counselors: 3.0 (806.0 to 1)
Current Spending: ($ per student per year):
Total: $6,269; Instruction: $4,043; Support Services: $1,982
Enrollment, Drop-out Rates and Diploma Recipients by Race/Ethnicity

Category	Total	White	Black	Asian	AIAN	Hisp.
Enrollment (%)	100.0	82.7	0.7	0.4	0.1	16.1
Drop-out Rate (%)	n/a	n/a	n/a	n/a	n/a	n/a
H.S. Diplomas (#)	137	125	0	1	0	11

Newaygo Public SD
360 S Mill St • Newaygo, MI 49337-0820
Mailing Address: PO Box 820 • Newaygo, MI 49337-0820
(231) 652-6984 • http://www.newaygo.net/
Grade Span: PK-12; **Agency Type:** 1
Schools: 5
1 Primary; 2 Middle; 1 High; 1 Other Level
4 Regular; 0 Special Education; 0 Vocational; 1 Alternative
0 Magnet; 0 Charter; 0 Title I Eligible; 0 School-wide Title I
Students: 2,432 (50.1% male; 49.9% female)
Individual Education Program: 274 (11.3%);
English Language Learner: n/a; Migrant: n/a
Eligible for Free Lunch Program: 571 (23.5%)
Eligible for Reduced-Price Lunch Program: 187 (7.7%)
Teachers: n/a
Librarians/Media Specialists: n/a
Guidance Counselors: n/a
Current Spending: ($ per student per year):
Total: $6,669; Instruction: $4,291; Support Services: $2,146
Enrollment, Drop-out Rates and Diploma Recipients by Race/Ethnicity

Category	Total	White	Black	Asian	AIAN	Hisp.
Enrollment (%)	100.0	91.2	0.6	0.3	0.4	7.1
Drop-out Rate (%)	n/a	n/a	n/a	n/a	n/a	n/a
H.S. Diplomas (#)	91	88	1	0	0	2

White Cloud Public Schools
553 Wilcox Ave • White Cloud, MI 49349-1003
Mailing Address: PO Box 1003 • White Cloud, MI 49349-1003
(231) 689-6591 • http://www.whitecloud.net/
Grade Span: KG-12; **Agency Type:** 1
Schools: 4
1 Primary; 1 Middle; 1 High; 0 Other Level
3 Regular; 0 Special Education; 0 Vocational; 0 Alternative
0 Magnet; 0 Charter; 1 Title I Eligible; 1 School-wide Title I
Students: 1,549 (51.1% male; 48.9% female)

Individual Education Program: 281 (18.1%);
English Language Learner: n/a; Migrant: n/a
Eligible for Free Lunch Program: 742 (47.9%)
Eligible for Reduced-Price Lunch Program: 195 (12.6%)
Teachers: 93.5 (16.6 to 1)
Librarians/Media Specialists: 1.0 (1,549.0 to 1)
Guidance Counselors: 2.0 (774.5 to 1)
Current Spending: ($ per student per year):
Total: $7,297; Instruction: $4,831; Support Services: $2,101
Enrollment, Drop-out Rates and Diploma Recipients by Race/Ethnicity

Category	Total	White	Black	Asian	AIAN	Hisp.
Enrollment (%)	100.0	92.7	4.2	1.0	0.6	1.5
Drop-out Rate (%)	n/a	n/a	n/a	n/a	n/a	n/a
H.S. Diplomas (#)	73	70	2	0	0	1

Oakland County

Avondale SD
260 S Squirrel Rd • Auburn Hills, MI 48326-3255
(248) 852-4411 • http://www.avondale.k12.mi.us/
Grade Span: PK-12; **Agency Type:** 1
Schools: 10
6 Primary; 2 Middle; 1 High; 1 Other Level
8 Regular; 1 Special Education; 0 Vocational; 1 Alternative
0 Magnet; 0 Charter; 3 Title I Eligible; 3 School-wide Title I
Students: 3,936 (51.0% male; 49.0% female)
Individual Education Program: 352 (8.9%);
English Language Learner: n/a; Migrant: n/a
Eligible for Free Lunch Program: 256 (6.5%)
Eligible for Reduced-Price Lunch Program: 100 (2.5%)
Teachers: 260.5 (15.1 to 1)
Librarians/Media Specialists: 6.0 (656.0 to 1)
Guidance Counselors: 8.0 (492.0 to 1)
Current Spending: ($ per student per year):
Total: $8,662; Instruction: $5,209; Support Services: $3,236
Enrollment, Drop-out Rates and Diploma Recipients by Race/Ethnicity

Category	Total	White	Black	Asian	AIAN	Hisp.
Enrollment (%)	100.0	75.6	12.9	7.3	0.4	3.5
Drop-out Rate (%)	n/a	n/a	n/a	n/a	n/a	n/a
H.S. Diplomas (#)	207	174	27	4	0	2

Berkley SD
2211 Oakshire St • Berkley, MI 48072-1290
(248) 837-8004 • http://www.berkley.k12.mi.us/
Grade Span: PK-12; **Agency Type:** 1
Schools: 10
7 Primary; 1 Middle; 1 High; 1 Other Level
9 Regular; 0 Special Education; 0 Vocational; 1 Alternative
0 Magnet; 0 Charter; 0 Title I Eligible; 0 School-wide Title I
Students: 4,505 (51.1% male; 48.9% female)
Individual Education Program: 506 (11.2%);
English Language Learner: 149 (3.3%); Migrant: n/a
Eligible for Free Lunch Program: 327 (7.3%)
Eligible for Reduced-Price Lunch Program: 150 (3.3%)
Teachers: 279.1 (16.1 to 1)
Librarians/Media Specialists: 6.0 (750.8 to 1)
Guidance Counselors: 8.0 (563.1 to 1)
Current Spending: ($ per student per year):
Total: $8,020; Instruction: $4,644; Support Services: $3,241
Enrollment, Drop-out Rates and Diploma Recipients by Race/Ethnicity

Category	Total	White	Black	Asian	AIAN	Hisp.
Enrollment (%)	100.0	84.4	12.4	1.7	0.6	0.8
Drop-out Rate (%)	n/a	n/a	n/a	n/a	n/a	n/a
H.S. Diplomas (#)	296	278	10	7	1	0

Birmingham City SD
550 W Merrill St • Birmingham, MI 48009-1443
(248) 203-3004 • http://www.birmingham.k12.mi.us/
Grade Span: PK-12; **Agency Type:** 1
Schools: 14
10 Primary; 2 Middle; 2 High; 0 Other Level
14 Regular; 0 Special Education; 0 Vocational; 0 Alternative
13 Magnet; 0 Charter; 0 Title I Eligible; 0 School-wide Title I
Students: 8,348 (51.4% male; 48.6% female)
Individual Education Program: 862 (10.3%);
English Language Learner: 180 (2.2%); Migrant: n/a
Eligible for Free Lunch Program: 163 (2.0%)
Eligible for Reduced-Price Lunch Program: 83 (1.0%)
Teachers: n/a
Librarians/Media Specialists: n/a
Guidance Counselors: n/a
Current Spending: ($ per student per year):
Total: $11,732; Instruction: $6,500; Support Services: $4,984

Enrollment, Drop-out Rates and Diploma Recipients by Race/Ethnicity

Category	Total	White	Black	Asian	AIAN	Hisp.
Enrollment (%)	100.0	90.4	6.3	2.3	0.2	0.8
Drop-out Rate (%)	n/a	n/a	n/a	n/a	n/a	n/a
H.S. Diplomas (#)	503	461	29	12	1	0

Bloomfield Hills SD
4175 Andover Rd • Bloomfield Hills, MI 48302-1903
Mailing Address: PO Box 816 • Bloomfield Hil, MI 48303-0816
(248) 341-5400 • http://www.bloomfield.org/
Grade Span: PK-12; **Agency Type:** 1
Schools: 14
7 Primary; 3 Middle; 3 High; 1 Other Level
12 Regular; 2 Special Education; 0 Vocational; 0 Alternative
0 Magnet; 0 Charter; 0 Title I Eligible; 0 School-wide Title I
Students: 6,465 (51.1% male; 48.9% female)
Individual Education Program: 902 (14.0%);
English Language Learner: 259 (4.0%); Migrant: n/a
Eligible for Free Lunch Program: 114 (1.8%)
Eligible for Reduced-Price Lunch Program: 31 (0.5%)
Teachers: 447.8 (14.4 to 1)
Librarians/Media Specialists: 10.5 (615.7 to 1)
Guidance Counselors: 16.6 (389.5 to 1)
Current Spending: ($ per student per year):
Total: $12,653; Instruction: $7,423; Support Services: $4,896
Enrollment, Drop-out Rates and Diploma Recipients by Race/Ethnicity

Category	Total	White	Black	Asian	AIAN	Hisp.
Enrollment (%)	100.0	81.2	7.1	10.4	0.5	0.9
Drop-out Rate (%)	n/a	n/a	n/a	n/a	n/a	n/a
H.S. Diplomas (#)	442	360	27	52	0	3

Brandon SD
1025 S Ortonville Rd • Ortonville, MI 48462-8547
(248) 627-1802 • http://www.brandon.k12.mi.us/splash.htm
Grade Span: PK-12; **Agency Type:** 1
Schools: 7
3 Primary; 2 Middle; 1 High; 1 Other Level
6 Regular; 0 Special Education; 0 Vocational; 1 Alternative
0 Magnet; 0 Charter; 0 Title I Eligible; 0 School-wide Title I
Students: 3,726 (50.6% male; 49.4% female)
Individual Education Program: 506 (13.6%);
English Language Learner: 12 (0.3%); Migrant: n/a
Eligible for Free Lunch Program: 355 (9.5%)
Eligible for Reduced-Price Lunch Program: 116 (3.1%)
Teachers: 192.0 (19.4 to 1)
Librarians/Media Specialists: 1.0 (3,726.0 to 1)
Guidance Counselors: 4.0 (931.5 to 1)
Current Spending: ($ per student per year):
Total: $6,591; Instruction: $3,925; Support Services: $2,458
Enrollment, Drop-out Rates and Diploma Recipients by Race/Ethnicity

Category	Total	White	Black	Asian	AIAN	Hisp.
Enrollment (%)	100.0	96.2	1.0	1.1	0.4	1.3
Drop-out Rate (%)	n/a	n/a	n/a	n/a	n/a	n/a
H.S. Diplomas (#)	237	232	1	1	1	2

Clarenceville SD
20210 Middlebelt Rd • Livonia, MI 48152-2002
(248) 473-8900 • http://www.clarenceville.k12.mi.us/
Grade Span: PK-12; **Agency Type:** 1
Schools: 4
2 Primary; 1 Middle; 1 High; 0 Other Level
4 Regular; 0 Special Education; 0 Vocational; 0 Alternative
0 Magnet; 0 Charter; 0 Title I Eligible; 0 School-wide Title I
Students: 1,989 (50.2% male; 49.8% female)
Individual Education Program: 271 (13.6%);
English Language Learner: n/a; Migrant: n/a
Eligible for Free Lunch Program: 363 (18.3%)
Eligible for Reduced-Price Lunch Program: 139 (7.0%)
Teachers: 112.4 (17.7 to 1)
Librarians/Media Specialists: 4.0 (497.3 to 1)
Guidance Counselors: 2.8 (710.4 to 1)
Current Spending: ($ per student per year):
Total: $8,102; Instruction: $4,529; Support Services: $3,348
Enrollment, Drop-out Rates and Diploma Recipients by Race/Ethnicity

Category	Total	White	Black	Asian	AIAN	Hisp.
Enrollment (%)	100.0	85.8	7.4	3.6	1.7	1.5
Drop-out Rate (%)	n/a	n/a	n/a	n/a	n/a	n/a
H.S. Diplomas (#)	94	80	8	2	0	4

Clarkston Community SD
6389 Clarkston Rd • Clarkston, MI 48347-1050
Mailing Address: PO Box 1050 • Clarkston, MI 48347-1050
(248) 623-5408 • http://www.clarkston.k12.mi.us/
Grade Span: PK-12; **Agency Type:** 1
Schools: 13

8 Primary; 2 Middle; 2 High; 1 Other Level
11 Regular; 1 Special Education; 0 Vocational; 1 Alternative
0 Magnet; 0 Charter; 4 Title I Eligible; 4 School-wide Title I
Students: 7,951 (51.6% male; 48.4% female)
Individual Education Program: 1,012 (12.7%);
English Language Learner: n/a; Migrant: n/a
Eligible for Free Lunch Program: 366 (4.6%)
Eligible for Reduced-Price Lunch Program: 152 (1.9%)
Teachers: 424.3 (18.7 to 1)
Librarians/Media Specialists: 10.0 (795.1 to 1)
Guidance Counselors: 10.0 (795.1 to 1)
Current Spending: ($ per student per year):
Total: $7,303; Instruction: $4,428; Support Services: $2,653
Enrollment, Drop-out Rates and Diploma Recipients by Race/Ethnicity

Category	Total	White	Black	Asian	AIAN	Hisp.
Enrollment (%)	100.0	94.3	1.5	1.4	0.2	2.4
Drop-out Rate (%)	n/a	n/a	n/a	n/a	n/a	n/a
H.S. Diplomas (#)	501	475	3	3	3	17

Clawson City SD

626 Phillips Ave • Clawson, MI 48017-1589
(248) 655-4400 • http://www.clawson.k12.mi.us/
Grade Span: PK-12; **Agency Type:** 1
Schools: 5
3 Primary; 1 Middle; 1 High; 0 Other Level
5 Regular; 0 Special Education; 0 Vocational; 0 Alternative
0 Magnet; 0 Charter; 0 Title I Eligible; 0 School-wide Title I
Students: 1,510 (53.6% male; 46.4% female)
Individual Education Program: 138 (9.1%);
English Language Learner: n/a; Migrant: n/a
Eligible for Free Lunch Program: 155 (10.3%)
Eligible for Reduced-Price Lunch Program: 62 (4.1%)
Teachers: 88.3 (17.1 to 1)
Librarians/Media Specialists: 2.0 (755.0 to 1)
Guidance Counselors: 1.8 (838.9 to 1)
Current Spending: ($ per student per year):
Total: $8,795; Instruction: $4,816; Support Services: $3,727
Enrollment, Drop-out Rates and Diploma Recipients by Race/Ethnicity

Category	Total	White	Black	Asian	AIAN	Hisp.
Enrollment (%)	100.0	96.2	0.9	1.7	0.0	0.4
Drop-out Rate (%)	n/a	n/a	n/a	n/a	n/a	n/a
H.S. Diplomas (#)	109	107	0	1	0	1

Farmington Public SD

32500 Shiawassee St • Farmington, MI 48336-2363
(248) 489-3300 • http://www.farmington.k12.mi.us/
Grade Span: PK-12; **Agency Type:** 1
Schools: 27
15 Primary; 4 Middle; 3 High; 5 Other Level
22 Regular; 4 Special Education; 0 Vocational; 1 Alternative
0 Magnet; 0 Charter; 0 Title I Eligible; 0 School-wide Title I
Students: 12,420 (51.8% male; 48.2% female)
Individual Education Program: 1,549 (12.5%);
English Language Learner: 2,496 (20.1%); Migrant: n/a
Eligible for Free Lunch Program: 768 (6.2%)
Eligible for Reduced-Price Lunch Program: 218 (1.8%)
Teachers: 764.0 (16.3 to 1)
Librarians/Media Specialists: 21.0 (591.4 to 1)
Guidance Counselors: 20.0 (621.0 to 1)
Current Spending: ($ per student per year):
Total: $11,057; Instruction: $6,130; Support Services: $4,685
Enrollment, Drop-out Rates and Diploma Recipients by Race/Ethnicity

Category	Total	White	Black	Asian	AIAN	Hisp.
Enrollment (%)	100.0	78.3	11.5	9.0	0.2	1.0
Drop-out Rate (%)	n/a	n/a	n/a	n/a	n/a	n/a
H.S. Diplomas (#)	847	704	81	56	0	6

Ferndale Public Schools

2920 Burdette • Ferndale, MI 48220-2356
(248) 586-8653 • http://www.ferndaleschools.org/
Grade Span: PK-12; **Agency Type:** 1
Schools: 7
4 Primary; 2 Middle; 1 High; 0 Other Level
7 Regular; 0 Special Education; 0 Vocational; 0 Alternative
0 Magnet; 0 Charter; 1 Title I Eligible; 1 School-wide Title I
Students: 3,935 (52.0% male; 48.0% female)
Individual Education Program: 391 (9.9%);
English Language Learner: n/a; Migrant: n/a
Eligible for Free Lunch Program: 925 (23.5%)
Eligible for Reduced-Price Lunch Program: 278 (7.1%)
Teachers: 176.5 (22.3 to 1)
Librarians/Media Specialists: 3.0 (1,311.7 to 1)
Guidance Counselors: 21.0 (187.4 to 1)
Current Spending: ($ per student per year):
Total: $8,390; Instruction: $4,555; Support Services: $3,578

Enrollment, Drop-out Rates and Diploma Recipients by Race/Ethnicity

Category	Total	White	Black	Asian	AIAN	Hisp.
Enrollment (%)	100.0	57.3	39.1	1.9	0.7	1.0
Drop-out Rate (%)	n/a	n/a	n/a	n/a	n/a	n/a
H.S. Diplomas (#)	202	118	78	5	0	1

Hazel Park City SD

23136 Hughes Ave • Hazel Park, MI 48030-1500
(248) 542-3910 • http://www.oakland.k12.mi.us/district/hazel.htm
Grade Span: PK-12; **Agency Type:** 1
Schools: 13
7 Primary; 2 Middle; 2 High; 2 Other Level
10 Regular; 2 Special Education; 0 Vocational; 1 Alternative
0 Magnet; 0 Charter; 8 Title I Eligible; 8 School-wide Title I
Students: 4,854 (52.7% male; 47.3% female)
Individual Education Program: 858 (17.7%);
English Language Learner: 379 (7.8%); Migrant: n/a
Eligible for Free Lunch Program: 1,872 (38.6%)
Eligible for Reduced-Price Lunch Program: 591 (12.2%)
Teachers: 278.0 (17.5 to 1)
Librarians/Media Specialists: 1.8 (2,696.7 to 1)
Guidance Counselors: 5.0 (970.8 to 1)
Current Spending: ($ per student per year):
Total: $9,100; Instruction: $5,305; Support Services: $3,507
Enrollment, Drop-out Rates and Diploma Recipients by Race/Ethnicity

Category	Total	White	Black	Asian	AIAN	Hisp.
Enrollment (%)	100.0	86.0	7.3	1.7	3.5	1.6
Drop-out Rate (%)	n/a	n/a	n/a	n/a	n/a	n/a
H.S. Diplomas (#)	157	132	2	2	17	4

Holly Area SD

111 College St • Holly, MI 48442-1720
(248) 328-3140 • http://www.hollyareaschools.com
Grade Span: PK-12; **Agency Type:** 1
Schools: 7
4 Primary; 1 Middle; 1 High; 1 Other Level
6 Regular; 1 Special Education; 0 Vocational; 0 Alternative
0 Magnet; 0 Charter; 0 Title I Eligible; 0 School-wide Title I
Students: 4,418 (52.1% male; 47.9% female)
Individual Education Program: 841 (19.0%);
English Language Learner: n/a; Migrant: n/a
Eligible for Free Lunch Program: 746 (16.9%)
Eligible for Reduced-Price Lunch Program: 240 (5.4%)
Teachers: 237.4 (18.6 to 1)
Librarians/Media Specialists: 2.0 (2,209.0 to 1)
Guidance Counselors: 9.0 (490.9 to 1)
Current Spending: ($ per student per year):
Total: $6,802; Instruction: $3,557; Support Services: $3,005
Enrollment, Drop-out Rates and Diploma Recipients by Race/Ethnicity

Category	Total	White	Black	Asian	AIAN	Hisp.
Enrollment (%)	100.0	93.7	3.3	0.9	0.2	1.9
Drop-out Rate (%)	n/a	n/a	n/a	n/a	n/a	n/a
H.S. Diplomas (#)	257	245	4	1	3	4

Huron Valley Schools

2390 S Milford Rd • Highland, MI 48357-4934
(248) 684-8000 • http://www.huronvalley.k12.mi.us/winindex.html
Grade Span: PK-12; **Agency Type:** 1
Schools: 18
11 Primary; 4 Middle; 3 High; 0 Other Level
18 Regular; 0 Special Education; 0 Vocational; 0 Alternative
0 Magnet; 0 Charter; 0 Title I Eligible; 0 School-wide Title I
Students: 10,965 (51.5% male; 48.5% female)
Individual Education Program: 1,411 (12.9%);
English Language Learner: n/a; Migrant: n/a
Eligible for Free Lunch Program: 886 (8.1%)
Eligible for Reduced-Price Lunch Program: 413 (3.8%)
Teachers: 578.4 (19.0 to 1)
Librarians/Media Specialists: 7.0 (1,566.4 to 1)
Guidance Counselors: 14.6 (751.0 to 1)
Current Spending: ($ per student per year):
Total: $6,838; Instruction: $3,747; Support Services: $2,896
Enrollment, Drop-out Rates and Diploma Recipients by Race/Ethnicity

Category	Total	White	Black	Asian	AIAN	Hisp.
Enrollment (%)	100.0	95.9	0.6	0.8	1.5	1.2
Drop-out Rate (%)	n/a	n/a	n/a	n/a	n/a	n/a
H.S. Diplomas (#)	622	597	2	6	9	8

Lake Orion Community Schools

315 N Lapeer St • Lake Orion, MI 48362-3165
(248) 693-5413 • http://www.lakeorion.k12.mi.us/
Grade Span: PK-12; **Agency Type:** 1
Schools: 12
7 Primary; 3 Middle; 2 High; 0 Other Level
11 Regular; 0 Special Education; 0 Vocational; 1 Alternative

0 Magnet; 0 Charter; 6 Title I Eligible; 6 School-wide Title I
Students: 7,840 (52.3% male; 47.7% female)
Individual Education Program: 783 (10.0%);
English Language Learner: 281 (3.6%); Migrant: n/a
Eligible for Free Lunch Program: 418 (5.3%)
Eligible for Reduced-Price Lunch Program: 211 (2.7%)
Teachers: 396.4 (19.8 to 1)
Librarians/Media Specialists: 11.0 (712.7 to 1)
Guidance Counselors: 11.0 (712.7 to 1)
Current Spending: ($ per student per year):
Total: $7,749; Instruction: $4,548; Support Services: $2,974
Enrollment, Drop-out Rates and Diploma Recipients by Race/Ethnicity

Category	Total	White	Black	Asian	AIAN	Hisp.
Enrollment (%)	100.0	93.7	2.0	1.4	1.0	1.9
Drop-out Rate (%)	n/a	n/a	n/a	n/a	n/a	n/a
H.S. Diplomas (#)	402	384	7	5	0	6

Lamphere Public Schools
31201 Dorchester St • Madison Heights, MI 48071-1099
(248) 589-1990 • http://www.lamphere.k12.mi.us/education/district/
Grade Span: PK-12; **Agency Type:** 1
Schools: 9
4 Primary; 1 Middle; 1 High; 3 Other Level
6 Regular; 2 Special Education; 0 Vocational; 1 Alternative
0 Magnet; 0 Charter; 0 Title I Eligible; 0 School-wide Title I
Students: 2,423 (51.7% male; 48.3% female)
Individual Education Program: 380 (15.7%);
English Language Learner: 236 (9.7%); Migrant: n/a
Eligible for Free Lunch Program: 450 (18.6%)
Eligible for Reduced-Price Lunch Program: 139 (5.7%)
Teachers: 147.7 (16.4 to 1)
Librarians/Media Specialists: 2.0 (1,211.5 to 1)
Guidance Counselors: 3.5 (692.3 to 1)
Current Spending: ($ per student per year):
Total: $10,613; Instruction: $5,826; Support Services: $4,531
Enrollment, Drop-out Rates and Diploma Recipients by Race/Ethnicity

Category	Total	White	Black	Asian	AIAN	Hisp.
Enrollment (%)	100.0	91.6	2.7	4.7	0.2	0.7
Drop-out Rate (%)	n/a	n/a	n/a	n/a	n/a	n/a
H.S. Diplomas (#)	167	162	2	1	0	2

Madison Public Schools (Oakland)
25421 Alger St • Madison Heights, MI 48071-3921
(248) 399-7800 • http://www.madisonschools.k12.mi.us/
Grade Span: PK-12; **Agency Type:** 1
Schools: 6
3 Primary; 1 Middle; 2 High; 0 Other Level
5 Regular; 0 Special Education; 0 Vocational; 1 Alternative
0 Magnet; 0 Charter; 0 Title I Eligible; 0 School-wide Title I
Students: 2,136 (51.4% male; 48.6% female)
Individual Education Program: 347 (16.2%);
English Language Learner: 232 (10.9%); Migrant: n/a
Eligible for Free Lunch Program: 601 (28.1%)
Eligible for Reduced-Price Lunch Program: 155 (7.3%)
Teachers: 129.3 (16.5 to 1)
Librarians/Media Specialists: 1.0 (2,136.0 to 1)
Guidance Counselors: 3.0 (712.0 to 1)
Current Spending: ($ per student per year):
Total: $7,413; Instruction: $4,322; Support Services: $2,808
Enrollment, Drop-out Rates and Diploma Recipients by Race/Ethnicity

Category	Total	White	Black	Asian	AIAN	Hisp.
Enrollment (%)	100.0	88.2	9.8	1.1	0.2	0.7
Drop-out Rate (%)	n/a	n/a	n/a	n/a	n/a	n/a
H.S. Diplomas (#)	86	81	5	0	0	0

Novi Community SD
25345 Taft Rd • Novi, MI 48374-2423
(248) 449-1200 • http://itc.novi.k12.mi.us/
Grade Span: PK-12; **Agency Type:** 1
Schools: 9
6 Primary; 2 Middle; 1 High; 0 Other Level
9 Regular; 0 Special Education; 0 Vocational; 0 Alternative
7 Magnet; 0 Charter; 0 Title I Eligible; 0 School-wide Title I
Students: 5,995 (51.6% male; 48.4% female)
Individual Education Program: 592 (9.9%);
English Language Learner: n/a; Migrant: n/a
Eligible for Free Lunch Program: 76 (1.3%)
Eligible for Reduced-Price Lunch Program: 26 (0.4%)
Teachers: n/a
Librarians/Media Specialists: n/a
Guidance Counselors: n/a
Current Spending: ($ per student per year):
Total: $8,636; Instruction: $5,477; Support Services: $2,893
Enrollment, Drop-out Rates and Diploma Recipients by Race/Ethnicity

Category	Total	White	Black	Asian	AIAN	Hisp.
Enrollment (%)	100.0	81.0	2.2	14.9	0.1	1.8
Drop-out Rate (%)	n/a	n/a	n/a	n/a	n/a	n/a
H.S. Diplomas (#)	389	345	5	34	0	5

Oak Park City SD
13900 Granzon St • Oak Park, MI 48237-2756
(248) 691-8400 • http://www.oakparkschools.org/
Grade Span: PK-12; **Agency Type:** 1
Schools: 8
6 Primary; 1 Middle; 1 High; 0 Other Level
8 Regular; 0 Special Education; 0 Vocational; 0 Alternative
0 Magnet; 0 Charter; 1 Title I Eligible; 1 School-wide Title I
Students: 4,141 (51.2% male; 48.8% female)
Individual Education Program: 373 (9.0%);
English Language Learner: 255 (6.2%); Migrant: n/a
Eligible for Free Lunch Program: 1,509 (36.4%)
Eligible for Reduced-Price Lunch Program: 325 (7.8%)
Teachers: 229.3 (18.1 to 1)
Librarians/Media Specialists: 4.0 (1,035.3 to 1)
Guidance Counselors: 5.0 (828.2 to 1)
Current Spending: ($ per student per year):
Total: $8,799; Instruction: $4,779; Support Services: $3,700
Enrollment, Drop-out Rates and Diploma Recipients by Race/Ethnicity

Category	Total	White	Black	Asian	AIAN	Hisp.
Enrollment (%)	100.0	9.3	88.2	1.2	0.8	0.4
Drop-out Rate (%)	n/a	n/a	n/a	n/a	n/a	n/a
H.S. Diplomas (#)	238	17	217	1	0	3

Oxford Area Community Schools
105 Pontiac St • Oxford, MI 48371-4863
(248) 969-5000 • http://www.oxford.k12.mi.us/
Grade Span: PK-12; **Agency Type:** 1
Schools: 8
5 Primary; 1 Middle; 1 High; 1 Other Level
7 Regular; 0 Special Education; 0 Vocational; 1 Alternative
0 Magnet; 0 Charter; 0 Title I Eligible; 0 School-wide Title I
Students: 4,047 (53.6% male; 46.4% female)
Individual Education Program: 438 (10.8%);
English Language Learner: n/a; Migrant: n/a
Eligible for Free Lunch Program: 336 (8.3%)
Eligible for Reduced-Price Lunch Program: 148 (3.7%)
Teachers: 211.5 (19.1 to 1)
Librarians/Media Specialists: 6.0 (674.5 to 1)
Guidance Counselors: 5.0 (809.4 to 1)
Current Spending: ($ per student per year):
Total: $7,405; Instruction: $4,295; Support Services: $2,900
Enrollment, Drop-out Rates and Diploma Recipients by Race/Ethnicity

Category	Total	White	Black	Asian	AIAN	Hisp.
Enrollment (%)	100.0	95.6	1.3	0.7	0.8	1.5
Drop-out Rate (%)	n/a	n/a	n/a	n/a	n/a	n/a
H.S. Diplomas (#)	235	225	3	5	1	1

Pontiac City SD
47200 Woodward • Pontiac, MI 48342-2243
(248) 451-6883 • http://www.pontiac.k12.mi.us/
Grade Span: PK-12; **Agency Type:** 1
Schools: 24
13 Primary; 4 Middle; 4 High; 3 Other Level
20 Regular; 2 Special Education; 0 Vocational; 2 Alternative
0 Magnet; 0 Charter; 0 Title I Eligible; 0 School-wide Title I
Students: 11,886 (51.3% male; 48.7% female)
Individual Education Program: 1,901 (16.0%);
English Language Learner: 1,832 (15.4%); Migrant: n/a
Eligible for Free Lunch Program: 7,455 (62.7%)
Eligible for Reduced-Price Lunch Program: 888 (7.5%)
Teachers: 684.0 (17.4 to 1)
Librarians/Media Specialists: 12.0 (990.5 to 1)
Guidance Counselors: 11.0 (1,080.5 to 1)
Current Spending: ($ per student per year):
Total: $8,902; Instruction: $5,191; Support Services: $3,406
Enrollment, Drop-out Rates and Diploma Recipients by Race/Ethnicity

Category	Total	White	Black	Asian	AIAN	Hisp.
Enrollment (%)	100.0	16.6	62.3	5.0	0.6	15.6
Drop-out Rate (%)	n/a	n/a	n/a	n/a	n/a	n/a
H.S. Diplomas (#)	416	60	284	17	12	43

Rochester Community SD
501 W University Dr • Rochester, MI 48307-1944
(248) 651-6210 • http://www.rochester.k12.mi.us/
Grade Span: KG-12; **Agency Type:** 1
Schools: 21
13 Primary; 4 Middle; 4 High; 0 Other Level
20 Regular; 0 Special Education; 0 Vocational; 1 Alternative

0 Magnet; 0 Charter; 0 Title I Eligible; 0 School-wide Title I
Students: 14,311 (51.0% male; 49.0% female)
Individual Education Program: 1,425 (10.0%);
English Language Learner: 907 (6.3%); Migrant: n/a
Eligible for Free Lunch Program: 423 (3.0%)
Eligible for Reduced-Price Lunch Program: 173 (1.2%)
Teachers: 706.6 (20.3 to 1)
Librarians/Media Specialists: 18.0 (795.1 to 1)
Guidance Counselors: 19.0 (753.2 to 1)
Current Spending: ($ per student per year):
Total: $7,792; Instruction: $4,637; Support Services: $2,946
Enrollment, Drop-out Rates and Diploma Recipients by Race/Ethnicity

Category	Total	White	Black	Asian	AIAN	Hisp.
Enrollment (%)	100.0	96.9	0.8	1.8	0.0	0.4
Drop-out Rate (%)	n/a	n/a	n/a	n/a	n/a	n/a
H.S. Diplomas (#)	1,009	894	28	72	1	14

School District of Royal Oak
1123 Lexington Blvd • Royal Oak, MI 48073-2438
(248) 435-8400 • http://www.rosd.k12.mi.us/
Grade Span: PK-12; **Agency Type:** 1
Schools: 15
11 Primary; 2 Middle; 2 High; 0 Other Level
15 Regular; 0 Special Education; 0 Vocational; 0 Alternative
0 Magnet; 0 Charter; 0 Title I Eligible; 0 School-wide Title I
Students: 6,840 (52.4% male; 47.6% female)
Individual Education Program: 895 (13.1%);
English Language Learner: 189 (2.8%); Migrant: n/a
Eligible for Free Lunch Program: 553 (8.1%)
Eligible for Reduced-Price Lunch Program: 207 (3.0%)
Teachers: 409.4 (16.7 to 1)
Librarians/Media Specialists: 3.8 (1,800.0 to 1)
Guidance Counselors: 10.4 (657.7 to 1)
Current Spending: ($ per student per year):
Total: $9,106; Instruction: $5,181; Support Services: $3,737
Enrollment, Drop-out Rates and Diploma Recipients by Race/Ethnicity

Category	Total	White	Black	Asian	AIAN	Hisp.
Enrollment (%)	100.0	92.0	5.8	1.3	0.2	0.6
Drop-out Rate (%)	n/a	n/a	n/a	n/a	n/a	n/a
H.S. Diplomas (#)	475	458	11	5	0	1

South Lyon Community Schools
345 S Warren St • South Lyon, MI 48178-1378
(248) 573-8127 • http://www.southlyon.k12.mi.us/portal.htm
Grade Span: PK-12; **Agency Type:** 1
Schools: 10
7 Primary; 2 Middle; 1 High; 0 Other Level
10 Regular; 0 Special Education; 0 Vocational; 0 Alternative
2 Magnet; 0 Charter; 0 Title I Eligible; 0 School-wide Title I
Students: 6,798 (51.5% male; 48.5% female)
Individual Education Program: 741 (10.9%);
English Language Learner: n/a; Migrant: n/a
Eligible for Free Lunch Program: 450 (6.6%)
Eligible for Reduced-Price Lunch Program: 233 (3.4%)
Teachers: 351.0 (19.4 to 1)
Librarians/Media Specialists: 7.0 (971.1 to 1)
Guidance Counselors: 9.0 (755.3 to 1)
Current Spending: ($ per student per year):
Total: $6,569; Instruction: $3,672; Support Services: $2,703
Enrollment, Drop-out Rates and Diploma Recipients by Race/Ethnicity

Category	Total	White	Black	Asian	AIAN	Hisp.
Enrollment (%)	100.0	95.3	1.4	1.3	0.6	1.4
Drop-out Rate (%)	n/a	n/a	n/a	n/a	n/a	n/a
H.S. Diplomas (#)	345	332	0	3	4	6

Southfield Public SD
24661 Lahser Rd • Southfield, MI 48034-3238
(248) 746-8550 • http://www.southfield.k12.mi.us/
Grade Span: PK-12; **Agency Type:** 1
Schools: 18
12 Primary; 3 Middle; 3 High; 0 Other Level
18 Regular; 0 Special Education; 0 Vocational; 0 Alternative
2 Magnet; 0 Charter; 0 Title I Eligible; 0 School-wide Title I
Students: 10,499 (50.8% male; 49.2% female)
Individual Education Program: 1,178 (11.2%);
English Language Learner: 549 (5.2%); Migrant: n/a
Eligible for Free Lunch Program: 2,503 (23.8%)
Eligible for Reduced-Price Lunch Program: 869 (8.3%)
Teachers: 615.8 (17.0 to 1)
Librarians/Media Specialists: 16.8 (624.9 to 1)
Guidance Counselors: 18.9 (555.5 to 1)
Current Spending: ($ per student per year):
Total: $11,759; Instruction: $6,740; Support Services: $4,776
Enrollment, Drop-out Rates and Diploma Recipients by Race/Ethnicity

Category	Total	White	Black	Asian	AIAN	Hisp.
Enrollment (%)	100.0	9.4	86.7	1.7	0.2	0.4
Drop-out Rate (%)	n/a	n/a	n/a	n/a	n/a	n/a
H.S. Diplomas (#)	534	61	457	9	0	7

Troy SD
4400 Livernois Rd • Troy, MI 48098-4799
(248) 823-4000 • http://www.troy.k12.mi.us/
Grade Span: PK-12; **Agency Type:** 1
Schools: 19
12 Primary; 4 Middle; 2 High; 1 Other Level
18 Regular; 0 Special Education; 0 Vocational; 1 Alternative
0 Magnet; 0 Charter; 0 Title I Eligible; 0 School-wide Title I
Students: 12,074 (51.8% male; 48.2% female)
Individual Education Program: 911 (7.5%);
English Language Learner: n/a; Migrant: n/a
Eligible for Free Lunch Program: 264 (2.2%)
Eligible for Reduced-Price Lunch Program: 96 (0.8%)
Teachers: 701.6 (17.2 to 1)
Librarians/Media Specialists: 20.0 (603.7 to 1)
Guidance Counselors: 24.0 (503.1 to 1)
Current Spending: ($ per student per year):
Total: $9,068; Instruction: $5,659; Support Services: $3,207
Enrollment, Drop-out Rates and Diploma Recipients by Race/Ethnicity

Category	Total	White	Black	Asian	AIAN	Hisp.
Enrollment (%)	100.0	76.4	3.2	18.7	0.4	1.3
Drop-out Rate (%)	n/a	n/a	n/a	n/a	n/a	n/a
H.S. Diplomas (#)	967	767	32	161	2	5

Walled Lake Consolidated Schools
850 Ladd Road, Building D • Walled Lake, MI 48390-3019
(248) 956-2000 • http://www.walledlake.k12.mi.us/
Grade Span: PK-12; **Agency Type:** 1
Schools: 23
14 Primary; 4 Middle; 2 High; 3 Other Level
21 Regular; 1 Special Education; 0 Vocational; 1 Alternative
0 Magnet; 0 Charter; 0 Title I Eligible; 0 School-wide Title I
Students: 14,960 (52.0% male; 48.0% female)
Individual Education Program: 1,770 (11.8%);
English Language Learner: 935 (6.3%); Migrant: n/a
Eligible for Free Lunch Program: 768 (5.1%)
Eligible for Reduced-Price Lunch Program: 338 (2.3%)
Teachers: 914.5 (16.4 to 1)
Librarians/Media Specialists: 1.0 (14,960.0 to 1)
Guidance Counselors: 4.0 (3,740.0 to 1)
Current Spending: ($ per student per year):
Total: $8,665; Instruction: $4,785; Support Services: $3,713
Enrollment, Drop-out Rates and Diploma Recipients by Race/Ethnicity

Category	Total	White	Black	Asian	AIAN	Hisp.
Enrollment (%)	100.0	90.5	2.8	4.6	0.5	1.6
Drop-out Rate (%)	n/a	n/a	n/a	n/a	n/a	n/a
H.S. Diplomas (#)	811	761	16	16	9	9

Waterford SD
6020 Pontiac Lake Rd • Waterford, MI 48327-1847
(248) 666-2222 • http://www.waterford.k12.mi.us/
Grade Span: PK-12; **Agency Type:** 1
Schools: 25
15 Primary; 4 Middle; 2 High; 4 Other Level
22 Regular; 2 Special Education; 0 Vocational; 1 Alternative
0 Magnet; 0 Charter; 3 Title I Eligible; 3 School-wide Title I
Students: 12,245 (51.7% male; 48.3% female)
Individual Education Program: 1,773 (14.5%);
English Language Learner: 416 (3.4%); Migrant: n/a
Eligible for Free Lunch Program: 1,639 (13.4%)
Eligible for Reduced-Price Lunch Program: 587 (4.8%)
Teachers: 372.4 (32.9 to 1)
Librarians/Media Specialists: 1.0 (12,245.0 to 1)
Guidance Counselors: 10.0 (1,224.5 to 1)
Current Spending: ($ per student per year):
Total: $8,009; Instruction: $4,572; Support Services: $3,158
Enrollment, Drop-out Rates and Diploma Recipients by Race/Ethnicity

Category	Total	White	Black	Asian	AIAN	Hisp.
Enrollment (%)	100.0	88.9	3.5	2.7	0.2	4.7
Drop-out Rate (%)	n/a	n/a	n/a	n/a	n/a	n/a
H.S. Diplomas (#)	555	513	17	13	0	12

West Bloomfield SD
5810 Commerce Rd • West Bloomfield, MI 48324-3200
(248) 865-6420 • http://www.westbloomfield.k12.mi.us/
Grade Span: PK-12; **Agency Type:** 1
Schools: 11
6 Primary; 2 Middle; 2 High; 1 Other Level
10 Regular; 0 Special Education; 0 Vocational; 1 Alternative

1 Magnet; 0 Charter; 0 Title I Eligible; 0 School-wide Title I
Students: 7,268 (52.8% male; 47.2% female)
Individual Education Program: 743 (10.2%);
English Language Learner: 474 (6.5%); Migrant: n/a
Eligible for Free Lunch Program: 368 (5.1%)
Eligible for Reduced-Price Lunch Program: 190 (2.6%)
Teachers: 391.8 (18.6 to 1)
Librarians/Media Specialists: 5.5 (1,321.5 to 1)
Guidance Counselors: 12.0 (605.7 to 1)
Current Spending: ($ per student per year):
Total: $9,450; Instruction: $5,343; Support Services: $3,863
Enrollment, Drop-out Rates and Diploma Recipients by Race/Ethnicity

Category	Total	White	Black	Asian	AIAN	Hisp.
Enrollment (%)	100.0	76.6	16.6	4.3	0.5	2.0
Drop-out Rate (%)	n/a	n/a	n/a	n/a	n/a	n/a
H.S. Diplomas (#)	418	340	34	43	1	0

Oceana County

Shelby Public Schools
525 N State St • Shelby, MI 49455-9601
(231) 861-5211 • http://hs.shelby.k12.mi.us/main/
Grade Span: PK-12; **Agency Type:** 1
Schools: 7
4 Primary; 1 Middle; 2 High; 0 Other Level
6 Regular; 0 Special Education; 0 Vocational; 1 Alternative
0 Magnet; 0 Charter; 4 Title I Eligible; 4 School-wide Title I
Students: 2,065 (53.5% male; 46.5% female)
Individual Education Program: 273 (13.2%);
English Language Learner: 231 (11.2%); Migrant: n/a
Eligible for Free Lunch Program: 680 (32.9%)
Eligible for Reduced-Price Lunch Program: 199 (9.6%)
Teachers: 108.7 (19.0 to 1)
Librarians/Media Specialists: 1.0 (2,065.0 to 1)
Guidance Counselors: 3.0 (688.3 to 1)
Current Spending: ($ per student per year):
Total: $6,838; Instruction: $4,824; Support Services: $1,772
Enrollment, Drop-out Rates and Diploma Recipients by Race/Ethnicity

Category	Total	White	Black	Asian	AIAN	Hisp.
Enrollment (%)	100.0	74.8	0.4	2.0	0.2	22.6
Drop-out Rate (%)	n/a	n/a	n/a	n/a	n/a	n/a
H.S. Diplomas (#)	91	80	0	2	0	9

Ogemaw County

West Branch-Rose City Area Schools
836 S M-33 • West Branch, MI 48661-0308
Mailing Address: PO Box 308 • West Branch, MI 48661-0308
(989) 343-2000 • http://www.westbranch.com/wb_rcschool.htm
Grade Span: PK-12; **Agency Type:** 1
Schools: 5
2 Primary; 2 Middle; 1 High; 0 Other Level
5 Regular; 0 Special Education; 0 Vocational; 0 Alternative
0 Magnet; 0 Charter; 4 Title I Eligible; 4 School-wide Title I
Students: 2,697 (52.2% male; 47.8% female)
Individual Education Program: 381 (14.1%);
English Language Learner: n/a; Migrant: n/a
Eligible for Free Lunch Program: 865 (32.1%)
Eligible for Reduced-Price Lunch Program: 322 (11.9%)
Teachers: 165.0 (16.3 to 1)
Librarians/Media Specialists: 4.0 (674.3 to 1)
Guidance Counselors: 13.0 (207.5 to 1)
Current Spending: ($ per student per year):
Total: $7,006; Instruction: $4,269; Support Services: $2,403
Enrollment, Drop-out Rates and Diploma Recipients by Race/Ethnicity

Category	Total	White	Black	Asian	AIAN	Hisp.
Enrollment (%)	100.0	97.9	0.2	0.6	0.4	0.7
Drop-out Rate (%)	n/a	n/a	n/a	n/a	n/a	n/a
H.S. Diplomas (#)	181	173	0	2	2	4

Osceola County

Reed City Area Public Schools
829 S Chestnut St • Reed City, MI 49677-1384
(231) 832-2201 • http://www.reedcity.k12.mi.us/
Grade Span: KG-12; **Agency Type:** 1
Schools: 6
2 Primary; 2 Middle; 1 High; 1 Other Level
5 Regular; 0 Special Education; 0 Vocational; 1 Alternative
0 Magnet; 0 Charter; 0 Title I Eligible; 0 School-wide Title I
Students: 2,060 (52.1% male; 47.9% female)
Individual Education Program: 385 (18.7%);
English Language Learner: n/a; Migrant: n/a
Eligible for Free Lunch Program: 590 (28.6%)
Eligible for Reduced-Price Lunch Program: 288 (14.0%)
Teachers: 113.2 (18.2 to 1)
Librarians/Media Specialists: 2.2 (936.4 to 1)
Guidance Counselors: 3.0 (686.7 to 1)
Current Spending: ($ per student per year):
Total: $6,397; Instruction: $3,891; Support Services: $2,238
Enrollment, Drop-out Rates and Diploma Recipients by Race/Ethnicity

Category	Total	White	Black	Asian	AIAN	Hisp.
Enrollment (%)	100.0	96.5	2.0	0.2	0.7	0.7
Drop-out Rate (%)	n/a	n/a	n/a	n/a	n/a	n/a
H.S. Diplomas (#)	145	137	3	4	0	1

Otsego County

Gaylord Community Schools
615 S Elm St • Gaylord, MI 49735-1253
(989) 705-3080 • http://www.gaylordschools.com/
Grade Span: KG-12; **Agency Type:** 1
Schools: 7
3 Primary; 2 Middle; 1 High; 1 Other Level
6 Regular; 0 Special Education; 0 Vocational; 1 Alternative
6 Magnet; 0 Charter; 0 Title I Eligible; 0 School-wide Title I
Students: 3,427 (50.0% male; 50.0% female)
Individual Education Program: 418 (12.2%);
English Language Learner: n/a; Migrant: n/a
Eligible for Free Lunch Program: 881 (25.7%)
Eligible for Reduced-Price Lunch Program: 272 (7.9%)
Teachers: 198.5 (17.3 to 1)
Librarians/Media Specialists: 3.0 (1,142.3 to 1)
Guidance Counselors: 7.0 (489.6 to 1)
Current Spending: ($ per student per year):
Total: $6,569; Instruction: $4,342; Support Services: $1,974
Enrollment, Drop-out Rates and Diploma Recipients by Race/Ethnicity

Category	Total	White	Black	Asian	AIAN	Hisp.
Enrollment (%)	100.0	97.4	0.3	0.6	0.9	0.8
Drop-out Rate (%)	n/a	n/a	n/a	n/a	n/a	n/a
H.S. Diplomas (#)	206	202	0	0	3	1

Ottawa County

Allendale Public SD
6561 Lake Michigan Dr • Allendale, MI 49401-0030
Mailing Address: PO Box 30 • Allendale, MI 49401-0030
(616) 895-4350 • http://www.allendale.k12.mi.us/
Grade Span: PK-12; **Agency Type:** 1
Schools: 5
2 Primary; 1 Middle; 1 High; 1 Other Level
4 Regular; 0 Special Education; 0 Vocational; 1 Alternative
0 Magnet; 0 Charter; 1 Title I Eligible; 1 School-wide Title I
Students: 2,020 (50.9% male; 49.1% female)
Individual Education Program: 240 (11.9%);
English Language Learner: 42 (2.1%); Migrant: n/a
Eligible for Free Lunch Program: 223 (11.0%)
Eligible for Reduced-Price Lunch Program: 149 (7.4%)
Teachers: 120.6 (16.7 to 1)
Librarians/Media Specialists: 2.0 (1,010.0 to 1)
Guidance Counselors: 1.0 (2,020.0 to 1)
Current Spending: ($ per student per year):
Total: $6,683; Instruction: $4,128; Support Services: $2,344
Enrollment, Drop-out Rates and Diploma Recipients by Race/Ethnicity

Category	Total	White	Black	Asian	AIAN	Hisp.
Enrollment (%)	100.0	91.8	2.0	1.9	0.4	3.9
Drop-out Rate (%)	n/a	n/a	n/a	n/a	n/a	n/a
H.S. Diplomas (#)	110	101	1	6	0	2

Coopersville Public SD
198 E St • Coopersville, MI 49404-1211
(616) 997-3200 • http://www.coopersvillebroncos.org/
Grade Span: PK-12; **Agency Type:** 1
Schools: 4
2 Primary; 1 Middle; 1 High; 0 Other Level
4 Regular; 0 Special Education; 0 Vocational; 0 Alternative
0 Magnet; 0 Charter; 0 Title I Eligible; 0 School-wide Title I
Students: 2,379 (51.8% male; 48.2% female)
Individual Education Program: 309 (13.0%);
English Language Learner: n/a; Migrant: n/a
Eligible for Free Lunch Program: 392 (16.5%)
Eligible for Reduced-Price Lunch Program: 187 (7.9%)
Teachers: 127.2 (18.7 to 1)
Librarians/Media Specialists: 1.0 (2,379.0 to 1)
Guidance Counselors: 2.0 (1,189.5 to 1)
Current Spending: ($ per student per year):
Total: $6,812; Instruction: $4,388; Support Services: $2,216

Enrollment, Drop-out Rates and Diploma Recipients by Race/Ethnicity

Category	Total	White	Black	Asian	AIAN	Hisp.
Enrollment (%)	100.0	96.4	0.3	0.4	0.1	2.8
Drop-out Rate (%)	n/a	n/a	n/a	n/a	n/a	n/a
H.S. Diplomas (#)	156	153	0	2	0	1

Grand Haven Area Public Schools

1415 S Beechtree St • Grand Haven, MI 49417-2843
(616) 850-5015 • http://www.ghaps.org/
Grade Span: PK-12; **Agency Type:** 1
Schools: 12
8 Primary; 2 Middle; 2 High; 0 Other Level
11 Regular; 0 Special Education; 0 Vocational; 1 Alternative
0 Magnet; 0 Charter; 0 Title I Eligible; 0 School-wide Title I
Students: 6,056 (53.3% male; 46.7% female)
Individual Education Program: 614 (10.1%);
English Language Learner: n/a; Migrant: n/a
Eligible for Free Lunch Program: 747 (12.3%)
Eligible for Reduced-Price Lunch Program: 409 (6.8%)
Teachers: 328.1 (18.5 to 1)
Librarians/Media Specialists: 8.0 (757.0 to 1)
Guidance Counselors: 14.8 (409.2 to 1)
Current Spending: ($ per student per year):
Total: $7,461; Instruction: $4,329; Support Services: $2,875
Enrollment, Drop-out Rates and Diploma Recipients by Race/Ethnicity

Category	Total	White	Black	Asian	AIAN	Hisp.
Enrollment (%)	100.0	93.2	0.8	1.2	0.7	3.4
Drop-out Rate (%)	n/a	n/a	n/a	n/a	n/a	n/a
H.S. Diplomas (#)	446	429	2	8	3	4

Holland City SD

372 S River Ave • Holland, MI 49423-3356
(616) 494-2000 • http://www.holland.k12.mi.us/
Grade Span: PK-12; **Agency Type:** 1
Schools: 13
9 Primary; 2 Middle; 2 High; 0 Other Level
12 Regular; 0 Special Education; 0 Vocational; 1 Alternative
0 Magnet; 0 Charter; 5 Title I Eligible; 5 School-wide Title I
Students: 5,572 (51.9% male; 48.1% female)
Individual Education Program: 729 (13.1%);
English Language Learner: 1,140 (20.5%); Migrant: n/a
Eligible for Free Lunch Program: 1,868 (33.5%)
Eligible for Reduced-Price Lunch Program: 563 (10.1%)
Teachers: 327.2 (17.0 to 1)
Librarians/Media Specialists: 7.0 (796.0 to 1)
Guidance Counselors: 8.0 (696.5 to 1)
Current Spending: ($ per student per year):
Total: $8,680; Instruction: $5,766; Support Services: $2,638
Enrollment, Drop-out Rates and Diploma Recipients by Race/Ethnicity

Category	Total	White	Black	Asian	AIAN	Hisp.
Enrollment (%)	100.0	53.4	5.5	5.5	0.4	35.2
Drop-out Rate (%)	n/a	n/a	n/a	n/a	n/a	n/a
H.S. Diplomas (#)	292	195	9	14	1	73

Hudsonville Public SD

3886 Van Buren St • Hudsonville, MI 49426-1038
(616) 669-1740 • http://www.hudsonville.k12.mi.us
Grade Span: KG-12; **Agency Type:** 1
Schools: 10
6 Primary; 2 Middle; 1 High; 1 Other Level
10 Regular; 0 Special Education; 0 Vocational; 0 Alternative
0 Magnet; 0 Charter; 0 Title I Eligible; 0 School-wide Title I
Students: 4,756 (50.9% male; 49.1% female)
Individual Education Program: 589 (12.4%);
English Language Learner: 5 (0.1%); Migrant: n/a
Eligible for Free Lunch Program: 306 (6.4%)
Eligible for Reduced-Price Lunch Program: 204 (4.3%)
Teachers: 268.4 (17.7 to 1)
Librarians/Media Specialists: 3.0 (1,585.3 to 1)
Guidance Counselors: 10.5 (453.0 to 1)
Current Spending: ($ per student per year):
Total: $5,998; Instruction: $3,825; Support Services: $2,173
Enrollment, Drop-out Rates and Diploma Recipients by Race/Ethnicity

Category	Total	White	Black	Asian	AIAN	Hisp.
Enrollment (%)	100.0	0.0	0.3	0.4	99.3	0.0
Drop-out Rate (%)	n/a	n/a	n/a	n/a	n/a	n/a
H.S. Diplomas (#)	260	253	2	3	0	2

Jenison Public Schools

8375 20th Ave • Jenison, MI 49428-9230
(616) 457-8890 • http://www.remc7.k12.mi.us/jps/
Grade Span: PK-12; **Agency Type:** 1
Schools: 8
6 Primary; 1 Middle; 1 High; 0 Other Level
8 Regular; 0 Special Education; 0 Vocational; 0 Alternative
0 Magnet; 0 Charter; 0 Title I Eligible; 0 School-wide Title I
Students: 4,791 (52.2% male; 47.8% female)
Individual Education Program: 797 (16.6%);
English Language Learner: 29 (0.6%); Migrant: n/a
Eligible for Free Lunch Program: 185 (3.9%)
Eligible for Reduced-Price Lunch Program: 204 (4.3%)
Teachers: 28.0 (171.1 to 1)
Librarians/Media Specialists: 3.0 (1,597.0 to 1)
Guidance Counselors: 2.0 (2,395.5 to 1)
Current Spending: ($ per student per year):
Total: $7,187; Instruction: $4,651; Support Services: $2,156
Enrollment, Drop-out Rates and Diploma Recipients by Race/Ethnicity

Category	Total	White	Black	Asian	AIAN	Hisp.
Enrollment (%)	100.0	93.8	1.3	1.8	0.6	2.5
Drop-out Rate (%)	n/a	n/a	n/a	n/a	n/a	n/a
H.S. Diplomas (#)	357	343	3	6	0	5

Spring Lake Public Schools

345 Hammond St • Spring Lake, MI 49456-2064
(616) 847-7919 • http://www.spring-lake.k12.mi.us
Grade Span: PK-12; **Agency Type:** 1
Schools: 6
2 Primary; 2 Middle; 2 High; 0 Other Level
5 Regular; 0 Special Education; 0 Vocational; 1 Alternative
0 Magnet; 0 Charter; 0 Title I Eligible; 0 School-wide Title I
Students: 2,149 (52.0% male; 48.0% female)
Individual Education Program: 258 (12.0%);
English Language Learner: 3 (0.1%); Migrant: n/a
Eligible for Free Lunch Program: 156 (7.3%)
Eligible for Reduced-Price Lunch Program: 134 (6.2%)
Teachers: 118.5 (18.1 to 1)
Librarians/Media Specialists: 1.0 (2,149.0 to 1)
Guidance Counselors: 4.0 (537.3 to 1)
Current Spending: ($ per student per year):
Total: $7,235; Instruction: $4,461; Support Services: $2,507
Enrollment, Drop-out Rates and Diploma Recipients by Race/Ethnicity

Category	Total	White	Black	Asian	AIAN	Hisp.
Enrollment (%)	100.0	96.8	0.7	1.2	0.2	1.0
Drop-out Rate (%)	n/a	n/a	n/a	n/a	n/a	n/a
H.S. Diplomas (#)	144	142	0	2	0	0

West Ottawa Public SD

1138 136th Ave • Holland, MI 49424-1997
(616) 738-5700 • http://www.westottawa.k12.mi.us/
Grade Span: PK-12; **Agency Type:** 1
Schools: 13
9 Primary; 1 Middle; 2 High; 1 Other Level
12 Regular; 0 Special Education; 0 Vocational; 1 Alternative
0 Magnet; 0 Charter; 0 Title I Eligible; 0 School-wide Title I
Students: 7,897 (51.3% male; 48.7% female)
Individual Education Program: 948 (12.0%);
English Language Learner: 999 (12.7%); Migrant: n/a
Eligible for Free Lunch Program: 1,681 (21.3%)
Eligible for Reduced-Price Lunch Program: 522 (6.6%)
Teachers: 432.9 (18.2 to 1)
Librarians/Media Specialists: 12.0 (658.1 to 1)
Guidance Counselors: 13.2 (598.3 to 1)
Current Spending: ($ per student per year):
Total: $6,977; Instruction: $4,280; Support Services: $2,364
Enrollment, Drop-out Rates and Diploma Recipients by Race/Ethnicity

Category	Total	White	Black	Asian	AIAN	Hisp.
Enrollment (%)	100.0	64.1	3.3	8.8	0.3	20.4
Drop-out Rate (%)	n/a	n/a	n/a	n/a	n/a	n/a
H.S. Diplomas (#)	416	328	8	39	3	38

Zeeland Public Schools

183 W Roosevelt • Zeeland, MI 49464-0110
Mailing Address: PO Box 110 • Zeeland, MI 49464-0110
(616) 748-3000 • http://www.zeeland.k12.mi.us/
Grade Span: PK-12; **Agency Type:** 1
Schools: 10
5 Primary; 2 Middle; 3 High; 0 Other Level
9 Regular; 0 Special Education; 0 Vocational; 1 Alternative
0 Magnet; 0 Charter; 0 Title I Eligible; 0 School-wide Title I
Students: 4,863 (51.2% male; 48.8% female)
Individual Education Program: 490 (10.1%);
English Language Learner: 111 (2.3%); Migrant: n/a
Eligible for Free Lunch Program: 426 (8.8%)
Eligible for Reduced-Price Lunch Program: 308 (6.3%)
Teachers: 30.7 (158.4 to 1)
Librarians/Media Specialists: n/a
Guidance Counselors: 1.0 (4,863.0 to 1)
Current Spending: ($ per student per year):
Total: $6,279; Instruction: $3,884; Support Services: $2,132

Enrollment, Drop-out Rates and Diploma Recipients by Race/Ethnicity

Category	Total	White	Black	Asian	AIAN	Hisp.
Enrollment (%)	100.0	87.4	1.2	4.0	0.3	7.1
Drop-out Rate (%)	n/a	n/a	n/a	n/a	n/a	n/a
H.S. Diplomas (#)	286	261	0	8	0	17

Roscommon County

Gerrish-Higgins SD

702 Lake St • Roscommon, MI 48653-8653
Mailing Address: PO Box 825 • Roscommon, MI 48653-0825
(989) 275-6600 • http://www.ghsd.k12.mi.us/
Grade Span: KG-12; **Agency Type:** 1
Schools: 5
2 Primary; 1 Middle; 1 High; 1 Other Level
4 Regular; 0 Special Education; 0 Vocational; 1 Alternative
0 Magnet; 0 Charter; 1 Title I Eligible; 1 School-wide Title I
Students: 1,899 (52.9% male; 47.1% female)
Individual Education Program: 271 (14.3%);
English Language Learner: n/a; Migrant: n/a
Eligible for Free Lunch Program: 577 (30.4%)
Eligible for Reduced-Price Lunch Program: 147 (7.7%)
Teachers: 98.7 (19.2 to 1)
Librarians/Media Specialists: 1.0 (1,899.0 to 1)
Guidance Counselors: 4.1 (463.2 to 1)
Current Spending: ($ per student per year):
Total: $6,949; Instruction: $4,543; Support Services: $2,063

Enrollment, Drop-out Rates and Diploma Recipients by Race/Ethnicity

Category	Total	White	Black	Asian	AIAN	Hisp.
Enrollment (%)	100.0	98.8	0.2	0.3	0.6	0.2
Drop-out Rate (%)	n/a	n/a	n/a	n/a	n/a	n/a
H.S. Diplomas (#)	102	102	0	0	0	0

Houghton Lake Community Schools

6001 W Houghton Lake Dr • Houghton Lake, MI 48629-9704
(989) 366-2000 • http://www.hlcs.k12.mi.us
Grade Span: PK-12; **Agency Type:** 1
Schools: 7
4 Primary; 1 Middle; 1 High; 1 Other Level
6 Regular; 0 Special Education; 0 Vocational; 1 Alternative
0 Magnet; 0 Charter; 3 Title I Eligible; 3 School-wide Title I
Students: 2,201 (52.3% male; 47.7% female)
Individual Education Program: 286 (13.0%);
English Language Learner: n/a; Migrant: n/a
Eligible for Free Lunch Program: 832 (37.8%)
Eligible for Reduced-Price Lunch Program: 175 (8.0%)
Teachers: 52.0 (42.3 to 1)
Librarians/Media Specialists: 1.0 (2,201.0 to 1)
Guidance Counselors: 4.0 (550.3 to 1)
Current Spending: ($ per student per year):
Total: $7,141; Instruction: $4,524; Support Services: $2,322

Enrollment, Drop-out Rates and Diploma Recipients by Race/Ethnicity

Category	Total	White	Black	Asian	AIAN	Hisp.
Enrollment (%)	100.0	97.4	0.9	0.3	0.8	0.6
Drop-out Rate (%)	n/a	n/a	n/a	n/a	n/a	n/a
H.S. Diplomas (#)	121	120	0	1	0	0

Saginaw County

Birch Run Area SD

12400 Church St • Birch Run, MI 48415-8759
(989) 624-9307 • http://www.birchrun.k12.mi.us/
Grade Span: PK-12; **Agency Type:** 1
Schools: 4
2 Primary; 1 Middle; 1 High; 0 Other Level
4 Regular; 0 Special Education; 0 Vocational; 0 Alternative
0 Magnet; 0 Charter; 0 Title I Eligible; 0 School-wide Title I
Students: 1,946 (52.7% male; 47.3% female)
Individual Education Program: 205 (10.5%);
English Language Learner: 2 (0.1%); Migrant: n/a
Eligible for Free Lunch Program: 327 (16.8%)
Eligible for Reduced-Price Lunch Program: 131 (6.7%)
Teachers: 105.8 (18.4 to 1)
Librarians/Media Specialists: 3.0 (648.7 to 1)
Guidance Counselors: 3.0 (648.7 to 1)
Current Spending: ($ per student per year):
Total: $6,329; Instruction: $3,691; Support Services: $2,382

Enrollment, Drop-out Rates and Diploma Recipients by Race/Ethnicity

Category	Total	White	Black	Asian	AIAN	Hisp.
Enrollment (%)	100.0	95.2	0.8	0.6	0.5	2.9
Drop-out Rate (%)	n/a	n/a	n/a	n/a	n/a	n/a
H.S. Diplomas (#)	112	106	2	2	2	0

Bridgeport-Spaulding Community SD

3878 Sherman St • Bridgeport, MI 48722-0657
Mailing Address: PO Box 657 • Bridgeport, MI 48722-0657
(989) 777-1770 • http://www.bscs.k12.mi.us/
Grade Span: KG-12; **Agency Type:** 1
Schools: 7
4 Primary; 1 Middle; 2 High; 0 Other Level
6 Regular; 0 Special Education; 0 Vocational; 1 Alternative
0 Magnet; 0 Charter; 0 Title I Eligible; 0 School-wide Title I
Students: 2,409 (51.4% male; 48.6% female)
Individual Education Program: 394 (16.4%);
English Language Learner: n/a; Migrant: n/a
Eligible for Free Lunch Program: 1,166 (48.4%)
Eligible for Reduced-Price Lunch Program: 247 (10.3%)
Teachers: 154.8 (15.6 to 1)
Librarians/Media Specialists: 1.0 (2,409.0 to 1)
Guidance Counselors: 4.0 (602.3 to 1)
Current Spending: ($ per student per year):
Total: $7,454; Instruction: $4,341; Support Services: $2,824

Enrollment, Drop-out Rates and Diploma Recipients by Race/Ethnicity

Category	Total	White	Black	Asian	AIAN	Hisp.
Enrollment (%)	100.0	51.7	32.8	0.6	1.0	13.9
Drop-out Rate (%)	n/a	n/a	n/a	n/a	n/a	n/a
H.S. Diplomas (#)	118	61	41	4	0	12

Carrollton SD

3211 Carla • Saginaw, MI 48604
Mailing Address: PO Box 517 • Carrollton, MI 48724-0517
(989) 754-1475
Grade Span: KG-12; **Agency Type:** 1
Schools: 3
1 Primary; 1 Middle; 1 High; 0 Other Level
3 Regular; 0 Special Education; 0 Vocational; 0 Alternative
0 Magnet; 0 Charter; 1 Title I Eligible; 1 School-wide Title I
Students: 1,518 (51.6% male; 48.4% female)
Individual Education Program: 458 (30.2%);
English Language Learner: n/a; Migrant: n/a
Eligible for Free Lunch Program: 476 (31.4%)
Eligible for Reduced-Price Lunch Program: 159 (10.5%)
Teachers: 112.5 (13.5 to 1)
Librarians/Media Specialists: 1.0 (1,518.0 to 1)
Guidance Counselors: 6.0 (253.0 to 1)
Current Spending: ($ per student per year):
Total: $7,067; Instruction: $4,454; Support Services: $2,349

Enrollment, Drop-out Rates and Diploma Recipients by Race/Ethnicity

Category	Total	White	Black	Asian	AIAN	Hisp.
Enrollment (%)	100.0	66.0	17.1	4.2	0.7	12.1
Drop-out Rate (%)	n/a	n/a	n/a	n/a	n/a	n/a
H.S. Diplomas (#)	80	67	7	0	0	6

Chesaning Union Schools

850 N 4th St • Chesaning, MI 48616
(989) 845-7020 • http://www.chesaning.k12.mi.us/
Grade Span: PK-12; **Agency Type:** 1
Schools: 5
3 Primary; 1 Middle; 1 High; 0 Other Level
5 Regular; 0 Special Education; 0 Vocational; 0 Alternative
0 Magnet; 0 Charter; 3 Title I Eligible; 3 School-wide Title I
Students: 2,092 (51.8% male; 48.2% female)
Individual Education Program: 360 (17.2%);
English Language Learner: n/a; Migrant: n/a
Eligible for Free Lunch Program: 451 (21.6%)
Eligible for Reduced-Price Lunch Program: 161 (7.7%)
Teachers: 113.5 (18.4 to 1)
Librarians/Media Specialists: 1.0 (2,092.0 to 1)
Guidance Counselors: 4.0 (523.0 to 1)
Current Spending: ($ per student per year):
Total: $6,553; Instruction: $4,209; Support Services: $2,101

Enrollment, Drop-out Rates and Diploma Recipients by Race/Ethnicity

Category	Total	White	Black	Asian	AIAN	Hisp.
Enrollment (%)	100.0	94.1	1.3	0.4	0.2	3.7
Drop-out Rate (%)	n/a	n/a	n/a	n/a	n/a	n/a
H.S. Diplomas (#)	139	133	0	2	0	4

Freeland Community SD

710 Powley Dr • Freeland, MI 48623-8106
(989) 695-5527 • http://www.freeland.k12.mi.us/
Grade Span: KG-12; **Agency Type:** 1
Schools: 3
2 Primary; 0 Middle; 1 High; 0 Other Level
3 Regular; 0 Special Education; 0 Vocational; 0 Alternative
0 Magnet; 0 Charter; 1 Title I Eligible; 1 School-wide Title I
Students: 1,649 (52.0% male; 48.0% female)
Individual Education Program: 170 (10.3%);
English Language Learner: n/a; Migrant: n/a

Eligible for Free Lunch Program: 68 (4.1%)
Eligible for Reduced-Price Lunch Program: 22 (1.3%)
Teachers: 85.0 (19.4 to 1)
Librarians/Media Specialists: 2.0 (824.5 to 1)
Guidance Counselors: 2.0 (824.5 to 1)
Current Spending: ($ per student per year):
Total: $5,264; Instruction: $3,209; Support Services: $1,878
Enrollment, Drop-out Rates and Diploma Recipients by Race/Ethnicity

Category	Total	White	Black	Asian	AIAN	Hisp.
Enrollment (%)	100.0	95.6	1.3	1.2	0.2	1.8
Drop-out Rate (%)	n/a	n/a	n/a	n/a	n/a	n/a
H.S. Diplomas (#)	86	80	2	2	0	2

Saginaw City SD
550 Millard St • Saginaw, MI 48607-1140
(989) 399-6500 • http://www.saginaw-city.k12.mi.us/
Grade Span: PK-12; **Agency Type:** 1
Schools: 35
24 Primary; 4 Middle; 3 High; 4 Other Level
31 Regular; 2 Special Education; 1 Vocational; 1 Alternative
1 Magnet; 0 Charter; 0 Title I Eligible; 0 School-wide Title I
Students: 13,312 (51.3% male; 48.7% female)
Individual Education Program: 2,434 (18.3%);
English Language Learner: 698 (5.2%); Migrant: n/a
Eligible for Free Lunch Program: 8,010 (60.2%)
Eligible for Reduced-Price Lunch Program: 715 (5.4%)
Teachers: 822.0 (16.2 to 1)
Librarians/Media Specialists: 8.0 (1,664.0 to 1)
Guidance Counselors: 21.0 (633.9 to 1)
Current Spending: ($ per student per year):
Total: $8,641; Instruction: $4,979; Support Services: $3,344
Enrollment, Drop-out Rates and Diploma Recipients by Race/Ethnicity

Category	Total	White	Black	Asian	AIAN	Hisp.
Enrollment (%)	100.0	24.6	61.2	0.9	0.2	13.2
Drop-out Rate (%)	n/a	n/a	n/a	n/a	n/a	n/a
H.S. Diplomas (#)	462	153	254	7	3	45

Saginaw Township Community Schools
3465 N Center Rd • Saginaw, MI 48603
Mailing Address: PO Box 6278 • Saginaw, MI 48608-6278
(989) 797-1800 • http://www.saginaw-twp.k12.mi.us/
Grade Span: KG-12; **Agency Type:** 1
Schools: 9
6 Primary; 1 Middle; 1 High; 1 Other Level
8 Regular; 0 Special Education; 0 Vocational; 1 Alternative
0 Magnet; 0 Charter; 0 Title I Eligible; 0 School-wide Title I
Students: 5,002 (50.4% male; 49.6% female)
Individual Education Program: 705 (14.1%);
English Language Learner: n/a; Migrant: n/a
Eligible for Free Lunch Program: 1,018 (20.4%)
Eligible for Reduced-Price Lunch Program: 234 (4.7%)
Teachers: 279.0 (17.9 to 1)
Librarians/Media Specialists: 2.0 (2,501.0 to 1)
Guidance Counselors: 13.0 (384.8 to 1)
Current Spending: ($ per student per year):
Total: $6,777; Instruction: $4,051; Support Services: $2,350
Enrollment, Drop-out Rates and Diploma Recipients by Race/Ethnicity

Category	Total	White	Black	Asian	AIAN	Hisp.
Enrollment (%)	100.0	78.9	10.0	2.9	0.9	7.3
Drop-out Rate (%)	n/a	n/a	n/a	n/a	n/a	n/a
H.S. Diplomas (#)	350	292	26	18	1	13

Swan Valley SD
8380 O'hern Rd • Saginaw, MI 48609-5199
(989) 921-3701 • http://www.swanvalley.k12.mi.us/
Grade Span: PK-12; **Agency Type:** 1
Schools: 4
2 Primary; 1 Middle; 1 High; 0 Other Level
4 Regular; 0 Special Education; 0 Vocational; 0 Alternative
0 Magnet; 0 Charter; 0 Title I Eligible; 0 School-wide Title I
Students: 1,677 (49.2% male; 50.8% female)
Individual Education Program: 247 (14.7%);
English Language Learner: n/a; Migrant: n/a
Eligible for Free Lunch Program: 249 (14.8%)
Eligible for Reduced-Price Lunch Program: 54 (3.2%)
Teachers: 91.6 (18.3 to 1)
Librarians/Media Specialists: 2.0 (838.5 to 1)
Guidance Counselors: 3.0 (559.0 to 1)
Current Spending: ($ per student per year):
Total: $6,156; Instruction: $3,786; Support Services: $2,363
Enrollment, Drop-out Rates and Diploma Recipients by Race/Ethnicity

Category	Total	White	Black	Asian	AIAN	Hisp.
Enrollment (%)	100.0	92.1	2.9	1.3	0.4	3.3
Drop-out Rate (%)	n/a	n/a	n/a	n/a	n/a	n/a
H.S. Diplomas (#)	113	107	6	0	0	0

Sanilac County

Croswell-Lexington Comm Schools
5407 E Peck Rd • Croswell, MI 48422-9108
(810) 679-1000 • http://www.cros-lex.k12.mi.us/
Grade Span: PK-12; **Agency Type:** 1
Schools: 5
2 Primary; 2 Middle; 1 High; 0 Other Level
5 Regular; 0 Special Education; 0 Vocational; 0 Alternative
0 Magnet; 0 Charter; 0 Title I Eligible; 0 School-wide Title I
Students: 2,509 (53.1% male; 46.9% female)
Individual Education Program: 297 (11.8%);
English Language Learner: n/a; Migrant: n/a
Eligible for Free Lunch Program: 486 (19.4%)
Eligible for Reduced-Price Lunch Program: 224 (8.9%)
Teachers: 143.5 (17.5 to 1)
Librarians/Media Specialists: 3.0 (836.3 to 1)
Guidance Counselors: 7.0 (358.4 to 1)
Current Spending: ($ per student per year):
Total: $6,190; Instruction: $3,715; Support Services: $2,209
Enrollment, Drop-out Rates and Diploma Recipients by Race/Ethnicity

Category	Total	White	Black	Asian	AIAN	Hisp.
Enrollment (%)	100.0	96.5	0.1	0.2	0.2	3.1
Drop-out Rate (%)	n/a	n/a	n/a	n/a	n/a	n/a
H.S. Diplomas (#)	158	152	0	0	1	5

Shiawassee County

Corunna Public SD
106 S Shiawassee St • Corunna, MI 48817-1359
(989) 743-6338 • http://corunna.k12.mi.us
Grade Span: PK-12; **Agency Type:** 1
Schools: 6
4 Primary; 1 Middle; 1 High; 0 Other Level
6 Regular; 0 Special Education; 0 Vocational; 0 Alternative
0 Magnet; 0 Charter; 0 Title I Eligible; 0 School-wide Title I
Students: 2,225 (51.3% male; 48.7% female)
Individual Education Program: 238 (10.7%);
English Language Learner: n/a; Migrant: n/a
Eligible for Free Lunch Program: 388 (17.4%)
Eligible for Reduced-Price Lunch Program: 177 (8.0%)
Teachers: 114.4 (19.4 to 1)
Librarians/Media Specialists: 3.0 (741.7 to 1)
Guidance Counselors: 3.0 (741.7 to 1)
Current Spending: ($ per student per year):
Total: $6,712; Instruction: $4,071; Support Services: $2,332
Enrollment, Drop-out Rates and Diploma Recipients by Race/Ethnicity

Category	Total	White	Black	Asian	AIAN	Hisp.
Enrollment (%)	100.0	96.4	0.4	0.6	0.9	1.5
Drop-out Rate (%)	n/a	n/a	n/a	n/a	n/a	n/a
H.S. Diplomas (#)	144	142	0	1	0	1

Durand Area Schools
310 N Saginaw St • Durand, MI 48429-1237
(989) 288-2681 • http://scnc.durand.k12.mi.us/
Grade Span: PK-12; **Agency Type:** 1
Schools: 6
4 Primary; 1 Middle; 1 High; 0 Other Level
6 Regular; 0 Special Education; 0 Vocational; 0 Alternative
0 Magnet; 0 Charter; 0 Title I Eligible; 0 School-wide Title I
Students: 2,060 (50.1% male; 49.9% female)
Individual Education Program: 251 (12.2%);
English Language Learner: n/a; Migrant: n/a
Eligible for Free Lunch Program: 383 (18.6%)
Eligible for Reduced-Price Lunch Program: 176 (8.5%)
Teachers: 107.8 (19.1 to 1)
Librarians/Media Specialists: 1.0 (2,060.0 to 1)
Guidance Counselors: 3.0 (686.7 to 1)
Current Spending: ($ per student per year):
Total: $6,881; Instruction: $4,471; Support Services: $2,126
Enrollment, Drop-out Rates and Diploma Recipients by Race/Ethnicity

Category	Total	White	Black	Asian	AIAN	Hisp.
Enrollment (%)	100.0	97.5	0.4	0.7	0.3	1.1
Drop-out Rate (%)	n/a	n/a	n/a	n/a	n/a	n/a
H.S. Diplomas (#)	100	98	1	0	0	1

Owosso Public Schools
1405 W N St • Owosso, MI 48867-0340
Mailing Address: PO Box 340 • Owosso, MI 48867-0340
(989) 723-8131 • http://www.owosso.k12.mi.us/
Grade Span: PK-12; **Agency Type:** 1
Schools: 9
7 Primary; 1 Middle; 1 High; 0 Other Level
9 Regular; 0 Special Education; 0 Vocational; 0 Alternative
0 Magnet; 0 Charter; 0 Title I Eligible; 0 School-wide Title I

Students: 4,222 (52.9% male; 47.1% female)
Individual Education Program: 569 (13.5%);
English Language Learner: n/a; Migrant: n/a
Eligible for Free Lunch Program: 1,110 (26.3%)
Eligible for Reduced-Price Lunch Program: 301 (7.1%)
Teachers: 225.5 (18.7 to 1)
Librarians/Media Specialists: 3.5 (1,206.3 to 1)
Guidance Counselors: 5.0 (844.4 to 1)
Current Spending: ($ per student per year):
Total: $6,646; Instruction: $4,309; Support Services: $2,081
Enrollment, Drop-out Rates and Diploma Recipients by Race/Ethnicity

Category	Total	White	Black	Asian	AIAN	Hisp.
Enrollment (%)	100.0	96.4	0.7	0.6	0.1	2.3
Drop-out Rate (%)	n/a	n/a	n/a	n/a	n/a	n/a
H.S. Diplomas (#)	244	234	0	4	0	6

Perry Public SD
2775 Britton Rd • Perry, MI 48872-0900
Mailing Address: PO Box 900 • Perry, MI 48872-0900
(517) 625-3108 • http://scnc.perry.k12.mi.us/main.html
Grade Span: PK-12; **Agency Type:** 1
Schools: 5
3 Primary; 1 Middle; 1 High; 0 Other Level
5 Regular; 0 Special Education; 0 Vocational; 0 Alternative
0 Magnet; 0 Charter; 0 Title I Eligible; 0 School-wide Title I
Students: 1,994 (50.2% male; 49.8% female)
Individual Education Program: 280 (14.0%);
English Language Learner: n/a; Migrant: n/a
Eligible for Free Lunch Program: 349 (17.5%)
Eligible for Reduced-Price Lunch Program: 120 (6.0%)
Teachers: 110.1 (18.1 to 1)
Librarians/Media Specialists: 2.0 (997.0 to 1)
Guidance Counselors: 5.0 (398.8 to 1)
Current Spending: ($ per student per year):
Total: $6,238; Instruction: $3,746; Support Services: $2,300
Enrollment, Drop-out Rates and Diploma Recipients by Race/Ethnicity

Category	Total	White	Black	Asian	AIAN	Hisp.
Enrollment (%)	100.0	97.8	0.6	0.7	0.1	0.9
Drop-out Rate (%)	n/a	n/a	n/a	n/a	n/a	n/a
H.S. Diplomas (#)	111	105	1	1	0	4

St. Clair County

Algonac Community SD
1216 St Clair Blvd • Algonac, MI 48001-1435
(810) 794-9364 • http://algonac.k12.mi.us/
Grade Span: PK-12; **Agency Type:** 1
Schools: 7
5 Primary; 1 Middle; 1 High; 0 Other Level
7 Regular; 0 Special Education; 0 Vocational; 0 Alternative
0 Magnet; 0 Charter; 0 Title I Eligible; 0 School-wide Title I
Students: 2,736 (51.7% male; 48.3% female)
Individual Education Program: 325 (11.9%);
English Language Learner: n/a; Migrant: n/a
Eligible for Free Lunch Program: 404 (14.8%)
Eligible for Reduced-Price Lunch Program: 204 (7.5%)
Teachers: 140.0 (19.5 to 1)
Librarians/Media Specialists: 2.0 (1,368.0 to 1)
Guidance Counselors: 3.0 (912.0 to 1)
Current Spending: ($ per student per year):
Total: $6,311; Instruction: $3,877; Support Services: $2,155
Enrollment, Drop-out Rates and Diploma Recipients by Race/Ethnicity

Category	Total	White	Black	Asian	AIAN	Hisp.
Enrollment (%)	100.0	94.8	0.4	0.8	2.9	0.9
Drop-out Rate (%)	n/a	n/a	n/a	n/a	n/a	n/a
H.S. Diplomas (#)	145	139	0	0	6	0

Capac Community SD
403 N Glassford St • Capac, MI 48014-0700
Mailing Address: PO Box 700 • Capac, MI 48014-0700
(810) 395-4321 • http://www.capac.k12.mi.us/
Grade Span: PK-12; **Agency Type:** 1
Schools: 3
1 Primary; 1 Middle; 1 High; 0 Other Level
3 Regular; 0 Special Education; 0 Vocational; 0 Alternative
0 Magnet; 0 Charter; 0 Title I Eligible; 0 School-wide Title I
Students: 1,958 (53.3% male; 46.7% female)
Individual Education Program: 291 (14.9%);
English Language Learner: n/a; Migrant: n/a
Eligible for Free Lunch Program: 289 (14.8%)
Eligible for Reduced-Price Lunch Program: 159 (8.1%)
Teachers: 106.0 (18.5 to 1)
Librarians/Media Specialists: 2.0 (979.0 to 1)
Guidance Counselors: 4.0 (489.5 to 1)
Current Spending: ($ per student per year):
Total: $6,465; Instruction: $3,952; Support Services: $2,273
Enrollment, Drop-out Rates and Diploma Recipients by Race/Ethnicity

Category	Total	White	Black	Asian	AIAN	Hisp.
Enrollment (%)	100.0	89.8	0.5	0.6	0.2	8.8
Drop-out Rate (%)	n/a	n/a	n/a	n/a	n/a	n/a
H.S. Diplomas (#)	118	111	1	0	1	5

East China SD
1585 Meisner Rd • East China, MI 48054-4143
(810) 676-1018 • http://www.east-china.k12.mi.us/
Grade Span: PK-12; **Agency Type:** 1
Schools: 11
6 Primary; 2 Middle; 3 High; 0 Other Level
10 Regular; 0 Special Education; 0 Vocational; 1 Alternative
11 Magnet; 0 Charter; 0 Title I Eligible; 0 School-wide Title I
Students: 5,960 (51.9% male; 48.1% female)
Individual Education Program: 588 (9.9%);
English Language Learner: n/a; Migrant: n/a
Eligible for Free Lunch Program: 605 (10.2%)
Eligible for Reduced-Price Lunch Program: 236 (4.0%)
Teachers: 320.8 (18.6 to 1)
Librarians/Media Specialists: 5.5 (1,083.6 to 1)
Guidance Counselors: 10.0 (596.0 to 1)
Current Spending: ($ per student per year):
Total: $7,492; Instruction: $4,269; Support Services: $3,008
Enrollment, Drop-out Rates and Diploma Recipients by Race/Ethnicity

Category	Total	White	Black	Asian	AIAN	Hisp.
Enrollment (%)	100.0	97.2	0.5	0.4	0.8	0.9
Drop-out Rate (%)	n/a	n/a	n/a	n/a	n/a	n/a
H.S. Diplomas (#)	404	394	1	1	3	5

Marysville Public Schools
1111 Delaware Ave • Marysville, MI 48040-1566
(810) 364-7731 • http://www.marysville.k12.mi.us/
Grade Span: PK-12; **Agency Type:** 1
Schools: 5
3 Primary; 1 Middle; 1 High; 0 Other Level
5 Regular; 0 Special Education; 0 Vocational; 0 Alternative
0 Magnet; 0 Charter; 0 Title I Eligible; 0 School-wide Title I
Students: 2,932 (53.2% male; 46.8% female)
Individual Education Program: 269 (9.2%);
English Language Learner: n/a; Migrant: n/a
Eligible for Free Lunch Program: 160 (5.5%)
Eligible for Reduced-Price Lunch Program: 76 (2.6%)
Teachers: 132.5 (22.1 to 1)
Librarians/Media Specialists: 2.0 (1,466.0 to 1)
Guidance Counselors: 4.0 (733.0 to 1)
Current Spending: ($ per student per year):
Total: $6,111; Instruction: $3,652; Support Services: $2,292
Enrollment, Drop-out Rates and Diploma Recipients by Race/Ethnicity

Category	Total	White	Black	Asian	AIAN	Hisp.
Enrollment (%)	100.0	96.1	0.6	0.9	1.1	1.2
Drop-out Rate (%)	n/a	n/a	n/a	n/a	n/a	n/a
H.S. Diplomas (#)	172	161	1	2	4	4

Port Huron Area SD
1925 Lapeer Ave • Port Huron, MI 48061-5013
Mailing Address: PO Box 5013 • Port Huron, MI 48061-5013
(810) 984-3101 • http://www.port-huron.k12.mi.us/phasd/
Grade Span: PK-12; **Agency Type:** 1
Schools: 22
14 Primary; 4 Middle; 2 High; 2 Other Level
20 Regular; 0 Special Education; 0 Vocational; 2 Alternative
0 Magnet; 0 Charter; 2 Title I Eligible; 2 School-wide Title I
Students: 13,214 (51.4% male; 48.6% female)
Individual Education Program: 1,678 (12.7%);
English Language Learner: 32 (0.2%); Migrant: n/a
Eligible for Free Lunch Program: 3,579 (27.1%)
Eligible for Reduced-Price Lunch Program: 956 (7.2%)
Teachers: 736.3 (17.9 to 1)
Librarians/Media Specialists: 9.0 (1,468.2 to 1)
Guidance Counselors: 20.0 (660.7 to 1)
Current Spending: ($ per student per year):
Total: $6,828; Instruction: $4,321; Support Services: $2,316
Enrollment, Drop-out Rates and Diploma Recipients by Race/Ethnicity

Category	Total	White	Black	Asian	AIAN	Hisp.
Enrollment (%)	100.0	85.9	8.5	0.8	2.0	2.5
Drop-out Rate (%)	n/a	n/a	n/a	n/a	n/a	n/a
H.S. Diplomas (#)	691	609	49	7	13	13

Yale Public Schools
198 School Dr • Yale, MI 48097-3342
(810) 387-4274 • http://www.yale.k12.mi.us/
Grade Span: PK-12; **Agency Type:** 1
Schools: 6
3 Primary; 1 Middle; 2 High; 0 Other Level

5 Regular; 0 Special Education; 0 Vocational; 1 Alternative
3 Magnet; 0 Charter; 0 Title I Eligible; 0 School-wide Title I
Students: 2,403 (52.2% male; 47.8% female)
Individual Education Program: 231 (9.6%);
English Language Learner: 5 (0.2%); Migrant: n/a
Eligible for Free Lunch Program: 385 (16.0%)
Eligible for Reduced-Price Lunch Program: 148 (6.2%)
Teachers: 111.3 (21.6 to 1)
Librarians/Media Specialists: 2.0 (1,201.5 to 1)
Guidance Counselors: 5.0 (480.6 to 1)
Current Spending: ($ per student per year):
Total: $6,538; Instruction: $3,719; Support Services: $2,550
Enrollment, Drop-out Rates and Diploma Recipients by Race/Ethnicity

Category	Total	White	Black	Asian	AIAN	Hisp.
Enrollment (%)	100.0	96.8	1.0	0.6	0.7	0.9
Drop-out Rate (%)	n/a	n/a	n/a	n/a	n/a	n/a
H.S. Diplomas (#)	143	137	2	0	3	1

St. Joseph County

Constantine Public SD
260 W 6th St • Constantine, MI 49042-1397
(269) 435-2015 • http://home.constps.org/
Grade Span: PK-12; **Agency Type:** 1
Schools: 4
2 Primary; 1 Middle; 1 High; 0 Other Level
4 Regular; 0 Special Education; 0 Vocational; 0 Alternative
0 Magnet; 0 Charter; 2 Title I Eligible; 2 School-wide Title I
Students: 1,555 (53.5% male; 46.5% female)
Individual Education Program: 183 (11.8%);
English Language Learner: n/a; Migrant: n/a
Eligible for Free Lunch Program: 308 (19.8%)
Eligible for Reduced-Price Lunch Program: 76 (4.9%)
Teachers: 90.6 (17.2 to 1)
Librarians/Media Specialists: 1.0 (1,555.0 to 1)
Guidance Counselors: 2.0 (777.5 to 1)
Current Spending: ($ per student per year):
Total: $6,459; Instruction: $4,424; Support Services: $1,780
Enrollment, Drop-out Rates and Diploma Recipients by Race/Ethnicity

Category	Total	White	Black	Asian	AIAN	Hisp.
Enrollment (%)	100.0	96.9	1.3	0.7	0.0	1.0
Drop-out Rate (%)	n/a	n/a	n/a	n/a	n/a	n/a
H.S. Diplomas (#)	101	100	1	0	0	0

Sturgis Public Schools
216 Vinewood Ave • Sturgis, MI 49091-9505
(269) 659-1500 • http://www.sturgis.k12.mi.us/
Grade Span: PK-12; **Agency Type:** 1
Schools: 10
6 Primary; 2 Middle; 1 High; 1 Other Level
9 Regular; 0 Special Education; 0 Vocational; 1 Alternative
0 Magnet; 0 Charter; 6 Title I Eligible; 6 School-wide Title I
Students: 3,107 (50.4% male; 49.6% female)
Individual Education Program: 338 (10.9%);
English Language Learner: 250 (8.0%); Migrant: n/a
Eligible for Free Lunch Program: 1,081 (34.8%)
Eligible for Reduced-Price Lunch Program: 246 (7.9%)
Teachers: 182.1 (17.1 to 1)
Librarians/Media Specialists: 4.0 (776.8 to 1)
Guidance Counselors: 6.0 (517.8 to 1)
Current Spending: ($ per student per year):
Total: $6,344; Instruction: $3,973; Support Services: $2,093
Enrollment, Drop-out Rates and Diploma Recipients by Race/Ethnicity

Category	Total	White	Black	Asian	AIAN	Hisp.
Enrollment (%)	100.0	82.0	1.9	1.2	0.1	14.9
Drop-out Rate (%)	n/a	n/a	n/a	n/a	n/a	n/a
H.S. Diplomas (#)	184	167	2	2	0	13

Three Rivers Community Schools
17601 6th Ave • Three Rivers, MI 49093-1700
(616) 279-1100 • http://www.trschools.org/
Grade Span: PK-12; **Agency Type:** 1
Schools: 9
6 Primary; 1 Middle; 1 High; 1 Other Level
8 Regular; 0 Special Education; 0 Vocational; 1 Alternative
0 Magnet; 0 Charter; 0 Title I Eligible; 0 School-wide Title I
Students: 3,109 (53.0% male; 47.0% female)
Individual Education Program: 423 (13.6%);
English Language Learner: n/a; Migrant: n/a
Eligible for Free Lunch Program: 847 (27.2%)
Eligible for Reduced-Price Lunch Program: 227 (7.3%)
Teachers: 174.3 (17.8 to 1)
Librarians/Media Specialists: 3.0 (1,036.3 to 1)
Guidance Counselors: 8.1 (383.8 to 1)
Current Spending: ($ per student per year):
Total: $6,335; Instruction: $3,958; Support Services: $2,089
Enrollment, Drop-out Rates and Diploma Recipients by Race/Ethnicity

Category	Total	White	Black	Asian	AIAN	Hisp.
Enrollment (%)	100.0	83.1	12.7	1.2	0.1	2.9
Drop-out Rate (%)	n/a	n/a	n/a	n/a	n/a	n/a
H.S. Diplomas (#)	159	143	9	2	2	3

Tuscola County

Caro Community Schools
301 N Hooper St • Caro, MI 48723-1474
(989) 673-3160 • http://www.caro.k12.mi.us/
Grade Span: KG-12; **Agency Type:** 1
Schools: 5
2 Primary; 1 Middle; 2 High; 0 Other Level
4 Regular; 0 Special Education; 0 Vocational; 1 Alternative
5 Magnet; 0 Charter; 2 Title I Eligible; 2 School-wide Title I
Students: 2,334 (52.9% male; 47.1% female)
Individual Education Program: 336 (14.4%);
English Language Learner: n/a; Migrant: n/a
Eligible for Free Lunch Program: 557 (23.9%)
Eligible for Reduced-Price Lunch Program: 209 (9.0%)
Teachers: 131.6 (17.7 to 1)
Librarians/Media Specialists: 3.0 (778.0 to 1)
Guidance Counselors: 4.0 (583.5 to 1)
Current Spending: ($ per student per year):
Total: $6,235; Instruction: $4,280; Support Services: $1,734
Enrollment, Drop-out Rates and Diploma Recipients by Race/Ethnicity

Category	Total	White	Black	Asian	AIAN	Hisp.
Enrollment (%)	100.0	94.8	0.8	0.7	0.0	3.7
Drop-out Rate (%)	n/a	n/a	n/a	n/a	n/a	n/a
H.S. Diplomas (#)	143	137	0	1	0	5

Cass City Public Schools
4868 N Seeger St • Cass City, MI 48726-9401
(989) 872-2200 • http://www.casscity.k12.mi.us/
Grade Span: PK-12; **Agency Type:** 1
Schools: 4
2 Primary; 1 Middle; 1 High; 0 Other Level
4 Regular; 0 Special Education; 0 Vocational; 0 Alternative
0 Magnet; 0 Charter; 0 Title I Eligible; 0 School-wide Title I
Students: 1,727 (53.9% male; 46.1% female)
Individual Education Program: 207 (12.0%);
English Language Learner: n/a; Migrant: n/a
Eligible for Free Lunch Program: 398 (23.0%)
Eligible for Reduced-Price Lunch Program: 147 (8.5%)
Teachers: 78.0 (22.1 to 1)
Librarians/Media Specialists: n/a
Guidance Counselors: 3.0 (575.7 to 1)
Current Spending: ($ per student per year):
Total: $6,488; Instruction: $4,121; Support Services: $2,065
Enrollment, Drop-out Rates and Diploma Recipients by Race/Ethnicity

Category	Total	White	Black	Asian	AIAN	Hisp.
Enrollment (%)	100.0	96.9	0.5	0.9	0.6	1.1
Drop-out Rate (%)	n/a	n/a	n/a	n/a	n/a	n/a
H.S. Diplomas (#)	125	122	0	3	0	0

Millington Community Schools
8655 Gleason Rd • Millington, MI 48746-2500
(989) 871-5201 • http://www.mcsdistrict.com/
Grade Span: KG-12; **Agency Type:** 1
Schools: 5
2 Primary; 1 Middle; 1 High; 0 Other Level
4 Regular; 0 Special Education; 0 Vocational; 0 Alternative
0 Magnet; 0 Charter; 0 Title I Eligible; 0 School-wide Title I
Students: 1,750 (51.1% male; 48.9% female)
Individual Education Program: 239 (13.7%);
English Language Learner: n/a; Migrant: n/a
Eligible for Free Lunch Program: 333 (19.0%)
Eligible for Reduced-Price Lunch Program: 122 (7.0%)
Teachers: 91.8 (19.1 to 1)
Librarians/Media Specialists: 1.0 (1,750.0 to 1)
Guidance Counselors: 3.0 (583.3 to 1)
Current Spending: ($ per student per year):
Total: $6,736; Instruction: $4,229; Support Services: $2,199
Enrollment, Drop-out Rates and Diploma Recipients by Race/Ethnicity

Category	Total	White	Black	Asian	AIAN	Hisp.
Enrollment (%)	100.0	97.9	0.6	0.3	0.3	0.9
Drop-out Rate (%)	n/a	n/a	n/a	n/a	n/a	n/a
H.S. Diplomas (#)	137	136	0	0	0	1

Vassar Public Schools
220 Athletic St • Vassar, MI 48768-1205
(989) 823-8535 • http://www.vassar.k12.mi.us/
Grade Span: KG-12; **Agency Type:** 1
Schools: 5

2 Primary; 1 Middle; 2 High; 0 Other Level
4 Regular; 0 Special Education; 0 Vocational; 1 Alternative
0 Magnet; 0 Charter; 0 Title I Eligible; 0 School-wide Title I
Students: 1,905 (58.5% male; 41.5% female)
Individual Education Program: 353 (18.5%);
English Language Learner: n/a; Migrant: n/a
Eligible for Free Lunch Program: 430 (22.6%)
Eligible for Reduced-Price Lunch Program: 154 (8.1%)
Teachers: n/a
Librarians/Media Specialists: n/a
Guidance Counselors: n/a
Current Spending: ($ per student per year):
Total: $6,096; Instruction: $4,181; Support Services: $1,624
Enrollment, Drop-out Rates and Diploma Recipients by Race/Ethnicity

Category	Total	White	Black	Asian	AIAN	Hisp.
Enrollment (%)	100.0	86.7	11.1	0.7	0.0	1.5
Drop-out Rate (%)	n/a	n/a	n/a	n/a	n/a	n/a
H.S. Diplomas (#)	93	87	5	1	0	0

Van Buren County

Bangor Public Schools (Van Buren)

801 W Arlington St • Bangor, MI 49013-1108
(616) 427-6800 • http://www.bangorvikings.org/
Grade Span: KG-12; **Agency Type:** 1
Schools: 5
2 Primary; 1 Middle; 1 High; 1 Other Level
4 Regular; 0 Special Education; 0 Vocational; 1 Alternative
0 Magnet; 0 Charter; 5 Title I Eligible; 5 School-wide Title I
Students: 1,524 (51.6% male; 48.4% female)
Individual Education Program: 111 (7.3%);
English Language Learner: n/a; Migrant: n/a
Eligible for Free Lunch Program: 883 (57.9%)
Eligible for Reduced-Price Lunch Program: 121 (7.9%)
Teachers: 89.5 (17.0 to 1)
Librarians/Media Specialists: 1.0 (1,524.0 to 1)
Guidance Counselors: 2.0 (762.0 to 1)
Current Spending: ($ per student per year):
Total: $7,218; Instruction: $4,539; Support Services: $2,339
Enrollment, Drop-out Rates and Diploma Recipients by Race/Ethnicity

Category	Total	White	Black	Asian	AIAN	Hisp.
Enrollment (%)	100.0	71.1	8.3	0.2	0.7	18.6
Drop-out Rate (%)	n/a	n/a	n/a	n/a	n/a	n/a
H.S. Diplomas (#)	103	81	6	0	0	16

Hartford Public SD

115-B School St • Hartford, MI 49057-1183
(269) 621-7000
Grade Span: PK-12; **Agency Type:** 1
Schools: 4
2 Primary; 1 Middle; 1 High; 0 Other Level
4 Regular; 0 Special Education; 0 Vocational; 0 Alternative
0 Magnet; 0 Charter; 4 Title I Eligible; 4 School-wide Title I
Students: 1,567 (51.8% male; 48.2% female)
Individual Education Program: 123 (7.8%);
English Language Learner: 214 (13.7%); Migrant: n/a
Eligible for Free Lunch Program: 546 (34.8%)
Eligible for Reduced-Price Lunch Program: 183 (11.7%)
Teachers: 99.3 (15.8 to 1)
Librarians/Media Specialists: 2.6 (602.7 to 1)
Guidance Counselors: 4.0 (391.8 to 1)
Current Spending: ($ per student per year):
Total: $7,405; Instruction: $4,584; Support Services: $2,490
Enrollment, Drop-out Rates and Diploma Recipients by Race/Ethnicity

Category	Total	White	Black	Asian	AIAN	Hisp.
Enrollment (%)	100.0	71.2	1.7	0.2	2.4	24.4
Drop-out Rate (%)	n/a	n/a	n/a	n/a	n/a	n/a
H.S. Diplomas (#)	90	63	3	3	1	20

Mattawan Consolidated School

56720 Murray St • Mattawan, MI 49071-9567
(269) 668-3361 • http://www.mattawan.k12.mi.us/
Grade Span: KG-12; **Agency Type:** 1
Schools: 4
2 Primary; 1 Middle; 1 High; 0 Other Level
4 Regular; 0 Special Education; 0 Vocational; 0 Alternative
0 Magnet; 0 Charter; 0 Title I Eligible; 0 School-wide Title I
Students: 3,490 (52.0% male; 48.0% female)
Individual Education Program: 120 (3.4%);
English Language Learner: n/a; Migrant: n/a
Eligible for Free Lunch Program: 234 (6.7%)
Eligible for Reduced-Price Lunch Program: 109 (3.1%)
Teachers: 178.7 (19.5 to 1)
Librarians/Media Specialists: 4.5 (775.6 to 1)
Guidance Counselors: 6.0 (581.7 to 1)
Current Spending: ($ per student per year):
Total: $5,932; Instruction: $3,674; Support Services: $2,046
Enrollment, Drop-out Rates and Diploma Recipients by Race/Ethnicity

Category	Total	White	Black	Asian	AIAN	Hisp.
Enrollment (%)	100.0	93.9	2.1	1.1	1.0	1.5
Drop-out Rate (%)	n/a	n/a	n/a	n/a	n/a	n/a
H.S. Diplomas (#)	217	198	7	6	4	2

Paw Paw Public SD

119 Johnson St • Paw Paw, MI 49079-1093
(269) 657-8800 • http://www.pawpaw.k12.mi.us/
Grade Span: PK-12; **Agency Type:** 1
Schools: 6
3 Primary; 1 Middle; 1 High; 1 Other Level
5 Regular; 0 Special Education; 0 Vocational; 1 Alternative
0 Magnet; 0 Charter; 0 Title I Eligible; 0 School-wide Title I
Students: 2,336 (52.3% male; 47.7% female)
Individual Education Program: 237 (10.1%);
English Language Learner: n/a; Migrant: n/a
Eligible for Free Lunch Program: 598 (25.6%)
Eligible for Reduced-Price Lunch Program: 143 (6.1%)
Teachers: 122.0 (19.1 to 1)
Librarians/Media Specialists: 3.0 (778.7 to 1)
Guidance Counselors: 2.0 (1,168.0 to 1)
Current Spending: ($ per student per year):
Total: $6,427; Instruction: $4,063; Support Services: $2,094
Enrollment, Drop-out Rates and Diploma Recipients by Race/Ethnicity

Category	Total	White	Black	Asian	AIAN	Hisp.
Enrollment (%)	100.0	93.8	2.0	1.2	0.5	2.4
Drop-out Rate (%)	n/a	n/a	n/a	n/a	n/a	n/a
H.S. Diplomas (#)	156	145	4	2	1	4

South Haven Public Schools

554 Green St • South Haven, MI 49090-1491
(269) 637-0520 • http://www.shps.org/
Grade Span: PK-12; **Agency Type:** 1
Schools: 5
3 Primary; 1 Middle; 1 High; 0 Other Level
5 Regular; 0 Special Education; 0 Vocational; 0 Alternative
0 Magnet; 0 Charter; 0 Title I Eligible; 0 School-wide Title I
Students: 2,515 (51.1% male; 48.9% female)
Individual Education Program: 213 (8.5%);
English Language Learner: 134 (5.3%); Migrant: n/a
Eligible for Free Lunch Program: 785 (31.2%)
Eligible for Reduced-Price Lunch Program: 192 (7.6%)
Teachers: 138.4 (18.2 to 1)
Librarians/Media Specialists: 1.0 (2,515.0 to 1)
Guidance Counselors: 3.0 (838.3 to 1)
Current Spending: ($ per student per year):
Total: $6,670; Instruction: $4,132; Support Services: $2,172
Enrollment, Drop-out Rates and Diploma Recipients by Race/Ethnicity

Category	Total	White	Black	Asian	AIAN	Hisp.
Enrollment (%)	100.0	77.4	12.2	0.6	0.9	8.7
Drop-out Rate (%)	n/a	n/a	n/a	n/a	n/a	n/a
H.S. Diplomas (#)	152	129	19	2	0	2

Washtenaw County

Ann Arbor Public Schools

2555 S State Rd • Ann Arbor, MI 48104
Mailing Address: PO Box 1188 • Ann Arbor, MI 48106-1188
(734) 994-2230 • http://aaps.k12.mi.us/
Grade Span: KG-12; **Agency Type:** 1
Schools: 33
21 Primary; 5 Middle; 6 High; 1 Other Level
29 Regular; 1 Special Education; 0 Vocational; 3 Alternative
0 Magnet; 0 Charter; 1 Title I Eligible; 1 School-wide Title I
Students: 16,774 (51.4% male; 48.6% female)
Individual Education Program: 1,946 (11.6%);
English Language Learner: 1,239 (7.4%); Migrant: n/a
Eligible for Free Lunch Program: 1,979 (11.8%)
Eligible for Reduced-Price Lunch Program: 652 (3.9%)
Teachers: 1,051.0 (16.0 to 1)
Librarians/Media Specialists: 33.9 (494.8 to 1)
Guidance Counselors: 37.2 (450.9 to 1)
Current Spending: ($ per student per year):
Total: $9,124; Instruction: $5,275; Support Services: $3,634
Enrollment, Drop-out Rates and Diploma Recipients by Race/Ethnicity

Category	Total	White	Black	Asian	AIAN	Hisp.
Enrollment (%)	100.0	68.5	15.0	12.5	0.5	3.5
Drop-out Rate (%)	n/a	n/a	n/a	n/a	n/a	n/a
H.S. Diplomas (#)	1,141	843	145	117	6	30

Chelsea SD

500 E Washington St • Chelsea, MI 48118-1144
(734) 433-2208 • http://chelsea.k12.mi.us/
Grade Span: PK-12; **Agency Type:** 1
Schools: 6
4 Primary; 1 Middle; 1 High; 0 Other Level
6 Regular; 0 Special Education; 0 Vocational; 0 Alternative
0 Magnet; 0 Charter; 5 Title I Eligible; 5 School-wide Title I
Students: 3,200 (52.2% male; 47.8% female)
Individual Education Program: 495 (15.5%);
English Language Learner: n/a; Migrant: n/a
Eligible for Free Lunch Program: 109 (3.4%)
Eligible for Reduced-Price Lunch Program: 56 (1.8%)
Teachers: 160.7 (19.9 to 1)
Librarians/Media Specialists: 5.0 (640.0 to 1)
Guidance Counselors: 5.0 (640.0 to 1)
Current Spending: ($ per student per year):
Total: $7,802; Instruction: $4,264; Support Services: $3,234
Enrollment, Drop-out Rates and Diploma Recipients by Race/Ethnicity

Category	Total	White	Black	Asian	AIAN	Hisp.
Enrollment (%)	100.0	96.9	0.3	1.3	0.5	1.0
Drop-out Rate (%)	n/a	n/a	n/a	n/a	n/a	n/a
H.S. Diplomas (#)	240	235	2	1	0	2

Dexter Community SD

7714 Ann Arbor St • Dexter, MI 48130-1534
(734) 424-4100 • http://web.dexter.k12.mi.us/
Grade Span: KG-12; **Agency Type:** 1
Schools: 6
3 Primary; 2 Middle; 1 High; 0 Other Level
6 Regular; 0 Special Education; 0 Vocational; 0 Alternative
0 Magnet; 0 Charter; 5 Title I Eligible; 5 School-wide Title I
Students: 3,359 (51.7% male; 48.3% female)
Individual Education Program: 410 (12.2%);
English Language Learner: n/a; Migrant: n/a
Eligible for Free Lunch Program: 120 (3.6%)
Eligible for Reduced-Price Lunch Program: 72 (2.1%)
Teachers: n/a
Librarians/Media Specialists: n/a
Guidance Counselors: n/a
Current Spending: ($ per student per year):
Total: $7,854; Instruction: $4,250; Support Services: $3,198
Enrollment, Drop-out Rates and Diploma Recipients by Race/Ethnicity

Category	Total	White	Black	Asian	AIAN	Hisp.
Enrollment (%)	100.0	97.4	0.5	1.4	0.1	0.5
Drop-out Rate (%)	n/a	n/a	n/a	n/a	n/a	n/a
H.S. Diplomas (#)	193	191	0	1	1	0

Lincoln Consolidated SD

8970 Whittaker Rd • Ypsilanti, MI 48197-9716
(734) 484-7001 • http://lincoln.k12.mi.us/
Grade Span: PK-12; **Agency Type:** 1
Schools: 7
5 Primary; 1 Middle; 1 High; 0 Other Level
7 Regular; 0 Special Education; 0 Vocational; 0 Alternative
6 Magnet; 0 Charter; 4 Title I Eligible; 4 School-wide Title I
Students: 4,761 (52.1% male; 47.9% female)
Individual Education Program: 710 (14.9%);
English Language Learner: n/a; Migrant: n/a
Eligible for Free Lunch Program: 851 (17.9%)
Eligible for Reduced-Price Lunch Program: 255 (5.4%)
Teachers: n/a
Librarians/Media Specialists: n/a
Guidance Counselors: n/a
Current Spending: ($ per student per year):
Total: $6,807; Instruction: $4,032; Support Services: $2,528
Enrollment, Drop-out Rates and Diploma Recipients by Race/Ethnicity

Category	Total	White	Black	Asian	AIAN	Hisp.
Enrollment (%)	100.0	71.6	23.9	1.9	0.4	2.1
Drop-out Rate (%)	n/a	n/a	n/a	n/a	n/a	n/a
H.S. Diplomas (#)	212	156	51	2	0	3

Milan Area Schools

920 N St • Milan, MI 48160-1199
(734) 439-5050 • http://scnc.milan.k12.mi.us/
Grade Span: KG-12; **Agency Type:** 1
Schools: 4
1 Primary; 1 Middle; 1 High; 0 Other Level
3 Regular; 0 Special Education; 0 Vocational; 0 Alternative
0 Magnet; 0 Charter; 0 Title I Eligible; 0 School-wide Title I
Students: 2,227 (52.3% male; 47.7% female)
Individual Education Program: 347 (15.6%);
English Language Learner: n/a; Migrant: n/a
Eligible for Free Lunch Program: 269 (12.1%)
Eligible for Reduced-Price Lunch Program: 78 (3.5%)
Teachers: n/a
Librarians/Media Specialists: n/a
Guidance Counselors: n/a
Current Spending: ($ per student per year):
Total: $7,537; Instruction: $4,522; Support Services: $2,720
Enrollment, Drop-out Rates and Diploma Recipients by Race/Ethnicity

Category	Total	White	Black	Asian	AIAN	Hisp.
Enrollment (%)	100.0	88.1	7.1	1.4	0.9	2.5
Drop-out Rate (%)	n/a	n/a	n/a	n/a	n/a	n/a
H.S. Diplomas (#)	125	111	9	2	0	3

Saline Area Schools

200 N Ann Arbor St • Saline, MI 48176-1168
(734) 429-8000 • http://www.salineschools.com/
Grade Span: KG-12; **Agency Type:** 1
Schools: 7
4 Primary; 2 Middle; 1 High; 0 Other Level
7 Regular; 0 Special Education; 0 Vocational; 0 Alternative
0 Magnet; 0 Charter; 0 Title I Eligible; 0 School-wide Title I
Students: 5,193 (50.9% male; 49.1% female)
Individual Education Program: 527 (10.1%);
English Language Learner: 102 (2.0%); Migrant: n/a
Eligible for Free Lunch Program: 114 (2.2%)
Eligible for Reduced-Price Lunch Program: 85 (1.6%)
Teachers: 268.5 (19.3 to 1)
Librarians/Media Specialists: 5.0 (1,038.6 to 1)
Guidance Counselors: 11.0 (472.1 to 1)
Current Spending: ($ per student per year):
Total: $7,307; Instruction: $4,361; Support Services: $2,704
Enrollment, Drop-out Rates and Diploma Recipients by Race/Ethnicity

Category	Total	White	Black	Asian	AIAN	Hisp.
Enrollment (%)	100.0	94.5	0.9	2.3	1.0	1.4
Drop-out Rate (%)	n/a	n/a	n/a	n/a	n/a	n/a
H.S. Diplomas (#)	359	339	1	7	0	12

School District of Ypsilanti

1885 Packard Rd • Ypsilanti, MI 48197-1846
(734) 714-1218 • http://scnc.yps.k12.mi.us/
Grade Span: PK-12; **Agency Type:** 1
Schools: 12
7 Primary; 2 Middle; 1 High; 2 Other Level
11 Regular; 0 Special Education; 0 Vocational; 1 Alternative
2 Magnet; 0 Charter; 0 Title I Eligible; 0 School-wide Title I
Students: 4,714 (51.9% male; 48.1% female)
Individual Education Program: 955 (20.3%);
English Language Learner: 335 (7.1%); Migrant: n/a
Eligible for Free Lunch Program: 2,106 (44.7%)
Eligible for Reduced-Price Lunch Program: 420 (8.9%)
Teachers: 291.2 (16.2 to 1)
Librarians/Media Specialists: 9.0 (523.8 to 1)
Guidance Counselors: 8.4 (561.2 to 1)
Current Spending: ($ per student per year):
Total: $9,925; Instruction: $5,376; Support Services: $4,239
Enrollment, Drop-out Rates and Diploma Recipients by Race/Ethnicity

Category	Total	White	Black	Asian	AIAN	Hisp.
Enrollment (%)	100.0	38.4	57.9	1.3	0.1	2.4
Drop-out Rate (%)	n/a	n/a	n/a	n/a	n/a	n/a
H.S. Diplomas (#)	235	120	102	7	1	5

Washtenaw ISD

1819 S Wagner Rd • Ann Arbor, MI 48106-1406
Mailing Address: PO Box 1406 • Ann Arbor, MI 48106-1406
(734) 994-8100
Grade Span: PK-12; **Agency Type:** 4
Schools: 4
1 Primary; 0 Middle; 1 High; 2 Other Level
1 Regular; 2 Special Education; 0 Vocational; 1 Alternative
0 Magnet; 0 Charter; 0 Title I Eligible; 0 School-wide Title I
Students: 1,943 (55.8% male; 44.2% female)
Individual Education Program: 328 (16.9%);
English Language Learner: n/a; Migrant: n/a
Eligible for Free Lunch Program: n/a
Eligible for Reduced-Price Lunch Program: n/a
Teachers: 59.8 (32.5 to 1)
Librarians/Media Specialists: n/a
Guidance Counselors: n/a
Current Spending: ($ per student per year):
Total: n/a; Instruction: n/a; Support Services: n/a
Enrollment, Drop-out Rates and Diploma Recipients by Race/Ethnicity

Category	Total	White	Black	Asian	AIAN	Hisp.
Enrollment (%)	100.0	64.9	10.1	7.5	0.1	3.9
Drop-out Rate (%)	n/a	n/a	n/a	n/a	n/a	n/a
H.S. Diplomas (#)	n/a	n/a	n/a	n/a	n/a	n/a

Willow Run Community Schools

2171 E Michigan Ave • Ypsilanti, MI 48198-6049
(734) 481-8200 • http://wrcs.k12.mi.us/splash.htm
Grade Span: PK-12; **Agency Type:** 1
Schools: 8
6 Primary; 1 Middle; 1 High; 0 Other Level
8 Regular; 0 Special Education; 0 Vocational; 0 Alternative
0 Magnet; 0 Charter; 7 Title I Eligible; 7 School-wide Title I
Students: 2,808 (51.3% male; 48.7% female)
Individual Education Program: 538 (19.2%);
English Language Learner: n/a; Migrant: n/a
Eligible for Free Lunch Program: 1,395 (49.7%)
Eligible for Reduced-Price Lunch Program: 370 (13.2%)
Teachers: 125.0 (22.5 to 1)
Librarians/Media Specialists: 1.0 (2,808.0 to 1)
Guidance Counselors: 3.0 (936.0 to 1)
Current Spending: ($ per student per year):
Total: $9,483; Instruction: $4,822; Support Services: $4,236
Enrollment, Drop-out Rates and Diploma Recipients by Race/Ethnicity

Category	Total	White	Black	Asian	AIAN	Hisp.
Enrollment (%)	100.0	43.9	53.6	1.0	0.3	1.2
Drop-out Rate (%)	n/a	n/a	n/a	n/a	n/a	n/a
H.S. Diplomas (#)	127	64	57	4	1	1

Wayne County

Allen Park Public Schools

9601 Vine Ave • Allen Park, MI 48101-2236
(313) 928-4667 • http://www.apps.k12.mi.us/
Grade Span: KG-12; **Agency Type:** 1
Schools: 6
3 Primary; 1 Middle; 1 High; 1 Other Level
5 Regular; 0 Special Education; 0 Vocational; 1 Alternative
0 Magnet; 0 Charter; 0 Title I Eligible; 0 School-wide Title I
Students: 3,490 (51.3% male; 48.7% female)
Individual Education Program: 265 (7.6%);
English Language Learner: n/a; Migrant: n/a
Eligible for Free Lunch Program: 188 (5.4%)
Eligible for Reduced-Price Lunch Program: 131 (3.8%)
Teachers: 173.8 (20.1 to 1)
Librarians/Media Specialists: 5.0 (698.0 to 1)
Guidance Counselors: 5.0 (698.0 to 1)
Current Spending: ($ per student per year):
Total: $7,155; Instruction: $4,412; Support Services: $2,484
Enrollment, Drop-out Rates and Diploma Recipients by Race/Ethnicity

Category	Total	White	Black	Asian	AIAN	Hisp.
Enrollment (%)	100.0	94.1	0.7	0.5	0.1	4.6
Drop-out Rate (%)	n/a	n/a	n/a	n/a	n/a	n/a
H.S. Diplomas (#)	198	182	1	3	0	12

Crestwood SD

1501 N Beech Daly Rd • Dearborn Heights, MI 48127-3495
(313) 278-0903 • http://www.crestwoodhigh.org/
Grade Span: PK-12; **Agency Type:** 1
Schools: 5
3 Primary; 1 Middle; 1 High; 0 Other Level
5 Regular; 0 Special Education; 0 Vocational; 0 Alternative
5 Magnet; 0 Charter; 0 Title I Eligible; 0 School-wide Title I
Students: 3,556 (53.0% male; 47.0% female)
Individual Education Program: 316 (8.9%);
English Language Learner: 141 (4.0%); Migrant: n/a
Eligible for Free Lunch Program: 603 (17.0%)
Eligible for Reduced-Price Lunch Program: 237 (6.7%)
Teachers: 167.3 (21.3 to 1)
Librarians/Media Specialists: 3.0 (1,185.3 to 1)
Guidance Counselors: 6.0 (592.7 to 1)
Current Spending: ($ per student per year):
Total: $6,527; Instruction: $3,887; Support Services: $2,380
Enrollment, Drop-out Rates and Diploma Recipients by Race/Ethnicity

Category	Total	White	Black	Asian	AIAN	Hisp.
Enrollment (%)	100.0	92.8	1.9	2.4	0.2	2.7
Drop-out Rate (%)	n/a	n/a	n/a	n/a	n/a	n/a
H.S. Diplomas (#)	216	197	1	6	2	10

Dearborn City SD

18700 Audette St • Dearborn, MI 48124-4295
(313) 730-3242 • http://www.dearbornschools.org/
Grade Span: PK-12; **Agency Type:** 1
Schools: 32
21 Primary; 5 Middle; 4 High; 2 Other Level
28 Regular; 2 Special Education; 0 Vocational; 2 Alternative
0 Magnet; 0 Charter; 13 Title I Eligible; 13 School-wide Title I
Students: 17,981 (51.6% male; 48.4% female)
Individual Education Program: 1,937 (10.8%);
English Language Learner: 6,472 (36.0%); Migrant: n/a
Eligible for Free Lunch Program: 5,833 (32.4%)
Eligible for Reduced-Price Lunch Program: 614 (3.4%)
Teachers: 1,111.1 (16.2 to 1)
Librarians/Media Specialists: 24.0 (749.2 to 1)
Guidance Counselors: 30.3 (593.4 to 1)
Current Spending: ($ per student per year):
Total: $9,342; Instruction: $5,496; Support Services: $3,598
Enrollment, Drop-out Rates and Diploma Recipients by Race/Ethnicity

Category	Total	White	Black	Asian	AIAN	Hisp.
Enrollment (%)	100.0	94.1	2.5	0.8	0.7	1.9
Drop-out Rate (%)	n/a	n/a	n/a	n/a	n/a	n/a
H.S. Diplomas (#)	1,014	983	5	7	3	16

Dearborn Heights SD #7

20629 Annapolis St • Dearborn Heights, MI 48125-2904
(313) 278-1900 • http://www.resa.net/district7/
Grade Span: KG-12; **Agency Type:** 1
Schools: 6
4 Primary; 1 Middle; 1 High; 0 Other Level
6 Regular; 0 Special Education; 0 Vocational; 0 Alternative
0 Magnet; 0 Charter; 2 Title I Eligible; 2 School-wide Title I
Students: 2,986 (51.3% male; 48.7% female)
Individual Education Program: 397 (13.3%);
English Language Learner: n/a; Migrant: n/a
Eligible for Free Lunch Program: 767 (25.7%)
Eligible for Reduced-Price Lunch Program: 316 (10.6%)
Teachers: 136.3 (21.9 to 1)
Librarians/Media Specialists: 6.0 (497.7 to 1)
Guidance Counselors: 4.0 (746.5 to 1)
Current Spending: ($ per student per year):
Total: $6,337; Instruction: $3,868; Support Services: $2,106
Enrollment, Drop-out Rates and Diploma Recipients by Race/Ethnicity

Category	Total	White	Black	Asian	AIAN	Hisp.
Enrollment (%)	100.0	89.4	4.4	1.0	0.7	4.6
Drop-out Rate (%)	n/a	n/a	n/a	n/a	n/a	n/a
H.S. Diplomas (#)	100	95	0	2	0	3

Detroit Academy of Arts and Sciences

2985 E Jefferson Ave • Detroit, MI 48207-4288
(313) 259-1744
Grade Span: KG-11; **Agency Type:** 7
Schools: 2
0 Primary; 0 Middle; 0 High; 2 Other Level
2 Regular; 0 Special Education; 0 Vocational; 0 Alternative
0 Magnet; 2 Charter; 2 Title I Eligible; 2 School-wide Title I
Students: 2,745 (48.0% male; 52.0% female)
Individual Education Program: 88 (3.2%);
English Language Learner: n/a; Migrant: n/a
Eligible for Free Lunch Program: 1,012 (36.9%)
Eligible for Reduced-Price Lunch Program: 170 (6.2%)
Teachers: n/a
Librarians/Media Specialists: n/a
Guidance Counselors: n/a
Current Spending: ($ per student per year):
Total: $6,839; Instruction: $2,758; Support Services: $3,767
Enrollment, Drop-out Rates and Diploma Recipients by Race/Ethnicity

Category	Total	White	Black	Asian	AIAN	Hisp.
Enrollment (%)	100.0	0.2	99.5	0.1	0.1	0.1
Drop-out Rate (%)	n/a	n/a	n/a	n/a	n/a	n/a
H.S. Diplomas (#)	n/a	n/a	n/a	n/a	n/a	n/a

Detroit City SD

3011 W Grand Blvd, Fisher 14th • Detroit, MI 48202-4050
(313) 873-7450 • http://www.detroit.k12.mi.us/
Grade Span: PK-12; **Agency Type:** 1
Schools: 273
183 Primary; 37 Middle; 33 High; 20 Other Level
253 Regular; 7 Special Education; 4 Vocational; 9 Alternative
0 Magnet; 0 Charter; 0 Title I Eligible; 0 School-wide Title I
Students: 173,742 (50.9% male; 49.1% female)
Individual Education Program: 20,089 (11.6%);
English Language Learner: 8,216 (4.7%); Migrant: n/a
Eligible for Free Lunch Program: 96,892 (55.8%)
Eligible for Reduced-Price Lunch Program: 6,070 (3.5%)
Teachers: 5,683.0 (30.6 to 1)
Librarians/Media Specialists: 44.0 (3,948.7 to 1)
Guidance Counselors: 252.0 (689.5 to 1)
Current Spending: ($ per student per year):
Total: $9,069; Instruction: $5,902; Support Services: $2,954
Enrollment, Drop-out Rates and Diploma Recipients by Race/Ethnicity

Category	Total	White	Black	Asian	AIAN	Hisp.
Enrollment (%)	100.0	3.3	90.6	0.8	0.3	4.9
Drop-out Rate (%)	n/a	n/a	n/a	n/a	n/a	n/a
H.S. Diplomas (#)	5,540	174	5,096	47	23	200

Flat Rock Community Schools
28639 Division • Flat Rock, MI 48134-1248
(734) 782-2451 • http://www.resa.net/flatrock/
Grade Span: PK-12; **Agency Type:** 1
Schools: 5
2 Primary; 2 Middle; 1 High; 0 Other Level
5 Regular; 0 Special Education; 0 Vocational; 0 Alternative
0 Magnet; 0 Charter; 1 Title I Eligible; 1 School-wide Title I
Students: 1,760 (48.8% male; 51.2% female)
Individual Education Program: 306 (17.4%);
English Language Learner: n/a; Migrant: n/a
Eligible for Free Lunch Program: 327 (18.6%)
Eligible for Reduced-Price Lunch Program: 82 (4.7%)
Teachers: 91.3 (19.3 to 1)
Librarians/Media Specialists: 1.0 (1,760.0 to 1)
Guidance Counselors: 2.0 (880.0 to 1)
Current Spending: ($ per student per year):
Total: $7,515; Instruction: $4,213; Support Services: $3,111
Enrollment, Drop-out Rates and Diploma Recipients by Race/Ethnicity

Category	Total	White	Black	Asian	AIAN	Hisp.
Enrollment (%)	100.0	94.5	1.9	0.8	0.3	2.4
Drop-out Rate (%)	n/a	n/a	n/a	n/a	n/a	n/a
H.S. Diplomas (#)	92	91	1	0	0	0

Garden City SD
1333 Radcliff St • Garden City, MI 48135-1198
(734) 762-8300 • http://www.resa.net/gardencity/
Grade Span: PK-12; **Agency Type:** 1
Schools: 10
5 Primary; 1 Middle; 2 High; 2 Other Level
7 Regular; 1 Special Education; 0 Vocational; 2 Alternative
0 Magnet; 0 Charter; 0 Title I Eligible; 0 School-wide Title I
Students: 5,178 (52.8% male; 47.2% female)
Individual Education Program: 1,148 (22.2%);
English Language Learner: n/a; Migrant: n/a
Eligible for Free Lunch Program: 619 (12.0%)
Eligible for Reduced-Price Lunch Program: 362 (7.0%)
Teachers: 351.5 (14.7 to 1)
Librarians/Media Specialists: 2.2 (2,353.6 to 1)
Guidance Counselors: 6.2 (835.2 to 1)
Current Spending: ($ per student per year):
Total: $9,601; Instruction: $6,121; Support Services: $3,480
Enrollment, Drop-out Rates and Diploma Recipients by Race/Ethnicity

Category	Total	White	Black	Asian	AIAN	Hisp.
Enrollment (%)	100.0	95.1	3.3	0.4	0.4	0.8
Drop-out Rate (%)	n/a	n/a	n/a	n/a	n/a	n/a
H.S. Diplomas (#)	275	269	2	1	0	3

Gibraltar SD
19370 Vreeland Rd • Woodhaven, MI 48183-4430
(734) 692-4002 • http://www.resa.net/gibraltar/
Grade Span: PK-12; **Agency Type:** 1
Schools: 8
5 Primary; 1 Middle; 2 High; 0 Other Level
7 Regular; 0 Special Education; 0 Vocational; 1 Alternative
0 Magnet; 0 Charter; 4 Title I Eligible; 4 School-wide Title I
Students: 3,032 (51.6% male; 48.4% female)
Individual Education Program: 407 (13.4%);
English Language Learner: n/a; Migrant: n/a
Eligible for Free Lunch Program: 363 (12.0%)
Eligible for Reduced-Price Lunch Program: 114 (3.8%)
Teachers: 158.9 (19.1 to 1)
Librarians/Media Specialists: 2.0 (1,516.0 to 1)
Guidance Counselors: 4.0 (758.0 to 1)
Current Spending: ($ per student per year):
Total: $7,121; Instruction: $4,104; Support Services: $2,695
Enrollment, Drop-out Rates and Diploma Recipients by Race/Ethnicity

Category	Total	White	Black	Asian	AIAN	Hisp.
Enrollment (%)	100.0	88.4	2.4	1.0	4.9	3.3
Drop-out Rate (%)	n/a	n/a	n/a	n/a	n/a	n/a
H.S. Diplomas (#)	200	182	1	2	11	4

Grosse Ile Township Schools
23276 E River Rd • Grosse Ile, MI 48138-1535
(734) 362-2555 • http://www.gischools.org/
Grade Span: KG-12; **Agency Type:** 1
Schools: 4
2 Primary; 1 Middle; 1 High; 0 Other Level
4 Regular; 0 Special Education; 0 Vocational; 0 Alternative
0 Magnet; 0 Charter; 0 Title I Eligible; 0 School-wide Title I
Students: 2,049 (50.4% male; 49.6% female)
Individual Education Program: 161 (7.9%);
English Language Learner: n/a; Migrant: n/a
Eligible for Free Lunch Program: 21 (1.0%)
Eligible for Reduced-Price Lunch Program: 25 (1.2%)
Teachers: 114.0 (18.0 to 1)
Librarians/Media Specialists: 3.0 (683.0 to 1)
Guidance Counselors: 4.0 (512.3 to 1)
Current Spending: ($ per student per year):
Total: $8,102; Instruction: $4,850; Support Services: $3,029
Enrollment, Drop-out Rates and Diploma Recipients by Race/Ethnicity

Category	Total	White	Black	Asian	AIAN	Hisp.
Enrollment (%)	100.0	93.5	0.1	2.7	2.2	1.4
Drop-out Rate (%)	n/a	n/a	n/a	n/a	n/a	n/a
H.S. Diplomas (#)	175	165	0	5	2	3

Grosse Pointe Public Schools
389 St Clair Ave • Grosse Pointe, MI 48230-1501
(313) 432-3000 • http://www.gp.k12.mi.us/
Grade Span: PK-12; **Agency Type:** 1
Schools: 16
10 Primary; 3 Middle; 2 High; 1 Other Level
15 Regular; 1 Special Education; 0 Vocational; 0 Alternative
0 Magnet; 0 Charter; 0 Title I Eligible; 0 School-wide Title I
Students: 8,940 (50.9% male; 49.1% female)
Individual Education Program: 1,063 (11.9%);
English Language Learner: 255 (2.9%); Migrant: n/a
Eligible for Free Lunch Program: 168 (1.9%)
Eligible for Reduced-Price Lunch Program: 60 (0.7%)
Teachers: 556.8 (16.1 to 1)
Librarians/Media Specialists: 12.1 (738.8 to 1)
Guidance Counselors: 17.0 (525.9 to 1)
Current Spending: ($ per student per year):
Total: $9,312; Instruction: $5,771; Support Services: $3,397
Enrollment, Drop-out Rates and Diploma Recipients by Race/Ethnicity

Category	Total	White	Black	Asian	AIAN	Hisp.
Enrollment (%)	100.0	91.2	5.8	1.9	0.2	0.9
Drop-out Rate (%)	n/a	n/a	n/a	n/a	n/a	n/a
H.S. Diplomas (#)	720	679	18	15	1	7

Hamtramck Public Schools
3201 Roosevelt • Hamtramck, MI 48212-0012
Mailing Address: PO Box 12012 • Hamtramck, MI 48212-0012
(313) 872-9270 • http://www.hamtramck.k12.mi.us/
Grade Span: PK-12; **Agency Type:** 1
Schools: 7
4 Primary; 1 Middle; 2 High; 0 Other Level
6 Regular; 0 Special Education; 0 Vocational; 1 Alternative
0 Magnet; 0 Charter; 7 Title I Eligible; 7 School-wide Title I
Students: 3,844 (54.3% male; 45.7% female)
Individual Education Program: 274 (7.1%);
English Language Learner: 2,555 (66.5%); Migrant: n/a
Eligible for Free Lunch Program: 2,964 (77.1%)
Eligible for Reduced-Price Lunch Program: 338 (8.8%)
Teachers: 216.0 (17.8 to 1)
Librarians/Media Specialists: 4.0 (961.0 to 1)
Guidance Counselors: 7.0 (549.1 to 1)
Current Spending: ($ per student per year):
Total: $7,323; Instruction: $4,182; Support Services: $2,865
Enrollment, Drop-out Rates and Diploma Recipients by Race/Ethnicity

Category	Total	White	Black	Asian	AIAN	Hisp.
Enrollment (%)	100.0	58.0	16.8	23.8	0.5	0.9
Drop-out Rate (%)	n/a	n/a	n/a	n/a	n/a	n/a
H.S. Diplomas (#)	162	102	12	47	1	0

Highland Park City Schools
20 Bartlett St • Highland Park, MI 48203-3779
(313) 957-3000 • http://www.resa.net/highlandpark/index.htm
Grade Span: KG-12; **Agency Type:** 1
Schools: 7
3 Primary; 1 Middle; 2 High; 1 Other Level
5 Regular; 0 Special Education; 0 Vocational; 2 Alternative
0 Magnet; 0 Charter; 0 Title I Eligible; 0 School-wide Title I
Students: 3,761 (48.9% male; 51.1% female)
Individual Education Program: 431 (11.5%);
English Language Learner: n/a; Migrant: n/a
Eligible for Free Lunch Program: 2,600 (69.1%)
Eligible for Reduced-Price Lunch Program: 106 (2.8%)
Teachers: n/a
Librarians/Media Specialists: n/a
Guidance Counselors: n/a
Current Spending: ($ per student per year):
Total: $8,593; Instruction: $4,480; Support Services: $3,818
Enrollment, Drop-out Rates and Diploma Recipients by Race/Ethnicity

Category	Total	White	Black	Asian	AIAN	Hisp.
Enrollment (%)	100.0	0.3	99.4	0.1	0.2	0.0
Drop-out Rate (%)	n/a	n/a	n/a	n/a	n/a	n/a
H.S. Diplomas (#)	81	1	80	0	0	0

Huron SD

32044 Huron River Dr • New Boston, MI 48164-9282
(734) 782-2441 • http://www.resa.net/huron/
Grade Span: KG-12; **Agency Type:** 1
Schools: 5
3 Primary; 1 Middle; 1 High; 0 Other Level
5 Regular; 0 Special Education; 0 Vocational; 0 Alternative
0 Magnet; 0 Charter; 1 Title I Eligible; 1 School-wide Title I
Students: 2,083 (51.0% male; 49.0% female)
Individual Education Program: 321 (15.4%);
English Language Learner: n/a; Migrant: n/a
Eligible for Free Lunch Program: 254 (12.2%)
Eligible for Reduced-Price Lunch Program: 91 (4.4%)
Teachers: 113.3 (18.4 to 1)
Librarians/Media Specialists: 2.0 (1,041.5 to 1)
Guidance Counselors: 4.0 (520.8 to 1)
Current Spending: ($ per student per year):
Total: $7,425; Instruction: $4,561; Support Services: $2,641
Enrollment, Drop-out Rates and Diploma Recipients by Race/Ethnicity

Category	Total	White	Black	Asian	AIAN	Hisp.
Enrollment (%)	100.0	95.3	0.5	0.6	1.4	2.2
Drop-out Rate (%)	n/a	n/a	n/a	n/a	n/a	n/a
H.S. Diplomas (#)	113	106	2	0	3	2

Lincoln Park Public Schools

1650 Champaign Rd • Lincoln Park, MI 48146-2322
(313) 389-0200 • http://www.resa.net/lincolnpark/index.htm
Grade Span: PK-12; **Agency Type:** 1
Schools: 13
9 Primary; 1 Middle; 1 High; 1 Other Level
10 Regular; 2 Special Education; 0 Vocational; 0 Alternative
0 Magnet; 0 Charter; 0 Title I Eligible; 0 School-wide Title I
Students: 5,324 (52.2% male; 47.8% female)
Individual Education Program: 679 (12.8%);
English Language Learner: n/a; Migrant: n/a
Eligible for Free Lunch Program: 1,507 (28.3%)
Eligible for Reduced-Price Lunch Program: 571 (10.7%)
Teachers: 278.9 (19.1 to 1)
Librarians/Media Specialists: 5.0 (1,064.8 to 1)
Guidance Counselors: 7.0 (760.6 to 1)
Current Spending: ($ per student per year):
Total: $7,362; Instruction: $4,630; Support Services: $2,479
Enrollment, Drop-out Rates and Diploma Recipients by Race/Ethnicity

Category	Total	White	Black	Asian	AIAN	Hisp.
Enrollment (%)	100.0	89.3	2.3	0.8	0.5	7.0
Drop-out Rate (%)	n/a	n/a	n/a	n/a	n/a	n/a
H.S. Diplomas (#)	260	237	7	2	1	13

Livonia Public Schools

15125 Farmington Rd • Livonia, MI 48154-5474
(734) 744-2525 • http://www.livonia.k12.mi.us/
Grade Span: PK-12; **Agency Type:** 1
Schools: 36
23 Primary; 4 Middle; 3 High; 6 Other Level
30 Regular; 2 Special Education; 2 Vocational; 2 Alternative
0 Magnet; 0 Charter; 0 Title I Eligible; 0 School-wide Title I
Students: 18,423 (51.7% male; 48.3% female)
Individual Education Program: 2,144 (11.6%);
English Language Learner: 149 (0.8%); Migrant: n/a
Eligible for Free Lunch Program: 805 (4.4%)
Eligible for Reduced-Price Lunch Program: 392 (2.1%)
Teachers: 1,019.5 (18.1 to 1)
Librarians/Media Specialists: 29.0 (635.3 to 1)
Guidance Counselors: 33.2 (554.9 to 1)
Current Spending: ($ per student per year):
Total: $8,447; Instruction: $4,651; Support Services: $3,532
Enrollment, Drop-out Rates and Diploma Recipients by Race/Ethnicity

Category	Total	White	Black	Asian	AIAN	Hisp.
Enrollment (%)	100.0	92.3	3.3	2.7	0.3	1.4
Drop-out Rate (%)	n/a	n/a	n/a	n/a	n/a	n/a
H.S. Diplomas (#)	1,315	1,258	16	27	2	12

Melvindale-North Allen Park Schools

18530 Prospect St • Melvindale, MI 48122-1508
(313) 389-3300 • http://www.melnap.k12.mi.us/
Grade Span: KG-12; **Agency Type:** 1
Schools: 6
4 Primary; 1 Middle; 1 High; 0 Other Level
6 Regular; 0 Special Education; 0 Vocational; 0 Alternative
0 Magnet; 0 Charter; 0 Title I Eligible; 0 School-wide Title I
Students: 2,498 (50.0% male; 50.0% female)
Individual Education Program: 307 (12.3%);
English Language Learner: 100 (4.0%); Migrant: n/a
Eligible for Free Lunch Program: 758 (30.3%)
Eligible for Reduced-Price Lunch Program: 299 (12.0%)
Teachers: 129.3 (19.3 to 1)
Librarians/Media Specialists: 3.0 (832.7 to 1)
Guidance Counselors: 3.0 (832.7 to 1)
Current Spending: ($ per student per year):
Total: $7,944; Instruction: $4,810; Support Services: $2,886
Enrollment, Drop-out Rates and Diploma Recipients by Race/Ethnicity

Category	Total	White	Black	Asian	AIAN	Hisp.
Enrollment (%)	100.0	82.4	5.2	0.3	1.6	10.6
Drop-out Rate (%)	n/a	n/a	n/a	n/a	n/a	n/a
H.S. Diplomas (#)	123	109	6	0	0	8

Northville Public Schools

501 W Main St • Northville, MI 48167-1583
(248) 349-3400 • http://www.northville.k12.mi.us/
Grade Span: PK-12; **Agency Type:** 1
Schools: 11
5 Primary; 2 Middle; 1 High; 2 Other Level
8 Regular; 2 Special Education; 0 Vocational; 0 Alternative
0 Magnet; 0 Charter; 0 Title I Eligible; 0 School-wide Title I
Students: 6,047 (50.8% male; 49.2% female)
Individual Education Program: 615 (10.2%);
English Language Learner: 101 (1.7%); Migrant: n/a
Eligible for Free Lunch Program: 116 (1.9%)
Eligible for Reduced-Price Lunch Program: 36 (0.6%)
Teachers: 384.4 (15.7 to 1)
Librarians/Media Specialists: 9.0 (671.9 to 1)
Guidance Counselors: 9.0 (671.9 to 1)
Current Spending: ($ per student per year):
Total: $9,374; Instruction: $5,555; Support Services: $3,542
Enrollment, Drop-out Rates and Diploma Recipients by Race/Ethnicity

Category	Total	White	Black	Asian	AIAN	Hisp.
Enrollment (%)	100.0	89.5	2.1	6.9	0.1	1.4
Drop-out Rate (%)	n/a	n/a	n/a	n/a	n/a	n/a
H.S. Diplomas (#)	331	303	2	24	0	2

Plymouth-Canton Community Schools

454 S Harvey St • Plymouth, MI 48170-1630
(734) 416-2700 • http://www.pccs.k12.mi.us/
Grade Span: PK-12; **Agency Type:** 1
Schools: 25
16 Primary; 5 Middle; 3 High; 1 Other Level
24 Regular; 1 Special Education; 0 Vocational; 0 Alternative
0 Magnet; 0 Charter; 0 Title I Eligible; 0 School-wide Title I
Students: 17,378 (50.3% male; 49.7% female)
Individual Education Program: 1,858 (10.7%);
English Language Learner: 712 (4.1%); Migrant: n/a
Eligible for Free Lunch Program: 841 (4.8%)
Eligible for Reduced-Price Lunch Program: 292 (1.7%)
Teachers: 888.0 (19.6 to 1)
Librarians/Media Specialists: 18.0 (965.4 to 1)
Guidance Counselors: 28.9 (601.3 to 1)
Current Spending: ($ per student per year):
Total: $7,021; Instruction: $4,037; Support Services: $2,803
Enrollment, Drop-out Rates and Diploma Recipients by Race/Ethnicity

Category	Total	White	Black	Asian	AIAN	Hisp.
Enrollment (%)	100.0	83.4	4.7	9.6	0.5	1.8
Drop-out Rate (%)	n/a	n/a	n/a	n/a	n/a	n/a
H.S. Diplomas (#)	1,008	887	37	72	3	9

Redford Union SD

18499 Beech Daly Rd • Redford, MI 48240-1897
(313) 592-3304 • http://www.steve-hatfield.com/redfordunion.htm
Grade Span: PK-12; **Agency Type:** 1
Schools: 11
6 Primary; 1 Middle; 1 High; 2 Other Level
7 Regular; 3 Special Education; 0 Vocational; 0 Alternative
0 Magnet; 0 Charter; 0 Title I Eligible; 0 School-wide Title I
Students: 4,570 (54.5% male; 45.5% female)
Individual Education Program: 1,116 (24.4%);
English Language Learner: n/a; Migrant: n/a
Eligible for Free Lunch Program: 1,043 (22.8%)
Eligible for Reduced-Price Lunch Program: 449 (9.8%)
Teachers: 219.0 (20.9 to 1)
Librarians/Media Specialists: 1.0 (4,570.0 to 1)
Guidance Counselors: 4.0 (1,142.5 to 1)
Current Spending: ($ per student per year):
Total: $8,399; Instruction: $4,997; Support Services: $3,147
Enrollment, Drop-out Rates and Diploma Recipients by Race/Ethnicity

Category	Total	White	Black	Asian	AIAN	Hisp.
Enrollment (%)	100.0	84.2	13.4	0.6	0.4	1.5
Drop-out Rate (%)	n/a	n/a	n/a	n/a	n/a	n/a
H.S. Diplomas (#)	205	181	18	1	1	4

River Rouge SD

1460 W Coolidge Hwy • River Rouge, MI 48218-1117
(313) 297-9600 • http://www.resa.net/riverrouge/
Grade Span: PK-12; **Agency Type:** 1
Schools: 5
3 Primary; 1 Middle; 1 High; 0 Other Level
5 Regular; 0 Special Education; 0 Vocational; 0 Alternative
0 Magnet; 0 Charter; 4 Title I Eligible; 4 School-wide Title I
Students: 2,705 (52.9% male; 47.1% female)
Individual Education Program: 403 (14.9%);
English Language Learner: n/a; Migrant: n/a
Eligible for Free Lunch Program: 1,924 (71.1%)
Eligible for Reduced-Price Lunch Program: 263 (9.7%)
Teachers: 132.6 (20.4 to 1)
Librarians/Media Specialists: 1.0 (2,705.0 to 1)
Guidance Counselors: 4.0 (676.3 to 1)
Current Spending: ($ per student per year):
Total: $8,751; Instruction: $4,939; Support Services: $3,381
Enrollment, Drop-out Rates and Diploma Recipients by Race/Ethnicity

Category	Total	White	Black	Asian	AIAN	Hisp.
Enrollment (%)	100.0	28.2	66.1	0.1	1.0	4.6
Drop-out Rate (%)	n/a	n/a	n/a	n/a	n/a	n/a
H.S. Diplomas (#)	136	32	97	0	0	7

Riverview Community SD

13425 Colvin St • Riverview, MI 48192-6628
(734) 285-9660 • http://www.resa.net/riverview/index.htm
Grade Span: KG-12; **Agency Type:** 1
Schools: 5
3 Primary; 1 Middle; 1 High; 0 Other Level
5 Regular; 0 Special Education; 0 Vocational; 0 Alternative
0 Magnet; 0 Charter; 0 Title I Eligible; 0 School-wide Title I
Students: 2,549 (50.9% male; 49.1% female)
Individual Education Program: 215 (8.4%);
English Language Learner: n/a; Migrant: n/a
Eligible for Free Lunch Program: 260 (10.2%)
Eligible for Reduced-Price Lunch Program: 120 (4.7%)
Teachers: 124.1 (20.5 to 1)
Librarians/Media Specialists: 3.0 (849.7 to 1)
Guidance Counselors: 3.5 (728.3 to 1)
Current Spending: ($ per student per year):
Total: $7,213; Instruction: $4,327; Support Services: $2,755
Enrollment, Drop-out Rates and Diploma Recipients by Race/Ethnicity

Category	Total	White	Black	Asian	AIAN	Hisp.
Enrollment (%)	100.0	94.7	2.0	0.8	0.2	2.2
Drop-out Rate (%)	n/a	n/a	n/a	n/a	n/a	n/a
H.S. Diplomas (#)	171	168	2	0	0	1

Romulus Community Schools

36540 Grant Rd • Romulus, MI 48174-1445
(734) 532-1600 • http://www.romulus.net/
Grade Span: PK-12; **Agency Type:** 1
Schools: 9
6 Primary; 1 Middle; 1 High; 1 Other Level
8 Regular; 0 Special Education; 0 Vocational; 1 Alternative
3 Magnet; 0 Charter; 6 Title I Eligible; 6 School-wide Title I
Students: 4,268 (50.9% male; 49.1% female)
Individual Education Program: 605 (14.2%);
English Language Learner: n/a; Migrant: n/a
Eligible for Free Lunch Program: 1,566 (36.7%)
Eligible for Reduced-Price Lunch Program: 361 (8.5%)
Teachers: 220.6 (19.3 to 1)
Librarians/Media Specialists: 2.0 (2,134.0 to 1)
Guidance Counselors: 5.6 (762.1 to 1)
Current Spending: ($ per student per year):
Total: $8,616; Instruction: $4,345; Support Services: $3,953
Enrollment, Drop-out Rates and Diploma Recipients by Race/Ethnicity

Category	Total	White	Black	Asian	AIAN	Hisp.
Enrollment (%)	100.0	47.1	50.5	0.3	0.7	1.5
Drop-out Rate (%)	n/a	n/a	n/a	n/a	n/a	n/a
H.S. Diplomas (#)	201	107	94	0	0	0

South Redford SD

26141 Schoolcraft • Redford, MI 48239-2791
(313) 535-4000 • http://southredford.net/
Grade Span: PK-12; **Agency Type:** 1
Schools: 7
5 Primary; 1 Middle; 1 High; 0 Other Level
7 Regular; 0 Special Education; 0 Vocational; 0 Alternative
0 Magnet; 0 Charter; 0 Title I Eligible; 0 School-wide Title I
Students: 3,521 (50.4% male; 49.6% female)
Individual Education Program: 409 (11.6%);
English Language Learner: n/a; Migrant: n/a
Eligible for Free Lunch Program: 505 (14.3%)
Eligible for Reduced-Price Lunch Program: 256 (7.3%)
Teachers: 189.7 (18.6 to 1)
Librarians/Media Specialists: 4.5 (782.4 to 1)
Guidance Counselors: 4.0 (880.3 to 1)
Current Spending: ($ per student per year):
Total: $7,630; Instruction: $4,001; Support Services: $3,549
Enrollment, Drop-out Rates and Diploma Recipients by Race/Ethnicity

Category	Total	White	Black	Asian	AIAN	Hisp.
Enrollment (%)	100.0	66.2	29.9	0.8	0.3	2.8
Drop-out Rate (%)	n/a	n/a	n/a	n/a	n/a	n/a
H.S. Diplomas (#)	199	148	37	4	0	10

Southgate Community SD

13201 Trenton Rd • Southgate, MI 48195-1822
(734) 246-4600 • http://www.southgateschools.com/
Grade Span: PK-12; **Agency Type:** 1
Schools: 11
6 Primary; 1 Middle; 1 High; 3 Other Level
9 Regular; 2 Special Education; 0 Vocational; 0 Alternative
0 Magnet; 0 Charter; 0 Title I Eligible; 0 School-wide Title I
Students: 4,987 (52.2% male; 47.8% female)
Individual Education Program: 724 (14.5%);
English Language Learner: n/a; Migrant: n/a
Eligible for Free Lunch Program: 624 (12.5%)
Eligible for Reduced-Price Lunch Program: 273 (5.5%)
Teachers: 284.7 (17.5 to 1)
Librarians/Media Specialists: 2.0 (2,493.5 to 1)
Guidance Counselors: 6.0 (831.2 to 1)
Current Spending: ($ per student per year):
Total: $8,107; Instruction: $4,630; Support Services: $3,270
Enrollment, Drop-out Rates and Diploma Recipients by Race/Ethnicity

Category	Total	White	Black	Asian	AIAN	Hisp.
Enrollment (%)	100.0	37.5	3.4	1.3	53.4	4.3
Drop-out Rate (%)	n/a	n/a	n/a	n/a	n/a	n/a
H.S. Diplomas (#)	284	262	4	2	2	14

Taylor SD

23033 Northline Rd • Taylor, MI 48180-4625
(734) 374-1200 • http://www.taylorschools.net/
Grade Span: PK-12; **Agency Type:** 1
Schools: 22
15 Primary; 3 Middle; 3 High; 1 Other Level
20 Regular; 0 Special Education; 1 Vocational; 1 Alternative
0 Magnet; 0 Charter; 16 Title I Eligible; 16 School-wide Title I
Students: 11,105 (50.4% male; 49.6% female)
Individual Education Program: 1,848 (16.6%);
English Language Learner: n/a; Migrant: n/a
Eligible for Free Lunch Program: 3,316 (29.9%)
Eligible for Reduced-Price Lunch Program: 1,050 (9.5%)
Teachers: 630.6 (17.6 to 1)
Librarians/Media Specialists: 4.0 (2,776.3 to 1)
Guidance Counselors: 20.0 (555.3 to 1)
Current Spending: ($ per student per year):
Total: $8,607; Instruction: $4,716; Support Services: $3,635
Enrollment, Drop-out Rates and Diploma Recipients by Race/Ethnicity

Category	Total	White	Black	Asian	AIAN	Hisp.
Enrollment (%)	100.0	79.9	15.6	1.2	0.9	2.4
Drop-out Rate (%)	n/a	n/a	n/a	n/a	n/a	n/a
H.S. Diplomas (#)	567	488	47	20	1	11

Trenton Public Schools

2603 Charlton Rd • Trenton, MI 48183-2490
(734) 676-8600 • http://www.trenton-mi.com/schools/schools.html
Grade Span: KG-12; **Agency Type:** 1
Schools: 6
4 Primary; 1 Middle; 1 High; 0 Other Level
6 Regular; 0 Special Education; 0 Vocational; 0 Alternative
0 Magnet; 0 Charter; 0 Title I Eligible; 0 School-wide Title I
Students: 3,170 (52.7% male; 47.3% female)
Individual Education Program: 471 (14.9%);
English Language Learner: n/a; Migrant: n/a
Eligible for Free Lunch Program: 172 (5.4%)
Eligible for Reduced-Price Lunch Program: 32 (1.0%)
Teachers: 209.8 (15.1 to 1)
Librarians/Media Specialists: 4.5 (704.4 to 1)
Guidance Counselors: 5.0 (634.0 to 1)
Current Spending: ($ per student per year):
Total: $8,761; Instruction: $5,591; Support Services: $3,004
Enrollment, Drop-out Rates and Diploma Recipients by Race/Ethnicity

Category	Total	White	Black	Asian	AIAN	Hisp.
Enrollment (%)	100.0	96.3	0.8	1.4	0.2	1.4
Drop-out Rate (%)	n/a	n/a	n/a	n/a	n/a	n/a
H.S. Diplomas (#)	216	214	0	0	0	2

Van Buren Public Schools

555 W Columbia Ave • Belleville, MI 48111-3999
(734) 697-9123 • http://www.resa.net/vanburen/
Grade Span: PK-12; **Agency Type:** 1
Schools: 10
6 Primary; 2 Middle; 1 High; 1 Other Level
9 Regular; 0 Special Education; 0 Vocational; 1 Alternative
0 Magnet; 0 Charter; 2 Title I Eligible; 2 School-wide Title I
Students: 6,315 (51.2% male; 48.8% female)
Individual Education Program: 826 (13.1%);
English Language Learner: n/a; Migrant: n/a
Eligible for Free Lunch Program: 1,337 (21.2%)
Eligible for Reduced-Price Lunch Program: 330 (5.2%)
Teachers: 354.1 (17.8 to 1)
Librarians/Media Specialists: 8.0 (789.4 to 1)
Guidance Counselors: 6.0 (1,052.5 to 1)
Current Spending: ($ per student per year):
Total: $7,163; Instruction: $4,109; Support Services: $2,803
Enrollment, Drop-out Rates and Diploma Recipients by Race/Ethnicity

Category	Total	White	Black	Asian	AIAN	Hisp.
Enrollment (%)	100.0	69.9	27.3	0.9	0.2	1.7
Drop-out Rate (%)	n/a	n/a	n/a	n/a	n/a	n/a
H.S. Diplomas (#)	363	264	90	6	1	2

Wayne-Westland Community SD

36745 Marquette St • Westland, MI 48185-3289
(734) 419-2000 • http://wwcsd.net/
Grade Span: PK-12; **Agency Type:** 1
Schools: 26
18 Primary; 4 Middle; 2 High; 2 Other Level
24 Regular; 0 Special Education; 1 Vocational; 1 Alternative
0 Magnet; 0 Charter; 11 Title I Eligible; 11 School-wide Title I
Students: 14,585 (50.8% male; 49.2% female)
Individual Education Program: 2,314 (15.9%);
English Language Learner: n/a; Migrant: n/a
Eligible for Free Lunch Program: 3,747 (25.7%)
Eligible for Reduced-Price Lunch Program: 1,357 (9.3%)
Teachers: 808.8 (18.0 to 1)
Librarians/Media Specialists: 12.5 (1,166.8 to 1)
Guidance Counselors: 31.0 (470.5 to 1)
Current Spending: ($ per student per year):
Total: $7,953; Instruction: $4,345; Support Services: $3,376
Enrollment, Drop-out Rates and Diploma Recipients by Race/Ethnicity

Category	Total	White	Black	Asian	AIAN	Hisp.
Enrollment (%)	100.0	77.0	18.0	1.7	1.0	2.2
Drop-out Rate (%)	n/a	n/a	n/a	n/a	n/a	n/a
H.S. Diplomas (#)	716	565	118	17	9	7

Westwood Community Schools

3335 S Beech Daly Rd • Dearborn Heights, MI 48125-3201
(313) 565-1900 • http://www.westwood.k12.mi.us/
Grade Span: KG-12; **Agency Type:** 1
Schools: 4
2 Primary; 1 Middle; 1 High; 0 Other Level
4 Regular; 0 Special Education; 0 Vocational; 0 Alternative
0 Magnet; 0 Charter; 3 Title I Eligible; 3 School-wide Title I
Students: 2,062 (52.7% male; 47.3% female)
Individual Education Program: 414 (20.1%);
English Language Learner: n/a; Migrant: n/a
Eligible for Free Lunch Program: 1,231 (59.7%)
Eligible for Reduced-Price Lunch Program: 207 (10.0%)
Teachers: 127.1 (16.2 to 1)
Librarians/Media Specialists: 3.0 (687.3 to 1)
Guidance Counselors: 6.0 (343.7 to 1)
Current Spending: ($ per student per year):
Total: $8,485; Instruction: $4,837; Support Services: $3,241
Enrollment, Drop-out Rates and Diploma Recipients by Race/Ethnicity

Category	Total	White	Black	Asian	AIAN	Hisp.
Enrollment (%)	100.0	21.9	75.1	1.5	0.3	1.2
Drop-out Rate (%)	n/a	n/a	n/a	n/a	n/a	n/a
H.S. Diplomas (#)	67	16	48	3	0	0

Woodhaven-Brownstown SD

24975 Van Horn Rd • Brownstown, MI 48134-9595
(734) 783-3300 • http://warrior.woodhaven.k12.mi.us/
Grade Span: KG-12; **Agency Type:** 1
Schools: 9
5 Primary; 1 Middle; 1 High; 2 Other Level
8 Regular; 1 Special Education; 0 Vocational; 0 Alternative
0 Magnet; 0 Charter; 0 Title I Eligible; 0 School-wide Title I
Students: 5,121 (50.9% male; 49.1% female)
Individual Education Program: 789 (15.4%);
English Language Learner: n/a; Migrant: n/a
Eligible for Free Lunch Program: 695 (13.6%)
Eligible for Reduced-Price Lunch Program: 181 (3.5%)
Teachers: 271.0 (18.9 to 1)
Librarians/Media Specialists: 7.0 (731.6 to 1)
Guidance Counselors: 7.0 (731.6 to 1)
Current Spending: ($ per student per year):
Total: $7,631; Instruction: $4,461; Support Services: $2,895
Enrollment, Drop-out Rates and Diploma Recipients by Race/Ethnicity

Category	Total	White	Black	Asian	AIAN	Hisp.
Enrollment (%)	100.0	82.2	6.1	4.3	2.4	5.0
Drop-out Rate (%)	n/a	n/a	n/a	n/a	n/a	n/a
H.S. Diplomas (#)	274	237	9	17	1	10

Wyandotte City SD

639 Oak St • Wyandotte, MI 48192-0130
Mailing Address: PO Box 130 • Wyandotte, MI 48192-0130
(734) 246-1000 • http://www.wyandotte.org/
Grade Span: PK-12; **Agency Type:** 1
Schools: 11
6 Primary; 1 Middle; 1 High; 3 Other Level
8 Regular; 3 Special Education; 0 Vocational; 0 Alternative
0 Magnet; 0 Charter; 1 Title I Eligible; 1 School-wide Title I
Students: 4,940 (51.2% male; 48.8% female)
Individual Education Program: 1,041 (21.1%);
English Language Learner: n/a; Migrant: n/a
Eligible for Free Lunch Program: 901 (18.2%)
Eligible for Reduced-Price Lunch Program: 284 (5.7%)
Teachers: 278.5 (17.7 to 1)
Librarians/Media Specialists: 2.0 (2,470.0 to 1)
Guidance Counselors: 6.0 (823.3 to 1)
Current Spending: ($ per student per year):
Total: $9,140; Instruction: $5,978; Support Services: $2,982
Enrollment, Drop-out Rates and Diploma Recipients by Race/Ethnicity

Category	Total	White	Black	Asian	AIAN	Hisp.
Enrollment (%)	100.0	93.7	2.4	0.5	0.6	2.7
Drop-out Rate (%)	n/a	n/a	n/a	n/a	n/a	n/a
H.S. Diplomas (#)	264	246	1	1	4	12

Wexford County

Cadillac Area Public Schools

421 S Mitchell St • Cadillac, MI 49601-2438
(231) 876-5000 • http://www.vikingnet.org/
Grade Span: KG-12; **Agency Type:** 1
Schools: 9
5 Primary; 1 Middle; 2 High; 1 Other Level
8 Regular; 0 Special Education; 0 Vocational; 1 Alternative
0 Magnet; 0 Charter; 5 Title I Eligible; 5 School-wide Title I
Students: 3,505 (52.6% male; 47.4% female)
Individual Education Program: 392 (11.2%);
English Language Learner: n/a; Migrant: n/a
Eligible for Free Lunch Program: 974 (27.8%)
Eligible for Reduced-Price Lunch Program: 361 (10.3%)
Teachers: 188.2 (18.6 to 1)
Librarians/Media Specialists: 2.4 (1,460.4 to 1)
Guidance Counselors: 11.0 (318.6 to 1)
Current Spending: ($ per student per year):
Total: $6,364; Instruction: $3,777; Support Services: $2,311
Enrollment, Drop-out Rates and Diploma Recipients by Race/Ethnicity

Category	Total	White	Black	Asian	AIAN	Hisp.
Enrollment (%)	100.0	96.7	1.0	0.5	0.7	1.0
Drop-out Rate (%)	n/a	n/a	n/a	n/a	n/a	n/a
H.S. Diplomas (#)	235	232	3	0	0	0

Number of Schools

Rank	Number	District Name	City
1	273	Detroit City SD	Detroit
2	94	Grand Rapids Public Schools	Grand Rapids
3	43	Flint City SD	Flint
3	43	Lansing Public SD	Lansing
3	43	Utica Community Schools	Sterling Hgts
6	36	Livonia Public Schools	Livonia
7	35	Saginaw City SD	Saginaw
8	33	Ann Arbor Public Schools	Ann Arbor
9	32	Dearborn City SD	Dearborn
10	29	Kalamazoo Public SD	Kalamazoo
11	28	Warren Consolidated Schools	Warren
12	27	Farmington Public SD	Farmington
13	26	Battle Creek Public Schools	Battle Creek
13	26	Wayne-Westland Community SD	Westland
15	25	Plymouth-Canton Community Schools	Plymouth
15	25	Waterford SD	Waterford
17	24	Pontiac City SD	Pontiac
18	23	Walled Lake Consolidated Schools	Walled Lake
19	22	Port Huron Area SD	Port Huron
19	22	Taylor SD	Taylor
19	22	Traverse City Area Public Schools	Traverse City
22	21	Rochester Community SD	Rochester
23	20	Midland Public Schools	Midland
24	19	L'anse Creuse Public Schools	Harrison Twp
24	19	Troy SD	Troy
26	18	Bay City SD	Bay City
26	18	Huron Valley Schools	Highland
26	18	Muskegon City SD	Muskegon
26	18	Southfield Public SD	Southfield
30	17	Chippewa Valley Schools	Clinton Twp
30	17	Kentwood Public Schools	Kentwood
32	16	Benton Harbor Area Schools	Benton Harbor
32	16	Grosse Pointe Public Schools	Grosse Pointe
32	16	Lapeer Community Schools	Lapeer
35	15	Forest Hills Public Schools	Grand Rapids
35	15	Jackson Public Schools	Jackson
35	15	School District of Royal Oak	Royal Oak
38	14	Birmingham City SD	Birmingham
38	14	Bloomfield Hills SD	Bloomfield Hls
38	14	Portage Public Schools	Portage
38	14	Roseville Community Schools	Roseville
42	13	Alpena Public Schools	Alpena
42	13	Anchor Bay SD	New Baltimore
42	13	Clarkston Community SD	Clarkston
42	13	Hazel Park City SD	Hazel Park
42	13	Holland City SD	Holland
42	13	Lincoln Park Public Schools	Lincoln Park
42	13	Monroe Public Schools	Monroe
42	13	Rockford Public Schools	Rockford
42	13	West Ottawa Public SD	Holland
42	13	Wyoming Public Schools	Wyoming
52	12	East Detroit Public Schools	Eastpointe
52	12	Grand Haven Area Public Schools	Grand Haven
52	12	Grandville Public Schools	Grandville
52	12	Lake Orion Community Schools	Lake Orion
52	12	School District of Ypsilanti	Ypsilanti
57	11	East China SD	East China
57	11	Grand Blanc Community Schools	Grand Blanc
57	11	Holt Public Schools	Holt
57	11	Mount Pleasant City SD	Mount Pleasant
57	11	Northville Public Schools	Northville
57	11	Redford Union SD	Redford
57	11	Romeo Community Schools	Romeo
57	11	Southgate Community SD	Southgate
57	11	Van Dyke Public Schools	Warren
57	11	West Bloomfield SD	West Bloomfield
57	11	Wyandotte City SD	Wyandotte
68	10	Adrian City SD	Adrian
68	10	Avondale SD	Auburn Hills
68	10	Berkley SD	Berkley
68	10	Carman-Ainsworth Community Schools	Flint
68	10	Fraser Public Schools	Fraser
68	10	Garden City SD	Garden City
68	10	Grand Ledge Public Schools	Grand Ledge
68	10	Howell Public Schools	Howell
68	10	Hudsonville Public SD	Hudsonville
68	10	Niles Community SD	Niles
68	10	South Lyon Community Schools	South Lyon
68	10	Sturgis Public Schools	Sturgis
68	10	Van Buren Public Schools	Belleville
68	10	Zeeland Public Schools	Zeeland
82	9	Brighton Area Schools	Brighton
82	9	Cadillac Area Public Schools	Cadillac
82	9	Davison Community Schools	Davison
82	9	Dowagiac Union SD	Dowagiac
82	9	East Lansing SD	East Lansing
82	9	Kenowa Hills Public Schools	Grand Rapids
82	9	Lamphere Public Schools	Madison Heights
82	9	Macomb ISD	Clinton Twp
82	9	Marshall Public Schools	Marshall
82	9	Novi Community SD	Novi
82	9	Okemos Public Schools	Okemos
82	9	Owosso Public Schools	Owosso
82	9	Pinckney Community Schools	Pinckney
82	9	Reeths-Puffer Schools	Muskegon
82	9	Romulus Community Schools	Romulus
82	9	Saginaw Township Community Schools	Saginaw
82	9	Three Rivers Community Schools	Three Rivers
82	9	Woodhaven-Brownstown SD	Brownstown
100	8	Byron Center Public Schools	Byron Center
100	8	Coldwater Community Schools	Coldwater
100	8	Escanaba Area Public Schools	Escanaba
100	8	Gibraltar SD	Woodhaven
100	8	Hartland Consolidated Schools	Hartland
100	8	Ionia Public Schools	Ionia
100	8	Jenison Public Schools	Jenison
100	8	Lakeview SD (Calhoun)	Battle Creek
100	8	Lakeville Community Schools	Otisville
100	8	Ludington Area SD	Ludington
100	8	Mount Clemens Community SD	Mount Clemens
100	8	Muskegon Heights SD	Muskegon Hgts
100	8	Oak Park City SD	Oak Park
100	8	Oxford Area Community Schools	Oxford
100	8	Saint Johns Public Schools	Saint Johns
100	8	Sault Sainte Marie Area Schools	Sault Ste Marie
100	8	Swartz Creek Community Schools	Swartz Creek
100	8	Willow Run Community Schools	Ypsilanti
118	7	Albion Public Schools	Albion
118	7	Algonac Community SD	Algonac
118	7	Allegan Public Schools	Allegan
118	7	Bedford Public Schools	Temperance
118	7	Beecher Community SD	Flint
118	7	Belding Area SD	Belding
118	7	Big Rapids Public Schools	Big Rapids
118	7	Brandon SD	Ortonville
118	7	Bridgeport-Spaulding Community SD	Bridgeport
118	7	Caledonia Community Schools	Caledonia
118	7	Center Line Public Schools	Center Line
118	7	Charlotte Public Schools	Charlotte
118	7	Chippewa Hills SD	Remus
118	7	Comstock Public Schools	Kalamazoo
118	7	Fenton Area Public Schools	Fenton
118	7	Ferndale Public Schools	Ferndale
118	7	Fitzgerald Public Schools	Warren
118	7	Gaylord Community Schools	Gaylord
118	7	Hamtramck Public Schools	Hamtramck
118	7	Hastings Area SD	Hastings
118	7	Highland Park City Schools	Highland Park
118	7	Holly Area SD	Holly
118	7	Houghton Lake Community Schools	Houghton Lake
118	7	Kearsley Community Schools	Flint
118	7	Kelloggsville Public Schools	Grand Rapids
118	7	Lakewood Public Schools	Lake Odessa
118	7	Lincoln Consolidated SD	Ypsilanti
118	7	Marquette Area Public Schools	Marquette
118	7	Mount Morris Consolidated Schools	Mount Morris
118	7	Northview Public SD	Grand Rapids
118	7	Public Schools of Petoskey	Petoskey
118	7	Saline Area Schools	Saline
118	7	Shelby Public Schools	Shelby
118	7	South Redford SD	Redford
118	7	Tecumseh Public Schools	Tecumseh
118	7	Warren Woods Public Schools	Warren
118	7	Waverly Community Schools	Lansing
118	7	Wayland Union Schools	Wayland
156	6	Airport Community SD	Carleton
156	6	Allen Park Public Schools	Allen Park
156	6	Bangor Township Schools	Bay City
156	6	Benzie County Central Schools	Benzonia
156	6	Cedar Springs Public Schools	Cedar Springs
156	6	Central Montcalm Public Schools	Stanton
156	6	Cheboygan Area Schools	Cheboygan
156	6	Chelsea SD	Chelsea
156	6	Coloma Community Schools	Coloma
156	6	Comstock Park Public Schools	Comstock Park
156	6	Corunna Public SD	Corunna
156	6	Dearborn Heights SD #7	Dearborn Hgts
156	6	Dewitt Public Schools	Dewitt
156	6	Dexter Community SD	Dexter
156	6	Durand Area Schools	Durand
156	6	Eaton Rapids Public Schools	Eaton Rapids
156	6	Edwardsburg Public Schools	Edwardsburg
156	6	Flushing Community Schools	Flushing
156	6	Fowlerville Community Schools	Fowlerville
156	6	Fremont Public SD	Fremont
156	6	Fruitport Community Schools	Fruitport
156	6	Godfrey-Lee Public Schools	Wyoming
156	6	Godwin Heights Public Schools	Wyoming
156	6	Greenville Public Schools	Greenville
156	6	Gull Lake Community Schools	Richland
156	6	Hamilton Community Schools	Hamilton
156	6	Harrison Community Schools	Harrison
156	6	Haslett Public Schools	Haslett
156	6	Jefferson Schools (Monroe)	Monroe
156	6	Kalkaska Public Schools	Kalkaska
156	6	Lakeview Public Schools (Macomb)	St Clair Shores
156	6	Lowell Area Schools	Lowell
156	6	Madison Public Schools (Oakland)	Madison Heights
156	6	Manistee Area Schools	Manistee
156	6	Mason County Central Schools	Scottville
156	6	Mason Public Schools (Ingham)	Mason
156	6	Melvindale-N Allen Park Schools	Melvindale
156	6	Menominee Area Public Schools	Menominee
156	6	Mona Shores Public SD	Norton Shores
156	6	Northwest Community Schools	Jackson
156	6	Orchard View Schools	Muskegon
156	6	Oscoda Area Schools	Oscoda
156	6	Ovid-Elsie Area Schools	Elsie
156	6	Parchment SD	Parchment
156	6	Paw Paw Public SD	Paw Paw
156	6	Pennfield SD	Battle Creek
156	6	Pinconning Area Schools	Pinconning
156	6	Plainwell Community Schools	Plainwell
156	6	Reed City Area Public Schools	Reed City
156	6	Saint Joseph Public Schools	Saint Joseph
156	6	South Lake Schools	St Clair Shores
156	6	Sparta Area Schools	Sparta
156	6	Spring Lake Public Schools	Spring Lake
156	6	Stockbridge Community Schools	Stockbridge
156	6	Thornapple Kellogg SD	Middleville
156	6	Trenton Public Schools	Trenton
156	6	Western SD	Parma
156	6	Yale Public Schools	Yale
214	5	Allendale Public SD	Allendale
214	5	Alma Public Schools	Alma
214	5	Armada Area Schools	Armada
214	5	Bangor Public Schools (Van Buren)	Bangor
214	5	Bendle Public Schools	Burton
214	5	Berrien Springs Public Schools	Berrien Springs
214	5	Brandywine Public SD	Niles
214	5	Buchanan Community Schools	Buchanan
214	5	Bullock Creek SD	Midland
214	5	Caro Community Schools	Caro
214	5	Chesaning Union Schools	Chesaning
214	5	Clawson City SD	Clawson
214	5	Clintondale Community Schools	Clinton Twp
214	5	Clio Area SD	Clio
214	5	Columbia SD	Brooklyn
214	5	Crawford Ausable Schools	Grayling
214	5	Crestwood SD	Dearborn Hgts
214	5	Croswell-Lexington Comm Schools	Croswell
214	5	East Grand Rapids Public Schools	E Grand Rapids
214	5	Essexville-Hampton Public Schools	Essexville
214	5	Fennville Public Schools	Fennville
214	5	Flat Rock Community Schools	Flat Rock
214	5	Gerrish-Higgins SD	Roscommon
214	5	Gladstone Area Schools	Gladstone
214	5	Gladwin Community Schools	Gladwin
214	5	Harper Creek Community Schools	Battle Creek
214	5	Hillsdale Community Schools	Hillsdale
214	5	Huron SD	New Boston
214	5	Imlay City Community Schools	Imlay City
214	5	Lake Shore Public Schools (Macomb)	St Clair Shores
214	5	Lakeshore SD (Berrien)	Stevensville
214	5	Lakeview Comm Schools (Montcalm)	Lakeview
214	5	Linden Community Schools	Linden
214	5	Maple Valley Schools	Vermontville
214	5	Marysville Public Schools	Marysville
214	5	Mason Consol Schools (Monroe)	Erie
214	5	Meridian Public Schools	Sanford
214	5	Millington Community Schools	Millington
214	5	Newaygo Public SD	Newaygo
214	5	North Branch Area Schools	North Branch
214	5	Oakridge Public Schools	Muskegon
214	5	Onsted Community Schools	Onsted
214	5	Otsego Public Schools	Otsego
214	5	Perry Public SD	Perry
214	5	Portland Public SD	Portland
214	5	River Rouge SD	River Rouge
214	5	Riverview Community SD	Riverview
214	5	Shepherd Public SD	Shepherd
214	5	South Haven Public Schools	South Haven
214	5	Tri County Area Schools	Howard City
214	5	Vassar Public Schools	Vassar
214	5	Vicksburg Community Schools	Vicksburg
214	5	West Branch-Rose City Area Schools	West Branch
267	4	Beaverton Rural Schools	Beaverton
267	4	Birch Run Area SD	Birch Run
267	4	Bronson Community SD	Bronson
267	4	Cass City Public Schools	Cass City
267	4	Clare Public Schools	Clare
267	4	Clarenceville SD	Livonia
267	4	Constantine Public SD	Constantine
267	4	Coopersville Public SD	Coopersville

Rank	Number	District Name	City
267	4	Delton-Kellogg SD	Delton
267	4	Dundee Community Schools	Dundee
267	4	East Jackson Community Schools	Jackson
267	4	Elk Rapids Schools	Elk Rapids
267	4	Goodrich Area Schools	Goodrich
267	4	Grant Public SD	Grant
267	4	Grosse Ile Township Schools	Grosse Ile
267	4	Hartford Public SD	Hartford
267	4	Mattawan Consolidated School	Mattawan
267	4	Michigan Center SD	Michigan Center
267	4	Milan Area Schools	Milan
267	4	Morley Stanwood Community Schools	Morley
267	4	Napoleon Community Schools	Napoleon
267	4	Public Schools of Calumet	Calumet
267	4	Standish-Sterling Comm Schools	Standish
267	4	Swan Valley SD	Saginaw
267	4	Tawas Area Schools	Tawas City
267	4	Washtenaw ISD	Ann Arbor
267	4	Westwood Community Schools	Dearborn Hgts
267	4	White Cloud Public Schools	White Cloud
267	4	Whitehall District Schools	Whitehall
267	4	Williamston Community Schools	Williamston
297	3	Almont Community Schools	Almont
297	3	Breitung Township Schools	Kingsford
297	3	Capac Community SD	Capac
297	3	Carrollton SD	Saginaw
297	3	Farwell Area Schools	Farwell
297	3	Freeland Community SD	Freeland
297	3	Ida Public SD	Ida
297	3	Montague Area Public Schools	Montague
297	3	Montrose Community Schools	Montrose
297	3	Quincy Community SD	Quincy
297	3	Richmond Community Schools	Richmond
308	2	Detroit Academy of Arts & Sci	Detroit

Number of Teachers

Rank	Number	District Name	City
1	5,683	Detroit City SD	Detroit
2	1,637	Grand Rapids Public Schools	Grand Rapids
3	1,524	Utica Community Schools	Sterling Hgts
4	1,321	Flint City SD	Flint
5	1,111	Dearborn City SD	Dearborn
6	1,051	Ann Arbor Public Schools	Ann Arbor
7	1,019	Livonia Public Schools	Livonia
8	914	Walled Lake Consolidated Schools	Walled Lake
9	888	Plymouth-Canton Community Schools	Plymouth
10	861	Warren Consolidated Schools	Warren
11	822	Saginaw City SD	Saginaw
12	808	Wayne-Westland Community SD	Westland
13	798	Kalamazoo Public SD	Kalamazoo
14	764	Farmington Public SD	Farmington
15	736	Port Huron Area SD	Port Huron
16	706	Rochester Community SD	Rochester
17	701	Troy SD	Troy
18	684	Pontiac City SD	Pontiac
19	644	Chippewa Valley Schools	Clinton Twp
20	630	Taylor SD	Taylor
21	615	Southfield Public SD	Southfield
22	610	Traverse City Area Public Schools	Traverse City
23	605	L'anse Creuse Public Schools	Harrison Twp
24	578	Huron Valley Schools	Highland
25	556	Grosse Pointe Public Schools	Grosse Pointe
26	545	Midland Public Schools	Midland
27	541	Battle Creek Public Schools	Battle Creek
28	537	Bay City SD	Bay City
29	519	Kentwood Public Schools	Kentwood
30	507	Forest Hills Public Schools	Grand Rapids
31	468	Portage Public Schools	Portage
32	447	Bloomfield Hills SD	Bloomfield Hls
33	432	West Ottawa Public SD	Holland
34	432	Howell Public Schools	Howell
35	424	Clarkston Community SD	Clarkston
36	409	School District of Royal Oak	Royal Oak
37	401	Muskegon City SD	Muskegon
38	396	Lake Orion Community Schools	Lake Orion
39	395	Rockford Public Schools	Rockford
40	391	West Bloomfield SD	West Bloomfield
41	384	Lapeer Community Schools	Lapeer
41	384	Northville Public Schools	Northville
43	383	Grand Blanc Community Schools	Grand Blanc
44	373	Brighton Area Schools	Brighton
45	372	Waterford SD	Waterford
46	370	Monroe Public Schools	Monroe
47	354	Van Buren Public Schools	Belleville
48	353	East Detroit Public Schools	Eastpointe
49	353	Roseville Community Schools	Roseville
50	351	Garden City SD	Garden City
51	351	South Lyon Community Schools	South Lyon
52	346	Wyoming Public Schools	Wyoming
53	340	Anchor Bay SD	New Baltimore
54	328	Grand Haven Area Public Schools	Grand Haven
55	327	Holland City SD	Holland
56	321	Grandville Public Schools	Grandville
57	320	East China SD	East China
58	309	Carman-Ainsworth Community Schools	Flint
59	305	Grand Ledge Public Schools	Grand Ledge
60	304	Benton Harbor Area Schools	Benton Harbor
61	298	Bedford Public Schools	Temperance
62	291	School District of Ypsilanti	Ypsilanti
63	285	Fraser Public Schools	Fraser
64	285	Alpena Public Schools	Alpena
65	284	Southgate Community SD	Southgate
66	281	Romeo Community Schools	Romeo
67	279	Berkley SD	Berkley
68	279	Saginaw Township Community Schools	Saginaw
69	278	Lincoln Park Public Schools	Lincoln Park
70	278	Wyandotte City SD	Wyandotte
71	278	Hazel Park City SD	Hazel Park
72	271	Woodhaven-Brownstown SD	Brownstown
73	268	Saline Area Schools	Saline
74	268	Hudsonville Public SD	Hudsonville
75	267	Pinckney Community Schools	Pinckney
76	266	Davison Community Schools	Davison
76	266	Saint Johns Public Schools	Saint Johns
78	260	Avondale SD	Auburn Hills
79	257	Reeths-Puffer Schools	Muskegon
80	252	Hartland Consolidated Schools	Hartland
81	240	Okemos Public Schools	Okemos
82	237	Holly Area SD	Holly
83	233	Adrian City SD	Adrian
84	229	Oak Park City SD	Oak Park
85	225	Owosso Public Schools	Owosso
86	221	Swartz Creek Community Schools	Swartz Creek
87	220	East Lansing SD	East Lansing
88	220	Romulus Community Schools	Romulus
89	220	Mount Clemens Community SD	Mount Clemens
90	219	Redford Union SD	Redford
91	217	Greenville Public Schools	Greenville
92	216	Hamtramck Public Schools	Hamtramck
93	214	Lowell Area Schools	Lowell
94	212	Ionia Public Schools	Ionia
95	211	Oxford Area Community Schools	Oxford
96	211	Flushing Community Schools	Flushing
97	209	Trenton Public Schools	Trenton
98	208	Marquette Area Public Schools	Marquette
99	204	Kenowa Hills Public Schools	Grand Rapids
100	203	Van Dyke Public Schools	Warren
101	199	Mona Shores Public SD	Norton Shores
102	198	Gaylord Community Schools	Gaylord
103	197	Hastings Area SD	Hastings
104	197	Macomb ISD	Clinton Twp
105	195	Lakeview SD (Calhoun)	Battle Creek
106	194	Fenton Area Public Schools	Fenton
107	192	Comstock Public Schools	Kalamazoo
108	192	Brandon SD	Ortonville
109	189	Caledonia Community Schools	Caledonia
110	189	South Redford SD	Redford
111	188	Mount Morris Consolidated Schools	Mount Morris
112	188	Kearsley Community Schools	Flint
113	188	Cadillac Area Public Schools	Cadillac
114	186	Eaton Rapids Public Schools	Eaton Rapids
115	183	Clio Area SD	Clio
116	182	Fruitport Community Schools	Fruitport
117	182	Sturgis Public Schools	Sturgis
118	181	Coldwater Community Schools	Coldwater
119	181	Lake Shore Public Schools (Macomb)	St Clair Shores
120	180	Airport Community SD	Carleton
121	180	Center Line Public Schools	Center Line
122	179	Mason Public Schools (Ingham)	Mason
123	178	Mattawan Consolidated School	Mattawan
124	178	Allegan Public Schools	Allegan
125	176	Haslett Public Schools	Haslett
126	176	Wayland Union Schools	Wayland
127	176	Ferndale Public Schools	Ferndale
128	176	Northview Public SD	Grand Rapids
129	175	Escanaba Area Public Schools	Escanaba
130	174	Sault Sainte Marie Area Schools	Sault Ste Marie
131	174	Three Rivers Community Schools	Three Rivers
132	173	Allen Park Public Schools	Allen Park
133	172	Warren Woods Public Schools	Warren
134	171	Gull Lake Community Schools	Richland
135	169	Fowlerville Community Schools	Fowlerville
136	167	Crestwood SD	Dearborn Hgts
137	166	Sparta Area Schools	Sparta
138	165	Fitzgerald Public Schools	Warren
139	165	Public Schools of Petoskey	Petoskey
140	165	Orchard View Schools	Muskegon
141	165	West Branch-Rose City Area Schools	West Branch
142	162	East Grand Rapids Public Schools	E Grand Rapids
143	160	Chelsea SD	Chelsea
144	160	Ludington Area SD	Ludington
145	158	Gibraltar SD	Woodhaven
146	158	Belding Area SD	Belding
147	157	Byron Center Public Schools	Byron Center
148	156	Plainwell Community Schools	Plainwell
149	156	Dowagiac Union SD	Dowagiac
150	155	Saint Joseph Public Schools	Saint Joseph
151	155	Muskegon Heights SD	Muskegon Hgts
152	154	Bridgeport-Spaulding Community SD	Bridgeport
153	154	Lakeview Public Schools (Macomb)	St Clair Shores
154	153	Clintondale Community Schools	Clinton Twp
154	153	Thornapple Kellogg SD	Middleville
156	151	Jefferson Schools (Monroe)	Monroe
157	150	Godwin Heights Public Schools	Wyoming
158	149	Chippewa Hills SD	Remus
159	148	Fremont Public SD	Fremont
160	147	Lamphere Public Schools	Madison Heights
161	147	Alma Public Schools	Alma
162	143	Dewitt Public Schools	Dewitt
163	143	Croswell-Lexington Comm Schools	Croswell
164	143	Western SD	Parma
165	143	Cheboygan Area Schools	Cheboygan
166	141	South Lake Schools	St Clair Shores
167	141	North Branch Area Schools	North Branch
168	140	Harper Creek Community Schools	Battle Creek
169	140	Marshall Public Schools	Marshall
170	140	Lakewood Public Schools	Lake Odessa
171	140	Algonac Community SD	Algonac
172	138	Lakeshore SD (Berrien)	Stevensville
173	138	South Haven Public Schools	South Haven
174	137	Vicksburg Community Schools	Vicksburg
175	136	Dearborn Heights SD #7	Dearborn Hgts
176	135	Coloma Community Schools	Coloma
177	134	Hamilton Community Schools	Hamilton
178	134	Grant Public SD	Grant
179	133	Tri County Area Schools	Howard City
180	132	River Rouge SD	River Rouge
181	132	Marysville Public Schools	Marysville
182	131	Caro Community Schools	Caro
183	131	Otsego Public Schools	Otsego
184	129	Whitehall District Schools	Whitehall
185	129	Madison Public Schools (Oakland)	Madison Heights
185	129	Melvindale-N Allen Park Schools	Melvindale
187	128	Bangor Township Schools	Bay City
188	127	Coopersville Public SD	Coopersville
189	127	Westwood Community Schools	Dearborn Hgts
190	126	Linden Community Schools	Linden
191	125	Harrison Community Schools	Harrison
192	125	Willow Run Community Schools	Ypsilanti
193	124	Bullock Creek SD	Midland
194	124	Holt Public Schools	Holt
195	124	Crawford Ausable Schools	Grayling
195	124	Riverview Community SD	Riverview
197	123	Delton-Kellogg SD	Delton
198	122	Paw Paw Public SD	Paw Paw
199	121	Kelloggsville Public Schools	Grand Rapids
200	120	Allendale Public SD	Allendale
201	120	Central Montcalm Public Schools	Stanton
202	119	Oakridge Public Schools	Muskegon
203	119	Big Rapids Public Schools	Big Rapids
203	119	Lansing Public SD	Lansing
205	118	Gladwin Community Schools	Gladwin
206	118	Spring Lake Public Schools	Spring Lake
207	116	Imlay City Community Schools	Imlay City
208	116	Breitung Township Schools	Kingsford
209	116	Parchment SD	Parchment
210	115	Edwardsburg Public Schools	Edwardsburg
211	115	Lakeville Community Schools	Otisville
212	114	Lakeview Comm Schools (Montcalm)	Lakeview
213	114	Corunna Public SD	Corunna
214	114	Grosse Ile Township Schools	Grosse Ile
215	113	Chesaning Union Schools	Chesaning
216	113	Huron SD	New Boston
216	113	Williamston Community Schools	Williamston
218	113	Reed City Area Public Schools	Reed City
219	112	Carrollton SD	Saginaw
220	112	Clarenceville SD	Livonia
221	111	Yale Public Schools	Yale
222	111	Benzie County Central Schools	Benzonia
222	111	Oscoda Area Schools	Oscoda
224	110	Portland Public SD	Portland
225	110	Perry Public SD	Perry
226	110	Pinconning Area Schools	Pinconning
227	109	Hillsdale Community Schools	Hillsdale
228	108	Shelby Public Schools	Shelby
229	108	Menominee Area Public Schools	Menominee
230	107	Durand Area Schools	Durand
231	107	Albion Public Schools	Albion
232	106	Richmond Community Schools	Richmond
233	106	Armada Area Schools	Armada
234	106	Berrien Springs Public Schools	Berrien Springs
235	106	Capac Community SD	Capac
235	106	Onsted Community Schools	Onsted
237	105	Birch Run Area SD	Birch Run
238	105	Beaverton Rural Schools	Beaverton
239	104	Goodrich Area Schools	Goodrich

239	104	Standish-Sterling Comm Schools	Standish
241	103	Shepherd Public SD	Shepherd
242	103	Essexville-Hampton Public Schools	Essexville
243	102	Gladstone Area Schools	Gladstone
244	100	Buchanan Community Schools	Buchanan
245	100	Columbia SD	Brooklyn
246	100	Pennfield SD	Battle Creek
247	99	Maple Valley Schools	Vermontville
248	99	Hartford Public SD	Hartford
249	98	Stockbridge Community Schools	Stockbridge
250	98	Gerrish-Higgins SD	Roscommon
251	98	Mason County Central Schools	Scottville
252	97	Brandywine Public SD	Niles
253	96	Napoleon Community Schools	Napoleon
254	95	Public Schools of Calumet	Calumet
255	94	Morley Stanwood Community Schools	Morley
256	93	Ida Public SD	Ida
256	93	White Cloud Public Schools	White Cloud
258	93	Fennville Public Schools	Fennville
259	93	Farwell Area Schools	Farwell
260	91	Millington Community Schools	Millington
261	91	Bendle Public Schools	Burton
261	91	Tawas Area Schools	Tawas City
263	91	Swan Valley SD	Saginaw
264	91	Flat Rock Community Schools	Flat Rock
265	90	Constantine Public SD	Constantine
266	89	Bangor Public Schools (Van Buren)	Bangor
266	89	East Jackson Community Schools	Jackson
268	88	Clawson City SD	Clawson
269	87	Clare Public Schools	Clare
270	87	Almont Community Schools	Almont
271	86	Quincy Community SD	Quincy
272	86	Tecumseh Public Schools	Tecumseh
273	85	Montague Area Public Schools	Montague
274	85	Freeland Community SD	Freeland
275	83	Elk Rapids Schools	Elk Rapids
276	79	Beecher Community SD	Flint
276	79	Michigan Center SD	Michigan Center
278	78	Cass City Public Schools	Cass City
279	69	Bronson Community SD	Bronson
280	63	Montrose Community Schools	Montrose
281	59	Washtenaw ISD	Ann Arbor
282	52	Houghton Lake Community Schools	Houghton Lake
283	39	Dundee Community Schools	Dundee
284	34	Ovid-Elsie Area Schools	Elsie
285	30	Zeeland Public Schools	Zeeland
286	28	Jenison Public Schools	Jenison
287	19	Charlotte Public Schools	Charlotte
288	17	Cedar Springs Public Schools	Cedar Springs
289	14	Meridian Public Schools	Sanford
290	n/a	Birmingham City SD	Birmingham
290	n/a	Comstock Park Public Schools	Comstock Park
290	n/a	Detroit Academy of Arts & Sci	Detroit
290	n/a	Dexter Community SD	Dexter
290	n/a	Godfrey-Lee Public Schools	Wyoming
290	n/a	Highland Park City Schools	Highland Park
290	n/a	Jackson Public Schools	Jackson
290	n/a	Kalkaska Public Schools	Kalkaska
290	n/a	Lincoln Consolidated SD	Ypsilanti
290	n/a	Manistee Area Schools	Manistee
290	n/a	Mason Consol Schools (Monroe)	Erie
290	n/a	Milan Area Schools	Milan
290	n/a	Mount Pleasant City SD	Mount Pleasant
290	n/a	Newaygo Public SD	Newaygo
290	n/a	Niles Community SD	Niles
290	n/a	Northwest Community Schools	Jackson
290	n/a	Novi Community SD	Novi
290	n/a	Vassar Public Schools	Vassar
290	n/a	Waverly Community Schools	Lansing

Number of Students

Rank	Number	District Name	City
1	173,742	Detroit City SD	Detroit
2	29,177	Utica Community Schools	Sterling Hgts
3	23,418	Grand Rapids Public Schools	Grand Rapids
4	21,443	Flint City SD	Flint
5	18,423	Livonia Public Schools	Livonia
6	17,981	Dearborn City SD	Dearborn
7	17,616	Lansing Public SD	Lansing
8	17,378	Plymouth-Canton Community Schools	Plymouth
9	16,774	Ann Arbor Public Schools	Ann Arbor
10	15,405	Warren Consolidated Schools	Warren
11	14,960	Walled Lake Consolidated Schools	Walled Lake
12	14,585	Wayne-Westland Community SD	Westland
13	14,311	Rochester Community SD	Rochester
14	13,312	Saginaw City SD	Saginaw
15	13,272	Chippewa Valley Schools	Clinton Twp
16	13,214	Port Huron Area SD	Port Huron
17	12,420	Farmington Public SD	Farmington
18	12,245	Waterford SD	Waterford
19	12,217	L'anse Creuse Public Schools	Harrison Twp
20	12,074	Troy SD	Troy
21	11,886	Pontiac City SD	Pontiac
22	11,536	Kalamazoo Public SD	Kalamazoo
23	11,339	Traverse City Area Public Schools	Traverse City
24	11,105	Taylor SD	Taylor
25	10,965	Huron Valley Schools	Highland
26	10,499	Southfield Public SD	Southfield
27	9,937	Bay City SD	Bay City
28	9,685	Midland Public Schools	Midland
29	9,218	Kentwood Public Schools	Kentwood
30	9,140	Portage Public Schools	Portage
31	8,940	Grosse Pointe Public Schools	Grosse Pointe
32	8,775	Forest Hills Public Schools	Grand Rapids
33	8,348	Birmingham City SD	Birmingham
34	8,255	Battle Creek Public Schools	Battle Creek
35	8,106	Howell Public Schools	Howell
36	7,951	Clarkston Community SD	Clarkston
37	7,897	West Ottawa Public SD	Holland
38	7,840	Lake Orion Community Schools	Lake Orion
39	7,687	Muskegon City SD	Muskegon
40	7,674	Lapeer Community Schools	Lapeer
41	7,590	Rockford Public Schools	Rockford
42	7,515	Jackson Public Schools	Jackson
43	7,268	West Bloomfield SD	West Bloomfield
44	7,226	Monroe Public Schools	Monroe
45	7,221	Brighton Area Schools	Brighton
46	6,840	School District of Royal Oak	Royal Oak
47	6,814	Grand Blanc Community Schools	Grand Blanc
48	6,798	South Lyon Community Schools	South Lyon
49	6,465	Bloomfield Hills SD	Bloomfield Hls
50	6,455	East Detroit Public Schools	Eastpointe
51	6,429	Anchor Bay SD	New Baltimore
52	6,409	Roseville Community Schools	Roseville
53	6,315	Van Buren Public Schools	Belleville
54	6,116	Grandville Public Schools	Grandville
55	6,056	Grand Haven Area Public Schools	Grand Haven
56	6,047	Northville Public Schools	Northville
57	5,995	Novi Community SD	Novi
58	5,960	East China SD	East China
59	5,911	Wyoming Public Schools	Wyoming
60	5,572	Holland City SD	Holland
61	5,570	Holt Public Schools	Holt
62	5,501	Grand Ledge Public Schools	Grand Ledge
63	5,492	Romeo Community Schools	Romeo
64	5,438	Bedford Public Schools	Temperance
65	5,324	Benton Harbor Area Schools	Benton Harbor
65	5,324	Lincoln Park Public Schools	Lincoln Park
67	5,317	Davison Community Schools	Davison
68	5,273	Carman-Ainsworth Community Schools	Flint
69	5,270	Alpena Public Schools	Alpena
70	5,193	Saline Area Schools	Saline
71	5,178	Garden City SD	Garden City
72	5,121	Woodhaven-Brownstown SD	Brownstown
73	5,078	Pinckney Community Schools	Pinckney
74	5,002	Saginaw Township Community Schools	Saginaw
75	4,987	Southgate Community SD	Southgate
76	4,964	Hartland Consolidated Schools	Hartland
77	4,940	Wyandotte City SD	Wyandotte
78	4,917	Fraser Public Schools	Fraser
79	4,863	Zeeland Public Schools	Zeeland
80	4,854	Hazel Park City SD	Hazel Park
81	4,791	Jenison Public Schools	Jenison
82	4,777	Flushing Community Schools	Flushing
83	4,761	Lincoln Consolidated SD	Ypsilanti
84	4,756	Hudsonville Public SD	Hudsonville
85	4,714	School District of Ypsilanti	Ypsilanti
86	4,570	Redford Union SD	Redford
87	4,546	Reeths-Puffer Schools	Muskegon
88	4,505	Berkley SD	Berkley
89	4,418	Holly Area SD	Holly
90	4,295	Mona Shores Public SD	Norton Shores
91	4,268	Romulus Community Schools	Romulus
92	4,222	Owosso Public Schools	Owosso
93	4,220	Niles Community SD	Niles
94	4,201	Van Dyke Public Schools	Warren
95	4,194	Okemos Public Schools	Okemos
96	4,167	Swartz Creek Community Schools	Swartz Creek
97	4,141	Oak Park City SD	Oak Park
98	4,068	Mount Pleasant City SD	Mount Pleasant
99	4,047	Oxford Area Community Schools	Oxford
100	4,032	Adrian City SD	Adrian
101	4,031	Clintondale Community Schools	Clinton Twp
102	4,004	Lowell Area Schools	Lowell
103	3,940	Kearsley Community Schools	Flint
104	3,936	Avondale SD	Auburn Hills
105	3,935	Ferndale Public Schools	Ferndale
106	3,930	Greenville Public Schools	Greenville
107	3,844	Hamtramck Public Schools	Hamtramck
108	3,805	Coldwater Community Schools	Coldwater
109	3,767	Marquette Area Public Schools	Marquette
110	3,761	Highland Park City Schools	Highland Park
111	3,727	Kenowa Hills Public Schools	Grand Rapids
112	3,726	Brandon SD	Ortonville
113	3,721	Fenton Area Public Schools	Fenton
114	3,693	Northwest Community Schools	Jackson
115	3,649	Clio Area SD	Clio
116	3,632	East Lansing SD	East Lansing
117	3,556	Crestwood SD	Dearborn Hgts
118	3,521	South Redford SD	Redford
119	3,505	Cadillac Area Public Schools	Cadillac
120	3,490	Allen Park Public Schools	Allen Park
120	3,490	Mattawan Consolidated School	Mattawan
122	3,489	Cedar Springs Public Schools	Cedar Springs
123	3,480	Mount Morris Consolidated Schools	Mount Morris
124	3,464	Airport Community SD	Carleton
125	3,460	Tecumseh Public Schools	Tecumseh
126	3,447	Northview Public SD	Grand Rapids
127	3,435	Ionia Public Schools	Ionia
128	3,427	Gaylord Community Schools	Gaylord
129	3,420	Waverly Community Schools	Lansing
130	3,409	Lakeview Public Schools (Macomb)	St Clair Shores
131	3,404	Saint Johns Public Schools	Saint Johns
132	3,388	Lakeview SD (Calhoun)	Battle Creek
133	3,385	Lake Shore Public Schools (Macomb)	St Clair Shores
134	3,370	Charlotte Public Schools	Charlotte
134	3,370	Hastings Area SD	Hastings
136	3,360	Fruitport Community Schools	Fruitport
137	3,359	Dexter Community SD	Dexter
138	3,343	Fitzgerald Public Schools	Warren
139	3,340	Caledonia Community Schools	Caledonia
140	3,335	Wayland Union Schools	Wayland
141	3,299	Mason Public Schools (Ingham)	Mason
142	3,268	Eaton Rapids Public Schools	Eaton Rapids
143	3,250	Sault Sainte Marie Area Schools	Sault Ste Marie
144	3,243	Warren Woods Public Schools	Warren
145	3,211	Fowlerville Community Schools	Fowlerville
146	3,205	Escanaba Area Public Schools	Escanaba
147	3,200	Chelsea SD	Chelsea
147	3,200	Mount Clemens Community SD	Mount Clemens
149	3,170	Trenton Public Schools	Trenton
150	3,109	Three Rivers Community Schools	Three Rivers
151	3,107	Sturgis Public Schools	Sturgis
152	3,091	Gull Lake Community Schools	Richland
153	3,033	Allegan Public Schools	Allegan
154	3,032	Gibraltar SD	Woodhaven
155	2,999	Public Schools of Petoskey	Petoskey
156	2,987	Comstock Public Schools	Kalamazoo
157	2,986	Dearborn Heights SD #7	Dearborn Hgts
158	2,968	Haslett Public Schools	Haslett
159	2,949	Center Line Public Schools	Center Line
160	2,934	Linden Community Schools	Linden
161	2,932	Marysville Public Schools	Marysville
162	2,897	Lakeshore SD (Berrien)	Stevensville
162	2,897	Plainwell Community Schools	Plainwell
164	2,895	Dowagiac Union SD	Dowagiac
165	2,894	Orchard View Schools	Muskegon
166	2,883	East Grand Rapids Public Schools	E Grand Rapids
167	2,866	Sparta Area Schools	Sparta
168	2,864	Saint Joseph Public Schools	Saint Joseph
169	2,863	Thornapple Kellogg SD	Middleville
170	2,818	Western SD	Parma
171	2,810	Byron Center Public Schools	Byron Center
172	2,808	Willow Run Community Schools	Ypsilanti
173	2,779	Vicksburg Community Schools	Vicksburg
174	2,747	Dewitt Public Schools	Dewitt
175	2,745	Detroit Academy of Arts & Sci	Detroit
176	2,736	Algonac Community SD	Algonac
177	2,720	Harper Creek Community Schools	Battle Creek
178	2,715	Jefferson Schools (Monroe)	Monroe
179	2,705	River Rouge SD	River Rouge
180	2,697	West Branch-Rose City Area Schools	West Branch
181	2,689	Hamilton Community Schools	Hamilton
182	2,664	North Branch Area Schools	North Branch
183	2,659	Fremont Public SD	Fremont
184	2,618	Belding Area SD	Belding
185	2,606	Lakewood Public Schools	Lake Odessa
186	2,601	Alma Public Schools	Alma
186	2,601	Chippewa Hills SD	Remus
188	2,560	Ludington Area SD	Ludington
189	2,549	Riverview Community SD	Riverview
190	2,515	South Haven Public Schools	South Haven
191	2,509	Croswell-Lexington Comm Schools	Croswell
192	2,498	Melvindale-N Allen Park Schools	Melvindale
193	2,473	Marshall Public Schools	Marshall
194	2,457	Bangor Township Schools	Bay City
195	2,439	South Lake Schools	St Clair Shores
196	2,432	Newaygo Public SD	Newaygo
197	2,430	Tri County Area Schools	Howard City
198	2,423	Lamphere Public Schools	Madison Heights
199	2,418	Grant Public SD	Grant
200	2,409	Bridgeport-Spaulding Community SD	Bridgeport
201	2,403	Yale Public Schools	Yale
202	2,390	Imlay City Community Schools	Imlay City
203	2,379	Coopersville Public SD	Coopersville
204	2,367	Cheboygan Area Schools	Cheboygan

205	2,341	Godwin Heights Public Schools	Wyoming
206	2,340	Muskegon Heights SD	Muskegon Hgts
207	2,336	Paw Paw Public SD	Paw Paw
208	2,334	Caro Community Schools	Caro
209	2,330	Otsego Public Schools	Otsego
210	2,273	Whitehall District Schools	Whitehall
211	2,262	Comstock Park Public Schools	Comstock Park
212	2,236	Edwardsburg Public Schools	Edwardsburg
212	2,236	Kelloggsville Public Schools	Grand Rapids
214	2,227	Milan Area Schools	Milan
215	2,225	Corunna Public SD	Corunna
216	2,202	Bullock Creek SD	Midland
217	2,201	Houghton Lake Community Schools	Houghton Lake
218	2,197	Big Rapids Public Schools	Big Rapids
219	2,161	Armada Area Schools	Armada
220	2,155	Lakeville Community Schools	Otisville
221	2,153	Harrison Community Schools	Harrison
222	2,149	Spring Lake Public Schools	Spring Lake
223	2,146	Crawford Ausable Schools	Grayling
224	2,136	Madison Public Schools (Oakland)	Madison Heights
225	2,123	Central Montcalm Public Schools	Stanton
226	2,120	Coloma Community Schools	Coloma
227	2,114	Breitung Township Schools	Kingsford
228	2,106	Gladwin Community Schools	Gladwin
229	2,092	Chesaning Union Schools	Chesaning
230	2,083	Huron SD	New Boston
231	2,071	Portland Public SD	Portland
232	2,066	Pinconning Area Schools	Pinconning
233	2,065	Shelby Public Schools	Shelby
234	2,062	Westwood Community Schools	Dearborn Hgts
235	2,060	Durand Area Schools	Durand
235	2,060	Reed City Area Public Schools	Reed City
237	2,059	Delton-Kellogg SD	Delton
238	2,056	Williamston Community Schools	Williamston
239	2,049	Grosse Ile Township Schools	Grosse Ile
240	2,039	Richmond Community Schools	Richmond
241	2,027	Menominee Area Public Schools	Menominee
242	2,022	Goodrich Area Schools	Goodrich
243	2,020	Allendale Public SD	Allendale
244	2,009	Beecher Community SD	Flint
245	2,008	Parchment SD	Parchment
246	2,006	Benzie County Central Schools	Benzonia
247	1,994	Perry Public SD	Perry
248	1,989	Clarenceville SD	Livonia
249	1,987	Oakridge Public Schools	Muskegon
250	1,979	Standish-Sterling Comm Schools	Standish
251	1,958	Capac Community SD	Capac
251	1,958	Hillsdale Community Schools	Hillsdale
253	1,956	Oscoda Area Schools	Oscoda
254	1,948	Lakeview Comm Schools (Montcalm)	Lakeview
255	1,946	Birch Run Area SD	Birch Run
256	1,943	Washtenaw ISD	Ann Arbor
257	1,926	Essexville-Hampton Public Schools	Essexville
258	1,924	Columbia SD	Brooklyn
259	1,905	Vassar Public Schools	Vassar
260	1,899	Gerrish-Higgins SD	Roscommon
261	1,891	Pennfield SD	Battle Creek
262	1,847	Albion Public Schools	Albion
263	1,841	Kalkaska Public Schools	Kalkaska
263	1,841	Onsted Community Schools	Onsted
265	1,824	Stockbridge Community Schools	Stockbridge
266	1,820	Napoleon Community Schools	Napoleon
267	1,803	Gladstone Area Schools	Gladstone
268	1,780	Ovid-Elsie Area Schools	Elsie
269	1,779	Maple Valley Schools	Vermontville
270	1,771	Buchanan Community Schools	Buchanan
271	1,760	Flat Rock Community Schools	Flat Rock
272	1,755	Almont Community Schools	Almont
272	1,755	Beaverton Rural Schools	Beaverton
274	1,750	Millington Community Schools	Millington
275	1,744	Manistee Area Schools	Manistee
276	1,734	Mason County Central Schools	Scottville
277	1,731	Shepherd Public SD	Shepherd
278	1,727	Cass City Public Schools	Cass City
279	1,710	Montrose Community Schools	Montrose
280	1,701	Bendle Public Schools	Burton
281	1,693	Farwell Area Schools	Farwell
282	1,683	Quincy Community SD	Quincy
283	1,677	Swan Valley SD	Saginaw
284	1,671	Ida Public SD	Ida
285	1,670	Clare Public Schools	Clare
286	1,657	Brandywine Public SD	Niles
287	1,652	Macomb ISD	Clinton Twp
288	1,649	Freeland Community SD	Freeland
289	1,646	Dundee Community Schools	Dundee
290	1,629	Tawas Area Schools	Tawas City
291	1,615	Morley Stanwood Community Schools	Morley
292	1,614	Public Schools of Calumet	Calumet
293	1,599	Montague Area Public Schools	Montague
294	1,597	Godfrey-Lee Public Schools	Wyoming
295	1,579	Berrien Springs Public Schools	Berrien Springs
296	1,571	Meridian Public Schools	Sanford
297	1,570	East Jackson Community Schools	Jackson
298	1,567	Hartford Public SD	Hartford
298	1,567	Mason Consol Schools (Monroe)	Erie
300	1,563	Fennville Public Schools	Fennville
301	1,555	Constantine Public SD	Constantine
302	1,549	White Cloud Public Schools	White Cloud
303	1,535	Michigan Center SD	Michigan Center
304	1,524	Bangor Public Schools (Van Buren)	Bangor
305	1,520	Elk Rapids Schools	Elk Rapids
306	1,518	Carrollton SD	Saginaw
307	1,510	Clawson City SD	Clawson
308	1,502	Bronson Community SD	Bronson

Male Students

Rank	Percent	District Name	City
1	69.9	Macomb ISD	Clinton Twp
2	58.5	Vassar Public Schools	Vassar
3	55.8	Washtenaw ISD	Ann Arbor
4	54.6	Mason County Central Schools	Scottville
5	54.5	Redford Union SD	Redford
6	54.3	Hamtramck Public Schools	Hamtramck
7	54.2	Buchanan Community Schools	Buchanan
7	54.2	Niles Community SD	Niles
9	53.9	Cass City Public Schools	Cass City
10	53.7	Caledonia Community Schools	Caledonia
11	53.6	Clawson City SD	Clawson
11	53.6	Clio Area SD	Clio
11	53.6	Fitzgerald Public Schools	Warren
11	53.6	Oxford Area Community Schools	Oxford
15	53.5	Constantine Public SD	Constantine
15	53.5	Ida Public SD	Ida
15	53.5	Shelby Public Schools	Shelby
18	53.3	Capac Community SD	Capac
18	53.3	Coldwater Community Schools	Coldwater
18	53.3	Grand Haven Area Public Schools	Grand Haven
21	53.2	Benzie County Central Schools	Benzonia
21	53.2	Marysville Public Schools	Marysville
21	53.2	Oakridge Public Schools	Muskegon
21	53.2	Ovid-Elsie Area Schools	Elsie
21	53.2	Quincy Community SD	Quincy
26	53.1	Albion Public Schools	Albion
26	53.1	Crawford Ausable Schools	Grayling
26	53.1	Croswell-Lexington Comm Schools	Croswell
26	53.1	Whitehall District Schools	Whitehall
30	53.0	Crestwood SD	Dearborn Hgts
30	53.0	Godwin Heights Public Schools	Wyoming
30	53.0	Montrose Community Schools	Montrose
30	53.0	Muskegon City SD	Muskegon
30	53.0	Three Rivers Community Schools	Three Rivers
35	52.9	Big Rapids Public Schools	Big Rapids
35	52.9	Caro Community Schools	Caro
35	52.9	Comstock Public Schools	Kalamazoo
35	52.9	Dundee Community Schools	Dundee
35	52.9	Gerrish-Higgins SD	Roscommon
35	52.9	Napoleon Community Schools	Napoleon
35	52.9	Onsted Community Schools	Onsted
35	52.9	Owosso Public Schools	Owosso
35	52.9	River Rouge SD	River Rouge
35	52.9	Roseville Community Schools	Roseville
45	52.8	Fowlerville Community Schools	Fowlerville
45	52.8	Garden City SD	Garden City
45	52.8	West Bloomfield SD	West Bloomfield
48	52.7	Bay City SD	Bay City
48	52.7	Bendle Public Schools	Burton
48	52.7	Birch Run Area SD	Birch Run
48	52.7	Grant Public SD	Grant
48	52.7	Hazel Park City SD	Hazel Park
48	52.7	Northview Public SD	Grand Rapids
48	52.7	Thornapple Kellogg SD	Middleville
48	52.7	Trenton Public Schools	Trenton
48	52.7	Westwood Community Schools	Dearborn Hgts
57	52.6	Armada Area Schools	Armada
57	52.6	Cadillac Area Public Schools	Cadillac
57	52.6	Public Schools of Petoskey	Petoskey
57	52.6	Saint Johns Public Schools	Saint Johns
61	52.5	Byron Center Public Schools	Byron Center
61	52.5	Dewitt Public Schools	Dewitt
61	52.5	Tri County Area Schools	Howard City
64	52.4	Berrien Springs Public Schools	Berrien Springs
64	52.4	School District of Royal Oak	Royal Oak
64	52.4	Van Dyke Public Schools	Warren
67	52.3	Escanaba Area Public Schools	Escanaba
67	52.3	Grand Rapids Public Schools	Grand Rapids
67	52.3	Houghton Lake Community Schools	Houghton Lake
67	52.3	Howell Public Schools	Howell
67	52.3	Lake Orion Community Schools	Lake Orion
67	52.3	Milan Area Schools	Milan
67	52.3	Paw Paw Public SD	Paw Paw
67	52.3	Public Schools of Calumet	Calumet
75	52.2	Airport Community SD	Carleton
75	52.2	Breitung Township Schools	Kingsford
75	52.2	Chelsea SD	Chelsea
75	52.2	Jenison Public Schools	Jenison
75	52.2	Lapeer Community Schools	Lapeer
75	52.2	Lincoln Park Public Schools	Lincoln Park
75	52.2	Otsego Public Schools	Otsego
75	52.2	Sault Sainte Marie Area Schools	Sault Ste Marie
75	52.2	Southgate Community SD	Southgate
75	52.2	Stockbridge Community Schools	Stockbridge
75	52.2	Utica Community Schools	Sterling Hgts
75	52.2	Waverly Community Schools	Lansing
75	52.2	West Branch-Rose City Area Schools	West Branch
75	52.2	Yale Public Schools	Yale
89	52.1	Beaverton Rural Schools	Beaverton
89	52.1	Bronson Community SD	Bronson
89	52.1	Clintondale Community Schools	Clinton Twp
89	52.1	Comstock Park Public Schools	Comstock Park
89	52.1	Fraser Public Schools	Fraser
89	52.1	Holly Area SD	Holly
89	52.1	Lincoln Consolidated SD	Ypsilanti
89	52.1	Reed City Area Public Schools	Reed City
89	52.1	Rockford Public Schools	Rockford
98	52.0	Almont Community Schools	Almont
98	52.0	Cheboygan Area Schools	Cheboygan
98	52.0	Dowagiac Union SD	Dowagiac
98	52.0	Edwardsburg Public Schools	Edwardsburg
98	52.0	Ferndale Public Schools	Ferndale
98	52.0	Freeland Community SD	Freeland
98	52.0	Goodrich Area Schools	Goodrich
98	52.0	Kalamazoo Public SD	Kalamazoo
98	52.0	Kenowa Hills Public Schools	Grand Rapids
98	52.0	Mattawan Consolidated School	Mattawan
98	52.0	Oscoda Area Schools	Oscoda
98	52.0	Reeths-Puffer Schools	Muskegon
98	52.0	Spring Lake Public Schools	Spring Lake
98	52.0	Swartz Creek Community Schools	Swartz Creek
98	52.0	Walled Lake Consolidated Schools	Walled Lake
98	52.0	Wyoming Public Schools	Wyoming
114	51.9	Brighton Area Schools	Brighton
114	51.9	East China SD	East China
114	51.9	Harrison Community Schools	Harrison
114	51.9	Haslett Public Schools	Haslett
114	51.9	Hillsdale Community Schools	Hillsdale
114	51.9	Holland City SD	Holland
114	51.9	Midland Public Schools	Midland
114	51.9	Monroe Public Schools	Monroe
114	51.9	North Branch Area Schools	North Branch
114	51.9	Saint Joseph Public Schools	Saint Joseph
114	51.9	School District of Ypsilanti	Ypsilanti
125	51.8	Brandywine Public SD	Niles
125	51.8	Chesaning Union Schools	Chesaning
125	51.8	Columbia SD	Brooklyn
125	51.8	Coopersville Public SD	Coopersville
125	51.8	Farmington Public SD	Farmington
125	51.8	Hartford Public SD	Hartford
125	51.8	Kalkaska Public Schools	Kalkaska
125	51.8	Kearsley Community Schools	Flint
125	51.8	Lakeview Comm Schools (Montcalm)	Lakeview
125	51.8	Marquette Area Public Schools	Marquette
125	51.8	Menominee Area Public Schools	Menominee
125	51.8	Parchment SD	Parchment
125	51.8	Troy SD	Troy
138	51.7	Algonac Community SD	Algonac
138	51.7	Dexter Community SD	Dexter
138	51.7	Eaton Rapids Public Schools	Eaton Rapids
138	51.7	Fennville Public Schools	Fennville
138	51.7	Lamphere Public Schools	Madison Heights
138	51.7	Livonia Public Schools	Livonia
138	51.7	Standish-Sterling Comm Schools	Standish
138	51.7	Waterford SD	Waterford
146	51.6	Bangor Public Schools (Van Buren)	Bangor
146	51.6	Carrollton SD	Saginaw
146	51.6	Center Line Public Schools	Center Line
146	51.6	Clarkston Community SD	Clarkston
146	51.6	Dearborn City SD	Dearborn
146	51.6	Gibraltar SD	Woodhaven
146	51.6	Gladwin Community Schools	Gladwin
146	51.6	Gull Lake Community Schools	Richland
146	51.6	Kentwood Public Schools	Kentwood
146	51.6	Lakeshore SD (Berrien)	Stevensville
146	51.6	Lakeville Community Schools	Otisville
146	51.6	Marshall Public Schools	Marshall
146	51.6	Mona Shores Public SD	Norton Shores
146	51.6	Mount Morris Consolidated Schools	Mount Morris
146	51.6	Novi Community SD	Novi
146	51.6	Sparta Area Schools	Sparta
162	51.5	Alma Public Schools	Alma
162	51.5	Coloma Community Schools	Coloma
162	51.5	Forest Hills Public Schools	Grand Rapids
162	51.5	Grand Ledge Public Schools	Grand Ledge
162	51.5	Harper Creek Community Schools	Battle Creek
162	51.5	Hartland Consolidated Schools	Hartland
162	51.5	Huron Valley Schools	Highland
162	51.5	Jefferson Schools (Monroe)	Monroe

162	51.5	Ludington Area SD	Ludington
162	51.5	Mason Consol Schools (Monroe)	Erie
162	51.5	South Lyon Community Schools	South Lyon
173	51.4	Ann Arbor Public Schools	Ann Arbor
173	51.4	Battle Creek Public Schools	Battle Creek
173	51.4	Birmingham City SD	Birmingham
173	51.4	Bridgeport-Spaulding Community SD	Bridgeport
173	51.4	Bullock Creek SD	Midland
173	51.4	East Grand Rapids Public Schools	E Grand Rapids
173	51.4	Greenville Public Schools	Greenville
173	51.4	Holt Public Schools	Holt
173	51.4	Madison Public Schools (Oakland)	Madison Heights
173	51.4	Manistee Area Schools	Manistee
173	51.4	Mount Pleasant City SD	Mount Pleasant
173	51.4	Port Huron Area SD	Port Huron
173	51.4	Richmond Community Schools	Richmond
173	51.4	Tawas Area Schools	Tawas City
187	51.3	Allen Park Public Schools	Allen Park
187	51.3	Alpena Public Schools	Alpena
187	51.3	Corunna Public SD	Corunna
187	51.3	Dearborn Heights SD #7	Dearborn Hgts
187	51.3	Delton-Kellogg SD	Delton
187	51.3	Jackson Public Schools	Jackson
187	51.3	Pontiac City SD	Pontiac
187	51.3	Portage Public Schools	Portage
187	51.3	Saginaw City SD	Saginaw
187	51.3	West Ottawa Public SD	Holland
187	51.3	Willow Run Community Schools	Ypsilanti
198	51.2	Adrian City SD	Adrian
198	51.2	Anchor Bay SD	New Baltimore
198	51.2	Carman-Ainsworth Community Schools	Flint
198	51.2	Elk Rapids Schools	Elk Rapids
198	51.2	Hamilton Community Schools	Hamilton
198	51.2	Ionia Public Schools	Ionia
198	51.2	Lake Shore Public Schools (Macomb)	St Clair Shores
198	51.2	Lansing Public SD	Lansing
198	51.2	Montague Area Public Schools	Montague
198	51.2	Oak Park City SD	Oak Park
198	51.2	Okemos Public Schools	Okemos
198	51.2	Van Buren Public Schools	Belleville
198	51.2	Wyandotte City SD	Wyandotte
198	51.2	Zeeland Public Schools	Zeeland
212	51.1	Bangor Township Schools	Bay City
212	51.1	Berkley SD	Berkley
212	51.1	Bloomfield Hills SD	Bloomfield Hls
212	51.1	Charlotte Public Schools	Charlotte
212	51.1	Gladstone Area Schools	Gladstone
212	51.1	Michigan Center SD	Michigan Center
212	51.1	Millington Community Schools	Millington
212	51.1	Pinckney Community Schools	Pinckney
212	51.1	Plainwell Community Schools	Plainwell
212	51.1	Romeo Community Schools	Romeo
212	51.1	Shepherd Public SD	Shepherd
212	51.1	South Haven Public Schools	South Haven
212	51.1	South Lake Schools	St Clair Shores
212	51.1	Traverse City Area Public Schools	Traverse City
212	51.1	White Cloud Public Schools	White Cloud
227	51.0	Avondale SD	Auburn Hills
227	51.0	East Detroit Public Schools	Eastpointe
227	51.0	Farwell Area Schools	Farwell
227	51.0	Fruitport Community Schools	Fruitport
227	51.0	Huron SD	New Boston
227	51.0	Morley Stanwood Community Schools	Morley
227	51.0	Rochester Community SD	Rochester
234	50.9	Allendale Public SD	Allendale
234	50.9	Detroit City SD	Detroit
234	50.9	Grandville Public Schools	Grandville
234	50.9	Grosse Pointe Public Schools	Grosse Pointe
234	50.9	Hudsonville Public SD	Hudsonville
234	50.9	Lakeview Public Schools (Macomb)	St Clair Shores
234	50.9	Lowell Area Schools	Lowell
234	50.9	Riverview Community SD	Riverview
234	50.9	Romulus Community Schools	Romulus
234	50.9	Saline Area Schools	Saline
234	50.9	Wayland Union Schools	Wayland
234	50.9	Woodhaven-Brownstown SD	Brownstown
246	50.8	East Lansing SD	East Lansing
246	50.8	Fenton Area Public Schools	Fenton
246	50.8	Northville Public Schools	Northville
246	50.8	Pennfield SD	Battle Creek
246	50.8	Southfield Public SD	Southfield
246	50.8	Wayne-Westland Community SD	Westland
252	50.7	Chippewa Valley Schools	Clinton Twp
252	50.7	Grand Blanc Community Schools	Grand Blanc
252	50.7	Kelloggsville Public Schools	Grand Rapids
252	50.7	Linden Community Schools	Linden
252	50.7	Orchard View Schools	Muskegon
252	50.7	Tecumseh Public Schools	Tecumseh
258	50.6	Brandon SD	Ortonville
258	50.6	Lakeview SD (Calhoun)	Battle Creek
258	50.6	Meridian Public Schools	Sanford
258	50.6	Muskegon Heights SD	Muskegon Hgts
258	50.6	Warren Consolidated Schools	Warren
263	50.5	Bedford Public Schools	Temperance
263	50.5	Chippewa Hills SD	Remus
263	50.5	Davison Community Schools	Davison
263	50.5	East Jackson Community Schools	Jackson
263	50.5	Imlay City Community Schools	Imlay City
263	50.5	Portland Public SD	Portland
269	50.4	Grosse Ile Township Schools	Grosse Ile
269	50.4	L'anse Creuse Public Schools	Harrison Twp
269	50.4	Northwest Community Schools	Jackson
269	50.4	Saginaw Township Community Schools	Saginaw
269	50.4	South Redford SD	Redford
269	50.4	Sturgis Public Schools	Sturgis
269	50.4	Taylor SD	Taylor
269	50.4	Vicksburg Community Schools	Vicksburg
269	50.4	Williamston Community Schools	Williamston
278	50.3	Allegan Public Schools	Allegan
278	50.3	Lakewood Public Schools	Lake Odessa
278	50.3	Maple Valley Schools	Vermontville
278	50.3	Mason Public Schools (Ingham)	Mason
278	50.3	Plymouth-Canton Community Schools	Plymouth
278	50.3	Warren Woods Public Schools	Warren
284	50.2	Clarenceville SD	Livonia
284	50.2	Flint City SD	Flint
284	50.2	Perry Public SD	Perry
287	50.1	Durand Area Schools	Durand
287	50.1	Hastings Area SD	Hastings
287	50.1	Newaygo Public SD	Newaygo
287	50.1	Western SD	Parma
291	50.0	Benton Harbor Area Schools	Benton Harbor
291	50.0	Flushing Community Schools	Flushing
291	50.0	Gaylord Community Schools	Gaylord
291	50.0	Melvindale-N Allen Park Schools	Melvindale
295	49.9	Cedar Springs Public Schools	Cedar Springs
295	49.9	Fremont Public SD	Fremont
297	49.8	Belding Area SD	Belding
297	49.8	Essexville-Hampton Public Schools	Essexville
297	49.8	Pinconning Area Schools	Pinconning
300	49.7	Mount Clemens Community SD	Mount Clemens
301	49.5	Godfrey-Lee Public Schools	Wyoming
302	49.4	Beecher Community SD	Flint
303	49.3	Central Montcalm Public Schools	Stanton
304	49.2	Swan Valley SD	Saginaw
305	48.9	Highland Park City Schools	Highland Park
306	48.8	Clare Public Schools	Clare
306	48.8	Flat Rock Community Schools	Flat Rock
308	48.0	Detroit Academy of Arts & Sci	Detroit

Female Students

Rank	Percent	District Name	City
1	52.0	Detroit Academy of Arts & Sci	Detroit
2	51.2	Clare Public Schools	Clare
2	51.2	Flat Rock Community Schools	Flat Rock
4	51.1	Highland Park City Schools	Highland Park
5	50.8	Swan Valley SD	Saginaw
6	50.7	Central Montcalm Public Schools	Stanton
7	50.6	Beecher Community SD	Flint
8	50.5	Godfrey-Lee Public Schools	Wyoming
9	50.3	Mount Clemens Community SD	Mount Clemens
10	50.2	Belding Area SD	Belding
10	50.2	Essexville-Hampton Public Schools	Essexville
10	50.2	Pinconning Area Schools	Pinconning
13	50.1	Cedar Springs Public Schools	Cedar Springs
13	50.1	Fremont Public SD	Fremont
15	50.0	Benton Harbor Area Schools	Benton Harbor
15	50.0	Flushing Community Schools	Flushing
15	50.0	Gaylord Community Schools	Gaylord
15	50.0	Melvindale-N Allen Park Schools	Melvindale
19	49.9	Durand Area Schools	Durand
19	49.9	Hastings Area SD	Hastings
19	49.9	Newaygo Public SD	Newaygo
19	49.9	Western SD	Parma
23	49.8	Clarenceville SD	Livonia
23	49.8	Flint City SD	Flint
23	49.8	Perry Public SD	Perry
26	49.7	Allegan Public Schools	Allegan
26	49.7	Lakewood Public Schools	Lake Odessa
26	49.7	Maple Valley Schools	Vermontville
26	49.7	Mason Public Schools (Ingham)	Mason
26	49.7	Plymouth-Canton Community Schools	Plymouth
26	49.7	Warren Woods Public Schools	Warren
32	49.6	Grosse Ile Township Schools	Grosse Ile
32	49.6	L'anse Creuse Public Schools	Harrison Twp
32	49.6	Northwest Community Schools	Jackson
32	49.6	Saginaw Township Community Schools	Saginaw
32	49.6	South Redford SD	Redford
32	49.6	Sturgis Public Schools	Sturgis
32	49.6	Taylor SD	Taylor
32	49.6	Vicksburg Community Schools	Vicksburg
32	49.6	Williamston Community Schools	Williamston
41	49.5	Bedford Public Schools	Temperance
41	49.5	Chippewa Hills SD	Remus
41	49.5	Davison Community Schools	Davison
41	49.5	East Jackson Community Schools	Jackson
41	49.5	Imlay City Community Schools	Imlay City
41	49.5	Portland Public SD	Portland
47	49.4	Brandon SD	Ortonville
47	49.4	Lakeview SD (Calhoun)	Battle Creek
47	49.4	Meridian Public Schools	Sanford
47	49.4	Muskegon Heights SD	Muskegon Hgts
47	49.4	Warren Consolidated Schools	Warren
52	49.3	Chippewa Valley Schools	Clinton Twp
52	49.3	Grand Blanc Community Schools	Grand Blanc
52	49.3	Kelloggsville Public Schools	Grand Rapids
52	49.3	Linden Community Schools	Linden
52	49.3	Orchard View Schools	Muskegon
52	49.3	Tecumseh Public Schools	Tecumseh
58	49.2	East Lansing SD	East Lansing
58	49.2	Fenton Area Public Schools	Fenton
58	49.2	Northville Public Schools	Northville
58	49.2	Pennfield SD	Battle Creek
58	49.2	Southfield Public SD	Southfield
58	49.2	Wayne-Westland Community SD	Westland
64	49.1	Allendale Public SD	Allendale
64	49.1	Detroit City SD	Detroit
64	49.1	Grandville Public Schools	Grandville
64	49.1	Grosse Pointe Public Schools	Grosse Pointe
64	49.1	Hudsonville Public SD	Hudsonville
64	49.1	Lakeview Public Schools (Macomb)	St Clair Shores
64	49.1	Lowell Area Schools	Lowell
64	49.1	Riverview Community SD	Riverview
64	49.1	Romulus Community Schools	Romulus
64	49.1	Saline Area Schools	Saline
64	49.1	Wayland Union Schools	Wayland
64	49.1	Woodhaven-Brownstown SD	Brownstown
76	49.0	Avondale SD	Auburn Hills
76	49.0	East Detroit Public Schools	Eastpointe
76	49.0	Farwell Area Schools	Farwell
76	49.0	Fruitport Community Schools	Fruitport
76	49.0	Huron SD	New Boston
76	49.0	Morley Stanwood Community Schools	Morley
76	49.0	Rochester Community SD	Rochester
83	48.9	Bangor Township Schools	Bay City
83	48.9	Berkley SD	Berkley
83	48.9	Bloomfield Hills SD	Bloomfield Hls
83	48.9	Charlotte Public Schools	Charlotte
83	48.9	Gladstone Area Schools	Gladstone
83	48.9	Michigan Center SD	Michigan Center
83	48.9	Millington Community Schools	Millington
83	48.9	Pinckney Community Schools	Pinckney
83	48.9	Plainwell Community Schools	Plainwell
83	48.9	Romeo Community Schools	Romeo
83	48.9	Shepherd Public SD	Shepherd
83	48.9	South Haven Public Schools	South Haven
83	48.9	South Lake Schools	St Clair Shores
83	48.9	Traverse City Area Public Schools	Traverse City
83	48.9	White Cloud Public Schools	White Cloud
98	48.8	Adrian City SD	Adrian
98	48.8	Anchor Bay SD	New Baltimore
98	48.8	Carman-Ainsworth Community Schools	Flint
98	48.8	Elk Rapids Schools	Elk Rapids
98	48.8	Hamilton Community Schools	Hamilton
98	48.8	Ionia Public Schools	Ionia
98	48.8	Lake Shore Public Schools (Macomb)	St Clair Shores
98	48.8	Lansing Public SD	Lansing
98	48.8	Montague Area Public Schools	Montague
98	48.8	Oak Park City SD	Oak Park
98	48.8	Okemos Public Schools	Okemos
98	48.8	Van Buren Public Schools	Belleville
98	48.8	Wyandotte City SD	Wyandotte
98	48.8	Zeeland Public Schools	Zeeland
112	48.7	Allen Park Public Schools	Allen Park
112	48.7	Alpena Public Schools	Alpena
112	48.7	Corunna Public SD	Corunna
112	48.7	Dearborn Heights SD #7	Dearborn Hgts
112	48.7	Delton-Kellogg SD	Delton
112	48.7	Jackson Public Schools	Jackson
112	48.7	Pontiac City SD	Pontiac
112	48.7	Portage Public Schools	Portage
112	48.7	Saginaw City SD	Saginaw
112	48.7	West Ottawa Public SD	Holland
112	48.7	Willow Run Community Schools	Ypsilanti
123	48.6	Ann Arbor Public Schools	Ann Arbor
123	48.6	Battle Creek Public Schools	Battle Creek
123	48.6	Birmingham City SD	Birmingham
123	48.6	Bridgeport-Spaulding Community SD	Bridgeport
123	48.6	Bullock Creek SD	Midland
123	48.6	East Grand Rapids Public Schools	E Grand Rapids
123	48.6	Greenville Public Schools	Greenville
123	48.6	Holt Public Schools	Holt
123	48.6	Madison Public Schools (Oakland)	Madison Heights
123	48.6	Manistee Area Schools	Manistee

123	48.6	Mount Pleasant City SD	Mount Pleasant
123	48.6	Port Huron Area SD	Port Huron
123	48.6	Richmond Community Schools	Richmond
123	48.6	Tawas Area Schools	Tawas City
137	48.5	Alma Public Schools	Alma
137	48.5	Coloma Community Schools	Coloma
137	48.5	Forest Hills Public Schools	Grand Rapids
137	48.5	Grand Ledge Public Schools	Grand Ledge
137	48.5	Harper Creek Community Schools	Battle Creek
137	48.5	Hartland Consolidated Schools	Hartland
137	48.5	Huron Valley Schools	Highland
137	48.5	Jefferson Schools (Monroe)	Monroe
137	48.5	Ludington Area SD	Ludington
137	48.5	Mason Consol Schools (Monroe)	Erie
137	48.5	South Lyon Community Schools	South Lyon
148	48.4	Bangor Public Schools (Van Buren)	Bangor
148	48.4	Carrollton SD	Saginaw
148	48.4	Center Line Public Schools	Center Line
148	48.4	Clarkston Community SD	Clarkston
148	48.4	Dearborn City SD	Dearborn
148	48.4	Gibraltar SD	Woodhaven
148	48.4	Gladwin Community Schools	Gladwin
148	48.4	Gull Lake Community Schools	Richland
148	48.4	Kentwood Public Schools	Kentwood
148	48.4	Lakeshore SD (Berrien)	Stevensville
148	48.4	Lakeville Community Schools	Otisville
148	48.4	Marshall Public Schools	Marshall
148	48.4	Mona Shores Public SD	Norton Shores
148	48.4	Mount Morris Consolidated Schools	Mount Morris
148	48.4	Novi Community SD	Novi
148	48.4	Sparta Area Schools	Sparta
164	48.3	Algonac Community SD	Algonac
164	48.3	Dexter Community SD	Dexter
164	48.3	Eaton Rapids Public Schools	Eaton Rapids
164	48.3	Fennville Public Schools	Fennville
164	48.3	Lamphere Public Schools	Madison Heights
164	48.3	Livonia Public Schools	Livonia
164	48.3	Standish-Sterling Comm Schools	Standish
164	48.3	Waterford SD	Waterford
172	48.2	Brandywine Public SD	Niles
172	48.2	Chesaning Union Schools	Chesaning
172	48.2	Columbia SD	Brooklyn
172	48.2	Coopersville Public SD	Coopersville
172	48.2	Farmington Public SD	Farmington
172	48.2	Hartford Public SD	Hartford
172	48.2	Kalkaska Public Schools	Kalkaska
172	48.2	Kearsley Community Schools	Flint
172	48.2	Lakeview Comm Schools (Montcalm)	Lakeview
172	48.2	Marquette Area Public Schools	Marquette
172	48.2	Menominee Area Public Schools	Menominee
172	48.2	Parchment SD	Parchment
172	48.2	Troy SD	Troy
185	48.1	Brighton Area Schools	Brighton
185	48.1	East China SD	East China
185	48.1	Harrison Community Schools	Harrison
185	48.1	Haslett Public Schools	Haslett
185	48.1	Hillsdale Community Schools	Hillsdale
185	48.1	Holland City SD	Holland
185	48.1	Midland Public Schools	Midland
185	48.1	Monroe Public Schools	Monroe
185	48.1	North Branch Area Schools	North Branch
185	48.1	Saint Joseph Public Schools	Saint Joseph
185	48.1	School District of Ypsilanti	Ypsilanti
196	48.0	Almont Community Schools	Almont
196	48.0	Cheboygan Area Schools	Cheboygan
196	48.0	Dowagiac Union SD	Dowagiac
196	48.0	Edwardsburg Public Schools	Edwardsburg
196	48.0	Ferndale Public Schools	Ferndale
196	48.0	Freeland Community SD	Freeland
196	48.0	Goodrich Area Schools	Goodrich
196	48.0	Kalamazoo Public SD	Kalamazoo
196	48.0	Kenowa Hills Public Schools	Grand Rapids
196	48.0	Mattawan Consolidated School	Mattawan
196	48.0	Oscoda Area Schools	Oscoda
196	48.0	Reeths-Puffer Schools	Muskegon
196	48.0	Spring Lake Public Schools	Spring Lake
196	48.0	Swartz Creek Community Schools	Swartz Creek
196	48.0	Walled Lake Consolidated Schools	Walled Lake
196	48.0	Wyoming Public Schools	Wyoming
212	47.9	Beaverton Rural Schools	Beaverton
212	47.9	Bronson Community SD	Bronson
212	47.9	Clintondale Community Schools	Clinton Twp
212	47.9	Comstock Park Public Schools	Comstock Park
212	47.9	Fraser Public Schools	Fraser
212	47.9	Holly Area SD	Holly
212	47.9	Lincoln Consolidated SD	Ypsilanti
212	47.9	Reed City Area Public Schools	Reed City
212	47.9	Rockford Public Schools	Rockford
221	47.8	Airport Community SD	Carleton
221	47.8	Breitung Township Schools	Kingsford
221	47.8	Chelsea SD	Chelsea
221	47.8	Jenison Public Schools	Jenison
221	47.8	Lapeer Community Schools	Lapeer
221	47.8	Lincoln Park Public Schools	Lincoln Park
221	47.8	Otsego Public Schools	Otsego
221	47.8	Sault Sainte Marie Area Schools	Sault Ste Marie
221	47.8	Southgate Community SD	Southgate
221	47.8	Stockbridge Community Schools	Stockbridge
221	47.8	Utica Community Schools	Sterling Hgts
221	47.8	Waverly Community Schools	Lansing
221	47.8	West Branch-Rose City Area Schools	West Branch
221	47.8	Yale Public Schools	Yale
235	47.7	Escanaba Area Public Schools	Escanaba
235	47.7	Grand Rapids Public Schools	Grand Rapids
235	47.7	Houghton Lake Community Schools	Houghton Lake
235	47.7	Howell Public Schools	Howell
235	47.7	Lake Orion Community Schools	Lake Orion
235	47.7	Milan Area Schools	Milan
235	47.7	Paw Paw Public SD	Paw Paw
235	47.7	Public Schools of Calumet	Calumet
243	47.6	Berrien Springs Public Schools	Berrien Springs
243	47.6	School District of Royal Oak	Royal Oak
243	47.6	Van Dyke Public Schools	Warren
246	47.5	Byron Center Public Schools	Byron Center
246	47.5	Dewitt Public Schools	Dewitt
246	47.5	Tri County Area Schools	Howard City
249	47.4	Armada Area Schools	Armada
249	47.4	Cadillac Area Public Schools	Cadillac
249	47.4	Public Schools of Petoskey	Petoskey
249	47.4	Saint Johns Public Schools	Saint Johns
253	47.3	Bay City SD	Bay City
253	47.3	Bendle Public Schools	Burton
253	47.3	Birch Run Area SD	Birch Run
253	47.3	Grant Public SD	Grant
253	47.3	Hazel Park City SD	Hazel Park
253	47.3	Northview Public SD	Grand Rapids
253	47.3	Thornapple Kellogg SD	Middleville
253	47.3	Trenton Public Schools	Trenton
253	47.3	Westwood Community Schools	Dearborn Hgts
262	47.2	Fowlerville Community Schools	Fowlerville
262	47.2	Garden City SD	Garden City
262	47.2	West Bloomfield SD	West Bloomfield
265	47.1	Big Rapids Public Schools	Big Rapids
265	47.1	Caro Community Schools	Caro
265	47.1	Comstock Public Schools	Kalamazoo
265	47.1	Dundee Community Schools	Dundee
265	47.1	Gerrish-Higgins SD	Roscommon
265	47.1	Napoleon Community Schools	Napoleon
265	47.1	Onsted Community Schools	Onsted
265	47.1	Owosso Public Schools	Owosso
265	47.1	River Rouge SD	River Rouge
265	47.1	Roseville Community Schools	Roseville
275	47.0	Crestwood SD	Dearborn Hgts
275	47.0	Godwin Heights Public Schools	Wyoming
275	47.0	Montrose Community Schools	Montrose
275	47.0	Muskegon City SD	Muskegon
275	47.0	Three Rivers Community Schools	Three Rivers
280	46.9	Albion Public Schools	Albion
280	46.9	Crawford Ausable Schools	Grayling
280	46.9	Croswell-Lexington Comm Schools	Croswell
280	46.9	Whitehall District Schools	Whitehall
284	46.8	Benzie County Central Schools	Benzonia
284	46.8	Marysville Public Schools	Marysville
284	46.8	Oakridge Public Schools	Muskegon
284	46.8	Ovid-Elsie Area Schools	Elsie
284	46.8	Quincy Community SD	Quincy
289	46.7	Capac Community SD	Capac
289	46.7	Coldwater Community Schools	Coldwater
289	46.7	Grand Haven Area Public Schools	Grand Haven
292	46.5	Constantine Public SD	Constantine
292	46.5	Ida Public SD	Ida
292	46.5	Shelby Public Schools	Shelby
295	46.4	Clawson City SD	Clawson
295	46.4	Clio Area SD	Clio
295	46.4	Fitzgerald Public Schools	Warren
295	46.4	Oxford Area Community Schools	Oxford
299	46.3	Caledonia Community Schools	Caledonia
300	46.1	Cass City Public Schools	Cass City
301	45.8	Buchanan Community Schools	Buchanan
301	45.8	Niles Community SD	Niles
303	45.7	Hamtramck Public Schools	Hamtramck
304	45.5	Redford Union SD	Redford
305	45.4	Mason County Central Schools	Scottville
306	44.2	Washtenaw ISD	Ann Arbor
307	41.5	Vassar Public Schools	Vassar
308	30.1	Macomb ISD	Clinton Twp

Individual Education Program Students

Rank	Percent	District Name	City
1	30.2	Carrollton SD	Saginaw
2	25.5	Grand Rapids Public Schools	Grand Rapids
3	24.4	Redford Union SD	Redford
4	22.2	Garden City SD	Garden City
5	21.1	Wyandotte City SD	Wyandotte
6	20.3	School District of Ypsilanti	Ypsilanti
7	20.1	Westwood Community Schools	Dearborn Hgts
8	19.9	Mount Clemens Community SD	Mount Clemens
9	19.2	Muskegon City SD	Muskegon
9	19.2	Willow Run Community Schools	Ypsilanti
11	19.0	Holly Area SD	Holly
12	18.8	Big Rapids Public Schools	Big Rapids
12	18.8	Harrison Community Schools	Harrison
12	18.8	Muskegon Heights SD	Muskegon Hgts
15	18.7	Reed City Area Public Schools	Reed City
16	18.5	Lansing Public SD	Lansing
16	18.5	Vassar Public Schools	Vassar
18	18.4	Adrian City SD	Adrian
19	18.3	Chippewa Hills SD	Remus
19	18.3	Saginaw City SD	Saginaw
21	18.1	White Cloud Public Schools	White Cloud
22	17.7	Hazel Park City SD	Hazel Park
23	17.4	Flat Rock Community Schools	Flat Rock
23	17.4	Niles Community SD	Niles
23	17.4	Sparta Area Schools	Sparta
26	17.2	Chesaning Union Schools	Chesaning
26	17.2	Ida Public SD	Ida
28	17.1	Fremont Public SD	Fremont
29	17.0	Shepherd Public SD	Shepherd
30	16.9	Buchanan Community Schools	Buchanan
30	16.9	Washtenaw ISD	Ann Arbor
32	16.6	Holt Public Schools	Holt
32	16.6	Ionia Public Schools	Ionia
32	16.6	Jenison Public Schools	Jenison
32	16.6	Oscoda Area Schools	Oscoda
32	16.6	Taylor SD	Taylor
37	16.5	Lakeview Comm Schools (Montcalm)	Lakeview
37	16.5	Meridian Public Schools	Sanford
39	16.4	Bridgeport-Spaulding Community SD	Bridgeport
39	16.4	Fruitport Community Schools	Fruitport
41	16.3	Richmond Community Schools	Richmond
42	16.2	Bullock Creek SD	Midland
42	16.2	Center Line Public Schools	Center Line
42	16.2	Madison Public Schools (Oakland)	Madison Heights
45	16.1	Eaton Rapids Public Schools	Eaton Rapids
45	16.1	Gladwin Community Schools	Gladwin
45	16.1	Marquette Area Public Schools	Marquette
48	16.0	Pontiac City SD	Pontiac
49	15.9	Portland Public SD	Portland
49	15.9	Wayne-Westland Community SD	Westland
51	15.8	Greenville Public Schools	Greenville
51	15.8	Van Dyke Public Schools	Warren
53	15.7	Lamphere Public Schools	Madison Heights
53	15.7	Wayland Union Schools	Wayland
55	15.6	Comstock Park Public Schools	Comstock Park
55	15.6	Crawford Ausable Schools	Grayling
55	15.6	Milan Area Schools	Milan
55	15.6	Stockbridge Community Schools	Stockbridge
59	15.5	Charlotte Public Schools	Charlotte
59	15.5	Chelsea SD	Chelsea
59	15.5	Godfrey-Lee Public Schools	Wyoming
62	15.4	Coloma Community Schools	Coloma
62	15.4	Grand Ledge Public Schools	Grand Ledge
62	15.4	Huron SD	New Boston
62	15.4	Kalkaska Public Schools	Kalkaska
62	15.4	Woodhaven-Brownstown SD	Brownstown
67	15.3	Beaverton Rural Schools	Beaverton
67	15.3	Godwin Heights Public Schools	Wyoming
67	15.3	Mount Morris Consolidated Schools	Mount Morris
70	15.2	Jackson Public Schools	Jackson
71	15.1	Lakewood Public Schools	Lake Odessa
71	15.1	Reeths-Puffer Schools	Muskegon
73	15.0	Belding Area SD	Belding
73	15.0	Roseville Community Schools	Roseville
75	14.9	Capac Community SD	Capac
75	14.9	Jefferson Schools (Monroe)	Monroe
75	14.9	Lincoln Consolidated SD	Ypsilanti
75	14.9	Ovid-Elsie Area Schools	Elsie
75	14.9	River Rouge SD	River Rouge
75	14.9	Trenton Public Schools	Trenton
81	14.8	Montague Area Public Schools	Montague
82	14.7	Swan Valley SD	Saginaw
83	14.6	Alma Public Schools	Alma
83	14.6	Byron Center Public Schools	Byron Center
83	14.6	Howell Public Schools	Howell
83	14.6	South Lake Schools	St Clair Shores
87	14.5	Berrien Springs Public Schools	Berrien Springs
87	14.5	Southgate Community SD	Southgate
87	14.5	Warren Woods Public Schools	Warren
87	14.5	Waterford SD	Waterford
91	14.4	Caro Community Schools	Caro
91	14.4	Haslett Public Schools	Haslett
91	14.4	Mason Consol Schools (Monroe)	Erie
91	14.4	Mount Pleasant City SD	Mount Pleasant
95	14.3	Battle Creek Public Schools	Battle Creek
95	14.3	Gerrish-Higgins SD	Roscommon
97	14.2	Romulus Community Schools	Romulus

98	14.1	Saginaw Township Community Schools	Saginaw
98	14.1	West Branch-Rose City Area Schools	West Branch
100	14.0	Bloomfield Hills SD	Bloomfield Hls
100	14.0	Morley Stanwood Community Schools	Morley
100	14.0	Perry Public SD	Perry
100	14.0	Wyoming Public Schools	Wyoming
104	13.9	Brandywine Public SD	Niles
104	13.9	Northview Public SD	Grand Rapids
106	13.8	Michigan Center SD	Michigan Center
106	13.8	Tri County Area Schools	Howard City
108	13.7	East Jackson Community Schools	Jackson
108	13.7	Fitzgerald Public Schools	Warren
108	13.7	Millington Community Schools	Millington
111	13.6	Brandon SD	Ortonville
111	13.6	Central Montcalm Public Schools	Stanton
111	13.6	Clarenceville SD	Livonia
111	13.6	Comstock Public Schools	Kalamazoo
111	13.6	East Detroit Public Schools	Eastpointe
111	13.6	Three Rivers Community Schools	Three Rivers
117	13.5	Carman-Ainsworth Community Schools	Flint
117	13.5	Owosso Public Schools	Owosso
119	13.4	Benton Harbor Area Schools	Benton Harbor
119	13.4	Gibraltar SD	Woodhaven
119	13.4	Grant Public SD	Grant
122	13.3	Anchor Bay SD	New Baltimore
122	13.3	Dearborn Heights SD #7	Dearborn Hgts
122	13.3	Kalamazoo Public SD	Kalamazoo
125	13.2	Albion Public Schools	Albion
125	13.2	Mason Public Schools (Ingham)	Mason
125	13.2	Shelby Public Schools	Shelby
128	13.1	Columbia SD	Brooklyn
128	13.1	Holland City SD	Holland
128	13.1	School District of Royal Oak	Royal Oak
128	13.1	Van Buren Public Schools	Belleville
128	13.1	Waverly Community Schools	Lansing
133	13.0	Coopersville Public SD	Coopersville
133	13.0	Houghton Lake Community Schools	Houghton Lake
133	13.0	Swartz Creek Community Schools	Swartz Creek
136	12.9	Huron Valley Schools	Highland
136	12.9	Lake Shore Public Schools (Macomb)	St Clair Shores
138	12.8	Allegan Public Schools	Allegan
138	12.8	Bedford Public Schools	Temperance
138	12.8	Bendle Public Schools	Burton
138	12.8	Brighton Area Schools	Brighton
138	12.8	Kenowa Hills Public Schools	Grand Rapids
138	12.8	Lincoln Park Public Schools	Lincoln Park
138	12.8	Ludington Area SD	Ludington
138	12.8	Maple Valley Schools	Vermontville
138	12.8	Monroe Public Schools	Monroe
138	12.8	Tawas Area Schools	Tawas City
148	12.7	Bay City SD	Bay City
148	12.7	Clarkston Community SD	Clarkston
148	12.7	Montrose Community Schools	Montrose
148	12.7	Northwest Community Schools	Jackson
148	12.7	Port Huron Area SD	Port Huron
148	12.7	Tecumseh Public Schools	Tecumseh
154	12.6	Bronson Community SD	Bronson
154	12.6	Clintondale Community Schools	Clinton Twp
154	12.6	Midland Public Schools	Midland
154	12.6	Pinckney Community Schools	Pinckney
154	12.6	Saint Johns Public Schools	Saint Johns
159	12.5	Farmington Public SD	Farmington
159	12.5	Fenton Area Public Schools	Fenton
159	12.5	Flint City SD	Flint
159	12.5	Forest Hills Public Schools	Grand Rapids
159	12.5	Kentwood Public Schools	Kentwood
164	12.4	Hudsonville Public SD	Hudsonville
164	12.4	Western SD	Parma
166	12.3	Caledonia Community Schools	Caledonia
166	12.3	Cedar Springs Public Schools	Cedar Springs
166	12.3	Grandville Public Schools	Grandville
166	12.3	Melvindale-N Allen Park Schools	Melvindale
166	12.3	Sault Sainte Marie Area Schools	Sault Ste Marie
171	12.2	Dexter Community SD	Dexter
171	12.2	Durand Area Schools	Durand
171	12.2	Fowlerville Community Schools	Fowlerville
171	12.2	Gaylord Community Schools	Gaylord
171	12.2	Menominee Area Public Schools	Menominee
171	12.2	Quincy Community SD	Quincy
177	12.1	Bangor Township Schools	Bay City
177	12.1	Dowagiac Union SD	Dowagiac
177	12.1	Lapeer Community Schools	Lapeer
177	12.1	Linden Community Schools	Linden
177	12.1	Mason County Central Schools	Scottville
177	12.1	Traverse City Area Public Schools	Traverse City
177	12.1	Whitehall District Schools	Whitehall
184	12.0	Cass City Public Schools	Cass City
184	12.0	Coldwater Community Schools	Coldwater
184	12.0	Spring Lake Public Schools	Spring Lake
184	12.0	West Ottawa Public SD	Holland
188	11.9	Airport Community SD	Carleton
188	11.9	Algonac Community SD	Algonac
188	11.9	Allendale Public SD	Allendale
188	11.9	Farwell Area Schools	Farwell
188	11.9	Grosse Pointe Public Schools	Grosse Pointe
188	11.9	Oakridge Public Schools	Muskegon
188	11.9	Standish-Sterling Comm Schools	Standish
195	11.8	Constantine Public SD	Constantine
195	11.8	Croswell-Lexington Comm Schools	Croswell
195	11.8	Walled Lake Consolidated Schools	Walled Lake
198	11.7	East Grand Rapids Public Schools	E Grand Rapids
199	11.6	Ann Arbor Public Schools	Ann Arbor
199	11.6	Detroit City SD	Detroit
199	11.6	Livonia Public Schools	Livonia
199	11.6	Lowell Area Schools	Lowell
199	11.6	North Branch Area Schools	North Branch
199	11.6	Romeo Community Schools	Romeo
199	11.6	South Redford SD	Redford
206	11.5	Highland Park City Schools	Highland Park
206	11.5	Marshall Public Schools	Marshall
206	11.5	Otsego Public Schools	Otsego
209	11.4	Clare Public Schools	Clare
209	11.4	Hartland Consolidated Schools	Hartland
211	11.3	Newaygo Public SD	Newaygo
211	11.3	Orchard View Schools	Muskegon
213	11.2	Berkley SD	Berkley
213	11.2	Cadillac Area Public Schools	Cadillac
213	11.2	Southfield Public SD	Southfield
213	11.2	Utica Community Schools	Sterling Hgts
217	11.1	Escanaba Area Public Schools	Escanaba
217	11.1	Imlay City Community Schools	Imlay City
217	11.1	Kelloggsville Public Schools	Grand Rapids
217	11.1	Lakeview Public Schools (Macomb)	St Clair Shores
221	11.0	Armada Area Schools	Armada
221	11.0	Hastings Area SD	Hastings
221	11.0	Plainwell Community Schools	Plainwell
224	10.9	Benzie County Central Schools	Benzonia
224	10.9	Davison Community Schools	Davison
224	10.9	Delton-Kellogg SD	Delton
224	10.9	South Lyon Community Schools	South Lyon
224	10.9	Sturgis Public Schools	Sturgis
229	10.8	Cheboygan Area Schools	Cheboygan
229	10.8	Dearborn City SD	Dearborn
229	10.8	Lakeshore SD (Berrien)	Stevensville
229	10.8	Oxford Area Community Schools	Oxford
233	10.7	Clio Area SD	Clio
233	10.7	Corunna Public SD	Corunna
233	10.7	Gladstone Area Schools	Gladstone
233	10.7	Mona Shores Public SD	Norton Shores
233	10.7	Plymouth-Canton Community Schools	Plymouth
238	10.6	Alpena Public Schools	Alpena
238	10.6	Williamston Community Schools	Williamston
240	10.5	Birch Run Area SD	Birch Run
240	10.5	Breitung Township Schools	Kingsford
240	10.5	L'anse Creuse Public Schools	Harrison Twp
240	10.5	Rockford Public Schools	Rockford
244	10.4	Lakeview SD (Calhoun)	Battle Creek
244	10.4	Warren Consolidated Schools	Warren
246	10.3	Birmingham City SD	Birmingham
246	10.3	Fraser Public Schools	Fraser
246	10.3	Freeland Community SD	Freeland
246	10.3	Hamilton Community Schools	Hamilton
246	10.3	Okemos Public Schools	Okemos
251	10.2	Flushing Community Schools	Flushing
251	10.2	Hillsdale Community Schools	Hillsdale
251	10.2	Lakeville Community Schools	Otisville
251	10.2	Northville Public Schools	Northville
251	10.2	Pinconning Area Schools	Pinconning
251	10.2	West Bloomfield SD	West Bloomfield
257	10.1	Elk Rapids Schools	Elk Rapids
257	10.1	Grand Haven Area Public Schools	Grand Haven
257	10.1	Paw Paw Public SD	Paw Paw
257	10.1	Saline Area Schools	Saline
257	10.1	Zeeland Public Schools	Zeeland
262	10.0	Beecher Community SD	Flint
262	10.0	Fennville Public Schools	Fennville
262	10.0	Lake Orion Community Schools	Lake Orion
262	10.0	Manistee Area Schools	Manistee
262	10.0	Rochester Community SD	Rochester
267	9.9	East China SD	East China
267	9.9	East Lansing SD	East Lansing
267	9.9	Ferndale Public Schools	Ferndale
267	9.9	Novi Community SD	Novi
271	9.8	Grand Blanc Community Schools	Grand Blanc
271	9.8	Onsted Community Schools	Onsted
271	9.8	Parchment SD	Parchment
271	9.8	Pennfield SD	Battle Creek
275	9.6	Chippewa Valley Schools	Clinton Twp
275	9.6	Kearsley Community Schools	Flint
275	9.6	Napoleon Community Schools	Napoleon
275	9.6	Yale Public Schools	Yale
279	9.5	Dundee Community Schools	Dundee
279	9.5	Goodrich Area Schools	Goodrich
281	9.4	Essexville-Hampton Public Schools	Essexville
282	9.3	Public Schools of Petoskey	Petoskey
283	9.2	Edwardsburg Public Schools	Edwardsburg
283	9.2	Marysville Public Schools	Marysville
285	9.1	Clawson City SD	Clawson
285	9.1	Dewitt Public Schools	Dewitt
285	9.1	Thornapple Kellogg SD	Middleville
288	9.0	Oak Park City SD	Oak Park
289	8.9	Avondale SD	Auburn Hills
289	8.9	Crestwood SD	Dearborn Hgts
289	8.9	Vicksburg Community Schools	Vicksburg
292	8.8	Gull Lake Community Schools	Richland
293	8.7	Portage Public Schools	Portage
294	8.6	Harper Creek Community Schools	Battle Creek
295	8.5	Public Schools of Calumet	Calumet
295	8.5	South Haven Public Schools	South Haven
297	8.4	Almont Community Schools	Almont
297	8.4	Riverview Community SD	Riverview
299	8.3	Saint Joseph Public Schools	Saint Joseph
300	7.9	Grosse Ile Township Schools	Grosse Ile
301	7.8	Hartford Public SD	Hartford
302	7.6	Allen Park Public Schools	Allen Park
303	7.5	Troy SD	Troy
304	7.3	Bangor Public Schools (Van Buren)	Bangor
305	7.1	Hamtramck Public Schools	Hamtramck
306	3.4	Mattawan Consolidated School	Mattawan
307	3.2	Detroit Academy of Arts & Sci	Detroit
308	n/a	Macomb ISD	Clinton Twp

English Language Learner Students

Rank	Percent	District Name	City
1	66.5	Hamtramck Public Schools	Hamtramck
2	51.2	Macomb ISD	Clinton Twp
3	36.0	Dearborn City SD	Dearborn
4	33.4	Godfrey-Lee Public Schools	Wyoming
5	25.2	Warren Consolidated Schools	Warren
6	20.6	Grand Rapids Public Schools	Grand Rapids
7	20.5	Holland City SD	Holland
8	20.1	Farmington Public SD	Farmington
9	15.7	East Lansing SD	East Lansing
10	15.4	Pontiac City SD	Pontiac
11	14.8	Adrian City SD	Adrian
12	13.7	Belding Area SD	Belding
12	13.7	Hartford Public SD	Hartford
14	12.7	West Ottawa Public SD	Holland
15	12.1	Godwin Heights Public Schools	Wyoming
16	11.5	Fennville Public Schools	Fennville
17	11.2	Shelby Public Schools	Shelby
18	10.9	Madison Public Schools (Oakland)	Madison Heights
19	10.4	Grant Public SD	Grant
20	9.7	Lamphere Public Schools	Madison Heights
21	9.0	Lansing Public SD	Lansing
22	8.5	Sparta Area Schools	Sparta
23	8.0	Sturgis Public Schools	Sturgis
24	7.8	Berrien Springs Public Schools	Berrien Springs
24	7.8	Coldwater Community Schools	Coldwater
24	7.8	Hazel Park City SD	Hazel Park
27	7.4	Ann Arbor Public Schools	Ann Arbor
28	7.2	Kalamazoo Public SD	Kalamazoo
29	7.1	Imlay City Community Schools	Imlay City
29	7.1	School District of Ypsilanti	Ypsilanti
31	6.6	Wyoming Public Schools	Wyoming
32	6.5	West Bloomfield SD	West Bloomfield
33	6.3	Rochester Community SD	Rochester
33	6.3	Walled Lake Consolidated Schools	Walled Lake
35	6.2	Oak Park City SD	Oak Park
36	5.7	Bay City SD	Bay City
37	5.3	South Haven Public Schools	South Haven
38	5.2	Saginaw City SD	Saginaw
38	5.2	Southfield Public SD	Southfield
40	4.8	Fitzgerald Public Schools	Warren
41	4.7	Detroit City SD	Detroit
42	4.2	Muskegon City SD	Muskegon
43	4.1	Plymouth-Canton Community Schools	Plymouth
44	4.0	Bloomfield Hills SD	Bloomfield Hls
44	4.0	Crestwood SD	Dearborn Hgts
44	4.0	Melvindale-N Allen Park Schools	Melvindale
47	3.9	Flint City SD	Flint
48	3.6	Lake Orion Community Schools	Lake Orion
49	3.4	Waterford SD	Waterford
50	3.3	Berkley SD	Berkley
50	3.3	Kenowa Hills Public Schools	Grand Rapids
52	3.1	Kentwood Public Schools	Kentwood
53	2.9	Grosse Pointe Public Schools	Grosse Pointe
54	2.8	School District of Royal Oak	Royal Oak
55	2.5	Jackson Public Schools	Jackson
56	2.4	Chippewa Valley Schools	Clinton Twp
57	2.3	Battle Creek Public Schools	Battle Creek
57	2.3	Zeeland Public Schools	Zeeland
59	2.2	Birmingham City SD	Birmingham
59	2.2	L'anse Creuse Public Schools	Harrison Twp
61	2.1	Allendale Public SD	Allendale
61	2.1	Utica Community Schools	Sterling Hgts

63	2.0	Forest Hills Public Schools	Grand Rapids
63	2.0	Saline Area Schools	Saline
65	1.7	Northville Public Schools	Northville
65	1.7	Waverly Community Schools	Lansing
67	1.5	East Detroit Public Schools	Eastpointe
68	1.3	Monroe Public Schools	Monroe
69	1.1	Thornapple Kellogg SD	Middleville
70	1.0	Sault Sainte Marie Area Schools	Sault Ste Marie
70	1.0	Traverse City Area Public Schools	Traverse City
72	0.9	Cedar Springs Public Schools	Cedar Springs
72	0.9	Hamilton Community Schools	Hamilton
74	0.8	Livonia Public Schools	Livonia
74	0.8	Otsego Public Schools	Otsego
76	0.7	Grand Blanc Community Schools	Grand Blanc
77	0.6	Jenison Public Schools	Jenison
77	0.6	Montague Area Public Schools	Montague
79	0.5	Haslett Public Schools	Haslett
79	0.5	Midland Public Schools	Midland
81	0.3	Brandon SD	Ortonville
81	0.3	Carman-Ainsworth Community Schools	Flint
81	0.3	Greenville Public Schools	Greenville
81	0.3	Lakewood Public Schools	Lake Odessa
81	0.3	Marquette Area Public Schools	Marquette
81	0.3	Stockbridge Community Schools	Stockbridge
87	0.2	Allegan Public Schools	Allegan
87	0.2	Harrison Community Schools	Harrison
87	0.2	Port Huron Area SD	Port Huron
87	0.2	Public Schools of Petoskey	Petoskey
87	0.2	Whitehall District Schools	Whitehall
87	0.2	Yale Public Schools	Yale
93	0.1	Birch Run Area SD	Birch Run
93	0.1	Clare Public Schools	Clare
93	0.1	Clio Area SD	Clio
93	0.1	Fenton Area Public Schools	Fenton
93	0.1	Hastings Area SD	Hastings
93	0.1	Hudsonville Public SD	Hudsonville
93	0.1	Lapeer Community Schools	Lapeer
93	0.1	Mount Morris Consolidated Schools	Mount Morris
93	0.1	Mount Pleasant City SD	Mount Pleasant
93	0.1	Oakridge Public Schools	Muskegon
93	0.1	Onsted Community Schools	Onsted
93	0.1	Spring Lake Public Schools	Spring Lake
105	0.0	Bullock Creek SD	Midland
105	0.0	Escanaba Area Public Schools	Escanaba
105	0.0	Linden Community Schools	Linden
105	0.0	Pinconning Area Schools	Pinconning
109	0.0	Beaverton Rural Schools	Beaverton
109	0.0	Farwell Area Schools	Farwell
109	0.0	Montrose Community Schools	Montrose
109	0.0	Standish-Sterling Comm Schools	Standish
113	n/a	Airport Community SD	Carleton
113	n/a	Albion Public Schools	Albion
113	n/a	Algonac Community SD	Algonac
113	n/a	Allen Park Public Schools	Allen Park
113	n/a	Alma Public Schools	Alma
113	n/a	Almont Community Schools	Almont
113	n/a	Alpena Public Schools	Alpena
113	n/a	Anchor Bay SD	New Baltimore
113	n/a	Armada Area Schools	Armada
113	n/a	Avondale SD	Auburn Hills
113	n/a	Bangor Public Schools (Van Buren)	Bangor
113	n/a	Bangor Township Schools	Bay City
113	n/a	Bedford Public Schools	Temperance
113	n/a	Beecher Community SD	Flint
113	n/a	Bendle Public Schools	Burton
113	n/a	Benton Harbor Area Schools	Benton Harbor
113	n/a	Benzie County Central Schools	Benzonia
113	n/a	Big Rapids Public Schools	Big Rapids
113	n/a	Brandywine Public SD	Niles
113	n/a	Breitung Township Schools	Kingsford
113	n/a	Bridgeport-Spaulding Community SD	Bridgeport
113	n/a	Brighton Area Schools	Brighton
113	n/a	Bronson Community SD	Bronson
113	n/a	Buchanan Community Schools	Buchanan
113	n/a	Byron Center Public Schools	Byron Center
113	n/a	Cadillac Area Public Schools	Cadillac
113	n/a	Caledonia Community Schools	Caledonia
113	n/a	Capac Community SD	Capac
113	n/a	Caro Community Schools	Caro
113	n/a	Carrollton SD	Saginaw
113	n/a	Cass City Public Schools	Cass City
113	n/a	Center Line Public Schools	Center Line
113	n/a	Central Montcalm Public Schools	Stanton
113	n/a	Charlotte Public Schools	Charlotte
113	n/a	Cheboygan Area Schools	Cheboygan
113	n/a	Chelsea SD	Chelsea
113	n/a	Chesaning Union Schools	Chesaning
113	n/a	Chippewa Hills SD	Remus
113	n/a	Clarenceville SD	Livonia
113	n/a	Clarkston Community SD	Clarkston
113	n/a	Clawson City SD	Clawson
113	n/a	Clintondale Community Schools	Clinton Twp
113	n/a	Coloma Community Schools	Coloma
113	n/a	Columbia SD	Brooklyn
113	n/a	Comstock Park Public Schools	Comstock Park
113	n/a	Comstock Public Schools	Kalamazoo
113	n/a	Constantine Public SD	Constantine
113	n/a	Coopersville Public SD	Coopersville
113	n/a	Corunna Public SD	Corunna
113	n/a	Crawford Ausable Schools	Grayling
113	n/a	Croswell-Lexington Comm Schools	Croswell
113	n/a	Davison Community Schools	Davison
113	n/a	Dearborn Heights SD #7	Dearborn Hgts
113	n/a	Delton-Kellogg SD	Delton
113	n/a	Detroit Academy of Arts & Sci	Detroit
113	n/a	Dewitt Public Schools	Dewitt
113	n/a	Dexter Community SD	Dexter
113	n/a	Dowagiac Union SD	Dowagiac
113	n/a	Dundee Community Schools	Dundee
113	n/a	Durand Area Schools	Durand
113	n/a	East China SD	East China
113	n/a	East Grand Rapids Public Schools	E Grand Rapids
113	n/a	East Jackson Community Schools	Jackson
113	n/a	Eaton Rapids Public Schools	Eaton Rapids
113	n/a	Edwardsburg Public Schools	Edwardsburg
113	n/a	Elk Rapids Schools	Elk Rapids
113	n/a	Essexville-Hampton Public Schools	Essexville
113	n/a	Ferndale Public Schools	Ferndale
113	n/a	Flat Rock Community Schools	Flat Rock
113	n/a	Flushing Community Schools	Flushing
113	n/a	Fowlerville Community Schools	Fowlerville
113	n/a	Fraser Public Schools	Fraser
113	n/a	Freeland Community SD	Freeland
113	n/a	Fremont Public SD	Fremont
113	n/a	Fruitport Community Schools	Fruitport
113	n/a	Garden City SD	Garden City
113	n/a	Gaylord Community Schools	Gaylord
113	n/a	Gerrish-Higgins SD	Roscommon
113	n/a	Gibraltar SD	Woodhaven
113	n/a	Gladstone Area Schools	Gladstone
113	n/a	Gladwin Community Schools	Gladwin
113	n/a	Goodrich Area Schools	Goodrich
113	n/a	Grand Haven Area Public Schools	Grand Haven
113	n/a	Grand Ledge Public Schools	Grand Ledge
113	n/a	Grandville Public Schools	Grandville
113	n/a	Grosse Ile Township Schools	Grosse Ile
113	n/a	Gull Lake Community Schools	Richland
113	n/a	Harper Creek Community Schools	Battle Creek
113	n/a	Hartland Consolidated Schools	Hartland
113	n/a	Highland Park City Schools	Highland Park
113	n/a	Hillsdale Community Schools	Hillsdale
113	n/a	Holly Area SD	Holly
113	n/a	Holt Public Schools	Holt
113	n/a	Houghton Lake Community Schools	Houghton Lake
113	n/a	Howell Public Schools	Howell
113	n/a	Huron SD	New Boston
113	n/a	Huron Valley Schools	Highland
113	n/a	Ida Public SD	Ida
113	n/a	Ionia Public Schools	Ionia
113	n/a	Jefferson Schools (Monroe)	Monroe
113	n/a	Kalkaska Public Schools	Kalkaska
113	n/a	Kearsley Community Schools	Flint
113	n/a	Kelloggsville Public Schools	Grand Rapids
113	n/a	Lake Shore Public Schools (Macomb)	St Clair Shores
113	n/a	Lakeshore SD (Berrien)	Stevensville
113	n/a	Lakeview Comm Schools (Montcalm)	Lakeview
113	n/a	Lakeview Public Schools (Macomb)	St Clair Shores
113	n/a	Lakeview SD (Calhoun)	Battle Creek
113	n/a	Lakeville Community Schools	Otisville
113	n/a	Lincoln Consolidated SD	Ypsilanti
113	n/a	Lincoln Park Public Schools	Lincoln Park
113	n/a	Lowell Area Schools	Lowell
113	n/a	Ludington Area SD	Ludington
113	n/a	Manistee Area Schools	Manistee
113	n/a	Maple Valley Schools	Vermontville
113	n/a	Marshall Public Schools	Marshall
113	n/a	Marysville Public Schools	Marysville
113	n/a	Mason Consol Schools (Monroe)	Erie
113	n/a	Mason County Central Schools	Scottville
113	n/a	Mason Public Schools (Ingham)	Mason
113	n/a	Mattawan Consolidated School	Mattawan
113	n/a	Menominee Area Public Schools	Menominee
113	n/a	Meridian Public Schools	Sanford
113	n/a	Michigan Center SD	Michigan Center
113	n/a	Milan Area Schools	Milan
113	n/a	Millington Community Schools	Millington
113	n/a	Mona Shores Public SD	Norton Shores
113	n/a	Morley Stanwood Community Schools	Morley
113	n/a	Mount Clemens Community SD	Mount Clemens
113	n/a	Muskegon Heights SD	Muskegon Hgts
113	n/a	Napoleon Community Schools	Napoleon
113	n/a	Newaygo Public SD	Newaygo
113	n/a	Niles Community SD	Niles
113	n/a	North Branch Area Schools	North Branch
113	n/a	Northview Public SD	Grand Rapids
113	n/a	Northwest Community Schools	Jackson
113	n/a	Novi Community SD	Novi
113	n/a	Okemos Public Schools	Okemos
113	n/a	Orchard View Schools	Muskegon
113	n/a	Oscoda Area Schools	Oscoda
113	n/a	Ovid-Elsie Area Schools	Elsie
113	n/a	Owosso Public Schools	Owosso
113	n/a	Oxford Area Community Schools	Oxford
113	n/a	Parchment SD	Parchment
113	n/a	Paw Paw Public SD	Paw Paw
113	n/a	Pennfield SD	Battle Creek
113	n/a	Perry Public SD	Perry
113	n/a	Pinckney Community Schools	Pinckney
113	n/a	Plainwell Community Schools	Plainwell
113	n/a	Portage Public Schools	Portage
113	n/a	Portland Public SD	Portland
113	n/a	Public Schools of Calumet	Calumet
113	n/a	Quincy Community SD	Quincy
113	n/a	Redford Union SD	Redford
113	n/a	Reed City Area Public Schools	Reed City
113	n/a	Reeths-Puffer Schools	Muskegon
113	n/a	Richmond Community Schools	Richmond
113	n/a	River Rouge SD	River Rouge
113	n/a	Riverview Community SD	Riverview
113	n/a	Rockford Public Schools	Rockford
113	n/a	Romeo Community Schools	Romeo
113	n/a	Romulus Community Schools	Romulus
113	n/a	Roseville Community Schools	Roseville
113	n/a	Saginaw Township Community Schools	Saginaw
113	n/a	Saint Johns Public Schools	Saint Johns
113	n/a	Saint Joseph Public Schools	Saint Joseph
113	n/a	Shepherd Public SD	Shepherd
113	n/a	South Lake Schools	St Clair Shores
113	n/a	South Lyon Community Schools	South Lyon
113	n/a	South Redford SD	Redford
113	n/a	Southgate Community SD	Southgate
113	n/a	Swan Valley SD	Saginaw
113	n/a	Swartz Creek Community Schools	Swartz Creek
113	n/a	Tawas Area Schools	Tawas City
113	n/a	Taylor SD	Taylor
113	n/a	Tecumseh Public Schools	Tecumseh
113	n/a	Three Rivers Community Schools	Three Rivers
113	n/a	Trenton Public Schools	Trenton
113	n/a	Tri County Area Schools	Howard City
113	n/a	Troy SD	Troy
113	n/a	Van Buren Public Schools	Belleville
113	n/a	Van Dyke Public Schools	Warren
113	n/a	Vassar Public Schools	Vassar
113	n/a	Vicksburg Community Schools	Vicksburg
113	n/a	Warren Woods Public Schools	Warren
113	n/a	Washtenaw ISD	Ann Arbor
113	n/a	Wayland Union Schools	Wayland
113	n/a	Wayne-Westland Community SD	Westland
113	n/a	West Branch-Rose City Area Schools	West Branch
113	n/a	Western SD	Parma
113	n/a	Westwood Community Schools	Dearborn Hgts
113	n/a	White Cloud Public Schools	White Cloud
113	n/a	Williamston Community Schools	Williamston
113	n/a	Willow Run Community Schools	Ypsilanti
113	n/a	Woodhaven-Brownstown SD	Brownstown
113	n/a	Wyandotte City SD	Wyandotte

Migrant Students

Rank	Percent	District Name	City
1	n/a	Adrian City SD	Adrian
1	n/a	Airport Community SD	Carleton
1	n/a	Albion Public Schools	Albion
1	n/a	Algonac Community SD	Algonac
1	n/a	Allegan Public Schools	Allegan
1	n/a	Allen Park Public Schools	Allen Park
1	n/a	Allendale Public SD	Allendale
1	n/a	Alma Public Schools	Alma
1	n/a	Almont Community Schools	Almont
1	n/a	Alpena Public Schools	Alpena
1	n/a	Anchor Bay SD	New Baltimore
1	n/a	Ann Arbor Public Schools	Ann Arbor
1	n/a	Armada Area Schools	Armada
1	n/a	Avondale SD	Auburn Hills
1	n/a	Bangor Public Schools (Van Buren)	Bangor
1	n/a	Bangor Township Schools	Bay City
1	n/a	Battle Creek Public Schools	Battle Creek
1	n/a	Bay City SD	Bay City
1	n/a	Beaverton Rural Schools	Beaverton
1	n/a	Bedford Public Schools	Temperance
1	n/a	Beecher Community SD	Flint
1	n/a	Belding Area SD	Belding
1	n/a	Bendle Public Schools	Burton
1	n/a	Benton Harbor Area Schools	Benton Harbor
1	n/a	Benzie County Central Schools	Benzonia
1	n/a	Berkley SD	Berkley

1 n/a Berrien Springs Public Schools Berrien Springs
1 n/a Big Rapids Public Schools Big Rapids
1 n/a Birch Run Area SD Birch Run
1 n/a Birmingham City SD Birmingham
1 n/a Bloomfield Hills SD Bloomfield Hls
1 n/a Brandon SD Ortonville
1 n/a Brandywine Public SD Niles
1 n/a Breitung Township Schools Kingsford
1 n/a Bridgeport-Spaulding Community SD Bridgeport
1 n/a Brighton Area Schools Brighton
1 n/a Bronson Community SD Bronson
1 n/a Buchanan Community Schools Buchanan
1 n/a Bullock Creek SD Midland
1 n/a Byron Center Public Schools Byron Center
1 n/a Cadillac Area Public Schools Cadillac
1 n/a Caledonia Community Schools Caledonia
1 n/a Capac Community SD Capac
1 n/a Carman-Ainsworth Community Schools
Flint
1 n/a Caro Community Schools Caro
1 n/a Carrollton SD Saginaw
1 n/a Cass City Public Schools Cass City
1 n/a Cedar Springs Public Schools Cedar Springs
1 n/a Center Line Public Schools Center Line
1 n/a Central Montcalm Public Schools Stanton
1 n/a Charlotte Public Schools Charlotte
1 n/a Cheboygan Area Schools Cheboygan
1 n/a Chelsea SD Chelsea
1 n/a Chesaning Union Schools Chesaning
1 n/a Chippewa Hills SD Remus
1 n/a Chippewa Valley Schools Clinton Twp
1 n/a Clare Public Schools Clare
1 n/a Clarenceville SD Livonia
1 n/a Clarkston Community SD Clarkston
1 n/a Clawson City SD Clawson
1 n/a Clintondale Community Schools Clinton Twp
1 n/a Clio Area SD Clio
1 n/a Coldwater Community Schools Coldwater
1 n/a Coloma Community Schools Coloma
1 n/a Columbia SD Brooklyn
1 n/a Comstock Park Public Schools Comstock Park
1 n/a Comstock Public Schools Kalamazoo
1 n/a Constantine Public SD Constantine
1 n/a Coopersville Public SD Coopersville
1 n/a Corunna Public SD Corunna
1 n/a Crawford Ausable Schools Grayling
1 n/a Crestwood SD Dearborn Hgts
1 n/a Croswell-Lexington Comm Schools Croswell
1 n/a Davison Community Schools Davison
1 n/a Dearborn City SD Dearborn
1 n/a Dearborn Heights SD #7 Dearborn Hgts
1 n/a Delton-Kellogg SD Delton
1 n/a Detroit Academy of Arts & Sci Detroit
1 n/a Detroit City SD Detroit
1 n/a Dewitt Public Schools Dewitt
1 n/a Dexter Community SD Dexter
1 n/a Dowagiac Union SD Dowagiac
1 n/a Dundee Community Schools Dundee
1 n/a Durand Area Schools Durand
1 n/a East China SD East China
1 n/a East Detroit Public Schools Eastpointe
1 n/a East Grand Rapids Public Schools E Grand Rapids
1 n/a East Jackson Community Schools Jackson
1 n/a East Lansing SD East Lansing
1 n/a Eaton Rapids Public Schools Eaton Rapids
1 n/a Edwardsburg Public Schools Edwardsburg
1 n/a Elk Rapids Schools Elk Rapids
1 n/a Escanaba Area Public Schools Escanaba
1 n/a Essexville-Hampton Public Schools Essexville
1 n/a Farmington Public SD Farmington
1 n/a Farwell Area Schools Farwell
1 n/a Fennville Public Schools Fennville
1 n/a Fenton Area Public Schools Fenton
1 n/a Ferndale Public Schools Ferndale
1 n/a Fitzgerald Public Schools Warren
1 n/a Flat Rock Community Schools Flat Rock
1 n/a Flint City SD Flint
1 n/a Flushing Community Schools Flushing
1 n/a Forest Hills Public Schools Grand Rapids
1 n/a Fowlerville Community Schools Fowlerville
1 n/a Fraser Public Schools Fraser
1 n/a Freeland Community SD Freeland
1 n/a Fremont Public SD Fremont
1 n/a Fruitport Community Schools Fruitport
1 n/a Garden City SD Garden City
1 n/a Gaylord Community Schools Gaylord
1 n/a Gerrish-Higgins SD Roscommon
1 n/a Gibraltar SD Woodhaven
1 n/a Gladstone Area Schools Gladstone
1 n/a Gladwin Community Schools Gladwin
1 n/a Godfrey-Lee Public Schools Wyoming
1 n/a Godwin Heights Public Schools Wyoming
1 n/a Goodrich Area Schools Goodrich
1 n/a Grand Blanc Community Schools Grand Blanc
1 n/a Grand Haven Area Public Schools Grand Haven
1 n/a Grand Ledge Public Schools Grand Ledge
1 n/a Grand Rapids Public Schools Grand Rapids
1 n/a Grandville Public Schools Grandville
1 n/a Grant Public SD Grant
1 n/a Greenville Public Schools Greenville
1 n/a Grosse Ile Township Schools Grosse Ile
1 n/a Grosse Pointe Public Schools Grosse Pointe
1 n/a Gull Lake Community Schools Richland
1 n/a Hamilton Community Schools Hamilton
1 n/a Hamtramck Public Schools Hamtramck
1 n/a Harper Creek Community Schools Battle Creek
1 n/a Harrison Community Schools Harrison
1 n/a Hartford Public SD Hartford
1 n/a Hartland Consolidated Schools Hartland
1 n/a Haslett Public Schools Haslett
1 n/a Hastings Area SD Hastings
1 n/a Hazel Park City SD Hazel Park
1 n/a Highland Park City Schools Highland Park
1 n/a Hillsdale Community Schools Hillsdale
1 n/a Holland City SD Holland
1 n/a Holly Area SD Holly
1 n/a Holt Public Schools Holt
1 n/a Houghton Lake Community Schools Houghton Lake
1 n/a Howell Public Schools Howell
1 n/a Hudsonville Public SD Hudsonville
1 n/a Huron SD New Boston
1 n/a Huron Valley Schools Highland
1 n/a Ida Public SD Ida
1 n/a Imlay City Community Schools Imlay City
1 n/a Ionia Public Schools Ionia
1 n/a Jackson Public Schools Jackson
1 n/a Jefferson Schools (Monroe) Monroe
1 n/a Jenison Public Schools Jenison
1 n/a Kalamazoo Public SD Kalamazoo
1 n/a Kalkaska Public Schools Kalkaska
1 n/a Kearsley Community Schools Flint
1 n/a Kelloggsville Public Schools Grand Rapids
1 n/a Kenowa Hills Public Schools Grand Rapids
1 n/a Kentwood Public Schools Kentwood
1 n/a L'anse Creuse Public Schools Harrison Twp
1 n/a Lake Orion Community Schools Lake Orion
1 n/a Lake Shore Public Schools (Macomb) St Clair Shores
1 n/a Lakeshore SD (Berrien) Stevensville
1 n/a Lakeview Comm Schools (Montcalm) Lakeview
1 n/a Lakeview Public Schools (Macomb) St Clair Shores
1 n/a Lakeview SD (Calhoun) Battle Creek
1 n/a Lakeville Community Schools Otisville
1 n/a Lakewood Public Schools Lake Odessa
1 n/a Lamphere Public Schools Madison Heights
1 n/a Lansing Public SD Lansing
1 n/a Lapeer Community Schools Lapeer
1 n/a Lincoln Consolidated SD Ypsilanti
1 n/a Lincoln Park Public Schools Lincoln Park
1 n/a Linden Community Schools Linden
1 n/a Livonia Public Schools Livonia
1 n/a Lowell Area Schools Lowell
1 n/a Ludington Area SD Ludington
1 n/a Macomb ISD Clinton Twp
1 n/a Madison Public Schools (Oakland) Madison Heights
1 n/a Manistee Area Schools Manistee
1 n/a Maple Valley Schools Vermontville
1 n/a Marquette Area Public Schools Marquette
1 n/a Marshall Public Schools Marshall
1 n/a Marysville Public Schools Marysville
1 n/a Mason Consol Schools (Monroe) Erie
1 n/a Mason County Central Schools Scottville
1 n/a Mason Public Schools (Ingham) Mason
1 n/a Mattawan Consolidated School Mattawan
1 n/a Melvindale-N Allen Park Schools Melvindale
1 n/a Menominee Area Public Schools Menominee
1 n/a Meridian Public Schools Sanford
1 n/a Michigan Center SD Michigan Center
1 n/a Midland Public Schools Midland
1 n/a Milan Area Schools Milan
1 n/a Millington Community Schools Millington
1 n/a Mona Shores Public SD Norton Shores
1 n/a Monroe Public Schools Monroe
1 n/a Montague Area Public Schools Montague
1 n/a Montrose Community Schools Montrose
1 n/a Morley Stanwood Community Schools Morley
1 n/a Mount Clemens Community SD Mount Clemens
1 n/a Mount Morris Consolidated Schools Mount Morris
1 n/a Mount Pleasant City SD Mount Pleasant
1 n/a Muskegon City SD Muskegon
1 n/a Muskegon Heights SD Muskegon Hgts
1 n/a Napoleon Community Schools Napoleon
1 n/a Newaygo Public SD Newaygo
1 n/a Niles Community SD Niles
1 n/a North Branch Area Schools North Branch
1 n/a Northview Public SD Grand Rapids
1 n/a Northville Public Schools Northville
1 n/a Northwest Community Schools Jackson
1 n/a Novi Community SD Novi
1 n/a Oak Park City SD Oak Park
1 n/a Oakridge Public Schools Muskegon
1 n/a Okemos Public Schools Okemos
1 n/a Onsted Community Schools Onsted
1 n/a Orchard View Schools Muskegon
1 n/a Oscoda Area Schools Oscoda
1 n/a Otsego Public Schools Otsego
1 n/a Ovid-Elsie Area Schools Elsie
1 n/a Owosso Public Schools Owosso
1 n/a Oxford Area Community Schools Oxford
1 n/a Parchment SD Parchment
1 n/a Paw Paw Public SD Paw Paw
1 n/a Pennfield SD Battle Creek
1 n/a Perry Public SD Perry
1 n/a Pinckney Community Schools Pinckney
1 n/a Pinconning Area Schools Pinconning
1 n/a Plainwell Community Schools Plainwell
1 n/a Plymouth-Canton Community Schools Plymouth
1 n/a Pontiac City SD Pontiac
1 n/a Port Huron Area SD Port Huron
1 n/a Portage Public Schools Portage
1 n/a Portland Public SD Portland
1 n/a Public Schools of Calumet Calumet
1 n/a Public Schools of Petoskey Petoskey
1 n/a Quincy Community SD Quincy
1 n/a Redford Union SD Redford
1 n/a Reed City Area Public Schools Reed City
1 n/a Reeths-Puffer Schools Muskegon
1 n/a Richmond Community Schools Richmond
1 n/a River Rouge SD River Rouge
1 n/a Riverview Community SD Riverview
1 n/a Rochester Community SD Rochester
1 n/a Rockford Public Schools Rockford
1 n/a Romeo Community Schools Romeo
1 n/a Romulus Community Schools Romulus
1 n/a Roseville Community Schools Roseville
1 n/a Saginaw City SD Saginaw
1 n/a Saginaw Township Community Schools
Saginaw
1 n/a Saint Johns Public Schools Saint Johns
1 n/a Saint Joseph Public Schools Saint Joseph
1 n/a Saline Area Schools Saline
1 n/a Sault Sainte Marie Area Schools Sault Ste Marie
1 n/a School District of Royal Oak Royal Oak
1 n/a School District of Ypsilanti Ypsilanti
1 n/a Shelby Public Schools Shelby
1 n/a Shepherd Public SD Shepherd
1 n/a South Haven Public Schools South Haven
1 n/a South Lake Schools St Clair Shores
1 n/a South Lyon Community Schools South Lyon
1 n/a South Redford SD Redford
1 n/a Southfield Public SD Southfield
1 n/a Southgate Community SD Southgate
1 n/a Sparta Area Schools Sparta
1 n/a Spring Lake Public Schools Spring Lake
1 n/a Standish-Sterling Comm Schools Standish
1 n/a Stockbridge Community Schools Stockbridge
1 n/a Sturgis Public Schools Sturgis
1 n/a Swan Valley SD Saginaw
1 n/a Swartz Creek Community Schools Swartz Creek
1 n/a Tawas Area Schools Tawas City
1 n/a Taylor SD Taylor
1 n/a Tecumseh Public Schools Tecumseh
1 n/a Thornapple Kellogg SD Middleville
1 n/a Three Rivers Community Schools Three Rivers
1 n/a Traverse City Area Public Schools Traverse City
1 n/a Trenton Public Schools Trenton
1 n/a Tri County Area Schools Howard City
1 n/a Troy SD Troy
1 n/a Utica Community Schools Sterling Hgts
1 n/a Van Buren Public Schools Belleville
1 n/a Van Dyke Public Schools Warren
1 n/a Vassar Public Schools Vassar
1 n/a Vicksburg Community Schools Vicksburg
1 n/a Walled Lake Consolidated Schools Walled Lake
1 n/a Warren Consolidated Schools Warren
1 n/a Warren Woods Public Schools Warren
1 n/a Washtenaw ISD Ann Arbor
1 n/a Waterford SD Waterford
1 n/a Waverly Community Schools Lansing
1 n/a Wayland Union Schools Wayland
1 n/a Wayne-Westland Community SD Westland
1 n/a West Bloomfield SD West Bloomfield
1 n/a West Branch-Rose City Area Schools West Branch
1 n/a West Ottawa Public SD Holland
1 n/a Western SD Parma
1 n/a Westwood Community Schools Dearborn Hgts
1 n/a White Cloud Public Schools White Cloud
1 n/a Whitehall District Schools Whitehall
1 n/a Williamston Community Schools Williamston

1	n/a	Willow Run Community Schools	Ypsilanti
1	n/a	Woodhaven-Brownstown SD	Brownstown
1	n/a	Wyandotte City SD	Wyandotte
1	n/a	Wyoming Public Schools	Wyoming
1	n/a	Yale Public Schools	Yale
1	n/a	Zeeland Public Schools	Zeeland

Students Eligible for Free Lunch

Rank	Percent	District Name	City
1	79.6	Muskegon Heights SD	Muskegon Hgts
2	77.1	Hamtramck Public Schools	Hamtramck
3	75.7	Benton Harbor Area Schools	Benton Harbor
4	71.1	River Rouge SD	River Rouge
5	69.1	Highland Park City Schools	Highland Park
6	68.4	Beecher Community SD	Flint
7	62.7	Pontiac City SD	Pontiac
8	61.7	Grand Rapids Public Schools	Grand Rapids
9	61.5	Flint City SD	Flint
10	60.2	Saginaw City SD	Saginaw
11	59.7	Westwood Community Schools	Dearborn Hgts
12	57.9	Bangor Public Schools (Van Buren)	Bangor
13	55.8	Detroit City SD	Detroit
14	55.5	Godfrey-Lee Public Schools	Wyoming
15	53.7	Muskegon City SD	Muskegon
16	53.5	Jackson Public Schools	Jackson
17	51.3	Mount Clemens Community SD	Mount Clemens
18	50.8	Kalamazoo Public SD	Kalamazoo
19	50.7	Albion Public Schools	Albion
20	49.7	Willow Run Community Schools	Ypsilanti
21	49.1	Van Dyke Public Schools	Warren
22	48.4	Battle Creek Public Schools	Battle Creek
22	48.4	Bridgeport-Spaulding Community SD	Bridgeport
24	48.3	Lansing Public SD	Lansing
25	47.9	White Cloud Public Schools	White Cloud
26	47.1	Harrison Community Schools	Harrison
27	46.9	Godwin Heights Public Schools	Wyoming
28	44.7	School District of Ypsilanti	Ypsilanti
29	43.2	Farwell Area Schools	Farwell
30	42.8	Oscoda Area Schools	Oscoda
31	41.6	Chippewa Hills SD	Remus
32	40.0	Orchard View Schools	Muskegon
33	38.6	Hazel Park City SD	Hazel Park
34	38.4	Carman-Ainsworth Community Schools	Flint
35	37.8	Houghton Lake Community Schools	Houghton Lake
36	37.6	Adrian City SD	Adrian
37	37.5	Public Schools of Calumet	Calumet
38	36.9	Detroit Academy of Arts & Sci	Detroit
39	36.7	Romulus Community Schools	Romulus
40	36.4	Oak Park City SD	Oak Park
41	36.3	Morley Stanwood Community Schools	Morley
42	34.8	Hartford Public SD	Hartford
42	34.8	Sturgis Public Schools	Sturgis
44	34.2	Bendle Public Schools	Burton
45	33.9	Crawford Ausable Schools	Grayling
45	33.9	Standish-Sterling Comm Schools	Standish
47	33.8	Kalkaska Public Schools	Kalkaska
48	33.5	Holland City SD	Holland
49	33.4	Berrien Springs Public Schools	Berrien Springs
50	32.9	Dowagiac Union SD	Dowagiac
50	32.9	Shelby Public Schools	Shelby
52	32.6	Big Rapids Public Schools	Big Rapids
53	32.4	Dearborn City SD	Dearborn
53	32.4	Escanaba Area Public Schools	Escanaba
55	32.2	Comstock Public Schools	Kalamazoo
56	32.1	West Branch-Rose City Area Schools	West Branch
57	31.7	Kelloggsville Public Schools	Grand Rapids
58	31.5	Mount Morris Consolidated Schools	Mount Morris
59	31.4	Carrollton SD	Saginaw
60	31.2	South Haven Public Schools	South Haven
61	31.0	Niles Community SD	Niles
62	30.6	Mason County Central Schools	Scottville
63	30.4	Fennville Public Schools	Fennville
63	30.4	Gerrish-Higgins SD	Roscommon
65	30.3	Melvindale-N Allen Park Schools	Melvindale
65	30.3	Oakridge Public Schools	Muskegon
67	29.9	Taylor SD	Taylor
68	29.8	Hillsdale Community Schools	Hillsdale
69	29.7	Cheboygan Area Schools	Cheboygan
70	29.5	Ionia Public Schools	Ionia
71	29.4	Fitzgerald Public Schools	Warren
72	29.2	Beaverton Rural Schools	Beaverton
73	29.0	East Jackson Community Schools	Jackson
74	28.9	Lakeview Comm Schools (Montcalm)	Lakeview
75	28.8	Bronson Community SD	Bronson
76	28.7	Alma Public Schools	Alma
76	28.7	Clare Public Schools	Clare
78	28.6	Reed City Area Public Schools	Reed City
79	28.5	Coloma Community Schools	Coloma
79	28.5	Grant Public SD	Grant
81	28.3	Lincoln Park Public Schools	Lincoln Park
82	28.1	Madison Public Schools (Oakland)	Madison Heights
82	28.1	Montague Area Public Schools	Montague
84	28.0	Bay City SD	Bay City
85	27.8	Cadillac Area Public Schools	Cadillac
86	27.7	Gladwin Community Schools	Gladwin
87	27.4	Buchanan Community Schools	Buchanan
88	27.2	Alpena Public Schools	Alpena
88	27.2	Belding Area SD	Belding
88	27.2	Three Rivers Community Schools	Three Rivers
91	27.1	Port Huron Area SD	Port Huron
92	26.8	Central Montcalm Public Schools	Stanton
93	26.6	Pinconning Area Schools	Pinconning
94	26.5	Fremont Public SD	Fremont
94	26.5	Wyoming Public Schools	Wyoming
96	26.3	Benzie County Central Schools	Benzonia
96	26.3	Owosso Public Schools	Owosso
98	26.2	Maple Valley Schools	Vermontville
98	26.2	Montrose Community Schools	Montrose
100	26.1	Parchment SD	Parchment
101	25.9	East Detroit Public Schools	Eastpointe
102	25.7	Dearborn Heights SD #7	Dearborn Hgts
102	25.7	Gaylord Community Schools	Gaylord
102	25.7	Wayne-Westland Community SD	Westland
105	25.6	Paw Paw Public SD	Paw Paw
106	24.9	Michigan Center SD	Michigan Center
107	24.8	Tawas Area Schools	Tawas City
108	24.7	Manistee Area Schools	Manistee
108	24.7	Meridian Public Schools	Sanford
110	23.9	Caro Community Schools	Caro
111	23.8	Southfield Public SD	Southfield
112	23.7	Kentwood Public Schools	Kentwood
112	23.7	Sault Sainte Marie Area Schools	Sault Ste Marie
114	23.6	Center Line Public Schools	Center Line
115	23.5	Ferndale Public Schools	Ferndale
115	23.5	Newaygo Public SD	Newaygo
117	23.4	Roseville Community Schools	Roseville
118	23.1	Gladstone Area Schools	Gladstone
119	23.0	Cass City Public Schools	Cass City
120	22.9	Brandywine Public SD	Niles
120	22.9	Whitehall District Schools	Whitehall
122	22.8	Monroe Public Schools	Monroe
122	22.8	Redford Union SD	Redford
124	22.6	Vassar Public Schools	Vassar
124	22.6	Western SD	Parma
126	22.4	Bullock Creek SD	Midland
126	22.4	Delton-Kellogg SD	Delton
126	22.4	Imlay City Community Schools	Imlay City
129	22.3	Northwest Community Schools	Jackson
130	22.1	Bangor Township Schools	Bay City
131	21.6	Chesaning Union Schools	Chesaning
132	21.5	Fruitport Community Schools	Fruitport
133	21.4	Allegan Public Schools	Allegan
134	21.3	West Ottawa Public SD	Holland
135	21.2	Ludington Area SD	Ludington
135	21.2	Van Buren Public Schools	Belleville
137	20.7	Clintondale Community Schools	Clinton Twp
138	20.4	Saginaw Township Community Schools	Saginaw
139	20.2	Mount Pleasant City SD	Mount Pleasant
140	20.1	Lakewood Public Schools	Lake Odessa
140	20.1	Menominee Area Public Schools	Menominee
142	19.9	Charlotte Public Schools	Charlotte
142	19.9	Sparta Area Schools	Sparta
142	19.9	Stockbridge Community Schools	Stockbridge
145	19.8	Constantine Public SD	Constantine
146	19.7	Cedar Springs Public Schools	Cedar Springs
146	19.7	Mason Consol Schools (Monroe)	Erie
148	19.6	Reeths-Puffer Schools	Muskegon
149	19.5	Greenville Public Schools	Greenville
149	19.5	Lakeville Community Schools	Otisville
151	19.4	Croswell-Lexington Comm Schools	Croswell
152	19.3	Kearsley Community Schools	Flint
153	19.1	Shepherd Public SD	Shepherd
153	19.1	Tri County Area Schools	Howard City
155	19.0	Millington Community Schools	Millington
156	18.6	Coldwater Community Schools	Coldwater
156	18.6	Durand Area Schools	Durand
156	18.6	Flat Rock Community Schools	Flat Rock
156	18.6	Lamphere Public Schools	Madison Heights
160	18.5	North Branch Area Schools	North Branch
161	18.3	Clarenceville SD	Livonia
162	18.2	Wyandotte City SD	Wyandotte
163	18.1	Airport Community SD	Carleton
164	17.9	Lincoln Consolidated SD	Ypsilanti
165	17.7	Ovid-Elsie Area Schools	Elsie
166	17.5	Perry Public SD	Perry
167	17.4	Clio Area SD	Clio
167	17.4	Corunna Public SD	Corunna
169	17.0	Crestwood SD	Dearborn Hgts
170	16.9	Essexville-Hampton Public Schools	Essexville
170	16.9	Holly Area SD	Holly
172	16.8	Birch Run Area SD	Birch Run
173	16.5	Coopersville Public SD	Coopersville
173	16.5	Traverse City Area Public Schools	Traverse City
173	16.5	Wayland Union Schools	Wayland
176	16.4	Kenowa Hills Public Schools	Grand Rapids
177	16.3	Pennfield SD	Battle Creek
178	16.2	Quincy Community SD	Quincy
179	16.1	Breitung Township Schools	Kingsford
180	16.0	Yale Public Schools	Yale
181	15.8	Edwardsburg Public Schools	Edwardsburg
181	15.8	Waverly Community Schools	Lansing
183	15.7	Davison Community Schools	Davison
183	15.7	Harper Creek Community Schools	Battle Creek
185	15.6	Public Schools of Petoskey	Petoskey
186	15.5	Elk Rapids Schools	Elk Rapids
187	15.2	Dundee Community Schools	Dundee
187	15.2	Warren Consolidated Schools	Warren
189	14.9	Lapeer Community Schools	Lapeer
190	14.8	Algonac Community SD	Algonac
190	14.8	Capac Community SD	Capac
190	14.8	Jefferson Schools (Monroe)	Monroe
190	14.8	Swan Valley SD	Saginaw
194	14.7	East Lansing SD	East Lansing
195	14.6	Marquette Area Public Schools	Marquette
196	14.3	South Redford SD	Redford
197	14.2	Hastings Area SD	Hastings
198	13.6	Eaton Rapids Public Schools	Eaton Rapids
198	13.6	Woodhaven-Brownstown SD	Brownstown
200	13.5	Otsego Public Schools	Otsego
201	13.4	Lakeview SD (Calhoun)	Battle Creek
201	13.4	Waterford SD	Waterford
203	13.2	Napoleon Community Schools	Napoleon
204	12.7	Plainwell Community Schools	Plainwell
205	12.6	Columbia SD	Brooklyn
206	12.5	Southgate Community SD	Southgate
207	12.3	Grand Haven Area Public Schools	Grand Haven
207	12.3	Marshall Public Schools	Marshall
209	12.2	Huron SD	New Boston
209	12.2	Swartz Creek Community Schools	Swartz Creek
211	12.1	Milan Area Schools	Milan
212	12.0	Garden City SD	Garden City
212	12.0	Gibraltar SD	Woodhaven
214	11.9	Fowlerville Community Schools	Fowlerville
215	11.8	Ann Arbor Public Schools	Ann Arbor
216	11.5	Mona Shores Public SD	Norton Shores
216	11.5	South Lake Schools	St Clair Shores
216	11.5	Vicksburg Community Schools	Vicksburg
219	11.4	L'anse Creuse Public Schools	Harrison Twp
220	11.0	Allendale Public SD	Allendale
220	11.0	Anchor Bay SD	New Baltimore
222	10.8	Holt Public Schools	Holt
223	10.6	Lowell Area Schools	Lowell
224	10.5	Midland Public Schools	Midland
224	10.5	Northview Public SD	Grand Rapids
226	10.3	Byron Center Public Schools	Byron Center
226	10.3	Clawson City SD	Clawson
226	10.3	Comstock Park Public Schools	Comstock Park
229	10.2	East China SD	East China
229	10.2	Riverview Community SD	Riverview
231	9.8	Thornapple Kellogg SD	Middleville
232	9.5	Brandon SD	Ortonville
232	9.5	Portage Public Schools	Portage
234	9.4	Warren Woods Public Schools	Warren
235	9.3	Almont Community Schools	Almont
235	9.3	Fraser Public Schools	Fraser
237	8.9	Tecumseh Public Schools	Tecumseh
238	8.8	Romeo Community Schools	Romeo
238	8.8	Saint Johns Public Schools	Saint Johns
238	8.8	Zeeland Public Schools	Zeeland
241	8.6	Fenton Area Public Schools	Fenton
241	8.6	Onsted Community Schools	Onsted
243	8.5	Grandville Public Schools	Grandville
243	8.5	Gull Lake Community Schools	Richland
243	8.5	Lake Shore Public Schools (Macomb)	St Clair Shores
246	8.3	Oxford Area Community Schools	Oxford
246	8.3	Richmond Community Schools	Richmond
248	8.2	Grand Ledge Public Schools	Grand Ledge
249	8.1	Huron Valley Schools	Highland
249	8.1	School District of Royal Oak	Royal Oak
251	8.0	Grand Blanc Community Schools	Grand Blanc
252	7.8	Lakeshore SD (Berrien)	Stevensville
253	7.7	Mason Public Schools (Ingham)	Mason
254	7.6	Howell Public Schools	Howell
255	7.3	Berkley SD	Berkley
255	7.3	Spring Lake Public Schools	Spring Lake
257	7.0	Utica Community Schools	Sterling Hgts
258	6.8	Linden Community Schools	Linden
259	6.7	Hamilton Community Schools	Hamilton
259	6.7	Mattawan Consolidated School	Mattawan
261	6.6	South Lyon Community Schools	South Lyon
262	6.5	Avondale SD	Auburn Hills
263	6.4	Hudsonville Public SD	Hudsonville
263	6.4	Portland Public SD	Portland
265	6.2	Bedford Public Schools	Temperance
265	6.2	Farmington Public SD	Farmington

267	6.0	Flushing Community Schools	Flushing
268	5.9	Williamston Community Schools	Williamston
269	5.8	Ida Public SD	Ida
270	5.6	Saint Joseph Public Schools	Saint Joseph
271	5.5	Marysville Public Schools	Marysville
272	5.4	Allen Park Public Schools	Allen Park
272	5.4	Chippewa Valley Schools	Clinton Twp
272	5.4	Trenton Public Schools	Trenton
275	5.3	Haslett Public Schools	Haslett
275	5.3	Lake Orion Community Schools	Lake Orion
277	5.2	Caledonia Community Schools	Caledonia
277	5.2	Lakeview Public Schools (Macomb)	St Clair Shores
279	5.1	Walled Lake Consolidated Schools	Walled Lake
279	5.1	West Bloomfield SD	West Bloomfield
281	5.0	Dewitt Public Schools	Dewitt
282	4.8	Plymouth-Canton Community Schools	Plymouth
283	4.6	Clarkston Community SD	Clarkston
284	4.4	Livonia Public Schools	Livonia
285	4.3	Pinckney Community Schools	Pinckney
286	4.2	Okemos Public Schools	Okemos
287	4.1	Armada Area Schools	Armada
287	4.1	Freeland Community SD	Freeland
289	3.9	Jenison Public Schools	Jenison
290	3.8	Rockford Public Schools	Rockford
291	3.6	Dexter Community SD	Dexter
292	3.4	Chelsea SD	Chelsea
293	3.1	Brighton Area Schools	Brighton
293	3.1	East Grand Rapids Public Schools	E Grand Rapids
295	3.0	Rochester Community SD	Rochester
296	2.9	Hartland Consolidated Schools	Hartland
297	2.4	Forest Hills Public Schools	Grand Rapids
297	2.4	Goodrich Area Schools	Goodrich
299	2.2	Saline Area Schools	Saline
299	2.2	Troy SD	Troy
301	2.0	Birmingham City SD	Birmingham
302	1.9	Grosse Pointe Public Schools	Grosse Pointe
302	1.9	Northville Public Schools	Northville
304	1.8	Bloomfield Hills SD	Bloomfield Hls
305	1.3	Novi Community SD	Novi
306	1.0	Grosse Ile Township Schools	Grosse Ile
307	n/a	Macomb ISD	Clinton Twp
307	n/a	Washtenaw ISD	Ann Arbor

Students Eligible for Reduced-Price Lunch

Rank	Percent	District Name	City
1	15.5	Van Dyke Public Schools	Warren
2	15.3	Oscoda Area Schools	Oscoda
3	14.9	Kalkaska Public Schools	Kalkaska
4	14.2	Oakridge Public Schools	Muskegon
5	14.0	Public Schools of Calumet	Calumet
5	14.0	Reed City Area Public Schools	Reed City
7	13.3	Orchard View Schools	Muskegon
8	13.2	Willow Run Community Schools	Ypsilanti
9	13.1	Tri County Area Schools	Howard City
10	13.0	Farwell Area Schools	Farwell
11	12.9	Parchment SD	Parchment
12	12.6	Belding Area SD	Belding
12	12.6	White Cloud Public Schools	White Cloud
14	12.5	Benzie County Central Schools	Benzonia
14	12.5	East Detroit Public Schools	Eastpointe
16	12.3	Godwin Heights Public Schools	Wyoming
16	12.3	Mason County Central Schools	Scottville
18	12.2	Hazel Park City SD	Hazel Park
19	12.1	Chippewa Hills SD	Remus
20	12.0	Hillsdale Community Schools	Hillsdale
20	12.0	Melvindale-N Allen Park Schools	Melvindale
22	11.9	West Branch-Rose City Area Schools	West Branch
23	11.8	Fennville Public Schools	Fennville
24	11.7	Hartford Public SD	Hartford
25	11.4	Kelloggsville Public Schools	Grand Rapids
26	10.9	Brandywine Public SD	Niles
27	10.8	Morley Stanwood Community Schools	Morley
28	10.7	Lincoln Park Public Schools	Lincoln Park
29	10.6	Dearborn Heights SD #7	Dearborn Hgts
30	10.5	Carrollton SD	Saginaw
31	10.4	Ionia Public Schools	Ionia
31	10.4	Manistee Area Schools	Manistee
31	10.4	Roseville Community Schools	Roseville
31	10.4	Standish-Sterling Comm Schools	Standish
35	10.3	Bridgeport-Spaulding Community SD	Bridgeport
35	10.3	Cadillac Area Public Schools	Cadillac
35	10.3	Lakeview Comm Schools (Montcalm)	Lakeview
38	10.1	Alma Public Schools	Alma
38	10.1	Alpena Public Schools	Alpena
38	10.1	Crawford Ausable Schools	Grayling
38	10.1	Holland City SD	Holland
42	10.0	Berrien Springs Public Schools	Berrien Springs
42	10.0	Westwood Community Schools	Dearborn Hgts
44	9.8	Clare Public Schools	Clare
44	9.8	Comstock Public Schools	Kalamazoo
44	9.8	Meridian Public Schools	Sanford
44	9.8	Redford Union SD	Redford
44	9.8	Stockbridge Community Schools	Stockbridge
49	9.7	Montague Area Public Schools	Montague
49	9.7	North Branch Area Schools	North Branch
49	9.7	River Rouge SD	River Rouge
52	9.6	Fruitport Community Schools	Fruitport
52	9.6	Shelby Public Schools	Shelby
54	9.5	Beaverton Rural Schools	Beaverton
54	9.5	Escanaba Area Public Schools	Escanaba
54	9.5	Sault Sainte Marie Area Schools	Sault Ste Marie
54	9.5	Tawas Area Schools	Tawas City
54	9.5	Taylor SD	Taylor
59	9.4	Gladstone Area Schools	Gladstone
59	9.4	Mount Clemens Community SD	Mount Clemens
61	9.3	Central Montcalm Public Schools	Stanton
61	9.3	Gladwin Community Schools	Gladwin
61	9.3	Wayne-Westland Community SD	Westland
61	9.3	Wyoming Public Schools	Wyoming
65	9.1	Allegan Public Schools	Allegan
65	9.1	Fitzgerald Public Schools	Warren
67	9.0	Breitung Township Schools	Kingsford
67	9.0	Caro Community Schools	Caro
67	9.0	Coloma Community Schools	Coloma
67	9.0	Dowagiac Union SD	Dowagiac
71	8.9	Cheboygan Area Schools	Cheboygan
71	8.9	Croswell-Lexington Comm Schools	Croswell
71	8.9	Harrison Community Schools	Harrison
71	8.9	School District of Ypsilanti	Ypsilanti
75	8.8	Hamtramck Public Schools	Hamtramck
75	8.8	Montrose Community Schools	Montrose
75	8.8	Niles Community SD	Niles
75	8.8	Pinconning Area Schools	Pinconning
75	8.8	Wayland Union Schools	Wayland
80	8.7	Buchanan Community Schools	Buchanan
81	8.5	Cass City Public Schools	Cass City
81	8.5	Durand Area Schools	Durand
81	8.5	Romulus Community Schools	Romulus
81	8.5	Shepherd Public SD	Shepherd
85	8.4	Lansing Public SD	Lansing
86	8.3	Bronson Community SD	Bronson
86	8.3	Grand Rapids Public Schools	Grand Rapids
86	8.3	Otsego Public Schools	Otsego
86	8.3	Southfield Public SD	Southfield
90	8.2	Grant Public SD	Grant
90	8.2	Lakewood Public Schools	Lake Odessa
92	8.1	Capac Community SD	Capac
92	8.1	Greenville Public Schools	Greenville
92	8.1	Menominee Area Public Schools	Menominee
92	8.1	Vassar Public Schools	Vassar
96	8.0	Corunna Public SD	Corunna
96	8.0	Houghton Lake Community Schools	Houghton Lake
98	7.9	Bangor Public Schools (Van Buren)	Bangor
98	7.9	Coopersville Public SD	Coopersville
98	7.9	Eaton Rapids Public Schools	Eaton Rapids
98	7.9	Gaylord Community Schools	Gaylord
98	7.9	Ludington Area SD	Ludington
98	7.9	Mount Morris Consolidated Schools	Mount Morris
98	7.9	Muskegon City SD	Muskegon
98	7.9	Sturgis Public Schools	Sturgis
106	7.8	Oak Park City SD	Oak Park
107	7.7	Adrian City SD	Adrian
107	7.7	Big Rapids Public Schools	Big Rapids
107	7.7	Chesaning Union Schools	Chesaning
107	7.7	Gerrish-Higgins SD	Roscommon
107	7.7	Jackson Public Schools	Jackson
107	7.7	Lakeville Community Schools	Otisville
107	7.7	Newaygo Public SD	Newaygo
107	7.7	Ovid-Elsie Area Schools	Elsie
107	7.7	Traverse City Area Public Schools	Traverse City
107	7.7	Western SD	Parma
117	7.6	Carman-Ainsworth Community Schools	Flint
117	7.6	Public Schools of Petoskey	Petoskey
117	7.6	South Haven Public Schools	South Haven
120	7.5	Algonac Community SD	Algonac
120	7.5	Battle Creek Public Schools	Battle Creek
120	7.5	Cedar Springs Public Schools	Cedar Springs
120	7.5	Pontiac City SD	Pontiac
124	7.4	Allendale Public SD	Allendale
125	7.3	Center Line Public Schools	Center Line
125	7.3	Hastings Area SD	Hastings
125	7.3	Imlay City Community Schools	Imlay City
125	7.3	Jefferson Schools (Monroe)	Monroe
125	7.3	Kenowa Hills Public Schools	Grand Rapids
125	7.3	Madison Public Schools (Oakland)	Madison Heights
125	7.3	South Redford SD	Redford
125	7.3	Three Rivers Community Schools	Three Rivers
133	7.2	Port Huron Area SD	Port Huron
134	7.1	Bay City SD	Bay City
134	7.1	Ferndale Public Schools	Ferndale
134	7.1	Fremont Public SD	Fremont
134	7.1	Kalamazoo Public SD	Kalamazoo
134	7.1	Owosso Public Schools	Owosso
134	7.1	Thornapple Kellogg SD	Middleville
140	7.0	Clarenceville SD	Livonia
140	7.0	Garden City SD	Garden City
140	7.0	Godfrey-Lee Public Schools	Wyoming
140	7.0	Millington Community Schools	Millington
144	6.9	Edwardsburg Public Schools	Edwardsburg
144	6.9	Kentwood Public Schools	Kentwood
144	6.9	Michigan Center SD	Michigan Center
147	6.8	Byron Center Public Schools	Byron Center
147	6.8	East Jackson Community Schools	Jackson
147	6.8	Elk Rapids Schools	Elk Rapids
147	6.8	Grand Haven Area Public Schools	Grand Haven
151	6.7	Birch Run Area SD	Birch Run
151	6.7	Crestwood SD	Dearborn Hgts
151	6.7	Delton-Kellogg SD	Delton
151	6.7	Quincy Community SD	Quincy
155	6.6	Albion Public Schools	Albion
155	6.6	Charlotte Public Schools	Charlotte
155	6.6	Sparta Area Schools	Sparta
155	6.6	West Ottawa Public SD	Holland
159	6.5	Beecher Community SD	Flint
159	6.5	Lowell Area Schools	Lowell
161	6.4	Muskegon Heights SD	Muskegon Hgts
161	6.4	Reeths-Puffer Schools	Muskegon
163	6.3	Columbia SD	Brooklyn
163	6.3	Lapeer Community Schools	Lapeer
163	6.3	Zeeland Public Schools	Zeeland
166	6.2	Detroit Academy of Arts & Sci	Detroit
166	6.2	Maple Valley Schools	Vermontville
166	6.2	Spring Lake Public Schools	Spring Lake
166	6.2	Yale Public Schools	Yale
170	6.1	Bullock Creek SD	Midland
170	6.1	Paw Paw Public SD	Paw Paw
172	6.0	Perry Public SD	Perry
173	5.9	Pennfield SD	Battle Creek
173	5.9	Plainwell Community Schools	Plainwell
175	5.8	Airport Community SD	Carleton
175	5.8	Mason Consol Schools (Monroe)	Erie
177	5.7	Bangor Township Schools	Bay City
177	5.7	Lamphere Public Schools	Madison Heights
177	5.7	Napoleon Community Schools	Napoleon
177	5.7	Wyandotte City SD	Wyandotte
181	5.5	Clio Area SD	Clio
181	5.5	Mona Shores Public SD	Norton Shores
181	5.5	Mount Pleasant City SD	Mount Pleasant
181	5.5	Southgate Community SD	Southgate
185	5.4	Davison Community Schools	Davison
185	5.4	Holly Area SD	Holly
185	5.4	Lincoln Consolidated SD	Ypsilanti
185	5.4	Northview Public SD	Grand Rapids
185	5.4	Saginaw City SD	Saginaw
190	5.2	Anchor Bay SD	New Baltimore
190	5.2	Monroe Public Schools	Monroe
190	5.2	Saint Johns Public Schools	Saint Johns
190	5.2	Van Buren Public Schools	Belleville
190	5.2	Whitehall District Schools	Whitehall
195	5.1	Northwest Community Schools	Jackson
195	5.1	Richmond Community Schools	Richmond
197	4.9	Bendle Public Schools	Burton
197	4.9	Constantine Public SD	Constantine
197	4.9	Vicksburg Community Schools	Vicksburg
200	4.8	Coldwater Community Schools	Coldwater
200	4.8	Waterford SD	Waterford
202	4.7	Clintondale Community Schools	Clinton Twp
202	4.7	Flat Rock Community Schools	Flat Rock
202	4.7	Hamilton Community Schools	Hamilton
202	4.7	Riverview Community SD	Riverview
202	4.7	Saginaw Township Community Schools	Saginaw
207	4.6	Holt Public Schools	Holt
207	4.6	South Lake Schools	St Clair Shores
209	4.5	Lake Shore Public Schools (Macomb)	St Clair Shores
209	4.5	Mason Public Schools (Ingham)	Mason
209	4.5	Waverly Community Schools	Lansing
212	4.4	Fowlerville Community Schools	Fowlerville
212	4.4	Grandville Public Schools	Grandville
212	4.4	Gull Lake Community Schools	Richland
212	4.4	Huron SD	New Boston
212	4.4	L'anse Creuse Public Schools	Harrison Twp
217	4.3	Hudsonville Public SD	Hudsonville
217	4.3	Jenison Public Schools	Jenison
217	4.3	Marquette Area Public Schools	Marquette
220	4.2	Benton Harbor Area Schools	Benton Harbor
220	4.2	East Lansing SD	East Lansing
220	4.2	Harper Creek Community Schools	Battle Creek
223	4.1	Clawson City SD	Clawson
223	4.1	Warren Consolidated Schools	Warren
225	4.0	East China SD	East China
225	4.0	Essexville-Hampton Public Schools	Essexville
225	4.0	Kearsley Community Schools	Flint
225	4.0	Portland Public SD	Portland
229	3.9	Ann Arbor Public Schools	Ann Arbor

229	3.9	Midland Public Schools	Midland
229	3.9	Portage Public Schools	Portage
232	3.8	Allen Park Public Schools	Allen Park
232	3.8	Fraser Public Schools	Fraser
232	3.8	Gibraltar SD	Woodhaven
232	3.8	Huron Valley Schools	Highland
232	3.8	Romeo Community Schools	Romeo
232	3.8	Warren Woods Public Schools	Warren
238	3.7	Oxford Area Community Schools	Oxford
239	3.6	Grand Ledge Public Schools	Grand Ledge
240	3.5	Caledonia Community Schools	Caledonia
240	3.5	Detroit City SD	Detroit
240	3.5	Lakeview SD (Calhoun)	Battle Creek
240	3.5	Milan Area Schools	Milan
240	3.5	Woodhaven-Brownstown SD	Brownstown
245	3.4	Dearborn City SD	Dearborn
245	3.4	Lakeshore SD (Berrien)	Stevensville
245	3.4	Saint Joseph Public Schools	Saint Joseph
245	3.4	South Lyon Community Schools	South Lyon
249	3.3	Berkley SD	Berkley
249	3.3	Flint City SD	Flint
249	3.3	Howell Public Schools	Howell
249	3.3	Marshall Public Schools	Marshall
249	3.3	Swartz Creek Community Schools	Swartz Creek
249	3.3	Tecumseh Public Schools	Tecumseh
249	3.3	Williamston Community Schools	Williamston
256	3.2	Comstock Park Public Schools	Comstock Park
256	3.2	Grand Blanc Community Schools	Grand Blanc
256	3.2	Ida Public SD	Ida
256	3.2	Swan Valley SD	Saginaw
260	3.1	Brandon SD	Ortonville
260	3.1	Mattawan Consolidated School	Mattawan
262	3.0	School District of Royal Oak	Royal Oak
263	2.9	Dundee Community Schools	Dundee
264	2.8	Fenton Area Public Schools	Fenton
264	2.8	Highland Park City Schools	Highland Park
264	2.8	Linden Community Schools	Linden
264	2.8	Onsted Community Schools	Onsted
268	2.7	Lake Orion Community Schools	Lake Orion
269	2.6	Chippewa Valley Schools	Clinton Twp
269	2.6	Marysville Public Schools	Marysville
269	2.6	West Bloomfield SD	West Bloomfield
272	2.5	Avondale SD	Auburn Hills
272	2.5	Bedford Public Schools	Temperance
274	2.4	Utica Community Schools	Sterling Hgts
275	2.3	Haslett Public Schools	Haslett
275	2.3	Lakeview Public Schools (Macomb)	St Clair Shores
275	2.3	Walled Lake Consolidated Schools	Walled Lake
278	2.2	Almont Community Schools	Almont
279	2.1	Dexter Community SD	Dexter
279	2.1	Livonia Public Schools	Livonia
281	1.9	Clarkston Community SD	Clarkston
282	1.8	Chelsea SD	Chelsea
282	1.8	Farmington Public SD	Farmington
284	1.7	Flushing Community Schools	Flushing
284	1.7	Plymouth-Canton Community Schools	Plymouth
286	1.6	Saline Area Schools	Saline
287	1.5	Dewitt Public Schools	Dewitt
287	1.5	Forest Hills Public Schools	Grand Rapids
287	1.5	Hartland Consolidated Schools	Hartland
290	1.4	Pinckney Community Schools	Pinckney
290	1.4	Rockford Public Schools	Rockford
292	1.3	Brighton Area Schools	Brighton
292	1.3	Freeland Community SD	Freeland
292	1.3	Goodrich Area Schools	Goodrich
295	1.2	Armada Area Schools	Armada
295	1.2	Grosse Ile Township Schools	Grosse Ile
295	1.2	Okemos Public Schools	Okemos
295	1.2	Rochester Community SD	Rochester
299	1.0	Birmingham City SD	Birmingham
299	1.0	Trenton Public Schools	Trenton
301	0.8	Troy SD	Troy
302	0.7	Grosse Pointe Public Schools	Grosse Pointe
303	0.6	Northville Public Schools	Northville
304	0.5	Bloomfield Hills SD	Bloomfield Hls
305	0.4	Novi Community SD	Novi
306	0.2	East Grand Rapids Public Schools	E Grand Rapids
307	n/a	Macomb ISD	Clinton Twp
307	n/a	Washtenaw ISD	Ann Arbor

Student/Teacher Ratio

Rank	Ratio	District Name	City
1	197.1	Cedar Springs Public Schools	Cedar Springs
2	177.4	Charlotte Public Schools	Charlotte
3	171.1	Jenison Public Schools	Jenison
4	158.4	Zeeland Public Schools	Zeeland
5	148.0	Lansing Public SD	Lansing
6	106.1	Meridian Public Schools	Sanford
7	51.6	Ovid-Elsie Area Schools	Elsie
8	44.8	Holt Public Schools	Holt
9	42.3	Houghton Lake Community Schools	Houghton Lake
10	42.2	Dundee Community Schools	Dundee
11	40.0	Tecumseh Public Schools	Tecumseh
12	32.9	Waterford SD	Waterford
13	32.5	Washtenaw ISD	Ann Arbor
14	30.6	Detroit City SD	Detroit
15	27.1	Montrose Community Schools	Montrose
16	26.3	Clintondale Community Schools	Clinton Twp
17	25.4	Beecher Community SD	Flint
18	23.3	Linden Community Schools	Linden
19	22.6	Flushing Community Schools	Flushing
20	22.5	Willow Run Community Schools	Ypsilanti
21	22.3	Ferndale Public Schools	Ferndale
22	22.1	Cass City Public Schools	Cass City
22	22.1	Lakeview Public Schools (Macomb)	St Clair Shores
22	22.1	Marysville Public Schools	Marysville
25	21.9	Dearborn Heights SD #7	Dearborn Hgts
26	21.6	Mona Shores Public SD	Norton Shores
26	21.6	Yale Public Schools	Yale
28	21.5	Bronson Community SD	Bronson
29	21.3	Crestwood SD	Dearborn Hgts
30	21.0	Coldwater Community Schools	Coldwater
31	20.9	Kearsley Community Schools	Flint
31	20.9	Lakeshore SD (Berrien)	Stevensville
31	20.9	Redford Union SD	Redford
34	20.6	Chippewa Valley Schools	Clinton Twp
34	20.6	Van Dyke Public Schools	Warren
36	20.5	Imlay City Community Schools	Imlay City
36	20.5	Riverview Community SD	Riverview
38	20.4	River Rouge SD	River Rouge
39	20.3	Armada Area Schools	Armada
39	20.3	Rochester Community SD	Rochester
39	20.3	Vicksburg Community Schools	Vicksburg
42	20.2	Fitzgerald Public Schools	Warren
42	20.2	L'anse Creuse Public Schools	Harrison Twp
44	20.1	Allen Park Public Schools	Allen Park
44	20.1	Almont Community Schools	Almont
46	20.0	Davison Community Schools	Davison
46	20.0	Hamilton Community Schools	Hamilton
46	20.0	Lapeer Community Schools	Lapeer
49	19.9	Chelsea SD	Chelsea
49	19.9	Clio Area SD	Clio
51	19.8	Lake Orion Community Schools	Lake Orion
52	19.7	Hartland Consolidated Schools	Hartland
52	19.7	Western SD	Parma
54	19.6	Northview Public SD	Grand Rapids
54	19.6	Plymouth-Canton Community Schools	Plymouth
56	19.5	Algonac Community SD	Algonac
56	19.5	Mattawan Consolidated School	Mattawan
56	19.5	Monroe Public Schools	Monroe
56	19.5	Portage Public Schools	Portage
56	19.5	Romeo Community Schools	Romeo
61	19.4	Brandon SD	Ortonville
61	19.4	Corunna Public SD	Corunna
61	19.4	Edwardsburg Public Schools	Edwardsburg
61	19.4	Freeland Community SD	Freeland
61	19.4	Goodrich Area Schools	Goodrich
61	19.4	Michigan Center SD	Michigan Center
61	19.4	Quincy Community SD	Quincy
61	19.4	South Lyon Community Schools	South Lyon
69	19.3	Brighton Area Schools	Brighton
69	19.3	Flat Rock Community Schools	Flat Rock
69	19.3	Harper Creek Community Schools	Battle Creek
69	19.3	Melvindale-N Allen Park Schools	Melvindale
69	19.3	Romulus Community Schools	Romulus
69	19.3	Saline Area Schools	Saline
75	19.2	Airport Community SD	Carleton
75	19.2	Fenton Area Public Schools	Fenton
75	19.2	Gerrish-Higgins SD	Roscommon
75	19.2	Muskegon City SD	Muskegon
75	19.2	Rockford Public Schools	Rockford
80	19.1	Bangor Township Schools	Bay City
80	19.1	Columbia SD	Brooklyn
80	19.1	Dewitt Public Schools	Dewitt
80	19.1	Durand Area Schools	Durand
80	19.1	Gibraltar SD	Woodhaven
80	19.1	Lincoln Park Public Schools	Lincoln Park
80	19.1	Millington Community Schools	Millington
80	19.1	Oxford Area Community Schools	Oxford
80	19.1	Paw Paw Public SD	Paw Paw
80	19.1	Richmond Community Schools	Richmond
80	19.1	Utica Community Schools	Sterling Hgts
91	19.0	Clare Public Schools	Clare
91	19.0	Grandville Public Schools	Grandville
91	19.0	Huron Valley Schools	Highland
91	19.0	Napoleon Community Schools	Napoleon
91	19.0	Pinckney Community Schools	Pinckney
91	19.0	Shelby Public Schools	Shelby
91	19.0	Standish-Sterling Comm Schools	Standish
98	18.9	Anchor Bay SD	New Baltimore
98	18.9	Fowlerville Community Schools	Fowlerville
98	18.9	North Branch Area Schools	North Branch
98	18.9	Wayland Union Schools	Wayland
98	18.9	Woodhaven-Brownstown SD	Brownstown
103	18.8	Howell Public Schools	Howell
103	18.8	Pennfield SD	Battle Creek
103	18.8	Pinconning Area Schools	Pinconning
103	18.8	Swartz Creek Community Schools	Swartz Creek
103	18.8	Warren Woods Public Schools	Warren
108	18.7	Clarkston Community SD	Clarkston
108	18.7	Coopersville Public SD	Coopersville
108	18.7	Essexville-Hampton Public Schools	Essexville
108	18.7	Lake Shore Public Schools (Macomb)	St Clair Shores
108	18.7	Lakeville Community Schools	Otisville
108	18.7	Lowell Area Schools	Lowell
108	18.7	Menominee Area Public Schools	Menominee
108	18.7	Montague Area Public Schools	Montague
108	18.7	Owosso Public Schools	Owosso
108	18.7	Portland Public SD	Portland
108	18.7	Thornapple Kellogg SD	Middleville
119	18.6	Cadillac Area Public Schools	Cadillac
119	18.6	East China SD	East China
119	18.6	Holly Area SD	Holly
119	18.6	Lakewood Public Schools	Lake Odessa
119	18.6	Sault Sainte Marie Area Schools	Sault Ste Marie
119	18.6	South Redford SD	Redford
119	18.6	Traverse City Area Public Schools	Traverse City
119	18.6	West Bloomfield SD	West Bloomfield
127	18.5	Bay City SD	Bay City
127	18.5	Bendle Public Schools	Burton
127	18.5	Big Rapids Public Schools	Big Rapids
127	18.5	Capac Community SD	Capac
127	18.5	Dowagiac Union SD	Dowagiac
127	18.5	Grand Haven Area Public Schools	Grand Haven
127	18.5	Mount Morris Consolidated Schools	Mount Morris
127	18.5	Plainwell Community Schools	Plainwell
127	18.5	Stockbridge Community Schools	Stockbridge
136	18.4	Alpena Public Schools	Alpena
136	18.4	Birch Run Area SD	Birch Run
136	18.4	Chesaning Union Schools	Chesaning
136	18.4	Fruitport Community Schools	Fruitport
136	18.4	Huron SD	New Boston
136	18.4	Kelloggsville Public Schools	Grand Rapids
136	18.4	Mason Public Schools (Ingham)	Mason
136	18.4	Saint Joseph Public Schools	Saint Joseph
144	18.3	East Detroit Public Schools	Eastpointe
144	18.3	Escanaba Area Public Schools	Escanaba
144	18.3	Kenowa Hills Public Schools	Grand Rapids
144	18.3	Swan Valley SD	Saginaw
148	18.2	Bedford Public Schools	Temperance
148	18.2	Elk Rapids Schools	Elk Rapids
148	18.2	Farwell Area Schools	Farwell
148	18.2	Reed City Area Public Schools	Reed City
148	18.2	Roseville Community Schools	Roseville
148	18.2	South Haven Public Schools	South Haven
148	18.2	Tri County Area Schools	Howard City
148	18.2	West Ottawa Public SD	Holland
156	18.1	Benzie County Central Schools	Benzonia
156	18.1	Breitung Township Schools	Kingsford
156	18.1	Greenville Public Schools	Greenville
156	18.1	Livonia Public Schools	Livonia
156	18.1	Marquette Area Public Schools	Marquette
156	18.1	Oak Park City SD	Oak Park
156	18.1	Perry Public SD	Perry
156	18.1	Public Schools of Petoskey	Petoskey
156	18.1	Spring Lake Public Schools	Spring Lake
156	18.1	Williamston Community Schools	Williamston
166	18.0	Grand Ledge Public Schools	Grand Ledge
166	18.0	Grant Public SD	Grant
166	18.0	Grosse Ile Township Schools	Grosse Ile
166	18.0	Gull Lake Community Schools	Richland
166	18.0	Wayne-Westland Community SD	Westland
171	17.9	Fremont Public SD	Fremont
171	17.9	Ida Public SD	Ida
171	17.9	Jefferson Schools (Monroe)	Monroe
171	17.9	Maple Valley Schools	Vermontville
171	17.9	Port Huron Area SD	Port Huron
171	17.9	Saginaw Township Community Schools	Saginaw
171	17.9	Warren Consolidated Schools	Warren
178	17.8	Byron Center Public Schools	Byron Center
178	17.8	Grand Blanc Community Schools	Grand Blanc
178	17.8	Hamtramck Public Schools	Hamtramck
178	17.8	Hillsdale Community Schools	Hillsdale
178	17.8	Midland Public Schools	Midland
178	17.8	Otsego Public Schools	Otsego
178	17.8	Tawas Area Schools	Tawas City
178	17.8	Three Rivers Community Schools	Three Rivers
178	17.8	Van Buren Public Schools	Belleville
187	17.7	Alma Public Schools	Alma
187	17.7	Bullock Creek SD	Midland
187	17.7	Caro Community Schools	Caro
187	17.7	Clarenceville SD	Livonia
187	17.7	East Grand Rapids Public Schools	E Grand Rapids
187	17.7	Gladwin Community Schools	Gladwin
187	17.7	Hudsonville Public SD	Hudsonville
187	17.7	Kentwood Public Schools	Kentwood

187	17.7	Wyandotte City SD	Wyandotte
196	17.6	Buchanan Community Schools	Buchanan
196	17.6	Caledonia Community Schools	Caledonia
196	17.6	Central Montcalm Public Schools	Stanton
196	17.6	Gladstone Area Schools	Gladstone
196	17.6	Marshall Public Schools	Marshall
196	17.6	Mason County Central Schools	Scottville
196	17.6	Oscoda Area Schools	Oscoda
196	17.6	Reeths-Puffer Schools	Muskegon
196	17.6	Taylor SD	Taylor
205	17.5	Benton Harbor Area Schools	Benton Harbor
205	17.5	Croswell-Lexington Comm Schools	Croswell
205	17.5	East Jackson Community Schools	Jackson
205	17.5	Eaton Rapids Public Schools	Eaton Rapids
205	17.5	Hazel Park City SD	Hazel Park
205	17.5	Orchard View Schools	Muskegon
205	17.5	Southgate Community SD	Southgate
205	17.5	Whitehall District Schools	Whitehall
213	17.4	Chippewa Hills SD	Remus
213	17.4	Okemos Public Schools	Okemos
213	17.4	Onsted Community Schools	Onsted
213	17.4	Pontiac City SD	Pontiac
217	17.3	Adrian City SD	Adrian
217	17.3	Albion Public Schools	Albion
217	17.3	Crawford Ausable Schools	Grayling
217	17.3	Forest Hills Public Schools	Grand Rapids
217	17.3	Gaylord Community Schools	Gaylord
217	17.3	Lakeview SD (Calhoun)	Battle Creek
217	17.3	Parchment SD	Parchment
217	17.3	South Lake Schools	St Clair Shores
225	17.2	Constantine Public SD	Constantine
225	17.2	Fraser Public Schools	Fraser
225	17.2	Sparta Area Schools	Sparta
225	17.2	Troy SD	Troy
229	17.1	Clawson City SD	Clawson
229	17.1	Harrison Community Schools	Harrison
229	17.1	Morley Stanwood Community Schools	Morley
229	17.1	Sturgis Public Schools	Sturgis
233	17.0	Allegan Public Schools	Allegan
233	17.0	Bangor Public Schools (Van Buren)	Bangor
233	17.0	Brandywine Public SD	Niles
233	17.0	Carman-Ainsworth Community Schools	Flint
233	17.0	Hastings Area SD	Hastings
233	17.0	Holland City SD	Holland
233	17.0	Lakeview Comm Schools (Montcalm)	Lakeview
233	17.0	Southfield Public SD	Southfield
233	17.0	Wyoming Public Schools	Wyoming
242	16.8	Fennville Public Schools	Fennville
242	16.8	Haslett Public Schools	Haslett
242	16.8	Public Schools of Calumet	Calumet
245	16.7	Allendale Public SD	Allendale
245	16.7	Beaverton Rural Schools	Beaverton
245	16.7	Delton-Kellogg SD	Delton
245	16.7	School District of Royal Oak	Royal Oak
245	16.7	Shepherd Public SD	Shepherd
250	16.6	Oakridge Public Schools	Muskegon
250	16.6	White Cloud Public Schools	White Cloud
252	16.5	Belding Area SD	Belding
252	16.5	Cheboygan Area Schools	Cheboygan
252	16.5	East Lansing SD	East Lansing
252	16.5	Madison Public Schools (Oakland)	Madison Heights
256	16.4	Center Line Public Schools	Center Line
256	16.4	Lamphere Public Schools	Madison Heights
256	16.4	Walled Lake Consolidated Schools	Walled Lake
259	16.3	Farmington Public SD	Farmington
259	16.3	West Branch-Rose City Area Schools	West Branch
261	16.2	Dearborn City SD	Dearborn
261	16.2	Flint City SD	Flint
261	16.2	Ionia Public Schools	Ionia
261	16.2	Saginaw City SD	Saginaw
261	16.2	School District of Ypsilanti	Ypsilanti
261	16.2	Westwood Community Schools	Dearborn Hgts
267	16.1	Berkley SD	Berkley
267	16.1	Grosse Pointe Public Schools	Grosse Pointe
269	16.0	Ann Arbor Public Schools	Ann Arbor
269	16.0	Ludington Area SD	Ludington
271	15.8	Hartford Public SD	Hartford
272	15.7	Northville Public Schools	Northville
273	15.6	Bridgeport-Spaulding Community SD	Bridgeport
273	15.6	Coloma Community Schools	Coloma
273	15.6	Godwin Heights Public Schools	Wyoming
276	15.5	Comstock Public Schools	Kalamazoo
277	15.3	Battle Creek Public Schools	Battle Creek
278	15.1	Avondale SD	Auburn Hills
278	15.1	Muskegon Heights SD	Muskegon Hgts
278	15.1	Trenton Public Schools	Trenton
281	14.9	Berrien Springs Public Schools	Berrien Springs
282	14.7	Garden City SD	Garden City
283	14.5	Kalamazoo Public SD	Kalamazoo
283	14.5	Mount Clemens Community SD	Mount Clemens
285	14.4	Bloomfield Hills SD	Bloomfield Hls
286	14.3	Grand Rapids Public Schools	Grand Rapids
287	13.5	Carrollton SD	Saginaw
288	12.8	Saint Johns Public Schools	Saint Johns
289	8.4	Macomb ISD	Clinton Twp
290	n/a	Birmingham City SD	Birmingham
290	n/a	Comstock Park Public Schools	Comstock Park
290	n/a	Detroit Academy of Arts & Sci	Detroit
290	n/a	Dexter Community SD	Dexter
290	n/a	Godfrey-Lee Public Schools	Wyoming
290	n/a	Highland Park City Schools	Highland Park
290	n/a	Jackson Public Schools	Jackson
290	n/a	Kalkaska Public Schools	Kalkaska
290	n/a	Lincoln Consolidated SD	Ypsilanti
290	n/a	Manistee Area Schools	Manistee
290	n/a	Mason Consol Schools (Monroe)	Erie
290	n/a	Milan Area Schools	Milan
290	n/a	Mount Pleasant City SD	Mount Pleasant
290	n/a	Newaygo Public SD	Newaygo
290	n/a	Niles Community SD	Niles
290	n/a	Northwest Community Schools	Jackson
290	n/a	Novi Community SD	Novi
290	n/a	Vassar Public Schools	Vassar
290	n/a	Waverly Community Schools	Lansing

Student/Librarian Ratio

Rank	Ratio	District Name	City
1	14,960.0	Walled Lake Consolidated Schools	Walled Lake
2	12,245.0	Waterford SD	Waterford
3	4,570.0	Redford Union SD	Redford
4	4,212.0	Gladwin Community Schools	Gladwin
5	4,053.0	Howell Public Schools	Howell
6	4,032.0	Adrian City SD	Adrian
7	4,031.0	Clintondale Community Schools	Clinton Twp
8	3,948.7	Detroit City SD	Detroit
9	3,726.0	Brandon SD	Ortonville
10	3,649.0	Clio Area SD	Clio
11	3,447.0	Northview Public SD	Grand Rapids
12	3,435.0	Ionia Public Schools	Ionia
13	3,360.0	Fruitport Community Schools	Fruitport
14	3,340.0	Caledonia Community Schools	Caledonia
15	3,033.0	Allegan Public Schools	Allegan
16	2,866.0	Sparta Area Schools	Sparta
17	2,810.0	Byron Center Public Schools	Byron Center
18	2,808.0	Willow Run Community Schools	Ypsilanti
19	2,776.3	Taylor SD	Taylor
20	2,751.7	Battle Creek Public Schools	Battle Creek
21	2,720.0	Harper Creek Community Schools	Battle Creek
22	2,705.0	River Rouge SD	River Rouge
23	2,696.7	Hazel Park City SD	Hazel Park
24	2,665.0	Montague Area Public Schools	Montague
25	2,618.0	Belding Area SD	Belding
26	2,606.0	Lakewood Public Schools	Lake Odessa
27	2,562.3	Muskegon City SD	Muskegon
28	2,560.0	Ludington Area SD	Ludington
29	2,558.0	Lapeer Community Schools	Lapeer
30	2,530.0	Rockford Public Schools	Rockford
31	2,515.0	South Haven Public Schools	South Haven
32	2,501.0	Saginaw Township Community Schools	Saginaw
33	2,493.5	Southgate Community SD	Southgate
34	2,470.0	Wyandotte City SD	Wyandotte
35	2,457.0	Bangor Township Schools	Bay City
36	2,409.0	Bridgeport-Spaulding Community SD	Bridgeport
37	2,390.0	Imlay City Community Schools	Imlay City
38	2,382.6	Flint City SD	Flint
39	2,379.0	Coopersville Public SD	Coopersville
40	2,367.0	Cheboygan Area Schools	Cheboygan
41	2,353.6	Garden City SD	Garden City
42	2,340.0	Muskegon Heights SD	Muskegon Hgts
43	2,273.0	Reeths-Puffer Schools	Muskegon
44	2,272.7	Lakeview Public Schools (Macomb)	St Clair Shores
45	2,270.0	East Lansing SD	East Lansing
46	2,267.8	Traverse City Area Public Schools	Traverse City
47	2,220.0	North Branch Area Schools	North Branch
48	2,215.9	Marquette Area Public Schools	Marquette
49	2,209.0	Holly Area SD	Holly
50	2,201.0	Houghton Lake Community Schools	Houghton Lake
51	2,168.3	Grand Rapids Public Schools	Grand Rapids
52	2,155.0	Lakeville Community Schools	Otisville
53	2,153.0	Harrison Community Schools	Harrison
54	2,149.0	Spring Lake Public Schools	Spring Lake
55	2,143.0	Anchor Bay SD	New Baltimore
56	2,136.0	Madison Public Schools (Oakland)	Madison Heights
57	2,134.0	Romulus Community Schools	Romulus
58	2,092.0	Chesaning Union Schools	Chesaning
59	2,083.5	Swartz Creek Community Schools	Swartz Creek
60	2,066.0	Pinconning Area Schools	Pinconning
61	2,065.0	Shelby Public Schools	Shelby
62	2,060.0	Durand Area Schools	Durand
63	2,059.0	Delton-Kellogg SD	Delton
64	2,056.0	Williamston Community Schools	Williamston
65	2,022.0	Goodrich Area Schools	Goodrich
66	2,006.0	Benzie County Central Schools	Benzonia
67	1,979.0	Standish-Sterling Comm Schools	Standish
68	1,958.0	Hillsdale Community Schools	Hillsdale
69	1,899.0	Gerrish-Higgins SD	Roscommon
70	1,896.0	Chippewa Valley Schools	Clinton Twp
71	1,885.3	Escanaba Area Public Schools	Escanaba
72	1,860.5	Fenton Area Public Schools	Fenton
73	1,856.7	Holt Public Schools	Holt
74	1,843.6	Kentwood Public Schools	Kentwood
75	1,833.7	Grand Ledge Public Schools	Grand Ledge
76	1,824.0	Stockbridge Community Schools	Stockbridge
77	1,806.5	Monroe Public Schools	Monroe
78	1,800.0	School District of Royal Oak	Royal Oak
79	1,780.0	Ovid-Elsie Area Schools	Elsie
80	1,779.0	Maple Valley Schools	Vermontville
81	1,772.3	Davison Community Schools	Davison
82	1,760.0	Flat Rock Community Schools	Flat Rock
83	1,755.0	Almont Community Schools	Almont
83	1,755.0	Forest Hills Public Schools	Grand Rapids
85	1,750.0	Millington Community Schools	Millington
86	1,732.0	Airport Community SD	Carleton
87	1,731.0	Shepherd Public SD	Shepherd
88	1,710.0	Montrose Community Schools	Montrose
89	1,701.0	Bendle Public Schools	Burton
90	1,692.7	Pinckney Community Schools	Pinckney
91	1,671.0	Ida Public SD	Ida
92	1,664.0	Saginaw City SD	Saginaw
93	1,657.0	Brandywine Public SD	Niles
94	1,649.5	Mason Public Schools (Ingham)	Mason
95	1,639.0	Fraser Public Schools	Fraser
96	1,629.0	Tawas Area Schools	Tawas City
97	1,615.0	Morley Stanwood Community Schools	Morley
98	1,614.0	Public Schools of Calumet	Calumet
99	1,597.0	Jenison Public Schools	Jenison
100	1,592.3	Flushing Community Schools	Flushing
101	1,585.3	Hudsonville Public SD	Hudsonville
102	1,579.0	Berrien Springs Public Schools	Berrien Springs
103	1,566.4	Huron Valley Schools	Highland
104	1,555.0	Constantine Public SD	Constantine
105	1,549.0	White Cloud Public Schools	White Cloud
106	1,524.0	Bangor Public Schools (Van Buren)	Bangor
107	1,518.0	Carrollton SD	Saginaw
108	1,516.0	Gibraltar SD	Woodhaven
109	1,502.0	Bronson Community SD	Bronson
110	1,499.5	Public Schools of Petoskey	Petoskey
111	1,484.0	Haslett Public Schools	Haslett
112	1,477.8	Wyoming Public Schools	Wyoming
113	1,474.5	Center Line Public Schools	Center Line
114	1,468.2	Port Huron Area SD	Port Huron
115	1,467.0	Linden Community Schools	Linden
116	1,466.0	Marysville Public Schools	Marysville
117	1,460.4	Cadillac Area Public Schools	Cadillac
118	1,448.5	Lakeshore SD (Berrien)	Stevensville
119	1,447.5	Dowagiac Union SD	Dowagiac
120	1,431.7	Mona Shores Public SD	Norton Shores
121	1,431.5	Thornapple Kellogg SD	Middleville
122	1,389.5	Vicksburg Community Schools	Vicksburg
123	1,368.0	Algonac Community SD	Algonac
124	1,341.9	Western SD	Parma
125	1,334.7	Lowell Area Schools	Lowell
126	1,321.5	West Bloomfield SD	West Bloomfield
127	1,313.3	Kearsley Community Schools	Flint
128	1,312.9	Brighton Area Schools	Brighton
129	1,311.7	Ferndale Public Schools	Ferndale
130	1,310.0	Greenville Public Schools	Greenville
131	1,300.5	Alma Public Schools	Alma
131	1,300.5	Chippewa Hills SD	Remus
133	1,253.5	East Grand Rapids Public Schools	E Grand Rapids
134	1,211.5	Lamphere Public Schools	Madison Heights
135	1,209.0	Grant Public SD	Grant
136	1,206.3	Owosso Public Schools	Owosso
137	1,201.5	Yale Public Schools	Yale
138	1,185.3	Crestwood SD	Dearborn Hgts
139	1,170.5	Godwin Heights Public Schools	Wyoming
140	1,166.8	Wayne-Westland Community SD	Westland
141	1,160.0	Mount Morris Consolidated Schools	Mount Morris
142	1,142.3	Gaylord Community Schools	Gaylord
143	1,136.5	Whitehall District Schools	Whitehall
144	1,134.7	Saint Johns Public Schools	Saint Johns
145	1,129.3	Lakeview SD (Calhoun)	Battle Creek
146	1,118.0	Edwardsburg Public Schools	Edwardsburg
146	1,118.0	Kelloggsville Public Schools	Grand Rapids
148	1,111.7	Wayland Union Schools	Wayland
149	1,110.6	L'anse Creuse Public Schools	Harrison Twp
150	1,087.1	Coldwater Community Schools	Coldwater
151	1,083.6	East China SD	East China
152	1,083.3	Sault Sainte Marie Area Schools	Sault Ste Marie
153	1,064.8	Benton Harbor Area Schools	Benton Harbor
153	1,064.8	Lincoln Park Public Schools	Lincoln Park
155	1,057.0	Breitung Township Schools	Kingsford
156	1,054.0	Alpena Public Schools	Alpena
157	1,048.7	Kalamazoo Public SD	Kalamazoo
158	1,048.5	Okemos Public Schools	Okemos

159	1,041.5	Huron SD	New Boston
160	1,038.6	Saline Area Schools	Saline
161	1,036.3	Three Rivers Community Schools	Three Rivers
162	1,035.3	Oak Park City SD	Oak Park
163	1,030.3	Gull Lake Community Schools	Richland
164	1,019.5	Richmond Community Schools	Richmond
165	1,019.3	Grandville Public Schools	Grandville
166	1,013.5	Menominee Area Public Schools	Menominee
167	1,010.0	Allendale Public SD	Allendale
168	997.0	Perry Public SD	Perry
169	993.5	Oakridge Public Schools	Muskegon
170	990.5	Pontiac City SD	Pontiac
171	984.8	Fremont Public SD	Fremont
172	979.0	Capac Community SD	Capac
173	978.0	Oscoda Area Schools	Oscoda
174	974.0	Lakeview Comm Schools (Montcalm)	Lakeview
175	971.1	South Lyon Community Schools	South Lyon
176	965.7	Plainwell Community Schools	Plainwell
177	965.4	Plymouth-Canton Community Schools	Plymouth
178	963.0	Essexville-Hampton Public Schools	Essexville
179	961.0	Hamtramck Public Schools	Hamtramck
180	954.7	Saint Joseph Public Schools	Saint Joseph
181	945.5	Pennfield SD	Battle Creek
182	936.4	Reed City Area Public Schools	Reed City
183	915.7	Dewitt Public Schools	Dewitt
184	906.3	Bedford Public Schools	Temperance
185	885.8	Quincy Community SD	Quincy
186	878.8	Carman-Ainsworth Community Schools	Flint
187	849.7	Riverview Community SD	Riverview
188	842.1	Bay City SD	Bay City
189	838.5	Swan Valley SD	Saginaw
190	836.3	Croswell-Lexington Comm Schools	Croswell
191	835.8	Fitzgerald Public Schools	Warren
192	832.7	Melvindale-N Allen Park Schools	Melvindale
193	830.9	Portage Public Schools	Portage
194	824.5	Freeland Community SD	Freeland
195	823.0	Dundee Community Schools	Dundee
196	817.0	Eaton Rapids Public Schools	Eaton Rapids
197	800.0	Mount Clemens Community SD	Mount Clemens
198	796.0	Holland City SD	Holland
199	795.1	Clarkston Community SD	Clarkston
199	795.1	Rochester Community SD	Rochester
201	789.4	Van Buren Public Schools	Belleville
202	782.4	South Redford SD	Redford
203	781.5	Fennville Public Schools	Fennville
204	778.7	Paw Paw Public SD	Paw Paw
205	778.0	Caro Community Schools	Caro
206	776.8	Sturgis Public Schools	Sturgis
207	776.7	Otsego Public Schools	Otsego
208	775.6	Mattawan Consolidated School	Mattawan
209	767.5	Michigan Center SD	Michigan Center
210	757.0	Grand Haven Area Public Schools	Grand Haven
211	755.0	Clawson City SD	Clawson
212	750.8	Berkley SD	Berkley
213	749.2	Dearborn City SD	Dearborn
214	745.4	Kenowa Hills Public Schools	Grand Rapids
215	741.7	Corunna Public SD	Corunna
216	738.8	Grosse Pointe Public Schools	Grosse Pointe
217	734.0	Bullock Creek SD	Midland
218	732.3	Big Rapids Public Schools	Big Rapids
219	731.6	Woodhaven-Brownstown SD	Brownstown
220	723.5	Orchard View Schools	Muskegon
221	720.3	Armada Area Schools	Armada
222	715.3	Crawford Ausable Schools	Grayling
223	714.5	Jefferson Schools (Monroe)	Monroe
224	712.7	Lake Orion Community Schools	Lake Orion
225	712.1	Roseville Community Schools	Roseville
226	709.1	Hartland Consolidated Schools	Hartland
227	707.7	Central Montcalm Public Schools	Stanton
228	704.4	Trenton Public Schools	Trenton
229	698.0	Allen Park Public Schools	Allen Park
230	687.3	Westwood Community Schools	Dearborn Hgts
231	683.0	Grosse Ile Township Schools	Grosse Ile
232	677.0	Lake Shore Public Schools (Macomb)	St Clair Shores
233	674.5	Oxford Area Community Schools	Oxford
234	674.3	West Branch-Rose City Area Schools	West Branch
235	674.0	Hastings Area SD	Hastings
236	672.3	Hamilton Community Schools	Hamilton
237	671.9	Northville Public Schools	Northville
238	669.3	Parchment SD	Parchment
239	658.1	West Ottawa Public SD	Holland
240	656.0	Avondale SD	Auburn Hills
241	655.7	Utica Community Schools	Sterling Hgts
242	648.7	Birch Run Area SD	Birch Run
243	648.6	Warren Woods Public Schools	Warren
244	642.2	Fowlerville Community Schools	Fowlerville
245	641.9	Warren Consolidated Schools	Warren
246	641.3	Columbia SD	Brooklyn
247	640.0	Chelsea SD	Chelsea
248	635.3	Livonia Public Schools	Livonia
249	624.9	Southfield Public SD	Southfield
250	615.7	Albion Public Schools	Albion
250	615.7	Bloomfield Hills SD	Bloomfield Hls
252	613.7	Onsted Community Schools	Onsted
253	610.2	Romeo Community Schools	Romeo
254	606.7	Napoleon Community Schools	Napoleon
255	603.7	Troy SD	Troy
256	602.7	Hartford Public SD	Hartford
257	600.1	Van Dyke Public Schools	Warren
258	591.4	Farmington Public SD	Farmington
259	590.3	Buchanan Community Schools	Buchanan
260	585.0	Beaverton Rural Schools	Beaverton
261	584.6	Elk Rapids Schools	Elk Rapids
262	583.4	Midland Public Schools	Midland
263	567.8	Grand Blanc Community Schools	Grand Blanc
264	564.3	Farwell Area Schools	Farwell
265	560.7	East Jackson Community Schools	Jackson
266	556.7	Clare Public Schools	Clare
267	523.8	School District of Ypsilanti	Ypsilanti
268	516.4	East Detroit Public Schools	Eastpointe
269	497.8	Comstock Public Schools	Kalamazoo
270	497.7	Dearborn Heights SD #7	Dearborn Hgts
271	497.3	Clarenceville SD	Livonia
272	494.8	Ann Arbor Public Schools	Ann Arbor
273	487.8	South Lake Schools	St Clair Shores
274	486.0	Tri County Area Schools	Howard City
275	415.7	Coloma Community Schools	Coloma
276	353.3	Marshall Public Schools	Marshall
277	n/a	Beecher Community SD	Flint
277	n/a	Birmingham City SD	Birmingham
277	n/a	Cass City Public Schools	Cass City
277	n/a	Cedar Springs Public Schools	Cedar Springs
277	n/a	Charlotte Public Schools	Charlotte
277	n/a	Comstock Park Public Schools	Comstock Park
277	n/a	Detroit Academy of Arts & Sci	Detroit
277	n/a	Dexter Community SD	Dexter
277	n/a	Gladstone Area Schools	Gladstone
277	n/a	Godfrey-Lee Public Schools	Wyoming
277	n/a	Highland Park City Schools	Highland Park
277	n/a	Jackson Public Schools	Jackson
277	n/a	Kalkaska Public Schools	Kalkaska
277	n/a	Lansing Public SD	Lansing
277	n/a	Lincoln Consolidated SD	Ypsilanti
277	n/a	Macomb ISD	Clinton Twp
277	n/a	Manistee Area Schools	Manistee
277	n/a	Mason Consol Schools (Monroe)	Erie
277	n/a	Mason County Central Schools	Scottville
277	n/a	Meridian Public Schools	Sanford
277	n/a	Milan Area Schools	Milan
277	n/a	Mount Pleasant City SD	Mount Pleasant
277	n/a	Newaygo Public SD	Newaygo
277	n/a	Niles Community SD	Niles
277	n/a	Northwest Community Schools	Jackson
277	n/a	Novi Community SD	Novi
277	n/a	Portland Public SD	Portland
277	n/a	Tecumseh Public Schools	Tecumseh
277	n/a	Vassar Public Schools	Vassar
277	n/a	Washtenaw ISD	Ann Arbor
277	n/a	Waverly Community Schools	Lansing
277	n/a	Zeeland Public Schools	Zeeland

Student/Counselor Ratio

Rank	Ratio	District Name	City
1	17,616.0	Lansing Public SD	Lansing
2	4,863.0	Zeeland Public Schools	Zeeland
3	3,740.0	Walled Lake Consolidated Schools	Walled Lake
4	3,489.0	Cedar Springs Public Schools	Cedar Springs
5	2,884.0	Kalamazoo Public SD	Kalamazoo
6	2,395.5	Jenison Public Schools	Jenison
7	2,020.0	Allendale Public SD	Allendale
8	2,009.0	Beecher Community SD	Flint
9	1,989.3	Holt Public Schools	Holt
10	1,803.0	Gladstone Area Schools	Gladstone
11	1,780.0	Ovid-Elsie Area Schools	Elsie
12	1,343.7	Clintondale Community Schools	Clinton Twp
13	1,336.0	Caledonia Community Schools	Caledonia
14	1,238.8	Gladwin Community Schools	Gladwin
15	1,224.5	Waterford SD	Waterford
16	1,215.0	Tri County Area Schools	Howard City
17	1,189.5	Coopersville Public SD	Coopersville
18	1,170.0	Muskegon Heights SD	Muskegon Hgts
19	1,168.0	Paw Paw Public SD	Paw Paw
20	1,158.0	Howell Public Schools	Howell
21	1,142.5	Redford Union SD	Redford
22	1,136.3	Lakeview Public Schools (Macomb)	St Clair Shores
23	1,135.7	Grand Blanc Community Schools	Grand Blanc
24	1,124.0	Byron Center Public Schools	Byron Center
25	1,081.0	Warren Woods Public Schools	Warren
26	1,080.5	Pontiac City SD	Pontiac
27	1,076.5	Harrison Community Schools	Harrison
28	1,071.5	Anchor Bay SD	New Baltimore
29	1,068.3	Escanaba Area Public Schools	Escanaba
30	1,066.7	Mount Clemens Community SD	Mount Clemens
31	1,052.5	Van Buren Public Schools	Belleville
32	1,050.3	Van Dyke Public Schools	Warren
33	1,001.0	Lowell Area Schools	Lowell
34	995.7	Comstock Public Schools	Kalamazoo
35	978.0	Linden Community Schools	Linden
36	970.8	Hazel Park City SD	Hazel Park
37	955.4	Flushing Community Schools	Flushing
38	954.6	Hartland Consolidated Schools	Hartland
39	936.0	Willow Run Community Schools	Ypsilanti
40	931.5	Brandon SD	Ortonville
41	912.0	Algonac Community SD	Algonac
42	909.2	Reeths-Puffer Schools	Muskegon
43	889.5	Maple Valley Schools	Vermontville
44	880.3	South Redford SD	Redford
45	880.0	Flat Rock Community Schools	Flat Rock
46	872.7	Belding Area SD	Belding
47	868.7	Lakewood Public Schools	Lake Odessa
48	859.0	Mona Shores Public SD	Norton Shores
49	844.4	Owosso Public Schools	Owosso
50	838.9	Clawson City SD	Clawson
51	838.3	South Haven Public Schools	South Haven
52	835.5	Ida Public SD	Ida
53	835.2	Garden City SD	Garden City
54	833.8	Wayland Union Schools	Wayland
55	832.7	Melvindale-N Allen Park Schools	Melvindale
56	831.2	Southgate Community SD	Southgate
57	828.2	Oak Park City SD	Oak Park
58	824.8	Mason Public Schools (Ingham)	Mason
59	824.5	Freeland Community SD	Freeland
60	823.3	Wyandotte City SD	Wyandotte
61	823.0	Dundee Community Schools	Dundee
62	819.5	Fraser Public Schools	Fraser
63	809.4	Oxford Area Community Schools	Oxford
64	807.5	Morley Stanwood Community Schools	Morley
65	807.0	Public Schools of Calumet	Calumet
66	806.4	Adrian City SD	Adrian
67	806.0	Grant Public SD	Grant
68	801.1	Roseville Community Schools	Roseville
69	798.5	Traverse City Area Public Schools	Traverse City
70	796.7	Imlay City Community Schools	Imlay City
71	795.1	Clarkston Community SD	Clarkston
72	789.5	Berrien Springs Public Schools	Berrien Springs
73	785.9	Grand Ledge Public Schools	Grand Ledge
74	783.4	Northview Public SD	Grand Rapids
75	781.5	Fennville Public Schools	Fennville
76	777.5	Constantine Public SD	Constantine
77	774.5	White Cloud Public Schools	White Cloud
78	768.7	Muskegon City SD	Muskegon
79	767.4	Lapeer Community Schools	Lapeer
80	764.5	Grandville Public Schools	Grandville
81	762.1	Romulus Community Schools	Romulus
82	762.0	Bangor Public Schools (Van Buren)	Bangor
83	760.6	Lincoln Park Public Schools	Lincoln Park
84	760.1	Brighton Area Schools	Brighton
85	760.0	Elk Rapids Schools	Elk Rapids
86	759.0	Rockford Public Schools	Rockford
87	758.0	Gibraltar SD	Woodhaven
88	755.3	Bedford Public Schools	Temperance
88	755.3	South Lyon Community Schools	South Lyon
90	753.2	Rochester Community SD	Rochester
91	751.0	Bronson Community SD	Bronson
91	751.0	Huron Valley Schools	Highland
93	746.5	Dearborn Heights SD #7	Dearborn Hgts
94	745.4	Kenowa Hills Public Schools	Grand Rapids
95	745.3	Edwardsburg Public Schools	Edwardsburg
96	744.2	Fenton Area Public Schools	Fenton
97	741.7	Corunna Public SD	Corunna
98	733.0	Marysville Public Schools	Marysville
99	732.3	Big Rapids Public Schools	Big Rapids
100	731.6	Woodhaven-Brownstown SD	Brownstown
101	729.8	Clio Area SD	Clio
102	728.3	Riverview Community SD	Riverview
103	725.4	Pinckney Community Schools	Pinckney
104	723.5	Orchard View Schools	Muskegon
105	720.8	East Grand Rapids Public Schools	E Grand Rapids
106	720.3	Armada Area Schools	Armada
107	718.3	Lakeville Community Schools	Otisville
108	717.2	East Detroit Public Schools	Eastpointe
109	712.7	Lake Orion Community Schools	Lake Orion
110	712.0	Madison Public Schools (Oakland)	Madison Heights
111	710.4	Clarenceville SD	Livonia
112	704.7	Breitung Township Schools	Kingsford
113	698.0	Allen Park Public Schools	Allen Park
114	696.5	Holland City SD	Holland
115	696.0	Mount Morris Consolidated Schools	Mount Morris
116	692.8	Airport Community SD	Carleton
117	692.3	Lamphere Public Schools	Madison Heights
118	689.5	Detroit City SD	Detroit
119	688.7	Pinconning Area Schools	Pinconning
120	688.3	Shelby Public Schools	Shelby
121	686.7	Durand Area Schools	Durand
121	686.7	Reed City Area Public Schools	Reed City
123	680.0	Harper Creek Community Schools	Battle Creek
124	679.7	Richmond Community Schools	Richmond

125	678.8	Jefferson Schools (Monroe)	Monroe
126	678.7	L'anse Creuse Public Schools	Harrison Twp
127	677.0	Lake Shore Public Schools (Macomb)	St Clair Shores
128	676.3	River Rouge SD	River Rouge
129	674.0	Goodrich Area Schools	Goodrich
130	672.3	Hamilton Community Schools	Hamilton
131	671.9	Northville Public Schools	Northville
132	671.0	Western SD	Parma
133	670.1	Flint City SD	Flint
134	669.1	Grand Rapids Public Schools	Grand Rapids
135	668.6	Fitzgerald Public Schools	Warren
136	666.0	North Branch Area Schools	North Branch
137	663.1	Utica Community Schools	Sterling Hgts
138	662.3	Oakridge Public Schools	Muskegon
139	660.7	Port Huron Area SD	Port Huron
140	659.7	Standish-Sterling Comm Schools	Standish
141	657.7	School District of Royal Oak	Royal Oak
142	650.0	Sault Sainte Marie Area Schools	Sault Ste Marie
143	648.7	Birch Run Area SD	Birch Run
144	641.3	Columbia SD	Brooklyn
145	640.0	Chelsea SD	Chelsea
145	640.0	Ludington Area SD	Ludington
147	634.2	Coldwater Community Schools	Coldwater
148	634.0	Trenton Public Schools	Trenton
149	633.9	Saginaw City SD	Saginaw
150	622.2	Wyoming Public Schools	Wyoming
151	621.0	Farmington Public SD	Farmington
152	618.2	Gull Lake Community Schools	Richland
153	614.3	Bangor Township Schools	Bay City
154	608.0	Stockbridge Community Schools	Stockbridge
155	605.7	West Bloomfield SD	West Bloomfield
156	602.3	Bridgeport-Spaulding Community SD	Bridgeport
157	601.3	Plymouth-Canton Community Schools	Plymouth
157	601.3	Portage Public Schools	Portage
159	599.8	Public Schools of Petoskey	Petoskey
160	598.3	West Ottawa Public SD	Holland
161	596.0	East China SD	East China
162	595.4	East Lansing SD	East Lansing
163	595.3	Swartz Creek Community Schools	Swartz Creek
164	593.4	Dearborn City SD	Dearborn
165	592.7	Crestwood SD	Dearborn Hgts
166	591.6	Benton Harbor Area Schools	Benton Harbor
167	590.9	Fremont Public SD	Fremont
168	585.6	Alpena Public Schools	Alpena
169	585.0	Almont Community Schools	Almont
169	585.0	Beaverton Rural Schools	Beaverton
171	583.5	Caro Community Schools	Caro
172	583.3	Millington Community Schools	Millington
173	581.7	Mattawan Consolidated School	Mattawan
174	577.0	Shepherd Public SD	Shepherd
175	576.7	Tecumseh Public Schools	Tecumseh
176	575.7	Cass City Public Schools	Cass City
177	572.8	Saint Joseph Public Schools	Saint Joseph
178	572.5	Ionia Public Schools	Ionia
179	570.0	Montrose Community Schools	Montrose
180	564.7	Lakeview SD (Calhoun)	Battle Creek
181	563.1	Berkley SD	Berkley
182	561.2	School District of Ypsilanti	Ypsilanti
183	561.0	Quincy Community SD	Quincy
184	559.0	Swan Valley SD	Saginaw
185	555.5	Southfield Public SD	Southfield
186	555.3	Taylor SD	Taylor
187	554.9	Livonia Public Schools	Livonia
188	550.3	Houghton Lake Community Schools	Houghton Lake
189	549.4	Dewitt Public Schools	Dewitt
190	549.1	Hamtramck Public Schools	Hamtramck
191	544.7	Eaton Rapids Public Schools	Eaton Rapids
192	543.0	Tawas Area Schools	Tawas City
193	542.2	Kentwood Public Schools	Kentwood
194	537.3	Spring Lake Public Schools	Spring Lake
195	536.5	Crawford Ausable Schools	Grayling
196	531.7	Davison Community Schools	Davison
197	526.0	Onsted Community Schools	Onsted
198	525.9	Grosse Pointe Public Schools	Grosse Pointe
199	523.0	Chesaning Union Schools	Chesaning
200	521.1	Sparta Area Schools	Sparta
201	520.8	Huron SD	New Boston
202	520.2	Alma Public Schools	Alma
203	520.0	Kelloggsville Public Schools	Grand Rapids
204	517.8	Portland Public SD	Portland
204	517.8	Sturgis Public Schools	Sturgis
206	514.8	Delton-Kellogg SD	Delton
207	512.3	Grosse Ile Township Schools	Grosse Ile
208	511.7	Michigan Center SD	Michigan Center
209	510.5	Chippewa Valley Schools	Clinton Twp
210	503.1	Troy SD	Troy
211	501.5	Benzie County Central Schools	Benzonia
212	495.4	Mason County Central Schools	Scottville
213	494.7	Haslett Public Schools	Haslett
214	492.0	Avondale SD	Auburn Hills
215	491.9	Bay City SD	Bay City
216	490.9	Holly Area SD	Holly
217	489.6	Gaylord Community Schools	Gaylord
218	489.5	Capac Community SD	Capac
218	489.5	Hillsdale Community Schools	Hillsdale
220	489.2	Marquette Area Public Schools	Marquette
221	487.0	Lakeview Comm Schools (Montcalm)	Lakeview
222	480.6	Yale Public Schools	Yale
223	480.0	Fruitport Community Schools	Fruitport
224	477.2	Thornapple Kellogg SD	Middleville
225	477.1	Clare Public Schools	Clare
226	472.9	Chippewa Hills SD	Remus
227	472.8	Pennfield SD	Battle Creek
228	472.1	Saline Area Schools	Saline
229	470.5	Wayne-Westland Community SD	Westland
230	466.0	Otsego Public Schools	Otsego
231	463.2	Gerrish-Higgins SD	Roscommon
232	461.8	Albion Public Schools	Albion
233	458.7	Fowlerville Community Schools	Fowlerville
234	455.0	Napoleon Community Schools	Napoleon
235	454.6	Whitehall District Schools	Whitehall
236	453.0	Hudsonville Public SD	Hudsonville
237	452.6	Midland Public Schools	Midland
238	450.9	Ann Arbor Public Schools	Ann Arbor
239	449.6	Marshall Public Schools	Marshall
240	438.8	Forest Hills Public Schools	Grand Rapids
241	436.7	Greenville Public Schools	Greenville
242	433.3	Allegan Public Schools	Allegan
243	428.7	Carman-Ainsworth Community Schools	Flint
244	427.5	Vicksburg Community Schools	Vicksburg
245	426.0	Plainwell Community Schools	Plainwell
246	425.3	Bendle Public Schools	Burton
247	424.6	Central Montcalm Public Schools	Stanton
248	421.3	Hastings Area SD	Hastings
249	413.6	Dowagiac Union SD	Dowagiac
250	411.2	Williamston Community Schools	Williamston
251	409.7	Warren Consolidated Schools	Warren
252	409.2	Grand Haven Area Public Schools	Grand Haven
253	406.8	Romeo Community Schools	Romeo
254	399.8	Montague Area Public Schools	Montague
255	398.8	Perry Public SD	Perry
256	391.8	Hartford Public SD	Hartford
257	391.2	Oscoda Area Schools	Oscoda
258	390.2	Godwin Heights Public Schools	Wyoming
259	389.5	Bloomfield Hills SD	Bloomfield Hls
260	385.2	Essexville-Hampton Public Schools	Essexville
261	384.8	Saginaw Township Community Schools	Saginaw
262	383.8	Three Rivers Community Schools	Three Rivers
263	368.6	Center Line Public Schools	Center Line
264	367.0	Bullock Creek SD	Midland
265	362.1	Lakeshore SD (Berrien)	Stevensville
266	361.3	Monroe Public Schools	Monroe
267	358.9	Battle Creek Public Schools	Battle Creek
268	358.4	Croswell-Lexington Comm Schools	Croswell
269	358.2	Kearsley Community Schools	Flint
270	348.4	South Lake Schools	St Clair Shores
271	346.2	Parchment SD	Parchment
272	343.7	Westwood Community Schools	Dearborn Hgts
273	340.4	Saint Johns Public Schools	Saint Johns
274	338.6	Farwell Area Schools	Farwell
275	337.8	Menominee Area Public Schools	Menominee
276	331.4	Brandywine Public SD	Niles
277	326.2	Coloma Community Schools	Coloma
278	318.6	Cadillac Area Public Schools	Cadillac
279	314.0	East Jackson Community Schools	Jackson
280	299.6	Okemos Public Schools	Okemos
281	295.9	Cheboygan Area Schools	Cheboygan
282	295.2	Buchanan Community Schools	Buchanan
283	253.0	Carrollton SD	Saginaw
284	207.5	West Branch-Rose City Area Schools	West Branch
285	187.4	Ferndale Public Schools	Ferndale
286	n/a	Birmingham City SD	Birmingham
286	n/a	Charlotte Public Schools	Charlotte
286	n/a	Comstock Park Public Schools	Comstock Park
286	n/a	Detroit Academy of Arts & Sci	Detroit
286	n/a	Dexter Community SD	Dexter
286	n/a	Godfrey-Lee Public Schools	Wyoming
286	n/a	Highland Park City Schools	Highland Park
286	n/a	Jackson Public Schools	Jackson
286	n/a	Kalkaska Public Schools	Kalkaska
286	n/a	Lincoln Consolidated SD	Ypsilanti
286	n/a	Macomb ISD	Clinton Twp
286	n/a	Manistee Area Schools	Manistee
286	n/a	Mason Consol Schools (Monroe)	Erie
286	n/a	Meridian Public Schools	Sanford
286	n/a	Milan Area Schools	Milan
286	n/a	Mount Pleasant City SD	Mount Pleasant
286	n/a	Newaygo Public SD	Newaygo
286	n/a	Niles Community SD	Niles
286	n/a	Northwest Community Schools	Jackson
286	n/a	Novi Community SD	Novi
286	n/a	Vassar Public Schools	Vassar
286	n/a	Washtenaw ISD	Ann Arbor
286	n/a	Waverly Community Schools	Lansing

Current Spending per Student in FY2001

Rank	Dollars	District Name	City
1	12,653	Bloomfield Hills SD	Bloomfield Hls
2	11,759	Southfield Public SD	Southfield
3	11,732	Birmingham City SD	Birmingham
4	11,057	Farmington Public SD	Farmington
5	10,613	Lamphere Public Schools	Madison Heights
6	10,539	Beecher Community SD	Flint
7	9,925	School District of Ypsilanti	Ypsilanti
8	9,691	Muskegon Heights SD	Muskegon Hgts
9	9,625	Grand Rapids Public Schools	Grand Rapids
10	9,601	Garden City SD	Garden City
11	9,544	Muskegon City SD	Muskegon
12	9,536	Benton Harbor Area Schools	Benton Harbor
13	9,483	Willow Run Community Schools	Ypsilanti
14	9,450	West Bloomfield SD	West Bloomfield
15	9,406	Lansing Public SD	Lansing
16	9,374	Northville Public Schools	Northville
17	9,342	Dearborn City SD	Dearborn
18	9,330	Kalamazoo Public SD	Kalamazoo
19	9,312	Grosse Pointe Public Schools	Grosse Pointe
20	9,260	Center Line Public Schools	Center Line
21	9,140	Wyandotte City SD	Wyandotte
22	9,124	Ann Arbor Public Schools	Ann Arbor
23	9,106	School District of Royal Oak	Royal Oak
24	9,100	Hazel Park City SD	Hazel Park
25	9,084	South Lake Schools	St Clair Shores
26	9,069	Detroit City SD	Detroit
27	9,068	Troy SD	Troy
28	8,995	Van Dyke Public Schools	Warren
29	8,982	East Lansing SD	East Lansing
30	8,970	Waverly Community Schools	Lansing
31	8,945	Warren Consolidated Schools	Warren
32	8,902	Pontiac City SD	Pontiac
33	8,887	Godwin Heights Public Schools	Wyoming
34	8,879	Flint City SD	Flint
35	8,799	Oak Park City SD	Oak Park
36	8,795	Clawson City SD	Clawson
37	8,775	Jefferson Schools (Monroe)	Monroe
38	8,761	Trenton Public Schools	Trenton
39	8,751	River Rouge SD	River Rouge
40	8,714	Warren Woods Public Schools	Warren
41	8,680	Holland City SD	Holland
41	8,680	Jackson Public Schools	Jackson
43	8,665	Walled Lake Consolidated Schools	Walled Lake
44	8,662	Avondale SD	Auburn Hills
45	8,641	Saginaw City SD	Saginaw
46	8,636	Novi Community SD	Novi
47	8,634	Fitzgerald Public Schools	Warren
48	8,616	Romulus Community Schools	Romulus
49	8,607	Taylor SD	Taylor
50	8,593	Highland Park City Schools	Highland Park
51	8,522	Armada Area Schools	Armada
52	8,485	Westwood Community Schools	Dearborn Hgts
53	8,447	Carman-Ainsworth Community Schools	Flint
53	8,447	Livonia Public Schools	Livonia
55	8,399	Redford Union SD	Redford
56	8,390	Ferndale Public Schools	Ferndale
57	8,329	Battle Creek Public Schools	Battle Creek
58	8,282	Midland Public Schools	Midland
59	8,217	Forest Hills Public Schools	Grand Rapids
60	8,204	Fraser Public Schools	Fraser
61	8,203	Okemos Public Schools	Okemos
62	8,177	Mount Clemens Community SD	Mount Clemens
63	8,107	Southgate Community SD	Southgate
64	8,102	Clarenceville SD	Livonia
64	8,102	Grosse Ile Township Schools	Grosse Ile
66	8,068	Berrien Springs Public Schools	Berrien Springs
67	8,020	Berkley SD	Berkley
68	8,009	Waterford SD	Waterford
69	7,953	Wayne-Westland Community SD	Westland
70	7,944	Melvindale-N Allen Park Schools	Melvindale
71	7,926	Albion Public Schools	Albion
72	7,910	Roseville Community Schools	Roseville
73	7,854	Dexter Community SD	Dexter
74	7,822	Caledonia Community Schools	Caledonia
75	7,809	Lake Shore Public Schools (Macomb)	St Clair Shores
76	7,802	Chelsea SD	Chelsea
77	7,792	Rochester Community SD	Rochester
78	7,749	Lake Orion Community Schools	Lake Orion
79	7,716	Wyoming Public Schools	Wyoming
80	7,712	Adrian City SD	Adrian
81	7,705	Mason County Central Schools	Scottville
82	7,631	Woodhaven-Brownstown SD	Brownstown
83	7,630	South Redford SD	Redford
84	7,609	East Grand Rapids Public Schools	E Grand Rapids
85	7,607	Lakeview Public Schools (Macomb)	St Clair Shores
86	7,573	East Detroit Public Schools	Eastpointe
87	7,537	Milan Area Schools	Milan

88	7,515	Flat Rock Community Schools	Flat Rock
89	7,511	Parchment SD	Parchment
90	7,492	East China SD	East China
91	7,461	Grand Haven Area Public Schools	Grand Haven
92	7,454	Bridgeport-Spaulding Community SD	Bridgeport
92	7,454	L'anse Creuse Public Schools	Harrison Twp
94	7,425	Huron SD	New Boston
95	7,413	Madison Public Schools (Oakland)	Madison Heights
96	7,405	Hartford Public SD	Hartford
96	7,405	Oxford Area Community Schools	Oxford
98	7,399	Kenowa Hills Public Schools	Grand Rapids
99	7,376	Saint Joseph Public Schools	Saint Joseph
100	7,374	Kentwood Public Schools	Kentwood
101	7,362	Lincoln Park Public Schools	Lincoln Park
102	7,336	Bay City SD	Bay City
103	7,333	Godfrey-Lee Public Schools	Wyoming
104	7,323	Hamtramck Public Schools	Hamtramck
105	7,316	Fruitport Community Schools	Fruitport
106	7,307	Saline Area Schools	Saline
107	7,303	Clarkston Community SD	Clarkston
108	7,297	White Cloud Public Schools	White Cloud
109	7,267	Niles Community SD	Niles
110	7,260	Comstock Public Schools	Kalamazoo
111	7,241	Kelloggsville Public Schools	Grand Rapids
112	7,235	Spring Lake Public Schools	Spring Lake
113	7,222	Manistee Area Schools	Manistee
114	7,218	Bangor Public Schools (Van Buren)	Bangor
115	7,213	Riverview Community SD	Riverview
116	7,208	Coloma Community Schools	Coloma
117	7,202	Fennville Public Schools	Fennville
118	7,201	Pinconning Area Schools	Pinconning
119	7,187	Jenison Public Schools	Jenison
120	7,175	Monroe Public Schools	Monroe
121	7,171	Holt Public Schools	Holt
122	7,169	Haslett Public Schools	Haslett
123	7,163	Van Buren Public Schools	Belleville
124	7,155	Allen Park Public Schools	Allen Park
125	7,151	Mount Pleasant City SD	Mount Pleasant
126	7,141	Houghton Lake Community Schools	Houghton Lake
127	7,133	Bangor Township Schools	Bay City
127	7,133	Montrose Community Schools	Montrose
129	7,129	Utica Community Schools	Sterling Hgts
130	7,121	Gibraltar SD	Woodhaven
130	7,121	Oscoda Area Schools	Oscoda
132	7,115	Orchard View Schools	Muskegon
133	7,091	Northview Public SD	Grand Rapids
134	7,067	Carrollton SD	Saginaw
135	7,058	Marshall Public Schools	Marshall
136	7,045	Alpena Public Schools	Alpena
137	7,039	Farwell Area Schools	Farwell
138	7,030	Mount Morris Consolidated Schools	Mount Morris
139	7,027	Rockford Public Schools	Rockford
140	7,021	Plymouth-Canton Community Schools	Plymouth
141	7,018	Reeths-Puffer Schools	Muskegon
142	7,016	Harrison Community Schools	Harrison
143	7,014	Mason Public Schools (Ingham)	Mason
144	7,006	West Branch-Rose City Area Schools	West Branch
145	7,004	Byron Center Public Schools	Byron Center
146	6,999	Ludington Area SD	Ludington
147	6,994	Alma Public Schools	Alma
148	6,986	Essexville-Hampton Public Schools	Essexville
149	6,978	Fenton Area Public Schools	Fenton
150	6,977	West Ottawa Public SD	Holland
151	6,971	Ionia Public Schools	Ionia
152	6,952	Meridian Public Schools	Sanford
153	6,950	Wayland Union Schools	Wayland
154	6,949	Gerrish-Higgins SD	Roscommon
155	6,931	Sault Sainte Marie Area Schools	Sault Ste Marie
156	6,901	Columbia SD	Brooklyn
157	6,898	Airport Community SD	Carleton
158	6,889	Lakeview SD (Calhoun)	Battle Creek
159	6,885	Oakridge Public Schools	Muskegon
160	6,881	Durand Area Schools	Durand
161	6,880	Elk Rapids Schools	Elk Rapids
161	6,880	Ida Public SD	Ida
163	6,871	Comstock Park Public Schools	Comstock Park
163	6,871	Crawford Ausable Schools	Grayling
165	6,863	Chippewa Valley Schools	Clinton Twp
166	6,839	Detroit Academy of Arts & Sci	Detroit
166	6,839	Shepherd Public SD	Shepherd
168	6,838	Huron Valley Schools	Highland
168	6,838	Shelby Public Schools	Shelby
170	6,830	Romeo Community Schools	Romeo
171	6,828	Port Huron Area SD	Port Huron
172	6,827	Clintondale Community Schools	Clinton Twp
173	6,812	Coopersville Public SD	Coopersville
174	6,807	Lincoln Consolidated SD	Ypsilanti
175	6,802	Holly Area SD	Holly
176	6,798	Coldwater Community Schools	Coldwater
177	6,797	Escanaba Area Public Schools	Escanaba
177	6,797	Hastings Area SD	Hastings
179	6,781	Vicksburg Community Schools	Vicksburg
180	6,777	Saginaw Township Community Schools	Saginaw
181	6,757	Ovid-Elsie Area Schools	Elsie
182	6,756	Marquette Area Public Schools	Marquette
183	6,748	Beaverton Rural Schools	Beaverton
184	6,747	Big Rapids Public Schools	Big Rapids
185	6,744	Fremont Public SD	Fremont
186	6,743	Belding Area SD	Belding
187	6,737	Grand Ledge Public Schools	Grand Ledge
188	6,736	Millington Community Schools	Millington
189	6,735	Whitehall District Schools	Whitehall
190	6,734	Portage Public Schools	Portage
191	6,718	Lowell Area Schools	Lowell
191	6,718	Pennfield SD	Battle Creek
193	6,712	Corunna Public SD	Corunna
194	6,709	Grand Blanc Community Schools	Grand Blanc
195	6,699	Anchor Bay SD	New Baltimore
196	6,695	Dowagiac Union SD	Dowagiac
197	6,690	Saint Johns Public Schools	Saint Johns
198	6,688	Chippewa Hills SD	Remus
199	6,687	Kalkaska Public Schools	Kalkaska
200	6,683	Allendale Public SD	Allendale
201	6,682	Harper Creek Community Schools	Battle Creek
201	6,682	Mason Consol Schools (Monroe)	Erie
203	6,673	Montague Area Public Schools	Montague
204	6,670	South Haven Public Schools	South Haven
205	6,669	Newaygo Public SD	Newaygo
206	6,666	Gladstone Area Schools	Gladstone
206	6,666	Williamston Community Schools	Williamston
208	6,665	Cedar Springs Public Schools	Cedar Springs
209	6,653	Clare Public Schools	Clare
210	6,650	Lakeville Community Schools	Otisville
210	6,650	Sparta Area Schools	Sparta
212	6,647	Public Schools of Petoskey	Petoskey
213	6,646	Owosso Public Schools	Owosso
214	6,627	Traverse City Area Public Schools	Traverse City
215	6,621	Allegan Public Schools	Allegan
216	6,618	Grandville Public Schools	Grandville
217	6,612	Lakeview Comm Schools (Montcalm)	Lakeview
218	6,599	Lakewood Public Schools	Lake Odessa
219	6,595	Swartz Creek Community Schools	Swartz Creek
220	6,591	Brandon SD	Ortonville
221	6,590	Brighton Area Schools	Brighton
222	6,583	Gladwin Community Schools	Gladwin
222	6,583	Richmond Community Schools	Richmond
224	6,582	Eaton Rapids Public Schools	Eaton Rapids
225	6,581	Cheboygan Area Schools	Cheboygan
226	6,572	Delton-Kellogg SD	Delton
226	6,572	Menominee Area Public Schools	Menominee
228	6,569	Gaylord Community Schools	Gaylord
228	6,569	South Lyon Community Schools	South Lyon
230	6,564	Central Montcalm Public Schools	Stanton
231	6,560	Fowlerville Community Schools	Fowlerville
232	6,553	Chesaning Union Schools	Chesaning
232	6,553	Stockbridge Community Schools	Stockbridge
234	6,551	Charlotte Public Schools	Charlotte
235	6,538	Yale Public Schools	Yale
236	6,532	Buchanan Community Schools	Buchanan
237	6,527	Crestwood SD	Dearborn Hgts
238	6,526	Bedford Public Schools	Temperance
239	6,515	Benzie County Central Schools	Benzonia
240	6,503	Kearsley Community Schools	Flint
241	6,493	Lapeer Community Schools	Lapeer
242	6,492	Napoleon Community Schools	Napoleon
243	6,488	Cass City Public Schools	Cass City
244	6,484	Greenville Public Schools	Greenville
244	6,484	Morley Stanwood Community Schools	Morley
246	6,476	East Jackson Community Schools	Jackson
247	6,474	Breitung Township Schools	Kingsford
248	6,473	Northwest Community Schools	Jackson
249	6,470	Maple Valley Schools	Vermontville
250	6,467	Bronson Community SD	Bronson
251	6,465	Capac Community SD	Capac
252	6,461	Hartland Consolidated Schools	Hartland
253	6,459	Constantine Public SD	Constantine
254	6,458	Thornapple Kellogg SD	Middleville
255	6,455	Bullock Creek SD	Midland
256	6,453	Linden Community Schools	Linden
257	6,435	Mona Shores Public SD	Norton Shores
258	6,433	Hillsdale Community Schools	Hillsdale
259	6,427	Paw Paw Public SD	Paw Paw
260	6,424	Lakeshore SD (Berrien)	Stevensville
261	6,412	Pinckney Community Schools	Pinckney
261	6,412	Tawas Area Schools	Tawas City
263	6,405	Portland Public SD	Portland
264	6,399	Plainwell Community Schools	Plainwell
265	6,397	Reed City Area Public Schools	Reed City
266	6,395	Imlay City Community Schools	Imlay City
267	6,386	Public Schools of Calumet	Calumet
268	6,364	Cadillac Area Public Schools	Cadillac
269	6,359	Gull Lake Community Schools	Richland
270	6,357	Clio Area SD	Clio
271	6,353	North Branch Area Schools	North Branch
272	6,350	Davison Community Schools	Davison
273	6,344	Sturgis Public Schools	Sturgis
274	6,341	Western SD	Parma
275	6,337	Dearborn Heights SD #7	Dearborn Hgts
276	6,336	Bendle Public Schools	Burton
277	6,335	Three Rivers Community Schools	Three Rivers
278	6,333	Quincy Community SD	Quincy
279	6,329	Birch Run Area SD	Birch Run
280	6,328	Dewitt Public Schools	Dewitt
280	6,328	Goodrich Area Schools	Goodrich
282	6,326	Tecumseh Public Schools	Tecumseh
283	6,317	Onsted Community Schools	Onsted
284	6,311	Algonac Community SD	Algonac
285	6,279	Zeeland Public Schools	Zeeland
286	6,269	Grant Public SD	Grant
287	6,252	Howell Public Schools	Howell
288	6,238	Perry Public SD	Perry
289	6,235	Caro Community Schools	Caro
290	6,214	Dundee Community Schools	Dundee
291	6,190	Croswell-Lexington Comm Schools	Croswell
292	6,175	Otsego Public Schools	Otsego
293	6,156	Swan Valley SD	Saginaw
294	6,138	Michigan Center SD	Michigan Center
295	6,111	Marysville Public Schools	Marysville
296	6,099	Tri County Area Schools	Howard City
297	6,096	Vassar Public Schools	Vassar
298	6,091	Brandywine Public SD	Niles
299	6,015	Standish-Sterling Comm Schools	Standish
300	6,011	Almont Community Schools	Almont
301	6,006	Hamilton Community Schools	Hamilton
302	5,998	Hudsonville Public SD	Hudsonville
303	5,932	Mattawan Consolidated School	Mattawan
304	5,928	Flushing Community Schools	Flushing
305	5,532	Edwardsburg Public Schools	Edwardsburg
306	5,264	Freeland Community SD	Freeland
307	n/a	Macomb ISD	Clinton Twp
307	n/a	Washtenaw ISD	Ann Arbor

Number of Diploma Recipients

Rank	Number	District Name	City
1	5,540	Detroit City SD	Detroit
2	1,867	Utica Community Schools	Sterling Hgts
3	1,315	Livonia Public Schools	Livonia
4	1,141	Ann Arbor Public Schools	Ann Arbor
5	1,014	Dearborn City SD	Dearborn
6	1,009	Rochester Community SD	Rochester
7	1,008	Plymouth-Canton Community Schools	Plymouth
8	970	Warren Consolidated Schools	Warren
9	967	Troy SD	Troy
10	847	Farmington Public SD	Farmington
11	811	Walled Lake Consolidated Schools	Walled Lake
12	778	Lansing Public SD	Lansing
13	762	Chippewa Valley Schools	Clinton Twp
14	760	Traverse City Area Public Schools	Traverse City
15	720	Grosse Pointe Public Schools	Grosse Pointe
16	716	Wayne-Westland Community SD	Westland
17	714	Flint City SD	Flint
18	708	Grand Rapids Public Schools	Grand Rapids
19	691	Port Huron Area SD	Port Huron
20	678	Midland Public Schools	Midland
21	659	Forest Hills Public Schools	Grand Rapids
22	622	Huron Valley Schools	Highland
23	616	Portage Public Schools	Portage
24	615	L'anse Creuse Public Schools	Harrison Twp
25	590	Bay City SD	Bay City
26	570	Kentwood Public Schools	Kentwood
27	567	Taylor SD	Taylor
28	559	Rockford Public Schools	Rockford
29	555	Waterford SD	Waterford
30	534	Southfield Public SD	Southfield
31	503	Birmingham City SD	Birmingham
32	501	Clarkston Community SD	Clarkston
33	485	Brighton Area Schools	Brighton
34	475	Lapeer Community Schools	Lapeer
34	475	School District of Royal Oak	Royal Oak
36	462	Saginaw City SD	Saginaw
37	446	Grand Haven Area Public Schools	Grand Haven
38	442	Bloomfield Hills SD	Bloomfield Hls
39	437	Howell Public Schools	Howell
40	434	Kalamazoo Public SD	Kalamazoo
41	418	West Bloomfield SD	West Bloomfield
42	416	Grand Blanc Community Schools	Grand Blanc
42	416	Pontiac City SD	Pontiac
42	416	West Ottawa Public SD	Holland
45	404	East China SD	East China
46	402	Lake Orion Community Schools	Lake Orion
47	392	Bedford Public Schools	Temperance
48	389	Novi Community SD	Novi
49	386	Grand Ledge Public Schools	Grand Ledge
49	386	Monroe Public Schools	Monroe
51	383	Alpena Public Schools	Alpena
52	371	Grandville Public Schools	Grandville

53	363	Van Buren Public Schools	Belleville
54	359	Saline Area Schools	Saline
55	357	Jenison Public Schools	Jenison
56	351	Okemos Public Schools	Okemos
57	350	Saginaw Township Community Schools	Saginaw
58	347	Wyoming Public Schools	Wyoming
59	345	South Lyon Community Schools	South Lyon
60	343	Romeo Community Schools	Romeo
61	342	East Detroit Public Schools	Eastpointe
62	333	Jackson Public Schools	Jackson
63	331	Marquette Area Public Schools	Marquette
63	331	Northville Public Schools	Northville
65	315	Flushing Community Schools	Flushing
66	308	Roseville Community Schools	Roseville
67	303	Mona Shores Public SD	Norton Shores
68	301	Holt Public Schools	Holt
68	301	Pinckney Community Schools	Pinckney
70	300	Fraser Public Schools	Fraser
71	296	Berkley SD	Berkley
71	296	Davison Community Schools	Davison
73	292	Holland City SD	Holland
74	286	Zeeland Public Schools	Zeeland
75	285	Hartland Consolidated Schools	Hartland
76	284	Southgate Community SD	Southgate
77	279	Reeths-Puffer Schools	Muskegon
78	278	Battle Creek Public Schools	Battle Creek
79	276	Anchor Bay SD	New Baltimore
80	275	Garden City SD	Garden City
81	274	Woodhaven-Brownstown SD	Brownstown
82	273	East Lansing SD	East Lansing
83	272	Carman-Ainsworth Community Schools	Flint
84	270	Mount Pleasant City SD	Mount Pleasant
85	268	Swartz Creek Community Schools	Swartz Creek
86	264	Wyandotte City SD	Wyandotte
87	263	Escanaba Area Public Schools	Escanaba
88	260	Hudsonville Public SD	Hudsonville
88	260	Lincoln Park Public Schools	Lincoln Park
90	258	Northview Public SD	Grand Rapids
91	257	Holly Area SD	Holly
92	255	Waverly Community Schools	Lansing
93	247	Kearsley Community Schools	Flint
93	247	Muskegon City SD	Muskegon
95	246	Adrian City SD	Adrian
96	244	Owosso Public Schools	Owosso
97	242	Greenville Public Schools	Greenville
98	240	Chelsea SD	Chelsea
99	238	Lakeview SD (Calhoun)	Battle Creek
99	238	Oak Park City SD	Oak Park
99	238	Saint Johns Public Schools	Saint Johns
102	237	Brandon SD	Ortonville
102	237	Eaton Rapids Public Schools	Eaton Rapids
102	237	Lakeshore SD (Berrien)	Stevensville
105	235	Cadillac Area Public Schools	Cadillac
105	235	Mason Public Schools (Ingham)	Mason
105	235	Oxford Area Community Schools	Oxford
105	235	School District of Ypsilanti	Ypsilanti
109	229	Fenton Area Public Schools	Fenton
110	224	Lowell Area Schools	Lowell
111	218	East Grand Rapids Public Schools	E Grand Rapids
111	218	Lakeview Public Schools (Macomb)	St Clair Shores
113	217	Kenowa Hills Public Schools	Grand Rapids
113	217	Mattawan Consolidated School	Mattawan
115	216	Crestwood SD	Dearborn Hgts
115	216	Haslett Public Schools	Haslett
115	216	Trenton Public Schools	Trenton
118	214	Tecumseh Public Schools	Tecumseh
119	213	Sault Sainte Marie Area Schools	Sault Ste Marie
120	212	Lincoln Consolidated SD	Ypsilanti
121	211	Coldwater Community Schools	Coldwater
122	210	Gull Lake Community Schools	Richland
122	210	Saint Joseph Public Schools	Saint Joseph
124	209	Thornapple Kellogg SD	Middleville
124	209	Vicksburg Community Schools	Vicksburg
124	209	Wayland Union Schools	Wayland
127	207	Avondale SD	Auburn Hills
127	207	Ionia Public Schools	Ionia
129	206	Fowlerville Community Schools	Fowlerville
129	206	Gaylord Community Schools	Gaylord
129	206	Northwest Community Schools	Jackson
132	205	Redford Union SD	Redford
133	203	Marshall Public Schools	Marshall
134	202	Caledonia Community Schools	Caledonia
134	202	Ferndale Public Schools	Ferndale
136	201	Benton Harbor Area Schools	Benton Harbor
136	201	Fruitport Community Schools	Fruitport
136	201	Romulus Community Schools	Romulus
139	200	Gibraltar SD	Woodhaven
140	199	South Redford SD	Redford
141	198	Allen Park Public Schools	Allen Park
142	194	Dewitt Public Schools	Dewitt
142	194	Lake Shore Public Schools (Macomb)	St Clair Shores
144	193	Dexter Community SD	Dexter
144	193	Fremont Public SD	Fremont
146	192	Hastings Area SD	Hastings
147	191	Warren Woods Public Schools	Warren
148	190	Sparta Area Schools	Sparta
149	189	Charlotte Public Schools	Charlotte
150	187	Plainwell Community Schools	Plainwell
151	185	Clio Area SD	Clio
152	184	Sturgis Public Schools	Sturgis
153	182	Lakewood Public Schools	Lake Odessa
154	181	West Branch-Rose City Area Schools	West Branch
155	178	Jefferson Schools (Monroe)	Monroe
155	178	Ludington Area SD	Ludington
157	175	Bangor Township Schools	Bay City
157	175	Grosse Ile Township Schools	Grosse Ile
159	172	Marysville Public Schools	Marysville
160	171	Airport Community SD	Carleton
160	171	Breitung Township Schools	Kingsford
160	171	Riverview Community SD	Riverview
163	170	Big Rapids Public Schools	Big Rapids
164	169	Fitzgerald Public Schools	Warren
164	169	North Branch Area Schools	North Branch
166	168	Otsego Public Schools	Otsego
167	167	Lamphere Public Schools	Madison Heights
168	165	Byron Center Public Schools	Byron Center
169	164	Cheboygan Area Schools	Cheboygan
169	164	Mount Morris Consolidated Schools	Mount Morris
171	163	Pinconning Area Schools	Pinconning
172	162	Hamtramck Public Schools	Hamtramck
173	160	Niles Community SD	Niles
174	159	Three Rivers Community Schools	Three Rivers
175	158	Croswell-Lexington Comm Schools	Croswell
176	157	Hazel Park City SD	Hazel Park
177	156	Coopersville Public SD	Coopersville
177	156	Harper Creek Community Schools	Battle Creek
177	156	Paw Paw Public SD	Paw Paw
180	155	South Lake Schools	St Clair Shores
180	155	Van Dyke Public Schools	Warren
182	154	Center Line Public Schools	Center Line
183	153	Portland Public SD	Portland
184	152	Belding Area SD	Belding
184	152	South Haven Public Schools	South Haven
186	151	Linden Community Schools	Linden
187	150	Allegan Public Schools	Allegan
188	149	Gladstone Area Schools	Gladstone
189	148	Western SD	Parma
190	147	Alma Public Schools	Alma
191	145	Algonac Community SD	Algonac
191	145	Reed City Area Public Schools	Reed City
191	145	Richmond Community Schools	Richmond
194	144	Corunna Public SD	Corunna
194	144	Menominee Area Public Schools	Menominee
194	144	Spring Lake Public Schools	Spring Lake
197	143	Caro Community Schools	Caro
197	143	Chippewa Hills SD	Remus
197	143	Comstock Public Schools	Kalamazoo
197	143	Yale Public Schools	Yale
201	142	Delton-Kellogg SD	Delton
202	141	Gladwin Community Schools	Gladwin
202	141	Lakeville Community Schools	Otisville
204	140	Dowagiac Union SD	Dowagiac
204	140	Imlay City Community Schools	Imlay City
206	139	Chesaning Union Schools	Chesaning
207	137	Essexville-Hampton Public Schools	Essexville
207	137	Grant Public SD	Grant
207	137	Millington Community Schools	Millington
210	136	River Rouge SD	River Rouge
211	135	Manistee Area Schools	Manistee
212	134	Tawas Area Schools	Tawas City
213	133	Oscoda Area Schools	Oscoda
214	132	Cedar Springs Public Schools	Cedar Springs
214	132	Coloma Community Schools	Coloma
214	132	Kalkaska Public Schools	Kalkaska
214	132	Whitehall District Schools	Whitehall
218	131	Armada Area Schools	Armada
218	131	Hamilton Community Schools	Hamilton
220	130	Williamston Community Schools	Williamston
221	129	Goodrich Area Schools	Goodrich
221	129	Standish-Sterling Comm Schools	Standish
223	128	Ida Public SD	Ida
224	127	Willow Run Community Schools	Ypsilanti
225	126	Orchard View Schools	Muskegon
226	125	Cass City Public Schools	Cass City
226	125	Milan Area Schools	Milan
226	125	Ovid-Elsie Area Schools	Elsie
229	123	Melvindale-N Allen Park Schools	Melvindale
230	122	Central Montcalm Public Schools	Stanton
230	122	Crawford Ausable Schools	Grayling
232	121	Houghton Lake Community Schools	Houghton Lake
233	120	Onsted Community Schools	Onsted
234	119	Clintondale Community Schools	Clinton Twp
234	119	Elk Rapids Schools	Elk Rapids
236	118	Beaverton Rural Schools	Beaverton
236	118	Bridgeport-Spaulding Community SD	Bridgeport
236	118	Bullock Creek SD	Midland
236	118	Capac Community SD	Capac
240	117	Hillsdale Community Schools	Hillsdale
241	116	Shepherd Public SD	Shepherd
242	115	Columbia SD	Brooklyn
242	115	Kelloggsville Public Schools	Grand Rapids
242	115	Lakeview Comm Schools (Montcalm)	Lakeview
245	114	Bronson Community SD	Bronson
245	114	Edwardsburg Public Schools	Edwardsburg
245	114	Godwin Heights Public Schools	Wyoming
245	114	Mason County Central Schools	Scottville
245	114	Pennfield SD	Battle Creek
250	113	Huron SD	New Boston
250	113	Mason Consol Schools (Monroe)	Erie
250	113	Swan Valley SD	Saginaw
253	112	Birch Run Area SD	Birch Run
254	111	Benzie County Central Schools	Benzonia
254	111	Perry Public SD	Perry
256	110	Allendale Public SD	Allendale
257	109	Clawson City SD	Clawson
258	108	Harrison Community Schools	Harrison
258	108	Public Schools of Calumet	Calumet
260	107	Clare Public Schools	Clare
260	107	Parchment SD	Parchment
262	106	Oakridge Public Schools	Muskegon
262	106	Stockbridge Community Schools	Stockbridge
264	104	Comstock Park Public Schools	Comstock Park
264	104	Montague Area Public Schools	Montague
266	103	Bangor Public Schools (Van Buren)	Bangor
267	102	Gerrish-Higgins SD	Roscommon
268	101	Albion Public Schools	Albion
268	101	Constantine Public SD	Constantine
270	100	Dearborn Heights SD #7	Dearborn Hgts
270	100	Durand Area Schools	Durand
272	98	Montrose Community Schools	Montrose
273	97	Brandywine Public SD	Niles
274	94	Clarenceville SD	Livonia
274	94	Napoleon Community Schools	Napoleon
276	93	Berrien Springs Public Schools	Berrien Springs
276	93	Buchanan Community Schools	Buchanan
276	93	Maple Valley Schools	Vermontville
276	93	Vassar Public Schools	Vassar
280	92	Flat Rock Community Schools	Flat Rock
281	91	Dundee Community Schools	Dundee
281	91	Meridian Public Schools	Sanford
281	91	Newaygo Public SD	Newaygo
281	91	Shelby Public Schools	Shelby
285	90	Hartford Public SD	Hartford
286	89	Mount Clemens Community SD	Mount Clemens
287	88	Almont Community Schools	Almont
287	88	East Jackson Community Schools	Jackson
287	88	Fennville Public Schools	Fennville
290	87	Farwell Area Schools	Farwell
290	87	Quincy Community SD	Quincy
292	86	Freeland Community SD	Freeland
292	86	Madison Public Schools (Oakland)	Madison Heights
292	86	Morley Stanwood Community Schools	Morley
295	81	Highland Park City Schools	Highland Park
296	80	Carrollton SD	Saginaw
297	73	Muskegon Heights SD	Muskegon Hgts
297	73	White Cloud Public Schools	White Cloud
299	70	Michigan Center SD	Michigan Center
300	69	Tri County Area Schools	Howard City
301	67	Westwood Community Schools	Dearborn Hgts
302	65	Bendle Public Schools	Burton
303	63	Beecher Community SD	Flint
304	46	Godfrey-Lee Public Schools	Wyoming
305	0	Public Schools of Petoskey	Petoskey
306	n/a	Detroit Academy of Arts & Sci	Detroit
306	n/a	Macomb ISD	Clinton Twp
306	n/a	Washtenaw ISD	Ann Arbor

High School Drop-out Rate

Rank	Percent	District Name	City
1	n/a	Adrian City SD	Adrian
1	n/a	Airport Community SD	Carleton
1	n/a	Albion Public Schools	Albion
1	n/a	Algonac Community SD	Algonac
1	n/a	Allegan Public Schools	Allegan
1	n/a	Allen Park Public Schools	Allen Park
1	n/a	Allendale Public SD	Allendale
1	n/a	Alma Public Schools	Alma
1	n/a	Almont Community Schools	Almont
1	n/a	Alpena Public Schools	Alpena
1	n/a	Anchor Bay SD	New Baltimore
1	n/a	Ann Arbor Public Schools	Ann Arbor
1	n/a	Armada Area Schools	Armada
1	n/a	Avondale SD	Auburn Hills
1	n/a	Bangor Public Schools (Van Buren)	Bangor
1	n/a	Bangor Township Schools	Bay City

1	n/a	Battle Creek Public Schools	Battle Creek
1	n/a	Bay City SD	Bay City
1	n/a	Beaverton Rural Schools	Beaverton
1	n/a	Bedford Public Schools	Temperance
1	n/a	Beecher Community SD	Flint
1	n/a	Belding Area SD	Belding
1	n/a	Bendle Public Schools	Burton
1	n/a	Benton Harbor Area Schools	Benton Harbor
1	n/a	Benzie County Central Schools	Benzonia
1	n/a	Berkley SD	Berkley
1	n/a	Berrien Springs Public Schools	Berrien Springs
1	n/a	Big Rapids Public Schools	Big Rapids
1	n/a	Birch Run Area SD	Birch Run
1	n/a	Birmingham City SD	Birmingham
1	n/a	Bloomfield Hills SD	Bloomfield Hls
1	n/a	Brandon SD	Ortonville
1	n/a	Brandywine Public SD	Niles
1	n/a	Breitung Township Schools	Kingsford
1	n/a	Bridgeport-Spaulding Community SD	Bridgeport
1	n/a	Brighton Area Schools	Brighton
1	n/a	Bronson Community SD	Bronson
1	n/a	Buchanan Community Schools	Buchanan
1	n/a	Bullock Creek SD	Midland
1	n/a	Byron Center Public Schools	Byron Center
1	n/a	Cadillac Area Public Schools	Cadillac
1	n/a	Caledonia Community Schools	Caledonia
1	n/a	Capac Community SD	Capac
1	n/a	Carman-Ainsworth Community Schools	Flint
1	n/a	Caro Community Schools	Caro
1	n/a	Carrollton SD	Saginaw
1	n/a	Cass City Public Schools	Cass City
1	n/a	Cedar Springs Public Schools	Cedar Springs
1	n/a	Center Line Public Schools	Center Line
1	n/a	Central Montcalm Public Schools	Stanton
1	n/a	Charlotte Public Schools	Charlotte
1	n/a	Cheboygan Area Schools	Cheboygan
1	n/a	Chelsea SD	Chelsea
1	n/a	Chesaning Union Schools	Chesaning
1	n/a	Chippewa Hills SD	Remus
1	n/a	Chippewa Valley Schools	Clinton Twp
1	n/a	Clare Public Schools	Clare
1	n/a	Clarenceville SD	Livonia
1	n/a	Clarkston Community SD	Clarkston
1	n/a	Clawson City SD	Clawson
1	n/a	Clintondale Community Schools	Clinton Twp
1	n/a	Clio Area SD	Clio
1	n/a	Coldwater Community Schools	Coldwater
1	n/a	Coloma Community Schools	Coloma
1	n/a	Columbia SD	Brooklyn
1	n/a	Comstock Park Public Schools	Comstock Park
1	n/a	Comstock Public Schools	Kalamazoo
1	n/a	Constantine Public SD	Constantine
1	n/a	Coopersville Public SD	Coopersville
1	n/a	Corunna Public SD	Corunna
1	n/a	Crawford Ausable Schools	Grayling
1	n/a	Crestwood SD	Dearborn Hgts
1	n/a	Croswell-Lexington Comm Schools	Croswell
1	n/a	Davison Community Schools	Davison
1	n/a	Dearborn City SD	Dearborn
1	n/a	Dearborn Heights SD #7	Dearborn Hgts
1	n/a	Delton-Kellogg SD	Delton
1	n/a	Detroit Academy of Arts & Sci	Detroit
1	n/a	Detroit City SD	Detroit
1	n/a	Dewitt Public Schools	Dewitt
1	n/a	Dexter Community SD	Dexter
1	n/a	Dowagiac Union SD	Dowagiac
1	n/a	Dundee Community Schools	Dundee
1	n/a	Durand Area Schools	Durand
1	n/a	East China SD	East China
1	n/a	East Detroit Public Schools	Eastpointe
1	n/a	East Grand Rapids Public Schools	E Grand Rapids
1	n/a	East Jackson Community Schools	Jackson
1	n/a	East Lansing SD	East Lansing
1	n/a	Eaton Rapids Public Schools	Eaton Rapids
1	n/a	Edwardsburg Public Schools	Edwardsburg
1	n/a	Elk Rapids Schools	Elk Rapids
1	n/a	Escanaba Area Public Schools	Escanaba
1	n/a	Essexville-Hampton Public Schools	Essexville
1	n/a	Farmington Public SD	Farmington
1	n/a	Farwell Area Schools	Farwell
1	n/a	Fennville Public Schools	Fennville
1	n/a	Fenton Area Public Schools	Fenton
1	n/a	Ferndale Public Schools	Ferndale
1	n/a	Fitzgerald Public Schools	Warren
1	n/a	Flat Rock Community Schools	Flat Rock
1	n/a	Flint City SD	Flint
1	n/a	Flushing Community Schools	Flushing
1	n/a	Forest Hills Public Schools	Grand Rapids
1	n/a	Fowlerville Community Schools	Fowlerville
1	n/a	Fraser Public Schools	Fraser
1	n/a	Freeland Community SD	Freeland
1	n/a	Fremont Public SD	Fremont
1	n/a	Fruitport Community Schools	Fruitport
1	n/a	Garden City SD	Garden City
1	n/a	Gaylord Community Schools	Gaylord
1	n/a	Gerrish-Higgins SD	Roscommon
1	n/a	Gibraltar SD	Woodhaven
1	n/a	Gladstone Area Schools	Gladstone
1	n/a	Gladwin Community Schools	Gladwin
1	n/a	Godfrey-Lee Public Schools	Wyoming
1	n/a	Godwin Heights Public Schools	Wyoming
1	n/a	Goodrich Area Schools	Goodrich
1	n/a	Grand Blanc Community Schools	Grand Blanc
1	n/a	Grand Haven Area Public Schools	Grand Haven
1	n/a	Grand Ledge Public Schools	Grand Ledge
1	n/a	Grand Rapids Public Schools	Grand Rapids
1	n/a	Grandville Public Schools	Grandville
1	n/a	Grant Public SD	Grant
1	n/a	Greenville Public Schools	Greenville
1	n/a	Grosse Ile Township Schools	Grosse Ile
1	n/a	Grosse Pointe Public Schools	Grosse Pointe
1	n/a	Gull Lake Community Schools	Richland
1	n/a	Hamilton Community Schools	Hamilton
1	n/a	Hamtramck Public Schools	Hamtramck
1	n/a	Harper Creek Community Schools	Battle Creek
1	n/a	Harrison Community Schools	Harrison
1	n/a	Hartford Public SD	Hartford
1	n/a	Hartland Consolidated Schools	Hartland
1	n/a	Haslett Public Schools	Haslett
1	n/a	Hastings Area SD	Hastings
1	n/a	Hazel Park City SD	Hazel Park
1	n/a	Highland Park City Schools	Highland Park
1	n/a	Hillsdale Community Schools	Hillsdale
1	n/a	Holland City SD	Holland
1	n/a	Holly Area SD	Holly
1	n/a	Holt Public Schools	Holt
1	n/a	Houghton Lake Community Schools	Houghton Lake
1	n/a	Howell Public Schools	Howell
1	n/a	Hudsonville Public SD	Hudsonville
1	n/a	Huron SD	New Boston
1	n/a	Huron Valley Schools	Highland
1	n/a	Ida Public SD	Ida
1	n/a	Imlay City Community Schools	Imlay City
1	n/a	Ionia Public Schools	Ionia
1	n/a	Jackson Public Schools	Jackson
1	n/a	Jefferson Schools (Monroe)	Monroe
1	n/a	Jenison Public Schools	Jenison
1	n/a	Kalamazoo Public SD	Kalamazoo
1	n/a	Kalkaska Public Schools	Kalkaska
1	n/a	Kearsley Community Schools	Flint
1	n/a	Kelloggsville Public Schools	Grand Rapids
1	n/a	Kenowa Hills Public Schools	Grand Rapids
1	n/a	Kentwood Public Schools	Kentwood
1	n/a	L'anse Creuse Public Schools	Harrison Twp
1	n/a	Lake Orion Community Schools	Lake Orion
1	n/a	Lake Shore Public Schools (Macomb)	St Clair Shores
1	n/a	Lakeshore SD (Berrien)	Stevensville
1	n/a	Lakeview Comm Schools (Montcalm)	Lakeview
1	n/a	Lakeview Public Schools (Macomb)	St Clair Shores
1	n/a	Lakeview SD (Calhoun)	Battle Creek
1	n/a	Lakeville Community Schools	Otisville
1	n/a	Lakewood Public Schools	Lake Odessa
1	n/a	Lamphere Public Schools	Madison Heights
1	n/a	Lansing Public SD	Lansing
1	n/a	Lapeer Community Schools	Lapeer
1	n/a	Lincoln Consolidated SD	Ypsilanti
1	n/a	Lincoln Park Public Schools	Lincoln Park
1	n/a	Linden Community Schools	Linden
1	n/a	Livonia Public Schools	Livonia
1	n/a	Lowell Area Schools	Lowell
1	n/a	Ludington Area SD	Ludington
1	n/a	Macomb ISD	Clinton Twp
1	n/a	Madison Public Schools (Oakland)	Madison Heights
1	n/a	Manistee Area Schools	Manistee
1	n/a	Maple Valley Schools	Vermontville
1	n/a	Marquette Area Public Schools	Marquette
1	n/a	Marshall Public Schools	Marshall
1	n/a	Marysville Public Schools	Marysville
1	n/a	Mason Consol Schools (Monroe)	Erie
1	n/a	Mason County Central Schools	Scottville
1	n/a	Mason Public Schools (Ingham)	Mason
1	n/a	Mattawan Consolidated School	Mattawan
1	n/a	Melvindale-N Allen Park Schools	Melvindale
1	n/a	Menominee Area Public Schools	Menominee
1	n/a	Meridian Public Schools	Sanford
1	n/a	Michigan Center SD	Michigan Center
1	n/a	Midland Public Schools	Midland
1	n/a	Milan Area Schools	Milan
1	n/a	Millington Community Schools	Millington
1	n/a	Mona Shores Public SD	Norton Shores
1	n/a	Monroe Public Schools	Monroe
1	n/a	Montague Area Public Schools	Montague
1	n/a	Montrose Community Schools	Montrose
1	n/a	Morley Stanwood Community Schools	Morley
1	n/a	Mount Clemens Community SD	Mount Clemens
1	n/a	Mount Morris Consolidated Schools	Mount Morris
1	n/a	Mount Pleasant City SD	Mount Pleasant
1	n/a	Muskegon City SD	Muskegon
1	n/a	Muskegon Heights SD	Muskegon Hgts
1	n/a	Napoleon Community Schools	Napoleon
1	n/a	Newaygo Public SD	Newaygo
1	n/a	Niles Community SD	Niles
1	n/a	North Branch Area Schools	North Branch
1	n/a	Northview Public SD	Grand Rapids
1	n/a	Northville Public Schools	Northville
1	n/a	Northwest Community Schools	Jackson
1	n/a	Novi Community SD	Novi
1	n/a	Oak Park City SD	Oak Park
1	n/a	Oakridge Public Schools	Muskegon
1	n/a	Okemos Public Schools	Okemos
1	n/a	Onsted Community Schools	Onsted
1	n/a	Orchard View Schools	Muskegon
1	n/a	Oscoda Area Schools	Oscoda
1	n/a	Otsego Public Schools	Otsego
1	n/a	Ovid-Elsie Area Schools	Elsie
1	n/a	Owosso Public Schools	Owosso
1	n/a	Oxford Area Community Schools	Oxford
1	n/a	Parchment SD	Parchment
1	n/a	Paw Paw Public SD	Paw Paw
1	n/a	Pennfield SD	Battle Creek
1	n/a	Perry Public SD	Perry
1	n/a	Pinckney Community Schools	Pinckney
1	n/a	Pinconning Area Schools	Pinconning
1	n/a	Plainwell Community Schools	Plainwell
1	n/a	Plymouth-Canton Community Schools	Plymouth
1	n/a	Pontiac City SD	Pontiac
1	n/a	Port Huron Area SD	Port Huron
1	n/a	Portage Public Schools	Portage
1	n/a	Portland Public SD	Portland
1	n/a	Public Schools of Calumet	Calumet
1	n/a	Public Schools of Petoskey	Petoskey
1	n/a	Quincy Community SD	Quincy
1	n/a	Redford Union SD	Redford
1	n/a	Reed City Area Public Schools	Reed City
1	n/a	Reeths-Puffer Schools	Muskegon
1	n/a	Richmond Community Schools	Richmond
1	n/a	River Rouge SD	River Rouge
1	n/a	Riverview Community SD	Riverview
1	n/a	Rochester Community SD	Rochester
1	n/a	Rockford Public Schools	Rockford
1	n/a	Romeo Community Schools	Romeo
1	n/a	Romulus Community Schools	Romulus
1	n/a	Roseville Community Schools	Roseville
1	n/a	Saginaw City SD	Saginaw
1	n/a	Saginaw Township Community Schools	Saginaw
1	n/a	Saint Johns Public Schools	Saint Johns
1	n/a	Saint Joseph Public Schools	Saint Joseph
1	n/a	Saline Area Schools	Saline
1	n/a	Sault Sainte Marie Area Schools	Sault Ste Marie
1	n/a	School District of Royal Oak	Royal Oak
1	n/a	School District of Ypsilanti	Ypsilanti
1	n/a	Shelby Public Schools	Shelby
1	n/a	Shepherd Public SD	Shepherd
1	n/a	South Haven Public Schools	South Haven
1	n/a	South Lake Schools	St Clair Shores
1	n/a	South Lyon Community Schools	South Lyon
1	n/a	South Redford SD	Redford
1	n/a	Southfield Public SD	Southfield
1	n/a	Southgate Community SD	Southgate
1	n/a	Sparta Area Schools	Sparta
1	n/a	Spring Lake Public Schools	Spring Lake
1	n/a	Standish-Sterling Comm Schools	Standish
1	n/a	Stockbridge Community Schools	Stockbridge
1	n/a	Sturgis Public Schools	Sturgis
1	n/a	Swan Valley SD	Saginaw
1	n/a	Swartz Creek Community Schools	Swartz Creek
1	n/a	Tawas Area Schools	Tawas City
1	n/a	Taylor SD	Taylor
1	n/a	Tecumseh Public Schools	Tecumseh
1	n/a	Thornapple Kellogg SD	Middleville
1	n/a	Three Rivers Community Schools	Three Rivers
1	n/a	Traverse City Area Public Schools	Traverse City
1	n/a	Trenton Public Schools	Trenton
1	n/a	Tri County Area Schools	Howard City
1	n/a	Troy SD	Troy
1	n/a	Utica Community Schools	Sterling Hgts
1	n/a	Van Buren Public Schools	Belleville
1	n/a	Van Dyke Public Schools	Warren
1	n/a	Vassar Public Schools	Vassar
1	n/a	Vicksburg Community Schools	Vicksburg
1	n/a	Walled Lake Consolidated Schools	Walled Lake
1	n/a	Warren Consolidated Schools	Warren
1	n/a	Warren Woods Public Schools	Warren
1	n/a	Washtenaw ISD	Ann Arbor
1	n/a	Waterford SD	Waterford
1	n/a	Waverly Community Schools	Lansing

1	n/a	Wayland Union Schools	Wayland
1	n/a	Wayne-Westland Community SD	Westland
1	n/a	West Bloomfield SD	West Bloomfield
1	n/a	West Branch-Rose City Area Schools	West Branch
1	n/a	West Ottawa Public SD	Holland
1	n/a	Western SD	Parma
1	n/a	Westwood Community Schools	Dearborn Hgts
1	n/a	White Cloud Public Schools	White Cloud
1	n/a	Whitehall District Schools	Whitehall
1	n/a	Williamston Community Schools	Williamston
1	n/a	Willow Run Community Schools	Ypsilanti
1	n/a	Woodhaven-Brownstown SD	Brownstown
1	n/a	Wyandotte City SD	Wyandotte
1	n/a	Wyoming Public Schools	Wyoming
1	n/a	Yale Public Schools	Yale
1	n/a	Zeeland Public Schools	Zeeland

Minnesota

Minnesota Public School Educational Profile

Category	Value	Category	Value
Schools *(2002-2003)*	2,507	**Diploma Recipients** *(2002-2003)*	57,440
Instructional Level		White, Non-Hispanic	51,052
Primary	1,085	Black, Non-Hispanic	2,122
Middle	302	Asian/Pacific Islander	2,573
High	713	American Indian/Alaskan Native	661
Other Level	407	Hispanic	1,032
Curriculum		**High School Drop-out Rate** (%) *(2000-2001)*	4.0
Regular	1,624	White, Non-Hispanic	2.9
Special Education	261	Black, Non-Hispanic	12.3
Vocational	13	Asian/Pacific Islander	5.5
Alternative	609	American Indian/Alaskan Native	15.1
Type		Hispanic	12.7
Magnet	65	**Staff** *(2002-2003)*	105,312.0
Charter	94	Teachers	52,808.0
Title I Eligible	984	Average Salary ($)	44,745
School-wide Title I	219	Librarians/Media Specialists	968.1
Students *(2002-2003)*	846,891	Guidance Counselors	1,063.1
Gender (%)		**Ratios** *(2002-2003)*	
Male	51.6	Student/Teacher Ratio	16.0 to 1
Female	48.4	Student/Librarian Ratio	874.8 to 1
Race/Ethnicity (%)		Student/Counselor Ratio	796.6 to 1
White, Non-Hispanic	81.1	**Current Spending** *($ per student in FY 2001)*	7,736
Black, Non-Hispanic	7.4	Instruction	4,924
Asian/Pacific Islander	5.3	Support Services	2,482
American Indian/Alaskan Native	2.1	**College Entrance Exam Scores** *(2003)*	
Hispanic	4.2	Scholastic Aptitude Test (SAT)	
Classification (%)		Participation Rate (%)	10
Individual Education Program (IEP)	13.2	Mean SAT I Verbal Score	582
Migrant	0.1	Mean SAT I Math Score	591
English Language Learner (ELL)	6.1	American College Testing Program (ACT)	
Eligible for Free Lunch Program	20.0	Participation Rate (%)	67
Eligible for Reduced-Price Lunch Program	7.4	Average Composite Score	22.0

Note: *For an explanation of data, please refer to the User's Guide in the front of the book; n/a indicates data not available*

Minnesota NAEP 2003 Test Scores

Reading		
Grade/Category	**Value**	**Rank**
4th Grade		
Average Proficiency	222.6 (1.1)	12/51
Proficiency by Gender/Race/Ethnicity		
Male	216.2 (1.3)	22/51
Female	229.3 (1.2)	4/51
White, Non-Hispanic	229.0 (1.0)	12/51
Black, Non-Hispanic	194.0 (3.4)	32/42
Asian, Non-Hispanic	195.3 (3.7)	35/41
American Indian, Non-Hispanic	197.1 (2.8)	25/25
Hispanic	n/a	n/a
Proficiency by Class Size		
Less than 16 Students	188.9 (7.3)	38/45
16 to 18 Students	*197.3 (4.3)*	43/48
19 to 20 Students	*214.3 (5.8)*	34/50
21 to 25 Students	225.0 (1.9)	15/51
Greater than 25 Students	226.4 (1.4)	5/49
Percent Attaining Achievement Levels		
Below Basic	31.3 (1.4)	38/51
Basic or Above	68.7 (1.4)	12/51
Proficient or Above	37.2 (1.3)	5/51
Advanced or Above	9.1 (0.8)	5/51
8th Grade		
Average Proficiency	267.7 (1.1)	10/51
Proficiency by Gender/Race/Ethnicity		
Male	261.2 (1.4)	17/51
Female	274.4 (1.4)	8/51
White, Non-Hispanic	272.5 (1.0)	11/50
Black, Non-Hispanic	243.0 (3.7)	27/41
Asian, Non-Hispanic	240.2 (5.3)	32/37
American Indian, Non-Hispanic	256.6 (3.9)	19/23
Hispanic	n/a	n/a
Proficiency by Parents Highest Level of Ed.		
Did Not Finish High School	247.1 (4.0)	21/50
Graduated High School	255.5 (2.6)	26/50
Some Education After High School	271.6 (1.8)	7/50
Graduated College	275.4 (1.1)	13/50
Percent Attaining Achievement Levels		
Below Basic	21.9 (1.3)	39/51
Basic or Above	78.1 (1.3)	13/51
Proficient or Above	37.2 (1.2)	6/51
Advanced or Above	3.0 (0.6)	15/51

Mathematics		
Grade/Category	**Value**	**Rank**
4th Grade		
Average Proficiency	241.9 (0.9)	3/51
Proficiency by Gender/Race/Ethnicity		
Male	243.5 (1.1)	4/51
Female	240.1 (1.0)	4/51
White, Non-Hispanic	246.3 (1.0)	7/51
Black, Non-Hispanic	218.8 (2.1)	13/42
Asian, Non-Hispanic	220.3 (3.3)	25/43
American Indian, Non-Hispanic	229.2 (2.8)	23/26
Hispanic	n/a	n/a
Proficiency by Class Size		
Less than 16 Students	*227.3 (6.1)*	17/47
16 to 18 Students	*222.5 (3.5)*	41/48
19 to 20 Students	*237.1 (3.0)*	14/50
21 to 25 Students	243.7 (1.5)	4/51
Greater than 25 Students	243.0 (1.6)	6/49
Percent Attaining Achievement Levels		
Below Basic	16.1 (0.9)	45/51
Basic or Above	83.9 (0.9)	7/51
Proficient or Above	41.8 (1.6)	3/51
Advanced or Above	6.8 (0.8)	1/51
8th Grade		
Average Proficiency	290.7 (1.1)	1/51
Proficiency by Gender/Race/Ethnicity		
Male	289.2 (1.4)	2/51
Female	292.1 (1.1)	1/51
White, Non-Hispanic	295.4 (1.0)	1/50
Black, Non-Hispanic	251.3 (5.6)	21/41
Asian, Non-Hispanic	262.5 (4.6)	12/37
American Indian, Non-Hispanic	284.5 (3.9)	16/23
Hispanic	n/a	n/a
Proficiency by Parents Highest Level of Ed.		
Did Not Finish High School	261.9 (6.6)	11/50
Graduated High School	279.2 (1.8)	1/50
Some Education After High School	294.6 (1.9)	1/50
Graduated College	298.2 (1.1)	1/50
Percent Attaining Achievement Levels		
Below Basic	18.1 (1.1)	51/51
Basic or Above	81.9 (1.1)	1/51
Proficient or Above	43.7 (1.4)	1/51
Advanced or Above	8.8 (0.8)	1/51

Note: *For an explanation of data, please refer to the User's Guide in the front of the book; values in italics indicate that the nature of the sample does not allow accurate determination of the variability of the statistic; n/a indicates data not available*

Anoka County

Anoka-Hennepin

11299 Hanson Blvd NW • Coon Rapids, MN 55433-3799
(763) 506-1000 • http://www.anoka.k12.mn.us/
Grade Span: PK-12; **Agency Type:** 1
Schools: 61
31 Primary; 8 Middle; 15 High; 7 Other Level
42 Regular; 4 Special Education; 1 Vocational; 14 Alternative
0 Magnet; 0 Charter; 17 Title I Eligible; 0 School-wide Title I
Students: 41,383 (51.3% male; 48.7% female)
Individual Education Program: 5,289 (12.8%);
English Language Learner: 1,590 (3.8%); Migrant: 0 (0.0%)
Eligible for Free Lunch Program: 4,536 (11.0%)
Eligible for Reduced-Price Lunch Program: 2,521 (6.1%)
Teachers: 2,234.2 (18.5 to 1)
Librarians/Media Specialists: 28.3 (1,462.3 to 1)
Guidance Counselors: 27.0 (1,532.7 to 1)
Current Spending: ($ per student per year):
Total: $6,579; Instruction: $4,270; Support Services: $1,991
Enrollment, Drop-out Rates and Diploma Recipients by Race/Ethnicity

Category	Total	White	Black	Asian	AIAN	Hisp.
Enrollment (%)	100.0	88.6	4.0	4.1	1.4	1.8
Drop-out Rate (%)	4.0	3.7	7.8	5.8	10.9	9.4
H.S. Diplomas (#)	2,372	2,184	36	84	39	29

Centennial

4707 N Rd • Circle Pines, MN 55014-1898
(763) 792-6000 • http://www.centennial.k12.mn.us/
Grade Span: PK-12; **Agency Type:** 1
Schools: 11
6 Primary; 1 Middle; 2 High; 2 Other Level
7 Regular; 1 Special Education; 0 Vocational; 3 Alternative
0 Magnet; 0 Charter; 5 Title I Eligible; 0 School-wide Title I
Students: 7,027 (51.1% male; 48.9% female)
Individual Education Program: 876 (12.5%);
English Language Learner: 46 (0.7%); Migrant: 0 (0.0%)
Eligible for Free Lunch Program: 468 (6.7%)
Eligible for Reduced-Price Lunch Program: 247 (3.5%)
Teachers: 380.6 (18.5 to 1)
Librarians/Media Specialists: 6.0 (1,171.2 to 1)
Guidance Counselors: 12.0 (585.6 to 1)
Current Spending: ($ per student per year):
Total: $6,572; Instruction: $4,310; Support Services: $1,961
Enrollment, Drop-out Rates and Diploma Recipients by Race/Ethnicity

Category	Total	White	Black	Asian	AIAN	Hisp.
Enrollment (%)	100.0	94.0	1.1	2.1	1.4	1.4
Drop-out Rate (%)	2.0	2.0	4.5	0.0	2.5	3.6
H.S. Diplomas (#)	340	326	1	5	3	5

Columbia Heights

1400 49th Ave NE • Columbia Heights, MN 55421-1992
(763) 528-4505 • http://www.colheights.k12.mn.us/
Grade Span: PK-12; **Agency Type:** 1
Schools: 8
4 Primary; 2 Middle; 2 High; 0 Other Level
5 Regular; 1 Special Education; 0 Vocational; 2 Alternative
0 Magnet; 0 Charter; 3 Title I Eligible; 0 School-wide Title I
Students: 3,030 (49.1% male; 50.9% female)
Individual Education Program: 377 (12.4%);
English Language Learner: 409 (13.5%); Migrant: 0 (0.0%)
Eligible for Free Lunch Program: 1,027 (33.9%)
Eligible for Reduced-Price Lunch Program: 240 (7.9%)
Teachers: 183.9 (16.5 to 1)
Librarians/Media Specialists: 4.0 (757.5 to 1)
Guidance Counselors: 4.0 (757.5 to 1)
Current Spending: ($ per student per year):
Total: $7,495; Instruction: $4,587; Support Services: $2,591
Enrollment, Drop-out Rates and Diploma Recipients by Race/Ethnicity

Category	Total	White	Black	Asian	AIAN	Hisp.
Enrollment (%)	100.0	67.1	15.5	6.2	3.7	7.5
Drop-out Rate (%)	9.5	7.8	19.0	8.2	15.4	12.8
H.S. Diplomas (#)	213	161	25	11	7	9

Fridley

6000 W Moore Lake Dr • Fridley, MN 55432-5698
(763) 502-5000 • http://www.fridley.k12.mn.us/
Grade Span: PK-12; **Agency Type:** 1
Schools: 8
3 Primary; 2 Middle; 3 High; 0 Other Level
4 Regular; 1 Special Education; 0 Vocational; 3 Alternative
0 Magnet; 0 Charter; 1 Title I Eligible; 0 School-wide Title I
Students: 2,593 (51.5% male; 48.5% female)
Individual Education Program: 288 (11.1%);
English Language Learner: 132 (5.1%); Migrant: 0 (0.0%)
Eligible for Free Lunch Program: 661 (25.5%)
Eligible for Reduced-Price Lunch Program: 239 (9.2%)
Teachers: 147.9 (17.5 to 1)
Librarians/Media Specialists: 3.7 (700.8 to 1)
Guidance Counselors: 6.0 (432.2 to 1)
Current Spending: ($ per student per year):
Total: $7,365; Instruction: $4,791; Support Services: $2,259
Enrollment, Drop-out Rates and Diploma Recipients by Race/Ethnicity

Category	Total	White	Black	Asian	AIAN	Hisp.
Enrollment (%)	100.0	74.5	12.5	7.0	2.9	3.1
Drop-out Rate (%)	3.5	3.4	2.2	2.4	12.5	5.6
H.S. Diplomas (#)	158	129	9	12	2	6

Saint Francis

4115 Ambassador Blvd • Saint Francis, MN 55070-9668
(763) 753-7059 • http://www.stfrancissd.com/
Grade Span: PK-12; **Agency Type:** 1
Schools: 10
4 Primary; 3 Middle; 2 High; 1 Other Level
7 Regular; 2 Special Education; 0 Vocational; 1 Alternative
0 Magnet; 0 Charter; 4 Title I Eligible; 0 School-wide Title I
Students: 5,973 (52.3% male; 47.7% female)
Individual Education Program: 619 (10.4%);
English Language Learner: 83 (1.4%); Migrant: 0 (0.0%)
Eligible for Free Lunch Program: 709 (11.9%)
Eligible for Reduced-Price Lunch Program: 338 (5.7%)
Teachers: 302.2 (19.8 to 1)
Librarians/Media Specialists: 0.7 (8,532.9 to 1)
Guidance Counselors: 5.0 (1,194.6 to 1)
Current Spending: ($ per student per year):
Total: $6,453; Instruction: $4,156; Support Services: $1,990
Enrollment, Drop-out Rates and Diploma Recipients by Race/Ethnicity

Category	Total	White	Black	Asian	AIAN	Hisp.
Enrollment (%)	100.0	94.1	1.4	1.7	1.4	1.3
Drop-out Rate (%)	2.5	2.3	0.0	3.4	10.0	0.0
H.S. Diplomas (#)	297	273	6	6	6	6

Spring Lake Park

8000 Hwy 65 NE • Spring Lake Park, MN 55432-2071
(763) 786-5570 • http://www.splkpark.k12.mn.us/mainsite/default.htm
Grade Span: PK-12; **Agency Type:** 1
Schools: 12
5 Primary; 1 Middle; 4 High; 2 Other Level
6 Regular; 1 Special Education; 0 Vocational; 5 Alternative
0 Magnet; 0 Charter; 3 Title I Eligible; 0 School-wide Title I
Students: 4,258 (50.3% male; 49.7% female)
Individual Education Program: 492 (11.6%);
English Language Learner: 170 (4.0%); Migrant: 0 (0.0%)
Eligible for Free Lunch Program: 624 (14.7%)
Eligible for Reduced-Price Lunch Program: 307 (7.2%)
Teachers: 220.3 (19.3 to 1)
Librarians/Media Specialists: 4.0 (1,064.5 to 1)
Guidance Counselors: 8.0 (532.3 to 1)
Current Spending: ($ per student per year):
Total: $7,305; Instruction: $4,540; Support Services: $2,476
Enrollment, Drop-out Rates and Diploma Recipients by Race/Ethnicity

Category	Total	White	Black	Asian	AIAN	Hisp.
Enrollment (%)	100.0	86.0	3.6	5.3	1.8	3.4
Drop-out Rate (%)	5.4	5.0	13.0	9.1	6.3	13.0
H.S. Diplomas (#)	275	252	5	13	0	5

Becker County

Detroit Lakes

702 Lake Ave • Detroit Lakes, MN 56501-3026
Mailing Address: Box 766, 702 Lake Ave • Detroit Lakes, MN 56501-3026
(218) 847-9271 • http://www.detroitlakes.com/schools/index2.html
Grade Span: PK-12; **Agency Type:** 1
Schools: 14
5 Primary; 1 Middle; 3 High; 5 Other Level
5 Regular; 0 Special Education; 0 Vocational; 9 Alternative
0 Magnet; 0 Charter; 3 Title I Eligible; 1 School-wide Title I
Students: 2,855 (50.0% male; 50.0% female)
Individual Education Program: 473 (16.6%);
English Language Learner: 0 (0.0%); Migrant: 0 (0.0%)
Eligible for Free Lunch Program: 651 (22.8%)
Eligible for Reduced-Price Lunch Program: 288 (10.1%)
Teachers: 207.7 (13.7 to 1)
Librarians/Media Specialists: 2.9 (984.5 to 1)
Guidance Counselors: 5.5 (519.1 to 1)
Current Spending: ($ per student per year):
Total: $6,881; Instruction: $4,528; Support Services: $2,066

Enrollment, Drop-out Rates and Diploma Recipients by Race/Ethnicity

Category	Total	White	Black	Asian	AIAN	Hisp.
Enrollment (%)	100.0	85.0	1.0	0.6	12.1	1.2
Drop-out Rate (%)	1.6	1.4	0.0	0.0	4.4	0.0
H.S. Diplomas (#)	213	201	0	1	9	2

Beltrami County

Bemidji

201 15th St NW • Bemidji, MN 56601-3865
(218) 333-3110 • http://www.bemidji.k12.mn.us/
Grade Span: PK-12; **Agency Type:** 1
Schools: 14
8 Primary; 1 Middle; 1 High; 4 Other Level
8 Regular; 3 Special Education; 0 Vocational; 3 Alternative
0 Magnet; 0 Charter; 9 Title I Eligible; 0 School-wide Title I
Students: 5,212 (52.8% male; 47.2% female)
Individual Education Program: 840 (16.1%);
English Language Learner: 0 (0.0%); Migrant: 0 (0.0%)
Eligible for Free Lunch Program: 1,735 (33.3%)
Eligible for Reduced-Price Lunch Program: 372 (7.1%)
Teachers: 322.6 (16.2 to 1)
Librarians/Media Specialists: 6.5 (801.8 to 1)
Guidance Counselors: 5.0 (1,042.4 to 1)
Current Spending: ($ per student per year):
Total: $7,688; Instruction: $5,190; Support Services: $2,125

Enrollment, Drop-out Rates and Diploma Recipients by Race/Ethnicity

Category	Total	White	Black	Asian	AIAN	Hisp.
Enrollment (%)	100.0	80.3	1.3	0.8	16.8	0.9
Drop-out Rate (%)	2.0	1.4	7.1	0.0	6.1	0.0
H.S. Diplomas (#)	340	313	2	4	18	3

Benton County

Foley

520 Dewey St • Foley, MN 56329
Mailing Address: Box 297 • Foley, MN 56329
(320) 968-7175 • http://www.foley.k12.mn.us/
Grade Span: PK-12; **Agency Type:** 1
Schools: 3
1 Primary; 1 Middle; 1 High; 0 Other Level
3 Regular; 0 Special Education; 0 Vocational; 0 Alternative
0 Magnet; 0 Charter; 2 Title I Eligible; 0 School-wide Title I
Students: 1,661 (52.0% male; 48.0% female)
Individual Education Program: 250 (15.1%);
English Language Learner: 0 (0.0%); Migrant: 0 (0.0%)
Eligible for Free Lunch Program: 235 (14.1%)
Eligible for Reduced-Price Lunch Program: 155 (9.3%)
Teachers: 112.1 (14.8 to 1)
Librarians/Media Specialists: 2.0 (830.5 to 1)
Guidance Counselors: 2.0 (830.5 to 1)
Current Spending: ($ per student per year):
Total: $6,297; Instruction: $3,907; Support Services: $2,086

Enrollment, Drop-out Rates and Diploma Recipients by Race/Ethnicity

Category	Total	White	Black	Asian	AIAN	Hisp.
Enrollment (%)	100.0	98.4	0.7	0.2	0.5	0.2
Drop-out Rate (%)	2.2	2.2	0.0	0.0	0.0	0.0
H.S. Diplomas (#)	136	136	0	0	0	0

Sauk Rapids

901 1st St S • Sauk Rapids, MN 56379-1916
(320) 253-4703 • http://www.isd47.org/
Grade Span: PK-12; **Agency Type:** 1
Schools: 5
2 Primary; 2 Middle; 1 High; 0 Other Level
5 Regular; 0 Special Education; 0 Vocational; 0 Alternative
0 Magnet; 0 Charter; 3 Title I Eligible; 0 School-wide Title I
Students: 3,600 (50.8% male; 49.2% female)
Individual Education Program: 515 (14.3%);
English Language Learner: 1 (<0.1%); Migrant: 0 (0.0%)
Eligible for Free Lunch Program: 422 (11.7%)
Eligible for Reduced-Price Lunch Program: 306 (8.5%)
Teachers: 216.4 (16.6 to 1)
Librarians/Media Specialists: 6.3 (571.4 to 1)
Guidance Counselors: 5.0 (720.0 to 1)
Current Spending: ($ per student per year):
Total: $6,308; Instruction: $3,776; Support Services: $2,198

Enrollment, Drop-out Rates and Diploma Recipients by Race/Ethnicity

Category	Total	White	Black	Asian	AIAN	Hisp.
Enrollment (%)	100.0	97.6	0.8	1.0	0.1	0.4
Drop-out Rate (%)	0.3	0.4	0.0	0.0	0.0	0.0
H.S. Diplomas (#)	230	224	2	2	1	1

Blue Earth County

Mankato

10 Civic Center Plaza, Ste 1 • Mankato, MN 56001
(507) 387-1868 • http://www.isd77.k12.mn.us/index.php3
Grade Span: PK-12; **Agency Type:** 1
Schools: 19
9 Primary; 2 Middle; 4 High; 4 Other Level
14 Regular; 1 Special Education; 0 Vocational; 4 Alternative
0 Magnet; 0 Charter; 8 Title I Eligible; 0 School-wide Title I
Students: 7,090 (51.4% male; 48.6% female)
Individual Education Program: 1,030 (14.5%);
English Language Learner: 202 (2.8%); Migrant: 0 (0.0%)
Eligible for Free Lunch Program: 1,311 (18.5%)
Eligible for Reduced-Price Lunch Program: 657 (9.3%)
Teachers: 417.2 (17.0 to 1)
Librarians/Media Specialists: 13.7 (517.5 to 1)
Guidance Counselors: 15.3 (463.4 to 1)
Current Spending: ($ per student per year):
Total: $6,692; Instruction: $4,527; Support Services: $1,886

Enrollment, Drop-out Rates and Diploma Recipients by Race/Ethnicity

Category	Total	White	Black	Asian	AIAN	Hisp.
Enrollment (%)	100.0	89.4	4.5	2.5	0.5	3.1
Drop-out Rate (%)	4.1	4.0	8.0	6.1	25.0	2.2
H.S. Diplomas (#)	606	560	14	21	2	9

Brown County

New Ulm

400 S Payne • New Ulm, MN 56073-3296
(507) 359-8401 • http://www.newulm.k12.mn.us/
Grade Span: PK-12; **Agency Type:** 1
Schools: 5
1 Primary; 2 Middle; 2 High; 0 Other Level
4 Regular; 0 Special Education; 0 Vocational; 1 Alternative
0 Magnet; 0 Charter; 2 Title I Eligible; 0 School-wide Title I
Students: 2,415 (52.5% male; 47.5% female)
Individual Education Program: 270 (11.2%);
English Language Learner: 12 (0.5%); Migrant: 0 (0.0%)
Eligible for Free Lunch Program: 308 (12.8%)
Eligible for Reduced-Price Lunch Program: 155 (6.4%)
Teachers: 158.0 (15.3 to 1)
Librarians/Media Specialists: 4.0 (603.8 to 1)
Guidance Counselors: 6.0 (402.5 to 1)
Current Spending: ($ per student per year):
Total: $6,620; Instruction: $4,137; Support Services: $2,231

Enrollment, Drop-out Rates and Diploma Recipients by Race/Ethnicity

Category	Total	White	Black	Asian	AIAN	Hisp.
Enrollment (%)	100.0	97.0	0.5	0.7	0.2	1.6
Drop-out Rate (%)	0.5	0.5	n/a	0.0	0.0	0.0
H.S. Diplomas (#)	215	210	0	0	0	5

Carlton County

Cloquet

509 Carlton Ave • Cloquet, MN 55720-1757
(218) 879-6721 • http://www.cloquet.k12.mn.us/
Grade Span: PK-12; **Agency Type:** 1
Schools: 8
5 Primary; 1 Middle; 1 High; 1 Other Level
4 Regular; 1 Special Education; 0 Vocational; 3 Alternative
0 Magnet; 0 Charter; 3 Title I Eligible; 0 School-wide Title I
Students: 2,381 (49.8% male; 50.2% female)
Individual Education Program: 306 (12.9%);
English Language Learner: 0 (0.0%); Migrant: 0 (0.0%)
Eligible for Free Lunch Program: 536 (22.5%)
Eligible for Reduced-Price Lunch Program: 200 (8.4%)
Teachers: 137.0 (17.4 to 1)
Librarians/Media Specialists: 2.2 (1,082.3 to 1)
Guidance Counselors: 5.4 (440.9 to 1)
Current Spending: ($ per student per year):
Total: $7,855; Instruction: $5,194; Support Services: $2,402

Enrollment, Drop-out Rates and Diploma Recipients by Race/Ethnicity

Category	Total	White	Black	Asian	AIAN	Hisp.
Enrollment (%)	100.0	82.1	0.7	0.9	15.5	0.8
Drop-out Rate (%)	4.1	3.5	0.0	0.0	8.3	0.0
H.S. Diplomas (#)	197	168	2	1	26	0

Carver County

Chaska

11 Peavey Rd • Chaska, MN 55318-2321
(952) 556-6100 • http://www.district112.org/
Grade Span: PK-12; **Agency Type:** 1
Schools: 12

7 Primary; 2 Middle; 2 High; 1 Other Level
11 Regular; 1 Special Education; 0 Vocational; 0 Alternative
0 Magnet; 0 Charter; 5 Title I Eligible; 0 School-wide Title I
Students: 7,804 (51.9% male; 48.1% female)
Individual Education Program: 840 (10.8%);
English Language Learner: 418 (5.4%); Migrant: 0 (0.0%)
Eligible for Free Lunch Program: 559 (7.2%)
Eligible for Reduced-Price Lunch Program: 220 (2.8%)
Teachers: 445.7 (17.5 to 1)
Librarians/Media Specialists: 10.0 (780.4 to 1)
Guidance Counselors: 14.0 (557.4 to 1)
Current Spending: ($ per student per year):
Total: $6,876; Instruction: $3,793; Support Services: $2,767
Enrollment, Drop-out Rates and Diploma Recipients by Race/Ethnicity

Category	Total	White	Black	Asian	AIAN	Hisp.
Enrollment (%)	100.0	90.6	1.7	2.9	0.2	4.7
Drop-out Rate (%)	1.1	0.8	10.0	0.0	16.7	9.6
H.S. Diplomas (#)	390	369	5	8	2	6

Waconia

24 S Walnut St • Waconia, MN 55387
(952) 442-0600 • http://www.waconia.k12.mn.us/waconia/
Grade Span: PK-12; **Agency Type:** 1
Schools: 4
2 Primary; 1 Middle; 1 High; 0 Other Level
4 Regular; 0 Special Education; 0 Vocational; 0 Alternative
0 Magnet; 0 Charter; 2 Title I Eligible; 0 School-wide Title I
Students: 2,327 (52.2% male; 47.8% female)
Individual Education Program: 279 (12.0%);
English Language Learner: 12 (0.5%); Migrant: 0 (0.0%)
Eligible for Free Lunch Program: 109 (4.7%)
Eligible for Reduced-Price Lunch Program: 80 (3.4%)
Teachers: 126.0 (18.5 to 1)
Librarians/Media Specialists: 2.0 (1,163.5 to 1)
Guidance Counselors: 3.0 (775.7 to 1)
Current Spending: ($ per student per year):
Total: $6,166; Instruction: $3,539; Support Services: $2,337
Enrollment, Drop-out Rates and Diploma Recipients by Race/Ethnicity

Category	Total	White	Black	Asian	AIAN	Hisp.
Enrollment (%)	100.0	95.2	1.2	1.5	0.5	1.5
Drop-out Rate (%)	0.6	0.6	0.0	0.0	0.0	0.0
H.S. Diplomas (#)	134	131	0	1	0	2

Chippewa County

Montevideo

2001 William Ave • Montevideo, MN 56265-2200
(320) 269-8833 • http://www.montevideoschools.com/
Grade Span: PK-12; **Agency Type:** 1
Schools: 4
2 Primary; 1 Middle; 1 High; 0 Other Level
4 Regular; 0 Special Education; 0 Vocational; 0 Alternative
0 Magnet; 0 Charter; 2 Title I Eligible; 0 School-wide Title I
Students: 1,528 (51.6% male; 48.4% female)
Individual Education Program: 210 (13.7%);
English Language Learner: 8 (0.5%); Migrant: 0 (0.0%)
Eligible for Free Lunch Program: 340 (22.3%)
Eligible for Reduced-Price Lunch Program: 186 (12.2%)
Teachers: 104.9 (14.6 to 1)
Librarians/Media Specialists: 2.0 (764.0 to 1)
Guidance Counselors: 1.0 (1,528.0 to 1)
Current Spending: ($ per student per year):
Total: $7,266; Instruction: $4,568; Support Services: $2,322
Enrollment, Drop-out Rates and Diploma Recipients by Race/Ethnicity

Category	Total	White	Black	Asian	AIAN	Hisp.
Enrollment (%)	100.0	94.8	0.6	0.7	0.1	3.8
Drop-out Rate (%)	0.0	0.0	0.0	0.0	n/a	0.0
H.S. Diplomas (#)	113	107	1	3	0	2

Chisago County

Chisago Lakes

13750 Lake Blvd • Lindstrom, MN 55045-0187
(651) 213-2096 • http://www.chisagolakes.k12.mn.us/
Grade Span: PK-12; **Agency Type:** 1
Schools: 7
4 Primary; 1 Middle; 1 High; 1 Other Level
5 Regular; 1 Special Education; 0 Vocational; 1 Alternative
0 Magnet; 0 Charter; 2 Title I Eligible; 0 School-wide Title I
Students: 3,526 (52.1% male; 47.9% female)
Individual Education Program: 337 (9.6%);
English Language Learner: 53 (1.5%); Migrant: 0 (0.0%)
Eligible for Free Lunch Program: 264 (7.5%)
Eligible for Reduced-Price Lunch Program: 190 (5.4%)
Teachers: 197.5 (17.9 to 1)
Librarians/Media Specialists: 5.0 (705.2 to 1)
Guidance Counselors: 4.7 (750.2 to 1)
Current Spending: ($ per student per year):
Total: $5,784; Instruction: $3,679; Support Services: $1,797
Enrollment, Drop-out Rates and Diploma Recipients by Race/Ethnicity

Category	Total	White	Black	Asian	AIAN	Hisp.
Enrollment (%)	100.0	95.3	1.1	2.1	0.6	0.9
Drop-out Rate (%)	1.9	1.9	0.0	7.1	0.0	0.0
H.S. Diplomas (#)	240	233	2	4	0	1

North Branch

6644 Main St • North Branch, MN 55056-0370
Mailing Address: Box 370, 6644 Main St • North Branch, MN 55056-0370
(651) 674-1000 • http://www.northbranch.k12.mn.us/
Grade Span: PK-12; **Agency Type:** 1
Schools: 8
3 Primary; 1 Middle; 1 High; 3 Other Level
4 Regular; 1 Special Education; 0 Vocational; 3 Alternative
0 Magnet; 0 Charter; 2 Title I Eligible; 0 School-wide Title I
Students: 3,897 (51.3% male; 48.7% female)
Individual Education Program: 501 (12.9%);
English Language Learner: 70 (1.8%); Migrant: 0 (0.0%)
Eligible for Free Lunch Program: 497 (12.8%)
Eligible for Reduced-Price Lunch Program: 240 (6.2%)
Teachers: 210.6 (18.5 to 1)
Librarians/Media Specialists: 3.5 (1,113.4 to 1)
Guidance Counselors: 4.0 (974.3 to 1)
Current Spending: ($ per student per year):
Total: $5,875; Instruction: $3,521; Support Services: $2,039
Enrollment, Drop-out Rates and Diploma Recipients by Race/Ethnicity

Category	Total	White	Black	Asian	AIAN	Hisp.
Enrollment (%)	100.0	95.7	0.8	1.5	0.8	1.3
Drop-out Rate (%)	3.7	3.8	0.0	0.0	0.0	0.0
H.S. Diplomas (#)	259	248	2	6	1	2

Clay County

Moorhead

810 4th Ave S • Moorhead, MN 56560
(218) 284-3335 • http://www.moorhead.k12.mn.us/
Grade Span: PK-12; **Agency Type:** 1
Schools: 12
4 Primary; 2 Middle; 3 High; 3 Other Level
7 Regular; 1 Special Education; 0 Vocational; 4 Alternative
0 Magnet; 0 Charter; 5 Title I Eligible; 1 School-wide Title I
Students: 5,547 (52.2% male; 47.8% female)
Individual Education Program: 961 (17.3%);
English Language Learner: 385 (6.9%); Migrant: 43 (0.8%)
Eligible for Free Lunch Program: 1,249 (22.5%)
Eligible for Reduced-Price Lunch Program: 286 (5.2%)
Teachers: 348.5 (15.9 to 1)
Librarians/Media Specialists: 7.0 (792.4 to 1)
Guidance Counselors: 10.0 (554.7 to 1)
Current Spending: ($ per student per year):
Total: $6,942; Instruction: $4,668; Support Services: $2,042
Enrollment, Drop-out Rates and Diploma Recipients by Race/Ethnicity

Category	Total	White	Black	Asian	AIAN	Hisp.
Enrollment (%)	100.0	84.8	1.9	1.5	3.1	8.7
Drop-out Rate (%)	2.0	1.7	0.0	0.0	2.5	8.7
H.S. Diplomas (#)	399	366	6	4	4	19

Crow Wing County

Brainerd

300 Quince St • Brainerd, MN 56401-4095
(218) 828-5300 • http://www.brainerd.k12.mn.us/
Grade Span: PK-12; **Agency Type:** 1
Schools: 19
9 Primary; 3 Middle; 3 High; 4 Other Level
12 Regular; 1 Special Education; 0 Vocational; 6 Alternative
1 Magnet; 0 Charter; 7 Title I Eligible; 0 School-wide Title I
Students: 7,303 (51.3% male; 48.7% female)
Individual Education Program: 1,081 (14.8%);
English Language Learner: 0 (0.0%); Migrant: 0 (0.0%)
Eligible for Free Lunch Program: 1,535 (21.0%)
Eligible for Reduced-Price Lunch Program: 771 (10.6%)
Teachers: 437.5 (16.7 to 1)
Librarians/Media Specialists: 11.0 (663.9 to 1)
Guidance Counselors: 8.0 (912.9 to 1)
Current Spending: ($ per student per year):
Total: $7,055; Instruction: $4,697; Support Services: $2,029

Enrollment, Drop-out Rates and Diploma Recipients by Race/Ethnicity

Category	Total	White	Black	Asian	AIAN	Hisp.
Enrollment (%)	100.0	96.9	0.8	0.4	1.3	0.5
Drop-out Rate (%)	7.0	6.5	20.0	5.0	37.1	5.9
H.S. Diplomas (#)	498	485	0	3	2	8

Crosby-Ironton

711 Poplar St • Crosby, MN 56441-1198
(218) 546-5165
Grade Span: PK-12; **Agency Type:** 1
Schools: 3
1 Primary; 0 Middle; 2 High; 0 Other Level
2 Regular; 0 Special Education; 0 Vocational; 1 Alternative
0 Magnet; 0 Charter; 1 Title I Eligible; 0 School-wide Title I
Students: 1,513 (49.5% male; 50.5% female)
Individual Education Program: 211 (13.9%);
English Language Learner: 0 (0.0%); Migrant: 0 (0.0%)
Eligible for Free Lunch Program: 404 (26.7%)
Eligible for Reduced-Price Lunch Program: 174 (11.5%)
Teachers: 100.8 (15.0 to 1)
Librarians/Media Specialists: 2.0 (756.5 to 1)
Guidance Counselors: 2.0 (756.5 to 1)
Current Spending: ($ per student per year):
Total: $6,811; Instruction: $4,317; Support Services: $2,207

Enrollment, Drop-out Rates and Diploma Recipients by Race/Ethnicity

Category	Total	White	Black	Asian	AIAN	Hisp.
Enrollment (%)	100.0	96.5	0.9	0.4	1.3	0.9
Drop-out Rate (%)	5.6	5.5	50.0	0.0	0.0	0.0
H.S. Diplomas (#)	84	83	0	1	0	0

Dakota County

Burnsville

100 River Ridge Ct • Burnsville, MN 55337-1613
(952) 707-2000 • http://www.rschooltoday.com/
Grade Span: PK-12; **Agency Type:** 1
Schools: 23
12 Primary; 3 Middle; 4 High; 4 Other Level
14 Regular; 3 Special Education; 0 Vocational; 6 Alternative
0 Magnet; 0 Charter; 9 Title I Eligible; 0 School-wide Title I
Students: 11,386 (51.5% male; 48.5% female)
Individual Education Program: 1,446 (12.7%);
English Language Learner: 816 (7.2%); Migrant: 0 (0.0%)
Eligible for Free Lunch Program: 1,340 (11.8%)
Eligible for Reduced-Price Lunch Program: 705 (6.2%)
Teachers: 642.5 (17.7 to 1)
Librarians/Media Specialists: 9.0 (1,265.1 to 1)
Guidance Counselors: 10.5 (1,084.4 to 1)
Current Spending: ($ per student per year):
Total: $7,434; Instruction: $4,723; Support Services: $2,399

Enrollment, Drop-out Rates and Diploma Recipients by Race/Ethnicity

Category	Total	White	Black	Asian	AIAN	Hisp.
Enrollment (%)	100.0	77.8	10.8	7.1	0.6	3.7
Drop-out Rate (%)	3.5	3.0	6.0	5.6	0.0	6.7
H.S. Diplomas (#)	751	641	41	56	1	12

Farmington

510 Walnut St • Farmington, MN 55024-1389
(651) 463-5011 • http://www.farmington.k12.mn.us/
Grade Span: PK-12; **Agency Type:** 1
Schools: 9
5 Primary; 1 Middle; 2 High; 1 Other Level
7 Regular; 0 Special Education; 0 Vocational; 2 Alternative
0 Magnet; 0 Charter; 4 Title I Eligible; 0 School-wide Title I
Students: 5,261 (52.2% male; 47.8% female)
Individual Education Program: 668 (12.7%);
English Language Learner: 105 (2.0%); Migrant: 0 (0.0%)
Eligible for Free Lunch Program: 268 (5.1%)
Eligible for Reduced-Price Lunch Program: 193 (3.7%)
Teachers: 297.3 (17.7 to 1)
Librarians/Media Specialists: 9.0 (584.6 to 1)
Guidance Counselors: 7.0 (751.6 to 1)
Current Spending: ($ per student per year):
Total: $6,141; Instruction: $3,520; Support Services: $2,332

Enrollment, Drop-out Rates and Diploma Recipients by Race/Ethnicity

Category	Total	White	Black	Asian	AIAN	Hisp.
Enrollment (%)	100.0	94.5	1.6	2.0	0.2	1.7
Drop-out Rate (%)	0.3	0.2	0.0	4.0	n/a	0.0
H.S. Diplomas (#)	283	271	4	6	0	2

Hastings

1000 W 10th St • Hastings, MN 55033-2116
Mailing Address: 1000 11th St W • Hastings, MN 55033-2597
(651) 437-6111 • http://www.hastings.k12.mn.us/
Grade Span: PK-12; **Agency Type:** 1
Schools: 12
8 Primary; 1 Middle; 2 High; 1 Other Level
7 Regular; 1 Special Education; 0 Vocational; 4 Alternative
0 Magnet; 0 Charter; 4 Title I Eligible; 0 School-wide Title I
Students: 5,155 (51.7% male; 48.3% female)
Individual Education Program: 664 (12.9%);
English Language Learner: 13 (0.3%); Migrant: 0 (0.0%)
Eligible for Free Lunch Program: 425 (8.2%)
Eligible for Reduced-Price Lunch Program: 242 (4.7%)
Teachers: 264.4 (19.5 to 1)
Librarians/Media Specialists: 5.4 (954.6 to 1)
Guidance Counselors: 7.0 (736.4 to 1)
Current Spending: ($ per student per year):
Total: $6,883; Instruction: $4,510; Support Services: $2,052

Enrollment, Drop-out Rates and Diploma Recipients by Race/Ethnicity

Category	Total	White	Black	Asian	AIAN	Hisp.
Enrollment (%)	100.0	94.4	1.6	1.2	1.0	1.9
Drop-out Rate (%)	0.8	0.8	0.0	0.0	0.0	0.0
H.S. Diplomas (#)	431	419	2	4	1	5

Inver Grove

9875 Inver Grove Tr E • Inver Grove Heights, MN 55075
Mailing Address: 2990 80th St E • Inver Grove Heights, MN 55076-3235
(651) 306-7825 • http://www.invergrove.k12.mn.us/
Grade Span: PK-12; **Agency Type:** 1
Schools: 9
6 Primary; 1 Middle; 2 High; 0 Other Level
7 Regular; 1 Special Education; 0 Vocational; 1 Alternative
0 Magnet; 0 Charter; 4 Title I Eligible; 0 School-wide Title I
Students: 3,951 (52.0% male; 48.0% female)
Individual Education Program: 617 (15.6%);
English Language Learner: 98 (2.5%); Migrant: 0 (0.0%)
Eligible for Free Lunch Program: 554 (14.0%)
Eligible for Reduced-Price Lunch Program: 262 (6.6%)
Teachers: 210.2 (18.8 to 1)
Librarians/Media Specialists: 6.0 (658.5 to 1)
Guidance Counselors: 5.0 (790.2 to 1)
Current Spending: ($ per student per year):
Total: $6,783; Instruction: $4,236; Support Services: $2,205

Enrollment, Drop-out Rates and Diploma Recipients by Race/Ethnicity

Category	Total	White	Black	Asian	AIAN	Hisp.
Enrollment (%)	100.0	85.8	4.8	3.1	0.4	5.8
Drop-out Rate (%)	1.5	1.3	5.4	2.8	0.0	1.6
H.S. Diplomas (#)	265	242	6	6	0	11

Lakeville

8670 210th St W • Lakeville, MN 55044-8501
(952) 469-7100 • http://www.isd194.k12.mn.us/
Grade Span: PK-12; **Agency Type:** 1
Schools: 15
9 Primary; 4 Middle; 2 High; 0 Other Level
13 Regular; 0 Special Education; 0 Vocational; 2 Alternative
0 Magnet; 0 Charter; 5 Title I Eligible; 0 School-wide Title I
Students: 10,154 (51.6% male; 48.4% female)
Individual Education Program: 1,162 (11.4%);
English Language Learner: 119 (1.2%); Migrant: 0 (0.0%)
Eligible for Free Lunch Program: 333 (3.3%)
Eligible for Reduced-Price Lunch Program: 166 (1.6%)
Teachers: 590.8 (17.2 to 1)
Librarians/Media Specialists: 13.0 (781.1 to 1)
Guidance Counselors: 9.0 (1,128.2 to 1)
Current Spending: ($ per student per year):
Total: $5,987; Instruction: $3,589; Support Services: $2,058

Enrollment, Drop-out Rates and Diploma Recipients by Race/Ethnicity

Category	Total	White	Black	Asian	AIAN	Hisp.
Enrollment (%)	100.0	95.5	1.5	1.6	0.3	1.1
Drop-out Rate (%)	2.6	2.4	3.6	4.1	33.3	12.5
H.S. Diplomas (#)	655	628	5	15	0	7

Rosemount-Apple Valley-Eagan

14445 Diamond Path W • Rosemount, MN 55068-4199
(651) 423-7700 • http://www.isd196.k12.mn.us/
Grade Span: PK-12; **Agency Type:** 1
Schools: 37
20 Primary; 7 Middle; 8 High; 2 Other Level
29 Regular; 4 Special Education; 0 Vocational; 4 Alternative
0 Magnet; 0 Charter; 9 Title I Eligible; 0 School-wide Title I
Students: 28,486 (51.3% male; 48.7% female)
Individual Education Program: 4,005 (14.1%);
English Language Learner: 859 (3.0%); Migrant: 0 (0.0%)

Eligible for Free Lunch Program: 1,612 (5.7%)
Eligible for Reduced-Price Lunch Program: 761 (2.7%)
Teachers: 1,745.3 (16.3 to 1)
Librarians/Media Specialists: 28.0 (1,017.4 to 1)
Guidance Counselors: 31.4 (907.2 to 1)
Current Spending: ($ per student per year):
Total: $6,240; Instruction: $4,122; Support Services: $1,842
Enrollment, Drop-out Rates and Diploma Recipients by Race/Ethnicity

Category	Total	White	Black	Asian	AIAN	Hisp.
Enrollment (%)	100.0	86.4	5.2	5.4	0.5	2.5
Drop-out Rate (%)	1.8	1.7	4.5	1.6	6.1	2.6
H.S. Diplomas (#)	1,865	1,684	48	97	7	29

South Saint Paul
104 5th Ave S • South Saint Paul, MN 55075-2332
(651) 457-9400
Grade Span: PK-12; **Agency Type:** 1
Schools: 7
4 Primary; 1 Middle; 2 High; 0 Other Level
3 Regular; 0 Special Education; 0 Vocational; 4 Alternative
0 Magnet; 0 Charter; 4 Title I Eligible; 0 School-wide Title I
Students: 3,432 (50.4% male; 49.6% female)
Individual Education Program: 422 (12.3%);
English Language Learner: 159 (4.6%); Migrant: 0 (0.0%)
Eligible for Free Lunch Program: 632 (18.4%)
Eligible for Reduced-Price Lunch Program: 312 (9.1%)
Teachers: 193.2 (17.8 to 1)
Librarians/Media Specialists: 2.0 (1,716.0 to 1)
Guidance Counselors: 0.0 (0.0 to 1)
Current Spending: ($ per student per year):
Total: $7,183; Instruction: $4,424; Support Services: $2,425
Enrollment, Drop-out Rates and Diploma Recipients by Race/Ethnicity

Category	Total	White	Black	Asian	AIAN	Hisp.
Enrollment (%)	100.0	85.1	3.1	1.3	0.7	9.8
Drop-out Rate (%)	7.6	6.8	6.3	16.0	60.0	16.1
H.S. Diplomas (#)	263	250	3	4	0	6

W Saint Paul-Mendota Height-Eagan
1897 Delaware Ave • Mendota Heights, MN 55118-4338
(651) 681-2396 •
http://rschooltoday.com/se3bin/clientschool.cgi?schoolname=school157
Grade Span: PK-12; **Agency Type:** 1
Schools: 10
5 Primary; 2 Middle; 2 High; 1 Other Level
8 Regular; 1 Special Education; 0 Vocational; 1 Alternative
0 Magnet; 0 Charter; 4 Title I Eligible; 0 School-wide Title I
Students: 4,783 (51.6% male; 48.4% female)
Individual Education Program: 800 (16.7%);
English Language Learner: 298 (6.2%); Migrant: 0 (0.0%)
Eligible for Free Lunch Program: 731 (15.3%)
Eligible for Reduced-Price Lunch Program: 337 (7.0%)
Teachers: 309.6 (15.4 to 1)
Librarians/Media Specialists: 6.8 (703.4 to 1)
Guidance Counselors: 9.5 (503.5 to 1)
Current Spending: ($ per student per year):
Total: $7,153; Instruction: $4,191; Support Services: $2,660
Enrollment, Drop-out Rates and Diploma Recipients by Race/Ethnicity

Category	Total	White	Black	Asian	AIAN	Hisp.
Enrollment (%)	100.0	75.8	7.0	5.0	0.9	11.4
Drop-out Rate (%)	2.0	1.3	0.0	8.3	28.6	5.3
H.S. Diplomas (#)	315	270	9	15	1	20

Dodge County

Kasson-Mantorville
101 16th St NE • Kasson, MN 55944-1610
(507) 634-1100 • http://komets.k12.mn.us/
Grade Span: PK-12; **Agency Type:** 1
Schools: 5
1 Primary; 2 Middle; 2 High; 0 Other Level
4 Regular; 0 Special Education; 0 Vocational; 1 Alternative
0 Magnet; 0 Charter; 1 Title I Eligible; 0 School-wide Title I
Students: 1,866 (50.5% male; 49.5% female)
Individual Education Program: 142 (7.6%);
English Language Learner: 20 (1.1%); Migrant: 0 (0.0%)
Eligible for Free Lunch Program: 132 (7.1%)
Eligible for Reduced-Price Lunch Program: 65 (3.5%)
Teachers: 109.9 (17.0 to 1)
Librarians/Media Specialists: 2.0 (933.0 to 1)
Guidance Counselors: 5.0 (373.2 to 1)
Current Spending: ($ per student per year):
Total: $5,666; Instruction: $3,600; Support Services: $1,801
Enrollment, Drop-out Rates and Diploma Recipients by Race/Ethnicity

Category	Total	White	Black	Asian	AIAN	Hisp.
Enrollment (%)	100.0	95.5	0.6	1.0	0.4	2.5
Drop-out Rate (%)	1.5	1.6	0.0	0.0	n/a	0.0
H.S. Diplomas (#)	98	95	1	0	0	2

Douglas County

Alexandria
14th & Jefferson St • Alexandria, MN 56308-0308
Mailing Address: Box 308 • Alexandria, MN 56308-0308
(320) 762-2141 • http://www.alexandria.k12.mn.us/
Grade Span: PK-12; **Agency Type:** 1
Schools: 8
6 Primary; 1 Middle; 1 High; 0 Other Level
8 Regular; 0 Special Education; 0 Vocational; 0 Alternative
1 Magnet; 0 Charter; 5 Title I Eligible; 0 School-wide Title I
Students: 4,100 (51.4% male; 48.6% female)
Individual Education Program: 587 (14.3%);
English Language Learner: 6 (0.1%); Migrant: 0 (0.0%)
Eligible for Free Lunch Program: 500 (12.2%)
Eligible for Reduced-Price Lunch Program: 404 (9.9%)
Teachers: 257.3 (15.9 to 1)
Librarians/Media Specialists: 5.9 (694.9 to 1)
Guidance Counselors: 5.0 (820.0 to 1)
Current Spending: ($ per student per year):
Total: $6,490; Instruction: $4,386; Support Services: $1,792
Enrollment, Drop-out Rates and Diploma Recipients by Race/Ethnicity

Category	Total	White	Black	Asian	AIAN	Hisp.
Enrollment (%)	100.0	97.6	1.0	0.7	0.2	0.6
Drop-out Rate (%)	0.3	0.3	20.0	0.0	n/a	0.0
H.S. Diplomas (#)	335	330	0	4	0	1

Freeborn County

Albert Lea
211 W Richway Dr • Albert Lea, MN 56007-2477
(507) 379-4800 • http://albertlea.k12.mn.us/
Grade Span: PK-12; **Agency Type:** 1
Schools: 8
5 Primary; 1 Middle; 2 High; 0 Other Level
6 Regular; 0 Special Education; 0 Vocational; 2 Alternative
0 Magnet; 0 Charter; 5 Title I Eligible; 0 School-wide Title I
Students: 3,713 (49.9% male; 50.1% female)
Individual Education Program: 634 (17.1%);
English Language Learner: 251 (6.8%); Migrant: 0 (0.0%)
Eligible for Free Lunch Program: 869 (23.4%)
Eligible for Reduced-Price Lunch Program: 332 (8.9%)
Teachers: 211.9 (17.5 to 1)
Librarians/Media Specialists: 3.5 (1,060.9 to 1)
Guidance Counselors: 4.0 (928.3 to 1)
Current Spending: ($ per student per year):
Total: $6,701; Instruction: $4,194; Support Services: $2,227
Enrollment, Drop-out Rates and Diploma Recipients by Race/Ethnicity

Category	Total	White	Black	Asian	AIAN	Hisp.
Enrollment (%)	100.0	84.8	0.7	1.0	0.1	13.4
Drop-out Rate (%)	4.9	4.1	0.0	8.3	n/a	14.6
H.S. Diplomas (#)	275	255	0	4	0	16

Goodhue County

Red Wing
2451 Eagle Ridge Dr • Red Wing, MN 55066-7444
(651) 385-4500 • http://www.redwing.k12.mn.us/
Grade Span: PK-12; **Agency Type:** 1
Schools: 9
4 Primary; 2 Middle; 3 High; 0 Other Level
5 Regular; 1 Special Education; 0 Vocational; 3 Alternative
0 Magnet; 0 Charter; 3 Title I Eligible; 0 School-wide Title I
Students: 3,168 (50.2% male; 49.8% female)
Individual Education Program: 419 (13.2%);
English Language Learner: 35 (1.1%); Migrant: 0 (0.0%)
Eligible for Free Lunch Program: 431 (13.6%)
Eligible for Reduced-Price Lunch Program: 121 (3.8%)
Teachers: 180.3 (17.6 to 1)
Librarians/Media Specialists: 3.8 (833.7 to 1)
Guidance Counselors: 0.0 (0.0 to 1)
Current Spending: ($ per student per year):
Total: $6,934; Instruction: $4,367; Support Services: $2,212
Enrollment, Drop-out Rates and Diploma Recipients by Race/Ethnicity

Category	Total	White	Black	Asian	AIAN	Hisp.
Enrollment (%)	100.0	90.3	2.7	1.5	3.5	2.0
Drop-out Rate (%)	4.1	3.7	13.3	0.0	23.1	20.0
H.S. Diplomas (#)	263	254	4	2	2	1

Hennepin County

Bloomington

1350 W 106th St • Bloomington, MN 55431
(952) 681-6400 • http://www.bloomington.k12.mn.us/
Grade Span: PK-12; **Agency Type:** 1
Schools: 16
10 Primary; 3 Middle; 2 High; 1 Other Level
15 Regular; 1 Special Education; 0 Vocational; 0 Alternative
0 Magnet; 0 Charter; 3 Title I Eligible; 1 School-wide Title I
Students: 10,690 (52.0% male; 48.0% female)
Individual Education Program: 1,221 (11.4%);
English Language Learner: 748 (7.0%); Migrant: 0 (0.0%)
Eligible for Free Lunch Program: 1,641 (15.4%)
Eligible for Reduced-Price Lunch Program: 724 (6.8%)
Teachers: 610.2 (17.5 to 1)
Librarians/Media Specialists: 16.7 (640.1 to 1)
Guidance Counselors: 16.0 (668.1 to 1)
Current Spending: ($ per student per year):
Total: $7,501; Instruction: $4,590; Support Services: $2,581
Enrollment, Drop-out Rates and Diploma Recipients by Race/Ethnicity

Category	Total	White	Black	Asian	AIAN	Hisp.
Enrollment (%)	100.0	73.6	10.9	8.7	0.8	5.9
Drop-out Rate (%)	1.1	0.9	2.5	1.5	6.9	1.0
H.S. Diplomas (#)	662	568	18	60	4	12

Brooklyn Center

6500 Humboldt Ave N • Brooklyn Center, MN 55430-1897
(763) 561-2120
Grade Span: PK-12; **Agency Type:** 1
Schools: 2
1 Primary; 0 Middle; 1 High; 0 Other Level
2 Regular; 0 Special Education; 0 Vocational; 0 Alternative
0 Magnet; 0 Charter; 1 Title I Eligible; 1 School-wide Title I
Students: 1,732 (52.7% male; 47.3% female)
Individual Education Program: 185 (10.7%);
English Language Learner: 364 (21.0%); Migrant: 0 (0.0%)
Eligible for Free Lunch Program: 735 (42.4%)
Eligible for Reduced-Price Lunch Program: 233 (13.5%)
Teachers: 100.0 (17.3 to 1)
Librarians/Media Specialists: 2.0 (866.0 to 1)
Guidance Counselors: 1.0 (1,732.0 to 1)
Current Spending: ($ per student per year):
Total: $8,293; Instruction: $5,176; Support Services: $2,724
Enrollment, Drop-out Rates and Diploma Recipients by Race/Ethnicity

Category	Total	White	Black	Asian	AIAN	Hisp.
Enrollment (%)	100.0	40.4	32.9	19.3	1.6	5.9
Drop-out Rate (%)	3.7	3.6	4.5	3.1	0.0	4.0
H.S. Diplomas (#)	121	55	35	27	0	4

Eden Prairie

8100 School Rd • Eden Prairie, MN 55344-2292
(952) 975-7000 • http://www.edenpr.k12.mn.us/
Grade Span: PK-12; **Agency Type:** 1
Schools: 11
7 Primary; 2 Middle; 2 High; 0 Other Level
8 Regular; 2 Special Education; 0 Vocational; 1 Alternative
0 Magnet; 0 Charter; 3 Title I Eligible; 0 School-wide Title I
Students: 10,441 (51.9% male; 48.1% female)
Individual Education Program: 1,036 (9.9%);
English Language Learner: 434 (4.2%); Migrant: 0 (0.0%)
Eligible for Free Lunch Program: 640 (6.1%)
Eligible for Reduced-Price Lunch Program: 268 (2.6%)
Teachers: 546.8 (19.1 to 1)
Librarians/Media Specialists: 8.0 (1,305.1 to 1)
Guidance Counselors: 12.4 (842.0 to 1)
Current Spending: ($ per student per year):
Total: $6,840; Instruction: $4,053; Support Services: $2,434
Enrollment, Drop-out Rates and Diploma Recipients by Race/Ethnicity

Category	Total	White	Black	Asian	AIAN	Hisp.
Enrollment (%)	100.0	87.9	4.6	5.5	1.0	1.1
Drop-out Rate (%)	0.8	0.7	2.5	0.0	0.0	4.0
H.S. Diplomas (#)	706	651	19	27	4	5

Edina

5701 Normandale Rd • Edina, MN 55435
(952) 848-3900 • http://www.edina.k12.mn.us/
Grade Span: PK-12; **Agency Type:** 1
Schools: 12
7 Primary; 2 Middle; 2 High; 1 Other Level
9 Regular; 2 Special Education; 0 Vocational; 1 Alternative
0 Magnet; 0 Charter; 3 Title I Eligible; 0 School-wide Title I
Students: 7,163 (50.1% male; 49.9% female)
Individual Education Program: 722 (10.1%);
English Language Learner: 148 (2.1%); Migrant: 0 (0.0%)
Eligible for Free Lunch Program: 237 (3.3%)
Eligible for Reduced-Price Lunch Program: 88 (1.2%)
Teachers: 412.4 (17.4 to 1)
Librarians/Media Specialists: 9.0 (795.9 to 1)
Guidance Counselors: 9.0 (795.9 to 1)
Current Spending: ($ per student per year):
Total: $7,687; Instruction: $4,773; Support Services: $2,620
Enrollment, Drop-out Rates and Diploma Recipients by Race/Ethnicity

Category	Total	White	Black	Asian	AIAN	Hisp.
Enrollment (%)	100.0	91.2	2.8	4.2	0.3	1.6
Drop-out Rate (%)	0.2	0.1	7.7	1.3	0.0	0.0
H.S. Diplomas (#)	499	469	4	21	1	4

Hopkins

1001 State Hwy 7 • Hopkins, MN 55343
(952) 988-4000 • http://www.hopkins.k12.mn.us/
Grade Span: PK-12; **Agency Type:** 1
Schools: 16
8 Primary; 2 Middle; 1 High; 5 Other Level
10 Regular; 1 Special Education; 0 Vocational; 5 Alternative
0 Magnet; 0 Charter; 7 Title I Eligible; 1 School-wide Title I
Students: 8,223 (52.2% male; 47.8% female)
Individual Education Program: 1,008 (12.3%);
English Language Learner: 549 (6.7%); Migrant: 0 (0.0%)
Eligible for Free Lunch Program: 861 (10.5%)
Eligible for Reduced-Price Lunch Program: 254 (3.1%)
Teachers: 547.9 (15.0 to 1)
Librarians/Media Specialists: 11.2 (734.2 to 1)
Guidance Counselors: 17.8 (462.0 to 1)
Current Spending: ($ per student per year):
Total: $8,654; Instruction: $5,351; Support Services: $2,968
Enrollment, Drop-out Rates and Diploma Recipients by Race/Ethnicity

Category	Total	White	Black	Asian	AIAN	Hisp.
Enrollment (%)	100.0	82.5	8.5	3.6	0.7	4.7
Drop-out Rate (%)	1.0	0.8	2.0	0.8	2.8	3.1
H.S. Diplomas (#)	656	580	33	28	3	12

Intermediate SD 287

1820 N Xenium Ln • Plymouth, MN 55441-3790
(763) 559-3535 • http://www.int287.k12.mn.us/
Grade Span: PK-12; **Agency Type:** 4
Schools: 162
11 Primary; 7 Middle; 59 High; 85 Other Level
0 Regular; 32 Special Education; 2 Vocational; 128 Alternative
0 Magnet; 0 Charter; 0 Title I Eligible; 0 School-wide Title I
Students: 2,165 (58.3% male; 41.7% female)
Individual Education Program: 754 (34.8%);
English Language Learner: 17 (0.8%); Migrant: 0 (0.0%)
Eligible for Free Lunch Program: 134 (6.2%)
Eligible for Reduced-Price Lunch Program: 44 (2.0%)
Teachers: 249.9 (8.7 to 1)
Librarians/Media Specialists: 0.0 (0.0 to 1)
Guidance Counselors: 0.0 (0.0 to 1)
Current Spending: ($ per student per year):
Total: n/a; Instruction: n/a; Support Services: n/a
Enrollment, Drop-out Rates and Diploma Recipients by Race/Ethnicity

Category	Total	White	Black	Asian	AIAN	Hisp.
Enrollment (%)	100.0	72.0	15.9	7.3	1.3	3.6
Drop-out Rate (%)	14.6	13.6	19.3	15.2	18.8	18.4
H.S. Diplomas (#)	132	113	11	7	0	1

Minneapolis

807 NE Broadway • Minneapolis, MN 55413-2398
(612) 668-0000 • http://www.mpls.k12.mn.us/
Grade Span: PK-12; **Agency Type:** 1
Schools: 144
72 Primary; 12 Middle; 39 High; 21 Other Level
81 Regular; 9 Special Education; 0 Vocational; 54 Alternative
20 Magnet; 0 Charter; 76 Title I Eligible; 76 School-wide Title I
Students: 46,037 (51.8% male; 48.2% female)
Individual Education Program: 6,456 (14.0%);
English Language Learner: 11,094 (24.1%); Migrant: 0 (0.0%)
Eligible for Free Lunch Program: 26,882 (58.4%)
Eligible for Reduced-Price Lunch Program: 4,109 (8.9%)
Teachers: 3,142.0 (14.7 to 1)
Librarians/Media Specialists: 73.6 (625.5 to 1)
Guidance Counselors: 42.2 (1,090.9 to 1)
Current Spending: ($ per student per year):
Total: $10,861; Instruction: $6,763; Support Services: $3,729
Enrollment, Drop-out Rates and Diploma Recipients by Race/Ethnicity

Category	Total	White	Black	Asian	AIAN	Hisp.
Enrollment (%)	100.0	26.4	42.9	13.9	4.2	12.6
Drop-out Rate (%)	13.7	8.3	16.6	8.3	26.7	22.7
H.S. Diplomas (#)	2,180	835	842	350	48	105

Minneapolis Area Office

311 S Second Ave, 7th Flr • Minneapolis, MN 55401
(612) 373-1000
Grade Span: KG-12; **Agency Type:** 6
Schools: 12
1 Primary; 0 Middle; 1 High; 10 Other Level
12 Regular; 0 Special Education; 0 Vocational; 0 Alternative
0 Magnet; 0 Charter; 12 Title I Eligible; 12 School-wide Title I
Students: 2,644 (n/a% male; n/a% female)
Individual Education Program: n/a;
English Language Learner: n/a; Migrant: n/a
Eligible for Free Lunch Program: n/a
Eligible for Reduced-Price Lunch Program: n/a
Teachers: n/a
Librarians/Media Specialists: n/a
Guidance Counselors: n/a
Current Spending: ($ per student per year):
Total: n/a; Instruction: n/a; Support Services: n/a
Enrollment, Drop-out Rates and Diploma Recipients by Race/Ethnicity

Category	Total	White	Black	Asian	AIAN	Hisp.
Enrollment (%)	100.0	0.0	0.0	0.0	100.0	0.0
Drop-out Rate (%)	n/a	n/a	n/a	n/a	n/a	n/a
H.S. Diplomas (#)	n/a	n/a	n/a	n/a	n/a	n/a

Minnetonka

5621 Hwy 101 • Excelsior, MN 55331
(952) 401-5000 • http://www.minnetonka.k12.mn.us/
Grade Span: PK-12; **Agency Type:** 1
Schools: 11
8 Primary; 2 Middle; 1 High; 0 Other Level
9 Regular; 0 Special Education; 0 Vocational; 2 Alternative
0 Magnet; 0 Charter; 4 Title I Eligible; 0 School-wide Title I
Students: 7,591 (51.0% male; 49.0% female)
Individual Education Program: 895 (11.8%);
English Language Learner: 44 (0.6%); Migrant: 0 (0.0%)
Eligible for Free Lunch Program: 127 (1.7%)
Eligible for Reduced-Price Lunch Program: 99 (1.3%)
Teachers: 462.2 (16.4 to 1)
Librarians/Media Specialists: 9.0 (843.4 to 1)
Guidance Counselors: 10.0 (759.1 to 1)
Current Spending: ($ per student per year):
Total: $7,265; Instruction: $4,424; Support Services: $2,497
Enrollment, Drop-out Rates and Diploma Recipients by Race/Ethnicity

Category	Total	White	Black	Asian	AIAN	Hisp.
Enrollment (%)	100.0	93.0	1.6	3.3	0.4	1.6
Drop-out Rate (%)	0.7	0.4	4.5	3.0	0.0	10.9
H.S. Diplomas (#)	492	472	4	8	1	7

Orono

685 Old Crystal Bay Rd • Long Lake, MN 55356-0046
Mailing Address: Box 46, 685 Old Crystal Bay Rd • Long Lake, MN 55356-0046
(952) 449-8300 • http://www.orono.k12.mn.us/
Grade Span: PK-12; **Agency Type:** 1
Schools: 5
3 Primary; 1 Middle; 1 High; 0 Other Level
4 Regular; 0 Special Education; 0 Vocational; 1 Alternative
0 Magnet; 0 Charter; 1 Title I Eligible; 0 School-wide Title I
Students: 2,486 (50.6% male; 49.4% female)
Individual Education Program: 215 (8.6%);
English Language Learner: 14 (0.6%); Migrant: 0 (0.0%)
Eligible for Free Lunch Program: 51 (2.1%)
Eligible for Reduced-Price Lunch Program: 35 (1.4%)
Teachers: 145.0 (17.1 to 1)
Librarians/Media Specialists: 3.0 (828.7 to 1)
Guidance Counselors: 3.0 (828.7 to 1)
Current Spending: ($ per student per year):
Total: $7,010; Instruction: $4,402; Support Services: $2,279
Enrollment, Drop-out Rates and Diploma Recipients by Race/Ethnicity

Category	Total	White	Black	Asian	AIAN	Hisp.
Enrollment (%)	100.0	95.9	0.9	1.5	0.2	1.4
Drop-out Rate (%)	0.5	0.5	0.0	0.0	0.0	0.0
H.S. Diplomas (#)	185	174	0	7	1	3

Osseo

11200 93rd Ave N • Osseo, MN 55369-6605
(763) 391-7000 • http://www.osseo.k12.mn.us/
Grade Span: PK-12; **Agency Type:** 1
Schools: 30
20 Primary; 4 Middle; 5 High; 1 Other Level
26 Regular; 2 Special Education; 0 Vocational; 2 Alternative
0 Magnet; 0 Charter; 6 Title I Eligible; 1 School-wide Title I
Students: 21,824 (51.4% male; 48.6% female)
Individual Education Program: 2,395 (11.0%);
English Language Learner: 1,723 (7.9%); Migrant: 0 (0.0%)
Eligible for Free Lunch Program: 3,647 (16.7%)
Eligible for Reduced-Price Lunch Program: 1,409 (6.5%)
Teachers: 1,193.1 (18.3 to 1)
Librarians/Media Specialists: 31.0 (704.0 to 1)
Guidance Counselors: 30.8 (708.6 to 1)
Current Spending: ($ per student per year):
Total: $7,221; Instruction: $4,677; Support Services: $2,232
Enrollment, Drop-out Rates and Diploma Recipients by Race/Ethnicity

Category	Total	White	Black	Asian	AIAN	Hisp.
Enrollment (%)	100.0	69.9	15.6	10.9	0.8	2.8
Drop-out Rate (%)	1.7	1.1	3.9	4.2	8.0	2.9
H.S. Diplomas (#)	1,342	1,099	100	118	3	22

Richfield

7001 Harriet Ave S • Richfield, MN 55423-3000
(612) 798-6000 • http://www.richfield.k12.mn.us/
Grade Span: PK-12; **Agency Type:** 1
Schools: 7
4 Primary; 1 Middle; 2 High; 0 Other Level
5 Regular; 2 Special Education; 0 Vocational; 0 Alternative
0 Magnet; 0 Charter; 2 Title I Eligible; 0 School-wide Title I
Students: 4,176 (53.1% male; 46.9% female)
Individual Education Program: 510 (12.2%);
English Language Learner: 634 (15.2%); Migrant: 0 (0.0%)
Eligible for Free Lunch Program: 1,056 (25.3%)
Eligible for Reduced-Price Lunch Program: 379 (9.1%)
Teachers: 251.2 (16.6 to 1)
Librarians/Media Specialists: 3.0 (1,392.0 to 1)
Guidance Counselors: 5.0 (835.2 to 1)
Current Spending: ($ per student per year):
Total: $7,623; Instruction: $4,707; Support Services: $2,644
Enrollment, Drop-out Rates and Diploma Recipients by Race/Ethnicity

Category	Total	White	Black	Asian	AIAN	Hisp.
Enrollment (%)	100.0	59.1	17.5	8.4	1.5	13.5
Drop-out Rate (%)	5.0	3.7	8.0	7.9	9.5	6.6
H.S. Diplomas (#)	261	198	29	23	1	10

Robbinsdale

4148 Winnetka Ave N • New Hope, MN 55427-1288
(763) 504-8011 • http://www.rdale.k12.mn.us/dist/
Grade Span: PK-12; **Agency Type:** 1
Schools: 25
15 Primary; 3 Middle; 2 High; 5 Other Level
18 Regular; 3 Special Education; 0 Vocational; 4 Alternative
2 Magnet; 0 Charter; 6 Title I Eligible; 0 School-wide Title I
Students: 13,656 (51.4% male; 48.6% female)
Individual Education Program: 1,374 (10.1%);
English Language Learner: 1,108 (8.1%); Migrant: 0 (0.0%)
Eligible for Free Lunch Program: 2,356 (17.3%)
Eligible for Reduced-Price Lunch Program: 1,118 (8.2%)
Teachers: 774.4 (17.6 to 1)
Librarians/Media Specialists: 15.9 (858.9 to 1)
Guidance Counselors: 16.8 (812.9 to 1)
Current Spending: ($ per student per year):
Total: $7,446; Instruction: $4,507; Support Services: $2,577
Enrollment, Drop-out Rates and Diploma Recipients by Race/Ethnicity

Category	Total	White	Black	Asian	AIAN	Hisp.
Enrollment (%)	100.0	70.7	15.8	6.4	1.3	5.8
Drop-out Rate (%)	1.6	1.0	3.5	4.0	3.4	1.8
H.S. Diplomas (#)	693	581	48	47	3	14

Saint Anthony-New Brighton

3303 33rd Ave NE • Saint Anthony, MN 55418-9971
(612) 706-1000
Grade Span: PK-12; **Agency Type:** 1
Schools: 3
1 Primary; 1 Middle; 1 High; 0 Other Level
3 Regular; 0 Special Education; 0 Vocational; 0 Alternative
0 Magnet; 0 Charter; 1 Title I Eligible; 0 School-wide Title I
Students: 1,528 (52.7% male; 47.3% female)
Individual Education Program: 124 (8.1%);
English Language Learner: 0 (0.0%); Migrant: 0 (0.0%)
Eligible for Free Lunch Program: 87 (5.7%)
Eligible for Reduced-Price Lunch Program: 57 (3.7%)
Teachers: 87.7 (17.4 to 1)
Librarians/Media Specialists: 2.0 (764.0 to 1)
Guidance Counselors: 3.0 (509.3 to 1)
Current Spending: ($ per student per year):
Total: $7,762; Instruction: $4,219; Support Services: $3,225
Enrollment, Drop-out Rates and Diploma Recipients by Race/Ethnicity

Category	Total	White	Black	Asian	AIAN	Hisp.
Enrollment (%)	100.0	84.4	4.5	8.0	1.2	1.9
Drop-out Rate (%)	1.9	1.8	4.2	0.0	0.0	12.5
H.S. Diplomas (#)	116	103	7	5	0	1

Saint Louis Park

6425 W 33rd St • Saint Louis Park, MN 55426-3498
(952) 928-6003 • http://www.stlpark.k12.mn.us/index.html
Grade Span: PK-12; **Agency Type:** 1
Schools: 10
6 Primary; 1 Middle; 2 High; 1 Other Level
7 Regular; 2 Special Education; 0 Vocational; 1 Alternative
0 Magnet; 0 Charter; 3 Title I Eligible; 0 School-wide Title I
Students: 4,238 (51.8% male; 48.2% female)
Individual Education Program: 665 (15.7%);
English Language Learner: 273 (6.4%); Migrant: 0 (0.0%)
Eligible for Free Lunch Program: 662 (15.6%)
Eligible for Reduced-Price Lunch Program: 217 (5.1%)
Teachers: 293.2 (14.5 to 1)
Librarians/Media Specialists: 7.0 (605.4 to 1)
Guidance Counselors: 6.8 (623.2 to 1)
Current Spending: ($ per student per year):
Total: $9,211; Instruction: $5,449; Support Services: $3,418
Enrollment, Drop-out Rates and Diploma Recipients by Race/Ethnicity

Category	Total	White	Black	Asian	AIAN	Hisp.
Enrollment (%)	100.0	77.8	11.9	4.8	0.7	4.8
Drop-out Rate (%)	2.7	2.1	7.8	1.8	25.0	4.3
H.S. Diplomas (#)	259	224	18	11	1	5

Wayzata

Box 660 • Wayzata, MN 55391-0660
(763) 745-5000 • http://www.wayzata.k12.mn.us/communications/
Grade Span: PK-12; **Agency Type:** 1
Schools: 11
7 Primary; 3 Middle; 1 High; 0 Other Level
11 Regular; 0 Special Education; 0 Vocational; 0 Alternative
0 Magnet; 0 Charter; 3 Title I Eligible; 0 School-wide Title I
Students: 9,534 (51.0% male; 49.0% female)
Individual Education Program: 886 (9.3%);
English Language Learner: 10 (0.1%); Migrant: 0 (0.0%)
Eligible for Free Lunch Program: 555 (5.8%)
Eligible for Reduced-Price Lunch Program: 236 (2.5%)
Teachers: 513.5 (18.6 to 1)
Librarians/Media Specialists: 12.0 (794.5 to 1)
Guidance Counselors: 8.0 (1,191.8 to 1)
Current Spending: ($ per student per year):
Total: $7,251; Instruction: $4,231; Support Services: $2,693
Enrollment, Drop-out Rates and Diploma Recipients by Race/Ethnicity

Category	Total	White	Black	Asian	AIAN	Hisp.
Enrollment (%)	100.0	88.9	3.9	5.5	0.2	1.5
Drop-out Rate (%)	0.7	0.5	5.7	1.3	11.1	0.0
H.S. Diplomas (#)	642	585	8	35	1	13

Westonka

2450 Wilshire Blvd Ste A • Mound, MN 55364-1697
(952) 491-8001 • http://www.westonka.k12.mn.us/
Grade Span: PK-12; **Agency Type:** 1
Schools: 5
2 Primary; 1 Middle; 1 High; 1 Other Level
4 Regular; 1 Special Education; 0 Vocational; 0 Alternative
0 Magnet; 0 Charter; 3 Title I Eligible; 0 School-wide Title I
Students: 2,201 (54.2% male; 45.8% female)
Individual Education Program: 255 (11.6%);
English Language Learner: 21 (1.0%); Migrant: 0 (0.0%)
Eligible for Free Lunch Program: 171 (7.8%)
Eligible for Reduced-Price Lunch Program: 107 (4.9%)
Teachers: 134.7 (16.3 to 1)
Librarians/Media Specialists: 4.0 (550.3 to 1)
Guidance Counselors: 3.0 (733.7 to 1)
Current Spending: ($ per student per year):
Total: $7,255; Instruction: $3,955; Support Services: $2,966
Enrollment, Drop-out Rates and Diploma Recipients by Race/Ethnicity

Category	Total	White	Black	Asian	AIAN	Hisp.
Enrollment (%)	100.0	97.4	0.6	1.0	0.2	0.7
Drop-out Rate (%)	2.1	2.1	0.0	0.0	0.0	11.1
H.S. Diplomas (#)	154	148	1	4	0	1

Houston County

Lacrescent-Hokah

703 S 11th St • Lacrescent, MN 55947-1315
(507) 895-4484 • http://www.isd300.k12.mn.us
Grade Span: PK-12; **Agency Type:** 1
Schools: 5
2 Primary; 0 Middle; 1 High; 2 Other Level
3 Regular; 0 Special Education; 0 Vocational; 2 Alternative
0 Magnet; 0 Charter; 2 Title I Eligible; 0 School-wide Title I
Students: 1,680 (50.4% male; 49.6% female)
Individual Education Program: 174 (10.4%);
English Language Learner: 0 (0.0%); Migrant: 0 (0.0%)
Eligible for Free Lunch Program: 140 (8.3%)
Eligible for Reduced-Price Lunch Program: 69 (4.1%)
Teachers: 99.7 (16.9 to 1)
Librarians/Media Specialists: 1.8 (933.3 to 1)
Guidance Counselors: 3.0 (560.0 to 1)
Current Spending: ($ per student per year):
Total: $6,511; Instruction: $3,981; Support Services: $2,184
Enrollment, Drop-out Rates and Diploma Recipients by Race/Ethnicity

Category	Total	White	Black	Asian	AIAN	Hisp.
Enrollment (%)	100.0	96.4	2.0	1.1	0.2	0.4
Drop-out Rate (%)	2.0	2.0	0.0	0.0	0.0	n/a
H.S. Diplomas (#)	162	159	1	2	0	0

Hubbard County

Park Rapids

Box 591 • Park Rapids, MN 56470-0591
(218) 237-6500 • http://www.parkrapids.k12.mn.us/
Grade Span: PK-12; **Agency Type:** 1
Schools: 4
1 Primary; 1 Middle; 2 High; 0 Other Level
3 Regular; 0 Special Education; 0 Vocational; 1 Alternative
0 Magnet; 0 Charter; 2 Title I Eligible; 0 School-wide Title I
Students: 1,820 (53.4% male; 46.6% female)
Individual Education Program: 327 (18.0%);
English Language Learner: 0 (0.0%); Migrant: 0 (0.0%)
Eligible for Free Lunch Program: 555 (30.5%)
Eligible for Reduced-Price Lunch Program: 262 (14.4%)
Teachers: 114.6 (15.9 to 1)
Librarians/Media Specialists: 2.0 (910.0 to 1)
Guidance Counselors: 2.0 (910.0 to 1)
Current Spending: ($ per student per year):
Total: $7,284; Instruction: $4,661; Support Services: $2,302
Enrollment, Drop-out Rates and Diploma Recipients by Race/Ethnicity

Category	Total	White	Black	Asian	AIAN	Hisp.
Enrollment (%)	100.0	90.9	0.5	0.4	7.3	0.9
Drop-out Rate (%)	10.3	9.0	0.0	0.0	30.3	28.6
H.S. Diplomas (#)	129	122	0	2	3	2

Isanti County

Cambridge-Isanti

430 NW 8th Ave • Cambridge, MN 55008-1269
Mailing Address: 315 7th Ln NE • Cambridge, MN 55008-1269
(763) 689-4988 • http://www.cambridge.k12.mn.us/
Grade Span: PK-12; **Agency Type:** 1
Schools: 7
3 Primary; 3 Middle; 1 High; 0 Other Level
7 Regular; 0 Special Education; 0 Vocational; 0 Alternative
0 Magnet; 0 Charter; 5 Title I Eligible; 0 School-wide Title I
Students: 4,866 (51.4% male; 48.6% female)
Individual Education Program: 470 (9.7%);
English Language Learner: 43 (0.9%); Migrant: 0 (0.0%)
Eligible for Free Lunch Program: 625 (12.8%)
Eligible for Reduced-Price Lunch Program: 382 (7.9%)
Teachers: 270.1 (18.0 to 1)
Librarians/Media Specialists: 5.0 (973.2 to 1)
Guidance Counselors: 6.5 (748.6 to 1)
Current Spending: ($ per student per year):
Total: $7,002; Instruction: $4,699; Support Services: $2,047
Enrollment, Drop-out Rates and Diploma Recipients by Race/Ethnicity

Category	Total	White	Black	Asian	AIAN	Hisp.
Enrollment (%)	100.0	95.4	1.0	1.2	1.3	1.0
Drop-out Rate (%)	1.7	1.6	11.1	0.0	12.5	0.0
H.S. Diplomas (#)	334	319	2	7	6	0

Itasca County

Grand Rapids

820 NW First Ave • Grand Rapids, MN 55744-2687
(218) 327-5704 • http://www.isd318.org/
Grade Span: PK-12; **Agency Type:** 1
Schools: 19
9 Primary; 1 Middle; 5 High; 4 Other Level
10 Regular; 1 Special Education; 0 Vocational; 8 Alternative
0 Magnet; 0 Charter; 10 Title I Eligible; 1 School-wide Title I
Students: 4,158 (52.5% male; 47.5% female)
Individual Education Program: 548 (13.2%);
English Language Learner: 0 (0.0%); Migrant: 0 (0.0%)
Eligible for Free Lunch Program: 892 (21.5%)
Eligible for Reduced-Price Lunch Program: 349 (8.4%)
Teachers: 237.8 (17.5 to 1)
Librarians/Media Specialists: 2.6 (1,599.2 to 1)
Guidance Counselors: 6.9 (602.6 to 1)

Current Spending: ($ per student per year):
Total: $7,673; Instruction: $5,079; Support Services: $2,348
Enrollment, Drop-out Rates and Diploma Recipients by Race/Ethnicity

Category	Total	White	Black	Asian	AIAN	Hisp.
Enrollment (%)	100.0	93.1	0.6	0.7	4.9	0.7
Drop-out Rate (%)	9.4	7.9	111.1	16.7	19.0	43.8
H.S. Diplomas (#)	356	339	0	2	13	2

Kanabec County

Mora
400 E Maple • Mora, MN 55051-1313
(320) 679-6200 • http://www.mora.k12.mn.us/
Grade Span: PK-12; **Agency Type:** 1
Schools: 4
1 Primary; 1 Middle; 2 High; 0 Other Level
3 Regular; 0 Special Education; 0 Vocational; 1 Alternative
0 Magnet; 0 Charter; 2 Title I Eligible; 0 School-wide Title I
Students: 1,949 (49.8% male; 50.2% female)
Individual Education Program: 180 (9.2%);
English Language Learner: 2 (0.1%); Migrant: 0 (0.0%)
Eligible for Free Lunch Program: 398 (20.4%)
Eligible for Reduced-Price Lunch Program: 221 (11.3%)
Teachers: 120.8 (16.1 to 1)
Librarians/Media Specialists: 3.0 (649.7 to 1)
Guidance Counselors: 2.0 (974.5 to 1)
Current Spending: ($ per student per year):
Total: $5,976; Instruction: $3,971; Support Services: $1,755
Enrollment, Drop-out Rates and Diploma Recipients by Race/Ethnicity

Category	Total	White	Black	Asian	AIAN	Hisp.
Enrollment (%)	100.0	94.8	0.7	1.1	1.7	1.6
Drop-out Rate (%)	3.6	3.4	33.3	0.0	0.0	11.1
H.S. Diplomas (#)	146	142	0	1	1	2

Kandiyohi County

New London-Spicer
Box 430 • New London, MN 56273
(320) 354-2252 • http://nls.k12.mn.us/
Grade Span: PK-12; **Agency Type:** 1
Schools: 6
2 Primary; 2 Middle; 2 High; 0 Other Level
4 Regular; 0 Special Education; 0 Vocational; 2 Alternative
0 Magnet; 0 Charter; 4 Title I Eligible; 0 School-wide Title I
Students: 1,769 (52.5% male; 47.5% female)
Individual Education Program: 233 (13.2%);
English Language Learner: 1 (0.1%); Migrant: 0 (0.0%)
Eligible for Free Lunch Program: 245 (13.8%)
Eligible for Reduced-Price Lunch Program: 147 (8.3%)
Teachers: 110.5 (16.0 to 1)
Librarians/Media Specialists: 2.0 (884.5 to 1)
Guidance Counselors: 2.0 (884.5 to 1)
Current Spending: ($ per student per year):
Total: $6,320; Instruction: $4,079; Support Services: $1,932
Enrollment, Drop-out Rates and Diploma Recipients by Race/Ethnicity

Category	Total	White	Black	Asian	AIAN	Hisp.
Enrollment (%)	100.0	99.3	0.3	0.2	0.2	0.1
Drop-out Rate (%)	3.0	3.0	0.0	0.0	0.0	n/a
H.S. Diplomas (#)	125	123	1	1	0	0

Willmar
611 5th St SW • Willmar, MN 56201-3297
(320) 231-8500 • http://www.willmar.k12.mn.us
Grade Span: PK-12; **Agency Type:** 1
Schools: 14
5 Primary; 2 Middle; 4 High; 3 Other Level
6 Regular; 3 Special Education; 0 Vocational; 5 Alternative
1 Magnet; 0 Charter; 3 Title I Eligible; 0 School-wide Title I
Students: 4,382 (50.6% male; 49.4% female)
Individual Education Program: 614 (14.0%);
English Language Learner: 568 (13.0%); Migrant: 145 (3.3%)
Eligible for Free Lunch Program: 1,400 (31.9%)
Eligible for Reduced-Price Lunch Program: 363 (8.3%)
Teachers: 299.5 (14.6 to 1)
Librarians/Media Specialists: 2.5 (1,752.8 to 1)
Guidance Counselors: 4.1 (1,068.8 to 1)
Current Spending: ($ per student per year):
Total: $7,647; Instruction: $4,942; Support Services: $2,397
Enrollment, Drop-out Rates and Diploma Recipients by Race/Ethnicity

Category	Total	White	Black	Asian	AIAN	Hisp.
Enrollment (%)	100.0	73.2	1.9	0.5	0.6	23.8
Drop-out Rate (%)	3.7	2.0	11.4	0.0	14.3	11.8
H.S. Diplomas (#)	269	244	2	3	0	20

Lake County

Lake Superior
405 4th Ave • Two Harbors, MN 55616
(218) 834-8216 • http://www.isd381.k12.mn.us/
Grade Span: PK-12; **Agency Type:** 1
Schools: 6
2 Primary; 1 Middle; 3 High; 0 Other Level
5 Regular; 0 Special Education; 0 Vocational; 1 Alternative
0 Magnet; 0 Charter; 3 Title I Eligible; 0 School-wide Title I
Students: 1,698 (51.4% male; 48.6% female)
Individual Education Program: 226 (13.3%);
English Language Learner: 1 (0.1%); Migrant: 0 (0.0%)
Eligible for Free Lunch Program: 241 (14.2%)
Eligible for Reduced-Price Lunch Program: 151 (8.9%)
Teachers: 100.6 (16.9 to 1)
Librarians/Media Specialists: 1.0 (1,698.0 to 1)
Guidance Counselors: 3.0 (566.0 to 1)
Current Spending: ($ per student per year):
Total: $7,248; Instruction: $4,099; Support Services: $2,916
Enrollment, Drop-out Rates and Diploma Recipients by Race/Ethnicity

Category	Total	White	Black	Asian	AIAN	Hisp.
Enrollment (%)	100.0	97.9	0.7	0.3	0.9	0.2
Drop-out Rate (%)	2.7	2.7	0.0	0.0	0.0	0.0
H.S. Diplomas (#)	140	139	0	0	0	1

Lyon County

Marshall
401 S Saratoga St • Marshall, MN 56258-1799
(507) 537-6924 • http://www.marshall.k12.mn.us/
Grade Span: PK-12; **Agency Type:** 1
Schools: 6
3 Primary; 1 Middle; 2 High; 0 Other Level
5 Regular; 0 Special Education; 0 Vocational; 1 Alternative
0 Magnet; 0 Charter; 3 Title I Eligible; 0 School-wide Title I
Students: 2,304 (48.7% male; 51.3% female)
Individual Education Program: 287 (12.5%);
English Language Learner: 138 (6.0%); Migrant: 0 (0.0%)
Eligible for Free Lunch Program: 428 (18.6%)
Eligible for Reduced-Price Lunch Program: 207 (9.0%)
Teachers: 165.2 (13.9 to 1)
Librarians/Media Specialists: 1.7 (1,355.3 to 1)
Guidance Counselors: 4.0 (576.0 to 1)
Current Spending: ($ per student per year):
Total: $7,004; Instruction: $4,556; Support Services: $2,075
Enrollment, Drop-out Rates and Diploma Recipients by Race/Ethnicity

Category	Total	White	Black	Asian	AIAN	Hisp.
Enrollment (%)	100.0	83.2	5.2	2.6	0.4	8.6
Drop-out Rate (%)	2.8	2.1	8.2	0.0	0.0	14.6
H.S. Diplomas (#)	243	220	10	6	0	7

Martin County

Fairmont Area Schools
115 S Park St • Fairmont, MN 56031-2287
(507) 238-4234 • http://fairmont.k12.mn.us/
Grade Span: KG-12; **Agency Type:** 1
Schools: 4
2 Primary; 1 Middle; 1 High; 0 Other Level
4 Regular; 0 Special Education; 0 Vocational; 0 Alternative
0 Magnet; 0 Charter; 3 Title I Eligible; 0 School-wide Title I
Students: 1,825 (51.9% male; 48.1% female)
Individual Education Program: 250 (13.7%);
English Language Learner: 5 (0.3%); Migrant: 0 (0.0%)
Eligible for Free Lunch Program: 452 (24.8%)
Eligible for Reduced-Price Lunch Program: 158 (8.7%)
Teachers: 116.2 (15.7 to 1)
Librarians/Media Specialists: 2.0 (912.5 to 1)
Guidance Counselors: 2.0 (912.5 to 1)
Current Spending: ($ per student per year):
Total: $6,413; Instruction: $3,554; Support Services: $2,494
Enrollment, Drop-out Rates and Diploma Recipients by Race/Ethnicity

Category	Total	White	Black	Asian	AIAN	Hisp.
Enrollment (%)	100.0	93.6	1.0	0.9	0.2	4.3
Drop-out Rate (%)	3.5	3.1	0.0	6.7	n/a	18.8
H.S. Diplomas (#)	167	161	0	4	0	2

Mcleod County

Glencoe-Silver Lake
1621 E 16th St • Glencoe, MN 55336-1799
(320) 864-2498 • http://gsl.k12.mn.us/
Grade Span: PK-12; **Agency Type:** 1
Schools: 5

2 Primary; 1 Middle; 2 High; 0 Other Level
4 Regular; 0 Special Education; 0 Vocational; 1 Alternative
0 Magnet; 0 Charter; 2 Title I Eligible; 0 School-wide Title I
Students: 1,777 (50.5% male; 49.5% female)
Individual Education Program: 191 (10.7%);
English Language Learner: 134 (7.5%); Migrant: 15 (0.8%)
Eligible for Free Lunch Program: 281 (15.8%)
Eligible for Reduced-Price Lunch Program: 156 (8.8%)
Teachers: 108.2 (16.4 to 1)
Librarians/Media Specialists: 1.0 (1,777.0 to 1)
Guidance Counselors: 2.0 (888.5 to 1)
Current Spending: ($ per student per year):
Total: $6,570; Instruction: $3,860; Support Services: $2,326
Enrollment, Drop-out Rates and Diploma Recipients by Race/Ethnicity

Category	Total	White	Black	Asian	AIAN	Hisp.
Enrollment (%)	100.0	85.0	0.2	0.3	0.3	14.2
Drop-out Rate (%)	2.9	2.1	0.0	33.3	n/a	14.6
H.S. Diplomas (#)	138	132	0	1	0	5

Hutchinson
30 Glen St N • Hutchinson, MN 55350-1696
(320) 587-2860 • http://www.hutch.k12.mn.us/tigers/html/indexnojava.html
Grade Span: PK-12; **Agency Type:** 1
Schools: 7
2 Primary; 2 Middle; 1 High; 2 Other Level
4 Regular; 1 Special Education; 0 Vocational; 2 Alternative
0 Magnet; 0 Charter; 2 Title I Eligible; 0 School-wide Title I
Students: 3,142 (52.2% male; 47.8% female)
Individual Education Program: 325 (10.3%);
English Language Learner: 92 (2.9%); Migrant: 0 (0.0%)
Eligible for Free Lunch Program: 395 (12.6%)
Eligible for Reduced-Price Lunch Program: 108 (3.4%)
Teachers: 191.3 (16.4 to 1)
Librarians/Media Specialists: 2.0 (1,571.0 to 1)
Guidance Counselors: 6.0 (523.7 to 1)
Current Spending: ($ per student per year):
Total: $5,760; Instruction: $3,534; Support Services: $1,919
Enrollment, Drop-out Rates and Diploma Recipients by Race/Ethnicity

Category	Total	White	Black	Asian	AIAN	Hisp.
Enrollment (%)	100.0	93.4	0.9	1.0	0.2	4.5
Drop-out Rate (%)	2.9	2.7	0.0	0.0	n/a	33.3
H.S. Diplomas (#)	228	226	0	2	0	0

Meeker County

Dassel-Cokato
4852 Reardon Ave SW • Cokato, MN 55321
Mailing Address: Box 1700 • Cokato, MN 55321
(320) 286-4100 • http://www.dc.k12.mn.us/
Grade Span: PK-12; **Agency Type:** 1
Schools: 6
2 Primary; 1 Middle; 2 High; 1 Other Level
4 Regular; 0 Special Education; 0 Vocational; 2 Alternative
0 Magnet; 0 Charter; 3 Title I Eligible; 0 School-wide Title I
Students: 2,264 (50.5% male; 49.5% female)
Individual Education Program: 222 (9.8%);
English Language Learner: 10 (0.4%); Migrant: 0 (0.0%)
Eligible for Free Lunch Program: 391 (17.3%)
Eligible for Reduced-Price Lunch Program: 144 (6.4%)
Teachers: 127.9 (17.7 to 1)
Librarians/Media Specialists: 4.0 (566.0 to 1)
Guidance Counselors: 1.0 (2,264.0 to 1)
Current Spending: ($ per student per year):
Total: $6,162; Instruction: $3,930; Support Services: $1,963
Enrollment, Drop-out Rates and Diploma Recipients by Race/Ethnicity

Category	Total	White	Black	Asian	AIAN	Hisp.
Enrollment (%)	100.0	96.6	0.6	0.8	0.4	1.7
Drop-out Rate (%)	2.2	2.1	0.0	0.0	0.0	11.1
H.S. Diplomas (#)	199	192	2	2	0	3

Litchfield
114 N Holcombe • Litchfield, MN 55355-1409
(320) 693-2444 • http://www.litchfield.k12.mn.us
Grade Span: PK-12; **Agency Type:** 1
Schools: 5
1 Primary; 2 Middle; 2 High; 0 Other Level
4 Regular; 0 Special Education; 0 Vocational; 1 Alternative
0 Magnet; 0 Charter; 2 Title I Eligible; 0 School-wide Title I
Students: 1,962 (53.0% male; 47.0% female)
Individual Education Program: 265 (13.5%);
English Language Learner: 23 (1.2%); Migrant: 0 (0.0%)
Eligible for Free Lunch Program: 322 (16.4%)
Eligible for Reduced-Price Lunch Program: 180 (9.2%)
Teachers: 122.1 (16.1 to 1)
Librarians/Media Specialists: 2.0 (981.0 to 1)
Guidance Counselors: 2.0 (981.0 to 1)
Current Spending: ($ per student per year):
Total: $6,411; Instruction: $4,048; Support Services: $2,073
Enrollment, Drop-out Rates and Diploma Recipients by Race/Ethnicity

Category	Total	White	Black	Asian	AIAN	Hisp.
Enrollment (%)	100.0	92.8	1.0	0.7	0.2	5.4
Drop-out Rate (%)	1.8	1.3	16.7	0.0	n/a	11.1
H.S. Diplomas (#)	162	151	1	3	0	7

Mille Lacs County

Milaca
500 SW 4th St • Milaca, MN 56353-1147
Mailing Address: 500 Hwy 23 W • Milaca, MN 56353-1147
(320) 982-7210 • http://www.milaca.k12.mn.us/
Grade Span: PK-12; **Agency Type:** 1
Schools: 5
2 Primary; 0 Middle; 2 High; 1 Other Level
2 Regular; 1 Special Education; 0 Vocational; 2 Alternative
0 Magnet; 0 Charter; 2 Title I Eligible; 0 School-wide Title I
Students: 1,944 (53.0% male; 47.0% female)
Individual Education Program: 217 (11.2%);
English Language Learner: 0 (0.0%); Migrant: 0 (0.0%)
Eligible for Free Lunch Program: 408 (21.0%)
Eligible for Reduced-Price Lunch Program: 178 (9.2%)
Teachers: 124.3 (15.6 to 1)
Librarians/Media Specialists: 2.0 (972.0 to 1)
Guidance Counselors: 1.0 (1,944.0 to 1)
Current Spending: ($ per student per year):
Total: $6,871; Instruction: $4,301; Support Services: $2,214
Enrollment, Drop-out Rates and Diploma Recipients by Race/Ethnicity

Category	Total	White	Black	Asian	AIAN	Hisp.
Enrollment (%)	100.0	95.3	0.7	1.3	2.0	0.7
Drop-out Rate (%)	1.5	1.6	0.0	0.0	0.0	n/a
H.S. Diplomas (#)	119	117	2	0	0	0

Princeton
706 1st St • Princeton, MN 55371-1820
(763) 389-2422 • http://www.princeton.k12.mn.us/
Grade Span: PK-12; **Agency Type:** 1
Schools: 4
2 Primary; 1 Middle; 1 High; 0 Other Level
4 Regular; 0 Special Education; 0 Vocational; 0 Alternative
0 Magnet; 0 Charter; 2 Title I Eligible; 0 School-wide Title I
Students: 3,355 (52.1% male; 47.9% female)
Individual Education Program: 391 (11.7%);
English Language Learner: 5 (0.1%); Migrant: 0 (0.0%)
Eligible for Free Lunch Program: 407 (12.1%)
Eligible for Reduced-Price Lunch Program: 223 (6.6%)
Teachers: 182.1 (18.4 to 1)
Librarians/Media Specialists: 4.0 (838.8 to 1)
Guidance Counselors: 5.0 (671.0 to 1)
Current Spending: ($ per student per year):
Total: $6,435; Instruction: $3,830; Support Services: $2,318
Enrollment, Drop-out Rates and Diploma Recipients by Race/Ethnicity

Category	Total	White	Black	Asian	AIAN	Hisp.
Enrollment (%)	100.0	96.6	1.0	0.5	0.9	0.9
Drop-out Rate (%)	0.6	0.6	0.0	0.0	0.0	0.0
H.S. Diplomas (#)	202	196	2	1	2	1

Morrison County

Little Falls
1001 SE 5th Ave • Little Falls, MN 56345-3398
(320) 632-2002 • http://www.lfalls.k12.mn.us/
Grade Span: PK-12; **Agency Type:** 1
Schools: 6
3 Primary; 1 Middle; 2 High; 0 Other Level
5 Regular; 0 Special Education; 0 Vocational; 1 Alternative
0 Magnet; 0 Charter; 3 Title I Eligible; 0 School-wide Title I
Students: 3,087 (50.8% male; 49.2% female)
Individual Education Program: 526 (17.0%);
English Language Learner: 11 (0.4%); Migrant: 0 (0.0%)
Eligible for Free Lunch Program: 712 (23.1%)
Eligible for Reduced-Price Lunch Program: 405 (13.1%)
Teachers: 194.4 (15.9 to 1)
Librarians/Media Specialists: 2.0 (1,543.5 to 1)
Guidance Counselors: 3.5 (882.0 to 1)
Current Spending: ($ per student per year):
Total: $6,590; Instruction: $4,025; Support Services: $2,280
Enrollment, Drop-out Rates and Diploma Recipients by Race/Ethnicity

Category	Total	White	Black	Asian	AIAN	Hisp.
Enrollment (%)	100.0	96.7	0.9	0.8	0.6	1.0
Drop-out Rate (%)	3.1	3.2	0.0	0.0	0.0	0.0
H.S. Diplomas (#)	302	301	0	0	1	0

Mower County

Austin

202 4th Ave NE • Austin, MN 55912
Mailing Address: 401 NW Third Ave • Austin, MN 55912
(507) 433-0966 • http://www.austin.k12.mn.us/
Grade Span: PK-12; **Agency Type:** 1
Schools: 15
6 Primary; 1 Middle; 2 High; 6 Other Level
6 Regular; 2 Special Education; 0 Vocational; 7 Alternative
0 Magnet; 0 Charter; 5 Title I Eligible; 0 School-wide Title I
Students: 4,131 (52.1% male; 47.9% female)
Individual Education Program: 569 (13.8%);
English Language Learner: 315 (7.6%); Migrant: 0 (0.0%)
Eligible for Free Lunch Program: 1,067 (25.8%)
Eligible for Reduced-Price Lunch Program: 426 (10.3%)
Teachers: 255.5 (16.2 to 1)
Librarians/Media Specialists: 4.0 (1,032.8 to 1)
Guidance Counselors: 4.0 (1,032.8 to 1)
Current Spending: ($ per student per year):
Total: $6,792; Instruction: $4,448; Support Services: $2,029
Enrollment, Drop-out Rates and Diploma Recipients by Race/Ethnicity

Category	Total	White	Black	Asian	AIAN	Hisp.
Enrollment (%)	100.0	83.3	2.6	3.3	0.3	10.5
Drop-out Rate (%)	8.8	8.1	21.4	9.8	50.0	15.1
H.S. Diplomas (#)	274	256	2	7	0	9

Nicollet County

Saint Peter

803 Davis St • Saint Peter, MN 56082-1657
(507) 934-5703 • http://www.stpeterschools.org/
Grade Span: PK-12; **Agency Type:** 1
Schools: 8
1 Primary; 2 Middle; 3 High; 2 Other Level
4 Regular; 0 Special Education; 0 Vocational; 4 Alternative
0 Magnet; 0 Charter; 2 Title I Eligible; 0 School-wide Title I
Students: 1,898 (53.1% male; 46.9% female)
Individual Education Program: 310 (16.3%);
English Language Learner: 64 (3.4%); Migrant: 0 (0.0%)
Eligible for Free Lunch Program: 353 (18.6%)
Eligible for Reduced-Price Lunch Program: 100 (5.3%)
Teachers: 128.3 (14.8 to 1)
Librarians/Media Specialists: 2.5 (759.2 to 1)
Guidance Counselors: 2.8 (677.9 to 1)
Current Spending: ($ per student per year):
Total: $7,041; Instruction: $4,498; Support Services: $2,211
Enrollment, Drop-out Rates and Diploma Recipients by Race/Ethnicity

Category	Total	White	Black	Asian	AIAN	Hisp.
Enrollment (%)	100.0	90.7	2.6	1.5	0.4	4.7
Drop-out Rate (%)	1.4	1.2	0.0	0.0	0.0	15.4
H.S. Diplomas (#)	151	144	2	0	2	3

Nobles County

Worthington

1117 Marine Ave • Worthington, MN 56187-1610
(507) 372-2172 • http://www.isd518.net/
Grade Span: PK-12; **Agency Type:** 1
Schools: 8
3 Primary; 1 Middle; 3 High; 1 Other Level
3 Regular; 2 Special Education; 0 Vocational; 3 Alternative
0 Magnet; 0 Charter; 2 Title I Eligible; 0 School-wide Title I
Students: 2,334 (51.5% male; 48.5% female)
Individual Education Program: 341 (14.6%);
English Language Learner: 391 (16.8%); Migrant: 0 (0.0%)
Eligible for Free Lunch Program: 781 (33.5%)
Eligible for Reduced-Price Lunch Program: 248 (10.6%)
Teachers: 160.3 (14.6 to 1)
Librarians/Media Specialists: 3.0 (778.0 to 1)
Guidance Counselors: 4.0 (583.5 to 1)
Current Spending: ($ per student per year):
Total: $7,728; Instruction: $5,156; Support Services: $2,263
Enrollment, Drop-out Rates and Diploma Recipients by Race/Ethnicity

Category	Total	White	Black	Asian	AIAN	Hisp.
Enrollment (%)	100.0	62.1	1.7	10.0	0.4	25.8
Drop-out Rate (%)	4.5	2.2	6.3	8.2	25.0	13.9
H.S. Diplomas (#)	192	156	4	18	0	14

Olmsted County

Byron

501 10th Ave NE • Byron, MN 55920
(507) 775-2383
Grade Span: PK-12; **Agency Type:** 1
Schools: 3
1 Primary; 1 Middle; 1 High; 0 Other Level
3 Regular; 0 Special Education; 0 Vocational; 0 Alternative
0 Magnet; 0 Charter; 1 Title I Eligible; 0 School-wide Title I
Students: 1,500 (51.5% male; 48.5% female)
Individual Education Program: 179 (11.9%);
English Language Learner: 0 (0.0%); Migrant: 0 (0.0%)
Eligible for Free Lunch Program: 80 (5.3%)
Eligible for Reduced-Price Lunch Program: 50 (3.3%)
Teachers: 91.6 (16.4 to 1)
Librarians/Media Specialists: 1.0 (1,500.0 to 1)
Guidance Counselors: 3.0 (500.0 to 1)
Current Spending: ($ per student per year):
Total: $5,754; Instruction: $3,722; Support Services: $1,769
Enrollment, Drop-out Rates and Diploma Recipients by Race/Ethnicity

Category	Total	White	Black	Asian	AIAN	Hisp.
Enrollment (%)	100.0	97.5	0.5	1.1	0.1	0.8
Drop-out Rate (%)	0.2	0.2	0.0	0.0	n/a	0.0
H.S. Diplomas (#)	106	102	1	3	0	0

Rochester

615 SW 7th St • Rochester, MN 55902
(507) 285-8551 • http://www.rochester.k12.mn.us/
Grade Span: PK-12; **Agency Type:** 1
Schools: 42
21 Primary; 5 Middle; 7 High; 9 Other Level
23 Regular; 5 Special Education; 0 Vocational; 14 Alternative
1 Magnet; 0 Charter; 9 Title I Eligible; 2 School-wide Title I
Students: 16,400 (51.9% male; 48.1% female)
Individual Education Program: 1,833 (11.2%);
English Language Learner: 2,164 (13.2%); Migrant: 1 (<0.1%)
Eligible for Free Lunch Program: 2,949 (18.0%)
Eligible for Reduced-Price Lunch Program: 863 (5.3%)
Teachers: 929.7 (17.6 to 1)
Librarians/Media Specialists: 17.7 (926.6 to 1)
Guidance Counselors: 33.1 (495.5 to 1)
Current Spending: ($ per student per year):
Total: $7,178; Instruction: $4,472; Support Services: $2,414
Enrollment, Drop-out Rates and Diploma Recipients by Race/Ethnicity

Category	Total	White	Black	Asian	AIAN	Hisp.
Enrollment (%)	100.0	78.0	9.2	8.5	0.4	3.9
Drop-out Rate (%)	4.0	2.9	9.1	8.2	5.3	12.3
H.S. Diplomas (#)	1,068	926	47	82	2	11

Stewartville

500 4th St SW • Stewartville, MN 55976-1198
(507) 533-1438 • http://stewartville.k12.mn.us/
Grade Span: PK-12; **Agency Type:** 1
Schools: 4
1 Primary; 2 Middle; 1 High; 0 Other Level
4 Regular; 0 Special Education; 0 Vocational; 0 Alternative
0 Magnet; 0 Charter; 1 Title I Eligible; 0 School-wide Title I
Students: 1,838 (49.5% male; 50.5% female)
Individual Education Program: 207 (11.3%);
English Language Learner: 3 (0.2%); Migrant: 0 (0.0%)
Eligible for Free Lunch Program: 135 (7.3%)
Eligible for Reduced-Price Lunch Program: 119 (6.5%)
Teachers: 104.2 (17.6 to 1)
Librarians/Media Specialists: 1.8 (1,021.1 to 1)
Guidance Counselors: 3.0 (612.7 to 1)
Current Spending: ($ per student per year):
Total: $5,906; Instruction: $3,662; Support Services: $1,923
Enrollment, Drop-out Rates and Diploma Recipients by Race/Ethnicity

Category	Total	White	Black	Asian	AIAN	Hisp.
Enrollment (%)	100.0	96.1	1.2	1.0	0.3	1.4
Drop-out Rate (%)	0.9	0.4	33.3	12.5	0.0	0.0
H.S. Diplomas (#)	129	127	0	0	1	1

Otter Tail County

Fergus Falls

600 Friberg Ave • Fergus Falls, MN 56537-4104
Mailing Address: 4B E Dr • Fergus Falls, MN 56537-4104
(218) 998-0544 • http://www.fergusfalls.k12.mn.us/
Grade Span: KG-12; **Agency Type:** 1
Schools: 7
4 Primary; 1 Middle; 2 High; 0 Other Level
6 Regular; 0 Special Education; 0 Vocational; 1 Alternative
0 Magnet; 0 Charter; 4 Title I Eligible; 0 School-wide Title I

Students: 2,841 (50.6% male; 49.4% female)
Individual Education Program: 422 (14.9%);
English Language Learner: 4 (0.1%); Migrant: 0 (0.0%)
Eligible for Free Lunch Program: 373 (13.1%)
Eligible for Reduced-Price Lunch Program: 148 (5.2%)
Teachers: 183.6 (15.5 to 1)
Librarians/Media Specialists: 3.1 (916.5 to 1)
Guidance Counselors: 5.9 (481.5 to 1)
Current Spending: ($ per student per year):
Total: $6,325; Instruction: $3,967; Support Services: $2,159
Enrollment, Drop-out Rates and Diploma Recipients by Race/Ethnicity

Category	Total	White	Black	Asian	AIAN	Hisp.
Enrollment (%)	100.0	95.1	1.7	1.0	1.2	1.1
Drop-out Rate (%)	5.2	5.1	0.0	0.0	20.0	13.3
H.S. Diplomas (#)	251	245	1	1	0	4

Perham
200 5th St SE Room D • Perham, MN 56573-1797
(218) 346-4501 • http://www.perham.k12.mn.us/
Grade Span: PK-12; **Agency Type:** 1
Schools: 7
2 Primary; 1 Middle; 4 High; 0 Other Level
4 Regular; 0 Special Education; 0 Vocational; 3 Alternative
0 Magnet; 0 Charter; 2 Title I Eligible; 1 School-wide Title I
Students: 1,658 (53.0% male; 47.0% female)
Individual Education Program: 213 (12.8%);
English Language Learner: 17 (1.0%); Migrant: 0 (0.0%)
Eligible for Free Lunch Program: 312 (18.8%)
Eligible for Reduced-Price Lunch Program: 202 (12.2%)
Teachers: 107.1 (15.5 to 1)
Librarians/Media Specialists: 2.0 (829.0 to 1)
Guidance Counselors: 2.0 (829.0 to 1)
Current Spending: ($ per student per year):
Total: $6,664; Instruction: $3,967; Support Services: $2,370
Enrollment, Drop-out Rates and Diploma Recipients by Race/Ethnicity

Category	Total	White	Black	Asian	AIAN	Hisp.
Enrollment (%)	100.0	96.4	0.8	0.4	0.7	1.7
Drop-out Rate (%)	6.5	6.6	0.0	0.0	0.0	0.0
H.S. Diplomas (#)	138	136	0	1	0	1

Pennington County

Thief River Falls
Zeh & Labree • Thief River Falls, MN 56701-2800
Mailing Address: 230 S Labree • Thief River Falls, MN 56701-2800
(218) 681-8711 • http://www.trf.k12.mn.us/
Grade Span: PK-12; **Agency Type:** 1
Schools: 5
2 Primary; 1 Middle; 1 High; 1 Other Level
3 Regular; 0 Special Education; 0 Vocational; 2 Alternative
0 Magnet; 0 Charter; 1 Title I Eligible; 0 School-wide Title I
Students: 2,123 (53.3% male; 46.7% female)
Individual Education Program: 328 (15.4%);
English Language Learner: 7 (0.3%); Migrant: 0 (0.0%)
Eligible for Free Lunch Program: 404 (19.0%)
Eligible for Reduced-Price Lunch Program: 198 (9.3%)
Teachers: 144.2 (14.7 to 1)
Librarians/Media Specialists: 3.0 (707.7 to 1)
Guidance Counselors: 4.0 (530.8 to 1)
Current Spending: ($ per student per year):
Total: $6,822; Instruction: $4,447; Support Services: $2,100
Enrollment, Drop-out Rates and Diploma Recipients by Race/Ethnicity

Category	Total	White	Black	Asian	AIAN	Hisp.
Enrollment (%)	100.0	94.0	0.9	0.5	2.2	2.4
Drop-out Rate (%)	0.6	0.4	0.0	0.0	8.3	20.0
H.S. Diplomas (#)	189	177	1	5	3	3

Pine County

Pine City
1400 6th St S • Pine City, MN 55063-2064
Mailing Address: 1400 Main St S • Pine City, MN 55063-2064
(320) 629-4000 • http://www.pinecity.k12.mn.us/
Grade Span: PK-12; **Agency Type:** 1
Schools: 4
2 Primary; 0 Middle; 2 High; 0 Other Level
2 Regular; 0 Special Education; 0 Vocational; 2 Alternative
0 Magnet; 0 Charter; 1 Title I Eligible; 0 School-wide Title I
Students: 1,742 (51.0% male; 49.0% female)
Individual Education Program: 142 (8.2%);
English Language Learner: 2 (0.1%); Migrant: 0 (0.0%)
Eligible for Free Lunch Program: 416 (23.9%)
Eligible for Reduced-Price Lunch Program: 194 (11.1%)
Teachers: 106.0 (16.4 to 1)
Librarians/Media Specialists: 2.0 (871.0 to 1)
Guidance Counselors: 1.7 (1,024.7 to 1)
Current Spending: ($ per student per year):
Total: $6,436; Instruction: $4,010; Support Services: $2,030
Enrollment, Drop-out Rates and Diploma Recipients by Race/Ethnicity

Category	Total	White	Black	Asian	AIAN	Hisp.
Enrollment (%)	100.0	97.9	0.6	0.3	0.6	0.5
Drop-out Rate (%)	6.2	6.1	14.3	0.0	16.7	0.0
H.S. Diplomas (#)	147	143	0	1	3	0

Polk County

Crookston
402 Fisher Ave #593 • Crookston, MN 56716-2099
(218) 281-5313 • http://www.crookston.k12.mn.us/
Grade Span: PK-12; **Agency Type:** 1
Schools: 6
3 Primary; 0 Middle; 2 High; 1 Other Level
4 Regular; 0 Special Education; 0 Vocational; 2 Alternative
0 Magnet; 0 Charter; 4 Title I Eligible; 0 School-wide Title I
Students: 1,593 (51.2% male; 48.8% female)
Individual Education Program: 232 (14.6%);
English Language Learner: 136 (8.5%); Migrant: 53 (3.3%)
Eligible for Free Lunch Program: 446 (28.0%)
Eligible for Reduced-Price Lunch Program: 172 (10.8%)
Teachers: 96.2 (16.6 to 1)
Librarians/Media Specialists: 0.0 (0.0 to 1)
Guidance Counselors: 1.0 (1,593.0 to 1)
Current Spending: ($ per student per year):
Total: $6,891; Instruction: $4,418; Support Services: $2,045
Enrollment, Drop-out Rates and Diploma Recipients by Race/Ethnicity

Category	Total	White	Black	Asian	AIAN	Hisp.
Enrollment (%)	100.0	79.2	0.9	0.4	3.0	16.6
Drop-out Rate (%)	6.8	4.5	0.0	0.0	23.8	21.2
H.S. Diplomas (#)	139	132	1	0	0	6

East Grand Forks
Box 151 • East Grand Forks, MN 56721-0151
(218) 773-3494 • http://www.ci.east-grand-forks.mn.us/schools.htm
Grade Span: PK-12; **Agency Type:** 1
Schools: 4
2 Primary; 1 Middle; 1 High; 0 Other Level
4 Regular; 0 Special Education; 0 Vocational; 0 Alternative
0 Magnet; 0 Charter; 2 Title I Eligible; 0 School-wide Title I
Students: 1,817 (52.1% male; 47.9% female)
Individual Education Program: 245 (13.5%);
English Language Learner: 36 (2.0%); Migrant: 0 (0.0%)
Eligible for Free Lunch Program: 380 (20.9%)
Eligible for Reduced-Price Lunch Program: 166 (9.1%)
Teachers: 126.2 (14.4 to 1)
Librarians/Media Specialists: 4.6 (395.0 to 1)
Guidance Counselors: 3.3 (550.6 to 1)
Current Spending: ($ per student per year):
Total: $7,128; Instruction: $4,448; Support Services: $2,310
Enrollment, Drop-out Rates and Diploma Recipients by Race/Ethnicity

Category	Total	White	Black	Asian	AIAN	Hisp.
Enrollment (%)	100.0	86.4	0.8	0.6	2.0	10.3
Drop-out Rate (%)	2.8	1.8	0.0	0.0	13.3	13.3
H.S. Diplomas (#)	116	108	0	4	2	2

Pope County

Minnewaska
25122 State Hwy 28 • Glenwood, MN 56334-9327
(320) 239-4820 • http://www.minnewaska.k12.mn.us/
Grade Span: PK-12; **Agency Type:** 1
Schools: 4
3 Primary; 0 Middle; 1 High; 0 Other Level
4 Regular; 0 Special Education; 0 Vocational; 0 Alternative
0 Magnet; 0 Charter; 3 Title I Eligible; 0 School-wide Title I
Students: 1,515 (52.4% male; 47.6% female)
Individual Education Program: 231 (15.2%);
English Language Learner: 1 (0.1%); Migrant: 0 (0.0%)
Eligible for Free Lunch Program: 330 (21.8%)
Eligible for Reduced-Price Lunch Program: 186 (12.3%)
Teachers: 105.3 (14.4 to 1)
Librarians/Media Specialists: 1.0 (1,515.0 to 1)
Guidance Counselors: 2.0 (757.5 to 1)
Current Spending: ($ per student per year):
Total: $6,996; Instruction: $4,572; Support Services: $2,003
Enrollment, Drop-out Rates and Diploma Recipients by Race/Ethnicity

Category	Total	White	Black	Asian	AIAN	Hisp.
Enrollment (%)	100.0	97.6	0.9	0.5	0.5	0.5
Drop-out Rate (%)	0.0	0.0	0.0	0.0	0.0	0.0
H.S. Diplomas (#)	137	136	0	0	1	0

Ramsey County

Mounds View

2959 Hamline Ave N • Roseville, MN 55113-1664
(651) 639-6212 • http://www.moundsviewschools.org
Grade Span: PK-12; **Agency Type:** 1
Schools: 26
13 Primary; 5 Middle; 5 High; 3 Other Level
13 Regular; 7 Special Education; 0 Vocational; 6 Alternative
0 Magnet; 0 Charter; 4 Title I Eligible; 0 School-wide Title I
Students: 11,187 (52.1% male; 47.9% female)
Individual Education Program: 1,228 (11.0%);
English Language Learner: 162 (1.4%); Migrant: 0 (0.0%)
Eligible for Free Lunch Program: 1,177 (10.5%)
Eligible for Reduced-Price Lunch Program: 529 (4.7%)
Teachers: 619.3 (18.1 to 1)
Librarians/Media Specialists: 7.7 (1,452.9 to 1)
Guidance Counselors: 12.8 (874.0 to 1)
Current Spending: ($ per student per year):
Total: $7,555; Instruction: $4,803; Support Services: $2,407
Enrollment, Drop-out Rates and Diploma Recipients by Race/Ethnicity

Category	Total	White	Black	Asian	AIAN	Hisp.
Enrollment (%)	100.0	85.5	4.4	6.6	1.0	2.5
Drop-out Rate (%)	2.8	2.5	6.1	2.5	10.6	7.8
H.S. Diplomas (#)	918	813	21	65	6	13

North Saint Paul-Maplewood

2520 E 12th Ave • Maplewood, MN 55109
(651) 748-7410 • http://www.isd622.org/
Grade Span: PK-12; **Agency Type:** 1
Schools: 18
11 Primary; 3 Middle; 4 High; 0 Other Level
14 Regular; 2 Special Education; 0 Vocational; 2 Alternative
0 Magnet; 0 Charter; 7 Title I Eligible; 0 School-wide Title I
Students: 11,458 (50.8% male; 49.2% female)
Individual Education Program: 1,456 (12.7%);
English Language Learner: 432 (3.8%); Migrant: 0 (0.0%)
Eligible for Free Lunch Program: 1,645 (14.4%)
Eligible for Reduced-Price Lunch Program: 900 (7.9%)
Teachers: 594.4 (19.3 to 1)
Librarians/Media Specialists: 14.6 (784.8 to 1)
Guidance Counselors: 17.0 (674.0 to 1)
Current Spending: ($ per student per year):
Total: $6,660; Instruction: $4,213; Support Services: $2,117
Enrollment, Drop-out Rates and Diploma Recipients by Race/Ethnicity

Category	Total	White	Black	Asian	AIAN	Hisp.
Enrollment (%)	100.0	81.2	6.9	7.3	1.3	3.4
Drop-out Rate (%)	1.7	1.5	2.0	2.7	13.6	2.6
H.S. Diplomas (#)	709	632	26	36	2	13

Roseville

1251 W County Rd B-2 • Roseville, MN 55113-3299
(651) 635-1600 • http://www.roseville.k12.mn.us/
Grade Span: PK-12; **Agency Type:** 1
Schools: 13
8 Primary; 1 Middle; 3 High; 1 Other Level
9 Regular; 1 Special Education; 0 Vocational; 3 Alternative
0 Magnet; 0 Charter; 4 Title I Eligible; 0 School-wide Title I
Students: 6,375 (51.2% male; 48.8% female)
Individual Education Program: 722 (11.3%);
English Language Learner: 406 (6.4%); Migrant: 0 (0.0%)
Eligible for Free Lunch Program: 825 (12.9%)
Eligible for Reduced-Price Lunch Program: 395 (6.2%)
Teachers: 354.3 (18.0 to 1)
Librarians/Media Specialists: 9.0 (708.3 to 1)
Guidance Counselors: 6.0 (1,062.5 to 1)
Current Spending: ($ per student per year):
Total: $7,611; Instruction: $4,539; Support Services: $2,764
Enrollment, Drop-out Rates and Diploma Recipients by Race/Ethnicity

Category	Total	White	Black	Asian	AIAN	Hisp.
Enrollment (%)	100.0	77.0	7.5	11.5	0.6	3.4
Drop-out Rate (%)	1.0	0.8	2.7	1.1	0.0	2.5
H.S. Diplomas (#)	498	419	23	43	5	8

Saint Paul

360 Colborne St • Saint Paul, MN 55102-3299
(651) 293-5100 • http://www.stpaul.k12.mn.us/
Grade Span: PK-12; **Agency Type:** 1
Schools: 125
74 Primary; 11 Middle; 21 High; 19 Other Level
71 Regular; 29 Special Education; 0 Vocational; 25 Alternative
32 Magnet; 0 Charter; 52 Title I Eligible; 45 School-wide Title I
Students: 43,923 (51.4% male; 48.6% female)
Individual Education Program: 6,944 (15.8%);
English Language Learner: 14,865 (33.8%); Migrant: 92 (0.2%)
Eligible for Free Lunch Program: 23,347 (53.2%)
Eligible for Reduced-Price Lunch Program: 5,144 (11.7%)
Teachers: 2,955.4 (14.9 to 1)
Librarians/Media Specialists: 48.1 (913.2 to 1)
Guidance Counselors: 74.5 (589.6 to 1)
Current Spending: ($ per student per year):
Total: $9,285; Instruction: $5,903; Support Services: $2,993
Enrollment, Drop-out Rates and Diploma Recipients by Race/Ethnicity

Category	Total	White	Black	Asian	AIAN	Hisp.
Enrollment (%)	100.0	30.8	26.6	29.7	1.8	11.0
Drop-out Rate (%)	8.8	6.3	12.3	7.1	22.7	15.1
H.S. Diplomas (#)	2,127	920	329	711	15	152

White Bear Lake

4855 Bloom Ave Ste 300 • White Bear Lake, MN 55110-2731
(651) 407-7500 • http://wblwww.whitebear.k12.mn.us/
Grade Span: PK-12; **Agency Type:** 1
Schools: 19
11 Primary; 4 Middle; 3 High; 1 Other Level
12 Regular; 2 Special Education; 0 Vocational; 5 Alternative
0 Magnet; 0 Charter; 9 Title I Eligible; 0 School-wide Title I
Students: 9,160 (51.3% male; 48.7% female)
Individual Education Program: 1,156 (12.6%);
English Language Learner: 261 (2.8%); Migrant: 0 (0.0%)
Eligible for Free Lunch Program: 932 (10.2%)
Eligible for Reduced-Price Lunch Program: 407 (4.4%)
Teachers: 458.4 (20.0 to 1)
Librarians/Media Specialists: 9.5 (964.2 to 1)
Guidance Counselors: 6.8 (1,347.1 to 1)
Current Spending: ($ per student per year):
Total: $6,640; Instruction: $4,302; Support Services: $2,020
Enrollment, Drop-out Rates and Diploma Recipients by Race/Ethnicity

Category	Total	White	Black	Asian	AIAN	Hisp.
Enrollment (%)	100.0	90.5	2.2	4.8	0.6	1.9
Drop-out Rate (%)	2.0	1.9	7.5	2.3	0.0	0.0
H.S. Diplomas (#)	831	775	10	34	2	10

Redwood County

Redwood Falls Area Schools

100 George Ramseth Dr • Redwood Falls, MN 56283-1938
(507) 644-3531
Grade Span: PK-12; **Agency Type:** 1
Schools: 4
1 Primary; 1 Middle; 2 High; 0 Other Level
3 Regular; 0 Special Education; 0 Vocational; 1 Alternative
0 Magnet; 0 Charter; 2 Title I Eligible; 0 School-wide Title I
Students: 1,501 (51.8% male; 48.2% female)
Individual Education Program: 181 (12.1%);
English Language Learner: 25 (1.7%); Migrant: 0 (0.0%)
Eligible for Free Lunch Program: 315 (21.0%)
Eligible for Reduced-Price Lunch Program: 150 (10.0%)
Teachers: 99.0 (15.2 to 1)
Librarians/Media Specialists: 2.0 (750.5 to 1)
Guidance Counselors: 2.0 (750.5 to 1)
Current Spending: ($ per student per year):
Total: n/a; Instruction: n/a; Support Services: n/a
Enrollment, Drop-out Rates and Diploma Recipients by Race/Ethnicity

Category	Total	White	Black	Asian	AIAN	Hisp.
Enrollment (%)	100.0	82.1	0.3	1.2	13.0	3.3
Drop-out Rate (%)	n/a	n/a	n/a	n/a	n/a	n/a
H.S. Diplomas (#)	102	97	0	1	3	1

Rice County

Faribault

2855 NW 1st Ave • Faribault, MN 55021-1908
(507) 333-6000 • http://www.faribault.k12.mn.us/
Grade Span: PK-12; **Agency Type:** 1
Schools: 10
5 Primary; 2 Middle; 2 High; 1 Other Level
5 Regular; 1 Special Education; 0 Vocational; 4 Alternative
0 Magnet; 0 Charter; 4 Title I Eligible; 0 School-wide Title I
Students: 3,969 (51.4% male; 48.6% female)
Individual Education Program: 621 (15.6%);
English Language Learner: 484 (12.2%); Migrant: 0 (0.0%)
Eligible for Free Lunch Program: 1,021 (25.7%)
Eligible for Reduced-Price Lunch Program: 375 (9.4%)
Teachers: 249.8 (15.9 to 1)
Librarians/Media Specialists: 5.0 (793.8 to 1)
Guidance Counselors: 5.0 (793.8 to 1)
Current Spending: ($ per student per year):
Total: $7,451; Instruction: $4,585; Support Services: $2,472

Enrollment, Drop-out Rates and Diploma Recipients by Race/Ethnicity

Category	Total	White	Black	Asian	AIAN	Hisp.
Enrollment (%)	100.0	82.1	1.7	2.3	0.2	13.7
Drop-out Rate (%)	5.5	4.2	10.0	6.7	50.0	25.0
H.S. Diplomas (#)	376	348	3	12	0	13

Northfield

1400 S Division • Northfield, MN 55057
(507) 663-0629 • http://www.nfld.k12.mn.us/
Grade Span: PK-12; **Agency Type:** 1
Schools: 7
4 Primary; 1 Middle; 2 High; 0 Other Level
6 Regular; 0 Special Education; 0 Vocational; 1 Alternative
0 Magnet; 0 Charter; 4 Title I Eligible; 0 School-wide Title I
Students: 3,911 (51.6% male; 48.4% female)
Individual Education Program: 529 (13.5%);
English Language Learner: 28 (0.7%); Migrant: 0 (0.0%)
Eligible for Free Lunch Program: 417 (10.7%)
Eligible for Reduced-Price Lunch Program: 237 (6.1%)
Teachers: 257.8 (15.2 to 1)
Librarians/Media Specialists: 4.1 (953.9 to 1)
Guidance Counselors: 4.6 (850.2 to 1)
Current Spending: ($ per student per year):
Total: $6,335; Instruction: $3,955; Support Services: $2,049
Enrollment, Drop-out Rates and Diploma Recipients by Race/Ethnicity

Category	Total	White	Black	Asian	AIAN	Hisp.
Enrollment (%)	100.0	91.3	0.9	1.6	0.2	6.0
Drop-out Rate (%)	5.3	4.9	11.1	3.0	0.0	19.4
H.S. Diplomas (#)	297	280	1	8	1	7

Roseau County

Roseau

509 3rd St NE • Roseau, MN 56751-1199
(218) 463-1471 • http://www.roseau.k12.mn.us/
Grade Span: PK-12; **Agency Type:** 1
Schools: 4
2 Primary; 1 Middle; 1 High; 0 Other Level
4 Regular; 0 Special Education; 0 Vocational; 0 Alternative
0 Magnet; 0 Charter; 3 Title I Eligible; 0 School-wide Title I
Students: 1,505 (51.8% male; 48.2% female)
Individual Education Program: 233 (15.5%);
English Language Learner: 1 (0.1%); Migrant: 0 (0.0%)
Eligible for Free Lunch Program: 189 (12.6%)
Eligible for Reduced-Price Lunch Program: 169 (11.2%)
Teachers: 82.2 (18.3 to 1)
Librarians/Media Specialists: 1.0 (1,505.0 to 1)
Guidance Counselors: 1.0 (1,505.0 to 1)
Current Spending: ($ per student per year):
Total: $6,228; Instruction: $3,899; Support Services: $2,095
Enrollment, Drop-out Rates and Diploma Recipients by Race/Ethnicity

Category	Total	White	Black	Asian	AIAN	Hisp.
Enrollment (%)	100.0	97.9	0.5	0.9	0.6	0.1
Drop-out Rate (%)	0.8	0.9	0.0	0.0	0.0	0.0
H.S. Diplomas (#)	120	118	0	2	0	0

Scott County

New Prague Area Schools

301 Lexington Ave S • New Prague, MN 56071-1439
(952) 758-1700 • http://www.np.k12.mn.us/
Grade Span: PK-12; **Agency Type:** 1
Schools: 5
2 Primary; 1 Middle; 1 High; 1 Other Level
4 Regular; 0 Special Education; 0 Vocational; 1 Alternative
0 Magnet; 0 Charter; 1 Title I Eligible; 0 School-wide Title I
Students: 2,705 (49.6% male; 50.4% female)
Individual Education Program: 205 (7.6%);
English Language Learner: 0 (0.0%); Migrant: 0 (0.0%)
Eligible for Free Lunch Program: 115 (4.3%)
Eligible for Reduced-Price Lunch Program: 114 (4.2%)
Teachers: 148.9 (18.2 to 1)
Librarians/Media Specialists: 4.0 (676.3 to 1)
Guidance Counselors: 3.0 (901.7 to 1)
Current Spending: ($ per student per year):
Total: $5,847; Instruction: $3,420; Support Services: $2,113
Enrollment, Drop-out Rates and Diploma Recipients by Race/Ethnicity

Category	Total	White	Black	Asian	AIAN	Hisp.
Enrollment (%)	100.0	97.9	0.3	1.0	0.1	0.7
Drop-out Rate (%)	0.2	0.2	0.0	0.0	0.0	0.0
H.S. Diplomas (#)	208	206	0	0	2	0

Prior Lake

5300 Westwood Dr • Prior Lake, MN 55372-0539
Mailing Address: Box 539 • Prior Lake, MN 55372-0539
(952) 447-2185 • http://www.priorlake-savage.k12.mn.us/welcome.htm
Grade Span: PK-12; **Agency Type:** 1
Schools: 9
5 Primary; 2 Middle; 1 High; 1 Other Level
7 Regular; 2 Special Education; 0 Vocational; 0 Alternative
0 Magnet; 0 Charter; 2 Title I Eligible; 0 School-wide Title I
Students: 5,220 (50.7% male; 49.3% female)
Individual Education Program: 394 (7.5%);
English Language Learner: 112 (2.1%); Migrant: 0 (0.0%)
Eligible for Free Lunch Program: 226 (4.3%)
Eligible for Reduced-Price Lunch Program: 125 (2.4%)
Teachers: 286.1 (18.2 to 1)
Librarians/Media Specialists: 6.3 (828.6 to 1)
Guidance Counselors: 1.9 (2,747.4 to 1)
Current Spending: ($ per student per year):
Total: $6,369; Instruction: $3,990; Support Services: $2,106
Enrollment, Drop-out Rates and Diploma Recipients by Race/Ethnicity

Category	Total	White	Black	Asian	AIAN	Hisp.
Enrollment (%)	100.0	92.1	1.5	3.7	1.3	1.4
Drop-out Rate (%)	1.2	1.2	0.0	0.0	0.0	12.5
H.S. Diplomas (#)	282	271	0	9	1	1

Shakopee

505 S Holmes St • Shakopee, MN 55379-1384
(952) 496-5005 • http://www.shakopee.k12.mn.us/shakopee/default.htm
Grade Span: PK-12; **Agency Type:** 1
Schools: 7
4 Primary; 2 Middle; 1 High; 0 Other Level
6 Regular; 0 Special Education; 0 Vocational; 1 Alternative
0 Magnet; 0 Charter; 6 Title I Eligible; 0 School-wide Title I
Students: 4,564 (52.2% male; 47.8% female)
Individual Education Program: 464 (10.2%);
English Language Learner: 541 (11.9%); Migrant: 0 (0.0%)
Eligible for Free Lunch Program: 673 (14.7%)
Eligible for Reduced-Price Lunch Program: 272 (6.0%)
Teachers: 263.9 (17.3 to 1)
Librarians/Media Specialists: 6.0 (760.7 to 1)
Guidance Counselors: 4.0 (1,141.0 to 1)
Current Spending: ($ per student per year):
Total: $7,080; Instruction: $4,592; Support Services: $2,196
Enrollment, Drop-out Rates and Diploma Recipients by Race/Ethnicity

Category	Total	White	Black	Asian	AIAN	Hisp.
Enrollment (%)	100.0	82.5	1.6	4.8	2.1	9.0
Drop-out Rate (%)	3.8	2.2	6.7	8.6	23.1	18.3
H.S. Diplomas (#)	201	194	1	2	1	3

Sherburne County

Becker

12000 Hancock St • Becker, MN 55308-9585
(763) 261-4502 • http://www.becker.k12.mn.us/
Grade Span: PK-12; **Agency Type:** 1
Schools: 4
2 Primary; 1 Middle; 1 High; 0 Other Level
4 Regular; 0 Special Education; 0 Vocational; 0 Alternative
0 Magnet; 0 Charter; 2 Title I Eligible; 0 School-wide Title I
Students: 2,358 (51.8% male; 48.2% female)
Individual Education Program: 305 (12.9%);
English Language Learner: 21 (0.9%); Migrant: 0 (0.0%)
Eligible for Free Lunch Program: 175 (7.4%)
Eligible for Reduced-Price Lunch Program: 116 (4.9%)
Teachers: 132.2 (17.8 to 1)
Librarians/Media Specialists: 4.0 (589.5 to 1)
Guidance Counselors: 2.0 (1,179.0 to 1)
Current Spending: ($ per student per year):
Total: $5,976; Instruction: $3,895; Support Services: $1,851
Enrollment, Drop-out Rates and Diploma Recipients by Race/Ethnicity

Category	Total	White	Black	Asian	AIAN	Hisp.
Enrollment (%)	100.0	97.6	0.7	0.9	0.2	0.6
Drop-out Rate (%)	0.3	0.4	0.0	0.0	0.0	0.0
H.S. Diplomas (#)	117	111	2	2	1	1

Big Lake

Box 407, 501 Minnesota Ave • Big Lake, MN 55309-0410
(763) 262-2536 • http://www.biglake.k12.mn.us/
Grade Span: PK-12; **Agency Type:** 1
Schools: 3
1 Primary; 1 Middle; 1 High; 0 Other Level
3 Regular; 0 Special Education; 0 Vocational; 0 Alternative
0 Magnet; 0 Charter; 2 Title I Eligible; 0 School-wide Title I
Students: 3,030 (51.2% male; 48.8% female)
Individual Education Program: 335 (11.1%);

English Language Learner: 29 (1.0%); Migrant: 0 (0.0%)
Eligible for Free Lunch Program: 310 (10.2%)
Eligible for Reduced-Price Lunch Program: 189 (6.2%)
Teachers: 178.2 (17.0 to 1)
Librarians/Media Specialists: 3.0 (1,010.0 to 1)
Guidance Counselors: 3.0 (1,010.0 to 1)
Current Spending: ($ per student per year):
Total: $5,709; Instruction: $3,407; Support Services: $2,065
Enrollment, Drop-out Rates and Diploma Recipients by Race/Ethnicity

Category	Total	White	Black	Asian	AIAN	Hisp.
Enrollment (%)	100.0	95.5	0.7	1.1	1.1	1.6
Drop-out Rate (%)	1.8	1.8	0.0	0.0	0.0	0.0
H.S. Diplomas (#)	125	123	2	0	0	0

Elk River

327 King Ave • Elk River, MN 55330-1391
(763) 241-3400 • http://www.elkriver.k12.mn.us/
Grade Span: PK-12; **Agency Type:** 1
Schools: 14
7 Primary; 4 Middle; 2 High; 1 Other Level
12 Regular; 0 Special Education; 0 Vocational; 2 Alternative
1 Magnet; 0 Charter; 6 Title I Eligible; 0 School-wide Title I
Students: 9,768 (51.1% male; 48.9% female)
Individual Education Program: 1,190 (12.2%);
English Language Learner: 101 (1.0%); Migrant: 0 (0.0%)
Eligible for Free Lunch Program: 614 (6.3%)
Eligible for Reduced-Price Lunch Program: 432 (4.4%)
Teachers: 475.7 (20.5 to 1)
Librarians/Media Specialists: 6.0 (1,628.0 to 1)
Guidance Counselors: 9.0 (1,085.3 to 1)
Current Spending: ($ per student per year):
Total: $6,621; Instruction: $4,353; Support Services: $1,971
Enrollment, Drop-out Rates and Diploma Recipients by Race/Ethnicity

Category	Total	White	Black	Asian	AIAN	Hisp.
Enrollment (%)	100.0	96.6	0.5	1.1	0.8	1.1
Drop-out Rate (%)	3.7	3.6	25.0	0.0	11.1	0.0
H.S. Diplomas (#)	595	574	1	5	8	7

St. Louis County

Duluth

Lake Ave & 2nd St • Duluth, MN 55802-2069
Mailing Address: 215 N 1st Ave E • Duluth, MN 55802-2069
(218) 723-4100 • http://www.duluth.k12.mn.us/
Grade Span: PK-12; **Agency Type:** 1
Schools: 39
15 Primary; 4 Middle; 7 High; 13 Other Level
19 Regular; 8 Special Education; 1 Vocational; 11 Alternative
3 Magnet; 0 Charter; 8 Title I Eligible; 4 School-wide Title I
Students: 11,603 (52.3% male; 47.7% female)
Individual Education Program: 1,617 (13.9%);
English Language Learner: 83 (0.7%); Migrant: 0 (0.0%)
Eligible for Free Lunch Program: 3,068 (26.4%)
Eligible for Reduced-Price Lunch Program: 880 (7.6%)
Teachers: 763.0 (15.2 to 1)
Librarians/Media Specialists: 16.4 (707.5 to 1)
Guidance Counselors: 16.7 (694.8 to 1)
Current Spending: ($ per student per year):
Total: $7,672; Instruction: $5,014; Support Services: $2,425
Enrollment, Drop-out Rates and Diploma Recipients by Race/Ethnicity

Category	Total	White	Black	Asian	AIAN	Hisp.
Enrollment (%)	100.0	87.4	4.2	2.3	4.9	1.2
Drop-out Rate (%)	8.5	7.6	28.2	4.1	18.8	4.5
H.S. Diplomas (#)	915	854	15	19	18	9

Hermantown

4190 Ugstad Rd • Duluth, MN 55811-1317
Mailing Address: 4307 Ugstad Rd • Hermantown, MN 55811-1317
(218) 729-9313 • http://www.hermantown.k12.mn.us/
Grade Span: PK-12; **Agency Type:** 1
Schools: 4
2 Primary; 1 Middle; 1 High; 0 Other Level
3 Regular; 1 Special Education; 0 Vocational; 0 Alternative
0 Magnet; 0 Charter; 2 Title I Eligible; 0 School-wide Title I
Students: 1,963 (51.9% male; 48.1% female)
Individual Education Program: 236 (12.0%);
English Language Learner: 0 (0.0%); Migrant: 0 (0.0%)
Eligible for Free Lunch Program: 127 (6.5%)
Eligible for Reduced-Price Lunch Program: 99 (5.0%)
Teachers: 107.9 (18.2 to 1)
Librarians/Media Specialists: 2.0 (981.5 to 1)
Guidance Counselors: 3.5 (560.9 to 1)
Current Spending: ($ per student per year):
Total: $6,076; Instruction: $3,706; Support Services: $2,149
Enrollment, Drop-out Rates and Diploma Recipients by Race/Ethnicity

Category	Total	White	Black	Asian	AIAN	Hisp.
Enrollment (%)	100.0	97.1	0.2	1.3	0.9	0.5
Drop-out Rate (%)	0.0	0.0	0.0	0.0	0.0	0.0
H.S. Diplomas (#)	149	144	1	0	1	3

Hibbing

800 E 21st St • Hibbing, MN 55746-1803
(218) 263-4850 • http://www.hibbing.k12.mn.us/
Grade Span: PK-12; **Agency Type:** 1
Schools: 8
4 Primary; 1 Middle; 1 High; 2 Other Level
5 Regular; 1 Special Education; 0 Vocational; 2 Alternative
0 Magnet; 0 Charter; 3 Title I Eligible; 0 School-wide Title I
Students: 2,774 (51.9% male; 48.1% female)
Individual Education Program: 334 (12.0%);
English Language Learner: 5 (0.2%); Migrant: 0 (0.0%)
Eligible for Free Lunch Program: 617 (22.2%)
Eligible for Reduced-Price Lunch Program: 191 (6.9%)
Teachers: 151.9 (18.3 to 1)
Librarians/Media Specialists: 5.0 (554.8 to 1)
Guidance Counselors: 4.0 (693.5 to 1)
Current Spending: ($ per student per year):
Total: $7,188; Instruction: $4,385; Support Services: $2,559
Enrollment, Drop-out Rates and Diploma Recipients by Race/Ethnicity

Category	Total	White	Black	Asian	AIAN	Hisp.
Enrollment (%)	100.0	96.7	0.4	0.3	2.1	0.6
Drop-out Rate (%)	4.8	4.8	0.0	0.0	33.3	0.0
H.S. Diplomas (#)	208	206	1	1	0	0

Proctor

131 9th Ave • Proctor, MN 55810-2797
(218) 628-4934 • http://www.proctor.k12.mn.us/
Grade Span: PK-12; **Agency Type:** 1
Schools: 7
3 Primary; 2 Middle; 2 High; 0 Other Level
6 Regular; 0 Special Education; 0 Vocational; 1 Alternative
0 Magnet; 0 Charter; 2 Title I Eligible; 0 School-wide Title I
Students: 1,873 (48.7% male; 51.3% female)
Individual Education Program: 216 (11.5%);
English Language Learner: 0 (0.0%); Migrant: 0 (0.0%)
Eligible for Free Lunch Program: 238 (12.7%)
Eligible for Reduced-Price Lunch Program: 165 (8.8%)
Teachers: 114.7 (16.3 to 1)
Librarians/Media Specialists: 2.0 (936.5 to 1)
Guidance Counselors: 2.5 (749.2 to 1)
Current Spending: ($ per student per year):
Total: $6,758; Instruction: $4,321; Support Services: $2,189
Enrollment, Drop-out Rates and Diploma Recipients by Race/Ethnicity

Category	Total	White	Black	Asian	AIAN	Hisp.
Enrollment (%)	100.0	98.0	0.3	0.5	0.7	0.4
Drop-out Rate (%)	0.3	0.3	0.0	0.0	0.0	0.0
H.S. Diplomas (#)	167	167	0	0	0	0

Saint Louis County

1701 N 9th Ave • Virginia, MN 55792-2172
(218) 749-8130 • http://www.isd2142.k12.mn.us/
Grade Span: PK-12; **Agency Type:** 1
Schools: 14
7 Primary; 0 Middle; 7 High; 0 Other Level
14 Regular; 0 Special Education; 0 Vocational; 0 Alternative
0 Magnet; 0 Charter; 7 Title I Eligible; 0 School-wide Title I
Students: 2,491 (52.1% male; 47.9% female)
Individual Education Program: 436 (17.5%);
English Language Learner: 0 (0.0%); Migrant: 0 (0.0%)
Eligible for Free Lunch Program: 586 (23.5%)
Eligible for Reduced-Price Lunch Program: 262 (10.5%)
Teachers: 190.4 (13.1 to 1)
Librarians/Media Specialists: 6.5 (383.2 to 1)
Guidance Counselors: 6.3 (395.4 to 1)
Current Spending: ($ per student per year):
Total: $8,755; Instruction: $5,607; Support Services: $2,851
Enrollment, Drop-out Rates and Diploma Recipients by Race/Ethnicity

Category	Total	White	Black	Asian	AIAN	Hisp.
Enrollment (%)	100.0	87.8	0.2	0.6	11.1	0.3
Drop-out Rate (%)	1.6	1.7	0.0	0.0	1.2	0.0
H.S. Diplomas (#)	211	193	0	1	15	2

Virginia

411 5th Ave S • Virginia, MN 55792-2734
(218) 749-5437 • http://www.virginia.k12.mn.us/
Grade Span: PK-12; **Agency Type:** 1
Schools: 3
1 Primary; 1 Middle; 1 High; 0 Other Level
3 Regular; 0 Special Education; 0 Vocational; 0 Alternative

0 Magnet; 0 Charter; 2 Title I Eligible; 0 School-wide Title I
Students: 1,748 (50.2% male; 49.8% female)
Individual Education Program: 196 (11.2%);
English Language Learner: 5 (0.3%); Migrant: 0 (0.0%)
Eligible for Free Lunch Program: 419 (24.0%)
Eligible for Reduced-Price Lunch Program: 147 (8.4%)
Teachers: 91.5 (19.1 to 1)
Librarians/Media Specialists: 2.0 (874.0 to 1)
Guidance Counselors: 2.0 (874.0 to 1)
Current Spending: ($ per student per year):
Total: $7,785; Instruction: $5,101; Support Services: $2,405
Enrollment, Drop-out Rates and Diploma Recipients by Race/Ethnicity

Category	Total	White	Black	Asian	AIAN	Hisp.
Enrollment (%)	100.0	92.8	1.6	1.1	3.7	0.7
Drop-out Rate (%)	1.5	1.2	n/a	11.1	7.1	0.0
H.S. Diplomas (#)	130	124	0	2	4	0

Stearns County

Albany
Box 330 • Albany, MN 56307-0330
(320) 845-2171 • http://www.albany.k12.mn.us
Grade Span: PK-12; **Agency Type:** 1
Schools: 4
2 Primary; 1 Middle; 1 High; 0 Other Level
4 Regular; 0 Special Education; 0 Vocational; 0 Alternative
0 Magnet; 0 Charter; 1 Title I Eligible; 0 School-wide Title I
Students: 1,625 (49.2% male; 50.8% female)
Individual Education Program: 211 (13.0%);
English Language Learner: 11 (0.7%); Migrant: 0 (0.0%)
Eligible for Free Lunch Program: 171 (10.5%)
Eligible for Reduced-Price Lunch Program: 115 (7.1%)
Teachers: 105.5 (15.4 to 1)
Librarians/Media Specialists: 2.0 (812.5 to 1)
Guidance Counselors: 2.0 (812.5 to 1)
Current Spending: ($ per student per year):
Total: $6,072; Instruction: $4,027; Support Services: $1,752
Enrollment, Drop-out Rates and Diploma Recipients by Race/Ethnicity

Category	Total	White	Black	Asian	AIAN	Hisp.
Enrollment (%)	100.0	97.7	0.6	0.4	0.2	1.1
Drop-out Rate (%)	1.0	1.0	0.0	0.0	n/a	0.0
H.S. Diplomas (#)	146	144	1	1	0	0

Melrose
546 N 5th Ave E • Melrose, MN 56352
(320) 256-4224 • http://www.melrose.k12.mn.us/
Grade Span: PK-12; **Agency Type:** 1
Schools: 2
1 Primary; 0 Middle; 1 High; 0 Other Level
2 Regular; 0 Special Education; 0 Vocational; 0 Alternative
0 Magnet; 0 Charter; 1 Title I Eligible; 0 School-wide Title I
Students: 1,533 (54.5% male; 45.5% female)
Individual Education Program: 171 (11.2%);
English Language Learner: 132 (8.6%); Migrant: 0 (0.0%)
Eligible for Free Lunch Program: 307 (20.0%)
Eligible for Reduced-Price Lunch Program: 173 (11.3%)
Teachers: 105.5 (14.5 to 1)
Librarians/Media Specialists: 2.0 (766.5 to 1)
Guidance Counselors: 1.0 (1,533.0 to 1)
Current Spending: ($ per student per year):
Total: $6,836; Instruction: $4,459; Support Services: $2,074
Enrollment, Drop-out Rates and Diploma Recipients by Race/Ethnicity

Category	Total	White	Black	Asian	AIAN	Hisp.
Enrollment (%)	100.0	90.0	0.3	0.1	0.0	9.5
Drop-out Rate (%)	0.6	0.7	n/a	0.0	n/a	0.0
H.S. Diplomas (#)	139	133	0	3	0	3

Rocori
Rocori High School • Cold Spring, MN 56320
Mailing Address: 534 N 5th Ave • Cold Spring, MN 56320
(320) 685-4901 • http://rocori.k12.mn.us/
Grade Span: PK-12; **Agency Type:** 1
Schools: 5
3 Primary; 1 Middle; 1 High; 0 Other Level
5 Regular; 0 Special Education; 0 Vocational; 0 Alternative
0 Magnet; 0 Charter; 2 Title I Eligible; 0 School-wide Title I
Students: 2,349 (54.1% male; 45.9% female)
Individual Education Program: 252 (10.7%);
English Language Learner: 18 (0.8%); Migrant: 0 (0.0%)
Eligible for Free Lunch Program: 242 (10.3%)
Eligible for Reduced-Price Lunch Program: 177 (7.5%)
Teachers: 136.8 (17.2 to 1)
Librarians/Media Specialists: 4.5 (522.0 to 1)
Guidance Counselors: 4.1 (572.9 to 1)
Current Spending: ($ per student per year):
Total: $6,715; Instruction: $4,328; Support Services: $2,047

Enrollment, Drop-out Rates and Diploma Recipients by Race/Ethnicity

Category	Total	White	Black	Asian	AIAN	Hisp.
Enrollment (%)	100.0	96.8	0.8	0.4	0.0	2.0
Drop-out Rate (%)	1.0	1.1	0.0	0.0	n/a	0.0
H.S. Diplomas (#)	192	189	0	2	0	1

Saint Cloud
628 Roosevelt Rd • Saint Cloud, MN 56301-4898
(320) 253-9333 • http://isd742.org/
Grade Span: PK-12; **Agency Type:** 1
Schools: 20
10 Primary; 4 Middle; 4 High; 2 Other Level
15 Regular; 3 Special Education; 0 Vocational; 2 Alternative
0 Magnet; 0 Charter; 8 Title I Eligible; 3 School-wide Title I
Students: 10,292 (51.9% male; 48.1% female)
Individual Education Program: 1,783 (17.3%);
English Language Learner: 545 (5.3%); Migrant: 0 (0.0%)
Eligible for Free Lunch Program: 2,174 (21.1%)
Eligible for Reduced-Price Lunch Program: 741 (7.2%)
Teachers: 660.2 (15.6 to 1)
Librarians/Media Specialists: 13.6 (756.8 to 1)
Guidance Counselors: 28.0 (367.6 to 1)
Current Spending: ($ per student per year):
Total: $7,999; Instruction: $5,141; Support Services: $2,555
Enrollment, Drop-out Rates and Diploma Recipients by Race/Ethnicity

Category	Total	White	Black	Asian	AIAN	Hisp.
Enrollment (%)	100.0	86.8	6.1	4.0	1.1	1.9
Drop-out Rate (%)	4.7	4.4	12.2	2.6	22.2	6.7
H.S. Diplomas (#)	834	790	12	23	4	5

Sartell
212 Third Ave N • Sartell, MN 56377-0328
(320) 656-3715 • http://www.sartell.k12.mn.us/
Grade Span: PK-12; **Agency Type:** 1
Schools: 4
2 Primary; 1 Middle; 1 High; 0 Other Level
4 Regular; 0 Special Education; 0 Vocational; 0 Alternative
0 Magnet; 0 Charter; 1 Title I Eligible; 0 School-wide Title I
Students: 2,737 (52.1% male; 47.9% female)
Individual Education Program: 297 (10.9%);
English Language Learner: 5 (0.2%); Migrant: 0 (0.0%)
Eligible for Free Lunch Program: 109 (4.0%)
Eligible for Reduced-Price Lunch Program: 95 (3.5%)
Teachers: 161.0 (17.0 to 1)
Librarians/Media Specialists: 3.0 (912.3 to 1)
Guidance Counselors: 3.0 (912.3 to 1)
Current Spending: ($ per student per year):
Total: $6,405; Instruction: $4,075; Support Services: $1,984
Enrollment, Drop-out Rates and Diploma Recipients by Race/Ethnicity

Category	Total	White	Black	Asian	AIAN	Hisp.
Enrollment (%)	100.0	97.0	0.5	1.9	0.1	0.5
Drop-out Rate (%)	0.2	0.2	n/a	n/a	n/a	n/a
H.S. Diplomas (#)	189	185	0	4	0	0

Steele County

Owatonna
515 W Bridge St • Owatonna, MN 55060-2816
(507) 444-8601 • http://www.owatonna.k12.mn.us/
Grade Span: PK-12; **Agency Type:** 1
Schools: 21
7 Primary; 2 Middle; 9 High; 3 Other Level
7 Regular; 1 Special Education; 0 Vocational; 13 Alternative
0 Magnet; 0 Charter; 10 Title I Eligible; 0 School-wide Title I
Students: 5,009 (52.2% male; 47.8% female)
Individual Education Program: 678 (13.5%);
English Language Learner: 345 (6.9%); Migrant: 8 (0.2%)
Eligible for Free Lunch Program: 785 (15.7%)
Eligible for Reduced-Price Lunch Program: 288 (5.7%)
Teachers: 288.9 (17.3 to 1)
Librarians/Media Specialists: 3.0 (1,669.7 to 1)
Guidance Counselors: 5.0 (1,001.8 to 1)
Current Spending: ($ per student per year):
Total: $6,595; Instruction: $4,097; Support Services: $2,183
Enrollment, Drop-out Rates and Diploma Recipients by Race/Ethnicity

Category	Total	White	Black	Asian	AIAN	Hisp.
Enrollment (%)	100.0	86.0	5.3	1.5	0.1	7.2
Drop-out Rate (%)	3.7	2.3	16.0	6.7	0.0	26.8
H.S. Diplomas (#)	359	344	6	3	0	6

Todd County

Staples-Motley

202 Pleasant Ave NE • Staples, MN 56479-2118
(218) 894-2430
Grade Span: PK-12; **Agency Type:** 1
Schools: 4
2 Primary; 1 Middle; 1 High; 0 Other Level
4 Regular; 0 Special Education; 0 Vocational; 0 Alternative
0 Magnet; 0 Charter; 3 Title I Eligible; 0 School-wide Title I
Students: 1,504 (49.8% male; 50.2% female)
Individual Education Program: 221 (14.7%);
English Language Learner: 25 (1.7%); Migrant: 0 (0.0%)
Eligible for Free Lunch Program: 522 (34.7%)
Eligible for Reduced-Price Lunch Program: 239 (15.9%)
Teachers: 108.8 (13.8 to 1)
Librarians/Media Specialists: 1.0 (1,504.0 to 1)
Guidance Counselors: 1.0 (1,504.0 to 1)
Current Spending: ($ per student per year):
Total: $7,796; Instruction: $4,654; Support Services: $2,735
Enrollment, Drop-out Rates and Diploma Recipients by Race/Ethnicity

Category	Total	White	Black	Asian	AIAN	Hisp.
Enrollment (%)	100.0	95.6	0.7	0.5	1.1	2.0
Drop-out Rate (%)	0.7	0.7	0.0	n/a	0.0	n/a
H.S. Diplomas (#)	124	122	0	0	1	1

Waseca County

Waseca

501 Elm Ave E • Waseca, MN 56093-3399
(507) 835-2500 • http://www.waseca.k12.mn.us/
Grade Span: PK-12; **Agency Type:** 1
Schools: 9
4 Primary; 2 Middle; 2 High; 1 Other Level
4 Regular; 1 Special Education; 0 Vocational; 4 Alternative
0 Magnet; 0 Charter; 2 Title I Eligible; 0 School-wide Title I
Students: 2,217 (51.9% male; 48.1% female)
Individual Education Program: 346 (15.6%);
English Language Learner: 101 (4.6%); Migrant: 0 (0.0%)
Eligible for Free Lunch Program: 405 (18.3%)
Eligible for Reduced-Price Lunch Program: 169 (7.6%)
Teachers: 136.5 (16.2 to 1)
Librarians/Media Specialists: 2.5 (886.8 to 1)
Guidance Counselors: 3.2 (692.8 to 1)
Current Spending: ($ per student per year):
Total: $7,044; Instruction: $4,388; Support Services: $2,326
Enrollment, Drop-out Rates and Diploma Recipients by Race/Ethnicity

Category	Total	White	Black	Asian	AIAN	Hisp.
Enrollment (%)	100.0	88.6	4.1	1.0	0.5	5.8
Drop-out Rate (%)	3.9	3.2	12.0	0.0	0.0	29.4
H.S. Diplomas (#)	151	143	3	4	0	1

Washington County

Forest Lake

6100 210th St N • Forest Lake, MN 55025-9796
(651) 982-8100 • http://www.forestlake.k12.mn.us/
Grade Span: PK-12; **Agency Type:** 1
Schools: 15
9 Primary; 1 Middle; 2 High; 3 Other Level
11 Regular; 1 Special Education; 0 Vocational; 3 Alternative
1 Magnet; 0 Charter; 4 Title I Eligible; 0 School-wide Title I
Students: 7,655 (52.1% male; 47.9% female)
Individual Education Program: 867 (11.3%);
English Language Learner: 31 (0.4%); Migrant: 0 (0.0%)
Eligible for Free Lunch Program: 636 (8.3%)
Eligible for Reduced-Price Lunch Program: 422 (5.5%)
Teachers: 421.9 (18.1 to 1)
Librarians/Media Specialists: 10.0 (765.5 to 1)
Guidance Counselors: 10.0 (765.5 to 1)
Current Spending: ($ per student per year):
Total: $6,933; Instruction: $4,175; Support Services: $2,394
Enrollment, Drop-out Rates and Diploma Recipients by Race/Ethnicity

Category	Total	White	Black	Asian	AIAN	Hisp.
Enrollment (%)	100.0	96.7	0.5	1.5	0.6	0.6
Drop-out Rate (%)	4.3	4.2	0.0	9.4	11.1	0.0
H.S. Diplomas (#)	570	548	5	9	4	4

Mahtomedi

814 Mahtomedi Ave • Mahtomedi, MN 55115-1900
Mailing Address: 1520 Mahtomedi Ave • Mahtomedi, MN 55115-1900
(651) 407-2000 • http://www.mahtomedi.k12.mn.us/
Grade Span: PK-12; **Agency Type:** 1
Schools: 6
3 Primary; 1 Middle; 2 High; 0 Other Level
4 Regular; 1 Special Education; 0 Vocational; 1 Alternative
0 Magnet; 0 Charter; 2 Title I Eligible; 0 School-wide Title I
Students: 3,093 (51.9% male; 48.1% female)
Individual Education Program: 318 (10.3%);
English Language Learner: 18 (0.6%); Migrant: 0 (0.0%)
Eligible for Free Lunch Program: 90 (2.9%)
Eligible for Reduced-Price Lunch Program: 38 (1.2%)
Teachers: 175.1 (17.7 to 1)
Librarians/Media Specialists: 4.0 (773.3 to 1)
Guidance Counselors: 4.9 (631.2 to 1)
Current Spending: ($ per student per year):
Total: $6,859; Instruction: $4,368; Support Services: $2,162
Enrollment, Drop-out Rates and Diploma Recipients by Race/Ethnicity

Category	Total	White	Black	Asian	AIAN	Hisp.
Enrollment (%)	100.0	94.8	1.7	1.9	0.2	1.4
Drop-out Rate (%)	0.7	0.7	0.0	0.0	0.0	0.0
H.S. Diplomas (#)	236	229	1	3	0	3

South Washington County

7362 E Point Douglas Rd S • Cottage Grove, MN 55016-3025
(651) 458-6301 • http://www.sowashco.k12.mn.us/
Grade Span: PK-12; **Agency Type:** 1
Schools: 24
15 Primary; 4 Middle; 5 High; 0 Other Level
20 Regular; 1 Special Education; 0 Vocational; 3 Alternative
0 Magnet; 0 Charter; 3 Title I Eligible; 0 School-wide Title I
Students: 15,400 (50.9% male; 49.1% female)
Individual Education Program: 1,841 (12.0%);
English Language Learner: 130 (0.8%); Migrant: 0 (0.0%)
Eligible for Free Lunch Program: 1,161 (7.5%)
Eligible for Reduced-Price Lunch Program: 439 (2.9%)
Teachers: 909.0 (16.9 to 1)
Librarians/Media Specialists: 15.0 (1,026.7 to 1)
Guidance Counselors: 21.0 (733.3 to 1)
Current Spending: ($ per student per year):
Total: $6,629; Instruction: $4,283; Support Services: $2,073
Enrollment, Drop-out Rates and Diploma Recipients by Race/Ethnicity

Category	Total	White	Black	Asian	AIAN	Hisp.
Enrollment (%)	100.0	86.9	4.7	5.0	0.6	2.9
Drop-out Rate (%)	2.7	2.7	4.1	1.2	3.3	5.1
H.S. Diplomas (#)	1,031	941	31	41	6	12

Stillwater

1875 S Greeley St • Stillwater, MN 55082-6094
(651) 351-8301 • http://www.stillwater.k12.mn.us/
Grade Span: PK-12; **Agency Type:** 1
Schools: 19
11 Primary; 2 Middle; 4 High; 2 Other Level
12 Regular; 2 Special Education; 0 Vocational; 5 Alternative
0 Magnet; 0 Charter; 4 Title I Eligible; 0 School-wide Title I
Students: 9,005 (52.2% male; 47.8% female)
Individual Education Program: 983 (10.9%);
English Language Learner: 50 (0.6%); Migrant: 0 (0.0%)
Eligible for Free Lunch Program: 473 (5.3%)
Eligible for Reduced-Price Lunch Program: 255 (2.8%)
Teachers: 450.6 (20.0 to 1)
Librarians/Media Specialists: 7.3 (1,233.6 to 1)
Guidance Counselors: 11.0 (818.6 to 1)
Current Spending: ($ per student per year):
Total: $6,910; Instruction: $4,585; Support Services: $2,086
Enrollment, Drop-out Rates and Diploma Recipients by Race/Ethnicity

Category	Total	White	Black	Asian	AIAN	Hisp.
Enrollment (%)	100.0	95.6	1.0	2.2	0.2	0.9
Drop-out Rate (%)	1.3	1.2	10.0	2.9	0.0	3.6
H.S. Diplomas (#)	704	671	5	21	1	6

Winona County

Winona Area Public Schools

654 Huff • Winona, MN 55987-3320
(507) 494-0861 • http://www.winona.k12.mn.us/
Grade Span: PK-12; **Agency Type:** 1
Schools: 12
8 Primary; 1 Middle; 1 High; 2 Other Level
9 Regular; 1 Special Education; 0 Vocational; 2 Alternative
0 Magnet; 0 Charter; 4 Title I Eligible; 0 School-wide Title I
Students: 4,129 (52.5% male; 47.5% female)
Individual Education Program: 669 (16.2%);
English Language Learner: 125 (3.0%); Migrant: 0 (0.0%)
Eligible for Free Lunch Program: 869 (21.0%)
Eligible for Reduced-Price Lunch Program: 384 (9.3%)
Teachers: 276.0 (15.0 to 1)
Librarians/Media Specialists: 2.2 (1,876.8 to 1)
Guidance Counselors: 9.0 (458.8 to 1)
Current Spending: ($ per student per year):
Total: $6,978; Instruction: $4,546; Support Services: $2,137

Enrollment, Drop-out Rates and Diploma Recipients by Race/Ethnicity

Category	Total	White	Black	Asian	AIAN	Hisp.
Enrollment (%)	100.0	91.1	2.3	4.7	0.3	1.7
Drop-out Rate (%)	3.1	3.2	3.8	2.0	0.0	0.0
H.S. Diplomas (#)	348	333	4	8	2	1

Wright County

Annandale

Box 190 • Annandale, MN 55302-0190
(320) 274-5602 • http://www.annandale.k12.mn.us/
Grade Span: PK-12; **Agency Type:** 1
Schools: 3
1 Primary; 1 Middle; 1 High; 0 Other Level
3 Regular; 0 Special Education; 0 Vocational; 0 Alternative
0 Magnet; 0 Charter; 2 Title I Eligible; 0 School-wide Title I
Students: 1,859 (50.8% male; 49.2% female)
Individual Education Program: 218 (11.7%);
English Language Learner: 3 (0.2%); Migrant: 0 (0.0%)
Eligible for Free Lunch Program: 249 (13.4%)
Eligible for Reduced-Price Lunch Program: 149 (8.0%)
Teachers: 107.9 (17.2 to 1)
Librarians/Media Specialists: 1.0 (1,859.0 to 1)
Guidance Counselors: 2.0 (929.5 to 1)
Current Spending: ($ per student per year):
Total: $6,363; Instruction: $4,025; Support Services: $2,045
Enrollment, Drop-out Rates and Diploma Recipients by Race/Ethnicity

Category	Total	White	Black	Asian	AIAN	Hisp.
Enrollment (%)	100.0	97.9	1.1	0.5	0.2	0.4
Drop-out Rate (%)	4.2	4.3	0.0	0.0	n/a	n/a
H.S. Diplomas (#)	117	116	1	0	0	0

Buffalo

214 NE 1st Ave • Buffalo, MN 55313-1697
(612) 682-5200 • http://www.buffalo.k12.mn.us/
Grade Span: PK-12; **Agency Type:** 1
Schools: 9
6 Primary; 1 Middle; 2 High; 0 Other Level
7 Regular; 1 Special Education; 0 Vocational; 1 Alternative
0 Magnet; 0 Charter; 3 Title I Eligible; 0 School-wide Title I
Students: 5,102 (51.4% male; 48.6% female)
Individual Education Program: 640 (12.5%);
English Language Learner: 37 (0.7%); Migrant: 0 (0.0%)
Eligible for Free Lunch Program: 542 (10.6%)
Eligible for Reduced-Price Lunch Program: 455 (8.9%)
Teachers: 279.6 (18.2 to 1)
Librarians/Media Specialists: 5.5 (927.6 to 1)
Guidance Counselors: 6.0 (850.3 to 1)
Current Spending: ($ per student per year):
Total: $6,616; Instruction: $4,208; Support Services: $2,059
Enrollment, Drop-out Rates and Diploma Recipients by Race/Ethnicity

Category	Total	White	Black	Asian	AIAN	Hisp.
Enrollment (%)	100.0	96.7	0.6	0.8	0.4	1.4
Drop-out Rate (%)	2.2	2.1	0.0	5.9	16.7	0.0
H.S. Diplomas (#)	341	334	3	2	1	1

Delano

700 Elm Ave E • Delano, MN 55328-9183
(763) 972-3365 • http://www.delano.k12.mn.us/
Grade Span: PK-12; **Agency Type:** 1
Schools: 3
1 Primary; 1 Middle; 1 High; 0 Other Level
3 Regular; 0 Special Education; 0 Vocational; 0 Alternative
0 Magnet; 0 Charter; 1 Title I Eligible; 0 School-wide Title I
Students: 1,925 (51.8% male; 48.2% female)
Individual Education Program: 234 (12.2%);
English Language Learner: 0 (0.0%); Migrant: 0 (0.0%)
Eligible for Free Lunch Program: 55 (2.9%)
Eligible for Reduced-Price Lunch Program: 90 (4.7%)
Teachers: 104.5 (18.4 to 1)
Librarians/Media Specialists: 3.0 (641.7 to 1)
Guidance Counselors: 2.0 (962.5 to 1)
Current Spending: ($ per student per year):
Total: $6,175; Instruction: $3,843; Support Services: $2,044
Enrollment, Drop-out Rates and Diploma Recipients by Race/Ethnicity

Category	Total	White	Black	Asian	AIAN	Hisp.
Enrollment (%)	100.0	96.4	0.9	1.2	0.6	0.8
Drop-out Rate (%)	0.5	0.5	0.0	0.0	0.0	0.0
H.S. Diplomas (#)	119	116	1	0	1	1

Monticello

302 Washington St • Monticello, MN 55362
(763) 271-0300 • http://www.monticello.k12.mn.us/
Grade Span: PK-12; **Agency Type:** 1
Schools: 6
3 Primary; 1 Middle; 2 High; 0 Other Level
5 Regular; 0 Special Education; 0 Vocational; 1 Alternative
0 Magnet; 0 Charter; 4 Title I Eligible; 0 School-wide Title I
Students: 3,924 (49.6% male; 50.4% female)
Individual Education Program: 620 (15.8%);
English Language Learner: 50 (1.3%); Migrant: 0 (0.0%)
Eligible for Free Lunch Program: 336 (8.6%)
Eligible for Reduced-Price Lunch Program: 208 (5.3%)
Teachers: 214.2 (18.3 to 1)
Librarians/Media Specialists: 5.0 (784.8 to 1)
Guidance Counselors: 3.0 (1,308.0 to 1)
Current Spending: ($ per student per year):
Total: $6,940; Instruction: $4,416; Support Services: $2,202
Enrollment, Drop-out Rates and Diploma Recipients by Race/Ethnicity

Category	Total	White	Black	Asian	AIAN	Hisp.
Enrollment (%)	100.0	96.8	0.8	1.0	0.1	1.3
Drop-out Rate (%)	3.2	3.2	0.0	0.0	100.0	0.0
H.S. Diplomas (#)	237	234	1	2	0	0

Rockford

Box 9 • Rockford, MN 55373-0009
(763) 477-9165 • http://www.rockford.k12.mn.us/
Grade Span: PK-12; **Agency Type:** 1
Schools: 5
1 Primary; 1 Middle; 2 High; 1 Other Level
3 Regular; 0 Special Education; 0 Vocational; 2 Alternative
0 Magnet; 0 Charter; 1 Title I Eligible; 0 School-wide Title I
Students: 1,762 (52.4% male; 47.6% female)
Individual Education Program: 244 (13.8%);
English Language Learner: 39 (2.2%); Migrant: 0 (0.0%)
Eligible for Free Lunch Program: 218 (12.4%)
Eligible for Reduced-Price Lunch Program: 117 (6.6%)
Teachers: 104.6 (16.8 to 1)
Librarians/Media Specialists: 2.0 (881.0 to 1)
Guidance Counselors: 2.0 (881.0 to 1)
Current Spending: ($ per student per year):
Total: $6,009; Instruction: $3,585; Support Services: $2,187
Enrollment, Drop-out Rates and Diploma Recipients by Race/Ethnicity

Category	Total	White	Black	Asian	AIAN	Hisp.
Enrollment (%)	100.0	95.1	1.3	1.8	0.5	1.4
Drop-out Rate (%)	1.2	1.2	0.0	0.0	0.0	0.0
H.S. Diplomas (#)	105	97	0	5	1	2

Saint Michael-Albertville

11343 50th St NE • Saint Michael, MN 55376
(763) 497-3180 • http://www.stma.k12.mn.us/
Grade Span: PK-12; **Agency Type:** 1
Schools: 5
2 Primary; 1 Middle; 2 High; 0 Other Level
4 Regular; 0 Special Education; 0 Vocational; 1 Alternative
0 Magnet; 0 Charter; 2 Title I Eligible; 0 School-wide Title I
Students: 3,351 (51.3% male; 48.7% female)
Individual Education Program: 320 (9.5%);
English Language Learner: 15 (0.4%); Migrant: 0 (0.0%)
Eligible for Free Lunch Program: 145 (4.3%)
Eligible for Reduced-Price Lunch Program: 94 (2.8%)
Teachers: 186.7 (17.9 to 1)
Librarians/Media Specialists: 4.0 (837.8 to 1)
Guidance Counselors: 4.0 (837.8 to 1)
Current Spending: ($ per student per year):
Total: $5,880; Instruction: $3,364; Support Services: $2,241
Enrollment, Drop-out Rates and Diploma Recipients by Race/Ethnicity

Category	Total	White	Black	Asian	AIAN	Hisp.
Enrollment (%)	100.0	96.0	0.7	2.2	0.2	0.9
Drop-out Rate (%)	0.4	0.4	0.0	0.0	n/a	0.0
H.S. Diplomas (#)	166	164	0	2	0	0

Number of Schools

Rank	Number	District Name	City
1	162	Intermediate SD 287	Plymouth
2	144	Minneapolis	Minneapolis
3	125	Saint Paul	Saint Paul
4	61	Anoka-Hennepin	Coon Rapids
5	42	Rochester	Rochester
6	39	Duluth	Duluth
7	37	Rosemount-Apple Valley-Eagan	Rosemount
8	30	Osseo	Osseo
9	26	Mounds View	Roseville
10	25	Robbinsdale	New Hope
11	24	South Washington County	Cottage Grove
12	23	Burnsville	Burnsville
13	21	Owatonna	Owatonna
14	20	Saint Cloud	Saint Cloud
15	19	Brainerd	Brainerd
15	19	Grand Rapids	Grand Rapids
15	19	Mankato	Mankato
15	19	Stillwater	Stillwater
15	19	White Bear Lake	White Bear Lake
20	18	North Saint Paul-Maplewood	Maplewood
21	16	Bloomington	Bloomington
21	16	Hopkins	Hopkins
23	15	Austin	Austin
23	15	Forest Lake	Forest Lake
23	15	Lakeville	Lakeville
26	14	Bemidji	Bemidji
26	14	Detroit Lakes	Detroit Lakes
26	14	Elk River	Elk River
26	14	Saint Louis County	Virginia
26	14	Willmar	Willmar
31	13	Roseville	Roseville
32	12	Chaska	Chaska
32	12	Edina	Edina
32	12	Hastings	Hastings
32	12	Minneapolis Area Office	Minneapolis
32	12	Moorhead	Moorhead
32	12	Spring Lake Park	Spring Lake Pk
32	12	Winona Area Public Schools	Winona
39	11	Centennial	Circle Pines
39	11	Eden Prairie	Eden Prairie
39	11	Minnetonka	Excelsior
39	11	Wayzata	Wayzata
43	10	Faribault	Faribault
43	10	Saint Francis	Saint Francis
43	10	Saint Louis Park	St Louis Park
43	10	W Saint Paul-Mendota Height-Eagan	Mendota Heights
47	9	Buffalo	Buffalo
47	9	Farmington	Farmington
47	9	Inver Grove	Inver Grove Hgts
47	9	Prior Lake	Prior Lake
47	9	Red Wing	Red Wing
47	9	Waseca	Waseca
53	8	Albert Lea	Albert Lea
53	8	Alexandria	Alexandria
53	8	Cloquet	Cloquet
53	8	Columbia Heights	Columbia Hgts
53	8	Fridley	Fridley
53	8	Hibbing	Hibbing
53	8	North Branch	North Branch
53	8	Saint Peter	Saint Peter
53	8	Worthington	Worthington
62	7	Cambridge-Isanti	Cambridge
62	7	Chisago Lakes	Lindstrom
62	7	Fergus Falls	Fergus Falls
62	7	Hutchinson	Hutchinson
62	7	Northfield	Northfield
62	7	Perham	Perham
62	7	Proctor	Proctor
62	7	Richfield	Richfield
62	7	Shakopee	Shakopee
62	7	South Saint Paul	S Saint Paul
72	6	Crookston	Crookston
72	6	Dassel-Cokato	Cokato
72	6	Lake Superior	Two Harbors
72	6	Little Falls	Little Falls
72	6	Mahtomedi	Mahtomedi
72	6	Marshall	Marshall
72	6	Monticello	Monticello
72	6	New London-Spicer	New London
80	5	Glencoe-Silver Lake	Glencoe
80	5	Kasson-Mantorville	Kasson
80	5	Lacrescent-Hokah	Lacrescent
80	5	Litchfield	Litchfield
80	5	Milaca	Milaca
80	5	New Prague Area Schools	New Prague
80	5	New Ulm	New Ulm
80	5	Orono	Long Lake
80	5	Rockford	Rockford
80	5	Rocori	Cold Spring
80	5	Saint Michael-Albertville	Saint Michael
80	5	Sauk Rapids	Sauk Rapids
80	5	Thief River Falls	Thief River Fls
80	5	Westonka	Mound
94	4	Albany	Albany
94	4	Becker	Becker
94	4	East Grand Forks	E Grand Forks
94	4	Fairmont Area Schools	Fairmont
94	4	Hermantown	Duluth
94	4	Minnewaska	Glenwood
94	4	Montevideo	Montevideo
94	4	Mora	Mora
94	4	Park Rapids	Park Rapids
94	4	Pine City	Pine City
94	4	Princeton	Princeton
94	4	Redwood Falls Area Schools	Redwood Falls
94	4	Roseau	Roseau
94	4	Sartell	Sartell
94	4	Staples-Motley	Staples
94	4	Stewartville	Stewartville
94	4	Waconia	Waconia
111	3	Annandale	Annandale
111	3	Big Lake	Big Lake
111	3	Byron	Byron
111	3	Crosby-Ironton	Crosby
111	3	Delano	Delano
111	3	Foley	Foley
111	3	Saint Anthony-New Brighton	Saint Anthony
111	3	Virginia	Virginia
119	2	Brooklyn Center	Brooklyn Center
119	2	Melrose	Melrose

Number of Teachers

Rank	Number	District Name	City
1	3,142	Minneapolis	Minneapolis
2	2,955	Saint Paul	Saint Paul
3	2,234	Anoka-Hennepin	Coon Rapids
4	1,745	Rosemount-Apple Valley-Eagan	Rosemount
5	1,193	Osseo	Osseo
6	929	Rochester	Rochester
7	909	South Washington County	Cottage Grove
8	774	Robbinsdale	New Hope
9	763	Duluth	Duluth
10	660	Saint Cloud	Saint Cloud
11	642	Burnsville	Burnsville
12	619	Mounds View	Roseville
13	610	Bloomington	Bloomington
14	594	North Saint Paul-Maplewood	Maplewood
15	590	Lakeville	Lakeville
16	547	Hopkins	Hopkins
17	546	Eden Prairie	Eden Prairie
18	513	Wayzata	Wayzata
19	475	Elk River	Elk River
20	462	Minnetonka	Excelsior
21	458	White Bear Lake	White Bear Lake
22	450	Stillwater	Stillwater
23	445	Chaska	Chaska
24	437	Brainerd	Brainerd
25	421	Forest Lake	Forest Lake
26	417	Mankato	Mankato
27	412	Edina	Edina
28	380	Centennial	Circle Pines
29	354	Roseville	Roseville
30	348	Moorhead	Moorhead
31	322	Bemidji	Bemidji
32	309	W Saint Paul-Mendota Height-Eagan	Mendota Heights
33	302	Saint Francis	Saint Francis
34	299	Willmar	Willmar
35	297	Farmington	Farmington
36	293	Saint Louis Park	St Louis Park
37	288	Owatonna	Owatonna
38	286	Prior Lake	Prior Lake
39	279	Buffalo	Buffalo
40	276	Winona Area Public Schools	Winona
41	270	Cambridge-Isanti	Cambridge
42	264	Hastings	Hastings
43	263	Shakopee	Shakopee
44	257	Northfield	Northfield
45	257	Alexandria	Alexandria
46	255	Austin	Austin
47	251	Richfield	Richfield
48	249	Intermediate SD 287	Plymouth
49	249	Faribault	Faribault
50	237	Grand Rapids	Grand Rapids
51	220	Spring Lake Park	Spring Lake Pk
52	216	Sauk Rapids	Sauk Rapids
53	214	Monticello	Monticello
54	211	Albert Lea	Albert Lea
55	210	North Branch	North Branch
56	210	Inver Grove	Inver Grove Hgts
57	207	Detroit Lakes	Detroit Lakes
58	197	Chisago Lakes	Lindstrom
59	194	Little Falls	Little Falls
60	193	South Saint Paul	S Saint Paul
61	191	Hutchinson	Hutchinson
62	190	Saint Louis County	Virginia
63	186	Saint Michael-Albertville	Saint Michael
64	183	Columbia Heights	Columbia Hgts
65	183	Fergus Falls	Fergus Falls
66	182	Princeton	Princeton
67	180	Red Wing	Red Wing
68	178	Big Lake	Big Lake
69	175	Mahtomedi	Mahtomedi
70	165	Marshall	Marshall
71	161	Sartell	Sartell
72	160	Worthington	Worthington
73	158	New Ulm	New Ulm
74	151	Hibbing	Hibbing
75	148	New Prague Area Schools	New Prague
76	147	Fridley	Fridley
77	145	Orono	Long Lake
78	144	Thief River Falls	Thief River Fls
79	137	Cloquet	Cloquet
80	136	Rocori	Cold Spring
81	136	Waseca	Waseca
82	134	Westonka	Mound
83	132	Becker	Becker
84	128	Saint Peter	Saint Peter
85	127	Dassel-Cokato	Cokato
86	126	East Grand Forks	E Grand Forks
87	126	Waconia	Waconia
88	124	Milaca	Milaca
89	122	Litchfield	Litchfield
90	120	Mora	Mora
91	116	Fairmont Area Schools	Fairmont
92	114	Proctor	Proctor
93	114	Park Rapids	Park Rapids
94	112	Foley	Foley
95	110	New London-Spicer	New London
96	109	Kasson-Mantorville	Kasson
97	108	Staples-Motley	Staples
98	108	Glencoe-Silver Lake	Glencoe
99	107	Annandale	Annandale
99	107	Hermantown	Duluth
101	107	Perham	Perham
102	106	Pine City	Pine City
103	105	Albany	Albany
103	105	Melrose	Melrose
105	105	Minnewaska	Glenwood
106	104	Montevideo	Montevideo
107	104	Rockford	Rockford
108	104	Delano	Delano
109	104	Stewartville	Stewartville
110	100	Crosby-Ironton	Crosby
111	100	Lake Superior	Two Harbors
112	100	Brooklyn Center	Brooklyn Center
113	99	Lacrescent-Hokah	Lacrescent
114	99	Redwood Falls Area Schools	Redwood Falls
115	96	Crookston	Crookston
116	91	Byron	Byron
117	91	Virginia	Virginia
118	87	Saint Anthony-New Brighton	Saint Anthony
119	82	Roseau	Roseau
120	n/a	Minneapolis Area Office	Minneapolis

Number of Students

Rank	Number	District Name	City
1	46,037	Minneapolis	Minneapolis
2	43,923	Saint Paul	Saint Paul
3	41,383	Anoka-Hennepin	Coon Rapids
4	28,486	Rosemount-Apple Valley-Eagan	Rosemount
5	21,824	Osseo	Osseo
6	16,400	Rochester	Rochester
7	15,400	South Washington County	Cottage Grove
8	13,656	Robbinsdale	New Hope
9	11,603	Duluth	Duluth
10	11,458	North Saint Paul-Maplewood	Maplewood
11	11,386	Burnsville	Burnsville
12	11,187	Mounds View	Roseville
13	10,690	Bloomington	Bloomington
14	10,441	Eden Prairie	Eden Prairie
15	10,292	Saint Cloud	Saint Cloud
16	10,154	Lakeville	Lakeville
17	9,768	Elk River	Elk River
18	9,534	Wayzata	Wayzata
19	9,160	White Bear Lake	White Bear Lake
20	9,005	Stillwater	Stillwater
21	8,223	Hopkins	Hopkins
22	7,804	Chaska	Chaska
23	7,655	Forest Lake	Forest Lake
24	7,591	Minnetonka	Excelsior
25	7,303	Brainerd	Brainerd
26	7,163	Edina	Edina
27	7,090	Mankato	Mankato
28	7,027	Centennial	Circle Pines

29	6,375	Roseville	Roseville
30	5,973	Saint Francis	Saint Francis
31	5,547	Moorhead	Moorhead
32	5,261	Farmington	Farmington
33	5,220	Prior Lake	Prior Lake
34	5,212	Bemidji	Bemidji
35	5,155	Hastings	Hastings
36	5,102	Buffalo	Buffalo
37	5,009	Owatonna	Owatonna
38	4,866	Cambridge-Isanti	Cambridge
39	4,783	W Saint Paul-Mendota Height-Eagan	Mendota Heights
40	4,564	Shakopee	Shakopee
41	4,382	Willmar	Willmar
42	4,258	Spring Lake Park	Spring Lake Pk
43	4,238	Saint Louis Park	St Louis Park
44	4,176	Richfield	Richfield
45	4,158	Grand Rapids	Grand Rapids
46	4,131	Austin	Austin
47	4,129	Winona Area Public Schools	Winona
48	4,100	Alexandria	Alexandria
49	3,969	Faribault	Faribault
50	3,951	Inver Grove	Inver Grove Hgts
51	3,924	Monticello	Monticello
52	3,911	Northfield	Northfield
53	3,897	North Branch	North Branch
54	3,713	Albert Lea	Albert Lea
55	3,600	Sauk Rapids	Sauk Rapids
56	3,526	Chisago Lakes	Lindstrom
57	3,432	South Saint Paul	S Saint Paul
58	3,355	Princeton	Princeton
59	3,351	Saint Michael-Albertville	Saint Michael
60	3,168	Red Wing	Red Wing
61	3,142	Hutchinson	Hutchinson
62	3,093	Mahtomedi	Mahtomedi
63	3,087	Little Falls	Little Falls
64	3,030	Big Lake	Big Lake
64	3,030	Columbia Heights	Columbia Hgts
66	2,855	Detroit Lakes	Detroit Lakes
67	2,841	Fergus Falls	Fergus Falls
68	2,774	Hibbing	Hibbing
69	2,737	Sartell	Sartell
70	2,705	New Prague Area Schools	New Prague
71	2,644	Minneapolis Area Office	Minneapolis
72	2,593	Fridley	Fridley
73	2,491	Saint Louis County	Virginia
74	2,486	Orono	Long Lake
75	2,415	New Ulm	New Ulm
76	2,381	Cloquet	Cloquet
77	2,358	Becker	Becker
78	2,349	Rocori	Cold Spring
79	2,334	Worthington	Worthington
80	2,327	Waconia	Waconia
81	2,304	Marshall	Marshall
82	2,264	Dassel-Cokato	Cokato
83	2,217	Waseca	Waseca
84	2,201	Westonka	Mound
85	2,165	Intermediate SD 287	Plymouth
86	2,123	Thief River Falls	Thief River Fls
87	1,963	Hermantown	Duluth
88	1,962	Litchfield	Litchfield
89	1,949	Mora	Mora
90	1,944	Milaca	Milaca
91	1,925	Delano	Delano
92	1,898	Saint Peter	Saint Peter
93	1,873	Proctor	Proctor
94	1,866	Kasson-Mantorville	Kasson
95	1,859	Annandale	Annandale
96	1,838	Stewartville	Stewartville
97	1,825	Fairmont Area Schools	Fairmont
98	1,820	Park Rapids	Park Rapids
99	1,817	East Grand Forks	E Grand Forks
100	1,777	Glencoe-Silver Lake	Glencoe
101	1,769	New London-Spicer	New London
102	1,762	Rockford	Rockford
103	1,748	Virginia	Virginia
104	1,742	Pine City	Pine City
105	1,732	Brooklyn Center	Brooklyn Center
106	1,698	Lake Superior	Two Harbors
107	1,680	Lacrescent-Hokah	Lacrescent
108	1,661	Foley	Foley
109	1,658	Perham	Perham
110	1,625	Albany	Albany
111	1,593	Crookston	Crookston
112	1,533	Melrose	Melrose
113	1,528	Montevideo	Montevideo
113	1,528	Saint Anthony-New Brighton	Saint Anthony
115	1,515	Minnewaska	Glenwood
116	1,513	Crosby-Ironton	Crosby
117	1,505	Roseau	Roseau
118	1,504	Staples-Motley	Staples
119	1,501	Redwood Falls Area Schools	Redwood Falls
120	1,500	Byron	Byron

Male Students

Rank	Percent	District Name	City
1	58.3	Intermediate SD 287	Plymouth
2	54.5	Melrose	Melrose
3	54.2	Westonka	Mound
4	54.1	Rocori	Cold Spring
5	53.4	Park Rapids	Park Rapids
6	53.3	Thief River Falls	Thief River Fls
7	53.1	Richfield	Richfield
7	53.1	Saint Peter	Saint Peter
9	53.0	Litchfield	Litchfield
9	53.0	Milaca	Milaca
9	53.0	Perham	Perham
12	52.8	Bemidji	Bemidji
13	52.7	Brooklyn Center	Brooklyn Center
13	52.7	Saint Anthony-New Brighton	Saint Anthony
15	52.5	Grand Rapids	Grand Rapids
15	52.5	New London-Spicer	New London
15	52.5	New Ulm	New Ulm
15	52.5	Winona Area Public Schools	Winona
19	52.4	Minnewaska	Glenwood
19	52.4	Rockford	Rockford
21	52.3	Duluth	Duluth
21	52.3	Saint Francis	Saint Francis
23	52.2	Farmington	Farmington
23	52.2	Hopkins	Hopkins
23	52.2	Hutchinson	Hutchinson
23	52.2	Moorhead	Moorhead
23	52.2	Owatonna	Owatonna
23	52.2	Shakopee	Shakopee
23	52.2	Stillwater	Stillwater
23	52.2	Waconia	Waconia
31	52.1	Austin	Austin
31	52.1	Chisago Lakes	Lindstrom
31	52.1	East Grand Forks	E Grand Forks
31	52.1	Forest Lake	Forest Lake
31	52.1	Mounds View	Roseville
31	52.1	Princeton	Princeton
31	52.1	Saint Louis County	Virginia
31	52.1	Sartell	Sartell
39	52.0	Bloomington	Bloomington
39	52.0	Foley	Foley
39	52.0	Inver Grove	Inver Grove Hgts
42	51.9	Chaska	Chaska
42	51.9	Eden Prairie	Eden Prairie
42	51.9	Fairmont Area Schools	Fairmont
42	51.9	Hermantown	Duluth
42	51.9	Hibbing	Hibbing
42	51.9	Mahtomedi	Mahtomedi
42	51.9	Rochester	Rochester
42	51.9	Saint Cloud	Saint Cloud
42	51.9	Waseca	Waseca
51	51.8	Becker	Becker
51	51.8	Delano	Delano
51	51.8	Minneapolis	Minneapolis
51	51.8	Redwood Falls Area Schools	Redwood Falls
51	51.8	Roseau	Roseau
51	51.8	Saint Louis Park	St Louis Park
57	51.7	Hastings	Hastings
58	51.6	Lakeville	Lakeville
58	51.6	Montevideo	Montevideo
58	51.6	Northfield	Northfield
58	51.6	W Saint Paul-Mendota Height-Eagan	Mendota Heights
62	51.5	Burnsville	Burnsville
62	51.5	Byron	Byron
62	51.5	Fridley	Fridley
62	51.5	Worthington	Worthington
66	51.4	Alexandria	Alexandria
66	51.4	Buffalo	Buffalo
66	51.4	Cambridge-Isanti	Cambridge
66	51.4	Faribault	Faribault
66	51.4	Lake Superior	Two Harbors
66	51.4	Mankato	Mankato
66	51.4	Osseo	Osseo
66	51.4	Robbinsdale	New Hope
66	51.4	Saint Paul	Saint Paul
75	51.3	Anoka-Hennepin	Coon Rapids
75	51.3	Brainerd	Brainerd
75	51.3	North Branch	North Branch
75	51.3	Rosemount-Apple Valley-Eagan	Rosemount
75	51.3	Saint Michael-Albertville	Saint Michael
75	51.3	White Bear Lake	White Bear Lake
81	51.2	Big Lake	Big Lake
81	51.2	Crookston	Crookston
81	51.2	Roseville	Roseville
84	51.1	Centennial	Circle Pines
84	51.1	Elk River	Elk River
86	51.0	Minnetonka	Excelsior
86	51.0	Pine City	Pine City
86	51.0	Wayzata	Wayzata
89	50.9	South Washington County	Cottage Grove
90	50.8	Annandale	Annandale
90	50.8	Little Falls	Little Falls
90	50.8	North Saint Paul-Maplewood	Maplewood
90	50.8	Sauk Rapids	Sauk Rapids
94	50.7	Prior Lake	Prior Lake
95	50.6	Fergus Falls	Fergus Falls
95	50.6	Orono	Long Lake
95	50.6	Willmar	Willmar
98	50.5	Dassel-Cokato	Cokato
98	50.5	Glencoe-Silver Lake	Glencoe
98	50.5	Kasson-Mantorville	Kasson
101	50.4	Lacrescent-Hokah	Lacrescent
101	50.4	South Saint Paul	S Saint Paul
103	50.3	Spring Lake Park	Spring Lake Pk
104	50.2	Red Wing	Red Wing
104	50.2	Virginia	Virginia
106	50.1	Edina	Edina
107	50.0	Detroit Lakes	Detroit Lakes
108	49.9	Albert Lea	Albert Lea
109	49.8	Cloquet	Cloquet
109	49.8	Mora	Mora
109	49.8	Staples-Motley	Staples
112	49.6	Monticello	Monticello
112	49.6	New Prague Area Schools	New Prague
114	49.5	Crosby-Ironton	Crosby
114	49.5	Stewartville	Stewartville
116	49.2	Albany	Albany
117	49.1	Columbia Heights	Columbia Hgts
118	48.7	Marshall	Marshall
118	48.7	Proctor	Proctor
120	n/a	Minneapolis Area Office	Minneapolis

Female Students

Rank	Percent	District Name	City
1	51.3	Marshall	Marshall
1	51.3	Proctor	Proctor
3	50.9	Columbia Heights	Columbia Hgts
4	50.8	Albany	Albany
5	50.5	Crosby-Ironton	Crosby
5	50.5	Stewartville	Stewartville
7	50.4	Monticello	Monticello
7	50.4	New Prague Area Schools	New Prague
9	50.2	Cloquet	Cloquet
9	50.2	Mora	Mora
9	50.2	Staples-Motley	Staples
12	50.1	Albert Lea	Albert Lea
13	50.0	Detroit Lakes	Detroit Lakes
14	49.9	Edina	Edina
15	49.8	Red Wing	Red Wing
15	49.8	Virginia	Virginia
17	49.7	Spring Lake Park	Spring Lake Pk
18	49.6	Lacrescent-Hokah	Lacrescent
18	49.6	South Saint Paul	S Saint Paul
20	49.5	Dassel-Cokato	Cokato
20	49.5	Glencoe-Silver Lake	Glencoe
20	49.5	Kasson-Mantorville	Kasson
23	49.4	Fergus Falls	Fergus Falls
23	49.4	Orono	Long Lake
23	49.4	Willmar	Willmar
26	49.3	Prior Lake	Prior Lake
27	49.2	Annandale	Annandale
27	49.2	Little Falls	Little Falls
27	49.2	North Saint Paul-Maplewood	Maplewood
27	49.2	Sauk Rapids	Sauk Rapids
31	49.1	South Washington County	Cottage Grove
32	49.0	Minnetonka	Excelsior
32	49.0	Pine City	Pine City
32	49.0	Wayzata	Wayzata
35	48.9	Centennial	Circle Pines
35	48.9	Elk River	Elk River
37	48.8	Big Lake	Big Lake
37	48.8	Crookston	Crookston
37	48.8	Roseville	Roseville
40	48.7	Anoka-Hennepin	Coon Rapids
40	48.7	Brainerd	Brainerd
40	48.7	North Branch	North Branch
40	48.7	Rosemount-Apple Valley-Eagan	Rosemount
40	48.7	Saint Michael-Albertville	Saint Michael
40	48.7	White Bear Lake	White Bear Lake
46	48.6	Alexandria	Alexandria
46	48.6	Buffalo	Buffalo
46	48.6	Cambridge-Isanti	Cambridge
46	48.6	Faribault	Faribault
46	48.6	Lake Superior	Two Harbors
46	48.6	Mankato	Mankato
46	48.6	Osseo	Osseo
46	48.6	Robbinsdale	New Hope
46	48.6	Saint Paul	Saint Paul
55	48.5	Burnsville	Burnsville
55	48.5	Byron	Byron
55	48.5	Fridley	Fridley
55	48.5	Worthington	Worthington
59	48.4	Lakeville	Lakeville

Rank	Percent	District Name	City
59	48.4	Montevideo	Montevideo
59	48.4	Northfield	Northfield
59	48.4	W Saint Paul-Mendota Height-Eagan	Mendota Heights
63	48.3	Hastings	Hastings
64	48.2	Becker	Becker
64	48.2	Delano	Delano
64	48.2	Minneapolis	Minneapolis
64	48.2	Redwood Falls Area Schools	Redwood Falls
64	48.2	Roseau	Roseau
64	48.2	Saint Louis Park	St Louis Park
70	48.1	Chaska	Chaska
70	48.1	Eden Prairie	Eden Prairie
70	48.1	Fairmont Area Schools	Fairmont
70	48.1	Hermantown	Duluth
70	48.1	Hibbing	Hibbing
70	48.1	Mahtomedi	Mahtomedi
70	48.1	Rochester	Rochester
70	48.1	Saint Cloud	Saint Cloud
70	48.1	Waseca	Waseca
79	48.0	Bloomington	Bloomington
79	48.0	Foley	Foley
79	48.0	Inver Grove	Inver Grove Hgts
82	47.9	Austin	Austin
82	47.9	Chisago Lakes	Lindstrom
82	47.9	East Grand Forks	E Grand Forks
82	47.9	Forest Lake	Forest Lake
82	47.9	Mounds View	Roseville
82	47.9	Princeton	Princeton
82	47.9	Saint Louis County	Virginia
82	47.9	Sartell	Sartell
90	47.8	Farmington	Farmington
90	47.8	Hopkins	Hopkins
90	47.8	Hutchinson	Hutchinson
90	47.8	Moorhead	Moorhead
90	47.8	Owatonna	Owatonna
90	47.8	Shakopee	Shakopee
90	47.8	Stillwater	Stillwater
90	47.8	Waconia	Waconia
98	47.7	Duluth	Duluth
98	47.7	Saint Francis	Saint Francis
100	47.6	Minnewaska	Glenwood
100	47.6	Rockford	Rockford
102	47.5	Grand Rapids	Grand Rapids
102	47.5	New London-Spicer	New London
102	47.5	New Ulm	New Ulm
102	47.5	Winona Area Public Schools	Winona
106	47.3	Brooklyn Center	Brooklyn Center
106	47.3	Saint Anthony-New Brighton	Saint Anthony
108	47.2	Bemidji	Bemidji
109	47.0	Litchfield	Litchfield
109	47.0	Milaca	Milaca
109	47.0	Perham	Perham
112	46.9	Richfield	Richfield
112	46.9	Saint Peter	Saint Peter
114	46.7	Thief River Falls	Thief River Fls
115	46.6	Park Rapids	Park Rapids
116	45.9	Rocori	Cold Spring
117	45.8	Westonka	Mound
118	45.5	Melrose	Melrose
119	41.7	Intermediate SD 287	Plymouth
120	n/a	Minneapolis Area Office	Minneapolis

Individual Education Program Students

Rank	Percent	District Name	City
1	34.8	Intermediate SD 287	Plymouth
2	18.0	Park Rapids	Park Rapids
3	17.5	Saint Louis County	Virginia
4	17.3	Moorhead	Moorhead
4	17.3	Saint Cloud	Saint Cloud
6	17.1	Albert Lea	Albert Lea
7	17.0	Little Falls	Little Falls
8	16.7	W Saint Paul-Mendota Height-Eagan	Mendota Heights
9	16.6	Detroit Lakes	Detroit Lakes
10	16.3	Saint Peter	Saint Peter
11	16.2	Winona Area Public Schools	Winona
12	16.1	Bemidji	Bemidji
13	15.8	Monticello	Monticello
13	15.8	Saint Paul	Saint Paul
15	15.7	Saint Louis Park	St Louis Park
16	15.6	Faribault	Faribault
16	15.6	Inver Grove	Inver Grove Hgts
16	15.6	Waseca	Waseca
19	15.5	Roseau	Roseau
20	15.4	Thief River Falls	Thief River Fls
21	15.2	Minnewaska	Glenwood
22	15.1	Foley	Foley
23	14.9	Fergus Falls	Fergus Falls
24	14.8	Brainerd	Brainerd
25	14.7	Staples-Motley	Staples
26	14.6	Crookston	Crookston
26	14.6	Worthington	Worthington
28	14.5	Mankato	Mankato
29	14.3	Alexandria	Alexandria
29	14.3	Sauk Rapids	Sauk Rapids
31	14.1	Rosemount-Apple Valley-Eagan	Rosemount
32	14.0	Minneapolis	Minneapolis
32	14.0	Willmar	Willmar
34	13.9	Crosby-Ironton	Crosby
34	13.9	Duluth	Duluth
36	13.8	Austin	Austin
36	13.8	Rockford	Rockford
38	13.7	Fairmont Area Schools	Fairmont
38	13.7	Montevideo	Montevideo
40	13.5	East Grand Forks	E Grand Forks
40	13.5	Litchfield	Litchfield
40	13.5	Northfield	Northfield
40	13.5	Owatonna	Owatonna
44	13.3	Lake Superior	Two Harbors
45	13.2	Grand Rapids	Grand Rapids
45	13.2	New London-Spicer	New London
45	13.2	Red Wing	Red Wing
48	13.0	Albany	Albany
49	12.9	Becker	Becker
49	12.9	Cloquet	Cloquet
49	12.9	Hastings	Hastings
49	12.9	North Branch	North Branch
53	12.8	Anoka-Hennepin	Coon Rapids
53	12.8	Perham	Perham
55	12.7	Burnsville	Burnsville
55	12.7	Farmington	Farmington
55	12.7	North Saint Paul-Maplewood	Maplewood
58	12.6	White Bear Lake	White Bear Lake
59	12.5	Buffalo	Buffalo
59	12.5	Centennial	Circle Pines
59	12.5	Marshall	Marshall
62	12.4	Columbia Heights	Columbia Hgts
63	12.3	Hopkins	Hopkins
63	12.3	South Saint Paul	S Saint Paul
65	12.2	Delano	Delano
65	12.2	Elk River	Elk River
65	12.2	Richfield	Richfield
68	12.1	Redwood Falls Area Schools	Redwood Falls
69	12.0	Hermantown	Duluth
69	12.0	Hibbing	Hibbing
69	12.0	South Washington County	Cottage Grove
69	12.0	Waconia	Waconia
73	11.9	Byron	Byron
74	11.8	Minnetonka	Excelsior
75	11.7	Annandale	Annandale
75	11.7	Princeton	Princeton
77	11.6	Spring Lake Park	Spring Lake Pk
77	11.6	Westonka	Mound
79	11.5	Proctor	Proctor
80	11.4	Bloomington	Bloomington
80	11.4	Lakeville	Lakeville
82	11.3	Forest Lake	Forest Lake
82	11.3	Roseville	Roseville
82	11.3	Stewartville	Stewartville
85	11.2	Melrose	Melrose
85	11.2	Milaca	Milaca
85	11.2	New Ulm	New Ulm
85	11.2	Rochester	Rochester
85	11.2	Virginia	Virginia
90	11.1	Big Lake	Big Lake
90	11.1	Fridley	Fridley
92	11.0	Mounds View	Roseville
92	11.0	Osseo	Osseo
94	10.9	Sartell	Sartell
94	10.9	Stillwater	Stillwater
96	10.8	Chaska	Chaska
97	10.7	Brooklyn Center	Brooklyn Center
97	10.7	Glencoe-Silver Lake	Glencoe
97	10.7	Rocori	Cold Spring
100	10.4	Lacrescent-Hokah	Lacrescent
100	10.4	Saint Francis	Saint Francis
102	10.3	Hutchinson	Hutchinson
102	10.3	Mahtomedi	Mahtomedi
104	10.2	Shakopee	Shakopee
105	10.1	Edina	Edina
105	10.1	Robbinsdale	New Hope
107	9.9	Eden Prairie	Eden Prairie
108	9.8	Dassel-Cokato	Cokato
109	9.7	Cambridge-Isanti	Cambridge
110	9.6	Chisago Lakes	Lindstrom
111	9.5	Saint Michael-Albertville	Saint Michael
112	9.3	Wayzata	Wayzata
113	9.2	Mora	Mora
114	8.6	Orono	Long Lake
115	8.2	Pine City	Pine City
116	8.1	Saint Anthony-New Brighton	Saint Anthony
117	7.6	Kasson-Mantorville	Kasson
117	7.6	New Prague Area Schools	New Prague
119	7.5	Prior Lake	Prior Lake
120	n/a	Minneapolis Area Office	Minneapolis

English Language Learner Students

Rank	Percent	District Name	City
1	33.8	Saint Paul	Saint Paul
2	24.1	Minneapolis	Minneapolis
3	21.0	Brooklyn Center	Brooklyn Center
4	16.8	Worthington	Worthington
5	15.2	Richfield	Richfield
6	13.5	Columbia Heights	Columbia Hgts
7	13.2	Rochester	Rochester
8	13.0	Willmar	Willmar
9	12.2	Faribault	Faribault
10	11.9	Shakopee	Shakopee
11	8.6	Melrose	Melrose
12	8.5	Crookston	Crookston
13	8.1	Robbinsdale	New Hope
14	7.9	Osseo	Osseo
15	7.6	Austin	Austin
16	7.5	Glencoe-Silver Lake	Glencoe
17	7.2	Burnsville	Burnsville
18	7.0	Bloomington	Bloomington
19	6.9	Moorhead	Moorhead
19	6.9	Owatonna	Owatonna
21	6.8	Albert Lea	Albert Lea
22	6.7	Hopkins	Hopkins
23	6.4	Roseville	Roseville
23	6.4	Saint Louis Park	St Louis Park
25	6.2	W Saint Paul-Mendota Height-Eagan	Mendota Heights
26	6.0	Marshall	Marshall
27	5.4	Chaska	Chaska
28	5.3	Saint Cloud	Saint Cloud
29	5.1	Fridley	Fridley
30	4.6	South Saint Paul	S Saint Paul
30	4.6	Waseca	Waseca
32	4.2	Eden Prairie	Eden Prairie
33	4.0	Spring Lake Park	Spring Lake Pk
34	3.8	Anoka-Hennepin	Coon Rapids
34	3.8	North Saint Paul-Maplewood	Maplewood
36	3.4	Saint Peter	Saint Peter
37	3.0	Rosemount-Apple Valley-Eagan	Rosemount
37	3.0	Winona Area Public Schools	Winona
39	2.9	Hutchinson	Hutchinson
40	2.8	Mankato	Mankato
40	2.8	White Bear Lake	White Bear Lake
42	2.5	Inver Grove	Inver Grove Hgts
43	2.2	Rockford	Rockford
44	2.1	Edina	Edina
44	2.1	Prior Lake	Prior Lake
46	2.0	East Grand Forks	E Grand Forks
46	2.0	Farmington	Farmington
48	1.8	North Branch	North Branch
49	1.7	Redwood Falls Area Schools	Redwood Falls
49	1.7	Staples-Motley	Staples
51	1.5	Chisago Lakes	Lindstrom
52	1.4	Mounds View	Roseville
52	1.4	Saint Francis	Saint Francis
54	1.3	Monticello	Monticello
55	1.2	Lakeville	Lakeville
55	1.2	Litchfield	Litchfield
57	1.1	Kasson-Mantorville	Kasson
57	1.1	Red Wing	Red Wing
59	1.0	Big Lake	Big Lake
59	1.0	Elk River	Elk River
59	1.0	Perham	Perham
59	1.0	Westonka	Mound
63	0.9	Becker	Becker
63	0.9	Cambridge-Isanti	Cambridge
65	0.8	Intermediate SD 287	Plymouth
65	0.8	Rocori	Cold Spring
65	0.8	South Washington County	Cottage Grove
68	0.7	Albany	Albany
68	0.7	Buffalo	Buffalo
68	0.7	Centennial	Circle Pines
68	0.7	Duluth	Duluth
68	0.7	Northfield	Northfield
73	0.6	Mahtomedi	Mahtomedi
73	0.6	Minnetonka	Excelsior
73	0.6	Orono	Long Lake
73	0.6	Stillwater	Stillwater
77	0.5	Montevideo	Montevideo
77	0.5	New Ulm	New Ulm
77	0.5	Waconia	Waconia
80	0.4	Dassel-Cokato	Cokato
80	0.4	Forest Lake	Forest Lake
80	0.4	Little Falls	Little Falls
80	0.4	Saint Michael-Albertville	Saint Michael
84	0.3	Fairmont Area Schools	Fairmont
84	0.3	Hastings	Hastings
84	0.3	Thief River Falls	Thief River Fls
84	0.3	Virginia	Virginia
88	0.2	Annandale	Annandale
88	0.2	Hibbing	Hibbing
88	0.2	Sartell	Sartell

88	0.2	Stewartville	Stewartville
92	0.1	Alexandria	Alexandria
92	0.1	Fergus Falls	Fergus Falls
92	0.1	Lake Superior	Two Harbors
92	0.1	Minnewaska	Glenwood
92	0.1	Mora	Mora
92	0.1	New London-Spicer	New London
92	0.1	Pine City	Pine City
92	0.1	Princeton	Princeton
92	0.1	Roseau	Roseau
92	0.1	Wayzata	Wayzata
102	0.0	Sauk Rapids	Sauk Rapids
103	0.0	Bemidji	Bemidji
103	0.0	Brainerd	Brainerd
103	0.0	Byron	Byron
103	0.0	Cloquet	Cloquet
103	0.0	Crosby-Ironton	Crosby
103	0.0	Delano	Delano
103	0.0	Detroit Lakes	Detroit Lakes
103	0.0	Foley	Foley
103	0.0	Grand Rapids	Grand Rapids
103	0.0	Hermantown	Duluth
103	0.0	Lacrescent-Hokah	Lacrescent
103	0.0	Milaca	Milaca
103	0.0	New Prague Area Schools	New Prague
103	0.0	Park Rapids	Park Rapids
103	0.0	Proctor	Proctor
103	0.0	Saint Anthony-New Brighton	Saint Anthony
103	0.0	Saint Louis County	Virginia
120	n/a	Minneapolis Area Office	Minneapolis

Migrant Students

Rank	Percent	District Name	City
1	3.3	Crookston	Crookston
1	3.3	Willmar	Willmar
3	0.8	Glencoe-Silver Lake	Glencoe
3	0.8	Moorhead	Moorhead
5	0.2	Owatonna	Owatonna
5	0.2	Saint Paul	Saint Paul
7	0.0	Rochester	Rochester
8	0.0	Albany	Albany
8	0.0	Albert Lea	Albert Lea
8	0.0	Alexandria	Alexandria
8	0.0	Annandale	Annandale
8	0.0	Anoka-Hennepin	Coon Rapids
8	0.0	Austin	Austin
8	0.0	Becker	Becker
8	0.0	Bemidji	Bemidji
8	0.0	Big Lake	Big Lake
8	0.0	Bloomington	Bloomington
8	0.0	Brainerd	Brainerd
8	0.0	Brooklyn Center	Brooklyn Center
8	0.0	Buffalo	Buffalo
8	0.0	Burnsville	Burnsville
8	0.0	Byron	Byron
8	0.0	Cambridge-Isanti	Cambridge
8	0.0	Centennial	Circle Pines
8	0.0	Chaska	Chaska
8	0.0	Chisago Lakes	Lindstrom
8	0.0	Cloquet	Cloquet
8	0.0	Columbia Heights	Columbia Hgts
8	0.0	Crosby-Ironton	Crosby
8	0.0	Dassel-Cokato	Cokato
8	0.0	Delano	Delano
8	0.0	Detroit Lakes	Detroit Lakes
8	0.0	Duluth	Duluth
8	0.0	East Grand Forks	E Grand Forks
8	0.0	Eden Prairie	Eden Prairie
8	0.0	Edina	Edina
8	0.0	Elk River	Elk River
8	0.0	Fairmont Area Schools	Fairmont
8	0.0	Faribault	Faribault
8	0.0	Farmington	Farmington
8	0.0	Fergus Falls	Fergus Falls
8	0.0	Foley	Foley
8	0.0	Forest Lake	Forest Lake
8	0.0	Fridley	Fridley
8	0.0	Grand Rapids	Grand Rapids
8	0.0	Hastings	Hastings
8	0.0	Hermantown	Duluth
8	0.0	Hibbing	Hibbing
8	0.0	Hopkins	Hopkins
8	0.0	Hutchinson	Hutchinson
8	0.0	Intermediate SD 287	Plymouth
8	0.0	Inver Grove	Inver Grove Hgts
8	0.0	Kasson-Mantorville	Kasson
8	0.0	Lacrescent-Hokah	Lacrescent
8	0.0	Lake Superior	Two Harbors
8	0.0	Lakeville	Lakeville
8	0.0	Litchfield	Litchfield
8	0.0	Little Falls	Little Falls
8	0.0	Mahtomedi	Mahtomedi
8	0.0	Mankato	Mankato
8	0.0	Marshall	Marshall
8	0.0	Melrose	Melrose
8	0.0	Milaca	Milaca
8	0.0	Minneapolis	Minneapolis
8	0.0	Minnetonka	Excelsior
8	0.0	Minnewaska	Glenwood
8	0.0	Montevideo	Montevideo
8	0.0	Monticello	Monticello
8	0.0	Mora	Mora
8	0.0	Mounds View	Roseville
8	0.0	New London-Spicer	New London
8	0.0	New Prague Area Schools	New Prague
8	0.0	New Ulm	New Ulm
8	0.0	North Branch	North Branch
8	0.0	North Saint Paul-Maplewood	Maplewood
8	0.0	Northfield	Northfield
8	0.0	Orono	Long Lake
8	0.0	Osseo	Osseo
8	0.0	Park Rapids	Park Rapids
8	0.0	Perham	Perham
8	0.0	Pine City	Pine City
8	0.0	Princeton	Princeton
8	0.0	Prior Lake	Prior Lake
8	0.0	Proctor	Proctor
8	0.0	Red Wing	Red Wing
8	0.0	Redwood Falls Area Schools	Redwood Falls
8	0.0	Richfield	Richfield
8	0.0	Robbinsdale	New Hope
8	0.0	Rockford	Rockford
8	0.0	Rocori	Cold Spring
8	0.0	Roseau	Roseau
8	0.0	Rosemount-Apple Valley-Eagan	Rosemount
8	0.0	Roseville	Roseville
8	0.0	Saint Anthony-New Brighton	Saint Anthony
8	0.0	Saint Cloud	Saint Cloud
8	0.0	Saint Francis	Saint Francis
8	0.0	Saint Louis County	Virginia
8	0.0	Saint Louis Park	St Louis Park
8	0.0	Saint Michael-Albertville	Saint Michael
8	0.0	Saint Peter	Saint Peter
8	0.0	Sartell	Sartell
8	0.0	Sauk Rapids	Sauk Rapids
8	0.0	Shakopee	Shakopee
8	0.0	South Saint Paul	S Saint Paul
8	0.0	South Washington County	Cottage Grove
8	0.0	Spring Lake Park	Spring Lake Pk
8	0.0	Staples-Motley	Staples
8	0.0	Stewartville	Stewartville
8	0.0	Stillwater	Stillwater
8	0.0	Thief River Falls	Thief River Fls
8	0.0	Virginia	Virginia
8	0.0	W Saint Paul-Mendota Height-Eagan	Mendota Heights
8	0.0	Waconia	Waconia
8	0.0	Waseca	Waseca
8	0.0	Wayzata	Wayzata
8	0.0	Westonka	Mound
8	0.0	White Bear Lake	White Bear Lake
8	0.0	Winona Area Public Schools	Winona
8	0.0	Worthington	Worthington
120	n/a	Minneapolis Area Office	Minneapolis

Students Eligible for Free Lunch

Rank	Percent	District Name	City
1	58.4	Minneapolis	Minneapolis
2	53.2	Saint Paul	Saint Paul
3	42.4	Brooklyn Center	Brooklyn Center
4	34.7	Staples-Motley	Staples
5	33.9	Columbia Heights	Columbia Hgts
6	33.5	Worthington	Worthington
7	33.3	Bemidji	Bemidji
8	31.9	Willmar	Willmar
9	30.5	Park Rapids	Park Rapids
10	28.0	Crookston	Crookston
11	26.7	Crosby-Ironton	Crosby
12	26.4	Duluth	Duluth
13	25.8	Austin	Austin
14	25.7	Faribault	Faribault
15	25.5	Fridley	Fridley
16	25.3	Richfield	Richfield
17	24.8	Fairmont Area Schools	Fairmont
18	24.0	Virginia	Virginia
19	23.9	Pine City	Pine City
20	23.5	Saint Louis County	Virginia
21	23.4	Albert Lea	Albert Lea
22	23.1	Little Falls	Little Falls
23	22.8	Detroit Lakes	Detroit Lakes
24	22.5	Cloquet	Cloquet
24	22.5	Moorhead	Moorhead
26	22.3	Montevideo	Montevideo
27	22.2	Hibbing	Hibbing
28	21.8	Minnewaska	Glenwood
29	21.5	Grand Rapids	Grand Rapids
30	21.1	Saint Cloud	Saint Cloud
31	21.0	Brainerd	Brainerd
31	21.0	Milaca	Milaca
31	21.0	Redwood Falls Area Schools	Redwood Falls
31	21.0	Winona Area Public Schools	Winona
35	20.9	East Grand Forks	E Grand Forks
36	20.4	Mora	Mora
37	20.0	Melrose	Melrose
38	19.0	Thief River Falls	Thief River Fls
39	18.8	Perham	Perham
40	18.6	Marshall	Marshall
40	18.6	Saint Peter	Saint Peter
42	18.5	Mankato	Mankato
43	18.4	South Saint Paul	S Saint Paul
44	18.3	Waseca	Waseca
45	18.0	Rochester	Rochester
46	17.3	Dassel-Cokato	Cokato
46	17.3	Robbinsdale	New Hope
48	16.7	Osseo	Osseo
49	16.4	Litchfield	Litchfield
50	15.8	Glencoe-Silver Lake	Glencoe
51	15.7	Owatonna	Owatonna
52	15.6	Saint Louis Park	St Louis Park
53	15.4	Bloomington	Bloomington
54	15.3	W Saint Paul-Mendota Height-Eagan	Mendota Heights
55	14.7	Shakopee	Shakopee
55	14.7	Spring Lake Park	Spring Lake Pk
57	14.4	North Saint Paul-Maplewood	Maplewood
58	14.2	Lake Superior	Two Harbors
59	14.1	Foley	Foley
60	14.0	Inver Grove	Inver Grove Hgts
61	13.8	New London-Spicer	New London
62	13.6	Red Wing	Red Wing
63	13.4	Annandale	Annandale
64	13.1	Fergus Falls	Fergus Falls
65	12.9	Roseville	Roseville
66	12.8	Cambridge-Isanti	Cambridge
66	12.8	New Ulm	New Ulm
66	12.8	North Branch	North Branch
69	12.7	Proctor	Proctor
70	12.6	Hutchinson	Hutchinson
70	12.6	Roseau	Roseau
72	12.4	Rockford	Rockford
73	12.2	Alexandria	Alexandria
74	12.1	Princeton	Princeton
75	11.9	Saint Francis	Saint Francis
76	11.8	Burnsville	Burnsville
77	11.7	Sauk Rapids	Sauk Rapids
78	11.0	Anoka-Hennepin	Coon Rapids
79	10.7	Northfield	Northfield
80	10.6	Buffalo	Buffalo
81	10.5	Albany	Albany
81	10.5	Hopkins	Hopkins
81	10.5	Mounds View	Roseville
84	10.3	Rocori	Cold Spring
85	10.2	Big Lake	Big Lake
85	10.2	White Bear Lake	White Bear Lake
87	8.6	Monticello	Monticello
88	8.3	Forest Lake	Forest Lake
88	8.3	Lacrescent-Hokah	Lacrescent
90	8.2	Hastings	Hastings
91	7.8	Westonka	Mound
92	7.5	Chisago Lakes	Lindstrom
92	7.5	South Washington County	Cottage Grove
94	7.4	Becker	Becker
95	7.3	Stewartville	Stewartville
96	7.2	Chaska	Chaska
97	7.1	Kasson-Mantorville	Kasson
98	6.7	Centennial	Circle Pines
99	6.5	Hermantown	Duluth
100	6.3	Elk River	Elk River
101	6.2	Intermediate SD 287	Plymouth
102	6.1	Eden Prairie	Eden Prairie
103	5.8	Wayzata	Wayzata
104	5.7	Rosemount-Apple Valley-Eagan	Rosemount
104	5.7	Saint Anthony-New Brighton	Saint Anthony
106	5.3	Byron	Byron
106	5.3	Stillwater	Stillwater
108	5.1	Farmington	Farmington
109	4.7	Waconia	Waconia
110	4.3	New Prague Area Schools	New Prague
110	4.3	Prior Lake	Prior Lake
110	4.3	Saint Michael-Albertville	Saint Michael
113	4.0	Sartell	Sartell
114	3.3	Edina	Edina
114	3.3	Lakeville	Lakeville
116	2.9	Delano	Delano
116	2.9	Mahtomedi	Mahtomedi
118	2.1	Orono	Long Lake
119	1.7	Minnetonka	Excelsior
120	n/a	Minneapolis Area Office	Minneapolis

Students Eligible for Reduced-Price Lunch

Rank	Percent	District Name	City
1	15.9	Staples-Motley	Staples
2	14.4	Park Rapids	Park Rapids
3	13.5	Brooklyn Center	Brooklyn Center
4	13.1	Little Falls	Little Falls
5	12.3	Minnewaska	Glenwood
6	12.2	Montevideo	Montevideo
6	12.2	Perham	Perham
8	11.7	Saint Paul	Saint Paul
9	11.5	Crosby-Ironton	Crosby
10	11.3	Melrose	Melrose
10	11.3	Mora	Mora
12	11.2	Roseau	Roseau
13	11.1	Pine City	Pine City
14	10.8	Crookston	Crookston
15	10.6	Brainerd	Brainerd
15	10.6	Worthington	Worthington
17	10.5	Saint Louis County	Virginia
18	10.3	Austin	Austin
19	10.1	Detroit Lakes	Detroit Lakes
20	10.0	Redwood Falls Area Schools	Redwood Falls
21	9.9	Alexandria	Alexandria
22	9.4	Faribault	Faribault
23	9.3	Foley	Foley
23	9.3	Mankato	Mankato
23	9.3	Thief River Falls	Thief River Fls
23	9.3	Winona Area Public Schools	Winona
27	9.2	Fridley	Fridley
27	9.2	Litchfield	Litchfield
27	9.2	Milaca	Milaca
30	9.1	East Grand Forks	E Grand Forks
30	9.1	Richfield	Richfield
30	9.1	South Saint Paul	S Saint Paul
33	9.0	Marshall	Marshall
34	8.9	Albert Lea	Albert Lea
34	8.9	Buffalo	Buffalo
34	8.9	Lake Superior	Two Harbors
34	8.9	Minneapolis	Minneapolis
38	8.8	Glencoe-Silver Lake	Glencoe
38	8.8	Proctor	Proctor
40	8.7	Fairmont Area Schools	Fairmont
41	8.5	Sauk Rapids	Sauk Rapids
42	8.4	Cloquet	Cloquet
42	8.4	Grand Rapids	Grand Rapids
42	8.4	Virginia	Virginia
45	8.3	New London-Spicer	New London
45	8.3	Willmar	Willmar
47	8.2	Robbinsdale	New Hope
48	8.0	Annandale	Annandale
49	7.9	Cambridge-Isanti	Cambridge
49	7.9	Columbia Heights	Columbia Hgts
49	7.9	North Saint Paul-Maplewood	Maplewood
52	7.6	Duluth	Duluth
52	7.6	Waseca	Waseca
54	7.5	Rocori	Cold Spring
55	7.2	Saint Cloud	Saint Cloud
55	7.2	Spring Lake Park	Spring Lake Pk
57	7.1	Albany	Albany
57	7.1	Bemidji	Bemidji
59	7.0	W Saint Paul-Mendota Height-Eagan	Mendota Heights
60	6.9	Hibbing	Hibbing
61	6.8	Bloomington	Bloomington
62	6.6	Inver Grove	Inver Grove Hgts
62	6.6	Princeton	Princeton
62	6.6	Rockford	Rockford
65	6.5	Osseo	Osseo
65	6.5	Stewartville	Stewartville
67	6.4	Dassel-Cokato	Cokato
67	6.4	New Ulm	New Ulm
69	6.2	Big Lake	Big Lake
69	6.2	Burnsville	Burnsville
69	6.2	North Branch	North Branch
69	6.2	Roseville	Roseville
73	6.1	Anoka-Hennepin	Coon Rapids
73	6.1	Northfield	Northfield
75	6.0	Shakopee	Shakopee
76	5.7	Owatonna	Owatonna
76	5.7	Saint Francis	Saint Francis
78	5.5	Forest Lake	Forest Lake
79	5.4	Chisago Lakes	Lindstrom
80	5.3	Monticello	Monticello
80	5.3	Rochester	Rochester
80	5.3	Saint Peter	Saint Peter
83	5.2	Fergus Falls	Fergus Falls
83	5.2	Moorhead	Moorhead
85	5.1	Saint Louis Park	St Louis Park
86	5.0	Hermantown	Duluth
87	4.9	Becker	Becker
87	4.9	Westonka	Mound
89	4.7	Delano	Delano
89	4.7	Hastings	Hastings
89	4.7	Mounds View	Roseville
92	4.4	Elk River	Elk River
92	4.4	White Bear Lake	White Bear Lake
94	4.2	New Prague Area Schools	New Prague
95	4.1	Lacrescent-Hokah	Lacrescent
96	3.8	Red Wing	Red Wing
97	3.7	Farmington	Farmington
97	3.7	Saint Anthony-New Brighton	Saint Anthony
99	3.5	Centennial	Circle Pines
99	3.5	Kasson-Mantorville	Kasson
99	3.5	Sartell	Sartell
102	3.4	Hutchinson	Hutchinson
102	3.4	Waconia	Waconia
104	3.3	Byron	Byron
105	3.1	Hopkins	Hopkins
106	2.9	South Washington County	Cottage Grove
107	2.8	Chaska	Chaska
107	2.8	Saint Michael-Albertville	Saint Michael
107	2.8	Stillwater	Stillwater
110	2.7	Rosemount-Apple Valley-Eagan	Rosemount
111	2.6	Eden Prairie	Eden Prairie
112	2.5	Wayzata	Wayzata
113	2.4	Prior Lake	Prior Lake
114	2.0	Intermediate SD 287	Plymouth
115	1.6	Lakeville	Lakeville
116	1.4	Orono	Long Lake
117	1.3	Minnetonka	Excelsior
118	1.2	Edina	Edina
118	1.2	Mahtomedi	Mahtomedi
120	n/a	Minneapolis Area Office	Minneapolis

Student/Teacher Ratio

Rank	Ratio	District Name	City
1	20.5	Elk River	Elk River
2	20.0	Stillwater	Stillwater
2	20.0	White Bear Lake	White Bear Lake
4	19.8	Saint Francis	Saint Francis
5	19.5	Hastings	Hastings
6	19.3	North Saint Paul-Maplewood	Maplewood
6	19.3	Spring Lake Park	Spring Lake Pk
8	19.1	Eden Prairie	Eden Prairie
8	19.1	Virginia	Virginia
10	18.8	Inver Grove	Inver Grove Hgts
11	18.6	Wayzata	Wayzata
12	18.5	Anoka-Hennepin	Coon Rapids
12	18.5	Centennial	Circle Pines
12	18.5	North Branch	North Branch
12	18.5	Waconia	Waconia
16	18.4	Delano	Delano
16	18.4	Princeton	Princeton
18	18.3	Hibbing	Hibbing
18	18.3	Monticello	Monticello
18	18.3	Osseo	Osseo
18	18.3	Roseau	Roseau
22	18.2	Buffalo	Buffalo
22	18.2	Hermantown	Duluth
22	18.2	New Prague Area Schools	New Prague
22	18.2	Prior Lake	Prior Lake
26	18.1	Forest Lake	Forest Lake
26	18.1	Mounds View	Roseville
28	18.0	Cambridge-Isanti	Cambridge
28	18.0	Roseville	Roseville
30	17.9	Chisago Lakes	Lindstrom
30	17.9	Saint Michael-Albertville	Saint Michael
32	17.8	Becker	Becker
32	17.8	South Saint Paul	S Saint Paul
34	17.7	Burnsville	Burnsville
34	17.7	Dassel-Cokato	Cokato
34	17.7	Farmington	Farmington
34	17.7	Mahtomedi	Mahtomedi
38	17.6	Red Wing	Red Wing
38	17.6	Robbinsdale	New Hope
38	17.6	Rochester	Rochester
38	17.6	Stewartville	Stewartville
42	17.5	Albert Lea	Albert Lea
42	17.5	Bloomington	Bloomington
42	17.5	Chaska	Chaska
42	17.5	Fridley	Fridley
42	17.5	Grand Rapids	Grand Rapids
47	17.4	Cloquet	Cloquet
47	17.4	Edina	Edina
47	17.4	Saint Anthony-New Brighton	Saint Anthony
50	17.3	Brooklyn Center	Brooklyn Center
50	17.3	Owatonna	Owatonna
50	17.3	Shakopee	Shakopee
53	17.2	Annandale	Annandale
53	17.2	Lakeville	Lakeville
53	17.2	Rocori	Cold Spring
56	17.1	Orono	Long Lake
57	17.0	Big Lake	Big Lake
57	17.0	Kasson-Mantorville	Kasson
57	17.0	Mankato	Mankato
57	17.0	Sartell	Sartell
61	16.9	Lacrescent-Hokah	Lacrescent
61	16.9	Lake Superior	Two Harbors
61	16.9	South Washington County	Cottage Grove
64	16.8	Rockford	Rockford
65	16.7	Brainerd	Brainerd
66	16.6	Crookston	Crookston
66	16.6	Richfield	Richfield
66	16.6	Sauk Rapids	Sauk Rapids
69	16.5	Columbia Heights	Columbia Hgts
70	16.4	Byron	Byron
70	16.4	Glencoe-Silver Lake	Glencoe
70	16.4	Hutchinson	Hutchinson
70	16.4	Minnetonka	Excelsior
70	16.4	Pine City	Pine City
75	16.3	Proctor	Proctor
75	16.3	Rosemount-Apple Valley-Eagan	Rosemount
75	16.3	Westonka	Mound
78	16.2	Austin	Austin
78	16.2	Bemidji	Bemidji
78	16.2	Waseca	Waseca
81	16.1	Litchfield	Litchfield
81	16.1	Mora	Mora
83	16.0	New London-Spicer	New London
84	15.9	Alexandria	Alexandria
84	15.9	Faribault	Faribault
84	15.9	Little Falls	Little Falls
84	15.9	Moorhead	Moorhead
84	15.9	Park Rapids	Park Rapids
89	15.7	Fairmont Area Schools	Fairmont
90	15.6	Milaca	Milaca
90	15.6	Saint Cloud	Saint Cloud
92	15.5	Fergus Falls	Fergus Falls
92	15.5	Perham	Perham
94	15.4	Albany	Albany
94	15.4	W Saint Paul-Mendota Height-Eagan	Mendota Heights
96	15.3	New Ulm	New Ulm
97	15.2	Duluth	Duluth
97	15.2	Northfield	Northfield
97	15.2	Redwood Falls Area Schools	Redwood Falls
100	15.0	Crosby-Ironton	Crosby
100	15.0	Hopkins	Hopkins
100	15.0	Winona Area Public Schools	Winona
103	14.9	Saint Paul	Saint Paul
104	14.8	Foley	Foley
104	14.8	Saint Peter	Saint Peter
106	14.7	Minneapolis	Minneapolis
106	14.7	Thief River Falls	Thief River Fls
108	14.6	Montevideo	Montevideo
108	14.6	Willmar	Willmar
108	14.6	Worthington	Worthington
111	14.5	Melrose	Melrose
111	14.5	Saint Louis Park	St Louis Park
113	14.4	East Grand Forks	E Grand Forks
113	14.4	Minnewaska	Glenwood
115	13.9	Marshall	Marshall
116	13.8	Staples-Motley	Staples
117	13.7	Detroit Lakes	Detroit Lakes
118	13.1	Saint Louis County	Virginia
119	8.7	Intermediate SD 287	Plymouth
120	n/a	Minneapolis Area Office	Minneapolis

Student/Librarian Ratio

Rank	Ratio	District Name	City
1	8,532.9	Saint Francis	Saint Francis
2	1,876.8	Winona Area Public Schools	Winona
3	1,859.0	Annandale	Annandale
4	1,777.0	Glencoe-Silver Lake	Glencoe
5	1,752.8	Willmar	Willmar
6	1,716.0	South Saint Paul	S Saint Paul
7	1,698.0	Lake Superior	Two Harbors
8	1,669.7	Owatonna	Owatonna
9	1,628.0	Elk River	Elk River
10	1,599.2	Grand Rapids	Grand Rapids
11	1,571.0	Hutchinson	Hutchinson
12	1,543.5	Little Falls	Little Falls
13	1,515.0	Minnewaska	Glenwood
14	1,505.0	Roseau	Roseau
15	1,504.0	Staples-Motley	Staples
16	1,500.0	Byron	Byron
17	1,462.3	Anoka-Hennepin	Coon Rapids
18	1,452.9	Mounds View	Roseville
19	1,392.0	Richfield	Richfield
20	1,355.3	Marshall	Marshall
21	1,305.1	Eden Prairie	Eden Prairie
22	1,265.1	Burnsville	Burnsville
23	1,233.6	Stillwater	Stillwater
24	1,171.2	Centennial	Circle Pines
25	1,163.5	Waconia	Waconia
26	1,113.4	North Branch	North Branch
27	1,082.3	Cloquet	Cloquet

28	1,064.5	Spring Lake Park	Spring Lake Pk
29	1,060.9	Albert Lea	Albert Lea
30	1,032.8	Austin	Austin
31	1,026.7	South Washington County	Cottage Grove
32	1,021.1	Stewartville	Stewartville
33	1,017.4	Rosemount-Apple Valley-Eagan	Rosemount
34	1,010.0	Big Lake	Big Lake
35	984.5	Detroit Lakes	Detroit Lakes
36	981.5	Hermantown	Duluth
37	981.0	Litchfield	Litchfield
38	973.2	Cambridge-Isanti	Cambridge
39	972.0	Milaca	Milaca
40	964.2	White Bear Lake	White Bear Lake
41	954.6	Hastings	Hastings
42	953.9	Northfield	Northfield
43	936.5	Proctor	Proctor
44	933.3	Lacrescent-Hokah	Lacrescent
45	933.0	Kasson-Mantorville	Kasson
46	927.6	Buffalo	Buffalo
47	926.6	Rochester	Rochester
48	916.5	Fergus Falls	Fergus Falls
49	913.2	Saint Paul	Saint Paul
50	912.5	Fairmont Area Schools	Fairmont
51	912.3	Sartell	Sartell
52	910.0	Park Rapids	Park Rapids
53	886.8	Waseca	Waseca
54	884.5	New London-Spicer	New London
55	881.0	Rockford	Rockford
56	874.0	Virginia	Virginia
57	871.0	Pine City	Pine City
58	866.0	Brooklyn Center	Brooklyn Center
59	858.9	Robbinsdale	New Hope
60	843.4	Minnetonka	Excelsior
61	838.8	Princeton	Princeton
62	837.8	Saint Michael-Albertville	Saint Michael
63	833.7	Red Wing	Red Wing
64	830.5	Foley	Foley
65	829.0	Perham	Perham
66	828.7	Orono	Long Lake
67	828.6	Prior Lake	Prior Lake
68	812.5	Albany	Albany
69	801.8	Bemidji	Bemidji
70	795.9	Edina	Edina
71	794.5	Wayzata	Wayzata
72	793.8	Faribault	Faribault
73	792.4	Moorhead	Moorhead
74	784.8	Monticello	Monticello
74	784.8	North Saint Paul-Maplewood	Maplewood
76	781.1	Lakeville	Lakeville
77	780.4	Chaska	Chaska
78	778.0	Worthington	Worthington
79	773.3	Mahtomedi	Mahtomedi
80	766.5	Melrose	Melrose
81	765.5	Forest Lake	Forest Lake
82	764.0	Montevideo	Montevideo
82	764.0	Saint Anthony-New Brighton	Saint Anthony
84	760.7	Shakopee	Shakopee
85	759.2	Saint Peter	Saint Peter
86	757.5	Columbia Heights	Columbia Hgts
87	756.8	Saint Cloud	Saint Cloud
88	756.5	Crosby-Ironton	Crosby
89	750.5	Redwood Falls Area Schools	Redwood Falls
90	734.2	Hopkins	Hopkins
91	708.3	Roseville	Roseville
92	707.7	Thief River Falls	Thief River Fls
93	707.5	Duluth	Duluth
94	705.2	Chisago Lakes	Lindstrom
95	704.0	Osseo	Osseo
96	703.4	W Saint Paul-Mendota Height-Eagan	Mendota Heights
97	700.8	Fridley	Fridley
98	694.9	Alexandria	Alexandria
99	676.3	New Prague Area Schools	New Prague
100	663.9	Brainerd	Brainerd
101	658.5	Inver Grove	Inver Grove Hgts
102	649.7	Mora	Mora
103	641.7	Delano	Delano
104	640.1	Bloomington	Bloomington
105	625.5	Minneapolis	Minneapolis
106	605.4	Saint Louis Park	St Louis Park
107	603.8	New Ulm	New Ulm
108	589.5	Becker	Becker
109	584.6	Farmington	Farmington
110	571.4	Sauk Rapids	Sauk Rapids
111	566.0	Dassel-Cokato	Cokato
112	554.8	Hibbing	Hibbing
113	550.3	Westonka	Mound
114	522.0	Rocori	Cold Spring
115	517.5	Mankato	Mankato
116	395.0	East Grand Forks	E Grand Forks
117	383.2	Saint Louis County	Virginia
118	0.0	Crookston	Crookston
118	0.0	Intermediate SD 287	Plymouth
120	n/a	Minneapolis Area Office	Minneapolis

Student/Counselor Ratio

Rank	Ratio	District Name	City
1	2,747.4	Prior Lake	Prior Lake
2	2,264.0	Dassel-Cokato	Cokato
3	1,944.0	Milaca	Milaca
4	1,732.0	Brooklyn Center	Brooklyn Center
5	1,593.0	Crookston	Crookston
6	1,533.0	Melrose	Melrose
7	1,532.7	Anoka-Hennepin	Coon Rapids
8	1,528.0	Montevideo	Montevideo
9	1,505.0	Roseau	Roseau
10	1,504.0	Staples-Motley	Staples
11	1,347.1	White Bear Lake	White Bear Lake
12	1,308.0	Monticello	Monticello
13	1,194.6	Saint Francis	Saint Francis
14	1,191.8	Wayzata	Wayzata
15	1,179.0	Becker	Becker
16	1,141.0	Shakopee	Shakopee
17	1,128.2	Lakeville	Lakeville
18	1,090.9	Minneapolis	Minneapolis
19	1,085.3	Elk River	Elk River
20	1,084.4	Burnsville	Burnsville
21	1,068.8	Willmar	Willmar
22	1,062.5	Roseville	Roseville
23	1,042.4	Bemidji	Bemidji
24	1,032.8	Austin	Austin
25	1,024.7	Pine City	Pine City
26	1,010.0	Big Lake	Big Lake
27	1,001.8	Owatonna	Owatonna
28	981.0	Litchfield	Litchfield
29	974.5	Mora	Mora
30	974.3	North Branch	North Branch
31	962.5	Delano	Delano
32	929.5	Annandale	Annandale
33	928.3	Albert Lea	Albert Lea
34	912.9	Brainerd	Brainerd
35	912.5	Fairmont Area Schools	Fairmont
36	912.3	Sartell	Sartell
37	910.0	Park Rapids	Park Rapids
38	907.2	Rosemount-Apple Valley-Eagan	Rosemount
39	901.7	New Prague Area Schools	New Prague
40	888.5	Glencoe-Silver Lake	Glencoe
41	884.5	New London-Spicer	New London
42	882.0	Little Falls	Little Falls
43	881.0	Rockford	Rockford
44	874.0	Mounds View	Roseville
44	874.0	Virginia	Virginia
46	850.3	Buffalo	Buffalo
47	850.2	Northfield	Northfield
48	842.0	Eden Prairie	Eden Prairie
49	837.8	Saint Michael-Albertville	Saint Michael
50	835.2	Richfield	Richfield
51	830.5	Foley	Foley
52	829.0	Perham	Perham
53	828.7	Orono	Long Lake
54	820.0	Alexandria	Alexandria
55	818.6	Stillwater	Stillwater
56	812.9	Robbinsdale	New Hope
57	812.5	Albany	Albany
58	795.9	Edina	Edina
59	793.8	Faribault	Faribault
60	790.2	Inver Grove	Inver Grove Hgts
61	775.7	Waconia	Waconia
62	765.5	Forest Lake	Forest Lake
63	759.1	Minnetonka	Excelsior
64	757.5	Columbia Heights	Columbia Hgts
64	757.5	Minnewaska	Glenwood
66	756.5	Crosby-Ironton	Crosby
67	751.6	Farmington	Farmington
68	750.5	Redwood Falls Area Schools	Redwood Falls
69	750.2	Chisago Lakes	Lindstrom
70	749.2	Proctor	Proctor
71	748.6	Cambridge-Isanti	Cambridge
72	736.4	Hastings	Hastings
73	733.7	Westonka	Mound
74	733.3	South Washington County	Cottage Grove
75	720.0	Sauk Rapids	Sauk Rapids
76	708.6	Osseo	Osseo
77	694.8	Duluth	Duluth
78	693.5	Hibbing	Hibbing
79	692.8	Waseca	Waseca
80	677.9	Saint Peter	Saint Peter
81	674.0	North Saint Paul-Maplewood	Maplewood
82	671.0	Princeton	Princeton
83	668.1	Bloomington	Bloomington
84	631.2	Mahtomedi	Mahtomedi
85	623.2	Saint Louis Park	St Louis Park
86	612.7	Stewartville	Stewartville
87	602.6	Grand Rapids	Grand Rapids
88	589.6	Saint Paul	Saint Paul
89	585.6	Centennial	Circle Pines
90	583.5	Worthington	Worthington
91	576.0	Marshall	Marshall
92	572.9	Rocori	Cold Spring
93	566.0	Lake Superior	Two Harbors
94	560.9	Hermantown	Duluth
95	560.0	Lacrescent-Hokah	Lacrescent
96	557.4	Chaska	Chaska
97	554.7	Moorhead	Moorhead
98	550.6	East Grand Forks	E Grand Forks
99	532.3	Spring Lake Park	Spring Lake Pk
100	530.8	Thief River Falls	Thief River Fls
101	523.7	Hutchinson	Hutchinson
102	519.1	Detroit Lakes	Detroit Lakes
103	509.3	Saint Anthony-New Brighton	Saint Anthony
104	503.5	W Saint Paul-Mendota Height-Eagan	Mendota Heights
105	500.0	Byron	Byron
106	495.5	Rochester	Rochester
107	481.5	Fergus Falls	Fergus Falls
108	463.4	Mankato	Mankato
109	462.0	Hopkins	Hopkins
110	458.8	Winona Area Public Schools	Winona
111	440.9	Cloquet	Cloquet
112	432.2	Fridley	Fridley
113	402.5	New Ulm	New Ulm
114	395.4	Saint Louis County	Virginia
115	373.2	Kasson-Mantorville	Kasson
116	367.6	Saint Cloud	Saint Cloud
117	0.0	Intermediate SD 287	Plymouth
117	0.0	Red Wing	Red Wing
117	0.0	South Saint Paul	S Saint Paul
120	n/a	Minneapolis Area Office	Minneapolis

Current Spending per Student in FY2001

Rank	Dollars	District Name	City
1	10,861	Minneapolis	Minneapolis
2	9,285	Saint Paul	Saint Paul
3	9,211	Saint Louis Park	St Louis Park
4	8,755	Saint Louis County	Virginia
5	8,654	Hopkins	Hopkins
6	8,293	Brooklyn Center	Brooklyn Center
7	7,999	Saint Cloud	Saint Cloud
8	7,855	Cloquet	Cloquet
9	7,796	Staples-Motley	Staples
10	7,785	Virginia	Virginia
11	7,762	Saint Anthony-New Brighton	Saint Anthony
12	7,728	Worthington	Worthington
13	7,688	Bemidji	Bemidji
14	7,687	Edina	Edina
15	7,673	Grand Rapids	Grand Rapids
16	7,672	Duluth	Duluth
17	7,647	Willmar	Willmar
18	7,623	Richfield	Richfield
19	7,611	Roseville	Roseville
20	7,555	Mounds View	Roseville
21	7,501	Bloomington	Bloomington
22	7,495	Columbia Heights	Columbia Hgts
23	7,451	Faribault	Faribault
24	7,446	Robbinsdale	New Hope
25	7,434	Burnsville	Burnsville
26	7,365	Fridley	Fridley
27	7,305	Spring Lake Park	Spring Lake Pk
28	7,284	Park Rapids	Park Rapids
29	7,266	Montevideo	Montevideo
30	7,265	Minnetonka	Excelsior
31	7,255	Westonka	Mound
32	7,251	Wayzata	Wayzata
33	7,248	Lake Superior	Two Harbors
34	7,221	Osseo	Osseo
35	7,188	Hibbing	Hibbing
36	7,183	South Saint Paul	S Saint Paul
37	7,178	Rochester	Rochester
38	7,153	W Saint Paul-Mendota Height-Eagan	Mendota Heights
39	7,128	East Grand Forks	E Grand Forks
40	7,080	Shakopee	Shakopee
41	7,055	Brainerd	Brainerd
42	7,044	Waseca	Waseca
43	7,041	Saint Peter	Saint Peter
44	7,010	Orono	Long Lake
45	7,004	Marshall	Marshall
46	7,002	Cambridge-Isanti	Cambridge
47	6,996	Minnewaska	Glenwood
48	6,978	Winona Area Public Schools	Winona
49	6,942	Moorhead	Moorhead
50	6,940	Monticello	Monticello
51	6,934	Red Wing	Red Wing
52	6,933	Forest Lake	Forest Lake
53	6,910	Stillwater	Stillwater
54	6,891	Crookston	Crookston
55	6,883	Hastings	Hastings
56	6,881	Detroit Lakes	Detroit Lakes
57	6,876	Chaska	Chaska
58	6,871	Milaca	Milaca
59	6,859	Mahtomedi	Mahtomedi

60	6,840	Eden Prairie	Eden Prairie
61	6,836	Melrose	Melrose
62	6,822	Thief River Falls	Thief River Fls
63	6,811	Crosby-Ironton	Crosby
64	6,792	Austin	Austin
65	6,783	Inver Grove	Inver Grove Hgts
66	6,758	Proctor	Proctor
67	6,715	Rocori	Cold Spring
68	6,701	Albert Lea	Albert Lea
69	6,692	Mankato	Mankato
70	6,664	Perham	Perham
71	6,660	North Saint Paul-Maplewood	Maplewood
72	6,640	White Bear Lake	White Bear Lake
73	6,629	South Washington County	Cottage Grove
74	6,621	Elk River	Elk River
75	6,620	New Ulm	New Ulm
76	6,616	Buffalo	Buffalo
77	6,595	Owatonna	Owatonna
78	6,590	Little Falls	Little Falls
79	6,579	Anoka-Hennepin	Coon Rapids
80	6,572	Centennial	Circle Pines
81	6,570	Glencoe-Silver Lake	Glencoe
82	6,511	Lacrescent-Hokah	Lacrescent
83	6,490	Alexandria	Alexandria
84	6,453	Saint Francis	Saint Francis
85	6,436	Pine City	Pine City
86	6,435	Princeton	Princeton
87	6,413	Fairmont Area Schools	Fairmont
88	6,411	Litchfield	Litchfield
89	6,405	Sartell	Sartell
90	6,369	Prior Lake	Prior Lake
91	6,363	Annandale	Annandale
92	6,335	Northfield	Northfield
93	6,325	Fergus Falls	Fergus Falls
94	6,320	New London-Spicer	New London
95	6,308	Sauk Rapids	Sauk Rapids
96	6,297	Foley	Foley
97	6,240	Rosemount-Apple Valley-Eagan	Rosemount
98	6,228	Roseau	Roseau
99	6,175	Delano	Delano
100	6,166	Waconia	Waconia
101	6,162	Dassel-Cokato	Cokato
102	6,141	Farmington	Farmington
103	6,076	Hermantown	Duluth
104	6,072	Albany	Albany
105	6,009	Rockford	Rockford
106	5,987	Lakeville	Lakeville
107	5,976	Becker	Becker
107	5,976	Mora	Mora
109	5,906	Stewartville	Stewartville
110	5,880	Saint Michael-Albertville	Saint Michael
111	5,875	North Branch	North Branch
112	5,847	New Prague Area Schools	New Prague
113	5,784	Chisago Lakes	Lindstrom
114	5,760	Hutchinson	Hutchinson
115	5,754	Byron	Byron
116	5,709	Big Lake	Big Lake
117	5,666	Kasson-Mantorville	Kasson
118	n/a	Intermediate SD 287	Plymouth
118	n/a	Minneapolis Area Office	Minneapolis
118	n/a	Redwood Falls Area Schools	Redwood Falls

Number of Diploma Recipients

Rank	Number	District Name	City
1	2,372	Anoka-Hennepin	Coon Rapids
2	2,180	Minneapolis	Minneapolis
3	2,127	Saint Paul	Saint Paul
4	1,865	Rosemount-Apple Valley-Eagan	Rosemount
5	1,342	Osseo	Osseo
6	1,068	Rochester	Rochester
7	1,031	South Washington County	Cottage Grove
8	918	Mounds View	Roseville
9	915	Duluth	Duluth
10	834	Saint Cloud	Saint Cloud
11	831	White Bear Lake	White Bear Lake
12	751	Burnsville	Burnsville
13	709	North Saint Paul-Maplewood	Maplewood
14	706	Eden Prairie	Eden Prairie
15	704	Stillwater	Stillwater
16	693	Robbinsdale	New Hope
17	662	Bloomington	Bloomington
18	656	Hopkins	Hopkins
19	655	Lakeville	Lakeville
20	642	Wayzata	Wayzata
21	606	Mankato	Mankato
22	595	Elk River	Elk River
23	570	Forest Lake	Forest Lake
24	499	Edina	Edina
25	498	Brainerd	Brainerd
25	498	Roseville	Roseville
27	492	Minnetonka	Excelsior
28	431	Hastings	Hastings
29	399	Moorhead	Moorhead
30	390	Chaska	Chaska
31	376	Faribault	Faribault
32	359	Owatonna	Owatonna
33	356	Grand Rapids	Grand Rapids
34	348	Winona Area Public Schools	Winona
35	341	Buffalo	Buffalo
36	340	Bemidji	Bemidji
36	340	Centennial	Circle Pines
38	335	Alexandria	Alexandria
39	334	Cambridge-Isanti	Cambridge
40	315	W Saint Paul-Mendota Height-Eagan	Mendota Heights
41	302	Little Falls	Little Falls
42	297	Northfield	Northfield
42	297	Saint Francis	Saint Francis
44	283	Farmington	Farmington
45	282	Prior Lake	Prior Lake
46	275	Albert Lea	Albert Lea
46	275	Spring Lake Park	Spring Lake Pk
48	274	Austin	Austin
49	269	Willmar	Willmar
50	265	Inver Grove	Inver Grove Hgts
51	263	Red Wing	Red Wing
51	263	South Saint Paul	S Saint Paul
53	261	Richfield	Richfield
54	259	North Branch	North Branch
54	259	Saint Louis Park	St Louis Park
56	251	Fergus Falls	Fergus Falls
57	243	Marshall	Marshall
58	240	Chisago Lakes	Lindstrom
59	237	Monticello	Monticello
60	236	Mahtomedi	Mahtomedi
61	230	Sauk Rapids	Sauk Rapids
62	228	Hutchinson	Hutchinson
63	215	New Ulm	New Ulm
64	213	Columbia Heights	Columbia Hgts
64	213	Detroit Lakes	Detroit Lakes
66	211	Saint Louis County	Virginia
67	208	Hibbing	Hibbing
67	208	New Prague Area Schools	New Prague
69	202	Princeton	Princeton
70	201	Shakopee	Shakopee
71	199	Dassel-Cokato	Cokato
72	197	Cloquet	Cloquet
73	192	Rocori	Cold Spring
73	192	Worthington	Worthington
75	189	Sartell	Sartell
75	189	Thief River Falls	Thief River Fls
77	185	Orono	Long Lake
78	167	Fairmont Area Schools	Fairmont
78	167	Proctor	Proctor
80	166	Saint Michael-Albertville	Saint Michael
81	162	Lacrescent-Hokah	Lacrescent
81	162	Litchfield	Litchfield
83	158	Fridley	Fridley
84	154	Westonka	Mound
85	151	Saint Peter	Saint Peter
85	151	Waseca	Waseca
87	149	Hermantown	Duluth
88	147	Pine City	Pine City
89	146	Albany	Albany
89	146	Mora	Mora
91	140	Lake Superior	Two Harbors
92	139	Crookston	Crookston
92	139	Melrose	Melrose
94	138	Glencoe-Silver Lake	Glencoe
94	138	Perham	Perham
96	137	Minnewaska	Glenwood
97	136	Foley	Foley
98	134	Waconia	Waconia
99	132	Intermediate SD 287	Plymouth
100	130	Virginia	Virginia
101	129	Park Rapids	Park Rapids
101	129	Stewartville	Stewartville
103	125	Big Lake	Big Lake
103	125	New London-Spicer	New London
105	124	Staples-Motley	Staples
106	121	Brooklyn Center	Brooklyn Center
107	120	Roseau	Roseau
108	119	Delano	Delano
108	119	Milaca	Milaca
110	117	Annandale	Annandale
110	117	Becker	Becker
112	116	East Grand Forks	E Grand Forks
112	116	Saint Anthony-New Brighton	Saint Anthony
114	113	Montevideo	Montevideo
115	106	Byron	Byron
116	105	Rockford	Rockford
117	102	Redwood Falls Area Schools	Redwood Falls
118	98	Kasson-Mantorville	Kasson
119	84	Crosby-Ironton	Crosby
120	n/a	Minneapolis Area Office	Minneapolis

High School Drop-out Rate

Rank	Percent	District Name	City
1	14.6	Intermediate SD 287	Plymouth
2	13.7	Minneapolis	Minneapolis
3	10.3	Park Rapids	Park Rapids
4	9.5	Columbia Heights	Columbia Hgts
5	9.4	Grand Rapids	Grand Rapids
6	8.8	Austin	Austin
6	8.8	Saint Paul	Saint Paul
8	8.5	Duluth	Duluth
9	7.6	South Saint Paul	S Saint Paul
10	7.0	Brainerd	Brainerd
11	6.8	Crookston	Crookston
12	6.5	Perham	Perham
13	6.2	Pine City	Pine City
14	5.6	Crosby-Ironton	Crosby
15	5.5	Faribault	Faribault
16	5.4	Spring Lake Park	Spring Lake Pk
17	5.3	Northfield	Northfield
18	5.2	Fergus Falls	Fergus Falls
19	5.0	Richfield	Richfield
20	4.9	Albert Lea	Albert Lea
21	4.8	Hibbing	Hibbing
22	4.7	Saint Cloud	Saint Cloud
23	4.5	Worthington	Worthington
24	4.3	Forest Lake	Forest Lake
25	4.2	Annandale	Annandale
26	4.1	Cloquet	Cloquet
26	4.1	Mankato	Mankato
26	4.1	Red Wing	Red Wing
29	4.0	Anoka-Hennepin	Coon Rapids
29	4.0	Rochester	Rochester
31	3.9	Waseca	Waseca
32	3.8	Shakopee	Shakopee
33	3.7	Brooklyn Center	Brooklyn Center
33	3.7	Elk River	Elk River
33	3.7	North Branch	North Branch
33	3.7	Owatonna	Owatonna
33	3.7	Willmar	Willmar
38	3.6	Mora	Mora
39	3.5	Burnsville	Burnsville
39	3.5	Fairmont Area Schools	Fairmont
39	3.5	Fridley	Fridley
42	3.2	Monticello	Monticello
43	3.1	Little Falls	Little Falls
43	3.1	Winona Area Public Schools	Winona
45	3.0	New London-Spicer	New London
46	2.9	Glencoe-Silver Lake	Glencoe
46	2.9	Hutchinson	Hutchinson
48	2.8	East Grand Forks	E Grand Forks
48	2.8	Marshall	Marshall
48	2.8	Mounds View	Roseville
51	2.7	Lake Superior	Two Harbors
51	2.7	Saint Louis Park	St Louis Park
51	2.7	South Washington County	Cottage Grove
54	2.6	Lakeville	Lakeville
55	2.5	Saint Francis	Saint Francis
56	2.2	Buffalo	Buffalo
56	2.2	Dassel-Cokato	Cokato
56	2.2	Foley	Foley
59	2.1	Westonka	Mound
60	2.0	Bemidji	Bemidji
60	2.0	Centennial	Circle Pines
60	2.0	Lacrescent-Hokah	Lacrescent
60	2.0	Moorhead	Moorhead
60	2.0	W Saint Paul-Mendota Height-Eagan	Mendota Heights
60	2.0	White Bear Lake	White Bear Lake
66	1.9	Chisago Lakes	Lindstrom
66	1.9	Saint Anthony-New Brighton	Saint Anthony
68	1.8	Big Lake	Big Lake
68	1.8	Litchfield	Litchfield
68	1.8	Rosemount-Apple Valley-Eagan	Rosemount
71	1.7	Cambridge-Isanti	Cambridge
71	1.7	North Saint Paul-Maplewood	Maplewood
71	1.7	Osseo	Osseo
74	1.6	Detroit Lakes	Detroit Lakes
74	1.6	Robbinsdale	New Hope
74	1.6	Saint Louis County	Virginia
77	1.5	Inver Grove	Inver Grove Hgts
77	1.5	Kasson-Mantorville	Kasson
77	1.5	Milaca	Milaca
77	1.5	Virginia	Virginia
81	1.4	Saint Peter	Saint Peter
82	1.3	Stillwater	Stillwater
83	1.2	Prior Lake	Prior Lake
83	1.2	Rockford	Rockford
85	1.1	Bloomington	Bloomington
85	1.1	Chaska	Chaska
87	1.0	Albany	Albany
87	1.0	Hopkins	Hopkins
87	1.0	Rocori	Cold Spring
87	1.0	Roseville	Roseville

91	0.9	Stewartville	Stewartville
92	0.8	Eden Prairie	Eden Prairie
92	0.8	Hastings	Hastings
92	0.8	Roseau	Roseau
95	0.7	Mahtomedi	Mahtomedi
95	0.7	Minnetonka	Excelsior
95	0.7	Staples-Motley	Staples
95	0.7	Wayzata	Wayzata
99	0.6	Melrose	Melrose
99	0.6	Princeton	Princeton
99	0.6	Thief River Falls	Thief River Fls
99	0.6	Waconia	Waconia
103	0.5	Delano	Delano
103	0.5	New Ulm	New Ulm
103	0.5	Orono	Long Lake
106	0.4	Saint Michael-Albertville	Saint Michael
107	0.3	Alexandria	Alexandria
107	0.3	Becker	Becker
107	0.3	Farmington	Farmington
107	0.3	Proctor	Proctor
107	0.3	Sauk Rapids	Sauk Rapids
112	0.2	Byron	Byron
112	0.2	Edina	Edina
112	0.2	New Prague Area Schools	New Prague
112	0.2	Sartell	Sartell
116	0.0	Hermantown	Duluth
116	0.0	Minnewaska	Glenwood
116	0.0	Montevideo	Montevideo
119	n/a	Minneapolis Area Office	Minneapolis
119	n/a	Redwood Falls Area Schools	Redwood Falls

Mississippi

Mississippi Public School Educational Profile

Category	Value	Category	Value
Schools *(2002-2003)*	1,048	**Diploma Recipients** *(2002-2003)*	23,740
Instructional Level		White, Non-Hispanic	12,174
Primary	450	Black, Non-Hispanic	11,195
Middle	182	Asian/Pacific Islander	219
High	280	American Indian/Alaskan Native	32
Other Level	136	Hispanic	120
Curriculum		**High School Drop-out Rate** (%) *(2000-2001)*	4.6
Regular	901	White, Non-Hispanic	3.8
Special Education	0	Black, Non-Hispanic	5.6
Vocational	86	Asian/Pacific Islander	1.8
Alternative	61	American Indian/Alaskan Native	3.9
Type		Hispanic	3.6
Magnet	5	**Staff** *(2002-2003)*	66,131.3
Charter	1	Teachers	31,593.2
Title I Eligible	684	Average Salary ($)	35,135
School-wide Title I	602	Librarians/Media Specialists	941.5
Students *(2002-2003)*	492,645	Guidance Counselors	965.7
Gender (%)		**Ratios** *(2002-2003)*	
Male	51.0	Student/Teacher Ratio	15.6 to 1
Female	49.0	Student/Librarian Ratio	523.3 to 1
Race/Ethnicity (%)		Student/Counselor Ratio	510.1 to 1
White, Non-Hispanic	47.3	**Current Spending** *($ per student in FY 2001)*	5,354
Black, Non-Hispanic	50.9	Instruction	3,224
Asian/Pacific Islander	0.7	Support Services	1,781
American Indian/Alaskan Native	0.2	**College Entrance Exam Scores** *(2003)*	
Hispanic	1.0	Scholastic Aptitude Test (SAT)	
Classification (%)		Participation Rate (%)	4
Individual Education Program (IEP)	12.9	Mean SAT I Verbal Score	565
Migrant	0.5	Mean SAT I Math Score	551
English Language Learner (ELL)	0.5	American College Testing Program (ACT)	
Eligible for Free Lunch Program	57.1	Participation Rate (%)	88
Eligible for Reduced-Price Lunch Program	8.2	Average Composite Score	18.7

Note: *For an explanation of data, please refer to the User's Guide in the front of the book; n/a indicates data not available*

Mississippi NAEP 2003 Test Scores

Reading			Mathematics		
Grade/Category	Value	Rank	Grade/Category	Value	Rank
4th Grade			**4th Grade**		
Average Proficiency	205.5 (1.3)	48/51	Average Proficiency	222.9 (1.0)	49/51
Proficiency by Gender/Race/Ethnicity			Proficiency by Gender/Race/Ethnicity		
Male	202.3 (1.5)	46/51	Male	223.0 (1.2)	50/51
Female	208.9 (1.5)	49/51	Female	222.8 (1.1)	49/51
White, Non-Hispanic	221.3 (1.3)	46/51	White, Non-Hispanic	236.2 (1.0)	45/51
Black, Non-Hispanic	191.9 (1.7)	35/42	Black, Non-Hispanic	212.0 (1.2)	31/42
Asian, Non-Hispanic	n/a	n/a	Asian, Non-Hispanic	n/a	n/a
American Indian, Non-Hispanic	n/a	n/a	American Indian, Non-Hispanic	n/a	n/a
Hispanic	n/a	n/a	Hispanic	n/a	n/a
Proficiency by Class Size			Proficiency by Class Size		
Less than 16 Students	*198.5 (12.7)*	31/45	Less than 16 Students	*215.7 (6.5)*	39/47
16 to 18 Students	*200.0 (5.7)*	42/48	16 to 18 Students	*215.1 (6.1)*	46/48
19 to 20 Students	200.1 (4.0)	49/50	19 to 20 Students	219.2 (2.1)	49/50
21 to 25 Students	206.0 (1.6)	48/51	21 to 25 Students	224.3 (1.4)	49/51
Greater than 25 Students	208.4 (3.1)	42/49	Greater than 25 Students	224.4 (2.5)	43/49
Percent Attaining Achievement Levels			Percent Attaining Achievement Levels		
Below Basic	51.4 (1.7)	3/51	Below Basic	37.6 (2.0)	2/51
Basic or Above	48.6 (1.7)	49/51	Basic or Above	62.4 (2.0)	50/51
Proficient or Above	18.3 (1.3)	50/51	Proficient or Above	17.0 (1.1)	50/51
Advanced or Above	3.1 (0.5)	50/51	Advanced or Above	0.8 (0.2)	51/51
8th Grade			**8th Grade**		
Average Proficiency	255.0 (1.4)	44/51	Average Proficiency	260.9 (1.1)	50/51
Proficiency by Gender/Race/Ethnicity			Proficiency by Gender/Race/Ethnicity		
Male	249.4 (1.5)	44/51	Male	262.1 (1.5)	50/51
Female	260.4 (1.5)	44/51	Female	259.7 (1.0)	50/51
White, Non-Hispanic	267.1 (1.4)	40/50	White, Non-Hispanic	275.3 (1.3)	46/50
Black, Non-Hispanic	242.5 (1.5)	28/41	Black, Non-Hispanic	246.3 (1.2)	33/41
Asian, Non-Hispanic	n/a	n/a	Asian, Non-Hispanic	n/a	n/a
American Indian, Non-Hispanic	n/a	n/a	American Indian, Non-Hispanic	n/a	n/a
Hispanic	n/a	n/a	Hispanic	n/a	n/a
Proficiency by Parents Highest Level of Ed.			Proficiency by Parents Highest Level of Ed.		
Did Not Finish High School	246.4 (2.5)	27/50	Did Not Finish High School	253.1 (2.3)	40/50
Graduated High School	249.4 (1.7)	40/50	Graduated High School	252.9 (1.7)	48/50
Some Education After High School	260.6 (1.7)	45/50	Some Education After High School	268.5 (1.9)	47/50
Graduated College	258.9 (2.0)	48/50	Graduated College	265.6 (1.6)	49/50
Percent Attaining Achievement Levels			Percent Attaining Achievement Levels		
Below Basic	34.5 (1.6)	8/51	Below Basic	52.8 (1.4)	2/51
Basic or Above	65.5 (1.6)	44/51	Basic or Above	47.2 (1.4)	50/51
Proficient or Above	20.9 (1.6)	48/51	Proficient or Above	12.3 (1.1)	50/51
Advanced or Above	1.2 (0.3)	49/51	Advanced or Above	1.0 (0.3)	51/51

***Note:** For an explanation of data, please refer to the User's Guide in the front of the book; values in italics indicate that the nature of the sample does not allow accurate determination of the variability of the statistic; n/a indicates data not available*

Adams County

Natchez-Adams SD

10 Homochitto St • Natchez, MS 39121-1188
Mailing Address: PO Box 1188 • Natchez, MS 39121-1188
(601) 445-2800 • http://natchez.k12.ms.us/
Grade Span: PK-12; **Agency Type:** 1
Schools: 8
4 Primary; 1 Middle; 2 High; 1 Other Level
6 Regular; 0 Special Education; 1 Vocational; 1 Alternative
0 Magnet; 0 Charter; 6 Title I Eligible; 5 School-wide Title I
Students: 4,796 (50.5% male; 49.5% female)
Individual Education Program: 519 (10.8%);
English Language Learner: 24 (0.5%); Migrant: 0 (0.0%)
Eligible for Free Lunch Program: 3,828 (79.8%)
Eligible for Reduced-Price Lunch Program: 275 (5.7%)
Teachers: 332.5 (14.4 to 1)
Librarians/Media Specialists: 8.0 (599.5 to 1)
Guidance Counselors: 14.0 (342.6 to 1)
Current Spending: ($ per student per year):
Total: $5,848; Instruction: $3,363; Support Services: $2,113
Enrollment, Drop-out Rates and Diploma Recipients by Race/Ethnicity

Category	Total	White	Black	Asian	AIAN	Hisp.
Enrollment (%)	100.0	12.4	86.9	0.3	0.0	0.4
Drop-out Rate (%)	4.5	8.1	3.9	0.0	n/a	0.0
H.S. Diplomas (#)	283	42	241	0	0	0

Alcorn County

Alcorn SD

Alcorn County Courthouse • Corinth, MS 38834-1420
Mailing Address: PO Box 1420 • Corinth, MS 38834-1420
(662) 286-5591 • http://www.alcorn.k12.ms.us/
Grade Span: KG-12; **Agency Type:** 1
Schools: 11
5 Primary; 1 Middle; 4 High; 1 Other Level
9 Regular; 0 Special Education; 1 Vocational; 1 Alternative
0 Magnet; 0 Charter; 8 Title I Eligible; 0 School-wide Title I
Students: 3,798 (52.0% male; 48.0% female)
Individual Education Program: 623 (16.4%);
English Language Learner: 14 (0.4%); Migrant: 4 (0.1%)
Eligible for Free Lunch Program: 1,354 (35.7%)
Eligible for Reduced-Price Lunch Program: 471 (12.4%)
Teachers: 261.8 (14.5 to 1)
Librarians/Media Specialists: 7.5 (506.4 to 1)
Guidance Counselors: 5.3 (716.6 to 1)
Current Spending: ($ per student per year):
Total: $5,279; Instruction: $3,624; Support Services: $1,369
Enrollment, Drop-out Rates and Diploma Recipients by Race/Ethnicity

Category	Total	White	Black	Asian	AIAN	Hisp.
Enrollment (%)	100.0	94.9	4.1	0.2	0.0	0.7
Drop-out Rate (%)	4.0	3.8	8.0	0.0	n/a	0.0
H.S. Diplomas (#)	223	214	7	1	0	1

Corinth SD

1204 N Harper Rd • Corinth, MS 38834-4500
(662) 287-2425 • http://www.corinth.k12.ms.us/
Grade Span: PK-12; **Agency Type:** 1
Schools: 5
2 Primary; 2 Middle; 1 High; 0 Other Level
5 Regular; 0 Special Education; 0 Vocational; 0 Alternative
0 Magnet; 0 Charter; 4 Title I Eligible; 4 School-wide Title I
Students: 1,781 (52.9% male; 47.1% female)
Individual Education Program: 263 (14.8%);
English Language Learner: 0 (0.0%); Migrant: 0 (0.0%)
Eligible for Free Lunch Program: 871 (48.9%)
Eligible for Reduced-Price Lunch Program: 124 (7.0%)
Teachers: 141.2 (12.6 to 1)
Librarians/Media Specialists: 2.1 (848.1 to 1)
Guidance Counselors: 2.3 (774.3 to 1)
Current Spending: ($ per student per year):
Total: $6,333; Instruction: $3,988; Support Services: $2,004
Enrollment, Drop-out Rates and Diploma Recipients by Race/Ethnicity

Category	Total	White	Black	Asian	AIAN	Hisp.
Enrollment (%)	100.0	53.5	43.1	0.9	0.1	2.4
Drop-out Rate (%)	2.6	0.4	6.6	0.0	0.0	0.0
H.S. Diplomas (#)	94	72	22	0	0	0

Attala County

Kosciusko SD

206 S Huntington • Kosciusko, MS 39090-3718
(662) 289-4771 • http://www2.mde.k12.ms.us/0420/stc.htm
Grade Span: KG-12; **Agency Type:** 1
Schools: 6
2 Primary; 2 Middle; 1 High; 1 Other Level
5 Regular; 0 Special Education; 0 Vocational; 1 Alternative
0 Magnet; 0 Charter; 3 Title I Eligible; 3 School-wide Title I
Students: 2,089 (51.8% male; 48.2% female)
Individual Education Program: 369 (17.7%);
English Language Learner: 16 (0.8%); Migrant: 2 (0.1%)
Eligible for Free Lunch Program: 1,030 (49.3%)
Eligible for Reduced-Price Lunch Program: 215 (10.3%)
Teachers: 135.1 (15.5 to 1)
Librarians/Media Specialists: 6.0 (348.2 to 1)
Guidance Counselors: 3.5 (596.9 to 1)
Current Spending: ($ per student per year):
Total: $5,171; Instruction: $2,941; Support Services: $1,912
Enrollment, Drop-out Rates and Diploma Recipients by Race/Ethnicity

Category	Total	White	Black	Asian	AIAN	Hisp.
Enrollment (%)	100.0	49.9	48.6	0.4	0.0	1.1
Drop-out Rate (%)	0.0	0.0	0.0	0.0	n/a	0.0
H.S. Diplomas (#)	123	76	46	1	0	0

Bolivar County

Cleveland SD

305 Merritt Dr • Cleveland, MS 38732-2247
(662) 843-3529 • http://www2.mde.k12.ms.us/csd/index_htm.html
Grade Span: PK-12; **Agency Type:** 1
Schools: 12
6 Primary; 2 Middle; 4 High; 0 Other Level
10 Regular; 0 Special Education; 1 Vocational; 1 Alternative
0 Magnet; 1 Charter; 6 Title I Eligible; 6 School-wide Title I
Students: 3,707 (50.1% male; 49.9% female)
Individual Education Program: 468 (12.6%);
English Language Learner: 14 (0.4%); Migrant: 2 (0.1%)
Eligible for Free Lunch Program: 2,386 (64.4%)
Eligible for Reduced-Price Lunch Program: 212 (5.7%)
Teachers: 270.3 (13.7 to 1)
Librarians/Media Specialists: 10.2 (363.4 to 1)
Guidance Counselors: 6.7 (553.3 to 1)
Current Spending: ($ per student per year):
Total: $5,683; Instruction: $3,112; Support Services: $2,219
Enrollment, Drop-out Rates and Diploma Recipients by Race/Ethnicity

Category	Total	White	Black	Asian	AIAN	Hisp.
Enrollment (%)	100.0	30.2	68.4	0.6	0.0	0.8
Drop-out Rate (%)	4.4	1.9	5.5	0.0	n/a	10.0
H.S. Diplomas (#)	200	66	131	0	0	3

Calhoun County

Calhoun County SD

119 W Main • Pittsboro, MS 38951-0058
Mailing Address: PO Box 58 • Pittsboro, MS 38951-0058
(662) 412-3152 • http://www2.mde.k12.ms.us/0700/index.htm
Grade Span: PK-12; **Agency Type:** 1
Schools: 7
3 Primary; 1 Middle; 2 High; 1 Other Level
7 Regular; 0 Special Education; 0 Vocational; 0 Alternative
0 Magnet; 0 Charter; 4 Title I Eligible; 4 School-wide Title I
Students: 2,587 (50.3% male; 49.7% female)
Individual Education Program: 426 (16.5%);
English Language Learner: 0 (0.0%); Migrant: 64 (2.5%)
Eligible for Free Lunch Program: 1,614 (62.4%)
Eligible for Reduced-Price Lunch Program: 251 (9.7%)
Teachers: 160.5 (16.1 to 1)
Librarians/Media Specialists: 6.7 (386.1 to 1)
Guidance Counselors: 4.0 (646.8 to 1)
Current Spending: ($ per student per year):
Total: $5,270; Instruction: $3,145; Support Services: $1,698
Enrollment, Drop-out Rates and Diploma Recipients by Race/Ethnicity

Category	Total	White	Black	Asian	AIAN	Hisp.
Enrollment (%)	100.0	52.5	43.2	0.1	0.0	4.2
Drop-out Rate (%)	1.9	1.9	1.9	0.0	n/a	0.0
H.S. Diplomas (#)	131	75	54	0	1	1

Chickasaw County

Houston SD

636 Starkville Rd • Houston, MS 38851-9303
Mailing Address: PO Drawer 351 • Houston, MS 38851-9303
(662) 456-3332 • http://www.houston.k12.ms.us/
Grade Span: KG-12; **Agency Type:** 1
Schools: 5
2 Primary; 1 Middle; 2 High; 0 Other Level
4 Regular; 0 Special Education; 1 Vocational; 0 Alternative
0 Magnet; 0 Charter; 4 Title I Eligible; 4 School-wide Title I
Students: 2,054 (49.9% male; 50.1% female)
Individual Education Program: 241 (11.7%);

English Language Learner: 58 (2.8%); Migrant: 7 (0.3%)
Eligible for Free Lunch Program: 1,224 (59.6%)
Eligible for Reduced-Price Lunch Program: 202 (9.8%)
Teachers: 131.6 (15.6 to 1)
Librarians/Media Specialists: 3.7 (555.1 to 1)
Guidance Counselors: 4.0 (513.5 to 1)
Current Spending: ($ per student per year):
Total: $4,661; Instruction: $2,842; Support Services: $1,467
Enrollment, Drop-out Rates and Diploma Recipients by Race/Ethnicity

Category	Total	White	Black	Asian	AIAN	Hisp.
Enrollment (%)	100.0	48.0	47.5	0.7	0.2	3.7
Drop-out Rate (%)	7.1	4.7	9.1	0.0	n/a	50.0
H.S. Diplomas (#)	77	44	33	0	0	0

Choctaw County

Choctaw County SD
126 E Quinn St • Ackerman, MS 39735-9768
(662) 285-6239 • http://www2.mde.k12.ms.us/1000/index.htm
Grade Span: PK-12; **Agency Type:** 1
Schools: 5
2 Primary; 0 Middle; 2 High; 1 Other Level
4 Regular; 0 Special Education; 1 Vocational; 0 Alternative
0 Magnet; 0 Charter; 3 Title I Eligible; 3 School-wide Title I
Students: 1,863 (51.0% male; 49.0% female)
Individual Education Program: 203 (10.9%);
English Language Learner: 0 (0.0%); Migrant: 0 (0.0%)
Eligible for Free Lunch Program: 1,102 (59.2%)
Eligible for Reduced-Price Lunch Program: 155 (8.3%)
Teachers: 128.9 (14.5 to 1)
Librarians/Media Specialists: 5.7 (326.8 to 1)
Guidance Counselors: 4.9 (380.2 to 1)
Current Spending: ($ per student per year):
Total: $5,252; Instruction: $3,211; Support Services: $1,662
Enrollment, Drop-out Rates and Diploma Recipients by Race/Ethnicity

Category	Total	White	Black	Asian	AIAN	Hisp.
Enrollment (%)	100.0	57.0	41.3	0.2	0.3	1.3
Drop-out Rate (%)	6.6	5.6	8.2	0.0	n/a	0.0
H.S. Diplomas (#)	96	55	41	0	0	0

Claiborne County

Claiborne County SD
404 Market St • Port Gibson, MS 39150
Mailing Address: PO Box 337 • Port Gibson, MS 39150
(601) 437-4232 • http://www2.mde.k12.ms.us/1100/index.htm
Grade Span: PK-12; **Agency Type:** 1
Schools: 4
1 Primary; 1 Middle; 2 High; 0 Other Level
3 Regular; 0 Special Education; 1 Vocational; 0 Alternative
0 Magnet; 0 Charter; 2 Title I Eligible; 2 School-wide Title I
Students: 1,866 (49.8% male; 50.2% female)
Individual Education Program: 146 (7.8%);
English Language Learner: 0 (0.0%); Migrant: 0 (0.0%)
Eligible for Free Lunch Program: 1,707 (91.5%)
Eligible for Reduced-Price Lunch Program: 63 (3.4%)
Teachers: 125.1 (14.9 to 1)
Librarians/Media Specialists: 2.3 (811.3 to 1)
Guidance Counselors: 2.0 (933.0 to 1)
Current Spending: ($ per student per year):
Total: $6,025; Instruction: $3,557; Support Services: $1,965
Enrollment, Drop-out Rates and Diploma Recipients by Race/Ethnicity

Category	Total	White	Black	Asian	AIAN	Hisp.
Enrollment (%)	100.0	0.5	99.4	0.1	0.0	0.0
Drop-out Rate (%)	2.3	n/a	2.3	n/a	n/a	n/a
H.S. Diplomas (#)	122	1	121	0	0	0

Clarke County

Quitman SD
312 E Franklin St • Quitman, MS 39355-2510
(601) 776-2186 • http://www.qsd.k12.ms.us/
Grade Span: KG-12; **Agency Type:** 1
Schools: 5
2 Primary; 1 Middle; 2 High; 0 Other Level
4 Regular; 0 Special Education; 1 Vocational; 0 Alternative
0 Magnet; 0 Charter; 3 Title I Eligible; 3 School-wide Title I
Students: 2,428 (51.4% male; 48.6% female)
Individual Education Program: 320 (13.2%);
English Language Learner: 0 (0.0%); Migrant: 4 (0.2%)
Eligible for Free Lunch Program: 1,466 (60.4%)
Eligible for Reduced-Price Lunch Program: 215 (8.9%)
Teachers: 153.6 (15.8 to 1)
Librarians/Media Specialists: 4.9 (495.5 to 1)
Guidance Counselors: 4.5 (539.6 to 1)
Current Spending: ($ per student per year):
Total: $5,070; Instruction: $2,770; Support Services: $1,933
Enrollment, Drop-out Rates and Diploma Recipients by Race/Ethnicity

Category	Total	White	Black	Asian	AIAN	Hisp.
Enrollment (%)	100.0	46.4	53.5	0.1	0.0	0.0
Drop-out Rate (%)	8.8	7.2	10.2	n/a	n/a	n/a
H.S. Diplomas (#)	122	51	71	0	0	0

Clay County

West Point SD
429 Commerce St • West Point, MS 39773-2924
Mailing Address: PO Box 656 • West Point, MS 39773-2924
(601) 494-4242 • http://westpoint.k12.ms.us/
Grade Span: PK-12; **Agency Type:** 1
Schools: 9
4 Primary; 2 Middle; 2 High; 1 Other Level
7 Regular; 0 Special Education; 1 Vocational; 1 Alternative
0 Magnet; 0 Charter; 5 Title I Eligible; 5 School-wide Title I
Students: 3,678 (50.0% male; 50.0% female)
Individual Education Program: 343 (9.3%);
English Language Learner: 11 (0.3%); Migrant: 0 (0.0%)
Eligible for Free Lunch Program: 2,773 (75.4%)
Eligible for Reduced-Price Lunch Program: 334 (9.1%)
Teachers: 207.9 (17.7 to 1)
Librarians/Media Specialists: 6.1 (603.0 to 1)
Guidance Counselors: 7.8 (471.5 to 1)
Current Spending: ($ per student per year):
Total: $4,489; Instruction: $2,584; Support Services: $1,515
Enrollment, Drop-out Rates and Diploma Recipients by Race/Ethnicity

Category	Total	White	Black	Asian	AIAN	Hisp.
Enrollment (%)	100.0	21.7	77.8	0.1	0.0	0.4
Drop-out Rate (%)	10.9	8.4	11.7	0.0	n/a	0.0
H.S. Diplomas (#)	153	37	114	0	0	2

Coahoma County

Clarksdale Municipal SD
101 Mcguire St • Clarksdale, MS 38614-2733
Mailing Address: PO Box 1088 • Clarksdale, MS 38614-2733
(662) 627-8500 • http://www.cdps.k12.ms.us/default.htm
Grade Span: KG-12; **Agency Type:** 1
Schools: 12
6 Primary; 3 Middle; 2 High; 1 Other Level
10 Regular; 0 Special Education; 1 Vocational; 1 Alternative
0 Magnet; 0 Charter; 8 Title I Eligible; 8 School-wide Title I
Students: 3,727 (49.6% male; 50.4% female)
Individual Education Program: 405 (10.9%);
English Language Learner: 24 (0.6%); Migrant: 1 (<0.1%)
Eligible for Free Lunch Program: 2,984 (80.1%)
Eligible for Reduced-Price Lunch Program: 234 (6.3%)
Teachers: 249.4 (14.9 to 1)
Librarians/Media Specialists: 6.8 (548.1 to 1)
Guidance Counselors: 6.4 (582.3 to 1)
Current Spending: ($ per student per year):
Total: $4,774; Instruction: $2,899; Support Services: $1,451
Enrollment, Drop-out Rates and Diploma Recipients by Race/Ethnicity

Category	Total	White	Black	Asian	AIAN	Hisp.
Enrollment (%)	100.0	10.7	88.7	0.5	0.0	0.2
Drop-out Rate (%)	4.2	7.8	3.6	0.0	n/a	0.0
H.S. Diplomas (#)	121	19	102	0	0	0

Coahoma County SD
1555 Lee Dr • Clarksdale, MS 38614-2915
(662) 624-5448 • http://www.coahoma.k12.ms.us/
Grade Span: KG-12; **Agency Type:** 1
Schools: 6
4 Primary; 1 Middle; 1 High; 0 Other Level
6 Regular; 0 Special Education; 0 Vocational; 0 Alternative
0 Magnet; 0 Charter; 5 Title I Eligible; 5 School-wide Title I
Students: 1,906 (50.5% male; 49.5% female)
Individual Education Program: 406 (21.3%);
English Language Learner: 15 (0.8%); Migrant: 27 (1.4%)
Eligible for Free Lunch Program: 1,786 (93.7%)
Eligible for Reduced-Price Lunch Program: 90 (4.7%)
Teachers: 153.7 (12.4 to 1)
Librarians/Media Specialists: 6.0 (317.7 to 1)
Guidance Counselors: 2.9 (657.2 to 1)
Current Spending: ($ per student per year):
Total: $5,401; Instruction: $3,273; Support Services: $1,714
Enrollment, Drop-out Rates and Diploma Recipients by Race/Ethnicity

Category	Total	White	Black	Asian	AIAN	Hisp.
Enrollment (%)	100.0	1.3	97.7	0.0	0.0	1.0
Drop-out Rate (%)	8.8	0.0	9.0	n/a	n/a	0.0
H.S. Diplomas (#)	63	1	61	0	0	1

Copiah County

Copiah County SD

254 W Gallatin St • Hazlehurst, MS 39083-3026
(601) 894-1341 • http://www2.mde.k12.ms.us/1500/
Grade Span: KG-12; **Agency Type:** 1
Schools: 4
1 Primary; 1 Middle; 1 High; 1 Other Level
4 Regular; 0 Special Education; 0 Vocational; 0 Alternative
0 Magnet; 0 Charter; 4 Title I Eligible; 4 School-wide Title I
Students: 3,160 (51.9% male; 48.1% female)
Individual Education Program: 245 (7.8%);
English Language Learner: 0 (0.0%); Migrant: 1 (<0.1%)
Eligible for Free Lunch Program: 2,031 (64.3%)
Eligible for Reduced-Price Lunch Program: 275 (8.7%)
Teachers: 187.8 (16.8 to 1)
Librarians/Media Specialists: 6.0 (526.7 to 1)
Guidance Counselors: 2.4 (1,316.7 to 1)
Current Spending: ($ per student per year):
Total: $5,028; Instruction: $2,638; Support Services: $1,921
Enrollment, Drop-out Rates and Diploma Recipients by Race/Ethnicity

Category	Total	White	Black	Asian	AIAN	Hisp.
Enrollment (%)	100.0	38.9	60.2	0.2	0.0	0.7
Drop-out Rate (%)	16.6	7.7	22.2	0.0	n/a	0.0
H.S. Diplomas (#)	157	62	95	0	0	0

Hazlehurst City SD

119 E Frost St • Hazlehurst, MS 39083-3407
(601) 894-1152 • http://www.hazlehurst.k12.ms.us/
Grade Span: PK-12; **Agency Type:** 1
Schools: 2
1 Primary; 0 Middle; 1 High; 0 Other Level
2 Regular; 0 Special Education; 0 Vocational; 0 Alternative
0 Magnet; 0 Charter; 1 Title I Eligible; 1 School-wide Title I
Students: 1,707 (51.7% male; 48.3% female)
Individual Education Program: 210 (12.3%);
English Language Learner: 0 (0.0%); Migrant: 0 (0.0%)
Eligible for Free Lunch Program: 1,563 (91.6%)
Eligible for Reduced-Price Lunch Program: 110 (6.4%)
Teachers: 110.2 (15.5 to 1)
Librarians/Media Specialists: 2.6 (656.5 to 1)
Guidance Counselors: 0.9 (1,896.7 to 1)
Current Spending: ($ per student per year):
Total: $5,139; Instruction: $3,115; Support Services: $1,546
Enrollment, Drop-out Rates and Diploma Recipients by Race/Ethnicity

Category	Total	White	Black	Asian	AIAN	Hisp.
Enrollment (%)	100.0	1.9	96.5	0.2	0.0	1.5
Drop-out Rate (%)	12.3	35.7	11.3	n/a	n/a	n/a
H.S. Diplomas (#)	97	3	94	0	0	0

Covington County

Covington County Schools

1211 S Dogwood St • Collins, MS 39428-1269
Mailing Address: PO Box 1269 • Collins, MS 39428-1269
(601) 765-8247 • http://www2.mde.k12.ms.us/1600/index.htm
Grade Span: KG-12; **Agency Type:** 1
Schools: 8
2 Primary; 1 Middle; 3 High; 2 Other Level
6 Regular; 0 Special Education; 1 Vocational; 1 Alternative
0 Magnet; 0 Charter; 6 Title I Eligible; 6 School-wide Title I
Students: 3,518 (50.3% male; 49.7% female)
Individual Education Program: 583 (16.6%);
English Language Learner: 0 (0.0%); Migrant: 43 (1.2%)
Eligible for Free Lunch Program: 2,413 (68.6%)
Eligible for Reduced-Price Lunch Program: 370 (10.5%)
Teachers: 224.2 (15.7 to 1)
Librarians/Media Specialists: 8.4 (418.8 to 1)
Guidance Counselors: 7.0 (502.6 to 1)
Current Spending: ($ per student per year):
Total: $4,893; Instruction: $3,006; Support Services: $1,520
Enrollment, Drop-out Rates and Diploma Recipients by Race/Ethnicity

Category	Total	White	Black	Asian	AIAN	Hisp.
Enrollment (%)	100.0	48.4	51.3	0.0	0.0	0.2
Drop-out Rate (%)	3.0	3.3	2.8	n/a	n/a	0.0
H.S. Diplomas (#)	161	73	88	0	0	0

De Soto County

Desoto County SD

Five E S St • Hernando, MS 38632-2348
(662) 429-5271 • http://www.desoto.k12.ms.us/
Grade Span: KG-12; **Agency Type:** 1
Schools: 25
12 Primary; 7 Middle; 5 High; 1 Other Level
23 Regular; 0 Special Education; 1 Vocational; 1 Alternative
0 Magnet; 0 Charter; 8 Title I Eligible; 2 School-wide Title I
Students: 22,145 (52.0% male; 48.0% female)
Individual Education Program: 2,627 (11.9%);
English Language Learner: 242 (1.1%); Migrant: 84 (0.4%)
Eligible for Free Lunch Program: 4,726 (21.3%)
Eligible for Reduced-Price Lunch Program: 1,630 (7.4%)
Teachers: 1,106.9 (20.0 to 1)
Librarians/Media Specialists: 26.8 (826.3 to 1)
Guidance Counselors: 37.7 (587.4 to 1)
Current Spending: ($ per student per year):
Total: $4,084; Instruction: $2,519; Support Services: $1,342
Enrollment, Drop-out Rates and Diploma Recipients by Race/Ethnicity

Category	Total	White	Black	Asian	AIAN	Hisp.
Enrollment (%)	100.0	77.1	18.8	0.9	0.1	3.0
Drop-out Rate (%)	0.1	0.0	0.5	0.0	0.0	0.0
H.S. Diplomas (#)	862	722	119	9	0	12

Forrest County

Forrest County SD

400 Forrest St • Hattiesburg, MS 39403-1977
Mailing Address: PO Box 1977 • Hattiesburg, MS 39403-1977
(601) 545-6055 • http://www2.mde.k12.ms.us/1800/index.html
Grade Span: PK-12; **Agency Type:** 1
Schools: 6
5 Primary; 0 Middle; 1 High; 0 Other Level
6 Regular; 0 Special Education; 0 Vocational; 0 Alternative
0 Magnet; 0 Charter; 5 Title I Eligible; 5 School-wide Title I
Students: 2,376 (51.8% male; 48.2% female)
Individual Education Program: 381 (16.0%);
English Language Learner: 22 (0.9%); Migrant: 0 (0.0%)
Eligible for Free Lunch Program: 1,353 (56.9%)
Eligible for Reduced-Price Lunch Program: 213 (9.0%)
Teachers: 192.6 (12.3 to 1)
Librarians/Media Specialists: 5.7 (416.8 to 1)
Guidance Counselors: 1.0 (2,376.0 to 1)
Current Spending: ($ per student per year):
Total: $5,628; Instruction: $3,583; Support Services: $1,701
Enrollment, Drop-out Rates and Diploma Recipients by Race/Ethnicity

Category	Total	White	Black	Asian	AIAN	Hisp.
Enrollment (%)	100.0	60.1	38.8	0.3	0.1	0.7
Drop-out Rate (%)	8.1	8.5	7.8	n/a	0.0	0.0
H.S. Diplomas (#)	57	32	24	0	0	1

Hattiesburg Public SD

301 Mamie St • Hattiesburg, MS 39403-1569
Mailing Address: PO Box 1569 • Hattiesburg, MS 39403-1569
(601) 584-6283 • http://www.hpsd.k12.ms.us/home.htm
Grade Span: KG-12; **Agency Type:** 1
Schools: 10
6 Primary; 1 Middle; 1 High; 2 Other Level
9 Regular; 0 Special Education; 0 Vocational; 1 Alternative
0 Magnet; 0 Charter; 7 Title I Eligible; 7 School-wide Title I
Students: 4,873 (50.5% male; 49.5% female)
Individual Education Program: 702 (14.4%);
English Language Learner: 17 (0.3%); Migrant: 12 (0.2%)
Eligible for Free Lunch Program: 3,927 (80.6%)
Eligible for Reduced-Price Lunch Program: 284 (5.8%)
Teachers: 251.7 (19.4 to 1)
Librarians/Media Specialists: 10.0 (487.3 to 1)
Guidance Counselors: 10.2 (477.7 to 1)
Current Spending: ($ per student per year):
Total: $6,115; Instruction: $3,604; Support Services: $2,165
Enrollment, Drop-out Rates and Diploma Recipients by Race/Ethnicity

Category	Total	White	Black	Asian	AIAN	Hisp.
Enrollment (%)	100.0	10.9	87.5	0.5	0.1	0.9
Drop-out Rate (%)	1.5	0.0	1.9	0.0	0.0	0.0
H.S. Diplomas (#)	226	52	171	2	1	0

Petal SD

115 Hwy 42 • Petal, MS 39465
Mailing Address: PO Box 523 • Petal, MS 39465
(601) 545-3002 • http://www.petalschools.com/
Grade Span: KG-12; **Agency Type:** 1
Schools: 4
2 Primary; 1 Middle; 1 High; 0 Other Level
4 Regular; 0 Special Education; 0 Vocational; 0 Alternative
0 Magnet; 0 Charter; 2 Title I Eligible; 0 School-wide Title I
Students: 3,679 (51.3% male; 48.7% female)
Individual Education Program: 633 (17.2%);
English Language Learner: 0 (0.0%); Migrant: 3 (0.1%)
Eligible for Free Lunch Program: 1,249 (33.9%)
Eligible for Reduced-Price Lunch Program: 429 (11.7%)
Teachers: 244.0 (15.1 to 1)
Librarians/Media Specialists: 5.0 (735.8 to 1)

Guidance Counselors: 5.0 (735.8 to 1)
Current Spending: ($ per student per year):
Total: $5,075; Instruction: $3,003; Support Services: $1,625
Enrollment, Drop-out Rates and Diploma Recipients by Race/Ethnicity

Category	Total	White	Black	Asian	AIAN	Hisp.
Enrollment (%)	100.0	87.5	11.4	0.2	0.2	0.7
Drop-out Rate (%)	2.7	2.5	4.7	0.0	n/a	0.0
H.S. Diplomas (#)	158	152	6	0	0	0

Franklin County

Franklin County SD

41 First St • Meadville, MS 39653-0605
Mailing Address: PO Box 605 • Meadville, MS 39653-0605
(601) 384-2340 • http://www2.mde.k12.ms.us/1900/index.htm
Grade Span: PK-12; **Agency Type:** 1
Schools: 5
2 Primary; 1 Middle; 2 High; 0 Other Level
4 Regular; 0 Special Education; 1 Vocational; 0 Alternative
0 Magnet; 0 Charter; 4 Title I Eligible; 4 School-wide Title I
Students: 1,609 (53.1% male; 46.9% female)
Individual Education Program: 294 (18.3%);
English Language Learner: 0 (0.0%); Migrant: 0 (0.0%)
Eligible for Free Lunch Program: 1,002 (62.3%)
Eligible for Reduced-Price Lunch Program: 154 (9.6%)
Teachers: 121.1 (13.3 to 1)
Librarians/Media Specialists: 4.0 (402.3 to 1)
Guidance Counselors: 3.8 (423.4 to 1)
Current Spending: ($ per student per year):
Total: $6,186; Instruction: $3,637; Support Services: $2,194
Enrollment, Drop-out Rates and Diploma Recipients by Race/Ethnicity

Category	Total	White	Black	Asian	AIAN	Hisp.
Enrollment (%)	100.0	48.9	51.1	0.0	0.0	0.0
Drop-out Rate (%)	5.1	4.6	5.6	n/a	n/a	n/a
H.S. Diplomas (#)	95	63	32	0	0	0

George County

George County SD

5152 Main St • Lucedale, MS 39452-6533
(601) 947-6993 • http://www.george.k12.ms.us/
Grade Span: PK-12; **Agency Type:** 1
Schools: 8
5 Primary; 2 Middle; 1 High; 0 Other Level
8 Regular; 0 Special Education; 0 Vocational; 0 Alternative
0 Magnet; 0 Charter; 7 Title I Eligible; 7 School-wide Title I
Students: 3,968 (52.2% male; 47.8% female)
Individual Education Program: 625 (15.8%);
English Language Learner: 7 (0.2%); Migrant: 5 (0.1%)
Eligible for Free Lunch Program: 1,831 (46.1%)
Eligible for Reduced-Price Lunch Program: 420 (10.6%)
Teachers: 248.6 (16.0 to 1)
Librarians/Media Specialists: 7.5 (529.1 to 1)
Guidance Counselors: 5.5 (721.5 to 1)
Current Spending: ($ per student per year):
Total: $4,265; Instruction: $2,718; Support Services: $1,177
Enrollment, Drop-out Rates and Diploma Recipients by Race/Ethnicity

Category	Total	White	Black	Asian	AIAN	Hisp.
Enrollment (%)	100.0	87.9	11.4	0.2	0.1	0.4
Drop-out Rate (%)	0.4	0.4	0.0	0.0	n/a	0.0
H.S. Diplomas (#)	207	174	32	0	0	1

Greene County

Greene County SD

528 Oak St • Leakesville, MS 39451-1329
(601) 394-2364 • http://www.schooltree.org/MS-GREENE.html
Grade Span: KG-12; **Agency Type:** 1
Schools: 6
3 Primary; 1 Middle; 2 High; 0 Other Level
5 Regular; 0 Special Education; 1 Vocational; 0 Alternative
0 Magnet; 0 Charter; 4 Title I Eligible; 4 School-wide Title I
Students: 1,910 (49.5% male; 50.5% female)
Individual Education Program: 297 (15.5%);
English Language Learner: 0 (0.0%); Migrant: 0 (0.0%)
Eligible for Free Lunch Program: 1,164 (60.9%)
Eligible for Reduced-Price Lunch Program: 196 (10.3%)
Teachers: 105.6 (18.1 to 1)
Librarians/Media Specialists: 1.7 (1,123.5 to 1)
Guidance Counselors: 3.1 (616.1 to 1)
Current Spending: ($ per student per year):
Total: $5,208; Instruction: $3,150; Support Services: $1,604

Enrollment, Drop-out Rates and Diploma Recipients by Race/Ethnicity

Category	Total	White	Black	Asian	AIAN	Hisp.
Enrollment (%)	100.0	78.5	21.3	0.2	0.0	0.1
Drop-out Rate (%)	2.7	3.1	1.5	n/a	n/a	n/a
H.S. Diplomas (#)	91	63	28	0	0	0

Grenada County

Grenada SD

1855 Jackson Ave • Grenada, MS 38902-1940
Mailing Address: PO Box 1940 • Grenada, MS 38901-5220
(601) 226-1606 • http://www.gsd.k12.ms.us/
Grade Span: PK-12; **Agency Type:** 1
Schools: 6
1 Primary; 2 Middle; 2 High; 1 Other Level
5 Regular; 0 Special Education; 1 Vocational; 0 Alternative
0 Magnet; 0 Charter; 2 Title I Eligible; 2 School-wide Title I
Students: 4,646 (50.4% male; 49.6% female)
Individual Education Program: 577 (12.4%);
English Language Learner: 6 (0.1%); Migrant: 0 (0.0%)
Eligible for Free Lunch Program: 2,503 (53.9%)
Eligible for Reduced-Price Lunch Program: 273 (5.9%)
Teachers: 261.6 (17.8 to 1)
Librarians/Media Specialists: 5.5 (844.7 to 1)
Guidance Counselors: 7.6 (611.3 to 1)
Current Spending: ($ per student per year):
Total: $4,594; Instruction: $2,812; Support Services: $1,498
Enrollment, Drop-out Rates and Diploma Recipients by Race/Ethnicity

Category	Total	White	Black	Asian	AIAN	Hisp.
Enrollment (%)	100.0	45.2	54.3	0.1	0.1	0.3
Drop-out Rate (%)	7.8	8.1	7.7	0.0	n/a	0.0
H.S. Diplomas (#)	180	89	89	0	0	2

Hancock County

Bay Saint Louis Waveland SD

201 Carroll Ave • Bay St Louis, MS 39520-4513
(228) 467-6621 • http://www.bwsd.org/
Grade Span: KG-12; **Agency Type:** 1
Schools: 5
2 Primary; 2 Middle; 1 High; 0 Other Level
5 Regular; 0 Special Education; 0 Vocational; 0 Alternative
0 Magnet; 0 Charter; 3 Title I Eligible; 3 School-wide Title I
Students: 2,208 (51.1% male; 48.9% female)
Individual Education Program: 333 (15.1%);
English Language Learner: 5 (0.2%); Migrant: 16 (0.7%)
Eligible for Free Lunch Program: 1,211 (54.8%)
Eligible for Reduced-Price Lunch Program: 232 (10.5%)
Teachers: 152.4 (14.5 to 1)
Librarians/Media Specialists: 6.0 (368.0 to 1)
Guidance Counselors: 4.6 (480.0 to 1)
Current Spending: ($ per student per year):
Total: $6,095; Instruction: $3,386; Support Services: $2,310
Enrollment, Drop-out Rates and Diploma Recipients by Race/Ethnicity

Category	Total	White	Black	Asian	AIAN	Hisp.
Enrollment (%)	100.0	76.7	19.9	1.4	0.5	1.5
Drop-out Rate (%)	4.2	5.1	0.9	0.0	0.0	0.0
H.S. Diplomas (#)	121	94	21	3	2	1

Hancock County SD

17304 Hwy 603 • Kiln, MS 39556-8210
(228) 255-0376 • http://www.hancock.k12.ms.us/
Grade Span: KG-12; **Agency Type:** 1
Schools: 7
4 Primary; 1 Middle; 2 High; 0 Other Level
6 Regular; 0 Special Education; 1 Vocational; 0 Alternative
0 Magnet; 0 Charter; 4 Title I Eligible; 4 School-wide Title I
Students: 4,307 (51.1% male; 48.9% female)
Individual Education Program: 641 (14.9%);
English Language Learner: 13 (0.3%); Migrant: 22 (0.5%)
Eligible for Free Lunch Program: 2,136 (49.6%)
Eligible for Reduced-Price Lunch Program: 510 (11.8%)
Teachers: 261.2 (16.5 to 1)
Librarians/Media Specialists: 6.4 (673.0 to 1)
Guidance Counselors: 9.0 (478.6 to 1)
Current Spending: ($ per student per year):
Total: $5,039; Instruction: $2,955; Support Services: $1,784
Enrollment, Drop-out Rates and Diploma Recipients by Race/Ethnicity

Category	Total	White	Black	Asian	AIAN	Hisp.
Enrollment (%)	100.0	93.8	4.1	0.7	0.2	1.1
Drop-out Rate (%)	5.3	5.3	9.5	0.0	n/a	0.0
H.S. Diplomas (#)	170	161	6	1	1	1

Harrison County

Biloxi Public SD

160 St Peter Ave • Biloxi, MS 39533-3404
Mailing Address: PO Box 168 • Biloxi, MS 39533-3404
(228) 374-1810 • http://www.biloxischools.net/
Grade Span: KG-12; **Agency Type:** 1
Schools: 12
7 Primary; 1 Middle; 2 High; 2 Other Level
10 Regular; 0 Special Education; 1 Vocational; 1 Alternative
0 Magnet; 0 Charter; 7 Title I Eligible; 6 School-wide Title I
Students: 6,171 (51.1% male; 48.9% female)
Individual Education Program: 901 (14.6%);
English Language Learner: 299 (4.8%); Migrant: 196 (3.2%)
Eligible for Free Lunch Program: 3,227 (52.3%)
Eligible for Reduced-Price Lunch Program: 795 (12.9%)
Teachers: 415.1 (14.9 to 1)
Librarians/Media Specialists: 14.0 (440.8 to 1)
Guidance Counselors: 5.0 (1,234.2 to 1)
Current Spending: ($ per student per year):
Total: $6,318; Instruction: $3,969; Support Services: $1,998
Enrollment, Drop-out Rates and Diploma Recipients by Race/Ethnicity

Category	Total	White	Black	Asian	AIAN	Hisp.
Enrollment (%)	100.0	54.8	32.7	8.6	0.4	3.5
Drop-out Rate (%)	3.3	2.2	5.2	4.1	0.0	0.0
H.S. Diplomas (#)	265	157	74	29	0	5

Gulfport SD

2010 15th St • Gulfport, MS 39502-0220
Mailing Address: PO Box 220 • Gulfport, MS 39502-0220
(228) 865-4600 • http://www.gulfport.k12.datasync.com/
Grade Span: KG-12; **Agency Type:** 1
Schools: 12
7 Primary; 2 Middle; 2 High; 1 Other Level
10 Regular; 0 Special Education; 1 Vocational; 1 Alternative
0 Magnet; 0 Charter; 7 Title I Eligible; 6 School-wide Title I
Students: 6,239 (50.1% male; 49.9% female)
Individual Education Program: 845 (13.5%);
English Language Learner: 28 (0.4%); Migrant: 52 (0.8%)
Eligible for Free Lunch Program: 3,619 (58.0%)
Eligible for Reduced-Price Lunch Program: 546 (8.8%)
Teachers: 450.0 (13.9 to 1)
Librarians/Media Specialists: 12.0 (519.9 to 1)
Guidance Counselors: 16.9 (369.2 to 1)
Current Spending: ($ per student per year):
Total: $6,227; Instruction: $3,666; Support Services: $2,178
Enrollment, Drop-out Rates and Diploma Recipients by Race/Ethnicity

Category	Total	White	Black	Asian	AIAN	Hisp.
Enrollment (%)	100.0	46.0	50.7	1.5	0.1	1.6
Drop-out Rate (%)	6.3	5.0	7.8	6.1	50.0	5.9
H.S. Diplomas (#)	336	180	142	7	2	5

Harrison County SD

11072 Hwy 49 • Gulfport, MS 39503-2983
(228) 539-6500 • http://www.harrison.k12.ms.us/site2/DesktopDefault.aspx
Grade Span: KG-12; **Agency Type:** 1
Schools: 20
11 Primary; 3 Middle; 4 High; 2 Other Level
18 Regular; 0 Special Education; 1 Vocational; 1 Alternative
0 Magnet; 0 Charter; 12 Title I Eligible; 12 School-wide Title I
Students: 13,018 (51.7% male; 48.3% female)
Individual Education Program: 1,722 (13.2%);
English Language Learner: 42 (0.3%); Migrant: 175 (1.3%)
Eligible for Free Lunch Program: 5,573 (42.8%)
Eligible for Reduced-Price Lunch Program: 1,345 (10.3%)
Teachers: 785.2 (16.6 to 1)
Librarians/Media Specialists: 19.1 (681.6 to 1)
Guidance Counselors: 14.0 (929.9 to 1)
Current Spending: ($ per student per year):
Total: $5,078; Instruction: $3,061; Support Services: $1,695
Enrollment, Drop-out Rates and Diploma Recipients by Race/Ethnicity

Category	Total	White	Black	Asian	AIAN	Hisp.
Enrollment (%)	100.0	70.7	25.4	2.4	0.2	1.2
Drop-out Rate (%)	6.9	7.3	6.5	2.0	0.0	6.5
H.S. Diplomas (#)	534	391	108	26	0	9

Long Beach SD

111 Quarles St • Long Beach, MS 39560-2618
(228) 864-1146 • http://www.lbsd.k12.ms.us/
Grade Span: KG-12; **Agency Type:** 1
Schools: 5
3 Primary; 1 Middle; 1 High; 0 Other Level
5 Regular; 0 Special Education; 0 Vocational; 0 Alternative
0 Magnet; 0 Charter; 2 Title I Eligible; 2 School-wide Title I
Students: 3,325 (50.4% male; 49.6% female)
Individual Education Program: 398 (12.0%);
English Language Learner: 0 (0.0%); Migrant: 33 (1.0%)
Eligible for Free Lunch Program: 1,012 (30.4%)
Eligible for Reduced-Price Lunch Program: 300 (9.0%)
Teachers: 231.0 (14.4 to 1)
Librarians/Media Specialists: 6.0 (554.2 to 1)
Guidance Counselors: 8.0 (415.6 to 1)
Current Spending: ($ per student per year):
Total: $4,889; Instruction: $3,049; Support Services: $1,600
Enrollment, Drop-out Rates and Diploma Recipients by Race/Ethnicity

Category	Total	White	Black	Asian	AIAN	Hisp.
Enrollment (%)	100.0	80.1	14.6	3.1	0.5	1.8
Drop-out Rate (%)	4.7	4.8	6.5	0.0	0.0	0.0
H.S. Diplomas (#)	218	192	13	7	0	6

Pass Christian Public SD

257 Davis Ave • Pass Christian, MS 39571-3522
Mailing Address: 701 W N St • Pass Christian, MS 39571-3522
(228) 452-7271 • http://welcome.to/pcps
Grade Span: KG-12; **Agency Type:** 1
Schools: 4
2 Primary; 1 Middle; 1 High; 0 Other Level
4 Regular; 0 Special Education; 0 Vocational; 0 Alternative
0 Magnet; 0 Charter; 2 Title I Eligible; 2 School-wide Title I
Students: 1,924 (49.8% male; 50.2% female)
Individual Education Program: 295 (15.3%);
English Language Learner: 0 (0.0%); Migrant: 58 (3.0%)
Eligible for Free Lunch Program: 978 (50.8%)
Eligible for Reduced-Price Lunch Program: 236 (12.3%)
Teachers: 136.4 (14.1 to 1)
Librarians/Media Specialists: 4.4 (437.3 to 1)
Guidance Counselors: 4.0 (481.0 to 1)
Current Spending: ($ per student per year):
Total: $5,948; Instruction: $3,589; Support Services: $1,984
Enrollment, Drop-out Rates and Diploma Recipients by Race/Ethnicity

Category	Total	White	Black	Asian	AIAN	Hisp.
Enrollment (%)	100.0	59.7	36.4	3.0	0.1	0.8
Drop-out Rate (%)	0.4	0.3	0.6	0.0	n/a	0.0
H.S. Diplomas (#)	109	65	37	7	0	0

Hinds County

Clinton Public SD

203 Easthaven Dr • Clinton, MS 39056-0300
Mailing Address: PO Box 300 • Clinton, MS 39060-0300
(601) 924-7533 • http://www2.mde.k12.ms.us/2521/district/index.htm
Grade Span: KG-12; **Agency Type:** 1
Schools: 9
2 Primary; 3 Middle; 2 High; 2 Other Level
7 Regular; 0 Special Education; 1 Vocational; 1 Alternative
0 Magnet; 0 Charter; 3 Title I Eligible; 0 School-wide Title I
Students: 4,956 (51.1% male; 48.9% female)
Individual Education Program: 418 (8.4%);
English Language Learner: 14 (0.3%); Migrant: 0 (0.0%)
Eligible for Free Lunch Program: 1,357 (27.4%)
Eligible for Reduced-Price Lunch Program: 364 (7.3%)
Teachers: 306.4 (16.2 to 1)
Librarians/Media Specialists: 8.0 (619.5 to 1)
Guidance Counselors: 11.5 (431.0 to 1)
Current Spending: ($ per student per year):
Total: $4,889; Instruction: $3,108; Support Services: $1,526
Enrollment, Drop-out Rates and Diploma Recipients by Race/Ethnicity

Category	Total	White	Black	Asian	AIAN	Hisp.
Enrollment (%)	100.0	56.4	41.2	1.9	0.1	0.5
Drop-out Rate (%)	2.5	2.2	3.1	0.0	0.0	0.0
H.S. Diplomas (#)	306	228	73	5	0	0

Hinds County SD

13192 Hwy 18 • Raymond, MS 39154-0100
(601) 857-5222 • http://www2.mde.k12.ms.us/hinds/
Grade Span: KG-12; **Agency Type:** 1
Schools: 11
5 Primary; 2 Middle; 3 High; 1 Other Level
9 Regular; 0 Special Education; 1 Vocational; 1 Alternative
0 Magnet; 0 Charter; 5 Title I Eligible; 4 School-wide Title I
Students: 5,769 (50.5% male; 49.5% female)
Individual Education Program: 519 (9.0%);
English Language Learner: 3 (0.1%); Migrant: 0 (0.0%)
Eligible for Free Lunch Program: 2,407 (41.7%)
Eligible for Reduced-Price Lunch Program: 399 (6.9%)
Teachers: 370.2 (15.6 to 1)
Librarians/Media Specialists: 9.0 (641.0 to 1)
Guidance Counselors: 14.5 (397.9 to 1)
Current Spending: ($ per student per year):
Total: $4,717; Instruction: $2,756; Support Services: $1,640

Enrollment, Drop-out Rates and Diploma Recipients by Race/Ethnicity

Category	Total	White	Black	Asian	AIAN	Hisp.
Enrollment (%)	100.0	43.0	56.4	0.1	0.0	0.4
Drop-out Rate (%)	8.7	11.4	6.1	25.0	n/a	25.0
H.S. Diplomas (#)	282	143	138	0	0	1

Jackson Public SD

662 S President St • Jackson, MS 39225-2338
(601) 960-8725 • http://www.jackson.k12.ms.us/
Grade Span: PK-12; **Agency Type:** 1
Schools: 61
37 Primary; 11 Middle; 9 High; 4 Other Level
57 Regular; 0 Special Education; 1 Vocational; 3 Alternative
4 Magnet; 0 Charter; 58 Title I Eligible; 56 School-wide Title I
Students: 31,529 (50.0% male; 50.0% female)
Individual Education Program: 3,112 (9.9%);
English Language Learner: 129 (0.4%); Migrant: 7 (<0.1%)
Eligible for Free Lunch Program: 24,114 (76.5%)
Eligible for Reduced-Price Lunch Program: 2,070 (6.6%)
Teachers: 1,883.0 (16.7 to 1)
Librarians/Media Specialists: 56.7 (556.1 to 1)
Guidance Counselors: 78.7 (400.6 to 1)
Current Spending: ($ per student per year):
Total: $5,890; Instruction: $3,364; Support Services: $2,111

Enrollment, Drop-out Rates and Diploma Recipients by Race/Ethnicity

Category	Total	White	Black	Asian	AIAN	Hisp.
Enrollment (%)	100.0	3.7	95.8	0.2	0.0	0.2
Drop-out Rate (%)	4.9	8.9	4.6	0.0	0.0	0.0
H.S. Diplomas (#)	1,239	81	1,149	9	0	0

Holmes County

Holmes County SD

313 Olive St • Lexington, MS 39095-0630
Mailing Address: PO Box 630 • Lexington, MS 39095-0630
(662) 834-2175 • http://www2.mde.k12.ms.us/2600/HCSD.html
Grade Span: KG-12; **Agency Type:** 1
Schools: 7
3 Primary; 0 Middle; 1 High; 3 Other Level
6 Regular; 0 Special Education; 1 Vocational; 0 Alternative
0 Magnet; 0 Charter; 6 Title I Eligible; 6 School-wide Title I
Students: 3,653 (49.8% male; 50.2% female)
Individual Education Program: 350 (9.6%);
English Language Learner: 0 (0.0%); Migrant: 1 (<0.1%)
Eligible for Free Lunch Program: 3,509 (96.1%)
Eligible for Reduced-Price Lunch Program: 115 (3.1%)
Teachers: 183.3 (19.9 to 1)
Librarians/Media Specialists: 8.5 (429.8 to 1)
Guidance Counselors: 6.1 (598.9 to 1)
Current Spending: ($ per student per year):
Total: $4,551; Instruction: $2,552; Support Services: $1,412

Enrollment, Drop-out Rates and Diploma Recipients by Race/Ethnicity

Category	Total	White	Black	Asian	AIAN	Hisp.
Enrollment (%)	100.0	0.0	99.9	0.0	0.0	0.0
Drop-out Rate (%)	2.3	n/a	2.3	n/a	n/a	n/a
H.S. Diplomas (#)	251	0	251	0	0	0

Humphreys County

Humphreys County SD

401 Fourth St • Belzoni, MS 39038-0678
Mailing Address: PO Box 678 • Belzoni, MS 39038-0678
(601) 247-3586 • http://www.mde.k12.ms.us/Districts/Humpreys.htm
Grade Span: KG-12; **Agency Type:** 1
Schools: 4
1 Primary; 1 Middle; 2 High; 0 Other Level
3 Regular; 0 Special Education; 1 Vocational; 0 Alternative
0 Magnet; 0 Charter; 3 Title I Eligible; 3 School-wide Title I
Students: 2,032 (50.4% male; 49.6% female)
Individual Education Program: 168 (8.3%);
English Language Learner: 8 (0.4%); Migrant: 25 (1.2%)
Eligible for Free Lunch Program: 1,861 (91.6%)
Eligible for Reduced-Price Lunch Program: 74 (3.6%)
Teachers: 109.6 (18.5 to 1)
Librarians/Media Specialists: 3.0 (677.3 to 1)
Guidance Counselors: 4.0 (508.0 to 1)
Current Spending: ($ per student per year):
Total: $4,793; Instruction: $2,633; Support Services: $1,729

Enrollment, Drop-out Rates and Diploma Recipients by Race/Ethnicity

Category	Total	White	Black	Asian	AIAN	Hisp.
Enrollment (%)	100.0	2.3	97.4	0.0	0.0	0.2
Drop-out Rate (%)	10.5	20.0	10.5	n/a	n/a	0.0
H.S. Diplomas (#)	74	0	74	0	0	0

Itawamba County

Itawamba County SD

605 S Cummings St • Fulton, MS 38843-1846
(662) 862-2159 • http://www2.mde.k12.ms.us/2900/index.htm
Grade Span: KG-12; **Agency Type:** 1
Schools: 8
3 Primary; 0 Middle; 2 High; 3 Other Level
6 Regular; 0 Special Education; 1 Vocational; 1 Alternative
0 Magnet; 0 Charter; 6 Title I Eligible; 3 School-wide Title I
Students: 3,781 (50.9% male; 49.1% female)
Individual Education Program: 537 (14.2%);
English Language Learner: 2 (0.1%); Migrant: 0 (0.0%)
Eligible for Free Lunch Program: 1,833 (48.5%)
Eligible for Reduced-Price Lunch Program: 429 (11.3%)
Teachers: 246.3 (15.4 to 1)
Librarians/Media Specialists: 8.4 (450.1 to 1)
Guidance Counselors: 6.6 (572.9 to 1)
Current Spending: ($ per student per year):
Total: $4,726; Instruction: $2,988; Support Services: $1,331

Enrollment, Drop-out Rates and Diploma Recipients by Race/Ethnicity

Category	Total	White	Black	Asian	AIAN	Hisp.
Enrollment (%)	100.0	91.4	7.8	0.3	0.0	0.6
Drop-out Rate (%)	4.0	4.2	2.3	n/a	n/a	0.0
H.S. Diplomas (#)	194	174	20	0	0	0

Jackson County

Jackson County SD

12210 Colonel Vickrey Rd • Vancleave, MS 39565-5069
(228) 826-1757 • http://www2.mde.k12.ms.us/3000/index.htm
Grade Span: PK-12; **Agency Type:** 1
Schools: 15
6 Primary; 4 Middle; 4 High; 1 Other Level
13 Regular; 0 Special Education; 1 Vocational; 1 Alternative
0 Magnet; 0 Charter; 7 Title I Eligible; 2 School-wide Title I
Students: 8,512 (51.8% male; 48.2% female)
Individual Education Program: 837 (9.8%);
English Language Learner: 38 (0.4%); Migrant: 219 (2.6%)
Eligible for Free Lunch Program: 2,870 (33.7%)
Eligible for Reduced-Price Lunch Program: 812 (9.5%)
Teachers: 458.1 (18.6 to 1)
Librarians/Media Specialists: 15.0 (567.5 to 1)
Guidance Counselors: 18.6 (457.6 to 1)
Current Spending: ($ per student per year):
Total: $4,554; Instruction: $2,718; Support Services: $1,552

Enrollment, Drop-out Rates and Diploma Recipients by Race/Ethnicity

Category	Total	White	Black	Asian	AIAN	Hisp.
Enrollment (%)	100.0	88.1	7.5	3.3	0.2	0.9
Drop-out Rate (%)	6.9	7.3	2.1	4.3	25.0	10.0
H.S. Diplomas (#)	466	420	32	12	1	1

Moss Point Separate SD

4924 Church St • Moss Point, MS 39563-2600
(228) 475-0691 • http://www.mphs.edu/
Grade Span: KG-12; **Agency Type:** 1
Schools: 11
6 Primary; 2 Middle; 3 High; 0 Other Level
9 Regular; 0 Special Education; 1 Vocational; 1 Alternative
0 Magnet; 0 Charter; 9 Title I Eligible; 9 School-wide Title I
Students: 4,125 (50.6% male; 49.4% female)
Individual Education Program: 661 (16.0%);
English Language Learner: 0 (0.0%); Migrant: 87 (2.1%)
Eligible for Free Lunch Program: 3,019 (73.2%)
Eligible for Reduced-Price Lunch Program: 353 (8.6%)
Teachers: 254.8 (16.2 to 1)
Librarians/Media Specialists: 8.7 (474.1 to 1)
Guidance Counselors: 10.0 (412.5 to 1)
Current Spending: ($ per student per year):
Total: $5,463; Instruction: $3,320; Support Services: $1,766

Enrollment, Drop-out Rates and Diploma Recipients by Race/Ethnicity

Category	Total	White	Black	Asian	AIAN	Hisp.
Enrollment (%)	100.0	32.1	67.0	0.3	0.0	0.5
Drop-out Rate (%)	1.7	1.5	1.7	0.0	n/a	0.0
H.S. Diplomas (#)	205	59	143	3	0	0

Ocean Springs SD

1600 Government • Ocean Springs, MS 39564-7002
Mailing Address: PO Box 7002 • Ocean Springs, MS 39564-7002
(228) 875-7706 • http://www2.mde.k12.ms.us/ossd/
Grade Span: PK-12; **Agency Type:** 1
Schools: 7
3 Primary; 2 Middle; 2 High; 0 Other Level
6 Regular; 0 Special Education; 1 Vocational; 0 Alternative
0 Magnet; 0 Charter; 3 Title I Eligible; 0 School-wide Title I

Students: 5,061 (51.6% male; 48.4% female)
Individual Education Program: 641 (12.7%);
English Language Learner: 22 (0.4%); Migrant: 56 (1.1%)
Eligible for Free Lunch Program: 859 (17.0%)
Eligible for Reduced-Price Lunch Program: 377 (7.4%)
Teachers: 293.9 (17.2 to 1)
Librarians/Media Specialists: 6.0 (843.5 to 1)
Guidance Counselors: 10.6 (477.5 to 1)
Current Spending: ($ per student per year):
Total: $4,726; Instruction: $2,958; Support Services: $1,559
Enrollment, Drop-out Rates and Diploma Recipients by Race/Ethnicity

Category	Total	White	Black	Asian	AIAN	Hisp.
Enrollment (%)	100.0	86.8	8.2	3.1	0.2	1.7
Drop-out Rate (%)	4.3	4.1	9.0	3.8	n/a	0.0
H.S. Diplomas (#)	251	214	26	6	0	5

Pascagoula Separate SD
1006 Communy Ave • Pascagoula, MS 39568-0250
Mailing Address: PO Box 250 • Pascagoula, MS 39568-0250
(228) 938-6491 • http://www.pascagoula.k12.ms.us/
Grade Span: KG-12; **Agency Type:** 1
Schools: 19
11 Primary; 3 Middle; 3 High; 2 Other Level
17 Regular; 0 Special Education; 1 Vocational; 1 Alternative
0 Magnet; 0 Charter; 17 Title I Eligible; 11 School-wide Title I
Students: 7,491 (51.1% male; 48.9% female)
Individual Education Program: 1,082 (14.4%);
English Language Learner: 101 (1.3%); Migrant: 94 (1.3%)
Eligible for Free Lunch Program: 4,073 (54.4%)
Eligible for Reduced-Price Lunch Program: 539 (7.2%)
Teachers: 468.8 (16.0 to 1)
Librarians/Media Specialists: 15.3 (489.6 to 1)
Guidance Counselors: 13.7 (546.8 to 1)
Current Spending: ($ per student per year):
Total: $5,784; Instruction: $3,453; Support Services: $2,012
Enrollment, Drop-out Rates and Diploma Recipients by Race/Ethnicity

Category	Total	White	Black	Asian	AIAN	Hisp.
Enrollment (%)	100.0	52.7	43.0	1.5	0.3	2.5
Drop-out Rate (%)	6.0	6.3	5.9	2.9	16.7	0.0
H.S. Diplomas (#)	365	234	116	10	1	4

Jasper County

West Jasper Consolidated Schools
510 Hwy 18 • Bay Springs, MS 39422-0610
Mailing Address: PO Box 610 • Bay Springs, MS 39422-0610
(601) 764-2280 • http://www.westjasper.k12.ms.us/
Grade Span: PK-12; **Agency Type:** 1
Schools: 6
1 Primary; 1 Middle; 2 High; 2 Other Level
4 Regular; 0 Special Education; 1 Vocational; 1 Alternative
0 Magnet; 0 Charter; 2 Title I Eligible; 2 School-wide Title I
Students: 1,808 (49.6% male; 50.4% female)
Individual Education Program: 301 (16.6%);
English Language Learner: 0 (0.0%); Migrant: 14 (0.8%)
Eligible for Free Lunch Program: 1,254 (69.4%)
Eligible for Reduced-Price Lunch Program: 177 (9.8%)
Teachers: 119.4 (15.1 to 1)
Librarians/Media Specialists: 2.9 (623.4 to 1)
Guidance Counselors: 2.5 (723.2 to 1)
Current Spending: ($ per student per year):
Total: $5,550; Instruction: $3,143; Support Services: $2,015
Enrollment, Drop-out Rates and Diploma Recipients by Race/Ethnicity

Category	Total	White	Black	Asian	AIAN	Hisp.
Enrollment (%)	100.0	38.9	60.6	0.1	0.2	0.2
Drop-out Rate (%)	4.2	4.0	4.4	0.0	0.0	0.0
H.S. Diplomas (#)	92	39	53	0	0	0

Jefferson County

Jefferson County SD
723 Main St • Fayette, MS 39069
Mailing Address: PO Box 157 • Fayette, MS 39069
(601) 786-3721 • http://www2.mde.k12.ms.us/
Grade Span: PK-12; **Agency Type:** 1
Schools: 5
1 Primary; 1 Middle; 3 High; 0 Other Level
3 Regular; 0 Special Education; 1 Vocational; 1 Alternative
0 Magnet; 0 Charter; 3 Title I Eligible; 3 School-wide Title I
Students: 1,653 (51.2% male; 48.8% female)
Individual Education Program: 231 (14.0%);
English Language Learner: 0 (0.0%); Migrant: 0 (0.0%)
Eligible for Free Lunch Program: 1,544 (93.4%)
Eligible for Reduced-Price Lunch Program: 46 (2.8%)
Teachers: 110.2 (15.0 to 1)
Librarians/Media Specialists: 4.0 (413.3 to 1)
Guidance Counselors: 3.5 (472.3 to 1)
Current Spending: ($ per student per year):
Total: $5,455; Instruction: $3,463; Support Services: $1,600
Enrollment, Drop-out Rates and Diploma Recipients by Race/Ethnicity

Category	Total	White	Black	Asian	AIAN	Hisp.
Enrollment (%)	100.0	0.0	99.9	0.1	0.0	0.0
Drop-out Rate (%)	12.6	0.0	12.6	n/a	n/a	n/a
H.S. Diplomas (#)	92	0	92	0	0	0

Jefferson Davis County SD
909 Leo St • Prentiss, MS 39474-1197
Mailing Address: PO Box 1197 • Prentiss, MS 39474-1197
(601) 792-4267 • http://www.mde.k12.ms.us/Districts/Jffdavis.htm
Grade Span: KG-12; **Agency Type:** 1
Schools: 5
2 Primary; 0 Middle; 1 High; 2 Other Level
4 Regular; 0 Special Education; 1 Vocational; 0 Alternative
0 Magnet; 0 Charter; 4 Title I Eligible; 4 School-wide Title I
Students: 2,320 (52.1% male; 47.9% female)
Individual Education Program: 407 (17.5%);
English Language Learner: 0 (0.0%); Migrant: 0 (0.0%)
Eligible for Free Lunch Program: 2,041 (88.0%)
Eligible for Reduced-Price Lunch Program: 171 (7.4%)
Teachers: 154.0 (15.1 to 1)
Librarians/Media Specialists: 5.7 (407.0 to 1)
Guidance Counselors: 5.0 (464.0 to 1)
Current Spending: ($ per student per year):
Total: $5,262; Instruction: $3,160; Support Services: $1,665
Enrollment, Drop-out Rates and Diploma Recipients by Race/Ethnicity

Category	Total	White	Black	Asian	AIAN	Hisp.
Enrollment (%)	100.0	13.6	86.2	0.2	0.0	0.0
Drop-out Rate (%)	6.8	11.5	5.9	n/a	0.0	n/a
H.S. Diplomas (#)	114	11	103	0	0	0

Jones County

Jones County SD
5204 Hwy 11 N • Ellisville, MS 39437-5049
(601) 649-5201 • http://jones.k12.ms.us/
Grade Span: KG-12; **Agency Type:** 1
Schools: 14
8 Primary; 1 Middle; 4 High; 1 Other Level
12 Regular; 0 Special Education; 1 Vocational; 1 Alternative
0 Magnet; 0 Charter; 8 Title I Eligible; 8 School-wide Title I
Students: 7,755 (52.4% male; 47.6% female)
Individual Education Program: 1,102 (14.2%);
English Language Learner: 66 (0.9%); Migrant: 209 (2.7%)
Eligible for Free Lunch Program: 3,697 (47.7%)
Eligible for Reduced-Price Lunch Program: 827 (10.7%)
Teachers: 512.8 (15.1 to 1)
Librarians/Media Specialists: 15.9 (487.7 to 1)
Guidance Counselors: 17.0 (456.2 to 1)
Current Spending: ($ per student per year):
Total: $5,000; Instruction: $3,242; Support Services: $1,430
Enrollment, Drop-out Rates and Diploma Recipients by Race/Ethnicity

Category	Total	White	Black	Asian	AIAN	Hisp.
Enrollment (%)	100.0	76.9	21.0	0.4	0.7	1.0
Drop-out Rate (%)	3.0	2.3	5.6	0.0	23.1	0.0
H.S. Diplomas (#)	437	331	102	1	2	1

Laurel SD
600 S 16th Ave • Laurel, MS 39440-4922
Mailing Address: PO Drawer 288 • Laurel, MS 39441-4922
(601) 649-6391 • http://www2.mde.k12.ms.us/3420/index.htm
Grade Span: PK-12; **Agency Type:** 1
Schools: 8
4 Primary; 1 Middle; 2 High; 1 Other Level
6 Regular; 0 Special Education; 1 Vocational; 1 Alternative
1 Magnet; 0 Charter; 5 Title I Eligible; 5 School-wide Title I
Students: 3,154 (50.2% male; 49.8% female)
Individual Education Program: 396 (12.6%);
English Language Learner: 21 (0.7%); Migrant: 101 (3.2%)
Eligible for Free Lunch Program: 2,624 (83.2%)
Eligible for Reduced-Price Lunch Program: 188 (6.0%)
Teachers: 250.5 (12.6 to 1)
Librarians/Media Specialists: 6.3 (500.6 to 1)
Guidance Counselors: 7.9 (399.2 to 1)
Current Spending: ($ per student per year):
Total: $5,855; Instruction: $3,440; Support Services: $1,992
Enrollment, Drop-out Rates and Diploma Recipients by Race/Ethnicity

Category	Total	White	Black	Asian	AIAN	Hisp.
Enrollment (%)	100.0	13.0	85.2	0.1	0.0	1.7
Drop-out Rate (%)	8.9	3.9	10.3	n/a	n/a	33.3
H.S. Diplomas (#)	172	45	126	0	0	1

Lafayette County

Lafayette County SD

100 Cr 404 • Oxford, MS 38655-0110
(662) 234-3271 • http://www.lafayette.k12.ms.us/index.php?id=main
Grade Span: KG-12; **Agency Type:** 1
Schools: 4
1 Primary; 1 Middle; 2 High; 0 Other Level
3 Regular; 0 Special Education; 1 Vocational; 0 Alternative
0 Magnet; 0 Charter; 2 Title I Eligible; 2 School-wide Title I
Students: 2,116 (52.6% male; 47.4% female)
Individual Education Program: 448 (21.2%);
English Language Learner: 0 (0.0%); Migrant: 0 (0.0%)
Eligible for Free Lunch Program: 959 (45.3%)
Eligible for Reduced-Price Lunch Program: 218 (10.3%)
Teachers: 156.1 (13.6 to 1)
Librarians/Media Specialists: 4.0 (529.0 to 1)
Guidance Counselors: 5.0 (423.2 to 1)
Current Spending: ($ per student per year):
Total: $6,034; Instruction: $3,510; Support Services: $2,212
Enrollment, Drop-out Rates and Diploma Recipients by Race/Ethnicity

Category	Total	White	Black	Asian	AIAN	Hisp.
Enrollment (%)	100.0	67.8	31.3	0.1	0.1	0.7
Drop-out Rate (%)	3.4	2.2	5.2	n/a	n/a	0.0
H.S. Diplomas (#)	95	64	31	0	0	0

Oxford SD

224 Bramlett Blvd • Oxford, MS 38655-3416
(662) 234-3541 • http://www.oxford.k12.ms.us/
Grade Span: PK-12; **Agency Type:** 1
Schools: 7
2 Primary; 2 Middle; 1 High; 2 Other Level
6 Regular; 0 Special Education; 0 Vocational; 1 Alternative
0 Magnet; 0 Charter; 5 Title I Eligible; 5 School-wide Title I
Students: 3,198 (51.0% male; 49.0% female)
Individual Education Program: 351 (11.0%);
English Language Learner: 38 (1.2%); Migrant: 0 (0.0%)
Eligible for Free Lunch Program: 1,267 (39.6%)
Eligible for Reduced-Price Lunch Program: 207 (6.5%)
Teachers: 215.5 (14.8 to 1)
Librarians/Media Specialists: 4.9 (652.7 to 1)
Guidance Counselors: 7.0 (456.9 to 1)
Current Spending: ($ per student per year):
Total: $5,363; Instruction: $3,426; Support Services: $1,626
Enrollment, Drop-out Rates and Diploma Recipients by Race/Ethnicity

Category	Total	White	Black	Asian	AIAN	Hisp.
Enrollment (%)	100.0	52.2	42.7	3.4	0.1	1.7
Drop-out Rate (%)	2.5	0.2	5.4	0.0	n/a	0.0
H.S. Diplomas (#)	150	91	57	2	0	0

Lamar County

Lamar County SD

300 N St • Purvis, MS 39475-0609
Mailing Address: PO Box 609 • Purvis, MS 39475-0609
(601) 794-1030 • http://www.lamar.k12.ms.us/
Grade Span: KG-12; **Agency Type:** 1
Schools: 13
4 Primary; 3 Middle; 2 High; 4 Other Level
11 Regular; 0 Special Education; 1 Vocational; 1 Alternative
0 Magnet; 0 Charter; 5 Title I Eligible; 3 School-wide Title I
Students: 6,757 (52.0% male; 48.0% female)
Individual Education Program: 1,001 (14.8%);
English Language Learner: 55 (0.8%); Migrant: 0 (0.0%)
Eligible for Free Lunch Program: 1,889 (28.0%)
Eligible for Reduced-Price Lunch Program: 670 (9.9%)
Teachers: 453.3 (14.9 to 1)
Librarians/Media Specialists: 10.4 (649.7 to 1)
Guidance Counselors: 10.3 (656.0 to 1)
Current Spending: ($ per student per year):
Total: $4,783; Instruction: $2,995; Support Services: $1,517
Enrollment, Drop-out Rates and Diploma Recipients by Race/Ethnicity

Category	Total	White	Black	Asian	AIAN	Hisp.
Enrollment (%)	100.0	84.5	13.5	1.0	0.1	0.9
Drop-out Rate (%)	2.8	2.7	3.9	0.0	0.0	14.3
H.S. Diplomas (#)	348	313	28	5	1	1

Lauderdale County

Lauderdale County SD

410 Constitution Ave • Meridian, MS 39302-5498
(601) 693-1683 • http://www.lauderdale.k12.ms.us/
Grade Span: KG-12; **Agency Type:** 1
Schools: 9
2 Primary; 2 Middle; 1 High; 4 Other Level
8 Regular; 0 Special Education; 0 Vocational; 1 Alternative
0 Magnet; 0 Charter; 5 Title I Eligible; 4 School-wide Title I
Students: 6,654 (52.0% male; 48.0% female)
Individual Education Program: 1,020 (15.3%);
English Language Learner: 0 (0.0%); Migrant: 4 (0.1%)
Eligible for Free Lunch Program: 2,513 (37.8%)
Eligible for Reduced-Price Lunch Program: 494 (7.4%)
Teachers: 411.5 (16.2 to 1)
Librarians/Media Specialists: 6.0 (1,109.0 to 1)
Guidance Counselors: 10.0 (665.4 to 1)
Current Spending: ($ per student per year):
Total: $4,941; Instruction: $3,031; Support Services: $1,629
Enrollment, Drop-out Rates and Diploma Recipients by Race/Ethnicity

Category	Total	White	Black	Asian	AIAN	Hisp.
Enrollment (%)	100.0	69.4	29.1	0.5	0.1	0.9
Drop-out Rate (%)	5.4	5.0	6.3	0.0	0.0	0.0
H.S. Diplomas (#)	338	240	94	1	0	3

Meridian Public SD

1019 25th Ave • Meridian, MS 39301
(601) 483-6271 • http://www.mpsd.k12.ms.us/
Grade Span: KG-12; **Agency Type:** 1
Schools: 15
7 Primary; 3 Middle; 2 High; 3 Other Level
13 Regular; 0 Special Education; 1 Vocational; 1 Alternative
0 Magnet; 0 Charter; 6 Title I Eligible; 6 School-wide Title I
Students: 6,695 (50.1% male; 49.9% female)
Individual Education Program: 803 (12.0%);
English Language Learner: 15 (0.2%); Migrant: 4 (0.1%)
Eligible for Free Lunch Program: 4,919 (73.5%)
Eligible for Reduced-Price Lunch Program: 331 (4.9%)
Teachers: 404.7 (16.5 to 1)
Librarians/Media Specialists: 10.3 (650.0 to 1)
Guidance Counselors: 22.5 (297.6 to 1)
Current Spending: ($ per student per year):
Total: $5,896; Instruction: $3,500; Support Services: $1,977
Enrollment, Drop-out Rates and Diploma Recipients by Race/Ethnicity

Category	Total	White	Black	Asian	AIAN	Hisp.
Enrollment (%)	100.0	20.3	78.6	0.4	0.1	0.7
Drop-out Rate (%)	4.9	3.5	5.5	0.0	0.0	11.1
H.S. Diplomas (#)	336	97	232	5	1	1

Lawrence County

Lawrence County SD

346 Thomas E Jolly Dr • Monticello, MS 39654-9301
(601) 587-2506 • http://www.lawrence.k12.ms.us/
Grade Span: KG-12; **Agency Type:** 1
Schools: 6
3 Primary; 1 Middle; 2 High; 0 Other Level
5 Regular; 0 Special Education; 1 Vocational; 0 Alternative
0 Magnet; 0 Charter; 5 Title I Eligible; 5 School-wide Title I
Students: 2,391 (50.4% male; 49.6% female)
Individual Education Program: 280 (11.7%);
English Language Learner: 0 (0.0%); Migrant: 0 (0.0%)
Eligible for Free Lunch Program: 1,205 (50.4%)
Eligible for Reduced-Price Lunch Program: 283 (11.8%)
Teachers: 164.7 (14.5 to 1)
Librarians/Media Specialists: 3.5 (683.1 to 1)
Guidance Counselors: 2.0 (1,195.5 to 1)
Current Spending: ($ per student per year):
Total: $5,120; Instruction: $3,143; Support Services: $1,580
Enrollment, Drop-out Rates and Diploma Recipients by Race/Ethnicity

Category	Total	White	Black	Asian	AIAN	Hisp.
Enrollment (%)	100.0	59.1	40.2	0.2	0.0	0.5
Drop-out Rate (%)	4.7	4.7	4.7	n/a	n/a	n/a
H.S. Diplomas (#)	120	80	40	0	0	0

Leake County

Leake County SD

123 Main St • Carthage, MS 39051-0478
Mailing Address: PO Drawer 478 • Carthage, MS 39051-0478
(601) 267-4579 • http://www.leakesd.k12.ms.us/
Grade Span: KG-12; **Agency Type:** 1
Schools: 8
2 Primary; 1 Middle; 3 High; 2 Other Level
7 Regular; 0 Special Education; 1 Vocational; 0 Alternative
0 Magnet; 0 Charter; 6 Title I Eligible; 6 School-wide Title I
Students: 3,318 (52.7% male; 47.3% female)
Individual Education Program: 494 (14.9%);
English Language Learner: 32 (1.0%); Migrant: 41 (1.2%)
Eligible for Free Lunch Program: 2,162 (65.2%)
Eligible for Reduced-Price Lunch Program: 341 (10.3%)
Teachers: 202.8 (16.4 to 1)

Librarians/Media Specialists: 5.0 (663.6 to 1)
Guidance Counselors: 7.9 (420.0 to 1)
Current Spending: ($ per student per year):
Total: $4,767; Instruction: $2,841; Support Services: $1,559
Enrollment, Drop-out Rates and Diploma Recipients by Race/Ethnicity

Category	Total	White	Black	Asian	AIAN	Hisp.
Enrollment (%)	100.0	38.3	58.6	0.2	1.3	1.7
Drop-out Rate (%)	5.8	6.1	5.6	0.0	7.7	0.0
H.S. Diplomas (#)	151	62	87	0	2	0

Lee County

Lee County SD

311 E Main • Tupelo, MS 38802-0832
Mailing Address: PO Box 832 • Tupelo, MS 38802-0832
(662) 841-9144 • http://www.lcs.k12.ms.us/default.asp
Grade Span: PK-12; **Agency Type:** 1
Schools: 9
5 Primary; 1 Middle; 1 High; 2 Other Level
9 Regular; 0 Special Education; 0 Vocational; 0 Alternative
0 Magnet; 0 Charter; 6 Title I Eligible; 3 School-wide Title I
Students: 6,241 (51.9% male; 48.1% female)
Individual Education Program: 1,064 (17.0%);
English Language Learner: 18 (0.3%); Migrant: 0 (0.0%)
Eligible for Free Lunch Program: 2,934 (47.0%)
Eligible for Reduced-Price Lunch Program: 490 (7.9%)
Teachers: 410.3 (15.2 to 1)
Librarians/Media Specialists: 11.7 (533.4 to 1)
Guidance Counselors: 12.0 (520.1 to 1)
Current Spending: ($ per student per year):
Total: $4,778; Instruction: $2,990; Support Services: $1,477
Enrollment, Drop-out Rates and Diploma Recipients by Race/Ethnicity

Category	Total	White	Black	Asian	AIAN	Hisp.
Enrollment (%)	100.0	69.2	29.9	0.3	0.0	0.6
Drop-out Rate (%)	6.3	4.8	9.7	0.0	0.0	0.0
H.S. Diplomas (#)	260	185	74	1	0	0

Tupelo Public SD

72 S Green St • Tupelo, MS 38802-0557
Mailing Address: PO Box 557 • Tupelo, MS 38802-0557
(662) 841-8850 • http://www.tupeloschools.com/
Grade Span: PK-12; **Agency Type:** 1
Schools: 16
8 Primary; 4 Middle; 3 High; 1 Other Level
14 Regular; 0 Special Education; 1 Vocational; 1 Alternative
0 Magnet; 0 Charter; 6 Title I Eligible; 0 School-wide Title I
Students: 7,282 (51.0% male; 49.0% female)
Individual Education Program: 961 (13.2%);
English Language Learner: 100 (1.4%); Migrant: 0 (0.0%)
Eligible for Free Lunch Program: 2,844 (39.1%)
Eligible for Reduced-Price Lunch Program: 378 (5.2%)
Teachers: 557.9 (13.1 to 1)
Librarians/Media Specialists: 12.5 (582.6 to 1)
Guidance Counselors: 18.4 (395.8 to 1)
Current Spending: ($ per student per year):
Total: $5,791; Instruction: $3,606; Support Services: $1,897
Enrollment, Drop-out Rates and Diploma Recipients by Race/Ethnicity

Category	Total	White	Black	Asian	AIAN	Hisp.
Enrollment (%)	100.0	56.1	41.7	1.1	0.0	1.0
Drop-out Rate (%)	2.9	1.9	5.0	0.0	n/a	12.5
H.S. Diplomas (#)	353	264	85	4	0	0

Leflore County

Greenwood Public SD

401 Howard St • Greenwood, MS 38935-1497
(662) 453-4231 • http://www2.mde.k12.ms.us/4220/
Grade Span: PK-12; **Agency Type:** 1
Schools: 8
4 Primary; 1 Middle; 2 High; 1 Other Level
6 Regular; 0 Special Education; 1 Vocational; 1 Alternative
0 Magnet; 0 Charter; 6 Title I Eligible; 6 School-wide Title I
Students: 3,486 (50.4% male; 49.6% female)
Individual Education Program: 392 (11.2%);
English Language Learner: 0 (0.0%); Migrant: 7 (0.2%)
Eligible for Free Lunch Program: 2,801 (80.4%)
Eligible for Reduced-Price Lunch Program: 167 (4.8%)
Teachers: 242.1 (14.4 to 1)
Librarians/Media Specialists: 8.0 (435.8 to 1)
Guidance Counselors: 8.0 (435.8 to 1)
Current Spending: ($ per student per year):
Total: $5,239; Instruction: $3,103; Support Services: $1,712
Enrollment, Drop-out Rates and Diploma Recipients by Race/Ethnicity

Category	Total	White	Black	Asian	AIAN	Hisp.
Enrollment (%)	100.0	10.8	88.7	0.3	0.0	0.2
Drop-out Rate (%)	12.1	32.0	11.6	0.0	n/a	25.0
H.S. Diplomas (#)	150	3	147	0	0	0

Leflore County SD

1901 Hwy 82 W • Greenwood, MS 38930-2722
(662) 453-8566 • http://www.mde.k12.ms.us/Districts/Leflore.htm
Grade Span: KG-12; **Agency Type:** 1
Schools: 8
4 Primary; 1 Middle; 3 High; 0 Other Level
7 Regular; 0 Special Education; 1 Vocational; 0 Alternative
0 Magnet; 0 Charter; 7 Title I Eligible; 7 School-wide Title I
Students: 3,050 (50.6% male; 49.4% female)
Individual Education Program: 549 (18.0%);
English Language Learner: 32 (1.0%); Migrant: 82 (2.7%)
Eligible for Free Lunch Program: 2,805 (92.0%)
Eligible for Reduced-Price Lunch Program: 168 (5.5%)
Teachers: 180.6 (16.9 to 1)
Librarians/Media Specialists: 6.4 (476.6 to 1)
Guidance Counselors: 5.6 (544.6 to 1)
Current Spending: ($ per student per year):
Total: $5,210; Instruction: $3,081; Support Services: $1,635
Enrollment, Drop-out Rates and Diploma Recipients by Race/Ethnicity

Category	Total	White	Black	Asian	AIAN	Hisp.
Enrollment (%)	100.0	1.9	96.8	0.0	0.0	1.3
Drop-out Rate (%)	8.7	28.6	8.5	n/a	n/a	0.0
H.S. Diplomas (#)	116	0	115	0	0	1

Lincoln County

Brookhaven SD

326 E Court St • Brookhaven, MS 39601
Mailing Address: PO Box 540 • Brookhaven, MS 39601
(601) 833-6661 • http://www.telapex.com/~bschool/index.html
Grade Span: KG-12; **Agency Type:** 1
Schools: 7
3 Primary; 1 Middle; 2 High; 1 Other Level
5 Regular; 0 Special Education; 1 Vocational; 1 Alternative
0 Magnet; 0 Charter; 4 Title I Eligible; 4 School-wide Title I
Students: 2,993 (49.0% male; 51.0% female)
Individual Education Program: 305 (10.2%);
English Language Learner: 0 (0.0%); Migrant: 0 (0.0%)
Eligible for Free Lunch Program: 1,705 (57.0%)
Eligible for Reduced-Price Lunch Program: 216 (7.2%)
Teachers: 219.8 (13.6 to 1)
Librarians/Media Specialists: 5.7 (525.1 to 1)
Guidance Counselors: 7.0 (427.6 to 1)
Current Spending: ($ per student per year):
Total: $5,247; Instruction: $3,123; Support Services: $1,794
Enrollment, Drop-out Rates and Diploma Recipients by Race/Ethnicity

Category	Total	White	Black	Asian	AIAN	Hisp.
Enrollment (%)	100.0	38.9	60.4	0.3	0.2	0.2
Drop-out Rate (%)	7.1	4.3	9.2	0.0	n/a	n/a
H.S. Diplomas (#)	166	79	87	0	0	0

Lincoln County SD

233 E Monticello St • Brookhaven, MS 39601-3328
(601) 835-0011 • http://lcsd.k12.ms.us/index2.asp
Grade Span: PK-12; **Agency Type:** 1
Schools: 5
0 Primary; 0 Middle; 0 High; 5 Other Level
4 Regular; 0 Special Education; 0 Vocational; 1 Alternative
0 Magnet; 0 Charter; 4 Title I Eligible; 0 School-wide Title I
Students: 2,826 (52.3% male; 47.7% female)
Individual Education Program: 354 (12.5%);
English Language Learner: 0 (0.0%); Migrant: 0 (0.0%)
Eligible for Free Lunch Program: 1,147 (40.6%)
Eligible for Reduced-Price Lunch Program: 324 (11.5%)
Teachers: 166.1 (17.0 to 1)
Librarians/Media Specialists: 8.0 (353.3 to 1)
Guidance Counselors: 4.0 (706.5 to 1)
Current Spending: ($ per student per year):
Total: $4,622; Instruction: $2,942; Support Services: $1,367
Enrollment, Drop-out Rates and Diploma Recipients by Race/Ethnicity

Category	Total	White	Black	Asian	AIAN	Hisp.
Enrollment (%)	100.0	82.8	16.5	0.2	0.1	0.4
Drop-out Rate (%)	5.8	5.2	8.6	0.0	n/a	0.0
H.S. Diplomas (#)	170	131	36	0	1	2

Lowndes County

Columbus Municipal SD
2630 Mcarthur Dr • Columbus, MS 39705
Mailing Address: PO Box 1308 • Columbus, MS 39703-1810
(601) 241-7400 • http://www2.mde.k12.ms.us/4420/
Grade Span: PK-12; **Agency Type:** 1
Schools: 13
8 Primary; 2 Middle; 2 High; 1 Other Level
11 Regular; 0 Special Education; 1 Vocational; 1 Alternative
0 Magnet; 0 Charter; 9 Title I Eligible; 9 School-wide Title I
Students: 5,097 (51.3% male; 48.7% female)
Individual Education Program: 621 (12.2%);
English Language Learner: 13 (0.3%); Migrant: 0 (0.0%)
Eligible for Free Lunch Program: 3,681 (72.2%)
Eligible for Reduced-Price Lunch Program: 377 (7.4%)
Teachers: 394.0 (12.9 to 1)
Librarians/Media Specialists: 14.0 (364.1 to 1)
Guidance Counselors: 13.5 (377.6 to 1)
Current Spending: ($ per student per year):
Total: $5,722; Instruction: $3,239; Support Services: $2,087
Enrollment, Drop-out Rates and Diploma Recipients by Race/Ethnicity

Category	Total	White	Black	Asian	AIAN	Hisp.
Enrollment (%)	100.0	16.0	82.5	0.6	0.1	0.7
Drop-out Rate (%)	4.0	3.7	4.1	0.0	0.0	0.0
H.S. Diplomas (#)	265	82	178	3	1	1

Lowndes County SD
1053 Hwy 45 S • Columbus, MS 39701-8480
(662) 329-5775 • http://www2.mde.k12.ms.us/4400/
Grade Span: KG-12; **Agency Type:** 1
Schools: 9
3 Primary; 3 Middle; 3 High; 0 Other Level
9 Regular; 0 Special Education; 0 Vocational; 0 Alternative
0 Magnet; 0 Charter; 7 Title I Eligible; 4 School-wide Title I
Students: 5,384 (50.5% male; 49.5% female)
Individual Education Program: 557 (10.3%);
English Language Learner: 9 (0.2%); Migrant: 0 (0.0%)
Eligible for Free Lunch Program: 2,181 (40.5%)
Eligible for Reduced-Price Lunch Program: 478 (8.9%)
Teachers: 336.3 (16.0 to 1)
Librarians/Media Specialists: 9.5 (566.7 to 1)
Guidance Counselors: 9.2 (585.2 to 1)
Current Spending: ($ per student per year):
Total: $4,720; Instruction: $2,964; Support Services: $1,459
Enrollment, Drop-out Rates and Diploma Recipients by Race/Ethnicity

Category	Total	White	Black	Asian	AIAN	Hisp.
Enrollment (%)	100.0	59.6	39.2	0.5	0.1	0.7
Drop-out Rate (%)	4.6	4.9	4.2	0.0	n/a	0.0
H.S. Diplomas (#)	268	178	88	2	0	0

Madison County

Canton Public SD
403 E Lincoln St • Canton, MS 39046-3215
(601) 859-4110 • http://www2.mde.k12.ms.us/4520/canton/main_index.htm
Grade Span: KG-12; **Agency Type:** 1
Schools: 6
2 Primary; 1 Middle; 2 High; 1 Other Level
4 Regular; 0 Special Education; 1 Vocational; 1 Alternative
0 Magnet; 0 Charter; 4 Title I Eligible; 4 School-wide Title I
Students: 3,560 (48.6% male; 51.4% female)
Individual Education Program: 381 (10.7%);
English Language Learner: 5 (0.1%); Migrant: 0 (0.0%)
Eligible for Free Lunch Program: 3,142 (88.3%)
Eligible for Reduced-Price Lunch Program: 111 (3.1%)
Teachers: 190.6 (18.7 to 1)
Librarians/Media Specialists: 4.9 (726.5 to 1)
Guidance Counselors: 6.5 (547.7 to 1)
Current Spending: ($ per student per year):
Total: $4,119; Instruction: $2,333; Support Services: $1,330
Enrollment, Drop-out Rates and Diploma Recipients by Race/Ethnicity

Category	Total	White	Black	Asian	AIAN	Hisp.
Enrollment (%)	100.0	0.2	99.6	0.0	0.0	0.2
Drop-out Rate (%)	5.6	0.0	5.7	n/a	n/a	0.0
H.S. Diplomas (#)	108	0	108	0	0	0

Madison County SD
117 Fourth St • Flora, MS 39071-9761
Mailing Address: PO Box 159 • Flora, MS 39071-9761
(601) 879-3025 • http://www.madison.k12.ms.us/
Grade Span: PK-12; **Agency Type:** 1
Schools: 17
8 Primary; 4 Middle; 4 High; 1 Other Level
15 Regular; 0 Special Education; 1 Vocational; 1 Alternative
0 Magnet; 0 Charter; 6 Title I Eligible; 6 School-wide Title I
Students: 9,423 (50.8% male; 49.2% female)
Individual Education Program: 792 (8.4%);
English Language Learner: 58 (0.6%); Migrant: 0 (0.0%)
Eligible for Free Lunch Program: 2,557 (27.1%)
Eligible for Reduced-Price Lunch Program: 419 (4.4%)
Teachers: 606.6 (15.5 to 1)
Librarians/Media Specialists: 16.8 (560.9 to 1)
Guidance Counselors: 22.9 (411.5 to 1)
Current Spending: ($ per student per year):
Total: $4,861; Instruction: $2,931; Support Services: $1,686
Enrollment, Drop-out Rates and Diploma Recipients by Race/Ethnicity

Category	Total	White	Black	Asian	AIAN	Hisp.
Enrollment (%)	100.0	59.9	37.3	2.0	0.0	0.7
Drop-out Rate (%)	0.7	0.7	0.9	0.0	0.0	0.0
H.S. Diplomas (#)	500	334	158	7	1	0

Marion County

Columbia SD
613 Bryan Ave • Columbia, MS 39429-3153
(601) 736-2366 • http://www.columbiaschools.org/
Grade Span: PK-12; **Agency Type:** 1
Schools: 4
1 Primary; 2 Middle; 1 High; 0 Other Level
4 Regular; 0 Special Education; 0 Vocational; 0 Alternative
0 Magnet; 0 Charter; 2 Title I Eligible; 2 School-wide Title I
Students: 1,863 (51.7% male; 48.3% female)
Individual Education Program: 320 (17.2%);
English Language Learner: 0 (0.0%); Migrant: 0 (0.0%)
Eligible for Free Lunch Program: 1,104 (59.3%)
Eligible for Reduced-Price Lunch Program: 177 (9.5%)
Teachers: 118.3 (15.7 to 1)
Librarians/Media Specialists: 4.6 (405.0 to 1)
Guidance Counselors: 4.4 (423.4 to 1)
Current Spending: ($ per student per year):
Total: $5,258; Instruction: $3,129; Support Services: $1,811
Enrollment, Drop-out Rates and Diploma Recipients by Race/Ethnicity

Category	Total	White	Black	Asian	AIAN	Hisp.
Enrollment (%)	100.0	53.7	45.1	0.6	0.1	0.5
Drop-out Rate (%)	2.0	1.7	2.4	0.0	n/a	n/a
H.S. Diplomas (#)	108	68	40	0	0	0

Marion County SD
600 Broad St • Columbia, MS 39429-3009
(601) 736-7193 • http://www2.mde.k12.ms.us/4600/index.htm
Grade Span: KG-12; **Agency Type:** 1
Schools: 9
3 Primary; 3 Middle; 3 High; 0 Other Level
8 Regular; 0 Special Education; 1 Vocational; 0 Alternative
0 Magnet; 0 Charter; 8 Title I Eligible; 8 School-wide Title I
Students: 2,594 (52.4% male; 47.6% female)
Individual Education Program: 496 (19.1%);
English Language Learner: 0 (0.0%); Migrant: 3 (0.1%)
Eligible for Free Lunch Program: 1,884 (72.6%)
Eligible for Reduced-Price Lunch Program: 307 (11.8%)
Teachers: 200.7 (12.9 to 1)
Librarians/Media Specialists: 3.8 (682.6 to 1)
Guidance Counselors: 3.0 (864.7 to 1)
Current Spending: ($ per student per year):
Total: $5,465; Instruction: $3,258; Support Services: $1,840
Enrollment, Drop-out Rates and Diploma Recipients by Race/Ethnicity

Category	Total	White	Black	Asian	AIAN	Hisp.
Enrollment (%)	100.0	53.3	46.2	0.1	0.0	0.4
Drop-out Rate (%)	8.6	8.9	8.4	n/a	n/a	0.0
H.S. Diplomas (#)	130	62	68	0	0	0

Marshall County

Holly Springs SD
840 Hwy 178 E • Holly Springs, MS 38635-2633
(662) 252-2183 • http://www2.mde.k12.ms.us/4720/
Grade Span: PK-12; **Agency Type:** 1
Schools: 5
1 Primary; 1 Middle; 2 High; 1 Other Level
3 Regular; 0 Special Education; 1 Vocational; 1 Alternative
0 Magnet; 0 Charter; 2 Title I Eligible; 2 School-wide Title I
Students: 1,893 (50.9% male; 49.1% female)
Individual Education Program: 329 (17.4%);
English Language Learner: 0 (0.0%); Migrant: 0 (0.0%)
Eligible for Free Lunch Program: 1,510 (79.8%)
Eligible for Reduced-Price Lunch Program: 173 (9.1%)
Teachers: 118.4 (16.0 to 1)
Librarians/Media Specialists: 3.6 (525.8 to 1)
Guidance Counselors: 4.8 (394.4 to 1)

Current Spending: ($ per student per year):
Total: $4,855; Instruction: $2,911; Support Services: $1,557
Enrollment, Drop-out Rates and Diploma Recipients by Race/Ethnicity

Category	Total	White	Black	Asian	AIAN	Hisp.
Enrollment (%)	100.0	3.0	96.5	0.3	0.0	0.3
Drop-out Rate (%)	3.1	4.8	3.0	0.0	n/a	n/a
H.S. Diplomas (#)	106	1	105	0	0	0

Marshall County SD
158 E College Ave • Holly Springs, MS 38635-3003
Mailing Address: PO Box 38 • Holly Springs, MS 38635-3003
(662) 252-4271 • http://www.mde.k12.ms.us/Districts/Marshall.htm#MARSHALL
Grade Span: PK-12; **Agency Type:** 1
Schools: 6
3 Primary; 0 Middle; 1 High; 2 Other Level
6 Regular; 0 Special Education; 0 Vocational; 0 Alternative
0 Magnet; 0 Charter; 6 Title I Eligible; 6 School-wide Title I
Students: 3,397 (51.5% male; 48.5% female)
Individual Education Program: 438 (12.9%);
English Language Learner: 46 (1.4%); Migrant: 16 (0.5%)
Eligible for Free Lunch Program: 2,278 (67.1%)
Eligible for Reduced-Price Lunch Program: 290 (8.5%)
Teachers: 191.7 (17.7 to 1)
Librarians/Media Specialists: 4.8 (707.7 to 1)
Guidance Counselors: 2.4 (1,415.4 to 1)
Current Spending: ($ per student per year):
Total: $4,510; Instruction: $2,693; Support Services: $1,384
Enrollment, Drop-out Rates and Diploma Recipients by Race/Ethnicity

Category	Total	White	Black	Asian	AIAN	Hisp.
Enrollment (%)	100.0	36.2	62.3	0.1	0.0	1.4
Drop-out Rate (%)	3.2	4.5	2.4	0.0	n/a	16.7
H.S. Diplomas (#)	122	31	88	1	0	2

Monroe County

Aberdeen SD
100 Bulldog Blvd • Aberdeen, MS 39730
Mailing Address: PO Drawer 607 • Aberdeen, MS 39730
(662) 369-4682 • http://www.aberdeen.k12.ms.us/
Grade Span: PK-12; **Agency Type:** 1
Schools: 7
2 Primary; 3 Middle; 2 High; 0 Other Level
6 Regular; 0 Special Education; 0 Vocational; 1 Alternative
0 Magnet; 0 Charter; 5 Title I Eligible; 5 School-wide Title I
Students: 1,798 (50.6% male; 49.4% female)
Individual Education Program: 278 (15.5%);
English Language Learner: 0 (0.0%); Migrant: 0 (0.0%)
Eligible for Free Lunch Program: 1,453 (80.8%)
Eligible for Reduced-Price Lunch Program: 127 (7.1%)
Teachers: 160.9 (11.2 to 1)
Librarians/Media Specialists: 4.2 (428.1 to 1)
Guidance Counselors: 2.5 (719.2 to 1)
Current Spending: ($ per student per year):
Total: $5,358; Instruction: $3,278; Support Services: $1,697
Enrollment, Drop-out Rates and Diploma Recipients by Race/Ethnicity

Category	Total	White	Black	Asian	AIAN	Hisp.
Enrollment (%)	100.0	9.9	89.4	0.2	0.2	0.4
Drop-out Rate (%)	1.5	0.0	1.8	n/a	n/a	n/a
H.S. Diplomas (#)	97	24	73	0	0	0

Amory SD
Sam Haskell Circle • Amory, MS 38821-0330
Mailing Address: PO Box 330 • Amory, MS 38821-0330
(662) 256-5991 • http://www.amoryschools.com/
Grade Span: KG-12; **Agency Type:** 1
Schools: 5
2 Primary; 1 Middle; 2 High; 0 Other Level
4 Regular; 0 Special Education; 1 Vocational; 0 Alternative
0 Magnet; 0 Charter; 4 Title I Eligible; 3 School-wide Title I
Students: 1,882 (51.3% male; 48.7% female)
Individual Education Program: 253 (13.4%);
English Language Learner: 1 (0.1%); Migrant: 0 (0.0%)
Eligible for Free Lunch Program: 832 (44.2%)
Eligible for Reduced-Price Lunch Program: 148 (7.9%)
Teachers: 122.4 (15.4 to 1)
Librarians/Media Specialists: 4.0 (470.5 to 1)
Guidance Counselors: 4.0 (470.5 to 1)
Current Spending: ($ per student per year):
Total: $5,055; Instruction: $3,140; Support Services: $1,451
Enrollment, Drop-out Rates and Diploma Recipients by Race/Ethnicity

Category	Total	White	Black	Asian	AIAN	Hisp.
Enrollment (%)	100.0	64.0	35.7	0.2	0.0	0.2
Drop-out Rate (%)	1.9	2.5	1.0	n/a	n/a	n/a
H.S. Diplomas (#)	107	70	35	0	0	2

Monroe County SD
1619 Hwy 25 N • Amory, MS 38821
(662) 257-2176 • http://www.monroe.k12.ms.us/
Grade Span: KG-12; **Agency Type:** 1
Schools: 5
1 Primary; 0 Middle; 1 High; 3 Other Level
4 Regular; 0 Special Education; 1 Vocational; 0 Alternative
0 Magnet; 0 Charter; 4 Title I Eligible; 3 School-wide Title I
Students: 2,619 (52.1% male; 47.9% female)
Individual Education Program: 383 (14.6%);
English Language Learner: 0 (0.0%); Migrant: 32 (1.2%)
Eligible for Free Lunch Program: 905 (34.6%)
Eligible for Reduced-Price Lunch Program: 390 (14.9%)
Teachers: 167.9 (15.6 to 1)
Librarians/Media Specialists: 6.8 (385.1 to 1)
Guidance Counselors: 4.6 (569.3 to 1)
Current Spending: ($ per student per year):
Total: $4,666; Instruction: $3,008; Support Services: $1,292
Enrollment, Drop-out Rates and Diploma Recipients by Race/Ethnicity

Category	Total	White	Black	Asian	AIAN	Hisp.
Enrollment (%)	100.0	88.3	9.7	0.2	0.0	1.8
Drop-out Rate (%)	4.6	5.0	2.3	n/a	n/a	0.0
H.S. Diplomas (#)	128	102	22	0	0	4

Neshoba County

Neshoba County SD
Main & Beacon St Courthouse • Philadelphia, MS 39350-0338
Mailing Address: PO Box 338 • Philadelphia, MS 39350-0338
(601) 656-3752 • http://www.neshoba.k12.ms.us/
Grade Span: KG-12; **Agency Type:** 1
Schools: 3
1 Primary; 1 Middle; 1 High; 0 Other Level
3 Regular; 0 Special Education; 0 Vocational; 0 Alternative
0 Magnet; 0 Charter; 2 Title I Eligible; 2 School-wide Title I
Students: 2,866 (49.5% male; 50.5% female)
Individual Education Program: 340 (11.9%);
English Language Learner: 0 (0.0%); Migrant: 8 (0.3%)
Eligible for Free Lunch Program: 1,260 (44.0%)
Eligible for Reduced-Price Lunch Program: 346 (12.1%)
Teachers: 209.4 (13.7 to 1)
Librarians/Media Specialists: 4.0 (716.5 to 1)
Guidance Counselors: 2.9 (988.3 to 1)
Current Spending: ($ per student per year):
Total: $5,121; Instruction: $3,321; Support Services: $1,381
Enrollment, Drop-out Rates and Diploma Recipients by Race/Ethnicity

Category	Total	White	Black	Asian	AIAN	Hisp.
Enrollment (%)	100.0	72.2	19.9	0.3	7.4	0.2
Drop-out Rate (%)	3.6	3.5	5.0	0.0	0.0	0.0
H.S. Diplomas (#)	125	94	20	1	10	0

Newton County

Newton County SD
15305 Hwy 15 S • Decatur, MS 39327-0097
Mailing Address: PO Box 97 • Decatur, MS 39327-0097
(601) 635-2317 • http://www.newton.k12.ms.us/index.html
Grade Span: PK-12; **Agency Type:** 1
Schools: 4
1 Primary; 0 Middle; 1 High; 2 Other Level
2 Regular; 0 Special Education; 1 Vocational; 1 Alternative
0 Magnet; 0 Charter; 1 Title I Eligible; 1 School-wide Title I
Students: 1,726 (52.0% male; 48.0% female)
Individual Education Program: 221 (12.8%);
English Language Learner: 5 (0.3%); Migrant: 0 (0.0%)
Eligible for Free Lunch Program: 809 (46.9%)
Eligible for Reduced-Price Lunch Program: 172 (10.0%)
Teachers: 120.6 (14.3 to 1)
Librarians/Media Specialists: 2.0 (863.0 to 1)
Guidance Counselors: 4.0 (431.5 to 1)
Current Spending: ($ per student per year):
Total: $4,912; Instruction: $2,857; Support Services: $1,580
Enrollment, Drop-out Rates and Diploma Recipients by Race/Ethnicity

Category	Total	White	Black	Asian	AIAN	Hisp.
Enrollment (%)	100.0	69.2	27.1	0.2	2.4	1.1
Drop-out Rate (%)	3.8	4.5	2.5	n/a	0.0	n/a
H.S. Diplomas (#)	74	56	18	0	0	0

Noxubee County

Noxubee County SD

505 S Jefferson St • Macon, MS 39341-3007
Mailing Address: PO Box 540 • Macon, MS 39341-3007
(601) 726-4527
Grade Span: KG-12; **Agency Type:** 1
Schools: 6
3 Primary; 1 Middle; 2 High; 0 Other Level
5 Regular; 0 Special Education; 1 Vocational; 0 Alternative
0 Magnet; 0 Charter; 5 Title I Eligible; 5 School-wide Title I
Students: 2,259 (49.3% male; 50.7% female)
Individual Education Program: 338 (15.0%);
English Language Learner: 0 (0.0%); Migrant: 0 (0.0%)
Eligible for Free Lunch Program: 2,046 (90.6%)
Eligible for Reduced-Price Lunch Program: 131 (5.8%)
Teachers: 139.6 (16.2 to 1)
Librarians/Media Specialists: 4.0 (564.8 to 1)
Guidance Counselors: 3.7 (610.5 to 1)
Current Spending: ($ per student per year):
Total: $5,436; Instruction: $3,010; Support Services: $1,964
Enrollment, Drop-out Rates and Diploma Recipients by Race/Ethnicity

Category	Total	White	Black	Asian	AIAN	Hisp.
Enrollment (%)	100.0	0.4	99.4	0.1	0.0	0.1
Drop-out Rate (%)	5.5	n/a	5.6	n/a	n/a	n/a
H.S. Diplomas (#)	127	0	127	0	0	0

Oktibbeha County

Starkville SD

401 Greensboro St • Starkville, MS 39759-2803
(662) 324-4050 • http://www2.mde.k12.ms.us/5320/
Grade Span: KG-12; **Agency Type:** 1
Schools: 9
2 Primary; 3 Middle; 3 High; 1 Other Level
7 Regular; 0 Special Education; 1 Vocational; 1 Alternative
0 Magnet; 0 Charter; 4 Title I Eligible; 4 School-wide Title I
Students: 3,837 (49.9% male; 50.1% female)
Individual Education Program: 472 (12.3%);
English Language Learner: 6 (0.2%); Migrant: 0 (0.0%)
Eligible for Free Lunch Program: 2,124 (55.4%)
Eligible for Reduced-Price Lunch Program: 295 (7.7%)
Teachers: 292.2 (13.1 to 1)
Librarians/Media Specialists: 8.6 (446.2 to 1)
Guidance Counselors: 10.2 (376.2 to 1)
Current Spending: ($ per student per year):
Total: $6,158; Instruction: $3,653; Support Services: $2,177
Enrollment, Drop-out Rates and Diploma Recipients by Race/Ethnicity

Category	Total	White	Black	Asian	AIAN	Hisp.
Enrollment (%)	100.0	33.0	63.5	2.4	0.3	0.9
Drop-out Rate (%)	1.8	0.9	2.5	0.0	n/a	0.0
H.S. Diplomas (#)	231	104	119	8	0	0

Panola County

North Panola Schools

470 Hwy 51 N • Sardis, MS 38666
Mailing Address: PO Box 334 • Sardis, MS 38666
(601) 487-2305 • http://www2.mde.k12.ms.us/5411/
Grade Span: PK-12; **Agency Type:** 1
Schools: 7
3 Primary; 1 Middle; 2 High; 1 Other Level
5 Regular; 0 Special Education; 1 Vocational; 1 Alternative
0 Magnet; 0 Charter; 5 Title I Eligible; 5 School-wide Title I
Students: 1,818 (50.7% male; 49.3% female)
Individual Education Program: 215 (11.8%);
English Language Learner: 1 (0.1%); Migrant: 5 (0.3%)
Eligible for Free Lunch Program: 1,553 (85.4%)
Eligible for Reduced-Price Lunch Program: 165 (9.1%)
Teachers: 135.0 (13.5 to 1)
Librarians/Media Specialists: 3.0 (606.0 to 1)
Guidance Counselors: 3.9 (466.2 to 1)
Current Spending: ($ per student per year):
Total: $5,095; Instruction: $3,020; Support Services: $1,644
Enrollment, Drop-out Rates and Diploma Recipients by Race/Ethnicity

Category	Total	White	Black	Asian	AIAN	Hisp.
Enrollment (%)	100.0	2.6	97.1	0.1	0.0	0.2
Drop-out Rate (%)	14.3	28.6	14.0	n/a	n/a	n/a
H.S. Diplomas (#)	53	0	53	0	0	0

South Panola SD

209 Boothe St • Batesville, MS 38606-2118
(662) 563-9361 • http://www.southpanola.k12.ms.us/
Grade Span: KG-12; **Agency Type:** 1
Schools: 7
3 Primary; 2 Middle; 1 High; 1 Other Level
6 Regular; 0 Special Education; 0 Vocational; 1 Alternative
0 Magnet; 0 Charter; 6 Title I Eligible; 6 School-wide Title I
Students: 4,592 (51.1% male; 48.9% female)
Individual Education Program: 551 (12.0%);
English Language Learner: 4 (0.1%); Migrant: 1 (<0.1%)
Eligible for Free Lunch Program: 3,126 (68.1%)
Eligible for Reduced-Price Lunch Program: 474 (10.3%)
Teachers: 289.6 (15.9 to 1)
Librarians/Media Specialists: 4.6 (998.3 to 1)
Guidance Counselors: 10.0 (459.2 to 1)
Current Spending: ($ per student per year):
Total: $4,938; Instruction: $3,043; Support Services: $1,548
Enrollment, Drop-out Rates and Diploma Recipients by Race/Ethnicity

Category	Total	White	Black	Asian	AIAN	Hisp.
Enrollment (%)	100.0	42.7	56.1	0.4	0.0	0.8
Drop-out Rate (%)	1.0	1.5	0.6	0.0	n/a	0.0
H.S. Diplomas (#)	191	90	100	0	0	1

Pearl River County

Pearl River County SD

7306 Hwy 11 • Carriere, MS 39426-9231
(601) 798-7744 • http://207.43.239.87/
Grade Span: KG-12; **Agency Type:** 1
Schools: 3
1 Primary; 1 Middle; 1 High; 0 Other Level
3 Regular; 0 Special Education; 0 Vocational; 0 Alternative
0 Magnet; 0 Charter; 2 Title I Eligible; 2 School-wide Title I
Students: 2,720 (51.4% male; 48.6% female)
Individual Education Program: 218 (8.0%);
English Language Learner: 0 (0.0%); Migrant: 0 (0.0%)
Eligible for Free Lunch Program: 1,179 (43.3%)
Eligible for Reduced-Price Lunch Program: 386 (14.2%)
Teachers: 168.4 (16.2 to 1)
Librarians/Media Specialists: 2.0 (1,360.0 to 1)
Guidance Counselors: 3.0 (906.7 to 1)
Current Spending: ($ per student per year):
Total: $4,093; Instruction: $2,537; Support Services: $1,263
Enrollment, Drop-out Rates and Diploma Recipients by Race/Ethnicity

Category	Total	White	Black	Asian	AIAN	Hisp.
Enrollment (%)	100.0	94.9	3.9	0.5	0.3	0.5
Drop-out Rate (%)	5.5	5.2	13.8	0.0	0.0	0.0
H.S. Diplomas (#)	115	105	6	3	1	0

Picayune SD

706 Goodyear Blvd • Picayune, MS 39466-3220
(601) 798-3230 • http://picayuneschools.datastar.net/
Grade Span: KG-12; **Agency Type:** 1
Schools: 9
5 Primary; 1 Middle; 2 High; 1 Other Level
7 Regular; 0 Special Education; 1 Vocational; 1 Alternative
0 Magnet; 0 Charter; 6 Title I Eligible; 0 School-wide Title I
Students: 3,770 (51.0% male; 49.0% female)
Individual Education Program: 493 (13.1%);
English Language Learner: 0 (0.0%); Migrant: 2 (0.1%)
Eligible for Free Lunch Program: 2,123 (56.3%)
Eligible for Reduced-Price Lunch Program: 268 (7.1%)
Teachers: 287.1 (13.1 to 1)
Librarians/Media Specialists: 7.0 (538.6 to 1)
Guidance Counselors: 4.8 (785.4 to 1)
Current Spending: ($ per student per year):
Total: $5,075; Instruction: $2,978; Support Services: $1,784
Enrollment, Drop-out Rates and Diploma Recipients by Race/Ethnicity

Category	Total	White	Black	Asian	AIAN	Hisp.
Enrollment (%)	100.0	69.1	29.2	0.2	0.2	1.3
Drop-out Rate (%)	3.5	4.1	2.4	0.0	0.0	0.0
H.S. Diplomas (#)	166	130	33	1	1	1

Poplarville Separate SD

804 S Julia St • Poplarville, MS 39470-3017
(601) 795-8477 • http://poplarville.k12.ms.us/testing/home.asp
Grade Span: KG-12; **Agency Type:** 1
Schools: 5
2 Primary; 1 Middle; 2 High; 0 Other Level
4 Regular; 0 Special Education; 1 Vocational; 0 Alternative
0 Magnet; 0 Charter; 3 Title I Eligible; 3 School-wide Title I
Students: 2,029 (50.8% male; 49.2% female)
Individual Education Program: 258 (12.7%);
English Language Learner: 0 (0.0%); Migrant: 0 (0.0%)
Eligible for Free Lunch Program: 1,078 (53.1%)
Eligible for Reduced-Price Lunch Program: 224 (11.0%)
Teachers: 133.9 (15.2 to 1)
Librarians/Media Specialists: 5.0 (405.8 to 1)
Guidance Counselors: 2.0 (1,014.5 to 1)

Current Spending: ($ per student per year):
Total: $5,296; Instruction: $3,184; Support Services: $1,741

Enrollment, Drop-out Rates and Diploma Recipients by Race/Ethnicity

Category	Total	White	Black	Asian	AIAN	Hisp.
Enrollment (%)	100.0	87.6	11.8	0.1	0.1	0.4
Drop-out Rate (%)	1.9	2.2	0.0	n/a	n/a	n/a
H.S. Diplomas (#)	111	98	13	0	0	0

Pike County

Mccomb SD

695 Minnesota Ave • Mccomb, MS 39649-0868
Mailing Address: PO Box 868 • Mccomb, MS 39648-4044
(601) 684-4661
Grade Span: KG-12; **Agency Type:** 1
Schools: 7
2 Primary; 2 Middle; 2 High; 1 Other Level
5 Regular; 0 Special Education; 1 Vocational; 1 Alternative
0 Magnet; 0 Charter; 3 Title I Eligible; 3 School-wide Title I
Students: 2,922 (48.9% male; 51.1% female)
Individual Education Program: 374 (12.8%);
English Language Learner: 18 (0.6%); Migrant: 0 (0.0%)
Eligible for Free Lunch Program: 2,137 (73.1%)
Eligible for Reduced-Price Lunch Program: 194 (6.6%)
Teachers: 220.5 (13.3 to 1)
Librarians/Media Specialists: 5.0 (584.4 to 1)
Guidance Counselors: 7.5 (389.6 to 1)
Current Spending: ($ per student per year):
Total: $6,145; Instruction: $3,496; Support Services: $2,216

Enrollment, Drop-out Rates and Diploma Recipients by Race/Ethnicity

Category	Total	White	Black	Asian	AIAN	Hisp.
Enrollment (%)	100.0	21.0	78.1	0.5	0.2	0.2
Drop-out Rate (%)	5.8	4.0	6.7	0.0	0.0	0.0
H.S. Diplomas (#)	161	40	120	1	0	0

North Pike SD

1036 Jaguar Tr • Summit, MS 39666-9196
(601) 276-2216
Grade Span: KG-12; **Agency Type:** 1
Schools: 3
1 Primary; 1 Middle; 1 High; 0 Other Level
3 Regular; 0 Special Education; 0 Vocational; 0 Alternative
0 Magnet; 0 Charter; 3 Title I Eligible; 3 School-wide Title I
Students: 1,727 (51.4% male; 48.6% female)
Individual Education Program: 172 (10.0%);
English Language Learner: 0 (0.0%); Migrant: 0 (0.0%)
Eligible for Free Lunch Program: 829 (48.0%)
Eligible for Reduced-Price Lunch Program: 176 (10.2%)
Teachers: 99.0 (17.4 to 1)
Librarians/Media Specialists: 3.0 (575.7 to 1)
Guidance Counselors: 1.5 (1,151.3 to 1)
Current Spending: ($ per student per year):
Total: $4,102; Instruction: $2,635; Support Services: $1,199

Enrollment, Drop-out Rates and Diploma Recipients by Race/Ethnicity

Category	Total	White	Black	Asian	AIAN	Hisp.
Enrollment (%)	100.0	67.3	32.1	0.5	0.1	0.1
Drop-out Rate (%)	3.9	3.8	4.3	n/a	0.0	n/a
H.S. Diplomas (#)	70	51	19	0	0	0

South Pike SD

250 W Bay St • Magnolia, MS 39652-2716
Mailing Address: PO Box 71 • Magnolia, MS 39652-2716
(601) 783-3742 • http://www.spike.k12.ms.us/
Grade Span: PK-12; **Agency Type:** 1
Schools: 7
2 Primary; 2 Middle; 2 High; 1 Other Level
5 Regular; 0 Special Education; 1 Vocational; 1 Alternative
0 Magnet; 0 Charter; 5 Title I Eligible; 4 School-wide Title I
Students: 2,244 (52.0% male; 48.0% female)
Individual Education Program: 256 (11.4%);
English Language Learner: 0 (0.0%); Migrant: 0 (0.0%)
Eligible for Free Lunch Program: 1,803 (80.3%)
Eligible for Reduced-Price Lunch Program: 198 (8.8%)
Teachers: 138.4 (16.2 to 1)
Librarians/Media Specialists: 8.0 (280.5 to 1)
Guidance Counselors: 3.9 (575.4 to 1)
Current Spending: ($ per student per year):
Total: $5,243; Instruction: $3,231; Support Services: $1,619

Enrollment, Drop-out Rates and Diploma Recipients by Race/Ethnicity

Category	Total	White	Black	Asian	AIAN	Hisp.
Enrollment (%)	100.0	23.7	76.2	0.2	0.0	0.0
Drop-out Rate (%)	8.3	10.1	7.7	0.0	n/a	n/a
H.S. Diplomas (#)	105	23	82	0	0	0

Pontotoc County

Pontotoc City Schools

132 N Main St • Pontotoc, MS 38863-2108
(662) 489-3336 • http://www.pontotoc.k12.ms.us/
Grade Span: KG-12; **Agency Type:** 1
Schools: 4
2 Primary; 1 Middle; 1 High; 0 Other Level
4 Regular; 0 Special Education; 0 Vocational; 0 Alternative
0 Magnet; 0 Charter; 2 Title I Eligible; 1 School-wide Title I
Students: 2,266 (50.6% male; 49.4% female)
Individual Education Program: 322 (14.2%);
English Language Learner: 27 (1.2%); Migrant: 0 (0.0%)
Eligible for Free Lunch Program: 857 (37.8%)
Eligible for Reduced-Price Lunch Program: 178 (7.9%)
Teachers: 141.6 (16.0 to 1)
Librarians/Media Specialists: 4.6 (492.6 to 1)
Guidance Counselors: 3.0 (755.3 to 1)
Current Spending: ($ per student per year):
Total: $4,805; Instruction: $3,042; Support Services: $1,469

Enrollment, Drop-out Rates and Diploma Recipients by Race/Ethnicity

Category	Total	White	Black	Asian	AIAN	Hisp.
Enrollment (%)	100.0	70.6	27.1	0.4	0.0	1.9
Drop-out Rate (%)	1.7	0.0	5.8	0.0	n/a	16.7
H.S. Diplomas (#)	106	79	25	1	0	1

Pontotoc County SD

285 Hwy 15 Bypass S • Pontotoc, MS 38863-3527
(662) 489-3932 • http://www2.mde.k12.ms.us/5800/default.htm
Grade Span: KG-12; **Agency Type:** 1
Schools: 7
2 Primary; 2 Middle; 3 High; 0 Other Level
6 Regular; 0 Special Education; 1 Vocational; 0 Alternative
0 Magnet; 0 Charter; 2 Title I Eligible; 2 School-wide Title I
Students: 3,035 (51.5% male; 48.5% female)
Individual Education Program: 402 (13.2%);
English Language Learner: 49 (1.6%); Migrant: 11 (0.4%)
Eligible for Free Lunch Program: 1,135 (37.4%)
Eligible for Reduced-Price Lunch Program: 360 (11.9%)
Teachers: 202.8 (15.0 to 1)
Librarians/Media Specialists: 6.1 (497.5 to 1)
Guidance Counselors: 6.0 (505.8 to 1)
Current Spending: ($ per student per year):
Total: $4,734; Instruction: $2,958; Support Services: $1,465

Enrollment, Drop-out Rates and Diploma Recipients by Race/Ethnicity

Category	Total	White	Black	Asian	AIAN	Hisp.
Enrollment (%)	100.0	87.1	10.3	0.1	0.2	2.3
Drop-out Rate (%)	0.1	0.1	0.0	0.0	n/a	0.0
H.S. Diplomas (#)	128	110	15	0	0	3

Prentiss County

Prentiss County SD

105 N College St • Booneville, MS 38829-0179
Mailing Address: PO Box 179 • Booneville, MS 38829-0179
(662) 728-4911 • http://www2.mde.k12.ms.us/5900/index.html
Grade Span: KG-12; **Agency Type:** 1
Schools: 8
2 Primary; 0 Middle; 2 High; 4 Other Level
6 Regular; 0 Special Education; 1 Vocational; 1 Alternative
0 Magnet; 0 Charter; 5 Title I Eligible; 1 School-wide Title I
Students: 2,251 (51.4% male; 48.6% female)
Individual Education Program: 551 (24.5%);
English Language Learner: 0 (0.0%); Migrant: 0 (0.0%)
Eligible for Free Lunch Program: 1,141 (50.7%)
Eligible for Reduced-Price Lunch Program: 356 (15.8%)
Teachers: 204.9 (11.0 to 1)
Librarians/Media Specialists: 6.8 (331.0 to 1)
Guidance Counselors: 7.4 (304.2 to 1)
Current Spending: ($ per student per year):
Total: $5,856; Instruction: $3,740; Support Services: $1,643

Enrollment, Drop-out Rates and Diploma Recipients by Race/Ethnicity

Category	Total	White	Black	Asian	AIAN	Hisp.
Enrollment (%)	100.0	93.6	6.1	0.1	0.0	0.1
Drop-out Rate (%)	0.9	0.8	2.2	0.0	n/a	0.0
H.S. Diplomas (#)	122	119	3	0	0	0

Quitman County

Quitman County SD

Drawer E • Marks, MS 38646
(662) 326-5451 • http://www2.mde.k12.ms.us/6000/
Grade Span: KG-12; **Agency Type:** 1
Schools: 4
1 Primary; 1 Middle; 2 High; 0 Other Level

3 Regular; 0 Special Education; 1 Vocational; 0 Alternative
0 Magnet; 0 Charter; 3 Title I Eligible; 3 School-wide Title I
Students: 1,596 (51.0% male; 49.0% female)
Individual Education Program: 232 (14.5%);
English Language Learner: 0 (0.0%); Migrant: 0 (0.0%)
Eligible for Free Lunch Program: 1,485 (93.0%)
Eligible for Reduced-Price Lunch Program: 102 (6.4%)
Teachers: 106.0 (15.1 to 1)
Librarians/Media Specialists: 3.8 (420.0 to 1)
Guidance Counselors: 2.9 (550.3 to 1)
Current Spending: ($ per student per year):
Total: $5,075; Instruction: $2,927; Support Services: $1,548
Enrollment, Drop-out Rates and Diploma Recipients by Race/Ethnicity

Category	Total	White	Black	Asian	AIAN	Hisp.
Enrollment (%)	100.0	1.4	97.9	0.1	0.1	0.5
Drop-out Rate (%)	6.2	50.0	5.8	0.0	n/a	n/a
H.S. Diplomas (#)	65	0	65	0	0	0

Rankin County

Pearl Public SD
3375 Hwy 80 E • Pearl, MS 39288-5750
(601) 932-7916 • http://www.pearl.k12.ms.us/
Grade Span: KG-12; **Agency Type:** 1
Schools: 5
2 Primary; 2 Middle; 1 High; 0 Other Level
5 Regular; 0 Special Education; 0 Vocational; 0 Alternative
0 Magnet; 0 Charter; 2 Title I Eligible; 2 School-wide Title I
Students: 3,718 (50.8% male; 49.2% female)
Individual Education Program: 384 (10.3%);
English Language Learner: 0 (0.0%); Migrant: 0 (0.0%)
Eligible for Free Lunch Program: 1,371 (36.9%)
Eligible for Reduced-Price Lunch Program: 374 (10.1%)
Teachers: 256.4 (14.5 to 1)
Librarians/Media Specialists: 6.0 (619.7 to 1)
Guidance Counselors: 8.0 (464.8 to 1)
Current Spending: ($ per student per year):
Total: $5,015; Instruction: $3,164; Support Services: $1,529
Enrollment, Drop-out Rates and Diploma Recipients by Race/Ethnicity

Category	Total	White	Black	Asian	AIAN	Hisp.
Enrollment (%)	100.0	71.9	25.1	0.8	0.1	2.1
Drop-out Rate (%)	3.5	3.6	2.7	0.0	n/a	11.8
H.S. Diplomas (#)	173	124	43	1	0	5

Rankin County SD
1220 Apple Park Place • Brandon, MS 39043-1359
Mailing Address: PO Box 1359 • Brandon, MS 39043-3056
(601) 825-5590 • http://www.rcsd.k12.ms.us/
Grade Span: PK-12; **Agency Type:** 1
Schools: 23
10 Primary; 4 Middle; 6 High; 3 Other Level
22 Regular; 0 Special Education; 0 Vocational; 1 Alternative
0 Magnet; 0 Charter; 8 Title I Eligible; 8 School-wide Title I
Students: 15,528 (51.6% male; 48.4% female)
Individual Education Program: 1,652 (10.6%);
English Language Learner: 36 (0.2%); Migrant: 17 (0.1%)
Eligible for Free Lunch Program: 4,277 (27.5%)
Eligible for Reduced-Price Lunch Program: 1,158 (7.5%)
Teachers: 1,000.0 (15.5 to 1)
Librarians/Media Specialists: 26.6 (583.8 to 1)
Guidance Counselors: 33.1 (469.1 to 1)
Current Spending: ($ per student per year):
Total: $4,621; Instruction: $2,931; Support Services: $1,347
Enrollment, Drop-out Rates and Diploma Recipients by Race/Ethnicity

Category	Total	White	Black	Asian	AIAN	Hisp.
Enrollment (%)	100.0	77.2	21.1	0.8	0.1	0.8
Drop-out Rate (%)	2.1	2.0	2.6	0.0	0.0	15.0
H.S. Diplomas (#)	795	633	151	6	1	4

Scott County

Forest Municipal SD
325 Cleveland St • Forest, MS 39074-3215
(601) 469-3250 • http://www2.mde.k12.ms.us/6220/
Grade Span: KG-12; **Agency Type:** 1
Schools: 3
1 Primary; 1 Middle; 1 High; 0 Other Level
3 Regular; 0 Special Education; 0 Vocational; 0 Alternative
0 Magnet; 0 Charter; 2 Title I Eligible; 2 School-wide Title I
Students: 1,645 (52.4% male; 47.6% female)
Individual Education Program: 238 (14.5%);
English Language Learner: 90 (5.5%); Migrant: 4 (0.2%)
Eligible for Free Lunch Program: 1,137 (69.1%)
Eligible for Reduced-Price Lunch Program: 139 (8.4%)
Teachers: 109.4 (15.0 to 1)
Librarians/Media Specialists: 4.0 (411.3 to 1)
Guidance Counselors: 3.0 (548.3 to 1)
Current Spending: ($ per student per year):
Total: $5,090; Instruction: $3,095; Support Services: $1,597
Enrollment, Drop-out Rates and Diploma Recipients by Race/Ethnicity

Category	Total	White	Black	Asian	AIAN	Hisp.
Enrollment (%)	100.0	25.7	65.0	0.5	0.0	8.8
Drop-out Rate (%)	2.2	2.0	2.1	0.0	n/a	5.6
H.S. Diplomas (#)	58	22	34	0	0	2

Scott County SD
100 E First St • Forest, MS 39074
(601) 469-3861 • http://scott.k12.ms.us/
Grade Span: KG-12; **Agency Type:** 1
Schools: 8
1 Primary; 2 Middle; 2 High; 3 Other Level
7 Regular; 0 Special Education; 1 Vocational; 0 Alternative
0 Magnet; 0 Charter; 6 Title I Eligible; 6 School-wide Title I
Students: 3,821 (51.3% male; 48.7% female)
Individual Education Program: 477 (12.5%);
English Language Learner: 37 (1.0%); Migrant: 163 (4.3%)
Eligible for Free Lunch Program: 2,428 (63.5%)
Eligible for Reduced-Price Lunch Program: 451 (11.8%)
Teachers: 236.3 (16.2 to 1)
Librarians/Media Specialists: 11.1 (344.2 to 1)
Guidance Counselors: 8.2 (466.0 to 1)
Current Spending: ($ per student per year):
Total: $4,496; Instruction: $2,850; Support Services: $1,290
Enrollment, Drop-out Rates and Diploma Recipients by Race/Ethnicity

Category	Total	White	Black	Asian	AIAN	Hisp.
Enrollment (%)	100.0	54.3	42.3	0.1	0.2	3.0
Drop-out Rate (%)	5.1	5.3	4.3	n/a	n/a	18.8
H.S. Diplomas (#)	163	92	69	0	0	2

Simpson County

Simpson County SD
111 Education Ln • Mendenhall, MS 39114-3636
(601) 847-1562 • http://www2.mde.k12.ms.us/6400/index.htm
Grade Span: KG-12; **Agency Type:** 1
Schools: 9
3 Primary; 2 Middle; 3 High; 1 Other Level
7 Regular; 0 Special Education; 1 Vocational; 1 Alternative
0 Magnet; 0 Charter; 5 Title I Eligible; 5 School-wide Title I
Students: 4,369 (51.9% male; 48.1% female)
Individual Education Program: 521 (11.9%);
English Language Learner: 0 (0.0%); Migrant: 23 (0.5%)
Eligible for Free Lunch Program: 2,875 (65.8%)
Eligible for Reduced-Price Lunch Program: 352 (8.1%)
Teachers: 268.4 (16.3 to 1)
Librarians/Media Specialists: 8.6 (508.0 to 1)
Guidance Counselors: 8.1 (539.4 to 1)
Current Spending: ($ per student per year):
Total: $4,811; Instruction: $3,014; Support Services: $1,385
Enrollment, Drop-out Rates and Diploma Recipients by Race/Ethnicity

Category	Total	White	Black	Asian	AIAN	Hisp.
Enrollment (%)	100.0	48.0	51.3	0.1	0.1	0.5
Drop-out Rate (%)	5.3	4.6	6.0	n/a	n/a	0.0
H.S. Diplomas (#)	218	108	110	0	0	0

Smith County

Smith County SD
212 Sylvarena Ave • Raleigh, MS 39153
Mailing Address: PO Box 308 • Raleigh, MS 39153
(601) 782-4296 • http://www2.mde.k12.ms.us/6500/index.html
Grade Span: PK-12; **Agency Type:** 1
Schools: 6
1 Primary; 0 Middle; 3 High; 2 Other Level
4 Regular; 0 Special Education; 1 Vocational; 1 Alternative
0 Magnet; 0 Charter; 4 Title I Eligible; 4 School-wide Title I
Students: 3,077 (52.0% male; 48.0% female)
Individual Education Program: 494 (16.1%);
English Language Learner: 3 (0.1%); Migrant: 19 (0.6%)
Eligible for Free Lunch Program: 1,519 (49.4%)
Eligible for Reduced-Price Lunch Program: 363 (11.8%)
Teachers: 191.1 (16.1 to 1)
Librarians/Media Specialists: 5.5 (559.5 to 1)
Guidance Counselors: 6.5 (473.4 to 1)
Current Spending: ($ per student per year):
Total: $4,839; Instruction: $2,977; Support Services: $1,553

Enrollment, Drop-out Rates and Diploma Recipients by Race/Ethnicity

Category	Total	White	Black	Asian	AIAN	Hisp.
Enrollment (%)	100.0	67.6	31.8	0.1	0.0	0.4
Drop-out Rate (%)	4.0	4.0	4.2	0.0	n/a	0.0
H.S. Diplomas (#)	147	102	44	1	0	0

Stone County

Stone County SD

214 Critz St • Wiggins, MS 39577-3218
(601) 928-7247 • http://www2.mde.k12.ms.us/6600/
Grade Span: KG-12; **Agency Type:** 1
Schools: 4
2 Primary; 1 Middle; 1 High; 0 Other Level
4 Regular; 0 Special Education; 0 Vocational; 0 Alternative
0 Magnet; 0 Charter; 3 Title I Eligible; 3 School-wide Title I
Students: 2,626 (50.6% male; 49.4% female)
Individual Education Program: 315 (12.0%);
English Language Learner: 0 (0.0%); Migrant: 5 (0.2%)
Eligible for Free Lunch Program: 1,190 (45.3%)
Eligible for Reduced-Price Lunch Program: 264 (10.1%)
Teachers: 171.7 (15.3 to 1)
Librarians/Media Specialists: 5.0 (525.2 to 1)
Guidance Counselors: 3.9 (673.3 to 1)
Current Spending: ($ per student per year):
Total: $4,958; Instruction: $3,034; Support Services: $1,600
Enrollment, Drop-out Rates and Diploma Recipients by Race/Ethnicity

Category	Total	White	Black	Asian	AIAN	Hisp.
Enrollment (%)	100.0	74.5	25.0	0.2	0.1	0.2
Drop-out Rate (%)	0.8	0.7	1.2	0.0	0.0	0.0
H.S. Diplomas (#)	125	94	31	0	0	0

Sunflower County

Indianola SD

702 Hwy 82 E • Indianola, MS 38751-2397
(601) 887-2654 • http://www2.mde.k12.ms.us/6721/
Grade Span: KG-12; **Agency Type:** 1
Schools: 6
3 Primary; 1 Middle; 1 High; 1 Other Level
6 Regular; 0 Special Education; 0 Vocational; 0 Alternative
0 Magnet; 0 Charter; 6 Title I Eligible; 6 School-wide Title I
Students: 2,793 (51.3% male; 48.7% female)
Individual Education Program: 343 (12.3%);
English Language Learner: 0 (0.0%); Migrant: 0 (0.0%)
Eligible for Free Lunch Program: 2,428 (86.9%)
Eligible for Reduced-Price Lunch Program: 228 (8.2%)
Teachers: 164.7 (17.0 to 1)
Librarians/Media Specialists: 6.0 (465.5 to 1)
Guidance Counselors: 4.4 (634.8 to 1)
Current Spending: ($ per student per year):
Total: $4,807; Instruction: $2,837; Support Services: $1,509
Enrollment, Drop-out Rates and Diploma Recipients by Race/Ethnicity

Category	Total	White	Black	Asian	AIAN	Hisp.
Enrollment (%)	100.0	4.8	94.2	0.3	0.0	0.7
Drop-out Rate (%)	4.0	0.0	4.0	n/a	n/a	0.0
H.S. Diplomas (#)	183	1	181	1	0	0

Sunflower County SD

Main St • Indianola, MS 38751
Mailing Address: PO Box 70 • Indianola, MS 38751
(662) 887-4919 • http://www2.mde.k12.ms.us/6700/scsd.html
Grade Span: KG-12; **Agency Type:** 1
Schools: 7
4 Primary; 2 Middle; 1 High; 0 Other Level
7 Regular; 0 Special Education; 0 Vocational; 0 Alternative
0 Magnet; 0 Charter; 7 Title I Eligible; 7 School-wide Title I
Students: 1,922 (50.9% male; 49.1% female)
Individual Education Program: 238 (12.4%);
English Language Learner: 23 (1.2%); Migrant: 25 (1.3%)
Eligible for Free Lunch Program: 1,708 (88.9%)
Eligible for Reduced-Price Lunch Program: 103 (5.4%)
Teachers: 125.2 (15.4 to 1)
Librarians/Media Specialists: 4.5 (427.1 to 1)
Guidance Counselors: 3.0 (640.7 to 1)
Current Spending: ($ per student per year):
Total: $5,516; Instruction: $3,400; Support Services: $1,658
Enrollment, Drop-out Rates and Diploma Recipients by Race/Ethnicity

Category	Total	White	Black	Asian	AIAN	Hisp.
Enrollment (%)	100.0	1.8	96.4	0.0	0.0	1.9
Drop-out Rate (%)	6.3	0.0	6.3	n/a	n/a	0.0
H.S. Diplomas (#)	56	0	56	0	0	0

Tallahatchie County

East Tallahatchie Consol SD

411 Chestnut St • Charleston, MS 38921
(662) 647-5524 • http://www2.mde.k12.ms.us/6811/index.htm
Grade Span: KG-12; **Agency Type:** 1
Schools: 4
1 Primary; 1 Middle; 2 High; 0 Other Level
3 Regular; 0 Special Education; 1 Vocational; 0 Alternative
0 Magnet; 0 Charter; 2 Title I Eligible; 2 School-wide Title I
Students: 1,623 (49.4% male; 50.6% female)
Individual Education Program: 228 (14.0%);
English Language Learner: 0 (0.0%); Migrant: 0 (0.0%)
Eligible for Free Lunch Program: 1,220 (75.2%)
Eligible for Reduced-Price Lunch Program: 146 (9.0%)
Teachers: 111.0 (14.6 to 1)
Librarians/Media Specialists: 3.7 (438.6 to 1)
Guidance Counselors: 2.0 (811.5 to 1)
Current Spending: ($ per student per year):
Total: $5,086; Instruction: $3,192; Support Services: $1,521
Enrollment, Drop-out Rates and Diploma Recipients by Race/Ethnicity

Category	Total	White	Black	Asian	AIAN	Hisp.
Enrollment (%)	100.0	32.4	67.3	0.1	0.0	0.1
Drop-out Rate (%)	6.2	7.0	5.8	n/a	n/a	0.0
H.S. Diplomas (#)	53	19	34	0	0	0

Tate County

Senatobia Municipal SD

104 Mckie St • Senatobia, MS 38668-2639
(662) 562-4897 • http://www.senatobia.k12.ms.us/
Grade Span: KG-12; **Agency Type:** 1
Schools: 4
1 Primary; 1 Middle; 1 High; 1 Other Level
3 Regular; 0 Special Education; 0 Vocational; 1 Alternative
0 Magnet; 0 Charter; 2 Title I Eligible; 1 School-wide Title I
Students: 1,682 (51.3% male; 48.7% female)
Individual Education Program: 267 (15.9%);
English Language Learner: 0 (0.0%); Migrant: 0 (0.0%)
Eligible for Free Lunch Program: 619 (36.8%)
Eligible for Reduced-Price Lunch Program: 124 (7.4%)
Teachers: 103.7 (16.2 to 1)
Librarians/Media Specialists: 4.0 (420.5 to 1)
Guidance Counselors: 3.0 (560.7 to 1)
Current Spending: ($ per student per year):
Total: $4,956; Instruction: $3,044; Support Services: $1,625
Enrollment, Drop-out Rates and Diploma Recipients by Race/Ethnicity

Category	Total	White	Black	Asian	AIAN	Hisp.
Enrollment (%)	100.0	62.1	36.6	0.2	0.1	1.1
Drop-out Rate (%)	3.9	3.4	5.4	0.0	n/a	0.0
H.S. Diplomas (#)	117	82	32	1	0	2

Tate County SD

107 Court St • Senatobia, MS 38668-2639
(662) 562-5861 • http://www.tcsd.k12.ms.us/
Grade Span: KG-12; **Agency Type:** 1
Schools: 6
3 Primary; 0 Middle; 3 High; 0 Other Level
5 Regular; 0 Special Education; 1 Vocational; 0 Alternative
0 Magnet; 0 Charter; 5 Title I Eligible; 5 School-wide Title I
Students: 2,845 (50.6% male; 49.4% female)
Individual Education Program: 417 (14.7%);
English Language Learner: 12 (0.4%); Migrant: 40 (1.4%)
Eligible for Free Lunch Program: 1,686 (59.3%)
Eligible for Reduced-Price Lunch Program: 334 (11.7%)
Teachers: 175.5 (16.2 to 1)
Librarians/Media Specialists: 6.0 (474.2 to 1)
Guidance Counselors: 5.0 (569.0 to 1)
Current Spending: ($ per student per year):
Total: $4,882; Instruction: $2,924; Support Services: $1,498
Enrollment, Drop-out Rates and Diploma Recipients by Race/Ethnicity

Category	Total	White	Black	Asian	AIAN	Hisp.
Enrollment (%)	100.0	51.3	47.2	0.1	0.0	1.4
Drop-out Rate (%)	5.5	6.0	5.1	0.0	n/a	0.0
H.S. Diplomas (#)	111	42	69	0	0	0

Tippah County

South Tippah SD

402 Greenlee St • Ripley, MS 38663-2609
Mailing Address: PO Box 439 • Ripley, MS 38663-2609
(662) 837-7156 • http://ww2.dixie-net.com/Ripley-HS/
Grade Span: PK-12; **Agency Type:** 1
Schools: 6
1 Primary; 1 Middle; 2 High; 2 Other Level

5 Regular; 0 Special Education; 1 Vocational; 0 Alternative
0 Magnet; 0 Charter; 3 Title I Eligible; 3 School-wide Title I
Students: 2,715 (50.4% male; 49.6% female)
Individual Education Program: 348 (12.8%);
English Language Learner: 42 (1.5%); Migrant: 1 (<0.1%)
Eligible for Free Lunch Program: 1,237 (45.6%)
Eligible for Reduced-Price Lunch Program: 300 (11.0%)
Teachers: 170.5 (15.9 to 1)
Librarians/Media Specialists: 6.4 (424.2 to 1)
Guidance Counselors: 5.4 (502.8 to 1)
Current Spending: ($ per student per year):
Total: $4,745; Instruction: $2,925; Support Services: $1,430
Enrollment, Drop-out Rates and Diploma Recipients by Race/Ethnicity

Category	Total	White	Black	Asian	AIAN	Hisp.
Enrollment (%)	100.0	71.7	23.9	0.2	0.0	4.2
Drop-out Rate (%)	3.9	2.8	8.0	n/a	n/a	0.0
H.S. Diplomas (#)	137	111	23	0	0	3

Tishomingo County

Tishomingo County Sp Mun SD
1620 Paul Edmondson Dr • Iuka, MS 38852-1904
(662) 423-3206 • http://www.tishomingo.k12.ms.us/
Grade Span: PK-12; **Agency Type:** 1
Schools: 8
3 Primary; 1 Middle; 1 High; 3 Other Level
6 Regular; 0 Special Education; 1 Vocational; 1 Alternative
0 Magnet; 0 Charter; 5 Title I Eligible; 5 School-wide Title I
Students: 3,245 (51.4% male; 48.6% female)
Individual Education Program: 443 (13.7%);
English Language Learner: 43 (1.3%); Migrant: 0 (0.0%)
Eligible for Free Lunch Program: 1,357 (41.8%)
Eligible for Reduced-Price Lunch Program: 346 (10.7%)
Teachers: 209.4 (15.5 to 1)
Librarians/Media Specialists: 6.3 (515.1 to 1)
Guidance Counselors: 7.3 (444.5 to 1)
Current Spending: ($ per student per year):
Total: $5,128; Instruction: $3,146; Support Services: $1,570
Enrollment, Drop-out Rates and Diploma Recipients by Race/Ethnicity

Category	Total	White	Black	Asian	AIAN	Hisp.
Enrollment (%)	100.0	94.7	3.2	0.0	0.0	2.0
Drop-out Rate (%)	1.1	1.0	0.0	0.0	n/a	10.0
H.S. Diplomas (#)	135	128	7	0	0	0

Tunica County

Tunica County SD
744 School St • Tunica, MS 38676-0758
(662) 363-2811 • http://www2.mde.k12.ms.us/7200/tcsd/
Grade Span: PK-12; **Agency Type:** 1
Schools: 6
3 Primary; 1 Middle; 2 High; 0 Other Level
5 Regular; 0 Special Education; 1 Vocational; 0 Alternative
0 Magnet; 0 Charter; 5 Title I Eligible; 5 School-wide Title I
Students: 2,106 (48.9% male; 51.1% female)
Individual Education Program: 158 (7.5%);
English Language Learner: 4 (0.2%); Migrant: 17 (0.8%)
Eligible for Free Lunch Program: 1,852 (87.9%)
Eligible for Reduced-Price Lunch Program: 122 (5.8%)
Teachers: 142.8 (14.7 to 1)
Librarians/Media Specialists: 6.0 (351.0 to 1)
Guidance Counselors: 6.7 (314.3 to 1)
Current Spending: ($ per student per year):
Total: $7,316; Instruction: $3,613; Support Services: $3,119
Enrollment, Drop-out Rates and Diploma Recipients by Race/Ethnicity

Category	Total	White	Black	Asian	AIAN	Hisp.
Enrollment (%)	100.0	1.9	97.1	0.1	0.0	1.0
Drop-out Rate (%)	7.8	25.0	7.7	n/a	n/a	n/a
H.S. Diplomas (#)	65	2	63	0	0	0

Union County

New Albany Public Schools
301 Hwy 15 N • New Albany, MS 38652-5519
Mailing Address: PO Box 1771 • New Albany, MS 38652-5519
(601) 534-1800 • http://www2.mde.k12.ms.us/7320/
Grade Span: PK-12; **Agency Type:** 1
Schools: 5
1 Primary; 1 Middle; 2 High; 1 Other Level
3 Regular; 0 Special Education; 1 Vocational; 1 Alternative
0 Magnet; 0 Charter; 0 Title I Eligible; 0 School-wide Title I
Students: 2,026 (52.0% male; 48.0% female)
Individual Education Program: 268 (13.2%);
English Language Learner: 60 (3.0%); Migrant: 10 (0.5%)
Eligible for Free Lunch Program: 847 (41.8%)
Eligible for Reduced-Price Lunch Program: 263 (13.0%)
Teachers: 139.8 (14.5 to 1)
Librarians/Media Specialists: 3.9 (519.5 to 1)
Guidance Counselors: 3.0 (675.3 to 1)
Current Spending: ($ per student per year):
Total: $5,957; Instruction: $3,579; Support Services: $2,013
Enrollment, Drop-out Rates and Diploma Recipients by Race/Ethnicity

Category	Total	White	Black	Asian	AIAN	Hisp.
Enrollment (%)	100.0	59.5	36.5	0.1	0.0	3.9
Drop-out Rate (%)	2.3	2.0	4.7	0.0	n/a	0.0
H.S. Diplomas (#)	92	66	23	1	0	2

Union County SD
250 Carter Ave • New Albany, MS 38652
Mailing Address: PO Box 939 • New Albany, MS 38652
(662) 534-1960 • http://www.union.k12.ms.us/
Grade Span: KG-12; **Agency Type:** 1
Schools: 4
0 Primary; 0 Middle; 0 High; 4 Other Level
4 Regular; 0 Special Education; 0 Vocational; 0 Alternative
0 Magnet; 0 Charter; 2 Title I Eligible; 2 School-wide Title I
Students: 2,697 (50.4% male; 49.6% female)
Individual Education Program: 373 (13.8%);
English Language Learner: 0 (0.0%); Migrant: 10 (0.4%)
Eligible for Free Lunch Program: 1,044 (38.7%)
Eligible for Reduced-Price Lunch Program: 328 (12.2%)
Teachers: 154.4 (17.5 to 1)
Librarians/Media Specialists: 7.5 (359.6 to 1)
Guidance Counselors: 3.9 (691.5 to 1)
Current Spending: ($ per student per year):
Total: $4,421; Instruction: $2,621; Support Services: $1,340
Enrollment, Drop-out Rates and Diploma Recipients by Race/Ethnicity

Category	Total	White	Black	Asian	AIAN	Hisp.
Enrollment (%)	100.0	92.2	7.2	0.1	0.0	0.5
Drop-out Rate (%)	3.0	3.3	0.0	n/a	n/a	0.0
H.S. Diplomas (#)	112	107	4	0	0	1

Walthall County

Walthall County SD
814 A Morse Ave • Tylertown, MS 39667-2130
(601) 876-3401 • http://www2.mde.k12.ms.us/7400/
Grade Span: KG-12; **Agency Type:** 1
Schools: 6
2 Primary; 0 Middle; 2 High; 2 Other Level
5 Regular; 0 Special Education; 0 Vocational; 1 Alternative
0 Magnet; 0 Charter; 5 Title I Eligible; 5 School-wide Title I
Students: 2,695 (52.9% male; 47.1% female)
Individual Education Program: 417 (15.5%);
English Language Learner: 3 (0.1%); Migrant: 0 (0.0%)
Eligible for Free Lunch Program: 1,904 (70.6%)
Eligible for Reduced-Price Lunch Program: 253 (9.4%)
Teachers: 191.4 (14.1 to 1)
Librarians/Media Specialists: 7.0 (385.0 to 1)
Guidance Counselors: 3.6 (748.6 to 1)
Current Spending: ($ per student per year):
Total: $5,279; Instruction: $3,526; Support Services: $1,357
Enrollment, Drop-out Rates and Diploma Recipients by Race/Ethnicity

Category	Total	White	Black	Asian	AIAN	Hisp.
Enrollment (%)	100.0	35.6	63.7	0.1	0.1	0.4
Drop-out Rate (%)	3.0	3.1	2.9	0.0	n/a	0.0
H.S. Diplomas (#)	148	54	94	0	0	0

Warren County

Vicksburg Warren SD
1500 Mission 66 • Vicksburg, MS 39180
(601) 638-5122 • http://www.vwsd.k12.ms.us/
Grade Span: PK-12; **Agency Type:** 1
Schools: 15
7 Primary; 4 Middle; 3 High; 1 Other Level
13 Regular; 0 Special Education; 0 Vocational; 2 Alternative
0 Magnet; 0 Charter; 9 Title I Eligible; 9 School-wide Title I
Students: 8,894 (50.0% male; 50.0% female)
Individual Education Program: 1,080 (12.1%);
English Language Learner: 22 (0.2%); Migrant: 0 (0.0%)
Eligible for Free Lunch Program: 4,985 (56.0%)
Eligible for Reduced-Price Lunch Program: 614 (6.9%)
Teachers: 423.6 (21.0 to 1)
Librarians/Media Specialists: 17.0 (523.2 to 1)
Guidance Counselors: 20.0 (444.7 to 1)
Current Spending: ($ per student per year):
Total: $5,331; Instruction: $3,089; Support Services: $1,864

Enrollment, Drop-out Rates and Diploma Recipients by Race/Ethnicity

Category	Total	White	Black	Asian	AIAN	Hisp.
Enrollment (%)	100.0	38.7	59.8	0.6	0.1	0.8
Drop-out Rate (%)	6.7	5.3	7.8	0.0	0.0	20.0
H.S. Diplomas (#)	441	207	225	7	0	2

Washington County

Greenville Public Schools

412 S Main St • Greenville, MS 38702-1619
Mailing Address: PO Box 1619 • Greenville, MS 38702-1619
(662) 334-7001 • http://members.tripod.com/gpsweb/
Grade Span: PK-12; **Agency Type:** 1
Schools: 16
11 Primary; 2 Middle; 2 High; 1 Other Level
14 Regular; 0 Special Education; 1 Vocational; 1 Alternative
0 Magnet; 0 Charter; 14 Title I Eligible; 14 School-wide Title I
Students: 7,401 (49.8% male; 50.2% female)
Individual Education Program: 834 (11.3%);
English Language Learner: 3 (<0.1%); Migrant: 9 (0.1%)
Eligible for Free Lunch Program: 6,353 (85.8%)
Eligible for Reduced-Price Lunch Program: 291 (3.9%)
Teachers: 322.2 (23.0 to 1)
Librarians/Media Specialists: 11.4 (649.2 to 1)
Guidance Counselors: 12.0 (616.8 to 1)
Current Spending: ($ per student per year):
Total: $5,019; Instruction: $3,036; Support Services: $1,564

Enrollment, Drop-out Rates and Diploma Recipients by Race/Ethnicity

Category	Total	White	Black	Asian	AIAN	Hisp.
Enrollment (%)	100.0	3.6	96.1	0.2	0.0	0.1
Drop-out Rate (%)	6.8	20.0	6.7	n/a	n/a	0.0
H.S. Diplomas (#)	300	0	300	0	0	0

Western Line SD

102 Maddox Rd • Avon, MS 38723-0050
Mailing Address: PO Box 50 • Avon, MS 38723-0050
(662) 335-7186 • http://www2.mde.k12.ms.us/7613/
Grade Span: KG-12; **Agency Type:** 1
Schools: 5
3 Primary; 0 Middle; 2 High; 0 Other Level
5 Regular; 0 Special Education; 0 Vocational; 0 Alternative
0 Magnet; 0 Charter; 3 Title I Eligible; 3 School-wide Title I
Students: 2,090 (52.7% male; 47.3% female)
Individual Education Program: 226 (10.8%);
English Language Learner: 2 (0.1%); Migrant: 44 (2.1%)
Eligible for Free Lunch Program: 1,552 (74.3%)
Eligible for Reduced-Price Lunch Program: 165 (7.9%)
Teachers: 135.9 (15.4 to 1)
Librarians/Media Specialists: 7.0 (298.6 to 1)
Guidance Counselors: 2.1 (995.2 to 1)
Current Spending: ($ per student per year):
Total: $4,955; Instruction: $2,984; Support Services: $1,607

Enrollment, Drop-out Rates and Diploma Recipients by Race/Ethnicity

Category	Total	White	Black	Asian	AIAN	Hisp.
Enrollment (%)	100.0	44.7	53.2	0.4	0.4	1.3
Drop-out Rate (%)	9.7	12.4	7.7	0.0	n/a	0.0
H.S. Diplomas (#)	115	44	70	0	0	1

Wayne County

Wayne County SD

810 Chickasawhay St • Waynesboro, MS 39367-2692
(601) 735-4871 • http://www2.mde.k12.ms.us/7700/
Grade Span: KG-12; **Agency Type:** 1
Schools: 8
4 Primary; 1 Middle; 2 High; 1 Other Level
6 Regular; 0 Special Education; 1 Vocational; 1 Alternative
0 Magnet; 0 Charter; 5 Title I Eligible; 5 School-wide Title I
Students: 3,941 (50.1% male; 49.9% female)
Individual Education Program: 536 (13.6%);
English Language Learner: 0 (0.0%); Migrant: 0 (0.0%)
Eligible for Free Lunch Program: 2,602 (66.0%)
Eligible for Reduced-Price Lunch Program: 366 (9.3%)
Teachers: 238.8 (16.5 to 1)
Librarians/Media Specialists: 5.0 (788.2 to 1)
Guidance Counselors: 3.2 (1,231.6 to 1)
Current Spending: ($ per student per year):
Total: $4,982; Instruction: $3,222; Support Services: $1,387

Enrollment, Drop-out Rates and Diploma Recipients by Race/Ethnicity

Category	Total	White	Black	Asian	AIAN	Hisp.
Enrollment (%)	100.0	46.6	52.9	0.3	0.1	0.2
Drop-out Rate (%)	4.7	3.4	5.9	0.0	n/a	0.0
H.S. Diplomas (#)	220	106	114	0	0	0

Webster County

Webster County SD

212 W Clark Ave • Eupora, MS 39744
(662) 258-5921
Grade Span: KG-12; **Agency Type:** 1
Schools: 5
2 Primary; 0 Middle; 3 High; 0 Other Level
4 Regular; 0 Special Education; 1 Vocational; 0 Alternative
0 Magnet; 0 Charter; 4 Title I Eligible; 4 School-wide Title I
Students: 1,873 (51.9% male; 48.1% female)
Individual Education Program: 232 (12.4%);
English Language Learner: 27 (1.4%); Migrant: 12 (0.6%)
Eligible for Free Lunch Program: 904 (48.3%)
Eligible for Reduced-Price Lunch Program: 220 (11.7%)
Teachers: 128.4 (14.6 to 1)
Librarians/Media Specialists: 5.0 (374.6 to 1)
Guidance Counselors: 2.9 (645.9 to 1)
Current Spending: ($ per student per year):
Total: $4,999; Instruction: $3,201; Support Services: $1,459

Enrollment, Drop-out Rates and Diploma Recipients by Race/Ethnicity

Category	Total	White	Black	Asian	AIAN	Hisp.
Enrollment (%)	100.0	69.0	30.1	0.0	0.0	0.9
Drop-out Rate (%)	4.7	5.2	3.8	n/a	n/a	0.0
H.S. Diplomas (#)	93	68	23	0	0	2

Wilkinson County

Wilkinson County SD

488 Main St • Woodville, MS 39669-0785
(601) 888-3582 • http://www2.mde.k12.ms.us/7900/default.htm
Grade Span: PK-12; **Agency Type:** 1
Schools: 4
2 Primary; 0 Middle; 2 High; 0 Other Level
3 Regular; 0 Special Education; 1 Vocational; 0 Alternative
0 Magnet; 0 Charter; 3 Title I Eligible; 3 School-wide Title I
Students: 1,537 (51.9% male; 48.1% female)
Individual Education Program: 216 (14.1%);
English Language Learner: 0 (0.0%); Migrant: 0 (0.0%)
Eligible for Free Lunch Program: 1,344 (87.4%)
Eligible for Reduced-Price Lunch Program: 85 (5.5%)
Teachers: 91.0 (16.9 to 1)
Librarians/Media Specialists: 4.0 (384.3 to 1)
Guidance Counselors: 3.5 (439.1 to 1)
Current Spending: ($ per student per year):
Total: $5,380; Instruction: $3,015; Support Services: $1,897

Enrollment, Drop-out Rates and Diploma Recipients by Race/Ethnicity

Category	Total	White	Black	Asian	AIAN	Hisp.
Enrollment (%)	100.0	0.7	99.3	0.0	0.0	0.0
Drop-out Rate (%)	4.7	0.0	4.7	n/a	n/a	n/a
H.S. Diplomas (#)	72	0	72	0	0	0

Winston County

Louisville Municipal SD

112 S Columbus Ave • Louisville, MS 39339-0909
(662) 773-3411 • http://www2.mde.k12.ms.us/8020/
Grade Span: KG-12; **Agency Type:** 1
Schools: 7
1 Primary; 2 Middle; 2 High; 2 Other Level
6 Regular; 0 Special Education; 1 Vocational; 0 Alternative
0 Magnet; 0 Charter; 6 Title I Eligible; 6 School-wide Title I
Students: 3,041 (52.7% male; 47.3% female)
Individual Education Program: 404 (13.3%);
English Language Learner: 0 (0.0%); Migrant: 0 (0.0%)
Eligible for Free Lunch Program: 2,053 (67.5%)
Eligible for Reduced-Price Lunch Program: 290 (9.5%)
Teachers: 225.3 (13.5 to 1)
Librarians/Media Specialists: 8.5 (357.8 to 1)
Guidance Counselors: 7.0 (434.4 to 1)
Current Spending: ($ per student per year):
Total: $5,149; Instruction: $3,232; Support Services: $1,531

Enrollment, Drop-out Rates and Diploma Recipients by Race/Ethnicity

Category	Total	White	Black	Asian	AIAN	Hisp.
Enrollment (%)	100.0	34.6	63.6	0.3	1.3	0.3
Drop-out Rate (%)	4.2	4.5	4.1	n/a	0.0	0.0
H.S. Diplomas (#)	186	64	120	1	1	0

Yazoo County

Yazoo City Municipal SD

1133 Calhoun • Yazoo City, MS 39194-2939
Mailing Address: PO Box 127 • Yazoo City, MS 39194-2939
(662) 746-2125 • http://www.yazoocity.k12.ms.us/
Grade Span: PK-12; **Agency Type:** 1
Schools: 6
2 Primary; 1 Middle; 2 High; 1 Other Level
4 Regular; 0 Special Education; 1 Vocational; 1 Alternative
0 Magnet; 0 Charter; 3 Title I Eligible; 3 School-wide Title I
Students: 2,939 (50.6% male; 49.4% female)
Individual Education Program: 328 (11.2%);
English Language Learner: 0 (0.0%); Migrant: 0 (0.0%)
Eligible for Free Lunch Program: 2,772 (94.3%)
Eligible for Reduced-Price Lunch Program: 112 (3.8%)
Teachers: 164.9 (17.8 to 1)
Librarians/Media Specialists: 5.0 (587.8 to 1)
Guidance Counselors: 4.0 (734.8 to 1)
Current Spending: ($ per student per year):
Total: $4,940; Instruction: $2,951; Support Services: $1,544

Enrollment, Drop-out Rates and Diploma Recipients by Race/Ethnicity

Category	Total	White	Black	Asian	AIAN	Hisp.
Enrollment (%)	100.0	1.6	97.6	0.3	0.1	0.4
Drop-out Rate (%)	8.0	8.7	8.1	0.0	n/a	0.0
H.S. Diplomas (#)	90	6	84	0	0	0

Yazoo County SD

119 W Jefferson • Yazoo City, MS 39194-4005
Mailing Address: PO Box 1088 • Yazoo City, MS 39194-4005
(662) 746-4672 • http://www.yazoo.k12.ms.us/
Grade Span: KG-12; **Agency Type:** 1
Schools: 3
2 Primary; 0 Middle; 1 High; 0 Other Level
3 Regular; 0 Special Education; 0 Vocational; 0 Alternative
0 Magnet; 0 Charter; 3 Title I Eligible; 3 School-wide Title I
Students: 1,811 (51.0% male; 49.0% female)
Individual Education Program: 265 (14.6%);
English Language Learner: 0 (0.0%); Migrant: 0 (0.0%)
Eligible for Free Lunch Program: 1,338 (73.9%)
Eligible for Reduced-Price Lunch Program: 154 (8.5%)
Teachers: 110.8 (16.3 to 1)
Librarians/Media Specialists: 3.0 (603.7 to 1)
Guidance Counselors: 4.3 (421.2 to 1)
Current Spending: ($ per student per year):
Total: $6,037; Instruction: $3,209; Support Services: $2,365

Enrollment, Drop-out Rates and Diploma Recipients by Race/Ethnicity

Category	Total	White	Black	Asian	AIAN	Hisp.
Enrollment (%)	100.0	43.6	55.7	0.4	0.0	0.4
Drop-out Rate (%)	7.7	13.0	4.5	n/a	n/a	0.0
H.S. Diplomas (#)	89	31	58	0	0	0

Number of Schools

Rank	Number	District Name	City
1	61	Jackson Public SD	Jackson
2	25	Desoto County SD	Hernando
3	23	Rankin County SD	Brandon
4	20	Harrison County SD	Gulfport
5	19	Pascagoula Separate SD	Pascagoula
6	17	Madison County SD	Flora
7	16	Greenville Public Schools	Greenville
7	16	Tupelo Public SD	Tupelo
9	15	Jackson County SD	Vancleave
9	15	Meridian Public SD	Meridian
9	15	Vicksburg Warren SD	Vicksburg
12	14	Jones County SD	Ellisville
13	13	Columbus Municipal SD	Columbus
13	13	Lamar County SD	Purvis
15	12	Biloxi Public SD	Biloxi
15	12	Clarksdale Municipal SD	Clarksdale
15	12	Cleveland SD	Cleveland
15	12	Gulfport SD	Gulfport
19	11	Alcorn SD	Corinth
19	11	Hinds County SD	Raymond
19	11	Moss Point Separate SD	Moss Point
22	10	Hattiesburg Public SD	Hattiesburg
23	9	Clinton Public SD	Clinton
23	9	Lauderdale County SD	Meridian
23	9	Lee County SD	Tupelo
23	9	Lowndes County SD	Columbus
23	9	Marion County SD	Columbia
23	9	Picayune SD	Picayune
23	9	Simpson County SD	Mendenhall
23	9	Starkville SD	Starkville
23	9	West Point SD	West Point
32	8	Covington County Schools	Collins
32	8	George County SD	Lucedale
32	8	Greenwood Public SD	Greenwood
32	8	Itawamba County SD	Fulton
32	8	Laurel SD	Laurel
32	8	Leake County SD	Carthage
32	8	Leflore County SD	Greenwood
32	8	Natchez-Adams SD	Natchez
32	8	Prentiss County SD	Booneville
32	8	Scott County SD	Forest
32	8	Tishomingo County Sp Mun SD	luka
32	8	Wayne County SD	Waynesboro
44	7	Aberdeen SD	Aberdeen
44	7	Brookhaven SD	Brookhaven
44	7	Calhoun County SD	Pittsboro
44	7	Hancock County SD	Kiln
44	7	Holmes County SD	Lexington
44	7	Louisville Municipal SD	Louisville
44	7	Mccomb SD	Mccomb
44	7	North Panola Schools	Sardis
44	7	Ocean Springs SD	Ocean Springs
44	7	Oxford SD	Oxford
44	7	Pontotoc County SD	Pontotoc
44	7	South Panola SD	Batesville
44	7	South Pike SD	Magnolia
44	7	Sunflower County SD	Indianola
58	6	Canton Public SD	Canton
58	6	Coahoma County SD	Clarksdale
58	6	Forrest County SD	Hattiesburg
58	6	Greene County SD	Leakesville
58	6	Grenada SD	Grenada
58	6	Indianola SD	Indianola
58	6	Kosciusko SD	Kosciusko
58	6	Lawrence County SD	Monticello
58	6	Marshall County SD	Holly Springs
58	6	Noxubee County SD	Macon
58	6	Smith County SD	Raleigh
58	6	South Tippah SD	Ripley
58	6	Tate County SD	Senatobia
58	6	Tunica County SD	Tunica
58	6	Walthall County SD	Tylertown
58	6	West Jasper Consolidated Schools	Bay Springs
58	6	Yazoo City Municipal SD	Yazoo City
75	5	Amory SD	Amory
75	5	Bay Saint Louis Waveland SD	Bay St Louis
75	5	Choctaw County SD	Ackerman
75	5	Corinth SD	Corinth
75	5	Franklin County SD	Meadville
75	5	Holly Springs SD	Holly Springs
75	5	Houston SD	Houston
75	5	Jefferson County SD	Fayette
75	5	Jefferson Davis County SD	Prentiss
75	5	Lincoln County SD	Brookhaven
75	5	Long Beach SD	Long Beach
75	5	Monroe County SD	Amory
75	5	New Albany Public Schools	New Albany
75	5	Pearl Public SD	Pearl
75	5	Poplarville Separate SD	Poplarville
75	5	Quitman SD	Quitman
75	5	Webster County SD	Eupora
75	5	Western Line SD	Avon
93	4	Claiborne County SD	Port Gibson
93	4	Columbia SD	Columbia
93	4	Copiah County SD	Hazlehurst
93	4	East Tallahatchie Consol SD	Charleston
93	4	Humphreys County SD	Belzoni
93	4	Lafayette County SD	Oxford
93	4	Newton County SD	Decatur
93	4	Pass Christian Public SD	Pass Christian
93	4	Petal SD	Petal
93	4	Pontotoc City Schools	Pontotoc
93	4	Quitman County SD	Marks
93	4	Senatobia Municipal SD	Senatobia
93	4	Stone County SD	Wiggins
93	4	Union County SD	New Albany
93	4	Wilkinson County SD	Woodville
108	3	Forest Municipal SD	Forest
108	3	Neshoba County SD	Philadelphia
108	3	North Pike SD	Summit
108	3	Pearl River County SD	Carriere
108	3	Yazoo County SD	Yazoo City
113	2	Hazlehurst City SD	Hazlehurst

Number of Teachers

Rank	Number	District Name	City
1	1,883	Jackson Public SD	Jackson
2	1,106	Desoto County SD	Hernando
3	1,000	Rankin County SD	Brandon
4	785	Harrison County SD	Gulfport
5	606	Madison County SD	Flora
6	557	Tupelo Public SD	Tupelo
7	512	Jones County SD	Ellisville
8	468	Pascagoula Separate SD	Pascagoula
9	458	Jackson County SD	Vancleave
10	453	Lamar County SD	Purvis
11	450	Gulfport SD	Gulfport
12	423	Vicksburg Warren SD	Vicksburg
13	415	Biloxi Public SD	Biloxi
14	411	Lauderdale County SD	Meridian
15	410	Lee County SD	Tupelo
16	404	Meridian Public SD	Meridian
17	394	Columbus Municipal SD	Columbus
18	370	Hinds County SD	Raymond
19	336	Lowndes County SD	Columbus
20	332	Natchez-Adams SD	Natchez
21	322	Greenville Public Schools	Greenville
22	306	Clinton Public SD	Clinton
23	293	Ocean Springs SD	Ocean Springs
24	292	Starkville SD	Starkville
25	289	South Panola SD	Batesville
26	287	Picayune SD	Picayune
27	270	Cleveland SD	Cleveland
28	268	Simpson County SD	Mendenhall
29	261	Alcorn SD	Corinth
30	261	Grenada SD	Grenada
31	261	Hancock County SD	Kiln
32	256	Pearl Public SD	Pearl
33	254	Moss Point Separate SD	Moss Point
34	251	Hattiesburg Public SD	Hattiesburg
35	250	Laurel SD	Laurel
36	249	Clarksdale Municipal SD	Clarksdale
37	248	George County SD	Lucedale
38	246	Itawamba County SD	Fulton
39	244	Petal SD	Petal
40	242	Greenwood Public SD	Greenwood
41	238	Wayne County SD	Waynesboro
42	236	Scott County SD	Forest
43	231	Long Beach SD	Long Beach
44	225	Louisville Municipal SD	Louisville
45	224	Covington County Schools	Collins
46	220	Mccomb SD	Mccomb
47	219	Brookhaven SD	Brookhaven
48	215	Oxford SD	Oxford
49	209	Neshoba County SD	Philadelphia
49	209	Tishomingo County Sp Mun SD	luka
51	207	West Point SD	West Point
52	204	Prentiss County SD	Booneville
53	202	Leake County SD	Carthage
53	202	Pontotoc County SD	Pontotoc
55	200	Marion County SD	Columbia
56	192	Forrest County SD	Hattiesburg
57	191	Marshall County SD	Holly Springs
58	191	Walthall County SD	Tylertown
59	191	Smith County SD	Raleigh
60	190	Canton Public SD	Canton
61	187	Copiah County SD	Hazlehurst
62	183	Holmes County SD	Lexington
63	180	Leflore County SD	Greenwood
64	175	Tate County SD	Senatobia
65	171	Stone County SD	Wiggins
66	170	South Tippah SD	Ripley
67	168	Pearl River County SD	Carriere
68	167	Monroe County SD	Amory
69	166	Lincoln County SD	Brookhaven
70	164	Yazoo City Municipal SD	Yazoo City
71	164	Indianola SD	Indianola
71	164	Lawrence County SD	Monticello
73	160	Aberdeen SD	Aberdeen
74	160	Calhoun County SD	Pittsboro
75	156	Lafayette County SD	Oxford
76	154	Union County SD	New Albany
77	154	Jefferson Davis County SD	Prentiss
78	153	Coahoma County SD	Clarksdale
79	153	Quitman SD	Quitman
80	152	Bay Saint Louis Waveland SD	Bay St Louis
81	142	Tunica County SD	Tunica
82	141	Pontotoc City Schools	Pontotoc
83	141	Corinth SD	Corinth
84	139	New Albany Public Schools	New Albany
85	139	Noxubee County SD	Macon
86	138	South Pike SD	Magnolia
87	136	Pass Christian Public SD	Pass Christian
88	135	Western Line SD	Avon
89	135	Kosciusko SD	Kosciusko
90	135	North Panola Schools	Sardis
91	133	Poplarville Separate SD	Poplarville
92	131	Houston SD	Houston
93	128	Choctaw County SD	Ackerman
94	128	Webster County SD	Eupora
95	125	Sunflower County SD	Indianola
96	125	Claiborne County SD	Port Gibson
97	122	Amory SD	Amory
98	121	Franklin County SD	Meadville
99	120	Newton County SD	Decatur
100	119	West Jasper Consolidated Schools	Bay Springs
101	118	Holly Springs SD	Holly Springs
102	118	Columbia SD	Columbia
103	111	East Tallahatchie Consol SD	Charleston
104	110	Yazoo County SD	Yazoo City
105	110	Hazlehurst City SD	Hazlehurst
105	110	Jefferson County SD	Fayette
107	109	Humphreys County SD	Belzoni
108	109	Forest Municipal SD	Forest
109	106	Quitman County SD	Marks
110	105	Greene County SD	Leakesville
111	103	Senatobia Municipal SD	Senatobia
112	99	North Pike SD	Summit
113	91	Wilkinson County SD	Woodville

Number of Students

Rank	Number	District Name	City
1	31,529	Jackson Public SD	Jackson
2	22,145	Desoto County SD	Hernando
3	15,528	Rankin County SD	Brandon
4	13,018	Harrison County SD	Gulfport
5	9,423	Madison County SD	Flora
6	8,894	Vicksburg Warren SD	Vicksburg
7	8,512	Jackson County SD	Vancleave
8	7,755	Jones County SD	Ellisville
9	7,491	Pascagoula Separate SD	Pascagoula
10	7,401	Greenville Public Schools	Greenville
11	7,282	Tupelo Public SD	Tupelo
12	6,757	Lamar County SD	Purvis
13	6,695	Meridian Public SD	Meridian
14	6,654	Lauderdale County SD	Meridian
15	6,241	Lee County SD	Tupelo
16	6,239	Gulfport SD	Gulfport
17	6,171	Biloxi Public SD	Biloxi
18	5,769	Hinds County SD	Raymond
19	5,384	Lowndes County SD	Columbus
20	5,097	Columbus Municipal SD	Columbus
21	5,061	Ocean Springs SD	Ocean Springs
22	4,956	Clinton Public SD	Clinton
23	4,873	Hattiesburg Public SD	Hattiesburg
24	4,796	Natchez-Adams SD	Natchez
25	4,646	Grenada SD	Grenada
26	4,592	South Panola SD	Batesville
27	4,369	Simpson County SD	Mendenhall
28	4,307	Hancock County SD	Kiln
29	4,125	Moss Point Separate SD	Moss Point
30	3,968	George County SD	Lucedale
31	3,941	Wayne County SD	Waynesboro
32	3,837	Starkville SD	Starkville
33	3,821	Scott County SD	Forest
34	3,798	Alcorn SD	Corinth
35	3,781	Itawamba County SD	Fulton
36	3,770	Picayune SD	Picayune
37	3,727	Clarksdale Municipal SD	Clarksdale
38	3,718	Pearl Public SD	Pearl
39	3,707	Cleveland SD	Cleveland
40	3,679	Petal SD	Petal
41	3,678	West Point SD	West Point
42	3,653	Holmes County SD	Lexington

Rank	Number	District Name	City
43	3,560	Canton Public SD	Canton
44	3,518	Covington County Schools	Collins
45	3,486	Greenwood Public SD	Greenwood
46	3,397	Marshall County SD	Holly Springs
47	3,325	Long Beach SD	Long Beach
48	3,318	Leake County SD	Carthage
49	3,245	Tishomingo County Sp Mun SD	Iuka
50	3,198	Oxford SD	Oxford
51	3,160	Copiah County SD	Hazlehurst
52	3,154	Laurel SD	Laurel
53	3,077	Smith County SD	Raleigh
54	3,050	Leflore County SD	Greenwood
55	3,041	Louisville Municipal SD	Louisville
56	3,035	Pontotoc County SD	Pontotoc
57	2,993	Brookhaven SD	Brookhaven
58	2,939	Yazoo City Municipal SD	Yazoo City
59	2,922	Mccomb SD	Mccomb
60	2,866	Neshoba County SD	Philadelphia
61	2,845	Tate County SD	Senatobia
62	2,826	Lincoln County SD	Brookhaven
63	2,793	Indianola SD	Indianola
64	2,720	Pearl River County SD	Carriere
65	2,715	South Tippah SD	Ripley
66	2,697	Union County SD	New Albany
67	2,695	Walthall County SD	Tylertown
68	2,626	Stone County SD	Wiggins
69	2,619	Monroe County SD	Amory
70	2,594	Marion County SD	Columbia
71	2,587	Calhoun County SD	Pittsboro
72	2,428	Quitman SD	Quitman
73	2,391	Lawrence County SD	Monticello
74	2,376	Forrest County SD	Hattiesburg
75	2,320	Jefferson Davis County SD	Prentiss
76	2,266	Pontotoc City Schools	Pontotoc
77	2,259	Noxubee County SD	Macon
78	2,251	Prentiss County SD	Booneville
79	2,244	South Pike SD	Magnolia
80	2,208	Bay Saint Louis Waveland SD	Bay St Louis
81	2,116	Lafayette County SD	Oxford
82	2,106	Tunica County SD	Tunica
83	2,090	Western Line SD	Avon
84	2,089	Kosciusko SD	Kosciusko
85	2,054	Houston SD	Houston
86	2,032	Humphreys County SD	Belzoni
87	2,029	Poplarville Separate SD	Poplarville
88	2,026	New Albany Public Schools	New Albany
89	1,924	Pass Christian Public SD	Pass Christian
90	1,922	Sunflower County SD	Indianola
91	1,910	Greene County SD	Leakesville
92	1,906	Coahoma County SD	Clarksdale
93	1,893	Holly Springs SD	Holly Springs
94	1,882	Amory SD	Amory
95	1,873	Webster County SD	Eupora
96	1,866	Claiborne County SD	Port Gibson
97	1,863	Choctaw County SD	Ackerman
97	1,863	Columbia SD	Columbia
99	1,818	North Panola Schools	Sardis
100	1,811	Yazoo County SD	Yazoo City
101	1,808	West Jasper Consolidated Schools	Bay Springs
102	1,798	Aberdeen SD	Aberdeen
103	1,781	Corinth SD	Corinth
104	1,727	North Pike SD	Summit
105	1,726	Newton County SD	Decatur
106	1,707	Hazlehurst City SD	Hazlehurst
107	1,682	Senatobia Municipal SD	Senatobia
108	1,653	Jefferson County SD	Fayette
109	1,645	Forest Municipal SD	Forest
110	1,623	East Tallahatchie Consol SD	Charleston
111	1,609	Franklin County SD	Meadville
112	1,596	Quitman County SD	Marks
113	1,537	Wilkinson County SD	Woodville

Male Students

Rank	Percent	District Name	City
1	53.1	Franklin County SD	Meadville
2	52.9	Corinth SD	Corinth
2	52.9	Walthall County SD	Tylertown
4	52.7	Leake County SD	Carthage
4	52.7	Louisville Municipal SD	Louisville
4	52.7	Western Line SD	Avon
7	52.6	Lafayette County SD	Oxford
8	52.4	Forest Municipal SD	Forest
8	52.4	Jones County SD	Ellisville
8	52.4	Marion County SD	Columbia
11	52.3	Lincoln County SD	Brookhaven
12	52.2	George County SD	Lucedale
13	52.1	Jefferson Davis County SD	Prentiss
13	52.1	Monroe County SD	Amory
15	52.0	Alcorn SD	Corinth
15	52.0	Desoto County SD	Hernando
15	52.0	Lamar County SD	Purvis
15	52.0	Lauderdale County SD	Meridian
15	52.0	New Albany Public Schools	New Albany
15	52.0	Newton County SD	Decatur
15	52.0	Smith County SD	Raleigh
15	52.0	South Pike SD	Magnolia
23	51.9	Copiah County SD	Hazlehurst
23	51.9	Lee County SD	Tupelo
23	51.9	Simpson County SD	Mendenhall
23	51.9	Webster County SD	Eupora
23	51.9	Wilkinson County SD	Woodville
28	51.8	Forrest County SD	Hattiesburg
28	51.8	Jackson County SD	Vancleave
28	51.8	Kosciusko SD	Kosciusko
31	51.7	Columbia SD	Columbia
31	51.7	Harrison County SD	Gulfport
31	51.7	Hazlehurst City SD	Hazlehurst
34	51.6	Ocean Springs SD	Ocean Springs
34	51.6	Rankin County SD	Brandon
36	51.5	Marshall County SD	Holly Springs
36	51.5	Pontotoc County SD	Pontotoc
38	51.4	North Pike SD	Summit
38	51.4	Pearl River County SD	Carriere
38	51.4	Prentiss County SD	Booneville
38	51.4	Quitman SD	Quitman
38	51.4	Tishomingo County Sp Mun SD	Iuka
43	51.3	Amory SD	Amory
43	51.3	Columbus Municipal SD	Columbus
43	51.3	Indianola SD	Indianola
43	51.3	Petal SD	Petal
43	51.3	Scott County SD	Forest
43	51.3	Senatobia Municipal SD	Senatobia
49	51.2	Jefferson County SD	Fayette
50	51.1	Bay Saint Louis Waveland SD	Bay St Louis
50	51.1	Biloxi Public SD	Biloxi
50	51.1	Clinton Public SD	Clinton
50	51.1	Hancock County SD	Kiln
50	51.1	Pascagoula Separate SD	Pascagoula
50	51.1	South Panola SD	Batesville
56	51.0	Choctaw County SD	Ackerman
56	51.0	Oxford SD	Oxford
56	51.0	Picayune SD	Picayune
56	51.0	Quitman County SD	Marks
56	51.0	Tupelo Public SD	Tupelo
56	51.0	Yazoo County SD	Yazoo City
62	50.9	Holly Springs SD	Holly Springs
62	50.9	Itawamba County SD	Fulton
62	50.9	Sunflower County SD	Indianola
65	50.8	Madison County SD	Flora
65	50.8	Pearl Public SD	Pearl
65	50.8	Poplarville Separate SD	Poplarville
68	50.7	North Panola Schools	Sardis
69	50.6	Aberdeen SD	Aberdeen
69	50.6	Leflore County SD	Greenwood
69	50.6	Moss Point Separate SD	Moss Point
69	50.6	Pontotoc City Schools	Pontotoc
69	50.6	Stone County SD	Wiggins
69	50.6	Tate County SD	Senatobia
69	50.6	Yazoo City Municipal SD	Yazoo City
76	50.5	Coahoma County SD	Clarksdale
76	50.5	Hattiesburg Public SD	Hattiesburg
76	50.5	Hinds County SD	Raymond
76	50.5	Lowndes County SD	Columbus
76	50.5	Natchez-Adams SD	Natchez
81	50.4	Greenwood Public SD	Greenwood
81	50.4	Grenada SD	Grenada
81	50.4	Humphreys County SD	Belzoni
81	50.4	Lawrence County SD	Monticello
81	50.4	Long Beach SD	Long Beach
81	50.4	South Tippah SD	Ripley
81	50.4	Union County SD	New Albany
88	50.3	Calhoun County SD	Pittsboro
88	50.3	Covington County Schools	Collins
90	50.2	Laurel SD	Laurel
91	50.1	Cleveland SD	Cleveland
91	50.1	Gulfport SD	Gulfport
91	50.1	Meridian Public SD	Meridian
91	50.1	Wayne County SD	Waynesboro
95	50.0	Jackson Public SD	Jackson
95	50.0	Vicksburg Warren SD	Vicksburg
95	50.0	West Point SD	West Point
98	49.9	Houston SD	Houston
98	49.9	Starkville SD	Starkville
100	49.8	Claiborne County SD	Port Gibson
100	49.8	Greenville Public Schools	Greenville
100	49.8	Holmes County SD	Lexington
100	49.8	Pass Christian Public SD	Pass Christian
104	49.6	Clarksdale Municipal SD	Clarksdale
104	49.6	West Jasper Consolidated Schools	Bay Springs
106	49.5	Greene County SD	Leakesville
106	49.5	Neshoba County SD	Philadelphia
108	49.4	East Tallahatchie Consol SD	Charleston
109	49.3	Noxubee County SD	Macon
110	49.0	Brookhaven SD	Brookhaven
111	48.9	Mccomb SD	Mccomb
111	48.9	Tunica County SD	Tunica
113	48.6	Canton Public SD	Canton

Female Students

Rank	Percent	District Name	City
1	51.4	Canton Public SD	Canton
2	51.1	Mccomb SD	Mccomb
2	51.1	Tunica County SD	Tunica
4	51.0	Brookhaven SD	Brookhaven
5	50.7	Noxubee County SD	Macon
6	50.6	East Tallahatchie Consol SD	Charleston
7	50.5	Greene County SD	Leakesville
7	50.5	Neshoba County SD	Philadelphia
9	50.4	Clarksdale Municipal SD	Clarksdale
9	50.4	West Jasper Consolidated Schools	Bay Springs
11	50.2	Claiborne County SD	Port Gibson
11	50.2	Greenville Public Schools	Greenville
11	50.2	Holmes County SD	Lexington
11	50.2	Pass Christian Public SD	Pass Christian
15	50.1	Houston SD	Houston
15	50.1	Starkville SD	Starkville
17	50.0	Jackson Public SD	Jackson
17	50.0	Vicksburg Warren SD	Vicksburg
17	50.0	West Point SD	West Point
20	49.9	Cleveland SD	Cleveland
20	49.9	Gulfport SD	Gulfport
20	49.9	Meridian Public SD	Meridian
20	49.9	Wayne County SD	Waynesboro
24	49.8	Laurel SD	Laurel
25	49.7	Calhoun County SD	Pittsboro
25	49.7	Covington County Schools	Collins
27	49.6	Greenwood Public SD	Greenwood
27	49.6	Grenada SD	Grenada
27	49.6	Humphreys County SD	Belzoni
27	49.6	Lawrence County SD	Monticello
27	49.6	Long Beach SD	Long Beach
27	49.6	South Tippah SD	Ripley
27	49.6	Union County SD	New Albany
34	49.5	Coahoma County SD	Clarksdale
34	49.5	Hattiesburg Public SD	Hattiesburg
34	49.5	Hinds County SD	Raymond
34	49.5	Lowndes County SD	Columbus
34	49.5	Natchez-Adams SD	Natchez
39	49.4	Aberdeen SD	Aberdeen
39	49.4	Leflore County SD	Greenwood
39	49.4	Moss Point Separate SD	Moss Point
39	49.4	Pontotoc City Schools	Pontotoc
39	49.4	Stone County SD	Wiggins
39	49.4	Tate County SD	Senatobia
39	49.4	Yazoo City Municipal SD	Yazoo City
46	49.3	North Panola Schools	Sardis
47	49.2	Madison County SD	Flora
47	49.2	Pearl Public SD	Pearl
47	49.2	Poplarville Separate SD	Poplarville
50	49.1	Holly Springs SD	Holly Springs
50	49.1	Itawamba County SD	Fulton
50	49.1	Sunflower County SD	Indianola
53	49.0	Choctaw County SD	Ackerman
53	49.0	Oxford SD	Oxford
53	49.0	Picayune SD	Picayune
53	49.0	Quitman County SD	Marks
53	49.0	Tupelo Public SD	Tupelo
53	49.0	Yazoo County SD	Yazoo City
59	48.9	Bay Saint Louis Waveland SD	Bay St Louis
59	48.9	Biloxi Public SD	Biloxi
59	48.9	Clinton Public SD	Clinton
59	48.9	Hancock County SD	Kiln
59	48.9	Pascagoula Separate SD	Pascagoula
59	48.9	South Panola SD	Batesville
65	48.8	Jefferson County SD	Fayette
66	48.7	Amory SD	Amory
66	48.7	Columbus Municipal SD	Columbus
66	48.7	Indianola SD	Indianola
66	48.7	Petal SD	Petal
66	48.7	Scott County SD	Forest
66	48.7	Senatobia Municipal SD	Senatobia
72	48.6	North Pike SD	Summit
72	48.6	Pearl River County SD	Carriere
72	48.6	Prentiss County SD	Booneville
72	48.6	Quitman SD	Quitman
72	48.6	Tishomingo County Sp Mun SD	Iuka
77	48.5	Marshall County SD	Holly Springs
77	48.5	Pontotoc County SD	Pontotoc
79	48.4	Ocean Springs SD	Ocean Springs
79	48.4	Rankin County SD	Brandon
81	48.3	Columbia SD	Columbia
81	48.3	Harrison County SD	Gulfport
81	48.3	Hazlehurst City SD	Hazlehurst
84	48.2	Forrest County SD	Hattiesburg
84	48.2	Jackson County SD	Vancleave
84	48.2	Kosciusko SD	Kosciusko

Rank	Percent	District Name	City
87	48.1	Copiah County SD	Hazlehurst
87	48.1	Lee County SD	Tupelo
87	48.1	Simpson County SD	Mendenhall
87	48.1	Webster County SD	Eupora
87	48.1	Wilkinson County SD	Woodville
92	48.0	Alcorn SD	Corinth
92	48.0	Desoto County SD	Hernando
92	48.0	Lamar County SD	Purvis
92	48.0	Lauderdale County SD	Meridian
92	48.0	New Albany Public Schools	New Albany
92	48.0	Newton County SD	Decatur
92	48.0	Smith County SD	Raleigh
92	48.0	South Pike SD	Magnolia
100	47.9	Jefferson Davis County SD	Prentiss
100	47.9	Monroe County SD	Amory
102	47.8	George County SD	Lucedale
103	47.7	Lincoln County SD	Brookhaven
104	47.6	Forest Municipal SD	Forest
104	47.6	Jones County SD	Ellisville
104	47.6	Marion County SD	Columbia
107	47.4	Lafayette County SD	Oxford
108	47.3	Leake County SD	Carthage
108	47.3	Louisville Municipal SD	Louisville
108	47.3	Western Line SD	Avon
111	47.1	Corinth SD	Corinth
111	47.1	Walthall County SD	Tylertown
113	46.9	Franklin County SD	Meadville

Individual Education Program Students

Rank	Percent	District Name	City
1	24.5	Prentiss County SD	Booneville
2	21.3	Coahoma County SD	Clarksdale
3	21.2	Lafayette County SD	Oxford
4	19.1	Marion County SD	Columbia
5	18.3	Franklin County SD	Meadville
6	18.0	Leflore County SD	Greenwood
7	17.7	Kosciusko SD	Kosciusko
8	17.5	Jefferson Davis County SD	Prentiss
9	17.4	Holly Springs SD	Holly Springs
10	17.2	Columbia SD	Columbia
10	17.2	Petal SD	Petal
12	17.0	Lee County SD	Tupelo
13	16.6	Covington County Schools	Collins
13	16.6	West Jasper Consolidated Schools	Bay Springs
15	16.5	Calhoun County SD	Pittsboro
16	16.4	Alcorn SD	Corinth
17	16.1	Smith County SD	Raleigh
18	16.0	Forrest County SD	Hattiesburg
18	16.0	Moss Point Separate SD	Moss Point
20	15.9	Senatobia Municipal SD	Senatobia
21	15.8	George County SD	Lucedale
22	15.5	Aberdeen SD	Aberdeen
22	15.5	Greene County SD	Leakesville
22	15.5	Walthall County SD	Tylertown
25	15.3	Lauderdale County SD	Meridian
25	15.3	Pass Christian Public SD	Pass Christian
27	15.1	Bay Saint Louis Waveland SD	Bay St Louis
28	15.0	Noxubee County SD	Macon
29	14.9	Hancock County SD	Kiln
29	14.9	Leake County SD	Carthage
31	14.8	Corinth SD	Corinth
31	14.8	Lamar County SD	Purvis
33	14.7	Tate County SD	Senatobia
34	14.6	Biloxi Public SD	Biloxi
34	14.6	Monroe County SD	Amory
34	14.6	Yazoo County SD	Yazoo City
37	14.5	Forest Municipal SD	Forest
37	14.5	Quitman County SD	Marks
39	14.4	Hattiesburg Public SD	Hattiesburg
39	14.4	Pascagoula Separate SD	Pascagoula
41	14.2	Itawamba County SD	Fulton
41	14.2	Jones County SD	Ellisville
41	14.2	Pontotoc City Schools	Pontotoc
44	14.1	Wilkinson County SD	Woodville
45	14.0	East Tallahatchie Consol SD	Charleston
45	14.0	Jefferson County SD	Fayette
47	13.8	Union County SD	New Albany
48	13.7	Tishomingo County Sp Mun SD	Iuka
49	13.6	Wayne County SD	Waynesboro
50	13.5	Gulfport SD	Gulfport
51	13.4	Amory SD	Amory
52	13.3	Louisville Municipal SD	Louisville
53	13.2	Harrison County SD	Gulfport
53	13.2	New Albany Public Schools	New Albany
53	13.2	Pontotoc County SD	Pontotoc
53	13.2	Quitman SD	Quitman
53	13.2	Tupelo Public SD	Tupelo
58	13.1	Picayune SD	Picayune
59	12.9	Marshall County SD	Holly Springs
60	12.8	Mccomb SD	Mccomb
60	12.8	Newton County SD	Decatur
60	12.8	South Tippah SD	Ripley
63	12.7	Ocean Springs SD	Ocean Springs
63	12.7	Poplarville Separate SD	Poplarville
65	12.6	Cleveland SD	Cleveland
65	12.6	Laurel SD	Laurel
67	12.5	Lincoln County SD	Brookhaven
67	12.5	Scott County SD	Forest
69	12.4	Grenada SD	Grenada
69	12.4	Sunflower County SD	Indianola
69	12.4	Webster County SD	Eupora
72	12.3	Hazlehurst City SD	Hazlehurst
72	12.3	Indianola SD	Indianola
72	12.3	Starkville SD	Starkville
75	12.2	Columbus Municipal SD	Columbus
76	12.1	Vicksburg Warren SD	Vicksburg
77	12.0	Long Beach SD	Long Beach
77	12.0	Meridian Public SD	Meridian
77	12.0	South Panola SD	Batesville
77	12.0	Stone County SD	Wiggins
81	11.9	Desoto County SD	Hernando
81	11.9	Neshoba County SD	Philadelphia
81	11.9	Simpson County SD	Mendenhall
84	11.8	North Panola Schools	Sardis
85	11.7	Houston SD	Houston
85	11.7	Lawrence County SD	Monticello
87	11.4	South Pike SD	Magnolia
88	11.3	Greenville Public Schools	Greenville
89	11.2	Greenwood Public SD	Greenwood
89	11.2	Yazoo City Municipal SD	Yazoo City
91	11.0	Oxford SD	Oxford
92	10.9	Choctaw County SD	Ackerman
92	10.9	Clarksdale Municipal SD	Clarksdale
94	10.8	Natchez-Adams SD	Natchez
94	10.8	Western Line SD	Avon
96	10.7	Canton Public SD	Canton
97	10.6	Rankin County SD	Brandon
98	10.3	Lowndes County SD	Columbus
98	10.3	Pearl Public SD	Pearl
100	10.2	Brookhaven SD	Brookhaven
101	10.0	North Pike SD	Summit
102	9.9	Jackson Public SD	Jackson
103	9.8	Jackson County SD	Vancleave
104	9.6	Holmes County SD	Lexington
105	9.3	West Point SD	West Point
106	9.0	Hinds County SD	Raymond
107	8.4	Clinton Public SD	Clinton
107	8.4	Madison County SD	Flora
109	8.3	Humphreys County SD	Belzoni
110	8.0	Pearl River County SD	Carriere
111	7.8	Claiborne County SD	Port Gibson
111	7.8	Copiah County SD	Hazlehurst
113	7.5	Tunica County SD	Tunica

English Language Learner Students

Rank	Percent	District Name	City
1	5.5	Forest Municipal SD	Forest
2	4.8	Biloxi Public SD	Biloxi
3	3.0	New Albany Public Schools	New Albany
4	2.8	Houston SD	Houston
5	1.6	Pontotoc County SD	Pontotoc
6	1.5	South Tippah SD	Ripley
7	1.4	Marshall County SD	Holly Springs
7	1.4	Tupelo Public SD	Tupelo
7	1.4	Webster County SD	Eupora
10	1.3	Pascagoula Separate SD	Pascagoula
10	1.3	Tishomingo County Sp Mun SD	Iuka
12	1.2	Oxford SD	Oxford
12	1.2	Pontotoc City Schools	Pontotoc
12	1.2	Sunflower County SD	Indianola
15	1.1	Desoto County SD	Hernando
16	1.0	Leake County SD	Carthage
16	1.0	Leflore County SD	Greenwood
16	1.0	Scott County SD	Forest
19	0.9	Forrest County SD	Hattiesburg
19	0.9	Jones County SD	Ellisville
21	0.8	Coahoma County SD	Clarksdale
21	0.8	Kosciusko SD	Kosciusko
21	0.8	Lamar County SD	Purvis
24	0.7	Laurel SD	Laurel
25	0.6	Clarksdale Municipal SD	Clarksdale
25	0.6	Madison County SD	Flora
25	0.6	Mccomb SD	Mccomb
28	0.5	Natchez-Adams SD	Natchez
29	0.4	Alcorn SD	Corinth
29	0.4	Cleveland SD	Cleveland
29	0.4	Gulfport SD	Gulfport
29	0.4	Humphreys County SD	Belzoni
29	0.4	Jackson County SD	Vancleave
29	0.4	Jackson Public SD	Jackson
29	0.4	Ocean Springs SD	Ocean Springs
29	0.4	Tate County SD	Senatobia
37	0.3	Clinton Public SD	Clinton
37	0.3	Columbus Municipal SD	Columbus
37	0.3	Hancock County SD	Kiln
37	0.3	Harrison County SD	Gulfport
37	0.3	Hattiesburg Public SD	Hattiesburg
37	0.3	Lee County SD	Tupelo
37	0.3	Newton County SD	Decatur
37	0.3	West Point SD	West Point
45	0.2	Bay Saint Louis Waveland SD	Bay St Louis
45	0.2	George County SD	Lucedale
45	0.2	Lowndes County SD	Columbus
45	0.2	Meridian Public SD	Meridian
45	0.2	Rankin County SD	Brandon
45	0.2	Starkville SD	Starkville
45	0.2	Tunica County SD	Tunica
45	0.2	Vicksburg Warren SD	Vicksburg
53	0.1	Amory SD	Amory
53	0.1	Canton Public SD	Canton
53	0.1	Grenada SD	Grenada
53	0.1	Hinds County SD	Raymond
53	0.1	Itawamba County SD	Fulton
53	0.1	North Panola Schools	Sardis
53	0.1	Smith County SD	Raleigh
53	0.1	South Panola SD	Batesville
53	0.1	Walthall County SD	Tylertown
53	0.1	Western Line SD	Avon
63	0.0	Greenville Public Schools	Greenville
64	0.0	Aberdeen SD	Aberdeen
64	0.0	Brookhaven SD	Brookhaven
64	0.0	Calhoun County SD	Pittsboro
64	0.0	Choctaw County SD	Ackerman
64	0.0	Claiborne County SD	Port Gibson
64	0.0	Columbia SD	Columbia
64	0.0	Copiah County SD	Hazlehurst
64	0.0	Corinth SD	Corinth
64	0.0	Covington County Schools	Collins
64	0.0	East Tallahatchie Consol SD	Charleston
64	0.0	Franklin County SD	Meadville
64	0.0	Greene County SD	Leakesville
64	0.0	Greenwood Public SD	Greenwood
64	0.0	Hazlehurst City SD	Hazlehurst
64	0.0	Holly Springs SD	Holly Springs
64	0.0	Holmes County SD	Lexington
64	0.0	Indianola SD	Indianola
64	0.0	Jefferson County SD	Fayette
64	0.0	Jefferson Davis County SD	Prentiss
64	0.0	Lafayette County SD	Oxford
64	0.0	Lauderdale County SD	Meridian
64	0.0	Lawrence County SD	Monticello
64	0.0	Lincoln County SD	Brookhaven
64	0.0	Long Beach SD	Long Beach
64	0.0	Louisville Municipal SD	Louisville
64	0.0	Marion County SD	Columbia
64	0.0	Monroe County SD	Amory
64	0.0	Moss Point Separate SD	Moss Point
64	0.0	Neshoba County SD	Philadelphia
64	0.0	North Pike SD	Summit
64	0.0	Noxubee County SD	Macon
64	0.0	Pass Christian Public SD	Pass Christian
64	0.0	Pearl Public SD	Pearl
64	0.0	Pearl River County SD	Carriere
64	0.0	Petal SD	Petal
64	0.0	Picayune SD	Picayune
64	0.0	Poplarville Separate SD	Poplarville
64	0.0	Prentiss County SD	Booneville
64	0.0	Quitman County SD	Marks
64	0.0	Quitman SD	Quitman
64	0.0	Senatobia Municipal SD	Senatobia
64	0.0	Simpson County SD	Mendenhall
64	0.0	South Pike SD	Magnolia
64	0.0	Stone County SD	Wiggins
64	0.0	Union County SD	New Albany
64	0.0	Wayne County SD	Waynesboro
64	0.0	West Jasper Consolidated Schools	Bay Springs
64	0.0	Wilkinson County SD	Woodville
64	0.0	Yazoo City Municipal SD	Yazoo City
64	0.0	Yazoo County SD	Yazoo City

Migrant Students

Rank	Percent	District Name	City
1	4.3	Scott County SD	Forest
2	3.2	Biloxi Public SD	Biloxi
2	3.2	Laurel SD	Laurel
4	3.0	Pass Christian Public SD	Pass Christian
5	2.7	Jones County SD	Ellisville
5	2.7	Leflore County SD	Greenwood
7	2.6	Jackson County SD	Vancleave
8	2.5	Calhoun County SD	Pittsboro
9	2.1	Moss Point Separate SD	Moss Point
9	2.1	Western Line SD	Avon
11	1.4	Coahoma County SD	Clarksdale
11	1.4	Tate County SD	Senatobia
13	1.3	Harrison County SD	Gulfport
13	1.3	Pascagoula Separate SD	Pascagoula

13	1.3	Sunflower County SD	Indianola
16	1.2	Covington County Schools	Collins
16	1.2	Humphreys County SD	Belzoni
16	1.2	Leake County SD	Carthage
16	1.2	Monroe County SD	Amory
20	1.1	Ocean Springs SD	Ocean Springs
21	1.0	Long Beach SD	Long Beach
22	0.8	Gulfport SD	Gulfport
22	0.8	Tunica County SD	Tunica
22	0.8	West Jasper Consolidated Schools	Bay Springs
25	0.7	Bay Saint Louis Waveland SD	Bay St Louis
26	0.6	Smith County SD	Raleigh
26	0.6	Webster County SD	Eupora
28	0.5	Hancock County SD	Kiln
28	0.5	Marshall County SD	Holly Springs
28	0.5	New Albany Public Schools	New Albany
28	0.5	Simpson County SD	Mendenhall
32	0.4	Desoto County SD	Hernando
32	0.4	Pontotoc County SD	Pontotoc
32	0.4	Union County SD	New Albany
35	0.3	Houston SD	Houston
35	0.3	Neshoba County SD	Philadelphia
35	0.3	North Panola Schools	Sardis
38	0.2	Forest Municipal SD	Forest
38	0.2	Greenwood Public SD	Greenwood
38	0.2	Hattiesburg Public SD	Hattiesburg
38	0.2	Quitman SD	Quitman
38	0.2	Stone County SD	Wiggins
43	0.1	Alcorn SD	Corinth
43	0.1	Cleveland SD	Cleveland
43	0.1	George County SD	Lucedale
43	0.1	Greenville Public Schools	Greenville
43	0.1	Kosciusko SD	Kosciusko
43	0.1	Lauderdale County SD	Meridian
43	0.1	Marion County SD	Columbia
43	0.1	Meridian Public SD	Meridian
43	0.1	Petal SD	Petal
43	0.1	Picayune SD	Picayune
43	0.1	Rankin County SD	Brandon
54	0.0	Clarksdale Municipal SD	Clarksdale
54	0.0	Copiah County SD	Hazlehurst
54	0.0	Holmes County SD	Lexington
54	0.0	Jackson Public SD	Jackson
54	0.0	South Panola SD	Batesville
54	0.0	South Tippah SD	Ripley
60	0.0	Aberdeen SD	Aberdeen
60	0.0	Amory SD	Amory
60	0.0	Brookhaven SD	Brookhaven
60	0.0	Canton Public SD	Canton
60	0.0	Choctaw County SD	Ackerman
60	0.0	Claiborne County SD	Port Gibson
60	0.0	Clinton Public SD	Clinton
60	0.0	Columbia SD	Columbia
60	0.0	Columbus Municipal SD	Columbus
60	0.0	Corinth SD	Corinth
60	0.0	East Tallahatchie Consol SD	Charleston
60	0.0	Forrest County SD	Hattiesburg
60	0.0	Franklin County SD	Meadville
60	0.0	Greene County SD	Leakesville
60	0.0	Grenada SD	Grenada
60	0.0	Hazlehurst City SD	Hazlehurst
60	0.0	Hinds County SD	Raymond
60	0.0	Holly Springs SD	Holly Springs
60	0.0	Indianola SD	Indianola
60	0.0	Itawamba County SD	Fulton
60	0.0	Jefferson County SD	Fayette
60	0.0	Jefferson Davis County SD	Prentiss
60	0.0	Lafayette County SD	Oxford
60	0.0	Lamar County SD	Purvis
60	0.0	Lawrence County SD	Monticello
60	0.0	Lee County SD	Tupelo
60	0.0	Lincoln County SD	Brookhaven
60	0.0	Louisville Municipal SD	Louisville
60	0.0	Lowndes County SD	Columbus
60	0.0	Madison County SD	Flora
60	0.0	Mccomb SD	Mccomb
60	0.0	Natchez-Adams SD	Natchez
60	0.0	Newton County SD	Decatur
60	0.0	North Pike SD	Summit
60	0.0	Noxubee County SD	Macon
60	0.0	Oxford SD	Oxford
60	0.0	Pearl Public SD	Pearl
60	0.0	Pearl River County SD	Carriere
60	0.0	Pontotoc City Schools	Pontotoc
60	0.0	Poplarville Separate SD	Poplarville
60	0.0	Prentiss County SD	Booneville
60	0.0	Quitman County SD	Marks
60	0.0	Senatobia Municipal SD	Senatobia
60	0.0	South Pike SD	Magnolia
60	0.0	Starkville SD	Starkville
60	0.0	Tishomingo County Sp Mun SD	Iuka
60	0.0	Tupelo Public SD	Tupelo
60	0.0	Vicksburg Warren SD	Vicksburg
60	0.0	Walthall County SD	Tylertown
60	0.0	Wayne County SD	Waynesboro
60	0.0	West Point SD	West Point
60	0.0	Wilkinson County SD	Woodville
60	0.0	Yazoo City Municipal SD	Yazoo City
60	0.0	Yazoo County SD	Yazoo City

Students Eligible for Free Lunch

Rank	Percent	District Name	City
1	96.1	Holmes County SD	Lexington
2	94.3	Yazoo City Municipal SD	Yazoo City
3	93.7	Coahoma County SD	Clarksdale
4	93.4	Jefferson County SD	Fayette
5	93.0	Quitman County SD	Marks
6	92.0	Leflore County SD	Greenwood
7	91.6	Hazlehurst City SD	Hazlehurst
7	91.6	Humphreys County SD	Belzoni
9	91.5	Claiborne County SD	Port Gibson
10	90.6	Noxubee County SD	Macon
11	88.9	Sunflower County SD	Indianola
12	88.3	Canton Public SD	Canton
13	88.0	Jefferson Davis County SD	Prentiss
14	87.9	Tunica County SD	Tunica
15	87.4	Wilkinson County SD	Woodville
16	86.9	Indianola SD	Indianola
17	85.8	Greenville Public Schools	Greenville
18	85.4	North Panola Schools	Sardis
19	83.2	Laurel SD	Laurel
20	80.8	Aberdeen SD	Aberdeen
21	80.6	Hattiesburg Public SD	Hattiesburg
22	80.4	Greenwood Public SD	Greenwood
23	80.3	South Pike SD	Magnolia
24	80.1	Clarksdale Municipal SD	Clarksdale
25	79.8	Holly Springs SD	Holly Springs
25	79.8	Natchez-Adams SD	Natchez
27	76.5	Jackson Public SD	Jackson
28	75.4	West Point SD	West Point
29	75.2	East Tallahatchie Consol SD	Charleston
30	74.3	Western Line SD	Avon
31	73.9	Yazoo County SD	Yazoo City
32	73.5	Meridian Public SD	Meridian
33	73.2	Moss Point Separate SD	Moss Point
34	73.1	Mccomb SD	Mccomb
35	72.6	Marion County SD	Columbia
36	72.2	Columbus Municipal SD	Columbus
37	70.6	Walthall County SD	Tylertown
38	69.4	West Jasper Consolidated Schools	Bay Springs
39	69.1	Forest Municipal SD	Forest
40	68.6	Covington County Schools	Collins
41	68.1	South Panola SD	Batesville
42	67.5	Louisville Municipal SD	Louisville
43	67.1	Marshall County SD	Holly Springs
44	66.0	Wayne County SD	Waynesboro
45	65.8	Simpson County SD	Mendenhall
46	65.2	Leake County SD	Carthage
47	64.4	Cleveland SD	Cleveland
48	64.3	Copiah County SD	Hazlehurst
49	63.5	Scott County SD	Forest
50	62.4	Calhoun County SD	Pittsboro
51	62.3	Franklin County SD	Meadville
52	60.9	Greene County SD	Leakesville
53	60.4	Quitman SD	Quitman
54	59.6	Houston SD	Houston
55	59.3	Columbia SD	Columbia
55	59.3	Tate County SD	Senatobia
57	59.2	Choctaw County SD	Ackerman
58	58.0	Gulfport SD	Gulfport
59	57.0	Brookhaven SD	Brookhaven
60	56.9	Forrest County SD	Hattiesburg
61	56.3	Picayune SD	Picayune
62	56.0	Vicksburg Warren SD	Vicksburg
63	55.4	Starkville SD	Starkville
64	54.8	Bay Saint Louis Waveland SD	Bay St Louis
65	54.4	Pascagoula Separate SD	Pascagoula
66	53.9	Grenada SD	Grenada
67	53.1	Poplarville Separate SD	Poplarville
68	52.3	Biloxi Public SD	Biloxi
69	50.8	Pass Christian Public SD	Pass Christian
70	50.7	Prentiss County SD	Booneville
71	50.4	Lawrence County SD	Monticello
72	49.6	Hancock County SD	Kiln
73	49.4	Smith County SD	Raleigh
74	49.3	Kosciusko SD	Kosciusko
75	48.9	Corinth SD	Corinth
76	48.5	Itawamba County SD	Fulton
77	48.3	Webster County SD	Eupora
78	48.0	North Pike SD	Summit
79	47.7	Jones County SD	Ellisville
80	47.0	Lee County SD	Tupelo
81	46.9	Newton County SD	Decatur
82	46.1	George County SD	Lucedale
83	45.6	South Tippah SD	Ripley
84	45.3	Lafayette County SD	Oxford
84	45.3	Stone County SD	Wiggins
86	44.2	Amory SD	Amory
87	44.0	Neshoba County SD	Philadelphia
88	43.3	Pearl River County SD	Carriere
89	42.8	Harrison County SD	Gulfport
90	41.8	New Albany Public Schools	New Albany
90	41.8	Tishomingo County Sp Mun SD	Iuka
92	41.7	Hinds County SD	Raymond
93	40.6	Lincoln County SD	Brookhaven
94	40.5	Lowndes County SD	Columbus
95	39.6	Oxford SD	Oxford
96	39.1	Tupelo Public SD	Tupelo
97	38.7	Union County SD	New Albany
98	37.8	Lauderdale County SD	Meridian
98	37.8	Pontotoc City Schools	Pontotoc
100	37.4	Pontotoc County SD	Pontotoc
101	36.9	Pearl Public SD	Pearl
102	36.8	Senatobia Municipal SD	Senatobia
103	35.7	Alcorn SD	Corinth
104	34.6	Monroe County SD	Amory
105	33.9	Petal SD	Petal
106	33.7	Jackson County SD	Vancleave
107	30.4	Long Beach SD	Long Beach
108	28.0	Lamar County SD	Purvis
109	27.5	Rankin County SD	Brandon
110	27.4	Clinton Public SD	Clinton
111	27.1	Madison County SD	Flora
112	21.3	Desoto County SD	Hernando
113	17.0	Ocean Springs SD	Ocean Springs

Students Eligible for Reduced-Price Lunch

Rank	Percent	District Name	City
1	15.8	Prentiss County SD	Booneville
2	14.9	Monroe County SD	Amory
3	14.2	Pearl River County SD	Carriere
4	13.0	New Albany Public Schools	New Albany
5	12.9	Biloxi Public SD	Biloxi
6	12.4	Alcorn SD	Corinth
7	12.3	Pass Christian Public SD	Pass Christian
8	12.2	Union County SD	New Albany
9	12.1	Neshoba County SD	Philadelphia
10	11.9	Pontotoc County SD	Pontotoc
11	11.8	Hancock County SD	Kiln
11	11.8	Lawrence County SD	Monticello
11	11.8	Marion County SD	Columbia
11	11.8	Scott County SD	Forest
11	11.8	Smith County SD	Raleigh
16	11.7	Petal SD	Petal
16	11.7	Tate County SD	Senatobia
16	11.7	Webster County SD	Eupora
19	11.5	Lincoln County SD	Brookhaven
20	11.3	Itawamba County SD	Fulton
21	11.0	Poplarville Separate SD	Poplarville
21	11.0	South Tippah SD	Ripley
23	10.7	Jones County SD	Ellisville
23	10.7	Tishomingo County Sp Mun SD	Iuka
25	10.6	George County SD	Lucedale
26	10.5	Bay Saint Louis Waveland SD	Bay St Louis
26	10.5	Covington County Schools	Collins
28	10.3	Greene County SD	Leakesville
28	10.3	Harrison County SD	Gulfport
28	10.3	Kosciusko SD	Kosciusko
28	10.3	Lafayette County SD	Oxford
28	10.3	Leake County SD	Carthage
28	10.3	South Panola SD	Batesville
34	10.2	North Pike SD	Summit
35	10.1	Pearl Public SD	Pearl
35	10.1	Stone County SD	Wiggins
37	10.0	Newton County SD	Decatur
38	9.9	Lamar County SD	Purvis
39	9.8	Houston SD	Houston
39	9.8	West Jasper Consolidated Schools	Bay Springs
41	9.7	Calhoun County SD	Pittsboro
42	9.6	Franklin County SD	Meadville
43	9.5	Columbia SD	Columbia
43	9.5	Jackson County SD	Vancleave
43	9.5	Louisville Municipal SD	Louisville
46	9.4	Walthall County SD	Tylertown
47	9.3	Wayne County SD	Waynesboro
48	9.1	Holly Springs SD	Holly Springs
48	9.1	North Panola Schools	Sardis
48	9.1	West Point SD	West Point
51	9.0	East Tallahatchie Consol SD	Charleston
51	9.0	Forrest County SD	Hattiesburg
51	9.0	Long Beach SD	Long Beach
54	8.9	Lowndes County SD	Columbus
54	8.9	Quitman SD	Quitman
56	8.8	Gulfport SD	Gulfport
56	8.8	South Pike SD	Magnolia

58	8.7	Copiah County SD	Hazlehurst
59	8.6	Moss Point Separate SD	Moss Point
60	8.5	Marshall County SD	Holly Springs
60	8.5	Yazoo County SD	Yazoo City
62	8.4	Forest Municipal SD	Forest
63	8.3	Choctaw County SD	Ackerman
64	8.2	Indianola SD	Indianola
65	8.1	Simpson County SD	Mendenhall
66	7.9	Amory SD	Amory
66	7.9	Lee County SD	Tupelo
66	7.9	Pontotoc City Schools	Pontotoc
66	7.9	Western Line SD	Avon
70	7.7	Starkville SD	Starkville
71	7.5	Rankin County SD	Brandon
72	7.4	Columbus Municipal SD	Columbus
72	7.4	Desoto County SD	Hernando
72	7.4	Jefferson Davis County SD	Prentiss
72	7.4	Lauderdale County SD	Meridian
72	7.4	Ocean Springs SD	Ocean Springs
72	7.4	Senatobia Municipal SD	Senatobia
78	7.3	Clinton Public SD	Clinton
79	7.2	Brookhaven SD	Brookhaven
79	7.2	Pascagoula Separate SD	Pascagoula
81	7.1	Aberdeen SD	Aberdeen
81	7.1	Picayune SD	Picayune
83	7.0	Corinth SD	Corinth
84	6.9	Hinds County SD	Raymond
84	6.9	Vicksburg Warren SD	Vicksburg
86	6.6	Jackson Public SD	Jackson
86	6.6	Mccomb SD	Mccomb
88	6.5	Oxford SD	Oxford
89	6.4	Hazlehurst City SD	Hazlehurst
89	6.4	Quitman County SD	Marks
91	6.3	Clarksdale Municipal SD	Clarksdale
92	6.0	Laurel SD	Laurel
93	5.9	Grenada SD	Grenada
94	5.8	Hattiesburg Public SD	Hattiesburg
94	5.8	Noxubee County SD	Macon
94	5.8	Tunica County SD	Tunica
97	5.7	Cleveland SD	Cleveland
97	5.7	Natchez-Adams SD	Natchez
99	5.5	Leflore County SD	Greenwood
99	5.5	Wilkinson County SD	Woodville
101	5.4	Sunflower County SD	Indianola
102	5.2	Tupelo Public SD	Tupelo
103	4.9	Meridian Public SD	Meridian
104	4.8	Greenwood Public SD	Greenwood
105	4.7	Coahoma County SD	Clarksdale
106	4.4	Madison County SD	Flora
107	3.9	Greenville Public Schools	Greenville
108	3.8	Yazoo City Municipal SD	Yazoo City
109	3.6	Humphreys County SD	Belzoni
110	3.4	Claiborne County SD	Port Gibson
111	3.1	Canton Public SD	Canton
111	3.1	Holmes County SD	Lexington
113	2.8	Jefferson County SD	Fayette

Student/Teacher Ratio

Rank	Ratio	District Name	City
1	23.0	Greenville Public Schools	Greenville
2	21.0	Vicksburg Warren SD	Vicksburg
3	20.0	Desoto County SD	Hernando
4	19.9	Holmes County SD	Lexington
5	19.4	Hattiesburg Public SD	Hattiesburg
6	18.7	Canton Public SD	Canton
7	18.6	Jackson County SD	Vancleave
8	18.5	Humphreys County SD	Belzoni
9	18.1	Greene County SD	Leakesville
10	17.8	Grenada SD	Grenada
10	17.8	Yazoo City Municipal SD	Yazoo City
12	17.7	Marshall County SD	Holly Springs
12	17.7	West Point SD	West Point
14	17.5	Union County SD	New Albany
15	17.4	North Pike SD	Summit
16	17.2	Ocean Springs SD	Ocean Springs
17	17.0	Indianola SD	Indianola
17	17.0	Lincoln County SD	Brookhaven
19	16.9	Leflore County SD	Greenwood
19	16.9	Wilkinson County SD	Woodville
21	16.8	Copiah County SD	Hazlehurst
22	16.7	Jackson Public SD	Jackson
23	16.6	Harrison County SD	Gulfport
24	16.5	Hancock County SD	Kiln
24	16.5	Meridian Public SD	Meridian
24	16.5	Wayne County SD	Waynesboro
27	16.4	Leake County SD	Carthage
28	16.3	Simpson County SD	Mendenhall
28	16.3	Yazoo County SD	Yazoo City
30	16.2	Clinton Public SD	Clinton
30	16.2	Lauderdale County SD	Meridian
30	16.2	Moss Point Separate SD	Moss Point
30	16.2	Noxubee County SD	Macon
30	16.2	Pearl River County SD	Carriere
30	16.2	Scott County SD	Forest
30	16.2	Senatobia Municipal SD	Senatobia
30	16.2	South Pike SD	Magnolia
30	16.2	Tate County SD	Senatobia
39	16.1	Calhoun County SD	Pittsboro
39	16.1	Smith County SD	Raleigh
41	16.0	George County SD	Lucedale
41	16.0	Holly Springs SD	Holly Springs
41	16.0	Lowndes County SD	Columbus
41	16.0	Pascagoula Separate SD	Pascagoula
41	16.0	Pontotoc City Schools	Pontotoc
46	15.9	South Panola SD	Batesville
46	15.9	South Tippah SD	Ripley
48	15.8	Quitman SD	Quitman
49	15.7	Columbia SD	Columbia
49	15.7	Covington County Schools	Collins
51	15.6	Hinds County SD	Raymond
51	15.6	Houston SD	Houston
51	15.6	Monroe County SD	Amory
54	15.5	Hazlehurst City SD	Hazlehurst
54	15.5	Kosciusko SD	Kosciusko
54	15.5	Madison County SD	Flora
54	15.5	Rankin County SD	Brandon
54	15.5	Tishomingo County Sp Mun SD	Iuka
59	15.4	Amory SD	Amory
59	15.4	Itawamba County SD	Fulton
59	15.4	Sunflower County SD	Indianola
59	15.4	Western Line SD	Avon
63	15.3	Stone County SD	Wiggins
64	15.2	Lee County SD	Tupelo
64	15.2	Poplarville Separate SD	Poplarville
66	15.1	Jefferson Davis County SD	Prentiss
66	15.1	Jones County SD	Ellisville
66	15.1	Petal SD	Petal
66	15.1	Quitman County SD	Marks
66	15.1	West Jasper Consolidated Schools	Bay Springs
71	15.0	Forest Municipal SD	Forest
71	15.0	Jefferson County SD	Fayette
71	15.0	Pontotoc County SD	Pontotoc
74	14.9	Biloxi Public SD	Biloxi
74	14.9	Claiborne County SD	Port Gibson
74	14.9	Clarksdale Municipal SD	Clarksdale
74	14.9	Lamar County SD	Purvis
78	14.8	Oxford SD	Oxford
79	14.7	Tunica County SD	Tunica
80	14.6	East Tallahatchie Consol SD	Charleston
80	14.6	Webster County SD	Eupora
82	14.5	Alcorn SD	Corinth
82	14.5	Bay Saint Louis Waveland SD	Bay St Louis
82	14.5	Choctaw County SD	Ackerman
82	14.5	Lawrence County SD	Monticello
82	14.5	New Albany Public Schools	New Albany
82	14.5	Pearl Public SD	Pearl
88	14.4	Greenwood Public SD	Greenwood
88	14.4	Long Beach SD	Long Beach
88	14.4	Natchez-Adams SD	Natchez
91	14.3	Newton County SD	Decatur
92	14.1	Pass Christian Public SD	Pass Christian
92	14.1	Walthall County SD	Tylertown
94	13.9	Gulfport SD	Gulfport
95	13.7	Cleveland SD	Cleveland
95	13.7	Neshoba County SD	Philadelphia
97	13.6	Brookhaven SD	Brookhaven
97	13.6	Lafayette County SD	Oxford
99	13.5	Louisville Municipal SD	Louisville
99	13.5	North Panola Schools	Sardis
101	13.3	Franklin County SD	Meadville
101	13.3	Mccomb SD	Mccomb
103	13.1	Picayune SD	Picayune
103	13.1	Starkville SD	Starkville
103	13.1	Tupelo Public SD	Tupelo
106	12.9	Columbus Municipal SD	Columbus
106	12.9	Marion County SD	Columbia
108	12.6	Corinth SD	Corinth
108	12.6	Laurel SD	Laurel
110	12.4	Coahoma County SD	Clarksdale
111	12.3	Forrest County SD	Hattiesburg
112	11.2	Aberdeen SD	Aberdeen
113	11.0	Prentiss County SD	Booneville

Student/Librarian Ratio

Rank	Ratio	District Name	City
1	1,360.0	Pearl River County SD	Carriere
2	1,123.5	Greene County SD	Leakesville
3	1,109.0	Lauderdale County SD	Meridian
4	998.3	South Panola SD	Batesville
5	863.0	Newton County SD	Decatur
6	848.1	Corinth SD	Corinth
7	844.7	Grenada SD	Grenada
8	843.5	Ocean Springs SD	Ocean Springs
9	826.3	Desoto County SD	Hernando
10	811.3	Claiborne County SD	Port Gibson
11	788.2	Wayne County SD	Waynesboro
12	735.8	Petal SD	Petal
13	726.5	Canton Public SD	Canton
14	716.5	Neshoba County SD	Philadelphia
15	707.7	Marshall County SD	Holly Springs
16	683.1	Lawrence County SD	Monticello
17	682.6	Marion County SD	Columbia
18	681.6	Harrison County SD	Gulfport
19	677.3	Humphreys County SD	Belzoni
20	673.0	Hancock County SD	Kiln
21	663.6	Leake County SD	Carthage
22	656.5	Hazlehurst City SD	Hazlehurst
23	652.7	Oxford SD	Oxford
24	650.0	Meridian Public SD	Meridian
25	649.7	Lamar County SD	Purvis
26	649.2	Greenville Public Schools	Greenville
27	641.0	Hinds County SD	Raymond
28	623.4	West Jasper Consolidated Schools	Bay Springs
29	619.7	Pearl Public SD	Pearl
30	619.5	Clinton Public SD	Clinton
31	606.0	North Panola Schools	Sardis
32	603.7	Yazoo County SD	Yazoo City
33	603.0	West Point SD	West Point
34	599.5	Natchez-Adams SD	Natchez
35	587.8	Yazoo City Municipal SD	Yazoo City
36	584.4	Mccomb SD	Mccomb
37	583.8	Rankin County SD	Brandon
38	582.6	Tupelo Public SD	Tupelo
39	575.7	North Pike SD	Summit
40	567.5	Jackson County SD	Vancleave
41	566.7	Lowndes County SD	Columbus
42	564.8	Noxubee County SD	Macon
43	560.9	Madison County SD	Flora
44	559.5	Smith County SD	Raleigh
45	556.1	Jackson Public SD	Jackson
46	555.1	Houston SD	Houston
47	554.2	Long Beach SD	Long Beach
48	548.1	Clarksdale Municipal SD	Clarksdale
49	538.6	Picayune SD	Picayune
50	533.4	Lee County SD	Tupelo
51	529.1	George County SD	Lucedale
52	529.0	Lafayette County SD	Oxford
53	526.7	Copiah County SD	Hazlehurst
54	525.8	Holly Springs SD	Holly Springs
55	525.2	Stone County SD	Wiggins
56	525.1	Brookhaven SD	Brookhaven
57	523.2	Vicksburg Warren SD	Vicksburg
58	519.9	Gulfport SD	Gulfport
59	519.5	New Albany Public Schools	New Albany
60	515.1	Tishomingo County Sp Mun SD	Iuka
61	508.0	Simpson County SD	Mendenhall
62	506.4	Alcorn SD	Corinth
63	500.6	Laurel SD	Laurel
64	497.5	Pontotoc County SD	Pontotoc
65	495.5	Quitman SD	Quitman
66	492.6	Pontotoc City Schools	Pontotoc
67	489.6	Pascagoula Separate SD	Pascagoula
68	487.7	Jones County SD	Ellisville
69	487.3	Hattiesburg Public SD	Hattiesburg
70	476.6	Leflore County SD	Greenwood
71	474.2	Tate County SD	Senatobia
72	474.1	Moss Point Separate SD	Moss Point
73	470.5	Amory SD	Amory
74	465.5	Indianola SD	Indianola
75	450.1	Itawamba County SD	Fulton
76	446.2	Starkville SD	Starkville
77	440.8	Biloxi Public SD	Biloxi
78	438.6	East Tallahatchie Consol SD	Charleston
79	437.3	Pass Christian Public SD	Pass Christian
80	435.8	Greenwood Public SD	Greenwood
81	429.8	Holmes County SD	Lexington
82	428.1	Aberdeen SD	Aberdeen
83	427.1	Sunflower County SD	Indianola
84	424.2	South Tippah SD	Ripley
85	420.5	Senatobia Municipal SD	Senatobia
86	420.0	Quitman County SD	Marks
87	418.8	Covington County Schools	Collins
88	416.8	Forrest County SD	Hattiesburg
89	413.3	Jefferson County SD	Fayette
90	411.3	Forest Municipal SD	Forest
91	407.0	Jefferson Davis County SD	Prentiss
92	405.8	Poplarville Separate SD	Poplarville
93	405.0	Columbia SD	Columbia
94	402.3	Franklin County SD	Meadville
95	386.1	Calhoun County SD	Pittsboro
96	385.1	Monroe County SD	Amory
97	385.0	Walthall County SD	Tylertown
98	384.3	Wilkinson County SD	Woodville
99	374.6	Webster County SD	Eupora
100	368.0	Bay Saint Louis Waveland SD	Bay St Louis
101	364.1	Columbus Municipal SD	Columbus
102	363.4	Cleveland SD	Cleveland

103	359.6	Union County SD	New Albany
104	357.8	Louisville Municipal SD	Louisville
105	353.3	Lincoln County SD	Brookhaven
106	351.0	Tunica County SD	Tunica
107	348.2	Kosciusko SD	Kosciusko
108	344.2	Scott County SD	Forest
109	331.0	Prentiss County SD	Booneville
110	326.8	Choctaw County SD	Ackerman
111	317.7	Coahoma County SD	Clarksdale
112	298.6	Western Line SD	Avon
113	280.5	South Pike SD	Magnolia

Student/Counselor Ratio

Rank	Ratio	District Name	City
1	2,376.0	Forrest County SD	Hattiesburg
2	1,896.7	Hazlehurst City SD	Hazlehurst
3	1,415.4	Marshall County SD	Holly Springs
4	1,316.7	Copiah County SD	Hazlehurst
5	1,234.2	Biloxi Public SD	Biloxi
6	1,231.6	Wayne County SD	Waynesboro
7	1,195.5	Lawrence County SD	Monticello
8	1,151.3	North Pike SD	Summit
9	1,014.5	Poplarville Separate SD	Poplarville
10	995.2	Western Line SD	Avon
11	988.3	Neshoba County SD	Philadelphia
12	933.0	Claiborne County SD	Port Gibson
13	929.9	Harrison County SD	Gulfport
14	906.7	Pearl River County SD	Carriere
15	864.7	Marion County SD	Columbia
16	811.5	East Tallahatchie Consol SD	Charleston
17	785.4	Picayune SD	Picayune
18	774.3	Corinth SD	Corinth
19	755.3	Pontotoc City Schools	Pontotoc
20	748.6	Walthall County SD	Tylertown
21	735.8	Petal SD	Petal
22	734.8	Yazoo City Municipal SD	Yazoo City
23	723.2	West Jasper Consolidated Schools	Bay Springs
24	721.5	George County SD	Lucedale
25	719.2	Aberdeen SD	Aberdeen
26	716.6	Alcorn SD	Corinth
27	706.5	Lincoln County SD	Brookhaven
28	691.5	Union County SD	New Albany
29	675.3	New Albany Public Schools	New Albany
30	673.3	Stone County SD	Wiggins
31	665.4	Lauderdale County SD	Meridian
32	657.2	Coahoma County SD	Clarksdale
33	656.0	Lamar County SD	Purvis
34	646.8	Calhoun County SD	Pittsboro
35	645.9	Webster County SD	Eupora
36	640.7	Sunflower County SD	Indianola
37	634.8	Indianola SD	Indianola
38	616.8	Greenville Public Schools	Greenville
39	616.1	Greene County SD	Leakesville
40	611.3	Grenada SD	Grenada
41	610.5	Noxubee County SD	Macon
42	598.9	Holmes County SD	Lexington
43	596.9	Kosciusko SD	Kosciusko
44	587.4	Desoto County SD	Hernando
45	585.2	Lowndes County SD	Columbus
46	582.3	Clarksdale Municipal SD	Clarksdale
47	575.4	South Pike SD	Magnolia
48	572.9	Itawamba County SD	Fulton
49	569.3	Monroe County SD	Amory
50	569.0	Tate County SD	Senatobia
51	560.7	Senatobia Municipal SD	Senatobia
52	553.3	Cleveland SD	Cleveland
53	550.3	Quitman County SD	Marks
54	548.3	Forest Municipal SD	Forest
55	547.7	Canton Public SD	Canton
56	546.8	Pascagoula Separate SD	Pascagoula
57	544.6	Leflore County SD	Greenwood
58	539.6	Quitman SD	Quitman
59	539.4	Simpson County SD	Mendenhall
60	520.1	Lee County SD	Tupelo
61	513.5	Houston SD	Houston
62	508.0	Humphreys County SD	Belzoni
63	505.8	Pontotoc County SD	Pontotoc
64	502.8	South Tippah SD	Ripley
65	502.6	Covington County Schools	Collins
66	481.0	Pass Christian Public SD	Pass Christian
67	480.0	Bay Saint Louis Waveland SD	Bay St Louis
68	478.6	Hancock County SD	Kiln
69	477.7	Hattiesburg Public SD	Hattiesburg
70	477.5	Ocean Springs SD	Ocean Springs
71	473.4	Smith County SD	Raleigh
72	472.3	Jefferson County SD	Fayette
73	471.5	West Point SD	West Point
74	470.5	Amory SD	Amory
75	469.1	Rankin County SD	Brandon
76	466.2	North Panola Schools	Sardis
77	466.0	Scott County SD	Forest
78	464.8	Pearl Public SD	Pearl
79	464.0	Jefferson Davis County SD	Prentiss
80	459.2	South Panola SD	Batesville
81	457.6	Jackson County SD	Vancleave
82	456.9	Oxford SD	Oxford
83	456.2	Jones County SD	Ellisville
84	444.7	Vicksburg Warren SD	Vicksburg
85	444.5	Tishomingo County Sp Mun SD	Iuka
86	439.1	Wilkinson County SD	Woodville
87	435.8	Greenwood Public SD	Greenwood
88	434.4	Louisville Municipal SD	Louisville
89	431.5	Newton County SD	Decatur
90	431.0	Clinton Public SD	Clinton
91	427.6	Brookhaven SD	Brookhaven
92	423.4	Columbia SD	Columbia
92	423.4	Franklin County SD	Meadville
94	423.2	Lafayette County SD	Oxford
95	421.2	Yazoo County SD	Yazoo City
96	420.0	Leake County SD	Carthage
97	415.6	Long Beach SD	Long Beach
98	412.5	Moss Point Separate SD	Moss Point
99	411.5	Madison County SD	Flora
100	400.6	Jackson Public SD	Jackson
101	399.2	Laurel SD	Laurel
102	397.9	Hinds County SD	Raymond
103	395.8	Tupelo Public SD	Tupelo
104	394.4	Holly Springs SD	Holly Springs
105	389.6	Mccomb SD	Mccomb
106	380.2	Choctaw County SD	Ackerman
107	377.6	Columbus Municipal SD	Columbus
108	376.2	Starkville SD	Starkville
109	369.2	Gulfport SD	Gulfport
110	342.6	Natchez-Adams SD	Natchez
111	314.3	Tunica County SD	Tunica
112	304.2	Prentiss County SD	Booneville
113	297.6	Meridian Public SD	Meridian

Current Spending per Student in FY2001

Rank	Dollars	District Name	City
1	7,316	Tunica County SD	Tunica
2	6,333	Corinth SD	Corinth
3	6,318	Biloxi Public SD	Biloxi
4	6,227	Gulfport SD	Gulfport
5	6,186	Franklin County SD	Meadville
6	6,158	Starkville SD	Starkville
7	6,145	Mccomb SD	Mccomb
8	6,115	Hattiesburg Public SD	Hattiesburg
9	6,095	Bay Saint Louis Waveland SD	Bay St Louis
10	6,037	Yazoo County SD	Yazoo City
11	6,034	Lafayette County SD	Oxford
12	6,025	Claiborne County SD	Port Gibson
13	5,957	New Albany Public Schools	New Albany
14	5,948	Pass Christian Public SD	Pass Christian
15	5,896	Meridian Public SD	Meridian
16	5,890	Jackson Public SD	Jackson
17	5,856	Prentiss County SD	Booneville
18	5,855	Laurel SD	Laurel
19	5,848	Natchez-Adams SD	Natchez
20	5,791	Tupelo Public SD	Tupelo
21	5,784	Pascagoula Separate SD	Pascagoula
22	5,722	Columbus Municipal SD	Columbus
23	5,683	Cleveland SD	Cleveland
24	5,628	Forrest County SD	Hattiesburg
25	5,550	West Jasper Consolidated Schools	Bay Springs
26	5,516	Sunflower County SD	Indianola
27	5,465	Marion County SD	Columbia
28	5,463	Moss Point Separate SD	Moss Point
29	5,455	Jefferson County SD	Fayette
30	5,436	Noxubee County SD	Macon
31	5,401	Coahoma County SD	Clarksdale
32	5,380	Wilkinson County SD	Woodville
33	5,363	Oxford SD	Oxford
34	5,358	Aberdeen SD	Aberdeen
35	5,331	Vicksburg Warren SD	Vicksburg
36	5,296	Poplarville Separate SD	Poplarville
37	5,279	Alcorn SD	Corinth
37	5,279	Walthall County SD	Tylertown
39	5,270	Calhoun County SD	Pittsboro
40	5,262	Jefferson Davis County SD	Prentiss
41	5,258	Columbia SD	Columbia
42	5,252	Choctaw County SD	Ackerman
43	5,247	Brookhaven SD	Brookhaven
44	5,243	South Pike SD	Magnolia
45	5,239	Greenwood Public SD	Greenwood
46	5,210	Leflore County SD	Greenwood
47	5,208	Greene County SD	Leakesville
48	5,171	Kosciusko SD	Kosciusko
49	5,149	Louisville Municipal SD	Louisville
50	5,139	Hazlehurst City SD	Hazlehurst
51	5,128	Tishomingo County Sp Mun SD	Iuka
52	5,121	Neshoba County SD	Philadelphia
53	5,120	Lawrence County SD	Monticello
54	5,095	North Panola Schools	Sardis
55	5,090	Forest Municipal SD	Forest
56	5,086	East Tallahatchie Consol SD	Charleston
57	5,078	Harrison County SD	Gulfport
58	5,075	Petal SD	Petal
58	5,075	Picayune SD	Picayune
58	5,075	Quitman County SD	Marks
61	5,070	Quitman SD	Quitman
62	5,055	Amory SD	Amory
63	5,039	Hancock County SD	Kiln
64	5,028	Copiah County SD	Hazlehurst
65	5,019	Greenville Public Schools	Greenville
66	5,015	Pearl Public SD	Pearl
67	5,000	Jones County SD	Ellisville
68	4,999	Webster County SD	Eupora
69	4,982	Wayne County SD	Waynesboro
70	4,958	Stone County SD	Wiggins
71	4,956	Senatobia Municipal SD	Senatobia
72	4,955	Western Line SD	Avon
73	4,941	Lauderdale County SD	Meridian
74	4,940	Yazoo City Municipal SD	Yazoo City
75	4,938	South Panola SD	Batesville
76	4,912	Newton County SD	Decatur
77	4,893	Covington County Schools	Collins
78	4,889	Clinton Public SD	Clinton
78	4,889	Long Beach SD	Long Beach
80	4,882	Tate County SD	Senatobia
81	4,861	Madison County SD	Flora
82	4,855	Holly Springs SD	Holly Springs
83	4,839	Smith County SD	Raleigh
84	4,811	Simpson County SD	Mendenhall
85	4,807	Indianola SD	Indianola
86	4,805	Pontotoc City Schools	Pontotoc
87	4,793	Humphreys County SD	Belzoni
88	4,783	Lamar County SD	Purvis
89	4,778	Lee County SD	Tupelo
90	4,774	Clarksdale Municipal SD	Clarksdale
91	4,767	Leake County SD	Carthage
92	4,745	South Tippah SD	Ripley
93	4,734	Pontotoc County SD	Pontotoc
94	4,726	Itawamba County SD	Fulton
94	4,726	Ocean Springs SD	Ocean Springs
96	4,720	Lowndes County SD	Columbus
97	4,717	Hinds County SD	Raymond
98	4,666	Monroe County SD	Amory
99	4,661	Houston SD	Houston
100	4,622	Lincoln County SD	Brookhaven
101	4,621	Rankin County SD	Brandon
102	4,594	Grenada SD	Grenada
103	4,554	Jackson County SD	Vancleave
104	4,551	Holmes County SD	Lexington
105	4,510	Marshall County SD	Holly Springs
106	4,496	Scott County SD	Forest
107	4,489	West Point SD	West Point
108	4,421	Union County SD	New Albany
109	4,265	George County SD	Lucedale
110	4,119	Canton Public SD	Canton
111	4,102	North Pike SD	Summit
112	4,093	Pearl River County SD	Carriere
113	4,084	Desoto County SD	Hernando

Number of Diploma Recipients

Rank	Number	District Name	City
1	1,239	Jackson Public SD	Jackson
2	862	Desoto County SD	Hernando
3	795	Rankin County SD	Brandon
4	534	Harrison County SD	Gulfport
5	500	Madison County SD	Flora
6	466	Jackson County SD	Vancleave
7	441	Vicksburg Warren SD	Vicksburg
8	437	Jones County SD	Ellisville
9	365	Pascagoula Separate SD	Pascagoula
10	353	Tupelo Public SD	Tupelo
11	348	Lamar County SD	Purvis
12	338	Lauderdale County SD	Meridian
13	336	Gulfport SD	Gulfport
13	336	Meridian Public SD	Meridian
15	306	Clinton Public SD	Clinton
16	300	Greenville Public Schools	Greenville
17	283	Natchez-Adams SD	Natchez
18	282	Hinds County SD	Raymond
19	268	Lowndes County SD	Columbus
20	265	Biloxi Public SD	Biloxi
20	265	Columbus Municipal SD	Columbus
22	260	Lee County SD	Tupelo
23	251	Holmes County SD	Lexington
23	251	Ocean Springs SD	Ocean Springs
25	231	Starkville SD	Starkville
26	226	Hattiesburg Public SD	Hattiesburg
27	223	Alcorn SD	Corinth
28	220	Wayne County SD	Waynesboro
29	218	Long Beach SD	Long Beach
29	218	Simpson County SD	Mendenhall

31	207	George County SD	Lucedale
32	205	Moss Point Separate SD	Moss Point
33	200	Cleveland SD	Cleveland
34	194	Itawamba County SD	Fulton
35	191	South Panola SD	Batesville
36	186	Louisville Municipal SD	Louisville
37	183	Indianola SD	Indianola
38	180	Grenada SD	Grenada
39	173	Pearl Public SD	Pearl
40	172	Laurel SD	Laurel
41	170	Hancock County SD	Kiln
41	170	Lincoln County SD	Brookhaven
43	166	Brookhaven SD	Brookhaven
43	166	Picayune SD	Picayune
45	163	Scott County SD	Forest
46	161	Covington County Schools	Collins
46	161	Mccomb SD	Mccomb
48	158	Petal SD	Petal
49	157	Copiah County SD	Hazlehurst
50	153	West Point SD	West Point
51	151	Leake County SD	Carthage
52	150	Greenwood Public SD	Greenwood
52	150	Oxford SD	Oxford
54	148	Walthall County SD	Tylertown
55	147	Smith County SD	Raleigh
56	137	South Tippah SD	Ripley
57	135	Tishomingo County Sp Mun SD	Iuka
58	131	Calhoun County SD	Pittsboro
59	130	Marion County SD	Columbia
60	128	Monroe County SD	Amory
60	128	Pontotoc County SD	Pontotoc
62	127	Noxubee County SD	Macon
63	125	Neshoba County SD	Philadelphia
63	125	Stone County SD	Wiggins
65	123	Kosciusko SD	Kosciusko
66	122	Claiborne County SD	Port Gibson
66	122	Marshall County SD	Holly Springs
66	122	Prentiss County SD	Booneville
66	122	Quitman SD	Quitman
70	121	Bay Saint Louis Waveland SD	Bay St Louis
70	121	Clarksdale Municipal SD	Clarksdale
72	120	Lawrence County SD	Monticello
73	117	Senatobia Municipal SD	Senatobia
74	116	Leflore County SD	Greenwood
75	115	Pearl River County SD	Carriere
75	115	Western Line SD	Avon
77	114	Jefferson Davis County SD	Prentiss
78	112	Union County SD	New Albany
79	111	Poplarville Separate SD	Poplarville
79	111	Tate County SD	Senatobia
81	109	Pass Christian Public SD	Pass Christian
82	108	Canton Public SD	Canton
82	108	Columbia SD	Columbia
84	107	Amory SD	Amory
85	106	Holly Springs SD	Holly Springs
85	106	Pontotoc City Schools	Pontotoc
87	105	South Pike SD	Magnolia
88	97	Aberdeen SD	Aberdeen
88	97	Hazlehurst City SD	Hazlehurst
90	96	Choctaw County SD	Ackerman
91	95	Franklin County SD	Meadville
91	95	Lafayette County SD	Oxford
93	94	Corinth SD	Corinth
94	93	Webster County SD	Eupora
95	92	Jefferson County SD	Fayette
95	92	New Albany Public Schools	New Albany
95	92	West Jasper Consolidated Schools	Bay Springs
98	91	Greene County SD	Leakesville
99	90	Yazoo City Municipal SD	Yazoo City
100	89	Yazoo County SD	Yazoo City
101	77	Houston SD	Houston
102	74	Humphreys County SD	Belzoni
102	74	Newton County SD	Decatur
104	72	Wilkinson County SD	Woodville
105	70	North Pike SD	Summit
106	65	Quitman County SD	Marks
106	65	Tunica County SD	Tunica
108	63	Coahoma County SD	Clarksdale
109	58	Forest Municipal SD	Forest
110	57	Forrest County SD	Hattiesburg
111	56	Sunflower County SD	Indianola
112	53	East Tallahatchie Consol SD	Charleston
112	53	North Panola Schools	Sardis

High School Drop-out Rate

Rank	Percent	District Name	City
1	16.6	Copiah County SD	Hazlehurst
2	14.3	North Panola Schools	Sardis
3	12.6	Jefferson County SD	Fayette
4	12.3	Hazlehurst City SD	Hazlehurst
5	12.1	Greenwood Public SD	Greenwood
6	10.9	West Point SD	West Point
7	10.5	Humphreys County SD	Belzoni
8	9.7	Western Line SD	Avon
9	8.9	Laurel SD	Laurel
10	8.8	Coahoma County SD	Clarksdale
10	8.8	Quitman SD	Quitman
12	8.7	Hinds County SD	Raymond
12	8.7	Leflore County SD	Greenwood
14	8.6	Marion County SD	Columbia
15	8.3	South Pike SD	Magnolia
16	8.1	Forrest County SD	Hattiesburg
17	8.0	Yazoo City Municipal SD	Yazoo City
18	7.8	Grenada SD	Grenada
18	7.8	Tunica County SD	Tunica
20	7.7	Yazoo County SD	Yazoo City
21	7.1	Brookhaven SD	Brookhaven
21	7.1	Houston SD	Houston
23	6.9	Harrison County SD	Gulfport
23	6.9	Jackson County SD	Vancleave
25	6.8	Greenville Public Schools	Greenville
25	6.8	Jefferson Davis County SD	Prentiss
27	6.7	Vicksburg Warren SD	Vicksburg
28	6.6	Choctaw County SD	Ackerman
29	6.3	Gulfport SD	Gulfport
29	6.3	Lee County SD	Tupelo
29	6.3	Sunflower County SD	Indianola
32	6.2	East Tallahatchie Consol SD	Charleston
32	6.2	Quitman County SD	Marks
34	6.0	Pascagoula Separate SD	Pascagoula
35	5.8	Leake County SD	Carthage
35	5.8	Lincoln County SD	Brookhaven
35	5.8	Mccomb SD	Mccomb
38	5.6	Canton Public SD	Canton
39	5.5	Noxubee County SD	Macon
39	5.5	Pearl River County SD	Carriere
39	5.5	Tate County SD	Senatobia
42	5.4	Lauderdale County SD	Meridian
43	5.3	Hancock County SD	Kiln
43	5.3	Simpson County SD	Mendenhall
45	5.1	Franklin County SD	Meadville
45	5.1	Scott County SD	Forest
47	4.9	Jackson Public SD	Jackson
47	4.9	Meridian Public SD	Meridian
49	4.7	Lawrence County SD	Monticello
49	4.7	Long Beach SD	Long Beach
49	4.7	Wayne County SD	Waynesboro
49	4.7	Webster County SD	Eupora
49	4.7	Wilkinson County SD	Woodville
54	4.6	Lowndes County SD	Columbus
54	4.6	Monroe County SD	Amory
56	4.5	Natchez-Adams SD	Natchez
57	4.4	Cleveland SD	Cleveland
58	4.3	Ocean Springs SD	Ocean Springs
59	4.2	Bay Saint Louis Waveland SD	Bay St Louis
59	4.2	Clarksdale Municipal SD	Clarksdale
59	4.2	Louisville Municipal SD	Louisville
59	4.2	West Jasper Consolidated Schools	Bay Springs
63	4.0	Alcorn SD	Corinth
63	4.0	Columbus Municipal SD	Columbus
63	4.0	Indianola SD	Indianola
63	4.0	Itawamba County SD	Fulton
63	4.0	Smith County SD	Raleigh
68	3.9	North Pike SD	Summit
68	3.9	Senatobia Municipal SD	Senatobia
68	3.9	South Tippah SD	Ripley
71	3.8	Newton County SD	Decatur
72	3.6	Neshoba County SD	Philadelphia
73	3.5	Pearl Public SD	Pearl
73	3.5	Picayune SD	Picayune
75	3.4	Lafayette County SD	Oxford
76	3.3	Biloxi Public SD	Biloxi
77	3.2	Marshall County SD	Holly Springs
78	3.1	Holly Springs SD	Holly Springs
79	3.0	Covington County Schools	Collins
79	3.0	Jones County SD	Ellisville
79	3.0	Union County SD	New Albany
79	3.0	Walthall County SD	Tylertown
83	2.9	Tupelo Public SD	Tupelo
84	2.8	Lamar County SD	Purvis
85	2.7	Greene County SD	Leakesville
85	2.7	Petal SD	Petal
87	2.6	Corinth SD	Corinth
88	2.5	Clinton Public SD	Clinton
88	2.5	Oxford SD	Oxford
90	2.3	Claiborne County SD	Port Gibson
90	2.3	Holmes County SD	Lexington
90	2.3	New Albany Public Schools	New Albany
93	2.2	Forest Municipal SD	Forest
94	2.1	Rankin County SD	Brandon
95	2.0	Columbia SD	Columbia
96	1.9	Amory SD	Amory
96	1.9	Calhoun County SD	Pittsboro
96	1.9	Poplarville Separate SD	Poplarville
99	1.8	Starkville SD	Starkville
100	1.7	Moss Point Separate SD	Moss Point
100	1.7	Pontotoc City Schools	Pontotoc
102	1.5	Aberdeen SD	Aberdeen
102	1.5	Hattiesburg Public SD	Hattiesburg
104	1.1	Tishomingo County Sp Mun SD	Iuka
105	1.0	South Panola SD	Batesville
106	0.9	Prentiss County SD	Booneville
107	0.8	Stone County SD	Wiggins
108	0.7	Madison County SD	Flora
109	0.4	George County SD	Lucedale
109	0.4	Pass Christian Public SD	Pass Christian
111	0.1	Desoto County SD	Hernando
111	0.1	Pontotoc County SD	Pontotoc
113	0.0	Kosciusko SD	Kosciusko

Missouri

Missouri Public School Educational Profile

Category	Value	Category	Value
Schools *(2002-2003)*	2,382	**Diploma Recipients** *(2002-2003)*	54,487
Instructional Level		White, Non-Hispanic	45,627
Primary	1,257	Black, Non-Hispanic	7,195
Middle	375	Asian/Pacific Islander	821
High	566	American Indian/Alaskan Native	148
Other Level	184	Hispanic	696
Curriculum		**High School Drop-out Rate** (%) *(2000-2001)*	4.2
Regular	2,177	White, Non-Hispanic	3.9
Special Education	62	Black, Non-Hispanic	6.2
Vocational	60	Asian/Pacific Islander	2.6
Alternative	83	American Indian/Alaskan Native	5.4
Type		Hispanic	7.4
Magnet	48	**Staff** *(2002-2003)*	127,960.0
Charter	25	Teachers	66,613.2
Title I Eligible	1,322	Average Salary ($)	37,641
School-wide Title I	404	Librarians/Media Specialists	1,646.6
Students *(2002-2003)*	926,648	Guidance Counselors	2,692.3
Gender (%)		**Ratios** *(2002-2003)*	
Male	51.5	Student/Teacher Ratio	13.9 to 1
Female	48.5	Student/Librarian Ratio	562.8 to 1
Race/Ethnicity (%)		Student/Counselor Ratio	344.2 to 1
White, Non-Hispanic	78.0	**Current Spending** *($ per student in FY 2001)*	7,135
Black, Non-Hispanic	18.1	Instruction	4,346
Asian/Pacific Islander	1.3	Support Services	2,472
American Indian/Alaskan Native	0.3	**College Entrance Exam Scores** *(2003)*	
Hispanic	2.3	Scholastic Aptitude Test (SAT)	
Classification (%)		Participation Rate (%)	8
Individual Education Program (IEP)	15.5	Mean SAT I Verbal Score	582
Migrant	0.5	Mean SAT I Math Score	583
English Language Learner (ELL)	1.4	American College Testing Program (ACT)	
Eligible for Free Lunch Program	29.1	Participation Rate (%)	69
Eligible for Reduced-Price Lunch Program	7.0	Average Composite Score	21.4

Note: *For an explanation of data, please refer to the User's Guide in the front of the book; n/a indicates data not available*

Missouri NAEP 2003 Test Scores

Reading			Mathematics		
Grade/Category	**Value**	**Rank**	**Grade/Category**	**Value**	**Rank**
4th Grade			**4th Grade**		
Average Proficiency	222.3 (1.2)	13/51	Average Proficiency	234.8 (0.9)	30/51
Proficiency by Gender/Race/Ethnicity			Proficiency by Gender/Race/Ethnicity		
Male	218.6 (1.5)	13/51	Male	234.7 (1.1)	31/51
Female	225.9 (1.4)	15/51	Female	235.0 (1.0)	21/51
White, Non-Hispanic	226.6 (1.3)	18/51	White, Non-Hispanic	239.7 (0.9)	35/51
Black, Non-Hispanic	203.0 (1.7)	9/42	Black, Non-Hispanic	216.0 (1.3)	22/42
Asian, Non-Hispanic	217.9 (4.2)	1/41	Asian, Non-Hispanic	*219.6 (3.7)*	26/43
American Indian, Non-Hispanic	n/a	n/a	American Indian, Non-Hispanic	n/a	n/a
Hispanic	n/a	n/a	Hispanic	n/a	n/a
Proficiency by Class Size			Proficiency by Class Size		
Less than 16 Students	*205.0 (6.2)*	22/45	Less than 16 Students	*216.9 (6.5)*	35/47
16 to 18 Students	*221.0 (2.9)*	13/48	16 to 18 Students	*230.6 (3.1)*	29/48
19 to 20 Students	220.3 (2.7)	24/50	19 to 20 Students	235.1 (2.6)	24/50
21 to 25 Students	224.5 (1.7)	16/51	21 to 25 Students	236.4 (1.2)	29/51
Greater than 25 Students	*227.3 (3.7)*	3/49	Greater than 25 Students	*238.4 (3.8)*	13/49
Percent Attaining Achievement Levels			Percent Attaining Achievement Levels		
Below Basic	32.0 (1.4)	35/51	Below Basic	20.9 (1.2)	27/51
Basic or Above	68.0 (1.4)	17/51	Basic or Above	79.1 (1.2)	25/51
Proficient or Above	34.2 (1.4)	12/51	Proficient or Above	29.9 (1.4)	35/51
Advanced or Above	8.1 (0.7)	11/51	Advanced or Above	2.8 (0.5)	34/51
8th Grade			**8th Grade**		
Average Proficiency	267.4 (1.0)	13/51	Average Proficiency	278.8 (1.1)	27/51
Proficiency by Gender/Race/Ethnicity			Proficiency by Gender/Race/Ethnicity		
Male	263.3 (1.2)	10/51	Male	280.0 (1.2)	29/51
Female	271.2 (1.3)	19/51	Female	277.5 (1.4)	27/51
White, Non-Hispanic	271.7 (1.0)	15/50	White, Non-Hispanic	284.2 (1.0)	33/50
Black, Non-Hispanic	243.5 (1.8)	24/41	Black, Non-Hispanic	250.3 (2.1)	23/41
Asian, Non-Hispanic	n/a	n/a	Asian, Non-Hispanic	n/a	n/a
American Indian, Non-Hispanic	n/a	n/a	American Indian, Non-Hispanic	n/a	n/a
Hispanic	n/a	n/a	Hispanic	n/a	n/a
Proficiency by Parents Highest Level of Ed.			Proficiency by Parents Highest Level of Ed.		
Did Not Finish High School	254.3 (3.1)	1/50	Did Not Finish High School	264.8 (2.6)	4/50
Graduated High School	261.4 (1.3)	4/50	Graduated High School	270.6 (1.7)	21/50
Some Education After High School	272.3 (1.5)	4/50	Some Education After High School	281.5 (1.5)	22/50
Graduated College	273.0 (1.4)	25/50	Graduated College	286.9 (1.5)	29/50
Percent Attaining Achievement Levels			Percent Attaining Achievement Levels		
Below Basic	20.5 (1.1)	44/51	Below Basic	29.3 (1.4)	28/51
Basic or Above	79.5 (1.1)	7/51	Basic or Above	70.7 (1.4)	24/51
Proficient or Above	34.4 (1.5)	19/51	Proficient or Above	28.0 (1.2)	30/51
Advanced or Above	2.6 (0.4)	25/51	Advanced or Above	4.1 (0.5)	35/51

Note: *For an explanation of data, please refer to the User's Guide in the front of the book; values in italics indicate that the nature of the sample does not allow accurate determination of the variability of the statistic; n/a indicates data not available*

Adair County

Kirksville R-III

1901 E Hamilton St • Kirksville, MO 63501-3904
(660) 665-7774 • http://www.kirksville.k12.mo.us/
Grade Span: PK-12; **Agency Type:** 1
Schools: 5
2 Primary; 1 Middle; 2 High; 0 Other Level
4 Regular; 0 Special Education; 1 Vocational; 0 Alternative
0 Magnet; 0 Charter; 3 Title I Eligible; 0 School-wide Title I
Students: 2,472 (51.9% male; 48.1% female)
Individual Education Program: 432 (17.5%);
English Language Learner: 2 (0.1%); Migrant: 3 (0.1%)
Eligible for Free Lunch Program: 617 (25.0%)
Eligible for Reduced-Price Lunch Program: 164 (6.6%)
Teachers: 189.2 (13.1 to 1)
Librarians/Media Specialists: 4.0 (618.0 to 1)
Guidance Counselors: 9.0 (274.7 to 1)
Current Spending: ($ per student per year):
Total: $5,844; Instruction: $3,532; Support Services: $2,047
Enrollment, Drop-out Rates and Diploma Recipients by Race/Ethnicity

Category	Total	White	Black	Asian	AIAN	Hisp.
Enrollment (%)	100.0	95.9	1.5	0.8	0.5	1.3
Drop-out Rate (%)	5.7	5.5	11.1	12.5	0.0	16.7
H.S. Diplomas (#)	171	166	1	2	0	2

Andrew County

Savannah R-III

507 1/2 W Main • Savannah, MO 64485-0151
Mailing Address: PO Box 151 • Savannah, MO 64485-0151
(816) 324-3144 • http://www.savannah.k12.mo.us
Grade Span: PK-12; **Agency Type:** 1
Schools: 6
4 Primary; 1 Middle; 1 High; 0 Other Level
6 Regular; 0 Special Education; 0 Vocational; 0 Alternative
0 Magnet; 0 Charter; 2 Title I Eligible; 1 School-wide Title I
Students: 2,398 (51.8% male; 48.2% female)
Individual Education Program: 287 (12.0%);
English Language Learner: 1 (<0.1%); Migrant: 0 (0.0%)
Eligible for Free Lunch Program: 490 (20.4%)
Eligible for Reduced-Price Lunch Program: 183 (7.6%)
Teachers: 166.2 (14.4 to 1)
Librarians/Media Specialists: 3.2 (749.4 to 1)
Guidance Counselors: 4.1 (584.9 to 1)
Current Spending: ($ per student per year):
Total: $5,527; Instruction: $3,536; Support Services: $1,694
Enrollment, Drop-out Rates and Diploma Recipients by Race/Ethnicity

Category	Total	White	Black	Asian	AIAN	Hisp.
Enrollment (%)	100.0	97.4	1.0	0.1	0.3	1.2
Drop-out Rate (%)	2.2	2.1	0.0	n/a	0.0	25.0
H.S. Diplomas (#)	164	161	1	0	1	1

Audrain County

Mexico 59

920 S Jefferson • Mexico, MO 65265-2599
(573) 581-3773 • http://www.mexicoschools.net/
Grade Span: PK-12; **Agency Type:** 1
Schools: 6
3 Primary; 1 Middle; 2 High; 0 Other Level
5 Regular; 0 Special Education; 1 Vocational; 0 Alternative
0 Magnet; 0 Charter; 2 Title I Eligible; 1 School-wide Title I
Students: 2,511 (50.9% male; 49.1% female)
Individual Education Program: 351 (14.0%);
English Language Learner: 8 (0.3%); Migrant: 18 (0.7%)
Eligible for Free Lunch Program: 786 (31.3%)
Eligible for Reduced-Price Lunch Program: 212 (8.4%)
Teachers: 178.0 (14.1 to 1)
Librarians/Media Specialists: 4.5 (558.0 to 1)
Guidance Counselors: 10.0 (251.1 to 1)
Current Spending: ($ per student per year):
Total: $5,533; Instruction: $3,418; Support Services: $1,810
Enrollment, Drop-out Rates and Diploma Recipients by Race/Ethnicity

Category	Total	White	Black	Asian	AIAN	Hisp.
Enrollment (%)	100.0	86.8	10.5	0.8	0.2	1.6
Drop-out Rate (%)	3.8	3.9	4.1	0.0	0.0	0.0
H.S. Diplomas (#)	184	157	20	1	3	3

Barry County

Cassville R-IV

1501 Main • Cassville, MO 65625-1154
(417) 847-2221 • http://wildcats.cassville.k12.mo.us/
Grade Span: PK-12; **Agency Type:** 1
Schools: 4
2 Primary; 1 Middle; 1 High; 0 Other Level
4 Regular; 0 Special Education; 0 Vocational; 0 Alternative
0 Magnet; 0 Charter; 3 Title I Eligible; 0 School-wide Title I
Students: 2,138 (53.1% male; 46.9% female)
Individual Education Program: 334 (15.6%);
English Language Learner: 37 (1.7%); Migrant: 69 (3.2%)
Eligible for Free Lunch Program: 688 (32.2%)
Eligible for Reduced-Price Lunch Program: 202 (9.4%)
Teachers: 125.5 (17.0 to 1)
Librarians/Media Specialists: 4.0 (534.5 to 1)
Guidance Counselors: 4.8 (445.4 to 1)
Current Spending: ($ per student per year):
Total: $5,226; Instruction: $3,417; Support Services: $1,509
Enrollment, Drop-out Rates and Diploma Recipients by Race/Ethnicity

Category	Total	White	Black	Asian	AIAN	Hisp.
Enrollment (%)	100.0	94.7	0.2	0.4	0.8	3.8
Drop-out Rate (%)	3.2	3.1	0.0	0.0	0.0	13.3
H.S. Diplomas (#)	135	130	0	1	2	2

Monett R-I

800 E Scott St • Monett, MO 65708-1741
(417) 235-7422 • http://hs1.monett.k12.mo.us/
Grade Span: PK-12; **Agency Type:** 1
Schools: 5
1 Primary; 2 Middle; 2 High; 0 Other Level
4 Regular; 0 Special Education; 1 Vocational; 0 Alternative
0 Magnet; 0 Charter; 3 Title I Eligible; 0 School-wide Title I
Students: 2,061 (50.6% male; 49.4% female)
Individual Education Program: 308 (14.9%);
English Language Learner: 237 (11.5%); Migrant: 310 (15.0%)
Eligible for Free Lunch Program: 757 (36.7%)
Eligible for Reduced-Price Lunch Program: 181 (8.8%)
Teachers: 148.3 (13.9 to 1)
Librarians/Media Specialists: 4.0 (515.3 to 1)
Guidance Counselors: 8.0 (257.6 to 1)
Current Spending: ($ per student per year):
Total: $6,277; Instruction: $4,313; Support Services: $1,711
Enrollment, Drop-out Rates and Diploma Recipients by Race/Ethnicity

Category	Total	White	Black	Asian	AIAN	Hisp.
Enrollment (%)	100.0	82.7	0.0	0.3	0.6	16.4
Drop-out Rate (%)	5.2	4.9	n/a	200.0	0.0	4.8
H.S. Diplomas (#)	123	112	0	0	0	11

Benton County

Warsaw R-IX

1 Wildcat Dr • Warsaw, MO 65355-0248
Mailing Address: PO Box 248 • Warsaw, MO 65355-0248
(660) 438-7120
Grade Span: PK-12; **Agency Type:** 1
Schools: 5
3 Primary; 1 Middle; 1 High; 0 Other Level
5 Regular; 0 Special Education; 0 Vocational; 0 Alternative
0 Magnet; 0 Charter; 2 Title I Eligible; 2 School-wide Title I
Students: 1,538 (49.2% male; 50.8% female)
Individual Education Program: 254 (16.5%);
English Language Learner: 0 (0.0%); Migrant: 10 (0.7%)
Eligible for Free Lunch Program: 652 (42.4%)
Eligible for Reduced-Price Lunch Program: 128 (8.3%)
Teachers: 90.4 (17.0 to 1)
Librarians/Media Specialists: 2.0 (769.0 to 1)
Guidance Counselors: 2.8 (549.3 to 1)
Current Spending: ($ per student per year):
Total: $5,644; Instruction: $3,572; Support Services: $1,745
Enrollment, Drop-out Rates and Diploma Recipients by Race/Ethnicity

Category	Total	White	Black	Asian	AIAN	Hisp.
Enrollment (%)	100.0	97.1	0.8	0.2	0.4	1.5
Drop-out Rate (%)	2.1	1.9	0.0	n/a	n/a	20.0
H.S. Diplomas (#)	102	99	0	1	0	2

Boone County

Columbia 93

1818 W Worley St • Columbia, MO 65203-1038
(573) 886-2100 • http://www.columbia.k12.mo.us/
Grade Span: PK-12; **Agency Type:** 1
Schools: 31
20 Primary; 3 Middle; 3 High; 5 Other Level

29 Regular; 0 Special Education; 1 Vocational; 1 Alternative
0 Magnet; 0 Charter; 12 Title I Eligible; 0 School-wide Title I
Students: 16,666 (51.8% male; 48.2% female)
Individual Education Program: 2,726 (16.4%);
English Language Learner: 352 (2.1%); Migrant: 0 (0.0%)
Eligible for Free Lunch Program: 3,975 (23.9%)
Eligible for Reduced-Price Lunch Program: 714 (4.3%)
Teachers: 1,255.1 (13.3 to 1)
Librarians/Media Specialists: 28.3 (588.9 to 1)
Guidance Counselors: 54.5 (305.8 to 1)
Current Spending: ($ per student per year):
Total: $6,847; Instruction: $4,261; Support Services: $2,317
Enrollment, Drop-out Rates and Diploma Recipients by Race/Ethnicity

Category	Total	White	Black	Asian	AIAN	Hisp.
Enrollment (%)	100.0	72.9	20.2	4.3	0.4	2.2
Drop-out Rate (%)	4.7	3.8	10.0	1.8	0.0	5.1
H.S. Diplomas (#)	1,039	834	135	55	1	14

Buchanan County

Saint Joseph
925 Felix • Saint Joseph, MO 64501-2706
(816) 671-4000 • http://www.sjsd.k12.mo.us/
Grade Span: PK-12; **Agency Type:** 1
Schools: 29
18 Primary; 4 Middle; 4 High; 3 Other Level
27 Regular; 1 Special Education; 1 Vocational; 0 Alternative
0 Magnet; 0 Charter; 8 Title I Eligible; 6 School-wide Title I
Students: 11,893 (50.8% male; 49.2% female)
Individual Education Program: 1,480 (12.4%);
English Language Learner: 42 (0.4%); Migrant: 0 (0.0%)
Eligible for Free Lunch Program: 4,522 (38.0%)
Eligible for Reduced-Price Lunch Program: 1,282 (10.8%)
Teachers: 812.7 (14.6 to 1)
Librarians/Media Specialists: 10.7 (1,111.5 to 1)
Guidance Counselors: 31.4 (378.8 to 1)
Current Spending: ($ per student per year):
Total: $6,079; Instruction: $3,896; Support Services: $1,862
Enrollment, Drop-out Rates and Diploma Recipients by Race/Ethnicity

Category	Total	White	Black	Asian	AIAN	Hisp.
Enrollment (%)	100.0	89.1	7.1	0.8	0.5	2.7
Drop-out Rate (%)	3.2	3.3	1.2	0.0	11.8	0.0
H.S. Diplomas (#)	711	659	31	9	2	10

Butler County

Poplar Bluff R-I
1110 N Westwood Blvd • Poplar Bluff, MO 63901-3336
(573) 785-7751 • http://www.pb.k12.mo.us/index.htm
Grade Span: PK-12; **Agency Type:** 1
Schools: 11
6 Primary; 2 Middle; 2 High; 1 Other Level
10 Regular; 0 Special Education; 1 Vocational; 0 Alternative
0 Magnet; 0 Charter; 6 Title I Eligible; 4 School-wide Title I
Students: 4,918 (51.0% male; 49.0% female)
Individual Education Program: 736 (15.0%);
English Language Learner: 4 (0.1%); Migrant: 0 (0.0%)
Eligible for Free Lunch Program: 2,041 (41.5%)
Eligible for Reduced-Price Lunch Program: 370 (7.5%)
Teachers: 307.0 (16.0 to 1)
Librarians/Media Specialists: 9.0 (546.4 to 1)
Guidance Counselors: 14.0 (351.3 to 1)
Current Spending: ($ per student per year):
Total: $5,461; Instruction: $3,452; Support Services: $1,741
Enrollment, Drop-out Rates and Diploma Recipients by Race/Ethnicity

Category	Total	White	Black	Asian	AIAN	Hisp.
Enrollment (%)	100.0	88.0	10.2	0.6	0.5	0.7
Drop-out Rate (%)	8.0	7.8	8.8	0.0	0.0	18.8
H.S. Diplomas (#)	312	272	36	0	2	2

Callaway County

Fulton 58
2 Hornet Dr • Fulton, MO 65251-2731
(573) 642-2206 • http://www.fulton.k12.mo.us/
Grade Span: PK-12; **Agency Type:** 1
Schools: 5
3 Primary; 1 Middle; 1 High; 0 Other Level
5 Regular; 0 Special Education; 0 Vocational; 0 Alternative
0 Magnet; 0 Charter; 4 Title I Eligible; 0 School-wide Title I
Students: 2,360 (51.6% male; 48.4% female)
Individual Education Program: 305 (12.9%);
English Language Learner: 5 (0.2%); Migrant: 0 (0.0%)
Eligible for Free Lunch Program: 708 (30.0%)
Eligible for Reduced-Price Lunch Program: 225 (9.5%)
Teachers: 174.4 (13.5 to 1)
Librarians/Media Specialists: 5.0 (472.0 to 1)
Guidance Counselors: 8.8 (268.2 to 1)
Current Spending: ($ per student per year):
Total: $5,932; Instruction: $3,557; Support Services: $2,015
Enrollment, Drop-out Rates and Diploma Recipients by Race/Ethnicity

Category	Total	White	Black	Asian	AIAN	Hisp.
Enrollment (%)	100.0	85.1	13.8	0.3	0.1	0.6
Drop-out Rate (%)	3.0	3.1	3.0	0.0	n/a	0.0
H.S. Diplomas (#)	131	118	11	2	0	0

Camden County

Camdenton R-III
Township Rd • Camdenton, MO 65020-1409
Mailing Address: PO Box 1409 • Camdenton, MO 65020-1409
(573) 346-9208 • http://schoolweb.missouri.edu/camdenton.k12.mo.us/
Grade Span: PK-12; **Agency Type:** 1
Schools: 8
3 Primary; 2 Middle; 2 High; 1 Other Level
6 Regular; 0 Special Education; 1 Vocational; 1 Alternative
0 Magnet; 0 Charter; 3 Title I Eligible; 0 School-wide Title I
Students: 4,095 (53.1% male; 46.9% female)
Individual Education Program: 576 (14.1%);
English Language Learner: 15 (0.4%); Migrant: 0 (0.0%)
Eligible for Free Lunch Program: 1,224 (29.9%)
Eligible for Reduced-Price Lunch Program: 386 (9.4%)
Teachers: 281.8 (14.5 to 1)
Librarians/Media Specialists: 5.0 (819.0 to 1)
Guidance Counselors: 13.0 (315.0 to 1)
Current Spending: ($ per student per year):
Total: $5,930; Instruction: $3,666; Support Services: $1,975
Enrollment, Drop-out Rates and Diploma Recipients by Race/Ethnicity

Category	Total	White	Black	Asian	AIAN	Hisp.
Enrollment (%)	100.0	97.4	0.5	0.7	0.3	1.1
Drop-out Rate (%)	2.4	2.4	0.0	0.0	0.0	0.0
H.S. Diplomas (#)	289	288	0	0	1	0

Cape Girardeau County

Cape Girardeau 63
301 N Clark St • Cape Girardeau, MO 63701-5101
(573) 335-1867 • http://www.cape.k12.mo.us/
Grade Span: PK-12; **Agency Type:** 1
Schools: 9
5 Primary; 2 Middle; 2 High; 0 Other Level
8 Regular; 0 Special Education; 1 Vocational; 0 Alternative
0 Magnet; 0 Charter; 6 Title I Eligible; 5 School-wide Title I
Students: 4,010 (50.1% male; 49.9% female)
Individual Education Program: 734 (18.3%);
English Language Learner: 32 (0.8%); Migrant: 0 (0.0%)
Eligible for Free Lunch Program: 1,416 (35.3%)
Eligible for Reduced-Price Lunch Program: 205 (5.1%)
Teachers: 323.3 (12.4 to 1)
Librarians/Media Specialists: 8.0 (501.3 to 1)
Guidance Counselors: 14.8 (270.9 to 1)
Current Spending: ($ per student per year):
Total: $5,921; Instruction: $3,827; Support Services: $1,869
Enrollment, Drop-out Rates and Diploma Recipients by Race/Ethnicity

Category	Total	White	Black	Asian	AIAN	Hisp.
Enrollment (%)	100.0	73.8	23.5	1.1	0.1	1.4
Drop-out Rate (%)	7.2	6.2	12.7	0.0	0.0	0.0
H.S. Diplomas (#)	275	236	34	3	1	1

Jackson R-II
614 E Adams St • Jackson, MO 63755-2150
(573) 243-9501 • http://www.jackson.k12.mo.us/
Grade Span: PK-12; **Agency Type:** 1
Schools: 10
6 Primary; 2 Middle; 1 High; 1 Other Level
10 Regular; 0 Special Education; 0 Vocational; 0 Alternative
0 Magnet; 0 Charter; 6 Title I Eligible; 0 School-wide Title I
Students: 4,664 (51.8% male; 48.2% female)
Individual Education Program: 599 (12.8%);
English Language Learner: 3 (0.1%); Migrant: 0 (0.0%)
Eligible for Free Lunch Program: 726 (15.6%)
Eligible for Reduced-Price Lunch Program: 271 (5.8%)
Teachers: 284.5 (16.4 to 1)
Librarians/Media Specialists: 7.8 (597.9 to 1)
Guidance Counselors: 11.9 (391.9 to 1)
Current Spending: ($ per student per year):
Total: $4,732; Instruction: $3,047; Support Services: $1,477

Enrollment, Drop-out Rates and Diploma Recipients by Race/Ethnicity

Category	Total	White	Black	Asian	AIAN	Hisp.
Enrollment (%)	100.0	97.4	1.7	0.5	0.0	0.4
Drop-out Rate (%)	2.6	2.4	7.4	25.0	n/a	0.0
H.S. Diplomas (#)	343	338	4	0	0	1

Cass County

Belton 124

110 W Walnut • Belton, MO 64012-4808
(816) 348-1000 • http://www.beltonschools.org/
Grade Span: PK-12; **Agency Type:** 1
Schools: 9
5 Primary; 2 Middle; 1 High; 1 Other Level
8 Regular; 1 Special Education; 0 Vocational; 0 Alternative
0 Magnet; 0 Charter; 4 Title I Eligible; 0 School-wide Title I
Students: 4,965 (52.7% male; 47.3% female)
Individual Education Program: 573 (11.5%);
English Language Learner: 83 (1.7%); Migrant: 17 (0.3%)
Eligible for Free Lunch Program: 889 (17.9%)
Eligible for Reduced-Price Lunch Program: 319 (6.4%)
Teachers: 297.8 (16.7 to 1)
Librarians/Media Specialists: 7.8 (636.5 to 1)
Guidance Counselors: 11.5 (431.7 to 1)
Current Spending: ($ per student per year):
Total: $5,915; Instruction: $3,598; Support Services: $2,036
Enrollment, Drop-out Rates and Diploma Recipients by Race/Ethnicity

Category	Total	White	Black	Asian	AIAN	Hisp.
Enrollment (%)	100.0	88.3	5.3	0.9	0.3	5.2
Drop-out Rate (%)	4.4	4.3	4.7	0.0	20.0	4.4
H.S. Diplomas (#)	261	232	8	4	2	15

Harrisonville R-IX

402 Eastwood Rd • Harrisonville, MO 64701-2599
(816) 380-2727 • http://www.harrisonvilleschools.org/
Grade Span: PK-12; **Agency Type:** 1
Schools: 7
3 Primary; 1 Middle; 2 High; 1 Other Level
5 Regular; 0 Special Education; 1 Vocational; 1 Alternative
0 Magnet; 0 Charter; 3 Title I Eligible; 0 School-wide Title I
Students: 2,544 (53.2% male; 46.8% female)
Individual Education Program: 263 (10.3%);
English Language Learner: 0 (0.0%); Migrant: 0 (0.0%)
Eligible for Free Lunch Program: 424 (16.7%)
Eligible for Reduced-Price Lunch Program: 132 (5.2%)
Teachers: 163.7 (15.5 to 1)
Librarians/Media Specialists: 4.0 (636.0 to 1)
Guidance Counselors: 7.3 (348.5 to 1)
Current Spending: ($ per student per year):
Total: $5,811; Instruction: $3,428; Support Services: $2,143
Enrollment, Drop-out Rates and Diploma Recipients by Race/Ethnicity

Category	Total	White	Black	Asian	AIAN	Hisp.
Enrollment (%)	100.0	91.3	1.3	0.6	0.5	6.3
Drop-out Rate (%)	3.6	3.4	0.0	28.6	0.0	16.7
H.S. Diplomas (#)	182	178	0	2	2	0

Pleasant Hill R-III

301 N Mckissock • Pleasant Hill, MO 64080-1445
(816) 540-3161 • http://pleasanthillschools.com/
Grade Span: PK-12; **Agency Type:** 1
Schools: 4
2 Primary; 1 Middle; 1 High; 0 Other Level
4 Regular; 0 Special Education; 0 Vocational; 0 Alternative
0 Magnet; 0 Charter; 2 Title I Eligible; 0 School-wide Title I
Students: 2,060 (52.2% male; 47.8% female)
Individual Education Program: 281 (13.6%);
English Language Learner: 0 (0.0%); Migrant: 0 (0.0%)
Eligible for Free Lunch Program: 220 (10.7%)
Eligible for Reduced-Price Lunch Program: 87 (4.2%)
Teachers: 122.5 (16.8 to 1)
Librarians/Media Specialists: 3.0 (686.7 to 1)
Guidance Counselors: 6.0 (343.3 to 1)
Current Spending: ($ per student per year):
Total: $5,849; Instruction: $3,480; Support Services: $2,146
Enrollment, Drop-out Rates and Diploma Recipients by Race/Ethnicity

Category	Total	White	Black	Asian	AIAN	Hisp.
Enrollment (%)	100.0	96.8	0.6	0.2	0.6	1.7
Drop-out Rate (%)	2.7	2.7	0.0	0.0	n/a	0.0
H.S. Diplomas (#)	124	120	0	2	0	2

Raymore-Peculiar R-II

208 W Walnut • Raymore, MO 64083-8800
(816) 331-0050 • http://www.raypec.k12.mo.us/
Grade Span: PK-12; **Agency Type:** 1
Schools: 7
4 Primary; 2 Middle; 1 High; 0 Other Level
7 Regular; 0 Special Education; 0 Vocational; 0 Alternative
0 Magnet; 0 Charter; 3 Title I Eligible; 0 School-wide Title I
Students: 4,643 (49.8% male; 50.2% female)
Individual Education Program: 394 (8.5%);
English Language Learner: 0 (0.0%); Migrant: 0 (0.0%)
Eligible for Free Lunch Program: 495 (10.7%)
Eligible for Reduced-Price Lunch Program: 162 (3.5%)
Teachers: 294.5 (15.8 to 1)
Librarians/Media Specialists: 7.3 (636.0 to 1)
Guidance Counselors: 10.0 (464.3 to 1)
Current Spending: ($ per student per year):
Total: $5,783; Instruction: $3,385; Support Services: $2,129
Enrollment, Drop-out Rates and Diploma Recipients by Race/Ethnicity

Category	Total	White	Black	Asian	AIAN	Hisp.
Enrollment (%)	100.0	94.6	3.1	0.6	0.3	1.4
Drop-out Rate (%)	2.9	2.6	0.0	0.0	50.0	18.2
H.S. Diplomas (#)	259	249	5	1	2	2

Christian County

Nixa R-II

205 N St • Nixa, MO 65714-8663
(417) 725-7400 • http://www.nixa.k12.mo.us/
Grade Span: PK-12; **Agency Type:** 1
Schools: 8
5 Primary; 2 Middle; 1 High; 0 Other Level
8 Regular; 0 Special Education; 0 Vocational; 0 Alternative
0 Magnet; 0 Charter; 4 Title I Eligible; 0 School-wide Title I
Students: 4,127 (50.5% male; 49.5% female)
Individual Education Program: 502 (12.2%);
English Language Learner: 1 (<0.1%); Migrant: 8 (0.2%)
Eligible for Free Lunch Program: 659 (16.0%)
Eligible for Reduced-Price Lunch Program: 312 (7.6%)
Teachers: 278.5 (14.8 to 1)
Librarians/Media Specialists: 7.4 (557.7 to 1)
Guidance Counselors: 10.5 (393.0 to 1)
Current Spending: ($ per student per year):
Total: $4,898; Instruction: $3,153; Support Services: $1,533
Enrollment, Drop-out Rates and Diploma Recipients by Race/Ethnicity

Category	Total	White	Black	Asian	AIAN	Hisp.
Enrollment (%)	100.0	96.1	1.0	0.8	0.4	1.7
Drop-out Rate (%)	3.6	3.6	0.0	9.1	0.0	0.0
H.S. Diplomas (#)	225	219	0	2	1	3

Ozark R-VI

302 N 4th Ave • Ozark, MO 65721-0166
Mailing Address: PO Box 166 • Ozark, MO 65721-0166
(417) 581-7694 • http://ozark.k12.mo.us/
Grade Span: PK-12; **Agency Type:** 1
Schools: 6
3 Primary; 2 Middle; 1 High; 0 Other Level
6 Regular; 0 Special Education; 0 Vocational; 0 Alternative
0 Magnet; 0 Charter; 3 Title I Eligible; 0 School-wide Title I
Students: 4,001 (52.1% male; 47.9% female)
Individual Education Program: 587 (14.7%);
English Language Learner: 6 (0.2%); Migrant: 2 (0.1%)
Eligible for Free Lunch Program: 559 (14.0%)
Eligible for Reduced-Price Lunch Program: 224 (5.6%)
Teachers: 251.0 (15.9 to 1)
Librarians/Media Specialists: 7.0 (571.6 to 1)
Guidance Counselors: 7.7 (519.6 to 1)
Current Spending: ($ per student per year):
Total: $5,220; Instruction: $3,323; Support Services: $1,627
Enrollment, Drop-out Rates and Diploma Recipients by Race/Ethnicity

Category	Total	White	Black	Asian	AIAN	Hisp.
Enrollment (%)	100.0	97.6	0.5	0.5	0.4	1.0
Drop-out Rate (%)	2.2	2.2	0.0	0.0	0.0	0.0
H.S. Diplomas (#)	221	215	0	2	1	3

Clay County

Excelsior Springs 40

100 N Thompson Ave • Excelsior Springs, MO 64024-0248
Mailing Address: PO Box 248 • Excelsior Springs, MO 64024-0248
(816) 630-9200 • http://estigers.k12.mo.us/
Grade Span: PK-12; **Agency Type:** 1
Schools: 7
3 Primary; 1 Middle; 3 High; 0 Other Level
6 Regular; 0 Special Education; 1 Vocational; 0 Alternative
0 Magnet; 0 Charter; 3 Title I Eligible; 0 School-wide Title I
Students: 3,344 (52.3% male; 47.7% female)
Individual Education Program: 386 (11.5%);
English Language Learner: 4 (0.1%); Migrant: 0 (0.0%)
Eligible for Free Lunch Program: 860 (25.7%)

Eligible for Reduced-Price Lunch Program: 214 (6.4%)
Teachers: 204.0 (16.4 to 1)
Librarians/Media Specialists: 4.0 (836.0 to 1)
Guidance Counselors: 9.0 (371.6 to 1)
Current Spending: ($ per student per year):
Total: $6,122; Instruction: $3,779; Support Services: $2,131
Enrollment, Drop-out Rates and Diploma Recipients by Race/Ethnicity

Category	Total	White	Black	Asian	AIAN	Hisp.
Enrollment (%)	100.0	89.3	7.4	0.6	0.5	2.2
Drop-out Rate (%)	20.7	13.7	60.2	0.0	14.3	33.3
H.S. Diplomas (#)	316	240	68	3	1	4

Kearney R-I

1002 S Jefferson • Kearney, MO 64060-8520
(816) 628-4116 • http://www.kearney.k12.mo.us/default.htm
Grade Span: PK-12; **Agency Type:** 1
Schools: 7
4 Primary; 2 Middle; 1 High; 0 Other Level
7 Regular; 0 Special Education; 0 Vocational; 0 Alternative
0 Magnet; 0 Charter; 2 Title I Eligible; 0 School-wide Title I
Students: 3,337 (50.9% male; 49.1% female)
Individual Education Program: 386 (11.6%);
English Language Learner: 0 (0.0%); Migrant: 0 (0.0%)
Eligible for Free Lunch Program: 148 (4.4%)
Eligible for Reduced-Price Lunch Program: 61 (1.8%)
Teachers: 194.9 (17.1 to 1)
Librarians/Media Specialists: 4.5 (741.6 to 1)
Guidance Counselors: 7.0 (476.7 to 1)
Current Spending: ($ per student per year):
Total: $4,690; Instruction: $2,957; Support Services: $1,494
Enrollment, Drop-out Rates and Diploma Recipients by Race/Ethnicity

Category	Total	White	Black	Asian	AIAN	Hisp.
Enrollment (%)	100.0	98.1	0.6	0.4	0.2	0.7
Drop-out Rate (%)	3.2	3.3	0.0	0.0	0.0	0.0
H.S. Diplomas (#)	199	195	2	0	0	2

Liberty 53

650 Conistor • Liberty, MO 64068-2323
(816) 415-5300 • http://liberty.k12.mo.us/
Grade Span: PK-12; **Agency Type:** 1
Schools: 15
8 Primary; 2 Middle; 3 High; 2 Other Level
13 Regular; 0 Special Education; 0 Vocational; 2 Alternative
0 Magnet; 0 Charter; 1 Title I Eligible; 0 School-wide Title I
Students: 7,733 (51.9% male; 48.1% female)
Individual Education Program: 865 (11.2%);
English Language Learner: 29 (0.4%); Migrant: 0 (0.0%)
Eligible for Free Lunch Program: 614 (7.9%)
Eligible for Reduced-Price Lunch Program: 223 (2.9%)
Teachers: 496.6 (15.6 to 1)
Librarians/Media Specialists: 12.8 (604.1 to 1)
Guidance Counselors: 20.4 (379.1 to 1)
Current Spending: ($ per student per year):
Total: $6,334; Instruction: $3,691; Support Services: $2,355
Enrollment, Drop-out Rates and Diploma Recipients by Race/Ethnicity

Category	Total	White	Black	Asian	AIAN	Hisp.
Enrollment (%)	100.0	91.8	4.3	1.0	0.5	2.5
Drop-out Rate (%)	3.9	3.7	1.3	15.8	33.3	7.9
H.S. Diplomas (#)	454	424	17	4	1	8

North Kansas City 74

2000 NE 46th St • Kansas City, MO 64116-2099
(816) 413-5000 • http://www.nkcsd.k12.mo.us/
Grade Span: PK-12; **Agency Type:** 1
Schools: 31
21 Primary; 5 Middle; 3 High; 2 Other Level
30 Regular; 0 Special Education; 0 Vocational; 1 Alternative
0 Magnet; 0 Charter; 8 Title I Eligible; 0 School-wide Title I
Students: 17,296 (51.6% male; 48.4% female)
Individual Education Program: 2,482 (14.4%);
English Language Learner: 314 (1.8%); Migrant: 0 (0.0%)
Eligible for Free Lunch Program: 3,019 (17.5%)
Eligible for Reduced-Price Lunch Program: 1,442 (8.3%)
Teachers: 1,189.0 (14.5 to 1)
Librarians/Media Specialists: 25.4 (680.9 to 1)
Guidance Counselors: 46.0 (376.0 to 1)
Current Spending: ($ per student per year):
Total: $6,355; Instruction: $4,194; Support Services: $1,956
Enrollment, Drop-out Rates and Diploma Recipients by Race/Ethnicity

Category	Total	White	Black	Asian	AIAN	Hisp.
Enrollment (%)	100.0	83.4	7.0	3.0	0.7	6.0
Drop-out Rate (%)	3.7	3.5	4.9	1.1	10.8	6.5
H.S. Diplomas (#)	1,137	954	63	47	20	53

Smithville R-II

645 S Commercial • Smithville, MO 64089-9381
(816) 532-0406 • http://www.smithville.k12.mo.us/
Grade Span: PK-12; **Agency Type:** 1
Schools: 4
2 Primary; 1 Middle; 1 High; 0 Other Level
4 Regular; 0 Special Education; 0 Vocational; 0 Alternative
0 Magnet; 0 Charter; 2 Title I Eligible; 0 School-wide Title I
Students: 1,804 (50.2% male; 49.8% female)
Individual Education Program: 198 (11.0%);
English Language Learner: 0 (0.0%); Migrant: 0 (0.0%)
Eligible for Free Lunch Program: 91 (5.0%)
Eligible for Reduced-Price Lunch Program: 47 (2.6%)
Teachers: 118.0 (15.3 to 1)
Librarians/Media Specialists: 5.0 (360.8 to 1)
Guidance Counselors: 5.0 (360.8 to 1)
Current Spending: ($ per student per year):
Total: $5,612; Instruction: $3,589; Support Services: $1,786
Enrollment, Drop-out Rates and Diploma Recipients by Race/Ethnicity

Category	Total	White	Black	Asian	AIAN	Hisp.
Enrollment (%)	100.0	96.2	0.3	1.4	0.7	1.3
Drop-out Rate (%)	3.6	3.1	n/a	16.7	0.0	22.2
H.S. Diplomas (#)	110	101	0	3	2	4

Clinton County

Cameron R-I

105 E Fifth St • Cameron, MO 64429-1714
(816) 632-2170 • http://www.cameron.k12.mo.us/
Grade Span: PK-12; **Agency Type:** 1
Schools: 5
2 Primary; 1 Middle; 2 High; 0 Other Level
5 Regular; 0 Special Education; 0 Vocational; 0 Alternative
0 Magnet; 0 Charter; 3 Title I Eligible; 0 School-wide Title I
Students: 1,643 (53.6% male; 46.4% female)
Individual Education Program: 263 (16.0%);
English Language Learner: 2 (0.1%); Migrant: 0 (0.0%)
Eligible for Free Lunch Program: 350 (21.3%)
Eligible for Reduced-Price Lunch Program: 136 (8.3%)
Teachers: 123.8 (13.3 to 1)
Librarians/Media Specialists: 3.0 (547.7 to 1)
Guidance Counselors: 4.3 (382.1 to 1)
Current Spending: ($ per student per year):
Total: $6,549; Instruction: $4,388; Support Services: $1,878
Enrollment, Drop-out Rates and Diploma Recipients by Race/Ethnicity

Category	Total	White	Black	Asian	AIAN	Hisp.
Enrollment (%)	100.0	96.7	1.4	0.9	0.4	0.7
Drop-out Rate (%)	1.6	1.5	9.1	0.0	n/a	0.0
H.S. Diplomas (#)	106	99	5	2	0	0

Cole County

Jefferson City

315 E Dunklin St • Jefferson City, MO 65101-3197
(573) 659-3000 • http://www.jcps.k12.mo.us/
Grade Span: PK-12; **Agency Type:** 1
Schools: 17
11 Primary; 2 Middle; 3 High; 1 Other Level
15 Regular; 0 Special Education; 1 Vocational; 1 Alternative
0 Magnet; 0 Charter; 8 Title I Eligible; 0 School-wide Title I
Students: 8,338 (50.3% male; 49.7% female)
Individual Education Program: 1,531 (18.4%);
English Language Learner: 280 (3.4%); Migrant: 0 (0.0%)
Eligible for Free Lunch Program: 2,162 (25.9%)
Eligible for Reduced-Price Lunch Program: 504 (6.0%)
Teachers: 573.1 (14.5 to 1)
Librarians/Media Specialists: 16.0 (521.1 to 1)
Guidance Counselors: 30.0 (277.9 to 1)
Current Spending: ($ per student per year):
Total: $5,745; Instruction: $3,749; Support Services: $1,697
Enrollment, Drop-out Rates and Diploma Recipients by Race/Ethnicity

Category	Total	White	Black	Asian	AIAN	Hisp.
Enrollment (%)	100.0	80.3	15.9	1.4	0.4	2.1
Drop-out Rate (%)	4.0	3.7	6.4	0.0	0.0	7.3
H.S. Diplomas (#)	509	453	48	4	2	2

Cooper County

Boonville R-I

736 Main St • Boonville, MO 65233-1656
(660) 882-7474
Grade Span: PK-12; **Agency Type:** 1
Schools: 5
2 Primary; 1 Middle; 2 High; 0 Other Level
4 Regular; 0 Special Education; 1 Vocational; 0 Alternative

0 Magnet; 0 Charter; 2 Title I Eligible; 0 School-wide Title I
Students: 1,504 (51.7% male; 48.3% female)
Individual Education Program: 185 (12.3%);
English Language Learner: 0 (0.0%); Migrant: 0 (0.0%)
Eligible for Free Lunch Program: 380 (25.3%)
Eligible for Reduced-Price Lunch Program: 173 (11.5%)
Teachers: 114.5 (13.1 to 1)
Librarians/Media Specialists: 3.0 (501.3 to 1)
Guidance Counselors: 5.0 (300.8 to 1)
Current Spending: ($ per student per year):
Total: $6,901; Instruction: $4,330; Support Services: $2,192
Enrollment, Drop-out Rates and Diploma Recipients by Race/Ethnicity

Category	Total	White	Black	Asian	AIAN	Hisp.
Enrollment (%)	100.0	86.2	11.8	1.0	0.3	0.7
Drop-out Rate (%)	3.7	3.1	7.0	0.0	n/a	33.3
H.S. Diplomas (#)	102	92	10	0	0	0

Dallas County

Dallas County R-I
309 W Commercial • Buffalo, MO 65622-0315
(417) 345-2222 • http://www.dallasr1.k12.mo.us/
Grade Span: PK-12; **Agency Type:** 1
Schools: 5
2 Primary; 1 Middle; 2 High; 0 Other Level
4 Regular; 0 Special Education; 1 Vocational; 0 Alternative
0 Magnet; 0 Charter; 3 Title I Eligible; 2 School-wide Title I
Students: 2,120 (52.8% male; 47.2% female)
Individual Education Program: 261 (12.3%);
English Language Learner: 4 (0.2%); Migrant: 1 (<0.1%)
Eligible for Free Lunch Program: 746 (35.2%)
Eligible for Reduced-Price Lunch Program: 170 (8.0%)
Teachers: 159.3 (13.3 to 1)
Librarians/Media Specialists: 2.8 (757.1 to 1)
Guidance Counselors: 7.0 (302.9 to 1)
Current Spending: ($ per student per year):
Total: $5,639; Instruction: $3,482; Support Services: $1,888
Enrollment, Drop-out Rates and Diploma Recipients by Race/Ethnicity

Category	Total	White	Black	Asian	AIAN	Hisp.
Enrollment (%)	100.0	97.5	0.3	0.2	0.7	1.4
Drop-out Rate (%)	6.8	6.9	0.0	0.0	0.0	0.0
H.S. Diplomas (#)	134	130	0	0	2	2

Dent County

Salem R-80
1400 W Third St • Salem, MO 65560-2730
(573) 729-6642 • http://www.salem.k12.mo.us/
Grade Span: PK-12; **Agency Type:** 1
Schools: 4
1 Primary; 2 Middle; 1 High; 0 Other Level
4 Regular; 0 Special Education; 0 Vocational; 0 Alternative
0 Magnet; 0 Charter; 3 Title I Eligible; 2 School-wide Title I
Students: 1,521 (52.6% male; 47.4% female)
Individual Education Program: 202 (13.3%);
English Language Learner: 0 (0.0%); Migrant: 0 (0.0%)
Eligible for Free Lunch Program: 447 (29.4%)
Eligible for Reduced-Price Lunch Program: 91 (6.0%)
Teachers: 108.0 (14.1 to 1)
Librarians/Media Specialists: 3.0 (507.0 to 1)
Guidance Counselors: 5.0 (304.2 to 1)
Current Spending: ($ per student per year):
Total: $5,092; Instruction: $3,324; Support Services: $1,488
Enrollment, Drop-out Rates and Diploma Recipients by Race/Ethnicity

Category	Total	White	Black	Asian	AIAN	Hisp.
Enrollment (%)	100.0	97.6	0.9	0.3	0.7	0.6
Drop-out Rate (%)	6.2	6.3	0.0	0.0	0.0	0.0
H.S. Diplomas (#)	128	127	1	0	0	0

Douglas County

Ava R-I
507 NE 3rd St • Ava, MO 65608-0338
Mailing Address: PO Box 338 • Ava, MO 65608-0338
(417) 683-4717
Grade Span: PK-12; **Agency Type:** 1
Schools: 3
1 Primary; 1 Middle; 1 High; 0 Other Level
3 Regular; 0 Special Education; 0 Vocational; 0 Alternative
0 Magnet; 0 Charter; 2 Title I Eligible; 2 School-wide Title I
Students: 1,633 (50.6% male; 49.4% female)
Individual Education Program: 224 (13.7%);
English Language Learner: 6 (0.4%); Migrant: 5 (0.3%)
Eligible for Free Lunch Program: 723 (44.3%)
Eligible for Reduced-Price Lunch Program: 180 (11.0%)
Teachers: 112.5 (14.5 to 1)
Librarians/Media Specialists: 3.0 (544.3 to 1)
Guidance Counselors: 3.9 (418.7 to 1)
Current Spending: ($ per student per year):
Total: $5,288; Instruction: $3,388; Support Services: $1,581
Enrollment, Drop-out Rates and Diploma Recipients by Race/Ethnicity

Category	Total	White	Black	Asian	AIAN	Hisp.
Enrollment (%)	100.0	98.8	0.3	0.2	0.1	0.6
Drop-out Rate (%)	1.7	1.7	n/a	0.0	0.0	n/a
H.S. Diplomas (#)	99	98	0	0	0	1

Dunklin County

Kennett 39
510 College Ave • Kennett, MO 63857-2006
(573) 717-1100 • http://www.kennett.k12.mo.us/
Grade Span: PK-12; **Agency Type:** 1
Schools: 9
4 Primary; 1 Middle; 3 High; 1 Other Level
7 Regular; 1 Special Education; 1 Vocational; 0 Alternative
0 Magnet; 0 Charter; 4 Title I Eligible; 4 School-wide Title I
Students: 2,192 (49.2% male; 50.8% female)
Individual Education Program: 334 (15.2%);
English Language Learner: 13 (0.6%); Migrant: 65 (3.0%)
Eligible for Free Lunch Program: 1,166 (53.2%)
Eligible for Reduced-Price Lunch Program: 93 (4.2%)
Teachers: 157.4 (13.9 to 1)
Librarians/Media Specialists: 3.1 (707.1 to 1)
Guidance Counselors: 7.9 (277.5 to 1)
Current Spending: ($ per student per year):
Total: $5,729; Instruction: $3,832; Support Services: $1,637
Enrollment, Drop-out Rates and Diploma Recipients by Race/Ethnicity

Category	Total	White	Black	Asian	AIAN	Hisp.
Enrollment (%)	100.0	71.0	26.1	0.5	0.1	2.3
Drop-out Rate (%)	5.0	5.0	4.5	n/a	0.0	16.7
H.S. Diplomas (#)	112	94	18	0	0	0

Franklin County

Meramec Valley R-III
126 N Payne St • Pacific, MO 63069-1224
(636) 271-1400 • http://info.csd.org/schools/meramec/
Grade Span: PK-12; **Agency Type:** 1
Schools: 9
6 Primary; 1 Middle; 1 High; 1 Other Level
9 Regular; 0 Special Education; 0 Vocational; 0 Alternative
0 Magnet; 0 Charter; 5 Title I Eligible; 0 School-wide Title I
Students: 3,903 (52.3% male; 47.7% female)
Individual Education Program: 661 (16.9%);
English Language Learner: 1 (<0.1%); Migrant: 3 (0.1%)
Eligible for Free Lunch Program: 873 (22.4%)
Eligible for Reduced-Price Lunch Program: 297 (7.6%)
Teachers: 254.1 (15.4 to 1)
Librarians/Media Specialists: 2.7 (1,445.6 to 1)
Guidance Counselors: 9.0 (433.7 to 1)
Current Spending: ($ per student per year):
Total: $5,145; Instruction: $3,209; Support Services: $1,710
Enrollment, Drop-out Rates and Diploma Recipients by Race/Ethnicity

Category	Total	White	Black	Asian	AIAN	Hisp.
Enrollment (%)	100.0	95.7	3.0	0.3	0.4	0.5
Drop-out Rate (%)	4.7	4.7	4.5	0.0	0.0	0.0
H.S. Diplomas (#)	242	232	2	4	1	3

Saint Clair R-XIII
905 Bardot St • Saint Clair, MO 63077-1700
(636) 629-3500 • http://stclair.k12.mo.us/
Grade Span: PK-12; **Agency Type:** 1
Schools: 5
2 Primary; 1 Middle; 1 High; 1 Other Level
4 Regular; 1 Special Education; 0 Vocational; 0 Alternative
0 Magnet; 0 Charter; 3 Title I Eligible; 0 School-wide Title I
Students: 2,455 (52.3% male; 47.7% female)
Individual Education Program: 364 (14.8%);
English Language Learner: 0 (0.0%); Migrant: 0 (0.0%)
Eligible for Free Lunch Program: 715 (29.1%)
Eligible for Reduced-Price Lunch Program: 167 (6.8%)
Teachers: 164.6 (14.9 to 1)
Librarians/Media Specialists: 3.0 (818.3 to 1)
Guidance Counselors: 5.2 (472.1 to 1)
Current Spending: ($ per student per year):
Total: $5,083; Instruction: $3,204; Support Services: $1,607

Enrollment, Drop-out Rates and Diploma Recipients by Race/Ethnicity

Category	Total	White	Black	Asian	AIAN	Hisp.
Enrollment (%)	100.0	97.6	2.0	0.3	0.0	0.1
Drop-out Rate (%)	4.4	4.5	0.0	0.0	n/a	0.0
H.S. Diplomas (#)	179	178	1	0	0	0

Sullivan C-2

138 Taylor St • Sullivan, MO 63080-1936
(573) 468-5171 • http://eagles.k12.mo.us./
Grade Span: PK-12; **Agency Type:** 1
Schools: 4
2 Primary; 1 Middle; 1 High; 0 Other Level
4 Regular; 0 Special Education; 0 Vocational; 0 Alternative
0 Magnet; 0 Charter; 2 Title I Eligible; 0 School-wide Title I
Students: 2,134 (52.5% male; 47.5% female)
Individual Education Program: 353 (16.5%);
English Language Learner: 1 (<0.1%); Migrant: 0 (0.0%)
Eligible for Free Lunch Program: 572 (26.8%)
Eligible for Reduced-Price Lunch Program: 154 (7.2%)
Teachers: 147.2 (14.5 to 1)
Librarians/Media Specialists: 3.0 (711.3 to 1)
Guidance Counselors: 5.0 (426.8 to 1)
Current Spending: ($ per student per year):
Total: $5,479; Instruction: $3,464; Support Services: $1,741
Enrollment, Drop-out Rates and Diploma Recipients by Race/Ethnicity

Category	Total	White	Black	Asian	AIAN	Hisp.
Enrollment (%)	100.0	98.2	0.0	0.2	0.4	1.2
Drop-out Rate (%)	5.4	5.4	n/a	0.0	n/a	n/a
H.S. Diplomas (#)	127	126	0	1	0	0

Union R-XI

770 Independence Dr • Union, MO 63084-0440
Mailing Address: PO Box 440 • Union, MO 63084-0440
(636) 583-8626 • http://union.k12.mo.us/
Grade Span: PK-12; **Agency Type:** 1
Schools: 5
2 Primary; 2 Middle; 1 High; 0 Other Level
5 Regular; 0 Special Education; 0 Vocational; 0 Alternative
0 Magnet; 0 Charter; 5 Title I Eligible; 0 School-wide Title I
Students: 3,029 (50.2% male; 49.8% female)
Individual Education Program: 434 (14.3%);
English Language Learner: 5 (0.2%); Migrant: 0 (0.0%)
Eligible for Free Lunch Program: 604 (19.9%)
Eligible for Reduced-Price Lunch Program: 253 (8.4%)
Teachers: 201.0 (15.1 to 1)
Librarians/Media Specialists: 4.0 (757.3 to 1)
Guidance Counselors: 8.5 (356.4 to 1)
Current Spending: ($ per student per year):
Total: $5,334; Instruction: $3,344; Support Services: $1,695
Enrollment, Drop-out Rates and Diploma Recipients by Race/Ethnicity

Category	Total	White	Black	Asian	AIAN	Hisp.
Enrollment (%)	100.0	98.3	0.7	0.3	0.0	0.7
Drop-out Rate (%)	3.8	3.8	0.0	0.0	n/a	0.0
H.S. Diplomas (#)	198	197	0	0	0	1

Washington

220 Locust St • Washington, MO 63090-0357
Mailing Address: PO Box 357 • Washington, MO 63090-0357
(636) 239-2727 • http://www.washington.k12.mo.us/
Grade Span: PK-12; **Agency Type:** 1
Schools: 12
9 Primary; 1 Middle; 2 High; 0 Other Level
11 Regular; 0 Special Education; 1 Vocational; 0 Alternative
0 Magnet; 0 Charter; 3 Title I Eligible; 0 School-wide Title I
Students: 4,078 (52.1% male; 47.9% female)
Individual Education Program: 836 (20.5%);
English Language Learner: 22 (0.5%); Migrant: 2 (<0.1%)
Eligible for Free Lunch Program: 486 (11.9%)
Eligible for Reduced-Price Lunch Program: 213 (5.2%)
Teachers: 271.7 (15.0 to 1)
Librarians/Media Specialists: 4.4 (926.8 to 1)
Guidance Counselors: 10.6 (384.7 to 1)
Current Spending: ($ per student per year):
Total: $6,104; Instruction: $3,726; Support Services: $2,099
Enrollment, Drop-out Rates and Diploma Recipients by Race/Ethnicity

Category	Total	White	Black	Asian	AIAN	Hisp.
Enrollment (%)	100.0	98.1	1.1	0.2	0.0	0.7
Drop-out Rate (%)	6.2	6.1	12.5	0.0	n/a	20.0
H.S. Diplomas (#)	281	278	1	0	0	2

Gasconade County

Gasconade County R-II

402 E Lincoln • Owensville, MO 65066-0536
Mailing Address: PO Box 536 • Owensville, MO 65066-0536
(573) 437-2177 • http://owensville.k12.mo.us/
Grade Span: KG-12; **Agency Type:** 1
Schools: 5
3 Primary; 1 Middle; 1 High; 0 Other Level
5 Regular; 0 Special Education; 0 Vocational; 0 Alternative
0 Magnet; 0 Charter; 3 Title I Eligible; 0 School-wide Title I
Students: 1,958 (49.6% male; 50.4% female)
Individual Education Program: 270 (13.8%);
English Language Learner: 1 (0.1%); Migrant: 0 (0.0%)
Eligible for Free Lunch Program: 413 (21.1%)
Eligible for Reduced-Price Lunch Program: 183 (9.3%)
Teachers: 131.5 (14.9 to 1)
Librarians/Media Specialists: 4.9 (399.6 to 1)
Guidance Counselors: 6.5 (301.2 to 1)
Current Spending: ($ per student per year):
Total: $5,236; Instruction: $3,304; Support Services: $1,688
Enrollment, Drop-out Rates and Diploma Recipients by Race/Ethnicity

Category	Total	White	Black	Asian	AIAN	Hisp.
Enrollment (%)	100.0	99.7	0.0	0.2	0.1	0.1
Drop-out Rate (%)	1.8	1.8	n/a	0.0	n/a	0.0
H.S. Diplomas (#)	147	146	0	0	1	0

Greene County

Greene County R-VIII

104 N Beatie St • Rogersville, MO 65742-1001
(417) 753-2891 • http://www.greene-r8.k12.mo.us/index.htm
Grade Span: PK-12; **Agency Type:** 1
Schools: 4
2 Primary; 1 Middle; 1 High; 0 Other Level
4 Regular; 0 Special Education; 0 Vocational; 0 Alternative
0 Magnet; 0 Charter; 2 Title I Eligible; 0 School-wide Title I
Students: 1,933 (54.5% male; 45.5% female)
Individual Education Program: 340 (17.6%);
English Language Learner: 0 (0.0%); Migrant: 0 (0.0%)
Eligible for Free Lunch Program: 272 (14.1%)
Eligible for Reduced-Price Lunch Program: 97 (5.0%)
Teachers: 120.2 (16.1 to 1)
Librarians/Media Specialists: 4.0 (483.3 to 1)
Guidance Counselors: 4.2 (460.2 to 1)
Current Spending: ($ per student per year):
Total: $4,911; Instruction: $3,245; Support Services: $1,485
Enrollment, Drop-out Rates and Diploma Recipients by Race/Ethnicity

Category	Total	White	Black	Asian	AIAN	Hisp.
Enrollment (%)	100.0	98.3	0.6	0.2	0.1	0.8
Drop-out Rate (%)	5.4	5.5	0.0	0.0	0.0	0.0
H.S. Diplomas (#)	132	130	1	0	0	1

Republic R-III

518 N Hampton • Republic, MO 65738-1323
(417) 732-3605 • http://www.republic.k12.mo.us/
Grade Span: PK-12; **Agency Type:** 1
Schools: 6
3 Primary; 2 Middle; 1 High; 0 Other Level
6 Regular; 0 Special Education; 0 Vocational; 0 Alternative
0 Magnet; 0 Charter; 4 Title I Eligible; 0 School-wide Title I
Students: 3,275 (50.4% male; 49.6% female)
Individual Education Program: 422 (12.9%);
English Language Learner: 0 (0.0%); Migrant: 0 (0.0%)
Eligible for Free Lunch Program: 701 (21.4%)
Eligible for Reduced-Price Lunch Program: 232 (7.1%)
Teachers: 181.4 (18.1 to 1)
Librarians/Media Specialists: 5.0 (655.0 to 1)
Guidance Counselors: 8.6 (380.8 to 1)
Current Spending: ($ per student per year):
Total: $5,129; Instruction: $3,215; Support Services: $1,635
Enrollment, Drop-out Rates and Diploma Recipients by Race/Ethnicity

Category	Total	White	Black	Asian	AIAN	Hisp.
Enrollment (%)	100.0	97.5	1.1	0.4	0.2	0.8
Drop-out Rate (%)	5.5	5.1	0.0	15.4	0.0	40.0
H.S. Diplomas (#)	183	178	3	2	0	0

Springfield R-XII

940 N Jefferson • Springfield, MO 65802-3718
(417) 864-3800 • http://sps.k12.mo.us/
Grade Span: PK-12; **Agency Type:** 1
Schools: 55
38 Primary; 9 Middle; 6 High; 2 Other Level
52 Regular; 0 Special Education; 0 Vocational; 3 Alternative
0 Magnet; 0 Charter; 21 Title I Eligible; 0 School-wide Title I

Students: 24,626 (50.7% male; 49.3% female)
Individual Education Program: 3,210 (13.0%);
English Language Learner: 175 (0.7%); Migrant: 132 (0.5%)
Eligible for Free Lunch Program: 7,095 (28.8%)
Eligible for Reduced-Price Lunch Program: 1,890 (7.7%)
Teachers: 1,521.0 (16.2 to 1)
Librarians/Media Specialists: 41.5 (593.4 to 1)
Guidance Counselors: 66.3 (371.4 to 1)
Current Spending: ($ per student per year):
Total: $5,760; Instruction: $3,597; Support Services: $1,885
Enrollment, Drop-out Rates and Diploma Recipients by Race/Ethnicity

Category	Total	White	Black	Asian	AIAN	Hisp.
Enrollment (%)	100.0	88.3	6.1	2.2	0.7	2.7
Drop-out Rate (%)	5.4	5.2	9.6	3.0	4.4	7.8
H.S. Diplomas (#)	1,464	1,353	56	38	4	13

Willard R-II
460 E Kime St • Willard, MO 65781-7233
(417) 742-2584 • http://www.willard.k12.mo.us/
Grade Span: PK-12; **Agency Type:** 1
Schools: 6
4 Primary; 1 Middle; 1 High; 0 Other Level
6 Regular; 0 Special Education; 0 Vocational; 0 Alternative
0 Magnet; 0 Charter; 5 Title I Eligible; 0 School-wide Title I
Students: 3,357 (50.5% male; 49.5% female)
Individual Education Program: 556 (16.6%);
English Language Learner: 16 (0.5%); Migrant: 5 (0.1%)
Eligible for Free Lunch Program: 625 (18.6%)
Eligible for Reduced-Price Lunch Program: 308 (9.2%)
Teachers: 241.1 (13.9 to 1)
Librarians/Media Specialists: 6.0 (559.5 to 1)
Guidance Counselors: 9.0 (373.0 to 1)
Current Spending: ($ per student per year):
Total: $5,125; Instruction: $3,430; Support Services: $1,446
Enrollment, Drop-out Rates and Diploma Recipients by Race/Ethnicity

Category	Total	White	Black	Asian	AIAN	Hisp.
Enrollment (%)	100.0	98.6	0.3	0.3	0.1	0.7
Drop-out Rate (%)	3.3	3.3	0.0	0.0	0.0	0.0
H.S. Diplomas (#)	205	201	1	2	0	1

Henry County

Clinton
701 S 8th St • Clinton, MO 64735-2901
(660) 885-2237 • http://clinton.k12.mo.us/
Grade Span: PK-12; **Agency Type:** 1
Schools: 5
2 Primary; 1 Middle; 2 High; 0 Other Level
4 Regular; 0 Special Education; 1 Vocational; 0 Alternative
0 Magnet; 0 Charter; 2 Title I Eligible; 0 School-wide Title I
Students: 2,092 (52.1% male; 47.9% female)
Individual Education Program: 340 (16.3%);
English Language Learner: 0 (0.0%); Migrant: 0 (0.0%)
Eligible for Free Lunch Program: 660 (31.5%)
Eligible for Reduced-Price Lunch Program: 104 (5.0%)
Teachers: 163.6 (12.8 to 1)
Librarians/Media Specialists: 3.0 (697.3 to 1)
Guidance Counselors: 7.0 (298.9 to 1)
Current Spending: ($ per student per year):
Total: $6,224; Instruction: $4,203; Support Services: $1,725
Enrollment, Drop-out Rates and Diploma Recipients by Race/Ethnicity

Category	Total	White	Black	Asian	AIAN	Hisp.
Enrollment (%)	100.0	95.8	3.2	0.0	0.1	0.8
Drop-out Rate (%)	4.4	4.2	11.8	0.0	n/a	0.0
H.S. Diplomas (#)	133	127	4	1	0	1

Howell County

West Plains R-VII
613 W First St • West Plains, MO 65775-2617
(417) 256-6150 • http://wphs.k12.mo.us/
Grade Span: PK-12; **Agency Type:** 1
Schools: 5
2 Primary; 1 Middle; 2 High; 0 Other Level
4 Regular; 0 Special Education; 1 Vocational; 0 Alternative
0 Magnet; 0 Charter; 3 Title I Eligible; 2 School-wide Title I
Students: 2,530 (51.4% male; 48.6% female)
Individual Education Program: 279 (11.0%);
English Language Learner: 23 (0.9%); Migrant: 0 (0.0%)
Eligible for Free Lunch Program: 973 (38.5%)
Eligible for Reduced-Price Lunch Program: 130 (5.1%)
Teachers: 177.4 (14.3 to 1)
Librarians/Media Specialists: 3.0 (843.3 to 1)
Guidance Counselors: 8.0 (316.3 to 1)
Current Spending: ($ per student per year):
Total: $5,841; Instruction: $3,884; Support Services: $1,709
Enrollment, Drop-out Rates and Diploma Recipients by Race/Ethnicity

Category	Total	White	Black	Asian	AIAN	Hisp.
Enrollment (%)	100.0	96.3	1.0	0.8	0.6	1.3
Drop-out Rate (%)	3.2	3.2	0.0	0.0	0.0	15.4
H.S. Diplomas (#)	265	260	1	1	0	3

Jackson County

Blue Springs R-IV
1801 NW Vesper • Blue Springs, MO 64015-3219
(816) 224-1300 •
http://www.bluesprings-schools.net/bluesprings/gen/blue_springs_generated_ns_pages/Home_Page_m1.html
Grade Span: PK-12; **Agency Type:** 1
Schools: 22
13 Primary; 4 Middle; 3 High; 2 Other Level
21 Regular; 1 Special Education; 0 Vocational; 0 Alternative
0 Magnet; 0 Charter; 8 Title I Eligible; 0 School-wide Title I
Students: 13,141 (51.6% male; 48.4% female)
Individual Education Program: 1,545 (11.8%);
English Language Learner: 63 (0.5%); Migrant: 0 (0.0%)
Eligible for Free Lunch Program: 902 (6.9%)
Eligible for Reduced-Price Lunch Program: 414 (3.2%)
Teachers: 816.8 (16.1 to 1)
Librarians/Media Specialists: 13.0 (1,010.8 to 1)
Guidance Counselors: 35.8 (367.1 to 1)
Current Spending: ($ per student per year):
Total: $6,122; Instruction: $3,760; Support Services: $2,095
Enrollment, Drop-out Rates and Diploma Recipients by Race/Ethnicity

Category	Total	White	Black	Asian	AIAN	Hisp.
Enrollment (%)	100.0	89.9	5.6	1.4	0.3	2.8
Drop-out Rate (%)	2.4	2.3	4.0	2.3	0.0	2.4
H.S. Diplomas (#)	808	730	33	23	3	19

Center 58
8701 Holmes Rd • Kansas City, MO 64131-2802
(816) 349-3300 • http://www.center.k12.mo.us/
Grade Span: PK-12; **Agency Type:** 1
Schools: 8
5 Primary; 1 Middle; 2 High; 0 Other Level
7 Regular; 0 Special Education; 0 Vocational; 1 Alternative
0 Magnet; 0 Charter; 4 Title I Eligible; 3 School-wide Title I
Students: 2,633 (51.2% male; 48.8% female)
Individual Education Program: 401 (15.2%);
English Language Learner: 47 (1.8%); Migrant: 0 (0.0%)
Eligible for Free Lunch Program: 1,080 (41.0%)
Eligible for Reduced-Price Lunch Program: 216 (8.2%)
Teachers: 203.7 (12.9 to 1)
Librarians/Media Specialists: 4.0 (658.3 to 1)
Guidance Counselors: 8.2 (321.1 to 1)
Current Spending: ($ per student per year):
Total: $8,530; Instruction: $5,044; Support Services: $3,192
Enrollment, Drop-out Rates and Diploma Recipients by Race/Ethnicity

Category	Total	White	Black	Asian	AIAN	Hisp.
Enrollment (%)	100.0	33.8	60.9	1.3	0.2	3.8
Drop-out Rate (%)	6.8	8.6	5.6	0.0	0.0	6.7
H.S. Diplomas (#)	155	49	97	0	1	8

Fort Osage R-I
2101 N Twyman Rd • Independence, MO 64058-3200
(816) 650-7000 • http://www.fortosage.k12.mo.us/
Grade Span: PK-12; **Agency Type:** 1
Schools: 10
5 Primary; 2 Middle; 3 High; 0 Other Level
9 Regular; 0 Special Education; 1 Vocational; 0 Alternative
0 Magnet; 0 Charter; 6 Title I Eligible; 0 School-wide Title I
Students: 5,004 (52.9% male; 47.1% female)
Individual Education Program: 840 (16.8%);
English Language Learner: 8 (0.2%); Migrant: 0 (0.0%)
Eligible for Free Lunch Program: 1,202 (24.0%)
Eligible for Reduced-Price Lunch Program: 456 (9.1%)
Teachers: 350.0 (14.3 to 1)
Librarians/Media Specialists: 5.5 (909.8 to 1)
Guidance Counselors: 15.0 (333.6 to 1)
Current Spending: ($ per student per year):
Total: $7,228; Instruction: $4,681; Support Services: $2,272
Enrollment, Drop-out Rates and Diploma Recipients by Race/Ethnicity

Category	Total	White	Black	Asian	AIAN	Hisp.
Enrollment (%)	100.0	88.6	5.5	2.3	0.6	3.0
Drop-out Rate (%)	2.4	2.4	2.2	0.0	0.0	2.6
H.S. Diplomas (#)	250	232	6	7	0	5

Grain Valley R-V

712 Main St • Grain Valley, MO 64029-0304
Mailing Address: PO Box 304 • Grain Valley, MO 64029-0304
(816) 847-5006 • http://www.grainvalley.k12.mo.us/
Grade Span: PK-12; **Agency Type:** 1
Schools: 4
2 Primary; 1 Middle; 1 High; 0 Other Level
4 Regular; 0 Special Education; 0 Vocational; 0 Alternative
0 Magnet; 0 Charter; 2 Title I Eligible; 0 School-wide Title I
Students: 2,047 (51.6% male; 48.4% female)
Individual Education Program: 232 (11.3%);
English Language Learner: 1 (<0.1%); Migrant: 0 (0.0%)
Eligible for Free Lunch Program: 204 (10.0%)
Eligible for Reduced-Price Lunch Program: 40 (2.0%)
Teachers: 130.5 (15.7 to 1)
Librarians/Media Specialists: 4.0 (511.8 to 1)
Guidance Counselors: 4.7 (435.5 to 1)
Current Spending: ($ per student per year):
Total: $5,336; Instruction: $3,153; Support Services: $1,937
Enrollment, Drop-out Rates and Diploma Recipients by Race/Ethnicity

Category	Total	White	Black	Asian	AIAN	Hisp.
Enrollment (%)	100.0	97.2	0.9	0.3	0.2	1.4
Drop-out Rate (%)	3.1	3.1	0.0	0.0	n/a	0.0
H.S. Diplomas (#)	90	88	1	0	0	1

Grandview C-4

724 Main St • Grandview, MO 64030-2329
(816) 316-5000 • http://www.csd4.k12.mo.us/
Grade Span: PK-12; **Agency Type:** 1
Schools: 10
6 Primary; 1 Middle; 1 High; 2 Other Level
9 Regular; 0 Special Education; 0 Vocational; 1 Alternative
0 Magnet; 0 Charter; 6 Title I Eligible; 3 School-wide Title I
Students: 4,299 (52.9% male; 47.1% female)
Individual Education Program: 556 (12.9%);
English Language Learner: 58 (1.3%); Migrant: 0 (0.0%)
Eligible for Free Lunch Program: 1,428 (33.2%)
Eligible for Reduced-Price Lunch Program: 291 (6.8%)
Teachers: 334.7 (12.8 to 1)
Librarians/Media Specialists: 8.5 (505.8 to 1)
Guidance Counselors: 15.4 (279.2 to 1)
Current Spending: ($ per student per year):
Total: $7,194; Instruction: $4,388; Support Services: $2,477
Enrollment, Drop-out Rates and Diploma Recipients by Race/Ethnicity

Category	Total	White	Black	Asian	AIAN	Hisp.
Enrollment (%)	100.0	40.5	51.7	0.9	0.4	6.5
Drop-out Rate (%)	5.7	6.2	2.8	5.6	20.0	35.9
H.S. Diplomas (#)	220	97	112	9	0	2

Hickman Mills C-1

9000 Old Santa Fe Rd • Kansas City, MO 64138-3913
(816) 316-7000 • http://schoolweb.missouri.edu/hickman.k12.mo.us/
Grade Span: PK-12; **Agency Type:** 1
Schools: 16
9 Primary; 2 Middle; 2 High; 3 Other Level
15 Regular; 0 Special Education; 0 Vocational; 1 Alternative
0 Magnet; 0 Charter; 11 Title I Eligible; 0 School-wide Title I
Students: 7,654 (52.8% male; 47.2% female)
Individual Education Program: 1,128 (14.7%);
English Language Learner: 161 (2.1%); Migrant: 0 (0.0%)
Eligible for Free Lunch Program: 3,360 (43.9%)
Eligible for Reduced-Price Lunch Program: 840 (11.0%)
Teachers: 559.2 (13.7 to 1)
Librarians/Media Specialists: 14.0 (546.7 to 1)
Guidance Counselors: 23.0 (332.8 to 1)
Current Spending: ($ per student per year):
Total: $7,600; Instruction: $4,683; Support Services: $2,573
Enrollment, Drop-out Rates and Diploma Recipients by Race/Ethnicity

Category	Total	White	Black	Asian	AIAN	Hisp.
Enrollment (%)	100.0	24.3	70.5	1.2	0.3	3.7
Drop-out Rate (%)	5.2	8.2	3.8	0.0	0.0	10.5
H.S. Diplomas (#)	394	105	275	4	3	7

Independence 30

218 N Pleasant • Independence, MO 64050-2655
(816) 521-2700 • http://www.indep.k12.mo.us/
Grade Span: PK-12; **Agency Type:** 1
Schools: 21
14 Primary; 2 Middle; 3 High; 2 Other Level
21 Regular; 0 Special Education; 0 Vocational; 0 Alternative
0 Magnet; 0 Charter; 10 Title I Eligible; 6 School-wide Title I
Students: 11,963 (51.2% male; 48.8% female)
Individual Education Program: 1,874 (15.7%);
English Language Learner: 180 (1.5%); Migrant: 0 (0.0%)
Eligible for Free Lunch Program: 3,040 (25.4%)
Eligible for Reduced-Price Lunch Program: 1,078 (9.0%)
Teachers: 781.1 (15.3 to 1)
Librarians/Media Specialists: 24.0 (498.5 to 1)
Guidance Counselors: 27.0 (443.1 to 1)
Current Spending: ($ per student per year):
Total: $7,234; Instruction: $4,362; Support Services: $2,311
Enrollment, Drop-out Rates and Diploma Recipients by Race/Ethnicity

Category	Total	White	Black	Asian	AIAN	Hisp.
Enrollment (%)	100.0	85.2	6.6	2.3	0.8	5.0
Drop-out Rate (%)	7.6	6.8	16.0	13.7	16.7	10.7
H.S. Diplomas (#)	666	579	25	21	8	33

Kansas City 33

1211 Mcgee • Kansas City, MO 64106-2416
(816) 418-7000 • http://www.kcmsd.k12.mo.us/
Grade Span: PK-12; **Agency Type:** 1
Schools: 90
60 Primary; 11 Middle; 12 High; 7 Other Level
83 Regular; 1 Special Education; 2 Vocational; 4 Alternative
16 Magnet; 18 Charter; 76 Title I Eligible; 46 School-wide Title I
Students: 38,521 (50.9% male; 49.1% female)
Individual Education Program: 4,422 (11.5%);
English Language Learner: 2,426 (6.3%); Migrant: 235 (0.6%)
Eligible for Free Lunch Program: 22,938 (59.5%)
Eligible for Reduced-Price Lunch Program: 2,940 (7.6%)
Teachers: 2,643.1 (14.6 to 1)
Librarians/Media Specialists: 75.0 (513.6 to 1)
Guidance Counselors: 111.4 (345.8 to 1)
Current Spending: ($ per student per year):
Total: $8,360; Instruction: $4,443; Support Services: $3,552
Enrollment, Drop-out Rates and Diploma Recipients by Race/Ethnicity

Category	Total	White	Black	Asian	AIAN	Hisp.
Enrollment (%)	100.0	13.7	72.0	2.0	0.2	12.1
Drop-out Rate (%)	6.7	9.1	5.9	4.3	20.8	9.1
H.S. Diplomas (#)	1,409	159	1,115	50	2	83

Lee's Summit R-VII

600 SE Miller • Lee's Summit, MO 64063-4297
(816) 986-1000 • http://www.leesummit.k12.mo.us/
Grade Span: PK-12; **Agency Type:** 1
Schools: 22
16 Primary; 3 Middle; 2 High; 1 Other Level
21 Regular; 0 Special Education; 0 Vocational; 1 Alternative
0 Magnet; 0 Charter; 1 Title I Eligible; 0 School-wide Title I
Students: 15,129 (51.7% male; 48.3% female)
Individual Education Program: 1,862 (12.3%);
English Language Learner: 99 (0.7%); Migrant: 5 (<0.1%)
Eligible for Free Lunch Program: 883 (5.8%)
Eligible for Reduced-Price Lunch Program: 347 (2.3%)
Teachers: 956.9 (15.8 to 1)
Librarians/Media Specialists: 23.6 (641.1 to 1)
Guidance Counselors: 35.0 (432.3 to 1)
Current Spending: ($ per student per year):
Total: $6,494; Instruction: $4,114; Support Services: $2,121
Enrollment, Drop-out Rates and Diploma Recipients by Race/Ethnicity

Category	Total	White	Black	Asian	AIAN	Hisp.
Enrollment (%)	100.0	88.6	7.1	1.7	0.1	2.4
Drop-out Rate (%)	2.3	2.2	6.0	0.0	0.0	1.6
H.S. Diplomas (#)	956	895	36	8	2	15

Oak Grove R-VI

1305 S Salem St • Oak Grove, MO 64075-7044
(816) 690-4156 • http://www.oakgrove.k12.mo.us/1024x768.htm
Grade Span: PK-12; **Agency Type:** 1
Schools: 4
2 Primary; 1 Middle; 1 High; 0 Other Level
4 Regular; 0 Special Education; 0 Vocational; 0 Alternative
0 Magnet; 0 Charter; 3 Title I Eligible; 0 School-wide Title I
Students: 2,017 (52.3% male; 47.7% female)
Individual Education Program: 262 (13.0%);
English Language Learner: 0 (0.0%); Migrant: 0 (0.0%)
Eligible for Free Lunch Program: 257 (12.7%)
Eligible for Reduced-Price Lunch Program: 105 (5.2%)
Teachers: 122.1 (16.5 to 1)
Librarians/Media Specialists: 4.0 (504.3 to 1)
Guidance Counselors: 5.0 (403.4 to 1)
Current Spending: ($ per student per year):
Total: $5,560; Instruction: $3,519; Support Services: $1,797
Enrollment, Drop-out Rates and Diploma Recipients by Race/Ethnicity

Category	Total	White	Black	Asian	AIAN	Hisp.
Enrollment (%)	100.0	98.4	0.7	0.1	0.1	0.7
Drop-out Rate (%)	1.3	1.3	0.0	0.0	0.0	0.0
H.S. Diplomas (#)	124	123	0	1	0	0

Raytown C-2

10500 E 60th Terr • Raytown, MO 64133-3999
(816) 268-7000 • http://www.raytown.k12.mo.us/
Grade Span: PK-12; **Agency Type:** 1
Schools: 17
10 Primary; 2 Middle; 3 High; 2 Other Level
14 Regular; 0 Special Education; 1 Vocational; 2 Alternative
0 Magnet; 0 Charter; 8 Title I Eligible; 1 School-wide Title I
Students: 8,801 (52.3% male; 47.7% female)
Individual Education Program: 1,029 (11.7%);
English Language Learner: 68 (0.8%); Migrant: 0 (0.0%)
Eligible for Free Lunch Program: 1,947 (22.1%)
Eligible for Reduced-Price Lunch Program: 688 (7.8%)
Teachers: 550.9 (16.0 to 1)
Librarians/Media Specialists: 8.7 (1,011.6 to 1)
Guidance Counselors: 19.8 (444.5 to 1)
Current Spending: ($ per student per year):
Total: $6,476; Instruction: $3,910; Support Services: $2,295
Enrollment, Drop-out Rates and Diploma Recipients by Race/Ethnicity

Category	Total	White	Black	Asian	AIAN	Hisp.
Enrollment (%)	100.0	62.4	31.8	1.4	0.4	4.0
Drop-out Rate (%)	8.3	8.8	6.2	2.6	7.1	17.1
H.S. Diplomas (#)	520	345	153	11	2	9

Jasper County

Carl Junction R-I

206 S Roney • Carl Junction, MO 64834-0004
Mailing Address: PO Box 4 • Carl Junction, MO 64834-0004
(417) 649-7026 • http://cj.k12.mo.us/
Grade Span: PK-12; **Agency Type:** 1
Schools: 6
2 Primary; 2 Middle; 1 High; 1 Other Level
5 Regular; 1 Special Education; 0 Vocational; 0 Alternative
0 Magnet; 0 Charter; 4 Title I Eligible; 0 School-wide Title I
Students: 2,726 (52.4% male; 47.6% female)
Individual Education Program: 412 (15.1%);
English Language Learner: 7 (0.3%); Migrant: 0 (0.0%)
Eligible for Free Lunch Program: 705 (25.9%)
Eligible for Reduced-Price Lunch Program: 244 (9.0%)
Teachers: 182.6 (14.9 to 1)
Librarians/Media Specialists: 4.7 (580.0 to 1)
Guidance Counselors: 6.5 (419.4 to 1)
Current Spending: ($ per student per year):
Total: $5,324; Instruction: $3,460; Support Services: $1,594
Enrollment, Drop-out Rates and Diploma Recipients by Race/Ethnicity

Category	Total	White	Black	Asian	AIAN	Hisp.
Enrollment (%)	100.0	96.8	0.6	0.4	1.1	1.1
Drop-out Rate (%)	7.4	7.6	0.0	0.0	0.0	0.0
H.S. Diplomas (#)	164	158	1	0	3	2

Carthage R-IX

710 Lyon St • Carthage, MO 64836-1700
(417) 359-7000 • http://carthage.k12.mo.us/
Grade Span: PK-12; **Agency Type:** 1
Schools: 8
5 Primary; 1 Middle; 2 High; 0 Other Level
7 Regular; 0 Special Education; 1 Vocational; 0 Alternative
0 Magnet; 0 Charter; 5 Title I Eligible; 3 School-wide Title I
Students: 3,661 (51.9% male; 48.1% female)
Individual Education Program: 462 (12.6%);
English Language Learner: 233 (6.4%); Migrant: 202 (5.5%)
Eligible for Free Lunch Program: 1,217 (33.2%)
Eligible for Reduced-Price Lunch Program: 242 (6.6%)
Teachers: 250.5 (14.6 to 1)
Librarians/Media Specialists: 7.0 (523.0 to 1)
Guidance Counselors: 10.0 (366.1 to 1)
Current Spending: ($ per student per year):
Total: $5,354; Instruction: $3,483; Support Services: $1,644
Enrollment, Drop-out Rates and Diploma Recipients by Race/Ethnicity

Category	Total	White	Black	Asian	AIAN	Hisp.
Enrollment (%)	100.0	84.7	2.1	0.2	0.9	12.0
Drop-out Rate (%)	7.9	7.2	19.2	0.0	9.1	13.8
H.S. Diplomas (#)	227	211	3	3	2	8

Joplin R-VIII

1717 E 15th St • Joplin, MO 64802-0128
Mailing Address: PO Box 128 • Joplin, MO 64802-0128
(417) 625-5200 • http://www.joplin.k12.mo.us/
Grade Span: PK-12; **Agency Type:** 1
Schools: 19
14 Primary; 3 Middle; 2 High; 0 Other Level
18 Regular; 0 Special Education; 1 Vocational; 0 Alternative
0 Magnet; 0 Charter; 10 Title I Eligible; 3 School-wide Title I
Students: 7,415 (50.8% male; 49.2% female)
Individual Education Program: 1,154 (15.6%);
English Language Learner: 76 (1.0%); Migrant: 41 (0.6%)
Eligible for Free Lunch Program: 2,836 (38.2%)
Eligible for Reduced-Price Lunch Program: 602 (8.1%)
Teachers: 514.5 (14.4 to 1)
Librarians/Media Specialists: 12.0 (617.9 to 1)
Guidance Counselors: 22.1 (335.5 to 1)
Current Spending: ($ per student per year):
Total: $5,511; Instruction: $3,574; Support Services: $1,677
Enrollment, Drop-out Rates and Diploma Recipients by Race/Ethnicity

Category	Total	White	Black	Asian	AIAN	Hisp.
Enrollment (%)	100.0	88.6	4.0	1.0	2.0	4.3
Drop-out Rate (%)	5.2	4.8	7.5	4.0	8.3	8.3
H.S. Diplomas (#)	306	277	13	6	3	7

Webb City R-VII

411 N Madison • Webb City, MO 64870-1238
(417) 673-6000 • http://www.wccards.k12.mo.us/
Grade Span: PK-12; **Agency Type:** 1
Schools: 10
7 Primary; 2 Middle; 1 High; 0 Other Level
10 Regular; 0 Special Education; 0 Vocational; 0 Alternative
0 Magnet; 0 Charter; 7 Title I Eligible; 0 School-wide Title I
Students: 3,687 (51.5% male; 48.5% female)
Individual Education Program: 492 (13.3%);
English Language Learner: 0 (0.0%); Migrant: 25 (0.7%)
Eligible for Free Lunch Program: 1,267 (34.4%)
Eligible for Reduced-Price Lunch Program: 387 (10.5%)
Teachers: 231.1 (16.0 to 1)
Librarians/Media Specialists: 6.0 (614.5 to 1)
Guidance Counselors: 9.0 (409.7 to 1)
Current Spending: ($ per student per year):
Total: $5,385; Instruction: $3,501; Support Services: $1,624
Enrollment, Drop-out Rates and Diploma Recipients by Race/Ethnicity

Category	Total	White	Black	Asian	AIAN	Hisp.
Enrollment (%)	100.0	93.8	1.7	0.5	1.3	2.7
Drop-out Rate (%)	6.3	6.4	0.0	0.0	0.0	11.1
H.S. Diplomas (#)	201	191	1	0	5	4

Jefferson County

Desoto 73

221 S Third • Desoto, MO 63020-2081
(636) 586-1000 • http://www.desotoschools.com/
Grade Span: KG-12; **Agency Type:** 1
Schools: 4
2 Primary; 1 Middle; 1 High; 0 Other Level
4 Regular; 0 Special Education; 0 Vocational; 0 Alternative
0 Magnet; 0 Charter; 2 Title I Eligible; 0 School-wide Title I
Students: 2,829 (52.3% male; 47.7% female)
Individual Education Program: 493 (17.4%);
English Language Learner: 0 (0.0%); Migrant: 0 (0.0%)
Eligible for Free Lunch Program: 753 (26.6%)
Eligible for Reduced-Price Lunch Program: 159 (5.6%)
Teachers: 172.4 (16.4 to 1)
Librarians/Media Specialists: 2.9 (975.5 to 1)
Guidance Counselors: 7.0 (404.1 to 1)
Current Spending: ($ per student per year):
Total: $6,534; Instruction: $4,117; Support Services: $2,189
Enrollment, Drop-out Rates and Diploma Recipients by Race/Ethnicity

Category	Total	White	Black	Asian	AIAN	Hisp.
Enrollment (%)	100.0	97.2	1.5	0.5	0.1	0.6
Drop-out Rate (%)	7.6	7.6	0.0	25.0	0.0	0.0
H.S. Diplomas (#)	188	186	2	0	0	0

Festus R-VI

1515 Mid-Meadow Ln • Festus, MO 63028-1598
(636) 937-4920 • http://info.csd.org/schools/festus/index.htm
Grade Span: KG-12; **Agency Type:** 1
Schools: 4
1 Primary; 2 Middle; 1 High; 0 Other Level
4 Regular; 0 Special Education; 0 Vocational; 0 Alternative
0 Magnet; 0 Charter; 1 Title I Eligible; 0 School-wide Title I
Students: 2,672 (50.1% male; 49.9% female)
Individual Education Program: 300 (11.2%);
English Language Learner: 0 (0.0%); Migrant: 0 (0.0%)
Eligible for Free Lunch Program: 578 (21.6%)
Eligible for Reduced-Price Lunch Program: 141 (5.3%)
Teachers: 152.4 (17.5 to 1)
Librarians/Media Specialists: 4.0 (668.0 to 1)
Guidance Counselors: 6.5 (411.1 to 1)
Current Spending: ($ per student per year):
Total: $4,637; Instruction: $3,091; Support Services: $1,332

Enrollment, Drop-out Rates and Diploma Recipients by Race/Ethnicity

Category	Total	White	Black	Asian	AIAN	Hisp.
Enrollment (%)	100.0	94.2	4.0	0.6	0.1	1.0
Drop-out Rate (%)	5.4	4.9	16.1	0.0	n/a	20.0
H.S. Diplomas (#)	161	152	8	1	0	0

Fox C-6

745 Jeffco Blvd • Arnold, MO 63010-1432
(636) 296-8000 • http://www.fox.k12.mo.us/
Grade Span: PK-12; **Agency Type:** 1
Schools: 15
11 Primary; 2 Middle; 2 High; 0 Other Level
15 Regular; 0 Special Education; 0 Vocational; 0 Alternative
0 Magnet; 0 Charter; 10 Title I Eligible; 0 School-wide Title I
Students: 11,341 (51.9% male; 48.1% female)
Individual Education Program: 1,952 (17.2%);
English Language Learner: 66 (0.6%); Migrant: 0 (0.0%)
Eligible for Free Lunch Program: 1,898 (16.7%)
Eligible for Reduced-Price Lunch Program: 688 (6.1%)
Teachers: 726.4 (15.6 to 1)
Librarians/Media Specialists: 18.0 (630.1 to 1)
Guidance Counselors: 26.6 (426.4 to 1)
Current Spending: ($ per student per year):
Total: $5,789; Instruction: $3,809; Support Services: $1,710
Enrollment, Drop-out Rates and Diploma Recipients by Race/Ethnicity

Category	Total	White	Black	Asian	AIAN	Hisp.
Enrollment (%)	100.0	97.6	0.8	0.6	0.1	0.8
Drop-out Rate (%)	5.6	5.6	0.0	0.0	0.0	0.0
H.S. Diplomas (#)	612	612	0	0	0	0

Hillsboro R-III

20 Hawk Dr • Hillsboro, MO 63050-5202
(636) 789-0000 • http://info.csd.org/schools/hills/home/hillsboro.htm
Grade Span: KG-12; **Agency Type:** 1
Schools: 6
2 Primary; 2 Middle; 1 High; 1 Other Level
5 Regular; 0 Special Education; 0 Vocational; 1 Alternative
0 Magnet; 0 Charter; 4 Title I Eligible; 0 School-wide Title I
Students: 3,592 (50.5% male; 49.5% female)
Individual Education Program: 524 (14.6%);
English Language Learner: 18 (0.5%); Migrant: 0 (0.0%)
Eligible for Free Lunch Program: 657 (18.3%)
Eligible for Reduced-Price Lunch Program: 217 (6.0%)
Teachers: 207.5 (17.3 to 1)
Librarians/Media Specialists: 5.0 (718.4 to 1)
Guidance Counselors: 7.7 (466.5 to 1)
Current Spending: ($ per student per year):
Total: $5,166; Instruction: $3,224; Support Services: $1,690
Enrollment, Drop-out Rates and Diploma Recipients by Race/Ethnicity

Category	Total	White	Black	Asian	AIAN	Hisp.
Enrollment (%)	100.0	98.7	0.3	0.4	0.3	0.4
Drop-out Rate (%)	2.8	2.6	n/a	0.0	25.0	25.0
H.S. Diplomas (#)	220	217	0	3	0	0

Northwest R-I

2843 Community Ln • House Springs, MO 63051-0500
Mailing Address: PO Box 500 • House Springs, MO 63051-0500
(636) 677-3473 • http://www.nwr1.k12.mo.us/
Grade Span: PK-12; **Agency Type:** 1
Schools: 11
7 Primary; 3 Middle; 1 High; 0 Other Level
11 Regular; 0 Special Education; 0 Vocational; 0 Alternative
0 Magnet; 0 Charter; 6 Title I Eligible; 0 School-wide Title I
Students: 7,572 (51.0% male; 49.0% female)
Individual Education Program: 1,338 (17.7%);
English Language Learner: 20 (0.3%); Migrant: 0 (0.0%)
Eligible for Free Lunch Program: 1,620 (21.4%)
Eligible for Reduced-Price Lunch Program: 564 (7.4%)
Teachers: 484.3 (15.6 to 1)
Librarians/Media Specialists: 13.8 (548.7 to 1)
Guidance Counselors: 16.0 (473.3 to 1)
Current Spending: ($ per student per year):
Total: $5,766; Instruction: $3,621; Support Services: $1,896
Enrollment, Drop-out Rates and Diploma Recipients by Race/Ethnicity

Category	Total	White	Black	Asian	AIAN	Hisp.
Enrollment (%)	100.0	98.6	0.5	0.5	0.1	0.4
Drop-out Rate (%)	5.0	4.9	11.1	12.5	0.0	8.3
H.S. Diplomas (#)	415	405	1	4	1	4

Windsor C-1

6208 Hwy 61-67 • Imperial, MO 63052-2311
(636) 464-4400 • http://www.windsor.k12.mo.us/district/
Grade Span: PK-12; **Agency Type:** 1
Schools: 4
2 Primary; 1 Middle; 1 High; 0 Other Level
4 Regular; 0 Special Education; 0 Vocational; 0 Alternative
0 Magnet; 0 Charter; 2 Title I Eligible; 0 School-wide Title I
Students: 3,031 (54.1% male; 45.9% female)
Individual Education Program: 409 (13.5%);
English Language Learner: 2 (0.1%); Migrant: 1 (<0.1%)
Eligible for Free Lunch Program: 372 (12.3%)
Eligible for Reduced-Price Lunch Program: 169 (5.6%)
Teachers: 229.7 (13.2 to 1)
Librarians/Media Specialists: 5.0 (606.2 to 1)
Guidance Counselors: 8.0 (378.9 to 1)
Current Spending: ($ per student per year):
Total: $5,458; Instruction: $3,362; Support Services: $1,824
Enrollment, Drop-out Rates and Diploma Recipients by Race/Ethnicity

Category	Total	White	Black	Asian	AIAN	Hisp.
Enrollment (%)	100.0	97.9	0.7	0.5	0.2	0.6
Drop-out Rate (%)	5.4	5.5	0.0	0.0	n/a	0.0
H.S. Diplomas (#)	193	190	0	1	0	2

Johnson County

Knob Noster R-VIII

401 E Wimer • Knob Noster, MO 65336-1444
(660) 563-3186 • http://knobnoster.k12.mo.us/
Grade Span: PK-12; **Agency Type:** 1
Schools: 4
2 Primary; 1 Middle; 1 High; 0 Other Level
4 Regular; 0 Special Education; 0 Vocational; 0 Alternative
0 Magnet; 0 Charter; 2 Title I Eligible; 0 School-wide Title I
Students: 1,863 (52.3% male; 47.7% female)
Individual Education Program: 276 (14.8%);
English Language Learner: 58 (3.1%); Migrant: 101 (5.4%)
Eligible for Free Lunch Program: 305 (16.4%)
Eligible for Reduced-Price Lunch Program: 302 (16.2%)
Teachers: 142.5 (13.1 to 1)
Librarians/Media Specialists: 4.0 (465.8 to 1)
Guidance Counselors: 9.0 (207.0 to 1)
Current Spending: ($ per student per year):
Total: $5,599; Instruction: $3,438; Support Services: $1,857
Enrollment, Drop-out Rates and Diploma Recipients by Race/Ethnicity

Category	Total	White	Black	Asian	AIAN	Hisp.
Enrollment (%)	100.0	78.3	11.4	3.6	0.9	5.9
Drop-out Rate (%)	2.1	1.8	3.6	5.3	n/a	0.0
H.S. Diplomas (#)	107	83	12	5	0	7

Warrensburg R-VI

438 E Market • Warrensburg, MO 64093-0638
Mailing Address: PO Box 638 • Warrensburg, MO 64093-0638
(660) 747-7823 • http://warrensburg.k12.mo.us/
Grade Span: PK-12; **Agency Type:** 1
Schools: 9
3 Primary; 2 Middle; 3 High; 1 Other Level
7 Regular; 0 Special Education; 1 Vocational; 1 Alternative
0 Magnet; 0 Charter; 3 Title I Eligible; 0 School-wide Title I
Students: 3,250 (50.0% male; 50.0% female)
Individual Education Program: 600 (18.5%);
English Language Learner: 53 (1.6%); Migrant: 12 (0.4%)
Eligible for Free Lunch Program: 610 (18.8%)
Eligible for Reduced-Price Lunch Program: 214 (6.6%)
Teachers: 243.5 (13.3 to 1)
Librarians/Media Specialists: 5.0 (650.0 to 1)
Guidance Counselors: 7.2 (451.4 to 1)
Current Spending: ($ per student per year):
Total: $5,977; Instruction: $3,590; Support Services: $2,145
Enrollment, Drop-out Rates and Diploma Recipients by Race/Ethnicity

Category	Total	White	Black	Asian	AIAN	Hisp.
Enrollment (%)	100.0	86.5	8.1	2.3	0.7	2.4
Drop-out Rate (%)	3.8	2.6	15.5	0.0	66.7	5.9
H.S. Diplomas (#)	217	200	8	1	1	7

Laclede County

Lebanon R-III

321 S Jefferson • Lebanon, MO 65536-3260
(417) 532-9141 • http://www.lebanon.k12.mo.us/
Grade Span: PK-12; **Agency Type:** 1
Schools: 8
2 Primary; 3 Middle; 3 High; 0 Other Level
6 Regular; 0 Special Education; 1 Vocational; 1 Alternative
0 Magnet; 0 Charter; 4 Title I Eligible; 0 School-wide Title I
Students: 4,578 (51.2% male; 48.8% female)
Individual Education Program: 569 (12.4%);
English Language Learner: 6 (0.1%); Migrant: 0 (0.0%)
Eligible for Free Lunch Program: 1,413 (30.9%)
Eligible for Reduced-Price Lunch Program: 373 (8.1%)
Teachers: 278.9 (16.4 to 1)

Librarians/Media Specialists: 6.0 (763.0 to 1)
Guidance Counselors: 11.0 (416.2 to 1)
Current Spending: ($ per student per year):
Total: $5,240; Instruction: $3,464; Support Services: $1,540
Enrollment, Drop-out Rates and Diploma Recipients by Race/Ethnicity

Category	Total	White	Black	Asian	AIAN	Hisp.
Enrollment (%)	100.0	97.1	0.7	0.6	0.3	1.2
Drop-out Rate (%)	4.0	4.0	0.0	0.0	0.0	50.0
H.S. Diplomas (#)	297	293	2	2	0	0

Lafayette County

Odessa R-VII

701 S Third • Odessa, MO 64076-1453
(816) 230-5316 • http://odessa.k12.mo.us/
Grade Span: PK-12; **Agency Type:** 1
Schools: 4
2 Primary; 1 Middle; 1 High; 0 Other Level
4 Regular; 0 Special Education; 0 Vocational; 0 Alternative
0 Magnet; 0 Charter; 2 Title I Eligible; 0 School-wide Title I
Students: 2,312 (53.4% male; 46.6% female)
Individual Education Program: 310 (13.4%);
English Language Learner: 8 (0.3%); Migrant: 0 (0.0%)
Eligible for Free Lunch Program: 477 (20.6%)
Eligible for Reduced-Price Lunch Program: 126 (5.4%)
Teachers: 156.8 (14.7 to 1)
Librarians/Media Specialists: 4.0 (578.0 to 1)
Guidance Counselors: 6.0 (385.3 to 1)
Current Spending: ($ per student per year):
Total: $5,709; Instruction: $3,846; Support Services: $1,620
Enrollment, Drop-out Rates and Diploma Recipients by Race/Ethnicity

Category	Total	White	Black	Asian	AIAN	Hisp.
Enrollment (%)	100.0	97.1	1.9	0.1	0.2	0.7
Drop-out Rate (%)	4.1	4.1	10.0	0.0	0.0	0.0
H.S. Diplomas (#)	161	149	6	1	0	5

Lawrence County

Aurora R-VIII

409 W Locust St • Aurora, MO 65605-1422
(417) 678-3373 • http://www.hdnet.k12.mo.us/
Grade Span: PK-12; **Agency Type:** 1
Schools: 4
1 Primary; 2 Middle; 1 High; 0 Other Level
4 Regular; 0 Special Education; 0 Vocational; 0 Alternative
0 Magnet; 0 Charter; 2 Title I Eligible; 2 School-wide Title I
Students: 2,123 (50.1% male; 49.9% female)
Individual Education Program: 250 (11.8%);
English Language Learner: 30 (1.4%); Migrant: 46 (2.2%)
Eligible for Free Lunch Program: 784 (36.9%)
Eligible for Reduced-Price Lunch Program: 156 (7.3%)
Teachers: 146.4 (14.5 to 1)
Librarians/Media Specialists: 3.0 (707.7 to 1)
Guidance Counselors: 5.5 (386.0 to 1)
Current Spending: ($ per student per year):
Total: $5,644; Instruction: $3,559; Support Services: $1,813
Enrollment, Drop-out Rates and Diploma Recipients by Race/Ethnicity

Category	Total	White	Black	Asian	AIAN	Hisp.
Enrollment (%)	100.0	96.8	0.2	0.3	0.6	2.1
Drop-out Rate (%)	5.1	5.1	0.0	0.0	0.0	0.0
H.S. Diplomas (#)	106	105	1	0	0	0

Lincoln County

Troy R-III

951 W College • Troy, MO 63379-1112
(636) 462-6098 • http://www.troy.k12.mo.us/index.htm
Grade Span: PK-12; **Agency Type:** 1
Schools: 6
4 Primary; 1 Middle; 1 High; 0 Other Level
6 Regular; 0 Special Education; 0 Vocational; 0 Alternative
0 Magnet; 0 Charter; 4 Title I Eligible; 0 School-wide Title I
Students: 4,932 (51.2% male; 48.8% female)
Individual Education Program: 813 (16.5%);
English Language Learner: 5 (0.1%); Migrant: 0 (0.0%)
Eligible for Free Lunch Program: 991 (20.1%)
Eligible for Reduced-Price Lunch Program: 274 (5.6%)
Teachers: 261.0 (18.9 to 1)
Librarians/Media Specialists: 4.0 (1,233.0 to 1)
Guidance Counselors: 9.3 (530.3 to 1)
Current Spending: ($ per student per year):
Total: $4,785; Instruction: $3,151; Support Services: $1,552
Enrollment, Drop-out Rates and Diploma Recipients by Race/Ethnicity

Category	Total	White	Black	Asian	AIAN	Hisp.
Enrollment (%)	100.0	95.2	3.3	0.4	0.3	0.9
Drop-out Rate (%)	3.3	3.4	0.0	0.0	0.0	0.0
H.S. Diplomas (#)	287	282	3	1	0	1

Winfield R-IV

701 Elm St • Winfield, MO 63389-9511
(636) 668-8188
Grade Span: PK-12; **Agency Type:** 1
Schools: 4
2 Primary; 1 Middle; 1 High; 0 Other Level
4 Regular; 0 Special Education; 0 Vocational; 0 Alternative
0 Magnet; 0 Charter; 1 Title I Eligible; 0 School-wide Title I
Students: 1,661 (51.5% male; 48.5% female)
Individual Education Program: 291 (17.5%);
English Language Learner: 0 (0.0%); Migrant: 0 (0.0%)
Eligible for Free Lunch Program: 489 (29.4%)
Eligible for Reduced-Price Lunch Program: 70 (4.2%)
Teachers: 100.9 (16.5 to 1)
Librarians/Media Specialists: 2.9 (572.8 to 1)
Guidance Counselors: 4.0 (415.3 to 1)
Current Spending: ($ per student per year):
Total: $5,012; Instruction: $2,960; Support Services: $1,663
Enrollment, Drop-out Rates and Diploma Recipients by Race/Ethnicity

Category	Total	White	Black	Asian	AIAN	Hisp.
Enrollment (%)	100.0	96.8	1.4	0.3	0.5	1.0
Drop-out Rate (%)	7.6	7.1	0.0	50.0	33.3	0.0
H.S. Diplomas (#)	88	88	0	0	0	0

Livingston County

Chillicothe R-II

1020 Old Hwy 36 W • Chillicothe, MO 64601-0530
Mailing Address: PO Box 530 • Chillicothe, MO 64601-0530
(660) 646-4566 • http://www.chillicothe.k12.mo.us/
Grade Span: PK-12; **Agency Type:** 1
Schools: 7
3 Primary; 2 Middle; 2 High; 0 Other Level
6 Regular; 0 Special Education; 1 Vocational; 0 Alternative
0 Magnet; 0 Charter; 4 Title I Eligible; 0 School-wide Title I
Students: 2,128 (51.1% male; 48.9% female)
Individual Education Program: 356 (16.7%);
English Language Learner: 0 (0.0%); Migrant: 0 (0.0%)
Eligible for Free Lunch Program: 462 (21.7%)
Eligible for Reduced-Price Lunch Program: 173 (8.1%)
Teachers: 153.3 (13.9 to 1)
Librarians/Media Specialists: 2.0 (1,064.0 to 1)
Guidance Counselors: 7.0 (304.0 to 1)
Current Spending: ($ per student per year):
Total: $6,952; Instruction: $4,919; Support Services: $1,754
Enrollment, Drop-out Rates and Diploma Recipients by Race/Ethnicity

Category	Total	White	Black	Asian	AIAN	Hisp.
Enrollment (%)	100.0	97.2	2.3	0.3	0.1	0.2
Drop-out Rate (%)	1.4	1.5	0.0	n/a	0.0	n/a
H.S. Diplomas (#)	143	140	1	1	0	1

Madison County

Fredericktown R-I

803 E Hwy 72 • Fredericktown, MO 63645-9620
(573) 783-2570 • http://fredericktown.k12.mo.us/
Grade Span: PK-12; **Agency Type:** 1
Schools: 4
2 Primary; 1 Middle; 1 High; 0 Other Level
4 Regular; 0 Special Education; 0 Vocational; 0 Alternative
0 Magnet; 0 Charter; 3 Title I Eligible; 0 School-wide Title I
Students: 1,906 (51.3% male; 48.7% female)
Individual Education Program: 214 (11.2%);
English Language Learner: 3 (0.2%); Migrant: 10 (0.5%)
Eligible for Free Lunch Program: 667 (35.0%)
Eligible for Reduced-Price Lunch Program: 225 (11.8%)
Teachers: 127.7 (14.9 to 1)
Librarians/Media Specialists: 4.0 (476.5 to 1)
Guidance Counselors: 6.0 (317.7 to 1)
Current Spending: ($ per student per year):
Total: $5,591; Instruction: $3,626; Support Services: $1,673
Enrollment, Drop-out Rates and Diploma Recipients by Race/Ethnicity

Category	Total	White	Black	Asian	AIAN	Hisp.
Enrollment (%)	100.0	98.9	0.3	0.1	0.0	0.7
Drop-out Rate (%)	3.9	4.0	n/a	0.0	n/a	n/a
H.S. Diplomas (#)	114	114	0	0	0	0

Marion County

Hannibal 60

4650 Mcmasters Ave • Hannibal, MO 63401-2244
(573) 221-1258 • http://www.hannibal.k12.mo.us/
Grade Span: PK-12; **Agency Type:** 1
Schools: 8
5 Primary; 1 Middle; 2 High; 0 Other Level
7 Regular; 0 Special Education; 1 Vocational; 0 Alternative
0 Magnet; 0 Charter; 5 Title I Eligible; 1 School-wide Title I
Students: 3,742 (49.7% male; 50.3% female)
Individual Education Program: 624 (16.7%);
English Language Learner: 0 (0.0%); Migrant: 1 (<0.1%)
Eligible for Free Lunch Program: 1,458 (39.0%)
Eligible for Reduced-Price Lunch Program: 283 (7.6%)
Teachers: 278.8 (13.4 to 1)
Librarians/Media Specialists: 4.0 (935.5 to 1)
Guidance Counselors: 14.5 (258.1 to 1)
Current Spending: ($ per student per year):
Total: $5,365; Instruction: $3,485; Support Services: $1,566
Enrollment, Drop-out Rates and Diploma Recipients by Race/Ethnicity

Category	Total	White	Black	Asian	AIAN	Hisp.
Enrollment (%)	100.0	88.8	9.8	0.7	0.2	0.5
Drop-out Rate (%)	5.0	4.8	7.1	7.7	0.0	0.0
H.S. Diplomas (#)	210	192	16	2	0	0

Mcdonald County

Mcdonald County R-I

100 Mustang Dr • Anderson, MO 64831-7305
(417) 845-3321 • http://mcdonaldco.k12.mo.us/
Grade Span: PK-12; **Agency Type:** 1
Schools: 7
6 Primary; 0 Middle; 1 High; 0 Other Level
7 Regular; 0 Special Education; 0 Vocational; 0 Alternative
0 Magnet; 0 Charter; 6 Title I Eligible; 6 School-wide Title I
Students: 3,623 (51.4% male; 48.6% female)
Individual Education Program: 402 (11.1%);
English Language Learner: 417 (11.5%); Migrant: 483 (13.3%)
Eligible for Free Lunch Program: 1,725 (47.6%)
Eligible for Reduced-Price Lunch Program: 362 (10.0%)
Teachers: 231.0 (15.7 to 1)
Librarians/Media Specialists: 4.0 (905.8 to 1)
Guidance Counselors: 9.0 (402.6 to 1)
Current Spending: ($ per student per year):
Total: $4,571; Instruction: $3,067; Support Services: $1,207
Enrollment, Drop-out Rates and Diploma Recipients by Race/Ethnicity

Category	Total	White	Black	Asian	AIAN	Hisp.
Enrollment (%)	100.0	83.6	0.3	0.1	1.5	14.5
Drop-out Rate (%)	4.6	4.8	0.0	0.0	0.0	3.2
H.S. Diplomas (#)	152	143	0	1	0	8

Miller County

Eldon R-I

110 S Oak • Eldon, MO 65026-1576
(573) 392-8000 • http://www.eldon.k12.mo.us/
Grade Span: PK-12; **Agency Type:** 1
Schools: 5
1 Primary; 2 Middle; 2 High; 0 Other Level
4 Regular; 0 Special Education; 1 Vocational; 0 Alternative
0 Magnet; 0 Charter; 3 Title I Eligible; 2 School-wide Title I
Students: 2,050 (51.7% male; 48.3% female)
Individual Education Program: 294 (14.3%);
English Language Learner: 7 (0.3%); Migrant: 0 (0.0%)
Eligible for Free Lunch Program: 705 (34.4%)
Eligible for Reduced-Price Lunch Program: 244 (11.9%)
Teachers: 155.1 (13.2 to 1)
Librarians/Media Specialists: 4.0 (512.5 to 1)
Guidance Counselors: 5.3 (386.8 to 1)
Current Spending: ($ per student per year):
Total: $5,549; Instruction: $3,608; Support Services: $1,684
Enrollment, Drop-out Rates and Diploma Recipients by Race/Ethnicity

Category	Total	White	Black	Asian	AIAN	Hisp.
Enrollment (%)	100.0	98.0	0.6	0.3	0.1	1.0
Drop-out Rate (%)	5.8	5.8	0.0	0.0	0.0	20.0
H.S. Diplomas (#)	133	128	0	2	1	2

School of The Osage R-II

1501 School Rd • Lake Ozark, MO 65049-1960
Mailing Address: PO Box 1960 • Lake Ozark, MO 65049-1960
(573) 365-4091 • http://www.osage.k12.mo.us/
Grade Span: PK-12; **Agency Type:** 1
Schools: 4
2 Primary; 1 Middle; 1 High; 0 Other Level
4 Regular; 0 Special Education; 0 Vocational; 0 Alternative
0 Magnet; 0 Charter; 3 Title I Eligible; 2 School-wide Title I
Students: 1,633 (51.2% male; 48.8% female)
Individual Education Program: 222 (13.6%);
English Language Learner: 1 (0.1%); Migrant: 0 (0.0%)
Eligible for Free Lunch Program: 626 (38.3%)
Eligible for Reduced-Price Lunch Program: 122 (7.5%)
Teachers: 118.6 (13.8 to 1)
Librarians/Media Specialists: 4.0 (408.3 to 1)
Guidance Counselors: 4.8 (340.2 to 1)
Current Spending: ($ per student per year):
Total: $6,100; Instruction: $3,796; Support Services: $1,998
Enrollment, Drop-out Rates and Diploma Recipients by Race/Ethnicity

Category	Total	White	Black	Asian	AIAN	Hisp.
Enrollment (%)	100.0	96.6	0.6	0.6	0.7	1.5
Drop-out Rate (%)	2.7	2.8	0.0	0.0	0.0	0.0
H.S. Diplomas (#)	108	105	0	0	0	3

Morgan County

Morgan County R-II

913 W Newton • Versailles, MO 65084-1363
(573) 378-4231 • http://schoolweb.missouri.edu/morganr2.k12.mo.us/
Grade Span: PK-12; **Agency Type:** 1
Schools: 4
2 Primary; 1 Middle; 1 High; 0 Other Level
4 Regular; 0 Special Education; 0 Vocational; 0 Alternative
0 Magnet; 0 Charter; 2 Title I Eligible; 2 School-wide Title I
Students: 1,664 (51.0% male; 49.0% female)
Individual Education Program: 228 (13.7%);
English Language Learner: 5 (0.3%); Migrant: 3 (0.2%)
Eligible for Free Lunch Program: 617 (37.1%)
Eligible for Reduced-Price Lunch Program: 211 (12.7%)
Teachers: 118.2 (14.1 to 1)
Librarians/Media Specialists: 4.6 (361.7 to 1)
Guidance Counselors: 5.0 (332.8 to 1)
Current Spending: ($ per student per year):
Total: $5,329; Instruction: $3,416; Support Services: $1,615
Enrollment, Drop-out Rates and Diploma Recipients by Race/Ethnicity

Category	Total	White	Black	Asian	AIAN	Hisp.
Enrollment (%)	100.0	97.8	1.1	0.4	0.2	0.5
Drop-out Rate (%)	4.0	4.1	0.0	0.0	0.0	0.0
H.S. Diplomas (#)	109	108	0	1	0	0

New Madrid County

New Madrid County R-I

310 US Hwy 61 • New Madrid, MO 63869-9753
(573) 688-2161 •
http://schoolweb.missouri.edu/newmadridco.k12.mo.us/index-old.html
Grade Span: PK-12; **Agency Type:** 1
Schools: 6
3 Primary; 1 Middle; 2 High; 0 Other Level
5 Regular; 0 Special Education; 1 Vocational; 0 Alternative
0 Magnet; 0 Charter; 4 Title I Eligible; 4 School-wide Title I
Students: 2,030 (52.5% male; 47.5% female)
Individual Education Program: 355 (17.5%);
English Language Learner: 0 (0.0%); Migrant: 3 (0.1%)
Eligible for Free Lunch Program: 1,022 (50.3%)
Eligible for Reduced-Price Lunch Program: 133 (6.6%)
Teachers: 159.0 (12.8 to 1)
Librarians/Media Specialists: 4.0 (507.5 to 1)
Guidance Counselors: 4.2 (483.3 to 1)
Current Spending: ($ per student per year):
Total: $6,427; Instruction: $3,784; Support Services: $2,349
Enrollment, Drop-out Rates and Diploma Recipients by Race/Ethnicity

Category	Total	White	Black	Asian	AIAN	Hisp.
Enrollment (%)	100.0	61.2	38.6	0.1	0.0	0.1
Drop-out Rate (%)	6.1	5.6	7.1	n/a	n/a	0.0
H.S. Diplomas (#)	101	64	37	0	0	0

Newton County

East Newton County R-VI

22808 E Hwy 86 • Granby, MO 64844-9998
(417) 472-6231
Grade Span: PK-12; **Agency Type:** 1
Schools: 3
2 Primary; 0 Middle; 1 High; 0 Other Level
3 Regular; 0 Special Education; 0 Vocational; 0 Alternative
0 Magnet; 0 Charter; 2 Title I Eligible; 2 School-wide Title I
Students: 1,509 (50.8% male; 49.2% female)
Individual Education Program: 217 (14.4%);
English Language Learner: 12 (0.8%); Migrant: 17 (1.1%)
Eligible for Free Lunch Program: 634 (42.0%)

Eligible for Reduced-Price Lunch Program: 164 (10.9%)
Teachers: 107.2 (14.1 to 1)
Librarians/Media Specialists: 3.0 (503.0 to 1)
Guidance Counselors: 3.4 (443.8 to 1)
Current Spending: ($ per student per year):
Total: $5,794; Instruction: $3,542; Support Services: $1,937
Enrollment, Drop-out Rates and Diploma Recipients by Race/Ethnicity

Category	Total	White	Black	Asian	AIAN	Hisp.
Enrollment (%)	100.0	98.3	0.5	0.5	0.3	0.5
Drop-out Rate (%)	3.4	3.5	n/a	n/a	n/a	0.0
H.S. Diplomas (#)	91	91	0	0	0	0

Neosho R-V
511 Neosho Blvd • Neosho, MO 64850-2098
(417) 451-8600 • http://www.neosho.k12.mo.us/
Grade Span: PK-12; **Agency Type:** 1
Schools: 8
5 Primary; 1 Middle; 1 High; 1 Other Level
8 Regular; 0 Special Education; 0 Vocational; 0 Alternative
0 Magnet; 0 Charter; 5 Title I Eligible; 3 School-wide Title I
Students: 4,483 (52.3% male; 47.7% female)
Individual Education Program: 619 (13.8%);
English Language Learner: 136 (3.0%); Migrant: 200 (4.5%)
Eligible for Free Lunch Program: 1,518 (33.9%)
Eligible for Reduced-Price Lunch Program: 430 (9.6%)
Teachers: 270.5 (16.6 to 1)
Librarians/Media Specialists: 5.0 (896.6 to 1)
Guidance Counselors: 9.0 (498.1 to 1)
Current Spending: ($ per student per year):
Total: $5,745; Instruction: $3,927; Support Services: $1,536
Enrollment, Drop-out Rates and Diploma Recipients by Race/Ethnicity

Category	Total	White	Black	Asian	AIAN	Hisp.
Enrollment (%)	100.0	89.0	1.4	1.3	1.7	6.6
Drop-out Rate (%)	4.8	4.8	0.0	0.0	12.5	7.1
H.S. Diplomas (#)	238	221	6	3	2	6

Seneca R-VII
914 Frisco St • Seneca, MO 64865-0469
Mailing Address: PO Box 469 • Seneca, MO 64865-0469
(417) 776-3426 • http://schoolweb.missouri.edu/seneca.k12.mo.us/
Grade Span: PK-12; **Agency Type:** 1
Schools: 3
1 Primary; 1 Middle; 1 High; 0 Other Level
3 Regular; 0 Special Education; 0 Vocational; 0 Alternative
0 Magnet; 0 Charter; 3 Title I Eligible; 0 School-wide Title I
Students: 1,698 (51.5% male; 48.5% female)
Individual Education Program: 238 (14.0%);
English Language Learner: 0 (0.0%); Migrant: 5 (0.3%)
Eligible for Free Lunch Program: 494 (29.1%)
Eligible for Reduced-Price Lunch Program: 184 (10.8%)
Teachers: 112.5 (15.1 to 1)
Librarians/Media Specialists: 3.0 (566.0 to 1)
Guidance Counselors: 4.5 (377.3 to 1)
Current Spending: ($ per student per year):
Total: $5,311; Instruction: $2,971; Support Services: $2,070
Enrollment, Drop-out Rates and Diploma Recipients by Race/Ethnicity

Category	Total	White	Black	Asian	AIAN	Hisp.
Enrollment (%)	100.0	89.8	0.5	0.3	9.0	0.5
Drop-out Rate (%)	3.4	3.9	n/a	0.0	0.0	0.0
H.S. Diplomas (#)	91	81	0	1	9	0

Pemiscot County

Caruthersville 18
1711 Ward Ave • Caruthersville, MO 63830-2555
(573) 333-6100 • http://caruthersville.k12.mo.us/
Grade Span: PK-12; **Agency Type:** 1
Schools: 3
1 Primary; 1 Middle; 1 High; 0 Other Level
3 Regular; 0 Special Education; 0 Vocational; 0 Alternative
0 Magnet; 0 Charter; 2 Title I Eligible; 2 School-wide Title I
Students: 1,755 (51.2% male; 48.8% female)
Individual Education Program: 251 (14.3%);
English Language Learner: 7 (0.4%); Migrant: 4 (0.2%)
Eligible for Free Lunch Program: 1,043 (59.4%)
Eligible for Reduced-Price Lunch Program: 59 (3.4%)
Teachers: 113.4 (15.5 to 1)
Librarians/Media Specialists: 4.0 (438.8 to 1)
Guidance Counselors: 4.0 (438.8 to 1)
Current Spending: ($ per student per year):
Total: $5,554; Instruction: $3,677; Support Services: $1,576
Enrollment, Drop-out Rates and Diploma Recipients by Race/Ethnicity

Category	Total	White	Black	Asian	AIAN	Hisp.
Enrollment (%)	100.0	50.7	48.2	0.2	0.2	0.8
Drop-out Rate (%)	3.6	4.6	2.0	0.0	0.0	0.0
H.S. Diplomas (#)	81	46	34	0	0	1

Perry County

Perry County 32
326 College St • Perryville, MO 63775-2699
(573) 547-7500 • http://www.perryville.k12.mo.us/
Grade Span: PK-12; **Agency Type:** 1
Schools: 5
2 Primary; 1 Middle; 2 High; 0 Other Level
4 Regular; 0 Special Education; 1 Vocational; 0 Alternative
0 Magnet; 0 Charter; 3 Title I Eligible; 1 School-wide Title I
Students: 2,323 (51.8% male; 48.2% female)
Individual Education Program: 483 (20.8%);
English Language Learner: 19 (0.8%); Migrant: 0 (0.0%)
Eligible for Free Lunch Program: 636 (27.4%)
Eligible for Reduced-Price Lunch Program: 257 (11.1%)
Teachers: 175.2 (13.3 to 1)
Librarians/Media Specialists: 3.0 (774.3 to 1)
Guidance Counselors: 8.6 (270.1 to 1)
Current Spending: ($ per student per year):
Total: $6,138; Instruction: $3,547; Support Services: $2,288
Enrollment, Drop-out Rates and Diploma Recipients by Race/Ethnicity

Category	Total	White	Black	Asian	AIAN	Hisp.
Enrollment (%)	100.0	99.1	0.0	0.6	0.0	0.2
Drop-out Rate (%)	6.0	6.0	0.0	0.0	n/a	n/a
H.S. Diplomas (#)	173	173	0	0	0	0

Pettis County

Sedalia 200
400 W Fourth St • Sedalia, MO 65301-4296
(660) 829-6450 • http://sedalia.k12.mo.us/
Grade Span: PK-12; **Agency Type:** 1
Schools: 9
6 Primary; 1 Middle; 1 High; 1 Other Level
8 Regular; 0 Special Education; 0 Vocational; 1 Alternative
0 Magnet; 0 Charter; 5 Title I Eligible; 1 School-wide Title I
Students: 4,166 (51.1% male; 48.9% female)
Individual Education Program: 696 (16.7%);
English Language Learner: 151 (3.6%); Migrant: 367 (8.8%)
Eligible for Free Lunch Program: 1,529 (36.7%)
Eligible for Reduced-Price Lunch Program: 333 (8.0%)
Teachers: 286.6 (14.5 to 1)
Librarians/Media Specialists: 7.0 (595.1 to 1)
Guidance Counselors: 12.2 (341.5 to 1)
Current Spending: ($ per student per year):
Total: $5,176; Instruction: $3,210; Support Services: $1,705
Enrollment, Drop-out Rates and Diploma Recipients by Race/Ethnicity

Category	Total	White	Black	Asian	AIAN	Hisp.
Enrollment (%)	100.0	85.5	7.4	0.7	0.1	6.2
Drop-out Rate (%)	5.5	4.9	10.1	0.0	0.0	16.1
H.S. Diplomas (#)	233	208	13	1	0	11

Phelps County

Rolla 31
708 N Main St • Rolla, MO 65401-3023
(573) 458-0100 • http://rolla.k12.mo.us/index.html
Grade Span: PK-12; **Agency Type:** 1
Schools: 8
3 Primary; 1 Middle; 3 High; 1 Other Level
6 Regular; 0 Special Education; 2 Vocational; 0 Alternative
0 Magnet; 0 Charter; 4 Title I Eligible; 0 School-wide Title I
Students: 4,130 (50.4% male; 49.6% female)
Individual Education Program: 538 (13.0%);
English Language Learner: 8 (0.2%); Migrant: 0 (0.0%)
Eligible for Free Lunch Program: 1,277 (30.9%)
Eligible for Reduced-Price Lunch Program: 311 (7.5%)
Teachers: 271.4 (15.2 to 1)
Librarians/Media Specialists: 6.0 (688.3 to 1)
Guidance Counselors: 13.0 (317.7 to 1)
Current Spending: ($ per student per year):
Total: $5,728; Instruction: $3,582; Support Services: $1,869
Enrollment, Drop-out Rates and Diploma Recipients by Race/Ethnicity

Category	Total	White	Black	Asian	AIAN	Hisp.
Enrollment (%)	100.0	92.1	3.4	2.8	0.4	1.3
Drop-out Rate (%)	2.8	2.7	2.9	2.5	0.0	13.3
H.S. Diplomas (#)	297	271	9	13	0	4

Saint James R-I

101 E Scioto St • Saint James, MO 65559-1717
(573) 265-3261 • http://stjames.k12.mo.us/index1024.html
Grade Span: PK-12; **Agency Type:** 1
Schools: 3
1 Primary; 1 Middle; 1 High; 0 Other Level
3 Regular; 0 Special Education; 0 Vocational; 0 Alternative
0 Magnet; 0 Charter; 1 Title I Eligible; 1 School-wide Title I
Students: 1,832 (49.5% male; 50.5% female)
Individual Education Program: 351 (19.2%);
English Language Learner: 6 (0.3%); Migrant: 0 (0.0%)
Eligible for Free Lunch Program: 683 (37.3%)
Eligible for Reduced-Price Lunch Program: 199 (10.9%)
Teachers: 122.9 (14.9 to 1)
Librarians/Media Specialists: 2.8 (654.3 to 1)
Guidance Counselors: 5.3 (345.7 to 1)
Current Spending: ($ per student per year):
Total: $5,553; Instruction: $3,686; Support Services: $1,559
Enrollment, Drop-out Rates and Diploma Recipients by Race/Ethnicity

Category	Total	White	Black	Asian	AIAN	Hisp.
Enrollment (%)	100.0	95.5	3.3	0.5	0.2	0.5
Drop-out Rate (%)	2.5	2.1	3.1	0.0	33.3	33.3
H.S. Diplomas (#)	126	122	1	3	0	0

Platte County

Park Hill

7703 NW Barry Rd • Kansas City, MO 64153-1731
(816) 741-1521 • http://www.parkhill.k12.mo.us/
Grade Span: PK-12; **Agency Type:** 1
Schools: 15
9 Primary; 3 Middle; 2 High; 1 Other Level
15 Regular; 0 Special Education; 0 Vocational; 0 Alternative
0 Magnet; 0 Charter; 6 Title I Eligible; 0 School-wide Title I
Students: 9,391 (51.3% male; 48.7% female)
Individual Education Program: 1,327 (14.1%);
English Language Learner: 201 (2.1%); Migrant: 0 (0.0%)
Eligible for Free Lunch Program: 990 (10.5%)
Eligible for Reduced-Price Lunch Program: 360 (3.8%)
Teachers: 627.3 (15.0 to 1)
Librarians/Media Specialists: 15.0 (626.1 to 1)
Guidance Counselors: 24.0 (391.3 to 1)
Current Spending: ($ per student per year):
Total: $6,750; Instruction: $3,890; Support Services: $2,546
Enrollment, Drop-out Rates and Diploma Recipients by Race/Ethnicity

Category	Total	White	Black	Asian	AIAN	Hisp.
Enrollment (%)	100.0	86.0	6.6	2.9	0.4	4.1
Drop-out Rate (%)	2.4	2.3	1.9	0.0	0.0	9.9
H.S. Diplomas (#)	640	570	34	19	4	13

Platte County R-III

1495 Branch & 92 Hwy • Platte City, MO 64079-1400
Mailing Address: PO Box 1400 • Platte City, MO 64079-1400
(816) 858-5420 • http://www.pcr3pirates.org/
Grade Span: PK-12; **Agency Type:** 1
Schools: 7
3 Primary; 2 Middle; 2 High; 0 Other Level
6 Regular; 0 Special Education; 1 Vocational; 0 Alternative
0 Magnet; 0 Charter; 4 Title I Eligible; 0 School-wide Title I
Students: 2,304 (51.3% male; 48.7% female)
Individual Education Program: 252 (10.9%);
English Language Learner: 13 (0.6%); Migrant: 6 (0.3%)
Eligible for Free Lunch Program: 262 (11.4%)
Eligible for Reduced-Price Lunch Program: 122 (5.3%)
Teachers: 166.0 (13.9 to 1)
Librarians/Media Specialists: 3.5 (658.3 to 1)
Guidance Counselors: 7.9 (291.6 to 1)
Current Spending: ($ per student per year):
Total: $6,546; Instruction: $4,419; Support Services: $1,959
Enrollment, Drop-out Rates and Diploma Recipients by Race/Ethnicity

Category	Total	White	Black	Asian	AIAN	Hisp.
Enrollment (%)	100.0	91.4	4.6	1.1	0.2	2.7
Drop-out Rate (%)	3.3	3.2	6.7	0.0	0.0	10.0
H.S. Diplomas (#)	148	140	5	0	0	3

Polk County

Bolivar R-I

524 W Madison • Bolivar, MO 65613-1945
(417) 326-5291 • http://www.bolivar-r1.k12.mo.us/
Grade Span: PK-12; **Agency Type:** 1
Schools: 6
2 Primary; 1 Middle; 1 High; 2 Other Level
5 Regular; 1 Special Education; 0 Vocational; 0 Alternative
0 Magnet; 0 Charter; 2 Title I Eligible; 2 School-wide Title I
Students: 2,496 (52.0% male; 48.0% female)
Individual Education Program: 366 (14.7%);
English Language Learner: 4 (0.2%); Migrant: 0 (0.0%)
Eligible for Free Lunch Program: 777 (31.1%)
Eligible for Reduced-Price Lunch Program: 225 (9.0%)
Teachers: 182.8 (13.7 to 1)
Librarians/Media Specialists: 4.0 (624.0 to 1)
Guidance Counselors: 6.4 (390.0 to 1)
Current Spending: ($ per student per year):
Total: $6,176; Instruction: $3,858; Support Services: $2,055
Enrollment, Drop-out Rates and Diploma Recipients by Race/Ethnicity

Category	Total	White	Black	Asian	AIAN	Hisp.
Enrollment (%)	100.0	97.2	1.1	0.2	0.4	1.1
Drop-out Rate (%)	4.9	4.9	50.0	0.0	0.0	0.0
H.S. Diplomas (#)	144	140	0	0	2	2

Pulaski County

Waynesville R-VI

200 Fleetwood Dr • Waynesville, MO 65583-2266
(573) 774-6497 • http://waynesville.k12.mo.us/
Grade Span: PK-12; **Agency Type:** 1
Schools: 12
7 Primary; 2 Middle; 2 High; 1 Other Level
11 Regular; 0 Special Education; 1 Vocational; 0 Alternative
0 Magnet; 0 Charter; 6 Title I Eligible; 0 School-wide Title I
Students: 5,368 (51.5% male; 48.5% female)
Individual Education Program: 777 (14.5%);
English Language Learner: 29 (0.5%); Migrant: 0 (0.0%)
Eligible for Free Lunch Program: 1,030 (19.2%)
Eligible for Reduced-Price Lunch Program: 854 (15.9%)
Teachers: 380.5 (14.1 to 1)
Librarians/Media Specialists: 13.5 (397.6 to 1)
Guidance Counselors: 18.0 (298.2 to 1)
Current Spending: ($ per student per year):
Total: $6,644; Instruction: $4,155; Support Services: $2,203
Enrollment, Drop-out Rates and Diploma Recipients by Race/Ethnicity

Category	Total	White	Black	Asian	AIAN	Hisp.
Enrollment (%)	100.0	64.7	23.5	3.8	1.0	7.0
Drop-out Rate (%)	3.4	4.0	2.1	1.7	0.0	2.5
H.S. Diplomas (#)	271	181	62	11	1	16

Randolph County

Moberly

926 Kwix Rd • Moberly, MO 65270-3813
(660) 269-2600 • http://www.moberly.k12.mo.us/
Grade Span: PK-12; **Agency Type:** 1
Schools: 7
3 Primary; 1 Middle; 3 High; 0 Other Level
6 Regular; 0 Special Education; 1 Vocational; 0 Alternative
0 Magnet; 0 Charter; 3 Title I Eligible; 1 School-wide Title I
Students: 2,316 (52.6% male; 47.4% female)
Individual Education Program: 426 (18.4%);
English Language Learner: 3 (0.1%); Migrant: 0 (0.0%)
Eligible for Free Lunch Program: 889 (38.4%)
Eligible for Reduced-Price Lunch Program: 220 (9.5%)
Teachers: 183.2 (12.6 to 1)
Librarians/Media Specialists: 4.0 (579.0 to 1)
Guidance Counselors: 8.4 (275.7 to 1)
Current Spending: ($ per student per year):
Total: $6,092; Instruction: $4,072; Support Services: $1,780
Enrollment, Drop-out Rates and Diploma Recipients by Race/Ethnicity

Category	Total	White	Black	Asian	AIAN	Hisp.
Enrollment (%)	100.0	87.5	11.1	0.5	0.1	0.9
Drop-out Rate (%)	9.4	10.4	2.6	0.0	0.0	0.0
H.S. Diplomas (#)	159	136	20	1	1	1

Ray County

Richmond R-XVI

749 Driskill Dr • Richmond, MO 64085-2202
(816) 776-6912 • http://richmond.k12.mo.us/
Grade Span: PK-12; **Agency Type:** 1
Schools: 4
2 Primary; 1 Middle; 1 High; 0 Other Level
4 Regular; 0 Special Education; 0 Vocational; 0 Alternative
0 Magnet; 0 Charter; 3 Title I Eligible; 0 School-wide Title I
Students: 1,784 (52.5% male; 47.5% female)
Individual Education Program: 242 (13.6%);
English Language Learner: 0 (0.0%); Migrant: 2 (0.1%)
Eligible for Free Lunch Program: 447 (25.1%)
Eligible for Reduced-Price Lunch Program: 138 (7.7%)
Teachers: 121.9 (14.6 to 1)
Librarians/Media Specialists: 4.0 (446.0 to 1)

Guidance Counselors: 5.0 (356.8 to 1)
Current Spending: ($ per student per year):
Total: $5,310; Instruction: $3,244; Support Services: $1,837
Enrollment, Drop-out Rates and Diploma Recipients by Race/Ethnicity

Category	Total	White	Black	Asian	AIAN	Hisp.
Enrollment (%)	100.0	93.4	5.0	0.2	0.4	0.9
Drop-out Rate (%)	2.7	2.6	6.3	n/a	0.0	0.0
H.S. Diplomas (#)	103	100	2	0	0	1

Ripley County

Doniphan R-I
309 Pine St • Doniphan, MO 63935-1703
(573) 996-3819 •
http://doniphanr1.k12.mo.us/education/district/district.php?sectionid=1
Grade Span: PK-12; **Agency Type:** 1
Schools: 4
1 Primary; 1 Middle; 2 High; 0 Other Level
3 Regular; 0 Special Education; 1 Vocational; 0 Alternative
0 Magnet; 0 Charter; 3 Title I Eligible; 3 School-wide Title I
Students: 1,685 (48.3% male; 51.7% female)
Individual Education Program: 224 (13.3%);
English Language Learner: 0 (0.0%); Migrant: 0 (0.0%)
Eligible for Free Lunch Program: 780 (46.3%)
Eligible for Reduced-Price Lunch Program: 212 (12.6%)
Teachers: 117.6 (14.3 to 1)
Librarians/Media Specialists: 2.0 (842.5 to 1)
Guidance Counselors: 5.0 (337.0 to 1)
Current Spending: ($ per student per year):
Total: $5,359; Instruction: $3,507; Support Services: $1,606
Enrollment, Drop-out Rates and Diploma Recipients by Race/Ethnicity

Category	Total	White	Black	Asian	AIAN	Hisp.
Enrollment (%)	100.0	99.3	0.2	0.2	0.1	0.1
Drop-out Rate (%)	3.3	3.4	0.0	0.0	0.0	0.0
H.S. Diplomas (#)	116	116	0	0	0	0

Saline County

Marshall
860 W Vest • Marshall, MO 65340-2139
(660) 886-7414 • http://www.marshallschools.com/
Grade Span: PK-12; **Agency Type:** 1
Schools: 7
4 Primary; 1 Middle; 2 High; 0 Other Level
6 Regular; 0 Special Education; 1 Vocational; 0 Alternative
0 Magnet; 0 Charter; 5 Title I Eligible; 0 School-wide Title I
Students: 2,451 (49.8% male; 50.2% female)
Individual Education Program: 535 (21.8%);
English Language Learner: 146 (6.0%); Migrant: 191 (7.8%)
Eligible for Free Lunch Program: 911 (37.2%)
Eligible for Reduced-Price Lunch Program: 171 (7.0%)
Teachers: 183.6 (13.3 to 1)
Librarians/Media Specialists: 3.0 (817.0 to 1)
Guidance Counselors: 5.9 (415.4 to 1)
Current Spending: ($ per student per year):
Total: $6,279; Instruction: $4,517; Support Services: $1,488
Enrollment, Drop-out Rates and Diploma Recipients by Race/Ethnicity

Category	Total	White	Black	Asian	AIAN	Hisp.
Enrollment (%)	100.0	81.3	9.2	1.0	0.0	8.5
Drop-out Rate (%)	8.1	6.8	13.9	0.0	0.0	17.5
H.S. Diplomas (#)	181	161	10	2	0	8

Scott County

Sikeston R-VI
1002 Virginia • Sikeston, MO 63801-3347
(573) 472-2581 • http://www.sikeston.k12.mo.us/
Grade Span: PK-12; **Agency Type:** 1
Schools: 10
5 Primary; 2 Middle; 2 High; 1 Other Level
9 Regular; 0 Special Education; 1 Vocational; 0 Alternative
0 Magnet; 0 Charter; 5 Title I Eligible; 0 School-wide Title I
Students: 3,915 (51.0% male; 49.0% female)
Individual Education Program: 329 (8.4%);
English Language Learner: 13 (0.3%); Migrant: 0 (0.0%)
Eligible for Free Lunch Program: 1,832 (46.8%)
Eligible for Reduced-Price Lunch Program: 178 (4.5%)
Teachers: 252.6 (15.5 to 1)
Librarians/Media Specialists: 5.5 (711.8 to 1)
Guidance Counselors: 13.8 (283.7 to 1)
Current Spending: ($ per student per year):
Total: $5,313; Instruction: $3,349; Support Services: $1,715
Enrollment, Drop-out Rates and Diploma Recipients by Race/Ethnicity

Category	Total	White	Black	Asian	AIAN	Hisp.
Enrollment (%)	100.0	65.4	32.7	0.5	0.3	1.1
Drop-out Rate (%)	5.3	4.6	7.3	0.0	0.0	0.0
H.S. Diplomas (#)	210	158	50	1	0	1

St. Charles County

Fort Zumwalt R-II
110 Virgil St • O'fallon, MO 63366-2637
(636) 240-2072 • http://www.fzschools.org/
Grade Span: PK-12; **Agency Type:** 1
Schools: 23
15 Primary; 4 Middle; 4 High; 0 Other Level
22 Regular; 0 Special Education; 0 Vocational; 1 Alternative
0 Magnet; 0 Charter; 8 Title I Eligible; 0 School-wide Title I
Students: 17,933 (51.0% male; 49.0% female)
Individual Education Program: 2,811 (15.7%);
English Language Learner: 42 (0.2%); Migrant: 0 (0.0%)
Eligible for Free Lunch Program: 1,172 (6.5%)
Eligible for Reduced-Price Lunch Program: 533 (3.0%)
Teachers: 1,077.3 (16.6 to 1)
Librarians/Media Specialists: 26.5 (676.7 to 1)
Guidance Counselors: 45.0 (398.5 to 1)
Current Spending: ($ per student per year):
Total: $5,884; Instruction: $3,677; Support Services: $1,997
Enrollment, Drop-out Rates and Diploma Recipients by Race/Ethnicity

Category	Total	White	Black	Asian	AIAN	Hisp.
Enrollment (%)	100.0	93.8	3.7	1.0	0.2	1.3
Drop-out Rate (%)	2.7	2.6	7.5	0.0	0.0	0.0
H.S. Diplomas (#)	1,073	1,030	25	9	1	8

Francis Howell R-III
4545 Central School Rd • Saint Charles, MO 63304-7113
(636) 441-0088 • http://www.fhsd.k12.mo.us/
Grade Span: PK-12; **Agency Type:** 1
Schools: 23
13 Primary; 5 Middle; 4 High; 1 Other Level
22 Regular; 0 Special Education; 0 Vocational; 1 Alternative
0 Magnet; 0 Charter; 8 Title I Eligible; 0 School-wide Title I
Students: 19,239 (52.0% male; 48.0% female)
Individual Education Program: 2,889 (15.0%);
English Language Learner: 112 (0.6%); Migrant: 0 (0.0%)
Eligible for Free Lunch Program: 860 (4.5%)
Eligible for Reduced-Price Lunch Program: 310 (1.6%)
Teachers: 1,203.3 (16.0 to 1)
Librarians/Media Specialists: 22.6 (851.3 to 1)
Guidance Counselors: 51.7 (372.1 to 1)
Current Spending: ($ per student per year):
Total: $5,679; Instruction: $3,520; Support Services: $1,932
Enrollment, Drop-out Rates and Diploma Recipients by Race/Ethnicity

Category	Total	White	Black	Asian	AIAN	Hisp.
Enrollment (%)	100.0	93.3	4.0	1.3	0.3	1.1
Drop-out Rate (%)	2.2	2.2	4.1	0.0	0.0	0.0
H.S. Diplomas (#)	1,232	1,184	29	12	1	6

Saint Charles R-VI
1025 Country Club Rd • Saint Charles, MO 63303-3346
(636) 724-5840 • http://www.stcharles.k12.mo.us/
Grade Span: KG-12; **Agency Type:** 1
Schools: 12
7 Primary; 2 Middle; 3 High; 0 Other Level
11 Regular; 0 Special Education; 1 Vocational; 0 Alternative
0 Magnet; 0 Charter; 6 Title I Eligible; 0 School-wide Title I
Students: 5,879 (52.1% male; 47.9% female)
Individual Education Program: 983 (16.7%);
English Language Learner: 123 (2.1%); Migrant: 70 (1.2%)
Eligible for Free Lunch Program: 1,102 (18.7%)
Eligible for Reduced-Price Lunch Program: 286 (4.9%)
Teachers: 448.3 (13.1 to 1)
Librarians/Media Specialists: 6.8 (864.6 to 1)
Guidance Counselors: 25.4 (231.5 to 1)
Current Spending: ($ per student per year):
Total: $7,053; Instruction: $4,412; Support Services: $2,384
Enrollment, Drop-out Rates and Diploma Recipients by Race/Ethnicity

Category	Total	White	Black	Asian	AIAN	Hisp.
Enrollment (%)	100.0	87.6	7.1	1.4	0.2	3.7
Drop-out Rate (%)	4.1	3.9	9.8	0.0	n/a	4.2
H.S. Diplomas (#)	416	395	16	5	0	0

Wentzville R-IV
One Campus Dr • Wentzville, MO 63385-3415
(636) 327-3800 • http://wentzville.k12.mo.us/
Grade Span: PK-12; **Agency Type:** 1
Schools: 9

5 Primary; 2 Middle; 2 High; 0 Other Level
9 Regular; 0 Special Education; 0 Vocational; 0 Alternative
0 Magnet; 0 Charter; 5 Title I Eligible; 0 School-wide Title I
Students: 7,275 (51.8% male; 48.2% female)
Individual Education Program: 1,244 (17.1%);
English Language Learner: 31 (0.4%); Migrant: 0 (0.0%)
Eligible for Free Lunch Program: 998 (13.7%)
Eligible for Reduced-Price Lunch Program: 253 (3.5%)
Teachers: 444.2 (16.4 to 1)
Librarians/Media Specialists: 7.1 (1,024.6 to 1)
Guidance Counselors: 16.2 (449.1 to 1)
Current Spending: ($ per student per year):
Total: $5,963; Instruction: $3,730; Support Services: $1,912
Enrollment, Drop-out Rates and Diploma Recipients by Race/Ethnicity

Category	Total	White	Black	Asian	AIAN	Hisp.
Enrollment (%)	100.0	90.3	7.7	0.9	0.2	0.9
Drop-out Rate (%)	4.9	4.6	9.2	6.7	0.0	7.7
H.S. Diplomas (#)	342	323	15	0	0	4

St. Francois County

Central R-III
200 High St • Park Hills, MO 63601-2524
(573) 431-2616 • http://www.central-ph.k12.mo.us/
Grade Span: PK-12; **Agency Type:** 1
Schools: 4
2 Primary; 1 Middle; 1 High; 0 Other Level
4 Regular; 0 Special Education; 0 Vocational; 0 Alternative
0 Magnet; 0 Charter; 4 Title I Eligible; 0 School-wide Title I
Students: 1,810 (49.3% male; 50.7% female)
Individual Education Program: 347 (19.2%);
English Language Learner: 3 (0.2%); Migrant: 0 (0.0%)
Eligible for Free Lunch Program: 813 (44.9%)
Eligible for Reduced-Price Lunch Program: 204 (11.3%)
Teachers: 131.3 (13.8 to 1)
Librarians/Media Specialists: 5.0 (362.0 to 1)
Guidance Counselors: 4.5 (402.2 to 1)
Current Spending: ($ per student per year):
Total: $6,112; Instruction: $3,569; Support Services: $2,205
Enrollment, Drop-out Rates and Diploma Recipients by Race/Ethnicity

Category	Total	White	Black	Asian	AIAN	Hisp.
Enrollment (%)	100.0	96.5	2.8	0.2	0.0	0.6
Drop-out Rate (%)	1.3	1.3	0.0	0.0	0.0	0.0
H.S. Diplomas (#)	111	108	2	1	0	0

Farmington R-VII
1022 Ste Genevieve • Farmington, MO 63640-0570
Mailing Address: PO Box 570 • Farmington, MO 63640-0570
(573) 701-1300 • http://www.farmington.k12.mo.us/
Grade Span: PK-12; **Agency Type:** 1
Schools: 10
5 Primary; 2 Middle; 1 High; 2 Other Level
10 Regular; 0 Special Education; 0 Vocational; 0 Alternative
0 Magnet; 0 Charter; 4 Title I Eligible; 0 School-wide Title I
Students: 3,818 (51.5% male; 48.5% female)
Individual Education Program: 640 (16.8%);
English Language Learner: 8 (0.2%); Migrant: 0 (0.0%)
Eligible for Free Lunch Program: 1,153 (30.2%)
Eligible for Reduced-Price Lunch Program: 390 (10.2%)
Teachers: 252.8 (15.1 to 1)
Librarians/Media Specialists: 6.0 (636.3 to 1)
Guidance Counselors: 9.0 (424.2 to 1)
Current Spending: ($ per student per year):
Total: $5,822; Instruction: $3,567; Support Services: $2,005
Enrollment, Drop-out Rates and Diploma Recipients by Race/Ethnicity

Category	Total	White	Black	Asian	AIAN	Hisp.
Enrollment (%)	100.0	96.6	2.0	0.7	0.1	0.6
Drop-out Rate (%)	2.5	2.5	7.7	0.0	n/a	0.0
H.S. Diplomas (#)	244	241	3	0	0	0

North Saint Francois County R-I
300 Berry Rd • Bonne Terre, MO 63628-4388
(573) 358-2247 • http://ncsd.k12.mo.us/
Grade Span: PK-12; **Agency Type:** 1
Schools: 7
3 Primary; 2 Middle; 2 High; 0 Other Level
6 Regular; 0 Special Education; 1 Vocational; 0 Alternative
0 Magnet; 0 Charter; 2 Title I Eligible; 0 School-wide Title I
Students: 3,236 (52.5% male; 47.5% female)
Individual Education Program: 439 (13.6%);
English Language Learner: 0 (0.0%); Migrant: 0 (0.0%)
Eligible for Free Lunch Program: 973 (30.1%)
Eligible for Reduced-Price Lunch Program: 300 (9.3%)
Teachers: 215.6 (15.0 to 1)
Librarians/Media Specialists: 5.0 (647.2 to 1)
Guidance Counselors: 8.5 (380.7 to 1)
Current Spending: ($ per student per year):
Total: $5,419; Instruction: $3,392; Support Services: $1,733
Enrollment, Drop-out Rates and Diploma Recipients by Race/Ethnicity

Category	Total	White	Black	Asian	AIAN	Hisp.
Enrollment (%)	100.0	98.4	0.8	0.3	0.1	0.5
Drop-out Rate (%)	4.6	4.7	0.0	0.0	n/a	0.0
H.S. Diplomas (#)	223	222	1	0	0	0

St. Louis County

Affton 101
8701 Mackenzie Rd • Saint Louis, MO 63123-3436
(314) 638-8770 • http://info.csd.org/affton.htm
Grade Span: KG-12; **Agency Type:** 1
Schools: 4
2 Primary; 1 Middle; 1 High; 0 Other Level
4 Regular; 0 Special Education; 0 Vocational; 0 Alternative
0 Magnet; 0 Charter; 1 Title I Eligible; 0 School-wide Title I
Students: 2,571 (50.7% male; 49.3% female)
Individual Education Program: 440 (17.1%);
English Language Learner: 131 (5.1%); Migrant: 0 (0.0%)
Eligible for Free Lunch Program: 243 (9.5%)
Eligible for Reduced-Price Lunch Program: 139 (5.4%)
Teachers: 159.7 (16.1 to 1)
Librarians/Media Specialists: 4.0 (642.8 to 1)
Guidance Counselors: 7.9 (325.4 to 1)
Current Spending: ($ per student per year):
Total: $6,252; Instruction: $3,710; Support Services: $2,351
Enrollment, Drop-out Rates and Diploma Recipients by Race/Ethnicity

Category	Total	White	Black	Asian	AIAN	Hisp.
Enrollment (%)	100.0	83.4	12.6	2.3	0.1	1.6
Drop-out Rate (%)	3.7	2.9	8.3	5.6	n/a	0.0
H.S. Diplomas (#)	181	158	17	3	0	3

Bayless
4530 Weber Rd • Saint Louis, MO 63123-5798
(314) 631-2244
Grade Span: PK-12; **Agency Type:** 1
Schools: 4
2 Primary; 1 Middle; 1 High; 0 Other Level
4 Regular; 0 Special Education; 0 Vocational; 0 Alternative
0 Magnet; 0 Charter; 4 Title I Eligible; 0 School-wide Title I
Students: 1,510 (49.1% male; 50.9% female)
Individual Education Program: 234 (15.5%);
English Language Learner: 145 (9.6%); Migrant: 0 (0.0%)
Eligible for Free Lunch Program: 267 (17.7%)
Eligible for Reduced-Price Lunch Program: 158 (10.5%)
Teachers: 87.0 (17.4 to 1)
Librarians/Media Specialists: 4.0 (377.5 to 1)
Guidance Counselors: 5.0 (302.0 to 1)
Current Spending: ($ per student per year):
Total: $4,975; Instruction: $2,997; Support Services: $1,868
Enrollment, Drop-out Rates and Diploma Recipients by Race/Ethnicity

Category	Total	White	Black	Asian	AIAN	Hisp.
Enrollment (%)	100.0	82.7	11.1	3.4	0.3	2.5
Drop-out Rate (%)	3.4	2.2	1.9	50.0	0.0	50.0
H.S. Diplomas (#)	94	81	8	1	0	4

Clayton
2 Mark Twain Cir • Clayton, MO 63105-1613
(314) 854-6000 • http://www.clayton.k12.mo.us/
Grade Span: PK-12; **Agency Type:** 1
Schools: 6
4 Primary; 1 Middle; 1 High; 0 Other Level
5 Regular; 0 Special Education; 0 Vocational; 1 Alternative
0 Magnet; 0 Charter; 1 Title I Eligible; 0 School-wide Title I
Students: 2,497 (51.1% male; 48.9% female)
Individual Education Program: 408 (16.3%);
English Language Learner: 118 (4.7%); Migrant: 0 (0.0%)
Eligible for Free Lunch Program: 76 (3.0%)
Eligible for Reduced-Price Lunch Program: 27 (1.1%)
Teachers: 218.5 (11.4 to 1)
Librarians/Media Specialists: 8.4 (297.3 to 1)
Guidance Counselors: 11.0 (227.0 to 1)
Current Spending: ($ per student per year):
Total: $12,914; Instruction: $7,272; Support Services: $5,316
Enrollment, Drop-out Rates and Diploma Recipients by Race/Ethnicity

Category	Total	White	Black	Asian	AIAN	Hisp.
Enrollment (%)	100.0	67.6	22.6	8.2	0.2	1.4
Drop-out Rate (%)	1.8	1.7	2.9	0.0	0.0	0.0
H.S. Diplomas (#)	189	135	35	18	0	1

Ferguson-Florissant R-II

1005 Waterford Dr • Florissant, MO 63033-3694
(314) 506-9000 • http://www.fergflor.k12.mo.us/index.htm
Grade Span: PK-12; **Agency Type:** 1
Schools: 25
18 Primary; 3 Middle; 3 High; 1 Other Level
24 Regular; 0 Special Education; 0 Vocational; 1 Alternative
0 Magnet; 0 Charter; 16 Title I Eligible; 5 School-wide Title I
Students: 12,984 (51.6% male; 48.4% female)
Individual Education Program: 2,273 (17.5%);
English Language Learner: 80 (0.6%); Migrant: 0 (0.0%)
Eligible for Free Lunch Program: 5,003 (38.5%)
Eligible for Reduced-Price Lunch Program: 1,147 (8.8%)
Teachers: 844.2 (15.4 to 1)
Librarians/Media Specialists: 26.0 (499.4 to 1)
Guidance Counselors: 37.6 (345.3 to 1)
Current Spending: ($ per student per year):
Total: $7,751; Instruction: $4,511; Support Services: $2,944
Enrollment, Drop-out Rates and Diploma Recipients by Race/Ethnicity

Category	Total	White	Black	Asian	AIAN	Hisp.
Enrollment (%)	100.0	32.9	64.9	0.8	0.2	1.2
Drop-out Rate (%)	2.6	3.1	2.3	0.0	0.0	0.0
H.S. Diplomas (#)	694	320	361	5	0	8

Hancock Place

9101 S Broadway • Saint Louis, MO 63125-1516
(314) 544-1300 • http://hancock.k12.mo.us/index.html
Grade Span: PK-12; **Agency Type:** 1
Schools: 3
1 Primary; 1 Middle; 1 High; 0 Other Level
3 Regular; 0 Special Education; 0 Vocational; 0 Alternative
0 Magnet; 0 Charter; 1 Title I Eligible; 0 School-wide Title I
Students: 1,862 (50.3% male; 49.7% female)
Individual Education Program: 284 (15.3%);
English Language Learner: 74 (4.0%); Migrant: 0 (0.0%)
Eligible for Free Lunch Program: 778 (41.8%)
Eligible for Reduced-Price Lunch Program: 175 (9.4%)
Teachers: 113.5 (16.4 to 1)
Librarians/Media Specialists: 2.0 (931.0 to 1)
Guidance Counselors: 4.4 (423.2 to 1)
Current Spending: ($ per student per year):
Total: $5,821; Instruction: $3,798; Support Services: $1,823
Enrollment, Drop-out Rates and Diploma Recipients by Race/Ethnicity

Category	Total	White	Black	Asian	AIAN	Hisp.
Enrollment (%)	100.0	77.7	19.7	0.3	0.1	2.3
Drop-out Rate (%)	5.5	6.6	1.4	0.0	n/a	0.0
H.S. Diplomas (#)	77	62	14	0	0	1

Hazelwood

15955 New Halls Ferry Rd • Florissant, MO 63031-1227
(314) 953-5000 • http://www.hazelwood.k12.mo.us/~mludwig/index.html
Grade Span: PK-12; **Agency Type:** 1
Schools: 25
20 Primary; 2 Middle; 3 High; 0 Other Level
24 Regular; 1 Special Education; 0 Vocational; 0 Alternative
0 Magnet; 0 Charter; 6 Title I Eligible; 0 School-wide Title I
Students: 19,721 (51.2% male; 48.8% female)
Individual Education Program: 3,265 (16.6%);
English Language Learner: 292 (1.5%); Migrant: 0 (0.0%)
Eligible for Free Lunch Program: 4,736 (24.0%)
Eligible for Reduced-Price Lunch Program: 1,211 (6.1%)
Teachers: 1,171.5 (16.8 to 1)
Librarians/Media Specialists: 29.8 (661.8 to 1)
Guidance Counselors: 53.0 (372.1 to 1)
Current Spending: ($ per student per year):
Total: $6,671; Instruction: $4,047; Support Services: $2,409
Enrollment, Drop-out Rates and Diploma Recipients by Race/Ethnicity

Category	Total	White	Black	Asian	AIAN	Hisp.
Enrollment (%)	100.0	42.7	55.3	1.0	0.1	0.9
Drop-out Rate (%)	3.4	3.3	3.6	1.5	0.0	2.4
H.S. Diplomas (#)	1,247	682	544	13	1	7

Jennings

2559 Dorwood • Jennings, MO 63136-4035
(314) 653-8000 • http://www.jenningsk12.net/
Grade Span: PK-12; **Agency Type:** 1
Schools: 7
4 Primary; 2 Middle; 1 High; 0 Other Level
7 Regular; 0 Special Education; 0 Vocational; 0 Alternative
0 Magnet; 0 Charter; 6 Title I Eligible; 4 School-wide Title I
Students: 3,153 (50.1% male; 49.9% female)
Individual Education Program: 542 (17.2%);
English Language Learner: 0 (0.0%); Migrant: 0 (0.0%)
Eligible for Free Lunch Program: 2,107 (66.8%)
Eligible for Reduced-Price Lunch Program: 331 (10.5%)
Teachers: 202.3 (15.6 to 1)
Librarians/Media Specialists: 2.9 (1,087.2 to 1)
Guidance Counselors: 8.0 (394.1 to 1)
Current Spending: ($ per student per year):
Total: $7,312; Instruction: $3,624; Support Services: $3,325
Enrollment, Drop-out Rates and Diploma Recipients by Race/Ethnicity

Category	Total	White	Black	Asian	AIAN	Hisp.
Enrollment (%)	100.0	4.6	95.2	0.0	0.0	0.1
Drop-out Rate (%)	3.4	5.9	3.2	0.0	0.0	0.0
H.S. Diplomas (#)	147	10	134	1	0	2

Kirkwood R-VII

11289 Manchester Rd • Kirkwood, MO 63122-1122
(314) 213-6101 • http://www.kirkwood.k12.mo.us/default.html
Grade Span: PK-12; **Agency Type:** 1
Schools: 8
5 Primary; 2 Middle; 1 High; 0 Other Level
8 Regular; 0 Special Education; 0 Vocational; 0 Alternative
0 Magnet; 0 Charter; 3 Title I Eligible; 0 School-wide Title I
Students: 5,188 (50.9% male; 49.1% female)
Individual Education Program: 1,010 (19.5%);
English Language Learner: 22 (0.4%); Migrant: 0 (0.0%)
Eligible for Free Lunch Program: 362 (7.0%)
Eligible for Reduced-Price Lunch Program: 111 (2.1%)
Teachers: 338.5 (15.3 to 1)
Librarians/Media Specialists: 11.0 (471.6 to 1)
Guidance Counselors: 16.0 (324.3 to 1)
Current Spending: ($ per student per year):
Total: $7,523; Instruction: $4,473; Support Services: $2,858
Enrollment, Drop-out Rates and Diploma Recipients by Race/Ethnicity

Category	Total	White	Black	Asian	AIAN	Hisp.
Enrollment (%)	100.0	74.0	24.1	1.1	0.1	0.8
Drop-out Rate (%)	3.0	2.2	5.4	10.0	n/a	0.0
H.S. Diplomas (#)	409	331	73	2	0	3

Ladue

9703 Conway Rd • Saint Louis, MO 63124-1646
(314) 994-7080 • http://www.ladue.k12.mo.us/
Grade Span: KG-12; **Agency Type:** 1
Schools: 6
4 Primary; 1 Middle; 1 High; 0 Other Level
6 Regular; 0 Special Education; 0 Vocational; 0 Alternative
0 Magnet; 0 Charter; 2 Title I Eligible; 0 School-wide Title I
Students: 3,272 (49.6% male; 50.4% female)
Individual Education Program: 490 (15.0%);
English Language Learner: 25 (0.8%); Migrant: 0 (0.0%)
Eligible for Free Lunch Program: 171 (5.2%)
Eligible for Reduced-Price Lunch Program: 46 (1.4%)
Teachers: 276.6 (11.8 to 1)
Librarians/Media Specialists: 7.0 (467.4 to 1)
Guidance Counselors: 12.0 (272.7 to 1)
Current Spending: ($ per student per year):
Total: $11,008; Instruction: $6,347; Support Services: $4,425
Enrollment, Drop-out Rates and Diploma Recipients by Race/Ethnicity

Category	Total	White	Black	Asian	AIAN	Hisp.
Enrollment (%)	100.0	75.1	17.9	5.7	0.2	1.2
Drop-out Rate (%)	1.2	1.3	1.1	0.0	n/a	0.0
H.S. Diplomas (#)	217	151	56	8	0	2

Lindbergh R-VIII

4900 S Lindbergh Blvd • Saint Louis, MO 63126-3235
(314) 729-2480 • http://www.lindbergh.k12.mo.us/
Grade Span: KG-12; **Agency Type:** 1
Schools: 7
5 Primary; 1 Middle; 1 High; 0 Other Level
7 Regular; 0 Special Education; 0 Vocational; 0 Alternative
0 Magnet; 0 Charter; 4 Title I Eligible; 0 School-wide Title I
Students: 5,289 (51.1% male; 48.9% female)
Individual Education Program: 866 (16.4%);
English Language Learner: 70 (1.3%); Migrant: 0 (0.0%)
Eligible for Free Lunch Program: 238 (4.5%)
Eligible for Reduced-Price Lunch Program: 121 (2.3%)
Teachers: 352.9 (15.0 to 1)
Librarians/Media Specialists: 7.0 (755.6 to 1)
Guidance Counselors: 15.5 (341.2 to 1)
Current Spending: ($ per student per year):
Total: $6,923; Instruction: $4,315; Support Services: $2,485
Enrollment, Drop-out Rates and Diploma Recipients by Race/Ethnicity

Category	Total	White	Black	Asian	AIAN	Hisp.
Enrollment (%)	100.0	84.0	13.6	1.7	0.0	0.7
Drop-out Rate (%)	2.0	2.4	0.0	4.2	n/a	0.0
H.S. Diplomas (#)	377	306	63	5	0	3

Mehlville R-IX

3120 Lemay Ferry Rd • Saint Louis, MO 63125-4416
(314) 467-5000 • http://info.csd.org/mehlville/index.html
Grade Span: PK-12; **Agency Type:** 1
Schools: 16
11 Primary; 3 Middle; 2 High; 0 Other Level
16 Regular; 0 Special Education; 0 Vocational; 0 Alternative
0 Magnet; 0 Charter; 4 Title I Eligible; 0 School-wide Title I
Students: 11,979 (51.2% male; 48.8% female)
Individual Education Program: 2,082 (17.4%);
English Language Learner: 265 (2.2%); Migrant: 3 (<0.1%)
Eligible for Free Lunch Program: 938 (7.8%)
Eligible for Reduced-Price Lunch Program: 308 (2.6%)
Teachers: 660.1 (18.1 to 1)
Librarians/Media Specialists: 16.4 (730.4 to 1)
Guidance Counselors: 30.7 (390.2 to 1)
Current Spending: ($ per student per year):
Total: $5,822; Instruction: $3,692; Support Services: $1,916
Enrollment, Drop-out Rates and Diploma Recipients by Race/Ethnicity

Category	Total	White	Black	Asian	AIAN	Hisp.
Enrollment (%)	100.0	84.8	13.1	1.6	0.1	0.4
Drop-out Rate (%)	3.2	2.9	5.0	1.9	0.0	5.6
H.S. Diplomas (#)	827	735	82	6	0	4

Normandy

3855 Lucas And Hunt Rd • Saint Louis, MO 63121-2919
(314) 493-0400 • http://www.normandy.k12.mo.us/
Grade Span: PK-12; **Agency Type:** 1
Schools: 12
8 Primary; 2 Middle; 2 High; 0 Other Level
12 Regular; 0 Special Education; 0 Vocational; 0 Alternative
0 Magnet; 0 Charter; 8 Title I Eligible; 8 School-wide Title I
Students: 5,941 (51.2% male; 48.8% female)
Individual Education Program: 882 (14.8%);
English Language Learner: 0 (0.0%); Migrant: 2 (<0.1%)
Eligible for Free Lunch Program: 4,282 (72.1%)
Eligible for Reduced-Price Lunch Program: 354 (6.0%)
Teachers: 344.5 (17.2 to 1)
Librarians/Media Specialists: 7.0 (848.7 to 1)
Guidance Counselors: 17.0 (349.5 to 1)
Current Spending: ($ per student per year):
Total: $7,117; Instruction: $4,120; Support Services: $2,665
Enrollment, Drop-out Rates and Diploma Recipients by Race/Ethnicity

Category	Total	White	Black	Asian	AIAN	Hisp.
Enrollment (%)	100.0	1.6	97.9	0.2	0.0	0.3
Drop-out Rate (%)	5.2	2.4	5.3	n/a	n/a	0.0
H.S. Diplomas (#)	312	18	289	1	0	4

Parkway C-2

455 N Woods Mill Rd • Chesterfield, MO 63017-3327
(314) 415-8100 • http://www.pkwy.k12.mo.us/
Grade Span: PK-12; **Agency Type:** 1
Schools: 28
18 Primary; 5 Middle; 5 High; 0 Other Level
28 Regular; 0 Special Education; 0 Vocational; 0 Alternative
0 Magnet; 0 Charter; 10 Title I Eligible; 0 School-wide Title I
Students: 20,354 (50.6% male; 49.4% female)
Individual Education Program: 3,413 (16.8%);
English Language Learner: 373 (1.8%); Migrant: 0 (0.0%)
Eligible for Free Lunch Program: 612 (3.0%)
Eligible for Reduced-Price Lunch Program: 237 (1.2%)
Teachers: 1,218.4 (16.7 to 1)
Librarians/Media Specialists: 30.6 (665.2 to 1)
Guidance Counselors: 65.1 (312.7 to 1)
Current Spending: ($ per student per year):
Total: $7,781; Instruction: $4,501; Support Services: $3,079
Enrollment, Drop-out Rates and Diploma Recipients by Race/Ethnicity

Category	Total	White	Black	Asian	AIAN	Hisp.
Enrollment (%)	100.0	72.6	17.0	8.6	0.1	1.6
Drop-out Rate (%)	1.8	2.0	1.4	1.0	0.0	1.7
H.S. Diplomas (#)	1,438	1,077	214	127	2	18

Pattonville R-III

11097 St Charles Rock Rd • Saint Ann, MO 63074-1509
(314) 213-8001 • http://www.pattonville.k12.mo.us/
Grade Span: PK-12; **Agency Type:** 1
Schools: 11
8 Primary; 2 Middle; 1 High; 0 Other Level
11 Regular; 0 Special Education; 0 Vocational; 0 Alternative
0 Magnet; 0 Charter; 5 Title I Eligible; 2 School-wide Title I
Students: 6,216 (51.8% male; 48.2% female)
Individual Education Program: 1,117 (18.0%);
English Language Learner: 143 (2.3%); Migrant: 0 (0.0%)
Eligible for Free Lunch Program: 1,076 (17.3%)
Eligible for Reduced-Price Lunch Program: 384 (6.2%)
Teachers: 482.2 (12.9 to 1)
Librarians/Media Specialists: 12.0 (518.0 to 1)
Guidance Counselors: 25.9 (240.0 to 1)
Current Spending: ($ per student per year):
Total: $9,071; Instruction: $5,221; Support Services: $3,607
Enrollment, Drop-out Rates and Diploma Recipients by Race/Ethnicity

Category	Total	White	Black	Asian	AIAN	Hisp.
Enrollment (%)	100.0	70.8	24.0	2.8	0.0	2.4
Drop-out Rate (%)	2.5	2.6	2.1	3.0	0.0	0.0
H.S. Diplomas (#)	428	322	94	8	0	4

Ritenour

2420 Woodson Rd • Saint Louis, MO 63114-5423
(314) 493-6010 • http://www.ritenour.k12.mo.us/
Grade Span: PK-12; **Agency Type:** 1
Schools: 9
6 Primary; 2 Middle; 1 High; 0 Other Level
9 Regular; 0 Special Education; 0 Vocational; 0 Alternative
0 Magnet; 0 Charter; 8 Title I Eligible; 0 School-wide Title I
Students: 6,350 (51.3% male; 48.7% female)
Individual Education Program: 1,104 (17.4%);
English Language Learner: 186 (2.9%); Migrant: 2 (<0.1%)
Eligible for Free Lunch Program: 2,344 (36.9%)
Eligible for Reduced-Price Lunch Program: 468 (7.4%)
Teachers: 363.4 (17.5 to 1)
Librarians/Media Specialists: 10.0 (635.0 to 1)
Guidance Counselors: 15.0 (423.3 to 1)
Current Spending: ($ per student per year):
Total: $6,223; Instruction: $3,664; Support Services: $2,320
Enrollment, Drop-out Rates and Diploma Recipients by Race/Ethnicity

Category	Total	White	Black	Asian	AIAN	Hisp.
Enrollment (%)	100.0	59.8	33.6	2.1	0.4	4.1
Drop-out Rate (%)	1.2	1.3	1.1	2.4	0.0	0.0
H.S. Diplomas (#)	296	209	75	8	1	3

Riverview Gardens

1370 Northumberland • Saint Louis, MO 63137-1413
(314) 869-2505 • http://www.rgsd.org/
Grade Span: PK-12; **Agency Type:** 1
Schools: 13
10 Primary; 2 Middle; 1 High; 0 Other Level
13 Regular; 0 Special Education; 0 Vocational; 0 Alternative
0 Magnet; 0 Charter; 12 Title I Eligible; 10 School-wide Title I
Students: 7,837 (51.1% male; 48.9% female)
Individual Education Program: 1,270 (16.2%);
English Language Learner: 7 (0.1%); Migrant: 0 (0.0%)
Eligible for Free Lunch Program: 5,089 (64.9%)
Eligible for Reduced-Price Lunch Program: 820 (10.5%)
Teachers: 437.3 (17.9 to 1)
Librarians/Media Specialists: 11.0 (712.5 to 1)
Guidance Counselors: 19.0 (412.5 to 1)
Current Spending: ($ per student per year):
Total: $6,294; Instruction: $3,853; Support Services: $2,155
Enrollment, Drop-out Rates and Diploma Recipients by Race/Ethnicity

Category	Total	White	Black	Asian	AIAN	Hisp.
Enrollment (%)	100.0	5.6	93.8	0.1	0.1	0.3
Drop-out Rate (%)	4.9	4.1	5.0	0.0	n/a	0.0
H.S. Diplomas (#)	306	34	272	0	0	0

Rockwood R-VI

111 E N St • Eureka, MO 63025-1229
(636) 938-2200 • http://www.rockwood.k12.mo.us/
Grade Span: PK-12; **Agency Type:** 1
Schools: 30
20 Primary; 6 Middle; 4 High; 0 Other Level
29 Regular; 0 Special Education; 0 Vocational; 1 Alternative
0 Magnet; 0 Charter; 15 Title I Eligible; 0 School-wide Title I
Students: 22,313 (51.1% male; 48.9% female)
Individual Education Program: 3,695 (16.6%);
English Language Learner: 225 (1.0%); Migrant: 4 (<0.1%)
Eligible for Free Lunch Program: 528 (2.4%)
Eligible for Reduced-Price Lunch Program: 250 (1.1%)
Teachers: 1,331.9 (16.8 to 1)
Librarians/Media Specialists: 32.8 (680.3 to 1)
Guidance Counselors: 64.4 (346.5 to 1)
Current Spending: ($ per student per year):
Total: $6,258; Instruction: $3,659; Support Services: $2,380
Enrollment, Drop-out Rates and Diploma Recipients by Race/Ethnicity

Category	Total	White	Black	Asian	AIAN	Hisp.
Enrollment (%)	100.0	83.8	12.2	2.8	0.2	1.0
Drop-out Rate (%)	2.4	2.0	5.0	2.1	0.0	1.7
H.S. Diplomas (#)	1,474	1,263	158	40	1	12

Special SD - Saint Louis County

12110 Clayton Rd • Town & Country, MO 63131-2516
(314) 989-8100 • http://ssd.k12.mo.us
Grade Span: PK-12; **Agency Type:** 1
Schools: 11
3 Primary; 0 Middle; 4 High; 4 Other Level
0 Regular; 9 Special Education; 2 Vocational; 0 Alternative
0 Magnet; 0 Charter; 5 Title I Eligible; 0 School-wide Title I
Students: 30,065 (n/a% male; n/a% female)
Individual Education Program: 28,129 (93.6%);
English Language Learner: n/a; Migrant: 0 (0.0%)
Eligible for Free Lunch Program: n/a
Eligible for Reduced-Price Lunch Program: n/a
Teachers: 2,165.8 (13.9 to 1)
Librarians/Media Specialists: n/a
Guidance Counselors: n/a
Current Spending: ($ per student per year):
Total: $28,881; Instruction: $18,823; Support Services: $9,939
Enrollment, Drop-out Rates and Diploma Recipients by Race/Ethnicity

Category	Total	White	Black	Asian	AIAN	Hisp.
Enrollment (%)	100.0	n/a	n/a	n/a	n/a	n/a
Drop-out Rate (%)	n/a	n/a	n/a	n/a	n/a	n/a
H.S. Diplomas (#)	n/a	n/a	n/a	n/a	n/a	n/a

University City

8346 Delcrest Dr • University City, MO 63124-2167
(314) 290-4001 • http://ucityschools.org/
Grade Span: PK-12; **Agency Type:** 1
Schools: 10
7 Primary; 2 Middle; 1 High; 0 Other Level
10 Regular; 0 Special Education; 0 Vocational; 0 Alternative
0 Magnet; 0 Charter; 6 Title I Eligible; 3 School-wide Title I
Students: 4,377 (50.4% male; 49.6% female)
Individual Education Program: 680 (15.5%);
English Language Learner: 35 (0.8%); Migrant: 0 (0.0%)
Eligible for Free Lunch Program: 1,896 (43.3%)
Eligible for Reduced-Price Lunch Program: 335 (7.7%)
Teachers: 290.3 (15.1 to 1)
Librarians/Media Specialists: 7.0 (625.3 to 1)
Guidance Counselors: 13.0 (336.7 to 1)
Current Spending: ($ per student per year):
Total: $7,169; Instruction: $3,857; Support Services: $3,027
Enrollment, Drop-out Rates and Diploma Recipients by Race/Ethnicity

Category	Total	White	Black	Asian	AIAN	Hisp.
Enrollment (%)	100.0	12.1	86.0	1.1	0.1	0.7
Drop-out Rate (%)	10.0	3.1	11.0	0.0	0.0	0.0
H.S. Diplomas (#)	168	19	148	0	0	1

Webster Groves

400 E Lockwood Ave • Webster Groves, MO 63119-3125
(314) 961-1233 • http://www.webster.k12.mo.us/
Grade Span: KG-12; **Agency Type:** 1
Schools: 10
7 Primary; 2 Middle; 1 High; 0 Other Level
10 Regular; 0 Special Education; 0 Vocational; 0 Alternative
0 Magnet; 0 Charter; 7 Title I Eligible; 0 School-wide Title I
Students: 4,116 (52.3% male; 47.7% female)
Individual Education Program: 666 (16.2%);
English Language Learner: 28 (0.7%); Migrant: 0 (0.0%)
Eligible for Free Lunch Program: 392 (9.5%)
Eligible for Reduced-Price Lunch Program: 90 (2.2%)
Teachers: 277.4 (14.8 to 1)
Librarians/Media Specialists: 8.7 (473.1 to 1)
Guidance Counselors: 15.5 (265.5 to 1)
Current Spending: ($ per student per year):
Total: $7,284; Instruction: $4,546; Support Services: $2,508
Enrollment, Drop-out Rates and Diploma Recipients by Race/Ethnicity

Category	Total	White	Black	Asian	AIAN	Hisp.
Enrollment (%)	100.0	72.3	25.4	1.5	0.2	0.8
Drop-out Rate (%)	3.7	3.2	5.2	0.0	n/a	0.0
H.S. Diplomas (#)	303	217	75	7	0	4

Saint Louis City

801 N 11th St • Saint Louis, MO 63101-1401
(314) 231-3720 • http://www.slps.org/
Grade Span: PK-12; **Agency Type:** 1
Schools: 124
75 Primary; 25 Middle; 16 High; 8 Other Level
120 Regular; 0 Special Education; 1 Vocational; 3 Alternative
32 Magnet; 7 Charter; 95 Title I Eligible; 87 School-wide Title I
Students: 45,480 (51.8% male; 48.2% female)
Individual Education Program: 7,303 (16.1%);
English Language Learner: 2,672 (5.9%); Migrant: 196 (0.4%)
Eligible for Free Lunch Program: 32,142 (70.7%)
Eligible for Reduced-Price Lunch Program: 2,069 (4.5%)
Teachers: 3,519.9 (12.9 to 1)
Librarians/Media Specialists: 88.0 (516.8 to 1)
Guidance Counselors: 151.0 (301.2 to 1)
Current Spending: ($ per student per year):
Total: $9,127; Instruction: $4,549; Support Services: $4,229
Enrollment, Drop-out Rates and Diploma Recipients by Race/Ethnicity

Category	Total	White	Black	Asian	AIAN	Hisp.
Enrollment (%)	100.0	15.6	81.7	1.3	0.1	1.3
Drop-out Rate (%)	9.4	7.9	10.0	4.3	0.0	10.5
H.S. Diplomas (#)	1,424	300	1,057	50	1	16

Ste. Genevieve County

Sainte Genevieve County R-II

375 N Fifth St • Ste Genevieve, MO 63670-1249
(573) 883-5720 • http://www.stegen.k12.mo.us/
Grade Span: PK-12; **Agency Type:** 1
Schools: 4
2 Primary; 1 Middle; 1 High; 0 Other Level
4 Regular; 0 Special Education; 0 Vocational; 0 Alternative
0 Magnet; 0 Charter; 2 Title I Eligible; 0 School-wide Title I
Students: 2,172 (51.2% male; 48.8% female)
Individual Education Program: 305 (14.0%);
English Language Learner: 2 (0.1%); Migrant: 0 (0.0%)
Eligible for Free Lunch Program: 574 (26.4%)
Eligible for Reduced-Price Lunch Program: 236 (10.9%)
Teachers: 133.5 (16.3 to 1)
Librarians/Media Specialists: 2.0 (1,086.0 to 1)
Guidance Counselors: 4.8 (452.5 to 1)
Current Spending: ($ per student per year):
Total: $5,710; Instruction: $3,663; Support Services: $1,745
Enrollment, Drop-out Rates and Diploma Recipients by Race/Ethnicity

Category	Total	White	Black	Asian	AIAN	Hisp.
Enrollment (%)	100.0	98.4	0.9	0.1	0.0	0.6
Drop-out Rate (%)	4.2	4.1	0.0	0.0	n/a	100.0
H.S. Diplomas (#)	143	141	1	1	0	0

Stoddard County

Dexter R-XI

1031 Brown Pilot Ln • Dexter, MO 63841-1803
(573) 614-1000 • http://dexter.k12.mo.us/
Grade Span: PK-12; **Agency Type:** 1
Schools: 4
2 Primary; 1 Middle; 1 High; 0 Other Level
4 Regular; 0 Special Education; 0 Vocational; 0 Alternative
0 Magnet; 0 Charter; 2 Title I Eligible; 0 School-wide Title I
Students: 2,089 (48.8% male; 51.2% female)
Individual Education Program: 341 (16.3%);
English Language Learner: 0 (0.0%); Migrant: 2 (0.1%)
Eligible for Free Lunch Program: 668 (32.0%)
Eligible for Reduced-Price Lunch Program: 244 (11.7%)
Teachers: 139.0 (15.0 to 1)
Librarians/Media Specialists: 3.0 (696.3 to 1)
Guidance Counselors: 5.0 (417.8 to 1)
Current Spending: ($ per student per year):
Total: $5,430; Instruction: $3,690; Support Services: $1,448
Enrollment, Drop-out Rates and Diploma Recipients by Race/Ethnicity

Category	Total	White	Black	Asian	AIAN	Hisp.
Enrollment (%)	100.0	98.5	0.3	0.2	0.0	1.0
Drop-out Rate (%)	4.9	5.0	n/a	n/a	n/a	0.0
H.S. Diplomas (#)	120	120	0	0	0	0

Stone County

Reeds Spring R-IV

22595 Main St • Reeds Spring, MO 65737-0358
Mailing Address: PO Box 358 • Reeds Spring, MO 65737-0358
(417) 272-8173 • http://www.wolves.k12.mo.us/
Grade Span: PK-12; **Agency Type:** 1
Schools: 6
2 Primary; 1 Middle; 2 High; 1 Other Level
4 Regular; 0 Special Education; 1 Vocational; 1 Alternative
0 Magnet; 0 Charter; 3 Title I Eligible; 1 School-wide Title I
Students: 2,136 (52.9% male; 47.1% female)
Individual Education Program: 354 (16.6%);
English Language Learner: 11 (0.5%); Migrant: 0 (0.0%)
Eligible for Free Lunch Program: 784 (36.7%)
Eligible for Reduced-Price Lunch Program: 239 (11.2%)
Teachers: 150.0 (14.2 to 1)
Librarians/Media Specialists: 4.0 (534.0 to 1)
Guidance Counselors: 7.0 (305.1 to 1)
Current Spending: ($ per student per year):
Total: $5,908; Instruction: $3,722; Support Services: $1,800

Enrollment, Drop-out Rates and Diploma Recipients by Race/Ethnicity

Category	Total	White	Black	Asian	AIAN	Hisp.
Enrollment (%)	100.0	96.5	0.5	0.8	0.5	1.7
Drop-out Rate (%)	5.5	5.6	0.0	0.0	n/a	0.0
H.S. Diplomas (#)	115	110	0	3	1	1

Taney County

Branson R-IV

400 Cedar Ridge Dr • Branson, MO 65616-8143
(417) 334-6541 • http://www.branson.k12.mo.us/
Grade Span: PK-12; **Agency Type:** 1
Schools: 6
3 Primary; 2 Middle; 1 High; 0 Other Level
6 Regular; 0 Special Education; 0 Vocational; 0 Alternative
0 Magnet; 0 Charter; 5 Title I Eligible; 0 School-wide Title I
Students: 3,151 (50.9% male; 49.1% female)
Individual Education Program: 410 (13.0%);
English Language Learner: 85 (2.7%); Migrant: 3 (0.1%)
Eligible for Free Lunch Program: 884 (28.1%)
Eligible for Reduced-Price Lunch Program: 334 (10.6%)
Teachers: 216.6 (14.5 to 1)
Librarians/Media Specialists: 4.0 (787.8 to 1)
Guidance Counselors: 7.0 (450.1 to 1)
Current Spending: ($ per student per year):
Total: $5,745; Instruction: $3,672; Support Services: $1,881
Enrollment, Drop-out Rates and Diploma Recipients by Race/Ethnicity

Category	Total	White	Black	Asian	AIAN	Hisp.
Enrollment (%)	100.0	91.7	0.8	1.4	1.0	5.2
Drop-out Rate (%)	4.6	4.4	n/a	0.0	14.3	5.6
H.S. Diplomas (#)	164	159	0	0	1	4

Vernon County

Nevada R-V

800 W Hickory • Nevada, MO 64772-2059
(417) 448-2000 • http://www.nevada.k12.mo.us/
Grade Span: PK-12; **Agency Type:** 1
Schools: 7
3 Primary; 1 Middle; 2 High; 1 Other Level
5 Regular; 0 Special Education; 1 Vocational; 1 Alternative
0 Magnet; 0 Charter; 4 Title I Eligible; 0 School-wide Title I
Students: 2,621 (52.3% male; 47.7% female)
Individual Education Program: 397 (15.1%);
English Language Learner: 4 (0.2%); Migrant: 3 (0.1%)
Eligible for Free Lunch Program: 931 (35.5%)
Eligible for Reduced-Price Lunch Program: 206 (7.9%)
Teachers: 186.7 (14.0 to 1)
Librarians/Media Specialists: 3.0 (873.7 to 1)
Guidance Counselors: 8.5 (308.4 to 1)
Current Spending: ($ per student per year):
Total: $6,099; Instruction: $4,005; Support Services: $1,784
Enrollment, Drop-out Rates and Diploma Recipients by Race/Ethnicity

Category	Total	White	Black	Asian	AIAN	Hisp.
Enrollment (%)	100.0	95.5	3.0	0.5	0.3	0.7
Drop-out Rate (%)	1.8	1.7	0.0	n/a	0.0	14.3
H.S. Diplomas (#)	170	166	3	1	0	0

Warren County

Warren County R-III

302 Kuhl Ave • Warrenton, MO 63383-2116
(636) 456-6901 • http://www.warrencor3.org/
Grade Span: PK-12; **Agency Type:** 1
Schools: 4
1 Primary; 2 Middle; 1 High; 0 Other Level
4 Regular; 0 Special Education; 0 Vocational; 0 Alternative
0 Magnet; 0 Charter; 2 Title I Eligible; 0 School-wide Title I
Students: 2,690 (51.1% male; 48.9% female)
Individual Education Program: 449 (16.7%);
English Language Learner: 4 (0.1%); Migrant: 1 (<0.1%)
Eligible for Free Lunch Program: 569 (21.2%)
Eligible for Reduced-Price Lunch Program: 196 (7.3%)
Teachers: 183.0 (14.7 to 1)
Librarians/Media Specialists: 4.0 (672.5 to 1)
Guidance Counselors: 7.0 (384.3 to 1)
Current Spending: ($ per student per year):
Total: $4,995; Instruction: $3,025; Support Services: $1,733
Enrollment, Drop-out Rates and Diploma Recipients by Race/Ethnicity

Category	Total	White	Black	Asian	AIAN	Hisp.
Enrollment (%)	100.0	94.7	2.6	0.6	0.9	1.3
Drop-out Rate (%)	3.0	3.1	0.0	0.0	0.0	0.0
H.S. Diplomas (#)	175	169	1	0	1	4

Washington County

Potosi R-III

400 N Mine • Potosi, MO 63664-1734
(573) 438-5485 • http://www.potosi.k12.mo.us/
Grade Span: PK-12; **Agency Type:** 1
Schools: 5
2 Primary; 2 Middle; 1 High; 0 Other Level
5 Regular; 0 Special Education; 0 Vocational; 0 Alternative
0 Magnet; 0 Charter; 3 Title I Eligible; 0 School-wide Title I
Students: 2,394 (50.3% male; 49.7% female)
Individual Education Program: 341 (14.2%);
English Language Learner: 5 (0.2%); Migrant: 0 (0.0%)
Eligible for Free Lunch Program: 930 (38.8%)
Eligible for Reduced-Price Lunch Program: 208 (8.7%)
Teachers: 154.5 (15.5 to 1)
Librarians/Media Specialists: 2.9 (825.5 to 1)
Guidance Counselors: 5.7 (420.0 to 1)
Current Spending: ($ per student per year):
Total: $5,092; Instruction: $3,000; Support Services: $1,819
Enrollment, Drop-out Rates and Diploma Recipients by Race/Ethnicity

Category	Total	White	Black	Asian	AIAN	Hisp.
Enrollment (%)	100.0	97.7	1.2	0.6	0.1	0.4
Drop-out Rate (%)	6.9	6.5	16.7	0.0	33.3	0.0
H.S. Diplomas (#)	161	157	3	1	0	0

Webster County

Marshfield R-I

114 E Commercial • Marshfield, MO 65706-2104
(417) 859-2120 • http://www.mr1.k12.mo.us/
Grade Span: PK-12; **Agency Type:** 1
Schools: 5
2 Primary; 2 Middle; 1 High; 0 Other Level
5 Regular; 0 Special Education; 0 Vocational; 0 Alternative
0 Magnet; 0 Charter; 4 Title I Eligible; 0 School-wide Title I
Students: 2,930 (50.9% male; 49.1% female)
Individual Education Program: 430 (14.7%);
English Language Learner: 0 (0.0%); Migrant: 0 (0.0%)
Eligible for Free Lunch Program: 712 (24.3%)
Eligible for Reduced-Price Lunch Program: 267 (9.1%)
Teachers: 196.6 (14.9 to 1)
Librarians/Media Specialists: 5.0 (586.0 to 1)
Guidance Counselors: 7.0 (418.6 to 1)
Current Spending: ($ per student per year):
Total: $5,152; Instruction: $3,194; Support Services: $1,721
Enrollment, Drop-out Rates and Diploma Recipients by Race/Ethnicity

Category	Total	White	Black	Asian	AIAN	Hisp.
Enrollment (%)	100.0	97.1	0.5	1.1	0.1	1.1
Drop-out Rate (%)	6.7	6.7	0.0	0.0	0.0	16.7
H.S. Diplomas (#)	169	169	0	0	0	0

Wright County

Mountain Grove R-III

207 E Fifth • Mountain Grove, MO 65711-0806
Mailing Address: PO Box 806 • Mountain Grove, MO 65711-0806
(417) 926-3177 • http://www.mgr3.k12.mo.us/
Grade Span: PK-12; **Agency Type:** 1
Schools: 5
1 Primary; 1 Middle; 3 High; 0 Other Level
3 Regular; 0 Special Education; 1 Vocational; 1 Alternative
0 Magnet; 0 Charter; 2 Title I Eligible; 2 School-wide Title I
Students: 1,632 (51.3% male; 48.7% female)
Individual Education Program: 256 (15.7%);
English Language Learner: 0 (0.0%); Migrant: 0 (0.0%)
Eligible for Free Lunch Program: 705 (43.2%)
Eligible for Reduced-Price Lunch Program: 199 (12.2%)
Teachers: 127.2 (12.8 to 1)
Librarians/Media Specialists: 2.8 (582.9 to 1)
Guidance Counselors: 6.0 (272.0 to 1)
Current Spending: ($ per student per year):
Total: $6,845; Instruction: $4,674; Support Services: $1,804
Enrollment, Drop-out Rates and Diploma Recipients by Race/Ethnicity

Category	Total	White	Black	Asian	AIAN	Hisp.
Enrollment (%)	100.0	99.1	0.1	0.4	0.0	0.4
Drop-out Rate (%)	5.6	5.8	0.0	0.0	0.0	0.0
H.S. Diplomas (#)	101	101	0	0	0	0

Number of Schools

Rank	Number	District Name	City
1	124	Saint Louis City	Saint Louis
2	90	Kansas City 33	Kansas City
3	55	Springfield R-XII	Springfield
4	31	Columbia 93	Columbia
4	31	North Kansas City 74	Kansas City
6	30	Rockwood R-VI	Eureka
7	29	Saint Joseph	Saint Joseph
8	28	Parkway C-2	Chesterfield
9	25	Ferguson-Florissant R-II	Florissant
9	25	Hazelwood	Florissant
11	23	Fort Zumwalt R-II	O'fallon
11	23	Francis Howell R-III	Saint Charles
13	22	Blue Springs R-IV	Blue Springs
13	22	Lee's Summit R-VII	Lee's Summit
15	21	Independence 30	Independence
16	19	Joplin R-VIII	Joplin
17	17	Jefferson City	Jefferson City
17	17	Raytown C-2	Raytown
19	16	Hickman Mills C-1	Kansas City
19	16	Mehlville R-IX	Saint Louis
21	15	Fox C-6	Arnold
21	15	Liberty 53	Liberty
21	15	Park Hill	Kansas City
24	13	Riverview Gardens	Saint Louis
25	12	Normandy	Saint Louis
25	12	Saint Charles R-VI	Saint Charles
25	12	Washington	Washington
25	12	Waynesville R-VI	Waynesville
29	11	Northwest R-I	House Springs
29	11	Pattonville R-III	Saint Ann
29	11	Poplar Bluff R-I	Poplar Bluff
29	11	Special SD - Saint Louis County	Town & Ctry
33	10	Farmington R-VII	Farmington
33	10	Fort Osage R-I	Independence
33	10	Grandview C-4	Grandview
33	10	Jackson R-II	Jackson
33	10	Sikeston R-VI	Sikeston
33	10	University City	University City
33	10	Webb City R-VII	Webb City
33	10	Webster Groves	Webster Groves
41	9	Belton 124	Belton
41	9	Cape Girardeau 63	Cape Girardeau
41	9	Kennett 39	Kennett
41	9	Meramec Valley R-III	Pacific
41	9	Ritenour	Saint Louis
41	9	Sedalia 200	Sedalia
41	9	Warrensburg R-VI	Warrensburg
41	9	Wentzville R-IV	Wentzville
49	8	Camdenton R-III	Camdenton
49	8	Carthage R-IX	Carthage
49	8	Center 58	Kansas City
49	8	Hannibal 60	Hannibal
49	8	Kirkwood R-VII	Kirkwood
49	8	Lebanon R-III	Lebanon
49	8	Neosho R-V	Neosho
49	8	Nixa R-II	Nixa
49	8	Rolla 31	Rolla
58	7	Chillicothe R-II	Chillicothe
58	7	Excelsior Springs 40	Excelsior Spgs
58	7	Harrisonville R-IX	Harrisonville
58	7	Jennings	Jennings
58	7	Kearney R-I	Kearney
58	7	Lindbergh R-VIII	Saint Louis
58	7	Marshall	Marshall
58	7	Mcdonald County R-I	Anderson
58	7	Moberly	Moberly
58	7	Nevada R-V	Nevada
58	7	North Saint Francois County R-I	Bonne Terre
58	7	Platte County R-III	Platte City
58	7	Raymore-Peculiar R-II	Raymore
71	6	Bolivar R-I	Bolivar
71	6	Branson R-IV	Branson
71	6	Carl Junction R-I	Carl Junction
71	6	Clayton	Clayton
71	6	Hillsboro R-III	Hillsboro
71	6	Ladue	Saint Louis
71	6	Mexico 59	Mexico
71	6	New Madrid County R-I	New Madrid
71	6	Ozark R-VI	Ozark
71	6	Reeds Spring R-IV	Reeds Spring
71	6	Republic R-III	Republic
71	6	Savannah R-III	Savannah
71	6	Troy R-III	Troy
71	6	Willard R-II	Willard
85	5	Boonville R-I	Boonville
85	5	Cameron R-I	Cameron
85	5	Clinton	Clinton
85	5	Dallas County R-I	Buffalo
85	5	Eldon R-I	Eldon
85	5	Fulton 58	Fulton
85	5	Gasconade County R-II	Owensville
85	5	Kirksville R-III	Kirksville
85	5	Marshfield R-I	Marshfield
85	5	Monett R-I	Monett
85	5	Mountain Grove R-III	Mountain Grove
85	5	Perry County 32	Perryville
85	5	Potosi R-III	Potosi
85	5	Saint Clair R-XIII	Saint Clair
85	5	Union R-XI	Union
85	5	Warsaw R-IX	Warsaw
85	5	West Plains R-VII	West Plains
102	4	Affton 101	Saint Louis
102	4	Aurora R-VIII	Aurora
102	4	Bayless	Saint Louis
102	4	Cassville R-IV	Cassville
102	4	Central R-III	Park Hills
102	4	Desoto 73	Desoto
102	4	Dexter R-XI	Dexter
102	4	Doniphan R-I	Doniphan
102	4	Festus R-VI	Festus
102	4	Fredericktown R-I	Fredericktown
102	4	Grain Valley R-V	Grain Valley
102	4	Greene County R-VIII	Rogersville
102	4	Knob Noster R-VIII	Knob Noster
102	4	Morgan County R-II	Versailles
102	4	Oak Grove R-VI	Oak Grove
102	4	Odessa R-VII	Odessa
102	4	Pleasant Hill R-III	Pleasant Hill
102	4	Richmond R-XVI	Richmond
102	4	Sainte Genevieve County R-II	Ste Genevieve
102	4	Salem R-80	Salem
102	4	School of The Osage R-II	Lake Ozark
102	4	Smithville R-II	Smithville
102	4	Sullivan C-2	Sullivan
102	4	Warren County R-III	Warrenton
102	4	Windsor C-1	Imperial
102	4	Winfield R-IV	Winfield
128	3	Ava R-I	Ava
128	3	Caruthersville 18	Caruthersville
128	3	East Newton County R-VI	Granby
128	3	Hancock Place	Saint Louis
128	3	Saint James R-I	Saint James
128	3	Seneca R-VII	Seneca

Number of Teachers

Rank	Number	District Name	City
1	3,519	Saint Louis City	Saint Louis
2	2,643	Kansas City 33	Kansas City
3	2,165	Special SD - Saint Louis County	Town & Ctry
4	1,521	Springfield R-XII	Springfield
5	1,331	Rockwood R-VI	Eureka
6	1,255	Columbia 93	Columbia
7	1,218	Parkway C-2	Chesterfield
8	1,203	Francis Howell R-III	Saint Charles
9	1,189	North Kansas City 74	Kansas City
10	1,171	Hazelwood	Florissant
11	1,077	Fort Zumwalt R-II	O'fallon
12	956	Lee's Summit R-VII	Lee's Summit
13	844	Ferguson-Florissant R-II	Florissant
14	816	Blue Springs R-IV	Blue Springs
15	812	Saint Joseph	Saint Joseph
16	781	Independence 30	Independence
17	726	Fox C-6	Arnold
18	660	Mehlville R-IX	Saint Louis
19	627	Park Hill	Kansas City
20	573	Jefferson City	Jefferson City
21	559	Hickman Mills C-1	Kansas City
22	550	Raytown C-2	Raytown
23	514	Joplin R-VIII	Joplin
24	496	Liberty 53	Liberty
25	484	Northwest R-I	House Springs
26	482	Pattonville R-III	Saint Ann
27	448	Saint Charles R-VI	Saint Charles
28	444	Wentzville R-IV	Wentzville
29	437	Riverview Gardens	Saint Louis
30	380	Waynesville R-VI	Waynesville
31	363	Ritenour	Saint Louis
32	352	Lindbergh R-VIII	Saint Louis
33	350	Fort Osage R-I	Independence
34	344	Normandy	Saint Louis
35	338	Kirkwood R-VII	Kirkwood
36	334	Grandview C-4	Grandview
37	323	Cape Girardeau 63	Cape Girardeau
38	307	Poplar Bluff R-I	Poplar Bluff
39	297	Belton 124	Belton
40	294	Raymore-Peculiar R-II	Raymore
41	290	University City	University City
42	286	Sedalia 200	Sedalia
43	284	Jackson R-II	Jackson
44	281	Camdenton R-III	Camdenton
45	278	Lebanon R-III	Lebanon
46	278	Hannibal 60	Hannibal
47	278	Nixa R-II	Nixa
48	277	Webster Groves	Webster Groves
49	276	Ladue	Saint Louis
50	271	Washington	Washington
51	271	Rolla 31	Rolla
52	270	Neosho R-V	Neosho
53	261	Troy R-III	Troy
54	254	Meramec Valley R-III	Pacific
55	252	Farmington R-VII	Farmington
56	252	Sikeston R-VI	Sikeston
57	251	Ozark R-VI	Ozark
58	250	Carthage R-IX	Carthage
59	243	Warrensburg R-VI	Warrensburg
60	241	Willard R-II	Willard
61	231	Webb City R-VII	Webb City
62	231	Mcdonald County R-I	Anderson
63	229	Windsor C-1	Imperial
64	218	Clayton	Clayton
65	216	Branson R-IV	Branson
66	215	North Saint Francois County R-I	Bonne Terre
67	207	Hillsboro R-III	Hillsboro
68	204	Excelsior Springs 40	Excelsior Spgs
69	203	Center 58	Kansas City
70	202	Jennings	Jennings
71	201	Union R-XI	Union
72	196	Marshfield R-I	Marshfield
73	194	Kearney R-I	Kearney
74	189	Kirksville R-III	Kirksville
75	186	Nevada R-V	Nevada
76	183	Marshall	Marshall
77	183	Moberly	Moberly
78	183	Warren County R-III	Warrenton
79	182	Bolivar R-I	Bolivar
80	182	Carl Junction R-I	Carl Junction
81	181	Republic R-III	Republic
82	178	Mexico 59	Mexico
83	177	West Plains R-VII	West Plains
84	175	Perry County 32	Perryville
85	174	Fulton 58	Fulton
86	172	Desoto 73	Desoto
87	166	Savannah R-III	Savannah
88	166	Platte County R-III	Platte City
89	164	Saint Clair R-XIII	Saint Clair
90	163	Harrisonville R-IX	Harrisonville
91	163	Clinton	Clinton
92	159	Affton 101	Saint Louis
93	159	Dallas County R-I	Buffalo
94	159	New Madrid County R-I	New Madrid
95	157	Kennett 39	Kennett
96	156	Odessa R-VII	Odessa
97	155	Eldon R-I	Eldon
98	154	Potosi R-III	Potosi
99	153	Chillicothe R-II	Chillicothe
100	152	Festus R-VI	Festus
101	150	Reeds Spring R-IV	Reeds Spring
102	148	Monett R-I	Monett
103	147	Sullivan C-2	Sullivan
104	146	Aurora R-VIII	Aurora
105	142	Knob Noster R-VIII	Knob Noster
106	139	Dexter R-XI	Dexter
107	133	Sainte Genevieve County R-II	Ste Genevieve
108	131	Gasconade County R-II	Owensville
109	131	Central R-III	Park Hills
110	130	Grain Valley R-V	Grain Valley
111	127	Fredericktown R-I	Fredericktown
112	127	Mountain Grove R-III	Mountain Grove
113	125	Cassville R-IV	Cassville
114	123	Cameron R-I	Cameron
115	122	Saint James R-I	Saint James
116	122	Pleasant Hill R-III	Pleasant Hill
117	122	Oak Grove R-VI	Oak Grove
118	121	Richmond R-XVI	Richmond
119	120	Greene County R-VIII	Rogersville
120	118	School of The Osage R-II	Lake Ozark
121	118	Morgan County R-II	Versailles
122	118	Smithville R-II	Smithville
123	117	Doniphan R-I	Doniphan
124	114	Boonville R-I	Boonville
125	113	Hancock Place	Saint Louis
126	113	Caruthersville 18	Caruthersville
127	112	Ava R-I	Ava
127	112	Seneca R-VII	Seneca
129	108	Salem R-80	Salem
130	107	East Newton County R-VI	Granby
131	100	Winfield R-IV	Winfield
132	90	Warsaw R-IX	Warsaw
133	87	Bayless	Saint Louis

Number of Students

Rank	Number	District Name	City
1	45,480	Saint Louis City	Saint Louis
2	38,521	Kansas City 33	Kansas City

3	30,065	Special SD - Saint Louis County	Town & Ctry
4	24,626	Springfield R-XII	Springfield
5	22,313	Rockwood R-VI	Eureka
6	20,354	Parkway C-2	Chesterfield
7	19,721	Hazelwood	Florissant
8	19,239	Francis Howell R-III	Saint Charles
9	17,933	Fort Zumwalt R-II	O'fallon
10	17,296	North Kansas City 74	Kansas City
11	16,666	Columbia 93	Columbia
12	15,129	Lee's Summit R-VII	Lee's Summit
13	13,141	Blue Springs R-IV	Blue Springs
14	12,984	Ferguson-Florissant R-II	Florissant
15	11,979	Mehlville R-IX	Saint Louis
16	11,963	Independence 30	Independence
17	11,893	Saint Joseph	Saint Joseph
18	11,341	Fox C-6	Arnold
19	9,391	Park Hill	Kansas City
20	8,801	Raytown C-2	Raytown
21	8,338	Jefferson City	Jefferson City
22	7,837	Riverview Gardens	Saint Louis
23	7,733	Liberty 53	Liberty
24	7,654	Hickman Mills C-1	Kansas City
25	7,572	Northwest R-I	House Springs
26	7,415	Joplin R-VIII	Joplin
27	7,275	Wentzville R-IV	Wentzville
28	6,350	Ritenour	Saint Louis
29	6,216	Pattonville R-III	Saint Ann
30	5,941	Normandy	Saint Louis
31	5,879	Saint Charles R-VI	Saint Charles
32	5,368	Waynesville R-VI	Waynesville
33	5,289	Lindbergh R-VIII	Saint Louis
34	5,188	Kirkwood R-VII	Kirkwood
35	5,004	Fort Osage R-I	Independence
36	4,965	Belton 124	Belton
37	4,932	Troy R-III	Troy
38	4,918	Poplar Bluff R-I	Poplar Bluff
39	4,664	Jackson R-II	Jackson
40	4,643	Raymore-Peculiar R-II	Raymore
41	4,578	Lebanon R-III	Lebanon
42	4,483	Neosho R-V	Neosho
43	4,377	University City	University City
44	4,299	Grandview C-4	Grandview
45	4,166	Sedalia 200	Sedalia
46	4,130	Rolla 31	Rolla
47	4,127	Nixa R-II	Nixa
48	4,116	Webster Groves	Webster Groves
49	4,095	Camdenton R-III	Camdenton
50	4,078	Washington	Washington
51	4,010	Cape Girardeau 63	Cape Girardeau
52	4,001	Ozark R-VI	Ozark
53	3,915	Sikeston R-VI	Sikeston
54	3,903	Meramec Valley R-III	Pacific
55	3,818	Farmington R-VII	Farmington
56	3,742	Hannibal 60	Hannibal
57	3,687	Webb City R-VII	Webb City
58	3,661	Carthage R-IX	Carthage
59	3,623	Mcdonald County R-I	Anderson
60	3,592	Hillsboro R-III	Hillsboro
61	3,357	Willard R-II	Willard
62	3,344	Excelsior Springs 40	Excelsior Spgs
63	3,337	Kearney R-I	Kearney
64	3,275	Republic R-III	Republic
65	3,272	Ladue	Saint Louis
66	3,250	Warrensburg R-VI	Warrensburg
67	3,236	North Saint Francois County R-I	Bonne Terre
68	3,153	Jennings	Jennings
69	3,151	Branson R-IV	Branson
70	3,031	Windsor C-1	Imperial
71	3,029	Union R-XI	Union
72	2,930	Marshfield R-I	Marshfield
73	2,829	Desoto 73	Desoto
74	2,726	Carl Junction R-I	Carl Junction
75	2,690	Warren County R-III	Warrenton
76	2,672	Festus R-VI	Festus
77	2,633	Center 58	Kansas City
78	2,621	Nevada R-V	Nevada
79	2,571	Affton 101	Saint Louis
80	2,544	Harrisonville R-IX	Harrisonville
81	2,530	West Plains R-VII	West Plains
82	2,511	Mexico 59	Mexico
83	2,497	Clayton	Clayton
84	2,496	Bolivar R-I	Bolivar
85	2,472	Kirksville R-III	Kirksville
86	2,455	Saint Clair R-XIII	Saint Clair
87	2,451	Marshall	Marshall
88	2,398	Savannah R-III	Savannah
89	2,394	Potosi R-III	Potosi
90	2,360	Fulton 58	Fulton
91	2,323	Perry County 32	Perryville
92	2,316	Moberly	Moberly
93	2,312	Odessa R-VII	Odessa
94	2,304	Platte County R-III	Platte City
95	2,192	Kennett 39	Kennett
96	2,172	Sainte Genevieve County R-II	Ste Genevieve
97	2,138	Cassville R-IV	Cassville
98	2,136	Reeds Spring R-IV	Reeds Spring
99	2,134	Sullivan C-2	Sullivan
100	2,128	Chillicothe R-II	Chillicothe
101	2,123	Aurora R-VIII	Aurora
102	2,120	Dallas County R-I	Buffalo
103	2,092	Clinton	Clinton
104	2,089	Dexter R-XI	Dexter
105	2,061	Monett R-I	Monett
106	2,060	Pleasant Hill R-III	Pleasant Hill
107	2,050	Eldon R-I	Eldon
108	2,047	Grain Valley R-V	Grain Valley
109	2,030	New Madrid County R-I	New Madrid
110	2,017	Oak Grove R-VI	Oak Grove
111	1,958	Gasconade County R-II	Owensville
112	1,933	Greene County R-VIII	Rogersville
113	1,906	Fredericktown R-I	Fredericktown
114	1,863	Knob Noster R-VIII	Knob Noster
115	1,862	Hancock Place	Saint Louis
116	1,832	Saint James R-I	Saint James
117	1,810	Central R-III	Park Hills
118	1,804	Smithville R-II	Smithville
119	1,784	Richmond R-XVI	Richmond
120	1,755	Caruthersville 18	Caruthersville
121	1,698	Seneca R-VII	Seneca
122	1,685	Doniphan R-I	Doniphan
123	1,664	Morgan County R-II	Versailles
124	1,661	Winfield R-IV	Winfield
125	1,643	Cameron R-I	Cameron
126	1,633	Ava R-I	Ava
126	1,633	School of The Osage R-II	Lake Ozark
128	1,632	Mountain Grove R-III	Mountain Grove
129	1,538	Warsaw R-IX	Warsaw
130	1,521	Salem R-80	Salem
131	1,510	Bayless	Saint Louis
132	1,509	East Newton County R-VI	Granby
133	1,504	Boonville R-I	Boonville

Male Students

Rank	Percent	District Name	City
1	54.5	Greene County R-VIII	Rogersville
2	54.1	Windsor C-1	Imperial
3	53.6	Cameron R-I	Cameron
4	53.4	Odessa R-VII	Odessa
5	53.2	Harrisonville R-IX	Harrisonville
6	53.1	Camdenton R-III	Camdenton
6	53.1	Cassville R-IV	Cassville
8	52.9	Fort Osage R-I	Independence
8	52.9	Grandview C-4	Grandview
8	52.9	Reeds Spring R-IV	Reeds Spring
11	52.8	Dallas County R-I	Buffalo
11	52.8	Hickman Mills C-1	Kansas City
13	52.7	Belton 124	Belton
14	52.6	Moberly	Moberly
14	52.6	Salem R-80	Salem
16	52.5	New Madrid County R-I	New Madrid
16	52.5	North Saint Francois County R-I	Bonne Terre
16	52.5	Richmond R-XVI	Richmond
16	52.5	Sullivan C-2	Sullivan
20	52.4	Carl Junction R-I	Carl Junction
21	52.3	Desoto 73	Desoto
21	52.3	Excelsior Springs 40	Excelsior Spgs
21	52.3	Knob Noster R-VIII	Knob Noster
21	52.3	Meramec Valley R-III	Pacific
21	52.3	Neosho R-V	Neosho
21	52.3	Nevada R-V	Nevada
21	52.3	Oak Grove R-VI	Oak Grove
21	52.3	Raytown C-2	Raytown
21	52.3	Saint Clair R-XIII	Saint Clair
21	52.3	Webster Groves	Webster Groves
31	52.2	Pleasant Hill R-III	Pleasant Hill
32	52.1	Clinton	Clinton
32	52.1	Ozark R-VI	Ozark
32	52.1	Saint Charles R-VI	Saint Charles
32	52.1	Washington	Washington
36	52.0	Bolivar R-I	Bolivar
36	52.0	Francis Howell R-III	Saint Charles
38	51.9	Carthage R-IX	Carthage
38	51.9	Fox C-6	Arnold
38	51.9	Kirksville R-III	Kirksville
38	51.9	Liberty 53	Liberty
42	51.8	Columbia 93	Columbia
42	51.8	Jackson R-II	Jackson
42	51.8	Pattonville R-III	Saint Ann
42	51.8	Perry County 32	Perryville
42	51.8	Saint Louis City	Saint Louis
42	51.8	Savannah R-III	Savannah
42	51.8	Wentzville R-IV	Wentzville
49	51.7	Boonville R-I	Boonville
49	51.7	Eldon R-I	Eldon
49	51.7	Lee's Summit R-VII	Lee's Summit
52	51.6	Blue Springs R-IV	Blue Springs
52	51.6	Ferguson-Florissant R-II	Florissant
52	51.6	Fulton 58	Fulton
52	51.6	Grain Valley R-V	Grain Valley
52	51.6	North Kansas City 74	Kansas City
57	51.5	Farmington R-VII	Farmington
57	51.5	Seneca R-VII	Seneca
57	51.5	Waynesville R-VI	Waynesville
57	51.5	Webb City R-VII	Webb City
57	51.5	Winfield R-IV	Winfield
62	51.4	Mcdonald County R-I	Anderson
62	51.4	West Plains R-VII	West Plains
64	51.3	Fredericktown R-I	Fredericktown
64	51.3	Mountain Grove R-III	Mountain Grove
64	51.3	Park Hill	Kansas City
64	51.3	Platte County R-III	Platte City
64	51.3	Ritenour	Saint Louis
69	51.2	Caruthersville 18	Caruthersville
69	51.2	Center 58	Kansas City
69	51.2	Hazelwood	Florissant
69	51.2	Independence 30	Independence
69	51.2	Lebanon R-III	Lebanon
69	51.2	Mehlville R-IX	Saint Louis
69	51.2	Normandy	Saint Louis
69	51.2	Sainte Genevieve County R-II	Ste Genevieve
69	51.2	School of The Osage R-II	Lake Ozark
69	51.2	Troy R-III	Troy
79	51.1	Chillicothe R-II	Chillicothe
79	51.1	Clayton	Clayton
79	51.1	Lindbergh R-VIII	Saint Louis
79	51.1	Riverview Gardens	Saint Louis
79	51.1	Rockwood R-VI	Eureka
79	51.1	Sedalia 200	Sedalia
79	51.1	Warren County R-III	Warrenton
86	51.0	Fort Zumwalt R-II	O'fallon
86	51.0	Morgan County R-II	Versailles
86	51.0	Northwest R-I	House Springs
86	51.0	Poplar Bluff R-I	Poplar Bluff
86	51.0	Sikeston R-VI	Sikeston
91	50.9	Branson R-IV	Branson
91	50.9	Kansas City 33	Kansas City
91	50.9	Kearney R-I	Kearney
91	50.9	Kirkwood R-VII	Kirkwood
91	50.9	Marshfield R-I	Marshfield
91	50.9	Mexico 59	Mexico
97	50.8	East Newton County R-VI	Granby
97	50.8	Joplin R-VIII	Joplin
97	50.8	Saint Joseph	Saint Joseph
100	50.7	Affton 101	Saint Louis
100	50.7	Springfield R-XII	Springfield
102	50.6	Ava R-I	Ava
102	50.6	Monett R-I	Monett
102	50.6	Parkway C-2	Chesterfield
105	50.5	Hillsboro R-III	Hillsboro
105	50.5	Nixa R-II	Nixa
105	50.5	Willard R-II	Willard
108	50.4	Republic R-III	Republic
108	50.4	Rolla 31	Rolla
108	50.4	University City	University City
111	50.3	Hancock Place	Saint Louis
111	50.3	Jefferson City	Jefferson City
111	50.3	Potosi R-III	Potosi
114	50.2	Smithville R-II	Smithville
114	50.2	Union R-XI	Union
116	50.1	Aurora R-VIII	Aurora
116	50.1	Cape Girardeau 63	Cape Girardeau
116	50.1	Festus R-VI	Festus
116	50.1	Jennings	Jennings
120	50.0	Warrensburg R-VI	Warrensburg
121	49.8	Marshall	Marshall
121	49.8	Raymore-Peculiar R-II	Raymore
123	49.7	Hannibal 60	Hannibal
124	49.6	Gasconade County R-II	Owensville
124	49.6	Ladue	Saint Louis
126	49.5	Saint James R-I	Saint James
127	49.3	Central R-III	Park Hills
128	49.2	Kennett 39	Kennett
128	49.2	Warsaw R-IX	Warsaw
130	49.1	Bayless	Saint Louis
131	48.8	Dexter R-XI	Dexter
132	48.3	Doniphan R-I	Doniphan
133	n/a	Special SD - Saint Louis County	Town & Ctry

Female Students

Rank	Percent	District Name	City
1	51.7	Doniphan R-I	Doniphan
2	51.2	Dexter R-XI	Dexter
3	50.9	Bayless	Saint Louis
4	50.8	Kennett 39	Kennett
4	50.8	Warsaw R-IX	Warsaw
6	50.7	Central R-III	Park Hills
7	50.5	Saint James R-I	Saint James

Rank	Percent	District Name	City
8	50.4	Gasconade County R-II	Owensville
8	50.4	Ladue	Saint Louis
10	50.3	Hannibal 60	Hannibal
11	50.2	Marshall	Marshall
11	50.2	Raymore-Peculiar R-II	Raymore
13	50.0	Warrensburg R-VI	Warrensburg
14	49.9	Aurora R-VIII	Aurora
14	49.9	Cape Girardeau 63	Cape Girardeau
14	49.9	Festus R-VI	Festus
14	49.9	Jennings	Jennings
18	49.8	Smithville R-II	Smithville
18	49.8	Union R-XI	Union
20	49.7	Hancock Place	Saint Louis
20	49.7	Jefferson City	Jefferson City
20	49.7	Potosi R-III	Potosi
23	49.6	Republic R-III	Republic
23	49.6	Rolla 31	Rolla
23	49.6	University City	University City
26	49.5	Hillsboro R-III	Hillsboro
26	49.5	Nixa R-II	Nixa
26	49.5	Willard R-II	Willard
29	49.4	Ava R-I	Ava
29	49.4	Monett R-I	Monett
29	49.4	Parkway C-2	Chesterfield
32	49.3	Affton 101	Saint Louis
32	49.3	Springfield R-XII	Springfield
34	49.2	East Newton County R-VI	Granby
34	49.2	Joplin R-VIII	Joplin
34	49.2	Saint Joseph	Saint Joseph
37	49.1	Branson R-IV	Branson
37	49.1	Kansas City 33	Kansas City
37	49.1	Kearney R-I	Kearney
37	49.1	Kirkwood R-VII	Kirkwood
37	49.1	Marshfield R-I	Marshfield
37	49.1	Mexico 59	Mexico
43	49.0	Fort Zumwalt R-II	O'fallon
43	49.0	Morgan County R-II	Versailles
43	49.0	Northwest R-I	House Springs
43	49.0	Poplar Bluff R-I	Poplar Bluff
43	49.0	Sikeston R-VI	Sikeston
48	48.9	Chillicothe R-II	Chillicothe
48	48.9	Clayton	Clayton
48	48.9	Lindbergh R-VIII	Saint Louis
48	48.9	Riverview Gardens	Saint Louis
48	48.9	Rockwood R-VI	Eureka
48	48.9	Sedalia 200	Sedalia
48	48.9	Warren County R-III	Warrenton
55	48.8	Caruthersville 18	Caruthersville
55	48.8	Center 58	Kansas City
55	48.8	Hazelwood	Florissant
55	48.8	Independence 30	Independence
55	48.8	Lebanon R-III	Lebanon
55	48.8	Mehlville R-IX	Saint Louis
55	48.8	Normandy	Saint Louis
55	48.8	Sainte Genevieve County R-II	Ste Genevieve
55	48.8	School of The Osage R-II	Lake Ozark
55	48.8	Troy R-III	Troy
65	48.7	Fredericktown R-I	Fredericktown
65	48.7	Mountain Grove R-III	Mountain Grove
65	48.7	Park Hill	Kansas City
65	48.7	Platte County R-III	Platte City
65	48.7	Ritenour	Saint Louis
70	48.6	Mcdonald County R-I	Anderson
70	48.6	West Plains R-VII	West Plains
72	48.5	Farmington R-VII	Farmington
72	48.5	Seneca R-VII	Seneca
72	48.5	Waynesville R-VI	Waynesville
72	48.5	Webb City R-VII	Webb City
72	48.5	Winfield R-IV	Winfield
77	48.4	Blue Springs R-IV	Blue Springs
77	48.4	Ferguson-Florissant R-II	Florissant
77	48.4	Fulton 58	Fulton
77	48.4	Grain Valley R-V	Grain Valley
77	48.4	North Kansas City 74	Kansas City
82	48.3	Boonville R-I	Boonville
82	48.3	Eldon R-I	Eldon
82	48.3	Lee's Summit R-VII	Lee's Summit
85	48.2	Columbia 93	Columbia
85	48.2	Jackson R-II	Jackson
85	48.2	Pattonville R-III	Saint Ann
85	48.2	Perry County 32	Perryville
85	48.2	Saint Louis City	Saint Louis
85	48.2	Savannah R-III	Savannah
85	48.2	Wentzville R-IV	Wentzville
92	48.1	Carthage R-IX	Carthage
92	48.1	Fox C-6	Arnold
92	48.1	Kirksville R-III	Kirksville
92	48.1	Liberty 53	Liberty
96	48.0	Bolivar R-I	Bolivar
96	48.0	Francis Howell R-III	Saint Charles
98	47.9	Clinton	Clinton
98	47.9	Ozark R-VI	Ozark
98	47.9	Saint Charles R-VI	Saint Charles
98	47.9	Washington	Washington
102	47.8	Pleasant Hill R-III	Pleasant Hill
103	47.7	Desoto 73	Desoto
103	47.7	Excelsior Springs 40	Excelsior Spgs
103	47.7	Knob Noster R-VIII	Knob Noster
103	47.7	Meramec Valley R-III	Pacific
103	47.7	Neosho R-V	Neosho
103	47.7	Nevada R-V	Nevada
103	47.7	Oak Grove R-VI	Oak Grove
103	47.7	Raytown C-2	Raytown
103	47.7	Saint Clair R-XIII	Saint Clair
103	47.7	Webster Groves	Webster Groves
113	47.6	Carl Junction R-I	Carl Junction
114	47.5	New Madrid County R-I	New Madrid
114	47.5	North Saint Francois County R-I	Bonne Terre
114	47.5	Richmond R-XVI	Richmond
114	47.5	Sullivan C-2	Sullivan
118	47.4	Moberly	Moberly
118	47.4	Salem R-80	Salem
120	47.3	Belton 124	Belton
121	47.2	Dallas County R-I	Buffalo
121	47.2	Hickman Mills C-1	Kansas City
123	47.1	Fort Osage R-I	Independence
123	47.1	Grandview C-4	Grandview
123	47.1	Reeds Spring R-IV	Reeds Spring
126	46.9	Camdenton R-III	Camdenton
126	46.9	Cassville R-IV	Cassville
128	46.8	Harrisonville R-IX	Harrisonville
129	46.6	Odessa R-VII	Odessa
130	46.4	Cameron R-I	Cameron
131	45.9	Windsor C-1	Imperial
132	45.5	Greene County R-VIII	Rogersville
133	n/a	Special SD - Saint Louis County	Town & Ctry

Individual Education Program Students

Rank	Percent	District Name	City
1	93.6	Special SD - Saint Louis County	Town & Ctry
2	21.8	Marshall	Marshall
3	20.8	Perry County 32	Perryville
4	20.5	Washington	Washington
5	19.5	Kirkwood R-VII	Kirkwood
6	19.2	Central R-III	Park Hills
6	19.2	Saint James R-I	Saint James
8	18.5	Warrensburg R-VI	Warrensburg
9	18.4	Jefferson City	Jefferson City
9	18.4	Moberly	Moberly
11	18.3	Cape Girardeau 63	Cape Girardeau
12	18.0	Pattonville R-III	Saint Ann
13	17.7	Northwest R-I	House Springs
14	17.6	Greene County R-VIII	Rogersville
15	17.5	Ferguson-Florissant R-II	Florissant
15	17.5	Kirksville R-III	Kirksville
15	17.5	New Madrid County R-I	New Madrid
15	17.5	Winfield R-IV	Winfield
19	17.4	Desoto 73	Desoto
19	17.4	Mehlville R-IX	Saint Louis
19	17.4	Ritenour	Saint Louis
22	17.2	Fox C-6	Arnold
22	17.2	Jennings	Jennings
24	17.1	Affton 101	Saint Louis
24	17.1	Wentzville R-IV	Wentzville
26	16.9	Meramec Valley R-III	Pacific
27	16.8	Farmington R-VII	Farmington
27	16.8	Fort Osage R-I	Independence
27	16.8	Parkway C-2	Chesterfield
30	16.7	Chillicothe R-II	Chillicothe
30	16.7	Hannibal 60	Hannibal
30	16.7	Saint Charles R-VI	Saint Charles
30	16.7	Sedalia 200	Sedalia
30	16.7	Warren County R-III	Warrenton
35	16.6	Hazelwood	Florissant
35	16.6	Reeds Spring R-IV	Reeds Spring
35	16.6	Rockwood R-VI	Eureka
35	16.6	Willard R-II	Willard
39	16.5	Sullivan C-2	Sullivan
39	16.5	Troy R-III	Troy
39	16.5	Warsaw R-IX	Warsaw
42	16.4	Columbia 93	Columbia
42	16.4	Lindbergh R-VIII	Saint Louis
44	16.3	Clayton	Clayton
44	16.3	Clinton	Clinton
44	16.3	Dexter R-XI	Dexter
47	16.2	Riverview Gardens	Saint Louis
47	16.2	Webster Groves	Webster Groves
49	16.1	Saint Louis City	Saint Louis
50	16.0	Cameron R-I	Cameron
51	15.7	Fort Zumwalt R-II	O'fallon
51	15.7	Independence 30	Independence
51	15.7	Mountain Grove R-III	Mountain Grove
54	15.6	Cassville R-IV	Cassville
54	15.6	Joplin R-VIII	Joplin
56	15.5	Bayless	Saint Louis
56	15.5	University City	University City
58	15.3	Hancock Place	Saint Louis
59	15.2	Center 58	Kansas City
59	15.2	Kennett 39	Kennett
61	15.1	Carl Junction R-I	Carl Junction
61	15.1	Nevada R-V	Nevada
63	15.0	Francis Howell R-III	Saint Charles
63	15.0	Ladue	Saint Louis
63	15.0	Poplar Bluff R-I	Poplar Bluff
66	14.9	Monett R-I	Monett
67	14.8	Knob Noster R-VIII	Knob Noster
67	14.8	Normandy	Saint Louis
67	14.8	Saint Clair R-XIII	Saint Clair
70	14.7	Bolivar R-I	Bolivar
70	14.7	Hickman Mills C-1	Kansas City
70	14.7	Marshfield R-I	Marshfield
70	14.7	Ozark R-VI	Ozark
74	14.6	Hillsboro R-III	Hillsboro
75	14.5	Waynesville R-VI	Waynesville
76	14.4	East Newton County R-VI	Granby
76	14.4	North Kansas City 74	Kansas City
78	14.3	Caruthersville 18	Caruthersville
78	14.3	Eldon R-I	Eldon
78	14.3	Union R-XI	Union
81	14.2	Potosi R-III	Potosi
82	14.1	Camdenton R-III	Camdenton
82	14.1	Park Hill	Kansas City
84	14.0	Mexico 59	Mexico
84	14.0	Sainte Genevieve County R-II	Ste Genevieve
84	14.0	Seneca R-VII	Seneca
87	13.8	Gasconade County R-II	Owensville
87	13.8	Neosho R-V	Neosho
89	13.7	Ava R-I	Ava
89	13.7	Morgan County R-II	Versailles
91	13.6	North Saint Francois County R-I	Bonne Terre
91	13.6	Pleasant Hill R-III	Pleasant Hill
91	13.6	Richmond R-XVI	Richmond
91	13.6	School of The Osage R-II	Lake Ozark
95	13.5	Windsor C-1	Imperial
96	13.4	Odessa R-VII	Odessa
97	13.3	Doniphan R-I	Doniphan
97	13.3	Salem R-80	Salem
97	13.3	Webb City R-VII	Webb City
100	13.0	Branson R-IV	Branson
100	13.0	Oak Grove R-VI	Oak Grove
100	13.0	Rolla 31	Rolla
100	13.0	Springfield R-XII	Springfield
104	12.9	Fulton 58	Fulton
104	12.9	Grandview C-4	Grandview
104	12.9	Republic R-III	Republic
107	12.8	Jackson R-II	Jackson
108	12.6	Carthage R-IX	Carthage
109	12.4	Lebanon R-III	Lebanon
109	12.4	Saint Joseph	Saint Joseph
111	12.3	Boonville R-I	Boonville
111	12.3	Dallas County R-I	Buffalo
111	12.3	Lee's Summit R-VII	Lee's Summit
114	12.2	Nixa R-II	Nixa
115	12.0	Savannah R-III	Savannah
116	11.8	Aurora R-VIII	Aurora
116	11.8	Blue Springs R-IV	Blue Springs
118	11.7	Raytown C-2	Raytown
119	11.6	Kearney R-I	Kearney
120	11.5	Belton 124	Belton
120	11.5	Excelsior Springs 40	Excelsior Spgs
120	11.5	Kansas City 33	Kansas City
123	11.3	Grain Valley R-V	Grain Valley
124	11.2	Festus R-VI	Festus
124	11.2	Fredericktown R-I	Fredericktown
124	11.2	Liberty 53	Liberty
127	11.1	Mcdonald County R-I	Anderson
128	11.0	Smithville R-II	Smithville
128	11.0	West Plains R-VII	West Plains
130	10.9	Platte County R-III	Platte City
131	10.3	Harrisonville R-IX	Harrisonville
132	8.5	Raymore-Peculiar R-II	Raymore
133	8.4	Sikeston R-VI	Sikeston

English Language Learner Students

Rank	Percent	District Name	City
1	11.5	Mcdonald County R-I	Anderson
1	11.5	Monett R-I	Monett
3	9.6	Bayless	Saint Louis
4	6.4	Carthage R-IX	Carthage
5	6.3	Kansas City 33	Kansas City
6	6.0	Marshall	Marshall
7	5.9	Saint Louis City	Saint Louis
8	5.1	Affton 101	Saint Louis
9	4.7	Clayton	Clayton
10	4.0	Hancock Place	Saint Louis
11	3.6	Sedalia 200	Sedalia
12	3.4	Jefferson City	Jefferson City

Rank	Percent	District Name	City
13	3.1	Knob Noster R-VIII	Knob Noster
14	3.0	Neosho R-V	Neosho
15	2.9	Ritenour	Saint Louis
16	2.7	Branson R-IV	Branson
17	2.3	Pattonville R-III	Saint Ann
18	2.2	Mehlville R-IX	Saint Louis
19	2.1	Columbia 93	Columbia
19	2.1	Hickman Mills C-1	Kansas City
19	2.1	Park Hill	Kansas City
19	2.1	Saint Charles R-VI	Saint Charles
23	1.8	Center 58	Kansas City
23	1.8	North Kansas City 74	Kansas City
23	1.8	Parkway C-2	Chesterfield
26	1.7	Belton 124	Belton
26	1.7	Cassville R-IV	Cassville
28	1.6	Warrensburg R-VI	Warrensburg
29	1.5	Hazelwood	Florissant
29	1.5	Independence 30	Independence
31	1.4	Aurora R-VIII	Aurora
32	1.3	Grandview C-4	Grandview
32	1.3	Lindbergh R-VIII	Saint Louis
34	1.0	Joplin R-VIII	Joplin
34	1.0	Rockwood R-VI	Eureka
36	0.9	West Plains R-VII	West Plains
37	0.8	Cape Girardeau 63	Cape Girardeau
37	0.8	East Newton County R-VI	Granby
37	0.8	Ladue	Saint Louis
37	0.8	Perry County 32	Perryville
37	0.8	Raytown C-2	Raytown
37	0.8	University City	University City
43	0.7	Lee's Summit R-VII	Lee's Summit
43	0.7	Springfield R-XII	Springfield
43	0.7	Webster Groves	Webster Groves
46	0.6	Ferguson-Florissant R-II	Florissant
46	0.6	Fox C-6	Arnold
46	0.6	Francis Howell R-III	Saint Charles
46	0.6	Kennett 39	Kennett
46	0.6	Platte County R-III	Platte City
51	0.5	Blue Springs R-IV	Blue Springs
51	0.5	Hillsboro R-III	Hillsboro
51	0.5	Reeds Spring R-IV	Reeds Spring
51	0.5	Washington	Washington
51	0.5	Waynesville R-VI	Waynesville
51	0.5	Willard R-II	Willard
57	0.4	Ava R-I	Ava
57	0.4	Camdenton R-III	Camdenton
57	0.4	Caruthersville 18	Caruthersville
57	0.4	Kirkwood R-VII	Kirkwood
57	0.4	Liberty 53	Liberty
57	0.4	Saint Joseph	Saint Joseph
57	0.4	Wentzville R-IV	Wentzville
64	0.3	Carl Junction R-I	Carl Junction
64	0.3	Eldon R-I	Eldon
64	0.3	Mexico 59	Mexico
64	0.3	Morgan County R-II	Versailles
64	0.3	Northwest R-I	House Springs
64	0.3	Odessa R-VII	Odessa
64	0.3	Saint James R-I	Saint James
64	0.3	Sikeston R-VI	Sikeston
72	0.2	Bolivar R-I	Bolivar
72	0.2	Central R-III	Park Hills
72	0.2	Dallas County R-I	Buffalo
72	0.2	Farmington R-VII	Farmington
72	0.2	Fort Osage R-I	Independence
72	0.2	Fort Zumwalt R-II	O'fallon
72	0.2	Fredericktown R-I	Fredericktown
72	0.2	Fulton 58	Fulton
72	0.2	Nevada R-V	Nevada
72	0.2	Ozark R-VI	Ozark
72	0.2	Potosi R-III	Potosi
72	0.2	Rolla 31	Rolla
72	0.2	Union R-XI	Union
85	0.1	Cameron R-I	Cameron
85	0.1	Excelsior Springs 40	Excelsior Spgs
85	0.1	Gasconade County R-II	Owensville
85	0.1	Jackson R-II	Jackson
85	0.1	Kirksville R-III	Kirksville
85	0.1	Lebanon R-III	Lebanon
85	0.1	Moberly	Moberly
85	0.1	Poplar Bluff R-I	Poplar Bluff
85	0.1	Riverview Gardens	Saint Louis
85	0.1	Sainte Genevieve County R-II	Ste Genevieve
85	0.1	School of The Osage R-II	Lake Ozark
85	0.1	Troy R-III	Troy
85	0.1	Warren County R-III	Warrenton
85	0.1	Windsor C-1	Imperial
99	0.0	Grain Valley R-V	Grain Valley
99	0.0	Meramec Valley R-III	Pacific
99	0.0	Nixa R-II	Nixa
99	0.0	Savannah R-III	Savannah
99	0.0	Sullivan C-2	Sullivan
104	0.0	Boonville R-I	Boonville
104	0.0	Chillicothe R-II	Chillicothe
104	0.0	Clinton	Clinton
104	0.0	Desoto 73	Desoto
104	0.0	Dexter R-XI	Dexter
104	0.0	Doniphan R-I	Doniphan
104	0.0	Festus R-VI	Festus
104	0.0	Greene County R-VIII	Rogersville
104	0.0	Hannibal 60	Hannibal
104	0.0	Harrisonville R-IX	Harrisonville
104	0.0	Jennings	Jennings
104	0.0	Kearney R-I	Kearney
104	0.0	Marshfield R-I	Marshfield
104	0.0	Mountain Grove R-III	Mountain Grove
104	0.0	New Madrid County R-I	New Madrid
104	0.0	Normandy	Saint Louis
104	0.0	North Saint Francois County R-I	Bonne Terre
104	0.0	Oak Grove R-VI	Oak Grove
104	0.0	Pleasant Hill R-III	Pleasant Hill
104	0.0	Raymore-Peculiar R-II	Raymore
104	0.0	Republic R-III	Republic
104	0.0	Richmond R-XVI	Richmond
104	0.0	Saint Clair R-XIII	Saint Clair
104	0.0	Salem R-80	Salem
104	0.0	Seneca R-VII	Seneca
104	0.0	Smithville R-II	Smithville
104	0.0	Warsaw R-IX	Warsaw
104	0.0	Webb City R-VII	Webb City
104	0.0	Winfield R-IV	Winfield
133	n/a	Special SD - Saint Louis County	Town & Ctry

Migrant Students

Rank	Percent	District Name	City
1	15.0	Monett R-I	Monett
2	13.3	Mcdonald County R-I	Anderson
3	8.8	Sedalia 200	Sedalia
4	7.8	Marshall	Marshall
5	5.5	Carthage R-IX	Carthage
6	5.4	Knob Noster R-VIII	Knob Noster
7	4.5	Neosho R-V	Neosho
8	3.2	Cassville R-IV	Cassville
9	3.0	Kennett 39	Kennett
10	2.2	Aurora R-VIII	Aurora
11	1.2	Saint Charles R-VI	Saint Charles
12	1.1	East Newton County R-VI	Granby
13	0.7	Mexico 59	Mexico
13	0.7	Warsaw R-IX	Warsaw
13	0.7	Webb City R-VII	Webb City
16	0.6	Joplin R-VIII	Joplin
16	0.6	Kansas City 33	Kansas City
18	0.5	Fredericktown R-I	Fredericktown
18	0.5	Springfield R-XII	Springfield
20	0.4	Saint Louis City	Saint Louis
20	0.4	Warrensburg R-VI	Warrensburg
22	0.3	Ava R-I	Ava
22	0.3	Belton 124	Belton
22	0.3	Platte County R-III	Platte City
22	0.3	Seneca R-VII	Seneca
26	0.2	Caruthersville 18	Caruthersville
26	0.2	Morgan County R-II	Versailles
26	0.2	Nixa R-II	Nixa
29	0.1	Branson R-IV	Branson
29	0.1	Dexter R-XI	Dexter
29	0.1	Kirksville R-III	Kirksville
29	0.1	Meramec Valley R-III	Pacific
29	0.1	Nevada R-V	Nevada
29	0.1	New Madrid County R-I	New Madrid
29	0.1	Ozark R-VI	Ozark
29	0.1	Richmond R-XVI	Richmond
29	0.1	Willard R-II	Willard
38	0.0	Dallas County R-I	Buffalo
38	0.0	Hannibal 60	Hannibal
38	0.0	Lee's Summit R-VII	Lee's Summit
38	0.0	Mehlville R-IX	Saint Louis
38	0.0	Normandy	Saint Louis
38	0.0	Ritenour	Saint Louis
38	0.0	Rockwood R-VI	Eureka
38	0.0	Warren County R-III	Warrenton
38	0.0	Washington	Washington
38	0.0	Windsor C-1	Imperial
48	0.0	Affton 101	Saint Louis
48	0.0	Bayless	Saint Louis
48	0.0	Blue Springs R-IV	Blue Springs
48	0.0	Bolivar R-I	Bolivar
48	0.0	Boonville R-I	Boonville
48	0.0	Camdenton R-III	Camdenton
48	0.0	Cameron R-I	Cameron
48	0.0	Cape Girardeau 63	Cape Girardeau
48	0.0	Carl Junction R-I	Carl Junction
48	0.0	Center 58	Kansas City
48	0.0	Central R-III	Park Hills
48	0.0	Chillicothe R-II	Chillicothe
48	0.0	Clayton	Clayton
48	0.0	Clinton	Clinton
48	0.0	Columbia 93	Columbia
48	0.0	Desoto 73	Desoto
48	0.0	Doniphan R-I	Doniphan
48	0.0	Eldon R-I	Eldon
48	0.0	Excelsior Springs 40	Excelsior Spgs
48	0.0	Farmington R-VII	Farmington
48	0.0	Ferguson-Florissant R-II	Florissant
48	0.0	Festus R-VI	Festus
48	0.0	Fort Osage R-I	Independence
48	0.0	Fort Zumwalt R-II	O'fallon
48	0.0	Fox C-6	Arnold
48	0.0	Francis Howell R-III	Saint Charles
48	0.0	Fulton 58	Fulton
48	0.0	Gasconade County R-II	Owensville
48	0.0	Grain Valley R-V	Grain Valley
48	0.0	Grandview C-4	Grandview
48	0.0	Greene County R-VIII	Rogersville
48	0.0	Hancock Place	Saint Louis
48	0.0	Harrisonville R-IX	Harrisonville
48	0.0	Hazelwood	Florissant
48	0.0	Hickman Mills C-1	Kansas City
48	0.0	Hillsboro R-III	Hillsboro
48	0.0	Independence 30	Independence
48	0.0	Jackson R-II	Jackson
48	0.0	Jefferson City	Jefferson City
48	0.0	Jennings	Jennings
48	0.0	Kearney R-I	Kearney
48	0.0	Kirkwood R-VII	Kirkwood
48	0.0	Ladue	Saint Louis
48	0.0	Lebanon R-III	Lebanon
48	0.0	Liberty 53	Liberty
48	0.0	Lindbergh R-VIII	Saint Louis
48	0.0	Marshfield R-I	Marshfield
48	0.0	Moberly	Moberly
48	0.0	Mountain Grove R-III	Mountain Grove
48	0.0	North Kansas City 74	Kansas City
48	0.0	North Saint Francois County R-I	Bonne Terre
48	0.0	Northwest R-I	House Springs
48	0.0	Oak Grove R-VI	Oak Grove
48	0.0	Odessa R-VII	Odessa
48	0.0	Park Hill	Kansas City
48	0.0	Parkway C-2	Chesterfield
48	0.0	Pattonville R-III	Saint Ann
48	0.0	Perry County 32	Perryville
48	0.0	Pleasant Hill R-III	Pleasant Hill
48	0.0	Poplar Bluff R-I	Poplar Bluff
48	0.0	Potosi R-III	Potosi
48	0.0	Raymore-Peculiar R-II	Raymore
48	0.0	Raytown C-2	Raytown
48	0.0	Reeds Spring R-IV	Reeds Spring
48	0.0	Republic R-III	Republic
48	0.0	Riverview Gardens	Saint Louis
48	0.0	Rolla 31	Rolla
48	0.0	Saint Clair R-XIII	Saint Clair
48	0.0	Saint James R-I	Saint James
48	0.0	Saint Joseph	Saint Joseph
48	0.0	Sainte Genevieve County R-II	Ste Genevieve
48	0.0	Salem R-80	Salem
48	0.0	Savannah R-III	Savannah
48	0.0	School of The Osage R-II	Lake Ozark
48	0.0	Sikeston R-VI	Sikeston
48	0.0	Smithville R-II	Smithville
48	0.0	Special SD - Saint Louis County	Town & Ctry
48	0.0	Sullivan C-2	Sullivan
48	0.0	Troy R-III	Troy
48	0.0	Union R-XI	Union
48	0.0	University City	University City
48	0.0	Waynesville R-VI	Waynesville
48	0.0	Webster Groves	Webster Groves
48	0.0	Wentzville R-IV	Wentzville
48	0.0	West Plains R-VII	West Plains
48	0.0	Winfield R-IV	Winfield

Students Eligible for Free Lunch

Rank	Percent	District Name	City
1	72.1	Normandy	Saint Louis
2	70.7	Saint Louis City	Saint Louis
3	66.8	Jennings	Jennings
4	64.9	Riverview Gardens	Saint Louis
5	59.5	Kansas City 33	Kansas City
6	59.4	Caruthersville 18	Caruthersville
7	53.2	Kennett 39	Kennett
8	50.3	New Madrid County R-I	New Madrid
9	47.6	Mcdonald County R-I	Anderson
10	46.8	Sikeston R-VI	Sikeston
11	46.3	Doniphan R-I	Doniphan
12	44.9	Central R-III	Park Hills
13	44.3	Ava R-I	Ava
14	43.9	Hickman Mills C-1	Kansas City
15	43.3	University City	University City
16	43.2	Mountain Grove R-III	Mountain Grove

17	42.4	Warsaw R-IX	Warsaw
18	42.0	East Newton County R-VI	Granby
19	41.8	Hancock Place	Saint Louis
20	41.5	Poplar Bluff R-I	Poplar Bluff
21	41.0	Center 58	Kansas City
22	39.0	Hannibal 60	Hannibal
23	38.8	Potosi R-III	Potosi
24	38.5	Ferguson-Florissant R-II	Florissant
24	38.5	West Plains R-VII	West Plains
26	38.4	Moberly	Moberly
27	38.3	School of The Osage R-II	Lake Ozark
28	38.2	Joplin R-VIII	Joplin
29	38.0	Saint Joseph	Saint Joseph
30	37.3	Saint James R-I	Saint James
31	37.2	Marshall	Marshall
32	37.1	Morgan County R-II	Versailles
33	36.9	Aurora R-VIII	Aurora
33	36.9	Ritenour	Saint Louis
35	36.7	Monett R-I	Monett
35	36.7	Reeds Spring R-IV	Reeds Spring
35	36.7	Sedalia 200	Sedalia
38	35.5	Nevada R-V	Nevada
39	35.3	Cape Girardeau 63	Cape Girardeau
40	35.2	Dallas County R-I	Buffalo
41	35.0	Fredericktown R-I	Fredericktown
42	34.4	Eldon R-I	Eldon
42	34.4	Webb City R-VII	Webb City
44	33.9	Neosho R-V	Neosho
45	33.2	Carthage R-IX	Carthage
45	33.2	Grandview C-4	Grandview
47	32.2	Cassville R-IV	Cassville
48	32.0	Dexter R-XI	Dexter
49	31.5	Clinton	Clinton
50	31.3	Mexico 59	Mexico
51	31.1	Bolivar R-I	Bolivar
52	30.9	Lebanon R-III	Lebanon
52	30.9	Rolla 31	Rolla
54	30.2	Farmington R-VII	Farmington
55	30.1	North Saint Francois County R-I	Bonne Terre
56	30.0	Fulton 58	Fulton
57	29.9	Camdenton R-III	Camdenton
58	29.4	Salem R-80	Salem
58	29.4	Winfield R-IV	Winfield
60	29.1	Saint Clair R-XIII	Saint Clair
60	29.1	Seneca R-VII	Seneca
62	28.8	Springfield R-XII	Springfield
63	28.1	Branson R-IV	Branson
64	27.4	Perry County 32	Perryville
65	26.8	Sullivan C-2	Sullivan
66	26.6	Desoto 73	Desoto
67	26.4	Sainte Genevieve County R-II	Ste Genevieve
68	25.9	Carl Junction R-I	Carl Junction
68	25.9	Jefferson City	Jefferson City
70	25.7	Excelsior Springs 40	Excelsior Spgs
71	25.4	Independence 30	Independence
72	25.3	Boonville R-I	Boonville
73	25.1	Richmond R-XVI	Richmond
74	25.0	Kirksville R-III	Kirksville
75	24.3	Marshfield R-I	Marshfield
76	24.0	Fort Osage R-I	Independence
76	24.0	Hazelwood	Florissant
78	23.9	Columbia 93	Columbia
79	22.4	Meramec Valley R-III	Pacific
80	22.1	Raytown C-2	Raytown
81	21.7	Chillicothe R-II	Chillicothe
82	21.6	Festus R-VI	Festus
83	21.4	Northwest R-I	House Springs
83	21.4	Republic R-III	Republic
85	21.3	Cameron R-I	Cameron
86	21.2	Warren County R-III	Warrenton
87	21.1	Gasconade County R-II	Owensville
88	20.6	Odessa R-VII	Odessa
89	20.4	Savannah R-III	Savannah
90	20.1	Troy R-III	Troy
91	19.9	Union R-XI	Union
92	19.2	Waynesville R-VI	Waynesville
93	18.8	Warrensburg R-VI	Warrensburg
94	18.7	Saint Charles R-VI	Saint Charles
95	18.6	Willard R-II	Willard
96	18.3	Hillsboro R-III	Hillsboro
97	17.9	Belton 124	Belton
98	17.7	Bayless	Saint Louis
99	17.5	North Kansas City 74	Kansas City
100	17.3	Pattonville R-III	Saint Ann
101	16.7	Fox C-6	Arnold
101	16.7	Harrisonville R-IX	Harrisonville
103	16.4	Knob Noster R-VIII	Knob Noster
104	16.0	Nixa R-II	Nixa
105	15.6	Jackson R-II	Jackson
106	14.1	Greene County R-VIII	Rogersville
107	14.0	Ozark R-VI	Ozark
108	13.7	Wentzville R-IV	Wentzville
109	12.7	Oak Grove R-VI	Oak Grove
110	12.3	Windsor C-1	Imperial
111	11.9	Washington	Washington
112	11.4	Platte County R-III	Platte City
113	10.7	Pleasant Hill R-III	Pleasant Hill
113	10.7	Raymore-Peculiar R-II	Raymore
115	10.5	Park Hill	Kansas City
116	10.0	Grain Valley R-V	Grain Valley
117	9.5	Affton 101	Saint Louis
117	9.5	Webster Groves	Webster Groves
119	7.9	Liberty 53	Liberty
120	7.8	Mehlville R-IX	Saint Louis
121	7.0	Kirkwood R-VII	Kirkwood
122	6.9	Blue Springs R-IV	Blue Springs
123	6.5	Fort Zumwalt R-II	O'fallon
124	5.8	Lee's Summit R-VII	Lee's Summit
125	5.2	Ladue	Saint Louis
126	5.0	Smithville R-II	Smithville
127	4.5	Francis Howell R-III	Saint Charles
127	4.5	Lindbergh R-VIII	Saint Louis
129	4.4	Kearney R-I	Kearney
130	3.0	Clayton	Clayton
130	3.0	Parkway C-2	Chesterfield
132	2.4	Rockwood R-VI	Eureka
133	n/a	Special SD - Saint Louis County	Town & Ctry

Students Eligible for Reduced-Price Lunch

Rank	Percent	District Name	City
1	16.2	Knob Noster R-VIII	Knob Noster
2	15.9	Waynesville R-VI	Waynesville
3	12.7	Morgan County R-II	Versailles
4	12.6	Doniphan R-I	Doniphan
5	12.2	Mountain Grove R-III	Mountain Grove
6	11.9	Eldon R-I	Eldon
7	11.8	Fredericktown R-I	Fredericktown
8	11.7	Dexter R-XI	Dexter
9	11.5	Boonville R-I	Boonville
10	11.3	Central R-III	Park Hills
11	11.2	Reeds Spring R-IV	Reeds Spring
12	11.1	Perry County 32	Perryville
13	11.0	Ava R-I	Ava
13	11.0	Hickman Mills C-1	Kansas City
15	10.9	East Newton County R-VI	Granby
15	10.9	Saint James R-I	Saint James
15	10.9	Sainte Genevieve County R-II	Ste Genevieve
18	10.8	Saint Joseph	Saint Joseph
18	10.8	Seneca R-VII	Seneca
20	10.6	Branson R-IV	Branson
21	10.5	Bayless	Saint Louis
21	10.5	Jennings	Jennings
21	10.5	Riverview Gardens	Saint Louis
21	10.5	Webb City R-VII	Webb City
25	10.2	Farmington R-VII	Farmington
26	10.0	Mcdonald County R-I	Anderson
27	9.6	Neosho R-V	Neosho
28	9.5	Fulton 58	Fulton
28	9.5	Moberly	Moberly
30	9.4	Camdenton R-III	Camdenton
30	9.4	Cassville R-IV	Cassville
30	9.4	Hancock Place	Saint Louis
33	9.3	Gasconade County R-II	Owensville
33	9.3	North Saint Francois County R-I	Bonne Terre
35	9.2	Willard R-II	Willard
36	9.1	Fort Osage R-I	Independence
36	9.1	Marshfield R-I	Marshfield
38	9.0	Bolivar R-I	Bolivar
38	9.0	Carl Junction R-I	Carl Junction
38	9.0	Independence 30	Independence
41	8.8	Ferguson-Florissant R-II	Florissant
41	8.8	Monett R-I	Monett
43	8.7	Potosi R-III	Potosi
44	8.4	Mexico 59	Mexico
44	8.4	Union R-XI	Union
46	8.3	Cameron R-I	Cameron
46	8.3	North Kansas City 74	Kansas City
46	8.3	Warsaw R-IX	Warsaw
49	8.2	Center 58	Kansas City
50	8.1	Chillicothe R-II	Chillicothe
50	8.1	Joplin R-VIII	Joplin
50	8.1	Lebanon R-III	Lebanon
53	8.0	Dallas County R-I	Buffalo
53	8.0	Sedalia 200	Sedalia
55	7.9	Nevada R-V	Nevada
56	7.8	Raytown C-2	Raytown
57	7.7	Richmond R-XVI	Richmond
57	7.7	Springfield R-XII	Springfield
57	7.7	University City	University City
60	7.6	Hannibal 60	Hannibal
60	7.6	Kansas City 33	Kansas City
60	7.6	Meramec Valley R-III	Pacific
60	7.6	Nixa R-II	Nixa
60	7.6	Savannah R-III	Savannah
65	7.5	Poplar Bluff R-I	Poplar Bluff
65	7.5	Rolla 31	Rolla
65	7.5	School of The Osage R-II	Lake Ozark
68	7.4	Northwest R-I	House Springs
68	7.4	Ritenour	Saint Louis
70	7.3	Aurora R-VIII	Aurora
70	7.3	Warren County R-III	Warrenton
72	7.2	Sullivan C-2	Sullivan
73	7.1	Republic R-III	Republic
74	7.0	Marshall	Marshall
75	6.8	Grandview C-4	Grandview
75	6.8	Saint Clair R-XIII	Saint Clair
77	6.6	Carthage R-IX	Carthage
77	6.6	Kirksville R-III	Kirksville
77	6.6	New Madrid County R-I	New Madrid
77	6.6	Warrensburg R-VI	Warrensburg
81	6.4	Belton 124	Belton
81	6.4	Excelsior Springs 40	Excelsior Spgs
83	6.2	Pattonville R-III	Saint Ann
84	6.1	Fox C-6	Arnold
84	6.1	Hazelwood	Florissant
86	6.0	Hillsboro R-III	Hillsboro
86	6.0	Jefferson City	Jefferson City
86	6.0	Normandy	Saint Louis
86	6.0	Salem R-80	Salem
90	5.8	Jackson R-II	Jackson
91	5.6	Desoto 73	Desoto
91	5.6	Ozark R-VI	Ozark
91	5.6	Troy R-III	Troy
91	5.6	Windsor C-1	Imperial
95	5.4	Affton 101	Saint Louis
95	5.4	Odessa R-VII	Odessa
97	5.3	Festus R-VI	Festus
97	5.3	Platte County R-III	Platte City
99	5.2	Harrisonville R-IX	Harrisonville
99	5.2	Oak Grove R-VI	Oak Grove
99	5.2	Washington	Washington
102	5.1	Cape Girardeau 63	Cape Girardeau
102	5.1	West Plains R-VII	West Plains
104	5.0	Clinton	Clinton
104	5.0	Greene County R-VIII	Rogersville
106	4.9	Saint Charles R-VI	Saint Charles
107	4.5	Saint Louis City	Saint Louis
107	4.5	Sikeston R-VI	Sikeston
109	4.3	Columbia 93	Columbia
110	4.2	Kennett 39	Kennett
110	4.2	Pleasant Hill R-III	Pleasant Hill
110	4.2	Winfield R-IV	Winfield
113	3.8	Park Hill	Kansas City
114	3.5	Raymore-Peculiar R-II	Raymore
114	3.5	Wentzville R-IV	Wentzville
116	3.4	Caruthersville 18	Caruthersville
117	3.2	Blue Springs R-IV	Blue Springs
118	3.0	Fort Zumwalt R-II	O'fallon
119	2.9	Liberty 53	Liberty
120	2.6	Mehlville R-IX	Saint Louis
120	2.6	Smithville R-II	Smithville
122	2.3	Lee's Summit R-VII	Lee's Summit
122	2.3	Lindbergh R-VIII	Saint Louis
124	2.2	Webster Groves	Webster Groves
125	2.1	Kirkwood R-VII	Kirkwood
126	2.0	Grain Valley R-V	Grain Valley
127	1.8	Kearney R-I	Kearney
128	1.6	Francis Howell R-III	Saint Charles
129	1.4	Ladue	Saint Louis
130	1.2	Parkway C-2	Chesterfield
131	1.1	Clayton	Clayton
131	1.1	Rockwood R-VI	Eureka
133	n/a	Special SD - Saint Louis County	Town & Ctry

Student/Teacher Ratio

Rank	Ratio	District Name	City
1	18.9	Troy R-III	Troy
2	18.1	Mehlville R-IX	Saint Louis
2	18.1	Republic R-III	Republic
4	17.9	Riverview Gardens	Saint Louis
5	17.5	Festus R-VI	Festus
5	17.5	Ritenour	Saint Louis
7	17.4	Bayless	Saint Louis
8	17.3	Hillsboro R-III	Hillsboro
9	17.2	Normandy	Saint Louis
10	17.1	Kearney R-I	Kearney
11	17.0	Cassville R-IV	Cassville
11	17.0	Warsaw R-IX	Warsaw
13	16.8	Hazelwood	Florissant
13	16.8	Pleasant Hill R-III	Pleasant Hill
13	16.8	Rockwood R-VI	Eureka
16	16.7	Belton 124	Belton
16	16.7	Parkway C-2	Chesterfield
18	16.6	Fort Zumwalt R-II	O'fallon

18	16.6	Neosho R-V	Neosho
20	16.5	Oak Grove R-VI	Oak Grove
20	16.5	Winfield R-IV	Winfield
22	16.4	Desoto 73	Desoto
22	16.4	Excelsior Springs 40	Excelsior Spgs
22	16.4	Hancock Place	Saint Louis
22	16.4	Jackson R-II	Jackson
22	16.4	Lebanon R-III	Lebanon
22	16.4	Wentzville R-IV	Wentzville
28	16.3	Sainte Genevieve County R-II	Ste Genevieve
29	16.2	Springfield R-XII	Springfield
30	16.1	Affton 101	Saint Louis
30	16.1	Blue Springs R-IV	Blue Springs
30	16.1	Greene County R-VIII	Rogersville
33	16.0	Francis Howell R-III	Saint Charles
33	16.0	Poplar Bluff R-I	Poplar Bluff
33	16.0	Raytown C-2	Raytown
33	16.0	Webb City R-VII	Webb City
37	15.9	Ozark R-VI	Ozark
38	15.8	Lee's Summit R-VII	Lee's Summit
38	15.8	Raymore-Peculiar R-II	Raymore
40	15.7	Grain Valley R-V	Grain Valley
40	15.7	Mcdonald County R-I	Anderson
42	15.6	Fox C-6	Arnold
42	15.6	Jennings	Jennings
42	15.6	Liberty 53	Liberty
42	15.6	Northwest R-I	House Springs
46	15.5	Caruthersville 18	Caruthersville
46	15.5	Harrisonville R-IX	Harrisonville
46	15.5	Potosi R-III	Potosi
46	15.5	Sikeston R-VI	Sikeston
50	15.4	Ferguson-Florissant R-II	Florissant
50	15.4	Meramec Valley R-III	Pacific
52	15.3	Independence 30	Independence
52	15.3	Kirkwood R-VII	Kirkwood
52	15.3	Smithville R-II	Smithville
55	15.2	Rolla 31	Rolla
56	15.1	Farmington R-VII	Farmington
56	15.1	Seneca R-VII	Seneca
56	15.1	Union R-XI	Union
56	15.1	University City	University City
60	15.0	Dexter R-XI	Dexter
60	15.0	Lindbergh R-VIII	Saint Louis
60	15.0	North Saint Francois County R-I	Bonne Terre
60	15.0	Park Hill	Kansas City
60	15.0	Washington	Washington
65	14.9	Carl Junction R-I	Carl Junction
65	14.9	Fredericktown R-I	Fredericktown
65	14.9	Gasconade County R-II	Owensville
65	14.9	Marshfield R-I	Marshfield
65	14.9	Saint Clair R-XIII	Saint Clair
65	14.9	Saint James R-I	Saint James
71	14.8	Nixa R-II	Nixa
71	14.8	Webster Groves	Webster Groves
73	14.7	Odessa R-VII	Odessa
73	14.7	Warren County R-III	Warrenton
75	14.6	Carthage R-IX	Carthage
75	14.6	Kansas City 33	Kansas City
75	14.6	Richmond R-XVI	Richmond
75	14.6	Saint Joseph	Saint Joseph
79	14.5	Aurora R-VIII	Aurora
79	14.5	Ava R-I	Ava
79	14.5	Branson R-IV	Branson
79	14.5	Camdenton R-III	Camdenton
79	14.5	Jefferson City	Jefferson City
79	14.5	North Kansas City 74	Kansas City
79	14.5	Sedalia 200	Sedalia
79	14.5	Sullivan C-2	Sullivan
87	14.4	Joplin R-VIII	Joplin
87	14.4	Savannah R-III	Savannah
89	14.3	Doniphan R-I	Doniphan
89	14.3	Fort Osage R-I	Independence
89	14.3	West Plains R-VII	West Plains
92	14.2	Reeds Spring R-IV	Reeds Spring
93	14.1	East Newton County R-VI	Granby
93	14.1	Mexico 59	Mexico
93	14.1	Morgan County R-II	Versailles
93	14.1	Salem R-80	Salem
93	14.1	Waynesville R-VI	Waynesville
98	14.0	Nevada R-V	Nevada
99	13.9	Chillicothe R-II	Chillicothe
99	13.9	Kennett 39	Kennett
99	13.9	Monett R-I	Monett
99	13.9	Platte County R-III	Platte City
99	13.9	Special SD - Saint Louis County	Town & Ctry
99	13.9	Willard R-II	Willard
105	13.8	Central R-III	Park Hills
105	13.8	School of The Osage R-II	Lake Ozark
107	13.7	Bolivar R-I	Bolivar
107	13.7	Hickman Mills C-1	Kansas City
109	13.5	Fulton 58	Fulton
110	13.4	Hannibal 60	Hannibal
111	13.3	Cameron R-I	Cameron
111	13.3	Columbia 93	Columbia
111	13.3	Dallas County R-I	Buffalo
111	13.3	Marshall	Marshall
111	13.3	Perry County 32	Perryville
111	13.3	Warrensburg R-VI	Warrensburg
117	13.2	Eldon R-I	Eldon
117	13.2	Windsor C-1	Imperial
119	13.1	Boonville R-I	Boonville
119	13.1	Kirksville R-III	Kirksville
119	13.1	Knob Noster R-VIII	Knob Noster
119	13.1	Saint Charles R-VI	Saint Charles
123	12.9	Center 58	Kansas City
123	12.9	Pattonville R-III	Saint Ann
123	12.9	Saint Louis City	Saint Louis
126	12.8	Clinton	Clinton
126	12.8	Grandview C-4	Grandview
126	12.8	Mountain Grove R-III	Mountain Grove
126	12.8	New Madrid County R-I	New Madrid
130	12.6	Moberly	Moberly
131	12.4	Cape Girardeau 63	Cape Girardeau
132	11.8	Ladue	Saint Louis
133	11.4	Clayton	Clayton

Student/Librarian Ratio

Rank	Ratio	District Name	City
1	1,445.6	Meramec Valley R-III	Pacific
2	1,233.0	Troy R-III	Troy
3	1,111.5	Saint Joseph	Saint Joseph
4	1,087.2	Jennings	Jennings
5	1,086.0	Sainte Genevieve County R-II	Ste Genevieve
6	1,064.0	Chillicothe R-II	Chillicothe
7	1,024.6	Wentzville R-IV	Wentzville
8	1,011.6	Raytown C-2	Raytown
9	1,010.8	Blue Springs R-IV	Blue Springs
10	975.5	Desoto 73	Desoto
11	935.5	Hannibal 60	Hannibal
12	931.0	Hancock Place	Saint Louis
13	926.8	Washington	Washington
14	909.8	Fort Osage R-I	Independence
15	905.8	Mcdonald County R-I	Anderson
16	896.6	Neosho R-V	Neosho
17	873.7	Nevada R-V	Nevada
18	864.6	Saint Charles R-VI	Saint Charles
19	851.3	Francis Howell R-III	Saint Charles
20	848.7	Normandy	Saint Louis
21	843.3	West Plains R-VII	West Plains
22	842.5	Doniphan R-I	Doniphan
23	836.0	Excelsior Springs 40	Excelsior Spgs
24	825.5	Potosi R-III	Potosi
25	819.0	Camdenton R-III	Camdenton
26	818.3	Saint Clair R-XIII	Saint Clair
27	817.0	Marshall	Marshall
28	787.8	Branson R-IV	Branson
29	774.3	Perry County 32	Perryville
30	769.0	Warsaw R-IX	Warsaw
31	763.0	Lebanon R-III	Lebanon
32	757.3	Union R-XI	Union
33	757.1	Dallas County R-I	Buffalo
34	755.6	Lindbergh R-VIII	Saint Louis
35	749.4	Savannah R-III	Savannah
36	741.6	Kearney R-I	Kearney
37	730.4	Mehlville R-IX	Saint Louis
38	718.4	Hillsboro R-III	Hillsboro
39	712.5	Riverview Gardens	Saint Louis
40	711.8	Sikeston R-VI	Sikeston
41	711.3	Sullivan C-2	Sullivan
42	707.7	Aurora R-VIII	Aurora
43	707.1	Kennett 39	Kennett
44	697.3	Clinton	Clinton
45	696.3	Dexter R-XI	Dexter
46	688.3	Rolla 31	Rolla
47	686.7	Pleasant Hill R-III	Pleasant Hill
48	680.9	North Kansas City 74	Kansas City
49	680.3	Rockwood R-VI	Eureka
50	676.7	Fort Zumwalt R-II	O'fallon
51	672.5	Warren County R-III	Warrenton
52	668.0	Festus R-VI	Festus
53	665.2	Parkway C-2	Chesterfield
54	661.8	Hazelwood	Florissant
55	658.3	Center 58	Kansas City
55	658.3	Platte County R-III	Platte City
57	655.0	Republic R-III	Republic
58	654.3	Saint James R-I	Saint James
59	650.0	Warrensburg R-VI	Warrensburg
60	647.2	North Saint Francois County R-I	Bonne Terre
61	642.8	Affton 101	Saint Louis
62	641.1	Lee's Summit R-VII	Lee's Summit
63	636.5	Belton 124	Belton
64	636.3	Farmington R-VII	Farmington
65	636.0	Harrisonville R-IX	Harrisonville
65	636.0	Raymore-Peculiar R-II	Raymore
67	635.0	Ritenour	Saint Louis
68	630.1	Fox C-6	Arnold
69	626.1	Park Hill	Kansas City
70	625.3	University City	University City
71	624.0	Bolivar R-I	Bolivar
72	618.0	Kirksville R-III	Kirksville
73	617.9	Joplin R-VIII	Joplin
74	614.5	Webb City R-VII	Webb City
75	606.2	Windsor C-1	Imperial
76	604.1	Liberty 53	Liberty
77	597.9	Jackson R-II	Jackson
78	595.1	Sedalia 200	Sedalia
79	593.4	Springfield R-XII	Springfield
80	588.9	Columbia 93	Columbia
81	586.0	Marshfield R-I	Marshfield
82	582.9	Mountain Grove R-III	Mountain Grove
83	580.0	Carl Junction R-I	Carl Junction
84	579.0	Moberly	Moberly
85	578.0	Odessa R-VII	Odessa
86	572.8	Winfield R-IV	Winfield
87	571.6	Ozark R-VI	Ozark
88	566.0	Seneca R-VII	Seneca
89	559.5	Willard R-II	Willard
90	558.0	Mexico 59	Mexico
91	557.7	Nixa R-II	Nixa
92	548.7	Northwest R-I	House Springs
93	547.7	Cameron R-I	Cameron
94	546.7	Hickman Mills C-1	Kansas City
95	546.4	Poplar Bluff R-I	Poplar Bluff
96	544.3	Ava R-I	Ava
97	534.5	Cassville R-IV	Cassville
98	534.0	Reeds Spring R-IV	Reeds Spring
99	523.0	Carthage R-IX	Carthage
100	521.1	Jefferson City	Jefferson City
101	518.0	Pattonville R-III	Saint Ann
102	516.8	Saint Louis City	Saint Louis
103	515.3	Monett R-I	Monett
104	513.6	Kansas City 33	Kansas City
105	512.5	Eldon R-I	Eldon
106	511.8	Grain Valley R-V	Grain Valley
107	507.5	New Madrid County R-I	New Madrid
108	507.0	Salem R-80	Salem
109	505.8	Grandview C-4	Grandview
110	504.3	Oak Grove R-VI	Oak Grove
111	503.0	East Newton County R-VI	Granby
112	501.3	Boonville R-I	Boonville
112	501.3	Cape Girardeau 63	Cape Girardeau
114	499.4	Ferguson-Florissant R-II	Florissant
115	498.5	Independence 30	Independence
116	483.3	Greene County R-VIII	Rogersville
117	476.5	Fredericktown R-I	Fredericktown
118	473.1	Webster Groves	Webster Groves
119	472.0	Fulton 58	Fulton
120	471.6	Kirkwood R-VII	Kirkwood
121	467.4	Ladue	Saint Louis
122	465.8	Knob Noster R-VIII	Knob Noster
123	446.0	Richmond R-XVI	Richmond
124	438.8	Caruthersville 18	Caruthersville
125	408.3	School of The Osage R-II	Lake Ozark
126	399.6	Gasconade County R-II	Owensville
127	397.6	Waynesville R-VI	Waynesville
128	377.5	Bayless	Saint Louis
129	362.0	Central R-III	Park Hills
130	361.7	Morgan County R-II	Versailles
131	360.8	Smithville R-II	Smithville
132	297.3	Clayton	Clayton
133	n/a	Special SD - Saint Louis County	Town & Ctry

Student/Counselor Ratio

Rank	Ratio	District Name	City
1	584.9	Savannah R-III	Savannah
2	549.3	Warsaw R-IX	Warsaw
3	530.3	Troy R-III	Troy
4	519.6	Ozark R-VI	Ozark
5	498.1	Neosho R-V	Neosho
6	483.3	New Madrid County R-I	New Madrid
7	476.7	Kearney R-I	Kearney
8	473.3	Northwest R-I	House Springs
9	472.1	Saint Clair R-XIII	Saint Clair
10	466.5	Hillsboro R-III	Hillsboro
11	464.3	Raymore-Peculiar R-II	Raymore
12	460.2	Greene County R-VIII	Rogersville
13	452.5	Sainte Genevieve County R-II	Ste Genevieve
14	451.4	Warrensburg R-VI	Warrensburg
15	450.1	Branson R-IV	Branson
16	449.1	Wentzville R-IV	Wentzville
17	445.4	Cassville R-IV	Cassville
18	444.5	Raytown C-2	Raytown
19	443.8	East Newton County R-VI	Granby
20	443.1	Independence 30	Independence
21	438.8	Caruthersville 18	Caruthersville
22	435.5	Grain Valley R-V	Grain Valley

23	433.7	Meramec Valley R-III	Pacific
24	432.3	Lee's Summit R-VII	Lee's Summit
25	431.7	Belton 124	Belton
26	426.8	Sullivan C-2	Sullivan
27	426.4	Fox C-6	Arnold
28	424.2	Farmington R-VII	Farmington
29	423.3	Ritenour	Saint Louis
30	423.2	Hancock Place	Saint Louis
31	420.0	Potosi R-III	Potosi
32	419.4	Carl Junction R-I	Carl Junction
33	418.7	Ava R-I	Ava
34	418.6	Marshfield R-I	Marshfield
35	417.8	Dexter R-XI	Dexter
36	416.2	Lebanon R-III	Lebanon
37	415.4	Marshall	Marshall
38	415.3	Winfield R-IV	Winfield
39	412.5	Riverview Gardens	Saint Louis
40	411.1	Festus R-VI	Festus
41	409.7	Webb City R-VII	Webb City
42	404.1	Desoto 73	Desoto
43	403.4	Oak Grove R-VI	Oak Grove
44	402.6	Mcdonald County R-I	Anderson
45	402.2	Central R-III	Park Hills
46	398.5	Fort Zumwalt R-II	O'fallon
47	394.1	Jennings	Jennings
48	393.0	Nixa R-II	Nixa
49	391.9	Jackson R-II	Jackson
50	391.3	Park Hill	Kansas City
51	390.2	Mehlville R-IX	Saint Louis
52	390.0	Bolivar R-I	Bolivar
53	386.8	Eldon R-I	Eldon
54	386.0	Aurora R-VIII	Aurora
55	385.3	Odessa R-VII	Odessa
56	384.7	Washington	Washington
57	384.3	Warren County R-III	Warrenton
58	382.1	Cameron R-I	Cameron
59	380.8	Republic R-III	Republic
60	380.7	North Saint Francois County R-I	Bonne Terre
61	379.1	Liberty 53	Liberty
62	378.9	Windsor C-1	Imperial
63	378.8	Saint Joseph	Saint Joseph
64	377.3	Seneca R-VII	Seneca
65	376.0	North Kansas City 74	Kansas City
66	373.0	Willard R-II	Willard
67	372.1	Francis Howell R-III	Saint Charles
67	372.1	Hazelwood	Florissant
69	371.6	Excelsior Springs 40	Excelsior Spgs
70	371.4	Springfield R-XII	Springfield
71	367.1	Blue Springs R-IV	Blue Springs
72	366.1	Carthage R-IX	Carthage
73	360.8	Smithville R-II	Smithville
74	356.8	Richmond R-XVI	Richmond
75	356.4	Union R-XI	Union
76	351.3	Poplar Bluff R-I	Poplar Bluff
77	349.5	Normandy	Saint Louis
78	348.5	Harrisonville R-IX	Harrisonville
79	346.5	Rockwood R-VI	Eureka
80	345.8	Kansas City 33	Kansas City
81	345.7	Saint James R-I	Saint James
82	345.3	Ferguson-Florissant R-II	Florissant
83	343.3	Pleasant Hill R-III	Pleasant Hill
84	341.5	Sedalia 200	Sedalia
85	341.2	Lindbergh R-VIII	Saint Louis
86	340.2	School of The Osage R-II	Lake Ozark
87	337.0	Doniphan R-I	Doniphan
88	336.7	University City	University City
89	335.5	Joplin R-VIII	Joplin
90	333.6	Fort Osage R-I	Independence
91	332.8	Hickman Mills C-1	Kansas City
91	332.8	Morgan County R-II	Versailles
93	325.4	Affton 101	Saint Louis
94	324.3	Kirkwood R-VII	Kirkwood
95	321.1	Center 58	Kansas City
96	317.7	Fredericktown R-I	Fredericktown
96	317.7	Rolla 31	Rolla
98	316.3	West Plains R-VII	West Plains
99	315.0	Camdenton R-III	Camdenton
100	312.7	Parkway C-2	Chesterfield
101	308.4	Nevada R-V	Nevada
102	305.8	Columbia 93	Columbia
103	305.1	Reeds Spring R-IV	Reeds Spring
104	304.2	Salem R-80	Salem
105	304.0	Chillicothe R-II	Chillicothe
106	302.9	Dallas County R-I	Buffalo
107	302.0	Bayless	Saint Louis
108	301.2	Gasconade County R-II	Owensville
108	301.2	Saint Louis City	Saint Louis
110	300.8	Boonville R-I	Boonville
111	298.9	Clinton	Clinton
112	298.2	Waynesville R-VI	Waynesville
113	291.6	Platte County R-III	Platte City
114	283.7	Sikeston R-VI	Sikeston
115	279.2	Grandview C-4	Grandview
116	277.9	Jefferson City	Jefferson City
117	277.5	Kennett 39	Kennett
118	275.7	Moberly	Moberly
119	274.7	Kirksville R-III	Kirksville
120	272.7	Ladue	Saint Louis
121	272.0	Mountain Grove R-III	Mountain Grove
122	270.9	Cape Girardeau 63	Cape Girardeau
123	270.1	Perry County 32	Perryville
124	268.2	Fulton 58	Fulton
125	265.5	Webster Groves	Webster Groves
126	258.1	Hannibal 60	Hannibal
127	257.6	Monett R-I	Monett
128	251.1	Mexico 59	Mexico
129	240.0	Pattonville R-III	Saint Ann
130	231.5	Saint Charles R-VI	Saint Charles
131	227.0	Clayton	Clayton
132	207.0	Knob Noster R-VIII	Knob Noster
133	n/a	Special SD - Saint Louis County	Town & Ctry

Current Spending per Student in FY2001

Rank	Dollars	District Name	City
1	28,881	Special SD - Saint Louis County	Town & Ctry
2	12,914	Clayton	Clayton
3	11,008	Ladue	Saint Louis
4	9,127	Saint Louis City	Saint Louis
5	9,071	Pattonville R-III	Saint Ann
6	8,530	Center 58	Kansas City
7	8,360	Kansas City 33	Kansas City
8	7,781	Parkway C-2	Chesterfield
9	7,751	Ferguson-Florissant R-II	Florissant
10	7,600	Hickman Mills C-1	Kansas City
11	7,523	Kirkwood R-VII	Kirkwood
12	7,312	Jennings	Jennings
13	7,284	Webster Groves	Webster Groves
14	7,234	Independence 30	Independence
15	7,228	Fort Osage R-I	Independence
16	7,194	Grandview C-4	Grandview
17	7,169	University City	University City
18	7,117	Normandy	Saint Louis
19	7,053	Saint Charles R-VI	Saint Charles
20	6,952	Chillicothe R-II	Chillicothe
21	6,923	Lindbergh R-VIII	Saint Louis
22	6,901	Boonville R-I	Boonville
23	6,847	Columbia 93	Columbia
24	6,845	Mountain Grove R-III	Mountain Grove
25	6,750	Park Hill	Kansas City
26	6,671	Hazelwood	Florissant
27	6,644	Waynesville R-VI	Waynesville
28	6,549	Cameron R-I	Cameron
29	6,546	Platte County R-III	Platte City
30	6,534	Desoto 73	Desoto
31	6,494	Lee's Summit R-VII	Lee's Summit
32	6,476	Raytown C-2	Raytown
33	6,427	New Madrid County R-I	New Madrid
34	6,355	North Kansas City 74	Kansas City
35	6,334	Liberty 53	Liberty
36	6,294	Riverview Gardens	Saint Louis
37	6,279	Marshall	Marshall
38	6,277	Monett R-I	Monett
39	6,258	Rockwood R-VI	Eureka
40	6,252	Affton 101	Saint Louis
41	6,224	Clinton	Clinton
42	6,223	Ritenour	Saint Louis
43	6,176	Bolivar R-I	Bolivar
44	6,138	Perry County 32	Perryville
45	6,122	Blue Springs R-IV	Blue Springs
45	6,122	Excelsior Springs 40	Excelsior Spgs
47	6,112	Central R-III	Park Hills
48	6,104	Washington	Washington
49	6,100	School of The Osage R-II	Lake Ozark
50	6,099	Nevada R-V	Nevada
51	6,092	Moberly	Moberly
52	6,079	Saint Joseph	Saint Joseph
53	5,977	Warrensburg R-VI	Warrensburg
54	5,963	Wentzville R-IV	Wentzville
55	5,932	Fulton 58	Fulton
56	5,930	Camdenton R-III	Camdenton
57	5,921	Cape Girardeau 63	Cape Girardeau
58	5,915	Belton 124	Belton
59	5,908	Reeds Spring R-IV	Reeds Spring
60	5,884	Fort Zumwalt R-II	O'fallon
61	5,849	Pleasant Hill R-III	Pleasant Hill
62	5,844	Kirksville R-III	Kirksville
63	5,841	West Plains R-VII	West Plains
64	5,822	Farmington R-VII	Farmington
64	5,822	Mehlville R-IX	Saint Louis
66	5,821	Hancock Place	Saint Louis
67	5,811	Harrisonville R-IX	Harrisonville
68	5,794	East Newton County R-VI	Granby
69	5,789	Fox C-6	Arnold
70	5,783	Raymore-Peculiar R-II	Raymore
71	5,766	Northwest R-I	House Springs
72	5,760	Springfield R-XII	Springfield
73	5,745	Branson R-IV	Branson
73	5,745	Jefferson City	Jefferson City
73	5,745	Neosho R-V	Neosho
76	5,729	Kennett 39	Kennett
77	5,728	Rolla 31	Rolla
78	5,710	Sainte Genevieve County R-II	Ste Genevieve
79	5,709	Odessa R-VII	Odessa
80	5,679	Francis Howell R-III	Saint Charles
81	5,644	Aurora R-VIII	Aurora
81	5,644	Warsaw R-IX	Warsaw
83	5,639	Dallas County R-I	Buffalo
84	5,612	Smithville R-II	Smithville
85	5,599	Knob Noster R-VIII	Knob Noster
86	5,591	Fredericktown R-I	Fredericktown
87	5,560	Oak Grove R-VI	Oak Grove
88	5,554	Caruthersville 18	Caruthersville
89	5,553	Saint James R-I	Saint James
90	5,549	Eldon R-I	Eldon
91	5,533	Mexico 59	Mexico
92	5,527	Savannah R-III	Savannah
93	5,511	Joplin R-VIII	Joplin
94	5,479	Sullivan C-2	Sullivan
95	5,461	Poplar Bluff R-I	Poplar Bluff
96	5,458	Windsor C-1	Imperial
97	5,430	Dexter R-XI	Dexter
98	5,419	North Saint Francois County R-I	Bonne Terre
99	5,385	Webb City R-VII	Webb City
100	5,365	Hannibal 60	Hannibal
101	5,359	Doniphan R-I	Doniphan
102	5,354	Carthage R-IX	Carthage
103	5,336	Grain Valley R-V	Grain Valley
104	5,334	Union R-XI	Union
105	5,329	Morgan County R-II	Versailles
106	5,324	Carl Junction R-I	Carl Junction
107	5,313	Sikeston R-VI	Sikeston
108	5,311	Seneca R-VII	Seneca
109	5,310	Richmond R-XVI	Richmond
110	5,288	Ava R-I	Ava
111	5,240	Lebanon R-III	Lebanon
112	5,236	Gasconade County R-II	Owensville
113	5,226	Cassville R-IV	Cassville
114	5,220	Ozark R-VI	Ozark
115	5,176	Sedalia 200	Sedalia
116	5,166	Hillsboro R-III	Hillsboro
117	5,152	Marshfield R-I	Marshfield
118	5,145	Meramec Valley R-III	Pacific
119	5,129	Republic R-III	Republic
120	5,125	Willard R-II	Willard
121	5,092	Potosi R-III	Potosi
121	5,092	Salem R-80	Salem
123	5,083	Saint Clair R-XIII	Saint Clair
124	5,012	Winfield R-IV	Winfield
125	4,995	Warren County R-III	Warrenton
126	4,975	Bayless	Saint Louis
127	4,911	Greene County R-VIII	Rogersville
128	4,898	Nixa R-II	Nixa
129	4,785	Troy R-III	Troy
130	4,732	Jackson R-II	Jackson
131	4,690	Kearney R-I	Kearney
132	4,637	Festus R-VI	Festus
133	4,571	Mcdonald County R-I	Anderson

Number of Diploma Recipients

Rank	Number	District Name	City
1	1,474	Rockwood R-VI	Eureka
2	1,464	Springfield R-XII	Springfield
3	1,438	Parkway C-2	Chesterfield
4	1,424	Saint Louis City	Saint Louis
5	1,409	Kansas City 33	Kansas City
6	1,247	Hazelwood	Florissant
7	1,232	Francis Howell R-III	Saint Charles
8	1,137	North Kansas City 74	Kansas City
9	1,073	Fort Zumwalt R-II	O'fallon
10	1,039	Columbia 93	Columbia
11	956	Lee's Summit R-VII	Lee's Summit
12	827	Mehlville R-IX	Saint Louis
13	808	Blue Springs R-IV	Blue Springs
14	711	Saint Joseph	Saint Joseph
15	694	Ferguson-Florissant R-II	Florissant
16	666	Independence 30	Independence
17	640	Park Hill	Kansas City
18	612	Fox C-6	Arnold
19	520	Raytown C-2	Raytown
20	509	Jefferson City	Jefferson City
21	454	Liberty 53	Liberty
22	428	Pattonville R-III	Saint Ann
23	416	Saint Charles R-VI	Saint Charles
24	415	Northwest R-I	House Springs
25	409	Kirkwood R-VII	Kirkwood
26	394	Hickman Mills C-1	Kansas City

27	377	Lindbergh R-VIII	Saint Louis
28	343	Jackson R-II	Jackson
29	342	Wentzville R-IV	Wentzville
30	316	Excelsior Springs 40	Excelsior Spgs
31	312	Normandy	Saint Louis
31	312	Poplar Bluff R-I	Poplar Bluff
33	306	Joplin R-VIII	Joplin
33	306	Riverview Gardens	Saint Louis
35	303	Webster Groves	Webster Groves
36	297	Lebanon R-III	Lebanon
36	297	Rolla 31	Rolla
38	296	Ritenour	Saint Louis
39	289	Camdenton R-III	Camdenton
40	287	Troy R-III	Troy
41	281	Washington	Washington
42	275	Cape Girardeau 63	Cape Girardeau
43	271	Waynesville R-VI	Waynesville
44	265	West Plains R-VII	West Plains
45	261	Belton 124	Belton
46	259	Raymore-Peculiar R-II	Raymore
47	250	Fort Osage R-I	Independence
48	244	Farmington R-VII	Farmington
49	242	Meramec Valley R-III	Pacific
50	238	Neosho R-V	Neosho
51	233	Sedalia 200	Sedalia
52	227	Carthage R-IX	Carthage
53	225	Nixa R-II	Nixa
54	223	North Saint Francois County R-I	Bonne Terre
55	221	Ozark R-VI	Ozark
56	220	Grandview C-4	Grandview
56	220	Hillsboro R-III	Hillsboro
58	217	Ladue	Saint Louis
58	217	Warrensburg R-VI	Warrensburg
60	210	Hannibal 60	Hannibal
60	210	Sikeston R-VI	Sikeston
62	205	Willard R-II	Willard
63	201	Webb City R-VII	Webb City
64	199	Kearney R-I	Kearney
65	198	Union R-XI	Union
66	193	Windsor C-1	Imperial
67	189	Clayton	Clayton
68	188	Desoto 73	Desoto
69	184	Mexico 59	Mexico
70	183	Republic R-III	Republic
71	182	Harrisonville R-IX	Harrisonville
72	181	Affton 101	Saint Louis
72	181	Marshall	Marshall
74	179	Saint Clair R-XIII	Saint Clair
75	175	Warren County R-III	Warrenton
76	173	Perry County 32	Perryville
77	171	Kirksville R-III	Kirksville
78	170	Nevada R-V	Nevada
79	169	Marshfield R-I	Marshfield
80	168	University City	University City
81	164	Branson R-IV	Branson
81	164	Carl Junction R-I	Carl Junction
81	164	Savannah R-III	Savannah
84	161	Festus R-VI	Festus
84	161	Odessa R-VII	Odessa
84	161	Potosi R-III	Potosi
87	159	Moberly	Moberly
88	155	Center 58	Kansas City
89	152	Mcdonald County R-I	Anderson
90	148	Platte County R-III	Platte City
91	147	Gasconade County R-II	Owensville
91	147	Jennings	Jennings
93	144	Bolivar R-I	Bolivar
94	143	Chillicothe R-II	Chillicothe
94	143	Sainte Genevieve County R-II	Ste Genevieve
96	135	Cassville R-IV	Cassville
97	134	Dallas County R-I	Buffalo
98	133	Clinton	Clinton
98	133	Eldon R-I	Eldon
100	132	Greene County R-VIII	Rogersville
101	131	Fulton 58	Fulton
102	128	Salem R-80	Salem
103	127	Sullivan C-2	Sullivan
104	126	Saint James R-I	Saint James
105	124	Oak Grove R-VI	Oak Grove
105	124	Pleasant Hill R-III	Pleasant Hill
107	123	Monett R-I	Monett
108	120	Dexter R-XI	Dexter
109	116	Doniphan R-I	Doniphan
110	115	Reeds Spring R-IV	Reeds Spring
111	114	Fredericktown R-I	Fredericktown
112	112	Kennett 39	Kennett
113	111	Central R-III	Park Hills
114	110	Smithville R-II	Smithville
115	109	Morgan County R-II	Versailles
116	108	School of The Osage R-II	Lake Ozark
117	107	Knob Noster R-VIII	Knob Noster
118	106	Aurora R-VIII	Aurora
118	106	Cameron R-I	Cameron
120	103	Richmond R-XVI	Richmond
121	102	Boonville R-I	Boonville
121	102	Warsaw R-IX	Warsaw
123	101	Mountain Grove R-III	Mountain Grove
123	101	New Madrid County R-I	New Madrid
125	99	Ava R-I	Ava
126	94	Bayless	Saint Louis
127	91	East Newton County R-VI	Granby
127	91	Seneca R-VII	Seneca
129	90	Grain Valley R-V	Grain Valley
130	88	Winfield R-IV	Winfield
131	81	Caruthersville 18	Caruthersville
132	77	Hancock Place	Saint Louis
133	n/a	Special SD - Saint Louis County	Town & Ctry

High School Drop-out Rate

Rank	Percent	District Name	City
1	20.7	Excelsior Springs 40	Excelsior Spgs
2	10.0	University City	University City
3	9.4	Moberly	Moberly
3	9.4	Saint Louis City	Saint Louis
5	8.3	Raytown C-2	Raytown
6	8.1	Marshall	Marshall
7	8.0	Poplar Bluff R-I	Poplar Bluff
8	7.9	Carthage R-IX	Carthage
9	7.6	Desoto 73	Desoto
9	7.6	Independence 30	Independence
9	7.6	Winfield R-IV	Winfield
12	7.4	Carl Junction R-I	Carl Junction
13	7.2	Cape Girardeau 63	Cape Girardeau
14	6.9	Potosi R-III	Potosi
15	6.8	Center 58	Kansas City
15	6.8	Dallas County R-I	Buffalo
17	6.7	Kansas City 33	Kansas City
17	6.7	Marshfield R-I	Marshfield
19	6.3	Webb City R-VII	Webb City
20	6.2	Salem R-80	Salem
20	6.2	Washington	Washington
22	6.1	New Madrid County R-I	New Madrid
23	6.0	Perry County 32	Perryville
24	5.8	Eldon R-I	Eldon
25	5.7	Grandview C-4	Grandview
25	5.7	Kirksville R-III	Kirksville
27	5.6	Fox C-6	Arnold
27	5.6	Mountain Grove R-III	Mountain Grove
29	5.5	Hancock Place	Saint Louis
29	5.5	Reeds Spring R-IV	Reeds Spring
29	5.5	Republic R-III	Republic
29	5.5	Sedalia 200	Sedalia
33	5.4	Festus R-VI	Festus
33	5.4	Greene County R-VIII	Rogersville
33	5.4	Springfield R-XII	Springfield
33	5.4	Sullivan C-2	Sullivan
33	5.4	Windsor C-1	Imperial
38	5.3	Sikeston R-VI	Sikeston
39	5.2	Hickman Mills C-1	Kansas City
39	5.2	Joplin R-VIII	Joplin
39	5.2	Monett R-I	Monett
39	5.2	Normandy	Saint Louis
43	5.1	Aurora R-VIII	Aurora
44	5.0	Hannibal 60	Hannibal
44	5.0	Kennett 39	Kennett
44	5.0	Northwest R-I	House Springs
47	4.9	Bolivar R-I	Bolivar
47	4.9	Dexter R-XI	Dexter
47	4.9	Riverview Gardens	Saint Louis
47	4.9	Wentzville R-IV	Wentzville
51	4.8	Neosho R-V	Neosho
52	4.7	Columbia 93	Columbia
52	4.7	Meramec Valley R-III	Pacific
54	4.6	Branson R-IV	Branson
54	4.6	Mcdonald County R-I	Anderson
54	4.6	North Saint Francois County R-I	Bonne Terre
57	4.4	Belton 124	Belton
57	4.4	Clinton	Clinton
57	4.4	Saint Clair R-XIII	Saint Clair
60	4.2	Sainte Genevieve County R-II	Ste Genevieve
61	4.1	Odessa R-VII	Odessa
61	4.1	Saint Charles R-VI	Saint Charles
63	4.0	Jefferson City	Jefferson City
63	4.0	Lebanon R-III	Lebanon
63	4.0	Morgan County R-II	Versailles
66	3.9	Fredericktown R-I	Fredericktown
66	3.9	Liberty 53	Liberty
68	3.8	Mexico 59	Mexico
68	3.8	Union R-XI	Union
68	3.8	Warrensburg R-VI	Warrensburg
71	3.7	Affton 101	Saint Louis
71	3.7	Boonville R-I	Boonville
71	3.7	North Kansas City 74	Kansas City
71	3.7	Webster Groves	Webster Groves
75	3.6	Caruthersville 18	Caruthersville
75	3.6	Harrisonville R-IX	Harrisonville
75	3.6	Nixa R-II	Nixa
75	3.6	Smithville R-II	Smithville
79	3.4	Bayless	Saint Louis
79	3.4	East Newton County R-VI	Granby
79	3.4	Hazelwood	Florissant
79	3.4	Jennings	Jennings
79	3.4	Seneca R-VII	Seneca
79	3.4	Waynesville R-VI	Waynesville
85	3.3	Doniphan R-I	Doniphan
85	3.3	Platte County R-III	Platte City
85	3.3	Troy R-III	Troy
85	3.3	Willard R-II	Willard
89	3.2	Cassville R-IV	Cassville
89	3.2	Kearney R-I	Kearney
89	3.2	Mehlville R-IX	Saint Louis
89	3.2	Saint Joseph	Saint Joseph
89	3.2	West Plains R-VII	West Plains
94	3.1	Grain Valley R-V	Grain Valley
95	3.0	Fulton 58	Fulton
95	3.0	Kirkwood R-VII	Kirkwood
95	3.0	Warren County R-III	Warrenton
98	2.9	Raymore-Peculiar R-II	Raymore
99	2.8	Hillsboro R-III	Hillsboro
99	2.8	Rolla 31	Rolla
101	2.7	Fort Zumwalt R-II	O'fallon
101	2.7	Pleasant Hill R-III	Pleasant Hill
101	2.7	Richmond R-XVI	Richmond
101	2.7	School of The Osage R-II	Lake Ozark
105	2.6	Ferguson-Florissant R-II	Florissant
105	2.6	Jackson R-II	Jackson
107	2.5	Farmington R-VII	Farmington
107	2.5	Pattonville R-III	Saint Ann
107	2.5	Saint James R-I	Saint James
110	2.4	Blue Springs R-IV	Blue Springs
110	2.4	Camdenton R-III	Camdenton
110	2.4	Fort Osage R-I	Independence
110	2.4	Park Hill	Kansas City
110	2.4	Rockwood R-VI	Eureka
115	2.3	Lee's Summit R-VII	Lee's Summit
116	2.2	Francis Howell R-III	Saint Charles
116	2.2	Ozark R-VI	Ozark
116	2.2	Savannah R-III	Savannah
119	2.1	Knob Noster R-VIII	Knob Noster
119	2.1	Warsaw R-IX	Warsaw
121	2.0	Lindbergh R-VIII	Saint Louis
122	1.8	Clayton	Clayton
122	1.8	Gasconade County R-II	Owensville
122	1.8	Nevada R-V	Nevada
122	1.8	Parkway C-2	Chesterfield
126	1.7	Ava R-I	Ava
127	1.6	Cameron R-I	Cameron
128	1.4	Chillicothe R-II	Chillicothe
129	1.3	Central R-III	Park Hills
129	1.3	Oak Grove R-VI	Oak Grove
131	1.2	Ladue	Saint Louis
131	1.2	Ritenour	Saint Louis
133	n/a	Special SD - Saint Louis County	Town & Ctry

Montana

Montana Public School Educational Profile

Category	Value	Category	Value
Schools *(2002-2003)*	872	**Diploma Recipients** *(2002-2003)*	10,554
Instructional Level		White, Non-Hispanic	9,537
Primary	451	Black, Non-Hispanic	34
Middle	241	Asian/Pacific Islander	112
High	176	American Indian/Alaskan Native	713
Other Level	4	Hispanic	158
Curriculum		**High School Drop-out Rate** (%) *(2000-2001)*	4.2
Regular	866	White, Non-Hispanic	3.5
Special Education	2	Black, Non-Hispanic	5.2
Vocational	0	Asian/Pacific Islander	3.6
Alternative	4	American Indian/Alaskan Native	11.0
Type		Hispanic	8.5
Magnet	0	**Staff** *(2002-2003)*	13,766.3
Charter	0	Teachers	10,362.3
Title I Eligible	695	Average Salary ($)	35,754
School-wide Title I	130	Librarians/Media Specialists	357.4
Students *(2002-2003)*	149,995	Guidance Counselors	432.4
Gender (%)		**Ratios** *(2002-2003)*	
Male	51.7	Student/Teacher Ratio	14.5 to 1
Female	48.3	Student/Librarian Ratio	419.7 to 1
Race/Ethnicity (%)		Student/Counselor Ratio	346.9 to 1
White, Non-Hispanic	85.4	**Current Spending** *($ per student in FY 2001)*	7,062
Black, Non-Hispanic	0.7	Instruction	4,374
Asian/Pacific Islander	1.1	Support Services	2,393
American Indian/Alaskan Native	10.9	**College Entrance Exam Scores** *(2003)*	
Hispanic	2.0	Scholastic Aptitude Test (SAT)	
Classification (%)		Participation Rate (%)	26
Individual Education Program (IEP)	12.8	Mean SAT I Verbal Score	538
Migrant	0.0	Mean SAT I Math Score	543
English Language Learner (ELL)	4.4	American College Testing Program (ACT)	
Eligible for Free Lunch Program	24.1	Participation Rate (%)	52
Eligible for Reduced-Price Lunch Program	7.8	Average Composite Score	21.7

Note: *For an explanation of data, please refer to the User's Guide in the front of the book; n/a indicates data not available*

Montana NAEP 2003 Test Scores

Reading			Mathematics		
Grade/Category	**Value**	**Rank**	**Grade/Category**	**Value**	**Rank**
4th Grade			**4th Grade**		
Average Proficiency	222.7 (1.2)	11/51	Average Proficiency	235.8 (0.8)	25/51
Proficiency by Gender/Race/Ethnicity			Proficiency by Gender/Race/Ethnicity		
Male	218.1 (1.4)	15/51	Male	236.5 (1.1)	29/51
Female	227.6 (1.4)	7/51	Female	235.0 (0.9)	21/51
White, Non-Hispanic	226.6 (1.0)	18/51	White, Non-Hispanic	238.0 (0.7)	39/51
Black, Non-Hispanic	n/a	n/a	Black, Non-Hispanic	n/a	n/a
Asian, Non-Hispanic	n/a	n/a	Asian, Non-Hispanic	235.8 (3.7)	1/43
American Indian, Non-Hispanic	n/a	n/a	American Indian, Non-Hispanic	n/a	n/a
Hispanic	194.6 (4.0)	7/12	Hispanic	216.9 (2.2)	7/12
Proficiency by Class Size			Proficiency by Class Size		
Less than 16 Students	217.8 (2.9)	6/45	Less than 16 Students	232.0 (2.5)	8/47
16 to 18 Students	211.5 (6.7)	31/48	16 to 18 Students	227.9 (2.9)	33/48
19 to 20 Students	*222.7 (2.5)*	12/50	19 to 20 Students	237.1 (1.9)	14/50
21 to 25 Students	226.0 (1.5)	8/51	21 to 25 Students	237.6 (1.2)	26/51
Greater than 25 Students	*226.7 (2.9)*	4/49	Greater than 25 Students	*237.4 (2.1)*	18/49
Percent Attaining Achievement Levels			Percent Attaining Achievement Levels		
Below Basic	30.6 (1.4)	42/51	Below Basic	18.6 (1.2)	36/51
Basic or Above	69.4 (1.4)	9/51	Basic or Above	81.4 (1.2)	16/51
Proficient or Above	34.9 (1.3)	10/51	Proficient or Above	31.1 (1.6)	30/51
Advanced or Above	8.0 (1.0)	14/51	Advanced or Above	2.5 (0.4)	35/51
8th Grade			**8th Grade**		
Average Proficiency	269.8 (1.0)	5/51	Average Proficiency	285.9 (0.8)	5/51
Proficiency by Gender/Race/Ethnicity			Proficiency by Gender/Race/Ethnicity		
Male	263.9 (1.2)	6/51	Male	285.9 (0.9)	5/51
Female	275.8 (1.2)	4/51	Female	286.0 (1.0)	3/51
White, Non-Hispanic	272.6 (1.0)	9/50	White, Non-Hispanic	288.8 (0.7)	17/50
Black, Non-Hispanic	n/a	n/a	Black, Non-Hispanic	n/a	n/a
Asian, Non-Hispanic	n/a	n/a	Asian, Non-Hispanic	n/a	n/a
American Indian, Non-Hispanic	n/a	n/a	American Indian, Non-Hispanic	n/a	n/a
Hispanic	246.5 (4.9)	3/10	Hispanic	260.0 (4.7)	6/11
Proficiency by Parents Highest Level of Ed.			Proficiency by Parents Highest Level of Ed.		
Did Not Finish High School	251.8 (3.4)	6/50	Did Not Finish High School	263.1 (4.8)	8/50
Graduated High School	262.1 (1.8)	2/50	Graduated High School	276.9 (1.8)	3/50
Some Education After High School	274.2 (1.5)	1/50	Some Education After High School	288.0 (1.7)	3/50
Graduated College	275.2 (1.3)	14/50	Graduated College	292.2 (0.9)	13/50
Percent Attaining Achievement Levels			Percent Attaining Achievement Levels		
Below Basic	18.2 (1.0)	51/51	Below Basic	20.9 (1.0)	49/51
Basic or Above	81.8 (1.0)	1/51	Basic or Above	79.1 (1.0)	3/51
Proficient or Above	37.2 (1.5)	6/51	Proficient or Above	34.9 (1.2)	7/51
Advanced or Above	3.0 (0.5)	15/51	Advanced or Above	5.7 (0.6)	17/51

***Note:** For an explanation of data, please refer to the User's Guide in the front of the book; values in italics indicate that the nature of the sample does not allow accurate determination of the variability of the statistic; n/a indicates data not available*

Cascade County

Great Falls Elem

1100 4th St So • Great Falls, MT 59403
Mailing Address: PO Box 2429 • Great Falls, MT 59403
(406) 268-6000 • http://www.gfps.k12.mt.us/
Grade Span: PK-08; **Agency Type:** 1
Schools: 18
15 Primary; 3 Middle; 0 High; 0 Other Level
18 Regular; 0 Special Education; 0 Vocational; 0 Alternative
0 Magnet; 0 Charter; 11 Title I Eligible; 3 School-wide Title I
Students: 7,690 (51.1% male; 48.9% female)
Individual Education Program: 905 (11.8%);
English Language Learner: 9 (0.1%); Migrant: n/a
Eligible for Free Lunch Program: 2,079 (27.0%)
Eligible for Reduced-Price Lunch Program: 755 (9.8%)
Teachers: 487.2 (15.8 to 1)
Librarians/Media Specialists: 12.0 (640.8 to 1)
Guidance Counselors: 18.9 (406.9 to 1)
Current Spending: ($ per student per year):
Total: $5,378; Instruction: $3,365; Support Services: $1,733
Enrollment, Drop-out Rates and Diploma Recipients by Race/Ethnicity

Category	Total	White	Black	Asian	AIAN	Hisp.
Enrollment (%)	100.0	86.0	1.7	1.1	9.5	1.7
Drop-out Rate (%)	n/a	n/a	n/a	n/a	n/a	n/a
H.S. Diplomas (#)	n/a	n/a	n/a	n/a	n/a	n/a

Great Falls HS

1100 4th St So • Great Falls, MT 59403
Mailing Address: PO Box 2429 • Great Falls, MT 59403
(406) 268-6051 • http://www.gfps.k12.mt.us/gfhs/index.html
Grade Span: 09-12; **Agency Type:** 1
Schools: 2
0 Primary; 0 Middle; 2 High; 0 Other Level
2 Regular; 0 Special Education; 0 Vocational; 0 Alternative
0 Magnet; 0 Charter; 1 Title I Eligible; 0 School-wide Title I
Students: 3,684 (50.2% male; 49.8% female)
Individual Education Program: 382 (10.4%);
English Language Learner: 2 (0.1%); Migrant: n/a
Eligible for Free Lunch Program: 420 (11.4%)
Eligible for Reduced-Price Lunch Program: 175 (4.8%)
Teachers: 231.6 (15.9 to 1)
Librarians/Media Specialists: 5.5 (669.8 to 1)
Guidance Counselors: 13.5 (272.9 to 1)
Current Spending: ($ per student per year):
Total: $6,762; Instruction: $4,604; Support Services: $2,158
Enrollment, Drop-out Rates and Diploma Recipients by Race/Ethnicity

Category	Total	White	Black	Asian	AIAN	Hisp.
Enrollment (%)	100.0	87.3	1.4	1.6	7.8	1.9
Drop-out Rate (%)	2.3	1.7	2.2	0.0	9.2	3.8
H.S. Diplomas (#)	803	727	9	13	49	5

Flathead County

Columbia Falls Elem

501 6th Ave W • Columbia Falls, MT 59912
Mailing Address: PO Box 1259 • Columbia Falls, MT 59912
(406) 892-6550
Grade Span: PK-08; **Agency Type:** 1
Schools: 5
3 Primary; 2 Middle; 0 High; 0 Other Level
5 Regular; 0 Special Education; 0 Vocational; 0 Alternative
0 Magnet; 0 Charter; 5 Title I Eligible; 1 School-wide Title I
Students: 1,671 (51.6% male; 48.4% female)
Individual Education Program: 252 (15.1%);
English Language Learner: 5 (0.3%); Migrant: n/a
Eligible for Free Lunch Program: 497 (29.7%)
Eligible for Reduced-Price Lunch Program: 157 (9.4%)
Teachers: 92.1 (18.1 to 1)
Librarians/Media Specialists: 3.0 (557.0 to 1)
Guidance Counselors: 4.2 (397.9 to 1)
Current Spending: ($ per student per year):
Total: $4,920; Instruction: $3,115; Support Services: $1,804
Enrollment, Drop-out Rates and Diploma Recipients by Race/Ethnicity

Category	Total	White	Black	Asian	AIAN	Hisp.
Enrollment (%)	100.0	93.7	0.9	0.9	3.0	1.6
Drop-out Rate (%)	n/a	n/a	n/a	n/a	n/a	n/a
H.S. Diplomas (#)	n/a	n/a	n/a	n/a	n/a	n/a

Flathead HS

233 First Ave E • Kalispell, MT 59901
(406) 751-3500 • http://www.sd5.k12.mt.us/fhs/index.htm
Grade Span: 09-12; **Agency Type:** 1
Schools: 2
0 Primary; 0 Middle; 1 High; 1 Other Level
2 Regular; 0 Special Education; 0 Vocational; 0 Alternative
0 Magnet; 0 Charter; 2 Title I Eligible; 0 School-wide Title I
Students: 2,452 (52.9% male; 47.1% female)
Individual Education Program: 180 (7.3%);
English Language Learner: 11 (0.4%); Migrant: n/a
Eligible for Free Lunch Program: 319 (13.0%)
Eligible for Reduced-Price Lunch Program: 116 (4.7%)
Teachers: 131.1 (18.7 to 1)
Librarians/Media Specialists: 3.5 (700.6 to 1)
Guidance Counselors: 6.9 (355.4 to 1)
Current Spending: ($ per student per year):
Total: $6,725; Instruction: $4,496; Support Services: $1,888
Enrollment, Drop-out Rates and Diploma Recipients by Race/Ethnicity

Category	Total	White	Black	Asian	AIAN	Hisp.
Enrollment (%)	100.0	98.0	0.4	0.4	0.7	0.5
Drop-out Rate (%)	3.9	3.7	14.3	25.0	7.1	28.6
H.S. Diplomas (#)	532	528	0	2	2	0

Kalispell Elem

233 First Ave E • Kalispell, MT 59901
(406) 751-3400 • http://www.sd5.k12.mt.us/
Grade Span: PK-08; **Agency Type:** 1
Schools: 7
5 Primary; 1 Middle; 0 High; 1 Other Level
7 Regular; 0 Special Education; 0 Vocational; 0 Alternative
0 Magnet; 0 Charter; 6 Title I Eligible; 0 School-wide Title I
Students: 2,473 (51.7% male; 48.3% female)
Individual Education Program: 320 (12.9%);
English Language Learner: 33 (1.3%); Migrant: n/a
Eligible for Free Lunch Program: 616 (24.9%)
Eligible for Reduced-Price Lunch Program: 263 (10.6%)
Teachers: 134.1 (18.4 to 1)
Librarians/Media Specialists: 8.0 (309.1 to 1)
Guidance Counselors: 6.4 (386.4 to 1)
Current Spending: ($ per student per year):
Total: $5,537; Instruction: $3,788; Support Services: $1,749
Enrollment, Drop-out Rates and Diploma Recipients by Race/Ethnicity

Category	Total	White	Black	Asian	AIAN	Hisp.
Enrollment (%)	100.0	95.0	0.6	0.9	1.9	1.6
Drop-out Rate (%)	n/a	n/a	n/a	n/a	n/a	n/a
H.S. Diplomas (#)	n/a	n/a	n/a	n/a	n/a	n/a

Gallatin County

Belgrade Elem

312 N Weaver • Belgrade, MT 59714
Mailing Address: PO Box 166 • Belgrade, MT 59714
(406) 388-6951
Grade Span: PK-08; **Agency Type:** 1
Schools: 4
2 Primary; 2 Middle; 0 High; 0 Other Level
4 Regular; 0 Special Education; 0 Vocational; 0 Alternative
0 Magnet; 0 Charter; 4 Title I Eligible; 0 School-wide Title I
Students: 1,747 (51.3% male; 48.7% female)
Individual Education Program: 195 (11.2%);
English Language Learner: 2 (0.1%); Migrant: n/a
Eligible for Free Lunch Program: 263 (15.1%)
Eligible for Reduced-Price Lunch Program: 142 (8.1%)
Teachers: 91.2 (19.2 to 1)
Librarians/Media Specialists: 3.0 (582.3 to 1)
Guidance Counselors: 4.0 (436.8 to 1)
Current Spending: ($ per student per year):
Total: $5,075; Instruction: $3,096; Support Services: $1,676
Enrollment, Drop-out Rates and Diploma Recipients by Race/Ethnicity

Category	Total	White	Black	Asian	AIAN	Hisp.
Enrollment (%)	100.0	95.3	0.6	1.0	1.9	1.3
Drop-out Rate (%)	n/a	n/a	n/a	n/a	n/a	n/a
H.S. Diplomas (#)	n/a	n/a	n/a	n/a	n/a	n/a

Bozeman Elem

404 W Main • Bozeman, MT 59715
Mailing Address: PO Box 520 • Bozeman, MT 59771
(406) 522-6042 • http://www.bozeman.k12.mt.us/welcome/18.elem.html
Grade Span: PK-08; **Agency Type:** 1
Schools: 8
6 Primary; 2 Middle; 0 High; 0 Other Level
8 Regular; 0 Special Education; 0 Vocational; 0 Alternative
0 Magnet; 0 Charter; 8 Title I Eligible; 0 School-wide Title I
Students: 3,228 (50.1% male; 49.9% female)
Individual Education Program: 338 (10.5%);
English Language Learner: 88 (2.7%); Migrant: n/a
Eligible for Free Lunch Program: 421 (13.0%)
Eligible for Reduced-Price Lunch Program: 176 (5.5%)
Teachers: 192.9 (16.7 to 1)
Librarians/Media Specialists: 7.7 (419.2 to 1)
Guidance Counselors: 3.7 (872.4 to 1)

Current Spending: ($ per student per year):
Total: $5,410; Instruction: $3,412; Support Services: $1,987
Enrollment, Drop-out Rates and Diploma Recipients by Race/Ethnicity

Category	Total	White	Black	Asian	AIAN	Hisp.
Enrollment (%)	100.0	93.8	0.4	2.1	2.4	1.4
Drop-out Rate (%)	n/a	n/a	n/a	n/a	n/a	n/a
H.S. Diplomas (#)	n/a	n/a	n/a	n/a	n/a	n/a

Bozeman HS

404 W Main • Bozeman, MT 59715
Mailing Address: PO Box 520 • Bozeman, MT 59771
(406) 522-6042 • http://www.bps.montana.edu/bhs/index.html
Grade Span: 09-12; **Agency Type:** 1
Schools: 1
0 Primary; 0 Middle; 1 High; 0 Other Level
1 Regular; 0 Special Education; 0 Vocational; 0 Alternative
0 Magnet; 0 Charter; 1 Title I Eligible; 0 School-wide Title I
Students: 1,873 (52.4% male; 47.6% female)
Individual Education Program: 144 (7.7%);
English Language Learner: 24 (1.3%); Migrant: n/a
Eligible for Free Lunch Program: 121 (6.5%)
Eligible for Reduced-Price Lunch Program: 48 (2.6%)
Teachers: 121.2 (15.5 to 1)
Librarians/Media Specialists: 2.7 (693.7 to 1)
Guidance Counselors: 6.0 (312.2 to 1)
Current Spending: ($ per student per year):
Total: $6,243; Instruction: $3,692; Support Services: $2,024
Enrollment, Drop-out Rates and Diploma Recipients by Race/Ethnicity

Category	Total	White	Black	Asian	AIAN	Hisp.
Enrollment (%)	100.0	95.2	0.6	1.9	1.4	1.0
Drop-out Rate (%)	3.1	3.2	0.0	4.0	0.0	0.0
H.S. Diplomas (#)	448	432	1	5	3	7

Lewis And Clark County

Helena Elem

55 S Rodney • Helena, MT 59601-5763
(406) 447-8510 • http://www.is.helena.k12.mt.us/
Grade Span: KG-08; **Agency Type:** 1
Schools: 13
11 Primary; 2 Middle; 0 High; 0 Other Level
13 Regular; 0 Special Education; 0 Vocational; 0 Alternative
0 Magnet; 0 Charter; 8 Title I Eligible; 1 School-wide Title I
Students: 5,020 (51.7% male; 48.3% female)
Individual Education Program: 671 (13.4%);
English Language Learner: 1 (<0.1%); Migrant: n/a
Eligible for Free Lunch Program: 1,018 (20.3%)
Eligible for Reduced-Price Lunch Program: 344 (6.9%)
Teachers: 262.7 (19.1 to 1)
Librarians/Media Specialists: 7.2 (697.2 to 1)
Guidance Counselors: 4.7 (1,068.1 to 1)
Current Spending: ($ per student per year):
Total: $5,753; Instruction: $3,537; Support Services: $1,876
Enrollment, Drop-out Rates and Diploma Recipients by Race/Ethnicity

Category	Total	White	Black	Asian	AIAN	Hisp.
Enrollment (%)	100.0	90.3	0.8	1.1	5.9	1.9
Drop-out Rate (%)	n/a	n/a	n/a	n/a	n/a	n/a
H.S. Diplomas (#)	n/a	n/a	n/a	n/a	n/a	n/a

Helena HS

55 S Rodney • Helena, MT 59601-5763
(406) 447-8510 • http://www.is.helena.k12.mt.us/
Grade Span: 09-12; **Agency Type:** 1
Schools: 2
0 Primary; 0 Middle; 2 High; 0 Other Level
2 Regular; 0 Special Education; 0 Vocational; 0 Alternative
0 Magnet; 0 Charter; 1 Title I Eligible; 0 School-wide Title I
Students: 3,070 (50.7% male; 49.3% female)
Individual Education Program: 243 (7.9%);
English Language Learner: 4 (0.1%); Migrant: n/a
Eligible for Free Lunch Program: 188 (6.1%)
Eligible for Reduced-Price Lunch Program: 60 (2.0%)
Teachers: 188.0 (16.3 to 1)
Librarians/Media Specialists: 4.6 (667.4 to 1)
Guidance Counselors: 7.0 (438.6 to 1)
Current Spending: ($ per student per year):
Total: $6,506; Instruction: $4,251; Support Services: $2,244
Enrollment, Drop-out Rates and Diploma Recipients by Race/Ethnicity

Category	Total	White	Black	Asian	AIAN	Hisp.
Enrollment (%)	100.0	93.5	0.2	1.5	3.7	1.1
Drop-out Rate (%)	5.0	4.5	0.0	0.0	18.4	41.7
H.S. Diplomas (#)	667	639	2	3	18	5

Lincoln County

Libby K-12 Schools

724 Louisiana Ave • Libby, MT 59923
(406) 293-8811
Grade Span: PK-12; **Agency Type:** 1
Schools: 4
2 Primary; 1 Middle; 1 High; 0 Other Level
4 Regular; 0 Special Education; 0 Vocational; 0 Alternative
0 Magnet; 0 Charter; 4 Title I Eligible; 0 School-wide Title I
Students: 1,700 (53.7% male; 46.3% female)
Individual Education Program: 256 (15.1%);
English Language Learner: 1 (0.1%); Migrant: n/a
Eligible for Free Lunch Program: 597 (35.1%)
Eligible for Reduced-Price Lunch Program: 186 (10.9%)
Teachers: 107.0 (15.9 to 1)
Librarians/Media Specialists: 3.5 (485.7 to 1)
Guidance Counselors: 5.0 (340.0 to 1)
Current Spending: ($ per student per year):
Total: $5,845; Instruction: $3,761; Support Services: $1,940
Enrollment, Drop-out Rates and Diploma Recipients by Race/Ethnicity

Category	Total	White	Black	Asian	AIAN	Hisp.
Enrollment (%)	100.0	93.9	0.7	0.6	2.4	2.4
Drop-out Rate (%)	3.9	3.9	0.0	n/a	0.0	0.0
H.S. Diplomas (#)	140	139	0	0	1	0

Missoula County

Missoula Elem

215 S 6th W • Missoula, MT 59801
(406) 728-2400 • http://www.mcps.k12.mt.us/
Grade Span: PK-08; **Agency Type:** 1
Schools: 14
9 Primary; 5 Middle; 0 High; 0 Other Level
14 Regular; 0 Special Education; 0 Vocational; 0 Alternative
0 Magnet; 0 Charter; 7 Title I Eligible; 3 School-wide Title I
Students: 5,135 (51.6% male; 48.4% female)
Individual Education Program: 872 (17.0%);
English Language Learner: 210 (4.1%); Migrant: n/a
Eligible for Free Lunch Program: 1,391 (27.1%)
Eligible for Reduced-Price Lunch Program: 404 (7.9%)
Teachers: 312.5 (16.4 to 1)
Librarians/Media Specialists: 14.0 (366.8 to 1)
Guidance Counselors: 8.0 (641.9 to 1)
Current Spending: ($ per student per year):
Total: $6,379; Instruction: $3,745; Support Services: $2,346
Enrollment, Drop-out Rates and Diploma Recipients by Race/Ethnicity

Category	Total	White	Black	Asian	AIAN	Hisp.
Enrollment (%)	100.0	91.3	0.9	1.6	4.5	1.7
Drop-out Rate (%)	n/a	n/a	n/a	n/a	n/a	n/a
H.S. Diplomas (#)	n/a	n/a	n/a	n/a	n/a	n/a

Missoula HS

215 S 6th W • Missoula, MT 59801
(406) 728-2400 • http://www.mcps.k12.mt.us/
Grade Span: 09-12; **Agency Type:** 1
Schools: 4
0 Primary; 0 Middle; 4 High; 0 Other Level
4 Regular; 0 Special Education; 0 Vocational; 0 Alternative
0 Magnet; 0 Charter; 3 Title I Eligible; 0 School-wide Title I
Students: 4,015 (50.1% male; 49.9% female)
Individual Education Program: 525 (13.1%);
English Language Learner: 245 (6.1%); Migrant: n/a
Eligible for Free Lunch Program: 563 (14.0%)
Eligible for Reduced-Price Lunch Program: 176 (4.4%)
Teachers: 265.0 (15.2 to 1)
Librarians/Media Specialists: 6.0 (669.2 to 1)
Guidance Counselors: 17.2 (233.4 to 1)
Current Spending: ($ per student per year):
Total: $7,204; Instruction: $4,647; Support Services: $2,320
Enrollment, Drop-out Rates and Diploma Recipients by Race/Ethnicity

Category	Total	White	Black	Asian	AIAN	Hisp.
Enrollment (%)	100.0	93.3	0.4	1.7	3.3	1.3
Drop-out Rate (%)	5.2	4.7	13.3	7.8	13.8	9.6
H.S. Diplomas (#)	838	785	2	17	22	12

Ravalli County

Hamilton K-12 Schools

217 Daly Ave • Hamilton, MT 59840
(406) 363-2280 • http://www.hsd3.org
Grade Span: PK-12; **Agency Type:** 1
Schools: 5
3 Primary; 1 Middle; 1 High; 0 Other Level
5 Regular; 0 Special Education; 0 Vocational; 0 Alternative

0 Magnet; 0 Charter; 5 Title I Eligible; 0 School-wide Title I
Students: 1,627 (50.6% male; 49.4% female)
Individual Education Program: 197 (12.1%);
English Language Learner: 2 (0.1%); Migrant: n/a
Eligible for Free Lunch Program: 391 (24.0%)
Eligible for Reduced-Price Lunch Program: 172 (10.6%)
Teachers: 93.7 (17.4 to 1)
Librarians/Media Specialists: 3.8 (428.2 to 1)
Guidance Counselors: 4.0 (406.8 to 1)
Current Spending: ($ per student per year):
Total: $5,444; Instruction: $3,433; Support Services: $1,777
Enrollment, Drop-out Rates and Diploma Recipients by Race/Ethnicity

Category	Total	White	Black	Asian	AIAN	Hisp.
Enrollment (%)	100.0	96.1	0.6	0.9	1.0	1.3
Drop-out Rate (%)	1.6	1.7	n/a	0.0	0.0	0.0
H.S. Diplomas (#)	123	119	0	3	0	1

Silver Bow County

Butte Elem
111 N Montana • Butte, MT 59701
(406) 533-2500 • http://www.butte.k12.mt.us/
Grade Span: PK-08; **Agency Type:** 1
Schools: 8
7 Primary; 1 Middle; 0 High; 0 Other Level
8 Regular; 0 Special Education; 0 Vocational; 0 Alternative
0 Magnet; 0 Charter; 6 Title I Eligible; 4 School-wide Title I
Students: 3,405 (51.2% male; 48.8% female)
Individual Education Program: 483 (14.2%);
English Language Learner: 3 (0.1%); Migrant: n/a
Eligible for Free Lunch Program: 1,103 (32.4%)
Eligible for Reduced-Price Lunch Program: 218 (6.4%)
Teachers: 203.1 (16.8 to 1)
Librarians/Media Specialists: 4.7 (724.5 to 1)
Guidance Counselors: 7.6 (448.0 to 1)
Current Spending: ($ per student per year):
Total: $5,439; Instruction: $3,070; Support Services: $2,102
Enrollment, Drop-out Rates and Diploma Recipients by Race/Ethnicity

Category	Total	White	Black	Asian	AIAN	Hisp.
Enrollment (%)	100.0	89.6	0.8	1.0	5.1	3.6
Drop-out Rate (%)	n/a	n/a	n/a	n/a	n/a	n/a
H.S. Diplomas (#)	n/a	n/a	n/a	n/a	n/a	n/a

Butte HS
111 N Montana • Butte, MT 59701
(406) 533-2500 • http://www.butte.k12.mt.us/
Grade Span: 09-12; **Agency Type:** 1
Schools: 1
0 Primary; 0 Middle; 1 High; 0 Other Level
1 Regular; 0 Special Education; 0 Vocational; 0 Alternative
0 Magnet; 0 Charter; 1 Title I Eligible; 0 School-wide Title I
Students: 1,531 (50.6% male; 49.4% female)
Individual Education Program: 179 (11.7%);
English Language Learner: 0 (0.0%); Migrant: n/a
Eligible for Free Lunch Program: 131 (8.6%)
Eligible for Reduced-Price Lunch Program: 16 (1.0%)
Teachers: 97.0 (15.8 to 1)
Librarians/Media Specialists: 2.7 (567.0 to 1)
Guidance Counselors: 4.0 (382.8 to 1)
Current Spending: ($ per student per year):
Total: $7,577; Instruction: $5,001; Support Services: $2,566
Enrollment, Drop-out Rates and Diploma Recipients by Race/Ethnicity

Category	Total	White	Black	Asian	AIAN	Hisp.
Enrollment (%)	100.0	93.3	0.1	0.7	4.1	1.8
Drop-out Rate (%)	6.2	6.3	0.0	0.0	2.1	12.5
H.S. Diplomas (#)	296	275	1	6	6	8

Yellowstone County

Billings Elem
415 N 30th St • Billings, MT 59101
(406) 247-3745 • http://www.billings.k12.mt.us/
Grade Span: PK-08; **Agency Type:** 1
Schools: 25
21 Primary; 4 Middle; 0 High; 0 Other Level
25 Regular; 0 Special Education; 0 Vocational; 0 Alternative
0 Magnet; 0 Charter; 11 Title I Eligible; 8 School-wide Title I
Students: 10,154 (51.8% male; 48.2% female)
Individual Education Program: 1,307 (12.9%);
English Language Learner: 28 (0.3%); Migrant: n/a
Eligible for Free Lunch Program: 2,496 (24.6%)
Eligible for Reduced-Price Lunch Program: 981 (9.7%)
Teachers: 623.0 (16.3 to 1)
Librarians/Media Specialists: 27.0 (376.1 to 1)
Guidance Counselors: 21.1 (481.2 to 1)
Current Spending: ($ per student per year):
Total: $5,576; Instruction: $3,663; Support Services: $1,914
Enrollment, Drop-out Rates and Diploma Recipients by Race/Ethnicity

Category	Total	White	Black	Asian	AIAN	Hisp.
Enrollment (%)	100.0	82.9	1.7	1.7	7.9	5.9
Drop-out Rate (%)	n/a	n/a	n/a	n/a	n/a	n/a
H.S. Diplomas (#)	n/a	n/a	n/a	n/a	n/a	n/a

Billings HS
415 N 30th St • Billings, MT 59101
(406) 247-3791 • http://www.billings.k12.mt.us/
Grade Span: 09-12; **Agency Type:** 1
Schools: 3
0 Primary; 0 Middle; 3 High; 0 Other Level
3 Regular; 0 Special Education; 0 Vocational; 0 Alternative
0 Magnet; 0 Charter; 1 Title I Eligible; 0 School-wide Title I
Students: 5,624 (52.2% male; 47.8% female)
Individual Education Program: 709 (12.6%);
English Language Learner: 27 (0.5%); Migrant: n/a
Eligible for Free Lunch Program: 639 (11.4%)
Eligible for Reduced-Price Lunch Program: 254 (4.5%)
Teachers: 316.7 (17.8 to 1)
Librarians/Media Specialists: 8.0 (703.0 to 1)
Guidance Counselors: 20.8 (270.4 to 1)
Current Spending: ($ per student per year):
Total: $6,643; Instruction: $3,913; Support Services: $2,140
Enrollment, Drop-out Rates and Diploma Recipients by Race/Ethnicity

Category	Total	White	Black	Asian	AIAN	Hisp.
Enrollment (%)	100.0	88.5	1.0	1.4	4.9	4.3
Drop-out Rate (%)	4.7	4.2	2.6	6.2	9.5	10.3
H.S. Diplomas (#)	1,167	1,072	10	15	36	34

Number of Schools

Rank	Number	District Name	City
1	25	Billings Elem	Billings
2	18	Great Falls Elem	Great Falls
3	14	Missoula Elem	Missoula
4	13	Helena Elem	Helena
5	8	Bozeman Elem	Bozeman
5	8	Butte Elem	Butte
7	7	Kalispell Elem	Kalispell
8	5	Columbia Falls Elem	Columbia Falls
8	5	Hamilton K-12 Schools	Hamilton
10	4	Belgrade Elem	Belgrade
10	4	Libby K-12 Schools	Libby
10	4	Missoula HS	Missoula
13	3	Billings HS	Billings
14	2	Flathead HS	Kalispell
14	2	Great Falls HS	Great Falls
14	2	Helena HS	Helena
17	1	Bozeman HS	Bozeman
17	1	Butte HS	Butte

Number of Teachers

Rank	Number	District Name	City
1	623	Billings Elem	Billings
2	487	Great Falls Elem	Great Falls
3	316	Billings HS	Billings
4	312	Missoula Elem	Missoula
5	265	Missoula HS	Missoula
6	262	Helena Elem	Helena
7	231	Great Falls HS	Great Falls
8	203	Butte Elem	Butte
9	192	Bozeman Elem	Bozeman
10	188	Helena HS	Helena
11	134	Kalispell Elem	Kalispell
12	131	Flathead HS	Kalispell
13	121	Bozeman HS	Bozeman
14	107	Libby K-12 Schools	Libby
15	97	Butte HS	Butte
16	93	Hamilton K-12 Schools	Hamilton
17	92	Columbia Falls Elem	Columbia Falls
18	91	Belgrade Elem	Belgrade

Number of Students

Rank	Number	District Name	City
1	10,154	Billings Elem	Billings
2	7,690	Great Falls Elem	Great Falls
3	5,624	Billings HS	Billings
4	5,135	Missoula Elem	Missoula
5	5,020	Helena Elem	Helena
6	4,015	Missoula HS	Missoula
7	3,684	Great Falls HS	Great Falls
8	3,405	Butte Elem	Butte
9	3,228	Bozeman Elem	Bozeman
10	3,070	Helena HS	Helena
11	2,473	Kalispell Elem	Kalispell
12	2,452	Flathead HS	Kalispell
13	1,873	Bozeman HS	Bozeman
14	1,747	Belgrade Elem	Belgrade
15	1,700	Libby K-12 Schools	Libby
16	1,671	Columbia Falls Elem	Columbia Falls
17	1,627	Hamilton K-12 Schools	Hamilton
18	1,531	Butte HS	Butte

Male Students

Rank	Percent	District Name	City
1	53.7	Libby K-12 Schools	Libby
2	52.9	Flathead HS	Kalispell
3	52.4	Bozeman HS	Bozeman
4	52.2	Billings HS	Billings
5	51.8	Billings Elem	Billings
6	51.7	Helena Elem	Helena
6	51.7	Kalispell Elem	Kalispell
8	51.6	Columbia Falls Elem	Columbia Falls
8	51.6	Missoula Elem	Missoula
10	51.3	Belgrade Elem	Belgrade
11	51.2	Butte Elem	Butte
12	51.1	Great Falls Elem	Great Falls
13	50.7	Helena HS	Helena
14	50.6	Butte HS	Butte
14	50.6	Hamilton K-12 Schools	Hamilton
16	50.2	Great Falls HS	Great Falls
17	50.1	Bozeman Elem	Bozeman
17	50.1	Missoula HS	Missoula

Female Students

Rank	Percent	District Name	City
1	49.9	Bozeman Elem	Bozeman
1	49.9	Missoula HS	Missoula
3	49.8	Great Falls HS	Great Falls
4	49.4	Butte HS	Butte
4	49.4	Hamilton K-12 Schools	Hamilton
6	49.3	Helena HS	Helena
7	48.9	Great Falls Elem	Great Falls
8	48.8	Butte Elem	Butte
9	48.7	Belgrade Elem	Belgrade
10	48.4	Columbia Falls Elem	Columbia Falls
10	48.4	Missoula Elem	Missoula
12	48.3	Helena Elem	Helena
12	48.3	Kalispell Elem	Kalispell
14	48.2	Billings Elem	Billings
15	47.8	Billings HS	Billings
16	47.6	Bozeman HS	Bozeman
17	47.1	Flathead HS	Kalispell
18	46.3	Libby K-12 Schools	Libby

Individual Education Program Students

Rank	Percent	District Name	City
1	17.0	Missoula Elem	Missoula
2	15.1	Columbia Falls Elem	Columbia Falls
2	15.1	Libby K-12 Schools	Libby
4	14.2	Butte Elem	Butte
5	13.4	Helena Elem	Helena
6	13.1	Missoula HS	Missoula
7	12.9	Billings Elem	Billings
7	12.9	Kalispell Elem	Kalispell
9	12.6	Billings HS	Billings
10	12.1	Hamilton K-12 Schools	Hamilton
11	11.8	Great Falls Elem	Great Falls
12	11.7	Butte HS	Butte
13	11.2	Belgrade Elem	Belgrade
14	10.5	Bozeman Elem	Bozeman
15	10.4	Great Falls HS	Great Falls
16	7.9	Helena HS	Helena
17	7.7	Bozeman HS	Bozeman
18	7.3	Flathead HS	Kalispell

English Language Learner Students

Rank	Percent	District Name	City
1	6.1	Missoula HS	Missoula
2	4.1	Missoula Elem	Missoula
3	2.7	Bozeman Elem	Bozeman
4	1.3	Bozeman HS	Bozeman
4	1.3	Kalispell Elem	Kalispell
6	0.5	Billings HS	Billings
7	0.4	Flathead HS	Kalispell
8	0.3	Billings Elem	Billings
8	0.3	Columbia Falls Elem	Columbia Falls
10	0.1	Belgrade Elem	Belgrade
10	0.1	Butte Elem	Butte
10	0.1	Great Falls Elem	Great Falls
10	0.1	Great Falls HS	Great Falls
10	0.1	Hamilton K-12 Schools	Hamilton
10	0.1	Helena HS	Helena
10	0.1	Libby K-12 Schools	Libby
17	0.0	Helena Elem	Helena
18	0.0	Butte HS	Butte

Migrant Students

Rank	Percent	District Name	City
1	n/a	Belgrade Elem	Belgrade
1	n/a	Billings Elem	Billings
1	n/a	Billings HS	Billings
1	n/a	Bozeman Elem	Bozeman
1	n/a	Bozeman HS	Bozeman
1	n/a	Butte Elem	Butte
1	n/a	Butte HS	Butte
1	n/a	Columbia Falls Elem	Columbia Falls
1	n/a	Flathead HS	Kalispell
1	n/a	Great Falls Elem	Great Falls
1	n/a	Great Falls HS	Great Falls
1	n/a	Hamilton K-12 Schools	Hamilton
1	n/a	Helena Elem	Helena
1	n/a	Helena HS	Helena
1	n/a	Kalispell Elem	Kalispell
1	n/a	Libby K-12 Schools	Libby
1	n/a	Missoula Elem	Missoula
1	n/a	Missoula HS	Missoula

Students Eligible for Free Lunch

Rank	Percent	District Name	City
1	35.1	Libby K-12 Schools	Libby
2	32.4	Butte Elem	Butte
3	29.7	Columbia Falls Elem	Columbia Falls
4	27.1	Missoula Elem	Missoula
5	27.0	Great Falls Elem	Great Falls
6	24.9	Kalispell Elem	Kalispell
7	24.6	Billings Elem	Billings
8	24.0	Hamilton K-12 Schools	Hamilton
9	20.3	Helena Elem	Helena
10	15.1	Belgrade Elem	Belgrade
11	14.0	Missoula HS	Missoula
12	13.0	Bozeman Elem	Bozeman
12	13.0	Flathead HS	Kalispell
14	11.4	Billings HS	Billings
14	11.4	Great Falls HS	Great Falls
16	8.6	Butte HS	Butte
17	6.5	Bozeman HS	Bozeman
18	6.1	Helena HS	Helena

Students Eligible for Reduced-Price Lunch

Rank	Percent	District Name	City
1	10.9	Libby K-12 Schools	Libby
2	10.6	Hamilton K-12 Schools	Hamilton
2	10.6	Kalispell Elem	Kalispell
4	9.8	Great Falls Elem	Great Falls
5	9.7	Billings Elem	Billings
6	9.4	Columbia Falls Elem	Columbia Falls
7	8.1	Belgrade Elem	Belgrade
8	7.9	Missoula Elem	Missoula
9	6.9	Helena Elem	Helena
10	6.4	Butte Elem	Butte
11	5.5	Bozeman Elem	Bozeman
12	4.8	Great Falls HS	Great Falls
13	4.7	Flathead HS	Kalispell
14	4.5	Billings HS	Billings
15	4.4	Missoula HS	Missoula
16	2.6	Bozeman HS	Bozeman
17	2.0	Helena HS	Helena
18	1.0	Butte HS	Butte

Student/Teacher Ratio

Rank	Ratio	District Name	City
1	19.2	Belgrade Elem	Belgrade
2	19.1	Helena Elem	Helena
3	18.7	Flathead HS	Kalispell
4	18.4	Kalispell Elem	Kalispell
5	18.1	Columbia Falls Elem	Columbia Falls
6	17.8	Billings HS	Billings
7	17.4	Hamilton K-12 Schools	Hamilton
8	16.8	Butte Elem	Butte
9	16.7	Bozeman Elem	Bozeman
10	16.4	Missoula Elem	Missoula
11	16.3	Billings Elem	Billings
11	16.3	Helena HS	Helena
13	15.9	Great Falls HS	Great Falls
13	15.9	Libby K-12 Schools	Libby
15	15.8	Butte HS	Butte
15	15.8	Great Falls Elem	Great Falls
17	15.5	Bozeman HS	Bozeman
18	15.2	Missoula HS	Missoula

Student/Librarian Ratio

Rank	Ratio	District Name	City
1	724.5	Butte Elem	Butte
2	703.0	Billings HS	Billings
3	700.6	Flathead HS	Kalispell
4	697.2	Helena Elem	Helena
5	693.7	Bozeman HS	Bozeman
6	669.8	Great Falls HS	Great Falls
7	669.2	Missoula HS	Missoula
8	667.4	Helena HS	Helena
9	640.8	Great Falls Elem	Great Falls
10	582.3	Belgrade Elem	Belgrade
11	567.0	Butte HS	Butte
12	557.0	Columbia Falls Elem	Columbia Falls
13	485.7	Libby K-12 Schools	Libby
14	428.2	Hamilton K-12 Schools	Hamilton
15	419.2	Bozeman Elem	Bozeman
16	376.1	Billings Elem	Billings
17	366.8	Missoula Elem	Missoula
18	309.1	Kalispell Elem	Kalispell

Student/Counselor Ratio

Rank	Ratio	District Name	City
1	1,068.1	Helena Elem	Helena
2	872.4	Bozeman Elem	Bozeman
3	641.9	Missoula Elem	Missoula
4	481.2	Billings Elem	Billings
5	448.0	Butte Elem	Butte
6	438.6	Helena HS	Helena
7	436.8	Belgrade Elem	Belgrade
8	406.9	Great Falls Elem	Great Falls
9	406.8	Hamilton K-12 Schools	Hamilton
10	397.9	Columbia Falls Elem	Columbia Falls
11	386.4	Kalispell Elem	Kalispell

Rank	Number	District Name	City
12	382.8	Butte HS	Butte
13	355.4	Flathead HS	Kalispell
14	340.0	Libby K-12 Schools	Libby
15	312.2	Bozeman HS	Bozeman
16	272.9	Great Falls HS	Great Falls
17	270.4	Billings HS	Billings
18	233.4	Missoula HS	Missoula

Current Spending per Student in FY2001

Rank	Dollars	District Name	City
1	7,577	Butte HS	Butte
2	7,204	Missoula HS	Missoula
3	6,762	Great Falls HS	Great Falls
4	6,725	Flathead HS	Kalispell
5	6,643	Billings HS	Billings
6	6,506	Helena HS	Helena
7	6,379	Missoula Elem	Missoula
8	6,243	Bozeman HS	Bozeman
9	5,845	Libby K-12 Schools	Libby
10	5,753	Helena Elem	Helena
11	5,576	Billings Elem	Billings
12	5,537	Kalispell Elem	Kalispell
13	5,444	Hamilton K-12 Schools	Hamilton
14	5,439	Butte Elem	Butte
15	5,410	Bozeman Elem	Bozeman
16	5,378	Great Falls Elem	Great Falls
17	5,075	Belgrade Elem	Belgrade
18	4,920	Columbia Falls Elem	Columbia Falls

Number of Diploma Recipients

Rank	Number	District Name	City
1	1,167	Billings HS	Billings
2	838	Missoula HS	Missoula
3	803	Great Falls HS	Great Falls
4	667	Helena HS	Helena
5	532	Flathead HS	Kalispell
6	448	Bozeman HS	Bozeman
7	296	Butte HS	Butte
8	140	Libby K-12 Schools	Libby
9	123	Hamilton K-12 Schools	Hamilton
10	n/a	Belgrade Elem	Belgrade
10	n/a	Billings Elem	Billings
10	n/a	Bozeman Elem	Bozeman
10	n/a	Butte Elem	Butte
10	n/a	Columbia Falls Elem	Columbia Falls
10	n/a	Great Falls Elem	Great Falls
10	n/a	Helena Elem	Helena
10	n/a	Kalispell Elem	Kalispell
10	n/a	Missoula Elem	Missoula

High School Drop-out Rate

Rank	Percent	District Name	City
1	6.2	Butte HS	Butte
2	5.2	Missoula HS	Missoula
3	5.0	Helena HS	Helena
4	4.7	Billings HS	Billings
5	3.9	Flathead HS	Kalispell
5	3.9	Libby K-12 Schools	Libby
7	3.1	Bozeman HS	Bozeman
8	2.3	Great Falls HS	Great Falls
9	1.6	Hamilton K-12 Schools	Hamilton
10	n/a	Belgrade Elem	Belgrade
10	n/a	Billings Elem	Billings
10	n/a	Bozeman Elem	Bozeman
10	n/a	Butte Elem	Butte
10	n/a	Columbia Falls Elem	Columbia Falls
10	n/a	Great Falls Elem	Great Falls
10	n/a	Helena Elem	Helena
10	n/a	Kalispell Elem	Kalispell
10	n/a	Missoula Elem	Missoula

Nebraska

Nebraska Public School Educational Profile

Category	Value	Category	Value
Schools *(2002-2003)*	1,281	**Diploma Recipients** *(2002-2003)*	19,910
Instructional Level		White, Non-Hispanic	17,851
Primary	825	Black, Non-Hispanic	796
Middle	98	Asian/Pacific Islander	357
High	308	American Indian/Alaskan Native	150
Other Level	50	Hispanic	756
Curriculum		**High School Drop-out Rate** (%) *(2000-2001)*	4.0
Regular	1,231	White, Non-Hispanic	2.9
Special Education	50	Black, Non-Hispanic	10.9
Vocational	0	Asian/Pacific Islander	3.8
Alternative	0	American Indian/Alaskan Native	13.9
Type		Hispanic	12.2
Magnet	0	**Staff** *(2002-2003)*	40,525.0
Charter	0	Teachers	21,043.3
Title I Eligible	497	Average Salary ($)	37,896
School-wide Title I	161	Librarians/Media Specialists	562.3
Students *(2002-2003)*	285,402	Guidance Counselors	776.5
Gender (%)		**Ratios** *(2002-2003)*	
Male	51.5	Student/Teacher Ratio	13.6 to 1
Female	48.5	Student/Librarian Ratio	507.6 to 1
Race/Ethnicity (%)		Student/Counselor Ratio	367.5 to 1
White, Non-Hispanic	80.6	**Current Spending** *($ per student in FY 2001)*	7,741
Black, Non-Hispanic	7.0	Instruction	4,879
Asian/Pacific Islander	1.6	Support Services	2,313
American Indian/Alaskan Native	1.6	**College Entrance Exam Scores** *(2003)*	
Hispanic	9.2	Scholastic Aptitude Test (SAT)	
Classification (%)		Participation Rate (%)	8
Individual Education Program (IEP)	15.8	Mean SAT I Verbal Score	573
Migrant	4.7	Mean SAT I Math Score	578
English Language Learner (ELL)	4.8	American College Testing Program (ACT)	
Eligible for Free Lunch Program	23.7	Participation Rate (%)	73
Eligible for Reduced-Price Lunch Program	8.7	Average Composite Score	21.7

Note: *For an explanation of data, please refer to the User's Guide in the front of the book; n/a indicates data not available*

Nebraska NAEP 2003 Test Scores

Reading			Mathematics		
Grade/Category	Value	Rank	Grade/Category	Value	Rank
4th Grade			**4th Grade**		
Average Proficiency	220.6 (1.0)	22/51	Average Proficiency	236.3 (0.8)	20/51
Proficiency by Gender/Race/Ethnicity			Proficiency by Gender/Race/Ethnicity		
Male	217.9 (1.3)	17/51	Male	237.8 (0.9)	22/51
Female	223.2 (1.3)	26/51	Female	234.7 (1.1)	24/51
White, Non-Hispanic	224.7 (1.1)	30/51	White, Non-Hispanic	241.5 (0.8)	29/51
Black, Non-Hispanic	203.3 (2.9)	8/42	Black, Non-Hispanic	210.8 (1.8)	34/42
Asian, Non-Hispanic	201.7 (2.7)	26/41	Asian, Non-Hispanic	212.9 (2.1)	41/43
American Indian, Non-Hispanic	n/a	n/a	American Indian, Non-Hispanic	n/a	n/a
Hispanic	n/a	n/a	Hispanic	218.8 (3.6)	5/12
Proficiency by Class Size			Proficiency by Class Size		
Less than 16 Students	216.7 (3.1)	7/45	Less than 16 Students	234.2 (2.3)	6/47
16 to 18 Students	216.7 (2.5)	23/48	16 to 18 Students	233.4 (1.7)	23/48
19 to 20 Students	218.6 (2.9)	27/50	19 to 20 Students	235.5 (2.9)	22/50
21 to 25 Students	225.3 (1.8)	14/51	21 to 25 Students	238.7 (1.9)	22/51
Greater than 25 Students	*219.4 (3.9)*	25/49	Greater than 25 Students	*237.7 (3.7)*	16/49
Percent Attaining Achievement Levels			Percent Attaining Achievement Levels		
Below Basic	33.7 (1.3)	31/51	Below Basic	20.1 (1.0)	31/51
Basic or Above	66.3 (1.3)	21/51	Basic or Above	79.9 (1.0)	21/51
Proficient or Above	32.3 (1.3)	24/51	Proficient or Above	33.6 (1.2)	22/51
Advanced or Above	7.9 (0.6)	15/51	Advanced or Above	3.2 (0.5)	28/51
8th Grade			**8th Grade**		
Average Proficiency	266.3 (0.9)	19/51	Average Proficiency	282.2 (0.9)	14/51
Proficiency by Gender/Race/Ethnicity			Proficiency by Gender/Race/Ethnicity		
Male	261.2 (1.1)	17/51	Male	283.7 (1.3)	13/51
Female	271.3 (1.1)	18/51	Female	280.5 (1.0)	19/51
White, Non-Hispanic	270.7 (0.9)	21/50	White, Non-Hispanic	287.3 (1.0)	19/50
Black, Non-Hispanic	239.0 (3.1)	34/41	Black, Non-Hispanic	246.7 (3.6)	32/41
Asian, Non-Hispanic	240.7 (3.1)	31/37	Asian, Non-Hispanic	254.6 (3.0)	28/37
American Indian, Non-Hispanic	n/a	n/a	American Indian, Non-Hispanic	n/a	n/a
Hispanic	n/a	n/a	Hispanic	n/a	n/a
Proficiency by Parents Highest Level of Ed.			Proficiency by Parents Highest Level of Ed.		
Did Not Finish High School	242.6 (3.2)	38/50	Did Not Finish High School	252.7 (3.8)	42/50
Graduated High School	255.1 (1.9)	27/50	Graduated High School	272.9 (1.7)	12/50
Some Education After High School	268.2 (2.0)	23/50	Some Education After High School	282.9 (1.7)	14/50
Graduated College	274.2 (1.1)	19/50	Graduated College	291.9 (1.1)	14/50
Percent Attaining Achievement Levels			Percent Attaining Achievement Levels		
Below Basic	22.7 (1.2)	35/51	Below Basic	25.6 (1.1)	39/51
Basic or Above	77.3 (1.2)	17/51	Basic or Above	74.4 (1.1)	13/51
Proficient or Above	35.0 (1.3)	16/51	Proficient or Above	32.3 (1.4)	14/51
Advanced or Above	2.5 (0.4)	26/51	Advanced or Above	5.1 (0.6)	22/51

***Note:** For an explanation of data, please refer to the User's Guide in the front of the book; values in italics indicate that the nature of the sample does not allow accurate determination of the variability of the statistic; n/a indicates data not available*

Adams County

Hastings Public Schools
714 W 5th • Hastings, NE 68901-5190
(402) 461-7500 • http://www1.hastings.esu9.k12.ne.us/
Grade Span: PK-12; **Agency Type:** 1
Schools: 8
6 Primary; 1 Middle; 1 High; 0 Other Level
8 Regular; 0 Special Education; 0 Vocational; 0 Alternative
0 Magnet; 0 Charter; 4 Title I Eligible; 2 School-wide Title I
Students: 3,264 (51.1% male; 48.9% female)
Individual Education Program: 615 (18.8%);
English Language Learner: 256 (7.8%); Migrant: 397 (12.2%)
Eligible for Free Lunch Program: 823 (25.2%)
Eligible for Reduced-Price Lunch Program: 327 (10.0%)
Teachers: 235.6 (13.9 to 1)
Librarians/Media Specialists: 5.0 (652.8 to 1)
Guidance Counselors: 11.0 (296.7 to 1)
Current Spending: ($ per student per year):
Total: $6,258; Instruction: $4,123; Support Services: $1,855
Enrollment, Drop-out Rates and Diploma Recipients by Race/Ethnicity

Category	Total	White	Black	Asian	AIAN	Hisp.
Enrollment (%)	100.0	83.7	1.3	2.1	0.9	12.0
Drop-out Rate (%)	4.6	3.5	50.0	3.2	0.0	18.5
H.S. Diplomas (#)	224	197	0	12	2	13

Box Butte County

Alliance Public Schools
1604 Sweetwater Ave • Alliance, NE 69301
(308) 762-5475 • http://www.aps.k12.ne.us/
Grade Span: PK-12; **Agency Type:** 1
Schools: 8
5 Primary; 1 Middle; 2 High; 0 Other Level
7 Regular; 1 Special Education; 0 Vocational; 0 Alternative
0 Magnet; 0 Charter; 3 Title I Eligible; 1 School-wide Title I
Students: 1,806 (54.3% male; 45.7% female)
Individual Education Program: 299 (16.6%);
English Language Learner: 20 (1.1%); Migrant: 280 (15.5%)
Eligible for Free Lunch Program: 397 (22.0%)
Eligible for Reduced-Price Lunch Program: 142 (7.9%)
Teachers: 136.0 (13.3 to 1)
Librarians/Media Specialists: 3.0 (602.0 to 1)
Guidance Counselors: 5.0 (361.2 to 1)
Current Spending: ($ per student per year):
Total: $6,624; Instruction: $4,420; Support Services: $1,979
Enrollment, Drop-out Rates and Diploma Recipients by Race/Ethnicity

Category	Total	White	Black	Asian	AIAN	Hisp.
Enrollment (%)	100.0	75.4	1.2	0.9	8.6	14.0
Drop-out Rate (%)	1.1	0.6	0.0	0.0	15.0	1.8
H.S. Diplomas (#)	169	153	1	0	0	15

Buffalo County

Kearney Public Schools
310 W 24th St • Kearney, NE 68845-5355
(308) 237-6000
Grade Span: PK-12; **Agency Type:** 1
Schools: 13
10 Primary; 2 Middle; 1 High; 0 Other Level
12 Regular; 1 Special Education; 0 Vocational; 0 Alternative
0 Magnet; 0 Charter; 6 Title I Eligible; 1 School-wide Title I
Students: 4,622 (51.6% male; 48.4% female)
Individual Education Program: 757 (16.4%);
English Language Learner: 129 (2.8%); Migrant: 172 (3.7%)
Eligible for Free Lunch Program: 978 (21.2%)
Eligible for Reduced-Price Lunch Program: 390 (8.4%)
Teachers: 302.6 (15.3 to 1)
Librarians/Media Specialists: 7.5 (616.3 to 1)
Guidance Counselors: 11.2 (412.7 to 1)
Current Spending: ($ per student per year):
Total: $5,985; Instruction: $3,815; Support Services: $1,755
Enrollment, Drop-out Rates and Diploma Recipients by Race/Ethnicity

Category	Total	White	Black	Asian	AIAN	Hisp.
Enrollment (%)	100.0	88.7	1.7	1.0	0.6	8.0
Drop-out Rate (%)	1.6	1.3	0.0	0.0	0.0	10.0
H.S. Diplomas (#)	317	305	1	2	1	8

Cass County

Plattsmouth Community Schools
1912 E Hwy 34 • Plattsmouth, NE 68048
(402) 296-3361 • http://www.plt.esu3.org
Grade Span: PK-12; **Agency Type:** 1
Schools: 5
2 Primary; 1 Middle; 2 High; 0 Other Level
4 Regular; 1 Special Education; 0 Vocational; 0 Alternative
0 Magnet; 0 Charter; 1 Title I Eligible; 1 School-wide Title I
Students: 1,635 (52.2% male; 47.8% female)
Individual Education Program: 381 (23.3%);
English Language Learner: 76 (4.6%); Migrant: 0 (0.0%)
Eligible for Free Lunch Program: 417 (25.5%)
Eligible for Reduced-Price Lunch Program: 154 (9.4%)
Teachers: 118.7 (13.8 to 1)
Librarians/Media Specialists: 2.5 (654.0 to 1)
Guidance Counselors: 3.0 (545.0 to 1)
Current Spending: ($ per student per year):
Total: $6,879; Instruction: $4,729; Support Services: $1,733
Enrollment, Drop-out Rates and Diploma Recipients by Race/Ethnicity

Category	Total	White	Black	Asian	AIAN	Hisp.
Enrollment (%)	100.0	94.0	0.6	1.2	0.8	3.4
Drop-out Rate (%)	4.3	4.2	n/a	0.0	0.0	12.5
H.S. Diplomas (#)	119	110	1	3	2	3

Dakota County

South Sioux City Community Schs
820 E 29th St Box 158 • So Sioux City, NE 68776-0158
(402) 494-2425 • http://www.sioux.esu1.k12.ne.us/
Grade Span: PK-12; **Agency Type:** 1
Schools: 10
7 Primary; 1 Middle; 1 High; 1 Other Level
9 Regular; 1 Special Education; 0 Vocational; 0 Alternative
0 Magnet; 0 Charter; 5 Title I Eligible; 3 School-wide Title I
Students: 3,457 (50.4% male; 49.6% female)
Individual Education Program: 547 (15.8%);
English Language Learner: 794 (23.0%); Migrant: 895 (25.9%)
Eligible for Free Lunch Program: 852 (24.6%)
Eligible for Reduced-Price Lunch Program: 334 (9.7%)
Teachers: 229.3 (15.1 to 1)
Librarians/Media Specialists: 5.0 (691.4 to 1)
Guidance Counselors: 8.4 (411.5 to 1)
Current Spending: ($ per student per year):
Total: $5,847; Instruction: $3,741; Support Services: $1,777
Enrollment, Drop-out Rates and Diploma Recipients by Race/Ethnicity

Category	Total	White	Black	Asian	AIAN	Hisp.
Enrollment (%)	100.0	47.3	1.2	3.6	3.7	44.2
Drop-out Rate (%)	7.8	5.4	25.0	3.9	22.2	13.1
H.S. Diplomas (#)	191	137	0	18	2	34

Dawson County

Lexington Public Schools
1610 N Washington Box 890 • Lexington, NE 68850-0890
(308) 324-4681 • http://www.lex.esu10.org/
Grade Span: PK-12; **Agency Type:** 1
Schools: 8
6 Primary; 1 Middle; 1 High; 0 Other Level
7 Regular; 1 Special Education; 0 Vocational; 0 Alternative
0 Magnet; 0 Charter; 4 Title I Eligible; 4 School-wide Title I
Students: 2,668 (52.4% male; 47.6% female)
Individual Education Program: 340 (12.7%);
English Language Learner: 644 (24.1%); Migrant: 1,914 (71.7%)
Eligible for Free Lunch Program: 1,069 (40.1%)
Eligible for Reduced-Price Lunch Program: 327 (12.3%)
Teachers: 163.9 (16.3 to 1)
Librarians/Media Specialists: 3.0 (889.3 to 1)
Guidance Counselors: 6.0 (444.7 to 1)
Current Spending: ($ per student per year):
Total: $5,314; Instruction: $3,467; Support Services: $1,512
Enrollment, Drop-out Rates and Diploma Recipients by Race/Ethnicity

Category	Total	White	Black	Asian	AIAN	Hisp.
Enrollment (%)	100.0	31.0	0.4	1.6	0.3	66.6
Drop-out Rate (%)	7.0	2.8	0.0	7.1	0.0	12.8
H.S. Diplomas (#)	126	71	0	2	0	53

Dodge County

Fremont Public Schools
957 N Pierce St • Fremont, NE 68025-3949
(402) 727-3000 • http://www.fpsweb.org/
Grade Span: PK-12; **Agency Type:** 1
Schools: 12
8 Primary; 1 Middle; 2 High; 1 Other Level
12 Regular; 0 Special Education; 0 Vocational; 0 Alternative
0 Magnet; 0 Charter; 3 Title I Eligible; 3 School-wide Title I
Students: 4,468 (49.8% male; 50.2% female)
Individual Education Program: 854 (19.1%);
English Language Learner: 217 (4.9%); Migrant: 394 (8.8%)
Eligible for Free Lunch Program: 1,058 (23.7%)

Eligible for Reduced-Price Lunch Program: 466 (10.4%)
Teachers: 279.8 (16.0 to 1)
Librarians/Media Specialists: 6.0 (744.7 to 1)
Guidance Counselors: 10.8 (413.7 to 1)
Current Spending: ($ per student per year):
Total: $5,875; Instruction: $3,589; Support Services: $1,984
Enrollment, Drop-out Rates and Diploma Recipients by Race/Ethnicity

Category	Total	White	Black	Asian	AIAN	Hisp.
Enrollment (%)	100.0	87.1	1.2	1.2	0.6	9.8
Drop-out Rate (%)	4.3	3.9	20.0	14.3	9.1	11.1
H.S. Diplomas (#)	287	272	2	3	1	9

Douglas County

Elkhorn Public Schools
502 Glenn St • Elkhorn, NE 68022-0439
Mailing Address: PO Box 439 • Elkhorn, NE 68022-0439
(402) 289-2579 • http://205.202.101.100/
Grade Span: PK-12; **Agency Type:** 1
Schools: 6
4 Primary; 1 Middle; 1 High; 0 Other Level
6 Regular; 0 Special Education; 0 Vocational; 0 Alternative
0 Magnet; 0 Charter; 2 Title I Eligible; 0 School-wide Title I
Students: 3,099 (53.1% male; 46.9% female)
Individual Education Program: 498 (16.1%);
English Language Learner: 40 (1.3%); Migrant: 2 (0.1%)
Eligible for Free Lunch Program: 221 (7.1%)
Eligible for Reduced-Price Lunch Program: 132 (4.3%)
Teachers: 207.4 (14.9 to 1)
Librarians/Media Specialists: 6.0 (516.5 to 1)
Guidance Counselors: 9.0 (344.3 to 1)
Current Spending: ($ per student per year):
Total: $5,937; Instruction: $3,933; Support Services: $1,707
Enrollment, Drop-out Rates and Diploma Recipients by Race/Ethnicity

Category	Total	White	Black	Asian	AIAN	Hisp.
Enrollment (%)	100.0	95.0	0.5	1.2	0.1	3.1
Drop-out Rate (%)	1.7	1.6	100.0	0.0	0.0	0.0
H.S. Diplomas (#)	200	193	0	0	2	5

Millard Public Schools
5606 S 147th St • Omaha, NE 68137-2604
(402) 895-8200 • http://www.mpsomaha.org/
Grade Span: PK-12; **Agency Type:** 1
Schools: 34
22 Primary; 6 Middle; 3 High; 3 Other Level
31 Regular; 3 Special Education; 0 Vocational; 0 Alternative
0 Magnet; 0 Charter; 3 Title I Eligible; 1 School-wide Title I
Students: 19,476 (52.0% male; 48.0% female)
Individual Education Program: 2,720 (14.0%);
English Language Learner: 130 (0.7%); Migrant: 0 (0.0%)
Eligible for Free Lunch Program: 877 (4.5%)
Eligible for Reduced-Price Lunch Program: 459 (2.4%)
Teachers: 1,240.5 (15.7 to 1)
Librarians/Media Specialists: 33.2 (586.6 to 1)
Guidance Counselors: 46.1 (422.5 to 1)
Current Spending: ($ per student per year):
Total: $6,133; Instruction: $3,869; Support Services: $1,973
Enrollment, Drop-out Rates and Diploma Recipients by Race/Ethnicity

Category	Total	White	Black	Asian	AIAN	Hisp.
Enrollment (%)	100.0	93.4	1.9	2.4	0.3	2.0
Drop-out Rate (%)	1.6	1.5	2.9	4.9	9.5	0.0
H.S. Diplomas (#)	1,513	1,433	17	36	5	22

Omaha Public Schools
3215 Cuming St • Omaha, NE 68131-2024
(402) 557-2222 • http://www.ops.org/
Grade Span: PK-12; **Agency Type:** 1
Schools: 84
60 Primary; 6 Middle; 10 High; 8 Other Level
81 Regular; 3 Special Education; 0 Vocational; 0 Alternative
0 Magnet; 0 Charter; 38 Title I Eligible; 38 School-wide Title I
Students: 45,986 (51.3% male; 48.7% female)
Individual Education Program: 7,011 (15.2%);
English Language Learner: 4,765 (10.4%); Migrant: 1,796 (3.9%)
Eligible for Free Lunch Program: 20,563 (44.7%)
Eligible for Reduced-Price Lunch Program: 4,373 (9.5%)
Teachers: 3,111.1 (14.8 to 1)
Librarians/Media Specialists: 89.0 (516.7 to 1)
Guidance Counselors: 143.3 (320.9 to 1)
Current Spending: ($ per student per year):
Total: $6,352; Instruction: $3,679; Support Services: $2,382
Enrollment, Drop-out Rates and Diploma Recipients by Race/Ethnicity

Category	Total	White	Black	Asian	AIAN	Hisp.
Enrollment (%)	100.0	49.0	31.2	1.7	1.4	16.6
Drop-out Rate (%)	9.9	7.8	11.6	2.5	24.7	16.9
H.S. Diplomas (#)	2,168	1,385	557	45	14	167

Ralston Public Schools
8545 Park Dr • Ralston, NE 68127-3690
(402) 331-4700 • http://www.ralstonschools.org/
Grade Span: PK-12; **Agency Type:** 1
Schools: 8
6 Primary; 1 Middle; 1 High; 0 Other Level
8 Regular; 0 Special Education; 0 Vocational; 0 Alternative
0 Magnet; 0 Charter; 4 Title I Eligible; 0 School-wide Title I
Students: 3,126 (52.3% male; 47.7% female)
Individual Education Program: 476 (15.2%);
English Language Learner: 85 (2.7%); Migrant: 0 (0.0%)
Eligible for Free Lunch Program: 533 (17.1%)
Eligible for Reduced-Price Lunch Program: 262 (8.4%)
Teachers: 201.6 (15.5 to 1)
Librarians/Media Specialists: 3.4 (919.4 to 1)
Guidance Counselors: 5.8 (539.0 to 1)
Current Spending: ($ per student per year):
Total: $7,072; Instruction: $4,969; Support Services: $1,811
Enrollment, Drop-out Rates and Diploma Recipients by Race/Ethnicity

Category	Total	White	Black	Asian	AIAN	Hisp.
Enrollment (%)	100.0	84.4	3.2	2.8	0.2	9.3
Drop-out Rate (%)	3.0	2.8	4.5	0.0	n/a	7.9
H.S. Diplomas (#)	204	190	6	4	0	4

Westside Community Schools
909 S 76th St • Omaha, NE 68114-4599
(402) 390-2100 • http://www.westside66.org/
Grade Span: PK-12; **Agency Type:** 1
Schools: 14
11 Primary; 1 Middle; 1 High; 1 Other Level
13 Regular; 1 Special Education; 0 Vocational; 0 Alternative
0 Magnet; 0 Charter; 4 Title I Eligible; 0 School-wide Title I
Students: 5,625 (52.1% male; 47.9% female)
Individual Education Program: 651 (11.6%);
English Language Learner: 146 (2.6%); Migrant: 0 (0.0%)
Eligible for Free Lunch Program: 649 (11.5%)
Eligible for Reduced-Price Lunch Program: 356 (6.3%)
Teachers: 410.8 (13.7 to 1)
Librarians/Media Specialists: 8.6 (654.1 to 1)
Guidance Counselors: 18.5 (304.1 to 1)
Current Spending: ($ per student per year):
Total: $7,541; Instruction: $4,811; Support Services: $2,402
Enrollment, Drop-out Rates and Diploma Recipients by Race/Ethnicity

Category	Total	White	Black	Asian	AIAN	Hisp.
Enrollment (%)	100.0	88.2	5.3	3.6	0.6	2.3
Drop-out Rate (%)	0.8	0.7	2.2	0.0	14.3	3.2
H.S. Diplomas (#)	338	315	4	11	1	7

Gage County

Beatrice Public Schools
320 N 5th St • Beatrice, NE 68310-2958
(402) 223-1500 • http://www.beatrice.k12.ne.us
Grade Span: PK-12; **Agency Type:** 1
Schools: 6
4 Primary; 1 Middle; 1 High; 0 Other Level
6 Regular; 0 Special Education; 0 Vocational; 0 Alternative
0 Magnet; 0 Charter; 4 Title I Eligible; 0 School-wide Title I
Students: 2,254 (52.0% male; 48.0% female)
Individual Education Program: 369 (16.4%);
English Language Learner: 2 (0.1%); Migrant: 2 (0.1%)
Eligible for Free Lunch Program: 479 (21.3%)
Eligible for Reduced-Price Lunch Program: 212 (9.4%)
Teachers: 145.9 (15.4 to 1)
Librarians/Media Specialists: 3.0 (751.3 to 1)
Guidance Counselors: 6.0 (375.7 to 1)
Current Spending: ($ per student per year):
Total: $6,038; Instruction: $3,868; Support Services: $1,752
Enrollment, Drop-out Rates and Diploma Recipients by Race/Ethnicity

Category	Total	White	Black	Asian	AIAN	Hisp.
Enrollment (%)	100.0	95.5	1.6	0.6	0.7	1.6
Drop-out Rate (%)	2.6	2.6	0.0	0.0	20.0	0.0
H.S. Diplomas (#)	180	176	1	1	0	2

Hall County

Grand Island Public Schools

123 S Webb Rd • Grand Island, NE 68802-4904
Mailing Address: PO Box 4904 • Grand Island, NE 68802-4904
(308) 385-5900 • http://www.gi.esu10.k12.ne.us/SDGI/Buildingweb.html
Grade Span: PK-12; **Agency Type:** 1
Schools: 21
14 Primary; 4 Middle; 2 High; 1 Other Level
20 Regular; 1 Special Education; 0 Vocational; 0 Alternative
0 Magnet; 0 Charter; 9 Title I Eligible; 9 School-wide Title I
Students: 7,690 (51.1% male; 48.9% female)
Individual Education Program: 1,247 (16.2%);
English Language Learner: 1,261 (16.4%); Migrant: 1,366 (17.8%)
Eligible for Free Lunch Program: 2,802 (36.4%)
Eligible for Reduced-Price Lunch Program: 815 (10.6%)
Teachers: 504.8 (15.2 to 1)
Librarians/Media Specialists: 17.3 (444.5 to 1)
Guidance Counselors: 17.6 (436.9 to 1)
Current Spending: ($ per student per year):
Total: $6,287; Instruction: $4,441; Support Services: $1,554
Enrollment, Drop-out Rates and Diploma Recipients by Race/Ethnicity

Category	Total	White	Black	Asian	AIAN	Hisp.
Enrollment (%)	100.0	67.8	1.4	1.9	0.4	28.5
Drop-out Rate (%)	6.8	4.5	0.0	8.2	75.0	16.2
H.S. Diplomas (#)	340	277	3	12	0	48

Lancaster County

Lincoln Public Schools

Box 82889 • Lincoln, NE 68501-2889
(402) 436-1000 • http://www.lps.org/
Grade Span: PK-12; **Agency Type:** 1
Schools: 65
40 Primary; 10 Middle; 12 High; 3 Other Level
63 Regular; 2 Special Education; 0 Vocational; 0 Alternative
0 Magnet; 0 Charter; 12 Title I Eligible; 12 School-wide Title I
Students: 31,867 (51.4% male; 48.6% female)
Individual Education Program: 5,315 (16.7%);
English Language Learner: 2,115 (6.6%); Migrant: 613 (1.9%)
Eligible for Free Lunch Program: 7,036 (22.1%)
Eligible for Reduced-Price Lunch Program: 1,852 (5.8%)
Teachers: 2,362.3 (13.5 to 1)
Librarians/Media Specialists: 54.9 (580.5 to 1)
Guidance Counselors: 73.8 (431.8 to 1)
Current Spending: ($ per student per year):
Total: $6,915; Instruction: $4,450; Support Services: $2,139
Enrollment, Drop-out Rates and Diploma Recipients by Race/Ethnicity

Category	Total	White	Black	Asian	AIAN	Hisp.
Enrollment (%)	100.0	83.3	7.0	3.7	1.3	4.6
Drop-out Rate (%)	6.5	5.7	11.1	6.6	11.5	19.5
H.S. Diplomas (#)	1,896	1,661	77	90	19	49

Norris SD 160

25211 S 68th St • Firth, NE 68358-9732
(402) 791-0000
Grade Span: PK-12; **Agency Type:** 1
Schools: 3
1 Primary; 1 Middle; 1 High; 0 Other Level
3 Regular; 0 Special Education; 0 Vocational; 0 Alternative
0 Magnet; 0 Charter; 1 Title I Eligible; 0 School-wide Title I
Students: 1,648 (53.5% male; 46.5% female)
Individual Education Program: 259 (15.7%);
English Language Learner: 6 (0.4%); Migrant: 3 (0.2%)
Eligible for Free Lunch Program: 104 (6.3%)
Eligible for Reduced-Price Lunch Program: 50 (3.0%)
Teachers: 92.2 (17.9 to 1)
Librarians/Media Specialists: 2.0 (824.0 to 1)
Guidance Counselors: 3.0 (549.3 to 1)
Current Spending: ($ per student per year):
Total: $5,813; Instruction: $3,457; Support Services: $2,117
Enrollment, Drop-out Rates and Diploma Recipients by Race/Ethnicity

Category	Total	White	Black	Asian	AIAN	Hisp.
Enrollment (%)	100.0	96.3	0.8	0.8	0.2	1.8
Drop-out Rate (%)	1.1	1.1	0.0	0.0	0.0	0.0
H.S. Diplomas (#)	120	116	2	0	1	1

Waverly SD 145

14511 Heywood Box 426 • Waverly, NE 68462-0426
(402) 786-2321 • http://www.dist145.esu6.org/whs/
Grade Span: PK-12; **Agency Type:** 1
Schools: 5
3 Primary; 1 Middle; 1 High; 0 Other Level
4 Regular; 1 Special Education; 0 Vocational; 0 Alternative
0 Magnet; 0 Charter; 1 Title I Eligible; 0 School-wide Title I
Students: 1,672 (53.1% male; 46.9% female)
Individual Education Program: 326 (19.5%);
English Language Learner: 42 (2.5%); Migrant: 3 (0.2%)
Eligible for Free Lunch Program: 167 (10.0%)
Eligible for Reduced-Price Lunch Program: 79 (4.7%)
Teachers: 120.1 (13.9 to 1)
Librarians/Media Specialists: 3.0 (557.3 to 1)
Guidance Counselors: 5.0 (334.4 to 1)
Current Spending: ($ per student per year):
Total: $7,016; Instruction: $4,084; Support Services: $2,123
Enrollment, Drop-out Rates and Diploma Recipients by Race/Ethnicity

Category	Total	White	Black	Asian	AIAN	Hisp.
Enrollment (%)	100.0	98.0	0.2	0.5	0.4	0.9
Drop-out Rate (%)	0.0	0.0	0.0	0.0	0.0	0.0
H.S. Diplomas (#)	131	130	0	0	0	1

Lincoln County

North Platte Public Schools

301 W F PO Box 1557 • North Platte, NE 69103-1557
(308) 535-7100 • http://www.nppsd.org/
Grade Span: PK-12; **Agency Type:** 1
Schools: 13
8 Primary; 3 Middle; 2 High; 0 Other Level
13 Regular; 0 Special Education; 0 Vocational; 0 Alternative
0 Magnet; 0 Charter; 5 Title I Eligible; 4 School-wide Title I
Students: 3,979 (51.8% male; 48.2% female)
Individual Education Program: 765 (19.2%);
English Language Learner: 16 (0.4%); Migrant: 0 (0.0%)
Eligible for Free Lunch Program: 1,024 (25.7%)
Eligible for Reduced-Price Lunch Program: 396 (10.0%)
Teachers: 269.5 (14.8 to 1)
Librarians/Media Specialists: 5.0 (795.8 to 1)
Guidance Counselors: 11.0 (361.7 to 1)
Current Spending: ($ per student per year):
Total: $6,261; Instruction: $4,079; Support Services: $1,871
Enrollment, Drop-out Rates and Diploma Recipients by Race/Ethnicity

Category	Total	White	Black	Asian	AIAN	Hisp.
Enrollment (%)	100.0	86.9	1.5	0.8	0.8	10.1
Drop-out Rate (%)	4.7	4.0	0.0	0.0	0.0	14.9
H.S. Diplomas (#)	344	317	4	1	1	21

Madison County

Norfolk Public Schools

512 Philip Ave • Norfolk, NE 68702-0139
Mailing Address: PO Box 139 • Norfolk, NE 68702-0139
(402) 644-2500 • http://www.norfolkpublicschools.org/
Grade Span: PK-12; **Agency Type:** 1
Schools: 15
10 Primary; 2 Middle; 2 High; 1 Other Level
13 Regular; 2 Special Education; 0 Vocational; 0 Alternative
0 Magnet; 0 Charter; 7 Title I Eligible; 3 School-wide Title I
Students: 4,232 (50.9% male; 49.1% female)
Individual Education Program: 757 (17.9%);
English Language Learner: 279 (6.6%); Migrant: 1,367 (32.3%)
Eligible for Free Lunch Program: 1,176 (27.8%)
Eligible for Reduced-Price Lunch Program: 401 (9.5%)
Teachers: 285.6 (14.8 to 1)
Librarians/Media Specialists: 5.0 (846.4 to 1)
Guidance Counselors: 11.5 (368.0 to 1)
Current Spending: ($ per student per year):
Total: $6,018; Instruction: $4,055; Support Services: $1,687
Enrollment, Drop-out Rates and Diploma Recipients by Race/Ethnicity

Category	Total	White	Black	Asian	AIAN	Hisp.
Enrollment (%)	100.0	74.9	3.6	0.5	3.4	17.6
Drop-out Rate (%)	3.0	2.2	3.4	0.0	5.4	11.4
H.S. Diplomas (#)	359	322	7	7	5	18

Platte County

Columbus Public Schools

2508 27th St Box 947 • Columbus, NE 68602-0947
(402) 563-7000 • http://www.discoverers.org/
Grade Span: PK-12; **Agency Type:** 1
Schools: 8
6 Primary; 1 Middle; 1 High; 0 Other Level
8 Regular; 0 Special Education; 0 Vocational; 0 Alternative
0 Magnet; 0 Charter; 3 Title I Eligible; 2 School-wide Title I
Students: 3,443 (50.2% male; 49.8% female)
Individual Education Program: 599 (17.4%);
English Language Learner: 433 (12.6%); Migrant: 551 (16.0%)
Eligible for Free Lunch Program: 663 (19.3%)
Eligible for Reduced-Price Lunch Program: 359 (10.4%)
Teachers: 220.4 (15.6 to 1)

Librarians/Media Specialists: 6.0 (573.8 to 1)
Guidance Counselors: 7.8 (441.4 to 1)
Current Spending: ($ per student per year):
Total: $5,894; Instruction: $3,966; Support Services: $1,589
Enrollment, Drop-out Rates and Diploma Recipients by Race/Ethnicity

Category	Total	White	Black	Asian	AIAN	Hisp.
Enrollment (%)	100.0	80.5	1.4	1.0	0.8	16.4
Drop-out Rate (%)	2.9	2.3	13.3	9.1	20.0	6.9
H.S. Diplomas (#)	279	261	2	3	1	12

Saline County

Crete Public Schools
920 Linden Ave • Crete, NE 68333-2292
(402) 471-3464
Grade Span: PK-12; **Agency Type:** 1
Schools: 2
1 Primary; 0 Middle; 1 High; 0 Other Level
2 Regular; 0 Special Education; 0 Vocational; 0 Alternative
0 Magnet; 0 Charter; 1 Title I Eligible; 0 School-wide Title I
Students: 1,522 (50.9% male; 49.1% female)
Individual Education Program: 170 (11.2%);
English Language Learner: 311 (20.4%); Migrant: 450 (29.6%)
Eligible for Free Lunch Program: 320 (21.0%)
Eligible for Reduced-Price Lunch Program: 134 (8.8%)
Teachers: 97.6 (15.6 to 1)
Librarians/Media Specialists: 1.9 (801.1 to 1)
Guidance Counselors: 2.6 (585.4 to 1)
Current Spending: ($ per student per year):
Total: $5,657; Instruction: $3,505; Support Services: $1,826
Enrollment, Drop-out Rates and Diploma Recipients by Race/Ethnicity

Category	Total	White	Black	Asian	AIAN	Hisp.
Enrollment (%)	100.0	71.7	1.7	3.4	0.2	23.0
Drop-out Rate (%)	1.6	1.4	0.0	0.0	0.0	6.7
H.S. Diplomas (#)	112	101	1	5	1	4

Sarpy County

Bellevue Public Schools
1600 Hwy 370 • Bellevue, NE 68005-3591
(402) 293-4000 •
http://www.esu3.k12.ne.us/districts/bellevue/bpshome.html
Grade Span: PK-12; **Agency Type:** 1
Schools: 19
14 Primary; 2 Middle; 2 High; 1 Other Level
18 Regular; 1 Special Education; 0 Vocational; 0 Alternative
0 Magnet; 0 Charter; 4 Title I Eligible; 4 School-wide Title I
Students: 8,886 (51.8% male; 48.2% female)
Individual Education Program: 1,315 (14.8%);
English Language Learner: 36 (0.4%); Migrant: 0 (0.0%)
Eligible for Free Lunch Program: 829 (9.3%)
Eligible for Reduced-Price Lunch Program: 676 (7.6%)
Teachers: 573.5 (15.5 to 1)
Librarians/Media Specialists: 15.0 (592.4 to 1)
Guidance Counselors: 22.0 (403.9 to 1)
Current Spending: ($ per student per year):
Total: $6,446; Instruction: $4,238; Support Services: $1,884
Enrollment, Drop-out Rates and Diploma Recipients by Race/Ethnicity

Category	Total	White	Black	Asian	AIAN	Hisp.
Enrollment (%)	100.0	80.5	9.5	3.5	1.0	5.5
Drop-out Rate (%)	1.8	1.8	1.7	0.0	25.0	0.9
H.S. Diplomas (#)	592	493	61	23	2	13

Gretna Public Schools
801 S St • Gretna, NE 68028-7865
(402) 332-3265
Grade Span: PK-12; **Agency Type:** 1
Schools: 3
1 Primary; 1 Middle; 1 High; 0 Other Level
3 Regular; 0 Special Education; 0 Vocational; 0 Alternative
0 Magnet; 0 Charter; 1 Title I Eligible; 0 School-wide Title I
Students: 1,571 (51.1% male; 48.9% female)
Individual Education Program: 236 (15.0%);
English Language Learner: 2 (0.1%); Migrant: 0 (0.0%)
Eligible for Free Lunch Program: 71 (4.5%)
Eligible for Reduced-Price Lunch Program: 32 (2.0%)
Teachers: 99.7 (15.8 to 1)
Librarians/Media Specialists: 3.0 (523.7 to 1)
Guidance Counselors: 3.0 (523.7 to 1)
Current Spending: ($ per student per year):
Total: $6,110; Instruction: $3,810; Support Services: $1,906

Enrollment, Drop-out Rates and Diploma Recipients by Race/Ethnicity

Category	Total	White	Black	Asian	AIAN	Hisp.
Enrollment (%)	100.0	97.8	0.1	1.2	0.3	0.6
Drop-out Rate (%)	0.0	0.0	n/a	0.0	n/a	0.0
H.S. Diplomas (#)	99	99	0	0	0	0

Papillion-La Vista Public Schools
420 S Washington • Papillion, NE 68046-2667
(402) 537-9998 • http://www.paplv.esu3.org/coadm/default2.html
Grade Span: PK-12; **Agency Type:** 1
Schools: 17
11 Primary; 2 Middle; 3 High; 1 Other Level
16 Regular; 1 Special Education; 0 Vocational; 0 Alternative
0 Magnet; 0 Charter; 5 Title I Eligible; 0 School-wide Title I
Students: 8,114 (50.9% male; 49.1% female)
Individual Education Program: 948 (11.7%);
English Language Learner: 42 (0.5%); Migrant: 0 (0.0%)
Eligible for Free Lunch Program: 611 (7.5%)
Eligible for Reduced-Price Lunch Program: 417 (5.1%)
Teachers: 499.2 (16.3 to 1)
Librarians/Media Specialists: 14.3 (567.4 to 1)
Guidance Counselors: 21.8 (372.2 to 1)
Current Spending: ($ per student per year):
Total: $5,837; Instruction: $3,974; Support Services: $1,608
Enrollment, Drop-out Rates and Diploma Recipients by Race/Ethnicity

Category	Total	White	Black	Asian	AIAN	Hisp.
Enrollment (%)	100.0	89.5	4.8	2.2	0.5	3.0
Drop-out Rate (%)	2.9	2.8	6.9	4.1	0.0	2.8
H.S. Diplomas (#)	534	482	12	22	2	16

Scotts Bluff County

Gering Public Schools
1800 8th St • Gering, NE 69341-2999
(308) 436-3125 • http://www.geringschools.net/
Grade Span: PK-12; **Agency Type:** 1
Schools: 5
3 Primary; 1 Middle; 1 High; 0 Other Level
5 Regular; 0 Special Education; 0 Vocational; 0 Alternative
0 Magnet; 0 Charter; 3 Title I Eligible; 0 School-wide Title I
Students: 1,879 (49.9% male; 50.1% female)
Individual Education Program: 217 (11.5%);
English Language Learner: 52 (2.8%); Migrant: 149 (7.9%)
Eligible for Free Lunch Program: 481 (25.6%)
Eligible for Reduced-Price Lunch Program: 196 (10.4%)
Teachers: 125.9 (14.9 to 1)
Librarians/Media Specialists: 2.9 (647.9 to 1)
Guidance Counselors: 4.9 (383.5 to 1)
Current Spending: ($ per student per year):
Total: $6,060; Instruction: $4,163; Support Services: $1,700
Enrollment, Drop-out Rates and Diploma Recipients by Race/Ethnicity

Category	Total	White	Black	Asian	AIAN	Hisp.
Enrollment (%)	100.0	72.0	0.4	0.7	3.7	23.2
Drop-out Rate (%)	4.3	3.0	n/a	0.0	9.1	9.6
H.S. Diplomas (#)	142	124	0	1	1	16

Scottsbluff Public Schools
2601 Broadway • Scottsbluff, NE 69361-1609
(308) 635-6200 • http://www.sbps.net/
Grade Span: PK-12; **Agency Type:** 1
Schools: 6
4 Primary; 1 Middle; 1 High; 0 Other Level
6 Regular; 0 Special Education; 0 Vocational; 0 Alternative
0 Magnet; 0 Charter; 3 Title I Eligible; 1 School-wide Title I
Students: 2,744 (49.5% male; 50.5% female)
Individual Education Program: 405 (14.8%);
English Language Learner: 114 (4.2%); Migrant: 12 (0.4%)
Eligible for Free Lunch Program: 912 (33.2%)
Eligible for Reduced-Price Lunch Program: 186 (6.8%)
Teachers: 184.0 (14.9 to 1)
Librarians/Media Specialists: 4.0 (686.0 to 1)
Guidance Counselors: 4.0 (686.0 to 1)
Current Spending: ($ per student per year):
Total: $5,907; Instruction: $3,972; Support Services: $1,680
Enrollment, Drop-out Rates and Diploma Recipients by Race/Ethnicity

Category	Total	White	Black	Asian	AIAN	Hisp.
Enrollment (%)	100.0	60.1	1.0	1.1	6.0	31.8
Drop-out Rate (%)	2.9	2.0	0.0	0.0	9.7	4.9
H.S. Diplomas (#)	195	158	0	1	1	35

Washington County

Blair Community Schools

140 S 16th • Blair, NE 68008-0288
Mailing Address: PO Box 288 • Blair, NE 68008-0288
(402) 426-2610
Grade Span: PK-12; **Agency Type:** 1
Schools: 6
4 Primary; 1 Middle; 1 High; 0 Other Level
6 Regular; 0 Special Education; 0 Vocational; 0 Alternative
0 Magnet; 0 Charter; 3 Title I Eligible; 0 School-wide Title I
Students: 2,245 (51.4% male; 48.6% female)
Individual Education Program: 376 (16.7%);
English Language Learner: 18 (0.8%); Migrant: 1 (<0.1%)
Eligible for Free Lunch Program: 254 (11.3%)
Eligible for Reduced-Price Lunch Program: 96 (4.3%)
Teachers: 140.5 (16.0 to 1)
Librarians/Media Specialists: 3.1 (724.2 to 1)
Guidance Counselors: 6.0 (374.2 to 1)
Current Spending: ($ per student per year):
Total: $5,955; Instruction: $3,770; Support Services: $1,868

Enrollment, Drop-out Rates and Diploma Recipients by Race/Ethnicity

Category	Total	White	Black	Asian	AIAN	Hisp.
Enrollment (%)	100.0	97.1	0.8	0.4	0.3	1.4
Drop-out Rate (%)	2.2	2.3	0.0	0.0	0.0	0.0
H.S. Diplomas (#)	160	159	0	1	0	0

Number of Schools

Rank	Number	District Name	City
1	84	Omaha Public Schools	Omaha
2	65	Lincoln Public Schools	Lincoln
3	34	Millard Public Schools	Omaha
4	21	Grand Island Public Schools	Grand Island
5	19	Bellevue Public Schools	Bellevue
6	17	Papillion-La Vista Public Schools	Papillion
7	15	Norfolk Public Schools	Norfolk
8	14	Westside Community Schools	Omaha
9	13	Kearney Public Schools	Kearney
9	13	North Platte Public Schools	North Platte
11	12	Fremont Public Schools	Fremont
12	10	South Sioux City Community Schs	So Sioux City
13	8	Alliance Public Schools	Alliance
13	8	Columbus Public Schools	Columbus
13	8	Hastings Public Schools	Hastings
13	8	Lexington Public Schools	Lexington
13	8	Ralston Public Schools	Ralston
18	6	Beatrice Public Schools	Beatrice
18	6	Blair Community Schools	Blair
18	6	Elkhorn Public Schools	Elkhorn
18	6	Scottsbluff Public Schools	Scottsbluff
22	5	Gering Public Schools	Gering
22	5	Plattsmouth Community Schools	Plattsmouth
22	5	Waverly SD 145	Waverly
25	3	Gretna Public Schools	Gretna
25	3	Norris SD 160	Firth
27	2	Crete Public Schools	Crete

Number of Teachers

Rank	Number	District Name	City
1	3,111	Omaha Public Schools	Omaha
2	2,362	Lincoln Public Schools	Lincoln
3	1,240	Millard Public Schools	Omaha
4	573	Bellevue Public Schools	Bellevue
5	504	Grand Island Public Schools	Grand Island
6	499	Papillion-La Vista Public Schools	Papillion
7	410	Westside Community Schools	Omaha
8	302	Kearney Public Schools	Kearney
9	285	Norfolk Public Schools	Norfolk
10	279	Fremont Public Schools	Fremont
11	269	North Platte Public Schools	North Platte
12	235	Hastings Public Schools	Hastings
13	229	South Sioux City Community Schs	So Sioux City
14	220	Columbus Public Schools	Columbus
15	207	Elkhorn Public Schools	Elkhorn
16	201	Ralston Public Schools	Ralston
17	184	Scottsbluff Public Schools	Scottsbluff
18	163	Lexington Public Schools	Lexington
19	145	Beatrice Public Schools	Beatrice
20	140	Blair Community Schools	Blair
21	136	Alliance Public Schools	Alliance
22	125	Gering Public Schools	Gering
23	120	Waverly SD 145	Waverly
24	118	Plattsmouth Community Schools	Plattsmouth
25	99	Gretna Public Schools	Gretna
26	97	Crete Public Schools	Crete
27	92	Norris SD 160	Firth

Number of Students

Rank	Number	District Name	City
1	45,986	Omaha Public Schools	Omaha
2	31,867	Lincoln Public Schools	Lincoln
3	19,476	Millard Public Schools	Omaha
4	8,886	Bellevue Public Schools	Bellevue
5	8,114	Papillion-La Vista Public Schools	Papillion
6	7,690	Grand Island Public Schools	Grand Island
7	5,625	Westside Community Schools	Omaha
8	4,622	Kearney Public Schools	Kearney
9	4,468	Fremont Public Schools	Fremont
10	4,232	Norfolk Public Schools	Norfolk
11	3,979	North Platte Public Schools	North Platte
12	3,457	South Sioux City Community Schs	So Sioux City
13	3,443	Columbus Public Schools	Columbus
14	3,264	Hastings Public Schools	Hastings
15	3,126	Ralston Public Schools	Ralston
16	3,099	Elkhorn Public Schools	Elkhorn
17	2,744	Scottsbluff Public Schools	Scottsbluff
18	2,668	Lexington Public Schools	Lexington
19	2,254	Beatrice Public Schools	Beatrice
20	2,245	Blair Community Schools	Blair
21	1,879	Gering Public Schools	Gering
22	1,806	Alliance Public Schools	Alliance
23	1,672	Waverly SD 145	Waverly
24	1,648	Norris SD 160	Firth
25	1,635	Plattsmouth Community Schools	Plattsmouth
26	1,571	Gretna Public Schools	Gretna
27	1,522	Crete Public Schools	Crete

Male Students

Rank	Percent	District Name	City
1	54.3	Alliance Public Schools	Alliance
2	53.5	Norris SD 160	Firth
3	53.1	Elkhorn Public Schools	Elkhorn
3	53.1	Waverly SD 145	Waverly
5	52.4	Lexington Public Schools	Lexington
6	52.3	Ralston Public Schools	Ralston
7	52.2	Plattsmouth Community Schools	Plattsmouth
8	52.1	Westside Community Schools	Omaha
9	52.0	Beatrice Public Schools	Beatrice
9	52.0	Millard Public Schools	Omaha
11	51.8	Bellevue Public Schools	Bellevue
11	51.8	North Platte Public Schools	North Platte
13	51.6	Kearney Public Schools	Kearney
14	51.4	Blair Community Schools	Blair
14	51.4	Lincoln Public Schools	Lincoln
16	51.3	Omaha Public Schools	Omaha
17	51.1	Grand Island Public Schools	Grand Island
17	51.1	Gretna Public Schools	Gretna
17	51.1	Hastings Public Schools	Hastings
20	50.9	Crete Public Schools	Crete
20	50.9	Norfolk Public Schools	Norfolk
20	50.9	Papillion-La Vista Public Schools	Papillion
23	50.4	South Sioux City Community Schs	So Sioux City
24	50.2	Columbus Public Schools	Columbus
25	49.9	Gering Public Schools	Gering
26	49.8	Fremont Public Schools	Fremont
27	49.5	Scottsbluff Public Schools	Scottsbluff

Female Students

Rank	Percent	District Name	City
1	50.5	Scottsbluff Public Schools	Scottsbluff
2	50.2	Fremont Public Schools	Fremont
3	50.1	Gering Public Schools	Gering
4	49.8	Columbus Public Schools	Columbus
5	49.6	South Sioux City Community Schs	So Sioux City
6	49.1	Crete Public Schools	Crete
6	49.1	Norfolk Public Schools	Norfolk
6	49.1	Papillion-La Vista Public Schools	Papillion
9	48.9	Grand Island Public Schools	Grand Island
9	48.9	Gretna Public Schools	Gretna
9	48.9	Hastings Public Schools	Hastings
12	48.7	Omaha Public Schools	Omaha
13	48.6	Blair Community Schools	Blair
13	48.6	Lincoln Public Schools	Lincoln
15	48.4	Kearney Public Schools	Kearney
16	48.2	Bellevue Public Schools	Bellevue
16	48.2	North Platte Public Schools	North Platte
18	48.0	Beatrice Public Schools	Beatrice
18	48.0	Millard Public Schools	Omaha
20	47.9	Westside Community Schools	Omaha
21	47.8	Plattsmouth Community Schools	Plattsmouth
22	47.7	Ralston Public Schools	Ralston
23	47.6	Lexington Public Schools	Lexington
24	46.9	Elkhorn Public Schools	Elkhorn
24	46.9	Waverly SD 145	Waverly
26	46.5	Norris SD 160	Firth
27	45.7	Alliance Public Schools	Alliance

Individual Education Program Students

Rank	Percent	District Name	City
1	23.3	Plattsmouth Community Schools	Plattsmouth
2	19.5	Waverly SD 145	Waverly
3	19.2	North Platte Public Schools	North Platte
4	19.1	Fremont Public Schools	Fremont
5	18.8	Hastings Public Schools	Hastings
6	17.9	Norfolk Public Schools	Norfolk
7	17.4	Columbus Public Schools	Columbus
8	16.7	Blair Community Schools	Blair
8	16.7	Lincoln Public Schools	Lincoln
10	16.6	Alliance Public Schools	Alliance
11	16.4	Beatrice Public Schools	Beatrice
11	16.4	Kearney Public Schools	Kearney
13	16.2	Grand Island Public Schools	Grand Island
14	16.1	Elkhorn Public Schools	Elkhorn
15	15.8	South Sioux City Community Schs	So Sioux City
16	15.7	Norris SD 160	Firth
17	15.2	Omaha Public Schools	Omaha
17	15.2	Ralston Public Schools	Ralston
19	15.0	Gretna Public Schools	Gretna
20	14.8	Bellevue Public Schools	Bellevue
20	14.8	Scottsbluff Public Schools	Scottsbluff
22	14.0	Millard Public Schools	Omaha
23	12.7	Lexington Public Schools	Lexington
24	11.7	Papillion-La Vista Public Schools	Papillion
25	11.6	Westside Community Schools	Omaha
26	11.5	Gering Public Schools	Gering
27	11.2	Crete Public Schools	Crete

English Language Learner Students

Rank	Percent	District Name	City
1	24.1	Lexington Public Schools	Lexington
2	23.0	South Sioux City Community Schs	So Sioux City
3	20.4	Crete Public Schools	Crete
4	16.4	Grand Island Public Schools	Grand Island
5	12.6	Columbus Public Schools	Columbus
6	10.4	Omaha Public Schools	Omaha
7	7.8	Hastings Public Schools	Hastings
8	6.6	Lincoln Public Schools	Lincoln
8	6.6	Norfolk Public Schools	Norfolk
10	4.9	Fremont Public Schools	Fremont
11	4.6	Plattsmouth Community Schools	Plattsmouth
12	4.2	Scottsbluff Public Schools	Scottsbluff
13	2.8	Gering Public Schools	Gering
13	2.8	Kearney Public Schools	Kearney
15	2.7	Ralston Public Schools	Ralston
16	2.6	Westside Community Schools	Omaha
17	2.5	Waverly SD 145	Waverly
18	1.3	Elkhorn Public Schools	Elkhorn
19	1.1	Alliance Public Schools	Alliance
20	0.8	Blair Community Schools	Blair
21	0.7	Millard Public Schools	Omaha
22	0.5	Papillion-La Vista Public Schools	Papillion
23	0.4	Bellevue Public Schools	Bellevue
23	0.4	Norris SD 160	Firth
23	0.4	North Platte Public Schools	North Platte
26	0.1	Beatrice Public Schools	Beatrice
26	0.1	Gretna Public Schools	Gretna

Migrant Students

Rank	Percent	District Name	City
1	71.7	Lexington Public Schools	Lexington
2	32.3	Norfolk Public Schools	Norfolk
3	29.6	Crete Public Schools	Crete
4	25.9	South Sioux City Community Schs	So Sioux City
5	17.8	Grand Island Public Schools	Grand Island
6	16.0	Columbus Public Schools	Columbus
7	15.5	Alliance Public Schools	Alliance
8	12.2	Hastings Public Schools	Hastings
9	8.8	Fremont Public Schools	Fremont
10	7.9	Gering Public Schools	Gering
11	3.9	Omaha Public Schools	Omaha
12	3.7	Kearney Public Schools	Kearney
13	1.9	Lincoln Public Schools	Lincoln
14	0.4	Scottsbluff Public Schools	Scottsbluff
15	0.2	Norris SD 160	Firth
15	0.2	Waverly SD 145	Waverly
17	0.1	Beatrice Public Schools	Beatrice
17	0.1	Elkhorn Public Schools	Elkhorn
19	0.0	Blair Community Schools	Blair
20	0.0	Bellevue Public Schools	Bellevue
20	0.0	Gretna Public Schools	Gretna
20	0.0	Millard Public Schools	Omaha
20	0.0	North Platte Public Schools	North Platte
20	0.0	Papillion-La Vista Public Schools	Papillion
20	0.0	Plattsmouth Community Schools	Plattsmouth
20	0.0	Ralston Public Schools	Ralston
20	0.0	Westside Community Schools	Omaha

Students Eligible for Free Lunch

Rank	Percent	District Name	City
1	44.7	Omaha Public Schools	Omaha
2	40.1	Lexington Public Schools	Lexington
3	36.4	Grand Island Public Schools	Grand Island
4	33.2	Scottsbluff Public Schools	Scottsbluff
5	27.8	Norfolk Public Schools	Norfolk
6	25.7	North Platte Public Schools	North Platte
7	25.6	Gering Public Schools	Gering
8	25.5	Plattsmouth Community Schools	Plattsmouth
9	25.2	Hastings Public Schools	Hastings
10	24.6	South Sioux City Community Schs	So Sioux City
11	23.7	Fremont Public Schools	Fremont
12	22.1	Lincoln Public Schools	Lincoln
13	22.0	Alliance Public Schools	Alliance
14	21.3	Beatrice Public Schools	Beatrice
15	21.2	Kearney Public Schools	Kearney
16	21.0	Crete Public Schools	Crete
17	19.3	Columbus Public Schools	Columbus
18	17.1	Ralston Public Schools	Ralston
19	11.5	Westside Community Schools	Omaha
20	11.3	Blair Community Schools	Blair
21	10.0	Waverly SD 145	Waverly
22	9.3	Bellevue Public Schools	Bellevue
23	7.5	Papillion-La Vista Public Schools	Papillion
24	7.1	Elkhorn Public Schools	Elkhorn
25	6.3	Norris SD 160	Firth
26	4.5	Gretna Public Schools	Gretna
26	4.5	Millard Public Schools	Omaha

Students Eligible for Reduced-Price Lunch

Rank	Percent	District Name	City
1	12.3	Lexington Public Schools	Lexington
2	10.6	Grand Island Public Schools	Grand Island
3	10.4	Columbus Public Schools	Columbus
3	10.4	Fremont Public Schools	Fremont
3	10.4	Gering Public Schools	Gering
6	10.0	Hastings Public Schools	Hastings
6	10.0	North Platte Public Schools	North Platte
8	9.7	South Sioux City Community Schs	So Sioux City
9	9.5	Norfolk Public Schools	Norfolk
9	9.5	Omaha Public Schools	Omaha
11	9.4	Beatrice Public Schools	Beatrice
11	9.4	Plattsmouth Community Schools	Plattsmouth
13	8.8	Crete Public Schools	Crete
14	8.4	Kearney Public Schools	Kearney
14	8.4	Ralston Public Schools	Ralston
16	7.9	Alliance Public Schools	Alliance
17	7.6	Bellevue Public Schools	Bellevue
18	6.8	Scottsbluff Public Schools	Scottsbluff
19	6.3	Westside Community Schools	Omaha
20	5.8	Lincoln Public Schools	Lincoln
21	5.1	Papillion-La Vista Public Schools	Papillion
22	4.7	Waverly SD 145	Waverly
23	4.3	Blair Community Schools	Blair
23	4.3	Elkhorn Public Schools	Elkhorn
25	3.0	Norris SD 160	Firth
26	2.4	Millard Public Schools	Omaha
27	2.0	Gretna Public Schools	Gretna

Student/Teacher Ratio

Rank	Ratio	District Name	City
1	17.9	Norris SD 160	Firth
2	16.3	Lexington Public Schools	Lexington
2	16.3	Papillion-La Vista Public Schools	Papillion
4	16.0	Blair Community Schools	Blair
4	16.0	Fremont Public Schools	Fremont
6	15.8	Gretna Public Schools	Gretna
7	15.7	Millard Public Schools	Omaha
8	15.6	Columbus Public Schools	Columbus
8	15.6	Crete Public Schools	Crete
10	15.5	Bellevue Public Schools	Bellevue
10	15.5	Ralston Public Schools	Ralston
12	15.4	Beatrice Public Schools	Beatrice
13	15.3	Kearney Public Schools	Kearney
14	15.2	Grand Island Public Schools	Grand Island
15	15.1	South Sioux City Community Schs	So Sioux City
16	14.9	Elkhorn Public Schools	Elkhorn
16	14.9	Gering Public Schools	Gering
16	14.9	Scottsbluff Public Schools	Scottsbluff
19	14.8	Norfolk Public Schools	Norfolk
19	14.8	North Platte Public Schools	North Platte
19	14.8	Omaha Public Schools	Omaha
22	13.9	Hastings Public Schools	Hastings
22	13.9	Waverly SD 145	Waverly
24	13.8	Plattsmouth Community Schools	Plattsmouth
25	13.7	Westside Community Schools	Omaha
26	13.5	Lincoln Public Schools	Lincoln
27	13.3	Alliance Public Schools	Alliance

Student/Librarian Ratio

Rank	Ratio	District Name	City
1	919.4	Ralston Public Schools	Ralston
2	889.3	Lexington Public Schools	Lexington
3	846.4	Norfolk Public Schools	Norfolk
4	824.0	Norris SD 160	Firth
5	801.1	Crete Public Schools	Crete
6	795.8	North Platte Public Schools	North Platte
7	751.3	Beatrice Public Schools	Beatrice
8	744.7	Fremont Public Schools	Fremont
9	724.2	Blair Community Schools	Blair
10	691.4	South Sioux City Community Schs	So Sioux City
11	686.0	Scottsbluff Public Schools	Scottsbluff
12	654.1	Westside Community Schools	Omaha
13	654.0	Plattsmouth Community Schools	Plattsmouth
14	652.8	Hastings Public Schools	Hastings
15	647.9	Gering Public Schools	Gering
16	616.3	Kearney Public Schools	Kearney
17	602.0	Alliance Public Schools	Alliance
18	592.4	Bellevue Public Schools	Bellevue
19	586.6	Millard Public Schools	Omaha
20	580.5	Lincoln Public Schools	Lincoln
21	573.8	Columbus Public Schools	Columbus
22	567.4	Papillion-La Vista Public Schools	Papillion
23	557.3	Waverly SD 145	Waverly
24	523.7	Gretna Public Schools	Gretna
25	516.7	Omaha Public Schools	Omaha
26	516.5	Elkhorn Public Schools	Elkhorn
27	444.5	Grand Island Public Schools	Grand Island

Student/Counselor Ratio

Rank	Ratio	District Name	City
1	686.0	Scottsbluff Public Schools	Scottsbluff
2	585.4	Crete Public Schools	Crete
3	549.3	Norris SD 160	Firth
4	545.0	Plattsmouth Community Schools	Plattsmouth
5	539.0	Ralston Public Schools	Ralston
6	523.7	Gretna Public Schools	Gretna
7	444.7	Lexington Public Schools	Lexington
8	441.4	Columbus Public Schools	Columbus
9	436.9	Grand Island Public Schools	Grand Island
10	431.8	Lincoln Public Schools	Lincoln
11	422.5	Millard Public Schools	Omaha
12	413.7	Fremont Public Schools	Fremont
13	412.7	Kearney Public Schools	Kearney
14	411.5	South Sioux City Community Schs	So Sioux City
15	403.9	Bellevue Public Schools	Bellevue
16	383.5	Gering Public Schools	Gering
17	375.7	Beatrice Public Schools	Beatrice
18	374.2	Blair Community Schools	Blair
19	372.2	Papillion-La Vista Public Schools	Papillion
20	368.0	Norfolk Public Schools	Norfolk
21	361.7	North Platte Public Schools	North Platte
22	361.2	Alliance Public Schools	Alliance
23	344.3	Elkhorn Public Schools	Elkhorn
24	334.4	Waverly SD 145	Waverly
25	320.9	Omaha Public Schools	Omaha
26	304.1	Westside Community Schools	Omaha
27	296.7	Hastings Public Schools	Hastings

Current Spending per Student in FY2001

Rank	Dollars	District Name	City
1	7,541	Westside Community Schools	Omaha
2	7,072	Ralston Public Schools	Ralston
3	7,016	Waverly SD 145	Waverly
4	6,915	Lincoln Public Schools	Lincoln
5	6,879	Plattsmouth Community Schools	Plattsmouth
6	6,624	Alliance Public Schools	Alliance
7	6,446	Bellevue Public Schools	Bellevue
8	6,352	Omaha Public Schools	Omaha
9	6,287	Grand Island Public Schools	Grand Island
10	6,261	North Platte Public Schools	North Platte
11	6,258	Hastings Public Schools	Hastings
12	6,133	Millard Public Schools	Omaha
13	6,110	Gretna Public Schools	Gretna
14	6,060	Gering Public Schools	Gering
15	6,038	Beatrice Public Schools	Beatrice
16	6,018	Norfolk Public Schools	Norfolk
17	5,985	Kearney Public Schools	Kearney
18	5,955	Blair Community Schools	Blair
19	5,937	Elkhorn Public Schools	Elkhorn
20	5,907	Scottsbluff Public Schools	Scottsbluff
21	5,894	Columbus Public Schools	Columbus
22	5,875	Fremont Public Schools	Fremont
23	5,847	South Sioux City Community Schs	So Sioux City
24	5,837	Papillion-La Vista Public Schools	Papillion
25	5,813	Norris SD 160	Firth
26	5,657	Crete Public Schools	Crete
27	5,314	Lexington Public Schools	Lexington

Number of Diploma Recipients

Rank	Number	District Name	City
1	2,168	Omaha Public Schools	Omaha
2	1,896	Lincoln Public Schools	Lincoln
3	1,513	Millard Public Schools	Omaha
4	592	Bellevue Public Schools	Bellevue
5	534	Papillion-La Vista Public Schools	Papillion
6	359	Norfolk Public Schools	Norfolk
7	344	North Platte Public Schools	North Platte
8	340	Grand Island Public Schools	Grand Island
9	338	Westside Community Schools	Omaha
10	317	Kearney Public Schools	Kearney
11	287	Fremont Public Schools	Fremont
12	279	Columbus Public Schools	Columbus
13	224	Hastings Public Schools	Hastings
14	204	Ralston Public Schools	Ralston
15	200	Elkhorn Public Schools	Elkhorn
16	195	Scottsbluff Public Schools	Scottsbluff
17	191	South Sioux City Community Schs	So Sioux City
18	180	Beatrice Public Schools	Beatrice
19	169	Alliance Public Schools	Alliance
20	160	Blair Community Schools	Blair
21	142	Gering Public Schools	Gering
22	131	Waverly SD 145	Waverly
23	126	Lexington Public Schools	Lexington
24	120	Norris SD 160	Firth
25	119	Plattsmouth Community Schools	Plattsmouth
26	112	Crete Public Schools	Crete
27	99	Gretna Public Schools	Gretna

High School Drop-out Rate

Rank	Percent	District Name	City
1	9.9	Omaha Public Schools	Omaha
2	7.8	South Sioux City Community Schs	So Sioux City
3	7.0	Lexington Public Schools	Lexington
4	6.8	Grand Island Public Schools	Grand Island
5	6.5	Lincoln Public Schools	Lincoln
6	4.7	North Platte Public Schools	North Platte
7	4.6	Hastings Public Schools	Hastings
8	4.3	Fremont Public Schools	Fremont
8	4.3	Gering Public Schools	Gering
8	4.3	Plattsmouth Community Schools	Plattsmouth
11	3.0	Norfolk Public Schools	Norfolk
11	3.0	Ralston Public Schools	Ralston
13	2.9	Columbus Public Schools	Columbus
13	2.9	Papillion-La Vista Public Schools	Papillion
13	2.9	Scottsbluff Public Schools	Scottsbluff
16	2.6	Beatrice Public Schools	Beatrice
17	2.2	Blair Community Schools	Blair
18	1.8	Bellevue Public Schools	Bellevue
19	1.7	Elkhorn Public Schools	Elkhorn
20	1.6	Crete Public Schools	Crete
20	1.6	Kearney Public Schools	Kearney
20	1.6	Millard Public Schools	Omaha
23	1.1	Alliance Public Schools	Alliance
23	1.1	Norris SD 160	Firth
25	0.8	Westside Community Schools	Omaha
26	0.0	Gretna Public Schools	Gretna
26	0.0	Waverly SD 145	Waverly

Nevada

Nevada Public School Educational Profile

Category	Value	Category	Value
Schools *(2002-2003)*	544	**Diploma Recipients** *(2002-2003)*	16,270
Instructional Level		White, Non-Hispanic	10,879
Primary	332	Black, Non-Hispanic	1,285
Middle	85	Asian/Pacific Islander	1,123
High	106	American Indian/Alaskan Native	255
Other Level	21	Hispanic	2,728
Curriculum		**High School Drop-out Rate** (%) *(2000-2001)*	5.2
Regular	489	White, Non-Hispanic	4.0
Special Education	13	Black, Non-Hispanic	6.8
Vocational	3	Asian/Pacific Islander	6.8
Alternative	39	American Indian/Alaskan Native	4.4
Type		Hispanic	8.0
Magnet	9	**Staff** *(2002-2003)*	34,855.3
Charter	13	Teachers	20,011.3
Title I Eligible	228	Average Salary ($)	41,795
School-wide Title I	83	Librarians/Media Specialists	327.0
Students *(2002-2003)*	369,498	Guidance Counselors	715.4
Gender (%)		**Ratios** *(2002-2003)*	
Male	51.4	Student/Teacher Ratio	18.5 to 1
Female	48.6	Student/Librarian Ratio	1,130.0 to 1
Race/Ethnicity (%)		Student/Counselor Ratio	516.5 to 1
White, Non-Hispanic	52.7	**Current Spending** *($ per student in FY 2001)*	6,079
Black, Non-Hispanic	10.5	Instruction	3,794
Asian/Pacific Islander	6.4	Support Services	2,086
American Indian/Alaskan Native	1.7	**College Entrance Exam Scores** *(2003)*	
Hispanic	28.7	Scholastic Aptitude Test (SAT)	
Classification (%)		Participation Rate (%)	36
Individual Education Program (IEP)	11.5	Mean SAT I Verbal Score	510
Migrant	0.1	Mean SAT I Math Score	517
English Language Learner (ELL)	15.9	American College Testing Program (ACT)	
Eligible for Free Lunch Program	27.6	Participation Rate (%)	34
Eligible for Reduced-Price Lunch Program	6.5	Average Composite Score	21.3

Note: *For an explanation of data, please refer to the User's Guide in the front of the book; n/a indicates data not available*

Nevada NAEP 2003 Test Scores

Reading			Mathematics		
Grade/Category	**Value**	**Rank**	**Grade/Category**	**Value**	**Rank**
4th Grade			**4th Grade**		
Average Proficiency	207.0 (1.2)	46/51	Average Proficiency	227.5 (0.8)	44/51
Proficiency by Gender/Race/Ethnicity			Proficiency by Gender/Race/Ethnicity		
Male	202.5 (1.4)	45/51	Male	228.5 (1.1)	43/51
Female	211.4 (1.6)	45/51	Female	226.4 (1.0)	44/51
White, Non-Hispanic	217.4 (1.5)	51/51	White, Non-Hispanic	236.1 (0.9)	46/51
Black, Non-Hispanic	192.6 (3.0)	34/42	Black, Non-Hispanic	214.6 (1.7)	27/42
Asian, Non-Hispanic	192.1 (2.0)	39/41	Asian, Non-Hispanic	215.7 (1.2)	40/43
American Indian, Non-Hispanic	214.2 (2.6)	20/25	American Indian, Non-Hispanic	236.6 (2.1)	20/26
Hispanic	*190.5 (6.0)*	8/12	Hispanic	*215.3 (4.0)*	9/12
Proficiency by Class Size			Proficiency by Class Size		
Less than 16 Students	n/a	n/a	Less than 16 Students	n/a	n/a
16 to 18 Students	n/a	n/a	16 to 18 Students	n/a	n/a
19 to 20 Students	*203.5 (11.0)*	46/50	19 to 20 Students	*228.4 (2.8)*	40/50
21 to 25 Students	207.2 (2.8)	46/51	21 to 25 Students	227.1 (1.8)	45/51
Greater than 25 Students	207.9 (1.5)	43/49	Greater than 25 Students	228.4 (1.0)	38/49
Percent Attaining Achievement Levels			Percent Attaining Achievement Levels		
Below Basic	48.0 (1.5)	6/51	Below Basic	30.5 (1.4)	8/51
Basic or Above	52.0 (1.5)	46/51	Basic or Above	69.5 (1.4)	44/51
Proficient or Above	20.4 (1.1)	47/51	Proficient or Above	23.1 (1.0)	44/51
Advanced or Above	3.4 (0.5)	49/51	Advanced or Above	1.5 (0.2)	46/51
8th Grade			**8th Grade**		
Average Proficiency	252.3 (0.8)	47/51	Average Proficiency	268.0 (0.8)	43/51
Proficiency by Gender/Race/Ethnicity			Proficiency by Gender/Race/Ethnicity		
Male	246.2 (1.3)	47/51	Male	268.1 (1.1)	42/51
Female	258.3 (1.1)	46/51	Female	268.0 (1.0)	43/51
White, Non-Hispanic	262.3 (1.0)	48/50	White, Non-Hispanic	278.1 (0.9)	43/50
Black, Non-Hispanic	233.0 (2.7)	40/41	Black, Non-Hispanic	248.3 (2.6)	30/41
Asian, Non-Hispanic	237.0 (1.2)	36/37	Asian, Non-Hispanic	249.6 (1.8)	33/37
American Indian, Non-Hispanic	260.1 (3.3)	18/23	American Indian, Non-Hispanic	279.5 (3.1)	19/23
Hispanic	n/a	n/a	Hispanic	n/a	n/a
Proficiency by Parents Highest Level of Ed.			Proficiency by Parents Highest Level of Ed.		
Did Not Finish High School	239.5 (2.4)	42/50	Did Not Finish High School	249.2 (2.7)	45/50
Graduated High School	249.2 (2.2)	41/50	Graduated High School	263.4 (1.9)	39/50
Some Education After High School	258.9 (1.3)	46/50	Some Education After High School	276.8 (1.6)	36/50
Graduated College	260.9 (1.4)	46/50	Graduated College	278.6 (1.3)	43/50
Percent Attaining Achievement Levels			Percent Attaining Achievement Levels		
Below Basic	36.7 (1.2)	5/51	Below Basic	41.0 (1.3)	10/51
Basic or Above	63.3 (1.2)	47/51	Basic or Above	59.0 (1.3)	42/51
Proficient or Above	20.6 (1.2)	49/51	Proficient or Above	20.3 (0.7)	42/51
Advanced or Above	1.1 (0.3)	51/51	Advanced or Above	2.8 (0.3)	41/51

***Note:** For an explanation of data, please refer to the User's Guide in the front of the book; values in italics indicate that the nature of the sample does not allow accurate determination of the variability of the statistic; n/a indicates data not available*

Carson City

Carson City SD

1402 W King St • Carson City, NV 89701-4554
(702) 885-6300 • http://www.carsoncityschools.com/index2.asp
Grade Span: PK-12; **Agency Type:** 1
Schools: 11
7 Primary; 2 Middle; 2 High; 0 Other Level
9 Regular; 1 Special Education; 0 Vocational; 1 Alternative
0 Magnet; 0 Charter; 5 Title I Eligible; 2 School-wide Title I
Students: 8,834 (51.3% male; 48.7% female)
Individual Education Program: 1,216 (13.8%);
English Language Learner: 1,534 (17.4%); Migrant: 31 (0.4%)
Eligible for Free Lunch Program: 2,325 (26.3%)
Eligible for Reduced-Price Lunch Program: 622 (7.0%)
Teachers: 475.0 (18.6 to 1)
Librarians/Media Specialists: 9.0 (981.6 to 1)
Guidance Counselors: 19.0 (464.9 to 1)
Current Spending: ($ per student per year):
Total: $6,606; Instruction: $4,004; Support Services: $2,411
Enrollment, Drop-out Rates and Diploma Recipients by Race/Ethnicity

Category	Total	White	Black	Asian	AIAN	Hisp.
Enrollment (%)	100.0	70.1	1.1	2.4	3.1	23.4
Drop-out Rate (%)	2.1	1.5	5.0	2.1	2.4	5.4
H.S. Diplomas (#)	543	441	8	13	13	68

Churchill County

Churchill County SD

545 E Richards St • Fallon, NV 89406-3430
(702) 423-5184 • http://www.churchill.k12.nv.us/
Grade Span: PK-12; **Agency Type:** 1
Schools: 10
5 Primary; 1 Middle; 3 High; 1 Other Level
8 Regular; 1 Special Education; 0 Vocational; 1 Alternative
0 Magnet; 1 Charter; 4 Title I Eligible; 0 School-wide Title I
Students: 4,610 (50.9% male; 49.1% female)
Individual Education Program: 668 (14.5%);
English Language Learner: 145 (3.1%); Migrant: 68 (1.5%)
Eligible for Free Lunch Program: 1,045 (22.7%)
Eligible for Reduced-Price Lunch Program: 410 (8.9%)
Teachers: 273.8 (16.8 to 1)
Librarians/Media Specialists: 4.0 (1,152.5 to 1)
Guidance Counselors: 10.0 (461.0 to 1)
Current Spending: ($ per student per year):
Total: $6,774; Instruction: $4,065; Support Services: $2,491
Enrollment, Drop-out Rates and Diploma Recipients by Race/Ethnicity

Category	Total	White	Black	Asian	AIAN	Hisp.
Enrollment (%)	100.0	75.2	2.4	5.0	7.1	10.3
Drop-out Rate (%)	2.2	1.9	2.9	0.0	1.1	7.5
H.S. Diplomas (#)	240	195	4	14	9	18

Clark County

Clark County SD

2832 E Flamingo Rd • Las Vegas, NV 89121-5205
(702) 799-5310 • http://www.ccsd.net/
Grade Span: PK-12; **Agency Type:** 1
Schools: 282
177 Primary; 47 Middle; 47 High; 11 Other Level
253 Regular; 8 Special Education; 2 Vocational; 19 Alternative
7 Magnet; 4 Charter; 121 Title I Eligible; 40 School-wide Title I
Students: 256,574 (51.3% male; 48.7% female)
Individual Education Program: 27,713 (10.8%);
English Language Learner: 46,772 (18.2%); Migrant: 116 (<0.1%)
Eligible for Free Lunch Program: 75,315 (29.4%)
Eligible for Reduced-Price Lunch Program: 14,870 (5.8%)
Teachers: 13,069.8 (19.6 to 1)
Librarians/Media Specialists: 244.0 (1,051.5 to 1)
Guidance Counselors: 445.1 (576.4 to 1)
Current Spending: ($ per student per year):
Total: $5,525; Instruction: $3,249; Support Services: $2,104
Enrollment, Drop-out Rates and Diploma Recipients by Race/Ethnicity

Category	Total	White	Black	Asian	AIAN	Hisp.
Enrollment (%)	100.0	46.0	14.0	7.4	0.8	31.7
Drop-out Rate (%)	6.1	4.6	6.8	7.9	4.3	8.5
H.S. Diplomas (#)	10,215	6,079	1,178	871	82	2,005

Douglas County

Douglas County SD

751 Mono Ave • Minden, NV 89423
(702) 782-5134 • http://dcsd.k12.nv.us/
Grade Span: PK-12; **Agency Type:** 1
Schools: 15
7 Primary; 3 Middle; 4 High; 1 Other Level
12 Regular; 0 Special Education; 0 Vocational; 3 Alternative
0 Magnet; 0 Charter; 4 Title I Eligible; 0 School-wide Title I
Students: 7,180 (51.5% male; 48.5% female)
Individual Education Program: 876 (12.2%);
English Language Learner: 384 (5.3%); Migrant: 0 (0.0%)
Eligible for Free Lunch Program: 1,001 (13.9%)
Eligible for Reduced-Price Lunch Program: 463 (6.4%)
Teachers: 379.0 (18.9 to 1)
Librarians/Media Specialists: 5.0 (1,436.0 to 1)
Guidance Counselors: 17.0 (422.4 to 1)
Current Spending: ($ per student per year):
Total: $6,967; Instruction: $3,985; Support Services: $2,769
Enrollment, Drop-out Rates and Diploma Recipients by Race/Ethnicity

Category	Total	White	Black	Asian	AIAN	Hisp.
Enrollment (%)	100.0	84.2	0.8	2.2	2.8	9.9
Drop-out Rate (%)	1.9	1.8	6.3	0.0	7.7	1.7
H.S. Diplomas (#)	426	394	2	5	4	21

Elko County

Elko County SD

1092 Burns Rd • Elko, NV 89801-3437
(702) 738-5196 • http://www.elko.k12.nv.us/
Grade Span: PK-12; **Agency Type:** 1
Schools: 26
17 Primary; 2 Middle; 7 High; 0 Other Level
25 Regular; 1 Special Education; 0 Vocational; 0 Alternative
0 Magnet; 0 Charter; 12 Title I Eligible; 6 School-wide Title I
Students: 9,694 (51.1% male; 48.9% female)
Individual Education Program: 1,107 (11.4%);
English Language Learner: 209 (2.2%); Migrant: 0 (0.0%)
Eligible for Free Lunch Program: 2,065 (21.3%)
Eligible for Reduced-Price Lunch Program: 720 (7.4%)
Teachers: 598.5 (16.2 to 1)
Librarians/Media Specialists: 16.0 (605.9 to 1)
Guidance Counselors: 21.0 (461.6 to 1)
Current Spending: ($ per student per year):
Total: $6,806; Instruction: $4,137; Support Services: $2,465
Enrollment, Drop-out Rates and Diploma Recipients by Race/Ethnicity

Category	Total	White	Black	Asian	AIAN	Hisp.
Enrollment (%)	100.0	68.0	0.6	0.9	7.0	23.5
Drop-out Rate (%)	2.6	1.6	12.5	2.2	1.5	6.3
H.S. Diplomas (#)	564	424	2	10	28	100

Humboldt County

Humboldt County SD

E 4th and Reinhart • Winnemucca, NV 89445
(702) 623-8100 • http://www.humboldt.k12.nv.us/
Grade Span: PK-12; **Agency Type:** 1
Schools: 16
10 Primary; 3 Middle; 2 High; 1 Other Level
14 Regular; 1 Special Education; 0 Vocational; 1 Alternative
0 Magnet; 0 Charter; 5 Title I Eligible; 1 School-wide Title I
Students: 3,504 (51.9% male; 48.1% female)
Individual Education Program: 524 (15.0%);
English Language Learner: 348 (9.9%); Migrant: 57 (1.6%)
Eligible for Free Lunch Program: 767 (21.9%)
Eligible for Reduced-Price Lunch Program: 286 (8.2%)
Teachers: 211.5 (16.6 to 1)
Librarians/Media Specialists: 1.0 (3,504.0 to 1)
Guidance Counselors: 8.0 (438.0 to 1)
Current Spending: ($ per student per year):
Total: $7,140; Instruction: $4,269; Support Services: $2,668
Enrollment, Drop-out Rates and Diploma Recipients by Race/Ethnicity

Category	Total	White	Black	Asian	AIAN	Hisp.
Enrollment (%)	100.0	69.6	0.5	0.8	4.8	24.3
Drop-out Rate (%)	3.1	2.8	0.0	0.0	2.7	4.5
H.S. Diplomas (#)	225	182	0	2	4	37

Lyon County

Lyon County SD

25 E Goldfield Ave • Yerington, NV 89447-2315
(702) 463-2205 • http://www.lyon.k12.nv.us/
Grade Span: PK-12; **Agency Type:** 1
Schools: 17
7 Primary; 4 Middle; 5 High; 1 Other Level
16 Regular; 0 Special Education; 0 Vocational; 1 Alternative
0 Magnet; 0 Charter; 6 Title I Eligible; 0 School-wide Title I
Students: 7,268 (52.6% male; 47.4% female)
Individual Education Program: 1,088 (15.0%);
English Language Learner: 443 (6.1%); Migrant: 33 (0.5%)
Eligible for Free Lunch Program: 2,213 (30.4%)

Eligible for Reduced-Price Lunch Program: 856 (11.8%)
Teachers: 428.0 (17.0 to 1)
Librarians/Media Specialists: 12.0 (605.7 to 1)
Guidance Counselors: 16.0 (454.3 to 1)
Current Spending: ($ per student per year):
Total: $6,450; Instruction: $3,670; Support Services: $2,539
Enrollment, Drop-out Rates and Diploma Recipients by Race/Ethnicity

Category	Total	White	Black	Asian	AIAN	Hisp.
Enrollment (%)	100.0	78.8	1.0	0.9	5.2	14.1
Drop-out Rate (%)	1.8	1.6	0.0	0.0	1.9	3.9
H.S. Diplomas (#)	355	293	0	5	18	39

Nye County

Nye County SD

Military Circle • TonOpah, NV 89049
(702) 482-6258 •
http://www.ezsdk.com/applications/website/outsideView.php?outVOU=527&pg=
Grade Span: PK-12; **Agency Type:** 1
Schools: 19
11 Primary; 2 Middle; 5 High; 1 Other Level
17 Regular; 0 Special Education; 0 Vocational; 2 Alternative
0 Magnet; 0 Charter; 7 Title I Eligible; 7 School-wide Title I
Students: 5,322 (51.0% male; 49.0% female)
Individual Education Program: 960 (18.0%);
English Language Learner: 279 (5.2%); Migrant: 35 (0.7%)
Eligible for Free Lunch Program: 1,685 (31.7%)
Eligible for Reduced-Price Lunch Program: 480 (9.0%)
Teachers: 331.5 (16.1 to 1)
Librarians/Media Specialists: 2.0 (2,661.0 to 1)
Guidance Counselors: 12.0 (443.5 to 1)
Current Spending: ($ per student per year):
Total: $6,927; Instruction: $4,214; Support Services: $2,468
Enrollment, Drop-out Rates and Diploma Recipients by Race/Ethnicity

Category	Total	White	Black	Asian	AIAN	Hisp.
Enrollment (%)	100.0	78.9	2.4	2.0	2.4	14.3
Drop-out Rate (%)	6.5	5.9	11.1	2.6	6.7	11.6
H.S. Diplomas (#)	293	245	4	9	5	30

Washoe County

Washoe County SD

425 E Ninth St • Reno, NV 89520-2800
(702) 348-0200 • http://www.washoe.k12.nv.us/
Grade Span: PK-12; **Agency Type:** 1
Schools: 100
67 Primary; 13 Middle; 15 High; 5 Other Level
92 Regular; 1 Special Education; 1 Vocational; 6 Alternative
2 Magnet; 8 Charter; 41 Title I Eligible; 21 School-wide Title I
Students: 60,384 (51.5% male; 48.5% female)
Individual Education Program: 7,369 (12.2%);
English Language Learner: 8,476 (14.0%); Migrant: 139 (0.2%)
Eligible for Free Lunch Program: 13,862 (23.0%)
Eligible for Reduced-Price Lunch Program: 4,645 (7.7%)
Teachers: 3,788.2 (15.9 to 1)
Librarians/Media Specialists: 25.0 (2,415.4 to 1)
Guidance Counselors: 147.0 (410.8 to 1)
Current Spending: ($ per student per year):
Total: $5,751; Instruction: $3,526; Support Services: $2,028
Enrollment, Drop-out Rates and Diploma Recipients by Race/Ethnicity

Category	Total	White	Black	Asian	AIAN	Hisp.
Enrollment (%)	100.0	62.1	3.6	5.8	2.7	25.8
Drop-out Rate (%)	4.3	3.6	5.6	3.6	6.2	7.0
H.S. Diplomas (#)	2,851	2,191	73	183	56	348

Number of Schools

Rank	Number	District Name	City
1	282	Clark County SD	Las Vegas
2	100	Washoe County SD	Reno
3	26	Elko County SD	Elko
4	19	Nye County SD	TonOpah
5	17	Lyon County SD	Yerington
6	16	Humboldt County SD	Winnemucca
7	15	Douglas County SD	Minden
8	11	Carson City SD	Carson City
9	10	Churchill County SD	Fallon

Number of Teachers

Rank	Number	District Name	City
1	13,069	Clark County SD	Las Vegas
2	3,788	Washoe County SD	Reno
3	598	Elko County SD	Elko
4	475	Carson City SD	Carson City
5	428	Lyon County SD	Yerington
6	379	Douglas County SD	Minden
7	331	Nye County SD	TonOpah
8	273	Churchill County SD	Fallon
9	211	Humboldt County SD	Winnemucca

Number of Students

Rank	Number	District Name	City
1	256,574	Clark County SD	Las Vegas
2	60,384	Washoe County SD	Reno
3	9,694	Elko County SD	Elko
4	8,834	Carson City SD	Carson City
5	7,268	Lyon County SD	Yerington
6	7,180	Douglas County SD	Minden
7	5,322	Nye County SD	TonOpah
8	4,610	Churchill County SD	Fallon
9	3,504	Humboldt County SD	Winnemucca

Male Students

Rank	Percent	District Name	City
1	52.6	Lyon County SD	Yerington
2	51.9	Humboldt County SD	Winnemucca
3	51.5	Douglas County SD	Minden
3	51.5	Washoe County SD	Reno
5	51.3	Carson City SD	Carson City
5	51.3	Clark County SD	Las Vegas
7	51.1	Elko County SD	Elko
8	51.0	Nye County SD	TonOpah
9	50.9	Churchill County SD	Fallon

Female Students

Rank	Percent	District Name	City
1	49.1	Churchill County SD	Fallon
2	49.0	Nye County SD	TonOpah
3	48.9	Elko County SD	Elko
4	48.7	Carson City SD	Carson City
4	48.7	Clark County SD	Las Vegas
6	48.5	Douglas County SD	Minden
6	48.5	Washoe County SD	Reno
8	48.1	Humboldt County SD	Winnemucca
9	47.4	Lyon County SD	Yerington

Individual Education Program Students

Rank	Percent	District Name	City
1	18.0	Nye County SD	TonOpah
2	15.0	Humboldt County SD	Winnemucca
2	15.0	Lyon County SD	Yerington
4	14.5	Churchill County SD	Fallon
5	13.8	Carson City SD	Carson City
6	12.2	Douglas County SD	Minden
6	12.2	Washoe County SD	Reno
8	11.4	Elko County SD	Elko
9	10.8	Clark County SD	Las Vegas

English Language Learner Students

Rank	Percent	District Name	City
1	18.2	Clark County SD	Las Vegas
2	17.4	Carson City SD	Carson City
3	14.0	Washoe County SD	Reno
4	9.9	Humboldt County SD	Winnemucca
5	6.1	Lyon County SD	Yerington
6	5.3	Douglas County SD	Minden
7	5.2	Nye County SD	TonOpah
8	3.1	Churchill County SD	Fallon
9	2.2	Elko County SD	Elko

Migrant Students

Rank	Percent	District Name	City
1	1.6	Humboldt County SD	Winnemucca
2	1.5	Churchill County SD	Fallon
3	0.7	Nye County SD	TonOpah
4	0.5	Lyon County SD	Yerington
5	0.4	Carson City SD	Carson City
6	0.2	Washoe County SD	Reno
7	0.0	Clark County SD	Las Vegas
8	0.0	Douglas County SD	Minden
8	0.0	Elko County SD	Elko

Students Eligible for Free Lunch

Rank	Percent	District Name	City
1	31.7	Nye County SD	TonOpah
2	30.4	Lyon County SD	Yerington
3	29.4	Clark County SD	Las Vegas
4	26.3	Carson City SD	Carson City
5	23.0	Washoe County SD	Reno
6	22.7	Churchill County SD	Fallon
7	21.9	Humboldt County SD	Winnemucca
8	21.3	Elko County SD	Elko
9	13.9	Douglas County SD	Minden

Students Eligible for Reduced-Price Lunch

Rank	Percent	District Name	City
1	11.8	Lyon County SD	Yerington
2	9.0	Nye County SD	TonOpah
3	8.9	Churchill County SD	Fallon
4	8.2	Humboldt County SD	Winnemucca
5	7.7	Washoe County SD	Reno
6	7.4	Elko County SD	Elko
7	7.0	Carson City SD	Carson City
8	6.4	Douglas County SD	Minden
9	5.8	Clark County SD	Las Vegas

Student/Teacher Ratio

Rank	Ratio	District Name	City
1	19.6	Clark County SD	Las Vegas
2	18.9	Douglas County SD	Minden
3	18.6	Carson City SD	Carson City
4	17.0	Lyon County SD	Yerington
5	16.8	Churchill County SD	Fallon
6	16.6	Humboldt County SD	Winnemucca
7	16.2	Elko County SD	Elko
8	16.1	Nye County SD	TonOpah
9	15.9	Washoe County SD	Reno

Student/Librarian Ratio

Rank	Ratio	District Name	City
1	3,504.0	Humboldt County SD	Winnemucca
2	2,661.0	Nye County SD	TonOpah
3	2,415.4	Washoe County SD	Reno
4	1,436.0	Douglas County SD	Minden
5	1,152.5	Churchill County SD	Fallon
6	1,051.5	Clark County SD	Las Vegas
7	981.6	Carson City SD	Carson City
8	605.9	Elko County SD	Elko
9	605.7	Lyon County SD	Yerington

Student/Counselor Ratio

Rank	Ratio	District Name	City
1	576.4	Clark County SD	Las Vegas
2	464.9	Carson City SD	Carson City
3	461.6	Elko County SD	Elko
4	461.0	Churchill County SD	Fallon
5	454.3	Lyon County SD	Yerington
6	443.5	Nye County SD	TonOpah
7	438.0	Humboldt County SD	Winnemucca
8	422.4	Douglas County SD	Minden
9	410.8	Washoe County SD	Reno

Current Spending per Student in FY2001

Rank	Dollars	District Name	City
1	7,140	Humboldt County SD	Winnemucca
2	6,967	Douglas County SD	Minden
3	6,927	Nye County SD	TonOpah
4	6,806	Elko County SD	Elko
5	6,774	Churchill County SD	Fallon
6	6,606	Carson City SD	Carson City
7	6,450	Lyon County SD	Yerington
8	5,751	Washoe County SD	Reno
9	5,525	Clark County SD	Las Vegas

Number of Diploma Recipients

Rank	Number	District Name	City
1	10,215	Clark County SD	Las Vegas
2	2,851	Washoe County SD	Reno
3	564	Elko County SD	Elko
4	543	Carson City SD	Carson City
5	426	Douglas County SD	Minden
6	355	Lyon County SD	Yerington
7	293	Nye County SD	TonOpah
8	240	Churchill County SD	Fallon
9	225	Humboldt County SD	Winnemucca

High School Drop-out Rate

Rank	Percent	District Name	City
1	6.5	Nye County SD	TonOpah
2	6.1	Clark County SD	Las Vegas
3	4.3	Washoe County SD	Reno
4	3.1	Humboldt County SD	Winnemucca
5	2.6	Elko County SD	Elko
6	2.2	Churchill County SD	Fallon
7	2.1	Carson City SD	Carson City
8	1.9	Douglas County SD	Minden
9	1.8	Lyon County SD	Yerington

New Hampshire

New Hampshire Public School Educational Profile

Category	Value	Category	Value
Schools *(2002-2003)*	474	**Diploma Recipients** *(2002-2003)*	12,452
Instructional Level		White, Non-Hispanic	0
Primary	298	Black, Non-Hispanic	0
Middle	96	Asian/Pacific Islander	0
High	78	American Indian/Alaskan Native	0
Other Level	2	Hispanic	0
Curriculum		**High School Drop-out Rate** (%) *(2000-2001)*	5.4
Regular	474	White, Non-Hispanic	5.2
Special Education	0	Black, Non-Hispanic	9.5
Vocational	0	Asian/Pacific Islander	4.3
Alternative	0	American Indian/Alaskan Native	7.8
Type		Hispanic	11.6
Magnet	0	**Staff** *(2002-2003)*	30,091.3
Charter	0	Teachers	14,977.9
Title I Eligible	265	Average Salary ($)	41,909
School-wide Title I	27	Librarians/Media Specialists	289.4
Students *(2002-2003)*	207,671	Guidance Counselors	772.4
Gender (%)		**Ratios** *(2002-2003)*	
Male	51.5	Student/Teacher Ratio	13.9 to 1
Female	48.5	Student/Librarian Ratio	717.6 to 1
Race/Ethnicity (%)		Student/Counselor Ratio	268.9 to 1
White, Non-Hispanic	94.4	**Current Spending** *($ per student in FY 2001)*	7,935
Black, Non-Hispanic	1.5	Instruction	5,148
Asian/Pacific Islander	1.6	Support Services	2,534
American Indian/Alaskan Native	0.3	**College Entrance Exam Scores** *(2003)*	
Hispanic	2.2	Scholastic Aptitude Test (SAT)	
Classification (%)		Participation Rate (%)	75
Individual Education Program (IEP)	14.1	Mean SAT I Verbal Score	522
Migrant	0.1	Mean SAT I Math Score	521
English Language Learner (ELL)	1.6	American College Testing Program (ACT)	
Eligible for Free Lunch Program	10.8	Participation Rate (%)	8
Eligible for Reduced-Price Lunch Program	4.7	Average Composite Score	22.2

Note: *For an explanation of data, please refer to the User's Guide in the front of the book; n/a indicates data not available*

New Hampshire NAEP 2003 Test Scores

Reading			Mathematics		
Grade/Category	Value	Rank	Grade/Category	Value	Rank
4th Grade			**4th Grade**		
Average Proficiency	227.8 (1.0)	2/51	Average Proficiency	243.1 (0.9)	1/51
Proficiency by Gender/Race/Ethnicity			Proficiency by Gender/Race/Ethnicity		
Male	223.8 (1.4)	3/51	Male	245.5 (1.0)	1/51
Female	231.7 (1.3)	2/51	Female	240.5 (1.0)	2/51
White, Non-Hispanic	228.6 (0.9)	13/51	White, Non-Hispanic	243.8 (0.9)	15/51
Black, Non-Hispanic	n/a	n/a	Black, Non-Hispanic	n/a	n/a
Asian, Non-Hispanic	205.8 (4.5)	16/41	Asian, Non-Hispanic	225.3 (3.0)	13/43
American Indian, Non-Hispanic	n/a	n/a	American Indian, Non-Hispanic	n/a	n/a
Hispanic	n/a	n/a	Hispanic	n/a	n/a
Proficiency by Class Size			Proficiency by Class Size		
Less than 16 Students	*216.5 (4.6)*	8/45	Less than 16 Students	*235.5 (2.9)*	5/47
16 to 18 Students	226.1 (2.6)	5/48	16 to 18 Students	242.9 (2.6)	3/48
19 to 20 Students	228.3 (2.3)	4/50	19 to 20 Students	243.8 (1.9)	3/50
21 to 25 Students	230.7 (1.3)	2/51	21 to 25 Students	244.1 (1.3)	2/51
Greater than 25 Students	*220.4 (4.8)*	22/49	Greater than 25 Students	*246.4 (3.4)*	1/49
Percent Attaining Achievement Levels			Percent Attaining Achievement Levels		
Below Basic	25.2 (1.1)	51/51	Below Basic	12.8 (1.0)	51/51
Basic or Above	74.8 (1.1)	1/51	Basic or Above	87.2 (1.0)	1/51
Proficient or Above	40.0 (1.5)	3/51	Proficient or Above	42.6 (1.4)	1/51
Advanced or Above	9.5 (0.8)	4/51	Advanced or Above	5.6 (0.5)	5/51
8th Grade			**8th Grade**		
Average Proficiency	270.7 (0.9)	2/51	Average Proficiency	286.2 (0.8)	4/51
Proficiency by Gender/Race/Ethnicity			Proficiency by Gender/Race/Ethnicity		
Male	265.2 (1.3)	2/51	Male	286.9 (1.0)	4/51
Female	276.0 (1.2)	3/51	Female	285.5 (1.1)	5/51
White, Non-Hispanic	271.6 (0.9)	16/50	White, Non-Hispanic	287.1 (0.8)	20/50
Black, Non-Hispanic	n/a	n/a	Black, Non-Hispanic	n/a	n/a
Asian, Non-Hispanic	n/a	n/a	Asian, Non-Hispanic	n/a	n/a
American Indian, Non-Hispanic	n/a	n/a	American Indian, Non-Hispanic	n/a	n/a
Hispanic	n/a	n/a	Hispanic	n/a	n/a
Proficiency by Parents Highest Level of Ed.			Proficiency by Parents Highest Level of Ed.		
Did Not Finish High School	253.1 (3.7)	2/50	Did Not Finish High School	260.5 (3.2)	15/50
Graduated High School	261.3 (1.5)	5/50	Graduated High School	276.0 (1.6)	7/50
Some Education After High School	272.9 (1.9)	2/50	Some Education After High School	287.3 (1.7)	5/50
Graduated College	278.1 (1.0)	3/50	Graduated College	294.7 (1.0)	5/50
Percent Attaining Achievement Levels			Percent Attaining Achievement Levels		
Below Basic	18.9 (1.2)	46/51	Below Basic	21.4 (1.1)	48/51
Basic or Above	81.1 (1.2)	6/51	Basic or Above	78.6 (1.1)	4/51
Proficient or Above	40.4 (1.5)	2/51	Proficient or Above	34.7 (1.2)	8/51
Advanced or Above	4.0 (0.4)	4/51	Advanced or Above	6.5 (0.8)	9/51

***Note:** For an explanation of data, please refer to the User's Guide in the front of the book; values in italics indicate that the nature of the sample does not allow accurate determination of the variability of the statistic; n/a indicates data not available*

Belknap County

Laconia SD

PO Box 309 • Laconia, NH 03247-0309
(603) 524-5710 • http://www.laconia.k12.nh.us/
Grade Span: PK-12; **Agency Type:** 2
Schools: 5
3 Primary; 1 Middle; 1 High; 0 Other Level
5 Regular; 0 Special Education; 0 Vocational; 0 Alternative
0 Magnet; 0 Charter; 3 Title I Eligible; 0 School-wide Title I
Students: 2,494 (50.5% male; 49.5% female)
Individual Education Program: 385 (15.4%);
English Language Learner: 99 (4.0%); Migrant: 0 (0.0%)
Eligible for Free Lunch Program: 561 (22.5%)
Eligible for Reduced-Price Lunch Program: 224 (9.0%)
Teachers: 196.0 (12.7 to 1)
Librarians/Media Specialists: 5.0 (498.8 to 1)
Guidance Counselors: 15.1 (165.2 to 1)
Current Spending: ($ per student per year):
Total: $7,376; Instruction: $4,843; Support Services: $2,235
Enrollment, Drop-out Rates and Diploma Recipients by Race/Ethnicity

Category	Total	White	Black	Asian	AIAN	Hisp.
Enrollment (%)	100.0	94.7	1.6	2.5	0.2	1.0
Drop-out Rate (%)	n/a	n/a	n/a	n/a	n/a	n/a
H.S. Diplomas (#)	154	n/a	n/a	n/a	n/a	n/a

Shaker Regional SD

58 School St • Belmont, NH 03220-4511
(603) 267-9233
Grade Span: PK-12; **Agency Type:** 2
Schools: 4
2 Primary; 1 Middle; 1 High; 0 Other Level
4 Regular; 0 Special Education; 0 Vocational; 0 Alternative
0 Magnet; 0 Charter; 2 Title I Eligible; 0 School-wide Title I
Students: 1,556 (50.6% male; 49.4% female)
Individual Education Program: 199 (12.8%);
English Language Learner: 2 (0.1%); Migrant: 0 (0.0%)
Eligible for Free Lunch Program: 176 (11.3%)
Eligible for Reduced-Price Lunch Program: 96 (6.2%)
Teachers: 108.7 (14.3 to 1)
Librarians/Media Specialists: 3.0 (518.7 to 1)
Guidance Counselors: 5.4 (288.1 to 1)
Current Spending: ($ per student per year):
Total: $7,213; Instruction: $4,259; Support Services: $2,646
Enrollment, Drop-out Rates and Diploma Recipients by Race/Ethnicity

Category	Total	White	Black	Asian	AIAN	Hisp.
Enrollment (%)	100.0	98.8	0.3	0.5	0.1	0.4
Drop-out Rate (%)	6.4	6.5	n/a	0.0	n/a	0.0
H.S. Diplomas (#)	72	n/a	n/a	n/a	n/a	n/a

Winnisquam Regional SD

48 Zion Hill Rd • Northfield, NH 03276-4021
(603) 286-4416 • http://www.winnisquam.k12.nh.us/
Grade Span: PK-12; **Agency Type:** 2
Schools: 5
3 Primary; 1 Middle; 1 High; 0 Other Level
5 Regular; 0 Special Education; 0 Vocational; 0 Alternative
0 Magnet; 0 Charter; 3 Title I Eligible; 0 School-wide Title I
Students: 1,786 (51.9% male; 48.1% female)
Individual Education Program: 253 (14.2%);
English Language Learner: 1 (0.1%); Migrant: 0 (0.0%)
Eligible for Free Lunch Program: 271 (15.2%)
Eligible for Reduced-Price Lunch Program: 91 (5.1%)
Teachers: 136.2 (13.1 to 1)
Librarians/Media Specialists: 2.0 (893.0 to 1)
Guidance Counselors: 7.0 (255.1 to 1)
Current Spending: ($ per student per year):
Total: $6,625; Instruction: $3,776; Support Services: $2,606
Enrollment, Drop-out Rates and Diploma Recipients by Race/Ethnicity

Category	Total	White	Black	Asian	AIAN	Hisp.
Enrollment (%)	100.0	98.5	0.4	0.5	0.3	0.3
Drop-out Rate (%)	n/a	n/a	n/a	n/a	n/a	n/a
H.S. Diplomas (#)	99	n/a	n/a	n/a	n/a	n/a

Carroll County

Conway SD

19 Pine St • North Conway, NH 03860-5556
(603) 356-5534 • http://www.kennett.k12.nh.us/
Grade Span: KG-12; **Agency Type:** 2
Schools: 5
3 Primary; 1 Middle; 1 High; 0 Other Level
5 Regular; 0 Special Education; 0 Vocational; 0 Alternative
0 Magnet; 0 Charter; 3 Title I Eligible; 1 School-wide Title I
Students: 2,180 (52.3% male; 47.7% female)
Individual Education Program: 199 (9.1%);
English Language Learner: 20 (0.9%); Migrant: 0 (0.0%)
Eligible for Free Lunch Program: 342 (15.7%)
Eligible for Reduced-Price Lunch Program: 131 (6.0%)
Teachers: 165.1 (13.2 to 1)
Librarians/Media Specialists: 1.9 (1,147.4 to 1)
Guidance Counselors: 9.0 (242.2 to 1)
Current Spending: ($ per student per year):
Total: $7,657; Instruction: $4,883; Support Services: $2,510
Enrollment, Drop-out Rates and Diploma Recipients by Race/Ethnicity

Category	Total	White	Black	Asian	AIAN	Hisp.
Enrollment (%)	100.0	97.2	0.7	1.2	0.3	0.6
Drop-out Rate (%)	6.0	5.9	12.5	0.0	0.0	50.0
H.S. Diplomas (#)	175	n/a	n/a	n/a	n/a	n/a

Governor Wentworth Reg SD

PO Box 190 • Wolfeboro Falls, NH 03896-0190
(603) 569-1658
Grade Span: PK-12; **Agency Type:** 2
Schools: 8
5 Primary; 2 Middle; 1 High; 0 Other Level
8 Regular; 0 Special Education; 0 Vocational; 0 Alternative
0 Magnet; 0 Charter; 4 Title I Eligible; 1 School-wide Title I
Students: 2,846 (51.1% male; 48.9% female)
Individual Education Program: 334 (11.7%);
English Language Learner: 8 (0.3%); Migrant: 0 (0.0%)
Eligible for Free Lunch Program: 416 (14.6%)
Eligible for Reduced-Price Lunch Program: 231 (8.1%)
Teachers: 217.0 (13.1 to 1)
Librarians/Media Specialists: 3.3 (862.4 to 1)
Guidance Counselors: 12.1 (235.2 to 1)
Current Spending: ($ per student per year):
Total: $7,781; Instruction: $5,076; Support Services: $2,422
Enrollment, Drop-out Rates and Diploma Recipients by Race/Ethnicity

Category	Total	White	Black	Asian	AIAN	Hisp.
Enrollment (%)	100.0	98.6	0.7	0.4	0.0	0.3
Drop-out Rate (%)	3.7	3.7	0.0	0.0	0.0	n/a
H.S. Diplomas (#)	218	n/a	n/a	n/a	n/a	n/a

Cheshire County

Jaffrey-Rindge Coop SD

10 Main St • Jaffrey, NH 03452-6142
(603) 532-8100 • http://www.sau47.k12.nh.us/
Grade Span: PK-12; **Agency Type:** 2
Schools: 4
2 Primary; 1 Middle; 1 High; 0 Other Level
4 Regular; 0 Special Education; 0 Vocational; 0 Alternative
0 Magnet; 0 Charter; 2 Title I Eligible; 0 School-wide Title I
Students: 1,667 (51.9% male; 48.1% female)
Individual Education Program: 265 (15.9%);
English Language Learner: 0 (0.0%); Migrant: 0 (0.0%)
Eligible for Free Lunch Program: 169 (10.1%)
Eligible for Reduced-Price Lunch Program: 58 (3.5%)
Teachers: 129.0 (12.9 to 1)
Librarians/Media Specialists: 4.0 (416.8 to 1)
Guidance Counselors: 5.8 (287.4 to 1)
Current Spending: ($ per student per year):
Total: $7,199; Instruction: $4,608; Support Services: $2,347
Enrollment, Drop-out Rates and Diploma Recipients by Race/Ethnicity

Category	Total	White	Black	Asian	AIAN	Hisp.
Enrollment (%)	100.0	96.5	0.9	1.3	0.5	0.8
Drop-out Rate (%)	2.9	2.7	n/a	0.0	100.0	0.0
H.S. Diplomas (#)	121	n/a	n/a	n/a	n/a	n/a

Keene SD

34 W St • Keene, NH 03431-3392
(603) 357-9002 • http://www.keene.k12.nh.us/
Grade Span: PK-12; **Agency Type:** 2
Schools: 7
5 Primary; 1 Middle; 1 High; 0 Other Level
7 Regular; 0 Special Education; 0 Vocational; 0 Alternative
0 Magnet; 0 Charter; 6 Title I Eligible; 0 School-wide Title I
Students: 3,818 (51.3% male; 48.7% female)
Individual Education Program: 517 (13.5%);
English Language Learner: 41 (1.1%); Migrant: 0 (0.0%)
Eligible for Free Lunch Program: 424 (11.1%)
Eligible for Reduced-Price Lunch Program: 272 (7.1%)
Teachers: 295.7 (12.9 to 1)
Librarians/Media Specialists: 7.0 (545.4 to 1)
Guidance Counselors: 27.0 (141.4 to 1)
Current Spending: ($ per student per year):
Total: $8,485; Instruction: $4,922; Support Services: $3,291

Enrollment, Drop-out Rates and Diploma Recipients by Race/Ethnicity

Category	Total	White	Black	Asian	AIAN	Hisp.
Enrollment (%)	100.0	96.9	0.8	1.3	0.3	0.8
Drop-out Rate (%)	3.2	3.3	0.0	0.0	0.0	0.0
H.S. Diplomas (#)	333	n/a	n/a	n/a	n/a	n/a

Monadnock Regional SD

600 Old Homestead Hwy • East Swanzey, NH 03446-2310
(603) 352-6955 • http://www.mrsd.org/LinkM.htm
Grade Span: PK-12; **Agency Type:** 2
Schools: 9
6 Primary; 2 Middle; 1 High; 0 Other Level
9 Regular; 0 Special Education; 0 Vocational; 0 Alternative
0 Magnet; 0 Charter; 6 Title I Eligible; 0 School-wide Title I
Students: 2,546 (52.1% male; 47.9% female)
Individual Education Program: 290 (11.4%);
English Language Learner: 1 (<0.1%); Migrant: 0 (0.0%)
Eligible for Free Lunch Program: 360 (14.1%)
Eligible for Reduced-Price Lunch Program: 186 (7.3%)
Teachers: 173.5 (14.7 to 1)
Librarians/Media Specialists: 2.6 (979.2 to 1)
Guidance Counselors: 12.0 (212.2 to 1)
Current Spending: ($ per student per year):
Total: $7,656; Instruction: $4,891; Support Services: $2,454
Enrollment, Drop-out Rates and Diploma Recipients by Race/Ethnicity

Category	Total	White	Black	Asian	AIAN	Hisp.
Enrollment (%)	100.0	97.4	0.5	0.4	0.5	1.1
Drop-out Rate (%)	3.7	3.6	0.0	50.0	n/a	0.0
H.S. Diplomas (#)	170	n/a	n/a	n/a	n/a	n/a

Coos County

Berlin SD

183 Hillside Ave • Berlin, NH 03570-1899
(603) 752-6500 • http://www.sau3.org/
Grade Span: KG-12; **Agency Type:** 2
Schools: 6
3 Primary; 2 Middle; 1 High; 0 Other Level
6 Regular; 0 Special Education; 0 Vocational; 0 Alternative
0 Magnet; 0 Charter; 3 Title I Eligible; 0 School-wide Title I
Students: 1,661 (54.6% male; 45.4% female)
Individual Education Program: 176 (10.6%);
English Language Learner: 0 (0.0%); Migrant: 0 (0.0%)
Eligible for Free Lunch Program: 455 (27.4%)
Eligible for Reduced-Price Lunch Program: 101 (6.1%)
Teachers: 109.2 (15.2 to 1)
Librarians/Media Specialists: 2.0 (830.5 to 1)
Guidance Counselors: 5.0 (332.2 to 1)
Current Spending: ($ per student per year):
Total: $6,342; Instruction: $4,021; Support Services: $2,081
Enrollment, Drop-out Rates and Diploma Recipients by Race/Ethnicity

Category	Total	White	Black	Asian	AIAN	Hisp.
Enrollment (%)	100.0	95.6	0.7	0.7	1.7	1.2
Drop-out Rate (%)	n/a	n/a	n/a	n/a	n/a	n/a
H.S. Diplomas (#)	102	n/a	n/a	n/a	n/a	n/a

Grafton County

Lebanon SD

84 Hanover St • Lebanon, NH 03766-0488
Mailing Address: PO Box 488 • Lebanon, NH 03766-0488
(603) 448-1634 • http://www.lebanon.k12.nh.us/
Grade Span: PK-12; **Agency Type:** 2
Schools: 7
4 Primary; 2 Middle; 1 High; 0 Other Level
7 Regular; 0 Special Education; 0 Vocational; 0 Alternative
0 Magnet; 0 Charter; 3 Title I Eligible; 0 School-wide Title I
Students: 2,059 (50.1% male; 49.9% female)
Individual Education Program: 266 (12.9%);
English Language Learner: 64 (3.1%); Migrant: 0 (0.0%)
Eligible for Free Lunch Program: 173 (8.4%)
Eligible for Reduced-Price Lunch Program: 68 (3.3%)
Teachers: 171.4 (12.0 to 1)
Librarians/Media Specialists: 5.7 (361.2 to 1)
Guidance Counselors: 8.6 (239.4 to 1)
Current Spending: ($ per student per year):
Total: $9,056; Instruction: $5,879; Support Services: $2,985
Enrollment, Drop-out Rates and Diploma Recipients by Race/Ethnicity

Category	Total	White	Black	Asian	AIAN	Hisp.
Enrollment (%)	100.0	91.7	2.2	3.8	0.6	1.6
Drop-out Rate (%)	3.7	3.9	0.0	0.0	0.0	0.0
H.S. Diplomas (#)	168	n/a	n/a	n/a	n/a	n/a

Mascoma Valley Reg SD

PO Box 789 • Enfield, NH 03748-0789
(603) 632-5563 • http://www.mascoma.k12.nh.us/
Grade Span: KG-12; **Agency Type:** 2
Schools: 4
2 Primary; 1 Middle; 1 High; 0 Other Level
4 Regular; 0 Special Education; 0 Vocational; 0 Alternative
0 Magnet; 0 Charter; 3 Title I Eligible; 0 School-wide Title I
Students: 1,512 (49.5% male; 50.5% female)
Individual Education Program: 206 (13.6%);
English Language Learner: 5 (0.3%); Migrant: 2 (0.1%)
Eligible for Free Lunch Program: 156 (10.3%)
Eligible for Reduced-Price Lunch Program: 76 (5.0%)
Teachers: 114.6 (13.2 to 1)
Librarians/Media Specialists: 3.0 (504.0 to 1)
Guidance Counselors: 7.0 (216.0 to 1)
Current Spending: ($ per student per year):
Total: $7,105; Instruction: $4,635; Support Services: $2,257
Enrollment, Drop-out Rates and Diploma Recipients by Race/Ethnicity

Category	Total	White	Black	Asian	AIAN	Hisp.
Enrollment (%)	100.0	97.8	0.7	0.6	0.4	0.5
Drop-out Rate (%)	4.2	4.2	0.0	n/a	n/a	n/a
H.S. Diplomas (#)	73	n/a	n/a	n/a	n/a	n/a

Newfound Area SD

20 N Main St • Bristol, NH 03222-1404
(603) 744-5555 • http://www.newfound.k12.nh.us/
Grade Span: PK-12; **Agency Type:** 2
Schools: 7
5 Primary; 1 Middle; 1 High; 0 Other Level
7 Regular; 0 Special Education; 0 Vocational; 0 Alternative
0 Magnet; 0 Charter; 4 Title I Eligible; 0 School-wide Title I
Students: 1,550 (52.9% male; 47.1% female)
Individual Education Program: 224 (14.5%);
English Language Learner: 8 (0.5%); Migrant: 0 (0.0%)
Eligible for Free Lunch Program: 250 (16.1%)
Eligible for Reduced-Price Lunch Program: 144 (9.3%)
Teachers: 118.9 (13.0 to 1)
Librarians/Media Specialists: 3.0 (516.7 to 1)
Guidance Counselors: 7.9 (196.2 to 1)
Current Spending: ($ per student per year):
Total: $7,437; Instruction: $4,301; Support Services: $2,817
Enrollment, Drop-out Rates and Diploma Recipients by Race/Ethnicity

Category	Total	White	Black	Asian	AIAN	Hisp.
Enrollment (%)	100.0	97.5	0.4	1.0	0.5	0.5
Drop-out Rate (%)	2.6	2.6	0.0	0.0	n/a	0.0
H.S. Diplomas (#)	91	n/a	n/a	n/a	n/a	n/a

Hillsborough County

Amherst SD

1 School St • Amherst, NH 03031-0849
Mailing Address: PO Box 849 • Amherst, NH 03031-0849
(603) 673-2690
Grade Span: KG-08; **Agency Type:** 2
Schools: 3
2 Primary; 1 Middle; 0 High; 0 Other Level
3 Regular; 0 Special Education; 0 Vocational; 0 Alternative
0 Magnet; 0 Charter; 2 Title I Eligible; 0 School-wide Title I
Students: 1,705 (51.4% male; 48.6% female)
Individual Education Program: 164 (9.6%);
English Language Learner: 3 (0.2%); Migrant: 0 (0.0%)
Eligible for Free Lunch Program: 37 (2.2%)
Eligible for Reduced-Price Lunch Program: 19 (1.1%)
Teachers: 119.0 (14.3 to 1)
Librarians/Media Specialists: 2.0 (852.5 to 1)
Guidance Counselors: 5.0 (341.0 to 1)
Current Spending: ($ per student per year):
Total: $7,662; Instruction: $5,454; Support Services: $1,970
Enrollment, Drop-out Rates and Diploma Recipients by Race/Ethnicity

Category	Total	White	Black	Asian	AIAN	Hisp.
Enrollment (%)	100.0	96.7	0.6	1.8	0.4	0.5
Drop-out Rate (%)	n/a	n/a	n/a	n/a	n/a	n/a
H.S. Diplomas (#)	n/a	n/a	n/a	n/a	n/a	n/a

Bedford SD

103 County Rd • Bedford, NH 03110-6202
(603) 472-3755 • http://www.sau25.net/index.ssi
Grade Span: PK-08; **Agency Type:** 2
Schools: 4
3 Primary; 1 Middle; 0 High; 0 Other Level
4 Regular; 0 Special Education; 0 Vocational; 0 Alternative
0 Magnet; 0 Charter; 3 Title I Eligible; 0 School-wide Title I
Students: 2,838 (52.7% male; 47.3% female)
Individual Education Program: 438 (15.4%);

English Language Learner: 53 (1.9%); Migrant: 0 (0.0%)
Eligible for Free Lunch Program: 32 (1.1%)
Eligible for Reduced-Price Lunch Program: 23 (0.8%)
Teachers: 185.0 (15.3 to 1)
Librarians/Media Specialists: 4.0 (709.5 to 1)
Guidance Counselors: 8.8 (322.5 to 1)
Current Spending: ($ per student per year):
Total: $7,468; Instruction: $4,555; Support Services: $2,714
Enrollment, Drop-out Rates and Diploma Recipients by Race/Ethnicity

Category	Total	White	Black	Asian	AIAN	Hisp.
Enrollment (%)	100.0	96.7	0.6	1.9	0.1	0.7
Drop-out Rate (%)	n/a	n/a	n/a	n/a	n/a	n/a
H.S. Diplomas (#)	n/a	n/a	n/a	n/a	n/a	n/a

Contoocook Valley SD
106 Hancock Rd • Peterborough, NH 03458-1197
(603) 924-3336 • http://www.conval.edu/
Grade Span: PK-12; **Agency Type:** 2
Schools: 12
9 Primary; 2 Middle; 1 High; 0 Other Level
12 Regular; 0 Special Education; 0 Vocational; 0 Alternative
0 Magnet; 0 Charter; 5 Title I Eligible; 0 School-wide Title I
Students: 3,186 (51.3% male; 48.7% female)
Individual Education Program: 511 (16.0%);
English Language Learner: 16 (0.5%); Migrant: 0 (0.0%)
Eligible for Free Lunch Program: 284 (8.9%)
Eligible for Reduced-Price Lunch Program: 162 (5.1%)
Teachers: 239.8 (13.3 to 1)
Librarians/Media Specialists: 6.6 (482.7 to 1)
Guidance Counselors: 11.5 (277.0 to 1)
Current Spending: ($ per student per year):
Total: $7,771; Instruction: $5,217; Support Services: $2,316
Enrollment, Drop-out Rates and Diploma Recipients by Race/Ethnicity

Category	Total	White	Black	Asian	AIAN	Hisp.
Enrollment (%)	100.0	97.0	0.9	1.4	0.2	0.5
Drop-out Rate (%)	1.4	1.4	0.0	0.0	n/a	n/a
H.S. Diplomas (#)	233	n/a	n/a	n/a	n/a	n/a

Goffstown SD
11 School St • Goffstown, NH 03045-1908
(603) 497-4818 • http://www.goffstown.k12.nh.us/
Grade Span: PK-12; **Agency Type:** 2
Schools: 4
2 Primary; 1 Middle; 1 High; 0 Other Level
4 Regular; 0 Special Education; 0 Vocational; 0 Alternative
0 Magnet; 0 Charter; 2 Title I Eligible; 0 School-wide Title I
Students: 2,998 (49.9% male; 50.1% female)
Individual Education Program: 300 (10.0%);
English Language Learner: 15 (0.5%); Migrant: 0 (0.0%)
Eligible for Free Lunch Program: 121 (4.0%)
Eligible for Reduced-Price Lunch Program: 83 (2.8%)
Teachers: 198.9 (15.1 to 1)
Librarians/Media Specialists: 3.2 (936.9 to 1)
Guidance Counselors: 8.8 (340.7 to 1)
Current Spending: ($ per student per year):
Total: $6,150; Instruction: $3,814; Support Services: $2,101
Enrollment, Drop-out Rates and Diploma Recipients by Race/Ethnicity

Category	Total	White	Black	Asian	AIAN	Hisp.
Enrollment (%)	100.0	98.4	0.3	0.6	0.1	0.5
Drop-out Rate (%)	2.3	2.3	0.0	n/a	n/a	n/a
H.S. Diplomas (#)	180	n/a	n/a	n/a	n/a	n/a

Hudson SD
20 Library St • Hudson, NH 03051-4260
(603) 883-7765 • http://ci.hudson.nh.us/schoolwelcome.html
Grade Span: 01-12; **Agency Type:** 2
Schools: 6
4 Primary; 1 Middle; 1 High; 0 Other Level
6 Regular; 0 Special Education; 0 Vocational; 0 Alternative
0 Magnet; 0 Charter; 4 Title I Eligible; 0 School-wide Title I
Students: 4,097 (51.3% male; 48.7% female)
Individual Education Program: 521 (12.7%);
English Language Learner: 39 (1.0%); Migrant: 0 (0.0%)
Eligible for Free Lunch Program: 153 (3.7%)
Eligible for Reduced-Price Lunch Program: 47 (1.1%)
Teachers: 245.0 (16.7 to 1)
Librarians/Media Specialists: 3.0 (1,365.7 to 1)
Guidance Counselors: 15.0 (273.1 to 1)
Current Spending: ($ per student per year):
Total: $6,481; Instruction: $4,118; Support Services: $2,138
Enrollment, Drop-out Rates and Diploma Recipients by Race/Ethnicity

Category	Total	White	Black	Asian	AIAN	Hisp.
Enrollment (%)	100.0	94.9	1.3	1.1	0.6	2.1
Drop-out Rate (%)	4.6	4.7	4.8	0.0	0.0	4.8
H.S. Diplomas (#)	402	n/a	n/a	n/a	n/a	n/a

Litchfield SD
20 Library St • Hudson, NH 03051-4260
(603) 883-7765
Grade Span: 01-12; **Agency Type:** 2
Schools: 3
1 Primary; 1 Middle; 1 High; 0 Other Level
3 Regular; 0 Special Education; 0 Vocational; 0 Alternative
0 Magnet; 0 Charter; 1 Title I Eligible; 0 School-wide Title I
Students: 1,597 (54.0% male; 46.0% female)
Individual Education Program: 271 (17.0%);
English Language Learner: 8 (0.5%); Migrant: 0 (0.0%)
Eligible for Free Lunch Program: 57 (3.6%)
Eligible for Reduced-Price Lunch Program: 25 (1.6%)
Teachers: 107.0 (14.9 to 1)
Librarians/Media Specialists: 3.0 (532.3 to 1)
Guidance Counselors: 4.0 (399.3 to 1)
Current Spending: ($ per student per year):
Total: $6,451; Instruction: $3,792; Support Services: $2,418
Enrollment, Drop-out Rates and Diploma Recipients by Race/Ethnicity

Category	Total	White	Black	Asian	AIAN	Hisp.
Enrollment (%)	100.0	96.4	0.5	0.6	1.1	1.4
Drop-out Rate (%)	0.4	0.4	0.0	0.0	n/a	0.0
H.S. Diplomas (#)	0	0	0	0	0	0

Manchester SD
196 Bridge St • Manchester, NH 03104-4985
(603) 624-6300 • http://www.mansd.org/
Grade Span: PK-12; **Agency Type:** 2
Schools: 22
15 Primary; 4 Middle; 3 High; 0 Other Level
22 Regular; 0 Special Education; 0 Vocational; 0 Alternative
0 Magnet; 0 Charter; 8 Title I Eligible; 4 School-wide Title I
Students: 17,576 (51.0% male; 49.0% female)
Individual Education Program: 2,591 (14.7%);
English Language Learner: 1,342 (7.6%); Migrant: 111 (0.6%)
Eligible for Free Lunch Program: 3,267 (18.6%)
Eligible for Reduced-Price Lunch Program: 991 (5.6%)
Teachers: 1,129.1 (15.6 to 1)
Librarians/Media Specialists: 18.1 (971.0 to 1)
Guidance Counselors: 54.3 (323.7 to 1)
Current Spending: ($ per student per year):
Total: $5,873; Instruction: $3,984; Support Services: $1,673
Enrollment, Drop-out Rates and Diploma Recipients by Race/Ethnicity

Category	Total	White	Black	Asian	AIAN	Hisp.
Enrollment (%)	100.0	84.3	4.1	2.4	0.5	8.7
Drop-out Rate (%)	7.5	7.1	16.8	7.4	5.3	12.3
H.S. Diplomas (#)	1,180	n/a	n/a	n/a	n/a	n/a

Merrimack SD
36 Mcelwain St • Merrimack, NH 03054-3693
(603) 424-6200 • http://www.merrimack.k12.nh.us/
Grade Span: 01-12; **Agency Type:** 2
Schools: 5
3 Primary; 1 Middle; 1 High; 0 Other Level
5 Regular; 0 Special Education; 0 Vocational; 0 Alternative
0 Magnet; 0 Charter; 4 Title I Eligible; 0 School-wide Title I
Students: 4,773 (51.8% male; 48.2% female)
Individual Education Program: 686 (14.4%);
English Language Learner: 44 (0.9%); Migrant: 0 (0.0%)
Eligible for Free Lunch Program: 113 (2.4%)
Eligible for Reduced-Price Lunch Program: 81 (1.7%)
Teachers: 339.8 (14.0 to 1)
Librarians/Media Specialists: 6.0 (795.5 to 1)
Guidance Counselors: 17.0 (280.8 to 1)
Current Spending: ($ per student per year):
Total: $6,705; Instruction: $4,398; Support Services: $2,108
Enrollment, Drop-out Rates and Diploma Recipients by Race/Ethnicity

Category	Total	White	Black	Asian	AIAN	Hisp.
Enrollment (%)	100.0	95.1	1.1	1.9	0.5	1.4
Drop-out Rate (%)	n/a	n/a	n/a	n/a	n/a	n/a
H.S. Diplomas (#)	316	n/a	n/a	n/a	n/a	n/a

Milford SD
100 W St • Milford, NH 03055-4871
(603) 673-2202 • http://www.milfordschools.net/district/index.php
Grade Span: PK-12; **Agency Type:** 2
Schools: 4
2 Primary; 1 Middle; 1 High; 0 Other Level
4 Regular; 0 Special Education; 0 Vocational; 0 Alternative
0 Magnet; 0 Charter; 3 Title I Eligible; 0 School-wide Title I
Students: 2,540 (52.4% male; 47.6% female)
Individual Education Program: 387 (15.2%);
English Language Learner: 23 (0.9%); Migrant: 0 (0.0%)
Eligible for Free Lunch Program: 246 (9.7%)
Eligible for Reduced-Price Lunch Program: 138 (5.4%)

Teachers: 178.0 (14.3 to 1)
Librarians/Media Specialists: 3.0 (846.7 to 1)
Guidance Counselors: 8.0 (317.5 to 1)
Current Spending: ($ per student per year):
Total: $7,441; Instruction: $4,845; Support Services: $2,358
Enrollment, Drop-out Rates and Diploma Recipients by Race/Ethnicity

Category	Total	White	Black	Asian	AIAN	Hisp.
Enrollment (%)	100.0	94.7	1.3	1.6	0.3	2.0
Drop-out Rate (%)	2.8	2.8	0.0	0.0	n/a	0.0
H.S. Diplomas (#)	165	n/a	n/a	n/a	n/a	n/a

Nashua SD

141 Ledge St • Nashua, NH 03061-0687
Mailing Address: PO Box 687 • Nashua, NH 03061-0687
(603) 594-4300 • http://district.nashua.edu/
Grade Span: PK-12; **Agency Type:** 2
Schools: 18
12 Primary; 4 Middle; 1 High; 1 Other Level
18 Regular; 0 Special Education; 0 Vocational; 0 Alternative
0 Magnet; 0 Charter; 5 Title I Eligible; 3 School-wide Title I
Students: 13,487 (51.9% male; 48.1% female)
Individual Education Program: 1,942 (14.4%);
English Language Learner: 655 (4.9%); Migrant: 2 (<0.1%)
Eligible for Free Lunch Program: 2,362 (17.5%)
Eligible for Reduced-Price Lunch Program: 788 (5.8%)
Teachers: 859.8 (15.7 to 1)
Librarians/Media Specialists: 15.0 (899.1 to 1)
Guidance Counselors: 37.0 (364.5 to 1)
Current Spending: ($ per student per year):
Total: $6,246; Instruction: $3,974; Support Services: $2,074
Enrollment, Drop-out Rates and Diploma Recipients by Race/Ethnicity

Category	Total	White	Black	Asian	AIAN	Hisp.
Enrollment (%)	100.0	81.5	3.0	4.1	0.4	11.1
Drop-out Rate (%)	10.7	10.2	9.3	6.3	21.4	16.4
H.S. Diplomas (#)	655	n/a	n/a	n/a	n/a	n/a

Pelham SD

19 Haverhill Rd • Windham, NH 03087-0510
Mailing Address: PO Box 510 • Windham, NH 03087-0510
(603) 425-1976 • http://www.windhamsd.org/SAU28/sau28.htm
Grade Span: 01-12; **Agency Type:** 2
Schools: 3
1 Primary; 1 Middle; 1 High; 0 Other Level
3 Regular; 0 Special Education; 0 Vocational; 0 Alternative
0 Magnet; 0 Charter; 2 Title I Eligible; 0 School-wide Title I
Students: 1,974 (50.6% male; 49.4% female)
Individual Education Program: 284 (14.4%);
English Language Learner: 16 (0.8%); Migrant: 0 (0.0%)
Eligible for Free Lunch Program: 67 (3.4%)
Eligible for Reduced-Price Lunch Program: 46 (2.3%)
Teachers: 122.2 (16.2 to 1)
Librarians/Media Specialists: 3.0 (658.0 to 1)
Guidance Counselors: 6.2 (318.4 to 1)
Current Spending: ($ per student per year):
Total: $6,559; Instruction: $4,151; Support Services: $2,061
Enrollment, Drop-out Rates and Diploma Recipients by Race/Ethnicity

Category	Total	White	Black	Asian	AIAN	Hisp.
Enrollment (%)	100.0	96.6	0.4	1.6	0.1	1.4
Drop-out Rate (%)	4.5	4.4	50.0	0.0	n/a	n/a
H.S. Diplomas (#)	104	n/a	n/a	n/a	n/a	n/a

Merrimack County

Bow SD

32 White Rock Hill Rd • Bow, NH 03304-4219
(603) 224-4728 • http://www.bow.k12.nh.us/
Grade Span: PK-12; **Agency Type:** 2
Schools: 3
1 Primary; 1 Middle; 1 High; 0 Other Level
3 Regular; 0 Special Education; 0 Vocational; 0 Alternative
0 Magnet; 0 Charter; 1 Title I Eligible; 0 School-wide Title I
Students: 1,820 (52.6% male; 47.4% female)
Individual Education Program: 91 (5.0%);
English Language Learner: 2 (0.1%); Migrant: 0 (0.0%)
Eligible for Free Lunch Program: 23 (1.3%)
Eligible for Reduced-Price Lunch Program: 5 (0.3%)
Teachers: 131.8 (13.8 to 1)
Librarians/Media Specialists: 3.0 (606.7 to 1)
Guidance Counselors: 6.0 (303.3 to 1)
Current Spending: ($ per student per year):
Total: $7,133; Instruction: $4,553; Support Services: $2,341
Enrollment, Drop-out Rates and Diploma Recipients by Race/Ethnicity

Category	Total	White	Black	Asian	AIAN	Hisp.
Enrollment (%)	100.0	97.9	0.0	1.4	0.1	0.6
Drop-out Rate (%)	1.1	1.1	n/a	0.0	0.0	0.0
H.S. Diplomas (#)	110	n/a	n/a	n/a	n/a	n/a

Concord SD

16 Rumford St • Concord, NH 03301-3999
(603) 225-0811 •
http://www.concord.k12.nh.us/comm/dropdownindex.html
Grade Span: PK-12; **Agency Type:** 2
Schools: 11
9 Primary; 1 Middle; 1 High; 0 Other Level
11 Regular; 0 Special Education; 0 Vocational; 0 Alternative
0 Magnet; 0 Charter; 5 Title I Eligible; 2 School-wide Title I
Students: 5,360 (51.2% male; 48.8% female)
Individual Education Program: 739 (13.8%);
English Language Learner: 118 (2.2%); Migrant: 2 (<0.1%)
Eligible for Free Lunch Program: 623 (11.6%)
Eligible for Reduced-Price Lunch Program: 243 (4.5%)
Teachers: 354.6 (15.1 to 1)
Librarians/Media Specialists: 7.3 (734.2 to 1)
Guidance Counselors: 17.4 (308.0 to 1)
Current Spending: ($ per student per year):
Total: $7,152; Instruction: $4,515; Support Services: $2,424
Enrollment, Drop-out Rates and Diploma Recipients by Race/Ethnicity

Category	Total	White	Black	Asian	AIAN	Hisp.
Enrollment (%)	100.0	93.5	2.6	2.5	0.3	1.1
Drop-out Rate (%)	n/a	n/a	n/a	n/a	n/a	n/a
H.S. Diplomas (#)	399	n/a	n/a	n/a	n/a	n/a

Kearsarge Regional SD

190 Main St • New London, NH 03257-4554
(603) 526-2051 • http://www.kearsarge.k12.nh.us/
Grade Span: KG-12; **Agency Type:** 2
Schools: 6
4 Primary; 1 Middle; 1 High; 0 Other Level
6 Regular; 0 Special Education; 0 Vocational; 0 Alternative
0 Magnet; 0 Charter; 4 Title I Eligible; 0 School-wide Title I
Students: 2,088 (52.8% male; 47.2% female)
Individual Education Program: 346 (16.6%);
English Language Learner: 9 (0.4%); Migrant: 0 (0.0%)
Eligible for Free Lunch Program: 137 (6.6%)
Eligible for Reduced-Price Lunch Program: 69 (3.3%)
Teachers: 160.8 (13.0 to 1)
Librarians/Media Specialists: 4.3 (485.6 to 1)
Guidance Counselors: 8.2 (254.6 to 1)
Current Spending: ($ per student per year):
Total: $8,428; Instruction: $5,072; Support Services: $3,119
Enrollment, Drop-out Rates and Diploma Recipients by Race/Ethnicity

Category	Total	White	Black	Asian	AIAN	Hisp.
Enrollment (%)	100.0	96.7	0.3	0.7	1.2	1.1
Drop-out Rate (%)	n/a	n/a	n/a	n/a	n/a	n/a
H.S. Diplomas (#)	129	n/a	n/a	n/a	n/a	n/a

Merrimack Valley SD

105 Community Dr • Penacook, NH 03303-1625
(603) 753-6561 • http://www.mv.k12.nh.us/
Grade Span: PK-12; **Agency Type:** 2
Schools: 7
5 Primary; 1 Middle; 1 High; 0 Other Level
7 Regular; 0 Special Education; 0 Vocational; 0 Alternative
0 Magnet; 0 Charter; 4 Title I Eligible; 0 School-wide Title I
Students: 2,755 (50.8% male; 49.2% female)
Individual Education Program: 367 (13.3%);
English Language Learner: 21 (0.8%); Migrant: 1 (<0.1%)
Eligible for Free Lunch Program: 264 (9.6%)
Eligible for Reduced-Price Lunch Program: 215 (7.8%)
Teachers: 195.5 (14.1 to 1)
Librarians/Media Specialists: 2.0 (1,377.5 to 1)
Guidance Counselors: 14.0 (196.8 to 1)
Current Spending: ($ per student per year):
Total: $6,431; Instruction: $3,821; Support Services: $2,339
Enrollment, Drop-out Rates and Diploma Recipients by Race/Ethnicity

Category	Total	White	Black	Asian	AIAN	Hisp.
Enrollment (%)	100.0	98.0	0.8	0.9	0.0	0.2
Drop-out Rate (%)	4.5	4.4	0.0	0.0	100.0	0.0
H.S. Diplomas (#)	160	n/a	n/a	n/a	n/a	n/a

Pembroke SD

267 Pembroke St • Pembroke, NH 03275-1343
(603) 485-5188 • http://www.sau53.org/sau53/districts/pembroke.htm
Grade Span: KG-12; **Agency Type:** 2
Schools: 4
2 Primary; 1 Middle; 1 High; 0 Other Level

4 Regular; 0 Special Education; 0 Vocational; 0 Alternative
0 Magnet; 0 Charter; 2 Title I Eligible; 0 School-wide Title I
Students: 1,815 (53.1% male; 46.9% female)
Individual Education Program: 212 (11.7%);
English Language Learner: 0 (0.0%); Migrant: 0 (0.0%)
Eligible for Free Lunch Program: 110 (6.1%)
Eligible for Reduced-Price Lunch Program: 65 (3.6%)
Teachers: 133.8 (13.6 to 1)
Librarians/Media Specialists: 1.0 (1,815.0 to 1)
Guidance Counselors: 6.0 (302.5 to 1)
Current Spending: ($ per student per year):
Total: $6,747; Instruction: $4,610; Support Services: $1,931
Enrollment, Drop-out Rates and Diploma Recipients by Race/Ethnicity

Category	Total	White	Black	Asian	AIAN	Hisp.
Enrollment (%)	100.0	97.7	1.0	0.4	0.4	0.4
Drop-out Rate (%)	6.6	6.7	0.0	0.0	n/a	0.0
H.S. Diplomas (#)	161	n/a	n/a	n/a	n/a	n/a

Rockingham County

Derry SD
18 S Main St • Derry, NH 03038-2197
(603) 432-1210 • http://www.derry.k12.nh.us/
Grade Span: 01-08; **Agency Type:** 2
Schools: 7
5 Primary; 2 Middle; 0 High; 0 Other Level
7 Regular; 0 Special Education; 0 Vocational; 0 Alternative
0 Magnet; 0 Charter; 4 Title I Eligible; 0 School-wide Title I
Students: 4,409 (51.6% male; 48.4% female)
Individual Education Program: 720 (16.3%);
English Language Learner: 28 (0.6%); Migrant: 2 (<0.1%)
Eligible for Free Lunch Program: 420 (9.5%)
Eligible for Reduced-Price Lunch Program: 268 (6.1%)
Teachers: 280.2 (15.7 to 1)
Librarians/Media Specialists: 2.0 (2,204.5 to 1)
Guidance Counselors: 14.3 (308.3 to 1)
Current Spending: ($ per student per year):
Total: $8,721; Instruction: $6,476; Support Services: $1,966
Enrollment, Drop-out Rates and Diploma Recipients by Race/Ethnicity

Category	Total	White	Black	Asian	AIAN	Hisp.
Enrollment (%)	100.0	95.8	1.5	1.2	0.1	1.4
Drop-out Rate (%)	n/a	n/a	n/a	n/a	n/a	n/a
H.S. Diplomas (#)	n/a	n/a	n/a	n/a	n/a	n/a

Exeter Region Cooperative SD
24 Front St • Exeter, NH 03833-2744
(603) 778-7772 • http://www.ercsd.k12.nh.us/
Grade Span: 06-12; **Agency Type:** 2
Schools: 2
0 Primary; 1 Middle; 1 High; 0 Other Level
2 Regular; 0 Special Education; 0 Vocational; 0 Alternative
0 Magnet; 0 Charter; 2 Title I Eligible; 0 School-wide Title I
Students: 2,892 (50.7% male; 49.3% female)
Individual Education Program: 397 (13.7%);
English Language Learner: 1 (<0.1%); Migrant: 0 (0.0%)
Eligible for Free Lunch Program: 83 (2.9%)
Eligible for Reduced-Price Lunch Program: 40 (1.4%)
Teachers: 208.1 (13.9 to 1)
Librarians/Media Specialists: 2.0 (1,446.0 to 1)
Guidance Counselors: 10.0 (289.2 to 1)
Current Spending: ($ per student per year):
Total: $7,813; Instruction: $4,912; Support Services: $2,639
Enrollment, Drop-out Rates and Diploma Recipients by Race/Ethnicity

Category	Total	White	Black	Asian	AIAN	Hisp.
Enrollment (%)	100.0	97.8	0.7	1.3	0.1	0.1
Drop-out Rate (%)	3.2	3.1	16.7	7.7	0.0	0.0
H.S. Diplomas (#)	319	n/a	n/a	n/a	n/a	n/a

Londonderry SD
268 Mammoth Rd • Londonderry, NH 03053-3096
(603) 432-6920 • http://www.londonderry.org/page.asp?Page_Id=103
Grade Span: PK-12; **Agency Type:** 2
Schools: 6
4 Primary; 1 Middle; 1 High; 0 Other Level
6 Regular; 0 Special Education; 0 Vocational; 0 Alternative
0 Magnet; 0 Charter; 2 Title I Eligible; 0 School-wide Title I
Students: 5,700 (50.9% male; 49.1% female)
Individual Education Program: 794 (13.9%);
English Language Learner: 13 (0.2%); Migrant: 0 (0.0%)
Eligible for Free Lunch Program: 133 (2.3%)
Eligible for Reduced-Price Lunch Program: 63 (1.1%)
Teachers: 392.6 (14.5 to 1)
Librarians/Media Specialists: 7.7 (740.3 to 1)
Guidance Counselors: 19.5 (292.3 to 1)
Current Spending: ($ per student per year):
Total: $6,935; Instruction: $4,368; Support Services: $2,412

Enrollment, Drop-out Rates and Diploma Recipients by Race/Ethnicity

Category	Total	White	Black	Asian	AIAN	Hisp.
Enrollment (%)	100.0	97.2	0.7	1.2	0.1	0.8
Drop-out Rate (%)	n/a	n/a	n/a	n/a	n/a	n/a
H.S. Diplomas (#)	371	n/a	n/a	n/a	n/a	n/a

Pinkerton Academy SD
5 Pinkerton St • Derry, NH 03038-1515
(603) 432-2588 • http://WWW.PINKERTONACADEMY.NET/
Grade Span: 09-12; **Agency Type:** 2
Schools: 1
0 Primary; 0 Middle; 1 High; 0 Other Level
1 Regular; 0 Special Education; 0 Vocational; 0 Alternative
0 Magnet; 0 Charter; 0 Title I Eligible; 0 School-wide Title I
Students: 3,297 (50.2% male; 49.8% female)
Individual Education Program: 0 (0.0%);
English Language Learner: 17 (0.5%); Migrant: 0 (0.0%)
Eligible for Free Lunch Program: 112 (3.4%)
Eligible for Reduced-Price Lunch Program: 60 (1.8%)
Teachers: 214.6 (15.4 to 1)
Librarians/Media Specialists: 2.0 (1,648.5 to 1)
Guidance Counselors: 14.5 (227.4 to 1)
Current Spending: ($ per student per year):
Total: n/a; Instruction: n/a; Support Services: n/a
Enrollment, Drop-out Rates and Diploma Recipients by Race/Ethnicity

Category	Total	White	Black	Asian	AIAN	Hisp.
Enrollment (%)	100.0	94.9	1.2	1.2	0.8	1.8
Drop-out Rate (%)	5.6	5.8	0.0	0.0	0.0	6.0
H.S. Diplomas (#)	614	n/a	n/a	n/a	n/a	n/a

Portsmouth SD
50 Clough Dr • Portsmouth, NH 03801-5296
(603) 431-5080 • http://www.ri.net/schools/Portsmouth/Admin/
Grade Span: PK-12; **Agency Type:** 2
Schools: 6
4 Primary; 1 Middle; 1 High; 0 Other Level
6 Regular; 0 Special Education; 0 Vocational; 0 Alternative
0 Magnet; 0 Charter; 2 Title I Eligible; 1 School-wide Title I
Students: 2,624 (51.7% male; 48.3% female)
Individual Education Program: 343 (13.1%);
English Language Learner: 68 (2.6%); Migrant: 0 (0.0%)
Eligible for Free Lunch Program: 410 (15.6%)
Eligible for Reduced-Price Lunch Program: 156 (5.9%)
Teachers: 237.2 (11.1 to 1)
Librarians/Media Specialists: 4.0 (656.0 to 1)
Guidance Counselors: 20.7 (126.8 to 1)
Current Spending: ($ per student per year):
Total: $10,136; Instruction: $6,081; Support Services: $3,798
Enrollment, Drop-out Rates and Diploma Recipients by Race/Ethnicity

Category	Total	White	Black	Asian	AIAN	Hisp.
Enrollment (%)	100.0	90.5	4.6	2.9	0.1	1.9
Drop-out Rate (%)	3.8	3.7	8.8	0.0	n/a	8.3
H.S. Diplomas (#)	229	n/a	n/a	n/a	n/a	n/a

Raymond SD
43 Harriman Hill Rd • Raymond, NH 03077-1509
(603) 895-4299 • http://raymond.k12.nh.us/District_General_Info.htm
Grade Span: 01-12; **Agency Type:** 2
Schools: 3
1 Primary; 1 Middle; 1 High; 0 Other Level
3 Regular; 0 Special Education; 0 Vocational; 0 Alternative
0 Magnet; 0 Charter; 1 Title I Eligible; 0 School-wide Title I
Students: 1,662 (51.4% male; 48.6% female)
Individual Education Program: 297 (17.9%);
English Language Learner: 2 (0.1%); Migrant: 0 (0.0%)
Eligible for Free Lunch Program: 211 (12.7%)
Eligible for Reduced-Price Lunch Program: 120 (7.2%)
Teachers: 129.4 (12.8 to 1)
Librarians/Media Specialists: 2.0 (831.0 to 1)
Guidance Counselors: 8.0 (207.8 to 1)
Current Spending: ($ per student per year):
Total: $6,818; Instruction: $4,006; Support Services: $2,484
Enrollment, Drop-out Rates and Diploma Recipients by Race/Ethnicity

Category	Total	White	Black	Asian	AIAN	Hisp.
Enrollment (%)	100.0	98.8	0.4	0.1	0.5	0.3
Drop-out Rate (%)	9.4	9.5	0.0	0.0	n/a	n/a
H.S. Diplomas (#)	126	n/a	n/a	n/a	n/a	n/a

Salem SD
38 Geremonty Dr • Salem, NH 03079-3313
(603) 893-7040 • http://www.salemschooldistrictnh.com/
Grade Span: 01-12; **Agency Type:** 2
Schools: 8
6 Primary; 1 Middle; 1 High; 0 Other Level
8 Regular; 0 Special Education; 0 Vocational; 0 Alternative

0 Magnet; 0 Charter; 4 Title I Eligible; 0 School-wide Title I
Students: 5,235 (51.8% male; 48.2% female)
Individual Education Program: 574 (11.0%);
English Language Learner: 26 (0.5%); Migrant: 0 (0.0%)
Eligible for Free Lunch Program: 248 (4.7%)
Eligible for Reduced-Price Lunch Program: 130 (2.5%)
Teachers: 306.0 (17.1 to 1)
Librarians/Media Specialists: 8.0 (654.4 to 1)
Guidance Counselors: 33.9 (154.4 to 1)
Current Spending: ($ per student per year):
Total: $6,474; Instruction: $4,163; Support Services: $2,049
Enrollment, Drop-out Rates and Diploma Recipients by Race/Ethnicity

Category	Total	White	Black	Asian	AIAN	Hisp.
Enrollment (%)	100.0	94.0	0.7	3.2	0.1	2.1
Drop-out Rate (%)	1.5	1.4	12.5	3.3	0.0	0.0
H.S. Diplomas (#)	411	n/a	n/a	n/a	n/a	n/a

Sanborn Regional SD
178 Main St • Kingston, NH 03848-3249
(603) 642-3688 • http://sanborn.k12.nh.us/
Grade Span: 01-12; **Agency Type:** 2
Schools: 4
2 Primary; 1 Middle; 1 High; 0 Other Level
4 Regular; 0 Special Education; 0 Vocational; 0 Alternative
0 Magnet; 0 Charter; 2 Title I Eligible; 0 School-wide Title I
Students: 1,821 (50.5% male; 49.5% female)
Individual Education Program: 269 (14.8%);
English Language Learner: 5 (0.3%); Migrant: 0 (0.0%)
Eligible for Free Lunch Program: 65 (3.6%)
Eligible for Reduced-Price Lunch Program: 38 (2.1%)
Teachers: 148.9 (12.2 to 1)
Librarians/Media Specialists: 4.0 (455.3 to 1)
Guidance Counselors: 6.0 (303.5 to 1)
Current Spending: ($ per student per year):
Total: $7,781; Instruction: $4,946; Support Services: $2,635
Enrollment, Drop-out Rates and Diploma Recipients by Race/Ethnicity

Category	Total	White	Black	Asian	AIAN	Hisp.
Enrollment (%)	100.0	97.7	0.7	0.4	0.3	0.9
Drop-out Rate (%)	5.1	5.0	0.0	0.0	n/a	100.0
H.S. Diplomas (#)	126	n/a	n/a	n/a	n/a	n/a

Timberlane Regional SD
30 Greenough Rd • Plaistow, NH 03865-2762
(603) 382-6119 • http://www.timberlane.net/
Grade Span: 01-12; **Agency Type:** 2
Schools: 7
4 Primary; 2 Middle; 1 High; 0 Other Level
7 Regular; 0 Special Education; 0 Vocational; 0 Alternative
0 Magnet; 0 Charter; 4 Title I Eligible; 0 School-wide Title I
Students: 4,384 (50.8% male; 49.2% female)
Individual Education Program: 721 (16.4%);
English Language Learner: 4 (0.1%); Migrant: 0 (0.0%)
Eligible for Free Lunch Program: 127 (2.9%)
Eligible for Reduced-Price Lunch Program: 78 (1.8%)
Teachers: 328.8 (13.3 to 1)
Librarians/Media Specialists: 4.6 (953.0 to 1)
Guidance Counselors: 17.0 (257.9 to 1)
Current Spending: ($ per student per year):
Total: $6,748; Instruction: $4,271; Support Services: $2,311
Enrollment, Drop-out Rates and Diploma Recipients by Race/Ethnicity

Category	Total	White	Black	Asian	AIAN	Hisp.
Enrollment (%)	100.0	98.3	0.5	0.3	0.3	0.6
Drop-out Rate (%)	5.2	5.2	0.0	0.0	0.0	0.0
H.S. Diplomas (#)	241	n/a	n/a	n/a	n/a	n/a

Windham SD
19 Haverhill Rd • Windham, NH 03087-0510
Mailing Address: PO Box 510 • Windham, NH 03087-0510
(603) 425-1976 • http://www.windhamsd.org/
Grade Span: PK-08; **Agency Type:** 2
Schools: 4
3 Primary; 1 Middle; 0 High; 0 Other Level
4 Regular; 0 Special Education; 0 Vocational; 0 Alternative
0 Magnet; 0 Charter; 3 Title I Eligible; 0 School-wide Title I
Students: 1,568 (52.6% male; 47.4% female)
Individual Education Program: 316 (20.2%);
English Language Learner: 15 (1.0%); Migrant: 0 (0.0%)
Eligible for Free Lunch Program: 17 (1.1%)
Eligible for Reduced-Price Lunch Program: 21 (1.3%)
Teachers: 113.0 (13.9 to 1)
Librarians/Media Specialists: 1.0 (1,568.0 to 1)
Guidance Counselors: 4.0 (392.0 to 1)
Current Spending: ($ per student per year):
Total: $7,204; Instruction: $4,404; Support Services: $2,656
Enrollment, Drop-out Rates and Diploma Recipients by Race/Ethnicity

Category	Total	White	Black	Asian	AIAN	Hisp.
Enrollment (%)	100.0	96.1	0.8	2.0	0.1	0.9
Drop-out Rate (%)	n/a	n/a	n/a	n/a	n/a	n/a
H.S. Diplomas (#)	n/a	n/a	n/a	n/a	n/a	n/a

Strafford County

Dover SD
288 Central Ave • Dover, NH 03820-4169
(603) 516-6800 • http://www.dover.k12.nh.us/
Grade Span: PK-12; **Agency Type:** 2
Schools: 5
3 Primary; 1 Middle; 1 High; 0 Other Level
5 Regular; 0 Special Education; 0 Vocational; 0 Alternative
0 Magnet; 0 Charter; 3 Title I Eligible; 1 School-wide Title I
Students: 3,970 (51.0% male; 49.0% female)
Individual Education Program: 440 (11.1%);
English Language Learner: 63 (1.6%); Migrant: 0 (0.0%)
Eligible for Free Lunch Program: 551 (13.9%)
Eligible for Reduced-Price Lunch Program: 187 (4.7%)
Teachers: 264.3 (15.0 to 1)
Librarians/Media Specialists: 5.0 (794.0 to 1)
Guidance Counselors: 14.6 (271.9 to 1)
Current Spending: ($ per student per year):
Total: $6,638; Instruction: $4,112; Support Services: $2,264
Enrollment, Drop-out Rates and Diploma Recipients by Race/Ethnicity

Category	Total	White	Black	Asian	AIAN	Hisp.
Enrollment (%)	100.0	93.4	2.2	3.2	0.0	1.1
Drop-out Rate (%)	6.4	6.4	4.3	5.7	n/a	9.1
H.S. Diplomas (#)	292	n/a	n/a	n/a	n/a	n/a

Oyster River Coop SD
36 Coe Dr • Durham, NH 03824-2200
(603) 868-5100 • http://www.orcsd.org/
Grade Span: KG-12; **Agency Type:** 2
Schools: 4
2 Primary; 1 Middle; 1 High; 0 Other Level
4 Regular; 0 Special Education; 0 Vocational; 0 Alternative
0 Magnet; 0 Charter; 3 Title I Eligible; 0 School-wide Title I
Students: 2,259 (52.5% male; 47.5% female)
Individual Education Program: 381 (16.9%);
English Language Learner: 58 (2.6%); Migrant: 0 (0.0%)
Eligible for Free Lunch Program: 88 (3.9%)
Eligible for Reduced-Price Lunch Program: 8 (0.4%)
Teachers: 165.2 (13.7 to 1)
Librarians/Media Specialists: 5.0 (451.8 to 1)
Guidance Counselors: 10.7 (211.1 to 1)
Current Spending: ($ per student per year):
Total: $7,949; Instruction: $5,013; Support Services: $2,733
Enrollment, Drop-out Rates and Diploma Recipients by Race/Ethnicity

Category	Total	White	Black	Asian	AIAN	Hisp.
Enrollment (%)	100.0	96.6	0.7	1.9	0.0	0.8
Drop-out Rate (%)	n/a	n/a	n/a	n/a	n/a	n/a
H.S. Diplomas (#)	160	n/a	n/a	n/a	n/a	n/a

Rochester SD
150 Wakefield St, Ste 8 • Rochester, NH 03867-1348
(603) 332-3678 • http://www.rochesterschools.com/
Grade Span: PK-12; **Agency Type:** 2
Schools: 10
8 Primary; 1 Middle; 1 High; 0 Other Level
10 Regular; 0 Special Education; 0 Vocational; 0 Alternative
0 Magnet; 0 Charter; 3 Title I Eligible; 3 School-wide Title I
Students: 4,790 (53.4% male; 46.6% female)
Individual Education Program: 997 (20.8%);
English Language Learner: 57 (1.2%); Migrant: 2 (<0.1%)
Eligible for Free Lunch Program: 801 (16.7%)
Eligible for Reduced-Price Lunch Program: 321 (6.7%)
Teachers: 340.1 (14.1 to 1)
Librarians/Media Specialists: 3.2 (1,496.9 to 1)
Guidance Counselors: 15.7 (305.1 to 1)
Current Spending: ($ per student per year):
Total: $6,326; Instruction: $4,339; Support Services: $1,777
Enrollment, Drop-out Rates and Diploma Recipients by Race/Ethnicity

Category	Total	White	Black	Asian	AIAN	Hisp.
Enrollment (%)	100.0	95.2	1.6	1.7	0.1	1.3
Drop-out Rate (%)	8.1	7.9	16.7	15.4	33.3	6.3
H.S. Diplomas (#)	306	n/a	n/a	n/a	n/a	n/a

Somersworth SD
51 W High St • Somersworth, NH 03878-1099
(603) 692-4450 • http://www.mw.somersworth.k12.nh.us/sau56/
Grade Span: PK-12; **Agency Type:** 2
Schools: 4

2 Primary; 1 Middle; 1 High; 0 Other Level
4 Regular; 0 Special Education; 0 Vocational; 0 Alternative
0 Magnet; 0 Charter; 3 Title I Eligible; 1 School-wide Title I

Students: 1,880 (51.5% male; 48.5% female)
Individual Education Program: 283 (15.1%);
English Language Learner: 33 (1.8%); Migrant: 0 (0.0%)
Eligible for Free Lunch Program: 324 (17.2%)
Eligible for Reduced-Price Lunch Program: 97 (5.2%)

Teachers: 131.1 (14.3 to 1)

Librarians/Media Specialists: 2.2 (854.5 to 1)

Guidance Counselors: 7.6 (247.4 to 1)

Current Spending: ($ per student per year):
Total: $6,481; Instruction: $4,049; Support Services: $2,212

Enrollment, Drop-out Rates and Diploma Recipients by Race/Ethnicity

Category	Total	White	Black	Asian	AIAN	Hisp.
Enrollment (%)	100.0	93.6	2.0	2.0	0.5	1.9
Drop-out Rate (%)	9.7	8.9	44.4	14.3	50.0	14.3
H.S. Diplomas (#)	122	n/a	n/a	n/a	n/a	n/a

Sullivan County

Claremont SD

165 Broad St • Claremont, NH 03743-2624
(603) 543-4200 • http://www.sau6.k12.nh.us/claremont/claremont.htm

Grade Span: PK-12; **Agency Type:** 2

Schools: 5
3 Primary; 1 Middle; 1 High; 0 Other Level
5 Regular; 0 Special Education; 0 Vocational; 0 Alternative
0 Magnet; 0 Charter; 3 Title I Eligible; 1 School-wide Title I

Students: 2,054 (50.5% male; 49.5% female)
Individual Education Program: 308 (15.0%);
English Language Learner: 14 (0.7%); Migrant: 5 (0.2%)
Eligible for Free Lunch Program: 380 (18.5%)
Eligible for Reduced-Price Lunch Program: 172 (8.4%)

Teachers: 170.7 (12.0 to 1)

Librarians/Media Specialists: 3.0 (684.7 to 1)

Guidance Counselors: 9.0 (228.2 to 1)

Current Spending: ($ per student per year):
Total: $8,267; Instruction: $5,614; Support Services: $2,423

Enrollment, Drop-out Rates and Diploma Recipients by Race/Ethnicity

Category	Total	White	Black	Asian	AIAN	Hisp.
Enrollment (%)	100.0	98.1	0.9	0.7	0.1	0.3
Drop-out Rate (%)	5.4	5.4	n/a	0.0	n/a	0.0
H.S. Diplomas (#)	128	n/a	n/a	n/a	n/a	n/a

Fall Mountain Regional SD

PO Box 600 • Charlestown, NH 03603-0600
(603) 826-7756 • http://www.fall-mountain.k12.nh.us/

Grade Span: PK-12; **Agency Type:** 2

Schools: 12
9 Primary; 2 Middle; 1 High; 0 Other Level
12 Regular; 0 Special Education; 0 Vocational; 0 Alternative
0 Magnet; 0 Charter; 5 Title I Eligible; 0 School-wide Title I

Students: 2,087 (51.1% male; 48.9% female)
Individual Education Program: 296 (14.2%);
English Language Learner: 0 (0.0%); Migrant: 3 (0.1%)
Eligible for Free Lunch Program: 228 (10.9%)
Eligible for Reduced-Price Lunch Program: 156 (7.5%)

Teachers: 160.6 (13.0 to 1)

Librarians/Media Specialists: 1.0 (2,087.0 to 1)

Guidance Counselors: 7.9 (264.2 to 1)

Current Spending: ($ per student per year):
Total: $7,092; Instruction: $4,499; Support Services: $2,314

Enrollment, Drop-out Rates and Diploma Recipients by Race/Ethnicity

Category	Total	White	Black	Asian	AIAN	Hisp.
Enrollment (%)	100.0	99.2	0.5	0.1	0.0	0.1
Drop-out Rate (%)	3.5	3.6	0.0	n/a	0.0	n/a
H.S. Diplomas (#)	133	n/a	n/a	n/a	n/a	n/a

Number of Schools

Rank	Number	District Name	City
1	22	Manchester SD	Manchester
2	18	Nashua SD	Nashua
3	12	Contoocook Valley SD	Peterborough
3	12	Fall Mountain Regional SD	Charlestown
5	11	Concord SD	Concord
6	10	Rochester SD	Rochester
7	9	Monadnock Regional SD	East Swanzey
8	8	Governor Wentworth Reg SD	Wolfeboro Falls
8	8	Salem SD	Salem
10	7	Derry SD	Derry
10	7	Keene SD	Keene
10	7	Lebanon SD	Lebanon
10	7	Merrimack Valley SD	Penacook
10	7	Newfound Area SD	Bristol
10	7	Timberlane Regional SD	Plaistow
16	6	Berlin SD	Berlin
16	6	Hudson SD	Hudson
16	6	Kearsarge Regional SD	New London
16	6	Londonderry SD	Londonderry
16	6	Portsmouth SD	Portsmouth
21	5	Claremont SD	Claremont
21	5	Conway SD	North Conway
21	5	Dover SD	Dover
21	5	Laconia SD	Laconia
21	5	Merrimack SD	Merrimack
21	5	Winnisquam Regional SD	Northfield
27	4	Bedford SD	Bedford
27	4	Goffstown SD	Goffstown
27	4	Jaffrey-Rindge Coop SD	Jaffrey
27	4	Mascoma Valley Reg SD	Enfield
27	4	Milford SD	Milford
27	4	Oyster River Coop SD	Durham
27	4	Pembroke SD	Pembroke
27	4	Sanborn Regional SD	Kingston
27	4	Shaker Regional SD	Belmont
27	4	Somersworth SD	Somersworth
27	4	Windham SD	Windham
38	3	Amherst SD	Amherst
38	3	Bow SD	Bow
38	3	Litchfield SD	Hudson
38	3	Pelham SD	Windham
38	3	Raymond SD	Raymond
43	2	Exeter Region Cooperative SD	Exeter
44	1	Pinkerton Academy SD	Derry

Number of Teachers

Rank	Number	District Name	City
1	1,129	Manchester SD	Manchester
2	859	Nashua SD	Nashua
3	392	Londonderry SD	Londonderry
4	354	Concord SD	Concord
5	340	Rochester SD	Rochester
6	339	Merrimack SD	Merrimack
7	328	Timberlane Regional SD	Plaistow
8	306	Salem SD	Salem
9	295	Keene SD	Keene
10	280	Derry SD	Derry
11	264	Dover SD	Dover
12	245	Hudson SD	Hudson
13	239	Contoocook Valley SD	Peterborough
14	237	Portsmouth SD	Portsmouth
15	217	Governor Wentworth Reg SD	Wolfeboro Falls
16	214	Pinkerton Academy SD	Derry
17	208	Exeter Region Cooperative SD	Exeter
18	198	Goffstown SD	Goffstown
19	196	Laconia SD	Laconia
20	195	Merrimack Valley SD	Penacook
21	185	Bedford SD	Bedford
22	178	Milford SD	Milford
23	173	Monadnock Regional SD	East Swanzey
24	171	Lebanon SD	Lebanon
25	170	Claremont SD	Claremont
26	165	Oyster River Coop SD	Durham
27	165	Conway SD	North Conway
28	160	Kearsarge Regional SD	New London
29	160	Fall Mountain Regional SD	Charlestown
30	148	Sanborn Regional SD	Kingston
31	136	Winnisquam Regional SD	Northfield
32	133	Pembroke SD	Pembroke
33	131	Bow SD	Bow
34	131	Somersworth SD	Somersworth
35	129	Raymond SD	Raymond
36	129	Jaffrey-Rindge Coop SD	Jaffrey
37	122	Pelham SD	Windham
38	119	Amherst SD	Amherst
39	118	Newfound Area SD	Bristol
40	114	Mascoma Valley Reg SD	Enfield
41	113	Windham SD	Windham
42	109	Berlin SD	Berlin
43	108	Shaker Regional SD	Belmont
44	107	Litchfield SD	Hudson

Number of Students

Rank	Number	District Name	City
1	17,576	Manchester SD	Manchester
2	13,487	Nashua SD	Nashua
3	5,700	Londonderry SD	Londonderry
4	5,360	Concord SD	Concord
5	5,235	Salem SD	Salem
6	4,790	Rochester SD	Rochester
7	4,773	Merrimack SD	Merrimack
8	4,409	Derry SD	Derry
9	4,384	Timberlane Regional SD	Plaistow
10	4,097	Hudson SD	Hudson
11	3,970	Dover SD	Dover
12	3,818	Keene SD	Keene
13	3,297	Pinkerton Academy SD	Derry
14	3,186	Contoocook Valley SD	Peterborough
15	2,998	Goffstown SD	Goffstown
16	2,892	Exeter Region Cooperative SD	Exeter
17	2,846	Governor Wentworth Reg SD	Wolfeboro Falls
18	2,838	Bedford SD	Bedford
19	2,755	Merrimack Valley SD	Penacook
20	2,624	Portsmouth SD	Portsmouth
21	2,546	Monadnock Regional SD	East Swanzey
22	2,540	Milford SD	Milford
23	2,494	Laconia SD	Laconia
24	2,259	Oyster River Coop SD	Durham
25	2,180	Conway SD	North Conway
26	2,088	Kearsarge Regional SD	New London
27	2,087	Fall Mountain Regional SD	Charlestown
28	2,059	Lebanon SD	Lebanon
29	2,054	Claremont SD	Claremont
30	1,974	Pelham SD	Windham
31	1,880	Somersworth SD	Somersworth
32	1,821	Sanborn Regional SD	Kingston
33	1,820	Bow SD	Bow
34	1,815	Pembroke SD	Pembroke
35	1,786	Winnisquam Regional SD	Northfield
36	1,705	Amherst SD	Amherst
37	1,667	Jaffrey-Rindge Coop SD	Jaffrey
38	1,662	Raymond SD	Raymond
39	1,661	Berlin SD	Berlin
40	1,597	Litchfield SD	Hudson
41	1,568	Windham SD	Windham
42	1,556	Shaker Regional SD	Belmont
43	1,550	Newfound Area SD	Bristol
44	1,512	Mascoma Valley Reg SD	Enfield

Male Students

Rank	Percent	District Name	City
1	54.6	Berlin SD	Berlin
2	54.0	Litchfield SD	Hudson
3	53.4	Rochester SD	Rochester
4	53.1	Pembroke SD	Pembroke
5	52.9	Newfound Area SD	Bristol
6	52.8	Kearsarge Regional SD	New London
7	52.7	Bedford SD	Bedford
8	52.6	Bow SD	Bow
8	52.6	Windham SD	Windham
10	52.5	Oyster River Coop SD	Durham
11	52.4	Milford SD	Milford
12	52.3	Conway SD	North Conway
13	52.1	Monadnock Regional SD	East Swanzey
14	51.9	Jaffrey-Rindge Coop SD	Jaffrey
14	51.9	Nashua SD	Nashua
14	51.9	Winnisquam Regional SD	Northfield
17	51.8	Merrimack SD	Merrimack
17	51.8	Salem SD	Salem
19	51.7	Portsmouth SD	Portsmouth
20	51.6	Derry SD	Derry
21	51.5	Somersworth SD	Somersworth
22	51.4	Amherst SD	Amherst
22	51.4	Raymond SD	Raymond
24	51.3	Contoocook Valley SD	Peterborough
24	51.3	Hudson SD	Hudson
24	51.3	Keene SD	Keene
27	51.2	Concord SD	Concord
28	51.1	Fall Mountain Regional SD	Charlestown
28	51.1	Governor Wentworth Reg SD	Wolfeboro Falls
30	51.0	Dover SD	Dover
30	51.0	Manchester SD	Manchester
32	50.9	Londonderry SD	Londonderry
33	50.8	Merrimack Valley SD	Penacook
33	50.8	Timberlane Regional SD	Plaistow
35	50.7	Exeter Region Cooperative SD	Exeter
36	50.6	Pelham SD	Windham
36	50.6	Shaker Regional SD	Belmont
38	50.5	Claremont SD	Claremont
38	50.5	Laconia SD	Laconia
38	50.5	Sanborn Regional SD	Kingston
41	50.2	Pinkerton Academy SD	Derry
42	50.1	Lebanon SD	Lebanon
43	49.9	Goffstown SD	Goffstown
44	49.5	Mascoma Valley Reg SD	Enfield

Female Students

Rank	Percent	District Name	City
1	50.5	Mascoma Valley Reg SD	Enfield
2	50.1	Goffstown SD	Goffstown
3	49.9	Lebanon SD	Lebanon
4	49.8	Pinkerton Academy SD	Derry
5	49.5	Claremont SD	Claremont
5	49.5	Laconia SD	Laconia
5	49.5	Sanborn Regional SD	Kingston
8	49.4	Pelham SD	Windham
8	49.4	Shaker Regional SD	Belmont
10	49.3	Exeter Region Cooperative SD	Exeter
11	49.2	Merrimack Valley SD	Penacook
11	49.2	Timberlane Regional SD	Plaistow
13	49.1	Londonderry SD	Londonderry
14	49.0	Dover SD	Dover
14	49.0	Manchester SD	Manchester
16	48.9	Fall Mountain Regional SD	Charlestown
16	48.9	Governor Wentworth Reg SD	Wolfeboro Falls
18	48.8	Concord SD	Concord
19	48.7	Contoocook Valley SD	Peterborough
19	48.7	Hudson SD	Hudson
19	48.7	Keene SD	Keene
22	48.6	Amherst SD	Amherst
22	48.6	Raymond SD	Raymond
24	48.5	Somersworth SD	Somersworth
25	48.4	Derry SD	Derry
26	48.3	Portsmouth SD	Portsmouth
27	48.2	Merrimack SD	Merrimack
27	48.2	Salem SD	Salem
29	48.1	Jaffrey-Rindge Coop SD	Jaffrey
29	48.1	Nashua SD	Nashua
29	48.1	Winnisquam Regional SD	Northfield
32	47.9	Monadnock Regional SD	East Swanzey
33	47.7	Conway SD	North Conway
34	47.6	Milford SD	Milford
35	47.5	Oyster River Coop SD	Durham
36	47.4	Bow SD	Bow
36	47.4	Windham SD	Windham
38	47.3	Bedford SD	Bedford
39	47.2	Kearsarge Regional SD	New London
40	47.1	Newfound Area SD	Bristol
41	46.9	Pembroke SD	Pembroke
42	46.6	Rochester SD	Rochester
43	46.0	Litchfield SD	Hudson
44	45.4	Berlin SD	Berlin

Individual Education Program Students

Rank	Percent	District Name	City
1	20.8	Rochester SD	Rochester
2	20.2	Windham SD	Windham
3	17.9	Raymond SD	Raymond
4	17.0	Litchfield SD	Hudson
5	16.9	Oyster River Coop SD	Durham
6	16.6	Kearsarge Regional SD	New London
7	16.4	Timberlane Regional SD	Plaistow
8	16.3	Derry SD	Derry
9	16.0	Contoocook Valley SD	Peterborough
10	15.9	Jaffrey-Rindge Coop SD	Jaffrey
11	15.4	Bedford SD	Bedford
11	15.4	Laconia SD	Laconia
13	15.2	Milford SD	Milford
14	15.1	Somersworth SD	Somersworth
15	15.0	Claremont SD	Claremont
16	14.8	Sanborn Regional SD	Kingston
17	14.7	Manchester SD	Manchester
18	14.5	Newfound Area SD	Bristol
19	14.4	Merrimack SD	Merrimack
19	14.4	Nashua SD	Nashua
19	14.4	Pelham SD	Windham
22	14.2	Fall Mountain Regional SD	Charlestown
22	14.2	Winnisquam Regional SD	Northfield
24	13.9	Londonderry SD	Londonderry
25	13.8	Concord SD	Concord
26	13.7	Exeter Region Cooperative SD	Exeter
27	13.6	Mascoma Valley Reg SD	Enfield
28	13.5	Keene SD	Keene
29	13.3	Merrimack Valley SD	Penacook
30	13.1	Portsmouth SD	Portsmouth
31	12.9	Lebanon SD	Lebanon
32	12.8	Shaker Regional SD	Belmont
33	12.7	Hudson SD	Hudson
34	11.7	Governor Wentworth Reg SD	Wolfeboro Falls
34	11.7	Pembroke SD	Pembroke
36	11.4	Monadnock Regional SD	East Swanzey

37	11.1	Dover SD	Dover
38	11.0	Salem SD	Salem
39	10.6	Berlin SD	Berlin
40	10.0	Goffstown SD	Goffstown
41	9.6	Amherst SD	Amherst
42	9.1	Conway SD	North Conway
43	5.0	Bow SD	Bow
44	0.0	Pinkerton Academy SD	Derry

English Language Learner Students

Rank	Percent	District Name	City
1	7.6	Manchester SD	Manchester
2	4.9	Nashua SD	Nashua
3	4.0	Laconia SD	Laconia
4	3.1	Lebanon SD	Lebanon
5	2.6	Oyster River Coop SD	Durham
5	2.6	Portsmouth SD	Portsmouth
7	2.2	Concord SD	Concord
8	1.9	Bedford SD	Bedford
9	1.8	Somersworth SD	Somersworth
10	1.6	Dover SD	Dover
11	1.2	Rochester SD	Rochester
12	1.1	Keene SD	Keene
13	1.0	Hudson SD	Hudson
13	1.0	Windham SD	Windham
15	0.9	Conway SD	North Conway
15	0.9	Merrimack SD	Merrimack
15	0.9	Milford SD	Milford
18	0.8	Merrimack Valley SD	Penacook
18	0.8	Pelham SD	Windham
20	0.7	Claremont SD	Claremont
21	0.6	Derry SD	Derry
22	0.5	Contoocook Valley SD	Peterborough
22	0.5	Goffstown SD	Goffstown
22	0.5	Litchfield SD	Hudson
22	0.5	Newfound Area SD	Bristol
22	0.5	Pinkerton Academy SD	Derry
22	0.5	Salem SD	Salem
28	0.4	Kearsarge Regional SD	New London
29	0.3	Governor Wentworth Reg SD	Wolfeboro Falls
29	0.3	Mascoma Valley Reg SD	Enfield
29	0.3	Sanborn Regional SD	Kingston
32	0.2	Amherst SD	Amherst
32	0.2	Londonderry SD	Londonderry
34	0.1	Bow SD	Bow
34	0.1	Raymond SD	Raymond
34	0.1	Shaker Regional SD	Belmont
34	0.1	Timberlane Regional SD	Plaistow
34	0.1	Winnisquam Regional SD	Northfield
39	0.0	Exeter Region Cooperative SD	Exeter
39	0.0	Monadnock Regional SD	East Swanzey
41	0.0	Berlin SD	Berlin
41	0.0	Fall Mountain Regional SD	Charlestown
41	0.0	Jaffrey-Rindge Coop SD	Jaffrey
41	0.0	Pembroke SD	Pembroke

Migrant Students

Rank	Percent	District Name	City
1	0.6	Manchester SD	Manchester
2	0.2	Claremont SD	Claremont
3	0.1	Fall Mountain Regional SD	Charlestown
3	0.1	Mascoma Valley Reg SD	Enfield
5	0.0	Concord SD	Concord
5	0.0	Derry SD	Derry
5	0.0	Merrimack Valley SD	Penacook
5	0.0	Nashua SD	Nashua
5	0.0	Rochester SD	Rochester
10	0.0	Amherst SD	Amherst
10	0.0	Bedford SD	Bedford
10	0.0	Berlin SD	Berlin
10	0.0	Bow SD	Bow
10	0.0	Contoocook Valley SD	Peterborough
10	0.0	Conway SD	North Conway
10	0.0	Dover SD	Dover
10	0.0	Exeter Region Cooperative SD	Exeter
10	0.0	Goffstown SD	Goffstown
10	0.0	Governor Wentworth Reg SD	Wolfeboro Falls
10	0.0	Hudson SD	Hudson
10	0.0	Jaffrey-Rindge Coop SD	Jaffrey
10	0.0	Kearsarge Regional SD	New London
10	0.0	Keene SD	Keene
10	0.0	Laconia SD	Laconia
10	0.0	Lebanon SD	Lebanon
10	0.0	Litchfield SD	Hudson
10	0.0	Londonderry SD	Londonderry
10	0.0	Merrimack SD	Merrimack
10	0.0	Milford SD	Milford
10	0.0	Monadnock Regional SD	East Swanzey
10	0.0	Newfound Area SD	Bristol
10	0.0	Oyster River Coop SD	Durham
10	0.0	Pelham SD	Windham
10	0.0	Pembroke SD	Pembroke
10	0.0	Pinkerton Academy SD	Derry
10	0.0	Portsmouth SD	Portsmouth
10	0.0	Raymond SD	Raymond
10	0.0	Salem SD	Salem
10	0.0	Sanborn Regional SD	Kingston
10	0.0	Shaker Regional SD	Belmont
10	0.0	Somersworth SD	Somersworth
10	0.0	Timberlane Regional SD	Plaistow
10	0.0	Windham SD	Windham
10	0.0	Winnisquam Regional SD	Northfield

Students Eligible for Free Lunch

Rank	Percent	District Name	City
1	27.4	Berlin SD	Berlin
2	22.5	Laconia SD	Laconia
3	18.6	Manchester SD	Manchester
4	18.5	Claremont SD	Claremont
5	17.5	Nashua SD	Nashua
6	17.2	Somersworth SD	Somersworth
7	16.7	Rochester SD	Rochester
8	16.1	Newfound Area SD	Bristol
9	15.7	Conway SD	North Conway
10	15.6	Portsmouth SD	Portsmouth
11	15.2	Winnisquam Regional SD	Northfield
12	14.6	Governor Wentworth Reg SD	Wolfeboro Falls
13	14.1	Monadnock Regional SD	East Swanzey
14	13.9	Dover SD	Dover
15	12.7	Raymond SD	Raymond
16	11.6	Concord SD	Concord
17	11.3	Shaker Regional SD	Belmont
18	11.1	Keene SD	Keene
19	10.9	Fall Mountain Regional SD	Charlestown
20	10.3	Mascoma Valley Reg SD	Enfield
21	10.1	Jaffrey-Rindge Coop SD	Jaffrey
22	9.7	Milford SD	Milford
23	9.6	Merrimack Valley SD	Penacook
24	9.5	Derry SD	Derry
25	8.9	Contoocook Valley SD	Peterborough
26	8.4	Lebanon SD	Lebanon
27	6.6	Kearsarge Regional SD	New London
28	6.1	Pembroke SD	Pembroke
29	4.7	Salem SD	Salem
30	4.0	Goffstown SD	Goffstown
31	3.9	Oyster River Coop SD	Durham
32	3.7	Hudson SD	Hudson
33	3.6	Litchfield SD	Hudson
33	3.6	Sanborn Regional SD	Kingston
35	3.4	Pelham SD	Windham
35	3.4	Pinkerton Academy SD	Derry
37	2.9	Exeter Region Cooperative SD	Exeter
37	2.9	Timberlane Regional SD	Plaistow
39	2.4	Merrimack SD	Merrimack
40	2.3	Londonderry SD	Londonderry
41	2.2	Amherst SD	Amherst
42	1.3	Bow SD	Bow
43	1.1	Bedford SD	Bedford
43	1.1	Windham SD	Windham

Students Eligible for Reduced-Price Lunch

Rank	Percent	District Name	City
1	9.3	Newfound Area SD	Bristol
2	9.0	Laconia SD	Laconia
3	8.4	Claremont SD	Claremont
4	8.1	Governor Wentworth Reg SD	Wolfeboro Falls
5	7.8	Merrimack Valley SD	Penacook
6	7.5	Fall Mountain Regional SD	Charlestown
7	7.3	Monadnock Regional SD	East Swanzey
8	7.2	Raymond SD	Raymond
9	7.1	Keene SD	Keene
10	6.7	Rochester SD	Rochester
11	6.2	Shaker Regional SD	Belmont
12	6.1	Berlin SD	Berlin
12	6.1	Derry SD	Derry
14	6.0	Conway SD	North Conway
15	5.9	Portsmouth SD	Portsmouth
16	5.8	Nashua SD	Nashua
17	5.6	Manchester SD	Manchester
18	5.4	Milford SD	Milford
19	5.2	Somersworth SD	Somersworth
20	5.1	Contoocook Valley SD	Peterborough
20	5.1	Winnisquam Regional SD	Northfield
22	5.0	Mascoma Valley Reg SD	Enfield
23	4.7	Dover SD	Dover
24	4.5	Concord SD	Concord
25	3.6	Pembroke SD	Pembroke
26	3.5	Jaffrey-Rindge Coop SD	Jaffrey
27	3.3	Kearsarge Regional SD	New London
27	3.3	Lebanon SD	Lebanon
29	2.8	Goffstown SD	Goffstown
30	2.5	Salem SD	Salem
31	2.3	Pelham SD	Windham
32	2.1	Sanborn Regional SD	Kingston
33	1.8	Pinkerton Academy SD	Derry
33	1.8	Timberlane Regional SD	Plaistow
35	1.7	Merrimack SD	Merrimack
36	1.6	Litchfield SD	Hudson
37	1.4	Exeter Region Cooperative SD	Exeter
38	1.3	Windham SD	Windham
39	1.1	Amherst SD	Amherst
39	1.1	Hudson SD	Hudson
39	1.1	Londonderry SD	Londonderry
42	0.8	Bedford SD	Bedford
43	0.4	Oyster River Coop SD	Durham
44	0.3	Bow SD	Bow

Student/Teacher Ratio

Rank	Ratio	District Name	City
1	17.1	Salem SD	Salem
2	16.7	Hudson SD	Hudson
3	16.2	Pelham SD	Windham
4	15.7	Derry SD	Derry
4	15.7	Nashua SD	Nashua
6	15.6	Manchester SD	Manchester
7	15.4	Pinkerton Academy SD	Derry
8	15.3	Bedford SD	Bedford
9	15.2	Berlin SD	Berlin
10	15.1	Concord SD	Concord
10	15.1	Goffstown SD	Goffstown
12	15.0	Dover SD	Dover
13	14.9	Litchfield SD	Hudson
14	14.7	Monadnock Regional SD	East Swanzey
15	14.5	Londonderry SD	Londonderry
16	14.3	Amherst SD	Amherst
16	14.3	Milford SD	Milford
16	14.3	Shaker Regional SD	Belmont
16	14.3	Somersworth SD	Somersworth
20	14.1	Merrimack Valley SD	Penacook
20	14.1	Rochester SD	Rochester
22	14.0	Merrimack SD	Merrimack
23	13.9	Exeter Region Cooperative SD	Exeter
23	13.9	Windham SD	Windham
25	13.8	Bow SD	Bow
26	13.7	Oyster River Coop SD	Durham
27	13.6	Pembroke SD	Pembroke
28	13.3	Contoocook Valley SD	Peterborough
28	13.3	Timberlane Regional SD	Plaistow
30	13.2	Conway SD	North Conway
30	13.2	Mascoma Valley Reg SD	Enfield
32	13.1	Governor Wentworth Reg SD	Wolfeboro Falls
32	13.1	Winnisquam Regional SD	Northfield
34	13.0	Fall Mountain Regional SD	Charlestown
34	13.0	Kearsarge Regional SD	New London
34	13.0	Newfound Area SD	Bristol
37	12.9	Jaffrey-Rindge Coop SD	Jaffrey
37	12.9	Keene SD	Keene
39	12.8	Raymond SD	Raymond
40	12.7	Laconia SD	Laconia
41	12.2	Sanborn Regional SD	Kingston
42	12.0	Claremont SD	Claremont
42	12.0	Lebanon SD	Lebanon
44	11.1	Portsmouth SD	Portsmouth

Student/Librarian Ratio

Rank	Ratio	District Name	City
1	2,204.5	Derry SD	Derry
2	2,087.0	Fall Mountain Regional SD	Charlestown
3	1,815.0	Pembroke SD	Pembroke
4	1,648.5	Pinkerton Academy SD	Derry
5	1,568.0	Windham SD	Windham
6	1,496.9	Rochester SD	Rochester
7	1,446.0	Exeter Region Cooperative SD	Exeter
8	1,377.5	Merrimack Valley SD	Penacook
9	1,365.7	Hudson SD	Hudson
10	1,147.4	Conway SD	North Conway
11	979.2	Monadnock Regional SD	East Swanzey
12	971.0	Manchester SD	Manchester
13	953.0	Timberlane Regional SD	Plaistow
14	936.9	Goffstown SD	Goffstown
15	899.1	Nashua SD	Nashua
16	893.0	Winnisquam Regional SD	Northfield
17	862.4	Governor Wentworth Reg SD	Wolfeboro Falls
18	854.5	Somersworth SD	Somersworth
19	852.5	Amherst SD	Amherst
20	846.7	Milford SD	Milford
21	831.0	Raymond SD	Raymond
22	830.5	Berlin SD	Berlin
23	795.5	Merrimack SD	Merrimack
24	794.0	Dover SD	Dover
25	740.3	Londonderry SD	Londonderry
26	734.2	Concord SD	Concord

27	709.5	Bedford SD	Bedford
28	684.7	Claremont SD	Claremont
29	658.0	Pelham SD	Windham
30	656.0	Portsmouth SD	Portsmouth
31	654.4	Salem SD	Salem
32	606.7	Bow SD	Bow
33	545.4	Keene SD	Keene
34	532.3	Litchfield SD	Hudson
35	518.7	Shaker Regional SD	Belmont
36	516.7	Newfound Area SD	Bristol
37	504.0	Mascoma Valley Reg SD	Enfield
38	498.8	Laconia SD	Laconia
39	485.6	Kearsarge Regional SD	New London
40	482.7	Contoocook Valley SD	Peterborough
41	455.3	Sanborn Regional SD	Kingston
42	451.8	Oyster River Coop SD	Durham
43	416.8	Jaffrey-Rindge Coop SD	Jaffrey
44	361.2	Lebanon SD	Lebanon

Student/Counselor Ratio

Rank	Ratio	District Name	City
1	399.3	Litchfield SD	Hudson
2	392.0	Windham SD	Windham
3	364.5	Nashua SD	Nashua
4	341.0	Amherst SD	Amherst
5	340.7	Goffstown SD	Goffstown
6	332.2	Berlin SD	Berlin
7	323.7	Manchester SD	Manchester
8	322.5	Bedford SD	Bedford
9	318.4	Pelham SD	Windham
10	317.5	Milford SD	Milford
11	308.3	Derry SD	Derry
12	308.0	Concord SD	Concord
13	305.1	Rochester SD	Rochester
14	303.5	Sanborn Regional SD	Kingston
15	303.3	Bow SD	Bow
16	302.5	Pembroke SD	Pembroke
17	292.3	Londonderry SD	Londonderry
18	289.2	Exeter Region Cooperative SD	Exeter
19	288.1	Shaker Regional SD	Belmont
20	287.4	Jaffrey-Rindge Coop SD	Jaffrey
21	280.8	Merrimack SD	Merrimack
22	277.0	Contoocook Valley SD	Peterborough
23	273.1	Hudson SD	Hudson
24	271.9	Dover SD	Dover
25	264.2	Fall Mountain Regional SD	Charlestown
26	257.9	Timberlane Regional SD	Plaistow
27	255.1	Winnisquam Regional SD	Northfield
28	254.6	Kearsarge Regional SD	New London
29	247.4	Somersworth SD	Somersworth
30	242.2	Conway SD	North Conway
31	239.4	Lebanon SD	Lebanon
32	235.2	Governor Wentworth Reg SD	Wolfeboro Falls
33	228.2	Claremont SD	Claremont
34	227.4	Pinkerton Academy SD	Derry
35	216.0	Mascoma Valley Reg SD	Enfield
36	212.2	Monadnock Regional SD	East Swanzey
37	211.1	Oyster River Coop SD	Durham
38	207.8	Raymond SD	Raymond
39	196.8	Merrimack Valley SD	Penacook
40	196.2	Newfound Area SD	Bristol
41	165.2	Laconia SD	Laconia
42	154.4	Salem SD	Salem
43	141.4	Keene SD	Keene
44	126.8	Portsmouth SD	Portsmouth

Current Spending per Student in FY2001

Rank	Dollars	District Name	City
1	10,136	Portsmouth SD	Portsmouth
2	9,056	Lebanon SD	Lebanon
3	8,721	Derry SD	Derry
4	8,485	Keene SD	Keene
5	8,428	Kearsarge Regional SD	New London
6	8,267	Claremont SD	Claremont
7	7,949	Oyster River Coop SD	Durham
8	7,813	Exeter Region Cooperative SD	Exeter
9	7,781	Governor Wentworth Reg SD	Wolfeboro Falls
9	7,781	Sanborn Regional SD	Kingston
11	7,771	Contoocook Valley SD	Peterborough
12	7,662	Amherst SD	Amherst
13	7,657	Conway SD	North Conway
14	7,656	Monadnock Regional SD	East Swanzey
15	7,468	Bedford SD	Bedford
16	7,441	Milford SD	Milford
17	7,437	Newfound Area SD	Bristol
18	7,376	Laconia SD	Laconia
19	7,213	Shaker Regional SD	Belmont
20	7,204	Windham SD	Windham
21	7,199	Jaffrey-Rindge Coop SD	Jaffrey
22	7,152	Concord SD	Concord
23	7,133	Bow SD	Bow
24	7,105	Mascoma Valley Reg SD	Enfield
25	7,092	Fall Mountain Regional SD	Charlestown
26	6,935	Londonderry SD	Londonderry
27	6,818	Raymond SD	Raymond
28	6,748	Timberlane Regional SD	Plaistow
29	6,747	Pembroke SD	Pembroke
30	6,705	Merrimack SD	Merrimack
31	6,638	Dover SD	Dover
32	6,625	Winnisquam Regional SD	Northfield
33	6,559	Pelham SD	Windham
34	6,481	Hudson SD	Hudson
34	6,481	Somersworth SD	Somersworth
36	6,474	Salem SD	Salem
37	6,451	Litchfield SD	Hudson
38	6,431	Merrimack Valley SD	Penacook
39	6,342	Berlin SD	Berlin
40	6,326	Rochester SD	Rochester
41	6,246	Nashua SD	Nashua
42	6,150	Goffstown SD	Goffstown
43	5,873	Manchester SD	Manchester
44	n/a	Pinkerton Academy SD	Derry

Number of Diploma Recipients

Rank	Number	District Name	City
1	1,180	Manchester SD	Manchester
2	655	Nashua SD	Nashua
3	614	Pinkerton Academy SD	Derry
4	411	Salem SD	Salem
5	402	Hudson SD	Hudson
6	399	Concord SD	Concord
7	371	Londonderry SD	Londonderry
8	333	Keene SD	Keene
9	319	Exeter Region Cooperative SD	Exeter
10	316	Merrimack SD	Merrimack
11	306	Rochester SD	Rochester
12	292	Dover SD	Dover
13	241	Timberlane Regional SD	Plaistow
14	233	Contoocook Valley SD	Peterborough
15	229	Portsmouth SD	Portsmouth
16	218	Governor Wentworth Reg SD	Wolfeboro Falls
17	180	Goffstown SD	Goffstown
18	175	Conway SD	North Conway
19	170	Monadnock Regional SD	East Swanzey
20	168	Lebanon SD	Lebanon
21	165	Milford SD	Milford
22	161	Pembroke SD	Pembroke
23	160	Merrimack Valley SD	Penacook
23	160	Oyster River Coop SD	Durham
25	154	Laconia SD	Laconia
26	133	Fall Mountain Regional SD	Charlestown
27	129	Kearsarge Regional SD	New London
28	128	Claremont SD	Claremont
29	126	Raymond SD	Raymond
29	126	Sanborn Regional SD	Kingston
31	122	Somersworth SD	Somersworth
32	121	Jaffrey-Rindge Coop SD	Jaffrey
33	110	Bow SD	Bow
34	104	Pelham SD	Windham
35	102	Berlin SD	Berlin
36	99	Winnisquam Regional SD	Northfield
37	91	Newfound Area SD	Bristol
38	73	Mascoma Valley Reg SD	Enfield
39	72	Shaker Regional SD	Belmont
40	0	Litchfield SD	Hudson
41	n/a	Amherst SD	Amherst
41	n/a	Bedford SD	Bedford
41	n/a	Derry SD	Derry
41	n/a	Windham SD	Windham

High School Drop-out Rate

Rank	Percent	District Name	City
1	10.7	Nashua SD	Nashua
2	9.7	Somersworth SD	Somersworth
3	9.4	Raymond SD	Raymond
4	8.1	Rochester SD	Rochester
5	7.5	Manchester SD	Manchester
6	6.6	Pembroke SD	Pembroke
7	6.4	Dover SD	Dover
7	6.4	Shaker Regional SD	Belmont
9	6.0	Conway SD	North Conway
10	5.6	Pinkerton Academy SD	Derry
11	5.4	Claremont SD	Claremont
12	5.2	Timberlane Regional SD	Plaistow
13	5.1	Sanborn Regional SD	Kingston
14	4.6	Hudson SD	Hudson
15	4.5	Merrimack Valley SD	Penacook
15	4.5	Pelham SD	Windham
17	4.2	Mascoma Valley Reg SD	Enfield
18	3.8	Portsmouth SD	Portsmouth
19	3.7	Governor Wentworth Reg SD	Wolfeboro Falls
19	3.7	Lebanon SD	Lebanon
19	3.7	Monadnock Regional SD	East Swanzey
22	3.5	Fall Mountain Regional SD	Charlestown
23	3.2	Exeter Region Cooperative SD	Exeter
23	3.2	Keene SD	Keene
25	2.9	Jaffrey-Rindge Coop SD	Jaffrey
26	2.8	Milford SD	Milford
27	2.6	Newfound Area SD	Bristol
28	2.3	Goffstown SD	Goffstown
29	1.5	Salem SD	Salem
30	1.4	Contoocook Valley SD	Peterborough
31	1.1	Bow SD	Bow
32	0.4	Litchfield SD	Hudson
33	n/a	Amherst SD	Amherst
33	n/a	Bedford SD	Bedford
33	n/a	Berlin SD	Berlin
33	n/a	Concord SD	Concord
33	n/a	Derry SD	Derry
33	n/a	Kearsarge Regional SD	New London
33	n/a	Laconia SD	Laconia
33	n/a	Londonderry SD	Londonderry
33	n/a	Merrimack SD	Merrimack
33	n/a	Oyster River Coop SD	Durham
33	n/a	Windham SD	Windham
33	n/a	Winnisquam Regional SD	Northfield

New Jersey

New Jersey Public School Educational Profile

Category	Value	Category	Value
Schools *(2002-2003)*	2,453	**Diploma Recipients** *(2002-2003)*	77,664
Instructional Level		White, Non-Hispanic	50,347
Primary	1,532	Black, Non-Hispanic	11,909
Middle	432	Asian/Pacific Islander	5,619
High	378	American Indian/Alaskan Native	132
Other Level	111	Hispanic	9,657
Curriculum		**High School Drop-out Rate** (%) *(2000-2001)*	2.8
Regular	2,294	White, Non-Hispanic	1.6
Special Education	86	Black, Non-Hispanic	5.7
Vocational	55	Asian/Pacific Islander	1.0
Alternative	18	American Indian/Alaskan Native	12.0
Type		Hispanic	5.6
Magnet	3	**Staff** *(2002-2003)*	199,376.0
Charter	50	Teachers	107,002.0
Title I Eligible	1,368	Average Salary ($)	53,872
School-wide Title I	256	Librarians/Media Specialists	1,854.5
Students *(2002-2003)*	1,367,449	Guidance Counselors	3,609.7
Gender (%)		**Ratios** *(2002-2003)*	
Male	51.4	Student/Teacher Ratio	12.8 to 1
Female	48.6	Student/Librarian Ratio	737.4 to 1
Race/Ethnicity (%)		Student/Counselor Ratio	378.8 to 1
White, Non-Hispanic	58.6	**Current Spending** *($ per student in FY 2001)*	11,793
Black, Non-Hispanic	17.8	Instruction	6,975
Asian/Pacific Islander	6.8	Support Services	4,454
American Indian/Alaskan Native	0.2	**College Entrance Exam Scores** *(2003)*	
Hispanic	16.6	Scholastic Aptitude Test (SAT)	
Classification (%)		Participation Rate (%)	85
Individual Education Program (IEP)	16.0	Mean SAT I Verbal Score	501
Migrant	0.1	Mean SAT I Math Score	515
English Language Learner (ELL)	4.2	American College Testing Program (ACT)	
Eligible for Free Lunch Program	20.9	Participation Rate (%)	6
Eligible for Reduced-Price Lunch Program	6.3	Average Composite Score	21.2

Note: *For an explanation of data, please refer to the User's Guide in the front of the book; n/a indicates data not available*

New Jersey NAEP 2003 Test Scores

Reading			Mathematics		
Grade/Category	**Value**	**Rank**	**Grade/Category**	**Value**	**Rank**
4th Grade			**4th Grade**		
Average Proficiency	225.1 (1.2)	5/51	Average Proficiency	238.8 (1.1)	10/51
Proficiency by Gender/Race/Ethnicity			Proficiency by Gender/Race/Ethnicity		
Male	221.8 (1.3)	5/51	Male	240.1 (1.3)	10/51
Female	228.5 (1.5)	6/51	Female	237.3 (1.1)	10/51
White, Non-Hispanic	235.3 (1.4)	3/51	White, Non-Hispanic	247.6 (0.9)	4/51
Black, Non-Hispanic	199.7 (3.3)	21/42	Black, Non-Hispanic	217.1 (2.0)	15/42
Asian, Non-Hispanic	211.5 (2.1)	5/41	Asian, Non-Hispanic	224.3 (1.7)	15/43
American Indian, Non-Hispanic	235.3 (3.3)	3/25	American Indian, Non-Hispanic	255.6 (1.8)	2/26
Hispanic	n/a	n/a	Hispanic	n/a	n/a
Proficiency by Class Size			Proficiency by Class Size		
Less than 16 Students	203.0 (5.1)	25/45	Less than 16 Students	218.3 (4.5)	33/47
16 to 18 Students	229.7 (3.9)	2/48	16 to 18 Students	242.2 (4.4)	4/48
19 to 20 Students	223.0 (2.6)	10/50	19 to 20 Students	235.8 (1.8)	20/50
21 to 25 Students	230.5 (2.2)	3/51	21 to 25 Students	243.7 (1.4)	4/51
Greater than 25 Students	*216.4 (3.9)*	33/49	Greater than 25 Students	*236.7 (3.7)*	21/49
Percent Attaining Achievement Levels			Percent Attaining Achievement Levels		
Below Basic	30.1 (1.4)	44/51	Below Basic	19.6 (1.4)	32/51
Basic or Above	69.9 (1.4)	8/51	Basic or Above	80.4 (1.4)	20/51
Proficient or Above	38.5 (1.7)	4/51	Proficient or Above	38.8 (1.4)	8/51
Advanced or Above	10.6 (1.0)	2/51	Advanced or Above	5.2 (0.8)	9/51
8th Grade			**8th Grade**		
Average Proficiency	267.8 (1.2)	9/51	Average Proficiency	281.4 (1.1)	18/51
Proficiency by Gender/Race/Ethnicity			Proficiency by Gender/Race/Ethnicity		
Male	263.5 (1.4)	8/51	Male	282.1 (1.3)	19/51
Female	272.3 (1.5)	14/51	Female	280.7 (1.4)	16/51
White, Non-Hispanic	276.7 (1.1)	3/50	White, Non-Hispanic	291.7 (1.0)	7/50
Black, Non-Hispanic	247.7 (2.1)	10/41	Black, Non-Hispanic	253.0 (2.2)	19/41
Asian, Non-Hispanic	248.4 (2.4)	14/37	Asian, Non-Hispanic	261.7 (2.6)	17/37
American Indian, Non-Hispanic	288.9 (2.4)	1/23	American Indian, Non-Hispanic	306.2 (3.1)	1/23
Hispanic	n/a	n/a	Hispanic	n/a	n/a
Proficiency by Parents Highest Level of Ed.			Proficiency by Parents Highest Level of Ed.		
Did Not Finish High School	246.0 (4.1)	28/50	Did Not Finish High School	259.6 (4.4)	19/50
Graduated High School	258.2 (1.6)	16/50	Graduated High School	268.8 (2.1)	28/50
Some Education After High School	265.0 (2.2)	33/50	Some Education After High School	279.7 (1.3)	30/50
Graduated College	277.3 (1.2)	4/50	Graduated College	291.6 (1.2)	17/50
Percent Attaining Achievement Levels			Percent Attaining Achievement Levels		
Below Basic	21.3 (1.4)	40/51	Below Basic	28.3 (1.2)	29/51
Basic or Above	78.7 (1.4)	12/51	Basic or Above	71.7 (1.2)	21/51
Proficient or Above	36.9 (1.3)	9/51	Proficient or Above	33.3 (1.3)	13/51
Advanced or Above	3.5 (0.5)	8/51	Advanced or Above	6.4 (0.7)	10/51

Note: *For an explanation of data, please refer to the User's Guide in the front of the book; values in italics indicate that the nature of the sample does not allow accurate determination of the variability of the statistic; n/a indicates data not available*

Atlantic County

Atlantic City

1809 Pacific Ave • Atlantic City, NJ 08401-6803
(609) 343-7200 • http://www.acboe.org
Grade Span: PK-12; **Agency Type:** 1
Schools: 11
8 Primary; 1 Middle; 1 High; 1 Other Level
11 Regular; 0 Special Education; 0 Vocational; 0 Alternative
0 Magnet; 0 Charter; 9 Title I Eligible; 5 School-wide Title I
Students: 7,116 (51.3% male; 48.7% female)
Individual Education Program: 908 (12.8%);
English Language Learner: 955 (13.4%); Migrant: 0 (0.0%)
Eligible for Free Lunch Program: 4,278 (60.1%)
Eligible for Reduced-Price Lunch Program: 830 (11.7%)
Teachers: 579.8 (12.3 to 1)
Librarians/Media Specialists: 10.0 (711.6 to 1)
Guidance Counselors: 18.0 (395.3 to 1)
Current Spending: ($ per student per year):
Total: $12,375; Instruction: $7,419; Support Services: $4,475
Enrollment, Drop-out Rates and Diploma Recipients by Race/Ethnicity

Category	Total	White	Black	Asian	AIAN	Hisp.
Enrollment (%)	100.0	10.8	46.7	9.6	0.6	32.4
Drop-out Rate (%)	9.3	5.9	10.5	4.4	0.0	13.9
H.S. Diplomas (#)	416	119	140	57	4	96

Buena Regional

Harding Hwy • Buena, NJ 08310-9701
Mailing Address: PO Box 309 • Buena, NJ 08310-9701
(856) 697-0800 • http://www.buena.k12.nj.us
Grade Span: PK-12; **Agency Type:** 1
Schools: 6
4 Primary; 1 Middle; 1 High; 0 Other Level
6 Regular; 0 Special Education; 0 Vocational; 0 Alternative
0 Magnet; 0 Charter; 5 Title I Eligible; 0 School-wide Title I
Students: 2,569 (50.5% male; 49.5% female)
Individual Education Program: 452 (17.6%);
English Language Learner: 54 (2.1%); Migrant: 16 (0.6%)
Eligible for Free Lunch Program: 664 (25.8%)
Eligible for Reduced-Price Lunch Program: 283 (11.0%)
Teachers: 194.0 (13.2 to 1)
Librarians/Media Specialists: 3.0 (856.3 to 1)
Guidance Counselors: 7.0 (367.0 to 1)
Current Spending: ($ per student per year):
Total: $10,315; Instruction: $6,227; Support Services: $3,692
Enrollment, Drop-out Rates and Diploma Recipients by Race/Ethnicity

Category	Total	White	Black	Asian	AIAN	Hisp.
Enrollment (%)	100.0	66.9	14.5	0.5	0.1	17.9
Drop-out Rate (%)	3.3	2.3	13.4	0.0	0.0	3.7
H.S. Diplomas (#)	188	146	19	0	0	23

Egg Harbor Twp

202 Naples Ave • West Atlantic City, NJ 08232-2928
Mailing Address: PO Box 31 • West Atlantic City, NJ 08232-2928
(609) 646-7911 • http://www.eht.k12.nj.us
Grade Span: PK-12; **Agency Type:** 1
Schools: 6
3 Primary; 2 Middle; 1 High; 0 Other Level
6 Regular; 0 Special Education; 0 Vocational; 0 Alternative
0 Magnet; 0 Charter; 3 Title I Eligible; 0 School-wide Title I
Students: 6,282 (51.8% male; 48.2% female)
Individual Education Program: 1,076 (17.1%);
English Language Learner: 119 (1.9%); Migrant: 0 (0.0%)
Eligible for Free Lunch Program: 924 (14.7%)
Eligible for Reduced-Price Lunch Program: 570 (9.1%)
Teachers: 455.1 (13.8 to 1)
Librarians/Media Specialists: 4.0 (1,570.5 to 1)
Guidance Counselors: 18.0 (349.0 to 1)
Current Spending: ($ per student per year):
Total: $8,943; Instruction: $5,311; Support Services: $3,282
Enrollment, Drop-out Rates and Diploma Recipients by Race/Ethnicity

Category	Total	White	Black	Asian	AIAN	Hisp.
Enrollment (%)	100.0	67.9	13.1	7.8	0.2	11.0
Drop-out Rate (%)	2.7	3.0	3.2	0.0	0.0	1.5
H.S. Diplomas (#)	347	240	52	25	0	30

Galloway Twp

101 S Reeds Rd • Galloway, NJ 08205
(609) 748-1250
Grade Span: PK-08; **Agency Type:** 1
Schools: 9
8 Primary; 1 Middle; 0 High; 0 Other Level
9 Regular; 0 Special Education; 0 Vocational; 0 Alternative
0 Magnet; 0 Charter; 5 Title I Eligible; 0 School-wide Title I
Students: 3,975 (50.3% male; 49.7% female)
Individual Education Program: 613 (15.4%);
English Language Learner: 146 (3.7%); Migrant: 0 (0.0%)
Eligible for Free Lunch Program: 562 (14.1%)
Eligible for Reduced-Price Lunch Program: 374 (9.4%)
Teachers: 321.5 (12.4 to 1)
Librarians/Media Specialists: 6.0 (662.5 to 1)
Guidance Counselors: 10.0 (397.5 to 1)
Current Spending: ($ per student per year):
Total: $8,694; Instruction: $5,037; Support Services: $3,220
Enrollment, Drop-out Rates and Diploma Recipients by Race/Ethnicity

Category	Total	White	Black	Asian	AIAN	Hisp.
Enrollment (%)	100.0	66.8	12.0	12.3	0.4	8.5
Drop-out Rate (%)	n/a	n/a	n/a	n/a	n/a	n/a
H.S. Diplomas (#)	n/a	n/a	n/a	n/a	n/a	n/a

Greater Egg Harbor Reg

1824 Dr Dennis Foreman Dr • Mays Landing, NJ 08330-2640
(609) 625-1456 • http://www.gehrhsd.net/
Grade Span: 09-12; **Agency Type:** 1
Schools: 2
0 Primary; 0 Middle; 2 High; 0 Other Level
2 Regular; 0 Special Education; 0 Vocational; 0 Alternative
0 Magnet; 0 Charter; 2 Title I Eligible; 0 School-wide Title I
Students: 3,486 (50.1% male; 49.9% female)
Individual Education Program: 633 (18.2%);
English Language Learner: 46 (1.3%); Migrant: 3 (0.1%)
Eligible for Free Lunch Program: 481 (13.8%)
Eligible for Reduced-Price Lunch Program: 306 (8.8%)
Teachers: 250.0 (13.9 to 1)
Librarians/Media Specialists: 3.8 (917.4 to 1)
Guidance Counselors: 15.8 (220.6 to 1)
Current Spending: ($ per student per year):
Total: $11,227; Instruction: $6,063; Support Services: $4,819
Enrollment, Drop-out Rates and Diploma Recipients by Race/Ethnicity

Category	Total	White	Black	Asian	AIAN	Hisp.
Enrollment (%)	100.0	62.7	17.8	8.6	0.4	10.4
Drop-out Rate (%)	2.8	2.7	3.0	1.1	0.0	4.5
H.S. Diplomas (#)	648	426	101	65	1	55

Hamilton Twp

5801 Third St • Mays Landing, NJ 08330-1717
(609) 625-6595 • http://www.hamilton.k12.nj.us/
Grade Span: PK-08; **Agency Type:** 1
Schools: 3
2 Primary; 1 Middle; 0 High; 0 Other Level
3 Regular; 0 Special Education; 0 Vocational; 0 Alternative
0 Magnet; 0 Charter; 3 Title I Eligible; 0 School-wide Title I
Students: 2,861 (51.9% male; 48.1% female)
Individual Education Program: 483 (16.9%);
English Language Learner: 83 (2.9%); Migrant: 2 (0.1%)
Eligible for Free Lunch Program: 561 (19.6%)
Eligible for Reduced-Price Lunch Program: 316 (11.0%)
Teachers: 233.5 (12.3 to 1)
Librarians/Media Specialists: 5.0 (572.2 to 1)
Guidance Counselors: 5.0 (572.2 to 1)
Current Spending: ($ per student per year):
Total: $8,569; Instruction: $4,938; Support Services: $3,314
Enrollment, Drop-out Rates and Diploma Recipients by Race/Ethnicity

Category	Total	White	Black	Asian	AIAN	Hisp.
Enrollment (%)	100.0	60.1	24.2	3.2	0.1	12.3
Drop-out Rate (%)	n/a	n/a	n/a	n/a	n/a	n/a
H.S. Diplomas (#)	n/a	n/a	n/a	n/a	n/a	n/a

Hammonton Town

601 N 4th St • Hammonton, NJ 08037-0308
(609) 567-7004
Grade Span: PK-12; **Agency Type:** 1
Schools: 3
1 Primary; 1 Middle; 1 High; 0 Other Level
3 Regular; 0 Special Education; 0 Vocational; 0 Alternative
0 Magnet; 0 Charter; 1 Title I Eligible; 0 School-wide Title I
Students: 3,139 (49.3% male; 50.7% female)
Individual Education Program: 378 (12.0%);
English Language Learner: 129 (4.1%); Migrant: 73 (2.3%)
Eligible for Free Lunch Program: 600 (19.1%)
Eligible for Reduced-Price Lunch Program: 174 (5.5%)
Teachers: 226.4 (13.9 to 1)
Librarians/Media Specialists: 3.0 (1,046.3 to 1)
Guidance Counselors: 9.0 (348.8 to 1)
Current Spending: ($ per student per year):
Total: $9,537; Instruction: $5,984; Support Services: $3,262

Enrollment, Drop-out Rates and Diploma Recipients by Race/Ethnicity

Category	Total	White	Black	Asian	AIAN	Hisp.
Enrollment (%)	100.0	81.9	3.2	1.2	0.1	13.6
Drop-out Rate (%)	1.7	1.3	0.0	0.0	n/a	4.8
H.S. Diplomas (#)	137	109	1	4	0	23

Mainland Regional

Oak Ave • Linwood, NJ 08221-1653
(609) 927-2461
Grade Span: 09-12; **Agency Type:** 1
Schools: 1
0 Primary; 0 Middle; 1 High; 0 Other Level
1 Regular; 0 Special Education; 0 Vocational; 0 Alternative
0 Magnet; 0 Charter; 1 Title I Eligible; 0 School-wide Title I
Students: 1,596 (50.4% male; 49.6% female)
Individual Education Program: 232 (14.5%);
English Language Learner: 9 (0.6%); Migrant: 0 (0.0%)
Eligible for Free Lunch Program: 123 (7.7%)
Eligible for Reduced-Price Lunch Program: 79 (4.9%)
Teachers: 127.9 (12.5 to 1)
Librarians/Media Specialists: 2.0 (798.0 to 1)
Guidance Counselors: 5.0 (319.2 to 1)
Current Spending: ($ per student per year):
Total: $10,536; Instruction: $6,509; Support Services: $3,218
Enrollment, Drop-out Rates and Diploma Recipients by Race/Ethnicity

Category	Total	White	Black	Asian	AIAN	Hisp.
Enrollment (%)	100.0	84.3	4.9	5.5	0.3	5.1
Drop-out Rate (%)	1.7	1.4	4.5	1.4	0.0	4.5
H.S. Diplomas (#)	302	260	15	15	0	12

Pleasantville City

900 W Leeds Ave • Pleasantville, NJ 08232-0960
Mailing Address: PO Box 960 • Pleasantville, NJ 08232-0960
(609) 383-6800 • http://www.pleasantville.k12.nj.us/
Grade Span: PK-12; **Agency Type:** 1
Schools: 6
4 Primary; 1 Middle; 1 High; 0 Other Level
6 Regular; 0 Special Education; 0 Vocational; 0 Alternative
0 Magnet; 0 Charter; 5 Title I Eligible; 0 School-wide Title I
Students: 3,627 (52.5% male; 47.5% female)
Individual Education Program: 746 (20.6%);
English Language Learner: 268 (7.4%); Migrant: 0 (0.0%)
Eligible for Free Lunch Program: 1,557 (42.9%)
Eligible for Reduced-Price Lunch Program: 524 (14.4%)
Teachers: 379.0 (9.6 to 1)
Librarians/Media Specialists: 7.0 (518.1 to 1)
Guidance Counselors: 9.0 (403.0 to 1)
Current Spending: ($ per student per year):
Total: $12,192; Instruction: $6,991; Support Services: $4,695
Enrollment, Drop-out Rates and Diploma Recipients by Race/Ethnicity

Category	Total	White	Black	Asian	AIAN	Hisp.
Enrollment (%)	100.0	3.0	65.4	1.2	0.1	30.3
Drop-out Rate (%)	6.4	2.3	5.8	0.0	0.0	10.3
H.S. Diplomas (#)	204	3	159	6	0	36

Somers Point City

Jordan Rd School • Somers Point, NJ 08244-1499
(609) 927-7161
Grade Span: PK-08; **Agency Type:** 1
Schools: 2
2 Primary; 0 Middle; 0 High; 0 Other Level
2 Regular; 0 Special Education; 0 Vocational; 0 Alternative
0 Magnet; 0 Charter; 1 Title I Eligible; 0 School-wide Title I
Students: 1,632 (52.5% male; 47.5% female)
Individual Education Program: 262 (16.1%);
English Language Learner: 11 (0.7%); Migrant: 0 (0.0%)
Eligible for Free Lunch Program: 319 (19.5%)
Eligible for Reduced-Price Lunch Program: 135 (8.3%)
Teachers: 93.0 (17.5 to 1)
Librarians/Media Specialists: 2.0 (816.0 to 1)
Guidance Counselors: 2.0 (816.0 to 1)
Current Spending: ($ per student per year):
Total: $8,513; Instruction: $5,422; Support Services: $2,957
Enrollment, Drop-out Rates and Diploma Recipients by Race/Ethnicity

Category	Total	White	Black	Asian	AIAN	Hisp.
Enrollment (%)	100.0	78.6	10.2	3.4	0.1	7.8
Drop-out Rate (%)	n/a	n/a	n/a	n/a	n/a	n/a
H.S. Diplomas (#)	n/a	n/a	n/a	n/a	n/a	n/a

Bergen County

Bergen County Vocational

327 E Ridgewood Ave • Paramus, NJ 07652-2915
(201) 967-2472 • http://www.bergen.org/
Grade Span: 09-12; **Agency Type:** 1
Schools: 6
0 Primary; 0 Middle; 5 High; 1 Other Level
0 Regular; 2 Special Education; 4 Vocational; 0 Alternative
1 Magnet; 0 Charter; 1 Title I Eligible; 0 School-wide Title I
Students: 1,951 (55.8% male; 44.2% female)
Individual Education Program: 354 (18.1%);
English Language Learner: 3 (0.2%); Migrant: 0 (0.0%)
Eligible for Free Lunch Program: 152 (7.8%)
Eligible for Reduced-Price Lunch Program: 79 (4.0%)
Teachers: 224.1 (8.7 to 1)
Librarians/Media Specialists: 0.0 (0.0 to 1)
Guidance Counselors: 14.5 (134.6 to 1)
Current Spending: ($ per student per year):
Total: $23,317; Instruction: $15,391; Support Services: $7,032
Enrollment, Drop-out Rates and Diploma Recipients by Race/Ethnicity

Category	Total	White	Black	Asian	AIAN	Hisp.
Enrollment (%)	100.0	53.5	7.1	26.4	0.3	12.7
Drop-out Rate (%)	0.0	0.0	0.0	0.0	0.0	0.0
H.S. Diplomas (#)	285	163	22	72	0	28

Bergenfield Boro

100 S Prospect Ave • Bergenfield, NJ 07621-1958
(201) 385-8202 • http://www.bergenfield.org
Grade Span: PK-12; **Agency Type:** 1
Schools: 7
5 Primary; 1 Middle; 1 High; 0 Other Level
7 Regular; 0 Special Education; 0 Vocational; 0 Alternative
0 Magnet; 0 Charter; 3 Title I Eligible; 0 School-wide Title I
Students: 3,828 (50.2% male; 49.8% female)
Individual Education Program: 694 (18.1%);
English Language Learner: 207 (5.4%); Migrant: 0 (0.0%)
Eligible for Free Lunch Program: 294 (7.7%)
Eligible for Reduced-Price Lunch Program: 244 (6.4%)
Teachers: 266.8 (14.3 to 1)
Librarians/Media Specialists: 3.0 (1,276.0 to 1)
Guidance Counselors: 6.9 (554.8 to 1)
Current Spending: ($ per student per year):
Total: $10,351; Instruction: $6,536; Support Services: $3,597
Enrollment, Drop-out Rates and Diploma Recipients by Race/Ethnicity

Category	Total	White	Black	Asian	AIAN	Hisp.
Enrollment (%)	100.0	35.1	7.3	30.3	0.0	27.2
Drop-out Rate (%)	2.7	2.2	2.7	0.7	n/a	6.5
H.S. Diplomas (#)	222	110	12	56	0	44

Cliffside Park Boro

525 Palisade Ave • Cliffside Park, NJ 07010-2914
(201) 313-2310 • http://www.cliffsidepark.edu
Grade Span: PK-12; **Agency Type:** 1
Schools: 5
4 Primary; 0 Middle; 1 High; 0 Other Level
5 Regular; 0 Special Education; 0 Vocational; 0 Alternative
0 Magnet; 0 Charter; 3 Title I Eligible; 0 School-wide Title I
Students: 2,682 (53.3% male; 46.7% female)
Individual Education Program: 258 (9.6%);
English Language Learner: 303 (11.3%); Migrant: 0 (0.0%)
Eligible for Free Lunch Program: 659 (24.6%)
Eligible for Reduced-Price Lunch Program: 290 (10.8%)
Teachers: 190.7 (14.1 to 1)
Librarians/Media Specialists: 3.0 (894.0 to 1)
Guidance Counselors: 4.5 (596.0 to 1)
Current Spending: ($ per student per year):
Total: $9,696; Instruction: $6,620; Support Services: $2,820
Enrollment, Drop-out Rates and Diploma Recipients by Race/Ethnicity

Category	Total	White	Black	Asian	AIAN	Hisp.
Enrollment (%)	100.0	53.4	2.4	8.4	0.0	35.9
Drop-out Rate (%)	1.3	1.5	5.9	0.0	n/a	1.1
H.S. Diplomas (#)	227	119	4	20	0	84

Dumont Boro

25 Depew St • Dumont, NJ 07628-3601
(201) 387-3082 • http://www2.cybernex.net/~dumont/
Grade Span: PK-12; **Agency Type:** 1
Schools: 5
4 Primary; 0 Middle; 1 High; 0 Other Level
5 Regular; 0 Special Education; 0 Vocational; 0 Alternative
0 Magnet; 0 Charter; 5 Title I Eligible; 0 School-wide Title I
Students: 2,689 (51.5% male; 48.5% female)
Individual Education Program: 371 (13.8%);
English Language Learner: 120 (4.5%); Migrant: 0 (0.0%)

Eligible for Free Lunch Program: 76 (2.8%)
Eligible for Reduced-Price Lunch Program: 40 (1.5%)
Teachers: 193.5 (13.9 to 1)
Librarians/Media Specialists: 3.0 (896.3 to 1)
Guidance Counselors: 6.1 (440.8 to 1)
Current Spending: ($ per student per year):
Total: $10,186; Instruction: $6,582; Support Services: $3,512
Enrollment, Drop-out Rates and Diploma Recipients by Race/Ethnicity

Category	Total	White	Black	Asian	AIAN	Hisp.
Enrollment (%)	100.0	75.5	1.3	12.3	0.1	10.8
Drop-out Rate (%)	1.3	1.4	20.0	2.1	n/a	0.0
H.S. Diplomas (#)	180	129	4	28	0	19

Elmwood Park
465 Blvd • Elmwood Park, NJ 07407-1622
(201) 794-2979 • http://www.epps.org
Grade Span: PK-12; **Agency Type:** 1
Schools: 5
3 Primary; 1 Middle; 1 High; 0 Other Level
5 Regular; 0 Special Education; 0 Vocational; 0 Alternative
0 Magnet; 0 Charter; 3 Title I Eligible; 0 School-wide Title I
Students: 2,021 (51.6% male; 48.4% female)
Individual Education Program: 325 (16.1%);
English Language Learner: 87 (4.3%); Migrant: 0 (0.0%)
Eligible for Free Lunch Program: 210 (10.4%)
Eligible for Reduced-Price Lunch Program: 180 (8.9%)
Teachers: 135.5 (14.9 to 1)
Librarians/Media Specialists: 2.0 (1,010.5 to 1)
Guidance Counselors: 5.8 (348.4 to 1)
Current Spending: ($ per student per year):
Total: $8,738; Instruction: $4,783; Support Services: $3,737
Enrollment, Drop-out Rates and Diploma Recipients by Race/Ethnicity

Category	Total	White	Black	Asian	AIAN	Hisp.
Enrollment (%)	100.0	61.5	3.4	13.7	0.1	21.3
Drop-out Rate (%)	2.6	1.7	20.0	2.9	n/a	3.9
H.S. Diplomas (#)	125	84	6	15	0	20

Englewood City
12 Tenafly Rd • Englewood, NJ 07631-2206
(201) 833-6060 • http://www.epsd.org
Grade Span: PK-12; **Agency Type:** 1
Schools: 5
3 Primary; 1 Middle; 1 High; 0 Other Level
4 Regular; 0 Special Education; 0 Vocational; 1 Alternative
0 Magnet; 0 Charter; 5 Title I Eligible; 0 School-wide Title I
Students: 2,727 (52.1% male; 47.9% female)
Individual Education Program: 475 (17.4%);
English Language Learner: 251 (9.2%); Migrant: 0 (0.0%)
Eligible for Free Lunch Program: 954 (35.0%)
Eligible for Reduced-Price Lunch Program: 307 (11.3%)
Teachers: 233.1 (11.7 to 1)
Librarians/Media Specialists: 3.0 (909.0 to 1)
Guidance Counselors: 8.0 (340.9 to 1)
Current Spending: ($ per student per year):
Total: $14,924; Instruction: $9,065; Support Services: $5,479
Enrollment, Drop-out Rates and Diploma Recipients by Race/Ethnicity

Category	Total	White	Black	Asian	AIAN	Hisp.
Enrollment (%)	100.0	3.1	60.4	2.9	0.1	33.5
Drop-out Rate (%)	4.7	0.0	5.4	3.4	n/a	3.2
H.S. Diplomas (#)	149	2	98	9	1	39

Fair Lawn Boro
37-01 Fair Lawn Ave • Fair Lawn, NJ 07410-4919
(201) 794-5510 • http://www.fairlawnschools.org/
Grade Span: PK-12; **Agency Type:** 1
Schools: 9
6 Primary; 2 Middle; 1 High; 0 Other Level
9 Regular; 0 Special Education; 0 Vocational; 0 Alternative
0 Magnet; 0 Charter; 4 Title I Eligible; 0 School-wide Title I
Students: 4,704 (51.1% male; 48.9% female)
Individual Education Program: 845 (18.0%);
English Language Learner: 156 (3.3%); Migrant: 0 (0.0%)
Eligible for Free Lunch Program: 139 (3.0%)
Eligible for Reduced-Price Lunch Program: 98 (2.1%)
Teachers: 352.7 (13.3 to 1)
Librarians/Media Specialists: 8.0 (588.0 to 1)
Guidance Counselors: 11.0 (427.6 to 1)
Current Spending: ($ per student per year):
Total: $11,559; Instruction: $7,009; Support Services: $4,335
Enrollment, Drop-out Rates and Diploma Recipients by Race/Ethnicity

Category	Total	White	Black	Asian	AIAN	Hisp.
Enrollment (%)	100.0	80.9	1.2	9.1	0.1	8.7
Drop-out Rate (%)	0.6	0.6	0.0	0.0	n/a	0.0
H.S. Diplomas (#)	348	318	1	19	0	10

Fort Lee Boro
255 Whiteman St • Fort Lee, NJ 07024-5629
(201) 585-4610 • http://www.fortlee-boe.net/
Grade Span: PK-12; **Agency Type:** 1
Schools: 6
4 Primary; 1 Middle; 1 High; 0 Other Level
6 Regular; 0 Special Education; 0 Vocational; 0 Alternative
0 Magnet; 0 Charter; 3 Title I Eligible; 0 School-wide Title I
Students: 3,453 (51.0% male; 49.0% female)
Individual Education Program: 468 (13.6%);
English Language Learner: 369 (10.7%); Migrant: 0 (0.0%)
Eligible for Free Lunch Program: 184 (5.3%)
Eligible for Reduced-Price Lunch Program: 149 (4.3%)
Teachers: 252.1 (13.7 to 1)
Librarians/Media Specialists: 7.0 (493.3 to 1)
Guidance Counselors: 9.0 (383.7 to 1)
Current Spending: ($ per student per year):
Total: $10,594; Instruction: $6,639; Support Services: $3,651
Enrollment, Drop-out Rates and Diploma Recipients by Race/Ethnicity

Category	Total	White	Black	Asian	AIAN	Hisp.
Enrollment (%)	100.0	39.9	3.2	44.4	0.0	12.5
Drop-out Rate (%)	2.9	2.7	0.0	3.4	n/a	2.3
H.S. Diplomas (#)	212	91	2	100	0	19

Garfield City
125 Outwater Ln • Garfield, NJ 07026-2637
(973) 340-5000 • http://www.garfield.k12.nj.us
Grade Span: PK-12; **Agency Type:** 1
Schools: 10
8 Primary; 1 Middle; 1 High; 0 Other Level
10 Regular; 0 Special Education; 0 Vocational; 0 Alternative
0 Magnet; 0 Charter; 7 Title I Eligible; 0 School-wide Title I
Students: 4,214 (52.3% male; 47.7% female)
Individual Education Program: 701 (16.6%);
English Language Learner: 530 (12.6%); Migrant: 0 (0.0%)
Eligible for Free Lunch Program: 1,262 (29.9%)
Eligible for Reduced-Price Lunch Program: 765 (18.2%)
Teachers: 329.0 (12.8 to 1)
Librarians/Media Specialists: 2.0 (2,107.0 to 1)
Guidance Counselors: 7.5 (561.9 to 1)
Current Spending: ($ per student per year):
Total: $11,731; Instruction: $7,935; Support Services: $3,502
Enrollment, Drop-out Rates and Diploma Recipients by Race/Ethnicity

Category	Total	White	Black	Asian	AIAN	Hisp.
Enrollment (%)	100.0	63.6	3.8	2.4	0.0	30.2
Drop-out Rate (%)	3.5	4.2	0.0	0.0	n/a	2.9
H.S. Diplomas (#)	213	139	14	7	0	53

Glen Rock Boro
620 Harristown Rd • Glen Rock, NJ 07452-2328
(201) 445-7700 • http://www.glenrocknj.org/
Grade Span: PK-12; **Agency Type:** 1
Schools: 6
4 Primary; 1 Middle; 1 High; 0 Other Level
6 Regular; 0 Special Education; 0 Vocational; 0 Alternative
0 Magnet; 0 Charter; 0 Title I Eligible; 0 School-wide Title I
Students: 2,338 (51.5% male; 48.5% female)
Individual Education Program: 340 (14.5%);
English Language Learner: 94 (4.0%); Migrant: 0 (0.0%)
Eligible for Free Lunch Program: 20 (0.9%)
Eligible for Reduced-Price Lunch Program: 6 (0.3%)
Teachers: 177.6 (13.2 to 1)
Librarians/Media Specialists: 2.0 (1,169.0 to 1)
Guidance Counselors: 4.0 (584.5 to 1)
Current Spending: ($ per student per year):
Total: $11,492; Instruction: $6,680; Support Services: $4,640
Enrollment, Drop-out Rates and Diploma Recipients by Race/Ethnicity

Category	Total	White	Black	Asian	AIAN	Hisp.
Enrollment (%)	100.0	86.9	1.7	9.0	0.0	2.4
Drop-out Rate (%)	0.2	0.2	0.0	0.0	n/a	0.0
H.S. Diplomas (#)	130	111	1	15	0	3

Hackensack City
355 State St • Hackensack, NJ 07601-5510
(201) 646-7830 • http://www.hackensackelementary.org
Grade Span: PK-12; **Agency Type:** 1
Schools: 7
4 Primary; 2 Middle; 1 High; 0 Other Level
7 Regular; 0 Special Education; 0 Vocational; 0 Alternative
0 Magnet; 0 Charter; 6 Title I Eligible; 1 School-wide Title I
Students: 5,023 (51.1% male; 48.9% female)
Individual Education Program: 843 (16.8%);
English Language Learner: 332 (6.6%); Migrant: 0 (0.0%)
Eligible for Free Lunch Program: 1,509 (30.0%)
Eligible for Reduced-Price Lunch Program: 580 (11.5%)

Teachers: 381.7 (13.2 to 1)
Librarians/Media Specialists: 6.0 (837.2 to 1)
Guidance Counselors: 10.0 (502.3 to 1)
Current Spending: ($ per student per year):
Total: $11,240; Instruction: $7,268; Support Services: $3,713
Enrollment, Drop-out Rates and Diploma Recipients by Race/Ethnicity

Category	Total	White	Black	Asian	AIAN	Hisp.
Enrollment (%)	100.0	19.5	34.0	6.3	0.2	40.0
Drop-out Rate (%)	4.6	4.0	4.7	3.1	0.0	5.2
H.S. Diplomas (#)	342	110	82	28	0	122

Hasbrouck Heights Boro

379 Blvd • Hasbrouck Heights, NJ 07604-1421
(201) 393-8145
Grade Span: PK-12; **Agency Type:** 1
Schools: 4
2 Primary; 1 Middle; 1 High; 0 Other Level
4 Regular; 0 Special Education; 0 Vocational; 0 Alternative
0 Magnet; 0 Charter; 0 Title I Eligible; 0 School-wide Title I
Students: 1,563 (50.0% male; 50.0% female)
Individual Education Program: 244 (15.6%);
English Language Learner: 32 (2.0%); Migrant: 0 (0.0%)
Eligible for Free Lunch Program: 38 (2.4%)
Eligible for Reduced-Price Lunch Program: 5 (0.3%)
Teachers: 117.2 (13.3 to 1)
Librarians/Media Specialists: 2.0 (781.5 to 1)
Guidance Counselors: 3.0 (521.0 to 1)
Current Spending: ($ per student per year):
Total: $10,110; Instruction: $6,359; Support Services: $3,620
Enrollment, Drop-out Rates and Diploma Recipients by Race/Ethnicity

Category	Total	White	Black	Asian	AIAN	Hisp.
Enrollment (%)	100.0	73.6	2.8	10.7	0.0	12.9
Drop-out Rate (%)	0.8	0.3	0.0	0.0	n/a	3.4
H.S. Diplomas (#)	99	73	3	8	0	15

Leonia Boro

570 Grand Ave • Leonia, NJ 07605-1537
(201) 947-5655 • http://www.bergen.org/edpartners/Leonia/
Grade Span: PK-12; **Agency Type:** 1
Schools: 3
1 Primary; 1 Middle; 1 High; 0 Other Level
3 Regular; 0 Special Education; 0 Vocational; 0 Alternative
0 Magnet; 0 Charter; 3 Title I Eligible; 0 School-wide Title I
Students: 1,701 (50.3% male; 49.7% female)
Individual Education Program: 206 (12.1%);
English Language Learner: 178 (10.5%); Migrant: 0 (0.0%)
Eligible for Free Lunch Program: 92 (5.4%)
Eligible for Reduced-Price Lunch Program: 47 (2.8%)
Teachers: 173.0 (9.8 to 1)
Librarians/Media Specialists: 3.0 (567.0 to 1)
Guidance Counselors: 6.3 (270.0 to 1)
Current Spending: ($ per student per year):
Total: $10,079; Instruction: $6,494; Support Services: $3,304
Enrollment, Drop-out Rates and Diploma Recipients by Race/Ethnicity

Category	Total	White	Black	Asian	AIAN	Hisp.
Enrollment (%)	100.0	45.1	3.4	36.6	0.0	15.0
Drop-out Rate (%)	0.5	0.7	0.0	0.5	n/a	0.0
H.S. Diplomas (#)	120	66	4	35	0	15

Lodi Borough

Lincoln School • Lodi, NJ 07644
(973) 778-4620 • http://www.njcommunity.com/sites/lodi
Grade Span: PK-12; **Agency Type:** 1
Schools: 7
5 Primary; 1 Middle; 1 High; 0 Other Level
7 Regular; 0 Special Education; 0 Vocational; 0 Alternative
0 Magnet; 0 Charter; 4 Title I Eligible; 0 School-wide Title I
Students: 3,083 (50.2% male; 49.8% female)
Individual Education Program: 412 (13.4%);
English Language Learner: 266 (8.6%); Migrant: 0 (0.0%)
Eligible for Free Lunch Program: 726 (23.5%)
Eligible for Reduced-Price Lunch Program: 389 (12.6%)
Teachers: 221.4 (13.9 to 1)
Librarians/Media Specialists: 6.0 (513.8 to 1)
Guidance Counselors: 9.0 (342.6 to 1)
Current Spending: ($ per student per year):
Total: $10,489; Instruction: $6,514; Support Services: $3,683
Enrollment, Drop-out Rates and Diploma Recipients by Race/Ethnicity

Category	Total	White	Black	Asian	AIAN	Hisp.
Enrollment (%)	100.0	51.3	4.8	14.0	0.0	30.0
Drop-out Rate (%)	1.9	3.0	0.0	0.0	n/a	0.9
H.S. Diplomas (#)	191	111	7	29	0	44

Lyndhurst Twp

Lincoln School • Lyndhurst, NJ 07071-1928
(201) 438-5683 • http://www.lyndhurstschools.org
Grade Span: PK-12; **Agency Type:** 1
Schools: 7
6 Primary; 0 Middle; 1 High; 0 Other Level
7 Regular; 0 Special Education; 0 Vocational; 0 Alternative
0 Magnet; 0 Charter; 6 Title I Eligible; 0 School-wide Title I
Students: 2,102 (51.5% male; 48.5% female)
Individual Education Program: 446 (21.2%);
English Language Learner: 52 (2.5%); Migrant: 0 (0.0%)
Eligible for Free Lunch Program: 180 (8.6%)
Eligible for Reduced-Price Lunch Program: 129 (6.1%)
Teachers: 147.8 (14.2 to 1)
Librarians/Media Specialists: 1.0 (2,102.0 to 1)
Guidance Counselors: 6.0 (350.3 to 1)
Current Spending: ($ per student per year):
Total: $10,164; Instruction: $6,255; Support Services: $3,663
Enrollment, Drop-out Rates and Diploma Recipients by Race/Ethnicity

Category	Total	White	Black	Asian	AIAN	Hisp.
Enrollment (%)	100.0	78.0	1.0	6.3	0.0	14.7
Drop-out Rate (%)	1.8	1.4	20.0	0.0	0.0	5.0
H.S. Diplomas (#)	134	108	0	10	0	16

Mahwah Twp

Admin Office, 60 Ridge Rd • Mahwah, NJ 07430
(201) 529-6803 • http://www.mahwah.k12.nj.us
Grade Span: PK-12; **Agency Type:** 1
Schools: 7
4 Primary; 2 Middle; 1 High; 0 Other Level
7 Regular; 0 Special Education; 0 Vocational; 0 Alternative
0 Magnet; 0 Charter; 3 Title I Eligible; 0 School-wide Title I
Students: 3,250 (51.8% male; 48.2% female)
Individual Education Program: 407 (12.5%);
English Language Learner: 40 (1.2%); Migrant: 0 (0.0%)
Eligible for Free Lunch Program: 116 (3.6%)
Eligible for Reduced-Price Lunch Program: 76 (2.3%)
Teachers: 246.2 (13.2 to 1)
Librarians/Media Specialists: 5.0 (650.0 to 1)
Guidance Counselors: 8.0 (406.3 to 1)
Current Spending: ($ per student per year):
Total: $11,294; Instruction: $6,648; Support Services: $4,439
Enrollment, Drop-out Rates and Diploma Recipients by Race/Ethnicity

Category	Total	White	Black	Asian	AIAN	Hisp.
Enrollment (%)	100.0	80.5	3.0	10.7	2.0	3.8
Drop-out Rate (%)	1.7	1.1	9.5	1.4	15.0	0.0
H.S. Diplomas (#)	174	142	4	14	4	10

New Milford Boro

145 Madison Ave • New Milford, NJ 07646-2707
(201) 261-2952 • http://www.newmilfordschools.org/
Grade Span: PK-12; **Agency Type:** 1
Schools: 4
2 Primary; 1 Middle; 1 High; 0 Other Level
4 Regular; 0 Special Education; 0 Vocational; 0 Alternative
0 Magnet; 0 Charter; 2 Title I Eligible; 0 School-wide Title I
Students: 1,917 (53.8% male; 46.2% female)
Individual Education Program: 296 (15.4%);
English Language Learner: 68 (3.5%); Migrant: 0 (0.0%)
Eligible for Free Lunch Program: 77 (4.0%)
Eligible for Reduced-Price Lunch Program: 58 (3.0%)
Teachers: 147.8 (13.0 to 1)
Librarians/Media Specialists: 2.2 (871.4 to 1)
Guidance Counselors: 2.8 (684.6 to 1)
Current Spending: ($ per student per year):
Total: $10,119; Instruction: $5,928; Support Services: $3,881
Enrollment, Drop-out Rates and Diploma Recipients by Race/Ethnicity

Category	Total	White	Black	Asian	AIAN	Hisp.
Enrollment (%)	100.0	63.4	2.7	21.5	0.0	12.4
Drop-out Rate (%)	0.5	0.3	0.0	2.0	n/a	0.0
H.S. Diplomas (#)	113	73	5	12	8	15

North Arlington Boro

222 Ridge Rd • North Arlington, NJ 07031-6036
(201) 955-5200 • http://www.narlington.k12.nj.us/
Grade Span: PK-12; **Agency Type:** 1
Schools: 5
3 Primary; 1 Middle; 1 High; 0 Other Level
5 Regular; 0 Special Education; 0 Vocational; 0 Alternative
0 Magnet; 0 Charter; 2 Title I Eligible; 0 School-wide Title I
Students: 1,515 (53.9% male; 46.1% female)
Individual Education Program: 276 (18.2%);
English Language Learner: 83 (5.5%); Migrant: 0 (0.0%)
Eligible for Free Lunch Program: 91 (6.0%)
Eligible for Reduced-Price Lunch Program: 67 (4.4%)

Teachers: 113.8 (13.3 to 1)
Librarians/Media Specialists: 1.0 (1,515.0 to 1)
Guidance Counselors: 4.0 (378.8 to 1)
Current Spending: ($ per student per year):
Total: $9,459; Instruction: $5,873; Support Services: $3,415
Enrollment, Drop-out Rates and Diploma Recipients by Race/Ethnicity

Category	Total	White	Black	Asian	AIAN	Hisp.
Enrollment (%)	100.0	83.0	0.6	4.7	0.1	11.6
Drop-out Rate (%)	2.9	2.0	n/a	18.8	n/a	5.4
H.S. Diplomas (#)	106	93	0	6	0	7

Northern Valley Regional
162 Knickerbocker Rd • Demarest, NJ 07627-1033
(201) 768-2200 • http://www.nvnet.org
Grade Span: 09-12; **Agency Type:** 1
Schools: 2
0 Primary; 0 Middle; 2 High; 0 Other Level
2 Regular; 0 Special Education; 0 Vocational; 0 Alternative
0 Magnet; 0 Charter; 0 Title I Eligible; 0 School-wide Title I
Students: 2,260 (50.0% male; 50.0% female)
Individual Education Program: 270 (11.9%);
English Language Learner: 38 (1.7%); Migrant: 0 (0.0%)
Eligible for Free Lunch Program: 5 (0.2%)
Eligible for Reduced-Price Lunch Program: 4 (0.2%)
Teachers: 190.6 (11.9 to 1)
Librarians/Media Specialists: 2.0 (1,130.0 to 1)
Guidance Counselors: 12.0 (188.3 to 1)
Current Spending: ($ per student per year):
Total: $14,512; Instruction: $8,465; Support Services: $5,671
Enrollment, Drop-out Rates and Diploma Recipients by Race/Ethnicity

Category	Total	White	Black	Asian	AIAN	Hisp.
Enrollment (%)	100.0	69.8	1.0	26.0	0.1	3.1
Drop-out Rate (%)	0.1	0.2	0.0	0.0	0.0	0.0
H.S. Diplomas (#)	486	345	9	125	0	7

Oakland Boro
315 Ramapo Valley Rd • Oakland, NJ 07436-1813
(201) 337-6156
Grade Span: PK-08; **Agency Type:** 1
Schools: 4
3 Primary; 1 Middle; 0 High; 0 Other Level
4 Regular; 0 Special Education; 0 Vocational; 0 Alternative
0 Magnet; 0 Charter; 4 Title I Eligible; 0 School-wide Title I
Students: 1,605 (49.7% male; 50.3% female)
Individual Education Program: 271 (16.9%);
English Language Learner: 11 (0.7%); Migrant: 0 (0.0%)
Eligible for Free Lunch Program: 13 (0.8%)
Eligible for Reduced-Price Lunch Program: 23 (1.4%)
Teachers: 122.2 (13.1 to 1)
Librarians/Media Specialists: 4.0 (401.3 to 1)
Guidance Counselors: 4.5 (356.7 to 1)
Current Spending: ($ per student per year):
Total: $10,985; Instruction: $7,208; Support Services: $3,556
Enrollment, Drop-out Rates and Diploma Recipients by Race/Ethnicity

Category	Total	White	Black	Asian	AIAN	Hisp.
Enrollment (%)	100.0	92.9	0.8	2.8	0.4	3.1
Drop-out Rate (%)	n/a	n/a	n/a	n/a	n/a	n/a
H.S. Diplomas (#)	n/a	n/a	n/a	n/a	n/a	n/a

Paramus Boro
145 Spring Valley Rd • Paramus, NJ 07652-5333
(201) 261-7800 • http://www.paramus.k12.nj.us/
Grade Span: PK-12; **Agency Type:** 1
Schools: 8
5 Primary; 2 Middle; 1 High; 0 Other Level
8 Regular; 0 Special Education; 0 Vocational; 0 Alternative
0 Magnet; 0 Charter; 4 Title I Eligible; 0 School-wide Title I
Students: 4,188 (51.6% male; 48.4% female)
Individual Education Program: 446 (10.6%);
English Language Learner: 185 (4.4%); Migrant: 0 (0.0%)
Eligible for Free Lunch Program: 55 (1.3%)
Eligible for Reduced-Price Lunch Program: 31 (0.7%)
Teachers: 332.0 (12.6 to 1)
Librarians/Media Specialists: 7.0 (598.3 to 1)
Guidance Counselors: 11.0 (380.7 to 1)
Current Spending: ($ per student per year):
Total: $11,054; Instruction: $6,578; Support Services: $4,298
Enrollment, Drop-out Rates and Diploma Recipients by Race/Ethnicity

Category	Total	White	Black	Asian	AIAN	Hisp.
Enrollment (%)	100.0	67.9	0.9	26.1	0.0	5.1
Drop-out Rate (%)	0.6	0.7	0.0	0.4	0.0	0.0
H.S. Diplomas (#)	307	205	4	76	0	22

Pascack Valley Regional
46 Akers Ave • Montvale, NJ 07645-2028
(201) 358-7005 • http://www.pascack.k12.nj.us
Grade Span: 09-12; **Agency Type:** 1
Schools: 2
0 Primary; 0 Middle; 2 High; 0 Other Level
2 Regular; 0 Special Education; 0 Vocational; 0 Alternative
0 Magnet; 0 Charter; 1 Title I Eligible; 0 School-wide Title I
Students: 1,548 (50.8% male; 49.2% female)
Individual Education Program: 216 (14.0%);
English Language Learner: 12 (0.8%); Migrant: 0 (0.0%)
Eligible for Free Lunch Program: 5 (0.3%)
Eligible for Reduced-Price Lunch Program: 0 (0.0%)
Teachers: 127.7 (12.1 to 1)
Librarians/Media Specialists: 2.0 (774.0 to 1)
Guidance Counselors: 8.0 (193.5 to 1)
Current Spending: ($ per student per year):
Total: $16,621; Instruction: $10,166; Support Services: $6,195
Enrollment, Drop-out Rates and Diploma Recipients by Race/Ethnicity

Category	Total	White	Black	Asian	AIAN	Hisp.
Enrollment (%)	100.0	90.2	0.3	6.0	0.1	3.4
Drop-out Rate (%)	0.1	0.2	0.0	0.0	0.0	0.0
H.S. Diplomas (#)	367	321	1	31	0	14

Ramapo-Indian Hill Reg
331 George St • Franklin Lakes, NJ 07417-3099
(201) 891-1505 • http://www.rih.org
Grade Span: 09-12; **Agency Type:** 1
Schools: 2
0 Primary; 0 Middle; 2 High; 0 Other Level
2 Regular; 0 Special Education; 0 Vocational; 0 Alternative
0 Magnet; 0 Charter; 0 Title I Eligible; 0 School-wide Title I
Students: 2,039 (47.7% male; 52.3% female)
Individual Education Program: 288 (14.1%);
English Language Learner: 9 (0.4%); Migrant: 0 (0.0%)
Eligible for Free Lunch Program: 0 (0.0%)
Eligible for Reduced-Price Lunch Program: 5 (0.2%)
Teachers: 187.9 (10.9 to 1)
Librarians/Media Specialists: 2.0 (1,019.5 to 1)
Guidance Counselors: 11.0 (185.4 to 1)
Current Spending: ($ per student per year):
Total: $15,868; Instruction: $9,209; Support Services: $6,298
Enrollment, Drop-out Rates and Diploma Recipients by Race/Ethnicity

Category	Total	White	Black	Asian	AIAN	Hisp.
Enrollment (%)	100.0	91.6	0.8	4.8	0.0	2.7
Drop-out Rate (%)	0.4	0.4	0.0	0.9	n/a	0.0
H.S. Diplomas (#)	439	398	2	29	0	10

Ramsey Boro
266 E Main St • Ramsey, NJ 07446-1927
(201) 785-2300 • http://www.ramsey.k12.nj.us
Grade Span: PK-12; **Agency Type:** 1
Schools: 5
2 Primary; 2 Middle; 1 High; 0 Other Level
5 Regular; 0 Special Education; 0 Vocational; 0 Alternative
0 Magnet; 0 Charter; 0 Title I Eligible; 0 School-wide Title I
Students: 2,871 (53.4% male; 46.6% female)
Individual Education Program: 428 (14.9%);
English Language Learner: 21 (0.7%); Migrant: 0 (0.0%)
Eligible for Free Lunch Program: 22 (0.8%)
Eligible for Reduced-Price Lunch Program: 34 (1.2%)
Teachers: 219.3 (13.1 to 1)
Librarians/Media Specialists: 4.3 (667.7 to 1)
Guidance Counselors: 6.0 (478.5 to 1)
Current Spending: ($ per student per year):
Total: $11,436; Instruction: $7,174; Support Services: $4,050
Enrollment, Drop-out Rates and Diploma Recipients by Race/Ethnicity

Category	Total	White	Black	Asian	AIAN	Hisp.
Enrollment (%)	100.0	88.1	1.0	7.7	0.1	3.1
Drop-out Rate (%)	0.4	0.2	8.3	0.0	n/a	3.3
H.S. Diplomas (#)	184	164	1	14	0	5

Ridgefield Boro
555 Chestnut St • Ridgefield, NJ 07657-1825
(201) 945-9236 • http://school.nj.com/school/rmhs
Grade Span: PK-12; **Agency Type:** 1
Schools: 4
2 Primary; 0 Middle; 1 High; 1 Other Level
3 Regular; 1 Special Education; 0 Vocational; 0 Alternative
0 Magnet; 0 Charter; 3 Title I Eligible; 0 School-wide Title I
Students: 2,092 (52.8% male; 47.2% female)
Individual Education Program: 170 (8.1%);
English Language Learner: 107 (5.1%); Migrant: 0 (0.0%)
Eligible for Free Lunch Program: 150 (7.2%)
Eligible for Reduced-Price Lunch Program: 118 (5.6%)

Teachers: 150.9 (13.9 to 1)
Librarians/Media Specialists: 2.0 (1,046.0 to 1)
Guidance Counselors: 4.0 (523.0 to 1)
Current Spending: ($ per student per year):
Total: $11,572; Instruction: $8,143; Support Services: $2,836
Enrollment, Drop-out Rates and Diploma Recipients by Race/Ethnicity

Category	Total	White	Black	Asian	AIAN	Hisp.
Enrollment (%)	100.0	50.3	3.2	28.2	0.0	18.3
Drop-out Rate (%)	0.2	0.0	0.0	1.0	n/a	0.0
H.S. Diplomas (#)	127	77	0	26	0	24

Ridgefield Park Twp

712 Lincoln Ave • Ridgefield Park, NJ 07660-1033
(201) 807-2638 • http://www.rpps.net/
Grade Span: PK-12; **Agency Type:** 1
Schools: 4
3 Primary; 0 Middle; 1 High; 0 Other Level
4 Regular; 0 Special Education; 0 Vocational; 0 Alternative
0 Magnet; 0 Charter; 3 Title I Eligible; 0 School-wide Title I
Students: 1,867 (52.2% male; 47.8% female)
Individual Education Program: 307 (16.4%);
English Language Learner: 98 (5.2%); Migrant: 0 (0.0%)
Eligible for Free Lunch Program: 279 (14.9%)
Eligible for Reduced-Price Lunch Program: 202 (10.8%)
Teachers: 167.2 (11.2 to 1)
Librarians/Media Specialists: 3.2 (583.4 to 1)
Guidance Counselors: 6.0 (311.2 to 1)
Current Spending: ($ per student per year):
Total: $11,230; Instruction: $6,946; Support Services: $4,019
Enrollment, Drop-out Rates and Diploma Recipients by Race/Ethnicity

Category	Total	White	Black	Asian	AIAN	Hisp.
Enrollment (%)	100.0	48.3	4.9	10.7	0.3	35.7
Drop-out Rate (%)	2.4	1.1	4.7	3.3	n/a	4.0
H.S. Diplomas (#)	158	75	11	28	0	44

Ridgewood Village

49 Cottage Place • Ridgewood, NJ 07451-3813
(201) 670-2700 • http://www.ridgewood.k12.nj.us
Grade Span: PK-12; **Agency Type:** 1
Schools: 10
6 Primary; 2 Middle; 1 High; 1 Other Level
10 Regular; 0 Special Education; 0 Vocational; 0 Alternative
0 Magnet; 0 Charter; 5 Title I Eligible; 0 School-wide Title I
Students: 5,393 (50.7% male; 49.3% female)
Individual Education Program: 669 (12.4%);
English Language Learner: 107 (2.0%); Migrant: 0 (0.0%)
Eligible for Free Lunch Program: 31 (0.6%)
Eligible for Reduced-Price Lunch Program: 24 (0.4%)
Teachers: 384.4 (14.0 to 1)
Librarians/Media Specialists: 9.5 (567.7 to 1)
Guidance Counselors: 15.4 (350.2 to 1)
Current Spending: ($ per student per year):
Total: $11,424; Instruction: $6,816; Support Services: $4,279
Enrollment, Drop-out Rates and Diploma Recipients by Race/Ethnicity

Category	Total	White	Black	Asian	AIAN	Hisp.
Enrollment (%)	100.0	80.5	1.3	14.8	0.0	3.4
Drop-out Rate (%)	1.0	0.9	0.0	1.0	n/a	9.4
H.S. Diplomas (#)	332	271	9	43	0	9

Rutherford Boro

176 Park Ave • Rutherford, NJ 07070-2310
(201) 939-1717 • http://www.rutherford.k12.nj.us
Grade Span: PK-12; **Agency Type:** 1
Schools: 6
5 Primary; 0 Middle; 1 High; 0 Other Level
6 Regular; 0 Special Education; 0 Vocational; 0 Alternative
0 Magnet; 0 Charter; 0 Title I Eligible; 0 School-wide Title I
Students: 2,312 (51.0% male; 49.0% female)
Individual Education Program: 321 (13.9%);
English Language Learner: 43 (1.9%); Migrant: 0 (0.0%)
Eligible for Free Lunch Program: 33 (1.4%)
Eligible for Reduced-Price Lunch Program: 35 (1.5%)
Teachers: 182.4 (12.7 to 1)
Librarians/Media Specialists: 3.0 (770.7 to 1)
Guidance Counselors: 4.6 (502.6 to 1)
Current Spending: ($ per student per year):
Total: $10,410; Instruction: $6,651; Support Services: $3,570
Enrollment, Drop-out Rates and Diploma Recipients by Race/Ethnicity

Category	Total	White	Black	Asian	AIAN	Hisp.
Enrollment (%)	100.0	70.3	2.9	16.1	0.0	10.6
Drop-out Rate (%)	0.3	0.0	3.4	0.0	n/a	1.9
H.S. Diplomas (#)	149	119	4	17	0	9

Saddle Brook Twp

355 Mayhill St • Saddle Brook, NJ 07663-4628
(201) 843-2133 • http://www.njcommunity.com/
Grade Span: PK-12; **Agency Type:** 1
Schools: 5
3 Primary; 0 Middle; 1 High; 1 Other Level
4 Regular; 1 Special Education; 0 Vocational; 0 Alternative
0 Magnet; 0 Charter; 3 Title I Eligible; 0 School-wide Title I
Students: 1,616 (49.3% male; 50.7% female)
Individual Education Program: 282 (17.5%);
English Language Learner: 37 (2.3%); Migrant: 0 (0.0%)
Eligible for Free Lunch Program: 52 (3.2%)
Eligible for Reduced-Price Lunch Program: 61 (3.8%)
Teachers: 119.8 (13.5 to 1)
Librarians/Media Specialists: 2.0 (808.0 to 1)
Guidance Counselors: 4.0 (404.0 to 1)
Current Spending: ($ per student per year):
Total: $11,236; Instruction: $6,848; Support Services: $3,831
Enrollment, Drop-out Rates and Diploma Recipients by Race/Ethnicity

Category	Total	White	Black	Asian	AIAN	Hisp.
Enrollment (%)	100.0	76.2	1.1	8.5	1.5	12.7
Drop-out Rate (%)	0.2	0.3	0.0	0.0	0.0	0.0
H.S. Diplomas (#)	111	89	2	9	0	11

Teaneck Twp

One Merrison St • Teaneck, NJ 07666-4616
(201) 833-5510 • http://www.teaneckschools.org/aboutus.asp?mid=27
Grade Span: PK-12; **Agency Type:** 1
Schools: 7
4 Primary; 2 Middle; 1 High; 0 Other Level
7 Regular; 0 Special Education; 0 Vocational; 0 Alternative
0 Magnet; 0 Charter; 6 Title I Eligible; 0 School-wide Title I
Students: 4,471 (50.3% male; 49.7% female)
Individual Education Program: 669 (15.0%);
English Language Learner: 105 (2.3%); Migrant: 0 (0.0%)
Eligible for Free Lunch Program: 407 (9.1%)
Eligible for Reduced-Price Lunch Program: 285 (6.4%)
Teachers: 355.3 (12.6 to 1)
Librarians/Media Specialists: 6.0 (745.2 to 1)
Guidance Counselors: 15.0 (298.1 to 1)
Current Spending: ($ per student per year):
Total: $13,717; Instruction: $8,197; Support Services: $5,186
Enrollment, Drop-out Rates and Diploma Recipients by Race/Ethnicity

Category	Total	White	Black	Asian	AIAN	Hisp.
Enrollment (%)	100.0	23.0	47.3	10.8	0.3	18.6
Drop-out Rate (%)	1.8	2.1	1.8	0.0	0.0	2.1
H.S. Diplomas (#)	314	101	144	35	0	34

Tenafly Boro

500 Tenafly Rd • Tenafly, NJ 07670-1727
(201) 816-4501 • http://www.tenafly.k12.nj.us
Grade Span: PK-12; **Agency Type:** 1
Schools: 6
4 Primary; 1 Middle; 1 High; 0 Other Level
6 Regular; 0 Special Education; 0 Vocational; 0 Alternative
0 Magnet; 0 Charter; 0 Title I Eligible; 0 School-wide Title I
Students: 2,935 (53.1% male; 46.9% female)
Individual Education Program: 412 (14.0%);
English Language Learner: 207 (7.1%); Migrant: 0 (0.0%)
Eligible for Free Lunch Program: 10 (0.3%)
Eligible for Reduced-Price Lunch Program: 3 (0.1%)
Teachers: 247.5 (11.9 to 1)
Librarians/Media Specialists: 6.0 (489.2 to 1)
Guidance Counselors: 7.0 (419.3 to 1)
Current Spending: ($ per student per year):
Total: $11,848; Instruction: $7,487; Support Services: $4,149
Enrollment, Drop-out Rates and Diploma Recipients by Race/Ethnicity

Category	Total	White	Black	Asian	AIAN	Hisp.
Enrollment (%)	100.0	68.7	1.0	27.1	0.0	3.2
Drop-out Rate (%)	0.3	0.0	0.0	0.7	n/a	2.9
H.S. Diplomas (#)	232	141	6	73	0	12

Waldwick Boro

155 Summit Ave • Waldwick, NJ 07463-2133
(201) 445-3131
Grade Span: PK-12; **Agency Type:** 1
Schools: 3
2 Primary; 0 Middle; 1 High; 0 Other Level
3 Regular; 0 Special Education; 0 Vocational; 0 Alternative
0 Magnet; 0 Charter; 0 Title I Eligible; 0 School-wide Title I
Students: 1,516 (51.5% male; 48.5% female)
Individual Education Program: 248 (16.4%);
English Language Learner: 38 (2.5%); Migrant: 0 (0.0%)
Eligible for Free Lunch Program: 16 (1.1%)
Eligible for Reduced-Price Lunch Program: 1 (0.1%)

Teachers: 111.2 (13.6 to 1)
Librarians/Media Specialists: 2.0 (758.0 to 1)
Guidance Counselors: 3.0 (505.3 to 1)
Current Spending: ($ per student per year):
Total: $11,025; Instruction: $7,023; Support Services: $3,837
Enrollment, Drop-out Rates and Diploma Recipients by Race/Ethnicity

Category	Total	White	Black	Asian	AIAN	Hisp.
Enrollment (%)	100.0	85.6	0.9	6.0	0.5	7.1
Drop-out Rate (%)	1.3	0.6	0.0	0.0	0.0	12.5
H.S. Diplomas (#)	84	68	1	9	2	4

Westwood Regional

701 Ridgewood Rd • Westwood, NJ 07675-4811
(201) 664-2765 • http://www.westwood.k12.nj.us
Grade Span: PK-12; **Agency Type:** 1
Schools: 6
4 Primary; 1 Middle; 1 High; 0 Other Level
6 Regular; 0 Special Education; 0 Vocational; 0 Alternative
0 Magnet; 0 Charter; 3 Title I Eligible; 0 School-wide Title I
Students: 2,440 (52.6% male; 47.4% female)
Individual Education Program: 536 (22.0%);
English Language Learner: 44 (1.8%); Migrant: 0 (0.0%)
Eligible for Free Lunch Program: 58 (2.4%)
Eligible for Reduced-Price Lunch Program: 29 (1.2%)
Teachers: 198.3 (12.3 to 1)
Librarians/Media Specialists: 4.0 (610.0 to 1)
Guidance Counselors: 5.0 (488.0 to 1)
Current Spending: ($ per student per year):
Total: $12,744; Instruction: $7,754; Support Services: $4,783
Enrollment, Drop-out Rates and Diploma Recipients by Race/Ethnicity

Category	Total	White	Black	Asian	AIAN	Hisp.
Enrollment (%)	100.0	85.0	4.7	5.4	0.0	4.9
Drop-out Rate (%)	0.9	0.8	2.9	0.0	n/a	0.0
H.S. Diplomas (#)	137	116	12	3	0	6

Wyckoff Twp

241 Morse Ave • Wyckoff, NJ 07481-1917
(201) 848-5701 • http://www.wyckoffschools.org
Grade Span: PK-08; **Agency Type:** 1
Schools: 5
4 Primary; 1 Middle; 0 High; 0 Other Level
5 Regular; 0 Special Education; 0 Vocational; 0 Alternative
0 Magnet; 0 Charter; 0 Title I Eligible; 0 School-wide Title I
Students: 2,422 (49.8% male; 50.2% female)
Individual Education Program: 261 (10.8%);
English Language Learner: 18 (0.7%); Migrant: 0 (0.0%)
Eligible for Free Lunch Program: 5 (0.2%)
Eligible for Reduced-Price Lunch Program: 1 (<0.1%)
Teachers: 164.0 (14.8 to 1)
Librarians/Media Specialists: 4.0 (605.5 to 1)
Guidance Counselors: 6.0 (403.7 to 1)
Current Spending: ($ per student per year):
Total: $9,129; Instruction: $5,361; Support Services: $3,663
Enrollment, Drop-out Rates and Diploma Recipients by Race/Ethnicity

Category	Total	White	Black	Asian	AIAN	Hisp.
Enrollment (%)	100.0	92.0	0.7	6.1	0.0	1.1
Drop-out Rate (%)	n/a	n/a	n/a	n/a	n/a	n/a
H.S. Diplomas (#)	n/a	n/a	n/a	n/a	n/a	n/a

Burlington County

Bordentown Regional

48 Dunns Mill Rd • Bordentown, NJ 08505-1768
(609) 298-0025 • http://www.bordentown.k12.nj.us
Grade Span: PK-12; **Agency Type:** 1
Schools: 4
2 Primary; 1 Middle; 1 High; 0 Other Level
4 Regular; 0 Special Education; 0 Vocational; 0 Alternative
0 Magnet; 0 Charter; 2 Title I Eligible; 0 School-wide Title I
Students: 2,046 (50.8% male; 49.2% female)
Individual Education Program: 427 (20.9%);
English Language Learner: 46 (2.2%); Migrant: 0 (0.0%)
Eligible for Free Lunch Program: 118 (5.8%)
Eligible for Reduced-Price Lunch Program: 99 (4.8%)
Teachers: 145.1 (14.1 to 1)
Librarians/Media Specialists: 4.0 (511.5 to 1)
Guidance Counselors: 7.0 (292.3 to 1)
Current Spending: ($ per student per year):
Total: $10,886; Instruction: $6,218; Support Services: $4,208
Enrollment, Drop-out Rates and Diploma Recipients by Race/Ethnicity

Category	Total	White	Black	Asian	AIAN	Hisp.
Enrollment (%)	100.0	77.7	12.5	3.9	1.2	4.7
Drop-out Rate (%)	2.0	2.2	1.6	0.0	n/a	0.0
H.S. Diplomas (#)	119	98	13	2	1	5

Burlington City

518 Locust Ave • Burlington, NJ 08016-4512
(609) 387-5874 • http://www.burlington-nj.net
Grade Span: PK-12; **Agency Type:** 1
Schools: 5
3 Primary; 1 Middle; 1 High; 0 Other Level
5 Regular; 0 Special Education; 0 Vocational; 0 Alternative
0 Magnet; 0 Charter; 5 Title I Eligible; 4 School-wide Title I
Students: 1,802 (53.4% male; 46.6% female)
Individual Education Program: 318 (17.6%);
English Language Learner: 80 (4.4%); Migrant: 0 (0.0%)
Eligible for Free Lunch Program: 600 (33.3%)
Eligible for Reduced-Price Lunch Program: 184 (10.2%)
Teachers: 171.0 (10.5 to 1)
Librarians/Media Specialists: 2.5 (720.8 to 1)
Guidance Counselors: 7.0 (257.4 to 1)
Current Spending: ($ per student per year):
Total: $12,112; Instruction: $7,824; Support Services: $3,933
Enrollment, Drop-out Rates and Diploma Recipients by Race/Ethnicity

Category	Total	White	Black	Asian	AIAN	Hisp.
Enrollment (%)	100.0	46.0	45.7	4.1	0.1	4.1
Drop-out Rate (%)	2.4	2.3	1.8	0.0	12.5	8.7
H.S. Diplomas (#)	112	62	38	11	0	1

Burlington County Vocational

695 Woodlane Rd • Westampton Twp, NJ 08060-9614
(609) 267-4226 • http://www.bcit.tec.nj.us
Grade Span: 09-12; **Agency Type:** 1
Schools: 2
0 Primary; 0 Middle; 2 High; 0 Other Level
0 Regular; 0 Special Education; 2 Vocational; 0 Alternative
0 Magnet; 0 Charter; 2 Title I Eligible; 0 School-wide Title I
Students: 1,726 (54.3% male; 45.7% female)
Individual Education Program: 553 (32.0%);
English Language Learner: 0 (0.0%); Migrant: 0 (0.0%)
Eligible for Free Lunch Program: 301 (17.4%)
Eligible for Reduced-Price Lunch Program: 164 (9.5%)
Teachers: 153.5 (11.2 to 1)
Librarians/Media Specialists: 2.0 (863.0 to 1)
Guidance Counselors: 9.0 (191.8 to 1)
Current Spending: ($ per student per year):
Total: $15,241; Instruction: $8,543; Support Services: $5,521
Enrollment, Drop-out Rates and Diploma Recipients by Race/Ethnicity

Category	Total	White	Black	Asian	AIAN	Hisp.
Enrollment (%)	100.0	58.1	34.4	0.6	0.5	6.4
Drop-out Rate (%)	0.6	0.7	0.3	0.0	0.0	1.3
H.S. Diplomas (#)	929	503	357	3	3	63

Burlington Twp

1508 Mt Holly Rd • Burlington, NJ 08016-0428
Mailing Address: PO Box 428 • Burlington, NJ 08016-0428
(609) 387-3955 • http://www.burltwpsch.org
Grade Span: PK-12; **Agency Type:** 1
Schools: 5
3 Primary; 1 Middle; 1 High; 0 Other Level
5 Regular; 0 Special Education; 0 Vocational; 0 Alternative
0 Magnet; 0 Charter; 4 Title I Eligible; 0 School-wide Title I
Students: 3,845 (49.7% male; 50.3% female)
Individual Education Program: 598 (15.6%);
English Language Learner: 89 (2.3%); Migrant: 0 (0.0%)
Eligible for Free Lunch Program: 270 (7.0%)
Eligible for Reduced-Price Lunch Program: 163 (4.2%)
Teachers: 281.7 (13.6 to 1)
Librarians/Media Specialists: 3.0 (1,281.7 to 1)
Guidance Counselors: 10.4 (369.7 to 1)
Current Spending: ($ per student per year):
Total: $8,011; Instruction: $4,917; Support Services: $2,857
Enrollment, Drop-out Rates and Diploma Recipients by Race/Ethnicity

Category	Total	White	Black	Asian	AIAN	Hisp.
Enrollment (%)	100.0	54.8	33.8	6.4	0.1	4.9
Drop-out Rate (%)	0.1	0.2	0.0	0.0	0.0	0.0
H.S. Diplomas (#)	145	88	40	11	0	6

Cinnaminson Twp

2195 Riverton Rd • Cinnaminson, NJ 08077-2496
Mailing Address: PO Box 224 • Cinnaminson, NJ 08077-2496
(856) 829-7600 • http://www.cinnaminson.com
Grade Span: PK-12; **Agency Type:** 1
Schools: 4
2 Primary; 1 Middle; 1 High; 0 Other Level
4 Regular; 0 Special Education; 0 Vocational; 0 Alternative
0 Magnet; 0 Charter; 2 Title I Eligible; 0 School-wide Title I
Students: 2,539 (52.4% male; 47.6% female)
Individual Education Program: 481 (18.9%);
English Language Learner: 12 (0.5%); Migrant: 0 (0.0%)

Eligible for Free Lunch Program: 94 (3.7%)
Eligible for Reduced-Price Lunch Program: 53 (2.1%)
Teachers: 202.7 (12.5 to 1)
Librarians/Media Specialists: 3.0 (846.3 to 1)
Guidance Counselors: 6.0 (423.2 to 1)
Current Spending: ($ per student per year):
Total: $9,669; Instruction: $6,155; Support Services: $3,194
Enrollment, Drop-out Rates and Diploma Recipients by Race/Ethnicity

Category	Total	White	Black	Asian	AIAN	Hisp.
Enrollment (%)	100.0	88.7	6.3	2.3	0.0	2.6
Drop-out Rate (%)	0.2	0.3	0.0	0.0	n/a	0.0
H.S. Diplomas (#)	200	187	7	6	0	0

Delran Twp
52 Hartford Rd • Delran, NJ 08075-1895
(856) 461-6800 • http://www.delran.k12.nj.us
Grade Span: PK-12; **Agency Type:** 1
Schools: 4
2 Primary; 1 Middle; 1 High; 0 Other Level
4 Regular; 0 Special Education; 0 Vocational; 0 Alternative
0 Magnet; 0 Charter; 2 Title I Eligible; 0 School-wide Title I
Students: 2,586 (51.4% male; 48.6% female)
Individual Education Program: 325 (12.6%);
English Language Learner: 57 (2.2%); Migrant: 0 (0.0%)
Eligible for Free Lunch Program: 151 (5.8%)
Eligible for Reduced-Price Lunch Program: 118 (4.6%)
Teachers: 179.2 (14.4 to 1)
Librarians/Media Specialists: 5.0 (517.2 to 1)
Guidance Counselors: 5.8 (445.9 to 1)
Current Spending: ($ per student per year):
Total: $8,754; Instruction: $5,104; Support Services: $3,399
Enrollment, Drop-out Rates and Diploma Recipients by Race/Ethnicity

Category	Total	White	Black	Asian	AIAN	Hisp.
Enrollment (%)	100.0	83.1	8.9	4.3	0.0	3.6
Drop-out Rate (%)	1.8	1.8	1.5	0.0	n/a	5.9
H.S. Diplomas (#)	181	155	17	5	0	4

Evesham Twp
25 S Maple Ave • Marlton, NJ 08053-2001
(856) 983-1800 • http://www.evesham.k12.nj.us
Grade Span: PK-08; **Agency Type:** 1
Schools: 9
7 Primary; 2 Middle; 0 High; 0 Other Level
9 Regular; 0 Special Education; 0 Vocational; 0 Alternative
0 Magnet; 0 Charter; 3 Title I Eligible; 0 School-wide Title I
Students: 5,415 (52.1% male; 47.9% female)
Individual Education Program: 1,005 (18.6%);
English Language Learner: 46 (0.8%); Migrant: 0 (0.0%)
Eligible for Free Lunch Program: 110 (2.0%)
Eligible for Reduced-Price Lunch Program: 101 (1.9%)
Teachers: 390.7 (13.9 to 1)
Librarians/Media Specialists: 9.0 (601.7 to 1)
Guidance Counselors: 12.2 (443.9 to 1)
Current Spending: ($ per student per year):
Total: $8,784; Instruction: $5,106; Support Services: $3,325
Enrollment, Drop-out Rates and Diploma Recipients by Race/Ethnicity

Category	Total	White	Black	Asian	AIAN	Hisp.
Enrollment (%)	100.0	89.3	3.5	5.5	0.3	1.4
Drop-out Rate (%)	n/a	n/a	n/a	n/a	n/a	n/a
H.S. Diplomas (#)	n/a	n/a	n/a	n/a	n/a	n/a

Florence Twp
Admin Bldg, 201 Cedar St • Florence, NJ 08518
(609) 499-4600 • http://www.florence.k12.nj.us
Grade Span: PK-12; **Agency Type:** 1
Schools: 4
2 Primary; 1 Middle; 1 High; 0 Other Level
4 Regular; 0 Special Education; 0 Vocational; 0 Alternative
0 Magnet; 0 Charter; 4 Title I Eligible; 0 School-wide Title I
Students: 1,560 (51.0% male; 49.0% female)
Individual Education Program: 326 (20.9%);
English Language Learner: 13 (0.8%); Migrant: 0 (0.0%)
Eligible for Free Lunch Program: 213 (13.7%)
Eligible for Reduced-Price Lunch Program: 91 (5.8%)
Teachers: 127.6 (12.2 to 1)
Librarians/Media Specialists: 3.0 (520.0 to 1)
Guidance Counselors: 5.0 (312.0 to 1)
Current Spending: ($ per student per year):
Total: $9,416; Instruction: $5,863; Support Services: $3,254
Enrollment, Drop-out Rates and Diploma Recipients by Race/Ethnicity

Category	Total	White	Black	Asian	AIAN	Hisp.
Enrollment (%)	100.0	76.3	17.2	3.7	0.0	2.8
Drop-out Rate (%)	2.3	1.9	4.7	0.0	n/a	14.3
H.S. Diplomas (#)	105	88	9	8	0	0

Lenape Regional
93 Willow Grove Rd • Shamong, NJ 08088-8961
(609) 268-2000 • http://www.lr.k12.nj.us
Grade Span: 09-12; **Agency Type:** 1
Schools: 3
0 Primary; 0 Middle; 3 High; 0 Other Level
3 Regular; 0 Special Education; 0 Vocational; 0 Alternative
0 Magnet; 0 Charter; 0 Title I Eligible; 0 School-wide Title I
Students: 6,793 (49.7% male; 50.3% female)
Individual Education Program: 1,022 (15.0%);
English Language Learner: 25 (0.4%); Migrant: 0 (0.0%)
Eligible for Free Lunch Program: 77 (1.1%)
Eligible for Reduced-Price Lunch Program: 44 (0.6%)
Teachers: 491.5 (13.8 to 1)
Librarians/Media Specialists: 7.5 (905.7 to 1)
Guidance Counselors: 30.5 (222.7 to 1)
Current Spending: ($ per student per year):
Total: $11,253; Instruction: $6,363; Support Services: $4,572
Enrollment, Drop-out Rates and Diploma Recipients by Race/Ethnicity

Category	Total	White	Black	Asian	AIAN	Hisp.
Enrollment (%)	100.0	89.0	4.5	4.2	0.4	1.9
Drop-out Rate (%)	0.7	0.7	1.4	0.0	0.0	0.0
H.S. Diplomas (#)	1,496	1,338	70	58	7	23

Lumberton Twp
30 Dimsdale Dr • Lumberton, NJ 08048
Mailing Address: PO Box 8 • Lumberton, NJ 08048
(609) 265-7709
Grade Span: PK-08; **Agency Type:** 1
Schools: 3
2 Primary; 1 Middle; 0 High; 0 Other Level
3 Regular; 0 Special Education; 0 Vocational; 0 Alternative
0 Magnet; 0 Charter; 2 Title I Eligible; 2 School-wide Title I
Students: 1,654 (51.7% male; 48.3% female)
Individual Education Program: 349 (21.1%);
English Language Learner: 12 (0.7%); Migrant: 0 (0.0%)
Eligible for Free Lunch Program: 85 (5.1%)
Eligible for Reduced-Price Lunch Program: 74 (4.5%)
Teachers: 120.7 (13.7 to 1)
Librarians/Media Specialists: 3.0 (551.3 to 1)
Guidance Counselors: 4.9 (337.6 to 1)
Current Spending: ($ per student per year):
Total: $8,763; Instruction: $5,018; Support Services: $3,343
Enrollment, Drop-out Rates and Diploma Recipients by Race/Ethnicity

Category	Total	White	Black	Asian	AIAN	Hisp.
Enrollment (%)	100.0	73.8	18.3	3.9	0.1	4.0
Drop-out Rate (%)	n/a	n/a	n/a	n/a	n/a	n/a
H.S. Diplomas (#)	n/a	n/a	n/a	n/a	n/a	n/a

Maple Shade Twp
Frederick And Clinton Ave • Maple Shade, NJ 08052-3299
(856) 779-1750 • http://www.mapleshade.org
Grade Span: PK-12; **Agency Type:** 1
Schools: 4
2 Primary; 1 Middle; 1 High; 0 Other Level
4 Regular; 0 Special Education; 0 Vocational; 0 Alternative
0 Magnet; 0 Charter; 4 Title I Eligible; 0 School-wide Title I
Students: 2,133 (52.0% male; 48.0% female)
Individual Education Program: 503 (23.6%);
English Language Learner: 43 (2.0%); Migrant: 0 (0.0%)
Eligible for Free Lunch Program: 273 (12.8%)
Eligible for Reduced-Price Lunch Program: 219 (10.3%)
Teachers: 155.3 (13.7 to 1)
Librarians/Media Specialists: 1.0 (2,133.0 to 1)
Guidance Counselors: 7.0 (304.7 to 1)
Current Spending: ($ per student per year):
Total: $9,495; Instruction: $6,053; Support Services: $3,168
Enrollment, Drop-out Rates and Diploma Recipients by Race/Ethnicity

Category	Total	White	Black	Asian	AIAN	Hisp.
Enrollment (%)	100.0	81.9	7.4	5.6	0.2	4.9
Drop-out Rate (%)	1.9	1.7	0.0	2.8	n/a	10.0
H.S. Diplomas (#)	126	109	5	8	0	4

Medford Twp
128 Route 70, Ste 1 • Medford, NJ 08055
(609) 654-6416 • http://www.medford.k12.nj.us
Grade Span: PK-08; **Agency Type:** 1
Schools: 5
4 Primary; 1 Middle; 0 High; 0 Other Level
5 Regular; 0 Special Education; 0 Vocational; 0 Alternative
0 Magnet; 0 Charter; 2 Title I Eligible; 0 School-wide Title I
Students: 2,965 (51.2% male; 48.8% female)
Individual Education Program: 441 (14.9%);
English Language Learner: 9 (0.3%); Migrant: 0 (0.0%)
Eligible for Free Lunch Program: 55 (1.9%)

Eligible for Reduced-Price Lunch Program: 30 (1.0%)
Teachers: 188.3 (15.7 to 1)
Librarians/Media Specialists: 5.0 (593.0 to 1)
Guidance Counselors: 7.0 (423.6 to 1)
Current Spending: ($ per student per year):
Total: $9,287; Instruction: $5,582; Support Services: $3,511
Enrollment, Drop-out Rates and Diploma Recipients by Race/Ethnicity

Category	Total	White	Black	Asian	AIAN	Hisp.
Enrollment (%)	100.0	96.6	1.0	1.6	0.0	0.8
Drop-out Rate (%)	n/a	n/a	n/a	n/a	n/a	n/a
H.S. Diplomas (#)	n/a	n/a	n/a	n/a	n/a	n/a

Moorestown Twp

803 N Stanwick Rd • Moorestown, NJ 08057-2034
(856) 778-6600 • http://www.mtps.com
Grade Span: PK-12; **Agency Type:** 1
Schools: 6
3 Primary; 2 Middle; 1 High; 0 Other Level
6 Regular; 0 Special Education; 0 Vocational; 0 Alternative
0 Magnet; 0 Charter; 3 Title I Eligible; 0 School-wide Title I
Students: 4,049 (51.2% male; 48.8% female)
Individual Education Program: 726 (17.9%);
English Language Learner: 22 (0.5%); Migrant: 0 (0.0%)
Eligible for Free Lunch Program: 108 (2.7%)
Eligible for Reduced-Price Lunch Program: 74 (1.8%)
Teachers: 278.6 (14.5 to 1)
Librarians/Media Specialists: 6.0 (674.8 to 1)
Guidance Counselors: 8.1 (499.9 to 1)
Current Spending: ($ per student per year):
Total: $10,066; Instruction: $6,313; Support Services: $3,511
Enrollment, Drop-out Rates and Diploma Recipients by Race/Ethnicity

Category	Total	White	Black	Asian	AIAN	Hisp.
Enrollment (%)	100.0	85.7	6.8	5.3	0.0	2.1
Drop-out Rate (%)	0.9	0.7	1.3	1.7	n/a	5.9
H.S. Diplomas (#)	222	190	20	11	0	1

Mount Laurel Twp

330 Moorestown-Mt Laurel • Mount Laurel, NJ 08054-9521
(856) 235-3387 • http://www.mountlaurel.k12.nj.us
Grade Span: PK-08; **Agency Type:** 1
Schools: 8
6 Primary; 2 Middle; 0 High; 0 Other Level
8 Regular; 0 Special Education; 0 Vocational; 0 Alternative
0 Magnet; 0 Charter; 7 Title I Eligible; 0 School-wide Title I
Students: 4,522 (51.5% male; 48.5% female)
Individual Education Program: 816 (18.0%);
English Language Learner: 49 (1.1%); Migrant: 0 (0.0%)
Eligible for Free Lunch Program: 172 (3.8%)
Eligible for Reduced-Price Lunch Program: 121 (2.7%)
Teachers: 339.5 (13.3 to 1)
Librarians/Media Specialists: 8.0 (565.3 to 1)
Guidance Counselors: 11.0 (411.1 to 1)
Current Spending: ($ per student per year):
Total: $8,892; Instruction: $5,394; Support Services: $3,306
Enrollment, Drop-out Rates and Diploma Recipients by Race/Ethnicity

Category	Total	White	Black	Asian	AIAN	Hisp.
Enrollment (%)	100.0	82.0	9.6	5.2	0.2	3.1
Drop-out Rate (%)	n/a	n/a	n/a	n/a	n/a	n/a
H.S. Diplomas (#)	n/a	n/a	n/a	n/a	n/a	n/a

Northern Burlington Reg

160 Mansfield Road, E • Columbus, NJ 08022-9738
(609) 298-3900 • http://www.nburlington.com
Grade Span: 07-12; **Agency Type:** 1
Schools: 2
0 Primary; 1 Middle; 1 High; 0 Other Level
2 Regular; 0 Special Education; 0 Vocational; 0 Alternative
0 Magnet; 0 Charter; 1 Title I Eligible; 0 School-wide Title I
Students: 1,854 (53.5% male; 46.5% female)
Individual Education Program: 296 (16.0%);
English Language Learner: 7 (0.4%); Migrant: 0 (0.0%)
Eligible for Free Lunch Program: 72 (3.9%)
Eligible for Reduced-Price Lunch Program: 100 (5.4%)
Teachers: 140.7 (13.2 to 1)
Librarians/Media Specialists: 2.0 (927.0 to 1)
Guidance Counselors: 9.0 (206.0 to 1)
Current Spending: ($ per student per year):
Total: $11,436; Instruction: $6,486; Support Services: $4,483
Enrollment, Drop-out Rates and Diploma Recipients by Race/Ethnicity

Category	Total	White	Black	Asian	AIAN	Hisp.
Enrollment (%)	100.0	78.4	12.0	4.4	0.4	4.9
Drop-out Rate (%)	1.7	1.8	2.1	0.0	0.0	0.0
H.S. Diplomas (#)	223	188	17	8	1	9

Pemberton Twp

One Egbert St • Pemberton, NJ 08068
(609) 893-8141
Grade Span: PK-12; **Agency Type:** 1
Schools: 11
7 Primary; 3 Middle; 1 High; 0 Other Level
11 Regular; 0 Special Education; 0 Vocational; 0 Alternative
0 Magnet; 0 Charter; 9 Title I Eligible; 0 School-wide Title I
Students: 5,827 (51.1% male; 48.9% female)
Individual Education Program: 1,384 (23.8%);
English Language Learner: 47 (0.8%); Migrant: 2 (<0.1%)
Eligible for Free Lunch Program: 1,362 (23.4%)
Eligible for Reduced-Price Lunch Program: 863 (14.8%)
Teachers: 510.0 (11.4 to 1)
Librarians/Media Specialists: 10.0 (582.7 to 1)
Guidance Counselors: 20.0 (291.4 to 1)
Current Spending: ($ per student per year):
Total: $11,966; Instruction: $7,138; Support Services: $4,443
Enrollment, Drop-out Rates and Diploma Recipients by Race/Ethnicity

Category	Total	White	Black	Asian	AIAN	Hisp.
Enrollment (%)	100.0	55.2	30.6	2.9	0.2	11.1
Drop-out Rate (%)	4.2	5.0	3.0	4.1	0.0	3.6
H.S. Diplomas (#)	310	180	88	9	0	33

Rancocas Valley Regional

520 Jacksonville Rd • Mount Holly, NJ 08060-9622
(609) 267-0830 • http://www.rancocasvalley.k12.nj.us
Grade Span: 09-12; **Agency Type:** 1
Schools: 2
0 Primary; 0 Middle; 2 High; 0 Other Level
1 Regular; 0 Special Education; 0 Vocational; 1 Alternative
0 Magnet; 0 Charter; 1 Title I Eligible; 0 School-wide Title I
Students: 2,150 (51.8% male; 48.2% female)
Individual Education Program: 427 (19.9%);
English Language Learner: 11 (0.5%); Migrant: 0 (0.0%)
Eligible for Free Lunch Program: 116 (5.4%)
Eligible for Reduced-Price Lunch Program: 48 (2.2%)
Teachers: 124.1 (17.3 to 1)
Librarians/Media Specialists: 1.6 (1,343.8 to 1)
Guidance Counselors: 7.6 (282.9 to 1)
Current Spending: ($ per student per year):
Total: $9,429; Instruction: $5,465; Support Services: $3,714
Enrollment, Drop-out Rates and Diploma Recipients by Race/Ethnicity

Category	Total	White	Black	Asian	AIAN	Hisp.
Enrollment (%)	100.0	66.8	22.7	3.4	0.2	6.9
Drop-out Rate (%)	2.2	2.0	2.7	0.0	0.0	3.2
H.S. Diplomas (#)	410	280	90	17	0	23

Willingboro Twp

Levitt Building • Willingboro, NJ 08046
(609) 835-8600 • http://www.willingboroschools.org/
Grade Span: PK-12; **Agency Type:** 1
Schools: 10
8 Primary; 1 Middle; 1 High; 0 Other Level
9 Regular; 1 Special Education; 0 Vocational; 0 Alternative
0 Magnet; 0 Charter; 6 Title I Eligible; 0 School-wide Title I
Students: 5,305 (51.3% male; 48.7% female)
Individual Education Program: 973 (18.3%);
English Language Learner: 14 (0.3%); Migrant: 0 (0.0%)
Eligible for Free Lunch Program: 1,457 (27.5%)
Eligible for Reduced-Price Lunch Program: 731 (13.8%)
Teachers: 455.0 (11.7 to 1)
Librarians/Media Specialists: 8.0 (663.1 to 1)
Guidance Counselors: 15.0 (353.7 to 1)
Current Spending: ($ per student per year):
Total: $11,259; Instruction: $6,682; Support Services: $4,007
Enrollment, Drop-out Rates and Diploma Recipients by Race/Ethnicity

Category	Total	White	Black	Asian	AIAN	Hisp.
Enrollment (%)	100.0	3.6	90.2	1.1	0.2	4.9
Drop-out Rate (%)	0.8	2.8	0.6	0.0	0.0	1.6
H.S. Diplomas (#)	295	13	262	7	0	13

Camden County

Audubon Boro

350 Edgewood Ave • Audubon, NJ 08106-2299
(856) 547-1325 • http://www.audubon.k12.nj.us/
Grade Span: PK-12; **Agency Type:** 1
Schools: 3
2 Primary; 0 Middle; 1 High; 0 Other Level
3 Regular; 0 Special Education; 0 Vocational; 0 Alternative
0 Magnet; 0 Charter; 3 Title I Eligible; 0 School-wide Title I
Students: 1,741 (53.8% male; 46.2% female)
Individual Education Program: 209 (12.0%);
English Language Learner: 9 (0.5%); Migrant: 0 (0.0%)

Eligible for Free Lunch Program: 127 (7.3%)
Eligible for Reduced-Price Lunch Program: 75 (4.3%)
Teachers: 126.5 (13.8 to 1)
Librarians/Media Specialists: 1.0 (1,741.0 to 1)
Guidance Counselors: 5.5 (316.5 to 1)
Current Spending: ($ per student per year):
Total: $8,610; Instruction: $5,669; Support Services: $2,618
Enrollment, Drop-out Rates and Diploma Recipients by Race/Ethnicity

Category	Total	White	Black	Asian	AIAN	Hisp.
Enrollment (%)	100.0	95.9	0.9	1.1	0.2	1.9
Drop-out Rate (%)	1.4	1.4	0.0	0.0	n/a	0.0
H.S. Diplomas (#)	157	152	1	1	0	3

Black Horse Pike Regional
580 Erial Raod • Blackwood, NJ 08012
(856) 227-4106 • http://www.bhprsd.org/
Grade Span: 09-12; **Agency Type:** 1
Schools: 3
0 Primary; 0 Middle; 3 High; 0 Other Level
3 Regular; 0 Special Education; 0 Vocational; 0 Alternative
0 Magnet; 0 Charter; 3 Title I Eligible; 0 School-wide Title I
Students: 3,888 (51.3% male; 48.7% female)
Individual Education Program: 618 (15.9%);
English Language Learner: 27 (0.7%); Migrant: 0 (0.0%)
Eligible for Free Lunch Program: 261 (6.7%)
Eligible for Reduced-Price Lunch Program: 174 (4.5%)
Teachers: 257.8 (15.1 to 1)
Librarians/Media Specialists: 7.3 (532.6 to 1)
Guidance Counselors: 17.2 (226.0 to 1)
Current Spending: ($ per student per year):
Total: $10,816; Instruction: $6,363; Support Services: $4,233
Enrollment, Drop-out Rates and Diploma Recipients by Race/Ethnicity

Category	Total	White	Black	Asian	AIAN	Hisp.
Enrollment (%)	100.0	79.2	13.5	3.7	0.3	3.4
Drop-out Rate (%)	3.7	3.5	3.8	5.1	8.3	5.0
H.S. Diplomas (#)	730	597	88	30	2	13

Camden City
201 N Front St • Camden, NJ 08102-1935
(856) 966-2040 • http://www.camden.k12.nj.us/
Grade Span: PK-12; **Agency Type:** 1
Schools: 33
22 Primary; 6 Middle; 4 High; 1 Other Level
32 Regular; 0 Special Education; 0 Vocational; 1 Alternative
0 Magnet; 0 Charter; 28 Title I Eligible; 0 School-wide Title I
Students: 17,266 (50.5% male; 49.5% female)
Individual Education Program: 3,208 (18.6%);
English Language Learner: 1,246 (7.2%); Migrant: 1 (<0.1%)
Eligible for Free Lunch Program: 13,311 (77.1%)
Eligible for Reduced-Price Lunch Program: 522 (3.0%)
Teachers: 1,480.5 (11.7 to 1)
Librarians/Media Specialists: 26.0 (664.1 to 1)
Guidance Counselors: 60.0 (287.8 to 1)
Current Spending: ($ per student per year):
Total: $14,177; Instruction: $8,896; Support Services: $4,815
Enrollment, Drop-out Rates and Diploma Recipients by Race/Ethnicity

Category	Total	White	Black	Asian	AIAN	Hisp.
Enrollment (%)	100.0	1.3	54.8	1.9	0.1	42.0
Drop-out Rate (%)	33.3	61.9	29.2	0.0	***.*	40.3
H.S. Diplomas (#)	505	1	316	23	0	165

Camden County Vocational
343 Berlin-Cross Keys Rd • Sicklerville, NJ 08081-0566
(856) 767-7000 • http://www.ccts.tec.nj.us/
Grade Span: 09-12; **Agency Type:** 1
Schools: 2
0 Primary; 0 Middle; 2 High; 0 Other Level
0 Regular; 0 Special Education; 2 Vocational; 0 Alternative
0 Magnet; 0 Charter; 2 Title I Eligible; 0 School-wide Title I
Students: 1,992 (54.8% male; 45.2% female)
Individual Education Program: 630 (31.6%);
English Language Learner: 7 (0.4%); Migrant: 0 (0.0%)
Eligible for Free Lunch Program: 1,016 (51.0%)
Eligible for Reduced-Price Lunch Program: 289 (14.5%)
Teachers: 174.7 (11.4 to 1)
Librarians/Media Specialists: 2.0 (996.0 to 1)
Guidance Counselors: 13.0 (153.2 to 1)
Current Spending: ($ per student per year):
Total: $16,637; Instruction: $9,219; Support Services: $6,884
Enrollment, Drop-out Rates and Diploma Recipients by Race/Ethnicity

Category	Total	White	Black	Asian	AIAN	Hisp.
Enrollment (%)	100.0	27.3	34.4	1.4	0.2	36.7
Drop-out Rate (%)	3.1	6.0	3.0	0.0	0.0	1.4
H.S. Diplomas (#)	314	96	106	3	1	108

Cherry Hill Twp
45 Ranoldo Terrace • Cherry Hill, NJ 08034-0391
(856) 429-5600 • http://www.cherryhill.k12.nj.us/
Grade Span: PK-12; **Agency Type:** 1
Schools: 19
13 Primary; 3 Middle; 2 High; 1 Other Level
17 Regular; 1 Special Education; 0 Vocational; 1 Alternative
0 Magnet; 0 Charter; 8 Title I Eligible; 0 School-wide Title I
Students: 11,364 (51.9% male; 48.1% female)
Individual Education Program: 1,498 (13.2%);
English Language Learner: 147 (1.3%); Migrant: 0 (0.0%)
Eligible for Free Lunch Program: 508 (4.5%)
Eligible for Reduced-Price Lunch Program: 345 (3.0%)
Teachers: 765.5 (14.8 to 1)
Librarians/Media Specialists: 18.0 (631.3 to 1)
Guidance Counselors: 29.5 (385.2 to 1)
Current Spending: ($ per student per year):
Total: $10,313; Instruction: $6,489; Support Services: $3,475
Enrollment, Drop-out Rates and Diploma Recipients by Race/Ethnicity

Category	Total	White	Black	Asian	AIAN	Hisp.
Enrollment (%)	100.0	76.4	6.9	13.3	0.0	3.4
Drop-out Rate (%)	0.5	0.5	1.0	0.0	n/a	2.0
H.S. Diplomas (#)	846	620	49	152	0	25

Collingswood Boro
200 Lees Ave • Collingswood, NJ 08108-3106
(856) 962-5732 • http://collingswood.k12.nj.us
Grade Span: PK-12; **Agency Type:** 1
Schools: 7
5 Primary; 1 Middle; 1 High; 0 Other Level
7 Regular; 0 Special Education; 0 Vocational; 0 Alternative
0 Magnet; 0 Charter; 5 Title I Eligible; 0 School-wide Title I
Students: 2,068 (51.8% male; 48.2% female)
Individual Education Program: 315 (15.2%);
English Language Learner: 49 (2.4%); Migrant: 0 (0.0%)
Eligible for Free Lunch Program: 306 (14.8%)
Eligible for Reduced-Price Lunch Program: 203 (9.8%)
Teachers: 164.4 (12.6 to 1)
Librarians/Media Specialists: 4.0 (517.0 to 1)
Guidance Counselors: 8.0 (258.5 to 1)
Current Spending: ($ per student per year):
Total: $10,213; Instruction: $6,058; Support Services: $3,884
Enrollment, Drop-out Rates and Diploma Recipients by Race/Ethnicity

Category	Total	White	Black	Asian	AIAN	Hisp.
Enrollment (%)	100.0	74.2	12.3	3.2	0.2	10.0
Drop-out Rate (%)	3.3	3.3	3.4	2.9	n/a	3.2
H.S. Diplomas (#)	162	126	17	5	0	14

Eastern Camden County Reg
Laurel Oak Rd • Voorhees, NJ 08043-0995
(856) 346-6740 • http://www.eastern.k12.nj.us
Grade Span: 09-12; **Agency Type:** 1
Schools: 2
0 Primary; 0 Middle; 1 High; 1 Other Level
2 Regular; 0 Special Education; 0 Vocational; 0 Alternative
0 Magnet; 0 Charter; 2 Title I Eligible; 0 School-wide Title I
Students: 2,195 (52.4% male; 47.6% female)
Individual Education Program: 268 (12.2%);
English Language Learner: 7 (0.3%); Migrant: 0 (0.0%)
Eligible for Free Lunch Program: 72 (3.3%)
Eligible for Reduced-Price Lunch Program: 60 (2.7%)
Teachers: 145.6 (15.1 to 1)
Librarians/Media Specialists: 2.0 (1,097.5 to 1)
Guidance Counselors: 10.0 (219.5 to 1)
Current Spending: ($ per student per year):
Total: $10,404; Instruction: $6,048; Support Services: $3,947
Enrollment, Drop-out Rates and Diploma Recipients by Race/Ethnicity

Category	Total	White	Black	Asian	AIAN	Hisp.
Enrollment (%)	100.0	77.6	8.0	11.8	0.2	2.4
Drop-out Rate (%)	1.3	1.2	0.6	0.8	0.0	5.1
H.S. Diplomas (#)	476	361	41	57	1	16

Gloucester City
520 Cumberland St • Gloucester City, NJ 08030-1999
(856) 456-9394 • http://www.gcsd.k12.nj.us/
Grade Span: PK-12; **Agency Type:** 1
Schools: 3
1 Primary; 1 Middle; 1 High; 0 Other Level
3 Regular; 0 Special Education; 0 Vocational; 0 Alternative
0 Magnet; 0 Charter; 3 Title I Eligible; 0 School-wide Title I
Students: 2,176 (50.2% male; 49.8% female)
Individual Education Program: 424 (19.5%);
English Language Learner: 21 (1.0%); Migrant: 0 (0.0%)
Eligible for Free Lunch Program: 573 (26.3%)
Eligible for Reduced-Price Lunch Program: 259 (11.9%)

Teachers: 218.4 (10.0 to 1)
Librarians/Media Specialists: 3.0 (725.3 to 1)
Guidance Counselors: 8.0 (272.0 to 1)
Current Spending: ($ per student per year):
Total: $11,892; Instruction: $7,383; Support Services: $4,122
Enrollment, Drop-out Rates and Diploma Recipients by Race/Ethnicity

Category	Total	White	Black	Asian	AIAN	Hisp.
Enrollment (%)	100.0	95.8	1.3	1.0	0.0	1.9
Drop-out Rate (%)	1.6	1.6	0.0	0.0	n/a	0.0
H.S. Diplomas (#)	150	147	1	2	0	0

Gloucester Twp
17 Erial Rd • Blackwood, NJ 08012-3964
(856) 227-1400 • http://www.jersey.net/~gtps
Grade Span: PK-08; **Agency Type:** 1
Schools: 12
9 Primary; 3 Middle; 0 High; 0 Other Level
12 Regular; 0 Special Education; 0 Vocational; 0 Alternative
0 Magnet; 0 Charter; 7 Title I Eligible; 0 School-wide Title I
Students: 7,988 (52.0% male; 48.0% female)
Individual Education Program: 1,295 (16.2%);
English Language Learner: 71 (0.9%); Migrant: 0 (0.0%)
Eligible for Free Lunch Program: 1,056 (13.2%)
Eligible for Reduced-Price Lunch Program: 590 (7.4%)
Teachers: 546.0 (14.6 to 1)
Librarians/Media Specialists: 9.0 (887.6 to 1)
Guidance Counselors: 14.5 (550.9 to 1)
Current Spending: ($ per student per year):
Total: $8,123; Instruction: $5,140; Support Services: $2,626
Enrollment, Drop-out Rates and Diploma Recipients by Race/Ethnicity

Category	Total	White	Black	Asian	AIAN	Hisp.
Enrollment (%)	100.0	74.5	18.2	3.3	0.1	3.9
Drop-out Rate (%)	n/a	n/a	n/a	n/a	n/a	n/a
H.S. Diplomas (#)	n/a	n/a	n/a	n/a	n/a	n/a

Haddon Twp
500 Rhoads Ave • Westmont, NJ 08108
(856) 869-7700 • http://www.haddon.k12.nj.us
Grade Span: PK-12; **Agency Type:** 1
Schools: 6
5 Primary; 0 Middle; 1 High; 0 Other Level
6 Regular; 0 Special Education; 0 Vocational; 0 Alternative
0 Magnet; 0 Charter; 2 Title I Eligible; 0 School-wide Title I
Students: 2,242 (51.9% male; 48.1% female)
Individual Education Program: 341 (15.2%);
English Language Learner: 6 (0.3%); Migrant: 0 (0.0%)
Eligible for Free Lunch Program: 81 (3.6%)
Eligible for Reduced-Price Lunch Program: 63 (2.8%)
Teachers: 151.8 (14.8 to 1)
Librarians/Media Specialists: 1.0 (2,242.0 to 1)
Guidance Counselors: 6.4 (350.3 to 1)
Current Spending: ($ per student per year):
Total: $8,948; Instruction: $5,755; Support Services: $2,913
Enrollment, Drop-out Rates and Diploma Recipients by Race/Ethnicity

Category	Total	White	Black	Asian	AIAN	Hisp.
Enrollment (%)	100.0	92.2	1.7	3.3	0.3	2.5
Drop-out Rate (%)	0.4	0.5	0.0	0.0	0.0	0.0
H.S. Diplomas (#)	160	156	1	2	0	1

Haddonfield Boro
One Lincoln Ave • Haddonfield, NJ 08033-1892
(856) 429-4130 • http://www.haddonfield.k12.nj.us
Grade Span: PK-12; **Agency Type:** 1
Schools: 5
3 Primary; 1 Middle; 1 High; 0 Other Level
5 Regular; 0 Special Education; 0 Vocational; 0 Alternative
0 Magnet; 0 Charter; 0 Title I Eligible; 0 School-wide Title I
Students: 2,282 (49.9% male; 50.1% female)
Individual Education Program: 324 (14.2%);
English Language Learner: 7 (0.3%); Migrant: 0 (0.0%)
Eligible for Free Lunch Program: 18 (0.8%)
Eligible for Reduced-Price Lunch Program: 9 (0.4%)
Teachers: 166.4 (13.7 to 1)
Librarians/Media Specialists: 3.0 (760.7 to 1)
Guidance Counselors: 8.8 (259.3 to 1)
Current Spending: ($ per student per year):
Total: $9,757; Instruction: $6,144; Support Services: $3,413
Enrollment, Drop-out Rates and Diploma Recipients by Race/Ethnicity

Category	Total	White	Black	Asian	AIAN	Hisp.
Enrollment (%)	100.0	96.4	1.2	1.5	0.0	0.9
Drop-out Rate (%)	0.3	0.3	0.0	0.0	0.0	0.0
H.S. Diplomas (#)	175	169	4	1	1	0

Lindenwold Boro
Admin Bldg, 1017 E Linden • Lindenwold, NJ 08021-1126
(856) 784-4071
Grade Span: PK-12; **Agency Type:** 1
Schools: 4
2 Primary; 1 Middle; 1 High; 0 Other Level
4 Regular; 0 Special Education; 0 Vocational; 0 Alternative
0 Magnet; 0 Charter; 2 Title I Eligible; 0 School-wide Title I
Students: 2,478 (51.1% male; 48.9% female)
Individual Education Program: 503 (20.3%);
English Language Learner: 72 (2.9%); Migrant: 0 (0.0%)
Eligible for Free Lunch Program: 777 (31.4%)
Eligible for Reduced-Price Lunch Program: 397 (16.0%)
Teachers: 215.9 (11.5 to 1)
Librarians/Media Specialists: 4.0 (619.5 to 1)
Guidance Counselors: 9.0 (275.3 to 1)
Current Spending: ($ per student per year):
Total: $10,379; Instruction: $6,599; Support Services: $3,419
Enrollment, Drop-out Rates and Diploma Recipients by Race/Ethnicity

Category	Total	White	Black	Asian	AIAN	Hisp.
Enrollment (%)	100.0	36.3	48.1	3.6	0.0	11.9
Drop-out Rate (%)	n/a	n/a	n/a	n/a	n/a	n/a
H.S. Diplomas (#)	0	0	0	0	0	0

Pennsauken Twp
1695 Hylton Rd • Pennsauken, NJ 08110-1313
(856) 662-8505 • http://www.pennsauken.net
Grade Span: PK-12; **Agency Type:** 1
Schools: 13
9 Primary; 2 Middle; 1 High; 1 Other Level
12 Regular; 1 Special Education; 0 Vocational; 0 Alternative
1 Magnet; 0 Charter; 7 Title I Eligible; 0 School-wide Title I
Students: 6,124 (51.9% male; 48.1% female)
Individual Education Program: 1,324 (21.6%);
English Language Learner: 185 (3.0%); Migrant: 0 (0.0%)
Eligible for Free Lunch Program: 1,886 (30.8%)
Eligible for Reduced-Price Lunch Program: 847 (13.8%)
Teachers: 419.7 (14.6 to 1)
Librarians/Media Specialists: 4.0 (1,531.0 to 1)
Guidance Counselors: 15.0 (408.3 to 1)
Current Spending: ($ per student per year):
Total: $10,193; Instruction: $6,268; Support Services: $3,646
Enrollment, Drop-out Rates and Diploma Recipients by Race/Ethnicity

Category	Total	White	Black	Asian	AIAN	Hisp.
Enrollment (%)	100.0	31.1	37.7	6.7	0.3	24.1
Drop-out Rate (%)	6.2	2.1	3.3	59.8	0.0	5.2
H.S. Diplomas (#)	385	162	141	19	0	63

Pine Hill Boro
1003 Turnervill Rd • Pine Hill, NJ 08021-6339
(856) 783-6900
Grade Span: PK-12; **Agency Type:** 1
Schools: 4
2 Primary; 1 Middle; 1 High; 0 Other Level
4 Regular; 0 Special Education; 0 Vocational; 0 Alternative
0 Magnet; 0 Charter; 3 Title I Eligible; 0 School-wide Title I
Students: 2,221 (50.6% male; 49.4% female)
Individual Education Program: 395 (17.8%);
English Language Learner: 15 (0.7%); Migrant: 0 (0.0%)
Eligible for Free Lunch Program: 491 (22.1%)
Eligible for Reduced-Price Lunch Program: 238 (10.7%)
Teachers: 192.9 (11.5 to 1)
Librarians/Media Specialists: 2.0 (1,110.5 to 1)
Guidance Counselors: 7.0 (317.3 to 1)
Current Spending: ($ per student per year):
Total: $8,996; Instruction: $5,233; Support Services: $3,403
Enrollment, Drop-out Rates and Diploma Recipients by Race/Ethnicity

Category	Total	White	Black	Asian	AIAN	Hisp.
Enrollment (%)	100.0	72.1	21.8	1.5	0.3	4.4
Drop-out Rate (%)	n/a	n/a	n/a	n/a	n/a	n/a
H.S. Diplomas (#)	370	226	122	10	0	12

Voorhees Twp
Admin Bldg, 329 Route 73 • Voorhees, NJ 08043
(856) 751-8446 • http://hamilton.voorhees.k12.nj.us
Grade Span: PK-08; **Agency Type:** 1
Schools: 5
4 Primary; 1 Middle; 0 High; 0 Other Level
5 Regular; 0 Special Education; 0 Vocational; 0 Alternative
0 Magnet; 0 Charter; 2 Title I Eligible; 0 School-wide Title I
Students: 3,586 (51.2% male; 48.8% female)
Individual Education Program: 567 (15.8%);
English Language Learner: 46 (1.3%); Migrant: 0 (0.0%)
Eligible for Free Lunch Program: 145 (4.0%)
Eligible for Reduced-Price Lunch Program: 83 (2.3%)

Teachers: 256.3 (14.0 to 1)
Librarians/Media Specialists: 6.0 (597.7 to 1)
Guidance Counselors: 7.0 (512.3 to 1)
Current Spending: ($ per student per year):
Total: $9,535; Instruction: $5,826; Support Services: $3,218
Enrollment, Drop-out Rates and Diploma Recipients by Race/Ethnicity

Category	Total	White	Black	Asian	AIAN	Hisp.
Enrollment (%)	100.0	74.2	10.2	13.2	0.2	2.3
Drop-out Rate (%)	n/a	n/a	n/a	n/a	n/a	n/a
H.S. Diplomas (#)	n/a	n/a	n/a	n/a	n/a	n/a

Winslow Twp
200 Cooper Folly Rd • Atco, NJ 08004-9554
(856) 767-2850
Grade Span: PK-12; **Agency Type:** 1
Schools: 9
6 Primary; 1 Middle; 1 High; 1 Other Level
8 Regular; 1 Special Education; 0 Vocational; 0 Alternative
0 Magnet; 0 Charter; 6 Title I Eligible; 0 School-wide Title I
Students: 6,312 (52.0% male; 48.0% female)
Individual Education Program: 1,294 (20.5%);
English Language Learner: 52 (0.8%); Migrant: 10 (0.2%)
Eligible for Free Lunch Program: 1,597 (25.3%)
Eligible for Reduced-Price Lunch Program: 596 (9.4%)
Teachers: 526.5 (12.0 to 1)
Librarians/Media Specialists: 8.0 (789.0 to 1)
Guidance Counselors: 15.0 (420.8 to 1)
Current Spending: ($ per student per year):
Total: $10,393; Instruction: $6,434; Support Services: $3,587
Enrollment, Drop-out Rates and Diploma Recipients by Race/Ethnicity

Category	Total	White	Black	Asian	AIAN	Hisp.
Enrollment (%)	100.0	44.8	48.4	1.2	0.2	5.3
Drop-out Rate (%)	n/a	n/a	n/a	n/a	n/a	n/a
H.S. Diplomas (#)	328	199	106	10	3	10

Cape May County

Lower Cape May Regional
687 Route 9 • Cape May, NJ 08204-4637
(609) 884-3475 • http://lcmr.capemayschools.com
Grade Span: 07-12; **Agency Type:** 1
Schools: 2
0 Primary; 1 Middle; 1 High; 0 Other Level
2 Regular; 0 Special Education; 0 Vocational; 0 Alternative
0 Magnet; 0 Charter; 1 Title I Eligible; 0 School-wide Title I
Students: 1,816 (51.2% male; 48.8% female)
Individual Education Program: 441 (24.3%);
English Language Learner: 9 (0.5%); Migrant: 0 (0.0%)
Eligible for Free Lunch Program: 426 (23.5%)
Eligible for Reduced-Price Lunch Program: 165 (9.1%)
Teachers: 148.5 (12.2 to 1)
Librarians/Media Specialists: 2.0 (908.0 to 1)
Guidance Counselors: 7.5 (242.1 to 1)
Current Spending: ($ per student per year):
Total: $10,251; Instruction: $6,251; Support Services: $3,561
Enrollment, Drop-out Rates and Diploma Recipients by Race/Ethnicity

Category	Total	White	Black	Asian	AIAN	Hisp.
Enrollment (%)	100.0	93.9	3.0	0.8	0.1	2.2
Drop-out Rate (%)	1.7	1.7	0.0	14.3	0.0	0.0
H.S. Diplomas (#)	256	234	16	0	0	6

Lower Twp
834 Seashore Rd • Cape May, NJ 08204-4650
(609) 884-9400 • http://lowertwp.capemayschools.com
Grade Span: PK-06; **Agency Type:** 1
Schools: 4
3 Primary; 1 Middle; 0 High; 0 Other Level
4 Regular; 0 Special Education; 0 Vocational; 0 Alternative
0 Magnet; 0 Charter; 4 Title I Eligible; 0 School-wide Title I
Students: 1,957 (55.0% male; 45.0% female)
Individual Education Program: 431 (22.0%);
English Language Learner: 15 (0.8%); Migrant: 0 (0.0%)
Eligible for Free Lunch Program: 428 (21.9%)
Eligible for Reduced-Price Lunch Program: 325 (16.6%)
Teachers: 151.2 (12.9 to 1)
Librarians/Media Specialists: 4.0 (489.3 to 1)
Guidance Counselors: 3.9 (501.8 to 1)
Current Spending: ($ per student per year):
Total: $9,901; Instruction: $5,522; Support Services: $3,811
Enrollment, Drop-out Rates and Diploma Recipients by Race/Ethnicity

Category	Total	White	Black	Asian	AIAN	Hisp.
Enrollment (%)	100.0	92.9	3.1	0.7	0.1	3.2
Drop-out Rate (%)	n/a	n/a	n/a	n/a	n/a	n/a
H.S. Diplomas (#)	n/a	n/a	n/a	n/a	n/a	n/a

Middle Twp
216 S Main St • Cape May Ct House, NJ 08210-2273
(609) 465-1800
Grade Span: PK-12; **Agency Type:** 1
Schools: 4
2 Primary; 1 Middle; 1 High; 0 Other Level
4 Regular; 0 Special Education; 0 Vocational; 0 Alternative
0 Magnet; 0 Charter; 4 Title I Eligible; 0 School-wide Title I
Students: 2,991 (52.4% male; 47.6% female)
Individual Education Program: 538 (18.0%);
English Language Learner: 18 (0.6%); Migrant: 0 (0.0%)
Eligible for Free Lunch Program: 575 (19.2%)
Eligible for Reduced-Price Lunch Program: 232 (7.8%)
Teachers: 231.1 (12.9 to 1)
Librarians/Media Specialists: 2.0 (1,495.5 to 1)
Guidance Counselors: 7.0 (427.3 to 1)
Current Spending: ($ per student per year):
Total: $9,425; Instruction: $5,974; Support Services: $3,182
Enrollment, Drop-out Rates and Diploma Recipients by Race/Ethnicity

Category	Total	White	Black	Asian	AIAN	Hisp.
Enrollment (%)	100.0	74.9	20.7	2.1	0.0	2.2
Drop-out Rate (%)	2.4	2.5	2.8	0.0	0.0	0.0
H.S. Diplomas (#)	232	200	28	2	0	2

Ocean City
801 Asbury Ave • Ocean City, NJ 08226-3625
(609) 399-5150 • http://www.ocean.city.k12.nj.us
Grade Span: PK-12; **Agency Type:** 1
Schools: 3
1 Primary; 1 Middle; 1 High; 0 Other Level
3 Regular; 0 Special Education; 0 Vocational; 0 Alternative
0 Magnet; 0 Charter; 2 Title I Eligible; 0 School-wide Title I
Students: 2,183 (51.0% male; 49.0% female)
Individual Education Program: 244 (11.2%);
English Language Learner: 10 (0.5%); Migrant: 0 (0.0%)
Eligible for Free Lunch Program: 212 (9.7%)
Eligible for Reduced-Price Lunch Program: 82 (3.8%)
Teachers: 207.4 (10.5 to 1)
Librarians/Media Specialists: 4.0 (545.8 to 1)
Guidance Counselors: 9.0 (242.6 to 1)
Current Spending: ($ per student per year):
Total: $12,813; Instruction: $8,805; Support Services: $3,753
Enrollment, Drop-out Rates and Diploma Recipients by Race/Ethnicity

Category	Total	White	Black	Asian	AIAN	Hisp.
Enrollment (%)	100.0	90.4	6.8	1.0	0.1	1.7
Drop-out Rate (%)	1.2	1.1	3.5	0.0	0.0	3.8
H.S. Diplomas (#)	299	279	13	2	1	4

Upper Twp
525 Perry Rd • Petersburg, NJ 08270-9633
(609) 628-3513
Grade Span: PK-08; **Agency Type:** 1
Schools: 3
1 Primary; 2 Middle; 0 High; 0 Other Level
3 Regular; 0 Special Education; 0 Vocational; 0 Alternative
0 Magnet; 0 Charter; 1 Title I Eligible; 0 School-wide Title I
Students: 1,793 (52.3% male; 47.7% female)
Individual Education Program: 424 (23.6%);
English Language Learner: 1 (0.1%); Migrant: 0 (0.0%)
Eligible for Free Lunch Program: 80 (4.5%)
Eligible for Reduced-Price Lunch Program: 87 (4.9%)
Teachers: 132.5 (13.5 to 1)
Librarians/Media Specialists: 3.0 (597.7 to 1)
Guidance Counselors: 3.0 (597.7 to 1)
Current Spending: ($ per student per year):
Total: $8,561; Instruction: $5,132; Support Services: $3,107
Enrollment, Drop-out Rates and Diploma Recipients by Race/Ethnicity

Category	Total	White	Black	Asian	AIAN	Hisp.
Enrollment (%)	100.0	97.8	0.8	0.8	0.0	0.5
Drop-out Rate (%)	n/a	n/a	n/a	n/a	n/a	n/a
H.S. Diplomas (#)	n/a	n/a	n/a	n/a	n/a	n/a

Cumberland County

Bridgeton City
41 Bank St • Bridgeton, NJ 08302-0482
Mailing Address: PO Box 657 • Bridgeton, NJ 08302-0482
(856) 455-8030 • http://www.bridgetonschools.org/
Grade Span: PK-12; **Agency Type:** 1
Schools: 7
5 Primary; 1 Middle; 1 High; 0 Other Level
7 Regular; 0 Special Education; 0 Vocational; 0 Alternative
0 Magnet; 0 Charter; 7 Title I Eligible; 7 School-wide Title I
Students: 4,245 (51.0% male; 49.0% female)
Individual Education Program: 865 (20.4%);

English Language Learner: 374 (8.8%); Migrant: 452 (10.6%)
Eligible for Free Lunch Program: 2,920 (68.8%)
Eligible for Reduced-Price Lunch Program: 463 (10.9%)
Teachers: 374.4 (11.3 to 1)
Librarians/Media Specialists: 6.0 (707.5 to 1)
Guidance Counselors: 7.0 (606.4 to 1)
Current Spending: ($ per student per year):
Total: $12,838; Instruction: $7,802; Support Services: $4,603
Enrollment, Drop-out Rates and Diploma Recipients by Race/Ethnicity

Category	Total	White	Black	Asian	AIAN	Hisp.
Enrollment (%)	100.0	15.7	51.4	0.4	0.1	32.4
Drop-out Rate (%)	7.3	5.7	6.9	0.0	n/a	10.9
H.S. Diplomas (#)	168	53	67	5	2	41

Millville City
110 N Third St • Millville, NJ 08332-3829
Mailing Address: PO Box 5010 • Millville, NJ 08332-3829
(856) 327-7575 • http://www.millville.org
Grade Span: PK-12; **Agency Type:** 1
Schools: 10
7 Primary; 1 Middle; 1 High; 1 Other Level
10 Regular; 0 Special Education; 0 Vocational; 0 Alternative
0 Magnet; 0 Charter; 8 Title I Eligible; 0 School-wide Title I
Students: 6,061 (50.2% male; 49.8% female)
Individual Education Program: 1,100 (18.1%);
English Language Learner: 94 (1.6%); Migrant: 7 (0.1%)
Eligible for Free Lunch Program: 2,318 (38.2%)
Eligible for Reduced-Price Lunch Program: 606 (10.0%)
Teachers: 498.0 (12.2 to 1)
Librarians/Media Specialists: 9.0 (673.4 to 1)
Guidance Counselors: 20.0 (303.1 to 1)
Current Spending: ($ per student per year):
Total: $10,914; Instruction: $6,532; Support Services: $3,973
Enrollment, Drop-out Rates and Diploma Recipients by Race/Ethnicity

Category	Total	White	Black	Asian	AIAN	Hisp.
Enrollment (%)	100.0	59.0	25.0	0.7	0.8	14.5
Drop-out Rate (%)	6.8	6.1	10.4	0.0	20.0	4.6
H.S. Diplomas (#)	451	311	93	0	1	46

Vineland City
625 Plum St • Vineland, NJ 08360-3708
(856) 794-6700 • http://www.vineland.org
Grade Span: PK-12; **Agency Type:** 1
Schools: 19
12 Primary; 5 Middle; 2 High; 0 Other Level
19 Regular; 0 Special Education; 0 Vocational; 0 Alternative
0 Magnet; 0 Charter; 11 Title I Eligible; 0 School-wide Title I
Students: 9,616 (52.4% male; 47.6% female)
Individual Education Program: 1,925 (20.0%);
English Language Learner: 572 (5.9%); Migrant: 85 (0.9%)
Eligible for Free Lunch Program: 4,106 (42.7%)
Eligible for Reduced-Price Lunch Program: 1,223 (12.7%)
Teachers: 868.3 (11.1 to 1)
Librarians/Media Specialists: 15.0 (641.1 to 1)
Guidance Counselors: 39.0 (246.6 to 1)
Current Spending: ($ per student per year):
Total: $12,727; Instruction: $7,915; Support Services: $4,402
Enrollment, Drop-out Rates and Diploma Recipients by Race/Ethnicity

Category	Total	White	Black	Asian	AIAN	Hisp.
Enrollment (%)	100.0	34.1	20.7	1.5	0.3	43.4
Drop-out Rate (%)	3.6	2.5	4.2	33.3	0.0	4.7
H.S. Diplomas (#)	562	255	89	10	2	206

Essex County

Belleville Town
102 Passaic Ave • Belleville, NJ 07109-3127
(973) 450-3447 • http://www.belleville.k12.nj.us
Grade Span: PK-12; **Agency Type:** 1
Schools: 9
7 Primary; 1 Middle; 1 High; 0 Other Level
9 Regular; 0 Special Education; 0 Vocational; 0 Alternative
0 Magnet; 0 Charter; 5 Title I Eligible; 0 School-wide Title I
Students: 4,547 (51.7% male; 48.3% female)
Individual Education Program: 777 (17.1%);
English Language Learner: 267 (5.9%); Migrant: 0 (0.0%)
Eligible for Free Lunch Program: 811 (17.8%)
Eligible for Reduced-Price Lunch Program: 385 (8.5%)
Teachers: 313.2 (14.5 to 1)
Librarians/Media Specialists: 6.0 (757.8 to 1)
Guidance Counselors: 12.0 (378.9 to 1)
Current Spending: ($ per student per year):
Total: $9,740; Instruction: $6,189; Support Services: $3,310
Enrollment, Drop-out Rates and Diploma Recipients by Race/Ethnicity

Category	Total	White	Black	Asian	AIAN	Hisp.
Enrollment (%)	100.0	36.6	6.2	14.4	0.0	42.8
Drop-out Rate (%)	3.7	3.0	1.3	2.1	n/a	5.5
H.S. Diplomas (#)	325	137	17	48	0	123

Bloomfield Twp
155 Broad St • Bloomfield, NJ 07003-2629
(973) 680-8555 • http://www.bloomfield.k12.nj.us
Grade Span: PK-12; **Agency Type:** 1
Schools: 11
8 Primary; 1 Middle; 1 High; 1 Other Level
10 Regular; 1 Special Education; 0 Vocational; 0 Alternative
0 Magnet; 0 Charter; 4 Title I Eligible; 0 School-wide Title I
Students: 6,027 (52.1% male; 47.9% female)
Individual Education Program: 951 (15.8%);
English Language Learner: 269 (4.5%); Migrant: 0 (0.0%)
Eligible for Free Lunch Program: 1,048 (17.4%)
Eligible for Reduced-Price Lunch Program: 657 (10.9%)
Teachers: 430.6 (14.0 to 1)
Librarians/Media Specialists: 5.8 (1,039.1 to 1)
Guidance Counselors: 14.0 (430.5 to 1)
Current Spending: ($ per student per year):
Total: $8,650; Instruction: $5,255; Support Services: $3,185
Enrollment, Drop-out Rates and Diploma Recipients by Race/Ethnicity

Category	Total	White	Black	Asian	AIAN	Hisp.
Enrollment (%)	100.0	44.2	18.8	10.6	0.3	26.2
Drop-out Rate (%)	3.3	1.2	4.6	0.0	5.9	8.4
H.S. Diplomas (#)	344	194	50	48	0	52

Caldwell-West Caldwell
Harrison Bldg Gray St • West Caldwell, NJ 07006-7696
(973) 228-6979 • http://www.cwcboe.org
Grade Span: PK-12; **Agency Type:** 1
Schools: 6
4 Primary; 1 Middle; 1 High; 0 Other Level
6 Regular; 0 Special Education; 0 Vocational; 0 Alternative
0 Magnet; 0 Charter; 0 Title I Eligible; 0 School-wide Title I
Students: 2,578 (50.9% male; 49.1% female)
Individual Education Program: 362 (14.0%);
English Language Learner: 15 (0.6%); Migrant: 0 (0.0%)
Eligible for Free Lunch Program: 7 (0.3%)
Eligible for Reduced-Price Lunch Program: 11 (0.4%)
Teachers: 187.1 (13.8 to 1)
Librarians/Media Specialists: 5.4 (477.4 to 1)
Guidance Counselors: 5.0 (515.6 to 1)
Current Spending: ($ per student per year):
Total: $10,824; Instruction: $6,187; Support Services: $4,332
Enrollment, Drop-out Rates and Diploma Recipients by Race/Ethnicity

Category	Total	White	Black	Asian	AIAN	Hisp.
Enrollment (%)	100.0	90.4	1.3	4.5	0.0	3.8
Drop-out Rate (%)	0.8	0.6	0.0	0.0	n/a	6.9
H.S. Diplomas (#)	161	147	2	9	0	3

City of Orange Twp
451 Lincoln Ave • Orange, NJ 07050-2704
(973) 677-4040 • http://www.orange.k12.nj.us
Grade Span: PK-12; **Agency Type:** 1
Schools: 9
7 Primary; 1 Middle; 1 High; 0 Other Level
9 Regular; 0 Special Education; 0 Vocational; 0 Alternative
0 Magnet; 0 Charter; 8 Title I Eligible; 8 School-wide Title I
Students: 4,671 (52.6% male; 47.4% female)
Individual Education Program: 733 (15.7%);
English Language Learner: 344 (7.4%); Migrant: 0 (0.0%)
Eligible for Free Lunch Program: 3,196 (68.4%)
Eligible for Reduced-Price Lunch Program: 487 (10.4%)
Teachers: 337.8 (13.8 to 1)
Librarians/Media Specialists: 6.0 (778.5 to 1)
Guidance Counselors: 12.0 (389.3 to 1)
Current Spending: ($ per student per year):
Total: $12,207; Instruction: $7,569; Support Services: $4,319
Enrollment, Drop-out Rates and Diploma Recipients by Race/Ethnicity

Category	Total	White	Black	Asian	AIAN	Hisp.
Enrollment (%)	100.0	0.3	88.6	0.6	0.0	10.4
Drop-out Rate (%)	8.7	0.0	8.5	20.0	n/a	10.8
H.S. Diplomas (#)	209	1	200	1	0	7

East Orange
715 Park Ave • East Orange, NJ 07017-1004
(973) 266-5760 • http://www.eastorange.K12.nj.us
Grade Span: PK-12; **Agency Type:** 1
Schools: 21
14 Primary; 3 Middle; 2 High; 2 Other Level
21 Regular; 0 Special Education; 0 Vocational; 0 Alternative

0 Magnet; 0 Charter; 12 Title I Eligible; 10 School-wide Title I
Students: 11,762 (49.9% male; 50.1% female)
Individual Education Program: 1,852 (15.7%);
English Language Learner: 383 (3.3%); Migrant: 0 (0.0%)
Eligible for Free Lunch Program: 6,566 (55.8%)
Eligible for Reduced-Price Lunch Program: 1,385 (11.8%)
Teachers: 902.8 (13.0 to 1)
Librarians/Media Specialists: 9.0 (1,306.9 to 1)
Guidance Counselors: 32.0 (367.6 to 1)
Current Spending: ($ per student per year):
Total: $12,494; Instruction: $7,052; Support Services: $5,025

Enrollment, Drop-out Rates and Diploma Recipients by Race/Ethnicity

Category	Total	White	Black	Asian	AIAN	Hisp.
Enrollment (%)	100.0	0.1	95.8	0.1	0.0	4.0
Drop-out Rate (%)	5.3	0.0	5.4	0.0	n/a	3.4
H.S. Diplomas (#)	462	0	449	2	1	10

Essex County Voc-Tech

61 Main St • West Orange, NJ 07052-1703
(973) 243-2926 • http://www.essextech.org
Grade Span: 09-12; **Agency Type:** 1
Schools: 4
0 Primary; 0 Middle; 4 High; 0 Other Level
0 Regular; 0 Special Education; 4 Vocational; 0 Alternative
0 Magnet; 0 Charter; 3 Title I Eligible; 3 School-wide Title I
Students: 2,011 (42.9% male; 57.1% female)
Individual Education Program: 282 (14.0%);
English Language Learner: 139 (6.9%); Migrant: 0 (0.0%)
Eligible for Free Lunch Program: 1,452 (72.2%)
Eligible for Reduced-Price Lunch Program: 262 (13.0%)
Teachers: 169.0 (11.9 to 1)
Librarians/Media Specialists: 3.0 (670.3 to 1)
Guidance Counselors: 8.7 (231.1 to 1)
Current Spending: ($ per student per year):
Total: $13,473; Instruction: $7,512; Support Services: $5,664

Enrollment, Drop-out Rates and Diploma Recipients by Race/Ethnicity

Category	Total	White	Black	Asian	AIAN	Hisp.
Enrollment (%)	100.0	1.6	50.7	0.9	0.0	46.8
Drop-out Rate (%)	0.0	0.0	0.0	0.0	0.0	0.0
H.S. Diplomas (#)	395	16	206	1	0	172

Glen Ridge Boro

12 High St • Glen Ridge, NJ 07028-1424
(973) 429-8302
Grade Span: PK-12; **Agency Type:** 1
Schools: 4
3 Primary; 0 Middle; 1 High; 0 Other Level
4 Regular; 0 Special Education; 0 Vocational; 0 Alternative
0 Magnet; 0 Charter; 0 Title I Eligible; 0 School-wide Title I
Students: 1,757 (51.3% male; 48.7% female)
Individual Education Program: 196 (11.2%);
English Language Learner: 3 (0.2%); Migrant: 0 (0.0%)
Eligible for Free Lunch Program: 0 (0.0%)
Eligible for Reduced-Price Lunch Program: 0 (0.0%)
Teachers: 122.8 (14.3 to 1)
Librarians/Media Specialists: 3.0 (585.7 to 1)
Guidance Counselors: 5.0 (351.4 to 1)
Current Spending: ($ per student per year):
Total: $10,130; Instruction: $6,205; Support Services: $3,597

Enrollment, Drop-out Rates and Diploma Recipients by Race/Ethnicity

Category	Total	White	Black	Asian	AIAN	Hisp.
Enrollment (%)	100.0	88.0	6.1	3.6	0.1	2.2
Drop-out Rate (%)	0.0	0.0	0.0	0.0	n/a	0.0
H.S. Diplomas (#)	87	71	7	1	0	8

Irvington Township

1150 Springfield Ave • Irvington, NJ 07111-2441
(973) 399-6801 • http://www.irvington.k12.nj.us
Grade Span: PK-12; **Agency Type:** 1
Schools: 12
8 Primary; 3 Middle; 1 High; 0 Other Level
12 Regular; 0 Special Education; 0 Vocational; 0 Alternative
0 Magnet; 0 Charter; 9 Title I Eligible; 9 School-wide Title I
Students: 8,307 (51.9% male; 48.1% female)
Individual Education Program: 1,326 (16.0%);
English Language Learner: 430 (5.2%); Migrant: 0 (0.0%)
Eligible for Free Lunch Program: 4,640 (55.9%)
Eligible for Reduced-Price Lunch Program: 997 (12.0%)
Teachers: 532.7 (15.6 to 1)
Librarians/Media Specialists: 14.0 (593.4 to 1)
Guidance Counselors: 20.0 (415.4 to 1)
Current Spending: ($ per student per year):
Total: $13,054; Instruction: $8,262; Support Services: $4,467

Enrollment, Drop-out Rates and Diploma Recipients by Race/Ethnicity

Category	Total	White	Black	Asian	AIAN	Hisp.
Enrollment (%)	100.0	0.3	93.0	0.4	0.1	6.1
Drop-out Rate (%)	4.8	6.3	4.8	0.0	n/a	3.7
H.S. Diplomas (#)	302	1	278	1	0	22

Livingston Twp

11 Foxcroft Dr • Livingston, NJ 07039-2613
(973) 535-8010 • http://www.livingston.org/
Grade Span: PK-12; **Agency Type:** 1
Schools: 9
6 Primary; 2 Middle; 1 High; 0 Other Level
9 Regular; 0 Special Education; 0 Vocational; 0 Alternative
0 Magnet; 0 Charter; 8 Title I Eligible; 0 School-wide Title I
Students: 5,003 (52.0% male; 48.0% female)
Individual Education Program: 835 (16.7%);
English Language Learner: 77 (1.5%); Migrant: 0 (0.0%)
Eligible for Free Lunch Program: 23 (0.5%)
Eligible for Reduced-Price Lunch Program: 15 (0.3%)
Teachers: 407.7 (12.3 to 1)
Librarians/Media Specialists: 10.0 (500.3 to 1)
Guidance Counselors: 15.0 (333.5 to 1)
Current Spending: ($ per student per year):
Total: $12,362; Instruction: $7,755; Support Services: $4,605

Enrollment, Drop-out Rates and Diploma Recipients by Race/Ethnicity

Category	Total	White	Black	Asian	AIAN	Hisp.
Enrollment (%)	100.0	76.4	1.4	19.5	0.1	2.6
Drop-out Rate (%)	0.0	0.0	0.0	0.0	n/a	0.0
H.S. Diplomas (#)	353	249	8	86	0	10

Millburn Twp

434 Millburn Ave • Millburn, NJ 07041-1210
(973) 376-3600 • http://schools.millburn.org/
Grade Span: PK-12; **Agency Type:** 1
Schools: 7
6 Primary; 0 Middle; 1 High; 0 Other Level
7 Regular; 0 Special Education; 0 Vocational; 0 Alternative
0 Magnet; 0 Charter; 0 Title I Eligible; 0 School-wide Title I
Students: 4,186 (51.5% male; 48.5% female)
Individual Education Program: 527 (12.6%);
English Language Learner: 57 (1.4%); Migrant: 0 (0.0%)
Eligible for Free Lunch Program: 24 (0.6%)
Eligible for Reduced-Price Lunch Program: 6 (0.1%)
Teachers: 330.6 (12.7 to 1)
Librarians/Media Specialists: 8.0 (523.3 to 1)
Guidance Counselors: 9.0 (465.1 to 1)
Current Spending: ($ per student per year):
Total: $10,735; Instruction: $6,366; Support Services: $4,223

Enrollment, Drop-out Rates and Diploma Recipients by Race/Ethnicity

Category	Total	White	Black	Asian	AIAN	Hisp.
Enrollment (%)	100.0	84.9	1.0	11.8	0.1	2.1
Drop-out Rate (%)	0.1	0.1	0.0	0.0	n/a	0.0
H.S. Diplomas (#)	218	189	2	25	0	2

Montclair Town

22 Valley Rd • Montclair, NJ 07042-2709
(973) 509-4010 • http://www.montclair.k12.nj.us
Grade Span: PK-12; **Agency Type:** 1
Schools: 11
7 Primary; 3 Middle; 1 High; 0 Other Level
11 Regular; 0 Special Education; 0 Vocational; 0 Alternative
0 Magnet; 0 Charter; 5 Title I Eligible; 0 School-wide Title I
Students: 6,363 (50.8% male; 49.2% female)
Individual Education Program: 1,128 (17.7%);
English Language Learner: 79 (1.2%); Migrant: 0 (0.0%)
Eligible for Free Lunch Program: 835 (13.1%)
Eligible for Reduced-Price Lunch Program: 313 (4.9%)
Teachers: 528.5 (12.0 to 1)
Librarians/Media Specialists: 8.8 (723.1 to 1)
Guidance Counselors: 13.0 (489.5 to 1)
Current Spending: ($ per student per year):
Total: $11,198; Instruction: $7,214; Support Services: $3,794

Enrollment, Drop-out Rates and Diploma Recipients by Race/Ethnicity

Category	Total	White	Black	Asian	AIAN	Hisp.
Enrollment (%)	100.0	47.3	43.0	4.4	0.3	5.1
Drop-out Rate (%)	0.9	0.5	0.9	1.5	n/a	4.3
H.S. Diplomas (#)	348	151	171	13	0	13

Newark City

2 Cedar St • Newark, NJ 07102-3015
(973) 733-7333 • http://www.nps.k12.nj.us
Grade Span: PK-12; **Agency Type:** 1
Schools: 77
52 Primary; 7 Middle; 11 High; 7 Other Level
71 Regular; 5 Special Education; 0 Vocational; 1 Alternative

0 Magnet; 0 Charter; 50 Title I Eligible; 50 School-wide Title I
Students: 42,395 (51.3% male; 48.7% female)
Individual Education Program: 6,630 (15.6%);
English Language Learner: 3,700 (8.7%); Migrant: 0 (0.0%)
Eligible for Free Lunch Program: 28,866 (68.1%)
Eligible for Reduced-Price Lunch Program: 3,507 (8.3%)
Teachers: 3,684.0 (11.5 to 1)
Librarians/Media Specialists: 63.0 (672.9 to 1)
Guidance Counselors: 119.0 (356.3 to 1)
Current Spending: ($ per student per year):
Total: $14,694; Instruction: $7,924; Support Services: $6,225

Enrollment, Drop-out Rates and Diploma Recipients by Race/Ethnicity

Category	Total	White	Black	Asian	AIAN	Hisp.
Enrollment (%)	100.0	8.2	59.1	0.9	0.1	31.7
Drop-out Rate (%)	6.5	2.3	8.3	1.0	0.0	4.0
H.S. Diplomas (#)	1,699	205	1,035	12	0	447

Nutley Town
375 Bloomfield Ave • Nutley, NJ 07110-2252
(973) 661-8798 • http://www.nutleyschools.org
Grade Span: PK-12; **Agency Type:** 1
Schools: 7
5 Primary; 1 Middle; 1 High; 0 Other Level
7 Regular; 0 Special Education; 0 Vocational; 0 Alternative
0 Magnet; 0 Charter; 2 Title I Eligible; 0 School-wide Title I
Students: 4,220 (51.2% male; 48.8% female)
Individual Education Program: 563 (13.3%);
English Language Learner: 68 (1.6%); Migrant: 0 (0.0%)
Eligible for Free Lunch Program: 111 (2.6%)
Eligible for Reduced-Price Lunch Program: 94 (2.2%)
Teachers: 269.6 (15.7 to 1)
Librarians/Media Specialists: 7.7 (548.1 to 1)
Guidance Counselors: 8.0 (527.5 to 1)
Current Spending: ($ per student per year):
Total: $9,360; Instruction: $5,965; Support Services: $3,214

Enrollment, Drop-out Rates and Diploma Recipients by Race/Ethnicity

Category	Total	White	Black	Asian	AIAN	Hisp.
Enrollment (%)	100.0	81.5	1.4	8.5	0.0	8.6
Drop-out Rate (%)	1.1	0.6	5.9	2.7	n/a	3.9
H.S. Diplomas (#)	266	226	4	28	0	8

South Orange-Maplewood
525 Academy St • Maplewood, NJ 07040-1311
(973) 378-9630 • http://www.somsd.k12.nj.us
Grade Span: PK-12; **Agency Type:** 1
Schools: 9
6 Primary; 2 Middle; 1 High; 0 Other Level
9 Regular; 0 Special Education; 0 Vocational; 0 Alternative
0 Magnet; 0 Charter; 4 Title I Eligible; 0 School-wide Title I
Students: 6,364 (51.4% male; 48.6% female)
Individual Education Program: 777 (12.2%);
English Language Learner: 91 (1.4%); Migrant: 0 (0.0%)
Eligible for Free Lunch Program: 708 (11.1%)
Eligible for Reduced-Price Lunch Program: 363 (5.7%)
Teachers: 463.0 (13.7 to 1)
Librarians/Media Specialists: 11.8 (539.3 to 1)
Guidance Counselors: 15.0 (424.3 to 1)
Current Spending: ($ per student per year):
Total: $10,538; Instruction: $5,729; Support Services: $4,605

Enrollment, Drop-out Rates and Diploma Recipients by Race/Ethnicity

Category	Total	White	Black	Asian	AIAN	Hisp.
Enrollment (%)	100.0	41.0	51.5	3.2	0.2	4.2
Drop-out Rate (%)	2.6	0.7	3.5	3.6	0.0	6.3
H.S. Diplomas (#)	417	157	226	21	0	13

Verona Boro
121 Fairview Ave • Verona, NJ 07044-1320
(973) 239-2100 • http://veronaschools.org
Grade Span: PK-12; **Agency Type:** 1
Schools: 6
4 Primary; 1 Middle; 1 High; 0 Other Level
6 Regular; 0 Special Education; 0 Vocational; 0 Alternative
0 Magnet; 0 Charter; 0 Title I Eligible; 0 School-wide Title I
Students: 2,010 (51.7% male; 48.3% female)
Individual Education Program: 343 (17.1%);
English Language Learner: 12 (0.6%); Migrant: 0 (0.0%)
Eligible for Free Lunch Program: 3 (0.1%)
Eligible for Reduced-Price Lunch Program: 6 (0.3%)
Teachers: 138.7 (14.5 to 1)
Librarians/Media Specialists: 4.0 (502.5 to 1)
Guidance Counselors: 5.0 (402.0 to 1)
Current Spending: ($ per student per year):
Total: $10,864; Instruction: $6,995; Support Services: $3,680

Enrollment, Drop-out Rates and Diploma Recipients by Race/Ethnicity

Category	Total	White	Black	Asian	AIAN	Hisp.
Enrollment (%)	100.0	89.9	1.9	4.6	0.2	3.3
Drop-out Rate (%)	0.2	0.2	0.0	0.0	n/a	0.0
H.S. Diplomas (#)	114	95	3	6	2	8

West Orange Town
179 Eagle Rock Ave • West Orange, NJ 07052-5007
(973) 669-5430 • http://www.westorange.k12.nj.us
Grade Span: PK-12; **Agency Type:** 1
Schools: 10
7 Primary; 2 Middle; 1 High; 0 Other Level
10 Regular; 0 Special Education; 0 Vocational; 0 Alternative
0 Magnet; 0 Charter; 3 Title I Eligible; 0 School-wide Title I
Students: 6,278 (51.9% male; 48.1% female)
Individual Education Program: 863 (13.7%);
English Language Learner: 279 (4.4%); Migrant: 0 (0.0%)
Eligible for Free Lunch Program: 716 (11.4%)
Eligible for Reduced-Price Lunch Program: 394 (6.3%)
Teachers: 499.0 (12.6 to 1)
Librarians/Media Specialists: 10.0 (627.8 to 1)
Guidance Counselors: 17.9 (350.7 to 1)
Current Spending: ($ per student per year):
Total: $11,577; Instruction: $7,048; Support Services: $4,293

Enrollment, Drop-out Rates and Diploma Recipients by Race/Ethnicity

Category	Total	White	Black	Asian	AIAN	Hisp.
Enrollment (%)	100.0	35.8	36.8	8.5	0.0	18.9
Drop-out Rate (%)	2.3	1.4	2.2	0.6	n/a	6.7
H.S. Diplomas (#)	355	166	108	34	0	47

Gloucester County

Clearview Regional
420 Cedar Rd • Mullica Hill, NJ 08062-9436
(856) 223-2765 • http://www.clearviewregional.edu/
Grade Span: 07-12; **Agency Type:** 1
Schools: 2
0 Primary; 1 Middle; 1 High; 0 Other Level
2 Regular; 0 Special Education; 0 Vocational; 0 Alternative
0 Magnet; 0 Charter; 1 Title I Eligible; 0 School-wide Title I
Students: 2,035 (50.8% male; 49.2% female)
Individual Education Program: 296 (14.5%);
English Language Learner: 0 (0.0%); Migrant: 0 (0.0%)
Eligible for Free Lunch Program: 58 (2.9%)
Eligible for Reduced-Price Lunch Program: 52 (2.6%)
Teachers: 147.8 (13.8 to 1)
Librarians/Media Specialists: 2.0 (1,017.5 to 1)
Guidance Counselors: 6.0 (339.2 to 1)
Current Spending: ($ per student per year):
Total: $9,923; Instruction: $5,966; Support Services: $3,602

Enrollment, Drop-out Rates and Diploma Recipients by Race/Ethnicity

Category	Total	White	Black	Asian	AIAN	Hisp.
Enrollment (%)	100.0	96.0	2.1	0.7	0.0	1.1
Drop-out Rate (%)	1.0	0.9	0.0	0.0	0.0	12.5
H.S. Diplomas (#)	257	245	6	4	0	2

Delsea Regional HS District
242 Fries Mill Rd • Franklinville, NJ 08322-9139
Mailing Address: PO Box 405 • Franklinville, NJ 08322-9139
(856) 694-0100 • http://www.delsea.k12.nj.us
Grade Span: 07-12; **Agency Type:** 1
Schools: 2
0 Primary; 1 Middle; 1 High; 0 Other Level
2 Regular; 0 Special Education; 0 Vocational; 0 Alternative
0 Magnet; 0 Charter; 2 Title I Eligible; 0 School-wide Title I
Students: 1,905 (52.1% male; 47.9% female)
Individual Education Program: 327 (17.2%);
English Language Learner: 8 (0.4%); Migrant: 4 (0.2%)
Eligible for Free Lunch Program: 219 (11.5%)
Eligible for Reduced-Price Lunch Program: 177 (9.3%)
Teachers: 136.0 (14.0 to 1)
Librarians/Media Specialists: 3.0 (635.0 to 1)
Guidance Counselors: 7.0 (272.1 to 1)
Current Spending: ($ per student per year):
Total: $10,675; Instruction: $6,375; Support Services: $3,964

Enrollment, Drop-out Rates and Diploma Recipients by Race/Ethnicity

Category	Total	White	Black	Asian	AIAN	Hisp.
Enrollment (%)	100.0	84.6	11.3	0.8	0.0	3.3
Drop-out Rate (%)	1.7	1.4	3.9	0.0	n/a	3.7
H.S. Diplomas (#)	253	223	21	1	0	8

Deptford Twp

2022 Good Intent Rd • Deptford, NJ 08096-4333
(856) 232-2700 • http://www.deptford.k12.nj.us
Grade Span: PK-12; **Agency Type:** 1
Schools: 9
6 Primary; 1 Middle; 1 High; 1 Other Level
8 Regular; 1 Special Education; 0 Vocational; 0 Alternative
0 Magnet; 0 Charter; 6 Title I Eligible; 0 School-wide Title I
Students: 4,196 (51.6% male; 48.4% female)
Individual Education Program: 792 (18.9%);
English Language Learner: 39 (0.9%); Migrant: 0 (0.0%)
Eligible for Free Lunch Program: 820 (19.5%)
Eligible for Reduced-Price Lunch Program: 421 (10.0%)
Teachers: 269.0 (15.6 to 1)
Librarians/Media Specialists: 8.0 (524.5 to 1)
Guidance Counselors: 8.0 (524.5 to 1)
Current Spending: ($ per student per year):
Total: $9,732; Instruction: $5,890; Support Services: $3,538
Enrollment, Drop-out Rates and Diploma Recipients by Race/Ethnicity

Category	Total	White	Black	Asian	AIAN	Hisp.
Enrollment (%)	100.0	74.3	20.1	2.1	0.2	3.3
Drop-out Rate (%)	2.6	2.2	4.4	0.0	0.0	4.0
H.S. Diplomas (#)	197	145	43	2	0	7

Glassboro

George Beach Adm Bldg • Glassboro, NJ 08028
(856) 881-0123 • http://www.glassboro.k12.nj.us
Grade Span: PK-12; **Agency Type:** 1
Schools: 5
2 Primary; 2 Middle; 1 High; 0 Other Level
5 Regular; 0 Special Education; 0 Vocational; 0 Alternative
0 Magnet; 0 Charter; 5 Title I Eligible; 0 School-wide Title I
Students: 2,485 (50.5% male; 49.5% female)
Individual Education Program: 522 (21.0%);
English Language Learner: 28 (1.1%); Migrant: 1 (<0.1%)
Eligible for Free Lunch Program: 658 (26.5%)
Eligible for Reduced-Price Lunch Program: 258 (10.4%)
Teachers: 197.0 (12.6 to 1)
Librarians/Media Specialists: 4.0 (621.3 to 1)
Guidance Counselors: 6.9 (360.1 to 1)
Current Spending: ($ per student per year):
Total: $10,035; Instruction: $5,947; Support Services: $3,824
Enrollment, Drop-out Rates and Diploma Recipients by Race/Ethnicity

Category	Total	White	Black	Asian	AIAN	Hisp.
Enrollment (%)	100.0	54.6	36.9	3.6	0.1	4.8
Drop-out Rate (%)	3.4	2.1	4.9	5.6	n/a	4.2
H.S. Diplomas (#)	139	75	56	4	0	4

Kingsway Regional

213 Kings Hwy • Woolwich Twp, NJ 08085-9608
(856) 467-4600
Grade Span: 07-12; **Agency Type:** 1
Schools: 2
0 Primary; 1 Middle; 1 High; 0 Other Level
2 Regular; 0 Special Education; 0 Vocational; 0 Alternative
0 Magnet; 0 Charter; 1 Title I Eligible; 0 School-wide Title I
Students: 1,660 (51.3% male; 48.7% female)
Individual Education Program: 192 (11.6%);
English Language Learner: 7 (0.4%); Migrant: 4 (0.2%)
Eligible for Free Lunch Program: 84 (5.1%)
Eligible for Reduced-Price Lunch Program: 61 (3.7%)
Teachers: 114.3 (14.5 to 1)
Librarians/Media Specialists: 2.0 (830.0 to 1)
Guidance Counselors: 7.0 (237.1 to 1)
Current Spending: ($ per student per year):
Total: $10,492; Instruction: $5,491; Support Services: $3,974
Enrollment, Drop-out Rates and Diploma Recipients by Race/Ethnicity

Category	Total	White	Black	Asian	AIAN	Hisp.
Enrollment (%)	100.0	84.0	11.1	1.6	0.0	3.3
Drop-out Rate (%)	1.8	1.6	3.7	0.0	n/a	0.0
H.S. Diplomas (#)	223	196	22	0	2	3

Monroe Twp

75 E Academy St • Williamstown, NJ 08094
(856) 629-6400 • http://www.monroetwp.k12.nj.us
Grade Span: PK-12; **Agency Type:** 1
Schools: 6
4 Primary; 1 Middle; 1 High; 0 Other Level
6 Regular; 0 Special Education; 0 Vocational; 0 Alternative
0 Magnet; 0 Charter; 4 Title I Eligible; 0 School-wide Title I
Students: 5,117 (51.5% male; 48.5% female)
Individual Education Program: 904 (17.7%);
English Language Learner: 27 (0.5%); Migrant: 2 (<0.1%)
Eligible for Free Lunch Program: 754 (14.7%)
Eligible for Reduced-Price Lunch Program: 351 (6.9%)
Teachers: 361.7 (14.1 to 1)
Librarians/Media Specialists: 4.5 (1,137.1 to 1)
Guidance Counselors: 11.5 (445.0 to 1)
Current Spending: ($ per student per year):
Total: $8,731; Instruction: $4,894; Support Services: $3,558
Enrollment, Drop-out Rates and Diploma Recipients by Race/Ethnicity

Category	Total	White	Black	Asian	AIAN	Hisp.
Enrollment (%)	100.0	77.7	17.0	1.7	0.2	3.4
Drop-out Rate (%)	2.9	3.1	2.1	0.0	0.0	5.0
H.S. Diplomas (#)	264	209	46	4	0	5

Paulsboro Boro

662 N Delaware St • Paulsboro, NJ 08066-1020
(856) 423-5515
Grade Span: PK-12; **Agency Type:** 1
Schools: 3
2 Primary; 0 Middle; 1 High; 0 Other Level
3 Regular; 0 Special Education; 0 Vocational; 0 Alternative
0 Magnet; 0 Charter; 3 Title I Eligible; 0 School-wide Title I
Students: 1,525 (52.5% male; 47.5% female)
Individual Education Program: 299 (19.6%);
English Language Learner: 0 (0.0%); Migrant: 0 (0.0%)
Eligible for Free Lunch Program: 649 (42.6%)
Eligible for Reduced-Price Lunch Program: 132 (8.7%)
Teachers: 113.0 (13.5 to 1)
Librarians/Media Specialists: 3.0 (508.3 to 1)
Guidance Counselors: 3.0 (508.3 to 1)
Current Spending: ($ per student per year):
Total: $9,468; Instruction: $5,795; Support Services: $3,293
Enrollment, Drop-out Rates and Diploma Recipients by Race/Ethnicity

Category	Total	White	Black	Asian	AIAN	Hisp.
Enrollment (%)	100.0	50.8	44.3	0.7	0.4	3.8
Drop-out Rate (%)	5.0	3.8	9.0	0.0	n/a	0.0
H.S. Diplomas (#)	111	84	27	0	0	0

Pitman Boro

420 Hudson Ave • Pitman, NJ 08071-0088
(856) 589-2145 • http://pitman.k12.nj.us
Grade Span: PK-12; **Agency Type:** 1
Schools: 5
3 Primary; 1 Middle; 1 High; 0 Other Level
5 Regular; 0 Special Education; 0 Vocational; 0 Alternative
0 Magnet; 0 Charter; 2 Title I Eligible; 0 School-wide Title I
Students: 1,662 (48.7% male; 51.3% female)
Individual Education Program: 326 (19.6%);
English Language Learner: 0 (0.0%); Migrant: 0 (0.0%)
Eligible for Free Lunch Program: 108 (6.5%)
Eligible for Reduced-Price Lunch Program: 86 (5.2%)
Teachers: 137.6 (12.1 to 1)
Librarians/Media Specialists: 3.0 (554.0 to 1)
Guidance Counselors: 5.0 (332.4 to 1)
Current Spending: ($ per student per year):
Total: $9,910; Instruction: $6,390; Support Services: $3,297
Enrollment, Drop-out Rates and Diploma Recipients by Race/Ethnicity

Category	Total	White	Black	Asian	AIAN	Hisp.
Enrollment (%)	100.0	97.2	0.7	1.3	0.0	0.8
Drop-out Rate (%)	2.7	2.8	0.0	0.0	n/a	0.0
H.S. Diplomas (#)	112	110	0	1	0	1

Washington Twp

206 E Holly Ave • Sewell, NJ 08080-9231
(856) 589-6644 • http://www.wtps.org
Grade Span: PK-12; **Agency Type:** 1
Schools: 11
7 Primary; 3 Middle; 1 High; 0 Other Level
11 Regular; 0 Special Education; 0 Vocational; 0 Alternative
0 Magnet; 0 Charter; 7 Title I Eligible; 0 School-wide Title I
Students: 9,746 (51.1% male; 48.9% female)
Individual Education Program: 1,751 (18.0%);
English Language Learner: 35 (0.4%); Migrant: 0 (0.0%)
Eligible for Free Lunch Program: 431 (4.4%)
Eligible for Reduced-Price Lunch Program: 288 (3.0%)
Teachers: 737.1 (13.2 to 1)
Librarians/Media Specialists: 12.0 (812.2 to 1)
Guidance Counselors: 30.0 (324.9 to 1)
Current Spending: ($ per student per year):
Total: $9,171; Instruction: $5,386; Support Services: $3,413
Enrollment, Drop-out Rates and Diploma Recipients by Race/Ethnicity

Category	Total	White	Black	Asian	AIAN	Hisp.
Enrollment (%)	100.0	88.6	6.1	3.7	0.0	1.6
Drop-out Rate (%)	1.7	1.7	1.7	0.0	n/a	3.0
H.S. Diplomas (#)	675	595	40	33	0	7

West Deptford Twp

675 Grove Road, Ste 804 • West Deptford, NJ 08066-1999
(856) 848-4300 • http://www.wdeptford.k12.nj.us/
Grade Span: PK-12; **Agency Type:** 1
Schools: 5
3 Primary; 1 Middle; 1 High; 0 Other Level
5 Regular; 0 Special Education; 0 Vocational; 0 Alternative
0 Magnet; 0 Charter; 3 Title I Eligible; 0 School-wide Title I
Students: 3,101 (53.1% male; 46.9% female)
Individual Education Program: 651 (21.0%);
English Language Learner: 8 (0.3%); Migrant: 0 (0.0%)
Eligible for Free Lunch Program: 251 (8.1%)
Eligible for Reduced-Price Lunch Program: 205 (6.6%)
Teachers: 208.6 (14.9 to 1)
Librarians/Media Specialists: 4.0 (775.3 to 1)
Guidance Counselors: 10.0 (310.1 to 1)
Current Spending: ($ per student per year):
Total: $9,412; Instruction: $5,344; Support Services: $3,763
Enrollment, Drop-out Rates and Diploma Recipients by Race/Ethnicity

Category	Total	White	Black	Asian	AIAN	Hisp.
Enrollment (%)	100.0	90.0	7.0	1.4	0.0	1.6
Drop-out Rate (%)	0.4	0.4	1.6	0.0	n/a	0.0
H.S. Diplomas (#)	227	205	13	4	0	5

Woodbury City

25 N Broad St • Woodbury, NJ 08096-4602
(856) 853-0123 • http://www.woodburysch.com/
Grade Span: PK-12; **Agency Type:** 1
Schools: 4
3 Primary; 0 Middle; 0 High; 1 Other Level
4 Regular; 0 Special Education; 0 Vocational; 0 Alternative
0 Magnet; 0 Charter; 2 Title I Eligible; 0 School-wide Title I
Students: 1,529 (52.1% male; 47.9% female)
Individual Education Program: 336 (22.0%);
English Language Learner: 3 (0.2%); Migrant: 0 (0.0%)
Eligible for Free Lunch Program: 513 (33.6%)
Eligible for Reduced-Price Lunch Program: 161 (10.5%)
Teachers: 144.1 (10.6 to 1)
Librarians/Media Specialists: 3.0 (509.7 to 1)
Guidance Counselors: 6.0 (254.8 to 1)
Current Spending: ($ per student per year):
Total: $11,855; Instruction: $7,411; Support Services: $4,150
Enrollment, Drop-out Rates and Diploma Recipients by Race/Ethnicity

Category	Total	White	Black	Asian	AIAN	Hisp.
Enrollment (%)	100.0	51.9	39.4	1.6	0.1	7.0
Drop-out Rate (%)	4.6	3.8	6.9	0.0	n/a	0.0
H.S. Diplomas (#)	103	70	27	3	0	3

Hudson County

Bayonne City

Ave A And 29th St • Bayonne, NJ 07002
(201) 858-5817 • http://www.bhs.bboed.org
Grade Span: PK-12; **Agency Type:** 1
Schools: 12
10 Primary; 1 Middle; 1 High; 0 Other Level
12 Regular; 0 Special Education; 0 Vocational; 0 Alternative
0 Magnet; 0 Charter; 6 Title I Eligible; 0 School-wide Title I
Students: 8,426 (52.3% male; 47.7% female)
Individual Education Program: 1,584 (18.8%);
English Language Learner: 291 (3.5%); Migrant: 0 (0.0%)
Eligible for Free Lunch Program: 2,517 (29.9%)
Eligible for Reduced-Price Lunch Program: 828 (9.8%)
Teachers: 616.0 (13.7 to 1)
Librarians/Media Specialists: 6.0 (1,404.3 to 1)
Guidance Counselors: 19.2 (438.9 to 1)
Current Spending: ($ per student per year):
Total: $10,419; Instruction: $6,665; Support Services: $3,486
Enrollment, Drop-out Rates and Diploma Recipients by Race/Ethnicity

Category	Total	White	Black	Asian	AIAN	Hisp.
Enrollment (%)	100.0	58.8	8.3	4.4	0.2	28.3
Drop-out Rate (%)	1.9	1.3	1.8	1.8	0.0	3.3
H.S. Diplomas (#)	440	262	41	30	0	107

Harrison Town

430 William St • Harrison, NJ 07029-1430
(973) 483-4627 • http://www.harrison.k12.nj.us
Grade Span: PK-12; **Agency Type:** 1
Schools: 3
1 Primary; 1 Middle; 1 High; 0 Other Level
3 Regular; 0 Special Education; 0 Vocational; 0 Alternative
0 Magnet; 0 Charter; 3 Title I Eligible; 0 School-wide Title I
Students: 1,943 (52.3% male; 47.7% female)
Individual Education Program: 224 (11.5%);
English Language Learner: 291 (15.0%); Migrant: 0 (0.0%)
Eligible for Free Lunch Program: 515 (26.5%)
Eligible for Reduced-Price Lunch Program: 136 (7.0%)
Teachers: 129.2 (15.0 to 1)
Librarians/Media Specialists: 0.4 (4,857.5 to 1)
Guidance Counselors: 3.6 (539.7 to 1)
Current Spending: ($ per student per year):
Total: $11,908; Instruction: $8,068; Support Services: $3,703
Enrollment, Drop-out Rates and Diploma Recipients by Race/Ethnicity

Category	Total	White	Black	Asian	AIAN	Hisp.
Enrollment (%)	100.0	37.0	0.6	7.1	0.4	55.0
Drop-out Rate (%)	1.0	1.4	0.0	0.0	n/a	0.8
H.S. Diplomas (#)	148	52	2	9	0	85

Hoboken City

1115 Clinton St • Hoboken, NJ 07030-3201
(201) 420-2151 • http://www.hobokenk12.powertolearn.net/
Grade Span: PK-12; **Agency Type:** 1
Schools: 6
3 Primary; 2 Middle; 1 High; 0 Other Level
6 Regular; 0 Special Education; 0 Vocational; 0 Alternative
0 Magnet; 0 Charter; 5 Title I Eligible; 0 School-wide Title I
Students: 2,121 (52.9% male; 47.1% female)
Individual Education Program: 435 (20.5%);
English Language Learner: 42 (2.0%); Migrant: 0 (0.0%)
Eligible for Free Lunch Program: 1,322 (62.3%)
Eligible for Reduced-Price Lunch Program: 140 (6.6%)
Teachers: 208.6 (10.2 to 1)
Librarians/Media Specialists: 3.0 (707.0 to 1)
Guidance Counselors: 6.0 (353.5 to 1)
Current Spending: ($ per student per year):
Total: $20,007; Instruction: $12,783; Support Services: $6,755
Enrollment, Drop-out Rates and Diploma Recipients by Race/Ethnicity

Category	Total	White	Black	Asian	AIAN	Hisp.
Enrollment (%)	100.0	16.0	16.4	1.8	0.0	65.8
Drop-out Rate (%)	2.7	0.0	2.9	0.0	n/a	3.4
H.S. Diplomas (#)	137	19	20	6	0	92

Jersey City

346 Claremont Ave • Jersey City, NJ 07305-1634
(201) 915-6202 • http://www.jerseycity.k12.nj.us
Grade Span: PK-12; **Agency Type:** 1
Schools: 40
29 Primary; 4 Middle; 6 High; 1 Other Level
38 Regular; 2 Special Education; 0 Vocational; 0 Alternative
0 Magnet; 0 Charter; 29 Title I Eligible; 29 School-wide Title I
Students: 31,259 (51.3% male; 48.7% female)
Individual Education Program: 5,110 (16.3%);
English Language Learner: 2,561 (8.2%); Migrant: 0 (0.0%)
Eligible for Free Lunch Program: 18,261 (58.4%)
Eligible for Reduced-Price Lunch Program: 4,247 (13.6%)
Teachers: 2,666.8 (11.7 to 1)
Librarians/Media Specialists: 41.0 (762.4 to 1)
Guidance Counselors: 127.0 (246.1 to 1)
Current Spending: ($ per student per year):
Total: $13,179; Instruction: $8,163; Support Services: $4,653
Enrollment, Drop-out Rates and Diploma Recipients by Race/Ethnicity

Category	Total	White	Black	Asian	AIAN	Hisp.
Enrollment (%)	100.0	9.5	36.3	14.0	0.9	39.3
Drop-out Rate (%)	6.1	7.5	5.8	0.0	107.4	7.5
H.S. Diplomas (#)	1,293	100	495	247	1	450

Kearny Town

100 Davis Ave • Kearny, NJ 07032-2612
(201) 955-5021 • http://www.kearnyschools.com/
Grade Span: PK-12; **Agency Type:** 1
Schools: 7
6 Primary; 0 Middle; 1 High; 0 Other Level
7 Regular; 0 Special Education; 0 Vocational; 0 Alternative
0 Magnet; 0 Charter; 3 Title I Eligible; 0 School-wide Title I
Students: 5,349 (51.9% male; 48.1% female)
Individual Education Program: 697 (13.0%);
English Language Learner: 416 (7.8%); Migrant: 0 (0.0%)
Eligible for Free Lunch Program: 1,118 (20.9%)
Eligible for Reduced-Price Lunch Program: 512 (9.6%)
Teachers: 372.5 (14.4 to 1)
Librarians/Media Specialists: 8.0 (668.6 to 1)
Guidance Counselors: 14.0 (382.1 to 1)
Current Spending: ($ per student per year):
Total: $10,598; Instruction: $7,275; Support Services: $3,128
Enrollment, Drop-out Rates and Diploma Recipients by Race/Ethnicity

Category	Total	White	Black	Asian	AIAN	Hisp.
Enrollment (%)	100.0	52.6	1.1	4.1	0.1	42.0
Drop-out Rate (%)	3.6	2.2	0.0	1.5	0.0	6.2
H.S. Diplomas (#)	375	250	11	12	3	99

North Bergen Twp

7317 Kennedy Blvd • North Bergen, NJ 07047-4097
(201) 295-3985 • http://www.northbergen.k12.nj.us
Grade Span: PK-12; **Agency Type:** 1
Schools: 7
6 Primary; 0 Middle; 1 High; 0 Other Level
7 Regular; 0 Special Education; 0 Vocational; 0 Alternative
0 Magnet; 0 Charter; 7 Title I Eligible; 0 School-wide Title I
Students: 7,419 (51.6% male; 48.4% female)
Individual Education Program: 878 (11.8%);
English Language Learner: 782 (10.5%); Migrant: 0 (0.0%)
Eligible for Free Lunch Program: 2,894 (39.0%)
Eligible for Reduced-Price Lunch Program: 955 (12.9%)
Teachers: 479.0 (15.5 to 1)
Librarians/Media Specialists: 4.0 (1,854.8 to 1)
Guidance Counselors: 15.0 (494.6 to 1)
Current Spending: ($ per student per year):
Total: $8,774; Instruction: $5,374; Support Services: $3,205
Enrollment, Drop-out Rates and Diploma Recipients by Race/Ethnicity

Category	Total	White	Black	Asian	AIAN	Hisp.
Enrollment (%)	100.0	16.6	1.4	5.6	0.0	76.4
Drop-out Rate (%)	4.2	4.0	0.0	0.0	0.0	4.8
H.S. Diplomas (#)	426	97	8	33	0	288

Secaucus Town

20 Centre Ave • Secaucus, NJ 07096-1496
Mailing Address: PO Box 149 • Secaucus, NJ 07096-1496
(201) 974-2004
Grade Span: PK-12; **Agency Type:** 1
Schools: 4
2 Primary; 1 Middle; 1 High; 0 Other Level
4 Regular; 0 Special Education; 0 Vocational; 0 Alternative
0 Magnet; 0 Charter; 3 Title I Eligible; 0 School-wide Title I
Students: 1,799 (51.4% male; 48.6% female)
Individual Education Program: 228 (12.7%);
English Language Learner: 39 (2.2%); Migrant: 0 (0.0%)
Eligible for Free Lunch Program: 231 (12.8%)
Eligible for Reduced-Price Lunch Program: 131 (7.3%)
Teachers: 135.2 (13.3 to 1)
Librarians/Media Specialists: 1.0 (1,799.0 to 1)
Guidance Counselors: 7.0 (257.0 to 1)
Current Spending: ($ per student per year):
Total: $11,425; Instruction: $6,640; Support Services: $4,346
Enrollment, Drop-out Rates and Diploma Recipients by Race/Ethnicity

Category	Total	White	Black	Asian	AIAN	Hisp.
Enrollment (%)	100.0	62.1	2.2	17.4	0.0	18.3
Drop-out Rate (%)	0.2	0.3	0.0	0.0	n/a	0.0
H.S. Diplomas (#)	120	72	3	20	0	25

Union City

3912 Bergen Turnpike • Union City, NJ 07087-2507
(201) 348-5851 • http://www.union-city.k12.nj.us
Grade Span: PK-12; **Agency Type:** 1
Schools: 11
8 Primary; 1 Middle; 2 High; 0 Other Level
11 Regular; 0 Special Education; 0 Vocational; 0 Alternative
0 Magnet; 0 Charter; 10 Title I Eligible; 10 School-wide Title I
Students: 10,024 (51.5% male; 48.5% female)
Individual Education Program: 1,176 (11.7%);
English Language Learner: 4,267 (42.6%); Migrant: 0 (0.0%)
Eligible for Free Lunch Program: 7,931 (79.1%)
Eligible for Reduced-Price Lunch Program: 826 (8.2%)
Teachers: 788.1 (12.7 to 1)
Librarians/Media Specialists: 4.2 (2,386.7 to 1)
Guidance Counselors: 17.0 (589.6 to 1)
Current Spending: ($ per student per year):
Total: $11,286; Instruction: $7,256; Support Services: $3,685
Enrollment, Drop-out Rates and Diploma Recipients by Race/Ethnicity

Category	Total	White	Black	Asian	AIAN	Hisp.
Enrollment (%)	100.0	3.8	0.7	1.2	0.1	94.2
Drop-out Rate (%)	2.5	0.8	6.7	0.0	n/a	2.6
H.S. Diplomas (#)	560	30	4	18	0	508

West New York Town

6028 Broadway • West New York, NJ 07093-5223
(201) 902-1123 • http://www.wnyschools.net/index2.htm
Grade Span: PK-12; **Agency Type:** 1
Schools: 8
7 Primary; 0 Middle; 1 High; 0 Other Level
8 Regular; 0 Special Education; 0 Vocational; 0 Alternative
0 Magnet; 0 Charter; 6 Title I Eligible; 0 School-wide Title I
Students: 6,591 (51.6% male; 48.4% female)
Individual Education Program: 982 (14.9%);
English Language Learner: 1,152 (17.5%); Migrant: 0 (0.0%)
Eligible for Free Lunch Program: 3,704 (56.2%)
Eligible for Reduced-Price Lunch Program: 957 (14.5%)
Teachers: 502.7 (13.1 to 1)
Librarians/Media Specialists: 6.0 (1,098.5 to 1)
Guidance Counselors: 13.2 (499.3 to 1)
Current Spending: ($ per student per year):
Total: $12,520; Instruction: $7,840; Support Services: $4,441
Enrollment, Drop-out Rates and Diploma Recipients by Race/Ethnicity

Category	Total	White	Black	Asian	AIAN	Hisp.
Enrollment (%)	100.0	4.1	0.5	1.1	0.0	94.3
Drop-out Rate (%)	0.6	1.1	0.0	0.0	0.0	0.6
H.S. Diplomas (#)	357	16	19	9	0	313

Hunterdon County

Clinton Twp

11 Humphrey Rd • Annandale, NJ 08801-0006
(908) 735-8320 • http://www.ctsd.k12.nj.us
Grade Span: PK-08; **Agency Type:** 1
Schools: 3
2 Primary; 1 Middle; 0 High; 0 Other Level
3 Regular; 0 Special Education; 0 Vocational; 0 Alternative
0 Magnet; 0 Charter; 0 Title I Eligible; 0 School-wide Title I
Students: 1,781 (48.6% male; 51.4% female)
Individual Education Program: 265 (14.9%);
English Language Learner: 9 (0.5%); Migrant: 0 (0.0%)
Eligible for Free Lunch Program: 14 (0.8%)
Eligible for Reduced-Price Lunch Program: 0 (0.0%)
Teachers: 133.3 (13.4 to 1)
Librarians/Media Specialists: 3.0 (593.7 to 1)
Guidance Counselors: 4.0 (445.3 to 1)
Current Spending: ($ per student per year):
Total: $8,861; Instruction: $5,126; Support Services: $3,735
Enrollment, Drop-out Rates and Diploma Recipients by Race/Ethnicity

Category	Total	White	Black	Asian	AIAN	Hisp.
Enrollment (%)	100.0	93.9	1.5	3.1	0.1	1.4
Drop-out Rate (%)	n/a	n/a	n/a	n/a	n/a	n/a
H.S. Diplomas (#)	n/a	n/a	n/a	n/a	n/a	n/a

Flemington-Raritan Reg

50 Court St • Flemington, NJ 08822-1325
(908) 284-7561 • http://www.frsd.k12.nj.us
Grade Span: PK-08; **Agency Type:** 1
Schools: 5
4 Primary; 1 Middle; 0 High; 0 Other Level
5 Regular; 0 Special Education; 0 Vocational; 0 Alternative
0 Magnet; 0 Charter; 3 Title I Eligible; 0 School-wide Title I
Students: 3,498 (51.4% male; 48.6% female)
Individual Education Program: 477 (13.6%);
English Language Learner: 82 (2.3%); Migrant: 0 (0.0%)
Eligible for Free Lunch Program: 106 (3.0%)
Eligible for Reduced-Price Lunch Program: 60 (1.7%)
Teachers: 245.0 (14.3 to 1)
Librarians/Media Specialists: 8.0 (437.3 to 1)
Guidance Counselors: 7.0 (499.7 to 1)
Current Spending: ($ per student per year):
Total: $9,062; Instruction: $5,215; Support Services: $3,674
Enrollment, Drop-out Rates and Diploma Recipients by Race/Ethnicity

Category	Total	White	Black	Asian	AIAN	Hisp.
Enrollment (%)	100.0	89.9	2.4	4.0	0.1	3.6
Drop-out Rate (%)	n/a	n/a	n/a	n/a	n/a	n/a
H.S. Diplomas (#)	n/a	n/a	n/a	n/a	n/a	n/a

Hunterdon Central Reg

84 Route 31 • Flemington, NJ 08822-1239
(908) 782-5727 • http://www.hcrhs.hunterdon.k12.nj.us/
Grade Span: 09-12; **Agency Type:** 1
Schools: 1
0 Primary; 0 Middle; 1 High; 0 Other Level
1 Regular; 0 Special Education; 0 Vocational; 0 Alternative
0 Magnet; 0 Charter; 1 Title I Eligible; 0 School-wide Title I
Students: 2,630 (50.3% male; 49.7% female)
Individual Education Program: 417 (15.9%);
English Language Learner: 16 (0.6%); Migrant: 0 (0.0%)
Eligible for Free Lunch Program: 41 (1.6%)
Eligible for Reduced-Price Lunch Program: 12 (0.5%)
Teachers: 203.5 (12.9 to 1)
Librarians/Media Specialists: 3.0 (876.7 to 1)
Guidance Counselors: 14.0 (187.9 to 1)
Current Spending: ($ per student per year):
Total: $14,315; Instruction: $7,587; Support Services: $5,505
Enrollment, Drop-out Rates and Diploma Recipients by Race/Ethnicity

Category	Total	White	Black	Asian	AIAN	Hisp.
Enrollment (%)	100.0	96.4	0.6	1.4	0.1	1.4
Drop-out Rate (%)	1.0	0.8	0.0	9.5	0.0	12.0
H.S. Diplomas (#)	500	465	7	12	4	12

North Hunt-Voorhees Regional

1445 State Route 31 • Annandale, NJ 08801-3117
(908) 735-2846 • http://www.nhvweb.net
Grade Span: 09-12; **Agency Type:** 1
Schools: 2
0 Primary; 0 Middle; 2 High; 0 Other Level
2 Regular; 0 Special Education; 0 Vocational; 0 Alternative
0 Magnet; 0 Charter; 1 Title I Eligible; 0 School-wide Title I
Students: 2,622 (50.9% male; 49.1% female)
Individual Education Program: 412 (15.7%);
English Language Learner: 3 (0.1%); Migrant: 0 (0.0%)
Eligible for Free Lunch Program: 14 (0.5%)
Eligible for Reduced-Price Lunch Program: 8 (0.3%)
Teachers: 208.0 (12.6 to 1)
Librarians/Media Specialists: 2.0 (1,311.0 to 1)
Guidance Counselors: 15.4 (170.3 to 1)
Current Spending: ($ per student per year):
Total: $14,157; Instruction: $8,584; Support Services: $5,246
Enrollment, Drop-out Rates and Diploma Recipients by Race/Ethnicity

Category	Total	White	Black	Asian	AIAN	Hisp.
Enrollment (%)	100.0	97.0	0.4	1.3	0.2	1.1
Drop-out Rate (%)	0.5	0.5	0.0	0.0	n/a	0.0
H.S. Diplomas (#)	521	504	2	10	0	5

Readington Twp

48 Readington Rd • Whitehouse Station, NJ 08889-0807
Mailing Address: PO Box 807 • Whitehouse Station, NJ 08889-0807
(908) 534-2195
Grade Span: PK-08; **Agency Type:** 1
Schools: 4
3 Primary; 1 Middle; 0 High; 0 Other Level
4 Regular; 0 Special Education; 0 Vocational; 0 Alternative
0 Magnet; 0 Charter; 0 Title I Eligible; 0 School-wide Title I
Students: 2,183 (49.4% male; 50.6% female)
Individual Education Program: 359 (16.4%);
English Language Learner: 11 (0.5%); Migrant: 0 (0.0%)
Eligible for Free Lunch Program: 24 (1.1%)
Eligible for Reduced-Price Lunch Program: 16 (0.7%)
Teachers: 165.3 (13.2 to 1)
Librarians/Media Specialists: 3.0 (727.7 to 1)
Guidance Counselors: 6.0 (363.8 to 1)
Current Spending: ($ per student per year):
Total: $9,512; Instruction: $5,556; Support Services: $3,750
Enrollment, Drop-out Rates and Diploma Recipients by Race/Ethnicity

Category	Total	White	Black	Asian	AIAN	Hisp.
Enrollment (%)	100.0	92.9	1.1	3.4	0.3	2.3
Drop-out Rate (%)	n/a	n/a	n/a	n/a	n/a	n/a
H.S. Diplomas (#)	n/a	n/a	n/a	n/a	n/a	n/a

Mercer County

East Windsor Regional

384 Stockton St • Hightstown, NJ 08520-4228
(609) 443-7704 • http://eastwindsor.expresspage.net/
Grade Span: PK-12; **Agency Type:** 1
Schools: 6
4 Primary; 1 Middle; 1 High; 0 Other Level
6 Regular; 0 Special Education; 0 Vocational; 0 Alternative
0 Magnet; 0 Charter; 3 Title I Eligible; 0 School-wide Title I
Students: 4,729 (53.0% male; 47.0% female)
Individual Education Program: 821 (17.4%);
English Language Learner: 283 (6.0%); Migrant: 0 (0.0%)
Eligible for Free Lunch Program: 511 (10.8%)
Eligible for Reduced-Price Lunch Program: 244 (5.2%)
Teachers: 357.4 (13.2 to 1)
Librarians/Media Specialists: 7.0 (675.6 to 1)
Guidance Counselors: 13.0 (363.8 to 1)
Current Spending: ($ per student per year):
Total: $10,650; Instruction: $6,347; Support Services: $4,107
Enrollment, Drop-out Rates and Diploma Recipients by Race/Ethnicity

Category	Total	White	Black	Asian	AIAN	Hisp.
Enrollment (%)	100.0	57.2	11.8	11.4	0.0	19.5
Drop-out Rate (%)	0.9	0.3	2.1	0.0	0.0	3.2
H.S. Diplomas (#)	225	143	12	44	1	25

Ewing Twp

1331 Lower Ferry Rd • Ewing, NJ 08618-1409
(609) 538-9800 • http://www.ewing.k12.nj.us
Grade Span: PK-12; **Agency Type:** 1
Schools: 5
3 Primary; 1 Middle; 1 High; 0 Other Level
5 Regular; 0 Special Education; 0 Vocational; 0 Alternative
0 Magnet; 0 Charter; 3 Title I Eligible; 0 School-wide Title I
Students: 3,826 (51.6% male; 48.4% female)
Individual Education Program: 781 (20.4%);
English Language Learner: 75 (2.0%); Migrant: 0 (0.0%)
Eligible for Free Lunch Program: 449 (11.7%)
Eligible for Reduced-Price Lunch Program: 325 (8.5%)
Teachers: 315.4 (12.1 to 1)
Librarians/Media Specialists: 7.0 (546.6 to 1)
Guidance Counselors: 13.0 (294.3 to 1)
Current Spending: ($ per student per year):
Total: $11,094; Instruction: $7,102; Support Services: $3,993
Enrollment, Drop-out Rates and Diploma Recipients by Race/Ethnicity

Category	Total	White	Black	Asian	AIAN	Hisp.
Enrollment (%)	100.0	46.7	43.3	3.3	0.1	6.6
Drop-out Rate (%)	3.4	3.6	3.3	0.0	n/a	4.1
H.S. Diplomas (#)	230	118	100	3	1	8

Hamilton Twp

90 Park Ave • Hamilton Square, NJ 08690-2024
(609) 890-3723 • http://www.hamilton.k12.nj.us
Grade Span: PK-12; **Agency Type:** 1
Schools: 23
17 Primary; 3 Middle; 3 High; 0 Other Level
23 Regular; 0 Special Education; 0 Vocational; 0 Alternative
0 Magnet; 0 Charter; 21 Title I Eligible; 0 School-wide Title I
Students: 13,223 (51.1% male; 48.9% female)
Individual Education Program: 2,931 (22.2%);
English Language Learner: 187 (1.4%); Migrant: 0 (0.0%)
Eligible for Free Lunch Program: 1,534 (11.6%)
Eligible for Reduced-Price Lunch Program: 756 (5.7%)
Teachers: 938.1 (14.1 to 1)
Librarians/Media Specialists: 15.0 (881.5 to 1)
Guidance Counselors: 51.0 (259.3 to 1)
Current Spending: ($ per student per year):
Total: $9,108; Instruction: $5,642; Support Services: $3,256
Enrollment, Drop-out Rates and Diploma Recipients by Race/Ethnicity

Category	Total	White	Black	Asian	AIAN	Hisp.
Enrollment (%)	100.0	74.2	14.3	3.7	0.2	7.6
Drop-out Rate (%)	4.2	2.8	12.9	0.0	0.0	7.9
H.S. Diplomas (#)	899	686	107	42	9	55

Hopewell Valley Regional

425 S Main St • Pennington, NJ 08534-2716
(609) 737-0105 • http://www.hvrsd.k12.nj.us/district/intro.htm
Grade Span: PK-12; **Agency Type:** 1
Schools: 6
4 Primary; 1 Middle; 1 High; 0 Other Level
6 Regular; 0 Special Education; 0 Vocational; 0 Alternative
0 Magnet; 0 Charter; 0 Title I Eligible; 0 School-wide Title I
Students: 3,806 (50.8% male; 49.2% female)
Individual Education Program: 564 (14.8%);
English Language Learner: 5 (0.1%); Migrant: 0 (0.0%)
Eligible for Free Lunch Program: 22 (0.6%)
Eligible for Reduced-Price Lunch Program: 33 (0.9%)
Teachers: 308.5 (12.3 to 1)
Librarians/Media Specialists: 6.5 (585.5 to 1)
Guidance Counselors: 15.5 (245.5 to 1)
Current Spending: ($ per student per year):
Total: $10,801; Instruction: $6,733; Support Services: $3,864
Enrollment, Drop-out Rates and Diploma Recipients by Race/Ethnicity

Category	Total	White	Black	Asian	AIAN	Hisp.
Enrollment (%)	100.0	91.5	1.4	5.2	0.1	1.8
Drop-out Rate (%)	0.7	0.7	7.1	0.0	0.0	0.0
H.S. Diplomas (#)	240	217	4	12	1	6

Lawrence Twp

2565 Princeton Pike • Lawrenceville, NJ 08648-3631
(609) 530-8609 • http://www.lawrence.k12.nj.us
Grade Span: PK-12; **Agency Type:** 1
Schools: 7
4 Primary; 2 Middle; 1 High; 0 Other Level
7 Regular; 0 Special Education; 0 Vocational; 0 Alternative
0 Magnet; 0 Charter; 2 Title I Eligible; 0 School-wide Title I
Students: 4,117 (51.3% male; 48.7% female)
Individual Education Program: 837 (20.3%);
English Language Learner: 168 (4.1%); Migrant: 0 (0.0%)
Eligible for Free Lunch Program: 216 (5.2%)
Eligible for Reduced-Price Lunch Program: 100 (2.4%)
Teachers: 305.4 (13.5 to 1)
Librarians/Media Specialists: 4.0 (1,029.3 to 1)
Guidance Counselors: 13.0 (316.7 to 1)
Current Spending: ($ per student per year):
Total: $11,078; Instruction: $6,845; Support Services: $3,998
Enrollment, Drop-out Rates and Diploma Recipients by Race/Ethnicity

Category	Total	White	Black	Asian	AIAN	Hisp.
Enrollment (%)	100.0	67.2	15.5	10.8	0.2	6.3
Drop-out Rate (%)	0.0	0.0	0.0	0.0	n/a	0.0
H.S. Diplomas (#)	311	235	35	22	0	19

Princeton Regional

25 Valley Rd • Princeton, NJ 08540-0711
(609) 924-9322 • http://www.prs.k12.nj.us
Grade Span: PK-12; **Agency Type:** 1
Schools: 6
4 Primary; 1 Middle; 1 High; 0 Other Level
6 Regular; 0 Special Education; 0 Vocational; 0 Alternative
0 Magnet; 0 Charter; 4 Title I Eligible; 0 School-wide Title I
Students: 3,322 (51.5% male; 48.5% female)
Individual Education Program: 476 (14.3%);
English Language Learner: 115 (3.5%); Migrant: 0 (0.0%)
Eligible for Free Lunch Program: 225 (6.8%)
Eligible for Reduced-Price Lunch Program: 73 (2.2%)
Teachers: 267.9 (12.4 to 1)
Librarians/Media Specialists: 6.0 (553.7 to 1)
Guidance Counselors: 10.4 (319.4 to 1)
Current Spending: ($ per student per year):
Total: $12,563; Instruction: $7,855; Support Services: $4,450
Enrollment, Drop-out Rates and Diploma Recipients by Race/Ethnicity

Category	Total	White	Black	Asian	AIAN	Hisp.
Enrollment (%)	100.0	71.7	9.7	10.7	0.0	7.9
Drop-out Rate (%)	1.5	0.4	5.2	0.0	0.0	11.8
H.S. Diplomas (#)	237	168	22	33	0	14

Trenton City

108 N Clinton Ave • Trenton, NJ 08609-1014
(609) 989-2744 • http://www.trenton.k12.nj.us
Grade Span: PK-12; **Agency Type:** 1
Schools: 24
18 Primary; 4 Middle; 2 High; 0 Other Level
24 Regular; 0 Special Education; 0 Vocational; 0 Alternative
0 Magnet; 0 Charter; 22 Title I Eligible; 22 School-wide Title I
Students: 13,231 (48.8% male; 51.2% female)
Individual Education Program: 2,693 (20.4%);
English Language Learner: 832 (6.3%); Migrant: 0 (0.0%)
Eligible for Free Lunch Program: 6,074 (45.9%)
Eligible for Reduced-Price Lunch Program: 1,150 (8.7%)
Teachers: 1,076.0 (12.3 to 1)
Librarians/Media Specialists: 17.0 (778.3 to 1)
Guidance Counselors: 42.0 (315.0 to 1)
Current Spending: ($ per student per year):
Total: $17,909; Instruction: $10,491; Support Services: $6,832
Enrollment, Drop-out Rates and Diploma Recipients by Race/Ethnicity

Category	Total	White	Black	Asian	AIAN	Hisp.
Enrollment (%)	100.0	3.9	66.7	0.6	0.1	28.7
Drop-out Rate (%)	5.4	9.2	5.6	0.0	0.0	4.2
H.S. Diplomas (#)	872	10	458	0	0	404

West Windsor-Plainsboro Reg

505 Village Road, W • Princeton Junction, NJ 08550-0248
Mailing Address: PO Box 505 • Princeton Junction, NJ 08550-0248
(609) 716-5040 • http://www.west-windsor-plainsboro.k12.nj.us/
Grade Span: PK-12; **Agency Type:** 1
Schools: 10
4 Primary; 4 Middle; 2 High; 0 Other Level
10 Regular; 0 Special Education; 0 Vocational; 0 Alternative
0 Magnet; 0 Charter; 5 Title I Eligible; 0 School-wide Title I
Students: 8,786 (51.7% male; 48.3% female)
Individual Education Program: 1,101 (12.5%);
English Language Learner: 262 (3.0%); Migrant: 0 (0.0%)
Eligible for Free Lunch Program: 126 (1.4%)
Eligible for Reduced-Price Lunch Program: 114 (1.3%)
Teachers: 693.8 (12.7 to 1)
Librarians/Media Specialists: 11.8 (744.6 to 1)
Guidance Counselors: 26.1 (336.6 to 1)
Current Spending: ($ per student per year):
Total: $11,251; Instruction: $6,416; Support Services: $4,379
Enrollment, Drop-out Rates and Diploma Recipients by Race/Ethnicity

Category	Total	White	Black	Asian	AIAN	Hisp.
Enrollment (%)	100.0	56.0	5.3	34.3	0.0	4.5
Drop-out Rate (%)	1.2	1.0	4.0	1.0	n/a	1.0
H.S. Diplomas (#)	554	335	42	149	0	28

Middlesex County

Carteret Boro

599 Roosevelt Ave • Carteret, NJ 07008-2912
(732) 541-8961 • http://www.ci.carteret.nj.us
Grade Span: PK-12; **Agency Type:** 1
Schools: 5
3 Primary; 1 Middle; 1 High; 0 Other Level
5 Regular; 0 Special Education; 0 Vocational; 0 Alternative
0 Magnet; 0 Charter; 4 Title I Eligible; 0 School-wide Title I
Students: 3,770 (51.5% male; 48.5% female)
Individual Education Program: 391 (10.4%);
English Language Learner: 230 (6.1%); Migrant: 0 (0.0%)
Eligible for Free Lunch Program: 1,248 (33.1%)
Eligible for Reduced-Price Lunch Program: 432 (11.5%)
Teachers: 265.1 (14.2 to 1)
Librarians/Media Specialists: 4.6 (819.6 to 1)
Guidance Counselors: 11.0 (342.7 to 1)
Current Spending: ($ per student per year):
Total: $10,386; Instruction: $6,412; Support Services: $3,755
Enrollment, Drop-out Rates and Diploma Recipients by Race/Ethnicity

Category	Total	White	Black	Asian	AIAN	Hisp.
Enrollment (%)	100.0	30.3	16.3	17.9	0.0	35.5
Drop-out Rate (%)	4.6	3.1	7.8	0.0	n/a	7.2
H.S. Diplomas (#)	200	118	10	23	0	49

East Brunswick Twp

760 Route #18 • East Brunswick, NJ 08816-3068
(732) 613-6705 • http://www.ebruns.k12.nj.us
Grade Span: PK-12; **Agency Type:** 1
Schools: 11
8 Primary; 1 Middle; 1 High; 1 Other Level
11 Regular; 0 Special Education; 0 Vocational; 0 Alternative
0 Magnet; 0 Charter; 6 Title I Eligible; 0 School-wide Title I
Students: 8,819 (51.3% male; 48.7% female)
Individual Education Program: 1,395 (15.8%);
English Language Learner: 193 (2.2%); Migrant: 0 (0.0%)
Eligible for Free Lunch Program: 208 (2.4%)
Eligible for Reduced-Price Lunch Program: 197 (2.2%)
Teachers: 638.2 (13.8 to 1)
Librarians/Media Specialists: 14.0 (629.9 to 1)
Guidance Counselors: 23.0 (383.4 to 1)
Current Spending: ($ per student per year):
Total: $10,482; Instruction: $6,212; Support Services: $4,037
Enrollment, Drop-out Rates and Diploma Recipients by Race/Ethnicity

Category	Total	White	Black	Asian	AIAN	Hisp.
Enrollment (%)	100.0	69.4	3.4	22.8	0.2	4.2
Drop-out Rate (%)	1.0	1.3	1.4	0.3	0.0	0.0
H.S. Diplomas (#)	646	462	15	145	0	24

Edison Twp

312 Pierson Ave • Edison, NJ 08837
(732) 452-4900 • http://www.edison.k12.nj.us
Grade Span: PK-12; **Agency Type:** 1
Schools: 17
11 Primary; 4 Middle; 2 High; 0 Other Level
17 Regular; 0 Special Education; 0 Vocational; 0 Alternative
0 Magnet; 0 Charter; 8 Title I Eligible; 0 School-wide Title I
Students: 12,920 (50.3% male; 49.7% female)
Individual Education Program: 1,676 (13.0%);
English Language Learner: 352 (2.7%); Migrant: 0 (0.0%)
Eligible for Free Lunch Program: 692 (5.4%)
Eligible for Reduced-Price Lunch Program: 413 (3.2%)
Teachers: 975.8 (13.2 to 1)
Librarians/Media Specialists: 6.0 (2,153.3 to 1)
Guidance Counselors: 32.5 (397.5 to 1)
Current Spending: ($ per student per year):
Total: $10,655; Instruction: $6,976; Support Services: $3,463
Enrollment, Drop-out Rates and Diploma Recipients by Race/Ethnicity

Category	Total	White	Black	Asian	AIAN	Hisp.
Enrollment (%)	100.0	43.5	8.0	41.1	0.1	7.3
Drop-out Rate (%)	0.4	0.4	0.3	0.2	0.0	1.3
H.S. Diplomas (#)	926	451	80	343	0	52

Highland Park Boro

435 Mansfield St • Highland Park, NJ 08904-2642
(732) 572-6990
Grade Span: PK-12; **Agency Type:** 1
Schools: 3
2 Primary; 0 Middle; 1 High; 0 Other Level
3 Regular; 0 Special Education; 0 Vocational; 0 Alternative
0 Magnet; 0 Charter; 3 Title I Eligible; 3 School-wide Title I
Students: 1,604 (52.9% male; 47.1% female)
Individual Education Program: 223 (13.9%);
English Language Learner: 63 (3.9%); Migrant: 0 (0.0%)
Eligible for Free Lunch Program: 347 (21.6%)
Eligible for Reduced-Price Lunch Program: 117 (7.3%)
Teachers: 127.3 (12.6 to 1)
Librarians/Media Specialists: 2.0 (802.0 to 1)
Guidance Counselors: 5.0 (320.8 to 1)
Current Spending: ($ per student per year):
Total: $11,474; Instruction: $6,980; Support Services: $4,221
Enrollment, Drop-out Rates and Diploma Recipients by Race/Ethnicity

Category	Total	White	Black	Asian	AIAN	Hisp.
Enrollment (%)	100.0	48.5	17.0	20.6	0.0	13.9
Drop-out Rate (%)	0.0	0.0	0.0	0.0	n/a	0.0
H.S. Diplomas (#)	108	62	14	15	0	17

Metuchen Boro

442 Main St • Metuchen, NJ 08840-1886
(732) 321-8714 • http://www.metuchenschools.org/metuchen
Grade Span: PK-12; **Agency Type:** 1
Schools: 4
2 Primary; 1 Middle; 1 High; 0 Other Level
4 Regular; 0 Special Education; 0 Vocational; 0 Alternative
0 Magnet; 0 Charter; 1 Title I Eligible; 0 School-wide Title I
Students: 1,827 (51.1% male; 48.9% female)
Individual Education Program: 264 (14.4%);
English Language Learner: 18 (1.0%); Migrant: 0 (0.0%)
Eligible for Free Lunch Program: 41 (2.2%)
Eligible for Reduced-Price Lunch Program: 34 (1.9%)
Teachers: 150.8 (12.1 to 1)
Librarians/Media Specialists: 3.0 (609.0 to 1)
Guidance Counselors: 6.0 (304.5 to 1)
Current Spending: ($ per student per year):
Total: $10,814; Instruction: $6,583; Support Services: $4,055
Enrollment, Drop-out Rates and Diploma Recipients by Race/Ethnicity

Category	Total	White	Black	Asian	AIAN	Hisp.
Enrollment (%)	100.0	76.1	9.1	10.1	0.0	4.7
Drop-out Rate (%)	0.2	0.2	0.0	0.0	n/a	0.0
H.S. Diplomas (#)	136	113	11	6	0	6

Middlesex Boro

HS Annex • Middlesex, NJ 08846-1489
(732) 317-6000 • http://www.middlesex.k12.nj.us/
Grade Span: PK-12; **Agency Type:** 1
Schools: 5
3 Primary; 1 Middle; 1 High; 0 Other Level
5 Regular; 0 Special Education; 0 Vocational; 0 Alternative
0 Magnet; 0 Charter; 2 Title I Eligible; 0 School-wide Title I
Students: 2,105 (51.0% male; 49.0% female)
Individual Education Program: 331 (15.7%);
English Language Learner: 78 (3.7%); Migrant: 0 (0.0%)
Eligible for Free Lunch Program: 163 (7.7%)
Eligible for Reduced-Price Lunch Program: 116 (5.5%)
Teachers: 163.0 (12.9 to 1)
Librarians/Media Specialists: 2.0 (1,052.5 to 1)
Guidance Counselors: 6.0 (350.8 to 1)
Current Spending: ($ per student per year):
Total: $9,815; Instruction: $6,394; Support Services: $3,165
Enrollment, Drop-out Rates and Diploma Recipients by Race/Ethnicity

Category	Total	White	Black	Asian	AIAN	Hisp.
Enrollment (%)	100.0	76.2	4.4	5.3	0.1	14.1
Drop-out Rate (%)	0.0	0.0	0.0	0.0	n/a	0.0
H.S. Diplomas (#)	108	89	5	9	0	5

Middlesex County Vocational

112 Rues Ln • East Brunswick, NJ 08816-0220
Mailing Address: PO Box 1070 • East Brunswick, NJ 08816-0220
(732) 257-3300 • http://www.mc-votech.org
Grade Span: 09-12; **Agency Type:** 1
Schools: 6
0 Primary; 0 Middle; 4 High; 2 Other Level
0 Regular; 0 Special Education; 6 Vocational; 0 Alternative
0 Magnet; 0 Charter; 3 Title I Eligible; 0 School-wide Title I
Students: 1,769 (59.8% male; 40.2% female)
Individual Education Program: 512 (28.9%);
English Language Learner: 44 (2.5%); Migrant: 0 (0.0%)
Eligible for Free Lunch Program: 546 (30.9%)
Eligible for Reduced-Price Lunch Program: 194 (11.0%)
Teachers: 205.0 (8.6 to 1)
Librarians/Media Specialists: 3.0 (589.7 to 1)
Guidance Counselors: 6.0 (294.8 to 1)
Current Spending: ($ per student per year):
Total: $19,318; Instruction: $10,976; Support Services: $8,000
Enrollment, Drop-out Rates and Diploma Recipients by Race/Ethnicity

Category	Total	White	Black	Asian	AIAN	Hisp.
Enrollment (%)	100.0	47.0	15.7	2.4	0.0	34.9
Drop-out Rate (%)	0.4	0.4	1.0	0.0	n/a	0.2
H.S. Diplomas (#)	258	121	47	1	0	89

Monroe Twp

423 Buckelew Ave • Monroe Township, NJ 08831-9802
(732) 521-2111
Grade Span: PK-12; **Agency Type:** 1
Schools: 6
3 Primary; 2 Middle; 1 High; 0 Other Level
6 Regular; 0 Special Education; 0 Vocational; 0 Alternative
0 Magnet; 0 Charter; 4 Title I Eligible; 0 School-wide Title I
Students: 3,757 (51.6% male; 48.4% female)
Individual Education Program: 614 (16.3%);
English Language Learner: 27 (0.7%); Migrant: 0 (0.0%)
Eligible for Free Lunch Program: 117 (3.1%)
Eligible for Reduced-Price Lunch Program: 84 (2.2%)
Teachers: 290.5 (12.9 to 1)
Librarians/Media Specialists: 4.0 (939.3 to 1)
Guidance Counselors: 13.0 (289.0 to 1)
Current Spending: ($ per student per year):
Total: $11,248; Instruction: $6,410; Support Services: $4,570
Enrollment, Drop-out Rates and Diploma Recipients by Race/Ethnicity

Category	Total	White	Black	Asian	AIAN	Hisp.
Enrollment (%)	100.0	85.6	3.3	6.9	0.2	4.0
Drop-out Rate (%)	1.2	1.0	9.4	0.0	0.0	0.0
H.S. Diplomas (#)	179	151	11	5	0	12

New Brunswick City

268 Baldwin St • New Brunswick, NJ 08903-2683
Mailing Address: PO Box 2683 • New Brunswick, NJ 08903-2683
(732) 745-5414 • http://www.nbps.k12.nj.us
Grade Span: PK-12; **Agency Type:** 1
Schools: 10
8 Primary; 0 Middle; 1 High; 1 Other Level
9 Regular; 0 Special Education; 0 Vocational; 1 Alternative
0 Magnet; 0 Charter; 9 Title I Eligible; 0 School-wide Title I
Students: 6,105 (52.0% male; 48.0% female)
Individual Education Program: 1,227 (20.1%);
English Language Learner: 1,529 (25.0%); Migrant: 51 (0.8%)
Eligible for Free Lunch Program: 4,208 (68.9%)
Eligible for Reduced-Price Lunch Program: 669 (11.0%)
Teachers: 515.5 (11.8 to 1)
Librarians/Media Specialists: 8.0 (763.1 to 1)
Guidance Counselors: 14.0 (436.1 to 1)
Current Spending: ($ per student per year):
Total: $15,718; Instruction: $9,444; Support Services: $5,821
Enrollment, Drop-out Rates and Diploma Recipients by Race/Ethnicity

Category	Total	White	Black	Asian	AIAN	Hisp.
Enrollment (%)	100.0	2.8	28.9	2.2	0.6	65.4
Drop-out Rate (%)	16.0	9.1	17.0	6.3	n/a	15.7
H.S. Diplomas (#)	158	2	66	4	0	86

North Brunswick Twp

Old Georges Rd • North Brunswick, NJ 08902-0407
Mailing Address: PO Box 6016 • North Brunswick, NJ 08902-0407
(732) 289-3030 • http://www.nbtschools.org
Grade Span: PK-12; **Agency Type:** 1
Schools: 6
4 Primary; 1 Middle; 1 High; 0 Other Level
6 Regular; 0 Special Education; 0 Vocational; 0 Alternative
0 Magnet; 0 Charter; 3 Title I Eligible; 0 School-wide Title I
Students: 5,275 (50.7% male; 49.3% female)
Individual Education Program: 685 (13.0%);
English Language Learner: 349 (6.6%); Migrant: 0 (0.0%)
Eligible for Free Lunch Program: 657 (12.5%)
Eligible for Reduced-Price Lunch Program: 298 (5.6%)
Teachers: 391.9 (13.5 to 1)
Librarians/Media Specialists: 6.0 (879.2 to 1)
Guidance Counselors: 12.0 (439.6 to 1)
Current Spending: ($ per student per year):
Total: $9,564; Instruction: $5,930; Support Services: $3,213
Enrollment, Drop-out Rates and Diploma Recipients by Race/Ethnicity

Category	Total	White	Black	Asian	AIAN	Hisp.
Enrollment (%)	100.0	44.5	20.9	19.7	0.0	14.9
Drop-out Rate (%)	1.0	1.0	0.7	0.0	n/a	3.3
H.S. Diplomas (#)	309	165	57	53	0	34

Old Bridge Twp

Admin Bldg, Route 516 • Matawan, NJ 07747-9641
(732) 290-3976 • http://www.oldbridgeschools.org
Grade Span: PK-12; **Agency Type:** 1
Schools: 15
12 Primary; 2 Middle; 1 High; 0 Other Level
15 Regular; 0 Special Education; 0 Vocational; 0 Alternative
0 Magnet; 0 Charter; 5 Title I Eligible; 0 School-wide Title I
Students: 9,940 (51.1% male; 48.9% female)
Individual Education Program: 1,177 (11.8%);
English Language Learner: 284 (2.9%); Migrant: 0 (0.0%)
Eligible for Free Lunch Program: 742 (7.5%)
Eligible for Reduced-Price Lunch Program: 474 (4.8%)
Teachers: 661.1 (15.0 to 1)
Librarians/Media Specialists: 14.5 (685.5 to 1)
Guidance Counselors: 20.0 (497.0 to 1)
Current Spending: ($ per student per year):
Total: $10,018; Instruction: $6,138; Support Services: $3,639
Enrollment, Drop-out Rates and Diploma Recipients by Race/Ethnicity

Category	Total	White	Black	Asian	AIAN	Hisp.
Enrollment (%)	100.0	69.1	6.6	16.5	0.0	7.7
Drop-out Rate (%)	3.2	3.5	2.1	1.7	n/a	4.5
H.S. Diplomas (#)	579	412	40	94	0	33

Perth Amboy City

178 Barracks St • Perth Amboy, NJ 08861-3402
(732) 376-6279 • http://www.perthamboy.k12.nj.us
Grade Span: PK-12; **Agency Type:** 1
Schools: 11
8 Primary; 2 Middle; 1 High; 0 Other Level
11 Regular; 0 Special Education; 0 Vocational; 0 Alternative
0 Magnet; 0 Charter; 6 Title I Eligible; 4 School-wide Title I
Students: 9,365 (52.1% male; 47.9% female)
Individual Education Program: 1,093 (11.7%);
English Language Learner: 1,519 (16.2%); Migrant: 0 (0.0%)
Eligible for Free Lunch Program: 5,847 (62.4%)
Eligible for Reduced-Price Lunch Program: 1,591 (17.0%)
Teachers: 691.2 (13.5 to 1)
Librarians/Media Specialists: 9.0 (1,040.6 to 1)
Guidance Counselors: 25.0 (374.6 to 1)
Current Spending: ($ per student per year):
Total: $11,173; Instruction: $7,316; Support Services: $3,510
Enrollment, Drop-out Rates and Diploma Recipients by Race/Ethnicity

Category	Total	White	Black	Asian	AIAN	Hisp.
Enrollment (%)	100.0	4.4	7.8	0.5	0.1	87.2
Drop-out Rate (%)	4.1	0.0	4.4	0.0	0.0	4.6
H.S. Diplomas (#)	322	18	35	0	9	260

Piscataway Twp

1515 Stelton Rd • Piscataway, NJ 08855-1332
Mailing Address: PO Box 1332 • Piscataway, NJ 08855-1332
(732) 572-2289 • http://www.familyeducation.com/nj/piscataway
Grade Span: PK-12; **Agency Type:** 1
Schools: 10
4 Primary; 5 Middle; 1 High; 0 Other Level
10 Regular; 0 Special Education; 0 Vocational; 0 Alternative
0 Magnet; 0 Charter; 9 Title I Eligible; 0 School-wide Title I
Students: 6,751 (51.3% male; 48.7% female)
Individual Education Program: 972 (14.4%);
English Language Learner: 276 (4.1%); Migrant: 0 (0.0%)
Eligible for Free Lunch Program: 664 (9.8%)
Eligible for Reduced-Price Lunch Program: 472 (7.0%)
Teachers: 498.5 (13.5 to 1)
Librarians/Media Specialists: 10.0 (675.1 to 1)
Guidance Counselors: 14.3 (472.1 to 1)
Current Spending: ($ per student per year):
Total: $10,350; Instruction: $6,137; Support Services: $3,774
Enrollment, Drop-out Rates and Diploma Recipients by Race/Ethnicity

Category	Total	White	Black	Asian	AIAN	Hisp.
Enrollment (%)	100.0	32.6	32.2	24.0	0.1	11.2
Drop-out Rate (%)	0.9	1.0	1.2	0.0	n/a	1.1
H.S. Diplomas (#)	428	136	142	104	0	46

Sayreville Boro

150 Lincoln St • Sayreville, NJ 08879-0997
Mailing Address: PO Box 997 • Sayreville, NJ 08872-0997
(732) 525-5224 • http://www.sayrevillek12.net
Grade Span: PK-12; **Agency Type:** 1
Schools: 7
4 Primary; 1 Middle; 1 High; 1 Other Level
6 Regular; 1 Special Education; 0 Vocational; 0 Alternative
0 Magnet; 0 Charter; 4 Title I Eligible; 0 School-wide Title I
Students: 5,583 (51.9% male; 48.1% female)
Individual Education Program: 873 (15.6%);
English Language Learner: 76 (1.4%); Migrant: 0 (0.0%)
Eligible for Free Lunch Program: 438 (7.8%)
Eligible for Reduced-Price Lunch Program: 362 (6.5%)
Teachers: 375.3 (14.9 to 1)
Librarians/Media Specialists: 7.0 (797.6 to 1)
Guidance Counselors: 13.0 (429.5 to 1)
Current Spending: ($ per student per year):
Total: $8,813; Instruction: $5,564; Support Services: $3,012
Enrollment, Drop-out Rates and Diploma Recipients by Race/Ethnicity

Category	Total	White	Black	Asian	AIAN	Hisp.
Enrollment (%)	100.0	61.6	11.8	16.0	0.1	10.5
Drop-out Rate (%)	2.6	2.6	2.9	0.6	0.0	4.4
H.S. Diplomas (#)	348	250	37	37	0	24

South Brunswick Twp

PO Box 181 • Monmouth Junction, NJ 08852-0181
(732) 297-7800 • http://www.sbschools.org
Grade Span: PK-12; **Agency Type:** 1
Schools: 12
9 Primary; 2 Middle; 1 High; 0 Other Level
12 Regular; 0 Special Education; 0 Vocational; 0 Alternative
0 Magnet; 0 Charter; 4 Title I Eligible; 0 School-wide Title I
Students: 8,151 (50.0% male; 50.0% female)
Individual Education Program: 1,083 (13.3%);
English Language Learner: 0 (0.0%); Migrant: 0 (0.0%)
Eligible for Free Lunch Program: 233 (2.9%)
Eligible for Reduced-Price Lunch Program: 221 (2.7%)
Teachers: 631.5 (12.9 to 1)
Librarians/Media Specialists: 13.0 (627.0 to 1)
Guidance Counselors: 16.7 (488.1 to 1)
Current Spending: ($ per student per year):
Total: $9,973; Instruction: $5,598; Support Services: $3,847
Enrollment, Drop-out Rates and Diploma Recipients by Race/Ethnicity

Category	Total	White	Black	Asian	AIAN	Hisp.
Enrollment (%)	100.0	59.2	9.6	25.8	0.0	5.3
Drop-out Rate (%)	0.8	1.1	0.4	0.0	0.0	1.6
H.S. Diplomas (#)	427	262	43	102	0	20

South Plainfield Boro

305 Cromwell Place • South Plainfield, NJ 07080-4107
(908) 754-4620 • http://www.spnet.k12.nj.us
Grade Span: PK-12; **Agency Type:** 1
Schools: 7
4 Primary; 2 Middle; 1 High; 0 Other Level
7 Regular; 0 Special Education; 0 Vocational; 0 Alternative
0 Magnet; 0 Charter; 4 Title I Eligible; 0 School-wide Title I
Students: 3,794 (52.0% male; 48.0% female)
Individual Education Program: 596 (15.7%);
English Language Learner: 72 (1.9%); Migrant: 0 (0.0%)
Eligible for Free Lunch Program: 221 (5.8%)
Eligible for Reduced-Price Lunch Program: 160 (4.2%)
Teachers: 282.1 (13.4 to 1)
Librarians/Media Specialists: 6.0 (632.3 to 1)
Guidance Counselors: 10.0 (379.4 to 1)
Current Spending: ($ per student per year):
Total: $10,081; Instruction: $6,032; Support Services: $3,675
Enrollment, Drop-out Rates and Diploma Recipients by Race/Ethnicity

Category	Total	White	Black	Asian	AIAN	Hisp.
Enrollment (%)	100.0	66.6	11.4	10.7	0.3	11.0
Drop-out Rate (%)	0.7	0.4	2.3	1.0	0.0	0.0
H.S. Diplomas (#)	236	159	40	20	0	17

South River Boro

Admin Bldg, 15 Montgomery St • South River, NJ 08882
(732) 613-4000 • http://www.sriver.k12.nj.us
Grade Span: PK-12; **Agency Type:** 1
Schools: 3
1 Primary; 1 Middle; 1 High; 0 Other Level
3 Regular; 0 Special Education; 0 Vocational; 0 Alternative
0 Magnet; 0 Charter; 2 Title I Eligible; 0 School-wide Title I
Students: 2,227 (52.2% male; 47.8% female)
Individual Education Program: 290 (13.0%);
English Language Learner: 129 (5.8%); Migrant: 0 (0.0%)
Eligible for Free Lunch Program: 364 (16.3%)
Eligible for Reduced-Price Lunch Program: 232 (10.4%)
Teachers: 147.0 (15.1 to 1)
Librarians/Media Specialists: 3.0 (742.3 to 1)
Guidance Counselors: 6.0 (371.2 to 1)
Current Spending: ($ per student per year):
Total: $7,904; Instruction: $4,951; Support Services: $2,692
Enrollment, Drop-out Rates and Diploma Recipients by Race/Ethnicity

Category	Total	White	Black	Asian	AIAN	Hisp.
Enrollment (%)	100.0	72.3	10.0	3.0	0.1	14.5
Drop-out Rate (%)	5.9	5.8	7.9	18.2	0.0	4.4
H.S. Diplomas (#)	148	111	9	4	0	24

Spotswood Boro

105 Summerhill Rd • Spotswood, NJ 08884
(732) 723-2236 • http://www.spotswood.k12.nj.us/
Grade Span: PK-12; **Agency Type:** 1
Schools: 4
2 Primary; 1 Middle; 1 High; 0 Other Level
4 Regular; 0 Special Education; 0 Vocational; 0 Alternative
0 Magnet; 0 Charter; 3 Title I Eligible; 0 School-wide Title I
Students: 1,684 (51.4% male; 48.6% female)
Individual Education Program: 170 (10.1%);
English Language Learner: 18 (1.1%); Migrant: 0 (0.0%)
Eligible for Free Lunch Program: 92 (5.5%)
Eligible for Reduced-Price Lunch Program: 70 (4.2%)
Teachers: 124.9 (13.5 to 1)
Librarians/Media Specialists: 1.0 (1,684.0 to 1)
Guidance Counselors: 6.6 (255.2 to 1)
Current Spending: ($ per student per year):
Total: $9,955; Instruction: $5,945; Support Services: $3,652
Enrollment, Drop-out Rates and Diploma Recipients by Race/Ethnicity

Category	Total	White	Black	Asian	AIAN	Hisp.
Enrollment (%)	100.0	89.2	2.8	3.1	0.1	4.8
Drop-out Rate (%)	1.2	0.8	0.0	4.3	n/a	6.7
H.S. Diplomas (#)	190	166	3	12	0	9

Woodbridge Twp

School St • Woodbridge, NJ 07095-0952
Mailing Address: PO Box 428 • Woodbridge, NJ 07095-0952
(732) 602-8549 • http://www.woodbridge.k12.nj.us
Grade Span: PK-12; **Agency Type:** 1
Schools: 24
16 Primary; 5 Middle; 3 High; 0 Other Level
24 Regular; 0 Special Education; 0 Vocational; 0 Alternative
0 Magnet; 0 Charter; 6 Title I Eligible; 0 School-wide Title I
Students: 13,175 (51.0% male; 49.0% female)
Individual Education Program: 1,889 (14.3%);
English Language Learner: 351 (2.7%); Migrant: 0 (0.0%)
Eligible for Free Lunch Program: 1,410 (10.7%)
Eligible for Reduced-Price Lunch Program: 778 (5.9%)
Teachers: 980.4 (13.4 to 1)
Librarians/Media Specialists: 18.0 (731.9 to 1)
Guidance Counselors: 31.2 (422.3 to 1)
Current Spending: ($ per student per year):
Total: $9,753; Instruction: $5,996; Support Services: $3,539
Enrollment, Drop-out Rates and Diploma Recipients by Race/Ethnicity

Category	Total	White	Black	Asian	AIAN	Hisp.
Enrollment (%)	100.0	58.1	11.0	18.2	0.1	12.5
Drop-out Rate (%)	1.1	1.0	1.3	1.6	0.0	1.0
H.S. Diplomas (#)	901	561	120	129	0	91

Monmouth County

Asbury Park City

407 Lake Ave • Asbury Park, NJ 07712-5493
(732) 776-2606 • http://www.asburypark.k12.nj.us/
Grade Span: PK-12; **Agency Type:** 1
Schools: 6
3 Primary; 1 Middle; 1 High; 1 Other Level
5 Regular; 1 Special Education; 0 Vocational; 0 Alternative
0 Magnet; 0 Charter; 4 Title I Eligible; 3 School-wide Title I
Students: 3,043 (50.4% male; 49.6% female)
Individual Education Program: 678 (22.3%);
English Language Learner: 149 (4.9%); Migrant: 0 (0.0%)
Eligible for Free Lunch Program: 2,258 (74.2%)
Eligible for Reduced-Price Lunch Program: 280 (9.2%)
Teachers: 324.0 (9.4 to 1)
Librarians/Media Specialists: 6.0 (507.2 to 1)
Guidance Counselors: 9.0 (338.1 to 1)
Current Spending: ($ per student per year):
Total: $17,491; Instruction: $10,598; Support Services: $5,834
Enrollment, Drop-out Rates and Diploma Recipients by Race/Ethnicity

Category	Total	White	Black	Asian	AIAN	Hisp.
Enrollment (%)	100.0	4.8	80.7	0.2	0.0	14.3
Drop-out Rate (%)	10.1	8.3	10.3	n/a	n/a	9.1
H.S. Diplomas (#)	118	1	102	0	0	15

Colts Neck Twp

70 Conover Rd • Colts Neck, NJ 07722-1250
(732) 946-0055
Grade Span: PK-08; **Agency Type:** 1
Schools: 3
2 Primary; 1 Middle; 0 High; 0 Other Level
3 Regular; 0 Special Education; 0 Vocational; 0 Alternative
0 Magnet; 0 Charter; 0 Title I Eligible; 0 School-wide Title I
Students: 1,501 (50.2% male; 49.8% female)
Individual Education Program: 192 (12.8%);
English Language Learner: 16 (1.1%); Migrant: 0 (0.0%)
Eligible for Free Lunch Program: 14 (0.9%)
Eligible for Reduced-Price Lunch Program: 9 (0.6%)
Teachers: 132.5 (11.3 to 1)
Librarians/Media Specialists: 2.0 (750.5 to 1)
Guidance Counselors: 2.5 (600.4 to 1)
Current Spending: ($ per student per year):
Total: $9,011; Instruction: $5,535; Support Services: $3,299
Enrollment, Drop-out Rates and Diploma Recipients by Race/Ethnicity

Category	Total	White	Black	Asian	AIAN	Hisp.
Enrollment (%)	100.0	95.5	0.7	2.9	0.0	0.9
Drop-out Rate (%)	n/a	n/a	n/a	n/a	n/a	n/a
H.S. Diplomas (#)	n/a	n/a	n/a	n/a	n/a	n/a

Freehold Regional

11 Pine St • Englishtown, NJ 07726-1595
(732) 792-7300 • http://www.frhsd.com
Grade Span: 09-12; **Agency Type:** 1
Schools: 6
0 Primary; 0 Middle; 6 High; 0 Other Level
6 Regular; 0 Special Education; 0 Vocational; 0 Alternative
0 Magnet; 0 Charter; 4 Title I Eligible; 0 School-wide Title I
Students: 10,308 (49.1% male; 50.9% female)
Individual Education Program: 1,254 (12.2%);
English Language Learner: 81 (0.8%); Migrant: 0 (0.0%)
Eligible for Free Lunch Program: 280 (2.7%)
Eligible for Reduced-Price Lunch Program: 173 (1.7%)
Teachers: 734.0 (14.0 to 1)
Librarians/Media Specialists: 11.0 (937.1 to 1)
Guidance Counselors: 35.0 (294.5 to 1)
Current Spending: ($ per student per year):
Total: $10,210; Instruction: $5,390; Support Services: $4,563
Enrollment, Drop-out Rates and Diploma Recipients by Race/Ethnicity

Category	Total	White	Black	Asian	AIAN	Hisp.
Enrollment (%)	100.0	85.6	3.3	6.7	0.1	4.4
Drop-out Rate (%)	1.3	1.2	2.4	0.5	0.0	2.8
H.S. Diplomas (#)	2,214	1,822	129	142	3	118

Freehold Twp

384 W Main St • Freehold, NJ 07728-3198
(732) 462-8400 • http://www.freeholdtwp.k12.nj.us
Grade Span: PK-08; **Agency Type:** 1
Schools: 7
5 Primary; 2 Middle; 0 High; 0 Other Level
7 Regular; 0 Special Education; 0 Vocational; 0 Alternative
0 Magnet; 0 Charter; 3 Title I Eligible; 0 School-wide Title I
Students: 4,443 (50.3% male; 49.7% female)
Individual Education Program: 642 (14.4%);
English Language Learner: 28 (0.6%); Migrant: 0 (0.0%)
Eligible for Free Lunch Program: 110 (2.5%)
Eligible for Reduced-Price Lunch Program: 100 (2.3%)
Teachers: 299.7 (14.8 to 1)
Librarians/Media Specialists: 6.5 (683.5 to 1)
Guidance Counselors: 8.0 (555.4 to 1)
Current Spending: ($ per student per year):
Total: $8,796; Instruction: $5,223; Support Services: $3,399
Enrollment, Drop-out Rates and Diploma Recipients by Race/Ethnicity

Category	Total	White	Black	Asian	AIAN	Hisp.
Enrollment (%)	100.0	84.3	3.4	7.4	0.1	4.8
Drop-out Rate (%)	n/a	n/a	n/a	n/a	n/a	n/a
H.S. Diplomas (#)	n/a	n/a	n/a	n/a	n/a	n/a

Hazlet Twp

421 Middle Rd • Hazlet, NJ 07730-2342
(732) 264-8402 • http://www.hazlet.org
Grade Span: PK-12; **Agency Type:** 1
Schools: 8
6 Primary; 1 Middle; 1 High; 0 Other Level
8 Regular; 0 Special Education; 0 Vocational; 0 Alternative
0 Magnet; 0 Charter; 3 Title I Eligible; 0 School-wide Title I
Students: 3,472 (49.3% male; 50.7% female)
Individual Education Program: 587 (16.9%);
English Language Learner: 16 (0.5%); Migrant: 0 (0.0%)
Eligible for Free Lunch Program: 161 (4.6%)
Eligible for Reduced-Price Lunch Program: 131 (3.8%)
Teachers: 261.1 (13.3 to 1)
Librarians/Media Specialists: 5.0 (694.4 to 1)
Guidance Counselors: 7.0 (496.0 to 1)
Current Spending: ($ per student per year):
Total: $10,511; Instruction: $6,434; Support Services: $3,893
Enrollment, Drop-out Rates and Diploma Recipients by Race/Ethnicity

Category	Total	White	Black	Asian	AIAN	Hisp.
Enrollment (%)	100.0	89.5	1.3	3.6	0.1	5.6
Drop-out Rate (%)	0.5	0.5	0.0	0.0	0.0	0.0
H.S. Diplomas (#)	207	183	8	8	0	8

Holmdel Twp

4 Crawford's Corner Rd • Holmdel, NJ 07733-0407
(732) 946-1800 • http://www.holmdel.k12.nj.us
Grade Span: PK-12; **Agency Type:** 1
Schools: 4
2 Primary; 1 Middle; 1 High; 0 Other Level
4 Regular; 0 Special Education; 0 Vocational; 0 Alternative
0 Magnet; 0 Charter; 0 Title I Eligible; 0 School-wide Title I
Students: 3,518 (51.7% male; 48.3% female)
Individual Education Program: 361 (10.3%);
English Language Learner: 21 (0.6%); Migrant: 0 (0.0%)
Eligible for Free Lunch Program: 10 (0.3%)
Eligible for Reduced-Price Lunch Program: 6 (0.2%)
Teachers: 239.3 (14.7 to 1)
Librarians/Media Specialists: 3.0 (1,172.7 to 1)
Guidance Counselors: 8.0 (439.8 to 1)
Current Spending: ($ per student per year):
Total: $9,596; Instruction: $5,779; Support Services: $3,523
Enrollment, Drop-out Rates and Diploma Recipients by Race/Ethnicity

Category	Total	White	Black	Asian	AIAN	Hisp.
Enrollment (%)	100.0	76.2	0.4	21.3	0.2	1.9
Drop-out Rate (%)	0.3	0.4	0.0	0.0	0.0	0.0
H.S. Diplomas (#)	218	162	2	51	1	2

Howell Twp

200 Squankum-Yellowbrook • Howell, NJ 07731-0579
(732) 751-2480 • http://www.howell.k12.nj.us
Grade Span: PK-08; **Agency Type:** 1
Schools: 10
8 Primary; 2 Middle; 0 High; 0 Other Level
10 Regular; 0 Special Education; 0 Vocational; 0 Alternative
0 Magnet; 0 Charter; 5 Title I Eligible; 0 School-wide Title I
Students: 7,424 (51.2% male; 48.8% female)
Individual Education Program: 1,107 (14.9%);
English Language Learner: 52 (0.7%); Migrant: 0 (0.0%)
Eligible for Free Lunch Program: 375 (5.1%)
Eligible for Reduced-Price Lunch Program: 214 (2.9%)
Teachers: 520.7 (14.3 to 1)
Librarians/Media Specialists: 11.0 (674.9 to 1)
Guidance Counselors: 11.3 (657.0 to 1)
Current Spending: ($ per student per year):
Total: $9,184; Instruction: $5,511; Support Services: $3,483
Enrollment, Drop-out Rates and Diploma Recipients by Race/Ethnicity

Category	Total	White	Black	Asian	AIAN	Hisp.
Enrollment (%)	100.0	87.7	4.2	3.3	0.2	4.6
Drop-out Rate (%)	n/a	n/a	n/a	n/a	n/a	n/a
H.S. Diplomas (#)	n/a	n/a	n/a	n/a	n/a	n/a

Keansburg Boro

100 Palmer Place • Keansburg, NJ 07734-2056
(732) 787-7578 • http://titans.khs.keansburg.k12.nj.us
Grade Span: PK-12; **Agency Type:** 1
Schools: 4
2 Primary; 1 Middle; 1 High; 0 Other Level
4 Regular; 0 Special Education; 0 Vocational; 0 Alternative
0 Magnet; 0 Charter; 3 Title I Eligible; 3 School-wide Title I
Students: 2,090 (52.1% male; 47.9% female)
Individual Education Program: 582 (27.8%);
English Language Learner: 10 (0.5%); Migrant: 0 (0.0%)
Eligible for Free Lunch Program: 885 (42.3%)
Eligible for Reduced-Price Lunch Program: 337 (16.1%)
Teachers: 218.8 (9.6 to 1)
Librarians/Media Specialists: 4.0 (522.5 to 1)
Guidance Counselors: 9.5 (220.0 to 1)
Current Spending: ($ per student per year):
Total: $13,649; Instruction: $8,313; Support Services: $4,997
Enrollment, Drop-out Rates and Diploma Recipients by Race/Ethnicity

Category	Total	White	Black	Asian	AIAN	Hisp.
Enrollment (%)	100.0	81.0	5.6	1.6	0.2	11.6
Drop-out Rate (%)	7.9	8.5	13.3	0.0	n/a	2.3
H.S. Diplomas (#)	85	72	3	3	0	7

Long Branch City

540 Broadway • Long Branch, NJ 07740-5108
(908) 571-2868 • http://www.longbranch.k12.nj.us
Grade Span: PK-12; **Agency Type:** 1
Schools: 9
7 Primary; 1 Middle; 1 High; 0 Other Level
9 Regular; 0 Special Education; 0 Vocational; 0 Alternative
0 Magnet; 0 Charter; 9 Title I Eligible; 0 School-wide Title I
Students: 4,998 (51.1% male; 48.9% female)
Individual Education Program: 866 (17.3%);
English Language Learner: 261 (5.2%); Migrant: 0 (0.0%)
Eligible for Free Lunch Program: 2,354 (47.1%)
Eligible for Reduced-Price Lunch Program: 723 (14.5%)
Teachers: 487.8 (10.2 to 1)
Librarians/Media Specialists: 5.0 (999.6 to 1)
Guidance Counselors: 17.0 (294.0 to 1)
Current Spending: ($ per student per year):
Total: $12,052; Instruction: $7,360; Support Services: $4,285
Enrollment, Drop-out Rates and Diploma Recipients by Race/Ethnicity

Category	Total	White	Black	Asian	AIAN	Hisp.
Enrollment (%)	100.0	35.8	33.6	0.9	0.5	29.2
Drop-out Rate (%)	2.6	1.0	3.0	0.0	0.0	4.5
H.S. Diplomas (#)	207	79	74	4	1	49

Manalapan-Englishtown Reg

54 Main St • Englishtown, NJ 07726-1599
(732) 446-5506 • http://www.mers.k12.nj.us
Grade Span: PK-08; **Agency Type:** 1
Schools: 7
3 Primary; 4 Middle; 0 High; 0 Other Level
7 Regular; 0 Special Education; 0 Vocational; 0 Alternative
0 Magnet; 0 Charter; 3 Title I Eligible; 0 School-wide Title I
Students: 5,568 (50.2% male; 49.8% female)
Individual Education Program: 803 (14.4%);
English Language Learner: 77 (1.4%); Migrant: 0 (0.0%)
Eligible for Free Lunch Program: 122 (2.2%)
Eligible for Reduced-Price Lunch Program: 90 (1.6%)
Teachers: 382.4 (14.6 to 1)
Librarians/Media Specialists: 7.0 (795.4 to 1)
Guidance Counselors: 9.5 (586.1 to 1)
Current Spending: ($ per student per year):
Total: $7,741; Instruction: $4,662; Support Services: $2,924
Enrollment, Drop-out Rates and Diploma Recipients by Race/Ethnicity

Category	Total	White	Black	Asian	AIAN	Hisp.
Enrollment (%)	100.0	89.1	2.2	5.5	0.1	3.1
Drop-out Rate (%)	n/a	n/a	n/a	n/a	n/a	n/a
H.S. Diplomas (#)	n/a	n/a	n/a	n/a	n/a	n/a

Manasquan Boro

169 Broad St • Manasquan, NJ 08736-2892
(732) 528-8800 • http://www.manasquanboe.org/public/default.asp
Grade Span: PK-12; **Agency Type:** 1
Schools: 2
1 Primary; 0 Middle; 1 High; 0 Other Level
2 Regular; 0 Special Education; 0 Vocational; 0 Alternative
0 Magnet; 0 Charter; 2 Title I Eligible; 0 School-wide Title I
Students: 1,747 (50.4% male; 49.6% female)
Individual Education Program: 116 (6.6%);
English Language Learner: 28 (1.6%); Migrant: 0 (0.0%)
Eligible for Free Lunch Program: 69 (3.9%)
Eligible for Reduced-Price Lunch Program: 25 (1.4%)
Teachers: 119.8 (14.6 to 1)
Librarians/Media Specialists: 2.0 (873.5 to 1)
Guidance Counselors: 5.8 (301.2 to 1)
Current Spending: ($ per student per year):
Total: $9,639; Instruction: $5,813; Support Services: $3,550
Enrollment, Drop-out Rates and Diploma Recipients by Race/Ethnicity

Category	Total	White	Black	Asian	AIAN	Hisp.
Enrollment (%)	100.0	93.2	2.1	0.3	0.7	3.6
Drop-out Rate (%)	2.4	2.2	4.0	0.0	n/a	9.1
H.S. Diplomas (#)	197	187	5	1	0	4

Marlboro Twp

1980 Township Dr • Marlboro, NJ 07746-2298
(732) 972-2015 • http://www.marlboro.k12.nj.us/
Grade Span: PK-08; **Agency Type:** 1
Schools: 8
6 Primary; 2 Middle; 0 High; 0 Other Level
8 Regular; 0 Special Education; 0 Vocational; 0 Alternative
0 Magnet; 0 Charter; 4 Title I Eligible; 0 School-wide Title I
Students: 5,825 (51.8% male; 48.2% female)
Individual Education Program: 736 (12.6%);
English Language Learner: 99 (1.7%); Migrant: 0 (0.0%)
Eligible for Free Lunch Program: 58 (1.0%)
Eligible for Reduced-Price Lunch Program: 53 (0.9%)
Teachers: 386.3 (15.1 to 1)
Librarians/Media Specialists: 7.0 (832.1 to 1)
Guidance Counselors: 9.0 (647.2 to 1)
Current Spending: ($ per student per year):
Total: $8,163; Instruction: $5,036; Support Services: $2,945
Enrollment, Drop-out Rates and Diploma Recipients by Race/Ethnicity

Category	Total	White	Black	Asian	AIAN	Hisp.
Enrollment (%)	100.0	76.5	1.8	18.8	0.1	2.8
Drop-out Rate (%)	n/a	n/a	n/a	n/a	n/a	n/a
H.S. Diplomas (#)	n/a	n/a	n/a	n/a	n/a	n/a

Matawan-Aberdeen Regional

Cambridge Park School • Aberdeen, NJ 07747-2286
(732) 290-2705 • http://www.marsd.k12.nj.us
Grade Span: PK-12; **Agency Type:** 1
Schools: 6
4 Primary; 1 Middle; 1 High; 0 Other Level
6 Regular; 0 Special Education; 0 Vocational; 0 Alternative
0 Magnet; 0 Charter; 4 Title I Eligible; 0 School-wide Title I
Students: 3,927 (50.8% male; 49.2% female)
Individual Education Program: 489 (12.5%);
English Language Learner: 67 (1.7%); Migrant: 0 (0.0%)
Eligible for Free Lunch Program: 454 (11.6%)
Eligible for Reduced-Price Lunch Program: 252 (6.4%)
Teachers: 290.4 (13.5 to 1)
Librarians/Media Specialists: 4.0 (981.8 to 1)
Guidance Counselors: 8.0 (490.9 to 1)
Current Spending: ($ per student per year):
Total: $11,361; Instruction: $6,930; Support Services: $4,144
Enrollment, Drop-out Rates and Diploma Recipients by Race/Ethnicity

Category	Total	White	Black	Asian	AIAN	Hisp.
Enrollment (%)	100.0	69.9	15.6	6.3	0.0	8.2
Drop-out Rate (%)	2.0	1.7	3.4	0.0	0.0	3.3
H.S. Diplomas (#)	191	132	32	6	0	21

Middletown Twp

59 Tindall Rd • Middletown, NJ 07748-2999
(732) 706-6002 • http://www.middletownk12.org
Grade Span: PK-12; **Agency Type:** 1
Schools: 17
12 Primary; 3 Middle; 2 High; 0 Other Level
17 Regular; 0 Special Education; 0 Vocational; 0 Alternative
0 Magnet; 0 Charter; 8 Title I Eligible; 0 School-wide Title I
Students: 10,363 (51.8% male; 48.2% female)
Individual Education Program: 1,776 (17.1%);
English Language Learner: 27 (0.3%); Migrant: 0 (0.0%)
Eligible for Free Lunch Program: 353 (3.4%)
Eligible for Reduced-Price Lunch Program: 239 (2.3%)
Teachers: 743.7 (13.9 to 1)
Librarians/Media Specialists: 9.0 (1,151.4 to 1)
Guidance Counselors: 23.0 (450.6 to 1)
Current Spending: ($ per student per year):
Total: $9,741; Instruction: $6,107; Support Services: $3,468
Enrollment, Drop-out Rates and Diploma Recipients by Race/Ethnicity

Category	Total	White	Black	Asian	AIAN	Hisp.
Enrollment (%)	100.0	91.8	1.6	2.5	0.8	3.2
Drop-out Rate (%)	1.1	0.9	7.4	0.0	0.0	5.9
H.S. Diplomas (#)	696	633	19	20	5	19

Millstone Twp

18 Schoolhouse Ln • Clarksburg, NJ 08510-9701
(732) 446-0890
Grade Span: PK-08; **Agency Type:** 1
Schools: 2
1 Primary; 1 Middle; 0 High; 0 Other Level
2 Regular; 0 Special Education; 0 Vocational; 0 Alternative
0 Magnet; 0 Charter; 1 Title I Eligible; 0 School-wide Title I
Students: 1,650 (50.9% male; 49.1% female)
Individual Education Program: 300 (18.2%);
English Language Learner: 14 (0.8%); Migrant: 0 (0.0%)
Eligible for Free Lunch Program: 40 (2.4%)
Eligible for Reduced-Price Lunch Program: 15 (0.9%)
Teachers: 112.7 (14.6 to 1)
Librarians/Media Specialists: 2.3 (717.4 to 1)
Guidance Counselors: 2.0 (825.0 to 1)
Current Spending: ($ per student per year):
Total: $8,434; Instruction: $4,828; Support Services: $3,372
Enrollment, Drop-out Rates and Diploma Recipients by Race/Ethnicity

Category	Total	White	Black	Asian	AIAN	Hisp.
Enrollment (%)	100.0	90.8	3.0	3.7	0.1	2.4
Drop-out Rate (%)	n/a	n/a	n/a	n/a	n/a	n/a
H.S. Diplomas (#)	n/a	n/a	n/a	n/a	n/a	n/a

Neptune Twp

2106 Bangs Ave • Neptune, NJ 07753-4596
(732) 776-2001 • http://www.neptune.k12.nj.us
Grade Span: PK-12; **Agency Type:** 1
Schools: 8
6 Primary; 1 Middle; 1 High; 0 Other Level
8 Regular; 0 Special Education; 0 Vocational; 0 Alternative
0 Magnet; 0 Charter; 5 Title I Eligible; 0 School-wide Title I
Students: 4,268 (52.4% male; 47.6% female)
Individual Education Program: 889 (20.8%);
English Language Learner: 34 (0.8%); Migrant: 0 (0.0%)
Eligible for Free Lunch Program: 1,394 (32.7%)
Eligible for Reduced-Price Lunch Program: 452 (10.6%)
Teachers: 326.1 (13.1 to 1)
Librarians/Media Specialists: 8.0 (533.5 to 1)
Guidance Counselors: 12.5 (341.4 to 1)
Current Spending: ($ per student per year):
Total: $12,740; Instruction: $8,087; Support Services: $4,325
Enrollment, Drop-out Rates and Diploma Recipients by Race/Ethnicity

Category	Total	White	Black	Asian	AIAN	Hisp.
Enrollment (%)	100.0	27.5	64.6	1.3	0.0	6.6
Drop-out Rate (%)	0.7	0.8	0.8	0.0	n/a	0.0
H.S. Diplomas (#)	233	100	117	5	0	11

Ocean Twp

163 Monmouth Rd • Oakhurst, NJ 07755-1597
(732) 531-5600 • http://www.ocean.k12.nj.us/
Grade Span: PK-12; **Agency Type:** 1
Schools: 5
3 Primary; 1 Middle; 1 High; 0 Other Level
5 Regular; 0 Special Education; 0 Vocational; 0 Alternative
0 Magnet; 0 Charter; 2 Title I Eligible; 0 School-wide Title I
Students: 4,494 (51.2% male; 48.8% female)
Individual Education Program: 665 (14.8%);
English Language Learner: 180 (4.0%); Migrant: 0 (0.0%)
Eligible for Free Lunch Program: 277 (6.2%)
Eligible for Reduced-Price Lunch Program: 179 (4.0%)
Teachers: 318.6 (14.1 to 1)
Librarians/Media Specialists: 5.0 (898.8 to 1)
Guidance Counselors: 10.0 (449.4 to 1)
Current Spending: ($ per student per year):
Total: $10,036; Instruction: $6,326; Support Services: $3,486
Enrollment, Drop-out Rates and Diploma Recipients by Race/Ethnicity

Category	Total	White	Black	Asian	AIAN	Hisp.
Enrollment (%)	100.0	78.1	6.8	8.0	0.0	7.0
Drop-out Rate (%)	0.2	0.1	1.0	0.0	n/a	2.3
H.S. Diplomas (#)	286	235	15	27	0	9

Tinton Falls

658 Tinton Ave • Tinton Falls, NJ 07724-3275
(732) 460-2404 • http://tfs.k12.nj.us/
Grade Span: PK-08; **Agency Type:** 1
Schools: 3
1 Primary; 2 Middle; 0 High; 0 Other Level
3 Regular; 0 Special Education; 0 Vocational; 0 Alternative
0 Magnet; 0 Charter; 1 Title I Eligible; 0 School-wide Title I
Students: 1,760 (50.5% male; 49.5% female)
Individual Education Program: 301 (17.1%);
English Language Learner: 19 (1.1%); Migrant: 0 (0.0%)
Eligible for Free Lunch Program: 148 (8.4%)
Eligible for Reduced-Price Lunch Program: 124 (7.0%)
Teachers: 142.6 (12.3 to 1)
Librarians/Media Specialists: 2.0 (880.0 to 1)
Guidance Counselors: 2.0 (880.0 to 1)
Current Spending: ($ per student per year):
Total: $9,487; Instruction: $5,259; Support Services: $3,902
Enrollment, Drop-out Rates and Diploma Recipients by Race/Ethnicity

Category	Total	White	Black	Asian	AIAN	Hisp.
Enrollment (%)	100.0	70.2	15.9	8.2	0.0	5.7
Drop-out Rate (%)	n/a	n/a	n/a	n/a	n/a	n/a
H.S. Diplomas (#)	n/a	n/a	n/a	n/a	n/a	n/a

Upper Freehold Regional

27 High St • Allentown, NJ 08501-0278
(609) 259-7292 • http://www.ufrsd.net/
Grade Span: PK-12; **Agency Type:** 1
Schools: 2
1 Primary; 0 Middle; 1 High; 0 Other Level
2 Regular; 0 Special Education; 0 Vocational; 0 Alternative
0 Magnet; 0 Charter; 1 Title I Eligible; 0 School-wide Title I
Students: 1,829 (52.3% male; 47.7% female)
Individual Education Program: 169 (9.2%);
English Language Learner: 42 (2.3%); Migrant: 0 (0.0%)
Eligible for Free Lunch Program: 38 (2.1%)
Eligible for Reduced-Price Lunch Program: 27 (1.5%)
Teachers: 126.6 (14.4 to 1)
Librarians/Media Specialists: 2.0 (914.5 to 1)
Guidance Counselors: 5.0 (365.8 to 1)
Current Spending: ($ per student per year):
Total: $10,197; Instruction: $5,935; Support Services: $3,847
Enrollment, Drop-out Rates and Diploma Recipients by Race/Ethnicity

Category	Total	White	Black	Asian	AIAN	Hisp.
Enrollment (%)	100.0	91.9	2.6	3.4	0.0	2.1
Drop-out Rate (%)	1.1	1.1	3.1	0.0	n/a	0.0
H.S. Diplomas (#)	235	227	5	1	0	2

Wall Twp

18th Avenue, New Bedford • Wall, NJ 07719-1199
Mailing Address: PO Box 1199 • Wall, NJ 07719-1199
(732) 556-2000 • http://www.wall.k12.nj.us
Grade Span: PK-12; **Agency Type:** 1
Schools: 7
4 Primary; 1 Middle; 1 High; 1 Other Level
7 Regular; 0 Special Education; 0 Vocational; 0 Alternative
0 Magnet; 0 Charter; 0 Title I Eligible; 0 School-wide Title I
Students: 4,254 (51.6% male; 48.4% female)
Individual Education Program: 751 (17.7%);
English Language Learner: 36 (0.8%); Migrant: 0 (0.0%)
Eligible for Free Lunch Program: 185 (4.3%)
Eligible for Reduced-Price Lunch Program: 100 (2.4%)
Teachers: 311.5 (13.7 to 1)
Librarians/Media Specialists: 2.0 (2,127.0 to 1)
Guidance Counselors: 12.0 (354.5 to 1)
Current Spending: ($ per student per year):
Total: $10,355; Instruction: $6,089; Support Services: $4,042
Enrollment, Drop-out Rates and Diploma Recipients by Race/Ethnicity

Category	Total	White	Black	Asian	AIAN	Hisp.
Enrollment (%)	100.0	94.3	2.6	1.0	0.0	2.1
Drop-out Rate (%)	1.5	1.5	0.0	0.0	n/a	0.0
H.S. Diplomas (#)	251	249	0	2	0	0

Morris County

Denville Twp
501 Openaki Rd • Denville, NJ 07834-9609
(973) 366-1001 • http://www.denville.org/
Grade Span: PK-08; **Agency Type:** 1
Schools: 3
2 Primary; 1 Middle; 0 High; 0 Other Level
3 Regular; 0 Special Education; 0 Vocational; 0 Alternative
0 Magnet; 0 Charter; 0 Title I Eligible; 0 School-wide Title I
Students: 1,821 (51.4% male; 48.6% female)
Individual Education Program: 308 (16.9%);
English Language Learner: 24 (1.3%); Migrant: 0 (0.0%)
Eligible for Free Lunch Program: 19 (1.0%)
Eligible for Reduced-Price Lunch Program: 0 (0.0%)
Teachers: 120.0 (15.2 to 1)
Librarians/Media Specialists: 3.0 (607.0 to 1)
Guidance Counselors: 4.0 (455.3 to 1)
Current Spending: ($ per student per year):
Total: $8,693; Instruction: $5,281; Support Services: $3,396
Enrollment, Drop-out Rates and Diploma Recipients by Race/Ethnicity

Category	Total	White	Black	Asian	AIAN	Hisp.
Enrollment (%)	100.0	88.7	1.5	6.8	0.4	2.6
Drop-out Rate (%)	n/a	n/a	n/a	n/a	n/a	n/a
H.S. Diplomas (#)	n/a	n/a	n/a	n/a	n/a	n/a

Dover Town
100 Grace St • Dover, NJ 07801-2699
(973) 989-2000 • http://www.dover-nj.org
Grade Span: PK-12; **Agency Type:** 1
Schools: 5
3 Primary; 1 Middle; 1 High; 0 Other Level
5 Regular; 0 Special Education; 0 Vocational; 0 Alternative
0 Magnet; 0 Charter; 5 Title I Eligible; 0 School-wide Title I
Students: 2,945 (51.7% male; 48.3% female)
Individual Education Program: 315 (10.7%);
English Language Learner: 487 (16.5%); Migrant: 0 (0.0%)
Eligible for Free Lunch Program: 976 (33.1%)
Eligible for Reduced-Price Lunch Program: 561 (19.0%)
Teachers: 214.6 (13.7 to 1)
Librarians/Media Specialists: 4.0 (736.3 to 1)
Guidance Counselors: 9.0 (327.2 to 1)
Current Spending: ($ per student per year):
Total: $9,617; Instruction: $6,103; Support Services: $3,220
Enrollment, Drop-out Rates and Diploma Recipients by Race/Ethnicity

Category	Total	White	Black	Asian	AIAN	Hisp.
Enrollment (%)	100.0	15.5	8.5	2.7	0.0	73.4
Drop-out Rate (%)	4.6	1.3	6.0	0.0	n/a	6.5
H.S. Diplomas (#)	171	65	21	6	0	79

Jefferson Twp
28 Bowling Green Pkwy • Lake Hopatcong, NJ 07849-2259
(973) 663-5780 • http://www.jefftwp.org/
Grade Span: PK-12; **Agency Type:** 1
Schools: 8
6 Primary; 1 Middle; 1 High; 0 Other Level
8 Regular; 0 Special Education; 0 Vocational; 0 Alternative
0 Magnet; 0 Charter; 4 Title I Eligible; 0 School-wide Title I
Students: 3,549 (51.4% male; 48.6% female)
Individual Education Program: 512 (14.4%);
English Language Learner: 16 (0.5%); Migrant: 0 (0.0%)
Eligible for Free Lunch Program: 129 (3.6%)
Eligible for Reduced-Price Lunch Program: 111 (3.1%)
Teachers: 251.1 (14.1 to 1)
Librarians/Media Specialists: 4.0 (887.3 to 1)
Guidance Counselors: 9.0 (394.3 to 1)
Current Spending: ($ per student per year):
Total: $9,911; Instruction: $5,767; Support Services: $3,822
Enrollment, Drop-out Rates and Diploma Recipients by Race/Ethnicity

Category	Total	White	Black	Asian	AIAN	Hisp.
Enrollment (%)	100.0	92.9	1.4	2.0	0.0	3.7
Drop-out Rate (%)	4.2	4.1	0.0	0.0	n/a	12.5
H.S. Diplomas (#)	230	211	4	7	0	8

Kinnelon Boro
109 Kiel Ave • Kinnelon, NJ 07405-1621
(973) 838-1418
Grade Span: PK-12; **Agency Type:** 1
Schools: 4
2 Primary; 1 Middle; 1 High; 0 Other Level
4 Regular; 0 Special Education; 0 Vocational; 0 Alternative
0 Magnet; 0 Charter; 0 Title I Eligible; 0 School-wide Title I
Students: 2,058 (51.8% male; 48.2% female)
Individual Education Program: 243 (11.8%);
English Language Learner: 6 (0.3%); Migrant: 0 (0.0%)
Eligible for Free Lunch Program: 7 (0.3%)
Eligible for Reduced-Price Lunch Program: 4 (0.2%)
Teachers: 148.2 (13.9 to 1)
Librarians/Media Specialists: 4.5 (457.3 to 1)
Guidance Counselors: 4.0 (514.5 to 1)
Current Spending: ($ per student per year):
Total: $10,548; Instruction: $6,319; Support Services: $3,912
Enrollment, Drop-out Rates and Diploma Recipients by Race/Ethnicity

Category	Total	White	Black	Asian	AIAN	Hisp.
Enrollment (%)	100.0	96.9	0.3	2.0	0.0	0.7
Drop-out Rate (%)	0.4	0.4	0.0	0.0	n/a	0.0
H.S. Diplomas (#)	113	108	3	2	0	0

Madison Boro
359 Woodland Rd • Madison, NJ 07940-2422
(973) 593-3100 • http://www.mendhamboro.org
Grade Span: PK-12; **Agency Type:** 1
Schools: 5
3 Primary; 1 Middle; 1 High; 0 Other Level
5 Regular; 0 Special Education; 0 Vocational; 0 Alternative
0 Magnet; 0 Charter; 2 Title I Eligible; 0 School-wide Title I
Students: 2,154 (51.1% male; 48.9% female)
Individual Education Program: 307 (14.3%);
English Language Learner: 44 (2.0%); Migrant: 0 (0.0%)
Eligible for Free Lunch Program: 95 (4.4%)
Eligible for Reduced-Price Lunch Program: 52 (2.4%)
Teachers: 166.6 (12.9 to 1)
Librarians/Media Specialists: 5.3 (406.4 to 1)
Guidance Counselors: 4.0 (538.5 to 1)
Current Spending: ($ per student per year):
Total: $11,603; Instruction: $7,252; Support Services: $4,128
Enrollment, Drop-out Rates and Diploma Recipients by Race/Ethnicity

Category	Total	White	Black	Asian	AIAN	Hisp.
Enrollment (%)	100.0	83.5	3.4	5.6	0.4	7.1
Drop-out Rate (%)	0.0	0.0	0.0	0.0	0.0	0.0
H.S. Diplomas (#)	139	118	6	9	0	6

Montville Twp
125 Changebridge Rd • Montville, NJ 07045
(973) 331-7117 • http://www.montville.net
Grade Span: PK-12; **Agency Type:** 1
Schools: 7
5 Primary; 1 Middle; 1 High; 0 Other Level
7 Regular; 0 Special Education; 0 Vocational; 0 Alternative
0 Magnet; 0 Charter; 0 Title I Eligible; 0 School-wide Title I
Students: 3,818 (51.0% male; 49.0% female)
Individual Education Program: 475 (12.4%);
English Language Learner: 65 (1.7%); Migrant: 0 (0.0%)
Eligible for Free Lunch Program: 28 (0.7%)
Eligible for Reduced-Price Lunch Program: 5 (0.1%)
Teachers: 282.6 (13.5 to 1)
Librarians/Media Specialists: 6.0 (636.3 to 1)
Guidance Counselors: 8.7 (438.9 to 1)
Current Spending: ($ per student per year):
Total: $10,761; Instruction: $6,420; Support Services: $4,063
Enrollment, Drop-out Rates and Diploma Recipients by Race/Ethnicity

Category	Total	White	Black	Asian	AIAN	Hisp.
Enrollment (%)	100.0	79.4	1.5	17.1	0.0	2.0
Drop-out Rate (%)	0.4	0.5	0.0	0.0	n/a	0.0
H.S. Diplomas (#)	208	163	3	36	0	6

Morris Hills Regional
48 Knoll Dr • Rockaway, NJ 07866-4088
(973) 664-2291 • http://www.mhrd.k12.nj.us
Grade Span: 09-12; **Agency Type:** 1
Schools: 2
0 Primary; 0 Middle; 2 High; 0 Other Level
2 Regular; 0 Special Education; 0 Vocational; 0 Alternative
0 Magnet; 0 Charter; 2 Title I Eligible; 0 School-wide Title I
Students: 2,461 (51.1% male; 48.9% female)
Individual Education Program: 336 (13.7%);
English Language Learner: 28 (1.1%); Migrant: 0 (0.0%)
Eligible for Free Lunch Program: 108 (4.4%)
Eligible for Reduced-Price Lunch Program: 48 (2.0%)
Teachers: 200.6 (12.3 to 1)
Librarians/Media Specialists: 3.0 (820.3 to 1)
Guidance Counselors: 16.0 (153.8 to 1)
Current Spending: ($ per student per year):
Total: $14,778; Instruction: $8,337; Support Services: $5,990
Enrollment, Drop-out Rates and Diploma Recipients by Race/Ethnicity

Category	Total	White	Black	Asian	AIAN	Hisp.
Enrollment (%)	100.0	79.8	2.8	6.5	0.2	10.6
Drop-out Rate (%)	1.1	1.0	0.0	2.1	0.0	1.3
H.S. Diplomas (#)	523	424	23	27	1	48

Morris SD

51 Hazel St • Morristown, NJ 07960-3802
(973) 292-2300 • http://www.morrisschooldistrict.org/
Grade Span: PK-12; **Agency Type:** 1
Schools: 10
7 Primary; 1 Middle; 1 High; 1 Other Level
9 Regular; 1 Special Education; 0 Vocational; 0 Alternative
0 Magnet; 0 Charter; 5 Title I Eligible; 0 School-wide Title I
Students: 4,634 (51.6% male; 48.4% female)
Individual Education Program: 945 (20.4%);
English Language Learner: 345 (7.4%); Migrant: 0 (0.0%)
Eligible for Free Lunch Program: 666 (14.4%)
Eligible for Reduced-Price Lunch Program: 353 (7.6%)
Teachers: 399.9 (11.6 to 1)
Librarians/Media Specialists: 9.0 (514.9 to 1)
Guidance Counselors: 10.0 (463.4 to 1)
Current Spending: ($ per student per year):
Total: $14,427; Instruction: $8,439; Support Services: $5,682
Enrollment, Drop-out Rates and Diploma Recipients by Race/Ethnicity

Category	Total	White	Black	Asian	AIAN	Hisp.
Enrollment (%)	100.0	56.2	17.5	5.0	0.0	21.2
Drop-out Rate (%)	1.1	0.1	1.8	0.0	n/a	4.2
H.S. Diplomas (#)	316	199	52	16	0	49

Mount Olive Twp

89 Route 46 • Budd Lake, NJ 07828-1793
(973) 691-4008 • http://www.mtoliveboe.org
Grade Span: PK-12; **Agency Type:** 1
Schools: 6
4 Primary; 1 Middle; 1 High; 0 Other Level
6 Regular; 0 Special Education; 0 Vocational; 0 Alternative
0 Magnet; 0 Charter; 5 Title I Eligible; 0 School-wide Title I
Students: 4,602 (52.3% male; 47.7% female)
Individual Education Program: 698 (15.2%);
English Language Learner: 130 (2.8%); Migrant: 0 (0.0%)
Eligible for Free Lunch Program: 194 (4.2%)
Eligible for Reduced-Price Lunch Program: 154 (3.3%)
Teachers: 325.0 (14.2 to 1)
Librarians/Media Specialists: 6.0 (767.0 to 1)
Guidance Counselors: 10.0 (460.2 to 1)
Current Spending: ($ per student per year):
Total: $11,051; Instruction: $6,303; Support Services: $4,460
Enrollment, Drop-out Rates and Diploma Recipients by Race/Ethnicity

Category	Total	White	Black	Asian	AIAN	Hisp.
Enrollment (%)	100.0	81.4	4.5	6.6	0.0	7.6
Drop-out Rate (%)	1.8	1.6	0.0	6.7	0.0	3.2
H.S. Diplomas (#)	231	222	3	3	0	3

Mountain Lakes Boro

400 Blvd • Mountain Lakes, NJ 07046-1520
(973) 334-8280 • http://www.mtlakes.org/Schools/
Grade Span: PK-12; **Agency Type:** 1
Schools: 4
1 Primary; 1 Middle; 1 High; 1 Other Level
3 Regular; 1 Special Education; 0 Vocational; 0 Alternative
0 Magnet; 0 Charter; 3 Title I Eligible; 0 School-wide Title I
Students: 1,667 (53.0% male; 47.0% female)
Individual Education Program: 204 (12.2%);
English Language Learner: 0 (0.0%); Migrant: 0 (0.0%)
Eligible for Free Lunch Program: 49 (2.9%)
Eligible for Reduced-Price Lunch Program: 20 (1.2%)
Teachers: 162.0 (10.3 to 1)
Librarians/Media Specialists: 4.0 (416.8 to 1)
Guidance Counselors: 4.6 (362.4 to 1)
Current Spending: ($ per student per year):
Total: $13,131; Instruction: $8,257; Support Services: $4,682
Enrollment, Drop-out Rates and Diploma Recipients by Race/Ethnicity

Category	Total	White	Black	Asian	AIAN	Hisp.
Enrollment (%)	100.0	89.6	1.7	5.6	0.0	3.0
Drop-out Rate (%)	0.1	0.2	0.0	0.0	n/a	0.0
H.S. Diplomas (#)	121	114	2	5	0	0

Parsippany-Troy Hills Twp

577 Vail Rd • Parsippany, NJ 07054-0052
Mailing Address: PO Box 52 • Parsippany, NJ 07054-0052
(973) 263-7250 • http://www.pthsd.k12.nj.us
Grade Span: PK-12; **Agency Type:** 1
Schools: 14
9 Primary; 2 Middle; 2 High; 1 Other Level
13 Regular; 1 Special Education; 0 Vocational; 0 Alternative
0 Magnet; 0 Charter; 6 Title I Eligible; 0 School-wide Title I
Students: 6,753 (52.2% male; 47.8% female)
Individual Education Program: 1,103 (16.3%);
English Language Learner: 400 (5.9%); Migrant: 0 (0.0%)
Eligible for Free Lunch Program: 302 (4.5%)
Eligible for Reduced-Price Lunch Program: 223 (3.3%)
Teachers: 574.5 (11.8 to 1)
Librarians/Media Specialists: 16.0 (422.1 to 1)
Guidance Counselors: 28.0 (241.2 to 1)
Current Spending: ($ per student per year):
Total: $12,128; Instruction: $7,260; Support Services: $4,624
Enrollment, Drop-out Rates and Diploma Recipients by Race/Ethnicity

Category	Total	White	Black	Asian	AIAN	Hisp.
Enrollment (%)	100.0	60.6	3.5	27.5	0.1	8.3
Drop-out Rate (%)	0.4	0.5	0.0	0.2	0.0	0.7
H.S. Diplomas (#)	526	342	18	128	0	38

Pequannock Twp

85 Sunset Rd • Pompton Plains, NJ 07444
(973) 616-6040 • http://www.morris.k12.nj.us/pequan
Grade Span: PK-12; **Agency Type:** 1
Schools: 5
3 Primary; 1 Middle; 1 High; 0 Other Level
5 Regular; 0 Special Education; 0 Vocational; 0 Alternative
0 Magnet; 0 Charter; 0 Title I Eligible; 0 School-wide Title I
Students: 2,459 (51.6% male; 48.4% female)
Individual Education Program: 360 (14.6%);
English Language Learner: 13 (0.5%); Migrant: 0 (0.0%)
Eligible for Free Lunch Program: 29 (1.2%)
Eligible for Reduced-Price Lunch Program: 20 (0.8%)
Teachers: 179.2 (13.7 to 1)
Librarians/Media Specialists: 5.0 (491.8 to 1)
Guidance Counselors: 5.0 (491.8 to 1)
Current Spending: ($ per student per year):
Total: $9,788; Instruction: $6,284; Support Services: $3,328
Enrollment, Drop-out Rates and Diploma Recipients by Race/Ethnicity

Category	Total	White	Black	Asian	AIAN	Hisp.
Enrollment (%)	100.0	94.3	0.5	1.9	0.0	3.3
Drop-out Rate (%)	0.1	0.2	0.0	0.0	n/a	0.0
H.S. Diplomas (#)	151	137	1	6	1	6

Randolph Twp

25 School House Rd • Randolph, NJ 07869-3199
(973) 328-2775 • http://www.rtnj.org
Grade Span: PK-12; **Agency Type:** 1
Schools: 6
4 Primary; 1 Middle; 1 High; 0 Other Level
6 Regular; 0 Special Education; 0 Vocational; 0 Alternative
0 Magnet; 0 Charter; 3 Title I Eligible; 0 School-wide Title I
Students: 5,451 (51.7% male; 48.3% female)
Individual Education Program: 721 (13.2%);
English Language Learner: 58 (1.1%); Migrant: 0 (0.0%)
Eligible for Free Lunch Program: 90 (1.7%)
Eligible for Reduced-Price Lunch Program: 79 (1.4%)
Teachers: 389.9 (14.0 to 1)
Librarians/Media Specialists: 8.0 (681.4 to 1)
Guidance Counselors: 9.0 (605.7 to 1)
Current Spending: ($ per student per year):
Total: $9,873; Instruction: $5,898; Support Services: $3,730
Enrollment, Drop-out Rates and Diploma Recipients by Race/Ethnicity

Category	Total	White	Black	Asian	AIAN	Hisp.
Enrollment (%)	100.0	82.9	2.5	8.9	0.1	5.6
Drop-out Rate (%)	0.6	0.4	0.0	0.0	n/a	8.2
H.S. Diplomas (#)	333	264	11	41	0	17

Rockaway Twp

PO Box 500 • Hibernia, NJ 07842
(973) 627-8200 • http://www.morris.k12.nj.us/rocktwp
Grade Span: PK-08; **Agency Type:** 1
Schools: 6
5 Primary; 1 Middle; 0 High; 0 Other Level
6 Regular; 0 Special Education; 0 Vocational; 0 Alternative
0 Magnet; 0 Charter; 1 Title I Eligible; 0 School-wide Title I
Students: 2,873 (53.6% male; 46.4% female)
Individual Education Program: 490 (17.1%);
English Language Learner: 33 (1.1%); Migrant: 0 (0.0%)
Eligible for Free Lunch Program: 96 (3.3%)
Eligible for Reduced-Price Lunch Program: 114 (4.0%)
Teachers: 243.6 (11.8 to 1)
Librarians/Media Specialists: 5.4 (532.0 to 1)
Guidance Counselors: 2.5 (1,149.2 to 1)
Current Spending: ($ per student per year):
Total: $11,346; Instruction: $6,598; Support Services: $4,475
Enrollment, Drop-out Rates and Diploma Recipients by Race/Ethnicity

Category	Total	White	Black	Asian	AIAN	Hisp.
Enrollment (%)	100.0	80.4	3.5	7.2	0.1	8.8
Drop-out Rate (%)	n/a	n/a	n/a	n/a	n/a	n/a
H.S. Diplomas (#)	n/a	n/a	n/a	n/a	n/a	n/a

Roxbury Twp

25 Meeker St • Succasunna, NJ 07876-1418
(973) 584-6867 • http://www.roxbury.org
Grade Span: PK-12; **Agency Type:** 1
Schools: 7
4 Primary; 2 Middle; 1 High; 0 Other Level
7 Regular; 0 Special Education; 0 Vocational; 0 Alternative
0 Magnet; 0 Charter; 4 Title I Eligible; 0 School-wide Title I
Students: 4,541 (52.0% male; 48.0% female)
Individual Education Program: 580 (12.8%);
English Language Learner: 55 (1.2%); Migrant: 0 (0.0%)
Eligible for Free Lunch Program: 151 (3.3%)
Eligible for Reduced-Price Lunch Program: 121 (2.7%)
Teachers: 337.8 (13.4 to 1)
Librarians/Media Specialists: 8.0 (567.6 to 1)
Guidance Counselors: 13.0 (349.3 to 1)
Current Spending: ($ per student per year):
Total: $10,199; Instruction: $6,156; Support Services: $3,735
Enrollment, Drop-out Rates and Diploma Recipients by Race/Ethnicity

Category	Total	White	Black	Asian	AIAN	Hisp.
Enrollment (%)	100.0	86.9	2.7	4.5	0.0	5.8
Drop-out Rate (%)	0.8	0.7	0.0	1.6	n/a	1.6
H.S. Diplomas (#)	325	287	7	16	0	15

SD of The Chathams

54 Fairmount Ave • Chatham, NJ 07928-2313
(973) 635-5656 • http://www.chatham-nj.org
Grade Span: PK-12; **Agency Type:** 1
Schools: 6
3 Primary; 2 Middle; 1 High; 0 Other Level
6 Regular; 0 Special Education; 0 Vocational; 0 Alternative
0 Magnet; 0 Charter; 0 Title I Eligible; 0 School-wide Title I
Students: 2,997 (51.8% male; 48.2% female)
Individual Education Program: 521 (17.4%);
English Language Learner: 15 (0.5%); Migrant: 0 (0.0%)
Eligible for Free Lunch Program: 12 (0.4%)
Eligible for Reduced-Price Lunch Program: 4 (0.1%)
Teachers: 232.7 (12.9 to 1)
Librarians/Media Specialists: 6.0 (499.5 to 1)
Guidance Counselors: 8.0 (374.6 to 1)
Current Spending: ($ per student per year):
Total: $10,812; Instruction: $6,569; Support Services: $4,095
Enrollment, Drop-out Rates and Diploma Recipients by Race/Ethnicity

Category	Total	White	Black	Asian	AIAN	Hisp.
Enrollment (%)	100.0	92.5	0.4	4.9	0.2	2.0
Drop-out Rate (%)	0.1	0.2	0.0	0.0	n/a	0.0
H.S. Diplomas (#)	166	151	0	5	0	10

Washington Twp

53 W Mill Rd • Long Valley, NJ 07853-9205
(908) 876-4172 • http://www.wtschools.org
Grade Span: PK-08; **Agency Type:** 1
Schools: 5
3 Primary; 2 Middle; 0 High; 0 Other Level
5 Regular; 0 Special Education; 0 Vocational; 0 Alternative
0 Magnet; 0 Charter; 0 Title I Eligible; 0 School-wide Title I
Students: 2,845 (49.4% male; 50.6% female)
Individual Education Program: 468 (16.4%);
English Language Learner: 7 (0.2%); Migrant: 0 (0.0%)
Eligible for Free Lunch Program: 29 (1.0%)
Eligible for Reduced-Price Lunch Program: 21 (0.7%)
Teachers: 195.5 (14.6 to 1)
Librarians/Media Specialists: 4.0 (711.3 to 1)
Guidance Counselors: 3.0 (948.3 to 1)
Current Spending: ($ per student per year):
Total: $9,612; Instruction: $5,887; Support Services: $3,532
Enrollment, Drop-out Rates and Diploma Recipients by Race/Ethnicity

Category	Total	White	Black	Asian	AIAN	Hisp.
Enrollment (%)	100.0	94.1	1.3	2.4	0.1	2.1
Drop-out Rate (%)	n/a	n/a	n/a	n/a	n/a	n/a
H.S. Diplomas (#)	n/a	n/a	n/a	n/a	n/a	n/a

West Morris Regional

Four Bridges Rd • Chester, NJ 07930
(908) 879-6404 • http://www.wmchs.org
Grade Span: 09-12; **Agency Type:** 1
Schools: 2
0 Primary; 0 Middle; 2 High; 0 Other Level
2 Regular; 0 Special Education; 0 Vocational; 0 Alternative
0 Magnet; 0 Charter; 0 Title I Eligible; 0 School-wide Title I
Students: 2,312 (50.5% male; 49.5% female)
Individual Education Program: 313 (13.5%);
English Language Learner: 5 (0.2%); Migrant: 0 (0.0%)
Eligible for Free Lunch Program: 8 (0.3%)
Eligible for Reduced-Price Lunch Program: 0 (0.0%)
Teachers: 185.4 (12.5 to 1)
Librarians/Media Specialists: 2.0 (1,156.0 to 1)
Guidance Counselors: 12.5 (185.0 to 1)
Current Spending: ($ per student per year):
Total: $13,609; Instruction: $7,418; Support Services: $5,908
Enrollment, Drop-out Rates and Diploma Recipients by Race/Ethnicity

Category	Total	White	Black	Asian	AIAN	Hisp.
Enrollment (%)	100.0	95.0	1.0	2.0	0.1	1.9
Drop-out Rate (%)	0.4	0.3	6.7	2.0	0.0	2.9
H.S. Diplomas (#)	512	488	1	16	0	7

Ocean County

Barnegat Twp

25 Birdsall St • Barnegat, NJ 08005-2497
(609) 698-5800 • http://barnegatschools.com/main/index.htm
Grade Span: PK-08; **Agency Type:** 1
Schools: 5
4 Primary; 1 Middle; 0 High; 0 Other Level
5 Regular; 0 Special Education; 0 Vocational; 0 Alternative
0 Magnet; 0 Charter; 4 Title I Eligible; 0 School-wide Title I
Students: 2,245 (50.7% male; 49.3% female)
Individual Education Program: 611 (27.2%);
English Language Learner: 11 (0.5%); Migrant: 0 (0.0%)
Eligible for Free Lunch Program: 278 (12.4%)
Eligible for Reduced-Price Lunch Program: 219 (9.8%)
Teachers: 174.4 (12.9 to 1)
Librarians/Media Specialists: 4.1 (547.6 to 1)
Guidance Counselors: 4.0 (561.3 to 1)
Current Spending: ($ per student per year):
Total: $9,456; Instruction: $5,325; Support Services: $3,914
Enrollment, Drop-out Rates and Diploma Recipients by Race/Ethnicity

Category	Total	White	Black	Asian	AIAN	Hisp.
Enrollment (%)	100.0	89.1	4.4	1.1	0.0	5.3
Drop-out Rate (%)	n/a	n/a	n/a	n/a	n/a	n/a
H.S. Diplomas (#)	n/a	n/a	n/a	n/a	n/a	n/a

Berkeley Twp

53 Central Pkwy • Bayville, NJ 08721-2414
(732) 269-2233
Grade Span: PK-06; **Agency Type:** 1
Schools: 3
3 Primary; 0 Middle; 0 High; 0 Other Level
3 Regular; 0 Special Education; 0 Vocational; 0 Alternative
0 Magnet; 0 Charter; 2 Title I Eligible; 0 School-wide Title I
Students: 1,903 (53.4% male; 46.6% female)
Individual Education Program: 275 (14.5%);
English Language Learner: 29 (1.5%); Migrant: 0 (0.0%)
Eligible for Free Lunch Program: 236 (12.4%)
Eligible for Reduced-Price Lunch Program: 112 (5.9%)
Teachers: 128.4 (14.8 to 1)
Librarians/Media Specialists: 3.0 (634.3 to 1)
Guidance Counselors: 3.0 (634.3 to 1)
Current Spending: ($ per student per year):
Total: $8,759; Instruction: $5,486; Support Services: $3,091
Enrollment, Drop-out Rates and Diploma Recipients by Race/Ethnicity

Category	Total	White	Black	Asian	AIAN	Hisp.
Enrollment (%)	100.0	87.5	5.8	1.2	0.0	5.5
Drop-out Rate (%)	n/a	n/a	n/a	n/a	n/a	n/a
H.S. Diplomas (#)	n/a	n/a	n/a	n/a	n/a	n/a

Brick Twp

101 Hendrickson Ave • Brick, NJ 08724-2599
(732) 785-3002
Grade Span: PK-12; **Agency Type:** 1
Schools: 12
8 Primary; 2 Middle; 2 High; 0 Other Level
12 Regular; 0 Special Education; 0 Vocational; 0 Alternative
0 Magnet; 0 Charter; 7 Title I Eligible; 0 School-wide Title I
Students: 11,544 (51.8% male; 48.2% female)
Individual Education Program: 2,221 (19.2%);
English Language Learner: 73 (0.6%); Migrant: 0 (0.0%)
Eligible for Free Lunch Program: 849 (7.4%)
Eligible for Reduced-Price Lunch Program: 599 (5.2%)
Teachers: 755.1 (15.3 to 1)
Librarians/Media Specialists: 13.9 (830.5 to 1)
Guidance Counselors: 19.0 (607.6 to 1)
Current Spending: ($ per student per year):
Total: $8,408; Instruction: $5,345; Support Services: $2,851
Enrollment, Drop-out Rates and Diploma Recipients by Race/Ethnicity

Category	Total	White	Black	Asian	AIAN	Hisp.
Enrollment (%)	100.0	92.6	1.6	1.6	0.1	4.1
Drop-out Rate (%)	4.2	4.0	3.3	6.0	0.0	10.0
H.S. Diplomas (#)	668	625	5	13	3	22

Central Regional

Forest Hills Pkwy • Bayville, NJ 08721-2799
(732) 269-1100 • http://www.centralreg.k12.nj.us
Grade Span: 07-12; **Agency Type:** 1
Schools: 2
0 Primary; 1 Middle; 1 High; 0 Other Level
2 Regular; 0 Special Education; 0 Vocational; 0 Alternative
0 Magnet; 0 Charter; 2 Title I Eligible; 0 School-wide Title I
Students: 2,413 (52.8% male; 47.2% female)
Individual Education Program: 414 (17.2%);
English Language Learner: 17 (0.7%); Migrant: 0 (0.0%)
Eligible for Free Lunch Program: 249 (10.3%)
Eligible for Reduced-Price Lunch Program: 139 (5.8%)
Teachers: 133.0 (18.1 to 1)
Librarians/Media Specialists: 3.0 (804.3 to 1)
Guidance Counselors: 9.0 (268.1 to 1)
Current Spending: ($ per student per year):
Total: $10,664; Instruction: $6,390; Support Services: $3,985
Enrollment, Drop-out Rates and Diploma Recipients by Race/Ethnicity

Category	Total	White	Black	Asian	AIAN	Hisp.
Enrollment (%)	100.0	92.0	3.3	0.4	0.1	4.2
Drop-out Rate (%)	3.4	3.5	0.0	0.0	n/a	5.4
H.S. Diplomas (#)	249	237	4	0	3	5

Jackson Twp

151 Don Connor Blvd • Jackson, NJ 08527-3497
(732) 833-4600 • http://www.jacksonsd.k12.nj.us
Grade Span: PK-12; **Agency Type:** 1
Schools: 8
5 Primary; 2 Middle; 1 High; 0 Other Level
8 Regular; 0 Special Education; 0 Vocational; 0 Alternative
0 Magnet; 0 Charter; 4 Title I Eligible; 0 School-wide Title I
Students: 9,099 (51.5% male; 48.5% female)
Individual Education Program: 1,735 (19.1%);
English Language Learner: 69 (0.8%); Migrant: 0 (0.0%)
Eligible for Free Lunch Program: 431 (4.7%)
Eligible for Reduced-Price Lunch Program: 321 (3.5%)
Teachers: 618.5 (14.7 to 1)
Librarians/Media Specialists: 8.0 (1,137.4 to 1)
Guidance Counselors: 21.0 (433.3 to 1)
Current Spending: ($ per student per year):
Total: $9,427; Instruction: $6,008; Support Services: $3,137
Enrollment, Drop-out Rates and Diploma Recipients by Race/Ethnicity

Category	Total	White	Black	Asian	AIAN	Hisp.
Enrollment (%)	100.0	86.9	5.4	2.5	0.1	5.0
Drop-out Rate (%)	0.4	0.3	1.6	0.0	0.0	1.0
H.S. Diplomas (#)	435	408	22	3	0	2

Lacey Twp

200 Western Blvd • Lanoka Harbor, NJ 08734-0216
(609) 971-2002 • http://www.lacey.k12.nj.us/
Grade Span: PK-12; **Agency Type:** 1
Schools: 6
3 Primary; 2 Middle; 1 High; 0 Other Level
6 Regular; 0 Special Education; 0 Vocational; 0 Alternative
0 Magnet; 0 Charter; 4 Title I Eligible; 0 School-wide Title I
Students: 5,047 (51.3% male; 48.7% female)
Individual Education Program: 907 (18.0%);
English Language Learner: 20 (0.4%); Migrant: 0 (0.0%)
Eligible for Free Lunch Program: 375 (7.4%)
Eligible for Reduced-Price Lunch Program: 258 (5.1%)
Teachers: 337.0 (15.0 to 1)
Librarians/Media Specialists: 6.0 (841.2 to 1)
Guidance Counselors: 11.0 (458.8 to 1)
Current Spending: ($ per student per year):
Total: $8,470; Instruction: $5,262; Support Services: $2,929
Enrollment, Drop-out Rates and Diploma Recipients by Race/Ethnicity

Category	Total	White	Black	Asian	AIAN	Hisp.
Enrollment (%)	100.0	97.2	0.4	0.8	0.1	1.5
Drop-out Rate (%)	0.9	1.0	0.0	0.0	0.0	0.0
H.S. Diplomas (#)	325	323	0	1	0	1

Lakewood Twp

655 Princeton Ave • Lakewood, NJ 08701-2895
(732) 905-3633 • http://www.lakewood.k12.nj.us/
Grade Span: PK-12; **Agency Type:** 1
Schools: 6
4 Primary; 1 Middle; 1 High; 0 Other Level
6 Regular; 0 Special Education; 0 Vocational; 0 Alternative
0 Magnet; 0 Charter; 5 Title I Eligible; 0 School-wide Title I
Students: 5,311 (50.5% male; 49.5% female)
Individual Education Program: 799 (15.0%);
English Language Learner: 432 (8.1%); Migrant: 4 (0.1%)
Eligible for Free Lunch Program: 2,525 (47.5%)
Eligible for Reduced-Price Lunch Program: 507 (9.5%)
Teachers: 449.4 (11.8 to 1)
Librarians/Media Specialists: 6.0 (885.2 to 1)
Guidance Counselors: 14.0 (379.4 to 1)
Current Spending: ($ per student per year):
Total: $12,289; Instruction: $7,806; Support Services: $4,139
Enrollment, Drop-out Rates and Diploma Recipients by Race/Ethnicity

Category	Total	White	Black	Asian	AIAN	Hisp.
Enrollment (%)	100.0	23.5	34.2	1.8	0.6	40.0
Drop-out Rate (%)	0.0	0.0	0.0	0.0	0.0	0.0
H.S. Diplomas (#)	268	122	85	6	4	51

Little Egg Harbor Twp

307 Frog Pond Rd • Little Egg Harbor, NJ 08087-9750
(609) 296-3295 • http://www.lehsd.k12.nj.us
Grade Span: PK-06; **Agency Type:** 1
Schools: 2
2 Primary; 0 Middle; 0 High; 0 Other Level
2 Regular; 0 Special Education; 0 Vocational; 0 Alternative
0 Magnet; 0 Charter; 2 Title I Eligible; 0 School-wide Title I
Students: 1,717 (51.4% male; 48.6% female)
Individual Education Program: 336 (19.6%);
English Language Learner: 20 (1.2%); Migrant: 0 (0.0%)
Eligible for Free Lunch Program: 317 (18.5%)
Eligible for Reduced-Price Lunch Program: 135 (7.9%)
Teachers: 135.3 (12.7 to 1)
Librarians/Media Specialists: 2.0 (858.5 to 1)
Guidance Counselors: 0.0 (0.0 to 1)
Current Spending: ($ per student per year):
Total: $8,999; Instruction: $5,380; Support Services: $3,364
Enrollment, Drop-out Rates and Diploma Recipients by Race/Ethnicity

Category	Total	White	Black	Asian	AIAN	Hisp.
Enrollment (%)	100.0	90.8	2.8	1.0	0.1	5.4
Drop-out Rate (%)	n/a	n/a	n/a	n/a	n/a	n/a
H.S. Diplomas (#)	n/a	n/a	n/a	n/a	n/a	n/a

Manchester Twp

121 Route 539 • Whiting, NJ 08759-1237
Mailing Address: 121 Route 539, Box 4100 • Whiting, NJ 08759-1237
(732) 350-5900 • http://www.manchestertwp.org
Grade Span: PK-12; **Agency Type:** 1
Schools: 6
3 Primary; 1 Middle; 1 High; 1 Other Level
5 Regular; 1 Special Education; 0 Vocational; 0 Alternative
0 Magnet; 0 Charter; 1 Title I Eligible; 0 School-wide Title I
Students: 3,351 (51.4% male; 48.6% female)
Individual Education Program: 573 (17.1%);
English Language Learner: 16 (0.5%); Migrant: 0 (0.0%)
Eligible for Free Lunch Program: 372 (11.1%)
Eligible for Reduced-Price Lunch Program: 181 (5.4%)
Teachers: 256.8 (13.0 to 1)
Librarians/Media Specialists: 5.0 (670.2 to 1)
Guidance Counselors: 7.0 (478.7 to 1)
Current Spending: ($ per student per year):
Total: $9,494; Instruction: $5,378; Support Services: $3,821
Enrollment, Drop-out Rates and Diploma Recipients by Race/Ethnicity

Category	Total	White	Black	Asian	AIAN	Hisp.
Enrollment (%)	100.0	79.8	11.0	2.1	0.3	6.8
Drop-out Rate (%)	2.3	2.1	2.9	3.4	0.0	3.8
H.S. Diplomas (#)	182	152	13	6	0	11

Pinelands Regional

520 Nugentown Rd • Tuckerton, NJ 08087-0248
(609) 296-3106 • http://www.pinelandsregional.org/
Grade Span: 07-12; **Agency Type:** 1
Schools: 2
0 Primary; 1 Middle; 1 High; 0 Other Level
2 Regular; 0 Special Education; 0 Vocational; 0 Alternative
0 Magnet; 0 Charter; 2 Title I Eligible; 0 School-wide Title I
Students: 1,925 (50.3% male; 49.7% female)
Individual Education Program: 477 (24.8%);
English Language Learner: 3 (0.2%); Migrant: 0 (0.0%)
Eligible for Free Lunch Program: 303 (15.7%)
Eligible for Reduced-Price Lunch Program: 212 (11.0%)
Teachers: 172.3 (11.2 to 1)
Librarians/Media Specialists: 3.0 (641.7 to 1)
Guidance Counselors: 8.0 (240.6 to 1)
Current Spending: ($ per student per year):
Total: $12,377; Instruction: $7,055; Support Services: $4,950
Enrollment, Drop-out Rates and Diploma Recipients by Race/Ethnicity

Category	Total	White	Black	Asian	AIAN	Hisp.
Enrollment (%)	100.0	97.1	0.7	0.4	0.1	1.7
Drop-out Rate (%)	4.6	4.6	0.0	0.0	n/a	0.0
H.S. Diplomas (#)	194	191	2	1	0	0

Plumsted Twp

117 Evergreen Rd • New Egypt, NJ 08533-1316
(609) 758-6800
Grade Span: PK-12; **Agency Type:** 1
Schools: 3
1 Primary; 1 Middle; 1 High; 0 Other Level
3 Regular; 0 Special Education; 0 Vocational; 0 Alternative
0 Magnet; 0 Charter; 3 Title I Eligible; 0 School-wide Title I
Students: 1,659 (51.7% male; 48.3% female)
Individual Education Program: 273 (16.5%);
English Language Learner: 16 (1.0%); Migrant: 1 (0.1%)
Eligible for Free Lunch Program: 117 (7.1%)
Eligible for Reduced-Price Lunch Program: 98 (5.9%)
Teachers: 121.5 (13.7 to 1)
Librarians/Media Specialists: 2.0 (829.5 to 1)
Guidance Counselors: 3.0 (553.0 to 1)
Current Spending: ($ per student per year):
Total: $8,543; Instruction: $4,590; Support Services: $3,536
Enrollment, Drop-out Rates and Diploma Recipients by Race/Ethnicity

Category	Total	White	Black	Asian	AIAN	Hisp.
Enrollment (%)	100.0	94.2	2.0	0.8	0.0	3.1
Drop-out Rate (%)	0.0	0.0	0.0	0.0	n/a	0.0
H.S. Diplomas (#)	0	0	0	0	0	0

Point Pleasant Boro

2100 Panther Path • Point Pleasant, NJ 08742-3770
(732) 701-1900 • http://www.pointpleasant.k12.nj.us
Grade Span: PK-12; **Agency Type:** 1
Schools: 4
2 Primary; 1 Middle; 1 High; 0 Other Level
4 Regular; 0 Special Education; 0 Vocational; 0 Alternative
0 Magnet; 0 Charter; 2 Title I Eligible; 0 School-wide Title I
Students: 3,190 (51.6% male; 48.4% female)
Individual Education Program: 410 (12.9%);
English Language Learner: 19 (0.6%); Migrant: 0 (0.0%)
Eligible for Free Lunch Program: 121 (3.8%)
Eligible for Reduced-Price Lunch Program: 80 (2.5%)
Teachers: 221.0 (14.4 to 1)
Librarians/Media Specialists: 4.0 (797.5 to 1)
Guidance Counselors: 7.0 (455.7 to 1)
Current Spending: ($ per student per year):
Total: $8,359; Instruction: $5,137; Support Services: $2,941
Enrollment, Drop-out Rates and Diploma Recipients by Race/Ethnicity

Category	Total	White	Black	Asian	AIAN	Hisp.
Enrollment (%)	100.0	97.1	0.3	0.5	0.2	1.9
Drop-out Rate (%)	0.3	0.2	0.0	0.0	n/a	4.2
H.S. Diplomas (#)	224	212	0	4	2	6

Southern Regional

105 Cedar Bridge Rd • Manahawkin, NJ 08050-3056
(609) 597-9481 • http://www.srsd.org/
Grade Span: 07-12; **Agency Type:** 1
Schools: 2
0 Primary; 1 Middle; 1 High; 0 Other Level
2 Regular; 0 Special Education; 0 Vocational; 0 Alternative
0 Magnet; 0 Charter; 2 Title I Eligible; 0 School-wide Title I
Students: 4,683 (49.4% male; 50.6% female)
Individual Education Program: 441 (9.4%);
English Language Learner: 30 (0.6%); Migrant: 0 (0.0%)
Eligible for Free Lunch Program: 284 (6.1%)
Eligible for Reduced-Price Lunch Program: 193 (4.1%)
Teachers: 266.6 (17.6 to 1)
Librarians/Media Specialists: 1.0 (4,683.0 to 1)
Guidance Counselors: 13.0 (360.2 to 1)
Current Spending: ($ per student per year):
Total: $11,388; Instruction: $6,723; Support Services: $4,387
Enrollment, Drop-out Rates and Diploma Recipients by Race/Ethnicity

Category	Total	White	Black	Asian	AIAN	Hisp.
Enrollment (%)	100.0	93.8	1.5	1.5	0.1	3.1
Drop-out Rate (%)	3.4	3.4	2.6	0.0	n/a	3.4
H.S. Diplomas (#)	615	597	12	0	0	6

Stafford Twp

775 E Bay Ave • Manahawkin, NJ 08050-2895
(609) 978-5708 • http://www.staffordschools.org
Grade Span: PK-06; **Agency Type:** 1
Schools: 4
3 Primary; 1 Middle; 0 High; 0 Other Level
4 Regular; 0 Special Education; 0 Vocational; 0 Alternative
0 Magnet; 0 Charter; 4 Title I Eligible; 0 School-wide Title I
Students: 2,368 (53.4% male; 46.6% female)
Individual Education Program: 443 (18.7%);
English Language Learner: 12 (0.5%); Migrant: 0 (0.0%)
Eligible for Free Lunch Program: 179 (7.6%)
Eligible for Reduced-Price Lunch Program: 155 (6.5%)
Teachers: 168.2 (14.1 to 1)
Librarians/Media Specialists: 4.0 (592.0 to 1)
Guidance Counselors: 3.0 (789.3 to 1)
Current Spending: ($ per student per year):
Total: $8,892; Instruction: $5,312; Support Services: $3,263
Enrollment, Drop-out Rates and Diploma Recipients by Race/Ethnicity

Category	Total	White	Black	Asian	AIAN	Hisp.
Enrollment (%)	100.0	95.3	1.8	1.1	0.0	1.8
Drop-out Rate (%)	n/a	n/a	n/a	n/a	n/a	n/a
H.S. Diplomas (#)	n/a	n/a	n/a	n/a	n/a	n/a

Toms River Regional

1144 Hooper Ave • Toms River, NJ 08753-7643
(732) 505-5510 • http://www.trschools.com/
Grade Span: PK-12; **Agency Type:** 1
Schools: 17
12 Primary; 2 Middle; 3 High; 0 Other Level
17 Regular; 0 Special Education; 0 Vocational; 0 Alternative
0 Magnet; 0 Charter; 8 Title I Eligible; 0 School-wide Title I
Students: 18,303 (51.2% male; 48.8% female)
Individual Education Program: 2,463 (13.5%);
English Language Learner: 120 (0.7%); Migrant: 0 (0.0%)
Eligible for Free Lunch Program: 1,534 (8.4%)
Eligible for Reduced-Price Lunch Program: 613 (3.3%)
Teachers: 1,159.4 (15.8 to 1)
Librarians/Media Specialists: 13.0 (1,407.9 to 1)
Guidance Counselors: 36.5 (501.5 to 1)
Current Spending: ($ per student per year):
Total: $9,116; Instruction: $5,512; Support Services: $3,361
Enrollment, Drop-out Rates and Diploma Recipients by Race/Ethnicity

Category	Total	White	Black	Asian	AIAN	Hisp.
Enrollment (%)	100.0	89.9	3.4	2.1	0.2	4.4
Drop-out Rate (%)	3.0	3.0	2.0	0.0	0.0	6.5
H.S. Diplomas (#)	1,188	1,095	33	30	0	30

Passaic County

Clifton City

745 Clifton Ave • Clifton, NJ 07015-2209
(973) 470-2260 • http://www.clifton.k12.nj.us
Grade Span: PK-12; **Agency Type:** 1
Schools: 16
13 Primary; 2 Middle; 1 High; 0 Other Level
16 Regular; 0 Special Education; 0 Vocational; 0 Alternative
0 Magnet; 0 Charter; 7 Title I Eligible; 0 School-wide Title I
Students: 10,283 (52.4% male; 47.6% female)
Individual Education Program: 1,382 (13.4%);
English Language Learner: 677 (6.6%); Migrant: 0 (0.0%)
Eligible for Free Lunch Program: 2,242 (21.8%)
Eligible for Reduced-Price Lunch Program: 358 (3.5%)
Teachers: 743.4 (13.8 to 1)
Librarians/Media Specialists: 18.0 (571.3 to 1)
Guidance Counselors: 25.7 (400.1 to 1)
Current Spending: ($ per student per year):
Total: $9,334; Instruction: $5,910; Support Services: $3,154
Enrollment, Drop-out Rates and Diploma Recipients by Race/Ethnicity

Category	Total	White	Black	Asian	AIAN	Hisp.
Enrollment (%)	100.0	51.2	3.4	8.4	0.1	36.8
Drop-out Rate (%)	4.1	3.6	3.9	1.5	0.0	5.9
H.S. Diplomas (#)	703	438	23	65	0	177

Hawthorne Boro

445 Lafayette Ave • Hawthorne, NJ 07507-0002
(973) 423-6401 • http://www.hawthorne.k12.nj.us
Grade Span: PK-12; **Agency Type:** 1
Schools: 5
3 Primary; 1 Middle; 1 High; 0 Other Level
5 Regular; 0 Special Education; 0 Vocational; 0 Alternative
0 Magnet; 0 Charter; 3 Title I Eligible; 0 School-wide Title I
Students: 2,295 (51.4% male; 48.6% female)
Individual Education Program: 352 (15.3%);
English Language Learner: 27 (1.2%); Migrant: 0 (0.0%)
Eligible for Free Lunch Program: 137 (6.0%)
Eligible for Reduced-Price Lunch Program: 91 (4.0%)
Teachers: 183.6 (12.5 to 1)
Librarians/Media Specialists: 4.0 (573.8 to 1)
Guidance Counselors: 5.1 (450.0 to 1)
Current Spending: ($ per student per year):
Total: $10,098; Instruction: $6,356; Support Services: $3,461
Enrollment, Drop-out Rates and Diploma Recipients by Race/Ethnicity

Category	Total	White	Black	Asian	AIAN	Hisp.
Enrollment (%)	100.0	85.3	1.0	1.1	0.0	12.6
Drop-out Rate (%)	1.1	1.2	0.0	0.0	n/a	0.0
H.S. Diplomas (#)	136	129	0	0	0	7

Passaic City

101 Passaic Ave • Passaic, NJ 07055-4828
(973) 470-5201 • http://www.passaic-city.k12.nj.us/
Grade Span: PK-12; **Agency Type:** 1
Schools: 16
11 Primary; 3 Middle; 1 High; 1 Other Level
16 Regular; 0 Special Education; 0 Vocational; 0 Alternative
0 Magnet; 0 Charter; 12 Title I Eligible; 1 School-wide Title I
Students: 11,267 (50.0% male; 50.0% female)
Individual Education Program: 2,457 (21.8%);
English Language Learner: 3,202 (28.4%); Migrant: 0 (0.0%)
Eligible for Free Lunch Program: 7,394 (65.6%)
Eligible for Reduced-Price Lunch Program: 1,102 (9.8%)
Teachers: 883.3 (12.8 to 1)
Librarians/Media Specialists: 10.0 (1,126.7 to 1)
Guidance Counselors: 30.4 (370.6 to 1)
Current Spending: ($ per student per year):
Total: $13,744; Instruction: $9,058; Support Services: $4,322
Enrollment, Drop-out Rates and Diploma Recipients by Race/Ethnicity

Category	Total	White	Black	Asian	AIAN	Hisp.
Enrollment (%)	100.0	2.4	13.0	4.7	0.0	79.8
Drop-out Rate (%)	7.2	16.7	6.6	4.0	0.0	7.3
H.S. Diplomas (#)	0	0	0	0	0	0

Passaic County Vocational

45 Reinhardt Rd • Wayne, NJ 07470-2210
(973) 389-4202 • http://www.pcti.tec.nj.us
Grade Span: 09-12; **Agency Type:** 1
Schools: 1
0 Primary; 0 Middle; 1 High; 0 Other Level
0 Regular; 0 Special Education; 1 Vocational; 0 Alternative
0 Magnet; 0 Charter; 1 Title I Eligible; 0 School-wide Title I
Students: 2,013 (48.7% male; 51.3% female)
Individual Education Program: 354 (17.6%);
English Language Learner: 48 (2.4%); Migrant: 0 (0.0%)
Eligible for Free Lunch Program: 888 (44.1%)
Eligible for Reduced-Price Lunch Program: 394 (19.6%)
Teachers: 199.0 (10.1 to 1)
Librarians/Media Specialists: 1.0 (2,013.0 to 1)
Guidance Counselors: 12.0 (167.8 to 1)
Current Spending: ($ per student per year):
Total: $18,881; Instruction: $10,453; Support Services: $7,865
Enrollment, Drop-out Rates and Diploma Recipients by Race/Ethnicity

Category	Total	White	Black	Asian	AIAN	Hisp.
Enrollment (%)	100.0	13.7	26.5	0.9	0.0	58.9
Drop-out Rate (%)	2.1	2.8	2.4	n/a	n/a	1.9
H.S. Diplomas (#)	451	67	111	1	0	272

Paterson City

33-35 Church St • Paterson, NJ 07505-1306
(973) 321-0980 • http://www.paterson.K12.nj.us
Grade Span: PK-12; **Agency Type:** 1
Schools: 36
31 Primary; 2 Middle; 3 High; 0 Other Level
36 Regular; 0 Special Education; 0 Vocational; 0 Alternative
0 Magnet; 0 Charter; 32 Title I Eligible; 32 School-wide Title I
Students: 26,193 (51.1% male; 48.9% female)
Individual Education Program: 4,288 (16.4%);
English Language Learner: 3,383 (12.9%); Migrant: 0 (0.0%)
Eligible for Free Lunch Program: 17,959 (68.6%)
Eligible for Reduced-Price Lunch Program: 2,977 (11.4%)
Teachers: 2,337.7 (11.2 to 1)
Librarians/Media Specialists: 37.0 (707.9 to 1)
Guidance Counselors: 80.5 (325.4 to 1)
Current Spending: ($ per student per year):
Total: $12,409; Instruction: $7,312; Support Services: $4,725
Enrollment, Drop-out Rates and Diploma Recipients by Race/Ethnicity

Category	Total	White	Black	Asian	AIAN	Hisp.
Enrollment (%)	100.0	6.3	37.5	2.6	0.1	53.5
Drop-out Rate (%)	14.2	4.6	13.6	7.4	0.0	16.8
H.S. Diplomas (#)	754	26	327	27	0	374

Pompton Lakes Boro

237 Van Ave • Pompton Lakes, NJ 07442-1343
(973) 835-4334 • http://www.plps.org
Grade Span: PK-12; **Agency Type:** 1
Schools: 4
2 Primary; 1 Middle; 1 High; 0 Other Level
4 Regular; 0 Special Education; 0 Vocational; 0 Alternative
0 Magnet; 0 Charter; 3 Title I Eligible; 0 School-wide Title I
Students: 1,870 (49.8% male; 50.2% female)
Individual Education Program: 313 (16.7%);
English Language Learner: 31 (1.7%); Migrant: 0 (0.0%)
Eligible for Free Lunch Program: 70 (3.7%)
Eligible for Reduced-Price Lunch Program: 50 (2.7%)
Teachers: 136.0 (13.8 to 1)
Librarians/Media Specialists: 4.0 (467.5 to 1)
Guidance Counselors: 6.0 (311.7 to 1)
Current Spending: ($ per student per year):
Total: $10,633; Instruction: $6,407; Support Services: $3,925
Enrollment, Drop-out Rates and Diploma Recipients by Race/Ethnicity

Category	Total	White	Black	Asian	AIAN	Hisp.
Enrollment (%)	100.0	88.9	1.2	3.3	0.1	6.5
Drop-out Rate (%)	0.9	0.8	0.0	4.3	n/a	0.0
H.S. Diplomas (#)	140	124	0	6	0	10

Wayne Twp

50 Nellis Dr • Wayne, NJ 07470-3562
(973) 633-3032 • http://wayneschools.com/wboe/dsp_home_page.cfm
Grade Span: PK-12; **Agency Type:** 1
Schools: 13
9 Primary; 2 Middle; 2 High; 0 Other Level
13 Regular; 0 Special Education; 0 Vocational; 0 Alternative
0 Magnet; 0 Charter; 3 Title I Eligible; 0 School-wide Title I
Students: 8,613 (51.6% male; 48.4% female)
Individual Education Program: 1,040 (12.1%);
English Language Learner: 111 (1.3%); Migrant: 0 (0.0%)
Eligible for Free Lunch Program: 234 (2.7%)
Eligible for Reduced-Price Lunch Program: 160 (1.9%)
Teachers: 622.4 (13.8 to 1)
Librarians/Media Specialists: 11.0 (783.0 to 1)
Guidance Counselors: 22.0 (391.5 to 1)
Current Spending: ($ per student per year):
Total: $10,707; Instruction: $6,786; Support Services: $3,699
Enrollment, Drop-out Rates and Diploma Recipients by Race/Ethnicity

Category	Total	White	Black	Asian	AIAN	Hisp.
Enrollment (%)	100.0	86.6	0.9	8.0	0.0	4.6
Drop-out Rate (%)	1.6	1.7	4.8	0.0	n/a	0.9
H.S. Diplomas (#)	578	489	17	39	0	33

West Milford Twp

46 Highlander Dr • West Milford, NJ 07480-1511
(973) 697-1700 • http://www.wmtps.org
Grade Span: PK-12; **Agency Type:** 1
Schools: 8
6 Primary; 1 Middle; 1 High; 0 Other Level
8 Regular; 0 Special Education; 0 Vocational; 0 Alternative
0 Magnet; 0 Charter; 8 Title I Eligible; 0 School-wide Title I
Students: 4,700 (52.7% male; 47.3% female)
Individual Education Program: 820 (17.4%);
English Language Learner: 17 (0.4%); Migrant: 0 (0.0%)
Eligible for Free Lunch Program: 188 (4.0%)
Eligible for Reduced-Price Lunch Program: 111 (2.4%)
Teachers: 331.6 (14.2 to 1)
Librarians/Media Specialists: 8.0 (587.5 to 1)
Guidance Counselors: 11.0 (427.3 to 1)
Current Spending: ($ per student per year):
Total: $10,482; Instruction: $6,250; Support Services: $3,896
Enrollment, Drop-out Rates and Diploma Recipients by Race/Ethnicity

Category	Total	White	Black	Asian	AIAN	Hisp.
Enrollment (%)	100.0	94.7	1.8	1.2	0.4	1.8
Drop-out Rate (%)	1.8	1.5	5.7	0.0	0.0	12.5
H.S. Diplomas (#)	294	283	5	1	0	5

Salem County

Penns Grove-Carney's Point Reg

113 W Harmony St • Penns Grove, NJ 08069-1369
(856) 299-4250 • http://www.pennsgrove.k12.nj.us
Grade Span: PK-12; **Agency Type:** 1
Schools: 5
2 Primary; 2 Middle; 1 High; 0 Other Level
5 Regular; 0 Special Education; 0 Vocational; 0 Alternative
0 Magnet; 0 Charter; 5 Title I Eligible; 0 School-wide Title I
Students: 2,261 (49.7% male; 50.3% female)
Individual Education Program: 340 (15.0%);
English Language Learner: 70 (3.1%); Migrant: 11 (0.5%)
Eligible for Free Lunch Program: 920 (40.7%)
Eligible for Reduced-Price Lunch Program: 203 (9.0%)
Teachers: 190.9 (11.8 to 1)
Librarians/Media Specialists: 4.7 (481.1 to 1)
Guidance Counselors: 6.9 (327.7 to 1)
Current Spending: ($ per student per year):
Total: $10,894; Instruction: $6,862; Support Services: $3,593
Enrollment, Drop-out Rates and Diploma Recipients by Race/Ethnicity

Category	Total	White	Black	Asian	AIAN	Hisp.
Enrollment (%)	100.0	45.6	39.0	1.0	0.1	14.4
Drop-out Rate (%)	2.7	1.8	4.3	0.0	n/a	3.0
H.S. Diplomas (#)	162	94	59	2	0	7

Pennsville

30 Church St • Pennsville, NJ 08070-2123
(856) 540-6210 • http://www.pennsville.k12.nj.us
Grade Span: PK-12; **Agency Type:** 1
Schools: 5
3 Primary; 1 Middle; 1 High; 0 Other Level
5 Regular; 0 Special Education; 0 Vocational; 0 Alternative
0 Magnet; 0 Charter; 3 Title I Eligible; 0 School-wide Title I
Students: 2,044 (49.2% male; 50.8% female)
Individual Education Program: 405 (19.8%);
English Language Learner: 7 (0.3%); Migrant: 0 (0.0%)
Eligible for Free Lunch Program: 164 (8.0%)
Eligible for Reduced-Price Lunch Program: 83 (4.1%)
Teachers: 167.6 (12.2 to 1)
Librarians/Media Specialists: 5.0 (408.8 to 1)
Guidance Counselors: 5.2 (393.1 to 1)
Current Spending: ($ per student per year):
Total: $10,522; Instruction: $6,292; Support Services: $3,914
Enrollment, Drop-out Rates and Diploma Recipients by Race/Ethnicity

Category	Total	White	Black	Asian	AIAN	Hisp.
Enrollment (%)	100.0	94.9	1.0	2.0	0.0	2.1
Drop-out Rate (%)	3.5	3.5	8.3	0.0	n/a	0.0
H.S. Diplomas (#)	124	120	0	3	0	1

Pittsgrove Twp

Admin Bldg, 1076 Almond Rd • Pittsgrove, NJ 08318-8903
(609) 358-3094 • http://www.pittsgrove.org
Grade Span: PK-12; **Agency Type:** 1
Schools: 4
2 Primary; 1 Middle; 1 High; 0 Other Level
4 Regular; 0 Special Education; 0 Vocational; 0 Alternative
0 Magnet; 0 Charter; 4 Title I Eligible; 0 School-wide Title I
Students: 1,892 (51.5% male; 48.5% female)
Individual Education Program: 302 (16.0%);
English Language Learner: 7 (0.4%); Migrant: 8 (0.4%)
Eligible for Free Lunch Program: 346 (18.3%)
Eligible for Reduced-Price Lunch Program: 128 (6.8%)
Teachers: 128.7 (14.7 to 1)
Librarians/Media Specialists: 2.0 (946.0 to 1)
Guidance Counselors: 6.0 (315.3 to 1)
Current Spending: ($ per student per year):
Total: $9,215; Instruction: $5,217; Support Services: $3,552
Enrollment, Drop-out Rates and Diploma Recipients by Race/Ethnicity

Category	Total	White	Black	Asian	AIAN	Hisp.
Enrollment (%)	100.0	85.7	9.9	0.8	0.1	3.4
Drop-out Rate (%)	1.7	1.6	1.8	0.0	n/a	0.0
H.S. Diplomas (#)	125	107	15	2	0	1

Woodstown-Pilesgrove Reg

135 E Ave • Woodstown, NJ 08098-1336
(856) 769-1664 • http://www.woodstown.org
Grade Span: PK-12; **Agency Type:** 1
Schools: 3
1 Primary; 1 Middle; 1 High; 0 Other Level
3 Regular; 0 Special Education; 0 Vocational; 0 Alternative
0 Magnet; 0 Charter; 3 Title I Eligible; 0 School-wide Title I
Students: 1,684 (51.5% male; 48.5% female)
Individual Education Program: 188 (11.2%);
English Language Learner: 7 (0.4%); Migrant: 6 (0.4%)
Eligible for Free Lunch Program: 113 (6.7%)
Eligible for Reduced-Price Lunch Program: 78 (4.6%)
Teachers: 122.0 (13.8 to 1)
Librarians/Media Specialists: 3.0 (561.3 to 1)
Guidance Counselors: 6.0 (280.7 to 1)
Current Spending: ($ per student per year):
Total: $9,108; Instruction: $5,442; Support Services: $3,399
Enrollment, Drop-out Rates and Diploma Recipients by Race/Ethnicity

Category	Total	White	Black	Asian	AIAN	Hisp.
Enrollment (%)	100.0	88.5	9.0	0.8	0.1	1.6
Drop-out Rate (%)	2.5	2.0	7.3	0.0	n/a	14.3
H.S. Diplomas (#)	166	152	12	0	0	2

Somerset County

Bernards Twp

101 Peachtree Rd • Basking Ridge, NJ 07920
(908) 204-2600 • http://www.bernardsboe.com
Grade Span: PK-12; **Agency Type:** 1
Schools: 6
4 Primary; 1 Middle; 1 High; 0 Other Level
6 Regular; 0 Special Education; 0 Vocational; 0 Alternative
0 Magnet; 0 Charter; 0 Title I Eligible; 0 School-wide Title I
Students: 4,767 (51.1% male; 48.9% female)
Individual Education Program: 540 (11.3%);
English Language Learner: 48 (1.0%); Migrant: 0 (0.0%)
Eligible for Free Lunch Program: 23 (0.5%)
Eligible for Reduced-Price Lunch Program: 21 (0.4%)
Teachers: 373.5 (12.8 to 1)
Librarians/Media Specialists: 6.0 (794.5 to 1)
Guidance Counselors: 13.0 (366.7 to 1)
Current Spending: ($ per student per year):
Total: $10,097; Instruction: $5,828; Support Services: $4,021
Enrollment, Drop-out Rates and Diploma Recipients by Race/Ethnicity

Category	Total	White	Black	Asian	AIAN	Hisp.
Enrollment (%)	100.0	84.9	1.1	12.2	0.0	1.7
Drop-out Rate (%)	0.0	0.0	0.0	0.0	n/a	0.0
H.S. Diplomas (#)	231	196	1	28	0	6

Bound Brook Boro

133 W Maple Ave • Bound Brook, NJ 08805-1330
(732) 271-2830
Grade Span: PK-12; **Agency Type:** 1
Schools: 3
2 Primary; 0 Middle; 1 High; 0 Other Level
3 Regular; 0 Special Education; 0 Vocational; 0 Alternative
0 Magnet; 0 Charter; 3 Title I Eligible; 0 School-wide Title I
Students: 1,613 (52.3% male; 47.7% female)
Individual Education Program: 229 (14.2%);
English Language Learner: 217 (13.5%); Migrant: 0 (0.0%)
Eligible for Free Lunch Program: 424 (26.3%)
Eligible for Reduced-Price Lunch Program: 214 (13.3%)
Teachers: 118.6 (13.6 to 1)
Librarians/Media Specialists: 3.0 (537.7 to 1)
Guidance Counselors: 5.5 (293.3 to 1)
Current Spending: ($ per student per year):
Total: $9,566; Instruction: $6,126; Support Services: $3,178
Enrollment, Drop-out Rates and Diploma Recipients by Race/Ethnicity

Category	Total	White	Black	Asian	AIAN	Hisp.
Enrollment (%)	100.0	34.4	3.4	4.9	0.0	57.3
Drop-out Rate (%)	0.0	0.0	0.0	0.0	n/a	0.0
H.S. Diplomas (#)	100	52	4	5	0	39

Branchburg Twp

3461 US Hwy 22 • Branchburg, NJ 08876-6021
(908) 722-3265 • http://www.branchburg.k12.nj.us
Grade Span: PK-08; **Agency Type:** 1
Schools: 4
2 Primary; 2 Middle; 0 High; 0 Other Level
4 Regular; 0 Special Education; 0 Vocational; 0 Alternative
0 Magnet; 0 Charter; 0 Title I Eligible; 0 School-wide Title I
Students: 1,910 (51.5% male; 48.5% female)
Individual Education Program: 377 (19.7%);
English Language Learner: 17 (0.9%); Migrant: 0 (0.0%)
Eligible for Free Lunch Program: 21 (1.1%)
Eligible for Reduced-Price Lunch Program: 18 (0.9%)
Teachers: 158.1 (12.1 to 1)
Librarians/Media Specialists: 4.0 (477.5 to 1)
Guidance Counselors: 4.0 (477.5 to 1)
Current Spending: ($ per student per year):
Total: $10,982; Instruction: $6,115; Support Services: $4,698
Enrollment, Drop-out Rates and Diploma Recipients by Race/Ethnicity

Category	Total	White	Black	Asian	AIAN	Hisp.
Enrollment (%)	100.0	90.1	1.6	6.2	0.1	2.0
Drop-out Rate (%)	n/a	n/a	n/a	n/a	n/a	n/a
H.S. Diplomas (#)	n/a	n/a	n/a	n/a	n/a	n/a

Bridgewater-Raritan Reg

836 Newmans Ln • Bridgewater, NJ 08807-0030
(908) 685-2777 • http://www.brrsd.k12.nj.us
Grade Span: PK-12; **Agency Type:** 1
Schools: 10
6 Primary; 3 Middle; 1 High; 0 Other Level
10 Regular; 0 Special Education; 0 Vocational; 0 Alternative
0 Magnet; 0 Charter; 2 Title I Eligible; 0 School-wide Title I
Students: 8,420 (51.0% male; 49.0% female)
Individual Education Program: 1,238 (14.7%);
English Language Learner: 168 (2.0%); Migrant: 0 (0.0%)
Eligible for Free Lunch Program: 223 (2.6%)
Eligible for Reduced-Price Lunch Program: 176 (2.1%)
Teachers: 608.8 (13.8 to 1)
Librarians/Media Specialists: 11.8 (713.6 to 1)
Guidance Counselors: 25.0 (336.8 to 1)
Current Spending: ($ per student per year):
Total: $10,250; Instruction: $6,253; Support Services: $3,743
Enrollment, Drop-out Rates and Diploma Recipients by Race/Ethnicity

Category	Total	White	Black	Asian	AIAN	Hisp.
Enrollment (%)	100.0	76.0	2.5	15.0	0.0	6.5
Drop-out Rate (%)	1.1	0.9	4.5	0.4	n/a	3.3
H.S. Diplomas (#)	455	343	12	69	0	31

Franklin Twp

1755 Amwell Rd • Somerset, NJ 08873-2793
(732) 873-2400 • http://www.franklinboe.org
Grade Span: PK-12; **Agency Type:** 1
Schools: 8
6 Primary; 1 Middle; 1 High; 0 Other Level
2 Regular; 0 Special Education; 0 Vocational; 6 Alternative
0 Magnet; 0 Charter; 5 Title I Eligible; 0 School-wide Title I
Students: 6,305 (51.6% male; 48.4% female)
Individual Education Program: 1,126 (17.9%);
English Language Learner: 269 (4.3%); Migrant: 0 (0.0%)
Eligible for Free Lunch Program: 1,266 (20.1%)
Eligible for Reduced-Price Lunch Program: 461 (7.3%)
Teachers: 494.1 (12.8 to 1)
Librarians/Media Specialists: 10.5 (600.5 to 1)
Guidance Counselors: 18.0 (350.3 to 1)
Current Spending: ($ per student per year):
Total: $11,770; Instruction: $6,824; Support Services: $4,644
Enrollment, Drop-out Rates and Diploma Recipients by Race/Ethnicity

Category	Total	White	Black	Asian	AIAN	Hisp.
Enrollment (%)	100.0	29.8	44.2	13.7	0.1	12.2
Drop-out Rate (%)	5.4	4.7	5.2	0.7	0.0	12.1
H.S. Diplomas (#)	287	96	114	47	0	30

Hillsborough Twp

555 Amwell Rd • Neshanic, NJ 08853-3409
(908) 369-0030 • http://www.hillsborough.k12.nj.us
Grade Span: PK-12; **Agency Type:** 1
Schools: 9
6 Primary; 2 Middle; 1 High; 0 Other Level
9 Regular; 0 Special Education; 0 Vocational; 0 Alternative
0 Magnet; 0 Charter; 0 Title I Eligible; 0 School-wide Title I
Students: 7,510 (52.8% male; 47.2% female)
Individual Education Program: 1,286 (17.1%);
English Language Learner: 0 (0.0%); Migrant: 0 (0.0%)
Eligible for Free Lunch Program: 179 (2.4%)
Eligible for Reduced-Price Lunch Program: 143 (1.9%)
Teachers: 620.3 (12.1 to 1)
Librarians/Media Specialists: 9.0 (834.4 to 1)
Guidance Counselors: 19.0 (395.3 to 1)
Current Spending: ($ per student per year):
Total: $9,212; Instruction: $5,678; Support Services: $3,323
Enrollment, Drop-out Rates and Diploma Recipients by Race/Ethnicity

Category	Total	White	Black	Asian	AIAN	Hisp.
Enrollment (%)	100.0	82.9	4.1	8.2	0.1	4.8
Drop-out Rate (%)	0.8	0.5	1.3	0.0	150.0	5.3
H.S. Diplomas (#)	429	359	23	29	0	18

Montgomery Twp

405 Burnt Hill Rd • Skillman, NJ 08558-1705
(908) 874-5201 • http://mtsd.k12.nj.us
Grade Span: PK-12; **Agency Type:** 1
Schools: 4
2 Primary; 1 Middle; 1 High; 0 Other Level
4 Regular; 0 Special Education; 0 Vocational; 0 Alternative
0 Magnet; 0 Charter; 0 Title I Eligible; 0 School-wide Title I
Students: 4,339 (51.9% male; 48.1% female)
Individual Education Program: 478 (11.0%);
English Language Learner: 27 (0.6%); Migrant: 0 (0.0%)
Eligible for Free Lunch Program: 36 (0.8%)
Eligible for Reduced-Price Lunch Program: 28 (0.6%)
Teachers: 309.1 (14.0 to 1)
Librarians/Media Specialists: 5.5 (788.9 to 1)
Guidance Counselors: 13.0 (333.8 to 1)
Current Spending: ($ per student per year):
Total: $8,868; Instruction: $5,036; Support Services: $3,640
Enrollment, Drop-out Rates and Diploma Recipients by Race/Ethnicity

Category	Total	White	Black	Asian	AIAN	Hisp.
Enrollment (%)	100.0	77.2	2.2	18.3	0.1	2.2
Drop-out Rate (%)	0.3	0.1	0.0	0.0	n/a	13.3
H.S. Diplomas (#)	203	163	3	34	0	3

North Plainfield Boro

33 Mountain Ave • North Plainfield, NJ 07060-5336
(908) 769-6060 • http://www.familyeducation.com/NJ/North_Plainfield/
Grade Span: PK-12; **Agency Type:** 1
Schools: 5
3 Primary; 1 Middle; 1 High; 0 Other Level
5 Regular; 0 Special Education; 0 Vocational; 0 Alternative
0 Magnet; 0 Charter; 3 Title I Eligible; 0 School-wide Title I
Students: 3,331 (50.6% male; 49.4% female)
Individual Education Program: 520 (15.6%);
English Language Learner: 287 (8.6%); Migrant: 0 (0.0%)
Eligible for Free Lunch Program: 602 (18.1%)
Eligible for Reduced-Price Lunch Program: 348 (10.4%)
Teachers: 273.4 (12.2 to 1)
Librarians/Media Specialists: 5.0 (666.2 to 1)
Guidance Counselors: 9.8 (339.9 to 1)
Current Spending: ($ per student per year):
Total: $10,269; Instruction: $6,350; Support Services: $3,691
Enrollment, Drop-out Rates and Diploma Recipients by Race/Ethnicity

Category	Total	White	Black	Asian	AIAN	Hisp.
Enrollment (%)	100.0	25.3	20.3	7.0	0.0	47.5
Drop-out Rate (%)	1.2	0.6	1.4	0.0	n/a	2.0
H.S. Diplomas (#)	165	61	29	18	0	57

Somerset Hills Regional

25 Olcott Ave • Bernardsville, NJ 07924-2307
(908) 630-3010 • http://www.shsd.org
Grade Span: PK-12; **Agency Type:** 1
Schools: 3
1 Primary; 1 Middle; 1 High; 0 Other Level
3 Regular; 0 Special Education; 0 Vocational; 0 Alternative
0 Magnet; 0 Charter; 0 Title I Eligible; 0 School-wide Title I
Students: 1,770 (51.1% male; 48.9% female)
Individual Education Program: 217 (12.3%);
English Language Learner: 34 (1.9%); Migrant: 0 (0.0%)
Eligible for Free Lunch Program: 28 (1.6%)
Eligible for Reduced-Price Lunch Program: 13 (0.7%)
Teachers: 144.3 (12.3 to 1)
Librarians/Media Specialists: 3.0 (590.0 to 1)
Guidance Counselors: 4.0 (442.5 to 1)
Current Spending: ($ per student per year):
Total: $12,310; Instruction: $7,247; Support Services: $4,823
Enrollment, Drop-out Rates and Diploma Recipients by Race/Ethnicity

Category	Total	White	Black	Asian	AIAN	Hisp.
Enrollment (%)	100.0	85.9	1.5	3.7	0.1	8.8
Drop-out Rate (%)	1.1	0.6	0.0	n/a	0.0	8.8
H.S. Diplomas (#)	123	112	1	3	0	7

Somerville Boro

51 W Cliff St • Somerville, NJ 08876-1903
(908) 218-4101
Grade Span: PK-12; **Agency Type:** 1
Schools: 3
1 Primary; 1 Middle; 1 High; 0 Other Level
3 Regular; 0 Special Education; 0 Vocational; 0 Alternative
0 Magnet; 0 Charter; 2 Title I Eligible; 0 School-wide Title I
Students: 2,189 (51.2% male; 48.8% female)
Individual Education Program: 265 (12.1%);
English Language Learner: 81 (3.7%); Migrant: 0 (0.0%)
Eligible for Free Lunch Program: 423 (19.3%)
Eligible for Reduced-Price Lunch Program: 167 (7.6%)
Teachers: 165.2 (13.3 to 1)
Librarians/Media Specialists: 3.0 (729.7 to 1)
Guidance Counselors: 6.2 (353.1 to 1)
Current Spending: ($ per student per year):
Total: $11,511; Instruction: $7,317; Support Services: $3,982
Enrollment, Drop-out Rates and Diploma Recipients by Race/Ethnicity

Category	Total	White	Black	Asian	AIAN	Hisp.
Enrollment (%)	100.0	53.4	16.9	8.9	0.0	20.8
Drop-out Rate (%)	0.2	0.2	1.0	0.0	n/a	0.0
H.S. Diplomas (#)	174	133	17	14	0	10

Warren Twp

213 Mt Horeb Rd • Warren, NJ 07059-5819
(732) 560-8700 • http://www.warrentboe.org
Grade Span: PK-08; **Agency Type:** 1
Schools: 5
4 Primary; 1 Middle; 0 High; 0 Other Level
5 Regular; 0 Special Education; 0 Vocational; 0 Alternative
0 Magnet; 0 Charter; 0 Title I Eligible; 0 School-wide Title I
Students: 2,155 (50.5% male; 49.5% female)
Individual Education Program: 371 (17.2%);
English Language Learner: 22 (1.0%); Migrant: 0 (0.0%)
Eligible for Free Lunch Program: 8 (0.4%)
Eligible for Reduced-Price Lunch Program: 0 (0.0%)
Teachers: 202.7 (10.6 to 1)
Librarians/Media Specialists: 5.0 (431.0 to 1)
Guidance Counselors: 6.0 (359.2 to 1)
Current Spending: ($ per student per year):
Total: $10,992; Instruction: $6,655; Support Services: $4,214
Enrollment, Drop-out Rates and Diploma Recipients by Race/Ethnicity

Category	Total	White	Black	Asian	AIAN	Hisp.
Enrollment (%)	100.0	81.3	0.9	14.9	0.0	2.8
Drop-out Rate (%)	n/a	n/a	n/a	n/a	n/a	n/a
H.S. Diplomas (#)	n/a	n/a	n/a	n/a	n/a	n/a

Watchung Hills Regional

108 Stirling Rd • Warren, NJ 07059
(908) 647-4890
Grade Span: 09-12; **Agency Type:** 1
Schools: 1
0 Primary; 0 Middle; 1 High; 0 Other Level
1 Regular; 0 Special Education; 0 Vocational; 0 Alternative
0 Magnet; 0 Charter; 0 Title I Eligible; 0 School-wide Title I
Students: 1,581 (52.7% male; 47.3% female)
Individual Education Program: 185 (11.7%);
English Language Learner: 6 (0.4%); Migrant: 0 (0.0%)
Eligible for Free Lunch Program: 4 (0.3%)
Eligible for Reduced-Price Lunch Program: 4 (0.3%)
Teachers: 116.9 (13.5 to 1)
Librarians/Media Specialists: 2.0 (790.5 to 1)
Guidance Counselors: 7.0 (225.9 to 1)
Current Spending: ($ per student per year):
Total: $13,075; Instruction: $7,517; Support Services: $5,147
Enrollment, Drop-out Rates and Diploma Recipients by Race/Ethnicity

Category	Total	White	Black	Asian	AIAN	Hisp.
Enrollment (%)	100.0	79.5	1.2	14.5	0.3	4.5
Drop-out Rate (%)	0.4	0.5	0.0	0.0	0.0	0.0
H.S. Diplomas (#)	358	307	3	36	0	12

Sussex County

Hopatcong

Windsor Ave • Hopatcong, NJ 07843-0829
Mailing Address: PO Box 1029 • Hopatcong, NJ 07843-0829
(973) 398-8801 • http://www.hopatcongschools.org
Grade Span: PK-12; **Agency Type:** 1
Schools: 5
2 Primary; 2 Middle; 1 High; 0 Other Level
5 Regular; 0 Special Education; 0 Vocational; 0 Alternative
0 Magnet; 0 Charter; 3 Title I Eligible; 0 School-wide Title I
Students: 2,779 (51.5% male; 48.5% female)
Individual Education Program: 626 (22.5%);
English Language Learner: 22 (0.8%); Migrant: 0 (0.0%)
Eligible for Free Lunch Program: 174 (6.3%)
Eligible for Reduced-Price Lunch Program: 195 (7.0%)
Teachers: 201.7 (13.8 to 1)
Librarians/Media Specialists: 4.0 (694.8 to 1)
Guidance Counselors: 7.7 (360.9 to 1)
Current Spending: ($ per student per year):
Total: $9,899; Instruction: $5,835; Support Services: $3,824
Enrollment, Drop-out Rates and Diploma Recipients by Race/Ethnicity

Category	Total	White	Black	Asian	AIAN	Hisp.
Enrollment (%)	100.0	86.7	3.3	2.1	0.1	7.8
Drop-out Rate (%)	3.3	3.2	0.0	0.0	0.0	11.1
H.S. Diplomas (#)	160	152	1	2	0	5

Newton Town

57 Trinity St • Newton, NJ 07860-1824
(973) 383-7392 • http://www.newtonnj.org
Grade Span: PK-12; **Agency Type:** 1
Schools: 3
1 Primary; 1 Middle; 1 High; 0 Other Level
3 Regular; 0 Special Education; 0 Vocational; 0 Alternative
0 Magnet; 0 Charter; 2 Title I Eligible; 0 School-wide Title I
Students: 1,689 (51.2% male; 48.8% female)
Individual Education Program: 220 (13.0%);
English Language Learner: 23 (1.4%); Migrant: 0 (0.0%)
Eligible for Free Lunch Program: 232 (13.7%)
Eligible for Reduced-Price Lunch Program: 97 (5.7%)
Teachers: 133.4 (12.7 to 1)
Librarians/Media Specialists: 3.0 (563.0 to 1)
Guidance Counselors: 4.6 (367.2 to 1)
Current Spending: ($ per student per year):
Total: $11,513; Instruction: $7,173; Support Services: $3,985
Enrollment, Drop-out Rates and Diploma Recipients by Race/Ethnicity

Category	Total	White	Black	Asian	AIAN	Hisp.
Enrollment (%)	100.0	86.5	5.6	2.2	1.3	4.4
Drop-out Rate (%)	2.8	2.8	0.0	0.0	0.0	16.7
H.S. Diplomas (#)	163	156	3	3	0	1

Sparta Twp

18 Mohawk Ave • Sparta, NJ 07871-1112
(973) 729-7886 • http://www.sparta.org
Grade Span: PK-12; **Agency Type:** 1
Schools: 5
2 Primary; 2 Middle; 1 High; 0 Other Level
5 Regular; 0 Special Education; 0 Vocational; 0 Alternative
0 Magnet; 0 Charter; 0 Title I Eligible; 0 School-wide Title I
Students: 3,889 (50.9% male; 49.1% female)
Individual Education Program: 484 (12.4%);
English Language Learner: 25 (0.6%); Migrant: 0 (0.0%)
Eligible for Free Lunch Program: 33 (0.8%)
Eligible for Reduced-Price Lunch Program: 25 (0.6%)
Teachers: 246.7 (15.8 to 1)
Librarians/Media Specialists: 4.0 (972.3 to 1)
Guidance Counselors: 11.0 (353.5 to 1)
Current Spending: ($ per student per year):
Total: $9,618; Instruction: $5,608; Support Services: $3,780
Enrollment, Drop-out Rates and Diploma Recipients by Race/Ethnicity

Category	Total	White	Black	Asian	AIAN	Hisp.
Enrollment (%)	100.0	93.8	0.8	2.6	0.1	2.7
Drop-out Rate (%)	0.1	0.1	0.0	0.0	n/a	0.0
H.S. Diplomas (#)	227	216	1	5	0	5

Sussex-Wantage Regional

31 Ryan Rd • Wantage, NJ 07461-1705
(973) 875-3175
Grade Span: PK-08; **Agency Type:** 1
Schools: 3
2 Primary; 1 Middle; 0 High; 0 Other Level
3 Regular; 0 Special Education; 0 Vocational; 0 Alternative
0 Magnet; 0 Charter; 3 Title I Eligible; 0 School-wide Title I
Students: 1,759 (48.9% male; 51.1% female)
Individual Education Program: 394 (22.4%);
English Language Learner: 4 (0.2%); Migrant: 0 (0.0%)
Eligible for Free Lunch Program: 166 (9.4%)
Eligible for Reduced-Price Lunch Program: 103 (5.9%)
Teachers: 133.2 (13.2 to 1)
Librarians/Media Specialists: 3.0 (586.3 to 1)
Guidance Counselors: 2.9 (606.6 to 1)
Current Spending: ($ per student per year):
Total: $9,889; Instruction: $5,985; Support Services: $3,641
Enrollment, Drop-out Rates and Diploma Recipients by Race/Ethnicity

Category	Total	White	Black	Asian	AIAN	Hisp.
Enrollment (%)	100.0	97.1	0.7	0.7	0.0	1.5
Drop-out Rate (%)	n/a	n/a	n/a	n/a	n/a	n/a
H.S. Diplomas (#)	n/a	n/a	n/a	n/a	n/a	n/a

Vernon Twp

Route 515 • Vernon, NJ 07462-0099
Mailing Address: PO Box 99 • Vernon, NJ 07462-0099
(973) 764-2900 • http://www.vtsd.com/
Grade Span: PK-12; **Agency Type:** 1
Schools: 6
3 Primary; 2 Middle; 1 High; 0 Other Level
6 Regular; 0 Special Education; 0 Vocational; 0 Alternative
0 Magnet; 0 Charter; 3 Title I Eligible; 0 School-wide Title I
Students: 5,455 (52.1% male; 47.9% female)
Individual Education Program: 611 (11.2%);
English Language Learner: 10 (0.2%); Migrant: 0 (0.0%)
Eligible for Free Lunch Program: 209 (3.8%)
Eligible for Reduced-Price Lunch Program: 171 (3.1%)
Teachers: 375.2 (14.5 to 1)
Librarians/Media Specialists: 6.0 (909.2 to 1)
Guidance Counselors: 17.2 (317.2 to 1)
Current Spending: ($ per student per year):
Total: $9,748; Instruction: $5,769; Support Services: $3,773
Enrollment, Drop-out Rates and Diploma Recipients by Race/Ethnicity

Category	Total	White	Black	Asian	AIAN	Hisp.
Enrollment (%)	100.0	93.2	1.3	0.7	0.1	4.7
Drop-out Rate (%)	3.1	3.1	0.0	0.0	n/a	3.0
H.S. Diplomas (#)	343	341	0	0	0	2

Union County

Berkeley Heights Twp

345 Plainfield Ave • Berkeley Heights, NJ 07922-1436
(908) 464-1718 • http://www.bhs.k12.nj.us
Grade Span: PK-12; **Agency Type:** 1
Schools: 6
4 Primary; 1 Middle; 1 High; 0 Other Level
6 Regular; 0 Special Education; 0 Vocational; 0 Alternative
0 Magnet; 0 Charter; 0 Title I Eligible; 0 School-wide Title I
Students: 2,753 (51.4% male; 48.6% female)
Individual Education Program: 298 (10.8%);
English Language Learner: 36 (1.3%); Migrant: 0 (0.0%)
Eligible for Free Lunch Program: 21 (0.8%)
Eligible for Reduced-Price Lunch Program: 13 (0.5%)
Teachers: 203.6 (13.5 to 1)
Librarians/Media Specialists: 5.0 (550.6 to 1)
Guidance Counselors: 8.0 (344.1 to 1)
Current Spending: ($ per student per year):
Total: $11,861; Instruction: $7,653; Support Services: $3,939

Enrollment, Drop-out Rates and Diploma Recipients by Race/Ethnicity

Category	Total	White	Black	Asian	AIAN	Hisp.
Enrollment (%)	100.0	85.9	0.7	8.5	0.0	4.9
Drop-out Rate (%)	0.5	0.5	0.0	0.0	n/a	3.0
H.S. Diplomas (#)	171	148	0	17	0	6

Clark Twp

10 Schindler Rd • Clark, NJ 07066-2499
(732) 574-9600 • http://www.clarkschools.org/
Grade Span: PK-12; **Agency Type:** 1
Schools: 4
2 Primary; 1 Middle; 1 High; 0 Other Level
4 Regular; 0 Special Education; 0 Vocational; 0 Alternative
0 Magnet; 0 Charter; 0 Title I Eligible; 0 School-wide Title I
Students: 2,502 (54.2% male; 45.8% female)
Individual Education Program: 289 (11.6%);
English Language Learner: 18 (0.7%); Migrant: 0 (0.0%)
Eligible for Free Lunch Program: 38 (1.5%)
Eligible for Reduced-Price Lunch Program: 19 (0.8%)
Teachers: 168.0 (14.9 to 1)
Librarians/Media Specialists: 4.0 (625.5 to 1)
Guidance Counselors: 8.0 (312.8 to 1)
Current Spending: ($ per student per year):
Total: $11,718; Instruction: $6,961; Support Services: $4,504

Enrollment, Drop-out Rates and Diploma Recipients by Race/Ethnicity

Category	Total	White	Black	Asian	AIAN	Hisp.
Enrollment (%)	100.0	92.7	0.3	3.0	0.1	3.9
Drop-out Rate (%)	0.3	0.3	n/a	0.0	n/a	0.0
H.S. Diplomas (#)	189	169	6	7	0	7

Cranford Twp

132 Thomas St • Cranford, NJ 07016-3134
(908) 709-6202 • http://www.cranfordschools.org
Grade Span: PK-12; **Agency Type:** 1
Schools: 7
6 Primary; 0 Middle; 1 High; 0 Other Level
7 Regular; 0 Special Education; 0 Vocational; 0 Alternative
0 Magnet; 0 Charter; 2 Title I Eligible; 0 School-wide Title I
Students: 3,425 (53.6% male; 46.4% female)
Individual Education Program: 545 (15.9%);
English Language Learner: 8 (0.2%); Migrant: 0 (0.0%)
Eligible for Free Lunch Program: 43 (1.3%)
Eligible for Reduced-Price Lunch Program: 51 (1.5%)
Teachers: 280.5 (12.2 to 1)
Librarians/Media Specialists: 4.6 (744.6 to 1)
Guidance Counselors: 5.0 (685.0 to 1)
Current Spending: ($ per student per year):
Total: $10,968; Instruction: $6,897; Support Services: $3,907

Enrollment, Drop-out Rates and Diploma Recipients by Race/Ethnicity

Category	Total	White	Black	Asian	AIAN	Hisp.
Enrollment (%)	100.0	90.7	3.8	2.4	0.0	3.2
Drop-out Rate (%)	1.6	1.4	0.0	15.4	n/a	3.6
H.S. Diplomas (#)	232	221	8	0	0	3

Elizabeth City

Mitchell Building, 500 N Broad • Elizabeth, NJ 07207
(908) 436-5010 • http://www.elizabeth.k12.nj.us
Grade Span: PK-12; **Agency Type:** 1
Schools: 26
19 Primary; 6 Middle; 1 High; 0 Other Level
26 Regular; 0 Special Education; 0 Vocational; 0 Alternative
0 Magnet; 0 Charter; 21 Title I Eligible; 21 School-wide Title I
Students: 21,024 (50.2% male; 49.8% female)
Individual Education Program: 2,430 (11.6%);
English Language Learner: 4,323 (20.6%); Migrant: 0 (0.0%)
Eligible for Free Lunch Program: 12,043 (57.3%)
Eligible for Reduced-Price Lunch Program: 3,120 (14.8%)
Teachers: 1,952.3 (10.8 to 1)
Librarians/Media Specialists: 23.0 (914.1 to 1)
Guidance Counselors: 53.0 (396.7 to 1)
Current Spending: ($ per student per year):
Total: $11,686; Instruction: $6,484; Support Services: $4,808

Enrollment, Drop-out Rates and Diploma Recipients by Race/Ethnicity

Category	Total	White	Black	Asian	AIAN	Hisp.
Enrollment (%)	100.0	11.4	23.9	2.3	0.0	62.4
Drop-out Rate (%)	6.3	5.6	8.2	0.8	0.0	6.0
H.S. Diplomas (#)	877	161	192	27	0	497

Hillside Twp

195 Virginia St • Hillside, NJ 07205-2742
(908) 352-7664
Grade Span: PK-12; **Agency Type:** 1
Schools: 6
4 Primary; 1 Middle; 1 High; 0 Other Level
6 Regular; 0 Special Education; 0 Vocational; 0 Alternative
0 Magnet; 0 Charter; 4 Title I Eligible; 0 School-wide Title I
Students: 3,338 (51.3% male; 48.7% female)
Individual Education Program: 503 (15.1%);
English Language Learner: 141 (4.2%); Migrant: 0 (0.0%)
Eligible for Free Lunch Program: 1,142 (34.2%)
Eligible for Reduced-Price Lunch Program: 628 (18.8%)
Teachers: 228.9 (14.6 to 1)
Librarians/Media Specialists: 5.0 (667.6 to 1)
Guidance Counselors: 5.0 (667.6 to 1)
Current Spending: ($ per student per year):
Total: $10,241; Instruction: $6,282; Support Services: $3,698

Enrollment, Drop-out Rates and Diploma Recipients by Race/Ethnicity

Category	Total	White	Black	Asian	AIAN	Hisp.
Enrollment (%)	100.0	15.7	65.2	2.3	0.0	16.8
Drop-out Rate (%)	5.8	9.8	4.5	6.3	n/a	7.0
H.S. Diplomas (#)	169	33	105	11	0	20

Linden City

2 E Gibbons St • Linden, NJ 07036-4064
(908) 486-5818 • http://www.geocities.com/lindenschool1/
Grade Span: PK-12; **Agency Type:** 1
Schools: 11
8 Primary; 2 Middle; 1 High; 0 Other Level
11 Regular; 0 Special Education; 0 Vocational; 0 Alternative
0 Magnet; 0 Charter; 6 Title I Eligible; 0 School-wide Title I
Students: 6,131 (50.8% male; 49.2% female)
Individual Education Program: 1,046 (17.1%);
English Language Learner: 364 (5.9%); Migrant: 0 (0.0%)
Eligible for Free Lunch Program: 1,715 (28.0%)
Eligible for Reduced-Price Lunch Program: 920 (15.0%)
Teachers: 430.4 (14.2 to 1)
Librarians/Media Specialists: 6.0 (1,021.8 to 1)
Guidance Counselors: 9.6 (638.6 to 1)
Current Spending: ($ per student per year):
Total: $10,271; Instruction: $6,117; Support Services: $3,875

Enrollment, Drop-out Rates and Diploma Recipients by Race/Ethnicity

Category	Total	White	Black	Asian	AIAN	Hisp.
Enrollment (%)	100.0	35.6	37.6	3.3	0.1	23.3
Drop-out Rate (%)	4.1	3.5	3.9	8.9	0.0	4.9
H.S. Diplomas (#)	373	159	126	14	0	74

New Providence Boro

356 Elkwood Ave • New Providence, NJ 07974-2322
(908) 464-9050 • http://www.npsd.k12.nj.us
Grade Span: PK-12; **Agency Type:** 1
Schools: 4
2 Primary; 1 Middle; 1 High; 0 Other Level
4 Regular; 0 Special Education; 0 Vocational; 0 Alternative
0 Magnet; 0 Charter; 0 Title I Eligible; 0 School-wide Title I
Students: 2,120 (51.7% male; 48.3% female)
Individual Education Program: 273 (12.9%);
English Language Learner: 39 (1.8%); Migrant: 0 (0.0%)
Eligible for Free Lunch Program: 11 (0.5%)
Eligible for Reduced-Price Lunch Program: 22 (1.0%)
Teachers: 167.9 (12.6 to 1)
Librarians/Media Specialists: 4.0 (530.0 to 1)
Guidance Counselors: 3.0 (706.7 to 1)
Current Spending: ($ per student per year):
Total: $10,303; Instruction: $6,504; Support Services: $3,595

Enrollment, Drop-out Rates and Diploma Recipients by Race/Ethnicity

Category	Total	White	Black	Asian	AIAN	Hisp.
Enrollment (%)	100.0	87.2	0.7	8.6	0.0	3.5
Drop-out Rate (%)	0.0	0.0	0.0	0.0	n/a	0.0
H.S. Diplomas (#)	134	123	0	8	0	3

Plainfield City

504 Madison Ave • Plainfield, NJ 07060-1540
(908) 731-4335 • http://www.plainfieldnjk12.org/
Grade Span: PK-12; **Agency Type:** 1
Schools: 13
10 Primary; 2 Middle; 1 High; 0 Other Level
13 Regular; 0 Special Education; 0 Vocational; 0 Alternative
0 Magnet; 0 Charter; 10 Title I Eligible; 10 School-wide Title I
Students: 7,816 (50.9% male; 49.1% female)
Individual Education Program: 956 (12.2%);
English Language Learner: 966 (12.4%); Migrant: 0 (0.0%)
Eligible for Free Lunch Program: 4,335 (55.5%)
Eligible for Reduced-Price Lunch Program: 1,135 (14.5%)
Teachers: 697.5 (11.2 to 1)
Librarians/Media Specialists: 10.5 (744.4 to 1)
Guidance Counselors: 14.0 (558.3 to 1)
Current Spending: ($ per student per year):
Total: $12,337; Instruction: $6,885; Support Services: $5,049

Enrollment, Drop-out Rates and Diploma Recipients by Race/Ethnicity

Category	Total	White	Black	Asian	AIAN	Hisp.
Enrollment (%)	100.0	0.6	69.7	0.5	0.0	29.2
Drop-out Rate (%)	4.2	9.1	4.1	0.0	n/a	4.7
H.S. Diplomas (#)	276	1	224	1	0	50

Rahway City

Rahway Middle School • Rahway, NJ 07065
(732) 396-1020 • http://www.rahway.net
Grade Span: PK-12; **Agency Type:** 1
Schools: 6
4 Primary; 1 Middle; 1 High; 0 Other Level
6 Regular; 0 Special Education; 0 Vocational; 0 Alternative
0 Magnet; 0 Charter; 1 Title I Eligible; 0 School-wide Title I
Students: 3,957 (52.3% male; 47.7% female)
Individual Education Program: 717 (18.1%);
English Language Learner: 113 (2.9%); Migrant: 0 (0.0%)
Eligible for Free Lunch Program: 1,136 (28.7%)
Eligible for Reduced-Price Lunch Program: 525 (13.3%)
Teachers: 294.5 (13.4 to 1)
Librarians/Media Specialists: 6.0 (659.5 to 1)
Guidance Counselors: 7.0 (565.3 to 1)
Current Spending: ($ per student per year):
Total: $9,835; Instruction: $6,115; Support Services: $3,445
Enrollment, Drop-out Rates and Diploma Recipients by Race/Ethnicity

Category	Total	White	Black	Asian	AIAN	Hisp.
Enrollment (%)	100.0	30.5	43.3	3.9	0.4	21.9
Drop-out Rate (%)	3.9	3.3	4.8	0.0	n/a	4.1
H.S. Diplomas (#)	227	99	86	10	0	32

Roselle Boro

710 Locust St • Roselle, NJ 07203-1919
(908) 298-2040 • http://www.roselleschools.com
Grade Span: PK-12; **Agency Type:** 1
Schools: 6
3 Primary; 2 Middle; 1 High; 0 Other Level
6 Regular; 0 Special Education; 0 Vocational; 0 Alternative
0 Magnet; 0 Charter; 5 Title I Eligible; 0 School-wide Title I
Students: 2,728 (51.4% male; 48.6% female)
Individual Education Program: 565 (20.7%);
English Language Learner: 245 (9.0%); Migrant: 0 (0.0%)
Eligible for Free Lunch Program: 824 (30.2%)
Eligible for Reduced-Price Lunch Program: 310 (11.4%)
Teachers: 193.6 (14.1 to 1)
Librarians/Media Specialists: 1.0 (2,728.0 to 1)
Guidance Counselors: 6.0 (454.7 to 1)
Current Spending: ($ per student per year):
Total: $11,148; Instruction: $7,148; Support Services: $3,777
Enrollment, Drop-out Rates and Diploma Recipients by Race/Ethnicity

Category	Total	White	Black	Asian	AIAN	Hisp.
Enrollment (%)	100.0	2.8	72.9	1.7	0.0	22.5
Drop-out Rate (%)	2.4	2.0	2.6	0.0	n/a	1.6
H.S. Diplomas (#)	162	10	129	2	0	21

Roselle Park Boro

510 Chestnut St • Roselle Park, NJ 07204-2495
(908) 245-1197 • http://www.roselleschools.com/
Grade Span: PK-12; **Agency Type:** 1
Schools: 5
3 Primary; 1 Middle; 1 High; 0 Other Level
5 Regular; 0 Special Education; 0 Vocational; 0 Alternative
0 Magnet; 0 Charter; 3 Title I Eligible; 0 School-wide Title I
Students: 1,993 (51.4% male; 48.6% female)
Individual Education Program: 334 (16.8%);
English Language Learner: 140 (7.0%); Migrant: 0 (0.0%)
Eligible for Free Lunch Program: 225 (11.3%)
Eligible for Reduced-Price Lunch Program: 151 (7.6%)
Teachers: 162.1 (12.3 to 1)
Librarians/Media Specialists: 2.0 (996.5 to 1)
Guidance Counselors: 7.0 (284.7 to 1)
Current Spending: ($ per student per year):
Total: $9,823; Instruction: $6,001; Support Services: $3,610
Enrollment, Drop-out Rates and Diploma Recipients by Race/Ethnicity

Category	Total	White	Black	Asian	AIAN	Hisp.
Enrollment (%)	100.0	62.8	2.6	11.7	0.0	22.9
Drop-out Rate (%)	0.4	0.5	0.0	0.0	n/a	0.0
H.S. Diplomas (#)	104	71	2	6	0	25

Scotch Plains-Fanwood Reg

Evergreen Ave & Cedar • Scotch Plains, NJ 07076-1955
(908) 232-6161 • http://www.njcommunity.org/spfnet/index.htm#Home
Grade Span: PK-12; **Agency Type:** 1
Schools: 8
5 Primary; 2 Middle; 1 High; 0 Other Level
8 Regular; 0 Special Education; 0 Vocational; 0 Alternative
0 Magnet; 0 Charter; 4 Title I Eligible; 0 School-wide Title I
Students: 4,811 (51.2% male; 48.8% female)
Individual Education Program: 808 (16.8%);
English Language Learner: 24 (0.5%); Migrant: 0 (0.0%)
Eligible for Free Lunch Program: 79 (1.6%)
Eligible for Reduced-Price Lunch Program: 31 (0.6%)
Teachers: 347.1 (13.9 to 1)
Librarians/Media Specialists: 9.0 (534.6 to 1)
Guidance Counselors: 9.5 (506.4 to 1)
Current Spending: ($ per student per year):
Total: $10,664; Instruction: $6,474; Support Services: $4,034
Enrollment, Drop-out Rates and Diploma Recipients by Race/Ethnicity

Category	Total	White	Black	Asian	AIAN	Hisp.
Enrollment (%)	100.0	77.6	11.6	6.3	0.0	4.6
Drop-out Rate (%)	0.3	0.4	0.0	0.0	n/a	0.0
H.S. Diplomas (#)	254	196	34	19	0	5

Springfield Twp

Springfield Public School • Springfield, NJ 07081-1786
(973) 376-1025 • http://www.springfieldschools.com
Grade Span: PK-12; **Agency Type:** 1
Schools: 5
3 Primary; 1 Middle; 1 High; 0 Other Level
5 Regular; 0 Special Education; 0 Vocational; 0 Alternative
0 Magnet; 0 Charter; 3 Title I Eligible; 0 School-wide Title I
Students: 2,004 (50.7% male; 49.3% female)
Individual Education Program: 297 (14.8%);
English Language Learner: 40 (2.0%); Migrant: 0 (0.0%)
Eligible for Free Lunch Program: 55 (2.7%)
Eligible for Reduced-Price Lunch Program: 48 (2.4%)
Teachers: 158.3 (12.7 to 1)
Librarians/Media Specialists: 5.0 (400.8 to 1)
Guidance Counselors: 9.0 (222.7 to 1)
Current Spending: ($ per student per year):
Total: $11,677; Instruction: $7,115; Support Services: $4,445
Enrollment, Drop-out Rates and Diploma Recipients by Race/Ethnicity

Category	Total	White	Black	Asian	AIAN	Hisp.
Enrollment (%)	100.0	80.6	5.8	5.8	0.1	7.7
Drop-out Rate (%)	0.7	0.5	0.0	0.0	0.0	3.8
H.S. Diplomas (#)	110	88	10	6	0	6

Summit City

90 Maple St • Summit, NJ 07901-2545
(908) 273-3023 • http://www.summit.k12.nj.us
Grade Span: PK-12; **Agency Type:** 1
Schools: 7
5 Primary; 1 Middle; 1 High; 0 Other Level
7 Regular; 0 Special Education; 0 Vocational; 0 Alternative
0 Magnet; 0 Charter; 7 Title I Eligible; 0 School-wide Title I
Students: 3,364 (51.8% male; 48.2% female)
Individual Education Program: 431 (12.8%);
English Language Learner: 126 (3.7%); Migrant: 0 (0.0%)
Eligible for Free Lunch Program: 219 (6.5%)
Eligible for Reduced-Price Lunch Program: 134 (4.0%)
Teachers: 264.6 (12.7 to 1)
Librarians/Media Specialists: 8.6 (391.2 to 1)
Guidance Counselors: 9.3 (361.7 to 1)
Current Spending: ($ per student per year):
Total: $11,353; Instruction: $7,366; Support Services: $3,699
Enrollment, Drop-out Rates and Diploma Recipients by Race/Ethnicity

Category	Total	White	Black	Asian	AIAN	Hisp.
Enrollment (%)	100.0	75.5	5.3	5.4	0.2	13.6
Drop-out Rate (%)	0.8	0.4	2.3	0.0	n/a	3.6
H.S. Diplomas (#)	171	128	8	15	0	20

Union Twp

2369 Morris Ave • Union, NJ 07083-5703
(908) 851-6420 • http://www.twpunionschools.org
Grade Span: PK-12; **Agency Type:** 1
Schools: 10
6 Primary; 3 Middle; 1 High; 0 Other Level
10 Regular; 0 Special Education; 0 Vocational; 0 Alternative
0 Magnet; 0 Charter; 4 Title I Eligible; 0 School-wide Title I
Students: 8,085 (51.9% male; 48.1% female)
Individual Education Program: 1,258 (15.6%);
English Language Learner: 183 (2.3%); Migrant: 0 (0.0%)
Eligible for Free Lunch Program: 922 (11.4%)
Eligible for Reduced-Price Lunch Program: 599 (7.4%)
Teachers: 557.1 (14.5 to 1)
Librarians/Media Specialists: 7.0 (1,155.0 to 1)
Guidance Counselors: 14.0 (577.5 to 1)
Current Spending: ($ per student per year):
Total: $9,070; Instruction: $5,454; Support Services: $3,351

Enrollment, Drop-out Rates and Diploma Recipients by Race/Ethnicity

Category	Total	White	Black	Asian	AIAN	Hisp.
Enrollment (%)	100.0	43.0	34.6	10.6	0.1	11.7
Drop-out Rate (%)	1.5	1.5	1.5	0.4	n/a	1.9
H.S. Diplomas (#)	482	241	153	45	0	43

Westfield Town

302 Elm St • Westfield, NJ 07090-3104
(908) 789-4420 • http://westfieldnj.com
Grade Span: PK-12; **Agency Type:** 1
Schools: 9
6 Primary; 2 Middle; 1 High; 0 Other Level
9 Regular; 0 Special Education; 0 Vocational; 0 Alternative
0 Magnet; 0 Charter; 3 Title I Eligible; 0 School-wide Title I
Students: 5,656 (52.1% male; 47.9% female)
Individual Education Program: 956 (16.9%);
English Language Learner: 31 (0.5%); Migrant: 0 (0.0%)
Eligible for Free Lunch Program: 61 (1.1%)
Eligible for Reduced-Price Lunch Program: 20 (0.4%)
Teachers: 430.9 (13.1 to 1)
Librarians/Media Specialists: 10.0 (565.6 to 1)
Guidance Counselors: 14.0 (404.0 to 1)
Current Spending: ($ per student per year):
Total: $10,889; Instruction: $6,957; Support Services: $3,770
Enrollment, Drop-out Rates and Diploma Recipients by Race/Ethnicity

Category	Total	White	Black	Asian	AIAN	Hisp.
Enrollment (%)	100.0	88.3	4.2	5.3	0.0	2.2
Drop-out Rate (%)	0.1	0.1	1.4	0.0	n/a	0.0
H.S. Diplomas (#)	327	285	16	15	0	11

Warren County

Hackettstown

315 Washington Ave • Hackettstown, NJ 07840-2235
(908) 850-6500 • http://www.gti.net/hackboe
Grade Span: PK-12; **Agency Type:** 1
Schools: 4
2 Primary; 1 Middle; 1 High; 0 Other Level
4 Regular; 0 Special Education; 0 Vocational; 0 Alternative
0 Magnet; 0 Charter; 3 Title I Eligible; 0 School-wide Title I
Students: 1,878 (51.0% male; 49.0% female)
Individual Education Program: 244 (13.0%);
English Language Learner: 43 (2.3%); Migrant: 0 (0.0%)
Eligible for Free Lunch Program: 144 (7.7%)
Eligible for Reduced-Price Lunch Program: 88 (4.7%)
Teachers: 151.1 (12.4 to 1)
Librarians/Media Specialists: 3.3 (569.1 to 1)
Guidance Counselors: 8.9 (211.0 to 1)
Current Spending: ($ per student per year):
Total: $9,997; Instruction: $5,986; Support Services: $3,779
Enrollment, Drop-out Rates and Diploma Recipients by Race/Ethnicity

Category	Total	White	Black	Asian	AIAN	Hisp.
Enrollment (%)	100.0	87.8	1.4	3.1	0.1	7.7
Drop-out Rate (%)	1.2	1.4	0.0	0.0	0.0	0.0
H.S. Diplomas (#)	232	217	3	5	0	7

Phillipsburg Town

445 Marshall St • Phillipsburg, NJ 08865-1656
(908) 454-3400 • http://www.pburg.k12.nj.us
Grade Span: PK-12; **Agency Type:** 1
Schools: 7
4 Primary; 1 Middle; 2 High; 0 Other Level
7 Regular; 0 Special Education; 0 Vocational; 0 Alternative
0 Magnet; 0 Charter; 4 Title I Eligible; 0 School-wide Title I
Students: 3,479 (52.3% male; 47.7% female)
Individual Education Program: 551 (15.8%);
English Language Learner: 74 (2.1%); Migrant: 0 (0.0%)
Eligible for Free Lunch Program: 954 (27.4%)
Eligible for Reduced-Price Lunch Program: 290 (8.3%)
Teachers: 331.5 (10.5 to 1)
Librarians/Media Specialists: 9.0 (386.6 to 1)
Guidance Counselors: 18.0 (193.3 to 1)
Current Spending: ($ per student per year):
Total: $12,546; Instruction: $7,905; Support Services: $4,368
Enrollment, Drop-out Rates and Diploma Recipients by Race/Ethnicity

Category	Total	White	Black	Asian	AIAN	Hisp.
Enrollment (%)	100.0	83.7	6.6	2.1	0.0	7.6
Drop-out Rate (%)	4.4	4.2	9.0	0.0	0.0	6.3
H.S. Diplomas (#)	280	242	14	6	0	18

Warren Hills Regional

89 Bowerstown Rd • Washington, NJ 07882-4123
(908) 689-3143 • http://www.warrenhills.org
Grade Span: 07-12; **Agency Type:** 1
Schools: 2
0 Primary; 1 Middle; 1 High; 0 Other Level
2 Regular; 0 Special Education; 0 Vocational; 0 Alternative
0 Magnet; 0 Charter; 0 Title I Eligible; 0 School-wide Title I
Students: 2,092 (52.8% male; 47.2% female)
Individual Education Program: 328 (15.7%);
English Language Learner: 18 (0.9%); Migrant: 0 (0.0%)
Eligible for Free Lunch Program: 116 (5.5%)
Eligible for Reduced-Price Lunch Program: 54 (2.6%)
Teachers: 149.8 (14.0 to 1)
Librarians/Media Specialists: 2.0 (1,046.0 to 1)
Guidance Counselors: 8.0 (261.5 to 1)
Current Spending: ($ per student per year):
Total: $10,752; Instruction: $6,214; Support Services: $4,283
Enrollment, Drop-out Rates and Diploma Recipients by Race/Ethnicity

Category	Total	White	Black	Asian	AIAN	Hisp.
Enrollment (%)	100.0	89.3	4.2	2.1	0.1	4.3
Drop-out Rate (%)	2.4	2.3	0.0	0.0	0.0	7.7
H.S. Diplomas (#)	288	271	6	4	0	7

Number of Schools

Rank	Number	District Name	City
1	77	Newark City	Newark
2	40	Jersey City	Jersey City
3	36	Paterson City	Paterson
4	33	Camden City	Camden
5	26	Elizabeth City	Elizabeth
6	24	Trenton City	Trenton
6	24	Woodbridge Twp	Woodbridge
8	23	Hamilton Twp	Hamilton Square
9	21	East Orange	East Orange
10	19	Cherry Hill Twp	Cherry Hill
10	19	Vineland City	Vineland
12	17	Edison Twp	Edison
12	17	Middletown Twp	Middletown
12	17	Toms River Regional	Toms River
15	16	Clifton City	Clifton
15	16	Passaic City	Passaic
17	15	Old Bridge Twp	Matawan
18	14	Parsippany-Troy Hills Twp	Parsippany
19	13	Pennsauken Twp	Pennsauken
19	13	Plainfield City	Plainfield
19	13	Wayne Twp	Wayne
22	12	Bayonne City	Bayonne
22	12	Brick Twp	Brick
22	12	Gloucester Twp	Blackwood
22	12	Irvington Township	Irvington
22	12	South Brunswick Twp	Monmouth Jct
27	11	Atlantic City	Atlantic City
27	11	Bloomfield Twp	Bloomfield
27	11	East Brunswick Twp	E Brunswick
27	11	Linden City	Linden
27	11	Montclair Town	Montclair
27	11	Pemberton Twp	Pemberton
27	11	Perth Amboy City	Perth Amboy
27	11	Union City	Union City
27	11	Washington Twp	Sewell
36	10	Bridgewater-Raritan Reg	Bridgewater
36	10	Garfield City	Garfield
36	10	Howell Twp	Howell
36	10	Millville City	Millville
36	10	Morris SD	Morristown
36	10	New Brunswick City	New Brunswick
36	10	Piscataway Twp	Piscataway
36	10	Ridgewood Village	Ridgewood
36	10	Union Twp	Union
36	10	West Orange Town	West Orange
36	10	West Windsor-Plainsboro Reg	Princeton Jct
36	10	Willingboro Twp	Willingboro
48	9	Belleville Town	Belleville
48	9	City of Orange Twp	Orange
48	9	Deptford Twp	Deptford
48	9	Evesham Twp	Marlton
48	9	Fair Lawn Boro	Fair Lawn
48	9	Galloway Twp	Galloway
48	9	Hillsborough Twp	Neshanic
48	9	Livingston Twp	Livingston
48	9	Long Branch City	Long Branch
48	9	South Orange-Maplewood	Maplewood
48	9	Westfield Town	Westfield
48	9	Winslow Twp	Atco
60	8	Franklin Twp	Somerset
60	8	Hazlet Twp	Hazlet
60	8	Jackson Twp	Jackson
60	8	Jefferson Twp	Lake Hopatcong
60	8	Marlboro Twp	Marlboro
60	8	Mount Laurel Twp	Mount Laurel
60	8	Neptune Twp	Neptune
60	8	Paramus Boro	Paramus
60	8	Scotch Plains-Fanwood Reg	Scotch Plains
60	8	West Milford Twp	West Milford
60	8	West New York Town	West New York
71	7	Bergenfield Boro	Bergenfield
71	7	Bridgeton City	Bridgeton
71	7	Collingswood Boro	Collingswood
71	7	Cranford Twp	Cranford
71	7	Freehold Twp	Freehold
71	7	Hackensack City	Hackensack
71	7	Kearny Town	Kearny
71	7	Lawrence Twp	Lawrenceville
71	7	Lodi Borough	Lodi
71	7	Lyndhurst Twp	Lyndhurst
71	7	Mahwah Twp	Mahwah
71	7	Manalapan-Englishtown Reg	Englishtown
71	7	Millburn Twp	Millburn
71	7	Montville Twp	Montville
71	7	North Bergen Twp	North Bergen
71	7	Nutley Town	Nutley
71	7	Phillipsburg Town	Phillipsburg
71	7	Roxbury Twp	Succasunna
71	7	Sayreville Boro	Sayreville
71	7	South Plainfield Boro	S Plainfield
71	7	Summit City	Summit
71	7	Teaneck Twp	Teaneck
71	7	Wall Twp	Wall
94	6	Asbury Park City	Asbury Park
94	6	Bergen County Vocational	Paramus
94	6	Berkeley Heights Twp	Berkeley Hgts
94	6	Bernards Twp	Basking Ridge
94	6	Buena Regional	Buena
94	6	Caldwell-West Caldwell	West Caldwell
94	6	East Windsor Regional	Hightstown
94	6	Egg Harbor Twp	W Atlantic City
94	6	Fort Lee Boro	Fort Lee
94	6	Freehold Regional	Englishtown
94	6	Glen Rock Boro	Glen Rock
94	6	Haddon Twp	Westmont
94	6	Hillside Twp	Hillside
94	6	Hoboken City	Hoboken
94	6	Hopewell Valley Regional	Pennington
94	6	Lacey Twp	Lanoka Harbor
94	6	Lakewood Twp	Lakewood
94	6	Manchester Twp	Whiting
94	6	Matawan-Aberdeen Regional	Aberdeen
94	6	Middlesex County Vocational	E Brunswick
94	6	Monroe Twp	Williamstown
94	6	Monroe Twp	Monroe Township
94	6	Moorestown Twp	Moorestown
94	6	Mount Olive Twp	Budd Lake
94	6	North Brunswick Twp	North Brunswick
94	6	Pleasantville City	Pleasantville
94	6	Princeton Regional	Princeton
94	6	Rahway City	Rahway
94	6	Randolph Twp	Randolph
94	6	Rockaway Twp	Hibernia
94	6	Roselle Boro	Roselle
94	6	Rutherford Boro	Rutherford
94	6	SD of The Chathams	Chatham
94	6	Tenafly Boro	Tenafly
94	6	Vernon Twp	Vernon
94	6	Verona Boro	Verona
94	6	Westwood Regional	Westwood
131	5	Barnegat Twp	Barnegat
131	5	Burlington City	Burlington
131	5	Burlington Twp	Burlington
131	5	Carteret Boro	Carteret
131	5	Cliffside Park Boro	Cliffside Park
131	5	Dover Town	Dover
131	5	Dumont Boro	Dumont
131	5	Elmwood Park	Elmwood Park
131	5	Englewood City	Englewood
131	5	Ewing Twp	Ewing
131	5	Flemington-Raritan Reg	Flemington
131	5	Glassboro	Glassboro
131	5	Haddonfield Boro	Haddonfield
131	5	Hawthorne Boro	Hawthorne
131	5	Hopatcong	Hopatcong
131	5	Madison Boro	Madison
131	5	Medford Twp	Medford
131	5	Middlesex Boro	Middlesex
131	5	North Arlington Boro	North Arlington
131	5	North Plainfield Boro	N Plainfield
131	5	Ocean Twp	Oakhurst
131	5	Penns Grove-Carney's Point Reg	Penns Grove
131	5	Pennsville	Pennsville
131	5	Pequannock Twp	Pompton Plains
131	5	Pitman Boro	Pitman
131	5	Ramsey Boro	Ramsey
131	5	Roselle Park Boro	Roselle Park
131	5	Saddle Brook Twp	Saddle Brook
131	5	Sparta Twp	Sparta
131	5	Springfield Twp	Springfield
131	5	Voorhees Twp	Voorhees
131	5	Warren Twp	Warren
131	5	Washington Twp	Long Valley
131	5	West Deptford Twp	West Deptford
131	5	Wyckoff Twp	Wyckoff
166	4	Bordentown Regional	Bordentown
166	4	Branchburg Twp	Branchburg
166	4	Cinnaminson Twp	Cinnaminson
166	4	Clark Twp	Clark
166	4	Delran Twp	Delran
166	4	Essex County Voc-Tech	West Orange
166	4	Florence Twp	Florence
166	4	Glen Ridge Boro	Glen Ridge
166	4	Hackettstown	Hackettstown
166	4	Hasbrouck Heights Boro	Hasbrouck Hgts
166	4	Holmdel Twp	Holmdel
166	4	Keansburg Boro	Keansburg
166	4	Kinnelon Boro	Kinnelon
166	4	Lindenwold Boro	Lindenwold
166	4	Lower Twp	Cape May
166	4	Maple Shade Twp	Maple Shade
166	4	Metuchen Boro	Metuchen
166	4	Middle Twp	Cape May Ct Hse
166	4	Montgomery Twp	Skillman
166	4	Mountain Lakes Boro	Mountain Lakes
166	4	New Milford Boro	New Milford
166	4	New Providence Boro	New Providence
166	4	Oakland Boro	Oakland
166	4	Pine Hill Boro	Pine Hill
166	4	Pittsgrove Twp	Pittsgrove
166	4	Point Pleasant Boro	Pt Pleasant
166	4	Pompton Lakes Boro	Pompton Lakes
166	4	Readington Twp	Whitehouse Stn
166	4	Ridgefield Boro	Ridgefield
166	4	Ridgefield Park Twp	Ridgefield Park
166	4	Secaucus Town	Secaucus
166	4	Spotswood Boro	Spotswood
166	4	Stafford Twp	Manahawkin
166	4	Woodbury City	Woodbury
200	3	Audubon Boro	Audubon
200	3	Berkeley Twp	Bayville
200	3	Black Horse Pike Regional	Blackwood
200	3	Bound Brook Boro	Bound Brook
200	3	Clinton Twp	Annandale
200	3	Colts Neck Twp	Colts Neck
200	3	Denville Twp	Denville
200	3	Gloucester City	Gloucester City
200	3	Hamilton Twp	Mays Landing
200	3	Hammonton Town	Hammonton
200	3	Harrison Town	Harrison
200	3	Highland Park Boro	Highland Park
200	3	Lenape Regional	Shamong
200	3	Leonia Boro	Leonia
200	3	Lumberton Twp	Lumberton
200	3	Newton Town	Newton
200	3	Ocean City	Ocean City
200	3	Paulsboro Boro	Paulsboro
200	3	Plumsted Twp	New Egypt
200	3	Somerset Hills Regional	Bernardsville
200	3	Somerville Boro	Somerville
200	3	South River Boro	South River
200	3	Sussex-Wantage Regional	Wantage
200	3	Tinton Falls	Tinton Falls
200	3	Upper Twp	Petersburg
200	3	Waldwick Boro	Waldwick
200	3	Woodstown-Pilesgrove Reg	Woodstown
227	2	Burlington County Vocational	Westampton Twp
227	2	Camden County Vocational	Sicklerville
227	2	Central Regional	Bayville
227	2	Clearview Regional	Mullica Hill
227	2	Delsea Regional HS District	Franklinville
227	2	Eastern Camden County Reg	Voorhees
227	2	Greater Egg Harbor Reg	Mays Landing
227	2	Kingsway Regional	Woolwich Twp
227	2	Little Egg Harbor Twp	Little Egg Hbr
227	2	Lower Cape May Regional	Cape May
227	2	Manasquan Boro	Manasquan
227	2	Millstone Twp	Clarksburg
227	2	Morris Hills Regional	Rockaway
227	2	North Hunt-Voorhees Regional	Annandale
227	2	Northern Burlington Reg	Columbus
227	2	Northern Valley Regional	Demarest
227	2	Pascack Valley Regional	Montvale
227	2	Pinelands Regional	Tuckerton
227	2	Ramapo-Indian Hill Reg	Franklin Lakes
227	2	Rancocas Valley Regional	Mount Holly
227	2	Somers Point City	Somers Point
227	2	Southern Regional	Manahawkin
227	2	Upper Freehold Regional	Allentown
227	2	Warren Hills Regional	Washington
227	2	West Morris Regional	Chester
252	1	Hunterdon Central Reg	Flemington
252	1	Mainland Regional	Linwood
252	1	Passaic County Vocational	Wayne
252	1	Watchung Hills Regional	Warren

Number of Teachers

Rank	Number	District Name	City
1	3,684	Newark City	Newark
2	2,666	Jersey City	Jersey City
3	2,337	Paterson City	Paterson
4	1,952	Elizabeth City	Elizabeth
5	1,480	Camden City	Camden
6	1,159	Toms River Regional	Toms River
7	1,076	Trenton City	Trenton
8	980	Woodbridge Twp	Woodbridge
9	975	Edison Twp	Edison
10	938	Hamilton Twp	Hamilton Square
11	902	East Orange	East Orange
12	883	Passaic City	Passaic
13	868	Vineland City	Vineland
14	788	Union City	Union City
15	765	Cherry Hill Twp	Cherry Hill
16	755	Brick Twp	Brick

17	743	Middletown Twp	Middletown
18	743	Clifton City	Clifton
19	737	Washington Twp	Sewell
20	734	Freehold Regional	Englishtown
21	697	Plainfield City	Plainfield
22	693	West Windsor-Plainsboro Reg	Princeton Jct
23	691	Perth Amboy City	Perth Amboy
24	661	Old Bridge Twp	Matawan
25	638	East Brunswick Twp	E Brunswick
26	631	South Brunswick Twp	Monmouth Jct
27	622	Wayne Twp	Wayne
28	620	Hillsborough Twp	Neshanic
29	618	Jackson Twp	Jackson
30	616	Bayonne City	Bayonne
31	608	Bridgewater-Raritan Reg	Bridgewater
32	579	Atlantic City	Atlantic City
33	574	Parsippany-Troy Hills Twp	Parsippany
34	557	Union Twp	Union
35	546	Gloucester Twp	Blackwood
36	532	Irvington Township	Irvington
37	528	Montclair Town	Montclair
38	526	Winslow Twp	Atco
39	520	Howell Twp	Howell
40	515	New Brunswick City	New Brunswick
41	510	Pemberton Twp	Pemberton
42	502	West New York Town	West New York
43	499	West Orange Town	West Orange
44	498	Piscataway Twp	Piscataway
45	498	Millville City	Millville
46	494	Franklin Twp	Somerset
47	491	Lenape Regional	Shamong
48	487	Long Branch City	Long Branch
49	479	North Bergen Twp	North Bergen
50	463	South Orange-Maplewood	Maplewood
51	455	Egg Harbor Twp	W Atlantic City
52	455	Willingboro Twp	Willingboro
53	449	Lakewood Twp	Lakewood
54	430	Westfield Town	Westfield
55	430	Bloomfield Twp	Bloomfield
56	430	Linden City	Linden
57	419	Pennsauken Twp	Pennsauken
58	407	Livingston Twp	Livingston
59	399	Morris SD	Morristown
60	391	North Brunswick Twp	North Brunswick
61	390	Evesham Twp	Marlton
62	389	Randolph Twp	Randolph
63	386	Marlboro Twp	Marlboro
64	384	Ridgewood Village	Ridgewood
65	382	Manalapan-Englishtown Reg	Englishtown
66	381	Hackensack City	Hackensack
67	379	Pleasantville City	Pleasantville
68	375	Sayreville Boro	Sayreville
69	375	Vernon Twp	Vernon
70	374	Bridgeton City	Bridgeton
71	373	Bernards Twp	Basking Ridge
72	372	Kearny Town	Kearny
73	361	Monroe Twp	Williamstown
74	357	East Windsor Regional	Hightstown
75	355	Teaneck Twp	Teaneck
76	352	Fair Lawn Boro	Fair Lawn
77	347	Scotch Plains-Fanwood Reg	Scotch Plains
78	339	Mount Laurel Twp	Mount Laurel
79	337	City of Orange Twp	Orange
79	337	Roxbury Twp	Succasunna
81	337	Lacey Twp	Lanoka Harbor
82	332	Paramus Boro	Paramus
83	331	West Milford Twp	West Milford
84	331	Phillipsburg Town	Phillipsburg
85	330	Millburn Twp	Millburn
86	329	Garfield City	Garfield
87	326	Neptune Twp	Neptune
88	325	Mount Olive Twp	Budd Lake
89	324	Asbury Park City	Asbury Park
90	321	Galloway Twp	Galloway
91	318	Ocean Twp	Oakhurst
92	315	Ewing Twp	Ewing
93	313	Belleville Town	Belleville
94	311	Wall Twp	Wall
95	309	Montgomery Twp	Skillman
96	308	Hopewell Valley Regional	Pennington
97	305	Lawrence Twp	Lawrenceville
98	299	Freehold Twp	Freehold
99	294	Rahway City	Rahway
100	290	Monroe Twp	Monroe Township
101	290	Matawan-Aberdeen Regional	Aberdeen
102	282	Montville Twp	Montville
103	282	South Plainfield Boro	S Plainfield
104	281	Burlington Twp	Burlington
105	280	Cranford Twp	Cranford
106	278	Moorestown Twp	Moorestown
107	273	North Plainfield Boro	N Plainfield
108	269	Nutley Town	Nutley
109	269	Deptford Twp	Deptford
110	267	Princeton Regional	Princeton
111	266	Bergenfield Boro	Bergenfield
112	266	Southern Regional	Manahawkin
113	265	Carteret Boro	Carteret
114	264	Summit City	Summit
115	261	Hazlet Twp	Hazlet
116	257	Black Horse Pike Regional	Blackwood
117	256	Manchester Twp	Whiting
118	256	Voorhees Twp	Voorhees
119	252	Fort Lee Boro	Fort Lee
120	251	Jefferson Twp	Lake Hopatcong
121	250	Greater Egg Harbor Reg	Mays Landing
122	247	Tenafly Boro	Tenafly
123	246	Sparta Twp	Sparta
124	246	Mahwah Twp	Mahwah
125	245	Flemington-Raritan Reg	Flemington
126	243	Rockaway Twp	Hibernia
127	239	Holmdel Twp	Holmdel
128	233	Hamilton Twp	Mays Landing
129	233	Englewood City	Englewood
130	232	SD of The Chathams	Chatham
131	231	Middle Twp	Cape May Ct Hse
132	228	Hillside Twp	Hillside
133	226	Hammonton Town	Hammonton
134	224	Bergen County Vocational	Paramus
135	221	Lodi Borough	Lodi
136	221	Point Pleasant Boro	Pt Pleasant
137	219	Ramsey Boro	Ramsey
138	218	Keansburg Boro	Keansburg
139	218	Gloucester City	Gloucester City
140	215	Lindenwold Boro	Lindenwold
141	214	Dover Town	Dover
142	208	Hoboken City	Hoboken
142	208	West Deptford Twp	West Deptford
144	208	North Hunt-Voorhees Regional	Annandale
145	207	Ocean City	Ocean City
146	205	Middlesex County Vocational	E Brunswick
147	203	Berkeley Heights Twp	Berkeley Hgts
148	203	Hunterdon Central Reg	Flemington
149	202	Cinnaminson Twp	Cinnaminson
149	202	Warren Twp	Warren
151	201	Hopatcong	Hopatcong
152	200	Morris Hills Regional	Rockaway
153	199	Passaic County Vocational	Wayne
154	198	Westwood Regional	Westwood
155	197	Glassboro	Glassboro
156	195	Washington Twp	Long Valley
157	194	Buena Regional	Buena
158	193	Roselle Boro	Roselle
159	193	Dumont Boro	Dumont
160	192	Pine Hill Boro	Pine Hill
161	190	Penns Grove-Carney's Point Reg	Penns Grove
162	190	Cliffside Park Boro	Cliffside Park
163	190	Northern Valley Regional	Demarest
164	188	Medford Twp	Medford
165	187	Ramapo-Indian Hill Reg	Franklin Lakes
166	187	Caldwell-West Caldwell	West Caldwell
167	185	West Morris Regional	Chester
168	183	Hawthorne Boro	Hawthorne
169	182	Rutherford Boro	Rutherford
170	179	Delran Twp	Delran
170	179	Pequannock Twp	Pompton Plains
172	177	Glen Rock Boro	Glen Rock
173	174	Camden County Vocational	Sicklerville
174	174	Barnegat Twp	Barnegat
175	173	Leonia Boro	Leonia
176	172	Pinelands Regional	Tuckerton
177	171	Burlington City	Burlington
178	169	Essex County Voc-Tech	West Orange
179	168	Stafford Twp	Manahawkin
180	168	Clark Twp	Clark
181	167	New Providence Boro	New Providence
182	167	Pennsville	Pennsville
183	167	Ridgefield Park Twp	Ridgefield Park
184	166	Madison Boro	Madison
185	166	Haddonfield Boro	Haddonfield
186	165	Readington Twp	Whitehouse Stn
187	165	Somerville Boro	Somerville
188	164	Collingswood Boro	Collingswood
189	164	Wyckoff Twp	Wyckoff
190	163	Middlesex Boro	Middlesex
191	162	Roselle Park Boro	Roselle Park
192	162	Mountain Lakes Boro	Mountain Lakes
193	158	Springfield Twp	Springfield
194	158	Branchburg Twp	Branchburg
195	155	Maple Shade Twp	Maple Shade
196	153	Burlington County Vocational	Westampton Twp
197	151	Haddon Twp	Westmont
198	151	Lower Twp	Cape May
199	151	Hackettstown	Hackettstown
200	150	Ridgefield Boro	Ridgefield
201	150	Metuchen Boro	Metuchen
202	149	Warren Hills Regional	Washington
203	148	Lower Cape May Regional	Cape May
204	148	Kinnelon Boro	Kinnelon
205	147	Clearview Regional	Mullica Hill
205	147	Lyndhurst Twp	Lyndhurst
205	147	New Milford Boro	New Milford
208	147	South River Boro	South River
209	145	Eastern Camden County Reg	Voorhees
210	145	Bordentown Regional	Bordentown
211	144	Somerset Hills Regional	Bernardsville
212	144	Woodbury City	Woodbury
213	142	Tinton Falls	Tinton Falls
214	140	Northern Burlington Reg	Columbus
215	138	Verona Boro	Verona
216	137	Pitman Boro	Pitman
217	136	Delsea Regional HS District	Franklinville
217	136	Pompton Lakes Boro	Pompton Lakes
219	135	Elmwood Park	Elmwood Park
220	135	Little Egg Harbor Twp	Little Egg Hbr
221	135	Secaucus Town	Secaucus
222	133	Newton Town	Newton
223	133	Clinton Twp	Annandale
224	133	Sussex-Wantage Regional	Wantage
225	133	Central Regional	Bayville
226	132	Colts Neck Twp	Colts Neck
226	132	Upper Twp	Petersburg
228	129	Harrison Town	Harrison
229	128	Pittsgrove Twp	Pittsgrove
230	128	Berkeley Twp	Bayville
231	127	Mainland Regional	Linwood
232	127	Pascack Valley Regional	Montvale
233	127	Florence Twp	Florence
234	127	Highland Park Boro	Highland Park
235	126	Upper Freehold Regional	Allentown
236	126	Audubon Boro	Audubon
237	124	Spotswood Boro	Spotswood
238	124	Rancocas Valley Regional	Mount Holly
239	122	Glen Ridge Boro	Glen Ridge
240	122	Oakland Boro	Oakland
241	122	Woodstown-Pilesgrove Reg	Woodstown
242	121	Plumsted Twp	New Egypt
243	120	Lumberton Twp	Lumberton
244	120	Denville Twp	Denville
245	119	Manasquan Boro	Manasquan
245	119	Saddle Brook Twp	Saddle Brook
247	118	Bound Brook Boro	Bound Brook
248	117	Hasbrouck Heights Boro	Hasbrouck Hgts
249	116	Watchung Hills Regional	Warren
250	114	Kingsway Regional	Woolwich Twp
251	113	North Arlington Boro	North Arlington
252	113	Paulsboro Boro	Paulsboro
253	112	Millstone Twp	Clarksburg
254	111	Waldwick Boro	Waldwick
255	93	Somers Point City	Somers Point

Number of Students

Rank	Number	District Name	City
1	42,395	Newark City	Newark
2	31,259	Jersey City	Jersey City
3	26,193	Paterson City	Paterson
4	21,024	Elizabeth City	Elizabeth
5	18,303	Toms River Regional	Toms River
6	17,266	Camden City	Camden
7	13,231	Trenton City	Trenton
8	13,223	Hamilton Twp	Hamilton Square
9	13,175	Woodbridge Twp	Woodbridge
10	12,920	Edison Twp	Edison
11	11,762	East Orange	East Orange
12	11,544	Brick Twp	Brick
13	11,364	Cherry Hill Twp	Cherry Hill
14	11,267	Passaic City	Passaic
15	10,363	Middletown Twp	Middletown
16	10,308	Freehold Regional	Englishtown
17	10,283	Clifton City	Clifton
18	10,024	Union City	Union City
19	9,940	Old Bridge Twp	Matawan
20	9,746	Washington Twp	Sewell
21	9,616	Vineland City	Vineland
22	9,365	Perth Amboy City	Perth Amboy
23	9,099	Jackson Twp	Jackson
24	8,819	East Brunswick Twp	E Brunswick
25	8,786	West Windsor-Plainsboro Reg	Princeton Jct
26	8,613	Wayne Twp	Wayne
27	8,426	Bayonne City	Bayonne
28	8,420	Bridgewater-Raritan Reg	Bridgewater
29	8,307	Irvington Township	Irvington
30	8,151	South Brunswick Twp	Monmouth Jct
31	8,085	Union Twp	Union
32	7,988	Gloucester Twp	Blackwood
33	7,816	Plainfield City	Plainfield
34	7,510	Hillsborough Twp	Neshanic

35	7,424	Howell Twp	Howell
36	7,419	North Bergen Twp	North Bergen
37	7,116	Atlantic City	Atlantic City
38	6,793	Lenape Regional	Shamong
39	6,753	Parsippany-Troy Hills Twp	Parsippany
40	6,751	Piscataway Twp	Piscataway
41	6,591	West New York Town	West New York
42	6,364	South Orange-Maplewood	Maplewood
43	6,363	Montclair Town	Montclair
44	6,312	Winslow Twp	Atco
45	6,305	Franklin Twp	Somerset
46	6,282	Egg Harbor Twp	W Atlantic City
47	6,278	West Orange Town	West Orange
48	6,131	Linden City	Linden
49	6,124	Pennsauken Twp	Pennsauken
50	6,105	New Brunswick City	New Brunswick
51	6,061	Millville City	Millville
52	6,027	Bloomfield Twp	Bloomfield
53	5,827	Pemberton Twp	Pemberton
54	5,825	Marlboro Twp	Marlboro
55	5,656	Westfield Town	Westfield
56	5,583	Sayreville Boro	Sayreville
57	5,568	Manalapan-Englishtown Reg	Englishtown
58	5,455	Vernon Twp	Vernon
59	5,451	Randolph Twp	Randolph
60	5,415	Evesham Twp	Marlton
61	5,393	Ridgewood Village	Ridgewood
62	5,349	Kearny Town	Kearny
63	5,311	Lakewood Twp	Lakewood
64	5,305	Willingboro Twp	Willingboro
65	5,275	North Brunswick Twp	North Brunswick
66	5,117	Monroe Twp	Williamstown
67	5,047	Lacey Twp	Lanoka Harbor
68	5,023	Hackensack City	Hackensack
69	5,003	Livingston Twp	Livingston
70	4,998	Long Branch City	Long Branch
71	4,811	Scotch Plains-Fanwood Reg	Scotch Plains
72	4,767	Bernards Twp	Basking Ridge
73	4,729	East Windsor Regional	Hightstown
74	4,704	Fair Lawn Boro	Fair Lawn
75	4,700	West Milford Twp	West Milford
76	4,683	Southern Regional	Manahawkin
77	4,671	City of Orange Twp	Orange
78	4,634	Morris SD	Morristown
79	4,602	Mount Olive Twp	Budd Lake
80	4,547	Belleville Town	Belleville
81	4,541	Roxbury Twp	Succasunna
82	4,522	Mount Laurel Twp	Mount Laurel
83	4,494	Ocean Twp	Oakhurst
84	4,471	Teaneck Twp	Teaneck
85	4,443	Freehold Twp	Freehold
86	4,339	Montgomery Twp	Skillman
87	4,268	Neptune Twp	Neptune
88	4,254	Wall Twp	Wall
89	4,245	Bridgeton City	Bridgeton
90	4,220	Nutley Town	Nutley
91	4,214	Garfield City	Garfield
92	4,196	Deptford Twp	Deptford
93	4,188	Paramus Boro	Paramus
94	4,186	Millburn Twp	Millburn
95	4,117	Lawrence Twp	Lawrenceville
96	4,049	Moorestown Twp	Moorestown
97	3,975	Galloway Twp	Galloway
98	3,957	Rahway City	Rahway
99	3,927	Matawan-Aberdeen Regional	Aberdeen
100	3,889	Sparta Twp	Sparta
101	3,888	Black Horse Pike Regional	Blackwood
102	3,845	Burlington Twp	Burlington
103	3,828	Bergenfield Boro	Bergenfield
104	3,826	Ewing Twp	Ewing
105	3,818	Montville Twp	Montville
106	3,806	Hopewell Valley Regional	Pennington
107	3,794	South Plainfield Boro	S Plainfield
108	3,770	Carteret Boro	Carteret
109	3,757	Monroe Twp	Monroe Township
110	3,627	Pleasantville City	Pleasantville
111	3,586	Voorhees Twp	Voorhees
112	3,549	Jefferson Twp	Lake Hopatcong
113	3,518	Holmdel Twp	Holmdel
114	3,498	Flemington-Raritan Reg	Flemington
115	3,486	Greater Egg Harbor Reg	Mays Landing
116	3,479	Phillipsburg Town	Phillipsburg
117	3,472	Hazlet Twp	Hazlet
118	3,453	Fort Lee Boro	Fort Lee
119	3,425	Cranford Twp	Cranford
120	3,364	Summit City	Summit
121	3,351	Manchester Twp	Whiting
122	3,338	Hillside Twp	Hillside
123	3,331	North Plainfield Boro	N Plainfield
124	3,322	Princeton Regional	Princeton
125	3,250	Mahwah Twp	Mahwah
126	3,190	Point Pleasant Boro	Pt Pleasant
127	3,139	Hammonton Town	Hammonton
128	3,101	West Deptford Twp	West Deptford
129	3,083	Lodi Borough	Lodi
130	3,043	Asbury Park City	Asbury Park
131	2,997	SD of The Chathams	Chatham
132	2,991	Middle Twp	Cape May Ct Hse
133	2,965	Medford Twp	Medford
134	2,945	Dover Town	Dover
135	2,935	Tenafly Boro	Tenafly
136	2,873	Rockaway Twp	Hibernia
137	2,871	Ramsey Boro	Ramsey
138	2,861	Hamilton Twp	Mays Landing
139	2,845	Washington Twp	Long Valley
140	2,779	Hopatcong	Hopatcong
141	2,753	Berkeley Heights Twp	Berkeley Hgts
142	2,728	Roselle Boro	Roselle
143	2,727	Englewood City	Englewood
144	2,689	Dumont Boro	Dumont
145	2,682	Cliffside Park Boro	Cliffside Park
146	2,630	Hunterdon Central Reg	Flemington
147	2,622	North Hunt-Voorhees Regional	Annandale
148	2,586	Delran Twp	Delran
149	2,578	Caldwell-West Caldwell	West Caldwell
150	2,569	Buena Regional	Buena
151	2,539	Cinnaminson Twp	Cinnaminson
152	2,502	Clark Twp	Clark
153	2,485	Glassboro	Glassboro
154	2,478	Lindenwold Boro	Lindenwold
155	2,461	Morris Hills Regional	Rockaway
156	2,459	Pequannock Twp	Pompton Plains
157	2,440	Westwood Regional	Westwood
158	2,422	Wyckoff Twp	Wyckoff
159	2,413	Central Regional	Bayville
160	2,368	Stafford Twp	Manahawkin
161	2,338	Glen Rock Boro	Glen Rock
162	2,312	Rutherford Boro	Rutherford
162	2,312	West Morris Regional	Chester
164	2,295	Hawthorne Boro	Hawthorne
165	2,282	Haddonfield Boro	Haddonfield
166	2,261	Penns Grove-Carney's Point Reg	Penns Grove
167	2,260	Northern Valley Regional	Demarest
168	2,245	Barnegat Twp	Barnegat
169	2,242	Haddon Twp	Westmont
170	2,227	South River Boro	South River
171	2,221	Pine Hill Boro	Pine Hill
172	2,195	Eastern Camden County Reg	Voorhees
173	2,189	Somerville Boro	Somerville
174	2,183	Ocean City	Ocean City
174	2,183	Readington Twp	Whitehouse Stn
176	2,176	Gloucester City	Gloucester City
177	2,155	Warren Twp	Warren
178	2,154	Madison Boro	Madison
179	2,150	Rancocas Valley Regional	Mount Holly
180	2,133	Maple Shade Twp	Maple Shade
181	2,121	Hoboken City	Hoboken
182	2,120	New Providence Boro	New Providence
183	2,105	Middlesex Boro	Middlesex
184	2,102	Lyndhurst Twp	Lyndhurst
185	2,092	Ridgefield Boro	Ridgefield
185	2,092	Warren Hills Regional	Washington
187	2,090	Keansburg Boro	Keansburg
188	2,068	Collingswood Boro	Collingswood
189	2,058	Kinnelon Boro	Kinnelon
190	2,046	Bordentown Regional	Bordentown
191	2,044	Pennsville	Pennsville
192	2,039	Ramapo-Indian Hill Reg	Franklin Lakes
193	2,035	Clearview Regional	Mullica Hill
194	2,021	Elmwood Park	Elmwood Park
195	2,013	Passaic County Vocational	Wayne
196	2,011	Essex County Voc-Tech	West Orange
197	2,010	Verona Boro	Verona
198	2,004	Springfield Twp	Springfield
199	1,993	Roselle Park Boro	Roselle Park
200	1,992	Camden County Vocational	Sicklerville
201	1,957	Lower Twp	Cape May
202	1,951	Bergen County Vocational	Paramus
203	1,943	Harrison Town	Harrison
204	1,925	Pinelands Regional	Tuckerton
205	1,917	New Milford Boro	New Milford
206	1,910	Branchburg Twp	Branchburg
207	1,905	Delsea Regional HS District	Franklinville
208	1,903	Berkeley Twp	Bayville
209	1,892	Pittsgrove Twp	Pittsgrove
210	1,878	Hackettstown	Hackettstown
211	1,870	Pompton Lakes Boro	Pompton Lakes
212	1,867	Ridgefield Park Twp	Ridgefield Park
213	1,854	Northern Burlington Reg	Columbus
214	1,829	Upper Freehold Regional	Allentown
215	1,827	Metuchen Boro	Metuchen
216	1,821	Denville Twp	Denville
217	1,816	Lower Cape May Regional	Cape May
218	1,802	Burlington City	Burlington
219	1,799	Secaucus Town	Secaucus
220	1,793	Upper Twp	Petersburg
221	1,781	Clinton Twp	Annandale
222	1,770	Somerset Hills Regional	Bernardsville
223	1,769	Middlesex County Vocational	E Brunswick
224	1,760	Tinton Falls	Tinton Falls
225	1,759	Sussex-Wantage Regional	Wantage
226	1,757	Glen Ridge Boro	Glen Ridge
227	1,747	Manasquan Boro	Manasquan
228	1,741	Audubon Boro	Audubon
229	1,726	Burlington County Vocational	Westampton Twp
230	1,717	Little Egg Harbor Twp	Little Egg Hbr
231	1,701	Leonia Boro	Leonia
232	1,689	Newton Town	Newton
233	1,684	Spotswood Boro	Spotswood
233	1,684	Woodstown-Pilesgrove Reg	Woodstown
235	1,667	Mountain Lakes Boro	Mountain Lakes
236	1,662	Pitman Boro	Pitman
237	1,660	Kingsway Regional	Woolwich Twp
238	1,659	Plumsted Twp	New Egypt
239	1,654	Lumberton Twp	Lumberton
240	1,650	Millstone Twp	Clarksburg
241	1,632	Somers Point City	Somers Point
242	1,616	Saddle Brook Twp	Saddle Brook
243	1,613	Bound Brook Boro	Bound Brook
244	1,605	Oakland Boro	Oakland
245	1,604	Highland Park Boro	Highland Park
246	1,596	Mainland Regional	Linwood
247	1,581	Watchung Hills Regional	Warren
248	1,563	Hasbrouck Heights Boro	Hasbrouck Hgts
249	1,560	Florence Twp	Florence
250	1,548	Pascack Valley Regional	Montvale
251	1,529	Woodbury City	Woodbury
252	1,525	Paulsboro Boro	Paulsboro
253	1,516	Waldwick Boro	Waldwick
254	1,515	North Arlington Boro	North Arlington
255	1,501	Colts Neck Twp	Colts Neck

Male Students

Rank	Percent	District Name	City
1	59.8	Middlesex County Vocational	E Brunswick
2	55.8	Bergen County Vocational	Paramus
3	55.0	Lower Twp	Cape May
4	54.8	Camden County Vocational	Sicklerville
5	54.3	Burlington County Vocational	Westampton Twp
6	54.2	Clark Twp	Clark
7	53.9	North Arlington Boro	North Arlington
8	53.8	Audubon Boro	Audubon
8	53.8	New Milford Boro	New Milford
10	53.6	Cranford Twp	Cranford
10	53.6	Rockaway Twp	Hibernia
12	53.5	Northern Burlington Reg	Columbus
13	53.4	Berkeley Twp	Bayville
13	53.4	Burlington City	Burlington
13	53.4	Ramsey Boro	Ramsey
13	53.4	Stafford Twp	Manahawkin
17	53.3	Cliffside Park Boro	Cliffside Park
18	53.1	Tenafly Boro	Tenafly
18	53.1	West Deptford Twp	West Deptford
20	53.0	East Windsor Regional	Hightstown
20	53.0	Mountain Lakes Boro	Mountain Lakes
22	52.9	Highland Park Boro	Highland Park
22	52.9	Hoboken City	Hoboken
24	52.8	Central Regional	Bayville
24	52.8	Hillsborough Twp	Neshanic
24	52.8	Ridgefield Boro	Ridgefield
24	52.8	Warren Hills Regional	Washington
28	52.7	Watchung Hills Regional	Warren
28	52.7	West Milford Twp	West Milford
30	52.6	City of Orange Twp	Orange
30	52.6	Westwood Regional	Westwood
32	52.5	Paulsboro Boro	Paulsboro
32	52.5	Pleasantville City	Pleasantville
32	52.5	Somers Point City	Somers Point
35	52.4	Cinnaminson Twp	Cinnaminson
35	52.4	Clifton City	Clifton
35	52.4	Eastern Camden County Reg	Voorhees
35	52.4	Middle Twp	Cape May Ct Hse
35	52.4	Neptune Twp	Neptune
35	52.4	Vineland City	Vineland
41	52.3	Bayonne City	Bayonne
41	52.3	Bound Brook Boro	Bound Brook
41	52.3	Garfield City	Garfield
41	52.3	Harrison Town	Harrison
41	52.3	Mount Olive Twp	Budd Lake
41	52.3	Phillipsburg Town	Phillipsburg
41	52.3	Rahway City	Rahway
41	52.3	Upper Freehold Regional	Allentown
41	52.3	Upper Twp	Petersburg
50	52.2	Parsippany-Troy Hills Twp	Parsippany
50	52.2	Ridgefield Park Twp	Ridgefield Park
50	52.2	South River Boro	South River

53	52.1	Bloomfield Twp	Bloomfield
53	52.1	Delsea Regional HS District	Franklinville
53	52.1	Englewood City	Englewood
53	52.1	Evesham Twp	Marlton
53	52.1	Keansburg Boro	Keansburg
53	52.1	Perth Amboy City	Perth Amboy
53	52.1	Vernon Twp	Vernon
53	52.1	Westfield Town	Westfield
53	52.1	Woodbury City	Woodbury
62	52.0	Gloucester Twp	Blackwood
62	52.0	Livingston Twp	Livingston
62	52.0	Maple Shade Twp	Maple Shade
62	52.0	New Brunswick City	New Brunswick
62	52.0	Roxbury Twp	Succasunna
62	52.0	South Plainfield Boro	S Plainfield
62	52.0	Winslow Twp	Atco
69	51.9	Cherry Hill Twp	Cherry Hill
69	51.9	Haddon Twp	Westmont
69	51.9	Hamilton Twp	Mays Landing
69	51.9	Irvington Township	Irvington
69	51.9	Kearny Town	Kearny
69	51.9	Montgomery Twp	Skillman
69	51.9	Pennsauken Twp	Pennsauken
69	51.9	Sayreville Boro	Sayreville
69	51.9	Union Twp	Union
69	51.9	West Orange Town	West Orange
79	51.8	Brick Twp	Brick
79	51.8	Collingswood Boro	Collingswood
79	51.8	Egg Harbor Twp	W Atlantic City
79	51.8	Kinnelon Boro	Kinnelon
79	51.8	Mahwah Twp	Mahwah
79	51.8	Marlboro Twp	Marlboro
79	51.8	Middletown Twp	Middletown
79	51.8	Rancocas Valley Regional	Mount Holly
79	51.8	SD of The Chathams	Chatham
79	51.8	Summit City	Summit
89	51.7	Belleville Town	Belleville
89	51.7	Dover Town	Dover
89	51.7	Holmdel Twp	Holmdel
89	51.7	Lumberton Twp	Lumberton
89	51.7	New Providence Boro	New Providence
89	51.7	Plumsted Twp	New Egypt
89	51.7	Randolph Twp	Randolph
89	51.7	Verona Boro	Verona
89	51.7	West Windsor-Plainsboro Reg	Princeton Jct
98	51.6	Deptford Twp	Deptford
98	51.6	Elmwood Park	Elmwood Park
98	51.6	Ewing Twp	Ewing
98	51.6	Franklin Twp	Somerset
98	51.6	Monroe Twp	Monroe Township
98	51.6	Morris SD	Morristown
98	51.6	North Bergen Twp	North Bergen
98	51.6	Paramus Boro	Paramus
98	51.6	Pequannock Twp	Pompton Plains
98	51.6	Point Pleasant Boro	Pt Pleasant
98	51.6	Wall Twp	Wall
98	51.6	Wayne Twp	Wayne
98	51.6	West New York Town	West New York
111	51.5	Branchburg Twp	Branchburg
111	51.5	Carteret Boro	Carteret
111	51.5	Dumont Boro	Dumont
111	51.5	Glen Rock Boro	Glen Rock
111	51.5	Hopatcong	Hopatcong
111	51.5	Jackson Twp	Jackson
111	51.5	Lyndhurst Twp	Lyndhurst
111	51.5	Millburn Twp	Millburn
111	51.5	Monroe Twp	Williamstown
111	51.5	Mount Laurel Twp	Mount Laurel
111	51.5	Pittsgrove Twp	Pittsgrove
111	51.5	Princeton Regional	Princeton
111	51.5	Union City	Union City
111	51.5	Waldwick Boro	Waldwick
111	51.5	Woodstown-Pilesgrove Reg	Woodstown
126	51.4	Berkeley Heights Twp	Berkeley Hgts
126	51.4	Delran Twp	Delran
126	51.4	Denville Twp	Denville
126	51.4	Flemington-Raritan Reg	Flemington
126	51.4	Hawthorne Boro	Hawthorne
126	51.4	Jefferson Twp	Lake Hopatcong
126	51.4	Little Egg Harbor Twp	Little Egg Hbr
126	51.4	Manchester Twp	Whiting
126	51.4	Roselle Boro	Roselle
126	51.4	Roselle Park Boro	Roselle Park
126	51.4	Secaucus Town	Secaucus
126	51.4	South Orange-Maplewood	Maplewood
126	51.4	Spotswood Boro	Spotswood
139	51.3	Atlantic City	Atlantic City
139	51.3	Black Horse Pike Regional	Blackwood
139	51.3	East Brunswick Twp	E Brunswick
139	51.3	Glen Ridge Boro	Glen Ridge
139	51.3	Hillside Twp	Hillside
139	51.3	Jersey City	Jersey City
139	51.3	Kingsway Regional	Woolwich Twp
139	51.3	Lacey Twp	Lanoka Harbor
139	51.3	Lawrence Twp	Lawrenceville
139	51.3	Newark City	Newark
139	51.3	Piscataway Twp	Piscataway
139	51.3	Willingboro Twp	Willingboro
151	51.2	Howell Twp	Howell
151	51.2	Lower Cape May Regional	Cape May
151	51.2	Medford Twp	Medford
151	51.2	Moorestown Twp	Moorestown
151	51.2	Newton Town	Newton
151	51.2	Nutley Town	Nutley
151	51.2	Ocean Twp	Oakhurst
151	51.2	Scotch Plains-Fanwood Reg	Scotch Plains
151	51.2	Somerville Boro	Somerville
151	51.2	Toms River Regional	Toms River
151	51.2	Voorhees Twp	Voorhees
162	51.1	Bernards Twp	Basking Ridge
162	51.1	Fair Lawn Boro	Fair Lawn
162	51.1	Hackensack City	Hackensack
162	51.1	Hamilton Twp	Hamilton Square
162	51.1	Lindenwold Boro	Lindenwold
162	51.1	Long Branch City	Long Branch
162	51.1	Madison Boro	Madison
162	51.1	Metuchen Boro	Metuchen
162	51.1	Morris Hills Regional	Rockaway
162	51.1	Old Bridge Twp	Matawan
162	51.1	Paterson City	Paterson
162	51.1	Pemberton Twp	Pemberton
162	51.1	Somerset Hills Regional	Bernardsville
162	51.1	Washington Twp	Sewell
176	51.0	Bridgeton City	Bridgeton
176	51.0	Bridgewater-Raritan Reg	Bridgewater
176	51.0	Florence Twp	Florence
176	51.0	Fort Lee Boro	Fort Lee
176	51.0	Hackettstown	Hackettstown
176	51.0	Middlesex Boro	Middlesex
176	51.0	Montville Twp	Montville
176	51.0	Ocean City	Ocean City
176	51.0	Rutherford Boro	Rutherford
176	51.0	Woodbridge Twp	Woodbridge
186	50.9	Caldwell-West Caldwell	West Caldwell
186	50.9	Millstone Twp	Clarksburg
186	50.9	North Hunt-Voorhees Regional	Annandale
186	50.9	Plainfield City	Plainfield
186	50.9	Sparta Twp	Sparta
191	50.8	Bordentown Regional	Bordentown
191	50.8	Clearview Regional	Mullica Hill
191	50.8	Hopewell Valley Regional	Pennington
191	50.8	Linden City	Linden
191	50.8	Matawan-Aberdeen Regional	Aberdeen
191	50.8	Montclair Town	Montclair
191	50.8	Pascack Valley Regional	Montvale
198	50.7	Barnegat Twp	Barnegat
198	50.7	North Brunswick Twp	North Brunswick
198	50.7	Ridgewood Village	Ridgewood
198	50.7	Springfield Twp	Springfield
202	50.6	North Plainfield Boro	N Plainfield
202	50.6	Pine Hill Boro	Pine Hill
204	50.5	Buena Regional	Buena
204	50.5	Camden City	Camden
204	50.5	Glassboro	Glassboro
204	50.5	Lakewood Twp	Lakewood
204	50.5	Tinton Falls	Tinton Falls
204	50.5	Warren Twp	Warren
204	50.5	West Morris Regional	Chester
211	50.4	Asbury Park City	Asbury Park
211	50.4	Mainland Regional	Linwood
211	50.4	Manasquan Boro	Manasquan
214	50.3	Edison Twp	Edison
214	50.3	Freehold Twp	Freehold
214	50.3	Galloway Twp	Galloway
214	50.3	Hunterdon Central Reg	Flemington
214	50.3	Leonia Boro	Leonia
214	50.3	Pinelands Regional	Tuckerton
214	50.3	Teaneck Twp	Teaneck
221	50.2	Bergenfield Boro	Bergenfield
221	50.2	Colts Neck Twp	Colts Neck
221	50.2	Elizabeth City	Elizabeth
221	50.2	Gloucester City	Gloucester City
221	50.2	Lodi Borough	Lodi
221	50.2	Manalapan-Englishtown Reg	Englishtown
221	50.2	Millville City	Millville
228	50.1	Greater Egg Harbor Reg	Mays Landing
229	50.0	Hasbrouck Heights Boro	Hasbrouck Hgts
229	50.0	Northern Valley Regional	Demarest
229	50.0	Passaic City	Passaic
229	50.0	South Brunswick Twp	Monmouth Jct
233	49.9	East Orange	East Orange
233	49.9	Haddonfield Boro	Haddonfield
235	49.8	Pompton Lakes Boro	Pompton Lakes
235	49.8	Wyckoff Twp	Wyckoff
237	49.7	Burlington Twp	Burlington
237	49.7	Lenape Regional	Shamong
237	49.7	Oakland Boro	Oakland
237	49.7	Penns Grove-Carney's Point Reg	Penns Grove
241	49.4	Readington Twp	Whitehouse Stn
241	49.4	Southern Regional	Manahawkin
241	49.4	Washington Twp	Long Valley
244	49.3	Hammonton Town	Hammonton
244	49.3	Hazlet Twp	Hazlet
244	49.3	Saddle Brook Twp	Saddle Brook
247	49.2	Pennsville	Pennsville
248	49.1	Freehold Regional	Englishtown
249	48.9	Sussex-Wantage Regional	Wantage
250	48.8	Trenton City	Trenton
251	48.7	Passaic County Vocational	Wayne
251	48.7	Pitman Boro	Pitman
253	48.6	Clinton Twp	Annandale
254	47.7	Ramapo-Indian Hill Reg	Franklin Lakes
255	42.9	Essex County Voc-Tech	West Orange

Female Students

Rank	Percent	District Name	City
1	57.1	Essex County Voc-Tech	West Orange
2	52.3	Ramapo-Indian Hill Reg	Franklin Lakes
3	51.4	Clinton Twp	Annandale
4	51.3	Passaic County Vocational	Wayne
4	51.3	Pitman Boro	Pitman
6	51.2	Trenton City	Trenton
7	51.1	Sussex-Wantage Regional	Wantage
8	50.9	Freehold Regional	Englishtown
9	50.8	Pennsville	Pennsville
10	50.7	Hammonton Town	Hammonton
10	50.7	Hazlet Twp	Hazlet
10	50.7	Saddle Brook Twp	Saddle Brook
13	50.6	Readington Twp	Whitehouse Stn
13	50.6	Southern Regional	Manahawkin
13	50.6	Washington Twp	Long Valley
16	50.3	Burlington Twp	Burlington
16	50.3	Lenape Regional	Shamong
16	50.3	Oakland Boro	Oakland
16	50.3	Penns Grove-Carney's Point Reg	Penns Grove
20	50.2	Pompton Lakes Boro	Pompton Lakes
20	50.2	Wyckoff Twp	Wyckoff
22	50.1	East Orange	East Orange
22	50.1	Haddonfield Boro	Haddonfield
24	50.0	Hasbrouck Heights Boro	Hasbrouck Hgts
24	50.0	Northern Valley Regional	Demarest
24	50.0	Passaic City	Passaic
24	50.0	South Brunswick Twp	Monmouth Jct
28	49.9	Greater Egg Harbor Reg	Mays Landing
29	49.8	Bergenfield Boro	Bergenfield
29	49.8	Colts Neck Twp	Colts Neck
29	49.8	Elizabeth City	Elizabeth
29	49.8	Gloucester City	Gloucester City
29	49.8	Lodi Borough	Lodi
29	49.8	Manalapan-Englishtown Reg	Englishtown
29	49.8	Millville City	Millville
36	49.7	Edison Twp	Edison
36	49.7	Freehold Twp	Freehold
36	49.7	Galloway Twp	Galloway
36	49.7	Hunterdon Central Reg	Flemington
36	49.7	Leonia Boro	Leonia
36	49.7	Pinelands Regional	Tuckerton
36	49.7	Teaneck Twp	Teaneck
43	49.6	Asbury Park City	Asbury Park
43	49.6	Mainland Regional	Linwood
43	49.6	Manasquan Boro	Manasquan
46	49.5	Buena Regional	Buena
46	49.5	Camden City	Camden
46	49.5	Glassboro	Glassboro
46	49.5	Lakewood Twp	Lakewood
46	49.5	Tinton Falls	Tinton Falls
46	49.5	Warren Twp	Warren
46	49.5	West Morris Regional	Chester
53	49.4	North Plainfield Boro	N Plainfield
53	49.4	Pine Hill Boro	Pine Hill
55	49.3	Barnegat Twp	Barnegat
55	49.3	North Brunswick Twp	North Brunswick
55	49.3	Ridgewood Village	Ridgewood
55	49.3	Springfield Twp	Springfield
59	49.2	Bordentown Regional	Bordentown
59	49.2	Clearview Regional	Mullica Hill
59	49.2	Hopewell Valley Regional	Pennington
59	49.2	Linden City	Linden
59	49.2	Matawan-Aberdeen Regional	Aberdeen
59	49.2	Montclair Town	Montclair
59	49.2	Pascack Valley Regional	Montvale
66	49.1	Caldwell-West Caldwell	West Caldwell
66	49.1	Millstone Twp	Clarksburg
66	49.1	North Hunt-Voorhees Regional	Annandale
66	49.1	Plainfield City	Plainfield
66	49.1	Sparta Twp	Sparta

71	49.0	Bridgeton City	Bridgeton
71	49.0	Bridgewater-Raritan Reg	Bridgewater
71	49.0	Florence Twp	Florence
71	49.0	Fort Lee Boro	Fort Lee
71	49.0	Hackettstown	Hackettstown
71	49.0	Middlesex Boro	Middlesex
71	49.0	Montville Twp	Montville
71	49.0	Ocean City	Ocean City
71	49.0	Rutherford Boro	Rutherford
71	49.0	Woodbridge Twp	Woodbridge
81	48.9	Bernards Twp	Basking Ridge
81	48.9	Fair Lawn Boro	Fair Lawn
81	48.9	Hackensack City	Hackensack
81	48.9	Hamilton Twp	Hamilton Square
81	48.9	Lindenwold Boro	Lindenwold
81	48.9	Long Branch City	Long Branch
81	48.9	Madison Boro	Madison
81	48.9	Metuchen Boro	Metuchen
81	48.9	Morris Hills Regional	Rockaway
81	48.9	Old Bridge Twp	Matawan
81	48.9	Paterson City	Paterson
81	48.9	Pemberton Twp	Pemberton
81	48.9	Somerset Hills Regional	Bernardsville
81	48.9	Washington Twp	Sewell
95	48.8	Howell Twp	Howell
95	48.8	Lower Cape May Regional	Cape May
95	48.8	Medford Twp	Medford
95	48.8	Moorestown Twp	Moorestown
95	48.8	Newton Town	Newton
95	48.8	Nutley Town	Nutley
95	48.8	Ocean Twp	Oakhurst
95	48.8	Scotch Plains-Fanwood Reg	Scotch Plains
95	48.8	Somerville Boro	Somerville
95	48.8	Toms River Regional	Toms River
95	48.8	Voorhees Twp	Voorhees
106	48.7	Atlantic City	Atlantic City
106	48.7	Black Horse Pike Regional	Blackwood
106	48.7	East Brunswick Twp	E Brunswick
106	48.7	Glen Ridge Boro	Glen Ridge
106	48.7	Hillside Twp	Hillside
106	48.7	Jersey City	Jersey City
106	48.7	Kingsway Regional	Woolwich Twp
106	48.7	Lacey Twp	Lanoka Harbor
106	48.7	Lawrence Twp	Lawrenceville
106	48.7	Newark City	Newark
106	48.7	Piscataway Twp	Piscataway
106	48.7	Willingboro Twp	Willingboro
118	48.6	Berkeley Heights Twp	Berkeley Hgts
118	48.6	Delran Twp	Delran
118	48.6	Denville Twp	Denville
118	48.6	Flemington-Raritan Reg	Flemington
118	48.6	Hawthorne Boro	Hawthorne
118	48.6	Jefferson Twp	Lake Hopatcong
118	48.6	Little Egg Harbor Twp	Little Egg Hbr
118	48.6	Manchester Twp	Whiting
118	48.6	Roselle Boro	Roselle
118	48.6	Roselle Park Boro	Roselle Park
118	48.6	Secaucus Town	Secaucus
118	48.6	South Orange-Maplewood	Maplewood
118	48.6	Spotswood Boro	Spotswood
131	48.5	Branchburg Twp	Branchburg
131	48.5	Carteret Boro	Carteret
131	48.5	Dumont Boro	Dumont
131	48.5	Glen Rock Boro	Glen Rock
131	48.5	Hopatcong	Hopatcong
131	48.5	Jackson Twp	Jackson
131	48.5	Lyndhurst Twp	Lyndhurst
131	48.5	Millburn Twp	Millburn
131	48.5	Monroe Twp	Williamstown
131	48.5	Mount Laurel Twp	Mount Laurel
131	48.5	Pittsgrove Twp	Pittsgrove
131	48.5	Princeton Regional	Princeton
131	48.5	Union City	Union City
131	48.5	Waldwick Boro	Waldwick
131	48.5	Woodstown-Pilesgrove Reg	Woodstown
146	48.4	Deptford Twp	Deptford
146	48.4	Elmwood Park	Elmwood Park
146	48.4	Ewing Twp	Ewing
146	48.4	Franklin Twp	Somerset
146	48.4	Monroe Twp	Monroe Township
146	48.4	Morris SD	Morristown
146	48.4	North Bergen Twp	North Bergen
146	48.4	Paramus Boro	Paramus
146	48.4	Pequannock Twp	Pompton Plains
146	48.4	Point Pleasant Boro	Pt Pleasant
146	48.4	Wall Twp	Wall
146	48.4	Wayne Twp	Wayne
146	48.4	West New York Town	West New York
159	48.3	Belleville Town	Belleville
159	48.3	Dover Town	Dover
159	48.3	Holmdel Twp	Holmdel
159	48.3	Lumberton Twp	Lumberton
159	48.3	New Providence Boro	New Providence
159	48.3	Plumsted Twp	New Egypt
159	48.3	Randolph Twp	Randolph
159	48.3	Verona Boro	Verona
159	48.3	West Windsor-Plainsboro Reg	Princeton Jct
168	48.2	Brick Twp	Brick
168	48.2	Collingswood Boro	Collingswood
168	48.2	Egg Harbor Twp	W Atlantic City
168	48.2	Kinnelon Boro	Kinnelon
168	48.2	Mahwah Twp	Mahwah
168	48.2	Marlboro Twp	Marlboro
168	48.2	Middletown Twp	Middletown
168	48.2	Rancocas Valley Regional	Mount Holly
168	48.2	SD of The Chathams	Chatham
168	48.2	Summit City	Summit
178	48.1	Cherry Hill Twp	Cherry Hill
178	48.1	Haddon Twp	Westmont
178	48.1	Hamilton Twp	Mays Landing
178	48.1	Irvington Township	Irvington
178	48.1	Kearny Town	Kearny
178	48.1	Montgomery Twp	Skillman
178	48.1	Pennsauken Twp	Pennsauken
178	48.1	Sayreville Boro	Sayreville
178	48.1	Union Twp	Union
178	48.1	West Orange Town	West Orange
188	48.0	Gloucester Twp	Blackwood
188	48.0	Livingston Twp	Livingston
188	48.0	Maple Shade Twp	Maple Shade
188	48.0	New Brunswick City	New Brunswick
188	48.0	Roxbury Twp	Succasunna
188	48.0	South Plainfield Boro	S Plainfield
188	48.0	Winslow Twp	Atco
195	47.9	Bloomfield Twp	Bloomfield
195	47.9	Delsea Regional HS District	Franklinville
195	47.9	Englewood City	Englewood
195	47.9	Evesham Twp	Marlton
195	47.9	Keansburg Boro	Keansburg
195	47.9	Perth Amboy City	Perth Amboy
195	47.9	Vernon Twp	Vernon
195	47.9	Westfield Town	Westfield
195	47.9	Woodbury City	Woodbury
204	47.8	Parsippany-Troy Hills Twp	Parsippany
204	47.8	Ridgefield Park Twp	Ridgefield Park
204	47.8	South River Boro	South River
207	47.7	Bayonne City	Bayonne
207	47.7	Bound Brook Boro	Bound Brook
207	47.7	Garfield City	Garfield
207	47.7	Harrison Town	Harrison
207	47.7	Mount Olive Twp	Budd Lake
207	47.7	Phillipsburg Town	Phillipsburg
207	47.7	Rahway City	Rahway
207	47.7	Upper Freehold Regional	Allentown
207	47.7	Upper Twp	Petersburg
216	47.6	Cinnaminson Twp	Cinnaminson
216	47.6	Clifton City	Clifton
216	47.6	Eastern Camden County Reg	Voorhees
216	47.6	Middle Twp	Cape May Ct Hse
216	47.6	Neptune Twp	Neptune
216	47.6	Vineland City	Vineland
222	47.5	Paulsboro Boro	Paulsboro
222	47.5	Pleasantville City	Pleasantville
222	47.5	Somers Point City	Somers Point
225	47.4	City of Orange Twp	Orange
225	47.4	Westwood Regional	Westwood
227	47.3	Watchung Hills Regional	Warren
227	47.3	West Milford Twp	West Milford
229	47.2	Central Regional	Bayville
229	47.2	Hillsborough Twp	Neshanic
229	47.2	Ridgefield Boro	Ridgefield
229	47.2	Warren Hills Regional	Washington
233	47.1	Highland Park Boro	Highland Park
233	47.1	Hoboken City	Hoboken
235	47.0	East Windsor Regional	Hightstown
235	47.0	Mountain Lakes Boro	Mountain Lakes
237	46.9	Tenafly Boro	Tenafly
237	46.9	West Deptford Twp	West Deptford
239	46.7	Cliffside Park Boro	Cliffside Park
240	46.6	Berkeley Twp	Bayville
240	46.6	Burlington City	Burlington
240	46.6	Ramsey Boro	Ramsey
240	46.6	Stafford Twp	Manahawkin
244	46.5	Northern Burlington Reg	Columbus
245	46.4	Cranford Twp	Cranford
245	46.4	Rockaway Twp	Hibernia
247	46.2	Audubon Boro	Audubon
247	46.2	New Milford Boro	New Milford
249	46.1	North Arlington Boro	North Arlington
250	45.8	Clark Twp	Clark
251	45.7	Burlington County Vocational	Westampton Twp
252	45.2	Camden County Vocational	Sicklerville
253	45.0	Lower Twp	Cape May
254	44.2	Bergen County Vocational	Paramus
255	40.2	Middlesex County Vocational	E Brunswick

Individual Education Program Students

Rank	Percent	District Name	City
1	32.0	Burlington County Vocational	Westampton Twp
2	31.6	Camden County Vocational	Sicklerville
3	28.9	Middlesex County Vocational	E Brunswick
4	27.8	Keansburg Boro	Keansburg
5	27.2	Barnegat Twp	Barnegat
6	24.8	Pinelands Regional	Tuckerton
7	24.3	Lower Cape May Regional	Cape May
8	23.8	Pemberton Twp	Pemberton
9	23.6	Maple Shade Twp	Maple Shade
9	23.6	Upper Twp	Petersburg
11	22.5	Hopatcong	Hopatcong
12	22.4	Sussex-Wantage Regional	Wantage
13	22.3	Asbury Park City	Asbury Park
14	22.2	Hamilton Twp	Hamilton Square
15	22.0	Lower Twp	Cape May
15	22.0	Westwood Regional	Westwood
15	22.0	Woodbury City	Woodbury
18	21.8	Passaic City	Passaic
19	21.6	Pennsauken Twp	Pennsauken
20	21.2	Lyndhurst Twp	Lyndhurst
21	21.1	Lumberton Twp	Lumberton
22	21.0	Glassboro	Glassboro
22	21.0	West Deptford Twp	West Deptford
24	20.9	Bordentown Regional	Bordentown
24	20.9	Florence Twp	Florence
26	20.8	Neptune Twp	Neptune
27	20.7	Roselle Boro	Roselle
28	20.6	Pleasantville City	Pleasantville
29	20.5	Hoboken City	Hoboken
29	20.5	Winslow Twp	Atco
31	20.4	Bridgeton City	Bridgeton
31	20.4	Ewing Twp	Ewing
31	20.4	Morris SD	Morristown
31	20.4	Trenton City	Trenton
35	20.3	Lawrence Twp	Lawrenceville
35	20.3	Lindenwold Boro	Lindenwold
37	20.1	New Brunswick City	New Brunswick
38	20.0	Vineland City	Vineland
39	19.9	Rancocas Valley Regional	Mount Holly
40	19.8	Pennsville	Pennsville
41	19.7	Branchburg Twp	Branchburg
42	19.6	Little Egg Harbor Twp	Little Egg Hbr
42	19.6	Paulsboro Boro	Paulsboro
42	19.6	Pitman Boro	Pitman
45	19.5	Gloucester City	Gloucester City
46	19.2	Brick Twp	Brick
47	19.1	Jackson Twp	Jackson
48	18.9	Cinnaminson Twp	Cinnaminson
48	18.9	Deptford Twp	Deptford
50	18.8	Bayonne City	Bayonne
51	18.7	Stafford Twp	Manahawkin
52	18.6	Camden City	Camden
52	18.6	Evesham Twp	Marlton
54	18.3	Willingboro Twp	Willingboro
55	18.2	Greater Egg Harbor Reg	Mays Landing
55	18.2	Millstone Twp	Clarksburg
55	18.2	North Arlington Boro	North Arlington
58	18.1	Bergen County Vocational	Paramus
58	18.1	Bergenfield Boro	Bergenfield
58	18.1	Millville City	Millville
58	18.1	Rahway City	Rahway
62	18.0	Fair Lawn Boro	Fair Lawn
62	18.0	Lacey Twp	Lanoka Harbor
62	18.0	Middle Twp	Cape May Ct Hse
62	18.0	Mount Laurel Twp	Mount Laurel
62	18.0	Washington Twp	Sewell
67	17.9	Franklin Twp	Somerset
67	17.9	Moorestown Twp	Moorestown
69	17.8	Pine Hill Boro	Pine Hill
70	17.7	Monroe Twp	Williamstown
70	17.7	Montclair Town	Montclair
70	17.7	Wall Twp	Wall
73	17.6	Buena Regional	Buena
73	17.6	Burlington City	Burlington
73	17.6	Passaic County Vocational	Wayne
76	17.5	Saddle Brook Twp	Saddle Brook
77	17.4	East Windsor Regional	Hightstown
77	17.4	Englewood City	Englewood
77	17.4	SD of The Chathams	Chatham
77	17.4	West Milford Twp	West Milford
81	17.3	Long Branch City	Long Branch
82	17.2	Central Regional	Bayville
82	17.2	Delsea Regional HS District	Franklinville
82	17.2	Warren Twp	Warren
85	17.1	Belleville Town	Belleville
85	17.1	Egg Harbor Twp	W Atlantic City
85	17.1	Hillsborough Twp	Neshanic
85	17.1	Linden City	Linden

85	17.1	Manchester Twp	Whiting
85	17.1	Middletown Twp	Middletown
85	17.1	Rockaway Twp	Hibernia
85	17.1	Tinton Falls	Tinton Falls
85	17.1	Verona Boro	Verona
94	16.9	Denville Twp	Denville
94	16.9	Hamilton Twp	Mays Landing
94	16.9	Hazlet Twp	Hazlet
94	16.9	Oakland Boro	Oakland
94	16.9	Westfield Town	Westfield
99	16.8	Hackensack City	Hackensack
99	16.8	Roselle Park Boro	Roselle Park
99	16.8	Scotch Plains-Fanwood Reg	Scotch Plains
102	16.7	Livingston Twp	Livingston
102	16.7	Pompton Lakes Boro	Pompton Lakes
104	16.6	Garfield City	Garfield
105	16.5	Plumsted Twp	New Egypt
106	16.4	Paterson City	Paterson
106	16.4	Readington Twp	Whitehouse Stn
106	16.4	Ridgefield Park Twp	Ridgefield Park
106	16.4	Waldwick Boro	Waldwick
106	16.4	Washington Twp	Long Valley
111	16.3	Jersey City	Jersey City
111	16.3	Monroe Twp	Monroe Township
111	16.3	Parsippany-Troy Hills Twp	Parsippany
114	16.2	Gloucester Twp	Blackwood
115	16.1	Elmwood Park	Elmwood Park
115	16.1	Somers Point City	Somers Point
117	16.0	Irvington Township	Irvington
117	16.0	Northern Burlington Reg	Columbus
117	16.0	Pittsgrove Twp	Pittsgrove
120	15.9	Black Horse Pike Regional	Blackwood
120	15.9	Cranford Twp	Cranford
120	15.9	Hunterdon Central Reg	Flemington
123	15.8	Bloomfield Twp	Bloomfield
123	15.8	East Brunswick Twp	E Brunswick
123	15.8	Phillipsburg Town	Phillipsburg
123	15.8	Voorhees Twp	Voorhees
127	15.7	City of Orange Twp	Orange
127	15.7	East Orange	East Orange
127	15.7	Middlesex Boro	Middlesex
127	15.7	North Hunt-Voorhees Regional	Annandale
127	15.7	South Plainfield Boro	S Plainfield
127	15.7	Warren Hills Regional	Washington
133	15.6	Burlington Twp	Burlington
133	15.6	Hasbrouck Heights Boro	Hasbrouck Hgts
133	15.6	Newark City	Newark
133	15.6	North Plainfield Boro	N Plainfield
133	15.6	Sayreville Boro	Sayreville
133	15.6	Union Twp	Union
139	15.4	Galloway Twp	Galloway
139	15.4	New Milford Boro	New Milford
141	15.3	Hawthorne Boro	Hawthorne
142	15.2	Collingswood Boro	Collingswood
142	15.2	Haddon Twp	Westmont
142	15.2	Mount Olive Twp	Budd Lake
145	15.1	Hillside Twp	Hillside
146	15.0	Lakewood Twp	Lakewood
146	15.0	Lenape Regional	Shamong
146	15.0	Penns Grove-Carney's Point Reg	Penns Grove
146	15.0	Teaneck Twp	Teaneck
150	14.9	Clinton Twp	Annandale
150	14.9	Howell Twp	Howell
150	14.9	Medford Twp	Medford
150	14.9	Ramsey Boro	Ramsey
150	14.9	West New York Town	West New York
155	14.8	Hopewell Valley Regional	Pennington
155	14.8	Ocean Twp	Oakhurst
155	14.8	Springfield Twp	Springfield
158	14.7	Bridgewater-Raritan Reg	Bridgewater
159	14.6	Pequannock Twp	Pompton Plains
160	14.5	Berkeley Twp	Bayville
160	14.5	Clearview Regional	Mullica Hill
160	14.5	Glen Rock Boro	Glen Rock
160	14.5	Mainland Regional	Linwood
164	14.4	Freehold Twp	Freehold
164	14.4	Jefferson Twp	Lake Hopatcong
164	14.4	Manalapan-Englishtown Reg	Englishtown
164	14.4	Metuchen Boro	Metuchen
164	14.4	Piscataway Twp	Piscataway
169	14.3	Madison Boro	Madison
169	14.3	Princeton Regional	Princeton
169	14.3	Woodbridge Twp	Woodbridge
172	14.2	Bound Brook Boro	Bound Brook
172	14.2	Haddonfield Boro	Haddonfield
174	14.1	Ramapo-Indian Hill Reg	Franklin Lakes
175	14.0	Caldwell-West Caldwell	West Caldwell
175	14.0	Essex County Voc-Tech	West Orange
175	14.0	Pascack Valley Regional	Montvale
175	14.0	Tenafly Boro	Tenafly
179	13.9	Highland Park Boro	Highland Park
179	13.9	Rutherford Boro	Rutherford
181	13.8	Dumont Boro	Dumont
182	13.7	Morris Hills Regional	Rockaway
182	13.7	West Orange Town	West Orange
184	13.6	Flemington-Raritan Reg	Flemington
184	13.6	Fort Lee Boro	Fort Lee
186	13.5	Toms River Regional	Toms River
186	13.5	West Morris Regional	Chester
188	13.4	Clifton City	Clifton
188	13.4	Lodi Borough	Lodi
190	13.3	Nutley Town	Nutley
190	13.3	South Brunswick Twp	Monmouth Jct
192	13.2	Cherry Hill Twp	Cherry Hill
192	13.2	Randolph Twp	Randolph
194	13.0	Edison Twp	Edison
194	13.0	Hackettstown	Hackettstown
194	13.0	Kearny Town	Kearny
194	13.0	Newton Town	Newton
194	13.0	North Brunswick Twp	North Brunswick
194	13.0	South River Boro	South River
200	12.9	New Providence Boro	New Providence
200	12.9	Point Pleasant Boro	Pt Pleasant
202	12.8	Atlantic City	Atlantic City
202	12.8	Colts Neck Twp	Colts Neck
202	12.8	Roxbury Twp	Succasunna
202	12.8	Summit City	Summit
206	12.7	Secaucus Town	Secaucus
207	12.6	Delran Twp	Delran
207	12.6	Marlboro Twp	Marlboro
207	12.6	Millburn Twp	Millburn
210	12.5	Mahwah Twp	Mahwah
210	12.5	Matawan-Aberdeen Regional	Aberdeen
210	12.5	West Windsor-Plainsboro Reg	Princeton Jct
213	12.4	Montville Twp	Montville
213	12.4	Ridgewood Village	Ridgewood
213	12.4	Sparta Twp	Sparta
216	12.3	Somerset Hills Regional	Bernardsville
217	12.2	Eastern Camden County Reg	Voorhees
217	12.2	Freehold Regional	Englishtown
217	12.2	Mountain Lakes Boro	Mountain Lakes
217	12.2	Plainfield City	Plainfield
217	12.2	South Orange-Maplewood	Maplewood
222	12.1	Leonia Boro	Leonia
222	12.1	Somerville Boro	Somerville
222	12.1	Wayne Twp	Wayne
225	12.0	Audubon Boro	Audubon
225	12.0	Hammonton Town	Hammonton
227	11.9	Northern Valley Regional	Demarest
228	11.8	Kinnelon Boro	Kinnelon
228	11.8	North Bergen Twp	North Bergen
228	11.8	Old Bridge Twp	Matawan
231	11.7	Perth Amboy City	Perth Amboy
231	11.7	Union City	Union City
231	11.7	Watchung Hills Regional	Warren
234	11.6	Clark Twp	Clark
234	11.6	Elizabeth City	Elizabeth
234	11.6	Kingsway Regional	Woolwich Twp
237	11.5	Harrison Town	Harrison
238	11.3	Bernards Twp	Basking Ridge
239	11.2	Glen Ridge Boro	Glen Ridge
239	11.2	Ocean City	Ocean City
239	11.2	Vernon Twp	Vernon
239	11.2	Woodstown-Pilesgrove Reg	Woodstown
243	11.0	Montgomery Twp	Skillman
244	10.8	Berkeley Heights Twp	Berkeley Hgts
244	10.8	Wyckoff Twp	Wyckoff
246	10.7	Dover Town	Dover
247	10.6	Paramus Boro	Paramus
248	10.4	Carteret Boro	Carteret
249	10.3	Holmdel Twp	Holmdel
250	10.1	Spotswood Boro	Spotswood
251	9.6	Cliffside Park Boro	Cliffside Park
252	9.4	Southern Regional	Manahawkin
253	9.2	Upper Freehold Regional	Allentown
254	8.1	Ridgefield Boro	Ridgefield
255	6.6	Manasquan Boro	Manasquan

English Language Learner Students

Rank	Percent	District Name	City
1	42.6	Union City	Union City
2	28.4	Passaic City	Passaic
3	25.0	New Brunswick City	New Brunswick
4	20.6	Elizabeth City	Elizabeth
5	17.5	West New York Town	West New York
6	16.5	Dover Town	Dover
7	16.2	Perth Amboy City	Perth Amboy
8	15.0	Harrison Town	Harrison
9	13.5	Bound Brook Boro	Bound Brook
10	13.4	Atlantic City	Atlantic City
11	12.9	Paterson City	Paterson
12	12.6	Garfield City	Garfield
13	12.4	Plainfield City	Plainfield
14	11.3	Cliffside Park Boro	Cliffside Park
15	10.7	Fort Lee Boro	Fort Lee
16	10.5	Leonia Boro	Leonia
16	10.5	North Bergen Twp	North Bergen
18	9.2	Englewood City	Englewood
19	9.0	Roselle Boro	Roselle
20	8.8	Bridgeton City	Bridgeton
21	8.7	Newark City	Newark
22	8.6	Lodi Borough	Lodi
22	8.6	North Plainfield Boro	N Plainfield
24	8.2	Jersey City	Jersey City
25	8.1	Lakewood Twp	Lakewood
26	7.8	Kearny Town	Kearny
27	7.4	City of Orange Twp	Orange
27	7.4	Morris SD	Morristown
27	7.4	Pleasantville City	Pleasantville
30	7.2	Camden City	Camden
31	7.1	Tenafly Boro	Tenafly
32	7.0	Roselle Park Boro	Roselle Park
33	6.9	Essex County Voc-Tech	West Orange
34	6.6	Clifton City	Clifton
34	6.6	Hackensack City	Hackensack
34	6.6	North Brunswick Twp	North Brunswick
37	6.3	Trenton City	Trenton
38	6.1	Carteret Boro	Carteret
39	6.0	East Windsor Regional	Hightstown
40	5.9	Belleville Town	Belleville
40	5.9	Linden City	Linden
40	5.9	Parsippany-Troy Hills Twp	Parsippany
40	5.9	Vineland City	Vineland
44	5.8	South River Boro	South River
45	5.5	North Arlington Boro	North Arlington
46	5.4	Bergenfield Boro	Bergenfield
47	5.2	Irvington Township	Irvington
47	5.2	Long Branch City	Long Branch
47	5.2	Ridgefield Park Twp	Ridgefield Park
50	5.1	Ridgefield Boro	Ridgefield
51	4.9	Asbury Park City	Asbury Park
52	4.5	Bloomfield Twp	Bloomfield
52	4.5	Dumont Boro	Dumont
54	4.4	Burlington City	Burlington
54	4.4	Paramus Boro	Paramus
54	4.4	West Orange Town	West Orange
57	4.3	Elmwood Park	Elmwood Park
57	4.3	Franklin Twp	Somerset
59	4.2	Hillside Twp	Hillside
60	4.1	Hammonton Town	Hammonton
60	4.1	Lawrence Twp	Lawrenceville
60	4.1	Piscataway Twp	Piscataway
63	4.0	Glen Rock Boro	Glen Rock
63	4.0	Ocean Twp	Oakhurst
65	3.9	Highland Park Boro	Highland Park
66	3.7	Galloway Twp	Galloway
66	3.7	Middlesex Boro	Middlesex
66	3.7	Somerville Boro	Somerville
66	3.7	Summit City	Summit
70	3.5	Bayonne City	Bayonne
70	3.5	New Milford Boro	New Milford
70	3.5	Princeton Regional	Princeton
73	3.3	East Orange	East Orange
73	3.3	Fair Lawn Boro	Fair Lawn
75	3.1	Penns Grove-Carney's Point Reg	Penns Grove
76	3.0	Pennsauken Twp	Pennsauken
76	3.0	West Windsor-Plainsboro Reg	Princeton Jct
78	2.9	Hamilton Twp	Mays Landing
78	2.9	Lindenwold Boro	Lindenwold
78	2.9	Old Bridge Twp	Matawan
78	2.9	Rahway City	Rahway
82	2.8	Mount Olive Twp	Budd Lake
83	2.7	Edison Twp	Edison
83	2.7	Woodbridge Twp	Woodbridge
85	2.5	Lyndhurst Twp	Lyndhurst
85	2.5	Middlesex County Vocational	E Brunswick
85	2.5	Waldwick Boro	Waldwick
88	2.4	Collingswood Boro	Collingswood
88	2.4	Passaic County Vocational	Wayne
90	2.3	Burlington Twp	Burlington
90	2.3	Flemington-Raritan Reg	Flemington
90	2.3	Hackettstown	Hackettstown
90	2.3	Saddle Brook Twp	Saddle Brook
90	2.3	Teaneck Twp	Teaneck
90	2.3	Union Twp	Union
90	2.3	Upper Freehold Regional	Allentown
97	2.2	Bordentown Regional	Bordentown
97	2.2	Delran Twp	Delran
97	2.2	East Brunswick Twp	E Brunswick
97	2.2	Secaucus Town	Secaucus
101	2.1	Buena Regional	Buena
101	2.1	Phillipsburg Town	Phillipsburg
103	2.0	Bridgewater-Raritan Reg	Bridgewater
103	2.0	Ewing Twp	Ewing
103	2.0	Hasbrouck Heights Boro	Hasbrouck Hgts
103	2.0	Hoboken City	Hoboken
103	2.0	Madison Boro	Madison

103	2.0	Maple Shade Twp	Maple Shade
103	2.0	Ridgewood Village	Ridgewood
103	2.0	Springfield Twp	Springfield
111	1.9	Egg Harbor Twp	W Atlantic City
111	1.9	Rutherford Boro	Rutherford
111	1.9	Somerset Hills Regional	Bernardsville
111	1.9	South Plainfield Boro	S Plainfield
115	1.8	New Providence Boro	New Providence
115	1.8	Westwood Regional	Westwood
117	1.7	Marlboro Twp	Marlboro
117	1.7	Matawan-Aberdeen Regional	Aberdeen
117	1.7	Montville Twp	Montville
117	1.7	Northern Valley Regional	Demarest
117	1.7	Pompton Lakes Boro	Pompton Lakes
122	1.6	Manasquan Boro	Manasquan
122	1.6	Millville City	Millville
122	1.6	Nutley Town	Nutley
125	1.5	Berkeley Twp	Bayville
125	1.5	Livingston Twp	Livingston
127	1.4	Hamilton Twp	Hamilton Square
127	1.4	Manalapan-Englishtown Reg	Englishtown
127	1.4	Millburn Twp	Millburn
127	1.4	Newton Town	Newton
127	1.4	Sayreville Boro	Sayreville
127	1.4	South Orange-Maplewood	Maplewood
133	1.3	Berkeley Heights Twp	Berkeley Hgts
133	1.3	Cherry Hill Twp	Cherry Hill
133	1.3	Denville Twp	Denville
133	1.3	Greater Egg Harbor Reg	Mays Landing
133	1.3	Voorhees Twp	Voorhees
133	1.3	Wayne Twp	Wayne
139	1.2	Hawthorne Boro	Hawthorne
139	1.2	Little Egg Harbor Twp	Little Egg Hbr
139	1.2	Mahwah Twp	Mahwah
139	1.2	Montclair Town	Montclair
139	1.2	Roxbury Twp	Succasunna
144	1.1	Colts Neck Twp	Colts Neck
144	1.1	Glassboro	Glassboro
144	1.1	Morris Hills Regional	Rockaway
144	1.1	Mount Laurel Twp	Mount Laurel
144	1.1	Randolph Twp	Randolph
144	1.1	Rockaway Twp	Hibernia
144	1.1	Spotswood Boro	Spotswood
144	1.1	Tinton Falls	Tinton Falls
152	1.0	Bernards Twp	Basking Ridge
152	1.0	Gloucester City	Gloucester City
152	1.0	Metuchen Boro	Metuchen
152	1.0	Plumsted Twp	New Egypt
152	1.0	Warren Twp	Warren
157	0.9	Branchburg Twp	Branchburg
157	0.9	Deptford Twp	Deptford
157	0.9	Gloucester Twp	Blackwood
157	0.9	Warren Hills Regional	Washington
161	0.8	Evesham Twp	Marlton
161	0.8	Florence Twp	Florence
161	0.8	Freehold Regional	Englishtown
161	0.8	Hopatcong	Hopatcong
161	0.8	Jackson Twp	Jackson
161	0.8	Lower Twp	Cape May
161	0.8	Millstone Twp	Clarksburg
161	0.8	Neptune Twp	Neptune
161	0.8	Pascack Valley Regional	Montvale
161	0.8	Pemberton Twp	Pemberton
161	0.8	Wall Twp	Wall
161	0.8	Winslow Twp	Atco
173	0.7	Black Horse Pike Regional	Blackwood
173	0.7	Central Regional	Bayville
173	0.7	Clark Twp	Clark
173	0.7	Howell Twp	Howell
173	0.7	Lumberton Twp	Lumberton
173	0.7	Monroe Twp	Monroe Township
173	0.7	Oakland Boro	Oakland
173	0.7	Pine Hill Boro	Pine Hill
173	0.7	Ramsey Boro	Ramsey
173	0.7	Somers Point City	Somers Point
173	0.7	Toms River Regional	Toms River
173	0.7	Wyckoff Twp	Wyckoff
185	0.6	Brick Twp	Brick
185	0.6	Caldwell-West Caldwell	West Caldwell
185	0.6	Freehold Twp	Freehold
185	0.6	Holmdel Twp	Holmdel
185	0.6	Hunterdon Central Reg	Flemington
185	0.6	Mainland Regional	Linwood
185	0.6	Middle Twp	Cape May Ct Hse
185	0.6	Montgomery Twp	Skillman
185	0.6	Point Pleasant Boro	Pt Pleasant
185	0.6	Southern Regional	Manahawkin
185	0.6	Sparta Twp	Sparta
185	0.6	Verona Boro	Verona
197	0.5	Audubon Boro	Audubon
197	0.5	Barnegat Twp	Barnegat
197	0.5	Cinnaminson Twp	Cinnaminson
197	0.5	Clinton Twp	Annandale
197	0.5	Hazlet Twp	Hazlet
197	0.5	Jefferson Twp	Lake Hopatcong
197	0.5	Keansburg Boro	Keansburg
197	0.5	Lower Cape May Regional	Cape May
197	0.5	Manchester Twp	Whiting
197	0.5	Monroe Twp	Williamstown
197	0.5	Moorestown Twp	Moorestown
197	0.5	Ocean City	Ocean City
197	0.5	Pequannock Twp	Pompton Plains
197	0.5	Rancocas Valley Regional	Mount Holly
197	0.5	Readington Twp	Whitehouse Stn
197	0.5	SD of The Chathams	Chatham
197	0.5	Scotch Plains-Fanwood Reg	Scotch Plains
197	0.5	Stafford Twp	Manahawkin
197	0.5	Westfield Town	Westfield
216	0.4	Camden County Vocational	Sicklerville
216	0.4	Delsea Regional HS District	Franklinville
216	0.4	Kingsway Regional	Woolwich Twp
216	0.4	Lacey Twp	Lanoka Harbor
216	0.4	Lenape Regional	Shamong
216	0.4	Northern Burlington Reg	Columbus
216	0.4	Pittsgrove Twp	Pittsgrove
216	0.4	Ramapo-Indian Hill Reg	Franklin Lakes
216	0.4	Washington Twp	Sewell
216	0.4	Watchung Hills Regional	Warren
216	0.4	West Milford Twp	West Milford
216	0.4	Woodstown-Pilesgrove Reg	Woodstown
228	0.3	Eastern Camden County Reg	Voorhees
228	0.3	Haddon Twp	Westmont
228	0.3	Haddonfield Boro	Haddonfield
228	0.3	Kinnelon Boro	Kinnelon
228	0.3	Medford Twp	Medford
228	0.3	Middletown Twp	Middletown
228	0.3	Pennsville	Pennsville
228	0.3	West Deptford Twp	West Deptford
228	0.3	Willingboro Twp	Willingboro
237	0.2	Bergen County Vocational	Paramus
237	0.2	Cranford Twp	Cranford
237	0.2	Glen Ridge Boro	Glen Ridge
237	0.2	Pinelands Regional	Tuckerton
237	0.2	Sussex-Wantage Regional	Wantage
237	0.2	Vernon Twp	Vernon
237	0.2	Washington Twp	Long Valley
237	0.2	West Morris Regional	Chester
237	0.2	Woodbury City	Woodbury
246	0.1	Hopewell Valley Regional	Pennington
246	0.1	North Hunt-Voorhees Regional	Annandale
246	0.1	Upper Twp	Petersburg
249	0.0	Burlington County Vocational	Westampton Twp
249	0.0	Clearview Regional	Mullica Hill
249	0.0	Hillsborough Twp	Neshanic
249	0.0	Mountain Lakes Boro	Mountain Lakes
249	0.0	Paulsboro Boro	Paulsboro
249	0.0	Pitman Boro	Pitman
249	0.0	South Brunswick Twp	Monmouth Jct

Migrant Students

Rank	Percent	District Name	City
1	10.6	Bridgeton City	Bridgeton
2	2.3	Hammonton Town	Hammonton
3	0.9	Vineland City	Vineland
4	0.8	New Brunswick City	New Brunswick
5	0.6	Buena Regional	Buena
6	0.5	Penns Grove-Carney's Point Reg	Penns Grove
7	0.4	Pittsgrove Twp	Pittsgrove
7	0.4	Woodstown-Pilesgrove Reg	Woodstown
9	0.2	Delsea Regional HS District	Franklinville
9	0.2	Kingsway Regional	Woolwich Twp
9	0.2	Winslow Twp	Atco
12	0.1	Greater Egg Harbor Reg	Mays Landing
12	0.1	Hamilton Twp	Mays Landing
12	0.1	Lakewood Twp	Lakewood
12	0.1	Millville City	Millville
12	0.1	Plumsted Twp	New Egypt
17	0.0	Camden City	Camden
17	0.0	Glassboro	Glassboro
17	0.0	Monroe Twp	Williamstown
17	0.0	Pemberton Twp	Pemberton
21	0.0	Asbury Park City	Asbury Park
21	0.0	Atlantic City	Atlantic City
21	0.0	Audubon Boro	Audubon
21	0.0	Barnegat Twp	Barnegat
21	0.0	Bayonne City	Bayonne
21	0.0	Belleville Town	Belleville
21	0.0	Bergen County Vocational	Paramus
21	0.0	Bergenfield Boro	Bergenfield
21	0.0	Berkeley Heights Twp	Berkeley Hgts
21	0.0	Berkeley Twp	Bayville
21	0.0	Bernards Twp	Basking Ridge
21	0.0	Black Horse Pike Regional	Blackwood
21	0.0	Bloomfield Twp	Bloomfield
21	0.0	Bordentown Regional	Bordentown
21	0.0	Bound Brook Boro	Bound Brook
21	0.0	Branchburg Twp	Branchburg
21	0.0	Brick Twp	Brick
21	0.0	Bridgewater-Raritan Reg	Bridgewater
21	0.0	Burlington City	Burlington
21	0.0	Burlington County Vocational	Westampton Twp
21	0.0	Burlington Twp	Burlington
21	0.0	Caldwell-West Caldwell	West Caldwell
21	0.0	Camden County Vocational	Sicklerville
21	0.0	Carteret Boro	Carteret
21	0.0	Central Regional	Bayville
21	0.0	Cherry Hill Twp	Cherry Hill
21	0.0	Cinnaminson Twp	Cinnaminson
21	0.0	City of Orange Twp	Orange
21	0.0	Clark Twp	Clark
21	0.0	Clearview Regional	Mullica Hill
21	0.0	Cliffside Park Boro	Cliffside Park
21	0.0	Clifton City	Clifton
21	0.0	Clinton Twp	Annandale
21	0.0	Collingswood Boro	Collingswood
21	0.0	Colts Neck Twp	Colts Neck
21	0.0	Cranford Twp	Cranford
21	0.0	Delran Twp	Delran
21	0.0	Denville Twp	Denville
21	0.0	Deptford Twp	Deptford
21	0.0	Dover Town	Dover
21	0.0	Dumont Boro	Dumont
21	0.0	East Brunswick Twp	E Brunswick
21	0.0	East Orange	East Orange
21	0.0	East Windsor Regional	Hightstown
21	0.0	Eastern Camden County Reg	Voorhees
21	0.0	Edison Twp	Edison
21	0.0	Egg Harbor Twp	W Atlantic City
21	0.0	Elizabeth City	Elizabeth
21	0.0	Elmwood Park	Elmwood Park
21	0.0	Englewood City	Englewood
21	0.0	Essex County Voc-Tech	West Orange
21	0.0	Evesham Twp	Marlton
21	0.0	Ewing Twp	Ewing
21	0.0	Fair Lawn Boro	Fair Lawn
21	0.0	Flemington-Raritan Reg	Flemington
21	0.0	Florence Twp	Florence
21	0.0	Fort Lee Boro	Fort Lee
21	0.0	Franklin Twp	Somerset
21	0.0	Freehold Regional	Englishtown
21	0.0	Freehold Twp	Freehold
21	0.0	Galloway Twp	Galloway
21	0.0	Garfield City	Garfield
21	0.0	Glen Ridge Boro	Glen Ridge
21	0.0	Glen Rock Boro	Glen Rock
21	0.0	Gloucester City	Gloucester City
21	0.0	Gloucester Twp	Blackwood
21	0.0	Hackensack City	Hackensack
21	0.0	Hackettstown	Hackettstown
21	0.0	Haddon Twp	Westmont
21	0.0	Haddonfield Boro	Haddonfield
21	0.0	Hamilton Twp	Hamilton Square
21	0.0	Harrison Town	Harrison
21	0.0	Hasbrouck Heights Boro	Hasbrouck Hgts
21	0.0	Hawthorne Boro	Hawthorne
21	0.0	Hazlet Twp	Hazlet
21	0.0	Highland Park Boro	Highland Park
21	0.0	Hillsborough Twp	Neshanic
21	0.0	Hillside Twp	Hillside
21	0.0	Hoboken City	Hoboken
21	0.0	Holmdel Twp	Holmdel
21	0.0	Hopatcong	Hopatcong
21	0.0	Hopewell Valley Regional	Pennington
21	0.0	Howell Twp	Howell
21	0.0	Hunterdon Central Reg	Flemington
21	0.0	Irvington Township	Irvington
21	0.0	Jackson Twp	Jackson
21	0.0	Jefferson Twp	Lake Hopatcong
21	0.0	Jersey City	Jersey City
21	0.0	Keansburg Boro	Keansburg
21	0.0	Kearny Town	Kearny
21	0.0	Kinnelon Boro	Kinnelon
21	0.0	Lacey Twp	Lanoka Harbor
21	0.0	Lawrence Twp	Lawrenceville
21	0.0	Lenape Regional	Shamong
21	0.0	Leonia Boro	Leonia
21	0.0	Linden City	Linden
21	0.0	Lindenwold Boro	Lindenwold
21	0.0	Little Egg Harbor Twp	Little Egg Hbr
21	0.0	Livingston Twp	Livingston
21	0.0	Lodi Borough	Lodi
21	0.0	Long Branch City	Long Branch
21	0.0	Lower Cape May Regional	Cape May
21	0.0	Lower Twp	Cape May
21	0.0	Lumberton Twp	Lumberton
21	0.0	Lyndhurst Twp	Lyndhurst
21	0.0	Madison Boro	Madison

21	0.0	Mahwah Twp	Mahwah
21	0.0	Mainland Regional	Linwood
21	0.0	Manalapan-Englishtown Reg	Englishtown
21	0.0	Manasquan Boro	Manasquan
21	0.0	Manchester Twp	Whiting
21	0.0	Maple Shade Twp	Maple Shade
21	0.0	Marlboro Twp	Marlboro
21	0.0	Matawan-Aberdeen Regional	Aberdeen
21	0.0	Medford Twp	Medford
21	0.0	Metuchen Boro	Metuchen
21	0.0	Middle Twp	Cape May Ct Hse
21	0.0	Middlesex Boro	Middlesex
21	0.0	Middlesex County Vocational	E Brunswick
21	0.0	Middletown Twp	Middletown
21	0.0	Millburn Twp	Millburn
21	0.0	Millstone Twp	Clarksburg
21	0.0	Monroe Twp	Monroe Township
21	0.0	Montclair Town	Montclair
21	0.0	Montgomery Twp	Skillman
21	0.0	Montville Twp	Montville
21	0.0	Moorestown Twp	Moorestown
21	0.0	Morris Hills Regional	Rockaway
21	0.0	Morris SD	Morristown
21	0.0	Mount Laurel Twp	Mount Laurel
21	0.0	Mount Olive Twp	Budd Lake
21	0.0	Mountain Lakes Boro	Mountain Lakes
21	0.0	Neptune Twp	Neptune
21	0.0	New Milford Boro	New Milford
21	0.0	New Providence Boro	New Providence
21	0.0	Newark City	Newark
21	0.0	Newton Town	Newton
21	0.0	North Arlington Boro	North Arlington
21	0.0	North Bergen Twp	North Bergen
21	0.0	North Brunswick Twp	North Brunswick
21	0.0	North Hunt-Voorhees Regional	Annandale
21	0.0	North Plainfield Boro	N Plainfield
21	0.0	Northern Burlington Reg	Columbus
21	0.0	Northern Valley Regional	Demarest
21	0.0	Nutley Town	Nutley
21	0.0	Oakland Boro	Oakland
21	0.0	Ocean City	Ocean City
21	0.0	Ocean Twp	Oakhurst
21	0.0	Old Bridge Twp	Matawan
21	0.0	Paramus Boro	Paramus
21	0.0	Parsippany-Troy Hills Twp	Parsippany
21	0.0	Pascack Valley Regional	Montvale
21	0.0	Passaic City	Passaic
21	0.0	Passaic County Vocational	Wayne
21	0.0	Paterson City	Paterson
21	0.0	Paulsboro Boro	Paulsboro
21	0.0	Pennsauken Twp	Pennsauken
21	0.0	Pennsville	Pennsville
21	0.0	Pequannock Twp	Pompton Plains
21	0.0	Perth Amboy City	Perth Amboy
21	0.0	Phillipsburg Town	Phillipsburg
21	0.0	Pine Hill Boro	Pine Hill
21	0.0	Pinelands Regional	Tuckerton
21	0.0	Piscataway Twp	Piscataway
21	0.0	Pitman Boro	Pitman
21	0.0	Plainfield City	Plainfield
21	0.0	Pleasantville City	Pleasantville
21	0.0	Point Pleasant Boro	Pt Pleasant
21	0.0	Pompton Lakes Boro	Pompton Lakes
21	0.0	Princeton Regional	Princeton
21	0.0	Rahway City	Rahway
21	0.0	Ramapo-Indian Hill Reg	Franklin Lakes
21	0.0	Ramsey Boro	Ramsey
21	0.0	Rancocas Valley Regional	Mount Holly
21	0.0	Randolph Twp	Randolph
21	0.0	Readington Twp	Whitehouse Stn
21	0.0	Ridgefield Boro	Ridgefield
21	0.0	Ridgefield Park Twp	Ridgefield Park
21	0.0	Ridgewood Village	Ridgewood
21	0.0	Rockaway Twp	Hibernia
21	0.0	Roselle Boro	Roselle
21	0.0	Roselle Park Boro	Roselle Park
21	0.0	Roxbury Twp	Succasunna
21	0.0	Rutherford Boro	Rutherford
21	0.0	SD of The Chathams	Chatham
21	0.0	Saddle Brook Twp	Saddle Brook
21	0.0	Sayreville Boro	Sayreville
21	0.0	Scotch Plains-Fanwood Reg	Scotch Plains
21	0.0	Secaucus Town	Secaucus
21	0.0	Somers Point City	Somers Point
21	0.0	Somerset Hills Regional	Bernardsville
21	0.0	Somerville Boro	Somerville
21	0.0	South Brunswick Twp	Monmouth Jct
21	0.0	South Orange-Maplewood	Maplewood
21	0.0	South Plainfield Boro	S Plainfield
21	0.0	South River Boro	South River
21	0.0	Southern Regional	Manahawkin
21	0.0	Sparta Twp	Sparta
21	0.0	Spotswood Boro	Spotswood
21	0.0	Springfield Twp	Springfield
21	0.0	Stafford Twp	Manahawkin
21	0.0	Summit City	Summit
21	0.0	Sussex-Wantage Regional	Wantage
21	0.0	Teaneck Twp	Teaneck
21	0.0	Tenafly Boro	Tenafly
21	0.0	Tinton Falls	Tinton Falls
21	0.0	Toms River Regional	Toms River
21	0.0	Trenton City	Trenton
21	0.0	Union City	Union City
21	0.0	Union Twp	Union
21	0.0	Upper Freehold Regional	Allentown
21	0.0	Upper Twp	Petersburg
21	0.0	Vernon Twp	Vernon
21	0.0	Verona Boro	Verona
21	0.0	Voorhees Twp	Voorhees
21	0.0	Waldwick Boro	Waldwick
21	0.0	Wall Twp	Wall
21	0.0	Warren Hills Regional	Washington
21	0.0	Warren Twp	Warren
21	0.0	Washington Twp	Long Valley
21	0.0	Washington Twp	Sewell
21	0.0	Watchung Hills Regional	Warren
21	0.0	Wayne Twp	Wayne
21	0.0	West Deptford Twp	West Deptford
21	0.0	West Milford Twp	West Milford
21	0.0	West Morris Regional	Chester
21	0.0	West New York Town	West New York
21	0.0	West Orange Town	West Orange
21	0.0	West Windsor-Plainsboro Reg	Princeton Jct
21	0.0	Westfield Town	Westfield
21	0.0	Westwood Regional	Westwood
21	0.0	Willingboro Twp	Willingboro
21	0.0	Woodbridge Twp	Woodbridge
21	0.0	Woodbury City	Woodbury
21	0.0	Wyckoff Twp	Wyckoff

Students Eligible for Free Lunch

Rank	Percent	District Name	City
1	79.1	Union City	Union City
2	77.1	Camden City	Camden
3	74.2	Asbury Park City	Asbury Park
4	72.2	Essex County Voc-Tech	West Orange
5	68.9	New Brunswick City	New Brunswick
6	68.8	Bridgeton City	Bridgeton
7	68.6	Paterson City	Paterson
8	68.4	City of Orange Twp	Orange
9	68.1	Newark City	Newark
10	65.6	Passaic City	Passaic
11	62.4	Perth Amboy City	Perth Amboy
12	62.3	Hoboken City	Hoboken
13	60.1	Atlantic City	Atlantic City
14	58.4	Jersey City	Jersey City
15	57.3	Elizabeth City	Elizabeth
16	56.2	West New York Town	West New York
17	55.9	Irvington Township	Irvington
18	55.8	East Orange	East Orange
19	55.5	Plainfield City	Plainfield
20	51.0	Camden County Vocational	Sicklerville
21	47.5	Lakewood Twp	Lakewood
22	47.1	Long Branch City	Long Branch
23	45.9	Trenton City	Trenton
24	44.1	Passaic County Vocational	Wayne
25	42.9	Pleasantville City	Pleasantville
26	42.7	Vineland City	Vineland
27	42.6	Paulsboro Boro	Paulsboro
28	42.3	Keansburg Boro	Keansburg
29	40.7	Penns Grove-Carney's Point Reg	Penns Grove
30	39.0	North Bergen Twp	North Bergen
31	38.2	Millville City	Millville
32	35.0	Englewood City	Englewood
33	34.2	Hillside Twp	Hillside
34	33.6	Woodbury City	Woodbury
35	33.3	Burlington City	Burlington
36	33.1	Carteret Boro	Carteret
36	33.1	Dover Town	Dover
38	32.7	Neptune Twp	Neptune
39	31.4	Lindenwold Boro	Lindenwold
40	30.9	Middlesex County Vocational	E Brunswick
41	30.8	Pennsauken Twp	Pennsauken
42	30.2	Roselle Boro	Roselle
43	30.0	Hackensack City	Hackensack
44	29.9	Bayonne City	Bayonne
44	29.9	Garfield City	Garfield
46	28.7	Rahway City	Rahway
47	28.0	Linden City	Linden
48	27.5	Willingboro Twp	Willingboro
49	27.4	Phillipsburg Town	Phillipsburg
50	26.5	Glassboro	Glassboro
50	26.5	Harrison Town	Harrison
52	26.3	Bound Brook Boro	Bound Brook
52	26.3	Gloucester City	Gloucester City
54	25.8	Buena Regional	Buena
55	25.3	Winslow Twp	Atco
56	24.6	Cliffside Park Boro	Cliffside Park
57	23.5	Lodi Borough	Lodi
57	23.5	Lower Cape May Regional	Cape May
59	23.4	Pemberton Twp	Pemberton
60	22.1	Pine Hill Boro	Pine Hill
61	21.9	Lower Twp	Cape May
62	21.8	Clifton City	Clifton
63	21.6	Highland Park Boro	Highland Park
64	20.9	Kearny Town	Kearny
65	20.1	Franklin Twp	Somerset
66	19.6	Hamilton Twp	Mays Landing
67	19.5	Deptford Twp	Deptford
67	19.5	Somers Point City	Somers Point
69	19.3	Somerville Boro	Somerville
70	19.2	Middle Twp	Cape May Ct Hse
71	19.1	Hammonton Town	Hammonton
72	18.5	Little Egg Harbor Twp	Little Egg Hbr
73	18.3	Pittsgrove Twp	Pittsgrove
74	18.1	North Plainfield Boro	N Plainfield
75	17.8	Belleville Town	Belleville
76	17.4	Bloomfield Twp	Bloomfield
76	17.4	Burlington County Vocational	Westampton Twp
78	16.3	South River Boro	South River
79	15.7	Pinelands Regional	Tuckerton
80	14.9	Ridgefield Park Twp	Ridgefield Park
81	14.8	Collingswood Boro	Collingswood
82	14.7	Egg Harbor Twp	W Atlantic City
82	14.7	Monroe Twp	Williamstown
84	14.4	Morris SD	Morristown
85	14.1	Galloway Twp	Galloway
86	13.8	Greater Egg Harbor Reg	Mays Landing
87	13.7	Florence Twp	Florence
87	13.7	Newton Town	Newton
89	13.2	Gloucester Twp	Blackwood
90	13.1	Montclair Town	Montclair
91	12.8	Maple Shade Twp	Maple Shade
91	12.8	Secaucus Town	Secaucus
93	12.5	North Brunswick Twp	North Brunswick
94	12.4	Barnegat Twp	Barnegat
94	12.4	Berkeley Twp	Bayville
96	11.7	Ewing Twp	Ewing
97	11.6	Hamilton Twp	Hamilton Square
97	11.6	Matawan-Aberdeen Regional	Aberdeen
99	11.5	Delsea Regional HS District	Franklinville
100	11.4	Union Twp	Union
100	11.4	West Orange Town	West Orange
102	11.3	Roselle Park Boro	Roselle Park
103	11.1	Manchester Twp	Whiting
103	11.1	South Orange-Maplewood	Maplewood
105	10.8	East Windsor Regional	Hightstown
106	10.7	Woodbridge Twp	Woodbridge
107	10.4	Elmwood Park	Elmwood Park
108	10.3	Central Regional	Bayville
109	9.8	Piscataway Twp	Piscataway
110	9.7	Ocean City	Ocean City
111	9.4	Sussex-Wantage Regional	Wantage
112	9.1	Teaneck Twp	Teaneck
113	8.6	Lyndhurst Twp	Lyndhurst
114	8.4	Tinton Falls	Tinton Falls
114	8.4	Toms River Regional	Toms River
116	8.1	West Deptford Twp	West Deptford
117	8.0	Pennsville	Pennsville
118	7.8	Bergen County Vocational	Paramus
118	7.8	Sayreville Boro	Sayreville
120	7.7	Bergenfield Boro	Bergenfield
120	7.7	Hackettstown	Hackettstown
120	7.7	Mainland Regional	Linwood
120	7.7	Middlesex Boro	Middlesex
124	7.6	Stafford Twp	Manahawkin
125	7.5	Old Bridge Twp	Matawan
126	7.4	Brick Twp	Brick
126	7.4	Lacey Twp	Lanoka Harbor
128	7.3	Audubon Boro	Audubon
129	7.2	Ridgefield Boro	Ridgefield
130	7.1	Plumsted Twp	New Egypt
131	7.0	Burlington Twp	Burlington
132	6.8	Princeton Regional	Princeton
133	6.7	Black Horse Pike Regional	Blackwood
133	6.7	Woodstown-Pilesgrove Reg	Woodstown
135	6.5	Pitman Boro	Pitman
135	6.5	Summit City	Summit
137	6.3	Hopatcong	Hopatcong
138	6.2	Ocean Twp	Oakhurst
139	6.1	Southern Regional	Manahawkin
140	6.0	Hawthorne Boro	Hawthorne
140	6.0	North Arlington Boro	North Arlington
142	5.8	Bordentown Regional	Bordentown
142	5.8	Delran Twp	Delran
142	5.8	South Plainfield Boro	S Plainfield

Rank	Percent	District Name	City
145	5.5	Spotswood Boro	Spotswood
145	5.5	Warren Hills Regional	Washington
147	5.4	Edison Twp	Edison
147	5.4	Leonia Boro	Leonia
147	5.4	Rancocas Valley Regional	Mount Holly
150	5.3	Fort Lee Boro	Fort Lee
151	5.2	Lawrence Twp	Lawrenceville
152	5.1	Howell Twp	Howell
152	5.1	Kingsway Regional	Woolwich Twp
152	5.1	Lumberton Twp	Lumberton
155	4.7	Jackson Twp	Jackson
156	4.6	Hazlet Twp	Hazlet
157	4.5	Cherry Hill Twp	Cherry Hill
157	4.5	Parsippany-Troy Hills Twp	Parsippany
157	4.5	Upper Twp	Petersburg
160	4.4	Madison Boro	Madison
160	4.4	Morris Hills Regional	Rockaway
160	4.4	Washington Twp	Sewell
163	4.3	Wall Twp	Wall
164	4.2	Mount Olive Twp	Budd Lake
165	4.0	New Milford Boro	New Milford
165	4.0	Voorhees Twp	Voorhees
165	4.0	West Milford Twp	West Milford
168	3.9	Manasquan Boro	Manasquan
168	3.9	Northern Burlington Reg	Columbus
170	3.8	Mount Laurel Twp	Mount Laurel
170	3.8	Point Pleasant Boro	Pt Pleasant
170	3.8	Vernon Twp	Vernon
173	3.7	Cinnaminson Twp	Cinnaminson
173	3.7	Pompton Lakes Boro	Pompton Lakes
175	3.6	Haddon Twp	Westmont
175	3.6	Jefferson Twp	Lake Hopatcong
175	3.6	Mahwah Twp	Mahwah
178	3.4	Middletown Twp	Middletown
179	3.3	Eastern Camden County Reg	Voorhees
179	3.3	Rockaway Twp	Hibernia
179	3.3	Roxbury Twp	Succasunna
182	3.2	Saddle Brook Twp	Saddle Brook
183	3.1	Monroe Twp	Monroe Township
184	3.0	Fair Lawn Boro	Fair Lawn
184	3.0	Flemington-Raritan Reg	Flemington
186	2.9	Clearview Regional	Mullica Hill
186	2.9	Mountain Lakes Boro	Mountain Lakes
186	2.9	South Brunswick Twp	Monmouth Jct
189	2.8	Dumont Boro	Dumont
190	2.7	Freehold Regional	Englishtown
190	2.7	Moorestown Twp	Moorestown
190	2.7	Springfield Twp	Springfield
190	2.7	Wayne Twp	Wayne
194	2.6	Bridgewater-Raritan Reg	Bridgewater
194	2.6	Nutley Town	Nutley
196	2.5	Freehold Twp	Freehold
197	2.4	East Brunswick Twp	E Brunswick
197	2.4	Hasbrouck Heights Boro	Hasbrouck Hgts
197	2.4	Hillsborough Twp	Neshanic
197	2.4	Millstone Twp	Clarksburg
197	2.4	Westwood Regional	Westwood
202	2.2	Manalapan-Englishtown Reg	Englishtown
202	2.2	Metuchen Boro	Metuchen
204	2.1	Upper Freehold Regional	Allentown
205	2.0	Evesham Twp	Marlton
206	1.9	Medford Twp	Medford
207	1.7	Randolph Twp	Randolph
208	1.6	Hunterdon Central Reg	Flemington
208	1.6	Scotch Plains-Fanwood Reg	Scotch Plains
208	1.6	Somerset Hills Regional	Bernardsville
211	1.5	Clark Twp	Clark
212	1.4	Rutherford Boro	Rutherford
212	1.4	West Windsor-Plainsboro Reg	Princeton Jct
214	1.3	Cranford Twp	Cranford
214	1.3	Paramus Boro	Paramus
216	1.2	Pequannock Twp	Pompton Plains
217	1.1	Branchburg Twp	Branchburg
217	1.1	Lenape Regional	Shamong
217	1.1	Readington Twp	Whitehouse Stn
217	1.1	Waldwick Boro	Waldwick
217	1.1	Westfield Town	Westfield
222	1.0	Denville Twp	Denville
222	1.0	Marlboro Twp	Marlboro
222	1.0	Washington Twp	Long Valley
225	0.9	Colts Neck Twp	Colts Neck
225	0.9	Glen Rock Boro	Glen Rock
227	0.8	Berkeley Heights Twp	Berkeley Hgts
227	0.8	Clinton Twp	Annandale
227	0.8	Haddonfield Boro	Haddonfield
227	0.8	Montgomery Twp	Skillman
227	0.8	Oakland Boro	Oakland
227	0.8	Ramsey Boro	Ramsey
227	0.8	Sparta Twp	Sparta
234	0.7	Montville Twp	Montville
235	0.6	Hopewell Valley Regional	Pennington
235	0.6	Millburn Twp	Millburn
235	0.6	Ridgewood Village	Ridgewood
238	0.5	Bernards Twp	Basking Ridge
238	0.5	Livingston Twp	Livingston
238	0.5	New Providence Boro	New Providence
238	0.5	North Hunt-Voorhees Regional	Annandale
242	0.4	SD of The Chathams	Chatham
242	0.4	Warren Twp	Warren
244	0.3	Caldwell-West Caldwell	West Caldwell
244	0.3	Holmdel Twp	Holmdel
244	0.3	Kinnelon Boro	Kinnelon
244	0.3	Pascack Valley Regional	Montvale
244	0.3	Tenafly Boro	Tenafly
244	0.3	Watchung Hills Regional	Warren
244	0.3	West Morris Regional	Chester
251	0.2	Northern Valley Regional	Demarest
251	0.2	Wyckoff Twp	Wyckoff
253	0.1	Verona Boro	Verona
254	0.0	Glen Ridge Boro	Glen Ridge
254	0.0	Ramapo-Indian Hill Reg	Franklin Lakes

Students Eligible for Reduced-Price Lunch

Rank	Percent	District Name	City
1	19.6	Passaic County Vocational	Wayne
2	19.0	Dover Town	Dover
3	18.8	Hillside Twp	Hillside
4	18.2	Garfield City	Garfield
5	17.0	Perth Amboy City	Perth Amboy
6	16.6	Lower Twp	Cape May
7	16.1	Keansburg Boro	Keansburg
8	16.0	Lindenwold Boro	Lindenwold
9	15.0	Linden City	Linden
10	14.8	Elizabeth City	Elizabeth
10	14.8	Pemberton Twp	Pemberton
12	14.5	Camden County Vocational	Sicklerville
12	14.5	Long Branch City	Long Branch
12	14.5	Plainfield City	Plainfield
12	14.5	West New York Town	West New York
16	14.4	Pleasantville City	Pleasantville
17	13.8	Pennsauken Twp	Pennsauken
17	13.8	Willingboro Twp	Willingboro
19	13.6	Jersey City	Jersey City
20	13.3	Bound Brook Boro	Bound Brook
20	13.3	Rahway City	Rahway
22	13.0	Essex County Voc-Tech	West Orange
23	12.9	North Bergen Twp	North Bergen
24	12.7	Vineland City	Vineland
25	12.6	Lodi Borough	Lodi
26	12.0	Irvington Township	Irvington
27	11.9	Gloucester City	Gloucester City
28	11.8	East Orange	East Orange
29	11.7	Atlantic City	Atlantic City
30	11.5	Carteret Boro	Carteret
30	11.5	Hackensack City	Hackensack
32	11.4	Paterson City	Paterson
32	11.4	Roselle Boro	Roselle
34	11.3	Englewood City	Englewood
35	11.0	Buena Regional	Buena
35	11.0	Hamilton Twp	Mays Landing
35	11.0	Middlesex County Vocational	E Brunswick
35	11.0	New Brunswick City	New Brunswick
35	11.0	Pinelands Regional	Tuckerton
40	10.9	Bloomfield Twp	Bloomfield
40	10.9	Bridgeton City	Bridgeton
42	10.8	Cliffside Park Boro	Cliffside Park
42	10.8	Ridgefield Park Twp	Ridgefield Park
44	10.7	Pine Hill Boro	Pine Hill
45	10.6	Neptune Twp	Neptune
46	10.5	Woodbury City	Woodbury
47	10.4	City of Orange Twp	Orange
47	10.4	Glassboro	Glassboro
47	10.4	North Plainfield Boro	N Plainfield
47	10.4	South River Boro	South River
51	10.3	Maple Shade Twp	Maple Shade
52	10.2	Burlington City	Burlington
53	10.0	Deptford Twp	Deptford
53	10.0	Millville City	Millville
55	9.8	Barnegat Twp	Barnegat
55	9.8	Bayonne City	Bayonne
55	9.8	Collingswood Boro	Collingswood
55	9.8	Passaic City	Passaic
59	9.6	Kearny Town	Kearny
60	9.5	Burlington County Vocational	Westampton Twp
60	9.5	Lakewood Twp	Lakewood
62	9.4	Galloway Twp	Galloway
62	9.4	Winslow Twp	Atco
64	9.3	Delsea Regional HS District	Franklinville
65	9.2	Asbury Park City	Asbury Park
66	9.1	Egg Harbor Twp	W Atlantic City
66	9.1	Lower Cape May Regional	Cape May
68	9.0	Penns Grove-Carney's Point Reg	Penns Grove
69	8.9	Elmwood Park	Elmwood Park
70	8.8	Greater Egg Harbor Reg	Mays Landing
71	8.7	Paulsboro Boro	Paulsboro
71	8.7	Trenton City	Trenton
73	8.5	Belleville Town	Belleville
73	8.5	Ewing Twp	Ewing
75	8.3	Newark City	Newark
75	8.3	Phillipsburg Town	Phillipsburg
75	8.3	Somers Point City	Somers Point
78	8.2	Union City	Union City
79	7.9	Little Egg Harbor Twp	Little Egg Hbr
80	7.8	Middle Twp	Cape May Ct Hse
81	7.6	Morris SD	Morristown
81	7.6	Roselle Park Boro	Roselle Park
81	7.6	Somerville Boro	Somerville
84	7.4	Gloucester Twp	Blackwood
84	7.4	Union Twp	Union
86	7.3	Franklin Twp	Somerset
86	7.3	Highland Park Boro	Highland Park
86	7.3	Secaucus Town	Secaucus
89	7.0	Harrison Town	Harrison
89	7.0	Hopatcong	Hopatcong
89	7.0	Piscataway Twp	Piscataway
89	7.0	Tinton Falls	Tinton Falls
93	6.9	Monroe Twp	Williamstown
94	6.8	Pittsgrove Twp	Pittsgrove
95	6.6	Hoboken City	Hoboken
95	6.6	West Deptford Twp	West Deptford
97	6.5	Sayreville Boro	Sayreville
97	6.5	Stafford Twp	Manahawkin
99	6.4	Bergenfield Boro	Bergenfield
99	6.4	Matawan-Aberdeen Regional	Aberdeen
99	6.4	Teaneck Twp	Teaneck
102	6.3	West Orange Town	West Orange
103	6.1	Lyndhurst Twp	Lyndhurst
104	5.9	Berkeley Twp	Bayville
104	5.9	Plumsted Twp	New Egypt
104	5.9	Sussex-Wantage Regional	Wantage
104	5.9	Woodbridge Twp	Woodbridge
108	5.8	Central Regional	Bayville
108	5.8	Florence Twp	Florence
110	5.7	Hamilton Twp	Hamilton Square
110	5.7	Newton Town	Newton
110	5.7	South Orange-Maplewood	Maplewood
113	5.6	North Brunswick Twp	North Brunswick
113	5.6	Ridgefield Boro	Ridgefield
115	5.5	Hammonton Town	Hammonton
115	5.5	Middlesex Boro	Middlesex
117	5.4	Manchester Twp	Whiting
117	5.4	Northern Burlington Reg	Columbus
119	5.2	Brick Twp	Brick
119	5.2	East Windsor Regional	Hightstown
119	5.2	Pitman Boro	Pitman
122	5.1	Lacey Twp	Lanoka Harbor
123	4.9	Mainland Regional	Linwood
123	4.9	Montclair Town	Montclair
123	4.9	Upper Twp	Petersburg
126	4.8	Bordentown Regional	Bordentown
126	4.8	Old Bridge Twp	Matawan
128	4.7	Hackettstown	Hackettstown
129	4.6	Delran Twp	Delran
129	4.6	Woodstown-Pilesgrove Reg	Woodstown
131	4.5	Black Horse Pike Regional	Blackwood
131	4.5	Lumberton Twp	Lumberton
133	4.4	North Arlington Boro	North Arlington
134	4.3	Audubon Boro	Audubon
134	4.3	Fort Lee Boro	Fort Lee
136	4.2	Burlington Twp	Burlington
136	4.2	South Plainfield Boro	S Plainfield
136	4.2	Spotswood Boro	Spotswood
139	4.1	Pennsville	Pennsville
139	4.1	Southern Regional	Manahawkin
141	4.0	Bergen County Vocational	Paramus
141	4.0	Hawthorne Boro	Hawthorne
141	4.0	Ocean Twp	Oakhurst
141	4.0	Rockaway Twp	Hibernia
141	4.0	Summit City	Summit
146	3.8	Hazlet Twp	Hazlet
146	3.8	Ocean City	Ocean City
146	3.8	Saddle Brook Twp	Saddle Brook
149	3.7	Kingsway Regional	Woolwich Twp
150	3.5	Clifton City	Clifton
150	3.5	Jackson Twp	Jackson
152	3.3	Mount Olive Twp	Budd Lake
152	3.3	Parsippany-Troy Hills Twp	Parsippany
152	3.3	Toms River Regional	Toms River
155	3.2	Edison Twp	Edison
156	3.1	Jefferson Twp	Lake Hopatcong
156	3.1	Vernon Twp	Vernon
158	3.0	Camden City	Camden
158	3.0	Cherry Hill Twp	Cherry Hill
158	3.0	New Milford Boro	New Milford
158	3.0	Washington Twp	Sewell

162	2.9	Howell Twp	Howell
163	2.8	Haddon Twp	Westmont
163	2.8	Leonia Boro	Leonia
165	2.7	Eastern Camden County Reg	Voorhees
165	2.7	Mount Laurel Twp	Mount Laurel
165	2.7	Pompton Lakes Boro	Pompton Lakes
165	2.7	Roxbury Twp	Succasunna
165	2.7	South Brunswick Twp	Monmouth Jct
170	2.6	Clearview Regional	Mullica Hill
170	2.6	Warren Hills Regional	Washington
172	2.5	Point Pleasant Boro	Pt Pleasant
173	2.4	Lawrence Twp	Lawrenceville
173	2.4	Madison Boro	Madison
173	2.4	Springfield Twp	Springfield
173	2.4	Wall Twp	Wall
173	2.4	West Milford Twp	West Milford
178	2.3	Freehold Twp	Freehold
178	2.3	Mahwah Twp	Mahwah
178	2.3	Middletown Twp	Middletown
178	2.3	Voorhees Twp	Voorhees
182	2.2	East Brunswick Twp	E Brunswick
182	2.2	Monroe Twp	Monroe Township
182	2.2	Nutley Town	Nutley
182	2.2	Princeton Regional	Princeton
182	2.2	Rancocas Valley Regional	Mount Holly
187	2.1	Bridgewater-Raritan Reg	Bridgewater
187	2.1	Cinnaminson Twp	Cinnaminson
187	2.1	Fair Lawn Boro	Fair Lawn
190	2.0	Morris Hills Regional	Rockaway
191	1.9	Evesham Twp	Marlton
191	1.9	Hillsborough Twp	Neshanic
191	1.9	Metuchen Boro	Metuchen
191	1.9	Wayne Twp	Wayne
195	1.8	Moorestown Twp	Moorestown
196	1.7	Flemington-Raritan Reg	Flemington
196	1.7	Freehold Regional	Englishtown
198	1.6	Manalapan-Englishtown Reg	Englishtown
199	1.5	Cranford Twp	Cranford
199	1.5	Dumont Boro	Dumont
199	1.5	Rutherford Boro	Rutherford
199	1.5	Upper Freehold Regional	Allentown
203	1.4	Manasquan Boro	Manasquan
203	1.4	Oakland Boro	Oakland
203	1.4	Randolph Twp	Randolph
206	1.3	West Windsor-Plainsboro Reg	Princeton Jct
207	1.2	Mountain Lakes Boro	Mountain Lakes
207	1.2	Ramsey Boro	Ramsey
207	1.2	Westwood Regional	Westwood
210	1.0	Medford Twp	Medford
210	1.0	New Providence Boro	New Providence
212	0.9	Branchburg Twp	Branchburg
212	0.9	Hopewell Valley Regional	Pennington
212	0.9	Marlboro Twp	Marlboro
212	0.9	Millstone Twp	Clarksburg
216	0.8	Clark Twp	Clark
216	0.8	Pequannock Twp	Pompton Plains
218	0.7	Paramus Boro	Paramus
218	0.7	Readington Twp	Whitehouse Stn
218	0.7	Somerset Hills Regional	Bernardsville
218	0.7	Washington Twp	Long Valley
222	0.6	Colts Neck Twp	Colts Neck
222	0.6	Lenape Regional	Shamong
222	0.6	Montgomery Twp	Skillman
222	0.6	Scotch Plains-Fanwood Reg	Scotch Plains
222	0.6	Sparta Twp	Sparta
227	0.5	Berkeley Heights Twp	Berkeley Hgts
227	0.5	Hunterdon Central Reg	Flemington
229	0.4	Bernards Twp	Basking Ridge
229	0.4	Caldwell-West Caldwell	West Caldwell
229	0.4	Haddonfield Boro	Haddonfield
229	0.4	Ridgewood Village	Ridgewood
229	0.4	Westfield Town	Westfield
234	0.3	Glen Rock Boro	Glen Rock
234	0.3	Hasbrouck Heights Boro	Hasbrouck Hgts
234	0.3	Livingston Twp	Livingston
234	0.3	North Hunt-Voorhees Regional	Annandale
234	0.3	Verona Boro	Verona
234	0.3	Watchung Hills Regional	Warren
240	0.2	Holmdel Twp	Holmdel
240	0.2	Kinnelon Boro	Kinnelon
240	0.2	Northern Valley Regional	Demarest
240	0.2	Ramapo-Indian Hill Reg	Franklin Lakes
244	0.1	Millburn Twp	Millburn
244	0.1	Montville Twp	Montville
244	0.1	SD of The Chathams	Chatham
244	0.1	Tenafly Boro	Tenafly
244	0.1	Waldwick Boro	Waldwick
249	0.0	Wyckoff Twp	Wyckoff
250	0.0	Clinton Twp	Annandale
250	0.0	Denville Twp	Denville
250	0.0	Glen Ridge Boro	Glen Ridge
250	0.0	Pascack Valley Regional	Montvale
250	0.0	Warren Twp	Warren
250	0.0	West Morris Regional	Chester

Student/Teacher Ratio

Rank	Ratio	District Name	City
1	18.1	Central Regional	Bayville
2	17.6	Southern Regional	Manahawkin
3	17.5	Somers Point City	Somers Point
4	17.3	Rancocas Valley Regional	Mount Holly
5	15.8	Sparta Twp	Sparta
5	15.8	Toms River Regional	Toms River
7	15.7	Medford Twp	Medford
7	15.7	Nutley Town	Nutley
9	15.6	Deptford Twp	Deptford
9	15.6	Irvington Township	Irvington
11	15.5	North Bergen Twp	North Bergen
12	15.3	Brick Twp	Brick
13	15.2	Denville Twp	Denville
14	15.1	Black Horse Pike Regional	Blackwood
14	15.1	Eastern Camden County Reg	Voorhees
14	15.1	Marlboro Twp	Marlboro
14	15.1	South River Boro	South River
18	15.0	Harrison Town	Harrison
18	15.0	Lacey Twp	Lanoka Harbor
18	15.0	Old Bridge Twp	Matawan
21	14.9	Clark Twp	Clark
21	14.9	Elmwood Park	Elmwood Park
21	14.9	Sayreville Boro	Sayreville
21	14.9	West Deptford Twp	West Deptford
25	14.8	Berkeley Twp	Bayville
25	14.8	Cherry Hill Twp	Cherry Hill
25	14.8	Freehold Twp	Freehold
25	14.8	Haddon Twp	Westmont
25	14.8	Wyckoff Twp	Wyckoff
30	14.7	Holmdel Twp	Holmdel
30	14.7	Jackson Twp	Jackson
30	14.7	Pittsgrove Twp	Pittsgrove
33	14.6	Gloucester Twp	Blackwood
33	14.6	Hillside Twp	Hillside
33	14.6	Manalapan-Englishtown Reg	Englishtown
33	14.6	Manasquan Boro	Manasquan
33	14.6	Millstone Twp	Clarksburg
33	14.6	Pennsauken Twp	Pennsauken
33	14.6	Washington Twp	Long Valley
40	14.5	Belleville Town	Belleville
40	14.5	Kingsway Regional	Woolwich Twp
40	14.5	Moorestown Twp	Moorestown
40	14.5	Union Twp	Union
40	14.5	Vernon Twp	Vernon
40	14.5	Verona Boro	Verona
46	14.4	Delran Twp	Delran
46	14.4	Kearny Town	Kearny
46	14.4	Point Pleasant Boro	Pt Pleasant
46	14.4	Upper Freehold Regional	Allentown
50	14.3	Bergenfield Boro	Bergenfield
50	14.3	Flemington-Raritan Reg	Flemington
50	14.3	Glen Ridge Boro	Glen Ridge
50	14.3	Howell Twp	Howell
54	14.2	Carteret Boro	Carteret
54	14.2	Linden City	Linden
54	14.2	Lyndhurst Twp	Lyndhurst
54	14.2	Mount Olive Twp	Budd Lake
54	14.2	West Milford Twp	West Milford
59	14.1	Bordentown Regional	Bordentown
59	14.1	Cliffside Park Boro	Cliffside Park
59	14.1	Hamilton Twp	Hamilton Square
59	14.1	Jefferson Twp	Lake Hopatcong
59	14.1	Monroe Twp	Williamstown
59	14.1	Ocean Twp	Oakhurst
59	14.1	Roselle Boro	Roselle
59	14.1	Stafford Twp	Manahawkin
67	14.0	Bloomfield Twp	Bloomfield
67	14.0	Delsea Regional HS District	Franklinville
67	14.0	Freehold Regional	Englishtown
67	14.0	Montgomery Twp	Skillman
67	14.0	Randolph Twp	Randolph
67	14.0	Ridgewood Village	Ridgewood
67	14.0	Voorhees Twp	Voorhees
67	14.0	Warren Hills Regional	Washington
75	13.9	Dumont Boro	Dumont
75	13.9	Evesham Twp	Marlton
75	13.9	Greater Egg Harbor Reg	Mays Landing
75	13.9	Hammonton Town	Hammonton
75	13.9	Kinnelon Boro	Kinnelon
75	13.9	Lodi Borough	Lodi
75	13.9	Middletown Twp	Middletown
75	13.9	Ridgefield Boro	Ridgefield
75	13.9	Scotch Plains-Fanwood Reg	Scotch Plains
84	13.8	Audubon Boro	Audubon
84	13.8	Bridgewater-Raritan Reg	Bridgewater
84	13.8	Caldwell-West Caldwell	West Caldwell
84	13.8	City of Orange Twp	Orange
84	13.8	Clearview Regional	Mullica Hill
84	13.8	Clifton City	Clifton
84	13.8	East Brunswick Twp	E Brunswick
84	13.8	Egg Harbor Twp	W Atlantic City
84	13.8	Hopatcong	Hopatcong
84	13.8	Lenape Regional	Shamong
84	13.8	Pompton Lakes Boro	Pompton Lakes
84	13.8	Wayne Twp	Wayne
84	13.8	Woodstown-Pilesgrove Reg	Woodstown
97	13.7	Bayonne City	Bayonne
97	13.7	Dover Town	Dover
97	13.7	Fort Lee Boro	Fort Lee
97	13.7	Haddonfield Boro	Haddonfield
97	13.7	Lumberton Twp	Lumberton
97	13.7	Maple Shade Twp	Maple Shade
97	13.7	Pequannock Twp	Pompton Plains
97	13.7	Plumsted Twp	New Egypt
97	13.7	South Orange-Maplewood	Maplewood
97	13.7	Wall Twp	Wall
107	13.6	Bound Brook Boro	Bound Brook
107	13.6	Burlington Twp	Burlington
107	13.6	Waldwick Boro	Waldwick
110	13.5	Berkeley Heights Twp	Berkeley Hgts
110	13.5	Lawrence Twp	Lawrenceville
110	13.5	Matawan-Aberdeen Regional	Aberdeen
110	13.5	Montville Twp	Montville
110	13.5	North Brunswick Twp	North Brunswick
110	13.5	Paulsboro Boro	Paulsboro
110	13.5	Perth Amboy City	Perth Amboy
110	13.5	Piscataway Twp	Piscataway
110	13.5	Saddle Brook Twp	Saddle Brook
110	13.5	Spotswood Boro	Spotswood
110	13.5	Upper Twp	Petersburg
110	13.5	Watchung Hills Regional	Warren
122	13.4	Clinton Twp	Annandale
122	13.4	Rahway City	Rahway
122	13.4	Roxbury Twp	Succasunna
122	13.4	South Plainfield Boro	S Plainfield
122	13.4	Woodbridge Twp	Woodbridge
127	13.3	Fair Lawn Boro	Fair Lawn
127	13.3	Hasbrouck Heights Boro	Hasbrouck Hgts
127	13.3	Hazlet Twp	Hazlet
127	13.3	Mount Laurel Twp	Mount Laurel
127	13.3	North Arlington Boro	North Arlington
127	13.3	Secaucus Town	Secaucus
127	13.3	Somerville Boro	Somerville
134	13.2	Buena Regional	Buena
134	13.2	East Windsor Regional	Hightstown
134	13.2	Edison Twp	Edison
134	13.2	Glen Rock Boro	Glen Rock
134	13.2	Hackensack City	Hackensack
134	13.2	Mahwah Twp	Mahwah
134	13.2	Northern Burlington Reg	Columbus
134	13.2	Readington Twp	Whitehouse Stn
134	13.2	Sussex-Wantage Regional	Wantage
134	13.2	Washington Twp	Sewell
144	13.1	Neptune Twp	Neptune
144	13.1	Oakland Boro	Oakland
144	13.1	Ramsey Boro	Ramsey
144	13.1	West New York Town	West New York
144	13.1	Westfield Town	Westfield
149	13.0	East Orange	East Orange
149	13.0	Manchester Twp	Whiting
149	13.0	New Milford Boro	New Milford
152	12.9	Barnegat Twp	Barnegat
152	12.9	Hunterdon Central Reg	Flemington
152	12.9	Lower Twp	Cape May
152	12.9	Madison Boro	Madison
152	12.9	Middle Twp	Cape May Ct Hse
152	12.9	Middlesex Boro	Middlesex
152	12.9	Monroe Twp	Monroe Township
152	12.9	SD of The Chathams	Chatham
152	12.9	South Brunswick Twp	Monmouth Jct
161	12.8	Bernards Twp	Basking Ridge
161	12.8	Franklin Twp	Somerset
161	12.8	Garfield City	Garfield
161	12.8	Passaic City	Passaic
165	12.7	Little Egg Harbor Twp	Little Egg Hbr
165	12.7	Millburn Twp	Millburn
165	12.7	Newton Town	Newton
165	12.7	Rutherford Boro	Rutherford
165	12.7	Springfield Twp	Springfield
165	12.7	Summit City	Summit
165	12.7	Union City	Union City
165	12.7	West Windsor-Plainsboro Reg	Princeton Jct
173	12.6	Collingswood Boro	Collingswood
173	12.6	Glassboro	Glassboro
173	12.6	Highland Park Boro	Highland Park
173	12.6	New Providence Boro	New Providence
173	12.6	North Hunt-Voorhees Regional	Annandale
173	12.6	Paramus Boro	Paramus
173	12.6	Teaneck Twp	Teaneck
173	12.6	West Orange Town	West Orange

181	12.5	Cinnaminson Twp	Cinnaminson
181	12.5	Hawthorne Boro	Hawthorne
181	12.5	Mainland Regional	Linwood
181	12.5	West Morris Regional	Chester
185	12.4	Galloway Twp	Galloway
185	12.4	Hackettstown	Hackettstown
185	12.4	Princeton Regional	Princeton
188	12.3	Atlantic City	Atlantic City
188	12.3	Hamilton Twp	Mays Landing
188	12.3	Hopewell Valley Regional	Pennington
188	12.3	Livingston Twp	Livingston
188	12.3	Morris Hills Regional	Rockaway
188	12.3	Roselle Park Boro	Roselle Park
188	12.3	Somerset Hills Regional	Bernardsville
188	12.3	Tinton Falls	Tinton Falls
188	12.3	Trenton City	Trenton
188	12.3	Westwood Regional	Westwood
198	12.2	Cranford Twp	Cranford
198	12.2	Florence Twp	Florence
198	12.2	Lower Cape May Regional	Cape May
198	12.2	Millville City	Millville
198	12.2	North Plainfield Boro	N Plainfield
198	12.2	Pennsville	Pennsville
204	12.1	Branchburg Twp	Branchburg
204	12.1	Ewing Twp	Ewing
204	12.1	Hillsborough Twp	Neshanic
204	12.1	Metuchen Boro	Metuchen
204	12.1	Pascack Valley Regional	Montvale
204	12.1	Pitman Boro	Pitman
210	12.0	Montclair Town	Montclair
210	12.0	Winslow Twp	Atco
212	11.9	Essex County Voc-Tech	West Orange
212	11.9	Northern Valley Regional	Demarest
212	11.9	Tenafly Boro	Tenafly
215	11.8	Lakewood Twp	Lakewood
215	11.8	New Brunswick City	New Brunswick
215	11.8	Parsippany-Troy Hills Twp	Parsippany
215	11.8	Penns Grove-Carney's Point Reg	Penns Grove
215	11.8	Rockaway Twp	Hibernia
220	11.7	Camden City	Camden
220	11.7	Englewood City	Englewood
220	11.7	Jersey City	Jersey City
220	11.7	Willingboro Twp	Willingboro
224	11.6	Morris SD	Morristown
225	11.5	Lindenwold Boro	Lindenwold
225	11.5	Newark City	Newark
225	11.5	Pine Hill Boro	Pine Hill
228	11.4	Camden County Vocational	Sicklerville
228	11.4	Pemberton Twp	Pemberton
230	11.3	Bridgeton City	Bridgeton
230	11.3	Colts Neck Twp	Colts Neck
232	11.2	Burlington County Vocational	Westampton Twp
232	11.2	Paterson City	Paterson
232	11.2	Pinelands Regional	Tuckerton
232	11.2	Plainfield City	Plainfield
232	11.2	Ridgefield Park Twp	Ridgefield Park
237	11.1	Vineland City	Vineland
238	10.9	Ramapo-Indian Hill Reg	Franklin Lakes
239	10.8	Elizabeth City	Elizabeth
240	10.6	Warren Twp	Warren
240	10.6	Woodbury City	Woodbury
242	10.5	Burlington City	Burlington
242	10.5	Ocean City	Ocean City
242	10.5	Phillipsburg Town	Phillipsburg
245	10.3	Mountain Lakes Boro	Mountain Lakes
246	10.2	Hoboken City	Hoboken
246	10.2	Long Branch City	Long Branch
248	10.1	Passaic County Vocational	Wayne
249	10.0	Gloucester City	Gloucester City
250	9.8	Leonia Boro	Leonia
251	9.6	Keansburg Boro	Keansburg
251	9.6	Pleasantville City	Pleasantville
253	9.4	Asbury Park City	Asbury Park
254	8.7	Bergen County Vocational	Paramus
255	8.6	Middlesex County Vocational	E Brunswick

Student/Librarian Ratio

Rank	Ratio	District Name	City
1	4,857.5	Harrison Town	Harrison
2	4,683.0	Southern Regional	Manahawkin
3	2,728.0	Roselle Boro	Roselle
4	2,386.7	Union City	Union City
5	2,242.0	Haddon Twp	Westmont
6	2,153.3	Edison Twp	Edison
7	2,133.0	Maple Shade Twp	Maple Shade
8	2,127.0	Wall Twp	Wall
9	2,107.0	Garfield City	Garfield
10	2,102.0	Lyndhurst Twp	Lyndhurst
11	2,013.0	Passaic County Vocational	Wayne
12	1,854.8	North Bergen Twp	North Bergen
13	1,799.0	Secaucus Town	Secaucus
14	1,741.0	Audubon Boro	Audubon
15	1,684.0	Spotswood Boro	Spotswood
16	1,570.5	Egg Harbor Twp	W Atlantic City
17	1,531.0	Pennsauken Twp	Pennsauken
18	1,515.0	North Arlington Boro	North Arlington
19	1,495.5	Middle Twp	Cape May Ct Hse
20	1,407.9	Toms River Regional	Toms River
21	1,404.3	Bayonne City	Bayonne
22	1,343.8	Rancocas Valley Regional	Mount Holly
23	1,311.0	North Hunt-Voorhees Regional	Annandale
24	1,306.9	East Orange	East Orange
25	1,281.7	Burlington Twp	Burlington
26	1,276.0	Bergenfield Boro	Bergenfield
27	1,172.7	Holmdel Twp	Holmdel
28	1,169.0	Glen Rock Boro	Glen Rock
29	1,156.0	West Morris Regional	Chester
30	1,155.0	Union Twp	Union
31	1,151.4	Middletown Twp	Middletown
32	1,137.4	Jackson Twp	Jackson
33	1,137.1	Monroe Twp	Williamstown
34	1,130.0	Northern Valley Regional	Demarest
35	1,126.7	Passaic City	Passaic
36	1,110.5	Pine Hill Boro	Pine Hill
37	1,098.5	West New York Town	West New York
38	1,097.5	Eastern Camden County Reg	Voorhees
39	1,052.5	Middlesex Boro	Middlesex
40	1,046.3	Hammonton Town	Hammonton
41	1,046.0	Ridgefield Boro	Ridgefield
41	1,046.0	Warren Hills Regional	Washington
43	1,040.6	Perth Amboy City	Perth Amboy
44	1,039.1	Bloomfield Twp	Bloomfield
45	1,029.3	Lawrence Twp	Lawrenceville
46	1,021.8	Linden City	Linden
47	1,019.5	Ramapo-Indian Hill Reg	Franklin Lakes
48	1,017.5	Clearview Regional	Mullica Hill
49	1,010.5	Elmwood Park	Elmwood Park
50	999.6	Long Branch City	Long Branch
51	996.5	Roselle Park Boro	Roselle Park
52	996.0	Camden County Vocational	Sicklerville
53	981.8	Matawan-Aberdeen Regional	Aberdeen
54	972.3	Sparta Twp	Sparta
55	946.0	Pittsgrove Twp	Pittsgrove
56	939.3	Monroe Twp	Monroe Township
57	937.1	Freehold Regional	Englishtown
58	927.0	Northern Burlington Reg	Columbus
59	917.4	Greater Egg Harbor Reg	Mays Landing
60	914.5	Upper Freehold Regional	Allentown
61	914.1	Elizabeth City	Elizabeth
62	909.2	Vernon Twp	Vernon
63	909.0	Englewood City	Englewood
64	908.0	Lower Cape May Regional	Cape May
65	905.7	Lenape Regional	Shamong
66	898.8	Ocean Twp	Oakhurst
67	896.3	Dumont Boro	Dumont
68	894.0	Cliffside Park Boro	Cliffside Park
69	887.6	Gloucester Twp	Blackwood
70	887.3	Jefferson Twp	Lake Hopatcong
71	885.2	Lakewood Twp	Lakewood
72	881.5	Hamilton Twp	Hamilton Square
73	880.0	Tinton Falls	Tinton Falls
74	879.2	North Brunswick Twp	North Brunswick
75	876.7	Hunterdon Central Reg	Flemington
76	873.5	Manasquan Boro	Manasquan
77	871.4	New Milford Boro	New Milford
78	863.0	Burlington County Vocational	Westampton Twp
79	858.5	Little Egg Harbor Twp	Little Egg Hbr
80	856.3	Buena Regional	Buena
81	846.3	Cinnaminson Twp	Cinnaminson
82	841.2	Lacey Twp	Lanoka Harbor
83	837.2	Hackensack City	Hackensack
84	834.4	Hillsborough Twp	Neshanic
85	832.1	Marlboro Twp	Marlboro
86	830.5	Brick Twp	Brick
87	830.0	Kingsway Regional	Woolwich Twp
88	829.5	Plumsted Twp	New Egypt
89	820.3	Morris Hills Regional	Rockaway
90	819.6	Carteret Boro	Carteret
91	816.0	Somers Point City	Somers Point
92	812.2	Washington Twp	Sewell
93	808.0	Saddle Brook Twp	Saddle Brook
94	804.3	Central Regional	Bayville
95	802.0	Highland Park Boro	Highland Park
96	798.0	Mainland Regional	Linwood
97	797.6	Sayreville Boro	Sayreville
98	797.5	Point Pleasant Boro	Pt Pleasant
99	795.4	Manalapan-Englishtown Reg	Englishtown
100	794.5	Bernards Twp	Basking Ridge
101	790.5	Watchung Hills Regional	Warren
102	789.0	Winslow Twp	Atco
103	788.9	Montgomery Twp	Skillman
104	783.0	Wayne Twp	Wayne
105	781.5	Hasbrouck Heights Boro	Hasbrouck Hgts
106	778.5	City of Orange Twp	Orange
107	778.3	Trenton City	Trenton
108	775.3	West Deptford Twp	West Deptford
109	774.0	Pascack Valley Regional	Montvale
110	770.7	Rutherford Boro	Rutherford
111	767.0	Mount Olive Twp	Budd Lake
112	763.1	New Brunswick City	New Brunswick
113	762.4	Jersey City	Jersey City
114	760.7	Haddonfield Boro	Haddonfield
115	758.0	Waldwick Boro	Waldwick
116	757.8	Belleville Town	Belleville
117	750.5	Colts Neck Twp	Colts Neck
118	745.2	Teaneck Twp	Teaneck
119	744.6	Cranford Twp	Cranford
119	744.6	West Windsor-Plainsboro Reg	Princeton Jct
121	744.4	Plainfield City	Plainfield
122	742.3	South River Boro	South River
123	736.3	Dover Town	Dover
124	731.9	Woodbridge Twp	Woodbridge
125	729.7	Somerville Boro	Somerville
126	727.7	Readington Twp	Whitehouse Stn
127	725.3	Gloucester City	Gloucester City
128	723.1	Montclair Town	Montclair
129	720.8	Burlington City	Burlington
130	717.4	Millstone Twp	Clarksburg
131	713.6	Bridgewater-Raritan Reg	Bridgewater
132	711.6	Atlantic City	Atlantic City
133	711.3	Washington Twp	Long Valley
134	707.9	Paterson City	Paterson
135	707.5	Bridgeton City	Bridgeton
136	707.0	Hoboken City	Hoboken
137	694.8	Hopatcong	Hopatcong
138	694.4	Hazlet Twp	Hazlet
139	685.5	Old Bridge Twp	Matawan
140	683.5	Freehold Twp	Freehold
141	681.4	Randolph Twp	Randolph
142	675.6	East Windsor Regional	Hightstown
143	675.1	Piscataway Twp	Piscataway
144	674.9	Howell Twp	Howell
145	674.8	Moorestown Twp	Moorestown
146	673.4	Millville City	Millville
147	672.9	Newark City	Newark
148	670.3	Essex County Voc-Tech	West Orange
149	670.2	Manchester Twp	Whiting
150	668.6	Kearny Town	Kearny
151	667.7	Ramsey Boro	Ramsey
152	667.6	Hillside Twp	Hillside
153	666.2	North Plainfield Boro	N Plainfield
154	664.1	Camden City	Camden
155	663.1	Willingboro Twp	Willingboro
156	662.5	Galloway Twp	Galloway
157	659.5	Rahway City	Rahway
158	650.0	Mahwah Twp	Mahwah
159	641.7	Pinelands Regional	Tuckerton
160	641.1	Vineland City	Vineland
161	636.3	Montville Twp	Montville
162	635.0	Delsea Regional HS District	Franklinville
163	634.3	Berkeley Twp	Bayville
164	632.3	South Plainfield Boro	S Plainfield
165	631.3	Cherry Hill Twp	Cherry Hill
166	629.9	East Brunswick Twp	E Brunswick
167	627.8	West Orange Town	West Orange
168	627.0	South Brunswick Twp	Monmouth Jct
169	625.5	Clark Twp	Clark
170	621.3	Glassboro	Glassboro
171	619.5	Lindenwold Boro	Lindenwold
172	610.0	Westwood Regional	Westwood
173	609.0	Metuchen Boro	Metuchen
174	607.0	Denville Twp	Denville
175	605.5	Wyckoff Twp	Wyckoff
176	601.7	Evesham Twp	Marlton
177	600.5	Franklin Twp	Somerset
178	598.3	Paramus Boro	Paramus
179	597.7	Upper Twp	Petersburg
179	597.7	Voorhees Twp	Voorhees
181	593.7	Clinton Twp	Annandale
182	593.4	Irvington Township	Irvington
183	593.0	Medford Twp	Medford
184	592.0	Stafford Twp	Manahawkin
185	590.0	Somerset Hills Regional	Bernardsville
186	589.7	Middlesex County Vocational	E Brunswick
187	588.0	Fair Lawn Boro	Fair Lawn
188	587.5	West Milford Twp	West Milford
189	586.3	Sussex-Wantage Regional	Wantage
190	585.7	Glen Ridge Boro	Glen Ridge
191	585.5	Hopewell Valley Regional	Pennington
192	583.4	Ridgefield Park Twp	Ridgefield Park
193	582.7	Pemberton Twp	Pemberton
194	573.8	Hawthorne Boro	Hawthorne
195	572.2	Hamilton Twp	Mays Landing
196	571.3	Clifton City	Clifton
197	569.1	Hackettstown	Hackettstown
198	567.7	Ridgewood Village	Ridgewood
199	567.6	Roxbury Twp	Succasunna

Rank	Value	District Name	City
200	567.0	Leonia Boro	Leonia
201	565.6	Westfield Town	Westfield
202	565.3	Mount Laurel Twp	Mount Laurel
203	563.0	Newton Town	Newton
204	561.3	Woodstown-Pilesgrove Reg	Woodstown
205	554.0	Pitman Boro	Pitman
206	553.7	Princeton Regional	Princeton
207	551.3	Lumberton Twp	Lumberton
208	550.6	Berkeley Heights Twp	Berkeley Hgts
209	548.1	Nutley Town	Nutley
210	547.6	Barnegat Twp	Barnegat
211	546.6	Ewing Twp	Ewing
212	545.8	Ocean City	Ocean City
213	539.3	South Orange-Maplewood	Maplewood
214	537.7	Bound Brook Boro	Bound Brook
215	534.6	Scotch Plains-Fanwood Reg	Scotch Plains
216	533.5	Neptune Twp	Neptune
217	532.6	Black Horse Pike Regional	Blackwood
218	532.0	Rockaway Twp	Hibernia
219	530.0	New Providence Boro	New Providence
220	524.5	Deptford Twp	Deptford
221	523.3	Millburn Twp	Millburn
222	522.5	Keansburg Boro	Keansburg
223	520.0	Florence Twp	Florence
224	518.1	Pleasantville City	Pleasantville
225	517.2	Delran Twp	Delran
226	517.0	Collingswood Boro	Collingswood
227	514.9	Morris SD	Morristown
228	513.8	Lodi Borough	Lodi
229	511.5	Bordentown Regional	Bordentown
230	509.7	Woodbury City	Woodbury
231	508.3	Paulsboro Boro	Paulsboro
232	507.2	Asbury Park City	Asbury Park
233	502.5	Verona Boro	Verona
234	500.3	Livingston Twp	Livingston
235	499.5	SD of The Chathams	Chatham
236	493.3	Fort Lee Boro	Fort Lee
237	491.8	Pequannock Twp	Pompton Plains
238	489.3	Lower Twp	Cape May
239	489.2	Tenafly Boro	Tenafly
240	481.1	Penns Grove-Carney's Point Reg	Penns Grove
241	477.5	Branchburg Twp	Branchburg
242	477.4	Caldwell-West Caldwell	West Caldwell
243	467.5	Pompton Lakes Boro	Pompton Lakes
244	457.3	Kinnelon Boro	Kinnelon
245	437.3	Flemington-Raritan Reg	Flemington
246	431.0	Warren Twp	Warren
247	422.1	Parsippany-Troy Hills Twp	Parsippany
248	416.8	Mountain Lakes Boro	Mountain Lakes
249	408.8	Pennsville	Pennsville
250	406.4	Madison Boro	Madison
251	401.3	Oakland Boro	Oakland
252	400.8	Springfield Twp	Springfield
253	391.2	Summit City	Summit
254	386.6	Phillipsburg Town	Phillipsburg
255	0.0	Bergen County Vocational	Paramus

Student/Counselor Ratio

Rank	Ratio	District Name	City
1	1,149.2	Rockaway Twp	Hibernia
2	948.3	Washington Twp	Long Valley
3	880.0	Tinton Falls	Tinton Falls
4	825.0	Millstone Twp	Clarksburg
5	816.0	Somers Point City	Somers Point
6	789.3	Stafford Twp	Manahawkin
7	706.7	New Providence Boro	New Providence
8	685.0	Cranford Twp	Cranford
9	684.6	New Milford Boro	New Milford
10	667.6	Hillside Twp	Hillside
11	657.0	Howell Twp	Howell
12	647.2	Marlboro Twp	Marlboro
13	638.6	Linden City	Linden
14	634.3	Berkeley Twp	Bayville
15	607.6	Brick Twp	Brick
16	606.6	Sussex-Wantage Regional	Wantage
17	606.4	Bridgeton City	Bridgeton
18	605.7	Randolph Twp	Randolph
19	600.4	Colts Neck Twp	Colts Neck
20	597.7	Upper Twp	Petersburg
21	596.0	Cliffside Park Boro	Cliffside Park
22	589.6	Union City	Union City
23	586.1	Manalapan-Englishtown Reg	Englishtown
24	584.5	Glen Rock Boro	Glen Rock
25	577.5	Union Twp	Union
26	572.2	Hamilton Twp	Mays Landing
27	565.3	Rahway City	Rahway
28	561.9	Garfield City	Garfield
29	561.3	Barnegat Twp	Barnegat
30	558.3	Plainfield City	Plainfield
31	555.4	Freehold Twp	Freehold
32	554.8	Bergenfield Boro	Bergenfield
33	553.0	Plumsted Twp	New Egypt
34	550.9	Gloucester Twp	Blackwood
35	539.7	Harrison Town	Harrison
36	538.5	Madison Boro	Madison
37	527.5	Nutley Town	Nutley
38	524.5	Deptford Twp	Deptford
39	523.0	Ridgefield Boro	Ridgefield
40	521.0	Hasbrouck Heights Boro	Hasbrouck Hgts
41	515.6	Caldwell-West Caldwell	West Caldwell
42	514.5	Kinnelon Boro	Kinnelon
43	512.3	Voorhees Twp	Voorhees
44	508.3	Paulsboro Boro	Paulsboro
45	506.4	Scotch Plains-Fanwood Reg	Scotch Plains
46	505.3	Waldwick Boro	Waldwick
47	502.6	Rutherford Boro	Rutherford
48	502.3	Hackensack City	Hackensack
49	501.8	Lower Twp	Cape May
50	501.5	Toms River Regional	Toms River
51	499.9	Moorestown Twp	Moorestown
52	499.7	Flemington-Raritan Reg	Flemington
53	499.3	West New York Town	West New York
54	497.0	Old Bridge Twp	Matawan
55	496.0	Hazlet Twp	Hazlet
56	494.6	North Bergen Twp	North Bergen
57	491.8	Pequannock Twp	Pompton Plains
58	490.9	Matawan-Aberdeen Regional	Aberdeen
59	489.5	Montclair Town	Montclair
60	488.1	South Brunswick Twp	Monmouth Jct
61	488.0	Westwood Regional	Westwood
62	478.7	Manchester Twp	Whiting
63	478.5	Ramsey Boro	Ramsey
64	477.5	Branchburg Twp	Branchburg
65	472.1	Piscataway Twp	Piscataway
66	465.1	Millburn Twp	Millburn
67	463.4	Morris SD	Morristown
68	460.2	Mount Olive Twp	Budd Lake
69	458.8	Lacey Twp	Lanoka Harbor
70	455.7	Point Pleasant Boro	Pt Pleasant
71	455.3	Denville Twp	Denville
72	454.7	Roselle Boro	Roselle
73	450.6	Middletown Twp	Middletown
74	450.0	Hawthorne Boro	Hawthorne
75	449.4	Ocean Twp	Oakhurst
76	445.9	Delran Twp	Delran
77	445.3	Clinton Twp	Annandale
78	445.0	Monroe Twp	Williamstown
79	443.9	Evesham Twp	Marlton
80	442.5	Somerset Hills Regional	Bernardsville
81	440.8	Dumont Boro	Dumont
82	439.8	Holmdel Twp	Holmdel
83	439.6	North Brunswick Twp	North Brunswick
84	438.9	Bayonne City	Bayonne
84	438.9	Montville Twp	Montville
86	436.1	New Brunswick City	New Brunswick
87	433.3	Jackson Twp	Jackson
88	430.5	Bloomfield Twp	Bloomfield
89	429.5	Sayreville Boro	Sayreville
90	427.6	Fair Lawn Boro	Fair Lawn
91	427.3	Middle Twp	Cape May Ct Hse
91	427.3	West Milford Twp	West Milford
93	424.3	South Orange-Maplewood	Maplewood
94	423.6	Medford Twp	Medford
95	423.2	Cinnaminson Twp	Cinnaminson
96	422.3	Woodbridge Twp	Woodbridge
97	420.8	Winslow Twp	Atco
98	419.3	Tenafly Boro	Tenafly
99	415.4	Irvington Township	Irvington
100	411.1	Mount Laurel Twp	Mount Laurel
101	408.3	Pennsauken Twp	Pennsauken
102	406.3	Mahwah Twp	Mahwah
103	404.0	Saddle Brook Twp	Saddle Brook
103	404.0	Westfield Town	Westfield
105	403.7	Wyckoff Twp	Wyckoff
106	403.0	Pleasantville City	Pleasantville
107	402.0	Verona Boro	Verona
108	400.1	Clifton City	Clifton
109	397.5	Edison Twp	Edison
109	397.5	Galloway Twp	Galloway
111	396.7	Elizabeth City	Elizabeth
112	395.3	Atlantic City	Atlantic City
112	395.3	Hillsborough Twp	Neshanic
114	394.3	Jefferson Twp	Lake Hopatcong
115	393.1	Pennsville	Pennsville
116	391.5	Wayne Twp	Wayne
117	389.3	City of Orange Twp	Orange
118	385.2	Cherry Hill Twp	Cherry Hill
119	383.7	Fort Lee Boro	Fort Lee
120	383.4	East Brunswick Twp	E Brunswick
121	382.1	Kearny Town	Kearny
122	380.7	Paramus Boro	Paramus
123	379.4	Lakewood Twp	Lakewood
123	379.4	South Plainfield Boro	S Plainfield
125	378.9	Belleville Town	Belleville
126	378.8	North Arlington Boro	North Arlington
127	374.6	Perth Amboy City	Perth Amboy
127	374.6	SD of The Chathams	Chatham
129	371.2	South River Boro	South River
130	370.6	Passaic City	Passaic
131	369.7	Burlington Twp	Burlington
132	367.6	East Orange	East Orange
133	367.2	Newton Town	Newton
134	367.0	Buena Regional	Buena
135	366.7	Bernards Twp	Basking Ridge
136	365.8	Upper Freehold Regional	Allentown
137	363.8	East Windsor Regional	Hightstown
137	363.8	Readington Twp	Whitehouse Stn
139	362.4	Mountain Lakes Boro	Mountain Lakes
140	361.7	Summit City	Summit
141	360.9	Hopatcong	Hopatcong
142	360.2	Southern Regional	Manahawkin
143	360.1	Glassboro	Glassboro
144	359.2	Warren Twp	Warren
145	356.7	Oakland Boro	Oakland
146	356.3	Newark City	Newark
147	354.5	Wall Twp	Wall
148	353.7	Willingboro Twp	Willingboro
149	353.5	Hoboken City	Hoboken
149	353.5	Sparta Twp	Sparta
151	353.1	Somerville Boro	Somerville
152	351.4	Glen Ridge Boro	Glen Ridge
153	350.8	Middlesex Boro	Middlesex
154	350.7	West Orange Town	West Orange
155	350.3	Franklin Twp	Somerset
155	350.3	Haddon Twp	Westmont
155	350.3	Lyndhurst Twp	Lyndhurst
158	350.2	Ridgewood Village	Ridgewood
159	349.3	Roxbury Twp	Succasunna
160	349.0	Egg Harbor Twp	W Atlantic City
161	348.8	Hammonton Town	Hammonton
162	348.4	Elmwood Park	Elmwood Park
163	344.1	Berkeley Heights Twp	Berkeley Hgts
164	342.7	Carteret Boro	Carteret
165	342.6	Lodi Borough	Lodi
166	341.4	Neptune Twp	Neptune
167	340.9	Englewood City	Englewood
168	339.9	North Plainfield Boro	N Plainfield
169	339.2	Clearview Regional	Mullica Hill
170	338.1	Asbury Park City	Asbury Park
171	337.6	Lumberton Twp	Lumberton
172	336.8	Bridgewater-Raritan Reg	Bridgewater
173	336.6	West Windsor-Plainsboro Reg	Princeton Jct
174	333.8	Montgomery Twp	Skillman
175	333.5	Livingston Twp	Livingston
176	332.4	Pitman Boro	Pitman
177	327.7	Penns Grove-Carney's Point Reg	Penns Grove
178	327.2	Dover Town	Dover
179	325.4	Paterson City	Paterson
180	324.9	Washington Twp	Sewell
181	320.8	Highland Park Boro	Highland Park
182	319.4	Princeton Regional	Princeton
183	319.2	Mainland Regional	Linwood
184	317.3	Pine Hill Boro	Pine Hill
185	317.2	Vernon Twp	Vernon
186	316.7	Lawrence Twp	Lawrenceville
187	316.5	Audubon Boro	Audubon
188	315.3	Pittsgrove Twp	Pittsgrove
189	315.0	Trenton City	Trenton
190	312.8	Clark Twp	Clark
191	312.0	Florence Twp	Florence
192	311.7	Pompton Lakes Boro	Pompton Lakes
193	311.2	Ridgefield Park Twp	Ridgefield Park
194	310.1	West Deptford Twp	West Deptford
195	304.7	Maple Shade Twp	Maple Shade
196	304.5	Metuchen Boro	Metuchen
197	303.1	Millville City	Millville
198	301.2	Manasquan Boro	Manasquan
199	298.1	Teaneck Twp	Teaneck
200	294.8	Middlesex County Vocational	E Brunswick
201	294.5	Freehold Regional	Englishtown
202	294.3	Ewing Twp	Ewing
203	294.0	Long Branch City	Long Branch
204	293.3	Bound Brook Boro	Bound Brook
205	292.3	Bordentown Regional	Bordentown
206	291.4	Pemberton Twp	Pemberton
207	289.0	Monroe Twp	Monroe Township
208	287.8	Camden City	Camden
209	284.7	Roselle Park Boro	Roselle Park
210	282.9	Rancocas Valley Regional	Mount Holly
211	280.7	Woodstown-Pilesgrove Reg	Woodstown
212	275.3	Lindenwold Boro	Lindenwold
213	272.1	Delsea Regional HS District	Franklinville
214	272.0	Gloucester City	Gloucester City
215	270.0	Leonia Boro	Leonia
216	268.1	Central Regional	Bayville
217	261.5	Warren Hills Regional	Washington
218	259.3	Haddonfield Boro	Haddonfield

218	259.3	Hamilton Twp	Hamilton Square
220	258.5	Collingswood Boro	Collingswood
221	257.4	Burlington City	Burlington
222	257.0	Secaucus Town	Secaucus
223	255.2	Spotswood Boro	Spotswood
224	254.8	Woodbury City	Woodbury
225	246.6	Vineland City	Vineland
226	246.1	Jersey City	Jersey City
227	245.5	Hopewell Valley Regional	Pennington
228	242.6	Ocean City	Ocean City
229	242.1	Lower Cape May Regional	Cape May
230	241.2	Parsippany-Troy Hills Twp	Parsippany
231	240.6	Pinelands Regional	Tuckerton
232	237.1	Kingsway Regional	Woolwich Twp
233	231.1	Essex County Voc-Tech	West Orange
234	226.0	Black Horse Pike Regional	Blackwood
235	225.9	Watchung Hills Regional	Warren
236	222.7	Lenape Regional	Shamong
236	222.7	Springfield Twp	Springfield
238	220.6	Greater Egg Harbor Reg	Mays Landing
239	220.0	Keansburg Boro	Keansburg
240	219.5	Eastern Camden County Reg	Voorhees
241	211.0	Hackettstown	Hackettstown
242	206.0	Northern Burlington Reg	Columbus
243	193.5	Pascack Valley Regional	Montvale
244	193.3	Phillipsburg Town	Phillipsburg
245	191.8	Burlington County Vocational	Westampton Twp
246	188.3	Northern Valley Regional	Demarest
247	187.9	Hunterdon Central Reg	Flemington
248	185.4	Ramapo-Indian Hill Reg	Franklin Lakes
249	185.0	West Morris Regional	Chester
250	170.3	North Hunt-Voorhees Regional	Annandale
251	167.8	Passaic County Vocational	Wayne
252	153.8	Morris Hills Regional	Rockaway
253	153.2	Camden County Vocational	Sicklerville
254	134.6	Bergen County Vocational	Paramus
255	0.0	Little Egg Harbor Twp	Little Egg Hbr

Current Spending per Student in FY2001

Rank	Dollars	District Name	City
1	23,317	Bergen County Vocational	Paramus
2	20,007	Hoboken City	Hoboken
3	19,318	Middlesex County Vocational	E Brunswick
4	18,881	Passaic County Vocational	Wayne
5	17,909	Trenton City	Trenton
6	17,491	Asbury Park City	Asbury Park
7	16,637	Camden County Vocational	Sicklerville
8	16,621	Pascack Valley Regional	Montvale
9	15,868	Ramapo-Indian Hill Reg	Franklin Lakes
10	15,718	New Brunswick City	New Brunswick
11	15,241	Burlington County Vocational	Westampton Twp
12	14,924	Englewood City	Englewood
13	14,778	Morris Hills Regional	Rockaway
14	14,694	Newark City	Newark
15	14,512	Northern Valley Regional	Demarest
16	14,427	Morris SD	Morristown
17	14,315	Hunterdon Central Reg	Flemington
18	14,177	Camden City	Camden
19	14,157	North Hunt-Voorhees Regional	Annandale
20	13,744	Passaic City	Passaic
21	13,717	Teaneck Twp	Teaneck
22	13,649	Keansburg Boro	Keansburg
23	13,609	West Morris Regional	Chester
24	13,473	Essex County Voc-Tech	West Orange
25	13,179	Jersey City	Jersey City
26	13,131	Mountain Lakes Boro	Mountain Lakes
27	13,075	Watchung Hills Regional	Warren
28	13,054	Irvington Township	Irvington
29	12,838	Bridgeton City	Bridgeton
30	12,813	Ocean City	Ocean City
31	12,744	Westwood Regional	Westwood
32	12,740	Neptune Twp	Neptune
33	12,727	Vineland City	Vineland
34	12,563	Princeton Regional	Princeton
35	12,546	Phillipsburg Town	Phillipsburg
36	12,520	West New York Town	West New York
37	12,494	East Orange	East Orange
38	12,409	Paterson City	Paterson
39	12,377	Pinelands Regional	Tuckerton
40	12,375	Atlantic City	Atlantic City
41	12,362	Livingston Twp	Livingston
42	12,337	Plainfield City	Plainfield
43	12,310	Somerset Hills Regional	Bernardsville
44	12,289	Lakewood Twp	Lakewood
45	12,207	City of Orange Twp	Orange
46	12,192	Pleasantville City	Pleasantville
47	12,128	Parsippany-Troy Hills Twp	Parsippany
48	12,112	Burlington City	Burlington
49	12,052	Long Branch City	Long Branch
50	11,966	Pemberton Twp	Pemberton
51	11,908	Harrison Town	Harrison
52	11,892	Gloucester City	Gloucester City
53	11,861	Berkeley Heights Twp	Berkeley Hgts
54	11,855	Woodbury City	Woodbury
55	11,848	Tenafly Boro	Tenafly
56	11,770	Franklin Twp	Somerset
57	11,731	Garfield City	Garfield
58	11,718	Clark Twp	Clark
59	11,686	Elizabeth City	Elizabeth
60	11,677	Springfield Twp	Springfield
61	11,603	Madison Boro	Madison
62	11,577	West Orange Town	West Orange
63	11,572	Ridgefield Boro	Ridgefield
64	11,559	Fair Lawn Boro	Fair Lawn
65	11,513	Newton Town	Newton
66	11,511	Somerville Boro	Somerville
67	11,492	Glen Rock Boro	Glen Rock
68	11,474	Highland Park Boro	Highland Park
69	11,436	Northern Burlington Reg	Columbus
69	11,436	Ramsey Boro	Ramsey
71	11,425	Secaucus Town	Secaucus
72	11,424	Ridgewood Village	Ridgewood
73	11,388	Southern Regional	Manahawkin
74	11,361	Matawan-Aberdeen Regional	Aberdeen
75	11,353	Summit City	Summit
76	11,346	Rockaway Twp	Hibernia
77	11,294	Mahwah Twp	Mahwah
78	11,286	Union City	Union City
79	11,259	Willingboro Twp	Willingboro
80	11,253	Lenape Regional	Shamong
81	11,251	West Windsor-Plainsboro Reg	Princeton Jct
82	11,248	Monroe Twp	Monroe Township
83	11,240	Hackensack City	Hackensack
84	11,236	Saddle Brook Twp	Saddle Brook
85	11,230	Ridgefield Park Twp	Ridgefield Park
86	11,227	Greater Egg Harbor Reg	Mays Landing
87	11,198	Montclair Town	Montclair
88	11,173	Perth Amboy City	Perth Amboy
89	11,148	Roselle Boro	Roselle
90	11,094	Ewing Twp	Ewing
91	11,078	Lawrence Twp	Lawrenceville
92	11,054	Paramus Boro	Paramus
93	11,051	Mount Olive Twp	Budd Lake
94	11,025	Waldwick Boro	Waldwick
95	10,992	Warren Twp	Warren
96	10,985	Oakland Boro	Oakland
97	10,982	Branchburg Twp	Branchburg
98	10,968	Cranford Twp	Cranford
99	10,914	Millville City	Millville
100	10,894	Penns Grove-Carney's Point Reg	Penns Grove
101	10,889	Westfield Town	Westfield
102	10,886	Bordentown Regional	Bordentown
103	10,864	Verona Boro	Verona
104	10,824	Caldwell-West Caldwell	West Caldwell
105	10,816	Black Horse Pike Regional	Blackwood
106	10,814	Metuchen Boro	Metuchen
107	10,812	SD of The Chathams	Chatham
108	10,801	Hopewell Valley Regional	Pennington
109	10,761	Montville Twp	Montville
110	10,752	Warren Hills Regional	Washington
111	10,735	Millburn Twp	Millburn
112	10,707	Wayne Twp	Wayne
113	10,675	Delsea Regional HS District	Franklinville
114	10,664	Central Regional	Bayville
114	10,664	Scotch Plains-Fanwood Reg	Scotch Plains
116	10,655	Edison Twp	Edison
117	10,650	East Windsor Regional	Hightstown
118	10,633	Pompton Lakes Boro	Pompton Lakes
119	10,598	Kearny Town	Kearny
120	10,594	Fort Lee Boro	Fort Lee
121	10,548	Kinnelon Boro	Kinnelon
122	10,538	South Orange-Maplewood	Maplewood
123	10,536	Mainland Regional	Linwood
124	10,522	Pennsville	Pennsville
125	10,511	Hazlet Twp	Hazlet
126	10,492	Kingsway Regional	Woolwich Twp
127	10,489	Lodi Borough	Lodi
128	10,482	East Brunswick Twp	E Brunswick
128	10,482	West Milford Twp	West Milford
130	10,419	Bayonne City	Bayonne
131	10,410	Rutherford Boro	Rutherford
132	10,404	Eastern Camden County Reg	Voorhees
133	10,393	Winslow Twp	Atco
134	10,386	Carteret Boro	Carteret
135	10,379	Lindenwold Boro	Lindenwold
136	10,355	Wall Twp	Wall
137	10,351	Bergenfield Boro	Bergenfield
138	10,350	Piscataway Twp	Piscataway
139	10,315	Buena Regional	Buena
140	10,313	Cherry Hill Twp	Cherry Hill
141	10,303	New Providence Boro	New Providence
142	10,271	Linden City	Linden
143	10,269	North Plainfield Boro	N Plainfield
144	10,251	Lower Cape May Regional	Cape May
145	10,250	Bridgewater-Raritan Reg	Bridgewater
146	10,241	Hillside Twp	Hillside
147	10,213	Collingswood Boro	Collingswood
148	10,210	Freehold Regional	Englishtown
149	10,199	Roxbury Twp	Succasunna
150	10,197	Upper Freehold Regional	Allentown
151	10,193	Pennsauken Twp	Pennsauken
152	10,186	Dumont Boro	Dumont
153	10,164	Lyndhurst Twp	Lyndhurst
154	10,130	Glen Ridge Boro	Glen Ridge
155	10,119	New Milford Boro	New Milford
156	10,110	Hasbrouck Heights Boro	Hasbrouck Hgts
157	10,098	Hawthorne Boro	Hawthorne
158	10,097	Bernards Twp	Basking Ridge
159	10,081	South Plainfield Boro	S Plainfield
160	10,079	Leonia Boro	Leonia
161	10,066	Moorestown Twp	Moorestown
162	10,036	Ocean Twp	Oakhurst
163	10,035	Glassboro	Glassboro
164	10,018	Old Bridge Twp	Matawan
165	9,997	Hackettstown	Hackettstown
166	9,973	South Brunswick Twp	Monmouth Jct
167	9,955	Spotswood Boro	Spotswood
168	9,923	Clearview Regional	Mullica Hill
169	9,911	Jefferson Twp	Lake Hopatcong
170	9,910	Pitman Boro	Pitman
171	9,901	Lower Twp	Cape May
172	9,899	Hopatcong	Hopatcong
173	9,889	Sussex-Wantage Regional	Wantage
174	9,873	Randolph Twp	Randolph
175	9,835	Rahway City	Rahway
176	9,823	Roselle Park Boro	Roselle Park
177	9,815	Middlesex Boro	Middlesex
178	9,788	Pequannock Twp	Pompton Plains
179	9,757	Haddonfield Boro	Haddonfield
180	9,753	Woodbridge Twp	Woodbridge
181	9,748	Vernon Twp	Vernon
182	9,741	Middletown Twp	Middletown
183	9,740	Belleville Town	Belleville
184	9,732	Deptford Twp	Deptford
185	9,696	Cliffside Park Boro	Cliffside Park
186	9,669	Cinnaminson Twp	Cinnaminson
187	9,639	Manasquan Boro	Manasquan
188	9,618	Sparta Twp	Sparta
189	9,617	Dover Town	Dover
190	9,612	Washington Twp	Long Valley
191	9,596	Holmdel Twp	Holmdel
192	9,566	Bound Brook Boro	Bound Brook
193	9,564	North Brunswick Twp	North Brunswick
194	9,537	Hammonton Town	Hammonton
195	9,535	Voorhees Twp	Voorhees
196	9,512	Readington Twp	Whitehouse Stn
197	9,495	Maple Shade Twp	Maple Shade
198	9,494	Manchester Twp	Whiting
199	9,487	Tinton Falls	Tinton Falls
200	9,468	Paulsboro Boro	Paulsboro
201	9,459	North Arlington Boro	North Arlington
202	9,456	Barnegat Twp	Barnegat
203	9,429	Rancocas Valley Regional	Mount Holly
204	9,427	Jackson Twp	Jackson
205	9,425	Middle Twp	Cape May Ct Hse
206	9,416	Florence Twp	Florence
207	9,412	West Deptford Twp	West Deptford
208	9,360	Nutley Town	Nutley
209	9,334	Clifton City	Clifton
210	9,287	Medford Twp	Medford
211	9,215	Pittsgrove Twp	Pittsgrove
212	9,212	Hillsborough Twp	Neshanic
213	9,184	Howell Twp	Howell
214	9,171	Washington Twp	Sewell
215	9,129	Wyckoff Twp	Wyckoff
216	9,116	Toms River Regional	Toms River
217	9,108	Hamilton Twp	Hamilton Square
217	9,108	Woodstown-Pilesgrove Reg	Woodstown
219	9,070	Union Twp	Union
220	9,062	Flemington-Raritan Reg	Flemington
221	9,011	Colts Neck Twp	Colts Neck
222	8,999	Little Egg Harbor Twp	Little Egg Hbr
223	8,996	Pine Hill Boro	Pine Hill
224	8,948	Haddon Twp	Westmont
225	8,943	Egg Harbor Twp	W Atlantic City
226	8,892	Mount Laurel Twp	Mount Laurel
226	8,892	Stafford Twp	Manahawkin
228	8,868	Montgomery Twp	Skillman
229	8,861	Clinton Twp	Annandale
230	8,813	Sayreville Boro	Sayreville
231	8,796	Freehold Twp	Freehold
232	8,784	Evesham Twp	Marlton
233	8,774	North Bergen Twp	North Bergen
234	8,763	Lumberton Twp	Lumberton
235	8,759	Berkeley Twp	Bayville
236	8,754	Delran Twp	Delran

237	8,738	Elmwood Park	Elmwood Park
238	8,731	Monroe Twp	Williamstown
239	8,694	Galloway Twp	Galloway
240	8,693	Denville Twp	Denville
241	8,650	Bloomfield Twp	Bloomfield
242	8,610	Audubon Boro	Audubon
243	8,569	Hamilton Twp	Mays Landing
244	8,561	Upper Twp	Petersburg
245	8,543	Plumsted Twp	New Egypt
246	8,513	Somers Point City	Somers Point
247	8,470	Lacey Twp	Lanoka Harbor
248	8,434	Millstone Twp	Clarksburg
249	8,408	Brick Twp	Brick
250	8,359	Point Pleasant Boro	Pt Pleasant
251	8,163	Marlboro Twp	Marlboro
252	8,123	Gloucester Twp	Blackwood
253	8,011	Burlington Twp	Burlington
254	7,904	South River Boro	South River
255	7,741	Manalapan-Englishtown Reg	Englishtown

Number of Diploma Recipients

Rank	Number	District Name	City
1	2,214	Freehold Regional	Englishtown
2	1,699	Newark City	Newark
3	1,496	Lenape Regional	Shamong
4	1,293	Jersey City	Jersey City
5	1,188	Toms River Regional	Toms River
6	929	Burlington County Vocational	Westampton Twp
7	926	Edison Twp	Edison
8	901	Woodbridge Twp	Woodbridge
9	899	Hamilton Twp	Hamilton Square
10	877	Elizabeth City	Elizabeth
11	872	Trenton City	Trenton
12	846	Cherry Hill Twp	Cherry Hill
13	754	Paterson City	Paterson
14	730	Black Horse Pike Regional	Blackwood
15	703	Clifton City	Clifton
16	696	Middletown Twp	Middletown
17	675	Washington Twp	Sewell
18	668	Brick Twp	Brick
19	648	Greater Egg Harbor Reg	Mays Landing
20	646	East Brunswick Twp	E Brunswick
21	615	Southern Regional	Manahawkin
22	579	Old Bridge Twp	Matawan
23	578	Wayne Twp	Wayne
24	562	Vineland City	Vineland
25	560	Union City	Union City
26	554	West Windsor-Plainsboro Reg	Princeton Jct
27	526	Parsippany-Troy Hills Twp	Parsippany
28	523	Morris Hills Regional	Rockaway
29	521	North Hunt-Voorhees Regional	Annandale
30	512	West Morris Regional	Chester
31	505	Camden City	Camden
32	500	Hunterdon Central Reg	Flemington
33	486	Northern Valley Regional	Demarest
34	482	Union Twp	Union
35	476	Eastern Camden County Reg	Voorhees
36	462	East Orange	East Orange
37	455	Bridgewater-Raritan Reg	Bridgewater
38	451	Millville City	Millville
38	451	Passaic County Vocational	Wayne
40	440	Bayonne City	Bayonne
41	439	Ramapo-Indian Hill Reg	Franklin Lakes
42	435	Jackson Twp	Jackson
43	429	Hillsborough Twp	Neshanic
44	428	Piscataway Twp	Piscataway
45	427	South Brunswick Twp	Monmouth Jct
46	426	North Bergen Twp	North Bergen
47	417	South Orange-Maplewood	Maplewood
48	416	Atlantic City	Atlantic City
49	410	Rancocas Valley Regional	Mount Holly
50	395	Essex County Voc-Tech	West Orange
51	385	Pennsauken Twp	Pennsauken
52	375	Kearny Town	Kearny
53	373	Linden City	Linden
54	370	Pine Hill Boro	Pine Hill
55	367	Pascack Valley Regional	Montvale
56	358	Watchung Hills Regional	Warren
57	357	West New York Town	West New York
58	355	West Orange Town	West Orange
59	353	Livingston Twp	Livingston
60	348	Fair Lawn Boro	Fair Lawn
60	348	Montclair Town	Montclair
60	348	Sayreville Boro	Sayreville
63	347	Egg Harbor Twp	W Atlantic City
64	344	Bloomfield Twp	Bloomfield
65	343	Vernon Twp	Vernon
66	342	Hackensack City	Hackensack
67	333	Randolph Twp	Randolph
68	332	Ridgewood Village	Ridgewood
69	328	Winslow Twp	Atco
70	327	Westfield Town	Westfield
71	325	Belleville Town	Belleville
71	325	Lacey Twp	Lanoka Harbor
71	325	Roxbury Twp	Succasunna
74	322	Perth Amboy City	Perth Amboy
75	316	Morris SD	Morristown
76	314	Camden County Vocational	Sicklerville
76	314	Teaneck Twp	Teaneck
78	311	Lawrence Twp	Lawrenceville
79	310	Pemberton Twp	Pemberton
80	309	North Brunswick Twp	North Brunswick
81	307	Paramus Boro	Paramus
82	302	Irvington Township	Irvington
82	302	Mainland Regional	Linwood
84	299	Ocean City	Ocean City
85	295	Willingboro Twp	Willingboro
86	294	West Milford Twp	West Milford
87	288	Warren Hills Regional	Washington
88	287	Franklin Twp	Somerset
89	286	Ocean Twp	Oakhurst
90	285	Bergen County Vocational	Paramus
91	280	Phillipsburg Town	Phillipsburg
92	276	Plainfield City	Plainfield
93	268	Lakewood Twp	Lakewood
94	266	Nutley Town	Nutley
95	264	Monroe Twp	Williamstown
96	258	Middlesex County Vocational	E Brunswick
97	257	Clearview Regional	Mullica Hill
98	256	Lower Cape May Regional	Cape May
99	254	Scotch Plains-Fanwood Reg	Scotch Plains
100	253	Delsea Regional HS District	Franklinville
101	251	Wall Twp	Wall
102	249	Central Regional	Bayville
103	240	Hopewell Valley Regional	Pennington
104	237	Princeton Regional	Princeton
105	236	South Plainfield Boro	S Plainfield
106	235	Upper Freehold Regional	Allentown
107	233	Neptune Twp	Neptune
108	232	Cranford Twp	Cranford
108	232	Hackettstown	Hackettstown
108	232	Middle Twp	Cape May Ct Hse
108	232	Tenafly Boro	Tenafly
112	231	Bernards Twp	Basking Ridge
112	231	Mount Olive Twp	Budd Lake
114	230	Ewing Twp	Ewing
114	230	Jefferson Twp	Lake Hopatcong
116	227	Cliffside Park Boro	Cliffside Park
116	227	Rahway City	Rahway
116	227	Sparta Twp	Sparta
116	227	West Deptford Twp	West Deptford
120	225	East Windsor Regional	Hightstown
121	224	Point Pleasant Boro	Pt Pleasant
122	223	Kingsway Regional	Woolwich Twp
122	223	Northern Burlington Reg	Columbus
124	222	Bergenfield Boro	Bergenfield
124	222	Moorestown Twp	Moorestown
126	218	Holmdel Twp	Holmdel
126	218	Millburn Twp	Millburn
128	213	Garfield City	Garfield
129	212	Fort Lee Boro	Fort Lee
130	209	City of Orange Twp	Orange
131	208	Montville Twp	Montville
132	207	Hazlet Twp	Hazlet
132	207	Long Branch City	Long Branch
134	204	Pleasantville City	Pleasantville
135	203	Montgomery Twp	Skillman
136	200	Carteret Boro	Carteret
136	200	Cinnaminson Twp	Cinnaminson
138	197	Deptford Twp	Deptford
138	197	Manasquan Boro	Manasquan
140	194	Pinelands Regional	Tuckerton
141	191	Lodi Borough	Lodi
141	191	Matawan-Aberdeen Regional	Aberdeen
143	190	Spotswood Boro	Spotswood
144	189	Clark Twp	Clark
145	188	Buena Regional	Buena
146	184	Ramsey Boro	Ramsey
147	182	Manchester Twp	Whiting
148	181	Delran Twp	Delran
149	180	Dumont Boro	Dumont
150	179	Monroe Twp	Monroe Township
151	175	Haddonfield Boro	Haddonfield
152	174	Mahwah Twp	Mahwah
152	174	Somerville Boro	Somerville
154	171	Berkeley Heights Twp	Berkeley Hgts
154	171	Dover Town	Dover
154	171	Summit City	Summit
157	169	Hillside Twp	Hillside
158	168	Bridgeton City	Bridgeton
159	166	SD of The Chathams	Chatham
159	166	Woodstown-Pilesgrove Reg	Woodstown
161	165	North Plainfield Boro	N Plainfield
162	163	Newton Town	Newton
163	162	Collingswood Boro	Collingswood
163	162	Penns Grove-Carney's Point Reg	Penns Grove
163	162	Roselle Boro	Roselle
166	161	Caldwell-West Caldwell	West Caldwell
167	160	Haddon Twp	Westmont
167	160	Hopatcong	Hopatcong
169	158	New Brunswick City	New Brunswick
169	158	Ridgefield Park Twp	Ridgefield Park
171	157	Audubon Boro	Audubon
172	151	Pequannock Twp	Pompton Plains
173	150	Gloucester City	Gloucester City
174	149	Englewood City	Englewood
174	149	Rutherford Boro	Rutherford
176	148	Harrison Town	Harrison
176	148	South River Boro	South River
178	145	Burlington Twp	Burlington
179	140	Pompton Lakes Boro	Pompton Lakes
180	139	Glassboro	Glassboro
180	139	Madison Boro	Madison
182	137	Hammonton Town	Hammonton
182	137	Hoboken City	Hoboken
182	137	Westwood Regional	Westwood
185	136	Hawthorne Boro	Hawthorne
185	136	Metuchen Boro	Metuchen
187	134	Lyndhurst Twp	Lyndhurst
187	134	New Providence Boro	New Providence
189	130	Glen Rock Boro	Glen Rock
190	127	Ridgefield Boro	Ridgefield
191	126	Maple Shade Twp	Maple Shade
192	125	Elmwood Park	Elmwood Park
192	125	Pittsgrove Twp	Pittsgrove
194	124	Pennsville	Pennsville
195	123	Somerset Hills Regional	Bernardsville
196	121	Mountain Lakes Boro	Mountain Lakes
197	120	Leonia Boro	Leonia
197	120	Secaucus Town	Secaucus
199	119	Bordentown Regional	Bordentown
200	118	Asbury Park City	Asbury Park
201	114	Verona Boro	Verona
202	113	Kinnelon Boro	Kinnelon
202	113	New Milford Boro	New Milford
204	112	Burlington City	Burlington
204	112	Pitman Boro	Pitman
206	111	Paulsboro Boro	Paulsboro
206	111	Saddle Brook Twp	Saddle Brook
208	110	Springfield Twp	Springfield
209	108	Highland Park Boro	Highland Park
209	108	Middlesex Boro	Middlesex
211	106	North Arlington Boro	North Arlington
212	105	Florence Twp	Florence
213	104	Roselle Park Boro	Roselle Park
214	103	Woodbury City	Woodbury
215	100	Bound Brook Boro	Bound Brook
216	99	Hasbrouck Heights Boro	Hasbrouck Hgts
217	87	Glen Ridge Boro	Glen Ridge
218	85	Keansburg Boro	Keansburg
219	84	Waldwick Boro	Waldwick
220	0	Lindenwold Boro	Lindenwold
220	0	Passaic City	Passaic
220	0	Plumsted Twp	New Egypt
223	n/a	Barnegat Twp	Barnegat
223	n/a	Berkeley Twp	Bayville
223	n/a	Branchburg Twp	Branchburg
223	n/a	Clinton Twp	Annandale
223	n/a	Colts Neck Twp	Colts Neck
223	n/a	Denville Twp	Denville
223	n/a	Evesham Twp	Marlton
223	n/a	Flemington-Raritan Reg	Flemington
223	n/a	Freehold Twp	Freehold
223	n/a	Galloway Twp	Galloway
223	n/a	Gloucester Twp	Blackwood
223	n/a	Hamilton Twp	Mays Landing
223	n/a	Howell Twp	Howell
223	n/a	Little Egg Harbor Twp	Little Egg Hbr
223	n/a	Lower Twp	Cape May
223	n/a	Lumberton Twp	Lumberton
223	n/a	Manalapan-Englishtown Reg	Englishtown
223	n/a	Marlboro Twp	Marlboro
223	n/a	Medford Twp	Medford
223	n/a	Millstone Twp	Clarksburg
223	n/a	Mount Laurel Twp	Mount Laurel
223	n/a	Oakland Boro	Oakland
223	n/a	Readington Twp	Whitehouse Stn
223	n/a	Rockaway Twp	Hibernia
223	n/a	Somers Point City	Somers Point
223	n/a	Stafford Twp	Manahawkin
223	n/a	Sussex-Wantage Regional	Wantage
223	n/a	Tinton Falls	Tinton Falls
223	n/a	Upper Twp	Petersburg
223	n/a	Voorhees Twp	Voorhees
223	n/a	Warren Twp	Warren
223	n/a	Washington Twp	Long Valley

223	n/a	Wyckoff Twp	Wyckoff

High School Drop-out Rate

Rank	Percent	District Name	City
1	33.3	Camden City	Camden
2	16.0	New Brunswick City	New Brunswick
3	14.2	Paterson City	Paterson
4	10.1	Asbury Park City	Asbury Park
5	9.3	Atlantic City	Atlantic City
6	8.7	City of Orange Twp	Orange
7	7.9	Keansburg Boro	Keansburg
8	7.3	Bridgeton City	Bridgeton
9	7.2	Passaic City	Passaic
10	6.8	Millville City	Millville
11	6.5	Newark City	Newark
12	6.4	Pleasantville City	Pleasantville
13	6.3	Elizabeth City	Elizabeth
14	6.2	Pennsauken Twp	Pennsauken
15	6.1	Jersey City	Jersey City
16	5.9	South River Boro	South River
17	5.8	Hillside Twp	Hillside
18	5.4	Franklin Twp	Somerset
18	5.4	Trenton City	Trenton
20	5.3	East Orange	East Orange
21	5.0	Paulsboro Boro	Paulsboro
22	4.8	Irvington Township	Irvington
23	4.7	Englewood City	Englewood
24	4.6	Carteret Boro	Carteret
24	4.6	Dover Town	Dover
24	4.6	Hackensack City	Hackensack
24	4.6	Pinelands Regional	Tuckerton
24	4.6	Woodbury City	Woodbury
29	4.4	Phillipsburg Town	Phillipsburg
30	4.2	Brick Twp	Brick
30	4.2	Hamilton Twp	Hamilton Square
30	4.2	Jefferson Twp	Lake Hopatcong
30	4.2	North Bergen Twp	North Bergen
30	4.2	Pemberton Twp	Pemberton
30	4.2	Plainfield City	Plainfield
36	4.1	Clifton City	Clifton
36	4.1	Linden City	Linden
36	4.1	Perth Amboy City	Perth Amboy
39	3.9	Rahway City	Rahway
40	3.7	Belleville Town	Belleville
40	3.7	Black Horse Pike Regional	Blackwood
42	3.6	Kearny Town	Kearny
42	3.6	Vineland City	Vineland
44	3.5	Garfield City	Garfield
44	3.5	Pennsville	Pennsville
46	3.4	Central Regional	Bayville
46	3.4	Ewing Twp	Ewing
46	3.4	Glassboro	Glassboro
46	3.4	Southern Regional	Manahawkin
50	3.3	Bloomfield Twp	Bloomfield
50	3.3	Buena Regional	Buena
50	3.3	Collingswood Boro	Collingswood
50	3.3	Hopatcong	Hopatcong
54	3.2	Old Bridge Twp	Matawan
55	3.1	Camden County Vocational	Sicklerville
55	3.1	Vernon Twp	Vernon
57	3.0	Toms River Regional	Toms River
58	2.9	Fort Lee Boro	Fort Lee
58	2.9	Monroe Twp	Williamstown
58	2.9	North Arlington Boro	North Arlington
61	2.8	Greater Egg Harbor Reg	Mays Landing
61	2.8	Newton Town	Newton
63	2.7	Bergenfield Boro	Bergenfield
63	2.7	Egg Harbor Twp	W Atlantic City
63	2.7	Hoboken City	Hoboken
63	2.7	Penns Grove-Carney's Point Reg	Penns Grove
63	2.7	Pitman Boro	Pitman
68	2.6	Deptford Twp	Deptford
68	2.6	Elmwood Park	Elmwood Park
68	2.6	Long Branch City	Long Branch
68	2.6	Sayreville Boro	Sayreville
68	2.6	South Orange-Maplewood	Maplewood
73	2.5	Union City	Union City
73	2.5	Woodstown-Pilesgrove Reg	Woodstown
75	2.4	Burlington City	Burlington
75	2.4	Manasquan Boro	Manasquan
75	2.4	Middle Twp	Cape May Ct Hse
75	2.4	Ridgefield Park Twp	Ridgefield Park
75	2.4	Roselle Boro	Roselle
75	2.4	Warren Hills Regional	Washington
81	2.3	Florence Twp	Florence
81	2.3	Manchester Twp	Whiting
81	2.3	West Orange Town	West Orange
84	2.2	Rancocas Valley Regional	Mount Holly
85	2.1	Passaic County Vocational	Wayne
86	2.0	Bordentown Regional	Bordentown
86	2.0	Matawan-Aberdeen Regional	Aberdeen
88	1.9	Bayonne City	Bayonne
88	1.9	Lodi Borough	Lodi
88	1.9	Maple Shade Twp	Maple Shade
91	1.8	Delran Twp	Delran
91	1.8	Kingsway Regional	Woolwich Twp
91	1.8	Lyndhurst Twp	Lyndhurst
91	1.8	Mount Olive Twp	Budd Lake
91	1.8	Teaneck Twp	Teaneck
91	1.8	West Milford Twp	West Milford
97	1.7	Delsea Regional HS District	Franklinville
97	1.7	Hammonton Town	Hammonton
97	1.7	Lower Cape May Regional	Cape May
97	1.7	Mahwah Twp	Mahwah
97	1.7	Mainland Regional	Linwood
97	1.7	Northern Burlington Reg	Columbus
97	1.7	Pittsgrove Twp	Pittsgrove
97	1.7	Washington Twp	Sewell
105	1.6	Cranford Twp	Cranford
105	1.6	Gloucester City	Gloucester City
105	1.6	Wayne Twp	Wayne
108	1.5	Princeton Regional	Princeton
108	1.5	Union Twp	Union
108	1.5	Wall Twp	Wall
111	1.4	Audubon Boro	Audubon
112	1.3	Cliffside Park Boro	Cliffside Park
112	1.3	Dumont Boro	Dumont
112	1.3	Eastern Camden County Reg	Voorhees
112	1.3	Freehold Regional	Englishtown
112	1.3	Waldwick Boro	Waldwick
117	1.2	Hackettstown	Hackettstown
117	1.2	Monroe Twp	Monroe Township
117	1.2	North Plainfield Boro	N Plainfield
117	1.2	Ocean City	Ocean City
117	1.2	Spotswood Boro	Spotswood
117	1.2	West Windsor-Plainsboro Reg	Princeton Jct
123	1.1	Bridgewater-Raritan Reg	Bridgewater
123	1.1	Hawthorne Boro	Hawthorne
123	1.1	Middletown Twp	Middletown
123	1.1	Morris Hills Regional	Rockaway
123	1.1	Morris SD	Morristown
123	1.1	Nutley Town	Nutley
123	1.1	Somerset Hills Regional	Bernardsville
123	1.1	Upper Freehold Regional	Allentown
123	1.1	Woodbridge Twp	Woodbridge
132	1.0	Clearview Regional	Mullica Hill
132	1.0	East Brunswick Twp	E Brunswick
132	1.0	Harrison Town	Harrison
132	1.0	Hunterdon Central Reg	Flemington
132	1.0	North Brunswick Twp	North Brunswick
132	1.0	Ridgewood Village	Ridgewood
138	0.9	East Windsor Regional	Hightstown
138	0.9	Lacey Twp	Lanoka Harbor
138	0.9	Montclair Town	Montclair
138	0.9	Moorestown Twp	Moorestown
138	0.9	Piscataway Twp	Piscataway
138	0.9	Pompton Lakes Boro	Pompton Lakes
138	0.9	Westwood Regional	Westwood
145	0.8	Caldwell-West Caldwell	West Caldwell
145	0.8	Hasbrouck Heights Boro	Hasbrouck Hgts
145	0.8	Hillsborough Twp	Neshanic
145	0.8	Roxbury Twp	Succasunna
145	0.8	South Brunswick Twp	Monmouth Jct
145	0.8	Summit City	Summit
145	0.8	Willingboro Twp	Willingboro
152	0.7	Hopewell Valley Regional	Pennington
152	0.7	Lenape Regional	Shamong
152	0.7	Neptune Twp	Neptune
152	0.7	South Plainfield Boro	S Plainfield
152	0.7	Springfield Twp	Springfield
157	0.6	Burlington County Vocational	Westampton Twp
157	0.6	Fair Lawn Boro	Fair Lawn
157	0.6	Paramus Boro	Paramus
157	0.6	Randolph Twp	Randolph
157	0.6	West New York Town	West New York
162	0.5	Berkeley Heights Twp	Berkeley Hgts
162	0.5	Cherry Hill Twp	Cherry Hill
162	0.5	Hazlet Twp	Hazlet
162	0.5	Leonia Boro	Leonia
162	0.5	New Milford Boro	New Milford
162	0.5	North Hunt-Voorhees Regional	Annandale
168	0.4	Edison Twp	Edison
168	0.4	Haddon Twp	Westmont
168	0.4	Jackson Twp	Jackson
168	0.4	Kinnelon Boro	Kinnelon
168	0.4	Middlesex County Vocational	E Brunswick
168	0.4	Montville Twp	Montville
168	0.4	Parsippany-Troy Hills Twp	Parsippany
168	0.4	Ramapo-Indian Hill Reg	Franklin Lakes
168	0.4	Ramsey Boro	Ramsey
168	0.4	Roselle Park Boro	Roselle Park
168	0.4	Watchung Hills Regional	Warren
168	0.4	West Deptford Twp	West Deptford
168	0.4	West Morris Regional	Chester
181	0.3	Clark Twp	Clark
181	0.3	Haddonfield Boro	Haddonfield
181	0.3	Holmdel Twp	Holmdel
181	0.3	Montgomery Twp	Skillman
181	0.3	Point Pleasant Boro	Pt Pleasant
181	0.3	Rutherford Boro	Rutherford
181	0.3	Scotch Plains-Fanwood Reg	Scotch Plains
181	0.3	Tenafly Boro	Tenafly
189	0.2	Cinnaminson Twp	Cinnaminson
189	0.2	Glen Rock Boro	Glen Rock
189	0.2	Metuchen Boro	Metuchen
189	0.2	Ocean Twp	Oakhurst
189	0.2	Ridgefield Boro	Ridgefield
189	0.2	Saddle Brook Twp	Saddle Brook
189	0.2	Secaucus Town	Secaucus
189	0.2	Somerville Boro	Somerville
189	0.2	Verona Boro	Verona
198	0.1	Burlington Twp	Burlington
198	0.1	Millburn Twp	Millburn
198	0.1	Mountain Lakes Boro	Mountain Lakes
198	0.1	Northern Valley Regional	Demarest
198	0.1	Pascack Valley Regional	Montvale
198	0.1	Pequannock Twp	Pompton Plains
198	0.1	SD of The Chathams	Chatham
198	0.1	Sparta Twp	Sparta
198	0.1	Westfield Town	Westfield
207	0.0	Bergen County Vocational	Paramus
207	0.0	Bernards Twp	Basking Ridge
207	0.0	Bound Brook Boro	Bound Brook
207	0.0	Essex County Voc-Tech	West Orange
207	0.0	Glen Ridge Boro	Glen Ridge
207	0.0	Highland Park Boro	Highland Park
207	0.0	Lakewood Twp	Lakewood
207	0.0	Lawrence Twp	Lawrenceville
207	0.0	Livingston Twp	Livingston
207	0.0	Madison Boro	Madison
207	0.0	Middlesex Boro	Middlesex
207	0.0	New Providence Boro	New Providence
207	0.0	Plumsted Twp	New Egypt
220	n/a	Barnegat Twp	Barnegat
220	n/a	Berkeley Twp	Bayville
220	n/a	Branchburg Twp	Branchburg
220	n/a	Clinton Twp	Annandale
220	n/a	Colts Neck Twp	Colts Neck
220	n/a	Denville Twp	Denville
220	n/a	Evesham Twp	Marlton
220	n/a	Flemington-Raritan Reg	Flemington
220	n/a	Freehold Twp	Freehold
220	n/a	Galloway Twp	Galloway
220	n/a	Gloucester Twp	Blackwood
220	n/a	Hamilton Twp	Mays Landing
220	n/a	Howell Twp	Howell
220	n/a	Lindenwold Boro	Lindenwold
220	n/a	Little Egg Harbor Twp	Little Egg Hbr
220	n/a	Lower Twp	Cape May
220	n/a	Lumberton Twp	Lumberton
220	n/a	Manalapan-Englishtown Reg	Englishtown
220	n/a	Marlboro Twp	Marlboro
220	n/a	Medford Twp	Medford
220	n/a	Millstone Twp	Clarksburg
220	n/a	Mount Laurel Twp	Mount Laurel
220	n/a	Oakland Boro	Oakland
220	n/a	Pine Hill Boro	Pine Hill
220	n/a	Readington Twp	Whitehouse Stn
220	n/a	Rockaway Twp	Hibernia
220	n/a	Somers Point City	Somers Point
220	n/a	Stafford Twp	Manahawkin
220	n/a	Sussex-Wantage Regional	Wantage
220	n/a	Tinton Falls	Tinton Falls
220	n/a	Upper Twp	Petersburg
220	n/a	Voorhees Twp	Voorhees
220	n/a	Warren Twp	Warren
220	n/a	Washington Twp	Long Valley
220	n/a	Winslow Twp	Atco
220	n/a	Wyckoff Twp	Wyckoff

New Mexico

New Mexico Public School Educational Profile

Category	Value	Category	Value
Schools *(2002-2003)*	854	**Diploma Recipients** *(2002-2003)*	18,094
Instructional Level		White, Non-Hispanic	0
Primary	476	Black, Non-Hispanic	0
Middle	164	Asian/Pacific Islander	0
High	168	American Indian/Alaskan Native	0
Other Level	46	Hispanic	0
Curriculum		**High School Drop-out Rate** (%) *(2000-2001)*	5.3
Regular	778	White, Non-Hispanic	3.6
Special Education	16	Black, Non-Hispanic	5.3
Vocational	0	Asian/Pacific Islander	2.4
Alternative	60	American Indian/Alaskan Native	5.9
Type		Hispanic	6.7
Magnet	1	**Staff** *(2002-2003)*	44,139.6
Charter	27	Teachers	21,166.7
Title I Eligible	570	Average Salary ($)	37,054
School-wide Title I	412	Librarians/Media Specialists	290.4
Students *(2002-2003)*	320,264	Guidance Counselors	774.3
Gender (%)		**Ratios** *(2002-2003)*	
Male	51.3	Student/Teacher Ratio	15.1 to 1
Female	48.7	Student/Librarian Ratio	1,102.8 to 1
Race/Ethnicity (%)		Student/Counselor Ratio	413.6 to 1
White, Non-Hispanic	33.6	**Current Spending** *($ per student in FY 2001)*	6,882
Black, Non-Hispanic	2.4	Instruction	3,848
Asian/Pacific Islander	1.1	Support Services	2,716
American Indian/Alaskan Native	11.2	**College Entrance Exam Scores** *(2003)*	
Hispanic	51.7	Scholastic Aptitude Test (SAT)	
Classification (%)		Participation Rate (%)	14
Individual Education Program (IEP)	19.9	Mean SAT I Verbal Score	548
Migrant	0.6	Mean SAT I Math Score	540
English Language Learner (ELL)	20.4	American College Testing Program (ACT)	
Eligible for Free Lunch Program	47.1	Participation Rate (%)	62
Eligible for Reduced-Price Lunch Program	9.9	Average Composite Score	19.9

Note: *For an explanation of data, please refer to the User's Guide in the front of the book; n/a indicates data not available*

New Mexico NAEP 2003 Test Scores

Reading			Mathematics		
Grade/Category	**Value**	**Rank**	**Grade/Category**	**Value**	**Rank**
4th Grade			**4th Grade**		
Average Proficiency	203.2 (1.5)	50/51	Average Proficiency	222.5 (1.1)	50/51
Proficiency by Gender/Race/Ethnicity			Proficiency by Gender/Race/Ethnicity		
Male	200.6 (1.8)	49/51	Male	223.9 (1.2)	48/51
Female	205.9 (1.8)	50/51	Female	221.1 (1.2)	50/51
White, Non-Hispanic	221.9 (2.0)	41/51	White, Non-Hispanic	236.9 (1.2)	44/51
Black, Non-Hispanic	202.0 (5.2)	15/42	Black, Non-Hispanic	216.4 (3.9)	20/42
Asian, Non-Hispanic	196.7 (1.9)	33/41	Asian, Non-Hispanic	216.6 (1.0)	36/43
American Indian, Non-Hispanic	n/a	n/a	American Indian, Non-Hispanic	n/a	n/a
Hispanic	181.8 (2.6)	12/12	Hispanic	210.3 (2.7)	11/12
Proficiency by Class Size			Proficiency by Class Size		
Less than 16 Students	192.5 (5.2)	34/45	Less than 16 Students	207.2 (3.6)	44/47
16 to 18 Students	*196.4 (3.4)*	45/48	16 to 18 Students	*219.6 (2.5)*	44/48
19 to 20 Students	202.5 (3.1)	48/50	19 to 20 Students	223.9 (2.1)	45/50
21 to 25 Students	205.2 (2.1)	49/51	21 to 25 Students	224.5 (1.4)	48/51
Greater than 25 Students	*215.2 (5.2)*	35/49	Greater than 25 Students	*235.8 (3.9)*	24/49
Percent Attaining Achievement Levels			Percent Attaining Achievement Levels		
Below Basic	52.7 (1.8)	2/51	Below Basic	37.0 (1.8)	3/51
Basic or Above	47.3 (1.8)	50/51	Basic or Above	63.0 (1.8)	49/51
Proficient or Above	18.8 (1.3)	49/51	Proficient or Above	17.2 (1.1)	49/51
Advanced or Above	3.7 (0.5)	47/51	Advanced or Above	1.2 (0.3)	47/51
8th Grade			**8th Grade**		
Average Proficiency	251.6 (0.9)	48/51	Average Proficiency	263.3 (1.0)	48/51
Proficiency by Gender/Race/Ethnicity			Proficiency by Gender/Race/Ethnicity		
Male	246.2 (1.2)	47/51	Male	264.0 (1.1)	48/51
Female	256.9 (1.0)	49/51	Female	262.5 (1.3)	48/51
White, Non-Hispanic	267.8 (1.1)	36/50	White, Non-Hispanic	282.0 (1.2)	39/50
Black, Non-Hispanic	246.3 (3.4)	14/41	Black, Non-Hispanic	253.6 (4.4)	17/41
Asian, Non-Hispanic	242.9 (1.0)	28/37	Asian, Non-Hispanic	254.3 (1.0)	29/37
American Indian, Non-Hispanic	n/a	n/a	American Indian, Non-Hispanic	n/a	n/a
Hispanic	242.0 (3.3)	7/10	Hispanic	244.9 (1.9)	11/11
Proficiency by Parents Highest Level of Ed.			Proficiency by Parents Highest Level of Ed.		
Did Not Finish High School	239.5 (1.9)	42/50	Did Not Finish High School	246.4 (1.9)	48/50
Graduated High School	243.3 (1.7)	49/50	Graduated High School	254.2 (1.5)	47/50
Some Education After High School	256.1 (1.7)	48/50	Some Education After High School	267.6 (1.6)	48/50
Graduated College	263.8 (1.2)	43/50	Graduated College	277.4 (1.2)	44/50
Percent Attaining Achievement Levels			Percent Attaining Achievement Levels		
Below Basic	37.6 (1.2)	4/51	Below Basic	47.6 (1.3)	3/51
Basic or Above	62.4 (1.2)	48/51	Basic or Above	52.4 (1.3)	49/51
Proficient or Above	19.7 (0.8)	50/51	Proficient or Above	15.1 (0.8)	49/51
Advanced or Above	1.4 (0.3)	48/51	Advanced or Above	1.7 (0.3)	49/51

Note: *For an explanation of data, please refer to the User's Guide in the front of the book; values in italics indicate that the nature of the sample does not allow accurate determination of the variability of the statistic; n/a indicates data not available*

Bernalillo County

Albuquerque Public Schools

725 University Blvd, SE • Albuquerque, NM 87125-0704
Mailing Address: PO Box 25704 • Albuquerque, NM 87125-0704
(505) 842-8211 • http://ww2.aps.edu/
Grade Span: PK-12; **Agency Type:** 1
Schools: 144
83 Primary; 27 Middle; 28 High; 6 Other Level
131 Regular; 1 Special Education; 0 Vocational; 12 Alternative
1 Magnet; 12 Charter; 68 Title I Eligible; 59 School-wide Title I
Students: 88,120 (51.4% male; 48.6% female)
Individual Education Program: 17,984 (20.4%);
English Language Learner: 13,314 (15.1%); Migrant: 0 (0.0%)
Eligible for Free Lunch Program: 33,333 (37.8%)
Eligible for Reduced-Price Lunch Program: 6,750 (7.7%)
Teachers: 5,968.3 (14.8 to 1)
Librarians/Media Specialists: 87.1 (1,011.7 to 1)
Guidance Counselors: 201.2 (438.0 to 1)
Current Spending: ($ per student per year):
Total: $5,703; Instruction: $3,418; Support Services: $2,035
Enrollment, Drop-out Rates and Diploma Recipients by Race/Ethnicity

Category	Total	White	Black	Asian	AIAN	Hisp.
Enrollment (%)	100.0	37.9	3.8	2.1	4.7	51.6
Drop-out Rate (%)	8.6	5.4	8.4	4.3	15.0	11.2
H.S. Diplomas (#)	4,708	n/a	n/a	n/a	n/a	n/a

Southern Pueblos Agency

PO Box 1667 • Albuquerque, NM 87103
(505) 766-3034
Grade Span: KG-12; **Agency Type:** 6
Schools: 9
6 Primary; 1 Middle; 0 High; 2 Other Level
9 Regular; 0 Special Education; 0 Vocational; 0 Alternative
0 Magnet; 0 Charter; 9 Title I Eligible; 9 School-wide Title I
Students: 2,756 (n/a% male; n/a% female)
Individual Education Program: n/a;
English Language Learner: n/a; Migrant: n/a
Eligible for Free Lunch Program: n/a
Eligible for Reduced-Price Lunch Program: n/a
Teachers: n/a
Librarians/Media Specialists: n/a
Guidance Counselors: n/a
Current Spending: ($ per student per year):
Total: n/a; Instruction: n/a; Support Services: n/a
Enrollment, Drop-out Rates and Diploma Recipients by Race/Ethnicity

Category	Total	White	Black	Asian	AIAN	Hisp.
Enrollment (%)	100.0	0.0	0.0	0.0	100.0	0.0
Drop-out Rate (%)	n/a	n/a	n/a	n/a	n/a	n/a
H.S. Diplomas (#)	n/a	n/a	n/a	n/a	n/a	n/a

Chaves County

Roswell Independent Schools

200 W Chisum • Roswell, NM 88202-1437
Mailing Address: PO Box 1437 • Roswell, NM 88202-1437
(505) 627-2511 • http://www.risd.k12.nm.us
Grade Span: PK-12; **Agency Type:** 1
Schools: 24
15 Primary; 5 Middle; 4 High; 0 Other Level
22 Regular; 0 Special Education; 0 Vocational; 2 Alternative
0 Magnet; 1 Charter; 19 Title I Eligible; 17 School-wide Title I
Students: 9,510 (50.7% male; 49.3% female)
Individual Education Program: 2,460 (25.9%);
English Language Learner: 778 (8.2%); Migrant: 174 (1.8%)
Eligible for Free Lunch Program: 4,854 (51.0%)
Eligible for Reduced-Price Lunch Program: 908 (9.5%)
Teachers: 612.1 (15.5 to 1)
Librarians/Media Specialists: 6.0 (1,585.0 to 1)
Guidance Counselors: 24.0 (396.3 to 1)
Current Spending: ($ per student per year):
Total: $5,736; Instruction: $3,292; Support Services: $2,157
Enrollment, Drop-out Rates and Diploma Recipients by Race/Ethnicity

Category	Total	White	Black	Asian	AIAN	Hisp.
Enrollment (%)	100.0	37.4	3.0	0.5	0.5	58.6
Drop-out Rate (%)	5.6	3.3	2.5	0.0	10.0	7.7
H.S. Diplomas (#)	527	273	16	2	2	234

Cibola County

Grants-Cibola County Schools

401 N Second St • Grants, NM 87020-0008
Mailing Address: PO Box 8 • Grants, NM 87020-0008
(505) 285-2603
Grade Span: PK-12; **Agency Type:** 1
Schools: 12
7 Primary; 2 Middle; 2 High; 1 Other Level
11 Regular; 0 Special Education; 0 Vocational; 1 Alternative
0 Magnet; 0 Charter; 11 Title I Eligible; 11 School-wide Title I
Students: 3,705 (51.3% male; 48.7% female)
Individual Education Program: 506 (13.7%);
English Language Learner: 882 (23.8%); Migrant: 0 (0.0%)
Eligible for Free Lunch Program: 2,343 (63.2%)
Eligible for Reduced-Price Lunch Program: 406 (11.0%)
Teachers: 249.1 (14.9 to 1)
Librarians/Media Specialists: 4.0 (926.3 to 1)
Guidance Counselors: 8.6 (430.8 to 1)
Current Spending: ($ per student per year):
Total: $6,376; Instruction: $3,524; Support Services: $2,572
Enrollment, Drop-out Rates and Diploma Recipients by Race/Ethnicity

Category	Total	White	Black	Asian	AIAN	Hisp.
Enrollment (%)	100.0	21.9	0.8	0.5	36.1	40.7
Drop-out Rate (%)	5.3	5.1	20.0	0.0	3.8	7.1
H.S. Diplomas (#)	202	39	1	1	90	71

Curry County

Clovis Municipal Schools

1009 Main St • Clovis, NM 88102-9000
Mailing Address: PO Box 19000 • Clovis, NM 88102-9000
(505) 769-4300 • http://www.cms.k12.nm.us
Grade Span: PK-12; **Agency Type:** 1
Schools: 19
14 Primary; 3 Middle; 2 High; 0 Other Level
17 Regular; 1 Special Education; 0 Vocational; 1 Alternative
0 Magnet; 0 Charter; 13 Title I Eligible; 11 School-wide Title I
Students: 8,225 (52.0% male; 48.0% female)
Individual Education Program: 1,683 (20.5%);
English Language Learner: 521 (6.3%); Migrant: 128 (1.6%)
Eligible for Free Lunch Program: 3,991 (48.5%)
Eligible for Reduced-Price Lunch Program: 1,173 (14.3%)
Teachers: 533.7 (15.4 to 1)
Librarians/Media Specialists: 5.0 (1,645.0 to 1)
Guidance Counselors: 11.7 (703.0 to 1)
Current Spending: ($ per student per year):
Total: $5,540; Instruction: $3,190; Support Services: $1,967
Enrollment, Drop-out Rates and Diploma Recipients by Race/Ethnicity

Category	Total	White	Black	Asian	AIAN	Hisp.
Enrollment (%)	100.0	45.5	10.1	1.7	1.1	41.5
Drop-out Rate (%)	4.1	2.7	1.9	2.1	7.7	6.7
H.S. Diplomas (#)	400	240	38	10	0	112

Dona Ana County

Gadsden Independent Schools

1325 W Washington • Anthony, NM 88021-0070
Mailing Address: PO Box 70 • Anthony, NM 88021-0070
(505) 882-6203 • http://www.gisd.k12.nm.us/
Grade Span: PK-12; **Agency Type:** 1
Schools: 20
13 Primary; 4 Middle; 2 High; 1 Other Level
18 Regular; 1 Special Education; 0 Vocational; 1 Alternative
0 Magnet; 0 Charter; 18 Title I Eligible; 16 School-wide Title I
Students: 13,454 (51.7% male; 48.3% female)
Individual Education Program: 1,991 (14.8%);
English Language Learner: 8,943 (66.5%); Migrant: 242 (1.8%)
Eligible for Free Lunch Program: 11,563 (85.9%)
Eligible for Reduced-Price Lunch Program: 635 (4.7%)
Teachers: 821.2 (16.4 to 1)
Librarians/Media Specialists: 6.0 (2,242.3 to 1)
Guidance Counselors: 31.0 (434.0 to 1)
Current Spending: ($ per student per year):
Total: $5,915; Instruction: $3,060; Support Services: $2,435
Enrollment, Drop-out Rates and Diploma Recipients by Race/Ethnicity

Category	Total	White	Black	Asian	AIAN	Hisp.
Enrollment (%)	100.0	5.1	0.4	0.2	0.2	94.2
Drop-out Rate (%)	4.8	2.1	0.0	0.0	0.0	5.1
H.S. Diplomas (#)	634	34	2	0	0	598

Hatch Valley Public Schools
400 Main And Reed • Hatch, NM 87937-0790
Mailing Address: PO Box 790 • Hatch, NM 87937-0790
(505) 267-8200
Grade Span: PK-12; **Agency Type:** 1
Schools: 6
3 Primary; 1 Middle; 2 High; 0 Other Level
5 Regular; 0 Special Education; 0 Vocational; 1 Alternative
0 Magnet; 0 Charter; 6 Title I Eligible; 6 School-wide Title I
Students: 1,514 (50.2% male; 49.8% female)
Individual Education Program: 159 (10.5%);
English Language Learner: 988 (65.3%); Migrant: 116 (7.7%)
Eligible for Free Lunch Program: 1,161 (76.7%)
Eligible for Reduced-Price Lunch Program: 134 (8.9%)
Teachers: 100.9 (15.0 to 1)
Librarians/Media Specialists: 1.0 (1,514.0 to 1)
Guidance Counselors: 4.0 (378.5 to 1)
Current Spending: ($ per student per year):
Total: $6,843; Instruction: $3,628; Support Services: $2,858
Enrollment, Drop-out Rates and Diploma Recipients by Race/Ethnicity

Category	Total	White	Black	Asian	AIAN	Hisp.
Enrollment (%)	100.0	10.3	0.1	0.0	0.0	89.6
Drop-out Rate (%)	7.6	0.0	n/a	0.0	50.0	8.5
H.S. Diplomas (#)	62	8	0	0	0	54

Las Cruces Public Schools
505 S Main, Ste 249 • Las Cruces, NM 88001-1243
(505) 527-5807 • http://lcps.k12.nm.us/
Grade Span: PK-12; **Agency Type:** 1
Schools: 37
22 Primary; 7 Middle; 4 High; 4 Other Level
32 Regular; 2 Special Education; 0 Vocational; 3 Alternative
0 Magnet; 0 Charter; 22 Title I Eligible; 15 School-wide Title I
Students: 22,800 (51.1% male; 48.9% female)
Individual Education Program: 5,695 (25.0%);
English Language Learner: 3,216 (14.1%); Migrant: 358 (1.6%)
Eligible for Free Lunch Program: 11,773 (51.6%)
Eligible for Reduced-Price Lunch Program: 2,235 (9.8%)
Teachers: 1,495.0 (15.3 to 1)
Librarians/Media Specialists: 12.0 (1,900.0 to 1)
Guidance Counselors: 42.0 (542.9 to 1)
Current Spending: ($ per student per year):
Total: $5,913; Instruction: $3,358; Support Services: $2,226
Enrollment, Drop-out Rates and Diploma Recipients by Race/Ethnicity

Category	Total	White	Black	Asian	AIAN	Hisp.
Enrollment (%)	100.0	28.4	2.4	1.0	0.8	67.4
Drop-out Rate (%)	5.4	3.0	4.3	0.0	15.6	6.8
H.S. Diplomas (#)	1,417	519	24	17	7	850

Eddy County

Artesia Public Schools
1105 W Quay Ave • Artesia, NM 88210-1826
Mailing Address: 1106 W Quay Ave • Artesia, NM 88210-1826
(505) 746-3585 • http://www.bulldogs.org
Grade Span: PK-12; **Agency Type:** 1
Schools: 11
7 Primary; 1 Middle; 1 High; 2 Other Level
10 Regular; 0 Special Education; 0 Vocational; 1 Alternative
0 Magnet; 0 Charter; 7 Title I Eligible; 0 School-wide Title I
Students: 3,601 (51.4% male; 48.6% female)
Individual Education Program: 721 (20.0%);
English Language Learner: 254 (7.1%); Migrant: 68 (1.9%)
Eligible for Free Lunch Program: 1,149 (31.9%)
Eligible for Reduced-Price Lunch Program: 312 (8.7%)
Teachers: 229.2 (15.7 to 1)
Librarians/Media Specialists: 3.0 (1,200.3 to 1)
Guidance Counselors: 7.0 (514.4 to 1)
Current Spending: ($ per student per year):
Total: $5,875; Instruction: $3,403; Support Services: $2,083
Enrollment, Drop-out Rates and Diploma Recipients by Race/Ethnicity

Category	Total	White	Black	Asian	AIAN	Hisp.
Enrollment (%)	100.0	45.9	1.3	0.1	0.2	52.5
Drop-out Rate (%)	1.7	0.5	0.0	0.0	0.0	3.1
H.S. Diplomas (#)	237	134	2	0	1	100

Carlsbad Municipal Schools
498 N Canyon St • Carlsbad, NM 88220-5812
Mailing Address: 408 N Canyon St • Carlsbad, NM 88220-5812
(505) 234-3300 • http://www.carlsbad.k12.nm.us
Grade Span: PK-12; **Agency Type:** 1
Schools: 15
12 Primary; 2 Middle; 1 High; 0 Other Level
15 Regular; 0 Special Education; 0 Vocational; 0 Alternative
0 Magnet; 1 Charter; 11 Title I Eligible; 10 School-wide Title I
Students: 6,212 (51.7% male; 48.3% female)
Individual Education Program: 1,672 (26.9%);
English Language Learner: 258 (4.2%); Migrant: 2 (<0.1%)
Eligible for Free Lunch Program: 2,791 (44.9%)
Eligible for Reduced-Price Lunch Program: 744 (12.0%)
Teachers: 380.8 (16.3 to 1)
Librarians/Media Specialists: 3.0 (2,070.7 to 1)
Guidance Counselors: 9.6 (647.1 to 1)
Current Spending: ($ per student per year):
Total: $6,153; Instruction: $3,552; Support Services: $2,189
Enrollment, Drop-out Rates and Diploma Recipients by Race/Ethnicity

Category	Total	White	Black	Asian	AIAN	Hisp.
Enrollment (%)	100.0	50.4	1.9	0.6	0.7	46.4
Drop-out Rate (%)	2.2	2.5	0.0	0.0	0.0	1.8
H.S. Diplomas (#)	360	218	11	2	1	128

Grant County

Cobre Consolidated Schools
207 N Central Ave • Bayard, NM 88023-1000
Mailing Address: PO Box 1000 • Bayard, NM 88023-1000
(505) 537-3371 • http://www.Cobre-High-School.homepagehere.com/
Grade Span: PK-12; **Agency Type:** 1
Schools: 6
4 Primary; 1 Middle; 1 High; 0 Other Level
6 Regular; 0 Special Education; 0 Vocational; 0 Alternative
0 Magnet; 0 Charter; 5 Title I Eligible; 5 School-wide Title I
Students: 1,698 (52.1% male; 47.9% female)
Individual Education Program: 389 (22.9%);
English Language Learner: 915 (53.9%); Migrant: 0 (0.0%)
Eligible for Free Lunch Program: 964 (56.8%)
Eligible for Reduced-Price Lunch Program: 303 (17.8%)
Teachers: 125.5 (13.5 to 1)
Librarians/Media Specialists: 1.0 (1,698.0 to 1)
Guidance Counselors: 4.9 (346.5 to 1)
Current Spending: ($ per student per year):
Total: $7,607; Instruction: $3,724; Support Services: $3,492
Enrollment, Drop-out Rates and Diploma Recipients by Race/Ethnicity

Category	Total	White	Black	Asian	AIAN	Hisp.
Enrollment (%)	100.0	14.8	0.6	0.1	0.9	83.6
Drop-out Rate (%)	2.4	2.1	50.0	n/a	0.0	2.3
H.S. Diplomas (#)	110	15	0	0	2	93

Silver City Consolidated Schl
2810 N Swan St • Silver City, NM 88061-5853
(505) 956-2002 • http://silverhigh.com/
Grade Span: PK-12; **Agency Type:** 1
Schools: 10
5 Primary; 1 Middle; 3 High; 1 Other Level
8 Regular; 0 Special Education; 0 Vocational; 2 Alternative
0 Magnet; 0 Charter; 6 Title I Eligible; 2 School-wide Title I
Students: 3,377 (53.0% male; 47.0% female)
Individual Education Program: 653 (19.3%);
English Language Learner: 503 (14.9%); Migrant: 0 (0.0%)
Eligible for Free Lunch Program: 1,563 (46.3%)
Eligible for Reduced-Price Lunch Program: 343 (10.2%)
Teachers: 226.4 (14.9 to 1)
Librarians/Media Specialists: 2.0 (1,688.5 to 1)
Guidance Counselors: 9.5 (355.5 to 1)
Current Spending: ($ per student per year):
Total: $6,678; Instruction: $3,743; Support Services: $2,661
Enrollment, Drop-out Rates and Diploma Recipients by Race/Ethnicity

Category	Total	White	Black	Asian	AIAN	Hisp.
Enrollment (%)	100.0	47.1	1.2	0.7	0.9	50.3
Drop-out Rate (%)	4.7	3.5	0.0	0.0	0.0	6.4
H.S. Diplomas (#)	231	131	5	0	0	95

Lea County

Hobbs Municipal Schools
1515 East Sanger • Hobbs, NM 88241-1040
Mailing Address: PO Box 1040 • Hobbs, NM 88241-1040
(505) 433-0100 • http://www.hobbsschools.net/
Grade Span: PK-12; **Agency Type:** 1
Schools: 18
13 Primary; 3 Middle; 2 High; 0 Other Level
16 Regular; 1 Special Education; 0 Vocational; 1 Alternative
0 Magnet; 0 Charter; 8 Title I Eligible; 8 School-wide Title I
Students: 7,626 (51.5% male; 48.5% female)
Individual Education Program: 1,351 (17.7%);
English Language Learner: 687 (9.0%); Migrant: 0 (0.0%)
Eligible for Free Lunch Program: 3,434 (45.0%)
Eligible for Reduced-Price Lunch Program: 660 (8.7%)
Teachers: 449.0 (17.0 to 1)
Librarians/Media Specialists: 4.0 (1,906.5 to 1)

Guidance Counselors: 10.0 (762.6 to 1)
Current Spending: ($ per student per year):
Total: $5,656; Instruction: $3,203; Support Services: $2,072
Enrollment, Drop-out Rates and Diploma Recipients by Race/Ethnicity

Category	Total	White	Black	Asian	AIAN	Hisp.
Enrollment (%)	100.0	40.5	6.3	0.6	0.3	52.3
Drop-out Rate (%)	2.4	1.7	1.2	0.0	0.0	3.4
H.S. Diplomas (#)	433	191	27	0	3	212

Lovington Public Schools

1310 N 5th St • Lovington, NM 88260-1537
Mailing Address: PO Box 1537 • Lovington, NM 88260-1537
(505) 739-2200 • http://lovschools.leaco.net/
Grade Span: PK-12; **Agency Type:** 1
Schools: 10
4 Primary; 2 Middle; 3 High; 1 Other Level
8 Regular; 0 Special Education; 0 Vocational; 2 Alternative
0 Magnet; 0 Charter; 7 Title I Eligible; 5 School-wide Title I
Students: 2,786 (51.0% male; 49.0% female)
Individual Education Program: 735 (26.4%);
English Language Learner: 554 (19.9%); Migrant: 95 (3.4%)
Eligible for Free Lunch Program: 1,429 (51.3%)
Eligible for Reduced-Price Lunch Program: 271 (9.7%)
Teachers: 172.6 (16.1 to 1)
Librarians/Media Specialists: 1.0 (2,786.0 to 1)
Guidance Counselors: 4.0 (696.5 to 1)
Current Spending: ($ per student per year):
Total: $6,297; Instruction: $3,692; Support Services: $2,299
Enrollment, Drop-out Rates and Diploma Recipients by Race/Ethnicity

Category	Total	White	Black	Asian	AIAN	Hisp.
Enrollment (%)	100.0	37.2	3.3	0.3	0.3	58.9
Drop-out Rate (%)	4.7	2.5	10.0	0.0	0.0	6.2
H.S. Diplomas (#)	203	90	1	2	0	110

Lincoln County

Ruidoso Municipal Schools

200 Horton Circle • Ruidoso, NM 88345-6032
(505) 257-4051 • http://www.ruidoso.k12.nm.us
Grade Span: PK-12; **Agency Type:** 1
Schools: 7
3 Primary; 2 Middle; 1 High; 1 Other Level
6 Regular; 1 Special Education; 0 Vocational; 0 Alternative
0 Magnet; 0 Charter; 3 Title I Eligible; 1 School-wide Title I
Students: 2,324 (51.1% male; 48.9% female)
Individual Education Program: 487 (21.0%);
English Language Learner: 381 (16.4%); Migrant: 0 (0.0%)
Eligible for Free Lunch Program: 1,151 (49.5%)
Eligible for Reduced-Price Lunch Program: 368 (15.8%)
Teachers: 155.0 (15.0 to 1)
Librarians/Media Specialists: 3.0 (774.7 to 1)
Guidance Counselors: 4.0 (581.0 to 1)
Current Spending: ($ per student per year):
Total: $6,867; Instruction: $3,938; Support Services: $2,493
Enrollment, Drop-out Rates and Diploma Recipients by Race/Ethnicity

Category	Total	White	Black	Asian	AIAN	Hisp.
Enrollment (%)	100.0	50.0	1.1	0.3	14.5	34.2
Drop-out Rate (%)	4.1	1.9	0.0	0.0	6.1	8.6
H.S. Diplomas (#)	120	65	0	1	21	33

Los Alamos County

Los Alamos Public Schools

751 Trinity Dr • Los Alamos, NM 87544-0090
Mailing Address: PO Box 90 • Los Alamos, NM 87544-0090
(505) 663-2230 • http://losalamos.k12.nm.us/
Grade Span: PK-12; **Agency Type:** 1
Schools: 7
5 Primary; 1 Middle; 1 High; 0 Other Level
7 Regular; 0 Special Education; 0 Vocational; 0 Alternative
0 Magnet; 0 Charter; 0 Title I Eligible; 0 School-wide Title I
Students: 3,655 (51.0% male; 49.0% female)
Individual Education Program: 1,109 (30.3%);
English Language Learner: 52 (1.4%); Migrant: 0 (0.0%)
Eligible for Free Lunch Program: 0 (0.0%)
Eligible for Reduced-Price Lunch Program: 0 (0.0%)
Teachers: 250.3 (14.6 to 1)
Librarians/Media Specialists: 7.5 (487.3 to 1)
Guidance Counselors: 10.0 (365.5 to 1)
Current Spending: ($ per student per year):
Total: $8,346; Instruction: $4,740; Support Services: $3,283
Enrollment, Drop-out Rates and Diploma Recipients by Race/Ethnicity

Category	Total	White	Black	Asian	AIAN	Hisp.
Enrollment (%)	100.0	77.3	0.6	4.2	0.7	17.2
Drop-out Rate (%)	0.6	0.4	0.0	0.0	0.0	1.6
H.S. Diplomas (#)	258	209	0	9	1	39

Luna County

Deming Public Schools

501 W Florida St • Deming, NM 88030-6302
(505) 546-8841 • http://www.demingps.org/
Grade Span: PK-12; **Agency Type:** 1
Schools: 13
8 Primary; 1 Middle; 3 High; 1 Other Level
10 Regular; 1 Special Education; 0 Vocational; 2 Alternative
0 Magnet; 0 Charter; 9 Title I Eligible; 9 School-wide Title I
Students: 5,384 (50.5% male; 49.5% female)
Individual Education Program: 536 (10.0%);
English Language Learner: 1,615 (30.0%); Migrant: 328 (6.1%)
Eligible for Free Lunch Program: 3,679 (68.3%)
Eligible for Reduced-Price Lunch Program: 456 (8.5%)
Teachers: 306.4 (17.6 to 1)
Librarians/Media Specialists: 4.0 (1,346.0 to 1)
Guidance Counselors: 11.0 (489.5 to 1)
Current Spending: ($ per student per year):
Total: $5,401; Instruction: $3,220; Support Services: $1,829
Enrollment, Drop-out Rates and Diploma Recipients by Race/Ethnicity

Category	Total	White	Black	Asian	AIAN	Hisp.
Enrollment (%)	100.0	19.1	0.9	0.3	0.3	79.4
Drop-out Rate (%)	1.6	1.9	6.3	0.0	0.0	1.4
H.S. Diplomas (#)	236	66	2	2	0	166

Mckinley County

Eastern Navajo Agency

PO Box 328 • Crownpoint, NM 87313
(505) 786-6150
Grade Span: KG-12; **Agency Type:** 6
Schools: 18
14 Primary; 0 Middle; 1 High; 3 Other Level
18 Regular; 0 Special Education; 0 Vocational; 0 Alternative
0 Magnet; 0 Charter; 18 Title I Eligible; 18 School-wide Title I
Students: 5,234 (n/a% male; n/a% female)
Individual Education Program: n/a;
English Language Learner: n/a; Migrant: n/a
Eligible for Free Lunch Program: n/a
Eligible for Reduced-Price Lunch Program: n/a
Teachers: n/a
Librarians/Media Specialists: n/a
Guidance Counselors: n/a
Current Spending: ($ per student per year):
Total: n/a; Instruction: n/a; Support Services: n/a
Enrollment, Drop-out Rates and Diploma Recipients by Race/Ethnicity

Category	Total	White	Black	Asian	AIAN	Hisp.
Enrollment (%)	100.0	0.0	0.0	0.0	100.0	0.0
Drop-out Rate (%)	n/a	n/a	n/a	n/a	n/a	n/a
H.S. Diplomas (#)	n/a	n/a	n/a	n/a	n/a	n/a

Gallup-Mckinley County School

700 S Boardman • Gallup, NM 87305-1318
Mailing Address: PO Box 1318 • Gallup, NM 87305-1318
(505) 722-7711 • http://www.gmcs.k12.nm.us/
Grade Span: PK-12; **Agency Type:** 1
Schools: 36
20 Primary; 5 Middle; 8 High; 3 Other Level
33 Regular; 1 Special Education; 0 Vocational; 2 Alternative
0 Magnet; 1 Charter; 34 Title I Eligible; 22 School-wide Title I
Students: 13,618 (50.6% male; 49.4% female)
Individual Education Program: 2,258 (16.6%);
English Language Learner: 4,896 (36.0%); Migrant: 5 (<0.1%)
Eligible for Free Lunch Program: 8,611 (63.2%)
Eligible for Reduced-Price Lunch Program: 1,315 (9.7%)
Teachers: 873.6 (15.6 to 1)
Librarians/Media Specialists: 14.0 (972.7 to 1)
Guidance Counselors: 54.0 (252.2 to 1)
Current Spending: ($ per student per year):
Total: $6,519; Instruction: $3,352; Support Services: $2,850
Enrollment, Drop-out Rates and Diploma Recipients by Race/Ethnicity

Category	Total	White	Black	Asian	AIAN	Hisp.
Enrollment (%)	100.0	7.7	0.4	0.4	80.6	11.0
Drop-out Rate (%)	3.0	0.7	0.0	5.3	3.1	3.6
H.S. Diplomas (#)	966	107	2	0	715	142

Zuni Public Schools

22 St Anthony Dr • Zuni, NM 87327-0166
Mailing Address: PO Box A • Zuni, NM 87327-0166
(505) 782-5511 • http://www.zuni.k12.nm.us/
Grade Span: PK-12; **Agency Type:** 1
Schools: 6
2 Primary; 2 Middle; 2 High; 0 Other Level
5 Regular; 0 Special Education; 0 Vocational; 1 Alternative
0 Magnet; 0 Charter; 6 Title I Eligible; 6 School-wide Title I
Students: 1,761 (50.0% male; 50.0% female)
Individual Education Program: 358 (20.3%);
English Language Learner: 871 (49.5%); Migrant: 0 (0.0%)
Eligible for Free Lunch Program: 1,187 (67.4%)
Eligible for Reduced-Price Lunch Program: 175 (9.9%)
Teachers: 116.9 (15.1 to 1)
Librarians/Media Specialists: 3.0 (587.0 to 1)
Guidance Counselors: 7.0 (251.6 to 1)
Current Spending: ($ per student per year):
Total: $9,017; Instruction: $4,751; Support Services: $3,788
Enrollment, Drop-out Rates and Diploma Recipients by Race/Ethnicity

Category	Total	White	Black	Asian	AIAN	Hisp.
Enrollment (%)	100.0	0.3	0.0	0.1	99.5	0.1
Drop-out Rate (%)	7.6	0.0	n/a	n/a	7.6	n/a
H.S. Diplomas (#)	55	0	0	0	55	0

Otero County

Alamogordo Public Schools

1222 Indiana Ave • Alamogordo, NM 88311-0617
Mailing Address: PO Box 650 • Alamogordo, NM 88311-0617
(505) 439-3270 • http://www.zianet.com/aps4jobs/main.html
Grade Span: PK-12; **Agency Type:** 1
Schools: 16
11 Primary; 3 Middle; 2 High; 0 Other Level
15 Regular; 0 Special Education; 0 Vocational; 1 Alternative
0 Magnet; 0 Charter; 10 Title I Eligible; 6 School-wide Title I
Students: 6,923 (52.2% male; 47.8% female)
Individual Education Program: 1,345 (19.4%);
English Language Learner: 221 (3.2%); Migrant: 0 (0.0%)
Eligible for Free Lunch Program: 2,152 (31.1%)
Eligible for Reduced-Price Lunch Program: 861 (12.4%)
Teachers: 416.4 (16.6 to 1)
Librarians/Media Specialists: 4.0 (1,730.8 to 1)
Guidance Counselors: 16.5 (419.6 to 1)
Current Spending: ($ per student per year):
Total: $5,290; Instruction: $2,972; Support Services: $2,009
Enrollment, Drop-out Rates and Diploma Recipients by Race/Ethnicity

Category	Total	White	Black	Asian	AIAN	Hisp.
Enrollment (%)	100.0	56.8	7.1	2.6	1.1	32.4
Drop-out Rate (%)	0.8	0.3	0.0	0.0	0.0	2.0
H.S. Diplomas (#)	482	305	39	14	0	124

Rio Arriba County

Espanola Municipal Schools

714 Calle Don Diego • Espanola, NM 87532-3414
(505) 753-2254 • http://www.k12espanola.org/
Grade Span: PK-12; **Agency Type:** 1
Schools: 16
12 Primary; 1 Middle; 1 High; 2 Other Level
15 Regular; 0 Special Education; 0 Vocational; 1 Alternative
0 Magnet; 0 Charter; 13 Title I Eligible; 0 School-wide Title I
Students: 4,894 (50.4% male; 49.6% female)
Individual Education Program: 500 (10.2%);
English Language Learner: 2,569 (52.5%); Migrant: 46 (0.9%)
Eligible for Free Lunch Program: 2,972 (60.7%)
Eligible for Reduced-Price Lunch Program: 631 (12.9%)
Teachers: 319.0 (15.3 to 1)
Librarians/Media Specialists: 6.0 (815.7 to 1)
Guidance Counselors: 13.5 (362.5 to 1)
Current Spending: ($ per student per year):
Total: $6,595; Instruction: $3,287; Support Services: $2,988
Enrollment, Drop-out Rates and Diploma Recipients by Race/Ethnicity

Category	Total	White	Black	Asian	AIAN	Hisp.
Enrollment (%)	100.0	3.8	0.3	0.2	7.2	88.5
Drop-out Rate (%)	9.9	4.5	0.0	n/a	16.7	9.7
H.S. Diplomas (#)	153	10	0	0	6	137

Roosevelt County

Portales Municipal Schools

501 S Abilene Ave • Portales, NM 88130-6380
(505) 356-6641 • http://www.portalesschools.com
Grade Span: PK-12; **Agency Type:** 1
Schools: 8
3 Primary; 3 Middle; 2 High; 0 Other Level
7 Regular; 0 Special Education; 0 Vocational; 1 Alternative
0 Magnet; 0 Charter; 6 Title I Eligible; 2 School-wide Title I
Students: 2,783 (50.3% male; 49.7% female)
Individual Education Program: 470 (16.9%);
English Language Learner: 123 (4.4%); Migrant: 115 (4.1%)
Eligible for Free Lunch Program: 1,510 (54.3%)
Eligible for Reduced-Price Lunch Program: 262 (9.4%)
Teachers: 171.4 (16.2 to 1)
Librarians/Media Specialists: 8.0 (347.9 to 1)
Guidance Counselors: 5.0 (556.6 to 1)
Current Spending: ($ per student per year):
Total: $6,081; Instruction: $3,202; Support Services: $2,458
Enrollment, Drop-out Rates and Diploma Recipients by Race/Ethnicity

Category	Total	White	Black	Asian	AIAN	Hisp.
Enrollment (%)	100.0	48.3	1.7	0.3	1.0	48.7
Drop-out Rate (%)	2.7	1.3	0.0	0.0	0.0	5.0
H.S. Diplomas (#)	145	98	5	0	0	42

San Juan County

Aztec Municipal Schools

1118 W Aztec Blvd • Aztec, NM 87410-1818
(505) 334-9474 • http://www.aztecschools.com
Grade Span: PK-12; **Agency Type:** 1
Schools: 8
3 Primary; 2 Middle; 2 High; 1 Other Level
5 Regular; 1 Special Education; 0 Vocational; 2 Alternative
0 Magnet; 0 Charter; 4 Title I Eligible; 1 School-wide Title I
Students: 3,266 (52.8% male; 47.2% female)
Individual Education Program: 711 (21.8%);
English Language Learner: 56 (1.7%); Migrant: 0 (0.0%)
Eligible for Free Lunch Program: 1,083 (33.2%)
Eligible for Reduced-Price Lunch Program: 317 (9.7%)
Teachers: 208.3 (15.7 to 1)
Librarians/Media Specialists: 3.0 (1,088.7 to 1)
Guidance Counselors: 7.4 (441.4 to 1)
Current Spending: ($ per student per year):
Total: $5,463; Instruction: $3,153; Support Services: $2,040
Enrollment, Drop-out Rates and Diploma Recipients by Race/Ethnicity

Category	Total	White	Black	Asian	AIAN	Hisp.
Enrollment (%)	100.0	66.2	0.3	0.5	12.3	20.7
Drop-out Rate (%)	1.8	2.3	0.0	0.0	0.0	1.6
H.S. Diplomas (#)	203	127	1	0	35	40

Bloomfield Municipal Schools

325 N Bergin Ln • Bloomfield, NM 87413-6729
(505) 632-4316 • http://www.bsin.k12.nm.us/
Grade Span: PK-12; **Agency Type:** 1
Schools: 8
4 Primary; 1 Middle; 2 High; 1 Other Level
7 Regular; 0 Special Education; 0 Vocational; 1 Alternative
0 Magnet; 0 Charter; 4 Title I Eligible; 4 School-wide Title I
Students: 3,280 (51.2% male; 48.8% female)
Individual Education Program: 746 (22.7%);
English Language Learner: 727 (22.2%); Migrant: 0 (0.0%)
Eligible for Free Lunch Program: 1,776 (54.1%)
Eligible for Reduced-Price Lunch Program: 417 (12.7%)
Teachers: 200.3 (16.4 to 1)
Librarians/Media Specialists: 6.0 (546.7 to 1)
Guidance Counselors: 5.0 (656.0 to 1)
Current Spending: ($ per student per year):
Total: $6,191; Instruction: $3,268; Support Services: $2,597
Enrollment, Drop-out Rates and Diploma Recipients by Race/Ethnicity

Category	Total	White	Black	Asian	AIAN	Hisp.
Enrollment (%)	100.0	36.3	0.4	0.2	33.4	29.7
Drop-out Rate (%)	3.0	1.1	0.0	0.0	3.4	5.4
H.S. Diplomas (#)	166	67	0	2	48	49

Central Consolidated Schools

Hwys 64 & Old High School Rd • Shiprock, NM 87420-1179
Mailing Address: PO Box 1179 • Shiprock, NM 87420-1179
(505) 368-4984 • http://bird.kchs.k12.nm.us/
Grade Span: PK-12; **Agency Type:** 1
Schools: 17
7 Primary; 6 Middle; 4 High; 0 Other Level
16 Regular; 0 Special Education; 0 Vocational; 1 Alternative
0 Magnet; 0 Charter; 17 Title I Eligible; 17 School-wide Title I
Students: 7,083 (51.0% male; 49.0% female)
Individual Education Program: 1,276 (18.0%);
English Language Learner: 3,754 (53.0%); Migrant: 64 (0.9%)
Eligible for Free Lunch Program: 4,599 (64.9%)
Eligible for Reduced-Price Lunch Program: 822 (11.6%)
Teachers: 493.4 (14.4 to 1)
Librarians/Media Specialists: 5.0 (1,416.6 to 1)
Guidance Counselors: 23.0 (308.0 to 1)

Current Spending: ($ per student per year):
Total: $7,287; Instruction: $4,048; Support Services: $2,860
Enrollment, Drop-out Rates and Diploma Recipients by Race/Ethnicity

Category	Total	White	Black	Asian	AIAN	Hisp.
Enrollment (%)	100.0	8.9	0.2	0.1	89.0	2.0
Drop-out Rate (%)	6.0	6.3	0.0	0.0	5.9	8.5
H.S. Diplomas (#)	433	42	1	0	382	8

Farmington Municipal Schools

2001 N Dustin • Farmington, NM 87499-5850
Mailing Address: PO Box 5850 • Farmington, NM 87499-5850
(505) 324-9840 • http://www.fms.k12.nm.us
Grade Span: PK-12; **Agency Type:** 1
Schools: 21
12 Primary; 4 Middle; 4 High; 1 Other Level
16 Regular; 1 Special Education; 0 Vocational; 4 Alternative
0 Magnet; 0 Charter; 9 Title I Eligible; 6 School-wide Title I
Students: 10,126 (50.8% male; 49.2% female)
Individual Education Program: 1,638 (16.2%);
English Language Learner: 2,524 (24.9%); Migrant: 0 (0.0%)
Eligible for Free Lunch Program: 3,689 (36.4%)
Eligible for Reduced-Price Lunch Program: 1,047 (10.3%)
Teachers: 642.9 (15.8 to 1)
Librarians/Media Specialists: 5.0 (2,025.2 to 1)
Guidance Counselors: 26.0 (389.5 to 1)
Current Spending: ($ per student per year):
Total: $5,145; Instruction: $3,140; Support Services: $1,772
Enrollment, Drop-out Rates and Diploma Recipients by Race/Ethnicity

Category	Total	White	Black	Asian	AIAN	Hisp.
Enrollment (%)	100.0	48.5	1.1	0.9	28.4	21.2
Drop-out Rate (%)	5.3	2.9	2.6	3.7	8.0	9.5
H.S. Diplomas (#)	558	333	8	9	107	101

Shiprock Agency

PO Box 3239 • Shiprock, NM 87420
(505) 368-3400 • http://www.centralschools.org/~shs/
Grade Span: KG-12; **Agency Type:** 6
Schools: 13
9 Primary; 0 Middle; 3 High; 1 Other Level
13 Regular; 0 Special Education; 0 Vocational; 0 Alternative
0 Magnet; 0 Charter; 13 Title I Eligible; 13 School-wide Title I
Students: 2,112 (n/a% male; n/a% female)
Individual Education Program: n/a;
English Language Learner: n/a; Migrant: n/a
Eligible for Free Lunch Program: n/a
Eligible for Reduced-Price Lunch Program: n/a
Teachers: n/a
Librarians/Media Specialists: n/a
Guidance Counselors: n/a
Current Spending: ($ per student per year):
Total: n/a; Instruction: n/a; Support Services: n/a
Enrollment, Drop-out Rates and Diploma Recipients by Race/Ethnicity

Category	Total	White	Black	Asian	AIAN	Hisp.
Enrollment (%)	100.0	0.0	0.0	0.0	100.0	0.0
Drop-out Rate (%)	n/a	n/a	n/a	n/a	n/a	n/a
H.S. Diplomas (#)	n/a	n/a	n/a	n/a	n/a	n/a

San Miguel County

Las Vegas City Public Schools

901 Douglas Ave • Las Vegas, NM 87701-3928
(505) 454-5700 • http://cybercardinal.com/
Grade Span: PK-12; **Agency Type:** 1
Schools: 9
6 Primary; 1 Middle; 1 High; 1 Other Level
8 Regular; 1 Special Education; 0 Vocational; 0 Alternative
0 Magnet; 1 Charter; 7 Title I Eligible; 0 School-wide Title I
Students: 2,277 (48.4% male; 51.6% female)
Individual Education Program: 431 (18.9%);
English Language Learner: 622 (27.3%); Migrant: 0 (0.0%)
Eligible for Free Lunch Program: 1,012 (44.4%)
Eligible for Reduced-Price Lunch Program: 329 (14.4%)
Teachers: 162.2 (14.0 to 1)
Librarians/Media Specialists: 2.8 (813.2 to 1)
Guidance Counselors: 7.5 (303.6 to 1)
Current Spending: ($ per student per year):
Total: $5,989; Instruction: $3,185; Support Services: $2,579
Enrollment, Drop-out Rates and Diploma Recipients by Race/Ethnicity

Category	Total	White	Black	Asian	AIAN	Hisp.
Enrollment (%)	100.0	10.1	0.8	1.2	0.5	87.4
Drop-out Rate (%)	1.0	1.1	0.0	0.0	0.0	1.1
H.S. Diplomas (#)	174	19	1	0	0	154

West Las Vegas Public Schools

179 Bridge St • Las Vegas, NM 87701-3426
(505) 426-2333
Grade Span: PK-12; **Agency Type:** 1
Schools: 11
6 Primary; 2 Middle; 1 High; 2 Other Level
9 Regular; 0 Special Education; 0 Vocational; 2 Alternative
0 Magnet; 0 Charter; 6 Title I Eligible; 5 School-wide Title I
Students: 2,056 (51.3% male; 48.7% female)
Individual Education Program: 288 (14.0%);
English Language Learner: 1,262 (61.4%); Migrant: 0 (0.0%)
Eligible for Free Lunch Program: 1,323 (64.3%)
Eligible for Reduced-Price Lunch Program: 278 (13.5%)
Teachers: 144.4 (14.2 to 1)
Librarians/Media Specialists: 3.0 (685.3 to 1)
Guidance Counselors: 6.9 (298.0 to 1)
Current Spending: ($ per student per year):
Total: $8,199; Instruction: $4,068; Support Services: $3,672
Enrollment, Drop-out Rates and Diploma Recipients by Race/Ethnicity

Category	Total	White	Black	Asian	AIAN	Hisp.
Enrollment (%)	100.0	5.0	0.5	0.0	0.4	94.1
Drop-out Rate (%)	2.3	7.7	0.0	n/a	0.0	2.0
H.S. Diplomas (#)	112	4	0	0	2	106

Sandoval County

Bernalillo Public Schools

224 N Camino Del Pueblo • Bernalillo, NM 87004-0640
(505) 867-2317 •
http://www.bernalillo.bps.k12.nm.us/education/district/district.php?sectionid=1
Grade Span: PK-12; **Agency Type:** 1
Schools: 11
6 Primary; 3 Middle; 1 High; 1 Other Level
10 Regular; 0 Special Education; 0 Vocational; 1 Alternative
0 Magnet; 0 Charter; 7 Title I Eligible; 7 School-wide Title I
Students: 3,428 (51.1% male; 48.9% female)
Individual Education Program: 541 (15.8%);
English Language Learner: 1,643 (47.9%); Migrant: 25 (0.7%)
Eligible for Free Lunch Program: 2,188 (63.8%)
Eligible for Reduced-Price Lunch Program: 474 (13.8%)
Teachers: 249.7 (13.7 to 1)
Librarians/Media Specialists: 5.0 (685.6 to 1)
Guidance Counselors: 11.0 (311.6 to 1)
Current Spending: ($ per student per year):
Total: $7,529; Instruction: $4,285; Support Services: $2,961
Enrollment, Drop-out Rates and Diploma Recipients by Race/Ethnicity

Category	Total	White	Black	Asian	AIAN	Hisp.
Enrollment (%)	100.0	10.3	0.5	0.1	43.0	46.1
Drop-out Rate (%)	4.9	9.0	0.0	n/a	4.6	4.5
H.S. Diplomas (#)	141	9	0	0	62	70

Rio Rancho Public Schools

500 Laser Road, NE • Rio Rancho, NM 87124-3765
(505) 896-0667 • http://www.rrps.net/
Grade Span: PK-12; **Agency Type:** 1
Schools: 13
7 Primary; 3 Middle; 2 High; 1 Other Level
12 Regular; 0 Special Education; 0 Vocational; 1 Alternative
0 Magnet; 0 Charter; 2 Title I Eligible; 1 School-wide Title I
Students: 11,063 (51.5% male; 48.5% female)
Individual Education Program: 1,954 (17.7%);
English Language Learner: 657 (5.9%); Migrant: 0 (0.0%)
Eligible for Free Lunch Program: 2,053 (18.6%)
Eligible for Reduced-Price Lunch Program: 1,191 (10.8%)
Teachers: 649.3 (17.0 to 1)
Librarians/Media Specialists: 12.0 (921.9 to 1)
Guidance Counselors: 20.0 (553.2 to 1)
Current Spending: ($ per student per year):
Total: $4,783; Instruction: $2,762; Support Services: $1,795
Enrollment, Drop-out Rates and Diploma Recipients by Race/Ethnicity

Category	Total	White	Black	Asian	AIAN	Hisp.
Enrollment (%)	100.0	56.2	3.7	1.9	4.0	34.2
Drop-out Rate (%)	5.5	4.9	6.5	0.0	11.3	6.5
H.S. Diplomas (#)	638	400	22	17	14	185

Santa Fe County

Pojoaque Valley Public Schools

1574 State Rd 502 • Santa Fe, NM 87501-0468
Mailing Address: PO Box 3468 Pojoaque Station • Santa Fe, NM 87501-0468
(505) 455-2282 • http://pvs.k12.nm.us/
Grade Span: PK-12; **Agency Type:** 1
Schools: 4

1 Primary; 2 Middle; 1 High; 0 Other Level
4 Regular; 0 Special Education; 0 Vocational; 0 Alternative
0 Magnet; 0 Charter; 1 Title I Eligible; 1 School-wide Title I
Students: 1,942 (48.6% male; 51.4% female)
Individual Education Program: 354 (18.2%);
English Language Learner: 697 (35.9%); Migrant: 0 (0.0%)
Eligible for Free Lunch Program: 630 (32.4%)
Eligible for Reduced-Price Lunch Program: 248 (12.8%)
Teachers: 120.2 (16.2 to 1)
Librarians/Media Specialists: 3.0 (647.3 to 1)
Guidance Counselors: 8.0 (242.8 to 1)
Current Spending: ($ per student per year):
Total: $6,348; Instruction: $3,217; Support Services: $2,661
Enrollment, Drop-out Rates and Diploma Recipients by Race/Ethnicity

Category	Total	White	Black	Asian	AIAN	Hisp.
Enrollment (%)	100.0	8.2	0.4	0.4	18.3	72.8
Drop-out Rate (%)	2.0	0.0	n/a	n/a	6.7	1.2
H.S. Diplomas (#)	142	16	0	0	28	98

Santa Fe Public Schools
610 Alta Vista St • Santa Fe, NM 87505-4149
(505) 954-2003 • http://www.sfps.k12.nm.us/
Grade Span: PK-12; **Agency Type:** 1
Schools: 34
22 Primary; 4 Middle; 5 High; 3 Other Level
29 Regular; 2 Special Education; 0 Vocational; 3 Alternative
0 Magnet; 3 Charter; 21 Title I Eligible; 18 School-wide Title I
Students: 13,557 (51.8% male; 48.2% female)
Individual Education Program: 2,421 (17.9%);
English Language Learner: 3,572 (26.3%); Migrant: 0 (0.0%)
Eligible for Free Lunch Program: 5,472 (40.4%)
Eligible for Reduced-Price Lunch Program: 1,469 (10.8%)
Teachers: 852.4 (15.9 to 1)
Librarians/Media Specialists: 5.8 (2,337.4 to 1)
Guidance Counselors: 34.5 (393.0 to 1)
Current Spending: ($ per student per year):
Total: $5,328; Instruction: $3,096; Support Services: $2,041
Enrollment, Drop-out Rates and Diploma Recipients by Race/Ethnicity

Category	Total	White	Black	Asian	AIAN	Hisp.
Enrollment (%)	100.0	25.7	0.6	1.1	3.0	69.4
Drop-out Rate (%)	7.5	3.8	6.1	1.9	7.6	9.5
H.S. Diplomas (#)	661	237	7	10	16	391

Sierra County

Truth Or Consequences Schools
180 N Date St • Truth or Consequences, NM 87901-0952
Mailing Address: PO Box 952 • Truth or Consequences, NM 87901-0952
(505) 894-7141
Grade Span: PK-12; **Agency Type:** 1
Schools: 6
2 Primary; 2 Middle; 2 High; 0 Other Level
5 Regular; 0 Special Education; 0 Vocational; 1 Alternative
0 Magnet; 0 Charter; 4 Title I Eligible; 4 School-wide Title I
Students: 1,687 (52.9% male; 47.1% female)
Individual Education Program: 356 (21.1%);
English Language Learner: 515 (30.5%); Migrant: 0 (0.0%)
Eligible for Free Lunch Program: 1,022 (60.6%)
Eligible for Reduced-Price Lunch Program: 207 (12.3%)
Teachers: 103.3 (16.3 to 1)
Librarians/Media Specialists: 1.0 (1,687.0 to 1)
Guidance Counselors: 3.0 (562.3 to 1)
Current Spending: ($ per student per year):
Total: $6,348; Instruction: $3,376; Support Services: $2,671
Enrollment, Drop-out Rates and Diploma Recipients by Race/Ethnicity

Category	Total	White	Black	Asian	AIAN	Hisp.
Enrollment (%)	100.0	53.9	0.8	0.2	0.9	44.2
Drop-out Rate (%)	8.4	9.1	0.0	n/a	0.0	7.5
H.S. Diplomas (#)	74	47	1	0	1	25

Socorro County

Socorro Consolidated Schools
700 Franklin • Socorro, NM 87801-1157
Mailing Address: PO Box 1157 • Socorro, NM 87801-1157
(505) 835-0300 • http://www.nmt.edu/mainpage/socorro/pubsch.html
Grade Span: PK-12; **Agency Type:** 1
Schools: 8
5 Primary; 2 Middle; 1 High; 0 Other Level
8 Regular; 0 Special Education; 0 Vocational; 0 Alternative
0 Magnet; 1 Charter; 6 Title I Eligible; 4 School-wide Title I
Students: 2,082 (51.4% male; 48.6% female)
Individual Education Program: 375 (18.0%);
English Language Learner: 208 (10.0%); Migrant: 0 (0.0%)
Eligible for Free Lunch Program: 987 (47.4%)
Eligible for Reduced-Price Lunch Program: 186 (8.9%)
Teachers: 137.0 (15.2 to 1)
Librarians/Media Specialists: 4.0 (520.5 to 1)
Guidance Counselors: 6.0 (347.0 to 1)
Current Spending: ($ per student per year):
Total: $6,362; Instruction: $3,274; Support Services: $2,689
Enrollment, Drop-out Rates and Diploma Recipients by Race/Ethnicity

Category	Total	White	Black	Asian	AIAN	Hisp.
Enrollment (%)	100.0	29.8	1.0	1.2	2.4	65.6
Drop-out Rate (%)	2.7	3.1	12.5	0.0	0.0	2.3
H.S. Diplomas (#)	113	33	2	1	2	75

Taos County

Taos Municipal Schools
213 Paseo Del Canon • Taos, NM 87571-6239
(505) 758-5202 • http://www.taosschools.org/
Grade Span: PK-12; **Agency Type:** 1
Schools: 10
5 Primary; 2 Middle; 2 High; 1 Other Level
8 Regular; 1 Special Education; 0 Vocational; 1 Alternative
0 Magnet; 2 Charter; 7 Title I Eligible; 2 School-wide Title I
Students: 3,289 (50.6% male; 49.4% female)
Individual Education Program: 710 (21.6%);
English Language Learner: 518 (15.7%); Migrant: 0 (0.0%)
Eligible for Free Lunch Program: 2,569 (78.1%)
Eligible for Reduced-Price Lunch Program: 92 (2.8%)
Teachers: 267.0 (12.3 to 1)
Librarians/Media Specialists: 4.0 (822.3 to 1)
Guidance Counselors: 17.0 (193.5 to 1)
Current Spending: ($ per student per year):
Total: $6,866; Instruction: $3,674; Support Services: $2,652
Enrollment, Drop-out Rates and Diploma Recipients by Race/Ethnicity

Category	Total	White	Black	Asian	AIAN	Hisp.
Enrollment (%)	100.0	22.8	0.4	0.5	5.8	70.4
Drop-out Rate (%)	4.2	4.1	0.0	0.0	6.3	4.1
H.S. Diplomas (#)	207	58	2	2	5	140

Torrance County

Moriarty Muncipal Schools
200 Center St • Moriarty, NM 87035-0020
Mailing Address: PO Box 20 • Moriarty, NM 87035-0020
(505) 832-4471 • http://www.moriarty.k12.nm.us/
Grade Span: PK-12; **Agency Type:** 1
Schools: 8
5 Primary; 2 Middle; 1 High; 0 Other Level
8 Regular; 0 Special Education; 0 Vocational; 0 Alternative
0 Magnet; 0 Charter; 4 Title I Eligible; 0 School-wide Title I
Students: 4,264 (52.0% male; 48.0% female)
Individual Education Program: 968 (22.7%);
English Language Learner: 348 (8.2%); Migrant: 0 (0.0%)
Eligible for Free Lunch Program: 1,421 (33.3%)
Eligible for Reduced-Price Lunch Program: 468 (11.0%)
Teachers: 275.1 (15.5 to 1)
Librarians/Media Specialists: 1.9 (2,244.2 to 1)
Guidance Counselors: 10.0 (426.4 to 1)
Current Spending: ($ per student per year):
Total: $6,116; Instruction: $3,281; Support Services: $2,590
Enrollment, Drop-out Rates and Diploma Recipients by Race/Ethnicity

Category	Total	White	Black	Asian	AIAN	Hisp.
Enrollment (%)	100.0	65.4	1.2	0.5	1.6	31.3
Drop-out Rate (%)	3.6	3.4	0.0	n/a	0.0	4.3
H.S. Diplomas (#)	241	181	0	0	3	57

Valencia County

Belen Consolidated Schools
520 N Main St • Belen, NM 87002-3720
(505) 966-1000 • http://www.belen.k12.nm.us/
Grade Span: PK-12; **Agency Type:** 1
Schools: 12
7 Primary; 2 Middle; 2 High; 1 Other Level
9 Regular; 0 Special Education; 0 Vocational; 3 Alternative
0 Magnet; 0 Charter; 9 Title I Eligible; 9 School-wide Title I
Students: 4,870 (51.7% male; 48.3% female)
Individual Education Program: 1,103 (22.6%);
English Language Learner: 343 (7.0%); Migrant: 0 (0.0%)
Eligible for Free Lunch Program: 2,521 (51.8%)
Eligible for Reduced-Price Lunch Program: 598 (12.3%)
Teachers: 293.6 (16.6 to 1)
Librarians/Media Specialists: 1.0 (4,870.0 to 1)
Guidance Counselors: 12.0 (405.8 to 1)
Current Spending: ($ per student per year):
Total: $5,958; Instruction: $3,180; Support Services: $2,476

Enrollment, Drop-out Rates and Diploma Recipients by Race/Ethnicity

Category	Total	White	Black	Asian	AIAN	Hisp.
Enrollment (%)	100.0	30.2	1.4	0.4	1.4	66.6
Drop-out Rate (%)	8.8	9.1	10.0	0.0	28.0	8.1
H.S. Diplomas (#)	239	64	3	0	1	171

Los Lunas Public Schools

343 Main St • Los Lunas, NM 87031-1300
Mailing Address: PO Box 1300 • Los Lunas, NM 87031-1300
(505) 865-9636 • http://llmain.loslunas.k12.nm.us/
Grade Span: PK-12; **Agency Type:** 1
Schools: 17
9 Primary; 5 Middle; 2 High; 1 Other Level
13 Regular; 0 Special Education; 0 Vocational; 4 Alternative
0 Magnet; 0 Charter; 13 Title I Eligible; 13 School-wide Title I
Students: 8,421 (51.4% male; 48.6% female)
Individual Education Program: 1,887 (22.4%);
English Language Learner: 990 (11.8%); Migrant: 0 (0.0%)
Eligible for Free Lunch Program: 4,262 (50.6%)
Eligible for Reduced-Price Lunch Program: 999 (11.9%)
Teachers: 533.1 (15.8 to 1)
Librarians/Media Specialists: 12.0 (701.8 to 1)
Guidance Counselors: 18.0 (467.8 to 1)
Current Spending: ($ per student per year):
Total: $5,914; Instruction: $3,054; Support Services: $2,508

Enrollment, Drop-out Rates and Diploma Recipients by Race/Ethnicity

Category	Total	White	Black	Asian	AIAN	Hisp.
Enrollment (%)	100.0	30.2	1.0	0.5	7.4	60.9
Drop-out Rate (%)	2.8	2.6	0.0	16.7	1.9	3.1
H.S. Diplomas (#)	390	135	5	0	32	218

Number of Schools

Rank	Number	District Name	City
1	144	Albuquerque Public Schools	Albuquerque
2	37	Las Cruces Public Schools	Las Cruces
3	36	Gallup-Mckinley County School	Gallup
4	34	Santa Fe Public Schools	Santa Fe
5	24	Roswell Independent Schools	Roswell
6	21	Farmington Municipal Schools	Farmington
7	20	Gadsden Independent Schools	Anthony
8	19	Clovis Municipal Schools	Clovis
9	18	Eastern Navajo Agency	Crownpoint
9	18	Hobbs Municipal Schools	Hobbs
11	17	Central Consolidated Schools	Shiprock
11	17	Los Lunas Public Schools	Los Lunas
13	16	Alamogordo Public Schools	Alamogordo
13	16	Espanola Municipal Schools	Espanola
15	15	Carlsbad Municipal Schools	Carlsbad
16	13	Deming Public Schools	Deming
16	13	Rio Rancho Public Schools	Rio Rancho
16	13	Shiprock Agency	Shiprock
19	12	Belen Consolidated Schools	Belen
19	12	Grants-Cibola County Schools	Grants
21	11	Artesia Public Schools	Artesia
21	11	Bernalillo Public Schools	Bernalillo
21	11	West Las Vegas Public Schools	Las Vegas
24	10	Lovington Public Schools	Lovington
24	10	Silver City Consolidated Schl	Silver City
24	10	Taos Municipal Schools	Taos
27	9	Las Vegas City Public Schools	Las Vegas
27	9	Southern Pueblos Agency	Albuquerque
29	8	Aztec Municipal Schools	Aztec
29	8	Bloomfield Municipal Schools	Bloomfield
29	8	Moriarty Muncipal Schools	Moriarty
29	8	Portales Municipal Schools	Portales
29	8	Socorro Consolidated Schools	Socorro
34	7	Los Alamos Public Schools	Los Alamos
34	7	Ruidoso Municipal Schools	Ruidoso
36	6	Cobre Consolidated Schools	Bayard
36	6	Hatch Valley Public Schools	Hatch
36	6	Truth Or Consequences Schools	Truth or Conseq
36	6	Zuni Public Schools	Zuni
40	4	Pojoaque Valley Public Schools	Santa Fe

Number of Teachers

Rank	Number	District Name	City
1	5,968	Albuquerque Public Schools	Albuquerque
2	1,495	Las Cruces Public Schools	Las Cruces
3	873	Gallup-Mckinley County School	Gallup
4	852	Santa Fe Public Schools	Santa Fe
5	821	Gadsden Independent Schools	Anthony
6	649	Rio Rancho Public Schools	Rio Rancho
7	642	Farmington Municipal Schools	Farmington
8	612	Roswell Independent Schools	Roswell
9	533	Clovis Municipal Schools	Clovis
10	533	Los Lunas Public Schools	Los Lunas
11	493	Central Consolidated Schools	Shiprock
12	449	Hobbs Municipal Schools	Hobbs
13	416	Alamogordo Public Schools	Alamogordo
14	380	Carlsbad Municipal Schools	Carlsbad
15	319	Espanola Municipal Schools	Espanola
16	306	Deming Public Schools	Deming
17	293	Belen Consolidated Schools	Belen
18	275	Moriarty Muncipal Schools	Moriarty
19	267	Taos Municipal Schools	Taos
20	250	Los Alamos Public Schools	Los Alamos
21	249	Bernalillo Public Schools	Bernalillo
22	249	Grants-Cibola County Schools	Grants
23	229	Artesia Public Schools	Artesia
24	226	Silver City Consolidated Schl	Silver City
25	208	Aztec Municipal Schools	Aztec
26	200	Bloomfield Municipal Schools	Bloomfield
27	172	Lovington Public Schools	Lovington
28	171	Portales Municipal Schools	Portales
29	162	Las Vegas City Public Schools	Las Vegas
30	155	Ruidoso Municipal Schools	Ruidoso
31	144	West Las Vegas Public Schools	Las Vegas
32	137	Socorro Consolidated Schools	Socorro
33	125	Cobre Consolidated Schools	Bayard
34	120	Pojoaque Valley Public Schools	Santa Fe
35	116	Zuni Public Schools	Zuni
36	103	Truth Or Consequences Schools	Truth or Conseq
37	100	Hatch Valley Public Schools	Hatch
38	n/a	Eastern Navajo Agency	Crownpoint
38	n/a	Shiprock Agency	Shiprock
38	n/a	Southern Pueblos Agency	Albuquerque

Number of Students

Rank	Number	District Name	City
1	88,120	Albuquerque Public Schools	Albuquerque
2	22,800	Las Cruces Public Schools	Las Cruces
3	13,618	Gallup-Mckinley County School	Gallup
4	13,557	Santa Fe Public Schools	Santa Fe
5	13,454	Gadsden Independent Schools	Anthony
6	11,063	Rio Rancho Public Schools	Rio Rancho
7	10,126	Farmington Municipal Schools	Farmington
8	9,510	Roswell Independent Schools	Roswell
9	8,421	Los Lunas Public Schools	Los Lunas
10	8,225	Clovis Municipal Schools	Clovis
11	7,626	Hobbs Municipal Schools	Hobbs
12	7,083	Central Consolidated Schools	Shiprock
13	6,923	Alamogordo Public Schools	Alamogordo
14	6,212	Carlsbad Municipal Schools	Carlsbad
15	5,384	Deming Public Schools	Deming
16	5,234	Eastern Navajo Agency	Crownpoint
17	4,894	Espanola Municipal Schools	Espanola
18	4,870	Belen Consolidated Schools	Belen
19	4,264	Moriarty Muncipal Schools	Moriarty
20	3,705	Grants-Cibola County Schools	Grants
21	3,655	Los Alamos Public Schools	Los Alamos
22	3,601	Artesia Public Schools	Artesia
23	3,428	Bernalillo Public Schools	Bernalillo
24	3,377	Silver City Consolidated Schl	Silver City
25	3,289	Taos Municipal Schools	Taos
26	3,280	Bloomfield Municipal Schools	Bloomfield
27	3,266	Aztec Municipal Schools	Aztec
28	2,786	Lovington Public Schools	Lovington
29	2,783	Portales Municipal Schools	Portales
30	2,756	Southern Pueblos Agency	Albuquerque
31	2,324	Ruidoso Municipal Schools	Ruidoso
32	2,277	Las Vegas City Public Schools	Las Vegas
33	2,112	Shiprock Agency	Shiprock
34	2,082	Socorro Consolidated Schools	Socorro
35	2,056	West Las Vegas Public Schools	Las Vegas
36	1,942	Pojoaque Valley Public Schools	Santa Fe
37	1,761	Zuni Public Schools	Zuni
38	1,698	Cobre Consolidated Schools	Bayard
39	1,687	Truth Or Consequences Schools	Truth or Conseq
40	1,514	Hatch Valley Public Schools	Hatch

Male Students

Rank	Percent	District Name	City
1	53.0	Silver City Consolidated Schl	Silver City
2	52.9	Truth Or Consequences Schools	Truth or Conseq
3	52.8	Aztec Municipal Schools	Aztec
4	52.2	Alamogordo Public Schools	Alamogordo
5	52.1	Cobre Consolidated Schools	Bayard
6	52.0	Clovis Municipal Schools	Clovis
6	52.0	Moriarty Muncipal Schools	Moriarty
8	51.8	Santa Fe Public Schools	Santa Fe
9	51.7	Belen Consolidated Schools	Belen
9	51.7	Carlsbad Municipal Schools	Carlsbad
9	51.7	Gadsden Independent Schools	Anthony
12	51.5	Hobbs Municipal Schools	Hobbs
12	51.5	Rio Rancho Public Schools	Rio Rancho
14	51.4	Albuquerque Public Schools	Albuquerque
14	51.4	Artesia Public Schools	Artesia
14	51.4	Los Lunas Public Schools	Los Lunas
14	51.4	Socorro Consolidated Schools	Socorro
18	51.3	Grants-Cibola County Schools	Grants
18	51.3	West Las Vegas Public Schools	Las Vegas
20	51.2	Bloomfield Municipal Schools	Bloomfield
21	51.1	Bernalillo Public Schools	Bernalillo
21	51.1	Las Cruces Public Schools	Las Cruces
21	51.1	Ruidoso Municipal Schools	Ruidoso
24	51.0	Central Consolidated Schools	Shiprock
24	51.0	Los Alamos Public Schools	Los Alamos
24	51.0	Lovington Public Schools	Lovington
27	50.8	Farmington Municipal Schools	Farmington
28	50.7	Roswell Independent Schools	Roswell
29	50.6	Gallup-Mckinley County School	Gallup
29	50.6	Taos Municipal Schools	Taos
31	50.5	Deming Public Schools	Deming
32	50.4	Espanola Municipal Schools	Espanola
33	50.3	Portales Municipal Schools	Portales
34	50.2	Hatch Valley Public Schools	Hatch
35	50.0	Zuni Public Schools	Zuni
36	48.6	Pojoaque Valley Public Schools	Santa Fe
37	48.4	Las Vegas City Public Schools	Las Vegas
38	n/a	Eastern Navajo Agency	Crownpoint
38	n/a	Shiprock Agency	Shiprock
38	n/a	Southern Pueblos Agency	Albuquerque

Female Students

Rank	Percent	District Name	City
1	51.6	Las Vegas City Public Schools	Las Vegas
2	51.4	Pojoaque Valley Public Schools	Santa Fe
3	50.0	Zuni Public Schools	Zuni
4	49.8	Hatch Valley Public Schools	Hatch
5	49.7	Portales Municipal Schools	Portales
6	49.6	Espanola Municipal Schools	Espanola
7	49.5	Deming Public Schools	Deming
8	49.4	Gallup-Mckinley County School	Gallup
8	49.4	Taos Municipal Schools	Taos
10	49.3	Roswell Independent Schools	Roswell
11	49.2	Farmington Municipal Schools	Farmington
12	49.0	Central Consolidated Schools	Shiprock
12	49.0	Los Alamos Public Schools	Los Alamos
12	49.0	Lovington Public Schools	Lovington
15	48.9	Bernalillo Public Schools	Bernalillo
15	48.9	Las Cruces Public Schools	Las Cruces
15	48.9	Ruidoso Municipal Schools	Ruidoso
18	48.8	Bloomfield Municipal Schools	Bloomfield
19	48.7	Grants-Cibola County Schools	Grants
19	48.7	West Las Vegas Public Schools	Las Vegas
21	48.6	Albuquerque Public Schools	Albuquerque
21	48.6	Artesia Public Schools	Artesia
21	48.6	Los Lunas Public Schools	Los Lunas
21	48.6	Socorro Consolidated Schools	Socorro
25	48.5	Hobbs Municipal Schools	Hobbs
25	48.5	Rio Rancho Public Schools	Rio Rancho
27	48.3	Belen Consolidated Schools	Belen
27	48.3	Carlsbad Municipal Schools	Carlsbad
27	48.3	Gadsden Independent Schools	Anthony
30	48.2	Santa Fe Public Schools	Santa Fe
31	48.0	Clovis Municipal Schools	Clovis
31	48.0	Moriarty Muncipal Schools	Moriarty
33	47.9	Cobre Consolidated Schools	Bayard
34	47.8	Alamogordo Public Schools	Alamogordo
35	47.2	Aztec Municipal Schools	Aztec
36	47.1	Truth Or Consequences Schools	Truth or Conseq
37	47.0	Silver City Consolidated Schl	Silver City
38	n/a	Eastern Navajo Agency	Crownpoint
38	n/a	Shiprock Agency	Shiprock
38	n/a	Southern Pueblos Agency	Albuquerque

Individual Education Program Students

Rank	Percent	District Name	City
1	30.3	Los Alamos Public Schools	Los Alamos
2	26.9	Carlsbad Municipal Schools	Carlsbad
3	26.4	Lovington Public Schools	Lovington
4	25.9	Roswell Independent Schools	Roswell
5	25.0	Las Cruces Public Schools	Las Cruces
6	22.9	Cobre Consolidated Schools	Bayard
7	22.7	Bloomfield Municipal Schools	Bloomfield
7	22.7	Moriarty Muncipal Schools	Moriarty
9	22.6	Belen Consolidated Schools	Belen
10	22.4	Los Lunas Public Schools	Los Lunas
11	21.8	Aztec Municipal Schools	Aztec
12	21.6	Taos Municipal Schools	Taos
13	21.1	Truth Or Consequences Schools	Truth or Conseq
14	21.0	Ruidoso Municipal Schools	Ruidoso
15	20.5	Clovis Municipal Schools	Clovis
16	20.4	Albuquerque Public Schools	Albuquerque
17	20.3	Zuni Public Schools	Zuni
18	20.0	Artesia Public Schools	Artesia
19	19.4	Alamogordo Public Schools	Alamogordo
20	19.3	Silver City Consolidated Schl	Silver City
21	18.9	Las Vegas City Public Schools	Las Vegas
22	18.2	Pojoaque Valley Public Schools	Santa Fe
23	18.0	Central Consolidated Schools	Shiprock
23	18.0	Socorro Consolidated Schools	Socorro
25	17.9	Santa Fe Public Schools	Santa Fe
26	17.7	Hobbs Municipal Schools	Hobbs
26	17.7	Rio Rancho Public Schools	Rio Rancho
28	16.9	Portales Municipal Schools	Portales
29	16.6	Gallup-Mckinley County School	Gallup
30	16.2	Farmington Municipal Schools	Farmington
31	15.8	Bernalillo Public Schools	Bernalillo
32	14.8	Gadsden Independent Schools	Anthony
33	14.0	West Las Vegas Public Schools	Las Vegas
34	13.7	Grants-Cibola County Schools	Grants
35	10.5	Hatch Valley Public Schools	Hatch
36	10.2	Espanola Municipal Schools	Espanola
37	10.0	Deming Public Schools	Deming
38	n/a	Eastern Navajo Agency	Crownpoint
38	n/a	Shiprock Agency	Shiprock
38	n/a	Southern Pueblos Agency	Albuquerque

English Language Learner Students

Rank	Percent	District Name	City
1	66.5	Gadsden Independent Schools	Anthony
2	65.3	Hatch Valley Public Schools	Hatch
3	61.4	West Las Vegas Public Schools	Las Vegas
4	53.9	Cobre Consolidated Schools	Bayard
5	53.0	Central Consolidated Schools	Shiprock
6	52.5	Espanola Municipal Schools	Espanola
7	49.5	Zuni Public Schools	Zuni
8	47.9	Bernalillo Public Schools	Bernalillo
9	36.0	Gallup-Mckinley County School	Gallup
10	35.9	Pojoaque Valley Public Schools	Santa Fe
11	30.5	Truth Or Consequences Schools	Truth or Conseq
12	30.0	Deming Public Schools	Deming

Rank	Percent	District Name	City
13	27.3	Las Vegas City Public Schools	Las Vegas
14	26.3	Santa Fe Public Schools	Santa Fe
15	24.9	Farmington Municipal Schools	Farmington
16	23.8	Grants-Cibola County Schools	Grants
17	22.2	Bloomfield Municipal Schools	Bloomfield
18	19.9	Lovington Public Schools	Lovington
19	16.4	Ruidoso Municipal Schools	Ruidoso
20	15.7	Taos Municipal Schools	Taos
21	15.1	Albuquerque Public Schools	Albuquerque
22	14.9	Silver City Consolidated Schl	Silver City
23	14.1	Las Cruces Public Schools	Las Cruces
24	11.8	Los Lunas Public Schools	Los Lunas
25	10.0	Socorro Consolidated Schools	Socorro
26	9.0	Hobbs Municipal Schools	Hobbs
27	8.2	Moriarty Muncipal Schools	Moriarty
27	8.2	Roswell Independent Schools	Roswell
29	7.1	Artesia Public Schools	Artesia
30	7.0	Belen Consolidated Schools	Belen
31	6.3	Clovis Municipal Schools	Clovis
32	5.9	Rio Rancho Public Schools	Rio Rancho
33	4.4	Portales Municipal Schools	Portales
34	4.2	Carlsbad Municipal Schools	Carlsbad
35	3.2	Alamogordo Public Schools	Alamogordo
36	1.7	Aztec Municipal Schools	Aztec
37	1.4	Los Alamos Public Schools	Los Alamos
38	n/a	Eastern Navajo Agency	Crownpoint
38	n/a	Shiprock Agency	Shiprock
38	n/a	Southern Pueblos Agency	Albuquerque

Migrant Students

Rank	Percent	District Name	City
1	7.7	Hatch Valley Public Schools	Hatch
2	6.1	Deming Public Schools	Deming
3	4.1	Portales Municipal Schools	Portales
4	3.4	Lovington Public Schools	Lovington
5	1.9	Artesia Public Schools	Artesia
6	1.8	Gadsden Independent Schools	Anthony
6	1.8	Roswell Independent Schools	Roswell
8	1.6	Clovis Municipal Schools	Clovis
8	1.6	Las Cruces Public Schools	Las Cruces
10	0.9	Central Consolidated Schools	Shiprock
10	0.9	Espanola Municipal Schools	Espanola
12	0.7	Bernalillo Public Schools	Bernalillo
13	0.0	Carlsbad Municipal Schools	Carlsbad
13	0.0	Gallup-Mckinley County School	Gallup
15	0.0	Alamogordo Public Schools	Alamogordo
15	0.0	Albuquerque Public Schools	Albuquerque
15	0.0	Aztec Municipal Schools	Aztec
15	0.0	Belen Consolidated Schools	Belen
15	0.0	Bloomfield Municipal Schools	Bloomfield
15	0.0	Cobre Consolidated Schools	Bayard
15	0.0	Farmington Municipal Schools	Farmington
15	0.0	Grants-Cibola County Schools	Grants
15	0.0	Hobbs Municipal Schools	Hobbs
15	0.0	Las Vegas City Public Schools	Las Vegas
15	0.0	Los Alamos Public Schools	Los Alamos
15	0.0	Los Lunas Public Schools	Los Lunas
15	0.0	Moriarty Muncipal Schools	Moriarty
15	0.0	Pojoaque Valley Public Schools	Santa Fe
15	0.0	Rio Rancho Public Schools	Rio Rancho
15	0.0	Ruidoso Municipal Schools	Ruidoso
15	0.0	Santa Fe Public Schools	Santa Fe
15	0.0	Silver City Consolidated Schl	Silver City
15	0.0	Socorro Consolidated Schools	Socorro
15	0.0	Taos Municipal Schools	Taos
15	0.0	Truth Or Consequences Schools	Truth or Conseq
15	0.0	West Las Vegas Public Schools	Las Vegas
15	0.0	Zuni Public Schools	Zuni
38	n/a	Eastern Navajo Agency	Crownpoint
38	n/a	Shiprock Agency	Shiprock
38	n/a	Southern Pueblos Agency	Albuquerque

Students Eligible for Free Lunch

Rank	Percent	District Name	City
1	85.9	Gadsden Independent Schools	Anthony
2	78.1	Taos Municipal Schools	Taos
3	76.7	Hatch Valley Public Schools	Hatch
4	68.3	Deming Public Schools	Deming
5	67.4	Zuni Public Schools	Zuni
6	64.9	Central Consolidated Schools	Shiprock
7	64.3	West Las Vegas Public Schools	Las Vegas
8	63.8	Bernalillo Public Schools	Bernalillo
9	63.2	Gallup-Mckinley County School	Gallup
9	63.2	Grants-Cibola County Schools	Grants
11	60.7	Espanola Municipal Schools	Espanola
12	60.6	Truth Or Consequences Schools	Truth or Conseq
13	56.8	Cobre Consolidated Schools	Bayard
14	54.3	Portales Municipal Schools	Portales
15	54.1	Bloomfield Municipal Schools	Bloomfield
16	51.8	Belen Consolidated Schools	Belen
17	51.6	Las Cruces Public Schools	Las Cruces
18	51.3	Lovington Public Schools	Lovington
19	51.0	Roswell Independent Schools	Roswell
20	50.6	Los Lunas Public Schools	Los Lunas
21	49.5	Ruidoso Municipal Schools	Ruidoso
22	48.5	Clovis Municipal Schools	Clovis
23	47.4	Socorro Consolidated Schools	Socorro
24	46.3	Silver City Consolidated Schl	Silver City
25	45.0	Hobbs Municipal Schools	Hobbs
26	44.9	Carlsbad Municipal Schools	Carlsbad
27	44.4	Las Vegas City Public Schools	Las Vegas
28	40.4	Santa Fe Public Schools	Santa Fe
29	37.8	Albuquerque Public Schools	Albuquerque
30	36.4	Farmington Municipal Schools	Farmington
31	33.3	Moriarty Muncipal Schools	Moriarty
32	33.2	Aztec Municipal Schools	Aztec
33	32.4	Pojoaque Valley Public Schools	Santa Fe
34	31.9	Artesia Public Schools	Artesia
35	31.1	Alamogordo Public Schools	Alamogordo
36	18.6	Rio Rancho Public Schools	Rio Rancho
37	0.0	Los Alamos Public Schools	Los Alamos
38	n/a	Eastern Navajo Agency	Crownpoint
38	n/a	Shiprock Agency	Shiprock
38	n/a	Southern Pueblos Agency	Albuquerque

Students Eligible for Reduced-Price Lunch

Rank	Percent	District Name	City
1	17.8	Cobre Consolidated Schools	Bayard
2	15.8	Ruidoso Municipal Schools	Ruidoso
3	14.4	Las Vegas City Public Schools	Las Vegas
4	14.3	Clovis Municipal Schools	Clovis
5	13.8	Bernalillo Public Schools	Bernalillo
6	13.5	West Las Vegas Public Schools	Las Vegas
7	12.9	Espanola Municipal Schools	Espanola
8	12.8	Pojoaque Valley Public Schools	Santa Fe
9	12.7	Bloomfield Municipal Schools	Bloomfield
10	12.4	Alamogordo Public Schools	Alamogordo
11	12.3	Belen Consolidated Schools	Belen
11	12.3	Truth Or Consequences Schools	Truth or Conseq
13	12.0	Carlsbad Municipal Schools	Carlsbad
14	11.9	Los Lunas Public Schools	Los Lunas
15	11.6	Central Consolidated Schools	Shiprock
16	11.0	Grants-Cibola County Schools	Grants
16	11.0	Moriarty Muncipal Schools	Moriarty
18	10.8	Rio Rancho Public Schools	Rio Rancho
18	10.8	Santa Fe Public Schools	Santa Fe
20	10.3	Farmington Municipal Schools	Farmington
21	10.2	Silver City Consolidated Schl	Silver City
22	9.9	Zuni Public Schools	Zuni
23	9.8	Las Cruces Public Schools	Las Cruces
24	9.7	Aztec Municipal Schools	Aztec
24	9.7	Gallup-Mckinley County School	Gallup
24	9.7	Lovington Public Schools	Lovington
27	9.5	Roswell Independent Schools	Roswell
28	9.4	Portales Municipal Schools	Portales
29	8.9	Hatch Valley Public Schools	Hatch
29	8.9	Socorro Consolidated Schools	Socorro
31	8.7	Artesia Public Schools	Artesia
31	8.7	Hobbs Municipal Schools	Hobbs
33	8.5	Deming Public Schools	Deming
34	7.7	Albuquerque Public Schools	Albuquerque
35	4.7	Gadsden Independent Schools	Anthony
36	2.8	Taos Municipal Schools	Taos
37	0.0	Los Alamos Public Schools	Los Alamos
38	n/a	Eastern Navajo Agency	Crownpoint
38	n/a	Shiprock Agency	Shiprock
38	n/a	Southern Pueblos Agency	Albuquerque

Student/Teacher Ratio

Rank	Ratio	District Name	City
1	17.6	Deming Public Schools	Deming
2	17.0	Hobbs Municipal Schools	Hobbs
2	17.0	Rio Rancho Public Schools	Rio Rancho
4	16.6	Alamogordo Public Schools	Alamogordo
4	16.6	Belen Consolidated Schools	Belen
6	16.4	Bloomfield Municipal Schools	Bloomfield
6	16.4	Gadsden Independent Schools	Anthony
8	16.3	Carlsbad Municipal Schools	Carlsbad
8	16.3	Truth Or Consequences Schools	Truth or Conseq
10	16.2	Pojoaque Valley Public Schools	Santa Fe
10	16.2	Portales Municipal Schools	Portales
12	16.1	Lovington Public Schools	Lovington
13	15.9	Santa Fe Public Schools	Santa Fe
14	15.8	Farmington Municipal Schools	Farmington
14	15.8	Los Lunas Public Schools	Los Lunas
16	15.7	Artesia Public Schools	Artesia
16	15.7	Aztec Municipal Schools	Aztec
18	15.6	Gallup-Mckinley County School	Gallup
19	15.5	Moriarty Muncipal Schools	Moriarty
19	15.5	Roswell Independent Schools	Roswell
21	15.4	Clovis Municipal Schools	Clovis
22	15.3	Espanola Municipal Schools	Espanola
22	15.3	Las Cruces Public Schools	Las Cruces
24	15.2	Socorro Consolidated Schools	Socorro
25	15.1	Zuni Public Schools	Zuni
26	15.0	Hatch Valley Public Schools	Hatch
26	15.0	Ruidoso Municipal Schools	Ruidoso
28	14.9	Grants-Cibola County Schools	Grants
28	14.9	Silver City Consolidated Schl	Silver City
30	14.8	Albuquerque Public Schools	Albuquerque
31	14.6	Los Alamos Public Schools	Los Alamos
32	14.4	Central Consolidated Schools	Shiprock
33	14.2	West Las Vegas Public Schools	Las Vegas
34	14.0	Las Vegas City Public Schools	Las Vegas
35	13.7	Bernalillo Public Schools	Bernalillo
36	13.5	Cobre Consolidated Schools	Bayard
37	12.3	Taos Municipal Schools	Taos
38	n/a	Eastern Navajo Agency	Crownpoint
38	n/a	Shiprock Agency	Shiprock
38	n/a	Southern Pueblos Agency	Albuquerque

Student/Librarian Ratio

Rank	Ratio	District Name	City
1	4,870.0	Belen Consolidated Schools	Belen
2	2,786.0	Lovington Public Schools	Lovington
3	2,337.4	Santa Fe Public Schools	Santa Fe
4	2,244.2	Moriarty Muncipal Schools	Moriarty
5	2,242.3	Gadsden Independent Schools	Anthony
6	2,070.7	Carlsbad Municipal Schools	Carlsbad
7	2,025.2	Farmington Municipal Schools	Farmington
8	1,906.5	Hobbs Municipal Schools	Hobbs
9	1,900.0	Las Cruces Public Schools	Las Cruces
10	1,730.8	Alamogordo Public Schools	Alamogordo
11	1,698.0	Cobre Consolidated Schools	Bayard
12	1,688.5	Silver City Consolidated Schl	Silver City
13	1,687.0	Truth Or Consequences Schools	Truth or Conseq
14	1,645.0	Clovis Municipal Schools	Clovis
15	1,585.0	Roswell Independent Schools	Roswell
16	1,514.0	Hatch Valley Public Schools	Hatch
17	1,416.6	Central Consolidated Schools	Shiprock
18	1,346.0	Deming Public Schools	Deming
19	1,200.3	Artesia Public Schools	Artesia
20	1,088.7	Aztec Municipal Schools	Aztec
21	1,011.7	Albuquerque Public Schools	Albuquerque
22	972.7	Gallup-Mckinley County School	Gallup
23	926.3	Grants-Cibola County Schools	Grants
24	921.9	Rio Rancho Public Schools	Rio Rancho
25	822.3	Taos Municipal Schools	Taos
26	815.7	Espanola Municipal Schools	Espanola
27	813.2	Las Vegas City Public Schools	Las Vegas
28	774.7	Ruidoso Municipal Schools	Ruidoso
29	701.8	Los Lunas Public Schools	Los Lunas
30	685.6	Bernalillo Public Schools	Bernalillo
31	685.3	West Las Vegas Public Schools	Las Vegas
32	647.3	Pojoaque Valley Public Schools	Santa Fe
33	587.0	Zuni Public Schools	Zuni
34	546.7	Bloomfield Municipal Schools	Bloomfield
35	520.5	Socorro Consolidated Schools	Socorro
36	487.3	Los Alamos Public Schools	Los Alamos
37	347.9	Portales Municipal Schools	Portales
38	n/a	Eastern Navajo Agency	Crownpoint
38	n/a	Shiprock Agency	Shiprock
38	n/a	Southern Pueblos Agency	Albuquerque

Student/Counselor Ratio

Rank	Ratio	District Name	City
1	762.6	Hobbs Municipal Schools	Hobbs
2	703.0	Clovis Municipal Schools	Clovis
3	696.5	Lovington Public Schools	Lovington
4	656.0	Bloomfield Municipal Schools	Bloomfield
5	647.1	Carlsbad Municipal Schools	Carlsbad
6	581.0	Ruidoso Municipal Schools	Ruidoso
7	562.3	Truth Or Consequences Schools	Truth or Conseq
8	556.6	Portales Municipal Schools	Portales
9	553.2	Rio Rancho Public Schools	Rio Rancho
10	542.9	Las Cruces Public Schools	Las Cruces
11	514.4	Artesia Public Schools	Artesia
12	489.5	Deming Public Schools	Deming
13	467.8	Los Lunas Public Schools	Los Lunas
14	441.4	Aztec Municipal Schools	Aztec
15	438.0	Albuquerque Public Schools	Albuquerque
16	434.0	Gadsden Independent Schools	Anthony
17	430.8	Grants-Cibola County Schools	Grants
18	426.4	Moriarty Muncipal Schools	Moriarty
19	419.6	Alamogordo Public Schools	Alamogordo
20	405.8	Belen Consolidated Schools	Belen
21	396.3	Roswell Independent Schools	Roswell
22	393.0	Santa Fe Public Schools	Santa Fe
23	389.5	Farmington Municipal Schools	Farmington
24	378.5	Hatch Valley Public Schools	Hatch
25	365.5	Los Alamos Public Schools	Los Alamos
26	362.5	Espanola Municipal Schools	Espanola

27	355.5	Silver City Consolidated Schl	Silver City
28	347.0	Socorro Consolidated Schools	Socorro
29	346.5	Cobre Consolidated Schools	Bayard
30	311.6	Bernalillo Public Schools	Bernalillo
31	308.0	Central Consolidated Schools	Shiprock
32	303.6	Las Vegas City Public Schools	Las Vegas
33	298.0	West Las Vegas Public Schools	Las Vegas
34	252.2	Gallup-Mckinley County School	Gallup
35	251.6	Zuni Public Schools	Zuni
36	242.8	Pojoaque Valley Public Schools	Santa Fe
37	193.5	Taos Municipal Schools	Taos
38	n/a	Eastern Navajo Agency	Crownpoint
38	n/a	Shiprock Agency	Shiprock
38	n/a	Southern Pueblos Agency	Albuquerque

Current Spending per Student in FY2001

Rank	Dollars	District Name	City
1	9,017	Zuni Public Schools	Zuni
2	8,346	Los Alamos Public Schools	Los Alamos
3	8,199	West Las Vegas Public Schools	Las Vegas
4	7,607	Cobre Consolidated Schools	Bayard
5	7,529	Bernalillo Public Schools	Bernalillo
6	7,287	Central Consolidated Schools	Shiprock
7	6,867	Ruidoso Municipal Schools	Ruidoso
8	6,866	Taos Municipal Schools	Taos
9	6,843	Hatch Valley Public Schools	Hatch
10	6,678	Silver City Consolidated Schl	Silver City
11	6,595	Espanola Municipal Schools	Espanola
12	6,519	Gallup-Mckinley County School	Gallup
13	6,376	Grants-Cibola County Schools	Grants
14	6,362	Socorro Consolidated Schools	Socorro
15	6,348	Pojoaque Valley Public Schools	Santa Fe
15	6,348	Truth Or Consequences Schools	Truth or Conseq
17	6,297	Lovington Public Schools	Lovington
18	6,191	Bloomfield Municipal Schools	Bloomfield
19	6,153	Carlsbad Municipal Schools	Carlsbad
20	6,116	Moriarty Muncipal Schools	Moriarty
21	6,081	Portales Municipal Schools	Portales
22	5,989	Las Vegas City Public Schools	Las Vegas
23	5,958	Belen Consolidated Schools	Belen
24	5,915	Gadsden Independent Schools	Anthony
25	5,914	Los Lunas Public Schools	Los Lunas
26	5,913	Las Cruces Public Schools	Las Cruces
27	5,875	Artesia Public Schools	Artesia
28	5,736	Roswell Independent Schools	Roswell
29	5,703	Albuquerque Public Schools	Albuquerque
30	5,656	Hobbs Municipal Schools	Hobbs
31	5,540	Clovis Municipal Schools	Clovis
32	5,463	Aztec Municipal Schools	Aztec
33	5,401	Deming Public Schools	Deming
34	5,328	Santa Fe Public Schools	Santa Fe
35	5,290	Alamogordo Public Schools	Alamogordo
36	5,145	Farmington Municipal Schools	Farmington
37	4,783	Rio Rancho Public Schools	Rio Rancho
38	n/a	Eastern Navajo Agency	Crownpoint
38	n/a	Shiprock Agency	Shiprock
38	n/a	Southern Pueblos Agency	Albuquerque

Number of Diploma Recipients

Rank	Number	District Name	City
1	4,708	Albuquerque Public Schools	Albuquerque
2	1,417	Las Cruces Public Schools	Las Cruces
3	966	Gallup-Mckinley County School	Gallup
4	661	Santa Fe Public Schools	Santa Fe
5	638	Rio Rancho Public Schools	Rio Rancho
6	634	Gadsden Independent Schools	Anthony
7	558	Farmington Municipal Schools	Farmington
8	527	Roswell Independent Schools	Roswell
9	482	Alamogordo Public Schools	Alamogordo
10	433	Central Consolidated Schools	Shiprock
10	433	Hobbs Municipal Schools	Hobbs
12	400	Clovis Municipal Schools	Clovis
13	390	Los Lunas Public Schools	Los Lunas
14	360	Carlsbad Municipal Schools	Carlsbad
15	258	Los Alamos Public Schools	Los Alamos
16	241	Moriarty Muncipal Schools	Moriarty
17	239	Belen Consolidated Schools	Belen
18	237	Artesia Public Schools	Artesia
19	236	Deming Public Schools	Deming
20	231	Silver City Consolidated Schl	Silver City
21	207	Taos Municipal Schools	Taos
22	203	Aztec Municipal Schools	Aztec
22	203	Lovington Public Schools	Lovington
24	202	Grants-Cibola County Schools	Grants
25	174	Las Vegas City Public Schools	Las Vegas
26	166	Bloomfield Municipal Schools	Bloomfield
27	153	Espanola Municipal Schools	Espanola
28	145	Portales Municipal Schools	Portales
29	142	Pojoaque Valley Public Schools	Santa Fe
30	141	Bernalillo Public Schools	Bernalillo
31	120	Ruidoso Municipal Schools	Ruidoso
32	113	Socorro Consolidated Schools	Socorro
33	112	West Las Vegas Public Schools	Las Vegas
34	110	Cobre Consolidated Schools	Bayard
35	74	Truth Or Consequences Schools	Truth or Conseq
36	62	Hatch Valley Public Schools	Hatch
37	55	Zuni Public Schools	Zuni
38	n/a	Eastern Navajo Agency	Crownpoint
38	n/a	Shiprock Agency	Shiprock
38	n/a	Southern Pueblos Agency	Albuquerque

High School Drop-out Rate

Rank	Percent	District Name	City
1	9.9	Espanola Municipal Schools	Espanola
2	8.8	Belen Consolidated Schools	Belen
3	8.6	Albuquerque Public Schools	Albuquerque
4	8.4	Truth Or Consequences Schools	Truth or Conseq
5	7.6	Hatch Valley Public Schools	Hatch
5	7.6	Zuni Public Schools	Zuni
7	7.5	Santa Fe Public Schools	Santa Fe
8	6.0	Central Consolidated Schools	Shiprock
9	5.6	Roswell Independent Schools	Roswell
10	5.5	Rio Rancho Public Schools	Rio Rancho
11	5.4	Las Cruces Public Schools	Las Cruces
12	5.3	Farmington Municipal Schools	Farmington
12	5.3	Grants-Cibola County Schools	Grants
14	4.9	Bernalillo Public Schools	Bernalillo
15	4.8	Gadsden Independent Schools	Anthony
16	4.7	Lovington Public Schools	Lovington
16	4.7	Silver City Consolidated Schl	Silver City
18	4.2	Taos Municipal Schools	Taos
19	4.1	Clovis Municipal Schools	Clovis
19	4.1	Ruidoso Municipal Schools	Ruidoso
21	3.6	Moriarty Muncipal Schools	Moriarty
22	3.0	Bloomfield Municipal Schools	Bloomfield
22	3.0	Gallup-Mckinley County School	Gallup
24	2.8	Los Lunas Public Schools	Los Lunas
25	2.7	Portales Municipal Schools	Portales
25	2.7	Socorro Consolidated Schools	Socorro
27	2.4	Cobre Consolidated Schools	Bayard
27	2.4	Hobbs Municipal Schools	Hobbs
29	2.3	West Las Vegas Public Schools	Las Vegas
30	2.2	Carlsbad Municipal Schools	Carlsbad
31	2.0	Pojoaque Valley Public Schools	Santa Fe
32	1.8	Aztec Municipal Schools	Aztec
33	1.7	Artesia Public Schools	Artesia
34	1.6	Deming Public Schools	Deming
35	1.0	Las Vegas City Public Schools	Las Vegas
36	0.8	Alamogordo Public Schools	Alamogordo
37	0.6	Los Alamos Public Schools	Los Alamos
38	n/a	Eastern Navajo Agency	Crownpoint
38	n/a	Shiprock Agency	Shiprock
38	n/a	Southern Pueblos Agency	Albuquerque

New York

New York Public School Educational Profile

Category	Value	Category	Value
Schools *(2002-2003)*	4,906	**Diploma Recipients** *(2002-2003)*	153,879
Instructional Level		White, Non-Hispanic	104,673
Primary	2,522	Black, Non-Hispanic	22,046
Middle	759	Asian/Pacific Islander	10,315
High	797	American Indian/Alaskan Native	565
Other Level	828	Hispanic	16,280
Curriculum		**High School Drop-out Rate** (%) *(2000-2001)*	3.8
Regular	4,203	White, Non-Hispanic	2.1
Special Education	76	Black, Non-Hispanic	6.3
Vocational	25	Asian/Pacific Islander	2.9
Alternative	602	American Indian/Alaskan Native	6.5
Type		Hispanic	7.2
Magnet	27	**Staff** *(2002-2003)*	427,743.0
Charter	44	Teachers	210,332.0
Title I Eligible	2,716	Average Salary ($)	53,017
School-wide Title I	0	Librarians/Media Specialists	3,229.8
Students *(2002-2003)*	2,914,574	Guidance Counselors	7,223.7
Gender (%)		**Ratios** *(2002-2003)*	
Male	51.5	Student/Teacher Ratio	13.9 to 1
Female	48.5	Student/Librarian Ratio	902.4 to 1
Race/Ethnicity (%)		Student/Counselor Ratio	403.5 to 1
White, Non-Hispanic	54.2	**Current Spending** *($ per student in FY 2001)*	11,218
Black, Non-Hispanic	20.0	Instruction	7,660
Asian/Pacific Islander	6.3	Support Services	3,256
American Indian/Alaskan Native	0.4	**College Entrance Exam Scores** *(2003)*	
Hispanic	19.0	Scholastic Aptitude Test (SAT)	
Classification (%)		Participation Rate (%)	82
Individual Education Program (IEP)	14.6	Mean SAT I Verbal Score	496
Migrant	0.0	Mean SAT I Math Score	510
English Language Learner (ELL)	6.2	American College Testing Program (ACT)	
Eligible for Free Lunch Program	12.6	Participation Rate (%)	15
Eligible for Reduced-Price Lunch Program	4.2	Average Composite Score	22.3

Note: *For an explanation of data, please refer to the User's Guide in the front of the book; n/a indicates data not available*

New York NAEP 2003 Test Scores

Reading			Mathematics		
Grade/Category	**Value**	**Rank**	**Grade/Category**	**Value**	**Rank**
4th Grade			**4th Grade**		
Average Proficiency	222.2 (1.1)	15/51	Average Proficiency	235.9 (0.9)	22/51
Proficiency by Gender/Race/Ethnicity			Proficiency by Gender/Race/Ethnicity		
Male	217.9 (1.4)	17/51	Male	237.2 (1.0)	25/51
Female	226.4 (1.1)	13/51	Female	234.7 (1.0)	24/51
White, Non-Hispanic	235.1 (1.3)	4/51	White, Non-Hispanic	245.7 (1.0)	10/51
Black, Non-Hispanic	202.6 (1.9)	11/42	Black, Non-Hispanic	219.2 (1.2)	12/42
Asian, Non-Hispanic	207.7 (1.9)	12/41	Asian, Non-Hispanic	221.0 (1.5)	23/43
American Indian, Non-Hispanic	230.5 (2.5)	10/25	American Indian, Non-Hispanic	249.5 (1.8)	8/26
Hispanic	n/a	n/a	Hispanic	n/a	n/a
Proficiency by Class Size			Proficiency by Class Size		
Less than 16 Students	*215.3 (5.2)*	9/45	Less than 16 Students	*229.3 (5.0)*	12/47
16 to 18 Students	*230.9 (4.1)*	1/48	16 to 18 Students	*243.8 (3.3)*	2/48
19 to 20 Students	225.5 (3.0)	7/50	19 to 20 Students	235.9 (2.0)	19/50
21 to 25 Students	226.4 (2.2)	7/51	21 to 25 Students	238.6 (1.6)	23/51
Greater than 25 Students	217.1 (2.0)	32/49	Greater than 25 Students	232.5 (2.0)	32/49
Percent Attaining Achievement Levels			Percent Attaining Achievement Levels		
Below Basic	32.8 (1.3)	32/51	Below Basic	21.3 (1.0)	24/51
Basic or Above	67.2 (1.3)	19/51	Basic or Above	78.7 (1.0)	28/51
Proficient or Above	34.2 (1.3)	12/51	Proficient or Above	32.9 (1.4)	24/51
Advanced or Above	8.4 (0.8)	10/51	Advanced or Above	3.9 (0.5)	18/51
8th Grade			**8th Grade**		
Average Proficiency	265.3 (1.3)	22/51	Average Proficiency	279.7 (1.1)	25/51
Proficiency by Gender/Race/Ethnicity			Proficiency by Gender/Race/Ethnicity		
Male	259.1 (1.6)	24/51	Male	281.0 (1.1)	23/51
Female	271.1 (1.4)	20/51	Female	278.5 (1.5)	25/51
White, Non-Hispanic	277.3 (1.4)	2/50	White, Non-Hispanic	292.8 (1.1)	4/50
Black, Non-Hispanic	245.7 (2.1)	15/41	Black, Non-Hispanic	255.4 (2.0)	14/41
Asian, Non-Hispanic	249.6 (2.4)	11/37	Asian, Non-Hispanic	261.8 (2.4)	14/37
American Indian, Non-Hispanic	269.8 (4.4)	10/23	American Indian, Non-Hispanic	290.0 (3.3)	11/23
Hispanic	n/a	n/a	Hispanic	n/a	n/a
Proficiency by Parents Highest Level of Ed.			Proficiency by Parents Highest Level of Ed.		
Did Not Finish High School	247.4 (3.2)	19/50	Did Not Finish High School	258.7 (3.3)	21/50
Graduated High School	257.6 (2.3)	17/50	Graduated High School	269.7 (1.9)	24/50
Some Education After High School	271.3 (1.6)	10/50	Some Education After High School	282.2 (1.7)	19/50
Graduated College	273.7 (1.5)	23/50	Graduated College	289.2 (1.3)	26/50
Percent Attaining Achievement Levels			Percent Attaining Achievement Levels		
Below Basic	24.8 (1.5)	23/51	Below Basic	29.5 (1.2)	27/51
Basic or Above	75.2 (1.5)	29/51	Basic or Above	70.5 (1.2)	25/51
Proficient or Above	35.1 (1.6)	15/51	Proficient or Above	32.0 (1.4)	18/51
Advanced or Above	3.7 (0.6)	6/51	Advanced or Above	5.9 (0.6)	14/51

***Note:** For an explanation of data, please refer to the User's Guide in the front of the book; values in italics indicate that the nature of the sample does not allow accurate determination of the variability of the statistic; n/a indicates data not available*

Albany County

Albany City SD

Academy Park • Albany, NY 12207-1099
(518) 462-7200 • http://www.albany.k12.ny.us/
Grade Span: PK-12; **Agency Type:** 1
Schools: 27
12 Primary; 2 Middle; 1 High; 12 Other Level
15 Regular; 0 Special Education; 0 Vocational; 12 Alternative
2 Magnet; 0 Charter; 13 Title I Eligible; 0 School-wide Title I
Students: 9,656 (51.7% male; 48.3% female)
Individual Education Program: 1,976 (20.5%);
English Language Learner: 324 (3.4%); Migrant: n/a
Eligible for Free Lunch Program: 5,841 (60.5%)
Eligible for Reduced-Price Lunch Program: 867 (9.0%)
Teachers: n/a
Librarians/Media Specialists: n/a
Guidance Counselors: n/a
Current Spending: ($ per student per year):
Total: $11,706; Instruction: $8,045; Support Services: $3,374
Enrollment, Drop-out Rates and Diploma Recipients by Race/Ethnicity

Category	Total	White	Black	Asian	AIAN	Hisp.
Enrollment (%)	100.0	23.8	64.0	2.7	0.3	9.2
Drop-out Rate (%)	5.9	3.4	7.4	3.8	0.0	7.7
H.S. Diplomas (#)	382	167	172	18	0	25

Bethlehem CSD

90 Adams Pl • Delmar, NY 12054-3297
(518) 439-7098 • http://bcsd.k12.ny.us/
Grade Span: KG-12; **Agency Type:** 1
Schools: 8
5 Primary; 1 Middle; 1 High; 1 Other Level
7 Regular; 0 Special Education; 0 Vocational; 1 Alternative
0 Magnet; 0 Charter; 5 Title I Eligible; 0 School-wide Title I
Students: 5,034 (52.4% male; 47.6% female)
Individual Education Program: 620 (12.3%);
English Language Learner: 49 (1.0%); Migrant: n/a
Eligible for Free Lunch Program: 79 (1.6%)
Eligible for Reduced-Price Lunch Program: 75 (1.5%)
Teachers: 340.4 (14.8 to 1)
Librarians/Media Specialists: 9.2 (547.2 to 1)
Guidance Counselors: 13.1 (384.3 to 1)
Current Spending: ($ per student per year):
Total: $9,263; Instruction: $5,642; Support Services: $3,499
Enrollment, Drop-out Rates and Diploma Recipients by Race/Ethnicity

Category	Total	White	Black	Asian	AIAN	Hisp.
Enrollment (%)	100.0	94.2	1.8	2.7	0.2	1.2
Drop-out Rate (%)	0.8	0.7	0.0	2.8	n/a	0.0
H.S. Diplomas (#)	357	335	6	11	0	5

Cohoes City SD

7 Bevan St • Cohoes, NY 12047-3299
(518) 237-0100 • http://cohoes.neric.org/
Grade Span: KG-12; **Agency Type:** 1
Schools: 6
3 Primary; 1 Middle; 1 High; 1 Other Level
5 Regular; 0 Special Education; 0 Vocational; 1 Alternative
0 Magnet; 0 Charter; 4 Title I Eligible; 0 School-wide Title I
Students: 2,117 (51.1% male; 48.9% female)
Individual Education Program: 345 (16.3%);
English Language Learner: 65 (3.1%); Migrant: n/a
Eligible for Free Lunch Program: 876 (41.4%)
Eligible for Reduced-Price Lunch Program: 270 (12.8%)
Teachers: 181.0 (11.7 to 1)
Librarians/Media Specialists: 3.0 (705.7 to 1)
Guidance Counselors: 4.0 (529.3 to 1)
Current Spending: ($ per student per year):
Total: $10,740; Instruction: $6,730; Support Services: $3,609
Enrollment, Drop-out Rates and Diploma Recipients by Race/Ethnicity

Category	Total	White	Black	Asian	AIAN	Hisp.
Enrollment (%)	100.0	91.5	6.1	0.7	0.1	1.6
Drop-out Rate (%)	3.9	3.8	9.1	0.0	n/a	0.0
H.S. Diplomas (#)	107	107	0	0	0	0

Guilderland CSD

6076 State Farm Rd • Guilderland, NY 12084-9533
(518) 456-6200 • http://www.gcsd.k12.ny.us/gcsddo/
Grade Span: KG-12; **Agency Type:** 1
Schools: 7
5 Primary; 1 Middle; 1 High; 0 Other Level
7 Regular; 0 Special Education; 0 Vocational; 0 Alternative
0 Magnet; 0 Charter; 5 Title I Eligible; 0 School-wide Title I
Students: 5,667 (51.0% male; 49.0% female)
Individual Education Program: 721 (12.7%);
English Language Learner: 98 (1.7%); Migrant: n/a
Eligible for Free Lunch Program: 174 (3.1%)
Eligible for Reduced-Price Lunch Program: 95 (1.7%)
Teachers: 422.9 (13.4 to 1)
Librarians/Media Specialists: 8.8 (644.0 to 1)
Guidance Counselors: 11.0 (515.2 to 1)
Current Spending: ($ per student per year):
Total: $9,617; Instruction: $6,228; Support Services: $3,197
Enrollment, Drop-out Rates and Diploma Recipients by Race/Ethnicity

Category	Total	White	Black	Asian	AIAN	Hisp.
Enrollment (%)	100.0	91.7	3.2	3.8	0.1	1.2
Drop-out Rate (%)	2.0	1.8	3.5	2.9	0.0	6.7
H.S. Diplomas (#)	374	345	10	4	8	7

North Colonie CSD

91 Fiddler's Ln • Latham, NY 12110-5349
(518) 785-8591
Grade Span: KG-12; **Agency Type:** 1
Schools: 8
6 Primary; 1 Middle; 1 High; 0 Other Level
8 Regular; 0 Special Education; 0 Vocational; 0 Alternative
0 Magnet; 0 Charter; 6 Title I Eligible; 0 School-wide Title I
Students: 5,619 (51.0% male; 49.0% female)
Individual Education Program: 615 (10.9%);
English Language Learner: 98 (1.7%); Migrant: n/a
Eligible for Free Lunch Program: 303 (5.4%)
Eligible for Reduced-Price Lunch Program: 184 (3.3%)
Teachers: 382.9 (14.7 to 1)
Librarians/Media Specialists: 10.2 (550.9 to 1)
Guidance Counselors: 15.2 (369.7 to 1)
Current Spending: ($ per student per year):
Total: $8,767; Instruction: $5,459; Support Services: $3,082
Enrollment, Drop-out Rates and Diploma Recipients by Race/Ethnicity

Category	Total	White	Black	Asian	AIAN	Hisp.
Enrollment (%)	100.0	87.6	4.0	6.6	0.1	1.7
Drop-out Rate (%)	1.0	1.1	0.0	0.0	n/a	3.2
H.S. Diplomas (#)	454	410	8	33	0	3

Ravena-Coeymans-Selkirk CSD

26 Thatcher St • Selkirk, NY 12158-0097
(518) 756-5201 • http://www.rcscsd.org/default_40.asp
Grade Span: PK-12; **Agency Type:** 1
Schools: 4
2 Primary; 1 Middle; 1 High; 0 Other Level
4 Regular; 0 Special Education; 0 Vocational; 0 Alternative
0 Magnet; 0 Charter; 4 Title I Eligible; 0 School-wide Title I
Students: 2,376 (50.9% male; 49.1% female)
Individual Education Program: 449 (18.9%);
English Language Learner: 19 (0.8%); Migrant: n/a
Eligible for Free Lunch Program: 375 (15.8%)
Eligible for Reduced-Price Lunch Program: 146 (6.1%)
Teachers: 188.8 (12.6 to 1)
Librarians/Media Specialists: 2.5 (950.4 to 1)
Guidance Counselors: 6.0 (396.0 to 1)
Current Spending: ($ per student per year):
Total: $11,583; Instruction: $7,549; Support Services: $3,787
Enrollment, Drop-out Rates and Diploma Recipients by Race/Ethnicity

Category	Total	White	Black	Asian	AIAN	Hisp.
Enrollment (%)	100.0	91.5	4.7	0.7	0.1	3.0
Drop-out Rate (%)	3.6	3.6	4.0	0.0	0.0	4.3
H.S. Diplomas (#)	167	156	2	2	0	7

South Colonie CSD

102 Loralee Dr • Albany, NY 12205-2298
(518) 869-3576 • http://family.knick.net/scolonie/
Grade Span: PK-12; **Agency Type:** 1
Schools: 10
5 Primary; 2 Middle; 1 High; 2 Other Level
8 Regular; 0 Special Education; 0 Vocational; 2 Alternative
0 Magnet; 0 Charter; 6 Title I Eligible; 0 School-wide Title I
Students: 5,788 (51.4% male; 48.6% female)
Individual Education Program: 668 (11.5%);
English Language Learner: 39 (0.7%); Migrant: n/a
Eligible for Free Lunch Program: 456 (7.9%)
Eligible for Reduced-Price Lunch Program: 246 (4.3%)
Teachers: 447.1 (12.9 to 1)
Librarians/Media Specialists: 8.2 (705.9 to 1)
Guidance Counselors: 11.6 (499.0 to 1)
Current Spending: ($ per student per year):
Total: $9,622; Instruction: $6,447; Support Services: $2,933
Enrollment, Drop-out Rates and Diploma Recipients by Race/Ethnicity

Category	Total	White	Black	Asian	AIAN	Hisp.
Enrollment (%)	100.0	88.6	5.7	3.6	0.5	1.6
Drop-out Rate (%)	2.7	2.4	6.8	0.0	9.1	8.3
H.S. Diplomas (#)	389	351	18	17	2	1

Broome County

Binghamton City SD

164 Hawley St • Binghamton, NY 13901-2126
(607) 762-8100 • http://www.bcsd.stier.org/welcome.html
Grade Span: PK-12; **Agency Type:** 1
Schools: 12
7 Primary; 2 Middle; 0 High; 3 Other Level
10 Regular; 0 Special Education; 0 Vocational; 2 Alternative
0 Magnet; 0 Charter; 10 Title I Eligible; 0 School-wide Title I
Students: 6,432 (49.9% male; 50.1% female)
Individual Education Program: 1,091 (17.0%);
English Language Learner: 316 (4.9%); Migrant: n/a
Eligible for Free Lunch Program: 2,971 (46.2%)
Eligible for Reduced-Price Lunch Program: 651 (10.1%)
Teachers: 547.8 (11.7 to 1)
Librarians/Media Specialists: 10.3 (624.5 to 1)
Guidance Counselors: 14.0 (459.4 to 1)
Current Spending: ($ per student per year):
Total: $9,964; Instruction: $6,759; Support Services: $2,809
Enrollment, Drop-out Rates and Diploma Recipients by Race/Ethnicity

Category	Total	White	Black	Asian	AIAN	Hisp.
Enrollment (%)	100.0	70.2	20.0	3.6	0.1	6.1
Drop-out Rate (%)	2.6	2.2	4.0	1.6	0.0	6.7
H.S. Diplomas (#)	253	214	26	9	0	4

Chenango Forks CSD

One Gordon Dr • Binghamton, NY 13901-5614
(607) 648-7543
Grade Span: PK-12; **Agency Type:** 1
Schools: 4
2 Primary; 1 Middle; 1 High; 0 Other Level
4 Regular; 0 Special Education; 0 Vocational; 0 Alternative
0 Magnet; 0 Charter; 2 Title I Eligible; 0 School-wide Title I
Students: 1,901 (51.8% male; 48.2% female)
Individual Education Program: 213 (11.2%);
English Language Learner: 4 (0.2%); Migrant: n/a
Eligible for Free Lunch Program: 331 (17.4%)
Eligible for Reduced-Price Lunch Program: 226 (11.9%)
Teachers: 139.0 (13.7 to 1)
Librarians/Media Specialists: 3.6 (528.1 to 1)
Guidance Counselors: 4.0 (475.3 to 1)
Current Spending: ($ per student per year):
Total: $9,553; Instruction: $6,086; Support Services: $3,201
Enrollment, Drop-out Rates and Diploma Recipients by Race/Ethnicity

Category	Total	White	Black	Asian	AIAN	Hisp.
Enrollment (%)	100.0	97.7	0.8	0.3	0.3	0.9
Drop-out Rate (%)	3.0	2.9	0.0	0.0	n/a	100.0
H.S. Diplomas (#)	128	128	0	0	0	0

Chenango Valley CSD

1160 Chenango St • Binghamton, NY 13901-1653
(607) 779-4710 • http://www.cvcsd.stier.org/
Grade Span: PK-12; **Agency Type:** 1
Schools: 4
1 Primary; 2 Middle; 1 High; 0 Other Level
4 Regular; 0 Special Education; 0 Vocational; 0 Alternative
0 Magnet; 0 Charter; 1 Title I Eligible; 0 School-wide Title I
Students: 2,009 (51.8% male; 48.2% female)
Individual Education Program: 318 (15.8%);
English Language Learner: 7 (0.3%); Migrant: n/a
Eligible for Free Lunch Program: 362 (18.0%)
Eligible for Reduced-Price Lunch Program: 178 (8.9%)
Teachers: 149.2 (13.5 to 1)
Librarians/Media Specialists: 2.9 (692.8 to 1)
Guidance Counselors: 4.0 (502.3 to 1)
Current Spending: ($ per student per year):
Total: $9,613; Instruction: $6,394; Support Services: $2,980
Enrollment, Drop-out Rates and Diploma Recipients by Race/Ethnicity

Category	Total	White	Black	Asian	AIAN	Hisp.
Enrollment (%)	100.0	96.1	2.2	0.6	0.1	1.0
Drop-out Rate (%)	1.2	1.2	0.0	0.0	n/a	0.0
H.S. Diplomas (#)	130	129	1	0	0	0

Johnson City CSD

666 Reynolds Rd • Johnson City, NY 13790-1398
(607) 763-1230 • http://www.tier.net/jcschools/
Grade Span: KG-12; **Agency Type:** 1
Schools: 5
2 Primary; 1 Middle; 1 High; 1 Other Level
4 Regular; 0 Special Education; 0 Vocational; 1 Alternative
0 Magnet; 0 Charter; 3 Title I Eligible; 0 School-wide Title I
Students: 2,556 (50.5% male; 49.5% female)
Individual Education Program: 441 (17.3%);
English Language Learner: 96 (3.8%); Migrant: n/a
Eligible for Free Lunch Program: 691 (27.0%)
Eligible for Reduced-Price Lunch Program: 203 (7.9%)
Teachers: 213.3 (12.0 to 1)
Librarians/Media Specialists: 3.5 (730.3 to 1)
Guidance Counselors: 8.0 (319.5 to 1)
Current Spending: ($ per student per year):
Total: $11,393; Instruction: $7,624; Support Services: $3,444
Enrollment, Drop-out Rates and Diploma Recipients by Race/Ethnicity

Category	Total	White	Black	Asian	AIAN	Hisp.
Enrollment (%)	100.0	82.7	7.2	6.4	0.8	2.9
Drop-out Rate (%)	3.4	2.9	9.1	3.6	0.0	9.1
H.S. Diplomas (#)	156	144	4	6	0	2

Maine-Endwell CSD

712 Farm-To-Market Rd • Endwell, NY 13760-1199
(607) 754-1400
Grade Span: KG-12; **Agency Type:** 1
Schools: 4
2 Primary; 1 Middle; 1 High; 0 Other Level
4 Regular; 0 Special Education; 0 Vocational; 0 Alternative
0 Magnet; 0 Charter; 3 Title I Eligible; 0 School-wide Title I
Students: 2,694 (50.5% male; 49.5% female)
Individual Education Program: 440 (16.3%);
English Language Learner: 5 (0.2%); Migrant: n/a
Eligible for Free Lunch Program: 313 (11.6%)
Eligible for Reduced-Price Lunch Program: 174 (6.5%)
Teachers: 211.1 (12.8 to 1)
Librarians/Media Specialists: 3.8 (708.9 to 1)
Guidance Counselors: 5.0 (538.8 to 1)
Current Spending: ($ per student per year):
Total: $9,622; Instruction: $6,168; Support Services: $3,233
Enrollment, Drop-out Rates and Diploma Recipients by Race/Ethnicity

Category	Total	White	Black	Asian	AIAN	Hisp.
Enrollment (%)	100.0	96.2	1.7	1.5	0.0	0.6
Drop-out Rate (%)	1.3	1.3	0.0	4.0	n/a	0.0
H.S. Diplomas (#)	139	134	0	4	0	1

Susquehanna Valley CSD

1040 Conklin Rd • Conklin, NY 13748-0200
(607) 775-9100 • http://www.sv.stier.org/
Grade Span: KG-12; **Agency Type:** 1
Schools: 5
3 Primary; 1 Middle; 1 High; 0 Other Level
5 Regular; 0 Special Education; 0 Vocational; 0 Alternative
0 Magnet; 0 Charter; 3 Title I Eligible; 0 School-wide Title I
Students: 2,159 (51.3% male; 48.7% female)
Individual Education Program: 305 (14.1%);
English Language Learner: 7 (0.3%); Migrant: n/a
Eligible for Free Lunch Program: 387 (17.9%)
Eligible for Reduced-Price Lunch Program: 154 (7.1%)
Teachers: 186.3 (11.6 to 1)
Librarians/Media Specialists: 3.0 (719.7 to 1)
Guidance Counselors: 5.0 (431.8 to 1)
Current Spending: ($ per student per year):
Total: $9,566; Instruction: $6,147; Support Services: $3,144
Enrollment, Drop-out Rates and Diploma Recipients by Race/Ethnicity

Category	Total	White	Black	Asian	AIAN	Hisp.
Enrollment (%)	100.0	96.2	2.1	0.6	0.1	0.8
Drop-out Rate (%)	0.6	0.7	0.0	0.0	0.0	0.0
H.S. Diplomas (#)	141	139	1	0	0	1

Union-Endicott CSD

1100 E Main St • Endicott, NY 13760-5271
(607) 757-2112 • http://www.uetigers.stier.org/
Grade Span: KG-12; **Agency Type:** 1
Schools: 7
4 Primary; 2 Middle; 1 High; 0 Other Level
7 Regular; 0 Special Education; 0 Vocational; 0 Alternative
0 Magnet; 0 Charter; 4 Title I Eligible; 0 School-wide Title I
Students: 4,563 (51.9% male; 48.1% female)
Individual Education Program: 696 (15.3%);
English Language Learner: 34 (0.7%); Migrant: n/a
Eligible for Free Lunch Program: 833 (18.3%)
Eligible for Reduced-Price Lunch Program: 336 (7.4%)
Teachers: 349.9 (13.0 to 1)
Librarians/Media Specialists: 5.6 (814.8 to 1)
Guidance Counselors: 8.0 (570.4 to 1)
Current Spending: ($ per student per year):
Total: $9,720; Instruction: $6,218; Support Services: $3,265
Enrollment, Drop-out Rates and Diploma Recipients by Race/Ethnicity

Category	Total	White	Black	Asian	AIAN	Hisp.
Enrollment (%)	100.0	90.2	5.6	2.4	0.2	1.6
Drop-out Rate (%)	2.6	2.4	3.8	0.0	0.0	42.9
H.S. Diplomas (#)	279	260	10	8	1	0

Vestal CSD

201 Main St • Vestal, NY 13850-1599
(607) 757-2241 • http://www.vestal.stier.org/
Grade Span: KG-12; **Agency Type:** 1
Schools: 7
5 Primary; 1 Middle; 1 High; 0 Other Level
7 Regular; 0 Special Education; 0 Vocational; 0 Alternative
0 Magnet; 0 Charter; 6 Title I Eligible; 0 School-wide Title I
Students: 4,372 (52.9% male; 47.1% female)
Individual Education Program: 494 (11.3%);
English Language Learner: 44 (1.0%); Migrant: n/a
Eligible for Free Lunch Program: 230 (5.3%)
Eligible for Reduced-Price Lunch Program: 152 (3.5%)
Teachers: 336.9 (13.0 to 1)
Librarians/Media Specialists: 7.0 (624.6 to 1)
Guidance Counselors: 12.9 (338.9 to 1)
Current Spending: ($ per student per year):
Total: $8,934; Instruction: $5,883; Support Services: $2,907
Enrollment, Drop-out Rates and Diploma Recipients by Race/Ethnicity

Category	Total	White	Black	Asian	AIAN	Hisp.
Enrollment (%)	100.0	90.7	2.8	5.1	0.3	1.0
Drop-out Rate (%)	0.8	0.9	0.0	0.0	n/a	0.0
H.S. Diplomas (#)	296	267	7	15	1	6

Whitney Point CSD

10 Keibel Rd • Whitney Point, NY 13862-0249
(607) 692-8202 • http://www.tier.net/whitneypoint/
Grade Span: PK-12; **Agency Type:** 1
Schools: 4
2 Primary; 1 Middle; 1 High; 0 Other Level
4 Regular; 0 Special Education; 0 Vocational; 0 Alternative
0 Magnet; 0 Charter; 2 Title I Eligible; 0 School-wide Title I
Students: 1,933 (49.9% male; 50.1% female)
Individual Education Program: 273 (14.1%);
English Language Learner: 2 (0.1%); Migrant: n/a
Eligible for Free Lunch Program: 460 (23.8%)
Eligible for Reduced-Price Lunch Program: 298 (15.4%)
Teachers: 161.6 (12.0 to 1)
Librarians/Media Specialists: 3.0 (644.3 to 1)
Guidance Counselors: 7.0 (276.1 to 1)
Current Spending: ($ per student per year):
Total: $8,617; Instruction: $5,989; Support Services: $2,357
Enrollment, Drop-out Rates and Diploma Recipients by Race/Ethnicity

Category	Total	White	Black	Asian	AIAN	Hisp.
Enrollment (%)	100.0	98.4	1.1	0.3	0.0	0.2
Drop-out Rate (%)	5.2	5.0	50.0	n/a	0.0	0.0
H.S. Diplomas (#)	98	97	0	1	0	0

Windsor CSD

215 Main St • Windsor, NY 13865-4134
(607) 655-8216 • http://www.windsor-csd.org/
Grade Span: KG-12; **Agency Type:** 1
Schools: 4
3 Primary; 0 Middle; 1 High; 0 Other Level
4 Regular; 0 Special Education; 0 Vocational; 0 Alternative
0 Magnet; 0 Charter; 3 Title I Eligible; 0 School-wide Title I
Students: 2,060 (49.7% male; 50.3% female)
Individual Education Program: 267 (13.0%);
English Language Learner: 3 (0.1%); Migrant: n/a
Eligible for Free Lunch Program: 386 (18.7%)
Eligible for Reduced-Price Lunch Program: 144 (7.0%)
Teachers: 159.2 (12.9 to 1)
Librarians/Media Specialists: 3.8 (542.1 to 1)
Guidance Counselors: 7.0 (294.3 to 1)
Current Spending: ($ per student per year):
Total: $8,835; Instruction: $5,832; Support Services: $2,722
Enrollment, Drop-out Rates and Diploma Recipients by Race/Ethnicity

Category	Total	White	Black	Asian	AIAN	Hisp.
Enrollment (%)	100.0	98.0	1.0	0.8	0.0	0.2
Drop-out Rate (%)	2.9	2.9	0.0	0.0	n/a	0.0
H.S. Diplomas (#)	111	108	0	3	0	0

Cattaraugus County

Gowanda CSD

10674 Prospect St • Gowanda, NY 14070-1384
(716) 532-3325
Grade Span: KG-12; **Agency Type:** 1
Schools: 5
1 Primary; 1 Middle; 1 High; 2 Other Level
3 Regular; 0 Special Education; 0 Vocational; 2 Alternative
0 Magnet; 0 Charter; 3 Title I Eligible; 0 School-wide Title I
Students: 1,513 (52.5% male; 47.5% female)
Individual Education Program: 228 (15.1%);
English Language Learner: 1 (0.1%); Migrant: n/a
Eligible for Free Lunch Program: 582 (38.5%)
Eligible for Reduced-Price Lunch Program: 197 (13.0%)
Teachers: 120.9 (12.5 to 1)
Librarians/Media Specialists: 3.0 (504.3 to 1)
Guidance Counselors: 5.0 (302.6 to 1)
Current Spending: ($ per student per year):
Total: $14,817; Instruction: $9,817; Support Services: $4,486
Enrollment, Drop-out Rates and Diploma Recipients by Race/Ethnicity

Category	Total	White	Black	Asian	AIAN	Hisp.
Enrollment (%)	100.0	70.8	1.6	0.5	26.3	0.9
Drop-out Rate (%)	3.8	2.0	0.0	0.0	10.0	0.0
H.S. Diplomas (#)	105	79	0	0	26	0

Olean City SD

410 W Sullivan St • Olean, NY 14760-2596
(716) 375-8018 • http://www.oleanschools.org/
Grade Span: PK-12; **Agency Type:** 1
Schools: 8
5 Primary; 1 Middle; 1 High; 1 Other Level
7 Regular; 0 Special Education; 0 Vocational; 1 Alternative
0 Magnet; 0 Charter; 5 Title I Eligible; 0 School-wide Title I
Students: 2,640 (49.2% male; 50.8% female)
Individual Education Program: 387 (14.7%);
English Language Learner: 3 (0.1%); Migrant: n/a
Eligible for Free Lunch Program: 743 (28.1%)
Eligible for Reduced-Price Lunch Program: 266 (10.1%)
Teachers: 197.1 (13.4 to 1)
Librarians/Media Specialists: 4.0 (660.0 to 1)
Guidance Counselors: 10.0 (264.0 to 1)
Current Spending: ($ per student per year):
Total: $8,932; Instruction: $6,222; Support Services: $2,434
Enrollment, Drop-out Rates and Diploma Recipients by Race/Ethnicity

Category	Total	White	Black	Asian	AIAN	Hisp.
Enrollment (%)	100.0	89.5	7.1	1.4	0.5	1.5
Drop-out Rate (%)	3.0	2.5	12.5	0.0	0.0	0.0
H.S. Diplomas (#)	141	134	3	3	0	1

Salamanca City SD

50 Iroquois Dr • Salamanca, NY 14779-1398
(716) 945-2403 •
http://rin.buffalo.edu/c_catt/educ/scho_publ/scho_sala.html
Grade Span: PK-12; **Agency Type:** 1
Schools: 5
2 Primary; 1 Middle; 1 High; 1 Other Level
4 Regular; 0 Special Education; 0 Vocational; 1 Alternative
0 Magnet; 0 Charter; 3 Title I Eligible; 0 School-wide Title I
Students: 1,586 (51.4% male; 48.6% female)
Individual Education Program: 209 (13.2%);
English Language Learner: 20 (1.3%); Migrant: n/a
Eligible for Free Lunch Program: 557 (35.1%)
Eligible for Reduced-Price Lunch Program: 157 (9.9%)
Teachers: 127.9 (12.4 to 1)
Librarians/Media Specialists: 2.9 (546.9 to 1)
Guidance Counselors: 8.0 (198.3 to 1)
Current Spending: ($ per student per year):
Total: $10,611; Instruction: $6,955; Support Services: $3,336
Enrollment, Drop-out Rates and Diploma Recipients by Race/Ethnicity

Category	Total	White	Black	Asian	AIAN	Hisp.
Enrollment (%)	100.0	67.0	1.3	0.1	29.8	1.8
Drop-out Rate (%)	4.3	4.1	0.0	0.0	6.1	0.0
H.S. Diplomas (#)	71	58	0	1	10	2

Yorkshire-Pioneer CSD

County Line Rd • Yorkshire, NY 14173-0579
(716) 492-9304
Grade Span: KG-12; **Agency Type:** 1
Schools: 4
2 Primary; 1 Middle; 1 High; 0 Other Level
4 Regular; 0 Special Education; 0 Vocational; 0 Alternative
0 Magnet; 0 Charter; 3 Title I Eligible; 0 School-wide Title I
Students: 3,029 (51.4% male; 48.6% female)
Individual Education Program: 565 (18.7%);
English Language Learner: 0 (0.0%); Migrant: n/a
Eligible for Free Lunch Program: 808 (26.7%)
Eligible for Reduced-Price Lunch Program: 480 (15.8%)
Teachers: 232.5 (13.0 to 1)
Librarians/Media Specialists: 2.8 (1,081.8 to 1)
Guidance Counselors: 7.0 (432.7 to 1)
Current Spending: ($ per student per year):
Total: $10,341; Instruction: $6,596; Support Services: $3,443
Enrollment, Drop-out Rates and Diploma Recipients by Race/Ethnicity

Category	Total	White	Black	Asian	AIAN	Hisp.
Enrollment (%)	100.0	97.7	0.5	0.5	0.8	0.4
Drop-out Rate (%)	4.3	4.3	0.0	0.0	16.7	0.0
H.S. Diplomas (#)	214	212	0	1	1	0

Cayuga County

Auburn City SD

78 Thornton Ave • Auburn, NY 13021-4698
(315) 255-8835 • http://www.auburn.cnyric.org/
Grade Span: KG-12; **Agency Type:** 1
Schools: 12
5 Primary; 3 Middle; 1 High; 3 Other Level
8 Regular; 0 Special Education; 0 Vocational; 4 Alternative
0 Magnet; 0 Charter; 5 Title I Eligible; 0 School-wide Title I
Students: 4,930 (51.6% male; 48.4% female)
Individual Education Program: 657 (13.3%);
English Language Learner: 8 (0.2%); Migrant: n/a
Eligible for Free Lunch Program: 1,251 (25.4%)
Eligible for Reduced-Price Lunch Program: 305 (6.2%)
Teachers: 366.7 (13.4 to 1)
Librarians/Media Specialists: 3.9 (1,264.1 to 1)
Guidance Counselors: 8.0 (616.3 to 1)
Current Spending: ($ per student per year):
Total: $8,901; Instruction: $6,252; Support Services: $2,426
Enrollment, Drop-out Rates and Diploma Recipients by Race/Ethnicity

Category	Total	White	Black	Asian	AIAN	Hisp.
Enrollment (%)	100.0	87.8	9.2	0.8	0.7	1.5
Drop-out Rate (%)	2.2	2.0	6.0	0.0	0.0	0.0
H.S. Diplomas (#)	278	264	12	2	0	0

Chautauqua County

Dunkirk City SD

620 Marauder Dr • Dunkirk, NY 14048-1396
(716) 366-9300
Grade Span: KG-12; **Agency Type:** 1
Schools: 6
4 Primary; 1 Middle; 1 High; 0 Other Level
6 Regular; 0 Special Education; 0 Vocational; 0 Alternative
0 Magnet; 0 Charter; 5 Title I Eligible; 0 School-wide Title I
Students: 2,113 (51.3% male; 48.7% female)
Individual Education Program: 296 (14.0%);
English Language Learner: 246 (11.6%); Migrant: n/a
Eligible for Free Lunch Program: 866 (41.0%)
Eligible for Reduced-Price Lunch Program: 148 (7.0%)
Teachers: 210.4 (10.0 to 1)
Librarians/Media Specialists: 3.0 (704.3 to 1)
Guidance Counselors: 7.0 (301.9 to 1)
Current Spending: ($ per student per year):
Total: $12,463; Instruction: $8,820; Support Services: $3,342
Enrollment, Drop-out Rates and Diploma Recipients by Race/Ethnicity

Category	Total	White	Black	Asian	AIAN	Hisp.
Enrollment (%)	100.0	56.6	9.3	0.5	0.6	32.9
Drop-out Rate (%)	3.2	1.8	5.7	n/a	0.0	7.2
H.S. Diplomas (#)	110	92	6	0	0	12

Fredonia CSD

425 E Main St • Fredonia, NY 14063-1496
(716) 679-1581 • http://www.fredonia.wnyric.org/
Grade Span: PK-12; **Agency Type:** 1
Schools: 4
2 Primary; 1 Middle; 1 High; 0 Other Level
4 Regular; 0 Special Education; 0 Vocational; 0 Alternative
0 Magnet; 0 Charter; 3 Title I Eligible; 0 School-wide Title I
Students: 1,925 (50.5% male; 49.5% female)
Individual Education Program: 231 (12.0%);
English Language Learner: 42 (2.2%); Migrant: n/a
Eligible for Free Lunch Program: 263 (13.7%)
Eligible for Reduced-Price Lunch Program: 139 (7.2%)
Teachers: 172.1 (11.2 to 1)
Librarians/Media Specialists: 1.5 (1,283.3 to 1)
Guidance Counselors: 5.0 (385.0 to 1)
Current Spending: ($ per student per year):
Total: $9,255; Instruction: $6,189; Support Services: $2,802
Enrollment, Drop-out Rates and Diploma Recipients by Race/Ethnicity

Category	Total	White	Black	Asian	AIAN	Hisp.
Enrollment (%)	100.0	93.9	1.3	1.7	0.2	3.0
Drop-out Rate (%)	0.8	0.8	0.0	0.0	n/a	0.0
H.S. Diplomas (#)	152	146	2	2	0	2

Jamestown City SD

201 E Fourth St • Jamestown, NY 14701-5397
(716) 483-4420 • http://www.jamestown.wnyric.org/
Grade Span: PK-12; **Agency Type:** 1
Schools: 11
6 Primary; 3 Middle; 1 High; 1 Other Level
10 Regular; 0 Special Education; 0 Vocational; 1 Alternative
0 Magnet; 0 Charter; 9 Title I Eligible; 0 School-wide Title I
Students: 5,225 (50.8% male; 49.2% female)
Individual Education Program: 841 (16.1%);
English Language Learner: 103 (2.0%); Migrant: n/a
Eligible for Free Lunch Program: 2,151 (41.2%)
Eligible for Reduced-Price Lunch Program: 492 (9.4%)
Teachers: 481.6 (10.8 to 1)
Librarians/Media Specialists: 11.6 (450.4 to 1)
Guidance Counselors: 19.4 (269.3 to 1)
Current Spending: ($ per student per year):
Total: $9,919; Instruction: $7,079; Support Services: $2,449
Enrollment, Drop-out Rates and Diploma Recipients by Race/Ethnicity

Category	Total	White	Black	Asian	AIAN	Hisp.
Enrollment (%)	100.0	82.6	6.9	0.8	1.0	8.7
Drop-out Rate (%)	6.0	5.8	9.8	20.0	0.0	6.2
H.S. Diplomas (#)	278	256	5	4	0	13

Southwestern CSD at Jamestown

600 Hunt Rd • Jamestown, NY 14701-5799
(716) 484-1136 • http://swcs.wnyric.org/
Grade Span: KG-12; **Agency Type:** 1
Schools: 3
1 Primary; 1 Middle; 1 High; 0 Other Level
3 Regular; 0 Special Education; 0 Vocational; 0 Alternative
0 Magnet; 0 Charter; 1 Title I Eligible; 0 School-wide Title I
Students: 1,738 (52.6% male; 47.4% female)
Individual Education Program: 141 (8.1%);
English Language Learner: 1 (0.1%); Migrant: n/a
Eligible for Free Lunch Program: 174 (10.0%)
Eligible for Reduced-Price Lunch Program: 87 (5.0%)
Teachers: 133.3 (13.0 to 1)
Librarians/Media Specialists: 3.6 (482.8 to 1)
Guidance Counselors: 4.0 (434.5 to 1)
Current Spending: ($ per student per year):
Total: $9,043; Instruction: $6,097; Support Services: $2,736
Enrollment, Drop-out Rates and Diploma Recipients by Race/Ethnicity

Category	Total	White	Black	Asian	AIAN	Hisp.
Enrollment (%)	100.0	96.7	0.7	1.6	0.3	0.7
Drop-out Rate (%)	2.0	2.0	0.0	0.0	n/a	0.0
H.S. Diplomas (#)	132	130	0	1	0	1

Chemung County

Elmira City SD

951 Hoffman St • Elmira, NY 14905-1715
(607) 735-3010 • http://www.elmiracityschools.com/index800.html
Grade Span: PK-12; **Agency Type:** 1
Schools: 17
9 Primary; 2 Middle; 2 High; 4 Other Level
13 Regular; 0 Special Education; 0 Vocational; 4 Alternative
0 Magnet; 0 Charter; 11 Title I Eligible; 0 School-wide Title I
Students: 7,539 (52.1% male; 47.9% female)
Individual Education Program: 1,253 (16.6%);
English Language Learner: 25 (0.3%); Migrant: n/a
Eligible for Free Lunch Program: 2,803 (37.2%)
Eligible for Reduced-Price Lunch Program: 781 (10.4%)
Teachers: 576.2 (13.1 to 1)
Librarians/Media Specialists: 12.1 (623.1 to 1)
Guidance Counselors: 18.0 (418.8 to 1)
Current Spending: ($ per student per year):
Total: $10,243; Instruction: $6,726; Support Services: $3,242
Enrollment, Drop-out Rates and Diploma Recipients by Race/Ethnicity

Category	Total	White	Black	Asian	AIAN	Hisp.
Enrollment (%)	100.0	81.9	15.1	0.7	0.2	2.0
Drop-out Rate (%)	8.5	8.5	9.5	0.0	0.0	3.7
H.S. Diplomas (#)	324	301	18	2	0	3

Horseheads CSD

One Raider Ln • Horseheads, NY 14845-2398
(607) 739-5601 • http://www.horseheadsdistrict.com/
Grade Span: KG-12; **Agency Type:** 1
Schools: 7
5 Primary; 1 Middle; 1 High; 0 Other Level
7 Regular; 0 Special Education; 0 Vocational; 0 Alternative
0 Magnet; 0 Charter; 4 Title I Eligible; 0 School-wide Title I
Students: 4,462 (50.2% male; 49.8% female)
Individual Education Program: 596 (13.4%);
English Language Learner: 8 (0.2%); Migrant: n/a
Eligible for Free Lunch Program: 553 (12.4%)
Eligible for Reduced-Price Lunch Program: 223 (5.0%)
Teachers: 307.8 (14.5 to 1)
Librarians/Media Specialists: 7.4 (603.0 to 1)
Guidance Counselors: 9.0 (495.8 to 1)
Current Spending: ($ per student per year):
Total: $9,276; Instruction: $5,730; Support Services: $3,291

Enrollment, Drop-out Rates and Diploma Recipients by Race/Ethnicity

Category	Total	White	Black	Asian	AIAN	Hisp.
Enrollment (%)	100.0	95.0	2.2	2.2	0.1	0.5
Drop-out Rate (%)	3.7	3.7	6.7	0.0	0.0	8.3
H.S. Diplomas (#)	320	306	2	9	0	3

Chenango County

Norwich City SD

19 Eaton Ave • Norwich, NY 13815-9964
(607) 334-1600 • http://www.ncs.stier.org/
Grade Span: PK-12; **Agency Type:** 1
Schools: 6
1 Primary; 2 Middle; 1 High; 2 Other Level
4 Regular; 0 Special Education; 0 Vocational; 2 Alternative
0 Magnet; 0 Charter; 2 Title I Eligible; 0 School-wide Title I
Students: 2,286 (49.9% male; 50.1% female)
Individual Education Program: 401 (17.5%);
English Language Learner: 1 (<0.1%); Migrant: n/a
Eligible for Free Lunch Program: 605 (26.5%)
Eligible for Reduced-Price Lunch Program: 187 (8.2%)
Teachers: 196.1 (11.7 to 1)
Librarians/Media Specialists: 3.7 (617.8 to 1)
Guidance Counselors: 8.9 (256.9 to 1)
Current Spending: ($ per student per year):
Total: $10,158; Instruction: $6,381; Support Services: $3,465
Enrollment, Drop-out Rates and Diploma Recipients by Race/Ethnicity

Category	Total	White	Black	Asian	AIAN	Hisp.
Enrollment (%)	100.0	96.3	1.7	0.7	0.2	1.2
Drop-out Rate (%)	3.4	3.4	5.3	0.0	0.0	0.0
H.S. Diplomas (#)	133	129	1	3	0	0

Sherburne-Earlville CSD

15 School St • Sherburne, NY 13460-0725
(607) 674-7300
Grade Span: KG-12; **Agency Type:** 2
Schools: 3
1 Primary; 1 Middle; 1 High; 0 Other Level
3 Regular; 0 Special Education; 0 Vocational; 0 Alternative
0 Magnet; 0 Charter; 2 Title I Eligible; 0 School-wide Title I
Students: 1,787 (50.0% male; 50.0% female)
Individual Education Program: 329 (18.4%);
English Language Learner: 1 (0.1%); Migrant: n/a
Eligible for Free Lunch Program: 502 (28.1%)
Eligible for Reduced-Price Lunch Program: 205 (11.5%)
Teachers: 165.5 (10.8 to 1)
Librarians/Media Specialists: 2.6 (687.3 to 1)
Guidance Counselors: 5.0 (357.4 to 1)
Current Spending: ($ per student per year):
Total: $9,476; Instruction: $5,886; Support Services: $3,240
Enrollment, Drop-out Rates and Diploma Recipients by Race/Ethnicity

Category	Total	White	Black	Asian	AIAN	Hisp.
Enrollment (%)	100.0	98.7	0.8	0.3	0.0	0.1
Drop-out Rate (%)	4.4	4.4	0.0	0.0	n/a	0.0
H.S. Diplomas (#)	100	100	0	0	0	0

Clinton County

Beekmantown CSD

6944 Rt 22 • Plattsburgh, NY 12901-0829
Mailing Address: PO Box 829 • Plattsburgh, NY 12901-0829
(518) 563-8250 • http://bcs.neric.org/
Grade Span: PK-12; **Agency Type:** 1
Schools: 4
2 Primary; 1 Middle; 1 High; 0 Other Level
4 Regular; 0 Special Education; 0 Vocational; 0 Alternative
0 Magnet; 0 Charter; 3 Title I Eligible; 0 School-wide Title I
Students: 2,116 (51.1% male; 48.9% female)
Individual Education Program: 327 (15.5%);
English Language Learner: 2 (0.1%); Migrant: n/a
Eligible for Free Lunch Program: 482 (22.8%)
Eligible for Reduced-Price Lunch Program: 282 (13.3%)
Teachers: 192.6 (11.0 to 1)
Librarians/Media Specialists: 3.6 (587.8 to 1)
Guidance Counselors: 6.0 (352.7 to 1)
Current Spending: ($ per student per year):
Total: $9,943; Instruction: $6,652; Support Services: $2,979
Enrollment, Drop-out Rates and Diploma Recipients by Race/Ethnicity

Category	Total	White	Black	Asian	AIAN	Hisp.
Enrollment (%)	100.0	96.8	1.7	0.6	0.2	0.8
Drop-out Rate (%)	4.5	4.4	0.0	0.0	0.0	16.7
H.S. Diplomas (#)	113	110	2	0	0	1

Northeastern Clinton CSD

103 Route 276 • Champlain, NY 12919-0339
(518) 298-8242 • http://www.nccscougars.org/
Grade Span: KG-12; **Agency Type:** 2
Schools: 5
3 Primary; 1 Middle; 1 High; 0 Other Level
5 Regular; 0 Special Education; 0 Vocational; 0 Alternative
0 Magnet; 0 Charter; 4 Title I Eligible; 0 School-wide Title I
Students: 1,692 (48.5% male; 51.5% female)
Individual Education Program: 324 (19.1%);
English Language Learner: 3 (0.2%); Migrant: n/a
Eligible for Free Lunch Program: 284 (16.8%)
Eligible for Reduced-Price Lunch Program: 163 (9.6%)
Teachers: 121.9 (13.9 to 1)
Librarians/Media Specialists: 3.0 (564.0 to 1)
Guidance Counselors: 5.4 (313.3 to 1)
Current Spending: ($ per student per year):
Total: $10,390; Instruction: $7,114; Support Services: $2,958
Enrollment, Drop-out Rates and Diploma Recipients by Race/Ethnicity

Category	Total	White	Black	Asian	AIAN	Hisp.
Enrollment (%)	100.0	97.9	0.6	0.5	0.5	0.5
Drop-out Rate (%)	4.2	4.4	0.0	0.0	0.0	0.0
H.S. Diplomas (#)	103	103	0	0	0	0

Peru CSD

17 School St • Peru, NY 12972-0068
(518) 643-6000 • http://www.perucsd.org/
Grade Span: KG-12; **Agency Type:** 1
Schools: 6
2 Primary; 1 Middle; 1 High; 2 Other Level
4 Regular; 0 Special Education; 0 Vocational; 2 Alternative
0 Magnet; 0 Charter; 3 Title I Eligible; 0 School-wide Title I
Students: 2,302 (51.9% male; 48.1% female)
Individual Education Program: 449 (19.5%);
English Language Learner: 0 (0.0%); Migrant: n/a
Eligible for Free Lunch Program: 591 (25.7%)
Eligible for Reduced-Price Lunch Program: 298 (12.9%)
Teachers: 182.6 (12.6 to 1)
Librarians/Media Specialists: 3.4 (677.1 to 1)
Guidance Counselors: 8.0 (287.8 to 1)
Current Spending: ($ per student per year):
Total: $12,003; Instruction: $7,209; Support Services: $4,495
Enrollment, Drop-out Rates and Diploma Recipients by Race/Ethnicity

Category	Total	White	Black	Asian	AIAN	Hisp.
Enrollment (%)	100.0	95.3	2.2	0.9	0.6	1.0
Drop-out Rate (%)	6.3	6.3	20.0	0.0	0.0	0.0
H.S. Diplomas (#)	149	143	1	3	0	2

Plattsburgh City SD

49 Broad St • Plattsburgh, NY 12901-3396
(518) 957-6002 • http://plattsburgh.neric.org/
Grade Span: PK-12; **Agency Type:** 1
Schools: 7
3 Primary; 1 Middle; 1 High; 2 Other Level
5 Regular; 0 Special Education; 0 Vocational; 2 Alternative
0 Magnet; 0 Charter; 3 Title I Eligible; 0 School-wide Title I
Students: 2,101 (51.5% male; 48.5% female)
Individual Education Program: 406 (19.3%);
English Language Learner: 8 (0.4%); Migrant: n/a
Eligible for Free Lunch Program: 524 (24.9%)
Eligible for Reduced-Price Lunch Program: 133 (6.3%)
Teachers: 196.6 (10.7 to 1)
Librarians/Media Specialists: 2.9 (724.5 to 1)
Guidance Counselors: 7.0 (300.1 to 1)
Current Spending: ($ per student per year):
Total: $11,542; Instruction: $7,775; Support Services: $3,460
Enrollment, Drop-out Rates and Diploma Recipients by Race/Ethnicity

Category	Total	White	Black	Asian	AIAN	Hisp.
Enrollment (%)	100.0	90.6	5.3	1.6	0.7	1.8
Drop-out Rate (%)	3.8	3.7	8.3	0.0	n/a	0.0
H.S. Diplomas (#)	155	141	3	4	3	4

Saranac CSD

32 Emmons St • Dannemora, NY 12929
(518) 565-5600
Grade Span: KG-12; **Agency Type:** 1
Schools: 7
4 Primary; 1 Middle; 1 High; 1 Other Level
6 Regular; 0 Special Education; 0 Vocational; 1 Alternative
0 Magnet; 0 Charter; 5 Title I Eligible; 0 School-wide Title I
Students: 1,892 (51.6% male; 48.4% female)
Individual Education Program: 407 (21.5%);
English Language Learner: 5 (0.3%); Migrant: n/a
Eligible for Free Lunch Program: 312 (16.5%)
Eligible for Reduced-Price Lunch Program: 156 (8.2%)

Teachers: 154.3 (12.3 to 1)
Librarians/Media Specialists: 3.0 (630.7 to 1)
Guidance Counselors: 5.0 (378.4 to 1)
Current Spending: ($ per student per year):
Total: $8,983; Instruction: $5,806; Support Services: $2,851
Enrollment, Drop-out Rates and Diploma Recipients by Race/Ethnicity

Category	Total	White	Black	Asian	AIAN	Hisp.
Enrollment (%)	100.0	95.2	3.0	0.5	0.0	1.4
Drop-out Rate (%)	2.7	2.7	0.0	0.0	n/a	0.0
H.S. Diplomas (#)	133	128	1	1	0	3

Columbia County

Chatham CSD
50 Woodbridge Ave • Chatham, NY 12037-1397
(518) 392-2400 • http://www.chathamcentralschools.com/
Grade Span: KG-12; **Agency Type:** 2
Schools: 3
1 Primary; 1 Middle; 1 High; 0 Other Level
3 Regular; 0 Special Education; 0 Vocational; 0 Alternative
0 Magnet; 0 Charter; 2 Title I Eligible; 0 School-wide Title I
Students: 1,511 (51.6% male; 48.4% female)
Individual Education Program: 206 (13.6%);
English Language Learner: 10 (0.7%); Migrant: n/a
Eligible for Free Lunch Program: 258 (17.1%)
Eligible for Reduced-Price Lunch Program: 159 (10.5%)
Teachers: 106.5 (14.2 to 1)
Librarians/Media Specialists: 1.8 (839.4 to 1)
Guidance Counselors: 3.0 (503.7 to 1)
Current Spending: ($ per student per year):
Total: $9,893; Instruction: $6,178; Support Services: $3,463
Enrollment, Drop-out Rates and Diploma Recipients by Race/Ethnicity

Category	Total	White	Black	Asian	AIAN	Hisp.
Enrollment (%)	100.0	94.8	2.5	1.3	0.1	1.3
Drop-out Rate (%)	3.3	3.4	0.0	0.0	n/a	0.0
H.S. Diplomas (#)	99	98	1	0	0	0

Hudson City SD
621 State Rt 23b • Hudson, NY 12534-4011
(518) 828-4360 • http://www.hudson.edu/
Grade Span: KG-12; **Agency Type:** 1
Schools: 9
2 Primary; 1 Middle; 3 High; 3 Other Level
4 Regular; 0 Special Education; 0 Vocational; 5 Alternative
0 Magnet; 0 Charter; 2 Title I Eligible; 0 School-wide Title I
Students: 2,256 (56.2% male; 43.8% female)
Individual Education Program: 392 (17.4%);
English Language Learner: 77 (3.4%); Migrant: n/a
Eligible for Free Lunch Program: 763 (33.8%)
Eligible for Reduced-Price Lunch Program: 258 (11.4%)
Teachers: 196.5 (11.5 to 1)
Librarians/Media Specialists: 2.6 (867.7 to 1)
Guidance Counselors: 3.0 (752.0 to 1)
Current Spending: ($ per student per year):
Total: $10,856; Instruction: $7,135; Support Services: $3,371
Enrollment, Drop-out Rates and Diploma Recipients by Race/Ethnicity

Category	Total	White	Black	Asian	AIAN	Hisp.
Enrollment (%)	100.0	59.4	28.7	3.9	0.0	8.0
Drop-out Rate (%)	6.5	5.3	11.9	5.6	n/a	8.8
H.S. Diplomas (#)	90	79	5	1	0	5

Kinderhook CSD
2910 Rt 9 • Valatie, NY 12184-0137
(518) 758-7575
Grade Span: KG-12; **Agency Type:** 2
Schools: 5
3 Primary; 1 Middle; 1 High; 0 Other Level
5 Regular; 0 Special Education; 0 Vocational; 0 Alternative
0 Magnet; 0 Charter; 3 Title I Eligible; 0 School-wide Title I
Students: 2,325 (50.0% male; 50.0% female)
Individual Education Program: 336 (14.5%);
English Language Learner: 22 (0.9%); Migrant: n/a
Eligible for Free Lunch Program: 297 (12.8%)
Eligible for Reduced-Price Lunch Program: 204 (8.8%)
Teachers: 172.2 (13.5 to 1)
Librarians/Media Specialists: 3.6 (645.8 to 1)
Guidance Counselors: 5.0 (465.0 to 1)
Current Spending: ($ per student per year):
Total: $9,036; Instruction: $5,853; Support Services: $2,944
Enrollment, Drop-out Rates and Diploma Recipients by Race/Ethnicity

Category	Total	White	Black	Asian	AIAN	Hisp.
Enrollment (%)	100.0	95.3	1.7	1.1	0.5	1.5
Drop-out Rate (%)	1.7	1.8	0.0	0.0	n/a	0.0
H.S. Diplomas (#)	143	142	0	0	0	1

Taconic Hills CSD
73 County Rt 11a • Craryville, NY 12521-5510
(518) 325-0313 • http://www.taconichills.k12.ny.us/
Grade Span: KG-12; **Agency Type:** 2
Schools: 4
2 Primary; 1 Middle; 1 High; 0 Other Level
4 Regular; 0 Special Education; 0 Vocational; 0 Alternative
0 Magnet; 0 Charter; 3 Title I Eligible; 0 School-wide Title I
Students: 1,874 (49.2% male; 50.8% female)
Individual Education Program: 244 (13.0%);
English Language Learner: 3 (0.2%); Migrant: n/a
Eligible for Free Lunch Program: 433 (23.1%)
Eligible for Reduced-Price Lunch Program: 202 (10.8%)
Teachers: 149.1 (12.6 to 1)
Librarians/Media Specialists: 2.7 (694.1 to 1)
Guidance Counselors: 5.0 (374.8 to 1)
Current Spending: ($ per student per year):
Total: $10,749; Instruction: $6,618; Support Services: $3,858
Enrollment, Drop-out Rates and Diploma Recipients by Race/Ethnicity

Category	Total	White	Black	Asian	AIAN	Hisp.
Enrollment (%)	100.0	94.6	2.5	0.9	0.2	1.9
Drop-out Rate (%)	3.7	3.9	0.0	0.0	0.0	0.0
H.S. Diplomas (#)	86	80	4	2	0	0

Cortland County

Cortland City SD
1 Valley View Dr • Cortland, NY 13045-3297
(607) 758-4100 • http://www.cortlandschools.org/hslt/
Grade Span: KG-12; **Agency Type:** 1
Schools: 7
5 Primary; 0 Middle; 1 High; 1 Other Level
6 Regular; 0 Special Education; 0 Vocational; 1 Alternative
0 Magnet; 0 Charter; 5 Title I Eligible; 0 School-wide Title I
Students: 2,805 (50.7% male; 49.3% female)
Individual Education Program: 535 (19.1%);
English Language Learner: 21 (0.7%); Migrant: n/a
Eligible for Free Lunch Program: 718 (25.6%)
Eligible for Reduced-Price Lunch Program: 191 (6.8%)
Teachers: 224.3 (12.5 to 1)
Librarians/Media Specialists: 5.7 (492.1 to 1)
Guidance Counselors: 6.0 (467.5 to 1)
Current Spending: ($ per student per year):
Total: $9,566; Instruction: $6,151; Support Services: $3,054
Enrollment, Drop-out Rates and Diploma Recipients by Race/Ethnicity

Category	Total	White	Black	Asian	AIAN	Hisp.
Enrollment (%)	100.0	93.8	4.0	0.7	0.2	1.3
Drop-out Rate (%)	3.5	3.6	0.0	0.0	0.0	0.0
H.S. Diplomas (#)	180	175	1	2	1	1

Homer CSD
80 SW St • Homer, NY 13077-0500
(607) 749-7241 • http://www.homer.cnyric.org/
Grade Span: KG-12; **Agency Type:** 1
Schools: 5
3 Primary; 1 Middle; 1 High; 0 Other Level
5 Regular; 0 Special Education; 0 Vocational; 0 Alternative
0 Magnet; 0 Charter; 1 Title I Eligible; 0 School-wide Title I
Students: 2,448 (51.6% male; 48.4% female)
Individual Education Program: 298 (12.2%);
English Language Learner: 19 (0.8%); Migrant: n/a
Eligible for Free Lunch Program: 322 (13.2%)
Eligible for Reduced-Price Lunch Program: 182 (7.4%)
Teachers: 193.4 (12.7 to 1)
Librarians/Media Specialists: 3.6 (680.0 to 1)
Guidance Counselors: 4.0 (612.0 to 1)
Current Spending: ($ per student per year):
Total: $8,778; Instruction: $5,722; Support Services: $2,824
Enrollment, Drop-out Rates and Diploma Recipients by Race/Ethnicity

Category	Total	White	Black	Asian	AIAN	Hisp.
Enrollment (%)	100.0	97.4	1.1	0.6	0.2	0.7
Drop-out Rate (%)	1.7	1.7	0.0	0.0	n/a	0.0
H.S. Diplomas (#)	176	173	2	1	0	0

Dutchess County

Arlington CSD
696 Dutchess Tpke • Poughkeepsie, NY 12603
(845) 486-4460 • http://arlingtonschools.org/
Grade Span: KG-12; **Agency Type:** 1
Schools: 13
8 Primary; 2 Middle; 1 High; 2 Other Level
11 Regular; 0 Special Education; 0 Vocational; 2 Alternative
0 Magnet; 0 Charter; 5 Title I Eligible; 0 School-wide Title I
Students: 9,993 (51.6% male; 48.4% female)

Individual Education Program: 1,256 (12.6%);
English Language Learner: 95 (1.0%); Migrant: n/a
Eligible for Free Lunch Program: 468 (4.7%)
Eligible for Reduced-Price Lunch Program: 249 (2.5%)
Teachers: 614.8 (16.3 to 1)
Librarians/Media Specialists: 11.8 (846.9 to 1)
Guidance Counselors: 15.5 (644.7 to 1)
Current Spending: ($ per student per year):
Total: $8,749; Instruction: $5,893; Support Services: $2,643
Enrollment, Drop-out Rates and Diploma Recipients by Race/Ethnicity

Category	Total	White	Black	Asian	AIAN	Hisp.
Enrollment (%)	100.0	86.5	5.3	3.5	0.0	4.7
Drop-out Rate (%)	2.3	2.5	1.8	0.0	0.0	1.1
H.S. Diplomas (#)	501	426	27	25	0	23

Beacon City SD
10 Education Dr • Beacon, NY 12508-3994
(845) 838-6900 • http://www.dcboces.org/bcsd/
Grade Span: PK-12; **Agency Type:** 1
Schools: 8
4 Primary; 1 Middle; 1 High; 2 Other Level
6 Regular; 0 Special Education; 0 Vocational; 2 Alternative
0 Magnet; 0 Charter; 3 Title I Eligible; 0 School-wide Title I
Students: 3,589 (51.6% male; 48.4% female)
Individual Education Program: 515 (14.3%);
English Language Learner: 103 (2.9%); Migrant: n/a
Eligible for Free Lunch Program: 945 (26.3%)
Eligible for Reduced-Price Lunch Program: 345 (9.6%)
Teachers: 242.9 (14.8 to 1)
Librarians/Media Specialists: 4.0 (897.3 to 1)
Guidance Counselors: 6.0 (598.2 to 1)
Current Spending: ($ per student per year):
Total: $9,693; Instruction: $6,783; Support Services: $2,653
Enrollment, Drop-out Rates and Diploma Recipients by Race/Ethnicity

Category	Total	White	Black	Asian	AIAN	Hisp.
Enrollment (%)	100.0	55.8	23.2	2.4	0.5	18.1
Drop-out Rate (%)	2.0	1.2	4.0	0.0	0.0	2.3
H.S. Diplomas (#)	144	86	33	1	0	24

Dover UFSD
2368 Rt 22 • Dover Plains, NY 12522-6311
(845) 832-4500 • http://www.doverplains.org/
Grade Span: KG-12; **Agency Type:** 2
Schools: 5
2 Primary; 1 Middle; 2 High; 0 Other Level
4 Regular; 0 Special Education; 0 Vocational; 1 Alternative
0 Magnet; 0 Charter; 3 Title I Eligible; 0 School-wide Title I
Students: 1,821 (53.9% male; 46.1% female)
Individual Education Program: 229 (12.6%);
English Language Learner: 10 (0.5%); Migrant: n/a
Eligible for Free Lunch Program: 301 (16.5%)
Eligible for Reduced-Price Lunch Program: 142 (7.8%)
Teachers: 111.8 (16.3 to 1)
Librarians/Media Specialists: 1.0 (1,821.0 to 1)
Guidance Counselors: 3.0 (607.0 to 1)
Current Spending: ($ per student per year):
Total: $9,003; Instruction: $5,644; Support Services: $3,142
Enrollment, Drop-out Rates and Diploma Recipients by Race/Ethnicity

Category	Total	White	Black	Asian	AIAN	Hisp.
Enrollment (%)	100.0	84.8	7.0	1.5	0.2	6.5
Drop-out Rate (%)	2.4	2.4	0.0	0.0	n/a	9.1
H.S. Diplomas (#)	104	93	3	2	0	6

Hyde Park CSD
386 Violet Ave • Poughkeepsie, NY 12601
(845) 483-3600
Grade Span: KG-12; **Agency Type:** 1
Schools: 9
5 Primary; 1 Middle; 1 High; 2 Other Level
7 Regular; 0 Special Education; 0 Vocational; 2 Alternative
0 Magnet; 0 Charter; 3 Title I Eligible; 0 School-wide Title I
Students: 4,729 (50.2% male; 49.8% female)
Individual Education Program: 652 (13.8%);
English Language Learner: 104 (2.2%); Migrant: n/a
Eligible for Free Lunch Program: 495 (10.5%)
Eligible for Reduced-Price Lunch Program: 289 (6.1%)
Teachers: 321.3 (14.7 to 1)
Librarians/Media Specialists: 7.0 (675.6 to 1)
Guidance Counselors: 8.0 (591.1 to 1)
Current Spending: ($ per student per year):
Total: $10,079; Instruction: $6,771; Support Services: $3,056
Enrollment, Drop-out Rates and Diploma Recipients by Race/Ethnicity

Category	Total	White	Black	Asian	AIAN	Hisp.
Enrollment (%)	100.0	84.1	10.4	1.7	0.0	3.8
Drop-out Rate (%)	1.8	1.3	5.4	5.0	0.0	6.1
H.S. Diplomas (#)	253	221	24	5	1	2

Poughkeepsie City SD
11 College Ave • Poughkeepsie, NY 12603-3313
(845) 451-4950 • http://www.pcsd.k12.ny.us/
Grade Span: PK-12; **Agency Type:** 1
Schools: 15
7 Primary; 1 Middle; 1 High; 6 Other Level
9 Regular; 0 Special Education; 0 Vocational; 6 Alternative
2 Magnet; 0 Charter; 7 Title I Eligible; 0 School-wide Title I
Students: 4,746 (50.1% male; 49.9% female)
Individual Education Program: 878 (18.5%);
English Language Learner: 362 (7.6%); Migrant: n/a
Eligible for Free Lunch Program: 2,726 (57.4%)
Eligible for Reduced-Price Lunch Program: 616 (13.0%)
Teachers: 347.6 (13.7 to 1)
Librarians/Media Specialists: 7.0 (678.0 to 1)
Guidance Counselors: 9.0 (527.3 to 1)
Current Spending: ($ per student per year):
Total: $12,110; Instruction: $8,887; Support Services: $2,897
Enrollment, Drop-out Rates and Diploma Recipients by Race/Ethnicity

Category	Total	White	Black	Asian	AIAN	Hisp.
Enrollment (%)	100.0	21.1	62.9	1.7	0.1	14.2
Drop-out Rate (%)	1.8	0.4	2.1	0.0	0.0	3.7
H.S. Diplomas (#)	153	35	102	1	0	15

Red Hook CSD
7401 S Broadway • Red Hook, NY 12571-9446
(845) 758-2241 • http://www.northerndutchess.com/redhookschool.htm
Grade Span: KG-12; **Agency Type:** 1
Schools: 6
2 Primary; 1 Middle; 1 High; 2 Other Level
4 Regular; 0 Special Education; 0 Vocational; 2 Alternative
0 Magnet; 0 Charter; 3 Title I Eligible; 0 School-wide Title I
Students: 2,332 (52.3% male; 47.7% female)
Individual Education Program: 341 (14.6%);
English Language Learner: 40 (1.7%); Migrant: n/a
Eligible for Free Lunch Program: 133 (5.7%)
Eligible for Reduced-Price Lunch Program: 63 (2.7%)
Teachers: 169.8 (13.7 to 1)
Librarians/Media Specialists: 3.7 (630.3 to 1)
Guidance Counselors: 4.0 (583.0 to 1)
Current Spending: ($ per student per year):
Total: $9,695; Instruction: $6,832; Support Services: $2,673
Enrollment, Drop-out Rates and Diploma Recipients by Race/Ethnicity

Category	Total	White	Black	Asian	AIAN	Hisp.
Enrollment (%)	100.0	91.9	2.0	3.2	0.1	2.8
Drop-out Rate (%)	3.0	3.0	9.1	0.0	n/a	0.0
H.S. Diplomas (#)	126	116	2	3	0	5

Spackenkill UFSD
15 Croft Rd • Poughkeepsie, NY 12603-5028
(845) 463-7800 • http://www.dcboces.org/sufsd/
Grade Span: KG-12; **Agency Type:** 2
Schools: 4
2 Primary; 1 Middle; 1 High; 0 Other Level
4 Regular; 0 Special Education; 0 Vocational; 0 Alternative
0 Magnet; 0 Charter; 1 Title I Eligible; 0 School-wide Title I
Students: 1,785 (51.2% male; 48.8% female)
Individual Education Program: 206 (11.5%);
English Language Learner: 17 (1.0%); Migrant: n/a
Eligible for Free Lunch Program: 99 (5.5%)
Eligible for Reduced-Price Lunch Program: 81 (4.5%)
Teachers: 147.1 (12.1 to 1)
Librarians/Media Specialists: 3.8 (469.7 to 1)
Guidance Counselors: 4.6 (388.0 to 1)
Current Spending: ($ per student per year):
Total: $11,712; Instruction: $7,729; Support Services: $3,720
Enrollment, Drop-out Rates and Diploma Recipients by Race/Ethnicity

Category	Total	White	Black	Asian	AIAN	Hisp.
Enrollment (%)	100.0	75.1	10.2	9.5	0.1	5.2
Drop-out Rate (%)	1.7	2.2	0.0	0.0	n/a	0.0
H.S. Diplomas (#)	111	85	11	10	0	5

Wappingers CSD
29 Marshall Rd • Wappingers Falls, NY 12590-3296
(845) 298-5000 • http://wappingersschools.org/
Grade Span: KG-12; **Agency Type:** 1
Schools: 19
9 Primary; 3 Middle; 2 High; 5 Other Level
14 Regular; 0 Special Education; 0 Vocational; 5 Alternative

0 Magnet; 0 Charter; 2 Title I Eligible; 0 School-wide Title I
Students: 12,125 (51.6% male; 48.4% female)
Individual Education Program: 1,503 (12.4%);
English Language Learner: 147 (1.2%); Migrant: n/a
Eligible for Free Lunch Program: 616 (5.1%)
Eligible for Reduced-Price Lunch Program: 460 (3.8%)
Teachers: 776.1 (15.6 to 1)
Librarians/Media Specialists: 14.7 (824.8 to 1)
Guidance Counselors: 18.0 (673.6 to 1)
Current Spending: ($ per student per year):
Total: $9,383; Instruction: $5,937; Support Services: $3,235
Enrollment, Drop-out Rates and Diploma Recipients by Race/Ethnicity

Category	Total	White	Black	Asian	AIAN	Hisp.
Enrollment (%)	100.0	82.8	5.3	4.8	0.1	6.9
Drop-out Rate (%)	1.5	1.3	2.2	0.0	n/a	5.0
H.S. Diplomas (#)	761	748	6	1	0	6

Erie County

Akron CSD
47 Bloomingdale Ave • Akron, NY 14001-1197
(716) 542-5101 • http://www.akronschools.org/
Grade Span: PK-12; **Agency Type:** 2
Schools: 3
1 Primary; 1 Middle; 1 High; 0 Other Level
3 Regular; 0 Special Education; 0 Vocational; 0 Alternative
0 Magnet; 0 Charter; 2 Title I Eligible; 0 School-wide Title I
Students: 1,704 (49.0% male; 51.0% female)
Individual Education Program: 217 (12.7%);
English Language Learner: 0 (0.0%); Migrant: n/a
Eligible for Free Lunch Program: 212 (12.4%)
Eligible for Reduced-Price Lunch Program: 162 (9.5%)
Teachers: 125.3 (13.6 to 1)
Librarians/Media Specialists: 1.8 (946.7 to 1)
Guidance Counselors: 3.6 (473.3 to 1)
Current Spending: ($ per student per year):
Total: $9,511; Instruction: $6,079; Support Services: $3,173
Enrollment, Drop-out Rates and Diploma Recipients by Race/Ethnicity

Category	Total	White	Black	Asian	AIAN	Hisp.
Enrollment (%)	100.0	90.4	0.8	0.0	8.5	0.4
Drop-out Rate (%)	1.1	1.2	n/a	n/a	0.0	n/a
H.S. Diplomas (#)	98	94	0	0	4	0

Alden CSD
13190 Park St • Alden, NY 14004-1099
(716) 937-9116 • http://www.alden.wnyric.org/
Grade Span: KG-12; **Agency Type:** 1
Schools: 6
2 Primary; 1 Middle; 1 High; 2 Other Level
4 Regular; 0 Special Education; 0 Vocational; 2 Alternative
0 Magnet; 0 Charter; 2 Title I Eligible; 0 School-wide Title I
Students: 2,066 (53.0% male; 47.0% female)
Individual Education Program: 262 (12.7%);
English Language Learner: 3 (0.1%); Migrant: n/a
Eligible for Free Lunch Program: 199 (9.6%)
Eligible for Reduced-Price Lunch Program: 206 (10.0%)
Teachers: 152.6 (13.5 to 1)
Librarians/Media Specialists: 3.6 (573.9 to 1)
Guidance Counselors: 4.0 (516.5 to 1)
Current Spending: ($ per student per year):
Total: $9,448; Instruction: $6,004; Support Services: $3,203
Enrollment, Drop-out Rates and Diploma Recipients by Race/Ethnicity

Category	Total	White	Black	Asian	AIAN	Hisp.
Enrollment (%)	100.0	97.6	1.7	0.4	0.0	0.3
Drop-out Rate (%)	1.6	1.6	0.0	0.0	n/a	0.0
H.S. Diplomas (#)	150	147	1	2	0	0

Amherst CSD
55 Kings Hwy • Amherst, NY 14226-4398
(716) 362-3051 • http://www.amherst.k12.ny.us/
Grade Span: KG-12; **Agency Type:** 1
Schools: 4
2 Primary; 1 Middle; 1 High; 0 Other Level
4 Regular; 0 Special Education; 0 Vocational; 0 Alternative
0 Magnet; 0 Charter; 1 Title I Eligible; 0 School-wide Title I
Students: 3,169 (50.6% male; 49.4% female)
Individual Education Program: 351 (11.1%);
English Language Learner: 31 (1.0%); Migrant: n/a
Eligible for Free Lunch Program: 289 (9.1%)
Eligible for Reduced-Price Lunch Program: 128 (4.0%)
Teachers: 243.6 (13.0 to 1)
Librarians/Media Specialists: 4.0 (792.3 to 1)
Guidance Counselors: 3.9 (812.6 to 1)
Current Spending: ($ per student per year):
Total: $10,115; Instruction: $6,182; Support Services: $3,725

Enrollment, Drop-out Rates and Diploma Recipients by Race/Ethnicity

Category	Total	White	Black	Asian	AIAN	Hisp.
Enrollment (%)	100.0	82.0	13.2	3.4	0.1	1.3
Drop-out Rate (%)	0.6	0.7	0.0	0.0	0.0	0.0
H.S. Diplomas (#)	212	189	10	8	1	4

Buffalo City SD
712 City Hall • Buffalo, NY 14202-3375
(716) 851-3575
Grade Span: PK-12; **Agency Type:** 1
Schools: 86
49 Primary; 7 Middle; 13 High; 17 Other Level
67 Regular; 1 Special Education; 5 Vocational; 13 Alternative
1 Magnet; 0 Charter; 51 Title I Eligible; 0 School-wide Title I
Students: 43,474 (50.9% male; 49.1% female)
Individual Education Program: 9,413 (21.7%);
English Language Learner: 2,767 (6.4%); Migrant: n/a
Eligible for Free Lunch Program: 27,414 (63.1%)
Eligible for Reduced-Price Lunch Program: 4,673 (10.7%)
Teachers: 3,229.2 (13.5 to 1)
Librarians/Media Specialists: 51.9 (837.6 to 1)
Guidance Counselors: 82.1 (529.5 to 1)
Current Spending: ($ per student per year):
Total: $12,424; Instruction: $7,813; Support Services: $4,192
Enrollment, Drop-out Rates and Diploma Recipients by Race/Ethnicity

Category	Total	White	Black	Asian	AIAN	Hisp.
Enrollment (%)	100.0	26.7	58.3	1.3	1.4	12.3
Drop-out Rate (%)	1.7	1.0	2.2	0.0	2.1	1.5
H.S. Diplomas (#)	1,638	656	794	40	22	126

Cheektowaga CSD
3600 Union Rd • Cheektowaga, NY 14225-5170
(716) 686-3606 • http://www.ccsd.wnyric.org/
Grade Span: KG-12; **Agency Type:** 1
Schools: 3
2 Primary; 0 Middle; 1 High; 0 Other Level
3 Regular; 0 Special Education; 0 Vocational; 0 Alternative
0 Magnet; 0 Charter; 1 Title I Eligible; 0 School-wide Title I
Students: 2,453 (52.1% male; 47.9% female)
Individual Education Program: 312 (12.7%);
English Language Learner: 32 (1.3%); Migrant: n/a
Eligible for Free Lunch Program: 465 (19.0%)
Eligible for Reduced-Price Lunch Program: 163 (6.6%)
Teachers: 181.0 (13.6 to 1)
Librarians/Media Specialists: 3.0 (817.7 to 1)
Guidance Counselors: 4.0 (613.3 to 1)
Current Spending: ($ per student per year):
Total: $9,216; Instruction: $5,663; Support Services: $3,353
Enrollment, Drop-out Rates and Diploma Recipients by Race/Ethnicity

Category	Total	White	Black	Asian	AIAN	Hisp.
Enrollment (%)	100.0	80.7	14.4	2.3	0.6	2.1
Drop-out Rate (%)	2.2	2.0	5.0	0.0	0.0	0.0
H.S. Diplomas (#)	165	156	6	2	0	1

Cheektowaga-Maryvale UFSD
1050 Maryvale Dr • Cheektowaga, NY 14225-2386
(716) 631-7407 • http://www.maryvale.wnyric.org/
Grade Span: PK-12; **Agency Type:** 1
Schools: 4
2 Primary; 1 Middle; 1 High; 0 Other Level
4 Regular; 0 Special Education; 0 Vocational; 0 Alternative
0 Magnet; 0 Charter; 2 Title I Eligible; 0 School-wide Title I
Students: 2,581 (50.1% male; 49.9% female)
Individual Education Program: 326 (12.6%);
English Language Learner: 35 (1.4%); Migrant: n/a
Eligible for Free Lunch Program: 341 (13.2%)
Eligible for Reduced-Price Lunch Program: 210 (8.1%)
Teachers: 187.6 (13.8 to 1)
Librarians/Media Specialists: 3.7 (697.6 to 1)
Guidance Counselors: 6.0 (430.2 to 1)
Current Spending: ($ per student per year):
Total: $11,117; Instruction: $7,348; Support Services: $3,543
Enrollment, Drop-out Rates and Diploma Recipients by Race/Ethnicity

Category	Total	White	Black	Asian	AIAN	Hisp.
Enrollment (%)	100.0	94.4	3.6	1.2	0.3	0.5
Drop-out Rate (%)	3.5	3.7	0.0	0.0	n/a	0.0
H.S. Diplomas (#)	160	156	1	2	0	1

Cheektowaga-Sloan UFSD
166 Halstead Ave • Sloan, NY 14212-2295
(716) 891-6402 • http://www.sloan.wnyric.org/
Grade Span: PK-12; **Agency Type:** 1
Schools: 4
2 Primary; 1 Middle; 1 High; 0 Other Level
4 Regular; 0 Special Education; 0 Vocational; 0 Alternative

0 Magnet; 0 Charter; 1 Title I Eligible; 0 School-wide Title I
Students: 1,531 (51.1% male; 48.9% female)
Individual Education Program: 233 (15.2%);
English Language Learner: 8 (0.5%); Migrant: n/a
Eligible for Free Lunch Program: 316 (20.6%)
Eligible for Reduced-Price Lunch Program: 311 (20.3%)
Teachers: 118.0 (13.0 to 1)
Librarians/Media Specialists: 1.8 (850.6 to 1)
Guidance Counselors: 2.0 (765.5 to 1)
Current Spending: ($ per student per year):
Total: $11,058; Instruction: $7,082; Support Services: $3,653
Enrollment, Drop-out Rates and Diploma Recipients by Race/Ethnicity

Category	Total	White	Black	Asian	AIAN	Hisp.
Enrollment (%)	100.0	97.2	1.5	0.4	0.3	0.7
Drop-out Rate (%)	2.9	3.0	0.0	0.0	0.0	0.0
H.S. Diplomas (#)	104	101	2	0	1	0

Clarence CSD
9625 Main St • Clarence, NY 14031-2083
(716) 407-9102 • http://www.clarence.wnyric.org/
Grade Span: KG-12; **Agency Type:** 1
Schools: 6
4 Primary; 1 Middle; 1 High; 0 Other Level
6 Regular; 0 Special Education; 0 Vocational; 0 Alternative
0 Magnet; 0 Charter; 4 Title I Eligible; 0 School-wide Title I
Students: 4,784 (51.2% male; 48.8% female)
Individual Education Program: 576 (12.0%);
English Language Learner: 17 (0.4%); Migrant: n/a
Eligible for Free Lunch Program: 133 (2.8%)
Eligible for Reduced-Price Lunch Program: 116 (2.4%)
Teachers: 338.8 (14.1 to 1)
Librarians/Media Specialists: 5.2 (920.0 to 1)
Guidance Counselors: 9.0 (531.6 to 1)
Current Spending: ($ per student per year):
Total: $8,666; Instruction: $5,631; Support Services: $2,856
Enrollment, Drop-out Rates and Diploma Recipients by Race/Ethnicity

Category	Total	White	Black	Asian	AIAN	Hisp.
Enrollment (%)	100.0	96.2	0.8	1.8	0.2	1.0
Drop-out Rate (%)	1.1	1.1	0.0	0.0	0.0	0.0
H.S. Diplomas (#)	339	330	2	4	0	3

Cleveland Hill UFSD
105 Mapleview Rd • Cheektowaga, NY 14225-1599
(716) 836-7200 • http://www.clevehill.wnyric.org/
Grade Span: KG-12; **Agency Type:** 2
Schools: 3
1 Primary; 1 Middle; 1 High; 0 Other Level
3 Regular; 0 Special Education; 0 Vocational; 0 Alternative
0 Magnet; 0 Charter; 2 Title I Eligible; 0 School-wide Title I
Students: 1,589 (53.7% male; 46.3% female)
Individual Education Program: 248 (15.6%);
English Language Learner: 12 (0.8%); Migrant: n/a
Eligible for Free Lunch Program: 343 (21.6%)
Eligible for Reduced-Price Lunch Program: 157 (9.9%)
Teachers: 119.7 (13.3 to 1)
Librarians/Media Specialists: 2.0 (794.5 to 1)
Guidance Counselors: 5.0 (317.8 to 1)
Current Spending: ($ per student per year):
Total: $10,175; Instruction: $6,393; Support Services: $3,586
Enrollment, Drop-out Rates and Diploma Recipients by Race/Ethnicity

Category	Total	White	Black	Asian	AIAN	Hisp.
Enrollment (%)	100.0	71.7	19.9	1.4	3.3	3.7
Drop-out Rate (%)	3.7	3.3	7.5	0.0	0.0	0.0
H.S. Diplomas (#)	78	64	10	0	1	3

Depew UFSD
591 Terrace Blvd • Depew, NY 14043-4535
(716) 686-2251
Grade Span: KG-12; **Agency Type:** 1
Schools: 3
1 Primary; 1 Middle; 1 High; 0 Other Level
3 Regular; 0 Special Education; 0 Vocational; 0 Alternative
0 Magnet; 0 Charter; 1 Title I Eligible; 0 School-wide Title I
Students: 2,417 (50.1% male; 49.9% female)
Individual Education Program: 244 (10.1%);
English Language Learner: 9 (0.4%); Migrant: n/a
Eligible for Free Lunch Program: 397 (16.4%)
Eligible for Reduced-Price Lunch Program: 278 (11.5%)
Teachers: 184.3 (13.1 to 1)
Librarians/Media Specialists: 3.0 (805.7 to 1)
Guidance Counselors: 9.0 (268.6 to 1)
Current Spending: ($ per student per year):
Total: $11,496; Instruction: $7,745; Support Services: $3,435
Enrollment, Drop-out Rates and Diploma Recipients by Race/Ethnicity

Category	Total	White	Black	Asian	AIAN	Hisp.
Enrollment (%)	100.0	96.7	1.4	1.0	0.5	0.4
Drop-out Rate (%)	3.6	3.7	0.0	0.0	0.0	0.0
H.S. Diplomas (#)	151	149	0	0	1	1

East Aurora UFSD
430 Main St • East Aurora, NY 14052-1786
(716) 687-2302 • http://www.eaur.wnyric.org/
Grade Span: KG-12; **Agency Type:** 1
Schools: 4
2 Primary; 1 Middle; 1 High; 0 Other Level
4 Regular; 0 Special Education; 0 Vocational; 0 Alternative
0 Magnet; 0 Charter; 1 Title I Eligible; 0 School-wide Title I
Students: 2,094 (51.1% male; 48.9% female)
Individual Education Program: 146 (7.0%);
English Language Learner: 11 (0.5%); Migrant: n/a
Eligible for Free Lunch Program: 69 (3.3%)
Eligible for Reduced-Price Lunch Program: 63 (3.0%)
Teachers: 141.6 (14.8 to 1)
Librarians/Media Specialists: 2.7 (775.6 to 1)
Guidance Counselors: 4.6 (455.2 to 1)
Current Spending: ($ per student per year):
Total: $9,015; Instruction: $5,738; Support Services: $3,138
Enrollment, Drop-out Rates and Diploma Recipients by Race/Ethnicity

Category	Total	White	Black	Asian	AIAN	Hisp.
Enrollment (%)	100.0	98.2	0.5	0.4	0.2	0.6
Drop-out Rate (%)	0.5	0.5	0.0	0.0	0.0	0.0
H.S. Diplomas (#)	150	149	0	1	0	0

Eden CSD
3150 Schoolview Rd • Eden, NY 14057-0267
(716) 992-3629 • http://www.edencentral.org/
Grade Span: PK-12; **Agency Type:** 1
Schools: 3
2 Primary; 0 Middle; 1 High; 0 Other Level
3 Regular; 0 Special Education; 0 Vocational; 0 Alternative
0 Magnet; 0 Charter; 1 Title I Eligible; 0 School-wide Title I
Students: 1,860 (51.6% male; 48.4% female)
Individual Education Program: 152 (8.2%);
English Language Learner: 0 (0.0%); Migrant: n/a
Eligible for Free Lunch Program: 104 (5.6%)
Eligible for Reduced-Price Lunch Program: 58 (3.1%)
Teachers: 133.2 (14.0 to 1)
Librarians/Media Specialists: 1.6 (1,162.5 to 1)
Guidance Counselors: 4.0 (465.0 to 1)
Current Spending: ($ per student per year):
Total: $8,248; Instruction: $5,486; Support Services: $2,604
Enrollment, Drop-out Rates and Diploma Recipients by Race/Ethnicity

Category	Total	White	Black	Asian	AIAN	Hisp.
Enrollment (%)	100.0	98.3	0.3	0.3	0.2	0.9
Drop-out Rate (%)	0.4	0.4	0.0	n/a	n/a	0.0
H.S. Diplomas (#)	111	111	0	0	0	0

Evans-Brant CSD (Lake Shore)
959 Beach Rd • Angola, NY 14006-9690
(716) 926-2201 • http://www.lakeshore.wnyric.org/
Grade Span: PK-12; **Agency Type:** 1
Schools: 7
5 Primary; 1 Middle; 1 High; 0 Other Level
7 Regular; 0 Special Education; 0 Vocational; 0 Alternative
0 Magnet; 0 Charter; 4 Title I Eligible; 0 School-wide Title I
Students: 3,413 (50.5% male; 49.5% female)
Individual Education Program: 426 (12.5%);
English Language Learner: 1 (<0.1%); Migrant: n/a
Eligible for Free Lunch Program: 532 (15.6%)
Eligible for Reduced-Price Lunch Program: 326 (9.6%)
Teachers: 260.9 (13.1 to 1)
Librarians/Media Specialists: 4.7 (726.2 to 1)
Guidance Counselors: 9.4 (363.1 to 1)
Current Spending: ($ per student per year):
Total: $9,577; Instruction: $6,387; Support Services: $2,972
Enrollment, Drop-out Rates and Diploma Recipients by Race/Ethnicity

Category	Total	White	Black	Asian	AIAN	Hisp.
Enrollment (%)	100.0	90.9	0.9	0.3	6.5	1.3
Drop-out Rate (%)	3.1	3.3	0.0	0.0	0.0	0.0
H.S. Diplomas (#)	188	185	0	0	2	1

Frontier CSD
S 5120 Orchard Ave • Hamburg, NY 14075-5657
(716) 926-1711 • http://www.frontier.wnyric.org/
Grade Span: KG-12; **Agency Type:** 1
Schools: 6
4 Primary; 1 Middle; 1 High; 0 Other Level
6 Regular; 0 Special Education; 0 Vocational; 0 Alternative

0 Magnet; 0 Charter; 4 Title I Eligible; 0 School-wide Title I
Students: 5,645 (50.0% male; 50.0% female)
Individual Education Program: 666 (11.8%);
English Language Learner: 21 (0.4%); Migrant: n/a
Eligible for Free Lunch Program: 563 (10.0%)
Eligible for Reduced-Price Lunch Program: 543 (9.6%)
Teachers: 421.3 (13.4 to 1)
Librarians/Media Specialists: 5.6 (1,008.0 to 1)
Guidance Counselors: 10.0 (564.5 to 1)
Current Spending: ($ per student per year):
Total: $8,667; Instruction: $5,526; Support Services: $2,894
Enrollment, Drop-out Rates and Diploma Recipients by Race/Ethnicity

Category	Total	White	Black	Asian	AIAN	Hisp.
Enrollment (%)	100.0	96.6	1.2	0.6	0.2	1.4
Drop-out Rate (%)	1.7	1.7	0.0	0.0	0.0	0.0
H.S. Diplomas (#)	340	332	0	4	2	2

Grand Island CSD
1100 Ransom Rd • Grand Island, NY 14072-1460
(716) 773-8800 • http://www.grandisland-cs.k12.ny.us/
Grade Span: KG-12; **Agency Type:** 1
Schools: 5
3 Primary; 1 Middle; 1 High; 0 Other Level
5 Regular; 0 Special Education; 0 Vocational; 0 Alternative
0 Magnet; 0 Charter; 1 Title I Eligible; 0 School-wide Title I
Students: 3,205 (52.0% male; 48.0% female)
Individual Education Program: 361 (11.3%);
English Language Learner: 32 (1.0%); Migrant: n/a
Eligible for Free Lunch Program: 178 (5.6%)
Eligible for Reduced-Price Lunch Program: 193 (6.0%)
Teachers: 233.1 (13.7 to 1)
Librarians/Media Specialists: 4.5 (712.2 to 1)
Guidance Counselors: 6.0 (534.2 to 1)
Current Spending: ($ per student per year):
Total: $9,466; Instruction: $6,283; Support Services: $2,938
Enrollment, Drop-out Rates and Diploma Recipients by Race/Ethnicity

Category	Total	White	Black	Asian	AIAN	Hisp.
Enrollment (%)	100.0	94.8	2.0	2.0	0.2	1.0
Drop-out Rate (%)	3.4	3.1	0.0	14.3	0.0	33.3
H.S. Diplomas (#)	195	189	1	5	0	0

Hamburg CSD
5305 Abbott Rd • Hamburg, NY 14075-1699
(716) 646-3220 • http://www.hamburg.wnyric.org/
Grade Span: PK-12; **Agency Type:** 1
Schools: 6
4 Primary; 1 Middle; 1 High; 0 Other Level
6 Regular; 0 Special Education; 0 Vocational; 0 Alternative
0 Magnet; 0 Charter; 5 Title I Eligible; 0 School-wide Title I
Students: 4,133 (50.2% male; 49.8% female)
Individual Education Program: 581 (14.1%);
English Language Learner: 19 (0.5%); Migrant: n/a
Eligible for Free Lunch Program: 302 (7.3%)
Eligible for Reduced-Price Lunch Program: 239 (5.8%)
Teachers: 335.6 (12.3 to 1)
Librarians/Media Specialists: 5.8 (712.6 to 1)
Guidance Counselors: 11.5 (359.4 to 1)
Current Spending: ($ per student per year):
Total: $9,499; Instruction: $6,086; Support Services: $3,208
Enrollment, Drop-out Rates and Diploma Recipients by Race/Ethnicity

Category	Total	White	Black	Asian	AIAN	Hisp.
Enrollment (%)	100.0	97.5	0.6	0.8	0.4	0.7
Drop-out Rate (%)	2.1	2.1	0.0	0.0	0.0	0.0
H.S. Diplomas (#)	319	309	2	3	1	4

Iroquois CSD
2111 Girdle Rd • Elma, NY 14059-0032
(716) 652-3000 • http://www.iroquois.wnyric.org/
Grade Span: KG-12; **Agency Type:** 1
Schools: 6
3 Primary; 2 Middle; 1 High; 0 Other Level
6 Regular; 0 Special Education; 0 Vocational; 0 Alternative
0 Magnet; 0 Charter; 3 Title I Eligible; 0 School-wide Title I
Students: 2,907 (52.1% male; 47.9% female)
Individual Education Program: 304 (10.5%);
English Language Learner: 2 (0.1%); Migrant: n/a
Eligible for Free Lunch Program: 110 (3.8%)
Eligible for Reduced-Price Lunch Program: 114 (3.9%)
Teachers: 199.2 (14.6 to 1)
Librarians/Media Specialists: 3.9 (745.4 to 1)
Guidance Counselors: 6.0 (484.5 to 1)
Current Spending: ($ per student per year):
Total: $8,633; Instruction: $5,492; Support Services: $3,003
Enrollment, Drop-out Rates and Diploma Recipients by Race/Ethnicity

Category	Total	White	Black	Asian	AIAN	Hisp.
Enrollment (%)	100.0	98.2	0.6	0.7	0.0	0.5
Drop-out Rate (%)	0.8	0.8	0.0	0.0	n/a	0.0
H.S. Diplomas (#)	222	221	0	0	0	1

Kenmore-Tonawanda UFSD
1500 Colvin Blvd • Buffalo, NY 14223-1196
(716) 874-8400 • http://www.kenton.k12.ny.us/
Grade Span: PK-12; **Agency Type:** 1
Schools: 14
9 Primary; 3 Middle; 2 High; 0 Other Level
14 Regular; 0 Special Education; 0 Vocational; 0 Alternative
0 Magnet; 0 Charter; 3 Title I Eligible; 0 School-wide Title I
Students: 9,100 (51.4% male; 48.6% female)
Individual Education Program: 1,486 (16.3%);
English Language Learner: 57 (0.6%); Migrant: n/a
Eligible for Free Lunch Program: 1,212 (13.3%)
Eligible for Reduced-Price Lunch Program: 775 (8.5%)
Teachers: 682.8 (13.3 to 1)
Librarians/Media Specialists: 13.8 (659.4 to 1)
Guidance Counselors: 23.0 (395.7 to 1)
Current Spending: ($ per student per year):
Total: $10,455; Instruction: $6,676; Support Services: $3,538
Enrollment, Drop-out Rates and Diploma Recipients by Race/Ethnicity

Category	Total	White	Black	Asian	AIAN	Hisp.
Enrollment (%)	100.0	94.2	3.0	1.0	0.3	1.4
Drop-out Rate (%)	1.3	1.3	3.6	0.0	0.0	0.0
H.S. Diplomas (#)	624	618	2	3	0	1

Lackawanna City SD
30 Johnson St • Lackawanna, NY 14218-3595
(716) 827-6767
Grade Span: PK-12; **Agency Type:** 1
Schools: 8
3 Primary; 2 Middle; 1 High; 2 Other Level
6 Regular; 0 Special Education; 0 Vocational; 2 Alternative
0 Magnet; 0 Charter; 3 Title I Eligible; 0 School-wide Title I
Students: 2,095 (53.3% male; 46.7% female)
Individual Education Program: 490 (23.4%);
English Language Learner: 85 (4.1%); Migrant: n/a
Eligible for Free Lunch Program: 1,236 (59.0%)
Eligible for Reduced-Price Lunch Program: 342 (16.3%)
Teachers: 174.6 (12.0 to 1)
Librarians/Media Specialists: 2.0 (1,047.5 to 1)
Guidance Counselors: 4.0 (523.8 to 1)
Current Spending: ($ per student per year):
Total: $11,988; Instruction: $8,179; Support Services: $3,419
Enrollment, Drop-out Rates and Diploma Recipients by Race/Ethnicity

Category	Total	White	Black	Asian	AIAN	Hisp.
Enrollment (%)	100.0	69.9	22.6	0.4	0.2	6.9
Drop-out Rate (%)	3.0	2.9	5.1	0.0	0.0	0.0
H.S. Diplomas (#)	109	91	14	0	0	4

Lancaster CSD
177 Central Ave • Lancaster, NY 14086-1897
(716) 686-3200
Grade Span: KG-12; **Agency Type:** 1
Schools: 8
5 Primary; 2 Middle; 1 High; 0 Other Level
8 Regular; 0 Special Education; 0 Vocational; 0 Alternative
0 Magnet; 0 Charter; 3 Title I Eligible; 0 School-wide Title I
Students: 6,109 (50.6% male; 49.4% female)
Individual Education Program: 760 (12.4%);
English Language Learner: 15 (0.2%); Migrant: n/a
Eligible for Free Lunch Program: 473 (7.7%)
Eligible for Reduced-Price Lunch Program: 402 (6.6%)
Teachers: 403.1 (15.2 to 1)
Librarians/Media Specialists: 7.8 (783.2 to 1)
Guidance Counselors: 9.0 (678.8 to 1)
Current Spending: ($ per student per year):
Total: $8,666; Instruction: $5,144; Support Services: $3,289
Enrollment, Drop-out Rates and Diploma Recipients by Race/Ethnicity

Category	Total	White	Black	Asian	AIAN	Hisp.
Enrollment (%)	100.0	97.3	1.0	0.7	0.3	0.7
Drop-out Rate (%)	0.9	0.9	0.0	0.0	0.0	0.0
H.S. Diplomas (#)	412	409	1	1	0	1

Orchard Park CSD
3330 Baker Rd • Orchard Park, NY 14127-1472
(716) 209-6280 • http://www.opcsd.wnyric.org/
Grade Span: KG-12; **Agency Type:** 1
Schools: 6
4 Primary; 1 Middle; 1 High; 0 Other Level
6 Regular; 0 Special Education; 0 Vocational; 0 Alternative

0 Magnet; 0 Charter; 1 Title I Eligible; 0 School-wide Title I
Students: 5,127 (51.5% male; 48.5% female)
Individual Education Program: 853 (16.6%);
English Language Learner: 14 (0.3%); Migrant: n/a
Eligible for Free Lunch Program: 122 (2.4%)
Eligible for Reduced-Price Lunch Program: 103 (2.0%)
Teachers: 408.4 (12.6 to 1)
Librarians/Media Specialists: 8.5 (603.2 to 1)
Guidance Counselors: 13.0 (394.4 to 1)
Current Spending: ($ per student per year):
Total: $9,677; Instruction: $6,566; Support Services: $2,978

Enrollment, Drop-out Rates and Diploma Recipients by Race/Ethnicity

Category	Total	White	Black	Asian	AIAN	Hisp.
Enrollment (%)	100.0	97.7	0.8	0.6	0.2	0.6
Drop-out Rate (%)	1.1	1.1	0.0	0.0	n/a	0.0
H.S. Diplomas (#)	406	406	0	0	0	0

Springville-Griffith Inst CSD

307 Newman St • Springville, NY 14141-1599
(716) 592-3236 • http://www.springvillegi.wnyric.org/
Grade Span: KG-12; **Agency Type:** 1
Schools: 4
2 Primary; 1 Middle; 1 High; 0 Other Level
4 Regular; 0 Special Education; 0 Vocational; 0 Alternative
0 Magnet; 0 Charter; 2 Title I Eligible; 0 School-wide Title I
Students: 2,388 (50.9% male; 49.1% female)
Individual Education Program: 299 (12.5%);
English Language Learner: 4 (0.2%); Migrant: n/a
Eligible for Free Lunch Program: 345 (14.4%)
Eligible for Reduced-Price Lunch Program: 173 (7.2%)
Teachers: 171.0 (14.0 to 1)
Librarians/Media Specialists: 3.8 (628.4 to 1)
Guidance Counselors: 4.0 (597.0 to 1)
Current Spending: ($ per student per year):
Total: $9,198; Instruction: $5,827; Support Services: $3,172

Enrollment, Drop-out Rates and Diploma Recipients by Race/Ethnicity

Category	Total	White	Black	Asian	AIAN	Hisp.
Enrollment (%)	100.0	97.9	0.9	0.5	0.3	0.4
Drop-out Rate (%)	2.6	2.7	0.0	0.0	0.0	0.0
H.S. Diplomas (#)	156	153	1	0	1	1

Sweet Home CSD

1901 Sweet Home Rd • Amherst, NY 14228-3399
(716) 250-1402 • http://www.sweethomeschools.com/
Grade Span: PK-12; **Agency Type:** 1
Schools: 6
4 Primary; 1 Middle; 1 High; 0 Other Level
6 Regular; 0 Special Education; 0 Vocational; 0 Alternative
0 Magnet; 0 Charter; 3 Title I Eligible; 0 School-wide Title I
Students: 3,917 (52.2% male; 47.8% female)
Individual Education Program: 344 (8.8%);
English Language Learner: 102 (2.6%); Migrant: n/a
Eligible for Free Lunch Program: 536 (13.7%)
Eligible for Reduced-Price Lunch Program: 276 (7.0%)
Teachers: 317.3 (12.3 to 1)
Librarians/Media Specialists: 5.6 (699.5 to 1)
Guidance Counselors: 13.0 (301.3 to 1)
Current Spending: ($ per student per year):
Total: $10,843; Instruction: $7,292; Support Services: $3,264

Enrollment, Drop-out Rates and Diploma Recipients by Race/Ethnicity

Category	Total	White	Black	Asian	AIAN	Hisp.
Enrollment (%)	100.0	84.4	9.7	4.6	0.1	1.2
Drop-out Rate (%)	0.8	0.7	0.0	3.5	0.0	0.0
H.S. Diplomas (#)	245	222	13	10	0	0

Tonawanda City SD

202 Broad St • Tonawanda, NY 14150-2098
(716) 694-7784 • http://www.tona.wnyric.org/default.htm
Grade Span: PK-12; **Agency Type:** 1
Schools: 6
4 Primary; 1 Middle; 1 High; 0 Other Level
6 Regular; 0 Special Education; 0 Vocational; 0 Alternative
0 Magnet; 0 Charter; 6 Title I Eligible; 0 School-wide Title I
Students: 2,437 (50.8% male; 49.2% female)
Individual Education Program: 290 (11.9%);
English Language Learner: 6 (0.2%); Migrant: n/a
Eligible for Free Lunch Program: 424 (17.4%)
Eligible for Reduced-Price Lunch Program: 180 (7.4%)
Teachers: 186.7 (13.1 to 1)
Librarians/Media Specialists: 5.8 (420.2 to 1)
Guidance Counselors: 5.0 (487.4 to 1)
Current Spending: ($ per student per year):
Total: $9,909; Instruction: $5,938; Support Services: $3,761

Enrollment, Drop-out Rates and Diploma Recipients by Race/Ethnicity

Category	Total	White	Black	Asian	AIAN	Hisp.
Enrollment (%)	100.0	97.5	0.7	0.1	0.3	1.4
Drop-out Rate (%)	0.8	0.8	0.0	0.0	n/a	0.0
H.S. Diplomas (#)	174	171	1	1	0	1

West Seneca CSD

1397 Orchard Park Rd • West Seneca, NY 14224-4098
(716) 677-3101 • http://www.westseneca.wnyric.org/
Grade Span: KG-12; **Agency Type:** 1
Schools: 14
7 Primary; 2 Middle; 3 High; 2 Other Level
12 Regular; 0 Special Education; 0 Vocational; 2 Alternative
0 Magnet; 0 Charter; 7 Title I Eligible; 0 School-wide Title I
Students: 7,637 (51.7% male; 48.3% female)
Individual Education Program: 1,067 (14.0%);
English Language Learner: 51 (0.7%); Migrant: n/a
Eligible for Free Lunch Program: 969 (12.7%)
Eligible for Reduced-Price Lunch Program: 654 (8.6%)
Teachers: 564.9 (13.5 to 1)
Librarians/Media Specialists: 9.5 (803.9 to 1)
Guidance Counselors: 13.0 (587.5 to 1)
Current Spending: ($ per student per year):
Total: $9,389; Instruction: $5,992; Support Services: $3,204

Enrollment, Drop-out Rates and Diploma Recipients by Race/Ethnicity

Category	Total	White	Black	Asian	AIAN	Hisp.
Enrollment (%)	100.0	97.3	1.1	0.7	0.3	0.6
Drop-out Rate (%)	1.2	1.2	0.0	0.0	0.0	0.0
H.S. Diplomas (#)	552	535	5	9	2	1

Williamsville CSD

105 Casey Rd • East Amherst, NY 14051-5000
(716) 626-8005
Grade Span: KG-12; **Agency Type:** 1
Schools: 14
6 Primary; 4 Middle; 3 High; 1 Other Level
13 Regular; 0 Special Education; 0 Vocational; 1 Alternative
0 Magnet; 0 Charter; 4 Title I Eligible; 0 School-wide Title I
Students: 10,726 (50.8% male; 49.2% female)
Individual Education Program: 1,234 (11.5%);
English Language Learner: 167 (1.6%); Migrant: n/a
Eligible for Free Lunch Program: 386 (3.6%)
Eligible for Reduced-Price Lunch Program: 245 (2.3%)
Teachers: 777.0 (13.8 to 1)
Librarians/Media Specialists: 12.2 (879.2 to 1)
Guidance Counselors: 27.0 (397.3 to 1)
Current Spending: ($ per student per year):
Total: $9,761; Instruction: $6,326; Support Services: $3,259

Enrollment, Drop-out Rates and Diploma Recipients by Race/Ethnicity

Category	Total	White	Black	Asian	AIAN	Hisp.
Enrollment (%)	100.0	89.3	3.3	6.1	0.3	1.0
Drop-out Rate (%)	0.9	1.0	2.1	0.0	0.0	0.0
H.S. Diplomas (#)	773	700	22	43	0	8

Franklin County

Malone CSD

64 W St • Malone, NY 12953-1118
(518) 483-7800 • http://www.fehb.org/malone.htm
Grade Span: PK-12; **Agency Type:** 1
Schools: 9
3 Primary; 1 Middle; 1 High; 4 Other Level
5 Regular; 0 Special Education; 0 Vocational; 4 Alternative
0 Magnet; 0 Charter; 3 Title I Eligible; 0 School-wide Title I
Students: 2,655 (52.7% male; 47.3% female)
Individual Education Program: 435 (16.4%);
English Language Learner: 2 (0.1%); Migrant: n/a
Eligible for Free Lunch Program: 960 (36.2%)
Eligible for Reduced-Price Lunch Program: 312 (11.8%)
Teachers: 216.5 (12.3 to 1)
Librarians/Media Specialists: 4.0 (663.8 to 1)
Guidance Counselors: 7.0 (379.3 to 1)
Current Spending: ($ per student per year):
Total: $10,904; Instruction: $7,546; Support Services: $3,026

Enrollment, Drop-out Rates and Diploma Recipients by Race/Ethnicity

Category	Total	White	Black	Asian	AIAN	Hisp.
Enrollment (%)	100.0	94.8	2.5	0.5	0.8	1.4
Drop-out Rate (%)	2.3	2.3	0.0	0.0	0.0	0.0
H.S. Diplomas (#)	188	181	2	3	0	2

Salmon River CSD

637 County Rte 1 • Fort Covington, NY 12937-9722
(518) 358-2215 • http://srk12.neric.org/
Grade Span: PK-12; **Agency Type:** 2
Schools: 3

2 Primary; 0 Middle; 1 High; 0 Other Level
3 Regular; 0 Special Education; 0 Vocational; 0 Alternative
0 Magnet; 0 Charter; 3 Title I Eligible; 0 School-wide Title I

Students: 1,536 (48.9% male; 51.1% female)
Individual Education Program: 276 (18.0%);
English Language Learner: 15 (1.0%); Migrant: n/a
Eligible for Free Lunch Program: 614 (40.0%)
Eligible for Reduced-Price Lunch Program: 231 (15.0%)

Teachers: 137.9 (11.1 to 1)
Librarians/Media Specialists: 2.7 (568.9 to 1)
Guidance Counselors: 5.0 (307.2 to 1)
Current Spending: ($ per student per year):
Total: $13,099; Instruction: $8,526; Support Services: $4,079

Enrollment, Drop-out Rates and Diploma Recipients by Race/Ethnicity

Category	Total	White	Black	Asian	AIAN	Hisp.
Enrollment (%)	100.0	42.9	0.7	0.3	55.6	0.5
Drop-out Rate (%)	4.9	2.2	0.0	n/a	7.5	0.0
H.S. Diplomas (#)	88	42	2	1	42	1

Saranac Lake CSD

99 Lapan Hwy • Saranac Lake, NY 12983-1500
(518) 891-5460 • http://www.slcs.org/
Grade Span: KG-12; **Agency Type:** 1
Schools: 8
4 Primary; 1 Middle; 1 High; 2 Other Level
6 Regular; 0 Special Education; 0 Vocational; 2 Alternative
0 Magnet; 0 Charter; 4 Title I Eligible; 0 School-wide Title I

Students: 1,680 (51.1% male; 48.9% female)
Individual Education Program: 247 (14.7%);
English Language Learner: 25 (1.5%); Migrant: n/a
Eligible for Free Lunch Program: 239 (14.2%)
Eligible for Reduced-Price Lunch Program: 123 (7.3%)

Teachers: 135.7 (12.4 to 1)
Librarians/Media Specialists: 4.0 (420.0 to 1)
Guidance Counselors: 2.2 (763.6 to 1)
Current Spending: ($ per student per year):
Total: $11,047; Instruction: $7,322; Support Services: $3,488

Enrollment, Drop-out Rates and Diploma Recipients by Race/Ethnicity

Category	Total	White	Black	Asian	AIAN	Hisp.
Enrollment (%)	100.0	97.9	1.0	0.5	0.2	0.4
Drop-out Rate (%)	1.8	1.8	0.0	0.0	n/a	0.0
H.S. Diplomas (#)	112	111	0	1	0	0

Fulton County

Broadalbin-Perth CSD

14 School St • Broadalbin, NY 12025-9997
(518) 954-2500 • http://www.bpcsd.org/
Grade Span: PK-12; **Agency Type:** 2
Schools: 5
1 Primary; 2 Middle; 2 High; 0 Other Level
4 Regular; 0 Special Education; 0 Vocational; 1 Alternative
0 Magnet; 0 Charter; 2 Title I Eligible; 0 School-wide Title I

Students: 2,178 (57.4% male; 42.6% female)
Individual Education Program: 232 (10.7%);
English Language Learner: 2 (0.1%); Migrant: n/a
Eligible for Free Lunch Program: 239 (11.0%)
Eligible for Reduced-Price Lunch Program: 124 (5.7%)

Teachers: 137.9 (15.8 to 1)
Librarians/Media Specialists: 3.7 (588.6 to 1)
Guidance Counselors: 2.0 (1,089.0 to 1)
Current Spending: ($ per student per year):
Total: $7,898; Instruction: $5,214; Support Services: $2,412

Enrollment, Drop-out Rates and Diploma Recipients by Race/Ethnicity

Category	Total	White	Black	Asian	AIAN	Hisp.
Enrollment (%)	100.0	88.4	6.9	0.7	0.1	3.9
Drop-out Rate (%)	4.2	4.1	0.0	n/a	n/a	100.0
H.S. Diplomas (#)	128	122	4	0	0	2

Gloversville City SD

243 Lincoln St • Gloversville, NY 12078-0005
(518) 775-5600
Grade Span: PK-12; **Agency Type:** 1
Schools: 7
5 Primary; 1 Middle; 1 High; 0 Other Level
7 Regular; 0 Special Education; 0 Vocational; 0 Alternative
0 Magnet; 0 Charter; 6 Title I Eligible; 0 School-wide Title I

Students: 3,284 (51.6% male; 48.4% female)
Individual Education Program: 515 (15.7%);
English Language Learner: 8 (0.2%); Migrant: n/a
Eligible for Free Lunch Program: 1,048 (31.9%)
Eligible for Reduced-Price Lunch Program: 324 (9.9%)

Teachers: 251.7 (13.0 to 1)
Librarians/Media Specialists: 3.8 (864.2 to 1)
Guidance Counselors: 9.0 (364.9 to 1)
Current Spending: ($ per student per year):
Total: $9,681; Instruction: $6,841; Support Services: $2,531

Enrollment, Drop-out Rates and Diploma Recipients by Race/Ethnicity

Category	Total	White	Black	Asian	AIAN	Hisp.
Enrollment (%)	100.0	94.0	3.2	0.9	0.0	1.8
Drop-out Rate (%)	3.6	3.7	6.3	0.0	n/a	0.0
H.S. Diplomas (#)	166	157	1	3	0	5

Johnstown City SD

2 Wright Dr Ste 101 • Johnstown, NY 12095-3099
(518) 762-4611
Grade Span: PK-12; **Agency Type:** 1
Schools: 13
4 Primary; 1 Middle; 2 High; 6 Other Level
6 Regular; 0 Special Education; 0 Vocational; 7 Alternative
0 Magnet; 0 Charter; 3 Title I Eligible; 0 School-wide Title I

Students: 2,124 (47.9% male; 52.1% female)
Individual Education Program: 318 (15.0%);
English Language Learner: 1 (<0.1%); Migrant: n/a
Eligible for Free Lunch Program: 502 (23.6%)
Eligible for Reduced-Price Lunch Program: 255 (12.0%)

Teachers: 149.1 (14.2 to 1)
Librarians/Media Specialists: 1.0 (2,124.0 to 1)
Guidance Counselors: 4.0 (531.0 to 1)
Current Spending: ($ per student per year):
Total: $8,593; Instruction: $5,769; Support Services: $2,496

Enrollment, Drop-out Rates and Diploma Recipients by Race/Ethnicity

Category	Total	White	Black	Asian	AIAN	Hisp.
Enrollment (%)	100.0	94.5	2.8	1.0	0.1	1.7
Drop-out Rate (%)	4.8	4.7	0.0	0.0	0.0	14.3
H.S. Diplomas (#)	140	135	0	4	0	1

Genesee County

Batavia City SD

39 Washington Ave • Batavia, NY 14021-0677
(585) 343-2480 • http://www.bataviacsd.org/
Grade Span: KG-12; **Agency Type:** 1
Schools: 10
3 Primary; 1 Middle; 1 High; 5 Other Level
5 Regular; 0 Special Education; 0 Vocational; 5 Alternative
0 Magnet; 0 Charter; 5 Title I Eligible; 0 School-wide Title I

Students: 2,703 (49.7% male; 50.3% female)
Individual Education Program: 443 (16.4%);
English Language Learner: 8 (0.3%); Migrant: n/a
Eligible for Free Lunch Program: 690 (25.5%)
Eligible for Reduced-Price Lunch Program: 227 (8.4%)

Teachers: 221.7 (12.2 to 1)
Librarians/Media Specialists: 4.8 (563.1 to 1)
Guidance Counselors: 10.0 (270.3 to 1)
Current Spending: ($ per student per year):
Total: $11,468; Instruction: $7,947; Support Services: $3,213

Enrollment, Drop-out Rates and Diploma Recipients by Race/Ethnicity

Category	Total	White	Black	Asian	AIAN	Hisp.
Enrollment (%)	100.0	86.0	10.2	1.4	0.4	2.0
Drop-out Rate (%)	3.0	2.8	4.5	0.0	0.0	7.7
H.S. Diplomas (#)	152	143	7	1	1	0

Greene County

Cairo-Durham CSD

424 Main St • Cairo, NY 12413-0780
(518) 622-8534 • http://www.cairodurham.org/
Grade Span: KG-12; **Agency Type:** 2
Schools: 4
2 Primary; 1 Middle; 1 High; 0 Other Level
4 Regular; 0 Special Education; 0 Vocational; 0 Alternative
0 Magnet; 0 Charter; 3 Title I Eligible; 0 School-wide Title I

Students: 1,819 (50.5% male; 49.5% female)
Individual Education Program: 278 (15.3%);
English Language Learner: 5 (0.3%); Migrant: n/a
Eligible for Free Lunch Program: 427 (23.5%)
Eligible for Reduced-Price Lunch Program: 151 (8.3%)

Teachers: 129.1 (14.1 to 1)
Librarians/Media Specialists: 1.2 (1,515.8 to 1)
Guidance Counselors: 3.0 (606.3 to 1)
Current Spending: ($ per student per year):
Total: $8,499; Instruction: $5,472; Support Services: $2,739

Enrollment, Drop-out Rates and Diploma Recipients by Race/Ethnicity

Category	Total	White	Black	Asian	AIAN	Hisp.
Enrollment (%)	100.0	95.0	1.3	0.7	0.4	2.6
Drop-out Rate (%)	0.4	0.4	0.0	0.0	n/a	0.0
H.S. Diplomas (#)	74	73	0	0	0	1

Catskill CSD

343 W Main St • Catskill, NY 12414-1699
(518) 943-4696
Grade Span: KG-12; **Agency Type:** 1
Schools: 3
1 Primary; 1 Middle; 1 High; 0 Other Level
3 Regular; 0 Special Education; 0 Vocational; 0 Alternative
0 Magnet; 0 Charter; 3 Title I Eligible; 0 School-wide Title I
Students: 1,786 (51.3% male; 48.7% female)
Individual Education Program: 248 (13.9%);
English Language Learner: 14 (0.8%); Migrant: n/a
Eligible for Free Lunch Program: 413 (23.1%)
Eligible for Reduced-Price Lunch Program: 120 (6.7%)
Teachers: 147.0 (12.1 to 1)
Librarians/Media Specialists: 3.7 (482.7 to 1)
Guidance Counselors: 3.0 (595.3 to 1)
Current Spending: ($ per student per year):
Total: $10,244; Instruction: $6,982; Support Services: $3,039
Enrollment, Drop-out Rates and Diploma Recipients by Race/Ethnicity

Category	Total	White	Black	Asian	AIAN	Hisp.
Enrollment (%)	100.0	78.9	13.3	1.4	0.1	6.3
Drop-out Rate (%)	5.6	4.6	16.7	11.1	n/a	5.6
H.S. Diplomas (#)	79	68	4	2	1	4

Coxsackie-Athens CSD

24 Sunset Blvd • Coxsackie, NY 12051-1199
(518) 731-1710 • http://www.coxsackie-athens.org/
Grade Span: KG-12; **Agency Type:** 2
Schools: 6
2 Primary; 1 Middle; 1 High; 2 Other Level
4 Regular; 0 Special Education; 0 Vocational; 2 Alternative
0 Magnet; 0 Charter; 2 Title I Eligible; 0 School-wide Title I
Students: 1,641 (69.1% male; 30.9% female)
Individual Education Program: 144 (8.8%);
English Language Learner: 11 (0.7%); Migrant: n/a
Eligible for Free Lunch Program: 221 (13.5%)
Eligible for Reduced-Price Lunch Program: 98 (6.0%)
Teachers: 131.3 (12.5 to 1)
Librarians/Media Specialists: 3.0 (547.0 to 1)
Guidance Counselors: 3.0 (547.0 to 1)
Current Spending: ($ per student per year):
Total: $8,737; Instruction: $5,295; Support Services: $3,147
Enrollment, Drop-out Rates and Diploma Recipients by Race/Ethnicity

Category	Total	White	Black	Asian	AIAN	Hisp.
Enrollment (%)	100.0	65.6	22.4	0.4	0.3	11.3
Drop-out Rate (%)	1.6	1.5	0.0	0.0	n/a	8.3
H.S. Diplomas (#)	98	94	2	0	0	2

Herkimer County

Ilion CSD

1 Golden Bomber Dr • Ilion, NY 13357-0480
(315) 894-9934 • http://www.moric.org/ilion/
Grade Span: PK-12; **Agency Type:** 1
Schools: 3
2 Primary; 0 Middle; 1 High; 0 Other Level
3 Regular; 0 Special Education; 0 Vocational; 0 Alternative
0 Magnet; 0 Charter; 2 Title I Eligible; 0 School-wide Title I
Students: 1,854 (49.6% male; 50.4% female)
Individual Education Program: 310 (16.7%);
English Language Learner: 12 (0.6%); Migrant: n/a
Eligible for Free Lunch Program: 489 (26.4%)
Eligible for Reduced-Price Lunch Program: 216 (11.7%)
Teachers: 135.5 (13.7 to 1)
Librarians/Media Specialists: 1.0 (1,854.0 to 1)
Guidance Counselors: 3.0 (618.0 to 1)
Current Spending: ($ per student per year):
Total: $8,036; Instruction: $6,004; Support Services: $1,782
Enrollment, Drop-out Rates and Diploma Recipients by Race/Ethnicity

Category	Total	White	Black	Asian	AIAN	Hisp.
Enrollment (%)	100.0	95.2	2.0	1.0	0.1	1.7
Drop-out Rate (%)	3.5	3.6	0.0	0.0	0.0	0.0
H.S. Diplomas (#)	114	108	1	0	2	3

Jefferson County

Carthage CSD

25059 County Rt 197 • Carthage, NY 13619-9527
(315) 493-5000 • http://www.carthagecsd.org/
Grade Span: KG-12; **Agency Type:** 1
Schools: 5
3 Primary; 1 Middle; 1 High; 0 Other Level
5 Regular; 0 Special Education; 0 Vocational; 0 Alternative
0 Magnet; 0 Charter; 4 Title I Eligible; 0 School-wide Title I
Students: 2,959 (50.6% male; 49.4% female)
Individual Education Program: 424 (14.3%);
English Language Learner: 9 (0.3%); Migrant: n/a
Eligible for Free Lunch Program: 618 (20.9%)
Eligible for Reduced-Price Lunch Program: 329 (11.1%)
Teachers: 205.3 (14.4 to 1)
Librarians/Media Specialists: 4.8 (616.5 to 1)
Guidance Counselors: 5.0 (591.8 to 1)
Current Spending: ($ per student per year):
Total: $9,380; Instruction: $6,061; Support Services: $2,999
Enrollment, Drop-out Rates and Diploma Recipients by Race/Ethnicity

Category	Total	White	Black	Asian	AIAN	Hisp.
Enrollment (%)	100.0	88.6	6.5	2.0	0.1	2.9
Drop-out Rate (%)	1.9	2.1	1.7	0.0	0.0	0.0
H.S. Diplomas (#)	193	177	9	4	2	1

General Brown CSD

17643 Cemetery Rd • Dexter, NY 13634-9731
(315) 639-4711 • http://www.moric.org/genbrown/gb_do.htm
Grade Span: PK-12; **Agency Type:** 2
Schools: 3
2 Primary; 0 Middle; 1 High; 0 Other Level
3 Regular; 0 Special Education; 0 Vocational; 0 Alternative
0 Magnet; 0 Charter; 3 Title I Eligible; 0 School-wide Title I
Students: 1,565 (50.9% male; 49.1% female)
Individual Education Program: 220 (14.1%);
English Language Learner: 1 (0.1%); Migrant: n/a
Eligible for Free Lunch Program: 332 (21.2%)
Eligible for Reduced-Price Lunch Program: 141 (9.0%)
Teachers: 111.2 (14.1 to 1)
Librarians/Media Specialists: 1.8 (869.4 to 1)
Guidance Counselors: 3.0 (521.7 to 1)
Current Spending: ($ per student per year):
Total: $7,918; Instruction: $5,358; Support Services: $2,280
Enrollment, Drop-out Rates and Diploma Recipients by Race/Ethnicity

Category	Total	White	Black	Asian	AIAN	Hisp.
Enrollment (%)	100.0	95.9	1.5	1.0	1.0	0.6
Drop-out Rate (%)	1.5	1.6	0.0	0.0	0.0	0.0
H.S. Diplomas (#)	121	118	1	2	0	0

Indian River CSD

32735-B Cnty Rte 29 • Philadelphia, NY 13673-0308
(315) 642-3481 • http://www.ircsd.org/
Grade Span: KG-12; **Agency Type:** 1
Schools: 8
5 Primary; 2 Middle; 1 High; 0 Other Level
8 Regular; 0 Special Education; 0 Vocational; 0 Alternative
0 Magnet; 0 Charter; 7 Title I Eligible; 0 School-wide Title I
Students: 3,478 (50.9% male; 49.1% female)
Individual Education Program: 493 (14.2%);
English Language Learner: 148 (4.3%); Migrant: n/a
Eligible for Free Lunch Program: 886 (25.5%)
Eligible for Reduced-Price Lunch Program: 629 (18.1%)
Teachers: 295.9 (11.8 to 1)
Librarians/Media Specialists: 6.0 (579.7 to 1)
Guidance Counselors: 10.0 (347.8 to 1)
Current Spending: ($ per student per year):
Total: $11,289; Instruction: $6,859; Support Services: $4,041
Enrollment, Drop-out Rates and Diploma Recipients by Race/Ethnicity

Category	Total	White	Black	Asian	AIAN	Hisp.
Enrollment (%)	100.0	76.4	14.0	1.7	0.6	7.3
Drop-out Rate (%)	2.0	2.3	0.0	0.0	0.0	0.0
H.S. Diplomas (#)	155	132	13	1	0	9

South Jefferson CSD

13180 U S Rt 11 • Adams Center, NY 13606-0010
(315) 583-6104 • http://www.spartanpride.org/
Grade Span: KG-12; **Agency Type:** 2
Schools: 4
3 Primary; 0 Middle; 1 High; 0 Other Level
4 Regular; 0 Special Education; 0 Vocational; 0 Alternative
0 Magnet; 0 Charter; 3 Title I Eligible; 0 School-wide Title I
Students: 1,991 (52.9% male; 47.1% female)
Individual Education Program: 282 (14.2%);
English Language Learner: 0 (0.0%); Migrant: n/a
Eligible for Free Lunch Program: 412 (20.7%)
Eligible for Reduced-Price Lunch Program: 202 (10.1%)
Teachers: 146.2 (13.6 to 1)
Librarians/Media Specialists: 1.8 (1,106.1 to 1)
Guidance Counselors: 5.0 (398.2 to 1)
Current Spending: ($ per student per year):
Total: $8,154; Instruction: $5,381; Support Services: $2,441

Enrollment, Drop-out Rates and Diploma Recipients by Race/Ethnicity

Category	Total	White	Black	Asian	AIAN	Hisp.
Enrollment (%)	100.0	98.2	0.8	0.5	0.3	0.3
Drop-out Rate (%)	3.3	3.3	n/a	0.0	n/a	0.0
H.S. Diplomas (#)	123	122	0	0	0	1

Watertown City SD

376 Butterfield Ave • Watertown, NY 13601-4593
(315) 785-3700 • http://watertown.k12.sd.us/
Grade Span: PK-12; **Agency Type:** 1
Schools: 10
5 Primary; 2 Middle; 1 High; 2 Other Level
8 Regular; 0 Special Education; 0 Vocational; 2 Alternative
0 Magnet; 0 Charter; 3 Title I Eligible; 0 School-wide Title I
Students: 4,229 (51.2% male; 48.8% female)
Individual Education Program: 682 (16.1%);
English Language Learner: 50 (1.2%); Migrant: n/a
Eligible for Free Lunch Program: 1,657 (39.2%)
Eligible for Reduced-Price Lunch Program: 512 (12.1%)
Teachers: 305.0 (13.9 to 1)
Librarians/Media Specialists: 5.0 (845.8 to 1)
Guidance Counselors: 7.0 (604.1 to 1)
Current Spending: ($ per student per year):
Total: $8,829; Instruction: $5,965; Support Services: $2,561

Enrollment, Drop-out Rates and Diploma Recipients by Race/Ethnicity

Category	Total	White	Black	Asian	AIAN	Hisp.
Enrollment (%)	100.0	81.7	11.3	2.3	0.8	3.9
Drop-out Rate (%)	5.0	5.3	4.8	0.0	0.0	2.0
H.S. Diplomas (#)	173	156	11	2	0	4

Kings County

New York City Public Schools

110 Livingston St • Brooklyn, NY 11201
(718) 935-2794 • http://www.nycenet.edu/
Grade Span: PK-12; **Agency Type:** 1
Schools: 1,429
708 Primary; 211 Middle; 192 High; 318 Other Level
1,095 Regular; 57 Special Education; 18 Vocational; 259 Alternative
4 Magnet; 0 Charter; 792 Title I Eligible; 0 School-wide Title I
Students: 1,077,381 (51.3% male; 48.7% female)
Individual Education Program: 144,040 (13.4%);
English Language Learner: 124,947 (11.6%); Migrant: n/a
Eligible for Free Lunch Program: n/a
Eligible for Reduced-Price Lunch Program: n/a
Teachers: 65,803.2 (16.4 to 1)
Librarians/Media Specialists: 764.0 (1,410.2 to 1)
Guidance Counselors: 2,851.0 (377.9 to 1)
Current Spending: ($ per student per year):
Total: $11,112; Instruction: $8,270; Support Services: $2,477

Enrollment, Drop-out Rates and Diploma Recipients by Race/Ethnicity

Category	Total	White	Black	Asian	AIAN	Hisp.
Enrollment (%)	100.0	15.0	34.0	12.4	0.4	38.2
Drop-out Rate (%)	6.5	3.7	7.4	3.7	9.4	8.0
H.S. Diplomas (#)	37,915	8,110	12,208	6,698	87	10,812

Note: *The New York City Public School System is actually comprised of 81 school districts spread across the five boroughs. The National Center for Education Statistics summarizes all the districts' data under this single entity.*

Livingston County

Dansville CSD

299 Main St • Dansville, NY 14437-1199
(585) 335-4000 • http://www.dansville.k12.ny.us/
Grade Span: PK-12; **Agency Type:** 1
Schools: 4
2 Primary; 1 Middle; 1 High; 0 Other Level
4 Regular; 0 Special Education; 0 Vocational; 0 Alternative
0 Magnet; 0 Charter; 2 Title I Eligible; 0 School-wide Title I
Students: 1,803 (51.6% male; 48.4% female)
Individual Education Program: 307 (17.0%);
English Language Learner: 3 (0.2%); Migrant: n/a
Eligible for Free Lunch Program: 358 (19.9%)
Eligible for Reduced-Price Lunch Program: 134 (7.4%)
Teachers: 144.4 (12.5 to 1)
Librarians/Media Specialists: 3.6 (500.8 to 1)
Guidance Counselors: 8.0 (225.4 to 1)
Current Spending: ($ per student per year):
Total: $9,351; Instruction: $6,236; Support Services: $2,894

Enrollment, Drop-out Rates and Diploma Recipients by Race/Ethnicity

Category	Total	White	Black	Asian	AIAN	Hisp.
Enrollment (%)	100.0	96.5	1.4	0.7	0.2	1.2
Drop-out Rate (%)	4.1	4.1	11.1	0.0	n/a	0.0
H.S. Diplomas (#)	107	100	4	2	0	1

Livonia CSD

6 Puppy Ln • Livonia, NY 14487-0489
(585) 346-4000 • http://www.livonia-csd.k12.ny.us/
Grade Span: KG-12; **Agency Type:** 1
Schools: 4
1 Primary; 2 Middle; 1 High; 0 Other Level
4 Regular; 0 Special Education; 0 Vocational; 0 Alternative
0 Magnet; 0 Charter; 3 Title I Eligible; 0 School-wide Title I
Students: 2,180 (50.6% male; 49.4% female)
Individual Education Program: 201 (9.2%);
English Language Learner: 1 (<0.1%); Migrant: n/a
Eligible for Free Lunch Program: 195 (8.9%)
Eligible for Reduced-Price Lunch Program: 93 (4.3%)
Teachers: 180.0 (12.1 to 1)
Librarians/Media Specialists: 3.7 (589.2 to 1)
Guidance Counselors: 5.0 (436.0 to 1)
Current Spending: ($ per student per year):
Total: $8,735; Instruction: $5,814; Support Services: $2,692

Enrollment, Drop-out Rates and Diploma Recipients by Race/Ethnicity

Category	Total	White	Black	Asian	AIAN	Hisp.
Enrollment (%)	100.0	97.9	1.1	0.4	0.1	0.5
Drop-out Rate (%)	1.7	1.8	0.0	0.0	0.0	0.0
H.S. Diplomas (#)	146	146	0	0	0	0

Madison County

Canastota CSD

120 Roberts St • Canastota, NY 13032-1198
(315) 697-2025
Grade Span: KG-12; **Agency Type:** 1
Schools: 4
2 Primary; 1 Middle; 1 High; 0 Other Level
4 Regular; 0 Special Education; 0 Vocational; 0 Alternative
0 Magnet; 0 Charter; 2 Title I Eligible; 0 School-wide Title I
Students: 1,570 (50.6% male; 49.4% female)
Individual Education Program: 247 (15.7%);
English Language Learner: 1 (0.1%); Migrant: n/a
Eligible for Free Lunch Program: 312 (19.9%)
Eligible for Reduced-Price Lunch Program: 134 (8.5%)
Teachers: 116.7 (13.5 to 1)
Librarians/Media Specialists: 2.0 (785.0 to 1)
Guidance Counselors: 3.0 (523.3 to 1)
Current Spending: ($ per student per year):
Total: $9,204; Instruction: $6,360; Support Services: $2,578

Enrollment, Drop-out Rates and Diploma Recipients by Race/Ethnicity

Category	Total	White	Black	Asian	AIAN	Hisp.
Enrollment (%)	100.0	97.0	1.6	0.6	0.1	0.7
Drop-out Rate (%)	3.8	3.6	n/a	0.0	n/a	33.3
H.S. Diplomas (#)	105	105	0	0	0	0

Cazenovia CSD

31 Emory Ave • Cazenovia, NY 13035-1098
(315) 655-1317 • http://www.caz.cnyric.org/
Grade Span: KG-12; **Agency Type:** 1
Schools: 3
1 Primary; 1 Middle; 1 High; 0 Other Level
3 Regular; 0 Special Education; 0 Vocational; 0 Alternative
0 Magnet; 0 Charter; 1 Title I Eligible; 0 School-wide Title I
Students: 1,822 (51.0% male; 49.0% female)
Individual Education Program: 200 (11.0%);
English Language Learner: 1 (0.1%); Migrant: n/a
Eligible for Free Lunch Program: 117 (6.4%)
Eligible for Reduced-Price Lunch Program: 61 (3.3%)
Teachers: 137.7 (13.2 to 1)
Librarians/Media Specialists: 2.8 (650.7 to 1)
Guidance Counselors: 5.0 (364.4 to 1)
Current Spending: ($ per student per year):
Total: $8,669; Instruction: $5,600; Support Services: $2,886

Enrollment, Drop-out Rates and Diploma Recipients by Race/Ethnicity

Category	Total	White	Black	Asian	AIAN	Hisp.
Enrollment (%)	100.0	97.4	0.8	0.8	0.1	0.9
Drop-out Rate (%)	1.7	1.7	0.0	0.0	n/a	0.0
H.S. Diplomas (#)	108	108	0	0	0	0

Chittenango CSD

1732 Fyler Rd • Chittenango, NY 13037-9520
(315) 687-2669
Grade Span: KG-12; **Agency Type:** 1
Schools: 5
3 Primary; 1 Middle; 1 High; 0 Other Level
5 Regular; 0 Special Education; 0 Vocational; 0 Alternative
0 Magnet; 0 Charter; 3 Title I Eligible; 0 School-wide Title I
Students: 2,580 (50.0% male; 50.0% female)
Individual Education Program: 358 (13.9%);
English Language Learner: 2 (0.1%); Migrant: n/a

Eligible for Free Lunch Program: 354 (13.7%)
Eligible for Reduced-Price Lunch Program: 196 (7.6%)
Teachers: 189.8 (13.6 to 1)
Librarians/Media Specialists: 4.5 (573.3 to 1)
Guidance Counselors: 7.2 (358.3 to 1)
Current Spending: ($ per student per year):
Total: $8,231; Instruction: $5,259; Support Services: $2,687
Enrollment, Drop-out Rates and Diploma Recipients by Race/Ethnicity

Category	Total	White	Black	Asian	AIAN	Hisp.
Enrollment (%)	100.0	98.1	0.8	0.5	0.3	0.2
Drop-out Rate (%)	1.1	1.1	0.0	0.0	0.0	0.0
H.S. Diplomas (#)	165	163	0	0	1	1

Oneida City SD
565 Sayles St • Oneida, NY 13421-0327
(315) 363-2550 • http://www.oneidany.org/
Grade Span: KG-12; **Agency Type:** 1
Schools: 8
6 Primary; 1 Middle; 1 High; 0 Other Level
8 Regular; 0 Special Education; 0 Vocational; 0 Alternative
0 Magnet; 0 Charter; 5 Title I Eligible; 0 School-wide Title I
Students: 2,589 (51.0% male; 49.0% female)
Individual Education Program: 353 (13.6%);
English Language Learner: 12 (0.5%); Migrant: n/a
Eligible for Free Lunch Program: 552 (21.3%)
Eligible for Reduced-Price Lunch Program: 225 (8.7%)
Teachers: 194.3 (13.3 to 1)
Librarians/Media Specialists: 6.5 (398.3 to 1)
Guidance Counselors: 4.0 (647.3 to 1)
Current Spending: ($ per student per year):
Total: $9,927; Instruction: $6,608; Support Services: $3,039
Enrollment, Drop-out Rates and Diploma Recipients by Race/Ethnicity

Category	Total	White	Black	Asian	AIAN	Hisp.
Enrollment (%)	100.0	96.5	0.8	0.9	1.2	0.6
Drop-out Rate (%)	4.0	3.9	0.0	0.0	11.8	0.0
H.S. Diplomas (#)	159	155	0	0	1	3

Monroe County

Boces Monroe 1
41 O'connor Rd • Fairport, NY 14450
(585) 383-2200 • http://www.monroe.edu/
Grade Span: PK-PK; **Agency Type:** 4
Schools: 1
1 Primary; 0 Middle; 0 High; 0 Other Level
1 Regular; 0 Special Education; 0 Vocational; 0 Alternative
0 Magnet; 0 Charter; 0 Title I Eligible; 0 School-wide Title I
Students: 1,521 (72.0% male; 28.0% female)
Individual Education Program: 1,265 (83.2%);
English Language Learner: n/a; Migrant: n/a
Eligible for Free Lunch Program: n/a
Eligible for Reduced-Price Lunch Program: n/a
Teachers: 344.2 (4.4 to 1)
Librarians/Media Specialists: 1.0 (1,521.0 to 1)
Guidance Counselors: 3.0 (507.0 to 1)
Current Spending: ($ per student per year):
Total: n/a; Instruction: n/a; Support Services: n/a
Enrollment, Drop-out Rates and Diploma Recipients by Race/Ethnicity

Category	Total	White	Black	Asian	AIAN	Hisp.
Enrollment (%)	100.0	67.5	18.8	4.9	0.3	8.5
Drop-out Rate (%)	n/a	n/a	n/a	n/a	n/a	n/a
H.S. Diplomas (#)	n/a	n/a	n/a	n/a	n/a	n/a

Brighton CSD
2035 Monroe Ave • Rochester, NY 14618-2027
(585) 242-5080 • http://www.bcsd.org/index_noflash.cfm
Grade Span: KG-12; **Agency Type:** 1
Schools: 5
2 Primary; 1 Middle; 1 High; 1 Other Level
4 Regular; 0 Special Education; 0 Vocational; 1 Alternative
0 Magnet; 0 Charter; 2 Title I Eligible; 0 School-wide Title I
Students: 3,593 (50.8% male; 49.2% female)
Individual Education Program: 378 (10.5%);
English Language Learner: 121 (3.4%); Migrant: n/a
Eligible for Free Lunch Program: 151 (4.2%)
Eligible for Reduced-Price Lunch Program: 93 (2.6%)
Teachers: 278.0 (12.9 to 1)
Librarians/Media Specialists: 3.6 (998.1 to 1)
Guidance Counselors: 11.2 (320.8 to 1)
Current Spending: ($ per student per year):
Total: $10,692; Instruction: $6,579; Support Services: $3,880

Enrollment, Drop-out Rates and Diploma Recipients by Race/Ethnicity

Category	Total	White	Black	Asian	AIAN	Hisp.
Enrollment (%)	100.0	78.0	5.7	13.3	0.4	2.7
Drop-out Rate (%)	1.0	0.8	1.7	2.2	0.0	0.0
H.S. Diplomas (#)	259	215	8	29	0	7

Brockport CSD
40 Allen St • Brockport, NY 14420-2296
(585) 637-1810 • http://www.brockport.k12.ny.us/
Grade Span: KG-12; **Agency Type:** 1
Schools: 6
3 Primary; 1 Middle; 1 High; 1 Other Level
5 Regular; 0 Special Education; 0 Vocational; 1 Alternative
0 Magnet; 0 Charter; 2 Title I Eligible; 0 School-wide Title I
Students: 4,573 (49.9% male; 50.1% female)
Individual Education Program: 619 (13.5%);
English Language Learner: 54 (1.2%); Migrant: n/a
Eligible for Free Lunch Program: 721 (15.8%)
Eligible for Reduced-Price Lunch Program: 409 (8.9%)
Teachers: 322.5 (14.2 to 1)
Librarians/Media Specialists: 4.9 (933.3 to 1)
Guidance Counselors: 13.0 (351.8 to 1)
Current Spending: ($ per student per year):
Total: $9,808; Instruction: $6,120; Support Services: $3,400
Enrollment, Drop-out Rates and Diploma Recipients by Race/Ethnicity

Category	Total	White	Black	Asian	AIAN	Hisp.
Enrollment (%)	100.0	91.5	3.9	1.2	0.5	3.0
Drop-out Rate (%)	2.1	1.9	6.7	0.0	0.0	3.7
H.S. Diplomas (#)	290	264	20	1	0	5

Churchville-Chili CSD
139 Fairbanks Rd • Churchville, NY 14428-9797
(585) 293-1800 • http://www.cccsd.org/
Grade Span: KG-12; **Agency Type:** 1
Schools: 6
3 Primary; 2 Middle; 1 High; 0 Other Level
6 Regular; 0 Special Education; 0 Vocational; 0 Alternative
0 Magnet; 0 Charter; 3 Title I Eligible; 0 School-wide Title I
Students: 4,515 (52.1% male; 47.9% female)
Individual Education Program: 401 (8.9%);
English Language Learner: 47 (1.0%); Migrant: n/a
Eligible for Free Lunch Program: 410 (9.1%)
Eligible for Reduced-Price Lunch Program: 234 (5.2%)
Teachers: 324.9 (13.9 to 1)
Librarians/Media Specialists: 6.8 (664.0 to 1)
Guidance Counselors: 12.0 (376.3 to 1)
Current Spending: ($ per student per year):
Total: $9,304; Instruction: $6,018; Support Services: $3,064
Enrollment, Drop-out Rates and Diploma Recipients by Race/Ethnicity

Category	Total	White	Black	Asian	AIAN	Hisp.
Enrollment (%)	100.0	91.0	5.6	1.7	0.1	1.5
Drop-out Rate (%)	0.5	0.5	0.0	0.0	0.0	0.0
H.S. Diplomas (#)	298	297	1	0	0	0

East Irondequoit CSD
600 Pardee Rd • Rochester, NY 14609-2898
(585) 339-1210 • http://www.eicsd.k12.ny.us/
Grade Span: KG-12; **Agency Type:** 1
Schools: 6
3 Primary; 2 Middle; 1 High; 0 Other Level
6 Regular; 0 Special Education; 0 Vocational; 0 Alternative
0 Magnet; 0 Charter; 3 Title I Eligible; 0 School-wide Title I
Students: 3,499 (50.4% male; 49.6% female)
Individual Education Program: 452 (12.9%);
English Language Learner: 97 (2.8%); Migrant: n/a
Eligible for Free Lunch Program: 639 (18.3%)
Eligible for Reduced-Price Lunch Program: 281 (8.0%)
Teachers: 265.8 (13.2 to 1)
Librarians/Media Specialists: 4.7 (744.5 to 1)
Guidance Counselors: 8.0 (437.4 to 1)
Current Spending: ($ per student per year):
Total: $10,073; Instruction: $5,909; Support Services: $3,910
Enrollment, Drop-out Rates and Diploma Recipients by Race/Ethnicity

Category	Total	White	Black	Asian	AIAN	Hisp.
Enrollment (%)	100.0	80.8	10.3	1.9	0.2	6.7
Drop-out Rate (%)	1.6	1.2	1.3	8.3	0.0	8.0
H.S. Diplomas (#)	203	177	9	1	0	16

Fairport CSD
38 W Church St • Fairport, NY 14450-2130
(585) 421-2004 • http://www.fairport.org/
Grade Span: KG-12; **Agency Type:** 1
Schools: 8
4 Primary; 2 Middle; 1 High; 1 Other Level
8 Regular; 0 Special Education; 0 Vocational; 0 Alternative

0 Magnet; 0 Charter; 3 Title I Eligible; 0 School-wide Title I
Students: 7,126 (50.6% male; 49.4% female)
Individual Education Program: 842 (11.8%);
English Language Learner: 57 (0.8%); Migrant: n/a
Eligible for Free Lunch Program: 288 (4.0%)
Eligible for Reduced-Price Lunch Program: 155 (2.2%)
Teachers: 508.1 (14.0 to 1)
Librarians/Media Specialists: 8.9 (800.7 to 1)
Guidance Counselors: 14.5 (491.4 to 1)
Current Spending: ($ per student per year):
Total: $9,478; Instruction: $6,437; Support Services: $2,800

Enrollment, Drop-out Rates and Diploma Recipients by Race/Ethnicity

Category	Total	White	Black	Asian	AIAN	Hisp.
Enrollment (%)	100.0	92.4	2.4	3.7	0.1	1.4
Drop-out Rate (%)	0.5	0.5	0.0	0.0	0.0	0.0
H.S. Diplomas (#)	489	455	12	17	0	5

Gates-Chili CSD

910 Wegman Rd • Rochester, NY 14624-1440
(585) 247-5050 • http://www.gateschili.org/
Grade Span: KG-12; **Agency Type:** 1
Schools: 7
5 Primary; 1 Middle; 1 High; 0 Other Level
7 Regular; 0 Special Education; 0 Vocational; 0 Alternative
0 Magnet; 0 Charter; 3 Title I Eligible; 0 School-wide Title I
Students: 5,124 (50.9% male; 49.1% female)
Individual Education Program: 659 (12.9%);
English Language Learner: 64 (1.2%); Migrant: n/a
Eligible for Free Lunch Program: 561 (10.9%)
Eligible for Reduced-Price Lunch Program: 360 (7.0%)
Teachers: 384.1 (13.3 to 1)
Librarians/Media Specialists: 8.8 (582.3 to 1)
Guidance Counselors: 12.0 (427.0 to 1)
Current Spending: ($ per student per year):
Total: $10,458; Instruction: $6,800; Support Services: $3,375

Enrollment, Drop-out Rates and Diploma Recipients by Race/Ethnicity

Category	Total	White	Black	Asian	AIAN	Hisp.
Enrollment (%)	100.0	83.9	10.0	2.8	0.2	3.1
Drop-out Rate (%)	0.9	0.8	0.6	0.0	0.0	5.6
H.S. Diplomas (#)	379	326	34	8	3	8

Greece CSD

750 Maiden Ln • Rochester, NY 14615-1296
(585) 621-1000
Grade Span: PK-12; **Agency Type:** 1
Schools: 21
13 Primary; 3 Middle; 3 High; 2 Other Level
21 Regular; 0 Special Education; 0 Vocational; 0 Alternative
0 Magnet; 0 Charter; 4 Title I Eligible; 0 School-wide Title I
Students: 13,730 (51.7% male; 48.3% female)
Individual Education Program: 1,516 (11.0%);
English Language Learner: 272 (2.0%); Migrant: n/a
Eligible for Free Lunch Program: 1,857 (13.5%)
Eligible for Reduced-Price Lunch Program: 990 (7.2%)
Teachers: 1,029.6 (13.3 to 1)
Librarians/Media Specialists: 17.4 (789.1 to 1)
Guidance Counselors: 37.4 (367.1 to 1)
Current Spending: ($ per student per year):
Total: $9,995; Instruction: $6,256; Support Services: $3,442

Enrollment, Drop-out Rates and Diploma Recipients by Race/Ethnicity

Category	Total	White	Black	Asian	AIAN	Hisp.
Enrollment (%)	100.0	88.7	5.2	2.0	0.5	3.5
Drop-out Rate (%)	0.6	0.6	1.1	0.0	0.0	0.7
H.S. Diplomas (#)	901	826	25	23	0	27

Hilton CSD

225 W Ave • Hilton, NY 14468-1283
(585) 392-1000 • http://www.hilton.k12.ny.us/
Grade Span: KG-12; **Agency Type:** 1
Schools: 5
3 Primary; 1 Middle; 1 High; 0 Other Level
5 Regular; 0 Special Education; 0 Vocational; 0 Alternative
0 Magnet; 0 Charter; 1 Title I Eligible; 0 School-wide Title I
Students: 4,438 (51.5% male; 48.5% female)
Individual Education Program: 536 (12.1%);
English Language Learner: 34 (0.8%); Migrant: n/a
Eligible for Free Lunch Program: 341 (7.7%)
Eligible for Reduced-Price Lunch Program: 273 (6.2%)
Teachers: 340.9 (13.0 to 1)
Librarians/Media Specialists: 5.0 (887.6 to 1)
Guidance Counselors: 12.9 (344.0 to 1)
Current Spending: ($ per student per year):
Total: $9,149; Instruction: $6,131; Support Services: $2,801

Enrollment, Drop-out Rates and Diploma Recipients by Race/Ethnicity

Category	Total	White	Black	Asian	AIAN	Hisp.
Enrollment (%)	100.0	96.1	1.6	0.9	0.3	1.0
Drop-out Rate (%)	1.3	1.3	4.0	0.0	0.0	0.0
H.S. Diplomas (#)	330	315	4	8	1	2

Honeoye Falls-Lima CSD

20 Church St • Honeoye Falls, NY 14472-1294
(585) 624-7010 • http://www.hfl.monroe.edu/
Grade Span: KG-12; **Agency Type:** 1
Schools: 4
2 Primary; 1 Middle; 1 High; 0 Other Level
4 Regular; 0 Special Education; 0 Vocational; 0 Alternative
0 Magnet; 0 Charter; 3 Title I Eligible; 0 School-wide Title I
Students: 2,606 (49.0% male; 51.0% female)
Individual Education Program: 304 (11.7%);
English Language Learner: 2 (0.1%); Migrant: n/a
Eligible for Free Lunch Program: 120 (4.6%)
Eligible for Reduced-Price Lunch Program: 69 (2.6%)
Teachers: 190.7 (13.7 to 1)
Librarians/Media Specialists: 1.9 (1,371.6 to 1)
Guidance Counselors: 6.0 (434.3 to 1)
Current Spending: ($ per student per year):
Total: $9,461; Instruction: $5,974; Support Services: $3,225

Enrollment, Drop-out Rates and Diploma Recipients by Race/Ethnicity

Category	Total	White	Black	Asian	AIAN	Hisp.
Enrollment (%)	100.0	97.4	0.8	1.0	0.2	0.7
Drop-out Rate (%)	0.8	0.8	0.0	0.0	0.0	0.0
H.S. Diplomas (#)	164	161	1	1	0	1

Penfield CSD

2590 Atlantic Ave • Penfield, NY 14526-0900
(585) 249-5700 • http://penfield.edu/
Grade Span: KG-12; **Agency Type:** 1
Schools: 6
4 Primary; 1 Middle; 1 High; 0 Other Level
6 Regular; 0 Special Education; 0 Vocational; 0 Alternative
0 Magnet; 0 Charter; 3 Title I Eligible; 0 School-wide Title I
Students: 5,058 (50.3% male; 49.7% female)
Individual Education Program: 560 (11.1%);
English Language Learner: 78 (1.5%); Migrant: n/a
Eligible for Free Lunch Program: 208 (4.1%)
Eligible for Reduced-Price Lunch Program: 113 (2.2%)
Teachers: 410.3 (12.3 to 1)
Librarians/Media Specialists: 6.5 (778.2 to 1)
Guidance Counselors: 13.2 (383.2 to 1)
Current Spending: ($ per student per year):
Total: $10,046; Instruction: $6,860; Support Services: $2,969

Enrollment, Drop-out Rates and Diploma Recipients by Race/Ethnicity

Category	Total	White	Black	Asian	AIAN	Hisp.
Enrollment (%)	100.0	90.5	3.5	3.6	0.4	2.0
Drop-out Rate (%)	1.1	1.2	0.0	0.0	n/a	0.0
H.S. Diplomas (#)	302	277	13	8	0	4

Pittsford CSD

42 W Jefferson Rd • Pittsford, NY 14534-1978
(585) 218-1004 • http://www.pittsfordschools.org/
Grade Span: KG-12; **Agency Type:** 1
Schools: 8
5 Primary; 1 Middle; 2 High; 0 Other Level
8 Regular; 0 Special Education; 0 Vocational; 0 Alternative
0 Magnet; 0 Charter; 0 Title I Eligible; 0 School-wide Title I
Students: 5,933 (50.8% male; 49.2% female)
Individual Education Program: 694 (11.7%);
English Language Learner: 35 (0.6%); Migrant: n/a
Eligible for Free Lunch Program: 83 (1.4%)
Eligible for Reduced-Price Lunch Program: 27 (0.5%)
Teachers: 451.1 (13.2 to 1)
Librarians/Media Specialists: 8.1 (732.5 to 1)
Guidance Counselors: 17.6 (337.1 to 1)
Current Spending: ($ per student per year):
Total: $10,800; Instruction: $7,536; Support Services: $3,067

Enrollment, Drop-out Rates and Diploma Recipients by Race/Ethnicity

Category	Total	White	Black	Asian	AIAN	Hisp.
Enrollment (%)	100.0	92.4	2.1	4.7	0.0	0.7
Drop-out Rate (%)	0.2	0.2	0.0	0.0	0.0	0.0
H.S. Diplomas (#)	443	410	21	8	0	4

Rochester City SD

131 W Broad St • Rochester, NY 14614-1187
(585) 262-8378 • http://www.rcsd-k12.org/
Grade Span: PK-12; **Agency Type:** 1
Schools: 69
40 Primary; 7 Middle; 7 High; 15 Other Level
59 Regular; 0 Special Education; 1 Vocational; 9 Alternative

1 Magnet; 0 Charter; 54 Title I Eligible; 0 School-wide Title I
Students: 35,659 (50.8% male; 49.2% female)
Individual Education Program: 6,770 (19.0%);
English Language Learner: 2,768 (7.8%); Migrant: n/a
Eligible for Free Lunch Program: 22,837 (64.0%)
Eligible for Reduced-Price Lunch Program: 2,562 (7.2%)
Teachers: 2,943.7 (12.1 to 1)
Librarians/Media Specialists: 48.1 (741.4 to 1)
Guidance Counselors: 66.2 (538.7 to 1)
Current Spending: ($ per student per year):
Total: $12,068; Instruction: $7,720; Support Services: $3,940
Enrollment, Drop-out Rates and Diploma Recipients by Race/Ethnicity

Category	Total	White	Black	Asian	AIAN	Hisp.
Enrollment (%)	100.0	14.4	63.9	1.8	0.3	19.6
Drop-out Rate (%)	9.9	9.5	9.1	6.5	15.8	13.4
H.S. Diplomas (#)	1,021	234	617	32	5	133

Rush-Henrietta CSD

2034 Lehigh Sta Rd • Henrietta, NY 14467-9692
(585) 359-5012 • http://www.rhnet.org/
Grade Span: KG-12; **Agency Type:** 1
Schools: 11
5 Primary; 2 Middle; 1 High; 3 Other Level
9 Regular; 0 Special Education; 0 Vocational; 2 Alternative
0 Magnet; 0 Charter; 4 Title I Eligible; 0 School-wide Title I
Students: 6,091 (52.3% male; 47.7% female)
Individual Education Program: 889 (14.6%);
English Language Learner: 152 (2.5%); Migrant: n/a
Eligible for Free Lunch Program: 720 (11.8%)
Eligible for Reduced-Price Lunch Program: 430 (7.1%)
Teachers: 493.7 (12.3 to 1)
Librarians/Media Specialists: 8.7 (700.1 to 1)
Guidance Counselors: 16.0 (380.7 to 1)
Current Spending: ($ per student per year):
Total: $12,452; Instruction: $7,749; Support Services: $4,396
Enrollment, Drop-out Rates and Diploma Recipients by Race/Ethnicity

Category	Total	White	Black	Asian	AIAN	Hisp.
Enrollment (%)	100.0	75.6	13.7	6.4	0.8	3.6
Drop-out Rate (%)	3.1	3.0	3.6	2.9	7.1	1.9
H.S. Diplomas (#)	349	271	45	24	3	6

Spencerport CSD

71 Lyell Ave • Spencerport, NY 14559-1899
(585) 349-5102 • http://www.spencerportschools.org/
Grade Span: KG-12; **Agency Type:** 1
Schools: 5
3 Primary; 1 Middle; 1 High; 0 Other Level
5 Regular; 0 Special Education; 0 Vocational; 0 Alternative
0 Magnet; 0 Charter; 4 Title I Eligible; 0 School-wide Title I
Students: 4,312 (52.0% male; 48.0% female)
Individual Education Program: 596 (13.8%);
English Language Learner: 44 (1.0%); Migrant: n/a
Eligible for Free Lunch Program: 297 (6.9%)
Eligible for Reduced-Price Lunch Program: 228 (5.3%)
Teachers: 314.7 (13.7 to 1)
Librarians/Media Specialists: 4.3 (1,002.8 to 1)
Guidance Counselors: 9.0 (479.1 to 1)
Current Spending: ($ per student per year):
Total: $9,531; Instruction: $6,686; Support Services: $2,601
Enrollment, Drop-out Rates and Diploma Recipients by Race/Ethnicity

Category	Total	White	Black	Asian	AIAN	Hisp.
Enrollment (%)	100.0	91.6	3.7	2.6	0.2	1.9
Drop-out Rate (%)	1.0	0.6	8.7	2.9	0.0	0.0
H.S. Diplomas (#)	292	268	12	9	0	3

Webster CSD

119 S Ave • Webster, NY 14580-3594
(585) 265-3600 • http://www.websterschools.org/
Grade Span: KG-12; **Agency Type:** 1
Schools: 12
7 Primary; 2 Middle; 1 High; 2 Other Level
11 Regular; 0 Special Education; 0 Vocational; 1 Alternative
0 Magnet; 0 Charter; 5 Title I Eligible; 0 School-wide Title I
Students: 8,471 (52.1% male; 47.9% female)
Individual Education Program: 1,059 (12.5%);
English Language Learner: 109 (1.3%); Migrant: n/a
Eligible for Free Lunch Program: 355 (4.2%)
Eligible for Reduced-Price Lunch Program: 183 (2.2%)
Teachers: 666.9 (12.7 to 1)
Librarians/Media Specialists: 9.6 (882.4 to 1)
Guidance Counselors: 21.5 (394.0 to 1)
Current Spending: ($ per student per year):
Total: $9,698; Instruction: $6,711; Support Services: $2,788

Enrollment, Drop-out Rates and Diploma Recipients by Race/Ethnicity

Category	Total	White	Black	Asian	AIAN	Hisp.
Enrollment (%)	100.0	94.8	2.1	2.2	0.0	0.9
Drop-out Rate (%)	0.8	0.8	0.0	0.0	0.0	5.3
H.S. Diplomas (#)	600	578	8	12	1	1

West Irondequoit CSD

370 Cooper Rd • Rochester, NY 14617-3093
(585) 342-5500 • http://www.westirondequoit.org/
Grade Span: KG-12; **Agency Type:** 1
Schools: 10
6 Primary; 3 Middle; 1 High; 0 Other Level
10 Regular; 0 Special Education; 0 Vocational; 0 Alternative
0 Magnet; 0 Charter; 2 Title I Eligible; 0 School-wide Title I
Students: 3,973 (50.0% male; 50.0% female)
Individual Education Program: 414 (10.4%);
English Language Learner: 39 (1.0%); Migrant: n/a
Eligible for Free Lunch Program: 224 (5.6%)
Eligible for Reduced-Price Lunch Program: 129 (3.2%)
Teachers: 262.2 (15.2 to 1)
Librarians/Media Specialists: 7.0 (567.6 to 1)
Guidance Counselors: 14.0 (283.8 to 1)
Current Spending: ($ per student per year):
Total: $9,274; Instruction: $5,493; Support Services: $3,547
Enrollment, Drop-out Rates and Diploma Recipients by Race/Ethnicity

Category	Total	White	Black	Asian	AIAN	Hisp.
Enrollment (%)	100.0	89.5	5.2	2.1	0.3	3.0
Drop-out Rate (%)	1.1	1.1	0.0	0.0	n/a	5.9
H.S. Diplomas (#)	315	286	12	9	0	8

Montgomery County

Amsterdam City SD

11 Liberty St • Amsterdam, NY 12010-0670
(518) 843-5217
Grade Span: KG-12; **Agency Type:** 1
Schools: 7
5 Primary; 1 Middle; 1 High; 0 Other Level
7 Regular; 0 Special Education; 0 Vocational; 0 Alternative
0 Magnet; 0 Charter; 4 Title I Eligible; 0 School-wide Title I
Students: 3,740 (51.2% male; 48.8% female)
Individual Education Program: 634 (17.0%);
English Language Learner: 132 (3.5%); Migrant: n/a
Eligible for Free Lunch Program: 1,087 (29.1%)
Eligible for Reduced-Price Lunch Program: 209 (5.6%)
Teachers: 297.1 (12.6 to 1)
Librarians/Media Specialists: 4.0 (935.0 to 1)
Guidance Counselors: 10.0 (374.0 to 1)
Current Spending: ($ per student per year):
Total: $9,215; Instruction: $6,364; Support Services: $2,624
Enrollment, Drop-out Rates and Diploma Recipients by Race/Ethnicity

Category	Total	White	Black	Asian	AIAN	Hisp.
Enrollment (%)	100.0	72.1	3.1	0.5	0.0	24.3
Drop-out Rate (%)	3.7	3.3	0.0	9.1	n/a	5.6
H.S. Diplomas (#)	0	0	0	0	0	0

Fonda-Fultonville CSD

112 Old Johnstown Rd • Fonda, NY 12068-1501
(518) 853-4415 • http://ffcs.neric.org/
Grade Span: KG-12; **Agency Type:** 2
Schools: 4
1 Primary; 1 Middle; 1 High; 1 Other Level
3 Regular; 0 Special Education; 0 Vocational; 1 Alternative
0 Magnet; 0 Charter; 3 Title I Eligible; 0 School-wide Title I
Students: 1,602 (52.9% male; 47.1% female)
Individual Education Program: 209 (13.0%);
English Language Learner: 1 (0.1%); Migrant: n/a
Eligible for Free Lunch Program: 299 (18.7%)
Eligible for Reduced-Price Lunch Program: 150 (9.4%)
Teachers: 125.0 (12.8 to 1)
Librarians/Media Specialists: 2.0 (801.0 to 1)
Guidance Counselors: 2.0 (801.0 to 1)
Current Spending: ($ per student per year):
Total: $10,127; Instruction: $6,599; Support Services: $3,221
Enrollment, Drop-out Rates and Diploma Recipients by Race/Ethnicity

Category	Total	White	Black	Asian	AIAN	Hisp.
Enrollment (%)	100.0	97.1	0.6	1.1	0.0	1.2
Drop-out Rate (%)	3.5	3.6	0.0	n/a	0.0	0.0
H.S. Diplomas (#)	121	120	1	0	0	0

Nassau County

Baldwin UFSD
960 Hastings St • Baldwin, NY 11510-4798
(516) 377-9271
Grade Span: KG-12; **Agency Type:** 1
Schools: 9
7 Primary; 1 Middle; 1 High; 0 Other Level
9 Regular; 0 Special Education; 0 Vocational; 0 Alternative
0 Magnet; 0 Charter; 2 Title I Eligible; 0 School-wide Title I
Students: 5,437 (52.0% male; 48.0% female)
Individual Education Program: 563 (10.4%);
English Language Learner: 159 (2.9%); Migrant: n/a
Eligible for Free Lunch Program: 0 (0.0%)
Eligible for Reduced-Price Lunch Program: 0 (0.0%)
Teachers: 423.7 (12.8 to 1)
Librarians/Media Specialists: 3.2 (1,699.1 to 1)
Guidance Counselors: 9.0 (604.1 to 1)
Current Spending: ($ per student per year):
Total: $11,827; Instruction: $7,829; Support Services: $3,836
Enrollment, Drop-out Rates and Diploma Recipients by Race/Ethnicity

Category	Total	White	Black	Asian	AIAN	Hisp.
Enrollment (%)	100.0	49.0	32.4	4.6	0.2	13.8
Drop-out Rate (%)	1.3	1.0	0.8	0.0	0.0	4.2
H.S. Diplomas (#)	346	218	95	9	0	24

Bellmore-Merrick Central HSD
1260 Meadowbrook Rd • North Merrick, NY 11566-9998
(516) 992-1001 • http://www.bellmore-merrick.k12.ny.us/
Grade Span: 07-12; **Agency Type:** 2
Schools: 5
0 Primary; 2 Middle; 3 High; 0 Other Level
5 Regular; 0 Special Education; 0 Vocational; 0 Alternative
0 Magnet; 0 Charter; 1 Title I Eligible; 0 School-wide Title I
Students: 5,681 (51.6% male; 48.4% female)
Individual Education Program: 665 (11.7%);
English Language Learner: 35 (0.6%); Migrant: n/a
Eligible for Free Lunch Program: 69 (1.2%)
Eligible for Reduced-Price Lunch Program: 39 (0.7%)
Teachers: 367.4 (15.5 to 1)
Librarians/Media Specialists: 5.0 (1,136.2 to 1)
Guidance Counselors: 21.6 (263.0 to 1)
Current Spending: ($ per student per year):
Total: $12,988; Instruction: $8,341; Support Services: $4,383
Enrollment, Drop-out Rates and Diploma Recipients by Race/Ethnicity

Category	Total	White	Black	Asian	AIAN	Hisp.
Enrollment (%)	100.0	92.8	1.1	3.8	0.0	2.2
Drop-out Rate (%)	0.7	0.7	2.0	0.8	n/a	0.9
H.S. Diplomas (#)	812	754	12	22	0	24

Bethpage UFSD
10 Cherry Ave • Bethpage, NY 11714-1596
(516) 644-4001 • http://www.bethpagecommunity.com/Schools/
Grade Span: KG-12; **Agency Type:** 1
Schools: 6
3 Primary; 1 Middle; 1 High; 1 Other Level
5 Regular; 0 Special Education; 0 Vocational; 1 Alternative
0 Magnet; 0 Charter; 4 Title I Eligible; 0 School-wide Title I
Students: 2,960 (52.2% male; 47.8% female)
Individual Education Program: 372 (12.6%);
English Language Learner: 72 (2.4%); Migrant: n/a
Eligible for Free Lunch Program: 97 (3.3%)
Eligible for Reduced-Price Lunch Program: 71 (2.4%)
Teachers: 235.1 (12.6 to 1)
Librarians/Media Specialists: 4.8 (616.7 to 1)
Guidance Counselors: 7.0 (422.9 to 1)
Current Spending: ($ per student per year):
Total: $13,915; Instruction: $8,739; Support Services: $4,965
Enrollment, Drop-out Rates and Diploma Recipients by Race/Ethnicity

Category	Total	White	Black	Asian	AIAN	Hisp.
Enrollment (%)	100.0	92.9	0.0	4.8	0.0	2.3
Drop-out Rate (%)	0.5	0.4	50.0	0.0	n/a	0.0
H.S. Diplomas (#)	180	159	1	15	0	5

Boces Nassau
71 Clinton Rd • Garden City, NY 11530-4757
(516) 396-2200
Grade Span: PK-PK; **Agency Type:** 4
Schools: 1
1 Primary; 0 Middle; 0 High; 0 Other Level
1 Regular; 0 Special Education; 0 Vocational; 0 Alternative
0 Magnet; 0 Charter; 0 Title I Eligible; 0 School-wide Title I
Students: 2,008 (74.0% male; 26.0% female)
Individual Education Program: 1,724 (85.9%);
English Language Learner: n/a; Migrant: n/a
Eligible for Free Lunch Program: n/a
Eligible for Reduced-Price Lunch Program: n/a
Teachers: 554.4 (3.6 to 1)
Librarians/Media Specialists: 2.0 (1,004.0 to 1)
Guidance Counselors: 8.0 (251.0 to 1)
Current Spending: ($ per student per year):
Total: n/a; Instruction: n/a; Support Services: n/a
Enrollment, Drop-out Rates and Diploma Recipients by Race/Ethnicity

Category	Total	White	Black	Asian	AIAN	Hisp.
Enrollment (%)	100.0	56.0	25.3	4.7	0.2	13.8
Drop-out Rate (%)	n/a	n/a	n/a	n/a	n/a	n/a
H.S. Diplomas (#)	n/a	n/a	n/a	n/a	n/a	n/a

Carle Place UFSD
168 Cherry Ln • Carle Place, NY 11514-1788
(516) 622-6442
Grade Span: KG-12; **Agency Type:** 1
Schools: 3
2 Primary; 0 Middle; 1 High; 0 Other Level
3 Regular; 0 Special Education; 0 Vocational; 0 Alternative
0 Magnet; 0 Charter; 0 Title I Eligible; 0 School-wide Title I
Students: 1,517 (49.9% male; 50.1% female)
Individual Education Program: 239 (15.8%);
English Language Learner: 84 (5.5%); Migrant: n/a
Eligible for Free Lunch Program: 41 (2.7%)
Eligible for Reduced-Price Lunch Program: 45 (3.0%)
Teachers: 137.5 (11.0 to 1)
Librarians/Media Specialists: 3.0 (505.7 to 1)
Guidance Counselors: 4.0 (379.3 to 1)
Current Spending: ($ per student per year):
Total: $15,751; Instruction: $9,613; Support Services: $5,898
Enrollment, Drop-out Rates and Diploma Recipients by Race/Ethnicity

Category	Total	White	Black	Asian	AIAN	Hisp.
Enrollment (%)	100.0	83.7	0.6	4.9	0.3	10.5
Drop-out Rate (%)	0.6	0.8	n/a	0.0	n/a	0.0
H.S. Diplomas (#)	103	89	0	8	0	6

East Meadow UFSD
718 The Plain Rd • Westbury, NY 11590
(516) 478-5776
Grade Span: KG-12; **Agency Type:** 1
Schools: 10
5 Primary; 2 Middle; 2 High; 1 Other Level
9 Regular; 0 Special Education; 0 Vocational; 1 Alternative
0 Magnet; 0 Charter; 6 Title I Eligible; 0 School-wide Title I
Students: 8,081 (50.8% male; 49.2% female)
Individual Education Program: 843 (10.4%);
English Language Learner: 325 (4.0%); Migrant: n/a
Eligible for Free Lunch Program: 318 (3.9%)
Eligible for Reduced-Price Lunch Program: 310 (3.8%)
Teachers: 620.6 (13.0 to 1)
Librarians/Media Specialists: 13.0 (621.6 to 1)
Guidance Counselors: 20.0 (404.1 to 1)
Current Spending: ($ per student per year):
Total: $12,984; Instruction: $8,626; Support Services: $4,165
Enrollment, Drop-out Rates and Diploma Recipients by Race/Ethnicity

Category	Total	White	Black	Asian	AIAN	Hisp.
Enrollment (%)	100.0	76.5	2.2	12.2	0.0	9.1
Drop-out Rate (%)	0.6	0.4	0.0	1.9	n/a	1.7
H.S. Diplomas (#)	507	434	3	44	0	26

East Williston UFSD
11 Bacon Rd • Old Westbury, NY 11568-1599
(516) 876-4740 • http://www.ewsdonline.org/
Grade Span: KG-12; **Agency Type:** 1
Schools: 3
1 Primary; 1 Middle; 1 High; 0 Other Level
3 Regular; 0 Special Education; 0 Vocational; 0 Alternative
0 Magnet; 0 Charter; 1 Title I Eligible; 0 School-wide Title I
Students: 1,752 (52.7% male; 47.3% female)
Individual Education Program: 210 (12.0%);
English Language Learner: 38 (2.2%); Migrant: n/a
Eligible for Free Lunch Program: 8 (0.5%)
Eligible for Reduced-Price Lunch Program: 0 (0.0%)
Teachers: 149.5 (11.7 to 1)
Librarians/Media Specialists: 3.0 (584.0 to 1)
Guidance Counselors: 7.0 (250.3 to 1)
Current Spending: ($ per student per year):
Total: $17,285; Instruction: $11,221; Support Services: $5,875
Enrollment, Drop-out Rates and Diploma Recipients by Race/Ethnicity

Category	Total	White	Black	Asian	AIAN	Hisp.
Enrollment (%)	100.0	86.9	0.2	9.8	0.0	3.1
Drop-out Rate (%)	0.0	0.0	0.0	0.0	n/a	0.0
H.S. Diplomas (#)	127	107	1	15	0	4

Elmont UFSD

135 Elmont Rd • Elmont, NY 11003-1609
(516) 326-5500
Grade Span: PK-06; **Agency Type:** 2
Schools: 6
6 Primary; 0 Middle; 0 High; 0 Other Level
6 Regular; 0 Special Education; 0 Vocational; 0 Alternative
0 Magnet; 0 Charter; 3 Title I Eligible; 0 School-wide Title I
Students: 4,338 (51.0% male; 49.0% female)
Individual Education Program: 533 (12.3%);
English Language Learner: 230 (5.3%); Migrant: n/a
Eligible for Free Lunch Program: 1,087 (25.1%)
Eligible for Reduced-Price Lunch Program: 587 (13.5%)
Teachers: 277.1 (15.7 to 1)
Librarians/Media Specialists: 5.7 (761.1 to 1)
Guidance Counselors: 0.0 (0.0 to 1)
Current Spending: ($ per student per year):
Total: $9,500; Instruction: $6,320; Support Services: $2,895
Enrollment, Drop-out Rates and Diploma Recipients by Race/Ethnicity

Category	Total	White	Black	Asian	AIAN	Hisp.
Enrollment (%)	100.0	19.2	49.8	12.6	0.3	18.1
Drop-out Rate (%)	n/a	n/a	n/a	n/a	n/a	n/a
H.S. Diplomas (#)	n/a	n/a	n/a	n/a	n/a	n/a

Farmingdale UFSD

50 Van Cott Ave • Farmingdale, NY 11735-3742
(516) 752-6510 • http://farmingdaleschools.org/fps/
Grade Span: KG-12; **Agency Type:** 1
Schools: 6
4 Primary; 1 Middle; 1 High; 0 Other Level
6 Regular; 0 Special Education; 0 Vocational; 0 Alternative
0 Magnet; 0 Charter; 3 Title I Eligible; 0 School-wide Title I
Students: 6,502 (52.7% male; 47.3% female)
Individual Education Program: 863 (13.3%);
English Language Learner: 179 (2.8%); Migrant: n/a
Eligible for Free Lunch Program: 485 (7.5%)
Eligible for Reduced-Price Lunch Program: 275 (4.2%)
Teachers: 524.7 (12.4 to 1)
Librarians/Media Specialists: 9.5 (684.4 to 1)
Guidance Counselors: 14.0 (464.4 to 1)
Current Spending: ($ per student per year):
Total: $12,954; Instruction: $8,151; Support Services: $4,609
Enrollment, Drop-out Rates and Diploma Recipients by Race/Ethnicity

Category	Total	White	Black	Asian	AIAN	Hisp.
Enrollment (%)	100.0	80.8	6.3	3.7	0.1	9.1
Drop-out Rate (%)	0.6	0.1	1.5	0.0	0.0	3.8
H.S. Diplomas (#)	367	299	22	18	0	28

Floral Park-Bellerose UFSD

One Poppy Pl • Floral Park, NY 11001-2398
(516) 327-9300 • http://www.floralpark.k12.ny.us/
Grade Span: PK-06; **Agency Type:** 2
Schools: 2
2 Primary; 0 Middle; 0 High; 0 Other Level
2 Regular; 0 Special Education; 0 Vocational; 0 Alternative
0 Magnet; 0 Charter; 1 Title I Eligible; 0 School-wide Title I
Students: 1,726 (51.7% male; 48.3% female)
Individual Education Program: 209 (12.1%);
English Language Learner: 45 (2.6%); Migrant: n/a
Eligible for Free Lunch Program: 39 (2.3%)
Eligible for Reduced-Price Lunch Program: 28 (1.6%)
Teachers: 104.1 (16.6 to 1)
Librarians/Media Specialists: 1.0 (1,726.0 to 1)
Guidance Counselors: 0.0 (0.0 to 1)
Current Spending: ($ per student per year):
Total: $9,026; Instruction: $6,745; Support Services: $2,188
Enrollment, Drop-out Rates and Diploma Recipients by Race/Ethnicity

Category	Total	White	Black	Asian	AIAN	Hisp.
Enrollment (%)	100.0	79.2	1.4	9.7	0.1	9.5
Drop-out Rate (%)	n/a	n/a	n/a	n/a	n/a	n/a
H.S. Diplomas (#)	n/a	n/a	n/a	n/a	n/a	n/a

Franklin Square UFSD

760 Washington St • Franklin Square, NY 11010-3898
(516) 481-4100
Grade Span: KG-06; **Agency Type:** 2
Schools: 3
3 Primary; 0 Middle; 0 High; 0 Other Level
3 Regular; 0 Special Education; 0 Vocational; 0 Alternative
0 Magnet; 0 Charter; 3 Title I Eligible; 0 School-wide Title I
Students: 1,940 (50.5% male; 49.5% female)
Individual Education Program: 226 (11.6%);
English Language Learner: 52 (2.7%); Migrant: n/a
Eligible for Free Lunch Program: 123 (6.3%)
Eligible for Reduced-Price Lunch Program: 86 (4.4%)
Teachers: 131.8 (14.7 to 1)
Librarians/Media Specialists: 1.7 (1,141.2 to 1)
Guidance Counselors: 0.0 (0.0 to 1)
Current Spending: ($ per student per year):
Total: $9,638; Instruction: $6,863; Support Services: $2,587
Enrollment, Drop-out Rates and Diploma Recipients by Race/Ethnicity

Category	Total	White	Black	Asian	AIAN	Hisp.
Enrollment (%)	100.0	87.6	0.7	3.5	0.1	8.1
Drop-out Rate (%)	n/a	n/a	n/a	n/a	n/a	n/a
H.S. Diplomas (#)	n/a	n/a	n/a	n/a	n/a	n/a

Freeport UFSD

235 N Ocean Ave • Freeport, NY 11520-0801
(516) 867-5205
Grade Span: PK-12; **Agency Type:** 1
Schools: 9
5 Primary; 2 Middle; 1 High; 1 Other Level
8 Regular; 0 Special Education; 0 Vocational; 1 Alternative
0 Magnet; 0 Charter; 6 Title I Eligible; 0 School-wide Title I
Students: 7,251 (50.1% male; 49.9% female)
Individual Education Program: 794 (11.0%);
English Language Learner: 994 (13.7%); Migrant: n/a
Eligible for Free Lunch Program: 2,196 (30.3%)
Eligible for Reduced-Price Lunch Program: 548 (7.6%)
Teachers: 522.3 (13.9 to 1)
Librarians/Media Specialists: 8.0 (906.4 to 1)
Guidance Counselors: 19.0 (381.6 to 1)
Current Spending: ($ per student per year):
Total: $11,321; Instruction: $7,608; Support Services: $3,503
Enrollment, Drop-out Rates and Diploma Recipients by Race/Ethnicity

Category	Total	White	Black	Asian	AIAN	Hisp.
Enrollment (%)	100.0	12.0	41.1	1.5	0.1	45.4
Drop-out Rate (%)	2.3	0.3	2.6	0.0	n/a	2.9
H.S. Diplomas (#)	281	63	124	7	0	87

Garden City UFSD

56 Cathedral Ave • Garden City, NY 11530-0216
(516) 294-3004
Grade Span: KG-12; **Agency Type:** 1
Schools: 7
5 Primary; 1 Middle; 1 High; 0 Other Level
7 Regular; 0 Special Education; 0 Vocational; 0 Alternative
0 Magnet; 0 Charter; 2 Title I Eligible; 0 School-wide Title I
Students: 4,058 (52.9% male; 47.1% female)
Individual Education Program: 484 (11.9%);
English Language Learner: 22 (0.5%); Migrant: n/a
Eligible for Free Lunch Program: 4 (0.1%)
Eligible for Reduced-Price Lunch Program: 1 (<0.1%)
Teachers: 312.6 (13.0 to 1)
Librarians/Media Specialists: 4.5 (901.8 to 1)
Guidance Counselors: 9.0 (450.9 to 1)
Current Spending: ($ per student per year):
Total: $13,126; Instruction: $8,543; Support Services: $4,459
Enrollment, Drop-out Rates and Diploma Recipients by Race/Ethnicity

Category	Total	White	Black	Asian	AIAN	Hisp.
Enrollment (%)	100.0	96.1	0.5	2.3	0.1	0.9
Drop-out Rate (%)	n/a	n/a	n/a	n/a	n/a	n/a
H.S. Diplomas (#)	214	197	2	9	3	3

Glen Cove City SD

Dosoris Ln • Glen Cove, NY 11542-1237
(516) 759-7217 • http://www.glencove.k12.ny.us/
Grade Span: PK-12; **Agency Type:** 1
Schools: 6
4 Primary; 1 Middle; 1 High; 0 Other Level
6 Regular; 0 Special Education; 0 Vocational; 0 Alternative
0 Magnet; 0 Charter; 2 Title I Eligible; 0 School-wide Title I
Students: 3,187 (51.9% male; 48.1% female)
Individual Education Program: 543 (17.0%);
English Language Learner: 307 (9.6%); Migrant: n/a
Eligible for Free Lunch Program: 598 (18.8%)
Eligible for Reduced-Price Lunch Program: 336 (10.5%)
Teachers: 254.3 (12.5 to 1)
Librarians/Media Specialists: 3.6 (885.3 to 1)
Guidance Counselors: 9.0 (354.1 to 1)
Current Spending: ($ per student per year):
Total: $13,595; Instruction: $8,663; Support Services: $4,658
Enrollment, Drop-out Rates and Diploma Recipients by Race/Ethnicity

Category	Total	White	Black	Asian	AIAN	Hisp.
Enrollment (%)	100.0	48.1	13.1	4.6	0.1	34.2
Drop-out Rate (%)	0.5	0.0	1.5	1.9	n/a	0.8
H.S. Diplomas (#)	192	110	20	13	0	49

Great Neck UFSD

345 Lakeville Rd • Great Neck, NY 11020-1606
(516) 773-1405 • http://www.greatneck.k12.ny.us/
Grade Span: PK-12; **Agency Type:** 1
Schools: 10
5 Primary; 2 Middle; 3 High; 0 Other Level
10 Regular; 0 Special Education; 0 Vocational; 0 Alternative
0 Magnet; 0 Charter; 4 Title I Eligible; 0 School-wide Title I
Students: 6,065 (52.3% male; 47.7% female)
Individual Education Program: 832 (13.7%);
English Language Learner: 380 (6.3%); Migrant: n/a
Eligible for Free Lunch Program: 362 (6.0%)
Eligible for Reduced-Price Lunch Program: 275 (4.5%)
Teachers: 554.7 (10.9 to 1)
Librarians/Media Specialists: 11.6 (522.8 to 1)
Guidance Counselors: 17.0 (356.8 to 1)
Current Spending: ($ per student per year):
Total: $17,891; Instruction: $11,547; Support Services: $6,076
Enrollment, Drop-out Rates and Diploma Recipients by Race/Ethnicity

Category	Total	White	Black	Asian	AIAN	Hisp.
Enrollment (%)	100.0	72.7	2.9	16.5	0.1	7.9
Drop-out Rate (%)	0.1	0.0	0.0	0.0	n/a	1.2
H.S. Diplomas (#)	516	402	10	75	0	29

Hempstead UFSD

185 Peninsula Blvd • Hempstead, NY 11550
(516) 292-7001
Grade Span: PK-12; **Agency Type:** 1
Schools: 12
8 Primary; 1 Middle; 1 High; 2 Other Level
10 Regular; 0 Special Education; 0 Vocational; 2 Alternative
0 Magnet; 0 Charter; 3 Title I Eligible; 0 School-wide Title I
Students: 7,218 (51.2% male; 48.8% female)
Individual Education Program: 792 (11.0%);
English Language Learner: 1,279 (17.7%); Migrant: n/a
Eligible for Free Lunch Program: 5,174 (71.7%)
Eligible for Reduced-Price Lunch Program: 1,208 (16.7%)
Teachers: 458.2 (15.8 to 1)
Librarians/Media Specialists: 8.3 (869.6 to 1)
Guidance Counselors: 7.0 (1,031.1 to 1)
Current Spending: ($ per student per year):
Total: $13,449; Instruction: $8,663; Support Services: $4,446
Enrollment, Drop-out Rates and Diploma Recipients by Race/Ethnicity

Category	Total	White	Black	Asian	AIAN	Hisp.
Enrollment (%)	100.0	0.5	55.9	0.4	0.1	43.0
Drop-out Rate (%)	10.4	6.7	9.8	0.0	0.0	11.7
H.S. Diplomas (#)	154	0	105	4	0	45

Herricks UFSD

99 Shelter Rock Rd • New Hyde Park, NY 11040-1355
(516) 248-3105 • http://www.herricks.org/
Grade Span: KG-12; **Agency Type:** 1
Schools: 5
3 Primary; 1 Middle; 1 High; 0 Other Level
5 Regular; 0 Special Education; 0 Vocational; 0 Alternative
0 Magnet; 0 Charter; 3 Title I Eligible; 0 School-wide Title I
Students: 3,874 (51.3% male; 48.7% female)
Individual Education Program: 523 (13.5%);
English Language Learner: 287 (7.4%); Migrant: n/a
Eligible for Free Lunch Program: 65 (1.7%)
Eligible for Reduced-Price Lunch Program: 43 (1.1%)
Teachers: 336.9 (11.5 to 1)
Librarians/Media Specialists: 5.8 (667.9 to 1)
Guidance Counselors: 7.5 (516.5 to 1)
Current Spending: ($ per student per year):
Total: $13,618; Instruction: $8,765; Support Services: $4,652
Enrollment, Drop-out Rates and Diploma Recipients by Race/Ethnicity

Category	Total	White	Black	Asian	AIAN	Hisp.
Enrollment (%)	100.0	56.9	0.4	38.3	0.1	4.3
Drop-out Rate (%)	0.2	0.1	0.0	0.5	n/a	0.0
H.S. Diplomas (#)	276	154	0	114	0	8

Hewlett-Woodmere UFSD

1 Johnson Pl • Woodmere, NY 11598-1312
(516) 374-8100
Grade Span: PK-12; **Agency Type:** 1
Schools: 5
3 Primary; 1 Middle; 1 High; 0 Other Level
5 Regular; 0 Special Education; 0 Vocational; 0 Alternative
0 Magnet; 0 Charter; 0 Title I Eligible; 0 School-wide Title I
Students: 3,370 (51.6% male; 48.4% female)
Individual Education Program: 530 (15.7%);
English Language Learner: 134 (4.0%); Migrant: n/a
Eligible for Free Lunch Program: 52 (1.5%)
Eligible for Reduced-Price Lunch Program: 44 (1.3%)
Teachers: 283.6 (11.9 to 1)
Librarians/Media Specialists: 3.0 (1,123.3 to 1)
Guidance Counselors: 9.0 (374.4 to 1)
Current Spending: ($ per student per year):
Total: $14,387; Instruction: $8,850; Support Services: $5,346
Enrollment, Drop-out Rates and Diploma Recipients by Race/Ethnicity

Category	Total	White	Black	Asian	AIAN	Hisp.
Enrollment (%)	100.0	85.8	1.5	6.8	0.0	5.8
Drop-out Rate (%)	0.0	0.0	0.0	0.0	n/a	0.0
H.S. Diplomas (#)	267	228	5	22	0	12

Hicksville UFSD

200 Division Ave-Adm • Hicksville, NY 11801-4800
(516) 733-6600
Grade Span: PK-12; **Agency Type:** 1
Schools: 9
7 Primary; 1 Middle; 1 High; 0 Other Level
9 Regular; 0 Special Education; 0 Vocational; 0 Alternative
0 Magnet; 0 Charter; 7 Title I Eligible; 0 School-wide Title I
Students: 5,161 (51.3% male; 48.7% female)
Individual Education Program: 851 (16.5%);
English Language Learner: 360 (7.0%); Migrant: n/a
Eligible for Free Lunch Program: 310 (6.0%)
Eligible for Reduced-Price Lunch Program: 199 (3.9%)
Teachers: 382.6 (13.5 to 1)
Librarians/Media Specialists: 9.0 (573.4 to 1)
Guidance Counselors: 10.0 (516.1 to 1)
Current Spending: ($ per student per year):
Total: $12,841; Instruction: $7,890; Support Services: $4,716
Enrollment, Drop-out Rates and Diploma Recipients by Race/Ethnicity

Category	Total	White	Black	Asian	AIAN	Hisp.
Enrollment (%)	100.0	66.6	2.3	15.4	0.1	15.6
Drop-out Rate (%)	0.5	0.4	0.0	0.5	n/a	1.1
H.S. Diplomas (#)	310	218	2	60	0	30

Island Trees UFSD

74 Farmedge Rd • Levittown, NY 11756-5205
(516) 520-2100
Grade Span: KG-12; **Agency Type:** 1
Schools: 4
2 Primary; 1 Middle; 1 High; 0 Other Level
4 Regular; 0 Special Education; 0 Vocational; 0 Alternative
0 Magnet; 0 Charter; 1 Title I Eligible; 0 School-wide Title I
Students: 2,783 (51.0% male; 49.0% female)
Individual Education Program: 271 (9.7%);
English Language Learner: 38 (1.4%); Migrant: n/a
Eligible for Free Lunch Program: 153 (5.5%)
Eligible for Reduced-Price Lunch Program: 82 (2.9%)
Teachers: 211.0 (13.2 to 1)
Librarians/Media Specialists: 4.0 (695.8 to 1)
Guidance Counselors: 7.6 (366.2 to 1)
Current Spending: ($ per student per year):
Total: $11,566; Instruction: $7,435; Support Services: $3,933
Enrollment, Drop-out Rates and Diploma Recipients by Race/Ethnicity

Category	Total	White	Black	Asian	AIAN	Hisp.
Enrollment (%)	100.0	88.1	0.4	3.6	0.0	7.9
Drop-out Rate (%)	0.5	0.5	0.0	0.0	n/a	0.0
H.S. Diplomas (#)	140	127	0	4	0	9

Jericho UFSD

99 Cedar Swamp Rd • Jericho, NY 11753-1202
(516) 681-4100 • http://www.bestschools.org/
Grade Span: KG-12; **Agency Type:** 1
Schools: 5
3 Primary; 1 Middle; 1 High; 0 Other Level
5 Regular; 0 Special Education; 0 Vocational; 0 Alternative
0 Magnet; 0 Charter; 3 Title I Eligible; 0 School-wide Title I
Students: 3,129 (51.7% male; 48.3% female)
Individual Education Program: 356 (11.4%);
English Language Learner: 80 (2.6%); Migrant: n/a
Eligible for Free Lunch Program: 34 (1.1%)
Eligible for Reduced-Price Lunch Program: 5 (0.2%)
Teachers: 304.0 (10.3 to 1)
Librarians/Media Specialists: 5.5 (568.9 to 1)
Guidance Counselors: 10.0 (312.9 to 1)
Current Spending: ($ per student per year):
Total: $18,670; Instruction: $11,515; Support Services: $6,884
Enrollment, Drop-out Rates and Diploma Recipients by Race/Ethnicity

Category	Total	White	Black	Asian	AIAN	Hisp.
Enrollment (%)	100.0	82.8	1.8	14.8	0.0	0.7
Drop-out Rate (%)	n/a	n/a	n/a	n/a	n/a	n/a
H.S. Diplomas (#)	191	161	2	26	0	2

Lawrence UFSD

195 Broadway • Lawrence, NY 11559-0477
(516) 295-7030 • http://www.lawrence.org/
Grade Span: PK-12; **Agency Type:** 1
Schools: 7
5 Primary; 1 Middle; 1 High; 0 Other Level
7 Regular; 0 Special Education; 0 Vocational; 0 Alternative
0 Magnet; 0 Charter; 2 Title I Eligible; 0 School-wide Title I
Students: 3,804 (50.9% male; 49.1% female)
Individual Education Program: 831 (21.8%);
English Language Learner: 273 (7.2%); Migrant: n/a
Eligible for Free Lunch Program: 732 (19.2%)
Eligible for Reduced-Price Lunch Program: 309 (8.1%)
Teachers: 355.9 (10.7 to 1)
Librarians/Media Specialists: 6.0 (634.0 to 1)
Guidance Counselors: 9.5 (400.4 to 1)
Current Spending: ($ per student per year):
Total: $19,485; Instruction: $12,171; Support Services: $7,056
Enrollment, Drop-out Rates and Diploma Recipients by Race/Ethnicity

Category	Total	White	Black	Asian	AIAN	Hisp.
Enrollment (%)	100.0	53.4	16.8	5.8	0.3	23.6
Drop-out Rate (%)	1.6	0.5	1.6	0.0	0.0	5.6
H.S. Diplomas (#)	241	153	34	9	0	45

Levittown UFSD

150 Abbey Ln • Levittown, NY 11756-4042
(516) 520-8300 • http://www.lawrence.org/
Grade Span: KG-12; **Agency Type:** 1
Schools: 11
6 Primary; 2 Middle; 2 High; 1 Other Level
10 Regular; 1 Special Education; 0 Vocational; 0 Alternative
0 Magnet; 0 Charter; 5 Title I Eligible; 0 School-wide Title I
Students: 8,015 (51.6% male; 48.4% female)
Individual Education Program: 1,070 (13.4%);
English Language Learner: 102 (1.3%); Migrant: n/a
Eligible for Free Lunch Program: 241 (3.0%)
Eligible for Reduced-Price Lunch Program: 188 (2.3%)
Teachers: 618.5 (13.0 to 1)
Librarians/Media Specialists: 9.8 (817.9 to 1)
Guidance Counselors: 16.0 (500.9 to 1)
Current Spending: ($ per student per year):
Total: $12,790; Instruction: $8,737; Support Services: $3,863
Enrollment, Drop-out Rates and Diploma Recipients by Race/Ethnicity

Category	Total	White	Black	Asian	AIAN	Hisp.
Enrollment (%)	100.0	89.9	0.6	3.8	0.0	5.7
Drop-out Rate (%)	0.2	0.2	5.0	0.0	n/a	0.0
H.S. Diplomas (#)	455	416	2	19	1	17

Locust Valley CSD

22 Horse Hollow Rd • Locust Valley, NY 11560-1118
(516) 674-6310 • http://www.lvcsd.k12.ny.us/
Grade Span: KG-12; **Agency Type:** 1
Schools: 4
2 Primary; 1 Middle; 1 High; 0 Other Level
4 Regular; 0 Special Education; 0 Vocational; 0 Alternative
0 Magnet; 0 Charter; 1 Title I Eligible; 0 School-wide Title I
Students: 2,231 (49.7% male; 50.3% female)
Individual Education Program: 360 (16.1%);
English Language Learner: 71 (3.2%); Migrant: n/a
Eligible for Free Lunch Program: 69 (3.1%)
Eligible for Reduced-Price Lunch Program: 41 (1.8%)
Teachers: 200.2 (11.1 to 1)
Librarians/Media Specialists: 5.3 (420.9 to 1)
Guidance Counselors: 5.0 (446.2 to 1)
Current Spending: ($ per student per year):
Total: $17,417; Instruction: $10,684; Support Services: $6,465
Enrollment, Drop-out Rates and Diploma Recipients by Race/Ethnicity

Category	Total	White	Black	Asian	AIAN	Hisp.
Enrollment (%)	100.0	89.5	2.0	2.4	0.1	6.0
Drop-out Rate (%)	0.0	0.0	0.0	0.0	n/a	0.0
H.S. Diplomas (#)	131	120	0	2	0	9

Long Beach City SD

235 Lido Blvd • Long Beach, NY 11561-5093
(516) 897-2104 • http://www.lbeach.org/
Grade Span: PK-12; **Agency Type:** 1
Schools: 7
5 Primary; 1 Middle; 1 High; 0 Other Level
7 Regular; 0 Special Education; 0 Vocational; 0 Alternative
0 Magnet; 0 Charter; 4 Title I Eligible; 0 School-wide Title I
Students: 4,536 (50.4% male; 49.6% female)
Individual Education Program: 633 (14.0%);
English Language Learner: 259 (5.7%); Migrant: n/a
Eligible for Free Lunch Program: 693 (15.3%)
Eligible for Reduced-Price Lunch Program: 197 (4.3%)
Teachers: 350.6 (12.9 to 1)
Librarians/Media Specialists: 5.3 (855.8 to 1)
Guidance Counselors: 14.0 (324.0 to 1)
Current Spending: ($ per student per year):
Total: $15,698; Instruction: $10,484; Support Services: $4,954
Enrollment, Drop-out Rates and Diploma Recipients by Race/Ethnicity

Category	Total	White	Black	Asian	AIAN	Hisp.
Enrollment (%)	100.0	64.0	12.4	4.1	0.0	19.5
Drop-out Rate (%)	1.5	1.2	1.7	0.0	n/a	2.4
H.S. Diplomas (#)	234	169	25	8	0	32

Lynbrook UFSD

111 Atlantic Ave • Lynbrook, NY 11563-3437
(516) 887-0253
Grade Span: KG-12; **Agency Type:** 1
Schools: 7
4 Primary; 2 Middle; 1 High; 0 Other Level
7 Regular; 0 Special Education; 0 Vocational; 0 Alternative
0 Magnet; 0 Charter; 4 Title I Eligible; 0 School-wide Title I
Students: 3,105 (51.0% male; 49.0% female)
Individual Education Program: 345 (11.1%);
English Language Learner: 81 (2.6%); Migrant: n/a
Eligible for Free Lunch Program: 31 (1.0%)
Eligible for Reduced-Price Lunch Program: 7 (0.2%)
Teachers: 254.2 (12.2 to 1)
Librarians/Media Specialists: 5.9 (526.3 to 1)
Guidance Counselors: 8.0 (388.1 to 1)
Current Spending: ($ per student per year):
Total: $12,408; Instruction: $8,103; Support Services: $4,237
Enrollment, Drop-out Rates and Diploma Recipients by Race/Ethnicity

Category	Total	White	Black	Asian	AIAN	Hisp.
Enrollment (%)	100.0	88.3	0.9	3.3	0.0	7.5
Drop-out Rate (%)	0.0	0.0	0.0	0.0	0.0	0.0
H.S. Diplomas (#)	188	161	0	11	1	15

Malverne UFSD

301 Wicks Ln • Malverne, NY 11565-2244
(516) 887-6405 • http://www.malverne.k12.ny.us/
Grade Span: KG-12; **Agency Type:** 1
Schools: 4
2 Primary; 1 Middle; 1 High; 0 Other Level
4 Regular; 0 Special Education; 0 Vocational; 0 Alternative
0 Magnet; 0 Charter; 3 Title I Eligible; 0 School-wide Title I
Students: 1,836 (52.0% male; 48.0% female)
Individual Education Program: 305 (16.6%);
English Language Learner: 47 (2.6%); Migrant: n/a
Eligible for Free Lunch Program: 276 (15.0%)
Eligible for Reduced-Price Lunch Program: 105 (5.7%)
Teachers: 163.4 (11.2 to 1)
Librarians/Media Specialists: 3.8 (483.2 to 1)
Guidance Counselors: 5.0 (367.2 to 1)
Current Spending: ($ per student per year):
Total: $15,109; Instruction: $9,583; Support Services: $5,259
Enrollment, Drop-out Rates and Diploma Recipients by Race/Ethnicity

Category	Total	White	Black	Asian	AIAN	Hisp.
Enrollment (%)	100.0	25.6	61.3	2.8	0.4	9.9
Drop-out Rate (%)	1.5	0.0	1.9	0.0	0.0	4.0
H.S. Diplomas (#)	107	28	61	4	1	13

Manhasset UFSD

200 Memorial Pl • Manhasset, NY 11030-2300
(516) 627-4400
Grade Span: KG-12; **Agency Type:** 1
Schools: 4
2 Primary; 1 Middle; 1 High; 0 Other Level
4 Regular; 0 Special Education; 0 Vocational; 0 Alternative
0 Magnet; 0 Charter; 3 Title I Eligible; 0 School-wide Title I
Students: 2,624 (51.2% male; 48.8% female)
Individual Education Program: 319 (12.2%);
English Language Learner: 61 (2.3%); Migrant: n/a
Eligible for Free Lunch Program: 87 (3.3%)
Eligible for Reduced-Price Lunch Program: 17 (0.6%)
Teachers: 234.8 (11.2 to 1)
Librarians/Media Specialists: 3.0 (874.7 to 1)
Guidance Counselors: 7.0 (374.9 to 1)
Current Spending: ($ per student per year):
Total: $19,480; Instruction: $12,182; Support Services: $7,111
Enrollment, Drop-out Rates and Diploma Recipients by Race/Ethnicity

Category	Total	White	Black	Asian	AIAN	Hisp.
Enrollment (%)	100.0	81.2	5.8	9.9	0.0	3.1
Drop-out Rate (%)	0.1	0.0	2.1	0.0	n/a	0.0
H.S. Diplomas (#)	170	131	8	25	0	6

Massapequa UFSD

4925 Merrick Rd • Massapequa, NY 11758-6298
(516) 797-6160 • http://www.msd.k12.ny.us/
Grade Span: KG-12; **Agency Type:** 1
Schools: 9
6 Primary; 1 Middle; 1 High; 1 Other Level
9 Regular; 0 Special Education; 0 Vocational; 0 Alternative
0 Magnet; 0 Charter; 5 Title I Eligible; 0 School-wide Title I
Students: 8,192 (51.5% male; 48.5% female)
Individual Education Program: 1,036 (12.6%);
English Language Learner: 20 (0.2%); Migrant: n/a
Eligible for Free Lunch Program: 137 (1.7%)
Eligible for Reduced-Price Lunch Program: 99 (1.2%)
Teachers: 600.7 (13.6 to 1)
Librarians/Media Specialists: 15.0 (546.1 to 1)
Guidance Counselors: 16.0 (512.0 to 1)
Current Spending: ($ per student per year):
Total: $11,931; Instruction: $8,110; Support Services: $3,643
Enrollment, Drop-out Rates and Diploma Recipients by Race/Ethnicity

Category	Total	White	Black	Asian	AIAN	Hisp.
Enrollment (%)	100.0	97.3	0.3	1.1	0.0	1.3
Drop-out Rate (%)	0.3	0.3	0.0	0.0	0.0	1.9
H.S. Diplomas (#)	496	496	0	0	0	0

Merrick UFSD

21 Babylon Rd • Merrick, NY 11566-4547
(516) 992-7240 • http://www.merrick.k12.ny.us/
Grade Span: KG-06; **Agency Type:** 2
Schools: 3
3 Primary; 0 Middle; 0 High; 0 Other Level
3 Regular; 0 Special Education; 0 Vocational; 0 Alternative
0 Magnet; 0 Charter; 2 Title I Eligible; 0 School-wide Title I
Students: 1,944 (50.4% male; 49.6% female)
Individual Education Program: 280 (14.4%);
English Language Learner: 19 (1.0%); Migrant: n/a
Eligible for Free Lunch Program: 0 (0.0%)
Eligible for Reduced-Price Lunch Program: 0 (0.0%)
Teachers: 143.0 (13.6 to 1)
Librarians/Media Specialists: 2.7 (720.0 to 1)
Guidance Counselors: 0.0 (0.0 to 1)
Current Spending: ($ per student per year):
Total: $10,708; Instruction: $7,584; Support Services: $3,122
Enrollment, Drop-out Rates and Diploma Recipients by Race/Ethnicity

Category	Total	White	Black	Asian	AIAN	Hisp.
Enrollment (%)	100.0	94.9	0.7	1.6	0.1	2.8
Drop-out Rate (%)	n/a	n/a	n/a	n/a	n/a	n/a
H.S. Diplomas (#)	n/a	n/a	n/a	n/a	n/a	n/a

Mineola UFSD

200 Emory Rd • Mineola, NY 11501-2361
(516) 741-5036 • http://mineola.ny.schoolwebpages.com/education/
Grade Span: PK-12; **Agency Type:** 1
Schools: 7
4 Primary; 1 Middle; 1 High; 1 Other Level
6 Regular; 0 Special Education; 0 Vocational; 1 Alternative
0 Magnet; 0 Charter; 4 Title I Eligible; 0 School-wide Title I
Students: 2,884 (51.2% male; 48.8% female)
Individual Education Program: 429 (14.9%);
English Language Learner: 304 (10.5%); Migrant: n/a
Eligible for Free Lunch Program: 255 (8.8%)
Eligible for Reduced-Price Lunch Program: 134 (4.6%)
Teachers: 264.4 (10.9 to 1)
Librarians/Media Specialists: 5.0 (576.8 to 1)
Guidance Counselors: 9.0 (320.4 to 1)
Current Spending: ($ per student per year):
Total: $18,380; Instruction: $11,061; Support Services: $7,108
Enrollment, Drop-out Rates and Diploma Recipients by Race/Ethnicity

Category	Total	White	Black	Asian	AIAN	Hisp.
Enrollment (%)	100.0	76.5	2.2	6.2	0.0	15.2
Drop-out Rate (%)	0.9	0.6	0.0	0.0	n/a	3.8
H.S. Diplomas (#)	201	158	6	17	0	20

New Hyde Pk-Garden City Pk UFSD

1950 Hillside Ave • New Hyde Park, NY 11040-2607
(516) 352-6257 • http://www.nhp-gcp.org/
Grade Span: PK-06; **Agency Type:** 2
Schools: 4
4 Primary; 0 Middle; 0 High; 0 Other Level
4 Regular; 0 Special Education; 0 Vocational; 0 Alternative
0 Magnet; 0 Charter; 0 Title I Eligible; 0 School-wide Title I
Students: 1,811 (51.5% male; 48.5% female)
Individual Education Program: 176 (9.7%);
English Language Learner: 67 (3.7%); Migrant: n/a
Eligible for Free Lunch Program: 0 (0.0%)
Eligible for Reduced-Price Lunch Program: 0 (0.0%)
Teachers: 116.9 (15.5 to 1)
Librarians/Media Specialists: 2.7 (670.7 to 1)
Guidance Counselors: 0.0 (0.0 to 1)
Current Spending: ($ per student per year):
Total: $9,189; Instruction: $5,940; Support Services: $3,237
Enrollment, Drop-out Rates and Diploma Recipients by Race/Ethnicity

Category	Total	White	Black	Asian	AIAN	Hisp.
Enrollment (%)	100.0	57.9	0.5	31.8	0.5	9.3
Drop-out Rate (%)	n/a	n/a	n/a	n/a	n/a	n/a
H.S. Diplomas (#)	n/a	n/a	n/a	n/a	n/a	n/a

North Bellmore UFSD

2616 Martin Ave • Bellmore, NY 11710-3199
(516) 221-2200
Grade Span: KG-06; **Agency Type:** 2
Schools: 6
6 Primary; 0 Middle; 0 High; 0 Other Level
6 Regular; 0 Special Education; 0 Vocational; 0 Alternative
0 Magnet; 0 Charter; 3 Title I Eligible; 0 School-wide Title I
Students: 2,542 (52.3% male; 47.7% female)
Individual Education Program: 285 (11.2%);
English Language Learner: 35 (1.4%); Migrant: n/a
Eligible for Free Lunch Program: 57 (2.2%)
Eligible for Reduced-Price Lunch Program: 38 (1.5%)
Teachers: 176.4 (14.4 to 1)
Librarians/Media Specialists: 5.5 (462.2 to 1)
Guidance Counselors: 0.0 (0.0 to 1)
Current Spending: ($ per student per year):
Total: $10,172; Instruction: $6,582; Support Services: $3,400
Enrollment, Drop-out Rates and Diploma Recipients by Race/Ethnicity

Category	Total	White	Black	Asian	AIAN	Hisp.
Enrollment (%)	100.0	90.4	2.1	4.1	0.0	3.4
Drop-out Rate (%)	n/a	n/a	n/a	n/a	n/a	n/a
H.S. Diplomas (#)	n/a	n/a	n/a	n/a	n/a	n/a

North Shore CSD

112 Franklin Ave • Sea Cliff, NY 11579-1706
(516) 705-0350 • http://www.northshore.k12.ny.us/
Grade Span: KG-12; **Agency Type:** 1
Schools: 6
3 Primary; 1 Middle; 1 High; 1 Other Level
5 Regular; 0 Special Education; 0 Vocational; 1 Alternative
0 Magnet; 0 Charter; 1 Title I Eligible; 0 School-wide Title I
Students: 2,623 (48.9% male; 51.1% female)
Individual Education Program: 471 (18.0%);
English Language Learner: 47 (1.8%); Migrant: n/a
Eligible for Free Lunch Program: 62 (2.4%)
Eligible for Reduced-Price Lunch Program: 60 (2.3%)
Teachers: 242.5 (10.8 to 1)
Librarians/Media Specialists: 5.6 (468.4 to 1)
Guidance Counselors: 5.5 (476.9 to 1)
Current Spending: ($ per student per year):
Total: $18,072; Instruction: $12,522; Support Services: $5,301
Enrollment, Drop-out Rates and Diploma Recipients by Race/Ethnicity

Category	Total	White	Black	Asian	AIAN	Hisp.
Enrollment (%)	100.0	91.0	1.1	4.8	0.0	3.1
Drop-out Rate (%)	1.1	0.7	0.0	0.0	n/a	12.5
H.S. Diplomas (#)	132	116	1	7	0	8

Oceanside UFSD

145 Merle Ave • Oceanside, NY 11572-2206
(516) 678-1215 • http://www.oceanside.k12.ny.us/
Grade Span: KG-12; **Agency Type:** 1
Schools: 9
7 Primary; 1 Middle; 1 High; 0 Other Level
9 Regular; 0 Special Education; 0 Vocational; 0 Alternative
0 Magnet; 0 Charter; 3 Title I Eligible; 0 School-wide Title I
Students: 6,320 (50.4% male; 49.6% female)
Individual Education Program: 668 (10.6%);
English Language Learner: 370 (5.9%); Migrant: n/a
Eligible for Free Lunch Program: 179 (2.8%)
Eligible for Reduced-Price Lunch Program: 95 (1.5%)
Teachers: 470.3 (13.4 to 1)
Librarians/Media Specialists: 8.3 (761.4 to 1)
Guidance Counselors: 13.9 (454.7 to 1)
Current Spending: ($ per student per year):
Total: $11,836; Instruction: $8,100; Support Services: $3,582
Enrollment, Drop-out Rates and Diploma Recipients by Race/Ethnicity

Category	Total	White	Black	Asian	AIAN	Hisp.
Enrollment (%)	100.0	92.3	0.8	1.4	0.0	5.6
Drop-out Rate (%)	0.5	0.6	0.0	0.0	0.0	0.0
H.S. Diplomas (#)	380	351	1	6	0	22

Oyster Bay-East Norwich CSD

1 Mccouns Ln • Oyster Bay, NY 11771-3105
(516) 624-6504 • http://oben.powertolearn.com/
Grade Span: PK-12; **Agency Type:** 1
Schools: 3
2 Primary; 0 Middle; 1 High; 0 Other Level
3 Regular; 0 Special Education; 0 Vocational; 0 Alternative
0 Magnet; 0 Charter; 2 Title I Eligible; 0 School-wide Title I
Students: 1,502 (51.4% male; 48.6% female)
Individual Education Program: 208 (13.8%);
English Language Learner: 80 (5.3%); Migrant: n/a
Eligible for Free Lunch Program: 188 (12.5%)
Eligible for Reduced-Price Lunch Program: 45 (3.0%)
Teachers: 142.5 (10.5 to 1)
Librarians/Media Specialists: 2.6 (577.7 to 1)
Guidance Counselors: 4.0 (375.5 to 1)
Current Spending: ($ per student per year):
Total: $18,146; Instruction: $11,083; Support Services: $6,889
Enrollment, Drop-out Rates and Diploma Recipients by Race/Ethnicity

Category	Total	White	Black	Asian	AIAN	Hisp.
Enrollment (%)	100.0	78.9	4.5	4.1	0.0	12.5
Drop-out Rate (%)	1.1	0.9	0.0	0.0	n/a	3.7
H.S. Diplomas (#)	108	88	4	4	0	12

Plainedge UFSD

241 Wyngate Dr • North Massapequa, NY 11758-0912
(516) 992-7455
Grade Span: PK-12; **Agency Type:** 1
Schools: 5
3 Primary; 1 Middle; 1 High; 0 Other Level
5 Regular; 0 Special Education; 0 Vocational; 0 Alternative
0 Magnet; 0 Charter; 0 Title I Eligible; 0 School-wide Title I
Students: 3,505 (49.6% male; 50.4% female)
Individual Education Program: 330 (9.4%);
English Language Learner: 47 (1.3%); Migrant: n/a
Eligible for Free Lunch Program: 146 (4.2%)
Eligible for Reduced-Price Lunch Program: 92 (2.6%)
Teachers: 245.7 (14.3 to 1)
Librarians/Media Specialists: 4.0 (876.3 to 1)
Guidance Counselors: 8.0 (438.1 to 1)
Current Spending: ($ per student per year):
Total: $11,953; Instruction: $7,301; Support Services: $4,474
Enrollment, Drop-out Rates and Diploma Recipients by Race/Ethnicity

Category	Total	White	Black	Asian	AIAN	Hisp.
Enrollment (%)	100.0	95.2	0.2	2.0	0.1	2.5
Drop-out Rate (%)	0.8	0.7	0.0	6.3	n/a	0.0
H.S. Diplomas (#)	203	188	2	6	0	7

Plainview-Old Bethpage CSD

106 Washington Ave • Plainview, NY 11803-3612
(516) 937-6301 • http://www.pob.k12.ny.us/
Grade Span: KG-12; **Agency Type:** 1
Schools: 8
5 Primary; 2 Middle; 1 High; 0 Other Level
8 Regular; 0 Special Education; 0 Vocational; 0 Alternative
0 Magnet; 0 Charter; 6 Title I Eligible; 0 School-wide Title I
Students: 4,874 (51.3% male; 48.7% female)
Individual Education Program: 805 (16.5%);
English Language Learner: 48 (1.0%); Migrant: n/a
Eligible for Free Lunch Program: 66 (1.4%)
Eligible for Reduced-Price Lunch Program: 48 (1.0%)
Teachers: 430.6 (11.3 to 1)
Librarians/Media Specialists: 8.0 (609.3 to 1)
Guidance Counselors: 15.0 (324.9 to 1)
Current Spending: ($ per student per year):
Total: $14,896; Instruction: $9,222; Support Services: $5,490
Enrollment, Drop-out Rates and Diploma Recipients by Race/Ethnicity

Category	Total	White	Black	Asian	AIAN	Hisp.
Enrollment (%)	100.0	92.6	0.2	5.8	0.0	1.4
Drop-out Rate (%)	0.0	0.0	0.0	0.0	n/a	0.0
H.S. Diplomas (#)	341	308	0	26	0	7

Port Washington UFSD

100 Campus Dr • Port Washington, NY 11050-3719
(516) 767-4326 • http://www.portnet.k12.ny.us/
Grade Span: KG-12; **Agency Type:** 1
Schools: 7
4 Primary; 1 Middle; 1 High; 1 Other Level
6 Regular; 0 Special Education; 0 Vocational; 1 Alternative
0 Magnet; 0 Charter; 5 Title I Eligible; 0 School-wide Title I
Students: 4,706 (50.7% male; 49.3% female)
Individual Education Program: 685 (14.6%);
English Language Learner: 395 (8.4%); Migrant: n/a
Eligible for Free Lunch Program: 272 (5.8%)
Eligible for Reduced-Price Lunch Program: 75 (1.6%)
Teachers: 400.9 (11.7 to 1)
Librarians/Media Specialists: 5.8 (811.4 to 1)
Guidance Counselors: 14.1 (333.8 to 1)
Current Spending: ($ per student per year):
Total: $16,387; Instruction: $11,184; Support Services: $5,004
Enrollment, Drop-out Rates and Diploma Recipients by Race/Ethnicity

Category	Total	White	Black	Asian	AIAN	Hisp.
Enrollment (%)	100.0	70.8	2.5	12.9	0.0	13.8
Drop-out Rate (%)	0.3	0.1	3.1	0.0	n/a	1.1
H.S. Diplomas (#)	282	192	5	36	1	48

Rockville Centre UFSD

128 Shepherd St • Rockville Centre, NY 11570-2298
(516) 255-8920
Grade Span: KG-12; **Agency Type:** 1
Schools: 7
5 Primary; 1 Middle; 1 High; 0 Other Level
7 Regular; 0 Special Education; 0 Vocational; 0 Alternative
0 Magnet; 0 Charter; 2 Title I Eligible; 0 School-wide Title I
Students: 3,643 (51.1% male; 48.9% female)
Individual Education Program: 434 (11.9%);
English Language Learner: 74 (2.0%); Migrant: n/a
Eligible for Free Lunch Program: 168 (4.6%)
Eligible for Reduced-Price Lunch Program: 53 (1.5%)
Teachers: 337.5 (10.8 to 1)
Librarians/Media Specialists: 2.5 (1,457.2 to 1)
Guidance Counselors: 8.6 (423.6 to 1)
Current Spending: ($ per student per year):
Total: $14,187; Instruction: $9,414; Support Services: $4,672
Enrollment, Drop-out Rates and Diploma Recipients by Race/Ethnicity

Category	Total	White	Black	Asian	AIAN	Hisp.
Enrollment (%)	100.0	79.9	7.3	2.9	0.1	9.9
Drop-out Rate (%)	0.6	0.5	0.0	0.0	0.0	1.7
H.S. Diplomas (#)	258	212	20	8	0	18

Roosevelt UFSD

240 Denton Pl • Roosevelt, NY 11575-1539
(516) 867-8616 • http://roughridersedu.net/
Grade Span: PK-12; **Agency Type:** 1
Schools: 6
5 Primary; 0 Middle; 1 High; 0 Other Level
6 Regular; 0 Special Education; 0 Vocational; 0 Alternative
0 Magnet; 0 Charter; 5 Title I Eligible; 0 School-wide Title I
Students: 2,940 (51.3% male; 48.7% female)
Individual Education Program: 351 (11.9%);
English Language Learner: 304 (10.3%); Migrant: n/a
Eligible for Free Lunch Program: 2,715 (92.3%)
Eligible for Reduced-Price Lunch Program: 70 (2.4%)
Teachers: 231.0 (12.7 to 1)
Librarians/Media Specialists: 4.0 (735.0 to 1)
Guidance Counselors: 6.0 (490.0 to 1)
Current Spending: ($ per student per year):
Total: $11,921; Instruction: $8,055; Support Services: $3,536
Enrollment, Drop-out Rates and Diploma Recipients by Race/Ethnicity

Category	Total	White	Black	Asian	AIAN	Hisp.
Enrollment (%)	100.0	0.2	84.3	0.0	0.1	15.3
Drop-out Rate (%)	n/a	n/a	n/a	n/a	n/a	n/a
H.S. Diplomas (#)	86	0	80	0	0	6

Roslyn UFSD

300 Harbor Hill Rd • Roslyn, NY 11576-1531
(516) 625-6303
Grade Span: PK-12; **Agency Type:** 1
Schools: 5
3 Primary; 1 Middle; 1 High; 0 Other Level
5 Regular; 0 Special Education; 0 Vocational; 0 Alternative
0 Magnet; 0 Charter; 2 Title I Eligible; 0 School-wide Title I
Students: 3,191 (52.3% male; 47.7% female)
Individual Education Program: 354 (11.1%);
English Language Learner: 103 (3.2%); Migrant: n/a
Eligible for Free Lunch Program: 155 (4.9%)
Eligible for Reduced-Price Lunch Program: 110 (3.4%)
Teachers: 253.7 (12.6 to 1)
Librarians/Media Specialists: 4.5 (709.1 to 1)
Guidance Counselors: 10.0 (319.1 to 1)
Current Spending: ($ per student per year):
Total: $17,893; Instruction: $10,861; Support Services: $6,726
Enrollment, Drop-out Rates and Diploma Recipients by Race/Ethnicity

Category	Total	White	Black	Asian	AIAN	Hisp.
Enrollment (%)	100.0	83.0	4.1	8.8	0.0	4.0
Drop-out Rate (%)	0.0	0.0	0.0	0.0	n/a	0.0
H.S. Diplomas (#)	209	161	16	24	0	8

Seaford UFSD

1600 Washington Ave • Seaford, NY 11783-1998
(516) 783-0711 • http://seaford.k12.ny.us/
Grade Span: KG-12; **Agency Type:** 1
Schools: 4
2 Primary; 1 Middle; 1 High; 0 Other Level
4 Regular; 0 Special Education; 0 Vocational; 0 Alternative
0 Magnet; 0 Charter; 0 Title I Eligible; 0 School-wide Title I
Students: 2,718 (51.8% male; 48.2% female)
Individual Education Program: 218 (8.0%);
English Language Learner: 15 (0.6%); Migrant: n/a
Eligible for Free Lunch Program: 50 (1.8%)
Eligible for Reduced-Price Lunch Program: 14 (0.5%)
Teachers: 195.2 (13.9 to 1)
Librarians/Media Specialists: 3.8 (715.3 to 1)
Guidance Counselors: 8.0 (339.8 to 1)
Current Spending: ($ per student per year):
Total: $12,226; Instruction: $7,826; Support Services: $4,232
Enrollment, Drop-out Rates and Diploma Recipients by Race/Ethnicity

Category	Total	White	Black	Asian	AIAN	Hisp.
Enrollment (%)	100.0	94.7	0.5	2.3	0.0	2.5
Drop-out Rate (%)	1.2	1.0	0.0	0.0	n/a	16.7
H.S. Diplomas (#)	166	156	1	2	1	6

Sewanhaka Central HSD

77 Landau Ave • Floral Park, NY 11001
(516) 488-9800
Grade Span: 07-12; **Agency Type:** 2
Schools: 5
0 Primary; 0 Middle; 5 High; 0 Other Level
5 Regular; 0 Special Education; 0 Vocational; 0 Alternative
0 Magnet; 0 Charter; 2 Title I Eligible; 0 School-wide Title I
Students: 8,266 (51.3% male; 48.7% female)
Individual Education Program: 996 (12.0%);
English Language Learner: 219 (2.6%); Migrant: n/a
Eligible for Free Lunch Program: 762 (9.2%)
Eligible for Reduced-Price Lunch Program: 346 (4.2%)
Teachers: 496.7 (16.6 to 1)
Librarians/Media Specialists: 10.7 (772.5 to 1)
Guidance Counselors: 38.0 (217.5 to 1)
Current Spending: ($ per student per year):
Total: $11,060; Instruction: $7,015; Support Services: $3,839
Enrollment, Drop-out Rates and Diploma Recipients by Race/Ethnicity

Category	Total	White	Black	Asian	AIAN	Hisp.
Enrollment (%)	100.0	50.5	25.0	12.0	0.0	12.4
Drop-out Rate (%)	0.3	0.3	0.1	0.0	n/a	1.3
H.S. Diplomas (#)	1,135	608	247	163	1	116

Syosset CSD

99 Pell Ln • Syosset, NY 11791-2998
(516) 364-5605 • http://www.syosset.k12.ny.us/
Grade Span: KG-12; **Agency Type:** 1
Schools: 11
7 Primary; 2 Middle; 1 High; 1 Other Level
10 Regular; 0 Special Education; 0 Vocational; 1 Alternative
0 Magnet; 0 Charter; 3 Title I Eligible; 0 School-wide Title I
Students: 6,472 (51.7% male; 48.3% female)
Individual Education Program: 800 (12.4%);
English Language Learner: 106 (1.6%); Migrant: n/a
Eligible for Free Lunch Program: 26 (0.4%)
Eligible for Reduced-Price Lunch Program: 12 (0.2%)
Teachers: 586.9 (11.0 to 1)
Librarians/Media Specialists: 11.0 (588.4 to 1)
Guidance Counselors: 16.0 (404.5 to 1)
Current Spending: ($ per student per year):
Total: $15,371; Instruction: $10,027; Support Services: $5,185
Enrollment, Drop-out Rates and Diploma Recipients by Race/Ethnicity

Category	Total	White	Black	Asian	AIAN	Hisp.
Enrollment (%)	100.0	80.5	0.4	17.9	0.0	1.3
Drop-out Rate (%)	n/a	n/a	n/a	n/a	n/a	n/a
H.S. Diplomas (#)	445	345	2	96	0	2

Uniondale UFSD

933 Goodrich St • Uniondale, NY 11553-2499
(516) 560-8824 • http://www.uniondale.k12.ny.us/
Grade Span: KG-12; **Agency Type:** 1
Schools: 8
5 Primary; 2 Middle; 1 High; 0 Other Level
8 Regular; 0 Special Education; 0 Vocational; 0 Alternative
0 Magnet; 0 Charter; 7 Title I Eligible; 0 School-wide Title I
Students: 6,325 (50.7% male; 49.3% female)
Individual Education Program: 695 (11.0%);
English Language Learner: 631 (10.0%); Migrant: n/a
Eligible for Free Lunch Program: 1,509 (23.9%)
Eligible for Reduced-Price Lunch Program: 498 (7.9%)
Teachers: 525.2 (12.0 to 1)
Librarians/Media Specialists: 11.3 (559.7 to 1)
Guidance Counselors: 14.0 (451.8 to 1)
Current Spending: ($ per student per year):
Total: $15,061; Instruction: $9,169; Support Services: $5,659
Enrollment, Drop-out Rates and Diploma Recipients by Race/Ethnicity

Category	Total	White	Black	Asian	AIAN	Hisp.
Enrollment (%)	100.0	1.7	69.0	1.0	0.3	28.0
Drop-out Rate (%)	2.1	2.9	1.8	0.0	n/a	3.3
H.S. Diplomas (#)	307	10	235	5	5	52

Valley Stream 13 UFSD

585 N Corona Ave • Valley Stream, NY 11580-2099
(516) 568-6100 • http://www.valleystream13.com/
Grade Span: PK-06; **Agency Type:** 2
Schools: 4
4 Primary; 0 Middle; 0 High; 0 Other Level
4 Regular; 0 Special Education; 0 Vocational; 0 Alternative
0 Magnet; 0 Charter; 1 Title I Eligible; 0 School-wide Title I
Students: 2,192 (53.1% male; 46.9% female)
Individual Education Program: 268 (12.2%);
English Language Learner: 103 (4.7%); Migrant: n/a
Eligible for Free Lunch Program: 114 (5.2%)
Eligible for Reduced-Price Lunch Program: 58 (2.6%)
Teachers: 165.0 (13.3 to 1)
Librarians/Media Specialists: 2.8 (782.9 to 1)
Guidance Counselors: 0.0 (0.0 to 1)
Current Spending: ($ per student per year):
Total: $10,170; Instruction: $7,097; Support Services: $3,073
Enrollment, Drop-out Rates and Diploma Recipients by Race/Ethnicity

Category	Total	White	Black	Asian	AIAN	Hisp.
Enrollment (%)	100.0	61.8	13.9	11.7	0.0	12.6
Drop-out Rate (%)	n/a	n/a	n/a	n/a	n/a	n/a
H.S. Diplomas (#)	n/a	n/a	n/a	n/a	n/a	n/a

Valley Stream 30 UFSD

175 N Central Ave • Valley Stream, NY 11580-3801
(516) 285-9881
Grade Span: KG-06; **Agency Type:** 2
Schools: 3
3 Primary; 0 Middle; 0 High; 0 Other Level
3 Regular; 0 Special Education; 0 Vocational; 0 Alternative
0 Magnet; 0 Charter; 2 Title I Eligible; 0 School-wide Title I
Students: 1,524 (50.2% male; 49.8% female)
Individual Education Program: 122 (8.0%);
English Language Learner: 202 (13.3%); Migrant: n/a
Eligible for Free Lunch Program: 153 (10.0%)
Eligible for Reduced-Price Lunch Program: 97 (6.4%)
Teachers: 112.0 (13.6 to 1)
Librarians/Media Specialists: 3.0 (508.0 to 1)
Guidance Counselors: 0.0 (0.0 to 1)
Current Spending: ($ per student per year):
Total: $11,639; Instruction: $8,122; Support Services: $3,518
Enrollment, Drop-out Rates and Diploma Recipients by Race/Ethnicity

Category	Total	White	Black	Asian	AIAN	Hisp.
Enrollment (%)	100.0	20.9	34.8	19.9	0.0	24.4
Drop-out Rate (%)	n/a	n/a	n/a	n/a	n/a	n/a
H.S. Diplomas (#)	n/a	n/a	n/a	n/a	n/a	n/a

Valley Stream Central HSD

One Kent Rd • Valley Stream, NY 11582-3007
(516) 872-5601 • http://www.valleystream30.com/
Grade Span: 07-12; **Agency Type:** 2
Schools: 4
0 Primary; 1 Middle; 3 High; 0 Other Level
4 Regular; 0 Special Education; 0 Vocational; 0 Alternative
0 Magnet; 0 Charter; 2 Title I Eligible; 0 School-wide Title I
Students: 4,488 (51.6% male; 48.4% female)
Individual Education Program: 504 (11.2%);
English Language Learner: 118 (2.6%); Migrant: n/a
Eligible for Free Lunch Program: 75 (1.7%)
Eligible for Reduced-Price Lunch Program: 47 (1.0%)
Teachers: 330.1 (13.6 to 1)
Librarians/Media Specialists: 3.0 (1,496.0 to 1)
Guidance Counselors: 20.0 (224.4 to 1)
Current Spending: ($ per student per year):
Total: $13,423; Instruction: $8,569; Support Services: $4,575
Enrollment, Drop-out Rates and Diploma Recipients by Race/Ethnicity

Category	Total	White	Black	Asian	AIAN	Hisp.
Enrollment (%)	100.0	57.3	15.6	11.7	0.1	15.4
Drop-out Rate (%)	1.9	1.8	2.5	0.8	n/a	2.5
H.S. Diplomas (#)	629	401	93	57	0	78

Wantagh UFSD

3301 Beltagh Ave • Wantagh, NY 11793-3395
(516) 679-6300 • http://www.wms.wantaghufsd.k12.ny.us/
Grade Span: KG-12; **Agency Type:** 1
Schools: 5
3 Primary; 1 Middle; 1 High; 0 Other Level
5 Regular; 0 Special Education; 0 Vocational; 0 Alternative
0 Magnet; 0 Charter; 4 Title I Eligible; 0 School-wide Title I
Students: 3,488 (50.6% male; 49.4% female)
Individual Education Program: 441 (12.6%);
English Language Learner: 13 (0.4%); Migrant: n/a
Eligible for Free Lunch Program: 17 (0.5%)
Eligible for Reduced-Price Lunch Program: 16 (0.5%)
Teachers: 255.2 (13.7 to 1)
Librarians/Media Specialists: 5.4 (645.9 to 1)
Guidance Counselors: 8.0 (436.0 to 1)
Current Spending: ($ per student per year):
Total: $11,545; Instruction: $7,400; Support Services: $3,965
Enrollment, Drop-out Rates and Diploma Recipients by Race/Ethnicity

Category	Total	White	Black	Asian	AIAN	Hisp.
Enrollment (%)	100.0	95.0	0.2	2.4	0.1	2.3
Drop-out Rate (%)	0.7	0.4	n/a	20.0	n/a	0.0
H.S. Diplomas (#)	191	183	0	7	0	1

West Hempstead UFSD

252 Chestnut St • West Hempstead, NY 11552-2455
(516) 390-3107 • http://www.westhempstead.k12.ny.us/
Grade Span: KG-12; **Agency Type:** 1
Schools: 6
3 Primary; 1 Middle; 1 High; 1 Other Level
5 Regular; 0 Special Education; 0 Vocational; 1 Alternative
0 Magnet; 0 Charter; 2 Title I Eligible; 0 School-wide Title I
Students: 2,405 (51.2% male; 48.8% female)
Individual Education Program: 303 (12.6%);
English Language Learner: 82 (3.4%); Migrant: n/a
Eligible for Free Lunch Program: 235 (9.8%)
Eligible for Reduced-Price Lunch Program: 70 (2.9%)
Teachers: 182.7 (13.2 to 1)
Librarians/Media Specialists: 3.8 (632.9 to 1)
Guidance Counselors: 8.0 (300.6 to 1)
Current Spending: ($ per student per year):
Total: $13,715; Instruction: $9,224; Support Services: $4,304
Enrollment, Drop-out Rates and Diploma Recipients by Race/Ethnicity

Category	Total	White	Black	Asian	AIAN	Hisp.
Enrollment (%)	100.0	62.5	14.6	4.4	0.0	18.5
Drop-out Rate (%)	0.5	0.6	0.0	0.0	n/a	0.0
H.S. Diplomas (#)	194	142	8	16	0	28

Westbury UFSD

2 Hitchcock Ln • Old Westbury, NY 11568-1624
(516) 876-5016
Grade Span: PK-12; **Agency Type:** 1
Schools: 8
4 Primary; 1 Middle; 1 High; 2 Other Level
6 Regular; 0 Special Education; 0 Vocational; 2 Alternative
0 Magnet; 0 Charter; 4 Title I Eligible; 0 School-wide Title I
Students: 4,069 (48.4% male; 51.6% female)
Individual Education Program: 464 (11.4%);
English Language Learner: 1,109 (27.3%); Migrant: n/a
Eligible for Free Lunch Program: 2,540 (62.4%)
Eligible for Reduced-Price Lunch Program: 317 (7.8%)
Teachers: 288.6 (14.1 to 1)
Librarians/Media Specialists: 3.9 (1,043.3 to 1)
Guidance Counselors: 11.0 (369.9 to 1)
Current Spending: ($ per student per year):
Total: $13,676; Instruction: $9,116; Support Services: $4,216
Enrollment, Drop-out Rates and Diploma Recipients by Race/Ethnicity

Category	Total	White	Black	Asian	AIAN	Hisp.
Enrollment (%)	100.0	1.4	47.4	2.3	0.0	48.8
Drop-out Rate (%)	3.0	0.0	1.5	0.0	n/a	6.4
H.S. Diplomas (#)	157	6	114	2	0	35

Niagara County

Lewiston-Porter CSD

4061 Creek Rd • Youngstown, NY 14174-9799
(716) 754-8281 • http://www.lewport.wnyric.org/
Grade Span: PK-12; **Agency Type:** 1
Schools: 4
2 Primary; 1 Middle; 1 High; 0 Other Level
4 Regular; 0 Special Education; 0 Vocational; 0 Alternative
0 Magnet; 0 Charter; 3 Title I Eligible; 0 School-wide Title I
Students: 2,428 (52.0% male; 48.0% female)
Individual Education Program: 332 (13.7%);
English Language Learner: 0 (0.0%); Migrant: n/a
Eligible for Free Lunch Program: 168 (6.9%)
Eligible for Reduced-Price Lunch Program: 114 (4.7%)
Teachers: 182.0 (13.3 to 1)
Librarians/Media Specialists: 3.0 (809.3 to 1)
Guidance Counselors: 6.5 (373.5 to 1)
Current Spending: ($ per student per year):
Total: $11,398; Instruction: $7,351; Support Services: $3,868
Enrollment, Drop-out Rates and Diploma Recipients by Race/Ethnicity

Category	Total	White	Black	Asian	AIAN	Hisp.
Enrollment (%)	100.0	98.1	0.5	0.5	0.5	0.4
Drop-out Rate (%)	1.1	1.1	0.0	0.0	0.0	0.0
H.S. Diplomas (#)	186	184	0	1	1	0

Lockport City SD

130 Beattie Ave • Lockport, NY 14094-5099
(716) 478-4835 • http://www.lockport.k12.ny.us/education/district/
Grade Span: PK-12; **Agency Type:** 1
Schools: 11
7 Primary; 2 Middle; 1 High; 1 Other Level
10 Regular; 0 Special Education; 0 Vocational; 1 Alternative
0 Magnet; 0 Charter; 7 Title I Eligible; 0 School-wide Title I
Students: 5,804 (51.8% male; 48.2% female)
Individual Education Program: 705 (12.1%);
English Language Learner: 55 (0.9%); Migrant: n/a
Eligible for Free Lunch Program: 1,238 (21.3%)
Eligible for Reduced-Price Lunch Program: 412 (7.1%)
Teachers: 446.6 (13.0 to 1)
Librarians/Media Specialists: 9.5 (610.9 to 1)
Guidance Counselors: 12.0 (483.7 to 1)
Current Spending: ($ per student per year):
Total: $9,436; Instruction: $6,475; Support Services: $2,765
Enrollment, Drop-out Rates and Diploma Recipients by Race/Ethnicity

Category	Total	White	Black	Asian	AIAN	Hisp.
Enrollment (%)	100.0	86.7	9.8	0.9	0.3	2.4
Drop-out Rate (%)	1.9	1.6	2.5	15.4	0.0	8.3
H.S. Diplomas (#)	302	280	16	1	1	4

Newfane CSD

6273 Charlottevile Rd • Newfane, NY 14108
(716) 778-6850 • http://www.newfane.wnyric.org/
Grade Span: PK-12; **Agency Type:** 1
Schools: 5
2 Primary; 2 Middle; 1 High; 0 Other Level
5 Regular; 0 Special Education; 0 Vocational; 0 Alternative
0 Magnet; 0 Charter; 3 Title I Eligible; 0 School-wide Title I
Students: 2,177 (51.5% male; 48.5% female)
Individual Education Program: 273 (12.5%);
English Language Learner: 7 (0.3%); Migrant: n/a
Eligible for Free Lunch Program: 193 (8.9%)
Eligible for Reduced-Price Lunch Program: 109 (5.0%)
Teachers: 153.9 (14.1 to 1)
Librarians/Media Specialists: 1.8 (1,209.4 to 1)
Guidance Counselors: 4.8 (453.5 to 1)
Current Spending: ($ per student per year):
Total: $9,156; Instruction: $5,968; Support Services: $2,938
Enrollment, Drop-out Rates and Diploma Recipients by Race/Ethnicity

Category	Total	White	Black	Asian	AIAN	Hisp.
Enrollment (%)	100.0	97.1	1.0	0.6	0.5	0.9
Drop-out Rate (%)	0.3	0.3	0.0	0.0	0.0	0.0
H.S. Diplomas (#)	156	152	1	1	1	1

Niagara Falls City SD

607 Walnut Ave • Niagara Falls, NY 14302-0399
(716) 286-4205 • http://www.nfschools.net/wsmgr.nsf
Grade Span: PK-12; **Agency Type:** 1
Schools: 13
9 Primary; 3 Middle; 1 High; 0 Other Level
13 Regular; 0 Special Education; 0 Vocational; 0 Alternative
1 Magnet; 0 Charter; 13 Title I Eligible; 0 School-wide Title I
Students: 8,929 (51.0% male; 49.0% female)
Individual Education Program: 1,535 (17.2%);
English Language Learner: 100 (1.1%); Migrant: n/a
Eligible for Free Lunch Program: 3,692 (41.3%)
Eligible for Reduced-Price Lunch Program: 895 (10.0%)
Teachers: 567.3 (15.7 to 1)
Librarians/Media Specialists: 5.0 (1,785.8 to 1)
Guidance Counselors: 14.1 (633.3 to 1)
Current Spending: ($ per student per year):
Total: $11,426; Instruction: $7,231; Support Services: $3,900
Enrollment, Drop-out Rates and Diploma Recipients by Race/Ethnicity

Category	Total	White	Black	Asian	AIAN	Hisp.
Enrollment (%)	100.0	58.9	34.5	1.3	3.3	2.1
Drop-out Rate (%)	0.0	0.0	0.0	0.0	0.0	0.0
H.S. Diplomas (#)	362	280	61	9	9	3

Niagara-Wheatfield CSD

6700 Shultz St • Niagara Falls, NY 14304
(716) 215-3003 • http://www.nwcsd.wnyric.org/
Grade Span: PK-12; **Agency Type:** 1
Schools: 6
4 Primary; 1 Middle; 1 High; 0 Other Level
6 Regular; 0 Special Education; 0 Vocational; 0 Alternative
0 Magnet; 0 Charter; 3 Title I Eligible; 0 School-wide Title I
Students: 4,004 (53.0% male; 47.0% female)
Individual Education Program: 435 (10.9%);
English Language Learner: 8 (0.2%); Migrant: n/a
Eligible for Free Lunch Program: 615 (15.4%)
Eligible for Reduced-Price Lunch Program: 281 (7.0%)
Teachers: 300.2 (13.3 to 1)
Librarians/Media Specialists: 5.5 (728.0 to 1)
Guidance Counselors: 10.5 (381.3 to 1)
Current Spending: ($ per student per year):
Total: $10,846; Instruction: $7,128; Support Services: $3,508
Enrollment, Drop-out Rates and Diploma Recipients by Race/Ethnicity

Category	Total	White	Black	Asian	AIAN	Hisp.
Enrollment (%)	100.0	88.4	2.5	0.9	7.4	0.8
Drop-out Rate (%)	1.8	1.7	0.0	0.0	5.2	0.0
H.S. Diplomas (#)	272	252	8	0	11	1

North Tonawanda City SD

175 Humphrey St • North Tonawanda, NY 14120-4097
(716) 807-3500
Grade Span: PK-12; **Agency Type:** 1
Schools: 9
6 Primary; 2 Middle; 1 High; 0 Other Level
9 Regular; 0 Special Education; 0 Vocational; 0 Alternative
0 Magnet; 0 Charter; 3 Title I Eligible; 0 School-wide Title I
Students: 4,864 (51.6% male; 48.4% female)
Individual Education Program: 688 (14.1%);
English Language Learner: 60 (1.2%); Migrant: n/a
Eligible for Free Lunch Program: 722 (14.8%)
Eligible for Reduced-Price Lunch Program: 350 (7.2%)
Teachers: 358.0 (13.6 to 1)
Librarians/Media Specialists: 5.9 (824.4 to 1)
Guidance Counselors: 9.0 (540.4 to 1)
Current Spending: ($ per student per year):
Total: $9,358; Instruction: $6,410; Support Services: $2,761
Enrollment, Drop-out Rates and Diploma Recipients by Race/Ethnicity

Category	Total	White	Black	Asian	AIAN	Hisp.
Enrollment (%)	100.0	97.0	0.5	0.7	0.9	1.0
Drop-out Rate (%)	2.1	2.1	0.0	0.0	0.0	22.2
H.S. Diplomas (#)	335	333	0	0	2	0

Royalton-Hartland CSD

54 State St • Middleport, NY 14105-1199
(716) 735-3031 • http://www.royhart.wnyric.org/
Grade Span: KG-12; **Agency Type:** 1
Schools: 3
2 Primary; 0 Middle; 1 High; 0 Other Level
3 Regular; 0 Special Education; 0 Vocational; 0 Alternative
0 Magnet; 0 Charter; 1 Title I Eligible; 0 School-wide Title I
Students: 1,717 (51.2% male; 48.8% female)
Individual Education Program: 205 (11.9%);
English Language Learner: 10 (0.6%); Migrant: n/a
Eligible for Free Lunch Program: 234 (13.6%)
Eligible for Reduced-Price Lunch Program: 90 (5.2%)
Teachers: 139.3 (12.3 to 1)
Librarians/Media Specialists: 2.7 (635.9 to 1)
Guidance Counselors: 4.0 (429.3 to 1)
Current Spending: ($ per student per year):
Total: $9,204; Instruction: $5,778; Support Services: $3,195
Enrollment, Drop-out Rates and Diploma Recipients by Race/Ethnicity

Category	Total	White	Black	Asian	AIAN	Hisp.
Enrollment (%)	100.0	97.4	1.5	0.3	0.1	0.8
Drop-out Rate (%)	1.4	1.4	0.0	n/a	0.0	0.0
H.S. Diplomas (#)	117	117	0	0	0	0

Starpoint CSD

4363 Mapleton Rd • Lockport, NY 14094-9623
(716) 210-2352 • http://www.starpoint.wnyric.org/
Grade Span: KG-12; **Agency Type:** 1
Schools: 3
1 Primary; 1 Middle; 1 High; 0 Other Level
3 Regular; 0 Special Education; 0 Vocational; 0 Alternative
0 Magnet; 0 Charter; 3 Title I Eligible; 0 School-wide Title I
Students: 2,804 (50.9% male; 49.1% female)
Individual Education Program: 340 (12.1%);
English Language Learner: 4 (0.1%); Migrant: n/a
Eligible for Free Lunch Program: 140 (5.0%)
Eligible for Reduced-Price Lunch Program: 136 (4.9%)
Teachers: 180.2 (15.6 to 1)
Librarians/Media Specialists: 3.7 (757.8 to 1)
Guidance Counselors: 6.0 (467.3 to 1)
Current Spending: ($ per student per year):
Total: $8,350; Instruction: $5,561; Support Services: $2,602
Enrollment, Drop-out Rates and Diploma Recipients by Race/Ethnicity

Category	Total	White	Black	Asian	AIAN	Hisp.
Enrollment (%)	100.0	98.4	0.6	0.2	0.2	0.5
Drop-out Rate (%)	3.2	3.3	0.0	0.0	0.0	0.0
H.S. Diplomas (#)	154	152	1	0	0	1

Wilson CSD

412 Lake St • Wilson, NY 14172-9799
(716) 751-9341 • http://www.wilson.wnyric.org/
Grade Span: PK-12; **Agency Type:** 1
Schools: 3
2 Primary; 0 Middle; 0 High; 1 Other Level
3 Regular; 0 Special Education; 0 Vocational; 0 Alternative
0 Magnet; 0 Charter; 2 Title I Eligible; 0 School-wide Title I
Students: 1,500 (50.5% male; 49.5% female)
Individual Education Program: 182 (12.1%);
English Language Learner: 1 (0.1%); Migrant: n/a
Eligible for Free Lunch Program: 213 (14.2%)
Eligible for Reduced-Price Lunch Program: 145 (9.7%)
Teachers: 126.4 (11.9 to 1)
Librarians/Media Specialists: 4.0 (375.0 to 1)
Guidance Counselors: 5.5 (272.7 to 1)
Current Spending: ($ per student per year):
Total: $10,146; Instruction: $6,229; Support Services: $3,628
Enrollment, Drop-out Rates and Diploma Recipients by Race/Ethnicity

Category	Total	White	Black	Asian	AIAN	Hisp.
Enrollment (%)	100.0	96.9	0.5	0.6	1.3	0.7
Drop-out Rate (%)	0.6	0.6	0.0	0.0	0.0	0.0
H.S. Diplomas (#)	114	112	0	0	1	1

Oneida County

Adirondack CSD

110 Ford St • Boonville, NY 13309-1200
(315) 942-9200 • http://www.pikeco.com/compulink/adirondack/
Grade Span: KG-12; **Agency Type:** 1
Schools: 5
3 Primary; 1 Middle; 1 High; 0 Other Level
5 Regular; 0 Special Education; 0 Vocational; 0 Alternative
0 Magnet; 0 Charter; 5 Title I Eligible; 0 School-wide Title I
Students: 1,617 (51.1% male; 48.9% female)
Individual Education Program: 245 (15.2%);
English Language Learner: 0 (0.0%); Migrant: n/a
Eligible for Free Lunch Program: 366 (22.6%)
Eligible for Reduced-Price Lunch Program: 173 (10.7%)
Teachers: 130.0 (12.4 to 1)
Librarians/Media Specialists: 1.0 (1,617.0 to 1)
Guidance Counselors: 2.0 (808.5 to 1)
Current Spending: ($ per student per year):
Total: $9,509; Instruction: $6,236; Support Services: $2,942
Enrollment, Drop-out Rates and Diploma Recipients by Race/Ethnicity

Category	Total	White	Black	Asian	AIAN	Hisp.
Enrollment (%)	100.0	99.2	0.3	0.4	0.1	0.0
Drop-out Rate (%)	2.5	2.5	n/a	0.0	0.0	n/a
H.S. Diplomas (#)	111	109	0	1	1	0

Camden CSD

51 Third St • Camden, NY 13316-1114
(315) 245-4075 • http://www.camdenschools.org/
Grade Span: KG-12; **Agency Type:** 2
Schools: 8
4 Primary; 1 Middle; 2 High; 1 Other Level
6 Regular; 0 Special Education; 0 Vocational; 2 Alternative
0 Magnet; 0 Charter; 5 Title I Eligible; 0 School-wide Title I
Students: 2,758 (51.0% male; 49.0% female)
Individual Education Program: 411 (14.9%);
English Language Learner: 0 (0.0%); Migrant: n/a
Eligible for Free Lunch Program: 863 (31.3%)
Eligible for Reduced-Price Lunch Program: 368 (13.3%)
Teachers: 202.5 (13.6 to 1)
Librarians/Media Specialists: 6.0 (459.7 to 1)
Guidance Counselors: 8.0 (344.8 to 1)
Current Spending: ($ per student per year):
Total: $8,733; Instruction: $5,767; Support Services: $2,621
Enrollment, Drop-out Rates and Diploma Recipients by Race/Ethnicity

Category	Total	White	Black	Asian	AIAN	Hisp.
Enrollment (%)	100.0	97.2	1.4	0.3	0.3	0.8
Drop-out Rate (%)	1.8	1.9	0.0	0.0	n/a	0.0
H.S. Diplomas (#)	159	158	1	0	0	0

Clinton CSD

75 Chenango Ave • Clinton, NY 13323-1395
(315) 853-5574 • http://www.clintoncsd.org/
Grade Span: KG-12; **Agency Type:** 1
Schools: 3
1 Primary; 1 Middle; 1 High; 0 Other Level
3 Regular; 0 Special Education; 0 Vocational; 0 Alternative
0 Magnet; 0 Charter; 1 Title I Eligible; 0 School-wide Title I
Students: 1,661 (51.7% male; 48.3% female)
Individual Education Program: 188 (11.3%);
English Language Learner: 6 (0.4%); Migrant: n/a
Eligible for Free Lunch Program: 131 (7.9%)
Eligible for Reduced-Price Lunch Program: 46 (2.8%)
Teachers: 127.9 (13.0 to 1)
Librarians/Media Specialists: 1.0 (1,661.0 to 1)
Guidance Counselors: 3.9 (425.9 to 1)
Current Spending: ($ per student per year):
Total: $8,016; Instruction: $5,551; Support Services: $2,449
Enrollment, Drop-out Rates and Diploma Recipients by Race/Ethnicity

Category	Total	White	Black	Asian	AIAN	Hisp.
Enrollment (%)	100.0	95.2	1.5	1.9	0.1	1.3
Drop-out Rate (%)	0.9	0.8	0.0	0.0	n/a	10.0
H.S. Diplomas (#)	148	143	2	1	0	2

Holland Patent CSD

9601 Main St • Holland Patent, NY 13354-4610
(315) 865-7221 • http://www.moric.org/hpknight/home.htm
Grade Span: KG-12; **Agency Type:** 1
Schools: 4
2 Primary; 1 Middle; 1 High; 0 Other Level
4 Regular; 0 Special Education; 0 Vocational; 0 Alternative
0 Magnet; 0 Charter; 3 Title I Eligible; 0 School-wide Title I
Students: 1,899 (51.0% male; 49.0% female)
Individual Education Program: 216 (11.4%);
English Language Learner: 0 (0.0%); Migrant: n/a
Eligible for Free Lunch Program: 195 (10.3%)
Eligible for Reduced-Price Lunch Program: 193 (10.2%)
Teachers: 142.7 (13.3 to 1)
Librarians/Media Specialists: 3.0 (633.0 to 1)
Guidance Counselors: 5.0 (379.8 to 1)
Current Spending: ($ per student per year):
Total: $9,301; Instruction: $6,062; Support Services: $2,994
Enrollment, Drop-out Rates and Diploma Recipients by Race/Ethnicity

Category	Total	White	Black	Asian	AIAN	Hisp.
Enrollment (%)	100.0	97.6	0.6	0.9	0.1	0.7
Drop-out Rate (%)	1.0	1.0	0.0	0.0	0.0	0.0
H.S. Diplomas (#)	129	126	0	1	0	2

New Hartford CSD

33 Oxford Rd • New Hartford, NY 13413-2699
(315) 624-1218 • http://www.myschoolonline.com/
Grade Span: KG-12; **Agency Type:** 1
Schools: 5
3 Primary; 1 Middle; 1 High; 0 Other Level
5 Regular; 0 Special Education; 0 Vocational; 0 Alternative
0 Magnet; 0 Charter; 3 Title I Eligible; 0 School-wide Title I
Students: 2,708 (51.4% male; 48.6% female)
Individual Education Program: 292 (10.8%);
English Language Learner: 2 (0.1%); Migrant: n/a
Eligible for Free Lunch Program: 122 (4.5%)
Eligible for Reduced-Price Lunch Program: 59 (2.2%)
Teachers: 206.6 (13.1 to 1)
Librarians/Media Specialists: 4.7 (576.2 to 1)
Guidance Counselors: 7.0 (386.9 to 1)
Current Spending: ($ per student per year):
Total: $10,122; Instruction: $6,887; Support Services: $3,221
Enrollment, Drop-out Rates and Diploma Recipients by Race/Ethnicity

Category	Total	White	Black	Asian	AIAN	Hisp.
Enrollment (%)	100.0	92.3	1.8	4.9	0.1	0.9
Drop-out Rate (%)	1.0	1.1	0.0	0.0	n/a	0.0
H.S. Diplomas (#)	222	209	2	9	0	2

Rome City SD

112 E Thomas St • Rome, NY 13440-5298
(315) 334-7400 • http://www.romecsd.org/
Grade Span: PK-12; **Agency Type:** 1
Schools: 15
9 Primary; 1 Middle; 1 High; 4 Other Level
12 Regular; 0 Special Education; 0 Vocational; 3 Alternative
0 Magnet; 0 Charter; 5 Title I Eligible; 0 School-wide Title I
Students: 6,275 (52.4% male; 47.6% female)
Individual Education Program: 918 (14.6%);
English Language Learner: 33 (0.5%); Migrant: n/a
Eligible for Free Lunch Program: 1,883 (30.0%)
Eligible for Reduced-Price Lunch Program: 489 (7.8%)
Teachers: 466.5 (13.5 to 1)
Librarians/Media Specialists: 11.5 (545.7 to 1)
Guidance Counselors: 17.0 (369.1 to 1)
Current Spending: ($ per student per year):
Total: $10,499; Instruction: $7,188; Support Services: $3,050
Enrollment, Drop-out Rates and Diploma Recipients by Race/Ethnicity

Category	Total	White	Black	Asian	AIAN	Hisp.
Enrollment (%)	100.0	87.5	6.9	1.5	0.7	3.4
Drop-out Rate (%)	2.6	2.7	2.9	0.0	0.0	0.0
H.S. Diplomas (#)	276	254	13	2	0	7

Sherrill City SD

5275 State Rt 31 • Verona, NY 13478-0128
(315) 829-2520
Grade Span: PK-12; **Agency Type:** 1
Schools: 5
3 Primary; 1 Middle; 1 High; 0 Other Level
5 Regular; 0 Special Education; 0 Vocational; 0 Alternative
0 Magnet; 0 Charter; 4 Title I Eligible; 0 School-wide Title I
Students: 2,465 (50.8% male; 49.2% female)
Individual Education Program: 274 (11.1%);
English Language Learner: 4 (0.2%); Migrant: n/a
Eligible for Free Lunch Program: 454 (18.4%)
Eligible for Reduced-Price Lunch Program: 241 (9.8%)
Teachers: 173.0 (14.2 to 1)
Librarians/Media Specialists: 4.7 (524.5 to 1)
Guidance Counselors: 4.0 (616.3 to 1)
Current Spending: ($ per student per year):
Total: $9,036; Instruction: $6,064; Support Services: $2,685
Enrollment, Drop-out Rates and Diploma Recipients by Race/Ethnicity

Category	Total	White	Black	Asian	AIAN	Hisp.
Enrollment (%)	100.0	97.6	1.0	0.9	0.2	0.3
Drop-out Rate (%)	1.5	1.5	0.0	0.0	0.0	0.0
H.S. Diplomas (#)	175	173	0	1	0	1

Utica City SD

1115 Mohawk St • Utica, NY 13501-3709
(315) 792-2222 • http://www.uticaschools.org/
Grade Span: KG-12; **Agency Type:** 1
Schools: 13
9 Primary; 2 Middle; 1 High; 1 Other Level
12 Regular; 0 Special Education; 0 Vocational; 1 Alternative
0 Magnet; 0 Charter; 12 Title I Eligible; 0 School-wide Title I
Students: 8,885 (51.1% male; 48.9% female)
Individual Education Program: 1,513 (17.0%);
English Language Learner: 1,143 (12.9%); Migrant: n/a
Eligible for Free Lunch Program: 5,539 (62.3%)
Eligible for Reduced-Price Lunch Program: 739 (8.3%)
Teachers: 620.8 (14.3 to 1)
Librarians/Media Specialists: 12.8 (694.1 to 1)
Guidance Counselors: 13.0 (683.5 to 1)
Current Spending: ($ per student per year):
Total: $9,527; Instruction: $6,363; Support Services: $2,856
Enrollment, Drop-out Rates and Diploma Recipients by Race/Ethnicity

Category	Total	White	Black	Asian	AIAN	Hisp.
Enrollment (%)	100.0	58.6	26.3	4.1	0.2	10.9
Drop-out Rate (%)	2.0	1.8	3.0	1.3	0.0	2.0
H.S. Diplomas (#)	341	250	59	10	1	21

Whitesboro CSD

67 Whtsbro St-Box 304 • Yorkville, NY 13495-0304
(315) 266-3303 •
http://www.wboro.org/education/district/district.php?sectionid=1
Grade Span: KG-12; **Agency Type:** 1
Schools: 10
4 Primary; 2 Middle; 1 High; 3 Other Level
7 Regular; 0 Special Education; 0 Vocational; 3 Alternative
0 Magnet; 0 Charter; 4 Title I Eligible; 0 School-wide Title I
Students: 3,872 (51.5% male; 48.5% female)
Individual Education Program: 606 (15.7%);
English Language Learner: 44 (1.1%); Migrant: n/a
Eligible for Free Lunch Program: 393 (10.1%)
Eligible for Reduced-Price Lunch Program: 199 (5.1%)
Teachers: 287.0 (13.5 to 1)
Librarians/Media Specialists: 4.0 (968.0 to 1)
Guidance Counselors: 7.0 (553.1 to 1)
Current Spending: ($ per student per year):
Total: $9,097; Instruction: $5,902; Support Services: $2,994
Enrollment, Drop-out Rates and Diploma Recipients by Race/Ethnicity

Category	Total	White	Black	Asian	AIAN	Hisp.
Enrollment (%)	100.0	95.8	2.4	0.8	0.0	1.0
Drop-out Rate (%)	1.7	1.7	0.0	0.0	n/a	0.0
H.S. Diplomas (#)	257	250	2	3	2	0

Onondaga County

Baldwinsville CSD
29 E Oneida St • Baldwinsville, NY 13027-2480
(315) 638-6043 • http://www.ocmboces.org/bville/
Grade Span: KG-12; **Agency Type:** 1
Schools: 9
5 Primary; 1 Middle; 1 High; 2 Other Level
8 Regular; 0 Special Education; 0 Vocational; 1 Alternative
0 Magnet; 0 Charter; 4 Title I Eligible; 0 School-wide Title I
Students: 5,800 (51.7% male; 48.3% female)
Individual Education Program: 916 (15.8%);
English Language Learner: 16 (0.3%); Migrant: n/a
Eligible for Free Lunch Program: 508 (8.8%)
Eligible for Reduced-Price Lunch Program: 244 (4.2%)
Teachers: 393.7 (14.7 to 1)
Librarians/Media Specialists: 7.3 (794.5 to 1)
Guidance Counselors: 12.0 (483.3 to 1)
Current Spending: ($ per student per year):
Total: $9,077; Instruction: $6,142; Support Services: $2,748
Enrollment, Drop-out Rates and Diploma Recipients by Race/Ethnicity

Category	Total	White	Black	Asian	AIAN	Hisp.
Enrollment (%)	100.0	96.7	1.4	0.8	0.3	0.7
Drop-out Rate (%)	0.3	0.4	0.0	0.0	n/a	0.0
H.S. Diplomas (#)	320	313	1	5	1	0

East Syracuse-Minoa CSD
407 Fremont Rd • East Syracuse, NY 13057-2631
(315) 656-7205 • http://www.esmschools.org/
Grade Span: PK-12; **Agency Type:** 1
Schools: 7
5 Primary; 1 Middle; 1 High; 0 Other Level
7 Regular; 0 Special Education; 0 Vocational; 0 Alternative
0 Magnet; 0 Charter; 4 Title I Eligible; 0 School-wide Title I
Students: 3,848 (51.6% male; 48.4% female)
Individual Education Program: 591 (15.4%);
English Language Learner: 41 (1.1%); Migrant: n/a
Eligible for Free Lunch Program: 511 (13.3%)
Eligible for Reduced-Price Lunch Program: 240 (6.2%)
Teachers: 325.4 (11.8 to 1)
Librarians/Media Specialists: 6.0 (641.3 to 1)
Guidance Counselors: 10.0 (384.8 to 1)
Current Spending: ($ per student per year):
Total: $10,869; Instruction: $7,197; Support Services: $3,459
Enrollment, Drop-out Rates and Diploma Recipients by Race/Ethnicity

Category	Total	White	Black	Asian	AIAN	Hisp.
Enrollment (%)	100.0	93.2	2.4	1.6	1.5	1.2
Drop-out Rate (%)	0.5	0.6	0.0	0.0	0.0	0.0
H.S. Diplomas (#)	274	265	2	5	1	1

Fayetteville-Manlius CSD
8199 E Seneca Tpke • Manlius, NY 13104-2140
(315) 682-1200 • http://www.fm.cnyric.org/
Grade Span: KG-12; **Agency Type:** 1
Schools: 6
3 Primary; 2 Middle; 1 High; 0 Other Level
6 Regular; 0 Special Education; 0 Vocational; 0 Alternative
0 Magnet; 0 Charter; 5 Title I Eligible; 0 School-wide Title I
Students: 4,605 (51.1% male; 48.9% female)
Individual Education Program: 459 (10.0%);
English Language Learner: 81 (1.8%); Migrant: n/a
Eligible for Free Lunch Program: 140 (3.0%)
Eligible for Reduced-Price Lunch Program: 49 (1.1%)
Teachers: 322.4 (14.3 to 1)
Librarians/Media Specialists: 6.4 (719.5 to 1)
Guidance Counselors: 14.0 (328.9 to 1)
Current Spending: ($ per student per year):
Total: $9,150; Instruction: $5,939; Support Services: $3,053
Enrollment, Drop-out Rates and Diploma Recipients by Race/Ethnicity

Category	Total	White	Black	Asian	AIAN	Hisp.
Enrollment (%)	100.0	92.7	1.8	4.6	0.0	1.0
Drop-out Rate (%)	0.0	0.0	0.0	0.0	0.0	0.0
H.S. Diplomas (#)	311	288	7	13	0	3

Jamesville-Dewitt CSD
6845 Edinger Dr • Dewitt, NY 13214-0606
(315) 445-8304 • http://www.jamesvilledewitt.org/index.tpl
Grade Span: KG-12; **Agency Type:** 1
Schools: 6
3 Primary; 1 Middle; 1 High; 1 Other Level
5 Regular; 0 Special Education; 0 Vocational; 1 Alternative
0 Magnet; 0 Charter; 4 Title I Eligible; 0 School-wide Title I
Students: 2,724 (49.7% male; 50.3% female)
Individual Education Program: 320 (11.7%);
English Language Learner: 41 (1.5%); Migrant: n/a
Eligible for Free Lunch Program: 198 (7.3%)
Eligible for Reduced-Price Lunch Program: 91 (3.3%)
Teachers: 225.6 (12.1 to 1)
Librarians/Media Specialists: 4.6 (592.2 to 1)
Guidance Counselors: 8.0 (340.5 to 1)
Current Spending: ($ per student per year):
Total: $10,315; Instruction: $6,736; Support Services: $3,330
Enrollment, Drop-out Rates and Diploma Recipients by Race/Ethnicity

Category	Total	White	Black	Asian	AIAN	Hisp.
Enrollment (%)	100.0	84.8	8.7	4.6	0.5	1.4
Drop-out Rate (%)	0.7	0.5	0.0	3.0	25.0	0.0
H.S. Diplomas (#)	179	149	15	12	2	1

Jordan-Elbridge CSD
9 Chappell St • Jordan, NY 13080-0902
(315) 689-3978
Grade Span: KG-12; **Agency Type:** 1
Schools: 4
2 Primary; 1 Middle; 1 High; 0 Other Level
4 Regular; 0 Special Education; 0 Vocational; 0 Alternative
0 Magnet; 0 Charter; 2 Title I Eligible; 0 School-wide Title I
Students: 1,736 (52.8% male; 47.2% female)
Individual Education Program: 162 (9.3%);
English Language Learner: 2 (0.1%); Migrant: n/a
Eligible for Free Lunch Program: 243 (14.0%)
Eligible for Reduced-Price Lunch Program: 116 (6.7%)
Teachers: 140.8 (12.3 to 1)
Librarians/Media Specialists: 4.0 (434.0 to 1)
Guidance Counselors: 5.0 (347.2 to 1)
Current Spending: ($ per student per year):
Total: $8,890; Instruction: $5,852; Support Services: $2,763
Enrollment, Drop-out Rates and Diploma Recipients by Race/Ethnicity

Category	Total	White	Black	Asian	AIAN	Hisp.
Enrollment (%)	100.0	97.6	0.6	0.8	0.8	0.2
Drop-out Rate (%)	3.2	3.3	0.0	0.0	n/a	0.0
H.S. Diplomas (#)	116	115	0	0	0	1

Liverpool CSD
800 Fourth St • Liverpool, NY 13088-4455
(315) 453-0225 • http://www.liverpool.k12.ny.us/
Grade Span: PK-12; **Agency Type:** 1
Schools: 14
10 Primary; 3 Middle; 1 High; 0 Other Level
14 Regular; 0 Special Education; 0 Vocational; 0 Alternative
0 Magnet; 0 Charter; 7 Title I Eligible; 0 School-wide Title I
Students: 8,613 (50.8% male; 49.2% female)
Individual Education Program: 1,423 (16.5%);
English Language Learner: 85 (1.0%); Migrant: n/a
Eligible for Free Lunch Program: 1,052 (12.2%)
Eligible for Reduced-Price Lunch Program: 486 (5.6%)
Teachers: 595.7 (14.5 to 1)
Librarians/Media Specialists: 13.8 (624.1 to 1)
Guidance Counselors: 23.5 (366.5 to 1)
Current Spending: ($ per student per year):
Total: $10,205; Instruction: $6,719; Support Services: $3,231
Enrollment, Drop-out Rates and Diploma Recipients by Race/Ethnicity

Category	Total	White	Black	Asian	AIAN	Hisp.
Enrollment (%)	100.0	88.3	6.5	2.8	0.6	1.7
Drop-out Rate (%)	1.5	1.4	2.4	0.0	9.5	6.5
H.S. Diplomas (#)	512	480	17	10	2	3

Marcellus CSD
2 Reed Pky • Marcellus, NY 13108-1199
(315) 673-0201 • http://mcs.rway.com/
Grade Span: KG-12; **Agency Type:** 1
Schools: 3
1 Primary; 1 Middle; 1 High; 0 Other Level
3 Regular; 0 Special Education; 0 Vocational; 0 Alternative
0 Magnet; 0 Charter; 2 Title I Eligible; 0 School-wide Title I
Students: 2,170 (51.2% male; 48.8% female)
Individual Education Program: 278 (12.8%);
English Language Learner: 5 (0.2%); Migrant: n/a
Eligible for Free Lunch Program: 104 (4.8%)
Eligible for Reduced-Price Lunch Program: 78 (3.6%)
Teachers: 142.2 (15.3 to 1)
Librarians/Media Specialists: 3.0 (723.3 to 1)
Guidance Counselors: 3.5 (620.0 to 1)
Current Spending: ($ per student per year):
Total: $8,093; Instruction: $5,524; Support Services: $2,343
Enrollment, Drop-out Rates and Diploma Recipients by Race/Ethnicity

Category	Total	White	Black	Asian	AIAN	Hisp.
Enrollment (%)	100.0	98.1	0.2	0.4	0.4	0.9
Drop-out Rate (%)	1.4	1.5	0.0	0.0	0.0	0.0
H.S. Diplomas (#)	132	128	0	4	0	0

North Syracuse CSD

5355 W Taft Rd • North Syracuse, NY 13212-2796
(315) 452-3128 • http://www.nscsd.k12.ny.us/
Grade Span: PK-12; **Agency Type:** 1
Schools: 11
7 Primary; 2 Middle; 1 High; 1 Other Level
11 Regular; 0 Special Education; 0 Vocational; 0 Alternative
0 Magnet; 0 Charter; 4 Title I Eligible; 0 School-wide Title I
Students: 10,202 (51.6% male; 48.4% female)
Individual Education Program: 1,268 (12.4%);
English Language Learner: 28 (0.3%); Migrant: n/a
Eligible for Free Lunch Program: 1,124 (11.0%)
Eligible for Reduced-Price Lunch Program: 891 (8.7%)
Teachers: 681.1 (15.0 to 1)
Librarians/Media Specialists: 10.8 (944.6 to 1)
Guidance Counselors: 18.0 (566.8 to 1)
Current Spending: ($ per student per year):
Total: $8,731; Instruction: $5,706; Support Services: $2,830
Enrollment, Drop-out Rates and Diploma Recipients by Race/Ethnicity

Category	Total	White	Black	Asian	AIAN	Hisp.
Enrollment (%)	100.0	93.7	2.8	1.7	1.1	0.7
Drop-out Rate (%)	2.0	2.0	1.2	0.0	6.7	4.3
H.S. Diplomas (#)	582	553	14	7	7	1

Skaneateles CSD

49 E Elizabeth St • Skaneateles, NY 13152-1398
(315) 291-2221 • http://www.scs.cnyric.org/
Grade Span: KG-12; **Agency Type:** 1
Schools: 4
2 Primary; 1 Middle; 1 High; 0 Other Level
4 Regular; 0 Special Education; 0 Vocational; 0 Alternative
0 Magnet; 0 Charter; 1 Title I Eligible; 0 School-wide Title I
Students: 1,875 (52.2% male; 47.8% female)
Individual Education Program: 164 (8.7%);
English Language Learner: 2 (0.1%); Migrant: n/a
Eligible for Free Lunch Program: 65 (3.5%)
Eligible for Reduced-Price Lunch Program: 33 (1.8%)
Teachers: 143.3 (13.1 to 1)
Librarians/Media Specialists: 3.4 (551.5 to 1)
Guidance Counselors: 5.0 (375.0 to 1)
Current Spending: ($ per student per year):
Total: $8,700; Instruction: $5,447; Support Services: $3,103
Enrollment, Drop-out Rates and Diploma Recipients by Race/Ethnicity

Category	Total	White	Black	Asian	AIAN	Hisp.
Enrollment (%)	100.0	98.7	0.1	0.8	0.1	0.3
Drop-out Rate (%)	0.3	0.3	n/a	0.0	0.0	n/a
H.S. Diplomas (#)	154	153	0	1	0	0

Solvay UFSD

103 3rd St • Solvay, NY 13209-1532
(315) 468-1111
Grade Span: KG-12; **Agency Type:** 1
Schools: 4
2 Primary; 1 Middle; 1 High; 0 Other Level
4 Regular; 0 Special Education; 0 Vocational; 0 Alternative
0 Magnet; 0 Charter; 2 Title I Eligible; 0 School-wide Title I
Students: 1,809 (52.1% male; 47.9% female)
Individual Education Program: 262 (14.5%);
English Language Learner: 99 (5.5%); Migrant: n/a
Eligible for Free Lunch Program: 342 (18.9%)
Eligible for Reduced-Price Lunch Program: 103 (5.7%)
Teachers: 136.5 (13.3 to 1)
Librarians/Media Specialists: 2.9 (623.8 to 1)
Guidance Counselors: 5.0 (361.8 to 1)
Current Spending: ($ per student per year):
Total: $8,400; Instruction: $5,767; Support Services: $2,405
Enrollment, Drop-out Rates and Diploma Recipients by Race/Ethnicity

Category	Total	White	Black	Asian	AIAN	Hisp.
Enrollment (%)	100.0	95.4	1.8	0.3	0.8	1.8
Drop-out Rate (%)	0.9	0.8	9.1	0.0	0.0	0.0
H.S. Diplomas (#)	116	114	0	1	1	0

Syracuse City SD

725 Harrison St • Syracuse, NY 13210-2325
(315) 435-4161 • http://www.syracusecityschools.com/
Grade Span: PK-12; **Agency Type:** 1
Schools: 43
24 Primary; 5 Middle; 4 High; 10 Other Level
33 Regular; 0 Special Education; 0 Vocational; 10 Alternative
7 Magnet; 0 Charter; 19 Title I Eligible; 0 School-wide Title I
Students: 22,455 (50.9% male; 49.1% female)
Individual Education Program: 4,572 (20.4%);
English Language Learner: 1,348 (6.0%); Migrant: n/a
Eligible for Free Lunch Program: 13,575 (60.5%)
Eligible for Reduced-Price Lunch Program: 2,066 (9.2%)
Teachers: 1,833.1 (12.2 to 1)
Librarians/Media Specialists: 28.6 (785.1 to 1)
Guidance Counselors: 41.2 (545.0 to 1)
Current Spending: ($ per student per year):
Total: $10,632; Instruction: $7,269; Support Services: $3,017
Enrollment, Drop-out Rates and Diploma Recipients by Race/Ethnicity

Category	Total	White	Black	Asian	AIAN	Hisp.
Enrollment (%)	100.0	43.5	46.7	1.4	1.1	7.2
Drop-out Rate (%)	5.5	4.7	6.4	5.4	12.2	6.0
H.S. Diplomas (#)	627	387	221	2	1	16

West Genesee CSD

300 Sanderson Dr • Camillus, NY 13031-1655
(315) 487-4562
Grade Span: KG-12; **Agency Type:** 1
Schools: 8
4 Primary; 2 Middle; 1 High; 1 Other Level
7 Regular; 0 Special Education; 0 Vocational; 1 Alternative
0 Magnet; 0 Charter; 5 Title I Eligible; 0 School-wide Title I
Students: 5,172 (52.0% male; 48.0% female)
Individual Education Program: 501 (9.7%);
English Language Learner: 76 (1.5%); Migrant: n/a
Eligible for Free Lunch Program: 358 (6.9%)
Eligible for Reduced-Price Lunch Program: 205 (4.0%)
Teachers: 354.2 (14.6 to 1)
Librarians/Media Specialists: 7.8 (663.1 to 1)
Guidance Counselors: 11.0 (470.2 to 1)
Current Spending: ($ per student per year):
Total: $7,967; Instruction: $5,289; Support Services: $2,484
Enrollment, Drop-out Rates and Diploma Recipients by Race/Ethnicity

Category	Total	White	Black	Asian	AIAN	Hisp.
Enrollment (%)	100.0	96.1	1.8	0.9	0.5	0.7
Drop-out Rate (%)	2.3	2.4	0.0	0.0	0.0	0.0
H.S. Diplomas (#)	390	384	4	0	1	1

Westhill CSD

400 Walberta Rd • Syracuse, NY 13219-2297
(315) 488-6322 • http://www.westhillschools.com/
Grade Span: KG-12; **Agency Type:** 1
Schools: 4
2 Primary; 1 Middle; 1 High; 0 Other Level
4 Regular; 0 Special Education; 0 Vocational; 0 Alternative
0 Magnet; 0 Charter; 2 Title I Eligible; 0 School-wide Title I
Students: 2,047 (52.2% male; 47.8% female)
Individual Education Program: 280 (13.7%);
English Language Learner: 41 (2.0%); Migrant: n/a
Eligible for Free Lunch Program: 78 (3.8%)
Eligible for Reduced-Price Lunch Program: 43 (2.1%)
Teachers: 146.5 (14.0 to 1)
Librarians/Media Specialists: 3.9 (524.9 to 1)
Guidance Counselors: 5.0 (409.4 to 1)
Current Spending: ($ per student per year):
Total: $8,642; Instruction: $5,358; Support Services: $3,092
Enrollment, Drop-out Rates and Diploma Recipients by Race/Ethnicity

Category	Total	White	Black	Asian	AIAN	Hisp.
Enrollment (%)	100.0	95.6	1.8	1.9	0.1	0.6
Drop-out Rate (%)	0.0	0.0	0.0	0.0	0.0	0.0
H.S. Diplomas (#)	167	157	2	5	0	3

Ontario County

Canandaigua City SD

143 N Pearl St • Canandaigua, NY 14424-1496
(585) 396-3700 • http://www.canandaigua.k12.ny.us/
Grade Span: PK-12; **Agency Type:** 1
Schools: 5
2 Primary; 1 Middle; 1 High; 1 Other Level
4 Regular; 0 Special Education; 0 Vocational; 1 Alternative
0 Magnet; 0 Charter; 1 Title I Eligible; 0 School-wide Title I
Students: 4,205 (50.9% male; 49.1% female)
Individual Education Program: 583 (13.9%);
English Language Learner: 1 (<0.1%); Migrant: n/a
Eligible for Free Lunch Program: 370 (8.8%)
Eligible for Reduced-Price Lunch Program: 210 (5.0%)
Teachers: 324.7 (13.0 to 1)
Librarians/Media Specialists: 4.8 (876.0 to 1)
Guidance Counselors: 12.0 (350.4 to 1)
Current Spending: ($ per student per year):
Total: $9,240; Instruction: $6,224; Support Services: $2,761
Enrollment, Drop-out Rates and Diploma Recipients by Race/Ethnicity

Category	Total	White	Black	Asian	AIAN	Hisp.
Enrollment (%)	100.0	95.8	2.3	1.1	0.1	0.7
Drop-out Rate (%)	1.1	1.2	0.0	0.0	0.0	0.0
H.S. Diplomas (#)	244	237	4	2	0	1

Geneva City SD

649 S Exchange St • Geneva, NY 14456-3492
(315) 781-0276 • http://www.genevacsd.org/
Grade Span: KG-12; **Agency Type:** 1
Schools: 4
2 Primary; 1 Middle; 1 High; 0 Other Level
4 Regular; 0 Special Education; 0 Vocational; 0 Alternative
0 Magnet; 0 Charter; 3 Title I Eligible; 0 School-wide Title I
Students: 2,625 (49.3% male; 50.7% female)
Individual Education Program: 556 (21.2%);
English Language Learner: 71 (2.7%); Migrant: n/a
Eligible for Free Lunch Program: 934 (35.6%)
Eligible for Reduced-Price Lunch Program: 250 (9.5%)
Teachers: 223.8 (11.7 to 1)
Librarians/Media Specialists: 3.8 (690.8 to 1)
Guidance Counselors: 6.0 (437.5 to 1)
Current Spending: ($ per student per year):
Total: $9,900; Instruction: $6,884; Support Services: $2,699
Enrollment, Drop-out Rates and Diploma Recipients by Race/Ethnicity

Category	Total	White	Black	Asian	AIAN	Hisp.
Enrollment (%)	100.0	68.7	19.1	1.3	0.1	10.9
Drop-out Rate (%)	4.9	4.0	10.2	0.0	0.0	8.7
H.S. Diplomas (#)	149	122	14	3	1	9

Gorham-Middlesex CSD

4100 Baldwin Rd • Rushville, NY 14544-9799
(585) 554-4848
Grade Span: KG-12; **Agency Type:** 1
Schools: 4
2 Primary; 1 Middle; 1 High; 0 Other Level
4 Regular; 0 Special Education; 0 Vocational; 0 Alternative
0 Magnet; 0 Charter; 3 Title I Eligible; 0 School-wide Title I
Students: 1,652 (50.4% male; 49.6% female)
Individual Education Program: 223 (13.5%);
English Language Learner: 3 (0.2%); Migrant: n/a
Eligible for Free Lunch Program: 248 (15.0%)
Eligible for Reduced-Price Lunch Program: 184 (11.1%)
Teachers: 129.2 (12.8 to 1)
Librarians/Media Specialists: 1.8 (917.8 to 1)
Guidance Counselors: 3.0 (550.7 to 1)
Current Spending: ($ per student per year):
Total: $10,560; Instruction: $6,963; Support Services: $3,246
Enrollment, Drop-out Rates and Diploma Recipients by Race/Ethnicity

Category	Total	White	Black	Asian	AIAN	Hisp.
Enrollment (%)	100.0	97.0	0.7	0.7	0.2	1.3
Drop-out Rate (%)	0.2	0.2	0.0	0.0	0.0	0.0
H.S. Diplomas (#)	99	96	0	1	0	2

Phelps-Clifton Springs CSD

1490 Rt 488 • Clifton Springs, NY 14432-9318
(315) 548-3480 • http://www.midlakes.org/
Grade Span: KG-12; **Agency Type:** 1
Schools: 4
2 Primary; 1 Middle; 1 High; 0 Other Level
4 Regular; 0 Special Education; 0 Vocational; 0 Alternative
0 Magnet; 0 Charter; 2 Title I Eligible; 0 School-wide Title I
Students: 2,120 (52.5% male; 47.5% female)
Individual Education Program: 317 (15.0%);
English Language Learner: 0 (0.0%); Migrant: n/a
Eligible for Free Lunch Program: 329 (15.5%)
Eligible for Reduced-Price Lunch Program: 228 (10.8%)
Teachers: 160.0 (13.3 to 1)
Librarians/Media Specialists: 2.9 (731.0 to 1)
Guidance Counselors: 5.0 (424.0 to 1)
Current Spending: ($ per student per year):
Total: $9,049; Instruction: $5,906; Support Services: $2,865
Enrollment, Drop-out Rates and Diploma Recipients by Race/Ethnicity

Category	Total	White	Black	Asian	AIAN	Hisp.
Enrollment (%)	100.0	97.1	0.9	0.6	0.4	1.0
Drop-out Rate (%)	5.0	5.1	0.0	0.0	0.0	0.0
H.S. Diplomas (#)	135	133	0	1	0	1

Victor CSD

953 High St • Victor, NY 14564-1167
(716) 924-3252 • http://www.victorschools.org/homeflash.cfm
Grade Span: PK-12; **Agency Type:** 1
Schools: 5
2 Primary; 2 Middle; 1 High; 0 Other Level
5 Regular; 0 Special Education; 0 Vocational; 0 Alternative
0 Magnet; 0 Charter; 3 Title I Eligible; 0 School-wide Title I
Students: 3,448 (51.6% male; 48.4% female)
Individual Education Program: 339 (9.8%);
English Language Learner: 28 (0.8%); Migrant: n/a
Eligible for Free Lunch Program: 174 (5.0%)
Eligible for Reduced-Price Lunch Program: 117 (3.4%)
Teachers: 241.1 (14.3 to 1)
Librarians/Media Specialists: 3.5 (985.1 to 1)
Guidance Counselors: 7.0 (492.6 to 1)
Current Spending: ($ per student per year):
Total: $9,357; Instruction: $6,202; Support Services: $2,913
Enrollment, Drop-out Rates and Diploma Recipients by Race/Ethnicity

Category	Total	White	Black	Asian	AIAN	Hisp.
Enrollment (%)	100.0	95.7	1.2	1.7	0.3	1.1
Drop-out Rate (%)	1.9	1.8	0.0	5.9	0.0	0.0
H.S. Diplomas (#)	199	190	1	6	1	1

Orange County

Cornwall CSD

24 Idlewild Ave • Cornwall On Hudson, NY 12520
(845) 534-8009
Grade Span: KG-12; **Agency Type:** 1
Schools: 5
2 Primary; 1 Middle; 1 High; 1 Other Level
4 Regular; 0 Special Education; 0 Vocational; 1 Alternative
0 Magnet; 0 Charter; 2 Title I Eligible; 0 School-wide Title I
Students: 2,983 (50.7% male; 49.3% female)
Individual Education Program: 287 (9.6%);
English Language Learner: 10 (0.3%); Migrant: n/a
Eligible for Free Lunch Program: 112 (3.8%)
Eligible for Reduced-Price Lunch Program: 76 (2.5%)
Teachers: 191.3 (15.6 to 1)
Librarians/Media Specialists: 3.5 (852.3 to 1)
Guidance Counselors: 7.0 (426.1 to 1)
Current Spending: ($ per student per year):
Total: $9,070; Instruction: $6,083; Support Services: $2,754
Enrollment, Drop-out Rates and Diploma Recipients by Race/Ethnicity

Category	Total	White	Black	Asian	AIAN	Hisp.
Enrollment (%)	100.0	88.4	3.0	1.6	0.2	6.8
Drop-out Rate (%)	1.3	1.3	5.0	0.0	0.0	0.0
H.S. Diplomas (#)	198	180	4	2	3	9

Goshen CSD

227 Main St • Goshen, NY 10924-2158
(845) 294-2410 • http://www.gcsny.org/
Grade Span: KG-12; **Agency Type:** 2
Schools: 8
2 Primary; 1 Middle; 2 High; 3 Other Level
4 Regular; 0 Special Education; 0 Vocational; 4 Alternative
0 Magnet; 0 Charter; 3 Title I Eligible; 0 School-wide Title I
Students: 2,965 (51.6% male; 48.4% female)
Individual Education Program: 261 (8.8%);
English Language Learner: 51 (1.7%); Migrant: n/a
Eligible for Free Lunch Program: 228 (7.7%)
Eligible for Reduced-Price Lunch Program: 147 (5.0%)
Teachers: 216.2 (13.7 to 1)
Librarians/Media Specialists: 3.6 (823.6 to 1)
Guidance Counselors: 6.0 (494.2 to 1)
Current Spending: ($ per student per year):
Total: $10,957; Instruction: $6,866; Support Services: $3,818
Enrollment, Drop-out Rates and Diploma Recipients by Race/Ethnicity

Category	Total	White	Black	Asian	AIAN	Hisp.
Enrollment (%)	100.0	84.2	6.0	1.7	0.2	7.8
Drop-out Rate (%)	1.2	0.8	0.0	0.0	n/a	8.7
H.S. Diplomas (#)	176	160	7	4	0	5

Middletown City SD

223 Wisner Ave Ext • Middletown, NY 10940-3240
(845) 341-5690 • http://www.middletown.k12.ny.us/
Grade Span: PK-12; **Agency Type:** 1
Schools: 14
5 Primary; 2 Middle; 1 High; 6 Other Level
8 Regular; 0 Special Education; 0 Vocational; 6 Alternative
0 Magnet; 0 Charter; 5 Title I Eligible; 0 School-wide Title I
Students: 6,491 (50.7% male; 49.3% female)
Individual Education Program: 904 (13.9%);
English Language Learner: 438 (6.7%); Migrant: n/a
Eligible for Free Lunch Program: 2,551 (39.3%)
Eligible for Reduced-Price Lunch Program: 1,020 (15.7%)
Teachers: 441.0 (14.7 to 1)
Librarians/Media Specialists: 7.4 (877.2 to 1)
Guidance Counselors: 14.0 (463.6 to 1)
Current Spending: ($ per student per year):
Total: $10,958; Instruction: $7,240; Support Services: $3,391
Enrollment, Drop-out Rates and Diploma Recipients by Race/Ethnicity

Category	Total	White	Black	Asian	AIAN	Hisp.
Enrollment (%)	100.0	38.3	25.3	2.2	0.2	34.1
Drop-out Rate (%)	3.9	2.9	4.1	2.4	0.0	6.3
H.S. Diplomas (#)	264	155	62	10	1	36

Minisink Valley CSD

Rt 6 • Slate Hill, NY 10973-0217
(845) 355-5110 • http://www.minisink.com/
Grade Span: KG-12; **Agency Type:** 2
Schools: 6
3 Primary; 1 Middle; 1 High; 1 Other Level
5 Regular; 0 Special Education; 0 Vocational; 1 Alternative
0 Magnet; 0 Charter; 1 Title I Eligible; 0 School-wide Title I
Students: 4,388 (51.7% male; 48.3% female)
Individual Education Program: 533 (12.1%);
English Language Learner: 25 (0.6%); Migrant: n/a
Eligible for Free Lunch Program: 310 (7.1%)
Eligible for Reduced-Price Lunch Program: 216 (4.9%)
Teachers: 295.0 (14.9 to 1)
Librarians/Media Specialists: 3.6 (1,218.9 to 1)
Guidance Counselors: 9.0 (487.6 to 1)
Current Spending: ($ per student per year):
Total: $9,347; Instruction: $6,552; Support Services: $2,593
Enrollment, Drop-out Rates and Diploma Recipients by Race/Ethnicity

Category	Total	White	Black	Asian	AIAN	Hisp.
Enrollment (%)	100.0	89.3	2.8	1.0	0.2	6.7
Drop-out Rate (%)	0.6	0.5	2.6	0.0	0.0	1.7
H.S. Diplomas (#)	246	228	8	3	2	5

Monroe-Woodbury CSD

278 Rte 32-Educ Ctr • Central Valley, NY 10917-1001
(845) 928-2321 • http://mw.k12.ny.us/
Grade Span: KG-12; **Agency Type:** 1
Schools: 7
5 Primary; 1 Middle; 1 High; 0 Other Level
7 Regular; 0 Special Education; 0 Vocational; 0 Alternative
0 Magnet; 0 Charter; 3 Title I Eligible; 0 School-wide Title I
Students: 7,164 (51.4% male; 48.6% female)
Individual Education Program: 1,069 (14.9%);
English Language Learner: 80 (1.1%); Migrant: n/a
Eligible for Free Lunch Program: 251 (3.5%)
Eligible for Reduced-Price Lunch Program: 182 (2.5%)
Teachers: 504.4 (14.2 to 1)
Librarians/Media Specialists: 9.7 (738.6 to 1)
Guidance Counselors: 14.4 (497.5 to 1)
Current Spending: ($ per student per year):
Total: $10,630; Instruction: $6,443; Support Services: $3,984
Enrollment, Drop-out Rates and Diploma Recipients by Race/Ethnicity

Category	Total	White	Black	Asian	AIAN	Hisp.
Enrollment (%)	100.0	81.5	3.3	3.6	0.6	11.0
Drop-out Rate (%)	0.3	0.2	0.0	0.0	0.0	1.1
H.S. Diplomas (#)	411	350	8	19	1	33

Newburgh City SD

124 Grand St • Newburgh, NY 12550-4600
(845) 563-3500 • http://www.newburgh.k12.ny.us/
Grade Span: PK-12; **Agency Type:** 1
Schools: 16
12 Primary; 3 Middle; 1 High; 0 Other Level
16 Regular; 0 Special Education; 0 Vocational; 0 Alternative
6 Magnet; 0 Charter; 14 Title I Eligible; 0 School-wide Title I
Students: 12,895 (51.3% male; 48.7% female)
Individual Education Program: 1,687 (13.1%);
English Language Learner: 1,305 (10.1%); Migrant: n/a
Eligible for Free Lunch Program: 5,664 (43.9%)
Eligible for Reduced-Price Lunch Program: 1,441 (11.2%)
Teachers: 941.0 (13.7 to 1)
Librarians/Media Specialists: 13.7 (941.2 to 1)
Guidance Counselors: 22.0 (586.1 to 1)
Current Spending: ($ per student per year):
Total: $10,343; Instruction: $6,732; Support Services: $3,311
Enrollment, Drop-out Rates and Diploma Recipients by Race/Ethnicity

Category	Total	White	Black	Asian	AIAN	Hisp.
Enrollment (%)	100.0	36.7	30.4	2.1	0.0	30.7
Drop-out Rate (%)	4.7	2.3	7.2	2.8	n/a	6.4
H.S. Diplomas (#)	482	279	91	12	0	100

Pine Bush CSD

156 State Rt 302 • Pine Bush, NY 12566-0700
(845) 744-2031 • http://www.pinebushschools.org/
Grade Span: PK-12; **Agency Type:** 1
Schools: 7
4 Primary; 2 Middle; 1 High; 0 Other Level
7 Regular; 0 Special Education; 0 Vocational; 0 Alternative
0 Magnet; 0 Charter; 4 Title I Eligible; 0 School-wide Title I
Students: 6,092 (50.2% male; 49.8% female)
Individual Education Program: 941 (15.4%);
English Language Learner: 90 (1.5%); Migrant: n/a
Eligible for Free Lunch Program: 763 (12.5%)
Eligible for Reduced-Price Lunch Program: 519 (8.5%)
Teachers: 417.9 (14.6 to 1)
Librarians/Media Specialists: 5.3 (1,149.4 to 1)
Guidance Counselors: 9.0 (676.9 to 1)
Current Spending: ($ per student per year):
Total: $9,753; Instruction: $6,511; Support Services: $3,010
Enrollment, Drop-out Rates and Diploma Recipients by Race/Ethnicity

Category	Total	White	Black	Asian	AIAN	Hisp.
Enrollment (%)	100.0	82.4	7.8	1.8	0.2	7.8
Drop-out Rate (%)	4.3	4.0	11.3	3.1	0.0	2.8
H.S. Diplomas (#)	306	262	20	3	1	20

Port Jervis City SD

9 Thompson St • Port Jervis, NY 12771-3058
(845) 858-3175 • http://www.portjerviscsd.k12.ny.us/
Grade Span: KG-12; **Agency Type:** 1
Schools: 5
3 Primary; 1 Middle; 1 High; 0 Other Level
5 Regular; 0 Special Education; 0 Vocational; 0 Alternative
0 Magnet; 0 Charter; 5 Title I Eligible; 0 School-wide Title I
Students: 3,432 (52.7% male; 47.3% female)
Individual Education Program: 427 (12.4%);
English Language Learner: 20 (0.6%); Migrant: n/a
Eligible for Free Lunch Program: 872 (25.4%)
Eligible for Reduced-Price Lunch Program: 369 (10.8%)
Teachers: 232.7 (14.7 to 1)
Librarians/Media Specialists: 4.3 (798.1 to 1)
Guidance Counselors: 7.0 (490.3 to 1)
Current Spending: ($ per student per year):
Total: $10,110; Instruction: $6,611; Support Services: $3,186
Enrollment, Drop-out Rates and Diploma Recipients by Race/Ethnicity

Category	Total	White	Black	Asian	AIAN	Hisp.
Enrollment (%)	100.0	88.3	5.4	0.5	0.3	5.6
Drop-out Rate (%)	5.6	5.0	15.1	0.0	0.0	5.7
H.S. Diplomas (#)	192	171	11	1	0	9

Valley CSD (Montgomery)

944 State Rt 17k • Montgomery, NY 12549-2240
(845) 457-2400 • http://www.vcsd.k12.ny.us/
Grade Span: KG-12; **Agency Type:** 1
Schools: 7
5 Primary; 1 Middle; 1 High; 0 Other Level
7 Regular; 0 Special Education; 0 Vocational; 0 Alternative
0 Magnet; 0 Charter; 5 Title I Eligible; 0 School-wide Title I
Students: 5,319 (51.8% male; 48.2% female)
Individual Education Program: 705 (13.3%);
English Language Learner: 47 (0.9%); Migrant: n/a
Eligible for Free Lunch Program: 835 (15.7%)
Eligible for Reduced-Price Lunch Program: 436 (8.2%)
Teachers: 367.7 (14.5 to 1)
Librarians/Media Specialists: 6.4 (831.1 to 1)
Guidance Counselors: 11.0 (483.5 to 1)
Current Spending: ($ per student per year):
Total: $8,957; Instruction: $5,844; Support Services: $2,863
Enrollment, Drop-out Rates and Diploma Recipients by Race/Ethnicity

Category	Total	White	Black	Asian	AIAN	Hisp.
Enrollment (%)	100.0	83.0	6.5	1.4	0.5	8.5
Drop-out Rate (%)	2.8	2.9	4.3	0.0	0.0	1.9
H.S. Diplomas (#)	308	263	17	5	2	21

Warwick Valley CSD

W St Ext • Warwick, NY 10990-0595
(845) 987-3010 • http://www.warwickvalleyschools.com/
Grade Span: KG-12; **Agency Type:** 1
Schools: 7
4 Primary; 1 Middle; 1 High; 1 Other Level
6 Regular; 0 Special Education; 0 Vocational; 1 Alternative
0 Magnet; 0 Charter; 5 Title I Eligible; 0 School-wide Title I
Students: 4,595 (52.2% male; 47.8% female)
Individual Education Program: 496 (10.8%);
English Language Learner: 30 (0.7%); Migrant: n/a
Eligible for Free Lunch Program: 229 (5.0%)
Eligible for Reduced-Price Lunch Program: 111 (2.4%)
Teachers: 304.9 (15.1 to 1)
Librarians/Media Specialists: 5.6 (820.5 to 1)
Guidance Counselors: 10.0 (459.5 to 1)
Current Spending: ($ per student per year):
Total: $9,823; Instruction: $6,298; Support Services: $3,284
Enrollment, Drop-out Rates and Diploma Recipients by Race/Ethnicity

Category	Total	White	Black	Asian	AIAN	Hisp.
Enrollment (%)	100.0	86.8	5.5	1.4	0.8	5.6
Drop-out Rate (%)	0.7	0.8	0.0	0.0	0.0	0.0
H.S. Diplomas (#)	257	241	6	3	0	7

Washingtonville CSD

52 W Main St • Washingtonville, NY 10992-1492
(845) 497-2200 • http://www.ws.k12.ny.us/
Grade Span: PK-12; **Agency Type:** 1
Schools: 5
3 Primary; 1 Middle; 1 High; 0 Other Level
5 Regular; 0 Special Education; 0 Vocational; 0 Alternative
0 Magnet; 0 Charter; 3 Title I Eligible; 0 School-wide Title I
Students: 5,158 (51.8% male; 48.2% female)
Individual Education Program: 544 (10.5%);
English Language Learner: 67 (1.3%); Migrant: n/a
Eligible for Free Lunch Program: 266 (5.2%)
Eligible for Reduced-Price Lunch Program: 229 (4.4%)
Teachers: 328.8 (15.7 to 1)
Librarians/Media Specialists: 5.0 (1,031.6 to 1)
Guidance Counselors: 13.0 (396.8 to 1)
Current Spending: ($ per student per year):
Total: $9,003; Instruction: $5,882; Support Services: $2,890
Enrollment, Drop-out Rates and Diploma Recipients by Race/Ethnicity

Category	Total	White	Black	Asian	AIAN	Hisp.
Enrollment (%)	100.0	82.3	5.8	1.6	0.3	9.9
Drop-out Rate (%)	1.0	1.0	2.7	0.0	0.0	0.9
H.S. Diplomas (#)	312	276	9	2	2	23

Orleans County

Albion CSD

324 E Ave • Albion, NY 14411-1697
(585) 589-2050 • http://www.albion.wnyric.org/
Grade Span: PK-12; **Agency Type:** 1
Schools: 6
1 Primary; 1 Middle; 1 High; 3 Other Level
3 Regular; 0 Special Education; 0 Vocational; 3 Alternative
0 Magnet; 0 Charter; 2 Title I Eligible; 0 School-wide Title I
Students: 2,820 (51.0% male; 49.0% female)
Individual Education Program: 315 (11.2%);
English Language Learner: 61 (2.2%); Migrant: n/a
Eligible for Free Lunch Program: 554 (19.6%)
Eligible for Reduced-Price Lunch Program: 225 (8.0%)
Teachers: 198.1 (14.2 to 1)
Librarians/Media Specialists: 3.0 (940.0 to 1)
Guidance Counselors: 6.0 (470.0 to 1)
Current Spending: ($ per student per year):
Total: $7,916; Instruction: $5,439; Support Services: $2,279
Enrollment, Drop-out Rates and Diploma Recipients by Race/Ethnicity

Category	Total	White	Black	Asian	AIAN	Hisp.
Enrollment (%)	100.0	83.1	9.0	1.2	1.0	5.7
Drop-out Rate (%)	1.0	1.1	0.0	0.0	0.0	0.0
H.S. Diplomas (#)	152	139	8	1	1	3

Medina CSD

One Mustang Dr • Medina, NY 14103-1845
(585) 798-2700 • http://www.medina.wnyric.org/
Grade Span: KG-12; **Agency Type:** 1
Schools: 4
2 Primary; 1 Middle; 1 High; 0 Other Level
4 Regular; 0 Special Education; 0 Vocational; 0 Alternative
0 Magnet; 0 Charter; 4 Title I Eligible; 0 School-wide Title I
Students: 1,997 (52.1% male; 47.9% female)
Individual Education Program: 299 (15.0%);
English Language Learner: 20 (1.0%); Migrant: n/a
Eligible for Free Lunch Program: 493 (24.7%)
Eligible for Reduced-Price Lunch Program: 130 (6.5%)
Teachers: 171.9 (11.6 to 1)
Librarians/Media Specialists: 3.1 (644.2 to 1)
Guidance Counselors: 5.0 (399.4 to 1)
Current Spending: ($ per student per year):
Total: $9,261; Instruction: $6,381; Support Services: $2,636
Enrollment, Drop-out Rates and Diploma Recipients by Race/Ethnicity

Category	Total	White	Black	Asian	AIAN	Hisp.
Enrollment (%)	100.0	89.7	6.4	0.9	0.5	2.6
Drop-out Rate (%)	5.9	5.2	15.8	0.0	0.0	25.0
H.S. Diplomas (#)	122	115	6	1	0	0

Oswego County

Altmar-Parish-Williamstown CSD

639 County Rt 22 • Parish, NY 13131-0097
(315) 625-5251 • http://www.apw.cnyric.org/
Grade Span: KG-12; **Agency Type:** 2
Schools: 5
3 Primary; 1 Middle; 1 High; 0 Other Level
5 Regular; 0 Special Education; 0 Vocational; 0 Alternative
0 Magnet; 0 Charter; 5 Title I Eligible; 0 School-wide Title I
Students: 1,690 (48.7% male; 51.3% female)
Individual Education Program: 259 (15.3%);
English Language Learner: 0 (0.0%); Migrant: n/a
Eligible for Free Lunch Program: 553 (32.7%)
Eligible for Reduced-Price Lunch Program: 248 (14.7%)
Teachers: 131.8 (12.8 to 1)
Librarians/Media Specialists: 3.0 (563.3 to 1)
Guidance Counselors: 4.0 (422.5 to 1)
Current Spending: ($ per student per year):
Total: $9,938; Instruction: $6,275; Support Services: $3,356
Enrollment, Drop-out Rates and Diploma Recipients by Race/Ethnicity

Category	Total	White	Black	Asian	AIAN	Hisp.
Enrollment (%)	100.0	98.9	0.5	0.2	0.1	0.3
Drop-out Rate (%)	4.5	4.4	0.0	0.0	33.3	0.0
H.S. Diplomas (#)	91	89	0	2	0	0

Central Square CSD

642 S Main St • Central Square, NY 13036-3511
(315) 668-4220 • http://www.centralsquareschools.org/
Grade Span: PK-12; **Agency Type:** 1
Schools: 8
6 Primary; 1 Middle; 1 High; 0 Other Level
8 Regular; 0 Special Education; 0 Vocational; 0 Alternative
0 Magnet; 0 Charter; 5 Title I Eligible; 0 School-wide Title I
Students: 4,985 (51.4% male; 48.6% female)
Individual Education Program: 637 (12.8%);
English Language Learner: 1 (<0.1%); Migrant: n/a
Eligible for Free Lunch Program: 808 (16.2%)
Eligible for Reduced-Price Lunch Program: 425 (8.5%)
Teachers: 351.5 (14.2 to 1)
Librarians/Media Specialists: 6.1 (817.2 to 1)
Guidance Counselors: 10.0 (498.5 to 1)
Current Spending: ($ per student per year):
Total: $8,473; Instruction: $5,333; Support Services: $2,867
Enrollment, Drop-out Rates and Diploma Recipients by Race/Ethnicity

Category	Total	White	Black	Asian	AIAN	Hisp.
Enrollment (%)	100.0	98.8	0.5	0.2	0.4	0.2
Drop-out Rate (%)	2.4	2.3	0.0	14.3	8.3	0.0
H.S. Diplomas (#)	249	245	0	2	1	1

Fulton City SD

167 S Fourth St • Fulton, NY 13069-1859
(315) 593-5510
Grade Span: KG-12; **Agency Type:** 1
Schools: 6
4 Primary; 1 Middle; 1 High; 0 Other Level
6 Regular; 0 Special Education; 0 Vocational; 0 Alternative
0 Magnet; 0 Charter; 6 Title I Eligible; 0 School-wide Title I
Students: 3,856 (49.1% male; 50.9% female)
Individual Education Program: 662 (17.2%);
English Language Learner: 24 (0.6%); Migrant: n/a
Eligible for Free Lunch Program: 1,301 (33.7%)
Eligible for Reduced-Price Lunch Program: 452 (11.7%)
Teachers: 297.3 (13.0 to 1)
Librarians/Media Specialists: 4.7 (820.4 to 1)
Guidance Counselors: 6.0 (642.7 to 1)
Current Spending: ($ per student per year):
Total: $10,023; Instruction: $6,674; Support Services: $3,061
Enrollment, Drop-out Rates and Diploma Recipients by Race/Ethnicity

Category	Total	White	Black	Asian	AIAN	Hisp.
Enrollment (%)	100.0	96.0	1.4	0.4	0.1	2.2
Drop-out Rate (%)	4.0	4.1	0.0	0.0	0.0	11.1
H.S. Diplomas (#)	213	210	0	1	0	2

Hannibal CSD

1051 Auburn St • Hannibal, NY 13074-0066
(315) 564-7902 • http://www.hannibal.cnyric.org/
Grade Span: KG-12; **Agency Type:** 2
Schools: 3
2 Primary; 0 Middle; 1 High; 0 Other Level
3 Regular; 0 Special Education; 0 Vocational; 0 Alternative
0 Magnet; 0 Charter; 2 Title I Eligible; 0 School-wide Title I
Students: 1,761 (49.9% male; 50.1% female)
Individual Education Program: 232 (13.2%);
English Language Learner: 0 (0.0%); Migrant: n/a
Eligible for Free Lunch Program: 499 (28.3%)
Eligible for Reduced-Price Lunch Program: 235 (13.3%)
Teachers: 127.4 (13.8 to 1)
Librarians/Media Specialists: 2.2 (800.5 to 1)
Guidance Counselors: 2.9 (607.2 to 1)
Current Spending: ($ per student per year):
Total: $9,038; Instruction: $5,891; Support Services: $2,822

Enrollment, Drop-out Rates and Diploma Recipients by Race/Ethnicity

Category	Total	White	Black	Asian	AIAN	Hisp.
Enrollment (%)	100.0	96.8	1.2	0.3	0.3	1.4
Drop-out Rate (%)	2.0	1.8	n/a	0.0	0.0	25.0
H.S. Diplomas (#)	94	93	0	0	0	1

Mexico CSD

40 Academy St • Mexico, NY 13114-3432
(315) 963-8400 • http://www.mexico.cnyric.org/
Grade Span: KG-12; **Agency Type:** 1
Schools: 6
3 Primary; 1 Middle; 1 High; 1 Other Level
5 Regular; 0 Special Education; 0 Vocational; 1 Alternative
0 Magnet; 0 Charter; 4 Title I Eligible; 0 School-wide Title I
Students: 2,688 (51.1% male; 48.9% female)
Individual Education Program: 389 (14.5%);
English Language Learner: 0 (0.0%); Migrant: n/a
Eligible for Free Lunch Program: 497 (18.5%)
Eligible for Reduced-Price Lunch Program: 303 (11.3%)
Teachers: 195.9 (13.7 to 1)
Librarians/Media Specialists: 2.0 (1,344.0 to 1)
Guidance Counselors: 5.0 (537.6 to 1)
Current Spending: ($ per student per year):
Total: $8,580; Instruction: $5,392; Support Services: $2,958
Enrollment, Drop-out Rates and Diploma Recipients by Race/Ethnicity

Category	Total	White	Black	Asian	AIAN	Hisp.
Enrollment (%)	100.0	97.0	0.5	0.4	1.3	0.7
Drop-out Rate (%)	4.1	4.3	0.0	0.0	0.0	0.0
H.S. Diplomas (#)	162	159	1	1	1	0

Oswego City SD

120 E 1st St • Oswego, NY 13126-2114
(315) 341-5885 • http://oswego.org/
Grade Span: KG-12; **Agency Type:** 1
Schools: 8
5 Primary; 1 Middle; 1 High; 1 Other Level
7 Regular; 0 Special Education; 0 Vocational; 1 Alternative
0 Magnet; 0 Charter; 5 Title I Eligible; 0 School-wide Title I
Students: 4,974 (51.5% male; 48.5% female)
Individual Education Program: 608 (12.2%);
English Language Learner: 39 (0.8%); Migrant: n/a
Eligible for Free Lunch Program: 885 (17.8%)
Eligible for Reduced-Price Lunch Program: 212 (4.3%)
Teachers: 371.4 (13.4 to 1)
Librarians/Media Specialists: 5.8 (857.6 to 1)
Guidance Counselors: 8.5 (585.2 to 1)
Current Spending: ($ per student per year):
Total: $10,582; Instruction: $6,837; Support Services: $3,500
Enrollment, Drop-out Rates and Diploma Recipients by Race/Ethnicity

Category	Total	White	Black	Asian	AIAN	Hisp.
Enrollment (%)	100.0	93.6	1.3	1.1	0.4	3.6
Drop-out Rate (%)	3.5	3.6	0.0	0.0	n/a	3.1
H.S. Diplomas (#)	253	244	1	3	0	5

Phoenix CSD

116 Volney St • Phoenix, NY 13135-9778
(315) 695-1555 • http://www.phoenix.k12.ny.us/
Grade Span: KG-12; **Agency Type:** 1
Schools: 3
1 Primary; 1 Middle; 1 High; 0 Other Level
3 Regular; 0 Special Education; 0 Vocational; 0 Alternative
0 Magnet; 0 Charter; 1 Title I Eligible; 0 School-wide Title I
Students: 2,488 (51.1% male; 48.9% female)
Individual Education Program: 469 (18.9%);
English Language Learner: 1 (<0.1%); Migrant: n/a
Eligible for Free Lunch Program: 490 (19.7%)
Eligible for Reduced-Price Lunch Program: 338 (13.6%)
Teachers: 204.9 (12.1 to 1)
Librarians/Media Specialists: 3.6 (691.1 to 1)
Guidance Counselors: 5.4 (460.7 to 1)
Current Spending: ($ per student per year):
Total: $10,528; Instruction: $7,084; Support Services: $3,172
Enrollment, Drop-out Rates and Diploma Recipients by Race/Ethnicity

Category	Total	White	Black	Asian	AIAN	Hisp.
Enrollment (%)	100.0	97.3	0.6	0.4	0.8	0.9
Drop-out Rate (%)	1.9	1.8	0.0	0.0	0.0	14.3
H.S. Diplomas (#)	174	173	0	1	0	0

Otsego County

Oneonta City SD

189 Main St-Ste 302 • Oneonta, NY 13820-1142
(607) 433-8232 • http://oneonta.k12.ny.us/districtwebpage.htm
Grade Span: PK-12; **Agency Type:** 1
Schools: 6
4 Primary; 1 Middle; 1 High; 0 Other Level
6 Regular; 0 Special Education; 0 Vocational; 0 Alternative
0 Magnet; 0 Charter; 4 Title I Eligible; 0 School-wide Title I
Students: 2,163 (50.9% male; 49.1% female)
Individual Education Program: 360 (16.6%);
English Language Learner: 14 (0.6%); Migrant: n/a
Eligible for Free Lunch Program: 433 (20.0%)
Eligible for Reduced-Price Lunch Program: 159 (7.4%)
Teachers: 176.1 (12.3 to 1)
Librarians/Media Specialists: 4.0 (540.8 to 1)
Guidance Counselors: 11.0 (196.6 to 1)
Current Spending: ($ per student per year):
Total: $10,047; Instruction: $6,683; Support Services: $3,158
Enrollment, Drop-out Rates and Diploma Recipients by Race/Ethnicity

Category	Total	White	Black	Asian	AIAN	Hisp.
Enrollment (%)	100.0	89.8	4.5	2.4	0.4	3.0
Drop-out Rate (%)	0.3	0.2	4.3	0.0	n/a	0.0
H.S. Diplomas (#)	148	141	4	0	1	2

Putnam County

Brewster CSD

30 Farm-To-Market Rd • Brewster, NY 10509-9956
(845) 279-8000 • http://www.brewsterschools.org/
Grade Span: KG-12; **Agency Type:** 1
Schools: 5
2 Primary; 2 Middle; 1 High; 0 Other Level
5 Regular; 0 Special Education; 0 Vocational; 0 Alternative
0 Magnet; 0 Charter; 1 Title I Eligible; 0 School-wide Title I
Students: 3,698 (53.3% male; 46.7% female)
Individual Education Program: 470 (12.7%);
English Language Learner: 75 (2.0%); Migrant: n/a
Eligible for Free Lunch Program: 232 (6.3%)
Eligible for Reduced-Price Lunch Program: 124 (3.4%)
Teachers: 274.1 (13.5 to 1)
Librarians/Media Specialists: 4.4 (840.5 to 1)
Guidance Counselors: 9.0 (410.9 to 1)
Current Spending: ($ per student per year):
Total: $12,942; Instruction: $8,629; Support Services: $4,041
Enrollment, Drop-out Rates and Diploma Recipients by Race/Ethnicity

Category	Total	White	Black	Asian	AIAN	Hisp.
Enrollment (%)	100.0	86.5	4.1	2.8	0.0	6.6
Drop-out Rate (%)	0.3	0.3	0.0	0.0	n/a	0.0
H.S. Diplomas (#)	203	184	4	5	1	9

Carmel CSD

81 S St • Patterson, NY 12563-0296
(845) 878-2094 • http://ccsd.k12.ny.us/
Grade Span: KG-12; **Agency Type:** 1
Schools: 7
3 Primary; 1 Middle; 1 High; 2 Other Level
5 Regular; 0 Special Education; 0 Vocational; 2 Alternative
0 Magnet; 0 Charter; 2 Title I Eligible; 0 School-wide Title I
Students: 4,956 (51.2% male; 48.8% female)
Individual Education Program: 591 (11.9%);
English Language Learner: 49 (1.0%); Migrant: n/a
Eligible for Free Lunch Program: 174 (3.5%)
Eligible for Reduced-Price Lunch Program: 130 (2.6%)
Teachers: 331.1 (15.0 to 1)
Librarians/Media Specialists: 3.5 (1,416.0 to 1)
Guidance Counselors: 9.5 (521.7 to 1)
Current Spending: ($ per student per year):
Total: $12,427; Instruction: $8,890; Support Services: $3,320
Enrollment, Drop-out Rates and Diploma Recipients by Race/Ethnicity

Category	Total	White	Black	Asian	AIAN	Hisp.
Enrollment (%)	100.0	88.5	2.3	1.2	0.1	7.8
Drop-out Rate (%)	1.2	1.1	0.0	0.0	n/a	2.1
H.S. Diplomas (#)	288	262	4	4	0	18

Mahopac CSD

179 E Lake Bouleva • Mahopac, NY 10541-1666
(845) 628-3415 • http://www.mahopac.k12.ny.us/
Grade Span: KG-12; **Agency Type:** 1
Schools: 6
4 Primary; 1 Middle; 1 High; 0 Other Level
6 Regular; 0 Special Education; 0 Vocational; 0 Alternative
0 Magnet; 0 Charter; 3 Title I Eligible; 0 School-wide Title I
Students: 5,255 (51.4% male; 48.6% female)
Individual Education Program: 792 (15.1%);
English Language Learner: 97 (1.8%); Migrant: n/a
Eligible for Free Lunch Program: 55 (1.0%)
Eligible for Reduced-Price Lunch Program: 64 (1.2%)
Teachers: 383.0 (13.7 to 1)
Librarians/Media Specialists: 3.0 (1,751.7 to 1)
Guidance Counselors: 12.0 (437.9 to 1)

Current Spending: ($ per student per year):
Total: $11,942; Instruction: $8,136; Support Services: $3,570
Enrollment, Drop-out Rates and Diploma Recipients by Race/Ethnicity

Category	Total	White	Black	Asian	AIAN	Hisp.
Enrollment (%)	100.0	93.2	1.3	1.2	0.1	4.3
Drop-out Rate (%)	0.9	0.8	0.0	0.0	0.0	4.2
H.S. Diplomas (#)	348	335	0	1	0	12

Putnam Valley CSD
146 Peekskll Hollw Rd • Putnam Valley, NY 10579-3238
(845) 528-8143
Grade Span: KG-11; **Agency Type:** 2
Schools: 3
1 Primary; 1 Middle; 0 High; 1 Other Level
3 Regular; 0 Special Education; 0 Vocational; 0 Alternative
0 Magnet; 0 Charter; 1 Title I Eligible; 0 School-wide Title I
Students: 1,764 (49.6% male; 50.4% female)
Individual Education Program: 220 (12.5%);
English Language Learner: 23 (1.3%); Migrant: n/a
Eligible for Free Lunch Program: 81 (4.6%)
Eligible for Reduced-Price Lunch Program: 59 (3.3%)
Teachers: 139.4 (12.7 to 1)
Librarians/Media Specialists: 1.0 (1,764.0 to 1)
Guidance Counselors: 4.0 (441.0 to 1)
Current Spending: ($ per student per year):
Total: $14,776; Instruction: $8,845; Support Services: $5,715
Enrollment, Drop-out Rates and Diploma Recipients by Race/Ethnicity

Category	Total	White	Black	Asian	AIAN	Hisp.
Enrollment (%)	100.0	86.3	2.8	1.5	0.1	9.3
Drop-out Rate (%)	n/a	n/a	n/a	n/a	n/a	n/a
H.S. Diplomas (#)	n/a	n/a	n/a	n/a	n/a	n/a

Rensselaer County

Averill Park CSD
8439 Miller Hill Rd • Averill Park, NY 12018-9798
(518) 674-7055 • http://www.averillpark.k12.ny.us/
Grade Span: KG-12; **Agency Type:** 1
Schools: 7
4 Primary; 1 Middle; 1 High; 1 Other Level
6 Regular; 0 Special Education; 0 Vocational; 1 Alternative
0 Magnet; 0 Charter; 4 Title I Eligible; 0 School-wide Title I
Students: 3,466 (51.0% male; 49.0% female)
Individual Education Program: 595 (17.2%);
English Language Learner: 5 (0.1%); Migrant: n/a
Eligible for Free Lunch Program: 247 (7.1%)
Eligible for Reduced-Price Lunch Program: 166 (4.8%)
Teachers: 266.0 (13.0 to 1)
Librarians/Media Specialists: 5.0 (693.2 to 1)
Guidance Counselors: 7.0 (495.1 to 1)
Current Spending: ($ per student per year):
Total: $9,251; Instruction: $5,974; Support Services: $3,018
Enrollment, Drop-out Rates and Diploma Recipients by Race/Ethnicity

Category	Total	White	Black	Asian	AIAN	Hisp.
Enrollment (%)	100.0	97.3	0.9	0.9	0.1	0.9
Drop-out Rate (%)	3.8	3.9	0.0	0.0	0.0	0.0
H.S. Diplomas (#)	219	216	0	3	0	0

East Greenbush CSD
29 Englewood Ave • East Greenbush, NY 12061-2213
(518) 477-2755 • http://www.egcsd.org/
Grade Span: KG-12; **Agency Type:** 1
Schools: 7
5 Primary; 1 Middle; 1 High; 0 Other Level
7 Regular; 0 Special Education; 0 Vocational; 0 Alternative
0 Magnet; 0 Charter; 1 Title I Eligible; 0 School-wide Title I
Students: 4,603 (49.4% male; 50.6% female)
Individual Education Program: 585 (12.7%);
English Language Learner: 17 (0.4%); Migrant: n/a
Eligible for Free Lunch Program: 253 (5.5%)
Eligible for Reduced-Price Lunch Program: 157 (3.4%)
Teachers: 337.7 (13.6 to 1)
Librarians/Media Specialists: 7.2 (639.3 to 1)
Guidance Counselors: 8.0 (575.4 to 1)
Current Spending: ($ per student per year):
Total: $10,105; Instruction: $6,087; Support Services: $3,802
Enrollment, Drop-out Rates and Diploma Recipients by Race/Ethnicity

Category	Total	White	Black	Asian	AIAN	Hisp.
Enrollment (%)	100.0	95.2	2.3	1.7	0.1	0.7
Drop-out Rate (%)	1.5	1.4	7.1	0.0	n/a	0.0
H.S. Diplomas (#)	281	268	7	5	0	1

Lansingburgh CSD
576 Fifth Ave • Troy, NY 12182-3295
(518) 235-4404
Grade Span: KG-12; **Agency Type:** 1
Schools: 4
2 Primary; 1 Middle; 1 High; 0 Other Level
4 Regular; 0 Special Education; 0 Vocational; 0 Alternative
0 Magnet; 0 Charter; 2 Title I Eligible; 0 School-wide Title I
Students: 2,458 (51.1% male; 48.9% female)
Individual Education Program: 448 (18.2%);
English Language Learner: 17 (0.7%); Migrant: n/a
Eligible for Free Lunch Program: 799 (32.5%)
Eligible for Reduced-Price Lunch Program: 260 (10.6%)
Teachers: 171.5 (14.3 to 1)
Librarians/Media Specialists: 1.8 (1,365.6 to 1)
Guidance Counselors: 4.0 (614.5 to 1)
Current Spending: ($ per student per year):
Total: $9,702; Instruction: $6,328; Support Services: $3,126
Enrollment, Drop-out Rates and Diploma Recipients by Race/Ethnicity

Category	Total	White	Black	Asian	AIAN	Hisp.
Enrollment (%)	100.0	81.7	14.5	0.7	0.0	3.0
Drop-out Rate (%)	4.0	3.7	8.3	0.0	n/a	11.1
H.S. Diplomas (#)	104	102	2	0	0	0

Troy City SD
1728 Tibbits Ave • Troy, NY 12180-7013
(518) 271-5210 • http://www.troy.k12.ny.us/
Grade Span: PK-12; **Agency Type:** 1
Schools: 13
6 Primary; 1 Middle; 2 High; 4 Other Level
8 Regular; 0 Special Education; 0 Vocational; 5 Alternative
0 Magnet; 0 Charter; 6 Title I Eligible; 0 School-wide Title I
Students: 5,093 (52.2% male; 47.8% female)
Individual Education Program: 949 (18.6%);
English Language Learner: 59 (1.2%); Migrant: n/a
Eligible for Free Lunch Program: 2,238 (43.9%)
Eligible for Reduced-Price Lunch Program: 490 (9.6%)
Teachers: 390.2 (13.1 to 1)
Librarians/Media Specialists: 5.2 (979.4 to 1)
Guidance Counselors: 10.5 (485.0 to 1)
Current Spending: ($ per student per year):
Total: $12,095; Instruction: $7,808; Support Services: $3,948
Enrollment, Drop-out Rates and Diploma Recipients by Race/Ethnicity

Category	Total	White	Black	Asian	AIAN	Hisp.
Enrollment (%)	100.0	62.0	28.2	1.9	0.2	7.8
Drop-out Rate (%)	2.5	1.9	3.1	0.0	0.0	8.9
H.S. Diplomas (#)	97	69	22	2	0	4

Rockland County

Clarkstown CSD
62 Old Middletown Rd • New City, NY 10956
(845) 639-6419 • http://www.ccsd.edu/
Grade Span: KG-12; **Agency Type:** 1
Schools: 18
10 Primary; 1 Middle; 2 High; 5 Other Level
13 Regular; 1 Special Education; 0 Vocational; 4 Alternative
0 Magnet; 0 Charter; 8 Title I Eligible; 0 School-wide Title I
Students: 9,196 (51.7% male; 48.3% female)
Individual Education Program: 1,403 (15.3%);
English Language Learner: 253 (2.8%); Migrant: n/a
Eligible for Free Lunch Program: 222 (2.4%)
Eligible for Reduced-Price Lunch Program: 187 (2.0%)
Teachers: 689.7 (13.3 to 1)
Librarians/Media Specialists: 13.0 (707.4 to 1)
Guidance Counselors: 16.3 (564.2 to 1)
Current Spending: ($ per student per year):
Total: $11,746; Instruction: $7,918; Support Services: $3,572
Enrollment, Drop-out Rates and Diploma Recipients by Race/Ethnicity

Category	Total	White	Black	Asian	AIAN	Hisp.
Enrollment (%)	100.0	81.0	2.8	10.5	0.0	5.7
Drop-out Rate (%)	0.4	0.2	0.0	1.0	n/a	1.9
H.S. Diplomas (#)	681	573	17	55	0	36

East Ramapo CSD (Spring Valley)
105 S Madison Ave • Spring Valley, NY 10977-5400
(845) 577-6011 • http://www.j51.com/eastramapo/
Grade Span: PK-12; **Agency Type:** 1
Schools: 17
6 Primary; 6 Middle; 2 High; 3 Other Level
14 Regular; 0 Special Education; 0 Vocational; 3 Alternative
0 Magnet; 0 Charter; 5 Title I Eligible; 0 School-wide Title I
Students: 9,362 (52.0% male; 48.0% female)
Individual Education Program: 1,630 (17.4%);
English Language Learner: 708 (7.6%); Migrant: n/a

Eligible for Free Lunch Program: 3,745 (40.0%)
Eligible for Reduced-Price Lunch Program: 1,331 (14.2%)
Teachers: 712.2 (13.1 to 1)
Librarians/Media Specialists: 10.7 (875.0 to 1)
Guidance Counselors: 21.0 (445.8 to 1)
Current Spending: ($ per student per year):
Total: $15,274; Instruction: $9,554; Support Services: $5,468
Enrollment, Drop-out Rates and Diploma Recipients by Race/Ethnicity

Category	Total	White	Black	Asian	AIAN	Hisp.
Enrollment (%)	100.0	15.7	60.4	9.9	0.1	13.8
Drop-out Rate (%)	2.8	1.6	3.1	0.0	0.0	7.2
H.S. Diplomas (#)	526	162	242	69	0	53

Haverstraw-Stony Point CSD

65 Chapel St • Garnerville, NY 10923-1280
(845) 942-3000
Grade Span: PK-12; **Agency Type:** 1
Schools: 12
3 Primary; 3 Middle; 1 High; 3 Other Level
9 Regular; 0 Special Education; 0 Vocational; 3 Alternative
0 Magnet; 0 Charter; 2 Title I Eligible; 0 School-wide Title I
Students: 8,219 (51.1% male; 48.9% female)
Individual Education Program: 1,313 (16.0%);
English Language Learner: 647 (7.9%); Migrant: n/a
Eligible for Free Lunch Program: 1,990 (24.2%)
Eligible for Reduced-Price Lunch Program: 780 (9.5%)
Teachers: 626.7 (13.1 to 1)
Librarians/Media Specialists: 8.0 (1,027.4 to 1)
Guidance Counselors: 15.6 (526.9 to 1)
Current Spending: ($ per student per year):
Total: $14,294; Instruction: $9,427; Support Services: $4,600
Enrollment, Drop-out Rates and Diploma Recipients by Race/Ethnicity

Category	Total	White	Black	Asian	AIAN	Hisp.
Enrollment (%)	100.0	51.8	10.8	3.8	0.2	33.5
Drop-out Rate (%)	3.5	1.8	2.2	2.9	0.0	7.0
H.S. Diplomas (#)	442	270	37	16	0	119

Nanuet UFSD

101 Church St • Nanuet, NY 10954-3000
(845) 627-9888 • http://nanunet.lhric.org/
Grade Span: KG-12; **Agency Type:** 1
Schools: 9
1 Primary; 2 Middle; 1 High; 5 Other Level
4 Regular; 0 Special Education; 0 Vocational; 5 Alternative
0 Magnet; 0 Charter; 3 Title I Eligible; 0 School-wide Title I
Students: 2,164 (51.8% male; 48.2% female)
Individual Education Program: 294 (13.6%);
English Language Learner: 57 (2.6%); Migrant: n/a
Eligible for Free Lunch Program: 74 (3.4%)
Eligible for Reduced-Price Lunch Program: 38 (1.8%)
Teachers: 182.6 (11.9 to 1)
Librarians/Media Specialists: 3.9 (554.9 to 1)
Guidance Counselors: 5.3 (408.3 to 1)
Current Spending: ($ per student per year):
Total: $15,995; Instruction: $9,745; Support Services: $5,990
Enrollment, Drop-out Rates and Diploma Recipients by Race/Ethnicity

Category	Total	White	Black	Asian	AIAN	Hisp.
Enrollment (%)	100.0	76.5	4.1	11.9	0.1	7.3
Drop-out Rate (%)	1.1	1.0	2.4	0.0	n/a	1.9
H.S. Diplomas (#)	120	79	6	27	0	8

Nyack UFSD

13a Dickinson Ave • Nyack, NY 10960-2914
(845) 353-7010
Grade Span: KG-12; **Agency Type:** 1
Schools: 7
3 Primary; 1 Middle; 1 High; 2 Other Level
5 Regular; 0 Special Education; 0 Vocational; 2 Alternative
0 Magnet; 0 Charter; 4 Title I Eligible; 0 School-wide Title I
Students: 2,906 (51.5% male; 48.5% female)
Individual Education Program: 317 (10.9%);
English Language Learner: 170 (5.9%); Migrant: n/a
Eligible for Free Lunch Program: 454 (15.6%)
Eligible for Reduced-Price Lunch Program: 170 (5.9%)
Teachers: 250.6 (11.6 to 1)
Librarians/Media Specialists: 2.0 (1,453.0 to 1)
Guidance Counselors: 8.0 (363.3 to 1)
Current Spending: ($ per student per year):
Total: $14,630; Instruction: $9,852; Support Services: $4,543
Enrollment, Drop-out Rates and Diploma Recipients by Race/Ethnicity

Category	Total	White	Black	Asian	AIAN	Hisp.
Enrollment (%)	100.0	55.4	28.7	8.3	0.0	7.6
Drop-out Rate (%)	1.2	0.6	1.8	1.2	n/a	3.8
H.S. Diplomas (#)	166	105	40	9	0	12

Pearl River UFSD

275 E Central Ave • Pearl River, NY 10965-2799
(845) 620-3900 • http://www.pearlriver.k12.ny.us/
Grade Span: KG-12; **Agency Type:** 1
Schools: 7
3 Primary; 1 Middle; 1 High; 2 Other Level
5 Regular; 0 Special Education; 0 Vocational; 2 Alternative
0 Magnet; 0 Charter; 5 Title I Eligible; 0 School-wide Title I
Students: 2,409 (49.9% male; 50.1% female)
Individual Education Program: 294 (12.2%);
English Language Learner: 28 (1.2%); Migrant: n/a
Eligible for Free Lunch Program: 45 (1.9%)
Eligible for Reduced-Price Lunch Program: 46 (1.9%)
Teachers: 181.3 (13.3 to 1)
Librarians/Media Specialists: 3.0 (803.0 to 1)
Guidance Counselors: 6.0 (401.5 to 1)
Current Spending: ($ per student per year):
Total: $13,065; Instruction: $8,275; Support Services: $4,638
Enrollment, Drop-out Rates and Diploma Recipients by Race/Ethnicity

Category	Total	White	Black	Asian	AIAN	Hisp.
Enrollment (%)	100.0	90.1	1.0	5.1	0.0	3.8
Drop-out Rate (%)	0.6	0.5	0.0	0.0	n/a	2.9
H.S. Diplomas (#)	177	155	0	9	0	13

Ramapo CSD (Suffern)

45 Mountain Ave • Hillburn, NY 10931-0935
(845) 357-7783 • http://www.ramapocentral.org/
Grade Span: KG-12; **Agency Type:** 1
Schools: 8
5 Primary; 1 Middle; 1 High; 1 Other Level
7 Regular; 0 Special Education; 0 Vocational; 1 Alternative
0 Magnet; 0 Charter; 2 Title I Eligible; 0 School-wide Title I
Students: 4,505 (51.0% male; 49.0% female)
Individual Education Program: 595 (13.2%);
English Language Learner: 93 (2.1%); Migrant: n/a
Eligible for Free Lunch Program: 197 (4.4%)
Eligible for Reduced-Price Lunch Program: 109 (2.4%)
Teachers: 358.0 (12.6 to 1)
Librarians/Media Specialists: 4.6 (979.3 to 1)
Guidance Counselors: 9.0 (500.6 to 1)
Current Spending: ($ per student per year):
Total: $14,037; Instruction: $9,731; Support Services: $4,123
Enrollment, Drop-out Rates and Diploma Recipients by Race/Ethnicity

Category	Total	White	Black	Asian	AIAN	Hisp.
Enrollment (%)	100.0	81.8	5.4	4.1	0.7	8.0
Drop-out Rate (%)	0.8	0.4	4.5	0.0	0.0	3.0
H.S. Diplomas (#)	277	223	15	18	2	19

South Orangetown CSD

160 Van Wyck Rd • Blauvelt, NY 10913-1299
(845) 680-1050 • http://www.socsd.k12.ny.us/
Grade Span: KG-12; **Agency Type:** 1
Schools: 6
2 Primary; 2 Middle; 1 High; 1 Other Level
5 Regular; 0 Special Education; 0 Vocational; 1 Alternative
0 Magnet; 0 Charter; 3 Title I Eligible; 0 School-wide Title I
Students: 3,258 (50.6% male; 49.4% female)
Individual Education Program: 398 (12.2%);
English Language Learner: 113 (3.5%); Migrant: n/a
Eligible for Free Lunch Program: 143 (4.4%)
Eligible for Reduced-Price Lunch Program: 95 (2.9%)
Teachers: 264.1 (12.3 to 1)
Librarians/Media Specialists: 3.8 (857.4 to 1)
Guidance Counselors: 6.5 (501.2 to 1)
Current Spending: ($ per student per year):
Total: $14,975; Instruction: $9,896; Support Services: $4,838
Enrollment, Drop-out Rates and Diploma Recipients by Race/Ethnicity

Category	Total	White	Black	Asian	AIAN	Hisp.
Enrollment (%)	100.0	78.3	2.9	12.2	0.1	6.4
Drop-out Rate (%)	1.1	1.2	2.4	0.7	n/a	0.0
H.S. Diplomas (#)	165	129	3	28	0	5

Saratoga County

Ballston Spa CSD

70 Malta Ave • Ballston Spa, NY 12020-1599
(518) 884-7195 • http://www.ballstonspa.k12.ny.us/
Grade Span: KG-12; **Agency Type:** 1
Schools: 8
3 Primary; 1 Middle; 1 High; 3 Other Level
5 Regular; 0 Special Education; 0 Vocational; 3 Alternative
0 Magnet; 0 Charter; 3 Title I Eligible; 0 School-wide Title I
Students: 4,477 (51.1% male; 48.9% female)
Individual Education Program: 549 (12.3%);
English Language Learner: 7 (0.2%); Migrant: n/a

Eligible for Free Lunch Program: 542 (12.1%)
Eligible for Reduced-Price Lunch Program: 270 (6.0%)
Teachers: 307.7 (14.5 to 1)
Librarians/Media Specialists: 4.6 (973.3 to 1)
Guidance Counselors: 8.8 (508.7 to 1)
Current Spending: ($ per student per year):
Total: $9,755; Instruction: $6,774; Support Services: $2,753
Enrollment, Drop-out Rates and Diploma Recipients by Race/Ethnicity

Category	Total	White	Black	Asian	AIAN	Hisp.
Enrollment (%)	100.0	96.4	1.1	0.9	0.1	1.4
Drop-out Rate (%)	3.1	3.0	7.7	25.0	0.0	0.0
H.S. Diplomas (#)	215	209	2	1	0	3

Burnt Hills-Ballston Lake CSD
50 Cypress Dr • Scotia, NY 12302-4398
(518) 399-6407 • http://www.bhbl.org/
Grade Span: KG-12; **Agency Type:** 1
Schools: 5
3 Primary; 1 Middle; 1 High; 0 Other Level
5 Regular; 0 Special Education; 0 Vocational; 0 Alternative
0 Magnet; 0 Charter; 4 Title I Eligible; 0 School-wide Title I
Students: 3,413 (51.2% male; 48.8% female)
Individual Education Program: 439 (12.9%);
English Language Learner: 2 (0.1%); Migrant: n/a
Eligible for Free Lunch Program: 111 (3.3%)
Eligible for Reduced-Price Lunch Program: 57 (1.7%)
Teachers: 243.5 (14.0 to 1)
Librarians/Media Specialists: 6.2 (550.5 to 1)
Guidance Counselors: 6.0 (568.8 to 1)
Current Spending: ($ per student per year):
Total: $9,585; Instruction: $6,606; Support Services: $2,793
Enrollment, Drop-out Rates and Diploma Recipients by Race/Ethnicity

Category	Total	White	Black	Asian	AIAN	Hisp.
Enrollment (%)	100.0	97.7	1.1	0.9	0.1	0.3
Drop-out Rate (%)	1.6	1.6	0.0	0.0	n/a	0.0
H.S. Diplomas (#)	213	207	0	3	0	3

Saratoga Springs City SD
5 Wells St • Saratoga Springs, NY 12866-1232
(518) 583-4708 • http://www.saratogaschools.org/
Grade Span: KG-12; **Agency Type:** 1
Schools: 11
6 Primary; 1 Middle; 1 High; 3 Other Level
9 Regular; 0 Special Education; 0 Vocational; 2 Alternative
0 Magnet; 0 Charter; 6 Title I Eligible; 0 School-wide Title I
Students: 6,905 (50.5% male; 49.5% female)
Individual Education Program: 849 (12.3%);
English Language Learner: 5 (0.1%); Migrant: n/a
Eligible for Free Lunch Program: 608 (8.8%)
Eligible for Reduced-Price Lunch Program: 251 (3.6%)
Teachers: 502.7 (13.7 to 1)
Librarians/Media Specialists: 9.1 (758.8 to 1)
Guidance Counselors: 10.1 (683.7 to 1)
Current Spending: ($ per student per year):
Total: $9,175; Instruction: $6,448; Support Services: $2,500
Enrollment, Drop-out Rates and Diploma Recipients by Race/Ethnicity

Category	Total	White	Black	Asian	AIAN	Hisp.
Enrollment (%)	100.0	95.2	3.1	0.8	0.0	0.9
Drop-out Rate (%)	1.5	1.6	0.0	0.0	0.0	0.0
H.S. Diplomas (#)	461	458	1	1	0	1

Schuylerville CSD
14 Spring St • Schuylerville, NY 12871-1098
(518) 695-3255 • http://www.schuylervilleschools.org/default_IE4.asp
Grade Span: KG-12; **Agency Type:** 2
Schools: 2
1 Primary; 0 Middle; 1 High; 0 Other Level
2 Regular; 0 Special Education; 0 Vocational; 0 Alternative
0 Magnet; 0 Charter; 2 Title I Eligible; 0 School-wide Title I
Students: 1,659 (51.2% male; 48.8% female)
Individual Education Program: 277 (16.7%);
English Language Learner: 10 (0.6%); Migrant: n/a
Eligible for Free Lunch Program: 242 (14.6%)
Eligible for Reduced-Price Lunch Program: 116 (7.0%)
Teachers: 128.2 (12.9 to 1)
Librarians/Media Specialists: 2.0 (829.5 to 1)
Guidance Counselors: 4.0 (414.8 to 1)
Current Spending: ($ per student per year):
Total: $11,583; Instruction: $7,985; Support Services: $3,293
Enrollment, Drop-out Rates and Diploma Recipients by Race/Ethnicity

Category	Total	White	Black	Asian	AIAN	Hisp.
Enrollment (%)	100.0	97.8	0.6	0.5	0.1	1.1
Drop-out Rate (%)	1.1	1.1	0.0	0.0	n/a	0.0
H.S. Diplomas (#)	114	114	0	0	0	0

Shenendehowa CSD
5 Chelsea Pl • Clifton Park, NY 12065-3240
(518) 881-0610 • http://www.shenet.org/
Grade Span: KG-12; **Agency Type:** 1
Schools: 11
7 Primary; 3 Middle; 1 High; 0 Other Level
11 Regular; 0 Special Education; 0 Vocational; 0 Alternative
0 Magnet; 0 Charter; 5 Title I Eligible; 0 School-wide Title I
Students: 9,233 (51.8% male; 48.2% female)
Individual Education Program: 1,203 (13.0%);
English Language Learner: 53 (0.6%); Migrant: n/a
Eligible for Free Lunch Program: 438 (4.7%)
Eligible for Reduced-Price Lunch Program: 345 (3.7%)
Teachers: 633.9 (14.6 to 1)
Librarians/Media Specialists: 13.8 (669.1 to 1)
Guidance Counselors: 28.0 (329.8 to 1)
Current Spending: ($ per student per year):
Total: $9,692; Instruction: $6,095; Support Services: $3,344
Enrollment, Drop-out Rates and Diploma Recipients by Race/Ethnicity

Category	Total	White	Black	Asian	AIAN	Hisp.
Enrollment (%)	100.0	93.2	2.2	3.1	0.2	1.3
Drop-out Rate (%)	3.7	3.6	10.8	0.0	0.0	10.3
H.S. Diplomas (#)	580	547	9	14	3	7

South Glens Falls CSD
6 Bluebird Rd • South Glens Falls, NY 12803-5704
(518) 793-9617 • http://www.sgfallssd.org/
Grade Span: KG-12; **Agency Type:** 2
Schools: 7
4 Primary; 1 Middle; 1 High; 1 Other Level
6 Regular; 0 Special Education; 0 Vocational; 1 Alternative
0 Magnet; 0 Charter; 5 Title I Eligible; 0 School-wide Title I
Students: 3,269 (50.4% male; 49.6% female)
Individual Education Program: 358 (11.0%);
English Language Learner: 0 (0.0%); Migrant: n/a
Eligible for Free Lunch Program: 342 (10.5%)
Eligible for Reduced-Price Lunch Program: 229 (7.0%)
Teachers: 244.3 (13.4 to 1)
Librarians/Media Specialists: 3.0 (1,089.7 to 1)
Guidance Counselors: 4.0 (817.3 to 1)
Current Spending: ($ per student per year):
Total: $8,915; Instruction: $6,194; Support Services: $2,457
Enrollment, Drop-out Rates and Diploma Recipients by Race/Ethnicity

Category	Total	White	Black	Asian	AIAN	Hisp.
Enrollment (%)	100.0	98.5	0.8	0.2	0.0	0.4
Drop-out Rate (%)	n/a	n/a	n/a	n/a	n/a	n/a
H.S. Diplomas (#)	161	160	0	0	1	0

Schenectady County

Niskayuna CSD
1239 Van Antwerp Rd • Schenectady, NY 12309-5317
(518) 377-4666 • http://www.nisk.k12.ny.us/
Grade Span: KG-12; **Agency Type:** 1
Schools: 8
5 Primary; 2 Middle; 1 High; 0 Other Level
8 Regular; 0 Special Education; 0 Vocational; 0 Alternative
0 Magnet; 0 Charter; 6 Title I Eligible; 0 School-wide Title I
Students: 4,224 (51.0% male; 49.0% female)
Individual Education Program: 466 (11.0%);
English Language Learner: 24 (0.6%); Migrant: n/a
Eligible for Free Lunch Program: 113 (2.7%)
Eligible for Reduced-Price Lunch Program: 56 (1.3%)
Teachers: 297.0 (14.2 to 1)
Librarians/Media Specialists: 9.2 (459.1 to 1)
Guidance Counselors: 11.2 (377.1 to 1)
Current Spending: ($ per student per year):
Total: $9,518; Instruction: $5,929; Support Services: $3,390
Enrollment, Drop-out Rates and Diploma Recipients by Race/Ethnicity

Category	Total	White	Black	Asian	AIAN	Hisp.
Enrollment (%)	100.0	90.4	1.9	6.6	0.1	1.0
Drop-out Rate (%)	0.7	0.7	4.3	0.0	0.0	0.0
H.S. Diplomas (#)	280	256	5	17	0	2

Rotterdam-Mohonasen CSD
2072 Curry Rd • Schenectady, NY 12303-4400
(518) 356-8200
Grade Span: KG-12; **Agency Type:** 1
Schools: 4
2 Primary; 1 Middle; 1 High; 0 Other Level
4 Regular; 0 Special Education; 0 Vocational; 0 Alternative
0 Magnet; 0 Charter; 3 Title I Eligible; 0 School-wide Title I
Students: 3,281 (51.7% male; 48.3% female)
Individual Education Program: 395 (12.0%);
English Language Learner: 11 (0.3%); Migrant: n/a

Eligible for Free Lunch Program: 240 (7.3%)
Eligible for Reduced-Price Lunch Program: 187 (5.7%)
Teachers: 219.4 (15.0 to 1)
Librarians/Media Specialists: 4.0 (820.3 to 1)
Guidance Counselors: 6.0 (546.8 to 1)
Current Spending: ($ per student per year):
Total: $8,075; Instruction: $5,407; Support Services: $2,422
Enrollment, Drop-out Rates and Diploma Recipients by Race/Ethnicity

Category	Total	White	Black	Asian	AIAN	Hisp.
Enrollment (%)	100.0	95.3	2.4	1.2	0.2	0.9
Drop-out Rate (%)	1.7	1.7	0.0	0.0	n/a	0.0
H.S. Diplomas (#)	201	195	2	4	0	0

Schalmont CSD
401 Duanesburg Rd • Schenectady, NY 12306-1981
(518) 355-9200 • http://www.schalmont.org/
Grade Span: KG-12; **Agency Type:** 1
Schools: 6
4 Primary; 1 Middle; 1 High; 0 Other Level
6 Regular; 0 Special Education; 0 Vocational; 0 Alternative
0 Magnet; 0 Charter; 1 Title I Eligible; 0 School-wide Title I
Students: 2,248 (50.6% male; 49.4% female)
Individual Education Program: 341 (15.2%);
English Language Learner: 0 (0.0%); Migrant: n/a
Eligible for Free Lunch Program: 127 (5.6%)
Eligible for Reduced-Price Lunch Program: 83 (3.7%)
Teachers: 175.0 (12.8 to 1)
Librarians/Media Specialists: 2.8 (802.9 to 1)
Guidance Counselors: 5.4 (416.3 to 1)
Current Spending: ($ per student per year):
Total: $11,000; Instruction: $7,450; Support Services: $3,305
Enrollment, Drop-out Rates and Diploma Recipients by Race/Ethnicity

Category	Total	White	Black	Asian	AIAN	Hisp.
Enrollment (%)	100.0	97.5	1.4	0.6	0.0	0.5
Drop-out Rate (%)	2.4	2.5	0.0	0.0	0.0	0.0
H.S. Diplomas (#)	161	158	2	1	0	0

Schenectady City SD
108 Education Dr • Schenectady, NY 12303-3442
(518) 370-8100 • http://www.schenectady.k12.ny.us/
Grade Span: PK-12; **Agency Type:** 1
Schools: 18
11 Primary; 3 Middle; 1 High; 3 Other Level
15 Regular; 0 Special Education; 0 Vocational; 3 Alternative
1 Magnet; 0 Charter; 13 Title I Eligible; 0 School-wide Title I
Students: 8,526 (50.8% male; 49.2% female)
Individual Education Program: 1,489 (17.5%);
English Language Learner: 233 (2.7%); Migrant: n/a
Eligible for Free Lunch Program: 4,011 (47.0%)
Eligible for Reduced-Price Lunch Program: 869 (10.2%)
Teachers: 639.2 (13.3 to 1)
Librarians/Media Specialists: 10.4 (819.8 to 1)
Guidance Counselors: 16.0 (532.9 to 1)
Current Spending: ($ per student per year):
Total: $10,015; Instruction: $7,193; Support Services: $2,561
Enrollment, Drop-out Rates and Diploma Recipients by Race/Ethnicity

Category	Total	White	Black	Asian	AIAN	Hisp.
Enrollment (%)	100.0	50.9	32.0	5.7	0.2	11.3
Drop-out Rate (%)	6.7	4.6	10.1	5.3	0.0	12.3
H.S. Diplomas (#)	358	224	92	20	0	22

Scotia-Glenville CSD
900 Preddice Pky • Scotia, NY 12302-1049
(518) 382-1215 • http://www.sgcsd.neric.org/
Grade Span: KG-12; **Agency Type:** 1
Schools: 7
4 Primary; 1 Middle; 1 High; 1 Other Level
6 Regular; 0 Special Education; 0 Vocational; 1 Alternative
0 Magnet; 0 Charter; 3 Title I Eligible; 0 School-wide Title I
Students: 3,011 (51.1% male; 48.9% female)
Individual Education Program: 479 (15.9%);
English Language Learner: 17 (0.6%); Migrant: n/a
Eligible for Free Lunch Program: 186 (6.2%)
Eligible for Reduced-Price Lunch Program: 157 (5.2%)
Teachers: 212.7 (14.2 to 1)
Librarians/Media Specialists: 5.8 (519.1 to 1)
Guidance Counselors: 7.0 (430.1 to 1)
Current Spending: ($ per student per year):
Total: $9,175; Instruction: $6,075; Support Services: $2,947
Enrollment, Drop-out Rates and Diploma Recipients by Race/Ethnicity

Category	Total	White	Black	Asian	AIAN	Hisp.
Enrollment (%)	100.0	96.6	1.1	1.1	0.3	0.9
Drop-out Rate (%)	0.4	0.4	0.0	0.0	0.0	0.0
H.S. Diplomas (#)	218	218	0	0	0	0

Schoharie County

Cobleskill-Richmondville CSD
155 Washington Ave • Cobleskill, NY 12043-1099
(518) 234-4032 • http://www.crcs.k12.ny.us/
Grade Span: KG-12; **Agency Type:** 1
Schools: 6
2 Primary; 2 Middle; 1 High; 1 Other Level
5 Regular; 0 Special Education; 0 Vocational; 1 Alternative
0 Magnet; 0 Charter; 2 Title I Eligible; 0 School-wide Title I
Students: 2,177 (51.9% male; 48.1% female)
Individual Education Program: 268 (12.3%);
English Language Learner: 12 (0.6%); Migrant: n/a
Eligible for Free Lunch Program: 461 (21.2%)
Eligible for Reduced-Price Lunch Program: 210 (9.6%)
Teachers: 183.6 (11.9 to 1)
Librarians/Media Specialists: 3.1 (702.3 to 1)
Guidance Counselors: 7.0 (311.0 to 1)
Current Spending: ($ per student per year):
Total: $10,423; Instruction: $6,875; Support Services: $3,275
Enrollment, Drop-out Rates and Diploma Recipients by Race/Ethnicity

Category	Total	White	Black	Asian	AIAN	Hisp.
Enrollment (%)	100.0	94.8	1.9	0.6	0.3	2.4
Drop-out Rate (%)	4.8	4.8	0.0	0.0	0.0	11.1
H.S. Diplomas (#)	140	136	0	3	0	1

Seneca County

Seneca Falls CSD
98 Clinton St • Seneca Falls, NY 13148-1497
(315) 568-5818
Grade Span: KG-12; **Agency Type:** 1
Schools: 4
2 Primary; 1 Middle; 1 High; 0 Other Level
4 Regular; 0 Special Education; 0 Vocational; 0 Alternative
0 Magnet; 0 Charter; 2 Title I Eligible; 0 School-wide Title I
Students: 1,536 (51.1% male; 48.9% female)
Individual Education Program: 233 (15.2%);
English Language Learner: 19 (1.2%); Migrant: n/a
Eligible for Free Lunch Program: 300 (19.5%)
Eligible for Reduced-Price Lunch Program: 84 (5.5%)
Teachers: 128.6 (11.9 to 1)
Librarians/Media Specialists: 2.0 (768.0 to 1)
Guidance Counselors: 3.0 (512.0 to 1)
Current Spending: ($ per student per year):
Total: $9,559; Instruction: $6,431; Support Services: $2,824
Enrollment, Drop-out Rates and Diploma Recipients by Race/Ethnicity

Category	Total	White	Black	Asian	AIAN	Hisp.
Enrollment (%)	100.0	93.5	2.2	1.9	1.1	1.3
Drop-out Rate (%)	4.6	4.6	0.0	0.0	100.0	0.0
H.S. Diplomas (#)	107	104	2	0	0	1

Waterloo CSD
212 Main St Shop Ctr • Waterloo, NY 13165-1397
(315) 539-1500 • http://www.flare.net/wcs/
Grade Span: PK-12; **Agency Type:** 1
Schools: 6
3 Primary; 1 Middle; 1 High; 1 Other Level
5 Regular; 0 Special Education; 0 Vocational; 1 Alternative
0 Magnet; 0 Charter; 3 Title I Eligible; 0 School-wide Title I
Students: 2,041 (49.5% male; 50.5% female)
Individual Education Program: 280 (13.7%);
English Language Learner: 4 (0.2%); Migrant: n/a
Eligible for Free Lunch Program: 542 (26.6%)
Eligible for Reduced-Price Lunch Program: 230 (11.3%)
Teachers: 150.3 (13.6 to 1)
Librarians/Media Specialists: 2.3 (887.4 to 1)
Guidance Counselors: 6.7 (304.6 to 1)
Current Spending: ($ per student per year):
Total: $9,074; Instruction: $5,671; Support Services: $3,118
Enrollment, Drop-out Rates and Diploma Recipients by Race/Ethnicity

Category	Total	White	Black	Asian	AIAN	Hisp.
Enrollment (%)	100.0	95.3	2.3	0.5	0.3	1.6
Drop-out Rate (%)	6.3	6.4	0.0	0.0	n/a	n/a
H.S. Diplomas (#)	100	100	0	0	0	0

St. Lawrence County

Canton CSD
99 State St • Canton, NY 13617-1099
(315) 386-8561
Grade Span: PK-12; **Agency Type:** 1
Schools: 4
1 Primary; 1 Middle; 1 High; 1 Other Level
3 Regular; 0 Special Education; 0 Vocational; 1 Alternative

0 Magnet; 0 Charter; 1 Title I Eligible; 0 School-wide Title I
Students: 1,559 (51.2% male; 48.8% female)
Individual Education Program: 253 (16.2%);
English Language Learner: 1 (0.1%); Migrant: n/a
Eligible for Free Lunch Program: 394 (25.3%)
Eligible for Reduced-Price Lunch Program: 131 (8.4%)
Teachers: 129.0 (12.1 to 1)
Librarians/Media Specialists: 2.0 (779.5 to 1)
Guidance Counselors: 5.0 (311.8 to 1)
Current Spending: ($ per student per year):
Total: $9,705; Instruction: $6,451; Support Services: $2,959
Enrollment, Drop-out Rates and Diploma Recipients by Race/Ethnicity

Category	Total	White	Black	Asian	AIAN	Hisp.
Enrollment (%)	100.0	97.0	1.2	1.0	0.3	0.5
Drop-out Rate (%)	3.6	3.7	0.0	0.0	0.0	0.0
H.S. Diplomas (#)	97	93	2	0	0	2

Gouverneur CSD
133 E Barney St • Gouverneur, NY 13642-1100
(315) 287-4870 • http://gcs.neric.org/
Grade Span: KG-12; **Agency Type:** 1
Schools: 5
3 Primary; 0 Middle; 0 High; 2 Other Level
4 Regular; 0 Special Education; 0 Vocational; 1 Alternative
0 Magnet; 0 Charter; 3 Title I Eligible; 0 School-wide Title I
Students: 1,774 (51.9% male; 48.1% female)
Individual Education Program: 322 (18.2%);
English Language Learner: 0 (0.0%); Migrant: n/a
Eligible for Free Lunch Program: 519 (29.3%)
Eligible for Reduced-Price Lunch Program: 196 (11.0%)
Teachers: 124.7 (14.2 to 1)
Librarians/Media Specialists: 1.0 (1,774.0 to 1)
Guidance Counselors: 6.0 (295.7 to 1)
Current Spending: ($ per student per year):
Total: $11,072; Instruction: $7,227; Support Services: $3,525
Enrollment, Drop-out Rates and Diploma Recipients by Race/Ethnicity

Category	Total	White	Black	Asian	AIAN	Hisp.
Enrollment (%)	100.0	95.4	2.1	0.6	0.2	1.7
Drop-out Rate (%)	3.9	4.0	0.0	0.0	0.0	0.0
H.S. Diplomas (#)	119	118	0	0	0	1

Massena CSD
84 Nightengale Ave • Massena, NY 13662-1999
(315) 764-3700 • http://www.mcs.k12.ny.us/
Grade Span: KG-12; **Agency Type:** 1
Schools: 5
3 Primary; 1 Middle; 1 High; 0 Other Level
5 Regular; 0 Special Education; 0 Vocational; 0 Alternative
0 Magnet; 0 Charter; 5 Title I Eligible; 0 School-wide Title I
Students: 2,839 (49.9% male; 50.1% female)
Individual Education Program: 418 (14.7%);
English Language Learner: 5 (0.2%); Migrant: n/a
Eligible for Free Lunch Program: 933 (32.9%)
Eligible for Reduced-Price Lunch Program: 325 (11.4%)
Teachers: 206.9 (13.7 to 1)
Librarians/Media Specialists: 4.8 (591.5 to 1)
Guidance Counselors: 7.7 (368.7 to 1)
Current Spending: ($ per student per year):
Total: $9,230; Instruction: $6,392; Support Services: $2,500
Enrollment, Drop-out Rates and Diploma Recipients by Race/Ethnicity

Category	Total	White	Black	Asian	AIAN	Hisp.
Enrollment (%)	100.0	87.1	0.6	1.1	10.7	0.5
Drop-out Rate (%)	3.7	3.7	50.0	0.0	1.8	0.0
H.S. Diplomas (#)	167	164	0	0	3	0

Ogdensburg City SD
1100 State St • Ogdensburg, NY 13669-3398
(315) 393-0900 • http://www.ogdensburg.neric.org/
Grade Span: PK-12; **Agency Type:** 1
Schools: 9
4 Primary; 1 Middle; 1 High; 3 Other Level
6 Regular; 0 Special Education; 0 Vocational; 3 Alternative
0 Magnet; 0 Charter; 4 Title I Eligible; 0 School-wide Title I
Students: 2,068 (52.9% male; 47.1% female)
Individual Education Program: 384 (18.6%);
English Language Learner: 1 (<0.1%); Migrant: n/a
Eligible for Free Lunch Program: 746 (36.1%)
Eligible for Reduced-Price Lunch Program: 299 (14.5%)
Teachers: 178.6 (11.6 to 1)
Librarians/Media Specialists: 3.2 (646.3 to 1)
Guidance Counselors: 5.0 (413.6 to 1)
Current Spending: ($ per student per year):
Total: $11,031; Instruction: $7,979; Support Services: $2,678
Enrollment, Drop-out Rates and Diploma Recipients by Race/Ethnicity

Category	Total	White	Black	Asian	AIAN	Hisp.
Enrollment (%)	100.0	97.0	1.8	0.8	0.1	0.2
Drop-out Rate (%)	7.9	8.1	0.0	0.0	n/a	n/a
H.S. Diplomas (#)	127	124	1	2	0	0

Steuben County

Bath CSD
25 Ellas Ave • Bath, NY 14810-1107
(607) 776-3301
Grade Span: PK-12; **Agency Type:** 1
Schools: 7
1 Primary; 2 Middle; 1 High; 3 Other Level
4 Regular; 0 Special Education; 0 Vocational; 3 Alternative
0 Magnet; 0 Charter; 3 Title I Eligible; 0 School-wide Title I
Students: 2,021 (54.6% male; 45.4% female)
Individual Education Program: 201 (9.9%);
English Language Learner: 0 (0.0%); Migrant: n/a
Eligible for Free Lunch Program: 568 (28.1%)
Eligible for Reduced-Price Lunch Program: 204 (10.1%)
Teachers: 150.6 (13.4 to 1)
Librarians/Media Specialists: 2.0 (1,010.5 to 1)
Guidance Counselors: 4.0 (505.3 to 1)
Current Spending: ($ per student per year):
Total: $8,766; Instruction: $5,827; Support Services: $2,626
Enrollment, Drop-out Rates and Diploma Recipients by Race/Ethnicity

Category	Total	White	Black	Asian	AIAN	Hisp.
Enrollment (%)	100.0	97.4	1.1	0.9	0.1	0.4
Drop-out Rate (%)	1.5	1.6	0.0	0.0	n/a	0.0
H.S. Diplomas (#)	134	130	2	0	0	2

Corning City SD
165 Charles St • Painted Post, NY 14870-1199
(607) 936-3704 • http://www.corningareaschools.com/
Grade Span: PK-12; **Agency Type:** 1
Schools: 14
9 Primary; 2 Middle; 2 High; 1 Other Level
13 Regular; 0 Special Education; 0 Vocational; 1 Alternative
0 Magnet; 0 Charter; 7 Title I Eligible; 0 School-wide Title I
Students: 5,806 (51.2% male; 48.8% female)
Individual Education Program: 634 (10.9%);
English Language Learner: 24 (0.4%); Migrant: n/a
Eligible for Free Lunch Program: 1,357 (23.4%)
Eligible for Reduced-Price Lunch Program: 537 (9.2%)
Teachers: 440.6 (13.2 to 1)
Librarians/Media Specialists: 10.0 (580.6 to 1)
Guidance Counselors: 16.0 (362.9 to 1)
Current Spending: ($ per student per year):
Total: $9,653; Instruction: $6,058; Support Services: $3,382
Enrollment, Drop-out Rates and Diploma Recipients by Race/Ethnicity

Category	Total	White	Black	Asian	AIAN	Hisp.
Enrollment (%)	100.0	92.9	3.7	2.1	0.4	1.0
Drop-out Rate (%)	4.3	4.5	0.0	0.0	0.0	0.0
H.S. Diplomas (#)	358	342	7	5	1	3

Hornell City SD
14 Allen St • Hornell, NY 14843-1504
(607) 324-1302 • http://www.hornell.wnyric.org/
Grade Span: KG-12; **Agency Type:** 1
Schools: 5
4 Primary; 0 Middle; 1 High; 0 Other Level
5 Regular; 0 Special Education; 0 Vocational; 0 Alternative
0 Magnet; 0 Charter; 3 Title I Eligible; 0 School-wide Title I
Students: 1,981 (54.1% male; 45.9% female)
Individual Education Program: 402 (20.3%);
English Language Learner: 1 (0.1%); Migrant: n/a
Eligible for Free Lunch Program: 790 (39.9%)
Eligible for Reduced-Price Lunch Program: 250 (12.6%)
Teachers: 163.9 (12.1 to 1)
Librarians/Media Specialists: 2.0 (990.5 to 1)
Guidance Counselors: 7.7 (257.3 to 1)
Current Spending: ($ per student per year):
Total: $9,260; Instruction: $6,265; Support Services: $2,587
Enrollment, Drop-out Rates and Diploma Recipients by Race/Ethnicity

Category	Total	White	Black	Asian	AIAN	Hisp.
Enrollment (%)	100.0	93.7	4.2	0.5	0.2	1.4
Drop-out Rate (%)	6.3	6.5	0.0	0.0	n/a	0.0
H.S. Diplomas (#)	104	102	0	2	0	0

Wayland-Cohocton CSD
2350 Rt 63 • Wayland, NY 14572-9404
(585) 728-2211 • http://www.wayland-cohocton.k12.ny.us/
Grade Span: PK-12; **Agency Type:** 2
Schools: 5

2 Primary; 1 Middle; 1 High; 1 Other Level
4 Regular; 0 Special Education; 0 Vocational; 1 Alternative
0 Magnet; 0 Charter; 3 Title I Eligible; 0 School-wide Title I
Students: 1,850 (50.6% male; 49.4% female)
Individual Education Program: 314 (17.0%);
English Language Learner: 0 (0.0%); Migrant: n/a
Eligible for Free Lunch Program: 366 (19.8%)
Eligible for Reduced-Price Lunch Program: 144 (7.8%)
Teachers: 156.8 (11.8 to 1)
Librarians/Media Specialists: 2.0 (925.0 to 1)
Guidance Counselors: 6.0 (308.3 to 1)
Current Spending: ($ per student per year):
Total: $9,722; Instruction: $6,429; Support Services: $3,052
Enrollment, Drop-out Rates and Diploma Recipients by Race/Ethnicity

Category	Total	White	Black	Asian	AIAN	Hisp.
Enrollment (%)	100.0	97.0	1.5	0.6	0.2	0.6
Drop-out Rate (%)	4.2	0.2	0.0	0.0	n/a	0.0
H.S. Diplomas (#)	141	139	1	1	0	0

Suffolk County

Amityville UFSD
150 Park Ave • Amityville, NY 11701-3195
(631) 598-6507
Grade Span: PK-12; **Agency Type:** 1
Schools: 5
3 Primary; 1 Middle; 1 High; 0 Other Level
5 Regular; 0 Special Education; 0 Vocational; 0 Alternative
0 Magnet; 0 Charter; 3 Title I Eligible; 0 School-wide Title I
Students: 3,240 (52.2% male; 47.8% female)
Individual Education Program: 511 (15.8%);
English Language Learner: 207 (6.4%); Migrant: n/a
Eligible for Free Lunch Program: 1,246 (38.5%)
Eligible for Reduced-Price Lunch Program: 280 (8.6%)
Teachers: 257.0 (12.6 to 1)
Librarians/Media Specialists: 3.9 (830.8 to 1)
Guidance Counselors: 7.0 (462.9 to 1)
Current Spending: ($ per student per year):
Total: $14,333; Instruction: $9,593; Support Services: $4,476
Enrollment, Drop-out Rates and Diploma Recipients by Race/Ethnicity

Category	Total	White	Black	Asian	AIAN	Hisp.
Enrollment (%)	100.0	14.0	64.3	1.5	0.1	20.1
Drop-out Rate (%)	3.9	2.0	3.5	n/a	n/a	9.3
H.S. Diplomas (#)	146	31	97	2	0	16

Babylon UFSD
50 Railroad Ave • Babylon, NY 11702-2221
(631) 893-7925
Grade Span: KG-12; **Agency Type:** 1
Schools: 3
2 Primary; 0 Middle; 1 High; 0 Other Level
3 Regular; 0 Special Education; 0 Vocational; 0 Alternative
0 Magnet; 0 Charter; 1 Title I Eligible; 0 School-wide Title I
Students: 2,001 (51.4% male; 48.6% female)
Individual Education Program: 226 (11.3%);
English Language Learner: 55 (2.7%); Migrant: n/a
Eligible for Free Lunch Program: 150 (7.5%)
Eligible for Reduced-Price Lunch Program: 85 (4.2%)
Teachers: 155.2 (12.9 to 1)
Librarians/Media Specialists: 2.0 (1,000.5 to 1)
Guidance Counselors: 4.0 (500.3 to 1)
Current Spending: ($ per student per year):
Total: $11,967; Instruction: $8,077; Support Services: $3,704
Enrollment, Drop-out Rates and Diploma Recipients by Race/Ethnicity

Category	Total	White	Black	Asian	AIAN	Hisp.
Enrollment (%)	100.0	86.2	5.1	3.2	0.2	5.3
Drop-out Rate (%)	0.3	0.4	0.0	0.0	0.0	0.0
H.S. Diplomas (#)	141	121	8	5	0	7

Bay Shore UFSD
75 W Perkal St • Bay Shore, NY 11706-6696
(631) 968-1117 • http://bayshore.k12.ny.us/
Grade Span: KG-12; **Agency Type:** 1
Schools: 9
5 Primary; 1 Middle; 1 High; 2 Other Level
7 Regular; 0 Special Education; 0 Vocational; 2 Alternative
0 Magnet; 0 Charter; 2 Title I Eligible; 0 School-wide Title I
Students: 5,724 (52.7% male; 47.3% female)
Individual Education Program: 829 (14.5%);
English Language Learner: 277 (4.8%); Migrant: n/a
Eligible for Free Lunch Program: 1,419 (24.8%)
Eligible for Reduced-Price Lunch Program: 502 (8.8%)
Teachers: 436.7 (13.1 to 1)
Librarians/Media Specialists: 6.6 (867.3 to 1)
Guidance Counselors: 12.0 (477.0 to 1)
Current Spending: ($ per student per year):
Total: $13,578; Instruction: $8,996; Support Services: $4,341
Enrollment, Drop-out Rates and Diploma Recipients by Race/Ethnicity

Category	Total	White	Black	Asian	AIAN	Hisp.
Enrollment (%)	100.0	52.3	21.2	2.8	0.1	23.6
Drop-out Rate (%)	0.7	0.1	1.9	0.0	0.0	1.1
H.S. Diplomas (#)	287	177	52	10	0	48

Bayport-Blue Point UFSD
189 Academy St • Bayport, NY 11705-1799
(631) 472-7860 • http://www.b-bp.k12.ny.us/district.htm
Grade Span: KG-12; **Agency Type:** 2
Schools: 5
3 Primary; 1 Middle; 1 High; 0 Other Level
5 Regular; 0 Special Education; 0 Vocational; 0 Alternative
0 Magnet; 0 Charter; 2 Title I Eligible; 0 School-wide Title I
Students: 2,447 (49.8% male; 50.2% female)
Individual Education Program: 323 (13.2%);
English Language Learner: 11 (0.4%); Migrant: n/a
Eligible for Free Lunch Program: 48 (2.0%)
Eligible for Reduced-Price Lunch Program: 49 (2.0%)
Teachers: 200.0 (12.2 to 1)
Librarians/Media Specialists: 4.8 (509.8 to 1)
Guidance Counselors: 6.0 (407.8 to 1)
Current Spending: ($ per student per year):
Total: $13,557; Instruction: $8,833; Support Services: $4,563
Enrollment, Drop-out Rates and Diploma Recipients by Race/Ethnicity

Category	Total	White	Black	Asian	AIAN	Hisp.
Enrollment (%)	100.0	94.5	1.2	1.3	0.5	2.5
Drop-out Rate (%)	0.3	0.2	0.0	0.0	0.0	8.3
H.S. Diplomas (#)	138	133	2	2	0	1

Boces Eastern Suffolk (Suffolk I)
201 Sunrise Hwy • Patchogue, NY 11772
(631) 289-2200 • http://www.sricboces.org/
Grade Span: UG-UG; **Agency Type:** 4
Schools: 1
0 Primary; 0 Middle; 0 High; 1 Other Level
1 Regular; 0 Special Education; 0 Vocational; 0 Alternative
0 Magnet; 0 Charter; 0 Title I Eligible; 0 School-wide Title I
Students: 2,042 (74.0% male; 26.0% female)
Individual Education Program: 2,042 (100.0%);
English Language Learner: n/a; Migrant: n/a
Eligible for Free Lunch Program: n/a
Eligible for Reduced-Price Lunch Program: n/a
Teachers: 646.1 (3.2 to 1)
Librarians/Media Specialists: 4.0 (510.5 to 1)
Guidance Counselors: 19.0 (107.5 to 1)
Current Spending: ($ per student per year):
Total: n/a; Instruction: n/a; Support Services: n/a
Enrollment, Drop-out Rates and Diploma Recipients by Race/Ethnicity

Category	Total	White	Black	Asian	AIAN	Hisp.
Enrollment (%)	100.0	64.2	21.1	1.5	0.4	12.8
Drop-out Rate (%)	n/a	n/a	n/a	n/a	n/a	n/a
H.S. Diplomas (#)	n/a	n/a	n/a	n/a	n/a	n/a

Brentwood UFSD
52 Third Ave • Brentwood, NY 11717-6198
(631) 434-2325 • http://www.brentwood.k12.ny.us/
Grade Span: PK-12; **Agency Type:** 1
Schools: 18
11 Primary; 4 Middle; 1 High; 2 Other Level
17 Regular; 0 Special Education; 0 Vocational; 1 Alternative
0 Magnet; 0 Charter; 15 Title I Eligible; 0 School-wide Title I
Students: 16,262 (52.3% male; 47.7% female)
Individual Education Program: 2,652 (16.3%);
English Language Learner: 2,877 (17.7%); Migrant: n/a
Eligible for Free Lunch Program: 8,248 (50.7%)
Eligible for Reduced-Price Lunch Program: 2,720 (16.7%)
Teachers: 1,040.7 (15.6 to 1)
Librarians/Media Specialists: 10.9 (1,491.9 to 1)
Guidance Counselors: 31.0 (524.6 to 1)
Current Spending: ($ per student per year):
Total: $12,150; Instruction: $8,080; Support Services: $3,778
Enrollment, Drop-out Rates and Diploma Recipients by Race/Ethnicity

Category	Total	White	Black	Asian	AIAN	Hisp.
Enrollment (%)	100.0	16.6	21.1	1.8	0.1	60.4
Drop-out Rate (%)	2.1	1.8	1.2	2.2	0.0	2.6
H.S. Diplomas (#)	641	140	134	20	0	347

Brookhaven-Comsewogue UFSD
290 Norwood Ave • Port Jefferson Stn, NY 11776-2999
(631) 474-8105
Grade Span: KG-12; **Agency Type:** 2
Schools: 6

4 Primary; 1 Middle; 1 High; 0 Other Level
6 Regular; 0 Special Education; 0 Vocational; 0 Alternative
0 Magnet; 0 Charter; 6 Title I Eligible; 0 School-wide Title I
Students: 3,896 (49.9% male; 50.1% female)
Individual Education Program: 580 (14.9%);
English Language Learner: 92 (2.4%); Migrant: n/a
Eligible for Free Lunch Program: 228 (5.9%)
Eligible for Reduced-Price Lunch Program: 110 (2.8%)
Teachers: 267.4 (14.6 to 1)
Librarians/Media Specialists: 4.9 (795.1 to 1)
Guidance Counselors: 7.5 (519.5 to 1)
Current Spending: ($ per student per year):
Total: $11,835; Instruction: $7,935; Support Services: $3,682
Enrollment, Drop-out Rates and Diploma Recipients by Race/Ethnicity

Category	Total	White	Black	Asian	AIAN	Hisp.
Enrollment (%)	100.0	84.0	1.8	3.6	0.0	10.5
Drop-out Rate (%)	3.6	2.8	3.4	8.3	n/a	7.5
H.S. Diplomas (#)	189	159	7	2	0	21

Central Islip UFSD
50 Wheeler Rd • Central Islip, NY 11722-9027
(631) 348-5001 • http://www.centralislip.k12.ny.us/
Grade Span: PK-12; **Agency Type:** 1
Schools: 8
6 Primary; 1 Middle; 1 High; 0 Other Level
8 Regular; 0 Special Education; 0 Vocational; 0 Alternative
0 Magnet; 0 Charter; 7 Title I Eligible; 0 School-wide Title I
Students: 6,628 (50.7% male; 49.3% female)
Individual Education Program: 1,100 (16.6%);
English Language Learner: 1,000 (15.1%); Migrant: n/a
Eligible for Free Lunch Program: 2,585 (39.0%)
Eligible for Reduced-Price Lunch Program: 1,068 (16.1%)
Teachers: 514.3 (12.9 to 1)
Librarians/Media Specialists: 7.0 (946.9 to 1)
Guidance Counselors: 10.0 (662.8 to 1)
Current Spending: ($ per student per year):
Total: $15,682; Instruction: $10,969; Support Services: $4,413
Enrollment, Drop-out Rates and Diploma Recipients by Race/Ethnicity

Category	Total	White	Black	Asian	AIAN	Hisp.
Enrollment (%)	100.0	15.4	34.7	4.0	1.0	45.0
Drop-out Rate (%)	11.9	6.2	11.6	1.6	0.0	16.3
H.S. Diplomas (#)	278	58	119	8	1	92

Cold Spring Harbor CSD
75 Goose Hill Rd • Cold Spring Harbor, NY 11724-9813
(631) 692-8036 • http://www.csh.k12.ny.us/
Grade Span: KG-12; **Agency Type:** 1
Schools: 4
3 Primary; 0 Middle; 1 High; 0 Other Level
4 Regular; 0 Special Education; 0 Vocational; 0 Alternative
0 Magnet; 0 Charter; 1 Title I Eligible; 0 School-wide Title I
Students: 2,047 (50.8% male; 49.2% female)
Individual Education Program: 225 (11.0%);
English Language Learner: 3 (0.1%); Migrant: n/a
Eligible for Free Lunch Program: 2 (0.1%)
Eligible for Reduced-Price Lunch Program: 0 (0.0%)
Teachers: 154.8 (13.2 to 1)
Librarians/Media Specialists: 2.2 (930.5 to 1)
Guidance Counselors: 3.0 (682.3 to 1)
Current Spending: ($ per student per year):
Total: $13,505; Instruction: $8,534; Support Services: $4,736
Enrollment, Drop-out Rates and Diploma Recipients by Race/Ethnicity

Category	Total	White	Black	Asian	AIAN	Hisp.
Enrollment (%)	100.0	96.4	0.5	2.1	0.0	0.9
Drop-out Rate (%)	0.2	0.2	0.0	0.0	0.0	n/a
H.S. Diplomas (#)	121	120	0	0	0	1

Commack UFSD
480 Clay Pitts Rd • East Northport, NY 11731-3828
(631) 912-2010
Grade Span: KG-12; **Agency Type:** 1
Schools: 8
6 Primary; 1 Middle; 1 High; 0 Other Level
8 Regular; 0 Special Education; 0 Vocational; 0 Alternative
0 Magnet; 0 Charter; 3 Title I Eligible; 0 School-wide Title I
Students: 7,321 (51.3% male; 48.7% female)
Individual Education Program: 862 (11.8%);
English Language Learner: 61 (0.8%); Migrant: n/a
Eligible for Free Lunch Program: 115 (1.6%)
Eligible for Reduced-Price Lunch Program: 78 (1.1%)
Teachers: 563.8 (13.0 to 1)
Librarians/Media Specialists: 10.7 (684.2 to 1)
Guidance Counselors: 16.1 (454.7 to 1)
Current Spending: ($ per student per year):
Total: $11,559; Instruction: $7,211; Support Services: $4,188

Enrollment, Drop-out Rates and Diploma Recipients by Race/Ethnicity

Category	Total	White	Black	Asian	AIAN	Hisp.
Enrollment (%)	100.0	90.8	0.9	5.8	0.1	2.4
Drop-out Rate (%)	0.7	0.7	0.0	0.9	0.0	0.0
H.S. Diplomas (#)	408	361	3	32	0	12

Connetquot CSD
780 Ocean Ave • Bohemia, NY 11716-3629
(631) 244-2211 • http://www.connetquot.k12.ny.us/
Grade Span: KG-12; **Agency Type:** 1
Schools: 10
7 Primary; 2 Middle; 1 High; 0 Other Level
10 Regular; 0 Special Education; 0 Vocational; 0 Alternative
0 Magnet; 0 Charter; 6 Title I Eligible; 0 School-wide Title I
Students: 7,064 (51.5% male; 48.5% female)
Individual Education Program: 1,129 (16.0%);
English Language Learner: 73 (1.0%); Migrant: n/a
Eligible for Free Lunch Program: 275 (3.9%)
Eligible for Reduced-Price Lunch Program: 265 (3.8%)
Teachers: 540.5 (13.1 to 1)
Librarians/Media Specialists: 8.3 (851.1 to 1)
Guidance Counselors: 13.0 (543.4 to 1)
Current Spending: ($ per student per year):
Total: $13,564; Instruction: $9,049; Support Services: $4,308
Enrollment, Drop-out Rates and Diploma Recipients by Race/Ethnicity

Category	Total	White	Black	Asian	AIAN	Hisp.
Enrollment (%)	100.0	92.4	0.8	2.7	0.2	3.9
Drop-out Rate (%)	0.6	0.6	0.0	0.0	0.0	0.0
H.S. Diplomas (#)	374	343	1	2	14	14

Copiague UFSD
2650 Great Neck Rd • Copiague, NY 11726-1699
(631) 842-4015 •
http://www.edutalk.com/leveltwo/sites/copiague/index.asp
Grade Span: KG-12; **Agency Type:** 1
Schools: 5
3 Primary; 1 Middle; 1 High; 0 Other Level
5 Regular; 0 Special Education; 0 Vocational; 0 Alternative
0 Magnet; 0 Charter; 3 Title I Eligible; 0 School-wide Title I
Students: 4,635 (51.5% male; 48.5% female)
Individual Education Program: 717 (15.5%);
English Language Learner: 342 (7.4%); Migrant: n/a
Eligible for Free Lunch Program: 1,350 (29.1%)
Eligible for Reduced-Price Lunch Program: 447 (9.6%)
Teachers: 301.2 (15.4 to 1)
Librarians/Media Specialists: 5.8 (799.1 to 1)
Guidance Counselors: 11.0 (421.4 to 1)
Current Spending: ($ per student per year):
Total: $12,832; Instruction: $8,808; Support Services: $3,702
Enrollment, Drop-out Rates and Diploma Recipients by Race/Ethnicity

Category	Total	White	Black	Asian	AIAN	Hisp.
Enrollment (%)	100.0	34.2	35.7	2.0	0.0	28.2
Drop-out Rate (%)	2.9	2.9	2.1	0.0	n/a	4.3
H.S. Diplomas (#)	205	101	60	1	0	43

Deer Park UFSD
1881 Deer Park Ave • Deer Park, NY 11729-4326
(631) 242-6505
Grade Span: PK-12; **Agency Type:** 1
Schools: 6
4 Primary; 1 Middle; 1 High; 0 Other Level
6 Regular; 0 Special Education; 0 Vocational; 0 Alternative
0 Magnet; 0 Charter; 2 Title I Eligible; 0 School-wide Title I
Students: 4,383 (52.5% male; 47.5% female)
Individual Education Program: 530 (12.1%);
English Language Learner: 166 (3.8%); Migrant: n/a
Eligible for Free Lunch Program: 418 (9.5%)
Eligible for Reduced-Price Lunch Program: 317 (7.2%)
Teachers: 374.5 (11.7 to 1)
Librarians/Media Specialists: 6.6 (664.1 to 1)
Guidance Counselors: 8.0 (547.9 to 1)
Current Spending: ($ per student per year):
Total: $13,167; Instruction: $8,679; Support Services: $4,268
Enrollment, Drop-out Rates and Diploma Recipients by Race/Ethnicity

Category	Total	White	Black	Asian	AIAN	Hisp.
Enrollment (%)	100.0	71.8	14.9	5.2	0.0	8.0
Drop-out Rate (%)	1.7	1.5	2.4	0.0	n/a	4.1
H.S. Diplomas (#)	198	150	32	8	0	8

East Hampton UFSD
76 Newtown Ln • East Hampton, NY 11937-2409
(631) 329-4104 • http://www.easthampton.k12.ny.us/
Grade Span: KG-12; **Agency Type:** 2
Schools: 3
1 Primary; 1 Middle; 1 High; 0 Other Level

3 Regular; 0 Special Education; 0 Vocational; 0 Alternative
0 Magnet; 0 Charter; 1 Title I Eligible; 0 School-wide Title I
Students: 1,988 (52.9% male; 47.1% female)
Individual Education Program: 226 (11.4%);
English Language Learner: 165 (8.3%); Migrant: n/a
Eligible for Free Lunch Program: 103 (5.2%)
Eligible for Reduced-Price Lunch Program: 35 (1.8%)
Teachers: 163.5 (12.2 to 1)
Librarians/Media Specialists: 2.3 (864.3 to 1)
Guidance Counselors: 7.5 (265.1 to 1)
Current Spending: ($ per student per year):
Total: $15,667; Instruction: $9,879; Support Services: $5,511
Enrollment, Drop-out Rates and Diploma Recipients by Race/Ethnicity

Category	Total	White	Black	Asian	AIAN	Hisp.
Enrollment (%)	100.0	70.7	5.6	1.5	0.2	22.0
Drop-out Rate (%)	2.3	0.9	0.0	0.0	n/a	7.5
H.S. Diplomas (#)	184	143	6	2	0	33

East Islip UFSD
1 C B Gariepy Ave • Islip Terrace, NY 11752-2820
(631) 581-1600 • http://www.eastislip.k12.ny.us/
Grade Span: PK-12; **Agency Type:** 1
Schools: 7
5 Primary; 1 Middle; 1 High; 0 Other Level
7 Regular; 0 Special Education; 0 Vocational; 0 Alternative
0 Magnet; 0 Charter; 3 Title I Eligible; 0 School-wide Title I
Students: 5,338 (53.6% male; 46.4% female)
Individual Education Program: 523 (9.8%);
English Language Learner: 61 (1.1%); Migrant: n/a
Eligible for Free Lunch Program: 193 (3.6%)
Eligible for Reduced-Price Lunch Program: 207 (3.9%)
Teachers: 378.4 (14.1 to 1)
Librarians/Media Specialists: 6.0 (889.7 to 1)
Guidance Counselors: 8.0 (667.3 to 1)
Current Spending: ($ per student per year):
Total: $11,726; Instruction: $8,247; Support Services: $3,320
Enrollment, Drop-out Rates and Diploma Recipients by Race/Ethnicity

Category	Total	White	Black	Asian	AIAN	Hisp.
Enrollment (%)	100.0	93.3	0.8	1.3	0.7	3.9
Drop-out Rate (%)	2.4	2.4	0.0	4.2	0.0	3.8
H.S. Diplomas (#)	300	288	0	7	0	5

Elwood UFSD
100 Kenneth Ave • Greenlawn, NY 11740-2900
(631) 266-5402 • http://www.elwood.k12.ny.us/
Grade Span: KG-12; **Agency Type:** 2
Schools: 4
2 Primary; 1 Middle; 1 High; 0 Other Level
4 Regular; 0 Special Education; 0 Vocational; 0 Alternative
0 Magnet; 0 Charter; 2 Title I Eligible; 0 School-wide Title I
Students: 2,462 (51.3% male; 48.7% female)
Individual Education Program: 197 (8.0%);
English Language Learner: 92 (3.7%); Migrant: n/a
Eligible for Free Lunch Program: 178 (7.2%)
Eligible for Reduced-Price Lunch Program: 69 (2.8%)
Teachers: 165.2 (14.9 to 1)
Librarians/Media Specialists: 2.9 (849.0 to 1)
Guidance Counselors: 5.0 (492.4 to 1)
Current Spending: ($ per student per year):
Total: $12,063; Instruction: $7,619; Support Services: $4,180
Enrollment, Drop-out Rates and Diploma Recipients by Race/Ethnicity

Category	Total	White	Black	Asian	AIAN	Hisp.
Enrollment (%)	100.0	76.6	10.4	6.0	0.1	6.9
Drop-out Rate (%)	0.8	0.7	2.0	0.0	n/a	0.0
H.S. Diplomas (#)	131	93	20	15	0	3

Half Hollow Hills CSD
525 Half Hollow Rd • Dix Hills, NY 11746-5899
(631) 592-3008 • http://www.halfhollowhills.k12.ny.us/
Grade Span: KG-12; **Agency Type:** 1
Schools: 14
7 Primary; 2 Middle; 2 High; 3 Other Level
11 Regular; 0 Special Education; 0 Vocational; 3 Alternative
0 Magnet; 0 Charter; 6 Title I Eligible; 0 School-wide Title I
Students: 9,192 (51.6% male; 48.4% female)
Individual Education Program: 1,183 (12.9%);
English Language Learner: 172 (1.9%); Migrant: n/a
Eligible for Free Lunch Program: 394 (4.3%)
Eligible for Reduced-Price Lunch Program: 190 (2.1%)
Teachers: 692.4 (13.3 to 1)
Librarians/Media Specialists: 10.1 (910.1 to 1)
Guidance Counselors: 25.8 (356.3 to 1)
Current Spending: ($ per student per year):
Total: $12,991; Instruction: $8,749; Support Services: $4,031
Enrollment, Drop-out Rates and Diploma Recipients by Race/Ethnicity

Category	Total	White	Black	Asian	AIAN	Hisp.
Enrollment (%)	100.0	74.8	11.6	9.3	0.1	4.1
Drop-out Rate (%)	0.4	0.4	0.8	0.0	0.0	0.0
H.S. Diplomas (#)	543	406	56	64	0	17

Hampton Bays UFSD
86 E Argonne Rd • Hampton Bays, NY 11946-1739
(631) 723-2100
Grade Span: KG-12; **Agency Type:** 2
Schools: 2
1 Primary; 0 Middle; 1 High; 0 Other Level
2 Regular; 0 Special Education; 0 Vocational; 0 Alternative
0 Magnet; 0 Charter; 1 Title I Eligible; 0 School-wide Title I
Students: 1,752 (53.1% male; 46.9% female)
Individual Education Program: 241 (13.8%);
English Language Learner: 167 (9.5%); Migrant: n/a
Eligible for Free Lunch Program: 274 (15.6%)
Eligible for Reduced-Price Lunch Program: 78 (4.5%)
Teachers: 132.9 (13.2 to 1)
Librarians/Media Specialists: 2.0 (876.0 to 1)
Guidance Counselors: 3.0 (584.0 to 1)
Current Spending: ($ per student per year):
Total: $11,256; Instruction: $7,457; Support Services: $3,575
Enrollment, Drop-out Rates and Diploma Recipients by Race/Ethnicity

Category	Total	White	Black	Asian	AIAN	Hisp.
Enrollment (%)	100.0	72.4	1.5	0.2	0.0	25.9
Drop-out Rate (%)	2.1	1.8	0.0	0.0	n/a	4.0
H.S. Diplomas (#)	0	0	0	0	0	0

Harborfields CSD
2 Oldfield Rd • Greenlawn, NY 11740-1200
(631) 754-5320 • http://www.harborfields.k12.ny.us/
Grade Span: KG-12; **Agency Type:** 1
Schools: 4
2 Primary; 1 Middle; 1 High; 0 Other Level
4 Regular; 0 Special Education; 0 Vocational; 0 Alternative
0 Magnet; 0 Charter; 1 Title I Eligible; 0 School-wide Title I
Students: 3,414 (51.7% male; 48.3% female)
Individual Education Program: 423 (12.4%);
English Language Learner: 50 (1.5%); Migrant: n/a
Eligible for Free Lunch Program: 78 (2.3%)
Eligible for Reduced-Price Lunch Program: 45 (1.3%)
Teachers: 229.7 (14.9 to 1)
Librarians/Media Specialists: 4.0 (853.5 to 1)
Guidance Counselors: 9.0 (379.3 to 1)
Current Spending: ($ per student per year):
Total: $11,104; Instruction: $7,243; Support Services: $3,640
Enrollment, Drop-out Rates and Diploma Recipients by Race/Ethnicity

Category	Total	White	Black	Asian	AIAN	Hisp.
Enrollment (%)	100.0	86.6	6.4	3.5	0.0	3.5
Drop-out Rate (%)	0.1	0.2	0.0	0.0	n/a	0.0
H.S. Diplomas (#)	189	152	18	18	0	1

Hauppauge UFSD
495 Hoffman Ln • Hauppauge, NY 11788-3103
(631) 265-3630 • http://www.hauppauge.k12.ny.us/
Grade Span: KG-12; **Agency Type:** 1
Schools: 5
3 Primary; 1 Middle; 1 High; 0 Other Level
5 Regular; 0 Special Education; 0 Vocational; 0 Alternative
0 Magnet; 0 Charter; 1 Title I Eligible; 0 School-wide Title I
Students: 4,014 (51.3% male; 48.7% female)
Individual Education Program: 492 (12.3%);
English Language Learner: 74 (1.8%); Migrant: n/a
Eligible for Free Lunch Program: 104 (2.6%)
Eligible for Reduced-Price Lunch Program: 61 (1.5%)
Teachers: 318.8 (12.6 to 1)
Librarians/Media Specialists: 7.0 (573.4 to 1)
Guidance Counselors: 11.0 (364.9 to 1)
Current Spending: ($ per student per year):
Total: $14,512; Instruction: $8,845; Support Services: $5,480
Enrollment, Drop-out Rates and Diploma Recipients by Race/Ethnicity

Category	Total	White	Black	Asian	AIAN	Hisp.
Enrollment (%)	100.0	90.3	1.4	4.4	0.1	3.7
Drop-out Rate (%)	1.1	1.2	0.0	0.0	n/a	0.0
H.S. Diplomas (#)	259	253	0	5	0	1

Huntington UFSD
50 Tower St • Huntington Station, NY 11746
(631) 673-2038
Grade Span: KG-12; **Agency Type:** 1
Schools: 8
4 Primary; 3 Middle; 1 High; 0 Other Level
8 Regular; 0 Special Education; 0 Vocational; 0 Alternative

0 Magnet; 0 Charter; 4 Title I Eligible; 0 School-wide Title I
Students: 4,104 (51.3% male; 48.7% female)
Individual Education Program: 618 (15.1%);
English Language Learner: 418 (10.2%); Migrant: n/a
Eligible for Free Lunch Program: 808 (19.7%)
Eligible for Reduced-Price Lunch Program: 199 (4.8%)
Teachers: 362.5 (11.3 to 1)
Librarians/Media Specialists: 6.5 (631.4 to 1)
Guidance Counselors: 9.0 (456.0 to 1)
Current Spending: ($ per student per year):
Total: $15,664; Instruction: $10,093; Support Services: $5,267
Enrollment, Drop-out Rates and Diploma Recipients by Race/Ethnicity

Category	Total	White	Black	Asian	AIAN	Hisp.
Enrollment (%)	100.0	63.6	13.5	1.5	0.0	21.4
Drop-out Rate (%)	3.6	1.2	2.4	0.0	n/a	12.6
H.S. Diplomas (#)	205	155	22	6	0	22

Islip UFSD
215 Main St • Islip, NY 11751-3435
(631) 859-2209
Grade Span: KG-12; **Agency Type:** 2
Schools: 5
3 Primary; 1 Middle; 1 High; 0 Other Level
5 Regular; 0 Special Education; 0 Vocational; 0 Alternative
0 Magnet; 0 Charter; 3 Title I Eligible; 0 School-wide Title I
Students: 3,617 (51.3% male; 48.7% female)
Individual Education Program: 438 (12.1%);
English Language Learner: 88 (2.4%); Migrant: n/a
Eligible for Free Lunch Program: 354 (9.8%)
Eligible for Reduced-Price Lunch Program: 193 (5.3%)
Teachers: 250.0 (14.5 to 1)
Librarians/Media Specialists: 2.0 (1,808.5 to 1)
Guidance Counselors: 7.0 (516.7 to 1)
Current Spending: ($ per student per year):
Total: $11,482; Instruction: $7,623; Support Services: $3,664
Enrollment, Drop-out Rates and Diploma Recipients by Race/Ethnicity

Category	Total	White	Black	Asian	AIAN	Hisp.
Enrollment (%)	100.0	85.3	4.3	2.1	0.2	8.2
Drop-out Rate (%)	1.0	0.9	0.0	100.0	n/a	1.3
H.S. Diplomas (#)	203	178	10	5	0	10

Kings Park CSD
101 Church St • Kings Park, NY 11754-1769
(631) 269-3210 • http://kpcsd.k12.ny.us/
Grade Span: KG-12; **Agency Type:** 1
Schools: 5
2 Primary; 2 Middle; 1 High; 0 Other Level
5 Regular; 0 Special Education; 0 Vocational; 0 Alternative
0 Magnet; 0 Charter; 5 Title I Eligible; 0 School-wide Title I
Students: 3,973 (50.3% male; 49.7% female)
Individual Education Program: 476 (12.0%);
English Language Learner: 59 (1.5%); Migrant: n/a
Eligible for Free Lunch Program: 52 (1.3%)
Eligible for Reduced-Price Lunch Program: 51 (1.3%)
Teachers: 316.3 (12.6 to 1)
Librarians/Media Specialists: 4.7 (845.3 to 1)
Guidance Counselors: 8.6 (462.0 to 1)
Current Spending: ($ per student per year):
Total: $11,494; Instruction: $7,391; Support Services: $3,930
Enrollment, Drop-out Rates and Diploma Recipients by Race/Ethnicity

Category	Total	White	Black	Asian	AIAN	Hisp.
Enrollment (%)	100.0	94.8	0.6	2.2	0.1	2.3
Drop-out Rate (%)	0.2	0.1	0.0	0.0	n/a	3.4
H.S. Diplomas (#)	247	227	2	11	0	7

Lindenhurst UFSD
350 Daniel St • Lindenhurst, NY 11757-0621
(631) 226-6511 • http://lhs.lindy.k12.ny.us/
Grade Span: KG-12; **Agency Type:** 1
Schools: 9
7 Primary; 1 Middle; 1 High; 0 Other Level
9 Regular; 0 Special Education; 0 Vocational; 0 Alternative
0 Magnet; 0 Charter; 4 Title I Eligible; 0 School-wide Title I
Students: 7,601 (51.4% male; 48.6% female)
Individual Education Program: 1,155 (15.2%);
English Language Learner: 192 (2.5%); Migrant: n/a
Eligible for Free Lunch Program: 563 (7.4%)
Eligible for Reduced-Price Lunch Program: 368 (4.8%)
Teachers: 527.6 (14.4 to 1)
Librarians/Media Specialists: 9.2 (826.2 to 1)
Guidance Counselors: 11.0 (691.0 to 1)
Current Spending: ($ per student per year):
Total: $10,565; Instruction: $7,090; Support Services: $3,223

Enrollment, Drop-out Rates and Diploma Recipients by Race/Ethnicity

Category	Total	White	Black	Asian	AIAN	Hisp.
Enrollment (%)	100.0	87.8	1.9	2.0	0.0	8.3
Drop-out Rate (%)	1.6	1.5	5.0	0.0	n/a	3.4
H.S. Diplomas (#)	419	385	3	7	0	24

Longwood CSD
35 Yaphnk-Mid Isl Rd • Middle Island, NY 11953-2369
(631) 345-2172 • http://www.longwood.k12.ny.us/
Grade Span: KG-12; **Agency Type:** 1
Schools: 8
4 Primary; 2 Middle; 1 High; 1 Other Level
7 Regular; 0 Special Education; 0 Vocational; 1 Alternative
0 Magnet; 0 Charter; 6 Title I Eligible; 0 School-wide Title I
Students: 9,867 (51.9% male; 48.1% female)
Individual Education Program: 1,488 (15.1%);
English Language Learner: 264 (2.7%); Migrant: n/a
Eligible for Free Lunch Program: 1,520 (15.4%)
Eligible for Reduced-Price Lunch Program: 564 (5.7%)
Teachers: 684.5 (14.4 to 1)
Librarians/Media Specialists: 11.2 (881.0 to 1)
Guidance Counselors: 22.0 (448.5 to 1)
Current Spending: ($ per student per year):
Total: $12,423; Instruction: $8,640; Support Services: $3,589
Enrollment, Drop-out Rates and Diploma Recipients by Race/Ethnicity

Category	Total	White	Black	Asian	AIAN	Hisp.
Enrollment (%)	100.0	65.1	19.7	3.4	0.5	11.4
Drop-out Rate (%)	1.1	1.1	1.6	2.4	0.0	0.3
H.S. Diplomas (#)	516	388	69	9	1	49

Mattituck-Cutchogue UFSD
385 Depot Ln • Cutchogue, NY 11935
(631) 298-4242
Grade Span: KG-12; **Agency Type:** 1
Schools: 2
1 Primary; 0 Middle; 1 High; 0 Other Level
2 Regular; 0 Special Education; 0 Vocational; 0 Alternative
0 Magnet; 0 Charter; 1 Title I Eligible; 0 School-wide Title I
Students: 1,562 (50.9% male; 49.1% female)
Individual Education Program: 127 (8.1%);
English Language Learner: 16 (1.0%); Migrant: n/a
Eligible for Free Lunch Program: 38 (2.4%)
Eligible for Reduced-Price Lunch Program: 25 (1.6%)
Teachers: 135.3 (11.5 to 1)
Librarians/Media Specialists: 3.0 (520.7 to 1)
Guidance Counselors: 5.0 (312.4 to 1)
Current Spending: ($ per student per year):
Total: $12,311; Instruction: $8,604; Support Services: $3,518
Enrollment, Drop-out Rates and Diploma Recipients by Race/Ethnicity

Category	Total	White	Black	Asian	AIAN	Hisp.
Enrollment (%)	100.0	95.1	2.5	0.7	0.1	1.7
Drop-out Rate (%)	2.4	2.3	8.3	0.0	n/a	0.0
H.S. Diplomas (#)	112	110	0	1	0	1

Middle Country CSD
8 43rd St - Adm Off • Centereach, NY 11720-2325
(631) 738-2714 • http://www.middlecountry.k12.ny.us/
Grade Span: PK-12; **Agency Type:** 1
Schools: 14
10 Primary; 2 Middle; 2 High; 0 Other Level
14 Regular; 0 Special Education; 0 Vocational; 0 Alternative
0 Magnet; 0 Charter; 5 Title I Eligible; 0 School-wide Title I
Students: 11,591 (51.8% male; 48.2% female)
Individual Education Program: 1,731 (14.9%);
English Language Learner: 225 (1.9%); Migrant: n/a
Eligible for Free Lunch Program: 765 (6.6%)
Eligible for Reduced-Price Lunch Program: 515 (4.4%)
Teachers: 777.1 (14.9 to 1)
Librarians/Media Specialists: 13.0 (891.6 to 1)
Guidance Counselors: 19.0 (610.1 to 1)
Current Spending: ($ per student per year):
Total: $10,358; Instruction: $6,928; Support Services: $3,238
Enrollment, Drop-out Rates and Diploma Recipients by Race/Ethnicity

Category	Total	White	Black	Asian	AIAN	Hisp.
Enrollment (%)	100.0	87.0	2.7	3.3	0.1	7.0
Drop-out Rate (%)	2.9	2.8	3.5	5.2	25.0	2.9
H.S. Diplomas (#)	670	586	19	21	1	43

Miller Place UFSD
275 Route 25a • Miller Place, NY 11764-2036
(631) 474-2733 • http://www.millerplace.k12.ny.us/
Grade Span: KG-12; **Agency Type:** 2
Schools: 4
2 Primary; 1 Middle; 1 High; 0 Other Level
4 Regular; 0 Special Education; 0 Vocational; 0 Alternative

0 Magnet; 0 Charter; 3 Title I Eligible; 0 School-wide Title I
Students: 2,974 (51.6% male; 48.4% female)
Individual Education Program: 383 (12.9%);
English Language Learner: 37 (1.2%); Migrant: n/a
Eligible for Free Lunch Program: 38 (1.3%)
Eligible for Reduced-Price Lunch Program: 16 (0.5%)
Teachers: 215.7 (13.8 to 1)
Librarians/Media Specialists: 3.6 (826.1 to 1)
Guidance Counselors: 6.0 (495.7 to 1)
Current Spending: ($ per student per year):
Total: $10,923; Instruction: $7,765; Support Services: $2,985
Enrollment, Drop-out Rates and Diploma Recipients by Race/Ethnicity

Category	Total	White	Black	Asian	AIAN	Hisp.
Enrollment (%)	100.0	96.7	0.7	1.2	0.1	1.2
Drop-out Rate (%)	0.0	0.0	0.0	0.0	0.0	0.0
H.S. Diplomas (#)	213	209	1	1	1	1

Mount Sinai UFSD

N Country Rd • Mount Sinai, NY 11766-0397
(631) 473-1991 • http://www.mtsinai.k12.ny.us/
Grade Span: KG-12; **Agency Type:** 2
Schools: 3
1 Primary; 1 Middle; 1 High; 0 Other Level
3 Regular; 0 Special Education; 0 Vocational; 0 Alternative
0 Magnet; 0 Charter; 3 Title I Eligible; 0 School-wide Title I
Students: 2,383 (48.5% male; 51.5% female)
Individual Education Program: 290 (12.2%);
English Language Learner: 3 (0.1%); Migrant: n/a
Eligible for Free Lunch Program: 21 (0.9%)
Eligible for Reduced-Price Lunch Program: 13 (0.5%)
Teachers: 166.3 (14.3 to 1)
Librarians/Media Specialists: 2.8 (851.1 to 1)
Guidance Counselors: 6.5 (366.6 to 1)
Current Spending: ($ per student per year):
Total: $12,096; Instruction: $7,814; Support Services: $4,110
Enrollment, Drop-out Rates and Diploma Recipients by Race/Ethnicity

Category	Total	White	Black	Asian	AIAN	Hisp.
Enrollment (%)	100.0	95.5	1.0	1.6	0.0	1.9
Drop-out Rate (%)	0.3	0.2	11.1	0.0	n/a	0.0
H.S. Diplomas (#)	143	133	3	3	0	4

North Babylon UFSD

5 Jardine Pl • North Babylon, NY 11703-4203
(631) 321-3226
Grade Span: KG-12; **Agency Type:** 1
Schools: 7
5 Primary; 1 Middle; 1 High; 0 Other Level
7 Regular; 0 Special Education; 0 Vocational; 0 Alternative
0 Magnet; 0 Charter; 6 Title I Eligible; 0 School-wide Title I
Students: 5,155 (50.2% male; 49.8% female)
Individual Education Program: 955 (18.5%);
English Language Learner: 91 (1.8%); Migrant: n/a
Eligible for Free Lunch Program: 597 (11.6%)
Eligible for Reduced-Price Lunch Program: 316 (6.1%)
Teachers: 357.9 (14.4 to 1)
Librarians/Media Specialists: 6.6 (781.1 to 1)
Guidance Counselors: 9.0 (572.8 to 1)
Current Spending: ($ per student per year):
Total: $11,453; Instruction: $7,492; Support Services: $3,738
Enrollment, Drop-out Rates and Diploma Recipients by Race/Ethnicity

Category	Total	White	Black	Asian	AIAN	Hisp.
Enrollment (%)	100.0	67.4	20.8	2.3	0.2	9.2
Drop-out Rate (%)	4.3	3.3	7.8	4.3	0.0	2.5
H.S. Diplomas (#)	385	255	86	7	0	37

Northport-East Northport UFSD

158 Laurel Ave • Northport, NY 11768-3455
(631) 262-6604 • http://northport.k12.ny.us/
Grade Span: PK-12; **Agency Type:** 1
Schools: 9
6 Primary; 2 Middle; 1 High; 0 Other Level
9 Regular; 0 Special Education; 0 Vocational; 0 Alternative
0 Magnet; 0 Charter; 6 Title I Eligible; 0 School-wide Title I
Students: 6,242 (50.9% male; 49.1% female)
Individual Education Program: 821 (13.2%);
English Language Learner: 92 (1.5%); Migrant: n/a
Eligible for Free Lunch Program: 200 (3.2%)
Eligible for Reduced-Price Lunch Program: 99 (1.6%)
Teachers: 535.3 (11.7 to 1)
Librarians/Media Specialists: 9.8 (636.9 to 1)
Guidance Counselors: 25.0 (249.7 to 1)
Current Spending: ($ per student per year):
Total: $13,267; Instruction: $8,459; Support Services: $4,598

Enrollment, Drop-out Rates and Diploma Recipients by Race/Ethnicity

Category	Total	White	Black	Asian	AIAN	Hisp.
Enrollment (%)	100.0	93.6	0.6	2.6	0.0	3.1
Drop-out Rate (%)	0.7	0.7	0.0	0.0	0.0	0.0
H.S. Diplomas (#)	329	307	4	14	1	3

Patchogue-Medford UFSD

241 S Ocean Ave • Patchogue, NY 11772-3787
(631) 758-1017 • http://www.pat-med.k12.ny.us/
Grade Span: PK-12; **Agency Type:** 1
Schools: 12
7 Primary; 3 Middle; 1 High; 1 Other Level
11 Regular; 0 Special Education; 0 Vocational; 1 Alternative
0 Magnet; 0 Charter; 5 Title I Eligible; 0 School-wide Title I
Students: 9,212 (50.8% male; 49.2% female)
Individual Education Program: 1,313 (14.3%);
English Language Learner: 386 (4.2%); Migrant: n/a
Eligible for Free Lunch Program: 1,391 (15.1%)
Eligible for Reduced-Price Lunch Program: 746 (8.1%)
Teachers: 621.8 (14.8 to 1)
Librarians/Media Specialists: 11.6 (794.1 to 1)
Guidance Counselors: 14.8 (622.4 to 1)
Current Spending: ($ per student per year):
Total: $11,458; Instruction: $7,921; Support Services: $3,262
Enrollment, Drop-out Rates and Diploma Recipients by Race/Ethnicity

Category	Total	White	Black	Asian	AIAN	Hisp.
Enrollment (%)	100.0	79.2	4.6	1.5	0.2	14.5
Drop-out Rate (%)	1.6	1.4	1.7	0.0	0.0	3.0
H.S. Diplomas (#)	496	434	16	7	0	39

Riverhead CSD

700 Osborne Ave • Riverhead, NY 11901-2996
(631) 369-6716
Grade Span: KG-12; **Agency Type:** 2
Schools: 8
4 Primary; 2 Middle; 1 High; 1 Other Level
7 Regular; 0 Special Education; 0 Vocational; 1 Alternative
0 Magnet; 0 Charter; 3 Title I Eligible; 0 School-wide Title I
Students: 4,897 (52.0% male; 48.0% female)
Individual Education Program: 724 (14.8%);
English Language Learner: 247 (5.0%); Migrant: n/a
Eligible for Free Lunch Program: 1,059 (21.6%)
Eligible for Reduced-Price Lunch Program: 341 (7.0%)
Teachers: 343.2 (14.3 to 1)
Librarians/Media Specialists: 5.6 (874.5 to 1)
Guidance Counselors: 5.3 (924.0 to 1)
Current Spending: ($ per student per year):
Total: $12,750; Instruction: $8,744; Support Services: $3,760
Enrollment, Drop-out Rates and Diploma Recipients by Race/Ethnicity

Category	Total	White	Black	Asian	AIAN	Hisp.
Enrollment (%)	100.0	62.6	25.9	1.1	0.7	9.7
Drop-out Rate (%)	2.8	1.8	4.9	0.0	0.0	6.1
H.S. Diplomas (#)	238	173	49	2	2	12

Rocky Point UFSD

170 Rt 25a • Rocky Point, NY 11778-8401
(631) 744-1600 • http://www.rockypointschools.org/
Grade Span: KG-12; **Agency Type:** 2
Schools: 4
2 Primary; 1 Middle; 1 High; 0 Other Level
4 Regular; 0 Special Education; 0 Vocational; 0 Alternative
0 Magnet; 0 Charter; 1 Title I Eligible; 0 School-wide Title I
Students: 3,656 (52.7% male; 47.3% female)
Individual Education Program: 556 (15.2%);
English Language Learner: 28 (0.8%); Migrant: n/a
Eligible for Free Lunch Program: 183 (5.0%)
Eligible for Reduced-Price Lunch Program: 111 (3.0%)
Teachers: 237.1 (15.4 to 1)
Librarians/Media Specialists: 3.6 (1,015.6 to 1)
Guidance Counselors: 6.0 (609.3 to 1)
Current Spending: ($ per student per year):
Total: $10,050; Instruction: $7,020; Support Services: $2,826
Enrollment, Drop-out Rates and Diploma Recipients by Race/Ethnicity

Category	Total	White	Black	Asian	AIAN	Hisp.
Enrollment (%)	100.0	95.5	1.2	0.8	0.0	2.5
Drop-out Rate (%)	3.2	3.3	0.0	0.0	n/a	0.0
H.S. Diplomas (#)	160	158	1	1	0	0

Sachem CSD

245 Union Ave • Holbrook, NY 11741-1890
(631) 471-1336 • http://www.sachem.k12.ny.us/
Grade Span: KG-12; **Agency Type:** 1
Schools: 15
12 Primary; 2 Middle; 1 High; 0 Other Level
15 Regular; 0 Special Education; 0 Vocational; 0 Alternative

0 Magnet; 0 Charter; 9 Title I Eligible; 0 School-wide Title I
Students: 15,311 (50.2% male; 49.8% female)
Individual Education Program: 1,905 (12.4%);
English Language Learner: 202 (1.3%); Migrant: n/a
Eligible for Free Lunch Program: 785 (5.1%)
Eligible for Reduced-Price Lunch Program: 582 (3.8%)
Teachers: 1,141.0 (13.4 to 1)
Librarians/Media Specialists: 17.8 (860.2 to 1)
Guidance Counselors: 33.0 (464.0 to 1)
Current Spending: ($ per student per year):
Total: $12,089; Instruction: $8,466; Support Services: $3,410
Enrollment, Drop-out Rates and Diploma Recipients by Race/Ethnicity

Category	Total	White	Black	Asian	AIAN	Hisp.
Enrollment (%)	100.0	90.4	1.0	3.3	0.1	5.1
Drop-out Rate (%)	1.7	1.6	6.8	0.0	0.0	4.4
H.S. Diplomas (#)	910	843	5	27	1	34

Sayville UFSD
99 Greeley Ave • Sayville, NY 11782-2698
(631) 244-6510
Grade Span: KG-12; **Agency Type:** 1
Schools: 5
3 Primary; 1 Middle; 1 High; 0 Other Level
5 Regular; 0 Special Education; 0 Vocational; 0 Alternative
0 Magnet; 0 Charter; 3 Title I Eligible; 0 School-wide Title I
Students: 3,629 (51.0% male; 49.0% female)
Individual Education Program: 438 (12.1%);
English Language Learner: 20 (0.6%); Migrant: n/a
Eligible for Free Lunch Program: 101 (2.8%)
Eligible for Reduced-Price Lunch Program: 59 (1.6%)
Teachers: 263.2 (13.8 to 1)
Librarians/Media Specialists: 4.1 (885.1 to 1)
Guidance Counselors: 7.0 (518.4 to 1)
Current Spending: ($ per student per year):
Total: $13,222; Instruction: $8,642; Support Services: $4,372
Enrollment, Drop-out Rates and Diploma Recipients by Race/Ethnicity

Category	Total	White	Black	Asian	AIAN	Hisp.
Enrollment (%)	100.0	95.1	0.9	2.6	0.0	1.4
Drop-out Rate (%)	n/a	n/a	n/a	n/a	n/a	n/a
H.S. Diplomas (#)	219	204	1	9	0	5

Shoreham-Wading River CSD
250b Rt 25a • Shoreham, NY 11786-2192
(631) 821-8105
Grade Span: KG-12; **Agency Type:** 2
Schools: 5
3 Primary; 1 Middle; 1 High; 0 Other Level
5 Regular; 0 Special Education; 0 Vocational; 0 Alternative
0 Magnet; 0 Charter; 2 Title I Eligible; 0 School-wide Title I
Students: 2,686 (51.8% male; 48.2% female)
Individual Education Program: 329 (12.2%);
English Language Learner: 10 (0.4%); Migrant: n/a
Eligible for Free Lunch Program: 4 (0.1%)
Eligible for Reduced-Price Lunch Program: 0 (0.0%)
Teachers: 201.6 (13.3 to 1)
Librarians/Media Specialists: 3.5 (767.4 to 1)
Guidance Counselors: 5.0 (537.2 to 1)
Current Spending: ($ per student per year):
Total: $13,088; Instruction: $8,161; Support Services: $4,916
Enrollment, Drop-out Rates and Diploma Recipients by Race/Ethnicity

Category	Total	White	Black	Asian	AIAN	Hisp.
Enrollment (%)	100.0	94.1	1.2	2.1	0.1	2.5
Drop-out Rate (%)	1.3	1.3	0.0	6.7	n/a	0.0
H.S. Diplomas (#)	169	154	3	7	0	5

Smithtown CSD
26 New York Ave • Smithtown, NY 11787-3435
(631) 382-2005 • http://www.smithtown.k12.ny.us/
Grade Span: KG-12; **Agency Type:** 1
Schools: 13
9 Primary; 2 Middle; 1 High; 1 Other Level
13 Regular; 0 Special Education; 0 Vocational; 0 Alternative
0 Magnet; 0 Charter; 3 Title I Eligible; 0 School-wide Title I
Students: 9,789 (51.9% male; 48.1% female)
Individual Education Program: 1,281 (13.1%);
English Language Learner: 73 (0.7%); Migrant: n/a
Eligible for Free Lunch Program: 174 (1.8%)
Eligible for Reduced-Price Lunch Program: 143 (1.5%)
Teachers: 721.1 (13.6 to 1)
Librarians/Media Specialists: 14.5 (675.1 to 1)
Guidance Counselors: 22.0 (445.0 to 1)
Current Spending: ($ per student per year):
Total: $12,759; Instruction: $8,030; Support Services: $4,574

Enrollment, Drop-out Rates and Diploma Recipients by Race/Ethnicity

Category	Total	White	Black	Asian	AIAN	Hisp.
Enrollment (%)	100.0	95.9	0.5	1.9	0.0	1.7
Drop-out Rate (%)	0.5	0.4	0.0	0.0	n/a	3.4
H.S. Diplomas (#)	556	522	1	22	0	11

South Country CSD
189 N Dunton Ave • East Patchogue, NY 11772-5598
(631) 286-4310 • http://www.southcountry.org/
Grade Span: PK-12; **Agency Type:** 1
Schools: 7
3 Primary; 2 Middle; 1 High; 1 Other Level
6 Regular; 1 Special Education; 0 Vocational; 0 Alternative
0 Magnet; 0 Charter; 2 Title I Eligible; 0 School-wide Title I
Students: 4,768 (50.3% male; 49.7% female)
Individual Education Program: 714 (15.0%);
English Language Learner: 161 (3.4%); Migrant: n/a
Eligible for Free Lunch Program: 1,264 (26.5%)
Eligible for Reduced-Price Lunch Program: 387 (8.1%)
Teachers: 375.9 (12.7 to 1)
Librarians/Media Specialists: 4.6 (1,036.5 to 1)
Guidance Counselors: 8.0 (596.0 to 1)
Current Spending: ($ per student per year):
Total: $14,621; Instruction: $10,099; Support Services: $4,241
Enrollment, Drop-out Rates and Diploma Recipients by Race/Ethnicity

Category	Total	White	Black	Asian	AIAN	Hisp.
Enrollment (%)	100.0	55.5	27.6	2.2	0.3	14.4
Drop-out Rate (%)	3.7	2.1	7.7	0.0	n/a	7.2
H.S. Diplomas (#)	283	192	47	7	0	37

South Huntington UFSD
60 Weston St • Huntington Station, NY 11746-4098
(631) 425-5300 • http://www.shuntington.k12.ny.us/
Grade Span: KG-12; **Agency Type:** 1
Schools: 6
4 Primary; 1 Middle; 1 High; 0 Other Level
6 Regular; 0 Special Education; 0 Vocational; 0 Alternative
0 Magnet; 0 Charter; 2 Title I Eligible; 0 School-wide Title I
Students: 6,248 (51.9% male; 48.1% female)
Individual Education Program: 759 (12.1%);
English Language Learner: 446 (7.1%); Migrant: n/a
Eligible for Free Lunch Program: 1,066 (17.1%)
Eligible for Reduced-Price Lunch Program: 345 (5.5%)
Teachers: 469.9 (13.3 to 1)
Librarians/Media Specialists: 6.7 (932.5 to 1)
Guidance Counselors: 14.7 (425.0 to 1)
Current Spending: ($ per student per year):
Total: $13,519; Instruction: $8,542; Support Services: $4,715
Enrollment, Drop-out Rates and Diploma Recipients by Race/Ethnicity

Category	Total	White	Black	Asian	AIAN	Hisp.
Enrollment (%)	100.0	69.2	11.7	5.5	0.0	13.7
Drop-out Rate (%)	2.0	0.7	5.5	0.0	n/a	10.8
H.S. Diplomas (#)	317	257	30	12	0	18

Southampton UFSD
70 Leland Ln • Southampton, NY 11968-5089
(631) 591-4510 • http://www.southampton.k12.ny.us/
Grade Span: PK-12; **Agency Type:** 1
Schools: 3
1 Primary; 1 Middle; 1 High; 0 Other Level
3 Regular; 0 Special Education; 0 Vocational; 0 Alternative
0 Magnet; 0 Charter; 3 Title I Eligible; 0 School-wide Title I
Students: 1,754 (51.2% male; 48.8% female)
Individual Education Program: 239 (13.6%);
English Language Learner: 117 (6.7%); Migrant: n/a
Eligible for Free Lunch Program: 89 (5.1%)
Eligible for Reduced-Price Lunch Program: 50 (2.9%)
Teachers: 163.3 (10.7 to 1)
Librarians/Media Specialists: 2.8 (626.4 to 1)
Guidance Counselors: 7.9 (222.0 to 1)
Current Spending: ($ per student per year):
Total: $18,074; Instruction: $10,805; Support Services: $6,990
Enrollment, Drop-out Rates and Diploma Recipients by Race/Ethnicity

Category	Total	White	Black	Asian	AIAN	Hisp.
Enrollment (%)	100.0	71.0	8.4	1.0	6.6	13.0
Drop-out Rate (%)	1.2	0.7	1.8	0.0	0.0	3.8
H.S. Diplomas (#)	151	108	12	0	9	22

Three Village CSD
200 Nicolls Rd • East Setauket, NY 11733-9050
(631) 474-7514 • http://www.3villagecsd.k12.ny.us/
Grade Span: KG-12; **Agency Type:** 1
Schools: 8
5 Primary; 2 Middle; 1 High; 0 Other Level
8 Regular; 0 Special Education; 0 Vocational; 0 Alternative

0 Magnet; 0 Charter; 8 Title I Eligible; 0 School-wide Title I
Students: 7,993 (51.2% male; 48.8% female)
Individual Education Program: 1,023 (12.8%);
English Language Learner: 58 (0.7%); Migrant: n/a
Eligible for Free Lunch Program: 128 (1.6%)
Eligible for Reduced-Price Lunch Program: 89 (1.1%)
Teachers: 579.3 (13.8 to 1)
Librarians/Media Specialists: 8.5 (940.4 to 1)
Guidance Counselors: 17.0 (470.2 to 1)
Current Spending: ($ per student per year):
Total: $12,383; Instruction: $7,961; Support Services: $4,223

Enrollment, Drop-out Rates and Diploma Recipients by Race/Ethnicity

Category	Total	White	Black	Asian	AIAN	Hisp.
Enrollment (%)	100.0	90.5	1.6	5.6	0.2	2.1
Drop-out Rate (%)	0.0	0.0	0.0	0.0	n/a	0.0
H.S. Diplomas (#)	472	416	5	39	0	12

West Babylon UFSD

10 Farmingdale Rd • West Babylon, NY 11704-6289
(631) 321-3142 • http://www.westbabylon.k12.ny.us/
Grade Span: KG-12; **Agency Type:** 1
Schools: 7
5 Primary; 1 Middle; 1 High; 0 Other Level
7 Regular; 0 Special Education; 0 Vocational; 0 Alternative
0 Magnet; 0 Charter; 3 Title I Eligible; 0 School-wide Title I
Students: 4,924 (51.1% male; 48.9% female)
Individual Education Program: 594 (12.1%);
English Language Learner: 107 (2.2%); Migrant: n/a
Eligible for Free Lunch Program: 470 (9.5%)
Eligible for Reduced-Price Lunch Program: 221 (4.5%)
Teachers: 337.7 (14.6 to 1)
Librarians/Media Specialists: 7.6 (647.9 to 1)
Guidance Counselors: 7.0 (703.4 to 1)
Current Spending: ($ per student per year):
Total: $11,499; Instruction: $7,810; Support Services: $3,441

Enrollment, Drop-out Rates and Diploma Recipients by Race/Ethnicity

Category	Total	White	Black	Asian	AIAN	Hisp.
Enrollment (%)	100.0	85.5	4.6	2.5	0.0	7.3
Drop-out Rate (%)	1.7	1.9	1.4	0.0	n/a	0.0
H.S. Diplomas (#)	280	238	18	10	0	14

West Islip UFSD

100 Sherman Ave • West Islip, NY 11795-3237
(631) 893-3200
Grade Span: KG-12; **Agency Type:** 1
Schools: 9
6 Primary; 2 Middle; 1 High; 0 Other Level
9 Regular; 0 Special Education; 0 Vocational; 0 Alternative
0 Magnet; 0 Charter; 3 Title I Eligible; 0 School-wide Title I
Students: 5,893 (51.3% male; 48.7% female)
Individual Education Program: 712 (12.1%);
English Language Learner: 17 (0.3%); Migrant: n/a
Eligible for Free Lunch Program: 130 (2.2%)
Eligible for Reduced-Price Lunch Program: 86 (1.5%)
Teachers: 432.4 (13.6 to 1)
Librarians/Media Specialists: 8.5 (693.3 to 1)
Guidance Counselors: 11.9 (495.2 to 1)
Current Spending: ($ per student per year):
Total: $10,895; Instruction: $7,090; Support Services: $3,594

Enrollment, Drop-out Rates and Diploma Recipients by Race/Ethnicity

Category	Total	White	Black	Asian	AIAN	Hisp.
Enrollment (%)	100.0	96.8	0.5	1.1	0.0	1.6
Drop-out Rate (%)	0.8	0.8	0.0	0.0	n/a	0.0
H.S. Diplomas (#)	302	296	0	4	0	2

Westhampton Beach UFSD

340 Mill Rd • Westhampton Beach, NY 11978-2045
(631) 288-3800 • http://www.westhamptonbeach.k12.ny.us/
Grade Span: KG-12; **Agency Type:** 2
Schools: 3
1 Primary; 1 Middle; 1 High; 0 Other Level
3 Regular; 0 Special Education; 0 Vocational; 0 Alternative
0 Magnet; 0 Charter; 2 Title I Eligible; 0 School-wide Title I
Students: 1,815 (49.9% male; 50.1% female)
Individual Education Program: 218 (12.0%);
English Language Learner: 41 (2.3%); Migrant: n/a
Eligible for Free Lunch Program: 99 (5.5%)
Eligible for Reduced-Price Lunch Program: 61 (3.4%)
Teachers: 158.0 (11.5 to 1)
Librarians/Media Specialists: 2.0 (907.5 to 1)
Guidance Counselors: 7.0 (259.3 to 1)
Current Spending: ($ per student per year):
Total: $13,868; Instruction: $9,124; Support Services: $4,509

Enrollment, Drop-out Rates and Diploma Recipients by Race/Ethnicity

Category	Total	White	Black	Asian	AIAN	Hisp.
Enrollment (%)	100.0	86.7	5.3	2.3	0.0	5.7
Drop-out Rate (%)	0.7	0.8	0.0	0.0	n/a	0.0
H.S. Diplomas (#)	211	192	8	5	0	6

William Floyd UFSD

240 Mastic Beach Rd • Mastic Beach, NY 11951-1099
(631) 874-1201 • http://www.wfsd.k12.ny.us/
Grade Span: KG-12; **Agency Type:** 1
Schools: 7
4 Primary; 2 Middle; 1 High; 0 Other Level
7 Regular; 0 Special Education; 0 Vocational; 0 Alternative
0 Magnet; 0 Charter; 6 Title I Eligible; 0 School-wide Title I
Students: 10,267 (51.9% male; 48.1% female)
Individual Education Program: 1,708 (16.6%);
English Language Learner: 163 (1.6%); Migrant: n/a
Eligible for Free Lunch Program: 3,241 (31.6%)
Eligible for Reduced-Price Lunch Program: 1,352 (13.2%)
Teachers: 607.2 (16.9 to 1)
Librarians/Media Specialists: 9.4 (1,092.2 to 1)
Guidance Counselors: 16.0 (641.7 to 1)
Current Spending: ($ per student per year):
Total: $11,681; Instruction: $8,020; Support Services: $3,457

Enrollment, Drop-out Rates and Diploma Recipients by Race/Ethnicity

Category	Total	White	Black	Asian	AIAN	Hisp.
Enrollment (%)	100.0	76.8	8.1	1.9	0.1	13.2
Drop-out Rate (%)	3.5	2.7	7.9	0.0	n/a	6.9
H.S. Diplomas (#)	455	382	26	10	0	37

Wyandanch UFSD

1445 Straight Path • Wyandanch, NY 11798-3997
(631) 491-1013
Grade Span: PK-12; **Agency Type:** 2
Schools: 3
1 Primary; 1 Middle; 1 High; 0 Other Level
3 Regular; 0 Special Education; 0 Vocational; 0 Alternative
0 Magnet; 0 Charter; 3 Title I Eligible; 0 School-wide Title I
Students: 2,281 (50.5% male; 49.5% female)
Individual Education Program: 489 (21.4%);
English Language Learner: 181 (7.9%); Migrant: n/a
Eligible for Free Lunch Program: 1,465 (64.2%)
Eligible for Reduced-Price Lunch Program: 154 (6.8%)
Teachers: 161.6 (14.1 to 1)
Librarians/Media Specialists: 1.9 (1,200.5 to 1)
Guidance Counselors: 2.0 (1,140.5 to 1)
Current Spending: ($ per student per year):
Total: $15,626; Instruction: $9,917; Support Services: $5,189

Enrollment, Drop-out Rates and Diploma Recipients by Race/Ethnicity

Category	Total	White	Black	Asian	AIAN	Hisp.
Enrollment (%)	100.0	0.0	83.4	0.0	0.0	16.5
Drop-out Rate (%)	6.5	0.0	6.8	n/a	n/a	1.9
H.S. Diplomas (#)	66	0	58	0	0	8

Sullivan County

Liberty CSD

115 Buckley St • Liberty, NY 12754-1600
(845) 292-6990 • http://www.libertyk12.org/
Grade Span: PK-12; **Agency Type:** 1
Schools: 5
2 Primary; 1 Middle; 1 High; 1 Other Level
4 Regular; 0 Special Education; 0 Vocational; 1 Alternative
0 Magnet; 0 Charter; 1 Title I Eligible; 0 School-wide Title I
Students: 1,923 (51.9% male; 48.1% female)
Individual Education Program: 316 (16.4%);
English Language Learner: 49 (2.5%); Migrant: n/a
Eligible for Free Lunch Program: 582 (30.3%)
Eligible for Reduced-Price Lunch Program: 182 (9.5%)
Teachers: 145.6 (13.2 to 1)
Librarians/Media Specialists: 2.0 (961.5 to 1)
Guidance Counselors: 7.0 (274.7 to 1)
Current Spending: ($ per student per year):
Total: $12,860; Instruction: $9,047; Support Services: $3,466

Enrollment, Drop-out Rates and Diploma Recipients by Race/Ethnicity

Category	Total	White	Black	Asian	AIAN	Hisp.
Enrollment (%)	100.0	70.9	12.1	1.5	0.4	15.2
Drop-out Rate (%)	3.2	3.5	3.8	0.0	n/a	1.6
H.S. Diplomas (#)	77	63	7	3	0	4

Monticello CSD

237 Forestburgh Rd • Monticello, NY 12701
(845) 794-7700 • http://www.catskill.net/monti/welcome.html
Grade Span: KG-12; **Agency Type:** 1
Schools: 8

4 Primary; 1 Middle; 1 High; 2 Other Level
6 Regular; 0 Special Education; 0 Vocational; 2 Alternative
0 Magnet; 0 Charter; 4 Title I Eligible; 0 School-wide Title I

Students: 3,592 (51.1% male; 48.9% female)
Individual Education Program: 600 (16.7%);
English Language Learner: 178 (5.0%); Migrant: n/a
Eligible for Free Lunch Program: 1,336 (37.2%)
Eligible for Reduced-Price Lunch Program: 347 (9.7%)

Teachers: 303.4 (11.8 to 1)
Librarians/Media Specialists: 2.9 (1,238.6 to 1)
Guidance Counselors: 7.0 (513.1 to 1)
Current Spending: ($ per student per year):
Total: $11,380; Instruction: $7,793; Support Services: $3,297

Enrollment, Drop-out Rates and Diploma Recipients by Race/Ethnicity

Category	Total	White	Black	Asian	AIAN	Hisp.
Enrollment (%)	100.0	58.7	21.1	2.1	0.3	17.8
Drop-out Rate (%)	5.5	5.5	6.1	5.0	0.0	5.0
H.S. Diplomas (#)	141	112	14	0	0	15

Sullivan West CSD

308 Schoolhouse Rd • Jeffersonville, NY 12748-0308
(845) 482-4610
Grade Span: KG-12; **Agency Type:** 2
Schools: 5
3 Primary; 0 Middle; 2 High; 0 Other Level
5 Regular; 0 Special Education; 0 Vocational; 0 Alternative
0 Magnet; 0 Charter; 2 Title I Eligible; 0 School-wide Title I

Students: 1,617 (50.0% male; 50.0% female)
Individual Education Program: 223 (13.8%);
English Language Learner: 6 (0.4%); Migrant: n/a
Eligible for Free Lunch Program: 241 (14.9%)
Eligible for Reduced-Price Lunch Program: 143 (8.8%)

Teachers: 146.2 (11.1 to 1)
Librarians/Media Specialists: 2.0 (808.5 to 1)
Guidance Counselors: 5.0 (323.4 to 1)
Current Spending: ($ per student per year):
Total: $12,154; Instruction: $8,245; Support Services: $3,602

Enrollment, Drop-out Rates and Diploma Recipients by Race/Ethnicity

Category	Total	White	Black	Asian	AIAN	Hisp.
Enrollment (%)	100.0	92.2	2.7	1.2	0.1	3.7
Drop-out Rate (%)	2.1	2.3	0.0	0.0	n/a	0.0
H.S. Diplomas (#)	119	110	1	3	0	5

Tioga County

Owego-Apalachin CSD

36 Talcott St • Owego, NY 13827-9965
(607) 687-6224 • http://www.oacsd.org/
Grade Span: PK-12; **Agency Type:** 1
Schools: 5
2 Primary; 1 Middle; 1 High; 1 Other Level
4 Regular; 0 Special Education; 0 Vocational; 1 Alternative
0 Magnet; 0 Charter; 3 Title I Eligible; 0 School-wide Title I

Students: 2,415 (52.3% male; 47.7% female)
Individual Education Program: 372 (15.4%);
English Language Learner: 7 (0.3%); Migrant: n/a
Eligible for Free Lunch Program: 427 (17.7%)
Eligible for Reduced-Price Lunch Program: 163 (6.7%)

Teachers: 176.6 (13.7 to 1)
Librarians/Media Specialists: 3.8 (635.5 to 1)
Guidance Counselors: 4.1 (589.0 to 1)
Current Spending: ($ per student per year):
Total: $10,051; Instruction: $6,517; Support Services: $3,226

Enrollment, Drop-out Rates and Diploma Recipients by Race/Ethnicity

Category	Total	White	Black	Asian	AIAN	Hisp.
Enrollment (%)	100.0	96.1	1.6	1.2	0.0	1.0
Drop-out Rate (%)	1.6	1.5	14.3	0.0	n/a	n/a
H.S. Diplomas (#)	166	160	2	3	1	0

Waverly CSD

15 Frederick St • Waverly, NY 14892-1294
(607) 565-2841 • http://www.sctboces.org/waverly/
Grade Span: KG-12; **Agency Type:** 1
Schools: 5
3 Primary; 1 Middle; 1 High; 0 Other Level
5 Regular; 0 Special Education; 0 Vocational; 0 Alternative
0 Magnet; 0 Charter; 4 Title I Eligible; 0 School-wide Title I

Students: 1,818 (52.4% male; 47.6% female)
Individual Education Program: 192 (10.6%);
English Language Learner: 0 (0.0%); Migrant: n/a
Eligible for Free Lunch Program: 398 (21.9%)
Eligible for Reduced-Price Lunch Program: 193 (10.6%)

Teachers: 130.8 (13.9 to 1)
Librarians/Media Specialists: 1.0 (1,818.0 to 1)
Guidance Counselors: 2.0 (909.0 to 1)
Current Spending: ($ per student per year):
Total: $8,630; Instruction: $5,719; Support Services: $2,627

Enrollment, Drop-out Rates and Diploma Recipients by Race/Ethnicity

Category	Total	White	Black	Asian	AIAN	Hisp.
Enrollment (%)	100.0	98.1	0.9	0.5	0.2	0.3
Drop-out Rate (%)	7.0	6.9	0.0	0.0	n/a	0.0
H.S. Diplomas (#)	95	95	0	0	0	0

Tompkins County

Dryden CSD

District Office • Dryden, NY 13053-0088
(607) 844-5361 • http://www.drydenschools.org/
Grade Span: KG-12; **Agency Type:** 1
Schools: 5
3 Primary; 1 Middle; 1 High; 0 Other Level
5 Regular; 0 Special Education; 0 Vocational; 0 Alternative
0 Magnet; 0 Charter; 2 Title I Eligible; 0 School-wide Title I

Students: 1,928 (52.0% male; 48.0% female)
Individual Education Program: 316 (16.4%);
English Language Learner: 7 (0.4%); Migrant: n/a
Eligible for Free Lunch Program: 394 (20.4%)
Eligible for Reduced-Price Lunch Program: 106 (5.5%)

Teachers: 173.7 (11.1 to 1)
Librarians/Media Specialists: 1.3 (1,483.1 to 1)
Guidance Counselors: 6.0 (321.3 to 1)
Current Spending: ($ per student per year):
Total: $10,223; Instruction: $6,315; Support Services: $3,580

Enrollment, Drop-out Rates and Diploma Recipients by Race/Ethnicity

Category	Total	White	Black	Asian	AIAN	Hisp.
Enrollment (%)	100.0	96.5	2.0	0.5	0.3	0.7
Drop-out Rate (%)	5.3	5.4	0.0	0.0	n/a	0.0
H.S. Diplomas (#)	106	105	0	0	0	1

Ithaca City SD

400 Lake St • Ithaca, NY 14851-0549
(607) 274-2101 • http://www.icsd.k12.ny.us/
Grade Span: PK-12; **Agency Type:** 1
Schools: 16
8 Primary; 2 Middle; 1 High; 5 Other Level
11 Regular; 0 Special Education; 0 Vocational; 5 Alternative
0 Magnet; 0 Charter; 5 Title I Eligible; 0 School-wide Title I

Students: 5,772 (52.1% male; 47.9% female)
Individual Education Program: 807 (14.0%);
English Language Learner: 348 (6.0%); Migrant: n/a
Eligible for Free Lunch Program: 1,292 (22.4%)
Eligible for Reduced-Price Lunch Program: 380 (6.6%)

Teachers: 489.4 (11.8 to 1)
Librarians/Media Specialists: 12.4 (465.5 to 1)
Guidance Counselors: 11.6 (497.6 to 1)
Current Spending: ($ per student per year):
Total: $11,601; Instruction: $7,725; Support Services: $3,559

Enrollment, Drop-out Rates and Diploma Recipients by Race/Ethnicity

Category	Total	White	Black	Asian	AIAN	Hisp.
Enrollment (%)	100.0	73.7	12.0	9.7	0.9	3.7
Drop-out Rate (%)	1.4	1.3	2.8	1.7	0.0	0.0
H.S. Diplomas (#)	326	282	15	23	1	5

Lansing CSD

264 Ridge Rd • Lansing, NY 14882-9021
(607) 533-4294
Grade Span: KG-12; **Agency Type:** 2
Schools: 5
1 Primary; 1 Middle; 3 High; 0 Other Level
3 Regular; 0 Special Education; 0 Vocational; 2 Alternative
0 Magnet; 0 Charter; 2 Title I Eligible; 0 School-wide Title I

Students: 1,583 (52.0% male; 48.0% female)
Individual Education Program: 167 (10.5%);
English Language Learner: 5 (0.3%); Migrant: n/a
Eligible for Free Lunch Program: 115 (7.3%)
Eligible for Reduced-Price Lunch Program: 40 (2.5%)

Teachers: 116.9 (13.5 to 1)
Librarians/Media Specialists: 3.0 (527.7 to 1)
Guidance Counselors: 2.0 (791.5 to 1)
Current Spending: ($ per student per year):
Total: $10,229; Instruction: $6,832; Support Services: $3,078

Enrollment, Drop-out Rates and Diploma Recipients by Race/Ethnicity

Category	Total	White	Black	Asian	AIAN	Hisp.
Enrollment (%)	100.0	83.9	10.0	2.3	0.1	3.6
Drop-out Rate (%)	1.6	1.4	20.0	0.0	n/a	0.0
H.S. Diplomas (#)	110	105	2	2	0	1

Ulster County

Ellenville CSD

28 Maple Ave • Ellenville, NY 12428-2000
(845) 647-0100 • http://www.ecs.k12.ny.us/
Grade Span: KG-12; **Agency Type:** 1
Schools: 5
1 Primary; 1 Middle; 1 High; 2 Other Level
3 Regular; 0 Special Education; 0 Vocational; 2 Alternative
0 Magnet; 0 Charter; 3 Title I Eligible; 0 School-wide Title I
Students: 1,878 (51.2% male; 48.8% female)
Individual Education Program: 230 (12.2%);
English Language Learner: 95 (5.1%); Migrant: n/a
Eligible for Free Lunch Program: 561 (29.9%)
Eligible for Reduced-Price Lunch Program: 182 (9.7%)
Teachers: 139.0 (13.5 to 1)
Librarians/Media Specialists: 3.8 (494.2 to 1)
Guidance Counselors: 4.0 (469.5 to 1)
Current Spending: ($ per student per year):
Total: $12,931; Instruction: $8,691; Support Services: $4,004
Enrollment, Drop-out Rates and Diploma Recipients by Race/Ethnicity

Category	Total	White	Black	Asian	AIAN	Hisp.
Enrollment (%)	100.0	64.2	10.5	1.2	0.5	23.6
Drop-out Rate (%)	1.3	1.0	1.6	0.0	n/a	2.2
H.S. Diplomas (#)	78	59	2	2	0	15

Highland CSD

320 Pancake Hollow Rd • Highland, NY 12528-2317
(845) 691-1012 • http://www.highland-k12.org/
Grade Span: KG-12; **Agency Type:** 2
Schools: 5
1 Primary; 1 Middle; 2 High; 1 Other Level
3 Regular; 0 Special Education; 0 Vocational; 2 Alternative
0 Magnet; 0 Charter; 1 Title I Eligible; 0 School-wide Title I
Students: 2,076 (54.9% male; 45.1% female)
Individual Education Program: 322 (15.5%);
English Language Learner: 16 (0.8%); Migrant: n/a
Eligible for Free Lunch Program: 256 (12.3%)
Eligible for Reduced-Price Lunch Program: 152 (7.3%)
Teachers: 128.6 (16.1 to 1)
Librarians/Media Specialists: 1.8 (1,153.3 to 1)
Guidance Counselors: 3.0 (692.0 to 1)
Current Spending: ($ per student per year):
Total: $10,652; Instruction: $7,292; Support Services: $3,082
Enrollment, Drop-out Rates and Diploma Recipients by Race/Ethnicity

Category	Total	White	Black	Asian	AIAN	Hisp.
Enrollment (%)	100.0	84.1	8.4	1.4	0.1	6.0
Drop-out Rate (%)	3.0	3.0	2.4	0.0	n/a	7.1
H.S. Diplomas (#)	140	123	12	1	0	4

Kingston City SD

61 Crown St • Kingston, NY 12401-3833
(845) 339-3000
Grade Span: PK-12; **Agency Type:** 1
Schools: 18
11 Primary; 2 Middle; 1 High; 4 Other Level
14 Regular; 0 Special Education; 0 Vocational; 4 Alternative
0 Magnet; 0 Charter; 5 Title I Eligible; 0 School-wide Title I
Students: 8,245 (50.5% male; 49.5% female)
Individual Education Program: 1,248 (15.1%);
English Language Learner: 125 (1.5%); Migrant: n/a
Eligible for Free Lunch Program: 2,147 (26.0%)
Eligible for Reduced-Price Lunch Program: 754 (9.1%)
Teachers: 585.4 (14.1 to 1)
Librarians/Media Specialists: 11.9 (692.9 to 1)
Guidance Counselors: 15.1 (546.0 to 1)
Current Spending: ($ per student per year):
Total: $10,340; Instruction: $7,328; Support Services: $2,785
Enrollment, Drop-out Rates and Diploma Recipients by Race/Ethnicity

Category	Total	White	Black	Asian	AIAN	Hisp.
Enrollment (%)	100.0	75.7	16.1	2.1	0.4	5.8
Drop-out Rate (%)	5.0	4.2	7.7	1.8	0.0	17.8
H.S. Diplomas (#)	485	418	44	13	2	8

Marlboro CSD

50 Cross Rd • Marlboro, NY 12542-6009
(845) 236-5802
Grade Span: KG-12; **Agency Type:** 1
Schools: 5
3 Primary; 1 Middle; 1 High; 0 Other Level
5 Regular; 0 Special Education; 0 Vocational; 0 Alternative
0 Magnet; 0 Charter; 2 Title I Eligible; 0 School-wide Title I
Students: 2,067 (50.0% male; 50.0% female)
Individual Education Program: 324 (15.7%);
English Language Learner: 46 (2.2%); Migrant: n/a
Eligible for Free Lunch Program: 176 (8.5%)
Eligible for Reduced-Price Lunch Program: 95 (4.6%)
Teachers: 157.1 (13.2 to 1)
Librarians/Media Specialists: 3.0 (689.0 to 1)
Guidance Counselors: 4.0 (516.8 to 1)
Current Spending: ($ per student per year):
Total: $11,342; Instruction: $7,609; Support Services: $3,500
Enrollment, Drop-out Rates and Diploma Recipients by Race/Ethnicity

Category	Total	White	Black	Asian	AIAN	Hisp.
Enrollment (%)	100.0	89.7	4.8	0.7	0.2	4.6
Drop-out Rate (%)	3.7	4.0	0.0	0.0	n/a	2.9
H.S. Diplomas (#)	106	98	2	2	0	4

New Paltz CSD

196 Main St • New Paltz, NY 12561-1200
(845) 256-4020 • http://www.newpaltz.k12.ny.us/
Grade Span: KG-12; **Agency Type:** 1
Schools: 5
2 Primary; 1 Middle; 1 High; 1 Other Level
4 Regular; 0 Special Education; 0 Vocational; 1 Alternative
0 Magnet; 0 Charter; 3 Title I Eligible; 0 School-wide Title I
Students: 2,386 (51.6% male; 48.4% female)
Individual Education Program: 364 (15.3%);
English Language Learner: 41 (1.7%); Migrant: n/a
Eligible for Free Lunch Program: 311 (13.0%)
Eligible for Reduced-Price Lunch Program: 107 (4.5%)
Teachers: 168.1 (14.2 to 1)
Librarians/Media Specialists: 4.0 (596.5 to 1)
Guidance Counselors: 6.0 (397.7 to 1)
Current Spending: ($ per student per year):
Total: $11,055; Instruction: $7,391; Support Services: $3,404
Enrollment, Drop-out Rates and Diploma Recipients by Race/Ethnicity

Category	Total	White	Black	Asian	AIAN	Hisp.
Enrollment (%)	100.0	85.2	6.0	2.8	0.1	5.9
Drop-out Rate (%)	1.5	1.5	4.0	0.0	0.0	0.0
H.S. Diplomas (#)	118	96	9	5	2	6

Onteora CSD

4166 Rt 28 • Boiceville, NY 12412-0300
(845) 657-6383 • http://www.onteora.k12.ny.us/
Grade Span: KG-12; **Agency Type:** 1
Schools: 6
4 Primary; 1 Middle; 1 High; 0 Other Level
6 Regular; 0 Special Education; 0 Vocational; 0 Alternative
0 Magnet; 0 Charter; 4 Title I Eligible; 0 School-wide Title I
Students: 2,228 (50.6% male; 49.4% female)
Individual Education Program: 362 (16.2%);
English Language Learner: 22 (1.0%); Migrant: n/a
Eligible for Free Lunch Program: 322 (14.5%)
Eligible for Reduced-Price Lunch Program: 160 (7.2%)
Teachers: 191.6 (11.6 to 1)
Librarians/Media Specialists: 3.8 (586.3 to 1)
Guidance Counselors: 5.0 (445.6 to 1)
Current Spending: ($ per student per year):
Total: $14,010; Instruction: $9,307; Support Services: $4,384
Enrollment, Drop-out Rates and Diploma Recipients by Race/Ethnicity

Category	Total	White	Black	Asian	AIAN	Hisp.
Enrollment (%)	100.0	91.2	3.2	2.3	0.3	3.0
Drop-out Rate (%)	5.3	6.0	0.0	0.0	n/a	0.0
H.S. Diplomas (#)	112	104	4	3	0	1

Rondout Valley CSD

122 Kyserike Rd • Accord, NY 12404-0009
(845) 687-2400 • http://rondout.k12.ny.us/
Grade Span: KG-12; **Agency Type:** 1
Schools: 6
3 Primary; 2 Middle; 1 High; 0 Other Level
6 Regular; 0 Special Education; 0 Vocational; 0 Alternative
0 Magnet; 0 Charter; 4 Title I Eligible; 0 School-wide Title I
Students: 2,801 (53.1% male; 46.9% female)
Individual Education Program: 504 (18.0%);
English Language Learner: 22 (0.8%); Migrant: n/a
Eligible for Free Lunch Program: 320 (11.4%)
Eligible for Reduced-Price Lunch Program: 227 (8.1%)
Teachers: 213.2 (13.1 to 1)
Librarians/Media Specialists: 4.7 (596.0 to 1)
Guidance Counselors: 10.5 (266.8 to 1)
Current Spending: ($ per student per year):
Total: $12,551; Instruction: $8,547; Support Services: $3,757
Enrollment, Drop-out Rates and Diploma Recipients by Race/Ethnicity

Category	Total	White	Black	Asian	AIAN	Hisp.
Enrollment (%)	100.0	92.1	2.9	1.1	0.2	3.7
Drop-out Rate (%)	2.3	2.2	0.0	0.0	n/a	22.2
H.S. Diplomas (#)	191	179	5	2	0	5

Saugerties CSD

Washington Ave Ext • Saugerties, NY 12477-0577
(845) 246-1043 • http://www.saugerties.k12.ny.us/
Grade Span: KG-12; **Agency Type:** 1
Schools: 6
4 Primary; 1 Middle; 1 High; 0 Other Level
6 Regular; 0 Special Education; 0 Vocational; 0 Alternative
0 Magnet; 0 Charter; 3 Title I Eligible; 0 School-wide Title I
Students: 3,413 (51.6% male; 48.4% female)
Individual Education Program: 371 (10.9%);
English Language Learner: 18 (0.5%); Migrant: n/a
Eligible for Free Lunch Program: 430 (12.6%)
Eligible for Reduced-Price Lunch Program: 216 (6.3%)
Teachers: 229.2 (14.9 to 1)
Librarians/Media Specialists: 5.8 (588.4 to 1)
Guidance Counselors: 7.0 (487.6 to 1)
Current Spending: ($ per student per year):
Total: $9,040; Instruction: $6,156; Support Services: $2,623
Enrollment, Drop-out Rates and Diploma Recipients by Race/Ethnicity

Category	Total	White	Black	Asian	AIAN	Hisp.
Enrollment (%)	100.0	93.7	2.6	1.5	0.1	2.2
Drop-out Rate (%)	2.2	2.2	3.4	0.0	n/a	0.0
H.S. Diplomas (#)	190	183	7	0	0	0

Wallkill CSD

19 Main St • Wallkill, NY 12589-0310
(845) 895-3301 • http://wallkillcsd.k12.ny.us/
Grade Span: KG-12; **Agency Type:** 1
Schools: 8
3 Primary; 1 Middle; 1 High; 3 Other Level
5 Regular; 0 Special Education; 0 Vocational; 3 Alternative
0 Magnet; 0 Charter; 3 Title I Eligible; 0 School-wide Title I
Students: 3,658 (51.8% male; 48.2% female)
Individual Education Program: 521 (14.2%);
English Language Learner: 54 (1.5%); Migrant: n/a
Eligible for Free Lunch Program: 374 (10.2%)
Eligible for Reduced-Price Lunch Program: 177 (4.8%)
Teachers: 248.5 (14.7 to 1)
Librarians/Media Specialists: 2.0 (1,829.0 to 1)
Guidance Counselors: 7.0 (522.6 to 1)
Current Spending: ($ per student per year):
Total: $10,313; Instruction: $6,839; Support Services: $3,209
Enrollment, Drop-out Rates and Diploma Recipients by Race/Ethnicity

Category	Total	White	Black	Asian	AIAN	Hisp.
Enrollment (%)	100.0	81.2	4.6	0.4	0.0	13.7
Drop-out Rate (%)	2.8	2.4	10.5	0.0	0.0	2.5
H.S. Diplomas (#)	203	172	10	1	0	20

Warren County

Glens Falls City SD

15 Quade St • Glens Falls, NY 12801-2724
(518) 792-1212 • http://www.gfsd.org/
Grade Span: KG-12; **Agency Type:** 1
Schools: 6
4 Primary; 1 Middle; 1 High; 0 Other Level
6 Regular; 0 Special Education; 0 Vocational; 0 Alternative
0 Magnet; 0 Charter; 3 Title I Eligible; 0 School-wide Title I
Students: 2,607 (51.4% male; 48.6% female)
Individual Education Program: 372 (14.3%);
English Language Learner: 3 (0.1%); Migrant: n/a
Eligible for Free Lunch Program: 515 (19.8%)
Eligible for Reduced-Price Lunch Program: 137 (5.3%)
Teachers: 208.1 (12.5 to 1)
Librarians/Media Specialists: 3.8 (686.1 to 1)
Guidance Counselors: 7.0 (372.4 to 1)
Current Spending: ($ per student per year):
Total: $8,939; Instruction: $6,374; Support Services: $2,291
Enrollment, Drop-out Rates and Diploma Recipients by Race/Ethnicity

Category	Total	White	Black	Asian	AIAN	Hisp.
Enrollment (%)	100.0	94.8	2.7	0.9	0.0	1.5
Drop-out Rate (%)	0.7	0.7	0.0	0.0	n/a	0.0
H.S. Diplomas (#)	147	140	3	1	0	3

Queensbury UFSD

429 Aviation Rd • Queensbury, NY 12804-2914
(518) 742-6000 • http://www.queensburyschool.org/
Grade Span: KG-12; **Agency Type:** 1
Schools: 6
1 Primary; 2 Middle; 1 High; 2 Other Level
4 Regular; 0 Special Education; 0 Vocational; 2 Alternative
0 Magnet; 0 Charter; 3 Title I Eligible; 0 School-wide Title I
Students: 3,836 (50.7% male; 49.3% female)
Individual Education Program: 458 (11.9%);
English Language Learner: 3 (0.1%); Migrant: n/a
Eligible for Free Lunch Program: 379 (9.9%)
Eligible for Reduced-Price Lunch Program: 161 (4.2%)
Teachers: 250.1 (15.3 to 1)
Librarians/Media Specialists: 3.8 (1,009.5 to 1)
Guidance Counselors: 9.0 (426.2 to 1)
Current Spending: ($ per student per year):
Total: $7,989; Instruction: $5,380; Support Services: $2,440
Enrollment, Drop-out Rates and Diploma Recipients by Race/Ethnicity

Category	Total	White	Black	Asian	AIAN	Hisp.
Enrollment (%)	100.0	96.3	1.4	1.1	0.0	1.1
Drop-out Rate (%)	3.4	3.5	0.0	0.0	0.0	0.0
H.S. Diplomas (#)	211	201	1	7	0	2

Washington County

Hudson Falls CSD

PO Box 710 • Hudson Falls, NY 12839-0710
(518) 747-2121 • http://www.hudsonfalls.k12.ny.us/
Grade Span: KG-12; **Agency Type:** 1
Schools: 5
2 Primary; 2 Middle; 1 High; 0 Other Level
5 Regular; 0 Special Education; 0 Vocational; 0 Alternative
0 Magnet; 0 Charter; 1 Title I Eligible; 0 School-wide Title I
Students: 2,361 (51.9% male; 48.1% female)
Individual Education Program: 391 (16.6%);
English Language Learner: 1 (<0.1%); Migrant: n/a
Eligible for Free Lunch Program: 688 (29.1%)
Eligible for Reduced-Price Lunch Program: 338 (14.3%)
Teachers: 165.9 (14.2 to 1)
Librarians/Media Specialists: 2.0 (1,180.5 to 1)
Guidance Counselors: 4.0 (590.3 to 1)
Current Spending: ($ per student per year):
Total: $9,573; Instruction: $6,058; Support Services: $3,180
Enrollment, Drop-out Rates and Diploma Recipients by Race/Ethnicity

Category	Total	White	Black	Asian	AIAN	Hisp.
Enrollment (%)	100.0	98.3	1.2	0.4	0.0	0.1
Drop-out Rate (%)	2.5	2.6	0.0	0.0	n/a	0.0
H.S. Diplomas (#)	128	128	0	0	0	0

Wayne County

Newark CSD

100 E Miller St • Newark, NY 14513-1599
(315) 332-3217 • http://www.newark.k12.ny.us/
Grade Span: PK-12; **Agency Type:** 1
Schools: 5
3 Primary; 1 Middle; 1 High; 0 Other Level
5 Regular; 0 Special Education; 0 Vocational; 0 Alternative
0 Magnet; 0 Charter; 2 Title I Eligible; 0 School-wide Title I
Students: 2,735 (51.0% male; 49.0% female)
Individual Education Program: 458 (16.7%);
English Language Learner: 58 (2.1%); Migrant: n/a
Eligible for Free Lunch Program: 551 (20.1%)
Eligible for Reduced-Price Lunch Program: 248 (9.1%)
Teachers: 222.3 (12.3 to 1)
Librarians/Media Specialists: 4.0 (683.8 to 1)
Guidance Counselors: 7.0 (390.7 to 1)
Current Spending: ($ per student per year):
Total: $10,125; Instruction: $6,861; Support Services: $3,022
Enrollment, Drop-out Rates and Diploma Recipients by Race/Ethnicity

Category	Total	White	Black	Asian	AIAN	Hisp.
Enrollment (%)	100.0	83.3	8.8	0.8	0.4	6.6
Drop-out Rate (%)	3.1	2.6	8.2	7.7	0.0	5.1
H.S. Diplomas (#)	165	154	5	2	0	4

North Rose-Wolcott CSD

11669 Saltr-Colvn Rd • Wolcott, NY 14590-9398
(315) 594-3141
Grade Span: KG-12; **Agency Type:** 1
Schools: 4
2 Primary; 1 Middle; 1 High; 0 Other Level
4 Regular; 0 Special Education; 0 Vocational; 0 Alternative
0 Magnet; 0 Charter; 2 Title I Eligible; 0 School-wide Title I
Students: 1,675 (50.9% male; 49.1% female)
Individual Education Program: 231 (13.8%);
English Language Learner: 30 (1.8%); Migrant: n/a
Eligible for Free Lunch Program: 443 (26.4%)
Eligible for Reduced-Price Lunch Program: 214 (12.8%)
Teachers: 148.9 (11.2 to 1)
Librarians/Media Specialists: 1.0 (1,675.0 to 1)
Guidance Counselors: 5.0 (335.0 to 1)
Current Spending: ($ per student per year):
Total: $10,213; Instruction: $6,358; Support Services: $3,602

Enrollment, Drop-out Rates and Diploma Recipients by Race/Ethnicity

Category	Total	White	Black	Asian	AIAN	Hisp.
Enrollment (%)	100.0	92.1	3.4	0.7	0.3	3.6
Drop-out Rate (%)	9.7	9.8	7.4	0.0	0.0	22.2
H.S. Diplomas (#)	95	89	2	2	0	2

Palmyra-Macedon CSD

151 Hyde Pky • Palmyra, NY 14522-1297
(315) 597-3401 • http://www.palmac.k12.ny.us/
Grade Span: KG-12; **Agency Type:** 1
Schools: 4
2 Primary; 1 Middle; 1 High; 0 Other Level
4 Regular; 0 Special Education; 0 Vocational; 0 Alternative
0 Magnet; 0 Charter; 3 Title I Eligible; 0 School-wide Title I
Students: 2,261 (52.8% male; 47.2% female)
Individual Education Program: 263 (11.6%);
English Language Learner: 19 (0.8%); Migrant: n/a
Eligible for Free Lunch Program: 226 (10.0%)
Eligible for Reduced-Price Lunch Program: 111 (4.9%)
Teachers: 185.7 (12.2 to 1)
Librarians/Media Specialists: 3.8 (595.0 to 1)
Guidance Counselors: 5.0 (452.2 to 1)
Current Spending: ($ per student per year):
Total: $9,726; Instruction: $6,007; Support Services: $3,482

Enrollment, Drop-out Rates and Diploma Recipients by Race/Ethnicity

Category	Total	White	Black	Asian	AIAN	Hisp.
Enrollment (%)	100.0	96.4	1.2	1.2	0.3	0.9
Drop-out Rate (%)	2.4	2.2	0.0	7.7	0.0	50.0
H.S. Diplomas (#)	139	139	0	0	0	0

Wayne CSD

6076 Ontario Ctr Rd • Ontario Center, NY 14520-0155
(315) 524-0201 • http://wayne.k12.ny.us/default.htm
Grade Span: KG-12; **Agency Type:** 1
Schools: 5
3 Primary; 1 Middle; 1 High; 0 Other Level
5 Regular; 0 Special Education; 0 Vocational; 0 Alternative
0 Magnet; 0 Charter; 2 Title I Eligible; 0 School-wide Title I
Students: 2,809 (52.9% male; 47.1% female)
Individual Education Program: 444 (15.8%);
English Language Learner: 1 (<0.1%); Migrant: n/a
Eligible for Free Lunch Program: 225 (8.0%)
Eligible for Reduced-Price Lunch Program: 148 (5.3%)
Teachers: 217.9 (12.9 to 1)
Librarians/Media Specialists: 4.6 (610.7 to 1)
Guidance Counselors: 11.3 (248.6 to 1)
Current Spending: ($ per student per year):
Total: $8,638; Instruction: $5,588; Support Services: $2,773

Enrollment, Drop-out Rates and Diploma Recipients by Race/Ethnicity

Category	Total	White	Black	Asian	AIAN	Hisp.
Enrollment (%)	100.0	96.8	1.8	0.0	0.5	0.9
Drop-out Rate (%)	3.2	3.2	4.8	0.0	0.0	0.0
H.S. Diplomas (#)	163	158	2	2	0	1

Westchester County

Ardsley UFSD

500 Farm Rd • Ardsley, NY 10502-1410
(914) 693-6300 • http://www.ardsleyschools.k12.ny.us/
Grade Span: KG-12; **Agency Type:** 1
Schools: 3
1 Primary; 1 Middle; 1 High; 0 Other Level
3 Regular; 0 Special Education; 0 Vocational; 0 Alternative
0 Magnet; 0 Charter; 1 Title I Eligible; 0 School-wide Title I
Students: 2,285 (53.0% male; 47.0% female)
Individual Education Program: 225 (9.8%);
English Language Learner: 36 (1.6%); Migrant: n/a
Eligible for Free Lunch Program: 28 (1.2%)
Eligible for Reduced-Price Lunch Program: 15 (0.7%)
Teachers: 180.0 (12.7 to 1)
Librarians/Media Specialists: 2.6 (878.8 to 1)
Guidance Counselors: 9.0 (253.9 to 1)
Current Spending: ($ per student per year):
Total: $12,841; Instruction: $8,507; Support Services: $4,149

Enrollment, Drop-out Rates and Diploma Recipients by Race/Ethnicity

Category	Total	White	Black	Asian	AIAN	Hisp.
Enrollment (%)	100.0	83.6	3.0	9.8	0.0	3.5
Drop-out Rate (%)	0.0	0.0	0.0	0.0	n/a	0.0
H.S. Diplomas (#)	123	102	3	15	0	3

Bedford CSD

Fox Ln Campus • Mount Kisco, NY 10549-0180
(914) 241-6010 • http://www.bedford.k12.ny.us/default.html
Grade Span: PK-12; **Agency Type:** 1
Schools: 10
5 Primary; 1 Middle; 1 High; 3 Other Level
7 Regular; 0 Special Education; 0 Vocational; 3 Alternative
0 Magnet; 0 Charter; 1 Title I Eligible; 0 School-wide Title I
Students: 4,075 (51.8% male; 48.2% female)
Individual Education Program: 526 (12.9%);
English Language Learner: 313 (7.7%); Migrant: n/a
Eligible for Free Lunch Program: 366 (9.0%)
Eligible for Reduced-Price Lunch Program: 191 (4.7%)
Teachers: 349.0 (11.7 to 1)
Librarians/Media Specialists: 6.6 (617.4 to 1)
Guidance Counselors: 9.6 (424.5 to 1)
Current Spending: ($ per student per year):
Total: $16,626; Instruction: $10,485; Support Services: $5,921

Enrollment, Drop-out Rates and Diploma Recipients by Race/Ethnicity

Category	Total	White	Black	Asian	AIAN	Hisp.
Enrollment (%)	100.0	73.9	6.2	4.2	0.2	15.4
Drop-out Rate (%)	0.9	0.4	5.3	2.2	n/a	0.7
H.S. Diplomas (#)	247	189	15	17	0	26

Briarcliff Manor UFSD

45 Ingham Rd • Briarcliff Manor, NY 10510-2221
(914) 941-8880
Grade Span: KG-12; **Agency Type:** 2
Schools: 3
1 Primary; 1 Middle; 1 High; 0 Other Level
3 Regular; 0 Special Education; 0 Vocational; 0 Alternative
0 Magnet; 0 Charter; 1 Title I Eligible; 0 School-wide Title I
Students: 1,690 (52.2% male; 47.8% female)
Individual Education Program: 176 (10.4%);
English Language Learner: 13 (0.8%); Migrant: n/a
Eligible for Free Lunch Program: 0 (0.0%)
Eligible for Reduced-Price Lunch Program: 6 (0.4%)
Teachers: 141.0 (12.0 to 1)
Librarians/Media Specialists: 3.0 (563.3 to 1)
Guidance Counselors: 3.0 (563.3 to 1)
Current Spending: ($ per student per year):
Total: $14,621; Instruction: $9,228; Support Services: $5,249

Enrollment, Drop-out Rates and Diploma Recipients by Race/Ethnicity

Category	Total	White	Black	Asian	AIAN	Hisp.
Enrollment (%)	100.0	93.0	1.0	4.9	0.0	1.1
Drop-out Rate (%)	n/a	n/a	n/a	n/a	n/a	n/a
H.S. Diplomas (#)	113	93	4	13	0	3

Byram Hills CSD

10 Tripp Ln • Armonk, NY 10504-2512
(914) 273-4082 • http://www.byramhills.org/
Grade Span: KG-12; **Agency Type:** 1
Schools: 4
2 Primary; 1 Middle; 1 High; 0 Other Level
4 Regular; 0 Special Education; 0 Vocational; 0 Alternative
0 Magnet; 0 Charter; 1 Title I Eligible; 0 School-wide Title I
Students: 2,657 (50.1% male; 49.9% female)
Individual Education Program: 333 (12.5%);
English Language Learner: 12 (0.5%); Migrant: n/a
Eligible for Free Lunch Program: 5 (0.2%)
Eligible for Reduced-Price Lunch Program: 0 (0.0%)
Teachers: 198.5 (13.4 to 1)
Librarians/Media Specialists: 4.6 (577.6 to 1)
Guidance Counselors: 6.0 (442.8 to 1)
Current Spending: ($ per student per year):
Total: $12,156; Instruction: $7,489; Support Services: $4,507

Enrollment, Drop-out Rates and Diploma Recipients by Race/Ethnicity

Category	Total	White	Black	Asian	AIAN	Hisp.
Enrollment (%)	100.0	94.4	0.3	3.7	0.0	1.7
Drop-out Rate (%)	0.0	0.0	0.0	0.0	n/a	0.0
H.S. Diplomas (#)	166	152	1	11	0	2

Chappaqua CSD

66 Roaring Brook Rd • Chappaqua, NY 10514-1703
(914) 238-7200 • http://www.chappaqua.k12.ny.us/ccsd/
Grade Span: KG-12; **Agency Type:** 1
Schools: 5
3 Primary; 1 Middle; 1 High; 0 Other Level
5 Regular; 0 Special Education; 0 Vocational; 0 Alternative
0 Magnet; 0 Charter; 5 Title I Eligible; 0 School-wide Title I
Students: 4,055 (51.8% male; 48.2% female)
Individual Education Program: 359 (8.9%);
English Language Learner: 31 (0.8%); Migrant: n/a
Eligible for Free Lunch Program: 15 (0.4%)
Eligible for Reduced-Price Lunch Program: 9 (0.2%)
Teachers: 332.0 (12.2 to 1)
Librarians/Media Specialists: 6.0 (675.8 to 1)
Guidance Counselors: 12.8 (316.8 to 1)
Current Spending: ($ per student per year):
Total: $14,357; Instruction: $9,028; Support Services: $5,050

Enrollment, Drop-out Rates and Diploma Recipients by Race/Ethnicity

Category	Total	White	Black	Asian	AIAN	Hisp.
Enrollment (%)	100.0	91.4	1.1	6.3	0.0	1.3
Drop-out Rate (%)	0.4	0.4	0.0	0.0	n/a	0.0
H.S. Diplomas (#)	257	224	1	22	0	10

Croton-Harmon UFSD

10 Gerstein St • Croton-On-Hudson, NY 10520-2303
(914) 271-4793
Grade Span: KG-12; **Agency Type:** 1
Schools: 3
1 Primary; 1 Middle; 1 High; 0 Other Level
3 Regular; 0 Special Education; 0 Vocational; 0 Alternative
0 Magnet; 0 Charter; 1 Title I Eligible; 0 School-wide Title I
Students: 1,520 (49.7% male; 50.3% female)
Individual Education Program: 191 (12.6%);
English Language Learner: 18 (1.2%); Migrant: n/a
Eligible for Free Lunch Program: 0 (0.0%)
Eligible for Reduced-Price Lunch Program: 0 (0.0%)
Teachers: 115.5 (13.2 to 1)
Librarians/Media Specialists: 2.0 (760.0 to 1)
Guidance Counselors: 3.0 (506.7 to 1)
Current Spending: ($ per student per year):
Total: $14,332; Instruction: $9,148; Support Services: $5,170

Enrollment, Drop-out Rates and Diploma Recipients by Race/Ethnicity

Category	Total	White	Black	Asian	AIAN	Hisp.
Enrollment (%)	100.0	88.3	2.7	3.0	0.1	5.9
Drop-out Rate (%)	0.8	0.6	0.0	0.0	n/a	6.3
H.S. Diplomas (#)	73	67	1	4	0	1

Eastchester UFSD

580 White Plains Rd • Eastchester, NY 10709
(914) 793-6130 • http://www.eastchester.k12.ny.us/
Grade Span: KG-12; **Agency Type:** 1
Schools: 5
3 Primary; 1 Middle; 1 High; 0 Other Level
5 Regular; 0 Special Education; 0 Vocational; 0 Alternative
0 Magnet; 0 Charter; 2 Title I Eligible; 0 School-wide Title I
Students: 2,611 (51.9% male; 48.1% female)
Individual Education Program: 212 (8.1%);
English Language Learner: 126 (4.8%); Migrant: n/a
Eligible for Free Lunch Program: 0 (0.0%)
Eligible for Reduced-Price Lunch Program: 0 (0.0%)
Teachers: 209.9 (12.4 to 1)
Librarians/Media Specialists: 3.0 (870.3 to 1)
Guidance Counselors: 8.0 (326.4 to 1)
Current Spending: ($ per student per year):
Total: $13,726; Instruction: $9,233; Support Services: $4,328

Enrollment, Drop-out Rates and Diploma Recipients by Race/Ethnicity

Category	Total	White	Black	Asian	AIAN	Hisp.
Enrollment (%)	100.0	84.5	1.1	10.9	0.0	3.4
Drop-out Rate (%)	0.0	0.0	0.0	0.0	0.0	0.0
H.S. Diplomas (#)	105	94	0	8	0	3

Edgemont UFSD

300 White Oak Ln • Scarsdale, NY 10583-1799
(914) 472-7768 • http://www.edgemont.org/
Grade Span: KG-12; **Agency Type:** 1
Schools: 3
2 Primary; 0 Middle; 1 High; 0 Other Level
3 Regular; 0 Special Education; 0 Vocational; 0 Alternative
0 Magnet; 0 Charter; 2 Title I Eligible; 0 School-wide Title I
Students: 1,798 (51.2% male; 48.8% female)
Individual Education Program: 186 (10.3%);
English Language Learner: 60 (3.3%); Migrant: n/a
Eligible for Free Lunch Program: 0 (0.0%)
Eligible for Reduced-Price Lunch Program: 0 (0.0%)
Teachers: 136.1 (13.2 to 1)
Librarians/Media Specialists: 3.0 (599.3 to 1)
Guidance Counselors: 4.0 (449.5 to 1)
Current Spending: ($ per student per year):
Total: $13,977; Instruction: $9,524; Support Services: $4,293

Enrollment, Drop-out Rates and Diploma Recipients by Race/Ethnicity

Category	Total	White	Black	Asian	AIAN	Hisp.
Enrollment (%)	100.0	80.1	0.9	17.0	0.0	2.0
Drop-out Rate (%)	0.2	0.3	0.0	0.0	n/a	0.0
H.S. Diplomas (#)	104	76	1	26	0	1

Greenburgh CSD

475 W Hartsdale Ave • Hartsdale, NY 10530-1398
(914) 761-6000 • http://www.greenburgh.k12.ny.us/
Grade Span: PK-12; **Agency Type:** 1
Schools: 6
3 Primary; 2 Middle; 1 High; 0 Other Level
6 Regular; 0 Special Education; 0 Vocational; 0 Alternative
0 Magnet; 0 Charter; 3 Title I Eligible; 0 School-wide Title I
Students: 2,016 (52.7% male; 47.3% female)
Individual Education Program: 248 (12.3%);
English Language Learner: 142 (7.0%); Migrant: n/a
Eligible for Free Lunch Program: 394 (19.5%)
Eligible for Reduced-Price Lunch Program: 251 (12.5%)
Teachers: 180.8 (11.2 to 1)
Librarians/Media Specialists: 3.4 (592.9 to 1)
Guidance Counselors: 4.0 (504.0 to 1)
Current Spending: ($ per student per year):
Total: $18,778; Instruction: $11,273; Support Services: $7,263

Enrollment, Drop-out Rates and Diploma Recipients by Race/Ethnicity

Category	Total	White	Black	Asian	AIAN	Hisp.
Enrollment (%)	100.0	15.5	56.0	6.5	0.0	22.0
Drop-out Rate (%)	0.0	0.0	0.0	0.0	n/a	0.0
H.S. Diplomas (#)	117	28	65	7	0	17

Harrison CSD

50 Union Ave • Harrison, NY 10528-2032
(914) 630-3002 • http://www.harrisoncsd.org/
Grade Span: KG-12; **Agency Type:** 1
Schools: 8
4 Primary; 1 Middle; 1 High; 2 Other Level
6 Regular; 0 Special Education; 0 Vocational; 2 Alternative
0 Magnet; 0 Charter; 2 Title I Eligible; 0 School-wide Title I
Students: 3,360 (51.1% male; 48.9% female)
Individual Education Program: 409 (12.2%);
English Language Learner: 193 (5.7%); Migrant: n/a
Eligible for Free Lunch Program: 124 (3.7%)
Eligible for Reduced-Price Lunch Program: 72 (2.1%)
Teachers: 309.8 (10.8 to 1)
Librarians/Media Specialists: 4.7 (714.9 to 1)
Guidance Counselors: 7.0 (480.0 to 1)
Current Spending: ($ per student per year):
Total: $15,047; Instruction: $9,733; Support Services: $5,081

Enrollment, Drop-out Rates and Diploma Recipients by Race/Ethnicity

Category	Total	White	Black	Asian	AIAN	Hisp.
Enrollment (%)	100.0	81.5	0.8	8.4	0.2	9.1
Drop-out Rate (%)	2.1	1.9	0.0	0.0	n/a	4.4
H.S. Diplomas (#)	163	139	0	9	0	15

Hastings-On-Hudson UFSD

27 Farragut Ave • Hastings-On-Hudson, NY 10706-2395
(914) 478-6200
Grade Span: KG-12; **Agency Type:** 1
Schools: 3
1 Primary; 1 Middle; 1 High; 0 Other Level
3 Regular; 0 Special Education; 0 Vocational; 0 Alternative
0 Magnet; 0 Charter; 0 Title I Eligible; 0 School-wide Title I
Students: 1,674 (50.4% male; 49.6% female)
Individual Education Program: 182 (10.9%);
English Language Learner: 35 (2.1%); Migrant: n/a
Eligible for Free Lunch Program: 38 (2.3%)
Eligible for Reduced-Price Lunch Program: 0 (0.0%)
Teachers: 141.6 (11.8 to 1)
Librarians/Media Specialists: 2.2 (760.9 to 1)
Guidance Counselors: 5.0 (334.8 to 1)
Current Spending: ($ per student per year):
Total: $13,163; Instruction: $8,598; Support Services: $4,330

Enrollment, Drop-out Rates and Diploma Recipients by Race/Ethnicity

Category	Total	White	Black	Asian	AIAN	Hisp.
Enrollment (%)	100.0	85.7	3.0	5.5	0.5	5.3
Drop-out Rate (%)	0.2	0.0	0.0	0.0	n/a	7.1
H.S. Diplomas (#)	74	64	2	6	0	2

Hendrick Hudson CSD

61 Trolley Rd • Montrose, NY 10548-1199
(914) 736-5200 • http://www2.lhric.org/henhud/
Grade Span: KG-12; **Agency Type:** 1
Schools: 5
3 Primary; 1 Middle; 1 High; 0 Other Level
5 Regular; 0 Special Education; 0 Vocational; 0 Alternative
0 Magnet; 0 Charter; 3 Title I Eligible; 0 School-wide Title I
Students: 2,833 (52.3% male; 47.7% female)
Individual Education Program: 370 (13.1%);
English Language Learner: 37 (1.3%); Migrant: n/a
Eligible for Free Lunch Program: 92 (3.2%)
Eligible for Reduced-Price Lunch Program: 41 (1.4%)
Teachers: 233.2 (12.1 to 1)
Librarians/Media Specialists: 4.8 (590.2 to 1)
Guidance Counselors: 7.0 (404.7 to 1)
Current Spending: ($ per student per year):
Total: $14,246; Instruction: $9,720; Support Services: $4,328

Enrollment, Drop-out Rates and Diploma Recipients by Race/Ethnicity

Category	Total	White	Black	Asian	AIAN	Hisp.
Enrollment (%)	100.0	86.9	3.6	4.1	0.0	5.4
Drop-out Rate (%)	0.4	0.5	0.0	0.0	n/a	0.0
H.S. Diplomas (#)	176	155	4	10	0	7

Irvington UFSD

40 N Broadway • Irvington, NY 10533-1328
(914) 591-8501 • http://www.irvingtonschools.org/
Grade Span: KG-12; **Agency Type:** 2
Schools: 4
1 Primary; 2 Middle; 1 High; 0 Other Level
4 Regular; 0 Special Education; 0 Vocational; 0 Alternative
0 Magnet; 0 Charter; 1 Title I Eligible; 0 School-wide Title I
Students: 1,931 (51.0% male; 49.0% female)
Individual Education Program: 171 (8.9%);
English Language Learner: 16 (0.8%); Migrant: n/a
Eligible for Free Lunch Program: 0 (0.0%)
Eligible for Reduced-Price Lunch Program: 0 (0.0%)
Teachers: 147.8 (13.1 to 1)
Librarians/Media Specialists: 2.0 (965.5 to 1)
Guidance Counselors: 4.0 (482.8 to 1)
Current Spending: ($ per student per year):
Total: $14,086; Instruction: $8,860; Support Services: $5,226
Enrollment, Drop-out Rates and Diploma Recipients by Race/Ethnicity

Category	Total	White	Black	Asian	AIAN	Hisp.
Enrollment (%)	100.0	82.9	3.6	10.5	0.1	3.0
Drop-out Rate (%)	0.2	0.0	0.0	0.0	n/a	6.7
H.S. Diplomas (#)	92	70	0	18	0	4

Katonah-Lewisboro UFSD

One Shady Ln Rt 123 • South Salem, NY 10590
(914) 763-7000 • http://www.klschools.org/public/
Grade Span: KG-12; **Agency Type:** 1
Schools: 6
4 Primary; 1 Middle; 1 High; 0 Other Level
6 Regular; 0 Special Education; 0 Vocational; 0 Alternative
0 Magnet; 0 Charter; 2 Title I Eligible; 0 School-wide Title I
Students: 4,112 (50.4% male; 49.6% female)
Individual Education Program: 544 (13.2%);
English Language Learner: 62 (1.5%); Migrant: n/a
Eligible for Free Lunch Program: 14 (0.3%)
Eligible for Reduced-Price Lunch Program: 14 (0.3%)
Teachers: 313.0 (13.1 to 1)
Librarians/Media Specialists: 5.6 (734.3 to 1)
Guidance Counselors: 12.0 (342.7 to 1)
Current Spending: ($ per student per year):
Total: $14,471; Instruction: $8,699; Support Services: $5,578
Enrollment, Drop-out Rates and Diploma Recipients by Race/Ethnicity

Category	Total	White	Black	Asian	AIAN	Hisp.
Enrollment (%)	100.0	94.5	1.3	2.1	0.0	2.1
Drop-out Rate (%)	0.5	0.4	10.0	0.0	n/a	0.0
H.S. Diplomas (#)	208	201	7	0	0	0

Lakeland CSD

1086 Main St • Shrub Oak, NY 10588-1507
(914) 245-1700 • http://www.lakelandschools.org/
Grade Span: KG-12; **Agency Type:** 1
Schools: 9
5 Primary; 1 Middle; 3 High; 0 Other Level
8 Regular; 0 Special Education; 0 Vocational; 1 Alternative
0 Magnet; 0 Charter; 3 Title I Eligible; 0 School-wide Title I
Students: 6,239 (50.8% male; 49.2% female)
Individual Education Program: 935 (15.0%);
English Language Learner: 63 (1.0%); Migrant: n/a
Eligible for Free Lunch Program: 198 (3.2%)
Eligible for Reduced-Price Lunch Program: 150 (2.4%)
Teachers: 451.6 (13.8 to 1)
Librarians/Media Specialists: 5.6 (1,114.1 to 1)
Guidance Counselors: 14.0 (445.6 to 1)
Current Spending: ($ per student per year):
Total: $12,066; Instruction: $7,680; Support Services: $4,147
Enrollment, Drop-out Rates and Diploma Recipients by Race/Ethnicity

Category	Total	White	Black	Asian	AIAN	Hisp.
Enrollment (%)	100.0	81.6	5.5	3.0	0.1	9.7
Drop-out Rate (%)	1.8	1.7	0.0	5.1	0.0	2.4
H.S. Diplomas (#)	472	377	32	11	0	52

Mamaroneck UFSD

1000 W Boston Post Rd • Mamaroneck, NY 10543-3399
(914) 698-9000 • http://www.mamkschools.org/
Grade Span: PK-12; **Agency Type:** 1
Schools: 6
4 Primary; 1 Middle; 1 High; 0 Other Level
6 Regular; 0 Special Education; 0 Vocational; 0 Alternative
0 Magnet; 0 Charter; 2 Title I Eligible; 0 School-wide Title I
Students: 4,712 (51.0% male; 49.0% female)
Individual Education Program: 686 (14.6%);
English Language Learner: 161 (3.4%); Migrant: n/a
Eligible for Free Lunch Program: 60 (1.3%)
Eligible for Reduced-Price Lunch Program: 26 (0.6%)
Teachers: 368.3 (12.8 to 1)
Librarians/Media Specialists: 4.3 (1,095.8 to 1)
Guidance Counselors: 11.0 (428.4 to 1)
Current Spending: ($ per student per year):
Total: $13,877; Instruction: $8,982; Support Services: $4,831
Enrollment, Drop-out Rates and Diploma Recipients by Race/Ethnicity

Category	Total	White	Black	Asian	AIAN	Hisp.
Enrollment (%)	100.0	79.2	3.7	3.1	0.1	14.0
Drop-out Rate (%)	1.0	0.3	2.6	0.0	0.0	4.7
H.S. Diplomas (#)	289	235	13	9	0	32

Mount Pleasant CSD

825 Westlake Dr • Thornwood, NY 10594-2120
(914) 769-5500 • http://www2.lhric.org/mpcsd/welcome.htm
Grade Span: KG-12; **Agency Type:** 1
Schools: 4
2 Primary; 1 Middle; 1 High; 0 Other Level
4 Regular; 0 Special Education; 0 Vocational; 0 Alternative
0 Magnet; 0 Charter; 0 Title I Eligible; 0 School-wide Title I
Students: 1,843 (51.2% male; 48.8% female)
Individual Education Program: 317 (17.2%);
English Language Learner: 35 (1.9%); Migrant: n/a
Eligible for Free Lunch Program: 39 (2.1%)
Eligible for Reduced-Price Lunch Program: 23 (1.2%)
Teachers: 163.7 (11.3 to 1)
Librarians/Media Specialists: 3.3 (558.5 to 1)
Guidance Counselors: 7.0 (263.3 to 1)
Current Spending: ($ per student per year):
Total: $15,040; Instruction: $10,068; Support Services: $4,799
Enrollment, Drop-out Rates and Diploma Recipients by Race/Ethnicity

Category	Total	White	Black	Asian	AIAN	Hisp.
Enrollment (%)	100.0	91.8	0.4	2.8	0.3	4.7
Drop-out Rate (%)	0.5	0.4	0.0	0.0	n/a	8.3
H.S. Diplomas (#)	118	107	1	5	0	5

Mount Vernon City SD

165 N Columbus Ave • Mount Vernon, NY 10553-1199
(914) 665-5201
Grade Span: PK-12; **Agency Type:** 1
Schools: 18
12 Primary; 2 Middle; 2 High; 2 Other Level
16 Regular; 0 Special Education; 0 Vocational; 2 Alternative
0 Magnet; 0 Charter; 14 Title I Eligible; 0 School-wide Title I
Students: 10,410 (50.2% male; 49.8% female)
Individual Education Program: 1,299 (12.5%);
English Language Learner: 1,048 (10.1%); Migrant: n/a
Eligible for Free Lunch Program: 4,670 (44.9%)
Eligible for Reduced-Price Lunch Program: 1,215 (11.7%)
Teachers: 676.5 (15.4 to 1)
Librarians/Media Specialists: 13.3 (782.7 to 1)
Guidance Counselors: 21.0 (495.7 to 1)
Current Spending: ($ per student per year):
Total: $11,510; Instruction: $8,049; Support Services: $3,211
Enrollment, Drop-out Rates and Diploma Recipients by Race/Ethnicity

Category	Total	White	Black	Asian	AIAN	Hisp.
Enrollment (%)	100.0	7.9	78.4	1.3	0.2	12.3
Drop-out Rate (%)	2.0	2.7	1.8	12.5	0.0	3.0
H.S. Diplomas (#)	337	16	294	0	2	25

New Rochelle City SD

515 N Ave • New Rochelle, NY 10801-3416
(914) 576-4200 • http://www.nred.org/
Grade Span: PK-12; **Agency Type:** 1
Schools: 12
7 Primary; 2 Middle; 1 High; 2 Other Level
10 Regular; 0 Special Education; 0 Vocational; 2 Alternative
0 Magnet; 0 Charter; 5 Title I Eligible; 0 School-wide Title I
Students: 10,299 (51.5% male; 48.5% female)
Individual Education Program: 1,408 (13.7%);
English Language Learner: 1,348 (13.1%); Migrant: n/a
Eligible for Free Lunch Program: 3,639 (35.3%)
Eligible for Reduced-Price Lunch Program: 937 (9.1%)
Teachers: 720.7 (14.3 to 1)
Librarians/Media Specialists: 7.6 (1,355.1 to 1)
Guidance Counselors: 21.0 (490.4 to 1)
Current Spending: ($ per student per year):
Total: $12,027; Instruction: $7,474; Support Services: $4,329

Enrollment, Drop-out Rates and Diploma Recipients by Race/Ethnicity

Category	Total	White	Black	Asian	AIAN	Hisp.
Enrollment (%)	100.0	40.2	26.1	3.7	0.1	30.0
Drop-out Rate (%)	0.6	0.2	0.2	1.0	0.0	1.8
H.S. Diplomas (#)	479	260	106	23	13	77

Ossining UFSD

190 Croton Ave • Ossining, NY 10562-4599
(914) 941-7700 • http://www.ossining.k12.ny.us/
Grade Span: PK-12; **Agency Type:** 1
Schools: 8
3 Primary; 2 Middle; 1 High; 2 Other Level
6 Regular; 0 Special Education; 0 Vocational; 2 Alternative
0 Magnet; 0 Charter; 1 Title I Eligible; 0 School-wide Title I
Students: 4,249 (52.8% male; 47.2% female)
Individual Education Program: 517 (12.2%);
English Language Learner: 396 (9.3%); Migrant: n/a
Eligible for Free Lunch Program: 845 (19.9%)
Eligible for Reduced-Price Lunch Program: 332 (7.8%)
Teachers: 329.3 (12.9 to 1)
Librarians/Media Specialists: 3.7 (1,148.4 to 1)
Guidance Counselors: 11.0 (386.3 to 1)
Current Spending: ($ per student per year):
Total: $13,407; Instruction: $8,574; Support Services: $4,623
Enrollment, Drop-out Rates and Diploma Recipients by Race/Ethnicity

Category	Total	White	Black	Asian	AIAN	Hisp.
Enrollment (%)	100.0	44.5	19.2	5.6	0.0	30.7
Drop-out Rate (%)	2.3	1.3	3.5	0.0	n/a	3.9
H.S. Diplomas (#)	203	122	36	14	0	31

Peekskill City SD

1031 Elm St • Peekskill, NY 10566-3499
(914) 737-3300
Grade Span: PK-12; **Agency Type:** 1
Schools: 10
3 Primary; 2 Middle; 2 High; 3 Other Level
7 Regular; 0 Special Education; 0 Vocational; 3 Alternative
0 Magnet; 0 Charter; 2 Title I Eligible; 0 School-wide Title I
Students: 2,974 (50.6% male; 49.4% female)
Individual Education Program: 502 (16.9%);
English Language Learner: 260 (8.7%); Migrant: n/a
Eligible for Free Lunch Program: 1,413 (47.5%)
Eligible for Reduced-Price Lunch Program: 382 (12.8%)
Teachers: 249.2 (11.9 to 1)
Librarians/Media Specialists: 5.0 (594.8 to 1)
Guidance Counselors: 5.0 (594.8 to 1)
Current Spending: ($ per student per year):
Total: $14,198; Instruction: $9,796; Support Services: $4,124
Enrollment, Drop-out Rates and Diploma Recipients by Race/Ethnicity

Category	Total	White	Black	Asian	AIAN	Hisp.
Enrollment (%)	100.0	24.1	46.5	1.1	0.4	27.8
Drop-out Rate (%)	1.2	0.4	1.9	0.0	n/a	1.1
H.S. Diplomas (#)	130	49	53	4	0	24

Pelham UFSD

661 Hillside Rd • Pelham, NY 10803-2147
(914) 738-3434 • http://www.pelham.k12.ny.us/
Grade Span: KG-12; **Agency Type:** 1
Schools: 6
4 Primary; 1 Middle; 1 High; 0 Other Level
6 Regular; 0 Special Education; 0 Vocational; 0 Alternative
0 Magnet; 0 Charter; 1 Title I Eligible; 0 School-wide Title I
Students: 2,473 (52.0% male; 48.0% female)
Individual Education Program: 313 (12.7%);
English Language Learner: 32 (1.3%); Migrant: n/a
Eligible for Free Lunch Program: 69 (2.8%)
Eligible for Reduced-Price Lunch Program: 30 (1.2%)
Teachers: 190.5 (13.0 to 1)
Librarians/Media Specialists: 2.0 (1,236.5 to 1)
Guidance Counselors: 7.0 (353.3 to 1)
Current Spending: ($ per student per year):
Total: $12,793; Instruction: $8,218; Support Services: $4,432
Enrollment, Drop-out Rates and Diploma Recipients by Race/Ethnicity

Category	Total	White	Black	Asian	AIAN	Hisp.
Enrollment (%)	100.0	82.4	6.1	5.5	0.0	6.0
Drop-out Rate (%)	0.0	0.0	0.0	0.0	n/a	0.0
H.S. Diplomas (#)	135	110	7	8	0	10

Pleasantville UFSD

60 Romer Ave • Pleasantville, NY 10570-3157
(914) 741-1400 • http://www2.lhric.org/pleasantville/
Grade Span: KG-12; **Agency Type:** 1
Schools: 4
1 Primary; 1 Middle; 1 High; 1 Other Level
3 Regular; 0 Special Education; 0 Vocational; 1 Alternative
0 Magnet; 0 Charter; 1 Title I Eligible; 0 School-wide Title I
Students: 1,699 (52.7% male; 47.3% female)
Individual Education Program: 288 (17.0%);
English Language Learner: 31 (1.8%); Migrant: n/a
Eligible for Free Lunch Program: 0 (0.0%)
Eligible for Reduced-Price Lunch Program: 0 (0.0%)
Teachers: 124.4 (13.7 to 1)
Librarians/Media Specialists: 1.9 (894.2 to 1)
Guidance Counselors: 5.0 (339.8 to 1)
Current Spending: ($ per student per year):
Total: $12,685; Instruction: $8,609; Support Services: $3,873
Enrollment, Drop-out Rates and Diploma Recipients by Race/Ethnicity

Category	Total	White	Black	Asian	AIAN	Hisp.
Enrollment (%)	100.0	90.4	1.4	4.1	0.1	4.0
Drop-out Rate (%)	0.0	0.0	0.0	0.0	0.0	0.0
H.S. Diplomas (#)	106	90	4	8	0	4

Port Chester-Rye UFSD

113 Bowman Ave • Port Chester, NY 10573-2851
(914) 934-7901 • http://www.portchester.k12.ny.us/
Grade Span: KG-12; **Agency Type:** 1
Schools: 6
4 Primary; 1 Middle; 1 High; 0 Other Level
6 Regular; 0 Special Education; 0 Vocational; 0 Alternative
1 Magnet; 0 Charter; 3 Title I Eligible; 0 School-wide Title I
Students: 3,527 (52.0% male; 48.0% female)
Individual Education Program: 510 (14.5%);
English Language Learner: 684 (19.4%); Migrant: n/a
Eligible for Free Lunch Program: 1,516 (43.0%)
Eligible for Reduced-Price Lunch Program: 426 (12.1%)
Teachers: 251.0 (14.1 to 1)
Librarians/Media Specialists: 3.5 (1,007.7 to 1)
Guidance Counselors: 9.0 (391.9 to 1)
Current Spending: ($ per student per year):
Total: $11,783; Instruction: $7,952; Support Services: $3,552
Enrollment, Drop-out Rates and Diploma Recipients by Race/Ethnicity

Category	Total	White	Black	Asian	AIAN	Hisp.
Enrollment (%)	100.0	23.9	10.0	0.8	0.0	65.3
Drop-out Rate (%)	9.8	3.0	10.8	0.0	0.0	14.0
H.S. Diplomas (#)	190	76	23	3	0	88

Rye City SD

324 Midland Ave • Rye, NY 10580-3899
(914) 967-6108 • http://ryecityschools.lhric.org/
Grade Span: KG-12; **Agency Type:** 1
Schools: 5
3 Primary; 1 Middle; 1 High; 0 Other Level
5 Regular; 0 Special Education; 0 Vocational; 0 Alternative
0 Magnet; 0 Charter; 2 Title I Eligible; 0 School-wide Title I
Students: 2,633 (52.9% male; 47.1% female)
Individual Education Program: 161 (6.1%);
English Language Learner: 110 (4.2%); Migrant: n/a
Eligible for Free Lunch Program: 41 (1.6%)
Eligible for Reduced-Price Lunch Program: 1 (<0.1%)
Teachers: 205.2 (12.8 to 1)
Librarians/Media Specialists: 4.8 (548.5 to 1)
Guidance Counselors: 6.6 (398.9 to 1)
Current Spending: ($ per student per year):
Total: $13,737; Instruction: $8,932; Support Services: $4,443
Enrollment, Drop-out Rates and Diploma Recipients by Race/Ethnicity

Category	Total	White	Black	Asian	AIAN	Hisp.
Enrollment (%)	100.0	88.6	1.1	6.2	0.0	4.1
Drop-out Rate (%)	0.2	0.0	0.0	0.0	0.0	3.4
H.S. Diplomas (#)	121	99	2	10	1	9

Scarsdale UFSD

2 Brewster Rd • Scarsdale, NY 10583-3049
(914) 721-2410 • http://www.scarsdaleschools.k12.ny.us/
Grade Span: KG-12; **Agency Type:** 1
Schools: 7
5 Primary; 1 Middle; 1 High; 0 Other Level
7 Regular; 0 Special Education; 0 Vocational; 0 Alternative
0 Magnet; 0 Charter; 0 Title I Eligible; 0 School-wide Title I
Students: 4,508 (51.8% male; 48.2% female)
Individual Education Program: 424 (9.4%);
English Language Learner: 144 (3.2%); Migrant: n/a
Eligible for Free Lunch Program: 0 (0.0%)
Eligible for Reduced-Price Lunch Program: 0 (0.0%)
Teachers: 369.2 (12.2 to 1)
Librarians/Media Specialists: 7.3 (617.5 to 1)
Guidance Counselors: 11.9 (378.8 to 1)
Current Spending: ($ per student per year):
Total: $14,878; Instruction: $10,187; Support Services: $4,545

Enrollment, Drop-out Rates and Diploma Recipients by Race/Ethnicity

Category	Total	White	Black	Asian	AIAN	Hisp.
Enrollment (%)	100.0	83.2	1.9	12.8	0.0	2.1
Drop-out Rate (%)	0.2	0.1	0.0	0.6	n/a	0.0
H.S. Diplomas (#)	267	207	9	44	0	7

Somers CSD

110 Prmrse • Lincolndale, NY 10540-0620
Mailing Address: PO Box 620 • Lincolndale, NY 10540-0620
(914) 248-7872 • http://www.somers.k12.ny.us/
Grade Span: KG-12; **Agency Type:** 1
Schools: 4
2 Primary; 1 Middle; 1 High; 0 Other Level
4 Regular; 0 Special Education; 0 Vocational; 0 Alternative
0 Magnet; 0 Charter; 3 Title I Eligible; 0 School-wide Title I
Students: 2,984 (50.3% male; 49.7% female)
Individual Education Program: 361 (12.1%);
English Language Learner: 12 (0.4%); Migrant: n/a
Eligible for Free Lunch Program: 64 (2.1%)
Eligible for Reduced-Price Lunch Program: 9 (0.3%)
Teachers: 233.3 (12.8 to 1)
Librarians/Media Specialists: 4.7 (634.9 to 1)
Guidance Counselors: 8.0 (373.0 to 1)
Current Spending: ($ per student per year):
Total: $14,013; Instruction: $9,053; Support Services: $4,735

Enrollment, Drop-out Rates and Diploma Recipients by Race/Ethnicity

Category	Total	White	Black	Asian	AIAN	Hisp.
Enrollment (%)	100.0	93.9	0.9	2.9	0.1	2.2
Drop-out Rate (%)	0.6	0.6	0.0	0.0	n/a	0.0
H.S. Diplomas (#)	171	154	2	7	0	8

UFSD - Tarrytowns

200 N Broadway • Sleepy Hollow, NY 10591-2696
(914) 631-9404 • http://www.tufsd.org/
Grade Span: PK-12; **Agency Type:** 1
Schools: 6
3 Primary; 1 Middle; 1 High; 1 Other Level
5 Regular; 0 Special Education; 0 Vocational; 1 Alternative
0 Magnet; 0 Charter; 2 Title I Eligible; 0 School-wide Title I
Students: 2,407 (50.4% male; 49.6% female)
Individual Education Program: 303 (12.6%);
English Language Learner: 472 (19.6%); Migrant: n/a
Eligible for Free Lunch Program: 772 (32.1%)
Eligible for Reduced-Price Lunch Program: 219 (9.1%)
Teachers: 195.0 (12.3 to 1)
Librarians/Media Specialists: 2.9 (830.0 to 1)
Guidance Counselors: 5.2 (462.9 to 1)
Current Spending: ($ per student per year):
Total: $14,390; Instruction: $9,713; Support Services: $4,440

Enrollment, Drop-out Rates and Diploma Recipients by Race/Ethnicity

Category	Total	White	Black	Asian	AIAN	Hisp.
Enrollment (%)	100.0	38.2	7.6	3.8	0.0	50.4
Drop-out Rate (%)	3.3	0.5	10.3	7.1	n/a	3.5
H.S. Diplomas (#)	111	49	5	1	0	56

White Plains City SD

5 Homeside Ln • White Plains, NY 10605-4299
(914) 422-2019 • http://www.wpcsd.k12.ny.us/
Grade Span: PK-12; **Agency Type:** 1
Schools: 11
6 Primary; 0 Middle; 1 High; 4 Other Level
7 Regular; 1 Special Education; 0 Vocational; 3 Alternative
0 Magnet; 0 Charter; 6 Title I Eligible; 0 School-wide Title I
Students: 6,775 (52.3% male; 47.7% female)
Individual Education Program: 776 (11.5%);
English Language Learner: 624 (9.2%); Migrant: n/a
Eligible for Free Lunch Program: 1,817 (26.8%)
Eligible for Reduced-Price Lunch Program: 590 (8.7%)
Teachers: 568.0 (11.9 to 1)
Librarians/Media Specialists: 4.9 (1,382.7 to 1)
Guidance Counselors: 19.0 (356.6 to 1)
Current Spending: ($ per student per year):
Total: $16,031; Instruction: $10,755; Support Services: $4,939

Enrollment, Drop-out Rates and Diploma Recipients by Race/Ethnicity

Category	Total	White	Black	Asian	AIAN	Hisp.
Enrollment (%)	100.0	37.3	22.1	2.8	0.0	37.7
Drop-out Rate (%)	0.9	0.4	1.4	0.0	n/a	1.1
H.S. Diplomas (#)	360	177	76	12	1	94

Yonkers City SD

1 Larkin Center • Yonkers, NY 10701-2756
(914) 376-8100 • http://www.yonkerspublicschools.org/
Grade Span: PK-12; **Agency Type:** 1
Schools: 43
30 Primary; 4 Middle; 4 High; 5 Other Level
38 Regular; 0 Special Education; 1 Vocational; 4 Alternative
1 Magnet; 0 Charter; 38 Title I Eligible; 0 School-wide Title I
Students: 26,398 (51.5% male; 48.5% female)
Individual Education Program: 3,434 (13.0%);
English Language Learner: 4,532 (17.2%); Migrant: n/a
Eligible for Free Lunch Program: 16,278 (61.7%)
Eligible for Reduced-Price Lunch Program: 1,978 (7.5%)
Teachers: 1,855.6 (14.2 to 1)
Librarians/Media Specialists: 24.2 (1,090.8 to 1)
Guidance Counselors: 63.0 (419.0 to 1)
Current Spending: ($ per student per year):
Total: $13,271; Instruction: $8,621; Support Services: $4,358

Enrollment, Drop-out Rates and Diploma Recipients by Race/Ethnicity

Category	Total	White	Black	Asian	AIAN	Hisp.
Enrollment (%)	100.0	18.9	29.7	5.6	0.2	45.7
Drop-out Rate (%)	1.9	1.2	2.3	0.0	0.0	2.4
H.S. Diplomas (#)	724	223	188	77	1	235

Yorktown CSD

2723 Crompond Rd • Yorktown Heights, NY 10598-3197
(914) 243-8000 • http://www.yorktown.org/
Grade Span: KG-12; **Agency Type:** 1
Schools: 6
4 Primary; 1 Middle; 1 High; 0 Other Level
6 Regular; 0 Special Education; 0 Vocational; 0 Alternative
0 Magnet; 0 Charter; 2 Title I Eligible; 0 School-wide Title I
Students: 4,183 (50.8% male; 49.2% female)
Individual Education Program: 551 (13.2%);
English Language Learner: 56 (1.3%); Migrant: n/a
Eligible for Free Lunch Program: 48 (1.1%)
Eligible for Reduced-Price Lunch Program: 13 (0.3%)
Teachers: 306.0 (13.7 to 1)
Librarians/Media Specialists: 4.6 (909.3 to 1)
Guidance Counselors: 10.2 (410.1 to 1)
Current Spending: ($ per student per year):
Total: $11,466; Instruction: $7,656; Support Services: $3,655

Enrollment, Drop-out Rates and Diploma Recipients by Race/Ethnicity

Category	Total	White	Black	Asian	AIAN	Hisp.
Enrollment (%)	100.0	90.5	1.4	4.3	0.0	3.8
Drop-out Rate (%)	0.5	0.5	0.0	0.0	n/a	0.0
H.S. Diplomas (#)	260	233	7	6	0	14

Wyoming County

Attica CSD

3338 E Main St • Attica, NY 14011-9699
(585) 591-0400 • http://www.atticacs.k12.ny.us/
Grade Span: KG-12; **Agency Type:** 1
Schools: 6
2 Primary; 1 Middle; 1 High; 2 Other Level
4 Regular; 0 Special Education; 0 Vocational; 2 Alternative
0 Magnet; 0 Charter; 3 Title I Eligible; 0 School-wide Title I
Students: 1,831 (54.1% male; 45.9% female)
Individual Education Program: 206 (11.3%);
English Language Learner: 2 (0.1%); Migrant: n/a
Eligible for Free Lunch Program: 273 (14.9%)
Eligible for Reduced-Price Lunch Program: 202 (11.0%)
Teachers: 143.7 (12.7 to 1)
Librarians/Media Specialists: 2.0 (915.5 to 1)
Guidance Counselors: 3.0 (610.3 to 1)
Current Spending: ($ per student per year):
Total: $8,566; Instruction: $5,855; Support Services: $2,478

Enrollment, Drop-out Rates and Diploma Recipients by Race/Ethnicity

Category	Total	White	Black	Asian	AIAN	Hisp.
Enrollment (%)	100.0	95.2	3.0	0.2	0.5	1.2
Drop-out Rate (%)	1.4	1.4	n/a	n/a	n/a	n/a
H.S. Diplomas (#)	145	145	0	0	0	0

Yates County

Penn Yan CSD

One School Dr • Pen, NY 14527-1099
(315) 536-3371 • http://www.pennyan.k12.ny.us/
Grade Span: PK-12; **Agency Type:** 1
Schools: 5
2 Primary; 1 Middle; 1 High; 1 Other Level
4 Regular; 0 Special Education; 0 Vocational; 1 Alternative
0 Magnet; 0 Charter; 3 Title I Eligible; 0 School-wide Title I
Students: 2,072 (49.5% male; 50.5% female)
Individual Education Program: 293 (14.1%);
English Language Learner: 7 (0.3%); Migrant: n/a
Eligible for Free Lunch Program: 392 (18.9%)
Eligible for Reduced-Price Lunch Program: 255 (12.3%)
Teachers: 171.0 (12.1 to 1)
Librarians/Media Specialists: 2.1 (986.7 to 1)

Guidance Counselors: 6.0 (345.3 to 1)
Current Spending: ($ per student per year):
Total: $9,644; Instruction: $6,641; Support Services: $2,696
Enrollment, Drop-out Rates and Diploma Recipients by Race/Ethnicity

Category	Total	White	Black	Asian	AIAN	Hisp.
Enrollment (%)	100.0	97.6	1.0	0.6	0.2	0.6
Drop-out Rate (%)	2.8	2.7	0.0	16.7	0.0	0.0
H.S. Diplomas (#)	152	148	0	2	1	1

Number of Schools

Rank	Number	District Name	City
1	1,429	New York City Public Schools	Brooklyn
2	86	Buffalo City SD	Buffalo
3	69	Rochester City SD	Rochester
4	43	Syracuse City SD	Syracuse
4	43	Yonkers City SD	Yonkers
6	27	Albany City SD	Albany
7	21	Greece CSD	Rochester
8	19	Wappingers CSD	Wappingers Fls
9	18	Brentwood UFSD	Brentwood
9	18	Clarkstown CSD	New City
9	18	Kingston City SD	Kingston
9	18	Mount Vernon City SD	Mount Vernon
9	18	Schenectady City SD	Schenectady
14	17	East Ramapo CSD (Spring Valley)	Spring Valley
14	17	Elmira City SD	Elmira
16	16	Ithaca City SD	Ithaca
16	16	Newburgh City SD	Newburgh
18	15	Poughkeepsie City SD	Poughkeepsie
18	15	Rome City SD	Rome
18	15	Sachem CSD	Holbrook
21	14	Corning City SD	Painted Post
21	14	Half Hollow Hills CSD	Dix Hills
21	14	Kenmore-Tonawanda UFSD	Buffalo
21	14	Liverpool CSD	Liverpool
21	14	Middle Country CSD	Centereach
21	14	Middletown City SD	Middletown
21	14	West Seneca CSD	West Seneca
21	14	Williamsville CSD	East Amherst
29	13	Arlington CSD	Poughkeepsie
29	13	Johnstown City SD	Johnstown
29	13	Niagara Falls City SD	Niagara Falls
29	13	Smithtown CSD	Smithtown
29	13	Troy City SD	Troy
29	13	Utica City SD	Utica
35	12	Auburn City SD	Auburn
35	12	Binghamton City SD	Binghamton
35	12	Haverstraw-Stony Point CSD	Garnerville
35	12	Hempstead UFSD	Hempstead
35	12	New Rochelle City SD	New Rochelle
35	12	Patchogue-Medford UFSD	Patchogue
35	12	Webster CSD	Webster
42	11	Jamestown City SD	Jamestown
42	11	Levittown UFSD	Levittown
42	11	Lockport City SD	Lockport
42	11	North Syracuse CSD	N Syracuse
42	11	Rush-Henrietta CSD	Henrietta
42	11	Saratoga Springs City SD	Saratoga Spgs
42	11	Shenendehowa CSD	Clifton Park
42	11	Syosset CSD	Syosset
42	11	White Plains City SD	White Plains
51	10	Batavia City SD	Batavia
51	10	Bedford CSD	Mount Kisco
51	10	Connetquot CSD	Bohemia
51	10	East Meadow UFSD	Westbury
51	10	Great Neck UFSD	Great Neck
51	10	Peekskill City SD	Peekskill
51	10	South Colonie CSD	Albany
51	10	Watertown City SD	Watertown
51	10	West Irondequoit CSD	Rochester
51	10	Whitesboro CSD	Yorkville
61	9	Baldwin UFSD	Baldwin
61	9	Baldwinsville CSD	Baldwinsville
61	9	Bay Shore UFSD	Bay Shore
61	9	Freeport UFSD	Freeport
61	9	Hicksville UFSD	Hicksville
61	9	Hudson City SD	Hudson
61	9	Hyde Park CSD	Poughkeepsie
61	9	Lakeland CSD	Shrub Oak
61	9	Lindenhurst UFSD	Lindenhurst
61	9	Malone CSD	Malone
61	9	Massapequa UFSD	Massapequa
61	9	Nanuet UFSD	Nanuet
61	9	North Tonawanda City SD	N Tonawanda
61	9	Northport-East Northport UFSD	Northport
61	9	Oceanside UFSD	Oceanside
61	9	Ogdensburg City SD	Ogdensburg
61	9	West Islip UFSD	West Islip
78	8	Ballston Spa CSD	Ballston Spa
78	8	Beacon City SD	Beacon
78	8	Bethlehem CSD	Delmar
78	8	Camden CSD	Camden
78	8	Central Islip UFSD	Central Islip
78	8	Central Square CSD	Central Square
78	8	Commack UFSD	E Northport
78	8	Fairport CSD	Fairport
78	8	Goshen CSD	Goshen
78	8	Harrison CSD	Harrison
78	8	Huntington UFSD	Huntington Stn
78	8	Indian River CSD	Philadelphia
78	8	Lackawanna City SD	Lackawanna
78	8	Lancaster CSD	Lancaster
78	8	Longwood CSD	Middle Island
78	8	Monticello CSD	Monticello
78	8	Niskayuna CSD	Schenectady
78	8	North Colonie CSD	Latham
78	8	Olean City SD	Olean
78	8	Oneida City SD	Oneida
78	8	Ossining UFSD	Ossining
78	8	Oswego City SD	Oswego
78	8	Pittsford CSD	Pittsford
78	8	Plainview-Old Bethpage CSD	Plainview
78	8	Ramapo CSD (Suffern)	Hillburn
78	8	Riverhead CSD	Riverhead
78	8	Saranac Lake CSD	Saranac Lake
78	8	Three Village CSD	East Setauket
78	8	Uniondale UFSD	Uniondale
78	8	Wallkill CSD	Wallkill
78	8	West Genesee CSD	Camillus
78	8	Westbury UFSD	Old Westbury
110	7	Amsterdam City SD	Amsterdam
110	7	Averill Park CSD	Averill Park
110	7	Bath CSD	Bath
110	7	Carmel CSD	Patterson
110	7	Cortland City SD	Cortland
110	7	East Greenbush CSD	E Greenbush
110	7	East Islip UFSD	Islip Terrace
110	7	East Syracuse-Minoa CSD	East Syracuse
110	7	Evans-Brant CSD (Lake Shore)	Angola
110	7	Garden City UFSD	Garden City
110	7	Gates-Chili CSD	Rochester
110	7	Gloversville City SD	Gloversville
110	7	Guilderland CSD	Guilderland
110	7	Horseheads CSD	Horseheads
110	7	Lawrence UFSD	Lawrence
110	7	Long Beach City SD	Long Beach
110	7	Lynbrook UFSD	Lynbrook
110	7	Mineola UFSD	Mineola
110	7	Monroe-Woodbury CSD	Central Valley
110	7	North Babylon UFSD	North Babylon
110	7	Nyack UFSD	Nyack
110	7	Pearl River UFSD	Pearl River
110	7	Pine Bush CSD	Pine Bush
110	7	Plattsburgh City SD	Plattsburgh
110	7	Port Washington UFSD	Pt Washington
110	7	Rockville Centre UFSD	Rockville Ctre
110	7	Saranac CSD	Dannemora
110	7	Scarsdale UFSD	Scarsdale
110	7	Scotia-Glenville CSD	Scotia
110	7	South Country CSD	E Patchogue
110	7	South Glens Falls CSD	S Glens Falls
110	7	Union-Endicott CSD	Endicott
110	7	Valley CSD (Montgomery)	Montgomery
110	7	Vestal CSD	Vestal
110	7	Warwick Valley CSD	Warwick
110	7	West Babylon UFSD	West Babylon
110	7	William Floyd UFSD	Mastic Beach
147	6	Albion CSD	Albion
147	6	Alden CSD	Alden
147	6	Attica CSD	Attica
147	6	Bethpage UFSD	Bethpage
147	6	Brockport CSD	Brockport
147	6	Brookhaven-Comsewogue UFSD	Pt Jefferson Stn
147	6	Churchville-Chili CSD	Churchville
147	6	Clarence CSD	Clarence
147	6	Cobleskill-Richmondville CSD	Cobleskill
147	6	Cohoes City SD	Cohoes
147	6	Coxsackie-Athens CSD	Coxsackie
147	6	Deer Park UFSD	Deer Park
147	6	Dunkirk City SD	Dunkirk
147	6	East Irondequoit CSD	Rochester
147	6	Elmont UFSD	Elmont
147	6	Farmingdale UFSD	Farmingdale
147	6	Fayetteville-Manlius CSD	Manlius
147	6	Frontier CSD	Hamburg
147	6	Fulton City SD	Fulton
147	6	Glen Cove City SD	Glen Cove
147	6	Glens Falls City SD	Glens Falls
147	6	Greenburgh CSD	Hartsdale
147	6	Hamburg CSD	Hamburg
147	6	Iroquois CSD	Elma
147	6	Jamesville-Dewitt CSD	Dewitt
147	6	Katonah-Lewisboro UFSD	South Salem
147	6	Mahopac CSD	Mahopac
147	6	Mamaroneck UFSD	Mamaroneck
147	6	Mexico CSD	Mexico
147	6	Minisink Valley CSD	Slate Hill
147	6	Niagara-Wheatfield CSD	Niagara Falls
147	6	North Bellmore UFSD	Bellmore
147	6	North Shore CSD	Sea Cliff
147	6	Norwich City SD	Norwich
147	6	Oneonta City SD	Oneonta
147	6	Onteora CSD	Boiceville
147	6	Orchard Park CSD	Orchard Park
147	6	Pelham UFSD	Pelham
147	6	Penfield CSD	Penfield
147	6	Peru CSD	Peru
147	6	Port Chester-Rye UFSD	Port Chester
147	6	Queensbury UFSD	Queensbury
147	6	Red Hook CSD	Red Hook
147	6	Rondout Valley CSD	Accord
147	6	Roosevelt UFSD	Roosevelt
147	6	Saugerties CSD	Saugerties
147	6	Schalmont CSD	Schenectady
147	6	South Huntington UFSD	Huntington Stn
147	6	South Orangetown CSD	Blauvelt
147	6	Sweet Home CSD	Amherst
147	6	Tonawanda City SD	Tonawanda
147	6	UFSD - Tarrytowns	Sleepy Hollow
147	6	Waterloo CSD	Waterloo
147	6	West Hempstead UFSD	W Hempstead
147	6	Yorktown CSD	Yorktown Hgts
202	5	Adirondack CSD	Boonville
202	5	Altmar-Parish-Williamstown CSD	Parish
202	5	Amityville UFSD	Amityville
202	5	Bayport-Blue Point UFSD	Bayport
202	5	Bellmore-Merrick Central HSD	North Merrick
202	5	Brewster CSD	Brewster
202	5	Brighton CSD	Rochester
202	5	Broadalbin-Perth CSD	Broadalbin
202	5	Burnt Hills-Ballston Lake CSD	Scotia
202	5	Canandaigua City SD	Canandaigua
202	5	Carthage CSD	Carthage
202	5	Chappaqua CSD	Chappaqua
202	5	Chittenango CSD	Chittenango
202	5	Copiague UFSD	Copiague
202	5	Cornwall CSD	Cornwall-on-Hud
202	5	Dover UFSD	Dover Plains
202	5	Dryden CSD	Dryden
202	5	Eastchester UFSD	Eastchester
202	5	Ellenville CSD	Ellenville
202	5	Gouverneur CSD	Gouverneur
202	5	Gowanda CSD	Gowanda
202	5	Grand Island CSD	Grand Island
202	5	Hauppauge UFSD	Hauppauge
202	5	Hendrick Hudson CSD	Montrose
202	5	Herricks UFSD	New Hyde Park
202	5	Hewlett-Woodmere UFSD	Woodmere
202	5	Highland CSD	Highland
202	5	Hilton CSD	Hilton
202	5	Homer CSD	Homer
202	5	Hornell City SD	Hornell
202	5	Hudson Falls CSD	Hudson Falls
202	5	Islip UFSD	Islip
202	5	Jericho UFSD	Jericho
202	5	Johnson City CSD	Johnson City
202	5	Kinderhook CSD	Valatie
202	5	Kings Park CSD	Kings Park
202	5	Lansing CSD	Lansing
202	5	Liberty CSD	Liberty
202	5	Marlboro CSD	Marlboro
202	5	Massena CSD	Massena
202	5	New Hartford CSD	New Hartford
202	5	New Paltz CSD	New Paltz
202	5	Newark CSD	Newark
202	5	Newfane CSD	Newfane
202	5	Northeastern Clinton CSD	Champlain
202	5	Owego-Apalachin CSD	Owego
202	5	Penn Yan CSD	Pen
202	5	Plainedge UFSD	N Massapequa
202	5	Port Jervis City SD	Port Jervis
202	5	Roslyn UFSD	Roslyn
202	5	Rye City SD	Rye
202	5	Salamanca City SD	Salamanca
202	5	Sayville UFSD	Sayville
202	5	Sewanhaka Central HSD	Floral Park
202	5	Sherrill City SD	Verona
202	5	Shoreham-Wading River CSD	Shoreham
202	5	Spencerport CSD	Spencerport
202	5	Sullivan West CSD	Jeffersonville
202	5	Susquehanna Valley CSD	Conklin
202	5	Victor CSD	Victor
202	5	Wantagh UFSD	Wantagh
202	5	Washingtonville CSD	Washingtonville
202	5	Waverly CSD	Waverly
202	5	Wayland-Cohocton CSD	Wayland
202	5	Wayne CSD	Ontario Center
267	4	Amherst CSD	Amherst
267	4	Beekmantown CSD	Plattsburgh
267	4	Byram Hills CSD	Armonk
267	4	Cairo-Durham CSD	Cairo
267	4	Canastota CSD	Canastota
267	4	Canton CSD	Canton
267	4	Cheektowaga-Maryvale UFSD	Cheektowaga
267	4	Cheektowaga-Sloan UFSD	Sloan
267	4	Chenango Forks CSD	Binghamton

267	4	Chenango Valley CSD	Binghamton
267	4	Cold Spring Harbor CSD	Cold Sprg Harbor
267	4	Dansville CSD	Dansville
267	4	East Aurora UFSD	East Aurora
267	4	Elwood UFSD	Greenlawn
267	4	Fonda-Fultonville CSD	Fonda
267	4	Fredonia CSD	Fredonia
267	4	Geneva City SD	Geneva
267	4	Gorham-Middlesex CSD	Rushville
267	4	Harborfields CSD	Greenlawn
267	4	Holland Patent CSD	Holland Patent
267	4	Honeoye Falls-Lima CSD	Honeoye Falls
267	4	Irvington UFSD	Irvington
267	4	Island Trees UFSD	Levittown
267	4	Jordan-Elbridge CSD	Jordan
267	4	Lansingburgh CSD	Troy
267	4	Lewiston-Porter CSD	Youngstown
267	4	Livonia CSD	Livonia
267	4	Locust Valley CSD	Locust Valley
267	4	Maine-Endwell CSD	Endwell
267	4	Malverne UFSD	Malverne
267	4	Manhasset UFSD	Manhasset
267	4	Medina CSD	Medina
267	4	Miller Place UFSD	Miller Place
267	4	Mount Pleasant CSD	Thornwood
267	4	New Hyde Pk-Garden City Pk UFSD	New Hyde Park
267	4	North Rose-Wolcott CSD	Wolcott
267	4	Palmyra-Macedon CSD	Palmyra
267	4	Phelps-Clifton Springs CSD	Clifton Spgs
267	4	Pleasantville UFSD	Pleasantville
267	4	Ravena-Coeymans-Selkirk CSD	Selkirk
267	4	Rocky Point UFSD	Rocky Point
267	4	Rotterdam-Mohonasen CSD	Schenectady
267	4	Seaford UFSD	Seaford
267	4	Seneca Falls CSD	Seneca Falls
267	4	Skaneateles CSD	Skaneateles
267	4	Solvay UFSD	Solvay
267	4	Somers CSD	Lincolndale
267	4	South Jefferson CSD	Adams Center
267	4	Spackenkill UFSD	Poughkeepsie
267	4	Springville-Griffith Inst CSD	Springville
267	4	Taconic Hills CSD	Craryville
267	4	Valley Stream 13 UFSD	Valley Stream
267	4	Valley Stream Central HSD	Valley Stream
267	4	Westhill CSD	Syracuse
267	4	Whitney Point CSD	Whitney Point
267	4	Windsor CSD	Windsor
267	4	Yorkshire-Pioneer CSD	Yorkshire
324	3	Akron CSD	Akron
324	3	Ardsley UFSD	Ardsley
324	3	Babylon UFSD	Babylon
324	3	Briarcliff Manor UFSD	Briarcliff Manor
324	3	Carle Place UFSD	Carle Place
324	3	Catskill CSD	Catskill
324	3	Cazenovia CSD	Cazenovia
324	3	Chatham CSD	Chatham
324	3	Cheektowaga CSD	Cheektowaga
324	3	Cleveland Hill UFSD	Cheektowaga
324	3	Clinton CSD	Clinton
324	3	Croton-Harmon UFSD	Croton-On-Hud
324	3	Depew UFSD	Depew
324	3	East Hampton UFSD	East Hampton
324	3	East Williston UFSD	Old Westbury
324	3	Eden CSD	Eden
324	3	Edgemont UFSD	Scarsdale
324	3	Franklin Square UFSD	Franklin Square
324	3	General Brown CSD	Dexter
324	3	Hannibal CSD	Hannibal
324	3	Hastings-On-Hudson UFSD	Hastings-on-Hud
324	3	Ilion CSD	Ilion
324	3	Marcellus CSD	Marcellus
324	3	Merrick UFSD	Merrick
324	3	Mount Sinai UFSD	Mount Sinai
324	3	Oyster Bay-East Norwich CSD	Oyster Bay
324	3	Phoenix CSD	Phoenix
324	3	Putnam Valley CSD	Putnam Valley
324	3	Royalton-Hartland CSD	Middleport
324	3	Salmon River CSD	Ft Covington
324	3	Sherburne-Earlville CSD	Sherburne
324	3	Southampton UFSD	Southampton
324	3	Southwestern CSD at Jamestown	Jamestown
324	3	Starpoint CSD	Lockport
324	3	Valley Stream 30 UFSD	Valley Stream
324	3	Westhampton Beach UFSD	Westhampton Bch
324	3	Wilson CSD	Wilson
324	3	Wyandanch UFSD	Wyandanch
362	2	Floral Park-Bellerose UFSD	Floral Park
362	2	Hampton Bays UFSD	Hampton Bays
362	2	Mattituck-Cutchogue UFSD	Cutchogue
362	2	Schuylerville CSD	Schuylerville
366	1	Boces Eastern Suffolk (Suffolk I)	Patchogue
366	1	Boces Monroe 1	Fairport
366	1	Boces Nassau	Garden City

Number of Teachers

Rank	Number	District Name	City
1	65,803	New York City Public Schools	Brooklyn
2	3,229	Buffalo City SD	Buffalo
3	2,943	Rochester City SD	Rochester
4	1,855	Yonkers City SD	Yonkers
5	1,833	Syracuse City SD	Syracuse
6	1,141	Sachem CSD	Holbrook
7	1,040	Brentwood UFSD	Brentwood
8	1,029	Greece CSD	Rochester
9	941	Newburgh City SD	Newburgh
10	777	Middle Country CSD	Centereach
11	777	Williamsville CSD	East Amherst
12	776	Wappingers CSD	Wappingers Fls
13	721	Smithtown CSD	Smithtown
14	720	New Rochelle City SD	New Rochelle
15	712	East Ramapo CSD (Spring Valley)	Spring Valley
16	692	Half Hollow Hills CSD	Dix Hills
17	689	Clarkstown CSD	New City
18	684	Longwood CSD	Middle Island
19	682	Kenmore-Tonawanda UFSD	Buffalo
20	681	North Syracuse CSD	N Syracuse
21	676	Mount Vernon City SD	Mount Vernon
22	666	Webster CSD	Webster
23	646	Boces Eastern Suffolk (Suffolk I)	Patchogue
24	639	Schenectady City SD	Schenectady
25	633	Shenendehowa CSD	Clifton Park
26	626	Haverstraw-Stony Point CSD	Garnerville
27	621	Patchogue-Medford UFSD	Patchogue
28	620	Utica City SD	Utica
29	620	East Meadow UFSD	Westbury
30	618	Levittown UFSD	Levittown
31	614	Arlington CSD	Poughkeepsie
32	607	William Floyd UFSD	Mastic Beach
33	600	Massapequa UFSD	Massapequa
34	595	Liverpool CSD	Liverpool
35	586	Syosset CSD	Syosset
36	585	Kingston City SD	Kingston
37	579	Three Village CSD	East Setauket
38	576	Elmira City SD	Elmira
39	568	White Plains City SD	White Plains
40	567	Niagara Falls City SD	Niagara Falls
41	564	West Seneca CSD	West Seneca
42	563	Commack UFSD	E Northport
43	554	Great Neck UFSD	Great Neck
44	554	Boces Nassau	Garden City
45	547	Binghamton City SD	Binghamton
46	540	Connetquot CSD	Bohemia
47	535	Northport-East Northport UFSD	Northport
48	527	Lindenhurst UFSD	Lindenhurst
49	525	Uniondale UFSD	Uniondale
50	524	Farmingdale UFSD	Farmingdale
51	522	Freeport UFSD	Freeport
52	514	Central Islip UFSD	Central Islip
53	508	Fairport CSD	Fairport
54	504	Monroe-Woodbury CSD	Central Valley
55	502	Saratoga Springs City SD	Saratoga Spgs
56	496	Sewanhaka Central HSD	Floral Park
57	493	Rush-Henrietta CSD	Henrietta
58	489	Ithaca City SD	Ithaca
59	481	Jamestown City SD	Jamestown
60	470	Oceanside UFSD	Oceanside
61	469	South Huntington UFSD	Huntington Stn
62	466	Rome City SD	Rome
63	458	Hempstead UFSD	Hempstead
64	451	Lakeland CSD	Shrub Oak
65	451	Pittsford CSD	Pittsford
66	447	South Colonie CSD	Albany
67	446	Lockport City SD	Lockport
68	441	Middletown City SD	Middletown
69	440	Corning City SD	Painted Post
70	436	Bay Shore UFSD	Bay Shore
71	432	West Islip UFSD	West Islip
72	430	Plainview-Old Bethpage CSD	Plainview
73	423	Baldwin UFSD	Baldwin
74	422	Guilderland CSD	Guilderland
75	421	Frontier CSD	Hamburg
76	417	Pine Bush CSD	Pine Bush
77	410	Penfield CSD	Penfield
78	408	Orchard Park CSD	Orchard Park
79	403	Lancaster CSD	Lancaster
80	400	Port Washington UFSD	Pt Washington
81	393	Baldwinsville CSD	Baldwinsville
82	390	Troy City SD	Troy
83	384	Gates-Chili CSD	Rochester
84	383	Mahopac CSD	Mahopac
85	382	North Colonie CSD	Latham
86	382	Hicksville UFSD	Hicksville
87	378	East Islip UFSD	Islip Terrace
88	375	South Country CSD	E Patchogue
89	374	Deer Park UFSD	Deer Park
90	371	Oswego City SD	Oswego
91	369	Scarsdale UFSD	Scarsdale
92	368	Mamaroneck UFSD	Mamaroneck
93	367	Valley CSD (Montgomery)	Montgomery
94	367	Bellmore-Merrick Central HSD	North Merrick
95	366	Auburn City SD	Auburn
96	362	Huntington UFSD	Huntington Stn
97	358	North Tonawanda City SD	N Tonawanda
97	358	Ramapo CSD (Suffern)	Hillburn
99	357	North Babylon UFSD	North Babylon
100	355	Lawrence UFSD	Lawrence
101	354	West Genesee CSD	Camillus
102	351	Central Square CSD	Central Square
103	350	Long Beach City SD	Long Beach
104	349	Union-Endicott CSD	Endicott
105	349	Bedford CSD	Mount Kisco
106	347	Poughkeepsie City SD	Poughkeepsie
107	344	Boces Monroe 1	Fairport
108	343	Riverhead CSD	Riverhead
109	340	Hilton CSD	Hilton
110	340	Bethlehem CSD	Delmar
111	338	Clarence CSD	Clarence
112	337	East Greenbush CSD	E Greenbush
112	337	West Babylon UFSD	West Babylon
114	337	Rockville Centre UFSD	Rockville Ctre
115	336	Herricks UFSD	New Hyde Park
115	336	Vestal CSD	Vestal
117	335	Hamburg CSD	Hamburg
118	332	Chappaqua CSD	Chappaqua
119	331	Carmel CSD	Patterson
120	330	Valley Stream Central HSD	Valley Stream
121	329	Ossining UFSD	Ossining
122	328	Washingtonville CSD	Washingtonville
123	325	East Syracuse-Minoa CSD	East Syracuse
124	324	Churchville-Chili CSD	Churchville
125	324	Canandaigua City SD	Canandaigua
126	322	Brockport CSD	Brockport
127	322	Fayetteville-Manlius CSD	Manlius
128	321	Hyde Park CSD	Poughkeepsie
129	318	Hauppauge UFSD	Hauppauge
130	317	Sweet Home CSD	Amherst
131	316	Kings Park CSD	Kings Park
132	314	Spencerport CSD	Spencerport
133	313	Katonah-Lewisboro UFSD	South Salem
134	312	Garden City UFSD	Garden City
135	309	Harrison CSD	Harrison
136	307	Horseheads CSD	Horseheads
137	307	Ballston Spa CSD	Ballston Spa
138	306	Yorktown CSD	Yorktown Hgts
139	305	Watertown City SD	Watertown
140	304	Warwick Valley CSD	Warwick
141	304	Jericho UFSD	Jericho
142	303	Monticello CSD	Monticello
143	301	Copiague UFSD	Copiague
144	300	Niagara-Wheatfield CSD	Niagara Falls
145	297	Fulton City SD	Fulton
146	297	Amsterdam City SD	Amsterdam
147	297	Niskayuna CSD	Schenectady
148	295	Indian River CSD	Philadelphia
149	295	Minisink Valley CSD	Slate Hill
150	288	Westbury UFSD	Old Westbury
151	287	Whitesboro CSD	Yorkville
152	283	Hewlett-Woodmere UFSD	Woodmere
153	278	Brighton CSD	Rochester
154	277	Elmont UFSD	Elmont
155	274	Brewster CSD	Brewster
156	267	Brookhaven-Comsewogue UFSD	Pt Jefferson Stn
157	266	Averill Park CSD	Averill Park
158	265	East Irondequoit CSD	Rochester
159	264	Mineola UFSD	Mineola
160	264	South Orangetown CSD	Blauvelt
161	263	Sayville UFSD	Sayville
162	262	West Irondequoit CSD	Rochester
163	260	Evans-Brant CSD (Lake Shore)	Angola
164	257	Amityville UFSD	Amityville
165	255	Wantagh UFSD	Wantagh
166	254	Glen Cove City SD	Glen Cove
167	254	Lynbrook UFSD	Lynbrook
168	253	Roslyn UFSD	Roslyn
169	251	Gloversville City SD	Gloversville
170	251	Port Chester-Rye UFSD	Port Chester
171	250	Nyack UFSD	Nyack
172	250	Queensbury UFSD	Queensbury
173	250	Islip UFSD	Islip
174	249	Peekskill City SD	Peekskill
175	248	Wallkill CSD	Wallkill
176	245	Plainedge UFSD	N Massapequa
177	244	South Glens Falls CSD	S Glens Falls
178	243	Amherst CSD	Amherst
179	243	Burnt Hills-Ballston Lake CSD	Scotia
180	242	Beacon City SD	Beacon

181	242	North Shore CSD	Sea Cliff
182	241	Victor CSD	Victor
183	237	Rocky Point UFSD	Rocky Point
184	235	Bethpage UFSD	Bethpage
185	234	Manhasset UFSD	Manhasset
186	233	Somers CSD	Lincolndale
187	233	Hendrick Hudson CSD	Montrose
188	233	Grand Island CSD	Grand Island
189	232	Port Jervis City SD	Port Jervis
190	232	Yorkshire-Pioneer CSD	Yorkshire
191	231	Roosevelt UFSD	Roosevelt
192	229	Harborfields CSD	Greenlawn
193	229	Saugerties CSD	Saugerties
194	225	Jamesville-Dewitt CSD	Dewitt
195	224	Cortland City SD	Cortland
196	223	Geneva City SD	Geneva
197	222	Newark CSD	Newark
198	221	Batavia City SD	Batavia
199	219	Rotterdam-Mohonasen CSD	Schenectady
200	217	Wayne CSD	Ontario Center
201	216	Malone CSD	Malone
202	216	Goshen CSD	Goshen
203	215	Miller Place UFSD	Miller Place
204	213	Johnson City CSD	Johnson City
205	213	Rondout Valley CSD	Accord
206	212	Scotia-Glenville CSD	Scotia
207	211	Maine-Endwell CSD	Endwell
208	211	Island Trees UFSD	Levittown
209	210	Dunkirk City SD	Dunkirk
210	209	Eastchester UFSD	Eastchester
211	208	Glens Falls City SD	Glens Falls
212	206	Massena CSD	Massena
213	206	New Hartford CSD	New Hartford
214	205	Carthage CSD	Carthage
215	205	Rye City SD	Rye
216	204	Phoenix CSD	Phoenix
217	202	Camden CSD	Camden
218	201	Shoreham-Wading River CSD	Shoreham
219	200	Locust Valley CSD	Locust Valley
220	200	Bayport-Blue Point UFSD	Bayport
221	199	Iroquois CSD	Elma
222	198	Byram Hills CSD	Armonk
223	198	Albion CSD	Albion
224	197	Olean City SD	Olean
225	196	Plattsburgh City SD	Plattsburgh
226	196	Hudson City SD	Hudson
227	196	Norwich City SD	Norwich
228	195	Mexico CSD	Mexico
229	195	Seaford UFSD	Seaford
230	195	UFSD - Tarrytowns	Sleepy Hollow
231	194	Oneida City SD	Oneida
232	193	Homer CSD	Homer
233	192	Beekmantown CSD	Plattsburgh
234	191	Onteora CSD	Boiceville
235	191	Cornwall CSD	Cornwall-on-Hud
236	190	Honeoye Falls-Lima CSD	Honeoye Falls
237	190	Pelham UFSD	Pelham
238	189	Chittenango CSD	Chittenango
239	188	Ravena-Coeymans-Selkirk CSD	Selkirk
240	187	Cheektowaga-Maryvale UFSD	Cheektowaga
241	186	Tonawanda City SD	Tonawanda
242	186	Susquehanna Valley CSD	Conklin
243	185	Palmyra-Macedon CSD	Palmyra
244	184	Depew UFSD	Depew
245	183	Cobleskill-Richmondville CSD	Cobleskill
246	182	West Hempstead UFSD	W Hempstead
247	182	Nanuet UFSD	Nanuet
247	182	Peru CSD	Peru
249	182	Lewiston-Porter CSD	Youngstown
250	181	Pearl River UFSD	Pearl River
251	181	Cheektowaga CSD	Cheektowaga
251	181	Cohoes City SD	Cohoes
253	180	Greenburgh CSD	Hartsdale
254	180	Starpoint CSD	Lockport
255	180	Ardsley UFSD	Ardsley
255	180	Livonia CSD	Livonia
257	178	Ogdensburg City SD	Ogdensburg
258	176	Owego-Apalachin CSD	Owego
259	176	North Bellmore UFSD	Bellmore
260	176	Oneonta City SD	Oneonta
261	175	Schalmont CSD	Schenectady
262	174	Lackawanna City SD	Lackawanna
263	173	Dryden CSD	Dryden
264	173	Sherrill City SD	Verona
265	172	Kinderhook CSD	Valatie
266	172	Fredonia CSD	Fredonia
267	171	Medina CSD	Medina
268	171	Lansingburgh CSD	Troy
269	171	Penn Yan CSD	Pen
269	171	Springville-Griffith Inst CSD	Springville
271	169	Red Hook CSD	Red Hook
272	168	New Paltz CSD	New Paltz
273	166	Mount Sinai UFSD	Mount Sinai
274	165	Hudson Falls CSD	Hudson Falls
275	165	Sherburne-Earlville CSD	Sherburne
276	165	Elwood UFSD	Greenlawn
277	165	Valley Stream 13 UFSD	Valley Stream
278	163	Hornell City SD	Hornell
279	163	Mount Pleasant CSD	Thornwood
280	163	East Hampton UFSD	East Hampton
281	163	Malverne UFSD	Malverne
282	163	Southampton UFSD	Southampton
283	161	Whitney Point CSD	Whitney Point
283	161	Wyandanch UFSD	Wyandanch
285	160	Phelps-Clifton Springs CSD	Clifton Spgs
286	159	Windsor CSD	Windsor
287	158	Westhampton Beach UFSD	Westhampton Bch
288	157	Marlboro CSD	Marlboro
289	156	Wayland-Cohocton CSD	Wayland
290	155	Babylon UFSD	Babylon
291	154	Cold Spring Harbor CSD	Cold Sprg Harbor
292	154	Saranac CSD	Dannemora
293	153	Newfane CSD	Newfane
294	152	Alden CSD	Alden
295	150	Bath CSD	Bath
296	150	Waterloo CSD	Waterloo
297	149	East Williston UFSD	Old Westbury
298	149	Chenango Valley CSD	Binghamton
299	149	Johnstown City SD	Johnstown
299	149	Taconic Hills CSD	Craryville
301	148	North Rose-Wolcott CSD	Wolcott
302	147	Irvington UFSD	Irvington
303	147	Spackenkill UFSD	Poughkeepsie
304	147	Catskill CSD	Catskill
305	146	Westhill CSD	Syracuse
306	146	South Jefferson CSD	Adams Center
306	146	Sullivan West CSD	Jeffersonville
308	145	Liberty CSD	Liberty
309	144	Dansville CSD	Dansville
310	143	Attica CSD	Attica
311	143	Skaneateles CSD	Skaneateles
312	143	Merrick UFSD	Merrick
313	142	Holland Patent CSD	Holland Patent
314	142	Oyster Bay-East Norwich CSD	Oyster Bay
315	142	Marcellus CSD	Marcellus
316	141	East Aurora UFSD	East Aurora
316	141	Hastings-On-Hudson UFSD	Hastings-on-Hud
318	141	Briarcliff Manor UFSD	Briarcliff Manor
319	140	Jordan-Elbridge CSD	Jordan
320	139	Putnam Valley CSD	Putnam Valley
321	139	Royalton-Hartland CSD	Middleport
322	139	Chenango Forks CSD	Binghamton
322	139	Ellenville CSD	Ellenville
324	137	Broadalbin-Perth CSD	Broadalbin
324	137	Salmon River CSD	Ft Covington
326	137	Cazenovia CSD	Cazenovia
327	137	Carle Place UFSD	Carle Place
328	136	Solvay UFSD	Solvay
329	136	Edgemont UFSD	Scarsdale
330	135	Saranac Lake CSD	Saranac Lake
331	135	Ilion CSD	Ilion
332	135	Mattituck-Cutchogue UFSD	Cutchogue
333	133	Southwestern CSD at Jamestown	Jamestown
334	133	Eden CSD	Eden
335	132	Hampton Bays UFSD	Hampton Bays
336	131	Altmar-Parish-Williamstown CSD	Parish
336	131	Franklin Square UFSD	Franklin Square
338	131	Coxsackie-Athens CSD	Coxsackie
339	130	Waverly CSD	Waverly
340	130	Adirondack CSD	Boonville
341	129	Gorham-Middlesex CSD	Rushville
342	129	Cairo-Durham CSD	Cairo
343	129	Canton CSD	Canton
344	128	Highland CSD	Highland
344	128	Seneca Falls CSD	Seneca Falls
346	128	Schuylerville CSD	Schuylerville
347	127	Clinton CSD	Clinton
347	127	Salamanca City SD	Salamanca
349	127	Hannibal CSD	Hannibal
350	126	Wilson CSD	Wilson
351	125	Akron CSD	Akron
352	125	Fonda-Fultonville CSD	Fonda
353	124	Gouverneur CSD	Gouverneur
354	124	Pleasantville UFSD	Pleasantville
355	121	Northeastern Clinton CSD	Champlain
356	120	Gowanda CSD	Gowanda
357	119	Cleveland Hill UFSD	Cheektowaga
358	118	Cheektowaga-Sloan UFSD	Sloan
359	116	Lansing CSD	Lansing
359	116	New Hyde Pk-Garden City Pk UFSD	New Hyde Park
361	116	Canastota CSD	Canastota
362	115	Croton-Harmon UFSD	Croton-On-Hud
363	112	Valley Stream 30 UFSD	Valley Stream
364	111	Dover UFSD	Dover Plains
365	111	General Brown CSD	Dexter
366	106	Chatham CSD	Chatham
367	104	Floral Park-Bellerose UFSD	Floral Park
368	n/a	Albany City SD	Albany

Number of Students

Rank	Number	District Name	City
1	1,077,381	New York City Public Schools	Brooklyn
2	43,474	Buffalo City SD	Buffalo
3	35,659	Rochester City SD	Rochester
4	26,398	Yonkers City SD	Yonkers
5	22,455	Syracuse City SD	Syracuse
6	16,262	Brentwood UFSD	Brentwood
7	15,311	Sachem CSD	Holbrook
8	13,730	Greece CSD	Rochester
9	12,895	Newburgh City SD	Newburgh
10	12,125	Wappingers CSD	Wappingers Fls
11	11,591	Middle Country CSD	Centereach
12	10,726	Williamsville CSD	East Amherst
13	10,410	Mount Vernon City SD	Mount Vernon
14	10,299	New Rochelle City SD	New Rochelle
15	10,267	William Floyd UFSD	Mastic Beach
16	10,202	North Syracuse CSD	N Syracuse
17	9,993	Arlington CSD	Poughkeepsie
18	9,867	Longwood CSD	Middle Island
19	9,789	Smithtown CSD	Smithtown
20	9,656	Albany City SD	Albany
21	9,362	East Ramapo CSD (Spring Valley)	Spring Valley
22	9,233	Shenendehowa CSD	Clifton Park
23	9,212	Patchogue-Medford UFSD	Patchogue
24	9,196	Clarkstown CSD	New City
25	9,192	Half Hollow Hills CSD	Dix Hills
26	9,100	Kenmore-Tonawanda UFSD	Buffalo
27	8,929	Niagara Falls City SD	Niagara Falls
28	8,885	Utica City SD	Utica
29	8,613	Liverpool CSD	Liverpool
30	8,526	Schenectady City SD	Schenectady
31	8,471	Webster CSD	Webster
32	8,266	Sewanhaka Central HSD	Floral Park
33	8,245	Kingston City SD	Kingston
34	8,219	Haverstraw-Stony Point CSD	Garnerville
35	8,192	Massapequa UFSD	Massapequa
36	8,081	East Meadow UFSD	Westbury
37	8,015	Levittown UFSD	Levittown
38	7,993	Three Village CSD	East Setauket
39	7,637	West Seneca CSD	West Seneca
40	7,601	Lindenhurst UFSD	Lindenhurst
41	7,539	Elmira City SD	Elmira
42	7,321	Commack UFSD	E Northport
43	7,251	Freeport UFSD	Freeport
44	7,218	Hempstead UFSD	Hempstead
45	7,164	Monroe-Woodbury CSD	Central Valley
46	7,126	Fairport CSD	Fairport
47	7,064	Connetquot CSD	Bohemia
48	6,905	Saratoga Springs City SD	Saratoga Spgs
49	6,775	White Plains City SD	White Plains
50	6,628	Central Islip UFSD	Central Islip
51	6,502	Farmingdale UFSD	Farmingdale
52	6,491	Middletown City SD	Middletown
53	6,472	Syosset CSD	Syosset
54	6,432	Binghamton City SD	Binghamton
55	6,325	Uniondale UFSD	Uniondale
56	6,320	Oceanside UFSD	Oceanside
57	6,275	Rome City SD	Rome
58	6,248	South Huntington UFSD	Huntington Stn
59	6,242	Northport-East Northport UFSD	Northport
60	6,239	Lakeland CSD	Shrub Oak
61	6,109	Lancaster CSD	Lancaster
62	6,092	Pine Bush CSD	Pine Bush
63	6,091	Rush-Henrietta CSD	Henrietta
64	6,065	Great Neck UFSD	Great Neck
65	5,933	Pittsford CSD	Pittsford
66	5,893	West Islip UFSD	West Islip
67	5,806	Corning City SD	Painted Post
68	5,804	Lockport City SD	Lockport
69	5,800	Baldwinsville CSD	Baldwinsville
70	5,788	South Colonie CSD	Albany
71	5,772	Ithaca City SD	Ithaca
72	5,724	Bay Shore UFSD	Bay Shore
73	5,681	Bellmore-Merrick Central HSD	North Merrick
74	5,667	Guilderland CSD	Guilderland
75	5,645	Frontier CSD	Hamburg
76	5,619	North Colonie CSD	Latham
77	5,437	Baldwin UFSD	Baldwin
78	5,338	East Islip UFSD	Islip Terrace
79	5,319	Valley CSD (Montgomery)	Montgomery
80	5,255	Mahopac CSD	Mahopac
81	5,225	Jamestown City SD	Jamestown
82	5,172	West Genesee CSD	Camillus
83	5,161	Hicksville UFSD	Hicksville
84	5,158	Washingtonville CSD	Washingtonville
85	5,155	North Babylon UFSD	North Babylon

Rank	Number	District	City
86	5,127	Orchard Park CSD	Orchard Park
87	5,124	Gates-Chili CSD	Rochester
88	5,093	Troy City SD	Troy
89	5,058	Penfield CSD	Penfield
90	5,034	Bethlehem CSD	Delmar
91	4,985	Central Square CSD	Central Square
92	4,974	Oswego City SD	Oswego
93	4,956	Carmel CSD	Patterson
94	4,930	Auburn City SD	Auburn
95	4,924	West Babylon UFSD	West Babylon
96	4,897	Riverhead CSD	Riverhead
97	4,874	Plainview-Old Bethpage CSD	Plainview
98	4,864	North Tonawanda City SD	N Tonawanda
99	4,784	Clarence CSD	Clarence
100	4,768	South Country CSD	E Patchogue
101	4,746	Poughkeepsie City SD	Poughkeepsie
102	4,729	Hyde Park CSD	Poughkeepsie
103	4,712	Mamaroneck UFSD	Mamaroneck
104	4,706	Port Washington UFSD	Pt Washington
105	4,635	Copiague UFSD	Copiague
106	4,605	Fayetteville-Manlius CSD	Manlius
107	4,603	East Greenbush CSD	E Greenbush
108	4,595	Warwick Valley CSD	Warwick
109	4,573	Brockport CSD	Brockport
110	4,563	Union-Endicott CSD	Endicott
111	4,536	Long Beach City SD	Long Beach
112	4,515	Churchville-Chili CSD	Churchville
113	4,508	Scarsdale UFSD	Scarsdale
114	4,505	Ramapo CSD (Suffern)	Hillburn
115	4,488	Valley Stream Central HSD	Valley Stream
116	4,477	Ballston Spa CSD	Ballston Spa
117	4,462	Horseheads CSD	Horseheads
118	4,438	Hilton CSD	Hilton
119	4,388	Minisink Valley CSD	Slate Hill
120	4,383	Deer Park UFSD	Deer Park
121	4,372	Vestal CSD	Vestal
122	4,338	Elmont UFSD	Elmont
123	4,312	Spencerport CSD	Spencerport
124	4,249	Ossining UFSD	Ossining
125	4,229	Watertown City SD	Watertown
126	4,224	Niskayuna CSD	Schenectady
127	4,205	Canandaigua City SD	Canandaigua
128	4,183	Yorktown CSD	Yorktown Hgts
129	4,133	Hamburg CSD	Hamburg
130	4,112	Katonah-Lewisboro UFSD	South Salem
131	4,104	Huntington UFSD	Huntington Stn
132	4,075	Bedford CSD	Mount Kisco
133	4,069	Westbury UFSD	Old Westbury
134	4,058	Garden City UFSD	Garden City
135	4,055	Chappaqua CSD	Chappaqua
136	4,014	Hauppauge UFSD	Hauppauge
137	4,004	Niagara-Wheatfield CSD	Niagara Falls
138	3,973	Kings Park CSD	Kings Park
138	3,973	West Irondequoit CSD	Rochester
140	3,917	Sweet Home CSD	Amherst
141	3,896	Brookhaven-Comsewogue UFSD	Pt Jefferson Stn
142	3,874	Herricks UFSD	New Hyde Park
143	3,872	Whitesboro CSD	Yorkville
144	3,856	Fulton City SD	Fulton
145	3,848	East Syracuse-Minoa CSD	East Syracuse
146	3,836	Queensbury UFSD	Queensbury
147	3,804	Lawrence UFSD	Lawrence
148	3,740	Amsterdam City SD	Amsterdam
149	3,698	Brewster CSD	Brewster
150	3,658	Wallkill CSD	Wallkill
151	3,656	Rocky Point UFSD	Rocky Point
152	3,643	Rockville Centre UFSD	Rockville Ctre
153	3,629	Sayville UFSD	Sayville
154	3,617	Islip UFSD	Islip
155	3,593	Brighton CSD	Rochester
156	3,592	Monticello CSD	Monticello
157	3,589	Beacon City SD	Beacon
158	3,527	Port Chester-Rye UFSD	Port Chester
159	3,505	Plainedge UFSD	N Massapequa
160	3,499	East Irondequoit CSD	Rochester
161	3,488	Wantagh UFSD	Wantagh
162	3,478	Indian River CSD	Philadelphia
163	3,466	Averill Park CSD	Averill Park
164	3,448	Victor CSD	Victor
165	3,432	Port Jervis City SD	Port Jervis
166	3,414	Harborfields CSD	Greenlawn
167	3,413	Burnt Hills-Ballston Lake CSD	Scotia
167	3,413	Evans-Brant CSD (Lake Shore)	Angola
167	3,413	Saugerties CSD	Saugerties
170	3,370	Hewlett-Woodmere UFSD	Woodmere
171	3,360	Harrison CSD	Harrison
172	3,284	Gloversville City SD	Gloversville
173	3,281	Rotterdam-Mohonasen CSD	Schenectady
174	3,269	South Glens Falls CSD	S Glens Falls
175	3,258	South Orangetown CSD	Blauvelt
176	3,240	Amityville UFSD	Amityville
177	3,205	Grand Island CSD	Grand Island
178	3,191	Roslyn UFSD	Roslyn
179	3,187	Glen Cove City SD	Glen Cove
180	3,169	Amherst CSD	Amherst
181	3,129	Jericho UFSD	Jericho
182	3,105	Lynbrook UFSD	Lynbrook
183	3,029	Yorkshire-Pioneer CSD	Yorkshire
184	3,011	Scotia-Glenville CSD	Scotia
185	2,984	Somers CSD	Lincolndale
186	2,983	Cornwall CSD	Cornwall-on-Hud
187	2,974	Miller Place UFSD	Miller Place
187	2,974	Peekskill City SD	Peekskill
189	2,965	Goshen CSD	Goshen
190	2,960	Bethpage UFSD	Bethpage
191	2,959	Carthage CSD	Carthage
192	2,940	Roosevelt UFSD	Roosevelt
193	2,907	Iroquois CSD	Elma
194	2,906	Nyack UFSD	Nyack
195	2,884	Mineola UFSD	Mineola
196	2,839	Massena CSD	Massena
197	2,833	Hendrick Hudson CSD	Montrose
198	2,820	Albion CSD	Albion
199	2,809	Wayne CSD	Ontario Center
200	2,805	Cortland City SD	Cortland
201	2,804	Starpoint CSD	Lockport
202	2,801	Rondout Valley CSD	Accord
203	2,783	Island Trees UFSD	Levittown
204	2,758	Camden CSD	Camden
205	2,735	Newark CSD	Newark
206	2,724	Jamesville-Dewitt CSD	Dewitt
207	2,718	Seaford UFSD	Seaford
208	2,708	New Hartford CSD	New Hartford
209	2,703	Batavia City SD	Batavia
210	2,694	Maine-Endwell CSD	Endwell
211	2,688	Mexico CSD	Mexico
212	2,686	Shoreham-Wading River CSD	Shoreham
213	2,657	Byram Hills CSD	Armonk
214	2,655	Malone CSD	Malone
215	2,640	Olean City SD	Olean
216	2,633	Rye City SD	Rye
217	2,625	Geneva City SD	Geneva
218	2,624	Manhasset UFSD	Manhasset
219	2,623	North Shore CSD	Sea Cliff
220	2,611	Eastchester UFSD	Eastchester
221	2,607	Glens Falls City SD	Glens Falls
222	2,606	Honeoye Falls-Lima CSD	Honeoye Falls
223	2,589	Oneida City SD	Oneida
224	2,581	Cheektowaga-Maryvale UFSD	Cheektowaga
225	2,580	Chittenango CSD	Chittenango
226	2,556	Johnson City CSD	Johnson City
227	2,542	North Bellmore UFSD	Bellmore
228	2,488	Phoenix CSD	Phoenix
229	2,473	Pelham UFSD	Pelham
230	2,465	Sherrill City SD	Verona
231	2,462	Elwood UFSD	Greenlawn
232	2,458	Lansingburgh CSD	Troy
233	2,453	Cheektowaga CSD	Cheektowaga
234	2,448	Homer CSD	Homer
235	2,447	Bayport-Blue Point UFSD	Bayport
236	2,437	Tonawanda City SD	Tonawanda
237	2,428	Lewiston-Porter CSD	Youngstown
238	2,417	Depew UFSD	Depew
239	2,415	Owego-Apalachin CSD	Owego
240	2,409	Pearl River UFSD	Pearl River
241	2,407	UFSD - Tarrytowns	Sleepy Hollow
242	2,405	West Hempstead UFSD	W Hempstead
243	2,388	Springville-Griffith Inst CSD	Springville
244	2,386	New Paltz CSD	New Paltz
245	2,383	Mount Sinai UFSD	Mount Sinai
246	2,376	Ravena-Coeymans-Selkirk CSD	Selkirk
247	2,361	Hudson Falls CSD	Hudson Falls
248	2,332	Red Hook CSD	Red Hook
249	2,325	Kinderhook CSD	Valatie
250	2,302	Peru CSD	Peru
251	2,286	Norwich City SD	Norwich
252	2,285	Ardsley UFSD	Ardsley
253	2,281	Wyandanch UFSD	Wyandanch
254	2,261	Palmyra-Macedon CSD	Palmyra
255	2,256	Hudson City SD	Hudson
256	2,248	Schalmont CSD	Schenectady
257	2,231	Locust Valley CSD	Locust Valley
258	2,228	Onteora CSD	Boiceville
259	2,192	Valley Stream 13 UFSD	Valley Stream
260	2,180	Livonia CSD	Livonia
261	2,178	Broadalbin-Perth CSD	Broadalbin
262	2,177	Cobleskill-Richmondville CSD	Cobleskill
262	2,177	Newfane CSD	Newfane
264	2,170	Marcellus CSD	Marcellus
265	2,164	Nanuet UFSD	Nanuet
266	2,163	Oneonta City SD	Oneonta
267	2,159	Susquehanna Valley CSD	Conklin
268	2,124	Johnstown City SD	Johnstown
269	2,120	Phelps-Clifton Springs CSD	Clifton Spgs
270	2,117	Cohoes City SD	Cohoes
271	2,116	Beekmantown CSD	Plattsburgh
272	2,113	Dunkirk City SD	Dunkirk
273	2,101	Plattsburgh City SD	Plattsburgh
274	2,095	Lackawanna City SD	Lackawanna
275	2,094	East Aurora UFSD	East Aurora
276	2,076	Highland CSD	Highland
277	2,072	Penn Yan CSD	Pen
278	2,068	Ogdensburg City SD	Ogdensburg
279	2,067	Marlboro CSD	Marlboro
280	2,066	Alden CSD	Alden
281	2,060	Windsor CSD	Windsor
282	2,047	Cold Spring Harbor CSD	Cold Sprg Harbor
282	2,047	Westhill CSD	Syracuse
284	2,042	Boces Eastern Suffolk (Suffolk I)	Patchogue
285	2,041	Waterloo CSD	Waterloo
286	2,021	Bath CSD	Bath
287	2,016	Greenburgh CSD	Hartsdale
288	2,009	Chenango Valley CSD	Binghamton
289	2,008	Boces Nassau	Garden City
290	2,001	Babylon UFSD	Babylon
291	1,997	Medina CSD	Medina
292	1,991	South Jefferson CSD	Adams Center
293	1,988	East Hampton UFSD	East Hampton
294	1,981	Hornell City SD	Hornell
295	1,944	Merrick UFSD	Merrick
296	1,940	Franklin Square UFSD	Franklin Square
297	1,933	Whitney Point CSD	Whitney Point
298	1,931	Irvington UFSD	Irvington
299	1,928	Dryden CSD	Dryden
300	1,925	Fredonia CSD	Fredonia
301	1,923	Liberty CSD	Liberty
302	1,901	Chenango Forks CSD	Binghamton
303	1,899	Holland Patent CSD	Holland Patent
304	1,892	Saranac CSD	Dannemora
305	1,878	Ellenville CSD	Ellenville
306	1,875	Skaneateles CSD	Skaneateles
307	1,874	Taconic Hills CSD	Craryville
308	1,860	Eden CSD	Eden
309	1,854	Ilion CSD	Ilion
310	1,850	Wayland-Cohocton CSD	Wayland
311	1,843	Mount Pleasant CSD	Thornwood
312	1,836	Malverne UFSD	Malverne
313	1,831	Attica CSD	Attica
314	1,822	Cazenovia CSD	Cazenovia
315	1,821	Dover UFSD	Dover Plains
316	1,819	Cairo-Durham CSD	Cairo
317	1,818	Waverly CSD	Waverly
318	1,815	Westhampton Beach UFSD	Westhampton Bch
319	1,811	New Hyde Pk-Garden City Pk UFSD	New Hyde Park
320	1,809	Solvay UFSD	Solvay
321	1,803	Dansville CSD	Dansville
322	1,798	Edgemont UFSD	Scarsdale
323	1,787	Sherburne-Earlville CSD	Sherburne
324	1,786	Catskill CSD	Catskill
325	1,785	Spackenkill UFSD	Poughkeepsie
326	1,774	Gouverneur CSD	Gouverneur
327	1,764	Putnam Valley CSD	Putnam Valley
328	1,761	Hannibal CSD	Hannibal
329	1,754	Southampton UFSD	Southampton
330	1,752	East Williston UFSD	Old Westbury
330	1,752	Hampton Bays UFSD	Hampton Bays
332	1,738	Southwestern CSD at Jamestown	Jamestown
333	1,736	Jordan-Elbridge CSD	Jordan
334	1,726	Floral Park-Bellerose UFSD	Floral Park
335	1,717	Royalton-Hartland CSD	Middleport
336	1,704	Akron CSD	Akron
337	1,699	Pleasantville UFSD	Pleasantville
338	1,692	Northeastern Clinton CSD	Champlain
339	1,690	Altmar-Parish-Williamstown CSD	Parish
339	1,690	Briarcliff Manor UFSD	Briarcliff Manor
341	1,680	Saranac Lake CSD	Saranac Lake
342	1,675	North Rose-Wolcott CSD	Wolcott
343	1,674	Hastings-On-Hudson UFSD	Hastings-on-Hud
344	1,661	Clinton CSD	Clinton
345	1,659	Schuylerville CSD	Schuylerville
346	1,652	Gorham-Middlesex CSD	Rushville
347	1,641	Coxsackie-Athens CSD	Coxsackie
348	1,617	Adirondack CSD	Boonville
348	1,617	Sullivan West CSD	Jeffersonville
350	1,602	Fonda-Fultonville CSD	Fonda
351	1,589	Cleveland Hill UFSD	Cheektowaga
352	1,586	Salamanca City SD	Salamanca
353	1,583	Lansing CSD	Lansing
354	1,570	Canastota CSD	Canastota
355	1,565	General Brown CSD	Dexter
356	1,562	Mattituck-Cutchogue UFSD	Cutchogue
357	1,559	Canton CSD	Canton
358	1,536	Salmon River CSD	Ft Covington
358	1,536	Seneca Falls CSD	Seneca Falls
360	1,531	Cheektowaga-Sloan UFSD	Sloan
361	1,524	Valley Stream 30 UFSD	Valley Stream
362	1,521	Boces Monroe 1	Fairport

363	1,520	Croton-Harmon UFSD	Croton-On-Hud
364	1,517	Carle Place UFSD	Carle Place
365	1,513	Gowanda CSD	Gowanda
366	1,511	Chatham CSD	Chatham
367	1,502	Oyster Bay-East Norwich CSD	Oyster Bay
368	1,500	Wilson CSD	Wilson

Male Students

Rank	Percent	District Name	City
1	74.0	Boces Eastern Suffolk (Suffolk I)	Patchogue
1	74.0	Boces Nassau	Garden City
3	72.0	Boces Monroe 1	Fairport
4	69.1	Coxsackie-Athens CSD	Coxsackie
5	57.4	Broadalbin-Perth CSD	Broadalbin
6	56.2	Hudson City SD	Hudson
7	54.9	Highland CSD	Highland
8	54.6	Bath CSD	Bath
9	54.1	Attica CSD	Attica
9	54.1	Hornell City SD	Hornell
11	53.9	Dover UFSD	Dover Plains
12	53.7	Cleveland Hill UFSD	Cheektowaga
13	53.6	East Islip UFSD	Islip Terrace
14	53.3	Brewster CSD	Brewster
14	53.3	Lackawanna City SD	Lackawanna
16	53.1	Hampton Bays UFSD	Hampton Bays
16	53.1	Rondout Valley CSD	Accord
16	53.1	Valley Stream 13 UFSD	Valley Stream
19	53.0	Alden CSD	Alden
19	53.0	Ardsley UFSD	Ardsley
19	53.0	Niagara-Wheatfield CSD	Niagara Falls
22	52.9	East Hampton UFSD	East Hampton
22	52.9	Fonda-Fultonville CSD	Fonda
22	52.9	Garden City UFSD	Garden City
22	52.9	Ogdensburg City SD	Ogdensburg
22	52.9	Rye City SD	Rye
22	52.9	South Jefferson CSD	Adams Center
22	52.9	Vestal CSD	Vestal
22	52.9	Wayne CSD	Ontario Center
30	52.8	Jordan-Elbridge CSD	Jordan
30	52.8	Ossining UFSD	Ossining
30	52.8	Palmyra-Macedon CSD	Palmyra
33	52.7	Bay Shore UFSD	Bay Shore
33	52.7	East Williston UFSD	Old Westbury
33	52.7	Farmingdale UFSD	Farmingdale
33	52.7	Greenburgh CSD	Hartsdale
33	52.7	Malone CSD	Malone
33	52.7	Pleasantville UFSD	Pleasantville
33	52.7	Port Jervis City SD	Port Jervis
33	52.7	Rocky Point UFSD	Rocky Point
41	52.6	Southwestern CSD at Jamestown	Jamestown
42	52.5	Deer Park UFSD	Deer Park
42	52.5	Gowanda CSD	Gowanda
42	52.5	Phelps-Clifton Springs CSD	Clifton Spgs
45	52.4	Bethlehem CSD	Delmar
45	52.4	Rome City SD	Rome
45	52.4	Waverly CSD	Waverly
48	52.3	Brentwood UFSD	Brentwood
48	52.3	Great Neck UFSD	Great Neck
48	52.3	Hendrick Hudson CSD	Montrose
48	52.3	North Bellmore UFSD	Bellmore
48	52.3	Owego-Apalachin CSD	Owego
48	52.3	Red Hook CSD	Red Hook
48	52.3	Roslyn UFSD	Roslyn
48	52.3	Rush-Henrietta CSD	Henrietta
48	52.3	White Plains City SD	White Plains
57	52.2	Amityville UFSD	Amityville
57	52.2	Bethpage UFSD	Bethpage
57	52.2	Briarcliff Manor UFSD	Briarcliff Manor
57	52.2	Skaneateles CSD	Skaneateles
57	52.2	Sweet Home CSD	Amherst
57	52.2	Troy City SD	Troy
57	52.2	Warwick Valley CSD	Warwick
57	52.2	Westhill CSD	Syracuse
65	52.1	Cheektowaga CSD	Cheektowaga
65	52.1	Churchville-Chili CSD	Churchville
65	52.1	Elmira City SD	Elmira
65	52.1	Iroquois CSD	Elma
65	52.1	Ithaca City SD	Ithaca
65	52.1	Medina CSD	Medina
65	52.1	Solvay UFSD	Solvay
65	52.1	Webster CSD	Webster
73	52.0	Baldwin UFSD	Baldwin
73	52.0	Dryden CSD	Dryden
73	52.0	East Ramapo CSD (Spring Valley)	Spring Valley
73	52.0	Grand Island CSD	Grand Island
73	52.0	Lansing CSD	Lansing
73	52.0	Lewiston-Porter CSD	Youngstown
73	52.0	Malverne UFSD	Malverne
73	52.0	Pelham UFSD	Pelham
73	52.0	Port Chester-Rye UFSD	Port Chester
73	52.0	Riverhead CSD	Riverhead
73	52.0	Spencerport CSD	Spencerport
73	52.0	West Genesee CSD	Camillus
85	51.9	Cobleskill-Richmondville CSD	Cobleskill
85	51.9	Eastchester UFSD	Eastchester
85	51.9	Glen Cove City SD	Glen Cove
85	51.9	Gouverneur CSD	Gouverneur
85	51.9	Hudson Falls CSD	Hudson Falls
85	51.9	Liberty CSD	Liberty
85	51.9	Longwood CSD	Middle Island
85	51.9	Peru CSD	Peru
85	51.9	Smithtown CSD	Smithtown
85	51.9	South Huntington UFSD	Huntington Stn
85	51.9	Union-Endicott CSD	Endicott
85	51.9	William Floyd UFSD	Mastic Beach
97	51.8	Bedford CSD	Mount Kisco
97	51.8	Chappaqua CSD	Chappaqua
97	51.8	Chenango Forks CSD	Binghamton
97	51.8	Chenango Valley CSD	Binghamton
97	51.8	Lockport City SD	Lockport
97	51.8	Middle Country CSD	Centereach
97	51.8	Nanuet UFSD	Nanuet
97	51.8	Scarsdale UFSD	Scarsdale
97	51.8	Seaford UFSD	Seaford
97	51.8	Shenendehowa CSD	Clifton Park
97	51.8	Shoreham-Wading River CSD	Shoreham
97	51.8	Valley CSD (Montgomery)	Montgomery
97	51.8	Wallkill CSD	Wallkill
97	51.8	Washingtonville CSD	Washingtonville
111	51.7	Albany City SD	Albany
111	51.7	Baldwinsville CSD	Baldwinsville
111	51.7	Clarkstown CSD	New City
111	51.7	Clinton CSD	Clinton
111	51.7	Floral Park-Bellerose UFSD	Floral Park
111	51.7	Greece CSD	Rochester
111	51.7	Harborfields CSD	Greenlawn
111	51.7	Jericho UFSD	Jericho
111	51.7	Minisink Valley CSD	Slate Hill
111	51.7	Rotterdam-Mohonasen CSD	Schenectady
111	51.7	Syosset CSD	Syosset
111	51.7	West Seneca CSD	West Seneca
123	51.6	Arlington CSD	Poughkeepsie
123	51.6	Auburn City SD	Auburn
123	51.6	Beacon City SD	Beacon
123	51.6	Bellmore-Merrick Central HSD	North Merrick
123	51.6	Chatham CSD	Chatham
123	51.6	Dansville CSD	Dansville
123	51.6	East Syracuse-Minoa CSD	East Syracuse
123	51.6	Eden CSD	Eden
123	51.6	Gloversville City SD	Gloversville
123	51.6	Goshen CSD	Goshen
123	51.6	Half Hollow Hills CSD	Dix Hills
123	51.6	Hewlett-Woodmere UFSD	Woodmere
123	51.6	Homer CSD	Homer
123	51.6	Levittown UFSD	Levittown
123	51.6	Miller Place UFSD	Miller Place
123	51.6	New Paltz CSD	New Paltz
123	51.6	North Syracuse CSD	N Syracuse
123	51.6	North Tonawanda City SD	N Tonawanda
123	51.6	Saranac CSD	Dannemora
123	51.6	Saugerties CSD	Saugerties
123	51.6	Valley Stream Central HSD	Valley Stream
123	51.6	Victor CSD	Victor
123	51.6	Wappingers CSD	Wappingers Fls
146	51.5	Connetquot CSD	Bohemia
146	51.5	Copiague UFSD	Copiague
146	51.5	Hilton CSD	Hilton
146	51.5	Massapequa UFSD	Massapequa
146	51.5	New Hyde Pk-Garden City Pk UFSD	New Hyde Park
146	51.5	New Rochelle City SD	New Rochelle
146	51.5	Newfane CSD	Newfane
146	51.5	Nyack UFSD	Nyack
146	51.5	Orchard Park CSD	Orchard Park
146	51.5	Oswego City SD	Oswego
146	51.5	Plattsburgh City SD	Plattsburgh
146	51.5	Whitesboro CSD	Yorkville
146	51.5	Yonkers City SD	Yonkers
159	51.4	Babylon UFSD	Babylon
159	51.4	Central Square CSD	Central Square
159	51.4	Glens Falls City SD	Glens Falls
159	51.4	Kenmore-Tonawanda UFSD	Buffalo
159	51.4	Lindenhurst UFSD	Lindenhurst
159	51.4	Mahopac CSD	Mahopac
159	51.4	Monroe-Woodbury CSD	Central Valley
159	51.4	New Hartford CSD	New Hartford
159	51.4	Oyster Bay-East Norwich CSD	Oyster Bay
159	51.4	Salamanca City SD	Salamanca
159	51.4	South Colonie CSD	Albany
159	51.4	Yorkshire-Pioneer CSD	Yorkshire
171	51.3	Catskill CSD	Catskill
171	51.3	Commack UFSD	E Northport
171	51.3	Dunkirk City SD	Dunkirk
171	51.3	Elwood UFSD	Greenlawn
171	51.3	Hauppauge UFSD	Hauppauge
171	51.3	Herricks UFSD	New Hyde Park
171	51.3	Hicksville UFSD	Hicksville
171	51.3	Huntington UFSD	Huntington Stn
171	51.3	Islip UFSD	Islip
171	51.3	New York City Public Schools	Brooklyn
171	51.3	Newburgh City SD	Newburgh
171	51.3	Plainview-Old Bethpage CSD	Plainview
171	51.3	Roosevelt UFSD	Roosevelt
171	51.3	Sewanhaka Central HSD	Floral Park
171	51.3	Susquehanna Valley CSD	Conklin
171	51.3	West Islip UFSD	West Islip
187	51.2	Amsterdam City SD	Amsterdam
187	51.2	Burnt Hills-Ballston Lake CSD	Scotia
187	51.2	Canton CSD	Canton
187	51.2	Carmel CSD	Patterson
187	51.2	Clarence CSD	Clarence
187	51.2	Corning City SD	Painted Post
187	51.2	Edgemont UFSD	Scarsdale
187	51.2	Ellenville CSD	Ellenville
187	51.2	Hempstead UFSD	Hempstead
187	51.2	Manhasset UFSD	Manhasset
187	51.2	Marcellus CSD	Marcellus
187	51.2	Mineola UFSD	Mineola
187	51.2	Mount Pleasant CSD	Thornwood
187	51.2	Royalton-Hartland CSD	Middleport
187	51.2	Schuylerville CSD	Schuylerville
187	51.2	Southampton UFSD	Southampton
187	51.2	Spackenkill UFSD	Poughkeepsie
187	51.2	Three Village CSD	East Setauket
187	51.2	Watertown City SD	Watertown
187	51.2	West Hempstead UFSD	W Hempstead
207	51.1	Adirondack CSD	Boonville
207	51.1	Ballston Spa CSD	Ballston Spa
207	51.1	Beekmantown CSD	Plattsburgh
207	51.1	Cheektowaga-Sloan UFSD	Sloan
207	51.1	Cohoes City SD	Cohoes
207	51.1	East Aurora UFSD	East Aurora
207	51.1	Fayetteville-Manlius CSD	Manlius
207	51.1	Harrison CSD	Harrison
207	51.1	Haverstraw-Stony Point CSD	Garnerville
207	51.1	Lansingburgh CSD	Troy
207	51.1	Mexico CSD	Mexico
207	51.1	Monticello CSD	Monticello
207	51.1	Phoenix CSD	Phoenix
207	51.1	Rockville Centre UFSD	Rockville Ctre
207	51.1	Saranac Lake CSD	Saranac Lake
207	51.1	Scotia-Glenville CSD	Scotia
207	51.1	Seneca Falls CSD	Seneca Falls
207	51.1	Utica City SD	Utica
207	51.1	West Babylon UFSD	West Babylon
226	51.0	Albion CSD	Albion
226	51.0	Averill Park CSD	Averill Park
226	51.0	Camden CSD	Camden
226	51.0	Cazenovia CSD	Cazenovia
226	51.0	Elmont UFSD	Elmont
226	51.0	Guilderland CSD	Guilderland
226	51.0	Holland Patent CSD	Holland Patent
226	51.0	Irvington UFSD	Irvington
226	51.0	Island Trees UFSD	Levittown
226	51.0	Lynbrook UFSD	Lynbrook
226	51.0	Mamaroneck UFSD	Mamaroneck
226	51.0	Newark CSD	Newark
226	51.0	Niagara Falls City SD	Niagara Falls
226	51.0	Niskayuna CSD	Schenectady
226	51.0	North Colonie CSD	Latham
226	51.0	Oneida City SD	Oneida
226	51.0	Ramapo CSD (Suffern)	Hillburn
226	51.0	Sayville UFSD	Sayville
244	50.9	Buffalo City SD	Buffalo
244	50.9	Canandaigua City SD	Canandaigua
244	50.9	Gates-Chili CSD	Rochester
244	50.9	General Brown CSD	Dexter
244	50.9	Indian River CSD	Philadelphia
244	50.9	Lawrence UFSD	Lawrence
244	50.9	Mattituck-Cutchogue UFSD	Cutchogue
244	50.9	North Rose-Wolcott CSD	Wolcott
244	50.9	Northport-East Northport UFSD	Northport
244	50.9	Oneonta City SD	Oneonta
244	50.9	Ravena-Coeymans-Selkirk CSD	Selkirk
244	50.9	Springville-Griffith Inst CSD	Springville
244	50.9	Starpoint CSD	Lockport
244	50.9	Syracuse City SD	Syracuse
258	50.8	Brighton CSD	Rochester
258	50.8	Cold Spring Harbor CSD	Cold Sprg Harbor
258	50.8	East Meadow UFSD	Westbury
258	50.8	Jamestown City SD	Jamestown
258	50.8	Lakeland CSD	Shrub Oak
258	50.8	Liverpool CSD	Liverpool
258	50.8	Patchogue-Medford UFSD	Patchogue
258	50.8	Pittsford CSD	Pittsford
258	50.8	Rochester City SD	Rochester
258	50.8	Schenectady City SD	Schenectady
258	50.8	Sherrill City SD	Verona

Rank	Percent	District Name	City
258	50.8	Tonawanda City SD	Tonawanda
258	50.8	Williamsville CSD	East Amherst
258	50.8	Yorktown CSD	Yorktown Hgts
272	50.7	Central Islip UFSD	Central Islip
272	50.7	Cornwall CSD	Cornwall-on-Hud
272	50.7	Cortland City SD	Cortland
272	50.7	Middletown City SD	Middletown
272	50.7	Port Washington UFSD	Pt Washington
272	50.7	Queensbury UFSD	Queensbury
272	50.7	Uniondale UFSD	Uniondale
279	50.6	Amherst CSD	Amherst
279	50.6	Canastota CSD	Canastota
279	50.6	Carthage CSD	Carthage
279	50.6	Fairport CSD	Fairport
279	50.6	Lancaster CSD	Lancaster
279	50.6	Livonia CSD	Livonia
279	50.6	Onteora CSD	Boiceville
279	50.6	Peekskill City SD	Peekskill
279	50.6	Schalmont CSD	Schenectady
279	50.6	South Orangetown CSD	Blauvelt
279	50.6	Wantagh UFSD	Wantagh
279	50.6	Wayland-Cohocton CSD	Wayland
291	50.5	Cairo-Durham CSD	Cairo
291	50.5	Evans-Brant CSD (Lake Shore)	Angola
291	50.5	Franklin Square UFSD	Franklin Square
291	50.5	Fredonia CSD	Fredonia
291	50.5	Johnson City CSD	Johnson City
291	50.5	Kingston City SD	Kingston
291	50.5	Maine-Endwell CSD	Endwell
291	50.5	Saratoga Springs City SD	Saratoga Spgs
291	50.5	Wilson CSD	Wilson
291	50.5	Wyandanch UFSD	Wyandanch
301	50.4	East Irondequoit CSD	Rochester
301	50.4	Gorham-Middlesex CSD	Rushville
301	50.4	Hastings-On-Hudson UFSD	Hastings-on-Hud
301	50.4	Katonah-Lewisboro UFSD	South Salem
301	50.4	Long Beach City SD	Long Beach
301	50.4	Merrick UFSD	Merrick
301	50.4	Oceanside UFSD	Oceanside
301	50.4	South Glens Falls CSD	S Glens Falls
301	50.4	UFSD - Tarrytowns	Sleepy Hollow
310	50.3	Kings Park CSD	Kings Park
310	50.3	Penfield CSD	Penfield
310	50.3	Somers CSD	Lincolndale
310	50.3	South Country CSD	E Patchogue
314	50.2	Hamburg CSD	Hamburg
314	50.2	Horseheads CSD	Horseheads
314	50.2	Hyde Park CSD	Poughkeepsie
314	50.2	Mount Vernon City SD	Mount Vernon
314	50.2	North Babylon UFSD	North Babylon
314	50.2	Pine Bush CSD	Pine Bush
314	50.2	Sachem CSD	Holbrook
314	50.2	Valley Stream 30 UFSD	Valley Stream
322	50.1	Byram Hills CSD	Armonk
322	50.1	Cheektowaga-Maryvale UFSD	Cheektowaga
322	50.1	Depew UFSD	Depew
322	50.1	Freeport UFSD	Freeport
322	50.1	Poughkeepsie City SD	Poughkeepsie
327	50.0	Chittenango CSD	Chittenango
327	50.0	Frontier CSD	Hamburg
327	50.0	Kinderhook CSD	Valatie
327	50.0	Marlboro CSD	Marlboro
327	50.0	Sherburne-Earlville CSD	Sherburne
327	50.0	Sullivan West CSD	Jeffersonville
327	50.0	West Irondequoit CSD	Rochester
334	49.9	Binghamton City SD	Binghamton
334	49.9	Brockport CSD	Brockport
334	49.9	Brookhaven-Comsewogue UFSD	Pt Jefferson Stn
334	49.9	Carle Place UFSD	Carle Place
334	49.9	Hannibal CSD	Hannibal
334	49.9	Massena CSD	Massena
334	49.9	Norwich City SD	Norwich
334	49.9	Pearl River UFSD	Pearl River
334	49.9	Westhampton Beach UFSD	Westhampton Bch
334	49.9	Whitney Point CSD	Whitney Point
344	49.8	Bayport-Blue Point UFSD	Bayport
345	49.7	Batavia City SD	Batavia
345	49.7	Croton-Harmon UFSD	Croton-On-Hud
345	49.7	Jamesville-Dewitt CSD	Dewitt
345	49.7	Locust Valley CSD	Locust Valley
345	49.7	Windsor CSD	Windsor
350	49.6	Ilion CSD	Ilion
350	49.6	Plainedge UFSD	N Massapequa
350	49.6	Putnam Valley CSD	Putnam Valley
353	49.5	Penn Yan CSD	Pen
353	49.5	Waterloo CSD	Waterloo
355	49.4	East Greenbush CSD	E Greenbush
356	49.3	Geneva City SD	Geneva
357	49.2	Olean City SD	Olean
357	49.2	Taconic Hills CSD	Craryville
359	49.1	Fulton City SD	Fulton
360	49.0	Akron CSD	Akron
360	49.0	Honeoye Falls-Lima CSD	Honeoye Falls
362	48.9	North Shore CSD	Sea Cliff
362	48.9	Salmon River CSD	Ft Covington
364	48.7	Altmar-Parish-Williamstown CSD	Parish
365	48.5	Mount Sinai UFSD	Mount Sinai
365	48.5	Northeastern Clinton CSD	Champlain
367	48.4	Westbury UFSD	Old Westbury
368	47.9	Johnston City SD	Johnstown

Female Students

Rank	Percent	District Name	City
1	52.1	Johnstown City SD	Johnstown
2	51.6	Westbury UFSD	Old Westbury
3	51.5	Mount Sinai UFSD	Mount Sinai
3	51.5	Northeastern Clinton CSD	Champlain
5	51.3	Altmar-Parish-Williamstown CSD	Parish
6	51.1	North Shore CSD	Sea Cliff
6	51.1	Salmon River CSD	Ft Covington
8	51.0	Akron CSD	Akron
8	51.0	Honeoye Falls-Lima CSD	Honeoye Falls
10	50.9	Fulton City SD	Fulton
11	50.8	Olean City SD	Olean
11	50.8	Taconic Hills CSD	Craryville
13	50.7	Geneva City SD	Geneva
14	50.6	East Greenbush CSD	E Greenbush
15	50.5	Penn Yan CSD	Pen
15	50.5	Waterloo CSD	Waterloo
17	50.4	Ilion CSD	Ilion
17	50.4	Plainedge UFSD	N Massapequa
17	50.4	Putnam Valley CSD	Putnam Valley
20	50.3	Batavia City SD	Batavia
20	50.3	Croton-Harmon UFSD	Croton-On-Hud
20	50.3	Jamesville-Dewitt CSD	Dewitt
20	50.3	Locust Valley CSD	Locust Valley
20	50.3	Windsor CSD	Windsor
25	50.2	Bayport-Blue Point UFSD	Bayport
26	50.1	Binghamton City SD	Binghamton
26	50.1	Brockport CSD	Brockport
26	50.1	Brookhaven-Comsewogue UFSD	Pt Jefferson Stn
26	50.1	Carle Place UFSD	Carle Place
26	50.1	Hannibal CSD	Hannibal
26	50.1	Massena CSD	Massena
26	50.1	Norwich City SD	Norwich
26	50.1	Pearl River UFSD	Pearl River
26	50.1	Westhampton Beach UFSD	Westhampton Bch
26	50.1	Whitney Point CSD	Whitney Point
36	50.0	Chittenango CSD	Chittenango
36	50.0	Frontier CSD	Hamburg
36	50.0	Kinderhook CSD	Valatie
36	50.0	Marlboro CSD	Marlboro
36	50.0	Sherburne-Earlville CSD	Sherburne
36	50.0	Sullivan West CSD	Jeffersonville
36	50.0	West Irondequoit CSD	Rochester
43	49.9	Byram Hills CSD	Armonk
43	49.9	Cheektowaga-Maryvale UFSD	Cheektowaga
43	49.9	Depew UFSD	Depew
43	49.9	Freeport UFSD	Freeport
43	49.9	Poughkeepsie City SD	Poughkeepsie
48	49.8	Hamburg CSD	Hamburg
48	49.8	Horseheads CSD	Horseheads
48	49.8	Hyde Park CSD	Poughkeepsie
48	49.8	Mount Vernon City SD	Mount Vernon
48	49.8	North Babylon UFSD	North Babylon
48	49.8	Pine Bush CSD	Pine Bush
48	49.8	Sachem CSD	Holbrook
48	49.8	Valley Stream 30 UFSD	Valley Stream
56	49.7	Kings Park CSD	Kings Park
56	49.7	Penfield CSD	Penfield
56	49.7	Somers CSD	Lincolndale
56	49.7	South Country CSD	E Patchogue
60	49.6	East Irondequoit CSD	Rochester
60	49.6	Gorham-Middlesex CSD	Rushville
60	49.6	Hastings-On-Hudson UFSD	Hastings-on-Hud
60	49.6	Katonah-Lewisboro UFSD	South Salem
60	49.6	Long Beach City SD	Long Beach
60	49.6	Merrick UFSD	Merrick
60	49.6	Oceanside UFSD	Oceanside
60	49.6	South Glens Falls CSD	S Glens Falls
60	49.6	UFSD - Tarrytowns	Sleepy Hollow
69	49.5	Cairo-Durham CSD	Cairo
69	49.5	Evans-Brant CSD (Lake Shore)	Angola
69	49.5	Franklin Square UFSD	Franklin Square
69	49.5	Fredonia CSD	Fredonia
69	49.5	Johnson City CSD	Johnson City
69	49.5	Kingston City SD	Kingston
69	49.5	Maine-Endwell CSD	Endwell
69	49.5	Saratoga Springs City SD	Saratoga Spgs
69	49.5	Wilson CSD	Wilson
69	49.5	Wyandanch UFSD	Wyandanch
79	49.4	Amherst CSD	Amherst
79	49.4	Canastota CSD	Canastota
79	49.4	Carthage CSD	Carthage
79	49.4	Fairport CSD	Fairport
79	49.4	Lancaster CSD	Lancaster
79	49.4	Livonia CSD	Livonia
79	49.4	Onteora CSD	Boiceville
79	49.4	Peekskill City SD	Peekskill
79	49.4	Schalmont CSD	Schenectady
79	49.4	South Orangetown CSD	Blauvelt
79	49.4	Wantagh UFSD	Wantagh
79	49.4	Wayland-Cohocton CSD	Wayland
91	49.3	Central Islip UFSD	Central Islip
91	49.3	Cornwall CSD	Cornwall-on-Hud
91	49.3	Cortland City SD	Cortland
91	49.3	Middletown City SD	Middletown
91	49.3	Port Washington UFSD	Pt Washington
91	49.3	Queensbury UFSD	Queensbury
91	49.3	Uniondale UFSD	Uniondale
98	49.2	Brighton CSD	Rochester
98	49.2	Cold Spring Harbor CSD	Cold Sprg Harbor
98	49.2	East Meadow UFSD	Westbury
98	49.2	Jamestown City SD	Jamestown
98	49.2	Lakeland CSD	Shrub Oak
98	49.2	Liverpool CSD	Liverpool
98	49.2	Patchogue-Medford UFSD	Patchogue
98	49.2	Pittsford CSD	Pittsford
98	49.2	Rochester City SD	Rochester
98	49.2	Schenectady City SD	Schenectady
98	49.2	Sherrill City SD	Verona
98	49.2	Tonawanda City SD	Tonawanda
98	49.2	Williamsville CSD	East Amherst
98	49.2	Yorktown CSD	Yorktown Hgts
112	49.1	Buffalo City SD	Buffalo
112	49.1	Canandaigua City SD	Canandaigua
112	49.1	Gates-Chili CSD	Rochester
112	49.1	General Brown CSD	Dexter
112	49.1	Indian River CSD	Philadelphia
112	49.1	Lawrence UFSD	Lawrence
112	49.1	Mattituck-Cutchogue UFSD	Cutchogue
112	49.1	North Rose-Wolcott CSD	Wolcott
112	49.1	Northport-East Northport UFSD	Northport
112	49.1	Oneonta City SD	Oneonta
112	49.1	Ravena-Coeymans-Selkirk CSD	Selkirk
112	49.1	Springville-Griffith Inst CSD	Springville
112	49.1	Starpoint CSD	Lockport
112	49.1	Syracuse City SD	Syracuse
126	49.0	Albion CSD	Albion
126	49.0	Averill Park CSD	Averill Park
126	49.0	Camden CSD	Camden
126	49.0	Cazenovia CSD	Cazenovia
126	49.0	Elmont UFSD	Elmont
126	49.0	Guilderland CSD	Guilderland
126	49.0	Holland Patent CSD	Holland Patent
126	49.0	Irvington UFSD	Irvington
126	49.0	Island Trees UFSD	Levittown
126	49.0	Lynbrook UFSD	Lynbrook
126	49.0	Mamaroneck UFSD	Mamaroneck
126	49.0	Newark CSD	Newark
126	49.0	Niagara Falls City SD	Niagara Falls
126	49.0	Niskayuna CSD	Schenectady
126	49.0	North Colonie CSD	Latham
126	49.0	Oneida City SD	Oneida
126	49.0	Ramapo CSD (Suffern)	Hillburn
126	49.0	Sayville UFSD	Sayville
144	48.9	Adirondack CSD	Boonville
144	48.9	Ballston Spa CSD	Ballston Spa
144	48.9	Beekmantown CSD	Plattsburgh
144	48.9	Cheektowaga-Sloan UFSD	Sloan
144	48.9	Cohoes City SD	Cohoes
144	48.9	East Aurora UFSD	East Aurora
144	48.9	Fayetteville-Manlius CSD	Manlius
144	48.9	Harrison CSD	Harrison
144	48.9	Haverstraw-Stony Point CSD	Garnerville
144	48.9	Lansingburgh CSD	Troy
144	48.9	Mexico CSD	Mexico
144	48.9	Monticello CSD	Monticello
144	48.9	Phoenix CSD	Phoenix
144	48.9	Rockville Centre UFSD	Rockville Ctre
144	48.9	Saranac Lake CSD	Saranac Lake
144	48.9	Scotia-Glenville CSD	Scotia
144	48.9	Seneca Falls CSD	Seneca Falls
144	48.9	Utica City SD	Utica
144	48.9	West Babylon UFSD	West Babylon
163	48.8	Amsterdam City SD	Amsterdam
163	48.8	Burnt Hills-Ballston Lake CSD	Scotia
163	48.8	Canton CSD	Canton
163	48.8	Carmel CSD	Patterson
163	48.8	Clarence CSD	Clarence
163	48.8	Corning City SD	Painted Post
163	48.8	Edgemont UFSD	Scarsdale
163	48.8	Ellenville CSD	Ellenville
163	48.8	Hempstead UFSD	Hempstead
163	48.8	Manhasset UFSD	Manhasset
163	48.8	Marcellus CSD	Marcellus
163	48.8	Mineola UFSD	Mineola

163	48.8	Mount Pleasant CSD	Thornwood
163	48.8	Royalton-Hartland CSD	Middleport
163	48.8	Schuylerville CSD	Schuylerville
163	48.8	Southampton UFSD	Southampton
163	48.8	Spackenkill UFSD	Poughkeepsie
163	48.8	Three Village CSD	East Setauket
163	48.8	Watertown City SD	Watertown
163	48.8	West Hempstead UFSD	W Hempstead
183	48.7	Catskill CSD	Catskill
183	48.7	Commack UFSD	E Northport
183	48.7	Dunkirk City SD	Dunkirk
183	48.7	Elwood UFSD	Greenlawn
183	48.7	Hauppauge UFSD	Hauppauge
183	48.7	Herricks UFSD	New Hyde Park
183	48.7	Hicksville UFSD	Hicksville
183	48.7	Huntington UFSD	Huntington Stn
183	48.7	Islip UFSD	Islip
183	48.7	New York City Public Schools	Brooklyn
183	48.7	Newburgh City SD	Newburgh
183	48.7	Plainview-Old Bethpage CSD	Plainview
183	48.7	Roosevelt UFSD	Roosevelt
183	48.7	Sewanhaka Central HSD	Floral Park
183	48.7	Susquehanna Valley CSD	Conklin
183	48.7	West Islip UFSD	West Islip
199	48.6	Babylon UFSD	Babylon
199	48.6	Central Square CSD	Central Square
199	48.6	Glens Falls City SD	Glens Falls
199	48.6	Kenmore-Tonawanda UFSD	Buffalo
199	48.6	Lindenhurst UFSD	Lindenhurst
199	48.6	Mahopac CSD	Mahopac
199	48.6	Monroe-Woodbury CSD	Central Valley
199	48.6	New Hartford CSD	New Hartford
199	48.6	Oyster Bay-East Norwich CSD	Oyster Bay
199	48.6	Salamanca City SD	Salamanca
199	48.6	South Colonie CSD	Albany
199	48.6	Yorkshire-Pioneer CSD	Yorkshire
211	48.5	Connetquot CSD	Bohemia
211	48.5	Copiague UFSD	Copiague
211	48.5	Hilton CSD	Hilton
211	48.5	Massapequa UFSD	Massapequa
211	48.5	New Hyde Pk-Garden City Pk UFSD	New Hyde Park
211	48.5	New Rochelle City SD	New Rochelle
211	48.5	Newfane CSD	Newfane
211	48.5	Nyack UFSD	Nyack
211	48.5	Orchard Park CSD	Orchard Park
211	48.5	Oswego City SD	Oswego
211	48.5	Plattsburgh City SD	Plattsburgh
211	48.5	Whitesboro CSD	Yorkville
211	48.5	Yonkers City SD	Yonkers
224	48.4	Arlington CSD	Poughkeepsie
224	48.4	Auburn City SD	Auburn
224	48.4	Beacon City SD	Beacon
224	48.4	Bellmore-Merrick Central HSD	North Merrick
224	48.4	Chatham CSD	Chatham
224	48.4	Dansville CSD	Dansville
224	48.4	East Syracuse-Minoa CSD	East Syracuse
224	48.4	Eden CSD	Eden
224	48.4	Gloversville City SD	Gloversville
224	48.4	Goshen CSD	Goshen
224	48.4	Half Hollow Hills CSD	Dix Hills
224	48.4	Hewlett-Woodmere UFSD	Woodmere
224	48.4	Homer CSD	Homer
224	48.4	Levittown UFSD	Levittown
224	48.4	Miller Place UFSD	Miller Place
224	48.4	New Paltz CSD	New Paltz
224	48.4	North Syracuse CSD	N Syracuse
224	48.4	North Tonawanda City SD	N Tonawanda
224	48.4	Saranac CSD	Dannemora
224	48.4	Saugerties CSD	Saugerties
224	48.4	Valley Stream Central HSD	Valley Stream
224	48.4	Victor CSD	Victor
224	48.4	Wappingers CSD	Wappingers Fls
247	48.3	Albany City SD	Albany
247	48.3	Baldwinsville CSD	Baldwinsville
247	48.3	Clarkstown CSD	New City
247	48.3	Clinton CSD	Clinton
247	48.3	Floral Park-Bellerose UFSD	Floral Park
247	48.3	Greece CSD	Rochester
247	48.3	Harborfields CSD	Greenlawn
247	48.3	Jericho UFSD	Jericho
247	48.3	Minisink Valley CSD	Slate Hill
247	48.3	Rotterdam-Mohonasen CSD	Schenectady
247	48.3	Syosset CSD	Syosset
247	48.3	West Seneca CSD	West Seneca
259	48.2	Bedford CSD	Mount Kisco
259	48.2	Chappaqua CSD	Chappaqua
259	48.2	Chenango Forks CSD	Binghamton
259	48.2	Chenango Valley CSD	Binghamton
259	48.2	Lockport City SD	Lockport
259	48.2	Middle Country CSD	Centereach
259	48.2	Nanuet UFSD	Nanuet
259	48.2	Scarsdale UFSD	Scarsdale
259	48.2	Seaford UFSD	Seaford
259	48.2	Shenendehowa CSD	Clifton Park
259	48.2	Shoreham-Wading River CSD	Shoreham
259	48.2	Valley CSD (Montgomery)	Montgomery
259	48.2	Wallkill CSD	Wallkill
259	48.2	Washingtonville CSD	Washingtonville
273	48.1	Cobleskill-Richmondville CSD	Cobleskill
273	48.1	Eastchester UFSD	Eastchester
273	48.1	Glen Cove City SD	Glen Cove
273	48.1	Gouverneur CSD	Gouverneur
273	48.1	Hudson Falls CSD	Hudson Falls
273	48.1	Liberty CSD	Liberty
273	48.1	Longwood CSD	Middle Island
273	48.1	Peru CSD	Peru
273	48.1	Smithtown CSD	Smithtown
273	48.1	South Huntington UFSD	Huntington Stn
273	48.1	Union-Endicott CSD	Endicott
273	48.1	William Floyd UFSD	Mastic Beach
285	48.0	Baldwin UFSD	Baldwin
285	48.0	Dryden CSD	Dryden
285	48.0	East Ramapo CSD (Spring Valley)	Spring Valley
285	48.0	Grand Island CSD	Grand Island
285	48.0	Lansing CSD	Lansing
285	48.0	Lewiston-Porter CSD	Youngstown
285	48.0	Malverne UFSD	Malverne
285	48.0	Pelham UFSD	Pelham
285	48.0	Port Chester-Rye UFSD	Port Chester
285	48.0	Riverhead CSD	Riverhead
285	48.0	Spencerport CSD	Spencerport
285	48.0	West Genesee CSD	Camillus
297	47.9	Cheektowaga CSD	Cheektowaga
297	47.9	Churchville-Chili CSD	Churchville
297	47.9	Elmira City SD	Elmira
297	47.9	Iroquois CSD	Elma
297	47.9	Ithaca City SD	Ithaca
297	47.9	Medina CSD	Medina
297	47.9	Solvay UFSD	Solvay
297	47.9	Webster CSD	Webster
305	47.8	Amityville UFSD	Amityville
305	47.8	Bethpage UFSD	Bethpage
305	47.8	Briarcliff Manor UFSD	Briarcliff Manor
305	47.8	Skaneateles CSD	Skaneateles
305	47.8	Sweet Home CSD	Amherst
305	47.8	Troy City SD	Troy
305	47.8	Warwick Valley CSD	Warwick
305	47.8	Westhill CSD	Syracuse
313	47.7	Brentwood UFSD	Brentwood
313	47.7	Great Neck UFSD	Great Neck
313	47.7	Hendrick Hudson CSD	Montrose
313	47.7	North Bellmore UFSD	Bellmore
313	47.7	Owego-Apalachin CSD	Owego
313	47.7	Red Hook CSD	Red Hook
313	47.7	Roslyn UFSD	Roslyn
313	47.7	Rush-Henrietta CSD	Henrietta
313	47.7	White Plains City SD	White Plains
322	47.6	Bethlehem CSD	Delmar
322	47.6	Rome City SD	Rome
322	47.6	Waverly CSD	Waverly
325	47.5	Deer Park UFSD	Deer Park
325	47.5	Gowanda CSD	Gowanda
325	47.5	Phelps-Clifton Springs CSD	Clifton Spgs
328	47.4	Southwestern CSD at Jamestown	Jamestown
329	47.3	Bay Shore UFSD	Bay Shore
329	47.3	East Williston UFSD	Old Westbury
329	47.3	Farmingdale UFSD	Farmingdale
329	47.3	Greenburgh CSD	Hartsdale
329	47.3	Malone CSD	Malone
329	47.3	Pleasantville UFSD	Pleasantville
329	47.3	Port Jervis City SD	Port Jervis
329	47.3	Rocky Point UFSD	Rocky Point
337	47.2	Jordan-Elbridge CSD	Jordan
337	47.2	Ossining UFSD	Ossining
337	47.2	Palmyra-Macedon CSD	Palmyra
340	47.1	East Hampton UFSD	East Hampton
340	47.1	Fonda-Fultonville CSD	Fonda
340	47.1	Garden City UFSD	Garden City
340	47.1	Ogdensburg City SD	Ogdensburg
340	47.1	Rye City SD	Rye
340	47.1	South Jefferson CSD	Adams Center
340	47.1	Vestal CSD	Vestal
340	47.1	Wayne CSD	Ontario Center
348	47.0	Alden CSD	Alden
348	47.0	Ardsley UFSD	Ardsley
348	47.0	Niagara-Wheatfield CSD	Niagara Falls
351	46.9	Hampton Bays UFSD	Hampton Bays
351	46.9	Rondout Valley CSD	Accord
351	46.9	Valley Stream 13 UFSD	Valley Stream
354	46.7	Brewster CSD	Brewster
354	46.7	Lackawanna City SD	Lackawanna
356	46.4	East Islip UFSD	Islip Terrace
357	46.3	Cleveland Hill UFSD	Cheektowaga
358	46.1	Dover UFSD	Dover Plains
359	45.9	Attica CSD	Attica
359	45.9	Hornell City SD	Hornell
361	45.4	Bath CSD	Bath
362	45.1	Highland CSD	Highland
363	43.8	Hudson City SD	Hudson
364	42.6	Broadalbin-Perth CSD	Broadalbin
365	30.9	Coxsackie-Athens CSD	Coxsackie
366	28.0	Boces Monroe 1	Fairport
367	26.0	Boces Eastern Suffolk (Suffolk I)	Patchogue
367	26.0	Boces Nassau	Garden City

Individual Education Program Students

Rank	Percent	District Name	City
1	100.0	Boces Eastern Suffolk (Suffolk I)	Patchogue
2	85.9	Boces Nassau	Garden City
3	83.2	Boces Monroe 1	Fairport
4	23.4	Lackawanna City SD	Lackawanna
5	21.8	Lawrence UFSD	Lawrence
6	21.7	Buffalo City SD	Buffalo
7	21.5	Saranac CSD	Dannemora
8	21.4	Wyandanch UFSD	Wyandanch
9	21.2	Geneva City SD	Geneva
10	20.5	Albany City SD	Albany
11	20.4	Syracuse City SD	Syracuse
12	20.3	Hornell City SD	Hornell
13	19.5	Peru CSD	Peru
14	19.3	Plattsburgh City SD	Plattsburgh
15	19.1	Cortland City SD	Cortland
15	19.1	Northeastern Clinton CSD	Champlain
17	19.0	Rochester City SD	Rochester
18	18.9	Phoenix CSD	Phoenix
18	18.9	Ravena-Coeymans-Selkirk CSD	Selkirk
20	18.7	Yorkshire-Pioneer CSD	Yorkshire
21	18.6	Ogdensburg City SD	Ogdensburg
21	18.6	Troy City SD	Troy
23	18.5	North Babylon UFSD	North Babylon
23	18.5	Poughkeepsie City SD	Poughkeepsie
25	18.4	Sherburne-Earlville CSD	Sherburne
26	18.2	Gouverneur CSD	Gouverneur
26	18.2	Lansingburgh CSD	Troy
28	18.0	North Shore CSD	Sea Cliff
28	18.0	Rondout Valley CSD	Accord
28	18.0	Salmon River CSD	Ft Covington
31	17.5	Norwich City SD	Norwich
31	17.5	Schenectady City SD	Schenectady
33	17.4	East Ramapo CSD (Spring Valley)	Spring Valley
33	17.4	Hudson City SD	Hudson
35	17.3	Johnson City CSD	Johnson City
36	17.2	Averill Park CSD	Averill Park
36	17.2	Fulton City SD	Fulton
36	17.2	Mount Pleasant CSD	Thornwood
36	17.2	Niagara Falls City SD	Niagara Falls
40	17.0	Amsterdam City SD	Amsterdam
40	17.0	Binghamton City SD	Binghamton
40	17.0	Dansville CSD	Dansville
40	17.0	Glen Cove City SD	Glen Cove
40	17.0	Pleasantville UFSD	Pleasantville
40	17.0	Utica City SD	Utica
40	17.0	Wayland-Cohocton CSD	Wayland
47	16.9	Peekskill City SD	Peekskill
48	16.7	Ilion CSD	Ilion
48	16.7	Monticello CSD	Monticello
48	16.7	Newark CSD	Newark
48	16.7	Schuylerville CSD	Schuylerville
52	16.6	Central Islip UFSD	Central Islip
52	16.6	Elmira City SD	Elmira
52	16.6	Hudson Falls CSD	Hudson Falls
52	16.6	Malverne UFSD	Malverne
52	16.6	Oneonta City SD	Oneonta
52	16.6	Orchard Park CSD	Orchard Park
52	16.6	William Floyd UFSD	Mastic Beach
59	16.5	Hicksville UFSD	Hicksville
59	16.5	Liverpool CSD	Liverpool
59	16.5	Plainview-Old Bethpage CSD	Plainview
62	16.4	Batavia City SD	Batavia
62	16.4	Dryden CSD	Dryden
62	16.4	Liberty CSD	Liberty
62	16.4	Malone CSD	Malone
66	16.3	Brentwood UFSD	Brentwood
66	16.3	Cohoes City SD	Cohoes
66	16.3	Kenmore-Tonawanda UFSD	Buffalo
66	16.3	Maine-Endwell CSD	Endwell
70	16.2	Canton CSD	Canton
70	16.2	Onteora CSD	Boiceville
72	16.1	Jamestown City SD	Jamestown
72	16.1	Locust Valley CSD	Locust Valley
72	16.1	Watertown City SD	Watertown
75	16.0	Connetquot CSD	Bohemia
75	16.0	Haverstraw-Stony Point CSD	Garnerville
77	15.9	Scotia-Glenville CSD	Scotia
78	15.8	Amityville UFSD	Amityville
78	15.8	Baldwinsville CSD	Baldwinsville
78	15.8	Carle Place UFSD	Carle Place

78	15.8	Chenango Valley CSD	Binghamton
78	15.8	Wayne CSD	Ontario Center
83	15.7	Canastota CSD	Canastota
83	15.7	Gloversville City SD	Gloversville
83	15.7	Hewlett-Woodmere UFSD	Woodmere
83	15.7	Marlboro CSD	Marlboro
83	15.7	Whitesboro CSD	Yorkville
88	15.6	Cleveland Hill UFSD	Cheektowaga
89	15.5	Beekmantown CSD	Plattsburgh
89	15.5	Copiague UFSD	Copiague
89	15.5	Highland CSD	Highland
92	15.4	East Syracuse-Minoa CSD	East Syracuse
92	15.4	Owego-Apalachin CSD	Owego
92	15.4	Pine Bush CSD	Pine Bush
95	15.3	Altmar-Parish-Williamstown CSD	Parish
95	15.3	Cairo-Durham CSD	Cairo
95	15.3	Clarkstown CSD	New City
95	15.3	New Paltz CSD	New Paltz
95	15.3	Union-Endicott CSD	Endicott
100	15.2	Adirondack CSD	Boonville
100	15.2	Cheektowaga-Sloan UFSD	Sloan
100	15.2	Lindenhurst UFSD	Lindenhurst
100	15.2	Rocky Point UFSD	Rocky Point
100	15.2	Schalmont CSD	Schenectady
100	15.2	Seneca Falls CSD	Seneca Falls
106	15.1	Gowanda CSD	Gowanda
106	15.1	Huntington UFSD	Huntington Stn
106	15.1	Kingston City SD	Kingston
106	15.1	Longwood CSD	Middle Island
106	15.1	Mahopac CSD	Mahopac
111	15.0	Johnstown City SD	Johnstown
111	15.0	Lakeland CSD	Shrub Oak
111	15.0	Medina CSD	Medina
111	15.0	Phelps-Clifton Springs CSD	Clifton Spgs
111	15.0	South Country CSD	E Patchogue
116	14.9	Brookhaven-Comsewogue UFSD	Pt Jefferson Stn
116	14.9	Camden CSD	Camden
116	14.9	Middle Country CSD	Centereach
116	14.9	Mineola UFSD	Mineola
116	14.9	Monroe-Woodbury CSD	Central Valley
121	14.8	Riverhead CSD	Riverhead
122	14.7	Massena CSD	Massena
122	14.7	Olean City SD	Olean
122	14.7	Saranac Lake CSD	Saranac Lake
125	14.6	Mamaroneck UFSD	Mamaroneck
125	14.6	Port Washington UFSD	Pt Washington
125	14.6	Red Hook CSD	Red Hook
125	14.6	Rome City SD	Rome
125	14.6	Rush-Henrietta CSD	Henrietta
130	14.5	Bay Shore UFSD	Bay Shore
130	14.5	Kinderhook CSD	Valatie
130	14.5	Mexico CSD	Mexico
130	14.5	Port Chester-Rye UFSD	Port Chester
130	14.5	Solvay UFSD	Solvay
135	14.4	Merrick UFSD	Merrick
136	14.3	Beacon City SD	Beacon
136	14.3	Carthage CSD	Carthage
136	14.3	Glens Falls City SD	Glens Falls
136	14.3	Patchogue-Medford UFSD	Patchogue
140	14.2	Indian River CSD	Philadelphia
140	14.2	South Jefferson CSD	Adams Center
140	14.2	Wallkill CSD	Wallkill
143	14.1	General Brown CSD	Dexter
143	14.1	Hamburg CSD	Hamburg
143	14.1	North Tonawanda City SD	N Tonawanda
143	14.1	Penn Yan CSD	Pen
143	14.1	Susquehanna Valley CSD	Conklin
143	14.1	Whitney Point CSD	Whitney Point
149	14.0	Dunkirk City SD	Dunkirk
149	14.0	Ithaca City SD	Ithaca
149	14.0	Long Beach City SD	Long Beach
149	14.0	West Seneca CSD	West Seneca
153	13.9	Canandaigua City SD	Canandaigua
153	13.9	Catskill CSD	Catskill
153	13.9	Chittenango CSD	Chittenango
153	13.9	Middletown City SD	Middletown
157	13.8	Hampton Bays UFSD	Hampton Bays
157	13.8	Hyde Park CSD	Poughkeepsie
157	13.8	North Rose-Wolcott CSD	Wolcott
157	13.8	Oyster Bay-East Norwich CSD	Oyster Bay
157	13.8	Spencerport CSD	Spencerport
157	13.8	Sullivan West CSD	Jeffersonville
163	13.7	Great Neck UFSD	Great Neck
163	13.7	Lewiston-Porter CSD	Youngstown
163	13.7	New Rochelle City SD	New Rochelle
163	13.7	Waterloo CSD	Waterloo
163	13.7	Westhill CSD	Syracuse
168	13.6	Chatham CSD	Chatham
168	13.6	Nanuet UFSD	Nanuet
168	13.6	Oneida City SD	Oneida
168	13.6	Southampton UFSD	Southampton
172	13.5	Brockport CSD	Brockport
172	13.5	Gorham-Middlesex CSD	Rushville
172	13.5	Herricks UFSD	New Hyde Park
175	13.4	Horseheads CSD	Horseheads
175	13.4	Levittown UFSD	Levittown
175	13.4	New York City Public Schools	Brooklyn
178	13.3	Auburn City SD	Auburn
178	13.3	Farmingdale UFSD	Farmingdale
178	13.3	Valley CSD (Montgomery)	Montgomery
181	13.2	Bayport-Blue Point UFSD	Bayport
181	13.2	Hannibal CSD	Hannibal
181	13.2	Katonah-Lewisboro UFSD	South Salem
181	13.2	Northport-East Northport UFSD	Northport
181	13.2	Ramapo CSD (Suffern)	Hillburn
181	13.2	Salamanca City SD	Salamanca
181	13.2	Yorktown CSD	Yorktown Hgts
188	13.1	Hendrick Hudson CSD	Montrose
188	13.1	Newburgh City SD	Newburgh
188	13.1	Smithtown CSD	Smithtown
191	13.0	Fonda-Fultonville CSD	Fonda
191	13.0	Shenendehowa CSD	Clifton Park
191	13.0	Taconic Hills CSD	Craryville
191	13.0	Windsor CSD	Windsor
191	13.0	Yonkers City SD	Yonkers
196	12.9	Bedford CSD	Mount Kisco
196	12.9	Burnt Hills-Ballston Lake CSD	Scotia
196	12.9	East Irondequoit CSD	Rochester
196	12.9	Gates-Chili CSD	Rochester
196	12.9	Half Hollow Hills CSD	Dix Hills
196	12.9	Miller Place UFSD	Miller Place
202	12.8	Central Square CSD	Central Square
202	12.8	Marcellus CSD	Marcellus
202	12.8	Three Village CSD	East Setauket
205	12.7	Akron CSD	Akron
205	12.7	Alden CSD	Alden
205	12.7	Brewster CSD	Brewster
205	12.7	Cheektowaga CSD	Cheektowaga
205	12.7	East Greenbush CSD	E Greenbush
205	12.7	Guilderland CSD	Guilderland
205	12.7	Pelham UFSD	Pelham
212	12.6	Arlington CSD	Poughkeepsie
212	12.6	Bethpage UFSD	Bethpage
212	12.6	Cheektowaga-Maryvale UFSD	Cheektowaga
212	12.6	Croton-Harmon UFSD	Croton-On-Hud
212	12.6	Dover UFSD	Dover Plains
212	12.6	Massapequa UFSD	Massapequa
212	12.6	UFSD - Tarrytowns	Sleepy Hollow
212	12.6	Wantagh UFSD	Wantagh
212	12.6	West Hempstead UFSD	W Hempstead
221	12.5	Byram Hills CSD	Armonk
221	12.5	Evans-Brant CSD (Lake Shore)	Angola
221	12.5	Mount Vernon City SD	Mount Vernon
221	12.5	Newfane CSD	Newfane
221	12.5	Putnam Valley CSD	Putnam Valley
221	12.5	Springville-Griffith Inst CSD	Springville
221	12.5	Webster CSD	Webster
228	12.4	Harborfields CSD	Greenlawn
228	12.4	Lancaster CSD	Lancaster
228	12.4	North Syracuse CSD	N Syracuse
228	12.4	Port Jervis City SD	Port Jervis
228	12.4	Sachem CSD	Holbrook
228	12.4	Syosset CSD	Syosset
228	12.4	Wappingers CSD	Wappingers Fls
235	12.3	Ballston Spa CSD	Ballston Spa
235	12.3	Bethlehem CSD	Delmar
235	12.3	Cobleskill-Richmondville CSD	Cobleskill
235	12.3	Elmont UFSD	Elmont
235	12.3	Greenburgh CSD	Hartsdale
235	12.3	Hauppauge UFSD	Hauppauge
235	12.3	Saratoga Springs City SD	Saratoga Spgs
242	12.2	Ellenville CSD	Ellenville
242	12.2	Harrison CSD	Harrison
242	12.2	Homer CSD	Homer
242	12.2	Manhasset UFSD	Manhasset
242	12.2	Mount Sinai UFSD	Mount Sinai
242	12.2	Ossining UFSD	Ossining
242	12.2	Oswego City SD	Oswego
242	12.2	Pearl River UFSD	Pearl River
242	12.2	Shoreham-Wading River CSD	Shoreham
242	12.2	South Orangetown CSD	Blauvelt
242	12.2	Valley Stream 13 UFSD	Valley Stream
253	12.1	Deer Park UFSD	Deer Park
253	12.1	Floral Park-Bellerose UFSD	Floral Park
253	12.1	Hilton CSD	Hilton
253	12.1	Islip UFSD	Islip
253	12.1	Lockport City SD	Lockport
253	12.1	Minisink Valley CSD	Slate Hill
253	12.1	Sayville UFSD	Sayville
253	12.1	Somers CSD	Lincolndale
253	12.1	South Huntington UFSD	Huntington Stn
253	12.1	Starpoint CSD	Lockport
253	12.1	West Babylon UFSD	West Babylon
253	12.1	West Islip UFSD	West Islip
253	12.1	Wilson CSD	Wilson
266	12.0	Clarence CSD	Clarence
266	12.0	East Williston UFSD	Old Westbury
266	12.0	Fredonia CSD	Fredonia
266	12.0	Kings Park CSD	Kings Park
266	12.0	Rotterdam-Mohonasen CSD	Schenectady
266	12.0	Sewanhaka Central HSD	Floral Park
266	12.0	Westhampton Beach UFSD	Westhampton Bch
273	11.9	Carmel CSD	Patterson
273	11.9	Garden City UFSD	Garden City
273	11.9	Queensbury UFSD	Queensbury
273	11.9	Rockville Centre UFSD	Rockville Ctre
273	11.9	Roosevelt UFSD	Roosevelt
273	11.9	Royalton-Hartland CSD	Middleport
273	11.9	Tonawanda City SD	Tonawanda
280	11.8	Commack UFSD	E Northport
280	11.8	Fairport CSD	Fairport
280	11.8	Frontier CSD	Hamburg
283	11.7	Bellmore-Merrick Central HSD	North Merrick
283	11.7	Honeoye Falls-Lima CSD	Honeoye Falls
283	11.7	Jamesville-Dewitt CSD	Dewitt
283	11.7	Pittsford CSD	Pittsford
287	11.6	Franklin Square UFSD	Franklin Square
287	11.6	Palmyra-Macedon CSD	Palmyra
289	11.5	South Colonie CSD	Albany
289	11.5	Spackenkill UFSD	Poughkeepsie
289	11.5	White Plains City SD	White Plains
289	11.5	Williamsville CSD	East Amherst
293	11.4	East Hampton UFSD	East Hampton
293	11.4	Holland Patent CSD	Holland Patent
293	11.4	Jericho UFSD	Jericho
293	11.4	Westbury UFSD	Old Westbury
297	11.3	Attica CSD	Attica
297	11.3	Babylon UFSD	Babylon
297	11.3	Clinton CSD	Clinton
297	11.3	Grand Island CSD	Grand Island
297	11.3	Vestal CSD	Vestal
302	11.2	Albion CSD	Albion
302	11.2	Chenango Forks CSD	Binghamton
302	11.2	North Bellmore UFSD	Bellmore
302	11.2	Valley Stream Central HSD	Valley Stream
306	11.1	Amherst CSD	Amherst
306	11.1	Lynbrook UFSD	Lynbrook
306	11.1	Penfield CSD	Penfield
306	11.1	Roslyn UFSD	Roslyn
306	11.1	Sherrill City SD	Verona
311	11.0	Cazenovia CSD	Cazenovia
311	11.0	Cold Spring Harbor CSD	Cold Sprg Harbor
311	11.0	Freeport UFSD	Freeport
311	11.0	Greece CSD	Rochester
311	11.0	Hempstead UFSD	Hempstead
311	11.0	Niskayuna CSD	Schenectady
311	11.0	South Glens Falls CSD	S Glens Falls
311	11.0	Uniondale UFSD	Uniondale
319	10.9	Corning City SD	Painted Post
319	10.9	Hastings-On-Hudson UFSD	Hastings-on-Hud
319	10.9	Niagara-Wheatfield CSD	Niagara Falls
319	10.9	North Colonie CSD	Latham
319	10.9	Nyack UFSD	Nyack
319	10.9	Saugerties CSD	Saugerties
325	10.8	New Hartford CSD	New Hartford
325	10.8	Warwick Valley CSD	Warwick
327	10.7	Broadalbin-Perth CSD	Broadalbin
328	10.6	Oceanside UFSD	Oceanside
328	10.6	Waverly CSD	Waverly
330	10.5	Brighton CSD	Rochester
330	10.5	Iroquois CSD	Elma
330	10.5	Lansing CSD	Lansing
330	10.5	Washingtonville CSD	Washingtonville
334	10.4	Baldwin UFSD	Baldwin
334	10.4	Briarcliff Manor UFSD	Briarcliff Manor
334	10.4	East Meadow UFSD	Westbury
334	10.4	West Irondequoit CSD	Rochester
338	10.3	Edgemont UFSD	Scarsdale
339	10.1	Depew UFSD	Depew
340	10.0	Fayetteville-Manlius CSD	Manlius
341	9.9	Bath CSD	Bath
342	9.8	Ardsley UFSD	Ardsley
342	9.8	East Islip UFSD	Islip Terrace
342	9.8	Victor CSD	Victor
345	9.7	Island Trees UFSD	Levittown
345	9.7	New Hyde Pk-Garden City Pk UFSD	New Hyde Park
345	9.7	West Genesee CSD	Camillus
348	9.6	Cornwall CSD	Cornwall-on-Hud
349	9.4	Plainedge UFSD	N Massapequa
349	9.4	Scarsdale UFSD	Scarsdale
351	9.3	Jordan-Elbridge CSD	Jordan
352	9.2	Livonia CSD	Livonia
353	8.9	Chappaqua CSD	Chappaqua
353	8.9	Churchville-Chili CSD	Churchville
353	8.9	Irvington UFSD	Irvington
356	8.8	Coxsackie-Athens CSD	Coxsackie
356	8.8	Goshen CSD	Goshen
356	8.8	Sweet Home CSD	Amherst

359	8.7	Skaneateles CSD	Skaneateles
360	8.2	Eden CSD	Eden
361	8.1	Eastchester UFSD	Eastchester
361	8.1	Mattituck-Cutchogue UFSD	Cutchogue
361	8.1	Southwestern CSD at Jamestown	Jamestown
364	8.0	Elwood UFSD	Greenlawn
364	8.0	Seaford UFSD	Seaford
364	8.0	Valley Stream 30 UFSD	Valley Stream
367	7.0	East Aurora UFSD	East Aurora
368	6.1	Rye City SD	Rye

English Language Learner Students

Rank	Percent	District Name	City
1	27.3	Westbury UFSD	Old Westbury
2	19.6	UFSD - Tarrytowns	Sleepy Hollow
3	19.4	Port Chester-Rye UFSD	Port Chester
4	17.7	Brentwood UFSD	Brentwood
4	17.7	Hempstead UFSD	Hempstead
6	17.2	Yonkers City SD	Yonkers
7	15.1	Central Islip UFSD	Central Islip
8	13.7	Freeport UFSD	Freeport
9	13.3	Valley Stream 30 UFSD	Valley Stream
10	13.1	New Rochelle City SD	New Rochelle
11	12.9	Utica City SD	Utica
12	11.6	Dunkirk City SD	Dunkirk
12	11.6	New York City Public Schools	Brooklyn
14	10.5	Mineola UFSD	Mineola
15	10.3	Roosevelt UFSD	Roosevelt
16	10.2	Huntington UFSD	Huntington Stn
17	10.1	Mount Vernon City SD	Mount Vernon
17	10.1	Newburgh City SD	Newburgh
19	10.0	Uniondale UFSD	Uniondale
20	9.6	Glen Cove City SD	Glen Cove
21	9.5	Hampton Bays UFSD	Hampton Bays
22	9.3	Ossining UFSD	Ossining
23	9.2	White Plains City SD	White Plains
24	8.7	Peekskill City SD	Peekskill
25	8.4	Port Washington UFSD	Pt Washington
26	8.3	East Hampton UFSD	East Hampton
27	7.9	Haverstraw-Stony Point CSD	Garnerville
27	7.9	Wyandanch UFSD	Wyandanch
29	7.8	Rochester City SD	Rochester
30	7.7	Bedford CSD	Mount Kisco
31	7.6	East Ramapo CSD (Spring Valley)	Spring Valley
31	7.6	Poughkeepsie City SD	Poughkeepsie
33	7.4	Copiague UFSD	Copiague
33	7.4	Herricks UFSD	New Hyde Park
35	7.2	Lawrence UFSD	Lawrence
36	7.1	South Huntington UFSD	Huntington Stn
37	7.0	Greenburgh CSD	Hartsdale
37	7.0	Hicksville UFSD	Hicksville
39	6.7	Middletown City SD	Middletown
39	6.7	Southampton UFSD	Southampton
41	6.4	Amityville UFSD	Amityville
41	6.4	Buffalo City SD	Buffalo
43	6.3	Great Neck UFSD	Great Neck
44	6.0	Ithaca City SD	Ithaca
44	6.0	Syracuse City SD	Syracuse
46	5.9	Nyack UFSD	Nyack
46	5.9	Oceanside UFSD	Oceanside
48	5.7	Harrison CSD	Harrison
48	5.7	Long Beach City SD	Long Beach
50	5.5	Carle Place UFSD	Carle Place
50	5.5	Solvay UFSD	Solvay
52	5.3	Elmont UFSD	Elmont
52	5.3	Oyster Bay-East Norwich CSD	Oyster Bay
54	5.1	Ellenville CSD	Ellenville
55	5.0	Monticello CSD	Monticello
55	5.0	Riverhead CSD	Riverhead
57	4.9	Binghamton City SD	Binghamton
58	4.8	Bay Shore UFSD	Bay Shore
58	4.8	Eastchester UFSD	Eastchester
60	4.7	Valley Stream 13 UFSD	Valley Stream
61	4.3	Indian River CSD	Philadelphia
62	4.2	Patchogue-Medford UFSD	Patchogue
62	4.2	Rye City SD	Rye
64	4.1	Lackawanna City SD	Lackawanna
65	4.0	East Meadow UFSD	Westbury
65	4.0	Hewlett-Woodmere UFSD	Woodmere
67	3.8	Deer Park UFSD	Deer Park
67	3.8	Johnson City CSD	Johnson City
69	3.7	Elwood UFSD	Greenlawn
69	3.7	New Hyde Pk-Garden City Pk UFSD	New Hyde Park
71	3.5	Amsterdam City SD	Amsterdam
71	3.5	South Orangetown CSD	Blauvelt
73	3.4	Albany City SD	Albany
73	3.4	Brighton CSD	Rochester
73	3.4	Hudson City SD	Hudson
73	3.4	Mamaroneck UFSD	Mamaroneck
73	3.4	South Country CSD	E Patchogue
73	3.4	West Hempstead UFSD	W Hempstead
79	3.3	Edgemont UFSD	Scarsdale
80	3.2	Locust Valley CSD	Locust Valley
80	3.2	Roslyn UFSD	Roslyn
80	3.2	Scarsdale UFSD	Scarsdale
83	3.1	Cohoes City SD	Cohoes
84	2.9	Baldwin UFSD	Baldwin
84	2.9	Beacon City SD	Beacon
86	2.8	Clarkstown CSD	New City
86	2.8	East Irondequoit CSD	Rochester
86	2.8	Farmingdale UFSD	Farmingdale
89	2.7	Babylon UFSD	Babylon
89	2.7	Franklin Square UFSD	Franklin Square
89	2.7	Geneva City SD	Geneva
89	2.7	Longwood CSD	Middle Island
89	2.7	Schenectady City SD	Schenectady
94	2.6	Floral Park-Bellerose UFSD	Floral Park
94	2.6	Jericho UFSD	Jericho
94	2.6	Lynbrook UFSD	Lynbrook
94	2.6	Malverne UFSD	Malverne
94	2.6	Nanuet UFSD	Nanuet
94	2.6	Sewanhaka Central HSD	Floral Park
94	2.6	Sweet Home CSD	Amherst
94	2.6	Valley Stream Central HSD	Valley Stream
102	2.5	Liberty CSD	Liberty
102	2.5	Lindenhurst UFSD	Lindenhurst
102	2.5	Rush-Henrietta CSD	Henrietta
105	2.4	Bethpage UFSD	Bethpage
105	2.4	Brookhaven-Comsewogue UFSD	Pt Jefferson Stn
105	2.4	Islip UFSD	Islip
108	2.3	Manhasset UFSD	Manhasset
108	2.3	Westhampton Beach UFSD	Westhampton Bch
110	2.2	Albion CSD	Albion
110	2.2	East Williston UFSD	Old Westbury
110	2.2	Fredonia CSD	Fredonia
110	2.2	Hyde Park CSD	Poughkeepsie
110	2.2	Marlboro CSD	Marlboro
110	2.2	West Babylon UFSD	West Babylon
116	2.1	Hastings-On-Hudson UFSD	Hastings-on-Hud
116	2.1	Newark CSD	Newark
116	2.1	Ramapo CSD (Suffern)	Hillburn
119	2.0	Brewster CSD	Brewster
119	2.0	Greece CSD	Rochester
119	2.0	Jamestown City SD	Jamestown
119	2.0	Rockville Centre UFSD	Rockville Ctre
119	2.0	Westhill CSD	Syracuse
124	1.9	Half Hollow Hills CSD	Dix Hills
124	1.9	Middle Country CSD	Centereach
124	1.9	Mount Pleasant CSD	Thornwood
127	1.8	Fayetteville-Manlius CSD	Manlius
127	1.8	Hauppauge UFSD	Hauppauge
127	1.8	Mahopac CSD	Mahopac
127	1.8	North Babylon UFSD	North Babylon
127	1.8	North Rose-Wolcott CSD	Wolcott
127	1.8	North Shore CSD	Sea Cliff
127	1.8	Pleasantville UFSD	Pleasantville
134	1.7	Goshen CSD	Goshen
134	1.7	Guilderland CSD	Guilderland
134	1.7	New Paltz CSD	New Paltz
134	1.7	North Colonie CSD	Latham
134	1.7	Red Hook CSD	Red Hook
139	1.6	Ardsley UFSD	Ardsley
139	1.6	Syosset CSD	Syosset
139	1.6	William Floyd UFSD	Mastic Beach
139	1.6	Williamsville CSD	East Amherst
143	1.5	Harborfields CSD	Greenlawn
143	1.5	Jamesville-Dewitt CSD	Dewitt
143	1.5	Katonah-Lewisboro UFSD	South Salem
143	1.5	Kings Park CSD	Kings Park
143	1.5	Kingston City SD	Kingston
143	1.5	Northport-East Northport UFSD	Northport
143	1.5	Penfield CSD	Penfield
143	1.5	Pine Bush CSD	Pine Bush
143	1.5	Saranac Lake CSD	Saranac Lake
143	1.5	Wallkill CSD	Wallkill
143	1.5	West Genesee CSD	Camillus
154	1.4	Cheektowaga-Maryvale UFSD	Cheektowaga
154	1.4	Island Trees UFSD	Levittown
154	1.4	North Bellmore UFSD	Bellmore
157	1.3	Cheektowaga CSD	Cheektowaga
157	1.3	Hendrick Hudson CSD	Montrose
157	1.3	Levittown UFSD	Levittown
157	1.3	Pelham UFSD	Pelham
157	1.3	Plainedge UFSD	N Massapequa
157	1.3	Putnam Valley CSD	Putnam Valley
157	1.3	Sachem CSD	Holbrook
157	1.3	Salamanca City SD	Salamanca
157	1.3	Washingtonville CSD	Washingtonville
157	1.3	Webster CSD	Webster
157	1.3	Yorktown CSD	Yorktown Hgts
168	1.2	Brockport CSD	Brockport
168	1.2	Croton-Harmon UFSD	Croton-On-Hud
168	1.2	Gates-Chili CSD	Rochester
168	1.2	Miller Place UFSD	Miller Place
168	1.2	North Tonawanda City SD	N Tonawanda
168	1.2	Pearl River UFSD	Pearl River
168	1.2	Seneca Falls CSD	Seneca Falls
168	1.2	Troy City SD	Troy
168	1.2	Wappingers CSD	Wappingers Fls
168	1.2	Watertown City SD	Watertown
178	1.1	East Islip UFSD	Islip Terrace
178	1.1	East Syracuse-Minoa CSD	East Syracuse
178	1.1	Monroe-Woodbury CSD	Central Valley
178	1.1	Niagara Falls City SD	Niagara Falls
178	1.1	Whitesboro CSD	Yorkville
183	1.0	Amherst CSD	Amherst
183	1.0	Arlington CSD	Poughkeepsie
183	1.0	Bethlehem CSD	Delmar
183	1.0	Carmel CSD	Patterson
183	1.0	Churchville-Chili CSD	Churchville
183	1.0	Connetquot CSD	Bohemia
183	1.0	Grand Island CSD	Grand Island
183	1.0	Lakeland CSD	Shrub Oak
183	1.0	Liverpool CSD	Liverpool
183	1.0	Mattituck-Cutchogue UFSD	Cutchogue
183	1.0	Medina CSD	Medina
183	1.0	Merrick UFSD	Merrick
183	1.0	Onteora CSD	Boiceville
183	1.0	Plainview-Old Bethpage CSD	Plainview
183	1.0	Salmon River CSD	Ft Covington
183	1.0	Spackenkill UFSD	Poughkeepsie
183	1.0	Spencerport CSD	Spencerport
183	1.0	Vestal CSD	Vestal
183	1.0	West Irondequoit CSD	Rochester
202	0.9	Kinderhook CSD	Valatie
202	0.9	Lockport City SD	Lockport
202	0.9	Valley CSD (Montgomery)	Montgomery
205	0.8	Briarcliff Manor UFSD	Briarcliff Manor
205	0.8	Catskill CSD	Catskill
205	0.8	Chappaqua CSD	Chappaqua
205	0.8	Cleveland Hill UFSD	Cheektowaga
205	0.8	Commack UFSD	E Northport
205	0.8	Fairport CSD	Fairport
205	0.8	Highland CSD	Highland
205	0.8	Hilton CSD	Hilton
205	0.8	Homer CSD	Homer
205	0.8	Irvington UFSD	Irvington
205	0.8	Oswego City SD	Oswego
205	0.8	Palmyra-Macedon CSD	Palmyra
205	0.8	Ravena-Coeymans-Selkirk CSD	Selkirk
205	0.8	Rocky Point UFSD	Rocky Point
205	0.8	Rondout Valley CSD	Accord
205	0.8	Victor CSD	Victor
221	0.7	Chatham CSD	Chatham
221	0.7	Cortland City SD	Cortland
221	0.7	Coxsackie-Athens CSD	Coxsackie
221	0.7	Lansingburgh CSD	Troy
221	0.7	Smithtown CSD	Smithtown
221	0.7	South Colonie CSD	Albany
221	0.7	Three Village CSD	East Setauket
221	0.7	Union-Endicott CSD	Endicott
221	0.7	Warwick Valley CSD	Warwick
221	0.7	West Seneca CSD	West Seneca
231	0.6	Bellmore-Merrick Central HSD	North Merrick
231	0.6	Cobleskill-Richmondville CSD	Cobleskill
231	0.6	Fulton City SD	Fulton
231	0.6	Ilion CSD	Ilion
231	0.6	Kenmore-Tonawanda UFSD	Buffalo
231	0.6	Minisink Valley CSD	Slate Hill
231	0.6	Niskayuna CSD	Schenectady
231	0.6	Oneonta City SD	Oneonta
231	0.6	Pittsford CSD	Pittsford
231	0.6	Port Jervis City SD	Port Jervis
231	0.6	Royalton-Hartland CSD	Middleport
231	0.6	Sayville UFSD	Sayville
231	0.6	Schuylerville CSD	Schuylerville
231	0.6	Scotia-Glenville CSD	Scotia
231	0.6	Seaford UFSD	Seaford
231	0.6	Shenendehowa CSD	Clifton Park
247	0.5	Byram Hills CSD	Armonk
247	0.5	Cheektowaga-Sloan UFSD	Sloan
247	0.5	Dover UFSD	Dover Plains
247	0.5	East Aurora UFSD	East Aurora
247	0.5	Garden City UFSD	Garden City
247	0.5	Hamburg CSD	Hamburg
247	0.5	Oneida City SD	Oneida
247	0.5	Rome City SD	Rome
247	0.5	Saugerties CSD	Saugerties
256	0.4	Bayport-Blue Point UFSD	Bayport
256	0.4	Clarence CSD	Clarence
256	0.4	Clinton CSD	Clinton
256	0.4	Corning City SD	Painted Post
256	0.4	Depew UFSD	Depew
256	0.4	Dryden CSD	Dryden
256	0.4	East Greenbush CSD	E Greenbush
256	0.4	Frontier CSD	Hamburg
256	0.4	Plattsburgh City SD	Plattsburgh

256	0.4	Shoreham-Wading River CSD	Shoreham
256	0.4	Somers CSD	Lincolndale
256	0.4	Sullivan West CSD	Jeffersonville
256	0.4	Wantagh UFSD	Wantagh
269	0.3	Baldwinsville CSD	Baldwinsville
269	0.3	Batavia City SD	Batavia
269	0.3	Cairo-Durham CSD	Cairo
269	0.3	Carthage CSD	Carthage
269	0.3	Chenango Valley CSD	Binghamton
269	0.3	Cornwall CSD	Cornwall-on-Hud
269	0.3	Elmira City SD	Elmira
269	0.3	Lansing CSD	Lansing
269	0.3	Newfane CSD	Newfane
269	0.3	North Syracuse CSD	N Syracuse
269	0.3	Orchard Park CSD	Orchard Park
269	0.3	Owego-Apalachin CSD	Owego
269	0.3	Penn Yan CSD	Pen
269	0.3	Rotterdam-Mohonasen CSD	Schenectady
269	0.3	Saranac CSD	Dannemora
269	0.3	Susquehanna Valley CSD	Conklin
269	0.3	West Islip UFSD	West Islip
286	0.2	Auburn City SD	Auburn
286	0.2	Ballston Spa CSD	Ballston Spa
286	0.2	Chenango Forks CSD	Binghamton
286	0.2	Dansville CSD	Dansville
286	0.2	Gloversville City SD	Gloversville
286	0.2	Gorham-Middlesex CSD	Rushville
286	0.2	Horseheads CSD	Horseheads
286	0.2	Lancaster CSD	Lancaster
286	0.2	Maine-Endwell CSD	Endwell
286	0.2	Marcellus CSD	Marcellus
286	0.2	Massapequa UFSD	Massapequa
286	0.2	Massena CSD	Massena
286	0.2	Niagara-Wheatfield CSD	Niagara Falls
286	0.2	Northeastern Clinton CSD	Champlain
286	0.2	Sherrill City SD	Verona
286	0.2	Springville-Griffith Inst CSD	Springville
286	0.2	Taconic Hills CSD	Craryville
286	0.2	Tonawanda City SD	Tonawanda
286	0.2	Waterloo CSD	Waterloo
305	0.1	Alden CSD	Alden
305	0.1	Attica CSD	Attica
305	0.1	Averill Park CSD	Averill Park
305	0.1	Beekmantown CSD	Plattsburgh
305	0.1	Broadalbin-Perth CSD	Broadalbin
305	0.1	Burnt Hills-Ballston Lake CSD	Scotia
305	0.1	Canastota CSD	Canastota
305	0.1	Canton CSD	Canton
305	0.1	Cazenovia CSD	Cazenovia
305	0.1	Chittenango CSD	Chittenango
305	0.1	Cold Spring Harbor CSD	Cold Sprg Harbor
305	0.1	Fonda-Fultonville CSD	Fonda
305	0.1	General Brown CSD	Dexter
305	0.1	Glens Falls City SD	Glens Falls
305	0.1	Gowanda CSD	Gowanda
305	0.1	Honeoye Falls-Lima CSD	Honeoye Falls
305	0.1	Hornell City SD	Hornell
305	0.1	Iroquois CSD	Elma
305	0.1	Jordan-Elbridge CSD	Jordan
305	0.1	Malone CSD	Malone
305	0.1	Mount Sinai UFSD	Mount Sinai
305	0.1	New Hartford CSD	New Hartford
305	0.1	Olean City SD	Olean
305	0.1	Queensbury UFSD	Queensbury
305	0.1	Saratoga Springs City SD	Saratoga Spgs
305	0.1	Sherburne-Earlville CSD	Sherburne
305	0.1	Skaneateles CSD	Skaneateles
305	0.1	Southwestern CSD at Jamestown	Jamestown
305	0.1	Starpoint CSD	Lockport
305	0.1	Whitney Point CSD	Whitney Point
305	0.1	Wilson CSD	Wilson
305	0.1	Windsor CSD	Windsor
337	0.0	Canandaigua City SD	Canandaigua
337	0.0	Central Square CSD	Central Square
337	0.0	Evans-Brant CSD (Lake Shore)	Angola
337	0.0	Hudson Falls CSD	Hudson Falls
337	0.0	Johnstown City SD	Johnstown
337	0.0	Livonia CSD	Livonia
337	0.0	Norwich City SD	Norwich
337	0.0	Ogdensburg City SD	Ogdensburg
337	0.0	Phoenix CSD	Phoenix
337	0.0	Wayne CSD	Ontario Center
347	0.0	Adirondack CSD	Boonville
347	0.0	Akron CSD	Akron
347	0.0	Altmar-Parish-Williamstown CSD	Parish
347	0.0	Bath CSD	Bath
347	0.0	Camden CSD	Camden
347	0.0	Eden CSD	Eden
347	0.0	Gouverneur CSD	Gouverneur
347	0.0	Hannibal CSD	Hannibal
347	0.0	Holland Patent CSD	Holland Patent
347	0.0	Lewiston-Porter CSD	Youngstown
347	0.0	Mexico CSD	Mexico
347	0.0	Peru CSD	Peru
347	0.0	Phelps-Clifton Springs CSD	Clifton Spgs
347	0.0	Schalmont CSD	Schenectady
347	0.0	South Glens Falls CSD	S Glens Falls
347	0.0	South Jefferson CSD	Adams Center
347	0.0	Waverly CSD	Waverly
347	0.0	Wayland-Cohocton CSD	Wayland
347	0.0	Yorkshire-Pioneer CSD	Yorkshire
366	n/a	Boces Eastern Suffolk (Suffolk I)	Patchogue
366	n/a	Boces Monroe 1	Fairport
366	n/a	Boces Nassau	Garden City

Migrant Students

Rank	Percent	District Name	City
1	n/a	Adirondack CSD	Boonville
1	n/a	Akron CSD	Akron
1	n/a	Albany City SD	Albany
1	n/a	Albion CSD	Albion
1	n/a	Alden CSD	Alden
1	n/a	Altmar-Parish-Williamstown CSD	Parish
1	n/a	Amherst CSD	Amherst
1	n/a	Amityville UFSD	Amityville
1	n/a	Amsterdam City SD	Amsterdam
1	n/a	Ardsley UFSD	Ardsley
1	n/a	Arlington CSD	Poughkeepsie
1	n/a	Attica CSD	Attica
1	n/a	Auburn City SD	Auburn
1	n/a	Averill Park CSD	Averill Park
1	n/a	Babylon UFSD	Babylon
1	n/a	Baldwin UFSD	Baldwin
1	n/a	Baldwinsville CSD	Baldwinsville
1	n/a	Ballston Spa CSD	Ballston Spa
1	n/a	Batavia City SD	Batavia
1	n/a	Bath CSD	Bath
1	n/a	Bay Shore UFSD	Bay Shore
1	n/a	Bayport-Blue Point UFSD	Bayport
1	n/a	Beacon City SD	Beacon
1	n/a	Bedford CSD	Mount Kisco
1	n/a	Beekmantown CSD	Plattsburgh
1	n/a	Bellmore-Merrick Central HSD	North Merrick
1	n/a	Bethlehem CSD	Delmar
1	n/a	Bethpage UFSD	Bethpage
1	n/a	Binghamton City SD	Binghamton
1	n/a	Boces Eastern Suffolk (Suffolk I)	Patchogue
1	n/a	Boces Monroe 1	Fairport
1	n/a	Boces Nassau	Garden City
1	n/a	Brentwood UFSD	Brentwood
1	n/a	Brewster CSD	Brewster
1	n/a	Briarcliff Manor UFSD	Briarcliff Manor
1	n/a	Brighton CSD	Rochester
1	n/a	Broadalbin-Perth CSD	Broadalbin
1	n/a	Brockport CSD	Brockport
1	n/a	Brookhaven-Comsewogue UFSD	Pt Jefferson Stn
1	n/a	Buffalo City SD	Buffalo
1	n/a	Burnt Hills-Ballston Lake CSD	Scotia
1	n/a	Byram Hills CSD	Armonk
1	n/a	Cairo-Durham CSD	Cairo
1	n/a	Camden CSD	Camden
1	n/a	Canandaigua City SD	Canandaigua
1	n/a	Canastota CSD	Canastota
1	n/a	Canton CSD	Canton
1	n/a	Carle Place UFSD	Carle Place
1	n/a	Carmel CSD	Patterson
1	n/a	Carthage CSD	Carthage
1	n/a	Catskill CSD	Catskill
1	n/a	Cazenovia CSD	Cazenovia
1	n/a	Central Islip UFSD	Central Islip
1	n/a	Central Square CSD	Central Square
1	n/a	Chappaqua CSD	Chappaqua
1	n/a	Chatham CSD	Chatham
1	n/a	Cheektowaga CSD	Cheektowaga
1	n/a	Cheektowaga-Maryvale UFSD	Cheektowaga
1	n/a	Cheektowaga-Sloan UFSD	Sloan
1	n/a	Chenango Forks CSD	Binghamton
1	n/a	Chenango Valley CSD	Binghamton
1	n/a	Chittenango CSD	Chittenango
1	n/a	Churchville-Chili CSD	Churchville
1	n/a	Clarence CSD	Clarence
1	n/a	Clarkstown CSD	New City
1	n/a	Cleveland Hill UFSD	Cheektowaga
1	n/a	Clinton CSD	Clinton
1	n/a	Cobleskill-Richmondville CSD	Cobleskill
1	n/a	Cohoes City SD	Cohoes
1	n/a	Cold Spring Harbor CSD	Cold Sprg Harbor
1	n/a	Commack UFSD	E Northport
1	n/a	Connetquot CSD	Bohemia
1	n/a	Copiague UFSD	Copiague
1	n/a	Corning City SD	Painted Post
1	n/a	Cornwall CSD	Cornwall-on-Hud
1	n/a	Cortland City SD	Cortland
1	n/a	Coxsackie-Athens CSD	Coxsackie
1	n/a	Croton-Harmon UFSD	Croton-On-Hud
1	n/a	Dansville CSD	Dansville
1	n/a	Deer Park UFSD	Deer Park
1	n/a	Depew UFSD	Depew
1	n/a	Dover UFSD	Dover Plains
1	n/a	Dryden CSD	Dryden
1	n/a	Dunkirk City SD	Dunkirk
1	n/a	East Aurora UFSD	East Aurora
1	n/a	East Greenbush CSD	E Greenbush
1	n/a	East Hampton UFSD	East Hampton
1	n/a	East Irondequoit CSD	Rochester
1	n/a	East Islip UFSD	Islip Terrace
1	n/a	East Meadow UFSD	Westbury
1	n/a	East Ramapo CSD (Spring Valley)	Spring Valley
1	n/a	East Syracuse-Minoa CSD	East Syracuse
1	n/a	East Williston UFSD	Old Westbury
1	n/a	Eastchester UFSD	Eastchester
1	n/a	Eden CSD	Eden
1	n/a	Edgemont UFSD	Scarsdale
1	n/a	Ellenville CSD	Ellenville
1	n/a	Elmira City SD	Elmira
1	n/a	Elmont UFSD	Elmont
1	n/a	Elwood UFSD	Greenlawn
1	n/a	Evans-Brant CSD (Lake Shore)	Angola
1	n/a	Fairport CSD	Fairport
1	n/a	Farmingdale UFSD	Farmingdale
1	n/a	Fayetteville-Manlius CSD	Manlius
1	n/a	Floral Park-Bellerose UFSD	Floral Park
1	n/a	Fonda-Fultonville CSD	Fonda
1	n/a	Franklin Square UFSD	Franklin Square
1	n/a	Fredonia CSD	Fredonia
1	n/a	Freeport UFSD	Freeport
1	n/a	Frontier CSD	Hamburg
1	n/a	Fulton City SD	Fulton
1	n/a	Garden City UFSD	Garden City
1	n/a	Gates-Chili CSD	Rochester
1	n/a	General Brown CSD	Dexter
1	n/a	Geneva City SD	Geneva
1	n/a	Glen Cove City SD	Glen Cove
1	n/a	Glens Falls City SD	Glens Falls
1	n/a	Gloversville City SD	Gloversville
1	n/a	Gorham-Middlesex CSD	Rushville
1	n/a	Goshen CSD	Goshen
1	n/a	Gouverneur CSD	Gouverneur
1	n/a	Gowanda CSD	Gowanda
1	n/a	Grand Island CSD	Grand Island
1	n/a	Great Neck UFSD	Great Neck
1	n/a	Greece CSD	Rochester
1	n/a	Greenburgh CSD	Hartsdale
1	n/a	Guilderland CSD	Guilderland
1	n/a	Half Hollow Hills CSD	Dix Hills
1	n/a	Hamburg CSD	Hamburg
1	n/a	Hampton Bays UFSD	Hampton Bays
1	n/a	Hannibal CSD	Hannibal
1	n/a	Harborfields CSD	Greenlawn
1	n/a	Harrison CSD	Harrison
1	n/a	Hastings-On-Hudson UFSD	Hastings-on-Hud
1	n/a	Hauppauge UFSD	Hauppauge
1	n/a	Haverstraw-Stony Point CSD	Garnerville
1	n/a	Hempstead UFSD	Hempstead
1	n/a	Hendrick Hudson CSD	Montrose
1	n/a	Herricks UFSD	New Hyde Park
1	n/a	Hewlett-Woodmere UFSD	Woodmere
1	n/a	Hicksville UFSD	Hicksville
1	n/a	Highland CSD	Highland
1	n/a	Hilton CSD	Hilton
1	n/a	Holland Patent CSD	Holland Patent
1	n/a	Homer CSD	Homer
1	n/a	Honeoye Falls-Lima CSD	Honeoye Falls
1	n/a	Hornell City SD	Hornell
1	n/a	Horseheads CSD	Horseheads
1	n/a	Hudson City SD	Hudson
1	n/a	Hudson Falls CSD	Hudson Falls
1	n/a	Huntington UFSD	Huntington Stn
1	n/a	Hyde Park CSD	Poughkeepsie
1	n/a	Ilion CSD	Ilion
1	n/a	Indian River CSD	Philadelphia
1	n/a	Iroquois CSD	Elma
1	n/a	Irvington UFSD	Irvington
1	n/a	Island Trees UFSD	Levittown
1	n/a	Islip UFSD	Islip
1	n/a	Ithaca City SD	Ithaca
1	n/a	Jamestown City SD	Jamestown
1	n/a	Jamesville-Dewitt CSD	Dewitt
1	n/a	Jericho UFSD	Jericho
1	n/a	Johnson City CSD	Johnson City
1	n/a	Johnstown City SD	Johnstown
1	n/a	Jordan-Elbridge CSD	Jordan
1	n/a	Katonah-Lewisboro UFSD	South Salem
1	n/a	Kenmore-Tonawanda UFSD	Buffalo
1	n/a	Kinderhook CSD	Valatie
1	n/a	Kings Park CSD	Kings Park

1	n/a	Kingston City SD	Kingston
1	n/a	Lackawanna City SD	Lackawanna
1	n/a	Lakeland CSD	Shrub Oak
1	n/a	Lancaster CSD	Lancaster
1	n/a	Lansing CSD	Lansing
1	n/a	Lansingburgh CSD	Troy
1	n/a	Lawrence UFSD	Lawrence
1	n/a	Levittown UFSD	Levittown
1	n/a	Lewiston-Porter CSD	Youngstown
1	n/a	Liberty CSD	Liberty
1	n/a	Lindenhurst UFSD	Lindenhurst
1	n/a	Liverpool CSD	Liverpool
1	n/a	Livonia CSD	Livonia
1	n/a	Lockport City SD	Lockport
1	n/a	Locust Valley CSD	Locust Valley
1	n/a	Long Beach City SD	Long Beach
1	n/a	Longwood CSD	Middle Island
1	n/a	Lynbrook UFSD	Lynbrook
1	n/a	Mahopac CSD	Mahopac
1	n/a	Maine-Endwell CSD	Endwell
1	n/a	Malone CSD	Malone
1	n/a	Malverne UFSD	Malverne
1	n/a	Mamaroneck UFSD	Mamaroneck
1	n/a	Manhasset UFSD	Manhasset
1	n/a	Marcellus CSD	Marcellus
1	n/a	Marlboro CSD	Marlboro
1	n/a	Massapequa UFSD	Massapequa
1	n/a	Massena CSD	Massena
1	n/a	Mattituck-Cutchogue UFSD	Cutchogue
1	n/a	Medina CSD	Medina
1	n/a	Merrick UFSD	Merrick
1	n/a	Mexico CSD	Mexico
1	n/a	Middle Country CSD	Centereach
1	n/a	Middletown City SD	Middletown
1	n/a	Miller Place UFSD	Miller Place
1	n/a	Mineola UFSD	Mineola
1	n/a	Minisink Valley CSD	Slate Hill
1	n/a	Monroe-Woodbury CSD	Central Valley
1	n/a	Monticello CSD	Monticello
1	n/a	Mount Pleasant CSD	Thornwood
1	n/a	Mount Sinai UFSD	Mount Sinai
1	n/a	Mount Vernon City SD	Mount Vernon
1	n/a	Nanuet UFSD	Nanuet
1	n/a	New Hartford CSD	New Hartford
1	n/a	New Hyde Pk-Garden City Pk UFSD	New Hyde Park
1	n/a	New Paltz CSD	New Paltz
1	n/a	New Rochelle City SD	New Rochelle
1	n/a	New York City Public Schools	Brooklyn
1	n/a	Newark CSD	Newark
1	n/a	Newburgh City SD	Newburgh
1	n/a	Newfane CSD	Newfane
1	n/a	Niagara Falls City SD	Niagara Falls
1	n/a	Niagara-Wheatfield CSD	Niagara Falls
1	n/a	Niskayuna CSD	Schenectady
1	n/a	North Babylon UFSD	North Babylon
1	n/a	North Bellmore UFSD	Bellmore
1	n/a	North Colonie CSD	Latham
1	n/a	North Rose-Wolcott CSD	Wolcott
1	n/a	North Shore CSD	Sea Cliff
1	n/a	North Syracuse CSD	N Syracuse
1	n/a	North Tonawanda City SD	N Tonawanda
1	n/a	Northeastern Clinton CSD	Champlain
1	n/a	Northport-East Northport UFSD	Northport
1	n/a	Norwich City SD	Norwich
1	n/a	Nyack UFSD	Nyack
1	n/a	Oceanside UFSD	Oceanside
1	n/a	Ogdensburg City SD	Ogdensburg
1	n/a	Olean City SD	Olean
1	n/a	Oneida City SD	Oneida
1	n/a	Oneonta City SD	Oneonta
1	n/a	Onteora CSD	Boiceville
1	n/a	Orchard Park CSD	Orchard Park
1	n/a	Ossining UFSD	Ossining
1	n/a	Oswego City SD	Oswego
1	n/a	Owego-Apalachin CSD	Owego
1	n/a	Oyster Bay-East Norwich CSD	Oyster Bay
1	n/a	Palmyra-Macedon CSD	Palmyra
1	n/a	Patchogue-Medford UFSD	Patchogue
1	n/a	Pearl River UFSD	Pearl River
1	n/a	Peekskill City SD	Peekskill
1	n/a	Pelham UFSD	Pelham
1	n/a	Penfield CSD	Penfield
1	n/a	Penn Yan CSD	Pen
1	n/a	Peru CSD	Peru
1	n/a	Phelps-Clifton Springs CSD	Clifton Spgs
1	n/a	Phoenix CSD	Phoenix
1	n/a	Pine Bush CSD	Pine Bush
1	n/a	Pittsford CSD	Pittsford
1	n/a	Plainedge UFSD	N Massapequa
1	n/a	Plainview-Old Bethpage CSD	Plainview
1	n/a	Plattsburgh City SD	Plattsburgh
1	n/a	Pleasantville UFSD	Pleasantville
1	n/a	Port Chester-Rye UFSD	Port Chester
1	n/a	Port Jervis City SD	Port Jervis
1	n/a	Port Washington UFSD	Pt Washington
1	n/a	Poughkeepsie City SD	Poughkeepsie
1	n/a	Putnam Valley CSD	Putnam Valley
1	n/a	Queensbury UFSD	Queensbury
1	n/a	Ramapo CSD (Suffern)	Hillburn
1	n/a	Ravena-Coeymans-Selkirk CSD	Selkirk
1	n/a	Red Hook CSD	Red Hook
1	n/a	Riverhead CSD	Riverhead
1	n/a	Rochester City SD	Rochester
1	n/a	Rockville Centre UFSD	Rockville Ctre
1	n/a	Rocky Point UFSD	Rocky Point
1	n/a	Rome City SD	Rome
1	n/a	Rondout Valley CSD	Accord
1	n/a	Roosevelt UFSD	Roosevelt
1	n/a	Roslyn UFSD	Roslyn
1	n/a	Rotterdam-Mohonasen CSD	Schenectady
1	n/a	Royalton-Hartland CSD	Middleport
1	n/a	Rush-Henrietta CSD	Henrietta
1	n/a	Rye City SD	Rye
1	n/a	Sachem CSD	Holbrook
1	n/a	Salamanca City SD	Salamanca
1	n/a	Salmon River CSD	Ft Covington
1	n/a	Saranac CSD	Dannemora
1	n/a	Saranac Lake CSD	Saranac Lake
1	n/a	Saratoga Springs City SD	Saratoga Spgs
1	n/a	Saugerties CSD	Saugerties
1	n/a	Sayville UFSD	Sayville
1	n/a	Scarsdale UFSD	Scarsdale
1	n/a	Schalmont CSD	Schenectady
1	n/a	Schenectady City SD	Schenectady
1	n/a	Schuylerville CSD	Schuylerville
1	n/a	Scotia-Glenville CSD	Scotia
1	n/a	Seaford UFSD	Seaford
1	n/a	Seneca Falls CSD	Seneca Falls
1	n/a	Sewanhaka Central HSD	Floral Park
1	n/a	Shenendehowa CSD	Clifton Park
1	n/a	Sherburne-Earlville CSD	Sherburne
1	n/a	Sherrill City SD	Verona
1	n/a	Shoreham-Wading River CSD	Shoreham
1	n/a	Skaneateles CSD	Skaneateles
1	n/a	Smithtown CSD	Smithtown
1	n/a	Solvay UFSD	Solvay
1	n/a	Somers CSD	Lincolndale
1	n/a	South Colonie CSD	Albany
1	n/a	South Country CSD	E Patchogue
1	n/a	South Glens Falls CSD	S Glens Falls
1	n/a	South Huntington UFSD	Huntington Stn
1	n/a	South Jefferson CSD	Adams Center
1	n/a	South Orangetown CSD	Blauvelt
1	n/a	Southampton UFSD	Southampton
1	n/a	Southwestern CSD at Jamestown	Jamestown
1	n/a	Spackenkill UFSD	Poughkeepsie
1	n/a	Spencerport CSD	Spencerport
1	n/a	Springville-Griffith Inst CSD	Springville
1	n/a	Starpoint CSD	Lockport
1	n/a	Sullivan West CSD	Jeffersonville
1	n/a	Susquehanna Valley CSD	Conklin
1	n/a	Sweet Home CSD	Amherst
1	n/a	Syosset CSD	Syosset
1	n/a	Syracuse City SD	Syracuse
1	n/a	Taconic Hills CSD	Craryville
1	n/a	Three Village CSD	East Setauket
1	n/a	Tonawanda City SD	Tonawanda
1	n/a	Troy City SD	Troy
1	n/a	UFSD - Tarrytowns	Sleepy Hollow
1	n/a	Union-Endicott CSD	Endicott
1	n/a	Uniondale UFSD	Uniondale
1	n/a	Utica City SD	Utica
1	n/a	Valley CSD (Montgomery)	Montgomery
1	n/a	Valley Stream 13 UFSD	Valley Stream
1	n/a	Valley Stream 30 UFSD	Valley Stream
1	n/a	Valley Stream Central HSD	Valley Stream
1	n/a	Vestal CSD	Vestal
1	n/a	Victor CSD	Victor
1	n/a	Wallkill CSD	Wallkill
1	n/a	Wantagh UFSD	Wantagh
1	n/a	Wappingers CSD	Wappingers Fls
1	n/a	Warwick Valley CSD	Warwick
1	n/a	Washingtonville CSD	Washingtonville
1	n/a	Waterloo CSD	Waterloo
1	n/a	Watertown City SD	Watertown
1	n/a	Waverly CSD	Waverly
1	n/a	Wayland-Cohocton CSD	Wayland
1	n/a	Wayne CSD	Ontario Center
1	n/a	Webster CSD	Webster
1	n/a	West Babylon UFSD	West Babylon
1	n/a	West Genesee CSD	Camillus
1	n/a	West Hempstead UFSD	W Hempstead
1	n/a	West Irondequoit CSD	Rochester
1	n/a	West Islip UFSD	West Islip
1	n/a	West Seneca CSD	West Seneca
1	n/a	Westbury UFSD	Old Westbury
1	n/a	Westhampton Beach UFSD	Westhampton Bch
1	n/a	Westhill CSD	Syracuse
1	n/a	White Plains City SD	White Plains
1	n/a	Whitesboro CSD	Yorkville
1	n/a	Whitney Point CSD	Whitney Point
1	n/a	William Floyd UFSD	Mastic Beach
1	n/a	Williamsville CSD	East Amherst
1	n/a	Wilson CSD	Wilson
1	n/a	Windsor CSD	Windsor
1	n/a	Wyandanch UFSD	Wyandanch
1	n/a	Yonkers City SD	Yonkers
1	n/a	Yorkshire-Pioneer CSD	Yorkshire
1	n/a	Yorktown CSD	Yorktown Hgts

Students Eligible for Free Lunch

Rank	Percent	District Name	City
1	92.3	Roosevelt UFSD	Roosevelt
2	71.7	Hempstead UFSD	Hempstead
3	64.2	Wyandanch UFSD	Wyandanch
4	64.0	Rochester City SD	Rochester
5	63.1	Buffalo City SD	Buffalo
6	62.4	Westbury UFSD	Old Westbury
7	62.3	Utica City SD	Utica
8	61.7	Yonkers City SD	Yonkers
9	60.5	Albany City SD	Albany
9	60.5	Syracuse City SD	Syracuse
11	59.0	Lackawanna City SD	Lackawanna
12	57.4	Poughkeepsie City SD	Poughkeepsie
13	50.7	Brentwood UFSD	Brentwood
14	47.5	Peekskill City SD	Peekskill
15	47.0	Schenectady City SD	Schenectady
16	46.2	Binghamton City SD	Binghamton
17	44.9	Mount Vernon City SD	Mount Vernon
18	43.9	Newburgh City SD	Newburgh
18	43.9	Troy City SD	Troy
20	43.0	Port Chester-Rye UFSD	Port Chester
21	41.4	Cohoes City SD	Cohoes
22	41.3	Niagara Falls City SD	Niagara Falls
23	41.2	Jamestown City SD	Jamestown
24	41.0	Dunkirk City SD	Dunkirk
25	40.0	East Ramapo CSD (Spring Valley)	Spring Valley
25	40.0	Salmon River CSD	Ft Covington
27	39.9	Hornell City SD	Hornell
28	39.3	Middletown City SD	Middletown
29	39.2	Watertown City SD	Watertown
30	39.0	Central Islip UFSD	Central Islip
31	38.5	Amityville UFSD	Amityville
31	38.5	Gowanda CSD	Gowanda
33	37.2	Elmira City SD	Elmira
33	37.2	Monticello CSD	Monticello
35	36.2	Malone CSD	Malone
36	36.1	Ogdensburg City SD	Ogdensburg
37	35.6	Geneva City SD	Geneva
38	35.3	New Rochelle City SD	New Rochelle
39	35.1	Salamanca City SD	Salamanca
40	33.8	Hudson City SD	Hudson
41	33.7	Fulton City SD	Fulton
42	32.9	Massena CSD	Massena
43	32.7	Altmar-Parish-Williamstown CSD	Parish
44	32.5	Lansingburgh CSD	Troy
45	32.1	UFSD - Tarrytowns	Sleepy Hollow
46	31.9	Gloversville City SD	Gloversville
47	31.6	William Floyd UFSD	Mastic Beach
48	31.3	Camden CSD	Camden
49	30.3	Freeport UFSD	Freeport
49	30.3	Liberty CSD	Liberty
51	30.0	Rome City SD	Rome
52	29.9	Ellenville CSD	Ellenville
53	29.3	Gouverneur CSD	Gouverneur
54	29.1	Amsterdam City SD	Amsterdam
54	29.1	Copiague UFSD	Copiague
54	29.1	Hudson Falls CSD	Hudson Falls
57	28.3	Hannibal CSD	Hannibal
58	28.1	Bath CSD	Bath
58	28.1	Olean City SD	Olean
58	28.1	Sherburne-Earlville CSD	Sherburne
61	27.0	Johnson City CSD	Johnson City
62	26.8	White Plains City SD	White Plains
63	26.7	Yorkshire-Pioneer CSD	Yorkshire
64	26.6	Waterloo CSD	Waterloo
65	26.5	Norwich City SD	Norwich
65	26.5	South Country CSD	E Patchogue
67	26.4	Ilion CSD	Ilion
67	26.4	North Rose-Wolcott CSD	Wolcott
69	26.3	Beacon City SD	Beacon
70	26.0	Kingston City SD	Kingston
71	25.7	Peru CSD	Peru
72	25.6	Cortland City SD	Cortland
73	25.5	Batavia City SD	Batavia
73	25.5	Indian River CSD	Philadelphia
75	25.4	Auburn City SD	Auburn

Rank	Value	District	City
75	25.4	Port Jervis City SD	Port Jervis
77	25.3	Canton CSD	Canton
78	25.1	Elmont UFSD	Elmont
79	24.9	Plattsburgh City SD	Plattsburgh
80	24.8	Bay Shore UFSD	Bay Shore
81	24.7	Medina CSD	Medina
82	24.2	Haverstraw-Stony Point CSD	Garnerville
83	23.9	Uniondale UFSD	Uniondale
84	23.8	Whitney Point CSD	Whitney Point
85	23.6	Johnstown City SD	Johnstown
86	23.5	Cairo-Durham CSD	Cairo
87	23.4	Corning City SD	Painted Post
88	23.1	Catskill CSD	Catskill
88	23.1	Taconic Hills CSD	Craryville
90	22.8	Beekmantown CSD	Plattsburgh
91	22.6	Adirondack CSD	Boonville
92	22.4	Ithaca City SD	Ithaca
93	21.9	Waverly CSD	Waverly
94	21.6	Cleveland Hill UFSD	Cheektowaga
94	21.6	Riverhead CSD	Riverhead
96	21.3	Lockport City SD	Lockport
96	21.3	Oneida City SD	Oneida
98	21.2	Cobleskill-Richmondville CSD	Cobleskill
98	21.2	General Brown CSD	Dexter
100	20.9	Carthage CSD	Carthage
101	20.7	South Jefferson CSD	Adams Center
102	20.6	Cheektowaga-Sloan UFSD	Sloan
103	20.4	Dryden CSD	Dryden
104	20.1	Newark CSD	Newark
105	20.0	Oneonta City SD	Oneonta
106	19.9	Canastota CSD	Canastota
106	19.9	Dansville CSD	Dansville
106	19.9	Ossining UFSD	Ossining
109	19.8	Glens Falls City SD	Glens Falls
109	19.8	Wayland-Cohocton CSD	Wayland
111	19.7	Huntington UFSD	Huntington Stn
111	19.7	Phoenix CSD	Phoenix
113	19.6	Albion CSD	Albion
114	19.5	Greenburgh CSD	Hartsdale
114	19.5	Seneca Falls CSD	Seneca Falls
116	19.2	Lawrence UFSD	Lawrence
117	19.0	Cheektowaga CSD	Cheektowaga
118	18.9	Penn Yan CSD	Pen
118	18.9	Solvay UFSD	Solvay
120	18.8	Glen Cove City SD	Glen Cove
121	18.7	Fonda-Fultonville CSD	Fonda
121	18.7	Windsor CSD	Windsor
123	18.5	Mexico CSD	Mexico
124	18.4	Sherrill City SD	Verona
125	18.3	East Irondequoit CSD	Rochester
125	18.3	Union-Endicott CSD	Endicott
127	18.0	Chenango Valley CSD	Binghamton
128	17.9	Susquehanna Valley CSD	Conklin
129	17.8	Oswego City SD	Oswego
130	17.7	Owego-Apalachin CSD	Owego
131	17.4	Chenango Forks CSD	Binghamton
131	17.4	Tonawanda City SD	Tonawanda
133	17.1	Chatham CSD	Chatham
133	17.1	South Huntington UFSD	Huntington Stn
135	16.8	Northeastern Clinton CSD	Champlain
136	16.5	Dover UFSD	Dover Plains
136	16.5	Saranac CSD	Dannemora
138	16.4	Depew UFSD	Depew
139	16.2	Central Square CSD	Central Square
140	15.8	Brockport CSD	Brockport
140	15.8	Ravena-Coeymans-Selkirk CSD	Selkirk
142	15.7	Valley CSD (Montgomery)	Montgomery
143	15.6	Evans-Brant CSD (Lake Shore)	Angola
143	15.6	Hampton Bays UFSD	Hampton Bays
143	15.6	Nyack UFSD	Nyack
146	15.5	Phelps-Clifton Springs CSD	Clifton Spgs
147	15.4	Longwood CSD	Middle Island
147	15.4	Niagara-Wheatfield CSD	Niagara Falls
149	15.3	Long Beach City SD	Long Beach
150	15.1	Patchogue-Medford UFSD	Patchogue
151	15.0	Gorham-Middlesex CSD	Rushville
151	15.0	Malverne UFSD	Malverne
153	14.9	Attica CSD	Attica
153	14.9	Sullivan West CSD	Jeffersonville
155	14.8	North Tonawanda City SD	N Tonawanda
156	14.6	Schuylerville CSD	Schuylerville
157	14.5	Onteora CSD	Boiceville
158	14.4	Springville-Griffith Inst CSD	Springville
159	14.2	Saranac Lake CSD	Saranac Lake
159	14.2	Wilson CSD	Wilson
161	14.0	Jordan-Elbridge CSD	Jordan
162	13.7	Chittenango CSD	Chittenango
162	13.7	Fredonia CSD	Fredonia
162	13.7	Sweet Home CSD	Amherst
165	13.6	Royalton-Hartland CSD	Middleport
166	13.5	Coxsackie-Athens CSD	Coxsackie
166	13.5	Greece CSD	Rochester
168	13.3	East Syracuse-Minoa CSD	East Syracuse
168	13.3	Kenmore-Tonawanda UFSD	Buffalo
170	13.2	Cheektowaga-Maryvale UFSD	Cheektowaga
170	13.2	Homer CSD	Homer
172	13.0	New Paltz CSD	New Paltz
173	12.8	Kinderhook CSD	Valatie
174	12.7	West Seneca CSD	West Seneca
175	12.6	Saugerties CSD	Saugerties
176	12.5	Oyster Bay-East Norwich CSD	Oyster Bay
176	12.5	Pine Bush CSD	Pine Bush
178	12.4	Akron CSD	Akron
178	12.4	Horseheads CSD	Horseheads
180	12.3	Highland CSD	Highland
181	12.2	Liverpool CSD	Liverpool
182	12.1	Ballston Spa CSD	Ballston Spa
183	11.8	Rush-Henrietta CSD	Henrietta
184	11.6	Maine-Endwell CSD	Endwell
184	11.6	North Babylon UFSD	North Babylon
186	11.4	Rondout Valley CSD	Accord
187	11.0	Broadalbin-Perth CSD	Broadalbin
187	11.0	North Syracuse CSD	N Syracuse
189	10.9	Gates-Chili CSD	Rochester
190	10.5	Hyde Park CSD	Poughkeepsie
190	10.5	South Glens Falls CSD	S Glens Falls
192	10.3	Holland Patent CSD	Holland Patent
193	10.2	Wallkill CSD	Wallkill
194	10.1	Whitesboro CSD	Yorkville
195	10.0	Frontier CSD	Hamburg
195	10.0	Palmyra-Macedon CSD	Palmyra
195	10.0	Southwestern CSD at Jamestown	Jamestown
195	10.0	Valley Stream 30 UFSD	Valley Stream
199	9.9	Queensbury UFSD	Queensbury
200	9.8	Islip UFSD	Islip
200	9.8	West Hempstead UFSD	W Hempstead
202	9.6	Alden CSD	Alden
203	9.5	Deer Park UFSD	Deer Park
203	9.5	West Babylon UFSD	West Babylon
205	9.2	Sewanhaka Central HSD	Floral Park
206	9.1	Amherst CSD	Amherst
206	9.1	Churchville-Chili CSD	Churchville
208	9.0	Bedford CSD	Mount Kisco
209	8.9	Livonia CSD	Livonia
209	8.9	Newfane CSD	Newfane
211	8.8	Baldwinsville CSD	Baldwinsville
211	8.8	Canandaigua City SD	Canandaigua
211	8.8	Mineola UFSD	Mineola
211	8.8	Saratoga Springs City SD	Saratoga Spgs
215	8.5	Marlboro CSD	Marlboro
216	8.0	Wayne CSD	Ontario Center
217	7.9	Clinton CSD	Clinton
217	7.9	South Colonie CSD	Albany
219	7.7	Goshen CSD	Goshen
219	7.7	Hilton CSD	Hilton
219	7.7	Lancaster CSD	Lancaster
222	7.5	Babylon UFSD	Babylon
222	7.5	Farmingdale UFSD	Farmingdale
224	7.4	Lindenhurst UFSD	Lindenhurst
225	7.3	Hamburg CSD	Hamburg
225	7.3	Jamesville-Dewitt CSD	Dewitt
225	7.3	Lansing CSD	Lansing
225	7.3	Rotterdam-Mohonasen CSD	Schenectady
229	7.2	Elwood UFSD	Greenlawn
230	7.1	Averill Park CSD	Averill Park
230	7.1	Minisink Valley CSD	Slate Hill
232	6.9	Lewiston-Porter CSD	Youngstown
232	6.9	Spencerport CSD	Spencerport
232	6.9	West Genesee CSD	Camillus
235	6.6	Middle Country CSD	Centereach
236	6.4	Cazenovia CSD	Cazenovia
237	6.3	Brewster CSD	Brewster
237	6.3	Franklin Square UFSD	Franklin Square
239	6.2	Scotia-Glenville CSD	Scotia
240	6.0	Great Neck UFSD	Great Neck
240	6.0	Hicksville UFSD	Hicksville
242	5.9	Brookhaven-Comsewogue UFSD	Pt Jefferson Stn
243	5.8	Port Washington UFSD	Pt Washington
244	5.7	Red Hook CSD	Red Hook
245	5.6	Eden CSD	Eden
245	5.6	Grand Island CSD	Grand Island
245	5.6	Schalmont CSD	Schenectady
245	5.6	West Irondequoit CSD	Rochester
249	5.5	East Greenbush CSD	E Greenbush
249	5.5	Island Trees UFSD	Levittown
249	5.5	Spackenkill UFSD	Poughkeepsie
249	5.5	Westhampton Beach UFSD	Westhampton Bch
253	5.4	North Colonie CSD	Latham
254	5.3	Vestal CSD	Vestal
255	5.2	East Hampton UFSD	East Hampton
255	5.2	Valley Stream 13 UFSD	Valley Stream
255	5.2	Washingtonville CSD	Washingtonville
258	5.1	Sachem CSD	Holbrook
258	5.1	Southampton UFSD	Southampton
258	5.1	Wappingers CSD	Wappingers Fls
261	5.0	Rocky Point UFSD	Rocky Point
261	5.0	Starpoint CSD	Lockport
261	5.0	Victor CSD	Victor
261	5.0	Warwick Valley CSD	Warwick
265	4.9	Roslyn UFSD	Roslyn
266	4.8	Marcellus CSD	Marcellus
267	4.7	Arlington CSD	Poughkeepsie
267	4.7	Shenendehowa CSD	Clifton Park
269	4.6	Honeoye Falls-Lima CSD	Honeoye Falls
269	4.6	Putnam Valley CSD	Putnam Valley
269	4.6	Rockville Centre UFSD	Rockville Ctre
272	4.5	New Hartford CSD	New Hartford
273	4.4	Ramapo CSD (Suffern)	Hillburn
273	4.4	South Orangetown CSD	Blauvelt
275	4.3	Half Hollow Hills CSD	Dix Hills
276	4.2	Brighton CSD	Rochester
276	4.2	Plainedge UFSD	N Massapequa
276	4.2	Webster CSD	Webster
279	4.1	Penfield CSD	Penfield
280	4.0	Fairport CSD	Fairport
281	3.9	Connetquot CSD	Bohemia
281	3.9	East Meadow UFSD	Westbury
283	3.8	Cornwall CSD	Cornwall-on-Hud
283	3.8	Iroquois CSD	Elma
283	3.8	Westhill CSD	Syracuse
286	3.7	Harrison CSD	Harrison
287	3.6	East Islip UFSD	Islip Terrace
287	3.6	Williamsville CSD	East Amherst
289	3.5	Carmel CSD	Patterson
289	3.5	Monroe-Woodbury CSD	Central Valley
289	3.5	Skaneateles CSD	Skaneateles
292	3.4	Nanuet UFSD	Nanuet
293	3.3	Bethpage UFSD	Bethpage
293	3.3	Burnt Hills-Ballston Lake CSD	Scotia
293	3.3	East Aurora UFSD	East Aurora
293	3.3	Manhasset UFSD	Manhasset
297	3.2	Hendrick Hudson CSD	Montrose
297	3.2	Lakeland CSD	Shrub Oak
297	3.2	Northport-East Northport UFSD	Northport
300	3.1	Guilderland CSD	Guilderland
300	3.1	Locust Valley CSD	Locust Valley
302	3.0	Fayetteville-Manlius CSD	Manlius
302	3.0	Levittown UFSD	Levittown
304	2.8	Clarence CSD	Clarence
304	2.8	Oceanside UFSD	Oceanside
304	2.8	Pelham UFSD	Pelham
304	2.8	Sayville UFSD	Sayville
308	2.7	Carle Place UFSD	Carle Place
308	2.7	Niskayuna CSD	Schenectady
310	2.6	Hauppauge UFSD	Hauppauge
311	2.4	Clarkstown CSD	New City
311	2.4	Mattituck-Cutchogue UFSD	Cutchogue
311	2.4	North Shore CSD	Sea Cliff
311	2.4	Orchard Park CSD	Orchard Park
315	2.3	Floral Park-Bellerose UFSD	Floral Park
315	2.3	Harborfields CSD	Greenlawn
315	2.3	Hastings-On-Hudson UFSD	Hastings-on-Hud
318	2.2	North Bellmore UFSD	Bellmore
318	2.2	West Islip UFSD	West Islip
320	2.1	Mount Pleasant CSD	Thornwood
320	2.1	Somers CSD	Lincolndale
322	2.0	Bayport-Blue Point UFSD	Bayport
323	1.9	Pearl River UFSD	Pearl River
324	1.8	Seaford UFSD	Seaford
324	1.8	Smithtown CSD	Smithtown
326	1.7	Herricks UFSD	New Hyde Park
326	1.7	Massapequa UFSD	Massapequa
326	1.7	Valley Stream Central HSD	Valley Stream
329	1.6	Bethlehem CSD	Delmar
329	1.6	Commack UFSD	E Northport
329	1.6	Rye City SD	Rye
329	1.6	Three Village CSD	East Setauket
333	1.5	Hewlett-Woodmere UFSD	Woodmere
334	1.4	Pittsford CSD	Pittsford
334	1.4	Plainview-Old Bethpage CSD	Plainview
336	1.3	Kings Park CSD	Kings Park
336	1.3	Mamaroneck UFSD	Mamaroneck
336	1.3	Miller Place UFSD	Miller Place
339	1.2	Ardsley UFSD	Ardsley
339	1.2	Bellmore-Merrick Central HSD	North Merrick
341	1.1	Jericho UFSD	Jericho
341	1.1	Yorktown CSD	Yorktown Hgts
343	1.0	Lynbrook UFSD	Lynbrook
343	1.0	Mahopac CSD	Mahopac
345	0.9	Mount Sinai UFSD	Mount Sinai
346	0.5	East Williston UFSD	Old Westbury
346	0.5	Wantagh UFSD	Wantagh
348	0.4	Chappaqua CSD	Chappaqua
348	0.4	Syosset CSD	Syosset
350	0.3	Katonah-Lewisboro UFSD	South Salem
351	0.2	Byram Hills CSD	Armonk
352	0.1	Cold Spring Harbor CSD	Cold Sprg Harbor
352	0.1	Garden City UFSD	Garden City

352	0.1	Shoreham-Wading River CSD	Shoreham
355	0.0	Baldwin UFSD	Baldwin
355	0.0	Briarcliff Manor UFSD	Briarcliff Manor
355	0.0	Croton-Harmon UFSD	Croton-On-Hud
355	0.0	Eastchester UFSD	Eastchester
355	0.0	Edgemont UFSD	Scarsdale
355	0.0	Irvington UFSD	Irvington
355	0.0	Merrick UFSD	Merrick
355	0.0	New Hyde Pk-Garden City Pk UFSD	New Hyde Park
355	0.0	Pleasantville UFSD	Pleasantville
355	0.0	Scarsdale UFSD	Scarsdale
365	n/a	Boces Eastern Suffolk (Suffolk I)	Patchogue
365	n/a	Boces Monroe 1	Fairport
365	n/a	Boces Nassau	Garden City
365	n/a	New York City Public Schools	Brooklyn

Students Eligible for Reduced-Price Lunch

Rank	Percent	District Name	City
1	20.3	Cheektowaga-Sloan UFSD	Sloan
2	18.1	Indian River CSD	Philadelphia
3	16.7	Brentwood UFSD	Brentwood
3	16.7	Hempstead UFSD	Hempstead
5	16.3	Lackawanna City SD	Lackawanna
6	16.1	Central Islip UFSD	Central Islip
7	15.8	Yorkshire-Pioneer CSD	Yorkshire
8	15.7	Middletown City SD	Middletown
9	15.4	Whitney Point CSD	Whitney Point
10	15.0	Salmon River CSD	Ft Covington
11	14.7	Altmar-Parish-Williamstown CSD	Parish
12	14.5	Ogdensburg City SD	Ogdensburg
13	14.3	Hudson Falls CSD	Hudson Falls
14	14.2	East Ramapo CSD (Spring Valley)	Spring Valley
15	13.6	Phoenix CSD	Phoenix
16	13.5	Elmont UFSD	Elmont
17	13.3	Beekmantown CSD	Plattsburgh
17	13.3	Camden CSD	Camden
17	13.3	Hannibal CSD	Hannibal
20	13.2	William Floyd UFSD	Mastic Beach
21	13.0	Gowanda CSD	Gowanda
21	13.0	Poughkeepsie City SD	Poughkeepsie
23	12.9	Peru CSD	Peru
24	12.8	Cohoes City SD	Cohoes
24	12.8	North Rose-Wolcott CSD	Wolcott
24	12.8	Peekskill City SD	Peekskill
27	12.6	Hornell City SD	Hornell
28	12.5	Greenburgh CSD	Hartsdale
29	12.3	Penn Yan CSD	Pen
30	12.1	Port Chester-Rye UFSD	Port Chester
30	12.1	Watertown City SD	Watertown
32	12.0	Johnstown City SD	Johnstown
33	11.9	Chenango Forks CSD	Binghamton
34	11.8	Malone CSD	Malone
35	11.7	Fulton City SD	Fulton
35	11.7	Ilion CSD	Ilion
35	11.7	Mount Vernon City SD	Mount Vernon
38	11.5	Depew UFSD	Depew
38	11.5	Sherburne-Earlville CSD	Sherburne
40	11.4	Hudson City SD	Hudson
40	11.4	Massena CSD	Massena
42	11.3	Mexico CSD	Mexico
42	11.3	Waterloo CSD	Waterloo
44	11.2	Newburgh City SD	Newburgh
45	11.1	Carthage CSD	Carthage
45	11.1	Gorham-Middlesex CSD	Rushville
47	11.0	Attica CSD	Attica
47	11.0	Gouverneur CSD	Gouverneur
49	10.8	Phelps-Clifton Springs CSD	Clifton Spgs
49	10.8	Port Jervis City SD	Port Jervis
49	10.8	Taconic Hills CSD	Craryville
52	10.7	Adirondack CSD	Boonville
52	10.7	Buffalo City SD	Buffalo
54	10.6	Lansingburgh CSD	Troy
54	10.6	Waverly CSD	Waverly
56	10.5	Chatham CSD	Chatham
56	10.5	Glen Cove City SD	Glen Cove
58	10.4	Elmira City SD	Elmira
59	10.2	Holland Patent CSD	Holland Patent
59	10.2	Schenectady City SD	Schenectady
61	10.1	Bath CSD	Bath
61	10.1	Binghamton City SD	Binghamton
61	10.1	Olean City SD	Olean
61	10.1	South Jefferson CSD	Adams Center
65	10.0	Alden CSD	Alden
65	10.0	Niagara Falls City SD	Niagara Falls
67	9.9	Cleveland Hill UFSD	Cheektowaga
67	9.9	Gloversville City SD	Gloversville
67	9.9	Salamanca City SD	Salamanca
70	9.8	Sherrill City SD	Verona
71	9.7	Ellenville CSD	Ellenville
71	9.7	Monticello CSD	Monticello
71	9.7	Wilson CSD	Wilson
74	9.6	Beacon City SD	Beacon
74	9.6	Cobleskill-Richmondville CSD	Cobleskill
74	9.6	Copiague UFSD	Copiague
74	9.6	Evans-Brant CSD (Lake Shore)	Angola
74	9.6	Frontier CSD	Hamburg
74	9.6	Northeastern Clinton CSD	Champlain
74	9.6	Troy City SD	Troy
81	9.5	Akron CSD	Akron
81	9.5	Geneva City SD	Geneva
81	9.5	Haverstraw-Stony Point CSD	Garnerville
81	9.5	Liberty CSD	Liberty
85	9.4	Fonda-Fultonville CSD	Fonda
85	9.4	Jamestown City SD	Jamestown
87	9.2	Corning City SD	Painted Post
87	9.2	Syracuse City SD	Syracuse
89	9.1	Kingston City SD	Kingston
89	9.1	New Rochelle City SD	New Rochelle
89	9.1	Newark CSD	Newark
89	9.1	UFSD - Tarrytowns	Sleepy Hollow
93	9.0	Albany City SD	Albany
93	9.0	General Brown CSD	Dexter
95	8.9	Brockport CSD	Brockport
95	8.9	Chenango Valley CSD	Binghamton
97	8.8	Bay Shore UFSD	Bay Shore
97	8.8	Kinderhook CSD	Valatie
97	8.8	Sullivan West CSD	Jeffersonville
100	8.7	North Syracuse CSD	N Syracuse
100	8.7	Oneida City SD	Oneida
100	8.7	White Plains City SD	White Plains
103	8.6	Amityville UFSD	Amityville
103	8.6	West Seneca CSD	West Seneca
105	8.5	Canastota CSD	Canastota
105	8.5	Central Square CSD	Central Square
105	8.5	Kenmore-Tonawanda UFSD	Buffalo
105	8.5	Pine Bush CSD	Pine Bush
109	8.4	Batavia City SD	Batavia
109	8.4	Canton CSD	Canton
111	8.3	Cairo-Durham CSD	Cairo
111	8.3	Utica City SD	Utica
113	8.2	Norwich City SD	Norwich
113	8.2	Saranac CSD	Dannemora
113	8.2	Valley CSD (Montgomery)	Montgomery
116	8.1	Cheektowaga-Maryvale UFSD	Cheektowaga
116	8.1	Lawrence UFSD	Lawrence
116	8.1	Patchogue-Medford UFSD	Patchogue
116	8.1	Rondout Valley CSD	Accord
116	8.1	South Country CSD	E Patchogue
121	8.0	Albion CSD	Albion
121	8.0	East Irondequoit CSD	Rochester
123	7.9	Johnson City CSD	Johnson City
123	7.9	Uniondale UFSD	Uniondale
125	7.8	Dover UFSD	Dover Plains
125	7.8	Ossining UFSD	Ossining
125	7.8	Rome City SD	Rome
125	7.8	Wayland-Cohocton CSD	Wayland
125	7.8	Westbury UFSD	Old Westbury
130	7.6	Chittenango CSD	Chittenango
130	7.6	Freeport UFSD	Freeport
132	7.5	Yonkers City SD	Yonkers
133	7.4	Dansville CSD	Dansville
133	7.4	Homer CSD	Homer
133	7.4	Oneonta City SD	Oneonta
133	7.4	Tonawanda City SD	Tonawanda
133	7.4	Union-Endicott CSD	Endicott
138	7.3	Highland CSD	Highland
138	7.3	Saranac Lake CSD	Saranac Lake
140	7.2	Deer Park UFSD	Deer Park
140	7.2	Fredonia CSD	Fredonia
140	7.2	Greece CSD	Rochester
140	7.2	North Tonawanda City SD	N Tonawanda
140	7.2	Onteora CSD	Boiceville
140	7.2	Rochester City SD	Rochester
140	7.2	Springville-Griffith Inst CSD	Springville
147	7.1	Lockport City SD	Lockport
147	7.1	Rush-Henrietta CSD	Henrietta
147	7.1	Susquehanna Valley CSD	Conklin
150	7.0	Dunkirk City SD	Dunkirk
150	7.0	Gates-Chili CSD	Rochester
150	7.0	Niagara-Wheatfield CSD	Niagara Falls
150	7.0	Riverhead CSD	Riverhead
150	7.0	Schuylerville CSD	Schuylerville
150	7.0	South Glens Falls CSD	S Glens Falls
150	7.0	Sweet Home CSD	Amherst
150	7.0	Windsor CSD	Windsor
158	6.8	Cortland City SD	Cortland
158	6.8	Wyandanch UFSD	Wyandanch
160	6.7	Catskill CSD	Catskill
160	6.7	Jordan-Elbridge CSD	Jordan
160	6.7	Owego-Apalachin CSD	Owego
163	6.6	Cheektowaga CSD	Cheektowaga
163	6.6	Ithaca City SD	Ithaca
163	6.6	Lancaster CSD	Lancaster
166	6.5	Maine-Endwell CSD	Endwell
166	6.5	Medina CSD	Medina
168	6.4	Valley Stream 30 UFSD	Valley Stream
169	6.3	Plattsburgh City SD	Plattsburgh
169	6.3	Saugerties CSD	Saugerties
171	6.2	Auburn City SD	Auburn
171	6.2	East Syracuse-Minoa CSD	East Syracuse
171	6.2	Hilton CSD	Hilton
174	6.1	Hyde Park CSD	Poughkeepsie
174	6.1	North Babylon UFSD	North Babylon
174	6.1	Ravena-Coeymans-Selkirk CSD	Selkirk
177	6.0	Ballston Spa CSD	Ballston Spa
177	6.0	Coxsackie-Athens CSD	Coxsackie
177	6.0	Grand Island CSD	Grand Island
180	5.9	Nyack UFSD	Nyack
181	5.8	Hamburg CSD	Hamburg
182	5.7	Broadalbin-Perth CSD	Broadalbin
182	5.7	Longwood CSD	Middle Island
182	5.7	Malverne UFSD	Malverne
182	5.7	Rotterdam-Mohonasen CSD	Schenectady
182	5.7	Solvay UFSD	Solvay
187	5.6	Amsterdam City SD	Amsterdam
187	5.6	Liverpool CSD	Liverpool
189	5.5	Dryden CSD	Dryden
189	5.5	Seneca Falls CSD	Seneca Falls
189	5.5	South Huntington UFSD	Huntington Stn
192	5.3	Glens Falls City SD	Glens Falls
192	5.3	Islip UFSD	Islip
192	5.3	Spencerport CSD	Spencerport
192	5.3	Wayne CSD	Ontario Center
196	5.2	Churchville-Chili CSD	Churchville
196	5.2	Royalton-Hartland CSD	Middleport
196	5.2	Scotia-Glenville CSD	Scotia
199	5.1	Whitesboro CSD	Yorkville
200	5.0	Canandaigua City SD	Canandaigua
200	5.0	Goshen CSD	Goshen
200	5.0	Horseheads CSD	Horseheads
200	5.0	Newfane CSD	Newfane
200	5.0	Southwestern CSD at Jamestown	Jamestown
205	4.9	Minisink Valley CSD	Slate Hill
205	4.9	Palmyra-Macedon CSD	Palmyra
205	4.9	Starpoint CSD	Lockport
208	4.8	Averill Park CSD	Averill Park
208	4.8	Huntington UFSD	Huntington Stn
208	4.8	Lindenhurst UFSD	Lindenhurst
208	4.8	Wallkill CSD	Wallkill
212	4.7	Bedford CSD	Mount Kisco
212	4.7	Lewiston-Porter CSD	Youngstown
214	4.6	Marlboro CSD	Marlboro
214	4.6	Mineola UFSD	Mineola
216	4.5	Great Neck UFSD	Great Neck
216	4.5	Hampton Bays UFSD	Hampton Bays
216	4.5	New Paltz CSD	New Paltz
216	4.5	Spackenkill UFSD	Poughkeepsie
216	4.5	West Babylon UFSD	West Babylon
221	4.4	Franklin Square UFSD	Franklin Square
221	4.4	Middle Country CSD	Centereach
221	4.4	Washingtonville CSD	Washingtonville
224	4.3	Livonia CSD	Livonia
224	4.3	Long Beach City SD	Long Beach
224	4.3	Oswego City SD	Oswego
224	4.3	South Colonie CSD	Albany
228	4.2	Babylon UFSD	Babylon
228	4.2	Baldwinsville CSD	Baldwinsville
228	4.2	Farmingdale UFSD	Farmingdale
228	4.2	Queensbury UFSD	Queensbury
228	4.2	Sewanhaka Central HSD	Floral Park
233	4.0	Amherst CSD	Amherst
233	4.0	West Genesee CSD	Camillus
235	3.9	East Islip UFSD	Islip Terrace
235	3.9	Hicksville UFSD	Hicksville
235	3.9	Iroquois CSD	Elma
238	3.8	Connetquot CSD	Bohemia
238	3.8	East Meadow UFSD	Westbury
238	3.8	Sachem CSD	Holbrook
238	3.8	Wappingers CSD	Wappingers Fls
242	3.7	Schalmont CSD	Schenectady
242	3.7	Shenendehowa CSD	Clifton Park
244	3.6	Marcellus CSD	Marcellus
244	3.6	Saratoga Springs City SD	Saratoga Spgs
246	3.5	Vestal CSD	Vestal
247	3.4	Brewster CSD	Brewster
247	3.4	East Greenbush CSD	E Greenbush
247	3.4	Roslyn UFSD	Roslyn
247	3.4	Victor CSD	Victor
247	3.4	Westhampton Beach UFSD	Westhampton Bch
252	3.3	Cazenovia CSD	Cazenovia
252	3.3	Jamesville-Dewitt CSD	Dewitt
252	3.3	North Colonie CSD	Latham
252	3.3	Putnam Valley CSD	Putnam Valley
256	3.2	West Irondequoit CSD	Rochester
257	3.1	Eden CSD	Eden

258	3.0	Carle Place UFSD	Carle Place
258	3.0	East Aurora UFSD	East Aurora
258	3.0	Oyster Bay-East Norwich CSD	Oyster Bay
258	3.0	Rocky Point UFSD	Rocky Point
262	2.9	Island Trees UFSD	Levittown
262	2.9	South Orangetown CSD	Blauvelt
262	2.9	Southampton UFSD	Southampton
262	2.9	West Hempstead UFSD	W Hempstead
266	2.8	Brookhaven-Comsewogue UFSD	Pt Jefferson Stn
266	2.8	Clinton CSD	Clinton
266	2.8	Elwood UFSD	Greenlawn
269	2.7	Red Hook CSD	Red Hook
270	2.6	Brighton CSD	Rochester
270	2.6	Carmel CSD	Patterson
270	2.6	Honeoye Falls-Lima CSD	Honeoye Falls
270	2.6	Plainedge UFSD	N Massapequa
270	2.6	Valley Stream 13 UFSD	Valley Stream
275	2.5	Arlington CSD	Poughkeepsie
275	2.5	Cornwall CSD	Cornwall-on-Hud
275	2.5	Lansing CSD	Lansing
275	2.5	Monroe-Woodbury CSD	Central Valley
279	2.4	Bethpage UFSD	Bethpage
279	2.4	Clarence CSD	Clarence
279	2.4	Lakeland CSD	Shrub Oak
279	2.4	Ramapo CSD (Suffern)	Hillburn
279	2.4	Roosevelt UFSD	Roosevelt
279	2.4	Warwick Valley CSD	Warwick
285	2.3	Levittown UFSD	Levittown
285	2.3	North Shore CSD	Sea Cliff
285	2.3	Williamsville CSD	East Amherst
288	2.2	Fairport CSD	Fairport
288	2.2	New Hartford CSD	New Hartford
288	2.2	Penfield CSD	Penfield
288	2.2	Webster CSD	Webster
292	2.1	Half Hollow Hills CSD	Dix Hills
292	2.1	Harrison CSD	Harrison
292	2.1	Westhill CSD	Syracuse
295	2.0	Bayport-Blue Point UFSD	Bayport
295	2.0	Clarkstown CSD	New City
295	2.0	Orchard Park CSD	Orchard Park
298	1.9	Pearl River UFSD	Pearl River
299	1.8	East Hampton UFSD	East Hampton
299	1.8	Locust Valley CSD	Locust Valley
299	1.8	Nanuet UFSD	Nanuet
299	1.8	Skaneateles CSD	Skaneateles
303	1.7	Burnt Hills-Ballston Lake CSD	Scotia
303	1.7	Guilderland CSD	Guilderland
305	1.6	Floral Park-Bellerose UFSD	Floral Park
305	1.6	Mattituck-Cutchogue UFSD	Cutchogue
305	1.6	Northport-East Northport UFSD	Northport
305	1.6	Port Washington UFSD	Pt Washington
305	1.6	Sayville UFSD	Sayville
310	1.5	Bethlehem CSD	Delmar
310	1.5	Hauppauge UFSD	Hauppauge
310	1.5	North Bellmore UFSD	Bellmore
310	1.5	Oceanside UFSD	Oceanside
310	1.5	Rockville Centre UFSD	Rockville Ctre
310	1.5	Smithtown CSD	Smithtown
310	1.5	West Islip UFSD	West Islip
317	1.4	Hendrick Hudson CSD	Montrose
318	1.3	Harborfields CSD	Greenlawn
318	1.3	Hewlett-Woodmere UFSD	Woodmere
318	1.3	Kings Park CSD	Kings Park
318	1.3	Niskayuna CSD	Schenectady
322	1.2	Mahopac CSD	Mahopac
322	1.2	Massapequa UFSD	Massapequa
322	1.2	Mount Pleasant CSD	Thornwood
322	1.2	Pelham UFSD	Pelham
326	1.1	Commack UFSD	E Northport
326	1.1	Fayetteville-Manlius CSD	Manlius
326	1.1	Herricks UFSD	New Hyde Park
326	1.1	Three Village CSD	East Setauket
330	1.0	Plainview-Old Bethpage CSD	Plainview
330	1.0	Valley Stream Central HSD	Valley Stream
332	0.7	Ardsley UFSD	Ardsley
332	0.7	Bellmore-Merrick Central HSD	North Merrick
334	0.6	Mamaroneck UFSD	Mamaroneck
334	0.6	Manhasset UFSD	Manhasset
336	0.5	Miller Place UFSD	Miller Place
336	0.5	Mount Sinai UFSD	Mount Sinai
336	0.5	Pittsford CSD	Pittsford
336	0.5	Seaford UFSD	Seaford
336	0.5	Wantagh UFSD	Wantagh
341	0.4	Briarcliff Manor UFSD	Briarcliff Manor
342	0.3	Katonah-Lewisboro UFSD	South Salem
342	0.3	Somers CSD	Lincolndale
342	0.3	Yorktown CSD	Yorktown Hgts
345	0.2	Chappaqua CSD	Chappaqua
345	0.2	Jericho UFSD	Jericho
345	0.2	Lynbrook UFSD	Lynbrook
345	0.2	Syosset CSD	Syosset
349	0.0	Garden City UFSD	Garden City
349	0.0	Rye City SD	Rye
351	0.0	Baldwin UFSD	Baldwin
351	0.0	Byram Hills CSD	Armonk
351	0.0	Cold Spring Harbor CSD	Cold Sprg Harbor
351	0.0	Croton-Harmon UFSD	Croton-On-Hud
351	0.0	East Williston UFSD	Old Westbury
351	0.0	Eastchester UFSD	Eastchester
351	0.0	Edgemont UFSD	Scarsdale
351	0.0	Hastings-On-Hudson UFSD	Hastings-on-Hud
351	0.0	Irvington UFSD	Irvington
351	0.0	Merrick UFSD	Merrick
351	0.0	New Hyde Pk-Garden City Pk UFSD	New Hyde Park
351	0.0	Pleasantville UFSD	Pleasantville
351	0.0	Scarsdale UFSD	Scarsdale
351	0.0	Shoreham-Wading River CSD	Shoreham
365	n/a	Boces Eastern Suffolk (Suffolk I)	Patchogue
365	n/a	Boces Monroe 1	Fairport
365	n/a	Boces Nassau	Garden City
365	n/a	New York City Public Schools	Brooklyn

Student/Teacher Ratio

Rank	Ratio	District Name	City
1	16.9	William Floyd UFSD	Mastic Beach
2	16.6	Floral Park-Bellerose UFSD	Floral Park
2	16.6	Sewanhaka Central HSD	Floral Park
4	16.4	New York City Public Schools	Brooklyn
5	16.3	Arlington CSD	Poughkeepsie
5	16.3	Dover UFSD	Dover Plains
7	16.1	Highland CSD	Highland
8	15.8	Broadalbin-Perth CSD	Broadalbin
8	15.8	Hempstead UFSD	Hempstead
10	15.7	Elmont UFSD	Elmont
10	15.7	Niagara Falls City SD	Niagara Falls
10	15.7	Washingtonville CSD	Washingtonville
13	15.6	Brentwood UFSD	Brentwood
13	15.6	Cornwall CSD	Cornwall-on-Hud
13	15.6	Starpoint CSD	Lockport
13	15.6	Wappingers CSD	Wappingers Fls
17	15.5	Bellmore-Merrick Central HSD	North Merrick
17	15.5	New Hyde Pk-Garden City Pk UFSD	New Hyde Park
19	15.4	Copiague UFSD	Copiague
19	15.4	Mount Vernon City SD	Mount Vernon
19	15.4	Rocky Point UFSD	Rocky Point
22	15.3	Marcellus CSD	Marcellus
22	15.3	Queensbury UFSD	Queensbury
24	15.2	Lancaster CSD	Lancaster
24	15.2	West Irondequoit CSD	Rochester
26	15.1	Warwick Valley CSD	Warwick
27	15.0	Carmel CSD	Patterson
27	15.0	North Syracuse CSD	N Syracuse
27	15.0	Rotterdam-Mohonasen CSD	Schenectady
30	14.9	Elwood UFSD	Greenlawn
30	14.9	Harborfields CSD	Greenlawn
30	14.9	Middle Country CSD	Centereach
30	14.9	Minisink Valley CSD	Slate Hill
30	14.9	Saugerties CSD	Saugerties
35	14.8	Beacon City SD	Beacon
35	14.8	Bethlehem CSD	Delmar
35	14.8	East Aurora UFSD	East Aurora
35	14.8	Patchogue-Medford UFSD	Patchogue
39	14.7	Baldwinsville CSD	Baldwinsville
39	14.7	Franklin Square UFSD	Franklin Square
39	14.7	Hyde Park CSD	Poughkeepsie
39	14.7	Middletown City SD	Middletown
39	14.7	North Colonie CSD	Latham
39	14.7	Port Jervis City SD	Port Jervis
39	14.7	Wallkill CSD	Wallkill
46	14.6	Brookhaven-Comsewogue UFSD	Pt Jefferson Stn
46	14.6	Iroquois CSD	Elma
46	14.6	Pine Bush CSD	Pine Bush
46	14.6	Shenendehowa CSD	Clifton Park
46	14.6	West Babylon UFSD	West Babylon
46	14.6	West Genesee CSD	Camillus
52	14.5	Ballston Spa CSD	Ballston Spa
52	14.5	Horseheads CSD	Horseheads
52	14.5	Islip UFSD	Islip
52	14.5	Liverpool CSD	Liverpool
52	14.5	Valley CSD (Montgomery)	Montgomery
57	14.4	Carthage CSD	Carthage
57	14.4	Lindenhurst UFSD	Lindenhurst
57	14.4	Longwood CSD	Middle Island
57	14.4	North Babylon UFSD	North Babylon
57	14.4	North Bellmore UFSD	Bellmore
62	14.3	Fayetteville-Manlius CSD	Manlius
62	14.3	Lansingburgh CSD	Troy
62	14.3	Mount Sinai UFSD	Mount Sinai
62	14.3	New Rochelle City SD	New Rochelle
62	14.3	Plainedge UFSD	N Massapequa
62	14.3	Riverhead CSD	Riverhead
62	14.3	Utica City SD	Utica
62	14.3	Victor CSD	Victor
70	14.2	Albion CSD	Albion
70	14.2	Brockport CSD	Brockport
70	14.2	Central Square CSD	Central Square
70	14.2	Chatham CSD	Chatham
70	14.2	Gouverneur CSD	Gouverneur
70	14.2	Hudson Falls CSD	Hudson Falls
70	14.2	Johnstown City SD	Johnstown
70	14.2	Monroe-Woodbury CSD	Central Valley
70	14.2	New Paltz CSD	New Paltz
70	14.2	Niskayuna CSD	Schenectady
70	14.2	Scotia-Glenville CSD	Scotia
70	14.2	Sherrill City SD	Verona
70	14.2	Yonkers City SD	Yonkers
83	14.1	Cairo-Durham CSD	Cairo
83	14.1	Clarence CSD	Clarence
83	14.1	East Islip UFSD	Islip Terrace
83	14.1	General Brown CSD	Dexter
83	14.1	Kingston City SD	Kingston
83	14.1	Newfane CSD	Newfane
83	14.1	Port Chester-Rye UFSD	Port Chester
83	14.1	Westbury UFSD	Old Westbury
83	14.1	Wyandanch UFSD	Wyandanch
92	14.0	Burnt Hills-Ballston Lake CSD	Scotia
92	14.0	Eden CSD	Eden
92	14.0	Fairport CSD	Fairport
92	14.0	Springville-Griffith Inst CSD	Springville
92	14.0	Westhill CSD	Syracuse
97	13.9	Churchville-Chili CSD	Churchville
97	13.9	Freeport UFSD	Freeport
97	13.9	Northeastern Clinton CSD	Champlain
97	13.9	Seaford UFSD	Seaford
97	13.9	Watertown City SD	Watertown
97	13.9	Waverly CSD	Waverly
103	13.8	Cheektowaga-Maryvale UFSD	Cheektowaga
103	13.8	Hannibal CSD	Hannibal
103	13.8	Lakeland CSD	Shrub Oak
103	13.8	Miller Place UFSD	Miller Place
103	13.8	Sayville UFSD	Sayville
103	13.8	Three Village CSD	East Setauket
103	13.8	Williamsville CSD	East Amherst
110	13.7	Chenango Forks CSD	Binghamton
110	13.7	Goshen CSD	Goshen
110	13.7	Grand Island CSD	Grand Island
110	13.7	Honeoye Falls-Lima CSD	Honeoye Falls
110	13.7	Ilion CSD	Ilion
110	13.7	Mahopac CSD	Mahopac
110	13.7	Massena CSD	Massena
110	13.7	Mexico CSD	Mexico
110	13.7	Newburgh City SD	Newburgh
110	13.7	Owego-Apalachin CSD	Owego
110	13.7	Pleasantville UFSD	Pleasantville
110	13.7	Poughkeepsie City SD	Poughkeepsie
110	13.7	Red Hook CSD	Red Hook
110	13.7	Saratoga Springs City SD	Saratoga Spgs
110	13.7	Spencerport CSD	Spencerport
110	13.7	Wantagh UFSD	Wantagh
110	13.7	Yorktown CSD	Yorktown Hgts
127	13.6	Akron CSD	Akron
127	13.6	Camden CSD	Camden
127	13.6	Cheektowaga CSD	Cheektowaga
127	13.6	Chittenango CSD	Chittenango
127	13.6	East Greenbush CSD	E Greenbush
127	13.6	Massapequa UFSD	Massapequa
127	13.6	Merrick UFSD	Merrick
127	13.6	North Tonawanda City SD	N Tonawanda
127	13.6	Smithtown CSD	Smithtown
127	13.6	South Jefferson CSD	Adams Center
127	13.6	Valley Stream 30 UFSD	Valley Stream
127	13.6	Valley Stream Central HSD	Valley Stream
127	13.6	Waterloo CSD	Waterloo
127	13.6	West Islip UFSD	West Islip
141	13.5	Alden CSD	Alden
141	13.5	Brewster CSD	Brewster
141	13.5	Buffalo City SD	Buffalo
141	13.5	Canastota CSD	Canastota
141	13.5	Chenango Valley CSD	Binghamton
141	13.5	Ellenville CSD	Ellenville
141	13.5	Hicksville UFSD	Hicksville
141	13.5	Kinderhook CSD	Valatie
141	13.5	Lansing CSD	Lansing
141	13.5	Rome City SD	Rome
141	13.5	West Seneca CSD	West Seneca
141	13.5	Whitesboro CSD	Yorkville
153	13.4	Auburn City SD	Auburn
153	13.4	Bath CSD	Bath
153	13.4	Byram Hills CSD	Armonk
153	13.4	Frontier CSD	Hamburg
153	13.4	Guilderland CSD	Guilderland
153	13.4	Oceanside UFSD	Oceanside
153	13.4	Olean City SD	Olean
153	13.4	Oswego City SD	Oswego
153	13.4	Sachem CSD	Holbrook
153	13.4	South Glens Falls CSD	S Glens Falls

163	13.3	Clarkstown CSD	New City
163	13.3	Cleveland Hill UFSD	Cheektowaga
163	13.3	Gates-Chili CSD	Rochester
163	13.3	Greece CSD	Rochester
163	13.3	Half Hollow Hills CSD	Dix Hills
163	13.3	Holland Patent CSD	Holland Patent
163	13.3	Kenmore-Tonawanda UFSD	Buffalo
163	13.3	Lewiston-Porter CSD	Youngstown
163	13.3	Niagara-Wheatfield CSD	Niagara Falls
163	13.3	Oneida City SD	Oneida
163	13.3	Pearl River UFSD	Pearl River
163	13.3	Phelps-Clifton Springs CSD	Clifton Spgs
163	13.3	Schenectady City SD	Schenectady
163	13.3	Shoreham-Wading River CSD	Shoreham
163	13.3	Solvay UFSD	Solvay
163	13.3	South Huntington UFSD	Huntington Stn
163	13.3	Valley Stream 13 UFSD	Valley Stream
180	13.2	Cazenovia CSD	Cazenovia
180	13.2	Cold Spring Harbor CSD	Cold Sprg Harbor
180	13.2	Corning City SD	Painted Post
180	13.2	Croton-Harmon UFSD	Croton-On-Hud
180	13.2	East Irondequoit CSD	Rochester
180	13.2	Edgemont UFSD	Scarsdale
180	13.2	Hampton Bays UFSD	Hampton Bays
180	13.2	Island Trees UFSD	Levittown
180	13.2	Liberty CSD	Liberty
180	13.2	Marlboro CSD	Marlboro
180	13.2	Pittsford CSD	Pittsford
180	13.2	West Hempstead UFSD	W Hempstead
192	13.1	Bay Shore UFSD	Bay Shore
192	13.1	Connetquot CSD	Bohemia
192	13.1	Depew UFSD	Depew
192	13.1	East Ramapo CSD (Spring Valley)	Spring Valley
192	13.1	Elmira City SD	Elmira
192	13.1	Evans-Brant CSD (Lake Shore)	Angola
192	13.1	Haverstraw-Stony Point CSD	Garnerville
192	13.1	Irvington UFSD	Irvington
192	13.1	Katonah-Lewisboro UFSD	South Salem
192	13.1	New Hartford CSD	New Hartford
192	13.1	Rondout Valley CSD	Accord
192	13.1	Skaneateles CSD	Skaneateles
192	13.1	Tonawanda City SD	Tonawanda
192	13.1	Troy City SD	Troy
206	13.0	Amherst CSD	Amherst
206	13.0	Averill Park CSD	Averill Park
206	13.0	Canandaigua City SD	Canandaigua
206	13.0	Cheektowaga-Sloan UFSD	Sloan
206	13.0	Clinton CSD	Clinton
206	13.0	Commack UFSD	E Northport
206	13.0	East Meadow UFSD	Westbury
206	13.0	Fulton City SD	Fulton
206	13.0	Garden City UFSD	Garden City
206	13.0	Gloversville City SD	Gloversville
206	13.0	Hilton CSD	Hilton
206	13.0	Levittown UFSD	Levittown
206	13.0	Lockport City SD	Lockport
206	13.0	Pelham UFSD	Pelham
206	13.0	Southwestern CSD at Jamestown	Jamestown
206	13.0	Union-Endicott CSD	Endicott
206	13.0	Vestal CSD	Vestal
206	13.0	Yorkshire-Pioneer CSD	Yorkshire
224	12.9	Babylon UFSD	Babylon
224	12.9	Brighton CSD	Rochester
224	12.9	Central Islip UFSD	Central Islip
224	12.9	Long Beach City SD	Long Beach
224	12.9	Ossining UFSD	Ossining
224	12.9	Schuylerville CSD	Schuylerville
224	12.9	South Colonie CSD	Albany
224	12.9	Wayne CSD	Ontario Center
224	12.9	Windsor CSD	Windsor
233	12.8	Altmar-Parish-Williamstown CSD	Parish
233	12.8	Baldwin UFSD	Baldwin
233	12.8	Fonda-Fultonville CSD	Fonda
233	12.8	Gorham-Middlesex CSD	Rushville
233	12.8	Maine-Endwell CSD	Endwell
233	12.8	Mamaroneck UFSD	Mamaroneck
233	12.8	Rye City SD	Rye
233	12.8	Schalmont CSD	Schenectady
233	12.8	Somers CSD	Lincolndale
242	12.7	Ardsley UFSD	Ardsley
242	12.7	Attica CSD	Attica
242	12.7	Homer CSD	Homer
242	12.7	Putnam Valley CSD	Putnam Valley
242	12.7	Roosevelt UFSD	Roosevelt
242	12.7	South Country CSD	E Patchogue
242	12.7	Webster CSD	Webster
249	12.6	Amityville UFSD	Amityville
249	12.6	Amsterdam City SD	Amsterdam
249	12.6	Bethpage UFSD	Bethpage
249	12.6	Hauppauge UFSD	Hauppauge
249	12.6	Kings Park CSD	Kings Park
249	12.6	Orchard Park CSD	Orchard Park
249	12.6	Peru CSD	Peru
249	12.6	Ramapo CSD (Suffern)	Hillburn
249	12.6	Ravena-Coeymans-Selkirk CSD	Selkirk
249	12.6	Roslyn UFSD	Roslyn
249	12.6	Taconic Hills CSD	Craryville
260	12.5	Cortland City SD	Cortland
260	12.5	Coxsackie-Athens CSD	Coxsackie
260	12.5	Dansville CSD	Dansville
260	12.5	Glen Cove City SD	Glen Cove
260	12.5	Glens Falls City SD	Glens Falls
260	12.5	Gowanda CSD	Gowanda
266	12.4	Adirondack CSD	Boonville
266	12.4	Eastchester UFSD	Eastchester
266	12.4	Farmingdale UFSD	Farmingdale
266	12.4	Salamanca City SD	Salamanca
266	12.4	Saranac Lake CSD	Saranac Lake
271	12.3	Hamburg CSD	Hamburg
271	12.3	Jordan-Elbridge CSD	Jordan
271	12.3	Malone CSD	Malone
271	12.3	Newark CSD	Newark
271	12.3	Oneonta City SD	Oneonta
271	12.3	Penfield CSD	Penfield
271	12.3	Royalton-Hartland CSD	Middleport
271	12.3	Rush-Henrietta CSD	Henrietta
271	12.3	Saranac CSD	Dannemora
271	12.3	South Orangetown CSD	Blauvelt
271	12.3	Sweet Home CSD	Amherst
271	12.3	UFSD - Tarrytowns	Sleepy Hollow
283	12.2	Batavia City SD	Batavia
283	12.2	Bayport-Blue Point UFSD	Bayport
283	12.2	Chappaqua CSD	Chappaqua
283	12.2	East Hampton UFSD	East Hampton
283	12.2	Lynbrook UFSD	Lynbrook
283	12.2	Palmyra-Macedon CSD	Palmyra
283	12.2	Scarsdale UFSD	Scarsdale
283	12.2	Syracuse City SD	Syracuse
291	12.1	Canton CSD	Canton
291	12.1	Catskill CSD	Catskill
291	12.1	Hendrick Hudson CSD	Montrose
291	12.1	Hornell City SD	Hornell
291	12.1	Jamesville-Dewitt CSD	Dewitt
291	12.1	Livonia CSD	Livonia
291	12.1	Penn Yan CSD	Pen
291	12.1	Phoenix CSD	Phoenix
291	12.1	Rochester City SD	Rochester
291	12.1	Spackenkill UFSD	Poughkeepsie
301	12.0	Briarcliff Manor UFSD	Briarcliff Manor
301	12.0	Johnson City CSD	Johnson City
301	12.0	Lackawanna City SD	Lackawanna
301	12.0	Uniondale UFSD	Uniondale
301	12.0	Whitney Point CSD	Whitney Point
306	11.9	Cobleskill-Richmondville CSD	Cobleskill
306	11.9	Hewlett-Woodmere UFSD	Woodmere
306	11.9	Nanuet UFSD	Nanuet
306	11.9	Peekskill City SD	Peekskill
306	11.9	Seneca Falls CSD	Seneca Falls
306	11.9	White Plains City SD	White Plains
306	11.9	Wilson CSD	Wilson
313	11.8	East Syracuse-Minoa CSD	East Syracuse
313	11.8	Hastings-On-Hudson UFSD	Hastings-on-Hud
313	11.8	Indian River CSD	Philadelphia
313	11.8	Ithaca City SD	Ithaca
313	11.8	Monticello CSD	Monticello
313	11.8	Wayland-Cohocton CSD	Wayland
319	11.7	Bedford CSD	Mount Kisco
319	11.7	Binghamton City SD	Binghamton
319	11.7	Cohoes City SD	Cohoes
319	11.7	Deer Park UFSD	Deer Park
319	11.7	East Williston UFSD	Old Westbury
319	11.7	Geneva City SD	Geneva
319	11.7	Northport-East Northport UFSD	Northport
319	11.7	Norwich City SD	Norwich
319	11.7	Port Washington UFSD	Pt Washington
328	11.6	Medina CSD	Medina
328	11.6	Nyack UFSD	Nyack
328	11.6	Ogdensburg City SD	Ogdensburg
328	11.6	Onteora CSD	Boiceville
328	11.6	Susquehanna Valley CSD	Conklin
333	11.5	Herricks UFSD	New Hyde Park
333	11.5	Hudson City SD	Hudson
333	11.5	Mattituck-Cutchogue UFSD	Cutchogue
333	11.5	Westhampton Beach UFSD	Westhampton Bch
337	11.3	Huntington UFSD	Huntington Stn
337	11.3	Mount Pleasant CSD	Thornwood
337	11.3	Plainview-Old Bethpage CSD	Plainview
340	11.2	Fredonia CSD	Fredonia
340	11.2	Greenburgh CSD	Hartsdale
340	11.2	Malverne UFSD	Malverne
340	11.2	Manhasset UFSD	Manhasset
340	11.2	North Rose-Wolcott CSD	Wolcott
345	11.1	Dryden CSD	Dryden
345	11.1	Locust Valley CSD	Locust Valley
345	11.1	Salmon River CSD	Ft Covington
345	11.1	Sullivan West CSD	Jeffersonville
349	11.0	Beekmantown CSD	Plattsburgh
349	11.0	Carle Place UFSD	Carle Place
349	11.0	Syosset CSD	Syosset
352	10.9	Great Neck UFSD	Great Neck
352	10.9	Mineola UFSD	Mineola
354	10.8	Harrison CSD	Harrison
354	10.8	Jamestown City SD	Jamestown
354	10.8	North Shore CSD	Sea Cliff
354	10.8	Rockville Centre UFSD	Rockville Ctre
354	10.8	Sherburne-Earlville CSD	Sherburne
359	10.7	Lawrence UFSD	Lawrence
359	10.7	Plattsburgh City SD	Plattsburgh
359	10.7	Southampton UFSD	Southampton
362	10.5	Oyster Bay-East Norwich CSD	Oyster Bay
363	10.3	Jericho UFSD	Jericho
364	10.0	Dunkirk City SD	Dunkirk
365	4.4	Boces Monroe 1	Fairport
366	3.6	Boces Nassau	Garden City
367	3.2	Boces Eastern Suffolk (Suffolk I)	Patchogue
368	n/a	Albany City SD	Albany

Student/Librarian Ratio

Rank	Ratio	District Name	City
1	2,124.0	Johnstown City SD	Johnstown
2	1,854.0	Ilion CSD	Ilion
3	1,829.0	Wallkill CSD	Wallkill
4	1,821.0	Dover UFSD	Dover Plains
5	1,818.0	Waverly CSD	Waverly
6	1,808.5	Islip UFSD	Islip
7	1,785.8	Niagara Falls City SD	Niagara Falls
8	1,774.0	Gouverneur CSD	Gouverneur
9	1,764.0	Putnam Valley CSD	Putnam Valley
10	1,751.7	Mahopac CSD	Mahopac
11	1,726.0	Floral Park-Bellerose UFSD	Floral Park
12	1,699.1	Baldwin UFSD	Baldwin
13	1,675.0	North Rose-Wolcott CSD	Wolcott
14	1,661.0	Clinton CSD	Clinton
15	1,617.0	Adirondack CSD	Boonville
16	1,521.0	Boces Monroe 1	Fairport
17	1,515.8	Cairo-Durham CSD	Cairo
18	1,496.0	Valley Stream Central HSD	Valley Stream
19	1,491.9	Brentwood UFSD	Brentwood
20	1,483.1	Dryden CSD	Dryden
21	1,457.2	Rockville Centre UFSD	Rockville Ctre
22	1,453.0	Nyack UFSD	Nyack
23	1,416.0	Carmel CSD	Patterson
24	1,410.2	New York City Public Schools	Brooklyn
25	1,382.7	White Plains City SD	White Plains
26	1,371.6	Honeoye Falls-Lima CSD	Honeoye Falls
27	1,365.6	Lansingburgh CSD	Troy
28	1,355.1	New Rochelle City SD	New Rochelle
29	1,344.0	Mexico CSD	Mexico
30	1,283.3	Fredonia CSD	Fredonia
31	1,264.1	Auburn City SD	Auburn
32	1,238.6	Monticello CSD	Monticello
33	1,236.5	Pelham UFSD	Pelham
34	1,218.9	Minisink Valley CSD	Slate Hill
35	1,209.4	Newfane CSD	Newfane
36	1,200.5	Wyandanch UFSD	Wyandanch
37	1,180.5	Hudson Falls CSD	Hudson Falls
38	1,162.5	Eden CSD	Eden
39	1,153.3	Highland CSD	Highland
40	1,149.4	Pine Bush CSD	Pine Bush
41	1,148.4	Ossining UFSD	Ossining
42	1,141.2	Franklin Square UFSD	Franklin Square
43	1,136.2	Bellmore-Merrick Central HSD	North Merrick
44	1,123.3	Hewlett-Woodmere UFSD	Woodmere
45	1,114.1	Lakeland CSD	Shrub Oak
46	1,106.1	South Jefferson CSD	Adams Center
47	1,095.8	Mamaroneck UFSD	Mamaroneck
48	1,092.2	William Floyd UFSD	Mastic Beach
49	1,090.8	Yonkers City SD	Yonkers
50	1,089.7	South Glens Falls CSD	S Glens Falls
51	1,081.8	Yorkshire-Pioneer CSD	Yorkshire
52	1,047.5	Lackawanna City SD	Lackawanna
53	1,043.3	Westbury UFSD	Old Westbury
54	1,036.5	South Country CSD	E Patchogue
55	1,031.6	Washingtonville CSD	Washingtonville
56	1,027.4	Haverstraw-Stony Point CSD	Garnerville
57	1,015.6	Rocky Point UFSD	Rocky Point
58	1,010.5	Bath CSD	Bath
59	1,009.5	Queensbury UFSD	Queensbury
60	1,008.0	Frontier CSD	Hamburg
61	1,007.7	Port Chester-Rye UFSD	Port Chester
62	1,004.0	Boces Nassau	Garden City
63	1,002.8	Spencerport CSD	Spencerport
64	1,000.5	Babylon UFSD	Babylon
65	998.1	Brighton CSD	Rochester
66	990.5	Hornell City SD	Hornell
67	986.7	Penn Yan CSD	Pen
68	985.1	Victor CSD	Victor

Rank	Value	District	City
69	979.4	Troy City SD	Troy
70	979.3	Ramapo CSD (Suffern)	Hillburn
71	973.3	Ballston Spa CSD	Ballston Spa
72	968.0	Whitesboro CSD	Yorkville
73	965.5	Irvington UFSD	Irvington
74	961.5	Liberty CSD	Liberty
75	950.4	Ravena-Coeymans-Selkirk CSD	Selkirk
76	946.9	Central Islip UFSD	Central Islip
77	946.7	Akron CSD	Akron
78	944.6	North Syracuse CSD	N Syracuse
79	941.2	Newburgh City SD	Newburgh
80	940.4	Three Village CSD	East Setauket
81	940.0	Albion CSD	Albion
82	935.0	Amsterdam City SD	Amsterdam
83	933.3	Brockport CSD	Brockport
84	932.5	South Huntington UFSD	Huntington Stn
85	930.5	Cold Spring Harbor CSD	Cold Sprg Harbor
86	925.0	Wayland-Cohocton CSD	Wayland
87	920.0	Clarence CSD	Clarence
88	917.8	Gorham-Middlesex CSD	Rushville
89	915.5	Attica CSD	Attica
90	910.1	Half Hollow Hills CSD	Dix Hills
91	909.3	Yorktown CSD	Yorktown Hgts
92	907.5	Westhampton Beach UFSD	Westhampton Bch
93	906.4	Freeport UFSD	Freeport
94	901.8	Garden City UFSD	Garden City
95	897.3	Beacon City SD	Beacon
96	894.2	Pleasantville UFSD	Pleasantville
97	891.6	Middle Country CSD	Centereach
98	889.7	East Islip UFSD	Islip Terrace
99	887.6	Hilton CSD	Hilton
100	887.4	Waterloo CSD	Waterloo
101	885.3	Glen Cove City SD	Glen Cove
102	885.1	Sayville UFSD	Sayville
103	882.4	Webster CSD	Webster
104	881.0	Longwood CSD	Middle Island
105	879.2	Williamsville CSD	East Amherst
106	878.8	Ardsley UFSD	Ardsley
107	877.2	Middletown City SD	Middletown
108	876.3	Plainedge UFSD	N Massapequa
109	876.0	Canandaigua City SD	Canandaigua
109	876.0	Hampton Bays UFSD	Hampton Bays
111	875.0	East Ramapo CSD (Spring Valley)	Spring Valley
112	874.7	Manhasset UFSD	Manhasset
113	874.5	Riverhead CSD	Riverhead
114	870.3	Eastchester UFSD	Eastchester
115	869.6	Hempstead UFSD	Hempstead
116	869.4	General Brown CSD	Dexter
117	867.7	Hudson City SD	Hudson
118	867.3	Bay Shore UFSD	Bay Shore
119	864.3	East Hampton UFSD	East Hampton
120	864.2	Gloversville City SD	Gloversville
121	860.2	Sachem CSD	Holbrook
122	857.6	Oswego City SD	Oswego
123	857.4	South Orangetown CSD	Blauvelt
124	855.8	Long Beach City SD	Long Beach
125	853.5	Harborfields CSD	Greenlawn
126	852.3	Cornwall CSD	Cornwall-on-Hud
127	851.1	Connetquot CSD	Bohemia
127	851.1	Mount Sinai UFSD	Mount Sinai
129	850.6	Cheektowaga-Sloan UFSD	Sloan
130	849.0	Elwood UFSD	Greenlawn
131	846.9	Arlington CSD	Poughkeepsie
132	845.8	Watertown City SD	Watertown
133	845.3	Kings Park CSD	Kings Park
134	840.5	Brewster CSD	Brewster
135	839.4	Chatham CSD	Chatham
136	837.6	Buffalo City SD	Buffalo
137	831.1	Valley CSD (Montgomery)	Montgomery
138	830.8	Amityville UFSD	Amityville
139	830.0	UFSD - Tarrytowns	Sleepy Hollow
140	829.5	Schuylerville CSD	Schuylerville
141	826.2	Lindenhurst UFSD	Lindenhurst
142	826.1	Miller Place UFSD	Miller Place
143	824.8	Wappingers CSD	Wappingers Fls
144	824.4	North Tonawanda City SD	N Tonawanda
145	823.6	Goshen CSD	Goshen
146	820.5	Warwick Valley CSD	Warwick
147	820.4	Fulton City SD	Fulton
148	820.3	Rotterdam-Mohonasen CSD	Schenectady
149	819.8	Schenectady City SD	Schenectady
150	817.9	Levittown UFSD	Levittown
151	817.7	Cheektowaga CSD	Cheektowaga
152	817.2	Central Square CSD	Central Square
153	814.8	Union-Endicott CSD	Endicott
154	811.4	Port Washington UFSD	Pt Washington
155	809.3	Lewiston-Porter CSD	Youngstown
156	808.5	Sullivan West CSD	Jeffersonville
157	805.7	Depew UFSD	Depew
158	803.9	West Seneca CSD	West Seneca
159	803.0	Pearl River UFSD	Pearl River
160	802.9	Schalmont CSD	Schenectady
161	801.0	Fonda-Fultonville CSD	Fonda
162	800.7	Fairport CSD	Fairport
163	800.5	Hannibal CSD	Hannibal
164	799.1	Copiague UFSD	Copiague
165	798.1	Port Jervis City SD	Port Jervis
166	795.1	Brookhaven-Comsewogue UFSD	Pt Jefferson Stn
167	794.5	Baldwinsville CSD	Baldwinsville
167	794.5	Cleveland Hill UFSD	Cheektowaga
169	794.1	Patchogue-Medford UFSD	Patchogue
170	792.3	Amherst CSD	Amherst
171	789.1	Greece CSD	Rochester
172	785.1	Syracuse City SD	Syracuse
173	785.0	Canastota CSD	Canastota
174	783.2	Lancaster CSD	Lancaster
175	782.9	Valley Stream 13 UFSD	Valley Stream
176	782.7	Mount Vernon City SD	Mount Vernon
177	781.1	North Babylon UFSD	North Babylon
178	779.5	Canton CSD	Canton
179	778.2	Penfield CSD	Penfield
180	775.6	East Aurora UFSD	East Aurora
181	772.5	Sewanhaka Central HSD	Floral Park
182	768.0	Seneca Falls CSD	Seneca Falls
183	767.4	Shoreham-Wading River CSD	Shoreham
184	761.4	Oceanside UFSD	Oceanside
185	761.1	Elmont UFSD	Elmont
186	760.9	Hastings-On-Hudson UFSD	Hastings-on-Hud
187	760.0	Croton-Harmon UFSD	Croton-On-Hud
188	758.8	Saratoga Springs City SD	Saratoga Spgs
189	757.8	Starpoint CSD	Lockport
190	745.4	Iroquois CSD	Elma
191	744.5	East Irondequoit CSD	Rochester
192	741.4	Rochester City SD	Rochester
193	738.6	Monroe-Woodbury CSD	Central Valley
194	735.0	Roosevelt UFSD	Roosevelt
195	734.3	Katonah-Lewisboro UFSD	South Salem
196	732.5	Pittsford CSD	Pittsford
197	731.0	Phelps-Clifton Springs CSD	Clifton Spgs
198	730.3	Johnson City CSD	Johnson City
199	728.0	Niagara-Wheatfield CSD	Niagara Falls
200	726.2	Evans-Brant CSD (Lake Shore)	Angola
201	724.5	Plattsburgh City SD	Plattsburgh
202	723.3	Marcellus CSD	Marcellus
203	720.0	Merrick UFSD	Merrick
204	719.7	Susquehanna Valley CSD	Conklin
205	719.5	Fayetteville-Manlius CSD	Manlius
206	715.3	Seaford UFSD	Seaford
207	714.9	Harrison CSD	Harrison
208	712.6	Hamburg CSD	Hamburg
209	712.2	Grand Island CSD	Grand Island
210	709.1	Roslyn UFSD	Roslyn
211	708.9	Maine-Endwell CSD	Endwell
212	707.4	Clarkstown CSD	New City
213	705.9	South Colonie CSD	Albany
214	705.7	Cohoes City SD	Cohoes
215	704.3	Dunkirk City SD	Dunkirk
216	702.3	Cobleskill-Richmondville CSD	Cobleskill
217	700.1	Rush-Henrietta CSD	Henrietta
218	699.5	Sweet Home CSD	Amherst
219	697.6	Cheektowaga-Maryvale UFSD	Cheektowaga
220	695.8	Island Trees UFSD	Levittown
221	694.1	Taconic Hills CSD	Craryville
221	694.1	Utica City SD	Utica
223	693.3	West Islip UFSD	West Islip
224	693.2	Averill Park CSD	Averill Park
225	692.9	Kingston City SD	Kingston
226	692.8	Chenango Valley CSD	Binghamton
227	691.1	Phoenix CSD	Phoenix
228	690.8	Geneva City SD	Geneva
229	689.0	Marlboro CSD	Marlboro
230	687.3	Sherburne-Earlville CSD	Sherburne
231	686.1	Glens Falls City SD	Glens Falls
232	684.4	Farmingdale UFSD	Farmingdale
233	684.2	Commack UFSD	E Northport
234	683.8	Newark CSD	Newark
235	680.0	Homer CSD	Homer
236	678.0	Poughkeepsie City SD	Poughkeepsie
237	677.1	Peru CSD	Peru
238	675.8	Chappaqua CSD	Chappaqua
239	675.6	Hyde Park CSD	Poughkeepsie
240	675.1	Smithtown CSD	Smithtown
241	670.7	New Hyde Pk-Garden City Pk UFSD	New Hyde Park
242	669.1	Shenendehowa CSD	Clifton Park
243	667.9	Herricks UFSD	New Hyde Park
244	664.1	Deer Park UFSD	Deer Park
245	664.0	Churchville-Chili CSD	Churchville
246	663.8	Malone CSD	Malone
247	663.1	West Genesee CSD	Camillus
248	660.0	Olean City SD	Olean
249	659.4	Kenmore-Tonawanda UFSD	Buffalo
250	650.7	Cazenovia CSD	Cazenovia
251	647.9	West Babylon UFSD	West Babylon
252	646.3	Ogdensburg City SD	Ogdensburg
253	645.9	Wantagh UFSD	Wantagh
254	645.8	Kinderhook CSD	Valatie
255	644.3	Whitney Point CSD	Whitney Point
256	644.2	Medina CSD	Medina
257	644.0	Guilderland CSD	Guilderland
258	641.3	East Syracuse-Minoa CSD	East Syracuse
259	639.3	East Greenbush CSD	E Greenbush
260	636.9	Northport-East Northport UFSD	Northport
261	635.9	Royalton-Hartland CSD	Middleport
262	635.5	Owego-Apalachin CSD	Owego
263	634.9	Somers CSD	Lincolndale
264	634.0	Lawrence UFSD	Lawrence
265	633.0	Holland Patent CSD	Holland Patent
266	632.9	West Hempstead UFSD	W Hempstead
267	631.4	Huntington UFSD	Huntington Stn
268	630.7	Saranac CSD	Dannemora
269	630.3	Red Hook CSD	Red Hook
270	628.4	Springville-Griffith Inst CSD	Springville
271	626.4	Southampton UFSD	Southampton
272	624.6	Vestal CSD	Vestal
273	624.5	Binghamton City SD	Binghamton
274	624.1	Liverpool CSD	Liverpool
275	623.8	Solvay UFSD	Solvay
276	623.1	Elmira City SD	Elmira
277	621.6	East Meadow UFSD	Westbury
278	617.8	Norwich City SD	Norwich
279	617.5	Scarsdale UFSD	Scarsdale
280	617.4	Bedford CSD	Mount Kisco
281	616.7	Bethpage UFSD	Bethpage
282	616.5	Carthage CSD	Carthage
283	610.9	Lockport City SD	Lockport
284	610.7	Wayne CSD	Ontario Center
285	609.3	Plainview-Old Bethpage CSD	Plainview
286	603.2	Orchard Park CSD	Orchard Park
287	603.0	Horseheads CSD	Horseheads
288	599.3	Edgemont UFSD	Scarsdale
289	596.5	New Paltz CSD	New Paltz
290	596.0	Rondout Valley CSD	Accord
291	595.0	Palmyra-Macedon CSD	Palmyra
292	594.8	Peekskill City SD	Peekskill
293	592.9	Greenburgh CSD	Hartsdale
294	592.2	Jamesville-Dewitt CSD	Dewitt
295	591.5	Massena CSD	Massena
296	590.2	Hendrick Hudson CSD	Montrose
297	589.2	Livonia CSD	Livonia
298	588.6	Broadalbin-Perth CSD	Broadalbin
299	588.4	Saugerties CSD	Saugerties
299	588.4	Syosset CSD	Syosset
301	587.8	Beekmantown CSD	Plattsburgh
302	586.3	Onteora CSD	Boiceville
303	584.0	East Williston UFSD	Old Westbury
304	582.3	Gates-Chili CSD	Rochester
305	580.6	Corning City SD	Painted Post
306	579.7	Indian River CSD	Philadelphia
307	577.7	Oyster Bay-East Norwich CSD	Oyster Bay
308	577.6	Byram Hills CSD	Armonk
309	576.8	Mineola UFSD	Mineola
310	576.2	New Hartford CSD	New Hartford
311	573.9	Alden CSD	Alden
312	573.4	Hauppauge UFSD	Hauppauge
312	573.4	Hicksville UFSD	Hicksville
314	573.3	Chittenango CSD	Chittenango
315	568.9	Jericho UFSD	Jericho
315	568.9	Salmon River CSD	Ft Covington
317	567.6	West Irondequoit CSD	Rochester
318	564.0	Northeastern Clinton CSD	Champlain
319	563.3	Altmar-Parish-Williamstown CSD	Parish
319	563.3	Briarcliff Manor UFSD	Briarcliff Manor
321	563.1	Batavia City SD	Batavia
322	559.7	Uniondale UFSD	Uniondale
323	558.5	Mount Pleasant CSD	Thornwood
324	554.9	Nanuet UFSD	Nanuet
325	551.5	Skaneateles CSD	Skaneateles
326	550.9	North Colonie CSD	Latham
327	550.5	Burnt Hills-Ballston Lake CSD	Scotia
328	548.5	Rye City SD	Rye
329	547.2	Bethlehem CSD	Delmar
330	547.0	Coxsackie-Athens CSD	Coxsackie
331	546.9	Salamanca City SD	Salamanca
332	546.1	Massapequa UFSD	Massapequa
333	545.7	Rome City SD	Rome
334	542.1	Windsor CSD	Windsor
335	540.8	Oneonta City SD	Oneonta
336	528.1	Chenango Forks CSD	Binghamton
337	527.7	Lansing CSD	Lansing
338	526.3	Lynbrook UFSD	Lynbrook
339	524.9	Westhill CSD	Syracuse
340	524.5	Sherrill City SD	Verona
341	522.8	Great Neck UFSD	Great Neck
342	520.7	Mattituck-Cutchogue UFSD	Cutchogue
343	519.1	Scotia-Glenville CSD	Scotia
344	510.5	Boces Eastern Suffolk (Suffolk I)	Patchogue
345	509.8	Bayport-Blue Point UFSD	Bayport
346	508.0	Valley Stream 30 UFSD	Valley Stream

347	505.7	Carle Place UFSD	Carle Place
348	504.3	Gowanda CSD	Gowanda
349	500.8	Dansville CSD	Dansville
350	494.2	Ellenville CSD	Ellenville
351	492.1	Cortland City SD	Cortland
352	483.2	Malverne UFSD	Malverne
353	482.8	Southwestern CSD at Jamestown	Jamestown
354	482.7	Catskill CSD	Catskill
355	469.7	Spackenkill UFSD	Poughkeepsie
356	468.4	North Shore CSD	Sea Cliff
357	465.5	Ithaca City SD	Ithaca
358	462.2	North Bellmore UFSD	Bellmore
359	459.7	Camden CSD	Camden
360	459.1	Niskayuna CSD	Schenectady
361	450.4	Jamestown City SD	Jamestown
362	434.0	Jordan-Elbridge CSD	Jordan
363	420.9	Locust Valley CSD	Locust Valley
364	420.2	Tonawanda City SD	Tonawanda
365	420.0	Saranac Lake CSD	Saranac Lake
366	398.3	Oneida City SD	Oneida
367	375.0	Wilson CSD	Wilson
368	n/a	Albany City SD	Albany

Student/Counselor Ratio

Rank	Ratio	District Name	City
1	1,140.5	Wyandanch UFSD	Wyandanch
2	1,089.0	Broadalbin-Perth CSD	Broadalbin
3	1,031.1	Hempstead UFSD	Hempstead
4	924.0	Riverhead CSD	Riverhead
5	909.0	Waverly CSD	Waverly
6	817.3	South Glens Falls CSD	S Glens Falls
7	812.6	Amherst CSD	Amherst
8	808.5	Adirondack CSD	Boonville
9	801.0	Fonda-Fultonville CSD	Fonda
10	791.5	Lansing CSD	Lansing
11	765.5	Cheektowaga-Sloan UFSD	Sloan
12	763.6	Saranac Lake CSD	Saranac Lake
13	752.0	Hudson City SD	Hudson
14	703.4	West Babylon UFSD	West Babylon
15	692.0	Highland CSD	Highland
16	691.0	Lindenhurst UFSD	Lindenhurst
17	683.7	Saratoga Springs City SD	Saratoga Spgs
18	683.5	Utica City SD	Utica
19	682.3	Cold Spring Harbor CSD	Cold Sprg Harbor
20	678.8	Lancaster CSD	Lancaster
21	676.9	Pine Bush CSD	Pine Bush
22	673.6	Wappingers CSD	Wappingers Fls
23	667.3	East Islip UFSD	Islip Terrace
24	662.8	Central Islip UFSD	Central Islip
25	647.3	Oneida City SD	Oneida
26	644.7	Arlington CSD	Poughkeepsie
27	642.7	Fulton City SD	Fulton
28	641.7	William Floyd UFSD	Mastic Beach
29	633.3	Niagara Falls City SD	Niagara Falls
30	622.4	Patchogue-Medford UFSD	Patchogue
31	620.0	Marcellus CSD	Marcellus
32	618.0	Ilion CSD	Ilion
33	616.3	Auburn City SD	Auburn
33	616.3	Sherrill City SD	Verona
35	614.5	Lansingburgh CSD	Troy
36	613.3	Cheektowaga CSD	Cheektowaga
37	612.0	Homer CSD	Homer
38	610.3	Attica CSD	Attica
39	610.1	Middle Country CSD	Centereach
40	609.3	Rocky Point UFSD	Rocky Point
41	607.2	Hannibal CSD	Hannibal
42	607.0	Dover UFSD	Dover Plains
43	606.3	Cairo-Durham CSD	Cairo
44	604.1	Baldwin UFSD	Baldwin
44	604.1	Watertown City SD	Watertown
46	598.2	Beacon City SD	Beacon
47	597.0	Springville-Griffith Inst CSD	Springville
48	596.0	South Country CSD	E Patchogue
49	595.3	Catskill CSD	Catskill
50	594.8	Peekskill City SD	Peekskill
51	591.8	Carthage CSD	Carthage
52	591.1	Hyde Park CSD	Poughkeepsie
53	590.3	Hudson Falls CSD	Hudson Falls
54	589.0	Owego-Apalachin CSD	Owego
55	587.5	West Seneca CSD	West Seneca
56	586.1	Newburgh City SD	Newburgh
57	585.2	Oswego City SD	Oswego
58	584.0	Hampton Bays UFSD	Hampton Bays
59	583.0	Red Hook CSD	Red Hook
60	575.4	East Greenbush CSD	E Greenbush
61	572.8	North Babylon UFSD	North Babylon
62	570.4	Union-Endicott CSD	Endicott
63	568.8	Burnt Hills-Ballston Lake CSD	Scotia
64	566.8	North Syracuse CSD	N Syracuse
65	564.5	Frontier CSD	Hamburg
66	564.2	Clarkstown CSD	New City
67	563.3	Briarcliff Manor UFSD	Briarcliff Manor
68	553.1	Whitesboro CSD	Yorkville
69	550.7	Gorham-Middlesex CSD	Rushville
70	547.9	Deer Park UFSD	Deer Park
71	547.0	Coxsackie-Athens CSD	Coxsackie
72	546.8	Rotterdam-Mohonasen CSD	Schenectady
73	546.0	Kingston City SD	Kingston
74	545.0	Syracuse City SD	Syracuse
75	543.4	Connetquot CSD	Bohemia
76	540.4	North Tonawanda City SD	N Tonawanda
77	538.8	Maine-Endwell CSD	Endwell
78	538.7	Rochester City SD	Rochester
79	537.6	Mexico CSD	Mexico
80	537.2	Shoreham-Wading River CSD	Shoreham
81	534.2	Grand Island CSD	Grand Island
82	532.9	Schenectady City SD	Schenectady
83	531.6	Clarence CSD	Clarence
84	531.0	Johnstown City SD	Johnstown
85	529.5	Buffalo City SD	Buffalo
86	529.3	Cohoes City SD	Cohoes
87	527.3	Poughkeepsie City SD	Poughkeepsie
88	526.9	Haverstraw-Stony Point CSD	Garnerville
89	524.6	Brentwood UFSD	Brentwood
90	523.8	Lackawanna City SD	Lackawanna
91	523.3	Canastota CSD	Canastota
92	522.6	Wallkill CSD	Wallkill
93	521.7	Carmel CSD	Patterson
93	521.7	General Brown CSD	Dexter
95	519.5	Brookhaven-Comsewogue UFSD	Pt Jefferson Stn
96	518.4	Sayville UFSD	Sayville
97	516.8	Marlboro CSD	Marlboro
98	516.7	Islip UFSD	Islip
99	516.5	Alden CSD	Alden
99	516.5	Herricks UFSD	New Hyde Park
101	516.1	Hicksville UFSD	Hicksville
102	515.2	Guilderland CSD	Guilderland
103	513.1	Monticello CSD	Monticello
104	512.0	Massapequa UFSD	Massapequa
104	512.0	Seneca Falls CSD	Seneca Falls
106	508.7	Ballston Spa CSD	Ballston Spa
107	507.0	Boces Monroe 1	Fairport
108	506.7	Croton-Harmon UFSD	Croton-On-Hud
109	505.3	Bath CSD	Bath
110	504.0	Greenburgh CSD	Hartsdale
111	503.7	Chatham CSD	Chatham
112	502.3	Chenango Valley CSD	Binghamton
113	501.2	South Orangetown CSD	Blauvelt
114	500.9	Levittown UFSD	Levittown
115	500.6	Ramapo CSD (Suffern)	Hillburn
116	500.3	Babylon UFSD	Babylon
117	499.0	South Colonie CSD	Albany
118	498.5	Central Square CSD	Central Square
119	497.6	Ithaca City SD	Ithaca
120	497.5	Monroe-Woodbury CSD	Central Valley
121	495.8	Horseheads CSD	Horseheads
122	495.7	Miller Place UFSD	Miller Place
122	495.7	Mount Vernon City SD	Mount Vernon
124	495.2	West Islip UFSD	West Islip
125	495.1	Averill Park CSD	Averill Park
126	494.2	Goshen CSD	Goshen
127	492.6	Victor CSD	Victor
128	492.4	Elwood UFSD	Greenlawn
129	491.4	Fairport CSD	Fairport
130	490.4	New Rochelle City SD	New Rochelle
131	490.3	Port Jervis City SD	Port Jervis
132	490.0	Roosevelt UFSD	Roosevelt
133	487.6	Minisink Valley CSD	Slate Hill
133	487.6	Saugerties CSD	Saugerties
135	487.4	Tonawanda City SD	Tonawanda
136	485.0	Troy City SD	Troy
137	484.5	Iroquois CSD	Elma
138	483.7	Lockport City SD	Lockport
139	483.5	Valley CSD (Montgomery)	Montgomery
140	483.3	Baldwinsville CSD	Baldwinsville
141	482.8	Irvington UFSD	Irvington
142	480.0	Harrison CSD	Harrison
143	479.1	Spencerport CSD	Spencerport
144	477.0	Bay Shore UFSD	Bay Shore
145	476.9	North Shore CSD	Sea Cliff
146	475.3	Chenango Forks CSD	Binghamton
147	473.3	Akron CSD	Akron
148	470.2	Three Village CSD	East Setauket
148	470.2	West Genesee CSD	Camillus
150	470.0	Albion CSD	Albion
151	469.5	Ellenville CSD	Ellenville
152	467.5	Cortland City SD	Cortland
153	467.3	Starpoint CSD	Lockport
154	465.0	Eden CSD	Eden
154	465.0	Kinderhook CSD	Valatie
156	464.4	Farmingdale UFSD	Farmingdale
157	464.0	Sachem CSD	Holbrook
158	463.6	Middletown City SD	Middletown
159	462.9	Amityville UFSD	Amityville
159	462.9	UFSD - Tarrytowns	Sleepy Hollow
161	462.0	Kings Park CSD	Kings Park
162	460.7	Phoenix CSD	Phoenix
163	459.5	Warwick Valley CSD	Warwick
164	459.4	Binghamton City SD	Binghamton
165	456.0	Huntington UFSD	Huntington Stn
166	455.2	East Aurora UFSD	East Aurora
167	454.7	Commack UFSD	E Northport
167	454.7	Oceanside UFSD	Oceanside
169	453.5	Newfane CSD	Newfane
170	452.2	Palmyra-Macedon CSD	Palmyra
171	451.8	Uniondale UFSD	Uniondale
172	450.9	Garden City UFSD	Garden City
173	449.5	Edgemont UFSD	Scarsdale
174	448.5	Longwood CSD	Middle Island
175	446.2	Locust Valley CSD	Locust Valley
176	445.8	East Ramapo CSD (Spring Valley)	Spring Valley
177	445.6	Lakeland CSD	Shrub Oak
177	445.6	Onteora CSD	Boiceville
179	445.0	Smithtown CSD	Smithtown
180	442.8	Byram Hills CSD	Armonk
181	441.0	Putnam Valley CSD	Putnam Valley
182	438.1	Plainedge UFSD	N Massapequa
183	437.9	Mahopac CSD	Mahopac
184	437.5	Geneva City SD	Geneva
185	437.4	East Irondequoit CSD	Rochester
186	436.0	Livonia CSD	Livonia
186	436.0	Wantagh UFSD	Wantagh
188	434.5	Southwestern CSD at Jamestown	Jamestown
189	434.3	Honeoye Falls-Lima CSD	Honeoye Falls
190	432.7	Yorkshire-Pioneer CSD	Yorkshire
191	431.8	Susquehanna Valley CSD	Conklin
192	430.2	Cheektowaga-Maryvale UFSD	Cheektowaga
193	430.1	Scotia-Glenville CSD	Scotia
194	429.3	Royalton-Hartland CSD	Middleport
195	428.4	Mamaroneck UFSD	Mamaroneck
196	427.0	Gates-Chili CSD	Rochester
197	426.2	Queensbury UFSD	Queensbury
198	426.1	Cornwall CSD	Cornwall-on-Hud
199	425.9	Clinton CSD	Clinton
200	425.0	South Huntington UFSD	Huntington Stn
201	424.5	Bedford CSD	Mount Kisco
202	424.0	Phelps-Clifton Springs CSD	Clifton Spgs
203	423.6	Rockville Centre UFSD	Rockville Ctre
204	422.9	Bethpage UFSD	Bethpage
205	422.5	Altmar-Parish-Williamstown CSD	Parish
206	421.4	Copiague UFSD	Copiague
207	419.0	Yonkers City SD	Yonkers
208	418.8	Elmira City SD	Elmira
209	416.3	Schalmont CSD	Schenectady
210	414.8	Schuylerville CSD	Schuylerville
211	413.6	Ogdensburg City SD	Ogdensburg
212	410.9	Brewster CSD	Brewster
213	410.1	Yorktown CSD	Yorktown Hgts
214	409.4	Westhill CSD	Syracuse
215	408.3	Nanuet UFSD	Nanuet
216	407.8	Bayport-Blue Point UFSD	Bayport
217	404.7	Hendrick Hudson CSD	Montrose
218	404.5	Syosset CSD	Syosset
219	404.1	East Meadow UFSD	Westbury
220	401.5	Pearl River UFSD	Pearl River
221	400.4	Lawrence UFSD	Lawrence
222	399.4	Medina CSD	Medina
223	398.9	Rye City SD	Rye
224	398.2	South Jefferson CSD	Adams Center
225	397.7	New Paltz CSD	New Paltz
226	397.3	Williamsville CSD	East Amherst
227	396.8	Washingtonville CSD	Washingtonville
228	396.0	Ravena-Coeymans-Selkirk CSD	Selkirk
229	395.7	Kenmore-Tonawanda UFSD	Buffalo
230	394.4	Orchard Park CSD	Orchard Park
231	394.0	Webster CSD	Webster
232	391.9	Port Chester-Rye UFSD	Port Chester
233	390.7	Newark CSD	Newark
234	388.1	Lynbrook UFSD	Lynbrook
235	388.0	Spackenkill UFSD	Poughkeepsie
236	386.9	New Hartford CSD	New Hartford
237	386.3	Ossining UFSD	Ossining
238	385.0	Fredonia CSD	Fredonia
239	384.8	East Syracuse-Minoa CSD	East Syracuse
240	384.3	Bethlehem CSD	Delmar
241	383.2	Penfield CSD	Penfield
242	381.6	Freeport UFSD	Freeport
243	381.3	Niagara-Wheatfield CSD	Niagara Falls
244	380.7	Rush-Henrietta CSD	Henrietta
245	379.8	Holland Patent CSD	Holland Patent
246	379.3	Carle Place UFSD	Carle Place
246	379.3	Harborfields CSD	Greenlawn
246	379.3	Malone CSD	Malone
249	378.8	Scarsdale UFSD	Scarsdale
250	378.4	Saranac CSD	Dannemora
251	377.9	New York City Public Schools	Brooklyn
252	377.1	Niskayuna CSD	Schenectady

253	376.3	Churchville-Chili CSD	Churchville
254	375.5	Oyster Bay-East Norwich CSD	Oyster Bay
255	375.0	Skaneateles CSD	Skaneateles
256	374.9	Manhasset UFSD	Manhasset
257	374.8	Taconic Hills CSD	Craryville
258	374.4	Hewlett-Woodmere UFSD	Woodmere
259	374.0	Amsterdam City SD	Amsterdam
260	373.5	Lewiston-Porter CSD	Youngstown
261	373.0	Somers CSD	Lincolndale
262	372.4	Glens Falls City SD	Glens Falls
263	369.9	Westbury UFSD	Old Westbury
264	369.7	North Colonie CSD	Latham
265	369.1	Rome City SD	Rome
266	368.7	Massena CSD	Massena
267	367.2	Malverne UFSD	Malverne
268	367.1	Greece CSD	Rochester
269	366.6	Mount Sinai UFSD	Mount Sinai
270	366.5	Liverpool CSD	Liverpool
271	366.2	Island Trees UFSD	Levittown
272	364.9	Gloversville City SD	Gloversville
272	364.9	Hauppauge UFSD	Hauppauge
274	364.4	Cazenovia CSD	Cazenovia
275	363.3	Nyack UFSD	Nyack
276	363.1	Evans-Brant CSD (Lake Shore)	Angola
277	362.9	Corning City SD	Painted Post
278	361.8	Solvay UFSD	Solvay
279	359.4	Hamburg CSD	Hamburg
280	358.3	Chittenango CSD	Chittenango
281	357.4	Sherburne-Earlville CSD	Sherburne
282	356.8	Great Neck UFSD	Great Neck
283	356.6	White Plains City SD	White Plains
284	356.3	Half Hollow Hills CSD	Dix Hills
285	354.1	Glen Cove City SD	Glen Cove
286	353.3	Pelham UFSD	Pelham
287	352.7	Beekmantown CSD	Plattsburgh
288	351.8	Brockport CSD	Brockport
289	350.4	Canandaigua City SD	Canandaigua
290	347.8	Indian River CSD	Philadelphia
291	347.2	Jordan-Elbridge CSD	Jordan
292	345.3	Penn Yan CSD	Pen
293	344.8	Camden CSD	Camden
294	344.0	Hilton CSD	Hilton
295	342.7	Katonah-Lewisboro UFSD	South Salem
296	340.5	Jamesville-Dewitt CSD	Dewitt
297	339.8	Pleasantville UFSD	Pleasantville
297	339.8	Seaford UFSD	Seaford
299	338.9	Vestal CSD	Vestal
300	337.1	Pittsford CSD	Pittsford
301	335.0	North Rose-Wolcott CSD	Wolcott
302	334.8	Hastings-On-Hudson UFSD	Hastings-on-Hud
303	333.8	Port Washington UFSD	Pt Washington
304	329.8	Shenendehowa CSD	Clifton Park
305	328.9	Fayetteville-Manlius CSD	Manlius
306	326.4	Eastchester UFSD	Eastchester
307	324.9	Plainview-Old Bethpage CSD	Plainview
308	324.0	Long Beach City SD	Long Beach
309	323.4	Sullivan West CSD	Jeffersonville
310	321.3	Dryden CSD	Dryden
311	320.8	Brighton CSD	Rochester
312	320.4	Mineola UFSD	Mineola
313	319.5	Johnson City CSD	Johnson City
314	319.1	Roslyn UFSD	Roslyn
315	317.8	Cleveland Hill UFSD	Cheektowaga
316	316.8	Chappaqua CSD	Chappaqua
317	313.3	Northeastern Clinton CSD	Champlain
318	312.9	Jericho UFSD	Jericho
319	312.4	Mattituck-Cutchogue UFSD	Cutchogue
320	311.8	Canton CSD	Canton
321	311.0	Cobleskill-Richmondville CSD	Cobleskill
322	308.3	Wayland-Cohocton CSD	Wayland
323	307.2	Salmon River CSD	Ft Covington
324	304.6	Waterloo CSD	Waterloo
325	302.6	Gowanda CSD	Gowanda
326	301.9	Dunkirk City SD	Dunkirk
327	301.3	Sweet Home CSD	Amherst
328	300.6	West Hempstead UFSD	W Hempstead
329	300.1	Plattsburgh City SD	Plattsburgh
330	295.7	Gouverneur CSD	Gouverneur
331	294.3	Windsor CSD	Windsor
332	287.8	Peru CSD	Peru
333	283.8	West Irondequoit CSD	Rochester
334	276.1	Whitney Point CSD	Whitney Point
335	274.7	Liberty CSD	Liberty
336	272.7	Wilson CSD	Wilson
337	270.3	Batavia City SD	Batavia
338	269.3	Jamestown City SD	Jamestown
339	268.6	Depew UFSD	Depew
340	266.8	Rondout Valley CSD	Accord
341	265.1	East Hampton UFSD	East Hampton
342	264.0	Olean City SD	Olean
343	263.3	Mount Pleasant CSD	Thornwood
344	263.0	Bellmore-Merrick Central HSD	North Merrick
345	259.3	Westhampton Beach UFSD	Westhampton Bch
346	257.3	Hornell City SD	Hornell
347	256.9	Norwich City SD	Norwich
348	253.9	Ardsley UFSD	Ardsley
349	251.0	Boces Nassau	Garden City
350	250.3	East Williston UFSD	Old Westbury
351	249.7	Northport-East Northport UFSD	Northport
352	248.6	Wayne CSD	Ontario Center
353	225.4	Dansville CSD	Dansville
354	224.4	Valley Stream Central HSD	Valley Stream
355	222.0	Southampton UFSD	Southampton
356	217.5	Sewanhaka Central HSD	Floral Park
357	198.3	Salamanca City SD	Salamanca
358	196.6	Oneonta City SD	Oneonta
359	107.5	Boces Eastern Suffolk (Suffolk I)	Patchogue
360	0.0	Elmont UFSD	Elmont
360	0.0	Floral Park-Bellerose UFSD	Floral Park
360	0.0	Franklin Square UFSD	Franklin Square
360	0.0	Merrick UFSD	Merrick
360	0.0	New Hyde Pk-Garden City Pk UFSD	New Hyde Park
360	0.0	North Bellmore UFSD	Bellmore
360	0.0	Valley Stream 13 UFSD	Valley Stream
360	0.0	Valley Stream 30 UFSD	Valley Stream
368	n/a	Albany City SD	Albany

Current Spending per Student in FY2001

Rank	Dollars	District Name	City
1	19,485	Lawrence UFSD	Lawrence
2	19,480	Manhasset UFSD	Manhasset
3	18,778	Greenburgh CSD	Hartsdale
4	18,670	Jericho UFSD	Jericho
5	18,380	Mineola UFSD	Mineola
6	18,146	Oyster Bay-East Norwich CSD	Oyster Bay
7	18,074	Southampton UFSD	Southampton
8	18,072	North Shore CSD	Sea Cliff
9	17,893	Roslyn UFSD	Roslyn
10	17,891	Great Neck UFSD	Great Neck
11	17,417	Locust Valley CSD	Locust Valley
12	17,285	East Williston UFSD	Old Westbury
13	16,626	Bedford CSD	Mount Kisco
14	16,387	Port Washington UFSD	Pt Washington
15	16,031	White Plains City SD	White Plains
16	15,995	Nanuet UFSD	Nanuet
17	15,751	Carle Place UFSD	Carle Place
18	15,698	Long Beach City SD	Long Beach
19	15,682	Central Islip UFSD	Central Islip
20	15,667	East Hampton UFSD	East Hampton
21	15,664	Huntington UFSD	Huntington Stn
22	15,626	Wyandanch UFSD	Wyandanch
23	15,371	Syosset CSD	Syosset
24	15,274	East Ramapo CSD (Spring Valley)	Spring Valley
25	15,109	Malverne UFSD	Malverne
26	15,061	Uniondale UFSD	Uniondale
27	15,047	Harrison CSD	Harrison
28	15,040	Mount Pleasant CSD	Thornwood
29	14,975	South Orangetown CSD	Blauvelt
30	14,896	Plainview-Old Bethpage CSD	Plainview
31	14,878	Scarsdale UFSD	Scarsdale
32	14,817	Gowanda CSD	Gowanda
33	14,776	Putnam Valley CSD	Putnam Valley
34	14,630	Nyack UFSD	Nyack
35	14,621	Briarcliff Manor UFSD	Briarcliff Manor
35	14,621	South Country CSD	E Patchogue
37	14,512	Hauppauge UFSD	Hauppauge
38	14,471	Katonah-Lewisboro UFSD	South Salem
39	14,390	UFSD - Tarrytowns	Sleepy Hollow
40	14,387	Hewlett-Woodmere UFSD	Woodmere
41	14,357	Chappaqua CSD	Chappaqua
42	14,333	Amityville UFSD	Amityville
43	14,332	Croton-Harmon UFSD	Croton-On-Hud
44	14,294	Haverstraw-Stony Point CSD	Garnerville
45	14,246	Hendrick Hudson CSD	Montrose
46	14,198	Peekskill City SD	Peekskill
47	14,187	Rockville Centre UFSD	Rockville Ctre
48	14,086	Irvington UFSD	Irvington
49	14,037	Ramapo CSD (Suffern)	Hillburn
50	14,013	Somers CSD	Lincolndale
51	14,010	Onteora CSD	Boiceville
52	13,977	Edgemont UFSD	Scarsdale
53	13,915	Bethpage UFSD	Bethpage
54	13,877	Mamaroneck UFSD	Mamaroneck
55	13,868	Westhampton Beach UFSD	Westhampton Bch
56	13,737	Rye City SD	Rye
57	13,726	Eastchester UFSD	Eastchester
58	13,715	West Hempstead UFSD	W Hempstead
59	13,676	Westbury UFSD	Old Westbury
60	13,618	Herricks UFSD	New Hyde Park
61	13,595	Glen Cove City SD	Glen Cove
62	13,578	Bay Shore UFSD	Bay Shore
63	13,564	Connetquot CSD	Bohemia
64	13,557	Bayport-Blue Point UFSD	Bayport
65	13,519	South Huntington UFSD	Huntington Stn
66	13,505	Cold Spring Harbor CSD	Cold Sprg Harbor
67	13,449	Hempstead UFSD	Hempstead
68	13,423	Valley Stream Central HSD	Valley Stream
69	13,407	Ossining UFSD	Ossining
70	13,271	Yonkers City SD	Yonkers
71	13,267	Northport-East Northport UFSD	Northport
72	13,222	Sayville UFSD	Sayville
73	13,167	Deer Park UFSD	Deer Park
74	13,163	Hastings-On-Hudson UFSD	Hastings-on-Hud
75	13,126	Garden City UFSD	Garden City
76	13,099	Salmon River CSD	Ft Covington
77	13,088	Shoreham-Wading River CSD	Shoreham
78	13,065	Pearl River UFSD	Pearl River
79	12,991	Half Hollow Hills CSD	Dix Hills
80	12,988	Bellmore-Merrick Central HSD	North Merrick
81	12,984	East Meadow UFSD	Westbury
82	12,954	Farmingdale UFSD	Farmingdale
83	12,942	Brewster CSD	Brewster
84	12,931	Ellenville CSD	Ellenville
85	12,860	Liberty CSD	Liberty
86	12,841	Ardsley UFSD	Ardsley
86	12,841	Hicksville UFSD	Hicksville
88	12,832	Copiague UFSD	Copiague
89	12,793	Pelham UFSD	Pelham
90	12,790	Levittown UFSD	Levittown
91	12,759	Smithtown CSD	Smithtown
92	12,750	Riverhead CSD	Riverhead
93	12,685	Pleasantville UFSD	Pleasantville
94	12,551	Rondout Valley CSD	Accord
95	12,463	Dunkirk City SD	Dunkirk
96	12,452	Rush-Henrietta CSD	Henrietta
97	12,427	Carmel CSD	Patterson
98	12,424	Buffalo City SD	Buffalo
99	12,423	Longwood CSD	Middle Island
100	12,408	Lynbrook UFSD	Lynbrook
101	12,383	Three Village CSD	East Setauket
102	12,311	Mattituck-Cutchogue UFSD	Cutchogue
103	12,226	Seaford UFSD	Seaford
104	12,156	Byram Hills CSD	Armonk
105	12,154	Sullivan West CSD	Jeffersonville
106	12,150	Brentwood UFSD	Brentwood
107	12,110	Poughkeepsie City SD	Poughkeepsie
108	12,096	Mount Sinai UFSD	Mount Sinai
109	12,095	Troy City SD	Troy
110	12,089	Sachem CSD	Holbrook
111	12,068	Rochester City SD	Rochester
112	12,066	Lakeland CSD	Shrub Oak
113	12,063	Elwood UFSD	Greenlawn
114	12,027	New Rochelle City SD	New Rochelle
115	12,003	Peru CSD	Peru
116	11,988	Lackawanna City SD	Lackawanna
117	11,967	Babylon UFSD	Babylon
118	11,953	Plainedge UFSD	N Massapequa
119	11,942	Mahopac CSD	Mahopac
120	11,931	Massapequa UFSD	Massapequa
121	11,921	Roosevelt UFSD	Roosevelt
122	11,836	Oceanside UFSD	Oceanside
123	11,835	Brookhaven-Comsewogue UFSD	Pt Jefferson Stn
124	11,827	Baldwin UFSD	Baldwin
125	11,783	Port Chester-Rye UFSD	Port Chester
126	11,746	Clarkstown CSD	New City
127	11,726	East Islip UFSD	Islip Terrace
128	11,712	Spackenkill UFSD	Poughkeepsie
129	11,706	Albany City SD	Albany
130	11,681	William Floyd UFSD	Mastic Beach
131	11,639	Valley Stream 30 UFSD	Valley Stream
132	11,601	Ithaca City SD	Ithaca
133	11,583	Ravena-Coeymans-Selkirk CSD	Selkirk
133	11,583	Schuylerville CSD	Schuylerville
135	11,566	Island Trees UFSD	Levittown
136	11,559	Commack UFSD	E Northport
137	11,545	Wantagh UFSD	Wantagh
138	11,542	Plattsburgh City SD	Plattsburgh
139	11,510	Mount Vernon City SD	Mount Vernon
140	11,499	West Babylon UFSD	West Babylon
141	11,496	Depew UFSD	Depew
142	11,494	Kings Park CSD	Kings Park
143	11,482	Islip UFSD	Islip
144	11,468	Batavia City SD	Batavia
145	11,466	Yorktown CSD	Yorktown Hgts
146	11,458	Patchogue-Medford UFSD	Patchogue
147	11,453	North Babylon UFSD	North Babylon
148	11,426	Niagara Falls City SD	Niagara Falls
149	11,398	Lewiston-Porter CSD	Youngstown
150	11,393	Johnson City CSD	Johnson City
151	11,380	Monticello CSD	Monticello
152	11,342	Marlboro CSD	Marlboro
153	11,321	Freeport UFSD	Freeport
154	11,289	Indian River CSD	Philadelphia
155	11,256	Hampton Bays UFSD	Hampton Bays
156	11,117	Cheektowaga-Maryvale UFSD	Cheektowaga
157	11,112	New York City Public Schools	Brooklyn

158	11,104	Harborfields CSD	Greenlawn
159	11,072	Gouverneur CSD	Gouverneur
160	11,060	Sewanhaka Central HSD	Floral Park
161	11,058	Cheektowaga-Sloan UFSD	Sloan
162	11,055	New Paltz CSD	New Paltz
163	11,047	Saranac Lake CSD	Saranac Lake
164	11,031	Ogdensburg City SD	Ogdensburg
165	11,000	Schalmont CSD	Schenectady
166	10,958	Middletown City SD	Middletown
167	10,957	Goshen CSD	Goshen
168	10,923	Miller Place UFSD	Miller Place
169	10,904	Malone CSD	Malone
170	10,895	West Islip UFSD	West Islip
171	10,869	East Syracuse-Minoa CSD	East Syracuse
172	10,856	Hudson City SD	Hudson
173	10,846	Niagara-Wheatfield CSD	Niagara Falls
174	10,843	Sweet Home CSD	Amherst
175	10,800	Pittsford CSD	Pittsford
176	10,749	Taconic Hills CSD	Craryville
177	10,740	Cohoes City SD	Cohoes
178	10,708	Merrick UFSD	Merrick
179	10,692	Brighton CSD	Rochester
180	10,652	Highland CSD	Highland
181	10,632	Syracuse City SD	Syracuse
182	10,630	Monroe-Woodbury CSD	Central Valley
183	10,611	Salamanca City SD	Salamanca
184	10,582	Oswego City SD	Oswego
185	10,565	Lindenhurst UFSD	Lindenhurst
186	10,560	Gorham-Middlesex CSD	Rushville
187	10,528	Phoenix CSD	Phoenix
188	10,499	Rome City SD	Rome
189	10,458	Gates-Chili CSD	Rochester
190	10,455	Kenmore-Tonawanda UFSD	Buffalo
191	10,423	Cobleskill-Richmondville CSD	Cobleskill
192	10,390	Northeastern Clinton CSD	Champlain
193	10,358	Middle Country CSD	Centereach
194	10,343	Newburgh City SD	Newburgh
195	10,341	Yorkshire-Pioneer CSD	Yorkshire
196	10,340	Kingston City SD	Kingston
197	10,315	Jamesville-Dewitt CSD	Dewitt
198	10,313	Wallkill CSD	Wallkill
199	10,244	Catskill CSD	Catskill
200	10,243	Elmira City SD	Elmira
201	10,229	Lansing CSD	Lansing
202	10,223	Dryden CSD	Dryden
203	10,213	North Rose-Wolcott CSD	Wolcott
204	10,205	Liverpool CSD	Liverpool
205	10,175	Cleveland Hill UFSD	Cheektowaga
206	10,172	North Bellmore UFSD	Bellmore
207	10,170	Valley Stream 13 UFSD	Valley Stream
208	10,158	Norwich City SD	Norwich
209	10,146	Wilson CSD	Wilson
210	10,127	Fonda-Fultonville CSD	Fonda
211	10,125	Newark CSD	Newark
212	10,122	New Hartford CSD	New Hartford
213	10,115	Amherst CSD	Amherst
214	10,110	Port Jervis City SD	Port Jervis
215	10,105	East Greenbush CSD	E Greenbush
216	10,079	Hyde Park CSD	Poughkeepsie
217	10,073	East Irondequoit CSD	Rochester
218	10,051	Owego-Apalachin CSD	Owego
219	10,050	Rocky Point UFSD	Rocky Point
220	10,047	Oneonta City SD	Oneonta
221	10,046	Penfield CSD	Penfield
222	10,023	Fulton City SD	Fulton
223	10,015	Schenectady City SD	Schenectady
224	9,995	Greece CSD	Rochester
225	9,964	Binghamton City SD	Binghamton
226	9,943	Beekmantown CSD	Plattsburgh
227	9,938	Altmar-Parish-Williamstown CSD	Parish
228	9,927	Oneida City SD	Oneida
229	9,919	Jamestown City SD	Jamestown
230	9,909	Tonawanda City SD	Tonawanda
231	9,900	Geneva City SD	Geneva
232	9,893	Chatham CSD	Chatham
233	9,823	Warwick Valley CSD	Warwick
234	9,808	Brockport CSD	Brockport
235	9,761	Williamsville CSD	East Amherst
236	9,755	Ballston Spa CSD	Ballston Spa
237	9,753	Pine Bush CSD	Pine Bush
238	9,726	Palmyra-Macedon CSD	Palmyra
239	9,722	Wayland-Cohocton CSD	Wayland
240	9,720	Union-Endicott CSD	Endicott
241	9,705	Canton CSD	Canton
242	9,702	Lansingburgh CSD	Troy
243	9,698	Webster CSD	Webster
244	9,695	Red Hook CSD	Red Hook
245	9,693	Beacon City SD	Beacon
246	9,692	Shenendehowa CSD	Clifton Park
247	9,681	Gloversville City SD	Gloversville
248	9,677	Orchard Park CSD	Orchard Park
249	9,653	Corning City SD	Painted Post
250	9,644	Penn Yan CSD	Pen
251	9,638	Franklin Square UFSD	Franklin Square
252	9,622	Maine-Endwell CSD	Endwell
252	9,622	South Colonie CSD	Albany
254	9,617	Guilderland CSD	Guilderland
255	9,613	Chenango Valley CSD	Binghamton
256	9,585	Burnt Hills-Ballston Lake CSD	Scotia
257	9,577	Evans-Brant CSD (Lake Shore)	Angola
258	9,573	Hudson Falls CSD	Hudson Falls
259	9,566	Cortland City SD	Cortland
259	9,566	Susquehanna Valley CSD	Conklin
261	9,559	Seneca Falls CSD	Seneca Falls
262	9,553	Chenango Forks CSD	Binghamton
263	9,531	Spencerport CSD	Spencerport
264	9,527	Utica City SD	Utica
265	9,518	Niskayuna CSD	Schenectady
266	9,511	Akron CSD	Akron
267	9,509	Adirondack CSD	Boonville
268	9,500	Elmont UFSD	Elmont
269	9,499	Hamburg CSD	Hamburg
270	9,478	Fairport CSD	Fairport
271	9,476	Sherburne-Earlville CSD	Sherburne
272	9,466	Grand Island CSD	Grand Island
273	9,461	Honeoye Falls-Lima CSD	Honeoye Falls
274	9,448	Alden CSD	Alden
275	9,436	Lockport City SD	Lockport
276	9,389	West Seneca CSD	West Seneca
277	9,383	Wappingers CSD	Wappingers Fls
278	9,380	Carthage CSD	Carthage
279	9,358	North Tonawanda City SD	N Tonawanda
280	9,357	Victor CSD	Victor
281	9,351	Dansville CSD	Dansville
282	9,347	Minisink Valley CSD	Slate Hill
283	9,304	Churchville-Chili CSD	Churchville
284	9,301	Holland Patent CSD	Holland Patent
285	9,276	Horseheads CSD	Horseheads
286	9,274	West Irondequoit CSD	Rochester
287	9,263	Bethlehem CSD	Delmar
288	9,261	Medina CSD	Medina
289	9,260	Hornell City SD	Hornell
290	9,255	Fredonia CSD	Fredonia
291	9,251	Averill Park CSD	Averill Park
292	9,240	Canandaigua City SD	Canandaigua
293	9,230	Massena CSD	Massena
294	9,216	Cheektowaga CSD	Cheektowaga
295	9,215	Amsterdam City SD	Amsterdam
296	9,204	Canastota CSD	Canastota
296	9,204	Royalton-Hartland CSD	Middleport
298	9,198	Springville-Griffith Inst CSD	Springville
299	9,189	New Hyde Pk-Garden City Pk UFSD	New Hyde Park
300	9,175	Saratoga Springs City SD	Saratoga Spgs
300	9,175	Scotia-Glenville CSD	Scotia
302	9,156	Newfane CSD	Newfane
303	9,150	Fayetteville-Manlius CSD	Manlius
304	9,149	Hilton CSD	Hilton
305	9,097	Whitesboro CSD	Yorkville
306	9,077	Baldwinsville CSD	Baldwinsville
307	9,074	Waterloo CSD	Waterloo
308	9,070	Cornwall CSD	Cornwall-on-Hud
309	9,049	Phelps-Clifton Springs CSD	Clifton Spgs
310	9,043	Southwestern CSD at Jamestown	Jamestown
311	9,040	Saugerties CSD	Saugerties
312	9,038	Hannibal CSD	Hannibal
313	9,036	Kinderhook CSD	Valatie
313	9,036	Sherrill City SD	Verona
315	9,026	Floral Park-Bellerose UFSD	Floral Park
316	9,015	East Aurora UFSD	East Aurora
317	9,003	Dover UFSD	Dover Plains
317	9,003	Washingtonville CSD	Washingtonville
319	8,983	Saranac CSD	Dannemora
320	8,957	Valley CSD (Montgomery)	Montgomery
321	8,939	Glens Falls City SD	Glens Falls
322	8,934	Vestal CSD	Vestal
323	8,932	Olean City SD	Olean
324	8,915	South Glens Falls CSD	S Glens Falls
325	8,901	Auburn City SD	Auburn
326	8,890	Jordan-Elbridge CSD	Jordan
327	8,835	Windsor CSD	Windsor
328	8,829	Watertown City SD	Watertown
329	8,778	Homer CSD	Homer
330	8,767	North Colonie CSD	Latham
331	8,766	Bath CSD	Bath
332	8,749	Arlington CSD	Poughkeepsie
333	8,737	Coxsackie-Athens CSD	Coxsackie
334	8,735	Livonia CSD	Livonia
335	8,733	Camden CSD	Camden
336	8,731	North Syracuse CSD	N Syracuse
337	8,700	Skaneateles CSD	Skaneateles
338	8,669	Cazenovia CSD	Cazenovia
339	8,667	Frontier CSD	Hamburg
340	8,666	Clarence CSD	Clarence
340	8,666	Lancaster CSD	Lancaster
342	8,642	Westhill CSD	Syracuse
343	8,638	Wayne CSD	Ontario Center
344	8,633	Iroquois CSD	Elma
345	8,630	Waverly CSD	Waverly
346	8,617	Whitney Point CSD	Whitney Point
347	8,593	Johnstown City SD	Johnstown
348	8,580	Mexico CSD	Mexico
349	8,566	Attica CSD	Attica
350	8,499	Cairo-Durham CSD	Cairo
351	8,473	Central Square CSD	Central Square
352	8,400	Solvay UFSD	Solvay
353	8,350	Starpoint CSD	Lockport
354	8,248	Eden CSD	Eden
355	8,231	Chittenango CSD	Chittenango
356	8,154	South Jefferson CSD	Adams Center
357	8,093	Marcellus CSD	Marcellus
358	8,075	Rotterdam-Mohonasen CSD	Schenectady
359	8,036	Ilion CSD	Ilion
360	8,016	Clinton CSD	Clinton
361	7,989	Queensbury UFSD	Queensbury
362	7,967	West Genesee CSD	Camillus
363	7,918	General Brown CSD	Dexter
364	7,916	Albion CSD	Albion
365	7,898	Broadalbin-Perth CSD	Broadalbin
366	n/a	Boces Eastern Suffolk (Suffolk I)	Patchogue
366	n/a	Boces Monroe 1	Fairport
366	n/a	Boces Nassau	Garden City

Number of Diploma Recipients

Rank	Number	District Name	City
1	37,915	New York City Public Schools	Brooklyn
2	1,638	Buffalo City SD	Buffalo
3	1,135	Sewanhaka Central HSD	Floral Park
4	1,021	Rochester City SD	Rochester
5	910	Sachem CSD	Holbrook
6	901	Greece CSD	Rochester
7	812	Bellmore-Merrick Central HSD	North Merrick
8	773	Williamsville CSD	East Amherst
9	761	Wappingers CSD	Wappingers Fls
10	724	Yonkers City SD	Yonkers
11	681	Clarkstown CSD	New City
12	670	Middle Country CSD	Centereach
13	641	Brentwood UFSD	Brentwood
14	629	Valley Stream Central HSD	Valley Stream
15	627	Syracuse City SD	Syracuse
16	624	Kenmore-Tonawanda UFSD	Buffalo
17	600	Webster CSD	Webster
18	582	North Syracuse CSD	N Syracuse
19	580	Shenendehowa CSD	Clifton Park
20	556	Smithtown CSD	Smithtown
21	552	West Seneca CSD	West Seneca
22	543	Half Hollow Hills CSD	Dix Hills
23	526	East Ramapo CSD (Spring Valley)	Spring Valley
24	516	Great Neck UFSD	Great Neck
24	516	Longwood CSD	Middle Island
26	512	Liverpool CSD	Liverpool
27	507	East Meadow UFSD	Westbury
28	501	Arlington CSD	Poughkeepsie
29	496	Massapequa UFSD	Massapequa
29	496	Patchogue-Medford UFSD	Patchogue
31	489	Fairport CSD	Fairport
32	485	Kingston City SD	Kingston
33	482	Newburgh City SD	Newburgh
34	479	New Rochelle City SD	New Rochelle
35	472	Lakeland CSD	Shrub Oak
35	472	Three Village CSD	East Setauket
37	461	Saratoga Springs City SD	Saratoga Spgs
38	455	Levittown UFSD	Levittown
38	455	William Floyd UFSD	Mastic Beach
40	454	North Colonie CSD	Latham
41	445	Syosset CSD	Syosset
42	443	Pittsford CSD	Pittsford
43	442	Haverstraw-Stony Point CSD	Garnerville
44	419	Lindenhurst UFSD	Lindenhurst
45	412	Lancaster CSD	Lancaster
46	411	Monroe-Woodbury CSD	Central Valley
47	408	Commack UFSD	E Northport
48	406	Orchard Park CSD	Orchard Park
49	390	West Genesee CSD	Camillus
50	389	South Colonie CSD	Albany
51	385	North Babylon UFSD	North Babylon
52	382	Albany City SD	Albany
53	380	Oceanside UFSD	Oceanside
54	379	Gates-Chili CSD	Rochester
55	374	Connetquot CSD	Bohemia
55	374	Guilderland CSD	Guilderland
57	367	Farmingdale UFSD	Farmingdale
58	362	Niagara Falls City SD	Niagara Falls
59	360	White Plains City SD	White Plains
60	358	Corning City SD	Painted Post
60	358	Schenectady City SD	Schenectady
62	357	Bethlehem CSD	Delmar
63	349	Rush-Henrietta CSD	Henrietta

64	348	Mahopac CSD	Mahopac
65	346	Baldwin UFSD	Baldwin
66	341	Plainview-Old Bethpage CSD	Plainview
66	341	Utica City SD	Utica
68	340	Frontier CSD	Hamburg
69	339	Clarence CSD	Clarence
70	337	Mount Vernon City SD	Mount Vernon
71	335	North Tonawanda City SD	N Tonawanda
72	330	Hilton CSD	Hilton
73	329	Northport-East Northport UFSD	Northport
74	326	Ithaca City SD	Ithaca
75	324	Elmira City SD	Elmira
76	320	Baldwinsville CSD	Baldwinsville
76	320	Horseheads CSD	Horseheads
78	319	Hamburg CSD	Hamburg
79	317	South Huntington UFSD	Huntington Stn
80	315	West Irondequoit CSD	Rochester
81	312	Washingtonville CSD	Washingtonville
82	311	Fayetteville-Manlius CSD	Manlius
83	310	Hicksville UFSD	Hicksville
84	308	Valley CSD (Montgomery)	Montgomery
85	307	Uniondale UFSD	Uniondale
86	306	Pine Bush CSD	Pine Bush
87	302	Lockport City SD	Lockport
87	302	Penfield CSD	Penfield
87	302	West Islip UFSD	West Islip
90	300	East Islip UFSD	Islip Terrace
91	298	Churchville-Chili CSD	Churchville
92	296	Vestal CSD	Vestal
93	292	Spencerport CSD	Spencerport
94	290	Brockport CSD	Brockport
95	289	Mamaroneck UFSD	Mamaroneck
96	288	Carmel CSD	Patterson
97	287	Bay Shore UFSD	Bay Shore
98	283	South Country CSD	E Patchogue
99	282	Port Washington UFSD	Pt Washington
100	281	East Greenbush CSD	E Greenbush
100	281	Freeport UFSD	Freeport
102	280	Niskayuna CSD	Schenectady
102	280	West Babylon UFSD	West Babylon
104	279	Union-Endicott CSD	Endicott
105	278	Auburn City SD	Auburn
105	278	Central Islip UFSD	Central Islip
105	278	Jamestown City SD	Jamestown
108	277	Ramapo CSD (Suffern)	Hillburn
109	276	Herricks UFSD	New Hyde Park
109	276	Rome City SD	Rome
111	274	East Syracuse-Minoa CSD	East Syracuse
112	272	Niagara-Wheatfield CSD	Niagara Falls
113	267	Hewlett-Woodmere UFSD	Woodmere
113	267	Scarsdale UFSD	Scarsdale
115	264	Middletown City SD	Middletown
116	260	Yorktown CSD	Yorktown Hgts
117	259	Brighton CSD	Rochester
117	259	Hauppauge UFSD	Hauppauge
119	258	Rockville Centre UFSD	Rockville Ctre
120	257	Chappaqua CSD	Chappaqua
120	257	Warwick Valley CSD	Warwick
120	257	Whitesboro CSD	Yorkville
123	253	Binghamton City SD	Binghamton
123	253	Hyde Park CSD	Poughkeepsie
123	253	Oswego City SD	Oswego
126	249	Central Square CSD	Central Square
127	247	Bedford CSD	Mount Kisco
127	247	Kings Park CSD	Kings Park
129	246	Minisink Valley CSD	Slate Hill
130	245	Sweet Home CSD	Amherst
131	244	Canandaigua City SD	Canandaigua
132	241	Lawrence UFSD	Lawrence
133	238	Riverhead CSD	Riverhead
134	234	Long Beach City SD	Long Beach
135	222	Iroquois CSD	Elma
135	222	New Hartford CSD	New Hartford
137	219	Averill Park CSD	Averill Park
137	219	Sayville UFSD	Sayville
139	218	Scotia-Glenville CSD	Scotia
140	215	Ballston Spa CSD	Ballston Spa
141	214	Garden City UFSD	Garden City
141	214	Yorkshire-Pioneer CSD	Yorkshire
143	213	Burnt Hills-Ballston Lake CSD	Scotia
143	213	Fulton City SD	Fulton
143	213	Miller Place UFSD	Miller Place
146	212	Amherst CSD	Amherst
147	211	Queensbury UFSD	Queensbury
147	211	Westhampton Beach UFSD	Westhampton Bch
149	209	Roslyn UFSD	Roslyn
150	208	Katonah-Lewisboro UFSD	South Salem
151	205	Copiague UFSD	Copiague
151	205	Huntington UFSD	Huntington Stn
153	203	Brewster CSD	Brewster
153	203	East Irondequoit CSD	Rochester
153	203	Islip UFSD	Islip
153	203	Ossining UFSD	Ossining

153	203	Plainedge UFSD	N Massapequa
153	203	Wallkill CSD	Wallkill
159	201	Mineola UFSD	Mineola
159	201	Rotterdam-Mohonasen CSD	Schenectady
161	199	Victor CSD	Victor
162	198	Cornwall CSD	Cornwall-on-Hud
162	198	Deer Park UFSD	Deer Park
164	195	Grand Island CSD	Grand Island
165	194	West Hempstead UFSD	W Hempstead
166	193	Carthage CSD	Carthage
167	192	Glen Cove City SD	Glen Cove
167	192	Port Jervis City SD	Port Jervis
169	191	Jericho UFSD	Jericho
169	191	Rondout Valley CSD	Accord
169	191	Wantagh UFSD	Wantagh
172	190	Port Chester-Rye UFSD	Port Chester
172	190	Saugerties CSD	Saugerties
174	189	Brookhaven-Comsewogue UFSD	Pt Jefferson Stn
174	189	Harborfields CSD	Greenlawn
176	188	Evans-Brant CSD (Lake Shore)	Angola
176	188	Lynbrook UFSD	Lynbrook
176	188	Malone CSD	Malone
179	186	Lewiston-Porter CSD	Youngstown
180	184	East Hampton UFSD	East Hampton
181	180	Bethpage UFSD	Bethpage
181	180	Cortland City SD	Cortland
183	179	Jamesville-Dewitt CSD	Dewitt
184	177	Pearl River UFSD	Pearl River
185	176	Goshen CSD	Goshen
185	176	Hendrick Hudson CSD	Montrose
185	176	Homer CSD	Homer
188	175	Sherrill City SD	Verona
189	174	Phoenix CSD	Phoenix
189	174	Tonawanda City SD	Tonawanda
191	173	Watertown City SD	Watertown
192	171	Somers CSD	Lincolndale
193	170	Manhasset UFSD	Manhasset
194	169	Shoreham-Wading River CSD	Shoreham
195	167	Massena CSD	Massena
195	167	Ravena-Coeymans-Selkirk CSD	Selkirk
195	167	Westhill CSD	Syracuse
198	166	Byram Hills CSD	Armonk
198	166	Gloversville City SD	Gloversville
198	166	Nyack UFSD	Nyack
198	166	Owego-Apalachin CSD	Owego
198	166	Seaford UFSD	Seaford
203	165	Cheektowaga CSD	Cheektowaga
203	165	Chittenango CSD	Chittenango
203	165	Newark CSD	Newark
203	165	South Orangetown CSD	Blauvelt
207	164	Honeoye Falls-Lima CSD	Honeoye Falls
208	163	Harrison CSD	Harrison
208	163	Wayne CSD	Ontario Center
210	162	Mexico CSD	Mexico
211	161	Schalmont CSD	Schenectady
211	161	South Glens Falls CSD	S Glens Falls
213	160	Cheektowaga-Maryvale UFSD	Cheektowaga
213	160	Rocky Point UFSD	Rocky Point
215	159	Camden CSD	Camden
215	159	Oneida City SD	Oneida
217	157	Westbury UFSD	Old Westbury
218	156	Johnson City CSD	Johnson City
218	156	Newfane CSD	Newfane
218	156	Springville-Griffith Inst CSD	Springville
221	155	Indian River CSD	Philadelphia
221	155	Plattsburgh City SD	Plattsburgh
223	154	Hempstead UFSD	Hempstead
223	154	Skaneateles CSD	Skaneateles
223	154	Starpoint CSD	Lockport
226	153	Poughkeepsie City SD	Poughkeepsie
227	152	Albion CSD	Albion
227	152	Batavia City SD	Batavia
227	152	Fredonia CSD	Fredonia
227	152	Penn Yan CSD	Pen
231	151	Depew UFSD	Depew
231	151	Southampton UFSD	Southampton
233	150	Alden CSD	Alden
233	150	East Aurora UFSD	East Aurora
235	149	Geneva City SD	Geneva
235	149	Peru CSD	Peru
237	148	Clinton CSD	Clinton
237	148	Oneonta City SD	Oneonta
239	147	Glens Falls City SD	Glens Falls
240	146	Amityville UFSD	Amityville
240	146	Livonia CSD	Livonia
242	145	Attica CSD	Attica
243	144	Beacon City SD	Beacon
244	143	Kinderhook CSD	Valatie
244	143	Mount Sinai UFSD	Mount Sinai
246	141	Babylon UFSD	Babylon
246	141	Monticello CSD	Monticello
246	141	Olean City SD	Olean

246	141	Susquehanna Valley CSD	Conklin
246	141	Wayland-Cohocton CSD	Wayland
251	140	Cobleskill-Richmondville CSD	Cobleskill
251	140	Highland CSD	Highland
251	140	Island Trees UFSD	Levittown
251	140	Johnstown City SD	Johnstown
255	139	Maine-Endwell CSD	Endwell
255	139	Palmyra-Macedon CSD	Palmyra
257	138	Bayport-Blue Point UFSD	Bayport
258	135	Pelham UFSD	Pelham
258	135	Phelps-Clifton Springs CSD	Clifton Spgs
260	134	Bath CSD	Bath
261	133	Norwich City SD	Norwich
261	133	Saranac CSD	Dannemora
263	132	Marcellus CSD	Marcellus
263	132	North Shore CSD	Sea Cliff
263	132	Southwestern CSD at Jamestown	Jamestown
266	131	Elwood UFSD	Greenlawn
266	131	Locust Valley CSD	Locust Valley
268	130	Chenango Valley CSD	Binghamton
268	130	Peekskill City SD	Peekskill
270	129	Holland Patent CSD	Holland Patent
271	128	Broadalbin-Perth CSD	Broadalbin
271	128	Chenango Forks CSD	Binghamton
271	128	Hudson Falls CSD	Hudson Falls
274	127	East Williston UFSD	Old Westbury
274	127	Ogdensburg City SD	Ogdensburg
276	126	Red Hook CSD	Red Hook
277	123	Ardsley UFSD	Ardsley
277	123	South Jefferson CSD	Adams Center
279	122	Medina CSD	Medina
280	121	Cold Spring Harbor CSD	Cold Sprg Harbor
280	121	Fonda-Fultonville CSD	Fonda
280	121	General Brown CSD	Dexter
280	121	Rye City SD	Rye
284	120	Nanuet UFSD	Nanuet
285	119	Gouverneur CSD	Gouverneur
285	119	Sullivan West CSD	Jeffersonville
287	118	Mount Pleasant CSD	Thornwood
287	118	New Paltz CSD	New Paltz
289	117	Greenburgh CSD	Hartsdale
289	117	Royalton-Hartland CSD	Middleport
291	116	Jordan-Elbridge CSD	Jordan
291	116	Solvay UFSD	Solvay
293	114	Ilion CSD	Ilion
293	114	Schuylerville CSD	Schuylerville
293	114	Wilson CSD	Wilson
296	113	Beekmantown CSD	Plattsburgh
296	113	Briarcliff Manor UFSD	Briarcliff Manor
298	112	Mattituck-Cutchogue UFSD	Cutchogue
298	112	Onteora CSD	Boiceville
298	112	Saranac Lake CSD	Saranac Lake
301	111	Adirondack CSD	Boonville
301	111	Eden CSD	Eden
301	111	Spackenkill UFSD	Poughkeepsie
301	111	UFSD - Tarrytowns	Sleepy Hollow
301	111	Windsor CSD	Windsor
306	110	Dunkirk City SD	Dunkirk
306	110	Lansing CSD	Lansing
308	109	Lackawanna City SD	Lackawanna
309	108	Cazenovia CSD	Cazenovia
309	108	Oyster Bay-East Norwich CSD	Oyster Bay
311	107	Cohoes City SD	Cohoes
311	107	Dansville CSD	Dansville
311	107	Malverne UFSD	Malverne
311	107	Seneca Falls CSD	Seneca Falls
315	106	Dryden CSD	Dryden
315	106	Marlboro CSD	Marlboro
315	106	Pleasantville UFSD	Pleasantville
318	105	Canastota CSD	Canastota
318	105	Eastchester UFSD	Eastchester
318	105	Gowanda CSD	Gowanda
321	104	Cheektowaga-Sloan UFSD	Sloan
321	104	Dover UFSD	Dover Plains
321	104	Edgemont UFSD	Scarsdale
321	104	Hornell City SD	Hornell
321	104	Lansingburgh CSD	Troy
326	103	Carle Place UFSD	Carle Place
326	103	Northeastern Clinton CSD	Champlain
328	100	Sherburne-Earlville CSD	Sherburne
328	100	Waterloo CSD	Waterloo
330	99	Chatham CSD	Chatham
330	99	Gorham-Middlesex CSD	Rushville
332	98	Akron CSD	Akron
332	98	Coxsackie-Athens CSD	Coxsackie
332	98	Whitney Point CSD	Whitney Point
335	97	Canton CSD	Canton
335	97	Troy City SD	Troy
337	95	North Rose-Wolcott CSD	Wolcott
337	95	Waverly CSD	Waverly
339	94	Hannibal CSD	Hannibal
340	92	Irvington UFSD	Irvington
341	91	Altmar-Parish-Williamstown CSD	Parish

342	90	Hudson City SD	Hudson
343	88	Salmon River CSD	Ft Covington
344	86	Roosevelt UFSD	Roosevelt
344	86	Taconic Hills CSD	Craryville
346	79	Catskill CSD	Catskill
347	78	Cleveland Hill UFSD	Cheektowaga
347	78	Ellenville CSD	Ellenville
349	77	Liberty CSD	Liberty
350	74	Cairo-Durham CSD	Cairo
350	74	Hastings-On-Hudson UFSD	Hastings-on-Hud
352	73	Croton-Harmon UFSD	Croton-On-Hud
353	71	Salamanca City SD	Salamanca
354	66	Wyandanch UFSD	Wyandanch
355	0	Amsterdam City SD	Amsterdam
355	0	Hampton Bays UFSD	Hampton Bays
357	n/a	Boces Eastern Suffolk (Suffolk I)	Patchogue
357	n/a	Boces Monroe 1	Fairport
357	n/a	Boces Nassau	Garden City
357	n/a	Elmont UFSD	Elmont
357	n/a	Floral Park-Bellerose UFSD	Floral Park
357	n/a	Franklin Square UFSD	Franklin Square
357	n/a	Merrick UFSD	Merrick
357	n/a	New Hyde Pk-Garden City Pk UFSD	New Hyde Park
357	n/a	North Bellmore UFSD	Bellmore
357	n/a	Putnam Valley CSD	Putnam Valley
357	n/a	Valley Stream 13 UFSD	Valley Stream
357	n/a	Valley Stream 30 UFSD	Valley Stream

High School Drop-out Rate

Rank	Percent	District Name	City
1	11.9	Central Islip UFSD	Central Islip
2	10.4	Hempstead UFSD	Hempstead
3	9.9	Rochester City SD	Rochester
4	9.8	Port Chester-Rye UFSD	Port Chester
5	9.7	North Rose-Wolcott CSD	Wolcott
6	8.5	Elmira City SD	Elmira
7	7.9	Ogdensburg City SD	Ogdensburg
8	7.0	Waverly CSD	Waverly
9	6.7	Schenectady City SD	Schenectady
10	6.5	Hudson City SD	Hudson
10	6.5	New York City Public Schools	Brooklyn
10	6.5	Wyandanch UFSD	Wyandanch
13	6.3	Hornell City SD	Hornell
13	6.3	Peru CSD	Peru
13	6.3	Waterloo CSD	Waterloo
16	6.0	Jamestown City SD	Jamestown
17	5.9	Albany City SD	Albany
17	5.9	Medina CSD	Medina
19	5.6	Catskill CSD	Catskill
19	5.6	Port Jervis City SD	Port Jervis
21	5.5	Monticello CSD	Monticello
21	5.5	Syracuse City SD	Syracuse
23	5.3	Dryden CSD	Dryden
23	5.3	Onteora CSD	Boiceville
25	5.2	Whitney Point CSD	Whitney Point
26	5.0	Kingston City SD	Kingston
26	5.0	Phelps-Clifton Springs CSD	Clifton Spgs
26	5.0	Watertown City SD	Watertown
29	4.9	Geneva City SD	Geneva
29	4.9	Salmon River CSD	Ft Covington
31	4.8	Cobleskill-Richmondville CSD	Cobleskill
31	4.8	Johnstown City SD	Johnstown
33	4.7	Newburgh City SD	Newburgh
34	4.6	Seneca Falls CSD	Seneca Falls
35	4.5	Altmar-Parish-Williamstown CSD	Parish
35	4.5	Beekmantown CSD	Plattsburgh
37	4.4	Sherburne-Earlville CSD	Sherburne
38	4.3	Corning City SD	Painted Post
38	4.3	North Babylon UFSD	North Babylon
38	4.3	Pine Bush CSD	Pine Bush
38	4.3	Salamanca City SD	Salamanca
38	4.3	Yorkshire-Pioneer CSD	Yorkshire
43	4.2	Broadalbin-Perth CSD	Broadalbin
43	4.2	Northeastern Clinton CSD	Champlain
43	4.2	Wayland-Cohocton CSD	Wayland
46	4.1	Dansville CSD	Dansville
46	4.1	Mexico CSD	Mexico
48	4.0	Fulton City SD	Fulton
48	4.0	Lansingburgh CSD	Troy
48	4.0	Oneida City SD	Oneida
51	3.9	Amityville UFSD	Amityville
51	3.9	Cohoes City SD	Cohoes
51	3.9	Gouverneur CSD	Gouverneur
51	3.9	Middletown City SD	Middletown
55	3.8	Averill Park CSD	Averill Park
55	3.8	Canastota CSD	Canastota
55	3.8	Gowanda CSD	Gowanda
55	3.8	Plattsburgh City SD	Plattsburgh
59	3.7	Amsterdam City SD	Amsterdam
59	3.7	Cleveland Hill UFSD	Cheektowaga
59	3.7	Horseheads CSD	Horseheads
59	3.7	Marlboro CSD	Marlboro
59	3.7	Massena CSD	Massena
59	3.7	Shenendehowa CSD	Clifton Park
59	3.7	South Country CSD	E Patchogue
59	3.7	Taconic Hills CSD	Craryville
67	3.6	Brookhaven-Comsewogue UFSD	Pt Jefferson Stn
67	3.6	Canton CSD	Canton
67	3.6	Depew UFSD	Depew
67	3.6	Gloversville City SD	Gloversville
67	3.6	Huntington UFSD	Huntington Stn
67	3.6	Ravena-Coeymans-Selkirk CSD	Selkirk
73	3.5	Cheektowaga-Maryvale UFSD	Cheektowaga
73	3.5	Cortland City SD	Cortland
73	3.5	Fonda-Fultonville CSD	Fonda
73	3.5	Haverstraw-Stony Point CSD	Garnerville
73	3.5	Ilion CSD	Ilion
73	3.5	Oswego City SD	Oswego
73	3.5	William Floyd UFSD	Mastic Beach
80	3.4	Grand Island CSD	Grand Island
80	3.4	Johnson City CSD	Johnson City
80	3.4	Norwich City SD	Norwich
80	3.4	Queensbury UFSD	Queensbury
84	3.3	Chatham CSD	Chatham
84	3.3	South Jefferson CSD	Adams Center
84	3.3	UFSD - Tarrytowns	Sleepy Hollow
87	3.2	Dunkirk City SD	Dunkirk
87	3.2	Jordan-Elbridge CSD	Jordan
87	3.2	Liberty CSD	Liberty
87	3.2	Rocky Point UFSD	Rocky Point
87	3.2	Starpoint CSD	Lockport
87	3.2	Wayne CSD	Ontario Center
93	3.1	Ballston Spa CSD	Ballston Spa
93	3.1	Evans-Brant CSD (Lake Shore)	Angola
93	3.1	Newark CSD	Newark
93	3.1	Rush-Henrietta CSD	Henrietta
97	3.0	Batavia City SD	Batavia
97	3.0	Chenango Forks CSD	Binghamton
97	3.0	Highland CSD	Highland
97	3.0	Lackawanna City SD	Lackawanna
97	3.0	Olean City SD	Olean
97	3.0	Red Hook CSD	Red Hook
97	3.0	Westbury UFSD	Old Westbury
104	2.9	Cheektowaga-Sloan UFSD	Sloan
104	2.9	Copiague UFSD	Copiague
104	2.9	Middle Country CSD	Centereach
104	2.9	Windsor CSD	Windsor
108	2.8	East Ramapo CSD (Spring Valley)	Spring Valley
108	2.8	Penn Yan CSD	Pen
108	2.8	Riverhead CSD	Riverhead
108	2.8	Valley CSD (Montgomery)	Montgomery
108	2.8	Wallkill CSD	Wallkill
113	2.7	Saranac CSD	Dannemora
113	2.7	South Colonie CSD	Albany
115	2.6	Binghamton City SD	Binghamton
115	2.6	Rome City SD	Rome
115	2.6	Springville-Griffith Inst CSD	Springville
115	2.6	Union-Endicott CSD	Endicott
119	2.5	Adirondack CSD	Boonville
119	2.5	Hudson Falls CSD	Hudson Falls
119	2.5	Troy City SD	Troy
122	2.4	Central Square CSD	Central Square
122	2.4	Dover UFSD	Dover Plains
122	2.4	East Islip UFSD	Islip Terrace
122	2.4	Mattituck-Cutchogue UFSD	Cutchogue
122	2.4	Palmyra-Macedon CSD	Palmyra
122	2.4	Schalmont CSD	Schenectady
128	2.3	Arlington CSD	Poughkeepsie
128	2.3	East Hampton UFSD	East Hampton
128	2.3	Freeport UFSD	Freeport
128	2.3	Malone CSD	Malone
128	2.3	Ossining UFSD	Ossining
128	2.3	Rondout Valley CSD	Accord
128	2.3	West Genesee CSD	Camillus
135	2.2	Auburn City SD	Auburn
135	2.2	Cheektowaga CSD	Cheektowaga
135	2.2	Saugerties CSD	Saugerties
138	2.1	Brentwood UFSD	Brentwood
138	2.1	Brockport CSD	Brockport
138	2.1	Hamburg CSD	Hamburg
138	2.1	Hampton Bays UFSD	Hampton Bays
138	2.1	Harrison CSD	Harrison
138	2.1	North Tonawanda City SD	N Tonawanda
138	2.1	Sullivan West CSD	Jeffersonville
138	2.1	Uniondale UFSD	Uniondale
146	2.0	Beacon City SD	Beacon
146	2.0	Guilderland CSD	Guilderland
146	2.0	Hannibal CSD	Hannibal
146	2.0	Indian River CSD	Philadelphia
146	2.0	Mount Vernon City SD	Mount Vernon
146	2.0	North Syracuse CSD	N Syracuse
146	2.0	South Huntington UFSD	Huntington Stn
146	2.0	Southwestern CSD at Jamestown	Jamestown
146	2.0	Utica City SD	Utica
155	1.9	Carthage CSD	Carthage
155	1.9	Lockport City SD	Lockport
155	1.9	Phoenix CSD	Phoenix
155	1.9	Valley Stream Central HSD	Valley Stream
155	1.9	Victor CSD	Victor
155	1.9	Yonkers City SD	Yonkers
161	1.8	Camden CSD	Camden
161	1.8	Hyde Park CSD	Poughkeepsie
161	1.8	Lakeland CSD	Shrub Oak
161	1.8	Niagara-Wheatfield CSD	Niagara Falls
161	1.8	Poughkeepsie City SD	Poughkeepsie
161	1.8	Saranac Lake CSD	Saranac Lake
167	1.7	Buffalo City SD	Buffalo
167	1.7	Cazenovia CSD	Cazenovia
167	1.7	Deer Park UFSD	Deer Park
167	1.7	Frontier CSD	Hamburg
167	1.7	Homer CSD	Homer
167	1.7	Kinderhook CSD	Valatie
167	1.7	Livonia CSD	Livonia
167	1.7	Rotterdam-Mohonasen CSD	Schenectady
167	1.7	Sachem CSD	Holbrook
167	1.7	Spackenkill UFSD	Poughkeepsie
167	1.7	West Babylon UFSD	West Babylon
167	1.7	Whitesboro CSD	Yorkville
179	1.6	Alden CSD	Alden
179	1.6	Burnt Hills-Ballston Lake CSD	Scotia
179	1.6	Coxsackie-Athens CSD	Coxsackie
179	1.6	East Irondequoit CSD	Rochester
179	1.6	Lansing CSD	Lansing
179	1.6	Lawrence UFSD	Lawrence
179	1.6	Lindenhurst UFSD	Lindenhurst
179	1.6	Owego-Apalachin CSD	Owego
179	1.6	Patchogue-Medford UFSD	Patchogue
188	1.5	Bath CSD	Bath
188	1.5	East Greenbush CSD	E Greenbush
188	1.5	General Brown CSD	Dexter
188	1.5	Liverpool CSD	Liverpool
188	1.5	Long Beach City SD	Long Beach
188	1.5	Malverne UFSD	Malverne
188	1.5	New Paltz CSD	New Paltz
188	1.5	Saratoga Springs City SD	Saratoga Spgs
188	1.5	Sherrill City SD	Verona
188	1.5	Wappingers CSD	Wappingers Fls
198	1.4	Attica CSD	Attica
198	1.4	Ithaca City SD	Ithaca
198	1.4	Marcellus CSD	Marcellus
198	1.4	Royalton-Hartland CSD	Middleport
202	1.3	Baldwin UFSD	Baldwin
202	1.3	Cornwall CSD	Cornwall-on-Hud
202	1.3	Ellenville CSD	Ellenville
202	1.3	Hilton CSD	Hilton
202	1.3	Kenmore-Tonawanda UFSD	Buffalo
202	1.3	Maine-Endwell CSD	Endwell
202	1.3	Shoreham-Wading River CSD	Shoreham
209	1.2	Carmel CSD	Patterson
209	1.2	Chenango Valley CSD	Binghamton
209	1.2	Goshen CSD	Goshen
209	1.2	Nyack UFSD	Nyack
209	1.2	Peekskill City SD	Peekskill
209	1.2	Seaford UFSD	Seaford
209	1.2	Southampton UFSD	Southampton
209	1.2	West Seneca CSD	West Seneca
217	1.1	Akron CSD	Akron
217	1.1	Canandaigua City SD	Canandaigua
217	1.1	Chittenango CSD	Chittenango
217	1.1	Clarence CSD	Clarence
217	1.1	Hauppauge UFSD	Hauppauge
217	1.1	Lewiston-Porter CSD	Youngstown
217	1.1	Longwood CSD	Middle Island
217	1.1	Nanuet UFSD	Nanuet
217	1.1	North Shore CSD	Sea Cliff
217	1.1	Orchard Park CSD	Orchard Park
217	1.1	Oyster Bay-East Norwich CSD	Oyster Bay
217	1.1	Penfield CSD	Penfield
217	1.1	Schuylerville CSD	Schuylerville
217	1.1	South Orangetown CSD	Blauvelt
217	1.1	West Irondequoit CSD	Rochester
232	1.0	Albion CSD	Albion
232	1.0	Brighton CSD	Rochester
232	1.0	Holland Patent CSD	Holland Patent
232	1.0	Islip UFSD	Islip
232	1.0	Mamaroneck UFSD	Mamaroneck
232	1.0	New Hartford CSD	New Hartford
232	1.0	North Colonie CSD	Latham
232	1.0	Spencerport CSD	Spencerport
232	1.0	Washingtonville CSD	Washingtonville
241	0.9	Bedford CSD	Mount Kisco
241	0.9	Clinton CSD	Clinton
241	0.9	Gates-Chili CSD	Rochester
241	0.9	Lancaster CSD	Lancaster
241	0.9	Mahopac CSD	Mahopac
241	0.9	Mineola UFSD	Mineola
241	0.9	Solvay UFSD	Solvay

Rank	Value	District	City
241	0.9	White Plains City SD	White Plains
241	0.9	Williamsville CSD	East Amherst
250	0.8	Bethlehem CSD	Delmar
250	0.8	Croton-Harmon UFSD	Croton-On-Hud
250	0.8	Elwood UFSD	Greenlawn
250	0.8	Fredonia CSD	Fredonia
250	0.8	Honeoye Falls-Lima CSD	Honeoye Falls
250	0.8	Iroquois CSD	Elma
250	0.8	Plainedge UFSD	N Massapequa
250	0.8	Ramapo CSD (Suffern)	Hillburn
250	0.8	Sweet Home CSD	Amherst
250	0.8	Tonawanda City SD	Tonawanda
250	0.8	Vestal CSD	Vestal
250	0.8	Webster CSD	Webster
250	0.8	West Islip UFSD	West Islip
263	0.7	Bay Shore UFSD	Bay Shore
263	0.7	Bellmore-Merrick Central HSD	North Merrick
263	0.7	Commack UFSD	E Northport
263	0.7	Glens Falls City SD	Glens Falls
263	0.7	Jamesville-Dewitt CSD	Dewitt
263	0.7	Niskayuna CSD	Schenectady
263	0.7	Northport-East Northport UFSD	Northport
263	0.7	Wantagh UFSD	Wantagh
263	0.7	Warwick Valley CSD	Warwick
263	0.7	Westhampton Beach UFSD	Westhampton Bch
273	0.6	Amherst CSD	Amherst
273	0.6	Carle Place UFSD	Carle Place
273	0.6	Connetquot CSD	Bohemia
273	0.6	East Meadow UFSD	Westbury
273	0.6	Farmingdale UFSD	Farmingdale
273	0.6	Greece CSD	Rochester
273	0.6	Minisink Valley CSD	Slate Hill
273	0.6	New Rochelle City SD	New Rochelle
273	0.6	Pearl River UFSD	Pearl River
273	0.6	Rockville Centre UFSD	Rockville Ctre
273	0.6	Somers CSD	Lincolndale
273	0.6	Susquehanna Valley CSD	Conklin
273	0.6	Wilson CSD	Wilson
286	0.5	Bethpage UFSD	Bethpage
286	0.5	Churchville-Chili CSD	Churchville
286	0.5	East Aurora UFSD	East Aurora
286	0.5	East Syracuse-Minoa CSD	East Syracuse
286	0.5	Fairport CSD	Fairport
286	0.5	Glen Cove City SD	Glen Cove
286	0.5	Hicksville UFSD	Hicksville
286	0.5	Island Trees UFSD	Levittown
286	0.5	Katonah-Lewisboro UFSD	South Salem
286	0.5	Mount Pleasant CSD	Thornwood
286	0.5	Oceanside UFSD	Oceanside
286	0.5	Smithtown CSD	Smithtown
286	0.5	West Hempstead UFSD	W Hempstead
286	0.5	Yorktown CSD	Yorktown Hgts
300	0.4	Cairo-Durham CSD	Cairo
300	0.4	Chappaqua CSD	Chappaqua
300	0.4	Clarkstown CSD	New City
300	0.4	Eden CSD	Eden
300	0.4	Half Hollow Hills CSD	Dix Hills
300	0.4	Hendrick Hudson CSD	Montrose
300	0.4	Scotia-Glenville CSD	Scotia
307	0.3	Babylon UFSD	Babylon
307	0.3	Baldwinsville CSD	Baldwinsville
307	0.3	Bayport-Blue Point UFSD	Bayport
307	0.3	Brewster CSD	Brewster
307	0.3	Massapequa UFSD	Massapequa
307	0.3	Monroe-Woodbury CSD	Central Valley
307	0.3	Mount Sinai UFSD	Mount Sinai
307	0.3	Newfane CSD	Newfane
307	0.3	Oneonta City SD	Oneonta
307	0.3	Port Washington UFSD	Pt Washington
307	0.3	Sewanhaka Central HSD	Floral Park
307	0.3	Skaneateles CSD	Skaneateles
319	0.2	Cold Spring Harbor CSD	Cold Sprg Harbor
319	0.2	Edgemont UFSD	Scarsdale
319	0.2	Gorham-Middlesex CSD	Rushville
319	0.2	Hastings-On-Hudson UFSD	Hastings-on-Hud
319	0.2	Herricks UFSD	New Hyde Park
319	0.2	Irvington UFSD	Irvington
319	0.2	Kings Park CSD	Kings Park
319	0.2	Levittown UFSD	Levittown
319	0.2	Pittsford CSD	Pittsford
319	0.2	Rye City SD	Rye
319	0.2	Scarsdale UFSD	Scarsdale
330	0.1	Great Neck UFSD	Great Neck
330	0.1	Harborfields CSD	Greenlawn
330	0.1	Manhasset UFSD	Manhasset
333	0.0	Ardsley UFSD	Ardsley
333	0.0	Byram Hills CSD	Armonk
333	0.0	East Williston UFSD	Old Westbury
333	0.0	Eastchester UFSD	Eastchester
333	0.0	Fayetteville-Manlius CSD	Manlius
333	0.0	Greenburgh CSD	Hartsdale
333	0.0	Hewlett-Woodmere UFSD	Woodmere
333	0.0	Locust Valley CSD	Locust Valley
333	0.0	Lynbrook UFSD	Lynbrook
333	0.0	Miller Place UFSD	Miller Place
333	0.0	Niagara Falls City SD	Niagara Falls
333	0.0	Pelham UFSD	Pelham
333	0.0	Plainview-Old Bethpage CSD	Plainview
333	0.0	Pleasantville UFSD	Pleasantville
333	0.0	Roslyn UFSD	Roslyn
333	0.0	Three Village CSD	East Setauket
333	0.0	Westhill CSD	Syracuse
350	n/a	Boces Eastern Suffolk (Suffolk I)	Patchogue
350	n/a	Boces Monroe 1	Fairport
350	n/a	Boces Nassau	Garden City
350	n/a	Briarcliff Manor UFSD	Briarcliff Manor
350	n/a	Elmont UFSD	Elmont
350	n/a	Floral Park-Bellerose UFSD	Floral Park
350	n/a	Franklin Square UFSD	Franklin Square
350	n/a	Garden City UFSD	Garden City
350	n/a	Jericho UFSD	Jericho
350	n/a	Merrick UFSD	Merrick
350	n/a	New Hyde Pk-Garden City Pk UFSD	New Hyde Park
350	n/a	North Bellmore UFSD	Bellmore
350	n/a	Putnam Valley CSD	Putnam Valley
350	n/a	Roosevelt UFSD	Roosevelt
350	n/a	Sayville UFSD	Sayville
350	n/a	South Glens Falls CSD	S Glens Falls
350	n/a	Syosset CSD	Syosset
350	n/a	Valley Stream 13 UFSD	Valley Stream
350	n/a	Valley Stream 30 UFSD	Valley Stream

North Carolina

North Carolina Public School Educational Profile

Category	Value	Category	Value
Schools *(2002-2003)*	2,274	**Diploma Recipients** *(2002-2003)*	65,955
Instructional Level		White, Non-Hispanic	44,888
Primary	1,337	Black, Non-Hispanic	17,385
Middle	466	Asian/Pacific Islander	1,410
High	369	American Indian/Alaskan Native	713
Other Level	102	Hispanic	1,559
Curriculum		**High School Drop-out Rate** (%) *(2000-2001)*	6.3
Regular	2,173	White, Non-Hispanic	5.4
Special Education	19	Black, Non-Hispanic	7.6
Vocational	7	Asian/Pacific Islander	4.6
Alternative	75	American Indian/Alaskan Native	11.7
Type		Hispanic	10.6
Magnet	180	**Staff** *(2002-2003)*	169,328.0
Charter	93	Teachers	87,677.0
Title I Eligible	1,127	Average Salary ($)	42,411
School-wide Title I	853	Librarians/Media Specialists	2,299.0
Students *(2002-2003)*	1,335,955	Guidance Counselors	3,422.0
Gender (%)		**Ratios** *(2002-2003)*	
Male	51.2	Student/Teacher Ratio	15.2 to 1
Female	48.8	Student/Librarian Ratio	581.1 to 1
Race/Ethnicity (%)		Student/Counselor Ratio	390.4 to 1
White, Non-Hispanic	59.2	**Current Spending** *($ per student in FY 2001)*	6,501
Black, Non-Hispanic	31.4	Instruction	4,115
Asian/Pacific Islander	2.0	Support Services	2,010
American Indian/Alaskan Native	1.5	**College Entrance Exam Scores** *(2003)*	
Hispanic	5.9	Scholastic Aptitude Test (SAT)	
Classification (%)		Participation Rate (%)	68
Individual Education Program (IEP)	14.2	Mean SAT I Verbal Score	495
Migrant	1.1	Mean SAT I Math Score	506
English Language Learner (ELL)	4.5	American College Testing Program (ACT)	
Eligible for Free Lunch Program	27.1	Participation Rate (%)	15
Eligible for Reduced-Price Lunch Program	6.8	Average Composite Score	19.9

Note: *For an explanation of data, please refer to the User's Guide in the front of the book; n/a indicates data not available*

North Carolina NAEP 2003 Test Scores

Reading			Mathematics		
Grade/Category	**Value**	**Rank**	**Grade/Category**	**Value**	**Rank**
4th Grade			**4th Grade**		
Average Proficiency	221.2 (1.0)	19/51	Average Proficiency	242.0 (0.8)	2/51
Proficiency by Gender/Race/Ethnicity			Proficiency by Gender/Race/Ethnicity		
Male	215.8 (1.3)	24/51	Male	242.7 (1.0)	7/51
Female	226.7 (1.4)	10/51	Female	241.4 (0.9)	1/51
White, Non-Hispanic	231.6 (1.1)	7/51	White, Non-Hispanic	251.2 (0.9)	2/51
Black, Non-Hispanic	202.6 (1.2)	11/42	Black, Non-Hispanic	224.9 (0.9)	2/42
Asian, Non-Hispanic	211.8 (2.8)	4/41	Asian, Non-Hispanic	234.6 (2.0)	2/43
American Indian, Non-Hispanic	227.4 (3.8)	13/25	American Indian, Non-Hispanic	254.8 (3.4)	3/26
Hispanic	*200.3 (5.5)*	5/12	Hispanic	n/a	n/a
Proficiency by Class Size			Proficiency by Class Size		
Less than 16 Students	*207.7 (6.9)*	16/45	Less than 16 Students	*224.7 (4.4)*	25/47
16 to 18 Students	*207.9 (4.5)*	35/48	16 to 18 Students	*233.0 (2.9)*	24/48
19 to 20 Students	213.9 (2.2)	35/50	19 to 20 Students	240.0 (1.7)	11/50
21 to 25 Students	224.4 (1.3)	17/51	21 to 25 Students	244.1 (1.3)	2/51
Greater than 25 Students	226.3 (2.6)	6/49	Greater than 25 Students	245.4 (2.0)	2/49
Percent Attaining Achievement Levels			Percent Attaining Achievement Levels		
Below Basic	34.4 (1.2)	27/51	Below Basic	15.2 (0.8)	47/51
Basic or Above	65.6 (1.2)	25/51	Basic or Above	84.8 (0.8)	4/51
Proficient or Above	32.7 (1.2)	20/51	Proficient or Above	40.8 (1.4)	7/51
Advanced or Above	8.5 (0.7)	9/51	Advanced or Above	6.2 (0.6)	2/51
8th Grade			**8th Grade**		
Average Proficiency	261.7 (1.0)	31/51	Average Proficiency	281.2 (1.0)	19/51
Proficiency by Gender/Race/Ethnicity			Proficiency by Gender/Race/Ethnicity		
Male	256.3 (1.3)	31/51	Male	280.6 (1.4)	24/51
Female	267.1 (1.1)	33/51	Female	281.9 (1.2)	14/51
White, Non-Hispanic	271.2 (1.1)	18/50	White, Non-Hispanic	293.6 (1.0)	2/50
Black, Non-Hispanic	246.9 (1.4)	11/41	Black, Non-Hispanic	259.9 (1.2)	6/41
Asian, Non-Hispanic	243.8 (3.7)	26/37	Asian, Non-Hispanic	263.2 (3.1)	10/37
American Indian, Non-Hispanic	266.9 (5.4)	12/23	American Indian, Non-Hispanic	297.3 (3.9)	6/23
Hispanic	*241.7 (7.9)*	8/10	Hispanic	*258.8 (5.3)*	8/11
Proficiency by Parents Highest Level of Ed.			Proficiency by Parents Highest Level of Ed.		
Did Not Finish High School	245.0 (2.7)	31/50	Did Not Finish High School	264.3 (2.8)	7/50
Graduated High School	250.6 (2.1)	37/50	Graduated High School	270.3 (1.8)	23/50
Some Education After High School	264.7 (1.5)	36/50	Some Education After High School	283.4 (1.3)	12/50
Graduated College	271.0 (1.2)	32/50	Graduated College	291.2 (1.3)	18/50
Percent Attaining Achievement Levels			Percent Attaining Achievement Levels		
Below Basic	27.6 (1.2)	20/51	Below Basic	28.3 (1.3)	29/51
Basic or Above	72.4 (1.2)	32/51	Basic or Above	71.7 (1.3)	21/51
Proficient or Above	28.7 (1.1)	34/51	Proficient or Above	32.2 (1.2)	17/51
Advanced or Above	2.5 (0.4)	26/51	Advanced or Above	7.1 (0.7)	5/51

***Note:** For an explanation of data, please refer to the User's Guide in the front of the book; values in italics indicate that the nature of the sample does not allow accurate determination of the variability of the statistic; n/a indicates data not available*

Alamance County

Alamance-Burlington Schools

1712 Vaughn Rd • Burlington, NC 27217-2916
(336) 570-6060 • http://abss.k12.nc.us/
Grade Span: PK-12; **Agency Type:** 1
Schools: 33
19 Primary; 7 Middle; 6 High; 1 Other Level
32 Regular; 0 Special Education; 0 Vocational; 1 Alternative
0 Magnet; 0 Charter; 10 Title I Eligible; 10 School-wide Title I
Students: 21,597 (51.1% male; 48.9% female)
Individual Education Program: 3,156 (14.6%);
English Language Learner: 1,788 (8.3%); Migrant: 704 (3.3%)
Eligible for Free Lunch Program: 7,544 (34.9%)
Eligible for Reduced-Price Lunch Program: 1,840 (8.5%)
Teachers: 1,401.0 (15.4 to 1)
Librarians/Media Specialists: 32.0 (674.9 to 1)
Guidance Counselors: 50.0 (431.9 to 1)
Current Spending: ($ per student per year):
Total: $5,899; Instruction: $3,760; Support Services: $1,782

Enrollment, Drop-out Rates and Diploma Recipients by Race/Ethnicity

Category	Total	White	Black	Asian	AIAN	Hisp.
Enrollment (%)	100.0	60.9	26.6	1.4	0.4	10.8
Drop-out Rate (%)	6.7	6.3	7.3	5.4	5.3	9.7
H.S. Diplomas (#)	1,081	768	251	21	3	38

Alexander County

Alexander County Schools

250 Liledoun Rd • Taylorsville, NC 28681-0128
Mailing Address: PO Box 128 • Taylorsville, NC 28681-0128
(828) 632-7001 • http://www.alexander.k12.nc.us/
Grade Span: PK-12; **Agency Type:** 1
Schools: 10
7 Primary; 2 Middle; 1 High; 0 Other Level
10 Regular; 0 Special Education; 0 Vocational; 0 Alternative
0 Magnet; 0 Charter; 7 Title I Eligible; 0 School-wide Title I
Students: 5,482 (51.6% male; 48.4% female)
Individual Education Program: 758 (13.8%);
English Language Learner: 406 (7.4%); Migrant: 0 (0.0%)
Eligible for Free Lunch Program: 1,327 (24.2%)
Eligible for Reduced-Price Lunch Program: 396 (7.2%)
Teachers: 326.0 (16.8 to 1)
Librarians/Media Specialists: 11.0 (498.4 to 1)
Guidance Counselors: 15.0 (365.5 to 1)
Current Spending: ($ per student per year):
Total: $5,711; Instruction: $3,549; Support Services: $1,737

Enrollment, Drop-out Rates and Diploma Recipients by Race/Ethnicity

Category	Total	White	Black	Asian	AIAN	Hisp.
Enrollment (%)	100.0	85.8	6.5	3.3	0.1	4.3
Drop-out Rate (%)	5.8	5.5	3.9	10.9	100.0	16.7
H.S. Diplomas (#)	322	298	15	7	0	2

Anson County

Anson County Schools

400 N Greene St • Wadesboro, NC 28170-1611
Mailing Address: PO Box 719 • Wadesboro, NC 28170-0719
(704) 694-4417 • http://www.anson.k12.nc.us/
Grade Span: PK-12; **Agency Type:** 1
Schools: 9
5 Primary; 2 Middle; 2 High; 0 Other Level
8 Regular; 0 Special Education; 0 Vocational; 1 Alternative
0 Magnet; 0 Charter; 5 Title I Eligible; 5 School-wide Title I
Students: 4,494 (50.4% male; 49.6% female)
Individual Education Program: 808 (18.0%);
English Language Learner: 58 (1.3%); Migrant: 0 (0.0%)
Eligible for Free Lunch Program: 2,502 (55.7%)
Eligible for Reduced-Price Lunch Program: 487 (10.8%)
Teachers: 297.0 (15.1 to 1)
Librarians/Media Specialists: 8.0 (561.8 to 1)
Guidance Counselors: 13.0 (345.7 to 1)
Current Spending: ($ per student per year):
Total: $6,660; Instruction: $4,146; Support Services: $2,094

Enrollment, Drop-out Rates and Diploma Recipients by Race/Ethnicity

Category	Total	White	Black	Asian	AIAN	Hisp.
Enrollment (%)	100.0	34.1	63.0	1.4	0.4	1.1
Drop-out Rate (%)	8.7	7.1	9.4	7.1	0.0	66.7
H.S. Diplomas (#)	207	67	137	2	1	0

Ashe County

Ashe County Schools

320 S St • Jefferson, NC 28640-0604
Mailing Address: PO Box 604 • Jefferson, NC 28640-0604
(336) 246-7175 • http://www.ashe.k12.nc.us/
Grade Span: PK-12; **Agency Type:** 1
Schools: 6
4 Primary; 1 Middle; 1 High; 0 Other Level
6 Regular; 0 Special Education; 0 Vocational; 0 Alternative
0 Magnet; 0 Charter; 4 Title I Eligible; 4 School-wide Title I
Students: 3,278 (51.9% male; 48.1% female)
Individual Education Program: 493 (15.0%);
English Language Learner: 71 (2.2%); Migrant: 69 (2.1%)
Eligible for Free Lunch Program: 1,122 (34.2%)
Eligible for Reduced-Price Lunch Program: 513 (15.6%)
Teachers: 236.0 (13.9 to 1)
Librarians/Media Specialists: 6.0 (546.3 to 1)
Guidance Counselors: 9.0 (364.2 to 1)
Current Spending: ($ per student per year):
Total: $7,085; Instruction: $4,346; Support Services: $2,275

Enrollment, Drop-out Rates and Diploma Recipients by Race/Ethnicity

Category	Total	White	Black	Asian	AIAN	Hisp.
Enrollment (%)	100.0	95.2	1.6	0.3	0.3	2.6
Drop-out Rate (%)	5.5	5.4	0.0	0.0	0.0	22.2
H.S. Diplomas (#)	188	185	1	0	0	2

Avery County

Avery County Schools

775 Cranberry St • Newland, NC 28657-1360
Mailing Address: PO Box 1360 • Newland, NC 28657-1360
(828) 733-6006 • http://www.avery.k12.nc.us/
Grade Span: PK-12; **Agency Type:** 1
Schools: 9
6 Primary; 2 Middle; 1 High; 0 Other Level
9 Regular; 0 Special Education; 0 Vocational; 0 Alternative
0 Magnet; 0 Charter; 6 Title I Eligible; 6 School-wide Title I
Students: 2,463 (52.7% male; 47.3% female)
Individual Education Program: 473 (19.2%);
English Language Learner: 58 (2.4%); Migrant: 0 (0.0%)
Eligible for Free Lunch Program: 850 (34.5%)
Eligible for Reduced-Price Lunch Program: 327 (13.3%)
Teachers: 182.0 (13.5 to 1)
Librarians/Media Specialists: 7.0 (351.9 to 1)
Guidance Counselors: 10.0 (246.3 to 1)
Current Spending: ($ per student per year):
Total: $7,662; Instruction: $4,664; Support Services: $2,627

Enrollment, Drop-out Rates and Diploma Recipients by Race/Ethnicity

Category	Total	White	Black	Asian	AIAN	Hisp.
Enrollment (%)	100.0	96.3	1.2	0.3	0.2	1.9
Drop-out Rate (%)	5.5	5.3	0.0	0.0	n/a	40.0
H.S. Diplomas (#)	133	131	1	1	0	0

Beaufort County

Beaufort County Schools

321 Smaw Rd • Washington, NC 27889-3937
(252) 946-6593 • http://www.beaufort.k12.nc.us/
Grade Span: PK-12; **Agency Type:** 1
Schools: 14
6 Primary; 4 Middle; 3 High; 1 Other Level
13 Regular; 0 Special Education; 0 Vocational; 1 Alternative
0 Magnet; 0 Charter; 5 Title I Eligible; 5 School-wide Title I
Students: 7,468 (51.2% male; 48.8% female)
Individual Education Program: 1,234 (16.5%);
English Language Learner: 230 (3.1%); Migrant: 104 (1.4%)
Eligible for Free Lunch Program: 0 (0.0%)
Eligible for Reduced-Price Lunch Program: 0 (0.0%)
Teachers: 537.0 (13.9 to 1)
Librarians/Media Specialists: 14.0 (533.4 to 1)
Guidance Counselors: 18.0 (414.9 to 1)
Current Spending: ($ per student per year):
Total: $6,529; Instruction: $4,123; Support Services: $2,035

Enrollment, Drop-out Rates and Diploma Recipients by Race/Ethnicity

Category	Total	White	Black	Asian	AIAN	Hisp.
Enrollment (%)	100.0	52.7	41.9	0.4	0.0	5.0
Drop-out Rate (%)	7.1	6.2	8.4	0.0	n/a	6.3
H.S. Diplomas (#)	380	247	126	3	0	4

Bertie County

Bertie County Schools

222 County Farm Rd • Windsor, NC 27983-0010
Mailing Address: PO Box 10 • Windsor, NC 27983-0010
(252) 794-3173 • http://www.bertieschools.com/
Grade Span: PK-12; **Agency Type:** 1
Schools: 10
6 Primary; 2 Middle; 1 High; 1 Other Level
9 Regular; 0 Special Education; 0 Vocational; 1 Alternative
0 Magnet; 0 Charter; 7 Title I Eligible; 7 School-wide Title I
Students: 3,555 (52.1% male; 47.9% female)
Individual Education Program: 517 (14.5%);
English Language Learner: 12 (0.3%); Migrant: 32 (0.9%)
Eligible for Free Lunch Program: 2,446 (68.8%)
Eligible for Reduced-Price Lunch Program: 557 (15.7%)
Teachers: 236.0 (15.1 to 1)
Librarians/Media Specialists: 9.0 (395.0 to 1)
Guidance Counselors: 8.0 (444.4 to 1)
Current Spending: ($ per student per year):
Total: $7,405; Instruction: $4,093; Support Services: $2,815
Enrollment, Drop-out Rates and Diploma Recipients by Race/Ethnicity

Category	Total	White	Black	Asian	AIAN	Hisp.
Enrollment (%)	100.0	14.1	84.8	0.2	0.4	0.6
Drop-out Rate (%)	6.0	5.5	6.1	0.0	0.0	0.0
H.S. Diplomas (#)	196	44	152	0	0	0

Bladen County

Bladen County Schools

Hwy 701 S • Elizabethtown, NC 28337-0037
Mailing Address: PO Box 37 • Elizabethtown, NC 28337-0037
(910) 862-4136 • http://bladen.schoolwebpages.com/education/district/
Grade Span: PK-12; **Agency Type:** 1
Schools: 14
7 Primary; 4 Middle; 2 High; 1 Other Level
13 Regular; 0 Special Education; 0 Vocational; 1 Alternative
0 Magnet; 0 Charter; 8 Title I Eligible; 8 School-wide Title I
Students: 5,811 (51.7% male; 48.3% female)
Individual Education Program: 704 (12.1%);
English Language Learner: 252 (4.3%); Migrant: 415 (7.1%)
Eligible for Free Lunch Program: 3,298 (56.8%)
Eligible for Reduced-Price Lunch Program: 583 (10.0%)
Teachers: 373.0 (15.6 to 1)
Librarians/Media Specialists: 13.0 (447.0 to 1)
Guidance Counselors: 13.0 (447.0 to 1)
Current Spending: ($ per student per year):
Total: $6,674; Instruction: $4,089; Support Services: $2,163
Enrollment, Drop-out Rates and Diploma Recipients by Race/Ethnicity

Category	Total	White	Black	Asian	AIAN	Hisp.
Enrollment (%)	100.0	44.3	50.3	0.1	0.9	4.3
Drop-out Rate (%)	4.9	4.7	4.9	0.0	18.2	5.9
H.S. Diplomas (#)	288	133	155	0	0	0

Brunswick County

Brunswick County Schools

35 Referendum Dr • Bolivia, NC 28422-0189
(910) 253-2900 • http://www.brunswickcountyschools.org/
Grade Span: PK-12; **Agency Type:** 1
Schools: 16
9 Primary; 3 Middle; 3 High; 1 Other Level
15 Regular; 0 Special Education; 0 Vocational; 1 Alternative
0 Magnet; 0 Charter; 9 Title I Eligible; 8 School-wide Title I
Students: 10,741 (51.0% male; 49.0% female)
Individual Education Program: 1,685 (15.7%);
English Language Learner: 216 (2.0%); Migrant: 102 (0.9%)
Eligible for Free Lunch Program: 0 (0.0%)
Eligible for Reduced-Price Lunch Program: 0 (0.0%)
Teachers: 709.0 (15.1 to 1)
Librarians/Media Specialists: 15.0 (716.1 to 1)
Guidance Counselors: 28.0 (383.6 to 1)
Current Spending: ($ per student per year):
Total: $7,027; Instruction: $4,221; Support Services: $2,451
Enrollment, Drop-out Rates and Diploma Recipients by Race/Ethnicity

Category	Total	White	Black	Asian	AIAN	Hisp.
Enrollment (%)	100.0	71.7	24.1	0.2	0.8	3.2
Drop-out Rate (%)	8.0	8.6	5.8	11.1	10.0	17.2
H.S. Diplomas (#)	474	325	137	3	0	9

Buncombe County

Asheville City Schools

85 Mountain St • Asheville, NC 28801
Mailing Address: PO Box 7347 • Asheville, NC 28802-7347
(828) 255-5304 • http://www.asheville.k12.nc.us/
Grade Span: KG-12; **Agency Type:** 1
Schools: 8
5 Primary; 2 Middle; 1 High; 0 Other Level
7 Regular; 0 Special Education; 0 Vocational; 1 Alternative
5 Magnet; 0 Charter; 5 Title I Eligible; 5 School-wide Title I
Students: 3,920 (51.1% male; 48.9% female)
Individual Education Program: 492 (12.6%);
English Language Learner: 56 (1.4%); Migrant: 0 (0.0%)
Eligible for Free Lunch Program: 1,728 (44.1%)
Eligible for Reduced-Price Lunch Program: 230 (5.9%)
Teachers: 325.0 (12.1 to 1)
Librarians/Media Specialists: 10.0 (392.0 to 1)
Guidance Counselors: 16.0 (245.0 to 1)
Current Spending: ($ per student per year):
Total: $9,418; Instruction: $5,856; Support Services: $3,160
Enrollment, Drop-out Rates and Diploma Recipients by Race/Ethnicity

Category	Total	White	Black	Asian	AIAN	Hisp.
Enrollment (%)	100.0	50.8	45.0	0.7	0.2	3.4
Drop-out Rate (%)	5.4	3.6	8.4	8.3	0.0	5.3
H.S. Diplomas (#)	249	172	71	2	0	4

Buncombe County Schools

175 Bingham Rd • Asheville, NC 28806-3800
(828) 255-5921 • http://www.buncombe.k12.nc.us/public/
Grade Span: PK-12; **Agency Type:** 1
Schools: 40
22 Primary; 9 Middle; 8 High; 1 Other Level
37 Regular; 0 Special Education; 1 Vocational; 2 Alternative
0 Magnet; 0 Charter; 18 Title I Eligible; 12 School-wide Title I
Students: 24,665 (51.3% male; 48.7% female)
Individual Education Program: 3,436 (13.9%);
English Language Learner: 624 (2.5%); Migrant: 98 (0.4%)
Eligible for Free Lunch Program: 6,483 (26.3%)
Eligible for Reduced-Price Lunch Program: 1,896 (7.7%)
Teachers: 1,587.0 (15.5 to 1)
Librarians/Media Specialists: 46.0 (536.2 to 1)
Guidance Counselors: 58.0 (425.3 to 1)
Current Spending: ($ per student per year):
Total: $6,356; Instruction: $4,040; Support Services: $1,959
Enrollment, Drop-out Rates and Diploma Recipients by Race/Ethnicity

Category	Total	White	Black	Asian	AIAN	Hisp.
Enrollment (%)	100.0	87.0	8.0	0.8	0.4	3.7
Drop-out Rate (%)	6.7	6.4	10.1	1.5	13.8	10.8
H.S. Diplomas (#)	1,370	1,261	72	13	3	21

Burke County

Burke County Schools

700 E Parker Rd • Morganton, NC 28655
Mailing Address: PO Drawer 989 • Morganton, NC 28680-0989
(828) 439-4321 • http://www.burke.k12.nc.us/
Grade Span: PK-12; **Agency Type:** 1
Schools: 25
17 Primary; 4 Middle; 2 High; 2 Other Level
23 Regular; 0 Special Education; 0 Vocational; 2 Alternative
0 Magnet; 0 Charter; 15 Title I Eligible; 15 School-wide Title I
Students: 14,752 (51.1% male; 48.9% female)
Individual Education Program: 2,426 (16.4%);
English Language Learner: 1,124 (7.6%); Migrant: 0 (0.0%)
Eligible for Free Lunch Program: 4,634 (31.4%)
Eligible for Reduced-Price Lunch Program: 1,783 (12.1%)
Teachers: 1,007.0 (14.6 to 1)
Librarians/Media Specialists: 23.0 (641.4 to 1)
Guidance Counselors: 37.0 (398.7 to 1)
Current Spending: ($ per student per year):
Total: $5,925; Instruction: $3,810; Support Services: $1,742
Enrollment, Drop-out Rates and Diploma Recipients by Race/Ethnicity

Category	Total	White	Black	Asian	AIAN	Hisp.
Enrollment (%)	100.0	78.3	8.5	9.1	0.1	4.0
Drop-out Rate (%)	6.4	6.5	6.4	5.4	0.0	6.3
H.S. Diplomas (#)	682	550	51	64	2	15

Cabarrus County

Cabarrus County Schools

660 Concord Pkwy N • Concord, NC 28027
Mailing Address: PO Box 388 • Concord, NC 28026-0388
(704) 786-6191 • http://www.cabarrus.k12.nc.us/
Grade Span: PK-12; **Agency Type:** 1
Schools: 28
15 Primary; 7 Middle; 5 High; 1 Other Level
27 Regular; 0 Special Education; 0 Vocational; 1 Alternative
1 Magnet; 0 Charter; 5 Title I Eligible; 3 School-wide Title I
Students: 20,939 (51.1% male; 48.9% female)
Individual Education Program: 2,969 (14.2%);
English Language Learner: 1,052 (5.0%); Migrant: 30 (0.1%)
Eligible for Free Lunch Program: 4,487 (21.4%)
Eligible for Reduced-Price Lunch Program: 1,342 (6.4%)
Teachers: 1,378.0 (15.2 to 1)
Librarians/Media Specialists: 27.0 (775.5 to 1)
Guidance Counselors: 57.0 (367.4 to 1)
Current Spending: ($ per student per year):
Total: $5,849; Instruction: $3,769; Support Services: $1,732
Enrollment, Drop-out Rates and Diploma Recipients by Race/Ethnicity

Category	Total	White	Black	Asian	AIAN	Hisp.
Enrollment (%)	100.0	76.0	15.9	1.2	0.3	6.5
Drop-out Rate (%)	4.9	4.0	7.7	8.3	4.3	20.8
H.S. Diplomas (#)	1,097	944	127	13	1	12

Kannapolis City Schools

100 Denver St • Kannapolis, NC 28083-3609
(704) 938-1131 • http://www.kannapolis.k12.nc.us/
Grade Span: PK-12; **Agency Type:** 1
Schools: 7
5 Primary; 1 Middle; 1 High; 0 Other Level
7 Regular; 0 Special Education; 0 Vocational; 0 Alternative
0 Magnet; 0 Charter; 5 Title I Eligible; 5 School-wide Title I
Students: 4,396 (52.4% male; 47.6% female)
Individual Education Program: 718 (16.3%);
English Language Learner: 571 (13.0%); Migrant: 0 (0.0%)
Eligible for Free Lunch Program: 0 (0.0%)
Eligible for Reduced-Price Lunch Program: 0 (0.0%)
Teachers: 325.0 (13.5 to 1)
Librarians/Media Specialists: 8.0 (549.5 to 1)
Guidance Counselors: 11.0 (399.6 to 1)
Current Spending: ($ per student per year):
Total: $6,643; Instruction: $4,153; Support Services: $2,062
Enrollment, Drop-out Rates and Diploma Recipients by Race/Ethnicity

Category	Total	White	Black	Asian	AIAN	Hisp.
Enrollment (%)	100.0	54.1	31.8	1.5	0.3	12.4
Drop-out Rate (%)	5.7	7.0	3.5	0.0	0.0	6.3
H.S. Diplomas (#)	231	138	83	2	0	8

Caldwell County

Caldwell County Schools

1914 Hickory Blvd SW • Lenoir, NC 28645-6404
(828) 728-8407 • http://205.152.116.5/CCSMainSite/
Grade Span: PK-12; **Agency Type:** 1
Schools: 25
16 Primary; 4 Middle; 5 High; 0 Other Level
22 Regular; 0 Special Education; 1 Vocational; 2 Alternative
0 Magnet; 0 Charter; 15 Title I Eligible; 15 School-wide Title I
Students: 12,744 (50.7% male; 49.3% female)
Individual Education Program: 1,511 (11.9%);
English Language Learner: 360 (2.8%); Migrant: 0 (0.0%)
Eligible for Free Lunch Program: 0 (0.0%)
Eligible for Reduced-Price Lunch Program: 0 (0.0%)
Teachers: 840.0 (15.2 to 1)
Librarians/Media Specialists: 23.0 (554.1 to 1)
Guidance Counselors: 39.0 (326.8 to 1)
Current Spending: ($ per student per year):
Total: $6,014; Instruction: $3,841; Support Services: $1,767
Enrollment, Drop-out Rates and Diploma Recipients by Race/Ethnicity

Category	Total	White	Black	Asian	AIAN	Hisp.
Enrollment (%)	100.0	87.6	8.5	0.8	0.1	3.1
Drop-out Rate (%)	6.8	6.8	7.6	5.0	0.0	2.2
H.S. Diplomas (#)	686	622	52	2	2	8

Carteret County

Carteret County Public Schools

107 Safrit Dr • Beaufort, NC 28516-9017
(252) 728-4583 • http://www.carteretcountyschools.org/
Grade Span: PK-12; **Agency Type:** 1
Schools: 16
8 Primary; 5 Middle; 3 High; 0 Other Level
16 Regular; 0 Special Education; 0 Vocational; 0 Alternative
0 Magnet; 0 Charter; 9 Title I Eligible; 8 School-wide Title I
Students: 8,251 (51.9% male; 48.1% female)
Individual Education Program: 1,491 (18.1%);
English Language Learner: 96 (1.2%); Migrant: 0 (0.0%)
Eligible for Free Lunch Program: 2,361 (28.6%)
Eligible for Reduced-Price Lunch Program: 816 (9.9%)
Teachers: 653.0 (12.6 to 1)
Librarians/Media Specialists: 16.0 (515.7 to 1)
Guidance Counselors: 29.0 (284.5 to 1)
Current Spending: ($ per student per year):
Total: $7,493; Instruction: $4,978; Support Services: $2,155
Enrollment, Drop-out Rates and Diploma Recipients by Race/Ethnicity

Category	Total	White	Black	Asian	AIAN	Hisp.
Enrollment (%)	100.0	85.6	11.6	0.7	0.3	1.8
Drop-out Rate (%)	5.9	6.4	3.3	0.0	7.1	0.0
H.S. Diplomas (#)	543	465	66	5	4	3

Caswell County

Caswell County Schools

353 County Home Rd • Yanceyville, NC 27379-0160
Mailing Address: PO Box 160 • Yanceyville, NC 27379-0160
(336) 694-4116 • http://www.caswellschools.org/
Grade Span: PK-12; **Agency Type:** 1
Schools: 6
4 Primary; 1 Middle; 1 High; 0 Other Level
6 Regular; 0 Special Education; 0 Vocational; 0 Alternative
0 Magnet; 0 Charter; 5 Title I Eligible; 3 School-wide Title I
Students: 3,563 (51.7% male; 48.3% female)
Individual Education Program: 515 (14.5%);
English Language Learner: 50 (1.4%); Migrant: 0 (0.0%)
Eligible for Free Lunch Program: 0 (0.0%)
Eligible for Reduced-Price Lunch Program: 0 (0.0%)
Teachers: 236.0 (15.1 to 1)
Librarians/Media Specialists: 12.0 (296.9 to 1)
Guidance Counselors: 10.0 (356.3 to 1)
Current Spending: ($ per student per year):
Total: $6,733; Instruction: $4,193; Support Services: $2,093
Enrollment, Drop-out Rates and Diploma Recipients by Race/Ethnicity

Category	Total	White	Black	Asian	AIAN	Hisp.
Enrollment (%)	100.0	52.7	44.3	0.3	0.2	2.5
Drop-out Rate (%)	3.9	4.9	2.9	n/a	0.0	0.0
H.S. Diplomas (#)	182	109	73	0	0	0

Catawba County

Catawba County Schools

10 E 25th St • Newton, NC 28658-1000
Mailing Address: PO Box 1000 • Newton, NC 28658-1000
(828) 464-8333 • http://www.catawba.k12.nc.us/
Grade Span: PK-12; **Agency Type:** 1
Schools: 25
14 Primary; 6 Middle; 5 High; 0 Other Level
25 Regular; 0 Special Education; 0 Vocational; 0 Alternative
0 Magnet; 0 Charter; 10 Title I Eligible; 1 School-wide Title I
Students: 16,620 (51.4% male; 48.6% female)
Individual Education Program: 2,462 (14.8%);
English Language Learner: 1,263 (7.6%); Migrant: 0 (0.0%)
Eligible for Free Lunch Program: 3,776 (22.7%)
Eligible for Reduced-Price Lunch Program: 1,453 (8.7%)
Teachers: 1,033.0 (16.1 to 1)
Librarians/Media Specialists: 27.0 (615.6 to 1)
Guidance Counselors: 43.0 (386.5 to 1)
Current Spending: ($ per student per year):
Total: $5,916; Instruction: $3,995; Support Services: $1,587
Enrollment, Drop-out Rates and Diploma Recipients by Race/Ethnicity

Category	Total	White	Black	Asian	AIAN	Hisp.
Enrollment (%)	100.0	78.8	8.1	7.3	0.2	5.5
Drop-out Rate (%)	6.5	6.3	6.5	5.4	0.0	15.1
H.S. Diplomas (#)	827	711	47	54	1	14

Hickory City Schools

432 4th Ave SW • Hickory, NC 28602-2805
(828) 322-2855 • http://www.hickory.k12.nc.us/
Grade Span: PK-12; **Agency Type:** 1
Schools: 10
5 Primary; 2 Middle; 1 High; 2 Other Level
8 Regular; 0 Special Education; 0 Vocational; 2 Alternative
0 Magnet; 0 Charter; 8 Title I Eligible; 6 School-wide Title I
Students: 4,458 (49.8% male; 50.2% female)
Individual Education Program: 563 (12.6%);
English Language Learner: 701 (15.7%); Migrant: 0 (0.0%)
Eligible for Free Lunch Program: 1,925 (43.2%)
Eligible for Reduced-Price Lunch Program: 424 (9.5%)

Teachers: 304.0 (14.7 to 1)
Librarians/Media Specialists: 9.0 (495.3 to 1)
Guidance Counselors: 15.0 (297.2 to 1)
Current Spending: ($ per student per year):
Total: $6,251; Instruction: $4,053; Support Services: $1,815
Enrollment, Drop-out Rates and Diploma Recipients by Race/Ethnicity

Category	Total	White	Black	Asian	AIAN	Hisp.
Enrollment (%)	100.0	52.0	28.3	8.6	0.1	11.0
Drop-out Rate (%)	10.6	9.1	13.4	10.9	n/a	15.4
H.S. Diplomas (#)	237	154	51	26	0	6

Newton Conover City Schools
605 N Ashe Ave • Newton, NC 28658-3120
(828) 464-3191 • http://www.nccs.k12.nc.us/
Grade Span: PK-12; **Agency Type:** 1
Schools: 6
4 Primary; 1 Middle; 1 High; 0 Other Level
5 Regular; 1 Special Education; 0 Vocational; 0 Alternative
0 Magnet; 0 Charter; 2 Title I Eligible; 2 School-wide Title I
Students: 2,848 (50.8% male; 49.2% female)
Individual Education Program: 424 (14.9%);
English Language Learner: 337 (11.8%); Migrant: 0 (0.0%)
Eligible for Free Lunch Program: 918 (32.2%)
Eligible for Reduced-Price Lunch Program: 301 (10.6%)
Teachers: 197.0 (14.5 to 1)
Librarians/Media Specialists: 5.0 (569.6 to 1)
Guidance Counselors: 8.0 (356.0 to 1)
Current Spending: ($ per student per year):
Total: $6,824; Instruction: $4,402; Support Services: $2,046
Enrollment, Drop-out Rates and Diploma Recipients by Race/Ethnicity

Category	Total	White	Black	Asian	AIAN	Hisp.
Enrollment (%)	100.0	60.8	20.1	7.3	0.2	11.6
Drop-out Rate (%)	3.8	3.4	4.4	6.1	n/a	3.6
H.S. Diplomas (#)	144	115	9	16	0	4

Chatham County

Chatham County Schools
369 W St • Pittsboro, NC 27312-0128
Mailing Address: PO Box 128 • Pittsboro, NC 27312-0128
(919) 542-3626 • http://www.chatham.k12.nc.us/index.nsf?OpenDatabase
Grade Span: PK-12; **Agency Type:** 1
Schools: 15
9 Primary; 2 Middle; 4 High; 0 Other Level
14 Regular; 0 Special Education; 0 Vocational; 1 Alternative
0 Magnet; 0 Charter; 3 Title I Eligible; 3 School-wide Title I
Students: 7,252 (52.3% male; 47.7% female)
Individual Education Program: 953 (13.1%);
English Language Learner: 824 (11.4%); Migrant: 662 (9.1%)
Eligible for Free Lunch Program: 0 (0.0%)
Eligible for Reduced-Price Lunch Program: 0 (0.0%)
Teachers: 493.0 (14.7 to 1)
Librarians/Media Specialists: 14.0 (518.0 to 1)
Guidance Counselors: 27.0 (268.6 to 1)
Current Spending: ($ per student per year):
Total: $6,844; Instruction: $4,177; Support Services: $2,294
Enrollment, Drop-out Rates and Diploma Recipients by Race/Ethnicity

Category	Total	White	Black	Asian	AIAN	Hisp.
Enrollment (%)	100.0	60.2	23.3	0.6	0.2	15.6
Drop-out Rate (%)	8.0	7.0	5.8	14.3	0.0	25.6
H.S. Diplomas (#)	306	202	87	2	0	15

Cherokee County

Cherokee County Schools
911 Andrews Rd • Murphy, NC 28906-2730
(828) 837-2722
Grade Span: PK-12; **Agency Type:** 1
Schools: 13
7 Primary; 2 Middle; 4 High; 0 Other Level
12 Regular; 0 Special Education; 0 Vocational; 1 Alternative
0 Magnet; 0 Charter; 7 Title I Eligible; 7 School-wide Title I
Students: 3,757 (52.5% male; 47.5% female)
Individual Education Program: 651 (17.3%);
English Language Learner: 4 (0.1%); Migrant: 0 (0.0%)
Eligible for Free Lunch Program: 1,354 (36.0%)
Eligible for Reduced-Price Lunch Program: 610 (16.2%)
Teachers: 277.0 (13.6 to 1)
Librarians/Media Specialists: 10.0 (375.7 to 1)
Guidance Counselors: 9.0 (417.4 to 1)
Current Spending: ($ per student per year):
Total: $6,908; Instruction: $4,445; Support Services: $1,981

Enrollment, Drop-out Rates and Diploma Recipients by Race/Ethnicity

Category	Total	White	Black	Asian	AIAN	Hisp.
Enrollment (%)	100.0	93.6	2.9	0.5	1.7	1.3
Drop-out Rate (%)	6.7	6.7	4.5	0.0	15.8	0.0
H.S. Diplomas (#)	236	228	4	0	4	0

Chowan County

Edenton-Chowan Schools
E King St • Edenton, NC 27932-0206
Mailing Address: PO Box 206 • Edenton, NC 27932-0206
(252) 482-4436 • http://www.ecps.k12.nc.us/
Grade Span: PK-12; **Agency Type:** 1
Schools: 4
2 Primary; 1 Middle; 1 High; 0 Other Level
4 Regular; 0 Special Education; 0 Vocational; 0 Alternative
0 Magnet; 0 Charter; 3 Title I Eligible; 3 School-wide Title I
Students: 2,544 (50.8% male; 49.2% female)
Individual Education Program: 315 (12.4%);
English Language Learner: 41 (1.6%); Migrant: 0 (0.0%)
Eligible for Free Lunch Program: 1,201 (47.2%)
Eligible for Reduced-Price Lunch Program: 217 (8.5%)
Teachers: 180.0 (14.1 to 1)
Librarians/Media Specialists: 4.0 (636.0 to 1)
Guidance Counselors: 7.0 (363.4 to 1)
Current Spending: ($ per student per year):
Total: $7,149; Instruction: $4,396; Support Services: $2,376
Enrollment, Drop-out Rates and Diploma Recipients by Race/Ethnicity

Category	Total	White	Black	Asian	AIAN	Hisp.
Enrollment (%)	100.0	48.8	49.1	0.2	0.2	1.7
Drop-out Rate (%)	5.0	3.3	6.9	n/a	0.0	0.0
H.S. Diplomas (#)	138	83	55	0	0	0

Cleveland County

Cleveland County Schools
130 S Post Rd Ste 2 • Shelby, NC 28152-6297
(704) 487-8581 • http://www.ccss.k12.nc.us/
Grade Span: PK-12; **Agency Type:** 1
Schools: 12
8 Primary; 2 Middle; 2 High; 0 Other Level
12 Regular; 0 Special Education; 0 Vocational; 0 Alternative
0 Magnet; 0 Charter; 6 Title I Eligible; 3 School-wide Title I
Students: 9,722 (51.5% male; 48.5% female)
Individual Education Program: 1,442 (14.8%);
English Language Learner: 128 (1.3%); Migrant: 0 (0.0%)
Eligible for Free Lunch Program: 0 (0.0%)
Eligible for Reduced-Price Lunch Program: 0 (0.0%)
Teachers: 632.0 (15.4 to 1)
Librarians/Media Specialists: 14.0 (694.4 to 1)
Guidance Counselors: 22.0 (441.9 to 1)
Current Spending: ($ per student per year):
Total: $6,007; Instruction: $3,973; Support Services: $1,708
Enrollment, Drop-out Rates and Diploma Recipients by Race/Ethnicity

Category	Total	White	Black	Asian	AIAN	Hisp.
Enrollment (%)	100.0	72.8	25.1	0.2	0.1	1.8
Drop-out Rate (%)	5.9	6.1	5.4	0.0	0.0	5.6
H.S. Diplomas (#)	442	355	83	0	0	4

Kings Mountain District
105 E Ridge St • Kings Mountain, NC 28086-0279
(704) 734-5637 • http://www.kmds.k12.nc.us/
Grade Span: PK-12; **Agency Type:** 1
Schools: 9
5 Primary; 2 Middle; 1 High; 1 Other Level
8 Regular; 0 Special Education; 0 Vocational; 1 Alternative
0 Magnet; 0 Charter; 5 Title I Eligible; 1 School-wide Title I
Students: 4,698 (50.6% male; 49.4% female)
Individual Education Program: 566 (12.0%);
English Language Learner: 31 (0.7%); Migrant: 0 (0.0%)
Eligible for Free Lunch Program: 0 (0.0%)
Eligible for Reduced-Price Lunch Program: 0 (0.0%)
Teachers: 293.0 (16.0 to 1)
Librarians/Media Specialists: 9.0 (522.0 to 1)
Guidance Counselors: 14.0 (335.6 to 1)
Current Spending: ($ per student per year):
Total: $6,817; Instruction: $4,310; Support Services: $2,114
Enrollment, Drop-out Rates and Diploma Recipients by Race/Ethnicity

Category	Total	White	Black	Asian	AIAN	Hisp.
Enrollment (%)	100.0	72.2	24.0	2.1	0.2	1.6
Drop-out Rate (%)	9.1	9.2	9.5	5.7	0.0	0.0
H.S. Diplomas (#)	184	138	38	7	0	1

Shelby City

315 Patton Dr • Shelby, NC 28150-5499
(704) 487-6367 • http://www.blueridge.net/scs/scs.htm
Grade Span: PK-12; **Agency Type:** 1
Schools: 7
4 Primary; 2 Middle; 1 High; 0 Other Level
6 Regular; 1 Special Education; 0 Vocational; 0 Alternative
0 Magnet; 0 Charter; 0 Title I Eligible; 0 School-wide Title I
Students: 3,296 (51.6% male; 48.4% female)
Individual Education Program: 557 (16.9%);
English Language Learner: 25 (0.8%); Migrant: 0 (0.0%)
Eligible for Free Lunch Program: 1,570 (47.6%)
Eligible for Reduced-Price Lunch Program: 200 (6.1%)
Teachers: 243.0 (13.6 to 1)
Librarians/Media Specialists: 6.0 (549.3 to 1)
Guidance Counselors: 7.0 (470.9 to 1)
Current Spending: ($ per student per year):
Total: $7,359; Instruction: $4,673; Support Services: $2,261
Enrollment, Drop-out Rates and Diploma Recipients by Race/Ethnicity

Category	Total	White	Black	Asian	AIAN	Hisp.
Enrollment (%)	100.0	39.3	58.5	0.5	0.1	1.6
Drop-out Rate (%)	6.2	3.5	9.3	0.0	n/a	33.3
H.S. Diplomas (#)	141	77	62	2	0	0

Columbus County

Columbus County Schools

817 Washington St • Whiteville, NC 28472-0729
Mailing Address: PO Box 729 • Whiteville, NC 28472-0729
(910) 642-5168 • http://www.columbus.k12.nc.us/
Grade Span: PK-12; **Agency Type:** 1
Schools: 19
10 Primary; 5 Middle; 3 High; 1 Other Level
18 Regular; 0 Special Education; 0 Vocational; 1 Alternative
0 Magnet; 0 Charter; 16 Title I Eligible; 16 School-wide Title I
Students: 7,102 (50.9% male; 49.1% female)
Individual Education Program: 969 (13.6%);
English Language Learner: 156 (2.2%); Migrant: 637 (9.0%)
Eligible for Free Lunch Program: 4,013 (56.5%)
Eligible for Reduced-Price Lunch Program: 767 (10.8%)
Teachers: 443.0 (16.0 to 1)
Librarians/Media Specialists: 17.0 (417.8 to 1)
Guidance Counselors: 21.0 (338.2 to 1)
Current Spending: ($ per student per year):
Total: $6,272; Instruction: $3,757; Support Services: $2,083
Enrollment, Drop-out Rates and Diploma Recipients by Race/Ethnicity

Category	Total	White	Black	Asian	AIAN	Hisp.
Enrollment (%)	100.0	50.6	40.4	0.0	5.8	3.1
Drop-out Rate (%)	7.3	7.1	7.4	0.0	6.1	26.7
H.S. Diplomas (#)	386	198	170	0	17	1

Whiteville City Schools

107 W Walter St • Whiteville, NC 28472-4019
Mailing Address: PO Box 609 • Whiteville, NC 28472-0609
(910) 642-4116 • http://www.whiteville.k12.nc.us/
Grade Span: PK-12; **Agency Type:** 1
Schools: 5
2 Primary; 1 Middle; 1 High; 1 Other Level
4 Regular; 0 Special Education; 0 Vocational; 1 Alternative
0 Magnet; 0 Charter; 3 Title I Eligible; 3 School-wide Title I
Students: 2,703 (50.3% male; 49.7% female)
Individual Education Program: 461 (17.1%);
English Language Learner: 39 (1.4%); Migrant: 134 (5.0%)
Eligible for Free Lunch Program: 0 (0.0%)
Eligible for Reduced-Price Lunch Program: 0 (0.0%)
Teachers: 196.0 (13.8 to 1)
Librarians/Media Specialists: 4.0 (675.8 to 1)
Guidance Counselors: 6.0 (450.5 to 1)
Current Spending: ($ per student per year):
Total: $6,306; Instruction: $3,951; Support Services: $1,980
Enrollment, Drop-out Rates and Diploma Recipients by Race/Ethnicity

Category	Total	White	Black	Asian	AIAN	Hisp.
Enrollment (%)	100.0	50.8	45.5	0.3	0.9	2.6
Drop-out Rate (%)	6.0	6.3	5.7	0.0	12.5	0.0
H.S. Diplomas (#)	132	77	54	1	0	0

Craven County

Craven County Schools

3600 Trent Rd • New Bern, NC 28562-2224
(252) 514-6300 • http://schools.craven.k12.nc.us/
Grade Span: PK-12; **Agency Type:** 1
Schools: 22
14 Primary; 5 Middle; 3 High; 0 Other Level
22 Regular; 0 Special Education; 0 Vocational; 0 Alternative
0 Magnet; 0 Charter; 18 Title I Eligible; 15 School-wide Title I
Students: 14,563 (50.5% male; 49.5% female)
Individual Education Program: 1,943 (13.3%);
English Language Learner: 206 (1.4%); Migrant: 0 (0.0%)
Eligible for Free Lunch Program: 5,289 (36.3%)
Eligible for Reduced-Price Lunch Program: 1,825 (12.5%)
Teachers: 993.0 (14.7 to 1)
Librarians/Media Specialists: 26.0 (560.1 to 1)
Guidance Counselors: 38.0 (383.2 to 1)
Current Spending: ($ per student per year):
Total: $6,111; Instruction: $3,860; Support Services: $1,929
Enrollment, Drop-out Rates and Diploma Recipients by Race/Ethnicity

Category	Total	White	Black	Asian	AIAN	Hisp.
Enrollment (%)	100.0	59.1	36.2	1.0	0.4	3.3
Drop-out Rate (%)	6.5	5.2	9.0	8.5	0.0	6.0
H.S. Diplomas (#)	816	521	263	11	0	21

Cumberland County

Cumberland County Schools

2465 Gillespie St • Fayetteville, NC 28306
Mailing Address: PO Box 2357 • Fayetteville, NC 28302-2357
(910) 678-2300 • http://www.ccs.k12.nc.us/
Grade Span: PK-12; **Agency Type:** 1
Schools: 84
54 Primary; 16 Middle; 12 High; 2 Other Level
80 Regular; 1 Special Education; 0 Vocational; 3 Alternative
0 Magnet; 0 Charter; 61 Title I Eligible; 61 School-wide Title I
Students: 52,094 (50.8% male; 49.2% female)
Individual Education Program: 6,771 (13.0%);
English Language Learner: 793 (1.5%); Migrant: 0 (0.0%)
Eligible for Free Lunch Program: 19,507 (37.4%)
Eligible for Reduced-Price Lunch Program: 6,211 (11.9%)
Teachers: 3,284.0 (15.9 to 1)
Librarians/Media Specialists: 93.0 (560.2 to 1)
Guidance Counselors: 133.0 (391.7 to 1)
Current Spending: ($ per student per year):
Total: $6,185; Instruction: $3,843; Support Services: $1,988
Enrollment, Drop-out Rates and Diploma Recipients by Race/Ethnicity

Category	Total	White	Black	Asian	AIAN	Hisp.
Enrollment (%)	100.0	41.3	49.6	1.7	1.7	5.7
Drop-out Rate (%)	4.8	4.7	5.0	2.4	10.1	3.6
H.S. Diplomas (#)	2,809	1,211	1,290	80	50	178

Fort Bragg District

PO Box 70089 • Fort Bragg, NC 28307-0089
(910) 436-5410
Grade Span: PK-10; **Agency Type:** 6
Schools: 9
7 Primary; 2 Middle; 0 High; 0 Other Level
9 Regular; 0 Special Education; 0 Vocational; 0 Alternative
0 Magnet; 0 Charter; 0 Title I Eligible; 0 School-wide Title I
Students: 4,537 (n/a% male; n/a% female)
Individual Education Program: 402 (8.9%);
English Language Learner: 242 (5.3%); Migrant: n/a
Eligible for Free Lunch Program: n/a
Eligible for Reduced-Price Lunch Program: n/a
Teachers: 295.0 (15.4 to 1)
Librarians/Media Specialists: 9.0 (504.1 to 1)
Guidance Counselors: 13.5 (336.1 to 1)
Current Spending: ($ per student per year):
Total: n/a; Instruction: n/a; Support Services: n/a
Enrollment, Drop-out Rates and Diploma Recipients by Race/Ethnicity

Category	Total	White	Black	Asian	AIAN	Hisp.
Enrollment (%)	100.0	47.3	28.9	2.8	1.2	16.9
Drop-out Rate (%)	n/a	n/a	n/a	n/a	n/a	n/a
H.S. Diplomas (#)	n/a	n/a	n/a	n/a	n/a	n/a

Currituck County

Currituck County Schools

2958 Caratoke Hwy • Currituck, NC 27929-0040
Mailing Address: PO Box 40 • Currituck, NC 27929-0040
(252) 232-2223 • http://www.currituck.k12.nc.us
Grade Span: KG-12; **Agency Type:** 1
Schools: 8
5 Primary; 2 Middle; 1 High; 0 Other Level
8 Regular; 0 Special Education; 0 Vocational; 0 Alternative
0 Magnet; 0 Charter; 4 Title I Eligible; 0 School-wide Title I
Students: 3,427 (50.0% male; 50.0% female)
Individual Education Program: 549 (16.0%);
English Language Learner: 6 (0.2%); Migrant: 0 (0.0%)
Eligible for Free Lunch Program: 647 (18.9%)
Eligible for Reduced-Price Lunch Program: 265 (7.7%)
Teachers: 241.0 (14.2 to 1)

Librarians/Media Specialists: 9.0 (380.8 to 1)
Guidance Counselors: 10.0 (342.7 to 1)
Current Spending: ($ per student per year):
Total: $7,194; Instruction: $4,367; Support Services: $2,498
Enrollment, Drop-out Rates and Diploma Recipients by Race/Ethnicity

Category	Total	White	Black	Asian	AIAN	Hisp.
Enrollment (%)	100.0	87.5	10.1	0.4	0.3	1.6
Drop-out Rate (%)	6.4	6.9	3.1	0.0	0.0	0.0
H.S. Diplomas (#)	195	170	23	1	0	1

Dare County

Dare County Schools

510 Budleigh St • Manteo, NC 27954-0640
Mailing Address: PO Box 640 • Manteo, NC 27954-0640
(252) 473-1151 • http://www.dare.k12.nc.us/
Grade Span: PK-12; **Agency Type:** 1
Schools: 9
4 Primary; 2 Middle; 2 High; 1 Other Level
8 Regular; 0 Special Education; 0 Vocational; 1 Alternative
0 Magnet; 0 Charter; 3 Title I Eligible; 0 School-wide Title I
Students: 4,724 (52.0% male; 48.0% female)
Individual Education Program: 551 (11.7%);
English Language Learner: 94 (2.0%); Migrant: 0 (0.0%)
Eligible for Free Lunch Program: 592 (12.5%)
Eligible for Reduced-Price Lunch Program: 283 (6.0%)
Teachers: 328.0 (14.4 to 1)
Librarians/Media Specialists: 9.0 (524.9 to 1)
Guidance Counselors: 15.0 (314.9 to 1)
Current Spending: ($ per student per year):
Total: $6,960; Instruction: $4,476; Support Services: $2,233
Enrollment, Drop-out Rates and Diploma Recipients by Race/Ethnicity

Category	Total	White	Black	Asian	AIAN	Hisp.
Enrollment (%)	100.0	91.3	4.9	0.4	0.1	3.2
Drop-out Rate (%)	7.9	7.7	7.0	33.3	0.0	13.8
H.S. Diplomas (#)	259	245	10	0	0	4

Davidson County

Davidson County Schools

250 County School Rd • Lexington, NC 27292
Mailing Address: PO Box 2057 • Lexington, NC 27293-2057
(336) 249-8182 • http://www.davidson.k12.nc.us/
Grade Span: PK-12; **Agency Type:** 1
Schools: 28
14 Primary; 6 Middle; 6 High; 2 Other Level
26 Regular; 1 Special Education; 0 Vocational; 1 Alternative
0 Magnet; 0 Charter; 10 Title I Eligible; 0 School-wide Title I
Students: 19,283 (50.9% male; 49.1% female)
Individual Education Program: 2,428 (12.6%);
English Language Learner: 102 (0.5%); Migrant: 0 (0.0%)
Eligible for Free Lunch Program: 3,519 (18.2%)
Eligible for Reduced-Price Lunch Program: 1,280 (6.6%)
Teachers: 1,156.0 (16.7 to 1)
Librarians/Media Specialists: 27.0 (714.2 to 1)
Guidance Counselors: 46.0 (419.2 to 1)
Current Spending: ($ per student per year):
Total: $5,425; Instruction: $3,494; Support Services: $1,590
Enrollment, Drop-out Rates and Diploma Recipients by Race/Ethnicity

Category	Total	White	Black	Asian	AIAN	Hisp.
Enrollment (%)	100.0	94.6	2.8	0.7	0.3	1.6
Drop-out Rate (%)	6.8	6.9	5.3	0.0	9.5	7.1
H.S. Diplomas (#)	1,046	1,010	22	5	1	8

Lexington City Schools

1010 Fair St • Lexington, NC 27292-1665
(336) 242-1527 • http://www.lexcs.org/
Grade Span: PK-12; **Agency Type:** 1
Schools: 6
3 Primary; 2 Middle; 1 High; 0 Other Level
6 Regular; 0 Special Education; 0 Vocational; 0 Alternative
0 Magnet; 0 Charter; 5 Title I Eligible; 5 School-wide Title I
Students: 3,313 (51.1% male; 48.9% female)
Individual Education Program: 492 (14.9%);
English Language Learner: 433 (13.1%); Migrant: 0 (0.0%)
Eligible for Free Lunch Program: 2,184 (65.9%)
Eligible for Reduced-Price Lunch Program: 390 (11.8%)
Teachers: 214.0 (15.5 to 1)
Librarians/Media Specialists: 6.0 (552.2 to 1)
Guidance Counselors: 8.0 (414.1 to 1)
Current Spending: ($ per student per year):
Total: $6,792; Instruction: $4,099; Support Services: $2,289

Enrollment, Drop-out Rates and Diploma Recipients by Race/Ethnicity

Category	Total	White	Black	Asian	AIAN	Hisp.
Enrollment (%)	100.0	29.2	45.6	5.5	0.3	19.3
Drop-out Rate (%)	8.0	10.2	5.7	11.5	0.0	9.8
H.S. Diplomas (#)	136	47	70	12	1	6

Thomasville City Schools

400 Turner St • Thomasville, NC 27360-3129
(336) 474-4200 • http://www.tcs.k12.nc.us/
Grade Span: PK-12; **Agency Type:** 1
Schools: 4
2 Primary; 1 Middle; 1 High; 0 Other Level
4 Regular; 0 Special Education; 0 Vocational; 0 Alternative
0 Magnet; 0 Charter; 2 Title I Eligible; 2 School-wide Title I
Students: 2,480 (51.7% male; 48.3% female)
Individual Education Program: 253 (10.2%);
English Language Learner: 230 (9.3%); Migrant: 0 (0.0%)
Eligible for Free Lunch Program: 1,555 (62.7%)
Eligible for Reduced-Price Lunch Program: 254 (10.2%)
Teachers: 177.0 (14.0 to 1)
Librarians/Media Specialists: 4.0 (620.0 to 1)
Guidance Counselors: 5.0 (496.0 to 1)
Current Spending: ($ per student per year):
Total: $7,280; Instruction: $4,700; Support Services: $2,058
Enrollment, Drop-out Rates and Diploma Recipients by Race/Ethnicity

Category	Total	White	Black	Asian	AIAN	Hisp.
Enrollment (%)	100.0	34.3	49.8	0.7	0.1	15.1
Drop-out Rate (%)	4.9	4.0	6.0	0.0	0.0	3.3
H.S. Diplomas (#)	91	37	48	1	0	5

Davie County

Davie County Schools

220 Cherry St • Mocksville, NC 27028-2206
(336) 751-5921 • http://www.davie.k12.nc.us/
Grade Span: PK-12; **Agency Type:** 1
Schools: 9
6 Primary; 2 Middle; 1 High; 0 Other Level
9 Regular; 0 Special Education; 0 Vocational; 0 Alternative
0 Magnet; 0 Charter; 5 Title I Eligible; 0 School-wide Title I
Students: 5,948 (51.5% male; 48.5% female)
Individual Education Program: 833 (14.0%);
English Language Learner: 213 (3.6%); Migrant: 0 (0.0%)
Eligible for Free Lunch Program: 1,225 (20.6%)
Eligible for Reduced-Price Lunch Program: 395 (6.6%)
Teachers: 394.0 (15.1 to 1)
Librarians/Media Specialists: 11.0 (540.7 to 1)
Guidance Counselors: 16.0 (371.8 to 1)
Current Spending: ($ per student per year):
Total: $6,120; Instruction: $3,903; Support Services: $1,839
Enrollment, Drop-out Rates and Diploma Recipients by Race/Ethnicity

Category	Total	White	Black	Asian	AIAN	Hisp.
Enrollment (%)	100.0	84.0	9.6	0.3	0.1	6.0
Drop-out Rate (%)	7.1	6.0	13.0	0.0	100.0	18.6
H.S. Diplomas (#)	327	288	29	3	0	7

Duplin County

Duplin County Schools

Hwy 11 N • Kenansville, NC 28349-0128
Mailing Address: PO Box 128 • Kenansville, NC 28349-0128
(910) 296-1521 • http://www.duplinschools.net/
Grade Span: PK-12; **Agency Type:** 1
Schools: 15
8 Primary; 3 Middle; 4 High; 0 Other Level
15 Regular; 0 Special Education; 0 Vocational; 0 Alternative
0 Magnet; 0 Charter; 9 Title I Eligible; 9 School-wide Title I
Students: 8,786 (50.9% male; 49.1% female)
Individual Education Program: 979 (11.1%);
English Language Learner: 1,134 (12.9%); Migrant: 413 (4.7%)
Eligible for Free Lunch Program: 4,961 (56.5%)
Eligible for Reduced-Price Lunch Program: 669 (7.6%)
Teachers: 583.0 (15.1 to 1)
Librarians/Media Specialists: 15.0 (585.7 to 1)
Guidance Counselors: 18.0 (488.1 to 1)
Current Spending: ($ per student per year):
Total: $5,912; Instruction: $3,773; Support Services: $1,741
Enrollment, Drop-out Rates and Diploma Recipients by Race/Ethnicity

Category	Total	White	Black	Asian	AIAN	Hisp.
Enrollment (%)	100.0	45.6	34.9	0.1	0.2	19.2
Drop-out Rate (%)	7.2	4.4	9.2	100.0	0.0	15.2
H.S. Diplomas (#)	442	273	145	0	0	24

Durham County

Durham Public Schools

511 Cleveland St • Durham, NC 27701
Mailing Address: PO Box 30002 • Durham, NC 27702-3002
(919) 560-2000 • http://www.dpsnc.net/
Grade Span: PK-12; **Agency Type:** 1
Schools: 44
27 Primary; 8 Middle; 5 High; 4 Other Level
41 Regular; 0 Special Education; 0 Vocational; 3 Alternative
7 Magnet; 0 Charter; 19 Title I Eligible; 15 School-wide Title I
Students: 30,794 (51.4% male; 48.6% female)
Individual Education Program: 3,944 (12.8%);
English Language Learner: 2,001 (6.5%); Migrant: 0 (0.0%)
Eligible for Free Lunch Program: 0 (0.0%)
Eligible for Reduced-Price Lunch Program: 0 (0.0%)
Teachers: 2,051.0 (15.0 to 1)
Librarians/Media Specialists: 48.0 (641.5 to 1)
Guidance Counselors: 87.0 (354.0 to 1)
Current Spending: ($ per student per year):
Total: $7,497; Instruction: $4,523; Support Services: $2,604
Enrollment, Drop-out Rates and Diploma Recipients by Race/Ethnicity

Category	Total	White	Black	Asian	AIAN	Hisp.
Enrollment (%)	100.0	29.2	59.3	2.4	0.3	8.9
Drop-out Rate (%)	4.8	2.9	6.2	1.1	8.7	6.3
H.S. Diplomas (#)	1,435	677	663	41	3	51

Edgecombe County

Edgecombe County Schools

412 Pearl St • Tarboro, NC 27886-7128
Mailing Address: PO Box 7128 • Tarboro, NC 27886-7128
(252) 641-2600 •
http://schools.eastnet.ecu.edu/edgecomb/visitschools.htm
Grade Span: PK-12; **Agency Type:** 1
Schools: 15
6 Primary; 5 Middle; 3 High; 1 Other Level
14 Regular; 0 Special Education; 0 Vocational; 1 Alternative
4 Magnet; 0 Charter; 7 Title I Eligible; 7 School-wide Title I
Students: 7,825 (51.0% male; 49.0% female)
Individual Education Program: 997 (12.7%);
English Language Learner: 362 (4.6%); Migrant: 232 (3.0%)
Eligible for Free Lunch Program: 4,104 (52.4%)
Eligible for Reduced-Price Lunch Program: 987 (12.6%)
Teachers: 525.0 (14.9 to 1)
Librarians/Media Specialists: 14.0 (558.9 to 1)
Guidance Counselors: 18.0 (434.7 to 1)
Current Spending: ($ per student per year):
Total: $6,495; Instruction: $4,030; Support Services: $2,110
Enrollment, Drop-out Rates and Diploma Recipients by Race/Ethnicity

Category	Total	White	Black	Asian	AIAN	Hisp.
Enrollment (%)	100.0	38.0	57.1	0.2	0.0	4.7
Drop-out Rate (%)	8.5	7.0	8.9	40.0	n/a	20.5
H.S. Diplomas (#)	391	158	230	0	0	3

Forsyth County

Forsyth County Schools

1605 Miller St • Winston Salem, NC 27103
Mailing Address: PO Box 2513 • Winston Salem, NC 27102-2513
(336) 727-2816 • http://mts.admin.wsfcs.k12.nc.us/
Grade Span: PK-12; **Agency Type:** 1
Schools: 68
40 Primary; 15 Middle; 10 High; 3 Other Level
61 Regular; 3 Special Education; 1 Vocational; 3 Alternative
51 Magnet; 0 Charter; 26 Title I Eligible; 19 School-wide Title I
Students: 46,806 (51.6% male; 48.4% female)
Individual Education Program: 6,357 (13.6%);
English Language Learner: 2,737 (5.8%); Migrant: 0 (0.0%)
Eligible for Free Lunch Program: 16,146 (34.5%)
Eligible for Reduced-Price Lunch Program: 2,623 (5.6%)
Teachers: 3,186.0 (14.7 to 1)
Librarians/Media Specialists: 62.0 (754.9 to 1)
Guidance Counselors: 97.0 (482.5 to 1)
Current Spending: ($ per student per year):
Total: $6,711; Instruction: $4,395; Support Services: $2,001
Enrollment, Drop-out Rates and Diploma Recipients by Race/Ethnicity

Category	Total	White	Black	Asian	AIAN	Hisp.
Enrollment (%)	100.0	51.0	37.7	1.2	0.2	9.8
Drop-out Rate (%)	6.3	5.5	6.7	3.8	3.8	17.1
H.S. Diplomas (#)	2,271	1,441	716	29	4	81

Franklin County

Franklin County Schools

105 S Bickett Blvd • Louisburg, NC 27549-0449
Mailing Address: PO Box 449 • Louisburg, NC 27549-0449
(919) 496-4159 • http://www.franklinco.k12.nc.us/
Grade Span: PK-12; **Agency Type:** 1
Schools: 14
8 Primary; 3 Middle; 3 High; 0 Other Level
14 Regular; 0 Special Education; 0 Vocational; 0 Alternative
1 Magnet; 0 Charter; 8 Title I Eligible; 7 School-wide Title I
Students: 7,914 (51.9% male; 48.1% female)
Individual Education Program: 869 (11.0%);
English Language Learner: 222 (2.8%); Migrant: 147 (1.9%)
Eligible for Free Lunch Program: 3,104 (39.2%)
Eligible for Reduced-Price Lunch Program: 810 (10.2%)
Teachers: 536.0 (14.8 to 1)
Librarians/Media Specialists: 14.0 (565.3 to 1)
Guidance Counselors: 18.0 (439.7 to 1)
Current Spending: ($ per student per year):
Total: $6,020; Instruction: $3,600; Support Services: $2,003
Enrollment, Drop-out Rates and Diploma Recipients by Race/Ethnicity

Category	Total	White	Black	Asian	AIAN	Hisp.
Enrollment (%)	100.0	53.2	39.6	0.5	0.3	6.5
Drop-out Rate (%)	7.0	4.9	9.8	10.0	0.0	8.6
H.S. Diplomas (#)	352	209	135	1	0	7

Gaston County

Gaston County Schools

943 Osceola St • Gastonia, NC 28054-1397
Mailing Address: PO Box 1397 • Gastonia, NC 28053-1397
(704) 866-6100 • http://www.gaston.k12.nc.us/
Grade Span: PK-12; **Agency Type:** 1
Schools: 52
30 Primary; 11 Middle; 9 High; 2 Other Level
50 Regular; 1 Special Education; 0 Vocational; 1 Alternative
0 Magnet; 0 Charter; 12 Title I Eligible; 12 School-wide Title I
Students: 31,258 (51.3% male; 48.7% female)
Individual Education Program: 3,889 (12.4%);
English Language Learner: 1,005 (3.2%); Migrant: 0 (0.0%)
Eligible for Free Lunch Program: 9,244 (29.6%)
Eligible for Reduced-Price Lunch Program: 2,560 (8.2%)
Teachers: 1,879.0 (16.6 to 1)
Librarians/Media Specialists: 53.0 (589.8 to 1)
Guidance Counselors: 68.0 (459.7 to 1)
Current Spending: ($ per student per year):
Total: $6,002; Instruction: $3,970; Support Services: $1,651
Enrollment, Drop-out Rates and Diploma Recipients by Race/Ethnicity

Category	Total	White	Black	Asian	AIAN	Hisp.
Enrollment (%)	100.0	73.9	20.6	1.4	0.2	4.0
Drop-out Rate (%)	7.1	6.6	9.2	5.7	6.3	5.6
H.S. Diplomas (#)	1,466	1,137	286	15	1	27

Gates County

Gates County Schools

205 Main St • Gatesville, NC 27938-0125
Mailing Address: PO Box 125 • Gatesville, NC 27938-0125
(252) 357-1113 • http://coserver.gates.k12.nc.us/
Grade Span: PK-12; **Agency Type:** 1
Schools: 5
3 Primary; 1 Middle; 1 High; 0 Other Level
5 Regular; 0 Special Education; 0 Vocational; 0 Alternative
0 Magnet; 0 Charter; 3 Title I Eligible; 3 School-wide Title I
Students: 1,993 (52.3% male; 47.7% female)
Individual Education Program: 419 (21.0%);
English Language Learner: 5 (0.3%); Migrant: 0 (0.0%)
Eligible for Free Lunch Program: 760 (38.1%)
Eligible for Reduced-Price Lunch Program: 252 (12.6%)
Teachers: 156.0 (12.8 to 1)
Librarians/Media Specialists: 5.0 (398.6 to 1)
Guidance Counselors: 7.0 (284.7 to 1)
Current Spending: ($ per student per year):
Total: $7,378; Instruction: $4,436; Support Services: $2,542
Enrollment, Drop-out Rates and Diploma Recipients by Race/Ethnicity

Category	Total	White	Black	Asian	AIAN	Hisp.
Enrollment (%)	100.0	55.9	42.5	0.5	0.1	1.0
Drop-out Rate (%)	5.1	4.8	5.6	0.0	n/a	n/a
H.S. Diplomas (#)	92	48	44	0	0	0

Granville County

Granville County Schools

101 Delacroix St • Oxford, NC 27565-2516
Mailing Address: PO Box 927 • Oxford, NC 27565-0927
(919) 693-4613 • http://eclipse.gcs.k12.nc.us/public/
Grade Span: PK-12; **Agency Type:** 1
Schools: 14
8 Primary; 4 Middle; 2 High; 0 Other Level
14 Regular; 0 Special Education; 0 Vocational; 0 Alternative
0 Magnet; 0 Charter; 6 Title I Eligible; 6 School-wide Title I
Students: 8,548 (50.8% male; 49.2% female)
Individual Education Program: 1,111 (13.0%);
English Language Learner: 394 (4.6%); Migrant: 136 (1.6%)
Eligible for Free Lunch Program: 2,984 (34.9%)
Eligible for Reduced-Price Lunch Program: 808 (9.5%)
Teachers: 524.0 (16.3 to 1)
Librarians/Media Specialists: 15.0 (569.9 to 1)
Guidance Counselors: 27.0 (316.6 to 1)
Current Spending: ($ per student per year):
Total: $5,956; Instruction: $3,716; Support Services: $1,893
Enrollment, Drop-out Rates and Diploma Recipients by Race/Ethnicity

Category	Total	White	Black	Asian	AIAN	Hisp.
Enrollment (%)	100.0	54.9	40.0	0.5	0.2	4.4
Drop-out Rate (%)	7.3	6.0	8.6	0.0	66.7	20.0
H.S. Diplomas (#)	328	201	117	2	0	8

Greene County

Greene County Schools

301 Kingold Blvd • Snow Hill, NC 28580-1393
(252) 747-3425 • http://www.greene.k12.nc.us/gc/greene.htm
Grade Span: PK-12; **Agency Type:** 1
Schools: 4
2 Primary; 1 Middle; 1 High; 0 Other Level
4 Regular; 0 Special Education; 0 Vocational; 0 Alternative
0 Magnet; 0 Charter; 3 Title I Eligible; 3 School-wide Title I
Students: 3,259 (53.8% male; 46.2% female)
Individual Education Program: 557 (17.1%);
English Language Learner: 387 (11.9%); Migrant: 149 (4.6%)
Eligible for Free Lunch Program: 1,828 (56.1%)
Eligible for Reduced-Price Lunch Program: 336 (10.3%)
Teachers: 235.0 (13.9 to 1)
Librarians/Media Specialists: 4.0 (814.8 to 1)
Guidance Counselors: 12.0 (271.6 to 1)
Current Spending: ($ per student per year):
Total: $6,669; Instruction: $4,020; Support Services: $2,235
Enrollment, Drop-out Rates and Diploma Recipients by Race/Ethnicity

Category	Total	White	Black	Asian	AIAN	Hisp.
Enrollment (%)	100.0	35.5	50.9	0.3	0.0	13.2
Drop-out Rate (%)	7.7	7.9	7.3	0.0	n/a	10.2
H.S. Diplomas (#)	117	53	60	0	0	4

Guilford County

Guilford County Schools

712 N Eugene St • Greensboro, NC 27401
Mailing Address: PO Box 880 • Greensboro, NC 27402-0880
(336) 370-8100 • http://www.guilford.k12.nc.us/
Grade Span: PK-12; **Agency Type:** 1
Schools: 102
64 Primary; 17 Middle; 18 High; 3 Other Level
99 Regular; 2 Special Education; 0 Vocational; 1 Alternative
13 Magnet; 0 Charter; 45 Title I Eligible; 45 School-wide Title I
Students: 65,677 (51.0% male; 49.0% female)
Individual Education Program: 10,506 (16.0%);
English Language Learner: 3,548 (5.4%); Migrant: 0 (0.0%)
Eligible for Free Lunch Program: 24,386 (37.1%)
Eligible for Reduced-Price Lunch Program: 5,106 (7.8%)
Teachers: 4,089.0 (16.1 to 1)
Librarians/Media Specialists: 108.0 (608.1 to 1)
Guidance Counselors: 184.0 (356.9 to 1)
Current Spending: ($ per student per year):
Total: $6,716; Instruction: $4,135; Support Services: $2,234
Enrollment, Drop-out Rates and Diploma Recipients by Race/Ethnicity

Category	Total	White	Black	Asian	AIAN	Hisp.
Enrollment (%)	100.0	46.8	43.5	4.3	0.7	4.8
Drop-out Rate (%)	4.6	3.3	6.1	5.9	20.0	6.2
H.S. Diplomas (#)	3,304	2,020	1,106	122	8	48

Halifax County

Halifax County Schools

9525 Hwy 301s • Halifax, NC 27839-0468
Mailing Address: PO Box 468 • Halifax, NC 27839-0468
(252) 583-5111 • http://www.schoollink.net/hcs/departments/index.html
Grade Span: PK-12; **Agency Type:** 1
Schools: 15
9 Primary; 4 Middle; 2 High; 0 Other Level
15 Regular; 0 Special Education; 0 Vocational; 0 Alternative
0 Magnet; 0 Charter; 15 Title I Eligible; 15 School-wide Title I
Students: 5,864 (51.7% male; 48.3% female)
Individual Education Program: 1,003 (17.1%);
English Language Learner: 56 (1.0%); Migrant: 154 (2.6%)
Eligible for Free Lunch Program: 4,065 (69.3%)
Eligible for Reduced-Price Lunch Program: 568 (9.7%)
Teachers: 360.0 (16.3 to 1)
Librarians/Media Specialists: 11.0 (533.1 to 1)
Guidance Counselors: 15.0 (390.9 to 1)
Current Spending: ($ per student per year):
Total: $7,068; Instruction: $4,396; Support Services: $2,224
Enrollment, Drop-out Rates and Diploma Recipients by Race/Ethnicity

Category	Total	White	Black	Asian	AIAN	Hisp.
Enrollment (%)	100.0	5.6	88.5	0.1	5.2	0.7
Drop-out Rate (%)	6.6	10.7	6.6	n/a	5.6	0.0
H.S. Diplomas (#)	267	7	249	0	11	0

Roanoke Rapids City Schools

536 Hamilton St • Roanoke Rapids, NC 27870-9990
(252) 535-3111 • http://www.rrgsd.org/
Grade Span: PK-12; **Agency Type:** 1
Schools: 4
2 Primary; 1 Middle; 1 High; 0 Other Level
4 Regular; 0 Special Education; 0 Vocational; 0 Alternative
0 Magnet; 0 Charter; 1 Title I Eligible; 1 School-wide Title I
Students: 3,065 (51.0% male; 49.0% female)
Individual Education Program: 405 (13.2%);
English Language Learner: 24 (0.8%); Migrant: 0 (0.0%)
Eligible for Free Lunch Program: 1,043 (34.0%)
Eligible for Reduced-Price Lunch Program: 264 (8.6%)
Teachers: 209.0 (14.7 to 1)
Librarians/Media Specialists: 4.0 (766.3 to 1)
Guidance Counselors: 9.0 (340.6 to 1)
Current Spending: ($ per student per year):
Total: $6,479; Instruction: $3,960; Support Services: $2,126
Enrollment, Drop-out Rates and Diploma Recipients by Race/Ethnicity

Category	Total	White	Black	Asian	AIAN	Hisp.
Enrollment (%)	100.0	74.2	22.7	1.5	0.4	1.2
Drop-out Rate (%)	6.9	7.0	6.5	5.6	0.0	10.0
H.S. Diplomas (#)	165	134	24	1	1	5

Harnett County

Harnett County Schools

1 W Harnett St • Lillington, NC 27546-1029
Mailing Address: PO Box 1029 • Lillington, NC 27546-1029
(910) 893-8151 • http://www.harnett.k12.nc.us/
Grade Span: PK-12; **Agency Type:** 1
Schools: 26
14 Primary; 8 Middle; 3 High; 1 Other Level
25 Regular; 0 Special Education; 0 Vocational; 1 Alternative
0 Magnet; 0 Charter; 23 Title I Eligible; 21 School-wide Title I
Students: 16,725 (51.0% male; 49.0% female)
Individual Education Program: 2,369 (14.2%);
English Language Learner: 1,382 (8.3%); Migrant: 598 (3.6%)
Eligible for Free Lunch Program: 6,727 (40.2%)
Eligible for Reduced-Price Lunch Program: 1,750 (10.5%)
Teachers: 1,052.0 (15.9 to 1)
Librarians/Media Specialists: 27.0 (619.4 to 1)
Guidance Counselors: 39.0 (428.8 to 1)
Current Spending: ($ per student per year):
Total: $5,638; Instruction: $3,803; Support Services: $1,472
Enrollment, Drop-out Rates and Diploma Recipients by Race/Ethnicity

Category	Total	White	Black	Asian	AIAN	Hisp.
Enrollment (%)	100.0	58.1	32.9	0.4	0.8	7.8
Drop-out Rate (%)	8.0	7.3	9.1	4.0	17.1	9.3
H.S. Diplomas (#)	759	522	191	7	8	31

Haywood County

Haywood County Schools

1230 N Main St • Waynesville, NC 28786-3461
(828) 456-2400 • http://www.haywood.k12.nc.us/
Grade Span: PK-12; **Agency Type:** 1
Schools: 15

9 Primary; 3 Middle; 3 High; 0 Other Level
14 Regular; 0 Special Education; 0 Vocational; 1 Alternative
0 Magnet; 0 Charter; 9 Title I Eligible; 6 School-wide Title I
Students: 7,869 (50.9% male; 49.1% female)
Individual Education Program: 1,242 (15.8%);
English Language Learner: 107 (1.4%); Migrant: 95 (1.2%)
Eligible for Free Lunch Program: 2,276 (28.9%)
Eligible for Reduced-Price Lunch Program: 735 (9.3%)
Teachers: 531.0 (14.8 to 1)
Librarians/Media Specialists: 15.0 (524.6 to 1)
Guidance Counselors: 21.0 (374.7 to 1)
Current Spending: ($ per student per year):
Total: $6,614; Instruction: $4,159; Support Services: $2,041
Enrollment, Drop-out Rates and Diploma Recipients by Race/Ethnicity

Category	Total	White	Black	Asian	AIAN	Hisp.
Enrollment (%)	100.0	94.7	2.1	0.3	0.7	2.1
Drop-out Rate (%)	6.5	6.6	0.0	0.0	33.3	5.9
H.S. Diplomas (#)	431	414	7	1	1	8

Henderson County

Henderson County Schools

414 4th Ave W • Hendersonville, NC 28739-4261
(828) 697-4733 • http://www.henderson.k12.nc.us/
Grade Span: PK-12; **Agency Type:** 1
Schools: 21
12 Primary; 4 Middle; 4 High; 1 Other Level
20 Regular; 0 Special Education; 0 Vocational; 1 Alternative
0 Magnet; 0 Charter; 9 Title I Eligible; 8 School-wide Title I
Students: 12,013 (52.1% male; 47.9% female)
Individual Education Program: 1,645 (13.7%);
English Language Learner: 930 (7.7%); Migrant: 452 (3.8%)
Eligible for Free Lunch Program: 3,357 (27.9%)
Eligible for Reduced-Price Lunch Program: 901 (7.5%)
Teachers: 759.0 (15.8 to 1)
Librarians/Media Specialists: 20.0 (600.7 to 1)
Guidance Counselors: 31.0 (387.5 to 1)
Current Spending: ($ per student per year):
Total: $6,278; Instruction: $4,126; Support Services: $1,813
Enrollment, Drop-out Rates and Diploma Recipients by Race/Ethnicity

Category	Total	White	Black	Asian	AIAN	Hisp.
Enrollment (%)	100.0	82.4	6.8	0.9	0.3	9.5
Drop-out Rate (%)	6.3	6.2	4.8	0.0	50.0	10.0
H.S. Diplomas (#)	650	577	46	7	0	20

Hertford County

Hertford County Schools

701 N Martin St • Winton, NC 27986-0158
Mailing Address: PO Box 158 • Winton, NC 27986-0158
(252) 358-1761
Grade Span: PK-12; **Agency Type:** 1
Schools: 6
3 Primary; 1 Middle; 1 High; 1 Other Level
6 Regular; 0 Special Education; 0 Vocational; 0 Alternative
0 Magnet; 0 Charter; 5 Title I Eligible; 4 School-wide Title I
Students: 3,950 (49.7% male; 50.3% female)
Individual Education Program: 624 (15.8%);
English Language Learner: 15 (0.4%); Migrant: 0 (0.0%)
Eligible for Free Lunch Program: 2,456 (62.2%)
Eligible for Reduced-Price Lunch Program: 379 (9.6%)
Teachers: 251.0 (15.7 to 1)
Librarians/Media Specialists: 5.0 (790.0 to 1)
Guidance Counselors: 11.0 (359.1 to 1)
Current Spending: ($ per student per year):
Total: $6,600; Instruction: $3,958; Support Services: $2,242
Enrollment, Drop-out Rates and Diploma Recipients by Race/Ethnicity

Category	Total	White	Black	Asian	AIAN	Hisp.
Enrollment (%)	100.0	17.3	80.6	0.6	1.1	0.5
Drop-out Rate (%)	5.3	4.6	5.6	n/a	0.0	0.0
H.S. Diplomas (#)	215	64	149	0	2	0

Hoke County

Hoke County Schools

310 Wooley St • Raeford, NC 28376-3299
Mailing Address: PO Box 370 • Raeford, NC 28376-0370
(910) 875-4106 • http://www.hcs.k12.nc.us/
Grade Span: PK-12; **Agency Type:** 1
Schools: 11
7 Primary; 2 Middle; 1 High; 1 Other Level
10 Regular; 0 Special Education; 0 Vocational; 1 Alternative
0 Magnet; 0 Charter; 7 Title I Eligible; 7 School-wide Title I
Students: 6,465 (50.8% male; 49.2% female)
Individual Education Program: 1,057 (16.3%);
English Language Learner: 221 (3.4%); Migrant: 233 (3.6%)
Eligible for Free Lunch Program: 3,065 (47.4%)
Eligible for Reduced-Price Lunch Program: 945 (14.6%)
Teachers: 371.0 (17.4 to 1)
Librarians/Media Specialists: 11.0 (587.7 to 1)
Guidance Counselors: 14.0 (461.8 to 1)
Current Spending: ($ per student per year):
Total: $5,766; Instruction: $3,659; Support Services: $1,732
Enrollment, Drop-out Rates and Diploma Recipients by Race/Ethnicity

Category	Total	White	Black	Asian	AIAN	Hisp.
Enrollment (%)	100.0	29.8	47.7	0.9	14.8	6.8
Drop-out Rate (%)	9.8	10.0	9.1	5.6	12.9	6.1
H.S. Diplomas (#)	263	84	138	4	30	7

Iredell County

Iredell-Statesville Schools

549 N Race St • Statesville, NC 28677
Mailing Address: PO Box 911 • Statesville, NC 28687-0911
(704) 872-8931 • http://www.iss.k12.nc.us/
Grade Span: PK-12; **Agency Type:** 1
Schools: 32
19 Primary; 7 Middle; 5 High; 1 Other Level
31 Regular; 0 Special Education; 0 Vocational; 1 Alternative
0 Magnet; 0 Charter; 13 Title I Eligible; 6 School-wide Title I
Students: 18,566 (51.1% male; 48.9% female)
Individual Education Program: 2,451 (13.2%);
English Language Learner: 670 (3.6%); Migrant: 0 (0.0%)
Eligible for Free Lunch Program: 4,410 (23.8%)
Eligible for Reduced-Price Lunch Program: 1,706 (9.2%)
Teachers: 1,075.0 (17.3 to 1)
Librarians/Media Specialists: 36.0 (515.7 to 1)
Guidance Counselors: 47.0 (395.0 to 1)
Current Spending: ($ per student per year):
Total: $6,146; Instruction: $3,821; Support Services: $1,951
Enrollment, Drop-out Rates and Diploma Recipients by Race/Ethnicity

Category	Total	White	Black	Asian	AIAN	Hisp.
Enrollment (%)	100.0	73.3	18.3	2.6	0.1	5.5
Drop-out Rate (%)	6.8	5.9	8.1	9.2	0.0	21.1
H.S. Diplomas (#)	821	637	138	23	2	21

Mooresville City Schools

305 N Main • Mooresville, NC 28115-2453
(704) 664-5553 • http://www.mgsd.k12.nc.us/
Grade Span: PK-12; **Agency Type:** 1
Schools: 6
2 Primary; 2 Middle; 2 High; 0 Other Level
5 Regular; 0 Special Education; 1 Vocational; 0 Alternative
0 Magnet; 0 Charter; 1 Title I Eligible; 0 School-wide Title I
Students: 4,208 (50.3% male; 49.7% female)
Individual Education Program: 530 (12.6%);
English Language Learner: 50 (1.2%); Migrant: 0 (0.0%)
Eligible for Free Lunch Program: 0 (0.0%)
Eligible for Reduced-Price Lunch Program: 0 (0.0%)
Teachers: 269.0 (15.6 to 1)
Librarians/Media Specialists: 6.0 (701.3 to 1)
Guidance Counselors: 11.0 (382.5 to 1)
Current Spending: ($ per student per year):
Total: $5,795; Instruction: $3,557; Support Services: $1,926
Enrollment, Drop-out Rates and Diploma Recipients by Race/Ethnicity

Category	Total	White	Black	Asian	AIAN	Hisp.
Enrollment (%)	100.0	77.2	18.9	1.8	0.2	1.9
Drop-out Rate (%)	6.1	5.0	10.8	0.0	0.0	33.3
H.S. Diplomas (#)	247	220	24	3	0	0

Jackson County

Jackson County Schools

398 Hospital Rd • Sylva, NC 28779-5196
(828) 586-2311 • http://www.main.nc.us/jackson/jc50educ.html
Grade Span: PK-12; **Agency Type:** 1
Schools: 7
4 Primary; 0 Middle; 1 High; 2 Other Level
6 Regular; 0 Special Education; 0 Vocational; 1 Alternative
0 Magnet; 0 Charter; 5 Title I Eligible; 4 School-wide Title I
Students: 3,720 (52.0% male; 48.0% female)
Individual Education Program: 583 (15.7%);
English Language Learner: 44 (1.2%); Migrant: 0 (0.0%)
Eligible for Free Lunch Program: 1,374 (36.9%)
Eligible for Reduced-Price Lunch Program: 492 (13.2%)
Teachers: 258.0 (14.4 to 1)
Librarians/Media Specialists: 6.0 (620.0 to 1)
Guidance Counselors: 11.0 (338.2 to 1)
Current Spending: ($ per student per year):
Total: $6,820; Instruction: $4,267; Support Services: $2,146

Enrollment, Drop-out Rates and Diploma Recipients by Race/Ethnicity

Category	Total	White	Black	Asian	AIAN	Hisp.
Enrollment (%)	100.0	84.8	2.0	0.7	10.2	2.2
Drop-out Rate (%)	5.9	5.3	10.0	0.0	12.6	0.0
H.S. Diplomas (#)	225	203	4	0	17	1

Johnston County

Johnston County Schools

2320 Hwy 70 E Business • Smithfield, NC 27577-1336
Mailing Address: PO Box 1336 • Smithfield, NC 27577-1336
(919) 934-6031 • http://www.johnston.k12.nc.us/
Grade Span: PK-12; **Agency Type:** 1
Schools: 32
17 Primary; 8 Middle; 4 High; 3 Other Level
31 Regular; 0 Special Education; 0 Vocational; 1 Alternative
0 Magnet; 0 Charter; 11 Title I Eligible; 10 School-wide Title I
Students: 23,506 (51.3% male; 48.7% female)
Individual Education Program: 3,725 (15.8%);
English Language Learner: 1,617 (6.9%); Migrant: 818 (3.5%)
Eligible for Free Lunch Program: 7,347 (31.3%)
Eligible for Reduced-Price Lunch Program: 1,727 (7.3%)
Teachers: 1,683.0 (14.0 to 1)
Librarians/Media Specialists: 34.0 (691.4 to 1)
Guidance Counselors: 61.0 (385.3 to 1)
Current Spending: ($ per student per year):
Total: $6,094; Instruction: $3,863; Support Services: $1,834

Enrollment, Drop-out Rates and Diploma Recipients by Race/Ethnicity

Category	Total	White	Black	Asian	AIAN	Hisp.
Enrollment (%)	100.0	66.9	22.6	0.4	0.3	9.9
Drop-out Rate (%)	6.0	4.8	9.4	0.0	13.3	9.8
H.S. Diplomas (#)	942	735	157	8	4	38

Jones County

Jones County Schools

320 W Jones St • Trenton, NC 28585-0187
Mailing Address: PO Box 187 • Trenton, NC 28585-0187
(252) 448-2531
Grade Span: PK-12; **Agency Type:** 1
Schools: 6
4 Primary; 1 Middle; 1 High; 0 Other Level
6 Regular; 0 Special Education; 0 Vocational; 0 Alternative
0 Magnet; 0 Charter; 5 Title I Eligible; 5 School-wide Title I
Students: 1,510 (51.5% male; 48.5% female)
Individual Education Program: 253 (16.8%);
English Language Learner: 48 (3.2%); Migrant: 0 (0.0%)
Eligible for Free Lunch Program: 878 (58.1%)
Eligible for Reduced-Price Lunch Program: 237 (15.7%)
Teachers: 115.0 (13.1 to 1)
Librarians/Media Specialists: 6.0 (251.7 to 1)
Guidance Counselors: 4.0 (377.5 to 1)
Current Spending: ($ per student per year):
Total: $8,054; Instruction: $4,390; Support Services: $3,125

Enrollment, Drop-out Rates and Diploma Recipients by Race/Ethnicity

Category	Total	White	Black	Asian	AIAN	Hisp.
Enrollment (%)	100.0	41.7	54.7	0.2	0.3	3.2
Drop-out Rate (%)	5.9	9.5	3.8	n/a	n/a	0.0
H.S. Diplomas (#)	51	16	35	0	0	0

Lee County

Lee County Schools

106 Gordon St • Sanford, NC 27330
Mailing Address: PO Box 1010 • Sanford, NC 27331-1010
(919) 774-6226 • http://www.lee.k12.nc.us/
Grade Span: PK-12; **Agency Type:** 1
Schools: 12
7 Primary; 2 Middle; 1 High; 2 Other Level
10 Regular; 1 Special Education; 0 Vocational; 1 Alternative
0 Magnet; 0 Charter; 7 Title I Eligible; 7 School-wide Title I
Students: 9,058 (51.3% male; 48.7% female)
Individual Education Program: 1,075 (11.9%);
English Language Learner: 1,200 (13.2%); Migrant: 476 (5.3%)
Eligible for Free Lunch Program: 3,522 (38.9%)
Eligible for Reduced-Price Lunch Program: 826 (9.1%)
Teachers: 582.0 (15.6 to 1)
Librarians/Media Specialists: 11.0 (823.5 to 1)
Guidance Counselors: 17.0 (532.8 to 1)
Current Spending: ($ per student per year):
Total: $6,218; Instruction: $4,085; Support Services: $1,773

Enrollment, Drop-out Rates and Diploma Recipients by Race/Ethnicity

Category	Total	White	Black	Asian	AIAN	Hisp.
Enrollment (%)	100.0	53.2	26.7	0.8	0.6	18.8
Drop-out Rate (%)	8.0	6.6	8.4	0.0	18.2	16.7
H.S. Diplomas (#)	429	302	96	2	1	28

Lenoir County

Lenoir County Public Schools

2017 W Vernon Ave • Kinston, NC 28504
Mailing Address: PO Box 729 • Kinston, NC 28502-0729
(252) 527-1109 • http://www.lenoir.k12.nc.us/
Grade Span: PK-12; **Agency Type:** 1
Schools: 20
9 Primary; 6 Middle; 3 High; 2 Other Level
18 Regular; 0 Special Education; 0 Vocational; 2 Alternative
0 Magnet; 0 Charter; 16 Title I Eligible; 13 School-wide Title I
Students: 10,249 (51.5% male; 48.5% female)
Individual Education Program: 1,471 (14.4%);
English Language Learner: 239 (2.3%); Migrant: 268 (2.6%)
Eligible for Free Lunch Program: 4,550 (44.4%)
Eligible for Reduced-Price Lunch Program: 827 (8.1%)
Teachers: 719.0 (14.3 to 1)
Librarians/Media Specialists: 19.0 (539.4 to 1)
Guidance Counselors: 28.0 (366.0 to 1)
Current Spending: ($ per student per year):
Total: $6,455; Instruction: $4,210; Support Services: $1,881

Enrollment, Drop-out Rates and Diploma Recipients by Race/Ethnicity

Category	Total	White	Black	Asian	AIAN	Hisp.
Enrollment (%)	100.0	43.5	51.7	0.4	0.1	4.3
Drop-out Rate (%)	7.0	4.9	9.2	0.0	0.0	3.8
H.S. Diplomas (#)	474	240	217	1	2	14

Lincoln County

Lincoln County Schools

353 N Generals Blvd • Lincolnton, NC 28092
Mailing Address: PO Box 400 • Lincolnton, NC 28093-0400
(704) 732-2261 • http://www.lincoln.k12.nc.us/
Grade Span: PK-12; **Agency Type:** 1
Schools: 19
10 Primary; 4 Middle; 5 High; 0 Other Level
17 Regular; 0 Special Education; 1 Vocational; 1 Alternative
0 Magnet; 0 Charter; 8 Title I Eligible; 7 School-wide Title I
Students: 11,106 (51.6% male; 48.4% female)
Individual Education Program: 1,640 (14.8%);
English Language Learner: 776 (7.0%); Migrant: 0 (0.0%)
Eligible for Free Lunch Program: 0 (0.0%)
Eligible for Reduced-Price Lunch Program: 0 (0.0%)
Teachers: 785.0 (14.1 to 1)
Librarians/Media Specialists: 17.0 (653.3 to 1)
Guidance Counselors: 29.0 (383.0 to 1)
Current Spending: ($ per student per year):
Total: $5,724; Instruction: $3,702; Support Services: $1,655

Enrollment, Drop-out Rates and Diploma Recipients by Race/Ethnicity

Category	Total	White	Black	Asian	AIAN	Hisp.
Enrollment (%)	100.0	82.0	10.0	0.4	0.3	7.3
Drop-out Rate (%)	6.6	6.1	5.6	0.0	28.6	14.3
H.S. Diplomas (#)	613	521	54	4	0	34

Macon County

Macon County Schools

1202 Old Murphy Rd • Franklin, NC 28734
Mailing Address: PO Box 1029 • Franklin, NC 28744-1029
(828) 524-3314 • http://www.mcsk-12.org/
Grade Span: PK-12; **Agency Type:** 1
Schools: 10
6 Primary; 1 Middle; 1 High; 2 Other Level
10 Regular; 0 Special Education; 0 Vocational; 0 Alternative
0 Magnet; 0 Charter; 8 Title I Eligible; 8 School-wide Title I
Students: 4,134 (51.7% male; 48.3% female)
Individual Education Program: 695 (16.8%);
English Language Learner: 70 (1.7%); Migrant: 0 (0.0%)
Eligible for Free Lunch Program: 1,305 (31.6%)
Eligible for Reduced-Price Lunch Program: 537 (13.0%)
Teachers: 288.0 (14.4 to 1)
Librarians/Media Specialists: 10.0 (413.4 to 1)
Guidance Counselors: 10.0 (413.4 to 1)
Current Spending: ($ per student per year):
Total: $6,776; Instruction: $4,299; Support Services: $2,000

Enrollment, Drop-out Rates and Diploma Recipients by Race/Ethnicity

Category	Total	White	Black	Asian	AIAN	Hisp.
Enrollment (%)	100.0	94.4	1.8	0.7	0.3	2.8
Drop-out Rate (%)	6.9	6.8	6.7	16.7	50.0	0.0
H.S. Diplomas (#)	247	238	4	4	0	1

Madison County

Madison County Schools

5738 US 25-70 Hwy • Marshall, NC 28753-9006
(828) 649-9276
Grade Span: PK-12; **Agency Type:** 1
Schools: 6
4 Primary; 1 Middle; 1 High; 0 Other Level
6 Regular; 0 Special Education; 0 Vocational; 0 Alternative
0 Magnet; 0 Charter; 4 Title I Eligible; 1 School-wide Title I
Students: 2,562 (53.7% male; 46.3% female)
Individual Education Program: 393 (15.3%);
English Language Learner: 21 (0.8%); Migrant: 0 (0.0%)
Eligible for Free Lunch Program: 881 (34.4%)
Eligible for Reduced-Price Lunch Program: 346 (13.5%)
Teachers: 209.0 (12.3 to 1)
Librarians/Media Specialists: 5.0 (512.4 to 1)
Guidance Counselors: 5.0 (512.4 to 1)
Current Spending: ($ per student per year):
Total: $7,132; Instruction: $4,192; Support Services: $2,492

Enrollment, Drop-out Rates and Diploma Recipients by Race/Ethnicity

Category	Total	White	Black	Asian	AIAN	Hisp.
Enrollment (%)	100.0	97.9	0.4	0.1	0.4	1.2
Drop-out Rate (%)	6.8	6.9	0.0	n/a	0.0	0.0
H.S. Diplomas (#)	129	129	0	0	0	0

Martin County

Martin County Schools

300 N Watts St • Williamston, NC 27892-2099
(252) 792-1575 • http://www.schoollink.net/martin/
Grade Span: PK-12; **Agency Type:** 1
Schools: 12
6 Primary; 2 Middle; 4 High; 0 Other Level
12 Regular; 0 Special Education; 0 Vocational; 0 Alternative
0 Magnet; 0 Charter; 8 Title I Eligible; 8 School-wide Title I
Students: 4,620 (51.3% male; 48.7% female)
Individual Education Program: 662 (14.3%);
English Language Learner: 20 (0.4%); Migrant: 0 (0.0%)
Eligible for Free Lunch Program: 2,407 (52.1%)
Eligible for Reduced-Price Lunch Program: 488 (10.6%)
Teachers: 332.0 (13.9 to 1)
Librarians/Media Specialists: 12.0 (385.0 to 1)
Guidance Counselors: 14.0 (330.0 to 1)
Current Spending: ($ per student per year):
Total: $6,835; Instruction: $4,366; Support Services: $2,066

Enrollment, Drop-out Rates and Diploma Recipients by Race/Ethnicity

Category	Total	White	Black	Asian	AIAN	Hisp.
Enrollment (%)	100.0	41.6	56.0	0.2	0.1	2.1
Drop-out Rate (%)	7.6	5.6	9.2	0.0	50.0	5.9
H.S. Diplomas (#)	270	130	137	1	0	2

Mcdowell County

Mcdowell County Schools

334 S Main St • Marion, NC 28752-0130
Mailing Address: PO Box 130 • Marion, NC 28752-0130
(828) 652-4535 • http://www.mcdowell.k12.nc.us/
Grade Span: KG-12; **Agency Type:** 1
Schools: 11
8 Primary; 2 Middle; 1 High; 0 Other Level
11 Regular; 0 Special Education; 0 Vocational; 0 Alternative
0 Magnet; 0 Charter; 8 Title I Eligible; 1 School-wide Title I
Students: 6,517 (51.2% male; 48.8% female)
Individual Education Program: 975 (15.0%);
English Language Learner: 271 (4.2%); Migrant: 0 (0.0%)
Eligible for Free Lunch Program: 2,158 (33.1%)
Eligible for Reduced-Price Lunch Program: 786 (12.1%)
Teachers: 417.0 (15.6 to 1)
Librarians/Media Specialists: 12.0 (543.1 to 1)
Guidance Counselors: 17.0 (383.4 to 1)
Current Spending: ($ per student per year):
Total: $6,156; Instruction: $4,010; Support Services: $1,701

Enrollment, Drop-out Rates and Diploma Recipients by Race/Ethnicity

Category	Total	White	Black	Asian	AIAN	Hisp.
Enrollment (%)	100.0	88.6	5.0	1.8	0.2	4.4
Drop-out Rate (%)	7.5	7.8	4.9	0.0	0.0	8.7
H.S. Diplomas (#)	306	279	15	10	0	2

Mecklenburg County

Charlotte-Mecklenburg Schools

701 E 2nd St • Charlotte, NC 28202-2825
Mailing Address: PO Box 30035 • Charlotte, NC 28230-0035
(704) 379-7000 • http://www.cms.k12.nc.us/
Grade Span: PK-12; **Agency Type:** 1
Schools: 134
86 Primary; 26 Middle; 17 High; 5 Other Level
129 Regular; 2 Special Education; 0 Vocational; 3 Alternative
53 Magnet; 0 Charter; 30 Title I Eligible; 30 School-wide Title I
Students: 109,767 (51.2% male; 48.8% female)
Individual Education Program: 13,220 (12.0%);
English Language Learner: 6,705 (6.1%); Migrant: 0 (0.0%)
Eligible for Free Lunch Program: 36,351 (33.1%)
Eligible for Reduced-Price Lunch Program: 7,404 (6.7%)
Teachers: 7,262.0 (15.1 to 1)
Librarians/Media Specialists: 159.0 (690.4 to 1)
Guidance Counselors: 297.0 (369.6 to 1)
Current Spending: ($ per student per year):
Total: $7,021; Instruction: $4,263; Support Services: $2,393

Enrollment, Drop-out Rates and Diploma Recipients by Race/Ethnicity

Category	Total	White	Black	Asian	AIAN	Hisp.
Enrollment (%)	100.0	43.3	44.0	4.3	0.6	7.8
Drop-out Rate (%)	7.4	4.9	10.1	7.0	14.6	11.1
H.S. Diplomas (#)	5,087	2,773	1,911	238	10	155

Mitchell County

Mitchell County Schools

72 Ledger School Rd • Bakersville, NC 28705-9533
(828) 688-4432 • http://central.mitchell.k12.nc.us/
Grade Span: PK-12; **Agency Type:** 1
Schools: 8
5 Primary; 2 Middle; 1 High; 0 Other Level
8 Regular; 0 Special Education; 0 Vocational; 0 Alternative
0 Magnet; 0 Charter; 7 Title I Eligible; 7 School-wide Title I
Students: 2,356 (52.8% male; 47.2% female)
Individual Education Program: 389 (16.5%);
English Language Learner: 90 (3.8%); Migrant: 56 (2.4%)
Eligible for Free Lunch Program: 874 (37.1%)
Eligible for Reduced-Price Lunch Program: 313 (13.3%)
Teachers: 164.0 (14.4 to 1)
Librarians/Media Specialists: 7.0 (336.6 to 1)
Guidance Counselors: 6.0 (392.7 to 1)
Current Spending: ($ per student per year):
Total: $6,892; Instruction: $4,107; Support Services: $2,401

Enrollment, Drop-out Rates and Diploma Recipients by Race/Ethnicity

Category	Total	White	Black	Asian	AIAN	Hisp.
Enrollment (%)	100.0	94.9	0.6	0.1	0.2	4.3
Drop-out Rate (%)	3.1	3.2	0.0	0.0	n/a	0.0
H.S. Diplomas (#)	150	144	1	1	0	4

Montgomery County

Montgomery County Schools

441 Page St • Troy, NC 27371-0427
Mailing Address: PO Box 427 • Troy, NC 27371-0427
(910) 576-6511 • http://www.montgomerycountyschool.org/
Grade Span: PK-12; **Agency Type:** 1
Schools: 10
5 Primary; 2 Middle; 3 High; 0 Other Level
9 Regular; 0 Special Education; 0 Vocational; 1 Alternative
0 Magnet; 0 Charter; 5 Title I Eligible; 5 School-wide Title I
Students: 4,561 (51.3% male; 48.7% female)
Individual Education Program: 600 (13.2%);
English Language Learner: 960 (21.0%); Migrant: 355 (7.8%)
Eligible for Free Lunch Program: 2,190 (48.0%)
Eligible for Reduced-Price Lunch Program: 454 (10.0%)
Teachers: 318.0 (14.3 to 1)
Librarians/Media Specialists: 9.0 (506.8 to 1)
Guidance Counselors: 10.0 (456.1 to 1)
Current Spending: ($ per student per year):
Total: $6,582; Instruction: $4,176; Support Services: $1,929

Enrollment, Drop-out Rates and Diploma Recipients by Race/Ethnicity

Category	Total	White	Black	Asian	AIAN	Hisp.
Enrollment (%)	100.0	51.0	28.4	2.8	0.1	17.7
Drop-out Rate (%)	6.7	5.8	7.5	0.0	0.0	13.4
H.S. Diplomas (#)	220	139	53	14	1	13

Moore County

Moore County Schools
Hwy 15-501 S • Carthage, NC 28327-1180
Mailing Address: PO Box 1180 • Carthage, NC 28327-1180
(910) 947-2976 • http://www.mcs.k12.nc.us/
Grade Span: KG-12; **Agency Type:** 1
Schools: 22
14 Primary; 4 Middle; 4 High; 0 Other Level
21 Regular; 0 Special Education; 0 Vocational; 1 Alternative
0 Magnet; 0 Charter; 10 Title I Eligible; 8 School-wide Title I
Students: 11,404 (50.9% male; 49.1% female)
Individual Education Program: 1,595 (14.0%);
English Language Learner: 519 (4.6%); Migrant: 202 (1.8%)
Eligible for Free Lunch Program: 3,720 (32.6%)
Eligible for Reduced-Price Lunch Program: 905 (7.9%)
Teachers: 786.0 (14.5 to 1)
Librarians/Media Specialists: 22.0 (518.4 to 1)
Guidance Counselors: 29.0 (393.2 to 1)
Current Spending: ($ per student per year):
Total: $6,517; Instruction: $4,042; Support Services: $2,166
Enrollment, Drop-out Rates and Diploma Recipients by Race/Ethnicity

Category	Total	White	Black	Asian	AIAN	Hisp.
Enrollment (%)	100.0	67.9	24.8	0.6	0.9	5.8
Drop-out Rate (%)	5.5	5.2	6.1	11.8	3.8	7.9
H.S. Diplomas (#)	625	479	135	0	4	7

Nash County

Nash-Rocky Mount Schools
930 Eastern Ave • Nashville, NC 27856-1716
(252) 459-5220 • http://www.nrms.k12.nc.us/
Grade Span: PK-12; **Agency Type:** 1
Schools: 29
18 Primary; 5 Middle; 5 High; 1 Other Level
28 Regular; 0 Special Education; 0 Vocational; 1 Alternative
0 Magnet; 0 Charter; 17 Title I Eligible; 17 School-wide Title I
Students: 18,464 (50.8% male; 49.2% female)
Individual Education Program: 2,925 (15.8%);
English Language Learner: 737 (4.0%); Migrant: 370 (2.0%)
Eligible for Free Lunch Program: 0 (0.0%)
Eligible for Reduced-Price Lunch Program: 0 (0.0%)
Teachers: 1,299.0 (14.2 to 1)
Librarians/Media Specialists: 31.0 (595.6 to 1)
Guidance Counselors: 67.0 (275.6 to 1)
Current Spending: ($ per student per year):
Total: $5,903; Instruction: $3,829; Support Services: $1,728
Enrollment, Drop-out Rates and Diploma Recipients by Race/Ethnicity

Category	Total	White	Black	Asian	AIAN	Hisp.
Enrollment (%)	100.0	39.0	54.8	1.1	0.4	4.7
Drop-out Rate (%)	7.9	6.6	9.0	2.4	9.1	8.9
H.S. Diplomas (#)	918	458	430	5	4	21

New Hanover County

New Hanover County Schools
6410 Carolina Beach Rd • Wilmington, NC 28412-6479
(910) 763-5431 • http://www.nhcs.k12.nc.us/
Grade Span: PK-12; **Agency Type:** 1
Schools: 34
22 Primary; 7 Middle; 4 High; 1 Other Level
33 Regular; 0 Special Education; 0 Vocational; 1 Alternative
1 Magnet; 0 Charter; 16 Title I Eligible; 16 School-wide Title I
Students: 21,861 (50.8% male; 49.2% female)
Individual Education Program: 2,944 (13.5%);
English Language Learner: 500 (2.3%); Migrant: 0 (0.0%)
Eligible for Free Lunch Program: 6,039 (27.6%)
Eligible for Reduced-Price Lunch Program: 1,327 (6.1%)
Teachers: 1,423.0 (15.4 to 1)
Librarians/Media Specialists: 38.0 (575.3 to 1)
Guidance Counselors: 56.0 (390.4 to 1)
Current Spending: ($ per student per year):
Total: $6,813; Instruction: $4,033; Support Services: $2,426
Enrollment, Drop-out Rates and Diploma Recipients by Race/Ethnicity

Category	Total	White	Black	Asian	AIAN	Hisp.
Enrollment (%)	100.0	66.5	29.9	1.1	0.4	2.1
Drop-out Rate (%)	5.6	4.7	8.5	1.2	0.0	6.0
H.S. Diplomas (#)	1,272	978	256	13	6	19

Northampton County

Northampton County Schools
320 Bagley Dr • Jackson, NC 27845-0158
Mailing Address: PO Box 158 • Jackson, NC 27845-0158
(252) 534-1371 • http://www.northampton.k12.nc.us/
Grade Span: PK-12; **Agency Type:** 1
Schools: 10
6 Primary; 2 Middle; 2 High; 0 Other Level
10 Regular; 0 Special Education; 0 Vocational; 0 Alternative
0 Magnet; 0 Charter; 8 Title I Eligible; 8 School-wide Title I
Students: 3,550 (52.0% male; 48.0% female)
Individual Education Program: 454 (12.8%);
English Language Learner: 21 (0.6%); Migrant: 184 (5.2%)
Eligible for Free Lunch Program: 2,390 (67.3%)
Eligible for Reduced-Price Lunch Program: 447 (12.6%)
Teachers: 239.0 (14.9 to 1)
Librarians/Media Specialists: 8.0 (443.8 to 1)
Guidance Counselors: 10.0 (355.0 to 1)
Current Spending: ($ per student per year):
Total: $6,962; Instruction: $4,222; Support Services: $2,273
Enrollment, Drop-out Rates and Diploma Recipients by Race/Ethnicity

Category	Total	White	Black	Asian	AIAN	Hisp.
Enrollment (%)	100.0	18.5	80.5	0.1	0.1	0.8
Drop-out Rate (%)	7.3	3.7	8.1	n/a	0.0	100.0
H.S. Diplomas (#)	181	48	133	0	0	0

Onslow County

Camp Lejeune District
855 Stone St, Building 855 • Camp Lejeune, NC 28547-2520
Mailing Address: 855 Stone Street, Building 855 • Camp Lejeune, NC 28547-2520
(910) 451-2461
Grade Span: PK-12; **Agency Type:** 6
Schools: 8
6 Primary; 0 Middle; 1 High; 1 Other Level
8 Regular; 0 Special Education; 0 Vocational; 0 Alternative
0 Magnet; 0 Charter; 0 Title I Eligible; 0 School-wide Title I
Students: 3,286 (n/a% male; n/a% female)
Individual Education Program: 404 (12.3%);
English Language Learner: 45 (1.4%); Migrant: n/a
Eligible for Free Lunch Program: n/a
Eligible for Reduced-Price Lunch Program: n/a
Teachers: 238.5 (13.8 to 1)
Librarians/Media Specialists: 8.0 (410.8 to 1)
Guidance Counselors: 9.5 (345.9 to 1)
Current Spending: ($ per student per year):
Total: n/a; Instruction: n/a; Support Services: n/a
Enrollment, Drop-out Rates and Diploma Recipients by Race/Ethnicity

Category	Total	White	Black	Asian	AIAN	Hisp.
Enrollment (%)	100.0	58.6	23.5	2.4	1.3	13.4
Drop-out Rate (%)	n/a	n/a	n/a	n/a	n/a	n/a
H.S. Diplomas (#)	93	0	26	1	0	10

Onslow County Schools
200 Broadhurst Rd • Jacksonville, NC 28540-3551
Mailing Address: PO Box 99 • Jacksonville, NC 28541-0099
(910) 455-2211 • http://www.onslow.k12.nc.us/
Grade Span: PK-12; **Agency Type:** 1
Schools: 33
18 Primary; 8 Middle; 7 High; 0 Other Level
33 Regular; 0 Special Education; 0 Vocational; 0 Alternative
0 Magnet; 0 Charter; 16 Title I Eligible; 10 School-wide Title I
Students: 21,580 (50.5% male; 49.5% female)
Individual Education Program: 3,107 (14.4%);
English Language Learner: 354 (1.6%); Migrant: 0 (0.0%)
Eligible for Free Lunch Program: 6,471 (30.0%)
Eligible for Reduced-Price Lunch Program: 2,630 (12.2%)
Teachers: 1,331.0 (16.2 to 1)
Librarians/Media Specialists: 42.0 (513.8 to 1)
Guidance Counselors: 48.0 (449.6 to 1)
Current Spending: ($ per student per year):
Total: $5,889; Instruction: $3,690; Support Services: $1,887
Enrollment, Drop-out Rates and Diploma Recipients by Race/Ethnicity

Category	Total	White	Black	Asian	AIAN	Hisp.
Enrollment (%)	100.0	63.9	29.1	1.4	1.1	4.5
Drop-out Rate (%)	5.1	4.8	5.3	8.0	7.1	6.5
H.S. Diplomas (#)	1,161	774	296	30	10	51

Orange County

Chapel Hill-Carrboro Schools

750 S Merritt Mill Rd • Chapel Hill, NC 27516-2878
(919) 967-8211 • http://www.chccs.k12.nc.us/
Grade Span: PK-12; **Agency Type:** 1
Schools: 15
8 Primary; 4 Middle; 2 High; 1 Other Level
14 Regular; 0 Special Education; 0 Vocational; 1 Alternative
0 Magnet; 0 Charter; 7 Title I Eligible; 0 School-wide Title I
Students: 10,360 (51.5% male; 48.5% female)
Individual Education Program: 1,345 (13.0%);
English Language Learner: 848 (8.2%); Migrant: 0 (0.0%)
Eligible for Free Lunch Program: 0 (0.0%)
Eligible for Reduced-Price Lunch Program: 0 (0.0%)
Teachers: 810.0 (12.8 to 1)
Librarians/Media Specialists: 14.0 (740.0 to 1)
Guidance Counselors: 34.0 (304.7 to 1)
Current Spending: ($ per student per year):
Total: $8,488; Instruction: $5,459; Support Services: $2,767
Enrollment, Drop-out Rates and Diploma Recipients by Race/Ethnicity

Category	Total	White	Black	Asian	AIAN	Hisp.
Enrollment (%)	100.0	64.3	18.9	10.0	0.3	6.4
Drop-out Rate (%)	2.0	1.3	3.5	0.0	0.0	15.0
H.S. Diplomas (#)	599	456	86	44	2	11

Orange County Schools

200 E King St • Hillsborough, NC 27278-2570
(919) 732-8126 • http://www.orange.k12.nc.us/
Grade Span: PK-12; **Agency Type:** 1
Schools: 11
7 Primary; 2 Middle; 2 High; 0 Other Level
11 Regular; 0 Special Education; 0 Vocational; 0 Alternative
0 Magnet; 0 Charter; 6 Title I Eligible; 0 School-wide Title I
Students: 6,360 (51.5% male; 48.5% female)
Individual Education Program: 1,262 (19.8%);
English Language Learner: 241 (3.8%); Migrant: 93 (1.5%)
Eligible for Free Lunch Program: 1,466 (23.1%)
Eligible for Reduced-Price Lunch Program: 478 (7.5%)
Teachers: 457.0 (13.9 to 1)
Librarians/Media Specialists: 11.0 (578.2 to 1)
Guidance Counselors: 17.0 (374.1 to 1)
Current Spending: ($ per student per year):
Total: $7,690; Instruction: $4,850; Support Services: $2,497
Enrollment, Drop-out Rates and Diploma Recipients by Race/Ethnicity

Category	Total	White	Black	Asian	AIAN	Hisp.
Enrollment (%)	100.0	70.7	24.1	0.7	0.3	4.1
Drop-out Rate (%)	4.7	3.5	7.2	0.0	25.0	18.2
H.S. Diplomas (#)	310	228	73	4	0	5

Pamlico County

Pamlico County Schools

507 Anderson Dr • Bayboro, NC 28515-9799
(252) 745-4171 • http://www.pamlico.k12.nc.us/
Grade Span: PK-12; **Agency Type:** 1
Schools: 4
2 Primary; 1 Middle; 1 High; 0 Other Level
4 Regular; 0 Special Education; 0 Vocational; 0 Alternative
0 Magnet; 0 Charter; 2 Title I Eligible; 2 School-wide Title I
Students: 1,788 (52.1% male; 47.9% female)
Individual Education Program: 370 (20.7%);
English Language Learner: 4 (0.2%); Migrant: 0 (0.0%)
Eligible for Free Lunch Program: 742 (41.5%)
Eligible for Reduced-Price Lunch Program: 206 (11.5%)
Teachers: 148.0 (12.1 to 1)
Librarians/Media Specialists: 4.0 (447.0 to 1)
Guidance Counselors: 4.0 (447.0 to 1)
Current Spending: ($ per student per year):
Total: $7,869; Instruction: $5,027; Support Services: $2,443
Enrollment, Drop-out Rates and Diploma Recipients by Race/Ethnicity

Category	Total	White	Black	Asian	AIAN	Hisp.
Enrollment (%)	100.0	64.0	34.1	0.4	0.7	0.8
Drop-out Rate (%)	4.2	5.5	2.3	0.0	0.0	0.0
H.S. Diplomas (#)	132	86	38	3	2	3

Pasquotank County

Pasquotank County Schools

1200 S Halstead Blvd • Elizabeth City, NC 27906-2247
Mailing Address: PO Box 2247 • Elizabeth City, NC 27906-2247
(252) 335-2981 • http://www.ecpps.com/
Grade Span: PK-12; **Agency Type:** 1
Schools: 12
7 Primary; 2 Middle; 2 High; 1 Other Level
11 Regular; 0 Special Education; 0 Vocational; 1 Alternative
0 Magnet; 0 Charter; 7 Title I Eligible; 7 School-wide Title I
Students: 6,036 (51.0% male; 49.0% female)
Individual Education Program: 859 (14.2%);
English Language Learner: 17 (0.3%); Migrant: 0 (0.0%)
Eligible for Free Lunch Program: 0 (0.0%)
Eligible for Reduced-Price Lunch Program: 0 (0.0%)
Teachers: 408.0 (14.8 to 1)
Librarians/Media Specialists: 11.0 (548.7 to 1)
Guidance Counselors: 15.0 (402.4 to 1)
Current Spending: ($ per student per year):
Total: $6,742; Instruction: $4,202; Support Services: $2,096
Enrollment, Drop-out Rates and Diploma Recipients by Race/Ethnicity

Category	Total	White	Black	Asian	AIAN	Hisp.
Enrollment (%)	100.0	47.2	51.1	0.6	0.1	1.0
Drop-out Rate (%)	7.6	8.0	7.2	9.1	50.0	0.0
H.S. Diplomas (#)	270	126	138	3	0	3

Pender County

Pender County Schools

925 Penderlea Hwy • Burgaw, NC 28425-4546
(910) 259-2187 • http://www.schoollink.net/pender/
Grade Span: PK-12; **Agency Type:** 1
Schools: 15
7 Primary; 4 Middle; 3 High; 1 Other Level
14 Regular; 0 Special Education; 0 Vocational; 1 Alternative
0 Magnet; 0 Charter; 9 Title I Eligible; 9 School-wide Title I
Students: 6,825 (51.8% male; 48.2% female)
Individual Education Program: 1,032 (15.1%);
English Language Learner: 330 (4.8%); Migrant: 652 (9.6%)
Eligible for Free Lunch Program: 2,811 (41.2%)
Eligible for Reduced-Price Lunch Program: 866 (12.7%)
Teachers: 479.0 (14.2 to 1)
Librarians/Media Specialists: 14.0 (487.5 to 1)
Guidance Counselors: 18.0 (379.2 to 1)
Current Spending: ($ per student per year):
Total: $6,312; Instruction: $3,861; Support Services: $2,120
Enrollment, Drop-out Rates and Diploma Recipients by Race/Ethnicity

Category	Total	White	Black	Asian	AIAN	Hisp.
Enrollment (%)	100.0	64.2	31.0	0.2	0.3	4.3
Drop-out Rate (%)	6.0	5.4	7.3	0.0	0.0	5.4
H.S. Diplomas (#)	305	199	98	1	3	4

Perquimans County

Perquimans County Schools

411 Edenton Rd St • Hertford, NC 27944-0337
Mailing Address: PO Box 337 • Hertford, NC 27944-0337
(252) 426-5741 • http://www.perquimans.k12.nc.us/
Grade Span: PK-12; **Agency Type:** 1
Schools: 4
2 Primary; 1 Middle; 1 High; 0 Other Level
4 Regular; 0 Special Education; 0 Vocational; 0 Alternative
0 Magnet; 0 Charter; 2 Title I Eligible; 2 School-wide Title I
Students: 1,824 (51.3% male; 48.7% female)
Individual Education Program: 283 (15.5%);
English Language Learner: 1 (0.1%); Migrant: 0 (0.0%)
Eligible for Free Lunch Program: 0 (0.0%)
Eligible for Reduced-Price Lunch Program: 0 (0.0%)
Teachers: 130.0 (14.0 to 1)
Librarians/Media Specialists: 4.0 (456.0 to 1)
Guidance Counselors: 5.0 (364.8 to 1)
Current Spending: ($ per student per year):
Total: $7,707; Instruction: $4,479; Support Services: $2,686
Enrollment, Drop-out Rates and Diploma Recipients by Race/Ethnicity

Category	Total	White	Black	Asian	AIAN	Hisp.
Enrollment (%)	100.0	60.0	38.8	0.1	0.3	0.9
Drop-out Rate (%)	9.2	10.4	7.6	0.0	0.0	0.0
H.S. Diplomas (#)	103	67	34	0	0	2

Person County

Person County Schools

304 S Morgan St Rm 25 • Roxboro, NC 27573-5245
(336) 599-2191 • http://www.person.k12.nc.us/
Grade Span: KG-12; **Agency Type:** 1
Schools: 10
7 Primary; 2 Middle; 1 High; 0 Other Level
10 Regular; 0 Special Education; 0 Vocational; 0 Alternative
0 Magnet; 0 Charter; 5 Title I Eligible; 4 School-wide Title I
Students: 5,796 (50.8% male; 49.2% female)
Individual Education Program: 963 (16.6%);
English Language Learner: 100 (1.7%); Migrant: 0 (0.0%)
Eligible for Free Lunch Program: 1,888 (32.6%)

Eligible for Reduced-Price Lunch Program: 568 (9.8%)
Teachers: 398.0 (14.6 to 1)
Librarians/Media Specialists: 12.0 (483.0 to 1)
Guidance Counselors: 14.0 (414.0 to 1)
Current Spending: ($ per student per year):
Total: $6,415; Instruction: $4,165; Support Services: $1,861
Enrollment, Drop-out Rates and Diploma Recipients by Race/Ethnicity

Category	Total	White	Black	Asian	AIAN	Hisp.
Enrollment (%)	100.0	57.8	38.7	0.2	0.5	2.8
Drop-out Rate (%)	7.3	7.7	6.3	0.0	0.0	16.7
H.S. Diplomas (#)	304	197	97	1	1	8

Pitt County

Pitt County Schools
1717 W 5th St • Greenville, NC 27834-1698
(252) 830-4200 • http://schools.eastnet.ecu.edu/pitt/pitt.htm
Grade Span: PK-12; **Agency Type:** 1
Schools: 33
20 Primary; 6 Middle; 6 High; 1 Other Level
32 Regular; 0 Special Education; 0 Vocational; 1 Alternative
0 Magnet; 0 Charter; 18 Title I Eligible; 2 School-wide Title I
Students: 20,929 (51.0% male; 49.0% female)
Individual Education Program: 2,962 (14.2%);
English Language Learner: 532 (2.5%); Migrant: 437 (2.1%)
Eligible for Free Lunch Program: 8,487 (40.6%)
Eligible for Reduced-Price Lunch Program: 1,351 (6.5%)
Teachers: 1,358.0 (15.4 to 1)
Librarians/Media Specialists: 28.0 (747.5 to 1)
Guidance Counselors: 62.0 (337.6 to 1)
Current Spending: ($ per student per year):
Total: $6,213; Instruction: $4,119; Support Services: $1,763
Enrollment, Drop-out Rates and Diploma Recipients by Race/Ethnicity

Category	Total	White	Black	Asian	AIAN	Hisp.
Enrollment (%)	100.0	43.1	51.8	1.2	0.1	3.7
Drop-out Rate (%)	8.3	5.7	11.2	1.3	0.0	20.0
H.S. Diplomas (#)	994	595	375	14	2	8

Polk County

Polk County Schools
125 E Mills St • Columbus, NC 28722-0638
Mailing Address: PO Box 638 • Columbus, NC 28722-0638
(828) 894-3051 • http://server.sec.polk.k12.nc.us/
Grade Span: PK-12; **Agency Type:** 1
Schools: 6
4 Primary; 1 Middle; 1 High; 0 Other Level
6 Regular; 0 Special Education; 0 Vocational; 0 Alternative
0 Magnet; 0 Charter; 0 Title I Eligible; 0 School-wide Title I
Students: 2,476 (50.4% male; 49.6% female)
Individual Education Program: 391 (15.8%);
English Language Learner: 111 (4.5%); Migrant: 0 (0.0%)
Eligible for Free Lunch Program: 714 (28.8%)
Eligible for Reduced-Price Lunch Program: 280 (11.3%)
Teachers: 176.0 (14.1 to 1)
Librarians/Media Specialists: 6.0 (412.7 to 1)
Guidance Counselors: 9.0 (275.1 to 1)
Current Spending: ($ per student per year):
Total: $6,740; Instruction: $4,356; Support Services: $2,024
Enrollment, Drop-out Rates and Diploma Recipients by Race/Ethnicity

Category	Total	White	Black	Asian	AIAN	Hisp.
Enrollment (%)	100.0	84.0	9.8	0.5	0.1	5.6
Drop-out Rate (%)	4.1	4.0	0.0	0.0	0.0	19.0
H.S. Diplomas (#)	117	105	10	0	0	2

Randolph County

Asheboro City Schools
1126 S Park St • Asheboro, NC 27203
Mailing Address: PO Box 1103 • Asheboro, NC 27204-1103
(336) 625-5104 • http://www.asheboro.k12.nc.us/
Grade Span: KG-12; **Agency Type:** 1
Schools: 8
5 Primary; 2 Middle; 1 High; 0 Other Level
8 Regular; 0 Special Education; 0 Vocational; 0 Alternative
0 Magnet; 0 Charter; 5 Title I Eligible; 4 School-wide Title I
Students: 4,388 (50.9% male; 49.1% female)
Individual Education Program: 569 (13.0%);
English Language Learner: 770 (17.5%); Migrant: 74 (1.7%)
Eligible for Free Lunch Program: 0 (0.0%)
Eligible for Reduced-Price Lunch Program: 0 (0.0%)
Teachers: 301.0 (14.6 to 1)
Librarians/Media Specialists: 8.0 (548.5 to 1)
Guidance Counselors: 9.0 (487.6 to 1)
Current Spending: ($ per student per year):
Total: $6,409; Instruction: $4,009; Support Services: $2,009
Enrollment, Drop-out Rates and Diploma Recipients by Race/Ethnicity

Category	Total	White	Black	Asian	AIAN	Hisp.
Enrollment (%)	100.0	57.1	16.9	2.6	0.2	23.1
Drop-out Rate (%)	7.8	6.9	10.7	8.3	0.0	10.4
H.S. Diplomas (#)	180	147	21	5	0	7

Randolph County Schools
2222-C S Fayetteville St • Asheboro, NC 27205-7379
(336) 318-6100 • http://www.randolph.k12.nc.us/
Grade Span: PK-12; **Agency Type:** 1
Schools: 28
17 Primary; 7 Middle; 4 High; 0 Other Level
28 Regular; 0 Special Education; 0 Vocational; 0 Alternative
0 Magnet; 0 Charter; 10 Title I Eligible; 0 School-wide Title I
Students: 18,144 (51.8% male; 48.2% female)
Individual Education Program: 2,430 (13.4%);
English Language Learner: 846 (4.7%); Migrant: 342 (1.9%)
Eligible for Free Lunch Program: 0 (0.0%)
Eligible for Reduced-Price Lunch Program: 0 (0.0%)
Teachers: 1,083.0 (16.8 to 1)
Librarians/Media Specialists: 31.0 (585.3 to 1)
Guidance Counselors: 40.0 (453.6 to 1)
Current Spending: ($ per student per year):
Total: $5,380; Instruction: $3,418; Support Services: $1,608
Enrollment, Drop-out Rates and Diploma Recipients by Race/Ethnicity

Category	Total	White	Black	Asian	AIAN	Hisp.
Enrollment (%)	100.0	85.9	6.3	0.7	0.4	6.7
Drop-out Rate (%)	7.0	6.7	8.1	4.0	15.0	12.6
H.S. Diplomas (#)	825	759	43	3	2	18

Richmond County

Richmond County Schools
522 W Hamlet Ave • Hamlet, NC 28345-2624
Mailing Address: PO Drawer 1259 • Hamlet, NC 28345-1259
(910) 582-5860 • http://www.richmond.k12.nc.us/
Grade Span: PK-12; **Agency Type:** 1
Schools: 18
8 Primary; 8 Middle; 1 High; 1 Other Level
16 Regular; 1 Special Education; 0 Vocational; 1 Alternative
0 Magnet; 0 Charter; 9 Title I Eligible; 9 School-wide Title I
Students: 8,375 (51.4% male; 48.6% female)
Individual Education Program: 1,138 (13.6%);
English Language Learner: 191 (2.3%); Migrant: 0 (0.0%)
Eligible for Free Lunch Program: 0 (0.0%)
Eligible for Reduced-Price Lunch Program: 0 (0.0%)
Teachers: 528.0 (15.9 to 1)
Librarians/Media Specialists: 16.0 (523.4 to 1)
Guidance Counselors: 20.0 (418.8 to 1)
Current Spending: ($ per student per year):
Total: $6,223; Instruction: $3,983; Support Services: $1,863
Enrollment, Drop-out Rates and Diploma Recipients by Race/Ethnicity

Category	Total	White	Black	Asian	AIAN	Hisp.
Enrollment (%)	100.0	52.7	41.1	0.8	2.0	3.3
Drop-out Rate (%)	6.8	6.5	6.7	0.0	27.3	8.3
H.S. Diplomas (#)	394	197	178	6	6	7

Robeson County

Robeson County Schools
410 Caton Rd • Lumberton, NC 28359-9767
Mailing Address: PO Drawer 2909 • Lumberton, NC 28359-2909
(910) 738-4841 • http://www.robeson.k12.nc.us/
Grade Span: PK-12; **Agency Type:** 1
Schools: 41
23 Primary; 11 Middle; 7 High; 0 Other Level
40 Regular; 0 Special Education; 1 Vocational; 0 Alternative
0 Magnet; 0 Charter; 33 Title I Eligible; 33 School-wide Title I
Students: 24,191 (51.3% male; 48.7% female)
Individual Education Program: 4,204 (17.4%);
English Language Learner: 856 (3.5%); Migrant: 646 (2.7%)
Eligible for Free Lunch Program: 0 (0.0%)
Eligible for Reduced-Price Lunch Program: 0 (0.0%)
Teachers: 1,498.0 (16.1 to 1)
Librarians/Media Specialists: 64.0 (378.0 to 1)
Guidance Counselors: 60.0 (403.2 to 1)
Current Spending: ($ per student per year):
Total: $5,718; Instruction: $3,588; Support Services: $1,706
Enrollment, Drop-out Rates and Diploma Recipients by Race/Ethnicity

Category	Total	White	Black	Asian	AIAN	Hisp.
Enrollment (%)	100.0	21.1	31.5	0.3	42.8	4.3
Drop-out Rate (%)	10.9	8.3	10.3	0.0	12.7	21.3
H.S. Diplomas (#)	963	252	308	5	393	5

Rockingham County

Rockingham County Schools

511 Harrington Hwy • Eden, NC 27288-7547
(336) 627-2600 • http://www.rock.k12.nc.us/
Grade Span: PK-12; **Agency Type:** 1
Schools: 25
15 Primary; 5 Middle; 4 High; 1 Other Level
24 Regular; 0 Special Education; 0 Vocational; 1 Alternative
0 Magnet; 0 Charter; 12 Title I Eligible; 12 School-wide Title I
Students: 14,871 (51.5% male; 48.5% female)
Individual Education Program: 2,335 (15.7%);
English Language Learner: 577 (3.9%); Migrant: 1,030 (6.9%)
Eligible for Free Lunch Program: 5,169 (34.8%)
Eligible for Reduced-Price Lunch Program: 1,393 (9.4%)
Teachers: 937.0 (15.9 to 1)
Librarians/Media Specialists: 31.0 (479.7 to 1)
Guidance Counselors: 31.0 (479.7 to 1)
Current Spending: ($ per student per year):
Total: $6,320; Instruction: $3,965; Support Services: $1,985
Enrollment, Drop-out Rates and Diploma Recipients by Race/Ethnicity

Category	Total	White	Black	Asian	AIAN	Hisp.
Enrollment (%)	100.0	68.0	27.0	0.4	0.2	4.4
Drop-out Rate (%)	6.3	5.5	8.1	3.7	15.4	15.7
H.S. Diplomas (#)	716	545	160	4	1	6

Rowan County

Rowan-Salisbury Schools

314 N Ellis St • Salisbury, NC 28144
Mailing Address: PO Box 2349 • Salisbury, NC 28145-2349
(704) 636-7500 • http://www.rss.k12.nc.us/menu/menu.asp
Grade Span: PK-12; **Agency Type:** 1
Schools: 30
17 Primary; 7 Middle; 6 High; 0 Other Level
29 Regular; 0 Special Education; 0 Vocational; 1 Alternative
0 Magnet; 0 Charter; 14 Title I Eligible; 5 School-wide Title I
Students: 20,843 (51.1% male; 48.9% female)
Individual Education Program: 2,985 (14.3%);
English Language Learner: 1,560 (7.5%); Migrant: 661 (3.2%)
Eligible for Free Lunch Program: 0 (0.0%)
Eligible for Reduced-Price Lunch Program: 0 (0.0%)
Teachers: 1,321.0 (15.8 to 1)
Librarians/Media Specialists: 31.0 (672.4 to 1)
Guidance Counselors: 64.0 (325.7 to 1)
Current Spending: ($ per student per year):
Total: $6,300; Instruction: $4,107; Support Services: $1,816
Enrollment, Drop-out Rates and Diploma Recipients by Race/Ethnicity

Category	Total	White	Black	Asian	AIAN	Hisp.
Enrollment (%)	100.0	69.9	23.3	1.3	0.3	5.2
Drop-out Rate (%)	5.8	5.9	4.9	3.5	5.6	9.7
H.S. Diplomas (#)	1,093	841	205	20	4	23

Rutherford County

Rutherford County Schools

382 W Main St • Forest City, NC 28043
(828) 286-2757
Grade Span: PK-12; **Agency Type:** 1
Schools: 19
13 Primary; 3 Middle; 3 High; 0 Other Level
17 Regular; 0 Special Education; 0 Vocational; 2 Alternative
0 Magnet; 0 Charter; 11 Title I Eligible; 11 School-wide Title I
Students: 10,188 (51.0% male; 49.0% female)
Individual Education Program: 1,471 (14.4%);
English Language Learner: 185 (1.8%); Migrant: 0 (0.0%)
Eligible for Free Lunch Program: 4,001 (39.3%)
Eligible for Reduced-Price Lunch Program: 907 (8.9%)
Teachers: 672.0 (15.2 to 1)
Librarians/Media Specialists: 19.0 (536.2 to 1)
Guidance Counselors: 28.0 (363.9 to 1)
Current Spending: ($ per student per year):
Total: $6,335; Instruction: $4,126; Support Services: $1,862
Enrollment, Drop-out Rates and Diploma Recipients by Race/Ethnicity

Category	Total	White	Black	Asian	AIAN	Hisp.
Enrollment (%)	100.0	79.2	17.7	0.4	0.1	2.6
Drop-out Rate (%)	8.9	8.7	10.1	0.0	n/a	10.0
H.S. Diplomas (#)	452	383	62	2	0	5

Sampson County

Clinton City Schools

606 College St • Clinton, NC 28328-4118
(910) 592-3132 • http://www.clinton.k12.nc.us/
Grade Span: PK-12; **Agency Type:** 1
Schools: 4
2 Primary; 1 Middle; 1 High; 0 Other Level
4 Regular; 0 Special Education; 0 Vocational; 0 Alternative
0 Magnet; 0 Charter; 3 Title I Eligible; 3 School-wide Title I
Students: 2,731 (49.9% male; 50.1% female)
Individual Education Program: 301 (11.0%);
English Language Learner: 88 (3.2%); Migrant: 0 (0.0%)
Eligible for Free Lunch Program: 0 (0.0%)
Eligible for Reduced-Price Lunch Program: 0 (0.0%)
Teachers: 186.0 (14.7 to 1)
Librarians/Media Specialists: 4.0 (682.8 to 1)
Guidance Counselors: 7.0 (390.1 to 1)
Current Spending: ($ per student per year):
Total: $6,325; Instruction: $3,910; Support Services: $1,966
Enrollment, Drop-out Rates and Diploma Recipients by Race/Ethnicity

Category	Total	White	Black	Asian	AIAN	Hisp.
Enrollment (%)	100.0	38.6	49.2	0.9	3.8	7.5
Drop-out Rate (%)	6.0	3.4	7.2	0.0	12.9	13.8
H.S. Diplomas (#)	146	79	57	1	5	4

Sampson County Schools

437 Rowan Rd • Clinton, NC 28328
Mailing Address: PO Box 439 • Clinton, NC 28329-0439
(910) 592-1401 • http://www.sampson.k12.nc.us/
Grade Span: PK-12; **Agency Type:** 1
Schools: 16
8 Primary; 4 Middle; 4 High; 0 Other Level
16 Regular; 0 Special Education; 0 Vocational; 0 Alternative
0 Magnet; 0 Charter; 14 Title I Eligible; 14 School-wide Title I
Students: 8,086 (52.1% male; 47.9% female)
Individual Education Program: 1,130 (14.0%);
English Language Learner: 909 (11.2%); Migrant: 654 (8.1%)
Eligible for Free Lunch Program: 4,610 (57.0%)
Eligible for Reduced-Price Lunch Program: 964 (11.9%)
Teachers: 543.0 (14.9 to 1)
Librarians/Media Specialists: 17.0 (475.6 to 1)
Guidance Counselors: 17.0 (475.6 to 1)
Current Spending: ($ per student per year):
Total: $6,079; Instruction: $3,850; Support Services: $1,777
Enrollment, Drop-out Rates and Diploma Recipients by Race/Ethnicity

Category	Total	White	Black	Asian	AIAN	Hisp.
Enrollment (%)	100.0	50.8	31.6	0.3	1.3	16.1
Drop-out Rate (%)	4.9	4.0	5.6	0.0	0.0	9.8
H.S. Diplomas (#)	357	231	107	0	4	15

Scotland County

Scotland County Schools

322 S Main St • Laurinburg, NC 28352-3855
(910) 276-1138 • http://www.scsnc.org/
Grade Span: PK-12; **Agency Type:** 1
Schools: 15
10 Primary; 3 Middle; 1 High; 1 Other Level
13 Regular; 0 Special Education; 0 Vocational; 2 Alternative
0 Magnet; 0 Charter; 8 Title I Eligible; 8 School-wide Title I
Students: 7,106 (50.9% male; 49.1% female)
Individual Education Program: 1,146 (16.1%);
English Language Learner: 54 (0.8%); Migrant: 82 (1.2%)
Eligible for Free Lunch Program: 3,861 (54.3%)
Eligible for Reduced-Price Lunch Program: 635 (8.9%)
Teachers: 547.0 (13.0 to 1)
Librarians/Media Specialists: 13.0 (546.6 to 1)
Guidance Counselors: 22.0 (323.0 to 1)
Current Spending: ($ per student per year):
Total: $6,800; Instruction: $4,329; Support Services: $2,076
Enrollment, Drop-out Rates and Diploma Recipients by Race/Ethnicity

Category	Total	White	Black	Asian	AIAN	Hisp.
Enrollment (%)	100.0	38.7	47.6	0.7	12.2	0.7
Drop-out Rate (%)	7.2	6.8	7.5	0.0	8.8	12.5
H.S. Diplomas (#)	339	174	137	4	23	1

Stanly County

Stanly County Schools

1000-4 N First St • Albemarle, NC 28001
(704) 983-5151 • http://www.scs.k12.nc.us/
Grade Span: PK-12; **Agency Type:** 1
Schools: 22
16 Primary; 2 Middle; 4 High; 0 Other Level

22 Regular; 0 Special Education; 0 Vocational; 0 Alternative
0 Magnet; 0 Charter; 5 Title I Eligible; 5 School-wide Title I
Students: 10,094 (52.5% male; 47.5% female)
Individual Education Program: 1,750 (17.3%);
English Language Learner: 473 (4.7%); Migrant: 0 (0.0%)
Eligible for Free Lunch Program: 0 (0.0%)
Eligible for Reduced-Price Lunch Program: 0 (0.0%)
Teachers: 646.0 (15.6 to 1)
Librarians/Media Specialists: 21.0 (480.7 to 1)
Guidance Counselors: 28.0 (360.5 to 1)
Current Spending: ($ per student per year):
Total: $5,941; Instruction: $3,939; Support Services: $1,636
Enrollment, Drop-out Rates and Diploma Recipients by Race/Ethnicity

Category	Total	White	Black	Asian	AIAN	Hisp.
Enrollment (%)	100.0	75.6	16.8	4.0	0.3	3.3
Drop-out Rate (%)	4.7	4.4	5.2	8.7	8.3	5.9
H.S. Diplomas (#)	569	476	68	20	1	4

Stokes County

Stokes County Schools
501 N Main St • Danbury, NC 27016-0050
Mailing Address: PO Box 50 • Danbury, NC 27016-0050
(336) 593-8146 • http://www.stokes.k12.nc.us/
Grade Span: PK-12; **Agency Type:** 1
Schools: 18
11 Primary; 3 Middle; 3 High; 1 Other Level
17 Regular; 0 Special Education; 0 Vocational; 1 Alternative
0 Magnet; 0 Charter; 10 Title I Eligible; 7 School-wide Title I
Students: 7,530 (51.9% male; 48.1% female)
Individual Education Program: 1,228 (16.3%);
English Language Learner: 46 (0.6%); Migrant: 0 (0.0%)
Eligible for Free Lunch Program: 1,548 (20.6%)
Eligible for Reduced-Price Lunch Program: 619 (8.2%)
Teachers: 523.0 (14.4 to 1)
Librarians/Media Specialists: 17.0 (442.9 to 1)
Guidance Counselors: 23.0 (327.4 to 1)
Current Spending: ($ per student per year):
Total: $6,418; Instruction: $3,936; Support Services: $2,047
Enrollment, Drop-out Rates and Diploma Recipients by Race/Ethnicity

Category	Total	White	Black	Asian	AIAN	Hisp.
Enrollment (%)	100.0	91.6	6.4	0.2	0.2	1.6
Drop-out Rate (%)	5.4	5.5	1.0	0.0	100.0	12.9
H.S. Diplomas (#)	414	379	28	0	0	7

Surry County

Mount Airy City Schools
130 Rawley Ave • Mount Airy, NC 27030-0710
Mailing Address: PO Drawer 710 • Mount Airy, NC 27030-0710
(910) 786-8355
Grade Span: PK-12; **Agency Type:** 1
Schools: 4
2 Primary; 1 Middle; 1 High; 0 Other Level
4 Regular; 0 Special Education; 0 Vocational; 0 Alternative
0 Magnet; 0 Charter; 2 Title I Eligible; 2 School-wide Title I
Students: 1,928 (50.2% male; 49.8% female)
Individual Education Program: 331 (17.2%);
English Language Learner: 171 (8.9%); Migrant: 0 (0.0%)
Eligible for Free Lunch Program: 743 (38.5%)
Eligible for Reduced-Price Lunch Program: 102 (5.3%)
Teachers: 143.0 (13.5 to 1)
Librarians/Media Specialists: 4.0 (482.0 to 1)
Guidance Counselors: 6.0 (321.3 to 1)
Current Spending: ($ per student per year):
Total: $7,762; Instruction: $4,816; Support Services: $2,438
Enrollment, Drop-out Rates and Diploma Recipients by Race/Ethnicity

Category	Total	White	Black	Asian	AIAN	Hisp.
Enrollment (%)	100.0	74.7	14.3	4.6	0.2	6.3
Drop-out Rate (%)	3.9	4.3	1.6	0.0	0.0	6.7
H.S. Diplomas (#)	87	70	9	5	0	3

Surry County Schools
209 N Crutchfield St • Dobson, NC 27017-0364
Mailing Address: PO Box 364 • Dobson, NC 27017-0364
(336) 386-8211 • http://surry.k12.nc.us/
Grade Span: PK-12; **Agency Type:** 1
Schools: 16
9 Primary; 4 Middle; 3 High; 0 Other Level
16 Regular; 0 Special Education; 0 Vocational; 0 Alternative
0 Magnet; 0 Charter; 8 Title I Eligible; 8 School-wide Title I
Students: 8,520 (51.6% male; 48.4% female)
Individual Education Program: 1,375 (16.1%);
English Language Learner: 706 (8.3%); Migrant: 393 (4.6%)
Eligible for Free Lunch Program: 3,170 (37.2%)
Eligible for Reduced-Price Lunch Program: 958 (11.2%)
Teachers: 568.0 (15.0 to 1)
Librarians/Media Specialists: 16.0 (532.5 to 1)
Guidance Counselors: 20.0 (426.0 to 1)
Current Spending: ($ per student per year):
Total: $6,512; Instruction: $4,193; Support Services: $1,908
Enrollment, Drop-out Rates and Diploma Recipients by Race/Ethnicity

Category	Total	White	Black	Asian	AIAN	Hisp.
Enrollment (%)	100.0	83.4	4.4	0.8	0.2	11.3
Drop-out Rate (%)	6.7	6.8	2.8	0.0	50.0	8.5
H.S. Diplomas (#)	476	431	19	3	0	23

Swain County

Swain County Schools
280 School Dr • Bryson City, NC 28713-2340
Mailing Address: PO Box 2340 • Bryson City, NC 28713-2340
(828) 488-3129 • http://www.swaincountyschools.com/
Grade Span: PK-12; **Agency Type:** 1
Schools: 5
2 Primary; 1 Middle; 1 High; 1 Other Level
5 Regular; 0 Special Education; 0 Vocational; 0 Alternative
0 Magnet; 0 Charter; 3 Title I Eligible; 3 School-wide Title I
Students: 1,794 (52.8% male; 47.2% female)
Individual Education Program: 327 (18.2%);
English Language Learner: 13 (0.7%); Migrant: 0 (0.0%)
Eligible for Free Lunch Program: 684 (38.1%)
Eligible for Reduced-Price Lunch Program: 284 (15.8%)
Teachers: 133.0 (13.5 to 1)
Librarians/Media Specialists: 4.0 (448.5 to 1)
Guidance Counselors: 4.0 (448.5 to 1)
Current Spending: ($ per student per year):
Total: $7,117; Instruction: $4,460; Support Services: $2,184
Enrollment, Drop-out Rates and Diploma Recipients by Race/Ethnicity

Category	Total	White	Black	Asian	AIAN	Hisp.
Enrollment (%)	100.0	76.0	0.9	0.3	21.5	1.3
Drop-out Rate (%)	7.5	7.0	0.0	0.0	8.9	25.0
H.S. Diplomas (#)	111	90	1	3	16	1

Transylvania County

Transylvania County Schools
400 Rosenwald Ln • Brevard, NC 28712-3239
(828) 884-6173 • http://www.transylvania.k12.nc.us/
Grade Span: KG-12; **Agency Type:** 1
Schools: 9
4 Primary; 2 Middle; 2 High; 1 Other Level
8 Regular; 0 Special Education; 0 Vocational; 1 Alternative
0 Magnet; 0 Charter; 4 Title I Eligible; 4 School-wide Title I
Students: 3,793 (51.7% male; 48.3% female)
Individual Education Program: 455 (12.0%);
English Language Learner: 60 (1.6%); Migrant: 0 (0.0%)
Eligible for Free Lunch Program: 1,138 (30.0%)
Eligible for Reduced-Price Lunch Program: 369 (9.7%)
Teachers: 271.0 (14.0 to 1)
Librarians/Media Specialists: 7.0 (541.9 to 1)
Guidance Counselors: 8.0 (474.1 to 1)
Current Spending: ($ per student per year):
Total: $6,866; Instruction: $4,342; Support Services: $2,117
Enrollment, Drop-out Rates and Diploma Recipients by Race/Ethnicity

Category	Total	White	Black	Asian	AIAN	Hisp.
Enrollment (%)	100.0	90.3	7.7	0.6	0.2	1.3
Drop-out Rate (%)	7.3	6.9	11.4	n/a	0.0	16.7
H.S. Diplomas (#)	252	234	18	0	0	0

Union County

Union County Public Schools
500 N Main St Ste 700 • Monroe, NC 28112-4730
(704) 283-3733 • http://www.ucps.k12.nc.us/
Grade Span: PK-12; **Agency Type:** 1
Schools: 34
19 Primary; 6 Middle; 7 High; 2 Other Level
32 Regular; 1 Special Education; 0 Vocational; 1 Alternative
0 Magnet; 0 Charter; 6 Title I Eligible; 4 School-wide Title I
Students: 25,636 (51.4% male; 48.6% female)
Individual Education Program: 3,125 (12.2%);
English Language Learner: 764 (3.0%); Migrant: 0 (0.0%)
Eligible for Free Lunch Program: 5,780 (22.5%)
Eligible for Reduced-Price Lunch Program: 1,715 (6.7%)
Teachers: 1,557.0 (16.5 to 1)
Librarians/Media Specialists: 39.0 (657.3 to 1)
Guidance Counselors: 60.0 (427.3 to 1)
Current Spending: ($ per student per year):
Total: $5,754; Instruction: $3,742; Support Services: $1,676

Enrollment, Drop-out Rates and Diploma Recipients by Race/Ethnicity

Category	Total	White	Black	Asian	AIAN	Hisp.
Enrollment (%)	100.0	74.1	17.5	0.8	0.3	7.3
Drop-out Rate (%)	5.0	4.0	7.2	0.0	30.8	15.3
H.S. Diplomas (#)	1,085	893	162	7	1	22

Vance County

Vance County Schools

128 Church St • Henderson, NC 27536-4295
Mailing Address: PO Box 7001 • Henderson, NC 27536-7001
(252) 492-2127 • http://www.vcs.k12.nc.us/
Grade Span: PK-12; **Agency Type:** 1
Schools: 15
10 Primary; 2 Middle; 2 High; 1 Other Level
14 Regular; 0 Special Education; 0 Vocational; 1 Alternative
0 Magnet; 0 Charter; 9 Title I Eligible; 9 School-wide Title I
Students: 8,584 (52.1% male; 47.9% female)
Individual Education Program: 1,045 (12.2%);
English Language Learner: 287 (3.3%); Migrant: 93 (1.1%)
Eligible for Free Lunch Program: 5,135 (59.8%)
Eligible for Reduced-Price Lunch Program: 795 (9.3%)
Teachers: 582.0 (14.7 to 1)
Librarians/Media Specialists: 16.0 (536.5 to 1)
Guidance Counselors: 21.0 (408.8 to 1)
Current Spending: ($ per student per year):
Total: $6,020; Instruction: $3,885; Support Services: $1,724

Enrollment, Drop-out Rates and Diploma Recipients by Race/Ethnicity

Category	Total	White	Black	Asian	AIAN	Hisp.
Enrollment (%)	100.0	28.4	65.3	0.3	0.1	5.8
Drop-out Rate (%)	7.6	6.4	8.1	7.7	0.0	17.2
H.S. Diplomas (#)	334	146	178	3	0	7

Wake County

Wake County Schools

3600 Wake Forest Rd • Raleigh, NC 27609-7329
Mailing Address: PO Box 28041 • Raleigh, NC 27611-8041
(919) 850-1600
Grade Span: PK-12; **Agency Type:** 1
Schools: 123
80 Primary; 25 Middle; 16 High; 2 Other Level
120 Regular; 0 Special Education; 0 Vocational; 3 Alternative
44 Magnet; 0 Charter; 47 Title I Eligible; 0 School-wide Title I
Students: 104,836 (51.1% male; 48.9% female)
Individual Education Program: 15,525 (14.8%);
English Language Learner: 4,447 (4.2%); Migrant: 580 (0.6%)
Eligible for Free Lunch Program: 19,719 (18.8%)
Eligible for Reduced-Price Lunch Program: 4,678 (4.5%)
Teachers: 6,789.0 (15.4 to 1)
Librarians/Media Specialists: 171.0 (613.1 to 1)
Guidance Counselors: 259.0 (404.8 to 1)
Current Spending: ($ per student per year):
Total: $6,496; Instruction: $4,037; Support Services: $2,202

Enrollment, Drop-out Rates and Diploma Recipients by Race/Ethnicity

Category	Total	White	Black	Asian	AIAN	Hisp.
Enrollment (%)	100.0	60.0	29.1	4.2	0.3	6.5
Drop-out Rate (%)	4.0	3.0	6.5	1.5	3.9	10.5
H.S. Diplomas (#)	5,411	3,845	1,170	234	10	152

Warren County

Warren County Schools

109 Cousin Lucy's Ln • Warrenton, NC 27589-0110
Mailing Address: PO Box 110 • Warrenton, NC 27589-0110
(252) 257-3184 • http://www.warren-county.k12.nc.us/
Grade Span: KG-12; **Agency Type:** 1
Schools: 6
4 Primary; 1 Middle; 1 High; 0 Other Level
6 Regular; 0 Special Education; 0 Vocational; 0 Alternative
0 Magnet; 0 Charter; 4 Title I Eligible; 4 School-wide Title I
Students: 3,183 (51.1% male; 48.9% female)
Individual Education Program: 516 (16.2%);
English Language Learner: 40 (1.3%); Migrant: 0 (0.0%)
Eligible for Free Lunch Program: 1,801 (56.6%)
Eligible for Reduced-Price Lunch Program: 413 (13.0%)
Teachers: 201.0 (15.8 to 1)
Librarians/Media Specialists: 4.0 (795.8 to 1)
Guidance Counselors: 7.0 (454.7 to 1)
Current Spending: ($ per student per year):
Total: $6,921; Instruction: $4,138; Support Services: $2,305

Enrollment, Drop-out Rates and Diploma Recipients by Race/Ethnicity

Category	Total	White	Black	Asian	AIAN	Hisp.
Enrollment (%)	100.0	19.1	73.9	0.1	4.8	2.1
Drop-out Rate (%)	11.3	13.5	10.7	n/a	10.2	0.0
H.S. Diplomas (#)	144	32	106	0	6	0

Washington County

Washington County Schools

802 Washington St • Plymouth, NC 27962-0747
(252) 793-5171 • http://www.washingtonco.k12.nc.us/
Grade Span: PK-12; **Agency Type:** 1
Schools: 5
2 Primary; 1 Middle; 2 High; 0 Other Level
5 Regular; 0 Special Education; 0 Vocational; 0 Alternative
0 Magnet; 0 Charter; 3 Title I Eligible; 3 School-wide Title I
Students: 2,365 (51.6% male; 48.4% female)
Individual Education Program: 427 (18.1%);
English Language Learner: 22 (0.9%); Migrant: 39 (1.6%)
Eligible for Free Lunch Program: 0 (0.0%)
Eligible for Reduced-Price Lunch Program: 0 (0.0%)
Teachers: 191.0 (12.4 to 1)
Librarians/Media Specialists: 4.0 (591.3 to 1)
Guidance Counselors: 4.0 (591.3 to 1)
Current Spending: ($ per student per year):
Total: $8,040; Instruction: $5,163; Support Services: $2,403

Enrollment, Drop-out Rates and Diploma Recipients by Race/Ethnicity

Category	Total	White	Black	Asian	AIAN	Hisp.
Enrollment (%)	100.0	24.6	73.7	0.2	0.0	1.5
Drop-out Rate (%)	5.5	4.9	5.9	0.0	n/a	0.0
H.S. Diplomas (#)	134	49	84	0	0	1

Watauga County

Watauga County Schools

175 Pioneer Dr • Boone, NC 28607-1790
Mailing Address: PO Box 1790 • Boone, NC 28607-1790
(828) 264-7190 • http://nt.watauga.k12.nc.us/co/default.htm
Grade Span: PK-12; **Agency Type:** 1
Schools: 9
8 Primary; 0 Middle; 1 High; 0 Other Level
9 Regular; 0 Special Education; 0 Vocational; 0 Alternative
0 Magnet; 0 Charter; 5 Title I Eligible; 2 School-wide Title I
Students: 4,734 (52.6% male; 47.4% female)
Individual Education Program: 769 (16.2%);
English Language Learner: 63 (1.3%); Migrant: 0 (0.0%)
Eligible for Free Lunch Program: 817 (17.3%)
Eligible for Reduced-Price Lunch Program: 355 (7.5%)
Teachers: 354.0 (13.4 to 1)
Librarians/Media Specialists: 12.0 (394.5 to 1)
Guidance Counselors: 14.0 (338.1 to 1)
Current Spending: ($ per student per year):
Total: $6,771; Instruction: $4,488; Support Services: $2,015

Enrollment, Drop-out Rates and Diploma Recipients by Race/Ethnicity

Category	Total	White	Black	Asian	AIAN	Hisp.
Enrollment (%)	100.0	95.6	2.3	0.8	0.1	1.2
Drop-out Rate (%)	5.5	5.6	5.0	0.0	n/a	0.0
H.S. Diplomas (#)	327	323	2	1	0	1

Wayne County

Wayne County Public Schools

2001 E Royall Ave • Goldsboro, NC 27534
Mailing Address: PO Drawer 1797 • Goldsboro, NC 27533-1797
(919) 731-5900 • http://www.waynecountyschools.org/
Grade Span: PK-12; **Agency Type:** 1
Schools: 31
14 Primary; 8 Middle; 5 High; 4 Other Level
28 Regular; 1 Special Education; 0 Vocational; 2 Alternative
0 Magnet; 0 Charter; 21 Title I Eligible; 19 School-wide Title I
Students: 19,155 (51.4% male; 48.6% female)
Individual Education Program: 2,949 (15.4%);
English Language Learner: 743 (3.9%); Migrant: 0 (0.0%)
Eligible for Free Lunch Program: 7,208 (37.6%)
Eligible for Reduced-Price Lunch Program: 2,040 (10.7%)
Teachers: 1,265.0 (15.1 to 1)
Librarians/Media Specialists: 36.0 (532.1 to 1)
Guidance Counselors: 45.0 (425.7 to 1)
Current Spending: ($ per student per year):
Total: $6,100; Instruction: $4,016; Support Services: $1,723

Enrollment, Drop-out Rates and Diploma Recipients by Race/Ethnicity

Category	Total	White	Black	Asian	AIAN	Hisp.
Enrollment (%)	100.0	48.4	44.4	1.0	0.1	6.1
Drop-out Rate (%)	5.2	4.5	6.0	1.2	16.7	6.8
H.S. Diplomas (#)	996	567	393	12	3	21

Wilkes County

Wilkes County Schools

201 W Main St • Wilkesboro, NC 28697-2424
(336) 667-1121 • http://www.wilkes.k12.nc.us/
Grade Span: PK-12; **Agency Type:** 1
Schools: 24
15 Primary; 4 Middle; 5 High; 0 Other Level
23 Regular; 0 Special Education; 1 Vocational; 0 Alternative
0 Magnet; 0 Charter; 11 Title I Eligible; 8 School-wide Title I
Students: 10,345 (50.6% male; 49.4% female)
Individual Education Program: 1,560 (15.1%);
English Language Learner: 440 (4.3%); Migrant: 402 (3.9%)
Eligible for Free Lunch Program: 3,376 (32.6%)
Eligible for Reduced-Price Lunch Program: 983 (9.5%)
Teachers: 677.0 (15.3 to 1)
Librarians/Media Specialists: 23.0 (449.8 to 1)
Guidance Counselors: 31.0 (333.7 to 1)
Current Spending: ($ per student per year):
Total: $6,315; Instruction: $3,987; Support Services: $1,903

Enrollment, Drop-out Rates and Diploma Recipients by Race/Ethnicity

Category	Total	White	Black	Asian	AIAN	Hisp.
Enrollment (%)	100.0	88.1	6.0	0.5	0.0	5.3
Drop-out Rate (%)	6.7	6.6	5.5	0.0	50.0	14.3
H.S. Diplomas (#)	536	501	28	3	0	4

Wilson County

Wilson County Schools

117 NE Tarboro St • Wilson, NC 27893-4016
Mailing Address: PO Box 2048 • Wilson, NC 27894-2048
(252) 399-7700 • http://schools.eastnet.ecu.edu/wilson/
Grade Span: PK-12; **Agency Type:** 1
Schools: 23
13 Primary; 6 Middle; 3 High; 1 Other Level
22 Regular; 0 Special Education; 0 Vocational; 1 Alternative
0 Magnet; 0 Charter; 12 Title I Eligible; 12 School-wide Title I
Students: 12,289 (51.4% male; 48.6% female)
Individual Education Program: 1,419 (11.5%);
English Language Learner: 417 (3.4%); Migrant: 234 (1.9%)
Eligible for Free Lunch Program: 5,779 (47.0%)
Eligible for Reduced-Price Lunch Program: 1,178 (9.6%)
Teachers: 768.0 (16.0 to 1)
Librarians/Media Specialists: 23.0 (534.3 to 1)
Guidance Counselors: 27.0 (455.1 to 1)
Current Spending: ($ per student per year):
Total: $6,451; Instruction: $4,174; Support Services: $1,888

Enrollment, Drop-out Rates and Diploma Recipients by Race/Ethnicity

Category	Total	White	Black	Asian	AIAN	Hisp.
Enrollment (%)	100.0	39.5	52.5	0.8	0.1	7.0
Drop-out Rate (%)	7.4	5.9	8.6	0.0	0.0	11.5
H.S. Diplomas (#)	594	295	278	6	0	15

Yadkin County

Yadkin County Schools

121 Washington St • Yadkinville, NC 27055-9806
(336) 679-2051 • http://www.yadkin.k12.nc.us/
Grade Span: PK-12; **Agency Type:** 1
Schools: 11
8 Primary; 0 Middle; 2 High; 1 Other Level
10 Regular; 0 Special Education; 0 Vocational; 1 Alternative
0 Magnet; 0 Charter; 5 Title I Eligible; 0 School-wide Title I
Students: 5,904 (51.1% male; 48.9% female)
Individual Education Program: 1,016 (17.2%);
English Language Learner: 291 (4.9%); Migrant: 131 (2.2%)
Eligible for Free Lunch Program: 1,217 (20.6%)
Eligible for Reduced-Price Lunch Program: 441 (7.5%)
Teachers: 356.0 (16.6 to 1)
Librarians/Media Specialists: 14.0 (421.7 to 1)
Guidance Counselors: 14.0 (421.7 to 1)
Current Spending: ($ per student per year):
Total: $6,249; Instruction: $3,856; Support Services: $1,955

Enrollment, Drop-out Rates and Diploma Recipients by Race/Ethnicity

Category	Total	White	Black	Asian	AIAN	Hisp.
Enrollment (%)	100.0	83.6	4.2	0.3	0.2	11.6
Drop-out Rate (%)	5.8	5.2	8.9	0.0	25.0	11.8
H.S. Diplomas (#)	304	281	9	1	1	12

Yancey County

Yancey County Schools

100 School Circle • Burnsville, NC 28714-0190
Mailing Address: PO Box 190 • Burnsville, NC 28714-0190
(828) 682-6101 • http://www.yanceync.net/
Grade Span: KG-12; **Agency Type:** 1
Schools: 9
6 Primary; 2 Middle; 1 High; 0 Other Level
9 Regular; 0 Special Education; 0 Vocational; 0 Alternative
0 Magnet; 0 Charter; 7 Title I Eligible; 5 School-wide Title I
Students: 2,509 (51.0% male; 49.0% female)
Individual Education Program: 436 (17.4%);
English Language Learner: 100 (4.0%); Migrant: 135 (5.4%)
Eligible for Free Lunch Program: 0 (0.0%)
Eligible for Reduced-Price Lunch Program: 0 (0.0%)
Teachers: 169.0 (14.8 to 1)
Librarians/Media Specialists: 7.0 (358.4 to 1)
Guidance Counselors: 7.0 (358.4 to 1)
Current Spending: ($ per student per year):
Total: $7,120; Instruction: $4,216; Support Services: $2,470

Enrollment, Drop-out Rates and Diploma Recipients by Race/Ethnicity

Category	Total	White	Black	Asian	AIAN	Hisp.
Enrollment (%)	100.0	94.4	1.2	0.3	0.2	4.0
Drop-out Rate (%)	4.9	5.0	0.0	0.0	0.0	0.0
H.S. Diplomas (#)	146	142	2	0	0	2

Number of Schools

Rank	Number	District Name	City
1	134	Charlotte-Mecklenburg Schools	Charlotte
2	123	Wake County Schools	Raleigh
3	102	Guilford County Schools	Greensboro
4	84	Cumberland County Schools	Fayetteville
5	68	Forsyth County Schools	Winston Salem
6	52	Gaston County Schools	Gastonia
7	44	Durham Public Schools	Durham
8	41	Robeson County Schools	Lumberton
9	40	Buncombe County Schools	Asheville
10	34	New Hanover County Schools	Wilmington
10	34	Union County Public Schools	Monroe
12	33	Alamance-Burlington Schools	Burlington
12	33	Onslow County Schools	Jacksonville
12	33	Pitt County Schools	Greenville
15	32	Iredell-Statesville Schools	Statesville
15	32	Johnston County Schools	Smithfield
17	31	Wayne County Public Schools	Goldsboro
18	30	Rowan-Salisbury Schools	Salisbury
19	29	Nash-Rocky Mount Schools	Nashville
20	28	Cabarrus County Schools	Concord
20	28	Davidson County Schools	Lexington
20	28	Randolph County Schools	Asheboro
23	26	Harnett County Schools	Lillington
24	25	Burke County Schools	Morganton
24	25	Caldwell County Schools	Lenoir
24	25	Catawba County Schools	Newton
24	25	Rockingham County Schools	Eden
28	24	Wilkes County Schools	Wilkesboro
29	23	Wilson County Schools	Wilson
30	22	Craven County Schools	New Bern
30	22	Moore County Schools	Carthage
30	22	Stanly County Schools	Albemarle
33	21	Henderson County Schools	Hendersonville
34	20	Lenoir County Public Schools	Kinston
35	19	Columbus County Schools	Whiteville
35	19	Lincoln County Schools	Lincolnton
35	19	Rutherford County Schools	Forest City
38	18	Richmond County Schools	Hamlet
38	18	Stokes County Schools	Danbury
40	16	Brunswick County Schools	Bolivia
40	16	Carteret County Public Schools	Beaufort
40	16	Sampson County Schools	Clinton
40	16	Surry County Schools	Dobson
44	15	Chapel Hill-Carrboro Schools	Chapel Hill
44	15	Chatham County Schools	Pittsboro
44	15	Duplin County Schools	Kenansville
44	15	Edgecombe County Schools	Tarboro
44	15	Halifax County Schools	Halifax
44	15	Haywood County Schools	Waynesville
44	15	Pender County Schools	Burgaw
44	15	Scotland County Schools	Laurinburg
44	15	Vance County Schools	Henderson
53	14	Beaufort County Schools	Washington
53	14	Bladen County Schools	Elizabethtown
53	14	Franklin County Schools	Louisburg
53	14	Granville County Schools	Oxford
57	13	Cherokee County Schools	Murphy
58	12	Cleveland County Schools	Shelby
58	12	Lee County Schools	Sanford
58	12	Martin County Schools	Williamston
58	12	Pasquotank County Schools	Elizabeth City
62	11	Hoke County Schools	Raeford
62	11	Mcdowell County Schools	Marion
62	11	Orange County Schools	Hillsborough
62	11	Yadkin County Schools	Yadkinville
66	10	Alexander County Schools	Taylorsville
66	10	Bertie County Schools	Windsor
66	10	Hickory City Schools	Hickory
66	10	Macon County Schools	Franklin
66	10	Montgomery County Schools	Troy
66	10	Northampton County Schools	Jackson
66	10	Person County Schools	Roxboro
73	9	Anson County Schools	Wadesboro
73	9	Avery County Schools	Newland
73	9	Dare County Schools	Manteo
73	9	Davie County Schools	Mocksville
73	9	Fort Bragg District	Fort Bragg
73	9	Kings Mountain District	Kings Mountain
73	9	Transylvania County Schools	Brevard
73	9	Watauga County Schools	Boone
73	9	Yancey County Schools	Burnsville
82	8	Asheboro City Schools	Asheboro
82	8	Asheville City Schools	Asheville
82	8	Camp Lejeune District	Camp Lejeune
82	8	Currituck County Schools	Currituck
82	8	Mitchell County Schools	Bakersville
87	7	Jackson County Schools	Sylva
87	7	Kannapolis City Schools	Kannapolis
87	7	Shelby City	Shelby
90	6	Ashe County Schools	Jefferson
90	6	Caswell County Schools	Yanceyville
90	6	Hertford County Schools	Winton
90	6	Jones County Schools	Trenton
90	6	Lexington City Schools	Lexington
90	6	Madison County Schools	Marshall
90	6	Mooresville City Schools	Mooresville
90	6	Newton Conover City Schools	Newton
90	6	Polk County Schools	Columbus
90	6	Warren County Schools	Warrenton
100	5	Gates County Schools	Gatesville
100	5	Swain County Schools	Bryson City
100	5	Washington County Schools	Plymouth
100	5	Whiteville City Schools	Whiteville
104	4	Clinton City Schools	Clinton
104	4	Edenton-Chowan Schools	Edenton
104	4	Greene County Schools	Snow Hill
104	4	Mount Airy City Schools	Mount Airy
104	4	Pamlico County Schools	Bayboro
104	4	Perquimans County Schools	Hertford
104	4	Roanoke Rapids City Schools	Roanoke Rapids
104	4	Thomasville City Schools	Thomasville

Number of Teachers

Rank	Number	District Name	City
1	7,262	Charlotte-Mecklenburg Schools	Charlotte
2	6,789	Wake County Schools	Raleigh
3	4,089	Guilford County Schools	Greensboro
4	3,284	Cumberland County Schools	Fayetteville
5	3,186	Forsyth County Schools	Winston Salem
6	2,051	Durham Public Schools	Durham
7	1,879	Gaston County Schools	Gastonia
8	1,683	Johnston County Schools	Smithfield
9	1,587	Buncombe County Schools	Asheville
10	1,557	Union County Public Schools	Monroe
11	1,498	Robeson County Schools	Lumberton
12	1,423	New Hanover County Schools	Wilmington
13	1,401	Alamance-Burlington Schools	Burlington
14	1,378	Cabarrus County Schools	Concord
15	1,358	Pitt County Schools	Greenville
16	1,331	Onslow County Schools	Jacksonville
17	1,321	Rowan-Salisbury Schools	Salisbury
18	1,299	Nash-Rocky Mount Schools	Nashville
19	1,265	Wayne County Public Schools	Goldsboro
20	1,156	Davidson County Schools	Lexington
21	1,083	Randolph County Schools	Asheboro
22	1,075	Iredell-Statesville Schools	Statesville
23	1,052	Harnett County Schools	Lillington
24	1,033	Catawba County Schools	Newton
25	1,007	Burke County Schools	Morganton
26	993	Craven County Schools	New Bern
27	937	Rockingham County Schools	Eden
28	840	Caldwell County Schools	Lenoir
29	810	Chapel Hill-Carrboro Schools	Chapel Hill
30	786	Moore County Schools	Carthage
31	785	Lincoln County Schools	Lincolnton
32	768	Wilson County Schools	Wilson
33	759	Henderson County Schools	Hendersonville
34	719	Lenoir County Public Schools	Kinston
35	709	Brunswick County Schools	Bolivia
36	677	Wilkes County Schools	Wilkesboro
37	672	Rutherford County Schools	Forest City
38	653	Carteret County Public Schools	Beaufort
39	646	Stanly County Schools	Albemarle
40	632	Cleveland County Schools	Shelby
41	583	Duplin County Schools	Kenansville
42	582	Lee County Schools	Sanford
42	582	Vance County Schools	Henderson
44	568	Surry County Schools	Dobson
45	547	Scotland County Schools	Laurinburg
46	543	Sampson County Schools	Clinton
47	537	Beaufort County Schools	Washington
48	536	Franklin County Schools	Louisburg
49	531	Haywood County Schools	Waynesville
50	528	Richmond County Schools	Hamlet
51	525	Edgecombe County Schools	Tarboro
52	524	Granville County Schools	Oxford
53	523	Stokes County Schools	Danbury
54	493	Chatham County Schools	Pittsboro
55	479	Pender County Schools	Burgaw
56	457	Orange County Schools	Hillsborough
57	443	Columbus County Schools	Whiteville
58	417	Mcdowell County Schools	Marion
59	408	Pasquotank County Schools	Elizabeth City
60	398	Person County Schools	Roxboro
61	394	Davie County Schools	Mocksville
62	373	Bladen County Schools	Elizabethtown
63	371	Hoke County Schools	Raeford
64	360	Halifax County Schools	Halifax
65	356	Yadkin County Schools	Yadkinville
66	354	Watauga County Schools	Boone
67	332	Martin County Schools	Williamston
68	328	Dare County Schools	Manteo
69	326	Alexander County Schools	Taylorsville
70	325	Asheville City Schools	Asheville
70	325	Kannapolis City Schools	Kannapolis
72	318	Montgomery County Schools	Troy
73	304	Hickory City Schools	Hickory
74	301	Asheboro City Schools	Asheboro
75	297	Anson County Schools	Wadesboro
76	295	Fort Bragg District	Fort Bragg
77	293	Kings Mountain District	Kings Mountain
78	288	Macon County Schools	Franklin
79	277	Cherokee County Schools	Murphy
80	271	Transylvania County Schools	Brevard
81	269	Mooresville City Schools	Mooresville
82	258	Jackson County Schools	Sylva
83	251	Hertford County Schools	Winton
84	243	Shelby City	Shelby
85	241	Currituck County Schools	Currituck
86	239	Northampton County Schools	Jackson
87	238	Camp Lejeune District	Camp Lejeune
88	236	Ashe County Schools	Jefferson
88	236	Bertie County Schools	Windsor
88	236	Caswell County Schools	Yanceyville
91	235	Greene County Schools	Snow Hill
92	214	Lexington City Schools	Lexington
93	209	Madison County Schools	Marshall
93	209	Roanoke Rapids City Schools	Roanoke Rapids
95	201	Warren County Schools	Warrenton
96	197	Newton Conover City Schools	Newton
97	196	Whiteville City Schools	Whiteville
98	191	Washington County Schools	Plymouth
99	186	Clinton City Schools	Clinton
100	182	Avery County Schools	Newland
101	180	Edenton-Chowan Schools	Edenton
102	177	Thomasville City Schools	Thomasville
103	176	Polk County Schools	Columbus
104	169	Yancey County Schools	Burnsville
105	164	Mitchell County Schools	Bakersville
106	156	Gates County Schools	Gatesville
107	148	Pamlico County Schools	Bayboro
108	143	Mount Airy City Schools	Mount Airy
109	133	Swain County Schools	Bryson City
110	130	Perquimans County Schools	Hertford
111	115	Jones County Schools	Trenton

Number of Students

Rank	Number	District Name	City
1	109,767	Charlotte-Mecklenburg Schools	Charlotte
2	104,836	Wake County Schools	Raleigh
3	65,677	Guilford County Schools	Greensboro
4	52,094	Cumberland County Schools	Fayetteville
5	46,806	Forsyth County Schools	Winston Salem
6	31,258	Gaston County Schools	Gastonia
7	30,794	Durham Public Schools	Durham
8	25,636	Union County Public Schools	Monroe
9	24,665	Buncombe County Schools	Asheville
10	24,191	Robeson County Schools	Lumberton
11	23,506	Johnston County Schools	Smithfield
12	21,861	New Hanover County Schools	Wilmington
13	21,597	Alamance-Burlington Schools	Burlington
14	21,580	Onslow County Schools	Jacksonville
15	20,939	Cabarrus County Schools	Concord
16	20,929	Pitt County Schools	Greenville
17	20,843	Rowan-Salisbury Schools	Salisbury
18	19,283	Davidson County Schools	Lexington
19	19,155	Wayne County Public Schools	Goldsboro
20	18,566	Iredell-Statesville Schools	Statesville
21	18,464	Nash-Rocky Mount Schools	Nashville
22	18,144	Randolph County Schools	Asheboro
23	16,725	Harnett County Schools	Lillington
24	16,620	Catawba County Schools	Newton
25	14,871	Rockingham County Schools	Eden
26	14,752	Burke County Schools	Morganton
27	14,563	Craven County Schools	New Bern
28	12,744	Caldwell County Schools	Lenoir
29	12,289	Wilson County Schools	Wilson
30	12,013	Henderson County Schools	Hendersonville
31	11,404	Moore County Schools	Carthage
32	11,106	Lincoln County Schools	Lincolnton
33	10,741	Brunswick County Schools	Bolivia
34	10,360	Chapel Hill-Carrboro Schools	Chapel Hill
35	10,345	Wilkes County Schools	Wilkesboro
36	10,249	Lenoir County Public Schools	Kinston
37	10,188	Rutherford County Schools	Forest City
38	10,094	Stanly County Schools	Albemarle
39	9,722	Cleveland County Schools	Shelby
40	9,058	Lee County Schools	Sanford
41	8,786	Duplin County Schools	Kenansville
42	8,584	Vance County Schools	Henderson
43	8,548	Granville County Schools	Oxford
44	8,520	Surry County Schools	Dobson
45	8,375	Richmond County Schools	Hamlet
46	8,251	Carteret County Public Schools	Beaufort

47	8,086	Sampson County Schools	Clinton
48	7,914	Franklin County Schools	Louisburg
49	7,869	Haywood County Schools	Waynesville
50	7,825	Edgecombe County Schools	Tarboro
51	7,530	Stokes County Schools	Danbury
52	7,468	Beaufort County Schools	Washington
53	7,252	Chatham County Schools	Pittsboro
54	7,106	Scotland County Schools	Laurinburg
55	7,102	Columbus County Schools	Whiteville
56	6,825	Pender County Schools	Burgaw
57	6,517	Mcdowell County Schools	Marion
58	6,465	Hoke County Schools	Raeford
59	6,360	Orange County Schools	Hillsborough
60	6,036	Pasquotank County Schools	Elizabeth City
61	5,948	Davie County Schools	Mocksville
62	5,904	Yadkin County Schools	Yadkinville
63	5,864	Halifax County Schools	Halifax
64	5,811	Bladen County Schools	Elizabethtown
65	5,796	Person County Schools	Roxboro
66	5,482	Alexander County Schools	Taylorsville
67	4,734	Watauga County Schools	Boone
68	4,724	Dare County Schools	Manteo
69	4,698	Kings Mountain District	Kings Mountain
70	4,620	Martin County Schools	Williamston
71	4,561	Montgomery County Schools	Troy
72	4,537	Fort Bragg District	Fort Bragg
73	4,494	Anson County Schools	Wadesboro
74	4,458	Hickory City Schools	Hickory
75	4,396	Kannapolis City Schools	Kannapolis
76	4,388	Asheboro City Schools	Asheboro
77	4,208	Mooresville City Schools	Mooresville
78	4,134	Macon County Schools	Franklin
79	3,950	Hertford County Schools	Winton
80	3,920	Asheville City Schools	Asheville
81	3,793	Transylvania County Schools	Brevard
82	3,757	Cherokee County Schools	Murphy
83	3,720	Jackson County Schools	Sylva
84	3,563	Caswell County Schools	Yanceyville
85	3,555	Bertie County Schools	Windsor
86	3,550	Northampton County Schools	Jackson
87	3,427	Currituck County Schools	Currituck
88	3,313	Lexington City Schools	Lexington
89	3,296	Shelby City	Shelby
90	3,286	Camp Lejeune District	Camp Lejeune
91	3,278	Ashe County Schools	Jefferson
92	3,259	Greene County Schools	Snow Hill
93	3,183	Warren County Schools	Warrenton
94	3,065	Roanoke Rapids City Schools	Roanoke Rapids
95	2,848	Newton Conover City Schools	Newton
96	2,731	Clinton City Schools	Clinton
97	2,703	Whiteville City Schools	Whiteville
98	2,562	Madison County Schools	Marshall
99	2,544	Edenton-Chowan Schools	Edenton
100	2,509	Yancey County Schools	Burnsville
101	2,480	Thomasville City Schools	Thomasville
102	2,476	Polk County Schools	Columbus
103	2,463	Avery County Schools	Newland
104	2,365	Washington County Schools	Plymouth
105	2,356	Mitchell County Schools	Bakersville
106	1,993	Gates County Schools	Gatesville
107	1,928	Mount Airy City Schools	Mount Airy
108	1,824	Perquimans County Schools	Hertford
109	1,794	Swain County Schools	Bryson City
110	1,788	Pamlico County Schools	Bayboro
111	1,510	Jones County Schools	Trenton

Male Students

Rank	Percent	District Name	City
1	53.8	Greene County Schools	Snow Hill
2	53.7	Madison County Schools	Marshall
3	52.8	Mitchell County Schools	Bakersville
3	52.8	Swain County Schools	Bryson City
5	52.7	Avery County Schools	Newland
6	52.6	Watauga County Schools	Boone
7	52.5	Cherokee County Schools	Murphy
7	52.5	Stanly County Schools	Albemarle
9	52.4	Kannapolis City Schools	Kannapolis
10	52.3	Chatham County Schools	Pittsboro
10	52.3	Gates County Schools	Gatesville
12	52.1	Bertie County Schools	Windsor
12	52.1	Henderson County Schools	Hendersonville
12	52.1	Pamlico County Schools	Bayboro
12	52.1	Sampson County Schools	Clinton
12	52.1	Vance County Schools	Henderson
17	52.0	Dare County Schools	Manteo
17	52.0	Jackson County Schools	Sylva
17	52.0	Northampton County Schools	Jackson
20	51.9	Ashe County Schools	Jefferson
20	51.9	Carteret County Public Schools	Beaufort
20	51.9	Franklin County Schools	Louisburg
20	51.9	Stokes County Schools	Danbury
24	51.8	Pender County Schools	Burgaw
24	51.8	Randolph County Schools	Asheboro
26	51.7	Bladen County Schools	Elizabethtown
26	51.7	Caswell County Schools	Yanceyville
26	51.7	Halifax County Schools	Halifax
26	51.7	Macon County Schools	Franklin
26	51.7	Thomasville City Schools	Thomasville
26	51.7	Transylvania County Schools	Brevard
32	51.6	Alexander County Schools	Taylorsville
32	51.6	Forsyth County Schools	Winston Salem
32	51.6	Lincoln County Schools	Lincolnton
32	51.6	Shelby City	Shelby
32	51.6	Surry County Schools	Dobson
32	51.6	Washington County Schools	Plymouth
38	51.5	Chapel Hill-Carrboro Schools	Chapel Hill
38	51.5	Cleveland County Schools	Shelby
38	51.5	Davie County Schools	Mocksville
38	51.5	Jones County Schools	Trenton
38	51.5	Lenoir County Public Schools	Kinston
38	51.5	Orange County Schools	Hillsborough
38	51.5	Rockingham County Schools	Eden
45	51.4	Catawba County Schools	Newton
45	51.4	Durham Public Schools	Durham
45	51.4	Richmond County Schools	Hamlet
45	51.4	Union County Public Schools	Monroe
45	51.4	Wayne County Public Schools	Goldsboro
45	51.4	Wilson County Schools	Wilson
51	51.3	Buncombe County Schools	Asheville
51	51.3	Gaston County Schools	Gastonia
51	51.3	Johnston County Schools	Smithfield
51	51.3	Lee County Schools	Sanford
51	51.3	Martin County Schools	Williamston
51	51.3	Montgomery County Schools	Troy
51	51.3	Perquimans County Schools	Hertford
51	51.3	Robeson County Schools	Lumberton
59	51.2	Beaufort County Schools	Washington
59	51.2	Charlotte-Mecklenburg Schools	Charlotte
59	51.2	Mcdowell County Schools	Marion
62	51.1	Alamance-Burlington Schools	Burlington
62	51.1	Asheville City Schools	Asheville
62	51.1	Burke County Schools	Morganton
62	51.1	Cabarrus County Schools	Concord
62	51.1	Iredell-Statesville Schools	Statesville
62	51.1	Lexington City Schools	Lexington
62	51.1	Rowan-Salisbury Schools	Salisbury
62	51.1	Wake County Schools	Raleigh
62	51.1	Warren County Schools	Warrenton
62	51.1	Yadkin County Schools	Yadkinville
72	51.0	Brunswick County Schools	Bolivia
72	51.0	Edgecombe County Schools	Tarboro
72	51.0	Guilford County Schools	Greensboro
72	51.0	Harnett County Schools	Lillington
72	51.0	Pasquotank County Schools	Elizabeth City
72	51.0	Pitt County Schools	Greenville
72	51.0	Roanoke Rapids City Schools	Roanoke Rapids
72	51.0	Rutherford County Schools	Forest City
72	51.0	Yancey County Schools	Burnsville
81	50.9	Asheboro City Schools	Asheboro
81	50.9	Columbus County Schools	Whiteville
81	50.9	Davidson County Schools	Lexington
81	50.9	Duplin County Schools	Kenansville
81	50.9	Haywood County Schools	Waynesville
81	50.9	Moore County Schools	Carthage
81	50.9	Scotland County Schools	Laurinburg
88	50.8	Cumberland County Schools	Fayetteville
88	50.8	Edenton-Chowan Schools	Edenton
88	50.8	Granville County Schools	Oxford
88	50.8	Hoke County Schools	Raeford
88	50.8	Nash-Rocky Mount Schools	Nashville
88	50.8	New Hanover County Schools	Wilmington
88	50.8	Newton Conover City Schools	Newton
88	50.8	Person County Schools	Roxboro
96	50.7	Caldwell County Schools	Lenoir
97	50.6	Kings Mountain District	Kings Mountain
97	50.6	Wilkes County Schools	Wilkesboro
99	50.5	Craven County Schools	New Bern
99	50.5	Onslow County Schools	Jacksonville
101	50.4	Anson County Schools	Wadesboro
101	50.4	Polk County Schools	Columbus
103	50.3	Mooresville City Schools	Mooresville
103	50.3	Whiteville City Schools	Whiteville
105	50.2	Mount Airy City Schools	Mount Airy
106	50.0	Currituck County Schools	Currituck
107	49.9	Clinton City Schools	Clinton
108	49.8	Hickory City Schools	Hickory
109	49.7	Hertford County Schools	Winton
110	n/a	Camp Lejeune District	Camp Lejeune
110	n/a	Fort Bragg District	Fort Bragg

Female Students

Rank	Percent	District Name	City
1	50.3	Hertford County Schools	Winton
2	50.2	Hickory City Schools	Hickory
3	50.1	Clinton City Schools	Clinton
4	50.0	Currituck County Schools	Currituck
5	49.8	Mount Airy City Schools	Mount Airy
6	49.7	Mooresville City Schools	Mooresville
6	49.7	Whiteville City Schools	Whiteville
8	49.6	Anson County Schools	Wadesboro
8	49.6	Polk County Schools	Columbus
10	49.5	Craven County Schools	New Bern
10	49.5	Onslow County Schools	Jacksonville
12	49.4	Kings Mountain District	Kings Mountain
12	49.4	Wilkes County Schools	Wilkesboro
14	49.3	Caldwell County Schools	Lenoir
15	49.2	Cumberland County Schools	Fayetteville
15	49.2	Edenton-Chowan Schools	Edenton
15	49.2	Granville County Schools	Oxford
15	49.2	Hoke County Schools	Raeford
15	49.2	Nash-Rocky Mount Schools	Nashville
15	49.2	New Hanover County Schools	Wilmington
15	49.2	Newton Conover City Schools	Newton
15	49.2	Person County Schools	Roxboro
23	49.1	Asheboro City Schools	Asheboro
23	49.1	Columbus County Schools	Whiteville
23	49.1	Davidson County Schools	Lexington
23	49.1	Duplin County Schools	Kenansville
23	49.1	Haywood County Schools	Waynesville
23	49.1	Moore County Schools	Carthage
23	49.1	Scotland County Schools	Laurinburg
30	49.0	Brunswick County Schools	Bolivia
30	49.0	Edgecombe County Schools	Tarboro
30	49.0	Guilford County Schools	Greensboro
30	49.0	Harnett County Schools	Lillington
30	49.0	Pasquotank County Schools	Elizabeth City
30	49.0	Pitt County Schools	Greenville
30	49.0	Roanoke Rapids City Schools	Roanoke Rapids
30	49.0	Rutherford County Schools	Forest City
30	49.0	Yancey County Schools	Burnsville
39	48.9	Alamance-Burlington Schools	Burlington
39	48.9	Asheville City Schools	Asheville
39	48.9	Burke County Schools	Morganton
39	48.9	Cabarrus County Schools	Concord
39	48.9	Iredell-Statesville Schools	Statesville
39	48.9	Lexington City Schools	Lexington
39	48.9	Rowan-Salisbury Schools	Salisbury
39	48.9	Wake County Schools	Raleigh
39	48.9	Warren County Schools	Warrenton
39	48.9	Yadkin County Schools	Yadkinville
49	48.8	Beaufort County Schools	Washington
49	48.8	Charlotte-Mecklenburg Schools	Charlotte
49	48.8	Mcdowell County Schools	Marion
52	48.7	Buncombe County Schools	Asheville
52	48.7	Gaston County Schools	Gastonia
52	48.7	Johnston County Schools	Smithfield
52	48.7	Lee County Schools	Sanford
52	48.7	Martin County Schools	Williamston
52	48.7	Montgomery County Schools	Troy
52	48.7	Perquimans County Schools	Hertford
52	48.7	Robeson County Schools	Lumberton
60	48.6	Catawba County Schools	Newton
60	48.6	Durham Public Schools	Durham
60	48.6	Richmond County Schools	Hamlet
60	48.6	Union County Public Schools	Monroe
60	48.6	Wayne County Public Schools	Goldsboro
60	48.6	Wilson County Schools	Wilson
66	48.5	Chapel Hill-Carrboro Schools	Chapel Hill
66	48.5	Cleveland County Schools	Shelby
66	48.5	Davie County Schools	Mocksville
66	48.5	Jones County Schools	Trenton
66	48.5	Lenoir County Public Schools	Kinston
66	48.5	Orange County Schools	Hillsborough
66	48.5	Rockingham County Schools	Eden
73	48.4	Alexander County Schools	Taylorsville
73	48.4	Forsyth County Schools	Winston Salem
73	48.4	Lincoln County Schools	Lincolnton
73	48.4	Shelby City	Shelby
73	48.4	Surry County Schools	Dobson
73	48.4	Washington County Schools	Plymouth
79	48.3	Bladen County Schools	Elizabethtown
79	48.3	Caswell County Schools	Yanceyville
79	48.3	Halifax County Schools	Halifax
79	48.3	Macon County Schools	Franklin
79	48.3	Thomasville City Schools	Thomasville
79	48.3	Transylvania County Schools	Brevard
85	48.2	Pender County Schools	Burgaw
85	48.2	Randolph County Schools	Asheboro
87	48.1	Ashe County Schools	Jefferson
87	48.1	Carteret County Public Schools	Beaufort
87	48.1	Franklin County Schools	Louisburg
87	48.1	Stokes County Schools	Danbury
91	48.0	Dare County Schools	Manteo
91	48.0	Jackson County Schools	Sylva
91	48.0	Northampton County Schools	Jackson
94	47.9	Bertie County Schools	Windsor
94	47.9	Henderson County Schools	Hendersonville

Rank	Percent	District Name	City
94	47.9	Pamlico County Schools	Bayboro
94	47.9	Sampson County Schools	Clinton
94	47.9	Vance County Schools	Henderson
99	47.7	Chatham County Schools	Pittsboro
99	47.7	Gates County Schools	Gatesville
101	47.6	Kannapolis City Schools	Kannapolis
102	47.5	Cherokee County Schools	Murphy
102	47.5	Stanly County Schools	Albemarle
104	47.4	Watauga County Schools	Boone
105	47.3	Avery County Schools	Newland
106	47.2	Mitchell County Schools	Bakersville
106	47.2	Swain County Schools	Bryson City
108	46.3	Madison County Schools	Marshall
109	46.2	Greene County Schools	Snow Hill
110	n/a	Camp Lejeune District	Camp Lejeune
110	n/a	Fort Bragg District	Fort Bragg

Individual Education Program Students

Rank	Percent	District Name	City
1	21.0	Gates County Schools	Gatesville
2	20.7	Pamlico County Schools	Bayboro
3	19.8	Orange County Schools	Hillsborough
4	19.2	Avery County Schools	Newland
5	18.2	Swain County Schools	Bryson City
6	18.1	Carteret County Public Schools	Beaufort
6	18.1	Washington County Schools	Plymouth
8	18.0	Anson County Schools	Wadesboro
9	17.4	Robeson County Schools	Lumberton
9	17.4	Yancey County Schools	Burnsville
11	17.3	Cherokee County Schools	Murphy
11	17.3	Stanly County Schools	Albemarle
13	17.2	Mount Airy City Schools	Mount Airy
13	17.2	Yadkin County Schools	Yadkinville
15	17.1	Greene County Schools	Snow Hill
15	17.1	Halifax County Schools	Halifax
15	17.1	Whiteville City Schools	Whiteville
18	16.9	Shelby City	Shelby
19	16.8	Jones County Schools	Trenton
19	16.8	Macon County Schools	Franklin
21	16.6	Person County Schools	Roxboro
22	16.5	Beaufort County Schools	Washington
22	16.5	Mitchell County Schools	Bakersville
24	16.4	Burke County Schools	Morganton
25	16.3	Hoke County Schools	Raeford
25	16.3	Kannapolis City Schools	Kannapolis
25	16.3	Stokes County Schools	Danbury
28	16.2	Warren County Schools	Warrenton
28	16.2	Watauga County Schools	Boone
30	16.1	Scotland County Schools	Laurinburg
30	16.1	Surry County Schools	Dobson
32	16.0	Currituck County Schools	Currituck
32	16.0	Guilford County Schools	Greensboro
34	15.8	Haywood County Schools	Waynesville
34	15.8	Hertford County Schools	Winton
34	15.8	Johnston County Schools	Smithfield
34	15.8	Nash-Rocky Mount Schools	Nashville
34	15.8	Polk County Schools	Columbus
39	15.7	Brunswick County Schools	Bolivia
39	15.7	Jackson County Schools	Sylva
39	15.7	Rockingham County Schools	Eden
42	15.5	Perquimans County Schools	Hertford
43	15.4	Wayne County Public Schools	Goldsboro
44	15.3	Madison County Schools	Marshall
45	15.1	Pender County Schools	Burgaw
45	15.1	Wilkes County Schools	Wilkesboro
47	15.0	Ashe County Schools	Jefferson
47	15.0	Mcdowell County Schools	Marion
49	14.9	Lexington City Schools	Lexington
49	14.9	Newton Conover City Schools	Newton
51	14.8	Catawba County Schools	Newton
51	14.8	Cleveland County Schools	Shelby
51	14.8	Lincoln County Schools	Lincolnton
51	14.8	Wake County Schools	Raleigh
55	14.6	Alamance-Burlington Schools	Burlington
56	14.5	Bertie County Schools	Windsor
56	14.5	Caswell County Schools	Yanceyville
58	14.4	Lenoir County Public Schools	Kinston
58	14.4	Onslow County Schools	Jacksonville
58	14.4	Rutherford County Schools	Forest City
61	14.3	Martin County Schools	Williamston
61	14.3	Rowan-Salisbury Schools	Salisbury
63	14.2	Cabarrus County Schools	Concord
63	14.2	Harnett County Schools	Lillington
63	14.2	Pasquotank County Schools	Elizabeth City
63	14.2	Pitt County Schools	Greenville
67	14.0	Davie County Schools	Mocksville
67	14.0	Moore County Schools	Carthage
67	14.0	Sampson County Schools	Clinton
70	13.9	Buncombe County Schools	Asheville
71	13.8	Alexander County Schools	Taylorsville
72	13.7	Henderson County Schools	Hendersonville
73	13.6	Columbus County Schools	Whiteville
73	13.6	Forsyth County Schools	Winston Salem
73	13.6	Richmond County Schools	Hamlet
76	13.5	New Hanover County Schools	Wilmington
77	13.4	Randolph County Schools	Asheboro
78	13.3	Craven County Schools	New Bern
79	13.2	Iredell-Statesville Schools	Statesville
79	13.2	Montgomery County Schools	Troy
79	13.2	Roanoke Rapids City Schools	Roanoke Rapids
82	13.1	Chatham County Schools	Pittsboro
83	13.0	Asheboro City Schools	Asheboro
83	13.0	Chapel Hill-Carrboro Schools	Chapel Hill
83	13.0	Cumberland County Schools	Fayetteville
83	13.0	Granville County Schools	Oxford
87	12.8	Durham Public Schools	Durham
87	12.8	Northampton County Schools	Jackson
89	12.7	Edgecombe County Schools	Tarboro
90	12.6	Asheville City Schools	Asheville
90	12.6	Davidson County Schools	Lexington
90	12.6	Hickory City Schools	Hickory
90	12.6	Mooresville City Schools	Mooresville
94	12.4	Edenton-Chowan Schools	Edenton
94	12.4	Gaston County Schools	Gastonia
96	12.3	Camp Lejeune District	Camp Lejeune
97	12.2	Union County Public Schools	Monroe
97	12.2	Vance County Schools	Henderson
99	12.1	Bladen County Schools	Elizabethtown
100	12.0	Charlotte-Mecklenburg Schools	Charlotte
100	12.0	Kings Mountain District	Kings Mountain
100	12.0	Transylvania County Schools	Brevard
103	11.9	Caldwell County Schools	Lenoir
103	11.9	Lee County Schools	Sanford
105	11.7	Dare County Schools	Manteo
106	11.5	Wilson County Schools	Wilson
107	11.1	Duplin County Schools	Kenansville
108	11.0	Clinton City Schools	Clinton
108	11.0	Franklin County Schools	Louisburg
110	10.2	Thomasville City Schools	Thomasville
111	8.9	Fort Bragg District	Fort Bragg

English Language Learner Students

Rank	Percent	District Name	City
1	21.0	Montgomery County Schools	Troy
2	17.5	Asheboro City Schools	Asheboro
3	15.7	Hickory City Schools	Hickory
4	13.2	Lee County Schools	Sanford
5	13.1	Lexington City Schools	Lexington
6	13.0	Kannapolis City Schools	Kannapolis
7	12.9	Duplin County Schools	Kenansville
8	11.9	Greene County Schools	Snow Hill
9	11.8	Newton Conover City Schools	Newton
10	11.4	Chatham County Schools	Pittsboro
11	11.2	Sampson County Schools	Clinton
12	9.3	Thomasville City Schools	Thomasville
13	8.9	Mount Airy City Schools	Mount Airy
14	8.3	Alamance-Burlington Schools	Burlington
14	8.3	Harnett County Schools	Lillington
14	8.3	Surry County Schools	Dobson
17	8.2	Chapel Hill-Carrboro Schools	Chapel Hill
18	7.7	Henderson County Schools	Hendersonville
19	7.6	Burke County Schools	Morganton
19	7.6	Catawba County Schools	Newton
21	7.5	Rowan-Salisbury Schools	Salisbury
22	7.4	Alexander County Schools	Taylorsville
23	7.0	Lincoln County Schools	Lincolnton
24	6.9	Johnston County Schools	Smithfield
25	6.5	Durham Public Schools	Durham
26	6.1	Charlotte-Mecklenburg Schools	Charlotte
27	5.8	Forsyth County Schools	Winston Salem
28	5.4	Guilford County Schools	Greensboro
29	5.3	Fort Bragg District	Fort Bragg
30	5.0	Cabarrus County Schools	Concord
31	4.9	Yadkin County Schools	Yadkinville
32	4.8	Pender County Schools	Burgaw
33	4.7	Randolph County Schools	Asheboro
33	4.7	Stanly County Schools	Albemarle
35	4.6	Edgecombe County Schools	Tarboro
35	4.6	Granville County Schools	Oxford
35	4.6	Moore County Schools	Carthage
38	4.5	Polk County Schools	Columbus
39	4.3	Bladen County Schools	Elizabethtown
39	4.3	Wilkes County Schools	Wilkesboro
41	4.2	Mcdowell County Schools	Marion
41	4.2	Wake County Schools	Raleigh
43	4.0	Nash-Rocky Mount Schools	Nashville
43	4.0	Yancey County Schools	Burnsville
45	3.9	Rockingham County Schools	Eden
45	3.9	Wayne County Public Schools	Goldsboro
47	3.8	Mitchell County Schools	Bakersville
47	3.8	Orange County Schools	Hillsborough
49	3.6	Davie County Schools	Mocksville
49	3.6	Iredell-Statesville Schools	Statesville
51	3.5	Robeson County Schools	Lumberton
52	3.4	Hoke County Schools	Raeford
52	3.4	Wilson County Schools	Wilson
54	3.3	Vance County Schools	Henderson
55	3.2	Clinton City Schools	Clinton
55	3.2	Gaston County Schools	Gastonia
55	3.2	Jones County Schools	Trenton
58	3.1	Beaufort County Schools	Washington
59	3.0	Union County Public Schools	Monroe
60	2.8	Caldwell County Schools	Lenoir
60	2.8	Franklin County Schools	Louisburg
62	2.5	Buncombe County Schools	Asheville
62	2.5	Pitt County Schools	Greenville
64	2.4	Avery County Schools	Newland
65	2.3	Lenoir County Public Schools	Kinston
65	2.3	New Hanover County Schools	Wilmington
65	2.3	Richmond County Schools	Hamlet
68	2.2	Ashe County Schools	Jefferson
68	2.2	Columbus County Schools	Whiteville
70	2.0	Brunswick County Schools	Bolivia
70	2.0	Dare County Schools	Manteo
72	1.8	Rutherford County Schools	Forest City
73	1.7	Macon County Schools	Franklin
73	1.7	Person County Schools	Roxboro
75	1.6	Edenton-Chowan Schools	Edenton
75	1.6	Onslow County Schools	Jacksonville
75	1.6	Transylvania County Schools	Brevard
78	1.5	Cumberland County Schools	Fayetteville
79	1.4	Asheville City Schools	Asheville
79	1.4	Camp Lejeune District	Camp Lejeune
79	1.4	Caswell County Schools	Yanceyville
79	1.4	Craven County Schools	New Bern
79	1.4	Haywood County Schools	Waynesville
79	1.4	Whiteville City Schools	Whiteville
85	1.3	Anson County Schools	Wadesboro
85	1.3	Cleveland County Schools	Shelby
85	1.3	Warren County Schools	Warrenton
85	1.3	Watauga County Schools	Boone
89	1.2	Carteret County Public Schools	Beaufort
89	1.2	Jackson County Schools	Sylva
89	1.2	Mooresville City Schools	Mooresville
92	1.0	Halifax County Schools	Halifax
93	0.9	Washington County Schools	Plymouth
94	0.8	Madison County Schools	Marshall
94	0.8	Roanoke Rapids City Schools	Roanoke Rapids
94	0.8	Scotland County Schools	Laurinburg
94	0.8	Shelby City	Shelby
98	0.7	Kings Mountain District	Kings Mountain
98	0.7	Swain County Schools	Bryson City
100	0.6	Northampton County Schools	Jackson
100	0.6	Stokes County Schools	Danbury
102	0.5	Davidson County Schools	Lexington
103	0.4	Hertford County Schools	Winton
103	0.4	Martin County Schools	Williamston
105	0.3	Bertie County Schools	Windsor
105	0.3	Gates County Schools	Gatesville
105	0.3	Pasquotank County Schools	Elizabeth City
108	0.2	Currituck County Schools	Currituck
108	0.2	Pamlico County Schools	Bayboro
110	0.1	Cherokee County Schools	Murphy
110	0.1	Perquimans County Schools	Hertford

Migrant Students

Rank	Percent	District Name	City
1	9.6	Pender County Schools	Burgaw
2	9.1	Chatham County Schools	Pittsboro
3	9.0	Columbus County Schools	Whiteville
4	8.1	Sampson County Schools	Clinton
5	7.8	Montgomery County Schools	Troy
6	7.1	Bladen County Schools	Elizabethtown
7	6.9	Rockingham County Schools	Eden
8	5.4	Yancey County Schools	Burnsville
9	5.3	Lee County Schools	Sanford
10	5.2	Northampton County Schools	Jackson
11	5.0	Whiteville City Schools	Whiteville
12	4.7	Duplin County Schools	Kenansville
13	4.6	Greene County Schools	Snow Hill
13	4.6	Surry County Schools	Dobson
15	3.9	Wilkes County Schools	Wilkesboro
16	3.8	Henderson County Schools	Hendersonville
17	3.6	Harnett County Schools	Lillington
17	3.6	Hoke County Schools	Raeford
19	3.5	Johnston County Schools	Smithfield
20	3.3	Alamance-Burlington Schools	Burlington
21	3.2	Rowan-Salisbury Schools	Salisbury
22	3.0	Edgecombe County Schools	Tarboro
23	2.7	Robeson County Schools	Lumberton
24	2.6	Halifax County Schools	Halifax
24	2.6	Lenoir County Public Schools	Kinston
26	2.4	Mitchell County Schools	Bakersville
27	2.2	Yadkin County Schools	Yadkinville
28	2.1	Ashe County Schools	Jefferson
28	2.1	Pitt County Schools	Greenville

30	2.0	Nash-Rocky Mount Schools	Nashville
31	1.9	Franklin County Schools	Louisburg
31	1.9	Randolph County Schools	Asheboro
31	1.9	Wilson County Schools	Wilson
34	1.8	Moore County Schools	Carthage
35	1.7	Asheboro City Schools	Asheboro
36	1.6	Granville County Schools	Oxford
36	1.6	Washington County Schools	Plymouth
38	1.5	Orange County Schools	Hillsborough
39	1.4	Beaufort County Schools	Washington
40	1.2	Haywood County Schools	Waynesville
40	1.2	Scotland County Schools	Laurinburg
42	1.1	Vance County Schools	Henderson
43	0.9	Bertie County Schools	Windsor
43	0.9	Brunswick County Schools	Bolivia
45	0.6	Wake County Schools	Raleigh
46	0.4	Buncombe County Schools	Asheville
47	0.1	Cabarrus County Schools	Concord
48	0.0	Alexander County Schools	Taylorsville
48	0.0	Anson County Schools	Wadesboro
48	0.0	Asheville City Schools	Asheville
48	0.0	Avery County Schools	Newland
48	0.0	Burke County Schools	Morganton
48	0.0	Caldwell County Schools	Lenoir
48	0.0	Carteret County Public Schools	Beaufort
48	0.0	Caswell County Schools	Yanceyville
48	0.0	Catawba County Schools	Newton
48	0.0	Chapel Hill-Carrboro Schools	Chapel Hill
48	0.0	Charlotte-Mecklenburg Schools	Charlotte
48	0.0	Cherokee County Schools	Murphy
48	0.0	Cleveland County Schools	Shelby
48	0.0	Clinton City Schools	Clinton
48	0.0	Craven County Schools	New Bern
48	0.0	Cumberland County Schools	Fayetteville
48	0.0	Currituck County Schools	Currituck
48	0.0	Dare County Schools	Manteo
48	0.0	Davidson County Schools	Lexington
48	0.0	Davie County Schools	Mocksville
48	0.0	Durham Public Schools	Durham
48	0.0	Edenton-Chowan Schools	Edenton
48	0.0	Forsyth County Schools	Winston Salem
48	0.0	Gaston County Schools	Gastonia
48	0.0	Gates County Schools	Gatesville
48	0.0	Guilford County Schools	Greensboro
48	0.0	Hertford County Schools	Winton
48	0.0	Hickory City Schools	Hickory
48	0.0	Iredell-Statesville Schools	Statesville
48	0.0	Jackson County Schools	Sylva
48	0.0	Jones County Schools	Trenton
48	0.0	Kannapolis City Schools	Kannapolis
48	0.0	Kings Mountain District	Kings Mountain
48	0.0	Lexington City Schools	Lexington
48	0.0	Lincoln County Schools	Lincolnton
48	0.0	Macon County Schools	Franklin
48	0.0	Madison County Schools	Marshall
48	0.0	Martin County Schools	Williamston
48	0.0	Mcdowell County Schools	Marion
48	0.0	Mooresville City Schools	Mooresville
48	0.0	Mount Airy City Schools	Mount Airy
48	0.0	New Hanover County Schools	Wilmington
48	0.0	Newton Conover City Schools	Newton
48	0.0	Onslow County Schools	Jacksonville
48	0.0	Pamlico County Schools	Bayboro
48	0.0	Pasquotank County Schools	Elizabeth City
48	0.0	Perquimans County Schools	Hertford
48	0.0	Person County Schools	Roxboro
48	0.0	Polk County Schools	Columbus
48	0.0	Richmond County Schools	Hamlet
48	0.0	Roanoke Rapids City Schools	Roanoke Rapids
48	0.0	Rutherford County Schools	Forest City
48	0.0	Shelby City	Shelby
48	0.0	Stanly County Schools	Albemarle
48	0.0	Stokes County Schools	Danbury
48	0.0	Swain County Schools	Bryson City
48	0.0	Thomasville City Schools	Thomasville
48	0.0	Transylvania County Schools	Brevard
48	0.0	Union County Public Schools	Monroe
48	0.0	Warren County Schools	Warrenton
48	0.0	Watauga County Schools	Boone
48	0.0	Wayne County Public Schools	Goldsboro
110	n/a	Camp Lejeune District	Camp Lejeune
110	n/a	Fort Bragg District	Fort Bragg

Students Eligible for Free Lunch

Rank	Percent	District Name	City
1	69.3	Halifax County Schools	Halifax
2	68.8	Bertie County Schools	Windsor
3	67.3	Northampton County Schools	Jackson
4	65.9	Lexington City Schools	Lexington
5	62.7	Thomasville City Schools	Thomasville
6	62.2	Hertford County Schools	Winton
7	59.8	Vance County Schools	Henderson
8	58.1	Jones County Schools	Trenton
9	57.0	Sampson County Schools	Clinton
10	56.8	Bladen County Schools	Elizabethtown
11	56.6	Warren County Schools	Warrenton
12	56.5	Columbus County Schools	Whiteville
12	56.5	Duplin County Schools	Kenansville
14	56.1	Greene County Schools	Snow Hill
15	55.7	Anson County Schools	Wadesboro
16	54.3	Scotland County Schools	Laurinburg
17	52.4	Edgecombe County Schools	Tarboro
18	52.1	Martin County Schools	Williamston
19	48.0	Montgomery County Schools	Troy
20	47.6	Shelby City	Shelby
21	47.4	Hoke County Schools	Raeford
22	47.2	Edenton-Chowan Schools	Edenton
23	47.0	Wilson County Schools	Wilson
24	44.4	Lenoir County Public Schools	Kinston
25	44.1	Asheville City Schools	Asheville
26	43.2	Hickory City Schools	Hickory
27	41.5	Pamlico County Schools	Bayboro
28	41.2	Pender County Schools	Burgaw
29	40.6	Pitt County Schools	Greenville
30	40.2	Harnett County Schools	Lillington
31	39.3	Rutherford County Schools	Forest City
32	39.2	Franklin County Schools	Louisburg
33	38.9	Lee County Schools	Sanford
34	38.5	Mount Airy City Schools	Mount Airy
35	38.1	Gates County Schools	Gatesville
35	38.1	Swain County Schools	Bryson City
37	37.6	Wayne County Public Schools	Goldsboro
38	37.4	Cumberland County Schools	Fayetteville
39	37.2	Surry County Schools	Dobson
40	37.1	Guilford County Schools	Greensboro
40	37.1	Mitchell County Schools	Bakersville
42	36.9	Jackson County Schools	Sylva
43	36.3	Craven County Schools	New Bern
44	36.0	Cherokee County Schools	Murphy
45	34.9	Alamance-Burlington Schools	Burlington
45	34.9	Granville County Schools	Oxford
47	34.8	Rockingham County Schools	Eden
48	34.5	Avery County Schools	Newland
48	34.5	Forsyth County Schools	Winston Salem
50	34.4	Madison County Schools	Marshall
51	34.2	Ashe County Schools	Jefferson
52	34.0	Roanoke Rapids City Schools	Roanoke Rapids
53	33.1	Charlotte-Mecklenburg Schools	Charlotte
53	33.1	Mcdowell County Schools	Marion
55	32.6	Moore County Schools	Carthage
55	32.6	Person County Schools	Roxboro
55	32.6	Wilkes County Schools	Wilkesboro
58	32.2	Newton Conover City Schools	Newton
59	31.6	Macon County Schools	Franklin
60	31.4	Burke County Schools	Morganton
61	31.3	Johnston County Schools	Smithfield
62	30.0	Onslow County Schools	Jacksonville
62	30.0	Transylvania County Schools	Brevard
64	29.6	Gaston County Schools	Gastonia
65	28.9	Haywood County Schools	Waynesville
66	28.8	Polk County Schools	Columbus
67	28.6	Carteret County Public Schools	Beaufort
68	27.9	Henderson County Schools	Hendersonville
69	27.6	New Hanover County Schools	Wilmington
70	26.3	Buncombe County Schools	Asheville
71	24.2	Alexander County Schools	Taylorsville
72	23.8	Iredell-Statesville Schools	Statesville
73	23.1	Orange County Schools	Hillsborough
74	22.7	Catawba County Schools	Newton
75	22.5	Union County Public Schools	Monroe
76	21.4	Cabarrus County Schools	Concord
77	20.6	Davie County Schools	Mocksville
77	20.6	Stokes County Schools	Danbury
77	20.6	Yadkin County Schools	Yadkinville
80	18.9	Currituck County Schools	Currituck
81	18.8	Wake County Schools	Raleigh
82	18.2	Davidson County Schools	Lexington
83	17.3	Watauga County Schools	Boone
84	12.5	Dare County Schools	Manteo
85	0.0	Asheboro City Schools	Asheboro
85	0.0	Beaufort County Schools	Washington
85	0.0	Brunswick County Schools	Bolivia
85	0.0	Caldwell County Schools	Lenoir
85	0.0	Caswell County Schools	Yanceyville
85	0.0	Chapel Hill-Carrboro Schools	Chapel Hill
85	0.0	Chatham County Schools	Pittsboro
85	0.0	Cleveland County Schools	Shelby
85	0.0	Clinton City Schools	Clinton
85	0.0	Durham Public Schools	Durham
85	0.0	Kannapolis City Schools	Kannapolis
85	0.0	Kings Mountain District	Kings Mountain
85	0.0	Lincoln County Schools	Lincolnton
85	0.0	Mooresville City Schools	Mooresville
85	0.0	Nash-Rocky Mount Schools	Nashville
85	0.0	Pasquotank County Schools	Elizabeth City
85	0.0	Perquimans County Schools	Hertford
85	0.0	Randolph County Schools	Asheboro
85	0.0	Richmond County Schools	Hamlet
85	0.0	Robeson County Schools	Lumberton
85	0.0	Rowan-Salisbury Schools	Salisbury
85	0.0	Stanly County Schools	Albemarle
85	0.0	Washington County Schools	Plymouth
85	0.0	Whiteville City Schools	Whiteville
85	0.0	Yancey County Schools	Burnsville
110	n/a	Camp Lejeune District	Camp Lejeune
110	n/a	Fort Bragg District	Fort Bragg

Students Eligible for Reduced-Price Lunch

Rank	Percent	District Name	City
1	16.2	Cherokee County Schools	Murphy
2	15.8	Swain County Schools	Bryson City
3	15.7	Bertie County Schools	Windsor
3	15.7	Jones County Schools	Trenton
5	15.6	Ashe County Schools	Jefferson
6	14.6	Hoke County Schools	Raeford
7	13.5	Madison County Schools	Marshall
8	13.3	Avery County Schools	Newland
8	13.3	Mitchell County Schools	Bakersville
10	13.2	Jackson County Schools	Sylva
11	13.0	Macon County Schools	Franklin
11	13.0	Warren County Schools	Warrenton
13	12.7	Pender County Schools	Burgaw
14	12.6	Edgecombe County Schools	Tarboro
14	12.6	Gates County Schools	Gatesville
14	12.6	Northampton County Schools	Jackson
17	12.5	Craven County Schools	New Bern
18	12.2	Onslow County Schools	Jacksonville
19	12.1	Burke County Schools	Morganton
19	12.1	Mcdowell County Schools	Marion
21	11.9	Cumberland County Schools	Fayetteville
21	11.9	Sampson County Schools	Clinton
23	11.8	Lexington City Schools	Lexington
24	11.5	Pamlico County Schools	Bayboro
25	11.3	Polk County Schools	Columbus
26	11.2	Surry County Schools	Dobson
27	10.8	Anson County Schools	Wadesboro
27	10.8	Columbus County Schools	Whiteville
29	10.7	Wayne County Public Schools	Goldsboro
30	10.6	Martin County Schools	Williamston
30	10.6	Newton Conover City Schools	Newton
32	10.5	Harnett County Schools	Lillington
33	10.3	Greene County Schools	Snow Hill
34	10.2	Franklin County Schools	Louisburg
34	10.2	Thomasville City Schools	Thomasville
36	10.0	Bladen County Schools	Elizabethtown
36	10.0	Montgomery County Schools	Troy
38	9.9	Carteret County Public Schools	Beaufort
39	9.8	Person County Schools	Roxboro
40	9.7	Halifax County Schools	Halifax
40	9.7	Transylvania County Schools	Brevard
42	9.6	Hertford County Schools	Winton
42	9.6	Wilson County Schools	Wilson
44	9.5	Granville County Schools	Oxford
44	9.5	Hickory City Schools	Hickory
44	9.5	Wilkes County Schools	Wilkesboro
47	9.4	Rockingham County Schools	Eden
48	9.3	Haywood County Schools	Waynesville
48	9.3	Vance County Schools	Henderson
50	9.2	Iredell-Statesville Schools	Statesville
51	9.1	Lee County Schools	Sanford
52	8.9	Rutherford County Schools	Forest City
52	8.9	Scotland County Schools	Laurinburg
54	8.7	Catawba County Schools	Newton
55	8.6	Roanoke Rapids City Schools	Roanoke Rapids
56	8.5	Alamance-Burlington Schools	Burlington
56	8.5	Edenton-Chowan Schools	Edenton
58	8.2	Gaston County Schools	Gastonia
58	8.2	Stokes County Schools	Danbury
60	8.1	Lenoir County Public Schools	Kinston
61	7.9	Moore County Schools	Carthage
62	7.8	Guilford County Schools	Greensboro
63	7.7	Buncombe County Schools	Asheville
63	7.7	Currituck County Schools	Currituck
65	7.6	Duplin County Schools	Kenansville
66	7.5	Henderson County Schools	Hendersonville
66	7.5	Orange County Schools	Hillsborough
66	7.5	Watauga County Schools	Boone
66	7.5	Yadkin County Schools	Yadkinville
70	7.3	Johnston County Schools	Smithfield
71	7.2	Alexander County Schools	Taylorsville
72	6.7	Charlotte-Mecklenburg Schools	Charlotte
72	6.7	Union County Public Schools	Monroe
74	6.6	Davidson County Schools	Lexington
74	6.6	Davie County Schools	Mocksville
76	6.5	Pitt County Schools	Greenville

77	6.4	Cabarrus County Schools	Concord
78	6.1	New Hanover County Schools	Wilmington
78	6.1	Shelby City	Shelby
80	6.0	Dare County Schools	Manteo
81	5.9	Asheville City Schools	Asheville
82	5.6	Forsyth County Schools	Winston Salem
83	5.3	Mount Airy City Schools	Mount Airy
84	4.5	Wake County Schools	Raleigh
85	0.0	Asheboro City Schools	Asheboro
85	0.0	Beaufort County Schools	Washington
85	0.0	Brunswick County Schools	Bolivia
85	0.0	Caldwell County Schools	Lenoir
85	0.0	Caswell County Schools	Yanceyville
85	0.0	Chapel Hill-Carrboro Schools	Chapel Hill
85	0.0	Chatham County Schools	Pittsboro
85	0.0	Cleveland County Schools	Shelby
85	0.0	Clinton City Schools	Clinton
85	0.0	Durham Public Schools	Durham
85	0.0	Kannapolis City Schools	Kannapolis
85	0.0	Kings Mountain District	Kings Mountain
85	0.0	Lincoln County Schools	Lincolnton
85	0.0	Mooresville City Schools	Mooresville
85	0.0	Nash-Rocky Mount Schools	Nashville
85	0.0	Pasquotank County Schools	Elizabeth City
85	0.0	Perquimans County Schools	Hertford
85	0.0	Randolph County Schools	Asheboro
85	0.0	Richmond County Schools	Hamlet
85	0.0	Robeson County Schools	Lumberton
85	0.0	Rowan-Salisbury Schools	Salisbury
85	0.0	Stanly County Schools	Albemarle
85	0.0	Washington County Schools	Plymouth
85	0.0	Whiteville City Schools	Whiteville
85	0.0	Yancey County Schools	Burnsville
110	n/a	Camp Lejeune District	Camp Lejeune
110	n/a	Fort Bragg District	Fort Bragg

Student/Teacher Ratio

Rank	Ratio	District Name	City
1	17.4	Hoke County Schools	Raeford
2	17.3	Iredell-Statesville Schools	Statesville
3	16.8	Alexander County Schools	Taylorsville
3	16.8	Randolph County Schools	Asheboro
5	16.7	Davidson County Schools	Lexington
6	16.6	Gaston County Schools	Gastonia
6	16.6	Yadkin County Schools	Yadkinville
8	16.5	Union County Public Schools	Monroe
9	16.3	Granville County Schools	Oxford
9	16.3	Halifax County Schools	Halifax
11	16.2	Onslow County Schools	Jacksonville
12	16.1	Catawba County Schools	Newton
12	16.1	Guilford County Schools	Greensboro
12	16.1	Robeson County Schools	Lumberton
15	16.0	Columbus County Schools	Whiteville
15	16.0	Kings Mountain District	Kings Mountain
15	16.0	Wilson County Schools	Wilson
18	15.9	Cumberland County Schools	Fayetteville
18	15.9	Harnett County Schools	Lillington
18	15.9	Richmond County Schools	Hamlet
18	15.9	Rockingham County Schools	Eden
22	15.8	Henderson County Schools	Hendersonville
22	15.8	Rowan-Salisbury Schools	Salisbury
22	15.8	Warren County Schools	Warrenton
25	15.7	Hertford County Schools	Winton
26	15.6	Bladen County Schools	Elizabethtown
26	15.6	Lee County Schools	Sanford
26	15.6	Mcdowell County Schools	Marion
26	15.6	Mooresville City Schools	Mooresville
26	15.6	Stanly County Schools	Albemarle
31	15.5	Buncombe County Schools	Asheville
31	15.5	Lexington City Schools	Lexington
33	15.4	Alamance-Burlington Schools	Burlington
33	15.4	Cleveland County Schools	Shelby
33	15.4	Fort Bragg District	Fort Bragg
33	15.4	New Hanover County Schools	Wilmington
33	15.4	Pitt County Schools	Greenville
33	15.4	Wake County Schools	Raleigh
39	15.3	Wilkes County Schools	Wilkesboro
40	15.2	Cabarrus County Schools	Concord
40	15.2	Caldwell County Schools	Lenoir
40	15.2	Rutherford County Schools	Forest City
43	15.1	Anson County Schools	Wadesboro
43	15.1	Bertie County Schools	Windsor
43	15.1	Brunswick County Schools	Bolivia
43	15.1	Caswell County Schools	Yanceyville
43	15.1	Charlotte-Mecklenburg Schools	Charlotte
43	15.1	Davie County Schools	Mocksville
43	15.1	Duplin County Schools	Kenansville
43	15.1	Wayne County Public Schools	Goldsboro
51	15.0	Durham Public Schools	Durham
51	15.0	Surry County Schools	Dobson
53	14.9	Edgecombe County Schools	Tarboro
53	14.9	Northampton County Schools	Jackson
53	14.9	Sampson County Schools	Clinton
56	14.8	Franklin County Schools	Louisburg
56	14.8	Haywood County Schools	Waynesville
56	14.8	Pasquotank County Schools	Elizabeth City
56	14.8	Yancey County Schools	Burnsville
60	14.7	Chatham County Schools	Pittsboro
60	14.7	Clinton City Schools	Clinton
60	14.7	Craven County Schools	New Bern
60	14.7	Forsyth County Schools	Winston Salem
60	14.7	Hickory City Schools	Hickory
60	14.7	Roanoke Rapids City Schools	Roanoke Rapids
60	14.7	Vance County Schools	Henderson
67	14.6	Asheboro City Schools	Asheboro
67	14.6	Burke County Schools	Morganton
67	14.6	Person County Schools	Roxboro
70	14.5	Moore County Schools	Carthage
70	14.5	Newton Conover City Schools	Newton
72	14.4	Dare County Schools	Manteo
72	14.4	Jackson County Schools	Sylva
72	14.4	Macon County Schools	Franklin
72	14.4	Mitchell County Schools	Bakersville
72	14.4	Stokes County Schools	Danbury
77	14.3	Lenoir County Public Schools	Kinston
77	14.3	Montgomery County Schools	Troy
79	14.2	Currituck County Schools	Currituck
79	14.2	Nash-Rocky Mount Schools	Nashville
79	14.2	Pender County Schools	Burgaw
82	14.1	Edenton-Chowan Schools	Edenton
82	14.1	Lincoln County Schools	Lincolnton
82	14.1	Polk County Schools	Columbus
85	14.0	Johnston County Schools	Smithfield
85	14.0	Perquimans County Schools	Hertford
85	14.0	Thomasville City Schools	Thomasville
85	14.0	Transylvania County Schools	Brevard
89	13.9	Ashe County Schools	Jefferson
89	13.9	Beaufort County Schools	Washington
89	13.9	Greene County Schools	Snow Hill
89	13.9	Martin County Schools	Williamston
89	13.9	Orange County Schools	Hillsborough
94	13.8	Camp Lejeune District	Camp Lejeune
94	13.8	Whiteville City Schools	Whiteville
96	13.6	Cherokee County Schools	Murphy
96	13.6	Shelby City	Shelby
98	13.5	Avery County Schools	Newland
98	13.5	Kannapolis City Schools	Kannapolis
98	13.5	Mount Airy City Schools	Mount Airy
98	13.5	Swain County Schools	Bryson City
102	13.4	Watauga County Schools	Boone
103	13.1	Jones County Schools	Trenton
104	13.0	Scotland County Schools	Laurinburg
105	12.8	Chapel Hill-Carrboro Schools	Chapel Hill
105	12.8	Gates County Schools	Gatesville
107	12.6	Carteret County Public Schools	Beaufort
108	12.4	Washington County Schools	Plymouth
109	12.3	Madison County Schools	Marshall
110	12.1	Asheville City Schools	Asheville
110	12.1	Pamlico County Schools	Bayboro

Student/Librarian Ratio

Rank	Ratio	District Name	City
1	823.5	Lee County Schools	Sanford
2	814.8	Greene County Schools	Snow Hill
3	795.8	Warren County Schools	Warrenton
4	790.0	Hertford County Schools	Winton
5	775.5	Cabarrus County Schools	Concord
6	766.3	Roanoke Rapids City Schools	Roanoke Rapids
7	754.9	Forsyth County Schools	Winston Salem
8	747.5	Pitt County Schools	Greenville
9	740.0	Chapel Hill-Carrboro Schools	Chapel Hill
10	716.1	Brunswick County Schools	Bolivia
11	714.2	Davidson County Schools	Lexington
12	701.3	Mooresville City Schools	Mooresville
13	694.4	Cleveland County Schools	Shelby
14	691.4	Johnston County Schools	Smithfield
15	690.4	Charlotte-Mecklenburg Schools	Charlotte
16	682.8	Clinton City Schools	Clinton
17	675.8	Whiteville City Schools	Whiteville
18	674.9	Alamance-Burlington Schools	Burlington
19	672.4	Rowan-Salisbury Schools	Salisbury
20	657.3	Union County Public Schools	Monroe
21	653.3	Lincoln County Schools	Lincolnton
22	641.5	Durham Public Schools	Durham
23	641.4	Burke County Schools	Morganton
24	636.0	Edenton-Chowan Schools	Edenton
25	620.0	Jackson County Schools	Sylva
25	620.0	Thomasville City Schools	Thomasville
27	619.4	Harnett County Schools	Lillington
28	615.6	Catawba County Schools	Newton
29	613.1	Wake County Schools	Raleigh
30	608.1	Guilford County Schools	Greensboro
31	600.7	Henderson County Schools	Hendersonville
32	595.6	Nash-Rocky Mount Schools	Nashville
33	591.3	Washington County Schools	Plymouth
34	589.8	Gaston County Schools	Gastonia
35	587.7	Hoke County Schools	Raeford
36	585.7	Duplin County Schools	Kenansville
37	585.3	Randolph County Schools	Asheboro
38	578.2	Orange County Schools	Hillsborough
39	575.3	New Hanover County Schools	Wilmington
40	569.9	Granville County Schools	Oxford
41	569.6	Newton Conover City Schools	Newton
42	565.3	Franklin County Schools	Louisburg
43	561.8	Anson County Schools	Wadesboro
44	560.2	Cumberland County Schools	Fayetteville
45	560.1	Craven County Schools	New Bern
46	558.9	Edgecombe County Schools	Tarboro
47	554.1	Caldwell County Schools	Lenoir
48	552.2	Lexington City Schools	Lexington
49	549.5	Kannapolis City Schools	Kannapolis
50	549.3	Shelby City	Shelby
51	548.7	Pasquotank County Schools	Elizabeth City
52	548.5	Asheboro City Schools	Asheboro
53	546.6	Scotland County Schools	Laurinburg
54	546.3	Ashe County Schools	Jefferson
55	543.1	Mcdowell County Schools	Marion
56	541.9	Transylvania County Schools	Brevard
57	540.7	Davie County Schools	Mocksville
58	539.4	Lenoir County Public Schools	Kinston
59	536.5	Vance County Schools	Henderson
60	536.2	Buncombe County Schools	Asheville
60	536.2	Rutherford County Schools	Forest City
62	534.3	Wilson County Schools	Wilson
63	533.4	Beaufort County Schools	Washington
64	533.1	Halifax County Schools	Halifax
65	532.5	Surry County Schools	Dobson
66	532.1	Wayne County Public Schools	Goldsboro
67	524.9	Dare County Schools	Manteo
68	524.6	Haywood County Schools	Waynesville
69	523.4	Richmond County Schools	Hamlet
70	522.0	Kings Mountain District	Kings Mountain
71	518.4	Moore County Schools	Carthage
72	518.0	Chatham County Schools	Pittsboro
73	515.7	Carteret County Public Schools	Beaufort
73	515.7	Iredell-Statesville Schools	Statesville
75	513.8	Onslow County Schools	Jacksonville
76	512.4	Madison County Schools	Marshall
77	506.8	Montgomery County Schools	Troy
78	504.1	Fort Bragg District	Fort Bragg
79	498.4	Alexander County Schools	Taylorsville
80	495.3	Hickory City Schools	Hickory
81	487.5	Pender County Schools	Burgaw
82	483.0	Person County Schools	Roxboro
83	482.0	Mount Airy City Schools	Mount Airy
84	480.7	Stanly County Schools	Albemarle
85	479.7	Rockingham County Schools	Eden
86	475.6	Sampson County Schools	Clinton
87	456.0	Perquimans County Schools	Hertford
88	449.8	Wilkes County Schools	Wilkesboro
89	448.5	Swain County Schools	Bryson City
90	447.0	Bladen County Schools	Elizabethtown
90	447.0	Pamlico County Schools	Bayboro
92	443.8	Northampton County Schools	Jackson
93	442.9	Stokes County Schools	Danbury
94	421.7	Yadkin County Schools	Yadkinville
95	417.8	Columbus County Schools	Whiteville
96	413.4	Macon County Schools	Franklin
97	412.7	Polk County Schools	Columbus
98	410.8	Camp Lejeune District	Camp Lejeune
99	398.6	Gates County Schools	Gatesville
100	395.0	Bertie County Schools	Windsor
101	394.5	Watauga County Schools	Boone
102	392.0	Asheville City Schools	Asheville
103	385.0	Martin County Schools	Williamston
104	380.8	Currituck County Schools	Currituck
105	378.0	Robeson County Schools	Lumberton
106	375.7	Cherokee County Schools	Murphy
107	358.4	Yancey County Schools	Burnsville
108	351.9	Avery County Schools	Newland
109	336.6	Mitchell County Schools	Bakersville
110	296.9	Caswell County Schools	Yanceyville
111	251.7	Jones County Schools	Trenton

Student/Counselor Ratio

Rank	Ratio	District Name	City
1	591.3	Washington County Schools	Plymouth
2	532.8	Lee County Schools	Sanford
3	512.4	Madison County Schools	Marshall
4	496.0	Thomasville City Schools	Thomasville
5	488.1	Duplin County Schools	Kenansville
6	487.6	Asheboro City Schools	Asheboro
7	482.5	Forsyth County Schools	Winston Salem
8	479.7	Rockingham County Schools	Eden
9	475.6	Sampson County Schools	Clinton
10	474.1	Transylvania County Schools	Brevard

11	470.9	Shelby City	Shelby
12	461.8	Hoke County Schools	Raeford
13	459.7	Gaston County Schools	Gastonia
14	456.1	Montgomery County Schools	Troy
15	455.1	Wilson County Schools	Wilson
16	454.7	Warren County Schools	Warrenton
17	453.6	Randolph County Schools	Asheboro
18	450.5	Whiteville City Schools	Whiteville
19	449.6	Onslow County Schools	Jacksonville
20	448.5	Swain County Schools	Bryson City
21	447.0	Bladen County Schools	Elizabethtown
21	447.0	Pamlico County Schools	Bayboro
23	444.4	Bertie County Schools	Windsor
24	441.9	Cleveland County Schools	Shelby
25	439.7	Franklin County Schools	Louisburg
26	434.7	Edgecombe County Schools	Tarboro
27	431.9	Alamance-Burlington Schools	Burlington
28	428.8	Harnett County Schools	Lillington
29	427.3	Union County Public Schools	Monroe
30	426.0	Surry County Schools	Dobson
31	425.7	Wayne County Public Schools	Goldsboro
32	425.3	Buncombe County Schools	Asheville
33	421.7	Yadkin County Schools	Yadkinville
34	419.2	Davidson County Schools	Lexington
35	418.8	Richmond County Schools	Hamlet
36	417.4	Cherokee County Schools	Murphy
37	414.9	Beaufort County Schools	Washington
38	414.1	Lexington City Schools	Lexington
39	414.0	Person County Schools	Roxboro
40	413.4	Macon County Schools	Franklin
41	408.8	Vance County Schools	Henderson
42	404.8	Wake County Schools	Raleigh
43	403.2	Robeson County Schools	Lumberton
44	402.4	Pasquotank County Schools	Elizabeth City
45	399.6	Kannapolis City Schools	Kannapolis
46	398.7	Burke County Schools	Morganton
47	395.0	Iredell-Statesville Schools	Statesville
48	393.2	Moore County Schools	Carthage
49	392.7	Mitchell County Schools	Bakersville
50	391.7	Cumberland County Schools	Fayetteville
51	390.9	Halifax County Schools	Halifax
52	390.4	New Hanover County Schools	Wilmington
53	390.1	Clinton City Schools	Clinton
54	387.5	Henderson County Schools	Hendersonville
55	386.5	Catawba County Schools	Newton
56	385.3	Johnston County Schools	Smithfield
57	383.6	Brunswick County Schools	Bolivia
58	383.4	Mcdowell County Schools	Marion
59	383.2	Craven County Schools	New Bern
60	383.0	Lincoln County Schools	Lincolnton
61	382.5	Mooresville City Schools	Mooresville
62	379.2	Pender County Schools	Burgaw
63	377.5	Jones County Schools	Trenton
64	374.7	Haywood County Schools	Waynesville
65	374.1	Orange County Schools	Hillsborough
66	371.8	Davie County Schools	Mocksville
67	369.6	Charlotte-Mecklenburg Schools	Charlotte
68	367.4	Cabarrus County Schools	Concord
69	366.0	Lenoir County Public Schools	Kinston
70	365.5	Alexander County Schools	Taylorsville
71	364.8	Perquimans County Schools	Hertford
72	364.2	Ashe County Schools	Jefferson
73	363.9	Rutherford County Schools	Forest City
74	363.4	Edenton-Chowan Schools	Edenton
75	360.5	Stanly County Schools	Albemarle
76	359.1	Hertford County Schools	Winton
77	358.4	Yancey County Schools	Burnsville
78	356.9	Guilford County Schools	Greensboro
79	356.3	Caswell County Schools	Yanceyville
80	356.0	Newton Conover City Schools	Newton
81	355.0	Northampton County Schools	Jackson
82	354.0	Durham Public Schools	Durham
83	345.9	Camp Lejeune District	Camp Lejeune
84	345.7	Anson County Schools	Wadesboro
85	342.7	Currituck County Schools	Currituck
86	340.6	Roanoke Rapids City Schools	Roanoke Rapids
87	338.2	Columbus County Schools	Whiteville
87	338.2	Jackson County Schools	Sylva
89	338.1	Watauga County Schools	Boone
90	337.6	Pitt County Schools	Greenville
91	336.1	Fort Bragg District	Fort Bragg
92	335.6	Kings Mountain District	Kings Mountain
93	333.7	Wilkes County Schools	Wilkesboro
94	330.0	Martin County Schools	Williamston
95	327.4	Stokes County Schools	Danbury
96	326.8	Caldwell County Schools	Lenoir
97	325.7	Rowan-Salisbury Schools	Salisbury
98	323.0	Scotland County Schools	Laurinburg
99	321.3	Mount Airy City Schools	Mount Airy
100	316.6	Granville County Schools	Oxford
101	314.9	Dare County Schools	Manteo
102	304.7	Chapel Hill-Carrboro Schools	Chapel Hill
103	297.2	Hickory City Schools	Hickory
104	284.7	Gates County Schools	Gatesville
105	284.5	Carteret County Public Schools	Beaufort
106	275.6	Nash-Rocky Mount Schools	Nashville
107	275.1	Polk County Schools	Columbus
108	271.6	Greene County Schools	Snow Hill
109	268.6	Chatham County Schools	Pittsboro
110	246.3	Avery County Schools	Newland
111	245.0	Asheville City Schools	Asheville

Current Spending per Student in FY2001

Rank	Dollars	District Name	City
1	9,418	Asheville City Schools	Asheville
2	8,488	Chapel Hill-Carrboro Schools	Chapel Hill
3	8,054	Jones County Schools	Trenton
4	8,040	Washington County Schools	Plymouth
5	7,869	Pamlico County Schools	Bayboro
6	7,762	Mount Airy City Schools	Mount Airy
7	7,707	Perquimans County Schools	Hertford
8	7,690	Orange County Schools	Hillsborough
9	7,662	Avery County Schools	Newland
10	7,497	Durham Public Schools	Durham
11	7,493	Carteret County Public Schools	Beaufort
12	7,405	Bertie County Schools	Windsor
13	7,378	Gates County Schools	Gatesville
14	7,359	Shelby City	Shelby
15	7,280	Thomasville City Schools	Thomasville
16	7,194	Currituck County Schools	Currituck
17	7,149	Edenton-Chowan Schools	Edenton
18	7,132	Madison County Schools	Marshall
19	7,120	Yancey County Schools	Burnsville
20	7,117	Swain County Schools	Bryson City
21	7,085	Ashe County Schools	Jefferson
22	7,068	Halifax County Schools	Halifax
23	7,027	Brunswick County Schools	Bolivia
24	7,021	Charlotte-Mecklenburg Schools	Charlotte
25	6,962	Northampton County Schools	Jackson
26	6,960	Dare County Schools	Manteo
27	6,921	Warren County Schools	Warrenton
28	6,908	Cherokee County Schools	Murphy
29	6,892	Mitchell County Schools	Bakersville
30	6,866	Transylvania County Schools	Brevard
31	6,844	Chatham County Schools	Pittsboro
32	6,835	Martin County Schools	Williamston
33	6,824	Newton Conover City Schools	Newton
34	6,820	Jackson County Schools	Sylva
35	6,817	Kings Mountain District	Kings Mountain
36	6,813	New Hanover County Schools	Wilmington
37	6,800	Scotland County Schools	Laurinburg
38	6,792	Lexington City Schools	Lexington
39	6,776	Macon County Schools	Franklin
40	6,771	Watauga County Schools	Boone
41	6,742	Pasquotank County Schools	Elizabeth City
42	6,740	Polk County Schools	Columbus
43	6,733	Caswell County Schools	Yanceyville
44	6,716	Guilford County Schools	Greensboro
45	6,711	Forsyth County Schools	Winston Salem
46	6,674	Bladen County Schools	Elizabethtown
47	6,669	Greene County Schools	Snow Hill
48	6,660	Anson County Schools	Wadesboro
49	6,643	Kannapolis City Schools	Kannapolis
50	6,614	Haywood County Schools	Waynesville
51	6,600	Hertford County Schools	Winton
52	6,582	Montgomery County Schools	Troy
53	6,529	Beaufort County Schools	Washington
54	6,517	Moore County Schools	Carthage
55	6,512	Surry County Schools	Dobson
56	6,496	Wake County Schools	Raleigh
57	6,495	Edgecombe County Schools	Tarboro
58	6,479	Roanoke Rapids City Schools	Roanoke Rapids
59	6,455	Lenoir County Public Schools	Kinston
60	6,451	Wilson County Schools	Wilson
61	6,418	Stokes County Schools	Danbury
62	6,415	Person County Schools	Roxboro
63	6,409	Asheboro City Schools	Asheboro
64	6,356	Buncombe County Schools	Asheville
65	6,335	Rutherford County Schools	Forest City
66	6,325	Clinton City Schools	Clinton
67	6,320	Rockingham County Schools	Eden
68	6,315	Wilkes County Schools	Wilkesboro
69	6,312	Pender County Schools	Burgaw
70	6,306	Whiteville City Schools	Whiteville
71	6,300	Rowan-Salisbury Schools	Salisbury
72	6,278	Henderson County Schools	Hendersonville
73	6,272	Columbus County Schools	Whiteville
74	6,251	Hickory City Schools	Hickory
75	6,249	Yadkin County Schools	Yadkinville
76	6,223	Richmond County Schools	Hamlet
77	6,218	Lee County Schools	Sanford
78	6,213	Pitt County Schools	Greenville
79	6,185	Cumberland County Schools	Fayetteville
80	6,156	Mcdowell County Schools	Marion
81	6,146	Iredell-Statesville Schools	Statesville
82	6,120	Davie County Schools	Mocksville
83	6,111	Craven County Schools	New Bern
84	6,100	Wayne County Public Schools	Goldsboro
85	6,094	Johnston County Schools	Smithfield
86	6,079	Sampson County Schools	Clinton
87	6,020	Franklin County Schools	Louisburg
87	6,020	Vance County Schools	Henderson
89	6,014	Caldwell County Schools	Lenoir
90	6,007	Cleveland County Schools	Shelby
91	6,002	Gaston County Schools	Gastonia
92	5,956	Granville County Schools	Oxford
93	5,941	Stanly County Schools	Albemarle
94	5,925	Burke County Schools	Morganton
95	5,916	Catawba County Schools	Newton
96	5,912	Duplin County Schools	Kenansville
97	5,903	Nash-Rocky Mount Schools	Nashville
98	5,899	Alamance-Burlington Schools	Burlington
99	5,889	Onslow County Schools	Jacksonville
100	5,849	Cabarrus County Schools	Concord
101	5,795	Mooresville City Schools	Mooresville
102	5,766	Hoke County Schools	Raeford
103	5,754	Union County Public Schools	Monroe
104	5,724	Lincoln County Schools	Lincolnton
105	5,718	Robeson County Schools	Lumberton
106	5,711	Alexander County Schools	Taylorsville
107	5,638	Harnett County Schools	Lillington
108	5,425	Davidson County Schools	Lexington
109	5,380	Randolph County Schools	Asheboro
110	n/a	Camp Lejeune District	Camp Lejeune
110	n/a	Fort Bragg District	Fort Bragg

Number of Diploma Recipients

Rank	Number	District Name	City
1	5,411	Wake County Schools	Raleigh
2	5,087	Charlotte-Mecklenburg Schools	Charlotte
3	3,304	Guilford County Schools	Greensboro
4	2,809	Cumberland County Schools	Fayetteville
5	2,271	Forsyth County Schools	Winston Salem
6	1,466	Gaston County Schools	Gastonia
7	1,435	Durham Public Schools	Durham
8	1,370	Buncombe County Schools	Asheville
9	1,272	New Hanover County Schools	Wilmington
10	1,161	Onslow County Schools	Jacksonville
11	1,097	Cabarrus County Schools	Concord
12	1,093	Rowan-Salisbury Schools	Salisbury
13	1,085	Union County Public Schools	Monroe
14	1,081	Alamance-Burlington Schools	Burlington
15	1,046	Davidson County Schools	Lexington
16	996	Wayne County Public Schools	Goldsboro
17	994	Pitt County Schools	Greenville
18	963	Robeson County Schools	Lumberton
19	942	Johnston County Schools	Smithfield
20	918	Nash-Rocky Mount Schools	Nashville
21	827	Catawba County Schools	Newton
22	825	Randolph County Schools	Asheboro
23	821	Iredell-Statesville Schools	Statesville
24	816	Craven County Schools	New Bern
25	759	Harnett County Schools	Lillington
26	716	Rockingham County Schools	Eden
27	686	Caldwell County Schools	Lenoir
28	682	Burke County Schools	Morganton
29	650	Henderson County Schools	Hendersonville
30	625	Moore County Schools	Carthage
31	613	Lincoln County Schools	Lincolnton
32	599	Chapel Hill-Carrboro Schools	Chapel Hill
33	594	Wilson County Schools	Wilson
34	569	Stanly County Schools	Albemarle
35	543	Carteret County Public Schools	Beaufort
36	536	Wilkes County Schools	Wilkesboro
37	476	Surry County Schools	Dobson
38	474	Brunswick County Schools	Bolivia
38	474	Lenoir County Public Schools	Kinston
40	452	Rutherford County Schools	Forest City
41	442	Cleveland County Schools	Shelby
41	442	Duplin County Schools	Kenansville
43	431	Haywood County Schools	Waynesville
44	429	Lee County Schools	Sanford
45	414	Stokes County Schools	Danbury
46	394	Richmond County Schools	Hamlet
47	391	Edgecombe County Schools	Tarboro
48	386	Columbus County Schools	Whiteville
49	380	Beaufort County Schools	Washington
50	357	Sampson County Schools	Clinton
51	352	Franklin County Schools	Louisburg
52	339	Scotland County Schools	Laurinburg
53	334	Vance County Schools	Henderson
54	328	Granville County Schools	Oxford
55	327	Davie County Schools	Mocksville
55	327	Watauga County Schools	Boone
57	322	Alexander County Schools	Taylorsville
58	310	Orange County Schools	Hillsborough

59	306	Chatham County Schools	Pittsboro
59	306	Mcdowell County Schools	Marion
61	305	Pender County Schools	Burgaw
62	304	Person County Schools	Roxboro
62	304	Yadkin County Schools	Yadkinville
64	288	Bladen County Schools	Elizabethtown
65	270	Martin County Schools	Williamston
65	270	Pasquotank County Schools	Elizabeth City
67	267	Halifax County Schools	Halifax
68	263	Hoke County Schools	Raeford
69	259	Dare County Schools	Manteo
70	252	Transylvania County Schools	Brevard
71	249	Asheville City Schools	Asheville
72	247	Macon County Schools	Franklin
72	247	Mooresville City Schools	Mooresville
74	237	Hickory City Schools	Hickory
75	236	Cherokee County Schools	Murphy
76	231	Kannapolis City Schools	Kannapolis
77	225	Jackson County Schools	Sylva
78	220	Montgomery County Schools	Troy
79	215	Hertford County Schools	Winton
80	207	Anson County Schools	Wadesboro
81	196	Bertie County Schools	Windsor
82	195	Currituck County Schools	Currituck
83	188	Ashe County Schools	Jefferson
84	184	Kings Mountain District	Kings Mountain
85	182	Caswell County Schools	Yanceyville
86	181	Northampton County Schools	Jackson
87	180	Asheboro City Schools	Asheboro
88	165	Roanoke Rapids City Schools	Roanoke Rapids
89	150	Mitchell County Schools	Bakersville
90	146	Clinton City Schools	Clinton
90	146	Yancey County Schools	Burnsville
92	144	Newton Conover City Schools	Newton
92	144	Warren County Schools	Warrenton
94	141	Shelby City	Shelby
95	138	Edenton-Chowan Schools	Edenton
96	136	Lexington City Schools	Lexington
97	134	Washington County Schools	Plymouth
98	133	Avery County Schools	Newland
99	132	Pamlico County Schools	Bayboro
99	132	Whiteville City Schools	Whiteville
101	129	Madison County Schools	Marshall
102	117	Greene County Schools	Snow Hill
102	117	Polk County Schools	Columbus
104	111	Swain County Schools	Bryson City
105	103	Perquimans County Schools	Hertford
106	93	Camp Lejeune District	Camp Lejeune
107	92	Gates County Schools	Gatesville
108	91	Thomasville City Schools	Thomasville
109	87	Mount Airy City Schools	Mount Airy
110	51	Jones County Schools	Trenton
111	n/a	Fort Bragg District	Fort Bragg

High School Drop-out Rate

Rank	Percent	District Name	City
1	11.3	Warren County Schools	Warrenton
2	10.9	Robeson County Schools	Lumberton
3	10.6	Hickory City Schools	Hickory
4	9.8	Hoke County Schools	Raeford
5	9.2	Perquimans County Schools	Hertford
6	9.1	Kings Mountain District	Kings Mountain
7	8.9	Rutherford County Schools	Forest City
8	8.7	Anson County Schools	Wadesboro
9	8.5	Edgecombe County Schools	Tarboro
10	8.3	Pitt County Schools	Greenville
11	8.0	Brunswick County Schools	Bolivia
11	8.0	Chatham County Schools	Pittsboro
11	8.0	Harnett County Schools	Lillington
11	8.0	Lee County Schools	Sanford
11	8.0	Lexington City Schools	Lexington
16	7.9	Dare County Schools	Manteo
16	7.9	Nash-Rocky Mount Schools	Nashville
18	7.8	Asheboro City Schools	Asheboro
19	7.7	Greene County Schools	Snow Hill
20	7.6	Martin County Schools	Williamston
20	7.6	Pasquotank County Schools	Elizabeth City
20	7.6	Vance County Schools	Henderson
23	7.5	Mcdowell County Schools	Marion
23	7.5	Swain County Schools	Bryson City
25	7.4	Charlotte-Mecklenburg Schools	Charlotte
25	7.4	Wilson County Schools	Wilson
27	7.3	Columbus County Schools	Whiteville
27	7.3	Granville County Schools	Oxford
27	7.3	Northampton County Schools	Jackson
27	7.3	Person County Schools	Roxboro
27	7.3	Transylvania County Schools	Brevard
32	7.2	Duplin County Schools	Kenansville
32	7.2	Scotland County Schools	Laurinburg
34	7.1	Beaufort County Schools	Washington
34	7.1	Davie County Schools	Mocksville
34	7.1	Gaston County Schools	Gastonia
37	7.0	Franklin County Schools	Louisburg
37	7.0	Lenoir County Public Schools	Kinston
37	7.0	Randolph County Schools	Asheboro
40	6.9	Macon County Schools	Franklin
40	6.9	Roanoke Rapids City Schools	Roanoke Rapids
42	6.8	Caldwell County Schools	Lenoir
42	6.8	Davidson County Schools	Lexington
42	6.8	Iredell-Statesville Schools	Statesville
42	6.8	Madison County Schools	Marshall
42	6.8	Richmond County Schools	Hamlet
47	6.7	Alamance-Burlington Schools	Burlington
47	6.7	Buncombe County Schools	Asheville
47	6.7	Cherokee County Schools	Murphy
47	6.7	Montgomery County Schools	Troy
47	6.7	Surry County Schools	Dobson
47	6.7	Wilkes County Schools	Wilkesboro
53	6.6	Halifax County Schools	Halifax
53	6.6	Lincoln County Schools	Lincolnton
55	6.5	Catawba County Schools	Newton
55	6.5	Craven County Schools	New Bern
55	6.5	Haywood County Schools	Waynesville
58	6.4	Burke County Schools	Morganton
58	6.4	Currituck County Schools	Currituck
60	6.3	Forsyth County Schools	Winston Salem
60	6.3	Henderson County Schools	Hendersonville
60	6.3	Rockingham County Schools	Eden
63	6.2	Shelby City	Shelby
64	6.1	Mooresville City Schools	Mooresville
65	6.0	Bertie County Schools	Windsor
65	6.0	Clinton City Schools	Clinton
65	6.0	Johnston County Schools	Smithfield
65	6.0	Pender County Schools	Burgaw
65	6.0	Whiteville City Schools	Whiteville
70	5.9	Carteret County Public Schools	Beaufort
70	5.9	Cleveland County Schools	Shelby
70	5.9	Jackson County Schools	Sylva
70	5.9	Jones County Schools	Trenton
74	5.8	Alexander County Schools	Taylorsville
74	5.8	Rowan-Salisbury Schools	Salisbury
74	5.8	Yadkin County Schools	Yadkinville
77	5.7	Kannapolis City Schools	Kannapolis
78	5.6	New Hanover County Schools	Wilmington
79	5.5	Ashe County Schools	Jefferson
79	5.5	Avery County Schools	Newland
79	5.5	Moore County Schools	Carthage
79	5.5	Washington County Schools	Plymouth
79	5.5	Watauga County Schools	Boone
84	5.4	Asheville City Schools	Asheville
84	5.4	Stokes County Schools	Danbury
86	5.3	Hertford County Schools	Winton
87	5.2	Wayne County Public Schools	Goldsboro
88	5.1	Gates County Schools	Gatesville
88	5.1	Onslow County Schools	Jacksonville
90	5.0	Edenton-Chowan Schools	Edenton
90	5.0	Union County Public Schools	Monroe
92	4.9	Bladen County Schools	Elizabethtown
92	4.9	Cabarrus County Schools	Concord
92	4.9	Sampson County Schools	Clinton
92	4.9	Thomasville City Schools	Thomasville
92	4.9	Yancey County Schools	Burnsville
97	4.8	Cumberland County Schools	Fayetteville
97	4.8	Durham Public Schools	Durham
99	4.7	Orange County Schools	Hillsborough
99	4.7	Stanly County Schools	Albemarle
101	4.6	Guilford County Schools	Greensboro
102	4.2	Pamlico County Schools	Bayboro
103	4.1	Polk County Schools	Columbus
104	4.0	Wake County Schools	Raleigh
105	3.9	Caswell County Schools	Yanceyville
105	3.9	Mount Airy City Schools	Mount Airy
107	3.8	Newton Conover City Schools	Newton
108	3.1	Mitchell County Schools	Bakersville
109	2.0	Chapel Hill-Carrboro Schools	Chapel Hill
110	n/a	Camp Lejeune District	Camp Lejeune
110	n/a	Fort Bragg District	Fort Bragg

North Dakota

North Dakota Public School Educational Profile

Category	Value	Category	Value
Schools *(2002-2003)*	577	**Diploma Recipients** *(2002-2003)*	8,114
Instructional Level		White, Non-Hispanic	7,564
Primary	309	Black, Non-Hispanic	58
Middle	39	Asian/Pacific Islander	62
High	189	American Indian/Alaskan Native	362
Other Level	40	Hispanic	68
Curriculum		**High School Drop-out Rate** (%) *(2000-2001)*	2.2
Regular	540	White, Non-Hispanic	1.5
Special Education	30	Black, Non-Hispanic	3.9
Vocational	7	Asian/Pacific Islander	3.2
Alternative	0	American Indian/Alaskan Native	10.0
Type		Hispanic	3.2
Magnet	0	**Staff** *(2002-2003)*	15,085.3
Charter	0	Teachers	8,077.5
Title I Eligible	456	Average Salary ($)	33,869
School-wide Title I	75	Librarians/Media Specialists	198.8
Students *(2002-2003)*	104,225	Guidance Counselors	278.3
Gender (%)		**Ratios** *(2002-2003)*	
Male	51.8	Student/Teacher Ratio	12.9 to 1
Female	48.2	Student/Librarian Ratio	524.3 to 1
Race/Ethnicity (%)		Student/Counselor Ratio	374.5 to 1
White, Non-Hispanic	88.6	**Current Spending** *($ per student in FY 2001)*	6,709
Black, Non-Hispanic	1.1	Instruction	4,117
Asian/Pacific Islander	0.9	Support Services	2,073
American Indian/Alaskan Native	8.1	**College Entrance Exam Scores** *(2003)*	
Hispanic	1.3	Scholastic Aptitude Test (SAT)	
Classification (%)		Participation Rate (%)	4
Individual Education Program (IEP)	13.1	Mean SAT I Verbal Score	602
Migrant	0.3	Mean SAT I Math Score	613
English Language Learner (ELL)	0.8	American College Testing Program (ACT)	
Eligible for Free Lunch Program	20.3	Participation Rate (%)	80
Eligible for Reduced-Price Lunch Program	7.8	Average Composite Score	21.3

Note: *For an explanation of data, please refer to the User's Guide in the front of the book; n/a indicates data not available*

North Dakota NAEP 2003 Test Scores

Reading			Mathematics		
Grade/Category	Value	Rank	Grade/Category	Value	Rank
4th Grade			**4th Grade**		
Average Proficiency	221.6 (0.9)	18/51	Average Proficiency	237.6 (0.7)	15/51
Proficiency by Gender/Race/Ethnicity			Proficiency by Gender/Race/Ethnicity		
Male	218.2 (1.1)	14/51	Male	239.6 (0.7)	13/51
Female	225.2 (1.1)	20/51	Female	235.4 (0.9)	18/51
White, Non-Hispanic	224.0 (0.9)	35/51	White, Non-Hispanic	240.0 (0.6)	34/51
Black, Non-Hispanic	n/a	n/a	Black, Non-Hispanic	n/a	n/a
Asian, Non-Hispanic	n/a	n/a	Asian, Non-Hispanic	n/a	n/a
American Indian, Non-Hispanic	n/a	n/a	American Indian, Non-Hispanic	n/a	n/a
Hispanic	202.1 (1.8)	4/12	Hispanic	215.2 (2.4)	10/12
Proficiency by Class Size			Proficiency by Class Size		
Less than 16 Students	219.3 (1.9)	5/45	Less than 16 Students	237.2 (1.6)	4/47
16 to 18 Students	220.7 (2.0)	15/48	16 to 18 Students	236.8 (1.6)	17/48
19 to 20 Students	221.2 (1.6)	21/50	19 to 20 Students	236.7 (1.5)	17/50
21 to 25 Students	223.1 (1.6)	21/51	21 to 25 Students	238.8 (1.0)	21/51
Greater than 25 Students	224.3 (2.6)	11/49	Greater than 25 Students	238.4 (2.8)	13/49
Percent Attaining Achievement Levels			Percent Attaining Achievement Levels		
Below Basic	31.3 (1.2)	38/51	Below Basic	16.8 (1.1)	43/51
Basic or Above	68.7 (1.2)	12/51	Basic or Above	83.2 (1.1)	8/51
Proficient or Above	31.8 (1.2)	27/51	Proficient or Above	34.1 (1.1)	18/51
Advanced or Above	5.9 (0.7)	38/51	Advanced or Above	2.4 (0.4)	36/51
8th Grade			**8th Grade**		
Average Proficiency	269.7 (0.8)	6/51	Average Proficiency	287.1 (0.8)	2/51
Proficiency by Gender/Race/Ethnicity			Proficiency by Gender/Race/Ethnicity		
Male	264.5 (1.0)	5/51	Male	287.3 (1.0)	3/51
Female	274.9 (1.2)	7/51	Female	287.0 (1.0)	2/51
White, Non-Hispanic	271.8 (0.9)	14/50	White, Non-Hispanic	289.9 (0.7)	13/50
Black, Non-Hispanic	n/a	n/a	Black, Non-Hispanic	n/a	n/a
Asian, Non-Hispanic	n/a	n/a	Asian, Non-Hispanic	n/a	n/a
American Indian, Non-Hispanic	n/a	n/a	American Indian, Non-Hispanic	n/a	n/a
Hispanic	243.5 (3.7)	5/10	Hispanic	260.8 (3.5)	5/11
Proficiency by Parents Highest Level of Ed.			Proficiency by Parents Highest Level of Ed.		
Did Not Finish High School	249.9 (7.0)	11/50	Did Not Finish High School	256.9 (6.6)	25/50
Graduated High School	260.4 (2.0)	7/50	Graduated High School	278.0 (1.8)	2/50
Some Education After High School	271.3 (1.8)	10/50	Some Education After High School	289.5 (1.7)	2/50
Graduated College	275.8 (1.0)	10/50	Graduated College	292.5 (0.9)	12/50
Percent Attaining Achievement Levels			Percent Attaining Achievement Levels		
Below Basic	18.5 (0.9)	49/51	Below Basic	18.8 (1.1)	50/51
Basic or Above	81.5 (0.9)	2/51	Basic or Above	81.2 (1.1)	2/51
Proficient or Above	38.2 (1.3)	5/51	Proficient or Above	36.3 (1.1)	3/51
Advanced or Above	2.5 (0.5)	26/51	Advanced or Above	4.9 (0.4)	26/51

***Note:** For an explanation of data, please refer to the User's Guide in the front of the book; values in italics indicate that the nature of the sample does not allow accurate determination of the variability of the statistic; n/a indicates data not available*

Burleigh County

Bismarck 1

806 N Washington St • Bismarck, ND 58501-3623
(701) 221-3710
Grade Span: PK-12; **Agency Type:** 1
Schools: 23
17 Primary; 3 Middle; 3 High; 0 Other Level
23 Regular; 0 Special Education; 0 Vocational; 0 Alternative
0 Magnet; 0 Charter; 9 Title I Eligible; 2 School-wide Title I
Students: 10,489 (50.6% male; 49.4% female)
Individual Education Program: 1,237 (11.8%);
English Language Learner: 18 (0.2%); Migrant: 0 (0.0%)
Eligible for Free Lunch Program: 1,397 (13.3%)
Eligible for Reduced-Price Lunch Program: 460 (4.4%)
Teachers: 650.3 (16.1 to 1)
Librarians/Media Specialists: 12.4 (845.9 to 1)
Guidance Counselors: 25.1 (417.9 to 1)
Current Spending: ($ per student per year):
Total: $5,696; Instruction: $3,674; Support Services: $1,648
Enrollment, Drop-out Rates and Diploma Recipients by Race/Ethnicity

Category	Total	White	Black	Asian	AIAN	Hisp.
Enrollment (%)	100.0	92.6	0.7	0.7	5.5	0.5
Drop-out Rate (%)	1.9	1.1	9.1	0.0	16.5	4.8
H.S. Diplomas (#)	828	800	2	11	13	2

Cass County

Fargo 1

415 4th St N • Fargo, ND 58102-4514
(701) 446-1000
Grade Span: PK-12; **Agency Type:** 1
Schools: 22
14 Primary; 3 Middle; 3 High; 2 Other Level
22 Regular; 0 Special Education; 0 Vocational; 0 Alternative
0 Magnet; 0 Charter; 10 Title I Eligible; 1 School-wide Title I
Students: 11,159 (51.0% male; 49.0% female)
Individual Education Program: 1,251 (11.2%);
English Language Learner: 440 (3.9%); Migrant: 0 (0.0%)
Eligible for Free Lunch Program: 1,307 (11.7%)
Eligible for Reduced-Price Lunch Program: 522 (4.7%)
Teachers: 705.2 (15.8 to 1)
Librarians/Media Specialists: 16.6 (672.2 to 1)
Guidance Counselors: 27.4 (407.3 to 1)
Current Spending: ($ per student per year):
Total: $6,699; Instruction: $4,388; Support Services: $1,977
Enrollment, Drop-out Rates and Diploma Recipients by Race/Ethnicity

Category	Total	White	Black	Asian	AIAN	Hisp.
Enrollment (%)	100.0	92.3	2.3	2.3	1.7	1.4
Drop-out Rate (%)	3.5	3.4	0.0	13.3	5.8	8.1
H.S. Diplomas (#)	781	727	19	22	8	5

West Fargo 6

207 Main Ave W • West Fargo, ND 58078-1793
(701) 356-2000
Grade Span: PK-12; **Agency Type:** 1
Schools: 9
7 Primary; 1 Middle; 1 High; 0 Other Level
9 Regular; 0 Special Education; 0 Vocational; 0 Alternative
0 Magnet; 0 Charter; 4 Title I Eligible; 0 School-wide Title I
Students: 5,262 (51.5% male; 48.5% female)
Individual Education Program: 609 (11.6%);
English Language Learner: 155 (2.9%); Migrant: 0 (0.0%)
Eligible for Free Lunch Program: 676 (12.8%)
Eligible for Reduced-Price Lunch Program: 330 (6.3%)
Teachers: 317.2 (16.6 to 1)
Librarians/Media Specialists: 4.6 (1,143.9 to 1)
Guidance Counselors: 11.2 (469.8 to 1)
Current Spending: ($ per student per year):
Total: $5,476; Instruction: $3,308; Support Services: $1,693
Enrollment, Drop-out Rates and Diploma Recipients by Race/Ethnicity

Category	Total	White	Black	Asian	AIAN	Hisp.
Enrollment (%)	100.0	91.9	2.7	1.0	2.8	1.7
Drop-out Rate (%)	2.6	2.4	12.5	12.5	16.7	0.0
H.S. Diplomas (#)	337	320	3	3	4	7

Grand Forks County

Grand Forks 1

2400 47th Ave S • Grand Forks, ND 58201
Mailing Address: PO Box 6000 • Grand Forks, ND 58206-6000
(701) 746-2200
Grade Span: PK-12; **Agency Type:** 1
Schools: 19
11 Primary; 5 Middle; 3 High; 0 Other Level
19 Regular; 0 Special Education; 0 Vocational; 0 Alternative
0 Magnet; 0 Charter; 11 Title I Eligible; 7 School-wide Title I
Students: 8,041 (52.0% male; 48.0% female)
Individual Education Program: 1,081 (13.4%);
English Language Learner: 65 (0.8%); Migrant: 0 (0.0%)
Eligible for Free Lunch Program: 1,484 (18.5%)
Eligible for Reduced-Price Lunch Program: 648 (8.1%)
Teachers: 599.0 (13.4 to 1)
Librarians/Media Specialists: 15.6 (515.4 to 1)
Guidance Counselors: 21.0 (382.9 to 1)
Current Spending: ($ per student per year):
Total: $6,187; Instruction: $4,108; Support Services: $1,793
Enrollment, Drop-out Rates and Diploma Recipients by Race/Ethnicity

Category	Total	White	Black	Asian	AIAN	Hisp.
Enrollment (%)	100.0	87.6	2.2	1.9	5.6	2.7
Drop-out Rate (%)	1.8	1.4	3.4	0.0	9.5	3.6
H.S. Diplomas (#)	540	507	9	7	8	9

Morton County

Mandan 1

309 Collins Ave • Mandan, ND 58554-3000
(701) 663-9531
Grade Span: PK-12; **Agency Type:** 1
Schools: 8
6 Primary; 1 Middle; 1 High; 0 Other Level
8 Regular; 0 Special Education; 0 Vocational; 0 Alternative
0 Magnet; 0 Charter; 4 Title I Eligible; 0 School-wide Title I
Students: 3,401 (52.3% male; 47.7% female)
Individual Education Program: 524 (15.4%);
English Language Learner: 0 (0.0%); Migrant: 0 (0.0%)
Eligible for Free Lunch Program: 594 (17.5%)
Eligible for Reduced-Price Lunch Program: 236 (6.9%)
Teachers: 212.0 (16.0 to 1)
Librarians/Media Specialists: 4.0 (850.3 to 1)
Guidance Counselors: 7.5 (453.5 to 1)
Current Spending: ($ per student per year):
Total: $4,929; Instruction: $3,097; Support Services: $1,485
Enrollment, Drop-out Rates and Diploma Recipients by Race/Ethnicity

Category	Total	White	Black	Asian	AIAN	Hisp.
Enrollment (%)	100.0	92.8	0.8	0.1	5.6	0.7
Drop-out Rate (%)	5.1	5.1	0.0	0.0	6.9	n/a
H.S. Diplomas (#)	248	246	0	0	2	0

Ramsey County

Devils Lake 1

1601 College Dr N • Devils Lake, ND 58301-1550
(701) 662-7640
Grade Span: PK-12; **Agency Type:** 1
Schools: 5
3 Primary; 1 Middle; 1 High; 0 Other Level
5 Regular; 0 Special Education; 0 Vocational; 0 Alternative
0 Magnet; 0 Charter; 4 Title I Eligible; 1 School-wide Title I
Students: 1,912 (51.4% male; 48.6% female)
Individual Education Program: 304 (15.9%);
English Language Learner: 0 (0.0%); Migrant: 0 (0.0%)
Eligible for Free Lunch Program: 487 (25.5%)
Eligible for Reduced-Price Lunch Program: 145 (7.6%)
Teachers: 131.4 (14.6 to 1)
Librarians/Media Specialists: 3.0 (637.3 to 1)
Guidance Counselors: 3.0 (637.3 to 1)
Current Spending: ($ per student per year):
Total: $5,390; Instruction: $3,141; Support Services: $1,693
Enrollment, Drop-out Rates and Diploma Recipients by Race/Ethnicity

Category	Total	White	Black	Asian	AIAN	Hisp.
Enrollment (%)	100.0	75.5	0.5	0.5	22.6	0.9
Drop-out Rate (%)	5.9	2.8	0.0	20.0	21.6	0.0
H.S. Diplomas (#)	159	140	2	0	16	1

Richland County

Wahpeton 37

1505 11th St N • Wahpeton, ND 58075-3551
(701) 642-6741
Grade Span: PK-12; **Agency Type:** 1
Schools: 4
2 Primary; 1 Middle; 1 High; 0 Other Level
4 Regular; 0 Special Education; 0 Vocational; 0 Alternative
0 Magnet; 0 Charter; 3 Title I Eligible; 0 School-wide Title I
Students: 1,543 (51.8% male; 48.2% female)
Individual Education Program: 207 (13.4%);
English Language Learner: 24 (1.6%); Migrant: 27 (1.7%)
Eligible for Free Lunch Program: 298 (19.3%)
Eligible for Reduced-Price Lunch Program: 89 (5.8%)

Teachers: 91.1 (16.9 to 1)
Librarians/Media Specialists: 2.0 (771.5 to 1)
Guidance Counselors: 2.0 (771.5 to 1)
Current Spending: ($ per student per year):
Total: $5,095; Instruction: $3,312; Support Services: $1,427
Enrollment, Drop-out Rates and Diploma Recipients by Race/Ethnicity

Category	Total	White	Black	Asian	AIAN	Hisp.
Enrollment (%)	100.0	91.6	0.5	0.8	5.0	2.0
Drop-out Rate (%)	3.0	2.4	100.0	0.0	21.4	0.0
H.S. Diplomas (#)	115	113	0	0	1	1

Rolette County

Belcourt 7

Hwy 5 E • Belcourt, ND 58316-0440
Mailing Address: PO Box 440 • Belcourt, ND 58316-0440
(701) 477-6471
Grade Span: KG-12; **Agency Type:** 1
Schools: 3
1 Primary; 1 Middle; 1 High; 0 Other Level
3 Regular; 0 Special Education; 0 Vocational; 0 Alternative
0 Magnet; 0 Charter; 3 Title I Eligible; 3 School-wide Title I
Students: 1,763 (50.4% male; 49.6% female)
Individual Education Program: 67 (3.8%);
English Language Learner: 0 (0.0%); Migrant: 0 (0.0%)
Eligible for Free Lunch Program: 1,409 (79.9%)
Eligible for Reduced-Price Lunch Program: 56 (3.2%)
Teachers: 190.5 (9.3 to 1)
Librarians/Media Specialists: 4.0 (440.8 to 1)
Guidance Counselors: 7.0 (251.9 to 1)
Current Spending: ($ per student per year):
Total: $6,642; Instruction: $3,982; Support Services: $2,284
Enrollment, Drop-out Rates and Diploma Recipients by Race/Ethnicity

Category	Total	White	Black	Asian	AIAN	Hisp.
Enrollment (%)	100.0	7.7	0.0	0.0	92.3	0.0
Drop-out Rate (%)	18.1	0.0	n/a	n/a	19.8	n/a
H.S. Diplomas (#)	100	0	0	0	100	0

Turtle Mountain Agency

PO Box 30 • Belcourt, ND 58316
(701) 477-3463
Grade Span: KG-12; **Agency Type:** 6
Schools: 9
4 Primary; 1 Middle; 1 High; 3 Other Level
9 Regular; 0 Special Education; 0 Vocational; 0 Alternative
0 Magnet; 0 Charter; 9 Title I Eligible; 9 School-wide Title I
Students: 2,424 (n/a% male; n/a% female)
Individual Education Program: n/a;
English Language Learner: n/a; Migrant: n/a
Eligible for Free Lunch Program: n/a
Eligible for Reduced-Price Lunch Program: n/a
Teachers: n/a
Librarians/Media Specialists: n/a
Guidance Counselors: n/a
Current Spending: ($ per student per year):
Total: n/a; Instruction: n/a; Support Services: n/a
Enrollment, Drop-out Rates and Diploma Recipients by Race/Ethnicity

Category	Total	White	Black	Asian	AIAN	Hisp.
Enrollment (%)	100.0	0.0	0.0	0.0	100.0	0.0
Drop-out Rate (%)	n/a	n/a	n/a	n/a	n/a	n/a
H.S. Diplomas (#)	n/a	n/a	n/a	n/a	n/a	n/a

Stark County

Dickinson 1

444 4th St W • Dickinson, ND 58601
Mailing Address: PO Box 1057 • Dickinson, ND 58602-1057
(701) 456-0002
Grade Span: PK-12; **Agency Type:** 1
Schools: 9
6 Primary; 1 Middle; 2 High; 0 Other Level
9 Regular; 0 Special Education; 0 Vocational; 0 Alternative
0 Magnet; 0 Charter; 7 Title I Eligible; 2 School-wide Title I
Students: 2,758 (52.1% male; 47.9% female)
Individual Education Program: 357 (12.9%);
English Language Learner: 0 (0.0%); Migrant: 0 (0.0%)
Eligible for Free Lunch Program: 501 (18.2%)
Eligible for Reduced-Price Lunch Program: 282 (10.2%)
Teachers: 183.6 (15.0 to 1)
Librarians/Media Specialists: 3.0 (919.3 to 1)
Guidance Counselors: 5.9 (467.5 to 1)
Current Spending: ($ per student per year):
Total: $5,269; Instruction: $3,457; Support Services: $1,334
Enrollment, Drop-out Rates and Diploma Recipients by Race/Ethnicity

Category	Total	White	Black	Asian	AIAN	Hisp.
Enrollment (%)	100.0	95.8	0.8	0.5	2.3	0.6
Drop-out Rate (%)	2.1	1.9	0.0	0.0	16.7	0.0
H.S. Diplomas (#)	216	215	0	0	1	0

Stutsman County

Jamestown 1

120 2nd St SE • Jamestown, ND 58401
Mailing Address: PO Box 269 • Jamestown, ND 58402-0269
(701) 252-1950
Grade Span: PK-12; **Agency Type:** 1
Schools: 8
5 Primary; 1 Middle; 2 High; 0 Other Level
8 Regular; 0 Special Education; 0 Vocational; 0 Alternative
0 Magnet; 0 Charter; 5 Title I Eligible; 0 School-wide Title I
Students: 2,570 (50.7% male; 49.3% female)
Individual Education Program: 391 (15.2%);
English Language Learner: 14 (0.5%); Migrant: 0 (0.0%)
Eligible for Free Lunch Program: 432 (16.8%)
Eligible for Reduced-Price Lunch Program: 221 (8.6%)
Teachers: 172.5 (14.9 to 1)
Librarians/Media Specialists: 3.0 (856.7 to 1)
Guidance Counselors: 6.0 (428.3 to 1)
Current Spending: ($ per student per year):
Total: $5,068; Instruction: $3,120; Support Services: $1,553
Enrollment, Drop-out Rates and Diploma Recipients by Race/Ethnicity

Category	Total	White	Black	Asian	AIAN	Hisp.
Enrollment (%)	100.0	94.7	0.9	0.9	2.1	1.4
Drop-out Rate (%)	0.9	1.0	0.0	0.0	0.0	0.0
H.S. Diplomas (#)	214	210	0	3	1	0

Ward County

Minot 1

215 2nd St SE • Minot, ND 58701-3985
(701) 857-4422
Grade Span: PK-12; **Agency Type:** 1
Schools: 19
13 Primary; 3 Middle; 2 High; 1 Other Level
19 Regular; 0 Special Education; 0 Vocational; 0 Alternative
0 Magnet; 0 Charter; 13 Title I Eligible; 2 School-wide Title I
Students: 7,015 (52.0% male; 48.0% female)
Individual Education Program: 1,109 (15.8%);
English Language Learner: 7 (0.1%); Migrant: 0 (0.0%)
Eligible for Free Lunch Program: 1,252 (17.8%)
Eligible for Reduced-Price Lunch Program: 634 (9.0%)
Teachers: 483.4 (14.5 to 1)
Librarians/Media Specialists: 4.5 (1,558.9 to 1)
Guidance Counselors: 20.7 (338.9 to 1)
Current Spending: ($ per student per year):
Total: $5,901; Instruction: $3,910; Support Services: $1,639
Enrollment, Drop-out Rates and Diploma Recipients by Race/Ethnicity

Category	Total	White	Black	Asian	AIAN	Hisp.
Enrollment (%)	100.0	88.6	3.4	1.6	4.7	1.7
Drop-out Rate (%)	1.8	1.7	3.2	0.0	3.4	0.0
H.S. Diplomas (#)	463	427	15	1	7	13

Williams County

Williston 1

502 Highland • Williston, ND 58802-1407
Mailing Address: PO Box 1407 • Williston, ND 58802-1407
(701) 572-1580
Grade Span: KG-12; **Agency Type:** 1
Schools: 6
4 Primary; 1 Middle; 1 High; 0 Other Level
6 Regular; 0 Special Education; 0 Vocational; 0 Alternative
0 Magnet; 0 Charter; 5 Title I Eligible; 2 School-wide Title I
Students: 2,345 (51.5% male; 48.5% female)
Individual Education Program: 349 (14.9%);
English Language Learner: 0 (0.0%); Migrant: 0 (0.0%)
Eligible for Free Lunch Program: 467 (19.9%)
Eligible for Reduced-Price Lunch Program: 170 (7.2%)
Teachers: 162.9 (14.4 to 1)
Librarians/Media Specialists: 3.2 (732.8 to 1)
Guidance Counselors: 7.7 (304.5 to 1)
Current Spending: ($ per student per year):
Total: $5,029; Instruction: $3,285; Support Services: $1,271

Enrollment, Drop-out Rates and Diploma Recipients by Race/Ethnicity

Category	Total	White	Black	Asian	AIAN	Hisp.
Enrollment (%)	100.0	91.1	0.2	0.0	7.4	1.2
Drop-out Rate (%)	0.8	0.8	0.0	0.0	1.9	0.0
H.S. Diplomas (#)	235	220	0	1	14	0

Number of Schools

Rank	Number	District Name	City
1	23	Bismarck 1	Bismarck
2	22	Fargo 1	Fargo
3	19	Grand Forks 1	Grand Forks
3	19	Minot 1	Minot
5	9	Dickinson 1	Dickinson
5	9	Turtle Mountain Agency	Belcourt
5	9	West Fargo 6	West Fargo
8	8	Jamestown 1	Jamestown
8	8	Mandan 1	Mandan
10	6	Williston 1	Williston
11	5	Devils Lake 1	Devils Lake
12	4	Wahpeton 37	Wahpeton
13	3	Belcourt 7	Belcourt

Number of Teachers

Rank	Number	District Name	City
1	705	Fargo 1	Fargo
2	650	Bismarck 1	Bismarck
3	599	Grand Forks 1	Grand Forks
4	483	Minot 1	Minot
5	317	West Fargo 6	West Fargo
6	212	Mandan 1	Mandan
7	190	Belcourt 7	Belcourt
8	183	Dickinson 1	Dickinson
9	172	Jamestown 1	Jamestown
10	162	Williston 1	Williston
11	131	Devils Lake 1	Devils Lake
12	91	Wahpeton 37	Wahpeton
13	n/a	Turtle Mountain Agency	Belcourt

Number of Students

Rank	Number	District Name	City
1	11,159	Fargo 1	Fargo
2	10,489	Bismarck 1	Bismarck
3	8,041	Grand Forks 1	Grand Forks
4	7,015	Minot 1	Minot
5	5,262	West Fargo 6	West Fargo
6	3,401	Mandan 1	Mandan
7	2,758	Dickinson 1	Dickinson
8	2,570	Jamestown 1	Jamestown
9	2,424	Turtle Mountain Agency	Belcourt
10	2,345	Williston 1	Williston
11	1,912	Devils Lake 1	Devils Lake
12	1,763	Belcourt 7	Belcourt
13	1,543	Wahpeton 37	Wahpeton

Male Students

Rank	Percent	District Name	City
1	52.3	Mandan 1	Mandan
2	52.1	Dickinson 1	Dickinson
3	52.0	Grand Forks 1	Grand Forks
3	52.0	Minot 1	Minot
5	51.8	Wahpeton 37	Wahpeton
6	51.5	West Fargo 6	West Fargo
6	51.5	Williston 1	Williston
8	51.4	Devils Lake 1	Devils Lake
9	51.0	Fargo 1	Fargo
10	50.7	Jamestown 1	Jamestown
11	50.6	Bismarck 1	Bismarck
12	50.4	Belcourt 7	Belcourt
13	n/a	Turtle Mountain Agency	Belcourt

Female Students

Rank	Percent	District Name	City
1	49.6	Belcourt 7	Belcourt
2	49.4	Bismarck 1	Bismarck
3	49.3	Jamestown 1	Jamestown
4	49.0	Fargo 1	Fargo
5	48.6	Devils Lake 1	Devils Lake
6	48.5	West Fargo 6	West Fargo
6	48.5	Williston 1	Williston
8	48.2	Wahpeton 37	Wahpeton
9	48.0	Grand Forks 1	Grand Forks
9	48.0	Minot 1	Minot
11	47.9	Dickinson 1	Dickinson
12	47.7	Mandan 1	Mandan
13	n/a	Turtle Mountain Agency	Belcourt

Individual Education Program Students

Rank	Percent	District Name	City
1	15.9	Devils Lake 1	Devils Lake
2	15.8	Minot 1	Minot
3	15.4	Mandan 1	Mandan
4	15.2	Jamestown 1	Jamestown
5	14.9	Williston 1	Williston
6	13.4	Grand Forks 1	Grand Forks
6	13.4	Wahpeton 37	Wahpeton
8	12.9	Dickinson 1	Dickinson
9	11.8	Bismarck 1	Bismarck
10	11.6	West Fargo 6	West Fargo
11	11.2	Fargo 1	Fargo
12	3.8	Belcourt 7	Belcourt
13	n/a	Turtle Mountain Agency	Belcourt

English Language Learner Students

Rank	Percent	District Name	City
1	3.9	Fargo 1	Fargo
2	2.9	West Fargo 6	West Fargo
3	1.6	Wahpeton 37	Wahpeton
4	0.8	Grand Forks 1	Grand Forks
5	0.5	Jamestown 1	Jamestown
6	0.2	Bismarck 1	Bismarck
7	0.1	Minot 1	Minot
8	0.0	Belcourt 7	Belcourt
8	0.0	Devils Lake 1	Devils Lake
8	0.0	Dickinson 1	Dickinson
8	0.0	Mandan 1	Mandan
8	0.0	Williston 1	Williston
13	n/a	Turtle Mountain Agency	Belcourt

Migrant Students

Rank	Percent	District Name	City
1	1.7	Wahpeton 37	Wahpeton
2	0.0	Belcourt 7	Belcourt
2	0.0	Bismarck 1	Bismarck
2	0.0	Devils Lake 1	Devils Lake
2	0.0	Dickinson 1	Dickinson
2	0.0	Fargo 1	Fargo
2	0.0	Grand Forks 1	Grand Forks
2	0.0	Jamestown 1	Jamestown
2	0.0	Mandan 1	Mandan
2	0.0	Minot 1	Minot
2	0.0	West Fargo 6	West Fargo
2	0.0	Williston 1	Williston
13	n/a	Turtle Mountain Agency	Belcourt

Students Eligible for Free Lunch

Rank	Percent	District Name	City
1	79.9	Belcourt 7	Belcourt
2	25.5	Devils Lake 1	Devils Lake
3	19.9	Williston 1	Williston
4	19.3	Wahpeton 37	Wahpeton
5	18.5	Grand Forks 1	Grand Forks
6	18.2	Dickinson 1	Dickinson
7	17.8	Minot 1	Minot
8	17.5	Mandan 1	Mandan
9	16.8	Jamestown 1	Jamestown
10	13.3	Bismarck 1	Bismarck
11	12.8	West Fargo 6	West Fargo
12	11.7	Fargo 1	Fargo
13	n/a	Turtle Mountain Agency	Belcourt

Students Eligible for Reduced-Price Lunch

Rank	Percent	District Name	City
1	10.2	Dickinson 1	Dickinson
2	9.0	Minot 1	Minot
3	8.6	Jamestown 1	Jamestown
4	8.1	Grand Forks 1	Grand Forks
5	7.6	Devils Lake 1	Devils Lake
6	7.2	Williston 1	Williston
7	6.9	Mandan 1	Mandan
8	6.3	West Fargo 6	West Fargo
9	5.8	Wahpeton 37	Wahpeton
10	4.7	Fargo 1	Fargo
11	4.4	Bismarck 1	Bismarck
12	3.2	Belcourt 7	Belcourt
13	n/a	Turtle Mountain Agency	Belcourt

Student/Teacher Ratio

Rank	Ratio	District Name	City
1	16.9	Wahpeton 37	Wahpeton
2	16.6	West Fargo 6	West Fargo
3	16.1	Bismarck 1	Bismarck
4	16.0	Mandan 1	Mandan
5	15.8	Fargo 1	Fargo
6	15.0	Dickinson 1	Dickinson
7	14.9	Jamestown 1	Jamestown
8	14.6	Devils Lake 1	Devils Lake
9	14.5	Minot 1	Minot
10	14.4	Williston 1	Williston
11	13.4	Grand Forks 1	Grand Forks
12	9.3	Belcourt 7	Belcourt
13	n/a	Turtle Mountain Agency	Belcourt

Student/Librarian Ratio

Rank	Ratio	District Name	City
1	1,558.9	Minot 1	Minot
2	1,143.9	West Fargo 6	West Fargo
3	919.3	Dickinson 1	Dickinson
4	856.7	Jamestown 1	Jamestown
5	850.3	Mandan 1	Mandan
6	845.9	Bismarck 1	Bismarck
7	771.5	Wahpeton 37	Wahpeton
8	732.8	Williston 1	Williston
9	672.2	Fargo 1	Fargo
10	637.3	Devils Lake 1	Devils Lake
11	515.4	Grand Forks 1	Grand Forks
12	440.8	Belcourt 7	Belcourt
13	n/a	Turtle Mountain Agency	Belcourt

Student/Counselor Ratio

Rank	Ratio	District Name	City
1	771.5	Wahpeton 37	Wahpeton
2	637.3	Devils Lake 1	Devils Lake
3	469.8	West Fargo 6	West Fargo
4	467.5	Dickinson 1	Dickinson
5	453.5	Mandan 1	Mandan
6	428.3	Jamestown 1	Jamestown
7	417.9	Bismarck 1	Bismarck
8	407.3	Fargo 1	Fargo
9	382.9	Grand Forks 1	Grand Forks
10	338.9	Minot 1	Minot
11	304.5	Williston 1	Williston
12	251.9	Belcourt 7	Belcourt
13	n/a	Turtle Mountain Agency	Belcourt

Current Spending per Student in FY2001

Rank	Dollars	District Name	City
1	6,699	Fargo 1	Fargo
2	6,642	Belcourt 7	Belcourt
3	6,187	Grand Forks 1	Grand Forks
4	5,901	Minot 1	Minot
5	5,696	Bismarck 1	Bismarck
6	5,476	West Fargo 6	West Fargo
7	5,390	Devils Lake 1	Devils Lake
8	5,269	Dickinson 1	Dickinson
9	5,095	Wahpeton 37	Wahpeton
10	5,068	Jamestown 1	Jamestown
11	5,029	Williston 1	Williston
12	4,929	Mandan 1	Mandan
13	n/a	Turtle Mountain Agency	Belcourt

Number of Diploma Recipients

Rank	Number	District Name	City
1	828	Bismarck 1	Bismarck
2	781	Fargo 1	Fargo
3	540	Grand Forks 1	Grand Forks
4	463	Minot 1	Minot
5	337	West Fargo 6	West Fargo
6	248	Mandan 1	Mandan
7	235	Williston 1	Williston
8	216	Dickinson 1	Dickinson
9	214	Jamestown 1	Jamestown
10	159	Devils Lake 1	Devils Lake
11	115	Wahpeton 37	Wahpeton
12	100	Belcourt 7	Belcourt
13	n/a	Turtle Mountain Agency	Belcourt

High School Drop-out Rate

Rank	Percent	District Name	City
1	18.1	Belcourt 7	Belcourt
2	5.9	Devils Lake 1	Devils Lake
3	5.1	Mandan 1	Mandan
4	3.5	Fargo 1	Fargo
5	3.0	Wahpeton 37	Wahpeton
6	2.6	West Fargo 6	West Fargo
7	2.1	Dickinson 1	Dickinson
8	1.9	Bismarck 1	Bismarck
9	1.8	Grand Forks 1	Grand Forks
9	1.8	Minot 1	Minot
11	0.9	Jamestown 1	Jamestown
12	0.8	Williston 1	Williston
13	n/a	Turtle Mountain Agency	Belcourt

Ohio

Ohio Public School Educational Profile

Category	Value	Category	Value
Schools *(2002-2003)*	3,973	**Diploma Recipients** *(2002-2003)*	110,608
Instructional Level		White, Non-Hispanic	95,036
Primary	2,218	Black, Non-Hispanic	11,945
Middle	758	Asian/Pacific Islander	1,568
High	778	American Indian/Alaskan Native	100
Other Level	219	Hispanic	1,441
Curriculum		**High School Drop-out Rate** (%) *(2000-2001)*	3.9
Regular	3,809	White, Non-Hispanic	3.0
Special Education	59	Black, Non-Hispanic	9.2
Vocational	90	Asian/Pacific Islander	2.4
Alternative	15	American Indian/Alaskan Native	7.6
Type		Hispanic	8.9
Magnet	0	**Staff** *(2002-2003)*	242,370.0
Charter	134	Teachers	125,371.0
Title I Eligible	2,615	Average Salary ($)	45,515
School-wide Title I	1,004	Librarians/Media Specialists	1,615.3
Students *(2002-2003)*	1,838,628	Guidance Counselors	3,586.3
Gender (%)		**Ratios** *(2002-2003)*	
Male	51.5	Student/Teacher Ratio	14.7 to 1
Female	48.5	Student/Librarian Ratio	1,138.3 to 1
Race/Ethnicity (%)		Student/Counselor Ratio	512.7 to 1
White, Non-Hispanic	78.4	**Current Spending** *($ per student in FY 2001)*	8,069
Black, Non-Hispanic	16.6	Instruction	4,683
Asian/Pacific Islander	1.2	Support Services	3,109
American Indian/Alaskan Native	0.1	**College Entrance Exam Scores** *(2003)*	
Hispanic	2.0	Scholastic Aptitude Test (SAT)	
Classification (%)		Participation Rate (%)	28
Individual Education Program (IEP)	13.6	Mean SAT I Verbal Score	536
Migrant	0.1	Mean SAT I Math Score	541
English Language Learner (ELL)	1.4	American College Testing Program (ACT)	
Eligible for Free Lunch Program	23.7	Participation Rate (%)	64
Eligible for Reduced-Price Lunch Program	5.6	Average Composite Score	21.4

Note: *For an explanation of data, please refer to the User's Guide in the front of the book; n/a indicates data not available*

Ohio NAEP 2003 Test Scores

Reading			Mathematics		
Grade/Category	Value	Rank	Grade/Category	Value	Rank
4th Grade			**4th Grade**		
Average Proficiency	221.9 (1.2)	17/51	Average Proficiency	237.8 (1.0)	14/51
Proficiency by Gender/Race/Ethnicity			Proficiency by Gender/Race/Ethnicity		
Male	218.0 (1.5)	16/51	Male	238.6 (1.3)	18/51
Female	225.7 (1.3)	17/51	Female	236.9 (1.0)	12/51
White, Non-Hispanic	226.5 (1.3)	20/51	White, Non-Hispanic	243.0 (1.1)	21/51
Black, Non-Hispanic	201.7 (2.4)	16/42	Black, Non-Hispanic	216.5 (1.7)	19/42
Asian, Non-Hispanic	207.1 (5.7)	13/41	Asian, Non-Hispanic	*224.6 (4.3)*	14/43
American Indian, Non-Hispanic	n/a	n/a	American Indian, Non-Hispanic	n/a	n/a
Hispanic	n/a	n/a	Hispanic	n/a	n/a
Proficiency by Class Size			Proficiency by Class Size		
Less than 16 Students	*207.1 (6.2)*	18/45	Less than 16 Students	*227.4 (5.1)*	16/47
16 to 18 Students	217.5 (3.7)	21/48	16 to 18 Students	*234.8 (2.9)*	22/48
19 to 20 Students	224.3 (4.1)	9/50	19 to 20 Students	235.8 (2.4)	20/50
21 to 25 Students	223.7 (1.8)	18/51	21 to 25 Students	240.0 (1.2)	15/51
Greater than 25 Students	*224.6 (4.4)*	10/49	Greater than 25 Students	*243.4 (3.6)*	5/49
Percent Attaining Achievement Levels			Percent Attaining Achievement Levels		
Below Basic	31.4 (1.3)	36/51	Below Basic	19.1 (1.4)	34/51
Basic or Above	68.6 (1.3)	15/51	Basic or Above	80.9 (1.4)	18/51
Proficient or Above	34.2 (1.3)	12/51	Proficient or Above	35.7 (1.7)	12/51
Advanced or Above	8.1 (0.8)	11/51	Advanced or Above	3.7 (0.5)	21/51
8th Grade			**8th Grade**		
Average Proficiency	266.6 (1.3)	16/51	Average Proficiency	281.6 (1.3)	17/51
Proficiency by Gender/Race/Ethnicity			Proficiency by Gender/Race/Ethnicity		
Male	263.1 (1.4)	11/51	Male	282.6 (1.5)	17/51
Female	269.8 (1.5)	25/51	Female	280.6 (1.4)	17/51
White, Non-Hispanic	270.8 (1.3)	20/50	White, Non-Hispanic	287.0 (1.2)	21/50
Black, Non-Hispanic	248.9 (1.6)	5/41	Black, Non-Hispanic	257.1 (2.1)	10/41
Asian, Non-Hispanic	*268.0 (5.1)*	1/37	Asian, Non-Hispanic	270.0 (5.5)	1/37
American Indian, Non-Hispanic	n/a	n/a	American Indian, Non-Hispanic	n/a	n/a
Hispanic	n/a	n/a	Hispanic	n/a	n/a
Proficiency by Parents Highest Level of Ed.			Proficiency by Parents Highest Level of Ed.		
Did Not Finish High School	243.8 (4.4)	35/50	Did Not Finish High School	260.0 (2.2)	17/50
Graduated High School	258.4 (1.7)	15/50	Graduated High School	275.7 (1.3)	9/50
Some Education After High School	268.5 (1.5)	22/50	Some Education After High School	281.3 (2.1)	23/50
Graduated College	275.9 (1.7)	9/50	Graduated College	290.9 (1.8)	20/50
Percent Attaining Achievement Levels			Percent Attaining Achievement Levels		
Below Basic	22.0 (1.4)	38/51	Below Basic	26.1 (1.5)	38/51
Basic or Above	78.0 (1.4)	14/51	Basic or Above	73.9 (1.5)	14/51
Proficient or Above	34.0 (1.8)	20/51	Proficient or Above	30.4 (1.8)	23/51
Advanced or Above	3.0 (0.5)	15/51	Advanced or Above	5.0 (0.8)	24/51

Note: *For an explanation of data, please refer to the User's Guide in the front of the book; values in italics indicate that the nature of the sample does not allow accurate determination of the variability of the statistic; n/a indicates data not available*

Adams County

Adams County-Ohio Valley Local SD

141 Lloyd Rd • West Union, OH 45693-8974
(937) 544-5586 • http://www.ohiovalley.k12.oh.us/
Grade Span: PK-12; **Agency Type:** 2
Schools: 10
4 Primary; 0 Middle; 5 High; 1 Other Level
8 Regular; 1 Special Education; 1 Vocational; 0 Alternative
0 Magnet; 0 Charter; 7 Title I Eligible; 4 School-wide Title I
Students: 5,016 (50.3% male; 49.7% female)
Individual Education Program: 764 (15.2%);
English Language Learner: 0 (0.0%); Migrant: n/a
Eligible for Free Lunch Program: 1,835 (36.6%)
Eligible for Reduced-Price Lunch Program: 487 (9.7%)
Teachers: 345.8 (14.5 to 1)
Librarians/Media Specialists: 4.0 (1,254.0 to 1)
Guidance Counselors: 9.0 (557.3 to 1)
Current Spending: ($ per student per year):
Total: $6,364; Instruction: $3,728; Support Services: $2,308
Enrollment, Drop-out Rates and Diploma Recipients by Race/Ethnicity

Category	Total	White	Black	Asian	AIAN	Hisp.
Enrollment (%)	100.0	98.7	0.3	0.1	0.1	0.5
Drop-out Rate (%)	3.8	3.7	n/a	0.0	0.0	16.7
H.S. Diplomas (#)	306	304	1	0	1	0

Allen County

Bath Local SD

2650 Bible Rd • Lima, OH 45801-2246
(419) 221-0807 • http://www.noacsc.org/allen/ba/
Grade Span: PK-12; **Agency Type:** 2
Schools: 3
1 Primary; 1 Middle; 1 High; 0 Other Level
3 Regular; 0 Special Education; 0 Vocational; 0 Alternative
0 Magnet; 0 Charter; 3 Title I Eligible; 0 School-wide Title I
Students: 2,030 (50.4% male; 49.6% female)
Individual Education Program: 210 (10.3%);
English Language Learner: 0 (0.0%); Migrant: n/a
Eligible for Free Lunch Program: 310 (15.3%)
Eligible for Reduced-Price Lunch Program: 146 (7.2%)
Teachers: 108.4 (18.7 to 1)
Librarians/Media Specialists: 2.0 (1,015.0 to 1)
Guidance Counselors: 4.0 (507.5 to 1)
Current Spending: ($ per student per year):
Total: $5,871; Instruction: $3,361; Support Services: $2,188
Enrollment, Drop-out Rates and Diploma Recipients by Race/Ethnicity

Category	Total	White	Black	Asian	AIAN	Hisp.
Enrollment (%)	100.0	94.0	3.0	1.2	0.0	1.1
Drop-out Rate (%)	2.4	2.4	5.9	0.0	0.0	0.0
H.S. Diplomas (#)	152	145	1	2	1	3

Elida Local SD

4380 Sunnydale St • Elida, OH 45807-9593
(419) 331-4155 • http://www.noacsc.org/allen/el/
Grade Span: PK-12; **Agency Type:** 2
Schools: 4
2 Primary; 1 Middle; 1 High; 0 Other Level
4 Regular; 0 Special Education; 0 Vocational; 0 Alternative
0 Magnet; 0 Charter; 3 Title I Eligible; 1 School-wide Title I
Students: 2,580 (51.4% male; 48.6% female)
Individual Education Program: 286 (11.1%);
English Language Learner: 11 (0.4%); Migrant: n/a
Eligible for Free Lunch Program: 475 (18.4%)
Eligible for Reduced-Price Lunch Program: 145 (5.6%)
Teachers: 143.0 (18.0 to 1)
Librarians/Media Specialists: 1.0 (2,580.0 to 1)
Guidance Counselors: 5.0 (516.0 to 1)
Current Spending: ($ per student per year):
Total: $5,774; Instruction: $3,547; Support Services: $1,915
Enrollment, Drop-out Rates and Diploma Recipients by Race/Ethnicity

Category	Total	White	Black	Asian	AIAN	Hisp.
Enrollment (%)	100.0	83.8	10.0	1.6	0.2	1.2
Drop-out Rate (%)	3.1	3.0	4.6	0.0	0.0	0.0
H.S. Diplomas (#)	187	168	14	2	0	1

Lima City SD

515 Calumet Ave • Lima, OH 45804-1405
(419) 998-2400 • http://www.limacityschools.org/
Grade Span: PK-12; **Agency Type:** 1
Schools: 12
7 Primary; 3 Middle; 2 High; 0 Other Level
11 Regular; 1 Special Education; 0 Vocational; 0 Alternative
0 Magnet; 0 Charter; 12 Title I Eligible; 10 School-wide Title I
Students: 5,253 (51.9% male; 48.1% female)
Individual Education Program: 1,075 (20.5%);
English Language Learner: 3 (0.1%); Migrant: n/a
Eligible for Free Lunch Program: 3,170 (60.3%)
Eligible for Reduced-Price Lunch Program: 336 (6.4%)
Teachers: 405.3 (13.0 to 1)
Librarians/Media Specialists: 3.0 (1,751.0 to 1)
Guidance Counselors: 8.6 (610.8 to 1)
Current Spending: ($ per student per year):
Total: $7,199; Instruction: $4,297; Support Services: $2,508
Enrollment, Drop-out Rates and Diploma Recipients by Race/Ethnicity

Category	Total	White	Black	Asian	AIAN	Hisp.
Enrollment (%)	100.0	48.5	42.6	0.1	0.2	1.1
Drop-out Rate (%)	12.4	11.2	13.4	0.0	n/a	31.6
H.S. Diplomas (#)	244	128	111	0	0	0

Shawnee Local SD

3255 Zurmehly Rd • Lima, OH 45806-1434
(419) 998-8031 • http://shawnee.noacsc.org/
Grade Span: PK-12; **Agency Type:** 2
Schools: 4
2 Primary; 1 Middle; 1 High; 0 Other Level
4 Regular; 0 Special Education; 0 Vocational; 0 Alternative
0 Magnet; 0 Charter; 3 Title I Eligible; 0 School-wide Title I
Students: 2,631 (51.3% male; 48.7% female)
Individual Education Program: 233 (8.9%);
English Language Learner: 0 (0.0%); Migrant: n/a
Eligible for Free Lunch Program: 254 (9.7%)
Eligible for Reduced-Price Lunch Program: 138 (5.2%)
Teachers: 137.3 (19.2 to 1)
Librarians/Media Specialists: 1.0 (2,631.0 to 1)
Guidance Counselors: 8.6 (305.9 to 1)
Current Spending: ($ per student per year):
Total: $6,199; Instruction: $3,332; Support Services: $2,595
Enrollment, Drop-out Rates and Diploma Recipients by Race/Ethnicity

Category	Total	White	Black	Asian	AIAN	Hisp.
Enrollment (%)	100.0	86.7	7.3	1.9	0.2	1.6
Drop-out Rate (%)	1.4	1.2	2.6	0.0	n/a	7.1
H.S. Diplomas (#)	171	146	16	5	0	2

Ashland County

Ashland City SD

PO Box 160 • Ashland, OH 44805-0160
(419) 289-1117 • http://www.ashland-city.k12.oh.us/index.asp
Grade Span: PK-12; **Agency Type:** 1
Schools: 8
5 Primary; 1 Middle; 2 High; 0 Other Level
8 Regular; 0 Special Education; 0 Vocational; 0 Alternative
0 Magnet; 0 Charter; 4 Title I Eligible; 2 School-wide Title I
Students: 3,846 (52.1% male; 47.9% female)
Individual Education Program: 571 (14.8%);
English Language Learner: 6 (0.2%); Migrant: n/a
Eligible for Free Lunch Program: 684 (17.8%)
Eligible for Reduced-Price Lunch Program: 264 (6.9%)
Teachers: 230.8 (16.7 to 1)
Librarians/Media Specialists: 3.0 (1,282.0 to 1)
Guidance Counselors: 7.0 (549.4 to 1)
Current Spending: ($ per student per year):
Total: $6,543; Instruction: $4,123; Support Services: $2,153
Enrollment, Drop-out Rates and Diploma Recipients by Race/Ethnicity

Category	Total	White	Black	Asian	AIAN	Hisp.
Enrollment (%)	100.0	95.6	1.3	0.9	0.2	0.7
Drop-out Rate (%)	2.0	2.0	5.9	0.0	0.0	0.0
H.S. Diplomas (#)	288	278	3	5	0	2

Ashtabula County

Ashtabula Area City SD

PO Box 290 • Ashtabula, OH 44005-0290
(440) 993-2500 • http://aacs.net/
Grade Span: KG-12; **Agency Type:** 1
Schools: 12
8 Primary; 2 Middle; 1 High; 1 Other Level
12 Regular; 0 Special Education; 0 Vocational; 0 Alternative
0 Magnet; 0 Charter; 11 Title I Eligible; 7 School-wide Title I
Students: 4,785 (51.9% male; 48.1% female)
Individual Education Program: 816 (17.1%);
English Language Learner: 137 (2.9%); Migrant: n/a
Eligible for Free Lunch Program: 1,875 (39.2%)
Eligible for Reduced-Price Lunch Program: 365 (7.6%)
Teachers: 335.0 (14.3 to 1)
Librarians/Media Specialists: 1.0 (4,785.0 to 1)
Guidance Counselors: 6.0 (797.5 to 1)
Current Spending: ($ per student per year):
Total: $6,936; Instruction: $4,375; Support Services: $2,269

Enrollment, Drop-out Rates and Diploma Recipients by Race/Ethnicity

Category	Total	White	Black	Asian	AIAN	Hisp.
Enrollment (%)	100.0	76.5	11.3	0.5	0.1	7.0
Drop-out Rate (%)	6.7	6.1	7.9	0.0	0.0	13.3
H.S. Diplomas (#)	240	190	40	1	0	8

Buckeye Local SD

3436 Edgewood Dr • Ashtabula, OH 44004-5967
(440) 998-4411
Grade Span: PK-12; **Agency Type:** 2
Schools: 6
4 Primary; 1 Middle; 1 High; 0 Other Level
6 Regular; 0 Special Education; 0 Vocational; 0 Alternative
0 Magnet; 0 Charter; 4 Title I Eligible; 3 School-wide Title I
Students: 2,270 (49.3% male; 50.7% female)
Individual Education Program: 214 (9.4%);
English Language Learner: 5 (0.2%); Migrant: n/a
Eligible for Free Lunch Program: 486 (21.4%)
Eligible for Reduced-Price Lunch Program: 228 (10.0%)
Teachers: 140.0 (16.2 to 1)
Librarians/Media Specialists: 1.0 (2,270.0 to 1)
Guidance Counselors: 3.0 (756.7 to 1)
Current Spending: ($ per student per year):
Total: $6,830; Instruction: $4,267; Support Services: $2,247

Enrollment, Drop-out Rates and Diploma Recipients by Race/Ethnicity

Category	Total	White	Black	Asian	AIAN	Hisp.
Enrollment (%)	100.0	96.6	1.5	0.5	0.1	0.3
Drop-out Rate (%)	3.9	4.0	0.0	0.0	n/a	0.0
H.S. Diplomas (#)	160	155	2	1	0	1

Conneaut Area City SD

263 Liberty St • Conneaut, OH 44030-2705
(440) 593-7200
Grade Span: PK-12; **Agency Type:** 1
Schools: 6
4 Primary; 1 Middle; 1 High; 0 Other Level
6 Regular; 0 Special Education; 0 Vocational; 0 Alternative
0 Magnet; 0 Charter; 5 Title I Eligible; 4 School-wide Title I
Students: 2,547 (52.7% male; 47.3% female)
Individual Education Program: 398 (15.6%);
English Language Learner: 0 (0.0%); Migrant: n/a
Eligible for Free Lunch Program: 925 (36.3%)
Eligible for Reduced-Price Lunch Program: 245 (9.6%)
Teachers: 150.5 (16.9 to 1)
Librarians/Media Specialists: 1.0 (2,547.0 to 1)
Guidance Counselors: 4.0 (636.8 to 1)
Current Spending: ($ per student per year):
Total: $5,850; Instruction: $3,629; Support Services: $1,998

Enrollment, Drop-out Rates and Diploma Recipients by Race/Ethnicity

Category	Total	White	Black	Asian	AIAN	Hisp.
Enrollment (%)	100.0	96.8	1.4	0.4	0.1	0.4
Drop-out Rate (%)	2.7	2.6	0.0	0.0	n/a	100.0
H.S. Diplomas (#)	162	158	3	0	0	0

Geneva Area City SD

135 S Eagle St • Geneva, OH 44041-1513
(440) 466-4831
Grade Span: PK-12; **Agency Type:** 1
Schools: 7
4 Primary; 2 Middle; 1 High; 0 Other Level
7 Regular; 0 Special Education; 0 Vocational; 0 Alternative
0 Magnet; 0 Charter; 4 Title I Eligible; 0 School-wide Title I
Students: 3,060 (52.9% male; 47.1% female)
Individual Education Program: 421 (13.8%);
English Language Learner: 24 (0.8%); Migrant: 1 (<0.1%)
Eligible for Free Lunch Program: 744 (24.3%)
Eligible for Reduced-Price Lunch Program: 321 (10.5%)
Teachers: 161.4 (19.0 to 1)
Librarians/Media Specialists: 0.9 (3,400.0 to 1)
Guidance Counselors: 6.0 (510.0 to 1)
Current Spending: ($ per student per year):
Total: $5,529; Instruction: $3,467; Support Services: $1,758

Enrollment, Drop-out Rates and Diploma Recipients by Race/Ethnicity

Category	Total	White	Black	Asian	AIAN	Hisp.
Enrollment (%)	100.0	94.1	0.7	0.1	0.0	4.7
Drop-out Rate (%)	2.7	2.8	0.0	0.0	n/a	2.9
H.S. Diplomas (#)	224	213	3	0	0	8

Jefferson Area Local SD

45 E Satin St • Jefferson, OH 44047-1416
(440) 576-9180 • http://www.west-jefferson.k12.oh.us/
Grade Span: PK-12; **Agency Type:** 2
Schools: 3
2 Primary; 0 Middle; 1 High; 0 Other Level
3 Regular; 0 Special Education; 0 Vocational; 0 Alternative
0 Magnet; 0 Charter; 2 Title I Eligible; 1 School-wide Title I
Students: 2,180 (51.7% male; 48.3% female)
Individual Education Program: 258 (11.8%);
English Language Learner: 3 (0.1%); Migrant: n/a
Eligible for Free Lunch Program: 371 (17.0%)
Eligible for Reduced-Price Lunch Program: 152 (7.0%)
Teachers: 122.6 (17.8 to 1)
Librarians/Media Specialists: 1.0 (2,180.0 to 1)
Guidance Counselors: 3.0 (726.7 to 1)
Current Spending: ($ per student per year):
Total: $5,645; Instruction: $3,281; Support Services: $2,092

Enrollment, Drop-out Rates and Diploma Recipients by Race/Ethnicity

Category	Total	White	Black	Asian	AIAN	Hisp.
Enrollment (%)	100.0	95.8	2.2	0.2	0.0	0.4
Drop-out Rate (%)	2.1	2.2	0.0	0.0	0.0	0.0
H.S. Diplomas (#)	139	138	1	0	0	0

Athens County

Alexander Local SD

6091 Ayers Rd • Albany, OH 45710-9492
(740) 698-8831
Grade Span: PK-12; **Agency Type:** 2
Schools: 4
1 Primary; 2 Middle; 1 High; 0 Other Level
4 Regular; 0 Special Education; 0 Vocational; 0 Alternative
0 Magnet; 0 Charter; 3 Title I Eligible; 2 School-wide Title I
Students: 1,652 (50.5% male; 49.5% female)
Individual Education Program: 326 (19.7%);
English Language Learner: 1 (0.1%); Migrant: n/a
Eligible for Free Lunch Program: 356 (21.5%)
Eligible for Reduced-Price Lunch Program: 110 (6.7%)
Teachers: 116.8 (14.1 to 1)
Librarians/Media Specialists: 1.0 (1,652.0 to 1)
Guidance Counselors: 3.0 (550.7 to 1)
Current Spending: ($ per student per year):
Total: $5,879; Instruction: $3,660; Support Services: $1,990

Enrollment, Drop-out Rates and Diploma Recipients by Race/Ethnicity

Category	Total	White	Black	Asian	AIAN	Hisp.
Enrollment (%)	100.0	98.3	0.7	0.1	0.1	0.2
Drop-out Rate (%)	4.0	4.1	0.0	0.0	0.0	0.0
H.S. Diplomas (#)	120	118	0	1	1	0

Athens City SD

25 S Plains Rd • The Plains, OH 45780-1333
(740) 797-4516
Grade Span: PK-12; **Agency Type:** 1
Schools: 7
5 Primary; 1 Middle; 1 High; 0 Other Level
7 Regular; 0 Special Education; 0 Vocational; 0 Alternative
0 Magnet; 0 Charter; 3 Title I Eligible; 3 School-wide Title I
Students: 2,955 (51.5% male; 48.5% female)
Individual Education Program: 397 (13.4%);
English Language Learner: 90 (3.0%); Migrant: n/a
Eligible for Free Lunch Program: 784 (26.5%)
Eligible for Reduced-Price Lunch Program: 164 (5.5%)
Teachers: 230.8 (12.8 to 1)
Librarians/Media Specialists: 1.0 (2,955.0 to 1)
Guidance Counselors: 5.0 (591.0 to 1)
Current Spending: ($ per student per year):
Total: $7,051; Instruction: $4,258; Support Services: $2,567

Enrollment, Drop-out Rates and Diploma Recipients by Race/Ethnicity

Category	Total	White	Black	Asian	AIAN	Hisp.
Enrollment (%)	100.0	89.3	2.4	4.9	0.3	1.0
Drop-out Rate (%)	4.5	4.8	0.0	0.0	0.0	0.0
H.S. Diplomas (#)	87	81	2	3	0	0

Auglaize County

Saint Marys City SD

101 W S St • Saint Marys, OH 45885-2523
(419) 394-4312
Grade Span: PK-12; **Agency Type:** 1
Schools: 6
3 Primary; 1 Middle; 1 High; 1 Other Level
6 Regular; 0 Special Education; 0 Vocational; 0 Alternative
0 Magnet; 0 Charter; 3 Title I Eligible; 0 School-wide Title I
Students: 2,614 (55.3% male; 44.7% female)
Individual Education Program: 446 (17.1%);
English Language Learner: 14 (0.5%); Migrant: n/a
Eligible for Free Lunch Program: 341 (13.0%)
Eligible for Reduced-Price Lunch Program: 149 (5.7%)
Teachers: 151.8 (17.2 to 1)
Librarians/Media Specialists: 3.0 (871.3 to 1)
Guidance Counselors: 5.0 (522.8 to 1)

Current Spending: ($ per student per year):
Total: $5,616; Instruction: $3,467; Support Services: $1,947
Enrollment, Drop-out Rates and Diploma Recipients by Race/Ethnicity

Category	Total	White	Black	Asian	AIAN	Hisp.
Enrollment (%)	100.0	97.2	0.2	0.9	0.0	0.4
Drop-out Rate (%)	0.5	0.5	0.0	0.0	0.0	0.0
H.S. Diplomas (#)	193	189	0	2	0	0

Wapakoneta City SD
1102 Gardenia Dr • Wapakoneta, OH 45895-1063
(419) 739-2900 • http://www.noacsc.org/auglaize/wk/
Grade Span: PK-12; **Agency Type:** 1
Schools: 6
3 Primary; 2 Middle; 1 High; 0 Other Level
6 Regular; 0 Special Education; 0 Vocational; 0 Alternative
0 Magnet; 0 Charter; 4 Title I Eligible; 0 School-wide Title I
Students: 3,180 (50.9% male; 49.1% female)
Individual Education Program: 482 (15.2%);
English Language Learner: 3 (0.1%); Migrant: n/a
Eligible for Free Lunch Program: 477 (15.0%)
Eligible for Reduced-Price Lunch Program: 199 (6.3%)
Teachers: 167.2 (19.0 to 1)
Librarians/Media Specialists: 1.0 (3,180.0 to 1)
Guidance Counselors: 6.5 (489.2 to 1)
Current Spending: ($ per student per year):
Total: $5,509; Instruction: $3,011; Support Services: $2,217
Enrollment, Drop-out Rates and Diploma Recipients by Race/Ethnicity

Category	Total	White	Black	Asian	AIAN	Hisp.
Enrollment (%)	100.0	98.2	0.2	0.2	0.1	0.8
Drop-out Rate (%)	2.3	2.2	0.0	0.0	n/a	8.3
H.S. Diplomas (#)	231	228	0	2	0	1

Belmont County

Bellaire Local SD
340 34th St • Bellaire, OH 43906-1589
(740) 676-1826
Grade Span: PK-12; **Agency Type:** 2
Schools: 3
1 Primary; 1 Middle; 1 High; 0 Other Level
3 Regular; 0 Special Education; 0 Vocational; 0 Alternative
0 Magnet; 0 Charter; 2 Title I Eligible; 2 School-wide Title I
Students: 1,592 (52.7% male; 47.3% female)
Individual Education Program: 337 (21.2%);
English Language Learner: 0 (0.0%); Migrant: n/a
Eligible for Free Lunch Program: 682 (42.8%)
Eligible for Reduced-Price Lunch Program: 119 (7.5%)
Teachers: 109.6 (14.5 to 1)
Librarians/Media Specialists: 1.0 (1,592.0 to 1)
Guidance Counselors: 3.0 (530.7 to 1)
Current Spending: ($ per student per year):
Total: $6,896; Instruction: $4,142; Support Services: $2,434
Enrollment, Drop-out Rates and Diploma Recipients by Race/Ethnicity

Category	Total	White	Black	Asian	AIAN	Hisp.
Enrollment (%)	100.0	93.0	4.6	0.1	0.0	0.1
Drop-out Rate (%)	4.2	3.8	9.7	n/a	n/a	0.0
H.S. Diplomas (#)	110	105	4	0	0	1

Saint Clairsville-Richland City
108 Woodrow Ave • Saint Clairsville, OH 43950-1567
(740) 695-1624
Grade Span: PK-12; **Agency Type:** 1
Schools: 3
1 Primary; 1 Middle; 1 High; 0 Other Level
3 Regular; 0 Special Education; 0 Vocational; 0 Alternative
0 Magnet; 0 Charter; 1 Title I Eligible; 0 School-wide Title I
Students: 1,612 (52.3% male; 47.7% female)
Individual Education Program: 192 (11.9%);
English Language Learner: 2 (0.1%); Migrant: n/a
Eligible for Free Lunch Program: 207 (12.8%)
Eligible for Reduced-Price Lunch Program: 64 (4.0%)
Teachers: 104.0 (15.5 to 1)
Librarians/Media Specialists: 1.0 (1,612.0 to 1)
Guidance Counselors: 3.0 (537.3 to 1)
Current Spending: ($ per student per year):
Total: $5,858; Instruction: $3,705; Support Services: $1,941
Enrollment, Drop-out Rates and Diploma Recipients by Race/Ethnicity

Category	Total	White	Black	Asian	AIAN	Hisp.
Enrollment (%)	100.0	96.8	2.2	0.4	0.0	0.3
Drop-out Rate (%)	2.4	2.3	7.1	0.0	n/a	n/a
H.S. Diplomas (#)	120	111	3	3	0	1

Union Local SD
PO Box 300 • Morristown, OH 43759-0300
(740) 695-5776
Grade Span: PK-12; **Agency Type:** 2
Schools: 3
1 Primary; 1 Middle; 1 High; 0 Other Level
3 Regular; 0 Special Education; 0 Vocational; 0 Alternative
0 Magnet; 0 Charter; 2 Title I Eligible; 0 School-wide Title I
Students: 1,530 (53.9% male; 46.1% female)
Individual Education Program: 208 (13.6%);
English Language Learner: 0 (0.0%); Migrant: n/a
Eligible for Free Lunch Program: 483 (31.6%)
Eligible for Reduced-Price Lunch Program: 107 (7.0%)
Teachers: 121.5 (12.6 to 1)
Librarians/Media Specialists: 2.0 (765.0 to 1)
Guidance Counselors: 3.0 (510.0 to 1)
Current Spending: ($ per student per year):
Total: $6,573; Instruction: $4,099; Support Services: $2,165
Enrollment, Drop-out Rates and Diploma Recipients by Race/Ethnicity

Category	Total	White	Black	Asian	AIAN	Hisp.
Enrollment (%)	100.0	98.6	0.3	0.1	0.0	0.0
Drop-out Rate (%)	2.2	2.2	0.0	n/a	0.0	n/a
H.S. Diplomas (#)	149	148	0	0	0	0

Brown County

Eastern Local SD
PO Box 500 • Sardinia, OH 45171-0500
(937) 378-3981
Grade Span: PK-12; **Agency Type:** 2
Schools: 4
2 Primary; 1 Middle; 1 High; 0 Other Level
4 Regular; 0 Special Education; 0 Vocational; 0 Alternative
0 Magnet; 0 Charter; 2 Title I Eligible; 2 School-wide Title I
Students: 1,582 (50.3% male; 49.7% female)
Individual Education Program: 158 (10.0%);
English Language Learner: 0 (0.0%); Migrant: n/a
Eligible for Free Lunch Program: 313 (19.8%)
Eligible for Reduced-Price Lunch Program: 126 (8.0%)
Teachers: 97.1 (16.3 to 1)
Librarians/Media Specialists: 2.0 (791.0 to 1)
Guidance Counselors: 2.0 (791.0 to 1)
Current Spending: ($ per student per year):
Total: $6,524; Instruction: $3,678; Support Services: $2,577
Enrollment, Drop-out Rates and Diploma Recipients by Race/Ethnicity

Category	Total	White	Black	Asian	AIAN	Hisp.
Enrollment (%)	100.0	98.5	0.3	0.1	0.2	0.1
Drop-out Rate (%)	1.4	1.4	n/a	n/a	n/a	0.0
H.S. Diplomas (#)	95	93	0	1	0	0

Western Brown Local SD
PO Box 455 • Mount Orab, OH 45154-0455
(937) 444-2044
Grade Span: PK-12; **Agency Type:** 2
Schools: 4
2 Primary; 1 Middle; 1 High; 0 Other Level
4 Regular; 0 Special Education; 0 Vocational; 0 Alternative
0 Magnet; 0 Charter; 2 Title I Eligible; 0 School-wide Title I
Students: 3,380 (51.9% male; 48.1% female)
Individual Education Program: 320 (9.5%);
English Language Learner: 0 (0.0%); Migrant: n/a
Eligible for Free Lunch Program: 652 (19.3%)
Eligible for Reduced-Price Lunch Program: 257 (7.6%)
Teachers: 192.3 (17.6 to 1)
Librarians/Media Specialists: 4.1 (824.4 to 1)
Guidance Counselors: 7.4 (456.8 to 1)
Current Spending: ($ per student per year):
Total: $5,021; Instruction: $3,002; Support Services: $1,775
Enrollment, Drop-out Rates and Diploma Recipients by Race/Ethnicity

Category	Total	White	Black	Asian	AIAN	Hisp.
Enrollment (%)	100.0	99.4	0.3	0.1	0.0	0.1
Drop-out Rate (%)	6.9	6.9	0.0	0.0	n/a	n/a
H.S. Diplomas (#)	143	142	1	0	0	0

Butler County

Edgewood City SD
3500 Busenbark Rd • Trenton, OH 45067-9566
(513) 863-4692
Grade Span: PK-12; **Agency Type:** 1
Schools: 6
4 Primary; 1 Middle; 1 High; 0 Other Level
6 Regular; 0 Special Education; 0 Vocational; 0 Alternative
0 Magnet; 0 Charter; 4 Title I Eligible; 0 School-wide Title I
Students: 3,364 (52.9% male; 47.1% female)

Individual Education Program: 546 (16.2%);
English Language Learner: 3 (0.1%); Migrant: n/a
Eligible for Free Lunch Program: 342 (10.2%)
Eligible for Reduced-Price Lunch Program: 152 (4.5%)

Teachers: 220.2 (15.3 to 1)
Librarians/Media Specialists: 7.0 (480.6 to 1)
Guidance Counselors: 10.0 (336.4 to 1)
Current Spending: ($ per student per year):
Total: $6,100; Instruction: $3,629; Support Services: $2,176

Enrollment, Drop-out Rates and Diploma Recipients by Race/Ethnicity

Category	Total	White	Black	Asian	AIAN	Hisp.
Enrollment (%)	100.0	98.5	0.7	0.1	0.0	0.2
Drop-out Rate (%)	2.8	2.8	0.0	0.0	n/a	0.0
H.S. Diplomas (#)	182	180	0	1	0	0

Fairfield City SD

211 Donald Dr • Fairfield, OH 45014-3006
(513) 829-6300
Grade Span: PK-12; **Agency Type:** 1
Schools: 10
6 Primary; 2 Middle; 2 High; 0 Other Level
10 Regular; 0 Special Education; 0 Vocational; 0 Alternative
0 Magnet; 0 Charter; 5 Title I Eligible; 0 School-wide Title I
Students: 9,395 (50.5% male; 49.5% female)
Individual Education Program: 1,058 (11.3%);
English Language Learner: 175 (1.9%); Migrant: n/a
Eligible for Free Lunch Program: 649 (6.9%)
Eligible for Reduced-Price Lunch Program: 286 (3.0%)
Teachers: 514.1 (18.3 to 1)
Librarians/Media Specialists: 7.0 (1,342.1 to 1)
Guidance Counselors: 11.3 (831.4 to 1)
Current Spending: ($ per student per year):
Total: $6,384; Instruction: $3,761; Support Services: $2,394

Enrollment, Drop-out Rates and Diploma Recipients by Race/Ethnicity

Category	Total	White	Black	Asian	AIAN	Hisp.
Enrollment (%)	100.0	86.2	7.6	1.9	0.1	1.8
Drop-out Rate (%)	3.0	3.2	2.0	0.0	0.0	3.4
H.S. Diplomas (#)	608	550	33	15	2	6

Hamilton City SD

PO Box 627 • Hamilton, OH 45012-0627
(513) 887-5000
Grade Span: PK-12; **Agency Type:** 1
Schools: 19
14 Primary; 2 Middle; 1 High; 1 Other Level
18 Regular; 0 Special Education; 0 Vocational; 0 Alternative
0 Magnet; 0 Charter; 14 Title I Eligible; 9 School-wide Title I
Students: 9,426 (51.9% male; 48.1% female)
Individual Education Program: 1,709 (18.1%);
English Language Learner: 199 (2.1%); Migrant: 29 (0.3%)
Eligible for Free Lunch Program: 3,820 (40.5%)
Eligible for Reduced-Price Lunch Program: 707 (7.5%)
Teachers: 563.3 (16.7 to 1)
Librarians/Media Specialists: 4.0 (2,356.5 to 1)
Guidance Counselors: 25.0 (377.0 to 1)
Current Spending: ($ per student per year):
Total: $6,685; Instruction: $3,979; Support Services: $2,393

Enrollment, Drop-out Rates and Diploma Recipients by Race/Ethnicity

Category	Total	White	Black	Asian	AIAN	Hisp.
Enrollment (%)	100.0	83.7	10.4	0.5	0.0	3.7
Drop-out Rate (%)	7.5	7.2	9.5	9.1	0.0	18.8
H.S. Diplomas (#)	524	459	52	5	0	4

Lakota Local SD

5572 Princeton Rd • Liberty Township, OH 45011-9726
(513) 874-5505
Grade Span: PK-12; **Agency Type:** 2
Schools: 19
11 Primary; 3 Middle; 2 High; 1 Other Level
17 Regular; 0 Special Education; 0 Vocational; 0 Alternative
0 Magnet; 0 Charter; 0 Title I Eligible; 0 School-wide Title I
Students: 15,844 (51.8% male; 48.2% female)
Individual Education Program: 1,398 (8.8%);
English Language Learner: 178 (1.1%); Migrant: n/a
Eligible for Free Lunch Program: 689 (4.3%)
Eligible for Reduced-Price Lunch Program: 256 (1.6%)
Teachers: 903.6 (17.5 to 1)
Librarians/Media Specialists: 16.0 (990.3 to 1)
Guidance Counselors: 23.9 (662.9 to 1)
Current Spending: ($ per student per year):
Total: $6,225; Instruction: $3,637; Support Services: $2,387

Enrollment, Drop-out Rates and Diploma Recipients by Race/Ethnicity

Category	Total	White	Black	Asian	AIAN	Hisp.
Enrollment (%)	100.0	86.2	6.0	4.3	0.1	1.7
Drop-out Rate (%)	0.5	0.5	1.1	0.0	0.0	0.0
H.S. Diplomas (#)	963	864	36	54	0	8

Madison Local SD

1324 Middletown Eaton Rd • Middletown, OH 45042-1525
(513) 420-4750
Grade Span: PK-12; **Agency Type:** 2
Schools: 3
2 Primary; 0 Middle; 1 High; 0 Other Level
3 Regular; 0 Special Education; 0 Vocational; 0 Alternative
0 Magnet; 0 Charter; 2 Title I Eligible; 0 School-wide Title I
Students: 1,576 (51.4% male; 48.6% female)
Individual Education Program: 208 (13.2%);
English Language Learner: 0 (0.0%); Migrant: n/a
Eligible for Free Lunch Program: 159 (10.1%)
Eligible for Reduced-Price Lunch Program: 36 (2.3%)
Teachers: 97.1 (16.2 to 1)
Librarians/Media Specialists: 1.0 (1,576.0 to 1)
Guidance Counselors: 4.6 (342.6 to 1)
Current Spending: ($ per student per year):
Total: $6,104; Instruction: $3,522; Support Services: $2,310

Enrollment, Drop-out Rates and Diploma Recipients by Race/Ethnicity

Category	Total	White	Black	Asian	AIAN	Hisp.
Enrollment (%)	100.0	98.4	0.5	0.2	0.1	0.1
Drop-out Rate (%)	3.6	3.6	n/a	n/a	n/a	0.0
H.S. Diplomas (#)	95	94	0	0	0	0

Middletown City SD

1515 Girard Ave • Middletown, OH 45044-4364
(513) 423-0781 • http://www.middletowncityschools.com/
Grade Span: PK-12; **Agency Type:** 1
Schools: 15
11 Primary; 2 Middle; 2 High; 0 Other Level
14 Regular; 1 Special Education; 0 Vocational; 0 Alternative
0 Magnet; 0 Charter; 11 Title I Eligible; 8 School-wide Title I
Students: 7,629 (51.9% male; 48.1% female)
Individual Education Program: 1,369 (17.9%);
English Language Learner: 79 (1.0%); Migrant: n/a
Eligible for Free Lunch Program: 2,264 (29.7%)
Eligible for Reduced-Price Lunch Program: 540 (7.1%)
Teachers: 512.6 (14.9 to 1)
Librarians/Media Specialists: 3.0 (2,543.0 to 1)
Guidance Counselors: 10.6 (719.7 to 1)
Current Spending: ($ per student per year):
Total: $6,175; Instruction: $3,513; Support Services: $2,373

Enrollment, Drop-out Rates and Diploma Recipients by Race/Ethnicity

Category	Total	White	Black	Asian	AIAN	Hisp.
Enrollment (%)	100.0	78.0	17.0	0.5	0.1	1.9
Drop-out Rate (%)	4.6	4.1	6.6	0.0	50.0	0.0
H.S. Diplomas (#)	360	281	72	4	0	2

Ross Local SD

3371 Hamilton Cleves Rd • Hamilton, OH 45013-9535
(513) 863-1253 • http://www.rosd.k12.oh.us/
Grade Span: PK-12; **Agency Type:** 2
Schools: 4
2 Primary; 1 Middle; 1 High; 0 Other Level
4 Regular; 0 Special Education; 0 Vocational; 0 Alternative
0 Magnet; 0 Charter; 3 Title I Eligible; 0 School-wide Title I
Students: 2,544 (54.0% male; 46.0% female)
Individual Education Program: 328 (12.9%);
English Language Learner: 0 (0.0%); Migrant: n/a
Eligible for Free Lunch Program: 179 (7.0%)
Eligible for Reduced-Price Lunch Program: 83 (3.3%)
Teachers: 146.4 (17.4 to 1)
Librarians/Media Specialists: 2.0 (1,272.0 to 1)
Guidance Counselors: 6.0 (424.0 to 1)
Current Spending: ($ per student per year):
Total: $5,631; Instruction: $3,448; Support Services: $1,898

Enrollment, Drop-out Rates and Diploma Recipients by Race/Ethnicity

Category	Total	White	Black	Asian	AIAN	Hisp.
Enrollment (%)	100.0	98.8	0.1	0.1	0.2	0.2
Drop-out Rate (%)	4.5	4.5	0.0	0.0	n/a	n/a
H.S. Diplomas (#)	169	165	0	1	0	0

Talawanda City SD

131 W Chestnut St • Oxford, OH 45056-2619
(513) 523-4716 • http://www.talawanda.net/
Grade Span: PK-12; **Agency Type:** 1
Schools: 5
2 Primary; 2 Middle; 1 High; 0 Other Level
5 Regular; 0 Special Education; 0 Vocational; 0 Alternative

0 Magnet; 0 Charter; 3 Title I Eligible; 0 School-wide Title I
Students: 3,219 (51.2% male; 48.8% female)
Individual Education Program: 351 (10.9%);
English Language Learner: 13 (0.4%); Migrant: n/a
Eligible for Free Lunch Program: 399 (12.4%)
Eligible for Reduced-Price Lunch Program: 111 (3.4%)
Teachers: 228.3 (14.1 to 1)
Librarians/Media Specialists: 2.0 (1,609.5 to 1)
Guidance Counselors: 7.5 (429.2 to 1)
Current Spending: ($ per student per year):
Total: $6,093; Instruction: $3,447; Support Services: $2,416
Enrollment, Drop-out Rates and Diploma Recipients by Race/Ethnicity

Category	Total	White	Black	Asian	AIAN	Hisp.
Enrollment (%)	100.0	93.7	3.0	1.8	0.1	0.3
Drop-out Rate (%)	3.1	3.0	7.1	5.6	n/a	0.0
H.S. Diplomas (#)	260	246	7	5	0	2

Carroll County

Carrollton Ex Vill SD

252 3rd St NE • Carrollton, OH 44615-1236
(330) 627-2181
Grade Span: PK-12; **Agency Type:** 1
Schools: 9
6 Primary; 2 Middle; 1 High; 0 Other Level
9 Regular; 0 Special Education; 0 Vocational; 0 Alternative
0 Magnet; 0 Charter; 7 Title I Eligible; 7 School-wide Title I
Students: 2,997 (50.0% male; 50.0% female)
Individual Education Program: 423 (14.1%);
English Language Learner: 0 (0.0%); Migrant: n/a
Eligible for Free Lunch Program: 664 (22.2%)
Eligible for Reduced-Price Lunch Program: 283 (9.4%)
Teachers: 163.1 (18.4 to 1)
Librarians/Media Specialists: 1.0 (2,997.0 to 1)
Guidance Counselors: 3.0 (999.0 to 1)
Current Spending: ($ per student per year):
Total: $4,962; Instruction: $2,903; Support Services: $1,785
Enrollment, Drop-out Rates and Diploma Recipients by Race/Ethnicity

Category	Total	White	Black	Asian	AIAN	Hisp.
Enrollment (%)	100.0	98.7	0.2	0.1	0.3	0.4
Drop-out Rate (%)	0.9	1.0	0.0	0.0	n/a	0.0
H.S. Diplomas (#)	199	197	0	1	0	1

Champaign County

Graham Local SD

370 E Main St • Saint Paris, OH 43072-9200
(937) 663-4123 • http://www.graham.k12.oh.us/
Grade Span: PK-12; **Agency Type:** 2
Schools: 4
2 Primary; 1 Middle; 1 High; 0 Other Level
4 Regular; 0 Special Education; 0 Vocational; 0 Alternative
0 Magnet; 0 Charter; 3 Title I Eligible; 0 School-wide Title I
Students: 2,201 (50.9% male; 49.1% female)
Individual Education Program: 326 (14.8%);
English Language Learner: 0 (0.0%); Migrant: n/a
Eligible for Free Lunch Program: 231 (10.5%)
Eligible for Reduced-Price Lunch Program: 111 (5.0%)
Teachers: 133.1 (16.5 to 1)
Librarians/Media Specialists: 3.5 (628.9 to 1)
Guidance Counselors: 5.0 (440.2 to 1)
Current Spending: ($ per student per year):
Total: $5,925; Instruction: $3,527; Support Services: $2,154
Enrollment, Drop-out Rates and Diploma Recipients by Race/Ethnicity

Category	Total	White	Black	Asian	AIAN	Hisp.
Enrollment (%)	100.0	97.9	0.2	0.2	0.3	0.5
Drop-out Rate (%)	1.3	1.4	0.0	n/a	n/a	0.0
H.S. Diplomas (#)	132	131	0	0	0	1

Urbana City SD

711 Wood St • Urbana, OH 43078-1498
(937) 653-1402 • http://www.urbana.k12.oh.us/
Grade Span: PK-12; **Agency Type:** 1
Schools: 6
3 Primary; 2 Middle; 1 High; 0 Other Level
6 Regular; 0 Special Education; 0 Vocational; 0 Alternative
0 Magnet; 0 Charter; 4 Title I Eligible; 0 School-wide Title I
Students: 2,388 (51.9% male; 48.1% female)
Individual Education Program: 428 (17.9%);
English Language Learner: 2 (0.1%); Migrant: 2 (0.1%)
Eligible for Free Lunch Program: 478 (20.0%)
Eligible for Reduced-Price Lunch Program: 189 (7.9%)
Teachers: 143.2 (16.7 to 1)
Librarians/Media Specialists: 1.0 (2,388.0 to 1)
Guidance Counselors: 5.0 (477.6 to 1)
Current Spending: ($ per student per year):
Total: $6,273; Instruction: $3,748; Support Services: $2,292
Enrollment, Drop-out Rates and Diploma Recipients by Race/Ethnicity

Category	Total	White	Black	Asian	AIAN	Hisp.
Enrollment (%)	100.0	87.7	6.0	0.7	0.0	1.3
Drop-out Rate (%)	2.8	2.7	3.1	11.1	0.0	0.0
H.S. Diplomas (#)	118	107	7	1	0	3

Clark County

Clark-Shawnee Local SD

1561 E Possum Rd • Springfield, OH 45502-7946
(937) 328-5378
Grade Span: PK-12; **Agency Type:** 2
Schools: 5
4 Primary; 0 Middle; 1 High; 0 Other Level
5 Regular; 0 Special Education; 0 Vocational; 0 Alternative
0 Magnet; 0 Charter; 3 Title I Eligible; 0 School-wide Title I
Students: 2,463 (51.1% male; 48.9% female)
Individual Education Program: 198 (8.0%);
English Language Learner: 0 (0.0%); Migrant: n/a
Eligible for Free Lunch Program: 237 (9.6%)
Eligible for Reduced-Price Lunch Program: 71 (2.9%)
Teachers: 131.4 (18.7 to 1)
Librarians/Media Specialists: 1.0 (2,463.0 to 1)
Guidance Counselors: 5.0 (492.6 to 1)
Current Spending: ($ per student per year):
Total: $6,296; Instruction: $3,924; Support Services: $2,122
Enrollment, Drop-out Rates and Diploma Recipients by Race/Ethnicity

Category	Total	White	Black	Asian	AIAN	Hisp.
Enrollment (%)	100.0	94.0	3.1	0.5	0.1	0.6
Drop-out Rate (%)	2.7	2.3	17.4	0.0	n/a	0.0
H.S. Diplomas (#)	203	201	1	1	0	0

Greenon Local SD

1215 Old Mill Rd • Springfield, OH 45506-4319
(937) 328-5351
Grade Span: PK-12; **Agency Type:** 2
Schools: 4
2 Primary; 1 Middle; 1 High; 0 Other Level
4 Regular; 0 Special Education; 0 Vocational; 0 Alternative
0 Magnet; 0 Charter; 3 Title I Eligible; 0 School-wide Title I
Students: 2,033 (51.0% male; 49.0% female)
Individual Education Program: 209 (10.3%);
English Language Learner: 4 (0.2%); Migrant: n/a
Eligible for Free Lunch Program: 150 (7.4%)
Eligible for Reduced-Price Lunch Program: 47 (2.3%)
Teachers: 118.9 (17.1 to 1)
Librarians/Media Specialists: 1.0 (2,033.0 to 1)
Guidance Counselors: 2.0 (1,016.5 to 1)
Current Spending: ($ per student per year):
Total: $5,655; Instruction: $3,222; Support Services: $2,220
Enrollment, Drop-out Rates and Diploma Recipients by Race/Ethnicity

Category	Total	White	Black	Asian	AIAN	Hisp.
Enrollment (%)	100.0	96.9	0.7	0.3	0.3	0.6
Drop-out Rate (%)	3.9	3.7	0.0	0.0	0.0	50.0
H.S. Diplomas (#)	146	135	2	4	1	1

Northeastern Local SD

1414 Bowman Rd • Springfield, OH 45502-8826
(937) 325-7615 • http://www.northeastern.k12.oh.us/
Grade Span: PK-12; **Agency Type:** 2
Schools: 7
3 Primary; 0 Middle; 2 High; 0 Other Level
5 Regular; 0 Special Education; 0 Vocational; 0 Alternative
0 Magnet; 0 Charter; 2 Title I Eligible; 0 School-wide Title I
Students: 3,601 (52.1% male; 47.9% female)
Individual Education Program: 306 (8.5%);
English Language Learner: 7 (0.2%); Migrant: n/a
Eligible for Free Lunch Program: 221 (6.1%)
Eligible for Reduced-Price Lunch Program: 84 (2.3%)
Teachers: 199.4 (18.1 to 1)
Librarians/Media Specialists: 4.0 (900.3 to 1)
Guidance Counselors: 7.6 (473.8 to 1)
Current Spending: ($ per student per year):
Total: $6,268; Instruction: $3,574; Support Services: $2,467
Enrollment, Drop-out Rates and Diploma Recipients by Race/Ethnicity

Category	Total	White	Black	Asian	AIAN	Hisp.
Enrollment (%)	100.0	96.1	0.8	0.9	0.0	0.5
Drop-out Rate (%)	2.9	2.9	0.0	0.0	n/a	0.0
H.S. Diplomas (#)	198	193	1	2	0	0

Northwestern Local SD

5610 Troy Rd • Springfield, OH 45502-9032
(937) 964-1318
Grade Span: PK-12; **Agency Type:** 2
Schools: 3
1 Primary; 1 Middle; 1 High; 0 Other Level
3 Regular; 0 Special Education; 0 Vocational; 0 Alternative
0 Magnet; 0 Charter; 2 Title I Eligible; 0 School-wide Title I
Students: 1,930 (49.7% male; 50.3% female)
Individual Education Program: 202 (10.5%);
English Language Learner: 2 (0.1%); Migrant: n/a
Eligible for Free Lunch Program: 179 (9.3%)
Eligible for Reduced-Price Lunch Program: 32 (1.7%)
Teachers: 107.7 (17.9 to 1)
Librarians/Media Specialists: 2.0 (965.0 to 1)
Guidance Counselors: 3.0 (643.3 to 1)
Current Spending: ($ per student per year):
Total: $5,981; Instruction: $3,744; Support Services: $1,990
Enrollment, Drop-out Rates and Diploma Recipients by Race/Ethnicity

Category	Total	White	Black	Asian	AIAN	Hisp.
Enrollment (%)	100.0	96.8	0.2	1.0	0.2	0.6
Drop-out Rate (%)	1.7	1.6	0.0	0.0	0.0	33.3
H.S. Diplomas (#)	135	134	0	0	0	1

Springfield City SD

49 E College Ave • Springfield, OH 45504-2502
(937) 328-2000
Grade Span: PK-12; **Agency Type:** 1
Schools: 22
13 Primary; 5 Middle; 3 High; 1 Other Level
21 Regular; 1 Special Education; 0 Vocational; 0 Alternative
0 Magnet; 0 Charter; 19 Title I Eligible; 9 School-wide Title I
Students: 9,599 (52.5% male; 47.5% female)
Individual Education Program: 1,481 (15.4%);
English Language Learner: 18 (0.2%); Migrant: 10 (0.1%)
Eligible for Free Lunch Program: 4,290 (44.7%)
Eligible for Reduced-Price Lunch Program: 449 (4.7%)
Teachers: 658.2 (14.6 to 1)
Librarians/Media Specialists: 8.0 (1,199.9 to 1)
Guidance Counselors: 29.0 (331.0 to 1)
Current Spending: ($ per student per year):
Total: $7,513; Instruction: $4,220; Support Services: $3,013
Enrollment, Drop-out Rates and Diploma Recipients by Race/Ethnicity

Category	Total	White	Black	Asian	AIAN	Hisp.
Enrollment (%)	100.0	67.9	25.7	0.5	0.1	1.0
Drop-out Rate (%)	8.0	7.8	8.9	0.0	0.0	8.7
H.S. Diplomas (#)	411	284	122	2	1	2

Tecumseh Local SD

9760 W National Rd • New Carlisle, OH 45344-9290
(937) 845-3576 • http://www.tecumseh.k12.oh.us/
Grade Span: PK-12; **Agency Type:** 2
Schools: 8
5 Primary; 2 Middle; 1 High; 0 Other Level
8 Regular; 0 Special Education; 0 Vocational; 0 Alternative
0 Magnet; 0 Charter; 5 Title I Eligible; 3 School-wide Title I
Students: 3,595 (51.2% male; 48.8% female)
Individual Education Program: 423 (11.8%);
English Language Learner: 0 (0.0%); Migrant: 84 (2.3%)
Eligible for Free Lunch Program: 690 (19.2%)
Eligible for Reduced-Price Lunch Program: 252 (7.0%)
Teachers: 227.3 (15.8 to 1)
Librarians/Media Specialists: 2.0 (1,797.5 to 1)
Guidance Counselors: 5.5 (653.6 to 1)
Current Spending: ($ per student per year):
Total: $6,552; Instruction: $3,643; Support Services: $2,590
Enrollment, Drop-out Rates and Diploma Recipients by Race/Ethnicity

Category	Total	White	Black	Asian	AIAN	Hisp.
Enrollment (%)	100.0	93.3	0.5	0.4	0.2	4.4
Drop-out Rate (%)	4.1	3.7	16.7	16.7	0.0	25.0
H.S. Diplomas (#)	224	216	0	0	1	4

Clermont County

Batavia Local SD

800 Bauer Ave • Batavia, OH 45103-2837
(513) 732-2343 • http://www.bataviaschools.org/
Grade Span: PK-12; **Agency Type:** 2
Schools: 3
1 Primary; 1 Middle; 1 High; 0 Other Level
3 Regular; 0 Special Education; 0 Vocational; 0 Alternative
0 Magnet; 0 Charter; 1 Title I Eligible; 1 School-wide Title I
Students: 1,926 (53.1% male; 46.9% female)
Individual Education Program: 191 (9.9%);
English Language Learner: 7 (0.4%); Migrant: n/a
Eligible for Free Lunch Program: 346 (18.0%)
Eligible for Reduced-Price Lunch Program: 138 (7.2%)
Teachers: 111.0 (17.4 to 1)
Librarians/Media Specialists: 2.0 (963.0 to 1)
Guidance Counselors: 3.0 (642.0 to 1)
Current Spending: ($ per student per year):
Total: $6,698; Instruction: $4,008; Support Services: $2,441
Enrollment, Drop-out Rates and Diploma Recipients by Race/Ethnicity

Category	Total	White	Black	Asian	AIAN	Hisp.
Enrollment (%)	100.0	96.0	1.6	0.3	0.0	0.8
Drop-out Rate (%)	4.1	3.9	11.1	0.0	n/a	0.0
H.S. Diplomas (#)	92	86	4	0	0	0

Bethel-Tate Local SD

112 N Union St • Bethel, OH 45106-1122
(513) 734-2238 • http://www.betheltate.org/
Grade Span: PK-12; **Agency Type:** 2
Schools: 5
2 Primary; 1 Middle; 1 High; 1 Other Level
5 Regular; 0 Special Education; 0 Vocational; 0 Alternative
0 Magnet; 0 Charter; 3 Title I Eligible; 0 School-wide Title I
Students: 1,932 (51.4% male; 48.6% female)
Individual Education Program: 88 (4.6%);
English Language Learner: 0 (0.0%); Migrant: n/a
Eligible for Free Lunch Program: 276 (14.3%)
Eligible for Reduced-Price Lunch Program: 72 (3.7%)
Teachers: 104.0 (18.6 to 1)
Librarians/Media Specialists: 3.0 (644.0 to 1)
Guidance Counselors: 1.0 (1,932.0 to 1)
Current Spending: ($ per student per year):
Total: $4,761; Instruction: $2,959; Support Services: $1,614
Enrollment, Drop-out Rates and Diploma Recipients by Race/Ethnicity

Category	Total	White	Black	Asian	AIAN	Hisp.
Enrollment (%)	100.0	98.3	0.2	0.1	0.4	0.4
Drop-out Rate (%)	5.4	5.4	n/a	0.0	n/a	0.0
H.S. Diplomas (#)	138	137	0	0	0	1

Clermont-Northeastern Local SD

2792 US Hwy 50 • Batavia, OH 45103-8532
(513) 625-5478
Grade Span: PK-12; **Agency Type:** 2
Schools: 4
1 Primary; 2 Middle; 1 High; 0 Other Level
4 Regular; 0 Special Education; 0 Vocational; 0 Alternative
0 Magnet; 0 Charter; 3 Title I Eligible; 0 School-wide Title I
Students: 2,036 (51.8% male; 48.2% female)
Individual Education Program: 279 (13.7%);
English Language Learner: 0 (0.0%); Migrant: n/a
Eligible for Free Lunch Program: 309 (15.2%)
Eligible for Reduced-Price Lunch Program: 70 (3.4%)
Teachers: 110.7 (18.4 to 1)
Librarians/Media Specialists: 2.0 (1,018.0 to 1)
Guidance Counselors: 2.9 (702.1 to 1)
Current Spending: ($ per student per year):
Total: $5,638; Instruction: $3,357; Support Services: $2,020
Enrollment, Drop-out Rates and Diploma Recipients by Race/Ethnicity

Category	Total	White	Black	Asian	AIAN	Hisp.
Enrollment (%)	100.0	98.4	0.1	0.0	0.1	0.6
Drop-out Rate (%)	5.9	5.9	n/a	n/a	n/a	0.0
H.S. Diplomas (#)	121	117	0	1	1	0

Goshen Local SD

6785 Goshen Rd • Goshen, OH 45122-9317
(513) 722-2222
Grade Span: PK-12; **Agency Type:** 2
Schools: 4
1 Primary; 2 Middle; 1 High; 0 Other Level
4 Regular; 0 Special Education; 0 Vocational; 0 Alternative
0 Magnet; 0 Charter; 2 Title I Eligible; 0 School-wide Title I
Students: 2,535 (52.0% male; 48.0% female)
Individual Education Program: 401 (15.8%);
English Language Learner: 1 (<0.1%); Migrant: n/a
Eligible for Free Lunch Program: 433 (17.1%)
Eligible for Reduced-Price Lunch Program: 160 (6.3%)
Teachers: 141.0 (18.0 to 1)
Librarians/Media Specialists: 2.0 (1,267.5 to 1)
Guidance Counselors: 5.0 (507.0 to 1)
Current Spending: ($ per student per year):
Total: $6,120; Instruction: $3,321; Support Services: $2,564
Enrollment, Drop-out Rates and Diploma Recipients by Race/Ethnicity

Category	Total	White	Black	Asian	AIAN	Hisp.
Enrollment (%)	100.0	98.3	0.4	0.1	0.0	0.2
Drop-out Rate (%)	6.1	6.1	0.0	0.0	0.0	16.7
H.S. Diplomas (#)	146	146	0	0	0	0

Milford Ex Vill SD

745 Center St Ste 300 • Milford, OH 45150-1300
(513) 831-1314 • http://www.milfordschools.org/
Grade Span: PK-12; **Agency Type:** 1
Schools: 11
4 Primary; 2 Middle; 1 High; 0 Other Level
7 Regular; 0 Special Education; 0 Vocational; 0 Alternative
0 Magnet; 0 Charter; 4 Title I Eligible; 0 School-wide Title I
Students: 6,071 (51.3% male; 48.7% female)
Individual Education Program: 655 (10.8%);
English Language Learner: 7 (0.1%); Migrant: n/a
Eligible for Free Lunch Program: 479 (7.9%)
Eligible for Reduced-Price Lunch Program: 190 (3.1%)
Teachers: 317.0 (19.2 to 1)
Librarians/Media Specialists: 3.0 (2,023.7 to 1)
Guidance Counselors: 7.0 (867.3 to 1)
Current Spending: ($ per student per year):
Total: $6,267; Instruction: $3,427; Support Services: $2,606
Enrollment, Drop-out Rates and Diploma Recipients by Race/Ethnicity

Category	Total	White	Black	Asian	AIAN	Hisp.
Enrollment (%)	100.0	96.8	1.8	0.4	0.0	0.5
Drop-out Rate (%)	2.7	2.5	5.9	7.1	0.0	22.2
H.S. Diplomas (#)	417	399	6	1	0	3

New Richmond Ex Vill SD

212 Market St Fl 3rd • New Richmond, OH 45157-1373
(513) 553-2616 • http://www.nrschools.org/
Grade Span: PK-12; **Agency Type:** 1
Schools: 5
3 Primary; 1 Middle; 1 High; 0 Other Level
5 Regular; 0 Special Education; 0 Vocational; 0 Alternative
0 Magnet; 0 Charter; 3 Title I Eligible; 2 School-wide Title I
Students: 2,524 (51.5% male; 48.5% female)
Individual Education Program: 193 (7.6%);
English Language Learner: 0 (0.0%); Migrant: n/a
Eligible for Free Lunch Program: 591 (23.4%)
Eligible for Reduced-Price Lunch Program: 115 (4.6%)
Teachers: 164.5 (15.3 to 1)
Librarians/Media Specialists: 1.0 (2,524.0 to 1)
Guidance Counselors: 6.0 (420.7 to 1)
Current Spending: ($ per student per year):
Total: $7,311; Instruction: $4,128; Support Services: $2,956
Enrollment, Drop-out Rates and Diploma Recipients by Race/Ethnicity

Category	Total	White	Black	Asian	AIAN	Hisp.
Enrollment (%)	100.0	97.2	1.0	0.3	0.2	0.6
Drop-out Rate (%)	8.2	8.2	0.0	n/a	0.0	0.0
H.S. Diplomas (#)	155	155	0	0	0	0

West Clermont Local SD

4578 E Tech Dr Ste 101 • Cincinnati, OH 45245-1054
(513) 943-5000
Grade Span: PK-12; **Agency Type:** 2
Schools: 12
8 Primary; 2 Middle; 2 High; 0 Other Level
12 Regular; 0 Special Education; 0 Vocational; 0 Alternative
0 Magnet; 0 Charter; 6 Title I Eligible; 1 School-wide Title I
Students: 9,176 (51.8% male; 48.2% female)
Individual Education Program: 1,030 (11.2%);
English Language Learner: 82 (0.9%); Migrant: n/a
Eligible for Free Lunch Program: 805 (8.8%)
Eligible for Reduced-Price Lunch Program: 287 (3.1%)
Teachers: 510.2 (18.0 to 1)
Librarians/Media Specialists: 2.0 (4,588.0 to 1)
Guidance Counselors: 11.0 (834.2 to 1)
Current Spending: ($ per student per year):
Total: $5,809; Instruction: $3,575; Support Services: $2,058
Enrollment, Drop-out Rates and Diploma Recipients by Race/Ethnicity

Category	Total	White	Black	Asian	AIAN	Hisp.
Enrollment (%)	100.0	96.5	0.8	1.0	0.1	0.7
Drop-out Rate (%)	6.6	6.7	0.0	0.0	0.0	10.0
H.S. Diplomas (#)	520	514	1	4	0	0

Clinton County

Blanchester Local SD

3580 State Route 28 • Blanchester, OH 45107-7846
(937) 783-3523 • http://www.blanchester.k12.oh.us/
Grade Span: PK-12; **Agency Type:** 2
Schools: 5
2 Primary; 2 Middle; 1 High; 0 Other Level
5 Regular; 0 Special Education; 0 Vocational; 0 Alternative
0 Magnet; 0 Charter; 2 Title I Eligible; 1 School-wide Title I
Students: 1,772 (50.3% male; 49.7% female)
Individual Education Program: 223 (12.6%);
English Language Learner: 0 (0.0%); Migrant: n/a
Eligible for Free Lunch Program: 232 (13.1%)
Eligible for Reduced-Price Lunch Program: 133 (7.5%)
Teachers: 101.1 (17.5 to 1)
Librarians/Media Specialists: 1.0 (1,772.0 to 1)
Guidance Counselors: 3.0 (590.7 to 1)
Current Spending: ($ per student per year):
Total: $8,733; Instruction: $5,350; Support Services: $3,114
Enrollment, Drop-out Rates and Diploma Recipients by Race/Ethnicity

Category	Total	White	Black	Asian	AIAN	Hisp.
Enrollment (%)	100.0	98.6	0.2	0.2	0.0	0.1
Drop-out Rate (%)	4.4	4.4	0.0	n/a	n/a	n/a
H.S. Diplomas (#)	93	92	1	0	0	0

Clinton-Massie Local SD

2556 Lebanon Rd • Clarksville, OH 45113-8201
(937) 289-2471 • http://www.clinton-massie.k12.oh.us/
Grade Span: PK-12; **Agency Type:** 2
Schools: 3
1 Primary; 1 Middle; 1 High; 0 Other Level
3 Regular; 0 Special Education; 0 Vocational; 0 Alternative
0 Magnet; 0 Charter; 2 Title I Eligible; 0 School-wide Title I
Students: 1,756 (52.3% male; 47.7% female)
Individual Education Program: 181 (10.3%);
English Language Learner: 0 (0.0%); Migrant: n/a
Eligible for Free Lunch Program: 133 (7.6%)
Eligible for Reduced-Price Lunch Program: 68 (3.9%)
Teachers: 88.8 (19.8 to 1)
Librarians/Media Specialists: 1.0 (1,756.0 to 1)
Guidance Counselors: 4.0 (439.0 to 1)
Current Spending: ($ per student per year):
Total: $5,482; Instruction: $3,220; Support Services: $2,050
Enrollment, Drop-out Rates and Diploma Recipients by Race/Ethnicity

Category	Total	White	Black	Asian	AIAN	Hisp.
Enrollment (%)	100.0	97.7	1.4	0.2	0.1	0.2
Drop-out Rate (%)	1.4	1.4	n/a	0.0	n/a	n/a
H.S. Diplomas (#)	117	116	0	1	0	0

East Clinton Local SD

97 College St • Lees Creek, OH 45138
(937) 584-2461 • http://www.east-clinton.k12.oh.us/
Grade Span: PK-12; **Agency Type:** 2
Schools: 4
2 Primary; 1 Middle; 1 High; 0 Other Level
4 Regular; 0 Special Education; 0 Vocational; 0 Alternative
0 Magnet; 0 Charter; 2 Title I Eligible; 0 School-wide Title I
Students: 1,561 (50.0% male; 50.0% female)
Individual Education Program: 199 (12.7%);
English Language Learner: 0 (0.0%); Migrant: n/a
Eligible for Free Lunch Program: 222 (14.2%)
Eligible for Reduced-Price Lunch Program: 90 (5.8%)
Teachers: 92.5 (16.9 to 1)
Librarians/Media Specialists: 1.0 (1,561.0 to 1)
Guidance Counselors: 1.0 (1,561.0 to 1)
Current Spending: ($ per student per year):
Total: $5,347; Instruction: $2,988; Support Services: $2,150
Enrollment, Drop-out Rates and Diploma Recipients by Race/Ethnicity

Category	Total	White	Black	Asian	AIAN	Hisp.
Enrollment (%)	100.0	97.9	0.5	0.6	0.1	0.4
Drop-out Rate (%)	2.4	2.5	0.0	n/a	n/a	0.0
H.S. Diplomas (#)	93	93	0	0	0	0

Wilmington City SD

341 S Nelson Ave • Wilmington, OH 45177-2034
(937) 382-1641
Grade Span: PK-12; **Agency Type:** 1
Schools: 5
3 Primary; 1 Middle; 1 High; 0 Other Level
5 Regular; 0 Special Education; 0 Vocational; 0 Alternative
0 Magnet; 0 Charter; 4 Title I Eligible; 0 School-wide Title I
Students: 3,179 (52.3% male; 47.7% female)
Individual Education Program: 319 (10.0%);
English Language Learner: 1 (<0.1%); Migrant: 1 (<0.1%)
Eligible for Free Lunch Program: 517 (16.3%)
Eligible for Reduced-Price Lunch Program: 240 (7.5%)
Teachers: 172.0 (18.5 to 1)
Librarians/Media Specialists: 1.0 (3,179.0 to 1)
Guidance Counselors: 4.0 (794.8 to 1)
Current Spending: ($ per student per year):
Total: $5,694; Instruction: $3,673; Support Services: $1,810
Enrollment, Drop-out Rates and Diploma Recipients by Race/Ethnicity

Category	Total	White	Black	Asian	AIAN	Hisp.
Enrollment (%)	100.0	91.9	4.2	0.6	0.2	0.5
Drop-out Rate (%)	0.8	0.9	0.0	0.0	n/a	0.0
H.S. Diplomas (#)	231	213	15	2	0	0

Columbiana County

Beaver Local SD

13093 State Route 7 • Lisbon, OH 44432-9559
(330) 385-6831 • http://www.beaver.k12.oh.us/
Grade Span: PK-12; **Agency Type:** 2
Schools: 5
3 Primary; 1 Middle; 1 High; 0 Other Level
5 Regular; 0 Special Education; 0 Vocational; 0 Alternative
0 Magnet; 0 Charter; 4 Title I Eligible; 3 School-wide Title I
Students: 2,492 (51.7% male; 48.3% female)
Individual Education Program: 305 (12.2%);
English Language Learner: 0 (0.0%); Migrant: n/a
Eligible for Free Lunch Program: 720 (28.9%)
Eligible for Reduced-Price Lunch Program: 252 (10.1%)
Teachers: 136.0 (18.3 to 1)
Librarians/Media Specialists: 2.0 (1,246.0 to 1)
Guidance Counselors: 4.0 (623.0 to 1)
Current Spending: ($ per student per year):
Total: $5,901; Instruction: $3,737; Support Services: $1,859
Enrollment, Drop-out Rates and Diploma Recipients by Race/Ethnicity

Category	Total	White	Black	Asian	AIAN	Hisp.
Enrollment (%)	100.0	97.8	0.2	0.3	0.2	0.4
Drop-out Rate (%)	3.0	2.9	33.3	0.0	n/a	0.0
H.S. Diplomas (#)	161	161	0	0	0	0

East Liverpool City SD

500 Maryland St • East Liverpool, OH 43920-2121
(330) 385-7132
Grade Span: PK-12; **Agency Type:** 1
Schools: 6
4 Primary; 1 Middle; 1 High; 0 Other Level
6 Regular; 0 Special Education; 0 Vocational; 0 Alternative
0 Magnet; 0 Charter; 5 Title I Eligible; 4 School-wide Title I
Students: 3,104 (50.9% male; 49.1% female)
Individual Education Program: 597 (19.2%);
English Language Learner: 0 (0.0%); Migrant: n/a
Eligible for Free Lunch Program: 1,189 (38.3%)
Eligible for Reduced-Price Lunch Program: 131 (4.2%)
Teachers: 224.0 (13.9 to 1)
Librarians/Media Specialists: 4.0 (776.0 to 1)
Guidance Counselors: 7.0 (443.4 to 1)
Current Spending: ($ per student per year):
Total: $7,359; Instruction: $4,489; Support Services: $2,575
Enrollment, Drop-out Rates and Diploma Recipients by Race/Ethnicity

Category	Total	White	Black	Asian	AIAN	Hisp.
Enrollment (%)	100.0	90.8	5.8	0.2	0.1	0.2
Drop-out Rate (%)	5.4	5.4	5.8	0.0	n/a	0.0
H.S. Diplomas (#)	185	170	15	0	0	0

Salem City SD

1226 E State St • Salem, OH 44460-2222
(330) 332-0316 • http://www.salem.k12.oh.us/
Grade Span: PK-12; **Agency Type:** 1
Schools: 7
2 Primary; 3 Middle; 1 High; 1 Other Level
6 Regular; 0 Special Education; 1 Vocational; 0 Alternative
0 Magnet; 0 Charter; 4 Title I Eligible; 0 School-wide Title I
Students: 2,472 (50.7% male; 49.3% female)
Individual Education Program: 306 (12.4%);
English Language Learner: 3 (0.1%); Migrant: n/a
Eligible for Free Lunch Program: 482 (19.5%)
Eligible for Reduced-Price Lunch Program: 94 (3.8%)
Teachers: 193.5 (12.8 to 1)
Librarians/Media Specialists: 2.0 (1,236.0 to 1)
Guidance Counselors: 4.0 (618.0 to 1)
Current Spending: ($ per student per year):
Total: $6,350; Instruction: $3,829; Support Services: $2,293
Enrollment, Drop-out Rates and Diploma Recipients by Race/Ethnicity

Category	Total	White	Black	Asian	AIAN	Hisp.
Enrollment (%)	100.0	97.3	0.5	0.5	0.2	0.4
Drop-out Rate (%)	3.1	3.0	16.7	0.0	n/a	0.0
H.S. Diplomas (#)	183	182	0	0	0	1

Coshocton County

Coshocton City SD

1207 Cambridge Rd • Coshocton, OH 43812-2742
(740) 622-1901 • http://www.coshoctonredskins.com/
Grade Span: PK-12; **Agency Type:** 1
Schools: 5
4 Primary; 0 Middle; 1 High; 0 Other Level
5 Regular; 0 Special Education; 0 Vocational; 0 Alternative
0 Magnet; 0 Charter; 3 Title I Eligible; 3 School-wide Title I
Students: 1,991 (50.7% male; 49.3% female)
Individual Education Program: 425 (21.3%);
English Language Learner: 0 (0.0%); Migrant: n/a
Eligible for Free Lunch Program: 697 (35.0%)
Eligible for Reduced-Price Lunch Program: 183 (9.2%)
Teachers: 125.6 (15.9 to 1)
Librarians/Media Specialists: 2.0 (995.5 to 1)
Guidance Counselors: 3.0 (663.7 to 1)
Current Spending: ($ per student per year):
Total: $6,287; Instruction: $3,841; Support Services: $2,149
Enrollment, Drop-out Rates and Diploma Recipients by Race/Ethnicity

Category	Total	White	Black	Asian	AIAN	Hisp.
Enrollment (%)	100.0	95.8	2.1	0.9	0.0	0.1
Drop-out Rate (%)	1.0	0.7	22.2	0.0	n/a	0.0
H.S. Diplomas (#)	122	112	4	5	0	0

River View Local SD

26496 State Route 60 • Warsaw, OH 43844-9714
(740) 824-3521
Grade Span: PK-12; **Agency Type:** 2
Schools: 7
5 Primary; 1 Middle; 1 High; 0 Other Level
6 Regular; 0 Special Education; 0 Vocational; 1 Alternative
0 Magnet; 0 Charter; 4 Title I Eligible; 3 School-wide Title I
Students: 2,665 (52.0% male; 48.0% female)
Individual Education Program: 430 (16.1%);
English Language Learner: 0 (0.0%); Migrant: n/a
Eligible for Free Lunch Program: 412 (15.5%)
Eligible for Reduced-Price Lunch Program: 131 (4.9%)
Teachers: 154.0 (17.3 to 1)
Librarians/Media Specialists: 1.0 (2,665.0 to 1)
Guidance Counselors: 3.0 (888.3 to 1)
Current Spending: ($ per student per year):
Total: $6,004; Instruction: $3,324; Support Services: $2,378
Enrollment, Drop-out Rates and Diploma Recipients by Race/Ethnicity

Category	Total	White	Black	Asian	AIAN	Hisp.
Enrollment (%)	100.0	98.5	1.2	0.0	0.0	0.0
Drop-out Rate (%)	2.3	2.3	0.0	n/a	n/a	n/a
H.S. Diplomas (#)	184	181	3	0	0	0

Crawford County

Bucyrus City SD

630 Jump St • Bucyrus, OH 44820-1525
(419) 562-4045
Grade Span: PK-12; **Agency Type:** 1
Schools: 7
4 Primary; 2 Middle; 1 High; 0 Other Level
7 Regular; 0 Special Education; 0 Vocational; 0 Alternative
0 Magnet; 0 Charter; 6 Title I Eligible; 6 School-wide Title I
Students: 1,936 (52.4% male; 47.6% female)
Individual Education Program: 359 (18.5%);
English Language Learner: 16 (0.8%); Migrant: n/a
Eligible for Free Lunch Program: 624 (32.2%)
Eligible for Reduced-Price Lunch Program: 265 (13.7%)
Teachers: 124.5 (15.6 to 1)
Librarians/Media Specialists: 2.0 (968.0 to 1)
Guidance Counselors: 1.0 (1,936.0 to 1)
Current Spending: ($ per student per year):
Total: $6,850; Instruction: $3,968; Support Services: $2,417
Enrollment, Drop-out Rates and Diploma Recipients by Race/Ethnicity

Category	Total	White	Black	Asian	AIAN	Hisp.
Enrollment (%)	100.0	96.0	0.5	1.5	0.2	0.6
Drop-out Rate (%)	4.9	5.0	0.0	0.0	0.0	0.0
H.S. Diplomas (#)	118	117	1	0	0	0

Galion City SD

200 W Church St • Galion, OH 44833-1707
(419) 468-3432 • http://www.galion-city.k12.oh.us/
Grade Span: PK-12; **Agency Type:** 1
Schools: 6
4 Primary; 1 Middle; 0 High; 1 Other Level
6 Regular; 0 Special Education; 0 Vocational; 0 Alternative
0 Magnet; 0 Charter; 3 Title I Eligible; 2 School-wide Title I
Students: 2,255 (47.5% male; 52.5% female)
Individual Education Program: 334 (14.8%);
English Language Learner: 4 (0.2%); Migrant: n/a
Eligible for Free Lunch Program: 475 (21.1%)
Eligible for Reduced-Price Lunch Program: 156 (6.9%)
Teachers: 141.9 (15.9 to 1)
Librarians/Media Specialists: 1.0 (2,255.0 to 1)
Guidance Counselors: 3.0 (751.7 to 1)
Current Spending: ($ per student per year):
Total: $5,966; Instruction: $3,804; Support Services: $1,942

Enrollment, Drop-out Rates and Diploma Recipients by Race/Ethnicity

Category	Total	White	Black	Asian	AIAN	Hisp.
Enrollment (%)	100.0	98.4	0.5	0.0	0.0	0.6
Drop-out Rate (%)	3.2	2.9	0.0	0.0	100.0	200.0
H.S. Diplomas (#)	170	168	0	1	1	0

Cuyahoga County

Bay Village City SD

377 Dover Center Rd • Bay Village, OH 44140-2304
(440) 617-7300 • http://www.bayvillageschools.com/
Grade Span: KG-12; **Agency Type:** 1
Schools: 4
2 Primary; 1 Middle; 1 High; 0 Other Level
4 Regular; 0 Special Education; 0 Vocational; 0 Alternative
0 Magnet; 0 Charter; 3 Title I Eligible; 0 School-wide Title I
Students: 2,406 (50.0% male; 50.0% female)
Individual Education Program: 307 (12.8%);
English Language Learner: 9 (0.4%); Migrant: 1 (<0.1%)
Eligible for Free Lunch Program: 58 (2.4%)
Eligible for Reduced-Price Lunch Program: 66 (2.7%)
Teachers: 160.5 (15.0 to 1)
Librarians/Media Specialists: 2.0 (1,203.0 to 1)
Guidance Counselors: 6.0 (401.0 to 1)
Current Spending: ($ per student per year):
Total: $8,394; Instruction: $4,750; Support Services: $3,413
Enrollment, Drop-out Rates and Diploma Recipients by Race/Ethnicity

Category	Total	White	Black	Asian	AIAN	Hisp.
Enrollment (%)	100.0	97.5	0.5	1.3	0.2	0.5
Drop-out Rate (%)	0.5	0.5	0.0	0.0	n/a	n/a
H.S. Diplomas (#)	168	163	1	2	0	2

Beachwood City SD

24601 Fairmount Blvd • Beachwood, OH 44122-2239
(216) 464-2600
Grade Span: PK-12; **Agency Type:** 1
Schools: 5
3 Primary; 1 Middle; 1 High; 0 Other Level
5 Regular; 0 Special Education; 0 Vocational; 0 Alternative
0 Magnet; 0 Charter; 0 Title I Eligible; 0 School-wide Title I
Students: 1,580 (53.8% male; 46.2% female)
Individual Education Program: 159 (10.1%);
English Language Learner: 5 (0.3%); Migrant: n/a
Eligible for Free Lunch Program: 35 (2.2%)
Eligible for Reduced-Price Lunch Program: 14 (0.9%)
Teachers: 164.7 (9.6 to 1)
Librarians/Media Specialists: 4.0 (395.0 to 1)
Guidance Counselors: 6.0 (263.3 to 1)
Current Spending: ($ per student per year):
Total: $17,180; Instruction: $8,831; Support Services: $8,009
Enrollment, Drop-out Rates and Diploma Recipients by Race/Ethnicity

Category	Total	White	Black	Asian	AIAN	Hisp.
Enrollment (%)	100.0	78.9	13.7	4.9	0.1	0.8
Drop-out Rate (%)	0.6	0.8	0.0	0.0	n/a	0.0
H.S. Diplomas (#)	142	122	14	3	0	1

Bedford City SD

475 Northfield Rd • Bedford, OH 44146-2201
(440) 439-1500 • http://www.bedford.k12.oh.us/
Grade Span: PK-12; **Agency Type:** 1
Schools: 7
4 Primary; 2 Middle; 1 High; 0 Other Level
7 Regular; 0 Special Education; 0 Vocational; 0 Alternative
0 Magnet; 0 Charter; 6 Title I Eligible; 4 School-wide Title I
Students: 3,822 (51.1% male; 48.9% female)
Individual Education Program: 536 (14.0%);
English Language Learner: 25 (0.7%); Migrant: n/a
Eligible for Free Lunch Program: 903 (23.6%)
Eligible for Reduced-Price Lunch Program: 297 (7.8%)
Teachers: 271.5 (14.1 to 1)
Librarians/Media Specialists: 5.0 (764.4 to 1)
Guidance Counselors: 10.0 (382.2 to 1)
Current Spending: ($ per student per year):
Total: $8,632; Instruction: $4,568; Support Services: $3,785
Enrollment, Drop-out Rates and Diploma Recipients by Race/Ethnicity

Category	Total	White	Black	Asian	AIAN	Hisp.
Enrollment (%)	100.0	28.6	64.4	0.9	0.1	0.9
Drop-out Rate (%)	7.9	9.4	7.0	7.7	n/a	10.0
H.S. Diplomas (#)	231	86	138	4	0	1

Berea City SD

390 Fair St • Berea, OH 44017-2308
(440) 243-6000 • http://berea.k12.oh.us/webmain/
Grade Span: PK-12; **Agency Type:** 1
Schools: 13
8 Primary; 2 Middle; 2 High; 1 Other Level
11 Regular; 1 Special Education; 0 Vocational; 1 Alternative
0 Magnet; 0 Charter; 7 Title I Eligible; 1 School-wide Title I
Students: 8,006 (52.8% male; 47.2% female)
Individual Education Program: 1,162 (14.5%);
English Language Learner: 100 (1.2%); Migrant: n/a
Eligible for Free Lunch Program: 747 (9.3%)
Eligible for Reduced-Price Lunch Program: 440 (5.5%)
Teachers: 509.4 (15.7 to 1)
Librarians/Media Specialists: 9.0 (889.6 to 1)
Guidance Counselors: 19.0 (421.4 to 1)
Current Spending: ($ per student per year):
Total: $8,119; Instruction: $4,466; Support Services: $3,423
Enrollment, Drop-out Rates and Diploma Recipients by Race/Ethnicity

Category	Total	White	Black	Asian	AIAN	Hisp.
Enrollment (%)	100.0	90.5	4.0	1.7	0.1	1.3
Drop-out Rate (%)	2.6	2.6	3.2	0.0	0.0	2.4
H.S. Diplomas (#)	611	560	20	9	1	12

Brecksville-Broadview Heights

6638 Mill Rd • Brecksville, OH 44141-1512
(440) 740-4010 • http://www.bbhcsd.org/
Grade Span: PK-12; **Agency Type:** 1
Schools: 6
4 Primary; 1 Middle; 1 High; 0 Other Level
6 Regular; 0 Special Education; 0 Vocational; 0 Alternative
0 Magnet; 0 Charter; 2 Title I Eligible; 0 School-wide Title I
Students: 4,513 (51.2% male; 48.8% female)
Individual Education Program: 466 (10.3%);
English Language Learner: 48 (1.1%); Migrant: n/a
Eligible for Free Lunch Program: 144 (3.2%)
Eligible for Reduced-Price Lunch Program: 68 (1.5%)
Teachers: 261.3 (17.3 to 1)
Librarians/Media Specialists: 4.0 (1,128.3 to 1)
Guidance Counselors: 9.0 (501.4 to 1)
Current Spending: ($ per student per year):
Total: $7,991; Instruction: $4,611; Support Services: $3,094
Enrollment, Drop-out Rates and Diploma Recipients by Race/Ethnicity

Category	Total	White	Black	Asian	AIAN	Hisp.
Enrollment (%)	100.0	93.0	1.2	3.6	0.0	0.7
Drop-out Rate (%)	0.8	0.9	0.0	0.0	0.0	0.0
H.S. Diplomas (#)	340	324	2	11	0	3

Chagrin Falls Ex Vill SD

400 E Washington St • Chagrin Falls, OH 44022-2924
(440) 247-5500
Grade Span: PK-12; **Agency Type:** 1
Schools: 4
1 Primary; 1 Middle; 2 High; 0 Other Level
4 Regular; 0 Special Education; 0 Vocational; 0 Alternative
0 Magnet; 0 Charter; 0 Title I Eligible; 0 School-wide Title I
Students: 1,967 (51.8% male; 48.2% female)
Individual Education Program: 205 (10.4%);
English Language Learner: 0 (0.0%); Migrant: n/a
Eligible for Free Lunch Program: 15 (0.8%)
Eligible for Reduced-Price Lunch Program: 2 (0.1%)
Teachers: 142.7 (13.8 to 1)
Librarians/Media Specialists: 2.0 (983.5 to 1)
Guidance Counselors: 5.0 (393.4 to 1)
Current Spending: ($ per student per year):
Total: $8,612; Instruction: $4,936; Support Services: $3,447
Enrollment, Drop-out Rates and Diploma Recipients by Race/Ethnicity

Category	Total	White	Black	Asian	AIAN	Hisp.
Enrollment (%)	100.0	97.8	0.7	0.3	0.0	0.2
Drop-out Rate (%)	0.8	0.7	0.0	0.0	n/a	16.7
H.S. Diplomas (#)	146	141	0	2	0	2

Cleveland Hts-Univ Hts City SD

2155 Miramar Blvd • University Heights, OH 44118-3301
(216) 371-7171
Grade Span: KG-12; **Agency Type:** 1
Schools: 14
8 Primary; 3 Middle; 1 High; 2 Other Level
13 Regular; 1 Special Education; 0 Vocational; 0 Alternative
0 Magnet; 0 Charter; 12 Title I Eligible; 0 School-wide Title I
Students: 7,044 (50.2% male; 49.8% female)
Individual Education Program: 964 (13.7%);
English Language Learner: 49 (0.7%); Migrant: n/a
Eligible for Free Lunch Program: 2,128 (30.2%)
Eligible for Reduced-Price Lunch Program: 477 (6.8%)
Teachers: 512.8 (13.7 to 1)
Librarians/Media Specialists: 11.6 (607.2 to 1)
Guidance Counselors: 23.1 (304.9 to 1)
Current Spending: ($ per student per year):
Total: $10,392; Instruction: $5,734; Support Services: $4,396

Enrollment, Drop-out Rates and Diploma Recipients by Race/Ethnicity

Category	Total	White	Black	Asian	AIAN	Hisp.
Enrollment (%)	100.0	19.1	75.0	1.3	0.1	0.9
Drop-out Rate (%)	5.2	2.6	6.2	3.3	0.0	0.0
H.S. Diplomas (#)	346	108	224	8	0	4

Cleveland Municipal SD

1380 E 6th St • Cleveland, OH 44114-1606
(216) 574-8000 • http://www.cmsdnet.net/
Grade Span: PK-12; **Agency Type:** 1
Schools: 129
79 Primary; 14 Middle; 16 High; 20 Other Level
129 Regular; 0 Special Education; 0 Vocational; 0 Alternative
0 Magnet; 0 Charter; 124 Title I Eligible; 110 School-wide Title I
Students: 71,616 (51.2% male; 48.8% female)
Individual Education Program: 12,494 (17.4%);
English Language Learner: 28 (<0.1%); Migrant: n/a
Eligible for Free Lunch Program: 52,050 (72.7%)
Eligible for Reduced-Price Lunch Program: 4,665 (6.5%)
Teachers: 6,670.7 (10.7 to 1)
Librarians/Media Specialists: 104.0 (688.6 to 1)
Guidance Counselors: 103.1 (694.6 to 1)
Current Spending: ($ per student per year):
Total: $8,735; Instruction: $4,883; Support Services: $3,500
Enrollment, Drop-out Rates and Diploma Recipients by Race/Ethnicity

Category	Total	White	Black	Asian	AIAN	Hisp.
Enrollment (%)	100.0	18.4	70.5	0.7	0.3	9.1
Drop-out Rate (%)	19.6	23.2	19.0	11.2	16.0	18.3
H.S. Diplomas (#)	2,443	405	1,796	34	7	194

East Cleveland City SD

15305 Terrace Rd • East Cleveland, OH 44112-2933
(216) 268-6570
Grade Span: PK-12; **Agency Type:** 1
Schools: 8
5 Primary; 1 Middle; 1 High; 1 Other Level
8 Regular; 0 Special Education; 0 Vocational; 0 Alternative
0 Magnet; 0 Charter; 8 Title I Eligible; 7 School-wide Title I
Students: 5,304 (49.6% male; 50.4% female)
Individual Education Program: 622 (11.7%);
English Language Learner: 0 (0.0%); Migrant: n/a
Eligible for Free Lunch Program: 3,299 (62.2%)
Eligible for Reduced-Price Lunch Program: 283 (5.3%)
Teachers: 370.4 (14.3 to 1)
Librarians/Media Specialists: 3.0 (1,768.0 to 1)
Guidance Counselors: 6.0 (884.0 to 1)
Current Spending: ($ per student per year):
Total: $9,685; Instruction: $5,445; Support Services: $3,862
Enrollment, Drop-out Rates and Diploma Recipients by Race/Ethnicity

Category	Total	White	Black	Asian	AIAN	Hisp.
Enrollment (%)	100.0	0.2	99.4	0.0	0.0	0.0
Drop-out Rate (%)	15.1	0.0	15.1	n/a	0.0	n/a
H.S. Diplomas (#)	252	0	252	0	0	0

Euclid City SD

651 E 222nd St • Euclid, OH 44123-2031
(216) 261-2900
Grade Span: PK-12; **Agency Type:** 1
Schools: 9
5 Primary; 2 Middle; 1 High; 1 Other Level
8 Regular; 0 Special Education; 1 Vocational; 0 Alternative
0 Magnet; 0 Charter; 8 Title I Eligible; 0 School-wide Title I
Students: 6,140 (51.9% male; 48.1% female)
Individual Education Program: 1,021 (16.6%);
English Language Learner: 41 (0.7%); Migrant: n/a
Eligible for Free Lunch Program: 2,455 (40.0%)
Eligible for Reduced-Price Lunch Program: 996 (16.2%)
Teachers: 390.8 (15.7 to 1)
Librarians/Media Specialists: 3.0 (2,046.7 to 1)
Guidance Counselors: 11.0 (558.2 to 1)
Current Spending: ($ per student per year):
Total: $8,933; Instruction: $4,973; Support Services: $3,716
Enrollment, Drop-out Rates and Diploma Recipients by Race/Ethnicity

Category	Total	White	Black	Asian	AIAN	Hisp.
Enrollment (%)	100.0	34.1	61.5	0.7	0.1	0.7
Drop-out Rate (%)	0.0	0.0	0.0	0.0	0.0	0.0
H.S. Diplomas (#)	363	192	165	1	0	2

Fairview Park City SD

20770 Lorain Rd • Fairview Park, OH 44126-2019
(440) 331-5500
Grade Span: PK-12; **Agency Type:** 1
Schools: 5
2 Primary; 2 Middle; 1 High; 0 Other Level
5 Regular; 0 Special Education; 0 Vocational; 0 Alternative
0 Magnet; 0 Charter; 4 Title I Eligible; 0 School-wide Title I
Students: 1,871 (51.1% male; 48.9% female)
Individual Education Program: 274 (14.6%);
English Language Learner: 63 (3.4%); Migrant: 1 (0.1%)
Eligible for Free Lunch Program: 196 (10.5%)
Eligible for Reduced-Price Lunch Program: 83 (4.4%)
Teachers: 135.8 (13.8 to 1)
Librarians/Media Specialists: 3.0 (623.7 to 1)
Guidance Counselors: 5.0 (374.2 to 1)
Current Spending: ($ per student per year):
Total: $8,358; Instruction: $4,978; Support Services: $3,254
Enrollment, Drop-out Rates and Diploma Recipients by Race/Ethnicity

Category	Total	White	Black	Asian	AIAN	Hisp.
Enrollment (%)	100.0	93.7	0.6	2.5	0.1	1.7
Drop-out Rate (%)	1.3	1.4	0.0	0.0	n/a	0.0
H.S. Diplomas (#)	167	161	1	3	0	2

Garfield Heights City SD

5640 Briarcliff Dr • Garfield Heights, OH 44125-4158
(216) 475-8100
Grade Span: PK-12; **Agency Type:** 1
Schools: 5
2 Primary; 2 Middle; 1 High; 0 Other Level
5 Regular; 0 Special Education; 0 Vocational; 0 Alternative
0 Magnet; 0 Charter; 4 Title I Eligible; 3 School-wide Title I
Students: 3,792 (52.5% male; 47.5% female)
Individual Education Program: 533 (14.1%);
English Language Learner: 13 (0.3%); Migrant: n/a
Eligible for Free Lunch Program: 826 (21.8%)
Eligible for Reduced-Price Lunch Program: 419 (11.0%)
Teachers: 206.0 (18.4 to 1)
Librarians/Media Specialists: 5.0 (758.4 to 1)
Guidance Counselors: 4.0 (948.0 to 1)
Current Spending: ($ per student per year):
Total: $7,152; Instruction: $4,130; Support Services: $2,789
Enrollment, Drop-out Rates and Diploma Recipients by Race/Ethnicity

Category	Total	White	Black	Asian	AIAN	Hisp.
Enrollment (%)	100.0	78.0	16.9	1.5	0.1	1.1
Drop-out Rate (%)	1.6	1.5	1.3	0.0	0.0	14.3
H.S. Diplomas (#)	263	223	30	4	0	3

Lakewood City SD

1470 Warren Rd • Lakewood, OH 44107-3918
(216) 529-4092 • http://www.lkwdpl.org/schools/
Grade Span: PK-12; **Agency Type:** 1
Schools: 14
10 Primary; 3 Middle; 1 High; 0 Other Level
14 Regular; 0 Special Education; 0 Vocational; 0 Alternative
0 Magnet; 0 Charter; 9 Title I Eligible; 6 School-wide Title I
Students: 6,949 (51.6% male; 48.4% female)
Individual Education Program: 1,033 (14.9%);
English Language Learner: 532 (7.7%); Migrant: n/a
Eligible for Free Lunch Program: 1,424 (20.5%)
Eligible for Reduced-Price Lunch Program: 436 (6.3%)
Teachers: 442.3 (15.7 to 1)
Librarians/Media Specialists: 7.0 (992.7 to 1)
Guidance Counselors: 14.5 (479.2 to 1)
Current Spending: ($ per student per year):
Total: $7,706; Instruction: $4,755; Support Services: $2,752
Enrollment, Drop-out Rates and Diploma Recipients by Race/Ethnicity

Category	Total	White	Black	Asian	AIAN	Hisp.
Enrollment (%)	100.0	89.3	3.3	1.5	0.4	2.0
Drop-out Rate (%)	3.6	3.6	2.1	2.4	16.7	3.7
H.S. Diplomas (#)	518	488	15	4	0	7

Maple Heights City SD

14605 Granger Rd • Maple Heights, OH 44137-1023
(216) 587-6100
Grade Span: PK-12; **Agency Type:** 1
Schools: 6
4 Primary; 1 Middle; 1 High; 0 Other Level
6 Regular; 0 Special Education; 0 Vocational; 0 Alternative
0 Magnet; 0 Charter; 5 Title I Eligible; 4 School-wide Title I
Students: 3,775 (52.1% male; 47.9% female)
Individual Education Program: 507 (13.4%);
English Language Learner: 21 (0.6%); Migrant: n/a
Eligible for Free Lunch Program: 1,141 (30.2%)
Eligible for Reduced-Price Lunch Program: 450 (11.9%)
Teachers: 224.0 (16.9 to 1)
Librarians/Media Specialists: 1.0 (3,775.0 to 1)
Guidance Counselors: 4.0 (943.8 to 1)
Current Spending: ($ per student per year):
Total: $6,808; Instruction: $3,912; Support Services: $2,610

Enrollment, Drop-out Rates and Diploma Recipients by Race/Ethnicity

Category	Total	White	Black	Asian	AIAN	Hisp.
Enrollment (%)	100.0	15.0	81.0	1.5	0.0	0.8
Drop-out Rate (%)	7.0	3.6	8.2	0.0	0.0	14.3
H.S. Diplomas (#)	189	44	141	2	0	1

Mayfield City SD

59 Alpha Park • Highland Heights, OH 44143-2202
(440) 995-6800
Grade Span: PK-12; **Agency Type:** 1
Schools: 7
5 Primary; 1 Middle; 1 High; 0 Other Level
6 Regular; 1 Special Education; 0 Vocational; 0 Alternative
0 Magnet; 0 Charter; 4 Title I Eligible; 0 School-wide Title I
Students: 4,264 (53.8% male; 46.2% female)
Individual Education Program: 679 (15.9%);
English Language Learner: 196 (4.6%); Migrant: n/a
Eligible for Free Lunch Program: 209 (4.9%)
Eligible for Reduced-Price Lunch Program: 89 (2.1%)
Teachers: 323.6 (13.2 to 1)
Librarians/Media Specialists: 3.0 (1,421.3 to 1)
Guidance Counselors: 10.0 (426.4 to 1)
Current Spending: ($ per student per year):
Total: $10,352; Instruction: $5,796; Support Services: $4,358
Enrollment, Drop-out Rates and Diploma Recipients by Race/Ethnicity

Category	Total	White	Black	Asian	AIAN	Hisp.
Enrollment (%)	100.0	85.0	6.8	5.0	0.1	1.0
Drop-out Rate (%)	1.3	1.3	1.7	0.0	0.0	0.0
H.S. Diplomas (#)	341	304	8	20	1	5

North Olmsted City SD

24100 Palm Dr • North Olmsted, OH 44070-2844
(440) 779-3549 • http://www.nocs.leeca.esu.k12.oh.us/
Grade Span: PK-12; **Agency Type:** 1
Schools: 9
6 Primary; 2 Middle; 1 High; 0 Other Level
9 Regular; 0 Special Education; 0 Vocational; 0 Alternative
0 Magnet; 0 Charter; 7 Title I Eligible; 0 School-wide Title I
Students: 4,665 (52.2% male; 47.8% female)
Individual Education Program: 572 (12.3%);
English Language Learner: 61 (1.3%); Migrant: 4 (0.1%)
Eligible for Free Lunch Program: 487 (10.4%)
Eligible for Reduced-Price Lunch Program: 227 (4.9%)
Teachers: 359.3 (13.0 to 1)
Librarians/Media Specialists: 2.0 (2,332.5 to 1)
Guidance Counselors: 12.0 (388.8 to 1)
Current Spending: ($ per student per year):
Total: $7,914; Instruction: $4,976; Support Services: $2,680
Enrollment, Drop-out Rates and Diploma Recipients by Race/Ethnicity

Category	Total	White	Black	Asian	AIAN	Hisp.
Enrollment (%)	100.0	92.3	1.2	3.1	0.1	1.6
Drop-out Rate (%)	2.3	2.2	8.3	2.0	0.0	0.0
H.S. Diplomas (#)	368	345	3	14	0	5

North Royalton City SD

6579 Royalton Rd • North Royalton, OH 44133-4925
(440) 237-8800 • http://www.lnoca.org/~nrcs/
Grade Span: PK-12; **Agency Type:** 1
Schools: 5
3 Primary; 1 Middle; 1 High; 0 Other Level
5 Regular; 0 Special Education; 0 Vocational; 0 Alternative
0 Magnet; 0 Charter; 3 Title I Eligible; 0 School-wide Title I
Students: 4,429 (50.6% male; 49.4% female)
Individual Education Program: 468 (10.6%);
English Language Learner: 52 (1.2%); Migrant: n/a
Eligible for Free Lunch Program: 180 (4.1%)
Eligible for Reduced-Price Lunch Program: 94 (2.1%)
Teachers: 247.6 (17.9 to 1)
Librarians/Media Specialists: 3.5 (1,265.4 to 1)
Guidance Counselors: 10.0 (442.9 to 1)
Current Spending: ($ per student per year):
Total: $7,232; Instruction: $4,224; Support Services: $2,751
Enrollment, Drop-out Rates and Diploma Recipients by Race/Ethnicity

Category	Total	White	Black	Asian	AIAN	Hisp.
Enrollment (%)	100.0	94.9	0.4	2.7	0.1	0.4
Drop-out Rate (%)	0.8	0.9	0.0	0.0	n/a	0.0
H.S. Diplomas (#)	335	324	0	10	0	1

Olmsted Falls City SD

PO Box 38010 • Olmsted Falls, OH 44138-0010
(440) 427-6000
Grade Span: PK-12; **Agency Type:** 1
Schools: 4
1 Primary; 2 Middle; 1 High; 0 Other Level
4 Regular; 0 Special Education; 0 Vocational; 0 Alternative
0 Magnet; 0 Charter; 3 Title I Eligible; 0 School-wide Title I
Students: 3,198 (51.3% male; 48.7% female)
Individual Education Program: 350 (10.9%);
English Language Learner: 2 (0.1%); Migrant: 1 (<0.1%)
Eligible for Free Lunch Program: 167 (5.2%)
Eligible for Reduced-Price Lunch Program: 110 (3.4%)
Teachers: 189.7 (16.9 to 1)
Librarians/Media Specialists: 3.0 (1,066.0 to 1)
Guidance Counselors: 6.6 (484.5 to 1)
Current Spending: ($ per student per year):
Total: $7,538; Instruction: $4,462; Support Services: $2,816
Enrollment, Drop-out Rates and Diploma Recipients by Race/Ethnicity

Category	Total	White	Black	Asian	AIAN	Hisp.
Enrollment (%)	100.0	95.9	1.3	1.0	0.1	1.2
Drop-out Rate (%)	1.3	1.3	0.0	0.0	n/a	0.0
H.S. Diplomas (#)	219	205	4	5	0	5

Orange City SD

32000 Chagrin Blvd • Cleveland, OH 44124-5922
(216) 831-8600 • http://www.orangeschools.org/
Grade Span: PK-12; **Agency Type:** 1
Schools: 4
2 Primary; 1 Middle; 1 High; 0 Other Level
3 Regular; 1 Special Education; 0 Vocational; 0 Alternative
0 Magnet; 0 Charter; 2 Title I Eligible; 0 School-wide Title I
Students: 2,363 (55.0% male; 45.0% female)
Individual Education Program: 274 (11.6%);
English Language Learner: 59 (2.5%); Migrant: n/a
Eligible for Free Lunch Program: 38 (1.6%)
Eligible for Reduced-Price Lunch Program: 9 (0.4%)
Teachers: 185.2 (12.8 to 1)
Librarians/Media Specialists: 4.0 (590.8 to 1)
Guidance Counselors: 7.0 (337.6 to 1)
Current Spending: ($ per student per year):
Total: $13,777; Instruction: $8,194; Support Services: $5,401
Enrollment, Drop-out Rates and Diploma Recipients by Race/Ethnicity

Category	Total	White	Black	Asian	AIAN	Hisp.
Enrollment (%)	100.0	74.3	17.3	5.0	0.3	0.4
Drop-out Rate (%)	0.7	0.7	0.9	0.0	0.0	0.0
H.S. Diplomas (#)	193	144	28	16	1	1

Parma City SD

6726 Ridge Rd • Parma, OH 44129-5703
(440) 842-5300
Grade Span: KG-12; **Agency Type:** 1
Schools: 21
15 Primary; 3 Middle; 3 High; 0 Other Level
21 Regular; 0 Special Education; 0 Vocational; 0 Alternative
0 Magnet; 0 Charter; 13 Title I Eligible; 0 School-wide Title I
Students: 13,441 (50.4% male; 49.6% female)
Individual Education Program: 2,117 (15.8%);
English Language Learner: 292 (2.2%); Migrant: n/a
Eligible for Free Lunch Program: 1,716 (12.8%)
Eligible for Reduced-Price Lunch Program: 968 (7.2%)
Teachers: 816.8 (16.5 to 1)
Librarians/Media Specialists: 8.0 (1,680.1 to 1)
Guidance Counselors: 21.0 (640.0 to 1)
Current Spending: ($ per student per year):
Total: $7,564; Instruction: $4,521; Support Services: $2,849
Enrollment, Drop-out Rates and Diploma Recipients by Race/Ethnicity

Category	Total	White	Black	Asian	AIAN	Hisp.
Enrollment (%)	100.0	93.5	1.5	2.3	0.1	1.5
Drop-out Rate (%)	5.7	5.6	7.7	4.3	n/a	15.2
H.S. Diplomas (#)	886	851	8	16	0	7

Rocky River City SD

21600 Center Ridge Rd • Rocky River, OH 44116-3918
(440) 333-6000
Grade Span: PK-12; **Agency Type:** 1
Schools: 4
2 Primary; 1 Middle; 1 High; 0 Other Level
4 Regular; 0 Special Education; 0 Vocational; 0 Alternative
0 Magnet; 0 Charter; 1 Title I Eligible; 0 School-wide Title I
Students: 2,575 (50.1% male; 49.9% female)
Individual Education Program: 352 (13.7%);
English Language Learner: 36 (1.4%); Migrant: n/a
Eligible for Free Lunch Program: 70 (2.7%)
Eligible for Reduced-Price Lunch Program: 23 (0.9%)
Teachers: 159.6 (16.1 to 1)
Librarians/Media Specialists: 3.0 (858.3 to 1)
Guidance Counselors: 7.0 (367.9 to 1)
Current Spending: ($ per student per year):
Total: $8,855; Instruction: $5,134; Support Services: $3,542

Enrollment, Drop-out Rates and Diploma Recipients by Race/Ethnicity

Category	Total	White	Black	Asian	AIAN	Hisp.
Enrollment (%)	100.0	94.1	0.5	1.5	0.3	1.5
Drop-out Rate (%)	0.5	0.6	0.0	0.0	0.0	0.0
H.S. Diplomas (#)	145	137	0	4	0	4

Shaker Heights City SD

15600 Parkland Dr • Shaker Heights, OH 44120-2529
(216) 295-4000 • http://www.shaker.org/
Grade Span: PK-12; **Agency Type:** 1
Schools: 9
6 Primary; 2 Middle; 1 High; 0 Other Level
9 Regular; 0 Special Education; 0 Vocational; 0 Alternative
0 Magnet; 0 Charter; 2 Title I Eligible; 0 School-wide Title I
Students: 5,612 (51.1% male; 48.9% female)
Individual Education Program: 829 (14.8%);
English Language Learner: 121 (2.2%); Migrant: n/a
Eligible for Free Lunch Program: 404 (7.2%)
Eligible for Reduced-Price Lunch Program: 83 (1.5%)
Teachers: 429.2 (13.1 to 1)
Librarians/Media Specialists: 9.0 (623.6 to 1)
Guidance Counselors: 11.0 (510.2 to 1)
Current Spending: ($ per student per year):
Total: $11,453; Instruction: $6,034; Support Services: $5,285

Enrollment, Drop-out Rates and Diploma Recipients by Race/Ethnicity

Category	Total	White	Black	Asian	AIAN	Hisp.
Enrollment (%)	100.0	40.5	51.0	3.2	0.0	1.3
Drop-out Rate (%)	0.1	0.1	0.1	0.0	n/a	0.0
H.S. Diplomas (#)	362	177	169	7	0	2

Solon City SD

33800 Inwood Dr • Solon, OH 44139-4133
(440) 248-1600
Grade Span: PK-12; **Agency Type:** 1
Schools: 7
4 Primary; 2 Middle; 1 High; 0 Other Level
7 Regular; 0 Special Education; 0 Vocational; 0 Alternative
0 Magnet; 0 Charter; 4 Title I Eligible; 0 School-wide Title I
Students: 5,115 (51.3% male; 48.7% female)
Individual Education Program: 599 (11.7%);
English Language Learner: 85 (1.7%); Migrant: n/a
Eligible for Free Lunch Program: 62 (1.2%)
Eligible for Reduced-Price Lunch Program: 64 (1.3%)
Teachers: 338.4 (15.1 to 1)
Librarians/Media Specialists: 7.0 (730.7 to 1)
Guidance Counselors: 12.0 (426.3 to 1)
Current Spending: ($ per student per year):
Total: $9,173; Instruction: $5,591; Support Services: $3,355

Enrollment, Drop-out Rates and Diploma Recipients by Race/Ethnicity

Category	Total	White	Black	Asian	AIAN	Hisp.
Enrollment (%)	100.0	82.0	8.1	7.3	0.0	0.6
Drop-out Rate (%)	0.8	0.6	2.6	0.0	0.0	14.3
H.S. Diplomas (#)	390	342	27	14	0	1

South Euclid-Lyndhurst City SD

5044 Mayfield Rd • Lyndhurst, OH 44124-2605
(216) 691-2000 •
http://www.sel.k12.oh.us/_vti_bin/owssvr.dll?Using=Default%2ehtm
Grade Span: PK-12; **Agency Type:** 1
Schools: 9
6 Primary; 2 Middle; 1 High; 0 Other Level
9 Regular; 0 Special Education; 0 Vocational; 0 Alternative
0 Magnet; 0 Charter; 5 Title I Eligible; 0 School-wide Title I
Students: 4,521 (52.1% male; 47.9% female)
Individual Education Program: 687 (15.2%);
English Language Learner: 14 (0.3%); Migrant: n/a
Eligible for Free Lunch Program: 495 (10.9%)
Eligible for Reduced-Price Lunch Program: 242 (5.4%)
Teachers: 314.3 (14.4 to 1)
Librarians/Media Specialists: 6.0 (753.5 to 1)
Guidance Counselors: 8.0 (565.1 to 1)
Current Spending: ($ per student per year):
Total: $8,983; Instruction: $5,246; Support Services: $3,503

Enrollment, Drop-out Rates and Diploma Recipients by Race/Ethnicity

Category	Total	White	Black	Asian	AIAN	Hisp.
Enrollment (%)	100.0	61.4	33.3	1.5	0.0	0.6
Drop-out Rate (%)	1.5	1.6	1.4	0.0	0.0	0.0
H.S. Diplomas (#)	342	250	76	13	0	2

Strongsville City SD

13200 Pearl Rd • Strongsville, OH 44136-3402
(440) 572-7000
Grade Span: PK-12; **Agency Type:** 1
Schools: 11
8 Primary; 2 Middle; 1 High; 0 Other Level
11 Regular; 0 Special Education; 0 Vocational; 0 Alternative
0 Magnet; 0 Charter; 5 Title I Eligible; 0 School-wide Title I
Students: 7,214 (52.2% male; 47.8% female)
Individual Education Program: 904 (12.5%);
English Language Learner: 67 (0.9%); Migrant: 2 (<0.1%)
Eligible for Free Lunch Program: 357 (4.9%)
Eligible for Reduced-Price Lunch Program: 235 (3.3%)
Teachers: 406.2 (17.8 to 1)
Librarians/Media Specialists: 6.0 (1,202.3 to 1)
Guidance Counselors: 11.0 (655.8 to 1)
Current Spending: ($ per student per year):
Total: $7,993; Instruction: $5,049; Support Services: $2,740

Enrollment, Drop-out Rates and Diploma Recipients by Race/Ethnicity

Category	Total	White	Black	Asian	AIAN	Hisp.
Enrollment (%)	100.0	91.3	1.5	4.0	0.0	1.0
Drop-out Rate (%)	1.2	1.2	3.2	0.0	0.0	0.0
H.S. Diplomas (#)	508	482	4	19	0	3

Warrensville Heights City SD

4500 Warrensville Center Rd • Warrensville Heights, OH 44128-4134
(216) 295-7710
Grade Span: PK-12; **Agency Type:** 1
Schools: 6
2 Primary; 1 Middle; 1 High; 2 Other Level
6 Regular; 0 Special Education; 0 Vocational; 0 Alternative
0 Magnet; 0 Charter; 5 Title I Eligible; 5 School-wide Title I
Students: 2,966 (49.6% male; 50.4% female)
Individual Education Program: 412 (13.9%);
English Language Learner: 0 (0.0%); Migrant: 2 (0.1%)
Eligible for Free Lunch Program: 1,588 (53.5%)
Eligible for Reduced-Price Lunch Program: 459 (15.5%)
Teachers: 219.0 (13.5 to 1)
Librarians/Media Specialists: 4.0 (741.5 to 1)
Guidance Counselors: 10.0 (296.6 to 1)
Current Spending: ($ per student per year):
Total: $8,661; Instruction: $4,688; Support Services: $3,757

Enrollment, Drop-out Rates and Diploma Recipients by Race/Ethnicity

Category	Total	White	Black	Asian	AIAN	Hisp.
Enrollment (%)	100.0	0.4	99.0	0.1	0.0	0.2
Drop-out Rate (%)	0.0	0.0	0.0	n/a	n/a	n/a
H.S. Diplomas (#)	160	0	159	0	0	0

Westlake City SD

27200 Hilliard Blvd • Westlake, OH 44145-3049
(440) 871-7300 • http://www.westlake.k12.oh.us/
Grade Span: PK-12; **Agency Type:** 1
Schools: 7
4 Primary; 2 Middle; 1 High; 0 Other Level
7 Regular; 0 Special Education; 0 Vocational; 0 Alternative
0 Magnet; 0 Charter; 6 Title I Eligible; 0 School-wide Title I
Students: 3,880 (51.7% male; 48.3% female)
Individual Education Program: 535 (13.8%);
English Language Learner: 16 (0.4%); Migrant: 3 (0.1%)
Eligible for Free Lunch Program: 121 (3.1%)
Eligible for Reduced-Price Lunch Program: 50 (1.3%)
Teachers: 244.3 (15.9 to 1)
Librarians/Media Specialists: 6.0 (646.7 to 1)
Guidance Counselors: 8.0 (485.0 to 1)
Current Spending: ($ per student per year):
Total: $9,014; Instruction: $5,381; Support Services: $3,434

Enrollment, Drop-out Rates and Diploma Recipients by Race/Ethnicity

Category	Total	White	Black	Asian	AIAN	Hisp.
Enrollment (%)	100.0	94.4	0.8	3.3	0.1	0.6
Drop-out Rate (%)	2.2	2.1	7.1	0.0	50.0	11.1
H.S. Diplomas (#)	276	258	3	12	0	3

Darke County

Greenville City SD

215 W 4th St • Greenville, OH 45331-1423
(937) 548-3185
Grade Span: PK-12; **Agency Type:** 1
Schools: 7
4 Primary; 2 Middle; 1 High; 0 Other Level
7 Regular; 0 Special Education; 0 Vocational; 0 Alternative
0 Magnet; 0 Charter; 5 Title I Eligible; 1 School-wide Title I
Students: 3,497 (51.2% male; 48.8% female)
Individual Education Program: 478 (13.7%);
English Language Learner: 1 (<0.1%); Migrant: 1 (<0.1%)
Eligible for Free Lunch Program: 633 (18.1%)
Eligible for Reduced-Price Lunch Program: 221 (6.3%)
Teachers: 230.3 (15.2 to 1)
Librarians/Media Specialists: 2.0 (1,748.5 to 1)
Guidance Counselors: 6.0 (582.8 to 1)
Current Spending: ($ per student per year):
Total: $5,995; Instruction: $3,843; Support Services: $1,980

Enrollment, Drop-out Rates and Diploma Recipients by Race/Ethnicity

Category	Total	White	Black	Asian	AIAN	Hisp.
Enrollment (%)	100.0	96.9	0.6	0.7	0.1	0.5
Drop-out Rate (%)	2.1	2.1	0.0	0.0	0.0	0.0
H.S. Diplomas (#)	267	263	2	2	0	0

Defiance County

Defiance City SD

629 Arabella St • Defiance, OH 43512-2856
(419) 782-0070 • http://www.defiance-city.k12.oh.us/
Grade Span: PK-12; **Agency Type:** 1
Schools: 7
4 Primary; 2 Middle; 1 High; 0 Other Level
7 Regular; 0 Special Education; 0 Vocational; 0 Alternative
0 Magnet; 0 Charter; 5 Title I Eligible; 0 School-wide Title I
Students: 2,592 (52.0% male; 48.0% female)
Individual Education Program: 407 (15.7%);
English Language Learner: 5 (0.2%); Migrant: n/a
Eligible for Free Lunch Program: 425 (16.4%)
Eligible for Reduced-Price Lunch Program: 83 (3.2%)
Teachers: 165.2 (15.7 to 1)
Librarians/Media Specialists: 2.0 (1,296.0 to 1)
Guidance Counselors: 7.0 (370.3 to 1)
Current Spending: ($ per student per year):
Total: $6,146; Instruction: $3,805; Support Services: $2,089

Enrollment, Drop-out Rates and Diploma Recipients by Race/Ethnicity

Category	Total	White	Black	Asian	AIAN	Hisp.
Enrollment (%)	100.0	75.3	4.2	0.5	0.1	16.7
Drop-out Rate (%)	6.8	5.4	10.0	0.0	n/a	15.2
H.S. Diplomas (#)	207	180	5	2	0	20

Delaware County

Big Walnut Local SD

PO Box 218 • Galena, OH 43021-0218
(740) 965-2706 • http://www.bigwalnut.k12.oh.us/
Grade Span: PK-12; **Agency Type:** 2
Schools: 5
3 Primary; 1 Middle; 1 High; 0 Other Level
5 Regular; 0 Special Education; 0 Vocational; 0 Alternative
0 Magnet; 0 Charter; 3 Title I Eligible; 0 School-wide Title I
Students: 2,668 (50.6% male; 49.4% female)
Individual Education Program: 328 (12.3%);
English Language Learner: 0 (0.0%); Migrant: n/a
Eligible for Free Lunch Program: 230 (8.6%)
Eligible for Reduced-Price Lunch Program: 86 (3.2%)
Teachers: 163.6 (16.3 to 1)
Librarians/Media Specialists: 1.0 (2,668.0 to 1)
Guidance Counselors: 6.0 (444.7 to 1)
Current Spending: ($ per student per year):
Total: $6,117; Instruction: $3,743; Support Services: $2,198

Enrollment, Drop-out Rates and Diploma Recipients by Race/Ethnicity

Category	Total	White	Black	Asian	AIAN	Hisp.
Enrollment (%)	100.0	98.3	0.6	0.2	0.0	0.5
Drop-out Rate (%)	2.4	2.3	14.3	0.0	n/a	0.0
H.S. Diplomas (#)	191	189	1	1	0	0

Buckeye Valley Local SD

679 Coover Rd • Delaware, OH 43015-9562
(740) 369-8735 • http://www.buckeyevalley.k12.oh.us/
Grade Span: PK-12; **Agency Type:** 2
Schools: 5
3 Primary; 1 Middle; 1 High; 0 Other Level
5 Regular; 0 Special Education; 0 Vocational; 0 Alternative
0 Magnet; 0 Charter; 2 Title I Eligible; 0 School-wide Title I
Students: 2,256 (52.6% male; 47.4% female)
Individual Education Program: 325 (14.4%);
English Language Learner: 0 (0.0%); Migrant: n/a
Eligible for Free Lunch Program: 160 (7.1%)
Eligible for Reduced-Price Lunch Program: 58 (2.6%)
Teachers: 138.5 (16.3 to 1)
Librarians/Media Specialists: 2.0 (1,128.0 to 1)
Guidance Counselors: 2.0 (1,128.0 to 1)
Current Spending: ($ per student per year):
Total: $6,545; Instruction: $3,703; Support Services: $2,583

Enrollment, Drop-out Rates and Diploma Recipients by Race/Ethnicity

Category	Total	White	Black	Asian	AIAN	Hisp.
Enrollment (%)	100.0	98.5	0.6	0.1	0.1	0.3
Drop-out Rate (%)	1.5	1.5	0.0	0.0	0.0	0.0
H.S. Diplomas (#)	157	153	1	0	1	2

Delaware City SD

248 N Washington St • Delaware, OH 43015-1649
(740) 833-1100 • http://www.dcs.k12.oh.us/
Grade Span: PK-12; **Agency Type:** 1
Schools: 9
5 Primary; 2 Middle; 1 High; 1 Other Level
9 Regular; 0 Special Education; 0 Vocational; 0 Alternative
0 Magnet; 0 Charter; 5 Title I Eligible; 1 School-wide Title I
Students: 4,479 (51.9% male; 48.1% female)
Individual Education Program: 842 (18.8%);
English Language Learner: 45 (1.0%); Migrant: 2 (<0.1%)
Eligible for Free Lunch Program: 662 (14.8%)
Eligible for Reduced-Price Lunch Program: 200 (4.5%)
Teachers: 294.7 (15.2 to 1)
Librarians/Media Specialists: 1.0 (4,479.0 to 1)
Guidance Counselors: 10.0 (447.9 to 1)
Current Spending: ($ per student per year):
Total: $7,670; Instruction: $4,648; Support Services: $2,789

Enrollment, Drop-out Rates and Diploma Recipients by Race/Ethnicity

Category	Total	White	Black	Asian	AIAN	Hisp.
Enrollment (%)	100.0	90.1	4.8	0.7	0.1	1.5
Drop-out Rate (%)	3.7	3.9	1.3	0.0	0.0	9.1
H.S. Diplomas (#)	261	240	14	3	1	2

Olentangy Local SD

814 Shanahan Rd Ste 100 • Lewis Center, OH 43035-9078
(740) 657-4050
Grade Span: PK-12; **Agency Type:** 2
Schools: 14
7 Primary; 2 Middle; 1 High; 0 Other Level
10 Regular; 0 Special Education; 0 Vocational; 0 Alternative
0 Magnet; 0 Charter; 3 Title I Eligible; 0 School-wide Title I
Students: 7,530 (51.1% male; 48.9% female)
Individual Education Program: 783 (10.4%);
English Language Learner: 87 (1.2%); Migrant: n/a
Eligible for Free Lunch Program: 274 (3.6%)
Eligible for Reduced-Price Lunch Program: 120 (1.6%)
Teachers: 460.3 (16.4 to 1)
Librarians/Media Specialists: 10.0 (753.0 to 1)
Guidance Counselors: 15.5 (485.8 to 1)
Current Spending: ($ per student per year):
Total: $7,305; Instruction: $4,260; Support Services: $2,768

Enrollment, Drop-out Rates and Diploma Recipients by Race/Ethnicity

Category	Total	White	Black	Asian	AIAN	Hisp.
Enrollment (%)	100.0	90.1	3.2	2.7	0.0	1.1
Drop-out Rate (%)	1.1	1.0	3.0	0.0	0.0	0.0
H.S. Diplomas (#)	315	301	7	4	0	2

Erie County

Berlin-Milan Local SD

140 Main St S • Milan, OH 44846-9735
(419) 499-4272
Grade Span: PK-12; **Agency Type:** 2
Schools: 4
2 Primary; 1 Middle; 1 High; 0 Other Level
4 Regular; 0 Special Education; 0 Vocational; 0 Alternative
0 Magnet; 0 Charter; 2 Title I Eligible; 0 School-wide Title I
Students: 1,872 (53.3% male; 46.7% female)
Individual Education Program: 260 (13.9%);
English Language Learner: 13 (0.7%); Migrant: 7 (0.4%)
Eligible for Free Lunch Program: 191 (10.2%)
Eligible for Reduced-Price Lunch Program: 69 (3.7%)
Teachers: 114.0 (16.4 to 1)
Librarians/Media Specialists: 1.0 (1,872.0 to 1)
Guidance Counselors: 2.0 (936.0 to 1)
Current Spending: ($ per student per year):
Total: $6,316; Instruction: $3,766; Support Services: $2,329

Enrollment, Drop-out Rates and Diploma Recipients by Race/Ethnicity

Category	Total	White	Black	Asian	AIAN	Hisp.
Enrollment (%)	100.0	95.2	0.4	0.4	0.1	2.2
Drop-out Rate (%)	1.0	1.1	0.0	0.0	n/a	0.0
H.S. Diplomas (#)	132	131	1	0	0	0

Huron City SD

712 Cleveland Rd E • Huron, OH 44839-1871
(419) 433-3911
Grade Span: PK-12; **Agency Type:** 1
Schools: 3
1 Primary; 1 Middle; 1 High; 0 Other Level
3 Regular; 0 Special Education; 0 Vocational; 0 Alternative
0 Magnet; 0 Charter; 1 Title I Eligible; 0 School-wide Title I
Students: 1,666 (50.5% male; 49.5% female)
Individual Education Program: 227 (13.6%);
English Language Learner: 0 (0.0%); Migrant: n/a

Eligible for Free Lunch Program: 140 (8.4%)
Eligible for Reduced-Price Lunch Program: 59 (3.5%)
Teachers: 102.2 (16.3 to 1)
Librarians/Media Specialists: 2.0 (833.0 to 1)
Guidance Counselors: 4.0 (416.5 to 1)
Current Spending: ($ per student per year):
Total: $6,979; Instruction: $4,149; Support Services: $2,528
Enrollment, Drop-out Rates and Diploma Recipients by Race/Ethnicity

Category	Total	White	Black	Asian	AIAN	Hisp.
Enrollment (%)	100.0	96.7	0.5	1.1	0.1	0.7
Drop-out Rate (%)	2.0	2.1	0.0	0.0	0.0	n/a
H.S. Diplomas (#)	136	135	0	0	0	1

Perkins Local SD

1210 E Bogart Rd • Sandusky, OH 44870-6411
(419) 625-0484 • http://www.perkins.k12.oh.us/
Grade Span: PK-12; **Agency Type:** 2
Schools: 4
2 Primary; 1 Middle; 1 High; 0 Other Level
4 Regular; 0 Special Education; 0 Vocational; 0 Alternative
0 Magnet; 0 Charter; 2 Title I Eligible; 0 School-wide Title I
Students: 2,246 (50.1% male; 49.9% female)
Individual Education Program: 348 (15.5%);
English Language Learner: 0 (0.0%); Migrant: n/a
Eligible for Free Lunch Program: 167 (7.4%)
Eligible for Reduced-Price Lunch Program: 76 (3.4%)
Teachers: 142.0 (15.8 to 1)
Librarians/Media Specialists: 2.0 (1,123.0 to 1)
Guidance Counselors: 6.0 (374.3 to 1)
Current Spending: ($ per student per year):
Total: $7,617; Instruction: $4,485; Support Services: $2,853
Enrollment, Drop-out Rates and Diploma Recipients by Race/Ethnicity

Category	Total	White	Black	Asian	AIAN	Hisp.
Enrollment (%)	100.0	89.7	6.4	0.8	0.1	0.6
Drop-out Rate (%)	1.6	1.4	2.2	8.3	n/a	0.0
H.S. Diplomas (#)	150	136	8	3	0	2

Sandusky City SD

407 Decatur St • Sandusky, OH 44870-2442
(419) 626-6940
Grade Span: PK-12; **Agency Type:** 1
Schools: 14
7 Primary; 2 Middle; 1 High; 4 Other Level
11 Regular; 1 Special Education; 2 Vocational; 0 Alternative
0 Magnet; 0 Charter; 11 Title I Eligible; 7 School-wide Title I
Students: 4,316 (51.7% male; 48.3% female)
Individual Education Program: 815 (18.9%);
English Language Learner: 2 (<0.1%); Migrant: n/a
Eligible for Free Lunch Program: 2,067 (47.9%)
Eligible for Reduced-Price Lunch Program: 379 (8.8%)
Teachers: 318.6 (13.5 to 1)
Librarians/Media Specialists: 3.0 (1,438.7 to 1)
Guidance Counselors: 9.0 (479.6 to 1)
Current Spending: ($ per student per year):
Total: $8,221; Instruction: $4,990; Support Services: $2,842
Enrollment, Drop-out Rates and Diploma Recipients by Race/Ethnicity

Category	Total	White	Black	Asian	AIAN	Hisp.
Enrollment (%)	100.0	53.8	33.9	0.0	0.0	2.6
Drop-out Rate (%)	5.6	3.6	8.2	0.0	n/a	15.6
H.S. Diplomas (#)	231	149	76	1	0	4

Vermilion Local SD

1230 Beechview Dr • Vermilion, OH 44089-1604
(440) 967-5210 • http://vermilionschools.org/
Grade Span: PK-12; **Agency Type:** 2
Schools: 4
2 Primary; 1 Middle; 1 High; 0 Other Level
4 Regular; 0 Special Education; 0 Vocational; 0 Alternative
0 Magnet; 0 Charter; 2 Title I Eligible; 0 School-wide Title I
Students: 2,569 (50.8% male; 49.2% female)
Individual Education Program: 366 (14.2%);
English Language Learner: 0 (0.0%); Migrant: 6 (0.2%)
Eligible for Free Lunch Program: 327 (12.7%)
Eligible for Reduced-Price Lunch Program: 187 (7.3%)
Teachers: 151.0 (17.0 to 1)
Librarians/Media Specialists: 1.0 (2,569.0 to 1)
Guidance Counselors: 4.0 (642.3 to 1)
Current Spending: ($ per student per year):
Total: $6,491; Instruction: $3,869; Support Services: $2,434
Enrollment, Drop-out Rates and Diploma Recipients by Race/Ethnicity

Category	Total	White	Black	Asian	AIAN	Hisp.
Enrollment (%)	100.0	96.8	0.3	0.2	0.3	1.7
Drop-out Rate (%)	3.4	3.2	0.0	0.0	0.0	14.3
H.S. Diplomas (#)	171	170	0	0	0	1

Fairfield County

Amanda-Clearcreek Local SD

328 E Main St • Amanda, OH 43102-9330
(740) 969-7250
Grade Span: PK-12; **Agency Type:** 2
Schools: 4
2 Primary; 1 Middle; 1 High; 0 Other Level
4 Regular; 0 Special Education; 0 Vocational; 0 Alternative
0 Magnet; 0 Charter; 2 Title I Eligible; 0 School-wide Title I
Students: 1,631 (51.9% male; 48.1% female)
Individual Education Program: 193 (11.8%);
English Language Learner: 0 (0.0%); Migrant: n/a
Eligible for Free Lunch Program: 243 (14.9%)
Eligible for Reduced-Price Lunch Program: 51 (3.1%)
Teachers: 88.0 (18.5 to 1)
Librarians/Media Specialists: 1.0 (1,631.0 to 1)
Guidance Counselors: 2.0 (815.5 to 1)
Current Spending: ($ per student per year):
Total: $5,684; Instruction: $3,557; Support Services: $1,883
Enrollment, Drop-out Rates and Diploma Recipients by Race/Ethnicity

Category	Total	White	Black	Asian	AIAN	Hisp.
Enrollment (%)	100.0	98.3	0.9	0.1	0.0	0.4
Drop-out Rate (%)	2.8	2.6	0.0	33.3	n/a	n/a
H.S. Diplomas (#)	87	87	0	0	0	0

Fairfield Union Local SD

PO Box 67 • West Rushville, OH 43163-0067
(740) 536-7384 • http://www.fairfield-union.k12.oh.us/
Grade Span: PK-12; **Agency Type:** 2
Schools: 5
2 Primary; 2 Middle; 1 High; 0 Other Level
5 Regular; 0 Special Education; 0 Vocational; 0 Alternative
0 Magnet; 0 Charter; 3 Title I Eligible; 0 School-wide Title I
Students: 1,888 (52.4% male; 47.6% female)
Individual Education Program: 139 (7.4%);
English Language Learner: 0 (0.0%); Migrant: n/a
Eligible for Free Lunch Program: 204 (10.8%)
Eligible for Reduced-Price Lunch Program: 47 (2.5%)
Teachers: 104.5 (18.1 to 1)
Librarians/Media Specialists: 1.0 (1,888.0 to 1)
Guidance Counselors: 3.0 (629.3 to 1)
Current Spending: ($ per student per year):
Total: $5,884; Instruction: $3,562; Support Services: $2,096
Enrollment, Drop-out Rates and Diploma Recipients by Race/Ethnicity

Category	Total	White	Black	Asian	AIAN	Hisp.
Enrollment (%)	100.0	99.2	0.3	0.1	0.2	0.1
Drop-out Rate (%)	1.5	1.5	0.0	n/a	n/a	0.0
H.S. Diplomas (#)	142	142	0	0	0	0

Lancaster City SD

111 S Broad St • Lancaster, OH 43130-4398
(740) 687-7300 • http://198.234.204.51/
Grade Span: PK-12; **Agency Type:** 1
Schools: 12
9 Primary; 2 Middle; 1 High; 0 Other Level
12 Regular; 0 Special Education; 0 Vocational; 0 Alternative
0 Magnet; 0 Charter; 8 Title I Eligible; 7 School-wide Title I
Students: 6,196 (52.4% male; 47.6% female)
Individual Education Program: 744 (12.0%);
English Language Learner: 2 (<0.1%); Migrant: n/a
Eligible for Free Lunch Program: 1,586 (25.6%)
Eligible for Reduced-Price Lunch Program: 501 (8.1%)
Teachers: 378.7 (16.4 to 1)
Librarians/Media Specialists: 7.0 (885.1 to 1)
Guidance Counselors: 9.0 (688.4 to 1)
Current Spending: ($ per student per year):
Total: $7,029; Instruction: $4,127; Support Services: $2,662
Enrollment, Drop-out Rates and Diploma Recipients by Race/Ethnicity

Category	Total	White	Black	Asian	AIAN	Hisp.
Enrollment (%)	100.0	97.5	0.7	0.4	0.1	0.4
Drop-out Rate (%)	4.4	4.4	0.0	8.3	33.3	0.0
H.S. Diplomas (#)	358	349	2	2	1	3

Pickerington Local SD

777 Long Rd • Pickerington, OH 43147-1061
(614) 833-2110
Grade Span: PK-12; **Agency Type:** 2
Schools: 11
5 Primary; 3 Middle; 1 High; 0 Other Level
9 Regular; 0 Special Education; 0 Vocational; 0 Alternative
0 Magnet; 0 Charter; 5 Title I Eligible; 0 School-wide Title I
Students: 8,440 (52.5% male; 47.5% female)
Individual Education Program: 718 (8.5%);
English Language Learner: 14 (0.2%); Migrant: n/a

Eligible for Free Lunch Program: 387 (4.6%)
Eligible for Reduced-Price Lunch Program: 207 (2.5%)
Teachers: 476.3 (17.7 to 1)
Librarians/Media Specialists: 5.5 (1,534.5 to 1)
Guidance Counselors: 18.0 (468.9 to 1)
Current Spending: ($ per student per year):
Total: $6,831; Instruction: $4,086; Support Services: $2,527
Enrollment, Drop-out Rates and Diploma Recipients by Race/Ethnicity

Category	Total	White	Black	Asian	AIAN	Hisp.
Enrollment (%)	100.0	81.9	10.9	2.3	0.1	1.4
Drop-out Rate (%)	1.4	1.1	2.9	6.8	n/a	4.5
H.S. Diplomas (#)	494	449	26	12	0	5

Fayette County

Miami Trace Local SD
1400 US Hwy 22 NW • Washington Ct House, OH 43160-8604
(740) 335-3010
Grade Span: PK-12; **Agency Type:** 2
Schools: 10
5 Primary; 3 Middle; 1 High; 1 Other Level
10 Regular; 0 Special Education; 0 Vocational; 0 Alternative
0 Magnet; 0 Charter; 8 Title I Eligible; 0 School-wide Title I
Students: 2,689 (51.5% male; 48.5% female)
Individual Education Program: 390 (14.5%);
English Language Learner: 3 (0.1%); Migrant: n/a
Eligible for Free Lunch Program: 430 (16.0%)
Eligible for Reduced-Price Lunch Program: 150 (5.6%)
Teachers: 162.8 (16.5 to 1)
Librarians/Media Specialists: 1.5 (1,792.7 to 1)
Guidance Counselors: 5.3 (507.4 to 1)
Current Spending: ($ per student per year):
Total: $6,191; Instruction: $3,382; Support Services: $2,498
Enrollment, Drop-out Rates and Diploma Recipients by Race/Ethnicity

Category	Total	White	Black	Asian	AIAN	Hisp.
Enrollment (%)	100.0	96.7	1.1	0.3	0.5	0.4
Drop-out Rate (%)	5.5	5.5	0.0	n/a	0.0	25.0
H.S. Diplomas (#)	170	168	0	0	0	2

Washington Court House City SD
306 Highland Ave • Washington Ct House, OH 43160-1819
(740) 335-6620
Grade Span: PK-12; **Agency Type:** 1
Schools: 7
5 Primary; 1 Middle; 1 High; 0 Other Level
7 Regular; 0 Special Education; 0 Vocational; 0 Alternative
0 Magnet; 0 Charter; 6 Title I Eligible; 1 School-wide Title I
Students: 2,348 (52.4% male; 47.6% female)
Individual Education Program: 300 (12.8%);
English Language Learner: 3 (0.1%); Migrant: n/a
Eligible for Free Lunch Program: 558 (23.8%)
Eligible for Reduced-Price Lunch Program: 164 (7.0%)
Teachers: 136.0 (17.3 to 1)
Librarians/Media Specialists: 2.0 (1,174.0 to 1)
Guidance Counselors: 6.0 (391.3 to 1)
Current Spending: ($ per student per year):
Total: $5,775; Instruction: $3,530; Support Services: $1,977
Enrollment, Drop-out Rates and Diploma Recipients by Race/Ethnicity

Category	Total	White	Black	Asian	AIAN	Hisp.
Enrollment (%)	100.0	92.7	3.4	1.0	0.0	1.0
Drop-out Rate (%)	3.6	3.6	0.0	100.0	n/a	0.0
H.S. Diplomas (#)	144	139	4	1	0	0

Franklin County

Bexley City SD
348 S Cassingham Rd • Bexley, OH 43209-1897
(614) 231-7611
Grade Span: PK-12; **Agency Type:** 1
Schools: 5
3 Primary; 1 Middle; 1 High; 0 Other Level
5 Regular; 0 Special Education; 0 Vocational; 0 Alternative
0 Magnet; 0 Charter; 2 Title I Eligible; 0 School-wide Title I
Students: 2,244 (51.7% male; 48.3% female)
Individual Education Program: 244 (10.9%);
English Language Learner: 20 (0.9%); Migrant: 1 (<0.1%)
Eligible for Free Lunch Program: 84 (3.7%)
Eligible for Reduced-Price Lunch Program: 30 (1.3%)
Teachers: 166.0 (13.5 to 1)
Librarians/Media Specialists: 4.0 (561.0 to 1)
Guidance Counselors: 6.8 (330.0 to 1)
Current Spending: ($ per student per year):
Total: $8,673; Instruction: $5,725; Support Services: $2,803
Enrollment, Drop-out Rates and Diploma Recipients by Race/Ethnicity

Category	Total	White	Black	Asian	AIAN	Hisp.
Enrollment (%)	100.0	91.5	4.6	1.4	0.0	0.6
Drop-out Rate (%)	1.2	1.3	0.0	0.0	n/a	0.0
H.S. Diplomas (#)	177	164	9	3	0	1

Canal Winchester Local SD
290 Washington St • Canal Winchester, OH 43110-1226
(614) 837-4533
Grade Span: PK-12; **Agency Type:** 2
Schools: 5
3 Primary; 1 Middle; 1 High; 0 Other Level
5 Regular; 0 Special Education; 0 Vocational; 0 Alternative
0 Magnet; 0 Charter; 4 Title I Eligible; 0 School-wide Title I
Students: 2,469 (51.7% male; 48.3% female)
Individual Education Program: 286 (11.6%);
English Language Learner: 21 (0.9%); Migrant: n/a
Eligible for Free Lunch Program: 291 (11.8%)
Eligible for Reduced-Price Lunch Program: 80 (3.2%)
Teachers: 162.7 (15.2 to 1)
Librarians/Media Specialists: 5.0 (493.8 to 1)
Guidance Counselors: 6.0 (411.5 to 1)
Current Spending: ($ per student per year):
Total: $7,614; Instruction: $4,322; Support Services: $3,020
Enrollment, Drop-out Rates and Diploma Recipients by Race/Ethnicity

Category	Total	White	Black	Asian	AIAN	Hisp.
Enrollment (%)	100.0	82.7	12.2	0.8	0.3	0.7
Drop-out Rate (%)	1.4	1.3	0.0	0.0	100.0	0.0
H.S. Diplomas (#)	135	123	10	1	0	1

Columbus City SD
270 E State St • Columbus, OH 43215-4312
(614) 365-5000 • http://www.columbus.k12.oh.us/
Grade Span: PK-12; **Agency Type:** 1
Schools: 151
96 Primary; 27 Middle; 22 High; 6 Other Level
136 Regular; 10 Special Education; 4 Vocational; 1 Alternative
0 Magnet; 0 Charter; 131 Title I Eligible; 115 School-wide Title I
Students: 64,175 (51.2% male; 48.8% female)
Individual Education Program: 8,813 (13.7%);
English Language Learner: 2,151 (3.4%); Migrant: 44 (0.1%)
Eligible for Free Lunch Program: 35,357 (55.1%)
Eligible for Reduced-Price Lunch Program: 4,653 (7.3%)
Teachers: 4,288.6 (15.0 to 1)
Librarians/Media Specialists: 69.0 (930.1 to 1)
Guidance Counselors: 128.5 (499.4 to 1)
Current Spending: ($ per student per year):
Total: $8,816; Instruction: $4,904; Support Services: $3,585
Enrollment, Drop-out Rates and Diploma Recipients by Race/Ethnicity

Category	Total	White	Black	Asian	AIAN	Hisp.
Enrollment (%)	100.0	33.2	61.6	2.1	0.3	2.8
Drop-out Rate (%)	10.1	11.4	9.3	9.6	15.6	11.6
H.S. Diplomas (#)	2,600	918	1,546	87	6	43

Dublin City SD
7030 Coffman Rd • Dublin, OH 43017-1068
(614) 764-5913 • http://the.dublinschools.net/
Grade Span: KG-12; **Agency Type:** 1
Schools: 18
11 Primary; 4 Middle; 2 High; 0 Other Level
17 Regular; 0 Special Education; 0 Vocational; 0 Alternative
0 Magnet; 0 Charter; 0 Title I Eligible; 0 School-wide Title I
Students: 12,046 (51.7% male; 48.3% female)
Individual Education Program: 1,209 (10.0%);
English Language Learner: 691 (5.7%); Migrant: 1 (<0.1%)
Eligible for Free Lunch Program: 296 (2.5%)
Eligible for Reduced-Price Lunch Program: 98 (0.8%)
Teachers: 834.3 (14.4 to 1)
Librarians/Media Specialists: 19.0 (634.0 to 1)
Guidance Counselors: 31.6 (381.2 to 1)
Current Spending: ($ per student per year):
Total: $8,158; Instruction: $5,059; Support Services: $2,866
Enrollment, Drop-out Rates and Diploma Recipients by Race/Ethnicity

Category	Total	White	Black	Asian	AIAN	Hisp.
Enrollment (%)	100.0	82.0	2.8	10.7	0.1	1.8
Drop-out Rate (%)	1.3	1.2	4.9	1.1	0.0	0.0
H.S. Diplomas (#)	767	654	19	79	0	11

Electronic Classroom of Tomorrow
3700 S High St Ste 95 • Columbus, OH 43207-4083
(614) 492-8884
Grade Span: KG-12; **Agency Type:** 7
Schools: 1
0 Primary; 0 Middle; 0 High; 1 Other Level
1 Regular; 0 Special Education; 0 Vocational; 0 Alternative

0 Magnet; 1 Charter; 1 Title I Eligible; 0 School-wide Title I
Students: 4,209 (49.3% male; 50.7% female)
Individual Education Program: 227 (5.4%);
English Language Learner: 0 (0.0%); Migrant: n/a
Eligible for Free Lunch Program: n/a
Eligible for Reduced-Price Lunch Program: n/a
Teachers: 85.2 (49.4 to 1)
Librarians/Media Specialists: 0.0 (0.0 to 1)
Guidance Counselors: 1.0 (4,209.0 to 1)
Current Spending: ($ per student per year):
Total: n/a; Instruction: n/a; Support Services: n/a
Enrollment, Drop-out Rates and Diploma Recipients by Race/Ethnicity

Category	Total	White	Black	Asian	AIAN	Hisp.
Enrollment (%)	100.0	79.3	14.5	0.3	0.6	0.7
Drop-out Rate (%)	0.0	0.0	0.0	0.0	0.0	0.0
H.S. Diplomas (#)	31	23	6	0	0	0

Gahanna-Jefferson City SD
160 S Hamilton Rd • Gahanna, OH 43230-2919
(614) 471-7065
Grade Span: PK-12; **Agency Type:** 1
Schools: 11
7 Primary; 3 Middle; 1 High; 0 Other Level
11 Regular; 0 Special Education; 0 Vocational; 0 Alternative
0 Magnet; 0 Charter; 6 Title I Eligible; 0 School-wide Title I
Students: 6,784 (52.4% male; 47.6% female)
Individual Education Program: 888 (13.1%);
English Language Learner: 57 (0.8%); Migrant: 1 (<0.1%)
Eligible for Free Lunch Program: 371 (5.5%)
Eligible for Reduced-Price Lunch Program: 196 (2.9%)
Teachers: 415.8 (16.3 to 1)
Librarians/Media Specialists: 12.0 (565.3 to 1)
Guidance Counselors: 11.0 (616.7 to 1)
Current Spending: ($ per student per year):
Total: $7,108; Instruction: $4,546; Support Services: $2,345
Enrollment, Drop-out Rates and Diploma Recipients by Race/Ethnicity

Category	Total	White	Black	Asian	AIAN	Hisp.
Enrollment (%)	100.0	81.4	11.9	2.6	0.1	1.2
Drop-out Rate (%)	0.6	0.6	0.9	0.0	0.0	3.7
H.S. Diplomas (#)	424	366	44	9	1	2

Groveport Madison Local SD
5055 S Hamilton Rd • Groveport, OH 43125-9336
(614) 836-5371
Grade Span: PK-12; **Agency Type:** 2
Schools: 10
6 Primary; 2 Middle; 1 High; 1 Other Level
10 Regular; 0 Special Education; 0 Vocational; 0 Alternative
0 Magnet; 0 Charter; 6 Title I Eligible; 0 School-wide Title I
Students: 6,318 (50.7% male; 49.3% female)
Individual Education Program: 1,026 (16.2%);
English Language Learner: 93 (1.5%); Migrant: n/a
Eligible for Free Lunch Program: 1,186 (18.8%)
Eligible for Reduced-Price Lunch Program: 457 (7.2%)
Teachers: 387.1 (16.3 to 1)
Librarians/Media Specialists: 9.0 (702.0 to 1)
Guidance Counselors: 11.0 (574.4 to 1)
Current Spending: ($ per student per year):
Total: $6,980; Instruction: $4,067; Support Services: $2,686
Enrollment, Drop-out Rates and Diploma Recipients by Race/Ethnicity

Category	Total	White	Black	Asian	AIAN	Hisp.
Enrollment (%)	100.0	73.3	21.1	1.4	0.2	1.8
Drop-out Rate (%)	4.7	5.1	2.4	3.8	20.0	6.7
H.S. Diplomas (#)	314	254	44	11	0	2

Hamilton Local SD
1055 Rathmell Rd • Columbus, OH 43207-4742
(614) 491-8044 • http://www.hamilton-local.k12.oh.us/
Grade Span: PK-12; **Agency Type:** 2
Schools: 5
2 Primary; 1 Middle; 1 High; 0 Other Level
4 Regular; 0 Special Education; 0 Vocational; 0 Alternative
0 Magnet; 0 Charter; 3 Title I Eligible; 1 School-wide Title I
Students: 2,905 (50.9% male; 49.1% female)
Individual Education Program: 335 (11.5%);
English Language Learner: 2 (0.1%); Migrant: n/a
Eligible for Free Lunch Program: 482 (16.6%)
Eligible for Reduced-Price Lunch Program: 172 (5.9%)
Teachers: 177.5 (16.4 to 1)
Librarians/Media Specialists: 2.0 (1,452.5 to 1)
Guidance Counselors: 4.5 (645.6 to 1)
Current Spending: ($ per student per year):
Total: $6,266; Instruction: $3,500; Support Services: $2,486

Enrollment, Drop-out Rates and Diploma Recipients by Race/Ethnicity

Category	Total	White	Black	Asian	AIAN	Hisp.
Enrollment (%)	100.0	86.8	10.3	0.9	0.2	0.9
Drop-out Rate (%)	5.6	5.7	7.0	0.0	n/a	0.0
H.S. Diplomas (#)	133	113	15	2	0	3

Hilliard City SD
5323 Cemetery Rd • Hilliard, OH 43026-1546
(614) 771-4273
Grade Span: PK-12; **Agency Type:** 1
Schools: 20
13 Primary; 5 Middle; 2 High; 0 Other Level
20 Regular; 0 Special Education; 0 Vocational; 0 Alternative
0 Magnet; 0 Charter; 9 Title I Eligible; 0 School-wide Title I
Students: 13,854 (51.5% male; 48.5% female)
Individual Education Program: 1,607 (11.6%);
English Language Learner: 450 (3.2%); Migrant: n/a
Eligible for Free Lunch Program: 944 (6.8%)
Eligible for Reduced-Price Lunch Program: 302 (2.2%)
Teachers: 955.1 (14.5 to 1)
Librarians/Media Specialists: 21.0 (659.7 to 1)
Guidance Counselors: 27.1 (511.2 to 1)
Current Spending: ($ per student per year):
Total: $7,124; Instruction: $4,351; Support Services: $2,537
Enrollment, Drop-out Rates and Diploma Recipients by Race/Ethnicity

Category	Total	White	Black	Asian	AIAN	Hisp.
Enrollment (%)	100.0	86.3	4.8	4.0	0.1	2.4
Drop-out Rate (%)	2.6	2.7	0.8	0.9	0.0	6.1
H.S. Diplomas (#)	785	717	19	36	1	4

Plain Local SD
99 W Main St Fl 2nd • New Albany, OH 43054-9270
(614) 855-2040
Grade Span: PK-12; **Agency Type:** 2
Schools: 4
1 Primary; 1 Middle; 1 High; 0 Other Level
3 Regular; 0 Special Education; 0 Vocational; 0 Alternative
0 Magnet; 0 Charter; 1 Title I Eligible; 0 School-wide Title I
Students: 2,592 (49.5% male; 50.5% female)
Individual Education Program: 216 (8.3%);
English Language Learner: 2 (0.1%); Migrant: n/a
Eligible for Free Lunch Program: 43 (1.7%)
Eligible for Reduced-Price Lunch Program: 46 (1.8%)
Teachers: 181.8 (14.3 to 1)
Librarians/Media Specialists: 4.0 (648.0 to 1)
Guidance Counselors: 5.0 (518.4 to 1)
Current Spending: ($ per student per year):
Total: $9,900; Instruction: $5,023; Support Services: $4,441
Enrollment, Drop-out Rates and Diploma Recipients by Race/Ethnicity

Category	Total	White	Black	Asian	AIAN	Hisp.
Enrollment (%)	100.0	86.2	4.8	5.0	0.1	1.4
Drop-out Rate (%)	2.4	2.3	0.0	0.0	n/a	20.0
H.S. Diplomas (#)	108	98	1	5	0	3

Reynoldsburg City SD
7244 E Main St • Reynoldsburg, OH 43068-2014
(614) 501-1020 • http://www.reynoldsburgcityschools.com/
Grade Span: PK-12; **Agency Type:** 1
Schools: 8
5 Primary; 2 Middle; 1 High; 0 Other Level
8 Regular; 0 Special Education; 0 Vocational; 0 Alternative
0 Magnet; 0 Charter; 5 Title I Eligible; 0 School-wide Title I
Students: 6,450 (50.9% male; 49.1% female)
Individual Education Program: 839 (13.0%);
English Language Learner: 80 (1.2%); Migrant: 52 (0.8%)
Eligible for Free Lunch Program: 497 (7.7%)
Eligible for Reduced-Price Lunch Program: 192 (3.0%)
Teachers: 426.0 (15.1 to 1)
Librarians/Media Specialists: 3.0 (2,150.0 to 1)
Guidance Counselors: 7.5 (860.0 to 1)
Current Spending: ($ per student per year):
Total: $6,347; Instruction: $3,887; Support Services: $2,266
Enrollment, Drop-out Rates and Diploma Recipients by Race/Ethnicity

Category	Total	White	Black	Asian	AIAN	Hisp.
Enrollment (%)	100.0	73.3	19.2	1.7	0.2	1.5
Drop-out Rate (%)	3.5	3.8	1.2	2.8	0.0	10.3
H.S. Diplomas (#)	458	372	62	10	1	6

South-Western City SD
3805 Marlane Dr • Grove City, OH 43123-9224
(614) 801-3000 • http://www.swcs.k12.oh.us/
Grade Span: PK-12; **Agency Type:** 1
Schools: 36
19 Primary; 9 Middle; 3 High; 4 Other Level
32 Regular; 2 Special Education; 1 Vocational; 0 Alternative

0 Magnet; 0 Charter; 15 Title I Eligible; 8 School-wide Title I
Students: 20,987 (51.1% male; 48.9% female)
Individual Education Program: 2,677 (12.8%);
English Language Learner: 994 (4.7%); Migrant: 172 (0.8%)
Eligible for Free Lunch Program: 5,213 (24.8%)
Eligible for Reduced-Price Lunch Program: 1,549 (7.4%)
Teachers: 1,310.3 (16.0 to 1)
Librarians/Media Specialists: 4.0 (5,246.8 to 1)
Guidance Counselors: 27.0 (777.3 to 1)
Current Spending: ($ per student per year):
Total: $7,158; Instruction: $3,902; Support Services: $2,981
Enrollment, Drop-out Rates and Diploma Recipients by Race/Ethnicity

Category	Total	White	Black	Asian	AIAN	Hisp.
Enrollment (%)	100.0	81.0	11.7	1.7	0.3	4.9
Drop-out Rate (%)	7.5	7.1	10.5	6.7	0.0	13.2
H.S. Diplomas (#)	1,003	921	57	18	0	7

Upper Arlington City SD
1950 N Mallway Dr • Upper Arlington, OH 43221-4326
(614) 487-5000 • http://www.uaschools.org/
Grade Span: KG-12; **Agency Type:** 1
Schools: 8
5 Primary; 2 Middle; 1 High; 0 Other Level
8 Regular; 0 Special Education; 0 Vocational; 0 Alternative
0 Magnet; 0 Charter; 0 Title I Eligible; 0 School-wide Title I
Students: 5,679 (51.3% male; 48.7% female)
Individual Education Program: 586 (10.3%);
English Language Learner: 108 (1.9%); Migrant: n/a
Eligible for Free Lunch Program: 22 (0.4%)
Eligible for Reduced-Price Lunch Program: 30 (0.5%)
Teachers: 418.8 (13.6 to 1)
Librarians/Media Specialists: 8.0 (709.9 to 1)
Guidance Counselors: 17.1 (332.1 to 1)
Current Spending: ($ per student per year):
Total: $9,151; Instruction: $5,516; Support Services: $3,454
Enrollment, Drop-out Rates and Diploma Recipients by Race/Ethnicity

Category	Total	White	Black	Asian	AIAN	Hisp.
Enrollment (%)	100.0	92.5	0.8	5.5	0.1	0.7
Drop-out Rate (%)	1.0	1.0	9.1	0.0	n/a	0.0
H.S. Diplomas (#)	421	397	2	18	0	3

Westerville City SD
336 S Otterbein Ave • Westerville, OH 43081-2334
(614) 797-5700 • http://www.westerville.k12.oh.us/
Grade Span: PK-12; **Agency Type:** 1
Schools: 23
16 Primary; 4 Middle; 2 High; 0 Other Level
22 Regular; 0 Special Education; 0 Vocational; 0 Alternative
0 Magnet; 0 Charter; 8 Title I Eligible; 0 School-wide Title I
Students: 14,044 (50.9% male; 49.1% female)
Individual Education Program: 1,436 (10.2%);
English Language Learner: 319 (2.3%); Migrant: n/a
Eligible for Free Lunch Program: 970 (6.9%)
Eligible for Reduced-Price Lunch Program: 298 (2.1%)
Teachers: 799.0 (17.6 to 1)
Librarians/Media Specialists: 15.0 (936.3 to 1)
Guidance Counselors: 27.0 (520.1 to 1)
Current Spending: ($ per student per year):
Total: $6,952; Instruction: $4,356; Support Services: $2,381
Enrollment, Drop-out Rates and Diploma Recipients by Race/Ethnicity

Category	Total	White	Black	Asian	AIAN	Hisp.
Enrollment (%)	100.0	78.0	13.9	2.4	0.2	1.4
Drop-out Rate (%)	2.7	2.5	4.2	0.9	0.0	11.1
H.S. Diplomas (#)	970	802	112	28	0	9

Whitehall City SD
625 S Yearling Rd • Whitehall, OH 43213-2861
(614) 417-5000
Grade Span: KG-12; **Agency Type:** 1
Schools: 5
3 Primary; 1 Middle; 1 High; 0 Other Level
5 Regular; 0 Special Education; 0 Vocational; 0 Alternative
0 Magnet; 0 Charter; 4 Title I Eligible; 3 School-wide Title I
Students: 3,042 (52.2% male; 47.8% female)
Individual Education Program: 491 (16.1%);
English Language Learner: 171 (5.6%); Migrant: n/a
Eligible for Free Lunch Program: 1,317 (43.3%)
Eligible for Reduced-Price Lunch Program: 358 (11.8%)
Teachers: 196.5 (15.5 to 1)
Librarians/Media Specialists: 4.0 (760.5 to 1)
Guidance Counselors: 3.0 (1,014.0 to 1)
Current Spending: ($ per student per year):
Total: $7,235; Instruction: $4,390; Support Services: $2,581
Enrollment, Drop-out Rates and Diploma Recipients by Race/Ethnicity

Category	Total	White	Black	Asian	AIAN	Hisp.
Enrollment (%)	100.0	64.6	23.9	2.2	0.3	4.5
Drop-out Rate (%)	7.9	7.9	8.9	0.0	0.0	0.0
H.S. Diplomas (#)	192	150	36	3	0	1

Worthington City SD
200 E Wilson Bridge Rd • Worthington, OH 43085-2332
(614) 883-3000
Grade Span: PK-12; **Agency Type:** 1
Schools: 18
12 Primary; 4 Middle; 2 High; 0 Other Level
18 Regular; 0 Special Education; 0 Vocational; 0 Alternative
0 Magnet; 0 Charter; 9 Title I Eligible; 0 School-wide Title I
Students: 9,941 (52.2% male; 47.8% female)
Individual Education Program: 923 (9.3%);
English Language Learner: 292 (2.9%); Migrant: n/a
Eligible for Free Lunch Program: 393 (4.0%)
Eligible for Reduced-Price Lunch Program: 227 (2.3%)
Teachers: 692.6 (14.4 to 1)
Librarians/Media Specialists: 20.0 (497.1 to 1)
Guidance Counselors: 22.5 (441.8 to 1)
Current Spending: ($ per student per year):
Total: $8,894; Instruction: $5,305; Support Services: $3,342
Enrollment, Drop-out Rates and Diploma Recipients by Race/Ethnicity

Category	Total	White	Black	Asian	AIAN	Hisp.
Enrollment (%)	100.0	84.3	5.7	7.0	0.2	2.2
Drop-out Rate (%)	1.5	1.7	0.6	0.8	0.0	2.3
H.S. Diplomas (#)	803	699	30	66	0	8

Fulton County

Pike-Delta-York Local SD
504 Fernwood St • Delta, OH 43515-1262
(419) 822-3391
Grade Span: PK-12; **Agency Type:** 2
Schools: 4
1 Primary; 2 Middle; 1 High; 0 Other Level
4 Regular; 0 Special Education; 0 Vocational; 0 Alternative
0 Magnet; 0 Charter; 2 Title I Eligible; 0 School-wide Title I
Students: 1,597 (51.6% male; 48.4% female)
Individual Education Program: 223 (14.0%);
English Language Learner: 6 (0.4%); Migrant: 1 (0.1%)
Eligible for Free Lunch Program: 257 (16.1%)
Eligible for Reduced-Price Lunch Program: 134 (8.4%)
Teachers: 93.4 (17.1 to 1)
Librarians/Media Specialists: 1.0 (1,597.0 to 1)
Guidance Counselors: 4.0 (399.3 to 1)
Current Spending: ($ per student per year):
Total: $6,692; Instruction: $3,930; Support Services: $2,504
Enrollment, Drop-out Rates and Diploma Recipients by Race/Ethnicity

Category	Total	White	Black	Asian	AIAN	Hisp.
Enrollment (%)	100.0	94.9	0.3	0.3	0.0	3.9
Drop-out Rate (%)	3.4	3.2	0.0	0.0	0.0	11.8
H.S. Diplomas (#)	116	111	0	1	0	4

Swanton Local SD
108 N Main St • Swanton, OH 43558-1032
(419) 826-7085 • http://www.swanton.k12.oh.us/
Grade Span: PK-12; **Agency Type:** 2
Schools: 5
2 Primary; 2 Middle; 1 High; 0 Other Level
5 Regular; 0 Special Education; 0 Vocational; 0 Alternative
0 Magnet; 0 Charter; 4 Title I Eligible; 0 School-wide Title I
Students: 1,597 (51.9% male; 48.1% female)
Individual Education Program: 226 (14.2%);
English Language Learner: 2 (0.1%); Migrant: n/a
Eligible for Free Lunch Program: 176 (11.0%)
Eligible for Reduced-Price Lunch Program: 75 (4.7%)
Teachers: 98.3 (16.2 to 1)
Librarians/Media Specialists: 2.0 (798.5 to 1)
Guidance Counselors: 4.0 (399.3 to 1)
Current Spending: ($ per student per year):
Total: $6,734; Instruction: $4,133; Support Services: $2,363
Enrollment, Drop-out Rates and Diploma Recipients by Race/Ethnicity

Category	Total	White	Black	Asian	AIAN	Hisp.
Enrollment (%)	100.0	93.6	1.1	0.0	0.8	2.4
Drop-out Rate (%)	3.6	3.4	33.3	0.0	0.0	5.6
H.S. Diplomas (#)	141	137	0	0	1	1

Wauseon Ex Vill SD
120 E Chestnut St • Wauseon, OH 43567-1443
(419) 335-6616
Grade Span: PK-12; **Agency Type:** 1
Schools: 4

2 Primary; 1 Middle; 1 High; 0 Other Level
4 Regular; 0 Special Education; 0 Vocational; 0 Alternative
0 Magnet; 0 Charter; 2 Title I Eligible; 0 School-wide Title I
Students: 2,132 (49.5% male; 50.5% female)
Individual Education Program: 219 (10.3%);
English Language Learner: 56 (2.6%); Migrant: 49 (2.3%)
Eligible for Free Lunch Program: 304 (14.3%)
Eligible for Reduced-Price Lunch Program: 128 (6.0%)
Teachers: 116.2 (18.3 to 1)
Librarians/Media Specialists: 1.0 (2,132.0 to 1)
Guidance Counselors: 4.0 (533.0 to 1)
Current Spending: ($ per student per year):
Total: $5,525; Instruction: $3,481; Support Services: $1,775
Enrollment, Drop-out Rates and Diploma Recipients by Race/Ethnicity

Category	Total	White	Black	Asian	AIAN	Hisp.
Enrollment (%)	100.0	86.4	0.5	1.3	0.1	10.6
Drop-out Rate (%)	2.1	2.0	0.0	0.0	n/a	3.8
H.S. Diplomas (#)	145	132	1	1	0	11

Gallia County

Gallia County Local SD
230 Shawnee Ln • Gallipolis, OH 45631-8594
(740) 446-7917
Grade Span: PK-12; **Agency Type:** 2
Schools: 8
5 Primary; 1 Middle; 2 High; 0 Other Level
8 Regular; 0 Special Education; 0 Vocational; 0 Alternative
0 Magnet; 0 Charter; 6 Title I Eligible; 6 School-wide Title I
Students: 2,679 (51.5% male; 48.5% female)
Individual Education Program: 474 (17.7%);
English Language Learner: 0 (0.0%); Migrant: n/a
Eligible for Free Lunch Program: 931 (34.8%)
Eligible for Reduced-Price Lunch Program: 160 (6.0%)
Teachers: 177.6 (15.1 to 1)
Librarians/Media Specialists: 2.0 (1,339.5 to 1)
Guidance Counselors: 4.0 (669.8 to 1)
Current Spending: ($ per student per year):
Total: $6,330; Instruction: $3,828; Support Services: $2,222
Enrollment, Drop-out Rates and Diploma Recipients by Race/Ethnicity

Category	Total	White	Black	Asian	AIAN	Hisp.
Enrollment (%)	100.0	96.2	2.9	0.2	0.1	0.3
Drop-out Rate (%)	4.0	4.1	0.0	0.0	0.0	0.0
H.S. Diplomas (#)	165	160	3	0	0	1

Gallipolis City SD
61 State St • Gallipolis, OH 45631-1131
(740) 446-3211 • http://gallianet.scoca-k12.org/
Grade Span: PK-12; **Agency Type:** 1
Schools: 5
3 Primary; 0 Middle; 1 High; 1 Other Level
4 Regular; 1 Special Education; 0 Vocational; 0 Alternative
0 Magnet; 0 Charter; 2 Title I Eligible; 2 School-wide Title I
Students: 2,446 (51.5% male; 48.5% female)
Individual Education Program: 496 (20.3%);
English Language Learner: 0 (0.0%); Migrant: n/a
Eligible for Free Lunch Program: 625 (25.6%)
Eligible for Reduced-Price Lunch Program: 78 (3.2%)
Teachers: 149.0 (16.4 to 1)
Librarians/Media Specialists: 1.0 (2,446.0 to 1)
Guidance Counselors: 2.0 (1,223.0 to 1)
Current Spending: ($ per student per year):
Total: $5,969; Instruction: $3,773; Support Services: $2,003
Enrollment, Drop-out Rates and Diploma Recipients by Race/Ethnicity

Category	Total	White	Black	Asian	AIAN	Hisp.
Enrollment (%)	100.0	93.2	5.2	0.6	0.1	0.4
Drop-out Rate (%)	3.2	3.2	3.4	0.0	0.0	0.0
H.S. Diplomas (#)	149	140	6	1	0	2

Geauga County

Chardon Local SD
428 N St • Chardon, OH 44024-1036
(440) 285-4052
Grade Span: PK-12; **Agency Type:** 2
Schools: 6
4 Primary; 1 Middle; 1 High; 0 Other Level
6 Regular; 0 Special Education; 0 Vocational; 0 Alternative
0 Magnet; 0 Charter; 5 Title I Eligible; 0 School-wide Title I
Students: 3,213 (51.5% male; 48.5% female)
Individual Education Program: 381 (11.9%);
English Language Learner: 4 (0.1%); Migrant: n/a
Eligible for Free Lunch Program: 241 (7.5%)
Eligible for Reduced-Price Lunch Program: 83 (2.6%)
Teachers: 190.2 (16.9 to 1)
Librarians/Media Specialists: 4.0 (803.3 to 1)
Guidance Counselors: 6.0 (535.5 to 1)
Current Spending: ($ per student per year):
Total: $6,994; Instruction: $3,889; Support Services: $2,877
Enrollment, Drop-out Rates and Diploma Recipients by Race/Ethnicity

Category	Total	White	Black	Asian	AIAN	Hisp.
Enrollment (%)	100.0	97.2	0.8	0.8	0.1	0.8
Drop-out Rate (%)	0.2	0.2	0.0	0.0	0.0	0.0
H.S. Diplomas (#)	232	229	1	2	0	0

Kenston Local SD
17419 Snyder Rd • Chagrin Falls, OH 44023-2730
(440) 543-9677
Grade Span: KG-12; **Agency Type:** 2
Schools: 5
3 Primary; 1 Middle; 1 High; 0 Other Level
5 Regular; 0 Special Education; 0 Vocational; 0 Alternative
0 Magnet; 0 Charter; 3 Title I Eligible; 0 School-wide Title I
Students: 3,181 (51.5% male; 48.5% female)
Individual Education Program: 311 (9.8%);
English Language Learner: 1 (<0.1%); Migrant: 1 (<0.1%)
Eligible for Free Lunch Program: 113 (3.6%)
Eligible for Reduced-Price Lunch Program: 47 (1.5%)
Teachers: 205.3 (15.5 to 1)
Librarians/Media Specialists: 1.0 (3,181.0 to 1)
Guidance Counselors: 7.0 (454.4 to 1)
Current Spending: ($ per student per year):
Total: $7,704; Instruction: $4,441; Support Services: $3,061
Enrollment, Drop-out Rates and Diploma Recipients by Race/Ethnicity

Category	Total	White	Black	Asian	AIAN	Hisp.
Enrollment (%)	100.0	92.4	4.7	0.7	0.0	0.4
Drop-out Rate (%)	0.9	0.9	0.0	0.0	n/a	0.0
H.S. Diplomas (#)	214	191	17	1	0	3

West Geauga Local SD
8615 Cedar Rd • Chesterland, OH 44026-3519
(440) 729-5900
Grade Span: KG-12; **Agency Type:** 2
Schools: 4
2 Primary; 1 Middle; 1 High; 0 Other Level
4 Regular; 0 Special Education; 0 Vocational; 0 Alternative
0 Magnet; 0 Charter; 2 Title I Eligible; 0 School-wide Title I
Students: 2,623 (53.0% male; 47.0% female)
Individual Education Program: 338 (12.9%);
English Language Learner: 0 (0.0%); Migrant: n/a
Eligible for Free Lunch Program: 37 (1.4%)
Eligible for Reduced-Price Lunch Program: 26 (1.0%)
Teachers: 163.8 (16.0 to 1)
Librarians/Media Specialists: 2.0 (1,311.5 to 1)
Guidance Counselors: 6.6 (397.4 to 1)
Current Spending: ($ per student per year):
Total: $7,188; Instruction: $4,069; Support Services: $2,963
Enrollment, Drop-out Rates and Diploma Recipients by Race/Ethnicity

Category	Total	White	Black	Asian	AIAN	Hisp.
Enrollment (%)	100.0	98.2	0.4	0.5	0.0	0.5
Drop-out Rate (%)	0.6	0.5	11.1	0.0	n/a	n/a
H.S. Diplomas (#)	195	188	5	1	0	0

Greene County

Beavercreek City SD
3040 Kemp Rd • Beavercreek, OH 45431-2644
(937) 426-1522
Grade Span: PK-12; **Agency Type:** 1
Schools: 8
5 Primary; 2 Middle; 1 High; 0 Other Level
8 Regular; 0 Special Education; 0 Vocational; 0 Alternative
0 Magnet; 0 Charter; 5 Title I Eligible; 0 School-wide Title I
Students: 6,891 (51.1% male; 48.9% female)
Individual Education Program: 805 (11.7%);
English Language Learner: 31 (0.4%); Migrant: n/a
Eligible for Free Lunch Program: 265 (3.8%)
Eligible for Reduced-Price Lunch Program: 133 (1.9%)
Teachers: 371.3 (18.6 to 1)
Librarians/Media Specialists: 5.0 (1,378.2 to 1)
Guidance Counselors: 18.0 (382.8 to 1)
Current Spending: ($ per student per year):
Total: $6,840; Instruction: $4,058; Support Services: $2,576
Enrollment, Drop-out Rates and Diploma Recipients by Race/Ethnicity

Category	Total	White	Black	Asian	AIAN	Hisp.
Enrollment (%)	100.0	90.1	1.6	4.9	0.1	1.3
Drop-out Rate (%)	1.7	1.7	8.0	0.0	0.0	0.0
H.S. Diplomas (#)	495	463	7	14	1	3

Fairborn City SD

306 E Whittier Ave • Fairborn, OH 45324-5313
(937) 878-3961
Grade Span: PK-12; **Agency Type:** 1
Schools: 7
5 Primary; 1 Middle; 1 High; 0 Other Level
7 Regular; 0 Special Education; 0 Vocational; 0 Alternative
0 Magnet; 0 Charter; 5 Title I Eligible; 2 School-wide Title I
Students: 5,553 (52.7% male; 47.3% female)
Individual Education Program: 696 (12.5%);
English Language Learner: 62 (1.1%); Migrant: 5 (0.1%)
Eligible for Free Lunch Program: 1,159 (20.9%)
Eligible for Reduced-Price Lunch Program: 349 (6.3%)
Teachers: 338.0 (16.4 to 1)
Librarians/Media Specialists: 2.0 (2,776.5 to 1)
Guidance Counselors: 9.0 (617.0 to 1)
Current Spending: ($ per student per year):
Total: $6,280; Instruction: $3,789; Support Services: $2,280
Enrollment, Drop-out Rates and Diploma Recipients by Race/Ethnicity

Category	Total	White	Black	Asian	AIAN	Hisp.
Enrollment (%)	100.0	84.3	7.5	2.3	0.3	2.0
Drop-out Rate (%)	3.3	2.9	5.9	5.7	11.1	10.0
H.S. Diplomas (#)	349	311	19	6	1	5

Greeneview Local SD

4 S Charleston Rd • Jamestown, OH 45335-1557
(937) 675-2728
Grade Span: PK-12; **Agency Type:** 2
Schools: 5
3 Primary; 1 Middle; 1 High; 0 Other Level
5 Regular; 0 Special Education; 0 Vocational; 0 Alternative
0 Magnet; 0 Charter; 4 Title I Eligible; 0 School-wide Title I
Students: 1,642 (52.0% male; 48.0% female)
Individual Education Program: 174 (10.6%);
English Language Learner: 1 (0.1%); Migrant: n/a
Eligible for Free Lunch Program: 168 (10.2%)
Eligible for Reduced-Price Lunch Program: 38 (2.3%)
Teachers: 90.0 (18.2 to 1)
Librarians/Media Specialists: 1.0 (1,642.0 to 1)
Guidance Counselors: 4.0 (410.5 to 1)
Current Spending: ($ per student per year):
Total: $5,746; Instruction: $3,016; Support Services: $2,537
Enrollment, Drop-out Rates and Diploma Recipients by Race/Ethnicity

Category	Total	White	Black	Asian	AIAN	Hisp.
Enrollment (%)	100.0	96.3	1.5	0.5	0.1	0.4
Drop-out Rate (%)	2.1	2.2	0.0	0.0	0.0	0.0
H.S. Diplomas (#)	102	95	3	1	1	0

Sugarcreek Local SD

60 E S St • Bellbrook, OH 45305-1944
(937) 848-6251
Grade Span: PK-12; **Agency Type:** 2
Schools: 5
2 Primary; 2 Middle; 1 High; 0 Other Level
5 Regular; 0 Special Education; 0 Vocational; 0 Alternative
0 Magnet; 0 Charter; 3 Title I Eligible; 0 School-wide Title I
Students: 2,750 (51.8% male; 48.2% female)
Individual Education Program: 266 (9.7%);
English Language Learner: 20 (0.7%); Migrant: n/a
Eligible for Free Lunch Program: 131 (4.8%)
Eligible for Reduced-Price Lunch Program: 31 (1.1%)
Teachers: 139.6 (19.7 to 1)
Librarians/Media Specialists: 0.0 (0.0 to 1)
Guidance Counselors: 5.4 (509.3 to 1)
Current Spending: ($ per student per year):
Total: $6,149; Instruction: $3,547; Support Services: $2,435
Enrollment, Drop-out Rates and Diploma Recipients by Race/Ethnicity

Category	Total	White	Black	Asian	AIAN	Hisp.
Enrollment (%)	100.0	94.0	1.9	1.6	0.3	0.7
Drop-out Rate (%)	1.9	1.7	33.3	0.0	0.0	0.0
H.S. Diplomas (#)	184	183	0	0	0	0

Xenia Community City SD

578 E Market St • Xenia, OH 45385-3145
(937) 376-2961 • http://www.xenia.k12.oh.us/
Grade Span: PK-12; **Agency Type:** 1
Schools: 10
7 Primary; 2 Middle; 1 High; 0 Other Level
10 Regular; 0 Special Education; 0 Vocational; 0 Alternative
0 Magnet; 0 Charter; 6 Title I Eligible; 3 School-wide Title I
Students: 5,264 (52.4% male; 47.6% female)
Individual Education Program: 743 (14.1%);
English Language Learner: 4 (0.1%); Migrant: n/a
Eligible for Free Lunch Program: 1,328 (25.2%)
Eligible for Reduced-Price Lunch Program: 283 (5.4%)
Teachers: 345.6 (15.2 to 1)
Librarians/Media Specialists: 4.0 (1,316.0 to 1)
Guidance Counselors: 12.4 (424.5 to 1)
Current Spending: ($ per student per year):
Total: $6,523; Instruction: $3,663; Support Services: $2,576
Enrollment, Drop-out Rates and Diploma Recipients by Race/Ethnicity

Category	Total	White	Black	Asian	AIAN	Hisp.
Enrollment (%)	100.0	80.1	15.1	0.5	0.2	0.9
Drop-out Rate (%)	6.8	6.4	8.8	0.0	25.0	11.1
H.S. Diplomas (#)	314	262	39	3	0	6

Guernsey County

Cambridge City SD

6111 Fairdale Dr • Cambridge, OH 43725-8865
(740) 439-5021 • http://www.cambridge.k12.oh.us/
Grade Span: PK-12; **Agency Type:** 1
Schools: 11
6 Primary; 1 Middle; 1 High; 0 Other Level
8 Regular; 0 Special Education; 0 Vocational; 0 Alternative
0 Magnet; 0 Charter; 7 Title I Eligible; 2 School-wide Title I
Students: 2,741 (52.1% male; 47.9% female)
Individual Education Program: 416 (15.2%);
English Language Learner: 2 (0.1%); Migrant: n/a
Eligible for Free Lunch Program: 881 (32.1%)
Eligible for Reduced-Price Lunch Program: 221 (8.1%)
Teachers: 180.4 (15.2 to 1)
Librarians/Media Specialists: 2.0 (1,370.5 to 1)
Guidance Counselors: 5.0 (548.2 to 1)
Current Spending: ($ per student per year):
Total: $6,334; Instruction: $4,000; Support Services: $2,053
Enrollment, Drop-out Rates and Diploma Recipients by Race/Ethnicity

Category	Total	White	Black	Asian	AIAN	Hisp.
Enrollment (%)	100.0	89.9	5.9	0.5	0.2	0.8
Drop-out Rate (%)	3.2	3.0	6.9	0.0	n/a	33.3
H.S. Diplomas (#)	154	138	13	2	0	1

Rolling Hills Local SD

PO Box 38 • Byesville, OH 43723-0038
(740) 432-5370 • http://www.omeresa.net/Schools/Meadowbrook/
Grade Span: PK-12; **Agency Type:** 2
Schools: 5
3 Primary; 1 Middle; 1 High; 0 Other Level
5 Regular; 0 Special Education; 0 Vocational; 0 Alternative
0 Magnet; 0 Charter; 4 Title I Eligible; 3 School-wide Title I
Students: 2,256 (50.1% male; 49.9% female)
Individual Education Program: 312 (13.8%);
English Language Learner: 1 (<0.1%); Migrant: n/a
Eligible for Free Lunch Program: 628 (27.8%)
Eligible for Reduced-Price Lunch Program: 190 (8.4%)
Teachers: 119.0 (19.0 to 1)
Librarians/Media Specialists: 0.0 (0.0 to 1)
Guidance Counselors: 4.0 (564.0 to 1)
Current Spending: ($ per student per year):
Total: $6,490; Instruction: $3,678; Support Services: $2,473
Enrollment, Drop-out Rates and Diploma Recipients by Race/Ethnicity

Category	Total	White	Black	Asian	AIAN	Hisp.
Enrollment (%)	100.0	98.2	0.1	0.1	0.0	0.1
Drop-out Rate (%)	5.0	5.0	n/a	0.0	n/a	n/a
H.S. Diplomas (#)	124	124	0	0	0	0

Hamilton County

Cincinnati City SD

PO Box 5381 • Cincinnati, OH 45201-5381
(513) 363-0000 • http://www.cpsboe.k12.oh.us/
Grade Span: PK-12; **Agency Type:** 1
Schools: 86
58 Primary; 2 Middle; 11 High; 14 Other Level
84 Regular; 0 Special Education; 1 Vocational; 0 Alternative
0 Magnet; 0 Charter; 67 Title I Eligible; 60 School-wide Title I
Students: 42,715 (49.8% male; 50.2% female)
Individual Education Program: 7,801 (18.3%);
English Language Learner: 3 (<0.1%); Migrant: 3 (<0.1%)
Eligible for Free Lunch Program: 25,115 (58.8%)
Eligible for Reduced-Price Lunch Program: 2,825 (6.6%)
Teachers: 3,548.6 (12.0 to 1)
Librarians/Media Specialists: 44.4 (962.0 to 1)
Guidance Counselors: 22.0 (1,941.6 to 1)
Current Spending: ($ per student per year):
Total: $8,353; Instruction: $5,143; Support Services: $2,939

Enrollment, Drop-out Rates and Diploma Recipients by Race/Ethnicity

Category	Total	White	Black	Asian	AIAN	Hisp.
Enrollment (%)	100.0	24.1	71.1	0.8	0.1	0.8
Drop-out Rate (%)	7.5	5.0	8.5	3.8	0.0	6.4
H.S. Diplomas (#)	1,305	454	814	13	2	4

Finneytown Local SD

8916 Fontainebleau Ter • Cincinnati, OH 45231-4806
(513) 728-3700 • http://www.finneytown.org/
Grade Span: PK-12; **Agency Type:** 2
Schools: 5
3 Primary; 1 Middle; 1 High; 0 Other Level
5 Regular; 0 Special Education; 0 Vocational; 0 Alternative
0 Magnet; 0 Charter; 4 Title I Eligible; 0 School-wide Title I
Students: 1,814 (53.3% male; 46.7% female)
Individual Education Program: 243 (13.4%);
English Language Learner: 18 (1.0%); Migrant: n/a
Eligible for Free Lunch Program: 230 (12.7%)
Eligible for Reduced-Price Lunch Program: 47 (2.6%)
Teachers: 123.9 (14.6 to 1)
Librarians/Media Specialists: 1.0 (1,814.0 to 1)
Guidance Counselors: 6.0 (302.3 to 1)
Current Spending: ($ per student per year):
Total: $7,178; Instruction: $4,376; Support Services: $2,588
Enrollment, Drop-out Rates and Diploma Recipients by Race/Ethnicity

Category	Total	White	Black	Asian	AIAN	Hisp.
Enrollment (%)	100.0	68.1	27.7	1.3	0.0	0.3
Drop-out Rate (%)	1.4	0.9	3.0	7.7	n/a	0.0
H.S. Diplomas (#)	141	114	19	5	0	1

Forest Hills Local SD

7550 Forest Rd • Cincinnati, OH 45255-4307
(513) 231-3600 • http://www.foresthills.edu/
Grade Span: PK-12; **Agency Type:** 2
Schools: 9
6 Primary; 1 Middle; 2 High; 0 Other Level
9 Regular; 0 Special Education; 0 Vocational; 0 Alternative
0 Magnet; 0 Charter; 3 Title I Eligible; 0 School-wide Title I
Students: 7,602 (50.7% male; 49.3% female)
Individual Education Program: 784 (10.3%);
English Language Learner: 19 (0.2%); Migrant: n/a
Eligible for Free Lunch Program: 176 (2.3%)
Eligible for Reduced-Price Lunch Program: 89 (1.2%)
Teachers: 438.0 (17.4 to 1)
Librarians/Media Specialists: 7.0 (1,086.0 to 1)
Guidance Counselors: 13.5 (563.1 to 1)
Current Spending: ($ per student per year):
Total: $6,386; Instruction: $4,048; Support Services: $2,152
Enrollment, Drop-out Rates and Diploma Recipients by Race/Ethnicity

Category	Total	White	Black	Asian	AIAN	Hisp.
Enrollment (%)	100.0	95.1	0.9	1.7	0.1	1.0
Drop-out Rate (%)	1.9	1.9	0.0	2.8	0.0	5.9
H.S. Diplomas (#)	585	558	12	11	0	3

Indian Hill Ex Vill SD

6855 Drake Rd • Cincinnati, OH 45243-2737
(513) 272-4500 • http://www.ih.k12.oh.us/
Grade Span: PK-12; **Agency Type:** 1
Schools: 4
2 Primary; 1 Middle; 1 High; 0 Other Level
4 Regular; 0 Special Education; 0 Vocational; 0 Alternative
0 Magnet; 0 Charter; 2 Title I Eligible; 0 School-wide Title I
Students: 2,273 (52.0% male; 48.0% female)
Individual Education Program: 164 (7.2%);
English Language Learner: 16 (0.7%); Migrant: n/a
Eligible for Free Lunch Program: 11 (0.5%)
Eligible for Reduced-Price Lunch Program: 9 (0.4%)
Teachers: 153.0 (14.9 to 1)
Librarians/Media Specialists: 4.0 (568.3 to 1)
Guidance Counselors: 7.8 (291.4 to 1)
Current Spending: ($ per student per year):
Total: $10,082; Instruction: $5,639; Support Services: $4,056
Enrollment, Drop-out Rates and Diploma Recipients by Race/Ethnicity

Category	Total	White	Black	Asian	AIAN	Hisp.
Enrollment (%)	100.0	88.5	2.4	7.0	0.0	0.7
Drop-out Rate (%)	0.5	0.5	0.0	0.0	n/a	0.0
H.S. Diplomas (#)	151	127	1	18	0	1

Loveland City SD

757 S Lebanon Rd • Loveland, OH 45140-9308
(513) 683-5600 • http://www.lovelandschools.onlinecommunity.com/
Grade Span: PK-12; **Agency Type:** 1
Schools: 6
3 Primary; 2 Middle; 1 High; 0 Other Level
6 Regular; 0 Special Education; 0 Vocational; 0 Alternative
0 Magnet; 0 Charter; 4 Title I Eligible; 0 School-wide Title I
Students: 4,194 (50.4% male; 49.6% female)
Individual Education Program: 358 (8.5%);
English Language Learner: 41 (1.0%); Migrant: n/a
Eligible for Free Lunch Program: 207 (4.9%)
Eligible for Reduced-Price Lunch Program: 75 (1.8%)
Teachers: 230.9 (18.2 to 1)
Librarians/Media Specialists: 3.0 (1,398.0 to 1)
Guidance Counselors: 6.5 (645.2 to 1)
Current Spending: ($ per student per year):
Total: $6,603; Instruction: $3,847; Support Services: $2,527
Enrollment, Drop-out Rates and Diploma Recipients by Race/Ethnicity

Category	Total	White	Black	Asian	AIAN	Hisp.
Enrollment (%)	100.0	95.7	1.4	1.5	0.0	0.5
Drop-out Rate (%)	1.4	1.5	0.0	0.0	n/a	0.0
H.S. Diplomas (#)	285	272	4	4	0	5

Mariemont City SD

6743 Chestnut St • Cincinnati, OH 45227-3600
(513) 272-7500 • http://www.mariemontschools.org/
Grade Span: PK-12; **Agency Type:** 1
Schools: 5
3 Primary; 1 Middle; 1 High; 0 Other Level
5 Regular; 0 Special Education; 0 Vocational; 0 Alternative
0 Magnet; 0 Charter; 3 Title I Eligible; 0 School-wide Title I
Students: 1,755 (51.1% male; 48.9% female)
Individual Education Program: 164 (9.3%);
English Language Learner: 0 (0.0%); Migrant: n/a
Eligible for Free Lunch Program: 72 (4.1%)
Eligible for Reduced-Price Lunch Program: 37 (2.1%)
Teachers: 118.1 (14.9 to 1)
Librarians/Media Specialists: 1.0 (1,755.0 to 1)
Guidance Counselors: 4.0 (438.8 to 1)
Current Spending: ($ per student per year):
Total: $8,088; Instruction: $4,776; Support Services: $3,138
Enrollment, Drop-out Rates and Diploma Recipients by Race/Ethnicity

Category	Total	White	Black	Asian	AIAN	Hisp.
Enrollment (%)	100.0	93.7	3.0	1.0	0.1	1.0
Drop-out Rate (%)	4.8	4.4	11.1	12.5	n/a	20.0
H.S. Diplomas (#)	113	113	0	0	0	0

Mount Healthy City SD

7615 Harrison Ave • Cincinnati, OH 45231-3107
(513) 729-0077 • http://www.hccanet.org/mhs
Grade Span: KG-12; **Agency Type:** 1
Schools: 8
5 Primary; 2 Middle; 1 High; 0 Other Level
8 Regular; 0 Special Education; 0 Vocational; 0 Alternative
0 Magnet; 0 Charter; 7 Title I Eligible; 5 School-wide Title I
Students: 3,892 (52.8% male; 47.2% female)
Individual Education Program: 652 (16.8%);
English Language Learner: 19 (0.5%); Migrant: n/a
Eligible for Free Lunch Program: 1,398 (35.9%)
Eligible for Reduced-Price Lunch Program: 362 (9.3%)
Teachers: 270.7 (14.4 to 1)
Librarians/Media Specialists: 3.0 (1,297.3 to 1)
Guidance Counselors: 9.0 (432.4 to 1)
Current Spending: ($ per student per year):
Total: $7,398; Instruction: $4,438; Support Services: $2,683
Enrollment, Drop-out Rates and Diploma Recipients by Race/Ethnicity

Category	Total	White	Black	Asian	AIAN	Hisp.
Enrollment (%)	100.0	32.4	63.7	0.5	0.0	0.8
Drop-out Rate (%)	7.1	7.0	7.3	0.0	n/a	0.0
H.S. Diplomas (#)	198	90	104	4	0	0

North College Hill City SD

1498 W Galbraith Rd • Cincinnati, OH 45231-5588
(513) 728-4770 • http://www.nchcityschools.org/
Grade Span: PK-12; **Agency Type:** 1
Schools: 4
3 Primary; 0 Middle; 1 High; 0 Other Level
4 Regular; 0 Special Education; 0 Vocational; 0 Alternative
0 Magnet; 0 Charter; 3 Title I Eligible; 3 School-wide Title I
Students: 1,542 (53.2% male; 46.8% female)
Individual Education Program: 256 (16.6%);
English Language Learner: 0 (0.0%); Migrant: n/a
Eligible for Free Lunch Program: 492 (31.9%)
Eligible for Reduced-Price Lunch Program: 117 (7.6%)
Teachers: 87.3 (17.7 to 1)
Librarians/Media Specialists: 1.0 (1,542.0 to 1)
Guidance Counselors: 2.6 (593.1 to 1)
Current Spending: ($ per student per year):
Total: $5,892; Instruction: $3,568; Support Services: $2,107

Enrollment, Drop-out Rates and Diploma Recipients by Race/Ethnicity

Category	Total	White	Black	Asian	AIAN	Hisp.
Enrollment (%)	100.0	41.0	54.2	0.4	0.1	0.6
Drop-out Rate (%)	4.2	2.9	5.9	0.0	n/a	0.0
H.S. Diplomas (#)	92	49	41	0	0	1

Northwest Local SD

3240 Banning Rd • Cincinnati, OH 45239-5207
(513) 923-1000
Grade Span: PK-12; **Agency Type:** 2
Schools: 14
8 Primary; 3 Middle; 2 High; 1 Other Level
14 Regular; 0 Special Education; 0 Vocational; 0 Alternative
0 Magnet; 0 Charter; 7 Title I Eligible; 3 School-wide Title I
Students: 10,678 (52.2% male; 47.8% female)
Individual Education Program: 1,096 (10.3%);
English Language Learner: 92 (0.9%); Migrant: n/a
Eligible for Free Lunch Program: 1,628 (15.2%)
Eligible for Reduced-Price Lunch Program: 790 (7.4%)
Teachers: 623.4 (17.1 to 1)
Librarians/Media Specialists: 5.0 (2,135.6 to 1)
Guidance Counselors: 19.0 (562.0 to 1)
Current Spending: ($ per student per year):
Total: $6,633; Instruction: $4,002; Support Services: $2,368
Enrollment, Drop-out Rates and Diploma Recipients by Race/Ethnicity

Category	Total	White	Black	Asian	AIAN	Hisp.
Enrollment (%)	100.0	78.9	16.0	0.9	0.2	0.9
Drop-out Rate (%)	4.9	4.8	5.6	0.0	0.0	10.5
H.S. Diplomas (#)	656	571	62	6	1	3

Norwood City SD

2132 Williams Ave • Norwood, OH 45212-3806
(513) 924-2500 • http://www.norwoodschools.org/
Grade Span: PK-12; **Agency Type:** 1
Schools: 7
4 Primary; 1 Middle; 1 High; 1 Other Level
7 Regular; 0 Special Education; 0 Vocational; 0 Alternative
0 Magnet; 0 Charter; 5 Title I Eligible; 4 School-wide Title I
Students: 2,835 (52.3% male; 47.7% female)
Individual Education Program: 335 (11.8%);
English Language Learner: 0 (0.0%); Migrant: n/a
Eligible for Free Lunch Program: 1,031 (36.4%)
Eligible for Reduced-Price Lunch Program: 246 (8.7%)
Teachers: 185.1 (15.3 to 1)
Librarians/Media Specialists: 1.0 (2,835.0 to 1)
Guidance Counselors: 5.0 (567.0 to 1)
Current Spending: ($ per student per year):
Total: $6,910; Instruction: $4,300; Support Services: $2,248
Enrollment, Drop-out Rates and Diploma Recipients by Race/Ethnicity

Category	Total	White	Black	Asian	AIAN	Hisp.
Enrollment (%)	100.0	89.2	2.7	1.2	0.6	3.2
Drop-out Rate (%)	8.3	8.5	0.0	0.0	0.0	0.0
H.S. Diplomas (#)	137	131	0	1	0	3

Oak Hills Local SD

6325 Rapid Run Rd • Cincinnati, OH 45233-4555
(513) 574-3200
Grade Span: PK-12; **Agency Type:** 2
Schools: 9
5 Primary; 3 Middle; 1 High; 0 Other Level
9 Regular; 0 Special Education; 0 Vocational; 0 Alternative
0 Magnet; 0 Charter; 4 Title I Eligible; 0 School-wide Title I
Students: 8,160 (52.8% male; 47.2% female)
Individual Education Program: 1,045 (12.8%);
English Language Learner: 30 (0.4%); Migrant: n/a
Eligible for Free Lunch Program: 104 (1.3%)
Eligible for Reduced-Price Lunch Program: 59 (0.7%)
Teachers: 448.2 (18.2 to 1)
Librarians/Media Specialists: 3.0 (2,720.0 to 1)
Guidance Counselors: 12.3 (663.4 to 1)
Current Spending: ($ per student per year):
Total: $5,948; Instruction: $3,718; Support Services: $1,976
Enrollment, Drop-out Rates and Diploma Recipients by Race/Ethnicity

Category	Total	White	Black	Asian	AIAN	Hisp.
Enrollment (%)	100.0	96.5	1.0	0.8	0.5	0.3
Drop-out Rate (%)	1.3	1.2	5.0	6.9	12.5	0.0
H.S. Diplomas (#)	633	616	3	8	4	1

Princeton City SD

25 W Sharon Rd • Cincinnati, OH 45246-4322
(513) 771-8560 • http://www.princeton.k12.oh.us/
Grade Span: PK-12; **Agency Type:** 1
Schools: 11
8 Primary; 2 Middle; 1 High; 0 Other Level
11 Regular; 0 Special Education; 0 Vocational; 0 Alternative
0 Magnet; 0 Charter; 6 Title I Eligible; 3 School-wide Title I
Students: 6,318 (52.2% male; 47.8% female)
Individual Education Program: 805 (12.7%);
English Language Learner: 163 (2.6%); Migrant: n/a
Eligible for Free Lunch Program: 2,269 (35.9%)
Eligible for Reduced-Price Lunch Program: 489 (7.7%)
Teachers: 488.2 (12.9 to 1)
Librarians/Media Specialists: 9.0 (702.0 to 1)
Guidance Counselors: 13.0 (486.0 to 1)
Current Spending: ($ per student per year):
Total: $9,423; Instruction: $4,910; Support Services: $4,222
Enrollment, Drop-out Rates and Diploma Recipients by Race/Ethnicity

Category	Total	White	Black	Asian	AIAN	Hisp.
Enrollment (%)	100.0	42.1	50.1	2.6	0.1	2.9
Drop-out Rate (%)	5.7	3.9	7.6	4.0	0.0	6.3
H.S. Diplomas (#)	403	213	170	12	0	7

Southwest Local SD

230 S Elm St • Harrison, OH 45030-1444
(513) 367-4139 • http://www.southwestschools.org/
Grade Span: PK-12; **Agency Type:** 2
Schools: 8
5 Primary; 2 Middle; 1 High; 0 Other Level
8 Regular; 0 Special Education; 0 Vocational; 0 Alternative
0 Magnet; 0 Charter; 5 Title I Eligible; 0 School-wide Title I
Students: 3,917 (52.5% male; 47.5% female)
Individual Education Program: 518 (13.2%);
English Language Learner: 4 (0.1%); Migrant: n/a
Eligible for Free Lunch Program: 466 (11.9%)
Eligible for Reduced-Price Lunch Program: 155 (4.0%)
Teachers: 211.4 (18.5 to 1)
Librarians/Media Specialists: 2.5 (1,566.8 to 1)
Guidance Counselors: 8.5 (460.8 to 1)
Current Spending: ($ per student per year):
Total: $5,945; Instruction: $3,492; Support Services: $2,146
Enrollment, Drop-out Rates and Diploma Recipients by Race/Ethnicity

Category	Total	White	Black	Asian	AIAN	Hisp.
Enrollment (%)	100.0	98.0	0.2	0.2	0.2	0.6
Drop-out Rate (%)	4.5	4.5	n/a	0.0	0.0	0.0
H.S. Diplomas (#)	277	277	0	0	0	0

Sycamore Community City SD

4881 Cooper Rd • Cincinnati, OH 45242-6902
(513) 791-4848 •
http://my.sycamoreschools.org/webapps/portal/frameset.jsp
Grade Span: PK-12; **Agency Type:** 1
Schools: 7
4 Primary; 2 Middle; 0 High; 1 Other Level
7 Regular; 0 Special Education; 0 Vocational; 0 Alternative
0 Magnet; 0 Charter; 4 Title I Eligible; 0 School-wide Title I
Students: 5,732 (51.2% male; 48.8% female)
Individual Education Program: 168 (2.9%);
English Language Learner: 274 (4.8%); Migrant: 1 (<0.1%)
Eligible for Free Lunch Program: 284 (5.0%)
Eligible for Reduced-Price Lunch Program: 98 (1.7%)
Teachers: 400.2 (14.3 to 1)
Librarians/Media Specialists: 8.0 (716.5 to 1)
Guidance Counselors: 16.5 (347.4 to 1)
Current Spending: ($ per student per year):
Total: $9,421; Instruction: $5,424; Support Services: $3,730
Enrollment, Drop-out Rates and Diploma Recipients by Race/Ethnicity

Category	Total	White	Black	Asian	AIAN	Hisp.
Enrollment (%)	100.0	80.5	6.4	9.3	0.3	1.2
Drop-out Rate (%)	1.4	1.2	6.2	0.0	0.0	0.0
H.S. Diplomas (#)	425	366	23	33	0	3

Three Rivers Local SD

92 Cleves Ave • Cleves, OH 45002-1368
(513) 941-6400 • http://www.threeriversschools.org/
Grade Span: PK-12; **Agency Type:** 2
Schools: 5
2 Primary; 2 Middle; 1 High; 0 Other Level
5 Regular; 0 Special Education; 0 Vocational; 0 Alternative
0 Magnet; 0 Charter; 3 Title I Eligible; 0 School-wide Title I
Students: 2,210 (53.9% male; 46.1% female)
Individual Education Program: 283 (12.8%);
English Language Learner: 0 (0.0%); Migrant: n/a
Eligible for Free Lunch Program: 307 (13.9%)
Eligible for Reduced-Price Lunch Program: 94 (4.3%)
Teachers: 125.4 (17.6 to 1)
Librarians/Media Specialists: 2.0 (1,105.0 to 1)
Guidance Counselors: 5.5 (401.8 to 1)
Current Spending: ($ per student per year):
Total: $6,767; Instruction: $4,113; Support Services: $2,399

Enrollment, Drop-out Rates and Diploma Recipients by Race/Ethnicity

Category	Total	White	Black	Asian	AIAN	Hisp.
Enrollment (%)	100.0	96.8	1.1	0.3	0.0	0.5
Drop-out Rate (%)	1.8	1.7	11.1	0.0	n/a	0.0
H.S. Diplomas (#)	136	129	3	1	0	0

Winton Woods City SD

1215 W Kemper Rd • Cincinnati, OH 45240-1617
(513) 825-5700
Grade Span: PK-12; **Agency Type:** 1
Schools: 7
5 Primary; 1 Middle; 1 High; 0 Other Level
7 Regular; 0 Special Education; 0 Vocational; 0 Alternative
0 Magnet; 0 Charter; 3 Title I Eligible; 1 School-wide Title I
Students: 4,191 (52.4% male; 47.6% female)
Individual Education Program: 689 (16.4%);
English Language Learner: 60 (1.4%); Migrant: n/a
Eligible for Free Lunch Program: 743 (17.7%)
Eligible for Reduced-Price Lunch Program: 202 (4.8%)
Teachers: 283.8 (14.8 to 1)
Librarians/Media Specialists: 4.0 (1,047.8 to 1)
Guidance Counselors: 5.5 (762.0 to 1)
Current Spending: ($ per student per year):
Total: $7,166; Instruction: $4,267; Support Services: $2,712
Enrollment, Drop-out Rates and Diploma Recipients by Race/Ethnicity

Category	Total	White	Black	Asian	AIAN	Hisp.
Enrollment (%)	100.0	27.5	62.8	1.8	0.1	2.0
Drop-out Rate (%)	5.1	5.0	5.1	6.3	0.0	7.1
H.S. Diplomas (#)	218	84	125	3	0	1

Wyoming City SD

420 Springfield Pike • Wyoming, OH 45215-4298
(513) 772-2343 • http://www.wyomingcityschools.org/
Grade Span: PK-12; **Agency Type:** 1
Schools: 5
3 Primary; 1 Middle; 1 High; 0 Other Level
5 Regular; 0 Special Education; 0 Vocational; 0 Alternative
0 Magnet; 0 Charter; 1 Title I Eligible; 0 School-wide Title I
Students: 1,984 (51.3% male; 48.7% female)
Individual Education Program: 187 (9.4%);
English Language Learner: 5 (0.3%); Migrant: n/a
Eligible for Free Lunch Program: 28 (1.4%)
Eligible for Reduced-Price Lunch Program: 10 (0.5%)
Teachers: 142.1 (14.0 to 1)
Librarians/Media Specialists: 2.0 (992.0 to 1)
Guidance Counselors: 4.0 (496.0 to 1)
Current Spending: ($ per student per year):
Total: $8,398; Instruction: $5,554; Support Services: $2,639
Enrollment, Drop-out Rates and Diploma Recipients by Race/Ethnicity

Category	Total	White	Black	Asian	AIAN	Hisp.
Enrollment (%)	100.0	85.5	9.7	1.7	0.1	0.8
Drop-out Rate (%)	0.0	0.0	0.0	0.0	0.0	0.0
H.S. Diplomas (#)	143	115	21	2	1	3

Hancock County

Findlay City SD

227 SW St • Findlay, OH 45840-3324
(419) 425-8212 • http://www.findlaycityschools.org/
Grade Span: PK-12; **Agency Type:** 1
Schools: 16
9 Primary; 3 Middle; 1 High; 3 Other Level
13 Regular; 2 Special Education; 1 Vocational; 0 Alternative
0 Magnet; 0 Charter; 9 Title I Eligible; 2 School-wide Title I
Students: 6,476 (50.9% male; 49.1% female)
Individual Education Program: 1,110 (17.1%);
English Language Learner: 98 (1.5%); Migrant: 1 (<0.1%)
Eligible for Free Lunch Program: 1,086 (16.8%)
Eligible for Reduced-Price Lunch Program: 333 (5.1%)
Teachers: 430.6 (15.0 to 1)
Librarians/Media Specialists: 2.0 (3,238.0 to 1)
Guidance Counselors: 12.0 (539.7 to 1)
Current Spending: ($ per student per year):
Total: $7,379; Instruction: $4,525; Support Services: $2,634
Enrollment, Drop-out Rates and Diploma Recipients by Race/Ethnicity

Category	Total	White	Black	Asian	AIAN	Hisp.
Enrollment (%)	100.0	88.3	1.9	2.3	0.1	3.8
Drop-out Rate (%)	3.8	3.7	6.5	0.0	0.0	6.2
H.S. Diplomas (#)	426	391	6	10	1	14

Hardin County

Kenton City SD

400 Decatur St • Kenton, OH 43326-2043
(419) 673-0775 • http://www.kentoncityschools.org/
Grade Span: PK-12; **Agency Type:** 1
Schools: 8
6 Primary; 1 Middle; 1 High; 0 Other Level
8 Regular; 0 Special Education; 0 Vocational; 0 Alternative
0 Magnet; 0 Charter; 5 Title I Eligible; 4 School-wide Title I
Students: 2,159 (51.9% male; 48.1% female)
Individual Education Program: 308 (14.3%);
English Language Learner: 1 (<0.1%); Migrant: n/a
Eligible for Free Lunch Program: 447 (20.7%)
Eligible for Reduced-Price Lunch Program: 172 (8.0%)
Teachers: 140.1 (15.4 to 1)
Librarians/Media Specialists: 2.0 (1,079.5 to 1)
Guidance Counselors: 4.0 (539.8 to 1)
Current Spending: ($ per student per year):
Total: $6,262; Instruction: $4,009; Support Services: $1,980
Enrollment, Drop-out Rates and Diploma Recipients by Race/Ethnicity

Category	Total	White	Black	Asian	AIAN	Hisp.
Enrollment (%)	100.0	96.6	0.4	0.5	0.3	0.4
Drop-out Rate (%)	2.8	2.8	0.0	0.0	n/a	0.0
H.S. Diplomas (#)	147	140	0	4	0	1

Harrison County

Harrison Hills City SD

PO Box 356 • Hopedale, OH 43976-0356
(740) 942-7800
Grade Span: PK-12; **Agency Type:** 1
Schools: 6
4 Primary; 1 Middle; 1 High; 0 Other Level
6 Regular; 0 Special Education; 0 Vocational; 0 Alternative
0 Magnet; 0 Charter; 5 Title I Eligible; 4 School-wide Title I
Students: 2,082 (53.3% male; 46.7% female)
Individual Education Program: 585 (28.1%);
English Language Learner: 0 (0.0%); Migrant: n/a
Eligible for Free Lunch Program: 648 (31.1%)
Eligible for Reduced-Price Lunch Program: 154 (7.4%)
Teachers: 136.8 (15.2 to 1)
Librarians/Media Specialists: 2.0 (1,041.0 to 1)
Guidance Counselors: 3.0 (694.0 to 1)
Current Spending: ($ per student per year):
Total: $6,412; Instruction: $4,000; Support Services: $2,096
Enrollment, Drop-out Rates and Diploma Recipients by Race/Ethnicity

Category	Total	White	Black	Asian	AIAN	Hisp.
Enrollment (%)	100.0	93.8	3.8	0.2	0.1	0.1
Drop-out Rate (%)	2.8	2.8	3.8	0.0	n/a	0.0
H.S. Diplomas (#)	138	132	6	0	0	0

Henry County

Napoleon Area City SD

701 Briarheath Ave Ste 108 • Napoleon, OH 43545-1251
(419) 599-7015
Grade Span: PK-12; **Agency Type:** 1
Schools: 5
3 Primary; 1 Middle; 1 High; 0 Other Level
5 Regular; 0 Special Education; 0 Vocational; 0 Alternative
0 Magnet; 0 Charter; 4 Title I Eligible; 0 School-wide Title I
Students: 2,334 (51.4% male; 48.6% female)
Individual Education Program: 473 (20.3%);
English Language Learner: 41 (1.8%); Migrant: 42 (1.8%)
Eligible for Free Lunch Program: 360 (15.4%)
Eligible for Reduced-Price Lunch Program: 109 (4.7%)
Teachers: 150.1 (15.5 to 1)
Librarians/Media Specialists: 2.0 (1,167.0 to 1)
Guidance Counselors: 7.0 (333.4 to 1)
Current Spending: ($ per student per year):
Total: $6,627; Instruction: $3,993; Support Services: $2,393
Enrollment, Drop-out Rates and Diploma Recipients by Race/Ethnicity

Category	Total	White	Black	Asian	AIAN	Hisp.
Enrollment (%)	100.0	89.0	0.6	0.9	0.2	8.8
Drop-out Rate (%)	3.4	3.0	11.1	0.0	n/a	10.0
H.S. Diplomas (#)	194	181	4	0	0	9

Highland County

Greenfield Ex Vill SD

200 N 5th St • Greenfield, OH 45123-1373
(937) 981-2152
Grade Span: PK-12; **Agency Type:** 1
Schools: 6

4 Primary; 1 Middle; 1 High; 0 Other Level
5 Regular; 1 Special Education; 0 Vocational; 0 Alternative
0 Magnet; 0 Charter; 5 Title I Eligible; 0 School-wide Title I
Students: 2,210 (52.7% male; 47.3% female)
Individual Education Program: 259 (11.7%);
English Language Learner: 0 (0.0%); Migrant: n/a
Eligible for Free Lunch Program: 483 (21.9%)
Eligible for Reduced-Price Lunch Program: 145 (6.6%)
Teachers: 130.8 (16.9 to 1)
Librarians/Media Specialists: 1.0 (2,210.0 to 1)
Guidance Counselors: 3.0 (736.7 to 1)
Current Spending: ($ per student per year):
Total: $5,745; Instruction: $3,453; Support Services: $2,075
Enrollment, Drop-out Rates and Diploma Recipients by Race/Ethnicity

Category	Total	White	Black	Asian	AIAN	Hisp.
Enrollment (%)	100.0	97.6	0.9	0.3	0.0	0.1
Drop-out Rate (%)	6.7	6.9	0.0	0.0	n/a	0.0
H.S. Diplomas (#)	132	128	4	0	0	0

Hillsboro City SD
338 W Main St • Hillsboro, OH 45133-1314
(937) 393-3475 • http://www.Hillsboro.k12.oh.us/
Grade Span: PK-12; **Agency Type:** 1
Schools: 6
2 Primary; 3 Middle; 1 High; 0 Other Level
6 Regular; 0 Special Education; 0 Vocational; 0 Alternative
0 Magnet; 0 Charter; 4 Title I Eligible; 2 School-wide Title I
Students: 2,870 (50.7% male; 49.3% female)
Individual Education Program: 147 (5.1%);
English Language Learner: 9 (0.3%); Migrant: n/a
Eligible for Free Lunch Program: 692 (24.1%)
Eligible for Reduced-Price Lunch Program: 202 (7.0%)
Teachers: 174.3 (16.5 to 1)
Librarians/Media Specialists: 3.0 (956.7 to 1)
Guidance Counselors: 5.0 (574.0 to 1)
Current Spending: ($ per student per year):
Total: $6,129; Instruction: $3,442; Support Services: $2,364
Enrollment, Drop-out Rates and Diploma Recipients by Race/Ethnicity

Category	Total	White	Black	Asian	AIAN	Hisp.
Enrollment (%)	100.0	93.6	3.4	0.5	0.1	0.3
Drop-out Rate (%)	3.5	3.3	6.3	25.0	0.0	0.0
H.S. Diplomas (#)	182	178	4	0	0	0

Hocking County

Logan-Hocking Local SD
57 S Walnut St • Logan, OH 43138-1317
(740) 385-8517
Grade Span: PK-12; **Agency Type:** 2
Schools: 10
8 Primary; 1 Middle; 1 High; 0 Other Level
10 Regular; 0 Special Education; 0 Vocational; 0 Alternative
0 Magnet; 0 Charter; 7 Title I Eligible; 7 School-wide Title I
Students: 3,958 (52.0% male; 48.0% female)
Individual Education Program: 607 (15.3%);
English Language Learner: 1 (<0.1%); Migrant: n/a
Eligible for Free Lunch Program: 972 (24.6%)
Eligible for Reduced-Price Lunch Program: 285 (7.2%)
Teachers: 223.5 (17.7 to 1)
Librarians/Media Specialists: 2.0 (1,979.0 to 1)
Guidance Counselors: 6.0 (659.7 to 1)
Current Spending: ($ per student per year):
Total: $6,056; Instruction: $3,282; Support Services: $2,485
Enrollment, Drop-out Rates and Diploma Recipients by Race/Ethnicity

Category	Total	White	Black	Asian	AIAN	Hisp.
Enrollment (%)	100.0	98.7	0.6	0.0	0.0	0.2
Drop-out Rate (%)	6.6	6.7	0.0	n/a	n/a	0.0
H.S. Diplomas (#)	227	225	2	0	0	0

Holmes County

East Holmes Local SD
PO Box 182 • Berlin, OH 44610-0182
(330) 893-2610
Grade Span: KG-12; **Agency Type:** 2
Schools: 10
8 Primary; 0 Middle; 1 High; 1 Other Level
10 Regular; 0 Special Education; 0 Vocational; 0 Alternative
0 Magnet; 0 Charter; 9 Title I Eligible; 9 School-wide Title I
Students: 1,873 (52.8% male; 47.2% female)
Individual Education Program: 225 (12.0%);
English Language Learner: 1,100 (58.7%); Migrant: n/a
Eligible for Free Lunch Program: 243 (13.0%)
Eligible for Reduced-Price Lunch Program: 185 (9.9%)
Teachers: 122.6 (15.3 to 1)
Librarians/Media Specialists: 1.0 (1,873.0 to 1)
Guidance Counselors: 2.0 (936.5 to 1)
Current Spending: ($ per student per year):
Total: $6,080; Instruction: $3,805; Support Services: $2,039
Enrollment, Drop-out Rates and Diploma Recipients by Race/Ethnicity

Category	Total	White	Black	Asian	AIAN	Hisp.
Enrollment (%)	100.0	99.0	0.6	0.1	0.0	0.0
Drop-out Rate (%)	0.4	0.4	n/a	n/a	n/a	n/a
H.S. Diplomas (#)	63	63	0	0	0	0

West Holmes Local SD
28 W Jackson St • Millersburg, OH 44654-1302
(330) 674-3546 • http://www.westholmes.k12.oh.us/
Grade Span: KG-12; **Agency Type:** 2
Schools: 7
5 Primary; 1 Middle; 1 High; 0 Other Level
7 Regular; 0 Special Education; 0 Vocational; 0 Alternative
0 Magnet; 0 Charter; 5 Title I Eligible; 5 School-wide Title I
Students: 2,787 (50.9% male; 49.1% female)
Individual Education Program: 422 (15.1%);
English Language Learner: 8 (0.3%); Migrant: n/a
Eligible for Free Lunch Program: 556 (19.9%)
Eligible for Reduced-Price Lunch Program: 315 (11.3%)
Teachers: 176.4 (15.8 to 1)
Librarians/Media Specialists: 1.0 (2,787.0 to 1)
Guidance Counselors: 4.0 (696.8 to 1)
Current Spending: ($ per student per year):
Total: $5,848; Instruction: $3,535; Support Services: $2,030
Enrollment, Drop-out Rates and Diploma Recipients by Race/Ethnicity

Category	Total	White	Black	Asian	AIAN	Hisp.
Enrollment (%)	100.0	98.2	0.3	0.2	0.0	0.8
Drop-out Rate (%)	2.9	2.9	n/a	0.0	n/a	0.0
H.S. Diplomas (#)	150	147	0	0	0	3

Huron County

Bellevue City SD
125 N St • Bellevue, OH 44811-1423
(419) 484-5000 • http://www.bellevueschools.org/district/mainindex.html
Grade Span: PK-12; **Agency Type:** 1
Schools: 7
5 Primary; 1 Middle; 1 High; 0 Other Level
7 Regular; 0 Special Education; 0 Vocational; 0 Alternative
0 Magnet; 0 Charter; 5 Title I Eligible; 2 School-wide Title I
Students: 2,334 (52.4% male; 47.6% female)
Individual Education Program: 397 (17.0%);
English Language Learner: 0 (0.0%); Migrant: n/a
Eligible for Free Lunch Program: 314 (13.5%)
Eligible for Reduced-Price Lunch Program: 175 (7.5%)
Teachers: 152.3 (15.3 to 1)
Librarians/Media Specialists: 2.0 (1,167.0 to 1)
Guidance Counselors: 4.0 (583.5 to 1)
Current Spending: ($ per student per year):
Total: $6,729; Instruction: $4,141; Support Services: $2,325
Enrollment, Drop-out Rates and Diploma Recipients by Race/Ethnicity

Category	Total	White	Black	Asian	AIAN	Hisp.
Enrollment (%)	100.0	96.3	0.4	0.3	0.0	2.1
Drop-out Rate (%)	2.8	2.9	n/a	0.0	n/a	0.0
H.S. Diplomas (#)	180	175	0	1	0	4

Norwalk City SD
134 Benedict Ave • Norwalk, OH 44857-2349
(419) 668-2779
Grade Span: PK-12; **Agency Type:** 1
Schools: 5
3 Primary; 1 Middle; 1 High; 0 Other Level
5 Regular; 0 Special Education; 0 Vocational; 0 Alternative
0 Magnet; 0 Charter; 3 Title I Eligible; 1 School-wide Title I
Students: 2,928 (52.5% male; 47.5% female)
Individual Education Program: 435 (14.9%);
English Language Learner: 1 (<0.1%); Migrant: n/a
Eligible for Free Lunch Program: 551 (18.8%)
Eligible for Reduced-Price Lunch Program: 213 (7.3%)
Teachers: 136.5 (21.5 to 1)
Librarians/Media Specialists: 3.0 (976.0 to 1)
Guidance Counselors: 5.0 (585.6 to 1)
Current Spending: ($ per student per year):
Total: $5,339; Instruction: $3,368; Support Services: $1,797
Enrollment, Drop-out Rates and Diploma Recipients by Race/Ethnicity

Category	Total	White	Black	Asian	AIAN	Hisp.
Enrollment (%)	100.0	91.2	3.5	0.2	0.1	4.4
Drop-out Rate (%)	2.4	2.4	0.0	0.0	n/a	5.0
H.S. Diplomas (#)	160	153	3	1	0	3

Willard City SD

955 S Main St • Willard, OH 44890-9598
(419) 935-1541
Grade Span: PK-12; **Agency Type:** 1
Schools: 6
4 Primary; 1 Middle; 1 High; 0 Other Level
6 Regular; 0 Special Education; 0 Vocational; 0 Alternative
0 Magnet; 0 Charter; 4 Title I Eligible; 0 School-wide Title I
Students: 2,314 (50.7% male; 49.3% female)
Individual Education Program: 325 (14.0%);
English Language Learner: 45 (1.9%); Migrant: 120 (5.2%)
Eligible for Free Lunch Program: 621 (26.8%)
Eligible for Reduced-Price Lunch Program: 125 (5.4%)
Teachers: 137.7 (16.8 to 1)
Librarians/Media Specialists: 1.0 (2,314.0 to 1)
Guidance Counselors: 5.0 (462.8 to 1)
Current Spending: ($ per student per year):
Total: $5,820; Instruction: $3,408; Support Services: $2,122
Enrollment, Drop-out Rates and Diploma Recipients by Race/Ethnicity

Category	Total	White	Black	Asian	AIAN	Hisp.
Enrollment (%)	100.0	82.5	1.6	0.3	0.0	14.4
Drop-out Rate (%)	3.2	3.1	0.0	0.0	n/a	4.8
H.S. Diplomas (#)	144	129	0	0	0	15

Jackson County

Jackson City SD

450 Vaughn St • Jackson, OH 45640-1944
(740) 286-6442 • http://www.jcs.k12.oh.us/
Grade Span: PK-12; **Agency Type:** 1
Schools: 9
6 Primary; 1 Middle; 1 High; 0 Other Level
8 Regular; 0 Special Education; 0 Vocational; 0 Alternative
0 Magnet; 0 Charter; 6 Title I Eligible; 5 School-wide Title I
Students: 2,736 (52.7% male; 47.3% female)
Individual Education Program: 367 (13.4%);
English Language Learner: 15 (0.5%); Migrant: n/a
Eligible for Free Lunch Program: 717 (26.2%)
Eligible for Reduced-Price Lunch Program: 160 (5.8%)
Teachers: 147.0 (18.6 to 1)
Librarians/Media Specialists: 1.0 (2,736.0 to 1)
Guidance Counselors: 4.0 (684.0 to 1)
Current Spending: ($ per student per year):
Total: $5,658; Instruction: $3,518; Support Services: $1,900
Enrollment, Drop-out Rates and Diploma Recipients by Race/Ethnicity

Category	Total	White	Black	Asian	AIAN	Hisp.
Enrollment (%)	100.0	97.7	0.5	0.2	0.1	0.8
Drop-out Rate (%)	2.5	2.5	0.0	0.0	0.0	0.0
H.S. Diplomas (#)	203	199	0	3	0	0

Wellston City SD

416 N Pennsylvania Ave • Wellston, OH 45692-1299
(740) 384-2152
Grade Span: PK-12; **Agency Type:** 1
Schools: 4
2 Primary; 1 Middle; 1 High; 0 Other Level
4 Regular; 0 Special Education; 0 Vocational; 0 Alternative
0 Magnet; 0 Charter; 3 Title I Eligible; 3 School-wide Title I
Students: 1,860 (51.5% male; 48.5% female)
Individual Education Program: 312 (16.8%);
English Language Learner: 0 (0.0%); Migrant: n/a
Eligible for Free Lunch Program: 608 (32.7%)
Eligible for Reduced-Price Lunch Program: 104 (5.6%)
Teachers: 119.3 (15.6 to 1)
Librarians/Media Specialists: 3.0 (620.0 to 1)
Guidance Counselors: 3.0 (620.0 to 1)
Current Spending: ($ per student per year):
Total: $5,857; Instruction: $3,617; Support Services: $2,026
Enrollment, Drop-out Rates and Diploma Recipients by Race/Ethnicity

Category	Total	White	Black	Asian	AIAN	Hisp.
Enrollment (%)	100.0	98.7	0.4	0.2	0.1	0.3
Drop-out Rate (%)	3.8	3.6	0.0	50.0	n/a	n/a
H.S. Diplomas (#)	78	77	0	1	0	0

Jefferson County

Buckeye Local SD

PO Box 300 • Rayland, OH 43943-0300
(740) 859-2114
Grade Span: PK-12; **Agency Type:** 2
Schools: 7
4 Primary; 2 Middle; 1 High; 0 Other Level
7 Regular; 0 Special Education; 0 Vocational; 0 Alternative
0 Magnet; 0 Charter; 7 Title I Eligible; 7 School-wide Title I
Students: 2,466 (52.2% male; 47.8% female)
Individual Education Program: 423 (17.2%);
English Language Learner: 8 (0.3%); Migrant: n/a
Eligible for Free Lunch Program: 718 (29.1%)
Eligible for Reduced-Price Lunch Program: 195 (7.9%)
Teachers: 165.0 (14.9 to 1)
Librarians/Media Specialists: 1.0 (2,466.0 to 1)
Guidance Counselors: 4.0 (616.5 to 1)
Current Spending: ($ per student per year):
Total: $6,078; Instruction: $3,820; Support Services: $1,970
Enrollment, Drop-out Rates and Diploma Recipients by Race/Ethnicity

Category	Total	White	Black	Asian	AIAN	Hisp.
Enrollment (%)	100.0	97.9	1.3	0.2	0.0	0.2
Drop-out Rate (%)	2.7	2.7	0.0	n/a	0.0	0.0
H.S. Diplomas (#)	183	181	0	0	0	2

Edison Local SD

14890 State Route 213 • Hammondsville, OH 43930-7902
(330) 532-3199
Grade Span: PK-12; **Agency Type:** 2
Schools: 7
4 Primary; 2 Middle; 1 High; 0 Other Level
7 Regular; 0 Special Education; 0 Vocational; 0 Alternative
0 Magnet; 0 Charter; 6 Title I Eligible; 6 School-wide Title I
Students: 2,697 (51.5% male; 48.5% female)
Individual Education Program: 332 (12.3%);
English Language Learner: 0 (0.0%); Migrant: n/a
Eligible for Free Lunch Program: 674 (25.0%)
Eligible for Reduced-Price Lunch Program: 314 (11.6%)
Teachers: 168.6 (16.0 to 1)
Librarians/Media Specialists: 1.0 (2,697.0 to 1)
Guidance Counselors: 4.0 (674.3 to 1)
Current Spending: ($ per student per year):
Total: $5,682; Instruction: $3,467; Support Services: $2,030
Enrollment, Drop-out Rates and Diploma Recipients by Race/Ethnicity

Category	Total	White	Black	Asian	AIAN	Hisp.
Enrollment (%)	100.0	98.4	0.5	0.4	0.0	0.5
Drop-out Rate (%)	2.3	2.4	0.0	0.0	n/a	0.0
H.S. Diplomas (#)	177	175	1	0	0	1

Indian Creek Local SD

587 Bantam Ridge Rd • Wintersville, OH 43953-4231
(740) 264-3502 • http://www.indian-creek.k12.oh.us/
Grade Span: PK-12; **Agency Type:** 2
Schools: 6
4 Primary; 1 Middle; 1 High; 0 Other Level
6 Regular; 0 Special Education; 0 Vocational; 0 Alternative
0 Magnet; 0 Charter; 4 Title I Eligible; 2 School-wide Title I
Students: 2,271 (52.6% male; 47.4% female)
Individual Education Program: 361 (15.9%);
English Language Learner: 0 (0.0%); Migrant: n/a
Eligible for Free Lunch Program: 572 (25.2%)
Eligible for Reduced-Price Lunch Program: 146 (6.4%)
Teachers: 138.0 (16.5 to 1)
Librarians/Media Specialists: 2.0 (1,135.5 to 1)
Guidance Counselors: 3.0 (757.0 to 1)
Current Spending: ($ per student per year):
Total: $6,869; Instruction: $4,021; Support Services: $2,618
Enrollment, Drop-out Rates and Diploma Recipients by Race/Ethnicity

Category	Total	White	Black	Asian	AIAN	Hisp.
Enrollment (%)	100.0	94.6	3.7	0.5	0.0	0.4
Drop-out Rate (%)	1.5	1.4	3.6	0.0	n/a	n/a
H.S. Diplomas (#)	132	124	7	0	0	1

Steubenville City SD

PO Box 189 • Steubenville, OH 43952-5189
(740) 283-3767
Grade Span: PK-12; **Agency Type:** 1
Schools: 8
6 Primary; 1 Middle; 0 High; 1 Other Level
8 Regular; 0 Special Education; 0 Vocational; 0 Alternative
0 Magnet; 0 Charter; 7 Title I Eligible; 7 School-wide Title I
Students: 2,464 (51.8% male; 48.2% female)
Individual Education Program: 315 (12.8%);
English Language Learner: 0 (0.0%); Migrant: n/a
Eligible for Free Lunch Program: 1,086 (44.1%)
Eligible for Reduced-Price Lunch Program: 148 (6.0%)
Teachers: 148.0 (16.6 to 1)
Librarians/Media Specialists: 0.0 (0.0 to 1)
Guidance Counselors: 4.0 (616.0 to 1)
Current Spending: ($ per student per year):
Total: $6,178; Instruction: $4,114; Support Services: $1,845

Enrollment, Drop-out Rates and Diploma Recipients by Race/Ethnicity

Category	Total	White	Black	Asian	AIAN	Hisp.
Enrollment (%)	100.0	58.1	32.8	0.8	0.0	0.4
Drop-out Rate (%)	4.7	4.4	4.9	25.0	n/a	0.0
H.S. Diplomas (#)	171	126	39	1	0	2

Knox County

Mount Vernon City SD

302 Martinsburg Rd • Mount Vernon, OH 43050-4252
(740) 397-7422 • http://www.mt-vernon.k12.oh.us/
Grade Span: PK-12; **Agency Type:** 1
Schools: 9
7 Primary; 1 Middle; 1 High; 0 Other Level
9 Regular; 0 Special Education; 0 Vocational; 0 Alternative
0 Magnet; 0 Charter; 5 Title I Eligible; 4 School-wide Title I
Students: 4,275 (51.3% male; 48.7% female)
Individual Education Program: 829 (19.4%);
English Language Learner: 4 (0.1%); Migrant: n/a
Eligible for Free Lunch Program: 830 (19.4%)
Eligible for Reduced-Price Lunch Program: 204 (4.8%)
Teachers: 253.0 (16.9 to 1)
Librarians/Media Specialists: 3.0 (1,425.0 to 1)
Guidance Counselors: 5.0 (855.0 to 1)
Current Spending: ($ per student per year):
Total: $5,777; Instruction: $3,574; Support Services: $2,007
Enrollment, Drop-out Rates and Diploma Recipients by Race/Ethnicity

Category	Total	White	Black	Asian	AIAN	Hisp.
Enrollment (%)	100.0	96.3	0.8	0.5	0.2	0.6
Drop-out Rate (%)	2.4	2.3	0.0	0.0	0.0	33.3
H.S. Diplomas (#)	284	272	6	4	0	2

Lake County

Madison Local SD

6741 N Ridge Rd • Madison, OH 44057-2656
(440) 428-2166 • http://www.madison-richland.k12.oh.us/
Grade Span: PK-12; **Agency Type:** 2
Schools: 5
3 Primary; 1 Middle; 1 High; 0 Other Level
5 Regular; 0 Special Education; 0 Vocational; 0 Alternative
0 Magnet; 0 Charter; 3 Title I Eligible; 0 School-wide Title I
Students: 3,749 (51.9% male; 48.1% female)
Individual Education Program: 407 (10.9%);
English Language Learner: 0 (0.0%); Migrant: n/a
Eligible for Free Lunch Program: 587 (15.7%)
Eligible for Reduced-Price Lunch Program: 262 (7.0%)
Teachers: 195.0 (19.2 to 1)
Librarians/Media Specialists: 1.0 (3,749.0 to 1)
Guidance Counselors: 5.0 (749.8 to 1)
Current Spending: ($ per student per year):
Total: $5,987; Instruction: $3,524; Support Services: $2,266
Enrollment, Drop-out Rates and Diploma Recipients by Race/Ethnicity

Category	Total	White	Black	Asian	AIAN	Hisp.
Enrollment (%)	100.0	97.9	0.3	0.5	0.1	0.7
Drop-out Rate (%)	4.4	4.4	0.0	20.0	0.0	0.0
H.S. Diplomas (#)	254	248	1	2	1	2

Mentor Ex Vill SD

6451 Center St • Mentor, OH 44060-4109
(440) 255-4444 • http://www.mentorschools.org/
Grade Span: PK-12; **Agency Type:** 1
Schools: 16
12 Primary; 3 Middle; 1 High; 0 Other Level
16 Regular; 0 Special Education; 0 Vocational; 0 Alternative
0 Magnet; 0 Charter; 9 Title I Eligible; 0 School-wide Title I
Students: 9,886 (50.7% male; 49.3% female)
Individual Education Program: 1,158 (11.7%);
English Language Learner: 9,844 (99.6%); Migrant: n/a
Eligible for Free Lunch Program: 590 (6.0%)
Eligible for Reduced-Price Lunch Program: 312 (3.2%)
Teachers: 637.7 (15.5 to 1)
Librarians/Media Specialists: 17.0 (581.5 to 1)
Guidance Counselors: 15.0 (659.1 to 1)
Current Spending: ($ per student per year):
Total: $7,855; Instruction: $4,810; Support Services: $2,836
Enrollment, Drop-out Rates and Diploma Recipients by Race/Ethnicity

Category	Total	White	Black	Asian	AIAN	Hisp.
Enrollment (%)	100.0	97.2	0.8	1.0	0.0	0.6
Drop-out Rate (%)	1.7	1.7	8.0	0.0	0.0	0.0
H.S. Diplomas (#)	730	711	8	8	0	3

Painesville City Local SD

58 Jefferson St • Painesville, OH 44077-3114
(440) 392-5060
Grade Span: KG-12; **Agency Type:** 2
Schools: 7
5 Primary; 1 Middle; 1 High; 0 Other Level
7 Regular; 0 Special Education; 0 Vocational; 0 Alternative
0 Magnet; 0 Charter; 7 Title I Eligible; 5 School-wide Title I
Students: 2,912 (51.8% male; 48.2% female)
Individual Education Program: 405 (13.9%);
English Language Learner: 507 (17.4%); Migrant: 358 (12.3%)
Eligible for Free Lunch Program: 1,618 (55.6%)
Eligible for Reduced-Price Lunch Program: 277 (9.5%)
Teachers: 172.5 (16.9 to 1)
Librarians/Media Specialists: 2.0 (1,456.0 to 1)
Guidance Counselors: 5.0 (582.4 to 1)
Current Spending: ($ per student per year):
Total: $7,933; Instruction: $4,351; Support Services: $3,316
Enrollment, Drop-out Rates and Diploma Recipients by Race/Ethnicity

Category	Total	White	Black	Asian	AIAN	Hisp.
Enrollment (%)	100.0	44.9	21.0	0.5	0.2	25.9
Drop-out Rate (%)	8.6	8.1	9.0	0.0	50.0	9.2
H.S. Diplomas (#)	88	53	23	3	0	7

Painesville Township Local SD

585 Riverside Dr • Painesville, OH 44077-5323
(440) 352-0668
Grade Span: PK-12; **Agency Type:** 2
Schools: 8
6 Primary; 1 Middle; 1 High; 0 Other Level
8 Regular; 0 Special Education; 0 Vocational; 0 Alternative
0 Magnet; 0 Charter; 4 Title I Eligible; 0 School-wide Title I
Students: 4,379 (51.5% male; 48.5% female)
Individual Education Program: 455 (10.4%);
English Language Learner: 9 (0.2%); Migrant: 2 (<0.1%)
Eligible for Free Lunch Program: 342 (7.8%)
Eligible for Reduced-Price Lunch Program: 178 (4.1%)
Teachers: 232.0 (18.9 to 1)
Librarians/Media Specialists: 2.0 (2,189.5 to 1)
Guidance Counselors: 7.0 (625.6 to 1)
Current Spending: ($ per student per year):
Total: $6,848; Instruction: $3,740; Support Services: $2,839
Enrollment, Drop-out Rates and Diploma Recipients by Race/Ethnicity

Category	Total	White	Black	Asian	AIAN	Hisp.
Enrollment (%)	100.0	95.9	1.5	0.6	0.1	0.8
Drop-out Rate (%)	2.9	2.9	0.0	0.0	n/a	0.0
H.S. Diplomas (#)	306	302	3	1	0	0

Perry Local SD

4325 Manchester Ave • Perry, OH 44081-9413
(440) 259-3881 • http://www.perry-lake.k12.oh.us/
Grade Span: KG-12; **Agency Type:** 2
Schools: 3
1 Primary; 1 Middle; 1 High; 0 Other Level
3 Regular; 0 Special Education; 0 Vocational; 0 Alternative
0 Magnet; 0 Charter; 2 Title I Eligible; 0 School-wide Title I
Students: 1,888 (49.8% male; 50.2% female)
Individual Education Program: 152 (8.1%);
English Language Learner: 0 (0.0%); Migrant: n/a
Eligible for Free Lunch Program: 106 (5.6%)
Eligible for Reduced-Price Lunch Program: 86 (4.6%)
Teachers: 123.0 (15.3 to 1)
Librarians/Media Specialists: 3.0 (629.3 to 1)
Guidance Counselors: 6.0 (314.7 to 1)
Current Spending: ($ per student per year):
Total: $13,223; Instruction: $6,566; Support Services: $6,154
Enrollment, Drop-out Rates and Diploma Recipients by Race/Ethnicity

Category	Total	White	Black	Asian	AIAN	Hisp.
Enrollment (%)	100.0	98.2	0.6	0.2	0.0	0.5
Drop-out Rate (%)	0.0	0.0	n/a	n/a	n/a	n/a
H.S. Diplomas (#)	132	132	0	0	0	0

Wickliffe City SD

2221 Rockefeller Rd • Wickliffe, OH 44092-2020
(440) 943-6900 • http://www.wickliffe-city.k12.oh.us/
Grade Span: PK-12; **Agency Type:** 1
Schools: 3
1 Primary; 1 Middle; 1 High; 0 Other Level
3 Regular; 0 Special Education; 0 Vocational; 0 Alternative
0 Magnet; 0 Charter; 2 Title I Eligible; 0 School-wide Title I
Students: 1,508 (54.8% male; 45.2% female)
Individual Education Program: 223 (14.8%);
English Language Learner: 0 (0.0%); Migrant: n/a
Eligible for Free Lunch Program: 162 (10.7%)
Eligible for Reduced-Price Lunch Program: 90 (6.0%)

Teachers: 110.7 (13.6 to 1)
Librarians/Media Specialists: 1.0 (1,508.0 to 1)
Guidance Counselors: 4.0 (377.0 to 1)
Current Spending: ($ per student per year):
Total: $9,207; Instruction: $5,087; Support Services: $3,879
Enrollment, Drop-out Rates and Diploma Recipients by Race/Ethnicity

Category	Total	White	Black	Asian	AIAN	Hisp.
Enrollment (%)	100.0	92.7	4.5	1.5	0.1	0.1
Drop-out Rate (%)	1.5	1.6	0.0	0.0	n/a	0.0
H.S. Diplomas (#)	117	112	4	0	0	1

Willoughby-Eastlake City SD

37047 Ridge Rd • Willoughby, OH 44094-4130
(440) 946-5000 • http://www.willoughby-eastlake.k12.oh.us/
Grade Span: PK-12; **Agency Type:** 1
Schools: 14
8 Primary; 3 Middle; 3 High; 0 Other Level
13 Regular; 0 Special Education; 1 Vocational; 0 Alternative
0 Magnet; 0 Charter; 7 Title I Eligible; 1 School-wide Title I
Students: 8,977 (51.4% male; 48.6% female)
Individual Education Program: 1,237 (13.8%);
English Language Learner: 168 (1.9%); Migrant: 6 (0.1%)
Eligible for Free Lunch Program: 931 (10.4%)
Eligible for Reduced-Price Lunch Program: 449 (5.0%)
Teachers: 534.5 (16.8 to 1)
Librarians/Media Specialists: 5.0 (1,795.4 to 1)
Guidance Counselors: 13.0 (690.5 to 1)
Current Spending: ($ per student per year):
Total: $7,114; Instruction: $4,318; Support Services: $2,563
Enrollment, Drop-out Rates and Diploma Recipients by Race/Ethnicity

Category	Total	White	Black	Asian	AIAN	Hisp.
Enrollment (%)	100.0	94.6	2.2	1.1	0.1	0.3
Drop-out Rate (%)	4.2	4.3	4.1	2.8	0.0	0.0
H.S. Diplomas (#)	637	616	7	8	0	4

Lawrence County

Fairland Local SD

228 Private Dr 10010 • Proctorville, OH 45669-8600
(740) 886-3100 • http://fairland.k12.oh.us/
Grade Span: KG-12; **Agency Type:** 2
Schools: 4
1 Primary; 1 Middle; 1 High; 0 Other Level
3 Regular; 0 Special Education; 0 Vocational; 0 Alternative
0 Magnet; 0 Charter; 2 Title I Eligible; 1 School-wide Title I
Students: 1,821 (50.9% male; 49.1% female)
Individual Education Program: 240 (13.2%);
English Language Learner: 0 (0.0%); Migrant: n/a
Eligible for Free Lunch Program: 381 (20.9%)
Eligible for Reduced-Price Lunch Program: 85 (4.7%)
Teachers: 100.8 (18.1 to 1)
Librarians/Media Specialists: 1.1 (1,655.5 to 1)
Guidance Counselors: 4.5 (404.7 to 1)
Current Spending: ($ per student per year):
Total: $5,375; Instruction: $3,410; Support Services: $1,782
Enrollment, Drop-out Rates and Diploma Recipients by Race/Ethnicity

Category	Total	White	Black	Asian	AIAN	Hisp.
Enrollment (%)	100.0	98.2	0.4	0.5	0.1	0.0
Drop-out Rate (%)	3.4	3.4	0.0	0.0	n/a	n/a
H.S. Diplomas (#)	115	114	0	1	0	0

Ironton City SD

105 S 5th St • Ironton, OH 45638-1426
(740) 532-4133 • http://www.tigertown.com/
Grade Span: PK-12; **Agency Type:** 1
Schools: 6
3 Primary; 2 Middle; 1 High; 0 Other Level
6 Regular; 0 Special Education; 0 Vocational; 0 Alternative
0 Magnet; 0 Charter; 5 Title I Eligible; 2 School-wide Title I
Students: 1,577 (52.8% male; 47.2% female)
Individual Education Program: 281 (17.8%);
English Language Learner: 1 (0.1%); Migrant: n/a
Eligible for Free Lunch Program: 538 (34.1%)
Eligible for Reduced-Price Lunch Program: 78 (4.9%)
Teachers: 104.5 (15.1 to 1)
Librarians/Media Specialists: 2.0 (788.5 to 1)
Guidance Counselors: 5.0 (315.4 to 1)
Current Spending: ($ per student per year):
Total: $6,524; Instruction: $3,768; Support Services: $2,424
Enrollment, Drop-out Rates and Diploma Recipients by Race/Ethnicity

Category	Total	White	Black	Asian	AIAN	Hisp.
Enrollment (%)	100.0	89.1	7.8	0.2	0.0	0.1
Drop-out Rate (%)	4.7	5.2	0.0	n/a	n/a	0.0
H.S. Diplomas (#)	128	115	12	0	0	0

Rock Hill Local SD

2273 County Rd 26 • Ironton, OH 45638-8386
(740) 532-7030 • http://rockhill.org/
Grade Span: KG-12; **Agency Type:** 2
Schools: 3
1 Primary; 1 Middle; 1 High; 0 Other Level
3 Regular; 0 Special Education; 0 Vocational; 0 Alternative
0 Magnet; 0 Charter; 3 Title I Eligible; 1 School-wide Title I
Students: 1,957 (52.4% male; 47.6% female)
Individual Education Program: 318 (16.2%);
English Language Learner: 0 (0.0%); Migrant: n/a
Eligible for Free Lunch Program: 699 (35.7%)
Eligible for Reduced-Price Lunch Program: 91 (4.7%)
Teachers: 130.3 (15.0 to 1)
Librarians/Media Specialists: 2.0 (978.5 to 1)
Guidance Counselors: 2.0 (978.5 to 1)
Current Spending: ($ per student per year):
Total: $6,131; Instruction: $3,682; Support Services: $2,131
Enrollment, Drop-out Rates and Diploma Recipients by Race/Ethnicity

Category	Total	White	Black	Asian	AIAN	Hisp.
Enrollment (%)	100.0	99.0	0.6	0.0	0.1	0.1
Drop-out Rate (%)	2.9	2.9	0.0	n/a	n/a	n/a
H.S. Diplomas (#)	100	99	1	0	0	0

South Point Local SD

203 Park Ave • South Point, OH 45680-9622
(740) 377-4315
Grade Span: PK-12; **Agency Type:** 2
Schools: 4
2 Primary; 1 Middle; 1 High; 0 Other Level
4 Regular; 0 Special Education; 0 Vocational; 0 Alternative
0 Magnet; 0 Charter; 3 Title I Eligible; 2 School-wide Title I
Students: 1,837 (50.1% male; 49.9% female)
Individual Education Program: 367 (20.0%);
English Language Learner: 0 (0.0%); Migrant: n/a
Eligible for Free Lunch Program: 636 (34.6%)
Eligible for Reduced-Price Lunch Program: 100 (5.4%)
Teachers: 115.0 (16.0 to 1)
Librarians/Media Specialists: 1.0 (1,837.0 to 1)
Guidance Counselors: 2.0 (918.5 to 1)
Current Spending: ($ per student per year):
Total: $5,560; Instruction: $3,331; Support Services: $1,958
Enrollment, Drop-out Rates and Diploma Recipients by Race/Ethnicity

Category	Total	White	Black	Asian	AIAN	Hisp.
Enrollment (%)	100.0	91.7	6.5	0.2	0.0	0.3
Drop-out Rate (%)	5.1	5.5	0.0	0.0	n/a	0.0
H.S. Diplomas (#)	105	93	12	0	0	0

Licking County

Granville Ex Vill SD

PO Box 417 • Granville, OH 43023-0417
(740) 587-0332
Grade Span: PK-12; **Agency Type:** 1
Schools: 4
2 Primary; 1 Middle; 1 High; 0 Other Level
4 Regular; 0 Special Education; 0 Vocational; 0 Alternative
0 Magnet; 0 Charter; 2 Title I Eligible; 0 School-wide Title I
Students: 2,049 (52.2% male; 47.8% female)
Individual Education Program: 212 (10.3%);
English Language Learner: 4 (0.2%); Migrant: n/a
Eligible for Free Lunch Program: 12 (0.6%)
Eligible for Reduced-Price Lunch Program: 13 (0.6%)
Teachers: 116.2 (17.6 to 1)
Librarians/Media Specialists: 3.0 (683.0 to 1)
Guidance Counselors: 4.0 (512.3 to 1)
Current Spending: ($ per student per year):
Total: $7,477; Instruction: $4,511; Support Services: $2,967
Enrollment, Drop-out Rates and Diploma Recipients by Race/Ethnicity

Category	Total	White	Black	Asian	AIAN	Hisp.
Enrollment (%)	100.0	97.5	0.7	1.4	0.0	0.4
Drop-out Rate (%)	0.3	0.3	0.0	0.0	n/a	0.0
H.S. Diplomas (#)	152	150	1	1	0	0

Heath City SD

107 Lancaster Dr • Heath, OH 43056-1220
(740) 522-2816
Grade Span: PK-12; **Agency Type:** 1
Schools: 4
2 Primary; 1 Middle; 1 High; 0 Other Level
4 Regular; 0 Special Education; 0 Vocational; 0 Alternative
0 Magnet; 0 Charter; 2 Title I Eligible; 0 School-wide Title I
Students: 1,686 (49.9% male; 50.1% female)
Individual Education Program: 173 (10.3%);
English Language Learner: 0 (0.0%); Migrant: n/a

Eligible for Free Lunch Program: 211 (12.5%)
Eligible for Reduced-Price Lunch Program: 82 (4.9%)
Teachers: 92.7 (18.2 to 1)
Librarians/Media Specialists: 2.0 (843.0 to 1)
Guidance Counselors: 3.0 (562.0 to 1)
Current Spending: ($ per student per year):
Total: $6,138; Instruction: $3,707; Support Services: $2,222
Enrollment, Drop-out Rates and Diploma Recipients by Race/Ethnicity

Category	Total	White	Black	Asian	AIAN	Hisp.
Enrollment (%)	100.0	91.7	2.4	1.2	0.4	0.7
Drop-out Rate (%)	2.7	2.7	9.1	0.0	0.0	0.0
H.S. Diplomas (#)	104	99	1	2	0	1

Lakewood Local SD

PO Box 70 • Hebron, OH 43025-0070
(740) 928-5878
Grade Span: PK-12; **Agency Type:** 2
Schools: 5
2 Primary; 2 Middle; 1 High; 0 Other Level
5 Regular; 0 Special Education; 0 Vocational; 0 Alternative
0 Magnet; 0 Charter; 3 Title I Eligible; 1 School-wide Title I
Students: 2,278 (52.1% male; 47.9% female)
Individual Education Program: 290 (12.7%);
English Language Learner: 3 (0.1%); Migrant: n/a
Eligible for Free Lunch Program: 452 (19.8%)
Eligible for Reduced-Price Lunch Program: 118 (5.2%)
Teachers: 155.0 (14.7 to 1)
Librarians/Media Specialists: 3.0 (759.3 to 1)
Guidance Counselors: 4.0 (569.5 to 1)
Current Spending: ($ per student per year):
Total: $6,180; Instruction: $3,562; Support Services: $2,318
Enrollment, Drop-out Rates and Diploma Recipients by Race/Ethnicity

Category	Total	White	Black	Asian	AIAN	Hisp.
Enrollment (%)	100.0	98.2	0.6	0.3	0.1	0.4
Drop-out Rate (%)	2.4	2.2	40.0	n/a	n/a	n/a
H.S. Diplomas (#)	155	155	0	0	0	0

Licking Heights Local SD

6539 Summit Rd SW • Summit Station, OH 43073-0027
(740) 927-6926
Grade Span: PK-12; **Agency Type:** 2
Schools: 4
2 Primary; 1 Middle; 1 High; 0 Other Level
4 Regular; 0 Special Education; 0 Vocational; 0 Alternative
0 Magnet; 0 Charter; 3 Title I Eligible; 0 School-wide Title I
Students: 1,675 (51.6% male; 48.4% female)
Individual Education Program: 186 (11.1%);
English Language Learner: 25 (1.5%); Migrant: n/a
Eligible for Free Lunch Program: 169 (10.1%)
Eligible for Reduced-Price Lunch Program: 65 (3.9%)
Teachers: 107.0 (15.7 to 1)
Librarians/Media Specialists: 1.0 (1,675.0 to 1)
Guidance Counselors: 3.5 (478.6 to 1)
Current Spending: ($ per student per year):
Total: $6,617; Instruction: $3,902; Support Services: $2,431
Enrollment, Drop-out Rates and Diploma Recipients by Race/Ethnicity

Category	Total	White	Black	Asian	AIAN	Hisp.
Enrollment (%)	100.0	83.5	13.0	0.3	0.2	1.3
Drop-out Rate (%)	2.0	1.4	5.0	0.0	n/a	50.0
H.S. Diplomas (#)	92	82	8	2	0	0

Licking Valley Local SD

1379 Licking Valley Rd • Newark, OH 43055-9450
(740) 763-3525 • http://www.lickingvalley.k12.oh.us/
Grade Span: PK-12; **Agency Type:** 2
Schools: 6
4 Primary; 1 Middle; 1 High; 0 Other Level
6 Regular; 0 Special Education; 0 Vocational; 0 Alternative
0 Magnet; 0 Charter; 5 Title I Eligible; 0 School-wide Title I
Students: 2,189 (50.9% male; 49.1% female)
Individual Education Program: 274 (12.5%);
English Language Learner: 0 (0.0%); Migrant: n/a
Eligible for Free Lunch Program: 306 (14.0%)
Eligible for Reduced-Price Lunch Program: 97 (4.4%)
Teachers: 127.9 (17.1 to 1)
Librarians/Media Specialists: 2.0 (1,094.5 to 1)
Guidance Counselors: 4.0 (547.3 to 1)
Current Spending: ($ per student per year):
Total: $6,341; Instruction: $3,465; Support Services: $2,628
Enrollment, Drop-out Rates and Diploma Recipients by Race/Ethnicity

Category	Total	White	Black	Asian	AIAN	Hisp.
Enrollment (%)	100.0	97.6	1.2	0.0	0.1	0.2
Drop-out Rate (%)	3.9	4.0	0.0	0.0	0.0	0.0
H.S. Diplomas (#)	115	113	0	0	1	0

Newark City SD

85 E Main St • Newark, OH 43055-5605
(740) 345-9891 • http://www.newarkcity.k12.oh.us/
Grade Span: PK-12; **Agency Type:** 1
Schools: 16
9 Primary; 6 Middle; 1 High; 0 Other Level
16 Regular; 0 Special Education; 0 Vocational; 0 Alternative
0 Magnet; 0 Charter; 11 Title I Eligible; 7 School-wide Title I
Students: 6,958 (51.1% male; 48.9% female)
Individual Education Program: 849 (12.2%);
English Language Learner: 26 (0.4%); Migrant: n/a
Eligible for Free Lunch Program: 1,704 (24.5%)
Eligible for Reduced-Price Lunch Program: 475 (6.8%)
Teachers: 428.8 (16.2 to 1)
Librarians/Media Specialists: 5.0 (1,391.6 to 1)
Guidance Counselors: 8.6 (809.1 to 1)
Current Spending: ($ per student per year):
Total: $6,161; Instruction: $3,639; Support Services: $2,242
Enrollment, Drop-out Rates and Diploma Recipients by Race/Ethnicity

Category	Total	White	Black	Asian	AIAN	Hisp.
Enrollment (%)	100.0	91.8	3.9	0.7	0.1	0.4
Drop-out Rate (%)	8.6	8.5	9.8	6.3	0.0	12.5
H.S. Diplomas (#)	389	368	8	5	3	3

North Fork Local SD

PO Box 497 • Utica, OH 43080-0497
(740) 892-3666
Grade Span: PK-12; **Agency Type:** 2
Schools: 4
2 Primary; 1 Middle; 1 High; 0 Other Level
4 Regular; 0 Special Education; 0 Vocational; 0 Alternative
0 Magnet; 0 Charter; 2 Title I Eligible; 0 School-wide Title I
Students: 1,887 (51.5% male; 48.5% female)
Individual Education Program: 232 (12.3%);
English Language Learner: 2 (0.1%); Migrant: n/a
Eligible for Free Lunch Program: 242 (12.8%)
Eligible for Reduced-Price Lunch Program: 149 (7.9%)
Teachers: 111.0 (17.0 to 1)
Librarians/Media Specialists: 2.0 (943.5 to 1)
Guidance Counselors: 4.0 (471.8 to 1)
Current Spending: ($ per student per year):
Total: $5,496; Instruction: $3,301; Support Services: $1,941
Enrollment, Drop-out Rates and Diploma Recipients by Race/Ethnicity

Category	Total	White	Black	Asian	AIAN	Hisp.
Enrollment (%)	100.0	98.9	0.2	0.1	0.0	0.3
Drop-out Rate (%)	3.6	3.6	n/a	n/a	n/a	0.0
H.S. Diplomas (#)	117	116	0	0	0	0

Southwest Licking Local SD

PO Box 180 • Etna, OH 43018-0180
(740) 927-3941 • http://www.swl.k12.oh.us/
Grade Span: PK-12; **Agency Type:** 2
Schools: 6
4 Primary; 1 Middle; 1 High; 0 Other Level
6 Regular; 0 Special Education; 0 Vocational; 0 Alternative
0 Magnet; 0 Charter; 4 Title I Eligible; 0 School-wide Title I
Students: 3,490 (51.3% male; 48.7% female)
Individual Education Program: 416 (11.9%);
English Language Learner: 5 (0.1%); Migrant: n/a
Eligible for Free Lunch Program: 248 (7.1%)
Eligible for Reduced-Price Lunch Program: 130 (3.7%)
Teachers: 203.1 (17.2 to 1)
Librarians/Media Specialists: 2.0 (1,745.0 to 1)
Guidance Counselors: 8.2 (425.6 to 1)
Current Spending: ($ per student per year):
Total: $6,284; Instruction: $3,710; Support Services: $2,359
Enrollment, Drop-out Rates and Diploma Recipients by Race/Ethnicity

Category	Total	White	Black	Asian	AIAN	Hisp.
Enrollment (%)	100.0	95.8	1.3	0.3	0.3	0.9
Drop-out Rate (%)	2.5	2.5	14.3	0.0	0.0	0.0
H.S. Diplomas (#)	233	227	1	0	1	4

Logan County

Bellefontaine City SD

820 Ludlow Rd • Bellefontaine, OH 43311-1852
(937) 593-9060 • http://www.bellefontaine.k12.oh.us/
Grade Span: KG-12; **Agency Type:** 1
Schools: 6
4 Primary; 1 Middle; 1 High; 0 Other Level
6 Regular; 0 Special Education; 0 Vocational; 0 Alternative
0 Magnet; 0 Charter; 4 Title I Eligible; 1 School-wide Title I
Students: 2,868 (51.0% male; 49.0% female)
Individual Education Program: 520 (18.1%);
English Language Learner: 22 (0.8%); Migrant: n/a

Eligible for Free Lunch Program: 626 (21.8%)
Eligible for Reduced-Price Lunch Program: 139 (4.8%)
Teachers: 187.6 (15.3 to 1)
Librarians/Media Specialists: 2.0 (1,434.0 to 1)
Guidance Counselors: 6.8 (421.8 to 1)
Current Spending: ($ per student per year):
Total: $6,264; Instruction: $3,921; Support Services: $2,103
Enrollment, Drop-out Rates and Diploma Recipients by Race/Ethnicity

Category	Total	White	Black	Asian	AIAN	Hisp.
Enrollment (%)	100.0	87.1	5.3	1.5	0.4	1.3
Drop-out Rate (%)	4.0	3.1	13.7	16.7	0.0	25.0
H.S. Diplomas (#)	199	183	15	0	0	1

Benjamin Logan Local SD

4626 County Rd 26 • Bellefontaine, OH 43311-9532
(937) 593-9211 •
http://www.benlogan.k12.oh.us/education/district/district.php?sectionid=1
Grade Span: KG-12; **Agency Type:** 2
Schools: 3
1 Primary; 1 Middle; 1 High; 0 Other Level
3 Regular; 0 Special Education; 0 Vocational; 0 Alternative
0 Magnet; 0 Charter; 2 Title I Eligible; 0 School-wide Title I
Students: 1,996 (51.5% male; 48.5% female)
Individual Education Program: 271 (13.6%);
English Language Learner: 1 (0.1%); Migrant: n/a
Eligible for Free Lunch Program: 137 (6.9%)
Eligible for Reduced-Price Lunch Program: 55 (2.8%)
Teachers: 109.4 (18.2 to 1)
Librarians/Media Specialists: 2.0 (998.0 to 1)
Guidance Counselors: 4.0 (499.0 to 1)
Current Spending: ($ per student per year):
Total: $4,991; Instruction: $3,007; Support Services: $1,723
Enrollment, Drop-out Rates and Diploma Recipients by Race/Ethnicity

Category	Total	White	Black	Asian	AIAN	Hisp.
Enrollment (%)	100.0	99.0	0.4	0.1	0.1	0.1
Drop-out Rate (%)	2.3	2.0	33.3	n/a	n/a	n/a
H.S. Diplomas (#)	131	128	1	0	0	1

Indian Lake Local SD

6210 State Route 235 N • Lewistown, OH 43333-9704
(937) 686-8601 • http://indianlake.k12.oh.us/
Grade Span: KG-12; **Agency Type:** 2
Schools: 4
2 Primary; 1 Middle; 1 High; 0 Other Level
4 Regular; 0 Special Education; 0 Vocational; 0 Alternative
0 Magnet; 0 Charter; 2 Title I Eligible; 1 School-wide Title I
Students: 2,036 (51.0% male; 49.0% female)
Individual Education Program: 367 (18.0%);
English Language Learner: 0 (0.0%); Migrant: n/a
Eligible for Free Lunch Program: 407 (20.0%)
Eligible for Reduced-Price Lunch Program: 100 (4.9%)
Teachers: 130.0 (15.7 to 1)
Librarians/Media Specialists: 1.0 (2,036.0 to 1)
Guidance Counselors: 4.0 (509.0 to 1)
Current Spending: ($ per student per year):
Total: $5,766; Instruction: $3,479; Support Services: $1,987
Enrollment, Drop-out Rates and Diploma Recipients by Race/Ethnicity

Category	Total	White	Black	Asian	AIAN	Hisp.
Enrollment (%)	100.0	98.9	0.1	0.3	0.1	0.3
Drop-out Rate (%)	4.2	4.1	n/a	0.0	n/a	0.0
H.S. Diplomas (#)	130	130	0	0	0	0

Lorain County

Amherst Ex Vill SD

185 Forest St • Amherst, OH 44001-1605
(440) 988-4406 • http://www.amherst.k12.oh.us/index.php
Grade Span: PK-12; **Agency Type:** 1
Schools: 6
3 Primary; 2 Middle; 1 High; 0 Other Level
6 Regular; 0 Special Education; 0 Vocational; 0 Alternative
0 Magnet; 0 Charter; 3 Title I Eligible; 0 School-wide Title I
Students: 3,967 (50.9% male; 49.1% female)
Individual Education Program: 495 (12.5%);
English Language Learner: 0 (0.0%); Migrant: 1 (<0.1%)
Eligible for Free Lunch Program: 228 (5.7%)
Eligible for Reduced-Price Lunch Program: 174 (4.4%)
Teachers: 211.7 (18.7 to 1)
Librarians/Media Specialists: 0.3 (13,223.3 to 1)
Guidance Counselors: 6.0 (661.2 to 1)
Current Spending: ($ per student per year):
Total: $5,912; Instruction: $3,672; Support Services: $2,022
Enrollment, Drop-out Rates and Diploma Recipients by Race/Ethnicity

Category	Total	White	Black	Asian	AIAN	Hisp.
Enrollment (%)	100.0	92.6	0.9	0.6	0.4	4.4
Drop-out Rate (%)	0.5	0.4	0.0	0.0	0.0	2.0
H.S. Diplomas (#)	281	249	8	3	1	19

Avon Lake City SD

175 Avon Belden Rd • Avon Lake, OH 44012-1600
(440) 933-6210
Grade Span: PK-12; **Agency Type:** 1
Schools: 7
4 Primary; 2 Middle; 1 High; 0 Other Level
7 Regular; 0 Special Education; 0 Vocational; 0 Alternative
0 Magnet; 0 Charter; 4 Title I Eligible; 0 School-wide Title I
Students: 3,352 (53.1% male; 46.9% female)
Individual Education Program: 299 (8.9%);
English Language Learner: 7 (0.2%); Migrant: 1 (<0.1%)
Eligible for Free Lunch Program: 73 (2.2%)
Eligible for Reduced-Price Lunch Program: 71 (2.1%)
Teachers: 216.7 (15.5 to 1)
Librarians/Media Specialists: 2.0 (1,676.0 to 1)
Guidance Counselors: 10.0 (335.2 to 1)
Current Spending: ($ per student per year):
Total: $7,541; Instruction: $4,393; Support Services: $2,977
Enrollment, Drop-out Rates and Diploma Recipients by Race/Ethnicity

Category	Total	White	Black	Asian	AIAN	Hisp.
Enrollment (%)	100.0	97.0	0.5	1.0	0.0	0.8
Drop-out Rate (%)	1.3	1.3	0.0	0.0	n/a	0.0
H.S. Diplomas (#)	243	240	1	0	0	2

Avon Local SD

3075 Stoney Ridge Rd • Avon, OH 44011-1821
(440) 934-6191 • http://www.avon.k12.oh.us/
Grade Span: KG-12; **Agency Type:** 2
Schools: 5
2 Primary; 2 Middle; 1 High; 0 Other Level
5 Regular; 0 Special Education; 0 Vocational; 0 Alternative
0 Magnet; 0 Charter; 3 Title I Eligible; 0 School-wide Title I
Students: 2,291 (50.3% male; 49.7% female)
Individual Education Program: 298 (13.0%);
English Language Learner: 3 (0.1%); Migrant: n/a
Eligible for Free Lunch Program: 143 (6.2%)
Eligible for Reduced-Price Lunch Program: 50 (2.2%)
Teachers: 138.5 (16.5 to 1)
Librarians/Media Specialists: 2.0 (1,145.5 to 1)
Guidance Counselors: 4.0 (572.8 to 1)
Current Spending: ($ per student per year):
Total: $6,454; Instruction: $3,757; Support Services: $2,447
Enrollment, Drop-out Rates and Diploma Recipients by Race/Ethnicity

Category	Total	White	Black	Asian	AIAN	Hisp.
Enrollment (%)	100.0	92.7	3.3	1.2	0.1	1.8
Drop-out Rate (%)	2.1	1.3	33.3	11.1	100.0	11.1
H.S. Diplomas (#)	117	109	1	2	0	5

Clearview Local SD

4700 Broadway • Lorain, OH 44052-5542
(440) 233-5412
Grade Span: PK-12; **Agency Type:** 2
Schools: 3
1 Primary; 1 Middle; 1 High; 0 Other Level
3 Regular; 0 Special Education; 0 Vocational; 0 Alternative
0 Magnet; 0 Charter; 3 Title I Eligible; 2 School-wide Title I
Students: 1,519 (49.3% male; 50.7% female)
Individual Education Program: 192 (12.6%);
English Language Learner: 13 (0.9%); Migrant: 1 (0.1%)
Eligible for Free Lunch Program: 680 (44.8%)
Eligible for Reduced-Price Lunch Program: 160 (10.5%)
Teachers: 100.6 (15.1 to 1)
Librarians/Media Specialists: 1.0 (1,519.0 to 1)
Guidance Counselors: 3.2 (474.7 to 1)
Current Spending: ($ per student per year):
Total: $7,369; Instruction: $4,451; Support Services: $2,567
Enrollment, Drop-out Rates and Diploma Recipients by Race/Ethnicity

Category	Total	White	Black	Asian	AIAN	Hisp.
Enrollment (%)	100.0	61.8	16.3	0.5	0.2	17.4
Drop-out Rate (%)	3.0	2.7	3.3	50.0	n/a	1.3
H.S. Diplomas (#)	97	59	17	0	0	18

Elyria City SD

42101 Griswold Rd • Elyria, OH 44035-2117
(440) 284-8000 • http://www.elyriaschools.k12.oh.us/
Grade Span: KG-12; **Agency Type:** 1
Schools: 18
12 Primary; 3 Middle; 1 High; 2 Other Level
17 Regular; 1 Special Education; 0 Vocational; 0 Alternative

0 Magnet; 0 Charter; 12 Title I Eligible; 9 School-wide Title I
Students: 8,348 (51.0% male; 49.0% female)
Individual Education Program: 1,252 (15.0%);
English Language Learner: 2 (<0.1%); Migrant: 6 (0.1%)
Eligible for Free Lunch Program: 2,716 (32.5%)
Eligible for Reduced-Price Lunch Program: 682 (8.2%)
Teachers: 575.0 (14.5 to 1)
Librarians/Media Specialists: 9.0 (927.6 to 1)
Guidance Counselors: 18.0 (463.8 to 1)
Current Spending: ($ per student per year):
Total: $7,370; Instruction: $4,320; Support Services: $2,758

Enrollment, Drop-out Rates and Diploma Recipients by Race/Ethnicity

Category	Total	White	Black	Asian	AIAN	Hisp.
Enrollment (%)	100.0	71.2	19.8	0.7	0.2	2.5
Drop-out Rate (%)	6.7	6.4	7.7	5.3	0.0	9.1
H.S. Diplomas (#)	362	288	55	4	1	7

Firelands Local SD

11970 Vermilion Rd • Oberlin, OH 44074-9495
(440) 965-5821 • http://www.firelandsschools.org/district/
Grade Span: PK-12; **Agency Type:** 2
Schools: 3
1 Primary; 1 Middle; 1 High; 0 Other Level
3 Regular; 0 Special Education; 0 Vocational; 0 Alternative
0 Magnet; 0 Charter; 2 Title I Eligible; 0 School-wide Title I
Students: 2,226 (51.5% male; 48.5% female)
Individual Education Program: 247 (11.1%);
English Language Learner: 0 (0.0%); Migrant: 2 (0.1%)
Eligible for Free Lunch Program: 195 (8.8%)
Eligible for Reduced-Price Lunch Program: 108 (4.9%)
Teachers: 121.7 (18.3 to 1)
Librarians/Media Specialists: 1.0 (2,226.0 to 1)
Guidance Counselors: 4.0 (556.5 to 1)
Current Spending: ($ per student per year):
Total: $6,035; Instruction: $3,571; Support Services: $2,273

Enrollment, Drop-out Rates and Diploma Recipients by Race/Ethnicity

Category	Total	White	Black	Asian	AIAN	Hisp.
Enrollment (%)	100.0	97.5	0.2	0.1	0.0	1.1
Drop-out Rate (%)	1.8	1.7	n/a	0.0	25.0	0.0
H.S. Diplomas (#)	140	138	0	0	2	0

Keystone Local SD

PO Box 65 • Lagrange, OH 44050-0065
(440) 355-5131
Grade Span: KG-12; **Agency Type:** 2
Schools: 4
2 Primary; 1 Middle; 1 High; 0 Other Level
4 Regular; 0 Special Education; 0 Vocational; 0 Alternative
0 Magnet; 0 Charter; 3 Title I Eligible; 0 School-wide Title I
Students: 1,854 (50.7% male; 49.3% female)
Individual Education Program: 196 (10.6%);
English Language Learner: 0 (0.0%); Migrant: n/a
Eligible for Free Lunch Program: 116 (6.3%)
Eligible for Reduced-Price Lunch Program: 84 (4.5%)
Teachers: 95.5 (19.4 to 1)
Librarians/Media Specialists: 1.0 (1,854.0 to 1)
Guidance Counselors: 5.0 (370.8 to 1)
Current Spending: ($ per student per year):
Total: $5,449; Instruction: $3,222; Support Services: $2,045

Enrollment, Drop-out Rates and Diploma Recipients by Race/Ethnicity

Category	Total	White	Black	Asian	AIAN	Hisp.
Enrollment (%)	100.0	98.1	0.3	0.2	0.1	0.5
Drop-out Rate (%)	0.9	0.9	0.0	0.0	0.0	0.0
H.S. Diplomas (#)	113	109	0	0	0	2

Lorain City SD

2350 Pole Ave • Lorain, OH 44052-4301
(440) 233-2271 • http://www.lorainschools.org/
Grade Span: PK-12; **Agency Type:** 1
Schools: 15
11 Primary; 2 Middle; 2 High; 0 Other Level
15 Regular; 0 Special Education; 0 Vocational; 0 Alternative
0 Magnet; 0 Charter; 15 Title I Eligible; 11 School-wide Title I
Students: 10,652 (51.8% male; 48.2% female)
Individual Education Program: 1,579 (14.8%);
English Language Learner: 207 (1.9%); Migrant: 7 (0.1%)
Eligible for Free Lunch Program: 5,750 (54.0%)
Eligible for Reduced-Price Lunch Program: 1,081 (10.1%)
Teachers: 739.3 (14.4 to 1)
Librarians/Media Specialists: 5.0 (2,130.4 to 1)
Guidance Counselors: 13.0 (819.4 to 1)
Current Spending: ($ per student per year):
Total: $7,899; Instruction: $5,191; Support Services: $2,306

Enrollment, Drop-out Rates and Diploma Recipients by Race/Ethnicity

Category	Total	White	Black	Asian	AIAN	Hisp.
Enrollment (%)	100.0	37.8	26.4	0.4	0.3	27.3
Drop-out Rate (%)	6.6	5.4	8.3	0.0	11.8	7.0
H.S. Diplomas (#)	476	203	113	1	4	148

Midview Local SD

1010 Vivian Dr • Grafton, OH 44044-1250
(440) 926-3737
Grade Span: KG-12; **Agency Type:** 2
Schools: 5
2 Primary; 2 Middle; 1 High; 0 Other Level
5 Regular; 0 Special Education; 0 Vocational; 0 Alternative
0 Magnet; 0 Charter; 4 Title I Eligible; 0 School-wide Title I
Students: 3,405 (51.9% male; 48.1% female)
Individual Education Program: 379 (11.1%);
English Language Learner: 16 (0.5%); Migrant: n/a
Eligible for Free Lunch Program: 365 (10.7%)
Eligible for Reduced-Price Lunch Program: 193 (5.7%)
Teachers: 175.0 (19.5 to 1)
Librarians/Media Specialists: 2.0 (1,702.5 to 1)
Guidance Counselors: 6.0 (567.5 to 1)
Current Spending: ($ per student per year):
Total: $5,532; Instruction: $3,217; Support Services: $2,145

Enrollment, Drop-out Rates and Diploma Recipients by Race/Ethnicity

Category	Total	White	Black	Asian	AIAN	Hisp.
Enrollment (%)	100.0	93.9	2.8	0.3	0.3	1.2
Drop-out Rate (%)	3.3	3.1	14.3	0.0	0.0	0.0
H.S. Diplomas (#)	208	200	6	0	0	1

North Ridgeville City SD

5490 Mills Creek Ln • North Ridgeville, OH 44039-2339
(440) 327-4444
Grade Span: KG-12; **Agency Type:** 1
Schools: 6
4 Primary; 1 Middle; 1 High; 0 Other Level
6 Regular; 0 Special Education; 0 Vocational; 0 Alternative
0 Magnet; 0 Charter; 4 Title I Eligible; 0 School-wide Title I
Students: 3,513 (51.8% male; 48.2% female)
Individual Education Program: 503 (14.3%);
English Language Learner: 0 (0.0%); Migrant: 3 (0.1%)
Eligible for Free Lunch Program: 303 (8.6%)
Eligible for Reduced-Price Lunch Program: 104 (3.0%)
Teachers: 222.0 (15.8 to 1)
Librarians/Media Specialists: 4.0 (878.3 to 1)
Guidance Counselors: 12.0 (292.8 to 1)
Current Spending: ($ per student per year):
Total: $6,964; Instruction: $4,344; Support Services: $2,400

Enrollment, Drop-out Rates and Diploma Recipients by Race/Ethnicity

Category	Total	White	Black	Asian	AIAN	Hisp.
Enrollment (%)	100.0	95.2	0.8	0.8	0.2	1.4
Drop-out Rate (%)	2.5	2.6	0.0	0.0	0.0	0.0
H.S. Diplomas (#)	198	191	1	3	0	3

Sheffield-Sheffield Lake City

1824 Harris Rd • Sheffield Village, OH 44054-2628
(440) 949-6181
Grade Span: PK-12; **Agency Type:** 1
Schools: 6
3 Primary; 2 Middle; 1 High; 0 Other Level
6 Regular; 0 Special Education; 0 Vocational; 0 Alternative
0 Magnet; 0 Charter; 4 Title I Eligible; 0 School-wide Title I
Students: 2,057 (48.9% male; 51.1% female)
Individual Education Program: 233 (11.3%);
English Language Learner: 0 (0.0%); Migrant: 1 (<0.1%)
Eligible for Free Lunch Program: 286 (13.9%)
Eligible for Reduced-Price Lunch Program: 130 (6.3%)
Teachers: 123.9 (16.6 to 1)
Librarians/Media Specialists: 1.0 (2,057.0 to 1)
Guidance Counselors: 5.0 (411.4 to 1)
Current Spending: ($ per student per year):
Total: $7,426; Instruction: $4,533; Support Services: $2,710

Enrollment, Drop-out Rates and Diploma Recipients by Race/Ethnicity

Category	Total	White	Black	Asian	AIAN	Hisp.
Enrollment (%)	100.0	92.2	1.1	0.3	0.6	3.7
Drop-out Rate (%)	2.3	1.9	27.3	0.0	0.0	0.0
H.S. Diplomas (#)	130	123	2	0	0	3

Wellington Ex Vill SD

201 S Main St • Wellington, OH 44090-1345
(440) 647-4286 • http://www.wellington.k12.oh.us/
Grade Span: KG-12; **Agency Type:** 1
Schools: 3
1 Primary; 1 Middle; 1 High; 0 Other Level
3 Regular; 0 Special Education; 0 Vocational; 0 Alternative

0 Magnet; 0 Charter; 2 Title I Eligible; 0 School-wide Title I
Students: 1,627 (51.7% male; 48.3% female)
Individual Education Program: 160 (9.8%);
English Language Learner: 2 (0.1%); Migrant: 2 (0.1%)
Eligible for Free Lunch Program: 237 (14.6%)
Eligible for Reduced-Price Lunch Program: 148 (9.1%)
Teachers: 92.9 (17.5 to 1)
Librarians/Media Specialists: 2.0 (813.5 to 1)
Guidance Counselors: 4.0 (406.8 to 1)
Current Spending: ($ per student per year):
Total: $5,752; Instruction: $3,612; Support Services: $1,905
Enrollment, Drop-out Rates and Diploma Recipients by Race/Ethnicity

Category	Total	White	Black	Asian	AIAN	Hisp.
Enrollment (%)	100.0	94.2	0.9	0.9	0.3	0.8
Drop-out Rate (%)	3.5	3.5	0.0	n/a	n/a	0.0
H.S. Diplomas (#)	109	107	1	0	0	1

Lucas County

Anthony Wayne Local SD
PO Box 2487 • Whitehouse, OH 43571-0487
(419) 877-5377 • http://198.234.116.31/
Grade Span: PK-12; **Agency Type:** 2
Schools: 6
3 Primary; 2 Middle; 1 High; 0 Other Level
6 Regular; 0 Special Education; 0 Vocational; 0 Alternative
0 Magnet; 0 Charter; 4 Title I Eligible; 0 School-wide Title I
Students: 3,711 (49.9% male; 50.1% female)
Individual Education Program: 271 (7.3%);
English Language Learner: 0 (0.0%); Migrant: n/a
Eligible for Free Lunch Program: 120 (3.2%)
Eligible for Reduced-Price Lunch Program: 35 (0.9%)
Teachers: 236.0 (15.7 to 1)
Librarians/Media Specialists: 2.0 (1,855.5 to 1)
Guidance Counselors: 8.1 (458.1 to 1)
Current Spending: ($ per student per year):
Total: $6,790; Instruction: $4,040; Support Services: $2,541
Enrollment, Drop-out Rates and Diploma Recipients by Race/Ethnicity

Category	Total	White	Black	Asian	AIAN	Hisp.
Enrollment (%)	100.0	96.7	0.4	0.6	0.2	1.7
Drop-out Rate (%)	3.3	3.3	25.0	0.0	0.0	0.0
H.S. Diplomas (#)	233	227	1	0	0	5

Maumee City SD
2345 Detroit Ave • Maumee, OH 43537-3712
(419) 893-3200 • http://www.maumee.k12.oh.us/
Grade Span: PK-12; **Agency Type:** 1
Schools: 6
4 Primary; 1 Middle; 1 High; 0 Other Level
6 Regular; 0 Special Education; 0 Vocational; 0 Alternative
0 Magnet; 0 Charter; 3 Title I Eligible; 0 School-wide Title I
Students: 2,909 (54.1% male; 45.9% female)
Individual Education Program: 424 (14.6%);
English Language Learner: 9 (0.3%); Migrant: n/a
Eligible for Free Lunch Program: 174 (6.0%)
Eligible for Reduced-Price Lunch Program: 101 (3.5%)
Teachers: 205.2 (14.2 to 1)
Librarians/Media Specialists: 3.0 (969.7 to 1)
Guidance Counselors: 8.0 (363.6 to 1)
Current Spending: ($ per student per year):
Total: $7,725; Instruction: $5,044; Support Services: $2,396
Enrollment, Drop-out Rates and Diploma Recipients by Race/Ethnicity

Category	Total	White	Black	Asian	AIAN	Hisp.
Enrollment (%)	100.0	91.6	3.9	1.2	0.2	2.4
Drop-out Rate (%)	2.4	2.3	4.8	7.7	n/a	0.0
H.S. Diplomas (#)	242	230	3	2	0	6

Oregon City SD
5721 Seaman St • Oregon, OH 43616-2631
(419) 693-0661
Grade Span: PK-12; **Agency Type:** 1
Schools: 7
4 Primary; 2 Middle; 1 High; 0 Other Level
7 Regular; 0 Special Education; 0 Vocational; 0 Alternative
0 Magnet; 0 Charter; 5 Title I Eligible; 0 School-wide Title I
Students: 3,879 (52.6% male; 47.4% female)
Individual Education Program: 456 (11.8%);
English Language Learner: 26 (0.7%); Migrant: n/a
Eligible for Free Lunch Program: 454 (11.7%)
Eligible for Reduced-Price Lunch Program: 273 (7.0%)
Teachers: 260.2 (14.9 to 1)
Librarians/Media Specialists: 3.0 (1,293.0 to 1)
Guidance Counselors: 8.0 (484.9 to 1)
Current Spending: ($ per student per year):
Total: $7,613; Instruction: $4,748; Support Services: $2,618
Enrollment, Drop-out Rates and Diploma Recipients by Race/Ethnicity

Category	Total	White	Black	Asian	AIAN	Hisp.
Enrollment (%)	100.0	90.2	0.8	1.2	0.0	5.2
Drop-out Rate (%)	3.6	3.4	22.2	0.0	n/a	5.4
H.S. Diplomas (#)	225	204	1	4	0	12

Springfield Local SD
6900 Hall St • Holland, OH 43528-9485
(419) 867-5600 • http://www.springfield.k12.oh.us/
Grade Span: PK-12; **Agency Type:** 2
Schools: 6
4 Primary; 1 Middle; 1 High; 0 Other Level
6 Regular; 0 Special Education; 0 Vocational; 0 Alternative
0 Magnet; 0 Charter; 5 Title I Eligible; 0 School-wide Title I
Students: 3,693 (52.2% male; 47.8% female)
Individual Education Program: 652 (17.7%);
English Language Learner: 36 (1.0%); Migrant: n/a
Eligible for Free Lunch Program: 691 (18.7%)
Eligible for Reduced-Price Lunch Program: 234 (6.3%)
Teachers: 231.7 (15.9 to 1)
Librarians/Media Specialists: 2.8 (1,318.9 to 1)
Guidance Counselors: 9.0 (410.3 to 1)
Current Spending: ($ per student per year):
Total: $7,242; Instruction: $4,480; Support Services: $2,492
Enrollment, Drop-out Rates and Diploma Recipients by Race/Ethnicity

Category	Total	White	Black	Asian	AIAN	Hisp.
Enrollment (%)	100.0	78.9	10.5	2.3	0.5	3.5
Drop-out Rate (%)	0.7	0.9	0.0	0.0	0.0	0.0
H.S. Diplomas (#)	236	208	15	6	0	4

Sylvania City SD
PO Box 608 • Sylvania, OH 43560-0608
(419) 824-8501 • http://www.sylvania.k12.oh.us/
Grade Span: PK-12; **Agency Type:** 1
Schools: 12
7 Primary; 3 Middle; 2 High; 0 Other Level
12 Regular; 0 Special Education; 0 Vocational; 0 Alternative
0 Magnet; 0 Charter; 7 Title I Eligible; 0 School-wide Title I
Students: 7,842 (51.5% male; 48.5% female)
Individual Education Program: 1,058 (13.5%);
English Language Learner: 48 (0.6%); Migrant: n/a
Eligible for Free Lunch Program: 459 (5.9%)
Eligible for Reduced-Price Lunch Program: 173 (2.2%)
Teachers: 510.3 (15.4 to 1)
Librarians/Media Specialists: 5.0 (1,568.4 to 1)
Guidance Counselors: 18.0 (435.7 to 1)
Current Spending: ($ per student per year):
Total: $7,352; Instruction: $4,286; Support Services: $2,848
Enrollment, Drop-out Rates and Diploma Recipients by Race/Ethnicity

Category	Total	White	Black	Asian	AIAN	Hisp.
Enrollment (%)	100.0	91.1	2.7	3.0	0.1	1.4
Drop-out Rate (%)	1.6	1.6	1.9	0.0	0.0	3.1
H.S. Diplomas (#)	599	567	13	12	0	6

Toledo City SD
420 E Manhattan Blvd • Toledo, OH 43608-1200
(419) 729-8200 • http://www.tps.org/
Grade Span: PK-12; **Agency Type:** 1
Schools: 69
47 Primary; 7 Middle; 9 High; 5 Other Level
63 Regular; 0 Special Education; 3 Vocational; 2 Alternative
0 Magnet; 0 Charter; 48 Title I Eligible; 21 School-wide Title I
Students: 35,742 (51.6% male; 48.4% female)
Individual Education Program: 5,833 (16.3%);
English Language Learner: 524 (1.5%); Migrant: n/a
Eligible for Free Lunch Program: 18,564 (51.9%)
Eligible for Reduced-Price Lunch Program: 1,663 (4.7%)
Teachers: 2,751.5 (13.0 to 1)
Librarians/Media Specialists: 26.0 (1,374.7 to 1)
Guidance Counselors: 64.0 (558.5 to 1)
Current Spending: ($ per student per year):
Total: $8,014; Instruction: $4,571; Support Services: $2,967
Enrollment, Drop-out Rates and Diploma Recipients by Race/Ethnicity

Category	Total	White	Black	Asian	AIAN	Hisp.
Enrollment (%)	100.0	43.5	46.7	0.7	0.1	7.2
Drop-out Rate (%)	7.8	6.9	8.3	2.9	14.3	11.5
H.S. Diplomas (#)	1,478	784	602	16	0	74

Washington Local SD
3505 W Lincolnshire Blvd • Toledo, OH 43606-1231
(419) 473-8220 • http://www.washloc.k12.oh.us/
Grade Span: PK-12; **Agency Type:** 2
Schools: 13
9 Primary; 1 Middle; 1 High; 2 Other Level
12 Regular; 1 Special Education; 0 Vocational; 0 Alternative

0 Magnet; 0 Charter; 9 Title I Eligible; 1 School-wide Title I
Students: 6,989 (52.8% male; 47.2% female)
Individual Education Program: 940 (13.4%);
English Language Learner: 95 (1.4%); Migrant: n/a
Eligible for Free Lunch Program: 1,258 (18.0%)
Eligible for Reduced-Price Lunch Program: 349 (5.0%)
Teachers: 458.8 (15.2 to 1)
Librarians/Media Specialists: 2.0 (3,494.5 to 1)
Guidance Counselors: 12.5 (559.1 to 1)
Current Spending: ($ per student per year):
Total: $7,180; Instruction: $4,340; Support Services: $2,630
Enrollment, Drop-out Rates and Diploma Recipients by Race/Ethnicity

Category	Total	White	Black	Asian	AIAN	Hisp.
Enrollment (%)	100.0	86.6	7.0	0.5	0.3	3.5
Drop-out Rate (%)	6.6	6.2	13.3	0.0	0.0	6.0
H.S. Diplomas (#)	448	404	22	5	1	14

Madison County

Jonathan Alder Local SD
6440 Kilbury Huber Rd • Plain City, OH 43064-9573
(614) 873-5621 • http://www.alder.k12.oh.us/metadot/index.pl
Grade Span: PK-12; **Agency Type:** 2
Schools: 4
2 Primary; 1 Middle; 1 High; 0 Other Level
4 Regular; 0 Special Education; 0 Vocational; 0 Alternative
0 Magnet; 0 Charter; 1 Title I Eligible; 0 School-wide Title I
Students: 1,805 (50.6% male; 49.4% female)
Individual Education Program: 216 (12.0%);
English Language Learner: 0 (0.0%); Migrant: n/a
Eligible for Free Lunch Program: 185 (10.2%)
Eligible for Reduced-Price Lunch Program: 64 (3.5%)
Teachers: 92.5 (19.5 to 1)
Librarians/Media Specialists: 1.0 (1,805.0 to 1)
Guidance Counselors: 4.0 (451.3 to 1)
Current Spending: ($ per student per year):
Total: $5,216; Instruction: $2,802; Support Services: $2,194
Enrollment, Drop-out Rates and Diploma Recipients by Race/Ethnicity

Category	Total	White	Black	Asian	AIAN	Hisp.
Enrollment (%)	100.0	98.0	1.1	0.2	0.1	0.5
Drop-out Rate (%)	3.2	3.2	0.0	0.0	n/a	n/a
H.S. Diplomas (#)	109	107	2	0	0	0

London City SD
60 S Walnut St • London, OH 43140-1246
(740) 852-5700 • http://www.london.k12.oh.us/
Grade Span: PK-12; **Agency Type:** 1
Schools: 6
4 Primary; 1 Middle; 1 High; 0 Other Level
6 Regular; 0 Special Education; 0 Vocational; 0 Alternative
0 Magnet; 0 Charter; 3 Title I Eligible; 2 School-wide Title I
Students: 2,045 (51.5% male; 48.5% female)
Individual Education Program: 302 (14.8%);
English Language Learner: 53 (2.6%); Migrant: n/a
Eligible for Free Lunch Program: 362 (17.7%)
Eligible for Reduced-Price Lunch Program: 98 (4.8%)
Teachers: 139.0 (14.7 to 1)
Librarians/Media Specialists: 1.0 (2,045.0 to 1)
Guidance Counselors: 3.0 (681.7 to 1)
Current Spending: ($ per student per year):
Total: $5,768; Instruction: $3,543; Support Services: $2,033
Enrollment, Drop-out Rates and Diploma Recipients by Race/Ethnicity

Category	Total	White	Black	Asian	AIAN	Hisp.
Enrollment (%)	100.0	86.5	9.4	1.5	0.0	1.4
Drop-out Rate (%)	4.3	4.3	5.5	0.0	n/a	0.0
H.S. Diplomas (#)	134	122	10	2	0	0

Madison-Plains Local SD
55 Linson Rd • London, OH 43140-9751
(740) 852-0290
Grade Span: KG-12; **Agency Type:** 2
Schools: 6
4 Primary; 1 Middle; 1 High; 0 Other Level
6 Regular; 0 Special Education; 0 Vocational; 0 Alternative
0 Magnet; 0 Charter; 3 Title I Eligible; 0 School-wide Title I
Students: 1,668 (51.6% male; 48.4% female)
Individual Education Program: 169 (10.1%);
English Language Learner: 7 (0.4%); Migrant: n/a
Eligible for Free Lunch Program: 132 (7.9%)
Eligible for Reduced-Price Lunch Program: 83 (5.0%)
Teachers: 98.0 (17.0 to 1)
Librarians/Media Specialists: 1.0 (1,668.0 to 1)
Guidance Counselors: 4.0 (417.0 to 1)
Current Spending: ($ per student per year):
Total: $6,265; Instruction: $3,594; Support Services: $2,404
Enrollment, Drop-out Rates and Diploma Recipients by Race/Ethnicity

Category	Total	White	Black	Asian	AIAN	Hisp.
Enrollment (%)	100.0	99.3	0.1	0.4	0.0	0.2
Drop-out Rate (%)	2.2	2.2	n/a	0.0	n/a	n/a
H.S. Diplomas (#)	127	127	0	0	0	0

Mahoning County

Austintown Local SD
225 Idaho Rd • Youngstown, OH 44515-3703
(330) 797-3900 • http://www.austintown.k12.oh.us/
Grade Span: PK-12; **Agency Type:** 2
Schools: 8
5 Primary; 2 Middle; 1 High; 0 Other Level
8 Regular; 0 Special Education; 0 Vocational; 0 Alternative
0 Magnet; 0 Charter; 5 Title I Eligible; 0 School-wide Title I
Students: 5,092 (51.1% male; 48.9% female)
Individual Education Program: 783 (15.4%);
English Language Learner: 21 (0.4%); Migrant: n/a
Eligible for Free Lunch Program: 857 (16.8%)
Eligible for Reduced-Price Lunch Program: 379 (7.4%)
Teachers: 299.3 (17.0 to 1)
Librarians/Media Specialists: 3.0 (1,697.3 to 1)
Guidance Counselors: 12.0 (424.3 to 1)
Current Spending: ($ per student per year):
Total: $6,698; Instruction: $4,111; Support Services: $2,339
Enrollment, Drop-out Rates and Diploma Recipients by Race/Ethnicity

Category	Total	White	Black	Asian	AIAN	Hisp.
Enrollment (%)	100.0	90.0	6.7	0.9	0.1	1.5
Drop-out Rate (%)	1.9	1.8	3.3	0.0	0.0	3.6
H.S. Diplomas (#)	351	318	21	5	0	6

Boardman Local SD
7410 Market St • Youngstown, OH 44512-5612
(330) 726-3404 • http://www.boardman.k12.oh.us/
Grade Span: PK-12; **Agency Type:** 2
Schools: 7
4 Primary; 2 Middle; 1 High; 0 Other Level
7 Regular; 0 Special Education; 0 Vocational; 0 Alternative
0 Magnet; 0 Charter; 5 Title I Eligible; 0 School-wide Title I
Students: 4,920 (51.0% male; 49.0% female)
Individual Education Program: 448 (9.1%);
English Language Learner: 40 (0.8%); Migrant: n/a
Eligible for Free Lunch Program: 578 (11.7%)
Eligible for Reduced-Price Lunch Program: 234 (4.8%)
Teachers: 299.6 (16.4 to 1)
Librarians/Media Specialists: 3.0 (1,640.0 to 1)
Guidance Counselors: 11.0 (447.3 to 1)
Current Spending: ($ per student per year):
Total: $6,952; Instruction: $4,186; Support Services: $2,522
Enrollment, Drop-out Rates and Diploma Recipients by Race/Ethnicity

Category	Total	White	Black	Asian	AIAN	Hisp.
Enrollment (%)	100.0	90.0	4.8	2.0	0.1	1.3
Drop-out Rate (%)	1.2	1.1	4.5	0.0	0.0	0.0
H.S. Diplomas (#)	380	357	7	8	0	8

Campbell City SD
280 6th St • Campbell, OH 44405-1325
(330) 799-8777
Grade Span: PK-12; **Agency Type:** 1
Schools: 3
1 Primary; 1 Middle; 1 High; 0 Other Level
3 Regular; 0 Special Education; 0 Vocational; 0 Alternative
0 Magnet; 0 Charter; 3 Title I Eligible; 3 School-wide Title I
Students: 1,591 (51.4% male; 48.6% female)
Individual Education Program: 239 (15.0%);
English Language Learner: 13 (0.8%); Migrant: n/a
Eligible for Free Lunch Program: 641 (40.3%)
Eligible for Reduced-Price Lunch Program: 124 (7.8%)
Teachers: 106.0 (15.0 to 1)
Librarians/Media Specialists: 1.0 (1,591.0 to 1)
Guidance Counselors: 2.0 (795.5 to 1)
Current Spending: ($ per student per year):
Total: $6,842; Instruction: $4,352; Support Services: $2,206
Enrollment, Drop-out Rates and Diploma Recipients by Race/Ethnicity

Category	Total	White	Black	Asian	AIAN	Hisp.
Enrollment (%)	100.0	49.3	29.1	0.1	0.0	14.8
Drop-out Rate (%)	0.0	0.0	0.0	n/a	n/a	0.0
H.S. Diplomas (#)	100	65	23	0	0	12

Canfield Local SD
100 Wadsworth St • Canfield, OH 44406-1451
(330) 533-3303 • http://canfield.access-k12.org/
Grade Span: PK-12; **Agency Type:** 2
Schools: 4

2 Primary; 1 Middle; 1 High; 0 Other Level
4 Regular; 0 Special Education; 0 Vocational; 0 Alternative
0 Magnet; 0 Charter; 0 Title I Eligible; 0 School-wide Title I
Students: 3,103 (51.0% male; 49.0% female)
Individual Education Program: 315 (10.2%);
English Language Learner: 10 (0.3%); Migrant: 1 (<0.1%)
Eligible for Free Lunch Program: 81 (2.6%)
Eligible for Reduced-Price Lunch Program: 41 (1.3%)
Teachers: 177.3 (17.5 to 1)
Librarians/Media Specialists: 2.0 (1,551.5 to 1)
Guidance Counselors: 4.0 (775.8 to 1)
Current Spending: ($ per student per year):
Total: $6,137; Instruction: $3,573; Support Services: $2,372
Enrollment, Drop-out Rates and Diploma Recipients by Race/Ethnicity

Category	Total	White	Black	Asian	AIAN	Hisp.
Enrollment (%)	100.0	96.1	0.7	2.1	0.0	0.5
Drop-out Rate (%)	0.3	0.3	0.0	0.0	n/a	0.0
H.S. Diplomas (#)	225	212	1	7	0	5

Poland Local SD
30 Riverside Dr • Poland, OH 44514-2049
(330) 757-7000 • http://www.polandbulldogs.com/
Grade Span: PK-12; **Agency Type:** 2
Schools: 6
4 Primary; 1 Middle; 1 High; 0 Other Level
6 Regular; 0 Special Education; 0 Vocational; 0 Alternative
0 Magnet; 0 Charter; 3 Title I Eligible; 0 School-wide Title I
Students: 2,525 (50.7% male; 49.3% female)
Individual Education Program: 271 (10.7%);
English Language Learner: 0 (0.0%); Migrant: n/a
Eligible for Free Lunch Program: 74 (2.9%)
Eligible for Reduced-Price Lunch Program: 54 (2.1%)
Teachers: 129.0 (19.6 to 1)
Librarians/Media Specialists: 1.0 (2,525.0 to 1)
Guidance Counselors: 4.8 (526.0 to 1)
Current Spending: ($ per student per year):
Total: $6,203; Instruction: $3,788; Support Services: $2,150
Enrollment, Drop-out Rates and Diploma Recipients by Race/Ethnicity

Category	Total	White	Black	Asian	AIAN	Hisp.
Enrollment (%)	100.0	97.3	0.4	0.5	0.3	0.9
Drop-out Rate (%)	0.7	0.7	0.0	0.0	0.0	0.0
H.S. Diplomas (#)	198	193	0	1	1	3

Struthers City SD
99 Euclid Ave • Struthers, OH 44471-1831
(330) 750-1061
Grade Span: PK-12; **Agency Type:** 1
Schools: 3
1 Primary; 1 Middle; 1 High; 0 Other Level
3 Regular; 0 Special Education; 0 Vocational; 0 Alternative
0 Magnet; 0 Charter; 3 Title I Eligible; 1 School-wide Title I
Students: 2,038 (51.1% male; 48.9% female)
Individual Education Program: 242 (11.9%);
English Language Learner: 0 (0.0%); Migrant: n/a
Eligible for Free Lunch Program: 847 (41.6%)
Eligible for Reduced-Price Lunch Program: 262 (12.9%)
Teachers: 123.8 (16.5 to 1)
Librarians/Media Specialists: 1.0 (2,038.0 to 1)
Guidance Counselors: 3.0 (679.3 to 1)
Current Spending: ($ per student per year):
Total: $6,481; Instruction: $4,229; Support Services: $2,012
Enrollment, Drop-out Rates and Diploma Recipients by Race/Ethnicity

Category	Total	White	Black	Asian	AIAN	Hisp.
Enrollment (%)	100.0	95.2	1.8	0.1	0.4	1.4
Drop-out Rate (%)	3.0	3.2	0.0	0.0	0.0	0.0
H.S. Diplomas (#)	123	121	1	0	0	1

West Branch Local SD
14277 S Main St • Beloit, OH 44609-9504
(330) 938-9324
Grade Span: PK-12; **Agency Type:** 2
Schools: 7
5 Primary; 1 Middle; 1 High; 0 Other Level
7 Regular; 0 Special Education; 0 Vocational; 0 Alternative
0 Magnet; 0 Charter; 5 Title I Eligible; 0 School-wide Title I
Students: 2,542 (52.3% male; 47.7% female)
Individual Education Program: 264 (10.4%);
English Language Learner: 3 (0.1%); Migrant: n/a
Eligible for Free Lunch Program: 406 (16.0%)
Eligible for Reduced-Price Lunch Program: 184 (7.2%)
Teachers: 137.0 (18.6 to 1)
Librarians/Media Specialists: 1.0 (2,542.0 to 1)
Guidance Counselors: 5.0 (508.4 to 1)
Current Spending: ($ per student per year):
Total: $5,542; Instruction: $3,277; Support Services: $2,003
Enrollment, Drop-out Rates and Diploma Recipients by Race/Ethnicity

Category	Total	White	Black	Asian	AIAN	Hisp.
Enrollment (%)	100.0	99.2	0.2	0.1	0.3	0.1
Drop-out Rate (%)	1.7	1.7	0.0	0.0	n/a	n/a
H.S. Diplomas (#)	187	185	1	0	1	0

Youngstown City SD
PO Box 550 • Youngstown, OH 44501-0550
(330) 744-6900 • http://www.youngstown.k12.oh.us/
Grade Span: KG-12; **Agency Type:** 1
Schools: 27
13 Primary; 4 Middle; 5 High; 5 Other Level
24 Regular; 0 Special Education; 2 Vocational; 1 Alternative
0 Magnet; 0 Charter; 21 Title I Eligible; 17 School-wide Title I
Students: 10,034 (51.7% male; 48.3% female)
Individual Education Program: 2,019 (20.1%);
English Language Learner: 67 (0.7%); Migrant: n/a
Eligible for Free Lunch Program: 6,348 (63.3%)
Eligible for Reduced-Price Lunch Program: 502 (5.0%)
Teachers: 742.1 (13.5 to 1)
Librarians/Media Specialists: 6.0 (1,672.3 to 1)
Guidance Counselors: 19.8 (506.8 to 1)
Current Spending: ($ per student per year):
Total: $8,411; Instruction: $4,749; Support Services: $3,365
Enrollment, Drop-out Rates and Diploma Recipients by Race/Ethnicity

Category	Total	White	Black	Asian	AIAN	Hisp.
Enrollment (%)	100.0	24.3	67.0	0.3	0.1	5.9
Drop-out Rate (%)	32.9	23.9	36.6	16.7	200.0	34.5
H.S. Diplomas (#)	421	134	262	1	0	22

Marion County

Elgin Local SD
4616 Larue Prospect Rd W • Marion, OH 43302-8859
(740) 382-1101 • http://www.treca.org/schools/elgin/
Grade Span: PK-12; **Agency Type:** 2
Schools: 4
2 Primary; 1 Middle; 1 High; 0 Other Level
4 Regular; 0 Special Education; 0 Vocational; 0 Alternative
0 Magnet; 0 Charter; 1 Title I Eligible; 0 School-wide Title I
Students: 1,681 (51.2% male; 48.8% female)
Individual Education Program: 190 (11.3%);
English Language Learner: 0 (0.0%); Migrant: n/a
Eligible for Free Lunch Program: 325 (19.3%)
Eligible for Reduced-Price Lunch Program: 136 (8.1%)
Teachers: 109.2 (15.4 to 1)
Librarians/Media Specialists: 2.0 (840.5 to 1)
Guidance Counselors: 7.0 (240.1 to 1)
Current Spending: ($ per student per year):
Total: $5,690; Instruction: $3,427; Support Services: $1,981
Enrollment, Drop-out Rates and Diploma Recipients by Race/Ethnicity

Category	Total	White	Black	Asian	AIAN	Hisp.
Enrollment (%)	100.0	98.6	0.1	0.1	0.0	0.4
Drop-out Rate (%)	1.7	1.7	n/a	n/a	n/a	n/a
H.S. Diplomas (#)	125	124	0	1	0	0

Marion City SD
910 E Church St • Marion, OH 43302-4317
(740) 387-3300 • http://www.marioncity.k12.oh.us/
Grade Span: PK-12; **Agency Type:** 1
Schools: 17
10 Primary; 4 Middle; 1 High; 0 Other Level
15 Regular; 0 Special Education; 0 Vocational; 0 Alternative
0 Magnet; 0 Charter; 11 Title I Eligible; 7 School-wide Title I
Students: 5,682 (52.2% male; 47.8% female)
Individual Education Program: 1,098 (19.3%);
English Language Learner: 20 (0.4%); Migrant: 3 (0.1%)
Eligible for Free Lunch Program: 1,811 (31.9%)
Eligible for Reduced-Price Lunch Program: 502 (8.8%)
Teachers: 374.7 (15.2 to 1)
Librarians/Media Specialists: 4.0 (1,420.5 to 1)
Guidance Counselors: 10.0 (568.2 to 1)
Current Spending: ($ per student per year):
Total: $6,589; Instruction: $4,316; Support Services: $1,961
Enrollment, Drop-out Rates and Diploma Recipients by Race/Ethnicity

Category	Total	White	Black	Asian	AIAN	Hisp.
Enrollment (%)	100.0	88.5	7.4	0.6	0.0	2.1
Drop-out Rate (%)	4.9	4.9	4.3	0.0	n/a	9.1
H.S. Diplomas (#)	280	251	22	0	0	4

River Valley Local SD
197 Brockelsby Rd • Caledonia, OH 43314
(740) 725-5400
Grade Span: PK-12; **Agency Type:** 2
Schools: 5

3 Primary; 1 Middle; 1 High; 0 Other Level
5 Regular; 0 Special Education; 0 Vocational; 0 Alternative
0 Magnet; 0 Charter; 2 Title I Eligible; 0 School-wide Title I
Students: 1,726 (53.6% male; 46.4% female)
Individual Education Program: 222 (12.9%);
English Language Learner: 0 (0.0%); Migrant: n/a
Eligible for Free Lunch Program: 199 (11.5%)
Eligible for Reduced-Price Lunch Program: 121 (7.0%)
Teachers: 107.2 (16.1 to 1)
Librarians/Media Specialists: 1.0 (1,726.0 to 1)
Guidance Counselors: 3.0 (575.3 to 1)
Current Spending: ($ per student per year):
Total: $6,546; Instruction: $3,930; Support Services: $2,367
Enrollment, Drop-out Rates and Diploma Recipients by Race/Ethnicity

Category	Total	White	Black	Asian	AIAN	Hisp.
Enrollment (%)	100.0	97.9	0.3	0.5	0.0	0.5
Drop-out Rate (%)	0.6	0.6	0.0	0.0	n/a	0.0
H.S. Diplomas (#)	139	137	0	1	0	1

Medina County

Black River Local SD

257 County Rd 40 - A • Sullivan, OH 44880-9731
(419) 736-3300 • http://www.leeca.esu.k12.oh.us/black_river/index.html
Grade Span: PK-12; **Agency Type:** 2
Schools: 3
1 Primary; 1 Middle; 1 High; 0 Other Level
3 Regular; 0 Special Education; 0 Vocational; 0 Alternative
0 Magnet; 0 Charter; 2 Title I Eligible; 0 School-wide Title I
Students: 1,676 (53.1% male; 46.9% female)
Individual Education Program: 189 (11.3%);
English Language Learner: 0 (0.0%); Migrant: 1 (0.1%)
Eligible for Free Lunch Program: 205 (12.2%)
Eligible for Reduced-Price Lunch Program: 123 (7.3%)
Teachers: 103.0 (16.3 to 1)
Librarians/Media Specialists: 1.0 (1,676.0 to 1)
Guidance Counselors: 8.0 (209.5 to 1)
Current Spending: ($ per student per year):
Total: $5,592; Instruction: $3,495; Support Services: $1,891
Enrollment, Drop-out Rates and Diploma Recipients by Race/Ethnicity

Category	Total	White	Black	Asian	AIAN	Hisp.
Enrollment (%)	100.0	96.7	1.6	0.5	0.1	0.6
Drop-out Rate (%)	2.4	2.5	0.0	n/a	0.0	0.0
H.S. Diplomas (#)	98	97	0	0	1	0

Brunswick City SD

3643 Center Rd • Brunswick, OH 44212-3619
(330) 225-7731 • http://www.bcsoh.org/
Grade Span: PK-12; **Agency Type:** 1
Schools: 11
7 Primary; 3 Middle; 1 High; 0 Other Level
11 Regular; 0 Special Education; 0 Vocational; 0 Alternative
0 Magnet; 0 Charter; 6 Title I Eligible; 1 School-wide Title I
Students: 7,270 (51.5% male; 48.5% female)
Individual Education Program: 809 (11.1%);
English Language Learner: 17 (0.2%); Migrant: n/a
Eligible for Free Lunch Program: 497 (6.8%)
Eligible for Reduced-Price Lunch Program: 335 (4.6%)
Teachers: 430.4 (16.9 to 1)
Librarians/Media Specialists: 4.0 (1,817.5 to 1)
Guidance Counselors: 12.0 (605.8 to 1)
Current Spending: ($ per student per year):
Total: $6,678; Instruction: $4,216; Support Services: $2,251
Enrollment, Drop-out Rates and Diploma Recipients by Race/Ethnicity

Category	Total	White	Black	Asian	AIAN	Hisp.
Enrollment (%)	100.0	96.2	0.6	0.7	0.2	1.0
Drop-out Rate (%)	1.4	1.4	0.0	0.0	n/a	7.1
H.S. Diplomas (#)	475	466	1	4	0	2

Buckeye Local SD

3044 Columbia Rd • Medina, OH 44256-9411
(330) 725-3735 • http://www.buckeye.k12.oh.us/
Grade Span: PK-12; **Agency Type:** 2
Schools: 5
3 Primary; 1 Middle; 1 High; 0 Other Level
5 Regular; 0 Special Education; 0 Vocational; 0 Alternative
0 Magnet; 0 Charter; 2 Title I Eligible; 0 School-wide Title I
Students: 2,437 (50.5% male; 49.5% female)
Individual Education Program: 284 (11.7%);
English Language Learner: 0 (0.0%); Migrant: n/a
Eligible for Free Lunch Program: 248 (10.2%)
Eligible for Reduced-Price Lunch Program: 64 (2.6%)
Teachers: 154.6 (15.8 to 1)
Librarians/Media Specialists: 2.0 (1,218.5 to 1)
Guidance Counselors: 6.0 (406.2 to 1)
Current Spending: ($ per student per year):
Total: $6,921; Instruction: $4,104; Support Services: $2,616
Enrollment, Drop-out Rates and Diploma Recipients by Race/Ethnicity

Category	Total	White	Black	Asian	AIAN	Hisp.
Enrollment (%)	100.0	95.4	2.1	0.6	0.2	0.4
Drop-out Rate (%)	2.3	2.4	0.0	0.0	0.0	n/a
H.S. Diplomas (#)	182	177	1	2	1	0

Cloverleaf Local SD

8525 Friendsville Rd • Lodi, OH 44254-9706
(330) 948-2500 • http://www.cls.k12.oh.us/
Grade Span: PK-12; **Agency Type:** 2
Schools: 7
5 Primary; 1 Middle; 1 High; 0 Other Level
7 Regular; 0 Special Education; 0 Vocational; 0 Alternative
0 Magnet; 0 Charter; 2 Title I Eligible; 0 School-wide Title I
Students: 3,609 (51.7% male; 48.3% female)
Individual Education Program: 436 (12.1%);
English Language Learner: 0 (0.0%); Migrant: 4 (0.1%)
Eligible for Free Lunch Program: 421 (11.7%)
Eligible for Reduced-Price Lunch Program: 280 (7.8%)
Teachers: 201.9 (17.9 to 1)
Librarians/Media Specialists: 3.0 (1,203.0 to 1)
Guidance Counselors: 7.0 (515.6 to 1)
Current Spending: ($ per student per year):
Total: $5,976; Instruction: $3,583; Support Services: $2,165
Enrollment, Drop-out Rates and Diploma Recipients by Race/Ethnicity

Category	Total	White	Black	Asian	AIAN	Hisp.
Enrollment (%)	100.0	98.3	0.1	0.2	0.2	0.6
Drop-out Rate (%)	2.4	2.4	0.0	0.0	n/a	0.0
H.S. Diplomas (#)	273	272	0	0	0	1

Highland Local SD

3880 Ridge Rd • Medina, OH 44256-7920
(330) 239-1901 • http://www.highlandschools.org/
Grade Span: PK-12; **Agency Type:** 2
Schools: 4
2 Primary; 0 Middle; 1 High; 1 Other Level
4 Regular; 0 Special Education; 0 Vocational; 0 Alternative
0 Magnet; 0 Charter; 3 Title I Eligible; 0 School-wide Title I
Students: 2,709 (52.0% male; 48.0% female)
Individual Education Program: 282 (10.4%);
English Language Learner: 0 (0.0%); Migrant: 2 (0.1%)
Eligible for Free Lunch Program: 68 (2.5%)
Eligible for Reduced-Price Lunch Program: 62 (2.3%)
Teachers: 157.1 (17.2 to 1)
Librarians/Media Specialists: 3.0 (903.0 to 1)
Guidance Counselors: 5.0 (541.8 to 1)
Current Spending: ($ per student per year):
Total: $6,425; Instruction: $3,831; Support Services: $2,353
Enrollment, Drop-out Rates and Diploma Recipients by Race/Ethnicity

Category	Total	White	Black	Asian	AIAN	Hisp.
Enrollment (%)	100.0	98.7	0.3	0.6	0.0	0.2
Drop-out Rate (%)	1.0	1.0	0.0	0.0	n/a	0.0
H.S. Diplomas (#)	196	195	0	1	0	0

Medina City SD

120 W Washington St • Medina, OH 44256-2260
(330) 636-3000 • http://www.mcsoh.org/
Grade Span: PK-12; **Agency Type:** 1
Schools: 9
7 Primary; 1 Middle; 1 High; 0 Other Level
9 Regular; 0 Special Education; 0 Vocational; 0 Alternative
0 Magnet; 0 Charter; 3 Title I Eligible; 0 School-wide Title I
Students: 7,030 (51.1% male; 48.9% female)
Individual Education Program: 1,037 (14.8%);
English Language Learner: 9 (0.1%); Migrant: 4 (0.1%)
Eligible for Free Lunch Program: 317 (4.5%)
Eligible for Reduced-Price Lunch Program: 177 (2.5%)
Teachers: 467.9 (15.0 to 1)
Librarians/Media Specialists: 7.0 (1,004.3 to 1)
Guidance Counselors: 13.0 (540.8 to 1)
Current Spending: ($ per student per year):
Total: $7,668; Instruction: $4,734; Support Services: $2,748
Enrollment, Drop-out Rates and Diploma Recipients by Race/Ethnicity

Category	Total	White	Black	Asian	AIAN	Hisp.
Enrollment (%)	100.0	94.3	2.1	1.0	0.2	0.7
Drop-out Rate (%)	0.6	0.5	4.5	0.0	n/a	0.0
H.S. Diplomas (#)	501	470	16	6	0	4

Wadsworth City SD

360 College St • Wadsworth, OH 44281-1146
(330) 336-3571 • http://www.wadsworth.k12.oh.us/
Grade Span: PK-12; **Agency Type:** 1
Schools: 8

5 Primary; 2 Middle; 1 High; 0 Other Level
8 Regular; 0 Special Education; 0 Vocational; 0 Alternative
0 Magnet; 0 Charter; 6 Title I Eligible; 0 School-wide Title I

Students: 4,630 (52.3% male; 47.7% female)
Individual Education Program: 439 (9.5%);
English Language Learner: 3 (0.1%); Migrant: n/a
Eligible for Free Lunch Program: 305 (6.6%)
Eligible for Reduced-Price Lunch Program: 159 (3.4%)

Teachers: 246.1 (18.8 to 1)
Librarians/Media Specialists: 2.0 (2,315.0 to 1)
Guidance Counselors: 8.0 (578.8 to 1)
Current Spending: ($ per student per year):
Total: $6,739; Instruction: $3,879; Support Services: $2,621

Enrollment, Drop-out Rates and Diploma Recipients by Race/Ethnicity

Category	Total	White	Black	Asian	AIAN	Hisp.
Enrollment (%)	100.0	97.6	0.5	0.7	0.2	0.3
Drop-out Rate (%)	1.5	1.5	0.0	0.0	0.0	0.0
H.S. Diplomas (#)	327	319	3	3	0	1

Meigs County

Meigs Local SD

PO Box 272 • Pomeroy, OH 45769-0272
(740) 992-2153
Grade Span: PK-12; **Agency Type:** 2
Schools: 10
5 Primary; 2 Middle; 1 High; 0 Other Level
8 Regular; 0 Special Education; 0 Vocational; 0 Alternative
0 Magnet; 0 Charter; 8 Title I Eligible; 2 School-wide Title I

Students: 2,179 (49.4% male; 50.6% female)
Individual Education Program: 415 (19.0%);
English Language Learner: 0 (0.0%); Migrant: n/a
Eligible for Free Lunch Program: 1,080 (49.6%)
Eligible for Reduced-Price Lunch Program: 220 (10.1%)

Teachers: 161.0 (13.5 to 1)
Librarians/Media Specialists: 0.0 (0.0 to 1)
Guidance Counselors: 4.0 (544.8 to 1)
Current Spending: ($ per student per year):
Total: $6,803; Instruction: $4,060; Support Services: $2,366

Enrollment, Drop-out Rates and Diploma Recipients by Race/Ethnicity

Category	Total	White	Black	Asian	AIAN	Hisp.
Enrollment (%)	100.0	97.2	1.9	0.0	0.1	0.0
Drop-out Rate (%)	1.7	1.7	0.0	n/a	n/a	0.0
H.S. Diplomas (#)	125	121	4	0	0	0

Mercer County

Celina City SD

585 E Livingston St • Celina, OH 45822-1742
(419) 586-8300 • http://www.noacsc.org/mercer/ce/
Grade Span: KG-12; **Agency Type:** 1
Schools: 6
3 Primary; 2 Middle; 1 High; 0 Other Level
6 Regular; 0 Special Education; 0 Vocational; 0 Alternative
0 Magnet; 0 Charter; 4 Title I Eligible; 0 School-wide Title I

Students: 3,354 (52.7% male; 47.3% female)
Individual Education Program: 580 (17.3%);
English Language Learner: 0 (0.0%); Migrant: n/a
Eligible for Free Lunch Program: 641 (19.1%)
Eligible for Reduced-Price Lunch Program: 180 (5.4%)

Teachers: 200.5 (16.7 to 1)
Librarians/Media Specialists: 1.0 (3,354.0 to 1)
Guidance Counselors: 5.0 (670.8 to 1)
Current Spending: ($ per student per year):
Total: $6,679; Instruction: $4,053; Support Services: $2,340

Enrollment, Drop-out Rates and Diploma Recipients by Race/Ethnicity

Category	Total	White	Black	Asian	AIAN	Hisp.
Enrollment (%)	100.0	97.8	0.2	0.5	0.1	0.9
Drop-out Rate (%)	2.7	2.5	0.0	0.0	0.0	21.4
H.S. Diplomas (#)	282	274	1	3	0	4

Coldwater Ex Vill SD

310 N 2nd St • Coldwater, OH 45828-1242
(419) 678-2611 • http://cw.noacsc.org/
Grade Span: PK-12; **Agency Type:** 1
Schools: 3
1 Primary; 1 Middle; 1 High; 0 Other Level
3 Regular; 0 Special Education; 0 Vocational; 0 Alternative
0 Magnet; 0 Charter; 2 Title I Eligible; 0 School-wide Title I

Students: 1,633 (52.4% male; 47.6% female)
Individual Education Program: 207 (12.7%);
English Language Learner: 0 (0.0%); Migrant: n/a
Eligible for Free Lunch Program: 108 (6.6%)
Eligible for Reduced-Price Lunch Program: 67 (4.1%)

Teachers: 96.6 (16.9 to 1)
Librarians/Media Specialists: 1.0 (1,633.0 to 1)
Guidance Counselors: 1.8 (907.2 to 1)
Current Spending: ($ per student per year):
Total: $5,833; Instruction: $3,988; Support Services: $1,639

Enrollment, Drop-out Rates and Diploma Recipients by Race/Ethnicity

Category	Total	White	Black	Asian	AIAN	Hisp.
Enrollment (%)	100.0	98.3	0.0	0.1	0.0	0.3
Drop-out Rate (%)	0.9	0.9	n/a	n/a	n/a	0.0
H.S. Diplomas (#)	124	123	0	0	0	1

Miami County

Milton-Union Ex Vill SD

112 S Spring St • West Milton, OH 45383-1609
(937) 884-7910
Grade Span: PK-12; **Agency Type:** 1
Schools: 3
1 Primary; 1 Middle; 1 High; 0 Other Level
3 Regular; 0 Special Education; 0 Vocational; 0 Alternative
0 Magnet; 0 Charter; 2 Title I Eligible; 0 School-wide Title I

Students: 1,832 (53.3% male; 46.7% female)
Individual Education Program: 213 (11.6%);
English Language Learner: 0 (0.0%); Migrant: n/a
Eligible for Free Lunch Program: 276 (15.1%)
Eligible for Reduced-Price Lunch Program: 86 (4.7%)

Teachers: 108.3 (16.9 to 1)
Librarians/Media Specialists: 2.0 (916.0 to 1)
Guidance Counselors: 3.0 (610.7 to 1)
Current Spending: ($ per student per year):
Total: $5,906; Instruction: $3,476; Support Services: $2,182

Enrollment, Drop-out Rates and Diploma Recipients by Race/Ethnicity

Category	Total	White	Black	Asian	AIAN	Hisp.
Enrollment (%)	100.0	98.1	0.1	0.2	0.2	0.3
Drop-out Rate (%)	2.6	2.4	0.0	0.0	n/a	33.3
H.S. Diplomas (#)	116	115	1	0	0	0

Piqua City SD

719 E Ash St • Piqua, OH 45356-2411
(937) 773-4321 • http://www.piqua.org/
Grade Span: PK-12; **Agency Type:** 1
Schools: 9
4 Primary; 4 Middle; 1 High; 0 Other Level
9 Regular; 0 Special Education; 0 Vocational; 0 Alternative
0 Magnet; 0 Charter; 6 Title I Eligible; 3 School-wide Title I

Students: 3,914 (53.7% male; 46.3% female)
Individual Education Program: 636 (16.2%);
English Language Learner: 11 (0.3%); Migrant: n/a
Eligible for Free Lunch Program: 1,002 (25.6%)
Eligible for Reduced-Price Lunch Program: 357 (9.1%)

Teachers: 191.6 (20.4 to 1)
Librarians/Media Specialists: 2.0 (1,957.0 to 1)
Guidance Counselors: 9.0 (434.9 to 1)
Current Spending: ($ per student per year):
Total: $6,311; Instruction: $3,832; Support Services: $2,203

Enrollment, Drop-out Rates and Diploma Recipients by Race/Ethnicity

Category	Total	White	Black	Asian	AIAN	Hisp.
Enrollment (%)	100.0	91.3	5.4	0.6	0.3	0.8
Drop-out Rate (%)	6.0	5.7	9.3	0.0	16.7	20.0
H.S. Diplomas (#)	228	211	16	0	1	0

Tipp City Ex Vill SD

90 S Tippecanoe Dr • Tipp City, OH 45371-1139
(937) 667-8444
Grade Span: KG-12; **Agency Type:** 1
Schools: 5
2 Primary; 2 Middle; 1 High; 0 Other Level
5 Regular; 0 Special Education; 0 Vocational; 0 Alternative
0 Magnet; 0 Charter; 4 Title I Eligible; 0 School-wide Title I

Students: 2,643 (51.7% male; 48.3% female)
Individual Education Program: 235 (8.9%);
English Language Learner: 25 (0.9%); Migrant: 27 (1.0%)
Eligible for Free Lunch Program: 146 (5.5%)
Eligible for Reduced-Price Lunch Program: 55 (2.1%)

Teachers: 152.3 (17.4 to 1)
Librarians/Media Specialists: 2.0 (1,321.5 to 1)
Guidance Counselors: 6.0 (440.5 to 1)
Current Spending: ($ per student per year):
Total: $5,524; Instruction: $3,438; Support Services: $1,884

Enrollment, Drop-out Rates and Diploma Recipients by Race/Ethnicity

Category	Total	White	Black	Asian	AIAN	Hisp.
Enrollment (%)	100.0	97.0	0.3	0.9	0.1	1.5
Drop-out Rate (%)	1.3	1.3	0.0	0.0	n/a	0.0
H.S. Diplomas (#)	175	173	1	1	0	0

Troy City SD

500 N Market St • Troy, OH 45373-1418
(937) 332-6700
Grade Span: KG-12; **Agency Type:** 1
Schools: 9
6 Primary; 1 Middle; 1 High; 1 Other Level
8 Regular; 1 Special Education; 0 Vocational; 0 Alternative
0 Magnet; 0 Charter; 6 Title I Eligible; 2 School-wide Title I
Students: 4,554 (52.3% male; 47.7% female)
Individual Education Program: 562 (12.3%);
English Language Learner: 53 (1.2%); Migrant: n/a
Eligible for Free Lunch Program: 587 (12.9%)
Eligible for Reduced-Price Lunch Program: 232 (5.1%)
Teachers: 243.1 (18.7 to 1)
Librarians/Media Specialists: 2.0 (2,277.0 to 1)
Guidance Counselors: 8.0 (569.3 to 1)
Current Spending: ($ per student per year):
Total: $6,314; Instruction: $4,087; Support Services: $1,932
Enrollment, Drop-out Rates and Diploma Recipients by Race/Ethnicity

Category	Total	White	Black	Asian	AIAN	Hisp.
Enrollment (%)	100.0	87.7	4.9	2.3	0.2	0.7
Drop-out Rate (%)	4.5	4.2	9.1	4.2	50.0	0.0
H.S. Diplomas (#)	294	263	17	9	0	3

Monroe County

Switzerland of Ohio Local SD

304 Mill St • Woodsfield, OH 43793-1256
(740) 472-5801
Grade Span: PK-12; **Agency Type:** 2
Schools: 10
6 Primary; 0 Middle; 4 High; 0 Other Level
9 Regular; 0 Special Education; 1 Vocational; 0 Alternative
0 Magnet; 0 Charter; 8 Title I Eligible; 0 School-wide Title I
Students: 2,812 (51.9% male; 48.1% female)
Individual Education Program: 460 (16.4%);
English Language Learner: 0 (0.0%); Migrant: n/a
Eligible for Free Lunch Program: 851 (30.3%)
Eligible for Reduced-Price Lunch Program: 260 (9.2%)
Teachers: 202.4 (13.9 to 1)
Librarians/Media Specialists: 3.0 (937.3 to 1)
Guidance Counselors: 4.0 (703.0 to 1)
Current Spending: ($ per student per year):
Total: $6,468; Instruction: $4,043; Support Services: $2,169
Enrollment, Drop-out Rates and Diploma Recipients by Race/Ethnicity

Category	Total	White	Black	Asian	AIAN	Hisp.
Enrollment (%)	100.0	98.8	0.3	0.0	0.0	0.0
Drop-out Rate (%)	3.4	3.4	0.0	n/a	n/a	n/a
H.S. Diplomas (#)	202	199	1	0	0	0

Montgomery County

Brookville Local SD

325 Simmons Ave • Brookville, OH 45309-1636
(937) 833-2181
Grade Span: PK-12; **Agency Type:** 2
Schools: 3
1 Primary; 1 Middle; 1 High; 0 Other Level
3 Regular; 0 Special Education; 0 Vocational; 0 Alternative
0 Magnet; 0 Charter; 2 Title I Eligible; 0 School-wide Title I
Students: 1,619 (52.9% male; 47.1% female)
Individual Education Program: 211 (13.0%);
English Language Learner: 0 (0.0%); Migrant: n/a
Eligible for Free Lunch Program: 169 (10.4%)
Eligible for Reduced-Price Lunch Program: 65 (4.0%)
Teachers: 85.0 (19.0 to 1)
Librarians/Media Specialists: 3.0 (539.7 to 1)
Guidance Counselors: 3.0 (539.7 to 1)
Current Spending: ($ per student per year):
Total: $6,124; Instruction: $3,537; Support Services: $2,294
Enrollment, Drop-out Rates and Diploma Recipients by Race/Ethnicity

Category	Total	White	Black	Asian	AIAN	Hisp.
Enrollment (%)	100.0	98.4	0.2	0.6	0.0	0.2
Drop-out Rate (%)	3.0	3.0	n/a	0.0	n/a	0.0
H.S. Diplomas (#)	104	102	0	2	0	0

Centerville City SD

111 Virginia Ave • Centerville, OH 45458-2249
(937) 433-8841
Grade Span: KG-12; **Agency Type:** 1
Schools: 11
7 Primary; 3 Middle; 1 High; 0 Other Level
11 Regular; 0 Special Education; 0 Vocational; 0 Alternative
0 Magnet; 0 Charter; 6 Title I Eligible; 0 School-wide Title I
Students: 7,899 (52.0% male; 48.0% female)
Individual Education Program: 992 (12.6%);
English Language Learner: 187 (2.4%); Migrant: 1 (<0.1%)
Eligible for Free Lunch Program: 307 (3.9%)
Eligible for Reduced-Price Lunch Program: 65 (0.8%)
Teachers: 522.6 (15.1 to 1)
Librarians/Media Specialists: 13.0 (607.6 to 1)
Guidance Counselors: 19.6 (403.0 to 1)
Current Spending: ($ per student per year):
Total: $7,333; Instruction: $4,590; Support Services: $2,534
Enrollment, Drop-out Rates and Diploma Recipients by Race/Ethnicity

Category	Total	White	Black	Asian	AIAN	Hisp.
Enrollment (%)	100.0	87.2	4.1	5.7	0.2	1.1
Drop-out Rate (%)	1.1	1.1	0.0	1.6	n/a	0.0
H.S. Diplomas (#)	590	539	15	27	1	7

Dayton City SD

348 W 1st St • Dayton, OH 45402-3006
(937) 542-3000 • http://www.dps.k12.oh.us/
Grade Span: PK-12; **Agency Type:** 1
Schools: 42
28 Primary; 6 Middle; 6 High; 2 Other Level
40 Regular; 1 Special Education; 1 Vocational; 0 Alternative
0 Magnet; 0 Charter; 41 Title I Eligible; 26 School-wide Title I
Students: 19,813 (50.8% male; 49.2% female)
Individual Education Program: 4,177 (21.1%);
English Language Learner: 60 (0.3%); Migrant: n/a
Eligible for Free Lunch Program: 12,771 (64.5%)
Eligible for Reduced-Price Lunch Program: 1,855 (9.4%)
Teachers: 1,455.7 (13.6 to 1)
Librarians/Media Specialists: 10.0 (1,981.3 to 1)
Guidance Counselors: 20.0 (990.7 to 1)
Current Spending: ($ per student per year):
Total: $8,282; Instruction: $4,172; Support Services: $3,625
Enrollment, Drop-out Rates and Diploma Recipients by Race/Ethnicity

Category	Total	White	Black	Asian	AIAN	Hisp.
Enrollment (%)	100.0	26.8	69.2	0.4	0.1	1.2
Drop-out Rate (%)	1.4	1.5	1.3	0.0	0.0	2.2
H.S. Diplomas (#)	858	166	674	8	0	4

Huber Heights City SD

5954 Longford Rd • Huber Heights, OH 45424-2943
(937) 237-6300 • http://www.huberheights.k12.oh.us/
Grade Span: PK-12; **Agency Type:** 1
Schools: 10
7 Primary; 2 Middle; 1 High; 0 Other Level
10 Regular; 0 Special Education; 0 Vocational; 0 Alternative
0 Magnet; 0 Charter; 8 Title I Eligible; 0 School-wide Title I
Students: 6,868 (51.4% male; 48.6% female)
Individual Education Program: 794 (11.6%);
English Language Learner: 111 (1.6%); Migrant: n/a
Eligible for Free Lunch Program: 739 (10.8%)
Eligible for Reduced-Price Lunch Program: 287 (4.2%)
Teachers: 435.0 (15.8 to 1)
Librarians/Media Specialists: 3.0 (2,289.3 to 1)
Guidance Counselors: 14.0 (490.6 to 1)
Current Spending: ($ per student per year):
Total: $6,140; Instruction: $3,840; Support Services: $2,028
Enrollment, Drop-out Rates and Diploma Recipients by Race/Ethnicity

Category	Total	White	Black	Asian	AIAN	Hisp.
Enrollment (%)	100.0	77.3	14.7	3.0	0.1	1.6
Drop-out Rate (%)	6.4	7.0	4.3	3.6	0.0	3.8
H.S. Diplomas (#)	437	337	75	18	0	5

Kettering City SD

3750 Far Hills Ave • Kettering, OH 45429-2506
(937) 296-7600 • http://www.kettering.k12.oh.us/
Grade Span: KG-12; **Agency Type:** 1
Schools: 12
9 Primary; 2 Middle; 1 High; 0 Other Level
12 Regular; 0 Special Education; 0 Vocational; 0 Alternative
0 Magnet; 0 Charter; 6 Title I Eligible; 2 School-wide Title I
Students: 7,902 (51.7% male; 48.3% female)
Individual Education Program: 1,055 (13.4%);
English Language Learner: 48 (0.6%); Migrant: n/a
Eligible for Free Lunch Program: 1,019 (12.9%)
Eligible for Reduced-Price Lunch Program: 432 (5.5%)
Teachers: 494.5 (16.0 to 1)
Librarians/Media Specialists: 3.0 (2,634.0 to 1)
Guidance Counselors: 25.2 (313.6 to 1)
Current Spending: ($ per student per year):
Total: $6,817; Instruction: $3,847; Support Services: $2,748

Enrollment, Drop-out Rates and Diploma Recipients by Race/Ethnicity

Category	Total	White	Black	Asian	AIAN	Hisp.
Enrollment (%)	100.0	93.9	2.4	1.5	0.2	0.8
Drop-out Rate (%)	0.9	0.8	2.4	5.4	n/a	0.0
H.S. Diplomas (#)	534	509	8	10	0	3

Mad River Local SD

801 Harshman Rd • Dayton, OH 45431-1238
(937) 259-6606
Grade Span: KG-12; **Agency Type:** 2
Schools: 7
4 Primary; 2 Middle; 1 High; 0 Other Level
7 Regular; 0 Special Education; 0 Vocational; 0 Alternative
0 Magnet; 0 Charter; 6 Title I Eligible; 2 School-wide Title I
Students: 3,707 (50.5% male; 49.5% female)
Individual Education Program: 550 (14.8%);
English Language Learner: 26 (0.7%); Migrant: 1 (<0.1%)
Eligible for Free Lunch Program: 871 (23.5%)
Eligible for Reduced-Price Lunch Program: 479 (12.9%)
Teachers: 253.7 (14.6 to 1)
Librarians/Media Specialists: 2.1 (1,765.2 to 1)
Guidance Counselors: 9.7 (382.2 to 1)
Current Spending: ($ per student per year):
Total: $6,662; Instruction: $4,218; Support Services: $2,167

Enrollment, Drop-out Rates and Diploma Recipients by Race/Ethnicity

Category	Total	White	Black	Asian	AIAN	Hisp.
Enrollment (%)	100.0	85.3	7.7	1.5	0.2	1.9
Drop-out Rate (%)	8.7	9.8	0.0	3.8	0.0	4.8
H.S. Diplomas (#)	182	159	14	6	0	2

Miamisburg City SD

540 E Park Ave • Miamisburg, OH 45342-2854
(937) 866-3381
Grade Span: PK-12; **Agency Type:** 1
Schools: 9
6 Primary; 2 Middle; 1 High; 0 Other Level
9 Regular; 0 Special Education; 0 Vocational; 0 Alternative
0 Magnet; 0 Charter; 7 Title I Eligible; 1 School-wide Title I
Students: 5,213 (51.8% male; 48.2% female)
Individual Education Program: 637 (12.2%);
English Language Learner: 15 (0.3%); Migrant: n/a
Eligible for Free Lunch Program: 802 (15.4%)
Eligible for Reduced-Price Lunch Program: 220 (4.2%)
Teachers: 310.9 (16.8 to 1)
Librarians/Media Specialists: 1.0 (5,213.0 to 1)
Guidance Counselors: 10.5 (496.5 to 1)
Current Spending: ($ per student per year):
Total: $6,500; Instruction: $3,757; Support Services: $2,446

Enrollment, Drop-out Rates and Diploma Recipients by Race/Ethnicity

Category	Total	White	Black	Asian	AIAN	Hisp.
Enrollment (%)	100.0	89.2	4.9	2.5	0.2	1.2
Drop-out Rate (%)	1.4	1.4	2.7	3.4	0.0	0.0
H.S. Diplomas (#)	330	303	5	12	2	4

Northmont City SD

4001 Old Salem Rd • Englewood, OH 45322-2681
(937) 832-5000 • http://www.northmont.k12.oh.us/
Grade Span: KG-12; **Agency Type:** 1
Schools: 9
7 Primary; 1 Middle; 1 High; 0 Other Level
9 Regular; 0 Special Education; 0 Vocational; 0 Alternative
0 Magnet; 0 Charter; 7 Title I Eligible; 0 School-wide Title I
Students: 5,801 (51.4% male; 48.6% female)
Individual Education Program: 658 (11.3%);
English Language Learner: 63 (1.1%); Migrant: n/a
Eligible for Free Lunch Program: 503 (8.7%)
Eligible for Reduced-Price Lunch Program: 332 (5.7%)
Teachers: 334.7 (17.3 to 1)
Librarians/Media Specialists: 1.0 (5,801.0 to 1)
Guidance Counselors: 12.0 (483.4 to 1)
Current Spending: ($ per student per year):
Total: $6,281; Instruction: $3,899; Support Services: $2,004

Enrollment, Drop-out Rates and Diploma Recipients by Race/Ethnicity

Category	Total	White	Black	Asian	AIAN	Hisp.
Enrollment (%)	100.0	86.6	8.0	1.3	0.2	0.5
Drop-out Rate (%)	1.9	1.9	2.3	0.0	0.0	0.0
H.S. Diplomas (#)	393	367	19	3	0	1

Northridge Local SD

2011 Timber Ln • Dayton, OH 45414-4528
(937) 278-5885 • http://northridge.k12.oh.us/
Grade Span: KG-12; **Agency Type:** 2
Schools: 5
3 Primary; 1 Middle; 1 High; 0 Other Level
5 Regular; 0 Special Education; 0 Vocational; 0 Alternative
0 Magnet; 0 Charter; 5 Title I Eligible; 4 School-wide Title I
Students: 2,060 (50.3% male; 49.7% female)
Individual Education Program: 281 (13.6%);
English Language Learner: 6 (0.3%); Migrant: n/a
Eligible for Free Lunch Program: 753 (36.6%)
Eligible for Reduced-Price Lunch Program: 166 (8.1%)
Teachers: 127.0 (16.2 to 1)
Librarians/Media Specialists: 1.0 (2,060.0 to 1)
Guidance Counselors: 3.0 (686.7 to 1)
Current Spending: ($ per student per year):
Total: $8,209; Instruction: $5,021; Support Services: $2,848

Enrollment, Drop-out Rates and Diploma Recipients by Race/Ethnicity

Category	Total	White	Black	Asian	AIAN	Hisp.
Enrollment (%)	100.0	81.4	15.8	0.7	0.2	0.5
Drop-out Rate (%)	9.7	9.3	17.1	0.0	0.0	n/a
H.S. Diplomas (#)	93	90	3	0	0	0

Oakwood City SD

20 Rubicon Rd • Dayton, OH 45409-2239
(937) 297-5332 • http://www.oakwood.k12.oh.us
Grade Span: KG-12; **Agency Type:** 1
Schools: 5
3 Primary; 1 Middle; 1 High; 0 Other Level
5 Regular; 0 Special Education; 0 Vocational; 0 Alternative
0 Magnet; 0 Charter; 2 Title I Eligible; 0 School-wide Title I
Students: 2,004 (49.4% male; 50.6% female)
Individual Education Program: 141 (7.0%);
English Language Learner: 11 (0.5%); Migrant: n/a
Eligible for Free Lunch Program: 8 (0.4%)
Eligible for Reduced-Price Lunch Program: 0 (0.0%)
Teachers: 164.4 (12.2 to 1)
Librarians/Media Specialists: 2.9 (691.0 to 1)
Guidance Counselors: 4.0 (501.0 to 1)
Current Spending: ($ per student per year):
Total: $7,536; Instruction: $4,870; Support Services: $2,553

Enrollment, Drop-out Rates and Diploma Recipients by Race/Ethnicity

Category	Total	White	Black	Asian	AIAN	Hisp.
Enrollment (%)	100.0	96.1	0.5	1.7	0.0	1.2
Drop-out Rate (%)	0.7	0.7	0.0	0.0	n/a	0.0
H.S. Diplomas (#)	140	137	1	1	0	1

Trotwood-Madison City SD

444 S Broadway St • Trotwood, OH 45426-3327
(937) 854-3050
Grade Span: PK-12; **Agency Type:** 1
Schools: 8
6 Primary; 1 Middle; 1 High; 0 Other Level
8 Regular; 0 Special Education; 0 Vocational; 0 Alternative
0 Magnet; 0 Charter; 8 Title I Eligible; 6 School-wide Title I
Students: 3,683 (51.7% male; 48.3% female)
Individual Education Program: 492 (13.4%);
English Language Learner: 1 (<0.1%); Migrant: n/a
Eligible for Free Lunch Program: 1,863 (50.6%)
Eligible for Reduced-Price Lunch Program: 260 (7.1%)
Teachers: 248.6 (14.8 to 1)
Librarians/Media Specialists: 3.0 (1,227.7 to 1)
Guidance Counselors: 5.0 (736.6 to 1)
Current Spending: ($ per student per year):
Total: $7,573; Instruction: $4,401; Support Services: $2,826

Enrollment, Drop-out Rates and Diploma Recipients by Race/Ethnicity

Category	Total	White	Black	Asian	AIAN	Hisp.
Enrollment (%)	100.0	14.6	81.3	0.2	0.0	0.6
Drop-out Rate (%)	5.6	8.7	5.1	0.0	n/a	0.0
H.S. Diplomas (#)	192	27	158	1	0	0

Valley View Local SD

64 Comstock St • Germantown, OH 45327-1004
(937) 855-6581
Grade Span: PK-12; **Agency Type:** 2
Schools: 4
2 Primary; 1 Middle; 1 High; 0 Other Level
4 Regular; 0 Special Education; 0 Vocational; 0 Alternative
0 Magnet; 0 Charter; 3 Title I Eligible; 0 School-wide Title I
Students: 2,038 (52.1% male; 47.9% female)
Individual Education Program: 209 (10.3%);
English Language Learner: 0 (0.0%); Migrant: n/a
Eligible for Free Lunch Program: 79 (3.9%)
Eligible for Reduced-Price Lunch Program: 28 (1.4%)
Teachers: 135.3 (15.1 to 1)
Librarians/Media Specialists: 2.0 (1,019.0 to 1)
Guidance Counselors: 3.0 (679.3 to 1)
Current Spending: ($ per student per year):
Total: $6,623; Instruction: $4,080; Support Services: $2,197

Enrollment, Drop-out Rates and Diploma Recipients by Race/Ethnicity

Category	Total	White	Black	Asian	AIAN	Hisp.
Enrollment (%)	100.0	99.1	0.5	0.1	0.0	0.0
Drop-out Rate (%)	3.2	3.0	0.0	0.0	n/a	n/a
H.S. Diplomas (#)	138	137	0	1	0	0

Vandalia-Butler City SD

306 S Dixie Dr • Vandalia, OH 45377-2128
(937) 415-6400
Grade Span: PK-12; **Agency Type:** 1
Schools: 6
3 Primary; 2 Middle; 1 High; 0 Other Level
6 Regular; 0 Special Education; 0 Vocational; 0 Alternative
0 Magnet; 0 Charter; 4 Title I Eligible; 0 School-wide Title I
Students: 3,476 (51.9% male; 48.1% female)
Individual Education Program: 468 (13.5%);
English Language Learner: 22 (0.6%); Migrant: 1 (<0.1%)
Eligible for Free Lunch Program: 253 (7.3%)
Eligible for Reduced-Price Lunch Program: 149 (4.3%)
Teachers: 229.0 (15.2 to 1)
Librarians/Media Specialists: 1.0 (3,476.0 to 1)
Guidance Counselors: 5.0 (695.2 to 1)
Current Spending: ($ per student per year):
Total: $6,932; Instruction: $4,235; Support Services: $2,484

Enrollment, Drop-out Rates and Diploma Recipients by Race/Ethnicity

Category	Total	White	Black	Asian	AIAN	Hisp.
Enrollment (%)	100.0	93.0	2.4	1.9	0.3	0.7
Drop-out Rate (%)	2.9	2.8	6.7	6.3	0.0	0.0
H.S. Diplomas (#)	244	234	0	4	2	3

West Carrollton City SD

430 E Pease Ave • West Carrollton, OH 45449-1357
(937) 859-5121
Grade Span: PK-12; **Agency Type:** 1
Schools: 7
5 Primary; 1 Middle; 1 High; 0 Other Level
7 Regular; 0 Special Education; 0 Vocational; 0 Alternative
0 Magnet; 0 Charter; 5 Title I Eligible; 1 School-wide Title I
Students: 3,933 (53.4% male; 46.6% female)
Individual Education Program: 468 (11.9%);
English Language Learner: 110 (2.8%); Migrant: n/a
Eligible for Free Lunch Program: 558 (14.2%)
Eligible for Reduced-Price Lunch Program: 196 (5.0%)
Teachers: 291.0 (13.5 to 1)
Librarians/Media Specialists: 2.0 (1,966.5 to 1)
Guidance Counselors: 7.0 (561.9 to 1)
Current Spending: ($ per student per year):
Total: $6,360; Instruction: $3,936; Support Services: $2,236

Enrollment, Drop-out Rates and Diploma Recipients by Race/Ethnicity

Category	Total	White	Black	Asian	AIAN	Hisp.
Enrollment (%)	100.0	86.5	6.4	3.2	0.3	1.4
Drop-out Rate (%)	3.8	4.1	0.0	0.0	0.0	9.1
H.S. Diplomas (#)	254	224	12	11	0	5

Morgan County

Morgan Local SD

PO Box 509 • Mc Connelsville, OH 43756-0509
(740) 962-2782
Grade Span: PK-12; **Agency Type:** 2
Schools: 5
3 Primary; 1 Middle; 1 High; 0 Other Level
5 Regular; 0 Special Education; 0 Vocational; 0 Alternative
0 Magnet; 0 Charter; 3 Title I Eligible; 3 School-wide Title I
Students: 2,322 (50.6% male; 49.4% female)
Individual Education Program: 285 (12.3%);
English Language Learner: 0 (0.0%); Migrant: n/a
Eligible for Free Lunch Program: 736 (31.7%)
Eligible for Reduced-Price Lunch Program: 166 (7.1%)
Teachers: 172.4 (13.5 to 1)
Librarians/Media Specialists: 5.0 (464.4 to 1)
Guidance Counselors: 3.0 (774.0 to 1)
Current Spending: ($ per student per year):
Total: $6,919; Instruction: $4,073; Support Services: $2,564

Enrollment, Drop-out Rates and Diploma Recipients by Race/Ethnicity

Category	Total	White	Black	Asian	AIAN	Hisp.
Enrollment (%)	100.0	92.8	4.0	0.0	0.3	0.1
Drop-out Rate (%)	5.5	5.7	0.0	n/a	0.0	0.0
H.S. Diplomas (#)	157	154	1	0	1	1

Morrow County

Highland Local SD

PO Box 98 • Sparta, OH 43350-0098
(419) 768-2206
Grade Span: PK-12; **Agency Type:** 2
Schools: 5
3 Primary; 1 Middle; 1 High; 0 Other Level
5 Regular; 0 Special Education; 0 Vocational; 0 Alternative
0 Magnet; 0 Charter; 3 Title I Eligible; 1 School-wide Title I
Students: 1,801 (52.9% male; 47.1% female)
Individual Education Program: 270 (15.0%);
English Language Learner: 0 (0.0%); Migrant: n/a
Eligible for Free Lunch Program: 313 (17.4%)
Eligible for Reduced-Price Lunch Program: 101 (5.6%)
Teachers: 105.0 (17.2 to 1)
Librarians/Media Specialists: 1.0 (1,801.0 to 1)
Guidance Counselors: 2.0 (900.5 to 1)
Current Spending: ($ per student per year):
Total: $5,866; Instruction: $3,401; Support Services: $2,195

Enrollment, Drop-out Rates and Diploma Recipients by Race/Ethnicity

Category	Total	White	Black	Asian	AIAN	Hisp.
Enrollment (%)	100.0	98.7	0.2	0.1	0.4	0.2
Drop-out Rate (%)	2.7	2.7	0.0	n/a	0.0	n/a
H.S. Diplomas (#)	106	104	0	0	2	0

Muskingum County

East Muskingum Local SD

13505 John Glenn School Rd • New Concord, OH 43762-9702
(740) 826-7655 •
http://www.east-muskingum.k12.oh.us/emsd/site/default.asp
Grade Span: PK-12; **Agency Type:** 2
Schools: 6
4 Primary; 1 Middle; 1 High; 0 Other Level
6 Regular; 0 Special Education; 0 Vocational; 0 Alternative
0 Magnet; 0 Charter; 4 Title I Eligible; 0 School-wide Title I
Students: 2,181 (53.0% male; 47.0% female)
Individual Education Program: 277 (12.7%);
English Language Learner: 0 (0.0%); Migrant: n/a
Eligible for Free Lunch Program: 299 (13.7%)
Eligible for Reduced-Price Lunch Program: 119 (5.5%)
Teachers: 125.2 (17.4 to 1)
Librarians/Media Specialists: 1.0 (2,181.0 to 1)
Guidance Counselors: 3.0 (727.0 to 1)
Current Spending: ($ per student per year):
Total: $5,579; Instruction: $3,517; Support Services: $1,802

Enrollment, Drop-out Rates and Diploma Recipients by Race/Ethnicity

Category	Total	White	Black	Asian	AIAN	Hisp.
Enrollment (%)	100.0	97.8	0.5	0.4	0.2	0.3
Drop-out Rate (%)	2.6	2.6	0.0	0.0	n/a	n/a
H.S. Diplomas (#)	177	171	2	2	0	0

Franklin Local SD

360 Cedar St • Duncan Falls, OH 43734-9710
Mailing Address: PO Box 428 • Duncan Falls, OH 43734-0428
(740) 674-5203
Grade Span: PK-12; **Agency Type:** 2
Schools: 5
2 Primary; 2 Middle; 1 High; 0 Other Level
5 Regular; 0 Special Education; 0 Vocational; 0 Alternative
0 Magnet; 0 Charter; 3 Title I Eligible; 3 School-wide Title I
Students: 2,428 (52.3% male; 47.7% female)
Individual Education Program: 329 (13.6%);
English Language Learner: 0 (0.0%); Migrant: n/a
Eligible for Free Lunch Program: 682 (28.1%)
Eligible for Reduced-Price Lunch Program: 217 (8.9%)
Teachers: 133.5 (18.2 to 1)
Librarians/Media Specialists: 1.0 (2,428.0 to 1)
Guidance Counselors: 3.0 (809.3 to 1)
Current Spending: ($ per student per year):
Total: $5,682; Instruction: $3,250; Support Services: $2,124

Enrollment, Drop-out Rates and Diploma Recipients by Race/Ethnicity

Category	Total	White	Black	Asian	AIAN	Hisp.
Enrollment (%)	100.0	98.4	0.4	0.2	0.2	0.0
Drop-out Rate (%)	2.8	2.8	0.0	0.0	0.0	n/a
H.S. Diplomas (#)	165	164	0	0	0	1

Maysville Local SD

PO Box 1818 • Zanesville, OH 43702-1818
(740) 453-0754
Grade Span: PK-12; **Agency Type:** 2
Schools: 3
1 Primary; 1 Middle; 1 High; 0 Other Level
3 Regular; 0 Special Education; 0 Vocational; 0 Alternative

0 Magnet; 0 Charter; 2 Title I Eligible; 1 School-wide Title I
Students: 2,274 (49.3% male; 50.7% female)
Individual Education Program: 293 (12.9%);
English Language Learner: 0 (0.0%); Migrant: n/a
Eligible for Free Lunch Program: 619 (27.2%)
Eligible for Reduced-Price Lunch Program: 168 (7.4%)
Teachers: 129.2 (17.6 to 1)
Librarians/Media Specialists: 2.0 (1,137.0 to 1)
Guidance Counselors: 4.0 (568.5 to 1)
Current Spending: ($ per student per year):
Total: $5,558; Instruction: $2,994; Support Services: $2,316
Enrollment, Drop-out Rates and Diploma Recipients by Race/Ethnicity

Category	Total	White	Black	Asian	AIAN	Hisp.
Enrollment (%)	100.0	98.2	1.3	0.0	0.0	0.0
Drop-out Rate (%)	2.2	1.9	25.0	0.0	n/a	n/a
H.S. Diplomas (#)	160	159	1	0	0	0

Tri-Valley Local SD
PO Box 125 • Dresden, OH 43821-0125
(740) 754-1572
Grade Span: PK-12; **Agency Type:** 2
Schools: 7
4 Primary; 2 Middle; 1 High; 0 Other Level
7 Regular; 0 Special Education; 0 Vocational; 0 Alternative
0 Magnet; 0 Charter; 4 Title I Eligible; 0 School-wide Title I
Students: 3,074 (50.4% male; 49.6% female)
Individual Education Program: 366 (11.9%);
English Language Learner: 0 (0.0%); Migrant: 1 (<0.1%)
Eligible for Free Lunch Program: 407 (13.2%)
Eligible for Reduced-Price Lunch Program: 127 (4.1%)
Teachers: 170.0 (18.1 to 1)
Librarians/Media Specialists: 2.0 (1,537.0 to 1)
Guidance Counselors: 5.0 (614.8 to 1)
Current Spending: ($ per student per year):
Total: $5,253; Instruction: $3,099; Support Services: $1,913
Enrollment, Drop-out Rates and Diploma Recipients by Race/Ethnicity

Category	Total	White	Black	Asian	AIAN	Hisp.
Enrollment (%)	100.0	98.0	1.2	0.1	0.0	0.3
Drop-out Rate (%)	3.1	3.0	33.3	n/a	n/a	0.0
H.S. Diplomas (#)	194	194	0	0	0	0

West Muskingum Local SD
4880 W Pike • Zanesville, OH 43701-9390
(740) 455-4052
Grade Span: PK-12; **Agency Type:** 2
Schools: 5
3 Primary; 1 Middle; 1 High; 0 Other Level
5 Regular; 0 Special Education; 0 Vocational; 0 Alternative
0 Magnet; 0 Charter; 4 Title I Eligible; 0 School-wide Title I
Students: 1,792 (49.9% male; 50.1% female)
Individual Education Program: 239 (13.3%);
English Language Learner: 4 (0.2%); Migrant: n/a
Eligible for Free Lunch Program: 273 (15.2%)
Eligible for Reduced-Price Lunch Program: 53 (3.0%)
Teachers: 102.3 (17.5 to 1)
Librarians/Media Specialists: 1.5 (1,194.7 to 1)
Guidance Counselors: 2.0 (896.0 to 1)
Current Spending: ($ per student per year):
Total: $5,756; Instruction: $3,496; Support Services: $2,023
Enrollment, Drop-out Rates and Diploma Recipients by Race/Ethnicity

Category	Total	White	Black	Asian	AIAN	Hisp.
Enrollment (%)	100.0	95.3	3.1	0.6	0.2	0.3
Drop-out Rate (%)	0.5	0.6	0.0	0.0	n/a	0.0
H.S. Diplomas (#)	142	134	6	1	1	0

Zanesville City SD
160 N 4th St • Zanesville, OH 43701-3518
(740) 454-9751 • http://www.zanesville.k12.oh.us/
Grade Span: PK-12; **Agency Type:** 1
Schools: 12
9 Primary; 2 Middle; 1 High; 0 Other Level
11 Regular; 0 Special Education; 0 Vocational; 1 Alternative
0 Magnet; 0 Charter; 10 Title I Eligible; 5 School-wide Title I
Students: 4,368 (49.3% male; 50.7% female)
Individual Education Program: 1,013 (23.2%);
English Language Learner: 0 (0.0%); Migrant: n/a
Eligible for Free Lunch Program: 2,131 (48.8%)
Eligible for Reduced-Price Lunch Program: 305 (7.0%)
Teachers: 307.3 (14.2 to 1)
Librarians/Media Specialists: 3.0 (1,456.0 to 1)
Guidance Counselors: 7.6 (574.7 to 1)
Current Spending: ($ per student per year):
Total: $7,380; Instruction: $4,656; Support Services: $2,390
Enrollment, Drop-out Rates and Diploma Recipients by Race/Ethnicity

Category	Total	White	Black	Asian	AIAN	Hisp.
Enrollment (%)	100.0	78.9	16.2	0.3	0.0	0.5
Drop-out Rate (%)	8.1	8.2	7.7	0.0	n/a	0.0
H.S. Diplomas (#)	181	146	29	2	0	2

Ottawa County

Benton Carroll Salem Local SD
11685 W State Route 163 • Oak Harbor, OH 43449-1278
(419) 898-6210 • http://www.bcs.k12.oh.us/
Grade Span: PK-12; **Agency Type:** 2
Schools: 6
4 Primary; 1 Middle; 1 High; 0 Other Level
6 Regular; 0 Special Education; 0 Vocational; 0 Alternative
0 Magnet; 0 Charter; 5 Title I Eligible; 0 School-wide Title I
Students: 2,065 (50.8% male; 49.2% female)
Individual Education Program: 297 (14.4%);
English Language Learner: 0 (0.0%); Migrant: 26 (1.3%)
Eligible for Free Lunch Program: 236 (11.4%)
Eligible for Reduced-Price Lunch Program: 136 (6.6%)
Teachers: 114.5 (18.0 to 1)
Librarians/Media Specialists: 2.0 (1,032.5 to 1)
Guidance Counselors: 5.0 (413.0 to 1)
Current Spending: ($ per student per year):
Total: $8,231; Instruction: $5,049; Support Services: $2,926
Enrollment, Drop-out Rates and Diploma Recipients by Race/Ethnicity

Category	Total	White	Black	Asian	AIAN	Hisp.
Enrollment (%)	100.0	93.9	0.2	0.1	0.1	2.1
Drop-out Rate (%)	1.6	1.5	0.0	0.0	0.0	6.7
H.S. Diplomas (#)	152	147	0	0	0	2

Genoa Area Local SD
2810 N Genoa Clay Center Rd • Genoa, OH 43430-9730
(419) 855-7741
Grade Span: PK-12; **Agency Type:** 2
Schools: 4
2 Primary; 1 Middle; 1 High; 0 Other Level
4 Regular; 0 Special Education; 0 Vocational; 0 Alternative
0 Magnet; 0 Charter; 2 Title I Eligible; 0 School-wide Title I
Students: 1,713 (54.1% male; 45.9% female)
Individual Education Program: 186 (10.9%);
English Language Learner: 0 (0.0%); Migrant: n/a
Eligible for Free Lunch Program: 139 (8.1%)
Eligible for Reduced-Price Lunch Program: 65 (3.8%)
Teachers: 93.0 (18.4 to 1)
Librarians/Media Specialists: 1.0 (1,713.0 to 1)
Guidance Counselors: 3.0 (571.0 to 1)
Current Spending: ($ per student per year):
Total: $5,936; Instruction: $3,820; Support Services: $1,865
Enrollment, Drop-out Rates and Diploma Recipients by Race/Ethnicity

Category	Total	White	Black	Asian	AIAN	Hisp.
Enrollment (%)	100.0	93.6	0.2	0.1	0.1	5.4
Drop-out Rate (%)	1.8	1.7	n/a	n/a	0.0	3.7
H.S. Diplomas (#)	127	122	0	0	0	5

Port Clinton City SD
431 Portage Dr • Port Clinton, OH 43452-1724
(419) 732-2102 • http://www.port-clinton.k12.oh.us/
Grade Span: PK-12; **Agency Type:** 1
Schools: 6
4 Primary; 1 Middle; 1 High; 0 Other Level
6 Regular; 0 Special Education; 0 Vocational; 0 Alternative
0 Magnet; 0 Charter; 4 Title I Eligible; 1 School-wide Title I
Students: 1,958 (52.8% male; 47.2% female)
Individual Education Program: 323 (16.5%);
English Language Learner: 0 (0.0%); Migrant: n/a
Eligible for Free Lunch Program: 400 (20.4%)
Eligible for Reduced-Price Lunch Program: 77 (3.9%)
Teachers: 131.3 (14.9 to 1)
Librarians/Media Specialists: 1.0 (1,958.0 to 1)
Guidance Counselors: 3.0 (652.7 to 1)
Current Spending: ($ per student per year):
Total: $7,774; Instruction: $4,639; Support Services: $2,887
Enrollment, Drop-out Rates and Diploma Recipients by Race/Ethnicity

Category	Total	White	Black	Asian	AIAN	Hisp.
Enrollment (%)	100.0	89.7	2.3	0.3	0.1	3.9
Drop-out Rate (%)	4.3	4.0	0.0	0.0	0.0	9.3
H.S. Diplomas (#)	169	153	1	1	0	12

Paulding County

Paulding Ex Vill SD

405 N Water St • Paulding, OH 45879-1251
(419) 399-4656
Grade Span: PK-12; **Agency Type:** 1
Schools: 4
2 Primary; 1 Middle; 1 High; 0 Other Level
4 Regular; 0 Special Education; 0 Vocational; 0 Alternative
0 Magnet; 0 Charter; 2 Title I Eligible; 0 School-wide Title I
Students: 1,855 (51.7% male; 48.3% female)
Individual Education Program: 320 (17.3%);
English Language Learner: 4 (0.2%); Migrant: n/a
Eligible for Free Lunch Program: 245 (13.2%)
Eligible for Reduced-Price Lunch Program: 84 (4.5%)
Teachers: 126.9 (14.6 to 1)
Librarians/Media Specialists: 1.0 (1,855.0 to 1)
Guidance Counselors: 3.0 (618.3 to 1)
Current Spending: ($ per student per year):
Total: $6,251; Instruction: $3,754; Support Services: $2,235
Enrollment, Drop-out Rates and Diploma Recipients by Race/Ethnicity

Category	Total	White	Black	Asian	AIAN	Hisp.
Enrollment (%)	100.0	92.9	1.2	0.1	0.0	3.8
Drop-out Rate (%)	1.5	1.5	0.0	0.0	n/a	0.0
H.S. Diplomas (#)	134	121	2	0	1	10

Perry County

New Lexington City SD

101 3rd Ave • New Lexington, OH 43764-1407
(740) 342-4133 • http://www.nlcs.k12.oh.us/
Grade Span: PK-12; **Agency Type:** 1
Schools: 4
2 Primary; 1 Middle; 1 High; 0 Other Level
4 Regular; 0 Special Education; 0 Vocational; 0 Alternative
0 Magnet; 0 Charter; 3 Title I Eligible; 2 School-wide Title I
Students: 1,997 (53.6% male; 46.4% female)
Individual Education Program: 290 (14.5%);
English Language Learner: 0 (0.0%); Migrant: n/a
Eligible for Free Lunch Program: 765 (38.3%)
Eligible for Reduced-Price Lunch Program: 239 (12.0%)
Teachers: 116.4 (17.2 to 1)
Librarians/Media Specialists: 3.0 (665.7 to 1)
Guidance Counselors: 2.8 (713.2 to 1)
Current Spending: ($ per student per year):
Total: $6,018; Instruction: $3,475; Support Services: $2,224
Enrollment, Drop-out Rates and Diploma Recipients by Race/Ethnicity

Category	Total	White	Black	Asian	AIAN	Hisp.
Enrollment (%)	100.0	99.4	0.1	0.1	0.2	0.1
Drop-out Rate (%)	6.2	6.2	n/a	n/a	n/a	n/a
H.S. Diplomas (#)	100	100	0	0	0	0

Northern Local SD

8700 Sheridan Dr • Thornville, OH 43076-9757
(740) 743-1303 • http://nlsd.k12.oh.us/
Grade Span: PK-12; **Agency Type:** 2
Schools: 5
3 Primary; 1 Middle; 1 High; 0 Other Level
5 Regular; 0 Special Education; 0 Vocational; 0 Alternative
0 Magnet; 0 Charter; 4 Title I Eligible; 2 School-wide Title I
Students: 2,313 (52.5% male; 47.5% female)
Individual Education Program: 326 (14.1%);
English Language Learner: 0 (0.0%); Migrant: n/a
Eligible for Free Lunch Program: 386 (16.7%)
Eligible for Reduced-Price Lunch Program: 151 (6.5%)
Teachers: 142.5 (16.2 to 1)
Librarians/Media Specialists: 1.0 (2,313.0 to 1)
Guidance Counselors: 4.0 (578.3 to 1)
Current Spending: ($ per student per year):
Total: $5,886; Instruction: $3,371; Support Services: $2,274
Enrollment, Drop-out Rates and Diploma Recipients by Race/Ethnicity

Category	Total	White	Black	Asian	AIAN	Hisp.
Enrollment (%)	100.0	99.1	0.3	0.1	0.0	0.0
Drop-out Rate (%)	1.4	1.4	0.0	0.0	0.0	n/a
H.S. Diplomas (#)	151	150	0	1	0	0

Pickaway County

Circleville City SD

388 Clark Dr • Circleville, OH 43113-1517
(740) 474-4340
Grade Span: PK-12; **Agency Type:** 1
Schools: 6
4 Primary; 1 Middle; 1 High; 0 Other Level
6 Regular; 0 Special Education; 0 Vocational; 0 Alternative
0 Magnet; 0 Charter; 2 Title I Eligible; 1 School-wide Title I
Students: 2,536 (51.1% male; 48.9% female)
Individual Education Program: 385 (15.2%);
English Language Learner: 0 (0.0%); Migrant: n/a
Eligible for Free Lunch Program: 638 (25.2%)
Eligible for Reduced-Price Lunch Program: 123 (4.9%)
Teachers: 153.5 (16.5 to 1)
Librarians/Media Specialists: 3.0 (845.3 to 1)
Guidance Counselors: 4.0 (634.0 to 1)
Current Spending: ($ per student per year):
Total: $6,295; Instruction: $3,863; Support Services: $2,185
Enrollment, Drop-out Rates and Diploma Recipients by Race/Ethnicity

Category	Total	White	Black	Asian	AIAN	Hisp.
Enrollment (%)	100.0	95.5	1.5	0.6	0.2	0.7
Drop-out Rate (%)	5.4	5.4	10.0	0.0	n/a	0.0
H.S. Diplomas (#)	142	135	2	0	0	1

Logan Elm Local SD

9579 Tarlton Rd • Circleville, OH 43113-9448
(740) 474-7501
Grade Span: PK-12; **Agency Type:** 2
Schools: 6
4 Primary; 1 Middle; 1 High; 0 Other Level
6 Regular; 0 Special Education; 0 Vocational; 0 Alternative
0 Magnet; 0 Charter; 2 Title I Eligible; 1 School-wide Title I
Students: 2,371 (52.7% male; 47.3% female)
Individual Education Program: 321 (13.5%);
English Language Learner: 0 (0.0%); Migrant: n/a
Eligible for Free Lunch Program: 369 (15.6%)
Eligible for Reduced-Price Lunch Program: 137 (5.8%)
Teachers: 147.2 (16.1 to 1)
Librarians/Media Specialists: 1.0 (2,371.0 to 1)
Guidance Counselors: 4.0 (592.8 to 1)
Current Spending: ($ per student per year):
Total: $6,292; Instruction: $3,616; Support Services: $2,400
Enrollment, Drop-out Rates and Diploma Recipients by Race/Ethnicity

Category	Total	White	Black	Asian	AIAN	Hisp.
Enrollment (%)	100.0	98.4	0.9	0.1	0.0	0.2
Drop-out Rate (%)	4.2	4.2	0.0	n/a	n/a	0.0
H.S. Diplomas (#)	167	165	2	0	0	0

Teays Valley Local SD

385 Circleville Ave • Ashville, OH 43103-9417
(740) 983-4111
Grade Span: PK-12; **Agency Type:** 2
Schools: 5
3 Primary; 0 Middle; 1 High; 1 Other Level
5 Regular; 0 Special Education; 0 Vocational; 0 Alternative
0 Magnet; 0 Charter; 4 Title I Eligible; 0 School-wide Title I
Students: 3,069 (52.5% male; 47.5% female)
Individual Education Program: 380 (12.4%);
English Language Learner: 1 (<0.1%); Migrant: n/a
Eligible for Free Lunch Program: 380 (12.4%)
Eligible for Reduced-Price Lunch Program: 138 (4.5%)
Teachers: 186.6 (16.4 to 1)
Librarians/Media Specialists: 2.0 (1,534.5 to 1)
Guidance Counselors: 3.0 (1,023.0 to 1)
Current Spending: ($ per student per year):
Total: $5,573; Instruction: $3,459; Support Services: $1,906
Enrollment, Drop-out Rates and Diploma Recipients by Race/Ethnicity

Category	Total	White	Black	Asian	AIAN	Hisp.
Enrollment (%)	100.0	98.3	0.3	0.2	0.1	0.3
Drop-out Rate (%)	4.6	4.6	0.0	0.0	0.0	0.0
H.S. Diplomas (#)	168	168	0	0	0	0

Westfall Local SD

19463 Pherson Pike • Williamsport, OH 43164-9745
(740) 986-3671
Grade Span: PK-12; **Agency Type:** 2
Schools: 6
1 Primary; 1 Middle; 1 High; 3 Other Level
6 Regular; 0 Special Education; 0 Vocational; 0 Alternative
0 Magnet; 0 Charter; 2 Title I Eligible; 0 School-wide Title I
Students: 1,682 (50.4% male; 49.6% female)
Individual Education Program: 167 (9.9%);
English Language Learner: 0 (0.0%); Migrant: n/a
Eligible for Free Lunch Program: 270 (16.1%)
Eligible for Reduced-Price Lunch Program: 62 (3.7%)
Teachers: 93.0 (18.1 to 1)
Librarians/Media Specialists: 1.0 (1,682.0 to 1)
Guidance Counselors: 3.0 (560.7 to 1)
Current Spending: ($ per student per year):
Total: $5,983; Instruction: $3,528; Support Services: $2,208

Enrollment, Drop-out Rates and Diploma Recipients by Race/Ethnicity

Category	Total	White	Black	Asian	AIAN	Hisp.
Enrollment (%)	100.0	99.3	0.2	0.1	0.0	0.2
Drop-out Rate (%)	3.5	3.5	0.0	n/a	n/a	0.0
H.S. Diplomas (#)	97	95	1	1	0	0

Pike County

Scioto Valley Local SD

PO Box 600 • Piketon, OH 45661-0600
(740) 289-4456
Grade Span: PK-12; **Agency Type:** 2
Schools: 3
2 Primary; 0 Middle; 1 High; 0 Other Level
3 Regular; 0 Special Education; 0 Vocational; 0 Alternative
0 Magnet; 0 Charter; 2 Title I Eligible; 2 School-wide Title I
Students: 1,660 (51.4% male; 48.6% female)
Individual Education Program: 254 (15.3%);
English Language Learner: 0 (0.0%); Migrant: n/a
Eligible for Free Lunch Program: 564 (34.0%)
Eligible for Reduced-Price Lunch Program: 103 (6.2%)
Teachers: 92.0 (18.0 to 1)
Librarians/Media Specialists: 1.0 (1,660.0 to 1)
Guidance Counselors: 3.0 (553.3 to 1)
Current Spending: ($ per student per year):
Total: $5,573; Instruction: $3,118; Support Services: $2,169

Enrollment, Drop-out Rates and Diploma Recipients by Race/Ethnicity

Category	Total	White	Black	Asian	AIAN	Hisp.
Enrollment (%)	100.0	99.3	0.3	0.0	0.0	0.2
Drop-out Rate (%)	6.2	6.2	0.0	0.0	n/a	n/a
H.S. Diplomas (#)	89	86	2	1	0	0

Waverly City SD

500 E 2nd St • Waverly, OH 45690-1286
(740) 947-4770
Grade Span: PK-12; **Agency Type:** 1
Schools: 4
2 Primary; 1 Middle; 0 High; 1 Other Level
4 Regular; 0 Special Education; 0 Vocational; 0 Alternative
0 Magnet; 0 Charter; 2 Title I Eligible; 2 School-wide Title I
Students: 2,152 (51.9% male; 48.1% female)
Individual Education Program: 301 (14.0%);
English Language Learner: 0 (0.0%); Migrant: n/a
Eligible for Free Lunch Program: 643 (29.9%)
Eligible for Reduced-Price Lunch Program: 98 (4.6%)
Teachers: 127.0 (16.9 to 1)
Librarians/Media Specialists: 1.0 (2,152.0 to 1)
Guidance Counselors: 3.0 (717.3 to 1)
Current Spending: ($ per student per year):
Total: $5,557; Instruction: $3,276; Support Services: $2,029

Enrollment, Drop-out Rates and Diploma Recipients by Race/Ethnicity

Category	Total	White	Black	Asian	AIAN	Hisp.
Enrollment (%)	100.0	96.5	2.6	0.3	0.0	0.5
Drop-out Rate (%)	4.8	4.6	18.2	0.0	n/a	n/a
H.S. Diplomas (#)	114	108	5	1	0	0

Portage County

Aurora City SD

102 E Garfield Rd • Aurora, OH 44202-8854
(330) 562-6106 • http://aurora.portage.k12.oh.us/
Grade Span: PK-12; **Agency Type:** 1
Schools: 4
2 Primary; 1 Middle; 1 High; 0 Other Level
4 Regular; 0 Special Education; 0 Vocational; 0 Alternative
0 Magnet; 0 Charter; 0 Title I Eligible; 0 School-wide Title I
Students: 2,711 (51.1% male; 48.9% female)
Individual Education Program: 223 (8.2%);
English Language Learner: 15 (0.6%); Migrant: n/a
Eligible for Free Lunch Program: 56 (2.1%)
Eligible for Reduced-Price Lunch Program: 29 (1.1%)
Teachers: 158.2 (17.1 to 1)
Librarians/Media Specialists: 2.8 (968.2 to 1)
Guidance Counselors: 6.5 (417.1 to 1)
Current Spending: ($ per student per year):
Total: $7,618; Instruction: $4,216; Support Services: $3,191

Enrollment, Drop-out Rates and Diploma Recipients by Race/Ethnicity

Category	Total	White	Black	Asian	AIAN	Hisp.
Enrollment (%)	100.0	95.9	2.3	1.3	0.1	0.2
Drop-out Rate (%)	0.9	0.8	5.6	0.0	n/a	0.0
H.S. Diplomas (#)	149	144	4	0	0	1

Crestwood Local SD

4565 W Prospect St • Mantua, OH 44255-9103
(330) 274-8511
Grade Span: PK-12; **Agency Type:** 2
Schools: 7
4 Primary; 1 Middle; 1 High; 1 Other Level
6 Regular; 1 Special Education; 0 Vocational; 0 Alternative
0 Magnet; 0 Charter; 4 Title I Eligible; 0 School-wide Title I
Students: 2,734 (52.6% male; 47.4% female)
Individual Education Program: 349 (12.8%);
English Language Learner: 1 (<0.1%); Migrant: n/a
Eligible for Free Lunch Program: 314 (11.5%)
Eligible for Reduced-Price Lunch Program: 139 (5.1%)
Teachers: 157.3 (17.4 to 1)
Librarians/Media Specialists: 3.0 (911.3 to 1)
Guidance Counselors: 4.0 (683.5 to 1)
Current Spending: ($ per student per year):
Total: $6,093; Instruction: $3,485; Support Services: $2,417

Enrollment, Drop-out Rates and Diploma Recipients by Race/Ethnicity

Category	Total	White	Black	Asian	AIAN	Hisp.
Enrollment (%)	100.0	98.2	1.0	0.3	0.0	0.1
Drop-out Rate (%)	2.6	2.6	0.0	n/a	n/a	n/a
H.S. Diplomas (#)	196	193	0	2	0	1

Field Local SD

1473 Saxe Rd • Mogadore, OH 44260-9790
(330) 673-2659 • http://156.63.123.52/fieldweb/index.html
Grade Span: PK-12; **Agency Type:** 2
Schools: 5
3 Primary; 1 Middle; 1 High; 0 Other Level
5 Regular; 0 Special Education; 0 Vocational; 0 Alternative
0 Magnet; 0 Charter; 1 Title I Eligible; 0 School-wide Title I
Students: 2,245 (52.9% male; 47.1% female)
Individual Education Program: 316 (14.1%);
English Language Learner: 9 (0.4%); Migrant: 2 (0.1%)
Eligible for Free Lunch Program: n/a
Eligible for Reduced-Price Lunch Program: n/a
Teachers: 139.6 (16.1 to 1)
Librarians/Media Specialists: 3.0 (748.3 to 1)
Guidance Counselors: 4.0 (561.3 to 1)
Current Spending: ($ per student per year):
Total: $6,138; Instruction: $3,674; Support Services: $2,269

Enrollment, Drop-out Rates and Diploma Recipients by Race/Ethnicity

Category	Total	White	Black	Asian	AIAN	Hisp.
Enrollment (%)	100.0	96.8	1.6	0.2	0.0	0.2
Drop-out Rate (%)	1.7	1.7	6.3	0.0	n/a	0.0
H.S. Diplomas (#)	175	167	5	2	0	1

James A Garfield Local SD

10235 State Route 88 • Garrettsville, OH 44231-9205
(330) 527-4336
Grade Span: PK-12; **Agency Type:** 2
Schools: 4
1 Primary; 2 Middle; 1 High; 0 Other Level
4 Regular; 0 Special Education; 0 Vocational; 0 Alternative
0 Magnet; 0 Charter; 2 Title I Eligible; 0 School-wide Title I
Students: 1,607 (50.7% male; 49.3% female)
Individual Education Program: 159 (9.9%);
English Language Learner: 0 (0.0%); Migrant: n/a
Eligible for Free Lunch Program: 207 (12.9%)
Eligible for Reduced-Price Lunch Program: 118 (7.3%)
Teachers: 95.6 (16.8 to 1)
Librarians/Media Specialists: 2.0 (803.5 to 1)
Guidance Counselors: 3.0 (535.7 to 1)
Current Spending: ($ per student per year):
Total: $6,004; Instruction: $3,239; Support Services: $2,503

Enrollment, Drop-out Rates and Diploma Recipients by Race/Ethnicity

Category	Total	White	Black	Asian	AIAN	Hisp.
Enrollment (%)	100.0	99.1	0.3	0.2	0.0	0.1
Drop-out Rate (%)	0.6	0.6	0.0	0.0	n/a	n/a
H.S. Diplomas (#)	101	99	2	0	0	0

Kent City SD

321 N Depeyster St • Kent, OH 44240-2514
(330) 673-6515
Grade Span: PK-12; **Agency Type:** 1
Schools: 7
5 Primary; 1 Middle; 1 High; 0 Other Level
7 Regular; 0 Special Education; 0 Vocational; 0 Alternative
0 Magnet; 0 Charter; 4 Title I Eligible; 0 School-wide Title I
Students: 3,786 (51.4% male; 48.6% female)
Individual Education Program: 501 (13.2%);
English Language Learner: 38 (1.0%); Migrant: n/a
Eligible for Free Lunch Program: 779 (20.6%)
Eligible for Reduced-Price Lunch Program: 178 (4.7%)

Teachers: 301.7 (12.5 to 1)
Librarians/Media Specialists: 5.0 (757.2 to 1)
Guidance Counselors: 7.0 (540.9 to 1)
Current Spending: ($ per student per year):
Total: $8,598; Instruction: $5,327; Support Services: $3,059
Enrollment, Drop-out Rates and Diploma Recipients by Race/Ethnicity

Category	Total	White	Black	Asian	AIAN	Hisp.
Enrollment (%)	100.0	80.5	11.5	2.7	0.2	0.8
Drop-out Rate (%)	3.6	3.5	4.7	0.0	n/a	14.3
H.S. Diplomas (#)	308	261	30	9	0	5

Ravenna City SD
507 E Main St • Ravenna, OH 44266-3257
(330) 296-9679 • http://www.ravenna.portage.k12.oh.us/
Grade Span: PK-12; **Agency Type:** 1
Schools: 8
5 Primary; 2 Middle; 1 High; 0 Other Level
8 Regular; 0 Special Education; 0 Vocational; 0 Alternative
0 Magnet; 0 Charter; 7 Title I Eligible; 7 School-wide Title I
Students: 3,287 (51.0% male; 49.0% female)
Individual Education Program: 570 (17.3%);
English Language Learner: 3 (0.1%); Migrant: n/a
Eligible for Free Lunch Program: 966 (29.4%)
Eligible for Reduced-Price Lunch Program: 315 (9.6%)
Teachers: 215.4 (15.3 to 1)
Librarians/Media Specialists: 2.0 (1,643.5 to 1)
Guidance Counselors: 8.0 (410.9 to 1)
Current Spending: ($ per student per year):
Total: $7,026; Instruction: $4,110; Support Services: $2,661
Enrollment, Drop-out Rates and Diploma Recipients by Race/Ethnicity

Category	Total	White	Black	Asian	AIAN	Hisp.
Enrollment (%)	100.0	89.4	7.3	0.2	0.0	2.1
Drop-out Rate (%)	4.7	4.7	3.0	0.0	n/a	20.0
H.S. Diplomas (#)	174	161	12	1	0	0

Southeast Local SD
8245 Tallmadge Rd • Ravenna, OH 44266-8547
(330) 654-5841 • http://pirate.portage.k12.oh.us/Main.html
Grade Span: PK-12; **Agency Type:** 2
Schools: 5
3 Primary; 1 Middle; 1 High; 0 Other Level
5 Regular; 0 Special Education; 0 Vocational; 0 Alternative
0 Magnet; 0 Charter; 3 Title I Eligible; 0 School-wide Title I
Students: 2,269 (51.8% male; 48.2% female)
Individual Education Program: 272 (12.0%);
English Language Learner: 0 (0.0%); Migrant: n/a
Eligible for Free Lunch Program: 301 (13.3%)
Eligible for Reduced-Price Lunch Program: 179 (7.9%)
Teachers: 129.5 (17.5 to 1)
Librarians/Media Specialists: 2.0 (1,134.5 to 1)
Guidance Counselors: 2.0 (1,134.5 to 1)
Current Spending: ($ per student per year):
Total: $6,062; Instruction: $3,662; Support Services: $2,173
Enrollment, Drop-out Rates and Diploma Recipients by Race/Ethnicity

Category	Total	White	Black	Asian	AIAN	Hisp.
Enrollment (%)	100.0	99.0	0.5	0.0	0.0	0.1
Drop-out Rate (%)	2.5	2.5	0.0	0.0	n/a	0.0
H.S. Diplomas (#)	171	167	2	1	0	1

Streetsboro City SD
9000 Kirby Ln • Streetsboro, OH 44241-1725
(330) 626-4900 • http://www.rockets.sparcc.org/
Grade Span: PK-12; **Agency Type:** 1
Schools: 5
2 Primary; 2 Middle; 1 High; 0 Other Level
5 Regular; 0 Special Education; 0 Vocational; 0 Alternative
0 Magnet; 0 Charter; 2 Title I Eligible; 0 School-wide Title I
Students: 2,048 (52.5% male; 47.5% female)
Individual Education Program: 232 (11.3%);
English Language Learner: 9 (0.4%); Migrant: n/a
Eligible for Free Lunch Program: 290 (14.2%)
Eligible for Reduced-Price Lunch Program: 145 (7.1%)
Teachers: 139.5 (14.7 to 1)
Librarians/Media Specialists: 1.0 (2,048.0 to 1)
Guidance Counselors: 3.0 (682.7 to 1)
Current Spending: ($ per student per year):
Total: $7,158; Instruction: $4,089; Support Services: $2,797
Enrollment, Drop-out Rates and Diploma Recipients by Race/Ethnicity

Category	Total	White	Black	Asian	AIAN	Hisp.
Enrollment (%)	100.0	92.5	4.3	1.9	0.3	0.5
Drop-out Rate (%)	1.6	1.6	0.0	0.0	n/a	0.0
H.S. Diplomas (#)	119	111	5	3	0	0

Preble County

Eaton City SD
307 N Cherry St • Eaton, OH 45320-1855
(937) 456-1107
Grade Span: PK-12; **Agency Type:** 1
Schools: 4
2 Primary; 1 Middle; 1 High; 0 Other Level
4 Regular; 0 Special Education; 0 Vocational; 0 Alternative
0 Magnet; 0 Charter; 3 Title I Eligible; 1 School-wide Title I
Students: 2,367 (52.2% male; 47.8% female)
Individual Education Program: 258 (10.9%);
English Language Learner: 8 (0.3%); Migrant: n/a
Eligible for Free Lunch Program: 347 (14.7%)
Eligible for Reduced-Price Lunch Program: 112 (4.7%)
Teachers: 131.1 (18.1 to 1)
Librarians/Media Specialists: 1.0 (2,367.0 to 1)
Guidance Counselors: 5.0 (473.4 to 1)
Current Spending: ($ per student per year):
Total: $5,670; Instruction: $3,469; Support Services: $1,980
Enrollment, Drop-out Rates and Diploma Recipients by Race/Ethnicity

Category	Total	White	Black	Asian	AIAN	Hisp.
Enrollment (%)	100.0	97.9	0.7	0.5	0.0	0.4
Drop-out Rate (%)	6.0	5.9	33.3	0.0	n/a	0.0
H.S. Diplomas (#)	135	135	0	0	0	0

Preble Shawnee Local SD
124 Bloomfield St • Camden, OH 45311-1154
(937) 452-3323
Grade Span: KG-12; **Agency Type:** 2
Schools: 4
2 Primary; 1 Middle; 1 High; 0 Other Level
4 Regular; 0 Special Education; 0 Vocational; 0 Alternative
0 Magnet; 0 Charter; 2 Title I Eligible; 0 School-wide Title I
Students: 1,747 (54.1% male; 45.9% female)
Individual Education Program: 174 (10.0%);
English Language Learner: 0 (0.0%); Migrant: n/a
Eligible for Free Lunch Program: 243 (13.9%)
Eligible for Reduced-Price Lunch Program: 129 (7.4%)
Teachers: 113.0 (15.5 to 1)
Librarians/Media Specialists: 2.0 (873.5 to 1)
Guidance Counselors: 0.0 (0.0 to 1)
Current Spending: ($ per student per year):
Total: $5,941; Instruction: $3,394; Support Services: $2,282
Enrollment, Drop-out Rates and Diploma Recipients by Race/Ethnicity

Category	Total	White	Black	Asian	AIAN	Hisp.
Enrollment (%)	100.0	99.5	0.2	0.1	0.0	0.0
Drop-out Rate (%)	2.7	2.7	0.0	0.0	n/a	n/a
H.S. Diplomas (#)	116	115	0	1	0	0

Putnam County

Ottawa-Glandorf Local SD
360 N Locust St • Ottawa, OH 45875-1432
(419) 523-5261
Grade Span: PK-12; **Agency Type:** 2
Schools: 4
3 Primary; 0 Middle; 1 High; 0 Other Level
4 Regular; 0 Special Education; 0 Vocational; 0 Alternative
0 Magnet; 0 Charter; 1 Title I Eligible; 0 School-wide Title I
Students: 1,764 (50.6% male; 49.4% female)
Individual Education Program: 220 (12.5%);
English Language Learner: 1 (0.1%); Migrant: 6 (0.3%)
Eligible for Free Lunch Program: 96 (5.4%)
Eligible for Reduced-Price Lunch Program: 29 (1.6%)
Teachers: 99.0 (17.8 to 1)
Librarians/Media Specialists: 1.0 (1,764.0 to 1)
Guidance Counselors: 3.0 (588.0 to 1)
Current Spending: ($ per student per year):
Total: $5,540; Instruction: $3,580; Support Services: $1,743
Enrollment, Drop-out Rates and Diploma Recipients by Race/Ethnicity

Category	Total	White	Black	Asian	AIAN	Hisp.
Enrollment (%)	100.0	92.3	0.3	0.4	0.0	4.6
Drop-out Rate (%)	2.4	1.4	n/a	50.0	n/a	21.1
H.S. Diplomas (#)	164	160	0	0	0	3

Richland County

Clear Fork Valley Local SD
92 Hines Ave • Bellville, OH 44813-1232
(419) 886-3855
Grade Span: PK-12; **Agency Type:** 2
Schools: 4
2 Primary; 1 Middle; 1 High; 0 Other Level
4 Regular; 0 Special Education; 0 Vocational; 0 Alternative

0 Magnet; 0 Charter; 3 Title I Eligible; 0 School-wide Title I
Students: 1,848 (50.2% male; 49.8% female)
Individual Education Program: 201 (10.9%);
English Language Learner: 0 (0.0%); Migrant: n/a
Eligible for Free Lunch Program: 239 (12.9%)
Eligible for Reduced-Price Lunch Program: 100 (5.4%)
Teachers: 116.5 (15.9 to 1)
Librarians/Media Specialists: 1.0 (1,848.0 to 1)
Guidance Counselors: 4.0 (462.0 to 1)
Current Spending: ($ per student per year):
Total: $5,524; Instruction: $3,054; Support Services: $2,194
Enrollment, Drop-out Rates and Diploma Recipients by Race/Ethnicity

Category	Total	White	Black	Asian	AIAN	Hisp.
Enrollment (%)	100.0	98.4	0.6	0.4	0.0	0.3
Drop-out Rate (%)	2.8	2.8	0.0	0.0	n/a	n/a
H.S. Diplomas (#)	139	139	0	0	0	0

Lexington Local SD
103 Clever Ln • Lexington, OH 44904-1209
(419) 884-2132 • http://www.lexington.k12.oh.us/
Grade Span: PK-12; **Agency Type:** 2
Schools: 5
2 Primary; 2 Middle; 1 High; 0 Other Level
5 Regular; 0 Special Education; 0 Vocational; 0 Alternative
0 Magnet; 0 Charter; 4 Title I Eligible; 0 School-wide Title I
Students: 2,828 (51.5% male; 48.5% female)
Individual Education Program: 330 (11.7%);
English Language Learner: 2 (0.1%); Migrant: n/a
Eligible for Free Lunch Program: 185 (6.5%)
Eligible for Reduced-Price Lunch Program: 89 (3.1%)
Teachers: 161.5 (17.5 to 1)
Librarians/Media Specialists: 3.0 (942.7 to 1)
Guidance Counselors: 3.0 (942.7 to 1)
Current Spending: ($ per student per year):
Total: $5,553; Instruction: $3,379; Support Services: $1,953
Enrollment, Drop-out Rates and Diploma Recipients by Race/Ethnicity

Category	Total	White	Black	Asian	AIAN	Hisp.
Enrollment (%)	100.0	94.5	2.8	1.7	0.0	0.4
Drop-out Rate (%)	0.9	0.9	0.0	0.0	n/a	0.0
H.S. Diplomas (#)	215	201	1	6	0	3

Madison Local SD
1379 Grace St • Mansfield, OH 44905-2742
(419) 589-2600
Grade Span: KG-12; **Agency Type:** 2
Schools: 6
4 Primary; 1 Middle; 1 High; 0 Other Level
6 Regular; 0 Special Education; 0 Vocational; 0 Alternative
0 Magnet; 0 Charter; 4 Title I Eligible; 0 School-wide Title I
Students: 3,563 (53.7% male; 46.3% female)
Individual Education Program: 533 (15.0%);
English Language Learner: 0 (0.0%); Migrant: n/a
Eligible for Free Lunch Program: 621 (17.4%)
Eligible for Reduced-Price Lunch Program: 284 (8.0%)
Teachers: 262.8 (13.6 to 1)
Librarians/Media Specialists: 2.0 (1,781.5 to 1)
Guidance Counselors: 7.0 (509.0 to 1)
Current Spending: ($ per student per year):
Total: $7,271; Instruction: $4,408; Support Services: $2,572
Enrollment, Drop-out Rates and Diploma Recipients by Race/Ethnicity

Category	Total	White	Black	Asian	AIAN	Hisp.
Enrollment (%)	100.0	93.3	3.6	0.2	0.2	0.9
Drop-out Rate (%)	5.2	5.4	4.4	0.0	0.0	0.0
H.S. Diplomas (#)	224	206	15	2	0	0

Mansfield City SD
PO Box 1448 • Mansfield, OH 44901-1448
(419) 525-6400 • http://www.mansfieldschools.org/
Grade Span: PK-12; **Agency Type:** 1
Schools: 14
9 Primary; 2 Middle; 2 High; 1 Other Level
14 Regular; 0 Special Education; 0 Vocational; 0 Alternative
0 Magnet; 0 Charter; 14 Title I Eligible; 9 School-wide Title I
Students: 5,997 (51.4% male; 48.6% female)
Individual Education Program: 1,160 (19.3%);
English Language Learner: 1 (<0.1%); Migrant: n/a
Eligible for Free Lunch Program: 3,470 (57.9%)
Eligible for Reduced-Price Lunch Program: 591 (9.9%)
Teachers: 484.8 (12.4 to 1)
Librarians/Media Specialists: 4.0 (1,499.3 to 1)
Guidance Counselors: 15.8 (379.6 to 1)
Current Spending: ($ per student per year):
Total: $8,444; Instruction: $5,035; Support Services: $3,063

Enrollment, Drop-out Rates and Diploma Recipients by Race/Ethnicity

Category	Total	White	Black	Asian	AIAN	Hisp.
Enrollment (%)	100.0	61.2	34.3	0.1	0.1	0.7
Drop-out Rate (%)	8.4	8.1	9.1	0.0	0.0	0.0
H.S. Diplomas (#)	258	172	86	0	0	0

Ontario Local SD
457 Shelby Ontario Rd • Mansfield, OH 44906-1029
(419) 747-4311
Grade Span: PK-12; **Agency Type:** 2
Schools: 4
2 Primary; 1 Middle; 1 High; 0 Other Level
4 Regular; 0 Special Education; 0 Vocational; 0 Alternative
0 Magnet; 0 Charter; 3 Title I Eligible; 0 School-wide Title I
Students: 1,747 (53.1% male; 46.9% female)
Individual Education Program: 141 (8.1%);
English Language Learner: 0 (0.0%); Migrant: n/a
Eligible for Free Lunch Program: 131 (7.5%)
Eligible for Reduced-Price Lunch Program: 46 (2.6%)
Teachers: 92.9 (18.8 to 1)
Librarians/Media Specialists: 2.0 (873.5 to 1)
Guidance Counselors: 3.0 (582.3 to 1)
Current Spending: ($ per student per year):
Total: $6,313; Instruction: $3,538; Support Services: $2,516
Enrollment, Drop-out Rates and Diploma Recipients by Race/Ethnicity

Category	Total	White	Black	Asian	AIAN	Hisp.
Enrollment (%)	100.0	94.0	3.3	1.3	0.0	0.2
Drop-out Rate (%)	1.2	0.9	18.2	0.0	n/a	0.0
H.S. Diplomas (#)	119	112	3	3	0	1

Shelby City SD
25 High School Ave • Shelby, OH 44875-1576
(419) 342-3520 • http://www.shelby-city.k12.oh.us/
Grade Span: KG-12; **Agency Type:** 1
Schools: 6
4 Primary; 1 Middle; 1 High; 0 Other Level
6 Regular; 0 Special Education; 0 Vocational; 0 Alternative
0 Magnet; 0 Charter; 4 Title I Eligible; 3 School-wide Title I
Students: 2,289 (51.9% male; 48.1% female)
Individual Education Program: 327 (14.3%);
English Language Learner: 0 (0.0%); Migrant: n/a
Eligible for Free Lunch Program: 347 (15.2%)
Eligible for Reduced-Price Lunch Program: 164 (7.2%)
Teachers: 144.7 (15.8 to 1)
Librarians/Media Specialists: 3.0 (763.0 to 1)
Guidance Counselors: 5.0 (457.8 to 1)
Current Spending: ($ per student per year):
Total: $6,595; Instruction: $3,998; Support Services: $2,272
Enrollment, Drop-out Rates and Diploma Recipients by Race/Ethnicity

Category	Total	White	Black	Asian	AIAN	Hisp.
Enrollment (%)	100.0	97.7	0.2	0.3	0.0	0.5
Drop-out Rate (%)	4.9	4.9	n/a	0.0	n/a	0.0
H.S. Diplomas (#)	171	166	0	2	0	2

Ross County

Chillicothe City SD
235 Cherry St • Chillicothe, OH 45601-2350
(740) 775-4250
Grade Span: PK-12; **Agency Type:** 1
Schools: 9
6 Primary; 2 Middle; 1 High; 0 Other Level
9 Regular; 0 Special Education; 0 Vocational; 0 Alternative
0 Magnet; 0 Charter; 5 Title I Eligible; 5 School-wide Title I
Students: 3,691 (51.8% male; 48.2% female)
Individual Education Program: 548 (14.8%);
English Language Learner: 1 (<0.1%); Migrant: n/a
Eligible for Free Lunch Program: 1,083 (29.3%)
Eligible for Reduced-Price Lunch Program: 206 (5.6%)
Teachers: 196.0 (18.8 to 1)
Librarians/Media Specialists: 3.0 (1,230.3 to 1)
Guidance Counselors: 6.0 (615.2 to 1)
Current Spending: ($ per student per year):
Total: $6,267; Instruction: $3,579; Support Services: $2,381
Enrollment, Drop-out Rates and Diploma Recipients by Race/Ethnicity

Category	Total	White	Black	Asian	AIAN	Hisp.
Enrollment (%)	100.0	84.3	9.3	0.8	0.1	0.7
Drop-out Rate (%)	4.3	4.2	6.4	0.0	0.0	0.0
H.S. Diplomas (#)	285	251	18	4	0	5

Union-Scioto Local SD
1432 Egypt Pike • Chillicothe, OH 45601-3905
(740) 773-4102
Grade Span: PK-12; **Agency Type:** 2
Schools: 4

1 Primary; 2 Middle; 1 High; 0 Other Level
4 Regular; 0 Special Education; 0 Vocational; 0 Alternative
0 Magnet; 0 Charter; 2 Title I Eligible; 0 School-wide Title I
Students: 1,918 (51.6% male; 48.4% female)
Individual Education Program: 217 (11.3%);
English Language Learner: 0 (0.0%); Migrant: n/a
Eligible for Free Lunch Program: 376 (19.6%)
Eligible for Reduced-Price Lunch Program: 96 (5.0%)
Teachers: 113.0 (17.0 to 1)
Librarians/Media Specialists: 1.0 (1,918.0 to 1)
Guidance Counselors: 3.0 (639.3 to 1)
Current Spending: ($ per student per year):
Total: $5,765; Instruction: $3,633; Support Services: $1,871
Enrollment, Drop-out Rates and Diploma Recipients by Race/Ethnicity

Category	Total	White	Black	Asian	AIAN	Hisp.
Enrollment (%)	100.0	94.9	1.8	0.7	0.4	0.3
Drop-out Rate (%)	5.4	5.0	23.1	0.0	n/a	n/a
H.S. Diplomas (#)	133	130	2	1	0	0

Zane Trace Local SD
946 State Route 180 • Chillicothe, OH 45601-8141
(740) 775-1355 • http://gsn.k12.oh.us/zanetrace/index.html
Grade Span: PK-12; **Agency Type:** 2
Schools: 3
1 Primary; 1 Middle; 1 High; 0 Other Level
3 Regular; 0 Special Education; 0 Vocational; 0 Alternative
0 Magnet; 0 Charter; 1 Title I Eligible; 0 School-wide Title I
Students: 1,522 (49.3% male; 50.7% female)
Individual Education Program: 152 (10.0%);
English Language Learner: 0 (0.0%); Migrant: n/a
Eligible for Free Lunch Program: 150 (9.9%)
Eligible for Reduced-Price Lunch Program: 49 (3.2%)
Teachers: 84.0 (18.1 to 1)
Librarians/Media Specialists: 1.0 (1,522.0 to 1)
Guidance Counselors: 3.0 (507.3 to 1)
Current Spending: ($ per student per year):
Total: $5,339; Instruction: $3,014; Support Services: $2,067
Enrollment, Drop-out Rates and Diploma Recipients by Race/Ethnicity

Category	Total	White	Black	Asian	AIAN	Hisp.
Enrollment (%)	100.0	98.7	0.3	0.3	0.0	0.1
Drop-out Rate (%)	2.4	2.4	0.0	0.0	0.0	n/a
H.S. Diplomas (#)	95	95	0	0	0	0

Sandusky County

Clyde-Green Springs Ex Vill SD
106 S Main St • Clyde, OH 43410-1633
(419) 547-0588 • http://www.clyde.k12.oh.us/
Grade Span: PK-12; **Agency Type:** 1
Schools: 5
3 Primary; 1 Middle; 1 High; 0 Other Level
5 Regular; 0 Special Education; 0 Vocational; 0 Alternative
0 Magnet; 0 Charter; 3 Title I Eligible; 0 School-wide Title I
Students: 2,300 (50.9% male; 49.1% female)
Individual Education Program: 317 (13.8%);
English Language Learner: 1 (<0.1%); Migrant: 6 (0.3%)
Eligible for Free Lunch Program: 366 (15.9%)
Eligible for Reduced-Price Lunch Program: 177 (7.7%)
Teachers: 137.0 (16.8 to 1)
Librarians/Media Specialists: 1.0 (2,300.0 to 1)
Guidance Counselors: 5.0 (460.0 to 1)
Current Spending: ($ per student per year):
Total: $6,061; Instruction: $3,646; Support Services: $2,173
Enrollment, Drop-out Rates and Diploma Recipients by Race/Ethnicity

Category	Total	White	Black	Asian	AIAN	Hisp.
Enrollment (%)	100.0	93.0	0.4	0.5	0.1	4.5
Drop-out Rate (%)	1.4	1.2	0.0	0.0	n/a	5.4
H.S. Diplomas (#)	171	165	0	2	0	4

Fremont City SD
1220 Cedar St Ste A • Fremont, OH 43420-5118
(419) 332-6454
Grade Span: PK-12; **Agency Type:** 1
Schools: 9
7 Primary; 1 Middle; 1 High; 0 Other Level
9 Regular; 0 Special Education; 0 Vocational; 0 Alternative
0 Magnet; 0 Charter; 7 Title I Eligible; 3 School-wide Title I
Students: 4,612 (51.1% male; 48.9% female)
Individual Education Program: 654 (14.2%);
English Language Learner: 41 (0.9%); Migrant: 61 (1.3%)
Eligible for Free Lunch Program: 1,292 (28.0%)
Eligible for Reduced-Price Lunch Program: 459 (10.0%)
Teachers: 267.1 (17.3 to 1)
Librarians/Media Specialists: 3.0 (1,537.3 to 1)
Guidance Counselors: 8.0 (576.5 to 1)
Current Spending: ($ per student per year):
Total: $6,187; Instruction: $3,801; Support Services: $2,113
Enrollment, Drop-out Rates and Diploma Recipients by Race/Ethnicity

Category	Total	White	Black	Asian	AIAN	Hisp.
Enrollment (%)	100.0	70.5	9.7	0.3	0.1	13.7
Drop-out Rate (%)	4.9	4.3	2.1	9.1	0.0	11.0
H.S. Diplomas (#)	325	254	22	2	1	37

Scioto County

Minford Local SD
PO Box 204 • Minford, OH 45653-0204
(740) 820-3896 • http://www.minford.k12.oh.us/
Grade Span: PK-12; **Agency Type:** 2
Schools: 3
1 Primary; 1 Middle; 1 High; 0 Other Level
3 Regular; 0 Special Education; 0 Vocational; 0 Alternative
0 Magnet; 0 Charter; 2 Title I Eligible; 0 School-wide Title I
Students: 1,638 (52.1% male; 47.9% female)
Individual Education Program: 167 (10.2%);
English Language Learner: 0 (0.0%); Migrant: n/a
Eligible for Free Lunch Program: 476 (29.1%)
Eligible for Reduced-Price Lunch Program: 140 (8.5%)
Teachers: 94.2 (17.4 to 1)
Librarians/Media Specialists: 3.0 (546.0 to 1)
Guidance Counselors: 3.0 (546.0 to 1)
Current Spending: ($ per student per year):
Total: $6,076; Instruction: $3,565; Support Services: $2,217
Enrollment, Drop-out Rates and Diploma Recipients by Race/Ethnicity

Category	Total	White	Black	Asian	AIAN	Hisp.
Enrollment (%)	100.0	98.3	0.2	0.1	0.2	0.3
Drop-out Rate (%)	2.0	2.0	n/a	n/a	n/a	0.0
H.S. Diplomas (#)	113	113	0	0	0	0

Northwest Local SD
800 Mohawk Dr • Mc Dermott, OH 45652-9000
(740) 259-5558
Grade Span: PK-12; **Agency Type:** 2
Schools: 3
1 Primary; 1 Middle; 1 High; 0 Other Level
3 Regular; 0 Special Education; 0 Vocational; 0 Alternative
0 Magnet; 0 Charter; 2 Title I Eligible; 1 School-wide Title I
Students: 1,781 (52.4% male; 47.6% female)
Individual Education Program: 254 (14.3%);
English Language Learner: 0 (0.0%); Migrant: n/a
Eligible for Free Lunch Program: 658 (36.9%)
Eligible for Reduced-Price Lunch Program: 179 (10.1%)
Teachers: 108.0 (16.5 to 1)
Librarians/Media Specialists: 3.0 (593.7 to 1)
Guidance Counselors: 4.0 (445.3 to 1)
Current Spending: ($ per student per year):
Total: $6,344; Instruction: $3,655; Support Services: $2,393
Enrollment, Drop-out Rates and Diploma Recipients by Race/Ethnicity

Category	Total	White	Black	Asian	AIAN	Hisp.
Enrollment (%)	100.0	99.6	0.0	0.2	0.0	0.0
Drop-out Rate (%)	3.0	2.9	n/a	0.0	n/a	n/a
H.S. Diplomas (#)	118	118	0	0	0	0

Portsmouth City SD
1149 Gallia St • Portsmouth, OH 45662-4159
(740) 354-4727
Grade Span: KG-12; **Agency Type:** 1
Schools: 9
3 Primary; 2 Middle; 1 High; 0 Other Level
6 Regular; 0 Special Education; 0 Vocational; 0 Alternative
0 Magnet; 0 Charter; 5 Title I Eligible; 5 School-wide Title I
Students: 2,185 (52.9% male; 47.1% female)
Individual Education Program: 322 (14.7%);
English Language Learner: 0 (0.0%); Migrant: n/a
Eligible for Free Lunch Program: 1,001 (45.8%)
Eligible for Reduced-Price Lunch Program: 126 (5.8%)
Teachers: 148.0 (14.8 to 1)
Librarians/Media Specialists: 2.0 (1,092.5 to 1)
Guidance Counselors: 5.0 (437.0 to 1)
Current Spending: ($ per student per year):
Total: $6,941; Instruction: $4,194; Support Services: $2,410
Enrollment, Drop-out Rates and Diploma Recipients by Race/Ethnicity

Category	Total	White	Black	Asian	AIAN	Hisp.
Enrollment (%)	100.0	88.3	7.9	0.5	0.2	0.2
Drop-out Rate (%)	4.4	4.3	4.1	33.3	n/a	0.0
H.S. Diplomas (#)	102	86	12	1	0	1

Washington-Nile Local SD

15332 US Hwy 52 • West Portsmouth, OH 45663-9093
(740) 858-1111
Grade Span: PK-12; **Agency Type:** 2
Schools: 3
1 Primary; 1 Middle; 1 High; 0 Other Level
3 Regular; 0 Special Education; 0 Vocational; 0 Alternative
0 Magnet; 0 Charter; 2 Title I Eligible; 2 School-wide Title I
Students: 1,728 (51.7% male; 48.3% female)
Individual Education Program: 178 (10.3%);
English Language Learner: 0 (0.0%); Migrant: n/a
Eligible for Free Lunch Program: 632 (36.6%)
Eligible for Reduced-Price Lunch Program: 110 (6.4%)
Teachers: 114.5 (15.1 to 1)
Librarians/Media Specialists: 2.0 (864.0 to 1)
Guidance Counselors: 5.0 (345.6 to 1)
Current Spending: ($ per student per year):
Total: $6,286; Instruction: $3,577; Support Services: $2,389
Enrollment, Drop-out Rates and Diploma Recipients by Race/Ethnicity

Category	Total	White	Black	Asian	AIAN	Hisp.
Enrollment (%)	100.0	98.7	0.2	0.1	0.1	0.3
Drop-out Rate (%)	4.0	4.0	0.0	n/a	0.0	n/a
H.S. Diplomas (#)	113	112	0	0	1	0

Seneca County

Fostoria City SD

500 Pkwy Dr • Fostoria, OH 44830-1513
(419) 435-8163
Grade Span: PK-12; **Agency Type:** 1
Schools: 5
3 Primary; 1 Middle; 1 High; 0 Other Level
5 Regular; 0 Special Education; 0 Vocational; 0 Alternative
0 Magnet; 0 Charter; 4 Title I Eligible; 4 School-wide Title I
Students: 2,351 (51.5% male; 48.5% female)
Individual Education Program: 435 (18.5%);
English Language Learner: 21 (0.9%); Migrant: n/a
Eligible for Free Lunch Program: 886 (37.7%)
Eligible for Reduced-Price Lunch Program: 267 (11.4%)
Teachers: 139.3 (16.9 to 1)
Librarians/Media Specialists: 1.0 (2,351.0 to 1)
Guidance Counselors: 6.0 (391.8 to 1)
Current Spending: ($ per student per year):
Total: $7,238; Instruction: $4,004; Support Services: $2,943
Enrollment, Drop-out Rates and Diploma Recipients by Race/Ethnicity

Category	Total	White	Black	Asian	AIAN	Hisp.
Enrollment (%)	100.0	69.9	7.4	0.3	0.1	8.5
Drop-out Rate (%)	6.2	6.3	7.7	0.0	0.0	5.5
H.S. Diplomas (#)	115	96	9	0	0	6

Tiffin City SD

244 S Monroe St • Tiffin, OH 44883-2906
(419) 447-2515 • http://www.tiffin.k12.oh.us/
Grade Span: PK-12; **Agency Type:** 1
Schools: 8
5 Primary; 1 Middle; 1 High; 1 Other Level
8 Regular; 0 Special Education; 0 Vocational; 0 Alternative
0 Magnet; 0 Charter; 5 Title I Eligible; 3 School-wide Title I
Students: 3,024 (51.8% male; 48.2% female)
Individual Education Program: 510 (16.9%);
English Language Learner: 5 (0.2%); Migrant: n/a
Eligible for Free Lunch Program: 472 (15.6%)
Eligible for Reduced-Price Lunch Program: 211 (7.0%)
Teachers: 181.7 (16.6 to 1)
Librarians/Media Specialists: 3.0 (1,008.0 to 1)
Guidance Counselors: 8.0 (378.0 to 1)
Current Spending: ($ per student per year):
Total: $5,974; Instruction: $3,659; Support Services: $2,129
Enrollment, Drop-out Rates and Diploma Recipients by Race/Ethnicity

Category	Total	White	Black	Asian	AIAN	Hisp.
Enrollment (%)	100.0	93.6	1.1	0.8	0.0	2.1
Drop-out Rate (%)	3.8	3.7	14.3	16.7	0.0	7.7
H.S. Diplomas (#)	247	237	1	3	0	2

Shelby County

Sidney City SD

232 N Miami Ave • Sidney, OH 45365-2708
(937) 497-2200 • http://www.sidney.k12.oh.us/
Grade Span: KG-12; **Agency Type:** 1
Schools: 9
6 Primary; 2 Middle; 1 High; 0 Other Level
9 Regular; 0 Special Education; 0 Vocational; 0 Alternative
0 Magnet; 0 Charter; 5 Title I Eligible; 3 School-wide Title I
Students: 3,948 (51.6% male; 48.4% female)
Individual Education Program: 702 (17.8%);
English Language Learner: 67 (1.7%); Migrant: n/a
Eligible for Free Lunch Program: 870 (22.0%)
Eligible for Reduced-Price Lunch Program: 275 (7.0%)
Teachers: 220.6 (17.9 to 1)
Librarians/Media Specialists: 3.0 (1,316.0 to 1)
Guidance Counselors: 11.0 (358.9 to 1)
Current Spending: ($ per student per year):
Total: $5,790; Instruction: $3,344; Support Services: $2,173
Enrollment, Drop-out Rates and Diploma Recipients by Race/Ethnicity

Category	Total	White	Black	Asian	AIAN	Hisp.
Enrollment (%)	100.0	88.6	3.9	2.6	0.1	0.7
Drop-out Rate (%)	4.3	4.3	7.0	0.0	0.0	16.7
H.S. Diplomas (#)	233	210	12	9	0	1

Stark County

Alliance City SD

200 Glamorgan St • Alliance, OH 44601-2946
(330) 821-2100 • http://www.aviators.stark.k12.oh.us/
Grade Span: PK-12; **Agency Type:** 1
Schools: 7
5 Primary; 1 Middle; 1 High; 0 Other Level
7 Regular; 0 Special Education; 0 Vocational; 0 Alternative
0 Magnet; 0 Charter; 7 Title I Eligible; 6 School-wide Title I
Students: 3,340 (51.7% male; 48.3% female)
Individual Education Program: 551 (16.5%);
English Language Learner: 8 (0.2%); Migrant: 4 (0.1%)
Eligible for Free Lunch Program: 1,559 (46.7%)
Eligible for Reduced-Price Lunch Program: 359 (10.7%)
Teachers: 263.7 (12.7 to 1)
Librarians/Media Specialists: 2.0 (1,670.0 to 1)
Guidance Counselors: 6.0 (556.7 to 1)
Current Spending: ($ per student per year):
Total: $7,150; Instruction: $4,696; Support Services: $2,160
Enrollment, Drop-out Rates and Diploma Recipients by Race/Ethnicity

Category	Total	White	Black	Asian	AIAN	Hisp.
Enrollment (%)	100.0	80.2	16.1	0.3	0.1	1.0
Drop-out Rate (%)	6.2	5.2	11.7	0.0	n/a	0.0
H.S. Diplomas (#)	213	185	25	0	0	3

Canton City SD

617 Mckinley Ave SW • Canton, OH 44707-4727
(330) 438-2500 • http://www.ccsdistrict.org/
Grade Span: PK-12; **Agency Type:** 1
Schools: 30
19 Primary; 4 Middle; 5 High; 2 Other Level
26 Regular; 0 Special Education; 1 Vocational; 3 Alternative
0 Magnet; 0 Charter; 23 Title I Eligible; 20 School-wide Title I
Students: 12,362 (51.4% male; 48.6% female)
Individual Education Program: 2,062 (16.7%);
English Language Learner: 43 (0.3%); Migrant: n/a
Eligible for Free Lunch Program: 6,260 (50.6%)
Eligible for Reduced-Price Lunch Program: 1,189 (9.6%)
Teachers: 929.2 (13.3 to 1)
Librarians/Media Specialists: 6.0 (2,060.3 to 1)
Guidance Counselors: 28.0 (441.5 to 1)
Current Spending: ($ per student per year):
Total: $7,999; Instruction: $4,694; Support Services: $3,034
Enrollment, Drop-out Rates and Diploma Recipients by Race/Ethnicity

Category	Total	White	Black	Asian	AIAN	Hisp.
Enrollment (%)	100.0	56.8	34.0	0.2	0.5	0.9
Drop-out Rate (%)	17.8	16.3	21.0	28.6	13.3	4.8
H.S. Diplomas (#)	495	324	162	2	1	1

Canton Local SD

4526 Ridge Ave SE • Canton, OH 44707-1118
(330) 484-8010 • http://www.cantonlocal.org/
Grade Span: PK-12; **Agency Type:** 2
Schools: 5
3 Primary; 1 Middle; 1 High; 0 Other Level
5 Regular; 0 Special Education; 0 Vocational; 0 Alternative
0 Magnet; 0 Charter; 2 Title I Eligible; 0 School-wide Title I
Students: 2,578 (55.0% male; 45.0% female)
Individual Education Program: 344 (13.3%);
English Language Learner: 1 (<0.1%); Migrant: n/a
Eligible for Free Lunch Program: 560 (21.7%)
Eligible for Reduced-Price Lunch Program: 211 (8.2%)
Teachers: 168.4 (15.3 to 1)
Librarians/Media Specialists: 1.0 (2,578.0 to 1)
Guidance Counselors: 4.6 (560.4 to 1)
Current Spending: ($ per student per year):
Total: $6,956; Instruction: $4,161; Support Services: $2,517

Enrollment, Drop-out Rates and Diploma Recipients by Race/Ethnicity

Category	Total	White	Black	Asian	AIAN	Hisp.
Enrollment (%)	100.0	90.5	7.3	0.2	0.1	0.5
Drop-out Rate (%)	0.7	0.7	0.0	n/a	n/a	0.0
H.S. Diplomas (#)	162	153	8	0	0	1

Fairless Local SD

11885 Navarre Rd SW • Navarre, OH 44662-9485
(330) 767-3577 • http://falcon.stark.k12.oh.us/FLocal/index.html
Grade Span: PK-12; **Agency Type:** 2
Schools: 5
3 Primary; 1 Middle; 1 High; 0 Other Level
5 Regular; 0 Special Education; 0 Vocational; 0 Alternative
0 Magnet; 0 Charter; 3 Title I Eligible; 2 School-wide Title I
Students: 1,914 (51.9% male; 48.1% female)
Individual Education Program: 289 (15.1%);
English Language Learner: 2 (0.1%); Migrant: n/a
Eligible for Free Lunch Program: 367 (19.2%)
Eligible for Reduced-Price Lunch Program: 239 (12.5%)
Teachers: 119.0 (16.1 to 1)
Librarians/Media Specialists: 1.0 (1,914.0 to 1)
Guidance Counselors: 1.0 (1,914.0 to 1)
Current Spending: ($ per student per year):
Total: $5,892; Instruction: $3,539; Support Services: $2,087
Enrollment, Drop-out Rates and Diploma Recipients by Race/Ethnicity

Category	Total	White	Black	Asian	AIAN	Hisp.
Enrollment (%)	100.0	98.2	0.3	0.3	0.1	0.7
Drop-out Rate (%)	1.8	1.8	0.0	0.0	n/a	0.0
H.S. Diplomas (#)	119	118	0	0	0	0

Jackson Local SD

7984 Fulton Dr NW • Massillon, OH 44646-9393
(330) 830-8000 • http://jackson.stark.k12.oh.us/
Grade Span: PK-12; **Agency Type:** 2
Schools: 6
4 Primary; 1 Middle; 1 High; 0 Other Level
6 Regular; 0 Special Education; 0 Vocational; 0 Alternative
0 Magnet; 0 Charter; 4 Title I Eligible; 0 School-wide Title I
Students: 5,380 (50.2% male; 49.8% female)
Individual Education Program: 429 (8.0%);
English Language Learner: 44 (0.8%); Migrant: n/a
Eligible for Free Lunch Program: 208 (3.9%)
Eligible for Reduced-Price Lunch Program: 112 (2.1%)
Teachers: 307.0 (17.5 to 1)
Librarians/Media Specialists: 3.0 (1,793.3 to 1)
Guidance Counselors: 11.0 (489.1 to 1)
Current Spending: ($ per student per year):
Total: $6,381; Instruction: $3,581; Support Services: $2,593
Enrollment, Drop-out Rates and Diploma Recipients by Race/Ethnicity

Category	Total	White	Black	Asian	AIAN	Hisp.
Enrollment (%)	100.0	94.5	2.2	2.6	0.0	0.5
Drop-out Rate (%)	1.6	1.7	0.0	0.0	n/a	0.0
H.S. Diplomas (#)	422	406	5	8	0	3

Lake Local SD

12077 Lisa St NW • Hartville, OH 44632-9670
(330) 877-9383 •
http://lakelocal.oh.schoolwebpages.com/education/district/district.php?sectionid=1
Grade Span: PK-12; **Agency Type:** 2
Schools: 5
2 Primary; 2 Middle; 1 High; 0 Other Level
5 Regular; 0 Special Education; 0 Vocational; 0 Alternative
0 Magnet; 0 Charter; 3 Title I Eligible; 0 School-wide Title I
Students: 3,346 (52.9% male; 47.1% female)
Individual Education Program: 351 (10.5%);
English Language Learner: 57 (1.7%); Migrant: n/a
Eligible for Free Lunch Program: 218 (6.5%)
Eligible for Reduced-Price Lunch Program: 87 (2.6%)
Teachers: 197.4 (17.0 to 1)
Librarians/Media Specialists: 2.0 (1,673.0 to 1)
Guidance Counselors: 5.0 (669.2 to 1)
Current Spending: ($ per student per year):
Total: $5,576; Instruction: $3,355; Support Services: $2,046
Enrollment, Drop-out Rates and Diploma Recipients by Race/Ethnicity

Category	Total	White	Black	Asian	AIAN	Hisp.
Enrollment (%)	100.0	98.7	0.2	0.4	0.0	0.6
Drop-out Rate (%)	1.3	1.3	0.0	0.0	n/a	0.0
H.S. Diplomas (#)	248	244	1	2	0	1

Louisville City SD

418 E Main St • Louisville, OH 44641-1420
(330) 875-1666 • http://leopard.stark.k12.oh.us/
Grade Span: PK-12; **Agency Type:** 1
Schools: 6
4 Primary; 1 Middle; 1 High; 0 Other Level
6 Regular; 0 Special Education; 0 Vocational; 0 Alternative
0 Magnet; 0 Charter; 4 Title I Eligible; 2 School-wide Title I
Students: 3,239 (49.6% male; 50.4% female)
Individual Education Program: 335 (10.3%);
English Language Learner: 8 (0.2%); Migrant: n/a
Eligible for Free Lunch Program: 402 (12.4%)
Eligible for Reduced-Price Lunch Program: 244 (7.5%)
Teachers: 192.5 (16.8 to 1)
Librarians/Media Specialists: 2.0 (1,619.5 to 1)
Guidance Counselors: 8.4 (385.6 to 1)
Current Spending: ($ per student per year):
Total: $5,879; Instruction: $3,779; Support Services: $1,821
Enrollment, Drop-out Rates and Diploma Recipients by Race/Ethnicity

Category	Total	White	Black	Asian	AIAN	Hisp.
Enrollment (%)	100.0	99.5	0.1	0.2	0.0	0.2
Drop-out Rate (%)	2.6	2.6	n/a	0.0	n/a	n/a
H.S. Diplomas (#)	199	198	0	1	0	0

Marlington Local SD

10320 Moulin Ave NE • Alliance, OH 44601-5906
(330) 823-7458 • http://dukes.stark.k12.oh.us/
Grade Span: PK-12; **Agency Type:** 2
Schools: 5
3 Primary; 1 Middle; 1 High; 0 Other Level
5 Regular; 0 Special Education; 0 Vocational; 0 Alternative
0 Magnet; 0 Charter; 3 Title I Eligible; 0 School-wide Title I
Students: 2,790 (49.0% male; 51.0% female)
Individual Education Program: 421 (15.1%);
English Language Learner: 28 (1.0%); Migrant: 24 (0.9%)
Eligible for Free Lunch Program: 379 (13.6%)
Eligible for Reduced-Price Lunch Program: 140 (5.0%)
Teachers: 164.0 (17.0 to 1)
Librarians/Media Specialists: 1.0 (2,790.0 to 1)
Guidance Counselors: 3.6 (775.0 to 1)
Current Spending: ($ per student per year):
Total: $6,035; Instruction: $3,639; Support Services: $2,191
Enrollment, Drop-out Rates and Diploma Recipients by Race/Ethnicity

Category	Total	White	Black	Asian	AIAN	Hisp.
Enrollment (%)	100.0	95.7	1.8	0.7	0.0	0.9
Drop-out Rate (%)	1.2	1.2	0.0	0.0	n/a	0.0
H.S. Diplomas (#)	171	168	2	0	0	1

Massillon City SD

207 Oak Ave SE • Massillon, OH 44646-6790
(330) 830-1810
Grade Span: PK-12; **Agency Type:** 1
Schools: 10
7 Primary; 2 Middle; 1 High; 0 Other Level
10 Regular; 0 Special Education; 0 Vocational; 0 Alternative
0 Magnet; 0 Charter; 8 Title I Eligible; 4 School-wide Title I
Students: 4,453 (53.5% male; 46.5% female)
Individual Education Program: 705 (15.8%);
English Language Learner: 12 (0.3%); Migrant: n/a
Eligible for Free Lunch Program: 1,544 (34.7%)
Eligible for Reduced-Price Lunch Program: 430 (9.7%)
Teachers: 337.5 (13.2 to 1)
Librarians/Media Specialists: 2.0 (2,226.5 to 1)
Guidance Counselors: 7.0 (636.1 to 1)
Current Spending: ($ per student per year):
Total: $6,582; Instruction: $3,851; Support Services: $2,480
Enrollment, Drop-out Rates and Diploma Recipients by Race/Ethnicity

Category	Total	White	Black	Asian	AIAN	Hisp.
Enrollment (%)	100.0	83.5	14.3	0.4	0.0	0.4
Drop-out Rate (%)	4.3	3.9	7.0	0.0	n/a	0.0
H.S. Diplomas (#)	255	227	28	0	0	0

Minerva Local SD

303 Latzer Ave • Minerva, OH 44657-1434
(330) 868-4332 • http://lion.stark.k12.oh.us/
Grade Span: KG-12; **Agency Type:** 2
Schools: 4
3 Primary; 0 Middle; 1 High; 0 Other Level
4 Regular; 0 Special Education; 0 Vocational; 0 Alternative
0 Magnet; 0 Charter; 2 Title I Eligible; 0 School-wide Title I
Students: 2,192 (52.6% male; 47.4% female)
Individual Education Program: 281 (12.8%);
English Language Learner: 8 (0.4%); Migrant: n/a
Eligible for Free Lunch Program: 481 (21.9%)
Eligible for Reduced-Price Lunch Program: 183 (8.3%)
Teachers: 132.5 (16.5 to 1)
Librarians/Media Specialists: 1.0 (2,192.0 to 1)
Guidance Counselors: 4.0 (548.0 to 1)
Current Spending: ($ per student per year):
Total: $6,075; Instruction: $3,844; Support Services: $2,006

Enrollment, Drop-out Rates and Diploma Recipients by Race/Ethnicity

Category	Total	White	Black	Asian	AIAN	Hisp.
Enrollment (%)	100.0	99.4	0.2	0.2	0.0	0.0
Drop-out Rate (%)	3.8	3.8	0.0	n/a	n/a	0.0
H.S. Diplomas (#)	145	144	0	0	0	1

North Canton City SD

525 7th St NE • North Canton, OH 44720-2012
(330) 497-5600
Grade Span: PK-12; **Agency Type:** 1
Schools: 7
5 Primary; 1 Middle; 1 High; 0 Other Level
7 Regular; 0 Special Education; 0 Vocational; 0 Alternative
0 Magnet; 0 Charter; 3 Title I Eligible; 0 School-wide Title I
Students: 4,863 (50.4% male; 49.6% female)
Individual Education Program: 534 (11.0%);
English Language Learner: 15 (0.3%); Migrant: n/a
Eligible for Free Lunch Program: 215 (4.4%)
Eligible for Reduced-Price Lunch Program: 170 (3.5%)
Teachers: 289.4 (16.8 to 1)
Librarians/Media Specialists: 2.0 (2,431.5 to 1)
Guidance Counselors: 11.3 (430.4 to 1)
Current Spending: ($ per student per year):
Total: $6,615; Instruction: $3,967; Support Services: $2,425
Enrollment, Drop-out Rates and Diploma Recipients by Race/Ethnicity

Category	Total	White	Black	Asian	AIAN	Hisp.
Enrollment (%)	100.0	95.1	1.3	1.5	0.2	0.8
Drop-out Rate (%)	1.1	1.1	0.0	0.0	0.0	0.0
H.S. Diplomas (#)	319	304	5	6	0	3

Northwest Local SD

104 Market St W • Canal Fulton, OH 44614-1050
(330) 854-2291
Grade Span: PK-12; **Agency Type:** 2
Schools: 5
2 Primary; 2 Middle; 1 High; 0 Other Level
5 Regular; 0 Special Education; 0 Vocational; 0 Alternative
0 Magnet; 0 Charter; 3 Title I Eligible; 0 School-wide Title I
Students: 2,426 (51.9% male; 48.1% female)
Individual Education Program: 334 (13.8%);
English Language Learner: 3 (0.1%); Migrant: n/a
Eligible for Free Lunch Program: 243 (10.0%)
Eligible for Reduced-Price Lunch Program: 120 (4.9%)
Teachers: 150.1 (16.2 to 1)
Librarians/Media Specialists: 1.0 (2,426.0 to 1)
Guidance Counselors: 4.5 (539.1 to 1)
Current Spending: ($ per student per year):
Total: $5,829; Instruction: $3,607; Support Services: $2,009
Enrollment, Drop-out Rates and Diploma Recipients by Race/Ethnicity

Category	Total	White	Black	Asian	AIAN	Hisp.
Enrollment (%)	100.0	98.1	1.2	0.4	0.0	0.3
Drop-out Rate (%)	0.7	0.7	0.0	0.0	n/a	0.0
H.S. Diplomas (#)	151	149	2	0	0	0

Perry Local SD

4201 13th St SW • Massillon, OH 44646-3447
(330) 477-8121
Grade Span: PK-12; **Agency Type:** 2
Schools: 9
6 Primary; 1 Middle; 1 High; 1 Other Level
9 Regular; 0 Special Education; 0 Vocational; 0 Alternative
0 Magnet; 0 Charter; 6 Title I Eligible; 1 School-wide Title I
Students: 4,900 (52.5% male; 47.5% female)
Individual Education Program: 703 (14.3%);
English Language Learner: 18 (0.4%); Migrant: n/a
Eligible for Free Lunch Program: 669 (13.7%)
Eligible for Reduced-Price Lunch Program: 294 (6.0%)
Teachers: 276.2 (17.7 to 1)
Librarians/Media Specialists: 3.0 (1,633.3 to 1)
Guidance Counselors: 15.0 (326.7 to 1)
Current Spending: ($ per student per year):
Total: $6,316; Instruction: $3,823; Support Services: $2,237
Enrollment, Drop-out Rates and Diploma Recipients by Race/Ethnicity

Category	Total	White	Black	Asian	AIAN	Hisp.
Enrollment (%)	100.0	94.3	3.5	0.4	0.1	0.4
Drop-out Rate (%)	0.5	0.6	0.0	0.0	n/a	0.0
H.S. Diplomas (#)	342	324	16	0	0	1

Plain Local SD

901 44th St NW • Canton, OH 44709-1611
(330) 492-3500 • http://eagle.stark.k12.oh.us/
Grade Span: PK-12; **Agency Type:** 2
Schools: 10
6 Primary; 3 Middle; 1 High; 0 Other Level
10 Regular; 0 Special Education; 0 Vocational; 0 Alternative
0 Magnet; 0 Charter; 6 Title I Eligible; 3 School-wide Title I
Students: 6,244 (50.8% male; 49.2% female)
Individual Education Program: 810 (13.0%);
English Language Learner: 20 (0.3%); Migrant: n/a
Eligible for Free Lunch Program: 1,130 (18.1%)
Eligible for Reduced-Price Lunch Program: 330 (5.3%)
Teachers: 392.4 (15.9 to 1)
Librarians/Media Specialists: 3.0 (2,081.3 to 1)
Guidance Counselors: 14.8 (421.9 to 1)
Current Spending: ($ per student per year):
Total: $6,063; Instruction: $3,724; Support Services: $2,127
Enrollment, Drop-out Rates and Diploma Recipients by Race/Ethnicity

Category	Total	White	Black	Asian	AIAN	Hisp.
Enrollment (%)	100.0	86.6	11.0	0.9	0.0	0.5
Drop-out Rate (%)	2.4	2.5	2.2	0.0	n/a	0.0
H.S. Diplomas (#)	390	358	27	3	0	2

Sandy Valley Local SD

5362 State Route 183 NE • Magnolia, OH 44643-8481
(330) 866-3339 • http://cardweb.stark.k12.oh.us/
Grade Span: PK-12; **Agency Type:** 2
Schools: 4
2 Primary; 1 Middle; 1 High; 0 Other Level
4 Regular; 0 Special Education; 0 Vocational; 0 Alternative
0 Magnet; 0 Charter; 4 Title I Eligible; 3 School-wide Title I
Students: 1,587 (52.7% male; 47.3% female)
Individual Education Program: 217 (13.7%);
English Language Learner: 2 (0.1%); Migrant: n/a
Eligible for Free Lunch Program: 306 (19.3%)
Eligible for Reduced-Price Lunch Program: 131 (8.3%)
Teachers: 101.2 (15.7 to 1)
Librarians/Media Specialists: 1.0 (1,587.0 to 1)
Guidance Counselors: 2.0 (793.5 to 1)
Current Spending: ($ per student per year):
Total: $6,025; Instruction: $3,729; Support Services: $2,003
Enrollment, Drop-out Rates and Diploma Recipients by Race/Ethnicity

Category	Total	White	Black	Asian	AIAN	Hisp.
Enrollment (%)	100.0	99.2	0.5	0.1	0.0	0.2
Drop-out Rate (%)	2.4	2.2	0.0	0.0	n/a	25.0
H.S. Diplomas (#)	113	108	3	0	0	2

Summit County

Akron City SD

70 N Broadway St • Akron, OH 44308-1911
(330) 761-1661 • http://www.akronschools.com/
Grade Span: KG-12; **Agency Type:** 1
Schools: 61
40 Primary; 10 Middle; 8 High; 3 Other Level
58 Regular; 0 Special Education; 1 Vocational; 2 Alternative
0 Magnet; 0 Charter; 47 Title I Eligible; 34 School-wide Title I
Students: 29,532 (50.8% male; 49.2% female)
Individual Education Program: 4,597 (15.6%);
English Language Learner: 341 (1.2%); Migrant: n/a
Eligible for Free Lunch Program: 14,149 (47.9%)
Eligible for Reduced-Price Lunch Program: 2,104 (7.1%)
Teachers: 2,550.1 (11.6 to 1)
Librarians/Media Specialists: 17.0 (1,737.2 to 1)
Guidance Counselors: 58.0 (509.2 to 1)
Current Spending: ($ per student per year):
Total: $8,093; Instruction: $4,847; Support Services: $2,988
Enrollment, Drop-out Rates and Diploma Recipients by Race/Ethnicity

Category	Total	White	Black	Asian	AIAN	Hisp.
Enrollment (%)	100.0	47.2	47.9	1.8	0.1	0.8
Drop-out Rate (%)	6.4	5.9	7.0	3.4	0.0	15.0
H.S. Diplomas (#)	1,526	805	651	49	2	16

Barberton City SD

479 Norton Ave • Barberton, OH 44203-1737
(330) 753-1025 • http://www.barberton.summit.k12.oh.us/
Grade Span: PK-12; **Agency Type:** 1
Schools: 11
7 Primary; 2 Middle; 2 High; 0 Other Level
10 Regular; 1 Special Education; 0 Vocational; 0 Alternative
0 Magnet; 0 Charter; 8 Title I Eligible; 8 School-wide Title I
Students: 4,616 (51.9% male; 48.1% female)
Individual Education Program: 679 (14.7%);
English Language Learner: 66 (1.4%); Migrant: n/a
Eligible for Free Lunch Program: 1,581 (34.3%)
Eligible for Reduced-Price Lunch Program: 471 (10.2%)
Teachers: 349.4 (13.2 to 1)
Librarians/Media Specialists: 3.0 (1,538.7 to 1)
Guidance Counselors: 8.0 (577.0 to 1)
Current Spending: ($ per student per year):
Total: $7,826; Instruction: $4,579; Support Services: $2,889

Enrollment, Drop-out Rates and Diploma Recipients by Race/Ethnicity

Category	Total	White	Black	Asian	AIAN	Hisp.
Enrollment (%)	100.0	85.7	11.8	0.4	0.1	0.6
Drop-out Rate (%)	6.3	5.9	10.2	0.0	0.0	50.0
H.S. Diplomas (#)	264	244	18	0	2	0

Copley-Fairlawn City SD

3797 Ridgewood Rd • Copley, OH 44321-1665
(330) 664-4800 • http://www.copley.summit.k12.oh.us/
Grade Span: PK-12; **Agency Type:** 1
Schools: 5
3 Primary; 1 Middle; 1 High; 0 Other Level
5 Regular; 0 Special Education; 0 Vocational; 0 Alternative
0 Magnet; 0 Charter; 3 Title I Eligible; 0 School-wide Title I
Students: 3,174 (50.9% male; 49.1% female)
Individual Education Program: 298 (9.4%);
English Language Learner: 174 (5.5%); Migrant: n/a
Eligible for Free Lunch Program: 168 (5.3%)
Eligible for Reduced-Price Lunch Program: 76 (2.4%)
Teachers: 196.6 (16.1 to 1)
Librarians/Media Specialists: 1.0 (3,174.0 to 1)
Guidance Counselors: 6.6 (480.9 to 1)
Current Spending: ($ per student per year):
Total: $7,785; Instruction: $4,664; Support Services: $2,885

Enrollment, Drop-out Rates and Diploma Recipients by Race/Ethnicity

Category	Total	White	Black	Asian	AIAN	Hisp.
Enrollment (%)	100.0	79.9	11.9	4.9	0.4	1.0
Drop-out Rate (%)	1.2	1.4	0.0	0.0	0.0	0.0
H.S. Diplomas (#)	211	167	32	5	0	2

Coventry Local SD

3257 Cormany Rd • Akron, OH 44319-1425
(330) 644-8489
Grade Span: PK-12; **Agency Type:** 2
Schools: 6
3 Primary; 1 Middle; 1 High; 1 Other Level
6 Regular; 0 Special Education; 0 Vocational; 0 Alternative
0 Magnet; 0 Charter; 6 Title I Eligible; 0 School-wide Title I
Students: 2,502 (50.2% male; 49.8% female)
Individual Education Program: 222 (8.9%);
English Language Learner: 0 (0.0%); Migrant: n/a
Eligible for Free Lunch Program: 376 (15.0%)
Eligible for Reduced-Price Lunch Program: 145 (5.8%)
Teachers: 141.4 (17.7 to 1)
Librarians/Media Specialists: 1.0 (2,502.0 to 1)
Guidance Counselors: 4.0 (625.5 to 1)
Current Spending: ($ per student per year):
Total: $6,075; Instruction: $3,571; Support Services: $2,254

Enrollment, Drop-out Rates and Diploma Recipients by Race/Ethnicity

Category	Total	White	Black	Asian	AIAN	Hisp.
Enrollment (%)	100.0	96.4	1.7	0.6	0.2	0.2
Drop-out Rate (%)	2.8	2.8	0.0	0.0	n/a	0.0
H.S. Diplomas (#)	178	175	2	1	0	0

Cuyahoga Falls City SD

PO Box 396 • Cuyahoga Falls, OH 44222-0396
(330) 926-3800
Grade Span: PK-12; **Agency Type:** 1
Schools: 13
7 Primary; 3 Middle; 1 High; 1 Other Level
11 Regular; 0 Special Education; 1 Vocational; 0 Alternative
0 Magnet; 0 Charter; 7 Title I Eligible; 0 School-wide Title I
Students: 5,411 (51.5% male; 48.5% female)
Individual Education Program: 713 (13.2%);
English Language Learner: 114 (2.1%); Migrant: n/a
Eligible for Free Lunch Program: 563 (10.4%)
Eligible for Reduced-Price Lunch Program: 386 (7.1%)
Teachers: 360.9 (15.0 to 1)
Librarians/Media Specialists: 4.0 (1,352.8 to 1)
Guidance Counselors: 9.0 (601.2 to 1)
Current Spending: ($ per student per year):
Total: $6,606; Instruction: $3,987; Support Services: $2,396

Enrollment, Drop-out Rates and Diploma Recipients by Race/Ethnicity

Category	Total	White	Black	Asian	AIAN	Hisp.
Enrollment (%)	100.0	96.3	1.7	1.1	0.2	0.4
Drop-out Rate (%)	2.6	2.6	0.0	0.0	25.0	0.0
H.S. Diplomas (#)	360	353	2	3	1	1

Green Local SD

PO Box 218 • Green, OH 44232-0218
(330) 896-7500 • http://green.summit.k12.oh.us/
Grade Span: PK-12; **Agency Type:** 2
Schools: 5
3 Primary; 1 Middle; 1 High; 0 Other Level
5 Regular; 0 Special Education; 0 Vocational; 0 Alternative
0 Magnet; 0 Charter; 4 Title I Eligible; 0 School-wide Title I
Students: 4,184 (52.8% male; 47.2% female)
Individual Education Program: 503 (12.0%);
English Language Learner: 33 (0.8%); Migrant: n/a
Eligible for Free Lunch Program: 280 (6.7%)
Eligible for Reduced-Price Lunch Program: 130 (3.1%)
Teachers: 257.6 (16.2 to 1)
Librarians/Media Specialists: 4.0 (1,046.0 to 1)
Guidance Counselors: 10.2 (410.2 to 1)
Current Spending: ($ per student per year):
Total: $6,447; Instruction: $3,926; Support Services: $2,283

Enrollment, Drop-out Rates and Diploma Recipients by Race/Ethnicity

Category	Total	White	Black	Asian	AIAN	Hisp.
Enrollment (%)	100.0	96.4	0.8	1.5	0.1	0.3
Drop-out Rate (%)	0.4	0.4	0.0	0.0	n/a	0.0
H.S. Diplomas (#)	247	243	0	4	0	0

Hudson City SD

2400 Hudson Aurora Rd • Hudson, OH 44236-2322
(330) 653-1200 • http://www.hudson.edu/hcsd/
Grade Span: PK-12; **Agency Type:** 1
Schools: 6
3 Primary; 2 Middle; 1 High; 0 Other Level
6 Regular; 0 Special Education; 0 Vocational; 0 Alternative
0 Magnet; 0 Charter; 0 Title I Eligible; 0 School-wide Title I
Students: 5,562 (53.2% male; 46.8% female)
Individual Education Program: 558 (10.0%);
English Language Learner: 24 (0.4%); Migrant: n/a
Eligible for Free Lunch Program: 62 (1.1%)
Eligible for Reduced-Price Lunch Program: 14 (0.3%)
Teachers: 355.8 (15.6 to 1)
Librarians/Media Specialists: 7.0 (794.6 to 1)
Guidance Counselors: 13.5 (412.0 to 1)
Current Spending: ($ per student per year):
Total: $8,116; Instruction: $4,755; Support Services: $3,122

Enrollment, Drop-out Rates and Diploma Recipients by Race/Ethnicity

Category	Total	White	Black	Asian	AIAN	Hisp.
Enrollment (%)	100.0	95.1	0.8	2.8	0.0	0.5
Drop-out Rate (%)	0.9	0.9	10.0	0.0	0.0	0.0
H.S. Diplomas (#)	381	364	2	14	1	0

Manchester Local SD

6075 Manchester Rd • Akron, OH 44319-4654
(330) 882-6926
Grade Span: PK-12; **Agency Type:** 2
Schools: 3
1 Primary; 1 Middle; 1 High; 0 Other Level
3 Regular; 0 Special Education; 0 Vocational; 0 Alternative
0 Magnet; 0 Charter; 2 Title I Eligible; 0 School-wide Title I
Students: 1,500 (49.6% male; 50.4% female)
Individual Education Program: 127 (8.5%);
English Language Learner: 0 (0.0%); Migrant: n/a
Eligible for Free Lunch Program: 86 (5.7%)
Eligible for Reduced-Price Lunch Program: 33 (2.2%)
Teachers: 84.6 (17.7 to 1)
Librarians/Media Specialists: 1.0 (1,500.0 to 1)
Guidance Counselors: 3.0 (500.0 to 1)
Current Spending: ($ per student per year):
Total: $6,362; Instruction: $3,575; Support Services: $2,598

Enrollment, Drop-out Rates and Diploma Recipients by Race/Ethnicity

Category	Total	White	Black	Asian	AIAN	Hisp.
Enrollment (%)	100.0	98.5	0.5	0.5	0.1	0.5
Drop-out Rate (%)	2.2	2.1	0.0	0.0	n/a	100.0
H.S. Diplomas (#)	133	131	1	1	0	0

Nordonia Hills City SD

9370 Olde Eight Rd • Northfield, OH 44067-2097
(330) 467-0580
Grade Span: PK-12; **Agency Type:** 1
Schools: 6
3 Primary; 2 Middle; 1 High; 0 Other Level
6 Regular; 0 Special Education; 0 Vocational; 0 Alternative
0 Magnet; 0 Charter; 3 Title I Eligible; 0 School-wide Title I
Students: 3,736 (51.5% male; 48.5% female)
Individual Education Program: 434 (11.6%);
English Language Learner: 52 (1.4%); Migrant: n/a
Eligible for Free Lunch Program: 199 (5.3%)
Eligible for Reduced-Price Lunch Program: 162 (4.3%)
Teachers: 242.6 (15.4 to 1)
Librarians/Media Specialists: 2.0 (1,868.0 to 1)
Guidance Counselors: 9.0 (415.1 to 1)
Current Spending: ($ per student per year):
Total: $7,545; Instruction: $4,229; Support Services: $3,057

Enrollment, Drop-out Rates and Diploma Recipients by Race/Ethnicity

Category	Total	White	Black	Asian	AIAN	Hisp.
Enrollment (%)	100.0	91.1	5.3	2.2	0.1	0.4
Drop-out Rate (%)	2.6	2.7	3.0	0.0	n/a	0.0
H.S. Diplomas (#)	309	281	15	11	0	1

Norton City SD

4128 Cleveland Massillon Rd • Norton, OH 44203-5633
(330) 825-0863
Grade Span: PK-12; **Agency Type:** 1
Schools: 6
4 Primary; 1 Middle; 1 High; 0 Other Level
6 Regular; 0 Special Education; 0 Vocational; 0 Alternative
0 Magnet; 0 Charter; 4 Title I Eligible; 0 School-wide Title I
Students: 2,598 (51.0% male; 49.0% female)
Individual Education Program: 242 (9.3%);
English Language Learner: 10 (0.4%); Migrant: n/a
Eligible for Free Lunch Program: 264 (10.2%)
Eligible for Reduced-Price Lunch Program: 132 (5.1%)
Teachers: 157.5 (16.5 to 1)
Librarians/Media Specialists: 1.0 (2,598.0 to 1)
Guidance Counselors: 3.0 (866.0 to 1)
Current Spending: ($ per student per year):
Total: $6,537; Instruction: $3,994; Support Services: $2,298
Enrollment, Drop-out Rates and Diploma Recipients by Race/Ethnicity

Category	Total	White	Black	Asian	AIAN	Hisp.
Enrollment (%)	100.0	97.1	1.1	0.5	0.1	0.5
Drop-out Rate (%)	1.5	1.0	20.0	25.0	n/a	33.3
H.S. Diplomas (#)	183	178	0	2	0	3

Revere Local SD

PO Box 340 • Bath, OH 44210-0340
(330) 666-4155 • http://www.edline.net/InterstitialLogin.page
Grade Span: KG-12; **Agency Type:** 2
Schools: 4
1 Primary; 2 Middle; 1 High; 0 Other Level
4 Regular; 0 Special Education; 0 Vocational; 0 Alternative
0 Magnet; 0 Charter; 2 Title I Eligible; 0 School-wide Title I
Students: 2,872 (52.0% male; 48.0% female)
Individual Education Program: 236 (8.2%);
English Language Learner: 9 (0.3%); Migrant: n/a
Eligible for Free Lunch Program: 57 (2.0%)
Eligible for Reduced-Price Lunch Program: 16 (0.6%)
Teachers: 176.1 (16.3 to 1)
Librarians/Media Specialists: 2.0 (1,436.0 to 1)
Guidance Counselors: 6.0 (478.7 to 1)
Current Spending: ($ per student per year):
Total: $7,282; Instruction: $4,502; Support Services: $2,594
Enrollment, Drop-out Rates and Diploma Recipients by Race/Ethnicity

Category	Total	White	Black	Asian	AIAN	Hisp.
Enrollment (%)	100.0	97.9	0.4	1.2	0.0	0.3
Drop-out Rate (%)	1.6	1.2	0.0	0.0	16.7	50.0
H.S. Diplomas (#)	225	218	1	4	0	1

Springfield Local SD

2960 Sanitarium Rd • Akron, OH 44312-4467
(330) 798-1111
Grade Span: PK-12; **Agency Type:** 2
Schools: 7
4 Primary; 2 Middle; 1 High; 0 Other Level
7 Regular; 0 Special Education; 0 Vocational; 0 Alternative
0 Magnet; 0 Charter; 5 Title I Eligible; 0 School-wide Title I
Students: 3,078 (51.0% male; 49.0% female)
Individual Education Program: 563 (18.3%);
English Language Learner: 0 (0.0%); Migrant: n/a
Eligible for Free Lunch Program: 683 (22.2%)
Eligible for Reduced-Price Lunch Program: 269 (8.7%)
Teachers: 205.9 (14.9 to 1)
Librarians/Media Specialists: 2.0 (1,539.0 to 1)
Guidance Counselors: 7.0 (439.7 to 1)
Current Spending: ($ per student per year):
Total: $6,498; Instruction: $3,861; Support Services: $2,425
Enrollment, Drop-out Rates and Diploma Recipients by Race/Ethnicity

Category	Total	White	Black	Asian	AIAN	Hisp.
Enrollment (%)	100.0	96.7	1.1	1.1	0.3	0.5
Drop-out Rate (%)	3.4	3.5	0.0	0.0	0.0	0.0
H.S. Diplomas (#)	191	188	2	1	0	0

Stow-Munroe Falls City SD

4350 Allen Rd • Stow, OH 44224-1032
(330) 689-5445
Grade Span: PK-12; **Agency Type:** 1
Schools: 9
6 Primary; 2 Middle; 1 High; 0 Other Level
9 Regular; 0 Special Education; 0 Vocational; 0 Alternative
0 Magnet; 0 Charter; 6 Title I Eligible; 0 School-wide Title I
Students: 5,963 (52.1% male; 47.9% female)
Individual Education Program: 618 (10.4%);
English Language Learner: 15 (0.3%); Migrant: n/a
Eligible for Free Lunch Program: 254 (4.3%)
Eligible for Reduced-Price Lunch Program: 166 (2.8%)
Teachers: 340.8 (17.5 to 1)
Librarians/Media Specialists: 6.0 (993.8 to 1)
Guidance Counselors: 9.2 (648.2 to 1)
Current Spending: ($ per student per year):
Total: $6,794; Instruction: $4,544; Support Services: $2,045
Enrollment, Drop-out Rates and Diploma Recipients by Race/Ethnicity

Category	Total	White	Black	Asian	AIAN	Hisp.
Enrollment (%)	100.0	94.7	1.7	2.1	0.0	0.5
Drop-out Rate (%)	1.6	1.6	0.0	0.0	0.0	0.0
H.S. Diplomas (#)	420	408	3	6	0	0

Tallmadge City SD

486 E Ave • Tallmadge, OH 44278-2000
(330) 633-3291
Grade Span: PK-12; **Agency Type:** 1
Schools: 5
2 Primary; 2 Middle; 1 High; 0 Other Level
5 Regular; 0 Special Education; 0 Vocational; 0 Alternative
0 Magnet; 0 Charter; 4 Title I Eligible; 0 School-wide Title I
Students: 2,743 (54.5% male; 45.5% female)
Individual Education Program: 315 (11.5%);
English Language Learner: 19 (0.7%); Migrant: n/a
Eligible for Free Lunch Program: 216 (7.9%)
Eligible for Reduced-Price Lunch Program: 68 (2.5%)
Teachers: 175.5 (15.6 to 1)
Librarians/Media Specialists: 2.0 (1,371.5 to 1)
Guidance Counselors: 6.0 (457.2 to 1)
Current Spending: ($ per student per year):
Total: $7,046; Instruction: $4,503; Support Services: $2,377
Enrollment, Drop-out Rates and Diploma Recipients by Race/Ethnicity

Category	Total	White	Black	Asian	AIAN	Hisp.
Enrollment (%)	100.0	94.9	2.5	1.0	0.1	0.5
Drop-out Rate (%)	1.4	1.4	0.0	0.0	0.0	0.0
H.S. Diplomas (#)	185	178	3	4	0	0

Twinsburg City SD

11136 Ravenna Rd • Twinsburg, OH 44087-1022
(330) 486-2000
Grade Span: PK-12; **Agency Type:** 1
Schools: 5
2 Primary; 2 Middle; 1 High; 0 Other Level
5 Regular; 0 Special Education; 0 Vocational; 0 Alternative
0 Magnet; 0 Charter; 4 Title I Eligible; 0 School-wide Title I
Students: 3,847 (51.5% male; 48.5% female)
Individual Education Program: 434 (11.3%);
English Language Learner: 8 (0.2%); Migrant: n/a
Eligible for Free Lunch Program: 313 (8.1%)
Eligible for Reduced-Price Lunch Program: 123 (3.2%)
Teachers: 234.2 (16.4 to 1)
Librarians/Media Specialists: 4.0 (961.8 to 1)
Guidance Counselors: 8.5 (452.6 to 1)
Current Spending: ($ per student per year):
Total: $8,078; Instruction: $5,016; Support Services: $2,809
Enrollment, Drop-out Rates and Diploma Recipients by Race/Ethnicity

Category	Total	White	Black	Asian	AIAN	Hisp.
Enrollment (%)	100.0	73.0	21.7	3.1	0.0	0.5
Drop-out Rate (%)	1.1	0.9	1.9	0.0	n/a	0.0
H.S. Diplomas (#)	206	162	36	4	0	2

Woodridge Local SD

4411 Quick Rd • Peninsula, OH 44264-9706
(330) 928-9074
Grade Span: PK-12; **Agency Type:** 2
Schools: 4
2 Primary; 1 Middle; 1 High; 0 Other Level
4 Regular; 0 Special Education; 0 Vocational; 0 Alternative
0 Magnet; 0 Charter; 3 Title I Eligible; 0 School-wide Title I
Students: 1,821 (52.0% male; 48.0% female)
Individual Education Program: 280 (15.4%);
English Language Learner: 20 (1.1%); Migrant: 58 (3.2%)
Eligible for Free Lunch Program: 402 (22.1%)
Eligible for Reduced-Price Lunch Program: 78 (4.3%)
Teachers: 131.7 (13.8 to 1)
Librarians/Media Specialists: 4.0 (455.3 to 1)
Guidance Counselors: 5.0 (364.2 to 1)
Current Spending: ($ per student per year):
Total: $7,833; Instruction: $4,409; Support Services: $3,193

Enrollment, Drop-out Rates and Diploma Recipients by Race/Ethnicity

Category	Total	White	Black	Asian	AIAN	Hisp.
Enrollment (%)	100.0	77.2	17.0	2.2	0.2	1.0
Drop-out Rate (%)	2.3	1.9	5.4	0.0	0.0	0.0
H.S. Diplomas (#)	96	87	7	1	1	0

Trumbull County

Brookfield Local SD

PO Box 209 • Brookfield, OH 44403-0209
(330) 448-4930 • http://www.brookfield.k12.oh.us/
Grade Span: PK-12; **Agency Type:** 2
Schools: 5
3 Primary; 0 Middle; 1 High; 1 Other Level
5 Regular; 0 Special Education; 0 Vocational; 0 Alternative
0 Magnet; 0 Charter; 4 Title I Eligible; 3 School-wide Title I
Students: 1,503 (52.9% male; 47.1% female)
Individual Education Program: 244 (16.2%);
English Language Learner: 0 (0.0%); Migrant: n/a
Eligible for Free Lunch Program: 408 (27.1%)
Eligible for Reduced-Price Lunch Program: 191 (12.7%)
Teachers: 92.5 (16.2 to 1)
Librarians/Media Specialists: 3.0 (501.0 to 1)
Guidance Counselors: 4.0 (375.8 to 1)
Current Spending: ($ per student per year):
Total: $6,443; Instruction: $4,031; Support Services: $2,169
Enrollment, Drop-out Rates and Diploma Recipients by Race/Ethnicity

Category	Total	White	Black	Asian	AIAN	Hisp.
Enrollment (%)	100.0	93.7	4.3	0.3	0.1	0.3
Drop-out Rate (%)	1.5	1.5	0.0	0.0	n/a	0.0
H.S. Diplomas (#)	118	108	7	1	0	0

Champion Local SD

5759 Mahoning Ave NW • Warren, OH 44483-1139
(330) 847-2330 • http://www.champion.k12.oh.us/
Grade Span: PK-12; **Agency Type:** 2
Schools: 3
1 Primary; 1 Middle; 1 High; 0 Other Level
3 Regular; 0 Special Education; 0 Vocational; 0 Alternative
0 Magnet; 0 Charter; 2 Title I Eligible; 0 School-wide Title I
Students: 1,753 (51.4% male; 48.6% female)
Individual Education Program: 198 (11.3%);
English Language Learner: 0 (0.0%); Migrant: n/a
Eligible for Free Lunch Program: 162 (9.2%)
Eligible for Reduced-Price Lunch Program: 85 (4.8%)
Teachers: 108.8 (16.1 to 1)
Librarians/Media Specialists: 3.0 (584.3 to 1)
Guidance Counselors: 4.0 (438.3 to 1)
Current Spending: ($ per student per year):
Total: $6,543; Instruction: $4,060; Support Services: $2,270
Enrollment, Drop-out Rates and Diploma Recipients by Race/Ethnicity

Category	Total	White	Black	Asian	AIAN	Hisp.
Enrollment (%)	100.0	98.9	0.6	0.2	0.0	0.1
Drop-out Rate (%)	1.2	1.2	0.0	0.0	n/a	n/a
H.S. Diplomas (#)	148	143	5	0	0	0

Girard City SD

31 N Ward Ave • Girard, OH 44420-2722
(330) 545-2596
Grade Span: PK-12; **Agency Type:** 1
Schools: 5
1 Primary; 2 Middle; 1 High; 0 Other Level
4 Regular; 0 Special Education; 0 Vocational; 0 Alternative
0 Magnet; 0 Charter; 2 Title I Eligible; 1 School-wide Title I
Students: 1,758 (51.9% male; 48.1% female)
Individual Education Program: 241 (13.7%);
English Language Learner: 11 (0.6%); Migrant: n/a
Eligible for Free Lunch Program: 471 (26.8%)
Eligible for Reduced-Price Lunch Program: 135 (7.7%)
Teachers: 103.0 (17.1 to 1)
Librarians/Media Specialists: 1.0 (1,758.0 to 1)
Guidance Counselors: 3.0 (586.0 to 1)
Current Spending: ($ per student per year):
Total: $6,353; Instruction: $4,240; Support Services: $1,863
Enrollment, Drop-out Rates and Diploma Recipients by Race/Ethnicity

Category	Total	White	Black	Asian	AIAN	Hisp.
Enrollment (%)	100.0	95.3	3.6	0.2	0.1	0.3
Drop-out Rate (%)	1.9	1.7	5.3	0.0	n/a	0.0
H.S. Diplomas (#)	119	114	4	1	0	0

Howland Local SD

8200 S St SE • Warren, OH 44484-2447
(330) 856-8200 • http://www.howlandschools.com/
Grade Span: PK-12; **Agency Type:** 2
Schools: 6
4 Primary; 1 Middle; 1 High; 0 Other Level
6 Regular; 0 Special Education; 0 Vocational; 0 Alternative
0 Magnet; 0 Charter; 4 Title I Eligible; 0 School-wide Title I
Students: 3,298 (51.2% male; 48.8% female)
Individual Education Program: 475 (14.4%);
English Language Learner: 15 (0.5%); Migrant: n/a
Eligible for Free Lunch Program: 311 (9.4%)
Eligible for Reduced-Price Lunch Program: 142 (4.3%)
Teachers: 202.4 (16.3 to 1)
Librarians/Media Specialists: 3.0 (1,099.3 to 1)
Guidance Counselors: 7.0 (471.1 to 1)
Current Spending: ($ per student per year):
Total: $6,705; Instruction: $3,966; Support Services: $2,530
Enrollment, Drop-out Rates and Diploma Recipients by Race/Ethnicity

Category	Total	White	Black	Asian	AIAN	Hisp.
Enrollment (%)	100.0	92.2	3.9	1.5	0.2	0.7
Drop-out Rate (%)	1.4	1.4	0.0	3.3	0.0	0.0
H.S. Diplomas (#)	230	215	6	5	1	1

Hubbard Ex Vill SD

150 Hall Ave • Hubbard, OH 44425-2065
(330) 534-1921
Grade Span: PK-12; **Agency Type:** 1
Schools: 3
2 Primary; 0 Middle; 1 High; 0 Other Level
3 Regular; 0 Special Education; 0 Vocational; 0 Alternative
0 Magnet; 0 Charter; 2 Title I Eligible; 0 School-wide Title I
Students: 2,301 (50.0% male; 50.0% female)
Individual Education Program: 248 (10.8%);
English Language Learner: 2 (0.1%); Migrant: n/a
Eligible for Free Lunch Program: 413 (17.9%)
Eligible for Reduced-Price Lunch Program: 245 (10.6%)
Teachers: 131.0 (17.6 to 1)
Librarians/Media Specialists: 3.0 (767.0 to 1)
Guidance Counselors: 5.0 (460.2 to 1)
Current Spending: ($ per student per year):
Total: $6,306; Instruction: $3,780; Support Services: $2,289
Enrollment, Drop-out Rates and Diploma Recipients by Race/Ethnicity

Category	Total	White	Black	Asian	AIAN	Hisp.
Enrollment (%)	100.0	94.4	3.3	0.5	0.1	0.5
Drop-out Rate (%)	2.4	2.4	4.2	0.0	n/a	0.0
H.S. Diplomas (#)	199	191	7	0	0	0

Labrae Local SD

1015 N Leavitt Rd • Leavittsburg, OH 44430-9644
(330) 898-1393
Grade Span: PK-12; **Agency Type:** 2
Schools: 4
3 Primary; 0 Middle; 1 High; 0 Other Level
4 Regular; 0 Special Education; 0 Vocational; 0 Alternative
0 Magnet; 0 Charter; 4 Title I Eligible; 0 School-wide Title I
Students: 1,534 (50.8% male; 49.2% female)
Individual Education Program: 205 (13.4%);
English Language Learner: 0 (0.0%); Migrant: n/a
Eligible for Free Lunch Program: 450 (29.3%)
Eligible for Reduced-Price Lunch Program: 201 (13.1%)
Teachers: 98.0 (15.7 to 1)
Librarians/Media Specialists: 1.0 (1,534.0 to 1)
Guidance Counselors: 3.0 (511.3 to 1)
Current Spending: ($ per student per year):
Total: $6,893; Instruction: $4,292; Support Services: $2,308
Enrollment, Drop-out Rates and Diploma Recipients by Race/Ethnicity

Category	Total	White	Black	Asian	AIAN	Hisp.
Enrollment (%)	100.0	92.8	5.4	0.1	0.0	0.2
Drop-out Rate (%)	3.9	4.3	0.0	n/a	n/a	0.0
H.S. Diplomas (#)	102	84	15	0	0	1

Lakeview Local SD

300 Hillman Dr • Cortland, OH 44410-1562
(330) 637-8741 • http://www.cboss.com/lakeview/
Grade Span: PK-12; **Agency Type:** 2
Schools: 4
2 Primary; 1 Middle; 1 High; 0 Other Level
4 Regular; 0 Special Education; 0 Vocational; 0 Alternative
0 Magnet; 0 Charter; 2 Title I Eligible; 0 School-wide Title I
Students: 2,242 (51.0% male; 49.0% female)
Individual Education Program: 218 (9.7%);
English Language Learner: 4 (0.2%); Migrant: n/a
Eligible for Free Lunch Program: 171 (7.6%)
Eligible for Reduced-Price Lunch Program: 68 (3.0%)
Teachers: 120.4 (18.6 to 1)
Librarians/Media Specialists: 3.0 (747.3 to 1)
Guidance Counselors: 5.0 (448.4 to 1)
Current Spending: ($ per student per year):
Total: $6,079; Instruction: $3,673; Support Services: $2,191

Enrollment, Drop-out Rates and Diploma Recipients by Race/Ethnicity

Category	Total	White	Black	Asian	AIAN	Hisp.
Enrollment (%)	100.0	96.8	0.9	0.4	0.1	0.7
Drop-out Rate (%)	1.1	1.1	0.0	0.0	n/a	n/a
H.S. Diplomas (#)	175	174	0	1	0	0

Liberty Local SD

4115 Shady Rd • Youngstown, OH 44505-1353
(330) 759-0807 • http://www.liberty.k12.oh.us/
Grade Span: PK-12; **Agency Type:** 2
Schools: 3
1 Primary; 1 Middle; 1 High; 0 Other Level
3 Regular; 0 Special Education; 0 Vocational; 0 Alternative
0 Magnet; 0 Charter; 2 Title I Eligible; 0 School-wide Title I
Students: 1,817 (52.7% male; 47.3% female)
Individual Education Program: 153 (8.4%);
English Language Learner: 0 (0.0%); Migrant: n/a
Eligible for Free Lunch Program: 408 (22.5%)
Eligible for Reduced-Price Lunch Program: 86 (4.7%)
Teachers: 107.7 (16.9 to 1)
Librarians/Media Specialists: 1.0 (1,817.0 to 1)
Guidance Counselors: 4.0 (454.3 to 1)
Current Spending: ($ per student per year):
Total: $6,599; Instruction: $3,952; Support Services: $2,427
Enrollment, Drop-out Rates and Diploma Recipients by Race/Ethnicity

Category	Total	White	Black	Asian	AIAN	Hisp.
Enrollment (%)	100.0	76.9	20.2	1.4	0.1	0.7
Drop-out Rate (%)	1.1	1.0	1.8	0.0	n/a	0.0
H.S. Diplomas (#)	150	120	22	6	0	2

Newton Falls Ex Vill SD

909 1/2 Milton Blvd • Newton Falls, OH 44444-9707
(330) 872-5445
Grade Span: PK-12; **Agency Type:** 1
Schools: 4
2 Primary; 1 Middle; 1 High; 0 Other Level
4 Regular; 0 Special Education; 0 Vocational; 0 Alternative
0 Magnet; 0 Charter; 3 Title I Eligible; 0 School-wide Title I
Students: 1,537 (51.5% male; 48.5% female)
Individual Education Program: 205 (13.3%);
English Language Learner: 0 (0.0%); Migrant: n/a
Eligible for Free Lunch Program: 299 (19.5%)
Eligible for Reduced-Price Lunch Program: 122 (7.9%)
Teachers: 89.1 (17.3 to 1)
Librarians/Media Specialists: 1.0 (1,537.0 to 1)
Guidance Counselors: 3.0 (512.3 to 1)
Current Spending: ($ per student per year):
Total: $5,933; Instruction: $3,660; Support Services: $2,019
Enrollment, Drop-out Rates and Diploma Recipients by Race/Ethnicity

Category	Total	White	Black	Asian	AIAN	Hisp.
Enrollment (%)	100.0	98.0	1.3	0.0	0.1	0.2
Drop-out Rate (%)	2.3	2.4	0.0	0.0	n/a	0.0
H.S. Diplomas (#)	89	89	0	0	0	0

Niles City SD

100 W St • Niles, OH 44446-2644
(330) 652-2509
Grade Span: PK-12; **Agency Type:** 1
Schools: 7
5 Primary; 1 Middle; 1 High; 0 Other Level
7 Regular; 0 Special Education; 0 Vocational; 0 Alternative
0 Magnet; 0 Charter; 5 Title I Eligible; 0 School-wide Title I
Students: 2,869 (50.9% male; 49.1% female)
Individual Education Program: 375 (13.1%);
English Language Learner: 0 (0.0%); Migrant: n/a
Eligible for Free Lunch Program: 862 (30.0%)
Eligible for Reduced-Price Lunch Program: 218 (7.6%)
Teachers: 185.0 (15.5 to 1)
Librarians/Media Specialists: 2.0 (1,434.5 to 1)
Guidance Counselors: 5.0 (573.8 to 1)
Current Spending: ($ per student per year):
Total: $6,229; Instruction: $3,868; Support Services: $2,055
Enrollment, Drop-out Rates and Diploma Recipients by Race/Ethnicity

Category	Total	White	Black	Asian	AIAN	Hisp.
Enrollment (%)	100.0	95.2	4.0	0.3	0.0	0.3
Drop-out Rate (%)	6.5	6.5	6.7	n/a	n/a	0.0
H.S. Diplomas (#)	210	207	2	0	0	0

Warren City SD

261 Monroe St NW • Warren, OH 44483-4810
(330) 841-2321 • http://www.warrenschools.k12.oh.us/
Grade Span: KG-12; **Agency Type:** 1
Schools: 18
12 Primary; 2 Middle; 0 High; 4 Other Level
17 Regular; 0 Special Education; 1 Vocational; 0 Alternative
0 Magnet; 0 Charter; 14 Title I Eligible; 6 School-wide Title I
Students: 6,918 (50.4% male; 49.6% female)
Individual Education Program: 1,335 (19.3%);
English Language Learner: 1 (<0.1%); Migrant: n/a
Eligible for Free Lunch Program: 3,162 (45.7%)
Eligible for Reduced-Price Lunch Program: 589 (8.5%)
Teachers: 558.9 (12.4 to 1)
Librarians/Media Specialists: 4.0 (1,729.5 to 1)
Guidance Counselors: 11.5 (601.6 to 1)
Current Spending: ($ per student per year):
Total: $7,924; Instruction: $4,539; Support Services: $3,169
Enrollment, Drop-out Rates and Diploma Recipients by Race/Ethnicity

Category	Total	White	Black	Asian	AIAN	Hisp.
Enrollment (%)	100.0	51.6	42.9	0.2	0.1	0.4
Drop-out Rate (%)	6.8	7.7	5.7	0.0	n/a	6.3
H.S. Diplomas (#)	352	211	138	1	0	1

Tuscarawas County

Claymont City SD

201 N 3rd St • Dennison, OH 44621-1237
Mailing Address: PO Box 111 • Dennison, OH 44621-0111
(740) 922-5478 • http://www.claymont.k12.oh.us/
Grade Span: PK-12; **Agency Type:** 1
Schools: 6
3 Primary; 2 Middle; 1 High; 0 Other Level
6 Regular; 0 Special Education; 0 Vocational; 0 Alternative
0 Magnet; 0 Charter; 4 Title I Eligible; 4 School-wide Title I
Students: 2,332 (53.0% male; 47.0% female)
Individual Education Program: 501 (21.5%);
English Language Learner: 0 (0.0%); Migrant: n/a
Eligible for Free Lunch Program: 603 (25.9%)
Eligible for Reduced-Price Lunch Program: 185 (7.9%)
Teachers: 136.8 (17.0 to 1)
Librarians/Media Specialists: 2.0 (1,166.0 to 1)
Guidance Counselors: 5.0 (466.4 to 1)
Current Spending: ($ per student per year):
Total: $5,967; Instruction: $3,653; Support Services: $2,076
Enrollment, Drop-out Rates and Diploma Recipients by Race/Ethnicity

Category	Total	White	Black	Asian	AIAN	Hisp.
Enrollment (%)	100.0	97.3	1.3	0.1	0.0	0.1
Drop-out Rate (%)	2.1	2.0	0.0	0.0	n/a	25.0
H.S. Diplomas (#)	145	142	2	0	0	1

Dover City SD

219 W 6th St • Dover, OH 44622-2803
(330) 364-1906 • http://www.dover.k12.oh.us/
Grade Span: PK-12; **Agency Type:** 1
Schools: 5
3 Primary; 1 Middle; 1 High; 0 Other Level
5 Regular; 0 Special Education; 0 Vocational; 0 Alternative
0 Magnet; 0 Charter; 4 Title I Eligible; 0 School-wide Title I
Students: 2,619 (51.5% male; 48.5% female)
Individual Education Program: 396 (15.1%);
English Language Learner: 5 (0.2%); Migrant: n/a
Eligible for Free Lunch Program: 168 (6.4%)
Eligible for Reduced-Price Lunch Program: 63 (2.4%)
Teachers: 174.0 (15.1 to 1)
Librarians/Media Specialists: 1.0 (2,619.0 to 1)
Guidance Counselors: 3.0 (873.0 to 1)
Current Spending: ($ per student per year):
Total: $5,954; Instruction: $3,664; Support Services: $2,092
Enrollment, Drop-out Rates and Diploma Recipients by Race/Ethnicity

Category	Total	White	Black	Asian	AIAN	Hisp.
Enrollment (%)	100.0	97.2	1.2	0.4	0.0	0.3
Drop-out Rate (%)	2.0	2.0	0.0	0.0	0.0	0.0
H.S. Diplomas (#)	240	235	2	2	0	0

Indian Valley Local SD

PO Box 171 • Gnadenhutten, OH 44629-0171
(740) 254-4334
Grade Span: PK-12; **Agency Type:** 2
Schools: 4
2 Primary; 1 Middle; 1 High; 0 Other Level
4 Regular; 0 Special Education; 0 Vocational; 0 Alternative
0 Magnet; 0 Charter; 3 Title I Eligible; 2 School-wide Title I
Students: 1,939 (51.6% male; 48.4% female)
Individual Education Program: 295 (15.2%);
English Language Learner: 0 (0.0%); Migrant: n/a
Eligible for Free Lunch Program: 458 (23.6%)
Eligible for Reduced-Price Lunch Program: 218 (11.2%)
Teachers: 125.0 (15.5 to 1)
Librarians/Media Specialists: 0.2 (9,695.0 to 1)
Guidance Counselors: 2.5 (775.6 to 1)
Current Spending: ($ per student per year):
Total: $5,632; Instruction: $3,373; Support Services: $1,985

Enrollment, Drop-out Rates and Diploma Recipients by Race/Ethnicity

Category	Total	White	Black	Asian	AIAN	Hisp.
Enrollment (%)	100.0	98.8	0.1	0.1	0.0	0.4
Drop-out Rate (%)	2.5	2.5	n/a	n/a	n/a	n/a
H.S. Diplomas (#)	122	122	0	0	0	0

New Philadelphia City SD

248 Front Ave SW • New Philadelphia, OH 44663-2150
(330) 364-0600 • http://www.new-phila.k12.oh.us/
Grade Span: PK-12; **Agency Type:** 1
Schools: 8
6 Primary; 1 Middle; 1 High; 0 Other Level
8 Regular; 0 Special Education; 0 Vocational; 0 Alternative
0 Magnet; 0 Charter; 6 Title I Eligible; 0 School-wide Title I
Students: 3,260 (51.8% male; 48.2% female)
Individual Education Program: 529 (16.2%);
English Language Learner: 15 (0.5%); Migrant: n/a
Eligible for Free Lunch Program: 433 (13.3%)
Eligible for Reduced-Price Lunch Program: 84 (2.6%)
Teachers: 208.3 (15.7 to 1)
Librarians/Media Specialists: 1.0 (3,260.0 to 1)
Guidance Counselors: 2.8 (1,164.3 to 1)
Current Spending: ($ per student per year):
Total: $5,641; Instruction: $3,574; Support Services: $1,885

Enrollment, Drop-out Rates and Diploma Recipients by Race/Ethnicity

Category	Total	White	Black	Asian	AIAN	Hisp.
Enrollment (%)	100.0	94.8	1.1	0.3	0.2	1.2
Drop-out Rate (%)	2.3	2.3	0.0	0.0	n/a	0.0
H.S. Diplomas (#)	238	236	2	0	0	0

Tuscarawas Valley Local SD

2637 Tuscarawas Valley Rd NE • Zoarville, OH 44656-9692
(330) 859-2213
Grade Span: PK-12; **Agency Type:** 2
Schools: 5
3 Primary; 1 Middle; 1 High; 0 Other Level
5 Regular; 0 Special Education; 0 Vocational; 0 Alternative
0 Magnet; 0 Charter; 2 Title I Eligible; 0 School-wide Title I
Students: 1,767 (53.1% male; 46.9% female)
Individual Education Program: 197 (11.1%);
English Language Learner: 0 (0.0%); Migrant: n/a
Eligible for Free Lunch Program: 230 (13.0%)
Eligible for Reduced-Price Lunch Program: 127 (7.2%)
Teachers: 103.3 (17.1 to 1)
Librarians/Media Specialists: 1.0 (1,767.0 to 1)
Guidance Counselors: 3.0 (589.0 to 1)
Current Spending: ($ per student per year):
Total: $5,375; Instruction: $3,276; Support Services: $1,866

Enrollment, Drop-out Rates and Diploma Recipients by Race/Ethnicity

Category	Total	White	Black	Asian	AIAN	Hisp.
Enrollment (%)	100.0	98.9	0.5	0.1	0.1	0.0
Drop-out Rate (%)	2.7	2.7	0.0	n/a	0.0	n/a
H.S. Diplomas (#)	108	105	1	0	2	0

Union County

Marysville Ex Vill SD

1000 Edgewood Dr • Marysville, OH 43040-2105
(937) 644-8105 • http://www.marysville.k12.oh.us/site/
Grade Span: KG-12; **Agency Type:** 1
Schools: 8
5 Primary; 2 Middle; 1 High; 0 Other Level
8 Regular; 0 Special Education; 0 Vocational; 0 Alternative
0 Magnet; 0 Charter; 4 Title I Eligible; 0 School-wide Title I
Students: 4,608 (51.7% male; 48.3% female)
Individual Education Program: 664 (14.4%);
English Language Learner: 64 (1.4%); Migrant: n/a
Eligible for Free Lunch Program: 396 (8.6%)
Eligible for Reduced-Price Lunch Program: 166 (3.6%)
Teachers: 295.2 (15.6 to 1)
Librarians/Media Specialists: 2.0 (2,304.0 to 1)
Guidance Counselors: 12.0 (384.0 to 1)
Current Spending: ($ per student per year):
Total: $7,150; Instruction: $4,030; Support Services: $2,842

Enrollment, Drop-out Rates and Diploma Recipients by Race/Ethnicity

Category	Total	White	Black	Asian	AIAN	Hisp.
Enrollment (%)	100.0	97.2	0.7	0.6	0.1	0.4
Drop-out Rate (%)	1.3	1.3	0.0	12.5	0.0	0.0
H.S. Diplomas (#)	257	253	2	1	0	0

Van Wert County

Van Wert City SD

641 N Jefferson St • Van Wert, OH 45891-1167
(419) 238-0648
Grade Span: PK-12; **Agency Type:** 1
Schools: 7
5 Primary; 1 Middle; 1 High; 0 Other Level
7 Regular; 0 Special Education; 0 Vocational; 0 Alternative
0 Magnet; 0 Charter; 4 Title I Eligible; 0 School-wide Title I
Students: 2,312 (51.1% male; 48.9% female)
Individual Education Program: 372 (16.1%);
English Language Learner: 0 (0.0%); Migrant: n/a
Eligible for Free Lunch Program: 383 (16.6%)
Eligible for Reduced-Price Lunch Program: 153 (6.6%)
Teachers: 151.8 (15.2 to 1)
Librarians/Media Specialists: 1.0 (2,312.0 to 1)
Guidance Counselors: 4.0 (578.0 to 1)
Current Spending: ($ per student per year):
Total: $5,845; Instruction: $3,711; Support Services: $1,912

Enrollment, Drop-out Rates and Diploma Recipients by Race/Ethnicity

Category	Total	White	Black	Asian	AIAN	Hisp.
Enrollment (%)	100.0	92.3	1.8	0.8	0.2	2.2
Drop-out Rate (%)	2.8	2.6	7.1	0.0	n/a	5.9
H.S. Diplomas (#)	153	145	1	2	0	3

Vinton County

Vinton County Local SD

307 W High St • Mc Arthur, OH 45651-1093
(740) 596-5218
Grade Span: PK-12; **Agency Type:** 2
Schools: 7
5 Primary; 1 Middle; 1 High; 0 Other Level
7 Regular; 0 Special Education; 0 Vocational; 0 Alternative
0 Magnet; 0 Charter; 7 Title I Eligible; 5 School-wide Title I
Students: 2,641 (52.5% male; 47.5% female)
Individual Education Program: 455 (17.2%);
English Language Learner: 1 (<0.1%); Migrant: n/a
Eligible for Free Lunch Program: 1,141 (43.2%)
Eligible for Reduced-Price Lunch Program: 263 (10.0%)
Teachers: 172.6 (15.3 to 1)
Librarians/Media Specialists: 1.0 (2,641.0 to 1)
Guidance Counselors: 2.0 (1,320.5 to 1)
Current Spending: ($ per student per year):
Total: $6,098; Instruction: $3,301; Support Services: $2,494

Enrollment, Drop-out Rates and Diploma Recipients by Race/Ethnicity

Category	Total	White	Black	Asian	AIAN	Hisp.
Enrollment (%)	100.0	99.5	0.1	0.1	0.0	0.0
Drop-out Rate (%)	5.3	5.3	0.0	n/a	n/a	n/a
H.S. Diplomas (#)	144	143	1	0	0	0

Warren County

Carlisle Local SD

724 Fairview Dr • Carlisle, OH 45005-3148
(937) 746-0710 • http://www.carlisle-local.k12.oh.us/
Grade Span: KG-12; **Agency Type:** 2
Schools: 4
2 Primary; 1 Middle; 1 High; 0 Other Level
4 Regular; 0 Special Education; 0 Vocational; 0 Alternative
0 Magnet; 0 Charter; 2 Title I Eligible; 0 School-wide Title I
Students: 1,764 (52.1% male; 47.9% female)
Individual Education Program: 185 (10.5%);
English Language Learner: 4 (0.2%); Migrant: n/a
Eligible for Free Lunch Program: 174 (9.9%)
Eligible for Reduced-Price Lunch Program: 55 (3.1%)
Teachers: 116.7 (15.1 to 1)
Librarians/Media Specialists: 2.0 (882.0 to 1)
Guidance Counselors: 3.9 (452.3 to 1)
Current Spending: ($ per student per year):
Total: $6,565; Instruction: $3,736; Support Services: $2,524

Enrollment, Drop-out Rates and Diploma Recipients by Race/Ethnicity

Category	Total	White	Black	Asian	AIAN	Hisp.
Enrollment (%)	100.0	97.8	0.7	0.3	0.1	0.2
Drop-out Rate (%)	1.1	1.1	0.0	n/a	n/a	0.0
H.S. Diplomas (#)	111	111	0	0	0	0

Franklin City SD

150 E 6th St • Franklin, OH 45005-2559
(937) 746-1699 • http://www.franklin-city.k12.oh.us/
Grade Span: KG-12; **Agency Type:** 1
Schools: 8
6 Primary; 1 Middle; 1 High; 0 Other Level
8 Regular; 0 Special Education; 0 Vocational; 0 Alternative

0 Magnet; 0 Charter; 4 Title I Eligible; 3 School-wide Title I
Students: 3,051 (51.8% male; 48.2% female)
Individual Education Program: 435 (14.3%);
English Language Learner: 3 (0.1%); Migrant: n/a
Eligible for Free Lunch Program: 448 (14.7%)
Eligible for Reduced-Price Lunch Program: 139 (4.6%)
Teachers: 178.0 (17.1 to 1)
Librarians/Media Specialists: 3.0 (1,017.0 to 1)
Guidance Counselors: 5.0 (610.2 to 1)
Current Spending: ($ per student per year):
Total: $6,292; Instruction: $3,829; Support Services: $2,192
Enrollment, Drop-out Rates and Diploma Recipients by Race/Ethnicity

Category	Total	White	Black	Asian	AIAN	Hisp.
Enrollment (%)	100.0	98.2	0.6	0.3	0.0	0.4
Drop-out Rate (%)	6.2	6.2	0.0	0.0	0.0	25.0
H.S. Diplomas (#)	190	184	2	3	0	1

Kings Local SD
1797 King Ave • Kings Mills, OH 45034
(513) 398-8050
Grade Span: PK-12; **Agency Type:** 2
Schools: 6
3 Primary; 2 Middle; 1 High; 0 Other Level
6 Regular; 0 Special Education; 0 Vocational; 0 Alternative
0 Magnet; 0 Charter; 2 Title I Eligible; 1 School-wide Title I
Students: 3,774 (53.1% male; 46.9% female)
Individual Education Program: 483 (12.8%);
English Language Learner: 28 (0.7%); Migrant: n/a
Eligible for Free Lunch Program: 192 (5.1%)
Eligible for Reduced-Price Lunch Program: 67 (1.8%)
Teachers: 213.2 (17.7 to 1)
Librarians/Media Specialists: 3.0 (1,258.0 to 1)
Guidance Counselors: 8.6 (438.8 to 1)
Current Spending: ($ per student per year):
Total: $6,894; Instruction: $3,957; Support Services: $2,717
Enrollment, Drop-out Rates and Diploma Recipients by Race/Ethnicity

Category	Total	White	Black	Asian	AIAN	Hisp.
Enrollment (%)	100.0	95.8	1.1	1.6	0.1	1.0
Drop-out Rate (%)	1.4	1.4	0.0	0.0	n/a	0.0
H.S. Diplomas (#)	223	219	0	4	0	0

Lebanon City SD
645 Oak St • Lebanon, OH 45036-1634
(513) 934-5770
Grade Span: PK-12; **Agency Type:** 1
Schools: 6
3 Primary; 2 Middle; 1 High; 0 Other Level
6 Regular; 0 Special Education; 0 Vocational; 0 Alternative
0 Magnet; 0 Charter; 5 Title I Eligible; 0 School-wide Title I
Students: 4,690 (50.2% male; 49.8% female)
Individual Education Program: 435 (9.3%);
English Language Learner: 28 (0.6%); Migrant: n/a
Eligible for Free Lunch Program: 490 (10.4%)
Eligible for Reduced-Price Lunch Program: 116 (2.5%)
Teachers: 242.0 (19.4 to 1)
Librarians/Media Specialists: 4.0 (1,172.5 to 1)
Guidance Counselors: 9.0 (521.1 to 1)
Current Spending: ($ per student per year):
Total: $6,024; Instruction: $3,330; Support Services: $2,439
Enrollment, Drop-out Rates and Diploma Recipients by Race/Ethnicity

Category	Total	White	Black	Asian	AIAN	Hisp.
Enrollment (%)	100.0	94.7	2.7	0.7	0.2	0.6
Drop-out Rate (%)	1.9	1.8	3.0	12.5	n/a	14.3
H.S. Diplomas (#)	279	275	3	0	0	1

Little Miami Local SD
5819 Morrow Rossburg Rd • Morrow, OH 45152-9426
(513) 899-2264
Grade Span: PK-12; **Agency Type:** 2
Schools: 6
3 Primary; 2 Middle; 1 High; 0 Other Level
6 Regular; 0 Special Education; 0 Vocational; 0 Alternative
0 Magnet; 0 Charter; 6 Title I Eligible; 0 School-wide Title I
Students: 3,033 (49.5% male; 50.5% female)
Individual Education Program: 329 (10.8%);
English Language Learner: 14 (0.5%); Migrant: n/a
Eligible for Free Lunch Program: 231 (7.6%)
Eligible for Reduced-Price Lunch Program: 65 (2.1%)
Teachers: 166.7 (18.2 to 1)
Librarians/Media Specialists: 1.0 (3,033.0 to 1)
Guidance Counselors: 5.0 (606.6 to 1)
Current Spending: ($ per student per year):
Total: $6,689; Instruction: $3,821; Support Services: $2,585
Enrollment, Drop-out Rates and Diploma Recipients by Race/Ethnicity

Category	Total	White	Black	Asian	AIAN	Hisp.
Enrollment (%)	100.0	97.6	0.5	0.4	0.0	1.0
Drop-out Rate (%)	4.0	4.0	n/a	0.0	n/a	0.0
H.S. Diplomas (#)	169	169	0	0	0	0

Mason City SD
211 NE St • Mason, OH 45040-1760
(513) 398-0474
Grade Span: PK-12; **Agency Type:** 1
Schools: 6
3 Primary; 2 Middle; 1 High; 0 Other Level
6 Regular; 0 Special Education; 0 Vocational; 0 Alternative
0 Magnet; 0 Charter; 4 Title I Eligible; 0 School-wide Title I
Students: 8,003 (51.6% male; 48.4% female)
Individual Education Program: 710 (8.9%);
English Language Learner: 66 (0.8%); Migrant: n/a
Eligible for Free Lunch Program: 135 (1.7%)
Eligible for Reduced-Price Lunch Program: 118 (1.5%)
Teachers: 464.0 (17.2 to 1)
Librarians/Media Specialists: 3.0 (2,667.7 to 1)
Guidance Counselors: 11.8 (678.2 to 1)
Current Spending: ($ per student per year):
Total: $6,805; Instruction: $3,668; Support Services: $2,881
Enrollment, Drop-out Rates and Diploma Recipients by Race/Ethnicity

Category	Total	White	Black	Asian	AIAN	Hisp.
Enrollment (%)	100.0	89.1	2.8	5.2	0.2	1.4
Drop-out Rate (%)	1.4	1.5	0.0	0.0	0.0	0.0
H.S. Diplomas (#)	367	342	11	8	0	4

Springboro Community City SD
1685 S Main St • Springboro, OH 45066-1524
(937) 748-3960
Grade Span: PK-12; **Agency Type:** 1
Schools: 5
2 Primary; 2 Middle; 1 High; 0 Other Level
5 Regular; 0 Special Education; 0 Vocational; 0 Alternative
0 Magnet; 0 Charter; 3 Title I Eligible; 0 School-wide Title I
Students: 4,051 (51.9% male; 48.1% female)
Individual Education Program: 382 (9.4%);
English Language Learner: 5 (0.1%); Migrant: n/a
Eligible for Free Lunch Program: 92 (2.3%)
Eligible for Reduced-Price Lunch Program: 42 (1.0%)
Teachers: 215.7 (18.8 to 1)
Librarians/Media Specialists: 2.0 (2,025.5 to 1)
Guidance Counselors: 7.0 (578.7 to 1)
Current Spending: ($ per student per year):
Total: $5,878; Instruction: $3,335; Support Services: $2,346
Enrollment, Drop-out Rates and Diploma Recipients by Race/Ethnicity

Category	Total	White	Black	Asian	AIAN	Hisp.
Enrollment (%)	100.0	95.4	0.8	1.3	0.2	0.6
Drop-out Rate (%)	1.4	1.4	0.0	0.0	0.0	25.0
H.S. Diplomas (#)	231	221	4	3	1	1

Washington County

Marietta City SD
701 3rd St • Marietta, OH 45750-1801
(740) 374-6500
Grade Span: PK-12; **Agency Type:** 1
Schools: 8
6 Primary; 1 Middle; 1 High; 0 Other Level
8 Regular; 0 Special Education; 0 Vocational; 0 Alternative
0 Magnet; 0 Charter; 4 Title I Eligible; 0 School-wide Title I
Students: 3,321 (51.8% male; 48.2% female)
Individual Education Program: 531 (16.0%);
English Language Learner: 1 (<0.1%); Migrant: n/a
Eligible for Free Lunch Program: 619 (18.6%)
Eligible for Reduced-Price Lunch Program: 129 (3.9%)
Teachers: 191.2 (17.4 to 1)
Librarians/Media Specialists: 2.0 (1,660.5 to 1)
Guidance Counselors: 5.0 (664.2 to 1)
Current Spending: ($ per student per year):
Total: $6,032; Instruction: $3,538; Support Services: $2,293
Enrollment, Drop-out Rates and Diploma Recipients by Race/Ethnicity

Category	Total	White	Black	Asian	AIAN	Hisp.
Enrollment (%)	100.0	98.0	0.9	0.3	0.2	0.5
Drop-out Rate (%)	1.1	1.0	16.7	0.0	n/a	0.0
H.S. Diplomas (#)	216	213	2	0	0	0

Warren Local SD
220 Sweetapple Rd • Vincent, OH 45784-5005
(740) 678-2366
Grade Span: PK-12; **Agency Type:** 2
Schools: 6

4 Primary; 1 Middle; 1 High; 0 Other Level
6 Regular; 0 Special Education; 0 Vocational; 0 Alternative
0 Magnet; 0 Charter; 5 Title I Eligible; 2 School-wide Title I
Students: 2,702 (53.0% male; 47.0% female)
Individual Education Program: 319 (11.8%);
English Language Learner: 1 (<0.1%); Migrant: n/a
Eligible for Free Lunch Program: 377 (14.0%)
Eligible for Reduced-Price Lunch Program: 172 (6.4%)
Teachers: 160.4 (16.8 to 1)
Librarians/Media Specialists: 1.0 (2,702.0 to 1)
Guidance Counselors: 6.0 (450.3 to 1)
Current Spending: ($ per student per year):
Total: $5,836; Instruction: $3,544; Support Services: $2,054
Enrollment, Drop-out Rates and Diploma Recipients by Race/Ethnicity

Category	Total	White	Black	Asian	AIAN	Hisp.
Enrollment (%)	100.0	96.8	1.0	0.2	0.0	0.3
Drop-out Rate (%)	2.3	2.1	28.6	0.0	0.0	0.0
H.S. Diplomas (#)	190	180	4	2	0	2

Wayne County

Orrville City SD
815 N Ella St • Orrville, OH 44667-1154
(330) 682-4651
Grade Span: PK-12; **Agency Type:** 1
Schools: 5
3 Primary; 1 Middle; 1 High; 0 Other Level
5 Regular; 0 Special Education; 0 Vocational; 0 Alternative
0 Magnet; 0 Charter; 4 Title I Eligible; 0 School-wide Title I
Students: 1,887 (54.0% male; 46.0% female)
Individual Education Program: 217 (11.5%);
English Language Learner: 0 (0.0%); Migrant: n/a
Eligible for Free Lunch Program: 327 (17.3%)
Eligible for Reduced-Price Lunch Program: 147 (7.8%)
Teachers: 117.6 (16.0 to 1)
Librarians/Media Specialists: 2.0 (943.5 to 1)
Guidance Counselors: 4.0 (471.8 to 1)
Current Spending: ($ per student per year):
Total: $6,140; Instruction: $3,720; Support Services: $2,180
Enrollment, Drop-out Rates and Diploma Recipients by Race/Ethnicity

Category	Total	White	Black	Asian	AIAN	Hisp.
Enrollment (%)	100.0	88.4	5.8	1.5	0.2	0.8
Drop-out Rate (%)	4.1	3.5	10.2	7.7	n/a	n/a
H.S. Diplomas (#)	127	118	5	4	0	0

Southeast Local SD
9048 Dover Rd • Apple Creek, OH 44606-9408
(330) 698-3001
Grade Span: PK-12; **Agency Type:** 2
Schools: 6
4 Primary; 1 Middle; 1 High; 0 Other Level
6 Regular; 0 Special Education; 0 Vocational; 0 Alternative
0 Magnet; 0 Charter; 6 Title I Eligible; 6 School-wide Title I
Students: 1,730 (53.4% male; 46.6% female)
Individual Education Program: 228 (13.2%);
English Language Learner: 6 (0.3%); Migrant: n/a
Eligible for Free Lunch Program: 305 (17.6%)
Eligible for Reduced-Price Lunch Program: 213 (12.3%)
Teachers: 110.2 (15.7 to 1)
Librarians/Media Specialists: 1.0 (1,730.0 to 1)
Guidance Counselors: 4.0 (432.5 to 1)
Current Spending: ($ per student per year):
Total: $6,785; Instruction: $4,232; Support Services: $2,287
Enrollment, Drop-out Rates and Diploma Recipients by Race/Ethnicity

Category	Total	White	Black	Asian	AIAN	Hisp.
Enrollment (%)	100.0	98.7	0.2	0.5	0.1	0.3
Drop-out Rate (%)	3.1	2.9	n/a	50.0	n/a	n/a
H.S. Diplomas (#)	96	96	0	0	0	0

Triway Local SD
3205 Shreve Rd • Wooster, OH 44691-4439
(330) 264-9491
Grade Span: PK-12; **Agency Type:** 2
Schools: 5
2 Primary; 1 Middle; 1 High; 1 Other Level
5 Regular; 0 Special Education; 0 Vocational; 0 Alternative
0 Magnet; 0 Charter; 3 Title I Eligible; 0 School-wide Title I
Students: 2,147 (50.9% male; 49.1% female)
Individual Education Program: 315 (14.7%);
English Language Learner: 4 (0.2%); Migrant: n/a
Eligible for Free Lunch Program: 278 (12.9%)
Eligible for Reduced-Price Lunch Program: 110 (5.1%)
Teachers: 137.9 (15.6 to 1)
Librarians/Media Specialists: 1.0 (2,147.0 to 1)
Guidance Counselors: 4.0 (536.8 to 1)
Current Spending: ($ per student per year):
Total: $6,077; Instruction: $3,708; Support Services: $2,110
Enrollment, Drop-out Rates and Diploma Recipients by Race/Ethnicity

Category	Total	White	Black	Asian	AIAN	Hisp.
Enrollment (%)	100.0	96.8	1.0	1.0	0.4	0.6
Drop-out Rate (%)	2.6	2.5	0.0	0.0	33.3	0.0
H.S. Diplomas (#)	146	144	0	2	0	0

Wooster City SD
144 N Market St • Wooster, OH 44691-4810
(330) 264-0869 • http://www.wooster.k12.oh.us/
Grade Span: PK-12; **Agency Type:** 1
Schools: 11
7 Primary; 1 Middle; 1 High; 2 Other Level
9 Regular; 2 Special Education; 0 Vocational; 0 Alternative
0 Magnet; 0 Charter; 5 Title I Eligible; 2 School-wide Title I
Students: 4,204 (52.6% male; 47.4% female)
Individual Education Program: 636 (15.1%);
English Language Learner: 8 (0.2%); Migrant: n/a
Eligible for Free Lunch Program: 999 (23.8%)
Eligible for Reduced-Price Lunch Program: 306 (7.3%)
Teachers: 312.2 (13.5 to 1)
Librarians/Media Specialists: 2.0 (2,102.0 to 1)
Guidance Counselors: 8.6 (488.8 to 1)
Current Spending: ($ per student per year):
Total: $7,756; Instruction: $4,733; Support Services: $2,737
Enrollment, Drop-out Rates and Diploma Recipients by Race/Ethnicity

Category	Total	White	Black	Asian	AIAN	Hisp.
Enrollment (%)	100.0	88.7	6.3	1.2	0.1	0.9
Drop-out Rate (%)	4.1	3.9	8.9	0.0	0.0	0.0
H.S. Diplomas (#)	281	259	9	7	1	3

Williams County

Bryan City SD
1350 Fountain Grove Dr • Bryan, OH 43506-8733
(419) 636-6973 • http://www.bryan.k12.oh.us/
Grade Span: PK-12; **Agency Type:** 1
Schools: 5
2 Primary; 1 Middle; 1 High; 1 Other Level
5 Regular; 0 Special Education; 0 Vocational; 0 Alternative
0 Magnet; 0 Charter; 3 Title I Eligible; 0 School-wide Title I
Students: 2,352 (51.6% male; 48.4% female)
Individual Education Program: 259 (11.0%);
English Language Learner: 4 (0.2%); Migrant: n/a
Eligible for Free Lunch Program: 241 (10.2%)
Eligible for Reduced-Price Lunch Program: 100 (4.3%)
Teachers: 144.7 (16.3 to 1)
Librarians/Media Specialists: 2.0 (1,176.0 to 1)
Guidance Counselors: 5.0 (470.4 to 1)
Current Spending: ($ per student per year):
Total: $6,434; Instruction: $4,109; Support Services: $2,100
Enrollment, Drop-out Rates and Diploma Recipients by Race/Ethnicity

Category	Total	White	Black	Asian	AIAN	Hisp.
Enrollment (%)	100.0	95.0	0.2	0.9	0.0	3.7
Drop-out Rate (%)	3.1	2.6	50.0	0.0	n/a	14.8
H.S. Diplomas (#)	149	139	0	6	0	4

Wood County

Bowling Green City SD
140 S Grove St • Bowling Green, OH 43402-2819
(419) 352-3576 • http://www.bgcs.k12.oh.us/
Grade Span: PK-12; **Agency Type:** 1
Schools: 9
6 Primary; 1 Middle; 1 High; 1 Other Level
8 Regular; 0 Special Education; 1 Vocational; 0 Alternative
0 Magnet; 0 Charter; 6 Title I Eligible; 0 School-wide Title I
Students: 3,245 (51.4% male; 48.6% female)
Individual Education Program: 392 (12.1%);
English Language Learner: 9 (0.3%); Migrant: 6 (0.2%)
Eligible for Free Lunch Program: 401 (12.4%)
Eligible for Reduced-Price Lunch Program: 95 (2.9%)
Teachers: 208.5 (15.6 to 1)
Librarians/Media Specialists: 4.0 (811.3 to 1)
Guidance Counselors: 8.0 (405.6 to 1)
Current Spending: ($ per student per year):
Total: $7,040; Instruction: $4,422; Support Services: $2,388
Enrollment, Drop-out Rates and Diploma Recipients by Race/Ethnicity

Category	Total	White	Black	Asian	AIAN	Hisp.
Enrollment (%)	100.0	87.4	1.4	1.4	0.2	5.3
Drop-out Rate (%)	2.1	1.8	6.7	0.0	33.3	8.3
H.S. Diplomas (#)	256	229	1	8	1	12

Eastwood Local SD

4800 Sugar Ridge Rd • Pemberville, OH 43450-9626
(419) 833-6411
Grade Span: PK-12; **Agency Type:** 2
Schools: 6
4 Primary; 1 Middle; 1 High; 0 Other Level
6 Regular; 0 Special Education; 0 Vocational; 0 Alternative
0 Magnet; 0 Charter; 4 Title I Eligible; 0 School-wide Title I
Students: 1,927 (51.5% male; 48.5% female)
Individual Education Program: 176 (9.1%);
English Language Learner: 1 (0.1%); Migrant: 4 (0.2%)
Eligible for Free Lunch Program: 138 (7.2%)
Eligible for Reduced-Price Lunch Program: 126 (6.5%)
Teachers: 95.1 (20.3 to 1)
Librarians/Media Specialists: 1.0 (1,927.0 to 1)
Guidance Counselors: 4.0 (481.8 to 1)
Current Spending: ($ per student per year):
Total: $6,763; Instruction: $3,711; Support Services: $2,793
Enrollment, Drop-out Rates and Diploma Recipients by Race/Ethnicity

Category	Total	White	Black	Asian	AIAN	Hisp.
Enrollment (%)	100.0	94.5	0.1	0.3	0.0	3.1
Drop-out Rate (%)	2.1	1.8	n/a	0.0	n/a	12.5
H.S. Diplomas (#)	140	135	0	2	0	3

Lake Local SD

PO Box 151 • Millbury, OH 43447-0151
(419) 836-2552 • http://www.lakelocal.k12.oh.us/
Grade Span: KG-12; **Agency Type:** 2
Schools: 4
2 Primary; 1 Middle; 1 High; 0 Other Level
4 Regular; 0 Special Education; 0 Vocational; 0 Alternative
0 Magnet; 0 Charter; 2 Title I Eligible; 0 School-wide Title I
Students: 1,863 (50.5% male; 49.5% female)
Individual Education Program: 176 (9.4%);
English Language Learner: 12 (0.6%); Migrant: 3 (0.2%)
Eligible for Free Lunch Program: 184 (9.9%)
Eligible for Reduced-Price Lunch Program: 126 (6.8%)
Teachers: 83.1 (22.4 to 1)
Librarians/Media Specialists: 1.0 (1,863.0 to 1)
Guidance Counselors: 4.0 (465.8 to 1)
Current Spending: ($ per student per year):
Total: $5,860; Instruction: $3,325; Support Services: $2,279
Enrollment, Drop-out Rates and Diploma Recipients by Race/Ethnicity

Category	Total	White	Black	Asian	AIAN	Hisp.
Enrollment (%)	100.0	92.1	1.6	0.1	0.4	5.1
Drop-out Rate (%)	1.9	1.8	0.0	0.0	0.0	3.8
H.S. Diplomas (#)	137	131	1	0	0	5

Otsego Local SD

PO Box 290 • Tontogany, OH 43565-0290
(419) 823-4381
Grade Span: PK-12; **Agency Type:** 2
Schools: 5
3 Primary; 1 Middle; 1 High; 0 Other Level
5 Regular; 0 Special Education; 0 Vocational; 0 Alternative
0 Magnet; 0 Charter; 2 Title I Eligible; 0 School-wide Title I
Students: 1,724 (50.7% male; 49.3% female)
Individual Education Program: 241 (14.0%);
English Language Learner: 0 (0.0%); Migrant: 11 (0.6%)
Eligible for Free Lunch Program: 150 (8.7%)
Eligible for Reduced-Price Lunch Program: 64 (3.7%)
Teachers: 93.1 (18.5 to 1)
Librarians/Media Specialists: 2.0 (862.0 to 1)
Guidance Counselors: 3.0 (574.7 to 1)
Current Spending: ($ per student per year):
Total: $6,123; Instruction: $3,825; Support Services: $2,052
Enrollment, Drop-out Rates and Diploma Recipients by Race/Ethnicity

Category	Total	White	Black	Asian	AIAN	Hisp.
Enrollment (%)	100.0	94.0	0.0	0.3	0.3	2.7
Drop-out Rate (%)	2.0	2.1	n/a	0.0	0.0	0.0
H.S. Diplomas (#)	117	113	0	0	0	4

Perrysburg Ex Vill SD

140 E Indiana Ave • Perrysburg, OH 43551-2261
(419) 874-9131
Grade Span: PK-12; **Agency Type:** 1
Schools: 6
4 Primary; 1 Middle; 1 High; 0 Other Level
6 Regular; 0 Special Education; 0 Vocational; 0 Alternative
0 Magnet; 0 Charter; 3 Title I Eligible; 0 School-wide Title I
Students: 4,379 (51.7% male; 48.3% female)
Individual Education Program: 357 (8.2%);
English Language Learner: 7 (0.2%); Migrant: 16 (0.4%)
Eligible for Free Lunch Program: 137 (3.1%)
Eligible for Reduced-Price Lunch Program: 89 (2.0%)
Teachers: 248.3 (17.6 to 1)
Librarians/Media Specialists: 2.0 (2,189.5 to 1)
Guidance Counselors: 9.0 (486.6 to 1)
Current Spending: ($ per student per year):
Total: $7,106; Instruction: $4,512; Support Services: $2,315
Enrollment, Drop-out Rates and Diploma Recipients by Race/Ethnicity

Category	Total	White	Black	Asian	AIAN	Hisp.
Enrollment (%)	100.0	90.6	1.3	2.9	0.1	3.2
Drop-out Rate (%)	0.6	0.6	0.0	0.0	0.0	0.0
H.S. Diplomas (#)	328	310	3	5	0	9

Rossford Ex Vill SD

601 Superior St • Rossford, OH 43460-1247
(419) 666-2010 • http://www.rossford.k12.oh.us/
Grade Span: PK-12; **Agency Type:** 1
Schools: 5
3 Primary; 1 Middle; 1 High; 0 Other Level
5 Regular; 0 Special Education; 0 Vocational; 0 Alternative
0 Magnet; 0 Charter; 2 Title I Eligible; 1 School-wide Title I
Students: 2,062 (51.8% male; 48.2% female)
Individual Education Program: 326 (15.8%);
English Language Learner: 1 (<0.1%); Migrant: n/a
Eligible for Free Lunch Program: 299 (14.5%)
Eligible for Reduced-Price Lunch Program: 157 (7.6%)
Teachers: 130.8 (15.8 to 1)
Librarians/Media Specialists: 0.0 (0.0 to 1)
Guidance Counselors: 4.0 (515.5 to 1)
Current Spending: ($ per student per year):
Total: $7,157; Instruction: $4,307; Support Services: $2,653
Enrollment, Drop-out Rates and Diploma Recipients by Race/Ethnicity

Category	Total	White	Black	Asian	AIAN	Hisp.
Enrollment (%)	100.0	92.6	1.7	0.6	0.1	2.3
Drop-out Rate (%)	4.0	4.1	0.0	0.0	n/a	0.0
H.S. Diplomas (#)	137	131	1	1	0	2

Wyandot County

Upper Sandusky Ex Vill SD

390 W Walker St • Upper Sandusky, OH 43351-1364
(419) 294-2307 • http://www.uppersandusky.k12.oh.us/
Grade Span: PK-12; **Agency Type:** 1
Schools: 5
4 Primary; 0 Middle; 1 High; 0 Other Level
5 Regular; 0 Special Education; 0 Vocational; 0 Alternative
0 Magnet; 0 Charter; 3 Title I Eligible; 0 School-wide Title I
Students: 1,832 (50.4% male; 49.6% female)
Individual Education Program: 292 (15.9%);
English Language Learner: 0 (0.0%); Migrant: 6 (0.3%)
Eligible for Free Lunch Program: 220 (12.0%)
Eligible for Reduced-Price Lunch Program: 101 (5.5%)
Teachers: 119.2 (15.4 to 1)
Librarians/Media Specialists: 2.0 (916.0 to 1)
Guidance Counselors: 3.0 (610.7 to 1)
Current Spending: ($ per student per year):
Total: $5,655; Instruction: $3,357; Support Services: $2,045
Enrollment, Drop-out Rates and Diploma Recipients by Race/Ethnicity

Category	Total	White	Black	Asian	AIAN	Hisp.
Enrollment (%)	100.0	96.3	0.1	0.3	0.3	2.0
Drop-out Rate (%)	2.6	2.7	n/a	0.0	0.0	0.0
H.S. Diplomas (#)	153	148	1	1	0	3

Number of Schools

Rank	Number	District Name	City
1	151	Columbus City SD	Columbus
2	129	Cleveland Municipal SD	Cleveland
3	86	Cincinnati City SD	Cincinnati
4	69	Toledo City SD	Toledo
5	61	Akron City SD	Akron
6	42	Dayton City SD	Dayton
7	36	South-Western City SD	Grove City
8	30	Canton City SD	Canton
9	27	Youngstown City SD	Youngstown
10	23	Westerville City SD	Westerville
11	22	Springfield City SD	Springfield
12	21	Parma City SD	Parma
13	20	Hilliard City SD	Hilliard
14	19	Hamilton City SD	Hamilton
14	19	Lakota Local SD	Liberty Twp
16	18	Dublin City SD	Dublin
16	18	Elyria City SD	Elyria
16	18	Warren City SD	Warren
16	18	Worthington City SD	Worthington
20	17	Marion City SD	Marion
21	16	Findlay City SD	Findlay
21	16	Mentor Ex Vill SD	Mentor
21	16	Newark City SD	Newark
24	15	Lorain City SD	Lorain
24	15	Middletown City SD	Middletown
26	14	Cleveland Hts-Univ Hts City SD	University Hgts
26	14	Lakewood City SD	Lakewood
26	14	Mansfield City SD	Mansfield
26	14	Northwest Local SD	Cincinnati
26	14	Olentangy Local SD	Lewis Center
26	14	Sandusky City SD	Sandusky
26	14	Willoughby-Eastlake City SD	Willoughby
33	13	Berea City SD	Berea
33	13	Cuyahoga Falls City SD	Cuyahoga Falls
33	13	Washington Local SD	Toledo
36	12	Ashtabula Area City SD	Ashtabula
36	12	Kettering City SD	Kettering
36	12	Lancaster City SD	Lancaster
36	12	Lima City SD	Lima
36	12	Sylvania City SD	Sylvania
36	12	West Clermont Local SD	Cincinnati
36	12	Zanesville City SD	Zanesville
43	11	Barberton City SD	Barberton
43	11	Brunswick City SD	Brunswick
43	11	Cambridge City SD	Cambridge
43	11	Centerville City SD	Centerville
43	11	Gahanna-Jefferson City SD	Gahanna
43	11	Milford Ex Vill SD	Milford
43	11	Pickerington Local SD	Pickerington
43	11	Princeton City SD	Cincinnati
43	11	Strongsville City SD	Strongsville
43	11	Wooster City SD	Wooster
53	10	Adams County-Ohio Valley Local SD	West Union
53	10	East Holmes Local SD	Berlin
53	10	Fairfield City SD	Fairfield
53	10	Groveport Madison Local SD	Groveport
53	10	Huber Heights City SD	Huber Heights
53	10	Logan-Hocking Local SD	Logan
53	10	Massillon City SD	Massillon
53	10	Meigs Local SD	Pomeroy
53	10	Miami Trace Local SD	Washington Ct Hse
53	10	Plain Local SD	Canton
53	10	Switzerland of Ohio Local SD	Woodsfield
53	10	Xenia Community City SD	Xenia
65	9	Bowling Green City SD	Bowling Green
65	9	Carrollton Ex Vill SD	Carrollton
65	9	Chillicothe City SD	Chillicothe
65	9	Delaware City SD	Delaware
65	9	Euclid City SD	Euclid
65	9	Forest Hills Local SD	Cincinnati
65	9	Fremont City SD	Fremont
65	9	Jackson City SD	Jackson
65	9	Medina City SD	Medina
65	9	Miamisburg City SD	Miamisburg
65	9	Mount Vernon City SD	Mount Vernon
65	9	North Olmsted City SD	North Olmsted
65	9	Northmont City SD	Englewood
65	9	Oak Hills Local SD	Cincinnati
65	9	Perry Local SD	Massillon
65	9	Piqua City SD	Piqua
65	9	Portsmouth City SD	Portsmouth
65	9	Shaker Heights City SD	Shaker Heights
65	9	Sidney City SD	Sidney
65	9	South Euclid-Lyndhurst City SD	Lyndhurst
65	9	Stow-Munroe Falls City SD	Stow
65	9	Troy City SD	Troy
87	8	Ashland City SD	Ashland
87	8	Austintown Local SD	Youngstown
87	8	Beavercreek City SD	Beavercreek
87	8	East Cleveland City SD	East Cleveland
87	8	Franklin City SD	Franklin
87	8	Gallia County Local SD	Gallipolis
87	8	Kenton City SD	Kenton
87	8	Marietta City SD	Marietta
87	8	Marysville Ex Vill SD	Marysville
87	8	Mount Healthy City SD	Cincinnati
87	8	New Philadelphia City SD	New Philadelphia
87	8	Painesville Township Local SD	Painesville
87	8	Ravenna City SD	Ravenna
87	8	Reynoldsburg City SD	Reynoldsburg
87	8	Southwest Local SD	Harrison
87	8	Steubenville City SD	Steubenville
87	8	Tecumseh Local SD	New Carlisle
87	8	Tiffin City SD	Tiffin
87	8	Trotwood-Madison City SD	Trotwood
87	8	Upper Arlington City SD	Upper Arlington
87	8	Wadsworth City SD	Wadsworth
108	7	Alliance City SD	Alliance
108	7	Athens City SD	The Plains
108	7	Avon Lake City SD	Avon Lake
108	7	Bedford City SD	Bedford
108	7	Bellevue City SD	Bellevue
108	7	Boardman Local SD	Youngstown
108	7	Buckeye Local SD	Rayland
108	7	Bucyrus City SD	Bucyrus
108	7	Cloverleaf Local SD	Lodi
108	7	Crestwood Local SD	Mantua
108	7	Defiance City SD	Defiance
108	7	Edison Local SD	Hammondsville
108	7	Fairborn City SD	Fairborn
108	7	Geneva Area City SD	Geneva
108	7	Greenville City SD	Greenville
108	7	Kent City SD	Kent
108	7	Mad River Local SD	Dayton
108	7	Mayfield City SD	Highland Hgts
108	7	Niles City SD	Niles
108	7	North Canton City SD	North Canton
108	7	Northeastern Local SD	Springfield
108	7	Norwood City SD	Norwood
108	7	Oregon City SD	Oregon
108	7	Painesville City Local SD	Painesville
108	7	River View Local SD	Warsaw
108	7	Salem City SD	Salem
108	7	Solon City SD	Solon
108	7	Springfield Local SD	Akron
108	7	Sycamore Community City SD	Cincinnati
108	7	Tri-Valley Local SD	Dresden
108	7	Van Wert City SD	Van Wert
108	7	Vinton County Local SD	Mc Arthur
108	7	Washington Court House City SD	Washington Ct Hse
108	7	West Branch Local SD	Beloit
108	7	West Carrollton City SD	West Carrollton
108	7	West Holmes Local SD	Millersburg
108	7	Westlake City SD	Westlake
108	7	Winton Woods City SD	Cincinnati
146	6	Amherst Ex Vill SD	Amherst
146	6	Anthony Wayne Local SD	Whitehouse
146	6	Bellefontaine City SD	Bellefontaine
146	6	Benton Carroll Salem Local SD	Oak Harbor
146	6	Brecksville-Broadview Heights	Brecksville
146	6	Buckeye Local SD	Ashtabula
146	6	Celina City SD	Celina
146	6	Chardon Local SD	Chardon
146	6	Circleville City SD	Circleville
146	6	Claymont City SD	Dennison
146	6	Conneaut Area City SD	Conneaut
146	6	Coventry Local SD	Akron
146	6	East Liverpool City SD	East Liverpool
146	6	East Muskingum Local SD	New Concord
146	6	Eastwood Local SD	Pemberville
146	6	Edgewood City SD	Trenton
146	6	Galion City SD	Galion
146	6	Greenfield Ex Vill SD	Greenfield
146	6	Harrison Hills City SD	Hopedale
146	6	Hillsboro City SD	Hillsboro
146	6	Howland Local SD	Warren
146	6	Hudson City SD	Hudson
146	6	Indian Creek Local SD	Wintersville
146	6	Ironton City SD	Ironton
146	6	Jackson Local SD	Massillon
146	6	Kings Local SD	Kings Mills
146	6	Lebanon City SD	Lebanon
146	6	Licking Valley Local SD	Newark
146	6	Little Miami Local SD	Morrow
146	6	Logan Elm Local SD	Circleville
146	6	London City SD	London
146	6	Louisville City SD	Louisville
146	6	Loveland City SD	Loveland
146	6	Madison Local SD	Mansfield
146	6	Madison-Plains Local SD	London
146	6	Maple Heights City SD	Maple Heights
146	6	Mason City SD	Mason
146	6	Maumee City SD	Maumee
146	6	Nordonia Hills City SD	Northfield
146	6	North Ridgeville City SD	N Ridgeville
146	6	Norton City SD	Norton
146	6	Perrysburg Ex Vill SD	Perrysburg
146	6	Poland Local SD	Poland
146	6	Port Clinton City SD	Port Clinton
146	6	Saint Marys City SD	Saint Marys
146	6	Sheffield-Sheffield Lake City	Sheffield Vlg
146	6	Shelby City SD	Shelby
146	6	Southeast Local SD	Apple Creek
146	6	Southwest Licking Local SD	Etna
146	6	Springfield Local SD	Holland
146	6	Urbana City SD	Urbana
146	6	Vandalia-Butler City SD	Vandalia
146	6	Wapakoneta City SD	Wapakoneta
146	6	Warren Local SD	Vincent
146	6	Warrensville Heights City SD	Warrensville Hgts
146	6	Westfall Local SD	Williamsport
146	6	Willard City SD	Willard
203	5	Avon Local SD	Avon
203	5	Beachwood City SD	Beachwood
203	5	Beaver Local SD	Lisbon
203	5	Bethel-Tate Local SD	Bethel
203	5	Bexley City SD	Bexley
203	5	Big Walnut Local SD	Galena
203	5	Blanchester Local SD	Blanchester
203	5	Brookfield Local SD	Brookfield
203	5	Bryan City SD	Bryan
203	5	Buckeye Local SD	Medina
203	5	Buckeye Valley Local SD	Delaware
203	5	Canal Winchester Local SD	Canal Winchester
203	5	Canton Local SD	Canton
203	5	Clark-Shawnee Local SD	Springfield
203	5	Clyde-Green Springs Ex Vill SD	Clyde
203	5	Copley-Fairlawn City SD	Copley
203	5	Coshocton City SD	Coshocton
203	5	Dover City SD	Dover
203	5	Fairfield Union Local SD	W Rushville
203	5	Fairless Local SD	Navarre
203	5	Fairview Park City SD	Fairview Park
203	5	Field Local SD	Mogadore
203	5	Finneytown Local SD	Cincinnati
203	5	Fostoria City SD	Fostoria
203	5	Franklin Local SD	Duncan Falls
203	5	Gallipolis City SD	Gallipolis
203	5	Garfield Heights City SD	Garfield Hgts
203	5	Girard City SD	Girard
203	5	Green Local SD	Green
203	5	Greeneview Local SD	Jamestown
203	5	Hamilton Local SD	Columbus
203	5	Highland Local SD	Sparta
203	5	Kenston Local SD	Chagrin Falls
203	5	Lake Local SD	Hartville
203	5	Lakewood Local SD	Hebron
203	5	Lexington Local SD	Lexington
203	5	Madison Local SD	Madison
203	5	Mariemont City SD	Cincinnati
203	5	Marlington Local SD	Alliance
203	5	Midview Local SD	Grafton
203	5	Morgan Local SD	McConnelsville
203	5	Napoleon Area City SD	Napoleon
203	5	New Richmond Ex Vill SD	New Richmond
203	5	North Royalton City SD	N Royalton
203	5	Northern Local SD	Thornville
203	5	Northridge Local SD	Dayton
203	5	Northwest Local SD	Canal Fulton
203	5	Norwalk City SD	Norwalk
203	5	Oakwood City SD	Dayton
203	5	Orrville City SD	Orrville
203	5	Otsego Local SD	Tontogany
203	5	River Valley Local SD	Caledonia
203	5	Rolling Hills Local SD	Byesville
203	5	Rossford Ex Vill SD	Rossford
203	5	Southeast Local SD	Ravenna
203	5	Springboro Community City SD	Springboro
203	5	Streetsboro City SD	Streetsboro
203	5	Sugarcreek Local SD	Bellbrook
203	5	Swanton Local SD	Swanton
203	5	Talawanda City SD	Oxford
203	5	Tallmadge City SD	Tallmadge
203	5	Teays Valley Local SD	Ashville
203	5	Three Rivers Local SD	Cleves
203	5	Tipp City Ex Vill SD	Tipp City
203	5	Triway Local SD	Wooster
203	5	Tuscarawas Valley Local SD	Zoarville
203	5	Twinsburg City SD	Twinsburg
203	5	Upper Sandusky Ex Vill SD	Upper Sandusky
203	5	West Muskingum Local SD	Zanesville
203	5	Whitehall City SD	Whitehall
203	5	Wilmington City SD	Wilmington
203	5	Wyoming City SD	Wyoming

275	4	Alexander Local SD	Albany
275	4	Amanda-Clearcreek Local SD	Amanda
275	4	Aurora City SD	Aurora
275	4	Bay Village City SD	Bay Village
275	4	Berlin-Milan Local SD	Milan
275	4	Canfield Local SD	Canfield
275	4	Carlisle Local SD	Carlisle
275	4	Chagrin Falls Ex Vill SD	Chagrin Falls
275	4	Clear Fork Valley Local SD	Bellville
275	4	Clermont-Northeastern Local SD	Batavia
275	4	East Clinton Local SD	Lees Creek
275	4	Eastern Local SD	Sardinia
275	4	Eaton City SD	Eaton
275	4	Elgin Local SD	Marion
275	4	Elida Local SD	Elida
275	4	Fairland Local SD	Proctorville
275	4	Genoa Area Local SD	Genoa
275	4	Goshen Local SD	Goshen
275	4	Graham Local SD	Saint Paris
275	4	Granville Ex Vill SD	Granville
275	4	Greenon Local SD	Springfield
275	4	Heath City SD	Heath
275	4	Highland Local SD	Medina
275	4	Indian Hill Ex Vill SD	Cincinnati
275	4	Indian Lake Local SD	Lewistown
275	4	Indian Valley Local SD	Gnadenhutten
275	4	James A Garfield Local SD	Garrettsville
275	4	Jonathan Alder Local SD	Plain City
275	4	Keystone Local SD	Lagrange
275	4	Labrae Local SD	Leavittsburg
275	4	Lake Local SD	Millbury
275	4	Lakeview Local SD	Cortland
275	4	Licking Heights Local SD	Summit Station
275	4	Minerva Local SD	Minerva
275	4	New Lexington City SD	New Lexington
275	4	Newton Falls Ex Vill SD	Newton Falls
275	4	North College Hill City SD	Cincinnati
275	4	North Fork Local SD	Utica
275	4	Olmsted Falls City SD	Olmsted Falls
275	4	Ontario Local SD	Mansfield
275	4	Orange City SD	Cleveland
275	4	Ottawa-Glandorf Local SD	Ottawa
275	4	Paulding Ex Vill SD	Paulding
275	4	Perkins Local SD	Sandusky
275	4	Pike-Delta-York Local SD	Delta
275	4	Plain Local SD	New Albany
275	4	Preble Shawnee Local SD	Camden
275	4	Revere Local SD	Bath
275	4	Rocky River City SD	Rocky River
275	4	Ross Local SD	Hamilton
275	4	Sandy Valley Local SD	Magnolia
275	4	Shawnee Local SD	Lima
275	4	South Point Local SD	South Point
275	4	Union-Scioto Local SD	Chillicothe
275	4	Valley View Local SD	Germantown
275	4	Vermilion Local SD	Vermilion
275	4	Wauseon Ex Vill SD	Wauseon
275	4	Waverly City SD	Waverly
275	4	Wellston City SD	Wellston
275	4	West Geauga Local SD	Chesterland
275	4	Western Brown Local SD	Mount Orab
275	4	Woodridge Local SD	Peninsula
337	3	Batavia Local SD	Batavia
337	3	Bath Local SD	Lima
337	3	Bellaire Local SD	Bellaire
337	3	Benjamin Logan Local SD	Bellefontaine
337	3	Black River Local SD	Sullivan
337	3	Brookville Local SD	Brookville
337	3	Campbell City SD	Campbell
337	3	Champion Local SD	Warren
337	3	Clearview Local SD	Lorain
337	3	Clinton-Massie Local SD	Clarksville
337	3	Coldwater Ex Vill SD	Coldwater
337	3	Firelands Local SD	Oberlin
337	3	Hubbard Ex Vill SD	Hubbard
337	3	Huron City SD	Huron
337	3	Jefferson Area Local SD	Jefferson
337	3	Liberty Local SD	Youngstown
337	3	Madison Local SD	Middletown
337	3	Manchester Local SD	Akron
337	3	Maysville Local SD	Zanesville
337	3	Milton-Union Ex Vill SD	West Milton
337	3	Minford Local SD	Minford
337	3	Northwest Local SD	Mc Dermott
337	3	Northwestern Local SD	Springfield
337	3	Perry Local SD	Perry
337	3	Rock Hill Local SD	Ironton
337	3	Saint Clairsville-Richland City	St Clairsville
337	3	Scioto Valley Local SD	Piketon
337	3	Struthers City SD	Struthers
337	3	Union Local SD	Morristown
337	3	Washington-Nile Local SD	West Portsmouth
337	3	Wellington Ex Vill SD	Wellington
337	3	Wickliffe City SD	Wickliffe
337	3	Zane Trace Local SD	Chillicothe
370	1	Electronic Classroom of Tomorrow	Columbus

Number of Teachers

Rank	Number	District Name	City
1	6,670	Cleveland Municipal SD	Cleveland
2	4,288	Columbus City SD	Columbus
3	3,548	Cincinnati City SD	Cincinnati
4	2,751	Toledo City SD	Toledo
5	2,550	Akron City SD	Akron
6	1,455	Dayton City SD	Dayton
7	1,310	South-Western City SD	Grove City
8	955	Hilliard City SD	Hilliard
9	929	Canton City SD	Canton
10	903	Lakota Local SD	Liberty Twp
11	834	Dublin City SD	Dublin
12	816	Parma City SD	Parma
13	799	Westerville City SD	Westerville
14	742	Youngstown City SD	Youngstown
15	739	Lorain City SD	Lorain
16	692	Worthington City SD	Worthington
17	658	Springfield City SD	Springfield
18	637	Mentor Ex Vill SD	Mentor
19	623	Northwest Local SD	Cincinnati
20	575	Elyria City SD	Elyria
21	563	Hamilton City SD	Hamilton
22	558	Warren City SD	Warren
23	534	Willoughby-Eastlake City SD	Willoughby
24	522	Centerville City SD	Centerville
25	514	Fairfield City SD	Fairfield
26	512	Cleveland Hts-Univ Hts City SD	University Hgts
27	512	Middletown City SD	Middletown
28	510	Sylvania City SD	Sylvania
29	510	West Clermont Local SD	Cincinnati
30	509	Berea City SD	Berea
31	494	Kettering City SD	Kettering
32	488	Princeton City SD	Cincinnati
33	484	Mansfield City SD	Mansfield
34	476	Pickerington Local SD	Pickerington
35	467	Medina City SD	Medina
36	464	Mason City SD	Mason
37	460	Olentangy Local SD	Lewis Center
38	458	Washington Local SD	Toledo
39	448	Oak Hills Local SD	Cincinnati
40	442	Lakewood City SD	Lakewood
41	438	Forest Hills Local SD	Cincinnati
42	435	Huber Heights City SD	Huber Heights
43	430	Findlay City SD	Findlay
44	430	Brunswick City SD	Brunswick
45	429	Shaker Heights City SD	Shaker Heights
46	428	Newark City SD	Newark
47	426	Reynoldsburg City SD	Reynoldsburg
48	418	Upper Arlington City SD	Upper Arlington
49	415	Gahanna-Jefferson City SD	Gahanna
50	406	Strongsville City SD	Strongsville
51	405	Lima City SD	Lima
52	400	Sycamore Community City SD	Cincinnati
53	392	Plain Local SD	Canton
54	390	Euclid City SD	Euclid
55	387	Groveport Madison Local SD	Groveport
56	378	Lancaster City SD	Lancaster
57	374	Marion City SD	Marion
58	371	Beavercreek City SD	Beavercreek
59	370	East Cleveland City SD	East Cleveland
60	360	Cuyahoga Falls City SD	Cuyahoga Falls
61	359	North Olmsted City SD	North Olmsted
62	355	Hudson City SD	Hudson
63	349	Barberton City SD	Barberton
64	345	Adams County-Ohio Valley Local SD	West Union
65	345	Xenia Community City SD	Xenia
66	340	Stow-Munroe Falls City SD	Stow
67	338	Solon City SD	Solon
68	338	Fairborn City SD	Fairborn
69	337	Massillon City SD	Massillon
70	335	Ashtabula Area City SD	Ashtabula
71	334	Northmont City SD	Englewood
72	323	Mayfield City SD	Highland Hgts
73	318	Sandusky City SD	Sandusky
74	317	Milford Ex Vill SD	Milford
75	314	South Euclid-Lyndhurst City SD	Lyndhurst
76	312	Wooster City SD	Wooster
77	310	Miamisburg City SD	Miamisburg
78	307	Zanesville City SD	Zanesville
79	307	Jackson Local SD	Massillon
80	301	Kent City SD	Kent
81	299	Boardman Local SD	Youngstown
82	299	Austintown Local SD	Youngstown
83	295	Marysville Ex Vill SD	Marysville
84	294	Delaware City SD	Delaware
85	291	West Carrollton City SD	West Carrollton
86	289	North Canton City SD	North Canton
87	283	Winton Woods City SD	Cincinnati
88	276	Perry Local SD	Massillon
89	271	Bedford City SD	Bedford
90	270	Mount Healthy City SD	Cincinnati
91	267	Fremont City SD	Fremont
92	263	Alliance City SD	Alliance
93	262	Madison Local SD	Mansfield
94	261	Brecksville-Broadview Heights	Brecksville
95	260	Oregon City SD	Oregon
96	257	Green Local SD	Green
97	253	Mad River Local SD	Dayton
98	253	Mount Vernon City SD	Mount Vernon
99	248	Trotwood-Madison City SD	Trotwood
100	248	Perrysburg Ex Vill SD	Perrysburg
101	247	North Royalton City SD	N Royalton
102	246	Wadsworth City SD	Wadsworth
103	244	Westlake City SD	Westlake
104	243	Troy City SD	Troy
105	242	Nordonia Hills City SD	Northfield
106	242	Lebanon City SD	Lebanon
107	236	Anthony Wayne Local SD	Whitehouse
108	234	Twinsburg City SD	Twinsburg
109	232	Painesville Township Local SD	Painesville
110	231	Springfield Local SD	Holland
111	230	Loveland City SD	Loveland
112	230	Ashland City SD	Ashland
112	230	Athens City SD	The Plains
114	230	Greenville City SD	Greenville
115	229	Vandalia-Butler City SD	Vandalia
116	228	Talawanda City SD	Oxford
117	227	Tecumseh Local SD	New Carlisle
118	224	East Liverpool City SD	East Liverpool
118	224	Maple Heights City SD	Maple Heights
120	223	Logan-Hocking Local SD	Logan
121	222	North Ridgeville City SD	N Ridgeville
122	220	Sidney City SD	Sidney
123	220	Edgewood City SD	Trenton
124	219	Warrensville Heights City SD	Warrensville Hgts
125	216	Avon Lake City SD	Avon Lake
126	215	Springboro Community City SD	Springboro
127	215	Ravenna City SD	Ravenna
128	213	Kings Local SD	Kings Mills
129	211	Amherst Ex Vill SD	Amherst
130	211	Southwest Local SD	Harrison
131	208	Bowling Green City SD	Bowling Green
132	208	New Philadelphia City SD	New Philadelphia
133	206	Garfield Heights City SD	Garfield Hgts
134	205	Springfield Local SD	Akron
135	205	Kenston Local SD	Chagrin Falls
136	205	Maumee City SD	Maumee
137	203	Southwest Licking Local SD	Etna
138	202	Howland Local SD	Warren
138	202	Switzerland of Ohio Local SD	Woodsfield
140	201	Cloverleaf Local SD	Lodi
141	200	Celina City SD	Celina
142	199	Northeastern Local SD	Springfield
143	197	Lake Local SD	Hartville
144	196	Copley-Fairlawn City SD	Copley
145	196	Whitehall City SD	Whitehall
146	196	Chillicothe City SD	Chillicothe
147	195	Madison Local SD	Madison
148	193	Salem City SD	Salem
149	192	Louisville City SD	Louisville
150	192	Western Brown Local SD	Mount Orab
151	191	Piqua City SD	Piqua
152	191	Marietta City SD	Marietta
153	190	Chardon Local SD	Chardon
154	189	Olmsted Falls City SD	Olmsted Falls
155	187	Bellefontaine City SD	Bellefontaine
156	186	Teays Valley Local SD	Ashville
157	185	Orange City SD	Cleveland
158	185	Norwood City SD	Norwood
159	185	Niles City SD	Niles
160	181	Plain Local SD	New Albany
161	181	Tiffin City SD	Tiffin
162	180	Cambridge City SD	Cambridge
163	178	Franklin City SD	Franklin
164	177	Gallia County Local SD	Gallipolis
165	177	Hamilton Local SD	Columbus
166	177	Canfield Local SD	Canfield
167	176	West Holmes Local SD	Millersburg
168	176	Revere Local SD	Bath
169	175	Tallmadge City SD	Tallmadge
170	175	Midview Local SD	Grafton
171	174	Hillsboro City SD	Hillsboro
172	174	Dover City SD	Dover
173	172	Vinton County Local SD	Mc Arthur
174	172	Painesville City Local SD	Painesville
175	172	Morgan Local SD	McConnelsville
176	172	Wilmington City SD	Wilmington
177	170	Tri-Valley Local SD	Dresden
178	168	Edison Local SD	Hammondsville

179	168	Canton Local SD	Canton
180	167	Wapakoneta City SD	Wapakoneta
181	166	Little Miami Local SD	Morrow
182	166	Bexley City SD	Bexley
183	165	Defiance City SD	Defiance
184	165	Buckeye Local SD	Rayland
185	164	Beachwood City SD	Beachwood
186	164	New Richmond Ex Vill SD	New Richmond
187	164	Oakwood City SD	Dayton
188	164	Marlington Local SD	Alliance
189	163	West Geauga Local SD	Chesterland
190	163	Big Walnut Local SD	Galena
191	163	Carrollton Ex Vill SD	Carrollton
192	162	Miami Trace Local SD	Washington Ct Hse
193	162	Canal Winchester Local SD	Canal Winchester
194	161	Lexington Local SD	Lexington
195	161	Geneva Area City SD	Geneva
196	161	Meigs Local SD	Pomeroy
197	160	Bay Village City SD	Bay Village
198	160	Warren Local SD	Vincent
199	159	Rocky River City SD	Rocky River
200	158	Aurora City SD	Aurora
201	157	Norton City SD	Norton
202	157	Crestwood Local SD	Mantua
203	157	Highland Local SD	Medina
204	155	Lakewood Local SD	Hebron
205	154	Buckeye Local SD	Medina
206	154	River View Local SD	Warsaw
207	153	Circleville City SD	Circleville
208	153	Indian Hill Ex Vill SD	Cincinnati
209	152	Bellevue City SD	Bellevue
209	152	Tipp City Ex Vill SD	Tipp City
211	151	Saint Marys City SD	Saint Marys
211	151	Van Wert City SD	Van Wert
213	151	Vermilion Local SD	Vermilion
214	150	Conneaut Area City SD	Conneaut
215	150	Napoleon Area City SD	Napoleon
215	150	Northwest Local SD	Canal Fulton
217	149	Gallipolis City SD	Gallipolis
218	148	Portsmouth City SD	Portsmouth
218	148	Steubenville City SD	Steubenville
220	147	Logan Elm Local SD	Circleville
221	147	Jackson City SD	Jackson
222	146	Ross Local SD	Hamilton
223	144	Bryan City SD	Bryan
223	144	Shelby City SD	Shelby
225	143	Urbana City SD	Urbana
226	143	Elida Local SD	Elida
227	142	Chagrin Falls Ex Vill SD	Chagrin Falls
228	142	Northern Local SD	Thornville
229	142	Wyoming City SD	Wyoming
230	142	Perkins Local SD	Sandusky
231	141	Galion City SD	Galion
232	141	Coventry Local SD	Akron
233	141	Goshen Local SD	Goshen
234	140	Kenton City SD	Kenton
235	140	Buckeye Local SD	Ashtabula
236	139	Field Local SD	Mogadore
236	139	Sugarcreek Local SD	Bellbrook
238	139	Streetsboro City SD	Streetsboro
239	139	Fostoria City SD	Fostoria
240	139	London City SD	London
241	138	Avon Local SD	Avon
241	138	Buckeye Valley Local SD	Delaware
243	138	Indian Creek Local SD	Wintersville
244	137	Triway Local SD	Wooster
245	137	Willard City SD	Willard
246	137	Shawnee Local SD	Lima
247	137	Clyde-Green Springs Ex Vill SD	Clyde
247	137	West Branch Local SD	Beloit
249	136	Claymont City SD	Dennison
249	136	Harrison Hills City SD	Hopedale
251	136	Norwalk City SD	Norwalk
252	136	Beaver Local SD	Lisbon
252	136	Washington Court House City SD	Washington Ct Hse
254	135	Fairview Park City SD	Fairview Park
255	135	Valley View Local SD	Germantown
256	133	Franklin Local SD	Duncan Falls
257	133	Graham Local SD	Saint Paris
258	132	Minerva Local SD	Minerva
259	131	Woodridge Local SD	Peninsula
260	131	Clark-Shawnee Local SD	Springfield
261	131	Port Clinton City SD	Port Clinton
262	131	Eaton City SD	Eaton
263	131	Hubbard Ex Vill SD	Hubbard
264	130	Greenfield Ex Vill SD	Greenfield
264	130	Rossford Ex Vill SD	Rossford
266	130	Rock Hill Local SD	Ironton
267	130	Indian Lake Local SD	Lewistown
268	129	Southeast Local SD	Ravenna
269	129	Maysville Local SD	Zanesville
270	129	Poland Local SD	Poland
271	128	Licking Valley Local SD	Newark
272	127	Northridge Local SD	Dayton
272	127	Waverly City SD	Waverly
274	126	Paulding Ex Vill SD	Paulding
275	125	Coshocton City SD	Coshocton
276	125	Three Rivers Local SD	Cleves
277	125	East Muskingum Local SD	New Concord
278	125	Indian Valley Local SD	Gnadenhutten
279	124	Bucyrus City SD	Bucyrus
280	123	Finneytown Local SD	Cincinnati
280	123	Sheffield-Sheffield Lake City	Sheffield Vlg
282	123	Struthers City SD	Struthers
283	123	Perry Local SD	Perry
284	122	East Holmes Local SD	Berlin
284	122	Jefferson Area Local SD	Jefferson
286	121	Firelands Local SD	Oberlin
287	121	Union Local SD	Morristown
288	120	Lakeview Local SD	Cortland
289	119	Wellston City SD	Wellston
290	119	Upper Sandusky Ex Vill SD	Upper Sandusky
291	119	Fairless Local SD	Navarre
291	119	Rolling Hills Local SD	Byesville
293	118	Greenon Local SD	Springfield
294	118	Mariemont City SD	Cincinnati
295	117	Orrville City SD	Orrville
296	116	Alexander Local SD	Albany
297	116	Carlisle Local SD	Carlisle
298	116	Clear Fork Valley Local SD	Bellville
299	116	New Lexington City SD	New Lexington
300	116	Granville Ex Vill SD	Granville
300	116	Wauseon Ex Vill SD	Wauseon
302	115	South Point Local SD	South Point
303	114	Benton Carroll Salem Local SD	Oak Harbor
303	114	Washington-Nile Local SD	West Portsmouth
305	114	Berlin-Milan Local SD	Milan
306	113	Preble Shawnee Local SD	Camden
306	113	Union-Scioto Local SD	Chillicothe
308	111	Batavia Local SD	Batavia
308	111	North Fork Local SD	Utica
310	110	Clermont-Northeastern Local SD	Batavia
310	110	Wickliffe City SD	Wickliffe
312	110	Southeast Local SD	Apple Creek
313	109	Bellaire Local SD	Bellaire
314	109	Benjamin Logan Local SD	Bellefontaine
315	109	Elgin Local SD	Marion
316	108	Champion Local SD	Warren
317	108	Bath Local SD	Lima
318	108	Milton-Union Ex Vill SD	West Milton
319	108	Northwest Local SD	Mc Dermott
320	107	Liberty Local SD	Youngstown
320	107	Northwestern Local SD	Springfield
322	107	River Valley Local SD	Caledonia
323	107	Licking Heights Local SD	Summit Station
324	106	Campbell City SD	Campbell
325	105	Highland Local SD	Sparta
326	104	Fairfield Union Local SD	W Rushville
326	104	Ironton City SD	Ironton
328	104	Bethel-Tate Local SD	Bethel
328	104	Saint Clairsville-Richland City	St Clairsville
330	103	Tuscarawas Valley Local SD	Zoarville
331	103	Black River Local SD	Sullivan
331	103	Girard City SD	Girard
333	102	West Muskingum Local SD	Zanesville
334	102	Huron City SD	Huron
335	101	Sandy Valley Local SD	Magnolia
336	101	Blanchester Local SD	Blanchester
337	100	Fairland Local SD	Proctorville
338	100	Clearview Local SD	Lorain
339	99	Ottawa-Glandorf Local SD	Ottawa
340	98	Swanton Local SD	Swanton
341	98	Labrae Local SD	Leavittsburg
341	98	Madison-Plains Local SD	London
343	97	Eastern Local SD	Sardinia
343	97	Madison Local SD	Middletown
345	96	Coldwater Ex Vill SD	Coldwater
346	95	James A Garfield Local SD	Garrettsville
347	95	Keystone Local SD	Lagrange
348	95	Eastwood Local SD	Pemberville
349	94	Minford Local SD	Minford
350	93	Pike-Delta-York Local SD	Delta
351	93	Otsego Local SD	Tontogany
352	93	Genoa Area Local SD	Genoa
352	93	Westfall Local SD	Williamsport
354	92	Ontario Local SD	Mansfield
354	92	Wellington Ex Vill SD	Wellington
356	92	Heath City SD	Heath
357	92	Brookfield Local SD	Brookfield
357	92	East Clinton Local SD	Lees Creek
357	92	Jonathan Alder Local SD	Plain City
360	92	Scioto Valley Local SD	Piketon
361	90	Greeneview Local SD	Jamestown
362	89	Newton Falls Ex Vill SD	Newton Falls
363	88	Clinton-Massie Local SD	Clarksville
364	88	Amanda-Clearcreek Local SD	Amanda
365	87	North College Hill City SD	Cincinnati
366	85	Electronic Classroom of Tomorrow	Columbus
367	85	Brookville Local SD	Brookville
368	84	Manchester Local SD	Akron
369	84	Zane Trace Local SD	Chillicothe
370	83	Lake Local SD	Millbury

Number of Students

Rank	Number	District Name	City
1	71,616	Cleveland Municipal SD	Cleveland
2	64,175	Columbus City SD	Columbus
3	42,715	Cincinnati City SD	Cincinnati
4	35,742	Toledo City SD	Toledo
5	29,532	Akron City SD	Akron
6	20,987	South-Western City SD	Grove City
7	19,813	Dayton City SD	Dayton
8	15,844	Lakota Local SD	Liberty Twp
9	14,044	Westerville City SD	Westerville
10	13,854	Hilliard City SD	Hilliard
11	13,441	Parma City SD	Parma
12	12,362	Canton City SD	Canton
13	12,046	Dublin City SD	Dublin
14	10,678	Northwest Local SD	Cincinnati
15	10,652	Lorain City SD	Lorain
16	10,034	Youngstown City SD	Youngstown
17	9,941	Worthington City SD	Worthington
18	9,886	Mentor Ex Vill SD	Mentor
19	9,599	Springfield City SD	Springfield
20	9,426	Hamilton City SD	Hamilton
21	9,395	Fairfield City SD	Fairfield
22	9,176	West Clermont Local SD	Cincinnati
23	8,977	Willoughby-Eastlake City SD	Willoughby
24	8,440	Pickerington Local SD	Pickerington
25	8,348	Elyria City SD	Elyria
26	8,160	Oak Hills Local SD	Cincinnati
27	8,006	Berea City SD	Berea
28	8,003	Mason City SD	Mason
29	7,902	Kettering City SD	Kettering
30	7,899	Centerville City SD	Centerville
31	7,842	Sylvania City SD	Sylvania
32	7,629	Middletown City SD	Middletown
33	7,602	Forest Hills Local SD	Cincinnati
34	7,530	Olentangy Local SD	Lewis Center
35	7,270	Brunswick City SD	Brunswick
36	7,214	Strongsville City SD	Strongsville
37	7,044	Cleveland Hts-Univ Hts City SD	University Hgts
38	7,030	Medina City SD	Medina
39	6,989	Washington Local SD	Toledo
40	6,958	Newark City SD	Newark
41	6,949	Lakewood City SD	Lakewood
42	6,918	Warren City SD	Warren
43	6,891	Beavercreek City SD	Beavercreek
44	6,868	Huber Heights City SD	Huber Heights
45	6,784	Gahanna-Jefferson City SD	Gahanna
46	6,476	Findlay City SD	Findlay
47	6,450	Reynoldsburg City SD	Reynoldsburg
48	6,318	Groveport Madison Local SD	Groveport
48	6,318	Princeton City SD	Cincinnati
50	6,244	Plain Local SD	Canton
51	6,196	Lancaster City SD	Lancaster
52	6,140	Euclid City SD	Euclid
53	6,071	Milford Ex Vill SD	Milford
54	5,997	Mansfield City SD	Mansfield
55	5,963	Stow-Munroe Falls City SD	Stow
56	5,801	Northmont City SD	Englewood
57	5,732	Sycamore Community City SD	Cincinnati
58	5,682	Marion City SD	Marion
59	5,679	Upper Arlington City SD	Upper Arlington
60	5,612	Shaker Heights City SD	Shaker Heights
61	5,562	Hudson City SD	Hudson
62	5,553	Fairborn City SD	Fairborn
63	5,411	Cuyahoga Falls City SD	Cuyahoga Falls
64	5,380	Jackson Local SD	Massillon
65	5,304	East Cleveland City SD	East Cleveland
66	5,264	Xenia Community City SD	Xenia
67	5,253	Lima City SD	Lima
68	5,213	Miamisburg City SD	Miamisburg
69	5,115	Solon City SD	Solon
70	5,092	Austintown Local SD	Youngstown
71	5,016	Adams County-Ohio Valley Local SD	West Union
72	4,920	Boardman Local SD	Youngstown
73	4,900	Perry Local SD	Massillon
74	4,863	North Canton City SD	North Canton
75	4,785	Ashtabula Area City SD	Ashtabula
76	4,690	Lebanon City SD	Lebanon
77	4,665	North Olmsted City SD	North Olmsted
78	4,630	Wadsworth City SD	Wadsworth
79	4,616	Barberton City SD	Barberton
80	4,612	Fremont City SD	Fremont

Rank	Number	District	City
81	4,608	Marysville Ex Vill SD	Marysville
82	4,554	Troy City SD	Troy
83	4,521	South Euclid-Lyndhurst City SD	Lyndhurst
84	4,513	Brecksville-Broadview Heights	Brecksville
85	4,479	Delaware City SD	Delaware
86	4,453	Massillon City SD	Massillon
87	4,429	North Royalton City SD	N Royalton
88	4,379	Painesville Township Local SD	Painesville
88	4,379	Perrysburg Ex Vill SD	Perrysburg
90	4,368	Zanesville City SD	Zanesville
91	4,316	Sandusky City SD	Sandusky
92	4,275	Mount Vernon City SD	Mount Vernon
93	4,264	Mayfield City SD	Highland Hgts
94	4,209	Electronic Classroom of Tomorrow	Columbus
95	4,204	Wooster City SD	Wooster
96	4,194	Loveland City SD	Loveland
97	4,191	Winton Woods City SD	Cincinnati
98	4,184	Green Local SD	Green
99	4,051	Springboro Community City SD	Springboro
100	3,967	Amherst Ex Vill SD	Amherst
101	3,958	Logan-Hocking Local SD	Logan
102	3,948	Sidney City SD	Sidney
103	3,933	West Carrollton City SD	West Carrollton
104	3,917	Southwest Local SD	Harrison
105	3,914	Piqua City SD	Piqua
106	3,892	Mount Healthy City SD	Cincinnati
107	3,880	Westlake City SD	Westlake
108	3,879	Oregon City SD	Oregon
109	3,847	Twinsburg City SD	Twinsburg
110	3,846	Ashland City SD	Ashland
111	3,822	Bedford City SD	Bedford
112	3,792	Garfield Heights City SD	Garfield Hgts
113	3,786	Kent City SD	Kent
114	3,775	Maple Heights City SD	Maple Heights
115	3,774	Kings Local SD	Kings Mills
116	3,749	Madison Local SD	Madison
117	3,736	Nordonia Hills City SD	Northfield
118	3,711	Anthony Wayne Local SD	Whitehouse
119	3,707	Mad River Local SD	Dayton
120	3,693	Springfield Local SD	Holland
121	3,691	Chillicothe City SD	Chillicothe
122	3,683	Trotwood-Madison City SD	Trotwood
123	3,609	Cloverleaf Local SD	Lodi
124	3,601	Northeastern Local SD	Springfield
125	3,595	Tecumseh Local SD	New Carlisle
126	3,563	Madison Local SD	Mansfield
127	3,513	North Ridgeville City SD	N Ridgeville
128	3,497	Greenville City SD	Greenville
129	3,490	Southwest Licking Local SD	Etna
130	3,476	Vandalia-Butler City SD	Vandalia
131	3,405	Midview Local SD	Grafton
132	3,380	Western Brown Local SD	Mount Orab
133	3,364	Edgewood City SD	Trenton
134	3,354	Celina City SD	Celina
135	3,352	Avon Lake City SD	Avon Lake
136	3,346	Lake Local SD	Hartville
137	3,340	Alliance City SD	Alliance
138	3,321	Marietta City SD	Marietta
139	3,298	Howland Local SD	Warren
140	3,287	Ravenna City SD	Ravenna
141	3,260	New Philadelphia City SD	New Philadelphia
142	3,245	Bowling Green City SD	Bowling Green
143	3,239	Louisville City SD	Louisville
144	3,219	Talawanda City SD	Oxford
145	3,213	Chardon Local SD	Chardon
146	3,198	Olmsted Falls City SD	Olmsted Falls
147	3,181	Kenston Local SD	Chagrin Falls
148	3,180	Wapakoneta City SD	Wapakoneta
149	3,179	Wilmington City SD	Wilmington
150	3,174	Copley-Fairlawn City SD	Copley
151	3,104	East Liverpool City SD	East Liverpool
152	3,103	Canfield Local SD	Canfield
153	3,078	Springfield Local SD	Akron
154	3,074	Tri-Valley Local SD	Dresden
155	3,069	Teays Valley Local SD	Ashville
156	3,060	Geneva Area City SD	Geneva
157	3,051	Franklin City SD	Franklin
158	3,042	Whitehall City SD	Whitehall
159	3,033	Little Miami Local SD	Morrow
160	3,024	Tiffin City SD	Tiffin
161	2,997	Carrollton Ex Vill SD	Carrollton
162	2,966	Warrensville Heights City SD	Warrensville Hgts
163	2,955	Athens City SD	The Plains
164	2,928	Norwalk City SD	Norwalk
165	2,912	Painesville City Local SD	Painesville
166	2,909	Maumee City SD	Maumee
167	2,905	Hamilton Local SD	Columbus
168	2,872	Revere Local SD	Bath
169	2,870	Hillsboro City SD	Hillsboro
170	2,869	Niles City SD	Niles
171	2,868	Bellefontaine City SD	Bellefontaine
172	2,835	Norwood City SD	Norwood
173	2,828	Lexington Local SD	Lexington
174	2,812	Switzerland of Ohio Local SD	Woodsfield
175	2,790	Marlington Local SD	Alliance
176	2,787	West Holmes Local SD	Millersburg
177	2,750	Sugarcreek Local SD	Bellbrook
178	2,743	Tallmadge City SD	Tallmadge
179	2,741	Cambridge City SD	Cambridge
180	2,736	Jackson City SD	Jackson
181	2,734	Crestwood Local SD	Mantua
182	2,711	Aurora City SD	Aurora
183	2,709	Highland Local SD	Medina
184	2,702	Warren Local SD	Vincent
185	2,697	Edison Local SD	Hammondsville
186	2,689	Miami Trace Local SD	Washington Ct Hse
187	2,679	Gallia County Local SD	Gallipolis
188	2,668	Big Walnut Local SD	Galena
189	2,665	River View Local SD	Warsaw
190	2,643	Tipp City Ex Vill SD	Tipp City
191	2,641	Vinton County Local SD	Mc Arthur
192	2,631	Shawnee Local SD	Lima
193	2,623	West Geauga Local SD	Chesterland
194	2,619	Dover City SD	Dover
195	2,614	Saint Marys City SD	Saint Marys
196	2,598	Norton City SD	Norton
197	2,592	Defiance City SD	Defiance
197	2,592	Plain Local SD	New Albany
199	2,580	Elida Local SD	Elida
200	2,578	Canton Local SD	Canton
201	2,575	Rocky River City SD	Rocky River
202	2,569	Vermilion Local SD	Vermilion
203	2,547	Conneaut Area City SD	Conneaut
204	2,544	Ross Local SD	Hamilton
205	2,542	West Branch Local SD	Beloit
206	2,536	Circleville City SD	Circleville
207	2,535	Goshen Local SD	Goshen
208	2,525	Poland Local SD	Poland
209	2,524	New Richmond Ex Vill SD	New Richmond
210	2,502	Coventry Local SD	Akron
211	2,492	Beaver Local SD	Lisbon
212	2,472	Salem City SD	Salem
213	2,469	Canal Winchester Local SD	Canal Winchester
214	2,466	Buckeye Local SD	Rayland
215	2,464	Steubenville City SD	Steubenville
216	2,463	Clark-Shawnee Local SD	Springfield
217	2,446	Gallipolis City SD	Gallipolis
218	2,437	Buckeye Local SD	Medina
219	2,428	Franklin Local SD	Duncan Falls
220	2,426	Northwest Local SD	Canal Fulton
221	2,406	Bay Village City SD	Bay Village
222	2,388	Urbana City SD	Urbana
223	2,371	Logan Elm Local SD	Circleville
224	2,367	Eaton City SD	Eaton
225	2,363	Orange City SD	Cleveland
226	2,352	Bryan City SD	Bryan
227	2,351	Fostoria City SD	Fostoria
228	2,348	Washington Court House City SD	Washington Ct Hse
229	2,334	Bellevue City SD	Bellevue
229	2,334	Napoleon Area City SD	Napoleon
231	2,332	Claymont City SD	Dennison
232	2,322	Morgan Local SD	McConnelsville
233	2,314	Willard City SD	Willard
234	2,313	Northern Local SD	Thornville
235	2,312	Van Wert City SD	Van Wert
236	2,301	Hubbard Ex Vill SD	Hubbard
237	2,300	Clyde-Green Springs Ex Vill SD	Clyde
238	2,291	Avon Local SD	Avon
239	2,289	Shelby City SD	Shelby
240	2,278	Lakewood Local SD	Hebron
241	2,274	Maysville Local SD	Zanesville
242	2,273	Indian Hill Ex Vill SD	Cincinnati
243	2,271	Indian Creek Local SD	Wintersville
244	2,270	Buckeye Local SD	Ashtabula
245	2,269	Southeast Local SD	Ravenna
246	2,256	Buckeye Valley Local SD	Delaware
246	2,256	Rolling Hills Local SD	Byesville
248	2,255	Galion City SD	Galion
249	2,246	Perkins Local SD	Sandusky
250	2,245	Field Local SD	Mogadore
251	2,244	Bexley City SD	Bexley
252	2,242	Lakeview Local SD	Cortland
253	2,226	Firelands Local SD	Oberlin
254	2,210	Greenfield Ex Vill SD	Greenfield
254	2,210	Three Rivers Local SD	Cleves
256	2,201	Graham Local SD	Saint Paris
257	2,192	Minerva Local SD	Minerva
258	2,189	Licking Valley Local SD	Newark
259	2,185	Portsmouth City SD	Portsmouth
260	2,181	East Muskingum Local SD	New Concord
261	2,180	Jefferson Area Local SD	Jefferson
262	2,179	Meigs Local SD	Pomeroy
263	2,159	Kenton City SD	Kenton
264	2,152	Waverly City SD	Waverly
265	2,147	Triway Local SD	Wooster
266	2,132	Wauseon Ex Vill SD	Wauseon
267	2,082	Harrison Hills City SD	Hopedale
268	2,065	Benton Carroll Salem Local SD	Oak Harbor
269	2,062	Rossford Ex Vill SD	Rossford
270	2,060	Northridge Local SD	Dayton
271	2,057	Sheffield-Sheffield Lake City	Sheffield Vlg
272	2,049	Granville Ex Vill SD	Granville
273	2,048	Streetsboro City SD	Streetsboro
274	2,045	London City SD	London
275	2,038	Struthers City SD	Struthers
275	2,038	Valley View Local SD	Germantown
277	2,036	Clermont-Northeastern Local SD	Batavia
277	2,036	Indian Lake Local SD	Lewistown
279	2,033	Greenon Local SD	Springfield
280	2,030	Bath Local SD	Lima
281	2,004	Oakwood City SD	Dayton
282	1,997	New Lexington City SD	New Lexington
283	1,996	Benjamin Logan Local SD	Bellefontaine
284	1,991	Coshocton City SD	Coshocton
285	1,984	Wyoming City SD	Wyoming
286	1,967	Chagrin Falls Ex Vill SD	Chagrin Falls
287	1,958	Port Clinton City SD	Port Clinton
288	1,957	Rock Hill Local SD	Ironton
289	1,939	Indian Valley Local SD	Gnadenhutten
290	1,936	Bucyrus City SD	Bucyrus
291	1,932	Bethel-Tate Local SD	Bethel
292	1,930	Northwestern Local SD	Springfield
293	1,927	Eastwood Local SD	Pemberville
294	1,926	Batavia Local SD	Batavia
295	1,918	Union-Scioto Local SD	Chillicothe
296	1,914	Fairless Local SD	Navarre
297	1,888	Fairfield Union Local SD	W Rushville
297	1,888	Perry Local SD	Perry
299	1,887	North Fork Local SD	Utica
299	1,887	Orrville City SD	Orrville
301	1,873	East Holmes Local SD	Berlin
302	1,872	Berlin-Milan Local SD	Milan
303	1,871	Fairview Park City SD	Fairview Park
304	1,863	Lake Local SD	Millbury
305	1,860	Wellston City SD	Wellston
306	1,855	Paulding Ex Vill SD	Paulding
307	1,854	Keystone Local SD	Lagrange
308	1,848	Clear Fork Valley Local SD	Bellville
309	1,837	South Point Local SD	South Point
310	1,832	Milton-Union Ex Vill SD	West Milton
310	1,832	Upper Sandusky Ex Vill SD	Upper Sandusky
312	1,821	Fairland Local SD	Proctorville
312	1,821	Woodridge Local SD	Peninsula
314	1,817	Liberty Local SD	Youngstown
315	1,814	Finneytown Local SD	Cincinnati
316	1,805	Jonathan Alder Local SD	Plain City
317	1,801	Highland Local SD	Sparta
318	1,792	West Muskingum Local SD	Zanesville
319	1,781	Northwest Local SD	Mc Dermott
320	1,772	Blanchester Local SD	Blanchester
321	1,767	Tuscarawas Valley Local SD	Zoarville
322	1,764	Carlisle Local SD	Carlisle
322	1,764	Ottawa-Glandorf Local SD	Ottawa
324	1,758	Girard City SD	Girard
325	1,756	Clinton-Massie Local SD	Clarksville
326	1,755	Mariemont City SD	Cincinnati
327	1,753	Champion Local SD	Warren
328	1,747	Ontario Local SD	Mansfield
328	1,747	Preble Shawnee Local SD	Camden
330	1,730	Southeast Local SD	Apple Creek
331	1,728	Washington-Nile Local SD	West Portsmouth
332	1,726	River Valley Local SD	Caledonia
333	1,724	Otsego Local SD	Tontogany
334	1,713	Genoa Area Local SD	Genoa
335	1,686	Heath City SD	Heath
336	1,682	Westfall Local SD	Williamsport
337	1,681	Elgin Local SD	Marion
338	1,676	Black River Local SD	Sullivan
339	1,675	Licking Heights Local SD	Summit Station
340	1,668	Madison-Plains Local SD	London
341	1,666	Huron City SD	Huron
342	1,660	Scioto Valley Local SD	Piketon
343	1,652	Alexander Local SD	Albany
344	1,642	Greeneview Local SD	Jamestown
345	1,638	Minford Local SD	Minford
346	1,633	Coldwater Ex Vill SD	Coldwater
347	1,631	Amanda-Clearcreek Local SD	Amanda
348	1,627	Wellington Ex Vill SD	Wellington
349	1,619	Brookville Local SD	Brookville
350	1,612	Saint Clairsville-Richland City	St Clairsville
351	1,607	James A Garfield Local SD	Garrettsville
352	1,597	Pike-Delta-York Local SD	Delta
352	1,597	Swanton Local SD	Swanton
354	1,592	Bellaire Local SD	Bellaire
355	1,591	Campbell City SD	Campbell
356	1,587	Sandy Valley Local SD	Magnolia

357	1,582	Eastern Local SD	Sardinia
358	1,580	Beachwood City SD	Beachwood
359	1,577	Ironton City SD	Ironton
360	1,576	Madison Local SD	Middletown
361	1,561	East Clinton Local SD	Lees Creek
362	1,542	North College Hill City SD	Cincinnati
363	1,537	Newton Falls Ex Vill SD	Newton Falls
364	1,534	Labrae Local SD	Leavittsburg
365	1,530	Union Local SD	Morristown
366	1,522	Zane Trace Local SD	Chillicothe
367	1,519	Clearview Local SD	Lorain
368	1,508	Wickliffe City SD	Wickliffe
369	1,503	Brookfield Local SD	Brookfield
370	1,500	Manchester Local SD	Akron

Male Students

Rank	Percent	District Name	City
1	55.3	Saint Marys City SD	Saint Marys
2	55.0	Canton Local SD	Canton
2	55.0	Orange City SD	Cleveland
4	54.8	Wickliffe City SD	Wickliffe
5	54.5	Tallmadge City SD	Tallmadge
6	54.1	Genoa Area Local SD	Genoa
6	54.1	Maumee City SD	Maumee
6	54.1	Preble Shawnee Local SD	Camden
9	54.0	Orrville City SD	Orrville
9	54.0	Ross Local SD	Hamilton
11	53.9	Three Rivers Local SD	Cleves
11	53.9	Union Local SD	Morristown
13	53.8	Beachwood City SD	Beachwood
13	53.8	Mayfield City SD	Highland Hgts
15	53.7	Madison Local SD	Mansfield
15	53.7	Piqua City SD	Piqua
17	53.6	New Lexington City SD	New Lexington
17	53.6	River Valley Local SD	Caledonia
19	53.5	Massillon City SD	Massillon
20	53.4	Southeast Local SD	Apple Creek
20	53.4	West Carrollton City SD	West Carrollton
22	53.3	Berlin-Milan Local SD	Milan
22	53.3	Finneytown Local SD	Cincinnati
22	53.3	Harrison Hills City SD	Hopedale
22	53.3	Milton-Union Ex Vill SD	West Milton
26	53.2	Hudson City SD	Hudson
26	53.2	North College Hill City SD	Cincinnati
28	53.1	Avon Lake City SD	Avon Lake
28	53.1	Batavia Local SD	Batavia
28	53.1	Black River Local SD	Sullivan
28	53.1	Kings Local SD	Kings Mills
28	53.1	Ontario Local SD	Mansfield
28	53.1	Tuscarawas Valley Local SD	Zoarville
34	53.0	Claymont City SD	Dennison
34	53.0	East Muskingum Local SD	New Concord
34	53.0	Warren Local SD	Vincent
34	53.0	West Geauga Local SD	Chesterland
38	52.9	Brookfield Local SD	Brookfield
38	52.9	Brookville Local SD	Brookville
38	52.9	Edgewood City SD	Trenton
38	52.9	Field Local SD	Mogadore
38	52.9	Geneva Area City SD	Geneva
38	52.9	Highland Local SD	Sparta
38	52.9	Lake Local SD	Hartville
38	52.9	Portsmouth City SD	Portsmouth
46	52.8	Berea City SD	Berea
46	52.8	East Holmes Local SD	Berlin
46	52.8	Green Local SD	Green
46	52.8	Ironton City SD	Ironton
46	52.8	Mount Healthy City SD	Cincinnati
46	52.8	Oak Hills Local SD	Cincinnati
46	52.8	Port Clinton City SD	Port Clinton
46	52.8	Washington Local SD	Toledo
54	52.7	Bellaire Local SD	Bellaire
54	52.7	Celina City SD	Celina
54	52.7	Conneaut Area City SD	Conneaut
54	52.7	Fairborn City SD	Fairborn
54	52.7	Greenfield Ex Vill SD	Greenfield
54	52.7	Jackson City SD	Jackson
54	52.7	Liberty Local SD	Youngstown
54	52.7	Logan Elm Local SD	Circleville
54	52.7	Sandy Valley Local SD	Magnolia
63	52.6	Buckeye Valley Local SD	Delaware
63	52.6	Crestwood Local SD	Mantua
63	52.6	Indian Creek Local SD	Wintersville
63	52.6	Minerva Local SD	Minerva
63	52.6	Oregon City SD	Oregon
63	52.6	Wooster City SD	Wooster
69	52.5	Garfield Heights City SD	Garfield Hgts
69	52.5	Northern Local SD	Thornville
69	52.5	Norwalk City SD	Norwalk
69	52.5	Perry Local SD	Massillon
69	52.5	Pickerington Local SD	Pickerington
69	52.5	Southwest Local SD	Harrison
69	52.5	Springfield City SD	Springfield
69	52.5	Streetsboro City SD	Streetsboro
69	52.5	Teays Valley Local SD	Ashville
69	52.5	Vinton County Local SD	Mc Arthur
79	52.4	Bellevue City SD	Bellevue
79	52.4	Bucyrus City SD	Bucyrus
79	52.4	Coldwater Ex Vill SD	Coldwater
79	52.4	Fairfield Union Local SD	W Rushville
79	52.4	Gahanna-Jefferson City SD	Gahanna
79	52.4	Lancaster City SD	Lancaster
79	52.4	Northwest Local SD	Mc Dermott
79	52.4	Rock Hill Local SD	Ironton
79	52.4	Washington Court House City SD	Washington Ct Hse
79	52.4	Winton Woods City SD	Cincinnati
79	52.4	Xenia Community City SD	Xenia
90	52.3	Clinton-Massie Local SD	Clarksville
90	52.3	Franklin Local SD	Duncan Falls
90	52.3	Norwood City SD	Norwood
90	52.3	Saint Clairsville-Richland City	St Clairsville
90	52.3	Troy City SD	Troy
90	52.3	Wadsworth City SD	Wadsworth
90	52.3	West Branch Local SD	Beloit
90	52.3	Wilmington City SD	Wilmington
98	52.2	Buckeye Local SD	Rayland
98	52.2	Eaton City SD	Eaton
98	52.2	Granville Ex Vill SD	Granville
98	52.2	Marion City SD	Marion
98	52.2	North Olmsted City SD	North Olmsted
98	52.2	Northwest Local SD	Cincinnati
98	52.2	Princeton City SD	Cincinnati
98	52.2	Springfield Local SD	Holland
98	52.2	Strongsville City SD	Strongsville
98	52.2	Whitehall City SD	Whitehall
98	52.2	Worthington City SD	Worthington
109	52.1	Ashland City SD	Ashland
109	52.1	Cambridge City SD	Cambridge
109	52.1	Carlisle Local SD	Carlisle
109	52.1	Lakewood Local SD	Hebron
109	52.1	Maple Heights City SD	Maple Heights
109	52.1	Minford Local SD	Minford
109	52.1	Northeastern Local SD	Springfield
109	52.1	South Euclid-Lyndhurst City SD	Lyndhurst
109	52.1	Stow-Munroe Falls City SD	Stow
109	52.1	Valley View Local SD	Germantown
119	52.0	Centerville City SD	Centerville
119	52.0	Defiance City SD	Defiance
119	52.0	Goshen Local SD	Goshen
119	52.0	Greeneview Local SD	Jamestown
119	52.0	Highland Local SD	Medina
119	52.0	Indian Hill Ex Vill SD	Cincinnati
119	52.0	Logan-Hocking Local SD	Logan
119	52.0	Revere Local SD	Bath
119	52.0	River View Local SD	Warsaw
119	52.0	Woodridge Local SD	Peninsula
129	51.9	Amanda-Clearcreek Local SD	Amanda
129	51.9	Ashtabula Area City SD	Ashtabula
129	51.9	Barberton City SD	Barberton
129	51.9	Delaware City SD	Delaware
129	51.9	Euclid City SD	Euclid
129	51.9	Fairless Local SD	Navarre
129	51.9	Girard City SD	Girard
129	51.9	Hamilton City SD	Hamilton
129	51.9	Kenton City SD	Kenton
129	51.9	Lima City SD	Lima
129	51.9	Madison Local SD	Madison
129	51.9	Middletown City SD	Middletown
129	51.9	Midview Local SD	Grafton
129	51.9	Northwest Local SD	Canal Fulton
129	51.9	Shelby City SD	Shelby
129	51.9	Springboro Community City SD	Springboro
129	51.9	Swanton Local SD	Swanton
129	51.9	Switzerland of Ohio Local SD	Woodsfield
129	51.9	Urbana City SD	Urbana
129	51.9	Vandalia-Butler City SD	Vandalia
129	51.9	Waverly City SD	Waverly
129	51.9	Western Brown Local SD	Mount Orab
151	51.8	Chagrin Falls Ex Vill SD	Chagrin Falls
151	51.8	Chillicothe City SD	Chillicothe
151	51.8	Clermont-Northeastern Local SD	Batavia
151	51.8	Franklin City SD	Franklin
151	51.8	Lakota Local SD	Liberty Twp
151	51.8	Lorain City SD	Lorain
151	51.8	Marietta City SD	Marietta
151	51.8	Miamisburg City SD	Miamisburg
151	51.8	New Philadelphia City SD	New Philadelphia
151	51.8	North Ridgeville City SD	N Ridgeville
151	51.8	Painesville City Local SD	Painesville
151	51.8	Rossford Ex Vill SD	Rossford
151	51.8	Southeast Local SD	Ravenna
151	51.8	Steubenville City SD	Steubenville
151	51.8	Sugarcreek Local SD	Bellbrook
151	51.8	Tiffin City SD	Tiffin
151	51.8	West Clermont Local SD	Cincinnati
168	51.7	Alliance City SD	Alliance
168	51.7	Beaver Local SD	Lisbon
168	51.7	Bexley City SD	Bexley
168	51.7	Canal Winchester Local SD	Canal Winchester
168	51.7	Cloverleaf Local SD	Lodi
168	51.7	Dublin City SD	Dublin
168	51.7	Jefferson Area Local SD	Jefferson
168	51.7	Kettering City SD	Kettering
168	51.7	Marysville Ex Vill SD	Marysville
168	51.7	Paulding Ex Vill SD	Paulding
168	51.7	Perrysburg Ex Vill SD	Perrysburg
168	51.7	Sandusky City SD	Sandusky
168	51.7	Tipp City Ex Vill SD	Tipp City
168	51.7	Trotwood-Madison City SD	Trotwood
168	51.7	Washington-Nile Local SD	West Portsmouth
168	51.7	Wellington Ex Vill SD	Wellington
168	51.7	Westlake City SD	Westlake
168	51.7	Youngstown City SD	Youngstown
186	51.6	Bryan City SD	Bryan
186	51.6	Indian Valley Local SD	Gnadenhutten
186	51.6	Lakewood City SD	Lakewood
186	51.6	Licking Heights Local SD	Summit Station
186	51.6	Madison-Plains Local SD	London
186	51.6	Mason City SD	Mason
186	51.6	Pike-Delta-York Local SD	Delta
186	51.6	Sidney City SD	Sidney
186	51.6	Toledo City SD	Toledo
186	51.6	Union-Scioto Local SD	Chillicothe
196	51.5	Athens City SD	The Plains
196	51.5	Benjamin Logan Local SD	Bellefontaine
196	51.5	Brunswick City SD	Brunswick
196	51.5	Chardon Local SD	Chardon
196	51.5	Cuyahoga Falls City SD	Cuyahoga Falls
196	51.5	Dover City SD	Dover
196	51.5	Eastwood Local SD	Pemberville
196	51.5	Edison Local SD	Hammondsville
196	51.5	Firelands Local SD	Oberlin
196	51.5	Fostoria City SD	Fostoria
196	51.5	Gallia County Local SD	Gallipolis
196	51.5	Gallipolis City SD	Gallipolis
196	51.5	Hilliard City SD	Hilliard
196	51.5	Kenston Local SD	Chagrin Falls
196	51.5	Lexington Local SD	Lexington
196	51.5	London City SD	London
196	51.5	Miami Trace Local SD	Washington Ct Hse
196	51.5	New Richmond Ex Vill SD	New Richmond
196	51.5	Newton Falls Ex Vill SD	Newton Falls
196	51.5	Nordonia Hills City SD	Northfield
196	51.5	North Fork Local SD	Utica
196	51.5	Painesville Township Local SD	Painesville
196	51.5	Sylvania City SD	Sylvania
196	51.5	Twinsburg City SD	Twinsburg
196	51.5	Wellston City SD	Wellston
221	51.4	Bethel-Tate Local SD	Bethel
221	51.4	Bowling Green City SD	Bowling Green
221	51.4	Campbell City SD	Campbell
221	51.4	Canton City SD	Canton
221	51.4	Champion Local SD	Warren
221	51.4	Elida Local SD	Elida
221	51.4	Huber Heights City SD	Huber Heights
221	51.4	Kent City SD	Kent
221	51.4	Madison Local SD	Middletown
221	51.4	Mansfield City SD	Mansfield
221	51.4	Napoleon Area City SD	Napoleon
221	51.4	Northmont City SD	Englewood
221	51.4	Scioto Valley Local SD	Piketon
221	51.4	Willoughby-Eastlake City SD	Willoughby
235	51.3	Milford Ex Vill SD	Milford
235	51.3	Mount Vernon City SD	Mount Vernon
235	51.3	Olmsted Falls City SD	Olmsted Falls
235	51.3	Shawnee Local SD	Lima
235	51.3	Solon City SD	Solon
235	51.3	Southwest Licking Local SD	Etna
235	51.3	Upper Arlington City SD	Upper Arlington
235	51.3	Wyoming City SD	Wyoming
243	51.2	Brecksville-Broadview Heights	Brecksville
243	51.2	Cleveland Municipal SD	Cleveland
243	51.2	Columbus City SD	Columbus
243	51.2	Elgin Local SD	Marion
243	51.2	Greenville City SD	Greenville
243	51.2	Howland Local SD	Warren
243	51.2	Sycamore Community City SD	Cincinnati
243	51.2	Talawanda City SD	Oxford
243	51.2	Tecumseh Local SD	New Carlisle
252	51.1	Aurora City SD	Aurora
252	51.1	Austintown Local SD	Youngstown
252	51.1	Beavercreek City SD	Beavercreek
252	51.1	Bedford City SD	Bedford
252	51.1	Circleville City SD	Circleville
252	51.1	Clark-Shawnee Local SD	Springfield
252	51.1	Fairview Park City SD	Fairview Park
252	51.1	Fremont City SD	Fremont

252	51.1	Mariemont City SD	Cincinnati
252	51.1	Medina City SD	Medina
252	51.1	Newark City SD	Newark
252	51.1	Olentangy Local SD	Lewis Center
252	51.1	Shaker Heights City SD	Shaker Heights
252	51.1	South-Western City SD	Grove City
252	51.1	Struthers City SD	Struthers
252	51.1	Van Wert City SD	Van Wert
268	51.0	Bellefontaine City SD	Bellefontaine
268	51.0	Boardman Local SD	Youngstown
268	51.0	Canfield Local SD	Canfield
268	51.0	Elyria City SD	Elyria
268	51.0	Greenon Local SD	Springfield
268	51.0	Indian Lake Local SD	Lewistown
268	51.0	Lakeview Local SD	Cortland
268	51.0	Norton City SD	Norton
268	51.0	Ravenna City SD	Ravenna
268	51.0	Springfield Local SD	Akron
278	50.9	Amherst Ex Vill SD	Amherst
278	50.9	Clyde-Green Springs Ex Vill SD	Clyde
278	50.9	Copley-Fairlawn City SD	Copley
278	50.9	East Liverpool City SD	East Liverpool
278	50.9	Fairland Local SD	Proctorville
278	50.9	Findlay City SD	Findlay
278	50.9	Graham Local SD	Saint Paris
278	50.9	Hamilton Local SD	Columbus
278	50.9	Licking Valley Local SD	Newark
278	50.9	Niles City SD	Niles
278	50.9	Reynoldsburg City SD	Reynoldsburg
278	50.9	Triway Local SD	Wooster
278	50.9	Wapakoneta City SD	Wapakoneta
278	50.9	West Holmes Local SD	Millersburg
278	50.9	Westerville City SD	Westerville
293	50.8	Akron City SD	Akron
293	50.8	Benton Carroll Salem Local SD	Oak Harbor
293	50.8	Dayton City SD	Dayton
293	50.8	Labrae Local SD	Leavittsburg
293	50.8	Plain Local SD	Canton
293	50.8	Vermilion Local SD	Vermilion
299	50.7	Coshocton City SD	Coshocton
299	50.7	Forest Hills Local SD	Cincinnati
299	50.7	Groveport Madison Local SD	Groveport
299	50.7	Hillsboro City SD	Hillsboro
299	50.7	James A Garfield Local SD	Garrettsville
299	50.7	Keystone Local SD	Lagrange
299	50.7	Mentor Ex Vill SD	Mentor
299	50.7	Otsego Local SD	Tontogany
299	50.7	Poland Local SD	Poland
299	50.7	Salem City SD	Salem
299	50.7	Willard City SD	Willard
310	50.6	Big Walnut Local SD	Galena
310	50.6	Jonathan Alder Local SD	Plain City
310	50.6	Morgan Local SD	McConnelsville
310	50.6	North Royalton City SD	N Royalton
310	50.6	Ottawa-Glandorf Local SD	Ottawa
315	50.5	Alexander Local SD	Albany
315	50.5	Buckeye Local SD	Medina
315	50.5	Fairfield City SD	Fairfield
315	50.5	Huron City SD	Huron
315	50.5	Lake Local SD	Millbury
315	50.5	Mad River Local SD	Dayton
321	50.4	Bath Local SD	Lima
321	50.4	Loveland City SD	Loveland
321	50.4	North Canton City SD	North Canton
321	50.4	Parma City SD	Parma
321	50.4	Tri-Valley Local SD	Dresden
321	50.4	Upper Sandusky Ex Vill SD	Upper Sandusky
321	50.4	Warren City SD	Warren
321	50.4	Westfall Local SD	Williamsport
329	50.3	Adams County-Ohio Valley Local SD	West Union
329	50.3	Avon Local SD	Avon
329	50.3	Blanchester Local SD	Blanchester
329	50.3	Eastern Local SD	Sardinia
329	50.3	Northridge Local SD	Dayton
334	50.2	Clear Fork Valley Local SD	Bellville
334	50.2	Cleveland Hts-Univ Hts City SD	University Hgts
334	50.2	Coventry Local SD	Akron
334	50.2	Jackson Local SD	Massillon
334	50.2	Lebanon City SD	Lebanon
339	50.1	Perkins Local SD	Sandusky
339	50.1	Rocky River City SD	Rocky River
339	50.1	Rolling Hills Local SD	Byesville
339	50.1	South Point Local SD	South Point
343	50.0	Bay Village City SD	Bay Village
343	50.0	Carrollton Ex Vill SD	Carrollton
343	50.0	East Clinton Local SD	Lees Creek
343	50.0	Hubbard Ex Vill SD	Hubbard
347	49.9	Anthony Wayne Local SD	Whitehouse
347	49.9	Heath City SD	Heath
347	49.9	West Muskingum Local SD	Zanesville
350	49.8	Cincinnati City SD	Cincinnati
350	49.8	Perry Local SD	Perry
352	49.7	Northwestern Local SD	Springfield
353	49.6	East Cleveland City SD	East Cleveland
353	49.6	Louisville City SD	Louisville
353	49.6	Manchester Local SD	Akron
353	49.6	Warrensville Heights City SD	Warrensville Hgts
357	49.5	Little Miami Local SD	Morrow
357	49.5	Plain Local SD	New Albany
357	49.5	Wauseon Ex Vill SD	Wauseon
360	49.4	Meigs Local SD	Pomeroy
360	49.4	Oakwood City SD	Dayton
362	49.3	Buckeye Local SD	Ashtabula
362	49.3	Clearview Local SD	Lorain
362	49.3	Electronic Classroom of Tomorrow	Columbus
362	49.3	Maysville Local SD	Zanesville
362	49.3	Zane Trace Local SD	Chillicothe
362	49.3	Zanesville City SD	Zanesville
368	49.0	Marlington Local SD	Alliance
369	48.9	Sheffield-Sheffield Lake City	Sheffield Vlg
370	47.5	Galion City SD	Galion

Female Students

Rank	Percent	District Name	City
1	52.5	Galion City SD	Galion
2	51.1	Sheffield-Sheffield Lake City	Sheffield Vlg
3	51.0	Marlington Local SD	Alliance
4	50.7	Buckeye Local SD	Ashtabula
4	50.7	Clearview Local SD	Lorain
4	50.7	Electronic Classroom of Tomorrow	Columbus
4	50.7	Maysville Local SD	Zanesville
4	50.7	Zane Trace Local SD	Chillicothe
4	50.7	Zanesville City SD	Zanesville
10	50.6	Meigs Local SD	Pomeroy
10	50.6	Oakwood City SD	Dayton
12	50.5	Little Miami Local SD	Morrow
12	50.5	Plain Local SD	New Albany
12	50.5	Wauseon Ex Vill SD	Wauseon
15	50.4	East Cleveland City SD	East Cleveland
15	50.4	Louisville City SD	Louisville
15	50.4	Manchester Local SD	Akron
15	50.4	Warrensville Heights City SD	Warrensville Hgts
19	50.3	Northwestern Local SD	Springfield
20	50.2	Cincinnati City SD	Cincinnati
20	50.2	Perry Local SD	Perry
22	50.1	Anthony Wayne Local SD	Whitehouse
22	50.1	Heath City SD	Heath
22	50.1	West Muskingum Local SD	Zanesville
25	50.0	Bay Village City SD	Bay Village
25	50.0	Carrollton Ex Vill SD	Carrollton
25	50.0	East Clinton Local SD	Lees Creek
25	50.0	Hubbard Ex Vill SD	Hubbard
29	49.9	Perkins Local SD	Sandusky
29	49.9	Rocky River City SD	Rocky River
29	49.9	Rolling Hills Local SD	Byesville
29	49.9	South Point Local SD	South Point
33	49.8	Clear Fork Valley Local SD	Bellville
33	49.8	Cleveland Hts-Univ Hts City SD	University Hgts
33	49.8	Coventry Local SD	Akron
33	49.8	Jackson Local SD	Massillon
33	49.8	Lebanon City SD	Lebanon
38	49.7	Adams County-Ohio Valley Local SD	West Union
38	49.7	Avon Local SD	Avon
38	49.7	Blanchester Local SD	Blanchester
38	49.7	Eastern Local SD	Sardinia
38	49.7	Northridge Local SD	Dayton
43	49.6	Bath Local SD	Lima
43	49.6	Loveland City SD	Loveland
43	49.6	North Canton City SD	North Canton
43	49.6	Parma City SD	Parma
43	49.6	Tri-Valley Local SD	Dresden
43	49.6	Upper Sandusky Ex Vill SD	Upper Sandusky
43	49.6	Warren City SD	Warren
43	49.6	Westfall Local SD	Williamsport
51	49.5	Alexander Local SD	Albany
51	49.5	Buckeye Local SD	Medina
51	49.5	Fairfield City SD	Fairfield
51	49.5	Huron City SD	Huron
51	49.5	Lake Local SD	Millbury
51	49.5	Mad River Local SD	Dayton
57	49.4	Big Walnut Local SD	Galena
57	49.4	Jonathan Alder Local SD	Plain City
57	49.4	Morgan Local SD	McConnelsville
57	49.4	North Royalton City SD	N Royalton
57	49.4	Ottawa-Glandorf Local SD	Ottawa
62	49.3	Coshocton City SD	Coshocton
62	49.3	Forest Hills Local SD	Cincinnati
62	49.3	Groveport Madison Local SD	Groveport
62	49.3	Hillsboro City SD	Hillsboro
62	49.3	James A Garfield Local SD	Garrettsville
62	49.3	Keystone Local SD	Lagrange
62	49.3	Mentor Ex Vill SD	Mentor
62	49.3	Otsego Local SD	Tontogany
62	49.3	Poland Local SD	Poland
62	49.3	Salem City SD	Salem
62	49.3	Willard City SD	Willard
73	49.2	Akron City SD	Akron
73	49.2	Benton Carroll Salem Local SD	Oak Harbor
73	49.2	Dayton City SD	Dayton
73	49.2	Labrae Local SD	Leavittsburg
73	49.2	Plain Local SD	Canton
73	49.2	Vermilion Local SD	Vermilion
79	49.1	Amherst Ex Vill SD	Amherst
79	49.1	Clyde-Green Springs Ex Vill SD	Clyde
79	49.1	Copley-Fairlawn City SD	Copley
79	49.1	East Liverpool City SD	East Liverpool
79	49.1	Fairland Local SD	Proctorville
79	49.1	Findlay City SD	Findlay
79	49.1	Graham Local SD	Saint Paris
79	49.1	Hamilton Local SD	Columbus
79	49.1	Licking Valley Local SD	Newark
79	49.1	Niles City SD	Niles
79	49.1	Reynoldsburg City SD	Reynoldsburg
79	49.1	Triway Local SD	Wooster
79	49.1	Wapakoneta City SD	Wapakoneta
79	49.1	West Holmes Local SD	Millersburg
79	49.1	Westerville City SD	Westerville
94	49.0	Bellefontaine City SD	Bellefontaine
94	49.0	Boardman Local SD	Youngstown
94	49.0	Canfield Local SD	Canfield
94	49.0	Elyria City SD	Elyria
94	49.0	Greenon Local SD	Springfield
94	49.0	Indian Lake Local SD	Lewistown
94	49.0	Lakeview Local SD	Cortland
94	49.0	Norton City SD	Norton
94	49.0	Ravenna City SD	Ravenna
94	49.0	Springfield Local SD	Akron
104	48.9	Aurora City SD	Aurora
104	48.9	Austintown Local SD	Youngstown
104	48.9	Beavercreek City SD	Beavercreek
104	48.9	Bedford City SD	Bedford
104	48.9	Circleville City SD	Circleville
104	48.9	Clark-Shawnee Local SD	Springfield
104	48.9	Fairview Park City SD	Fairview Park
104	48.9	Fremont City SD	Fremont
104	48.9	Mariemont City SD	Cincinnati
104	48.9	Medina City SD	Medina
104	48.9	Newark City SD	Newark
104	48.9	Olentangy Local SD	Lewis Center
104	48.9	Shaker Heights City SD	Shaker Heights
104	48.9	South-Western City SD	Grove City
104	48.9	Struthers City SD	Struthers
104	48.9	Van Wert City SD	Van Wert
120	48.8	Brecksville-Broadview Heights	Brecksville
120	48.8	Cleveland Municipal SD	Cleveland
120	48.8	Columbus City SD	Columbus
120	48.8	Elgin Local SD	Marion
120	48.8	Greenville City SD	Greenville
120	48.8	Howland Local SD	Warren
120	48.8	Sycamore Community City SD	Cincinnati
120	48.8	Talawanda City SD	Oxford
120	48.8	Tecumseh Local SD	New Carlisle
129	48.7	Milford Ex Vill SD	Milford
129	48.7	Mount Vernon City SD	Mount Vernon
129	48.7	Olmsted Falls City SD	Olmsted Falls
129	48.7	Shawnee Local SD	Lima
129	48.7	Solon City SD	Solon
129	48.7	Southwest Licking Local SD	Etna
129	48.7	Upper Arlington City SD	Upper Arlington
129	48.7	Wyoming City SD	Wyoming
137	48.6	Bethel-Tate Local SD	Bethel
137	48.6	Bowling Green City SD	Bowling Green
137	48.6	Campbell City SD	Campbell
137	48.6	Canton City SD	Canton
137	48.6	Champion Local SD	Warren
137	48.6	Elida Local SD	Elida
137	48.6	Huber Heights City SD	Huber Heights
137	48.6	Kent City SD	Kent
137	48.6	Madison Local SD	Middletown
137	48.6	Mansfield City SD	Mansfield
137	48.6	Napoleon Area City SD	Napoleon
137	48.6	Northmont City SD	Englewood
137	48.6	Scioto Valley Local SD	Piketon
137	48.6	Willoughby-Eastlake City SD	Willoughby
151	48.5	Athens City SD	The Plains
151	48.5	Benjamin Logan Local SD	Bellefontaine
151	48.5	Brunswick City SD	Brunswick
151	48.5	Chardon Local SD	Chardon
151	48.5	Cuyahoga Falls City SD	Cuyahoga Falls
151	48.5	Dover City SD	Dover
151	48.5	Eastwood Local SD	Pemberville
151	48.5	Edison Local SD	Hammondsville
151	48.5	Firelands Local SD	Oberlin
151	48.5	Fostoria City SD	Fostoria
151	48.5	Gallia County Local SD	Gallipolis
151	48.5	Gallipolis City SD	Gallipolis
151	48.5	Hilliard City SD	Hilliard

151	48.5	Kenston Local SD	Chagrin Falls
151	48.5	Lexington Local SD	Lexington
151	48.5	London City SD	London
151	48.5	Miami Trace Local SD	Washington Ct Hse
151	48.5	New Richmond Ex Vill SD	New Richmond
151	48.5	Newton Falls Ex Vill SD	Newton Falls
151	48.5	Nordonia Hills City SD	Northfield
151	48.5	North Fork Local SD	Utica
151	48.5	Painesville Township Local SD	Painesville
151	48.5	Sylvania City SD	Sylvania
151	48.5	Twinsburg City SD	Twinsburg
151	48.5	Wellston City SD	Wellston
176	48.4	Bryan City SD	Bryan
176	48.4	Indian Valley Local SD	Gnadenhutten
176	48.4	Lakewood City SD	Lakewood
176	48.4	Licking Heights Local SD	Summit Station
176	48.4	Madison-Plains Local SD	London
176	48.4	Mason City SD	Mason
176	48.4	Pike-Delta-York Local SD	Delta
176	48.4	Sidney City SD	Sidney
176	48.4	Toledo City SD	Toledo
176	48.4	Union-Scioto Local SD	Chillicothe
186	48.3	Alliance City SD	Alliance
186	48.3	Beaver Local SD	Lisbon
186	48.3	Bexley City SD	Bexley
186	48.3	Canal Winchester Local SD	Canal Winchester
186	48.3	Cloverleaf Local SD	Lodi
186	48.3	Dublin City SD	Dublin
186	48.3	Jefferson Area Local SD	Jefferson
186	48.3	Kettering City SD	Kettering
186	48.3	Marysville Ex Vill SD	Marysville
186	48.3	Paulding Ex Vill SD	Paulding
186	48.3	Perrysburg Ex Vill SD	Perrysburg
186	48.3	Sandusky City SD	Sandusky
186	48.3	Tipp City Ex Vill SD	Tipp City
186	48.3	Trotwood-Madison City SD	Trotwood
186	48.3	Washington-Nile Local SD	West Portsmouth
186	48.3	Wellington Ex Vill SD	Wellington
186	48.3	Westlake City SD	Westlake
186	48.3	Youngstown City SD	Youngstown
204	48.2	Chagrin Falls Ex Vill SD	Chagrin Falls
204	48.2	Chillicothe City SD	Chillicothe
204	48.2	Clermont-Northeastern Local SD	Batavia
204	48.2	Franklin City SD	Franklin
204	48.2	Lakota Local SD	Liberty Twp
204	48.2	Lorain City SD	Lorain
204	48.2	Marietta City SD	Marietta
204	48.2	Miamisburg City SD	Miamisburg
204	48.2	New Philadelphia City SD	New Philadelphia
204	48.2	North Ridgeville City SD	N Ridgeville
204	48.2	Painesville City Local SD	Painesville
204	48.2	Rossford Ex Vill SD	Rossford
204	48.2	Southeast Local SD	Ravenna
204	48.2	Steubenville City SD	Steubenville
204	48.2	Sugarcreek Local SD	Bellbrook
204	48.2	Tiffin City SD	Tiffin
204	48.2	West Clermont Local SD	Cincinnati
221	48.1	Amanda-Clearcreek Local SD	Amanda
221	48.1	Ashtabula Area City SD	Ashtabula
221	48.1	Barberton City SD	Barberton
221	48.1	Delaware City SD	Delaware
221	48.1	Euclid City SD	Euclid
221	48.1	Fairless Local SD	Navarre
221	48.1	Girard City SD	Girard
221	48.1	Hamilton City SD	Hamilton
221	48.1	Kenton City SD	Kenton
221	48.1	Lima City SD	Lima
221	48.1	Madison Local SD	Madison
221	48.1	Middletown City SD	Middletown
221	48.1	Midview Local SD	Grafton
221	48.1	Northwest Local SD	Canal Fulton
221	48.1	Shelby City SD	Shelby
221	48.1	Springboro Community City SD	Springboro
221	48.1	Swanton Local SD	Swanton
221	48.1	Switzerland of Ohio Local SD	Woodsfield
221	48.1	Urbana City SD	Urbana
221	48.1	Vandalia-Butler City SD	Vandalia
221	48.1	Waverly City SD	Waverly
221	48.1	Western Brown Local SD	Mount Orab
243	48.0	Centerville City SD	Centerville
243	48.0	Defiance City SD	Defiance
243	48.0	Goshen Local SD	Goshen
243	48.0	Greeneview Local SD	Jamestown
243	48.0	Highland Local SD	Medina
243	48.0	Indian Hill Ex Vill SD	Cincinnati
243	48.0	Logan-Hocking Local SD	Logan
243	48.0	Revere Local SD	Bath
243	48.0	River View Local SD	Warsaw
243	48.0	Woodridge Local SD	Peninsula
253	47.9	Ashland City SD	Ashland
253	47.9	Cambridge City SD	Cambridge
253	47.9	Carlisle Local SD	Carlisle
253	47.9	Lakewood Local SD	Hebron
253	47.9	Maple Heights City SD	Maple Heights
253	47.9	Minford Local SD	Minford
253	47.9	Northeastern Local SD	Springfield
253	47.9	South Euclid-Lyndhurst City SD	Lyndhurst
253	47.9	Stow-Munroe Falls City SD	Stow
253	47.9	Valley View Local SD	Germantown
263	47.8	Buckeye Local SD	Rayland
263	47.8	Eaton City SD	Eaton
263	47.8	Granville Ex Vill SD	Granville
263	47.8	Marion City SD	Marion
263	47.8	North Olmsted City SD	North Olmsted
263	47.8	Northwest Local SD	Cincinnati
263	47.8	Princeton City SD	Cincinnati
263	47.8	Springfield Local SD	Holland
263	47.8	Strongsville City SD	Strongsville
263	47.8	Whitehall City SD	Whitehall
263	47.8	Worthington City SD	Worthington
274	47.7	Clinton-Massie Local SD	Clarksville
274	47.7	Franklin Local SD	Duncan Falls
274	47.7	Norwood City SD	Norwood
274	47.7	Saint Clairsville-Richland City	St Clairsville
274	47.7	Troy City SD	Troy
274	47.7	Wadsworth City SD	Wadsworth
274	47.7	West Branch Local SD	Beloit
274	47.7	Wilmington City SD	Wilmington
282	47.6	Bellevue City SD	Bellevue
282	47.6	Bucyrus City SD	Bucyrus
282	47.6	Coldwater Ex Vill SD	Coldwater
282	47.6	Fairfield Union Local SD	W Rushville
282	47.6	Gahanna-Jefferson City SD	Gahanna
282	47.6	Lancaster City SD	Lancaster
282	47.6	Northwest Local SD	Mc Dermott
282	47.6	Rock Hill Local SD	Ironton
282	47.6	Washington Court House City SD	Washington Ct Hse
282	47.6	Winton Woods City SD	Cincinnati
282	47.6	Xenia Community City SD	Xenia
293	47.5	Garfield Heights City SD	Garfield Hgts
293	47.5	Northern Local SD	Thornville
293	47.5	Norwalk City SD	Norwalk
293	47.5	Perry Local SD	Massillon
293	47.5	Pickerington Local SD	Pickerington
293	47.5	Southwest Local SD	Harrison
293	47.5	Springfield City SD	Springfield
293	47.5	Streetsboro City SD	Streetsboro
293	47.5	Teays Valley Local SD	Ashville
293	47.5	Vinton County Local SD	Mc Arthur
303	47.4	Buckeye Valley Local SD	Delaware
303	47.4	Crestwood Local SD	Mantua
303	47.4	Indian Creek Local SD	Wintersville
303	47.4	Minerva Local SD	Minerva
303	47.4	Oregon City SD	Oregon
303	47.4	Wooster City SD	Wooster
309	47.3	Bellaire Local SD	Bellaire
309	47.3	Celina City SD	Celina
309	47.3	Conneaut Area City SD	Conneaut
309	47.3	Fairborn City SD	Fairborn
309	47.3	Greenfield Ex Vill SD	Greenfield
309	47.3	Jackson City SD	Jackson
309	47.3	Liberty Local SD	Youngstown
309	47.3	Logan Elm Local SD	Circleville
309	47.3	Sandy Valley Local SD	Magnolia
318	47.2	Berea City SD	Berea
318	47.2	East Holmes Local SD	Berlin
318	47.2	Green Local SD	Green
318	47.2	Ironton City SD	Ironton
318	47.2	Mount Healthy City SD	Cincinnati
318	47.2	Oak Hills Local SD	Cincinnati
318	47.2	Port Clinton City SD	Port Clinton
318	47.2	Washington Local SD	Toledo
326	47.1	Brookfield Local SD	Brookfield
326	47.1	Brookville Local SD	Brookville
326	47.1	Edgewood City SD	Trenton
326	47.1	Field Local SD	Mogadore
326	47.1	Geneva Area City SD	Geneva
326	47.1	Highland Local SD	Sparta
326	47.1	Lake Local SD	Hartville
326	47.1	Portsmouth City SD	Portsmouth
334	47.0	Claymont City SD	Dennison
334	47.0	East Muskingum Local SD	New Concord
334	47.0	Warren Local SD	Vincent
334	47.0	West Geauga Local SD	Chesterland
338	46.9	Avon Lake City SD	Avon Lake
338	46.9	Batavia Local SD	Batavia
338	46.9	Black River Local SD	Sullivan
338	46.9	Kings Local SD	Kings Mills
338	46.9	Ontario Local SD	Mansfield
338	46.9	Tuscarawas Valley Local SD	Zoarville
344	46.8	Hudson City SD	Hudson
344	46.8	North College Hill City SD	Cincinnati
346	46.7	Berlin-Milan Local SD	Milan
346	46.7	Finneytown Local SD	Cincinnati
346	46.7	Harrison Hills City SD	Hopedale
346	46.7	Milton-Union Ex Vill SD	West Milton
350	46.6	Southeast Local SD	Apple Creek
350	46.6	West Carrollton City SD	West Carrollton
352	46.5	Massillon City SD	Massillon
353	46.4	New Lexington City SD	New Lexington
353	46.4	River Valley Local SD	Caledonia
355	46.3	Madison Local SD	Mansfield
355	46.3	Piqua City SD	Piqua
357	46.2	Beachwood City SD	Beachwood
357	46.2	Mayfield City SD	Highland Hgts
359	46.1	Three Rivers Local SD	Cleves
359	46.1	Union Local SD	Morristown
361	46.0	Orrville City SD	Orrville
361	46.0	Ross Local SD	Hamilton
363	45.9	Genoa Area Local SD	Genoa
363	45.9	Maumee City SD	Maumee
363	45.9	Preble Shawnee Local SD	Camden
366	45.5	Tallmadge City SD	Tallmadge
367	45.2	Wickliffe City SD	Wickliffe
368	45.0	Canton Local SD	Canton
368	45.0	Orange City SD	Cleveland
370	44.7	Saint Marys City SD	Saint Marys

Individual Education Program Students

Rank	Percent	District Name	City
1	28.1	Harrison Hills City SD	Hopedale
2	23.2	Zanesville City SD	Zanesville
3	21.5	Claymont City SD	Dennison
4	21.3	Coshocton City SD	Coshocton
5	21.2	Bellaire Local SD	Bellaire
6	21.1	Dayton City SD	Dayton
7	20.5	Lima City SD	Lima
8	20.3	Gallipolis City SD	Gallipolis
8	20.3	Napoleon Area City SD	Napoleon
10	20.1	Youngstown City SD	Youngstown
11	20.0	South Point Local SD	South Point
12	19.7	Alexander Local SD	Albany
13	19.4	Mount Vernon City SD	Mount Vernon
14	19.3	Mansfield City SD	Mansfield
14	19.3	Marion City SD	Marion
14	19.3	Warren City SD	Warren
17	19.2	East Liverpool City SD	East Liverpool
18	19.0	Meigs Local SD	Pomeroy
19	18.9	Sandusky City SD	Sandusky
20	18.8	Delaware City SD	Delaware
21	18.5	Bucyrus City SD	Bucyrus
21	18.5	Fostoria City SD	Fostoria
23	18.3	Cincinnati City SD	Cincinnati
23	18.3	Springfield Local SD	Akron
25	18.1	Bellefontaine City SD	Bellefontaine
25	18.1	Hamilton City SD	Hamilton
27	18.0	Indian Lake Local SD	Lewistown
28	17.9	Middletown City SD	Middletown
28	17.9	Urbana City SD	Urbana
30	17.8	Ironton City SD	Ironton
30	17.8	Sidney City SD	Sidney
32	17.7	Gallia County Local SD	Gallipolis
32	17.7	Springfield Local SD	Holland
34	17.4	Cleveland Municipal SD	Cleveland
35	17.3	Celina City SD	Celina
35	17.3	Paulding Ex Vill SD	Paulding
35	17.3	Ravenna City SD	Ravenna
38	17.2	Buckeye Local SD	Rayland
38	17.2	Vinton County Local SD	Mc Arthur
40	17.1	Ashtabula Area City SD	Ashtabula
40	17.1	Findlay City SD	Findlay
40	17.1	Saint Marys City SD	Saint Marys
43	17.0	Bellevue City SD	Bellevue
44	16.9	Tiffin City SD	Tiffin
45	16.8	Mount Healthy City SD	Cincinnati
45	16.8	Wellston City SD	Wellston
47	16.7	Canton City SD	Canton
48	16.6	Euclid City SD	Euclid
48	16.6	North College Hill City SD	Cincinnati
50	16.5	Alliance City SD	Alliance
50	16.5	Port Clinton City SD	Port Clinton
52	16.4	Switzerland of Ohio Local SD	Woodsfield
52	16.4	Winton Woods City SD	Cincinnati
54	16.3	Toledo City SD	Toledo
55	16.2	Brookfield Local SD	Brookfield
55	16.2	Edgewood City SD	Trenton
55	16.2	Groveport Madison Local SD	Groveport
55	16.2	New Philadelphia City SD	New Philadelphia
55	16.2	Piqua City SD	Piqua
55	16.2	Rock Hill Local SD	Ironton
61	16.1	River View Local SD	Warsaw
61	16.1	Van Wert City SD	Van Wert
61	16.1	Whitehall City SD	Whitehall
64	16.0	Marietta City SD	Marietta
65	15.9	Indian Creek Local SD	Wintersville
65	15.9	Mayfield City SD	Highland Hgts

65	15.9	Upper Sandusky Ex Vill SD	Upper Sandusky
68	15.8	Goshen Local SD	Goshen
68	15.8	Massillon City SD	Massillon
68	15.8	Parma City SD	Parma
68	15.8	Rossford Ex Vill SD	Rossford
72	15.7	Defiance City SD	Defiance
73	15.6	Akron City SD	Akron
73	15.6	Conneaut Area City SD	Conneaut
75	15.5	Perkins Local SD	Sandusky
76	15.4	Austintown Local SD	Youngstown
76	15.4	Springfield City SD	Springfield
76	15.4	Woodridge Local SD	Peninsula
79	15.3	Logan-Hocking Local SD	Logan
79	15.3	Scioto Valley Local SD	Piketon
81	15.2	Adams County-Ohio Valley Local SD	West Union
81	15.2	Cambridge City SD	Cambridge
81	15.2	Circleville City SD	Circleville
81	15.2	Indian Valley Local SD	Gnadenhutten
81	15.2	South Euclid-Lyndhurst City SD	Lyndhurst
81	15.2	Wapakoneta City SD	Wapakoneta
87	15.1	Dover City SD	Dover
87	15.1	Fairless Local SD	Navarre
87	15.1	Marlington Local SD	Alliance
87	15.1	West Holmes Local SD	Millersburg
87	15.1	Wooster City SD	Wooster
92	15.0	Campbell City SD	Campbell
92	15.0	Elyria City SD	Elyria
92	15.0	Highland Local SD	Sparta
92	15.0	Madison Local SD	Mansfield
96	14.9	Lakewood City SD	Lakewood
96	14.9	Norwalk City SD	Norwalk
98	14.8	Ashland City SD	Ashland
98	14.8	Chillicothe City SD	Chillicothe
98	14.8	Galion City SD	Galion
98	14.8	Graham Local SD	Saint Paris
98	14.8	London City SD	London
98	14.8	Lorain City SD	Lorain
98	14.8	Mad River Local SD	Dayton
98	14.8	Medina City SD	Medina
98	14.8	Shaker Heights City SD	Shaker Heights
98	14.8	Wickliffe City SD	Wickliffe
108	14.7	Barberton City SD	Barberton
108	14.7	Portsmouth City SD	Portsmouth
108	14.7	Triway Local SD	Wooster
111	14.6	Fairview Park City SD	Fairview Park
111	14.6	Maumee City SD	Maumee
113	14.5	Berea City SD	Berea
113	14.5	Miami Trace Local SD	Washington Ct Hse
113	14.5	New Lexington City SD	New Lexington
116	14.4	Benton Carroll Salem Local SD	Oak Harbor
116	14.4	Buckeye Valley Local SD	Delaware
116	14.4	Howland Local SD	Warren
116	14.4	Marysville Ex Vill SD	Marysville
120	14.3	Franklin City SD	Franklin
120	14.3	Kenton City SD	Kenton
120	14.3	North Ridgeville City SD	N Ridgeville
120	14.3	Northwest Local SD	Mc Dermott
120	14.3	Perry Local SD	Massillon
120	14.3	Shelby City SD	Shelby
126	14.2	Fremont City SD	Fremont
126	14.2	Swanton Local SD	Swanton
126	14.2	Vermilion Local SD	Vermilion
129	14.1	Carrollton Ex Vill SD	Carrollton
129	14.1	Field Local SD	Mogadore
129	14.1	Garfield Heights City SD	Garfield Hgts
129	14.1	Northern Local SD	Thornville
129	14.1	Xenia Community City SD	Xenia
134	14.0	Bedford City SD	Bedford
134	14.0	Otsego Local SD	Tontogany
134	14.0	Pike-Delta-York Local SD	Delta
134	14.0	Waverly City SD	Waverly
134	14.0	Willard City SD	Willard
139	13.9	Berlin-Milan Local SD	Milan
139	13.9	Painesville City Local SD	Painesville
139	13.9	Warrensville Heights City SD	Warrensville Hgts
142	13.8	Clyde-Green Springs Ex Vill SD	Clyde
142	13.8	Geneva Area City SD	Geneva
142	13.8	Northwest Local SD	Canal Fulton
142	13.8	Rolling Hills Local SD	Byesville
142	13.8	Westlake City SD	Westlake
142	13.8	Willoughby-Eastlake City SD	Willoughby
148	13.7	Clermont-Northeastern Local SD	Batavia
148	13.7	Cleveland Hts-Univ Hts City SD	University Hgts
148	13.7	Columbus City SD	Columbus
148	13.7	Girard City SD	Girard
148	13.7	Greenville City SD	Greenville
148	13.7	Rocky River City SD	Rocky River
148	13.7	Sandy Valley Local SD	Magnolia
155	13.6	Benjamin Logan Local SD	Bellefontaine
155	13.6	Franklin Local SD	Duncan Falls
155	13.6	Huron City SD	Huron
155	13.6	Northridge Local SD	Dayton
155	13.6	Union Local SD	Morristown
160	13.5	Logan Elm Local SD	Circleville
160	13.5	Sylvania City SD	Sylvania
160	13.5	Vandalia-Butler City SD	Vandalia
163	13.4	Athens City SD	The Plains
163	13.4	Finneytown Local SD	Cincinnati
163	13.4	Jackson City SD	Jackson
163	13.4	Kettering City SD	Kettering
163	13.4	Labrae Local SD	Leavittsburg
163	13.4	Maple Heights City SD	Maple Heights
163	13.4	Trotwood-Madison City SD	Trotwood
163	13.4	Washington Local SD	Toledo
171	13.3	Canton Local SD	Canton
171	13.3	Newton Falls Ex Vill SD	Newton Falls
171	13.3	West Muskingum Local SD	Zanesville
174	13.2	Cuyahoga Falls City SD	Cuyahoga Falls
174	13.2	Fairland Local SD	Proctorville
174	13.2	Kent City SD	Kent
174	13.2	Madison Local SD	Middletown
174	13.2	Southeast Local SD	Apple Creek
174	13.2	Southwest Local SD	Harrison
180	13.1	Gahanna-Jefferson City SD	Gahanna
180	13.1	Niles City SD	Niles
182	13.0	Avon Local SD	Avon
182	13.0	Brookville Local SD	Brookville
182	13.0	Plain Local SD	Canton
182	13.0	Reynoldsburg City SD	Reynoldsburg
186	12.9	Maysville Local SD	Zanesville
186	12.9	River Valley Local SD	Caledonia
186	12.9	Ross Local SD	Hamilton
186	12.9	West Geauga Local SD	Chesterland
190	12.8	Bay Village City SD	Bay Village
190	12.8	Crestwood Local SD	Mantua
190	12.8	Kings Local SD	Kings Mills
190	12.8	Minerva Local SD	Minerva
190	12.8	Oak Hills Local SD	Cincinnati
190	12.8	South-Western City SD	Grove City
190	12.8	Steubenville City SD	Steubenville
190	12.8	Three Rivers Local SD	Cleves
190	12.8	Washington Court House City SD	Washington Ct Hse
199	12.7	Coldwater Ex Vill SD	Coldwater
199	12.7	East Clinton Local SD	Lees Creek
199	12.7	East Muskingum Local SD	New Concord
199	12.7	Lakewood Local SD	Hebron
199	12.7	Princeton City SD	Cincinnati
204	12.6	Blanchester Local SD	Blanchester
204	12.6	Centerville City SD	Centerville
204	12.6	Clearview Local SD	Lorain
207	12.5	Amherst Ex Vill SD	Amherst
207	12.5	Fairborn City SD	Fairborn
207	12.5	Licking Valley Local SD	Newark
207	12.5	Ottawa-Glandorf Local SD	Ottawa
207	12.5	Strongsville City SD	Strongsville
212	12.4	Salem City SD	Salem
212	12.4	Teays Valley Local SD	Ashville
214	12.3	Big Walnut Local SD	Galena
214	12.3	Edison Local SD	Hammondsville
214	12.3	Morgan Local SD	McConnelsville
214	12.3	North Fork Local SD	Utica
214	12.3	North Olmsted City SD	North Olmsted
214	12.3	Troy City SD	Troy
220	12.2	Beaver Local SD	Lisbon
220	12.2	Miamisburg City SD	Miamisburg
220	12.2	Newark City SD	Newark
223	12.1	Bowling Green City SD	Bowling Green
223	12.1	Cloverleaf Local SD	Lodi
225	12.0	East Holmes Local SD	Berlin
225	12.0	Green Local SD	Green
225	12.0	Jonathan Alder Local SD	Plain City
225	12.0	Lancaster City SD	Lancaster
225	12.0	Southeast Local SD	Ravenna
230	11.9	Chardon Local SD	Chardon
230	11.9	Saint Clairsville-Richland City	St Clairsville
230	11.9	Southwest Licking Local SD	Etna
230	11.9	Struthers City SD	Struthers
230	11.9	Tri-Valley Local SD	Dresden
230	11.9	West Carrollton City SD	West Carrollton
236	11.8	Amanda-Clearcreek Local SD	Amanda
236	11.8	Jefferson Area Local SD	Jefferson
236	11.8	Norwood City SD	Norwood
236	11.8	Oregon City SD	Oregon
236	11.8	Tecumseh Local SD	New Carlisle
236	11.8	Warren Local SD	Vincent
242	11.7	Beavercreek City SD	Beavercreek
242	11.7	Buckeye Local SD	Medina
242	11.7	East Cleveland City SD	East Cleveland
242	11.7	Greenfield Ex Vill SD	Greenfield
242	11.7	Lexington Local SD	Lexington
242	11.7	Mentor Ex Vill SD	Mentor
242	11.7	Solon City SD	Solon
249	11.6	Canal Winchester Local SD	Canal Winchester
249	11.6	Hilliard City SD	Hilliard
249	11.6	Huber Heights City SD	Huber Heights
249	11.6	Milton-Union Ex Vill SD	West Milton
249	11.6	Nordonia Hills City SD	Northfield
249	11.6	Orange City SD	Cleveland
255	11.5	Hamilton Local SD	Columbus
255	11.5	Orrville City SD	Orrville
255	11.5	Tallmadge City SD	Tallmadge
258	11.3	Black River Local SD	Sullivan
258	11.3	Champion Local SD	Warren
258	11.3	Elgin Local SD	Marion
258	11.3	Fairfield City SD	Fairfield
258	11.3	Northmont City SD	Englewood
258	11.3	Sheffield-Sheffield Lake City	Sheffield Vlg
258	11.3	Streetsboro City SD	Streetsboro
258	11.3	Twinsburg City SD	Twinsburg
258	11.3	Union-Scioto Local SD	Chillicothe
267	11.2	West Clermont Local SD	Cincinnati
268	11.1	Brunswick City SD	Brunswick
268	11.1	Elida Local SD	Elida
268	11.1	Firelands Local SD	Oberlin
268	11.1	Licking Heights Local SD	Summit Station
268	11.1	Midview Local SD	Grafton
268	11.1	Tuscarawas Valley Local SD	Zoarville
274	11.0	Bryan City SD	Bryan
274	11.0	North Canton City SD	North Canton
276	10.9	Bexley City SD	Bexley
276	10.9	Clear Fork Valley Local SD	Bellville
276	10.9	Eaton City SD	Eaton
276	10.9	Genoa Area Local SD	Genoa
276	10.9	Madison Local SD	Madison
276	10.9	Olmsted Falls City SD	Olmsted Falls
276	10.9	Talawanda City SD	Oxford
283	10.8	Hubbard Ex Vill SD	Hubbard
283	10.8	Little Miami Local SD	Morrow
283	10.8	Milford Ex Vill SD	Milford
286	10.7	Poland Local SD	Poland
287	10.6	Greeneview Local SD	Jamestown
287	10.6	Keystone Local SD	Lagrange
287	10.6	North Royalton City SD	N Royalton
290	10.5	Carlisle Local SD	Carlisle
290	10.5	Lake Local SD	Hartville
290	10.5	Northwestern Local SD	Springfield
293	10.4	Chagrin Falls Ex Vill SD	Chagrin Falls
293	10.4	Highland Local SD	Medina
293	10.4	Olentangy Local SD	Lewis Center
293	10.4	Painesville Township Local SD	Painesville
293	10.4	Stow-Munroe Falls City SD	Stow
293	10.4	West Branch Local SD	Beloit
299	10.3	Bath Local SD	Lima
299	10.3	Brecksville-Broadview Heights	Brecksville
299	10.3	Clinton-Massie Local SD	Clarksville
299	10.3	Forest Hills Local SD	Cincinnati
299	10.3	Granville Ex Vill SD	Granville
299	10.3	Greenon Local SD	Springfield
299	10.3	Heath City SD	Heath
299	10.3	Louisville City SD	Louisville
299	10.3	Northwest Local SD	Cincinnati
299	10.3	Upper Arlington City SD	Upper Arlington
299	10.3	Valley View Local SD	Germantown
299	10.3	Washington-Nile Local SD	West Portsmouth
299	10.3	Wauseon Ex Vill SD	Wauseon
312	10.2	Canfield Local SD	Canfield
312	10.2	Minford Local SD	Minford
312	10.2	Westerville City SD	Westerville
315	10.1	Beachwood City SD	Beachwood
315	10.1	Madison-Plains Local SD	London
317	10.0	Dublin City SD	Dublin
317	10.0	Eastern Local SD	Sardinia
317	10.0	Hudson City SD	Hudson
317	10.0	Preble Shawnee Local SD	Camden
317	10.0	Wilmington City SD	Wilmington
317	10.0	Zane Trace Local SD	Chillicothe
323	9.9	Batavia Local SD	Batavia
323	9.9	James A Garfield Local SD	Garrettsville
323	9.9	Westfall Local SD	Williamsport
326	9.8	Kenston Local SD	Chagrin Falls
326	9.8	Wellington Ex Vill SD	Wellington
328	9.7	Lakeview Local SD	Cortland
328	9.7	Sugarcreek Local SD	Bellbrook
330	9.5	Wadsworth City SD	Wadsworth
330	9.5	Western Brown Local SD	Mount Orab
332	9.4	Buckeye Local SD	Ashtabula
332	9.4	Copley-Fairlawn City SD	Copley
332	9.4	Lake Local SD	Millbury
332	9.4	Springboro Community City SD	Springboro
332	9.4	Wyoming City SD	Wyoming
337	9.3	Lebanon City SD	Lebanon
337	9.3	Mariemont City SD	Cincinnati
337	9.3	Norton City SD	Norton
337	9.3	Worthington City SD	Worthington
341	9.1	Boardman Local SD	Youngstown
341	9.1	Eastwood Local SD	Pemberville

343	8.9	Avon Lake City SD	Avon Lake
343	8.9	Coventry Local SD	Akron
343	8.9	Mason City SD	Mason
343	8.9	Shawnee Local SD	Lima
343	8.9	Tipp City Ex Vill SD	Tipp City
348	8.8	Lakota Local SD	Liberty Twp
349	8.5	Loveland City SD	Loveland
349	8.5	Manchester Local SD	Akron
349	8.5	Northeastern Local SD	Springfield
349	8.5	Pickerington Local SD	Pickerington
353	8.4	Liberty Local SD	Youngstown
354	8.3	Plain Local SD	New Albany
355	8.2	Aurora City SD	Aurora
355	8.2	Perrysburg Ex Vill SD	Perrysburg
355	8.2	Revere Local SD	Bath
358	8.1	Ontario Local SD	Mansfield
358	8.1	Perry Local SD	Perry
360	8.0	Clark-Shawnee Local SD	Springfield
360	8.0	Jackson Local SD	Massillon
362	7.6	New Richmond Ex Vill SD	New Richmond
363	7.4	Fairfield Union Local SD	W Rushville
364	7.3	Anthony Wayne Local SD	Whitehouse
365	7.2	Indian Hill Ex Vill SD	Cincinnati
366	7.0	Oakwood City SD	Dayton
367	5.4	Electronic Classroom of Tomorrow	Columbus
368	5.1	Hillsboro City SD	Hillsboro
369	4.6	Bethel-Tate Local SD	Bethel
370	2.9	Sycamore Community City SD	Cincinnati

English Language Learner Students

Rank	Percent	District Name	City
1	99.6	Mentor Ex Vill SD	Mentor
2	58.7	East Holmes Local SD	Berlin
3	17.4	Painesville City Local SD	Painesville
4	7.7	Lakewood City SD	Lakewood
5	5.7	Dublin City SD	Dublin
6	5.6	Whitehall City SD	Whitehall
7	5.5	Copley-Fairlawn City SD	Copley
8	4.8	Sycamore Community City SD	Cincinnati
9	4.7	South-Western City SD	Grove City
10	4.6	Mayfield City SD	Highland Hgts
11	3.4	Columbus City SD	Columbus
11	3.4	Fairview Park City SD	Fairview Park
13	3.2	Hilliard City SD	Hilliard
14	3.0	Athens City SD	The Plains
15	2.9	Ashtabula Area City SD	Ashtabula
15	2.9	Worthington City SD	Worthington
17	2.8	West Carrollton City SD	West Carrollton
18	2.6	London City SD	London
18	2.6	Princeton City SD	Cincinnati
18	2.6	Wauseon Ex Vill SD	Wauseon
21	2.5	Orange City SD	Cleveland
22	2.4	Centerville City SD	Centerville
23	2.3	Westerville City SD	Westerville
24	2.2	Parma City SD	Parma
24	2.2	Shaker Heights City SD	Shaker Heights
26	2.1	Cuyahoga Falls City SD	Cuyahoga Falls
26	2.1	Hamilton City SD	Hamilton
28	1.9	Fairfield City SD	Fairfield
28	1.9	Lorain City SD	Lorain
28	1.9	Upper Arlington City SD	Upper Arlington
28	1.9	Willard City SD	Willard
28	1.9	Willoughby-Eastlake City SD	Willoughby
33	1.8	Napoleon Area City SD	Napoleon
34	1.7	Lake Local SD	Hartville
34	1.7	Sidney City SD	Sidney
34	1.7	Solon City SD	Solon
37	1.6	Huber Heights City SD	Huber Heights
38	1.5	Findlay City SD	Findlay
38	1.5	Groveport Madison Local SD	Groveport
38	1.5	Licking Heights Local SD	Summit Station
38	1.5	Toledo City SD	Toledo
42	1.4	Barberton City SD	Barberton
42	1.4	Marysville Ex Vill SD	Marysville
42	1.4	Nordonia Hills City SD	Northfield
42	1.4	Rocky River City SD	Rocky River
42	1.4	Washington Local SD	Toledo
42	1.4	Winton Woods City SD	Cincinnati
48	1.3	North Olmsted City SD	North Olmsted
49	1.2	Akron City SD	Akron
49	1.2	Berea City SD	Berea
49	1.2	North Royalton City SD	N Royalton
49	1.2	Olentangy Local SD	Lewis Center
49	1.2	Reynoldsburg City SD	Reynoldsburg
49	1.2	Troy City SD	Troy
55	1.1	Brecksville-Broadview Heights	Brecksville
55	1.1	Fairborn City SD	Fairborn
55	1.1	Lakota Local SD	Liberty Twp
55	1.1	Northmont City SD	Englewood
55	1.1	Woodridge Local SD	Peninsula
60	1.0	Delaware City SD	Delaware
60	1.0	Finneytown Local SD	Cincinnati
60	1.0	Kent City SD	Kent
60	1.0	Loveland City SD	Loveland
60	1.0	Marlington Local SD	Alliance
60	1.0	Middletown City SD	Middletown
60	1.0	Springfield Local SD	Holland
67	0.9	Bexley City SD	Bexley
67	0.9	Canal Winchester Local SD	Canal Winchester
67	0.9	Clearview Local SD	Lorain
67	0.9	Fostoria City SD	Fostoria
67	0.9	Fremont City SD	Fremont
67	0.9	Northwest Local SD	Cincinnati
67	0.9	Strongsville City SD	Strongsville
67	0.9	Tipp City Ex Vill SD	Tipp City
67	0.9	West Clermont Local SD	Cincinnati
76	0.8	Bellefontaine City SD	Bellefontaine
76	0.8	Boardman Local SD	Youngstown
76	0.8	Bucyrus City SD	Bucyrus
76	0.8	Campbell City SD	Campbell
76	0.8	Gahanna-Jefferson City SD	Gahanna
76	0.8	Geneva Area City SD	Geneva
76	0.8	Green Local SD	Green
76	0.8	Jackson Local SD	Massillon
76	0.8	Mason City SD	Mason
85	0.7	Bedford City SD	Bedford
85	0.7	Berlin-Milan Local SD	Milan
85	0.7	Cleveland Hts-Univ Hts City SD	University Hgts
85	0.7	Euclid City SD	Euclid
85	0.7	Indian Hill Ex Vill SD	Cincinnati
85	0.7	Kings Local SD	Kings Mills
85	0.7	Mad River Local SD	Dayton
85	0.7	Oregon City SD	Oregon
85	0.7	Sugarcreek Local SD	Bellbrook
85	0.7	Tallmadge City SD	Tallmadge
85	0.7	Youngstown City SD	Youngstown
96	0.6	Aurora City SD	Aurora
96	0.6	Girard City SD	Girard
96	0.6	Kettering City SD	Kettering
96	0.6	Lake Local SD	Millbury
96	0.6	Lebanon City SD	Lebanon
96	0.6	Maple Heights City SD	Maple Heights
96	0.6	Sylvania City SD	Sylvania
96	0.6	Vandalia-Butler City SD	Vandalia
104	0.5	Howland Local SD	Warren
104	0.5	Jackson City SD	Jackson
104	0.5	Little Miami Local SD	Morrow
104	0.5	Midview Local SD	Grafton
104	0.5	Mount Healthy City SD	Cincinnati
104	0.5	New Philadelphia City SD	New Philadelphia
104	0.5	Oakwood City SD	Dayton
104	0.5	Saint Marys City SD	Saint Marys
112	0.4	Austintown Local SD	Youngstown
112	0.4	Batavia Local SD	Batavia
112	0.4	Bay Village City SD	Bay Village
112	0.4	Beavercreek City SD	Beavercreek
112	0.4	Elida Local SD	Elida
112	0.4	Field Local SD	Mogadore
112	0.4	Hudson City SD	Hudson
112	0.4	Madison-Plains Local SD	London
112	0.4	Marion City SD	Marion
112	0.4	Minerva Local SD	Minerva
112	0.4	Newark City SD	Newark
112	0.4	Norton City SD	Norton
112	0.4	Oak Hills Local SD	Cincinnati
112	0.4	Perry Local SD	Massillon
112	0.4	Pike-Delta-York Local SD	Delta
112	0.4	Streetsboro City SD	Streetsboro
112	0.4	Talawanda City SD	Oxford
112	0.4	Westlake City SD	Westlake
130	0.3	Beachwood City SD	Beachwood
130	0.3	Bowling Green City SD	Bowling Green
130	0.3	Buckeye Local SD	Rayland
130	0.3	Canfield Local SD	Canfield
130	0.3	Canton City SD	Canton
130	0.3	Dayton City SD	Dayton
130	0.3	Eaton City SD	Eaton
130	0.3	Garfield Heights City SD	Garfield Hgts
130	0.3	Hillsboro City SD	Hillsboro
130	0.3	Massillon City SD	Massillon
130	0.3	Maumee City SD	Maumee
130	0.3	Miamisburg City SD	Miamisburg
130	0.3	North Canton City SD	North Canton
130	0.3	Northridge Local SD	Dayton
130	0.3	Piqua City SD	Piqua
130	0.3	Plain Local SD	Canton
130	0.3	Revere Local SD	Bath
130	0.3	South Euclid-Lyndhurst City SD	Lyndhurst
130	0.3	Southeast Local SD	Apple Creek
130	0.3	Stow-Munroe Falls City SD	Stow
130	0.3	West Holmes Local SD	Millersburg
130	0.3	Wyoming City SD	Wyoming
152	0.2	Alliance City SD	Alliance
152	0.2	Ashland City SD	Ashland
152	0.2	Avon Lake City SD	Avon Lake
152	0.2	Brunswick City SD	Brunswick
152	0.2	Bryan City SD	Bryan
152	0.2	Buckeye Local SD	Ashtabula
152	0.2	Carlisle Local SD	Carlisle
152	0.2	Defiance City SD	Defiance
152	0.2	Dover City SD	Dover
152	0.2	Forest Hills Local SD	Cincinnati
152	0.2	Galion City SD	Galion
152	0.2	Granville Ex Vill SD	Granville
152	0.2	Greenon Local SD	Springfield
152	0.2	Lakeview Local SD	Cortland
152	0.2	Louisville City SD	Louisville
152	0.2	Northeastern Local SD	Springfield
152	0.2	Painesville Township Local SD	Painesville
152	0.2	Paulding Ex Vill SD	Paulding
152	0.2	Perrysburg Ex Vill SD	Perrysburg
152	0.2	Pickerington Local SD	Pickerington
152	0.2	Springfield City SD	Springfield
152	0.2	Tiffin City SD	Tiffin
152	0.2	Triway Local SD	Wooster
152	0.2	Twinsburg City SD	Twinsburg
152	0.2	West Muskingum Local SD	Zanesville
152	0.2	Wooster City SD	Wooster
178	0.1	Alexander Local SD	Albany
178	0.1	Avon Local SD	Avon
178	0.1	Benjamin Logan Local SD	Bellefontaine
178	0.1	Cambridge City SD	Cambridge
178	0.1	Chardon Local SD	Chardon
178	0.1	Eastwood Local SD	Pemberville
178	0.1	Edgewood City SD	Trenton
178	0.1	Fairless Local SD	Navarre
178	0.1	Franklin City SD	Franklin
178	0.1	Greeneview Local SD	Jamestown
178	0.1	Hamilton Local SD	Columbus
178	0.1	Hubbard Ex Vill SD	Hubbard
178	0.1	Ironton City SD	Ironton
178	0.1	Jefferson Area Local SD	Jefferson
178	0.1	Lakewood Local SD	Hebron
178	0.1	Lexington Local SD	Lexington
178	0.1	Lima City SD	Lima
178	0.1	Medina City SD	Medina
178	0.1	Miami Trace Local SD	Washington Ct Hse
178	0.1	Milford Ex Vill SD	Milford
178	0.1	Mount Vernon City SD	Mount Vernon
178	0.1	North Fork Local SD	Utica
178	0.1	Northwest Local SD	Canal Fulton
178	0.1	Northwestern Local SD	Springfield
178	0.1	Olmsted Falls City SD	Olmsted Falls
178	0.1	Ottawa-Glandorf Local SD	Ottawa
178	0.1	Plain Local SD	New Albany
178	0.1	Ravenna City SD	Ravenna
178	0.1	Saint Clairsville-Richland City	St Clairsville
178	0.1	Salem City SD	Salem
178	0.1	Sandy Valley Local SD	Magnolia
178	0.1	Southwest Licking Local SD	Etna
178	0.1	Southwest Local SD	Harrison
178	0.1	Springboro Community City SD	Springboro
178	0.1	Swanton Local SD	Swanton
178	0.1	Urbana City SD	Urbana
178	0.1	Wadsworth City SD	Wadsworth
178	0.1	Wapakoneta City SD	Wapakoneta
178	0.1	Washington Court House City SD	Washington Ct Hse
178	0.1	Wellington Ex Vill SD	Wellington
178	0.1	West Branch Local SD	Beloit
178	0.1	Xenia Community City SD	Xenia
220	0.0	Canton Local SD	Canton
220	0.0	Chillicothe City SD	Chillicothe
220	0.0	Cincinnati City SD	Cincinnati
220	0.0	Cleveland Municipal SD	Cleveland
220	0.0	Clyde-Green Springs Ex Vill SD	Clyde
220	0.0	Crestwood Local SD	Mantua
220	0.0	Elyria City SD	Elyria
220	0.0	Goshen Local SD	Goshen
220	0.0	Greenville City SD	Greenville
220	0.0	Kenston Local SD	Chagrin Falls
220	0.0	Kenton City SD	Kenton
220	0.0	Lancaster City SD	Lancaster
220	0.0	Logan-Hocking Local SD	Logan
220	0.0	Mansfield City SD	Mansfield
220	0.0	Marietta City SD	Marietta
220	0.0	Norwalk City SD	Norwalk
220	0.0	Rolling Hills Local SD	Byesville
220	0.0	Rossford Ex Vill SD	Rossford
220	0.0	Sandusky City SD	Sandusky
220	0.0	Teays Valley Local SD	Ashville
220	0.0	Trotwood-Madison City SD	Trotwood
220	0.0	Vinton County Local SD	Mc Arthur
220	0.0	Warren City SD	Warren
220	0.0	Warren Local SD	Vincent
220	0.0	Wilmington City SD	Wilmington
245	0.0	Adams County-Ohio Valley Local SD	West Union

245	0.0	Amanda-Clearcreek Local SD	Amanda
245	0.0	Amherst Ex Vill SD	Amherst
245	0.0	Anthony Wayne Local SD	Whitehouse
245	0.0	Bath Local SD	Lima
245	0.0	Beaver Local SD	Lisbon
245	0.0	Bellaire Local SD	Bellaire
245	0.0	Bellevue City SD	Bellevue
245	0.0	Benton Carroll Salem Local SD	Oak Harbor
245	0.0	Bethel-Tate Local SD	Bethel
245	0.0	Big Walnut Local SD	Galena
245	0.0	Black River Local SD	Sullivan
245	0.0	Blanchester Local SD	Blanchester
245	0.0	Brookfield Local SD	Brookfield
245	0.0	Brookville Local SD	Brookville
245	0.0	Buckeye Local SD	Medina
245	0.0	Buckeye Valley Local SD	Delaware
245	0.0	Carrollton Ex Vill SD	Carrollton
245	0.0	Celina City SD	Celina
245	0.0	Chagrin Falls Ex Vill SD	Chagrin Falls
245	0.0	Champion Local SD	Warren
245	0.0	Circleville City SD	Circleville
245	0.0	Clark-Shawnee Local SD	Springfield
245	0.0	Claymont City SD	Dennison
245	0.0	Clear Fork Valley Local SD	Bellville
245	0.0	Clermont-Northeastern Local SD	Batavia
245	0.0	Clinton-Massie Local SD	Clarksville
245	0.0	Cloverleaf Local SD	Lodi
245	0.0	Coldwater Ex Vill SD	Coldwater
245	0.0	Conneaut Area City SD	Conneaut
245	0.0	Coshocton City SD	Coshocton
245	0.0	Coventry Local SD	Akron
245	0.0	East Cleveland City SD	East Cleveland
245	0.0	East Clinton Local SD	Lees Creek
245	0.0	East Liverpool City SD	East Liverpool
245	0.0	East Muskingum Local SD	New Concord
245	0.0	Eastern Local SD	Sardinia
245	0.0	Edison Local SD	Hammondsville
245	0.0	Electronic Classroom of Tomorrow	Columbus
245	0.0	Elgin Local SD	Marion
245	0.0	Fairfield Union Local SD	W Rushville
245	0.0	Fairland Local SD	Proctorville
245	0.0	Firelands Local SD	Oberlin
245	0.0	Franklin Local SD	Duncan Falls
245	0.0	Gallia County Local SD	Gallipolis
245	0.0	Gallipolis City SD	Gallipolis
245	0.0	Genoa Area Local SD	Genoa
245	0.0	Graham Local SD	Saint Paris
245	0.0	Greenfield Ex Vill SD	Greenfield
245	0.0	Harrison Hills City SD	Hopedale
245	0.0	Heath City SD	Heath
245	0.0	Highland Local SD	Sparta
245	0.0	Highland Local SD	Medina
245	0.0	Huron City SD	Huron
245	0.0	Indian Creek Local SD	Wintersville
245	0.0	Indian Lake Local SD	Lewistown
245	0.0	Indian Valley Local SD	Gnadenhutten
245	0.0	James A Garfield Local SD	Garrettsville
245	0.0	Jonathan Alder Local SD	Plain City
245	0.0	Keystone Local SD	Lagrange
245	0.0	Labrae Local SD	Leavittsburg
245	0.0	Liberty Local SD	Youngstown
245	0.0	Licking Valley Local SD	Newark
245	0.0	Logan Elm Local SD	Circleville
245	0.0	Madison Local SD	Mansfield
245	0.0	Madison Local SD	Madison
245	0.0	Madison Local SD	Middletown
245	0.0	Manchester Local SD	Akron
245	0.0	Mariemont City SD	Cincinnati
245	0.0	Maysville Local SD	Zanesville
245	0.0	Meigs Local SD	Pomeroy
245	0.0	Milton-Union Ex Vill SD	West Milton
245	0.0	Minford Local SD	Minford
245	0.0	Morgan Local SD	McConnelsville
245	0.0	New Lexington City SD	New Lexington
245	0.0	New Richmond Ex Vill SD	New Richmond
245	0.0	Newton Falls Ex Vill SD	Newton Falls
245	0.0	Niles City SD	Niles
245	0.0	North College Hill City SD	Cincinnati
245	0.0	North Ridgeville City SD	N Ridgeville
245	0.0	Northern Local SD	Thornville
245	0.0	Northwest Local SD	Mc Dermott
245	0.0	Norwood City SD	Norwood
245	0.0	Ontario Local SD	Mansfield
245	0.0	Orrville City SD	Orrville
245	0.0	Otsego Local SD	Tontogany
245	0.0	Perkins Local SD	Sandusky
245	0.0	Perry Local SD	Perry
245	0.0	Poland Local SD	Poland
245	0.0	Port Clinton City SD	Port Clinton
245	0.0	Portsmouth City SD	Portsmouth
245	0.0	Preble Shawnee Local SD	Camden
245	0.0	River Valley Local SD	Caledonia
245	0.0	River View Local SD	Warsaw
245	0.0	Rock Hill Local SD	Ironton
245	0.0	Ross Local SD	Hamilton
245	0.0	Scioto Valley Local SD	Piketon
245	0.0	Shawnee Local SD	Lima
245	0.0	Sheffield-Sheffield Lake City	Sheffield Vlg
245	0.0	Shelby City SD	Shelby
245	0.0	South Point Local SD	South Point
245	0.0	Southeast Local SD	Ravenna
245	0.0	Springfield Local SD	Akron
245	0.0	Steubenville City SD	Steubenville
245	0.0	Struthers City SD	Struthers
245	0.0	Switzerland of Ohio Local SD	Woodsfield
245	0.0	Tecumseh Local SD	New Carlisle
245	0.0	Three Rivers Local SD	Cleves
245	0.0	Tri-Valley Local SD	Dresden
245	0.0	Tuscarawas Valley Local SD	Zoarville
245	0.0	Union Local SD	Morristown
245	0.0	Union-Scioto Local SD	Chillicothe
245	0.0	Upper Sandusky Ex Vill SD	Upper Sandusky
245	0.0	Valley View Local SD	Germantown
245	0.0	Van Wert City SD	Van Wert
245	0.0	Vermilion Local SD	Vermilion
245	0.0	Warrensville Heights City SD	Warrensville Hgts
245	0.0	Washington-Nile Local SD	West Portsmouth
245	0.0	Waverly City SD	Waverly
245	0.0	Wellston City SD	Wellston
245	0.0	West Geauga Local SD	Chesterland
245	0.0	Western Brown Local SD	Mount Orab
245	0.0	Westfall Local SD	Williamsport
245	0.0	Wickliffe City SD	Wickliffe
245	0.0	Zane Trace Local SD	Chillicothe
245	0.0	Zanesville City SD	Zanesville

Migrant Students

Rank	Percent	District Name	City
1	12.3	Painesville City Local SD	Painesville
2	5.2	Willard City SD	Willard
3	3.2	Woodridge Local SD	Peninsula
4	2.3	Tecumseh Local SD	New Carlisle
4	2.3	Wauseon Ex Vill SD	Wauseon
6	1.8	Napoleon Area City SD	Napoleon
7	1.3	Benton Carroll Salem Local SD	Oak Harbor
7	1.3	Fremont City SD	Fremont
9	1.0	Tipp City Ex Vill SD	Tipp City
10	0.9	Marlington Local SD	Alliance
11	0.8	Reynoldsburg City SD	Reynoldsburg
11	0.8	South-Western City SD	Grove City
13	0.6	Otsego Local SD	Tontogany
14	0.4	Berlin-Milan Local SD	Milan
14	0.4	Perrysburg Ex Vill SD	Perrysburg
16	0.3	Clyde-Green Springs Ex Vill SD	Clyde
16	0.3	Hamilton City SD	Hamilton
16	0.3	Ottawa-Glandorf Local SD	Ottawa
16	0.3	Upper Sandusky Ex Vill SD	Upper Sandusky
20	0.2	Bowling Green City SD	Bowling Green
20	0.2	Eastwood Local SD	Pemberville
20	0.2	Lake Local SD	Millbury
20	0.2	Vermilion Local SD	Vermilion
24	0.1	Alliance City SD	Alliance
24	0.1	Black River Local SD	Sullivan
24	0.1	Clearview Local SD	Lorain
24	0.1	Cloverleaf Local SD	Lodi
24	0.1	Columbus City SD	Columbus
24	0.1	Elyria City SD	Elyria
24	0.1	Fairborn City SD	Fairborn
24	0.1	Fairview Park City SD	Fairview Park
24	0.1	Field Local SD	Mogadore
24	0.1	Firelands Local SD	Oberlin
24	0.1	Highland Local SD	Medina
24	0.1	Lorain City SD	Lorain
24	0.1	Marion City SD	Marion
24	0.1	Medina City SD	Medina
24	0.1	North Olmsted City SD	North Olmsted
24	0.1	North Ridgeville City SD	N Ridgeville
24	0.1	Pike-Delta-York Local SD	Delta
24	0.1	Springfield City SD	Springfield
24	0.1	Urbana City SD	Urbana
24	0.1	Warrensville Heights City SD	Warrensville Hgts
24	0.1	Wellington Ex Vill SD	Wellington
24	0.1	Westlake City SD	Westlake
24	0.1	Willoughby-Eastlake City SD	Willoughby
47	0.0	Amherst Ex Vill SD	Amherst
47	0.0	Avon Lake City SD	Avon Lake
47	0.0	Bay Village City SD	Bay Village
47	0.0	Bexley City SD	Bexley
47	0.0	Canfield Local SD	Canfield
47	0.0	Centerville City SD	Centerville
47	0.0	Cincinnati City SD	Cincinnati
47	0.0	Delaware City SD	Delaware
47	0.0	Dublin City SD	Dublin
47	0.0	Findlay City SD	Findlay
47	0.0	Gahanna-Jefferson City SD	Gahanna
47	0.0	Geneva Area City SD	Geneva
47	0.0	Greenville City SD	Greenville
47	0.0	Kenston Local SD	Chagrin Falls
47	0.0	Mad River Local SD	Dayton
47	0.0	Olmsted Falls City SD	Olmsted Falls
47	0.0	Painesville Township Local SD	Painesville
47	0.0	Sheffield-Sheffield Lake City	Sheffield Vlg
47	0.0	Strongsville City SD	Strongsville
47	0.0	Sycamore Community City SD	Cincinnati
47	0.0	Tri-Valley Local SD	Dresden
47	0.0	Vandalia-Butler City SD	Vandalia
47	0.0	Wilmington City SD	Wilmington
70	n/a	Adams County-Ohio Valley Local SD	West Union
70	n/a	Akron City SD	Akron
70	n/a	Alexander Local SD	Albany
70	n/a	Amanda-Clearcreek Local SD	Amanda
70	n/a	Anthony Wayne Local SD	Whitehouse
70	n/a	Ashland City SD	Ashland
70	n/a	Ashtabula Area City SD	Ashtabula
70	n/a	Athens City SD	The Plains
70	n/a	Aurora City SD	Aurora
70	n/a	Austintown Local SD	Youngstown
70	n/a	Avon Local SD	Avon
70	n/a	Barberton City SD	Barberton
70	n/a	Batavia Local SD	Batavia
70	n/a	Bath Local SD	Lima
70	n/a	Beachwood City SD	Beachwood
70	n/a	Beaver Local SD	Lisbon
70	n/a	Beavercreek City SD	Beavercreek
70	n/a	Bedford City SD	Bedford
70	n/a	Bellaire Local SD	Bellaire
70	n/a	Bellefontaine City SD	Bellefontaine
70	n/a	Bellevue City SD	Bellevue
70	n/a	Benjamin Logan Local SD	Bellefontaine
70	n/a	Berea City SD	Berea
70	n/a	Bethel-Tate Local SD	Bethel
70	n/a	Big Walnut Local SD	Galena
70	n/a	Blanchester Local SD	Blanchester
70	n/a	Boardman Local SD	Youngstown
70	n/a	Brecksville-Broadview Heights	Brecksville
70	n/a	Brookfield Local SD	Brookfield
70	n/a	Brookville Local SD	Brookville
70	n/a	Brunswick City SD	Brunswick
70	n/a	Bryan City SD	Bryan
70	n/a	Buckeye Local SD	Rayland
70	n/a	Buckeye Local SD	Medina
70	n/a	Buckeye Local SD	Ashtabula
70	n/a	Buckeye Valley Local SD	Delaware
70	n/a	Bucyrus City SD	Bucyrus
70	n/a	Cambridge City SD	Cambridge
70	n/a	Campbell City SD	Campbell
70	n/a	Canal Winchester Local SD	Canal Winchester
70	n/a	Canton City SD	Canton
70	n/a	Canton Local SD	Canton
70	n/a	Carlisle Local SD	Carlisle
70	n/a	Carrollton Ex Vill SD	Carrollton
70	n/a	Celina City SD	Celina
70	n/a	Chagrin Falls Ex Vill SD	Chagrin Falls
70	n/a	Champion Local SD	Warren
70	n/a	Chardon Local SD	Chardon
70	n/a	Chillicothe City SD	Chillicothe
70	n/a	Circleville City SD	Circleville
70	n/a	Clark-Shawnee Local SD	Springfield
70	n/a	Claymont City SD	Dennison
70	n/a	Clear Fork Valley Local SD	Bellville
70	n/a	Clermont-Northeastern Local SD	Batavia
70	n/a	Cleveland Hts-Univ Hts City SD	University Hgts
70	n/a	Cleveland Municipal SD	Cleveland
70	n/a	Clinton-Massie Local SD	Clarksville
70	n/a	Coldwater Ex Vill SD	Coldwater
70	n/a	Conneaut Area City SD	Conneaut
70	n/a	Copley-Fairlawn City SD	Copley
70	n/a	Coshocton City SD	Coshocton
70	n/a	Coventry Local SD	Akron
70	n/a	Crestwood Local SD	Mantua
70	n/a	Cuyahoga Falls City SD	Cuyahoga Falls
70	n/a	Dayton City SD	Dayton
70	n/a	Defiance City SD	Defiance
70	n/a	Dover City SD	Dover
70	n/a	East Cleveland City SD	East Cleveland
70	n/a	East Clinton Local SD	Lees Creek
70	n/a	East Holmes Local SD	Berlin
70	n/a	East Liverpool City SD	East Liverpool
70	n/a	East Muskingum Local SD	New Concord
70	n/a	Eastern Local SD	Sardinia
70	n/a	Eaton City SD	Eaton
70	n/a	Edgewood City SD	Trenton
70	n/a	Edison Local SD	Hammondsville
70	n/a	Electronic Classroom of Tomorrow	Columbus
70	n/a	Elgin Local SD	Marion
70	n/a	Elida Local SD	Elida
70	n/a	Euclid City SD	Euclid

Rank	Percent	District Name	City
70	n/a	Fairfield City SD	Fairfield
70	n/a	Fairfield Union Local SD	W Rushville
70	n/a	Fairland Local SD	Proctorville
70	n/a	Fairless Local SD	Navarre
70	n/a	Finneytown Local SD	Cincinnati
70	n/a	Forest Hills Local SD	Cincinnati
70	n/a	Fostoria City SD	Fostoria
70	n/a	Franklin City SD	Franklin
70	n/a	Franklin Local SD	Duncan Falls
70	n/a	Galion City SD	Galion
70	n/a	Gallia County Local SD	Gallipolis
70	n/a	Gallipolis City SD	Gallipolis
70	n/a	Garfield Heights City SD	Garfield Hgts
70	n/a	Genoa Area Local SD	Genoa
70	n/a	Girard City SD	Girard
70	n/a	Goshen Local SD	Goshen
70	n/a	Graham Local SD	Saint Paris
70	n/a	Granville Ex Vill SD	Granville
70	n/a	Green Local SD	Green
70	n/a	Greeneview Local SD	Jamestown
70	n/a	Greenfield Ex Vill SD	Greenfield
70	n/a	Greenon Local SD	Springfield
70	n/a	Groveport Madison Local SD	Groveport
70	n/a	Hamilton Local SD	Columbus
70	n/a	Harrison Hills City SD	Hopedale
70	n/a	Heath City SD	Heath
70	n/a	Highland Local SD	Sparta
70	n/a	Hilliard City SD	Hilliard
70	n/a	Hillsboro City SD	Hillsboro
70	n/a	Howland Local SD	Warren
70	n/a	Hubbard Ex Vill SD	Hubbard
70	n/a	Huber Heights City SD	Huber Heights
70	n/a	Hudson City SD	Hudson
70	n/a	Huron City SD	Huron
70	n/a	Indian Creek Local SD	Wintersville
70	n/a	Indian Hill Ex Vill SD	Cincinnati
70	n/a	Indian Lake Local SD	Lewistown
70	n/a	Indian Valley Local SD	Gnadenhutten
70	n/a	Ironton City SD	Ironton
70	n/a	Jackson City SD	Jackson
70	n/a	Jackson Local SD	Massillon
70	n/a	James A Garfield Local SD	Garrettsville
70	n/a	Jefferson Area Local SD	Jefferson
70	n/a	Jonathan Alder Local SD	Plain City
70	n/a	Kent City SD	Kent
70	n/a	Kenton City SD	Kenton
70	n/a	Kettering City SD	Kettering
70	n/a	Keystone Local SD	Lagrange
70	n/a	Kings Local SD	Kings Mills
70	n/a	Labrae Local SD	Leavittsburg
70	n/a	Lake Local SD	Hartville
70	n/a	Lakeview Local SD	Cortland
70	n/a	Lakewood City SD	Lakewood
70	n/a	Lakewood Local SD	Hebron
70	n/a	Lakota Local SD	Liberty Twp
70	n/a	Lancaster City SD	Lancaster
70	n/a	Lebanon City SD	Lebanon
70	n/a	Lexington Local SD	Lexington
70	n/a	Liberty Local SD	Youngstown
70	n/a	Licking Heights Local SD	Summit Station
70	n/a	Licking Valley Local SD	Newark
70	n/a	Lima City SD	Lima
70	n/a	Little Miami Local SD	Morrow
70	n/a	Logan Elm Local SD	Circleville
70	n/a	Logan-Hocking Local SD	Logan
70	n/a	London City SD	London
70	n/a	Louisville City SD	Louisville
70	n/a	Loveland City SD	Loveland
70	n/a	Madison Local SD	Madison
70	n/a	Madison Local SD	Mansfield
70	n/a	Madison Local SD	Middletown
70	n/a	Madison-Plains Local SD	London
70	n/a	Manchester Local SD	Akron
70	n/a	Mansfield City SD	Mansfield
70	n/a	Maple Heights City SD	Maple Heights
70	n/a	Mariemont City SD	Cincinnati
70	n/a	Marietta City SD	Marietta
70	n/a	Marysville Ex Vill SD	Marysville
70	n/a	Mason City SD	Mason
70	n/a	Massillon City SD	Massillon
70	n/a	Maumee City SD	Maumee
70	n/a	Mayfield City SD	Highland Hgts
70	n/a	Maysville Local SD	Zanesville
70	n/a	Meigs Local SD	Pomeroy
70	n/a	Mentor Ex Vill SD	Mentor
70	n/a	Miami Trace Local SD	Washington Ct Hse
70	n/a	Miamisburg City SD	Miamisburg
70	n/a	Middletown City SD	Middletown
70	n/a	Midview Local SD	Grafton
70	n/a	Milford Ex Vill SD	Milford
70	n/a	Milton-Union Ex Vill SD	West Milton
70	n/a	Minerva Local SD	Minerva
70	n/a	Minford Local SD	Minford
70	n/a	Morgan Local SD	McConnelsville
70	n/a	Mount Healthy City SD	Cincinnati
70	n/a	Mount Vernon City SD	Mount Vernon
70	n/a	New Lexington City SD	New Lexington
70	n/a	New Philadelphia City SD	New Philadelphia
70	n/a	New Richmond Ex Vill SD	New Richmond
70	n/a	Newark City SD	Newark
70	n/a	Newton Falls Ex Vill SD	Newton Falls
70	n/a	Niles City SD	Niles
70	n/a	Nordonia Hills City SD	Northfield
70	n/a	North Canton City SD	North Canton
70	n/a	North College Hill City SD	Cincinnati
70	n/a	North Fork Local SD	Utica
70	n/a	North Royalton City SD	N Royalton
70	n/a	Northeastern Local SD	Springfield
70	n/a	Northern Local SD	Thornville
70	n/a	Northmont City SD	Englewood
70	n/a	Northridge Local SD	Dayton
70	n/a	Northwest Local SD	Cincinnati
70	n/a	Northwest Local SD	Canal Fulton
70	n/a	Northwest Local SD	Mc Dermott
70	n/a	Northwestern Local SD	Springfield
70	n/a	Norton City SD	Norton
70	n/a	Norwalk City SD	Norwalk
70	n/a	Norwood City SD	Norwood
70	n/a	Oak Hills Local SD	Cincinnati
70	n/a	Oakwood City SD	Dayton
70	n/a	Olentangy Local SD	Lewis Center
70	n/a	Ontario Local SD	Mansfield
70	n/a	Orange City SD	Cleveland
70	n/a	Oregon City SD	Oregon
70	n/a	Orrville City SD	Orrville
70	n/a	Parma City SD	Parma
70	n/a	Paulding Ex Vill SD	Paulding
70	n/a	Perkins Local SD	Sandusky
70	n/a	Perry Local SD	Perry
70	n/a	Perry Local SD	Massillon
70	n/a	Pickerington Local SD	Pickerington
70	n/a	Piqua City SD	Piqua
70	n/a	Plain Local SD	New Albany
70	n/a	Plain Local SD	Canton
70	n/a	Poland Local SD	Poland
70	n/a	Port Clinton City SD	Port Clinton
70	n/a	Portsmouth City SD	Portsmouth
70	n/a	Preble Shawnee Local SD	Camden
70	n/a	Princeton City SD	Cincinnati
70	n/a	Ravenna City SD	Ravenna
70	n/a	Revere Local SD	Bath
70	n/a	River Valley Local SD	Caledonia
70	n/a	River View Local SD	Warsaw
70	n/a	Rock Hill Local SD	Ironton
70	n/a	Rocky River City SD	Rocky River
70	n/a	Rolling Hills Local SD	Byesville
70	n/a	Ross Local SD	Hamilton
70	n/a	Rossford Ex Vill SD	Rossford
70	n/a	Saint Clairsville-Richland City	St Clairsville
70	n/a	Saint Marys City SD	Saint Marys
70	n/a	Salem City SD	Salem
70	n/a	Sandusky City SD	Sandusky
70	n/a	Sandy Valley Local SD	Magnolia
70	n/a	Scioto Valley Local SD	Piketon
70	n/a	Shaker Heights City SD	Shaker Heights
70	n/a	Shawnee Local SD	Lima
70	n/a	Shelby City SD	Shelby
70	n/a	Sidney City SD	Sidney
70	n/a	Solon City SD	Solon
70	n/a	South Euclid-Lyndhurst City SD	Lyndhurst
70	n/a	South Point Local SD	South Point
70	n/a	Southeast Local SD	Apple Creek
70	n/a	Southeast Local SD	Ravenna
70	n/a	Southwest Licking Local SD	Etna
70	n/a	Southwest Local SD	Harrison
70	n/a	Springboro Community City SD	Springboro
70	n/a	Springfield Local SD	Holland
70	n/a	Springfield Local SD	Akron
70	n/a	Steubenville City SD	Steubenville
70	n/a	Stow-Munroe Falls City SD	Stow
70	n/a	Streetsboro City SD	Streetsboro
70	n/a	Struthers City SD	Struthers
70	n/a	Sugarcreek Local SD	Bellbrook
70	n/a	Swanton Local SD	Swanton
70	n/a	Switzerland of Ohio Local SD	Woodsfield
70	n/a	Sylvania City SD	Sylvania
70	n/a	Talawanda City SD	Oxford
70	n/a	Tallmadge City SD	Tallmadge
70	n/a	Teays Valley Local SD	Ashville
70	n/a	Three Rivers Local SD	Cleves
70	n/a	Tiffin City SD	Tiffin
70	n/a	Toledo City SD	Toledo
70	n/a	Triway Local SD	Wooster
70	n/a	Trotwood-Madison City SD	Trotwood
70	n/a	Troy City SD	Troy
70	n/a	Tuscarawas Valley Local SD	Zoarville
70	n/a	Twinsburg City SD	Twinsburg
70	n/a	Union Local SD	Morristown
70	n/a	Union-Scioto Local SD	Chillicothe
70	n/a	Upper Arlington City SD	Upper Arlington
70	n/a	Valley View Local SD	Germantown
70	n/a	Van Wert City SD	Van Wert
70	n/a	Vinton County Local SD	Mc Arthur
70	n/a	Wadsworth City SD	Wadsworth
70	n/a	Wapakoneta City SD	Wapakoneta
70	n/a	Warren City SD	Warren
70	n/a	Warren Local SD	Vincent
70	n/a	Washington Court House City SD	Washington Ct Hse
70	n/a	Washington Local SD	Toledo
70	n/a	Washington-Nile Local SD	West Portsmouth
70	n/a	Waverly City SD	Waverly
70	n/a	Wellston City SD	Wellston
70	n/a	West Branch Local SD	Beloit
70	n/a	West Carrollton City SD	West Carrollton
70	n/a	West Clermont Local SD	Cincinnati
70	n/a	West Geauga Local SD	Chesterland
70	n/a	West Holmes Local SD	Millersburg
70	n/a	West Muskingum Local SD	Zanesville
70	n/a	Western Brown Local SD	Mount Orab
70	n/a	Westerville City SD	Westerville
70	n/a	Westfall Local SD	Williamsport
70	n/a	Whitehall City SD	Whitehall
70	n/a	Wickliffe City SD	Wickliffe
70	n/a	Winton Woods City SD	Cincinnati
70	n/a	Wooster City SD	Wooster
70	n/a	Worthington City SD	Worthington
70	n/a	Wyoming City SD	Wyoming
70	n/a	Xenia Community City SD	Xenia
70	n/a	Youngstown City SD	Youngstown
70	n/a	Zane Trace Local SD	Chillicothe
70	n/a	Zanesville City SD	Zanesville

Students Eligible for Free Lunch

Rank	Percent	District Name	City
1	72.7	Cleveland Municipal SD	Cleveland
2	64.5	Dayton City SD	Dayton
3	63.3	Youngstown City SD	Youngstown
4	62.2	East Cleveland City SD	East Cleveland
5	60.3	Lima City SD	Lima
6	58.8	Cincinnati City SD	Cincinnati
7	57.9	Mansfield City SD	Mansfield
8	55.6	Painesville City Local SD	Painesville
9	55.1	Columbus City SD	Columbus
10	54.0	Lorain City SD	Lorain
11	53.5	Warrensville Heights City SD	Warrensville Hgts
12	51.9	Toledo City SD	Toledo
13	50.6	Canton City SD	Canton
13	50.6	Trotwood-Madison City SD	Trotwood
15	49.6	Meigs Local SD	Pomeroy
16	48.8	Zanesville City SD	Zanesville
17	47.9	Akron City SD	Akron
17	47.9	Sandusky City SD	Sandusky
19	46.7	Alliance City SD	Alliance
20	45.8	Portsmouth City SD	Portsmouth
21	45.7	Warren City SD	Warren
22	44.8	Clearview Local SD	Lorain
23	44.7	Springfield City SD	Springfield
24	44.1	Steubenville City SD	Steubenville
25	43.3	Whitehall City SD	Whitehall
26	43.2	Vinton County Local SD	Mc Arthur
27	42.8	Bellaire Local SD	Bellaire
28	41.6	Struthers City SD	Struthers
29	40.5	Hamilton City SD	Hamilton
30	40.3	Campbell City SD	Campbell
31	40.0	Euclid City SD	Euclid
32	39.2	Ashtabula Area City SD	Ashtabula
33	38.3	East Liverpool City SD	East Liverpool
33	38.3	New Lexington City SD	New Lexington
35	37.7	Fostoria City SD	Fostoria
36	36.9	Northwest Local SD	Mc Dermott
37	36.6	Adams County-Ohio Valley Local SD	West Union
37	36.6	Northridge Local SD	Dayton
37	36.6	Washington-Nile Local SD	West Portsmouth
40	36.4	Norwood City SD	Norwood
41	36.3	Conneaut Area City SD	Conneaut
42	35.9	Mount Healthy City SD	Cincinnati
42	35.9	Princeton City SD	Cincinnati
44	35.7	Rock Hill Local SD	Ironton
45	35.0	Coshocton City SD	Coshocton
46	34.8	Gallia County Local SD	Gallipolis
47	34.7	Massillon City SD	Massillon
48	34.6	South Point Local SD	South Point
49	34.3	Barberton City SD	Barberton
50	34.1	Ironton City SD	Ironton
51	34.0	Scioto Valley Local SD	Piketon
52	32.7	Wellston City SD	Wellston

Rank	Percent	District	City
53	32.5	Elyria City SD	Elyria
54	32.2	Bucyrus City SD	Bucyrus
55	32.1	Cambridge City SD	Cambridge
56	31.9	Marion City SD	Marion
56	31.9	North College Hill City SD	Cincinnati
58	31.7	Morgan Local SD	McConnelsville
59	31.6	Union Local SD	Morristown
60	31.1	Harrison Hills City SD	Hopedale
61	30.3	Switzerland of Ohio Local SD	Woodsfield
62	30.2	Cleveland Hts-Univ Hts City SD	University Hgts
62	30.2	Maple Heights City SD	Maple Heights
64	30.0	Niles City SD	Niles
65	29.9	Waverly City SD	Waverly
66	29.7	Middletown City SD	Middletown
67	29.4	Ravenna City SD	Ravenna
68	29.3	Chillicothe City SD	Chillicothe
68	29.3	Labrae Local SD	Leavittsburg
70	29.1	Buckeye Local SD	Rayland
70	29.1	Minford Local SD	Minford
72	28.9	Beaver Local SD	Lisbon
73	28.1	Franklin Local SD	Duncan Falls
74	28.0	Fremont City SD	Fremont
75	27.8	Rolling Hills Local SD	Byesville
76	27.2	Maysville Local SD	Zanesville
77	27.1	Brookfield Local SD	Brookfield
78	26.8	Girard City SD	Girard
78	26.8	Willard City SD	Willard
80	26.5	Athens City SD	The Plains
81	26.2	Jackson City SD	Jackson
82	25.9	Claymont City SD	Dennison
83	25.6	Gallipolis City SD	Gallipolis
83	25.6	Lancaster City SD	Lancaster
83	25.6	Piqua City SD	Piqua
86	25.2	Circleville City SD	Circleville
86	25.2	Indian Creek Local SD	Wintersville
86	25.2	Xenia Community City SD	Xenia
89	25.0	Edison Local SD	Hammondsville
90	24.8	South-Western City SD	Grove City
91	24.6	Logan-Hocking Local SD	Logan
92	24.5	Newark City SD	Newark
93	24.3	Geneva Area City SD	Geneva
94	24.1	Hillsboro City SD	Hillsboro
95	23.8	Washington Court House City SD	Washington Ct Hse
95	23.8	Wooster City SD	Wooster
97	23.6	Bedford City SD	Bedford
97	23.6	Indian Valley Local SD	Gnadenhutten
99	23.5	Mad River Local SD	Dayton
100	23.4	New Richmond Ex Vill SD	New Richmond
101	22.5	Liberty Local SD	Youngstown
102	22.2	Carrollton Ex Vill SD	Carrollton
102	22.2	Springfield Local SD	Akron
104	22.1	Woodridge Local SD	Peninsula
105	22.0	Sidney City SD	Sidney
106	21.9	Greenfield Ex Vill SD	Greenfield
106	21.9	Minerva Local SD	Minerva
108	21.8	Bellefontaine City SD	Bellefontaine
108	21.8	Garfield Heights City SD	Garfield Hgts
110	21.7	Canton Local SD	Canton
111	21.5	Alexander Local SD	Albany
112	21.4	Buckeye Local SD	Ashtabula
113	21.1	Galion City SD	Galion
114	20.9	Fairborn City SD	Fairborn
114	20.9	Fairland Local SD	Proctorville
116	20.7	Kenton City SD	Kenton
117	20.6	Kent City SD	Kent
118	20.5	Lakewood City SD	Lakewood
119	20.4	Port Clinton City SD	Port Clinton
120	20.0	Indian Lake Local SD	Lewistown
120	20.0	Urbana City SD	Urbana
122	19.9	West Holmes Local SD	Millersburg
123	19.8	Eastern Local SD	Sardinia
123	19.8	Lakewood Local SD	Hebron
125	19.6	Union-Scioto Local SD	Chillicothe
126	19.5	Newton Falls Ex Vill SD	Newton Falls
126	19.5	Salem City SD	Salem
128	19.4	Mount Vernon City SD	Mount Vernon
129	19.3	Elgin Local SD	Marion
129	19.3	Sandy Valley Local SD	Magnolia
129	19.3	Western Brown Local SD	Mount Orab
132	19.2	Fairless Local SD	Navarre
132	19.2	Tecumseh Local SD	New Carlisle
134	19.1	Celina City SD	Celina
135	18.8	Groveport Madison Local SD	Groveport
135	18.8	Norwalk City SD	Norwalk
137	18.7	Springfield Local SD	Holland
138	18.6	Marietta City SD	Marietta
139	18.4	Elida Local SD	Elida
140	18.1	Greenville City SD	Greenville
140	18.1	Plain Local SD	Canton
142	18.0	Batavia Local SD	Batavia
142	18.0	Washington Local SD	Toledo
144	17.9	Hubbard Ex Vill SD	Hubbard
145	17.8	Ashland City SD	Ashland
146	17.7	London City SD	London
146	17.7	Winton Woods City SD	Cincinnati
148	17.6	Southeast Local SD	Apple Creek
149	17.4	Highland Local SD	Sparta
149	17.4	Madison Local SD	Mansfield
151	17.3	Orrville City SD	Orrville
152	17.1	Goshen Local SD	Goshen
153	17.0	Jefferson Area Local SD	Jefferson
154	16.8	Austintown Local SD	Youngstown
154	16.8	Findlay City SD	Findlay
156	16.7	Northern Local SD	Thornville
157	16.6	Hamilton Local SD	Columbus
157	16.6	Van Wert City SD	Van Wert
159	16.4	Defiance City SD	Defiance
160	16.3	Wilmington City SD	Wilmington
161	16.1	Pike-Delta-York Local SD	Delta
161	16.1	Westfall Local SD	Williamsport
163	16.0	Miami Trace Local SD	Washington Ct Hse
163	16.0	West Branch Local SD	Beloit
165	15.9	Clyde-Green Springs Ex Vill SD	Clyde
166	15.7	Madison Local SD	Madison
167	15.6	Logan Elm Local SD	Circleville
167	15.6	Tiffin City SD	Tiffin
169	15.5	River View Local SD	Warsaw
170	15.4	Miamisburg City SD	Miamisburg
170	15.4	Napoleon Area City SD	Napoleon
172	15.3	Bath Local SD	Lima
173	15.2	Clermont-Northeastern Local SD	Batavia
173	15.2	Northwest Local SD	Cincinnati
173	15.2	Shelby City SD	Shelby
173	15.2	West Muskingum Local SD	Zanesville
177	15.1	Milton-Union Ex Vill SD	West Milton
178	15.0	Coventry Local SD	Akron
178	15.0	Wapakoneta City SD	Wapakoneta
180	14.9	Amanda-Clearcreek Local SD	Amanda
181	14.8	Delaware City SD	Delaware
182	14.7	Eaton City SD	Eaton
182	14.7	Franklin City SD	Franklin
184	14.6	Wellington Ex Vill SD	Wellington
185	14.5	Rossford Ex Vill SD	Rossford
186	14.3	Bethel-Tate Local SD	Bethel
186	14.3	Wauseon Ex Vill SD	Wauseon
188	14.2	East Clinton Local SD	Lees Creek
188	14.2	Streetsboro City SD	Streetsboro
188	14.2	West Carrollton City SD	West Carrollton
191	14.0	Licking Valley Local SD	Newark
191	14.0	Warren Local SD	Vincent
193	13.9	Preble Shawnee Local SD	Camden
193	13.9	Sheffield-Sheffield Lake City	Sheffield Vlg
193	13.9	Three Rivers Local SD	Cleves
196	13.7	East Muskingum Local SD	New Concord
196	13.7	Perry Local SD	Massillon
198	13.6	Marlington Local SD	Alliance
199	13.5	Bellevue City SD	Bellevue
200	13.3	New Philadelphia City SD	New Philadelphia
200	13.3	Southeast Local SD	Ravenna
202	13.2	Paulding Ex Vill SD	Paulding
202	13.2	Tri-Valley Local SD	Dresden
204	13.1	Blanchester Local SD	Blanchester
205	13.0	East Holmes Local SD	Berlin
205	13.0	Saint Marys City SD	Saint Marys
205	13.0	Tuscarawas Valley Local SD	Zoarville
208	12.9	Clear Fork Valley Local SD	Bellville
208	12.9	James A Garfield Local SD	Garrettsville
208	12.9	Kettering City SD	Kettering
208	12.9	Triway Local SD	Wooster
208	12.9	Troy City SD	Troy
213	12.8	North Fork Local SD	Utica
213	12.8	Parma City SD	Parma
213	12.8	Saint Clairsville-Richland City	St Clairsville
216	12.7	Finneytown Local SD	Cincinnati
216	12.7	Vermilion Local SD	Vermilion
218	12.5	Heath City SD	Heath
219	12.4	Bowling Green City SD	Bowling Green
219	12.4	Louisville City SD	Louisville
219	12.4	Talawanda City SD	Oxford
219	12.4	Teays Valley Local SD	Ashville
223	12.2	Black River Local SD	Sullivan
224	12.0	Upper Sandusky Ex Vill SD	Upper Sandusky
225	11.9	Southwest Local SD	Harrison
226	11.8	Canal Winchester Local SD	Canal Winchester
227	11.7	Boardman Local SD	Youngstown
227	11.7	Cloverleaf Local SD	Lodi
227	11.7	Oregon City SD	Oregon
230	11.5	Crestwood Local SD	Mantua
230	11.5	River Valley Local SD	Caledonia
232	11.4	Benton Carroll Salem Local SD	Oak Harbor
233	11.0	Swanton Local SD	Swanton
234	10.9	South Euclid-Lyndhurst City SD	Lyndhurst
235	10.8	Fairfield Union Local SD	W Rushville
235	10.8	Huber Heights City SD	Huber Heights
237	10.7	Midview Local SD	Grafton
237	10.7	Wickliffe City SD	Wickliffe
239	10.5	Fairview Park City SD	Fairview Park
239	10.5	Graham Local SD	Saint Paris
241	10.4	Brookville Local SD	Brookville
241	10.4	Cuyahoga Falls City SD	Cuyahoga Falls
241	10.4	Lebanon City SD	Lebanon
241	10.4	North Olmsted City SD	North Olmsted
241	10.4	Willoughby-Eastlake City SD	Willoughby
246	10.2	Berlin-Milan Local SD	Milan
246	10.2	Bryan City SD	Bryan
246	10.2	Buckeye Local SD	Medina
246	10.2	Edgewood City SD	Trenton
246	10.2	Greeneview Local SD	Jamestown
246	10.2	Jonathan Alder Local SD	Plain City
246	10.2	Norton City SD	Norton
253	10.1	Licking Heights Local SD	Summit Station
253	10.1	Madison Local SD	Middletown
255	10.0	Northwest Local SD	Canal Fulton
256	9.9	Carlisle Local SD	Carlisle
256	9.9	Lake Local SD	Millbury
256	9.9	Zane Trace Local SD	Chillicothe
259	9.7	Shawnee Local SD	Lima
260	9.6	Clark-Shawnee Local SD	Springfield
261	9.4	Howland Local SD	Warren
262	9.3	Berea City SD	Berea
262	9.3	Northwestern Local SD	Springfield
264	9.2	Champion Local SD	Warren
265	8.8	Firelands Local SD	Oberlin
265	8.8	West Clermont Local SD	Cincinnati
267	8.7	Northmont City SD	Englewood
267	8.7	Otsego Local SD	Tontogany
269	8.6	Big Walnut Local SD	Galena
269	8.6	Marysville Ex Vill SD	Marysville
269	8.6	North Ridgeville City SD	N Ridgeville
272	8.4	Huron City SD	Huron
273	8.1	Genoa Area Local SD	Genoa
273	8.1	Twinsburg City SD	Twinsburg
275	7.9	Madison-Plains Local SD	London
275	7.9	Milford Ex Vill SD	Milford
275	7.9	Tallmadge City SD	Tallmadge
278	7.8	Painesville Township Local SD	Painesville
279	7.7	Reynoldsburg City SD	Reynoldsburg
280	7.6	Clinton-Massie Local SD	Clarksville
280	7.6	Lakeview Local SD	Cortland
280	7.6	Little Miami Local SD	Morrow
283	7.5	Chardon Local SD	Chardon
283	7.5	Ontario Local SD	Mansfield
285	7.4	Greenon Local SD	Springfield
285	7.4	Perkins Local SD	Sandusky
287	7.3	Vandalia-Butler City SD	Vandalia
288	7.2	Eastwood Local SD	Pemberville
288	7.2	Shaker Heights City SD	Shaker Heights
290	7.1	Buckeye Valley Local SD	Delaware
290	7.1	Southwest Licking Local SD	Etna
292	7.0	Ross Local SD	Hamilton
293	6.9	Benjamin Logan Local SD	Bellefontaine
293	6.9	Fairfield City SD	Fairfield
293	6.9	Westerville City SD	Westerville
296	6.8	Brunswick City SD	Brunswick
296	6.8	Hilliard City SD	Hilliard
298	6.7	Green Local SD	Green
299	6.6	Coldwater Ex Vill SD	Coldwater
299	6.6	Wadsworth City SD	Wadsworth
301	6.5	Lake Local SD	Hartville
301	6.5	Lexington Local SD	Lexington
303	6.4	Dover City SD	Dover
304	6.3	Keystone Local SD	Lagrange
305	6.2	Avon Local SD	Avon
306	6.1	Northeastern Local SD	Springfield
307	6.0	Maumee City SD	Maumee
307	6.0	Mentor Ex Vill SD	Mentor
309	5.9	Sylvania City SD	Sylvania
310	5.7	Amherst Ex Vill SD	Amherst
310	5.7	Manchester Local SD	Akron
312	5.6	Perry Local SD	Perry
313	5.5	Gahanna-Jefferson City SD	Gahanna
313	5.5	Tipp City Ex Vill SD	Tipp City
315	5.4	Ottawa-Glandorf Local SD	Ottawa
316	5.3	Copley-Fairlawn City SD	Copley
316	5.3	Nordonia Hills City SD	Northfield
318	5.2	Olmsted Falls City SD	Olmsted Falls
319	5.1	Kings Local SD	Kings Mills
320	5.0	Sycamore Community City SD	Cincinnati
321	4.9	Loveland City SD	Loveland
321	4.9	Mayfield City SD	Highland Hgts
321	4.9	Strongsville City SD	Strongsville
324	4.8	Sugarcreek Local SD	Bellbrook
325	4.6	Pickerington Local SD	Pickerington
326	4.5	Medina City SD	Medina
327	4.4	North Canton City SD	North Canton
328	4.3	Lakota Local SD	Liberty Twp
328	4.3	Stow-Munroe Falls City SD	Stow

330	4.1	Mariemont City SD	Cincinnati
330	4.1	North Royalton City SD	N Royalton
332	4.0	Worthington City SD	Worthington
333	3.9	Centerville City SD	Centerville
333	3.9	Jackson Local SD	Massillon
333	3.9	Valley View Local SD	Germantown
336	3.8	Beavercreek City SD	Beavercreek
337	3.7	Bexley City SD	Bexley
338	3.6	Kenston Local SD	Chagrin Falls
338	3.6	Olentangy Local SD	Lewis Center
340	3.2	Anthony Wayne Local SD	Whitehouse
340	3.2	Brecksville-Broadview Heights	Brecksville
342	3.1	Perrysburg Ex Vill SD	Perrysburg
342	3.1	Westlake City SD	Westlake
344	2.9	Poland Local SD	Poland
345	2.7	Rocky River City SD	Rocky River
346	2.6	Canfield Local SD	Canfield
347	2.5	Dublin City SD	Dublin
347	2.5	Highland Local SD	Medina
349	2.4	Bay Village City SD	Bay Village
350	2.3	Forest Hills Local SD	Cincinnati
350	2.3	Springboro Community City SD	Springboro
352	2.2	Avon Lake City SD	Avon Lake
352	2.2	Beachwood City SD	Beachwood
354	2.1	Aurora City SD	Aurora
355	2.0	Revere Local SD	Bath
356	1.7	Mason City SD	Mason
356	1.7	Plain Local SD	New Albany
358	1.6	Orange City SD	Cleveland
359	1.4	West Geauga Local SD	Chesterland
359	1.4	Wyoming City SD	Wyoming
361	1.3	Oak Hills Local SD	Cincinnati
362	1.2	Solon City SD	Solon
363	1.1	Hudson City SD	Hudson
364	0.8	Chagrin Falls Ex Vill SD	Chagrin Falls
365	0.6	Granville Ex Vill SD	Granville
366	0.5	Indian Hill Ex Vill SD	Cincinnati
367	0.4	Oakwood City SD	Dayton
367	0.4	Upper Arlington City SD	Upper Arlington
369	n/a	Electronic Classroom of Tomorrow	Columbus
369	n/a	Field Local SD	Mogadore

Students Eligible for Reduced-Price Lunch

Rank	Percent	District Name	City
1	16.2	Euclid City SD	Euclid
2	15.5	Warrensville Heights City SD	Warrensville Hgts
3	13.7	Bucyrus City SD	Bucyrus
4	13.1	Labrae Local SD	Leavittsburg
5	12.9	Mad River Local SD	Dayton
5	12.9	Struthers City SD	Struthers
7	12.7	Brookfield Local SD	Brookfield
8	12.5	Fairless Local SD	Navarre
9	12.3	Southeast Local SD	Apple Creek
10	12.0	New Lexington City SD	New Lexington
11	11.9	Maple Heights City SD	Maple Heights
12	11.8	Whitehall City SD	Whitehall
13	11.6	Edison Local SD	Hammondsville
14	11.4	Fostoria City SD	Fostoria
15	11.3	West Holmes Local SD	Millersburg
16	11.2	Indian Valley Local SD	Gnadenhutten
17	11.0	Garfield Heights City SD	Garfield Hgts
18	10.7	Alliance City SD	Alliance
19	10.6	Hubbard Ex Vill SD	Hubbard
20	10.5	Clearview Local SD	Lorain
20	10.5	Geneva Area City SD	Geneva
22	10.2	Barberton City SD	Barberton
23	10.1	Beaver Local SD	Lisbon
23	10.1	Lorain City SD	Lorain
23	10.1	Meigs Local SD	Pomeroy
23	10.1	Northwest Local SD	Mc Dermott
27	10.0	Buckeye Local SD	Ashtabula
27	10.0	Fremont City SD	Fremont
27	10.0	Vinton County Local SD	Mc Arthur
30	9.9	East Holmes Local SD	Berlin
30	9.9	Mansfield City SD	Mansfield
32	9.7	Adams County-Ohio Valley Local SD	West Union
32	9.7	Massillon City SD	Massillon
34	9.6	Canton City SD	Canton
34	9.6	Conneaut Area City SD	Conneaut
34	9.6	Ravenna City SD	Ravenna
37	9.5	Painesville City Local SD	Painesville
38	9.4	Carrollton Ex Vill SD	Carrollton
38	9.4	Dayton City SD	Dayton
40	9.3	Mount Healthy City SD	Cincinnati
41	9.2	Coshocton City SD	Coshocton
41	9.2	Switzerland of Ohio Local SD	Woodsfield
43	9.1	Piqua City SD	Piqua
43	9.1	Wellington Ex Vill SD	Wellington
45	8.9	Franklin Local SD	Duncan Falls
46	8.8	Marion City SD	Marion
46	8.8	Sandusky City SD	Sandusky
48	8.7	Norwood City SD	Norwood
48	8.7	Springfield Local SD	Akron
50	8.5	Minford Local SD	Minford
50	8.5	Warren City SD	Warren
52	8.4	Pike-Delta-York Local SD	Delta
52	8.4	Rolling Hills Local SD	Byesville
54	8.3	Minerva Local SD	Minerva
54	8.3	Sandy Valley Local SD	Magnolia
56	8.2	Canton Local SD	Canton
56	8.2	Elyria City SD	Elyria
58	8.1	Cambridge City SD	Cambridge
58	8.1	Elgin Local SD	Marion
58	8.1	Lancaster City SD	Lancaster
58	8.1	Northridge Local SD	Dayton
62	8.0	Eastern Local SD	Sardinia
62	8.0	Kenton City SD	Kenton
62	8.0	Madison Local SD	Mansfield
65	7.9	Buckeye Local SD	Rayland
65	7.9	Claymont City SD	Dennison
65	7.9	Newton Falls Ex Vill SD	Newton Falls
65	7.9	North Fork Local SD	Utica
65	7.9	Southeast Local SD	Ravenna
65	7.9	Urbana City SD	Urbana
71	7.8	Bedford City SD	Bedford
71	7.8	Campbell City SD	Campbell
71	7.8	Cloverleaf Local SD	Lodi
71	7.8	Orrville City SD	Orrville
75	7.7	Clyde-Green Springs Ex Vill SD	Clyde
75	7.7	Girard City SD	Girard
75	7.7	Princeton City SD	Cincinnati
78	7.6	Ashtabula Area City SD	Ashtabula
78	7.6	Niles City SD	Niles
78	7.6	North College Hill City SD	Cincinnati
78	7.6	Rossford Ex Vill SD	Rossford
78	7.6	Western Brown Local SD	Mount Orab
83	7.5	Bellaire Local SD	Bellaire
83	7.5	Bellevue City SD	Bellevue
83	7.5	Blanchester Local SD	Blanchester
83	7.5	Hamilton City SD	Hamilton
83	7.5	Louisville City SD	Louisville
83	7.5	Wilmington City SD	Wilmington
89	7.4	Austintown Local SD	Youngstown
89	7.4	Harrison Hills City SD	Hopedale
89	7.4	Maysville Local SD	Zanesville
89	7.4	Northwest Local SD	Cincinnati
89	7.4	Preble Shawnee Local SD	Camden
89	7.4	South-Western City SD	Grove City
95	7.3	Black River Local SD	Sullivan
95	7.3	Columbus City SD	Columbus
95	7.3	James A Garfield Local SD	Garrettsville
95	7.3	Norwalk City SD	Norwalk
95	7.3	Vermilion Local SD	Vermilion
95	7.3	Wooster City SD	Wooster
101	7.2	Batavia Local SD	Batavia
101	7.2	Bath Local SD	Lima
101	7.2	Groveport Madison Local SD	Groveport
101	7.2	Logan-Hocking Local SD	Logan
101	7.2	Parma City SD	Parma
101	7.2	Shelby City SD	Shelby
101	7.2	Tuscarawas Valley Local SD	Zoarville
101	7.2	West Branch Local SD	Beloit
109	7.1	Akron City SD	Akron
109	7.1	Cuyahoga Falls City SD	Cuyahoga Falls
109	7.1	Middletown City SD	Middletown
109	7.1	Morgan Local SD	McConnelsville
109	7.1	Streetsboro City SD	Streetsboro
109	7.1	Trotwood-Madison City SD	Trotwood
115	7.0	Hillsboro City SD	Hillsboro
115	7.0	Jefferson Area Local SD	Jefferson
115	7.0	Madison Local SD	Madison
115	7.0	Oregon City SD	Oregon
115	7.0	River Valley Local SD	Caledonia
115	7.0	Sidney City SD	Sidney
115	7.0	Tecumseh Local SD	New Carlisle
115	7.0	Tiffin City SD	Tiffin
115	7.0	Union Local SD	Morristown
115	7.0	Washington Court House City SD	Washington Ct Hse
115	7.0	Zanesville City SD	Zanesville
126	6.9	Ashland City SD	Ashland
126	6.9	Galion City SD	Galion
128	6.8	Cleveland Hts-Univ Hts City SD	University Hgts
128	6.8	Lake Local SD	Millbury
128	6.8	Newark City SD	Newark
131	6.7	Alexander Local SD	Albany
132	6.6	Benton Carroll Salem Local SD	Oak Harbor
132	6.6	Cincinnati City SD	Cincinnati
132	6.6	Greenfield Ex Vill SD	Greenfield
132	6.6	Van Wert City SD	Van Wert
136	6.5	Cleveland Municipal SD	Cleveland
136	6.5	Eastwood Local SD	Pemberville
136	6.5	Northern Local SD	Thornville
139	6.4	Indian Creek Local SD	Wintersville
139	6.4	Lima City SD	Lima
139	6.4	Warren Local SD	Vincent
139	6.4	Washington-Nile Local SD	West Portsmouth
143	6.3	Fairborn City SD	Fairborn
143	6.3	Goshen Local SD	Goshen
143	6.3	Greenville City SD	Greenville
143	6.3	Lakewood City SD	Lakewood
143	6.3	Sheffield-Sheffield Lake City	Sheffield Vlg
143	6.3	Springfield Local SD	Holland
143	6.3	Wapakoneta City SD	Wapakoneta
150	6.2	Scioto Valley Local SD	Piketon
151	6.0	Gallia County Local SD	Gallipolis
151	6.0	Perry Local SD	Massillon
151	6.0	Steubenville City SD	Steubenville
151	6.0	Wauseon Ex Vill SD	Wauseon
151	6.0	Wickliffe City SD	Wickliffe
156	5.9	Hamilton Local SD	Columbus
157	5.8	Coventry Local SD	Akron
157	5.8	East Clinton Local SD	Lees Creek
157	5.8	Jackson City SD	Jackson
157	5.8	Logan Elm Local SD	Circleville
157	5.8	Portsmouth City SD	Portsmouth
162	5.7	Midview Local SD	Grafton
162	5.7	Northmont City SD	Englewood
162	5.7	Saint Marys City SD	Saint Marys
165	5.6	Chillicothe City SD	Chillicothe
165	5.6	Elida Local SD	Elida
165	5.6	Highland Local SD	Sparta
165	5.6	Miami Trace Local SD	Washington Ct Hse
165	5.6	Wellston City SD	Wellston
170	5.5	Athens City SD	The Plains
170	5.5	Berea City SD	Berea
170	5.5	East Muskingum Local SD	New Concord
170	5.5	Kettering City SD	Kettering
170	5.5	Upper Sandusky Ex Vill SD	Upper Sandusky
175	5.4	Celina City SD	Celina
175	5.4	Clear Fork Valley Local SD	Bellville
175	5.4	South Euclid-Lyndhurst City SD	Lyndhurst
175	5.4	South Point Local SD	South Point
175	5.4	Willard City SD	Willard
175	5.4	Xenia Community City SD	Xenia
181	5.3	East Cleveland City SD	East Cleveland
181	5.3	Plain Local SD	Canton
183	5.2	Lakewood Local SD	Hebron
183	5.2	Shawnee Local SD	Lima
185	5.1	Crestwood Local SD	Mantua
185	5.1	Findlay City SD	Findlay
185	5.1	Norton City SD	Norton
185	5.1	Triway Local SD	Wooster
185	5.1	Troy City SD	Troy
190	5.0	Graham Local SD	Saint Paris
190	5.0	Madison-Plains Local SD	London
190	5.0	Marlington Local SD	Alliance
190	5.0	Union-Scioto Local SD	Chillicothe
190	5.0	Washington Local SD	Toledo
190	5.0	West Carrollton City SD	West Carrollton
190	5.0	Willoughby-Eastlake City SD	Willoughby
190	5.0	Youngstown City SD	Youngstown
198	4.9	Circleville City SD	Circleville
198	4.9	Firelands Local SD	Oberlin
198	4.9	Heath City SD	Heath
198	4.9	Indian Lake Local SD	Lewistown
198	4.9	Ironton City SD	Ironton
198	4.9	North Olmsted City SD	North Olmsted
198	4.9	Northwest Local SD	Canal Fulton
198	4.9	River View Local SD	Warsaw
206	4.8	Bellefontaine City SD	Bellefontaine
206	4.8	Boardman Local SD	Youngstown
206	4.8	Champion Local SD	Warren
206	4.8	London City SD	London
206	4.8	Mount Vernon City SD	Mount Vernon
206	4.8	Winton Woods City SD	Cincinnati
212	4.7	Eaton City SD	Eaton
212	4.7	Fairland Local SD	Proctorville
212	4.7	Kent City SD	Kent
212	4.7	Liberty Local SD	Youngstown
212	4.7	Milton-Union Ex Vill SD	West Milton
212	4.7	Napoleon Area City SD	Napoleon
212	4.7	Rock Hill Local SD	Ironton
212	4.7	Springfield City SD	Springfield
212	4.7	Swanton Local SD	Swanton
212	4.7	Toledo City SD	Toledo
222	4.6	Brunswick City SD	Brunswick
222	4.6	Franklin City SD	Franklin
222	4.6	New Richmond Ex Vill SD	New Richmond
222	4.6	Perry Local SD	Perry
222	4.6	Waverly City SD	Waverly
227	4.5	Delaware City SD	Delaware
227	4.5	Edgewood City SD	Trenton
227	4.5	Keystone Local SD	Lagrange
227	4.5	Paulding Ex Vill SD	Paulding

227	4.5	Teays Valley Local SD	Ashville
232	4.4	Amherst Ex Vill SD	Amherst
232	4.4	Fairview Park City SD	Fairview Park
232	4.4	Licking Valley Local SD	Newark
235	4.3	Bryan City SD	Bryan
235	4.3	Howland Local SD	Warren
235	4.3	Nordonia Hills City SD	Northfield
235	4.3	Three Rivers Local SD	Cleves
235	4.3	Vandalia-Butler City SD	Vandalia
235	4.3	Woodridge Local SD	Peninsula
241	4.2	East Liverpool City SD	East Liverpool
241	4.2	Huber Heights City SD	Huber Heights
241	4.2	Miamisburg City SD	Miamisburg
244	4.1	Coldwater Ex Vill SD	Coldwater
244	4.1	Painesville Township Local SD	Painesville
244	4.1	Tri-Valley Local SD	Dresden
247	4.0	Brookville Local SD	Brookville
247	4.0	Saint Clairsville-Richland City	St Clairsville
247	4.0	Southwest Local SD	Harrison
250	3.9	Clinton-Massie Local SD	Clarksville
250	3.9	Licking Heights Local SD	Summit Station
250	3.9	Marietta City SD	Marietta
250	3.9	Port Clinton City SD	Port Clinton
254	3.8	Genoa Area Local SD	Genoa
254	3.8	Salem City SD	Salem
256	3.7	Berlin-Milan Local SD	Milan
256	3.7	Bethel-Tate Local SD	Bethel
256	3.7	Otsego Local SD	Tontogany
256	3.7	Southwest Licking Local SD	Etna
256	3.7	Westfall Local SD	Williamsport
261	3.6	Marysville Ex Vill SD	Marysville
262	3.5	Huron City SD	Huron
262	3.5	Jonathan Alder Local SD	Plain City
262	3.5	Maumee City SD	Maumee
262	3.5	North Canton City SD	North Canton
266	3.4	Clermont-Northeastern Local SD	Batavia
266	3.4	Olmsted Falls City SD	Olmsted Falls
266	3.4	Perkins Local SD	Sandusky
266	3.4	Talawanda City SD	Oxford
266	3.4	Wadsworth City SD	Wadsworth
271	3.3	Ross Local SD	Hamilton
271	3.3	Strongsville City SD	Strongsville
273	3.2	Big Walnut Local SD	Galena
273	3.2	Canal Winchester Local SD	Canal Winchester
273	3.2	Defiance City SD	Defiance
273	3.2	Gallipolis City SD	Gallipolis
273	3.2	Mentor Ex Vill SD	Mentor
273	3.2	Twinsburg City SD	Twinsburg
273	3.2	Zane Trace Local SD	Chillicothe
280	3.1	Amanda-Clearcreek Local SD	Amanda
280	3.1	Carlisle Local SD	Carlisle
280	3.1	Green Local SD	Green
280	3.1	Lexington Local SD	Lexington
280	3.1	Milford Ex Vill SD	Milford
280	3.1	West Clermont Local SD	Cincinnati
286	3.0	Fairfield City SD	Fairfield
286	3.0	Lakeview Local SD	Cortland
286	3.0	North Ridgeville City SD	N Ridgeville
286	3.0	Reynoldsburg City SD	Reynoldsburg
286	3.0	West Muskingum Local SD	Zanesville
291	2.9	Bowling Green City SD	Bowling Green
291	2.9	Clark-Shawnee Local SD	Springfield
291	2.9	Gahanna-Jefferson City SD	Gahanna
294	2.8	Benjamin Logan Local SD	Bellefontaine
294	2.8	Stow-Munroe Falls City SD	Stow
296	2.7	Bay Village City SD	Bay Village
297	2.6	Buckeye Local SD	Medina
297	2.6	Buckeye Valley Local SD	Delaware
297	2.6	Chardon Local SD	Chardon
297	2.6	Finneytown Local SD	Cincinnati
297	2.6	Lake Local SD	Hartville
297	2.6	New Philadelphia City SD	New Philadelphia
297	2.6	Ontario Local SD	Mansfield
304	2.5	Fairfield Union Local SD	W Rushville
304	2.5	Lebanon City SD	Lebanon
304	2.5	Medina City SD	Medina
304	2.5	Pickerington Local SD	Pickerington
304	2.5	Tallmadge City SD	Tallmadge
309	2.4	Copley-Fairlawn City SD	Copley
309	2.4	Dover City SD	Dover
311	2.3	Greeneview Local SD	Jamestown
311	2.3	Greenon Local SD	Springfield
311	2.3	Highland Local SD	Medina
311	2.3	Madison Local SD	Middletown
311	2.3	Northeastern Local SD	Springfield
311	2.3	Worthington City SD	Worthington
317	2.2	Avon Local SD	Avon
317	2.2	Hilliard City SD	Hilliard
317	2.2	Manchester Local SD	Akron
317	2.2	Sylvania City SD	Sylvania
321	2.1	Avon Lake City SD	Avon Lake
321	2.1	Jackson Local SD	Massillon
321	2.1	Little Miami Local SD	Morrow
321	2.1	Mariemont City SD	Cincinnati
321	2.1	Mayfield City SD	Highland Hgts
321	2.1	North Royalton City SD	N Royalton
321	2.1	Poland Local SD	Poland
321	2.1	Tipp City Ex Vill SD	Tipp City
321	2.1	Westerville City SD	Westerville
330	2.0	Perrysburg Ex Vill SD	Perrysburg
331	1.9	Beavercreek City SD	Beavercreek
332	1.8	Kings Local SD	Kings Mills
332	1.8	Loveland City SD	Loveland
332	1.8	Plain Local SD	New Albany
335	1.7	Northwestern Local SD	Springfield
335	1.7	Sycamore Community City SD	Cincinnati
337	1.6	Lakota Local SD	Liberty Twp
337	1.6	Olentangy Local SD	Lewis Center
337	1.6	Ottawa-Glandorf Local SD	Ottawa
340	1.5	Brecksville-Broadview Heights	Brecksville
340	1.5	Kenston Local SD	Chagrin Falls
340	1.5	Mason City SD	Mason
340	1.5	Shaker Heights City SD	Shaker Heights
344	1.4	Valley View Local SD	Germantown
345	1.3	Bexley City SD	Bexley
345	1.3	Canfield Local SD	Canfield
345	1.3	Solon City SD	Solon
345	1.3	Westlake City SD	Westlake
349	1.2	Forest Hills Local SD	Cincinnati
350	1.1	Aurora City SD	Aurora
350	1.1	Sugarcreek Local SD	Bellbrook
352	1.0	Springboro Community City SD	Springboro
352	1.0	West Geauga Local SD	Chesterland
354	0.9	Anthony Wayne Local SD	Whitehouse
354	0.9	Beachwood City SD	Beachwood
354	0.9	Rocky River City SD	Rocky River
357	0.8	Centerville City SD	Centerville
357	0.8	Dublin City SD	Dublin
359	0.7	Oak Hills Local SD	Cincinnati
360	0.6	Granville Ex Vill SD	Granville
360	0.6	Revere Local SD	Bath
362	0.5	Upper Arlington City SD	Upper Arlington
362	0.5	Wyoming City SD	Wyoming
364	0.4	Indian Hill Ex Vill SD	Cincinnati
364	0.4	Orange City SD	Cleveland
366	0.3	Hudson City SD	Hudson
367	0.1	Chagrin Falls Ex Vill SD	Chagrin Falls
368	0.0	Oakwood City SD	Dayton
369	n/a	Electronic Classroom of Tomorrow	Columbus
369	n/a	Field Local SD	Mogadore

Student/Teacher Ratio

Rank	Ratio	District Name	City
1	49.4	Electronic Classroom of Tomorrow	Columbus
2	22.4	Lake Local SD	Millbury
3	21.5	Norwalk City SD	Norwalk
4	20.4	Piqua City SD	Piqua
5	20.3	Eastwood Local SD	Pemberville
6	19.8	Clinton-Massie Local SD	Clarksville
7	19.7	Sugarcreek Local SD	Bellbrook
8	19.6	Poland Local SD	Poland
9	19.5	Jonathan Alder Local SD	Plain City
9	19.5	Midview Local SD	Grafton
11	19.4	Keystone Local SD	Lagrange
11	19.4	Lebanon City SD	Lebanon
13	19.2	Madison Local SD	Madison
13	19.2	Milford Ex Vill SD	Milford
13	19.2	Shawnee Local SD	Lima
16	19.0	Brookville Local SD	Brookville
16	19.0	Geneva Area City SD	Geneva
16	19.0	Rolling Hills Local SD	Byesville
16	19.0	Wapakoneta City SD	Wapakoneta
20	18.9	Painesville Township Local SD	Painesville
21	18.8	Chillicothe City SD	Chillicothe
21	18.8	Ontario Local SD	Mansfield
21	18.8	Springboro Community City SD	Springboro
21	18.8	Wadsworth City SD	Wadsworth
25	18.7	Amherst Ex Vill SD	Amherst
25	18.7	Bath Local SD	Lima
25	18.7	Clark-Shawnee Local SD	Springfield
25	18.7	Troy City SD	Troy
29	18.6	Beavercreek City SD	Beavercreek
29	18.6	Bethel-Tate Local SD	Bethel
29	18.6	Jackson City SD	Jackson
29	18.6	Lakeview Local SD	Cortland
29	18.6	West Branch Local SD	Beloit
34	18.5	Amanda-Clearcreek Local SD	Amanda
34	18.5	Otsego Local SD	Tontogany
34	18.5	Southwest Local SD	Harrison
34	18.5	Wilmington City SD	Wilmington
38	18.4	Carrollton Ex Vill SD	Carrollton
38	18.4	Clermont-Northeastern Local SD	Batavia
38	18.4	Garfield Heights City SD	Garfield Hgts
38	18.4	Genoa Area Local SD	Genoa
42	18.3	Beaver Local SD	Lisbon
42	18.3	Fairfield City SD	Fairfield
42	18.3	Firelands Local SD	Oberlin
42	18.3	Wauseon Ex Vill SD	Wauseon
46	18.2	Benjamin Logan Local SD	Bellefontaine
46	18.2	Franklin Local SD	Duncan Falls
46	18.2	Greeneview Local SD	Jamestown
46	18.2	Heath City SD	Heath
46	18.2	Little Miami Local SD	Morrow
46	18.2	Loveland City SD	Loveland
46	18.2	Oak Hills Local SD	Cincinnati
53	18.1	Eaton City SD	Eaton
53	18.1	Fairfield Union Local SD	W Rushville
53	18.1	Fairland Local SD	Proctorville
53	18.1	Northeastern Local SD	Springfield
53	18.1	Tri-Valley Local SD	Dresden
53	18.1	Westfall Local SD	Williamsport
53	18.1	Zane Trace Local SD	Chillicothe
60	18.0	Benton Carroll Salem Local SD	Oak Harbor
60	18.0	Elida Local SD	Elida
60	18.0	Goshen Local SD	Goshen
60	18.0	Scioto Valley Local SD	Piketon
60	18.0	West Clermont Local SD	Cincinnati
65	17.9	Cloverleaf Local SD	Lodi
65	17.9	North Royalton City SD	N Royalton
65	17.9	Northwestern Local SD	Springfield
65	17.9	Sidney City SD	Sidney
69	17.8	Jefferson Area Local SD	Jefferson
69	17.8	Ottawa-Glandorf Local SD	Ottawa
69	17.8	Strongsville City SD	Strongsville
72	17.7	Coventry Local SD	Akron
72	17.7	Kings Local SD	Kings Mills
72	17.7	Logan-Hocking Local SD	Logan
72	17.7	Manchester Local SD	Akron
72	17.7	North College Hill City SD	Cincinnati
72	17.7	Perry Local SD	Massillon
72	17.7	Pickerington Local SD	Pickerington
79	17.6	Granville Ex Vill SD	Granville
79	17.6	Hubbard Ex Vill SD	Hubbard
79	17.6	Maysville Local SD	Zanesville
79	17.6	Perrysburg Ex Vill SD	Perrysburg
79	17.6	Three Rivers Local SD	Cleves
79	17.6	Western Brown Local SD	Mount Orab
79	17.6	Westerville City SD	Westerville
86	17.5	Blanchester Local SD	Blanchester
86	17.5	Canfield Local SD	Canfield
86	17.5	Jackson Local SD	Massillon
86	17.5	Lakota Local SD	Liberty Twp
86	17.5	Lexington Local SD	Lexington
86	17.5	Southeast Local SD	Ravenna
86	17.5	Stow-Munroe Falls City SD	Stow
86	17.5	Wellington Ex Vill SD	Wellington
86	17.5	West Muskingum Local SD	Zanesville
95	17.4	Batavia Local SD	Batavia
95	17.4	Crestwood Local SD	Mantua
95	17.4	East Muskingum Local SD	New Concord
95	17.4	Forest Hills Local SD	Cincinnati
95	17.4	Marietta City SD	Marietta
95	17.4	Minford Local SD	Minford
95	17.4	Ross Local SD	Hamilton
95	17.4	Tipp City Ex Vill SD	Tipp City
103	17.3	Brecksville-Broadview Heights	Brecksville
103	17.3	Fremont City SD	Fremont
103	17.3	Newton Falls Ex Vill SD	Newton Falls
103	17.3	Northmont City SD	Englewood
103	17.3	River View Local SD	Warsaw
103	17.3	Washington Court House City SD	Washington Ct Hse
109	17.2	Highland Local SD	Sparta
109	17.2	Highland Local SD	Medina
109	17.2	Mason City SD	Mason
109	17.2	New Lexington City SD	New Lexington
109	17.2	Saint Marys City SD	Saint Marys
109	17.2	Southwest Licking Local SD	Etna
115	17.1	Aurora City SD	Aurora
115	17.1	Franklin City SD	Franklin
115	17.1	Girard City SD	Girard
115	17.1	Greenon Local SD	Springfield
115	17.1	Licking Valley Local SD	Newark
115	17.1	Northwest Local SD	Cincinnati
115	17.1	Pike-Delta-York Local SD	Delta
115	17.1	Tuscarawas Valley Local SD	Zoarville
123	17.0	Austintown Local SD	Youngstown
123	17.0	Claymont City SD	Dennison
123	17.0	Lake Local SD	Hartville
123	17.0	Madison-Plains Local SD	London
123	17.0	Marlington Local SD	Alliance
123	17.0	North Fork Local SD	Utica
123	17.0	Union-Scioto Local SD	Chillicothe
123	17.0	Vermilion Local SD	Vermilion
131	16.9	Brunswick City SD	Brunswick
131	16.9	Chardon Local SD	Chardon
131	16.9	Coldwater Ex Vill SD	Coldwater
131	16.9	Conneaut Area City SD	Conneaut

131	16.9	East Clinton Local SD	Lees Creek
131	16.9	Fostoria City SD	Fostoria
131	16.9	Greenfield Ex Vill SD	Greenfield
131	16.9	Liberty Local SD	Youngstown
131	16.9	Maple Heights City SD	Maple Heights
131	16.9	Milton-Union Ex Vill SD	West Milton
131	16.9	Mount Vernon City SD	Mount Vernon
131	16.9	Olmsted Falls City SD	Olmsted Falls
131	16.9	Painesville City Local SD	Painesville
131	16.9	Waverly City SD	Waverly
145	16.8	Clyde-Green Springs Ex Vill SD	Clyde
145	16.8	James A Garfield Local SD	Garrettsville
145	16.8	Louisville City SD	Louisville
145	16.8	Miamisburg City SD	Miamisburg
145	16.8	North Canton City SD	North Canton
145	16.8	Warren Local SD	Vincent
145	16.8	Willard City SD	Willard
145	16.8	Willoughby-Eastlake City SD	Willoughby
153	16.7	Ashland City SD	Ashland
153	16.7	Celina City SD	Celina
153	16.7	Hamilton City SD	Hamilton
153	16.7	Urbana City SD	Urbana
157	16.6	Sheffield-Sheffield Lake City	Sheffield Vlg
157	16.6	Steubenville City SD	Steubenville
157	16.6	Tiffin City SD	Tiffin
160	16.5	Avon Local SD	Avon
160	16.5	Circleville City SD	Circleville
160	16.5	Graham Local SD	Saint Paris
160	16.5	Hillsboro City SD	Hillsboro
160	16.5	Indian Creek Local SD	Wintersville
160	16.5	Miami Trace Local SD	Washington Ct Hse
160	16.5	Minerva Local SD	Minerva
160	16.5	Northwest Local SD	Mc Dermott
160	16.5	Norton City SD	Norton
160	16.5	Parma City SD	Parma
160	16.5	Struthers City SD	Struthers
171	16.4	Berlin-Milan Local SD	Milan
171	16.4	Boardman Local SD	Youngstown
171	16.4	Fairborn City SD	Fairborn
171	16.4	Gallipolis City SD	Gallipolis
171	16.4	Hamilton Local SD	Columbus
171	16.4	Lancaster City SD	Lancaster
171	16.4	Olentangy Local SD	Lewis Center
171	16.4	Teays Valley Local SD	Ashville
171	16.4	Twinsburg City SD	Twinsburg
180	16.3	Big Walnut Local SD	Galena
180	16.3	Black River Local SD	Sullivan
180	16.3	Bryan City SD	Bryan
180	16.3	Buckeye Valley Local SD	Delaware
180	16.3	Eastern Local SD	Sardinia
180	16.3	Gahanna-Jefferson City SD	Gahanna
180	16.3	Groveport Madison Local SD	Groveport
180	16.3	Howland Local SD	Warren
180	16.3	Huron City SD	Huron
180	16.3	Revere Local SD	Bath
190	16.2	Brookfield Local SD	Brookfield
190	16.2	Buckeye Local SD	Ashtabula
190	16.2	Green Local SD	Green
190	16.2	Madison Local SD	Middletown
190	16.2	Newark City SD	Newark
190	16.2	Northern Local SD	Thornville
190	16.2	Northridge Local SD	Dayton
190	16.2	Northwest Local SD	Canal Fulton
190	16.2	Swanton Local SD	Swanton
199	16.1	Champion Local SD	Warren
199	16.1	Copley-Fairlawn City SD	Copley
199	16.1	Fairless Local SD	Navarre
199	16.1	Field Local SD	Mogadore
199	16.1	Logan Elm Local SD	Circleville
199	16.1	River Valley Local SD	Caledonia
199	16.1	Rocky River City SD	Rocky River
206	16.0	Edison Local SD	Hammondsville
206	16.0	Kettering City SD	Kettering
206	16.0	Orrville City SD	Orrville
206	16.0	South Point Local SD	South Point
206	16.0	South-Western City SD	Grove City
206	16.0	West Geauga Local SD	Chesterland
212	15.9	Clear Fork Valley Local SD	Bellville
212	15.9	Coshocton City SD	Coshocton
212	15.9	Galion City SD	Galion
212	15.9	Plain Local SD	Canton
212	15.9	Springfield Local SD	Holland
212	15.9	Westlake City SD	Westlake
218	15.8	Buckeye Local SD	Medina
218	15.8	Huber Heights City SD	Huber Heights
218	15.8	North Ridgeville City SD	N Ridgeville
218	15.8	Perkins Local SD	Sandusky
218	15.8	Rossford Ex Vill SD	Rossford
218	15.8	Shelby City SD	Shelby
218	15.8	Tecumseh Local SD	New Carlisle
218	15.8	West Holmes Local SD	Millersburg
226	15.7	Anthony Wayne Local SD	Whitehouse
226	15.7	Berea City SD	Berea
226	15.7	Defiance City SD	Defiance
226	15.7	Euclid City SD	Euclid
226	15.7	Indian Lake Local SD	Lewistown
226	15.7	Labrae Local SD	Leavittsburg
226	15.7	Lakewood City SD	Lakewood
226	15.7	Licking Heights Local SD	Summit Station
226	15.7	New Philadelphia City SD	New Philadelphia
226	15.7	Sandy Valley Local SD	Magnolia
226	15.7	Southeast Local SD	Apple Creek
237	15.6	Bowling Green City SD	Bowling Green
237	15.6	Bucyrus City SD	Bucyrus
237	15.6	Hudson City SD	Hudson
237	15.6	Marysville Ex Vill SD	Marysville
237	15.6	Tallmadge City SD	Tallmadge
237	15.6	Triway Local SD	Wooster
237	15.6	Wellston City SD	Wellston
244	15.5	Avon Lake City SD	Avon Lake
244	15.5	Indian Valley Local SD	Gnadenhutten
244	15.5	Kenston Local SD	Chagrin Falls
244	15.5	Mentor Ex Vill SD	Mentor
244	15.5	Napoleon Area City SD	Napoleon
244	15.5	Niles City SD	Niles
244	15.5	Preble Shawnee Local SD	Camden
244	15.5	Saint Clairsville-Richland City	St Clairsville
244	15.5	Whitehall City SD	Whitehall
253	15.4	Elgin Local SD	Marion
253	15.4	Kenton City SD	Kenton
253	15.4	Nordonia Hills City SD	Northfield
253	15.4	Sylvania City SD	Sylvania
253	15.4	Upper Sandusky Ex Vill SD	Upper Sandusky
258	15.3	Bellefontaine City SD	Bellefontaine
258	15.3	Bellevue City SD	Bellevue
258	15.3	Canton Local SD	Canton
258	15.3	East Holmes Local SD	Berlin
258	15.3	Edgewood City SD	Trenton
258	15.3	New Richmond Ex Vill SD	New Richmond
258	15.3	Norwood City SD	Norwood
258	15.3	Perry Local SD	Perry
258	15.3	Ravenna City SD	Ravenna
258	15.3	Vinton County Local SD	Mc Arthur
268	15.2	Cambridge City SD	Cambridge
268	15.2	Canal Winchester Local SD	Canal Winchester
268	15.2	Delaware City SD	Delaware
268	15.2	Greenville City SD	Greenville
268	15.2	Harrison Hills City SD	Hopedale
268	15.2	Marion City SD	Marion
268	15.2	Van Wert City SD	Van Wert
268	15.2	Vandalia-Butler City SD	Vandalia
268	15.2	Washington Local SD	Toledo
268	15.2	Xenia Community City SD	Xenia
278	15.1	Carlisle Local SD	Carlisle
278	15.1	Centerville City SD	Centerville
278	15.1	Clearview Local SD	Lorain
278	15.1	Dover City SD	Dover
278	15.1	Gallia County Local SD	Gallipolis
278	15.1	Ironton City SD	Ironton
278	15.1	Reynoldsburg City SD	Reynoldsburg
278	15.1	Solon City SD	Solon
278	15.1	Valley View Local SD	Germantown
278	15.1	Washington-Nile Local SD	West Portsmouth
288	15.0	Bay Village City SD	Bay Village
288	15.0	Campbell City SD	Campbell
288	15.0	Columbus City SD	Columbus
288	15.0	Cuyahoga Falls City SD	Cuyahoga Falls
288	15.0	Findlay City SD	Findlay
288	15.0	Medina City SD	Medina
288	15.0	Rock Hill Local SD	Ironton
295	14.9	Buckeye Local SD	Rayland
295	14.9	Indian Hill Ex Vill SD	Cincinnati
295	14.9	Mariemont City SD	Cincinnati
295	14.9	Middletown City SD	Middletown
295	14.9	Oregon City SD	Oregon
295	14.9	Port Clinton City SD	Port Clinton
295	14.9	Springfield Local SD	Akron
302	14.8	Portsmouth City SD	Portsmouth
302	14.8	Trotwood-Madison City SD	Trotwood
302	14.8	Winton Woods City SD	Cincinnati
305	14.7	Lakewood Local SD	Hebron
305	14.7	London City SD	London
305	14.7	Streetsboro City SD	Streetsboro
308	14.6	Finneytown Local SD	Cincinnati
308	14.6	Mad River Local SD	Dayton
308	14.6	Paulding Ex Vill SD	Paulding
308	14.6	Springfield City SD	Springfield
312	14.5	Adams County-Ohio Valley Local SD	West Union
312	14.5	Bellaire Local SD	Bellaire
312	14.5	Elyria City SD	Elyria
312	14.5	Hilliard City SD	Hilliard
316	14.4	Dublin City SD	Dublin
316	14.4	Lorain City SD	Lorain
316	14.4	Mount Healthy City SD	Cincinnati
316	14.4	South Euclid-Lyndhurst City SD	Lyndhurst
316	14.4	Worthington City SD	Worthington
321	14.3	Ashtabula Area City SD	Ashtabula
321	14.3	East Cleveland City SD	East Cleveland
321	14.3	Plain Local SD	New Albany
321	14.3	Sycamore Community City SD	Cincinnati
325	14.2	Maumee City SD	Maumee
325	14.2	Zanesville City SD	Zanesville
327	14.1	Alexander Local SD	Albany
327	14.1	Bedford City SD	Bedford
327	14.1	Talawanda City SD	Oxford
330	14.0	Wyoming City SD	Wyoming
331	13.9	East Liverpool City SD	East Liverpool
331	13.9	Switzerland of Ohio Local SD	Woodsfield
333	13.8	Chagrin Falls Ex Vill SD	Chagrin Falls
333	13.8	Fairview Park City SD	Fairview Park
333	13.8	Woodridge Local SD	Peninsula
336	13.7	Cleveland Hts-Univ Hts City SD	University Hgts
337	13.6	Dayton City SD	Dayton
337	13.6	Madison Local SD	Mansfield
337	13.6	Upper Arlington City SD	Upper Arlington
337	13.6	Wickliffe City SD	Wickliffe
341	13.5	Bexley City SD	Bexley
341	13.5	Meigs Local SD	Pomeroy
341	13.5	Morgan Local SD	McConnelsville
341	13.5	Sandusky City SD	Sandusky
341	13.5	Warrensville Heights City SD	Warrensville Hgts
341	13.5	West Carrollton City SD	West Carrollton
341	13.5	Wooster City SD	Wooster
341	13.5	Youngstown City SD	Youngstown
349	13.3	Canton City SD	Canton
350	13.2	Barberton City SD	Barberton
350	13.2	Massillon City SD	Massillon
350	13.2	Mayfield City SD	Highland Hgts
353	13.1	Shaker Heights City SD	Shaker Heights
354	13.0	Lima City SD	Lima
354	13.0	North Olmsted City SD	North Olmsted
354	13.0	Toledo City SD	Toledo
357	12.9	Princeton City SD	Cincinnati
358	12.8	Athens City SD	The Plains
358	12.8	Orange City SD	Cleveland
358	12.8	Salem City SD	Salem
361	12.7	Alliance City SD	Alliance
362	12.6	Union Local SD	Morristown
363	12.5	Kent City SD	Kent
364	12.4	Mansfield City SD	Mansfield
364	12.4	Warren City SD	Warren
366	12.2	Oakwood City SD	Dayton
367	12.0	Cincinnati City SD	Cincinnati
368	11.6	Akron City SD	Akron
369	10.7	Cleveland Municipal SD	Cleveland
370	9.6	Beachwood City SD	Beachwood

Student/Librarian Ratio

Rank	Ratio	District Name	City
1	13,223.3	Amherst Ex Vill SD	Amherst
2	9,695.0	Indian Valley Local SD	Gnadenhutten
3	5,801.0	Northmont City SD	Englewood
4	5,246.8	South-Western City SD	Grove City
5	5,213.0	Miamisburg City SD	Miamisburg
6	4,785.0	Ashtabula Area City SD	Ashtabula
7	4,588.0	West Clermont Local SD	Cincinnati
8	4,479.0	Delaware City SD	Delaware
9	3,775.0	Maple Heights City SD	Maple Heights
10	3,749.0	Madison Local SD	Madison
11	3,494.5	Washington Local SD	Toledo
12	3,476.0	Vandalia-Butler City SD	Vandalia
13	3,400.0	Geneva Area City SD	Geneva
14	3,354.0	Celina City SD	Celina
15	3,260.0	New Philadelphia City SD	New Philadelphia
16	3,238.0	Findlay City SD	Findlay
17	3,181.0	Kenston Local SD	Chagrin Falls
18	3,180.0	Wapakoneta City SD	Wapakoneta
19	3,179.0	Wilmington City SD	Wilmington
20	3,174.0	Copley-Fairlawn City SD	Copley
21	3,033.0	Little Miami Local SD	Morrow
22	2,997.0	Carrollton Ex Vill SD	Carrollton
23	2,955.0	Athens City SD	The Plains
24	2,835.0	Norwood City SD	Norwood
25	2,790.0	Marlington Local SD	Alliance
26	2,787.0	West Holmes Local SD	Millersburg
27	2,776.5	Fairborn City SD	Fairborn
28	2,736.0	Jackson City SD	Jackson
29	2,720.0	Oak Hills Local SD	Cincinnati
30	2,702.0	Warren Local SD	Vincent
31	2,697.0	Edison Local SD	Hammondsville
32	2,668.0	Big Walnut Local SD	Galena
33	2,667.7	Mason City SD	Mason
34	2,665.0	River View Local SD	Warsaw
35	2,641.0	Vinton County Local SD	Mc Arthur
36	2,634.0	Kettering City SD	Kettering
37	2,631.0	Shawnee Local SD	Lima

Rank	Number	District	City
38	2,619.0	Dover City SD	Dover
39	2,598.0	Norton City SD	Norton
40	2,580.0	Elida Local SD	Elida
41	2,578.0	Canton Local SD	Canton
42	2,569.0	Vermilion Local SD	Vermilion
43	2,547.0	Conneaut Area City SD	Conneaut
44	2,543.0	Middletown City SD	Middletown
45	2,542.0	West Branch Local SD	Beloit
46	2,525.0	Poland Local SD	Poland
47	2,524.0	New Richmond Ex Vill SD	New Richmond
48	2,502.0	Coventry Local SD	Akron
49	2,466.0	Buckeye Local SD	Rayland
50	2,463.0	Clark-Shawnee Local SD	Springfield
51	2,446.0	Gallipolis City SD	Gallipolis
52	2,431.5	North Canton City SD	North Canton
53	2,428.0	Franklin Local SD	Duncan Falls
54	2,426.0	Northwest Local SD	Canal Fulton
55	2,388.0	Urbana City SD	Urbana
56	2,371.0	Logan Elm Local SD	Circleville
57	2,367.0	Eaton City SD	Eaton
58	2,356.5	Hamilton City SD	Hamilton
59	2,351.0	Fostoria City SD	Fostoria
60	2,332.5	North Olmsted City SD	North Olmsted
61	2,315.0	Wadsworth City SD	Wadsworth
62	2,314.0	Willard City SD	Willard
63	2,313.0	Northern Local SD	Thornville
64	2,312.0	Van Wert City SD	Van Wert
65	2,304.0	Marysville Ex Vill SD	Marysville
66	2,300.0	Clyde-Green Springs Ex Vill SD	Clyde
67	2,289.3	Huber Heights City SD	Huber Heights
68	2,277.0	Troy City SD	Troy
69	2,270.0	Buckeye Local SD	Ashtabula
70	2,255.0	Galion City SD	Galion
71	2,226.5	Massillon City SD	Massillon
72	2,226.0	Firelands Local SD	Oberlin
73	2,210.0	Greenfield Ex Vill SD	Greenfield
74	2,192.0	Minerva Local SD	Minerva
75	2,189.5	Painesville Township Local SD	Painesville
75	2,189.5	Perrysburg Ex Vill SD	Perrysburg
77	2,181.0	East Muskingum Local SD	New Concord
78	2,180.0	Jefferson Area Local SD	Jefferson
79	2,152.0	Waverly City SD	Waverly
80	2,150.0	Reynoldsburg City SD	Reynoldsburg
81	2,147.0	Triway Local SD	Wooster
82	2,135.6	Northwest Local SD	Cincinnati
83	2,132.0	Wauseon Ex Vill SD	Wauseon
84	2,130.4	Lorain City SD	Lorain
85	2,102.0	Wooster City SD	Wooster
86	2,081.3	Plain Local SD	Canton
87	2,060.3	Canton City SD	Canton
88	2,060.0	Northridge Local SD	Dayton
89	2,057.0	Sheffield-Sheffield Lake City	Sheffield Vlg
90	2,048.0	Streetsboro City SD	Streetsboro
91	2,046.7	Euclid City SD	Euclid
92	2,045.0	London City SD	London
93	2,038.0	Struthers City SD	Struthers
94	2,036.0	Indian Lake Local SD	Lewistown
95	2,033.0	Greenon Local SD	Springfield
96	2,025.5	Springboro Community City SD	Springboro
97	2,023.7	Milford Ex Vill SD	Milford
98	1,981.3	Dayton City SD	Dayton
99	1,979.0	Logan-Hocking Local SD	Logan
100	1,966.5	West Carrollton City SD	West Carrollton
101	1,958.0	Port Clinton City SD	Port Clinton
102	1,957.0	Piqua City SD	Piqua
103	1,927.0	Eastwood Local SD	Pemberville
104	1,918.0	Union-Scioto Local SD	Chillicothe
105	1,914.0	Fairless Local SD	Navarre
106	1,888.0	Fairfield Union Local SD	W Rushville
107	1,873.0	East Holmes Local SD	Berlin
108	1,872.0	Berlin-Milan Local SD	Milan
109	1,868.0	Nordonia Hills City SD	Northfield
110	1,863.0	Lake Local SD	Millbury
111	1,855.5	Anthony Wayne Local SD	Whitehouse
112	1,855.0	Paulding Ex Vill SD	Paulding
113	1,854.0	Keystone Local SD	Lagrange
114	1,848.0	Clear Fork Valley Local SD	Bellville
115	1,837.0	South Point Local SD	South Point
116	1,817.5	Brunswick City SD	Brunswick
117	1,817.0	Liberty Local SD	Youngstown
118	1,814.0	Finneytown Local SD	Cincinnati
119	1,805.0	Jonathan Alder Local SD	Plain City
120	1,801.0	Highland Local SD	Sparta
121	1,797.5	Tecumseh Local SD	New Carlisle
122	1,795.4	Willoughby-Eastlake City SD	Willoughby
123	1,793.3	Jackson Local SD	Massillon
124	1,792.7	Miami Trace Local SD	Washington Ct Hse
125	1,781.5	Madison Local SD	Mansfield
126	1,772.0	Blanchester Local SD	Blanchester
127	1,768.0	East Cleveland City SD	East Cleveland
128	1,767.0	Tuscarawas Valley Local SD	Zoarville
129	1,765.2	Mad River Local SD	Dayton
130	1,764.0	Ottawa-Glandorf Local SD	Ottawa
131	1,758.0	Girard City SD	Girard
132	1,756.0	Clinton-Massie Local SD	Clarksville
133	1,755.0	Mariemont City SD	Cincinnati
134	1,751.0	Lima City SD	Lima
135	1,748.5	Greenville City SD	Greenville
136	1,745.0	Southwest Licking Local SD	Etna
137	1,737.2	Akron City SD	Akron
138	1,730.0	Southeast Local SD	Apple Creek
139	1,729.5	Warren City SD	Warren
140	1,726.0	River Valley Local SD	Caledonia
141	1,713.0	Genoa Area Local SD	Genoa
142	1,702.5	Midview Local SD	Grafton
143	1,697.3	Austintown Local SD	Youngstown
144	1,682.0	Westfall Local SD	Williamsport
145	1,680.1	Parma City SD	Parma
146	1,676.0	Avon Lake City SD	Avon Lake
146	1,676.0	Black River Local SD	Sullivan
148	1,675.0	Licking Heights Local SD	Summit Station
149	1,673.0	Lake Local SD	Hartville
150	1,672.3	Youngstown City SD	Youngstown
151	1,670.0	Alliance City SD	Alliance
152	1,668.0	Madison-Plains Local SD	London
153	1,660.5	Marietta City SD	Marietta
154	1,660.0	Scioto Valley Local SD	Piketon
155	1,655.5	Fairland Local SD	Proctorville
156	1,652.0	Alexander Local SD	Albany
157	1,643.5	Ravenna City SD	Ravenna
158	1,642.0	Greeneview Local SD	Jamestown
159	1,640.0	Boardman Local SD	Youngstown
160	1,633.3	Perry Local SD	Massillon
161	1,633.0	Coldwater Ex Vill SD	Coldwater
162	1,631.0	Amanda-Clearcreek Local SD	Amanda
163	1,619.5	Louisville City SD	Louisville
164	1,612.0	Saint Clairsville-Richland City	St Clairsville
165	1,609.5	Talawanda City SD	Oxford
166	1,597.0	Pike-Delta-York Local SD	Delta
167	1,592.0	Bellaire Local SD	Bellaire
168	1,591.0	Campbell City SD	Campbell
169	1,587.0	Sandy Valley Local SD	Magnolia
170	1,576.0	Madison Local SD	Middletown
171	1,568.4	Sylvania City SD	Sylvania
172	1,566.8	Southwest Local SD	Harrison
173	1,561.0	East Clinton Local SD	Lees Creek
174	1,551.5	Canfield Local SD	Canfield
175	1,542.0	North College Hill City SD	Cincinnati
176	1,539.0	Springfield Local SD	Akron
177	1,538.7	Barberton City SD	Barberton
178	1,537.3	Fremont City SD	Fremont
179	1,537.0	Newton Falls Ex Vill SD	Newton Falls
179	1,537.0	Tri-Valley Local SD	Dresden
181	1,534.5	Pickerington Local SD	Pickerington
181	1,534.5	Teays Valley Local SD	Ashville
183	1,534.0	Labrae Local SD	Leavittsburg
184	1,522.0	Zane Trace Local SD	Chillicothe
185	1,519.0	Clearview Local SD	Lorain
186	1,508.0	Wickliffe City SD	Wickliffe
187	1,500.0	Manchester Local SD	Akron
188	1,499.3	Mansfield City SD	Mansfield
189	1,456.0	Painesville City Local SD	Painesville
189	1,456.0	Zanesville City SD	Zanesville
191	1,452.5	Hamilton Local SD	Columbus
192	1,438.7	Sandusky City SD	Sandusky
193	1,436.0	Revere Local SD	Bath
194	1,434.5	Niles City SD	Niles
195	1,434.0	Bellefontaine City SD	Bellefontaine
196	1,425.0	Mount Vernon City SD	Mount Vernon
197	1,421.3	Mayfield City SD	Highland Hgts
198	1,420.5	Marion City SD	Marion
199	1,398.0	Loveland City SD	Loveland
200	1,391.6	Newark City SD	Newark
201	1,378.2	Beavercreek City SD	Beavercreek
202	1,374.7	Toledo City SD	Toledo
203	1,371.5	Tallmadge City SD	Tallmadge
204	1,370.5	Cambridge City SD	Cambridge
205	1,352.8	Cuyahoga Falls City SD	Cuyahoga Falls
206	1,342.1	Fairfield City SD	Fairfield
207	1,339.5	Gallia County Local SD	Gallipolis
208	1,321.5	Tipp City Ex Vill SD	Tipp City
209	1,318.9	Springfield Local SD	Holland
210	1,316.0	Sidney City SD	Sidney
210	1,316.0	Xenia Community City SD	Xenia
212	1,311.5	West Geauga Local SD	Chesterland
213	1,297.3	Mount Healthy City SD	Cincinnati
214	1,296.0	Defiance City SD	Defiance
215	1,293.0	Oregon City SD	Oregon
216	1,282.0	Ashland City SD	Ashland
217	1,272.0	Ross Local SD	Hamilton
218	1,267.5	Goshen Local SD	Goshen
219	1,265.4	North Royalton City SD	N Royalton
220	1,258.0	Kings Local SD	Kings Mills
221	1,254.0	Adams County-Ohio Valley Local SD	West Union
222	1,246.0	Beaver Local SD	Lisbon
223	1,236.0	Salem City SD	Salem
224	1,230.3	Chillicothe City SD	Chillicothe
225	1,227.7	Trotwood-Madison City SD	Trotwood
226	1,218.5	Buckeye Local SD	Medina
227	1,203.0	Bay Village City SD	Bay Village
227	1,203.0	Cloverleaf Local SD	Lodi
229	1,202.3	Strongsville City SD	Strongsville
230	1,199.9	Springfield City SD	Springfield
231	1,194.7	West Muskingum Local SD	Zanesville
232	1,176.0	Bryan City SD	Bryan
233	1,174.0	Washington Court House City SD	Washington Ct Hse
234	1,172.5	Lebanon City SD	Lebanon
235	1,167.0	Bellevue City SD	Bellevue
235	1,167.0	Napoleon Area City SD	Napoleon
237	1,166.0	Claymont City SD	Dennison
238	1,145.5	Avon Local SD	Avon
239	1,137.0	Maysville Local SD	Zanesville
240	1,135.5	Indian Creek Local SD	Wintersville
241	1,134.5	Southeast Local SD	Ravenna
242	1,128.3	Brecksville-Broadview Heights	Brecksville
243	1,128.0	Buckeye Valley Local SD	Delaware
244	1,123.0	Perkins Local SD	Sandusky
245	1,105.0	Three Rivers Local SD	Cleves
246	1,099.3	Howland Local SD	Warren
247	1,094.5	Licking Valley Local SD	Newark
248	1,092.5	Portsmouth City SD	Portsmouth
249	1,086.0	Forest Hills Local SD	Cincinnati
250	1,079.5	Kenton City SD	Kenton
251	1,066.0	Olmsted Falls City SD	Olmsted Falls
252	1,047.8	Winton Woods City SD	Cincinnati
253	1,046.0	Green Local SD	Green
254	1,041.0	Harrison Hills City SD	Hopedale
255	1,032.5	Benton Carroll Salem Local SD	Oak Harbor
256	1,019.0	Valley View Local SD	Germantown
257	1,018.0	Clermont-Northeastern Local SD	Batavia
258	1,017.0	Franklin City SD	Franklin
259	1,015.0	Bath Local SD	Lima
260	1,008.0	Tiffin City SD	Tiffin
261	1,004.3	Medina City SD	Medina
262	998.0	Benjamin Logan Local SD	Bellefontaine
263	995.5	Coshocton City SD	Coshocton
264	993.8	Stow-Munroe Falls City SD	Stow
265	992.7	Lakewood City SD	Lakewood
266	992.0	Wyoming City SD	Wyoming
267	990.3	Lakota Local SD	Liberty Twp
268	983.5	Chagrin Falls Ex Vill SD	Chagrin Falls
269	978.5	Rock Hill Local SD	Ironton
270	976.0	Norwalk City SD	Norwalk
271	969.7	Maumee City SD	Maumee
272	968.2	Aurora City SD	Aurora
273	968.0	Bucyrus City SD	Bucyrus
274	965.0	Northwestern Local SD	Springfield
275	963.0	Batavia Local SD	Batavia
276	962.0	Cincinnati City SD	Cincinnati
277	961.8	Twinsburg City SD	Twinsburg
278	956.7	Hillsboro City SD	Hillsboro
279	943.5	North Fork Local SD	Utica
279	943.5	Orrville City SD	Orrville
281	942.7	Lexington Local SD	Lexington
282	937.3	Switzerland of Ohio Local SD	Woodsfield
283	936.3	Westerville City SD	Westerville
284	930.1	Columbus City SD	Columbus
285	927.6	Elyria City SD	Elyria
286	916.0	Milton-Union Ex Vill SD	West Milton
286	916.0	Upper Sandusky Ex Vill SD	Upper Sandusky
288	911.3	Crestwood Local SD	Mantua
289	903.0	Highland Local SD	Medina
290	900.3	Northeastern Local SD	Springfield
291	889.6	Berea City SD	Berea
292	885.1	Lancaster City SD	Lancaster
293	882.0	Carlisle Local SD	Carlisle
294	878.3	North Ridgeville City SD	N Ridgeville
295	873.5	Ontario Local SD	Mansfield
295	873.5	Preble Shawnee Local SD	Camden
297	871.3	Saint Marys City SD	Saint Marys
298	864.0	Washington-Nile Local SD	West Portsmouth
299	862.0	Otsego Local SD	Tontogany
300	858.3	Rocky River City SD	Rocky River
301	845.3	Circleville City SD	Circleville
302	843.0	Heath City SD	Heath
303	840.5	Elgin Local SD	Marion
304	833.0	Huron City SD	Huron
305	824.4	Western Brown Local SD	Mount Orab
306	813.5	Wellington Ex Vill SD	Wellington
307	811.3	Bowling Green City SD	Bowling Green
308	803.5	James A Garfield Local SD	Garrettsville
309	803.3	Chardon Local SD	Chardon
310	798.5	Swanton Local SD	Swanton
311	794.6	Hudson City SD	Hudson
312	791.0	Eastern Local SD	Sardinia
313	788.5	Ironton City SD	Ironton
314	776.0	East Liverpool City SD	East Liverpool

315	767.0	Hubbard Ex Vill SD	Hubbard
316	765.0	Union Local SD	Morristown
317	764.4	Bedford City SD	Bedford
318	763.0	Shelby City SD	Shelby
319	760.5	Whitehall City SD	Whitehall
320	759.3	Lakewood Local SD	Hebron
321	758.4	Garfield Heights City SD	Garfield Hgts
322	757.2	Kent City SD	Kent
323	753.5	South Euclid-Lyndhurst City SD	Lyndhurst
324	753.0	Olentangy Local SD	Lewis Center
325	748.3	Field Local SD	Mogadore
326	747.3	Lakeview Local SD	Cortland
327	741.5	Warrensville Heights City SD	Warrensville Hgts
328	730.7	Solon City SD	Solon
329	716.5	Sycamore Community City SD	Cincinnati
330	709.9	Upper Arlington City SD	Upper Arlington
331	702.0	Groveport Madison Local SD	Groveport
331	702.0	Princeton City SD	Cincinnati
333	691.0	Oakwood City SD	Dayton
334	688.6	Cleveland Municipal SD	Cleveland
335	683.0	Granville Ex Vill SD	Granville
336	665.7	New Lexington City SD	New Lexington
337	659.7	Hilliard City SD	Hilliard
338	648.0	Plain Local SD	New Albany
339	646.7	Westlake City SD	Westlake
340	644.0	Bethel-Tate Local SD	Bethel
341	634.0	Dublin City SD	Dublin
342	629.3	Perry Local SD	Perry
343	628.9	Graham Local SD	Saint Paris
344	623.7	Fairview Park City SD	Fairview Park
345	623.6	Shaker Heights City SD	Shaker Heights
346	620.0	Wellston City SD	Wellston
347	607.6	Centerville City SD	Centerville
348	607.2	Cleveland Hts-Univ Hts City SD	University Hgts
349	593.7	Northwest Local SD	Mc Dermott
350	590.8	Orange City SD	Cleveland
351	584.3	Champion Local SD	Warren
352	581.5	Mentor Ex Vill SD	Mentor
353	568.3	Indian Hill Ex Vill SD	Cincinnati
354	565.3	Gahanna-Jefferson City SD	Gahanna
355	561.0	Bexley City SD	Bexley
356	546.0	Minford Local SD	Minford
357	539.7	Brookville Local SD	Brookville
358	501.0	Brookfield Local SD	Brookfield
359	497.1	Worthington City SD	Worthington
360	493.8	Canal Winchester Local SD	Canal Winchester
361	480.6	Edgewood City SD	Trenton
362	464.4	Morgan Local SD	McConnelsville
363	455.3	Woodridge Local SD	Peninsula
364	395.0	Beachwood City SD	Beachwood
365	0.0	Electronic Classroom of Tomorrow	Columbus
365	0.0	Meigs Local SD	Pomeroy
365	0.0	Rolling Hills Local SD	Byesville
365	0.0	Rossford Ex Vill SD	Rossford
365	0.0	Steubenville City SD	Steubenville
365	0.0	Sugarcreek Local SD	Bellbrook

Student/Counselor Ratio

Rank	Ratio	District Name	City
1	4,209.0	Electronic Classroom of Tomorrow	Columbus
2	1,941.6	Cincinnati City SD	Cincinnati
3	1,936.0	Bucyrus City SD	Bucyrus
4	1,932.0	Bethel-Tate Local SD	Bethel
5	1,914.0	Fairless Local SD	Navarre
6	1,561.0	East Clinton Local SD	Lees Creek
7	1,320.5	Vinton County Local SD	Mc Arthur
8	1,223.0	Gallipolis City SD	Gallipolis
9	1,164.3	New Philadelphia City SD	New Philadelphia
10	1,134.5	Southeast Local SD	Ravenna
11	1,128.0	Buckeye Valley Local SD	Delaware
12	1,023.0	Teays Valley Local SD	Ashville
13	1,016.5	Greenon Local SD	Springfield
14	1,014.0	Whitehall City SD	Whitehall
15	999.0	Carrollton Ex Vill SD	Carrollton
16	990.7	Dayton City SD	Dayton
17	978.5	Rock Hill Local SD	Ironton
18	948.0	Garfield Heights City SD	Garfield Hgts
19	943.8	Maple Heights City SD	Maple Heights
20	942.7	Lexington Local SD	Lexington
21	936.5	East Holmes Local SD	Berlin
22	936.0	Berlin-Milan Local SD	Milan
23	918.5	South Point Local SD	South Point
24	907.2	Coldwater Ex Vill SD	Coldwater
25	900.5	Highland Local SD	Sparta
26	896.0	West Muskingum Local SD	Zanesville
27	888.3	River View Local SD	Warsaw
28	884.0	East Cleveland City SD	East Cleveland
29	873.0	Dover City SD	Dover
30	867.3	Milford Ex Vill SD	Milford
31	866.0	Norton City SD	Norton
32	860.0	Reynoldsburg City SD	Reynoldsburg
33	855.0	Mount Vernon City SD	Mount Vernon
34	834.2	West Clermont Local SD	Cincinnati
35	831.4	Fairfield City SD	Fairfield
36	819.4	Lorain City SD	Lorain
37	815.5	Amanda-Clearcreek Local SD	Amanda
38	809.3	Franklin Local SD	Duncan Falls
39	809.1	Newark City SD	Newark
40	797.5	Ashtabula Area City SD	Ashtabula
41	795.5	Campbell City SD	Campbell
42	794.8	Wilmington City SD	Wilmington
43	793.5	Sandy Valley Local SD	Magnolia
44	791.0	Eastern Local SD	Sardinia
45	777.3	South-Western City SD	Grove City
46	775.8	Canfield Local SD	Canfield
47	775.6	Indian Valley Local SD	Gnadenhutten
48	775.0	Marlington Local SD	Alliance
49	774.0	Morgan Local SD	McConnelsville
50	762.0	Winton Woods City SD	Cincinnati
51	757.0	Indian Creek Local SD	Wintersville
52	756.7	Buckeye Local SD	Ashtabula
53	751.7	Galion City SD	Galion
54	749.8	Madison Local SD	Madison
55	736.7	Greenfield Ex Vill SD	Greenfield
56	736.6	Trotwood-Madison City SD	Trotwood
57	727.0	East Muskingum Local SD	New Concord
58	726.7	Jefferson Area Local SD	Jefferson
59	719.7	Middletown City SD	Middletown
60	717.3	Waverly City SD	Waverly
61	713.2	New Lexington City SD	New Lexington
62	703.0	Switzerland of Ohio Local SD	Woodsfield
63	702.1	Clermont-Northeastern Local SD	Batavia
64	696.8	West Holmes Local SD	Millersburg
65	695.2	Vandalia-Butler City SD	Vandalia
66	694.6	Cleveland Municipal SD	Cleveland
67	694.0	Harrison Hills City SD	Hopedale
68	690.5	Willoughby-Eastlake City SD	Willoughby
69	688.4	Lancaster City SD	Lancaster
70	686.7	Northridge Local SD	Dayton
71	684.0	Jackson City SD	Jackson
72	683.5	Crestwood Local SD	Mantua
73	682.7	Streetsboro City SD	Streetsboro
74	681.7	London City SD	London
75	679.3	Struthers City SD	Struthers
75	679.3	Valley View Local SD	Germantown
77	678.2	Mason City SD	Mason
78	674.3	Edison Local SD	Hammondsville
79	670.8	Celina City SD	Celina
80	669.8	Gallia County Local SD	Gallipolis
81	669.2	Lake Local SD	Hartville
82	664.2	Marietta City SD	Marietta
83	663.7	Coshocton City SD	Coshocton
84	663.4	Oak Hills Local SD	Cincinnati
85	662.9	Lakota Local SD	Liberty Twp
86	661.2	Amherst Ex Vill SD	Amherst
87	659.7	Logan-Hocking Local SD	Logan
88	659.1	Mentor Ex Vill SD	Mentor
89	655.8	Strongsville City SD	Strongsville
90	653.6	Tecumseh Local SD	New Carlisle
91	652.7	Port Clinton City SD	Port Clinton
92	648.2	Stow-Munroe Falls City SD	Stow
93	645.6	Hamilton Local SD	Columbus
94	645.2	Loveland City SD	Loveland
95	643.3	Northwestern Local SD	Springfield
96	642.3	Vermilion Local SD	Vermilion
97	642.0	Batavia Local SD	Batavia
98	640.0	Parma City SD	Parma
99	639.3	Union-Scioto Local SD	Chillicothe
100	636.8	Conneaut Area City SD	Conneaut
101	636.1	Massillon City SD	Massillon
102	634.0	Circleville City SD	Circleville
103	629.3	Fairfield Union Local SD	W Rushville
104	625.6	Painesville Township Local SD	Painesville
105	625.5	Coventry Local SD	Akron
106	623.0	Beaver Local SD	Lisbon
107	620.0	Wellston City SD	Wellston
108	618.3	Paulding Ex Vill SD	Paulding
109	618.0	Salem City SD	Salem
110	617.0	Fairborn City SD	Fairborn
111	616.7	Gahanna-Jefferson City SD	Gahanna
112	616.5	Buckeye Local SD	Rayland
113	616.0	Steubenville City SD	Steubenville
114	615.2	Chillicothe City SD	Chillicothe
115	614.8	Tri-Valley Local SD	Dresden
116	610.8	Lima City SD	Lima
117	610.7	Milton-Union Ex Vill SD	West Milton
117	610.7	Upper Sandusky Ex Vill SD	Upper Sandusky
119	610.2	Franklin City SD	Franklin
120	606.6	Little Miami Local SD	Morrow
121	605.8	Brunswick City SD	Brunswick
122	601.6	Warren City SD	Warren
123	601.2	Cuyahoga Falls City SD	Cuyahoga Falls
124	593.1	North College Hill City SD	Cincinnati
125	592.8	Logan Elm Local SD	Circleville
126	591.0	Athens City SD	The Plains
127	590.7	Blanchester Local SD	Blanchester
128	589.0	Tuscarawas Valley Local SD	Zoarville
129	588.0	Ottawa-Glandorf Local SD	Ottawa
130	586.0	Girard City SD	Girard
131	585.6	Norwalk City SD	Norwalk
132	583.5	Bellevue City SD	Bellevue
133	582.8	Greenville City SD	Greenville
134	582.4	Painesville City Local SD	Painesville
135	582.3	Ontario Local SD	Mansfield
136	578.8	Wadsworth City SD	Wadsworth
137	578.7	Springboro Community City SD	Springboro
138	578.3	Northern Local SD	Thornville
139	578.0	Van Wert City SD	Van Wert
140	577.0	Barberton City SD	Barberton
141	576.5	Fremont City SD	Fremont
142	575.3	River Valley Local SD	Caledonia
143	574.7	Otsego Local SD	Tontogany
143	574.7	Zanesville City SD	Zanesville
145	574.4	Groveport Madison Local SD	Groveport
146	574.0	Hillsboro City SD	Hillsboro
147	573.8	Niles City SD	Niles
148	572.8	Avon Local SD	Avon
149	571.0	Genoa Area Local SD	Genoa
150	569.5	Lakewood Local SD	Hebron
151	569.3	Troy City SD	Troy
152	568.5	Maysville Local SD	Zanesville
153	568.2	Marion City SD	Marion
154	567.5	Midview Local SD	Grafton
155	567.0	Norwood City SD	Norwood
156	565.1	South Euclid-Lyndhurst City SD	Lyndhurst
157	564.0	Rolling Hills Local SD	Byesville
158	563.1	Forest Hills Local SD	Cincinnati
159	562.0	Heath City SD	Heath
159	562.0	Northwest Local SD	Cincinnati
161	561.9	West Carrollton City SD	West Carrollton
162	561.3	Field Local SD	Mogadore
163	560.7	Westfall Local SD	Williamsport
164	560.4	Canton Local SD	Canton
165	559.1	Washington Local SD	Toledo
166	558.5	Toledo City SD	Toledo
167	558.2	Euclid City SD	Euclid
168	557.3	Adams County-Ohio Valley Local SD	West Union
169	556.7	Alliance City SD	Alliance
170	556.5	Firelands Local SD	Oberlin
171	553.3	Scioto Valley Local SD	Piketon
172	550.7	Alexander Local SD	Albany
173	549.4	Ashland City SD	Ashland
174	548.2	Cambridge City SD	Cambridge
175	548.0	Minerva Local SD	Minerva
176	547.3	Licking Valley Local SD	Newark
177	546.0	Minford Local SD	Minford
178	544.8	Meigs Local SD	Pomeroy
179	541.8	Highland Local SD	Medina
180	540.9	Kent City SD	Kent
181	540.8	Medina City SD	Medina
182	539.8	Kenton City SD	Kenton
183	539.7	Brookville Local SD	Brookville
183	539.7	Findlay City SD	Findlay
185	539.1	Northwest Local SD	Canal Fulton
186	537.3	Saint Clairsville-Richland City	St Clairsville
187	536.8	Triway Local SD	Wooster
188	535.7	James A Garfield Local SD	Garrettsville
189	535.5	Chardon Local SD	Chardon
190	533.0	Wauseon Ex Vill SD	Wauseon
191	530.7	Bellaire Local SD	Bellaire
192	526.0	Poland Local SD	Poland
193	522.8	Saint Marys City SD	Saint Marys
194	521.1	Lebanon City SD	Lebanon
195	520.1	Westerville City SD	Westerville
196	518.4	Plain Local SD	New Albany
197	516.0	Elida Local SD	Elida
198	515.6	Cloverleaf Local SD	Lodi
199	515.5	Rossford Ex Vill SD	Rossford
200	512.3	Granville Ex Vill SD	Granville
200	512.3	Newton Falls Ex Vill SD	Newton Falls
202	511.3	Labrae Local SD	Leavittsburg
203	511.2	Hilliard City SD	Hilliard
204	510.2	Shaker Heights City SD	Shaker Heights
205	510.0	Geneva Area City SD	Geneva
205	510.0	Union Local SD	Morristown
207	509.3	Sugarcreek Local SD	Bellbrook
208	509.2	Akron City SD	Akron
209	509.0	Indian Lake Local SD	Lewistown
209	509.0	Madison Local SD	Mansfield
211	508.4	West Branch Local SD	Beloit
212	507.5	Bath Local SD	Lima
213	507.4	Miami Trace Local SD	Washington Ct Hse
214	507.3	Zane Trace Local SD	Chillicothe
215	507.0	Goshen Local SD	Goshen
216	506.8	Youngstown City SD	Youngstown
217	501.4	Brecksville-Broadview Heights	Brecksville
218	501.0	Oakwood City SD	Dayton

219	500.0	Manchester Local SD	Akron
220	499.4	Columbus City SD	Columbus
221	499.0	Benjamin Logan Local SD	Bellefontaine
222	496.5	Miamisburg City SD	Miamisburg
223	496.0	Wyoming City SD	Wyoming
224	492.6	Clark-Shawnee Local SD	Springfield
225	490.6	Huber Heights City SD	Huber Heights
226	489.2	Wapakoneta City SD	Wapakoneta
227	489.1	Jackson Local SD	Massillon
228	488.8	Wooster City SD	Wooster
229	486.6	Perrysburg Ex Vill SD	Perrysburg
230	486.0	Princeton City SD	Cincinnati
231	485.8	Olentangy Local SD	Lewis Center
232	485.0	Westlake City SD	Westlake
233	484.9	Oregon City SD	Oregon
234	484.5	Olmsted Falls City SD	Olmsted Falls
235	483.4	Northmont City SD	Englewood
236	481.8	Eastwood Local SD	Pemberville
237	480.9	Copley-Fairlawn City SD	Copley
238	479.6	Sandusky City SD	Sandusky
239	479.2	Lakewood City SD	Lakewood
240	478.7	Revere Local SD	Bath
241	478.6	Licking Heights Local SD	Summit Station
242	477.6	Urbana City SD	Urbana
243	474.7	Clearview Local SD	Lorain
244	473.8	Northeastern Local SD	Springfield
245	473.4	Eaton City SD	Eaton
246	471.8	North Fork Local SD	Utica
246	471.8	Orrville City SD	Orrville
248	471.1	Howland Local SD	Warren
249	470.4	Bryan City SD	Bryan
250	468.9	Pickerington Local SD	Pickerington
251	466.4	Claymont City SD	Dennison
252	465.8	Lake Local SD	Millbury
253	463.8	Elyria City SD	Elyria
254	462.8	Willard City SD	Willard
255	462.0	Clear Fork Valley Local SD	Bellville
256	460.8	Southwest Local SD	Harrison
257	460.2	Hubbard Ex Vill SD	Hubbard
258	460.0	Clyde-Green Springs Ex Vill SD	Clyde
259	458.1	Anthony Wayne Local SD	Whitehouse
260	457.8	Shelby City SD	Shelby
261	457.2	Tallmadge City SD	Tallmadge
262	456.8	Western Brown Local SD	Mount Orab
263	454.4	Kenston Local SD	Chagrin Falls
264	454.3	Liberty Local SD	Youngstown
265	452.6	Twinsburg City SD	Twinsburg
266	452.3	Carlisle Local SD	Carlisle
267	451.3	Jonathan Alder Local SD	Plain City
268	450.3	Warren Local SD	Vincent
269	448.4	Lakeview Local SD	Cortland
270	447.9	Delaware City SD	Delaware
271	447.3	Boardman Local SD	Youngstown
272	445.3	Northwest Local SD	Mc Dermott
273	444.7	Big Walnut Local SD	Galena
274	443.4	East Liverpool City SD	East Liverpool
275	442.9	North Royalton City SD	N Royalton
276	441.8	Worthington City SD	Worthington
277	441.5	Canton City SD	Canton
278	440.5	Tipp City Ex Vill SD	Tipp City
279	440.2	Graham Local SD	Saint Paris
280	439.7	Springfield Local SD	Akron
281	439.0	Clinton-Massie Local SD	Clarksville
282	438.8	Kings Local SD	Kings Mills
282	438.8	Mariemont City SD	Cincinnati
284	438.3	Champion Local SD	Warren
285	437.0	Portsmouth City SD	Portsmouth
286	435.7	Sylvania City SD	Sylvania
287	434.9	Piqua City SD	Piqua
288	432.5	Southeast Local SD	Apple Creek
289	432.4	Mount Healthy City SD	Cincinnati
290	430.4	North Canton City SD	North Canton
291	429.2	Talawanda City SD	Oxford
292	426.4	Mayfield City SD	Highland Hgts
293	426.3	Solon City SD	Solon
294	425.6	Southwest Licking Local SD	Etna
295	424.5	Xenia Community City SD	Xenia
296	424.3	Austintown Local SD	Youngstown
297	424.0	Ross Local SD	Hamilton
298	421.9	Plain Local SD	Canton
299	421.8	Bellefontaine City SD	Bellefontaine
300	421.4	Berea City SD	Berea
301	420.7	New Richmond Ex Vill SD	New Richmond
302	417.1	Aurora City SD	Aurora
303	417.0	Madison-Plains Local SD	London
304	416.5	Huron City SD	Huron
305	415.1	Nordonia Hills City SD	Northfield
306	413.0	Benton Carroll Salem Local SD	Oak Harbor
307	412.0	Hudson City SD	Hudson
308	411.5	Canal Winchester Local SD	Canal Winchester
309	411.4	Sheffield-Sheffield Lake City	Sheffield Vlg
310	410.9	Ravenna City SD	Ravenna
311	410.5	Greeneview Local SD	Jamestown
312	410.3	Springfield Local SD	Holland
313	410.2	Green Local SD	Green
314	406.8	Wellington Ex Vill SD	Wellington
315	406.2	Buckeye Local SD	Medina
316	405.6	Bowling Green City SD	Bowling Green
317	404.7	Fairland Local SD	Proctorville
318	403.0	Centerville City SD	Centerville
319	401.8	Three Rivers Local SD	Cleves
320	401.0	Bay Village City SD	Bay Village
321	399.3	Pike-Delta-York Local SD	Delta
321	399.3	Swanton Local SD	Swanton
323	397.4	West Geauga Local SD	Chesterland
324	393.4	Chagrin Falls Ex Vill SD	Chagrin Falls
325	391.8	Fostoria City SD	Fostoria
326	391.3	Washington Court House City SD	Washington Ct Hse
327	388.8	North Olmsted City SD	North Olmsted
328	385.6	Louisville City SD	Louisville
329	384.0	Marysville Ex Vill SD	Marysville
330	382.8	Beavercreek City SD	Beavercreek
331	382.2	Bedford City SD	Bedford
331	382.2	Mad River Local SD	Dayton
333	381.2	Dublin City SD	Dublin
334	379.6	Mansfield City SD	Mansfield
335	378.0	Tiffin City SD	Tiffin
336	377.0	Hamilton City SD	Hamilton
336	377.0	Wickliffe City SD	Wickliffe
338	375.8	Brookfield Local SD	Brookfield
339	374.3	Perkins Local SD	Sandusky
340	374.2	Fairview Park City SD	Fairview Park
341	370.8	Keystone Local SD	Lagrange
342	370.3	Defiance City SD	Defiance
343	367.9	Rocky River City SD	Rocky River
344	364.2	Woodridge Local SD	Peninsula
345	363.6	Maumee City SD	Maumee
346	358.9	Sidney City SD	Sidney
347	347.4	Sycamore Community City SD	Cincinnati
348	345.6	Washington-Nile Local SD	West Portsmouth
349	342.6	Madison Local SD	Middletown
350	337.6	Orange City SD	Cleveland
351	336.4	Edgewood City SD	Trenton
352	335.2	Avon Lake City SD	Avon Lake
353	333.4	Napoleon Area City SD	Napoleon
354	332.1	Upper Arlington City SD	Upper Arlington
355	331.0	Springfield City SD	Springfield
356	330.0	Bexley City SD	Bexley
357	326.7	Perry Local SD	Massillon
358	315.4	Ironton City SD	Ironton
359	314.7	Perry Local SD	Perry
360	313.6	Kettering City SD	Kettering
361	305.9	Shawnee Local SD	Lima
362	304.9	Cleveland Hts-Univ Hts City SD	University Hgts
363	302.3	Finneytown Local SD	Cincinnati
364	296.6	Warrensville Heights City SD	Warrensville Hgts
365	292.8	North Ridgeville City SD	N Ridgeville
366	291.4	Indian Hill Ex Vill SD	Cincinnati
367	263.3	Beachwood City SD	Beachwood
368	240.1	Elgin Local SD	Marion
369	209.5	Black River Local SD	Sullivan
370	0.0	Preble Shawnee Local SD	Camden

Current Spending per Student in FY2001

Rank	Dollars	District Name	City
1	17,180	Beachwood City SD	Beachwood
2	13,777	Orange City SD	Cleveland
3	13,223	Perry Local SD	Perry
4	11,453	Shaker Heights City SD	Shaker Heights
5	10,392	Cleveland Hts-Univ Hts City SD	University Hgts
6	10,352	Mayfield City SD	Highland Hgts
7	10,082	Indian Hill Ex Vill SD	Cincinnati
8	9,900	Plain Local SD	New Albany
9	9,685	East Cleveland City SD	East Cleveland
10	9,423	Princeton City SD	Cincinnati
11	9,421	Sycamore Community City SD	Cincinnati
12	9,207	Wickliffe City SD	Wickliffe
13	9,173	Solon City SD	Solon
14	9,151	Upper Arlington City SD	Upper Arlington
15	9,014	Westlake City SD	Westlake
16	8,983	South Euclid-Lyndhurst City SD	Lyndhurst
17	8,933	Euclid City SD	Euclid
18	8,894	Worthington City SD	Worthington
19	8,855	Rocky River City SD	Rocky River
20	8,816	Columbus City SD	Columbus
21	8,735	Cleveland Municipal SD	Cleveland
22	8,733	Blanchester Local SD	Blanchester
23	8,673	Bexley City SD	Bexley
24	8,661	Warrensville Heights City SD	Warrensville Hgts
25	8,632	Bedford City SD	Bedford
26	8,612	Chagrin Falls Ex Vill SD	Chagrin Falls
27	8,598	Kent City SD	Kent
28	8,444	Mansfield City SD	Mansfield
29	8,411	Youngstown City SD	Youngstown
30	8,398	Wyoming City SD	Wyoming
31	8,394	Bay Village City SD	Bay Village
32	8,358	Fairview Park City SD	Fairview Park
33	8,353	Cincinnati City SD	Cincinnati
34	8,282	Dayton City SD	Dayton
35	8,231	Benton Carroll Salem Local SD	Oak Harbor
36	8,221	Sandusky City SD	Sandusky
37	8,209	Northridge Local SD	Dayton
38	8,158	Dublin City SD	Dublin
39	8,119	Berea City SD	Berea
40	8,116	Hudson City SD	Hudson
41	8,093	Akron City SD	Akron
42	8,088	Mariemont City SD	Cincinnati
43	8,078	Twinsburg City SD	Twinsburg
44	8,014	Toledo City SD	Toledo
45	7,999	Canton City SD	Canton
46	7,993	Strongsville City SD	Strongsville
47	7,991	Brecksville-Broadview Heights	Brecksville
48	7,933	Painesville City Local SD	Painesville
49	7,924	Warren City SD	Warren
50	7,914	North Olmsted City SD	North Olmsted
51	7,899	Lorain City SD	Lorain
52	7,855	Mentor Ex Vill SD	Mentor
53	7,833	Woodridge Local SD	Peninsula
54	7,826	Barberton City SD	Barberton
55	7,785	Copley-Fairlawn City SD	Copley
56	7,774	Port Clinton City SD	Port Clinton
57	7,756	Wooster City SD	Wooster
58	7,725	Maumee City SD	Maumee
59	7,706	Lakewood City SD	Lakewood
60	7,704	Kenston Local SD	Chagrin Falls
61	7,670	Delaware City SD	Delaware
62	7,668	Medina City SD	Medina
63	7,618	Aurora City SD	Aurora
64	7,617	Perkins Local SD	Sandusky
65	7,614	Canal Winchester Local SD	Canal Winchester
66	7,613	Oregon City SD	Oregon
67	7,573	Trotwood-Madison City SD	Trotwood
68	7,564	Parma City SD	Parma
69	7,545	Nordonia Hills City SD	Northfield
70	7,541	Avon Lake City SD	Avon Lake
71	7,538	Olmsted Falls City SD	Olmsted Falls
72	7,536	Oakwood City SD	Dayton
73	7,513	Springfield City SD	Springfield
74	7,477	Granville Ex Vill SD	Granville
75	7,426	Sheffield-Sheffield Lake City	Sheffield Vlg
76	7,398	Mount Healthy City SD	Cincinnati
77	7,380	Zanesville City SD	Zanesville
78	7,379	Findlay City SD	Findlay
79	7,370	Elyria City SD	Elyria
80	7,369	Clearview Local SD	Lorain
81	7,359	East Liverpool City SD	East Liverpool
82	7,352	Sylvania City SD	Sylvania
83	7,333	Centerville City SD	Centerville
84	7,311	New Richmond Ex Vill SD	New Richmond
85	7,305	Olentangy Local SD	Lewis Center
86	7,282	Revere Local SD	Bath
87	7,271	Madison Local SD	Mansfield
88	7,242	Springfield Local SD	Holland
89	7,238	Fostoria City SD	Fostoria
90	7,235	Whitehall City SD	Whitehall
91	7,232	North Royalton City SD	N Royalton
92	7,199	Lima City SD	Lima
93	7,188	West Geauga Local SD	Chesterland
94	7,180	Washington Local SD	Toledo
95	7,178	Finneytown Local SD	Cincinnati
96	7,166	Winton Woods City SD	Cincinnati
97	7,158	South-Western City SD	Grove City
97	7,158	Streetsboro City SD	Streetsboro
99	7,157	Rossford Ex Vill SD	Rossford
100	7,152	Garfield Heights City SD	Garfield Hgts
101	7,150	Alliance City SD	Alliance
101	7,150	Marysville Ex Vill SD	Marysville
103	7,124	Hilliard City SD	Hilliard
104	7,114	Willoughby-Eastlake City SD	Willoughby
105	7,108	Gahanna-Jefferson City SD	Gahanna
106	7,106	Perrysburg Ex Vill SD	Perrysburg
107	7,051	Athens City SD	The Plains
108	7,046	Tallmadge City SD	Tallmadge
109	7,040	Bowling Green City SD	Bowling Green
110	7,029	Lancaster City SD	Lancaster
111	7,026	Ravenna City SD	Ravenna
112	6,994	Chardon Local SD	Chardon
113	6,980	Groveport Madison Local SD	Groveport
114	6,979	Huron City SD	Huron
115	6,964	North Ridgeville City SD	N Ridgeville
116	6,956	Canton Local SD	Canton
117	6,952	Boardman Local SD	Youngstown
117	6,952	Westerville City SD	Westerville
119	6,941	Portsmouth City SD	Portsmouth
120	6,936	Ashtabula Area City SD	Ashtabula
121	6,932	Vandalia-Butler City SD	Vandalia

122	6,921	Buckeye Local SD	Medina
123	6,919	Morgan Local SD	McConnelsville
124	6,910	Norwood City SD	Norwood
125	6,896	Bellaire Local SD	Bellaire
126	6,894	Kings Local SD	Kings Mills
127	6,893	Labrae Local SD	Leavittsburg
128	6,869	Indian Creek Local SD	Wintersville
129	6,850	Bucyrus City SD	Bucyrus
130	6,848	Painesville Township Local SD	Painesville
131	6,842	Campbell City SD	Campbell
132	6,840	Beavercreek City SD	Beavercreek
133	6,831	Pickerington Local SD	Pickerington
134	6,830	Buckeye Local SD	Ashtabula
135	6,817	Kettering City SD	Kettering
136	6,808	Maple Heights City SD	Maple Heights
137	6,805	Mason City SD	Mason
138	6,803	Meigs Local SD	Pomeroy
139	6,794	Stow-Munroe Falls City SD	Stow
140	6,790	Anthony Wayne Local SD	Whitehouse
141	6,785	Southeast Local SD	Apple Creek
142	6,767	Three Rivers Local SD	Cleves
143	6,763	Eastwood Local SD	Pemberville
144	6,739	Wadsworth City SD	Wadsworth
145	6,734	Swanton Local SD	Swanton
146	6,729	Bellevue City SD	Bellevue
147	6,705	Howland Local SD	Warren
148	6,698	Austintown Local SD	Youngstown
148	6,698	Batavia Local SD	Batavia
150	6,692	Pike-Delta-York Local SD	Delta
151	6,689	Little Miami Local SD	Morrow
152	6,685	Hamilton City SD	Hamilton
153	6,679	Celina City SD	Celina
154	6,678	Brunswick City SD	Brunswick
155	6,662	Mad River Local SD	Dayton
156	6,633	Northwest Local SD	Cincinnati
157	6,627	Napoleon Area City SD	Napoleon
158	6,623	Valley View Local SD	Germantown
159	6,617	Licking Heights Local SD	Summit Station
160	6,615	North Canton City SD	North Canton
161	6,606	Cuyahoga Falls City SD	Cuyahoga Falls
162	6,603	Loveland City SD	Loveland
163	6,599	Liberty Local SD	Youngstown
164	6,595	Shelby City SD	Shelby
165	6,589	Marion City SD	Marion
166	6,582	Massillon City SD	Massillon
167	6,573	Union Local SD	Morristown
168	6,565	Carlisle Local SD	Carlisle
169	6,552	Tecumseh Local SD	New Carlisle
170	6,546	River Valley Local SD	Caledonia
171	6,545	Buckeye Valley Local SD	Delaware
172	6,543	Ashland City SD	Ashland
172	6,543	Champion Local SD	Warren
174	6,537	Norton City SD	Norton
175	6,524	Eastern Local SD	Sardinia
175	6,524	Ironton City SD	Ironton
177	6,523	Xenia Community City SD	Xenia
178	6,500	Miamisburg City SD	Miamisburg
179	6,498	Springfield Local SD	Akron
180	6,491	Vermilion Local SD	Vermilion
181	6,490	Rolling Hills Local SD	Byesville
182	6,481	Struthers City SD	Struthers
183	6,468	Switzerland of Ohio Local SD	Woodsfield
184	6,454	Avon Local SD	Avon
185	6,447	Green Local SD	Green
186	6,443	Brookfield Local SD	Brookfield
187	6,434	Bryan City SD	Bryan
188	6,425	Highland Local SD	Medina
189	6,412	Harrison Hills City SD	Hopedale
190	6,386	Forest Hills Local SD	Cincinnati
191	6,384	Fairfield City SD	Fairfield
192	6,381	Jackson Local SD	Massillon
193	6,364	Adams County-Ohio Valley Local SD	West Union
194	6,362	Manchester Local SD	Akron
195	6,360	West Carrollton City SD	West Carrollton
196	6,353	Girard City SD	Girard
197	6,350	Salem City SD	Salem
198	6,347	Reynoldsburg City SD	Reynoldsburg
199	6,344	Northwest Local SD	Mc Dermott
200	6,341	Licking Valley Local SD	Newark
201	6,334	Cambridge City SD	Cambridge
202	6,330	Gallia County Local SD	Gallipolis
203	6,316	Berlin-Milan Local SD	Milan
203	6,316	Perry Local SD	Massillon
205	6,314	Troy City SD	Troy
206	6,313	Ontario Local SD	Mansfield
207	6,311	Piqua City SD	Piqua
208	6,306	Hubbard Ex Vill SD	Hubbard
209	6,296	Clark-Shawnee Local SD	Springfield
210	6,295	Circleville City SD	Circleville
211	6,292	Franklin City SD	Franklin
211	6,292	Logan Elm Local SD	Circleville
213	6,287	Coshocton City SD	Coshocton
214	6,286	Washington-Nile Local SD	West Portsmouth
215	6,284	Southwest Licking Local SD	Etna
216	6,281	Northmont City SD	Englewood
217	6,280	Fairborn City SD	Fairborn
218	6,273	Urbana City SD	Urbana
219	6,268	Northeastern Local SD	Springfield
220	6,267	Chillicothe City SD	Chillicothe
220	6,267	Milford Ex Vill SD	Milford
222	6,266	Hamilton Local SD	Columbus
223	6,265	Madison-Plains Local SD	London
224	6,264	Bellefontaine City SD	Bellefontaine
225	6,262	Kenton City SD	Kenton
226	6,251	Paulding Ex Vill SD	Paulding
227	6,229	Niles City SD	Niles
228	6,225	Lakota Local SD	Liberty Twp
229	6,203	Poland Local SD	Poland
230	6,199	Shawnee Local SD	Lima
231	6,191	Miami Trace Local SD	Washington Ct Hse
232	6,187	Fremont City SD	Fremont
233	6,180	Lakewood Local SD	Hebron
234	6,178	Steubenville City SD	Steubenville
235	6,175	Middletown City SD	Middletown
236	6,161	Newark City SD	Newark
237	6,149	Sugarcreek Local SD	Bellbrook
238	6,146	Defiance City SD	Defiance
239	6,140	Huber Heights City SD	Huber Heights
239	6,140	Orrville City SD	Orrville
241	6,138	Field Local SD	Mogadore
241	6,138	Heath City SD	Heath
243	6,137	Canfield Local SD	Canfield
244	6,131	Rock Hill Local SD	Ironton
245	6,129	Hillsboro City SD	Hillsboro
246	6,124	Brookville Local SD	Brookville
247	6,123	Otsego Local SD	Tontogany
248	6,120	Goshen Local SD	Goshen
249	6,117	Big Walnut Local SD	Galena
250	6,104	Madison Local SD	Middletown
251	6,100	Edgewood City SD	Trenton
252	6,098	Vinton County Local SD	Mc Arthur
253	6,093	Crestwood Local SD	Mantua
253	6,093	Talawanda City SD	Oxford
255	6,080	East Holmes Local SD	Berlin
256	6,079	Lakeview Local SD	Cortland
257	6,078	Buckeye Local SD	Rayland
258	6,077	Triway Local SD	Wooster
259	6,076	Minford Local SD	Minford
260	6,075	Coventry Local SD	Akron
260	6,075	Minerva Local SD	Minerva
262	6,063	Plain Local SD	Canton
263	6,062	Southeast Local SD	Ravenna
264	6,061	Clyde-Green Springs Ex Vill SD	Clyde
265	6,056	Logan-Hocking Local SD	Logan
266	6,035	Firelands Local SD	Oberlin
266	6,035	Marlington Local SD	Alliance
268	6,032	Marietta City SD	Marietta
269	6,025	Sandy Valley Local SD	Magnolia
270	6,024	Lebanon City SD	Lebanon
271	6,018	New Lexington City SD	New Lexington
272	6,004	James A Garfield Local SD	Garrettsville
272	6,004	River View Local SD	Warsaw
274	5,995	Greenville City SD	Greenville
275	5,987	Madison Local SD	Madison
276	5,983	Westfall Local SD	Williamsport
277	5,981	Northwestern Local SD	Springfield
278	5,976	Cloverleaf Local SD	Lodi
279	5,974	Tiffin City SD	Tiffin
280	5,969	Gallipolis City SD	Gallipolis
281	5,967	Claymont City SD	Dennison
282	5,966	Galion City SD	Galion
283	5,954	Dover City SD	Dover
284	5,948	Oak Hills Local SD	Cincinnati
285	5,945	Southwest Local SD	Harrison
286	5,941	Preble Shawnee Local SD	Camden
287	5,936	Genoa Area Local SD	Genoa
288	5,933	Newton Falls Ex Vill SD	Newton Falls
289	5,925	Graham Local SD	Saint Paris
290	5,912	Amherst Ex Vill SD	Amherst
291	5,906	Milton-Union Ex Vill SD	West Milton
292	5,901	Beaver Local SD	Lisbon
293	5,892	Fairless Local SD	Navarre
293	5,892	North College Hill City SD	Cincinnati
295	5,886	Northern Local SD	Thornville
296	5,884	Fairfield Union Local SD	W Rushville
297	5,879	Alexander Local SD	Albany
297	5,879	Louisville City SD	Louisville
299	5,878	Springboro Community City SD	Springboro
300	5,871	Bath Local SD	Lima
301	5,866	Highland Local SD	Sparta
302	5,860	Lake Local SD	Millbury
303	5,858	Saint Clairsville-Richland City	St Clairsville
304	5,857	Wellston City SD	Wellston
305	5,850	Conneaut Area City SD	Conneaut
306	5,848	West Holmes Local SD	Millersburg
307	5,845	Van Wert City SD	Van Wert
308	5,836	Warren Local SD	Vincent
309	5,833	Coldwater Ex Vill SD	Coldwater
310	5,829	Northwest Local SD	Canal Fulton
311	5,820	Willard City SD	Willard
312	5,809	West Clermont Local SD	Cincinnati
313	5,790	Sidney City SD	Sidney
314	5,777	Mount Vernon City SD	Mount Vernon
315	5,775	Washington Court House City SD	Washington Ct Hse
316	5,774	Elida Local SD	Elida
317	5,768	London City SD	London
318	5,766	Indian Lake Local SD	Lewistown
319	5,765	Union-Scioto Local SD	Chillicothe
320	5,756	West Muskingum Local SD	Zanesville
321	5,752	Wellington Ex Vill SD	Wellington
322	5,746	Greeneview Local SD	Jamestown
323	5,745	Greenfield Ex Vill SD	Greenfield
324	5,694	Wilmington City SD	Wilmington
325	5,690	Elgin Local SD	Marion
326	5,684	Amanda-Clearcreek Local SD	Amanda
327	5,682	Edison Local SD	Hammondsville
327	5,682	Franklin Local SD	Duncan Falls
329	5,670	Eaton City SD	Eaton
330	5,658	Jackson City SD	Jackson
331	5,655	Greenon Local SD	Springfield
331	5,655	Upper Sandusky Ex Vill SD	Upper Sandusky
333	5,645	Jefferson Area Local SD	Jefferson
334	5,641	New Philadelphia City SD	New Philadelphia
335	5,638	Clermont-Northeastern Local SD	Batavia
336	5,632	Indian Valley Local SD	Gnadenhutten
337	5,631	Ross Local SD	Hamilton
338	5,616	Saint Marys City SD	Saint Marys
339	5,592	Black River Local SD	Sullivan
340	5,579	East Muskingum Local SD	New Concord
341	5,576	Lake Local SD	Hartville
342	5,573	Scioto Valley Local SD	Piketon
342	5,573	Teays Valley Local SD	Ashville
344	5,560	South Point Local SD	South Point
345	5,558	Maysville Local SD	Zanesville
346	5,557	Waverly City SD	Waverly
347	5,553	Lexington Local SD	Lexington
348	5,542	West Branch Local SD	Beloit
349	5,540	Ottawa-Glandorf Local SD	Ottawa
350	5,532	Midview Local SD	Grafton
351	5,529	Geneva Area City SD	Geneva
352	5,525	Wauseon Ex Vill SD	Wauseon
353	5,524	Clear Fork Valley Local SD	Bellville
353	5,524	Tipp City Ex Vill SD	Tipp City
355	5,509	Wapakoneta City SD	Wapakoneta
356	5,496	North Fork Local SD	Utica
357	5,482	Clinton-Massie Local SD	Clarksville
358	5,449	Keystone Local SD	Lagrange
359	5,375	Fairland Local SD	Proctorville
359	5,375	Tuscarawas Valley Local SD	Zoarville
361	5,347	East Clinton Local SD	Lees Creek
362	5,339	Norwalk City SD	Norwalk
362	5,339	Zane Trace Local SD	Chillicothe
364	5,253	Tri-Valley Local SD	Dresden
365	5,216	Jonathan Alder Local SD	Plain City
366	5,021	Western Brown Local SD	Mount Orab
367	4,991	Benjamin Logan Local SD	Bellefontaine
368	4,962	Carrollton Ex Vill SD	Carrollton
369	4,761	Bethel-Tate Local SD	Bethel
370	n/a	Electronic Classroom of Tomorrow	Columbus

Number of Diploma Recipients

Rank	Number	District Name	City
1	2,600	Columbus City SD	Columbus
2	2,443	Cleveland Municipal SD	Cleveland
3	1,526	Akron City SD	Akron
4	1,478	Toledo City SD	Toledo
5	1,305	Cincinnati City SD	Cincinnati
6	1,003	South-Western City SD	Grove City
7	970	Westerville City SD	Westerville
8	963	Lakota Local SD	Liberty Twp
9	886	Parma City SD	Parma
10	858	Dayton City SD	Dayton
11	803	Worthington City SD	Worthington
12	785	Hilliard City SD	Hilliard
13	767	Dublin City SD	Dublin
14	730	Mentor Ex Vill SD	Mentor
15	656	Northwest Local SD	Cincinnati
16	637	Willoughby-Eastlake City SD	Willoughby
17	633	Oak Hills Local SD	Cincinnati
18	611	Berea City SD	Berea
19	608	Fairfield City SD	Fairfield
20	599	Sylvania City SD	Sylvania
21	590	Centerville City SD	Centerville
22	585	Forest Hills Local SD	Cincinnati
23	534	Kettering City SD	Kettering
24	524	Hamilton City SD	Hamilton

25	520	West Clermont Local SD	Cincinnati
26	518	Lakewood City SD	Lakewood
27	508	Strongsville City SD	Strongsville
28	501	Medina City SD	Medina
29	495	Beavercreek City SD	Beavercreek
29	495	Canton City SD	Canton
31	494	Pickerington Local SD	Pickerington
32	476	Lorain City SD	Lorain
33	475	Brunswick City SD	Brunswick
34	458	Reynoldsburg City SD	Reynoldsburg
35	448	Washington Local SD	Toledo
36	437	Huber Heights City SD	Huber Heights
37	426	Findlay City SD	Findlay
38	425	Sycamore Community City SD	Cincinnati
39	424	Gahanna-Jefferson City SD	Gahanna
40	422	Jackson Local SD	Massillon
41	421	Upper Arlington City SD	Upper Arlington
41	421	Youngstown City SD	Youngstown
43	420	Stow-Munroe Falls City SD	Stow
44	417	Milford Ex Vill SD	Milford
45	411	Springfield City SD	Springfield
46	403	Princeton City SD	Cincinnati
47	393	Northmont City SD	Englewood
48	390	Plain Local SD	Canton
48	390	Solon City SD	Solon
50	389	Newark City SD	Newark
51	381	Hudson City SD	Hudson
52	380	Boardman Local SD	Youngstown
53	368	North Olmsted City SD	North Olmsted
54	367	Mason City SD	Mason
55	363	Euclid City SD	Euclid
56	362	Elyria City SD	Elyria
56	362	Shaker Heights City SD	Shaker Heights
58	360	Cuyahoga Falls City SD	Cuyahoga Falls
58	360	Middletown City SD	Middletown
60	358	Lancaster City SD	Lancaster
61	352	Warren City SD	Warren
62	351	Austintown Local SD	Youngstown
63	349	Fairborn City SD	Fairborn
64	346	Cleveland Hts-Univ Hts City SD	University Hgts
65	342	Perry Local SD	Massillon
65	342	South Euclid-Lyndhurst City SD	Lyndhurst
67	341	Mayfield City SD	Highland Hgts
68	340	Brecksville-Broadview Heights	Brecksville
69	335	North Royalton City SD	N Royalton
70	330	Miamisburg City SD	Miamisburg
71	328	Perrysburg Ex Vill SD	Perrysburg
72	327	Wadsworth City SD	Wadsworth
73	325	Fremont City SD	Fremont
74	319	North Canton City SD	North Canton
75	315	Olentangy Local SD	Lewis Center
76	314	Groveport Madison Local SD	Groveport
76	314	Xenia Community City SD	Xenia
78	309	Nordonia Hills City SD	Northfield
79	308	Kent City SD	Kent
80	306	Adams County-Ohio Valley Local SD	West Union
80	306	Painesville Township Local SD	Painesville
82	294	Troy City SD	Troy
83	288	Ashland City SD	Ashland
84	285	Chillicothe City SD	Chillicothe
84	285	Loveland City SD	Loveland
86	284	Mount Vernon City SD	Mount Vernon
87	282	Celina City SD	Celina
88	281	Amherst Ex Vill SD	Amherst
88	281	Wooster City SD	Wooster
90	280	Marion City SD	Marion
91	279	Lebanon City SD	Lebanon
92	277	Southwest Local SD	Harrison
93	276	Westlake City SD	Westlake
94	273	Cloverleaf Local SD	Lodi
95	267	Greenville City SD	Greenville
96	264	Barberton City SD	Barberton
97	263	Garfield Heights City SD	Garfield Hgts
98	261	Delaware City SD	Delaware
99	260	Talawanda City SD	Oxford
100	258	Mansfield City SD	Mansfield
101	257	Marysville Ex Vill SD	Marysville
102	256	Bowling Green City SD	Bowling Green
103	255	Massillon City SD	Massillon
104	254	Madison Local SD	Madison
104	254	West Carrollton City SD	West Carrollton
106	252	East Cleveland City SD	East Cleveland
107	248	Lake Local SD	Hartville
108	247	Green Local SD	Green
108	247	Tiffin City SD	Tiffin
110	244	Lima City SD	Lima
110	244	Vandalia-Butler City SD	Vandalia
112	243	Avon Lake City SD	Avon Lake
113	242	Maumee City SD	Maumee
114	240	Ashtabula Area City SD	Ashtabula
114	240	Dover City SD	Dover
116	238	New Philadelphia City SD	New Philadelphia
117	236	Springfield Local SD	Holland
118	233	Anthony Wayne Local SD	Whitehouse
118	233	Sidney City SD	Sidney
118	233	Southwest Licking Local SD	Etna
121	232	Chardon Local SD	Chardon
122	231	Bedford City SD	Bedford
122	231	Sandusky City SD	Sandusky
122	231	Springboro Community City SD	Springboro
122	231	Wapakoneta City SD	Wapakoneta
122	231	Wilmington City SD	Wilmington
127	230	Howland Local SD	Warren
128	228	Piqua City SD	Piqua
129	227	Logan-Hocking Local SD	Logan
130	225	Canfield Local SD	Canfield
130	225	Oregon City SD	Oregon
130	225	Revere Local SD	Bath
133	224	Geneva Area City SD	Geneva
133	224	Madison Local SD	Mansfield
133	224	Tecumseh Local SD	New Carlisle
136	223	Kings Local SD	Kings Mills
137	219	Olmsted Falls City SD	Olmsted Falls
138	218	Winton Woods City SD	Cincinnati
139	216	Marietta City SD	Marietta
140	215	Lexington Local SD	Lexington
141	214	Kenston Local SD	Chagrin Falls
142	213	Alliance City SD	Alliance
143	211	Copley-Fairlawn City SD	Copley
144	210	Niles City SD	Niles
145	208	Midview Local SD	Grafton
146	207	Defiance City SD	Defiance
147	206	Twinsburg City SD	Twinsburg
148	203	Clark-Shawnee Local SD	Springfield
148	203	Jackson City SD	Jackson
150	202	Switzerland of Ohio Local SD	Woodsfield
151	199	Bellefontaine City SD	Bellefontaine
151	199	Carrollton Ex Vill SD	Carrollton
151	199	Hubbard Ex Vill SD	Hubbard
151	199	Louisville City SD	Louisville
155	198	Mount Healthy City SD	Cincinnati
155	198	North Ridgeville City SD	N Ridgeville
155	198	Northeastern Local SD	Springfield
155	198	Poland Local SD	Poland
159	196	Crestwood Local SD	Mantua
159	196	Highland Local SD	Medina
161	195	West Geauga Local SD	Chesterland
162	194	Napoleon Area City SD	Napoleon
162	194	Tri-Valley Local SD	Dresden
164	193	Orange City SD	Cleveland
164	193	Saint Marys City SD	Saint Marys
166	192	Trotwood-Madison City SD	Trotwood
166	192	Whitehall City SD	Whitehall
168	191	Big Walnut Local SD	Galena
168	191	Springfield Local SD	Akron
170	190	Franklin City SD	Franklin
170	190	Warren Local SD	Vincent
172	189	Maple Heights City SD	Maple Heights
173	187	Elida Local SD	Elida
173	187	West Branch Local SD	Beloit
175	185	East Liverpool City SD	East Liverpool
175	185	Tallmadge City SD	Tallmadge
177	184	River View Local SD	Warsaw
177	184	Sugarcreek Local SD	Bellbrook
179	183	Buckeye Local SD	Rayland
179	183	Norton City SD	Norton
179	183	Salem City SD	Salem
182	182	Buckeye Local SD	Medina
182	182	Edgewood City SD	Trenton
182	182	Hillsboro City SD	Hillsboro
182	182	Mad River Local SD	Dayton
186	181	Zanesville City SD	Zanesville
187	180	Bellevue City SD	Bellevue
188	178	Coventry Local SD	Akron
189	177	Bexley City SD	Bexley
189	177	East Muskingum Local SD	New Concord
189	177	Edison Local SD	Hammondsville
192	175	Field Local SD	Mogadore
192	175	Lakeview Local SD	Cortland
192	175	Tipp City Ex Vill SD	Tipp City
195	174	Ravenna City SD	Ravenna
196	171	Clyde-Green Springs Ex Vill SD	Clyde
196	171	Marlington Local SD	Alliance
196	171	Shawnee Local SD	Lima
196	171	Shelby City SD	Shelby
196	171	Southeast Local SD	Ravenna
196	171	Steubenville City SD	Steubenville
196	171	Vermilion Local SD	Vermilion
203	170	Galion City SD	Galion
203	170	Miami Trace Local SD	Washington Ct Hse
205	169	Little Miami Local SD	Morrow
205	169	Port Clinton City SD	Port Clinton
205	169	Ross Local SD	Hamilton
208	168	Bay Village City SD	Bay Village
208	168	Teays Valley Local SD	Ashville
210	167	Fairview Park City SD	Fairview Park
210	167	Logan Elm Local SD	Circleville
212	165	Franklin Local SD	Duncan Falls
212	165	Gallia County Local SD	Gallipolis
214	164	Ottawa-Glandorf Local SD	Ottawa
215	162	Canton Local SD	Canton
215	162	Conneaut Area City SD	Conneaut
217	161	Beaver Local SD	Lisbon
218	160	Buckeye Local SD	Ashtabula
218	160	Maysville Local SD	Zanesville
218	160	Norwalk City SD	Norwalk
218	160	Warrensville Heights City SD	Warrensville Hgts
222	157	Buckeye Valley Local SD	Delaware
222	157	Morgan Local SD	McConnelsville
224	155	Lakewood Local SD	Hebron
224	155	New Richmond Ex Vill SD	New Richmond
226	154	Cambridge City SD	Cambridge
227	153	Upper Sandusky Ex Vill SD	Upper Sandusky
227	153	Van Wert City SD	Van Wert
229	152	Bath Local SD	Lima
229	152	Benton Carroll Salem Local SD	Oak Harbor
229	152	Granville Ex Vill SD	Granville
232	151	Indian Hill Ex Vill SD	Cincinnati
232	151	Northern Local SD	Thornville
232	151	Northwest Local SD	Canal Fulton
235	150	Liberty Local SD	Youngstown
235	150	Perkins Local SD	Sandusky
235	150	West Holmes Local SD	Millersburg
238	149	Aurora City SD	Aurora
238	149	Bryan City SD	Bryan
238	149	Gallipolis City SD	Gallipolis
238	149	Union Local SD	Morristown
242	148	Champion Local SD	Warren
243	147	Kenton City SD	Kenton
244	146	Chagrin Falls Ex Vill SD	Chagrin Falls
244	146	Goshen Local SD	Goshen
244	146	Greenon Local SD	Springfield
244	146	Triway Local SD	Wooster
248	145	Claymont City SD	Dennison
248	145	Minerva Local SD	Minerva
248	145	Rocky River City SD	Rocky River
248	145	Wauseon Ex Vill SD	Wauseon
252	144	Vinton County Local SD	Mc Arthur
252	144	Washington Court House City SD	Washington Ct Hse
252	144	Willard City SD	Willard
255	143	Western Brown Local SD	Mount Orab
255	143	Wyoming City SD	Wyoming
257	142	Beachwood City SD	Beachwood
257	142	Circleville City SD	Circleville
257	142	Fairfield Union Local SD	W Rushville
257	142	West Muskingum Local SD	Zanesville
261	141	Finneytown Local SD	Cincinnati
261	141	Swanton Local SD	Swanton
263	140	Eastwood Local SD	Pemberville
263	140	Firelands Local SD	Oberlin
263	140	Oakwood City SD	Dayton
266	139	Clear Fork Valley Local SD	Bellville
266	139	Jefferson Area Local SD	Jefferson
266	139	River Valley Local SD	Caledonia
269	138	Bethel-Tate Local SD	Bethel
269	138	Harrison Hills City SD	Hopedale
269	138	Valley View Local SD	Germantown
272	137	Lake Local SD	Millbury
272	137	Norwood City SD	Norwood
272	137	Rossford Ex Vill SD	Rossford
275	136	Huron City SD	Huron
275	136	Three Rivers Local SD	Cleves
277	135	Canal Winchester Local SD	Canal Winchester
277	135	Eaton City SD	Eaton
277	135	Northwestern Local SD	Springfield
280	134	London City SD	London
280	134	Paulding Ex Vill SD	Paulding
282	133	Hamilton Local SD	Columbus
282	133	Manchester Local SD	Akron
282	133	Union-Scioto Local SD	Chillicothe
285	132	Berlin-Milan Local SD	Milan
285	132	Graham Local SD	Saint Paris
285	132	Greenfield Ex Vill SD	Greenfield
285	132	Indian Creek Local SD	Wintersville
285	132	Perry Local SD	Perry
290	131	Benjamin Logan Local SD	Bellefontaine
291	130	Indian Lake Local SD	Lewistown
291	130	Sheffield-Sheffield Lake City	Sheffield Vlg
293	128	Ironton City SD	Ironton
294	127	Genoa Area Local SD	Genoa
294	127	Madison-Plains Local SD	London
294	127	Orrville City SD	Orrville
297	125	Elgin Local SD	Marion
297	125	Meigs Local SD	Pomeroy
299	124	Coldwater Ex Vill SD	Coldwater
299	124	Rolling Hills Local SD	Byesville

301	123	Struthers City SD	Struthers
302	122	Coshocton City SD	Coshocton
302	122	Indian Valley Local SD	Gnadenhutten
304	121	Clermont-Northeastern Local SD	Batavia
305	120	Alexander Local SD	Albany
305	120	Saint Clairsville-Richland City	St Clairsville
307	119	Fairless Local SD	Navarre
307	119	Girard City SD	Girard
307	119	Ontario Local SD	Mansfield
307	119	Streetsboro City SD	Streetsboro
311	118	Brookfield Local SD	Brookfield
311	118	Bucyrus City SD	Bucyrus
311	118	Northwest Local SD	Mc Dermott
311	118	Urbana City SD	Urbana
315	117	Avon Local SD	Avon
315	117	Clinton-Massie Local SD	Clarksville
315	117	North Fork Local SD	Utica
315	117	Otsego Local SD	Tontogany
315	117	Wickliffe City SD	Wickliffe
320	116	Milton-Union Ex Vill SD	West Milton
320	116	Pike-Delta-York Local SD	Delta
320	116	Preble Shawnee Local SD	Camden
323	115	Fairland Local SD	Proctorville
323	115	Fostoria City SD	Fostoria
323	115	Licking Valley Local SD	Newark
326	114	Waverly City SD	Waverly
327	113	Keystone Local SD	Lagrange
327	113	Mariemont City SD	Cincinnati
327	113	Minford Local SD	Minford
327	113	Sandy Valley Local SD	Magnolia
327	113	Washington-Nile Local SD	West Portsmouth
332	111	Carlisle Local SD	Carlisle
333	110	Bellaire Local SD	Bellaire
334	109	Jonathan Alder Local SD	Plain City
334	109	Wellington Ex Vill SD	Wellington
336	108	Plain Local SD	New Albany
336	108	Tuscarawas Valley Local SD	Zoarville
338	106	Highland Local SD	Sparta
339	105	South Point Local SD	South Point
340	104	Brookville Local SD	Brookville
340	104	Heath City SD	Heath
342	102	Greeneview Local SD	Jamestown
342	102	Labrae Local SD	Leavittsburg
342	102	Portsmouth City SD	Portsmouth
345	101	James A Garfield Local SD	Garrettsville
346	100	Campbell City SD	Campbell
346	100	New Lexington City SD	New Lexington
346	100	Rock Hill Local SD	Ironton
349	98	Black River Local SD	Sullivan
350	97	Clearview Local SD	Lorain
350	97	Westfall Local SD	Williamsport
352	96	Southeast Local SD	Apple Creek
352	96	Woodridge Local SD	Peninsula
354	95	Eastern Local SD	Sardinia
354	95	Madison Local SD	Middletown
354	95	Zane Trace Local SD	Chillicothe
357	93	Blanchester Local SD	Blanchester
357	93	East Clinton Local SD	Lees Creek
357	93	Northridge Local SD	Dayton
360	92	Batavia Local SD	Batavia
360	92	Licking Heights Local SD	Summit Station
360	92	North College Hill City SD	Cincinnati
363	89	Newton Falls Ex Vill SD	Newton Falls
363	89	Scioto Valley Local SD	Piketon
365	88	Painesville City Local SD	Painesville
366	87	Amanda-Clearcreek Local SD	Amanda
366	87	Athens City SD	The Plains
368	78	Wellston City SD	Wellston
369	63	East Holmes Local SD	Berlin
370	31	Electronic Classroom of Tomorrow	Columbus

High School Drop-out Rate

Rank	Percent	District Name	City
1	32.9	Youngstown City SD	Youngstown
2	19.6	Cleveland Municipal SD	Cleveland
3	17.8	Canton City SD	Canton
4	15.1	East Cleveland City SD	East Cleveland
5	12.4	Lima City SD	Lima
6	10.1	Columbus City SD	Columbus
7	9.7	Northridge Local SD	Dayton
8	8.7	Mad River Local SD	Dayton
9	8.6	Newark City SD	Newark
9	8.6	Painesville City Local SD	Painesville
11	8.4	Mansfield City SD	Mansfield
12	8.3	Norwood City SD	Norwood
13	8.2	New Richmond Ex Vill SD	New Richmond
14	8.1	Zanesville City SD	Zanesville
15	8.0	Springfield City SD	Springfield
16	7.9	Bedford City SD	Bedford
16	7.9	Whitehall City SD	Whitehall
18	7.8	Toledo City SD	Toledo
19	7.5	Cincinnati City SD	Cincinnati
19	7.5	Hamilton City SD	Hamilton
19	7.5	South-Western City SD	Grove City
22	7.1	Mount Healthy City SD	Cincinnati
23	7.0	Maple Heights City SD	Maple Heights
24	6.9	Western Brown Local SD	Mount Orab
25	6.8	Defiance City SD	Defiance
25	6.8	Warren City SD	Warren
25	6.8	Xenia Community City SD	Xenia
28	6.7	Ashtabula Area City SD	Ashtabula
28	6.7	Elyria City SD	Elyria
28	6.7	Greenfield Ex Vill SD	Greenfield
31	6.6	Logan-Hocking Local SD	Logan
31	6.6	Lorain City SD	Lorain
31	6.6	Washington Local SD	Toledo
31	6.6	West Clermont Local SD	Cincinnati
35	6.5	Niles City SD	Niles
36	6.4	Akron City SD	Akron
36	6.4	Huber Heights City SD	Huber Heights
38	6.3	Barberton City SD	Barberton
39	6.2	Alliance City SD	Alliance
39	6.2	Fostoria City SD	Fostoria
39	6.2	Franklin City SD	Franklin
39	6.2	New Lexington City SD	New Lexington
39	6.2	Scioto Valley Local SD	Piketon
44	6.1	Goshen Local SD	Goshen
45	6.0	Eaton City SD	Eaton
45	6.0	Piqua City SD	Piqua
47	5.9	Clermont-Northeastern Local SD	Batavia
48	5.7	Parma City SD	Parma
48	5.7	Princeton City SD	Cincinnati
50	5.6	Hamilton Local SD	Columbus
50	5.6	Sandusky City SD	Sandusky
50	5.6	Trotwood-Madison City SD	Trotwood
53	5.5	Miami Trace Local SD	Washington Ct Hse
53	5.5	Morgan Local SD	McConnelsville
55	5.4	Bethel-Tate Local SD	Bethel
55	5.4	Circleville City SD	Circleville
55	5.4	East Liverpool City SD	East Liverpool
55	5.4	Union-Scioto Local SD	Chillicothe
59	5.3	Vinton County Local SD	Mc Arthur
60	5.2	Cleveland Hts-Univ Hts City SD	University Hgts
60	5.2	Madison Local SD	Mansfield
62	5.1	South Point Local SD	South Point
62	5.1	Winton Woods City SD	Cincinnati
64	5.0	Rolling Hills Local SD	Byesville
65	4.9	Bucyrus City SD	Bucyrus
65	4.9	Fremont City SD	Fremont
65	4.9	Marion City SD	Marion
65	4.9	Northwest Local SD	Cincinnati
65	4.9	Shelby City SD	Shelby
70	4.8	Mariemont City SD	Cincinnati
70	4.8	Waverly City SD	Waverly
72	4.7	Groveport Madison Local SD	Groveport
72	4.7	Ironton City SD	Ironton
72	4.7	Ravenna City SD	Ravenna
72	4.7	Steubenville City SD	Steubenville
76	4.6	Middletown City SD	Middletown
76	4.6	Teays Valley Local SD	Ashville
78	4.5	Athens City SD	The Plains
78	4.5	Ross Local SD	Hamilton
78	4.5	Southwest Local SD	Harrison
78	4.5	Troy City SD	Troy
82	4.4	Blanchester Local SD	Blanchester
82	4.4	Lancaster City SD	Lancaster
82	4.4	Madison Local SD	Madison
82	4.4	Portsmouth City SD	Portsmouth
86	4.3	Chillicothe City SD	Chillicothe
86	4.3	London City SD	London
86	4.3	Massillon City SD	Massillon
86	4.3	Port Clinton City SD	Port Clinton
86	4.3	Sidney City SD	Sidney
91	4.2	Bellaire Local SD	Bellaire
91	4.2	Indian Lake Local SD	Lewistown
91	4.2	Logan Elm Local SD	Circleville
91	4.2	North College Hill City SD	Cincinnati
91	4.2	Willoughby-Eastlake City SD	Willoughby
96	4.1	Batavia Local SD	Batavia
96	4.1	Orrville City SD	Orrville
96	4.1	Tecumseh Local SD	New Carlisle
96	4.1	Wooster City SD	Wooster
100	4.0	Alexander Local SD	Albany
100	4.0	Bellefontaine City SD	Bellefontaine
100	4.0	Gallia County Local SD	Gallipolis
100	4.0	Little Miami Local SD	Morrow
100	4.0	Rossford Ex Vill SD	Rossford
100	4.0	Washington-Nile Local SD	West Portsmouth
106	3.9	Buckeye Local SD	Ashtabula
106	3.9	Greenon Local SD	Springfield
106	3.9	Labrae Local SD	Leavittsburg
106	3.9	Licking Valley Local SD	Newark
110	3.8	Adams County-Ohio Valley Local SD	West Union
110	3.8	Findlay City SD	Findlay
110	3.8	Minerva Local SD	Minerva
110	3.8	Tiffin City SD	Tiffin
110	3.8	Wellston City SD	Wellston
110	3.8	West Carrollton City SD	West Carrollton
116	3.7	Delaware City SD	Delaware
117	3.6	Kent City SD	Kent
117	3.6	Lakewood City SD	Lakewood
117	3.6	Madison Local SD	Middletown
117	3.6	North Fork Local SD	Utica
117	3.6	Oregon City SD	Oregon
117	3.6	Swanton Local SD	Swanton
117	3.6	Washington Court House City SD	Washington Ct Hse
124	3.5	Hillsboro City SD	Hillsboro
124	3.5	Reynoldsburg City SD	Reynoldsburg
124	3.5	Wellington Ex Vill SD	Wellington
124	3.5	Westfall Local SD	Williamsport
128	3.4	Fairland Local SD	Proctorville
128	3.4	Napoleon Area City SD	Napoleon
128	3.4	Pike-Delta-York Local SD	Delta
128	3.4	Springfield Local SD	Akron
128	3.4	Switzerland of Ohio Local SD	Woodsfield
128	3.4	Vermilion Local SD	Vermilion
134	3.3	Anthony Wayne Local SD	Whitehouse
134	3.3	Fairborn City SD	Fairborn
134	3.3	Midview Local SD	Grafton
137	3.2	Cambridge City SD	Cambridge
137	3.2	Galion City SD	Galion
137	3.2	Gallipolis City SD	Gallipolis
137	3.2	Jonathan Alder Local SD	Plain City
137	3.2	Valley View Local SD	Germantown
137	3.2	Willard City SD	Willard
143	3.1	Bryan City SD	Bryan
143	3.1	Elida Local SD	Elida
143	3.1	Salem City SD	Salem
143	3.1	Southeast Local SD	Apple Creek
143	3.1	Talawanda City SD	Oxford
143	3.1	Tri-Valley Local SD	Dresden
149	3.0	Beaver Local SD	Lisbon
149	3.0	Brookville Local SD	Brookville
149	3.0	Clearview Local SD	Lorain
149	3.0	Fairfield City SD	Fairfield
149	3.0	Northwest Local SD	Mc Dermott
149	3.0	Struthers City SD	Struthers
155	2.9	Northeastern Local SD	Springfield
155	2.9	Painesville Township Local SD	Painesville
155	2.9	Rock Hill Local SD	Ironton
155	2.9	Vandalia-Butler City SD	Vandalia
155	2.9	West Holmes Local SD	Millersburg
160	2.8	Amanda-Clearcreek Local SD	Amanda
160	2.8	Bellevue City SD	Bellevue
160	2.8	Clear Fork Valley Local SD	Bellville
160	2.8	Coventry Local SD	Akron
160	2.8	Edgewood City SD	Trenton
160	2.8	Franklin Local SD	Duncan Falls
160	2.8	Harrison Hills City SD	Hopedale
160	2.8	Kenton City SD	Kenton
160	2.8	Urbana City SD	Urbana
160	2.8	Van Wert City SD	Van Wert
170	2.7	Buckeye Local SD	Rayland
170	2.7	Celina City SD	Celina
170	2.7	Clark-Shawnee Local SD	Springfield
170	2.7	Conneaut Area City SD	Conneaut
170	2.7	Geneva Area City SD	Geneva
170	2.7	Heath City SD	Heath
170	2.7	Highland Local SD	Sparta
170	2.7	Milford Ex Vill SD	Milford
170	2.7	Preble Shawnee Local SD	Camden
170	2.7	Tuscarawas Valley Local SD	Zoarville
170	2.7	Westerville City SD	Westerville
181	2.6	Berea City SD	Berea
181	2.6	Crestwood Local SD	Mantua
181	2.6	Cuyahoga Falls City SD	Cuyahoga Falls
181	2.6	East Muskingum Local SD	New Concord
181	2.6	Hilliard City SD	Hilliard
181	2.6	Louisville City SD	Louisville
181	2.6	Milton-Union Ex Vill SD	West Milton
181	2.6	Nordonia Hills City SD	Northfield
181	2.6	Triway Local SD	Wooster
181	2.6	Upper Sandusky Ex Vill SD	Upper Sandusky
191	2.5	Indian Valley Local SD	Gnadenhutten
191	2.5	Jackson City SD	Jackson
191	2.5	North Ridgeville City SD	N Ridgeville
191	2.5	Southeast Local SD	Ravenna
191	2.5	Southwest Licking Local SD	Etna
196	2.4	Bath Local SD	Lima
196	2.4	Big Walnut Local SD	Galena
196	2.4	Black River Local SD	Sullivan
196	2.4	Cloverleaf Local SD	Lodi
196	2.4	East Clinton Local SD	Lees Creek
196	2.4	Hubbard Ex Vill SD	Hubbard
196	2.4	Lakewood Local SD	Hebron
196	2.4	Maumee City SD	Maumee

196	2.4	Mount Vernon City SD	Mount Vernon
196	2.4	Norwalk City SD	Norwalk
196	2.4	Ottawa-Glandorf Local SD	Ottawa
196	2.4	Plain Local SD	Canton
196	2.4	Plain Local SD	New Albany
196	2.4	Saint Clairsville-Richland City	St Clairsville
196	2.4	Sandy Valley Local SD	Magnolia
196	2.4	Zane Trace Local SD	Chillicothe
212	2.3	Benjamin Logan Local SD	Bellefontaine
212	2.3	Buckeye Local SD	Medina
212	2.3	Edison Local SD	Hammondsville
212	2.3	New Philadelphia City SD	New Philadelphia
212	2.3	Newton Falls Ex Vill SD	Newton Falls
212	2.3	North Olmsted City SD	North Olmsted
212	2.3	River View Local SD	Warsaw
212	2.3	Sheffield-Sheffield Lake City	Sheffield Vlg
212	2.3	Wapakoneta City SD	Wapakoneta
212	2.3	Warren Local SD	Vincent
212	2.3	Woodridge Local SD	Peninsula
223	2.2	Madison-Plains Local SD	London
223	2.2	Manchester Local SD	Akron
223	2.2	Maysville Local SD	Zanesville
223	2.2	Union Local SD	Morristown
223	2.2	Westlake City SD	Westlake
228	2.1	Avon Local SD	Avon
228	2.1	Bowling Green City SD	Bowling Green
228	2.1	Claymont City SD	Dennison
228	2.1	Eastwood Local SD	Pemberville
228	2.1	Greeneview Local SD	Jamestown
228	2.1	Greenville City SD	Greenville
228	2.1	Jefferson Area Local SD	Jefferson
228	2.1	Wauseon Ex Vill SD	Wauseon
236	2.0	Ashland City SD	Ashland
236	2.0	Dover City SD	Dover
236	2.0	Huron City SD	Huron
236	2.0	Licking Heights Local SD	Summit Station
236	2.0	Minford Local SD	Minford
236	2.0	Otsego Local SD	Tontogany
242	1.9	Austintown Local SD	Youngstown
242	1.9	Forest Hills Local SD	Cincinnati
242	1.9	Girard City SD	Girard
242	1.9	Lake Local SD	Millbury
242	1.9	Lebanon City SD	Lebanon
242	1.9	Northmont City SD	Englewood
242	1.9	Sugarcreek Local SD	Bellbrook
249	1.8	Fairless Local SD	Navarre
249	1.8	Firelands Local SD	Oberlin
249	1.8	Genoa Area Local SD	Genoa
249	1.8	Three Rivers Local SD	Cleves
253	1.7	Beavercreek City SD	Beavercreek
253	1.7	Elgin Local SD	Marion
253	1.7	Field Local SD	Mogadore
253	1.7	Meigs Local SD	Pomeroy
253	1.7	Mentor Ex Vill SD	Mentor
253	1.7	Northwestern Local SD	Springfield
253	1.7	West Branch Local SD	Beloit
260	1.6	Benton Carroll Salem Local SD	Oak Harbor
260	1.6	Garfield Heights City SD	Garfield Hgts
260	1.6	Jackson Local SD	Massillon
260	1.6	Perkins Local SD	Sandusky
260	1.6	Revere Local SD	Bath
260	1.6	Stow-Munroe Falls City SD	Stow
260	1.6	Streetsboro City SD	Streetsboro
260	1.6	Sylvania City SD	Sylvania
268	1.5	Brookfield Local SD	Brookfield
268	1.5	Buckeye Valley Local SD	Delaware
268	1.5	Fairfield Union Local SD	W Rushville
268	1.5	Indian Creek Local SD	Wintersville
268	1.5	Norton City SD	Norton
268	1.5	Paulding Ex Vill SD	Paulding
268	1.5	South Euclid-Lyndhurst City SD	Lyndhurst
268	1.5	Wadsworth City SD	Wadsworth
268	1.5	Wickliffe City SD	Wickliffe
268	1.5	Worthington City SD	Worthington
278	1.4	Brunswick City SD	Brunswick
278	1.4	Canal Winchester Local SD	Canal Winchester
278	1.4	Clinton-Massie Local SD	Clarksville
278	1.4	Clyde-Green Springs Ex Vill SD	Clyde
278	1.4	Dayton City SD	Dayton
278	1.4	Eastern Local SD	Sardinia
278	1.4	Finneytown Local SD	Cincinnati
278	1.4	Howland Local SD	Warren
278	1.4	Kings Local SD	Kings Mills
278	1.4	Loveland City SD	Loveland
278	1.4	Mason City SD	Mason
278	1.4	Miamisburg City SD	Miamisburg
278	1.4	Northern Local SD	Thornville
278	1.4	Pickerington Local SD	Pickerington
278	1.4	Shawnee Local SD	Lima
278	1.4	Springboro Community City SD	Springboro
278	1.4	Sycamore Community City SD	Cincinnati
278	1.4	Tallmadge City SD	Tallmadge

296	1.3	Avon Lake City SD	Avon Lake
296	1.3	Dublin City SD	Dublin
296	1.3	Fairview Park City SD	Fairview Park
296	1.3	Graham Local SD	Saint Paris
296	1.3	Lake Local SD	Hartville
296	1.3	Marysville Ex Vill SD	Marysville
296	1.3	Mayfield City SD	Highland Hgts
296	1.3	Oak Hills Local SD	Cincinnati
296	1.3	Olmsted Falls City SD	Olmsted Falls
296	1.3	Tipp City Ex Vill SD	Tipp City
306	1.2	Bexley City SD	Bexley
306	1.2	Boardman Local SD	Youngstown
306	1.2	Champion Local SD	Warren
306	1.2	Copley-Fairlawn City SD	Copley
306	1.2	Marlington Local SD	Alliance
306	1.2	Ontario Local SD	Mansfield
306	1.2	Strongsville City SD	Strongsville
313	1.1	Carlisle Local SD	Carlisle
313	1.1	Centerville City SD	Centerville
313	1.1	Lakeview Local SD	Cortland
313	1.1	Liberty Local SD	Youngstown
313	1.1	Marietta City SD	Marietta
313	1.1	North Canton City SD	North Canton
313	1.1	Olentangy Local SD	Lewis Center
313	1.1	Twinsburg City SD	Twinsburg
321	1.0	Berlin-Milan Local SD	Milan
321	1.0	Coshocton City SD	Coshocton
321	1.0	Highland Local SD	Medina
321	1.0	Upper Arlington City SD	Upper Arlington
325	0.9	Aurora City SD	Aurora
325	0.9	Carrollton Ex Vill SD	Carrollton
325	0.9	Coldwater Ex Vill SD	Coldwater
325	0.9	Hudson City SD	Hudson
325	0.9	Kenston Local SD	Chagrin Falls
325	0.9	Kettering City SD	Kettering
325	0.9	Keystone Local SD	Lagrange
325	0.9	Lexington Local SD	Lexington
333	0.8	Brecksville-Broadview Heights	Brecksville
333	0.8	Chagrin Falls Ex Vill SD	Chagrin Falls
333	0.8	North Royalton City SD	N Royalton
333	0.8	Solon City SD	Solon
333	0.8	Wilmington City SD	Wilmington
338	0.7	Canton Local SD	Canton
338	0.7	Northwest Local SD	Canal Fulton
338	0.7	Oakwood City SD	Dayton
338	0.7	Orange City SD	Cleveland
338	0.7	Poland Local SD	Poland
338	0.7	Springfield Local SD	Holland
344	0.6	Beachwood City SD	Beachwood
344	0.6	Gahanna-Jefferson City SD	Gahanna
344	0.6	James A Garfield Local SD	Garrettsville
344	0.6	Medina City SD	Medina
344	0.6	Perrysburg Ex Vill SD	Perrysburg
344	0.6	River Valley Local SD	Caledonia
344	0.6	West Geauga Local SD	Chesterland
351	0.5	Amherst Ex Vill SD	Amherst
351	0.5	Bay Village City SD	Bay Village
351	0.5	Indian Hill Ex Vill SD	Cincinnati
351	0.5	Lakota Local SD	Liberty Twp
351	0.5	Perry Local SD	Massillon
351	0.5	Rocky River City SD	Rocky River
351	0.5	Saint Marys City SD	Saint Marys
351	0.5	West Muskingum Local SD	Zanesville
359	0.4	East Holmes Local SD	Berlin
359	0.4	Green Local SD	Green
361	0.3	Canfield Local SD	Canfield
361	0.3	Granville Ex Vill SD	Granville
363	0.2	Chardon Local SD	Chardon
364	0.1	Shaker Heights City SD	Shaker Heights
365	0.0	Campbell City SD	Campbell
365	0.0	Electronic Classroom of Tomorrow	Columbus
365	0.0	Euclid City SD	Euclid
365	0.0	Perry Local SD	Perry
365	0.0	Warrensville Heights City SD	Warrensville Hgts
365	0.0	Wyoming City SD	Wyoming

Oklahoma

Oklahoma Public School Educational Profile

Category	Value	Category	Value
Schools *(2002-2003)*	1,821	**Diploma Recipients** *(2002-2003)*	36,852
Instructional Level		White, Non-Hispanic	25,385
Primary	979	Black, Non-Hispanic	3,299
Middle	341	Asian/Pacific Islander	650
High	467	American Indian/Alaskan Native	5,956
Other Level	34	Hispanic	1,562
Curriculum		**High School Drop-out Rate** (%) *(2000-2001)*	5.2
Regular	1,817	White, Non-Hispanic	4.6
Special Education	1	Black, Non-Hispanic	7.9
Vocational	0	Asian/Pacific Islander	3.9
Alternative	3	American Indian/Alaskan Native	4.8
Type		Hispanic	10.6
Magnet	0	**Staff** *(2002-2003)*	74,179.7
Charter	10	Teachers	40,469.2
Title I Eligible	1,192	Average Salary ($)	33,277
School-wide Title I	849	Librarians/Media Specialists	1,030.3
Students *(2002-2003)*	624,548	Guidance Counselors	1,561.5
Gender (%)		**Ratios** *(2002-2003)*	
Male	51.5	Student/Teacher Ratio	15.4 to 1
Female	48.5	Student/Librarian Ratio	606.2 to 1
Race/Ethnicity (%)		Student/Counselor Ratio	400.0 to 1
White, Non-Hispanic	62.6	**Current Spending** *($ per student in FY 2001)*	6,229
Black, Non-Hispanic	10.9	Instruction	3,600
Asian/Pacific Islander	1.5	Support Services	2,223
American Indian/Alaskan Native	17.9	**College Entrance Exam Scores** *(2003)*	
Hispanic	7.0	Scholastic Aptitude Test (SAT)	
Classification (%)		Participation Rate (%)	8
Individual Education Program (IEP)	14.6	Mean SAT I Verbal Score	569
Migrant	0.0	Mean SAT I Math Score	562
English Language Learner (ELL)	6.4	American College Testing Program (ACT)	
Eligible for Free Lunch Program	41.1	Participation Rate (%)	69
Eligible for Reduced-Price Lunch Program	10.3	Average Composite Score	20.5

***Note:** For an explanation of data, please refer to the User's Guide in the front of the book; n/a indicates data not available*

Oklahoma NAEP 2003 Test Scores

Reading			Mathematics		
Grade/Category	**Value**	**Rank**	**Grade/Category**	**Value**	**Rank**
4th Grade			**4th Grade**		
Average Proficiency	213.6 (1.2)	38/51	Average Proficiency	229.1 (1.0)	39/51
Proficiency by Gender/Race/Ethnicity			Proficiency by Gender/Race/Ethnicity		
Male	210.1 (1.5)	38/51	Male	230.3 (1.1)	40/51
Female	217.0 (1.5)	41/51	Female	227.9 (1.2)	40/51
White, Non-Hispanic	220.4 (1.3)	47/51	White, Non-Hispanic	234.7 (1.0)	48/51
Black, Non-Hispanic	195.4 (2.5)	30/42	Black, Non-Hispanic	211.2 (2.0)	33/42
Asian, Non-Hispanic	199.8 (3.0)	29/41	Asian, Non-Hispanic	219.5 (2.3)	27/43
American Indian, Non-Hispanic	n/a	n/a	American Indian, Non-Hispanic	246.6 (4.8)	14/26
Hispanic	205.9 (2.9)	3/12	Hispanic	224.7 (1.8)	2/12
Proficiency by Class Size			Proficiency by Class Size		
Less than 16 Students	196.7 (4.3)	33/45	Less than 16 Students	215.8 (3.0)	38/47
16 to 18 Students	206.1 (4.4)	39/48	16 to 18 Students	224.2 (2.6)	38/48
19 to 20 Students	218.6 (3.3)	27/50	19 to 20 Students	232.8 (1.8)	33/50
21 to 25 Students	217.3 (1.3)	39/51	21 to 25 Students	231.8 (1.2)	38/51
Greater than 25 Students	*218.8 (10.7)*	26/49	Greater than 25 Students	*230.3 (5.6)*	35/49
Percent Attaining Achievement Levels			Percent Attaining Achievement Levels		
Below Basic	39.7 (1.7)	16/51	Below Basic	26.4 (1.5)	17/51
Basic or Above	60.3 (1.7)	36/51	Basic or Above	73.6 (1.5)	35/51
Proficient or Above	25.9 (1.2)	41/51	Proficient or Above	22.6 (1.4)	45/51
Advanced or Above	4.7 (0.6)	43/51	Advanced or Above	1.2 (0.3)	47/51
8th Grade			**8th Grade**		
Average Proficiency	261.7 (0.9)	31/51	Average Proficiency	271.9 (1.1)	37/51
Proficiency by Gender/Race/Ethnicity			Proficiency by Gender/Race/Ethnicity		
Male	255.6 (1.2)	32/51	Male	272.2 (1.4)	38/51
Female	267.6 (1.2)	32/51	Female	271.6 (1.2)	36/51
White, Non-Hispanic	266.8 (1.1)	41/50	White, Non-Hispanic	278.4 (1.0)	42/50
Black, Non-Hispanic	240.3 (4.0)	31/41	Black, Non-Hispanic	249.2 (3.4)	28/41
Asian, Non-Hispanic	250.4 (2.8)	9/37	Asian, Non-Hispanic	257.6 (3.0)	24/37
American Indian, Non-Hispanic	n/a	n/a	American Indian, Non-Hispanic	n/a	n/a
Hispanic	256.7 (2.3)	1/10	Hispanic	265.5 (2.4)	1/11
Proficiency by Parents Highest Level of Ed.			Proficiency by Parents Highest Level of Ed.		
Did Not Finish High School	251.9 (2.2)	5/50	Did Not Finish High School	253.5 (2.7)	37/50
Graduated High School	252.2 (1.9)	32/50	Graduated High School	261.9 (1.7)	40/50
Some Education After High School	269.5 (1.3)	19/50	Some Education After High School	275.3 (1.4)	39/50
Graduated College	269.0 (1.4)	34/50	Graduated College	282.1 (1.3)	37/50
Percent Attaining Achievement Levels			Percent Attaining Achievement Levels		
Below Basic	25.8 (1.5)	21/51	Below Basic	35.5 (1.5)	16/51
Basic or Above	74.2 (1.5)	31/51	Basic or Above	64.5 (1.5)	36/51
Proficient or Above	29.8 (1.3)	33/51	Proficient or Above	20.1 (1.1)	43/51
Advanced or Above	2.0 (0.3)	35/51	Advanced or Above	2.0 (0.4)	45/51

Note: *For an explanation of data, please refer to the User's Guide in the front of the book; values in italics indicate that the nature of the sample does not allow accurate determination of the variability of the statistic; n/a indicates data not available*

Beckham County

Elk City

222 W Broadway Ave • Elk City, OK 73644-4742
(580) 225-0175 • http://www.elkcityschools.com/
Grade Span: PK-12; **Agency Type:** 1
Schools: 6
3 Primary; 2 Middle; 1 High; 0 Other Level
6 Regular; 0 Special Education; 0 Vocational; 0 Alternative
0 Magnet; 0 Charter; 0 Title I Eligible; 0 School-wide Title I
Students: 2,124 (49.9% male; 50.1% female)
Individual Education Program: 236 (11.1%);
English Language Learner: 113 (5.3%); Migrant: n/a
Eligible for Free Lunch Program: 808 (38.0%)
Eligible for Reduced-Price Lunch Program: 184 (8.7%)
Teachers: 148.7 (14.3 to 1)
Librarians/Media Specialists: 3.0 (708.0 to 1)
Guidance Counselors: 7.4 (287.0 to 1)
Current Spending: ($ per student per year):
Total: $5,614; Instruction: $3,635; Support Services: $1,696
Enrollment, Drop-out Rates and Diploma Recipients by Race/Ethnicity

Category	Total	White	Black	Asian	AIAN	Hisp.
Enrollment (%)	100.0	75.7	3.6	0.5	10.9	9.3
Drop-out Rate (%)	8.0	6.3	18.8	0.0	12.0	25.0
H.S. Diplomas (#)	123	111	3	1	4	4

Bryan County

Durant

PO Box 1160 • Durant, OK 74702-1160
(580) 924-1276 • http://www.durantisd.org/
Grade Span: PK-12; **Agency Type:** 1
Schools: 7
4 Primary; 2 Middle; 1 High; 0 Other Level
7 Regular; 0 Special Education; 0 Vocational; 0 Alternative
0 Magnet; 0 Charter; 4 Title I Eligible; 4 School-wide Title I
Students: 3,126 (51.6% male; 48.4% female)
Individual Education Program: 422 (13.5%);
English Language Learner: 54 (1.7%); Migrant: n/a
Eligible for Free Lunch Program: 1,539 (49.2%)
Eligible for Reduced-Price Lunch Program: 363 (11.6%)
Teachers: 193.0 (16.2 to 1)
Librarians/Media Specialists: 6.0 (521.0 to 1)
Guidance Counselors: 9.3 (336.1 to 1)
Current Spending: ($ per student per year):
Total: $5,820; Instruction: $3,622; Support Services: $1,775
Enrollment, Drop-out Rates and Diploma Recipients by Race/Ethnicity

Category	Total	White	Black	Asian	AIAN	Hisp.
Enrollment (%)	100.0	65.1	1.9	1.1	29.1	2.8
Drop-out Rate (%)	7.6	11.0	0.0	0.0	0.0	4.3
H.S. Diplomas (#)	152	104	1	2	40	5

Caddo County

Anadarko

1400 S Mission St • Anadarko, OK 73005-5813
(405) 247-6605
Grade Span: PK-12; **Agency Type:** 1
Schools: 5
3 Primary; 1 Middle; 1 High; 0 Other Level
5 Regular; 0 Special Education; 0 Vocational; 0 Alternative
0 Magnet; 0 Charter; 5 Title I Eligible; 5 School-wide Title I
Students: 2,183 (50.2% male; 49.8% female)
Individual Education Program: 416 (19.1%);
English Language Learner: 273 (12.5%); Migrant: n/a
Eligible for Free Lunch Program: 1,428 (65.4%)
Eligible for Reduced-Price Lunch Program: 258 (11.8%)
Teachers: 151.8 (14.4 to 1)
Librarians/Media Specialists: 5.0 (436.6 to 1)
Guidance Counselors: 6.0 (363.8 to 1)
Current Spending: ($ per student per year):
Total: $6,527; Instruction: $3,788; Support Services: $2,316
Enrollment, Drop-out Rates and Diploma Recipients by Race/Ethnicity

Category	Total	White	Black	Asian	AIAN	Hisp.
Enrollment (%)	100.0	26.3	5.6	0.0	61.4	6.6
Drop-out Rate (%)	7.0	4.3	6.5	0.0	0.7	112.5
H.S. Diplomas (#)	115	48	4	0	56	7

Canadian County

El Reno

PO Box 580 • El Reno, OK 73036-0580
(405) 262-1703 • http://www.elreno.k12.ok.us/
Grade Span: PK-12; **Agency Type:** 1
Schools: 7
4 Primary; 1 Middle; 1 High; 1 Other Level
7 Regular; 0 Special Education; 0 Vocational; 0 Alternative
0 Magnet; 0 Charter; 5 Title I Eligible; 5 School-wide Title I
Students: 2,628 (51.9% male; 48.1% female)
Individual Education Program: 389 (14.8%);
English Language Learner: 224 (8.5%); Migrant: n/a
Eligible for Free Lunch Program: 1,409 (53.6%)
Eligible for Reduced-Price Lunch Program: 306 (11.6%)
Teachers: 171.1 (15.4 to 1)
Librarians/Media Specialists: 4.0 (657.0 to 1)
Guidance Counselors: 7.0 (375.4 to 1)
Current Spending: ($ per student per year):
Total: $5,732; Instruction: $3,250; Support Services: $2,119
Enrollment, Drop-out Rates and Diploma Recipients by Race/Ethnicity

Category	Total	White	Black	Asian	AIAN	Hisp.
Enrollment (%)	100.0	69.7	7.3	0.5	13.5	8.9
Drop-out Rate (%)	3.6	3.6	1.5	0.0	3.9	6.3
H.S. Diplomas (#)	173	128	12	3	21	9

Mustang

906 S Heights Dr • Mustang, OK 73064-3542
(405) 376-2461
Grade Span: KG-12; **Agency Type:** 1
Schools: 9
5 Primary; 2 Middle; 1 High; 1 Other Level
9 Regular; 0 Special Education; 0 Vocational; 0 Alternative
0 Magnet; 0 Charter; 4 Title I Eligible; 0 School-wide Title I
Students: 6,802 (51.2% male; 48.8% female)
Individual Education Program: 610 (9.0%);
English Language Learner: 348 (5.1%); Migrant: n/a
Eligible for Free Lunch Program: 722 (10.6%)
Eligible for Reduced-Price Lunch Program: 564 (8.3%)
Teachers: 396.9 (17.1 to 1)
Librarians/Media Specialists: 8.9 (764.3 to 1)
Guidance Counselors: 20.0 (340.1 to 1)
Current Spending: ($ per student per year):
Total: $4,829; Instruction: $2,777; Support Services: $1,745
Enrollment, Drop-out Rates and Diploma Recipients by Race/Ethnicity

Category	Total	White	Black	Asian	AIAN	Hisp.
Enrollment (%)	100.0	84.0	1.6	5.7	5.6	3.2
Drop-out Rate (%)	3.4	3.6	0.0	0.8	2.7	6.4
H.S. Diplomas (#)	456	375	7	32	28	14

Piedmont

713 Piedmont Rd N • Piedmont, OK 73078-9248
(405) 373-2311
Grade Span: KG-12; **Agency Type:** 1
Schools: 4
2 Primary; 1 Middle; 1 High; 0 Other Level
4 Regular; 0 Special Education; 0 Vocational; 0 Alternative
0 Magnet; 0 Charter; 1 Title I Eligible; 0 School-wide Title I
Students: 1,549 (51.5% male; 48.5% female)
Individual Education Program: 164 (10.6%);
English Language Learner: 18 (1.2%); Migrant: n/a
Eligible for Free Lunch Program: 96 (6.2%)
Eligible for Reduced-Price Lunch Program: 50 (3.2%)
Teachers: 90.3 (17.2 to 1)
Librarians/Media Specialists: 3.0 (516.3 to 1)
Guidance Counselors: 3.0 (516.3 to 1)
Current Spending: ($ per student per year):
Total: $4,769; Instruction: $2,909; Support Services: $1,528
Enrollment, Drop-out Rates and Diploma Recipients by Race/Ethnicity

Category	Total	White	Black	Asian	AIAN	Hisp.
Enrollment (%)	100.0	81.1	3.0	1.5	12.3	2.1
Drop-out Rate (%)	3.6	4.3	0.0	0.0	0.0	0.0
H.S. Diplomas (#)	94	67	9	1	14	3

Yukon

600 Maple St • Yukon, OK 73099-2533
(405) 354-2587 • http://www.yukonps.com/
Grade Span: PK-12; **Agency Type:** 1
Schools: 10
7 Primary; 2 Middle; 1 High; 0 Other Level
10 Regular; 0 Special Education; 0 Vocational; 0 Alternative
0 Magnet; 0 Charter; 4 Title I Eligible; 0 School-wide Title I
Students: 5,792 (50.4% male; 49.6% female)
Individual Education Program: 576 (9.9%);
English Language Learner: 142 (2.5%); Migrant: n/a
Eligible for Free Lunch Program: 822 (14.2%)
Eligible for Reduced-Price Lunch Program: 371 (6.4%)
Teachers: 342.9 (16.9 to 1)
Librarians/Media Specialists: 8.0 (724.0 to 1)
Guidance Counselors: 16.7 (346.8 to 1)
Current Spending: ($ per student per year):
Total: $5,097; Instruction: $3,039; Support Services: $1,750

Enrollment, Drop-out Rates and Diploma Recipients by Race/Ethnicity

Category	Total	White	Black	Asian	AIAN	Hisp.
Enrollment (%)	100.0	87.6	1.1	2.4	5.2	3.7
Drop-out Rate (%)	2.3	2.3	6.3	0.0	4.1	0.0
H.S. Diplomas (#)	467	423	3	10	18	13

Carter County

Ardmore

PO Box 1709 • Ardmore, OK 73402-1709
(580) 226-7650 • http://www.ardmore.k12.ok.us/
Grade Span: PK-12; **Agency Type:** 1
Schools: 7
5 Primary; 1 Middle; 1 High; 0 Other Level
7 Regular; 0 Special Education; 0 Vocational; 0 Alternative
0 Magnet; 0 Charter; 6 Title I Eligible; 4 School-wide Title I
Students: 3,218 (52.1% male; 47.9% female)
Individual Education Program: 684 (21.3%);
English Language Learner: 67 (2.1%); Migrant: n/a
Eligible for Free Lunch Program: 1,803 (56.0%)
Eligible for Reduced-Price Lunch Program: 309 (9.6%)
Teachers: 203.3 (15.8 to 1)
Librarians/Media Specialists: 5.0 (643.6 to 1)
Guidance Counselors: 10.3 (312.4 to 1)
Current Spending: ($ per student per year):
Total: $6,551; Instruction: $3,445; Support Services: $2,653

Enrollment, Drop-out Rates and Diploma Recipients by Race/Ethnicity

Category	Total	White	Black	Asian	AIAN	Hisp.
Enrollment (%)	100.0	51.4	22.7	1.5	17.7	6.8
Drop-out Rate (%)	4.8	4.1	5.5	0.0	7.7	2.9
H.S. Diplomas (#)	183	106	42	3	21	11

Cherokee County

Tahlequah

PO Box 517 • Tahlequah, OK 74465-0517
(918) 458-4100 • http://www.tahlequah.k12.ok.us/
Grade Span: PK-12; **Agency Type:** 1
Schools: 6
3 Primary; 2 Middle; 1 High; 0 Other Level
6 Regular; 0 Special Education; 0 Vocational; 0 Alternative
0 Magnet; 0 Charter; 6 Title I Eligible; 4 School-wide Title I
Students: 3,731 (52.8% male; 47.2% female)
Individual Education Program: 577 (15.5%);
English Language Learner: 267 (7.2%); Migrant: n/a
Eligible for Free Lunch Program: 1,857 (49.8%)
Eligible for Reduced-Price Lunch Program: 507 (13.6%)
Teachers: 241.0 (15.5 to 1)
Librarians/Media Specialists: 6.0 (621.8 to 1)
Guidance Counselors: 13.0 (287.0 to 1)
Current Spending: ($ per student per year):
Total: $6,037; Instruction: $3,464; Support Services: $2,222

Enrollment, Drop-out Rates and Diploma Recipients by Race/Ethnicity

Category	Total	White	Black	Asian	AIAN	Hisp.
Enrollment (%)	100.0	33.4	1.8	0.5	57.5	6.8
Drop-out Rate (%)	5.9	5.5	15.8	0.0	6.3	3.2
H.S. Diplomas (#)	318	119	5	1	189	4

Cleveland County

Moore

1500 SE 4th St • Moore, OK 73160-8232
(405) 793-3188 • http://moore.k12.ok.us/
Grade Span: PK-12; **Agency Type:** 1
Schools: 27
20 Primary; 5 Middle; 2 High; 0 Other Level
27 Regular; 0 Special Education; 0 Vocational; 0 Alternative
0 Magnet; 0 Charter; 8 Title I Eligible; 2 School-wide Title I
Students: 18,458 (51.8% male; 48.2% female)
Individual Education Program: 2,306 (12.5%);
English Language Learner: 928 (5.0%); Migrant: n/a
Eligible for Free Lunch Program: 3,690 (20.0%)
Eligible for Reduced-Price Lunch Program: 1,589 (8.6%)
Teachers: 1,114.1 (16.6 to 1)
Librarians/Media Specialists: 27.8 (664.0 to 1)
Guidance Counselors: 50.9 (362.6 to 1)
Current Spending: ($ per student per year):
Total: $5,115; Instruction: $3,030; Support Services: $1,791

Enrollment, Drop-out Rates and Diploma Recipients by Race/Ethnicity

Category	Total	White	Black	Asian	AIAN	Hisp.
Enrollment (%)	100.0	70.9	5.6	4.1	14.0	5.4
Drop-out Rate (%)	5.3	5.6	7.4	1.2	4.2	7.2
H.S. Diplomas (#)	1,137	835	46	56	159	41

Noble

PO Box 499 • Noble, OK 73068-0499
(405) 872-3452 • http://www.nobleps.com/
Grade Span: PK-12; **Agency Type:** 1
Schools: 5
2 Primary; 2 Middle; 1 High; 0 Other Level
5 Regular; 0 Special Education; 0 Vocational; 0 Alternative
0 Magnet; 0 Charter; 5 Title I Eligible; 3 School-wide Title I
Students: 2,743 (51.3% male; 48.7% female)
Individual Education Program: 373 (13.6%);
English Language Learner: 0 (0.0%); Migrant: n/a
Eligible for Free Lunch Program: 987 (36.0%)
Eligible for Reduced-Price Lunch Program: 392 (14.3%)
Teachers: 166.7 (16.5 to 1)
Librarians/Media Specialists: 3.0 (914.3 to 1)
Guidance Counselors: 6.0 (457.2 to 1)
Current Spending: ($ per student per year):
Total: $5,088; Instruction: $2,983; Support Services: $1,845

Enrollment, Drop-out Rates and Diploma Recipients by Race/Ethnicity

Category	Total	White	Black	Asian	AIAN	Hisp.
Enrollment (%)	100.0	89.1	0.7	0.3	7.0	2.9
Drop-out Rate (%)	5.0	4.8	25.0	0.0	0.0	35.7
H.S. Diplomas (#)	165	152	0	1	11	1

Norman

131 S Flood Ave • Norman, OK 73069-5463
(405) 364-1339 • http://www.norman.k12.ok.us/
Grade Span: PK-12; **Agency Type:** 1
Schools: 23
16 Primary; 4 Middle; 3 High; 0 Other Level
23 Regular; 0 Special Education; 0 Vocational; 0 Alternative
0 Magnet; 0 Charter; 10 Title I Eligible; 6 School-wide Title I
Students: 12,657 (52.0% male; 48.0% female)
Individual Education Program: 1,813 (14.3%);
English Language Learner: 384 (3.0%); Migrant: n/a
Eligible for Free Lunch Program: 2,956 (23.4%)
Eligible for Reduced-Price Lunch Program: 821 (6.5%)
Teachers: 793.9 (15.9 to 1)
Librarians/Media Specialists: 24.0 (527.4 to 1)
Guidance Counselors: 38.2 (331.3 to 1)
Current Spending: ($ per student per year):
Total: $5,488; Instruction: $3,150; Support Services: $2,084

Enrollment, Drop-out Rates and Diploma Recipients by Race/Ethnicity

Category	Total	White	Black	Asian	AIAN	Hisp.
Enrollment (%)	100.0	78.4	6.6	3.1	7.2	4.7
Drop-out Rate (%)	6.8	6.6	7.3	4.2	10.5	7.5
H.S. Diplomas (#)	867	713	43	28	51	32

Comanche County

Lawton

PO Box 1009 • Lawton, OK 73502-1009
(580) 357-6900 • http://www.lawtonps.org/
Grade Span: PK-12; **Agency Type:** 1
Schools: 37
30 Primary; 4 Middle; 3 High; 0 Other Level
37 Regular; 0 Special Education; 0 Vocational; 0 Alternative
0 Magnet; 0 Charter; 16 Title I Eligible; 15 School-wide Title I
Students: 16,986 (51.5% male; 48.5% female)
Individual Education Program: 2,472 (14.6%);
English Language Learner: 1,553 (9.1%); Migrant: n/a
Eligible for Free Lunch Program: 6,432 (37.9%)
Eligible for Reduced-Price Lunch Program: 2,242 (13.2%)
Teachers: 1,033.8 (16.4 to 1)
Librarians/Media Specialists: 15.0 (1,132.4 to 1)
Guidance Counselors: 47.7 (356.1 to 1)
Current Spending: ($ per student per year):
Total: $5,660; Instruction: $3,117; Support Services: $2,198

Enrollment, Drop-out Rates and Diploma Recipients by Race/Ethnicity

Category	Total	White	Black	Asian	AIAN	Hisp.
Enrollment (%)	100.0	50.6	31.7	2.2	6.7	8.7
Drop-out Rate (%)	2.8	2.6	2.0	5.3	5.4	3.9
H.S. Diplomas (#)	894	476	257	40	28	93

Craig County

Vinita

PO Box 408 • Vinita, OK 74301-0408
(918) 256-6778 • http://www.vinita.k12.ok.us/
Grade Span: PK-12; **Agency Type:** 1
Schools: 5
2 Primary; 1 Middle; 1 High; 1 Other Level
4 Regular; 1 Special Education; 0 Vocational; 0 Alternative
0 Magnet; 0 Charter; 2 Title I Eligible; 2 School-wide Title I
Students: 1,674 (52.6% male; 47.4% female)

Individual Education Program: 302 (18.0%);
English Language Learner: 0 (0.0%); Migrant: n/a
Eligible for Free Lunch Program: 656 (39.2%)
Eligible for Reduced-Price Lunch Program: 249 (14.9%)
Teachers: 105.6 (15.9 to 1)
Librarians/Media Specialists: 4.0 (418.5 to 1)
Guidance Counselors: 5.0 (334.8 to 1)
Current Spending: ($ per student per year):
Total: $5,931; Instruction: $3,409; Support Services: $2,136
Enrollment, Drop-out Rates and Diploma Recipients by Race/Ethnicity

Category	Total	White	Black	Asian	AIAN	Hisp.
Enrollment (%)	100.0	46.8	2.3	0.5	49.2	1.1
Drop-out Rate (%)	7.7	7.9	15.4	33.3	6.5	14.3
H.S. Diplomas (#)	88	38	4	0	46	0

Creek County

Bristow
134 W 9th Ave • Bristow, OK 74010-2499
(918) 367-5555 • http://www.bristow.k12.ok.us/
Grade Span: PK-12; **Agency Type:** 1
Schools: 4
1 Primary; 2 Middle; 1 High; 0 Other Level
4 Regular; 0 Special Education; 0 Vocational; 0 Alternative
0 Magnet; 0 Charter; 3 Title I Eligible; 3 School-wide Title I
Students: 1,709 (51.7% male; 48.3% female)
Individual Education Program: 257 (15.0%);
English Language Learner: 9 (0.5%); Migrant: n/a
Eligible for Free Lunch Program: 1,048 (61.3%)
Eligible for Reduced-Price Lunch Program: 290 (17.0%)
Teachers: 107.8 (15.9 to 1)
Librarians/Media Specialists: 4.0 (427.3 to 1)
Guidance Counselors: 3.0 (569.7 to 1)
Current Spending: ($ per student per year):
Total: $5,548; Instruction: $3,203; Support Services: $1,954
Enrollment, Drop-out Rates and Diploma Recipients by Race/Ethnicity

Category	Total	White	Black	Asian	AIAN	Hisp.
Enrollment (%)	100.0	60.6	10.2	0.0	27.9	1.3
Drop-out Rate (%)	5.9	4.4	11.1	n/a	5.9	66.7
H.S. Diplomas (#)	90	60	6	0	24	0

Mannford
PO Box 100 • Mannford, OK 74044-0100
(918) 865-4062
Grade Span: PK-12; **Agency Type:** 1
Schools: 4
1 Primary; 2 Middle; 1 High; 0 Other Level
4 Regular; 0 Special Education; 0 Vocational; 0 Alternative
0 Magnet; 0 Charter; 4 Title I Eligible; 0 School-wide Title I
Students: 1,678 (51.9% male; 48.1% female)
Individual Education Program: 190 (11.3%);
English Language Learner: 0 (0.0%); Migrant: n/a
Eligible for Free Lunch Program: 524 (31.2%)
Eligible for Reduced-Price Lunch Program: 231 (13.8%)
Teachers: 92.7 (18.1 to 1)
Librarians/Media Specialists: 3.0 (559.3 to 1)
Guidance Counselors: 3.0 (559.3 to 1)
Current Spending: ($ per student per year):
Total: $4,660; Instruction: $2,633; Support Services: $1,803
Enrollment, Drop-out Rates and Diploma Recipients by Race/Ethnicity

Category	Total	White	Black	Asian	AIAN	Hisp.
Enrollment (%)	100.0	71.9	0.7	0.5	26.0	0.8
Drop-out Rate (%)	7.1	7.0	n/a	0.0	7.4	n/a
H.S. Diplomas (#)	94	73	0	0	21	0

Sapulpa
1 S Mission St • Sapulpa, OK 74066-4633
(918) 224-3400 • http://www.sapulpa.k12.ok.us/
Grade Span: PK-12; **Agency Type:** 1
Schools: 9
6 Primary; 1 Middle; 1 High; 1 Other Level
9 Regular; 0 Special Education; 0 Vocational; 0 Alternative
0 Magnet; 0 Charter; 5 Title I Eligible; 5 School-wide Title I
Students: 4,216 (50.7% male; 49.3% female)
Individual Education Program: 565 (13.4%);
English Language Learner: 82 (1.9%); Migrant: n/a
Eligible for Free Lunch Program: 1,627 (38.6%)
Eligible for Reduced-Price Lunch Program: 532 (12.6%)
Teachers: 251.0 (16.8 to 1)
Librarians/Media Specialists: 6.0 (702.7 to 1)
Guidance Counselors: 11.9 (354.3 to 1)
Current Spending: ($ per student per year):
Total: $5,501; Instruction: $3,131; Support Services: $2,016
Enrollment, Drop-out Rates and Diploma Recipients by Race/Ethnicity

Category	Total	White	Black	Asian	AIAN	Hisp.
Enrollment (%)	100.0	73.9	5.4	0.6	17.1	3.0
Drop-out Rate (%)	5.7	5.5	3.8	10.0	7.6	5.6
H.S. Diplomas (#)	275	232	4	3	33	3

Custer County

Clinton
PO Box 729 • Clinton, OK 73601-0729
(580) 323-1800 • http://www.clinton.k12.ok.us/
Grade Span: PK-12; **Agency Type:** 1
Schools: 5
2 Primary; 2 Middle; 1 High; 0 Other Level
5 Regular; 0 Special Education; 0 Vocational; 0 Alternative
0 Magnet; 0 Charter; 4 Title I Eligible; 4 School-wide Title I
Students: 1,853 (51.4% male; 48.6% female)
Individual Education Program: 216 (11.7%);
English Language Learner: 413 (22.3%); Migrant: n/a
Eligible for Free Lunch Program: 1,330 (71.8%)
Eligible for Reduced-Price Lunch Program: 309 (16.7%)
Teachers: 135.8 (13.6 to 1)
Librarians/Media Specialists: 5.0 (370.6 to 1)
Guidance Counselors: 6.0 (308.8 to 1)
Current Spending: ($ per student per year):
Total: $6,211; Instruction: $3,646; Support Services: $2,190
Enrollment, Drop-out Rates and Diploma Recipients by Race/Ethnicity

Category	Total	White	Black	Asian	AIAN	Hisp.
Enrollment (%)	100.0	50.5	11.2	0.9	9.0	28.4
Drop-out Rate (%)	3.3	1.7	7.8	0.0	8.6	3.4
H.S. Diplomas (#)	112	87	4	1	7	13

Weatherford
516 N Broadway St • Weatherford, OK 73096-4910
(580) 772-3327
Grade Span: PK-12; **Agency Type:** 1
Schools: 5
2 Primary; 2 Middle; 1 High; 0 Other Level
5 Regular; 0 Special Education; 0 Vocational; 0 Alternative
0 Magnet; 0 Charter; 4 Title I Eligible; 0 School-wide Title I
Students: 1,774 (50.7% male; 49.3% female)
Individual Education Program: 228 (12.9%);
English Language Learner: 69 (3.9%); Migrant: n/a
Eligible for Free Lunch Program: 578 (32.6%)
Eligible for Reduced-Price Lunch Program: 167 (9.4%)
Teachers: 117.2 (15.1 to 1)
Librarians/Media Specialists: 3.3 (537.6 to 1)
Guidance Counselors: 4.0 (443.5 to 1)
Current Spending: ($ per student per year):
Total: $5,895; Instruction: $3,324; Support Services: $2,139
Enrollment, Drop-out Rates and Diploma Recipients by Race/Ethnicity

Category	Total	White	Black	Asian	AIAN	Hisp.
Enrollment (%)	100.0	81.3	1.3	1.0	10.1	6.2
Drop-out Rate (%)	9.2	8.0	0.0	0.0	21.4	17.6
H.S. Diplomas (#)	162	146	2	1	10	3

Delaware County

Grove
PO Box 450789 • Grove, OK 74345-0789
(918) 786-3003
Grade Span: PK-12; **Agency Type:** 1
Schools: 4
1 Primary; 2 Middle; 1 High; 0 Other Level
4 Regular; 0 Special Education; 0 Vocational; 0 Alternative
0 Magnet; 0 Charter; 1 Title I Eligible; 1 School-wide Title I
Students: 2,375 (49.9% male; 50.1% female)
Individual Education Program: 352 (14.8%);
English Language Learner: 29 (1.2%); Migrant: n/a
Eligible for Free Lunch Program: 901 (37.9%)
Eligible for Reduced-Price Lunch Program: 337 (14.2%)
Teachers: 147.5 (16.1 to 1)
Librarians/Media Specialists: 3.0 (791.7 to 1)
Guidance Counselors: 9.0 (263.9 to 1)
Current Spending: ($ per student per year):
Total: $5,754; Instruction: $3,530; Support Services: $1,918
Enrollment, Drop-out Rates and Diploma Recipients by Race/Ethnicity

Category	Total	White	Black	Asian	AIAN	Hisp.
Enrollment (%)	100.0	69.0	0.7	0.7	28.2	1.5
Drop-out Rate (%)	9.1	10.9	0.0	150.0	1.0	0.0
H.S. Diplomas (#)	138	88	0	2	45	3

Jay

PO Box 630 • Jay, OK 74346-0630
(918) 253-4293 • http://www.brightok.net/~jayschl
Grade Span: PK-12; **Agency Type:** 1
Schools: 3
1 Primary; 1 Middle; 1 High; 0 Other Level
3 Regular; 0 Special Education; 0 Vocational; 0 Alternative
0 Magnet; 0 Charter; 3 Title I Eligible; 3 School-wide Title I
Students: 1,713 (51.4% male; 48.6% female)
Individual Education Program: 291 (17.0%);
English Language Learner: 238 (13.9%); Migrant: n/a
Eligible for Free Lunch Program: 951 (55.5%)
Eligible for Reduced-Price Lunch Program: 298 (17.4%)
Teachers: 113.4 (15.1 to 1)
Librarians/Media Specialists: 3.0 (571.0 to 1)
Guidance Counselors: 5.0 (342.6 to 1)
Current Spending: ($ per student per year):
Total: $5,902; Instruction: $3,444; Support Services: $2,033

Enrollment, Drop-out Rates and Diploma Recipients by Race/Ethnicity

Category	Total	White	Black	Asian	AIAN	Hisp.
Enrollment (%)	100.0	37.1	0.3	0.2	58.9	3.5
Drop-out Rate (%)	7.7	4.4	0.0	0.0	9.4	18.2
H.S. Diplomas (#)	96	27	0	1	65	3

Garfield County

Enid

500 S Independence St • Enid, OK 73701-5693
(580) 234-5270
Grade Span: PK-12; **Agency Type:** 1
Schools: 14
10 Primary; 3 Middle; 1 High; 0 Other Level
14 Regular; 0 Special Education; 0 Vocational; 0 Alternative
0 Magnet; 0 Charter; 8 Title I Eligible; 2 School-wide Title I
Students: 6,378 (51.3% male; 48.7% female)
Individual Education Program: 927 (14.5%);
English Language Learner: 557 (8.7%); Migrant: n/a
Eligible for Free Lunch Program: 2,630 (41.2%)
Eligible for Reduced-Price Lunch Program: 501 (7.9%)
Teachers: 429.1 (14.9 to 1)
Librarians/Media Specialists: 13.0 (490.6 to 1)
Guidance Counselors: 19.0 (335.7 to 1)
Current Spending: ($ per student per year):
Total: $5,862; Instruction: $3,535; Support Services: $2,051

Enrollment, Drop-out Rates and Diploma Recipients by Race/Ethnicity

Category	Total	White	Black	Asian	AIAN	Hisp.
Enrollment (%)	100.0	72.2	7.6	3.4	7.6	9.3
Drop-out Rate (%)	5.6	5.6	5.5	0.0	7.5	6.5
H.S. Diplomas (#)	406	314	23	15	35	19

Grady County

Chickasha

900 W Choctaw Ave • Chickasha, OK 73018-2213
(405) 222-6500
Grade Span: PK-12; **Agency Type:** 1
Schools: 7
4 Primary; 2 Middle; 1 High; 0 Other Level
7 Regular; 0 Special Education; 0 Vocational; 0 Alternative
0 Magnet; 0 Charter; 4 Title I Eligible; 4 School-wide Title I
Students: 2,840 (51.3% male; 48.7% female)
Individual Education Program: 458 (16.1%);
English Language Learner: 49 (1.7%); Migrant: n/a
Eligible for Free Lunch Program: 795 (28.0%)
Eligible for Reduced-Price Lunch Program: 176 (6.2%)
Teachers: 181.4 (15.7 to 1)
Librarians/Media Specialists: 5.5 (516.4 to 1)
Guidance Counselors: 8.0 (355.0 to 1)
Current Spending: ($ per student per year):
Total: $5,952; Instruction: $3,524; Support Services: $2,116

Enrollment, Drop-out Rates and Diploma Recipients by Race/Ethnicity

Category	Total	White	Black	Asian	AIAN	Hisp.
Enrollment (%)	100.0	74.9	12.7	0.6	7.1	4.7
Drop-out Rate (%)	4.3	3.3	5.7	0.0	12.0	11.5
H.S. Diplomas (#)	190	153	20	4	5	8

Jackson County

Altus

PO Box 558 • Altus, OK 73522-0558
(580) 481-2100 • http://www.altusschools.k12.ok.us/
Grade Span: PK-12; **Agency Type:** 1
Schools: 9
6 Primary; 1 Middle; 1 High; 1 Other Level
9 Regular; 0 Special Education; 0 Vocational; 0 Alternative
0 Magnet; 0 Charter; 6 Title I Eligible; 1 School-wide Title I
Students: 4,309 (52.6% male; 47.4% female)
Individual Education Program: 443 (10.3%);
English Language Learner: 706 (16.4%); Migrant: n/a
Eligible for Free Lunch Program: 1,697 (39.4%)
Eligible for Reduced-Price Lunch Program: 432 (10.0%)
Teachers: 295.1 (14.6 to 1)
Librarians/Media Specialists: 5.0 (861.8 to 1)
Guidance Counselors: 11.0 (391.7 to 1)
Current Spending: ($ per student per year):
Total: $5,723; Instruction: $3,543; Support Services: $1,853

Enrollment, Drop-out Rates and Diploma Recipients by Race/Ethnicity

Category	Total	White	Black	Asian	AIAN	Hisp.
Enrollment (%)	100.0	59.2	13.2	2.1	2.0	23.5
Drop-out Rate (%)	3.2	2.3	2.4	0.0	7.1	7.1
H.S. Diplomas (#)	295	196	44	6	3	46

Kay County

Blackwell

1034 S 1st St • Blackwell, OK 74631-4399
(580) 363-2570 • http://www.blackwell.k12.ok.us/
Grade Span: PK-12; **Agency Type:** 1
Schools: 5
2 Primary; 2 Middle; 1 High; 0 Other Level
5 Regular; 0 Special Education; 0 Vocational; 0 Alternative
0 Magnet; 0 Charter; 3 Title I Eligible; 2 School-wide Title I
Students: 1,579 (50.7% male; 49.3% female)
Individual Education Program: 254 (16.1%);
English Language Learner: 74 (4.7%); Migrant: n/a
Eligible for Free Lunch Program: 700 (44.3%)
Eligible for Reduced-Price Lunch Program: 199 (12.6%)
Teachers: 95.5 (16.5 to 1)
Librarians/Media Specialists: 2.0 (789.5 to 1)
Guidance Counselors: 4.0 (394.8 to 1)
Current Spending: ($ per student per year):
Total: $5,618; Instruction: $3,489; Support Services: $1,893

Enrollment, Drop-out Rates and Diploma Recipients by Race/Ethnicity

Category	Total	White	Black	Asian	AIAN	Hisp.
Enrollment (%)	100.0	56.3	0.3	0.6	36.0	6.8
Drop-out Rate (%)	7.1	5.5	0.0	0.0	10.0	26.3
H.S. Diplomas (#)	101	91	0	0	7	3

Ponca City

111 W Grand Ave • Ponca City, OK 74601-5211
(580) 767-8000 • http://www.poncacity.k12.ok.us/
Grade Span: PK-12; **Agency Type:** 1
Schools: 11
8 Primary; 1 Middle; 1 High; 1 Other Level
11 Regular; 0 Special Education; 0 Vocational; 0 Alternative
0 Magnet; 0 Charter; 7 Title I Eligible; 7 School-wide Title I
Students: 5,631 (52.2% male; 47.8% female)
Individual Education Program: 802 (14.2%);
English Language Learner: 163 (2.9%); Migrant: n/a
Eligible for Free Lunch Program: 2,531 (44.9%)
Eligible for Reduced-Price Lunch Program: 618 (11.0%)
Teachers: 355.0 (15.9 to 1)
Librarians/Media Specialists: 10.0 (563.1 to 1)
Guidance Counselors: 13.6 (414.0 to 1)
Current Spending: ($ per student per year):
Total: $5,339; Instruction: $3,208; Support Services: $1,723

Enrollment, Drop-out Rates and Diploma Recipients by Race/Ethnicity

Category	Total	White	Black	Asian	AIAN	Hisp.
Enrollment (%)	100.0	72.1	4.8	1.1	16.4	5.6
Drop-out Rate (%)	9.8	7.4	17.6	0.0	22.6	13.4
H.S. Diplomas (#)	387	300	12	5	52	18

Le Flore County

Poteau

100 Mockingbird Ln • Poteau, OK 74953-2602
(918) 647-7700 • http://www.poteau.k12.ok.us/
Grade Span: PK-12; **Agency Type:** 1
Schools: 4
2 Primary; 1 Middle; 1 High; 0 Other Level
4 Regular; 0 Special Education; 0 Vocational; 0 Alternative
0 Magnet; 0 Charter; 4 Title I Eligible; 4 School-wide Title I
Students: 1,982 (49.8% male; 50.2% female)
Individual Education Program: 301 (15.2%);
English Language Learner: 64 (3.2%); Migrant: n/a
Eligible for Free Lunch Program: 1,043 (52.6%)
Eligible for Reduced-Price Lunch Program: 233 (11.8%)
Teachers: 134.3 (14.8 to 1)
Librarians/Media Specialists: 3.0 (660.7 to 1)
Guidance Counselors: 5.0 (396.4 to 1)

Current Spending: ($ per student per year):
Total: $5,632; Instruction: $3,705; Support Services: $1,662

Enrollment, Drop-out Rates and Diploma Recipients by Race/Ethnicity

Category	Total	White	Black	Asian	AIAN	Hisp.
Enrollment (%)	100.0	77.0	1.6	0.8	17.0	3.6
Drop-out Rate (%)	5.3	5.3	0.0	0.0	7.2	0.0
H.S. Diplomas (#)	119	100	0	0	18	1

Logan County

Guthrie

802 E Vilas Ave • Guthrie, OK 73044-5228
(405) 282-8900 • http://www.guthrie.k12.ok.us/
Grade Span: PK-12; **Agency Type:** 1
Schools: 6
3 Primary; 2 Middle; 1 High; 0 Other Level
6 Regular; 0 Special Education; 0 Vocational; 0 Alternative
0 Magnet; 0 Charter; 5 Title I Eligible; 5 School-wide Title I
Students: 3,143 (51.3% male; 48.7% female)
Individual Education Program: 455 (14.5%);
English Language Learner: 43 (1.4%); Migrant: n/a
Eligible for Free Lunch Program: 1,437 (45.7%)
Eligible for Reduced-Price Lunch Program: 362 (11.5%)
Teachers: 208.7 (15.1 to 1)
Librarians/Media Specialists: 4.0 (785.8 to 1)
Guidance Counselors: 6.0 (523.8 to 1)
Current Spending: ($ per student per year):
Total: $5,748; Instruction: $3,300; Support Services: $2,029

Enrollment, Drop-out Rates and Diploma Recipients by Race/Ethnicity

Category	Total	White	Black	Asian	AIAN	Hisp.
Enrollment (%)	100.0	76.9	11.5	0.6	6.2	4.8
Drop-out Rate (%)	4.9	5.3	1.8	0.0	3.8	8.3
H.S. Diplomas (#)	181	138	25	1	14	3

Marshall County

Madill

601 W Mcarthur St • Madill, OK 73446-2846
(580) 795-3303
Grade Span: PK-12; **Agency Type:** 1
Schools: 3
1 Primary; 1 Middle; 1 High; 0 Other Level
3 Regular; 0 Special Education; 0 Vocational; 0 Alternative
0 Magnet; 0 Charter; 3 Title I Eligible; 3 School-wide Title I
Students: 1,542 (51.9% male; 48.1% female)
Individual Education Program: 128 (8.3%);
English Language Learner: 342 (22.2%); Migrant: n/a
Eligible for Free Lunch Program: 770 (49.9%)
Eligible for Reduced-Price Lunch Program: 179 (11.6%)
Teachers: 95.5 (16.1 to 1)
Librarians/Media Specialists: 3.0 (514.0 to 1)
Guidance Counselors: 5.0 (308.4 to 1)
Current Spending: ($ per student per year):
Total: $5,430; Instruction: $3,260; Support Services: $1,868

Enrollment, Drop-out Rates and Diploma Recipients by Race/Ethnicity

Category	Total	White	Black	Asian	AIAN	Hisp.
Enrollment (%)	100.0	50.5	3.1	0.2	21.9	24.4
Drop-out Rate (%)	1.0	0.9	0.0	0.0	0.0	3.0
H.S. Diplomas (#)	76	46	4	1	18	7

Mayes County

Pryor

PO Box 548 • Pryor, OK 74362-0548
(918) 825-1255 • http://www.pryor.k12.ok.us/
Grade Span: PK-12; **Agency Type:** 1
Schools: 6
4 Primary; 1 Middle; 1 High; 0 Other Level
6 Regular; 0 Special Education; 0 Vocational; 0 Alternative
0 Magnet; 0 Charter; 5 Title I Eligible; 0 School-wide Title I
Students: 2,365 (50.7% male; 49.3% female)
Individual Education Program: 222 (9.4%);
English Language Learner: 54 (2.3%); Migrant: n/a
Eligible for Free Lunch Program: 836 (35.3%)
Eligible for Reduced-Price Lunch Program: 241 (10.2%)
Teachers: 138.9 (17.0 to 1)
Librarians/Media Specialists: 6.0 (394.2 to 1)
Guidance Counselors: 7.8 (303.2 to 1)
Current Spending: ($ per student per year):
Total: $5,555; Instruction: $3,291; Support Services: $2,046

Enrollment, Drop-out Rates and Diploma Recipients by Race/Ethnicity

Category	Total	White	Black	Asian	AIAN	Hisp.
Enrollment (%)	100.0	60.0	0.2	0.6	36.2	3.1
Drop-out Rate (%)	9.7	9.4	0.0	0.0	9.5	28.6
H.S. Diplomas (#)	147	104	1	1	38	3

Mccurtain County

Broken Bow

108 W 5th St • Broken Bow, OK 74728-2912
(580) 584-3306 • http://www.bbisd.org/
Grade Span: PK-12; **Agency Type:** 1
Schools: 4
2 Primary; 1 Middle; 1 High; 0 Other Level
4 Regular; 0 Special Education; 0 Vocational; 0 Alternative
0 Magnet; 0 Charter; 4 Title I Eligible; 4 School-wide Title I
Students: 1,719 (53.6% male; 46.4% female)
Individual Education Program: 253 (14.7%);
English Language Learner: 91 (5.3%); Migrant: n/a
Eligible for Free Lunch Program: 1,095 (63.7%)
Eligible for Reduced-Price Lunch Program: 206 (12.0%)
Teachers: 119.6 (14.4 to 1)
Librarians/Media Specialists: 3.0 (573.0 to 1)
Guidance Counselors: 5.9 (291.4 to 1)
Current Spending: ($ per student per year):
Total: $6,430; Instruction: $3,735; Support Services: $2,253

Enrollment, Drop-out Rates and Diploma Recipients by Race/Ethnicity

Category	Total	White	Black	Asian	AIAN	Hisp.
Enrollment (%)	100.0	59.0	10.8	0.1	26.1	4.0
Drop-out Rate (%)	4.2	3.9	4.2	0.0	4.3	14.3
H.S. Diplomas (#)	125	90	8	1	23	3

Idabel

200 NE Ave C • Idabel, OK 74745-0029
(580) 286-7639
Grade Span: PK-12; **Agency Type:** 1
Schools: 5
3 Primary; 1 Middle; 1 High; 0 Other Level
5 Regular; 0 Special Education; 0 Vocational; 0 Alternative
0 Magnet; 0 Charter; 4 Title I Eligible; 4 School-wide Title I
Students: 1,666 (51.1% male; 48.9% female)
Individual Education Program: 246 (14.8%);
English Language Learner: 55 (3.3%); Migrant: n/a
Eligible for Free Lunch Program: 1,140 (68.4%)
Eligible for Reduced-Price Lunch Program: 126 (7.6%)
Teachers: 114.4 (14.6 to 1)
Librarians/Media Specialists: 3.0 (555.3 to 1)
Guidance Counselors: 3.0 (555.3 to 1)
Current Spending: ($ per student per year):
Total: $6,094; Instruction: $3,510; Support Services: $2,216

Enrollment, Drop-out Rates and Diploma Recipients by Race/Ethnicity

Category	Total	White	Black	Asian	AIAN	Hisp.
Enrollment (%)	100.0	39.9	34.3	0.4	18.8	6.5
Drop-out Rate (%)	7.9	9.0	5.0	0.0	7.5	21.4
H.S. Diplomas (#)	94	53	29	1	11	0

Mcintosh County

Checotah

PO Box 289 • Checotah, OK 74426-0289
(918) 473-5610 • http://www.checotah.k12.ok.us/
Grade Span: PK-12; **Agency Type:** 1
Schools: 4
1 Primary; 2 Middle; 1 High; 0 Other Level
4 Regular; 0 Special Education; 0 Vocational; 0 Alternative
0 Magnet; 0 Charter; 4 Title I Eligible; 4 School-wide Title I
Students: 1,592 (49.9% male; 50.1% female)
Individual Education Program: 251 (15.8%);
English Language Learner: 30 (1.9%); Migrant: n/a
Eligible for Free Lunch Program: 952 (59.8%)
Eligible for Reduced-Price Lunch Program: 239 (15.0%)
Teachers: 100.0 (15.9 to 1)
Librarians/Media Specialists: 3.0 (530.7 to 1)
Guidance Counselors: 5.0 (318.4 to 1)
Current Spending: ($ per student per year):
Total: $5,620; Instruction: $3,176; Support Services: $2,038

Enrollment, Drop-out Rates and Diploma Recipients by Race/Ethnicity

Category	Total	White	Black	Asian	AIAN	Hisp.
Enrollment (%)	100.0	59.7	7.0	0.2	31.4	1.7
Drop-out Rate (%)	7.2	7.9	0.0	n/a	1.3	200.0
H.S. Diplomas (#)	88	49	3	0	36	0

Muskogee County

Fort Gibson

500 S Ross Ave • Fort Gibson, OK 74434-8422
(918) 478-2474
Grade Span: PK-12; **Agency Type:** 1
Schools: 4
2 Primary; 1 Middle; 1 High; 0 Other Level
4 Regular; 0 Special Education; 0 Vocational; 0 Alternative
0 Magnet; 0 Charter; 2 Title I Eligible; 0 School-wide Title I
Students: 1,798 (51.7% male; 48.3% female)
Individual Education Program: 224 (12.5%);
English Language Learner: 41 (2.3%); Migrant: n/a
Eligible for Free Lunch Program: 530 (29.5%)
Eligible for Reduced-Price Lunch Program: 179 (10.0%)
Teachers: 114.2 (15.7 to 1)
Librarians/Media Specialists: 3.0 (599.3 to 1)
Guidance Counselors: 4.0 (449.5 to 1)
Current Spending: ($ per student per year):
Total: $6,149; Instruction: $3,782; Support Services: $1,966
Enrollment, Drop-out Rates and Diploma Recipients by Race/Ethnicity

Category	Total	White	Black	Asian	AIAN	Hisp.
Enrollment (%)	100.0	50.7	0.9	0.3	44.3	3.7
Drop-out Rate (%)	4.9	4.8	11.8	0.0	4.3	11.1
H.S. Diplomas (#)	135	76	4	0	52	3

Hilldale

500 E Smith Ferry Rd • Muskogee, OK 74403-8639
(918) 683-0273 • http://www.hilldale.k12.ok.us/
Grade Span: PK-12; **Agency Type:** 1
Schools: 4
2 Primary; 1 Middle; 1 High; 0 Other Level
4 Regular; 0 Special Education; 0 Vocational; 0 Alternative
0 Magnet; 0 Charter; 3 Title I Eligible; 0 School-wide Title I
Students: 1,731 (51.8% male; 48.2% female)
Individual Education Program: 242 (14.0%);
English Language Learner: 177 (10.2%); Migrant: n/a
Eligible for Free Lunch Program: 439 (25.4%)
Eligible for Reduced-Price Lunch Program: 183 (10.6%)
Teachers: 105.1 (16.5 to 1)
Librarians/Media Specialists: 2.0 (865.5 to 1)
Guidance Counselors: 3.0 (577.0 to 1)
Current Spending: ($ per student per year):
Total: $4,704; Instruction: $2,788; Support Services: $1,648
Enrollment, Drop-out Rates and Diploma Recipients by Race/Ethnicity

Category	Total	White	Black	Asian	AIAN	Hisp.
Enrollment (%)	100.0	52.1	2.1	1.8	42.7	1.4
Drop-out Rate (%)	3.9	2.9	0.0	11.1	0.8	116.7
H.S. Diplomas (#)	107	68	6	2	31	0

Muskogee

202 W Broadway St • Muskogee, OK 74401-6651
(918) 684-3700 • http://www.mpsi20.org/
Grade Span: PK-12; **Agency Type:** 1
Schools: 13
11 Primary; 1 Middle; 1 High; 0 Other Level
13 Regular; 0 Special Education; 0 Vocational; 0 Alternative
0 Magnet; 0 Charter; 13 Title I Eligible; 12 School-wide Title I
Students: 6,383 (51.2% male; 48.8% female)
Individual Education Program: 843 (13.2%);
English Language Learner: 232 (3.6%); Migrant: n/a
Eligible for Free Lunch Program: 3,648 (57.2%)
Eligible for Reduced-Price Lunch Program: 634 (9.9%)
Teachers: 382.8 (16.7 to 1)
Librarians/Media Specialists: 13.5 (472.8 to 1)
Guidance Counselors: 18.7 (341.3 to 1)
Current Spending: ($ per student per year):
Total: $5,866; Instruction: $3,270; Support Services: $2,157
Enrollment, Drop-out Rates and Diploma Recipients by Race/Ethnicity

Category	Total	White	Black	Asian	AIAN	Hisp.
Enrollment (%)	100.0	38.9	27.7	0.8	28.5	4.2
Drop-out Rate (%)	3.9	4.4	4.7	0.0	2.3	5.0
H.S. Diplomas (#)	319	151	74	5	79	10

Oklahoma County

Choctaw-Nicoma Park

12880 NE 10th St • Choctaw, OK 73020-8129
(405) 769-4859 • http://www.cnpschools.org/
Grade Span: KG-12; **Agency Type:** 1
Schools: 9
5 Primary; 3 Middle; 1 High; 0 Other Level
9 Regular; 0 Special Education; 0 Vocational; 0 Alternative
0 Magnet; 0 Charter; 0 Title I Eligible; 0 School-wide Title I
Students: 4,416 (53.0% male; 47.0% female)
Individual Education Program: 613 (13.9%);
English Language Learner: 19 (0.4%); Migrant: n/a
Eligible for Free Lunch Program: 924 (20.9%)
Eligible for Reduced-Price Lunch Program: 340 (7.7%)
Teachers: 269.6 (16.4 to 1)
Librarians/Media Specialists: 9.0 (490.7 to 1)
Guidance Counselors: 10.0 (441.6 to 1)
Current Spending: ($ per student per year):
Total: $5,174; Instruction: $3,036; Support Services: $1,862
Enrollment, Drop-out Rates and Diploma Recipients by Race/Ethnicity

Category	Total	White	Black	Asian	AIAN	Hisp.
Enrollment (%)	100.0	79.4	3.7	1.0	12.7	3.2
Drop-out Rate (%)	2.6	2.6	2.1	0.0	3.7	2.0
H.S. Diplomas (#)	308	248	8	4	35	13

Deer Creek

20825 N Macarthur Blvd • Edmond, OK 73003-9342
(405) 348-6100 • http://www.deercreek.k12.ok.us/
Grade Span: KG-12; **Agency Type:** 1
Schools: 4
2 Primary; 1 Middle; 1 High; 0 Other Level
4 Regular; 0 Special Education; 0 Vocational; 0 Alternative
0 Magnet; 0 Charter; 1 Title I Eligible; 0 School-wide Title I
Students: 1,883 (53.4% male; 46.6% female)
Individual Education Program: 258 (13.7%);
English Language Learner: 35 (1.9%); Migrant: n/a
Eligible for Free Lunch Program: 56 (3.0%)
Eligible for Reduced-Price Lunch Program: 27 (1.4%)
Teachers: 118.8 (15.9 to 1)
Librarians/Media Specialists: 4.0 (470.8 to 1)
Guidance Counselors: 5.0 (376.6 to 1)
Current Spending: ($ per student per year):
Total: $5,071; Instruction: $2,926; Support Services: $1,803
Enrollment, Drop-out Rates and Diploma Recipients by Race/Ethnicity

Category	Total	White	Black	Asian	AIAN	Hisp.
Enrollment (%)	100.0	85.2	3.1	2.1	6.6	3.0
Drop-out Rate (%)	1.6	1.6	9.1	0.0	0.0	0.0
H.S. Diplomas (#)	98	85	2	3	6	2

Edmond

1001 W Danforth Rd • Edmond, OK 73003-4801
(405) 340-2828 • http://www.edmond.k12.ok.us/
Grade Span: PK-12; **Agency Type:** 1
Schools: 22
14 Primary; 5 Middle; 3 High; 0 Other Level
22 Regular; 0 Special Education; 0 Vocational; 0 Alternative
0 Magnet; 0 Charter; 6 Title I Eligible; 0 School-wide Title I
Students: 17,872 (51.3% male; 48.7% female)
Individual Education Program: 2,403 (13.4%);
English Language Learner: 306 (1.7%); Migrant: n/a
Eligible for Free Lunch Program: 1,903 (10.6%)
Eligible for Reduced-Price Lunch Program: 754 (4.2%)
Teachers: 1,027.8 (17.4 to 1)
Librarians/Media Specialists: 24.0 (744.7 to 1)
Guidance Counselors: 45.7 (391.1 to 1)
Current Spending: ($ per student per year):
Total: $6,161; Instruction: $3,000; Support Services: $2,855
Enrollment, Drop-out Rates and Diploma Recipients by Race/Ethnicity

Category	Total	White	Black	Asian	AIAN	Hisp.
Enrollment (%)	100.0	82.5	7.9	2.8	3.7	3.0
Drop-out Rate (%)	3.1	2.7	9.2	3.2	3.9	3.0
H.S. Diplomas (#)	1,267	1,104	80	17	47	19

Harrah

20670 Walker St • Harrah, OK 73045-9782
(405) 454-6244
Grade Span: KG-12; **Agency Type:** 1
Schools: 6
2 Primary; 2 Middle; 1 High; 1 Other Level
6 Regular; 0 Special Education; 0 Vocational; 0 Alternative
0 Magnet; 0 Charter; 4 Title I Eligible; 0 School-wide Title I
Students: 2,215 (50.7% male; 49.3% female)
Individual Education Program: 382 (17.2%);
English Language Learner: 12 (0.5%); Migrant: n/a
Eligible for Free Lunch Program: 639 (28.8%)
Eligible for Reduced-Price Lunch Program: 233 (10.5%)
Teachers: 136.2 (16.3 to 1)
Librarians/Media Specialists: 4.0 (553.8 to 1)
Guidance Counselors: 6.0 (369.2 to 1)
Current Spending: ($ per student per year):
Total: $5,443; Instruction: $3,096; Support Services: $2,004

Enrollment, Drop-out Rates and Diploma Recipients by Race/Ethnicity

Category	Total	White	Black	Asian	AIAN	Hisp.
Enrollment (%)	100.0	76.7	0.9	0.5	20.4	1.5
Drop-out Rate (%)	2.2	2.1	0.0	0.0	2.1	11.1
H.S. Diplomas (#)	163	122	1	1	38	1

MWC-Del City

PO Box 10630 • Midwest City, OK 73140-1630
(405) 737-4461
Grade Span: PK-12; **Agency Type:** 1
Schools: 26
17 Primary; 5 Middle; 3 High; 1 Other Level
26 Regular; 0 Special Education; 0 Vocational; 0 Alternative
0 Magnet; 0 Charter; 14 Title I Eligible; 13 School-wide Title I
Students: 14,347 (52.1% male; 47.9% female)
Individual Education Program: 1,958 (13.6%);
English Language Learner: 428 (3.0%); Migrant: n/a
Eligible for Free Lunch Program: 4,996 (34.8%)
Eligible for Reduced-Price Lunch Program: 1,278 (8.9%)
Teachers: 914.0 (15.7 to 1)
Librarians/Media Specialists: 27.0 (531.4 to 1)
Guidance Counselors: 38.0 (377.6 to 1)
Current Spending: ($ per student per year):
Total: $5,815; Instruction: $3,286; Support Services: $2,191
Enrollment, Drop-out Rates and Diploma Recipients by Race/Ethnicity

Category	Total	White	Black	Asian	AIAN	Hisp.
Enrollment (%)	100.0	59.7	27.7	2.1	6.6	3.8
Drop-out Rate (%)	5.2	5.3	4.0	0.9	8.8	8.3
H.S. Diplomas (#)	1,076	633	295	33	73	42

Oklahoma City

900 N Klein Ave • Oklahoma City, OK 73106-7036
(405) 587-0000 • http://www.okcps.k12.ok.us/
Grade Span: PK-12; **Agency Type:** 1
Schools: 94
64 Primary; 16 Middle; 11 High; 3 Other Level
94 Regular; 0 Special Education; 0 Vocational; 0 Alternative
0 Magnet; 7 Charter; 77 Title I Eligible; 50 School-wide Title I
Students: 40,856 (51.2% male; 48.8% female)
Individual Education Program: 6,251 (15.3%);
English Language Learner: 9,266 (22.7%); Migrant: n/a
Eligible for Free Lunch Program: 29,938 (73.3%)
Eligible for Reduced-Price Lunch Program: 3,046 (7.5%)
Teachers: 2,529.3 (16.2 to 1)
Librarians/Media Specialists: 49.0 (833.8 to 1)
Guidance Counselors: 78.9 (517.8 to 1)
Current Spending: ($ per student per year):
Total: $6,300; Instruction: $3,448; Support Services: $2,436
Enrollment, Drop-out Rates and Diploma Recipients by Race/Ethnicity

Category	Total	White	Black	Asian	AIAN	Hisp.
Enrollment (%)	100.0	29.1	35.7	2.7	5.7	26.8
Drop-out Rate (%)	12.5	12.2	12.4	5.8	14.5	13.8
H.S. Diplomas (#)	1,441	382	733	53	51	222

Putnam City

5401 NW 40th St • Warr Acres, OK 73122-3302
(405) 495-5200 • http://www.putnamcityschools.org/
Grade Span: PK-12; **Agency Type:** 1
Schools: 27
18 Primary; 5 Middle; 3 High; 1 Other Level
26 Regular; 0 Special Education; 0 Vocational; 1 Alternative
0 Magnet; 0 Charter; 8 Title I Eligible; 8 School-wide Title I
Students: 19,356 (51.0% male; 49.0% female)
Individual Education Program: 2,320 (12.0%);
English Language Learner: 1,522 (7.9%); Migrant: n/a
Eligible for Free Lunch Program: 5,985 (30.9%)
Eligible for Reduced-Price Lunch Program: 1,391 (7.2%)
Teachers: 1,188.8 (16.3 to 1)
Librarians/Media Specialists: 29.0 (667.4 to 1)
Guidance Counselors: 39.1 (495.0 to 1)
Current Spending: ($ per student per year):
Total: $5,337; Instruction: $3,040; Support Services: $1,995
Enrollment, Drop-out Rates and Diploma Recipients by Race/Ethnicity

Category	Total	White	Black	Asian	AIAN	Hisp.
Enrollment (%)	100.0	63.9	19.9	4.0	3.9	8.2
Drop-out Rate (%)	6.7	5.5	9.3	3.8	7.6	16.8
H.S. Diplomas (#)	1,185	882	129	66	41	67

Western Heights

8401 SW 44th St • Oklahoma City, OK 73179-4010
(405) 350-3410 • http://westernheights.k12.ok.us/
Grade Span: PK-12; **Agency Type:** 1
Schools: 6
4 Primary; 1 Middle; 1 High; 0 Other Level
6 Regular; 0 Special Education; 0 Vocational; 0 Alternative
0 Magnet; 0 Charter; 5 Title I Eligible; 2 School-wide Title I
Students: 3,132 (49.8% male; 50.2% female)
Individual Education Program: 475 (15.2%);
English Language Learner: 399 (12.7%); Migrant: n/a
Eligible for Free Lunch Program: 1,798 (57.4%)
Eligible for Reduced-Price Lunch Program: 380 (12.1%)
Teachers: 208.0 (15.1 to 1)
Librarians/Media Specialists: 4.5 (696.0 to 1)
Guidance Counselors: 6.7 (467.5 to 1)
Current Spending: ($ per student per year):
Total: $5,944; Instruction: $3,213; Support Services: $2,354
Enrollment, Drop-out Rates and Diploma Recipients by Race/Ethnicity

Category	Total	White	Black	Asian	AIAN	Hisp.
Enrollment (%)	100.0	52.6	20.2	6.1	9.2	11.9
Drop-out Rate (%)	7.0	7.1	9.9	5.3	4.2	6.9
H.S. Diplomas (#)	164	100	20	14	15	15

Okmulgee County

Okmulgee

PO Box 1346 • Okmulgee, OK 74447-1346
(918) 758-2000
Grade Span: PK-12; **Agency Type:** 1
Schools: 4
2 Primary; 1 Middle; 1 High; 0 Other Level
4 Regular; 0 Special Education; 0 Vocational; 0 Alternative
0 Magnet; 0 Charter; 4 Title I Eligible; 4 School-wide Title I
Students: 1,958 (53.5% male; 46.5% female)
Individual Education Program: 305 (15.6%);
English Language Learner: 60 (3.1%); Migrant: n/a
Eligible for Free Lunch Program: 1,181 (60.3%)
Eligible for Reduced-Price Lunch Program: 291 (14.9%)
Teachers: 134.2 (14.6 to 1)
Librarians/Media Specialists: 4.0 (489.5 to 1)
Guidance Counselors: 5.9 (331.9 to 1)
Current Spending: ($ per student per year):
Total: $6,458; Instruction: $3,651; Support Services: $2,391
Enrollment, Drop-out Rates and Diploma Recipients by Race/Ethnicity

Category	Total	White	Black	Asian	AIAN	Hisp.
Enrollment (%)	100.0	42.4	34.0	0.2	22.0	1.5
Drop-out Rate (%)	7.5	9.0	4.8	0.0	9.9	0.0
H.S. Diplomas (#)	94	41	39	0	10	4

Ottawa County

Miami

418 G St SE • Miami, OK 74354-8218
(918) 542-8455
Grade Span: PK-12; **Agency Type:** 1
Schools: 8
6 Primary; 1 Middle; 1 High; 0 Other Level
8 Regular; 0 Special Education; 0 Vocational; 0 Alternative
0 Magnet; 0 Charter; 5 Title I Eligible; 5 School-wide Title I
Students: 2,448 (51.6% male; 48.4% female)
Individual Education Program: 249 (10.2%);
English Language Learner: 39 (1.6%); Migrant: n/a
Eligible for Free Lunch Program: 1,222 (49.9%)
Eligible for Reduced-Price Lunch Program: 332 (13.6%)
Teachers: 144.0 (17.0 to 1)
Librarians/Media Specialists: 5.0 (489.6 to 1)
Guidance Counselors: 7.0 (349.7 to 1)
Current Spending: ($ per student per year):
Total: $5,628; Instruction: $3,570; Support Services: $1,687
Enrollment, Drop-out Rates and Diploma Recipients by Race/Ethnicity

Category	Total	White	Black	Asian	AIAN	Hisp.
Enrollment (%)	100.0	55.0	1.3	0.7	39.7	3.4
Drop-out Rate (%)	3.9	5.1	0.0	12.5	2.2	0.0
H.S. Diplomas (#)	112	57	1	1	50	3

Pawnee County

Cleveland

600 N Gilbert St • Cleveland, OK 74020-1023
(918) 358-2210 • http://www.cleveland.k12.ok.us/
Grade Span: PK-12; **Agency Type:** 1
Schools: 4
2 Primary; 1 Middle; 1 High; 0 Other Level
4 Regular; 0 Special Education; 0 Vocational; 0 Alternative
0 Magnet; 0 Charter; 4 Title I Eligible; 4 School-wide Title I
Students: 1,718 (50.8% male; 49.2% female)
Individual Education Program: 243 (14.1%);
English Language Learner: 1 (0.1%); Migrant: n/a
Eligible for Free Lunch Program: 617 (35.9%)
Eligible for Reduced-Price Lunch Program: 223 (13.0%)
Teachers: 103.4 (16.6 to 1)

Librarians/Media Specialists: 2.0 (859.0 to 1)
Guidance Counselors: 3.0 (572.7 to 1)
Current Spending: ($ per student per year):
Total: $5,056; Instruction: $2,834; Support Services: $1,849
Enrollment, Drop-out Rates and Diploma Recipients by Race/Ethnicity

Category	Total	White	Black	Asian	AIAN	Hisp.
Enrollment (%)	100.0	82.4	0.6	0.9	14.0	2.2
Drop-out Rate (%)	7.6	8.4	n/a	0.0	3.3	0.0
H.S. Diplomas (#)	69	57	0	0	12	0

Payne County

Cushing
PO Box 1609 • Cushing, OK 74023-1609
(918) 225-3425
Grade Span: PK-12; **Agency Type:** 1
Schools: 7
5 Primary; 1 Middle; 1 High; 0 Other Level
7 Regular; 0 Special Education; 0 Vocational; 0 Alternative
0 Magnet; 0 Charter; 5 Title I Eligible; 0 School-wide Title I
Students: 1,923 (50.9% male; 49.1% female)
Individual Education Program: 296 (15.4%);
English Language Learner: 0 (0.0%); Migrant: n/a
Eligible for Free Lunch Program: 772 (40.1%)
Eligible for Reduced-Price Lunch Program: 253 (13.2%)
Teachers: 128.9 (14.9 to 1)
Librarians/Media Specialists: 5.0 (384.6 to 1)
Guidance Counselors: 5.0 (384.6 to 1)
Current Spending: ($ per student per year):
Total: $7,931; Instruction: $4,115; Support Services: $3,442
Enrollment, Drop-out Rates and Diploma Recipients by Race/Ethnicity

Category	Total	White	Black	Asian	AIAN	Hisp.
Enrollment (%)	100.0	77.5	4.0	0.6	16.4	1.5
Drop-out Rate (%)	6.3	5.6	7.7	0.0	10.7	16.7
H.S. Diplomas (#)	133	117	3	0	11	2

Stillwater
PO Box 879 • Stillwater, OK 74076-0879
(405) 533-6300 • http://www.stillwater.k12.ok.us/
Grade Span: PK-12; **Agency Type:** 1
Schools: 9
6 Primary; 1 Middle; 1 High; 1 Other Level
9 Regular; 0 Special Education; 0 Vocational; 0 Alternative
0 Magnet; 0 Charter; 4 Title I Eligible; 3 School-wide Title I
Students: 5,343 (50.9% male; 49.1% female)
Individual Education Program: 906 (17.0%);
English Language Learner: 254 (4.8%); Migrant: n/a
Eligible for Free Lunch Program: 1,238 (23.2%)
Eligible for Reduced-Price Lunch Program: 328 (6.1%)
Teachers: 310.8 (17.2 to 1)
Librarians/Media Specialists: 9.0 (593.7 to 1)
Guidance Counselors: 13.8 (387.2 to 1)
Current Spending: ($ per student per year):
Total: $5,862; Instruction: $3,054; Support Services: $2,374
Enrollment, Drop-out Rates and Diploma Recipients by Race/Ethnicity

Category	Total	White	Black	Asian	AIAN	Hisp.
Enrollment (%)	100.0	81.0	6.5	3.4	6.9	2.1
Drop-out Rate (%)	2.3	2.0	12.3	0.0	2.9	0.0
H.S. Diplomas (#)	380	332	10	11	19	8

Pittsburg County

Mc Alester
PO Box 1027 • Mcalester, OK 74502-1027
(918) 423-4771
Grade Span: PK-12; **Agency Type:** 1
Schools: 9
6 Primary; 1 Middle; 1 High; 1 Other Level
9 Regular; 0 Special Education; 0 Vocational; 0 Alternative
0 Magnet; 0 Charter; 7 Title I Eligible; 5 School-wide Title I
Students: 2,857 (51.9% male; 48.1% female)
Individual Education Program: 573 (20.1%);
English Language Learner: 55 (1.9%); Migrant: n/a
Eligible for Free Lunch Program: 1,297 (45.4%)
Eligible for Reduced-Price Lunch Program: 317 (11.1%)
Teachers: 190.6 (15.0 to 1)
Librarians/Media Specialists: 5.0 (571.4 to 1)
Guidance Counselors: 8.5 (336.1 to 1)
Current Spending: ($ per student per year):
Total: $6,134; Instruction: $3,451; Support Services: $2,189
Enrollment, Drop-out Rates and Diploma Recipients by Race/Ethnicity

Category	Total	White	Black	Asian	AIAN	Hisp.
Enrollment (%)	100.0	66.9	9.6	0.7	19.4	3.5
Drop-out Rate (%)	8.8	8.8	6.3	0.0	9.4	17.4
H.S. Diplomas (#)	167	113	20	5	26	3

Pontotoc County

Ada
PO Box 1359 • Ada, OK 74821-1359
(580) 310-7200 • http://www.adapss.com/
Grade Span: PK-12; **Agency Type:** 1
Schools: 6
3 Primary; 2 Middle; 1 High; 0 Other Level
6 Regular; 0 Special Education; 0 Vocational; 0 Alternative
0 Magnet; 0 Charter; 4 Title I Eligible; 4 School-wide Title I
Students: 2,551 (51.2% male; 48.8% female)
Individual Education Program: 389 (15.2%);
English Language Learner: 75 (2.9%); Migrant: n/a
Eligible for Free Lunch Program: 1,181 (46.3%)
Eligible for Reduced-Price Lunch Program: 254 (10.0%)
Teachers: 181.8 (14.0 to 1)
Librarians/Media Specialists: 2.0 (1,275.5 to 1)
Guidance Counselors: 7.0 (364.4 to 1)
Current Spending: ($ per student per year):
Total: $6,168; Instruction: $3,837; Support Services: $1,962
Enrollment, Drop-out Rates and Diploma Recipients by Race/Ethnicity

Category	Total	White	Black	Asian	AIAN	Hisp.
Enrollment (%)	100.0	61.2	4.5	0.5	31.1	2.7
Drop-out Rate (%)	7.7	6.7	12.0	0.0	9.7	6.7
H.S. Diplomas (#)	159	107	5	0	46	1

Byng
RR 3 Box 215 • Ada, OK 74820-9517
(580) 310-6751 • http://www.byngschools.com/
Grade Span: PK-12; **Agency Type:** 1
Schools: 5
2 Primary; 2 Middle; 1 High; 0 Other Level
5 Regular; 0 Special Education; 0 Vocational; 0 Alternative
0 Magnet; 0 Charter; 5 Title I Eligible; 5 School-wide Title I
Students: 1,666 (47.1% male; 52.9% female)
Individual Education Program: 271 (16.3%);
English Language Learner: 24 (1.4%); Migrant: n/a
Eligible for Free Lunch Program: 810 (48.6%)
Eligible for Reduced-Price Lunch Program: 208 (12.5%)
Teachers: 113.0 (14.7 to 1)
Librarians/Media Specialists: 3.0 (555.3 to 1)
Guidance Counselors: 5.0 (333.2 to 1)
Current Spending: ($ per student per year):
Total: $5,873; Instruction: $3,504; Support Services: $1,912
Enrollment, Drop-out Rates and Diploma Recipients by Race/Ethnicity

Category	Total	White	Black	Asian	AIAN	Hisp.
Enrollment (%)	100.0	56.0	1.9	0.1	39.9	2.0
Drop-out Rate (%)	2.6	0.8	0.0	0.0	3.2	50.0
H.S. Diplomas (#)	103	61	1	1	36	4

Pottawatomie County

Mc Loud
PO Box 240 • Mcloud, OK 74851-0240
(405) 964-3314
Grade Span: PK-12; **Agency Type:** 1
Schools: 3
1 Primary; 1 Middle; 1 High; 0 Other Level
3 Regular; 0 Special Education; 0 Vocational; 0 Alternative
0 Magnet; 0 Charter; 3 Title I Eligible; 3 School-wide Title I
Students: 1,779 (51.7% male; 48.3% female)
Individual Education Program: 209 (11.7%);
English Language Learner: 37 (2.1%); Migrant: n/a
Eligible for Free Lunch Program: 627 (35.2%)
Eligible for Reduced-Price Lunch Program: 179 (10.1%)
Teachers: 114.4 (15.6 to 1)
Librarians/Media Specialists: 2.0 (889.5 to 1)
Guidance Counselors: 5.0 (355.8 to 1)
Current Spending: ($ per student per year):
Total: $4,917; Instruction: $3,006; Support Services: $1,641
Enrollment, Drop-out Rates and Diploma Recipients by Race/Ethnicity

Category	Total	White	Black	Asian	AIAN	Hisp.
Enrollment (%)	100.0	76.8	1.2	0.9	18.2	2.9
Drop-out Rate (%)	5.5	4.5	33.3	0.0	9.2	7.1
H.S. Diplomas (#)	133	110	3	0	16	4

Shawnee
326 N Union St • Shawnee, OK 74801-7053
(405) 273-0653 • http://www.shawnee.k12.ok.us/
Grade Span: PK-12; **Agency Type:** 1
Schools: 9
5 Primary; 1 Middle; 1 High; 2 Other Level
9 Regular; 0 Special Education; 0 Vocational; 0 Alternative
0 Magnet; 0 Charter; 7 Title I Eligible; 6 School-wide Title I
Students: 3,805 (51.6% male; 48.4% female)

Individual Education Program: 574 (15.1%);
English Language Learner: 161 (4.2%); Migrant: n/a
Eligible for Free Lunch Program: 1,806 (47.5%)
Eligible for Reduced-Price Lunch Program: 331 (8.7%)
Teachers: 246.8 (15.4 to 1)
Librarians/Media Specialists: 7.0 (543.6 to 1)
Guidance Counselors: 12.0 (317.1 to 1)
Current Spending: ($ per student per year):
Total: $6,187; Instruction: $3,595; Support Services: $2,232
Enrollment, Drop-out Rates and Diploma Recipients by Race/Ethnicity

Category	Total	White	Black	Asian	AIAN	Hisp.
Enrollment (%)	100.0	61.4	7.3	0.9	27.3	3.0
Drop-out Rate (%)	10.3	7.3	9.6	87.5	14.1	13.0
H.S. Diplomas (#)	239	185	7	1	44	2

Tecumseh
302 S 9th St • Tecumseh, OK 74873-4021
(405) 598-3739
Grade Span: PK-12; **Agency Type:** 1
Schools: 6
3 Primary; 1 Middle; 2 High; 0 Other Level
6 Regular; 0 Special Education; 0 Vocational; 0 Alternative
0 Magnet; 0 Charter; 3 Title I Eligible; 3 School-wide Title I
Students: 2,171 (53.4% male; 46.6% female)
Individual Education Program: 304 (14.0%);
English Language Learner: 34 (1.6%); Migrant: n/a
Eligible for Free Lunch Program: 976 (45.0%)
Eligible for Reduced-Price Lunch Program: 238 (11.0%)
Teachers: 142.0 (15.3 to 1)
Librarians/Media Specialists: 4.0 (542.8 to 1)
Guidance Counselors: 5.0 (434.2 to 1)
Current Spending: ($ per student per year):
Total: $5,647; Instruction: $3,350; Support Services: $1,934
Enrollment, Drop-out Rates and Diploma Recipients by Race/Ethnicity

Category	Total	White	Black	Asian	AIAN	Hisp.
Enrollment (%)	100.0	67.4	3.2	0.5	27.0	1.8
Drop-out Rate (%)	4.0	4.3	0.0	0.0	3.5	12.5
H.S. Diplomas (#)	137	98	4	0	31	4

Rogers County

Catoosa
2000 S Cherokee St • Catoosa, OK 74015-3232
(918) 266-8603
Grade Span: PK-12; **Agency Type:** 1
Schools: 5
2 Primary; 2 Middle; 1 High; 0 Other Level
5 Regular; 0 Special Education; 0 Vocational; 0 Alternative
0 Magnet; 0 Charter; 4 Title I Eligible; 0 School-wide Title I
Students: 2,344 (51.3% male; 48.7% female)
Individual Education Program: 383 (16.3%);
English Language Learner: 0 (0.0%); Migrant: n/a
Eligible for Free Lunch Program: 714 (30.5%)
Eligible for Reduced-Price Lunch Program: 253 (10.8%)
Teachers: 147.9 (15.8 to 1)
Librarians/Media Specialists: 3.0 (781.3 to 1)
Guidance Counselors: 7.0 (334.9 to 1)
Current Spending: ($ per student per year):
Total: $5,394; Instruction: $3,107; Support Services: $1,923
Enrollment, Drop-out Rates and Diploma Recipients by Race/Ethnicity

Category	Total	White	Black	Asian	AIAN	Hisp.
Enrollment (%)	100.0	58.7	0.6	0.4	38.0	2.3
Drop-out Rate (%)	4.1	7.5	0.0	n/a	0.3	9.1
H.S. Diplomas (#)	139	81	1	1	56	0

Claremore
310 N Weenonah Ave • Claremore, OK 74017-7007
(918) 341-2213 • http://www.claremore.k12.ok.us/
Grade Span: PK-12; **Agency Type:** 1
Schools: 7
3 Primary; 2 Middle; 1 High; 1 Other Level
6 Regular; 0 Special Education; 0 Vocational; 1 Alternative
0 Magnet; 0 Charter; 3 Title I Eligible; 0 School-wide Title I
Students: 4,051 (51.3% male; 48.7% female)
Individual Education Program: 556 (13.7%);
English Language Learner: 120 (3.0%); Migrant: n/a
Eligible for Free Lunch Program: 1,123 (27.7%)
Eligible for Reduced-Price Lunch Program: 374 (9.2%)
Teachers: 247.8 (16.3 to 1)
Librarians/Media Specialists: 6.0 (675.2 to 1)
Guidance Counselors: 11.0 (368.3 to 1)
Current Spending: ($ per student per year):
Total: $5,503; Instruction: $3,282; Support Services: $1,963
Enrollment, Drop-out Rates and Diploma Recipients by Race/Ethnicity

Category	Total	White	Black	Asian	AIAN	Hisp.
Enrollment (%)	100.0	66.7	2.1	0.8	26.3	4.1
Drop-out Rate (%)	3.0	3.0	4.5	0.0	2.9	6.9
H.S. Diplomas (#)	270	207	6	2	49	6

Oologah-Talala
PO Box 189 • Oologah, OK 74053-0189
(918) 443-6079 • http://www.oologah.k12.ok.us/
Grade Span: KG-12; **Agency Type:** 1
Schools: 4
2 Primary; 1 Middle; 1 High; 0 Other Level
4 Regular; 0 Special Education; 0 Vocational; 0 Alternative
0 Magnet; 0 Charter; 2 Title I Eligible; 0 School-wide Title I
Students: 1,667 (51.6% male; 48.4% female)
Individual Education Program: 231 (13.9%);
English Language Learner: 0 (0.0%); Migrant: n/a
Eligible for Free Lunch Program: 306 (18.4%)
Eligible for Reduced-Price Lunch Program: 169 (10.1%)
Teachers: 98.5 (16.9 to 1)
Librarians/Media Specialists: 2.0 (833.5 to 1)
Guidance Counselors: 3.0 (555.7 to 1)
Current Spending: ($ per student per year):
Total: $5,219; Instruction: $2,879; Support Services: $1,985
Enrollment, Drop-out Rates and Diploma Recipients by Race/Ethnicity

Category	Total	White	Black	Asian	AIAN	Hisp.
Enrollment (%)	100.0	65.0	0.4	0.9	33.1	0.7
Drop-out Rate (%)	0.6	0.3	0.0	0.0	1.3	0.0
H.S. Diplomas (#)	103	62	1	0	40	0

Seminole County

Seminole
PO Box 1031 • Seminole, OK 74818-1031
(405) 382-5085
Grade Span: PK-12; **Agency Type:** 1
Schools: 5
3 Primary; 1 Middle; 1 High; 0 Other Level
5 Regular; 0 Special Education; 0 Vocational; 0 Alternative
0 Magnet; 0 Charter; 5 Title I Eligible; 5 School-wide Title I
Students: 1,510 (52.1% male; 47.9% female)
Individual Education Program: 184 (12.2%);
English Language Learner: 42 (2.8%); Migrant: n/a
Eligible for Free Lunch Program: 806 (53.4%)
Eligible for Reduced-Price Lunch Program: 145 (9.6%)
Teachers: 98.2 (15.4 to 1)
Librarians/Media Specialists: 4.0 (377.5 to 1)
Guidance Counselors: 5.0 (302.0 to 1)
Current Spending: ($ per student per year):
Total: $5,392; Instruction: $3,106; Support Services: $1,965
Enrollment, Drop-out Rates and Diploma Recipients by Race/Ethnicity

Category	Total	White	Black	Asian	AIAN	Hisp.
Enrollment (%)	100.0	62.0	7.2	0.6	28.1	2.1
Drop-out Rate (%)	10.8	8.6	8.0	0.0	17.9	16.7
H.S. Diplomas (#)	94	65	5	1	20	3

Sequoyah County

Muldrow
PO Box 660 • Muldrow, OK 74948-0660
(918) 427-7406
Grade Span: PK-12; **Agency Type:** 1
Schools: 3
1 Primary; 1 Middle; 1 High; 0 Other Level
3 Regular; 0 Special Education; 0 Vocational; 0 Alternative
0 Magnet; 0 Charter; 3 Title I Eligible; 3 School-wide Title I
Students: 1,575 (52.5% male; 47.5% female)
Individual Education Program: 188 (11.9%);
English Language Learner: 148 (9.4%); Migrant: n/a
Eligible for Free Lunch Program: 732 (46.5%)
Eligible for Reduced-Price Lunch Program: 202 (12.8%)
Teachers: 102.6 (15.4 to 1)
Librarians/Media Specialists: 2.0 (787.5 to 1)
Guidance Counselors: 3.0 (525.0 to 1)
Current Spending: ($ per student per year):
Total: $5,481; Instruction: $3,185; Support Services: $1,902
Enrollment, Drop-out Rates and Diploma Recipients by Race/Ethnicity

Category	Total	White	Black	Asian	AIAN	Hisp.
Enrollment (%)	100.0	60.3	2.0	1.1	31.6	5.0
Drop-out Rate (%)	2.9	1.0	0.0	0.0	5.8	11.1
H.S. Diplomas (#)	114	55	2	1	55	1

Sallisaw

701 J T Stites Blvd • Sallisaw, OK 74955-9304
(918) 775-5544
Grade Span: KG-12; **Agency Type:** 1
Schools: 4
2 Primary; 1 Middle; 1 High; 0 Other Level
4 Regular; 0 Special Education; 0 Vocational; 0 Alternative
0 Magnet; 0 Charter; 4 Title I Eligible; 2 School-wide Title I
Students: 1,896 (53.7% male; 46.3% female)
Individual Education Program: 354 (18.7%);
English Language Learner: 43 (2.3%); Migrant: n/a
Eligible for Free Lunch Program: 904 (47.7%)
Eligible for Reduced-Price Lunch Program: 220 (11.6%)
Teachers: 126.2 (15.0 to 1)
Librarians/Media Specialists: 2.0 (948.0 to 1)
Guidance Counselors: 4.0 (474.0 to 1)
Current Spending: ($ per student per year):
Total: $5,461; Instruction: $3,208; Support Services: $1,945
Enrollment, Drop-out Rates and Diploma Recipients by Race/Ethnicity

Category	Total	White	Black	Asian	AIAN	Hisp.
Enrollment (%)	100.0	54.3	2.1	0.4	40.8	2.4
Drop-out Rate (%)	2.1	2.1	0.0	0.0	0.4	100.0
H.S. Diplomas (#)	108	65	1	0	41	1

Stephens County

Duncan

PO Box 1548 • Duncan, OK 73534-1548
(580) 255-0686
Grade Span: PK-12; **Agency Type:** 1
Schools: 10
7 Primary; 2 Middle; 1 High; 0 Other Level
10 Regular; 0 Special Education; 0 Vocational; 0 Alternative
0 Magnet; 0 Charter; 6 Title I Eligible; 4 School-wide Title I
Students: 3,683 (51.7% male; 48.3% female)
Individual Education Program: 409 (11.1%);
English Language Learner: 277 (7.5%); Migrant: n/a
Eligible for Free Lunch Program: 1,592 (43.2%)
Eligible for Reduced-Price Lunch Program: 242 (6.6%)
Teachers: 217.9 (16.9 to 1)
Librarians/Media Specialists: 6.0 (613.8 to 1)
Guidance Counselors: 10.3 (357.6 to 1)
Current Spending: ($ per student per year):
Total: $5,841; Instruction: $3,359; Support Services: $2,164
Enrollment, Drop-out Rates and Diploma Recipients by Race/Ethnicity

Category	Total	White	Black	Asian	AIAN	Hisp.
Enrollment (%)	100.0	73.9	7.7	1.0	5.9	11.5
Drop-out Rate (%)	8.4	8.8	2.7	20.0	7.9	8.7
H.S. Diplomas (#)	245	197	15	0	6	27

Texas County

Guymon

PO Box 1307 • Guymon, OK 73942-1307
(580) 338-4340 • http://www.ptsi.net/user/guymonhs/
Grade Span: PK-12; **Agency Type:** 1
Schools: 8
5 Primary; 2 Middle; 1 High; 0 Other Level
8 Regular; 0 Special Education; 0 Vocational; 0 Alternative
0 Magnet; 0 Charter; 5 Title I Eligible; 5 School-wide Title I
Students: 2,271 (50.0% male; 50.0% female)
Individual Education Program: 230 (10.1%);
English Language Learner: 852 (37.5%); Migrant: n/a
Eligible for Free Lunch Program: 1,086 (47.8%)
Eligible for Reduced-Price Lunch Program: 271 (11.9%)
Teachers: 164.7 (13.8 to 1)
Librarians/Media Specialists: 3.9 (582.3 to 1)
Guidance Counselors: 5.9 (384.9 to 1)
Current Spending: ($ per student per year):
Total: $6,372; Instruction: $3,779; Support Services: $2,099
Enrollment, Drop-out Rates and Diploma Recipients by Race/Ethnicity

Category	Total	White	Black	Asian	AIAN	Hisp.
Enrollment (%)	100.0	46.8	0.7	1.2	0.6	50.8
Drop-out Rate (%)	4.1	2.2	66.7	0.0	0.0	5.1
H.S. Diplomas (#)	150	94	2	0	0	54

Tulsa County

Bixby

109 N Armstrong St • Bixby, OK 74008-4449
(918) 366-2200 • http://www.bixby.k12.ok.us/
Grade Span: PK-12; **Agency Type:** 1
Schools: 5
2 Primary; 2 Middle; 1 High; 0 Other Level
5 Regular; 0 Special Education; 0 Vocational; 0 Alternative
0 Magnet; 0 Charter; 3 Title I Eligible; 0 School-wide Title I
Students: 3,803 (52.0% male; 48.0% female)
Individual Education Program: 460 (12.1%);
English Language Learner: 82 (2.2%); Migrant: n/a
Eligible for Free Lunch Program: 596 (15.7%)
Eligible for Reduced-Price Lunch Program: 224 (5.9%)
Teachers: 199.5 (19.1 to 1)
Librarians/Media Specialists: 5.0 (760.6 to 1)
Guidance Counselors: 11.0 (345.7 to 1)
Current Spending: ($ per student per year):
Total: $4,788; Instruction: $2,622; Support Services: $1,899
Enrollment, Drop-out Rates and Diploma Recipients by Race/Ethnicity

Category	Total	White	Black	Asian	AIAN	Hisp.
Enrollment (%)	100.0	83.4	1.5	0.4	10.9	3.8
Drop-out Rate (%)	3.9	3.6	7.7	9.1	3.4	11.8
H.S. Diplomas (#)	286	248	2	2	22	12

Broken Arrow

601 S Main St • Broken Arrow, OK 74012-4334
(918) 259-4300 • http://www.ba.k12.ok.us/
Grade Span: PK-12; **Agency Type:** 1
Schools: 22
14 Primary; 5 Middle; 2 High; 1 Other Level
22 Regular; 0 Special Education; 0 Vocational; 0 Alternative
0 Magnet; 0 Charter; 8 Title I Eligible; 0 School-wide Title I
Students: 14,741 (51.8% male; 48.2% female)
Individual Education Program: 2,072 (14.1%);
English Language Learner: 392 (2.7%); Migrant: n/a
Eligible for Free Lunch Program: 2,400 (16.3%)
Eligible for Reduced-Price Lunch Program: 1,222 (8.3%)
Teachers: 866.9 (17.0 to 1)
Librarians/Media Specialists: 21.5 (685.6 to 1)
Guidance Counselors: 38.1 (386.9 to 1)
Current Spending: ($ per student per year):
Total: $5,315; Instruction: $2,798; Support Services: $2,164
Enrollment, Drop-out Rates and Diploma Recipients by Race/Ethnicity

Category	Total	White	Black	Asian	AIAN	Hisp.
Enrollment (%)	100.0	82.0	4.8	1.6	8.3	3.4
Drop-out Rate (%)	3.7	3.5	6.8	3.9	3.8	7.8
H.S. Diplomas (#)	885	781	29	9	56	10

Collinsville

1119 W Broadway St • Collinsville, OK 74021-2339
(918) 371-2326 • http://www.collinsville.k12.ok.us/
Grade Span: PK-12; **Agency Type:** 1
Schools: 5
3 Primary; 1 Middle; 1 High; 0 Other Level
5 Regular; 0 Special Education; 0 Vocational; 0 Alternative
0 Magnet; 0 Charter; 3 Title I Eligible; 0 School-wide Title I
Students: 2,016 (50.8% male; 49.2% female)
Individual Education Program: 233 (11.6%);
English Language Learner: 0 (0.0%); Migrant: n/a
Eligible for Free Lunch Program: 398 (19.7%)
Eligible for Reduced-Price Lunch Program: 196 (9.7%)
Teachers: 106.1 (19.0 to 1)
Librarians/Media Specialists: 4.0 (504.0 to 1)
Guidance Counselors: 4.0 (504.0 to 1)
Current Spending: ($ per student per year):
Total: $5,170; Instruction: $3,109; Support Services: $1,768
Enrollment, Drop-out Rates and Diploma Recipients by Race/Ethnicity

Category	Total	White	Black	Asian	AIAN	Hisp.
Enrollment (%)	100.0	56.3	0.4	0.0	40.5	2.7
Drop-out Rate (%)	3.0	3.0	0.0	n/a	3.2	0.0
H.S. Diplomas (#)	128	73	0	0	51	4

Glenpool

PO Box 1149 • Glenpool, OK 74033-1149
(918) 322-9500 • http://www.glenpool.k12.ok.us/
Grade Span: PK-12; **Agency Type:** 1
Schools: 3
1 Primary; 1 Middle; 1 High; 0 Other Level
3 Regular; 0 Special Education; 0 Vocational; 0 Alternative
0 Magnet; 0 Charter; 1 Title I Eligible; 0 School-wide Title I
Students: 2,073 (51.3% male; 48.7% female)
Individual Education Program: 269 (13.0%);
English Language Learner: 55 (2.7%); Migrant: n/a
Eligible for Free Lunch Program: 504 (24.3%)
Eligible for Reduced-Price Lunch Program: 296 (14.3%)
Teachers: 131.8 (15.7 to 1)
Librarians/Media Specialists: 3.0 (691.0 to 1)
Guidance Counselors: 5.0 (414.6 to 1)
Current Spending: ($ per student per year):
Total: $5,034; Instruction: $3,035; Support Services: $1,667

Enrollment, Drop-out Rates and Diploma Recipients by Race/Ethnicity

Category	Total	White	Black	Asian	AIAN	Hisp.
Enrollment (%)	100.0	65.4	3.7	1.2	25.7	4.1
Drop-out Rate (%)	3.5	2.3	4.0	0.0	6.7	5.3
H.S. Diplomas (#)	130	89	4	0	36	1

Jenks

205 E B St • Jenks, OK 74037-3906
(918) 299-4411
Grade Span: PK-12; **Agency Type:** 1
Schools: 9
4 Primary; 3 Middle; 1 High; 1 Other Level
9 Regular; 0 Special Education; 0 Vocational; 0 Alternative
0 Magnet; 0 Charter; 5 Title I Eligible; 0 School-wide Title I
Students: 9,300 (51.3% male; 48.7% female)
Individual Education Program: 1,418 (15.2%);
English Language Learner: 514 (5.5%); Migrant: n/a
Eligible for Free Lunch Program: 1,162 (12.5%)
Eligible for Reduced-Price Lunch Program: 346 (3.7%)
Teachers: 524.5 (17.7 to 1)
Librarians/Media Specialists: 11.0 (845.5 to 1)
Guidance Counselors: 19.9 (467.3 to 1)
Current Spending: ($ per student per year):
Total: $5,667; Instruction: $2,817; Support Services: $2,570
Enrollment, Drop-out Rates and Diploma Recipients by Race/Ethnicity

Category	Total	White	Black	Asian	AIAN	Hisp.
Enrollment (%)	100.0	78.5	5.5	2.9	7.7	5.4
Drop-out Rate (%)	2.6	2.2	3.0	2.8	6.6	3.1
H.S. Diplomas (#)	625	522	28	19	30	26

Owasso

1501 N Ash St • Owasso, OK 74055-4920
(918) 272-5367 • http://www.owasso.k12.ok.us/
Grade Span: PK-12; **Agency Type:** 1
Schools: 12
7 Primary; 2 Middle; 1 High; 2 Other Level
12 Regular; 0 Special Education; 0 Vocational; 0 Alternative
0 Magnet; 0 Charter; 4 Title I Eligible; 0 School-wide Title I
Students: 7,217 (50.6% male; 49.4% female)
Individual Education Program: 729 (10.1%);
English Language Learner: 184 (2.5%); Migrant: n/a
Eligible for Free Lunch Program: 719 (10.0%)
Eligible for Reduced-Price Lunch Program: 342 (4.7%)
Teachers: 418.6 (17.2 to 1)
Librarians/Media Specialists: 13.4 (538.6 to 1)
Guidance Counselors: 14.0 (515.5 to 1)
Current Spending: ($ per student per year):
Total: $4,718; Instruction: $2,771; Support Services: $1,619
Enrollment, Drop-out Rates and Diploma Recipients by Race/Ethnicity

Category	Total	White	Black	Asian	AIAN	Hisp.
Enrollment (%)	100.0	84.2	1.7	1.2	9.2	3.7
Drop-out Rate (%)	3.4	3.2	3.3	3.4	1.5	13.8
H.S. Diplomas (#)	408	347	10	5	31	15

Sand Springs

PO Box 970 • Sand Springs, OK 74063-0970
(918) 246-1400 • http://www.sandsprings.k12.ok.us/
Grade Span: PK-12; **Agency Type:** 1
Schools: 11
6 Primary; 3 Middle; 2 High; 0 Other Level
11 Regular; 0 Special Education; 0 Vocational; 0 Alternative
0 Magnet; 0 Charter; 8 Title I Eligible; 3 School-wide Title I
Students: 5,172 (52.5% male; 47.5% female)
Individual Education Program: 918 (17.7%);
English Language Learner: 60 (1.2%); Migrant: n/a
Eligible for Free Lunch Program: 1,668 (32.3%)
Eligible for Reduced-Price Lunch Program: 639 (12.4%)
Teachers: 329.3 (15.7 to 1)
Librarians/Media Specialists: 6.5 (795.7 to 1)
Guidance Counselors: 14.0 (369.4 to 1)
Current Spending: ($ per student per year):
Total: $5,614; Instruction: $3,283; Support Services: $2,069
Enrollment, Drop-out Rates and Diploma Recipients by Race/Ethnicity

Category	Total	White	Black	Asian	AIAN	Hisp.
Enrollment (%)	100.0	75.6	4.1	0.4	17.7	2.2
Drop-out Rate (%)	2.5	2.4	0.0	0.0	4.1	0.0
H.S. Diplomas (#)	349	255	18	0	69	7

Skiatook

355 S Osage St • Skiatook, OK 74070-2015
(918) 396-5702
Grade Span: PK-12; **Agency Type:** 1
Schools: 5
2 Primary; 2 Middle; 1 High; 0 Other Level
5 Regular; 0 Special Education; 0 Vocational; 0 Alternative
0 Magnet; 0 Charter; 2 Title I Eligible; 0 School-wide Title I
Students: 2,328 (52.1% male; 47.9% female)
Individual Education Program: 274 (11.8%);
English Language Learner: 0 (0.0%); Migrant: n/a
Eligible for Free Lunch Program: 631 (27.1%)
Eligible for Reduced-Price Lunch Program: 222 (9.5%)
Teachers: 141.0 (16.5 to 1)
Librarians/Media Specialists: 3.0 (776.0 to 1)
Guidance Counselors: 6.0 (388.0 to 1)
Current Spending: ($ per student per year):
Total: $4,870; Instruction: $2,884; Support Services: $1,672
Enrollment, Drop-out Rates and Diploma Recipients by Race/Ethnicity

Category	Total	White	Black	Asian	AIAN	Hisp.
Enrollment (%)	100.0	67.2	0.5	0.2	30.6	1.5
Drop-out Rate (%)	6.2	5.5	0.0	0.0	7.4	25.0
H.S. Diplomas (#)	158	105	1	0	51	1

Tulsa

PO Box 470208 • Tulsa, OK 74147-0208
(918) 746-6303 • http://www.tulsaschools.org/
Grade Span: PK-12; **Agency Type:** 1
Schools: 86
60 Primary; 15 Middle; 10 High; 1 Other Level
86 Regular; 0 Special Education; 0 Vocational; 0 Alternative
0 Magnet; 3 Charter; 45 Title I Eligible; 45 School-wide Title I
Students: 43,029 (50.8% male; 49.2% female)
Individual Education Program: 7,531 (17.5%);
English Language Learner: 3,793 (8.8%); Migrant: n/a
Eligible for Free Lunch Program: 26,715 (62.1%)
Eligible for Reduced-Price Lunch Program: 4,770 (11.1%)
Teachers: 2,669.8 (16.1 to 1)
Librarians/Media Specialists: 78.3 (549.5 to 1)
Guidance Counselors: 149.6 (287.6 to 1)
Current Spending: ($ per student per year):
Total: $6,095; Instruction: $3,197; Support Services: $2,546
Enrollment, Drop-out Rates and Diploma Recipients by Race/Ethnicity

Category	Total	White	Black	Asian	AIAN	Hisp.
Enrollment (%)	100.0	41.3	35.7	1.4	8.7	12.9
Drop-out Rate (%)	9.6	8.4	10.2	6.0	13.2	12.1
H.S. Diplomas (#)	1,758	900	596	33	115	114

Union

5656 S 129th E Ave • Tulsa, OK 74134-6715
(918) 459-5432 • http://www.unionps.org/
Grade Span: PK-12; **Agency Type:** 1
Schools: 15
11 Primary; 1 Middle; 1 High; 2 Other Level
15 Regular; 0 Special Education; 0 Vocational; 0 Alternative
0 Magnet; 0 Charter; 3 Title I Eligible; 1 School-wide Title I
Students: 13,517 (50.5% male; 49.5% female)
Individual Education Program: 1,109 (8.2%);
English Language Learner: 1,600 (11.8%); Migrant: n/a
Eligible for Free Lunch Program: 2,081 (15.4%)
Eligible for Reduced-Price Lunch Program: 606 (4.5%)
Teachers: 695.5 (19.4 to 1)
Librarians/Media Specialists: 17.2 (785.9 to 1)
Guidance Counselors: 25.0 (540.7 to 1)
Current Spending: ($ per student per year):
Total: $5,147; Instruction: $2,968; Support Services: $1,954
Enrollment, Drop-out Rates and Diploma Recipients by Race/Ethnicity

Category	Total	White	Black	Asian	AIAN	Hisp.
Enrollment (%)	100.0	65.6	10.2	5.4	9.6	9.2
Drop-out Rate (%)	4.9	4.0	8.4	2.3	6.6	10.9
H.S. Diplomas (#)	768	553	57	52	63	43

Wagoner County

Coweta

PO Box 550 • Coweta, OK 74429-0550
(918) 486-6506
Grade Span: KG-12; **Agency Type:** 1
Schools: 6
3 Primary; 2 Middle; 1 High; 0 Other Level
6 Regular; 0 Special Education; 0 Vocational; 0 Alternative
0 Magnet; 0 Charter; 3 Title I Eligible; 0 School-wide Title I
Students: 2,635 (50.8% male; 49.2% female)
Individual Education Program: 427 (16.2%);
English Language Learner: 51 (1.9%); Migrant: n/a
Eligible for Free Lunch Program: 695 (26.4%)
Eligible for Reduced-Price Lunch Program: 256 (9.7%)
Teachers: 168.4 (15.6 to 1)
Librarians/Media Specialists: 5.0 (527.0 to 1)
Guidance Counselors: 8.0 (329.4 to 1)
Current Spending: ($ per student per year):
Total: $5,135; Instruction: $3,053; Support Services: $1,685

Enrollment, Drop-out Rates and Diploma Recipients by Race/Ethnicity

Category	Total	White	Black	Asian	AIAN	Hisp.
Enrollment (%)	100.0	64.3	4.1	0.2	29.5	1.9
Drop-out Rate (%)	5.9	5.6	0.0	100.0	6.4	20.0
H.S. Diplomas (#)	154	95	9	0	50	0

Wagoner

PO Box 707 • Wagoner, OK 74477-0707
(918) 485-4046 • http://www.wagoner.k12.ok.us/
Grade Span: PK-12; **Agency Type:** 1
Schools: 6
3 Primary; 2 Middle; 1 High; 0 Other Level
6 Regular; 0 Special Education; 0 Vocational; 0 Alternative
0 Magnet; 0 Charter; 6 Title I Eligible; 6 School-wide Title I
Students: 2,448 (51.9% male; 48.1% female)
Individual Education Program: 414 (16.9%);
English Language Learner: 11 (0.4%); Migrant: n/a
Eligible for Free Lunch Program: 1,643 (67.1%)
Eligible for Reduced-Price Lunch Program: 253 (10.3%)
Teachers: 165.4 (14.8 to 1)
Librarians/Media Specialists: 2.0 (1,224.0 to 1)
Guidance Counselors: 7.0 (349.7 to 1)
Current Spending: ($ per student per year):
Total: $5,635; Instruction: $3,502; Support Services: $1,720

Enrollment, Drop-out Rates and Diploma Recipients by Race/Ethnicity

Category	Total	White	Black	Asian	AIAN	Hisp.
Enrollment (%)	100.0	61.4	11.2	0.7	25.4	1.4
Drop-out Rate (%)	5.1	5.2	3.1	0.0	6.5	0.0
H.S. Diplomas (#)	133	97	17	1	17	1

Washington County

Bartlesville

PO Box 1357 • Bartlesville, OK 74005-1357
(918) 336-8600 • http://www.bartlesville.k12.ok.us/
Grade Span: PK-12; **Agency Type:** 1
Schools: 12
7 Primary; 2 Middle; 1 High; 2 Other Level
11 Regular; 0 Special Education; 0 Vocational; 1 Alternative
0 Magnet; 0 Charter; 4 Title I Eligible; 4 School-wide Title I
Students: 6,019 (52.5% male; 47.5% female)
Individual Education Program: 732 (12.2%);
English Language Learner: 123 (2.0%); Migrant: n/a
Eligible for Free Lunch Program: 1,559 (25.9%)
Eligible for Reduced-Price Lunch Program: 449 (7.5%)
Teachers: 398.3 (15.1 to 1)
Librarians/Media Specialists: 9.1 (661.4 to 1)
Guidance Counselors: 19.0 (316.8 to 1)
Current Spending: ($ per student per year):
Total: $5,916; Instruction: $3,401; Support Services: $2,245

Enrollment, Drop-out Rates and Diploma Recipients by Race/Ethnicity

Category	Total	White	Black	Asian	AIAN	Hisp.
Enrollment (%)	100.0	78.7	5.2	1.1	10.7	4.2
Drop-out Rate (%)	6.0	5.4	12.9	0.0	9.2	7.8
H.S. Diplomas (#)	421	346	22	8	37	8

Woodward County

Woodward

PO Box 668 • Woodward, OK 73802-0668
(580) 256-6063 • http://www.woodward.k12.ok.us/
Grade Span: PK-12; **Agency Type:** 1
Schools: 8
4 Primary; 2 Middle; 1 High; 1 Other Level
8 Regular; 0 Special Education; 0 Vocational; 0 Alternative
0 Magnet; 0 Charter; 4 Title I Eligible; 0 School-wide Title I
Students: 2,526 (51.5% male; 48.5% female)
Individual Education Program: 311 (12.3%);
English Language Learner: 141 (5.6%); Migrant: n/a
Eligible for Free Lunch Program: 738 (29.2%)
Eligible for Reduced-Price Lunch Program: 240 (9.5%)
Teachers: 170.0 (14.9 to 1)
Librarians/Media Specialists: 5.0 (505.2 to 1)
Guidance Counselors: 8.0 (315.8 to 1)
Current Spending: ($ per student per year):
Total: $5,201; Instruction: $3,046; Support Services: $1,865

Enrollment, Drop-out Rates and Diploma Recipients by Race/Ethnicity

Category	Total	White	Black	Asian	AIAN	Hisp.
Enrollment (%)	100.0	86.0	1.3	1.0	2.9	8.8
Drop-out Rate (%)	8.5	7.7	0.0	0.0	23.1	22.5
H.S. Diplomas (#)	160	150	0	3	1	6

Number of Schools

Rank	Number	District Name	City
1	94	Oklahoma City	Oklahoma City
2	86	Tulsa	Tulsa
3	37	Lawton	Lawton
4	27	Moore	Moore
4	27	Putnam City	Warr Acres
6	26	MWC-Del City	Midwest City
7	23	Norman	Norman
8	22	Broken Arrow	Broken Arrow
8	22	Edmond	Edmond
10	15	Union	Tulsa
11	14	Enid	Enid
12	13	Muskogee	Muskogee
13	12	Bartlesville	Bartlesville
13	12	Owasso	Owasso
15	11	Ponca City	Ponca City
15	11	Sand Springs	Sand Springs
17	10	Duncan	Duncan
17	10	Yukon	Yukon
19	9	Altus	Altus
19	9	Choctaw-Nicoma Park	Choctaw
19	9	Jenks	Jenks
19	9	Mc Alester	Mcalester
19	9	Mustang	Mustang
19	9	Sapulpa	Sapulpa
19	9	Shawnee	Shawnee
19	9	Stillwater	Stillwater
27	8	Guymon	Guymon
27	8	Miami	Miami
27	8	Woodward	Woodward
30	7	Ardmore	Ardmore
30	7	Chickasha	Chickasha
30	7	Claremore	Claremore
30	7	Cushing	Cushing
30	7	Durant	Durant
30	7	El Reno	El Reno
36	6	Ada	Ada
36	6	Coweta	Coweta
36	6	Elk City	Elk City
36	6	Guthrie	Guthrie
36	6	Harrah	Harrah
36	6	Pryor	Pryor
36	6	Tahlequah	Tahlequah
36	6	Tecumseh	Tecumseh
36	6	Wagoner	Wagoner
36	6	Western Heights	Oklahoma City
46	5	Anadarko	Anadarko
46	5	Bixby	Bixby
46	5	Blackwell	Blackwell
46	5	Byng	Ada
46	5	Catoosa	Catoosa
46	5	Clinton	Clinton
46	5	Collinsville	Collinsville
46	5	Idabel	Idabel
46	5	Noble	Noble
46	5	Seminole	Seminole
46	5	Skiatook	Skiatook
46	5	Vinita	Vinita
46	5	Weatherford	Weatherford
59	4	Bristow	Bristow
59	4	Broken Bow	Broken Bow
59	4	Checotah	Checotah
59	4	Cleveland	Cleveland
59	4	Deer Creek	Edmond
59	4	Fort Gibson	Fort Gibson
59	4	Grove	Grove
59	4	Hilldale	Muskogee
59	4	Mannford	Mannford
59	4	Okmulgee	Okmulgee
59	4	Oologah-Talala	Oologah
59	4	Piedmont	Piedmont
59	4	Poteau	Poteau
59	4	Sallisaw	Sallisaw
73	3	Glenpool	Glenpool
73	3	Jay	Jay
73	3	Madill	Madill
73	3	Mc Loud	Mcloud
73	3	Muldrow	Muldrow

Number of Teachers

Rank	Number	District Name	City
1	2,669	Tulsa	Tulsa
2	2,529	Oklahoma City	Oklahoma City
3	1,188	Putnam City	Warr Acres
4	1,114	Moore	Moore
5	1,033	Lawton	Lawton
6	1,027	Edmond	Edmond
7	914	MWC-Del City	Midwest City
8	866	Broken Arrow	Broken Arrow
9	793	Norman	Norman
10	695	Union	Tulsa
11	524	Jenks	Jenks
12	429	Enid	Enid
13	418	Owasso	Owasso
14	398	Bartlesville	Bartlesville
15	396	Mustang	Mustang
16	382	Muskogee	Muskogee
17	355	Ponca City	Ponca City
18	342	Yukon	Yukon
19	329	Sand Springs	Sand Springs
20	310	Stillwater	Stillwater
21	295	Altus	Altus
22	269	Choctaw-Nicoma Park	Choctaw
23	251	Sapulpa	Sapulpa
24	247	Claremore	Claremore
25	246	Shawnee	Shawnee
26	241	Tahlequah	Tahlequah
27	217	Duncan	Duncan
28	208	Guthrie	Guthrie
29	208	Western Heights	Oklahoma City
30	203	Ardmore	Ardmore
31	199	Bixby	Bixby
32	193	Durant	Durant
33	190	Mc Alester	Mcalester
34	181	Ada	Ada
35	181	Chickasha	Chickasha
36	171	El Reno	El Reno
37	170	Woodward	Woodward
38	168	Coweta	Coweta
39	166	Noble	Noble
40	165	Wagoner	Wagoner
41	164	Guymon	Guymon
42	151	Anadarko	Anadarko
43	148	Elk City	Elk City
44	147	Catoosa	Catoosa
45	147	Grove	Grove
46	144	Miami	Miami
47	142	Tecumseh	Tecumseh
48	141	Skiatook	Skiatook
49	138	Pryor	Pryor
50	136	Harrah	Harrah
51	135	Clinton	Clinton
52	134	Poteau	Poteau
53	134	Okmulgee	Okmulgee
54	131	Glenpool	Glenpool
55	128	Cushing	Cushing
56	126	Sallisaw	Sallisaw
57	119	Broken Bow	Broken Bow
58	118	Deer Creek	Edmond
59	117	Weatherford	Weatherford
60	114	Idabel	Idabel
60	114	Mc Loud	Mcloud
62	114	Fort Gibson	Fort Gibson
63	113	Jay	Jay
64	113	Byng	Ada
65	107	Bristow	Bristow
66	106	Collinsville	Collinsville
67	105	Vinita	Vinita
68	105	Hilldale	Muskogee
69	103	Cleveland	Cleveland
70	102	Muldrow	Muldrow
71	100	Checotah	Checotah
72	98	Oologah-Talala	Oologah
73	98	Seminole	Seminole
74	95	Blackwell	Blackwell
74	95	Madill	Madill
76	92	Mannford	Mannford
77	90	Piedmont	Piedmont

Number of Students

Rank	Number	District Name	City
1	43,029	Tulsa	Tulsa
2	40,856	Oklahoma City	Oklahoma City
3	19,356	Putnam City	Warr Acres
4	18,458	Moore	Moore
5	17,872	Edmond	Edmond
6	16,986	Lawton	Lawton
7	14,741	Broken Arrow	Broken Arrow
8	14,347	MWC-Del City	Midwest City
9	13,517	Union	Tulsa
10	12,657	Norman	Norman
11	9,300	Jenks	Jenks
12	7,217	Owasso	Owasso
13	6,802	Mustang	Mustang
14	6,383	Muskogee	Muskogee
15	6,378	Enid	Enid
16	6,019	Bartlesville	Bartlesville
17	5,792	Yukon	Yukon
18	5,631	Ponca City	Ponca City
19	5,343	Stillwater	Stillwater
20	5,172	Sand Springs	Sand Springs
21	4,416	Choctaw-Nicoma Park	Choctaw
22	4,309	Altus	Altus
23	4,216	Sapulpa	Sapulpa
24	4,051	Claremore	Claremore
25	3,805	Shawnee	Shawnee
26	3,803	Bixby	Bixby
27	3,731	Tahlequah	Tahlequah
28	3,683	Duncan	Duncan
29	3,218	Ardmore	Ardmore
30	3,143	Guthrie	Guthrie
31	3,132	Western Heights	Oklahoma City
32	3,126	Durant	Durant
33	2,857	Mc Alester	Mcalester
34	2,840	Chickasha	Chickasha
35	2,743	Noble	Noble
36	2,635	Coweta	Coweta
37	2,628	El Reno	El Reno
38	2,551	Ada	Ada
39	2,526	Woodward	Woodward
40	2,448	Miami	Miami
40	2,448	Wagoner	Wagoner
42	2,375	Grove	Grove
43	2,365	Pryor	Pryor
44	2,344	Catoosa	Catoosa
45	2,328	Skiatook	Skiatook
46	2,271	Guymon	Guymon
47	2,215	Harrah	Harrah
48	2,183	Anadarko	Anadarko
49	2,171	Tecumseh	Tecumseh
50	2,124	Elk City	Elk City
51	2,073	Glenpool	Glenpool
52	2,016	Collinsville	Collinsville
53	1,982	Poteau	Poteau
54	1,958	Okmulgee	Okmulgee
55	1,923	Cushing	Cushing
56	1,896	Sallisaw	Sallisaw
57	1,883	Deer Creek	Edmond
58	1,853	Clinton	Clinton
59	1,798	Fort Gibson	Fort Gibson
60	1,779	Mc Loud	Mcloud
61	1,774	Weatherford	Weatherford
62	1,731	Hilldale	Muskogee
63	1,719	Broken Bow	Broken Bow
64	1,718	Cleveland	Cleveland
65	1,713	Jay	Jay
66	1,709	Bristow	Bristow
67	1,678	Mannford	Mannford
68	1,674	Vinita	Vinita
69	1,667	Oologah-Talala	Oologah
70	1,666	Byng	Ada
70	1,666	Idabel	Idabel
72	1,592	Checotah	Checotah
73	1,579	Blackwell	Blackwell
74	1,575	Muldrow	Muldrow
75	1,549	Piedmont	Piedmont
76	1,542	Madill	Madill
77	1,510	Seminole	Seminole

Male Students

Rank	Percent	District Name	City
1	53.7	Sallisaw	Sallisaw
2	53.6	Broken Bow	Broken Bow
3	53.5	Okmulgee	Okmulgee
4	53.4	Deer Creek	Edmond
4	53.4	Tecumseh	Tecumseh
6	53.0	Choctaw-Nicoma Park	Choctaw
7	52.8	Tahlequah	Tahlequah
8	52.6	Altus	Altus
8	52.6	Vinita	Vinita
10	52.5	Bartlesville	Bartlesville
10	52.5	Muldrow	Muldrow
10	52.5	Sand Springs	Sand Springs
13	52.2	Ponca City	Ponca City
14	52.1	Ardmore	Ardmore
14	52.1	MWC-Del City	Midwest City
14	52.1	Seminole	Seminole
14	52.1	Skiatook	Skiatook
18	52.0	Bixby	Bixby
18	52.0	Norman	Norman
20	51.9	El Reno	El Reno
20	51.9	Madill	Madill
20	51.9	Mannford	Mannford
20	51.9	Mc Alester	Mcalester
20	51.9	Wagoner	Wagoner
25	51.8	Broken Arrow	Broken Arrow
25	51.8	Hilldale	Muskogee
25	51.8	Moore	Moore
28	51.7	Bristow	Bristow
28	51.7	Duncan	Duncan
28	51.7	Fort Gibson	Fort Gibson
28	51.7	Mc Loud	Mcloud
32	51.6	Durant	Durant
32	51.6	Miami	Miami

Rank	Percent	District Name	City
32	51.6	Oologah-Talala	Oologah
32	51.6	Shawnee	Shawnee
36	51.5	Lawton	Lawton
36	51.5	Piedmont	Piedmont
36	51.5	Woodward	Woodward
39	51.4	Clinton	Clinton
39	51.4	Jay	Jay
41	51.3	Catoosa	Catoosa
41	51.3	Chickasha	Chickasha
41	51.3	Claremore	Claremore
41	51.3	Edmond	Edmond
41	51.3	Enid	Enid
41	51.3	Glenpool	Glenpool
41	51.3	Guthrie	Guthrie
41	51.3	Jenks	Jenks
41	51.3	Noble	Noble
50	51.2	Ada	Ada
50	51.2	Muskogee	Muskogee
50	51.2	Mustang	Mustang
50	51.2	Oklahoma City	Oklahoma City
54	51.1	Idabel	Idabel
55	51.0	Putnam City	Warr Acres
56	50.9	Cushing	Cushing
56	50.9	Stillwater	Stillwater
58	50.8	Cleveland	Cleveland
58	50.8	Collinsville	Collinsville
58	50.8	Coweta	Coweta
58	50.8	Tulsa	Tulsa
62	50.7	Blackwell	Blackwell
62	50.7	Harrah	Harrah
62	50.7	Pryor	Pryor
62	50.7	Sapulpa	Sapulpa
62	50.7	Weatherford	Weatherford
67	50.6	Owasso	Owasso
68	50.5	Union	Tulsa
69	50.4	Yukon	Yukon
70	50.2	Anadarko	Anadarko
71	50.0	Guymon	Guymon
72	49.9	Checotah	Checotah
72	49.9	Elk City	Elk City
72	49.9	Grove	Grove
75	49.8	Poteau	Poteau
75	49.8	Western Heights	Oklahoma City
77	47.1	Byng	Ada

Female Students

Rank	Percent	District Name	City
1	52.9	Byng	Ada
2	50.2	Poteau	Poteau
2	50.2	Western Heights	Oklahoma City
4	50.1	Checotah	Checotah
4	50.1	Elk City	Elk City
4	50.1	Grove	Grove
7	50.0	Guymon	Guymon
8	49.8	Anadarko	Anadarko
9	49.6	Yukon	Yukon
10	49.5	Union	Tulsa
11	49.4	Owasso	Owasso
12	49.3	Blackwell	Blackwell
12	49.3	Harrah	Harrah
12	49.3	Pryor	Pryor
12	49.3	Sapulpa	Sapulpa
12	49.3	Weatherford	Weatherford
17	49.2	Cleveland	Cleveland
17	49.2	Collinsville	Collinsville
17	49.2	Coweta	Coweta
17	49.2	Tulsa	Tulsa
21	49.1	Cushing	Cushing
21	49.1	Stillwater	Stillwater
23	49.0	Putnam City	Warr Acres
24	48.9	Idabel	Idabel
25	48.8	Ada	Ada
25	48.8	Muskogee	Muskogee
25	48.8	Mustang	Mustang
25	48.8	Oklahoma City	Oklahoma City
29	48.7	Catoosa	Catoosa
29	48.7	Chickasha	Chickasha
29	48.7	Claremore	Claremore
29	48.7	Edmond	Edmond
29	48.7	Enid	Enid
29	48.7	Glenpool	Glenpool
29	48.7	Guthrie	Guthrie
29	48.7	Jenks	Jenks
29	48.7	Noble	Noble
38	48.6	Clinton	Clinton
38	48.6	Jay	Jay
40	48.5	Lawton	Lawton
40	48.5	Piedmont	Piedmont
40	48.5	Woodward	Woodward
43	48.4	Durant	Durant
43	48.4	Miami	Miami
43	48.4	Oologah-Talala	Oologah
43	48.4	Shawnee	Shawnee
47	48.3	Bristow	Bristow
47	48.3	Duncan	Duncan
47	48.3	Fort Gibson	Fort Gibson
47	48.3	Mc Loud	Mcloud
51	48.2	Broken Arrow	Broken Arrow
51	48.2	Hilldale	Muskogee
51	48.2	Moore	Moore
54	48.1	El Reno	El Reno
54	48.1	Madill	Madill
54	48.1	Mannford	Mannford
54	48.1	Mc Alester	Mcalester
54	48.1	Wagoner	Wagoner
59	48.0	Bixby	Bixby
59	48.0	Norman	Norman
61	47.9	Ardmore	Ardmore
61	47.9	MWC-Del City	Midwest City
61	47.9	Seminole	Seminole
61	47.9	Skiatook	Skiatook
65	47.8	Ponca City	Ponca City
66	47.5	Bartlesville	Bartlesville
66	47.5	Muldrow	Muldrow
66	47.5	Sand Springs	Sand Springs
69	47.4	Altus	Altus
69	47.4	Vinita	Vinita
71	47.2	Tahlequah	Tahlequah
72	47.0	Choctaw-Nicoma Park	Choctaw
73	46.6	Deer Creek	Edmond
73	46.6	Tecumseh	Tecumseh
75	46.5	Okmulgee	Okmulgee
76	46.4	Broken Bow	Broken Bow
77	46.3	Sallisaw	Sallisaw

Individual Education Program Students

Rank	Percent	District Name	City
1	21.3	Ardmore	Ardmore
2	20.1	Mc Alester	Mcalester
3	19.1	Anadarko	Anadarko
4	18.7	Sallisaw	Sallisaw
5	18.0	Vinita	Vinita
6	17.7	Sand Springs	Sand Springs
7	17.5	Tulsa	Tulsa
8	17.2	Harrah	Harrah
9	17.0	Jay	Jay
9	17.0	Stillwater	Stillwater
11	16.9	Wagoner	Wagoner
12	16.3	Byng	Ada
12	16.3	Catoosa	Catoosa
14	16.2	Coweta	Coweta
15	16.1	Blackwell	Blackwell
15	16.1	Chickasha	Chickasha
17	15.8	Checotah	Checotah
18	15.6	Okmulgee	Okmulgee
19	15.5	Tahlequah	Tahlequah
20	15.4	Cushing	Cushing
21	15.3	Oklahoma City	Oklahoma City
22	15.2	Ada	Ada
22	15.2	Jenks	Jenks
22	15.2	Poteau	Poteau
22	15.2	Western Heights	Oklahoma City
26	15.1	Shawnee	Shawnee
27	15.0	Bristow	Bristow
28	14.8	El Reno	El Reno
28	14.8	Grove	Grove
28	14.8	Idabel	Idabel
31	14.7	Broken Bow	Broken Bow
32	14.6	Lawton	Lawton
33	14.5	Enid	Enid
33	14.5	Guthrie	Guthrie
35	14.3	Norman	Norman
36	14.2	Ponca City	Ponca City
37	14.1	Broken Arrow	Broken Arrow
37	14.1	Cleveland	Cleveland
39	14.0	Hilldale	Muskogee
39	14.0	Tecumseh	Tecumseh
41	13.9	Choctaw-Nicoma Park	Choctaw
41	13.9	Oologah-Talala	Oologah
43	13.7	Claremore	Claremore
43	13.7	Deer Creek	Edmond
45	13.6	MWC-Del City	Midwest City
45	13.6	Noble	Noble
47	13.5	Durant	Durant
48	13.4	Edmond	Edmond
48	13.4	Sapulpa	Sapulpa
50	13.2	Muskogee	Muskogee
51	13.0	Glenpool	Glenpool
52	12.9	Weatherford	Weatherford
53	12.5	Fort Gibson	Fort Gibson
53	12.5	Moore	Moore
55	12.3	Woodward	Woodward
56	12.2	Bartlesville	Bartlesville
56	12.2	Seminole	Seminole
58	12.1	Bixby	Bixby
59	12.0	Putnam City	Warr Acres
60	11.9	Muldrow	Muldrow
61	11.8	Skiatook	Skiatook
62	11.7	Clinton	Clinton
62	11.7	Mc Loud	Mcloud
64	11.6	Collinsville	Collinsville
65	11.3	Mannford	Mannford
66	11.1	Duncan	Duncan
66	11.1	Elk City	Elk City
68	10.6	Piedmont	Piedmont
69	10.3	Altus	Altus
70	10.2	Miami	Miami
71	10.1	Guymon	Guymon
71	10.1	Owasso	Owasso
73	9.9	Yukon	Yukon
74	9.4	Pryor	Pryor
75	9.0	Mustang	Mustang
76	8.3	Madill	Madill
77	8.2	Union	Tulsa

English Language Learner Students

Rank	Percent	District Name	City
1	37.5	Guymon	Guymon
2	22.7	Oklahoma City	Oklahoma City
3	22.3	Clinton	Clinton
4	22.2	Madill	Madill
5	16.4	Altus	Altus
6	13.9	Jay	Jay
7	12.7	Western Heights	Oklahoma City
8	12.5	Anadarko	Anadarko
9	11.8	Union	Tulsa
10	10.2	Hilldale	Muskogee
11	9.4	Muldrow	Muldrow
12	9.1	Lawton	Lawton
13	8.8	Tulsa	Tulsa
14	8.7	Enid	Enid
15	8.5	El Reno	El Reno
16	7.9	Putnam City	Warr Acres
17	7.5	Duncan	Duncan
18	7.2	Tahlequah	Tahlequah
19	5.6	Woodward	Woodward
20	5.5	Jenks	Jenks
21	5.3	Broken Bow	Broken Bow
21	5.3	Elk City	Elk City
23	5.1	Mustang	Mustang
24	5.0	Moore	Moore
25	4.8	Stillwater	Stillwater
26	4.7	Blackwell	Blackwell
27	4.2	Shawnee	Shawnee
28	3.9	Weatherford	Weatherford
29	3.6	Muskogee	Muskogee
30	3.3	Idabel	Idabel
31	3.2	Poteau	Poteau
32	3.1	Okmulgee	Okmulgee
33	3.0	Claremore	Claremore
33	3.0	MWC-Del City	Midwest City
33	3.0	Norman	Norman
36	2.9	Ada	Ada
36	2.9	Ponca City	Ponca City
38	2.8	Seminole	Seminole
39	2.7	Broken Arrow	Broken Arrow
39	2.7	Glenpool	Glenpool
41	2.5	Owasso	Owasso
41	2.5	Yukon	Yukon
43	2.3	Fort Gibson	Fort Gibson
43	2.3	Pryor	Pryor
43	2.3	Sallisaw	Sallisaw
46	2.2	Bixby	Bixby
47	2.1	Ardmore	Ardmore
47	2.1	Mc Loud	Mcloud
49	2.0	Bartlesville	Bartlesville
50	1.9	Checotah	Checotah
50	1.9	Coweta	Coweta
50	1.9	Deer Creek	Edmond
50	1.9	Mc Alester	Mcalester
50	1.9	Sapulpa	Sapulpa
55	1.7	Chickasha	Chickasha
55	1.7	Durant	Durant
55	1.7	Edmond	Edmond
58	1.6	Miami	Miami
58	1.6	Tecumseh	Tecumseh
60	1.4	Byng	Ada
60	1.4	Guthrie	Guthrie
62	1.2	Grove	Grove
62	1.2	Piedmont	Piedmont
62	1.2	Sand Springs	Sand Springs
65	0.5	Bristow	Bristow
65	0.5	Harrah	Harrah
67	0.4	Choctaw-Nicoma Park	Choctaw
67	0.4	Wagoner	Wagoner
69	0.1	Cleveland	Cleveland

Rank	Percent	District Name	City
70	0.0	Catoosa	Catoosa
70	0.0	Collinsville	Collinsville
70	0.0	Cushing	Cushing
70	0.0	Mannford	Mannford
70	0.0	Noble	Noble
70	0.0	Oologah-Talala	Oologah
70	0.0	Skiatook	Skiatook
70	0.0	Vinita	Vinita

Migrant Students

Rank	Percent	District Name	City
1	n/a	Ada	Ada
1	n/a	Altus	Altus
1	n/a	Anadarko	Anadarko
1	n/a	Ardmore	Ardmore
1	n/a	Bartlesville	Bartlesville
1	n/a	Bixby	Bixby
1	n/a	Blackwell	Blackwell
1	n/a	Bristow	Bristow
1	n/a	Broken Arrow	Broken Arrow
1	n/a	Broken Bow	Broken Bow
1	n/a	Byng	Ada
1	n/a	Catoosa	Catoosa
1	n/a	Checotah	Checotah
1	n/a	Chickasha	Chickasha
1	n/a	Choctaw-Nicoma Park	Choctaw
1	n/a	Claremore	Claremore
1	n/a	Cleveland	Cleveland
1	n/a	Clinton	Clinton
1	n/a	Collinsville	Collinsville
1	n/a	Coweta	Coweta
1	n/a	Cushing	Cushing
1	n/a	Deer Creek	Edmond
1	n/a	Duncan	Duncan
1	n/a	Durant	Durant
1	n/a	Edmond	Edmond
1	n/a	El Reno	El Reno
1	n/a	Elk City	Elk City
1	n/a	Enid	Enid
1	n/a	Fort Gibson	Fort Gibson
1	n/a	Glenpool	Glenpool
1	n/a	Grove	Grove
1	n/a	Guthrie	Guthrie
1	n/a	Guymon	Guymon
1	n/a	Harrah	Harrah
1	n/a	Hilldale	Muskogee
1	n/a	Idabel	Idabel
1	n/a	Jay	Jay
1	n/a	Jenks	Jenks
1	n/a	Lawton	Lawton
1	n/a	MWC-Del City	Midwest City
1	n/a	Madill	Madill
1	n/a	Mannford	Mannford
1	n/a	Mc Alester	Mcalester
1	n/a	Mc Loud	Mcloud
1	n/a	Miami	Miami
1	n/a	Moore	Moore
1	n/a	Muldrow	Muldrow
1	n/a	Muskogee	Muskogee
1	n/a	Mustang	Mustang
1	n/a	Noble	Noble
1	n/a	Norman	Norman
1	n/a	Oklahoma City	Oklahoma City
1	n/a	Okmulgee	Okmulgee
1	n/a	Oologah-Talala	Oologah
1	n/a	Owasso	Owasso
1	n/a	Piedmont	Piedmont
1	n/a	Ponca City	Ponca City
1	n/a	Poteau	Poteau
1	n/a	Pryor	Pryor
1	n/a	Putnam City	Warr Acres
1	n/a	Sallisaw	Sallisaw
1	n/a	Sand Springs	Sand Springs
1	n/a	Sapulpa	Sapulpa
1	n/a	Seminole	Seminole
1	n/a	Shawnee	Shawnee
1	n/a	Skiatook	Skiatook
1	n/a	Stillwater	Stillwater
1	n/a	Tahlequah	Tahlequah
1	n/a	Tecumseh	Tecumseh
1	n/a	Tulsa	Tulsa
1	n/a	Union	Tulsa
1	n/a	Vinita	Vinita
1	n/a	Wagoner	Wagoner
1	n/a	Weatherford	Weatherford
1	n/a	Western Heights	Oklahoma City
1	n/a	Woodward	Woodward
1	n/a	Yukon	Yukon

Students Eligible for Free Lunch

Rank	Percent	District Name	City
1	73.3	Oklahoma City	Oklahoma City
2	71.8	Clinton	Clinton
3	68.4	Idabel	Idabel
4	67.1	Wagoner	Wagoner
5	65.4	Anadarko	Anadarko
6	63.7	Broken Bow	Broken Bow
7	62.1	Tulsa	Tulsa
8	61.3	Bristow	Bristow
9	60.3	Okmulgee	Okmulgee
10	59.8	Checotah	Checotah
11	57.4	Western Heights	Oklahoma City
12	57.2	Muskogee	Muskogee
13	56.0	Ardmore	Ardmore
14	55.5	Jay	Jay
15	53.6	El Reno	El Reno
16	53.4	Seminole	Seminole
17	52.6	Poteau	Poteau
18	49.9	Madill	Madill
18	49.9	Miami	Miami
20	49.8	Tahlequah	Tahlequah
21	49.2	Durant	Durant
22	48.6	Byng	Ada
23	47.8	Guymon	Guymon
24	47.7	Sallisaw	Sallisaw
25	47.5	Shawnee	Shawnee
26	46.5	Muldrow	Muldrow
27	46.3	Ada	Ada
28	45.7	Guthrie	Guthrie
29	45.4	Mc Alester	Mcalester
30	45.0	Tecumseh	Tecumseh
31	44.9	Ponca City	Ponca City
32	44.3	Blackwell	Blackwell
33	43.2	Duncan	Duncan
34	41.2	Enid	Enid
35	40.1	Cushing	Cushing
36	39.4	Altus	Altus
37	39.2	Vinita	Vinita
38	38.6	Sapulpa	Sapulpa
39	38.0	Elk City	Elk City
40	37.9	Grove	Grove
40	37.9	Lawton	Lawton
42	36.0	Noble	Noble
43	35.9	Cleveland	Cleveland
44	35.3	Pryor	Pryor
45	35.2	Mc Loud	Mcloud
46	34.8	MWC-Del City	Midwest City
47	32.6	Weatherford	Weatherford
48	32.3	Sand Springs	Sand Springs
49	31.2	Mannford	Mannford
50	30.9	Putnam City	Warr Acres
51	30.5	Catoosa	Catoosa
52	29.5	Fort Gibson	Fort Gibson
53	29.2	Woodward	Woodward
54	28.8	Harrah	Harrah
55	28.0	Chickasha	Chickasha
56	27.7	Claremore	Claremore
57	27.1	Skiatook	Skiatook
58	26.4	Coweta	Coweta
59	25.9	Bartlesville	Bartlesville
60	25.4	Hilldale	Muskogee
61	24.3	Glenpool	Glenpool
62	23.4	Norman	Norman
63	23.2	Stillwater	Stillwater
64	20.9	Choctaw-Nicoma Park	Choctaw
65	20.0	Moore	Moore
66	19.7	Collinsville	Collinsville
67	18.4	Oologah-Talala	Oologah
68	16.3	Broken Arrow	Broken Arrow
69	15.7	Bixby	Bixby
70	15.4	Union	Tulsa
71	14.2	Yukon	Yukon
72	12.5	Jenks	Jenks
73	10.6	Edmond	Edmond
73	10.6	Mustang	Mustang
75	10.0	Owasso	Owasso
76	6.2	Piedmont	Piedmont
77	3.0	Deer Creek	Edmond

Students Eligible for Reduced-Price Lunch

Rank	Percent	District Name	City
1	17.4	Jay	Jay
2	17.0	Bristow	Bristow
3	16.7	Clinton	Clinton
4	15.0	Checotah	Checotah
5	14.9	Okmulgee	Okmulgee
5	14.9	Vinita	Vinita
7	14.3	Glenpool	Glenpool
7	14.3	Noble	Noble
9	14.2	Grove	Grove
10	13.8	Mannford	Mannford
11	13.6	Miami	Miami
11	13.6	Tahlequah	Tahlequah
13	13.2	Cushing	Cushing
13	13.2	Lawton	Lawton
15	13.0	Cleveland	Cleveland
16	12.8	Muldrow	Muldrow
17	12.6	Blackwell	Blackwell
17	12.6	Sapulpa	Sapulpa
19	12.5	Byng	Ada
20	12.4	Sand Springs	Sand Springs
21	12.1	Western Heights	Oklahoma City
22	12.0	Broken Bow	Broken Bow
23	11.9	Guymon	Guymon
24	11.8	Anadarko	Anadarko
24	11.8	Poteau	Poteau
26	11.6	Durant	Durant
26	11.6	El Reno	El Reno
26	11.6	Madill	Madill
26	11.6	Sallisaw	Sallisaw
30	11.5	Guthrie	Guthrie
31	11.1	Mc Alester	Mcalester
31	11.1	Tulsa	Tulsa
33	11.0	Ponca City	Ponca City
33	11.0	Tecumseh	Tecumseh
35	10.8	Catoosa	Catoosa
36	10.6	Hilldale	Muskogee
37	10.5	Harrah	Harrah
38	10.3	Wagoner	Wagoner
39	10.2	Pryor	Pryor
40	10.1	Mc Loud	Mcloud
40	10.1	Oologah-Talala	Oologah
42	10.0	Ada	Ada
42	10.0	Altus	Altus
42	10.0	Fort Gibson	Fort Gibson
45	9.9	Muskogee	Muskogee
46	9.7	Collinsville	Collinsville
46	9.7	Coweta	Coweta
48	9.6	Ardmore	Ardmore
48	9.6	Seminole	Seminole
50	9.5	Skiatook	Skiatook
50	9.5	Woodward	Woodward
52	9.4	Weatherford	Weatherford
53	9.2	Claremore	Claremore
54	8.9	MWC-Del City	Midwest City
55	8.7	Elk City	Elk City
55	8.7	Shawnee	Shawnee
57	8.6	Moore	Moore
58	8.3	Broken Arrow	Broken Arrow
58	8.3	Mustang	Mustang
60	7.9	Enid	Enid
61	7.7	Choctaw-Nicoma Park	Choctaw
62	7.6	Idabel	Idabel
63	7.5	Bartlesville	Bartlesville
63	7.5	Oklahoma City	Oklahoma City
65	7.2	Putnam City	Warr Acres
66	6.6	Duncan	Duncan
67	6.5	Norman	Norman
68	6.4	Yukon	Yukon
69	6.2	Chickasha	Chickasha
70	6.1	Stillwater	Stillwater
71	5.9	Bixby	Bixby
72	4.7	Owasso	Owasso
73	4.5	Union	Tulsa
74	4.2	Edmond	Edmond
75	3.7	Jenks	Jenks
76	3.2	Piedmont	Piedmont
77	1.4	Deer Creek	Edmond

Student/Teacher Ratio

Rank	Ratio	District Name	City
1	19.4	Union	Tulsa
2	19.1	Bixby	Bixby
3	19.0	Collinsville	Collinsville
4	18.1	Mannford	Mannford
5	17.7	Jenks	Jenks
6	17.4	Edmond	Edmond
7	17.2	Owasso	Owasso
7	17.2	Piedmont	Piedmont
7	17.2	Stillwater	Stillwater
10	17.1	Mustang	Mustang
11	17.0	Broken Arrow	Broken Arrow
11	17.0	Miami	Miami
11	17.0	Pryor	Pryor
14	16.9	Duncan	Duncan
14	16.9	Oologah-Talala	Oologah
14	16.9	Yukon	Yukon
17	16.8	Sapulpa	Sapulpa
18	16.7	Muskogee	Muskogee
19	16.6	Cleveland	Cleveland
19	16.6	Moore	Moore
21	16.5	Blackwell	Blackwell
21	16.5	Hilldale	Muskogee

21	16.5	Noble	Noble
21	16.5	Skiatook	Skiatook
25	16.4	Choctaw-Nicoma Park	Choctaw
25	16.4	Lawton	Lawton
27	16.3	Claremore	Claremore
27	16.3	Harrah	Harrah
27	16.3	Putnam City	Warr Acres
30	16.2	Durant	Durant
30	16.2	Oklahoma City	Oklahoma City
32	16.1	Grove	Grove
32	16.1	Madill	Madill
32	16.1	Tulsa	Tulsa
35	15.9	Bristow	Bristow
35	15.9	Checotah	Checotah
35	15.9	Deer Creek	Edmond
35	15.9	Norman	Norman
35	15.9	Ponca City	Ponca City
35	15.9	Vinita	Vinita
41	15.8	Ardmore	Ardmore
41	15.8	Catoosa	Catoosa
43	15.7	Chickasha	Chickasha
43	15.7	Fort Gibson	Fort Gibson
43	15.7	Glenpool	Glenpool
43	15.7	MWC-Del City	Midwest City
43	15.7	Sand Springs	Sand Springs
48	15.6	Coweta	Coweta
48	15.6	Mc Loud	Mcloud
50	15.5	Tahlequah	Tahlequah
51	15.4	El Reno	El Reno
51	15.4	Muldrow	Muldrow
51	15.4	Seminole	Seminole
51	15.4	Shawnee	Shawnee
55	15.3	Tecumseh	Tecumseh
56	15.1	Bartlesville	Bartlesville
56	15.1	Guthrie	Guthrie
56	15.1	Jay	Jay
56	15.1	Weatherford	Weatherford
56	15.1	Western Heights	Oklahoma City
61	15.0	Mc Alester	Mcalester
61	15.0	Sallisaw	Sallisaw
63	14.9	Cushing	Cushing
63	14.9	Enid	Enid
63	14.9	Woodward	Woodward
66	14.8	Poteau	Poteau
66	14.8	Wagoner	Wagoner
68	14.7	Byng	Ada
69	14.6	Altus	Altus
69	14.6	Idabel	Idabel
69	14.6	Okmulgee	Okmulgee
72	14.4	Anadarko	Anadarko
72	14.4	Broken Bow	Broken Bow
74	14.3	Elk City	Elk City
75	14.0	Ada	Ada
76	13.8	Guymon	Guymon
77	13.6	Clinton	Clinton

Student/Librarian Ratio

Rank	Ratio	District Name	City
1	1,275.5	Ada	Ada
2	1,224.0	Wagoner	Wagoner
3	1,132.4	Lawton	Lawton
4	948.0	Sallisaw	Sallisaw
5	914.3	Noble	Noble
6	889.5	Mc Loud	Mcloud
7	865.5	Hilldale	Muskogee
8	861.8	Altus	Altus
9	859.0	Cleveland	Cleveland
10	845.5	Jenks	Jenks
11	833.8	Oklahoma City	Oklahoma City
12	833.5	Oologah-Talala	Oologah
13	795.7	Sand Springs	Sand Springs
14	791.7	Grove	Grove
15	789.5	Blackwell	Blackwell
16	787.5	Muldrow	Muldrow
17	785.9	Union	Tulsa
18	785.8	Guthrie	Guthrie
19	781.3	Catoosa	Catoosa
20	776.0	Skiatook	Skiatook
21	764.3	Mustang	Mustang
22	760.6	Bixby	Bixby
23	744.7	Edmond	Edmond
24	724.0	Yukon	Yukon
25	708.0	Elk City	Elk City
26	702.7	Sapulpa	Sapulpa
27	696.0	Western Heights	Oklahoma City
28	691.0	Glenpool	Glenpool
29	685.6	Broken Arrow	Broken Arrow
30	675.2	Claremore	Claremore
31	667.4	Putnam City	Warr Acres
32	664.0	Moore	Moore
33	661.4	Bartlesville	Bartlesville
34	660.7	Poteau	Poteau
35	657.0	El Reno	El Reno
36	643.6	Ardmore	Ardmore
37	621.8	Tahlequah	Tahlequah
38	613.8	Duncan	Duncan
39	599.3	Fort Gibson	Fort Gibson
40	593.7	Stillwater	Stillwater
41	582.3	Guymon	Guymon
42	573.0	Broken Bow	Broken Bow
43	571.4	Mc Alester	Mcalester
44	571.0	Jay	Jay
45	563.1	Ponca City	Ponca City
46	559.3	Mannford	Mannford
47	555.3	Byng	Ada
47	555.3	Idabel	Idabel
49	553.8	Harrah	Harrah
50	549.5	Tulsa	Tulsa
51	543.6	Shawnee	Shawnee
52	542.8	Tecumseh	Tecumseh
53	538.6	Owasso	Owasso
54	537.6	Weatherford	Weatherford
55	531.4	MWC-Del City	Midwest City
56	530.7	Checotah	Checotah
57	527.4	Norman	Norman
58	527.0	Coweta	Coweta
59	521.0	Durant	Durant
60	516.4	Chickasha	Chickasha
61	516.3	Piedmont	Piedmont
62	514.0	Madill	Madill
63	505.2	Woodward	Woodward
64	504.0	Collinsville	Collinsville
65	490.7	Choctaw-Nicoma Park	Choctaw
66	490.6	Enid	Enid
67	489.6	Miami	Miami
68	489.5	Okmulgee	Okmulgee
69	472.8	Muskogee	Muskogee
70	470.8	Deer Creek	Edmond
71	436.6	Anadarko	Anadarko
72	427.3	Bristow	Bristow
73	418.5	Vinita	Vinita
74	394.2	Pryor	Pryor
75	384.6	Cushing	Cushing
76	377.5	Seminole	Seminole
77	370.6	Clinton	Clinton

Student/Counselor Ratio

Rank	Ratio	District Name	City
1	577.0	Hilldale	Muskogee
2	572.7	Cleveland	Cleveland
3	569.7	Bristow	Bristow
4	559.3	Mannford	Mannford
5	555.7	Oologah-Talala	Oologah
6	555.3	Idabel	Idabel
7	540.7	Union	Tulsa
8	525.0	Muldrow	Muldrow
9	523.8	Guthrie	Guthrie
10	517.8	Oklahoma City	Oklahoma City
11	516.3	Piedmont	Piedmont
12	515.5	Owasso	Owasso
13	504.0	Collinsville	Collinsville
14	495.0	Putnam City	Warr Acres
15	474.0	Sallisaw	Sallisaw
16	467.5	Western Heights	Oklahoma City
17	467.3	Jenks	Jenks
18	457.2	Noble	Noble
19	449.5	Fort Gibson	Fort Gibson
20	443.5	Weatherford	Weatherford
21	441.6	Choctaw-Nicoma Park	Choctaw
22	434.2	Tecumseh	Tecumseh
23	414.6	Glenpool	Glenpool
24	414.0	Ponca City	Ponca City
25	396.4	Poteau	Poteau
26	394.8	Blackwell	Blackwell
27	391.7	Altus	Altus
28	391.1	Edmond	Edmond
29	388.0	Skiatook	Skiatook
30	387.2	Stillwater	Stillwater
31	386.9	Broken Arrow	Broken Arrow
32	384.9	Guymon	Guymon
33	384.6	Cushing	Cushing
34	377.6	MWC-Del City	Midwest City
35	376.6	Deer Creek	Edmond
36	375.4	El Reno	El Reno
37	369.4	Sand Springs	Sand Springs
38	369.2	Harrah	Harrah
39	368.3	Claremore	Claremore
40	364.4	Ada	Ada
41	363.8	Anadarko	Anadarko
42	362.6	Moore	Moore
43	357.6	Duncan	Duncan
44	356.1	Lawton	Lawton
45	355.8	Mc Loud	Mcloud
46	355.0	Chickasha	Chickasha
47	354.3	Sapulpa	Sapulpa
48	349.7	Miami	Miami
48	349.7	Wagoner	Wagoner
50	346.8	Yukon	Yukon
51	345.7	Bixby	Bixby
52	342.6	Jay	Jay
53	341.3	Muskogee	Muskogee
54	340.1	Mustang	Mustang
55	336.1	Durant	Durant
55	336.1	Mc Alester	Mcalester
57	335.7	Enid	Enid
58	334.9	Catoosa	Catoosa
59	334.8	Vinita	Vinita
60	333.2	Byng	Ada
61	331.9	Okmulgee	Okmulgee
62	331.3	Norman	Norman
63	329.4	Coweta	Coweta
64	318.4	Checotah	Checotah
65	317.1	Shawnee	Shawnee
66	316.8	Bartlesville	Bartlesville
67	315.8	Woodward	Woodward
68	312.4	Ardmore	Ardmore
69	308.8	Clinton	Clinton
70	308.4	Madill	Madill
71	303.2	Pryor	Pryor
72	302.0	Seminole	Seminole
73	291.4	Broken Bow	Broken Bow
74	287.6	Tulsa	Tulsa
75	287.0	Elk City	Elk City
75	287.0	Tahlequah	Tahlequah
77	263.9	Grove	Grove

Current Spending per Student in FY2001

Rank	Dollars	District Name	City
1	7,931	Cushing	Cushing
2	6,551	Ardmore	Ardmore
3	6,527	Anadarko	Anadarko
4	6,458	Okmulgee	Okmulgee
5	6,430	Broken Bow	Broken Bow
6	6,372	Guymon	Guymon
7	6,300	Oklahoma City	Oklahoma City
8	6,211	Clinton	Clinton
9	6,187	Shawnee	Shawnee
10	6,168	Ada	Ada
11	6,161	Edmond	Edmond
12	6,149	Fort Gibson	Fort Gibson
13	6,134	Mc Alester	Mcalester
14	6,095	Tulsa	Tulsa
15	6,094	Idabel	Idabel
16	6,037	Tahlequah	Tahlequah
17	5,952	Chickasha	Chickasha
18	5,944	Western Heights	Oklahoma City
19	5,931	Vinita	Vinita
20	5,916	Bartlesville	Bartlesville
21	5,902	Jay	Jay
22	5,895	Weatherford	Weatherford
23	5,873	Byng	Ada
24	5,866	Muskogee	Muskogee
25	5,862	Enid	Enid
25	5,862	Stillwater	Stillwater
27	5,841	Duncan	Duncan
28	5,820	Durant	Durant
29	5,815	MWC-Del City	Midwest City
30	5,754	Grove	Grove
31	5,748	Guthrie	Guthrie
32	5,732	El Reno	El Reno
33	5,723	Altus	Altus
34	5,667	Jenks	Jenks
35	5,660	Lawton	Lawton
36	5,647	Tecumseh	Tecumseh
37	5,635	Wagoner	Wagoner
38	5,632	Poteau	Poteau
39	5,628	Miami	Miami
40	5,620	Checotah	Checotah
41	5,618	Blackwell	Blackwell
42	5,614	Elk City	Elk City
42	5,614	Sand Springs	Sand Springs
44	5,555	Pryor	Pryor
45	5,548	Bristow	Bristow
46	5,503	Claremore	Claremore
47	5,501	Sapulpa	Sapulpa
48	5,488	Norman	Norman
49	5,481	Muldrow	Muldrow
50	5,461	Sallisaw	Sallisaw
51	5,443	Harrah	Harrah
52	5,430	Madill	Madill
53	5,394	Catoosa	Catoosa
54	5,392	Seminole	Seminole
55	5,339	Ponca City	Ponca City
56	5,337	Putnam City	Warr Acres
57	5,315	Broken Arrow	Broken Arrow
58	5,219	Oologah-Talala	Oologah

Rank	Number	District Name	City
59	5,201	Woodward	Woodward
60	5,174	Choctaw-Nicoma Park	Choctaw
61	5,170	Collinsville	Collinsville
62	5,147	Union	Tulsa
63	5,135	Coweta	Coweta
64	5,115	Moore	Moore
65	5,097	Yukon	Yukon
66	5,088	Noble	Noble
67	5,071	Deer Creek	Edmond
68	5,056	Cleveland	Cleveland
69	5,034	Glenpool	Glenpool
70	4,917	Mc Loud	Mcloud
71	4,870	Skiatook	Skiatook
72	4,829	Mustang	Mustang
73	4,788	Bixby	Bixby
74	4,769	Piedmont	Piedmont
75	4,718	Owasso	Owasso
76	4,704	Hilldale	Muskogee
77	4,660	Mannford	Mannford

Number of Diploma Recipients

Rank	Number	District Name	City
1	1,758	Tulsa	Tulsa
2	1,441	Oklahoma City	Oklahoma City
3	1,267	Edmond	Edmond
4	1,185	Putnam City	Warr Acres
5	1,137	Moore	Moore
6	1,076	MWC-Del City	Midwest City
7	894	Lawton	Lawton
8	885	Broken Arrow	Broken Arrow
9	867	Norman	Norman
10	768	Union	Tulsa
11	625	Jenks	Jenks
12	467	Yukon	Yukon
13	456	Mustang	Mustang
14	421	Bartlesville	Bartlesville
15	408	Owasso	Owasso
16	406	Enid	Enid
17	387	Ponca City	Ponca City
18	380	Stillwater	Stillwater
19	349	Sand Springs	Sand Springs
20	319	Muskogee	Muskogee
21	318	Tahlequah	Tahlequah
22	308	Choctaw-Nicoma Park	Choctaw
23	295	Altus	Altus
24	286	Bixby	Bixby
25	275	Sapulpa	Sapulpa
26	270	Claremore	Claremore
27	245	Duncan	Duncan
28	239	Shawnee	Shawnee
29	190	Chickasha	Chickasha
30	183	Ardmore	Ardmore
31	181	Guthrie	Guthrie
32	173	El Reno	El Reno
33	167	Mc Alester	Mcalester
34	165	Noble	Noble
35	164	Western Heights	Oklahoma City
36	163	Harrah	Harrah
37	162	Weatherford	Weatherford
38	160	Woodward	Woodward
39	159	Ada	Ada
40	158	Skiatook	Skiatook
41	154	Coweta	Coweta
42	152	Durant	Durant
43	150	Guymon	Guymon
44	147	Pryor	Pryor
45	139	Catoosa	Catoosa
46	138	Grove	Grove
47	137	Tecumseh	Tecumseh
48	135	Fort Gibson	Fort Gibson
49	133	Cushing	Cushing
49	133	Mc Loud	Mcloud
49	133	Wagoner	Wagoner
52	130	Glenpool	Glenpool
53	128	Collinsville	Collinsville
54	125	Broken Bow	Broken Bow
55	123	Elk City	Elk City
56	119	Poteau	Poteau
57	115	Anadarko	Anadarko
58	114	Muldrow	Muldrow
59	112	Clinton	Clinton
59	112	Miami	Miami
61	108	Sallisaw	Sallisaw
62	107	Hilldale	Muskogee
63	103	Byng	Ada
63	103	Oologah-Talala	Oologah
65	101	Blackwell	Blackwell
66	98	Deer Creek	Edmond
67	96	Jay	Jay
68	94	Idabel	Idabel
68	94	Mannford	Mannford
68	94	Okmulgee	Okmulgee
68	94	Piedmont	Piedmont
68	94	Seminole	Seminole
73	90	Bristow	Bristow
74	88	Checotah	Checotah
74	88	Vinita	Vinita
76	76	Madill	Madill
77	69	Cleveland	Cleveland

High School Drop-out Rate

Rank	Percent	District Name	City
1	12.5	Oklahoma City	Oklahoma City
2	10.8	Seminole	Seminole
3	10.3	Shawnee	Shawnee
4	9.8	Ponca City	Ponca City
5	9.7	Pryor	Pryor
6	9.6	Tulsa	Tulsa
7	9.2	Weatherford	Weatherford
8	9.1	Grove	Grove
9	8.8	Mc Alester	Mcalester
10	8.5	Woodward	Woodward
11	8.4	Duncan	Duncan
12	8.0	Elk City	Elk City
13	7.9	Idabel	Idabel
14	7.7	Ada	Ada
14	7.7	Jay	Jay
14	7.7	Vinita	Vinita
17	7.6	Cleveland	Cleveland
17	7.6	Durant	Durant
19	7.5	Okmulgee	Okmulgee
20	7.2	Checotah	Checotah
21	7.1	Blackwell	Blackwell
21	7.1	Mannford	Mannford
23	7.0	Anadarko	Anadarko
23	7.0	Western Heights	Oklahoma City
25	6.8	Norman	Norman
26	6.7	Putnam City	Warr Acres
27	6.3	Cushing	Cushing
28	6.2	Skiatook	Skiatook
29	6.0	Bartlesville	Bartlesville
30	5.9	Bristow	Bristow
30	5.9	Coweta	Coweta
30	5.9	Tahlequah	Tahlequah
33	5.7	Sapulpa	Sapulpa
34	5.6	Enid	Enid
35	5.5	Mc Loud	Mcloud
36	5.3	Moore	Moore
36	5.3	Poteau	Poteau
38	5.2	MWC-Del City	Midwest City
39	5.1	Wagoner	Wagoner
40	5.0	Noble	Noble
41	4.9	Fort Gibson	Fort Gibson
41	4.9	Guthrie	Guthrie
41	4.9	Union	Tulsa
44	4.8	Ardmore	Ardmore
45	4.3	Chickasha	Chickasha
46	4.2	Broken Bow	Broken Bow
47	4.1	Catoosa	Catoosa
47	4.1	Guymon	Guymon
49	4.0	Tecumseh	Tecumseh
50	3.9	Bixby	Bixby
50	3.9	Hilldale	Muskogee
50	3.9	Miami	Miami
50	3.9	Muskogee	Muskogee
54	3.7	Broken Arrow	Broken Arrow
55	3.6	El Reno	El Reno
55	3.6	Piedmont	Piedmont
57	3.5	Glenpool	Glenpool
58	3.4	Mustang	Mustang
58	3.4	Owasso	Owasso
60	3.3	Clinton	Clinton
61	3.2	Altus	Altus
62	3.1	Edmond	Edmond
63	3.0	Claremore	Claremore
63	3.0	Collinsville	Collinsville
65	2.9	Muldrow	Muldrow
66	2.8	Lawton	Lawton
67	2.6	Byng	Ada
67	2.6	Choctaw-Nicoma Park	Choctaw
67	2.6	Jenks	Jenks
70	2.5	Sand Springs	Sand Springs
71	2.3	Stillwater	Stillwater
71	2.3	Yukon	Yukon
73	2.2	Harrah	Harrah
74	2.1	Sallisaw	Sallisaw
75	1.6	Deer Creek	Edmond
76	1.0	Madill	Madill
77	0.6	Oologah-Talala	Oologah

Oregon

Oregon Public School Educational Profile

Category	Value	Category	Value
Schools *(2002-2003)*	1,265	**Diploma Recipients** *(2002-2003)*	31,153
Instructional Level		White, Non-Hispanic	26,464
Primary	748	Black, Non-Hispanic	594
Middle	221	Asian/Pacific Islander	1,283
High	246	American Indian/Alaskan Native	490
Other Level	50	Hispanic	1,990
Curriculum		**High School Drop-out Rate** (%) *(2000-2001)*	5.3
Regular	1,184	White, Non-Hispanic	4.5
Special Education	10	Black, Non-Hispanic	11.7
Vocational	0	Asian/Pacific Islander	4.4
Alternative	71	American Indian/Alaskan Native	8.4
Type		Hispanic	11.5
Magnet	4	**Staff** *(2002-2003)*	55,043.5
Charter	21	Teachers	27,158.3
Title I Eligible	583	Average Salary ($)	47,463
School-wide Title I	259	Librarians/Media Specialists	510.3
Students *(2002-2003)*	554,071	Guidance Counselors	1,171.7
Gender (%)		**Ratios** *(2002-2003)*	
Male	n/a	Student/Teacher Ratio	20.4 to 1
Female	n/a	Student/Librarian Ratio	1,085.8 to 1
Race/Ethnicity (%)		Student/Counselor Ratio	472.9 to 1
White, Non-Hispanic	76.3	**Current Spending** *($ per student in FY 2001)*	7,642
Black, Non-Hispanic	2.9	Instruction	4,490
Asian/Pacific Islander	4.1	Support Services	2,896
American Indian/Alaskan Native	2.2	**College Entrance Exam Scores** *(2003)*	
Hispanic	12.2	Scholastic Aptitude Test (SAT)	
Classification (%)		Participation Rate (%)	57
Individual Education Program (IEP)	13.0	Mean SAT I Verbal Score	526
Migrant	3.7	Mean SAT I Math Score	527
English Language Learner (ELL)	9.5	American College Testing Program (ACT)	
Eligible for Free Lunch Program	30.0	Participation Rate (%)	12
Eligible for Reduced-Price Lunch Program	8.5	Average Composite Score	22.6

Note: *For an explanation of data, please refer to the User's Guide in the front of the book; n/a indicates data not available*

Oregon NAEP 2003 Test Scores

Reading			Mathematics		
Grade/Category	**Value**	**Rank**	**Grade/Category**	**Value**	**Rank**
4th Grade			**4th Grade**		
Average Proficiency	217.6 (1.3)	33/51	Average Proficiency	236.3 (0.9)	20/51
Proficiency by Gender/Race/Ethnicity			Proficiency by Gender/Race/Ethnicity		
Male	212.7 (1.5)	35/51	Male	237.4 (1.0)	23/51
Female	222.8 (1.6)	27/51	Female	235.2 (1.1)	20/51
White, Non-Hispanic	221.6 (1.2)	42/51	White, Non-Hispanic	239.7 (0.8)	35/51
Black, Non-Hispanic	202.1 (5.1)	14/42	Black, Non-Hispanic	223.0 (3.4)	3/42
Asian, Non-Hispanic	198.5 (2.3)	31/41	Asian, Non-Hispanic	218.2 (1.9)	30/43
American Indian, Non-Hispanic	219.4 (4.0)	18/25	American Indian, Non-Hispanic	245.3 (3.8)	16/26
Hispanic	n/a	n/a	Hispanic	n/a	n/a
Proficiency by Class Size			Proficiency by Class Size		
Less than 16 Students	n/a	n/a	Less than 16 Students	n/a	n/a
16 to 18 Students	n/a	n/a	16 to 18 Students	n/a	n/a
19 to 20 Students	n/a	n/a	19 to 20 Students	n/a	n/a
21 to 25 Students	217.6 (2.5)	37/51	21 to 25 Students	236.4 (1.4)	29/51
Greater than 25 Students	218.3 (1.4)	28/49	Greater than 25 Students	236.8 (1.3)	20/49
Percent Attaining Achievement Levels			Percent Attaining Achievement Levels		
Below Basic	36.8 (1.6)	21/51	Below Basic	21.1 (1.2)	25/51
Basic or Above	63.2 (1.6)	31/51	Basic or Above	78.9 (1.2)	27/51
Proficient or Above	30.5 (1.5)	32/51	Proficient or Above	33.2 (1.4)	23/51
Advanced or Above	6.5 (0.7)	30/51	Advanced or Above	4.2 (0.5)	15/51
8th Grade			**8th Grade**		
Average Proficiency	264.0 (1.2)	30/51	Average Proficiency	280.9 (1.3)	22/51
Proficiency by Gender/Race/Ethnicity			Proficiency by Gender/Race/Ethnicity		
Male	258.7 (1.6)	27/51	Male	282.0 (1.5)	20/51
Female	269.5 (1.2)	28/51	Female	279.8 (1.6)	22/51
White, Non-Hispanic	266.6 (1.2)	43/50	White, Non-Hispanic	284.4 (1.3)	32/50
Black, Non-Hispanic	251.5 (4.2)	2/41	Black, Non-Hispanic	264.8 (3.6)	1/41
Asian, Non-Hispanic	249.3 (2.7)	12/37	Asian, Non-Hispanic	258.2 (2.2)	22/37
American Indian, Non-Hispanic	265.3 (5.5)	15/23	American Indian, Non-Hispanic	291.8 (4.7)	9/23
Hispanic	n/a	n/a	Hispanic	263.2 (5.7)	3/11
Proficiency by Parents Highest Level of Ed.			Proficiency by Parents Highest Level of Ed.		
Did Not Finish High School	243.8 (3.7)	35/50	Did Not Finish High School	261.3 (2.6)	14/50
Graduated High School	257.2 (2.2)	19/50	Graduated High School	270.8 (1.9)	20/50
Some Education After High School	267.0 (2.0)	29/50	Some Education After High School	282.6 (1.8)	16/50
Graduated College	274.7 (1.4)	16/50	Graduated College	292.6 (1.4)	10/50
Percent Attaining Achievement Levels			Percent Attaining Achievement Levels		
Below Basic	25.4 (1.3)	22/51	Below Basic	29.7 (1.3)	26/51
Basic or Above	74.6 (1.3)	30/51	Basic or Above	70.3 (1.3)	26/51
Proficient or Above	33.1 (1.5)	23/51	Proficient or Above	32.0 (1.5)	18/51
Advanced or Above	3.2 (0.6)	13/51	Advanced or Above	6.7 (0.8)	8/51

Note: *For an explanation of data, please refer to the User's Guide in the front of the book; values in italics indicate that the nature of the sample does not allow accurate determination of the variability of the statistic; n/a indicates data not available*

Baker County

Baker SD 05J

2090 Fourth St • Baker City, OR 97814-3391
(541) 523-5814 • http://www.baker.k12.or.us
Grade Span: KG-12; **Agency Type:** 1
Schools: 7
5 Primary; 1 Middle; 1 High; 0 Other Level
7 Regular; 0 Special Education; 0 Vocational; 0 Alternative
0 Magnet; 0 Charter; 5 Title I Eligible; 2 School-wide Title I
Students: 2,151 (n/a% male; n/a% female)
Individual Education Program: 317 (14.7%);
English Language Learner: 22 (1.0%); Migrant: 0 (0.0%)
Eligible for Free Lunch Program: 682 (31.7%)
Eligible for Reduced-Price Lunch Program: 193 (9.0%)
Teachers: 108.5 (19.8 to 1)
Librarians/Media Specialists: 1.0 (2,151.0 to 1)
Guidance Counselors: 6.5 (330.9 to 1)
Current Spending: ($ per student per year):
Total: $7,080; Instruction: $4,196; Support Services: $2,653
Enrollment, Drop-out Rates and Diploma Recipients by Race/Ethnicity

Category	Total	White	Black	Asian	AIAN	Hisp.
Enrollment (%)	100.0	92.3	0.2	1.1	1.5	3.1
Drop-out Rate (%)	2.2	2.2	0.0	0.0	0.0	3.6
H.S. Diplomas (#)	137	133	0	0	0	3

Benton County

Corvallis SD 509J

1555 SW 35th St • Corvallis, OR 97333-1198
Mailing Address: PO Box 3509J • Corvallis, OR 97339-1198
(541) 757-5811 • http://www.corvallis.k12.or.us/
Grade Span: KG-12; **Agency Type:** 1
Schools: 14
9 Primary; 2 Middle; 2 High; 1 Other Level
13 Regular; 0 Special Education; 0 Vocational; 1 Alternative
0 Magnet; 0 Charter; 4 Title I Eligible; 2 School-wide Title I
Students: 7,169 (n/a% male; n/a% female)
Individual Education Program: 854 (11.9%);
English Language Learner: 448 (6.2%); Migrant: 79 (1.1%)
Eligible for Free Lunch Program: 1,303 (18.2%)
Eligible for Reduced-Price Lunch Program: 390 (5.4%)
Teachers: 318.4 (22.5 to 1)
Librarians/Media Specialists: 3.0 (2,389.7 to 1)
Guidance Counselors: 21.4 (335.0 to 1)
Current Spending: ($ per student per year):
Total: $7,134; Instruction: $3,827; Support Services: $2,985
Enrollment, Drop-out Rates and Diploma Recipients by Race/Ethnicity

Category	Total	White	Black	Asian	AIAN	Hisp.
Enrollment (%)	100.0	80.4	1.8	6.6	0.7	6.9
Drop-out Rate (%)	2.2	1.9	0.0	2.7	8.7	7.4
H.S. Diplomas (#)	491	446	7	20	2	16

Philomath SD 17J

1620 Applegate • Philomath, OR 97370-9328
(541) 929-3169 • http://www.philomath.k12.or.us/
Grade Span: KG-12; **Agency Type:** 1
Schools: 6
4 Primary; 1 Middle; 1 High; 0 Other Level
6 Regular; 0 Special Education; 0 Vocational; 0 Alternative
0 Magnet; 1 Charter; 4 Title I Eligible; 0 School-wide Title I
Students: 1,961 (n/a% male; n/a% female)
Individual Education Program: 215 (11.0%);
English Language Learner: 13 (0.7%); Migrant: 3 (0.2%)
Eligible for Free Lunch Program: 358 (18.3%)
Eligible for Reduced-Price Lunch Program: 111 (5.7%)
Teachers: 95.8 (20.5 to 1)
Librarians/Media Specialists: 2.0 (980.5 to 1)
Guidance Counselors: 4.0 (490.3 to 1)
Current Spending: ($ per student per year):
Total: $6,328; Instruction: $3,753; Support Services: $2,498
Enrollment, Drop-out Rates and Diploma Recipients by Race/Ethnicity

Category	Total	White	Black	Asian	AIAN	Hisp.
Enrollment (%)	100.0	88.8	0.3	2.4	1.5	3.4
Drop-out Rate (%)	3.5	2.9	0.0	14.3	10.0	12.5
H.S. Diplomas (#)	135	117	0	4	2	5

Clackamas County

Canby SD 086

811 SW 5th Ave • Canby, OR 97013-3838
(503) 266-7861 • http://www.canby.k12.or.us/
Grade Span: KG-12; **Agency Type:** 1
Schools: 7
5 Primary; 1 Middle; 1 High; 0 Other Level
7 Regular; 0 Special Education; 0 Vocational; 0 Alternative
0 Magnet; 0 Charter; 5 Title I Eligible; 0 School-wide Title I
Students: 5,257 (n/a% male; n/a% female)
Individual Education Program: 558 (10.6%);
English Language Learner: 913 (17.4%); Migrant: 389 (7.4%)
Eligible for Free Lunch Program: 1,238 (23.5%)
Eligible for Reduced-Price Lunch Program: 365 (6.9%)
Teachers: 251.8 (20.9 to 1)
Librarians/Media Specialists: 2.0 (2,628.5 to 1)
Guidance Counselors: 13.5 (389.4 to 1)
Current Spending: ($ per student per year):
Total: $6,516; Instruction: $3,949; Support Services: $2,328
Enrollment, Drop-out Rates and Diploma Recipients by Race/Ethnicity

Category	Total	White	Black	Asian	AIAN	Hisp.
Enrollment (%)	100.0	81.1	0.5	1.5	0.6	15.3
Drop-out Rate (%)	2.6	1.9	0.0	0.0	0.0	11.8
H.S. Diplomas (#)	352	322	0	4	0	26

Estacada SD 108

PO Box 519 • Estacada, OR 97023-0519
(503) 630-6871 • http://www.estacada.k12.or.us/
Grade Span: KG-12; **Agency Type:** 1
Schools: 5
3 Primary; 1 Middle; 1 High; 0 Other Level
5 Regular; 0 Special Education; 0 Vocational; 0 Alternative
0 Magnet; 0 Charter; 3 Title I Eligible; 0 School-wide Title I
Students: 2,320 (n/a% male; n/a% female)
Individual Education Program: 410 (17.7%);
English Language Learner: 183 (7.9%); Migrant: 42 (1.8%)
Eligible for Free Lunch Program: 694 (29.9%)
Eligible for Reduced-Price Lunch Program: 269 (11.6%)
Teachers: 98.0 (23.7 to 1)
Librarians/Media Specialists: 0.0 (0.0 to 1)
Guidance Counselors: 5.0 (464.0 to 1)
Current Spending: ($ per student per year):
Total: $6,754; Instruction: $3,807; Support Services: $2,663
Enrollment, Drop-out Rates and Diploma Recipients by Race/Ethnicity

Category	Total	White	Black	Asian	AIAN	Hisp.
Enrollment (%)	100.0	92.2	0.4	1.0	0.2	5.4
Drop-out Rate (%)	4.0	2.9	33.3	0.0	0.0	38.1
H.S. Diplomas (#)	149	143	1	1	2	2

Gladstone SD 115

17789 Webster Rd • Gladstone, OR 97027-1498
(503) 655-2777 • http://www.gladstone.k12.or.us/
Grade Span: KG-12; **Agency Type:** 1
Schools: 3
1 Primary; 1 Middle; 1 High; 0 Other Level
3 Regular; 0 Special Education; 0 Vocational; 0 Alternative
0 Magnet; 0 Charter; 1 Title I Eligible; 0 School-wide Title I
Students: 2,408 (n/a% male; n/a% female)
Individual Education Program: 292 (12.1%);
English Language Learner: 171 (7.1%); Migrant: 16 (0.7%)
Eligible for Free Lunch Program: 482 (20.0%)
Eligible for Reduced-Price Lunch Program: 197 (8.2%)
Teachers: 106.6 (22.6 to 1)
Librarians/Media Specialists: 2.5 (963.2 to 1)
Guidance Counselors: 6.0 (401.3 to 1)
Current Spending: ($ per student per year):
Total: $6,486; Instruction: $4,015; Support Services: $2,218
Enrollment, Drop-out Rates and Diploma Recipients by Race/Ethnicity

Category	Total	White	Black	Asian	AIAN	Hisp.
Enrollment (%)	100.0	85.2	1.1	3.3	1.4	6.0
Drop-out Rate (%)	1.5	1.0	0.0	0.0	0.0	22.7
H.S. Diplomas (#)	178	178	0	0	0	0

Lake Oswego SD 07J

2455 SW Country Club Rd • Lake Oswego, OR 97034-0070
Mailing Address: PO Box 70 • Lake Oswego, OR 97034-0070
(503) 636-7691 • http://www.loswego.k12.or.us/
Grade Span: KG-12; **Agency Type:** 1
Schools: 13
9 Primary; 2 Middle; 2 High; 0 Other Level
13 Regular; 0 Special Education; 0 Vocational; 0 Alternative
0 Magnet; 0 Charter; 1 Title I Eligible; 0 School-wide Title I
Students: 7,005 (n/a% male; n/a% female)
Individual Education Program: 709 (10.1%);
English Language Learner: 83 (1.2%); Migrant: 2 (<0.1%)
Eligible for Free Lunch Program: 208 (3.0%)
Eligible for Reduced-Price Lunch Program: 142 (2.0%)
Teachers: 340.4 (20.6 to 1)
Librarians/Media Specialists: 9.9 (707.6 to 1)
Guidance Counselors: 15.1 (463.9 to 1)
Current Spending: ($ per student per year):
Total: $7,099; Instruction: $4,216; Support Services: $2,445

Enrollment, Drop-out Rates and Diploma Recipients by Race/Ethnicity

Category	Total	White	Black	Asian	AIAN	Hisp.
Enrollment (%)	100.0	88.4	0.8	6.8	0.4	2.4
Drop-out Rate (%)	2.4	2.4	0.0	1.4	0.0	3.6
H.S. Diplomas (#)	489	445	1	31	1	7

Molalla River SD 035

412 Swegle • Molalla, OR 97038-0188
Mailing Address: PO Box 188 • Molalla, OR 97038-0188
(503) 829-2359 • http://www.molallariv.k12.or.us/
Grade Span: KG-12; **Agency Type:** 1
Schools: 8
6 Primary; 1 Middle; 1 High; 0 Other Level
8 Regular; 0 Special Education; 0 Vocational; 0 Alternative
0 Magnet; 0 Charter; 3 Title I Eligible; 1 School-wide Title I
Students: 2,864 (n/a% male; n/a% female)
Individual Education Program: 430 (15.0%);
English Language Learner: 271 (9.5%); Migrant: 168 (5.9%)
Eligible for Free Lunch Program: 678 (23.7%)
Eligible for Reduced-Price Lunch Program: 281 (9.8%)
Teachers: 138.7 (20.6 to 1)
Librarians/Media Specialists: 1.0 (2,864.0 to 1)
Guidance Counselors: 3.0 (954.7 to 1)
Current Spending: ($ per student per year):
Total: $7,307; Instruction: $4,072; Support Services: $3,021
Enrollment, Drop-out Rates and Diploma Recipients by Race/Ethnicity

Category	Total	White	Black	Asian	AIAN	Hisp.
Enrollment (%)	100.0	86.6	1.0	0.8	1.4	8.8
Drop-out Rate (%)	6.8	6.5	33.3	7.1	0.0	10.9
H.S. Diplomas (#)	111	101	0	2	0	8

North Clackamas SD 012

4444 SE Lake Rd • Milwaukie, OR 97222-4799
(503) 653-3600 • http://www.nclack.k12.or.us/
Grade Span: KG-12; **Agency Type:** 1
Schools: 25
19 Primary; 3 Middle; 3 High; 0 Other Level
24 Regular; 0 Special Education; 0 Vocational; 1 Alternative
0 Magnet; 0 Charter; 7 Title I Eligible; 2 School-wide Title I
Students: 15,777 (n/a% male; n/a% female)
Individual Education Program: 1,751 (11.1%);
English Language Learner: 1,867 (11.8%); Migrant: 51 (0.3%)
Eligible for Free Lunch Program: 3,358 (21.3%)
Eligible for Reduced-Price Lunch Program: 1,109 (7.0%)
Teachers: 774.2 (20.4 to 1)
Librarians/Media Specialists: 22.5 (701.2 to 1)
Guidance Counselors: 31.5 (500.9 to 1)
Current Spending: ($ per student per year):
Total: $7,253; Instruction: $3,966; Support Services: $2,994
Enrollment, Drop-out Rates and Diploma Recipients by Race/Ethnicity

Category	Total	White	Black	Asian	AIAN	Hisp.
Enrollment (%)	100.0	78.2	1.7	2.0	0.9	5.5
Drop-out Rate (%)	4.4	3.7	5.5	3.9	5.7	9.5
H.S. Diplomas (#)	789	682	7	0	7	27

Oregon City SD 062

PO Box 2110 • Oregon City, OR 97045-5010
(503) 656-4283 • http://www.orecity.k12.or.us/
Grade Span: KG-12; **Agency Type:** 1
Schools: 13
10 Primary; 2 Middle; 1 High; 0 Other Level
13 Regular; 0 Special Education; 0 Vocational; 0 Alternative
0 Magnet; 0 Charter; 7 Title I Eligible; 0 School-wide Title I
Students: 7,662 (n/a% male; n/a% female)
Individual Education Program: 1,287 (16.8%);
English Language Learner: 455 (5.9%); Migrant: 67 (0.9%)
Eligible for Free Lunch Program: 1,519 (19.8%)
Eligible for Reduced-Price Lunch Program: 468 (6.1%)
Teachers: 340.0 (22.5 to 1)
Librarians/Media Specialists: 2.0 (3,831.0 to 1)
Guidance Counselors: 17.5 (437.8 to 1)
Current Spending: ($ per student per year):
Total: $6,760; Instruction: $4,304; Support Services: $2,200
Enrollment, Drop-out Rates and Diploma Recipients by Race/Ethnicity

Category	Total	White	Black	Asian	AIAN	Hisp.
Enrollment (%)	100.0	88.8	1.3	1.4	1.1	5.7
Drop-out Rate (%)	0.9	0.9	8.3	2.3	0.0	0.8
H.S. Diplomas (#)	344	310	3	6	12	12

Oregon Trail SD 046

PO Box 547 • Sandy, OR 97055-0547
(503) 668-5541 • http://www.ortrail.k12.or.us/
Grade Span: KG-12; **Agency Type:** 1
Schools: 11
7 Primary; 3 Middle; 1 High; 0 Other Level
11 Regular; 0 Special Education; 0 Vocational; 0 Alternative
0 Magnet; 0 Charter; 4 Title I Eligible; 2 School-wide Title I
Students: 4,190 (n/a% male; n/a% female)
Individual Education Program: 563 (13.4%);
English Language Learner: 239 (5.7%); Migrant: 38 (0.9%)
Eligible for Free Lunch Program: 824 (19.7%)
Eligible for Reduced-Price Lunch Program: 355 (8.5%)
Teachers: 179.5 (23.3 to 1)
Librarians/Media Specialists: 1.0 (4,190.0 to 1)
Guidance Counselors: 9.4 (445.7 to 1)
Current Spending: ($ per student per year):
Total: $6,427; Instruction: $3,796; Support Services: $2,389
Enrollment, Drop-out Rates and Diploma Recipients by Race/Ethnicity

Category	Total	White	Black	Asian	AIAN	Hisp.
Enrollment (%)	100.0	89.2	0.9	1.6	1.8	6.3
Drop-out Rate (%)	2.2	1.8	16.7	8.3	18.2	4.3
H.S. Diplomas (#)	297	278	0	3	4	12

West Linn SD 03J

PO Box 35 • West Linn, OR 97068-0035
(503) 673-7000 • http://www.wlwv.k12.or.us/
Grade Span: PK-12; **Agency Type:** 1
Schools: 13
7 Primary; 4 Middle; 2 High; 0 Other Level
13 Regular; 0 Special Education; 0 Vocational; 0 Alternative
0 Magnet; 1 Charter; 3 Title I Eligible; 0 School-wide Title I
Students: 7,821 (n/a% male; n/a% female)
Individual Education Program: 862 (11.0%);
English Language Learner: 201 (2.6%); Migrant: 6 (0.1%)
Eligible for Free Lunch Program: 493 (6.3%)
Eligible for Reduced-Price Lunch Program: 182 (2.3%)
Teachers: 364.4 (21.5 to 1)
Librarians/Media Specialists: 11.5 (680.1 to 1)
Guidance Counselors: 15.3 (511.2 to 1)
Current Spending: ($ per student per year):
Total: $6,691; Instruction: $4,209; Support Services: $2,316
Enrollment, Drop-out Rates and Diploma Recipients by Race/Ethnicity

Category	Total	White	Black	Asian	AIAN	Hisp.
Enrollment (%)	100.0	88.6	0.9	3.8	0.6	4.9
Drop-out Rate (%)	2.3	2.1	0.0	11.1	0.0	7.3
H.S. Diplomas (#)	476	452	2	11	0	8

Clatsop County

Astoria SD 001

3196 Marine Dr • Astoria, OR 97103-2798
(503) 325-6441 • http://www.astoriaschools.org/
Grade Span: KG-12; **Agency Type:** 1
Schools: 5
3 Primary; 1 Middle; 1 High; 0 Other Level
5 Regular; 0 Special Education; 0 Vocational; 0 Alternative
0 Magnet; 0 Charter; 4 Title I Eligible; 2 School-wide Title I
Students: 2,224 (n/a% male; n/a% female)
Individual Education Program: 304 (13.7%);
English Language Learner: 100 (4.5%); Migrant: 0 (0.0%)
Eligible for Free Lunch Program: 613 (27.6%)
Eligible for Reduced-Price Lunch Program: 192 (8.6%)
Teachers: 117.5 (18.9 to 1)
Librarians/Media Specialists: 4.0 (556.0 to 1)
Guidance Counselors: 6.5 (342.2 to 1)
Current Spending: ($ per student per year):
Total: $7,484; Instruction: $4,645; Support Services: $2,583
Enrollment, Drop-out Rates and Diploma Recipients by Race/Ethnicity

Category	Total	White	Black	Asian	AIAN	Hisp.
Enrollment (%)	100.0	89.2	1.1	1.7	0.7	7.0
Drop-out Rate (%)	2.7	2.0	0.0	7.1	0.0	20.0
H.S. Diplomas (#)	146	141	0	3	0	1

Seaside SD 010

1801 S Franklin St • Seaside, OR 97138-5299
(503) 738-5591 • http://www.seaside.k12.or.us/
Grade Span: KG-12; **Agency Type:** 1
Schools: 5
3 Primary; 1 Middle; 1 High; 0 Other Level
5 Regular; 0 Special Education; 0 Vocational; 0 Alternative
0 Magnet; 0 Charter; 2 Title I Eligible; 0 School-wide Title I
Students: 1,707 (n/a% male; n/a% female)
Individual Education Program: 242 (14.2%);
English Language Learner: 127 (7.4%); Migrant: 0 (0.0%)
Eligible for Free Lunch Program: 467 (27.4%)
Eligible for Reduced-Price Lunch Program: 158 (9.3%)
Teachers: 90.3 (18.9 to 1)
Librarians/Media Specialists: 1.7 (1,004.1 to 1)
Guidance Counselors: 5.0 (341.4 to 1)
Current Spending: ($ per student per year):
Total: $6,792; Instruction: $4,223; Support Services: $2,329

Enrollment, Drop-out Rates and Diploma Recipients by Race/Ethnicity

Category	Total	White	Black	Asian	AIAN	Hisp.
Enrollment (%)	100.0	88.6	0.5	1.3	0.2	8.5
Drop-out Rate (%)	4.5	4.1	0.0	0.0	0.0	18.8
H.S. Diplomas (#)	88	86	0	0	0	2

Columbia County

Saint Helens SD 502

474 N 16th St • Saint Helens, OR 97051-1340
(503) 397-3085 • http://www.sthelens.k12.or.us/sthelens/
Grade Span: KG-12; **Agency Type:** 1
Schools: 6
4 Primary; 1 Middle; 1 High; 0 Other Level
6 Regular; 0 Special Education; 0 Vocational; 0 Alternative
0 Magnet; 0 Charter; 3 Title I Eligible; 1 School-wide Title I
Students: 3,436 (n/a% male; n/a% female)
Individual Education Program: 538 (15.7%);
English Language Learner: 9 (0.3%); Migrant: 0 (0.0%)
Eligible for Free Lunch Program: 777 (22.6%)
Eligible for Reduced-Price Lunch Program: 263 (7.7%)
Teachers: 175.4 (19.6 to 1)
Librarians/Media Specialists: 3.6 (954.4 to 1)
Guidance Counselors: 11.0 (312.4 to 1)
Current Spending: ($ per student per year):
Total: $6,607; Instruction: $3,956; Support Services: $2,416
Enrollment, Drop-out Rates and Diploma Recipients by Race/Ethnicity

Category	Total	White	Black	Asian	AIAN	Hisp.
Enrollment (%)	100.0	89.8	0.8	2.5	1.9	4.7
Drop-out Rate (%)	4.4	3.8	11.1	3.3	0.0	19.4
H.S. Diplomas (#)	176	159	2	6	4	5

Scappoose SD 01J

33589 High School Way • Scappoose, OR 97056-3326
(503) 543-6374 • http://www.scappoose.k12.or.us/
Grade Span: KG-12; **Agency Type:** 1
Schools: 6
3 Primary; 2 Middle; 1 High; 0 Other Level
6 Regular; 0 Special Education; 0 Vocational; 0 Alternative
0 Magnet; 0 Charter; 4 Title I Eligible; 0 School-wide Title I
Students: 2,192 (n/a% male; n/a% female)
Individual Education Program: 255 (11.6%);
English Language Learner: 6 (0.3%); Migrant: 0 (0.0%)
Eligible for Free Lunch Program: 294 (13.4%)
Eligible for Reduced-Price Lunch Program: 115 (5.2%)
Teachers: 115.3 (19.0 to 1)
Librarians/Media Specialists: 2.0 (1,096.0 to 1)
Guidance Counselors: 5.6 (391.4 to 1)
Current Spending: ($ per student per year):
Total: $6,718; Instruction: $3,830; Support Services: $2,687
Enrollment, Drop-out Rates and Diploma Recipients by Race/Ethnicity

Category	Total	White	Black	Asian	AIAN	Hisp.
Enrollment (%)	100.0	92.2	0.5	0.9	2.7	3.5
Drop-out Rate (%)	2.4	2.4	0.0	0.0	12.5	0.0
H.S. Diplomas (#)	142	136	0	1	2	3

Coos County

Coos Bay SD 009

PO Box 509 • Coos Bay, OR 97420-0102
(541) 267-3104 • http://www.coos-bay.k12.or.us/
Grade Span: KG-12; **Agency Type:** 1
Schools: 7
3 Primary; 2 Middle; 2 High; 0 Other Level
7 Regular; 0 Special Education; 0 Vocational; 0 Alternative
0 Magnet; 1 Charter; 3 Title I Eligible; 3 School-wide Title I
Students: 3,791 (n/a% male; n/a% female)
Individual Education Program: 578 (15.2%);
English Language Learner: 73 (1.9%); Migrant: 0 (0.0%)
Eligible for Free Lunch Program: 1,497 (39.5%)
Eligible for Reduced-Price Lunch Program: 339 (8.9%)
Teachers: 176.0 (21.5 to 1)
Librarians/Media Specialists: 2.9 (1,307.2 to 1)
Guidance Counselors: 7.0 (541.6 to 1)
Current Spending: ($ per student per year):
Total: $7,380; Instruction: $3,885; Support Services: $3,197
Enrollment, Drop-out Rates and Diploma Recipients by Race/Ethnicity

Category	Total	White	Black	Asian	AIAN	Hisp.
Enrollment (%)	100.0	75.7	0.7	1.9	16.1	5.5
Drop-out Rate (%)	4.4	4.1	0.0	2.9	5.8	8.6
H.S. Diplomas (#)	239	195	0	3	33	8

North Bend SD 013

1913 Meade St • North Bend, OR 97459-3432
(541) 756-2521 • http://www.nbend.k12.or.us/
Grade Span: KG-12; **Agency Type:** 1
Schools: 7
4 Primary; 2 Middle; 1 High; 0 Other Level
6 Regular; 1 Special Education; 0 Vocational; 0 Alternative
0 Magnet; 1 Charter; 4 Title I Eligible; 3 School-wide Title I
Students: 2,311 (n/a% male; n/a% female)
Individual Education Program: 326 (14.1%);
English Language Learner: 6 (0.3%); Migrant: 0 (0.0%)
Eligible for Free Lunch Program: 753 (32.6%)
Eligible for Reduced-Price Lunch Program: 207 (9.0%)
Teachers: 111.7 (20.7 to 1)
Librarians/Media Specialists: 2.0 (1,155.5 to 1)
Guidance Counselors: 3.0 (770.3 to 1)
Current Spending: ($ per student per year):
Total: $7,171; Instruction: $3,934; Support Services: $2,996
Enrollment, Drop-out Rates and Diploma Recipients by Race/Ethnicity

Category	Total	White	Black	Asian	AIAN	Hisp.
Enrollment (%)	100.0	88.7	1.0	2.6	4.9	2.7
Drop-out Rate (%)	2.9	2.5	33.3	0.0	5.0	20.0
H.S. Diplomas (#)	166	156	1	5	3	1

Crook County

Crook County SD

1390 SE 2nd St • Prineville, OR 97754-2498
(541) 447-5664 • http://www.crookcounty.k12.or.us/
Grade Span: KG-12; **Agency Type:** 1
Schools: 7
5 Primary; 1 Middle; 1 High; 0 Other Level
7 Regular; 0 Special Education; 0 Vocational; 0 Alternative
0 Magnet; 0 Charter; 5 Title I Eligible; 1 School-wide Title I
Students: 3,133 (n/a% male; n/a% female)
Individual Education Program: 396 (12.6%);
English Language Learner: 134 (4.3%); Migrant: 166 (5.3%)
Eligible for Free Lunch Program: 1,083 (34.6%)
Eligible for Reduced-Price Lunch Program: 361 (11.5%)
Teachers: 161.5 (19.4 to 1)
Librarians/Media Specialists: 2.5 (1,253.2 to 1)
Guidance Counselors: 7.0 (447.6 to 1)
Current Spending: ($ per student per year):
Total: $7,263; Instruction: $4,081; Support Services: $2,911
Enrollment, Drop-out Rates and Diploma Recipients by Race/Ethnicity

Category	Total	White	Black	Asian	AIAN	Hisp.
Enrollment (%)	100.0	89.1	0.3	0.6	0.9	9.1
Drop-out Rate (%)	2.9	2.8	100.0	0.0	0.0	3.2
H.S. Diplomas (#)	179	164	0	0	0	15

Curry County

Brookings-Harbor SD 17

564 Fern St • Brookings, OR 97415-9657
(541) 469-7443 • http://www.brookings.k12.or.us/
Grade Span: KG-12; **Agency Type:** 1
Schools: 4
1 Primary; 2 Middle; 1 High; 0 Other Level
4 Regular; 0 Special Education; 0 Vocational; 0 Alternative
0 Magnet; 0 Charter; 1 Title I Eligible; 1 School-wide Title I
Students: 1,849 (n/a% male; n/a% female)
Individual Education Program: 273 (14.8%);
English Language Learner: 40 (2.2%); Migrant: 0 (0.0%)
Eligible for Free Lunch Program: 718 (38.8%)
Eligible for Reduced-Price Lunch Program: 270 (14.6%)
Teachers: 93.0 (19.9 to 1)
Librarians/Media Specialists: 1.0 (1,849.0 to 1)
Guidance Counselors: 5.0 (369.8 to 1)
Current Spending: ($ per student per year):
Total: $6,772; Instruction: $4,393; Support Services: $2,137
Enrollment, Drop-out Rates and Diploma Recipients by Race/Ethnicity

Category	Total	White	Black	Asian	AIAN	Hisp.
Enrollment (%)	100.0	84.1	0.2	1.6	4.2	6.4
Drop-out Rate (%)	6.2	5.9	0.0	10.0	2.6	19.0
H.S. Diplomas (#)	121	102	1	1	13	4

Deschutes County

Bend Admin SD 1

520 NW Wall St • Bend, OR 97701-2699
(541) 383-6000 • http://www.bend.k12.or.us/
Grade Span: KG-12; **Agency Type:** 1
Schools: 23
12 Primary; 6 Middle; 5 High; 0 Other Level
22 Regular; 0 Special Education; 0 Vocational; 1 Alternative

0 Magnet; 1 Charter; 8 Title I Eligible; 1 School-wide Title I
Students: 13,671 (n/a% male; n/a% female)
Individual Education Program: 1,965 (14.4%);
English Language Learner: 328 (2.4%); Migrant: 77 (0.6%)
Eligible for Free Lunch Program: 3,218 (23.5%)
Eligible for Reduced-Price Lunch Program: 1,175 (8.6%)
Teachers: 646.0 (21.2 to 1)
Librarians/Media Specialists: 8.3 (1,647.1 to 1)
Guidance Counselors: 28.2 (484.8 to 1)
Current Spending: ($ per student per year):
Total: $6,603; Instruction: $4,038; Support Services: $2,352
Enrollment, Drop-out Rates and Diploma Recipients by Race/Ethnicity

Category	Total	White	Black	Asian	AIAN	Hisp.
Enrollment (%)	100.0	92.0	0.6	1.1	1.1	5.0
Drop-out Rate (%)	5.0	4.8	0.0	3.3	0.0	11.1
H.S. Diplomas (#)	805	766	2	5	0	32

Redmond SD 02J

145 SE Salmon Ave • Redmond, OR 97756-8422
(541) 923-5437 • http://www.redmond.k12.or.us/
Grade Span: KG-12; **Agency Type:** 1
Schools: 10
6 Primary; 2 Middle; 2 High; 0 Other Level
9 Regular; 0 Special Education; 0 Vocational; 1 Alternative
0 Magnet; 0 Charter; 5 Title I Eligible; 0 School-wide Title I
Students: 6,040 (n/a% male; n/a% female)
Individual Education Program: 729 (12.1%);
English Language Learner: 161 (2.7%); Migrant: 112 (1.9%)
Eligible for Free Lunch Program: 1,719 (28.5%)
Eligible for Reduced-Price Lunch Program: 526 (8.7%)
Teachers: 276.4 (21.9 to 1)
Librarians/Media Specialists: 1.0 (6,040.0 to 1)
Guidance Counselors: 16.8 (359.5 to 1)
Current Spending: ($ per student per year):
Total: $6,323; Instruction: $3,815; Support Services: $2,253
Enrollment, Drop-out Rates and Diploma Recipients by Race/Ethnicity

Category	Total	White	Black	Asian	AIAN	Hisp.
Enrollment (%)	100.0	92.1	0.5	1.1	1.0	5.0
Drop-out Rate (%)	3.4	3.3	0.0	8.3	0.0	4.1
H.S. Diplomas (#)	304	286	2	2	3	11

Douglas County

Roseburg SD 4

1419 NW Valley View Dr • Roseburg, OR 97470-1767
(541) 440-4015 • http://www.roseburg.k12.or.us/
Grade Span: KG-12; **Agency Type:** 1
Schools: 12
8 Primary; 3 Middle; 1 High; 0 Other Level
12 Regular; 0 Special Education; 0 Vocational; 0 Alternative
0 Magnet; 0 Charter; 7 Title I Eligible; 4 School-wide Title I
Students: 6,788 (n/a% male; n/a% female)
Individual Education Program: 863 (12.7%);
English Language Learner: 129 (1.9%); Migrant: 0 (0.0%)
Eligible for Free Lunch Program: 1,850 (27.3%)
Eligible for Reduced-Price Lunch Program: 641 (9.4%)
Teachers: 312.7 (21.7 to 1)
Librarians/Media Specialists: 3.0 (2,262.7 to 1)
Guidance Counselors: 18.0 (377.1 to 1)
Current Spending: ($ per student per year):
Total: $6,674; Instruction: $4,130; Support Services: $2,287
Enrollment, Drop-out Rates and Diploma Recipients by Race/Ethnicity

Category	Total	White	Black	Asian	AIAN	Hisp.
Enrollment (%)	100.0	89.2	0.7	1.7	2.4	4.9
Drop-out Rate (%)	6.3	5.7	55.6	5.6	8.1	13.1
H.S. Diplomas (#)	399	366	0	3	12	18

South Umpqua SD 019

558 SW Chadwick Ln • Myrtle Creek, OR 97457-9798
(541) 863-3115
Grade Span: KG-12; **Agency Type:** 1
Schools: 5
3 Primary; 1 Middle; 1 High; 0 Other Level
5 Regular; 0 Special Education; 0 Vocational; 0 Alternative
0 Magnet; 0 Charter; 3 Title I Eligible; 0 School-wide Title I
Students: 1,927 (n/a% male; n/a% female)
Individual Education Program: 298 (15.5%);
English Language Learner: 10 (0.5%); Migrant: 0 (0.0%)
Eligible for Free Lunch Program: 827 (42.9%)
Eligible for Reduced-Price Lunch Program: 225 (11.7%)
Teachers: 100.1 (19.3 to 1)
Librarians/Media Specialists: 0.9 (2,141.1 to 1)
Guidance Counselors: 5.0 (385.4 to 1)
Current Spending: ($ per student per year):
Total: $6,539; Instruction: $3,715; Support Services: $2,462

Enrollment, Drop-out Rates and Diploma Recipients by Race/Ethnicity

Category	Total	White	Black	Asian	AIAN	Hisp.
Enrollment (%)	100.0	88.4	0.8	1.3	5.1	4.0
Drop-out Rate (%)	7.8	7.0	n/a	0.0	25.0	21.1
H.S. Diplomas (#)	116	108	0	2	1	5

Sutherlin SD 130

730 W Central Ave • Sutherlin, OR 97479-9472
(541) 459-2228
Grade Span: KG-12; **Agency Type:** 1
Schools: 4
1 Primary; 2 Middle; 1 High; 0 Other Level
4 Regular; 0 Special Education; 0 Vocational; 0 Alternative
0 Magnet; 0 Charter; 2 Title I Eligible; 2 School-wide Title I
Students: 1,531 (n/a% male; n/a% female)
Individual Education Program: 207 (13.5%);
English Language Learner: 12 (0.8%); Migrant: 0 (0.0%)
Eligible for Free Lunch Program: 608 (39.7%)
Eligible for Reduced-Price Lunch Program: 191 (12.5%)
Teachers: 76.7 (20.0 to 1)
Librarians/Media Specialists: 0.0 (0.0 to 1)
Guidance Counselors: 4.0 (382.8 to 1)
Current Spending: ($ per student per year):
Total: $6,409; Instruction: $3,959; Support Services: $2,269
Enrollment, Drop-out Rates and Diploma Recipients by Race/Ethnicity

Category	Total	White	Black	Asian	AIAN	Hisp.
Enrollment (%)	100.0	90.1	0.4	1.2	2.4	5.6
Drop-out Rate (%)	3.7	3.6	n/a	0.0	0.0	7.7
H.S. Diplomas (#)	68	61	0	0	6	1

Winston-Dillard SD 116

165 Dyke Rd • Winston, OR 97496-8501
(541) 679-3000 • http://www.wdsd.org/
Grade Span: PK-12; **Agency Type:** 1
Schools: 6
3 Primary; 1 Middle; 1 High; 1 Other Level
5 Regular; 1 Special Education; 0 Vocational; 0 Alternative
0 Magnet; 0 Charter; 4 Title I Eligible; 2 School-wide Title I
Students: 1,622 (n/a% male; n/a% female)
Individual Education Program: 282 (17.4%);
English Language Learner: 0 (0.0%); Migrant: 0 (0.0%)
Eligible for Free Lunch Program: 619 (38.2%)
Eligible for Reduced-Price Lunch Program: 195 (12.0%)
Teachers: 109.7 (14.8 to 1)
Librarians/Media Specialists: 2.0 (811.0 to 1)
Guidance Counselors: 4.0 (405.5 to 1)
Current Spending: ($ per student per year):
Total: $7,032; Instruction: $4,194; Support Services: $2,565
Enrollment, Drop-out Rates and Diploma Recipients by Race/Ethnicity

Category	Total	White	Black	Asian	AIAN	Hisp.
Enrollment (%)	100.0	94.1	0.4	0.6	1.9	3.0
Drop-out Rate (%)	8.2	8.5	0.0	0.0	0.0	0.0
H.S. Diplomas (#)	81	79	0	0	0	2

Hood River County

Hood River County SD 1

PO Box 920 • Hood River, OR 97031-0030
(541) 386-2511 • http://www.hoodriver.k12.or.us/index.htm
Grade Span: KG-12; **Agency Type:** 1
Schools: 9
5 Primary; 2 Middle; 1 High; 1 Other Level
9 Regular; 0 Special Education; 0 Vocational; 0 Alternative
0 Magnet; 0 Charter; 5 Title I Eligible; 0 School-wide Title I
Students: 3,867 (n/a% male; n/a% female)
Individual Education Program: 494 (12.8%);
English Language Learner: 697 (18.0%); Migrant: 836 (21.6%)
Eligible for Free Lunch Program: 1,473 (38.1%)
Eligible for Reduced-Price Lunch Program: 358 (9.3%)
Teachers: 219.8 (17.6 to 1)
Librarians/Media Specialists: 1.6 (2,416.9 to 1)
Guidance Counselors: 5.5 (703.1 to 1)
Current Spending: ($ per student per year):
Total: $7,685; Instruction: $4,842; Support Services: $2,536
Enrollment, Drop-out Rates and Diploma Recipients by Race/Ethnicity

Category	Total	White	Black	Asian	AIAN	Hisp.
Enrollment (%)	100.0	59.2	0.6	1.4	0.7	38.1
Drop-out Rate (%)	2.1	1.3	0.0	0.0	14.3	4.1
H.S. Diplomas (#)	231	172	1	8	3	47

Jackson County

Ashland SD 005
885 Siskiyou Blvd • Ashland, OR 97520-2197
(541) 482-2811 • http://www.ashland.k12.or.us/splash/
Grade Span: KG-12; **Agency Type:** 1
Schools: 8
6 Primary; 1 Middle; 1 High; 0 Other Level
7 Regular; 0 Special Education; 0 Vocational; 1 Alternative
0 Magnet; 0 Charter; 3 Title I Eligible; 3 School-wide Title I
Students: 3,190 (n/a% male; n/a% female)
Individual Education Program: 331 (10.4%);
English Language Learner: 69 (2.2%); Migrant: 17 (0.5%)
Eligible for Free Lunch Program: 568 (17.8%)
Eligible for Reduced-Price Lunch Program: 159 (5.0%)
Teachers: 160.8 (19.8 to 1)
Librarians/Media Specialists: 2.8 (1,139.3 to 1)
Guidance Counselors: 9.2 (346.7 to 1)
Current Spending: ($ per student per year):
Total: $7,275; Instruction: $4,688; Support Services: $2,437
Enrollment, Drop-out Rates and Diploma Recipients by Race/Ethnicity

Category	Total	White	Black	Asian	AIAN	Hisp.
Enrollment (%)	100.0	87.6	1.7	3.1	1.7	5.0
Drop-out Rate (%)	3.1	3.0	16.7	0.0	10.5	2.7
H.S. Diplomas (#)	255	244	1	2	3	5

Central Point SD 006
451 N 2nd St • Central Point, OR 97502-1699
(541) 664-6611 • http://www.district6.org/
Grade Span: KG-12; **Agency Type:** 1
Schools: 8
5 Primary; 2 Middle; 1 High; 0 Other Level
8 Regular; 0 Special Education; 0 Vocational; 0 Alternative
0 Magnet; 0 Charter; 5 Title I Eligible; 0 School-wide Title I
Students: 4,643 (n/a% male; n/a% female)
Individual Education Program: 566 (12.2%);
English Language Learner: 115 (2.5%); Migrant: 24 (0.5%)
Eligible for Free Lunch Program: 1,145 (24.7%)
Eligible for Reduced-Price Lunch Program: 416 (9.0%)
Teachers: 186.4 (24.9 to 1)
Librarians/Media Specialists: 1.7 (2,731.2 to 1)
Guidance Counselors: 11.0 (422.1 to 1)
Current Spending: ($ per student per year):
Total: $6,203; Instruction: $3,839; Support Services: $2,147
Enrollment, Drop-out Rates and Diploma Recipients by Race/Ethnicity

Category	Total	White	Black	Asian	AIAN	Hisp.
Enrollment (%)	100.0	83.3	0.5	1.6	1.9	6.8
Drop-out Rate (%)	5.9	6.3	0.0	7.4	0.0	3.4
H.S. Diplomas (#)	273	242	1	4	7	15

Eagle Point SD 009
11 N Royal Ave • Eagle Point, OR 97524-0548
Mailing Address: PO Box 548 • Eagle Point, OR 97524-0548
(541) 830-1200 • http://www.eaglepnt.k12.or.us/
Grade Span: KG-12; **Agency Type:** 1
Schools: 9
7 Primary; 1 Middle; 1 High; 0 Other Level
9 Regular; 0 Special Education; 0 Vocational; 0 Alternative
0 Magnet; 0 Charter; 9 Title I Eligible; 8 School-wide Title I
Students: 4,134 (n/a% male; n/a% female)
Individual Education Program: 512 (12.4%);
English Language Learner: 314 (7.6%); Migrant: 53 (1.3%)
Eligible for Free Lunch Program: 1,479 (35.8%)
Eligible for Reduced-Price Lunch Program: 631 (15.3%)
Teachers: 176.0 (23.5 to 1)
Librarians/Media Specialists: 1.0 (4,134.0 to 1)
Guidance Counselors: 7.0 (590.6 to 1)
Current Spending: ($ per student per year):
Total: $6,814; Instruction: $4,041; Support Services: $2,534
Enrollment, Drop-out Rates and Diploma Recipients by Race/Ethnicity

Category	Total	White	Black	Asian	AIAN	Hisp.
Enrollment (%)	100.0	76.1	0.7	1.2	2.2	13.2
Drop-out Rate (%)	7.3	6.8	33.3	0.0	0.0	8.7
H.S. Diplomas (#)	241	216	0	2	0	23

Medford SD 549
500 Monroe St • Medford, OR 97501-3522
(541) 776-8600 • http://www.medford.k12.or.us/
Grade Span: KG-12; **Agency Type:** 1
Schools: 19
14 Primary; 2 Middle; 3 High; 0 Other Level
18 Regular; 0 Special Education; 0 Vocational; 1 Alternative
0 Magnet; 0 Charter; 7 Title I Eligible; 5 School-wide Title I
Students: 13,014 (n/a% male; n/a% female)
Individual Education Program: 1,437 (11.0%);
English Language Learner: 1,206 (9.3%); Migrant: 336 (2.6%)
Eligible for Free Lunch Program: 3,624 (27.8%)
Eligible for Reduced-Price Lunch Program: 1,040 (8.0%)
Teachers: 560.4 (23.2 to 1)
Librarians/Media Specialists: 18.6 (699.7 to 1)
Guidance Counselors: 22.2 (586.2 to 1)
Current Spending: ($ per student per year):
Total: $6,275; Instruction: $4,000; Support Services: $2,113
Enrollment, Drop-out Rates and Diploma Recipients by Race/Ethnicity

Category	Total	White	Black	Asian	AIAN	Hisp.
Enrollment (%)	100.0	82.1	1.3	2.0	1.5	13.1
Drop-out Rate (%)	8.2	7.2	20.0	7.8	16.3	14.8
H.S. Diplomas (#)	660	568	1	23	5	63

Phoenix-Talent SD 004
PO Box 698 • Phoenix, OR 97535-0698
(541) 535-1517 • http://www.phoenix.k12.or.us/
Grade Span: KG-12; **Agency Type:** 1
Schools: 6
3 Primary; 1 Middle; 1 High; 1 Other Level
5 Regular; 0 Special Education; 0 Vocational; 1 Alternative
0 Magnet; 1 Charter; 2 Title I Eligible; 2 School-wide Title I
Students: 2,833 (n/a% male; n/a% female)
Individual Education Program: 285 (10.1%);
English Language Learner: 410 (14.5%); Migrant: 155 (5.5%)
Eligible for Free Lunch Program: 1,047 (37.0%)
Eligible for Reduced-Price Lunch Program: 297 (10.5%)
Teachers: 145.2 (19.5 to 1)
Librarians/Media Specialists: 3.0 (944.3 to 1)
Guidance Counselors: 3.5 (809.4 to 1)
Current Spending: ($ per student per year):
Total: $6,729; Instruction: $4,228; Support Services: $2,288
Enrollment, Drop-out Rates and Diploma Recipients by Race/Ethnicity

Category	Total	White	Black	Asian	AIAN	Hisp.
Enrollment (%)	100.0	74.0	1.9	1.7	1.5	20.3
Drop-out Rate (%)	11.0	10.7	0.0	21.1	26.7	5.9
H.S. Diplomas (#)	127	112	2	1	1	11

Jefferson County

Jefferson County SD 509J
445 SE Buff St • Madras, OR 97741-1595
(541) 475-6192 • http://www.whitebuffalos.net/
Grade Span: KG-12; **Agency Type:** 1
Schools: 7
5 Primary; 1 Middle; 1 High; 0 Other Level
7 Regular; 0 Special Education; 0 Vocational; 0 Alternative
0 Magnet; 0 Charter; 4 Title I Eligible; 1 School-wide Title I
Students: 3,195 (n/a% male; n/a% female)
Individual Education Program: 410 (12.8%);
English Language Learner: 1,068 (33.4%); Migrant: 645 (20.2%)
Eligible for Free Lunch Program: 1,768 (55.3%)
Eligible for Reduced-Price Lunch Program: 380 (11.9%)
Teachers: 181.5 (17.6 to 1)
Librarians/Media Specialists: 3.2 (998.4 to 1)
Guidance Counselors: 8.3 (384.9 to 1)
Current Spending: ($ per student per year):
Total: $8,393; Instruction: $4,890; Support Services: $3,094
Enrollment, Drop-out Rates and Diploma Recipients by Race/Ethnicity

Category	Total	White	Black	Asian	AIAN	Hisp.
Enrollment (%)	100.0	38.9	0.5	0.6	33.1	26.4
Drop-out Rate (%)	5.6	2.3	0.0	0.0	8.3	8.4
H.S. Diplomas (#)	127	67	1	0	35	24

Josephine County

Grants Pass SD 007
725 NE Dean Dr • Grants Pass, OR 97526-1649
(541) 474-5700 • http://www.grantspass.k12.or.us/
Grade Span: PK-12; **Agency Type:** 1
Schools: 10
7 Primary; 2 Middle; 1 High; 0 Other Level
9 Regular; 0 Special Education; 0 Vocational; 1 Alternative
0 Magnet; 0 Charter; 6 Title I Eligible; 4 School-wide Title I
Students: 5,540 (n/a% male; n/a% female)
Individual Education Program: 534 (9.6%);
English Language Learner: 73 (1.3%); Migrant: 4 (0.1%)
Eligible for Free Lunch Program: 2,031 (36.7%)
Eligible for Reduced-Price Lunch Program: 766 (13.8%)
Teachers: 273.7 (20.2 to 1)
Librarians/Media Specialists: 4.0 (1,385.0 to 1)
Guidance Counselors: 11.0 (503.6 to 1)
Current Spending: ($ per student per year):
Total: $6,455; Instruction: $4,203; Support Services: $2,022

Enrollment, Drop-out Rates and Diploma Recipients by Race/Ethnicity

Category	Total	White	Black	Asian	AIAN	Hisp.
Enrollment (%)	100.0	86.3	0.7	1.6	2.0	6.9
Drop-out Rate (%)	6.0	5.3	66.7	0.0	150.0	13.8
H.S. Diplomas (#)	287	268	0	6	1	12

Three Rivers SD

PO Box 160 • Murphy, OR 97533-0160
(541) 862-3111 •
http://www.threerivers.k12.or.us/public2003/district/index.htm
Grade Span: KG-12; **Agency Type:** 1
Schools: 17
9 Primary; 3 Middle; 3 High; 2 Other Level
15 Regular; 0 Special Education; 0 Vocational; 2 Alternative
0 Magnet; 0 Charter; 10 Title I Eligible; 10 School-wide Title I
Students: 6,120 (n/a% male; n/a% female)
Individual Education Program: 750 (12.3%);
English Language Learner: 63 (1.0%); Migrant: 10 (0.2%)
Eligible for Free Lunch Program: 2,493 (40.7%)
Eligible for Reduced-Price Lunch Program: 777 (12.7%)
Teachers: 294.8 (20.8 to 1)
Librarians/Media Specialists: 1.0 (6,120.0 to 1)
Guidance Counselors: 8.0 (765.0 to 1)
Current Spending: ($ per student per year):
Total: $7,163; Instruction: $4,421; Support Services: $2,475
Enrollment, Drop-out Rates and Diploma Recipients by Race/Ethnicity

Category	Total	White	Black	Asian	AIAN	Hisp.
Enrollment (%)	100.0	89.5	0.9	1.3	2.7	5.4
Drop-out Rate (%)	4.7	4.5	0.0	0.0	1.7	9.2
H.S. Diplomas (#)	358	331	1	7	9	10

Klamath County

Klamath County SD

10501 Washburn Way • Klamath Falls, OR 97603-8626
(541) 883-5000 • http://www.kcsd.k12.or.us/
Grade Span: KG-12; **Agency Type:** 1
Schools: 19
12 Primary; 2 Middle; 3 High; 2 Other Level
19 Regular; 0 Special Education; 0 Vocational; 0 Alternative
0 Magnet; 0 Charter; 14 Title I Eligible; 8 School-wide Title I
Students: 6,722 (n/a% male; n/a% female)
Individual Education Program: 1,017 (15.1%);
English Language Learner: 286 (4.3%); Migrant: 307 (4.6%)
Eligible for Free Lunch Program: 2,666 (39.7%)
Eligible for Reduced-Price Lunch Program: 782 (11.6%)
Teachers: 352.8 (19.1 to 1)
Librarians/Media Specialists: 2.0 (3,361.0 to 1)
Guidance Counselors: 14.8 (454.2 to 1)
Current Spending: ($ per student per year):
Total: $6,917; Instruction: $4,190; Support Services: $2,410
Enrollment, Drop-out Rates and Diploma Recipients by Race/Ethnicity

Category	Total	White	Black	Asian	AIAN	Hisp.
Enrollment (%)	100.0	77.0	1.1	1.3	8.6	11.9
Drop-out Rate (%)	2.5	2.0	0.0	0.0	1.7	10.2
H.S. Diplomas (#)	223	185	2	7	13	16

Klamath Falls City Schools

1336 Avalon • Klamath Falls, OR 97603-4423
(541) 883-4700 • http://www.kfalls.k12.or.us/
Grade Span: KG-12; **Agency Type:** 1
Schools: 10
6 Primary; 1 Middle; 2 High; 1 Other Level
9 Regular; 1 Special Education; 0 Vocational; 0 Alternative
0 Magnet; 0 Charter; 8 Title I Eligible; 8 School-wide Title I
Students: 3,985 (n/a% male; n/a% female)
Individual Education Program: 621 (15.6%);
English Language Learner: 799 (20.1%); Migrant: 209 (5.2%)
Eligible for Free Lunch Program: 2,099 (52.7%)
Eligible for Reduced-Price Lunch Program: 404 (10.1%)
Teachers: 212.7 (18.7 to 1)
Librarians/Media Specialists: 6.0 (664.2 to 1)
Guidance Counselors: 13.0 (306.5 to 1)
Current Spending: ($ per student per year):
Total: $8,381; Instruction: $5,349; Support Services: $2,768
Enrollment, Drop-out Rates and Diploma Recipients by Race/Ethnicity

Category	Total	White	Black	Asian	AIAN	Hisp.
Enrollment (%)	100.0	78.3	1.8	1.7	6.2	11.8
Drop-out Rate (%)	4.4	3.8	3.7	0.0	4.7	9.8
H.S. Diplomas (#)	306	254	4	4	10	33

Lane County

Bethel SD 052

4640 Barger Dr • Eugene, OR 97402-1297
(541) 689-3280 • http://www.bethel.k12.or.us/
Grade Span: KG-12; **Agency Type:** 1
Schools: 11
7 Primary; 2 Middle; 2 High; 0 Other Level
11 Regular; 0 Special Education; 0 Vocational; 0 Alternative
0 Magnet; 0 Charter; 6 Title I Eligible; 1 School-wide Title I
Students: 5,507 (n/a% male; n/a% female)
Individual Education Program: 835 (15.2%);
English Language Learner: 86 (1.6%); Migrant: 38 (0.7%)
Eligible for Free Lunch Program: 1,775 (32.2%)
Eligible for Reduced-Price Lunch Program: 580 (10.5%)
Teachers: 222.9 (24.7 to 1)
Librarians/Media Specialists: 1.0 (5,507.0 to 1)
Guidance Counselors: 12.6 (437.1 to 1)
Current Spending: ($ per student per year):
Total: $6,823; Instruction: $4,290; Support Services: $2,318
Enrollment, Drop-out Rates and Diploma Recipients by Race/Ethnicity

Category	Total	White	Black	Asian	AIAN	Hisp.
Enrollment (%)	100.0	83.9	3.4	2.3	2.1	7.5
Drop-out Rate (%)	6.2	5.9	0.0	9.1	15.0	10.3
H.S. Diplomas (#)	224	208	1	3	2	10

Eugene SD 04J

200 N Monroe St • Eugene, OR 97402-4295
(541) 687-3123 • http://www.4j.lane.edu/
Grade Span: KG-12; **Agency Type:** 1
Schools: 47
31 Primary; 8 Middle; 7 High; 1 Other Level
34 Regular; 0 Special Education; 0 Vocational; 13 Alternative
0 Magnet; 3 Charter; 9 Title I Eligible; 1 School-wide Title I
Students: 18,735 (n/a% male; n/a% female)
Individual Education Program: 2,419 (12.9%);
English Language Learner: 344 (1.8%); Migrant: 70 (0.4%)
Eligible for Free Lunch Program: 3,932 (21.0%)
Eligible for Reduced-Price Lunch Program: 878 (4.7%)
Teachers: 826.3 (22.7 to 1)
Librarians/Media Specialists: 10.3 (1,818.9 to 1)
Guidance Counselors: 23.7 (790.5 to 1)
Current Spending: ($ per student per year):
Total: $7,203; Instruction: $4,368; Support Services: $2,633
Enrollment, Drop-out Rates and Diploma Recipients by Race/Ethnicity

Category	Total	White	Black	Asian	AIAN	Hisp.
Enrollment (%)	100.0	76.6	2.8	5.1	2.5	6.1
Drop-out Rate (%)	3.0	2.6	3.6	3.2	6.4	5.4
H.S. Diplomas (#)	1,378	1,176	26	45	25	51

Fern Ridge SD 28J

88834 Territorial Rd • Elmira, OR 97437-9756
(541) 935-2253 • http://www.fernridge.k12.or.us/
Grade Span: KG-12; **Agency Type:** 1
Schools: 4
2 Primary; 1 Middle; 1 High; 0 Other Level
4 Regular; 0 Special Education; 0 Vocational; 0 Alternative
0 Magnet; 0 Charter; 3 Title I Eligible; 0 School-wide Title I
Students: 1,685 (n/a% male; n/a% female)
Individual Education Program: 282 (16.7%);
English Language Learner: 0 (0.0%); Migrant: 0 (0.0%)
Eligible for Free Lunch Program: 559 (33.2%)
Eligible for Reduced-Price Lunch Program: 191 (11.3%)
Teachers: 81.5 (20.7 to 1)
Librarians/Media Specialists: 0.6 (2,808.3 to 1)
Guidance Counselors: 2.3 (732.6 to 1)
Current Spending: ($ per student per year):
Total: $7,474; Instruction: $4,236; Support Services: $2,905
Enrollment, Drop-out Rates and Diploma Recipients by Race/Ethnicity

Category	Total	White	Black	Asian	AIAN	Hisp.
Enrollment (%)	100.0	84.5	0.4	1.7	6.5	2.6
Drop-out Rate (%)	4.2	4.0	0.0	0.0	0.0	27.3
H.S. Diplomas (#)	112	108	0	2	1	1

Junction City SD 069

325 Maple St • Junction City, OR 97448-1359
(541) 998-6311 • http://www.junctioncity.k12.or.us/
Grade Span: KG-12; **Agency Type:** 1
Schools: 4
2 Primary; 1 Middle; 1 High; 0 Other Level
4 Regular; 0 Special Education; 0 Vocational; 0 Alternative
0 Magnet; 0 Charter; 2 Title I Eligible; 0 School-wide Title I
Students: 1,873 (n/a% male; n/a% female)
Individual Education Program: 283 (15.1%);
English Language Learner: 44 (2.3%); Migrant: 34 (1.8%)

Eligible for Free Lunch Program: 523 (27.9%)
Eligible for Reduced-Price Lunch Program: 181 (9.7%)
Teachers: 95.9 (19.5 to 1)
Librarians/Media Specialists: 3.2 (585.3 to 1)
Guidance Counselors: 6.5 (288.2 to 1)
Current Spending: ($ per student per year):
Total: $6,717; Instruction: $4,034; Support Services: $2,395
Enrollment, Drop-out Rates and Diploma Recipients by Race/Ethnicity

Category	Total	White	Black	Asian	AIAN	Hisp.
Enrollment (%)	100.0	89.1	1.0	0.9	2.2	6.4
Drop-out Rate (%)	1.4	1.5	0.0	0.0	0.0	0.0
H.S. Diplomas (#)	146	136	1	1	0	5

Siuslaw SD 97J
2111 Oak St • Florence, OR 97439-9618
(541) 997-2651 • http://www.siuslaw.k12.or.us/
Grade Span: KG-12; **Agency Type:** 1
Schools: 4
2 Primary; 1 Middle; 1 High; 0 Other Level
4 Regular; 0 Special Education; 0 Vocational; 0 Alternative
0 Magnet; 0 Charter; 1 Title I Eligible; 0 School-wide Title I
Students: 1,578 (n/a% male; n/a% female)
Individual Education Program: 208 (13.2%);
English Language Learner: 104 (6.6%); Migrant: 0 (0.0%)
Eligible for Free Lunch Program: 479 (30.4%)
Eligible for Reduced-Price Lunch Program: 124 (7.9%)
Teachers: 84.7 (18.6 to 1)
Librarians/Media Specialists: 2.0 (789.0 to 1)
Guidance Counselors: 4.0 (394.5 to 1)
Current Spending: ($ per student per year):
Total: $7,079; Instruction: $4,383; Support Services: $2,547
Enrollment, Drop-out Rates and Diploma Recipients by Race/Ethnicity

Category	Total	White	Black	Asian	AIAN	Hisp.
Enrollment (%)	100.0	86.9	0.6	1.1	8.4	2.9
Drop-out Rate (%)	4.9	4.9	0.0	0.0	5.7	0.0
H.S. Diplomas (#)	83	72	1	4	6	0

South Lane SD 45J
455 Adams • Cottage Grove, OR 97424-0218
Mailing Address: PO Box 218 • Cottage Grove, OR 97424-0218
(541) 942-3381 • http://www.slane.k12.or.us/dsc/index.html
Grade Span: KG-12; **Agency Type:** 1
Schools: 9
6 Primary; 1 Middle; 1 High; 1 Other Level
8 Regular; 0 Special Education; 0 Vocational; 1 Alternative
0 Magnet; 0 Charter; 6 Title I Eligible; 1 School-wide Title I
Students: 2,858 (n/a% male; n/a% female)
Individual Education Program: 489 (17.1%);
English Language Learner: 84 (2.9%); Migrant: 56 (2.0%)
Eligible for Free Lunch Program: 1,124 (39.3%)
Eligible for Reduced-Price Lunch Program: 383 (13.4%)
Teachers: 134.3 (21.3 to 1)
Librarians/Media Specialists: 2.0 (1,429.0 to 1)
Guidance Counselors: 4.0 (714.5 to 1)
Current Spending: ($ per student per year):
Total: $6,985; Instruction: $3,878; Support Services: $2,778
Enrollment, Drop-out Rates and Diploma Recipients by Race/Ethnicity

Category	Total	White	Black	Asian	AIAN	Hisp.
Enrollment (%)	100.0	90.9	0.4	1.0	2.0	5.4
Drop-out Rate (%)	4.9	4.3	50.0	0.0	7.7	10.5
H.S. Diplomas (#)	163	151	1	2	3	5

Springfield SD 019
525 Mill St • Springfield, OR 97477-4598
(541) 747-3331 • http://www.sps.lane.edu/index.html
Grade Span: PK-12; **Agency Type:** 1
Schools: 25
17 Primary; 5 Middle; 3 High; 0 Other Level
23 Regular; 0 Special Education; 0 Vocational; 2 Alternative
0 Magnet; 0 Charter; 9 Title I Eligible; 6 School-wide Title I
Students: 11,154 (n/a% male; n/a% female)
Individual Education Program: 1,802 (16.2%);
English Language Learner: 545 (4.9%); Migrant: 109 (1.0%)
Eligible for Free Lunch Program: 4,132 (37.0%)
Eligible for Reduced-Price Lunch Program: 870 (7.8%)
Teachers: 523.0 (21.3 to 1)
Librarians/Media Specialists: 14.0 (796.7 to 1)
Guidance Counselors: 21.7 (514.0 to 1)
Current Spending: ($ per student per year):
Total: $6,955; Instruction: $4,071; Support Services: $2,693
Enrollment, Drop-out Rates and Diploma Recipients by Race/Ethnicity

Category	Total	White	Black	Asian	AIAN	Hisp.
Enrollment (%)	100.0	84.3	1.6	2.0	2.0	9.3
Drop-out Rate (%)	5.0	4.6	4.0	3.8	1.5	15.7
H.S. Diplomas (#)	586	499	4	15	16	29

Lincoln County

Lincoln County SD
PO Box 1110 • Newport, OR 97365-0088
(541) 265-9211 • http://www.lincoln.k12.or.us/
Grade Span: KG-12; **Agency Type:** 1
Schools: 21
11 Primary; 5 Middle; 5 High; 0 Other Level
19 Regular; 0 Special Education; 0 Vocational; 2 Alternative
1 Magnet; 1 Charter; 9 Title I Eligible; 6 School-wide Title I
Students: 6,117 (n/a% male; n/a% female)
Individual Education Program: 994 (16.2%);
English Language Learner: 309 (5.1%); Migrant: 176 (2.9%)
Eligible for Free Lunch Program: 2,397 (39.2%)
Eligible for Reduced-Price Lunch Program: 628 (10.3%)
Teachers: 277.9 (22.0 to 1)
Librarians/Media Specialists: 3.0 (2,039.0 to 1)
Guidance Counselors: 9.0 (679.7 to 1)
Current Spending: ($ per student per year):
Total: $6,908; Instruction: $3,938; Support Services: $2,704
Enrollment, Drop-out Rates and Diploma Recipients by Race/Ethnicity

Category	Total	White	Black	Asian	AIAN	Hisp.
Enrollment (%)	100.0	74.5	0.8	1.9	7.8	7.1
Drop-out Rate (%)	8.3	7.8	0.0	4.3	10.9	14.5
H.S. Diplomas (#)	406	337	0	12	24	13

Linn County

Greater Albany SD 8J
718 SW 7th St • Albany, OR 97321-2320
(541) 967-4501 • http://www.8j.net/
Grade Span: KG-12; **Agency Type:** 1
Schools: 19
14 Primary; 3 Middle; 2 High; 0 Other Level
19 Regular; 0 Special Education; 0 Vocational; 0 Alternative
0 Magnet; 0 Charter; 7 Title I Eligible; 1 School-wide Title I
Students: 8,226 (n/a% male; n/a% female)
Individual Education Program: 1,126 (13.7%);
English Language Learner: 191 (2.3%); Migrant: 125 (1.5%)
Eligible for Free Lunch Program: 2,245 (27.3%)
Eligible for Reduced-Price Lunch Program: 638 (7.8%)
Teachers: 366.4 (22.5 to 1)
Librarians/Media Specialists: 9.5 (865.9 to 1)
Guidance Counselors: 15.0 (548.4 to 1)
Current Spending: ($ per student per year):
Total: $6,657; Instruction: $3,974; Support Services: $2,430
Enrollment, Drop-out Rates and Diploma Recipients by Race/Ethnicity

Category	Total	White	Black	Asian	AIAN	Hisp.
Enrollment (%)	100.0	86.0	1.0	2.1	1.0	8.4
Drop-out Rate (%)	6.3	6.1	6.3	0.0	12.5	11.1
H.S. Diplomas (#)	417	383	2	10	6	16

Lebanon Community SD 009
485 S 5th St • Lebanon, OR 97355-2602
(541) 451-8511 • http://www.lebanon.k12.or.us/
Grade Span: KG-12; **Agency Type:** 1
Schools: 9
6 Primary; 1 Middle; 1 High; 1 Other Level
9 Regular; 0 Special Education; 0 Vocational; 0 Alternative
0 Magnet; 1 Charter; 6 Title I Eligible; 3 School-wide Title I
Students: 4,451 (n/a% male; n/a% female)
Individual Education Program: 535 (12.0%);
English Language Learner: 125 (2.8%); Migrant: 15 (0.3%)
Eligible for Free Lunch Program: 1,848 (41.5%)
Eligible for Reduced-Price Lunch Program: 547 (12.3%)
Teachers: 213.0 (20.9 to 1)
Librarians/Media Specialists: 1.5 (2,967.3 to 1)
Guidance Counselors: 11.0 (404.6 to 1)
Current Spending: ($ per student per year):
Total: $6,288; Instruction: $3,841; Support Services: $2,235
Enrollment, Drop-out Rates and Diploma Recipients by Race/Ethnicity

Category	Total	White	Black	Asian	AIAN	Hisp.
Enrollment (%)	100.0	91.0	0.7	1.6	1.8	4.3
Drop-out Rate (%)	6.2	6.1	0.0	5.6	4.5	10.3
H.S. Diplomas (#)	236	225	1	5	2	3

Sweet Home SD 055
1920 Long St • Sweet Home, OR 97386-2395
(541) 367-6111 • http://www.sweethome.k12.or.us/
Grade Span: KG-12; **Agency Type:** 1
Schools: 7
5 Primary; 1 Middle; 1 High; 0 Other Level
7 Regular; 0 Special Education; 0 Vocational; 0 Alternative
0 Magnet; 0 Charter; 6 Title I Eligible; 0 School-wide Title I
Students: 2,466 (n/a% male; n/a% female)

Individual Education Program: 429 (17.4%);
English Language Learner: 13 (0.5%); Migrant: 0 (0.0%)
Eligible for Free Lunch Program: 1,053 (42.7%)
Eligible for Reduced-Price Lunch Program: 298 (12.1%)
Teachers: 114.4 (21.6 to 1)
Librarians/Media Specialists: 0.0 (0.0 to 1)
Guidance Counselors: 7.0 (352.3 to 1)
Current Spending: ($ per student per year):
Total: $6,980; Instruction: $4,047; Support Services: $2,650
Enrollment, Drop-out Rates and Diploma Recipients by Race/Ethnicity

Category	Total	White	Black	Asian	AIAN	Hisp.
Enrollment (%)	100.0	91.2	0.3	0.9	1.6	2.8
Drop-out Rate (%)	6.4	5.7	50.0	12.5	0.0	11.1
H.S. Diplomas (#)	152	145	1	2	1	3

Malheur County

Ontario SD 008
195 SW 3rd Ave • Ontario, OR 97914-2768
(541) 889-5374 • http://www.ontario.k12.or.us/
Grade Span: KG-12; **Agency Type:** 1
Schools: 7
5 Primary; 1 Middle; 1 High; 0 Other Level
7 Regular; 0 Special Education; 0 Vocational; 0 Alternative
0 Magnet; 0 Charter; 5 Title I Eligible; 4 School-wide Title I
Students: 2,795 (n/a% male; n/a% female)
Individual Education Program: 356 (12.7%);
English Language Learner: 805 (28.8%); Migrant: 953 (34.1%)
Eligible for Free Lunch Program: 1,447 (51.8%)
Eligible for Reduced-Price Lunch Program: 240 (8.6%)
Teachers: 148.5 (18.8 to 1)
Librarians/Media Specialists: 5.0 (559.0 to 1)
Guidance Counselors: 14.0 (199.6 to 1)
Current Spending: ($ per student per year):
Total: $7,098; Instruction: $4,181; Support Services: $2,635
Enrollment, Drop-out Rates and Diploma Recipients by Race/Ethnicity

Category	Total	White	Black	Asian	AIAN	Hisp.
Enrollment (%)	100.0	47.8	1.0	2.5	0.9	47.8
Drop-out Rate (%)	3.7	2.8	0.0	0.0	0.0	5.9
H.S. Diplomas (#)	123	89	0	6	0	28

Marion County

Cascade SD 005
10226 Marion Rd SE • Turner, OR 97392-9721
(503) 749-8488 • http://www.cascade.k12.or.us/
Grade Span: KG-12; **Agency Type:** 1
Schools: 6
4 Primary; 0 Middle; 1 High; 1 Other Level
6 Regular; 0 Special Education; 0 Vocational; 0 Alternative
0 Magnet; 0 Charter; 4 Title I Eligible; 0 School-wide Title I
Students: 2,298 (n/a% male; n/a% female)
Individual Education Program: 339 (14.8%);
English Language Learner: 121 (5.3%); Migrant: 71 (3.1%)
Eligible for Free Lunch Program: 728 (31.7%)
Eligible for Reduced-Price Lunch Program: 219 (9.5%)
Teachers: 113.2 (20.3 to 1)
Librarians/Media Specialists: 2.4 (957.5 to 1)
Guidance Counselors: 5.6 (410.4 to 1)
Current Spending: ($ per student per year):
Total: $6,887; Instruction: $4,019; Support Services: $2,566
Enrollment, Drop-out Rates and Diploma Recipients by Race/Ethnicity

Category	Total	White	Black	Asian	AIAN	Hisp.
Enrollment (%)	100.0	85.2	0.4	1.3	2.0	9.2
Drop-out Rate (%)	5.4	5.6	100.0	0.0	n/a	3.7
H.S. Diplomas (#)	118	100	0	4	0	14

North Marion SD 015
20256 Grim Rd NE • Aurora, OR 97002-9499
(503) 678-5835 • http://www.nmarion.k12.or.us/
Grade Span: KG-12; **Agency Type:** 1
Schools: 4
2 Primary; 1 Middle; 1 High; 0 Other Level
4 Regular; 0 Special Education; 0 Vocational; 0 Alternative
0 Magnet; 0 Charter; 4 Title I Eligible; 2 School-wide Title I
Students: 1,765 (n/a% male; n/a% female)
Individual Education Program: 209 (11.8%);
English Language Learner: 326 (18.5%); Migrant: 216 (12.2%)
Eligible for Free Lunch Program: 667 (37.8%)
Eligible for Reduced-Price Lunch Program: 189 (10.7%)
Teachers: 91.8 (19.2 to 1)
Librarians/Media Specialists: 1.0 (1,765.0 to 1)
Guidance Counselors: 5.0 (353.0 to 1)
Current Spending: ($ per student per year):
Total: $7,182; Instruction: $4,200; Support Services: $2,646
Enrollment, Drop-out Rates and Diploma Recipients by Race/Ethnicity

Category	Total	White	Black	Asian	AIAN	Hisp.
Enrollment (%)	100.0	68.6	1.0	1.6	1.8	26.5
Drop-out Rate (%)	1.0	1.1	0.0	0.0	0.0	0.8
H.S. Diplomas (#)	113	83	0	0	1	29

North Santiam SD 29J
1155 N 3rd Ave • Stayton, OR 97383-1801
(503) 769-6924 • http://www.northsantiamsd.com/
Grade Span: KG-12; **Agency Type:** 1
Schools: 5
3 Primary; 1 Middle; 1 High; 0 Other Level
5 Regular; 0 Special Education; 0 Vocational; 0 Alternative
0 Magnet; 0 Charter; 0 Title I Eligible; 0 School-wide Title I
Students: 2,417 (n/a% male; n/a% female)
Individual Education Program: 344 (14.2%);
English Language Learner: 131 (5.4%); Migrant: 102 (4.2%)
Eligible for Free Lunch Program: 688 (28.5%)
Eligible for Reduced-Price Lunch Program: 279 (11.5%)
Teachers: 120.8 (20.0 to 1)
Librarians/Media Specialists: 1.8 (1,342.8 to 1)
Guidance Counselors: 4.9 (493.3 to 1)
Current Spending: ($ per student per year):
Total: $6,501; Instruction: $3,901; Support Services: $2,309
Enrollment, Drop-out Rates and Diploma Recipients by Race/Ethnicity

Category	Total	White	Black	Asian	AIAN	Hisp.
Enrollment (%)	100.0	83.4	0.7	1.6	2.9	10.3
Drop-out Rate (%)	6.6	6.6	0.0	7.1	10.5	6.0
H.S. Diplomas (#)	130	123	2	3	0	2

Salem-Keizer SD 24J
PO Box 12024 • Salem, OR 97309-0024
(503) 399-3000 • http://www.salkeiz.k12.or.us/
Grade Span: KG-12; **Agency Type:** 1
Schools: 66
47 Primary; 11 Middle; 7 High; 1 Other Level
63 Regular; 0 Special Education; 0 Vocational; 3 Alternative
0 Magnet; 3 Charter; 24 Title I Eligible; 14 School-wide Title I
Students: 37,137 (n/a% male; n/a% female)
Individual Education Program: 4,411 (11.9%);
English Language Learner: 4,662 (12.6%); Migrant: 2,648 (7.1%)
Eligible for Free Lunch Program: 13,423 (36.1%)
Eligible for Reduced-Price Lunch Program: 3,270 (8.8%)
Teachers: 1,640.7 (22.6 to 1)
Librarians/Media Specialists: 48.9 (759.4 to 1)
Guidance Counselors: 84.5 (439.5 to 1)
Current Spending: ($ per student per year):
Total: $6,611; Instruction: $4,215; Support Services: $2,158
Enrollment, Drop-out Rates and Diploma Recipients by Race/Ethnicity

Category	Total	White	Black	Asian	AIAN	Hisp.
Enrollment (%)	100.0	61.2	1.4	3.1	1.4	19.5
Drop-out Rate (%)	7.5	5.8	14.1	5.9	9.0	13.7
H.S. Diplomas (#)	1,810	1,465	14	57	16	185

Silver Falls SD 4J
210 E C St • Silverton, OR 97381-1444
(503) 873-5303 • http://www.silverfalls.k12.or.us/
Grade Span: KG-12; **Agency Type:** 1
Schools: 13
10 Primary; 2 Middle; 1 High; 0 Other Level
13 Regular; 0 Special Education; 0 Vocational; 0 Alternative
0 Magnet; 0 Charter; 6 Title I Eligible; 1 School-wide Title I
Students: 3,675 (n/a% male; n/a% female)
Individual Education Program: 407 (11.1%);
English Language Learner: 412 (11.2%); Migrant: 254 (6.9%)
Eligible for Free Lunch Program: 959 (26.1%)
Eligible for Reduced-Price Lunch Program: 246 (6.7%)
Teachers: 194.6 (18.9 to 1)
Librarians/Media Specialists: 4.0 (918.8 to 1)
Guidance Counselors: 6.5 (565.4 to 1)
Current Spending: ($ per student per year):
Total: $6,997; Instruction: $4,236; Support Services: $2,553
Enrollment, Drop-out Rates and Diploma Recipients by Race/Ethnicity

Category	Total	White	Black	Asian	AIAN	Hisp.
Enrollment (%)	100.0	84.7	0.2	1.5	1.0	12.3
Drop-out Rate (%)	6.4	6.0	0.0	4.3	13.3	10.5
H.S. Diplomas (#)	214	195	1	5	3	10

Woodburn SD 103
965 N Boones Ferry Rd • Woodburn, OR 97071-9602
(503) 981-9555 • http://www.woodburn.k12.or.us/
Grade Span: KG-12; **Agency Type:** 1
Schools: 7
4 Primary; 2 Middle; 1 High; 0 Other Level
7 Regular; 0 Special Education; 0 Vocational; 0 Alternative

0 Magnet; 0 Charter; 7 Title I Eligible; 7 School-wide Title I
Students: 4,517 (n/a% male; n/a% female)
Individual Education Program: 545 (12.1%);
English Language Learner: 2,638 (58.4%); Migrant: 1,347 (29.8%)
Eligible for Free Lunch Program: 3,430 (75.9%)
Eligible for Reduced-Price Lunch Program: 438 (9.7%)
Teachers: 276.0 (16.4 to 1)
Librarians/Media Specialists: 7.0 (645.3 to 1)
Guidance Counselors: 10.0 (451.7 to 1)
Current Spending: ($ per student per year):
Total: $8,085; Instruction: $4,921; Support Services: $2,803
Enrollment, Drop-out Rates and Diploma Recipients by Race/Ethnicity

Category	Total	White	Black	Asian	AIAN	Hisp.
Enrollment (%)	100.0	30.6	0.4	0.3	0.3	68.3
Drop-out Rate (%)	9.6	7.1	0.0	0.0	33.3	11.6
H.S. Diplomas (#)	207	99	2	1	0	105

Morrow County

Morrow SD 001
PO Box 368 • Lexington, OR 97839-0368
(541) 989-8202 • http://www.morrow.k12.or.us/
Grade Span: KG-12; **Agency Type:** 1
Schools: 7
3 Primary; 1 Middle; 2 High; 1 Other Level
7 Regular; 0 Special Education; 0 Vocational; 0 Alternative
0 Magnet; 0 Charter; 3 Title I Eligible; 3 School-wide Title I
Students: 2,273 (n/a% male; n/a% female)
Individual Education Program: 290 (12.8%);
English Language Learner: 755 (33.2%); Migrant: 652 (28.7%)
Eligible for Free Lunch Program: 1,004 (44.2%)
Eligible for Reduced-Price Lunch Program: 279 (12.3%)
Teachers: 141.5 (16.1 to 1)
Librarians/Media Specialists: 0.0 (0.0 to 1)
Guidance Counselors: 3.0 (757.7 to 1)
Current Spending: ($ per student per year):
Total: $7,117; Instruction: $4,382; Support Services: $2,469
Enrollment, Drop-out Rates and Diploma Recipients by Race/Ethnicity

Category	Total	White	Black	Asian	AIAN	Hisp.
Enrollment (%)	100.0	62.2	0.4	0.4	0.8	36.2
Drop-out Rate (%)	2.8	3.2	0.0	0.0	0.0	1.7
H.S. Diplomas (#)	119	87	0	2	2	28

Multnomah County

Centennial SD 28J
18135 SE Brooklyn St • Portland, OR 97236-1099
(503) 760-7990 • http://www.centennial.k12.or.us/home.htm
Grade Span: KG-12; **Agency Type:** 1
Schools: 9
5 Primary; 2 Middle; 2 High; 0 Other Level
8 Regular; 0 Special Education; 0 Vocational; 1 Alternative
0 Magnet; 0 Charter; 5 Title I Eligible; 2 School-wide Title I
Students: 6,255 (n/a% male; n/a% female)
Individual Education Program: 728 (11.6%);
English Language Learner: 809 (12.9%); Migrant: 76 (1.2%)
Eligible for Free Lunch Program: 2,006 (32.1%)
Eligible for Reduced-Price Lunch Program: 627 (10.0%)
Teachers: 299.0 (20.9 to 1)
Librarians/Media Specialists: 8.0 (781.9 to 1)
Guidance Counselors: 7.0 (893.6 to 1)
Current Spending: ($ per student per year):
Total: $6,737; Instruction: $4,015; Support Services: $2,475
Enrollment, Drop-out Rates and Diploma Recipients by Race/Ethnicity

Category	Total	White	Black	Asian	AIAN	Hisp.
Enrollment (%)	100.0	76.9	3.6	9.1	0.8	9.5
Drop-out Rate (%)	8.5	8.1	2.6	7.8	0.0	21.7
H.S. Diplomas (#)	326	262	9	43	4	8

David Douglas SD 40
1500 SE 130th Ave • Portland, OR 97233-1799
(503) 252-2900 • http://www.ddouglas.k12.or.us/
Grade Span: KG-12; **Agency Type:** 1
Schools: 14
10 Primary; 2 Middle; 2 High; 0 Other Level
13 Regular; 0 Special Education; 0 Vocational; 1 Alternative
0 Magnet; 1 Charter; 9 Title I Eligible; 5 School-wide Title I
Students: 8,901 (n/a% male; n/a% female)
Individual Education Program: 1,049 (11.8%);
English Language Learner: 2,013 (22.6%); Migrant: 66 (0.7%)
Eligible for Free Lunch Program: 3,879 (43.6%)
Eligible for Reduced-Price Lunch Program: 958 (10.8%)
Teachers: 440.0 (20.2 to 1)
Librarians/Media Specialists: 12.0 (741.8 to 1)
Guidance Counselors: 17.8 (500.1 to 1)
Current Spending: ($ per student per year):
Total: $6,799; Instruction: $4,137; Support Services: $2,344
Enrollment, Drop-out Rates and Diploma Recipients by Race/Ethnicity

Category	Total	White	Black	Asian	AIAN	Hisp.
Enrollment (%)	100.0	70.4	5.5	10.6	1.4	12.1
Drop-out Rate (%)	3.9	3.7	5.5	2.3	0.0	11.1
H.S. Diplomas (#)	360	293	6	44	1	16

Gresham-Barlow SD 10J
1331 NW Eastman Pkwy • Gresham, OR 97030-3825
(503) 618-2450 • http://district.gresham.k12.or.us/
Grade Span: KG-12; **Agency Type:** 1
Schools: 19
11 Primary; 5 Middle; 3 High; 0 Other Level
19 Regular; 0 Special Education; 0 Vocational; 0 Alternative
0 Magnet; 0 Charter; 6 Title I Eligible; 2 School-wide Title I
Students: 11,712 (n/a% male; n/a% female)
Individual Education Program: 1,403 (12.0%);
English Language Learner: 1,008 (8.6%); Migrant: 171 (1.5%)
Eligible for Free Lunch Program: 2,633 (22.5%)
Eligible for Reduced-Price Lunch Program: 779 (6.7%)
Teachers: 552.3 (21.2 to 1)
Librarians/Media Specialists: 4.7 (2,491.9 to 1)
Guidance Counselors: 33.0 (354.9 to 1)
Current Spending: ($ per student per year):
Total: $6,675; Instruction: $4,080; Support Services: $2,385
Enrollment, Drop-out Rates and Diploma Recipients by Race/Ethnicity

Category	Total	White	Black	Asian	AIAN	Hisp.
Enrollment (%)	100.0	83.2	2.3	3.1	0.9	9.8
Drop-out Rate (%)	4.5	4.0	11.5	6.8	14.3	9.4
H.S. Diplomas (#)	721	641	9	30	9	32

Parkrose SD 003
10636 NE Prescott St • Portland, OR 97220-2699
(503) 408-2100 • http://www.parkrose.k12.or.us/
Grade Span: KG-12; **Agency Type:** 1
Schools: 6
4 Primary; 1 Middle; 1 High; 0 Other Level
6 Regular; 0 Special Education; 0 Vocational; 0 Alternative
0 Magnet; 0 Charter; 3 Title I Eligible; 2 School-wide Title I
Students: 3,647 (n/a% male; n/a% female)
Individual Education Program: 456 (12.5%);
English Language Learner: 719 (19.7%); Migrant: 20 (0.5%)
Eligible for Free Lunch Program: 1,503 (41.2%)
Eligible for Reduced-Price Lunch Program: 406 (11.1%)
Teachers: 160.0 (22.8 to 1)
Librarians/Media Specialists: 1.0 (3,647.0 to 1)
Guidance Counselors: 7.5 (486.3 to 1)
Current Spending: ($ per student per year):
Total: $6,845; Instruction: $4,026; Support Services: $2,503
Enrollment, Drop-out Rates and Diploma Recipients by Race/Ethnicity

Category	Total	White	Black	Asian	AIAN	Hisp.
Enrollment (%)	100.0	62.8	9.8	15.4	1.4	10.6
Drop-out Rate (%)	5.6	4.8	8.3	2.0	5.6	18.7
H.S. Diplomas (#)	190	157	6	21	2	4

Portland Area Office
911 NE 11 Ave • Portland, OR 97232-4169
(503) 872-2743
Grade Span: KG-12; **Agency Type:** 6
Schools: 12
3 Primary; 0 Middle; 5 High; 4 Other Level
12 Regular; 0 Special Education; 0 Vocational; 0 Alternative
0 Magnet; 0 Charter; 12 Title I Eligible; 12 School-wide Title I
Students: 2,061 (n/a% male; n/a% female)
Individual Education Program: n/a;
English Language Learner: n/a; Migrant: n/a
Eligible for Free Lunch Program: n/a
Eligible for Reduced-Price Lunch Program: n/a
Teachers: n/a
Librarians/Media Specialists: n/a
Guidance Counselors: n/a
Current Spending: ($ per student per year):
Total: n/a; Instruction: n/a; Support Services: n/a
Enrollment, Drop-out Rates and Diploma Recipients by Race/Ethnicity

Category	Total	White	Black	Asian	AIAN	Hisp.
Enrollment (%)	100.0	0.0	0.0	0.0	100.0	0.0
Drop-out Rate (%)	n/a	n/a	n/a	n/a	n/a	n/a
H.S. Diplomas (#)	n/a	n/a	n/a	n/a	n/a	n/a

Portland SD 1J
PO Box 3107 • Portland, OR 97208-3107
(503) 916-2000 • http://www.pps.k12.or.us/
Grade Span: PK-12; **Agency Type:** 1
Schools: 104

65 Primary; 19 Middle; 18 High; 2 Other Level
90 Regular; 2 Special Education; 0 Vocational; 12 Alternative
0 Magnet; 2 Charter; 51 Title I Eligible; 45 School-wide Title I
Students: 51,654 (n/a% male; n/a% female)
Individual Education Program: 6,497 (12.6%);
English Language Learner: 5,994 (11.6%); Migrant: 699 (1.4%)
Eligible for Free Lunch Program: 17,391 (33.7%)
Eligible for Reduced-Price Lunch Program: 3,865 (7.5%)
Teachers: 2,760.0 (18.7 to 1)
Librarians/Media Specialists: 26.0 (1,986.7 to 1)
Guidance Counselors: 65.9 (783.8 to 1)
Current Spending: ($ per student per year):
Total: $8,533; Instruction: $5,021; Support Services: $3,259
Enrollment, Drop-out Rates and Diploma Recipients by Race/Ethnicity

Category	Total	White	Black	Asian	AIAN	Hisp.
Enrollment (%)	100.0	60.1	16.7	10.3	2.3	10.7
Drop-out Rate (%)	11.9	9.7	15.3	7.8	25.1	26.3
H.S. Diplomas (#)	2,592	1,789	347	284	43	129

Reynolds SD 007

1204 NE 201st Ave • Fairview, OR 97024-9642
(503) 661-7200 • http://www.reynolds.k12.or.us/
Grade Span: KG-12; **Agency Type:** 1
Schools: 16
11 Primary; 3 Middle; 1 High; 1 Other Level
15 Regular; 1 Special Education; 0 Vocational; 0 Alternative
0 Magnet; 1 Charter; 4 Title I Eligible; 1 School-wide Title I
Students: 10,288 (n/a% male; n/a% female)
Individual Education Program: 1,563 (15.2%);
English Language Learner: 2,029 (19.7%); Migrant: 305 (3.0%)
Eligible for Free Lunch Program: 4,142 (40.3%)
Eligible for Reduced-Price Lunch Program: 999 (9.7%)
Teachers: 491.0 (21.0 to 1)
Librarians/Media Specialists: 13.5 (762.1 to 1)
Guidance Counselors: 27.5 (374.1 to 1)
Current Spending: ($ per student per year):
Total: $7,069; Instruction: $4,313; Support Services: $2,516
Enrollment, Drop-out Rates and Diploma Recipients by Race/Ethnicity

Category	Total	White	Black	Asian	AIAN	Hisp.
Enrollment (%)	100.0	66.3	5.7	5.8	1.0	21.2
Drop-out Rate (%)	4.6	4.4	0.0	0.0	11.1	8.6
H.S. Diplomas (#)	358	310	6	19	3	20

Polk County

Central SD 13J

1610 Monmouth St • Independence, OR 97351-1096
(503) 838-0030 • http://www.central.k12.or.us/
Grade Span: KG-12; **Agency Type:** 1
Schools: 8
4 Primary; 2 Middle; 1 High; 1 Other Level
7 Regular; 0 Special Education; 0 Vocational; 1 Alternative
0 Magnet; 0 Charter; 5 Title I Eligible; 3 School-wide Title I
Students: 2,588 (n/a% male; n/a% female)
Individual Education Program: 362 (14.0%);
English Language Learner: 497 (19.2%); Migrant: 294 (11.4%)
Eligible for Free Lunch Program: 1,174 (45.4%)
Eligible for Reduced-Price Lunch Program: 292 (11.3%)
Teachers: 131.2 (19.7 to 1)
Librarians/Media Specialists: 1.0 (2,588.0 to 1)
Guidance Counselors: 7.0 (369.7 to 1)
Current Spending: ($ per student per year):
Total: $7,055; Instruction: $4,464; Support Services: $2,356
Enrollment, Drop-out Rates and Diploma Recipients by Race/Ethnicity

Category	Total	White	Black	Asian	AIAN	Hisp.
Enrollment (%)	100.0	63.0	0.9	1.7	0.9	32.7
Drop-out Rate (%)	5.7	4.6	0.0	0.0	20.0	7.8
H.S. Diplomas (#)	143	97	4	4	3	32

Dallas SD 2

111 SW Ash St • Dallas, OR 97338-2299
(503) 623-5594 • http://www.dallas.k12.or.us/
Grade Span: KG-12; **Agency Type:** 1
Schools: 9
5 Primary; 2 Middle; 2 High; 0 Other Level
8 Regular; 0 Special Education; 0 Vocational; 1 Alternative
0 Magnet; 1 Charter; 3 Title I Eligible; 0 School-wide Title I
Students: 3,203 (n/a% male; n/a% female)
Individual Education Program: 422 (13.2%);
English Language Learner: 63 (2.0%); Migrant: 18 (0.6%)
Eligible for Free Lunch Program: 727 (22.7%)
Eligible for Reduced-Price Lunch Program: 223 (7.0%)
Teachers: 168.4 (19.0 to 1)
Librarians/Media Specialists: 5.1 (628.0 to 1)
Guidance Counselors: 9.0 (355.9 to 1)
Current Spending: ($ per student per year):
Total: $6,334; Instruction: $3,887; Support Services: $2,254
Enrollment, Drop-out Rates and Diploma Recipients by Race/Ethnicity

Category	Total	White	Black	Asian	AIAN	Hisp.
Enrollment (%)	100.0	88.8	1.0	1.4	3.1	5.6
Drop-out Rate (%)	10.2	10.9	0.0	0.0	13.3	10.0
H.S. Diplomas (#)	202	188	3	2	3	5

Tillamook County

Tillamook SD 9

6825 Officers' Row • Tillamook, OR 97141-9699
(503) 842-4414 • http://www.tillamook.k12.or.us/
Grade Span: KG-12; **Agency Type:** 1
Schools: 5
2 Primary; 2 Middle; 1 High; 0 Other Level
5 Regular; 0 Special Education; 0 Vocational; 0 Alternative
0 Magnet; 0 Charter; 3 Title I Eligible; 0 School-wide Title I
Students: 2,165 (n/a% male; n/a% female)
Individual Education Program: 315 (14.5%);
English Language Learner: 211 (9.7%); Migrant: 0 (0.0%)
Eligible for Free Lunch Program: 746 (34.5%)
Eligible for Reduced-Price Lunch Program: 220 (10.2%)
Teachers: 104.8 (20.7 to 1)
Librarians/Media Specialists: 1.8 (1,202.8 to 1)
Guidance Counselors: 4.0 (541.3 to 1)
Current Spending: ($ per student per year):
Total: $7,265; Instruction: $4,298; Support Services: $2,692
Enrollment, Drop-out Rates and Diploma Recipients by Race/Ethnicity

Category	Total	White	Black	Asian	AIAN	Hisp.
Enrollment (%)	100.0	79.9	0.6	1.9	2.2	15.3
Drop-out Rate (%)	5.6	5.6	n/a	0.0	0.0	11.1
H.S. Diplomas (#)	162	144	1	4	8	5

Umatilla County

Hermiston SD 008

341 NE 3rd St • Hermiston, OR 97838-1890
(541) 667-6000 • http://www.hermiston.k12.or.us/
Grade Span: KG-12; **Agency Type:** 1
Schools: 8
5 Primary; 2 Middle; 1 High; 0 Other Level
8 Regular; 0 Special Education; 0 Vocational; 0 Alternative
0 Magnet; 0 Charter; 5 Title I Eligible; 3 School-wide Title I
Students: 4,305 (n/a% male; n/a% female)
Individual Education Program: 601 (14.0%);
English Language Learner: 1,167 (27.1%); Migrant: 735 (17.1%)
Eligible for Free Lunch Program: 1,565 (36.4%)
Eligible for Reduced-Price Lunch Program: 430 (10.0%)
Teachers: 234.9 (18.3 to 1)
Librarians/Media Specialists: 5.5 (782.7 to 1)
Guidance Counselors: 12.0 (358.8 to 1)
Current Spending: ($ per student per year):
Total: $7,108; Instruction: $4,706; Support Services: $2,136
Enrollment, Drop-out Rates and Diploma Recipients by Race/Ethnicity

Category	Total	White	Black	Asian	AIAN	Hisp.
Enrollment (%)	100.0	64.1	1.7	1.5	0.8	31.8
Drop-out Rate (%)	4.4	3.4	0.0	4.3	0.0	7.5
H.S. Diplomas (#)	183	146	1	3	1	32

Milton-Freewater SD 007

138 S Main St • Milton-Freewater, OR 97862-1343
(541) 938-3551
Grade Span: KG-12; **Agency Type:** 1
Schools: 5
3 Primary; 1 Middle; 1 High; 0 Other Level
5 Regular; 0 Special Education; 0 Vocational; 0 Alternative
0 Magnet; 0 Charter; 4 Title I Eligible; 3 School-wide Title I
Students: 1,898 (n/a% male; n/a% female)
Individual Education Program: 228 (12.0%);
English Language Learner: 416 (21.9%); Migrant: 248 (13.1%)
Eligible for Free Lunch Program: 988 (52.1%)
Eligible for Reduced-Price Lunch Program: 172 (9.1%)
Teachers: 106.4 (17.8 to 1)
Librarians/Media Specialists: 2.4 (790.8 to 1)
Guidance Counselors: 5.3 (358.1 to 1)
Current Spending: ($ per student per year):
Total: $6,402; Instruction: $3,997; Support Services: $2,093
Enrollment, Drop-out Rates and Diploma Recipients by Race/Ethnicity

Category	Total	White	Black	Asian	AIAN	Hisp.
Enrollment (%)	100.0	52.9	0.4	0.2	0.3	46.0
Drop-out Rate (%)	7.5	4.3	0.0	0.0	0.0	13.8
H.S. Diplomas (#)	91	70	0	0	0	21

Pendleton SD 016

1207 SW Frazer Ave • Pendleton, OR 97801-2899
(541) 276-6711 • http://www.pendleton.k12.or.us/
Grade Span: KG-12; **Agency Type:** 1
Schools: 7
5 Primary; 1 Middle; 1 High; 0 Other Level
7 Regular; 0 Special Education; 0 Vocational; 0 Alternative
0 Magnet; 0 Charter; 3 Title I Eligible; 0 School-wide Title I
Students: 3,452 (n/a% male; n/a% female)
Individual Education Program: 494 (14.3%);
English Language Learner: 39 (1.1%); Migrant: 13 (0.4%)
Eligible for Free Lunch Program: 881 (25.5%)
Eligible for Reduced-Price Lunch Program: 275 (8.0%)
Teachers: 167.4 (20.6 to 1)
Librarians/Media Specialists: 4.0 (863.0 to 1)
Guidance Counselors: 9.6 (359.6 to 1)
Current Spending: ($ per student per year):
Total: $6,507; Instruction: $4,001; Support Services: $2,259
Enrollment, Drop-out Rates and Diploma Recipients by Race/Ethnicity

Category	Total	White	Black	Asian	AIAN	Hisp.
Enrollment (%)	100.0	78.8	1.3	1.2	11.4	6.6
Drop-out Rate (%)	5.6	4.8	0.0	0.0	13.6	9.3
H.S. Diplomas (#)	173	153	1	3	8	8

Union County

La Grande SD 001

2802 Adams Ave • La Grande, OR 97850-2179
(541) 663-3202 • http://www.lagrande.k12.or.us/
Grade Span: KG-12; **Agency Type:** 1
Schools: 6
4 Primary; 1 Middle; 1 High; 0 Other Level
6 Regular; 0 Special Education; 0 Vocational; 0 Alternative
0 Magnet; 0 Charter; 3 Title I Eligible; 1 School-wide Title I
Students: 2,297 (n/a% male; n/a% female)
Individual Education Program: 398 (17.3%);
English Language Learner: 25 (1.1%); Migrant: 0 (0.0%)
Eligible for Free Lunch Program: 594 (25.9%)
Eligible for Reduced-Price Lunch Program: 203 (8.8%)
Teachers: 125.5 (18.3 to 1)
Librarians/Media Specialists: 5.0 (459.4 to 1)
Guidance Counselors: 6.0 (382.8 to 1)
Current Spending: ($ per student per year):
Total: $6,773; Instruction: $4,058; Support Services: $2,468
Enrollment, Drop-out Rates and Diploma Recipients by Race/Ethnicity

Category	Total	White	Black	Asian	AIAN	Hisp.
Enrollment (%)	100.0	92.6	1.2	2.0	2.0	2.3
Drop-out Rate (%)	5.1	4.3	0.0	23.5	12.5	13.3
H.S. Diplomas (#)	152	140	0	0	1	11

Wasco County

The Dalles SD 012

1413 E 12th St • The Dalles, OR 97058-4096
(541) 296-6134 • http://www.thedalles.k12.or.us/
Grade Span: KG-12; **Agency Type:** 1
Schools: 4
2 Primary; 1 Middle; 1 High; 0 Other Level
4 Regular; 0 Special Education; 0 Vocational; 0 Alternative
0 Magnet; 0 Charter; 3 Title I Eligible; 3 School-wide Title I
Students: 2,053 (n/a% male; n/a% female)
Individual Education Program: 315 (15.3%);
English Language Learner: 254 (12.4%); Migrant: 254 (12.4%)
Eligible for Free Lunch Program: 767 (37.4%)
Eligible for Reduced-Price Lunch Program: 160 (7.8%)
Teachers: 105.0 (19.6 to 1)
Librarians/Media Specialists: 1.0 (2,053.0 to 1)
Guidance Counselors: 6.0 (342.2 to 1)
Current Spending: ($ per student per year):
Total: $6,948; Instruction: $4,261; Support Services: $2,504
Enrollment, Drop-out Rates and Diploma Recipients by Race/Ethnicity

Category	Total	White	Black	Asian	AIAN	Hisp.
Enrollment (%)	100.0	74.5	0.9	4.0	2.6	17.9
Drop-out Rate (%)	6.8	5.3	0.0	5.0	7.1	15.5
H.S. Diplomas (#)	142	115	2	5	3	17

Washington County

Beaverton SD 48J

16550 SW Merlo Rd • Beaverton, OR 97006-5152
(503) 591-8000 • http://www.beaverton.k12.or.us/
Grade Span: KG-12; **Agency Type:** 1
Schools: 49
31 Primary; 9 Middle; 9 High; 0 Other Level
47 Regular; 0 Special Education; 0 Vocational; 2 Alternative
3 Magnet; 0 Charter; 10 Title I Eligible; 5 School-wide Title I
Students: 35,320 (n/a% male; n/a% female)
Individual Education Program: 4,204 (11.9%);
English Language Learner: 4,234 (12.0%); Migrant: 753 (2.1%)
Eligible for Free Lunch Program: 6,265 (17.7%)
Eligible for Reduced-Price Lunch Program: 2,318 (6.6%)
Teachers: 1,655.8 (21.3 to 1)
Librarians/Media Specialists: 43.3 (815.7 to 1)
Guidance Counselors: 78.1 (452.2 to 1)
Current Spending: ($ per student per year):
Total: $6,238; Instruction: $3,719; Support Services: $2,280
Enrollment, Drop-out Rates and Diploma Recipients by Race/Ethnicity

Category	Total	White	Black	Asian	AIAN	Hisp.
Enrollment (%)	100.0	69.2	3.0	12.1	0.8	12.6
Drop-out Rate (%)	5.6	4.4	10.6	3.4	19.7	15.4
H.S. Diplomas (#)	1,957	1,495	32	270	11	96

Forest Grove SD 015

1728 Main St • Forest Grove, OR 97116-2737
(503) 357-6171 • http://www.fgsd.k12.or.us/
Grade Span: KG-12; **Agency Type:** 1
Schools: 10
6 Primary; 2 Middle; 1 High; 1 Other Level
9 Regular; 0 Special Education; 0 Vocational; 1 Alternative
0 Magnet; 0 Charter; 4 Title I Eligible; 1 School-wide Title I
Students: 5,773 (n/a% male; n/a% female)
Individual Education Program: 728 (12.6%);
English Language Learner: 1,164 (20.2%); Migrant: 693 (12.0%)
Eligible for Free Lunch Program: 2,275 (39.4%)
Eligible for Reduced-Price Lunch Program: 594 (10.3%)
Teachers: 285.2 (20.2 to 1)
Librarians/Media Specialists: 2.0 (2,886.5 to 1)
Guidance Counselors: 17.0 (339.6 to 1)
Current Spending: ($ per student per year):
Total: $6,990; Instruction: $4,296; Support Services: $2,436
Enrollment, Drop-out Rates and Diploma Recipients by Race/Ethnicity

Category	Total	White	Black	Asian	AIAN	Hisp.
Enrollment (%)	100.0	62.5	0.8	1.4	0.5	34.9
Drop-out Rate (%)	5.9	5.7	11.1	4.0	0.0	6.5
H.S. Diplomas (#)	260	202	3	5	2	48

Hillsboro SD 01J

215 SE 6th Ave • Hillsboro, OR 97123-4108
(503) 648-1126 • http://www.hsd.k12.or.us/default.asp
Grade Span: KG-12; **Agency Type:** 1
Schools: 30
23 Primary; 4 Middle; 3 High; 0 Other Level
30 Regular; 0 Special Education; 0 Vocational; 0 Alternative
0 Magnet; 0 Charter; 8 Title I Eligible; 3 School-wide Title I
Students: 18,850 (n/a% male; n/a% female)
Individual Education Program: 2,296 (12.2%);
English Language Learner: 2,807 (14.9%); Migrant: 1,623 (8.6%)
Eligible for Free Lunch Program: 4,481 (23.8%)
Eligible for Reduced-Price Lunch Program: 1,372 (7.3%)
Teachers: 867.9 (21.7 to 1)
Librarians/Media Specialists: 23.8 (792.0 to 1)
Guidance Counselors: 46.1 (408.9 to 1)
Current Spending: ($ per student per year):
Total: $6,810; Instruction: $3,947; Support Services: $2,650
Enrollment, Drop-out Rates and Diploma Recipients by Race/Ethnicity

Category	Total	White	Black	Asian	AIAN	Hisp.
Enrollment (%)	100.0	67.7	1.9	6.6	0.6	22.6
Drop-out Rate (%)	3.2	2.0	4.3	0.6	0.0	9.8
H.S. Diplomas (#)	888	701	13	68	9	97

Sherwood SD 88J

23295 S Sherwood Blvd • Sherwood, OR 97140-9104
(503) 625-8100 • http://www.sherwood.k12.or.us/
Grade Span: KG-12; **Agency Type:** 1
Schools: 5
3 Primary; 1 Middle; 1 High; 0 Other Level
5 Regular; 0 Special Education; 0 Vocational; 0 Alternative
0 Magnet; 0 Charter; 1 Title I Eligible; 0 School-wide Title I
Students: 3,250 (n/a% male; n/a% female)
Individual Education Program: 327 (10.1%);
English Language Learner: 79 (2.4%); Migrant: 0 (0.0%)
Eligible for Free Lunch Program: 186 (5.7%)
Eligible for Reduced-Price Lunch Program: 86 (2.6%)
Teachers: 149.4 (21.8 to 1)
Librarians/Media Specialists: 4.1 (792.7 to 1)
Guidance Counselors: 6.0 (541.7 to 1)
Current Spending: ($ per student per year):
Total: $6,233; Instruction: $3,583; Support Services: $2,433

Enrollment, Drop-out Rates and Diploma Recipients by Race/Ethnicity

Category	Total	White	Black	Asian	AIAN	Hisp.
Enrollment (%)	100.0	90.4	0.9	3.0	0.3	4.5
Drop-out Rate (%)	4.0	2.4	0.0	12.5	50.0	10.0
H.S. Diplomas (#)	137	130	1	1	0	5

Tigard-Tualatin SD 23J

6960 SW Sandburg St • Tigard, OR 97223-8039
(503) 620-1620 • http://www.ttsd.k12.or.us/ttsdwebsite/
Grade Span: KG-12; **Agency Type:** 1
Schools: 15
10 Primary; 3 Middle; 2 High; 0 Other Level
15 Regular; 0 Special Education; 0 Vocational; 0 Alternative
0 Magnet; 1 Charter; 6 Title I Eligible; 0 School-wide Title I
Students: 11,981 (n/a% male; n/a% female)
Individual Education Program: 1,184 (9.9%);
English Language Learner: 1,389 (11.6%); Migrant: 0 (0.0%)
Eligible for Free Lunch Program: 2,005 (16.7%)
Eligible for Reduced-Price Lunch Program: 578 (4.8%)
Teachers: 546.4 (21.9 to 1)
Librarians/Media Specialists: 11.7 (1,024.0 to 1)
Guidance Counselors: 24.0 (499.2 to 1)
Current Spending: ($ per student per year):
Total: $6,824; Instruction: $4,137; Support Services: $2,466

Enrollment, Drop-out Rates and Diploma Recipients by Race/Ethnicity

Category	Total	White	Black	Asian	AIAN	Hisp.
Enrollment (%)	100.0	78.3	2.2	6.5	0.8	12.2
Drop-out Rate (%)	3.8	2.6	0.0	2.8	14.3	19.8
H.S. Diplomas (#)	743	646	6	48	3	40

Yamhill County

Mcminnville SD 040

1500 NE Baker St • Mcminnville, OR 97128-3004
(503) 434-6551
Grade Span: KG-12; **Agency Type:** 1
Schools: 9
6 Primary; 2 Middle; 1 High; 0 Other Level
9 Regular; 0 Special Education; 0 Vocational; 0 Alternative
0 Magnet; 0 Charter; 5 Title I Eligible; 4 School-wide Title I
Students: 5,706 (n/a% male; n/a% female)
Individual Education Program: 731 (12.8%);
English Language Learner: 830 (14.5%); Migrant: 450 (7.9%)
Eligible for Free Lunch Program: 1,921 (33.7%)
Eligible for Reduced-Price Lunch Program: 498 (8.7%)
Teachers: 261.4 (21.8 to 1)
Librarians/Media Specialists: 6.0 (951.0 to 1)
Guidance Counselors: 14.0 (407.6 to 1)
Current Spending: ($ per student per year):
Total: $6,039; Instruction: $3,598; Support Services: $2,207

Enrollment, Drop-out Rates and Diploma Recipients by Race/Ethnicity

Category	Total	White	Black	Asian	AIAN	Hisp.
Enrollment (%)	100.0	74.7	0.9	1.6	0.9	20.8
Drop-out Rate (%)	6.6	6.3	14.3	2.6	0.0	9.0
H.S. Diplomas (#)	314	268	1	4	3	38

Newberg SD 29J

714 E 6th St • Newberg, OR 97132-3498
(503) 554-5000
Grade Span: KG-12; **Agency Type:** 1
Schools: 8
5 Primary; 2 Middle; 1 High; 0 Other Level
8 Regular; 0 Special Education; 0 Vocational; 0 Alternative
0 Magnet; 0 Charter; 3 Title I Eligible; 1 School-wide Title I
Students: 5,002 (n/a% male; n/a% female)
Individual Education Program: 615 (12.3%);
English Language Learner: 437 (8.7%); Migrant: 235 (4.7%)
Eligible for Free Lunch Program: 1,080 (21.6%)
Eligible for Reduced-Price Lunch Program: 384 (7.7%)
Teachers: 230.6 (21.7 to 1)
Librarians/Media Specialists: 3.0 (1,667.3 to 1)
Guidance Counselors: 11.7 (427.5 to 1)
Current Spending: ($ per student per year):
Total: $6,459; Instruction: $3,905; Support Services: $2,305

Enrollment, Drop-out Rates and Diploma Recipients by Race/Ethnicity

Category	Total	White	Black	Asian	AIAN	Hisp.
Enrollment (%)	100.0	85.6	1.0	1.6	0.5	11.2
Drop-out Rate (%)	6.5	5.6	42.9	0.0	16.7	14.8
H.S. Diplomas (#)	318	290	1	3	1	23

Number of Schools

Rank	Number	District Name	City
1	104	Portland SD 1J	Portland
2	66	Salem-Keizer SD 24J	Salem
3	49	Beaverton SD 48J	Beaverton
4	47	Eugene SD 04J	Eugene
5	30	Hillsboro SD 01J	Hillsboro
6	25	North Clackamas SD 012	Milwaukie
6	25	Springfield SD 019	Springfield
8	23	Bend Admin SD 1	Bend
9	21	Lincoln County SD	Newport
10	19	Greater Albany SD 8J	Albany
10	19	Gresham-Barlow SD 10J	Gresham
10	19	Klamath County SD	Klamath Falls
10	19	Medford SD 549	Medford
14	17	Three Rivers SD	Murphy
15	16	Reynolds SD 007	Fairview
16	15	Tigard-Tualatin SD 23J	Tigard
17	14	Corvallis SD 509J	Corvallis
17	14	David Douglas SD 40	Portland
19	13	Lake Oswego SD 07J	Lake Oswego
19	13	Oregon City SD 062	Oregon City
19	13	Silver Falls SD 4J	Silverton
19	13	West Linn SD 03J	West Linn
23	12	Portland Area Office	Portland
23	12	Roseburg SD 4	Roseburg
25	11	Bethel SD 052	Eugene
25	11	Oregon Trail SD 046	Sandy
27	10	Forest Grove SD 015	Forest Grove
27	10	Grants Pass SD 007	Grants Pass
27	10	Klamath Falls City Schools	Klamath Falls
27	10	Redmond SD 02J	Redmond
31	9	Centennial SD 28J	Portland
31	9	Dallas SD 2	Dallas
31	9	Eagle Point SD 009	Eagle Point
31	9	Hood River County SD 1	Hood River
31	9	Lebanon Community SD 009	Lebanon
31	9	Mcminnville SD 040	Mcminnville
31	9	South Lane SD 45J	Cottage Grove
38	8	Ashland SD 005	Ashland
38	8	Central Point SD 006	Central Point
38	8	Central SD 13J	Independence
38	8	Hermiston SD 008	Hermiston
38	8	Molalla River SD 035	Molalla
38	8	Newberg SD 29J	Newberg
44	7	Baker SD 05J	Baker City
44	7	Canby SD 086	Canby
44	7	Coos Bay SD 009	Coos Bay
44	7	Crook County SD	Prineville
44	7	Jefferson County SD 509J	Madras
44	7	Morrow SD 001	Lexington
44	7	North Bend SD 013	North Bend
44	7	Ontario SD 008	Ontario
44	7	Pendleton SD 016	Pendleton
44	7	Sweet Home SD 055	Sweet Home
44	7	Woodburn SD 103	Woodburn
55	6	Cascade SD 005	Turner
55	6	La Grande SD 001	La Grande
55	6	Parkrose SD 003	Portland
55	6	Philomath SD 17J	Philomath
55	6	Phoenix-Talent SD 004	Phoenix
55	6	Saint Helens SD 502	Saint Helens
55	6	Scappoose SD 01J	Scappoose
55	6	Winston-Dillard SD 116	Winston
63	5	Astoria SD 001	Astoria
63	5	Estacada SD 108	Estacada
63	5	Milton-Freewater SD 007	Milton-Freewater
63	5	North Santiam SD 29J	Stayton
63	5	Seaside SD 010	Seaside
63	5	Sherwood SD 88J	Sherwood
63	5	South Umpqua SD 019	Myrtle Creek
63	5	Tillamook SD 9	Tillamook
71	4	Brookings-Harbor SD 17	Brookings
71	4	Fern Ridge SD 28J	Elmira
71	4	Junction City SD 069	Junction City
71	4	North Marion SD 015	Aurora
71	4	Siuslaw SD 97J	Florence
71	4	Sutherlin SD 130	Sutherlin
71	4	The Dalles SD 012	The Dalles
78	3	Gladstone SD 115	Gladstone

Number of Teachers

Rank	Number	District Name	City
1	2,760	Portland SD 1J	Portland
2	1,655	Beaverton SD 48J	Beaverton
3	1,640	Salem-Keizer SD 24J	Salem
4	867	Hillsboro SD 01J	Hillsboro
5	826	Eugene SD 04J	Eugene
6	774	North Clackamas SD 012	Milwaukie
7	646	Bend Admin SD 1	Bend
8	560	Medford SD 549	Medford
9	552	Gresham-Barlow SD 10J	Gresham
10	546	Tigard-Tualatin SD 23J	Tigard
11	523	Springfield SD 019	Springfield
12	491	Reynolds SD 007	Fairview
13	440	David Douglas SD 40	Portland
14	366	Greater Albany SD 8J	Albany
15	364	West Linn SD 03J	West Linn
16	352	Klamath County SD	Klamath Falls
17	340	Lake Oswego SD 07J	Lake Oswego
18	340	Oregon City SD 062	Oregon City
19	318	Corvallis SD 509J	Corvallis
20	312	Roseburg SD 4	Roseburg
21	299	Centennial SD 28J	Portland
22	294	Three Rivers SD	Murphy
23	285	Forest Grove SD 015	Forest Grove
24	277	Lincoln County SD	Newport
25	276	Redmond SD 02J	Redmond
26	276	Woodburn SD 103	Woodburn
27	273	Grants Pass SD 007	Grants Pass
28	261	Mcminnville SD 040	Mcminnville
29	251	Canby SD 086	Canby
30	234	Hermiston SD 008	Hermiston
31	230	Newberg SD 29J	Newberg
32	222	Bethel SD 052	Eugene
33	219	Hood River County SD 1	Hood River
34	213	Lebanon Community SD 009	Lebanon
35	212	Klamath Falls City Schools	Klamath Falls
36	194	Silver Falls SD 4J	Silverton
37	186	Central Point SD 006	Central Point
38	181	Jefferson County SD 509J	Madras
39	179	Oregon Trail SD 046	Sandy
40	176	Coos Bay SD 009	Coos Bay
40	176	Eagle Point SD 009	Eagle Point
42	175	Saint Helens SD 502	Saint Helens
43	168	Dallas SD 2	Dallas
44	167	Pendleton SD 016	Pendleton
45	161	Crook County SD	Prineville
46	160	Ashland SD 005	Ashland
47	160	Parkrose SD 003	Portland
48	149	Sherwood SD 88J	Sherwood
49	148	Ontario SD 008	Ontario
50	145	Phoenix-Talent SD 004	Phoenix
51	141	Morrow SD 001	Lexington
52	138	Molalla River SD 035	Molalla
53	134	South Lane SD 45J	Cottage Grove
54	131	Central SD 13J	Independence
55	125	La Grande SD 001	La Grande
56	120	North Santiam SD 29J	Stayton
57	117	Astoria SD 001	Astoria
58	115	Scappoose SD 01J	Scappoose
59	114	Sweet Home SD 055	Sweet Home
60	113	Cascade SD 005	Turner
61	111	North Bend SD 013	North Bend
62	109	Winston-Dillard SD 116	Winston
63	108	Baker SD 05J	Baker City
64	106	Gladstone SD 115	Gladstone
65	106	Milton-Freewater SD 007	Milton-Freewater
66	105	The Dalles SD 012	The Dalles
67	104	Tillamook SD 9	Tillamook
68	100	South Umpqua SD 019	Myrtle Creek
69	98	Estacada SD 108	Estacada
70	95	Junction City SD 069	Junction City
71	95	Philomath SD 17J	Philomath
72	93	Brookings-Harbor SD 17	Brookings
73	91	North Marion SD 015	Aurora
74	90	Seaside SD 010	Seaside
75	84	Siuslaw SD 97J	Florence
76	81	Fern Ridge SD 28J	Elmira
77	76	Sutherlin SD 130	Sutherlin
78	n/a	Portland Area Office	Portland

Number of Students

Rank	Number	District Name	City
1	51,654	Portland SD 1J	Portland
2	37,137	Salem-Keizer SD 24J	Salem
3	35,320	Beaverton SD 48J	Beaverton
4	18,850	Hillsboro SD 01J	Hillsboro
5	18,735	Eugene SD 04J	Eugene
6	15,777	North Clackamas SD 012	Milwaukie
7	13,671	Bend Admin SD 1	Bend
8	13,014	Medford SD 549	Medford
9	11,981	Tigard-Tualatin SD 23J	Tigard
10	11,712	Gresham-Barlow SD 10J	Gresham
11	11,154	Springfield SD 019	Springfield
12	10,288	Reynolds SD 007	Fairview
13	8,901	David Douglas SD 40	Portland
14	8,226	Greater Albany SD 8J	Albany
15	7,821	West Linn SD 03J	West Linn
16	7,662	Oregon City SD 062	Oregon City
17	7,169	Corvallis SD 509J	Corvallis
18	7,005	Lake Oswego SD 07J	Lake Oswego
19	6,788	Roseburg SD 4	Roseburg
20	6,722	Klamath County SD	Klamath Falls
21	6,255	Centennial SD 28J	Portland
22	6,120	Three Rivers SD	Murphy
23	6,117	Lincoln County SD	Newport
24	6,040	Redmond SD 02J	Redmond
25	5,773	Forest Grove SD 015	Forest Grove
26	5,706	Mcminnville SD 040	Mcminnville
27	5,540	Grants Pass SD 007	Grants Pass
28	5,507	Bethel SD 052	Eugene
29	5,257	Canby SD 086	Canby
30	5,002	Newberg SD 29J	Newberg
31	4,643	Central Point SD 006	Central Point
32	4,517	Woodburn SD 103	Woodburn
33	4,451	Lebanon Community SD 009	Lebanon
34	4,305	Hermiston SD 008	Hermiston
35	4,190	Oregon Trail SD 046	Sandy
36	4,134	Eagle Point SD 009	Eagle Point
37	3,985	Klamath Falls City Schools	Klamath Falls
38	3,867	Hood River County SD 1	Hood River
39	3,791	Coos Bay SD 009	Coos Bay
40	3,675	Silver Falls SD 4J	Silverton
41	3,647	Parkrose SD 003	Portland
42	3,452	Pendleton SD 016	Pendleton
43	3,436	Saint Helens SD 502	Saint Helens
44	3,250	Sherwood SD 88J	Sherwood
45	3,203	Dallas SD 2	Dallas
46	3,195	Jefferson County SD 509J	Madras
47	3,190	Ashland SD 005	Ashland
48	3,133	Crook County SD	Prineville
49	2,864	Molalla River SD 035	Molalla
50	2,858	South Lane SD 45J	Cottage Grove
51	2,833	Phoenix-Talent SD 004	Phoenix
52	2,795	Ontario SD 008	Ontario
53	2,588	Central SD 13J	Independence
54	2,466	Sweet Home SD 055	Sweet Home
55	2,417	North Santiam SD 29J	Stayton
56	2,408	Gladstone SD 115	Gladstone
57	2,320	Estacada SD 108	Estacada
58	2,311	North Bend SD 013	North Bend
59	2,298	Cascade SD 005	Turner
60	2,297	La Grande SD 001	La Grande
61	2,273	Morrow SD 001	Lexington
62	2,224	Astoria SD 001	Astoria
63	2,192	Scappoose SD 01J	Scappoose
64	2,165	Tillamook SD 9	Tillamook
65	2,151	Baker SD 05J	Baker City
66	2,061	Portland Area Office	Portland
67	2,053	The Dalles SD 012	The Dalles
68	1,961	Philomath SD 17J	Philomath
69	1,927	South Umpqua SD 019	Myrtle Creek
70	1,898	Milton-Freewater SD 007	Milton-Freewater
71	1,873	Junction City SD 069	Junction City
72	1,849	Brookings-Harbor SD 17	Brookings
73	1,765	North Marion SD 015	Aurora
74	1,707	Seaside SD 010	Seaside
75	1,685	Fern Ridge SD 28J	Elmira
76	1,622	Winston-Dillard SD 116	Winston
77	1,578	Siuslaw SD 97J	Florence
78	1,531	Sutherlin SD 130	Sutherlin

Male Students

Rank	Percent	District Name	City
1	n/a	Ashland SD 005	Ashland
1	n/a	Astoria SD 001	Astoria
1	n/a	Baker SD 05J	Baker City
1	n/a	Beaverton SD 48J	Beaverton
1	n/a	Bend Admin SD 1	Bend
1	n/a	Bethel SD 052	Eugene
1	n/a	Brookings-Harbor SD 17	Brookings
1	n/a	Canby SD 086	Canby
1	n/a	Cascade SD 005	Turner
1	n/a	Centennial SD 28J	Portland
1	n/a	Central Point SD 006	Central Point
1	n/a	Central SD 13J	Independence
1	n/a	Coos Bay SD 009	Coos Bay
1	n/a	Corvallis SD 509J	Corvallis
1	n/a	Crook County SD	Prineville
1	n/a	Dallas SD 2	Dallas
1	n/a	David Douglas SD 40	Portland
1	n/a	Eagle Point SD 009	Eagle Point
1	n/a	Estacada SD 108	Estacada
1	n/a	Eugene SD 04J	Eugene
1	n/a	Fern Ridge SD 28J	Elmira
1	n/a	Forest Grove SD 015	Forest Grove
1	n/a	Gladstone SD 115	Gladstone
1	n/a	Grants Pass SD 007	Grants Pass
1	n/a	Greater Albany SD 8J	Albany
1	n/a	Gresham-Barlow SD 10J	Gresham
1	n/a	Hermiston SD 008	Hermiston
1	n/a	Hillsboro SD 01J	Hillsboro
1	n/a	Hood River County SD 1	Hood River
1	n/a	Jefferson County SD 509J	Madras

Rank	Percent	District Name	City
1	n/a	Junction City SD 069	Junction City
1	n/a	Klamath County SD	Klamath Falls
1	n/a	Klamath Falls City Schools	Klamath Falls
1	n/a	La Grande SD 001	La Grande
1	n/a	Lake Oswego SD 07J	Lake Oswego
1	n/a	Lebanon Community SD 009	Lebanon
1	n/a	Lincoln County SD	Newport
1	n/a	Mcminnville SD 040	Mcminnville
1	n/a	Medford SD 549	Medford
1	n/a	Milton-Freewater SD 007	Milton-Freewater
1	n/a	Molalla River SD 035	Molalla
1	n/a	Morrow SD 001	Lexington
1	n/a	Newberg SD 29J	Newberg
1	n/a	North Bend SD 013	North Bend
1	n/a	North Clackamas SD 012	Milwaukie
1	n/a	North Marion SD 015	Aurora
1	n/a	North Santiam SD 29J	Stayton
1	n/a	Ontario SD 008	Ontario
1	n/a	Oregon City SD 062	Oregon City
1	n/a	Oregon Trail SD 046	Sandy
1	n/a	Parkrose SD 003	Portland
1	n/a	Pendleton SD 016	Pendleton
1	n/a	Philomath SD 17J	Philomath
1	n/a	Phoenix-Talent SD 004	Phoenix
1	n/a	Portland Area Office	Portland
1	n/a	Portland SD 1J	Portland
1	n/a	Redmond SD 02J	Redmond
1	n/a	Reynolds SD 007	Fairview
1	n/a	Roseburg SD 4	Roseburg
1	n/a	Saint Helens SD 502	Saint Helens
1	n/a	Salem-Keizer SD 24J	Salem
1	n/a	Scappoose SD 01J	Scappoose
1	n/a	Seaside SD 010	Seaside
1	n/a	Sherwood SD 88J	Sherwood
1	n/a	Silver Falls SD 4J	Silverton
1	n/a	Siuslaw SD 97J	Florence
1	n/a	South Lane SD 45J	Cottage Grove
1	n/a	South Umpqua SD 019	Myrtle Creek
1	n/a	Springfield SD 019	Springfield
1	n/a	Sutherlin SD 130	Sutherlin
1	n/a	Sweet Home SD 055	Sweet Home
1	n/a	The Dalles SD 012	The Dalles
1	n/a	Three Rivers SD	Murphy
1	n/a	Tigard-Tualatin SD 23J	Tigard
1	n/a	Tillamook SD 9	Tillamook
1	n/a	West Linn SD 03J	West Linn
1	n/a	Winston-Dillard SD 116	Winston
1	n/a	Woodburn SD 103	Woodburn

Female Students

Rank	Percent	District Name	City
1	n/a	Ashland SD 005	Ashland
1	n/a	Astoria SD 001	Astoria
1	n/a	Baker SD 05J	Baker City
1	n/a	Beaverton SD 48J	Beaverton
1	n/a	Bend Admin SD 1	Bend
1	n/a	Bethel SD 052	Eugene
1	n/a	Brookings-Harbor SD 17	Brookings
1	n/a	Canby SD 086	Canby
1	n/a	Cascade SD 005	Turner
1	n/a	Centennial SD 28J	Portland
1	n/a	Central Point SD 006	Central Point
1	n/a	Central SD 13J	Independence
1	n/a	Coos Bay SD 009	Coos Bay
1	n/a	Corvallis SD 509J	Corvallis
1	n/a	Crook County SD	Prineville
1	n/a	Dallas SD 2	Dallas
1	n/a	David Douglas SD 40	Portland
1	n/a	Eagle Point SD 009	Eagle Point
1	n/a	Estacada SD 108	Estacada
1	n/a	Eugene SD 04J	Eugene
1	n/a	Fern Ridge SD 28J	Elmira
1	n/a	Forest Grove SD 015	Forest Grove
1	n/a	Gladstone SD 115	Gladstone
1	n/a	Grants Pass SD 007	Grants Pass
1	n/a	Greater Albany SD 8J	Albany
1	n/a	Gresham-Barlow SD 10J	Gresham
1	n/a	Hermiston SD 008	Hermiston
1	n/a	Hillsboro SD 01J	Hillsboro
1	n/a	Hood River County SD 1	Hood River
1	n/a	Jefferson County SD 509J	Madras
1	n/a	Junction City SD 069	Junction City
1	n/a	Klamath County SD	Klamath Falls
1	n/a	Klamath Falls City Schools	Klamath Falls
1	n/a	La Grande SD 001	La Grande
1	n/a	Lake Oswego SD 07J	Lake Oswego
1	n/a	Lebanon Community SD 009	Lebanon
1	n/a	Lincoln County SD	Newport
1	n/a	Mcminnville SD 040	Mcminnville
1	n/a	Medford SD 549	Medford
1	n/a	Milton-Freewater SD 007	Milton-Freewater
1	n/a	Molalla River SD 035	Molalla
1	n/a	Morrow SD 001	Lexington
1	n/a	Newberg SD 29J	Newberg
1	n/a	North Bend SD 013	North Bend
1	n/a	North Clackamas SD 012	Milwaukie
1	n/a	North Marion SD 015	Aurora
1	n/a	North Santiam SD 29J	Stayton
1	n/a	Ontario SD 008	Ontario
1	n/a	Oregon City SD 062	Oregon City
1	n/a	Oregon Trail SD 046	Sandy
1	n/a	Parkrose SD 003	Portland
1	n/a	Pendleton SD 016	Pendleton
1	n/a	Philomath SD 17J	Philomath
1	n/a	Phoenix-Talent SD 004	Phoenix
1	n/a	Portland Area Office	Portland
1	n/a	Portland SD 1J	Portland
1	n/a	Redmond SD 02J	Redmond
1	n/a	Reynolds SD 007	Fairview
1	n/a	Roseburg SD 4	Roseburg
1	n/a	Saint Helens SD 502	Saint Helens
1	n/a	Salem-Keizer SD 24J	Salem
1	n/a	Scappoose SD 01J	Scappoose
1	n/a	Seaside SD 010	Seaside
1	n/a	Sherwood SD 88J	Sherwood
1	n/a	Silver Falls SD 4J	Silverton
1	n/a	Siuslaw SD 97J	Florence
1	n/a	South Lane SD 45J	Cottage Grove
1	n/a	South Umpqua SD 019	Myrtle Creek
1	n/a	Springfield SD 019	Springfield
1	n/a	Sutherlin SD 130	Sutherlin
1	n/a	Sweet Home SD 055	Sweet Home
1	n/a	The Dalles SD 012	The Dalles
1	n/a	Three Rivers SD	Murphy
1	n/a	Tigard-Tualatin SD 23J	Tigard
1	n/a	Tillamook SD 9	Tillamook
1	n/a	West Linn SD 03J	West Linn
1	n/a	Winston-Dillard SD 116	Winston
1	n/a	Woodburn SD 103	Woodburn

Individual Education Program Students

Rank	Percent	District Name	City
1	17.7	Estacada SD 108	Estacada
2	17.4	Sweet Home SD 055	Sweet Home
2	17.4	Winston-Dillard SD 116	Winston
4	17.3	La Grande SD 001	La Grande
5	17.1	South Lane SD 45J	Cottage Grove
6	16.8	Oregon City SD 062	Oregon City
7	16.7	Fern Ridge SD 28J	Elmira
8	16.2	Lincoln County SD	Newport
8	16.2	Springfield SD 019	Springfield
10	15.7	Saint Helens SD 502	Saint Helens
11	15.6	Klamath Falls City Schools	Klamath Falls
12	15.5	South Umpqua SD 019	Myrtle Creek
13	15.3	The Dalles SD 012	The Dalles
14	15.2	Bethel SD 052	Eugene
14	15.2	Coos Bay SD 009	Coos Bay
14	15.2	Reynolds SD 007	Fairview
17	15.1	Junction City SD 069	Junction City
17	15.1	Klamath County SD	Klamath Falls
19	15.0	Molalla River SD 035	Molalla
20	14.8	Brookings-Harbor SD 17	Brookings
20	14.8	Cascade SD 005	Turner
22	14.7	Baker SD 05J	Baker City
23	14.5	Tillamook SD 9	Tillamook
24	14.4	Bend Admin SD 1	Bend
25	14.3	Pendleton SD 016	Pendleton
26	14.2	North Santiam SD 29J	Stayton
26	14.2	Seaside SD 010	Seaside
28	14.1	North Bend SD 013	North Bend
29	14.0	Central SD 13J	Independence
29	14.0	Hermiston SD 008	Hermiston
31	13.7	Astoria SD 001	Astoria
31	13.7	Greater Albany SD 8J	Albany
33	13.5	Sutherlin SD 130	Sutherlin
34	13.4	Oregon Trail SD 046	Sandy
35	13.2	Dallas SD 2	Dallas
35	13.2	Siuslaw SD 97J	Florence
37	12.9	Eugene SD 04J	Eugene
38	12.8	Hood River County SD 1	Hood River
38	12.8	Jefferson County SD 509J	Madras
38	12.8	Mcminnville SD 040	Mcminnville
38	12.8	Morrow SD 001	Lexington
42	12.7	Ontario SD 008	Ontario
42	12.7	Roseburg SD 4	Roseburg
44	12.6	Crook County SD	Prineville
44	12.6	Forest Grove SD 015	Forest Grove
44	12.6	Portland SD 1J	Portland
47	12.5	Parkrose SD 003	Portland
48	12.4	Eagle Point SD 009	Eagle Point
49	12.3	Newberg SD 29J	Newberg
49	12.3	Three Rivers SD	Murphy
51	12.2	Central Point SD 006	Central Point
51	12.2	Hillsboro SD 01J	Hillsboro
53	12.1	Gladstone SD 115	Gladstone
53	12.1	Redmond SD 02J	Redmond
53	12.1	Woodburn SD 103	Woodburn
56	12.0	Gresham-Barlow SD 10J	Gresham
56	12.0	Lebanon Community SD 009	Lebanon
56	12.0	Milton-Freewater SD 007	Milton-Freewater
59	11.9	Beaverton SD 48J	Beaverton
59	11.9	Corvallis SD 509J	Corvallis
59	11.9	Salem-Keizer SD 24J	Salem
62	11.8	David Douglas SD 40	Portland
62	11.8	North Marion SD 015	Aurora
64	11.6	Centennial SD 28J	Portland
64	11.6	Scappoose SD 01J	Scappoose
66	11.1	North Clackamas SD 012	Milwaukie
66	11.1	Silver Falls SD 4J	Silverton
68	11.0	Medford SD 549	Medford
68	11.0	Philomath SD 17J	Philomath
68	11.0	West Linn SD 03J	West Linn
71	10.6	Canby SD 086	Canby
72	10.4	Ashland SD 005	Ashland
73	10.1	Lake Oswego SD 07J	Lake Oswego
73	10.1	Phoenix-Talent SD 004	Phoenix
73	10.1	Sherwood SD 88J	Sherwood
76	9.9	Tigard-Tualatin SD 23J	Tigard
77	9.6	Grants Pass SD 007	Grants Pass
78	n/a	Portland Area Office	Portland

English Language Learner Students

Rank	Percent	District Name	City
1	58.4	Woodburn SD 103	Woodburn
2	33.4	Jefferson County SD 509J	Madras
3	33.2	Morrow SD 001	Lexington
4	28.8	Ontario SD 008	Ontario
5	27.1	Hermiston SD 008	Hermiston
6	22.6	David Douglas SD 40	Portland
7	21.9	Milton-Freewater SD 007	Milton-Freewater
8	20.2	Forest Grove SD 015	Forest Grove
9	20.1	Klamath Falls City Schools	Klamath Falls
10	19.7	Parkrose SD 003	Portland
10	19.7	Reynolds SD 007	Fairview
12	19.2	Central SD 13J	Independence
13	18.5	North Marion SD 015	Aurora
14	18.0	Hood River County SD 1	Hood River
15	17.4	Canby SD 086	Canby
16	14.9	Hillsboro SD 01J	Hillsboro
17	14.5	Mcminnville SD 040	Mcminnville
17	14.5	Phoenix-Talent SD 004	Phoenix
19	12.9	Centennial SD 28J	Portland
20	12.6	Salem-Keizer SD 24J	Salem
21	12.4	The Dalles SD 012	The Dalles
22	12.0	Beaverton SD 48J	Beaverton
23	11.8	North Clackamas SD 012	Milwaukie
24	11.6	Portland SD 1J	Portland
24	11.6	Tigard-Tualatin SD 23J	Tigard
26	11.2	Silver Falls SD 4J	Silverton
27	9.7	Tillamook SD 9	Tillamook
28	9.5	Molalla River SD 035	Molalla
29	9.3	Medford SD 549	Medford
30	8.7	Newberg SD 29J	Newberg
31	8.6	Gresham-Barlow SD 10J	Gresham
32	7.9	Estacada SD 108	Estacada
33	7.6	Eagle Point SD 009	Eagle Point
34	7.4	Seaside SD 010	Seaside
35	7.1	Gladstone SD 115	Gladstone
36	6.6	Siuslaw SD 97J	Florence
37	6.2	Corvallis SD 509J	Corvallis
38	5.9	Oregon City SD 062	Oregon City
39	5.7	Oregon Trail SD 046	Sandy
40	5.4	North Santiam SD 29J	Stayton
41	5.3	Cascade SD 005	Turner
42	5.1	Lincoln County SD	Newport
43	4.9	Springfield SD 019	Springfield
44	4.5	Astoria SD 001	Astoria
45	4.3	Crook County SD	Prineville
45	4.3	Klamath County SD	Klamath Falls
47	2.9	South Lane SD 45J	Cottage Grove
48	2.8	Lebanon Community SD 009	Lebanon
49	2.7	Redmond SD 02J	Redmond
50	2.6	West Linn SD 03J	West Linn
51	2.5	Central Point SD 006	Central Point
52	2.4	Bend Admin SD 1	Bend
52	2.4	Sherwood SD 88J	Sherwood
54	2.3	Greater Albany SD 8J	Albany
54	2.3	Junction City SD 069	Junction City
56	2.2	Ashland SD 005	Ashland
56	2.2	Brookings-Harbor SD 17	Brookings
58	2.0	Dallas SD 2	Dallas
59	1.9	Coos Bay SD 009	Coos Bay
59	1.9	Roseburg SD 4	Roseburg
61	1.8	Eugene SD 04J	Eugene
62	1.6	Bethel SD 052	Eugene
63	1.3	Grants Pass SD 007	Grants Pass

Rank	Percent	District Name	City
64	1.2	Lake Oswego SD 07J	Lake Oswego
65	1.1	La Grande SD 001	La Grande
65	1.1	Pendleton SD 016	Pendleton
67	1.0	Baker SD 05J	Baker City
67	1.0	Three Rivers SD	Murphy
69	0.8	Sutherlin SD 130	Sutherlin
70	0.7	Philomath SD 17J	Philomath
71	0.5	South Umpqua SD 019	Myrtle Creek
71	0.5	Sweet Home SD 055	Sweet Home
73	0.3	North Bend SD 013	North Bend
73	0.3	Saint Helens SD 502	Saint Helens
73	0.3	Scappoose SD 01J	Scappoose
76	0.0	Fern Ridge SD 28J	Elmira
76	0.0	Winston-Dillard SD 116	Winston
78	n/a	Portland Area Office	Portland

Migrant Students

Rank	Percent	District Name	City
1	34.1	Ontario SD 008	Ontario
2	29.8	Woodburn SD 103	Woodburn
3	28.7	Morrow SD 001	Lexington
4	21.6	Hood River County SD 1	Hood River
5	20.2	Jefferson County SD 509J	Madras
6	17.1	Hermiston SD 008	Hermiston
7	13.1	Milton-Freewater SD 007	Milton-Freewater
8	12.4	The Dalles SD 012	The Dalles
9	12.2	North Marion SD 015	Aurora
10	12.0	Forest Grove SD 015	Forest Grove
11	11.4	Central SD 13J	Independence
12	8.6	Hillsboro SD 01J	Hillsboro
13	7.9	Mcminnville SD 040	Mcminnville
14	7.4	Canby SD 086	Canby
15	7.1	Salem-Keizer SD 24J	Salem
16	6.9	Silver Falls SD 4J	Silverton
17	5.9	Molalla River SD 035	Molalla
18	5.5	Phoenix-Talent SD 004	Phoenix
19	5.3	Crook County SD	Prineville
20	5.2	Klamath Falls City Schools	Klamath Falls
21	4.7	Newberg SD 29J	Newberg
22	4.6	Klamath County SD	Klamath Falls
23	4.2	North Santiam SD 29J	Stayton
24	3.1	Cascade SD 005	Turner
25	3.0	Reynolds SD 007	Fairview
26	2.9	Lincoln County SD	Newport
27	2.6	Medford SD 549	Medford
28	2.1	Beaverton SD 48J	Beaverton
29	2.0	South Lane SD 45J	Cottage Grove
30	1.9	Redmond SD 02J	Redmond
31	1.8	Estacada SD 108	Estacada
31	1.8	Junction City SD 069	Junction City
33	1.5	Greater Albany SD 8J	Albany
33	1.5	Gresham-Barlow SD 10J	Gresham
35	1.4	Portland SD 1J	Portland
36	1.3	Eagle Point SD 009	Eagle Point
37	1.2	Centennial SD 28J	Portland
38	1.1	Corvallis SD 509J	Corvallis
39	1.0	Springfield SD 019	Springfield
40	0.9	Oregon City SD 062	Oregon City
40	0.9	Oregon Trail SD 046	Sandy
42	0.7	Bethel SD 052	Eugene
42	0.7	David Douglas SD 40	Portland
42	0.7	Gladstone SD 115	Gladstone
45	0.6	Bend Admin SD 1	Bend
45	0.6	Dallas SD 2	Dallas
47	0.5	Ashland SD 005	Ashland
47	0.5	Central Point SD 006	Central Point
47	0.5	Parkrose SD 003	Portland
50	0.4	Eugene SD 04J	Eugene
50	0.4	Pendleton SD 016	Pendleton
52	0.3	Lebanon Community SD 009	Lebanon
52	0.3	North Clackamas SD 012	Milwaukie
54	0.2	Philomath SD 17J	Philomath
54	0.2	Three Rivers SD	Murphy
56	0.1	Grants Pass SD 007	Grants Pass
56	0.1	West Linn SD 03J	West Linn
58	0.0	Lake Oswego SD 07J	Lake Oswego
59	0.0	Astoria SD 001	Astoria
59	0.0	Baker SD 05J	Baker City
59	0.0	Brookings-Harbor SD 17	Brookings
59	0.0	Coos Bay SD 009	Coos Bay
59	0.0	Fern Ridge SD 28J	Elmira
59	0.0	La Grande SD 001	La Grande
59	0.0	North Bend SD 013	North Bend
59	0.0	Roseburg SD 4	Roseburg
59	0.0	Saint Helens SD 502	Saint Helens
59	0.0	Scappoose SD 01J	Scappoose
59	0.0	Seaside SD 010	Seaside
59	0.0	Sherwood SD 88J	Sherwood
59	0.0	Siuslaw SD 97J	Florence
59	0.0	South Umpqua SD 019	Myrtle Creek
59	0.0	Sutherlin SD 130	Sutherlin
59	0.0	Sweet Home SD 055	Sweet Home
59	0.0	Tigard-Tualatin SD 23J	Tigard
59	0.0	Tillamook SD 9	Tillamook
59	0.0	Winston-Dillard SD 116	Winston
78	n/a	Portland Area Office	Portland

Students Eligible for Free Lunch

Rank	Percent	District Name	City
1	75.9	Woodburn SD 103	Woodburn
2	55.3	Jefferson County SD 509J	Madras
3	52.7	Klamath Falls City Schools	Klamath Falls
4	52.1	Milton-Freewater SD 007	Milton-Freewater
5	51.8	Ontario SD 008	Ontario
6	45.4	Central SD 13J	Independence
7	44.2	Morrow SD 001	Lexington
8	43.6	David Douglas SD 40	Portland
9	42.9	South Umpqua SD 019	Myrtle Creek
10	42.7	Sweet Home SD 055	Sweet Home
11	41.5	Lebanon Community SD 009	Lebanon
12	41.2	Parkrose SD 003	Portland
13	40.7	Three Rivers SD	Murphy
14	40.3	Reynolds SD 007	Fairview
15	39.7	Klamath County SD	Klamath Falls
15	39.7	Sutherlin SD 130	Sutherlin
17	39.5	Coos Bay SD 009	Coos Bay
18	39.4	Forest Grove SD 015	Forest Grove
19	39.3	South Lane SD 45J	Cottage Grove
20	39.2	Lincoln County SD	Newport
21	38.8	Brookings-Harbor SD 17	Brookings
22	38.2	Winston-Dillard SD 116	Winston
23	38.1	Hood River County SD 1	Hood River
24	37.8	North Marion SD 015	Aurora
25	37.4	The Dalles SD 012	The Dalles
26	37.0	Phoenix-Talent SD 004	Phoenix
26	37.0	Springfield SD 019	Springfield
28	36.7	Grants Pass SD 007	Grants Pass
29	36.4	Hermiston SD 008	Hermiston
30	36.1	Salem-Keizer SD 24J	Salem
31	35.8	Eagle Point SD 009	Eagle Point
32	34.6	Crook County SD	Prineville
33	34.5	Tillamook SD 9	Tillamook
34	33.7	Mcminnville SD 040	Mcminnville
34	33.7	Portland SD 1J	Portland
36	33.2	Fern Ridge SD 28J	Elmira
37	32.6	North Bend SD 013	North Bend
38	32.2	Bethel SD 052	Eugene
39	32.1	Centennial SD 28J	Portland
40	31.7	Baker SD 05J	Baker City
40	31.7	Cascade SD 005	Turner
42	30.4	Siuslaw SD 97J	Florence
43	29.9	Estacada SD 108	Estacada
44	28.5	North Santiam SD 29J	Stayton
44	28.5	Redmond SD 02J	Redmond
46	27.9	Junction City SD 069	Junction City
47	27.8	Medford SD 549	Medford
48	27.6	Astoria SD 001	Astoria
49	27.4	Seaside SD 010	Seaside
50	27.3	Greater Albany SD 8J	Albany
50	27.3	Roseburg SD 4	Roseburg
52	26.1	Silver Falls SD 4J	Silverton
53	25.9	La Grande SD 001	La Grande
54	25.5	Pendleton SD 016	Pendleton
55	24.7	Central Point SD 006	Central Point
56	23.8	Hillsboro SD 01J	Hillsboro
57	23.7	Molalla River SD 035	Molalla
58	23.5	Bend Admin SD 1	Bend
58	23.5	Canby SD 086	Canby
60	22.7	Dallas SD 2	Dallas
61	22.6	Saint Helens SD 502	Saint Helens
62	22.5	Gresham-Barlow SD 10J	Gresham
63	21.6	Newberg SD 29J	Newberg
64	21.3	North Clackamas SD 012	Milwaukie
65	21.0	Eugene SD 04J	Eugene
66	20.0	Gladstone SD 115	Gladstone
67	19.8	Oregon City SD 062	Oregon City
68	19.7	Oregon Trail SD 046	Sandy
69	18.3	Philomath SD 17J	Philomath
70	18.2	Corvallis SD 509J	Corvallis
71	17.8	Ashland SD 005	Ashland
72	17.7	Beaverton SD 48J	Beaverton
73	16.7	Tigard-Tualatin SD 23J	Tigard
74	13.4	Scappoose SD 01J	Scappoose
75	6.3	West Linn SD 03J	West Linn
76	5.7	Sherwood SD 88J	Sherwood
77	3.0	Lake Oswego SD 07J	Lake Oswego
78	n/a	Portland Area Office	Portland

Students Eligible for Reduced-Price Lunch

Rank	Percent	District Name	City
1	15.3	Eagle Point SD 009	Eagle Point
2	14.6	Brookings-Harbor SD 17	Brookings
3	13.8	Grants Pass SD 007	Grants Pass
4	13.4	South Lane SD 45J	Cottage Grove
5	12.7	Three Rivers SD	Murphy
6	12.5	Sutherlin SD 130	Sutherlin
7	12.3	Lebanon Community SD 009	Lebanon
7	12.3	Morrow SD 001	Lexington
9	12.1	Sweet Home SD 055	Sweet Home
10	12.0	Winston-Dillard SD 116	Winston
11	11.9	Jefferson County SD 509J	Madras
12	11.7	South Umpqua SD 019	Myrtle Creek
13	11.6	Estacada SD 108	Estacada
13	11.6	Klamath County SD	Klamath Falls
15	11.5	Crook County SD	Prineville
15	11.5	North Santiam SD 29J	Stayton
17	11.3	Central SD 13J	Independence
17	11.3	Fern Ridge SD 28J	Elmira
19	11.1	Parkrose SD 003	Portland
20	10.8	David Douglas SD 40	Portland
21	10.7	North Marion SD 015	Aurora
22	10.5	Bethel SD 052	Eugene
22	10.5	Phoenix-Talent SD 004	Phoenix
24	10.3	Forest Grove SD 015	Forest Grove
24	10.3	Lincoln County SD	Newport
26	10.2	Tillamook SD 9	Tillamook
27	10.1	Klamath Falls City Schools	Klamath Falls
28	10.0	Centennial SD 28J	Portland
28	10.0	Hermiston SD 008	Hermiston
30	9.8	Molalla River SD 035	Molalla
31	9.7	Junction City SD 069	Junction City
31	9.7	Reynolds SD 007	Fairview
31	9.7	Woodburn SD 103	Woodburn
34	9.5	Cascade SD 005	Turner
35	9.4	Roseburg SD 4	Roseburg
36	9.3	Hood River County SD 1	Hood River
36	9.3	Seaside SD 010	Seaside
38	9.1	Milton-Freewater SD 007	Milton-Freewater
39	9.0	Baker SD 05J	Baker City
39	9.0	Central Point SD 006	Central Point
39	9.0	North Bend SD 013	North Bend
42	8.9	Coos Bay SD 009	Coos Bay
43	8.8	La Grande SD 001	La Grande
43	8.8	Salem-Keizer SD 24J	Salem
45	8.7	Mcminnville SD 040	Mcminnville
45	8.7	Redmond SD 02J	Redmond
47	8.6	Astoria SD 001	Astoria
47	8.6	Bend Admin SD 1	Bend
47	8.6	Ontario SD 008	Ontario
50	8.5	Oregon Trail SD 046	Sandy
51	8.2	Gladstone SD 115	Gladstone
52	8.0	Medford SD 549	Medford
52	8.0	Pendleton SD 016	Pendleton
54	7.9	Siuslaw SD 97J	Florence
55	7.8	Greater Albany SD 8J	Albany
55	7.8	Springfield SD 019	Springfield
55	7.8	The Dalles SD 012	The Dalles
58	7.7	Newberg SD 29J	Newberg
58	7.7	Saint Helens SD 502	Saint Helens
60	7.5	Portland SD 1J	Portland
61	7.3	Hillsboro SD 01J	Hillsboro
62	7.0	Dallas SD 2	Dallas
62	7.0	North Clackamas SD 012	Milwaukie
64	6.9	Canby SD 086	Canby
65	6.7	Gresham-Barlow SD 10J	Gresham
65	6.7	Silver Falls SD 4J	Silverton
67	6.6	Beaverton SD 48J	Beaverton
68	6.1	Oregon City SD 062	Oregon City
69	5.7	Philomath SD 17J	Philomath
70	5.4	Corvallis SD 509J	Corvallis
71	5.2	Scappoose SD 01J	Scappoose
72	5.0	Ashland SD 005	Ashland
73	4.8	Tigard-Tualatin SD 23J	Tigard
74	4.7	Eugene SD 04J	Eugene
75	2.6	Sherwood SD 88J	Sherwood
76	2.3	West Linn SD 03J	West Linn
77	2.0	Lake Oswego SD 07J	Lake Oswego
78	n/a	Portland Area Office	Portland

Student/Teacher Ratio

Rank	Ratio	District Name	City
1	24.9	Central Point SD 006	Central Point
2	24.7	Bethel SD 052	Eugene
3	23.7	Estacada SD 108	Estacada
4	23.5	Eagle Point SD 009	Eagle Point
5	23.3	Oregon Trail SD 046	Sandy
6	23.2	Medford SD 549	Medford
7	22.8	Parkrose SD 003	Portland
8	22.7	Eugene SD 04J	Eugene
9	22.6	Gladstone SD 115	Gladstone
9	22.6	Salem-Keizer SD 24J	Salem
11	22.5	Corvallis SD 509J	Corvallis
11	22.5	Greater Albany SD 8J	Albany
11	22.5	Oregon City SD 062	Oregon City

14	22.0	Lincoln County SD	Newport
15	21.9	Redmond SD 02J	Redmond
15	21.9	Tigard-Tualatin SD 23J	Tigard
17	21.8	Mcminnville SD 040	Mcminnville
17	21.8	Sherwood SD 88J	Sherwood
19	21.7	Hillsboro SD 01J	Hillsboro
19	21.7	Newberg SD 29J	Newberg
19	21.7	Roseburg SD 4	Roseburg
22	21.6	Sweet Home SD 055	Sweet Home
23	21.5	Coos Bay SD 009	Coos Bay
23	21.5	West Linn SD 03J	West Linn
25	21.3	Beaverton SD 48J	Beaverton
25	21.3	South Lane SD 45J	Cottage Grove
25	21.3	Springfield SD 019	Springfield
28	21.2	Bend Admin SD 1	Bend
28	21.2	Gresham-Barlow SD 10J	Gresham
30	21.0	Reynolds SD 007	Fairview
31	20.9	Canby SD 086	Canby
31	20.9	Centennial SD 28J	Portland
31	20.9	Lebanon Community SD 009	Lebanon
34	20.8	Three Rivers SD	Murphy
35	20.7	Fern Ridge SD 28J	Elmira
35	20.7	North Bend SD 013	North Bend
35	20.7	Tillamook SD 9	Tillamook
38	20.6	Lake Oswego SD 07J	Lake Oswego
38	20.6	Molalla River SD 035	Molalla
38	20.6	Pendleton SD 016	Pendleton
41	20.5	Philomath SD 17J	Philomath
42	20.4	North Clackamas SD 012	Milwaukie
43	20.3	Cascade SD 005	Turner
44	20.2	David Douglas SD 40	Portland
44	20.2	Forest Grove SD 015	Forest Grove
44	20.2	Grants Pass SD 007	Grants Pass
47	20.0	North Santiam SD 29J	Stayton
47	20.0	Sutherlin SD 130	Sutherlin
49	19.9	Brookings-Harbor SD 17	Brookings
50	19.8	Ashland SD 005	Ashland
50	19.8	Baker SD 05J	Baker City
52	19.7	Central SD 13J	Independence
53	19.6	Saint Helens SD 502	Saint Helens
53	19.6	The Dalles SD 012	The Dalles
55	19.5	Junction City SD 069	Junction City
55	19.5	Phoenix-Talent SD 004	Phoenix
57	19.4	Crook County SD	Prineville
58	19.3	South Umpqua SD 019	Myrtle Creek
59	19.2	North Marion SD 015	Aurora
60	19.1	Klamath County SD	Klamath Falls
61	19.0	Dallas SD 2	Dallas
61	19.0	Scappoose SD 01J	Scappoose
63	18.9	Astoria SD 001	Astoria
63	18.9	Seaside SD 010	Seaside
63	18.9	Silver Falls SD 4J	Silverton
66	18.8	Ontario SD 008	Ontario
67	18.7	Klamath Falls City Schools	Klamath Falls
67	18.7	Portland SD 1J	Portland
69	18.6	Siuslaw SD 97J	Florence
70	18.3	Hermiston SD 008	Hermiston
70	18.3	La Grande SD 001	La Grande
72	17.8	Milton-Freewater SD 007	Milton-Freewater
73	17.6	Hood River County SD 1	Hood River
73	17.6	Jefferson County SD 509J	Madras
75	16.4	Woodburn SD 103	Woodburn
76	16.1	Morrow SD 001	Lexington
77	14.8	Winston-Dillard SD 116	Winston
78	n/a	Portland Area Office	Portland

Student/Librarian Ratio

Rank	Ratio	District Name	City
1	6,120.0	Three Rivers SD	Murphy
2	6,040.0	Redmond SD 02J	Redmond
3	5,507.0	Bethel SD 052	Eugene
4	4,190.0	Oregon Trail SD 046	Sandy
5	4,134.0	Eagle Point SD 009	Eagle Point
6	3,831.0	Oregon City SD 062	Oregon City
7	3,647.0	Parkrose SD 003	Portland
8	3,361.0	Klamath County SD	Klamath Falls
9	2,967.3	Lebanon Community SD 009	Lebanon
10	2,886.5	Forest Grove SD 015	Forest Grove
11	2,864.0	Molalla River SD 035	Molalla
12	2,808.3	Fern Ridge SD 28J	Elmira
13	2,731.2	Central Point SD 006	Central Point
14	2,628.5	Canby SD 086	Canby
15	2,588.0	Central SD 13J	Independence
16	2,491.9	Gresham-Barlow SD 10J	Gresham
17	2,416.9	Hood River County SD 1	Hood River
18	2,389.7	Corvallis SD 509J	Corvallis
19	2,262.7	Roseburg SD 4	Roseburg
20	2,151.0	Baker SD 05J	Baker City
21	2,141.1	South Umpqua SD 019	Myrtle Creek
22	2,053.0	The Dalles SD 012	The Dalles
23	2,039.0	Lincoln County SD	Newport
24	1,986.7	Portland SD 1J	Portland
25	1,849.0	Brookings-Harbor SD 17	Brookings
26	1,818.9	Eugene SD 04J	Eugene
27	1,765.0	North Marion SD 015	Aurora
28	1,667.3	Newberg SD 29J	Newberg
29	1,647.1	Bend Admin SD 1	Bend
30	1,429.0	South Lane SD 45J	Cottage Grove
31	1,385.0	Grants Pass SD 007	Grants Pass
32	1,342.8	North Santiam SD 29J	Stayton
33	1,307.2	Coos Bay SD 009	Coos Bay
34	1,253.2	Crook County SD	Prineville
35	1,202.8	Tillamook SD 9	Tillamook
36	1,155.5	North Bend SD 013	North Bend
37	1,139.3	Ashland SD 005	Ashland
38	1,096.0	Scappoose SD 01J	Scappoose
39	1,024.0	Tigard-Tualatin SD 23J	Tigard
40	1,004.1	Seaside SD 010	Seaside
41	998.4	Jefferson County SD 509J	Madras
42	980.5	Philomath SD 17J	Philomath
43	963.2	Gladstone SD 115	Gladstone
44	957.5	Cascade SD 005	Turner
45	954.4	Saint Helens SD 502	Saint Helens
46	951.0	Mcminnville SD 040	Mcminnville
47	944.3	Phoenix-Talent SD 004	Phoenix
48	918.8	Silver Falls SD 4J	Silverton
49	865.9	Greater Albany SD 8J	Albany
50	863.0	Pendleton SD 016	Pendleton
51	815.7	Beaverton SD 48J	Beaverton
52	811.0	Winston-Dillard SD 116	Winston
53	796.7	Springfield SD 019	Springfield
54	792.7	Sherwood SD 88J	Sherwood
55	792.0	Hillsboro SD 01J	Hillsboro
56	790.8	Milton-Freewater SD 007	Milton-Freewater
57	789.0	Siuslaw SD 97J	Florence
58	782.7	Hermiston SD 008	Hermiston
59	781.9	Centennial SD 28J	Portland
60	762.1	Reynolds SD 007	Fairview
61	759.4	Salem-Keizer SD 24J	Salem
62	741.8	David Douglas SD 40	Portland
63	707.6	Lake Oswego SD 07J	Lake Oswego
64	701.2	North Clackamas SD 012	Milwaukie
65	699.7	Medford SD 549	Medford
66	680.1	West Linn SD 03J	West Linn
67	664.2	Klamath Falls City Schools	Klamath Falls
68	645.3	Woodburn SD 103	Woodburn
69	628.0	Dallas SD 2	Dallas
70	585.3	Junction City SD 069	Junction City
71	559.0	Ontario SD 008	Ontario
72	556.0	Astoria SD 001	Astoria
73	459.4	La Grande SD 001	La Grande
74	0.0	Estacada SD 108	Estacada
74	0.0	Morrow SD 001	Lexington
74	0.0	Sutherlin SD 130	Sutherlin
74	0.0	Sweet Home SD 055	Sweet Home
78	n/a	Portland Area Office	Portland

Student/Counselor Ratio

Rank	Ratio	District Name	City
1	954.7	Molalla River SD 035	Molalla
2	893.6	Centennial SD 28J	Portland
3	809.4	Phoenix-Talent SD 004	Phoenix
4	790.5	Eugene SD 04J	Eugene
5	783.8	Portland SD 1J	Portland
6	770.3	North Bend SD 013	North Bend
7	765.0	Three Rivers SD	Murphy
8	757.7	Morrow SD 001	Lexington
9	732.6	Fern Ridge SD 28J	Elmira
10	714.5	South Lane SD 45J	Cottage Grove
11	703.1	Hood River County SD 1	Hood River
12	679.7	Lincoln County SD	Newport
13	590.6	Eagle Point SD 009	Eagle Point
14	586.2	Medford SD 549	Medford
15	565.4	Silver Falls SD 4J	Silverton
16	548.4	Greater Albany SD 8J	Albany
17	541.7	Sherwood SD 88J	Sherwood
18	541.6	Coos Bay SD 009	Coos Bay
19	541.3	Tillamook SD 9	Tillamook
20	514.0	Springfield SD 019	Springfield
21	511.2	West Linn SD 03J	West Linn
22	503.6	Grants Pass SD 007	Grants Pass
23	500.9	North Clackamas SD 012	Milwaukie
24	500.1	David Douglas SD 40	Portland
25	499.2	Tigard-Tualatin SD 23J	Tigard
26	493.3	North Santiam SD 29J	Stayton
27	490.3	Philomath SD 17J	Philomath
28	486.3	Parkrose SD 003	Portland
29	484.8	Bend Admin SD 1	Bend
30	464.0	Estacada SD 108	Estacada
31	463.9	Lake Oswego SD 07J	Lake Oswego
32	454.2	Klamath County SD	Klamath Falls
33	452.2	Beaverton SD 48J	Beaverton
34	451.7	Woodburn SD 103	Woodburn
35	447.6	Crook County SD	Prineville
36	445.7	Oregon Trail SD 046	Sandy
37	439.5	Salem-Keizer SD 24J	Salem
38	437.8	Oregon City SD 062	Oregon City
39	437.1	Bethel SD 052	Eugene
40	427.5	Newberg SD 29J	Newberg
41	422.1	Central Point SD 006	Central Point
42	410.4	Cascade SD 005	Turner
43	408.9	Hillsboro SD 01J	Hillsboro
44	407.6	Mcminnville SD 040	Mcminnville
45	405.5	Winston-Dillard SD 116	Winston
46	404.6	Lebanon Community SD 009	Lebanon
47	401.3	Gladstone SD 115	Gladstone
48	394.5	Siuslaw SD 97J	Florence
49	391.4	Scappoose SD 01J	Scappoose
50	389.4	Canby SD 086	Canby
51	385.4	South Umpqua SD 019	Myrtle Creek
52	384.9	Jefferson County SD 509J	Madras
53	382.8	La Grande SD 001	La Grande
53	382.8	Sutherlin SD 130	Sutherlin
55	377.1	Roseburg SD 4	Roseburg
56	374.1	Reynolds SD 007	Fairview
57	369.8	Brookings-Harbor SD 17	Brookings
58	369.7	Central SD 13J	Independence
59	359.6	Pendleton SD 016	Pendleton
60	359.5	Redmond SD 02J	Redmond
61	358.8	Hermiston SD 008	Hermiston
62	358.1	Milton-Freewater SD 007	Milton-Freewater
63	355.9	Dallas SD 2	Dallas
64	354.9	Gresham-Barlow SD 10J	Gresham
65	353.0	North Marion SD 015	Aurora
66	352.3	Sweet Home SD 055	Sweet Home
67	346.7	Ashland SD 005	Ashland
68	342.2	Astoria SD 001	Astoria
68	342.2	The Dalles SD 012	The Dalles
70	341.4	Seaside SD 010	Seaside
71	339.6	Forest Grove SD 015	Forest Grove
72	335.0	Corvallis SD 509J	Corvallis
73	330.9	Baker SD 05J	Baker City
74	312.4	Saint Helens SD 502	Saint Helens
75	306.5	Klamath Falls City Schools	Klamath Falls
76	288.2	Junction City SD 069	Junction City
77	199.6	Ontario SD 008	Ontario
78	n/a	Portland Area Office	Portland

Current Spending per Student in FY2001

Rank	Dollars	District Name	City
1	8,533	Portland SD 1J	Portland
2	8,393	Jefferson County SD 509J	Madras
3	8,381	Klamath Falls City Schools	Klamath Falls
4	8,085	Woodburn SD 103	Woodburn
5	7,685	Hood River County SD 1	Hood River
6	7,484	Astoria SD 001	Astoria
7	7,474	Fern Ridge SD 28J	Elmira
8	7,380	Coos Bay SD 009	Coos Bay
9	7,307	Molalla River SD 035	Molalla
10	7,275	Ashland SD 005	Ashland
11	7,265	Tillamook SD 9	Tillamook
12	7,263	Crook County SD	Prineville
13	7,253	North Clackamas SD 012	Milwaukie
14	7,203	Eugene SD 04J	Eugene
15	7,182	North Marion SD 015	Aurora
16	7,171	North Bend SD 013	North Bend
17	7,163	Three Rivers SD	Murphy
18	7,134	Corvallis SD 509J	Corvallis
19	7,117	Morrow SD 001	Lexington
20	7,108	Hermiston SD 008	Hermiston
21	7,099	Lake Oswego SD 07J	Lake Oswego
22	7,098	Ontario SD 008	Ontario
23	7,080	Baker SD 05J	Baker City
24	7,079	Siuslaw SD 97J	Florence
25	7,069	Reynolds SD 007	Fairview
26	7,055	Central SD 13J	Independence
27	7,032	Winston-Dillard SD 116	Winston
28	6,997	Silver Falls SD 4J	Silverton
29	6,990	Forest Grove SD 015	Forest Grove
30	6,985	South Lane SD 45J	Cottage Grove
31	6,980	Sweet Home SD 055	Sweet Home
32	6,955	Springfield SD 019	Springfield
33	6,948	The Dalles SD 012	The Dalles
34	6,917	Klamath County SD	Klamath Falls
35	6,908	Lincoln County SD	Newport
36	6,887	Cascade SD 005	Turner
37	6,845	Parkrose SD 003	Portland
38	6,824	Tigard-Tualatin SD 23J	Tigard
39	6,823	Bethel SD 052	Eugene
40	6,814	Eagle Point SD 009	Eagle Point
41	6,810	Hillsboro SD 01J	Hillsboro
42	6,799	David Douglas SD 40	Portland
43	6,792	Seaside SD 010	Seaside
44	6,773	La Grande SD 001	La Grande
45	6,772	Brookings-Harbor SD 17	Brookings
46	6,760	Oregon City SD 062	Oregon City

47	6,754	Estacada SD 108	Estacada
48	6,737	Centennial SD 28J	Portland
49	6,729	Phoenix-Talent SD 004	Phoenix
50	6,718	Scappoose SD 01J	Scappoose
51	6,717	Junction City SD 069	Junction City
52	6,691	West Linn SD 03J	West Linn
53	6,675	Gresham-Barlow SD 10J	Gresham
54	6,674	Roseburg SD 4	Roseburg
55	6,657	Greater Albany SD 8J	Albany
56	6,611	Salem-Keizer SD 24J	Salem
57	6,607	Saint Helens SD 502	Saint Helens
58	6,603	Bend Admin SD 1	Bend
59	6,539	South Umpqua SD 019	Myrtle Creek
60	6,516	Canby SD 086	Canby
61	6,507	Pendleton SD 016	Pendleton
62	6,501	North Santiam SD 29J	Stayton
63	6,486	Gladstone SD 115	Gladstone
64	6,459	Newberg SD 29J	Newberg
65	6,455	Grants Pass SD 007	Grants Pass
66	6,427	Oregon Trail SD 046	Sandy
67	6,409	Sutherlin SD 130	Sutherlin
68	6,402	Milton-Freewater SD 007	Milton-Freewater
69	6,334	Dallas SD 2	Dallas
70	6,328	Philomath SD 17J	Philomath
71	6,323	Redmond SD 02J	Redmond
72	6,288	Lebanon Community SD 009	Lebanon
73	6,275	Medford SD 549	Medford
74	6,238	Beaverton SD 48J	Beaverton
75	6,233	Sherwood SD 88J	Sherwood
76	6,203	Central Point SD 006	Central Point
77	6,039	Mcminnville SD 040	Mcminnville
78	n/a	Portland Area Office	Portland

Number of Diploma Recipients

Rank	Number	District Name	City
1	2,592	Portland SD 1J	Portland
2	1,957	Beaverton SD 48J	Beaverton
3	1,810	Salem-Keizer SD 24J	Salem
4	1,378	Eugene SD 04J	Eugene
5	888	Hillsboro SD 01J	Hillsboro
6	805	Bend Admin SD 1	Bend
7	789	North Clackamas SD 012	Milwaukie
8	743	Tigard-Tualatin SD 23J	Tigard
9	721	Gresham-Barlow SD 10J	Gresham
10	660	Medford SD 549	Medford
11	586	Springfield SD 019	Springfield
12	491	Corvallis SD 509J	Corvallis
13	489	Lake Oswego SD 07J	Lake Oswego
14	476	West Linn SD 03J	West Linn
15	417	Greater Albany SD 8J	Albany
16	406	Lincoln County SD	Newport
17	399	Roseburg SD 4	Roseburg
18	360	David Douglas SD 40	Portland
19	358	Reynolds SD 007	Fairview
19	358	Three Rivers SD	Murphy
21	352	Canby SD 086	Canby
22	344	Oregon City SD 062	Oregon City
23	326	Centennial SD 28J	Portland
24	318	Newberg SD 29J	Newberg
25	314	Mcminnville SD 040	Mcminnville
26	306	Klamath Falls City Schools	Klamath Falls
27	304	Redmond SD 02J	Redmond
28	297	Oregon Trail SD 046	Sandy
29	287	Grants Pass SD 007	Grants Pass
30	273	Central Point SD 006	Central Point
31	260	Forest Grove SD 015	Forest Grove
32	255	Ashland SD 005	Ashland
33	241	Eagle Point SD 009	Eagle Point
34	239	Coos Bay SD 009	Coos Bay
35	236	Lebanon Community SD 009	Lebanon
36	231	Hood River County SD 1	Hood River
37	224	Bethel SD 052	Eugene
38	223	Klamath County SD	Klamath Falls
39	214	Silver Falls SD 4J	Silverton
40	207	Woodburn SD 103	Woodburn
41	202	Dallas SD 2	Dallas
42	190	Parkrose SD 003	Portland
43	183	Hermiston SD 008	Hermiston
44	179	Crook County SD	Prineville
45	178	Gladstone SD 115	Gladstone
46	176	Saint Helens SD 502	Saint Helens
47	173	Pendleton SD 016	Pendleton
48	166	North Bend SD 013	North Bend
49	163	South Lane SD 45J	Cottage Grove
50	162	Tillamook SD 9	Tillamook
51	152	La Grande SD 001	La Grande
51	152	Sweet Home SD 055	Sweet Home
53	149	Estacada SD 108	Estacada
54	146	Astoria SD 001	Astoria
54	146	Junction City SD 069	Junction City
56	143	Central SD 13J	Independence
57	142	Scappoose SD 01J	Scappoose
57	142	The Dalles SD 012	The Dalles
59	137	Baker SD 05J	Baker City
59	137	Sherwood SD 88J	Sherwood
61	135	Philomath SD 17J	Philomath
62	130	North Santiam SD 29J	Stayton
63	127	Jefferson County SD 509J	Madras
63	127	Phoenix-Talent SD 004	Phoenix
65	123	Ontario SD 008	Ontario
66	121	Brookings-Harbor SD 17	Brookings
67	119	Morrow SD 001	Lexington
68	118	Cascade SD 005	Turner
69	116	South Umpqua SD 019	Myrtle Creek
70	113	North Marion SD 015	Aurora
71	112	Fern Ridge SD 28J	Elmira
72	111	Molalla River SD 035	Molalla
73	91	Milton-Freewater SD 007	Milton-Freewater
74	88	Seaside SD 010	Seaside
75	83	Siuslaw SD 97J	Florence
76	81	Winston-Dillard SD 116	Winston
77	68	Sutherlin SD 130	Sutherlin
78	n/a	Portland Area Office	Portland

High School Drop-out Rate

Rank	Percent	District Name	City
1	11.9	Portland SD 1J	Portland
2	11.0	Phoenix-Talent SD 004	Phoenix
3	10.2	Dallas SD 2	Dallas
4	9.6	Woodburn SD 103	Woodburn
5	8.5	Centennial SD 28J	Portland
6	8.3	Lincoln County SD	Newport
7	8.2	Medford SD 549	Medford
7	8.2	Winston-Dillard SD 116	Winston
9	7.8	South Umpqua SD 019	Myrtle Creek
10	7.5	Milton-Freewater SD 007	Milton-Freewater
10	7.5	Salem-Keizer SD 24J	Salem
12	7.3	Eagle Point SD 009	Eagle Point
13	6.8	Molalla River SD 035	Molalla
13	6.8	The Dalles SD 012	The Dalles
15	6.6	Mcminnville SD 040	Mcminnville
15	6.6	North Santiam SD 29J	Stayton
17	6.5	Newberg SD 29J	Newberg
18	6.4	Silver Falls SD 4J	Silverton
18	6.4	Sweet Home SD 055	Sweet Home
20	6.3	Greater Albany SD 8J	Albany
20	6.3	Roseburg SD 4	Roseburg
22	6.2	Bethel SD 052	Eugene
22	6.2	Brookings-Harbor SD 17	Brookings
22	6.2	Lebanon Community SD 009	Lebanon
25	6.0	Grants Pass SD 007	Grants Pass
26	5.9	Central Point SD 006	Central Point
26	5.9	Forest Grove SD 015	Forest Grove
28	5.7	Central SD 13J	Independence
29	5.6	Beaverton SD 48J	Beaverton
29	5.6	Jefferson County SD 509J	Madras
29	5.6	Parkrose SD 003	Portland
29	5.6	Pendleton SD 016	Pendleton
29	5.6	Tillamook SD 9	Tillamook
34	5.4	Cascade SD 005	Turner
35	5.1	La Grande SD 001	La Grande
36	5.0	Bend Admin SD 1	Bend
36	5.0	Springfield SD 019	Springfield
38	4.9	Siuslaw SD 97J	Florence
38	4.9	South Lane SD 45J	Cottage Grove
40	4.7	Three Rivers SD	Murphy
41	4.6	Reynolds SD 007	Fairview
42	4.5	Gresham-Barlow SD 10J	Gresham
42	4.5	Seaside SD 010	Seaside
44	4.4	Coos Bay SD 009	Coos Bay
44	4.4	Hermiston SD 008	Hermiston
44	4.4	Klamath Falls City Schools	Klamath Falls
44	4.4	North Clackamas SD 012	Milwaukie
44	4.4	Saint Helens SD 502	Saint Helens
49	4.2	Fern Ridge SD 28J	Elmira
50	4.0	Estacada SD 108	Estacada
50	4.0	Sherwood SD 88J	Sherwood
52	3.9	David Douglas SD 40	Portland
53	3.8	Tigard-Tualatin SD 23J	Tigard
54	3.7	Ontario SD 008	Ontario
54	3.7	Sutherlin SD 130	Sutherlin
56	3.5	Philomath SD 17J	Philomath
57	3.4	Redmond SD 02J	Redmond
58	3.2	Hillsboro SD 01J	Hillsboro
59	3.1	Ashland SD 005	Ashland
60	3.0	Eugene SD 04J	Eugene
61	2.9	Crook County SD	Prineville
61	2.9	North Bend SD 013	North Bend
63	2.8	Morrow SD 001	Lexington
64	2.7	Astoria SD 001	Astoria
65	2.6	Canby SD 086	Canby
66	2.5	Klamath County SD	Klamath Falls
67	2.4	Lake Oswego SD 07J	Lake Oswego
67	2.4	Scappoose SD 01J	Scappoose
69	2.3	West Linn SD 03J	West Linn
70	2.2	Baker SD 05J	Baker City
70	2.2	Corvallis SD 509J	Corvallis
70	2.2	Oregon Trail SD 046	Sandy
73	2.1	Hood River County SD 1	Hood River
74	1.5	Gladstone SD 115	Gladstone
75	1.4	Junction City SD 069	Junction City
76	1.0	North Marion SD 015	Aurora
77	0.9	Oregon City SD 062	Oregon City
78	n/a	Portland Area Office	Portland

Pennsylvania

Pennsylvania Public School Educational Profile

Category	Value	Category	Value
Schools *(2002-2003)*	3,254	**Diploma Recipients** *(2002-2003)*	114,943
Instructional Level		White, Non-Hispanic	97,397
Primary	1,921	Black, Non-Hispanic	11,655
Middle	569	Asian/Pacific Islander	2,696
High	612	American Indian/Alaskan Native	102
Other Level	152	Hispanic	3,093
Curriculum		**High School Drop-out Rate** (%) *(2000-2001)*	3.6
Regular	3,148	White, Non-Hispanic	2.7
Special Education	12	Black, Non-Hispanic	7.4
Vocational	81	Asian/Pacific Islander	2.9
Alternative	13	American Indian/Alaskan Native	5.7
Type		Hispanic	8.9
Magnet	14	**Staff** *(2002-2003)*	231,275.0
Charter	91	Teachers	118,261.0
Title I Eligible	2,179	Average Salary ($)	51,425
School-wide Title I	547	Librarians/Media Specialists	2,226.7
Students *(2002-2003)*	1,816,747	Guidance Counselors	4,292.4
Gender (%)		**Ratios** *(2002-2003)*	
Male	n/a	Student/Teacher Ratio	15.4 to 1
Female	n/a	Student/Librarian Ratio	815.9 to 1
Race/Ethnicity (%)		Student/Counselor Ratio	423.2 to 1
White, Non-Hispanic	77.1	**Current Spending** *($ per student in FY 2001)*	8,537
Black, Non-Hispanic	15.5	Instruction	5,318
Asian/Pacific Islander	2.2	Support Services	2,894
American Indian/Alaskan Native	0.1	**College Entrance Exam Scores** *(2003)*	
Hispanic	5.2	Scholastic Aptitude Test (SAT)	
Classification (%)		Participation Rate (%)	73
Individual Education Program (IEP)	13.4	Mean SAT I Verbal Score	500
Migrant	0.5	Mean SAT I Math Score	502
English Language Learner (ELL)	0.0	American College Testing Program (ACT)	
Eligible for Free Lunch Program	22.9	Participation Rate (%)	8
Eligible for Reduced-Price Lunch Program	6.2	Average Composite Score	21.5

Note: *For an explanation of data, please refer to the User's Guide in the front of the book; n/a indicates data not available*

Pennsylvania NAEP 2003 Test Scores

Reading			Mathematics		
Grade/Category	**Value**	**Rank**	**Grade/Category**	**Value**	**Rank**
4th Grade			**4th Grade**		
Average Proficiency	218.7 (1.3)	29/51	Average Proficiency	235.9 (1.1)	22/51
Proficiency by Gender/Race/Ethnicity			Proficiency by Gender/Race/Ethnicity		
Male	215.4 (1.6)	27/51	Male	237.9 (1.2)	21/51
Female	222.1 (1.4)	31/51	Female	234.0 (1.3)	27/51
White, Non-Hispanic	227.1 (1.2)	17/51	White, Non-Hispanic	243.1 (0.9)	20/51
Black, Non-Hispanic	191.3 (2.3)	36/42	Black, Non-Hispanic	212.0 (1.6)	31/42
Asian, Non-Hispanic	*195.3 (4.4)*	35/41	Asian, Non-Hispanic	*215.9 (2.9)*	37/43
American Indian, Non-Hispanic	n/a	n/a	American Indian, Non-Hispanic	n/a	n/a
Hispanic	n/a	n/a	Hispanic	n/a	n/a
Proficiency by Class Size			Proficiency by Class Size		
Less than 16 Students	187.0 (7.1)	39/45	Less than 16 Students	*221.3 (5.2)*	29/47
16 to 18 Students	*211.0 (5.6)*	32/48	16 to 18 Students	*229.9 (3.9)*	30/48
19 to 20 Students	*225.5 (3.9)*	7/50	19 to 20 Students	239.8 (2.7)	12/50
21 to 25 Students	226.0 (1.7)	8/51	21 to 25 Students	241.8 (1.3)	10/51
Greater than 25 Students	214.0 (3.1)	36/49	Greater than 25 Students	228.0 (2.8)	39/49
Percent Attaining Achievement Levels			Percent Attaining Achievement Levels		
Below Basic	35.1 (1.5)	25/51	Below Basic	22.5 (1.4)	23/51
Basic or Above	64.9 (1.5)	26/51	Basic or Above	77.5 (1.4)	29/51
Proficient or Above	32.8 (1.5)	18/51	Proficient or Above	35.7 (1.6)	12/51
Advanced or Above	7.1 (0.7)	25/51	Advanced or Above	4.1 (0.5)	17/51
8th Grade			**8th Grade**		
Average Proficiency	264.3 (1.2)	28/51	Average Proficiency	278.5 (1.1)	28/51
Proficiency by Gender/Race/Ethnicity			Proficiency by Gender/Race/Ethnicity		
Male	258.6 (1.4)	28/51	Male	280.3 (1.2)	26/51
Female	270.1 (1.3)	24/51	Female	276.8 (1.3)	28/51
White, Non-Hispanic	268.4 (1.3)	31/50	White, Non-Hispanic	284.9 (1.2)	29/50
Black, Non-Hispanic	243.3 (2.5)	25/41	Black, Non-Hispanic	247.1 (2.1)	31/41
Asian, Non-Hispanic	257.4 (6.0)	3/37	Asian, Non-Hispanic	253.1 (3.8)	30/37
American Indian, Non-Hispanic	n/a	n/a	American Indian, Non-Hispanic	n/a	n/a
Hispanic	n/a	n/a	Hispanic	n/a	n/a
Proficiency by Parents Highest Level of Ed.			Proficiency by Parents Highest Level of Ed.		
Did Not Finish High School	247.0 (4.2)	23/50	Did Not Finish High School	251.7 (3.2)	44/50
Graduated High School	258.9 (1.7)	14/50	Graduated High School	269.3 (1.7)	26/50
Some Education After High School	265.3 (1.8)	32/50	Some Education After High School	280.0 (1.8)	29/50
Graduated College	272.7 (1.4)	27/50	Graduated College	289.4 (1.3)	25/50
Percent Attaining Achievement Levels			Percent Attaining Achievement Levels		
Below Basic	24.0 (1.4)	26/51	Below Basic	31.3 (1.5)	24/51
Basic or Above	76.0 (1.4)	26/51	Basic or Above	68.7 (1.5)	28/51
Proficient or Above	32.1 (1.8)	29/51	Proficient or Above	29.9 (1.3)	25/51
Advanced or Above	2.1 (0.4)	33/51	Advanced or Above	5.1 (0.5)	22/51

Note: *For an explanation of data, please refer to the User's Guide in the front of the book; values in italics indicate that the nature of the sample does not allow accurate determination of the variability of the statistic; n/a indicates data not available*

Adams County

Bermudian Springs SD
PO Box 501 • York Springs, PA 17372-0501
(717) 528-4113 • http://www.bermudian.k12.pa.us
Grade Span: KG-12; **Agency Type:** 1
Schools: 3
1 Primary; 1 Middle; 1 High; 0 Other Level
3 Regular; 0 Special Education; 0 Vocational; 0 Alternative
0 Magnet; 0 Charter; 3 Title I Eligible; 0 School-wide Title I
Students: 2,161 (n/a% male; n/a% female)
Individual Education Program: 169 (7.8%);
English Language Learner: n/a; Migrant: 99 (4.6%)
Eligible for Free Lunch Program: 212 (9.8%)
Eligible for Reduced-Price Lunch Program: 182 (8.4%)
Teachers: 126.9 (17.0 to 1)
Librarians/Media Specialists: 3.0 (720.3 to 1)
Guidance Counselors: 4.0 (540.3 to 1)
Current Spending: ($ per student per year):
Total: $5,845; Instruction: $3,623; Support Services: $1,955
Enrollment, Drop-out Rates and Diploma Recipients by Race/Ethnicity

Category	Total	White	Black	Asian	AIAN	Hisp.
Enrollment (%)	100.0	92.5	0.4	0.9	0.0	6.2
Drop-out Rate (%)	1.9	1.6	0.0	0.0	0.0	25.0
H.S. Diplomas (#)	140	137	1	0	1	1

Conewago Valley SD
130 Berlin Rd • New Oxford, PA 17350-1206
(717) 624-2157 • http://www.conewago.k12.pa.us
Grade Span: KG-12; **Agency Type:** 1
Schools: 4
2 Primary; 1 Middle; 1 High; 0 Other Level
4 Regular; 0 Special Education; 0 Vocational; 0 Alternative
0 Magnet; 0 Charter; 3 Title I Eligible; 0 School-wide Title I
Students: 3,682 (n/a% male; n/a% female)
Individual Education Program: 482 (13.1%);
English Language Learner: n/a; Migrant: 137 (3.7%)
Eligible for Free Lunch Program: 531 (14.4%)
Eligible for Reduced-Price Lunch Program: 321 (8.7%)
Teachers: 194.9 (18.9 to 1)
Librarians/Media Specialists: 4.0 (920.5 to 1)
Guidance Counselors: 6.0 (613.7 to 1)
Current Spending: ($ per student per year):
Total: $5,347; Instruction: $3,374; Support Services: $1,679
Enrollment, Drop-out Rates and Diploma Recipients by Race/Ethnicity

Category	Total	White	Black	Asian	AIAN	Hisp.
Enrollment (%)	100.0	90.4	1.4	1.1	0.0	7.1
Drop-out Rate (%)	1.2	1.3	0.0	0.0	n/a	0.0
H.S. Diplomas (#)	217	195	1	2	0	19

Gettysburg Area SD
900 Biglerville Rd • Gettysburg, PA 17325-8007
(717) 334-6254 • http://www.gettysburg.k12.pa.us
Grade Span: KG-12; **Agency Type:** 1
Schools: 7
4 Primary; 2 Middle; 1 High; 0 Other Level
7 Regular; 0 Special Education; 0 Vocational; 0 Alternative
0 Magnet; 0 Charter; 5 Title I Eligible; 0 School-wide Title I
Students: 3,501 (n/a% male; n/a% female)
Individual Education Program: 510 (14.6%);
English Language Learner: n/a; Migrant: 169 (4.8%)
Eligible for Free Lunch Program: 668 (19.1%)
Eligible for Reduced-Price Lunch Program: 245 (7.0%)
Teachers: 229.8 (15.2 to 1)
Librarians/Media Specialists: 5.0 (700.2 to 1)
Guidance Counselors: 11.0 (318.3 to 1)
Current Spending: ($ per student per year):
Total: $7,453; Instruction: $4,429; Support Services: $2,735
Enrollment, Drop-out Rates and Diploma Recipients by Race/Ethnicity

Category	Total	White	Black	Asian	AIAN	Hisp.
Enrollment (%)	100.0	83.8	6.4	1.2	0.2	8.3
Drop-out Rate (%)	3.1	2.9	3.8	0.0	0.0	7.1
H.S. Diplomas (#)	256	225	14	8	0	9

Littlestown Area SD
Maple Ave • Littlestown, PA 17340-1343
(717) 359-4146 • http://www.lasd.k12.pa.us
Grade Span: KG-12; **Agency Type:** 1
Schools: 3
1 Primary; 1 Middle; 1 High; 0 Other Level
3 Regular; 0 Special Education; 0 Vocational; 0 Alternative
0 Magnet; 0 Charter; 3 Title I Eligible; 0 School-wide Title I
Students: 2,338 (n/a% male; n/a% female)
Individual Education Program: 283 (12.1%);
English Language Learner: n/a; Migrant: 3 (0.1%)
Eligible for Free Lunch Program: 281 (12.0%)
Eligible for Reduced-Price Lunch Program: 154 (6.6%)
Teachers: 133.0 (17.6 to 1)
Librarians/Media Specialists: 3.0 (779.3 to 1)
Guidance Counselors: 4.0 (584.5 to 1)
Current Spending: ($ per student per year):
Total: $5,531; Instruction: $3,633; Support Services: $1,630
Enrollment, Drop-out Rates and Diploma Recipients by Race/Ethnicity

Category	Total	White	Black	Asian	AIAN	Hisp.
Enrollment (%)	100.0	96.4	1.4	0.8	0.3	1.1
Drop-out Rate (%)	4.9	4.6	33.3	0.0	n/a	22.2
H.S. Diplomas (#)	146	140	0	5	0	1

Upper Adams SD
161 N Main Street • Biglerville, PA 17307-0847
Mailing Address: PO Box 847 • Biglerville, PA 17307-0847
(717) 677-7191 • http://www.uasd.k12.pa.us
Grade Span: KG-12; **Agency Type:** 1
Schools: 5
3 Primary; 1 Middle; 1 High; 0 Other Level
5 Regular; 0 Special Education; 0 Vocational; 0 Alternative
0 Magnet; 0 Charter; 4 Title I Eligible; 0 School-wide Title I
Students: 1,735 (n/a% male; n/a% female)
Individual Education Program: 287 (16.5%);
English Language Learner: n/a; Migrant: 206 (11.9%)
Eligible for Free Lunch Program: 374 (21.6%)
Eligible for Reduced-Price Lunch Program: 184 (10.6%)
Teachers: 108.0 (16.1 to 1)
Librarians/Media Specialists: 2.0 (867.5 to 1)
Guidance Counselors: 4.0 (433.8 to 1)
Current Spending: ($ per student per year):
Total: $6,229; Instruction: $3,672; Support Services: $2,219
Enrollment, Drop-out Rates and Diploma Recipients by Race/Ethnicity

Category	Total	White	Black	Asian	AIAN	Hisp.
Enrollment (%)	100.0	83.5	1.2	0.1	0.1	15.2
Drop-out Rate (%)	5.8	5.2	0.0	n/a	0.0	12.0
H.S. Diplomas (#)	114	107	2	0	0	5

Allegheny County

Baldwin-Whitehall SD
4900 Curry Rd • Pittsburgh, PA 15236-1817
(412) 885-7810 • http://www.baldwin.k12.pa.us
Grade Span: KG-12; **Agency Type:** 1
Schools: 5
3 Primary; 1 Middle; 1 High; 0 Other Level
5 Regular; 0 Special Education; 0 Vocational; 0 Alternative
0 Magnet; 0 Charter; 3 Title I Eligible; 0 School-wide Title I
Students: 4,741 (n/a% male; n/a% female)
Individual Education Program: 547 (11.5%);
English Language Learner: n/a; Migrant: 0 (0.0%)
Eligible for Free Lunch Program: 591 (12.5%)
Eligible for Reduced-Price Lunch Program: 267 (5.6%)
Teachers: 280.0 (16.9 to 1)
Librarians/Media Specialists: 5.5 (862.0 to 1)
Guidance Counselors: 7.0 (677.3 to 1)
Current Spending: ($ per student per year):
Total: $7,941; Instruction: $4,658; Support Services: $2,990
Enrollment, Drop-out Rates and Diploma Recipients by Race/Ethnicity

Category	Total	White	Black	Asian	AIAN	Hisp.
Enrollment (%)	100.0	90.9	7.5	0.9	0.1	0.5
Drop-out Rate (%)	1.5	1.5	1.8	0.0	0.0	0.0
H.S. Diplomas (#)	395	385	8	2	0	0

Bethel Park SD
301 Church Rd • Bethel Park, PA 15102-1607
(412) 833-5000 • http://www.bpsd.k12.pa.us
Grade Span: KG-12; **Agency Type:** 1
Schools: 8
5 Primary; 2 Middle; 1 High; 0 Other Level
8 Regular; 0 Special Education; 0 Vocational; 0 Alternative
0 Magnet; 0 Charter; 4 Title I Eligible; 0 School-wide Title I
Students: 5,277 (n/a% male; n/a% female)
Individual Education Program: 594 (11.3%);
English Language Learner: n/a; Migrant: 0 (0.0%)
Eligible for Free Lunch Program: 182 (3.4%)
Eligible for Reduced-Price Lunch Program: 139 (2.6%)
Teachers: 351.0 (15.0 to 1)
Librarians/Media Specialists: 9.0 (586.3 to 1)
Guidance Counselors: 10.0 (527.7 to 1)
Current Spending: ($ per student per year):
Total: $7,908; Instruction: $5,267; Support Services: $2,427

Enrollment, Drop-out Rates and Diploma Recipients by Race/Ethnicity

Category	Total	White	Black	Asian	AIAN	Hisp.
Enrollment (%)	100.0	97.2	1.4	1.0	0.1	0.3
Drop-out Rate (%)	0.7	0.6	0.0	3.4	n/a	7.7
H.S. Diplomas (#)	402	387	4	8	0	3

Carlynton SD

435 Kings Hwy • Carnegie, PA 15106-1043
(412) 429-8400 • http://www.carlynton.k12.pa.us
Grade Span: KG-12; **Agency Type:** 1
Schools: 3
2 Primary; 0 Middle; 1 High; 0 Other Level
3 Regular; 0 Special Education; 0 Vocational; 0 Alternative
0 Magnet; 0 Charter; 2 Title I Eligible; 0 School-wide Title I
Students: 1,650 (n/a% male; n/a% female)
Individual Education Program: 201 (12.2%);
English Language Learner: n/a; Migrant: 0 (0.0%)
Eligible for Free Lunch Program: 256 (15.5%)
Eligible for Reduced-Price Lunch Program: 75 (4.5%)
Teachers: 101.0 (16.3 to 1)
Librarians/Media Specialists: 2.0 (825.0 to 1)
Guidance Counselors: 2.0 (825.0 to 1)
Current Spending: ($ per student per year):
Total: $9,098; Instruction: $5,897; Support Services: $2,950

Enrollment, Drop-out Rates and Diploma Recipients by Race/Ethnicity

Category	Total	White	Black	Asian	AIAN	Hisp.
Enrollment (%)	100.0	88.2	9.9	0.9	0.3	0.7
Drop-out Rate (%)	1.8	1.6	5.1	0.0	0.0	0.0
H.S. Diplomas (#)	120	105	12	3	0	0

Chartiers Valley SD

2030 Swallow Hill Rd • Pittsburgh, PA 15220-1699
(412) 429-2201 • http://www.chartiersvalley.k12.pa.us
Grade Span: KG-12; **Agency Type:** 1
Schools: 4
2 Primary; 1 Middle; 1 High; 0 Other Level
4 Regular; 0 Special Education; 0 Vocational; 0 Alternative
0 Magnet; 0 Charter; 4 Title I Eligible; 0 School-wide Title I
Students: 3,439 (n/a% male; n/a% female)
Individual Education Program: 352 (10.2%);
English Language Learner: n/a; Migrant: 0 (0.0%)
Eligible for Free Lunch Program: 443 (12.9%)
Eligible for Reduced-Price Lunch Program: 175 (5.1%)
Teachers: 226.5 (15.2 to 1)
Librarians/Media Specialists: 4.0 (859.8 to 1)
Guidance Counselors: 8.0 (429.9 to 1)
Current Spending: ($ per student per year):
Total: $8,214; Instruction: $4,772; Support Services: $3,150

Enrollment, Drop-out Rates and Diploma Recipients by Race/Ethnicity

Category	Total	White	Black	Asian	AIAN	Hisp.
Enrollment (%)	100.0	92.6	3.4	3.5	0.0	0.5
Drop-out Rate (%)	2.0	2.0	2.6	0.0	n/a	0.0
H.S. Diplomas (#)	234	221	6	6	0	1

Deer Lakes SD

PO Box 10 • Russellton, PA 15076-0010
(724) 265-5300 • http://www.dlsd.k12.pa.us
Grade Span: KG-12; **Agency Type:** 1
Schools: 4
2 Primary; 1 Middle; 1 High; 0 Other Level
4 Regular; 0 Special Education; 0 Vocational; 0 Alternative
0 Magnet; 0 Charter; 3 Title I Eligible; 0 School-wide Title I
Students: 2,103 (n/a% male; n/a% female)
Individual Education Program: 294 (14.0%);
English Language Learner: n/a; Migrant: 0 (0.0%)
Eligible for Free Lunch Program: 218 (10.4%)
Eligible for Reduced-Price Lunch Program: 129 (6.1%)
Teachers: 135.5 (15.5 to 1)
Librarians/Media Specialists: 4.0 (525.8 to 1)
Guidance Counselors: 2.0 (1,051.5 to 1)
Current Spending: ($ per student per year):
Total: $8,010; Instruction: $4,856; Support Services: $2,852

Enrollment, Drop-out Rates and Diploma Recipients by Race/Ethnicity

Category	Total	White	Black	Asian	AIAN	Hisp.
Enrollment (%)	100.0	98.6	0.6	0.1	0.1	0.5
Drop-out Rate (%)	1.3	1.3	0.0	0.0	n/a	0.0
H.S. Diplomas (#)	170	170	0	0	0	0

East Allegheny SD

1150 Jacks Run Rd • North Versailles, PA 15137-2797
(412) 824-8012
Grade Span: KG-12; **Agency Type:** 1
Schools: 3
2 Primary; 0 Middle; 1 High; 0 Other Level
3 Regular; 0 Special Education; 0 Vocational; 0 Alternative
0 Magnet; 0 Charter; 2 Title I Eligible; 0 School-wide Title I
Students: 2,002 (n/a% male; n/a% female)
Individual Education Program: 302 (15.1%);
English Language Learner: n/a; Migrant: 0 (0.0%)
Eligible for Free Lunch Program: 593 (29.6%)
Eligible for Reduced-Price Lunch Program: 156 (7.8%)
Teachers: 117.3 (17.1 to 1)
Librarians/Media Specialists: 2.5 (800.8 to 1)
Guidance Counselors: 4.0 (500.5 to 1)
Current Spending: ($ per student per year):
Total: $7,673; Instruction: $4,407; Support Services: $2,886

Enrollment, Drop-out Rates and Diploma Recipients by Race/Ethnicity

Category	Total	White	Black	Asian	AIAN	Hisp.
Enrollment (%)	100.0	83.6	15.3	0.6	0.1	0.4
Drop-out Rate (%)	4.3	4.3	4.4	0.0	0.0	0.0
H.S. Diplomas (#)	119	105	13	1	0	0

Elizabeth Forward SD

401 Rock Run Rd • Elizabeth, PA 15037-2416
(412) 896-2300 • http://www.efsd.net
Grade Span: KG-12; **Agency Type:** 1
Schools: 7
5 Primary; 1 Middle; 1 High; 0 Other Level
7 Regular; 0 Special Education; 0 Vocational; 0 Alternative
0 Magnet; 0 Charter; 4 Title I Eligible; 0 School-wide Title I
Students: 2,966 (n/a% male; n/a% female)
Individual Education Program: 396 (13.4%);
English Language Learner: n/a; Migrant: 0 (0.0%)
Eligible for Free Lunch Program: 373 (12.6%)
Eligible for Reduced-Price Lunch Program: 213 (7.2%)
Teachers: 185.0 (16.0 to 1)
Librarians/Media Specialists: 3.0 (988.7 to 1)
Guidance Counselors: 3.0 (988.7 to 1)
Current Spending: ($ per student per year):
Total: $7,367; Instruction: $4,750; Support Services: $2,342

Enrollment, Drop-out Rates and Diploma Recipients by Race/Ethnicity

Category	Total	White	Black	Asian	AIAN	Hisp.
Enrollment (%)	100.0	97.3	2.0	0.4	0.1	0.3
Drop-out Rate (%)	2.4	2.3	6.7	0.0	0.0	0.0
H.S. Diplomas (#)	197	191	5	1	0	0

Fox Chapel Area SD

611 Field Club Rd • Pittsburgh, PA 15238-2406
(412) 963-9600 • http://www.fcasd.edu
Grade Span: KG-12; **Agency Type:** 1
Schools: 6
4 Primary; 1 Middle; 1 High; 0 Other Level
6 Regular; 0 Special Education; 0 Vocational; 0 Alternative
0 Magnet; 0 Charter; 3 Title I Eligible; 0 School-wide Title I
Students: 4,598 (n/a% male; n/a% female)
Individual Education Program: 525 (11.4%);
English Language Learner: n/a; Migrant: 0 (0.0%)
Eligible for Free Lunch Program: 310 (6.7%)
Eligible for Reduced-Price Lunch Program: 129 (2.8%)
Teachers: 370.5 (12.4 to 1)
Librarians/Media Specialists: 6.0 (766.3 to 1)
Guidance Counselors: 12.0 (383.2 to 1)
Current Spending: ($ per student per year):
Total: $9,631; Instruction: $6,236; Support Services: $3,194

Enrollment, Drop-out Rates and Diploma Recipients by Race/Ethnicity

Category	Total	White	Black	Asian	AIAN	Hisp.
Enrollment (%)	100.0	94.2	1.1	3.7	0.1	0.9
Drop-out Rate (%)	0.9	0.9	5.0	0.0	0.0	0.0
H.S. Diplomas (#)	318	298	2	15	0	3

Gateway SD

9000 Gateway Campus Blvd • Monroeville, PA 15146-3378
(412) 372-5300 • http://gator.gasd.k12.pa.us/
Grade Span: KG-12; **Agency Type:** 1
Schools: 8
5 Primary; 2 Middle; 1 High; 0 Other Level
8 Regular; 0 Special Education; 0 Vocational; 0 Alternative
0 Magnet; 0 Charter; 4 Title I Eligible; 0 School-wide Title I
Students: 4,397 (n/a% male; n/a% female)
Individual Education Program: 609 (13.9%);
English Language Learner: n/a; Migrant: 0 (0.0%)
Eligible for Free Lunch Program: 606 (13.8%)
Eligible for Reduced-Price Lunch Program: 316 (7.2%)
Teachers: 304.0 (14.5 to 1)
Librarians/Media Specialists: 5.0 (879.4 to 1)
Guidance Counselors: 11.0 (399.7 to 1)
Current Spending: ($ per student per year):
Total: $10,046; Instruction: $6,409; Support Services: $3,275

Enrollment, Drop-out Rates and Diploma Recipients by Race/Ethnicity

Category	Total	White	Black	Asian	AIAN	Hisp.
Enrollment (%)	100.0	81.4	11.9	5.8	0.1	0.8
Drop-out Rate (%)	1.7	1.9	1.3	0.0	n/a	0.0
H.S. Diplomas (#)	340	282	36	22	0	0

Hampton Township SD

2919 E Hardies Rd • Gibsonia, PA 15044-8423
(724) 449-8888 • http://www.htsd.k12.pa.us
Grade Span: KG-12; **Agency Type:** 1
Schools: 5
3 Primary; 1 Middle; 1 High; 0 Other Level
5 Regular; 0 Special Education; 0 Vocational; 0 Alternative
0 Magnet; 0 Charter; 3 Title I Eligible; 0 School-wide Title I
Students: 3,229 (n/a% male; n/a% female)
Individual Education Program: 331 (10.3%);
English Language Learner: n/a; Migrant: 0 (0.0%)
Eligible for Free Lunch Program: 112 (3.5%)
Eligible for Reduced-Price Lunch Program: 68 (2.1%)
Teachers: 196.9 (16.4 to 1)
Librarians/Media Specialists: 5.0 (645.8 to 1)
Guidance Counselors: 5.0 (645.8 to 1)
Current Spending: ($ per student per year):
Total: $7,651; Instruction: $5,015; Support Services: $2,361
Enrollment, Drop-out Rates and Diploma Recipients by Race/Ethnicity

Category	Total	White	Black	Asian	AIAN	Hisp.
Enrollment (%)	100.0	98.0	0.8	0.9	0.0	0.2
Drop-out Rate (%)	0.8	0.9	0.0	0.0	n/a	0.0
H.S. Diplomas (#)	252	245	1	5	0	1

Highlands SD

PO Box 288 • Natrona Heights, PA 15065-0288
(724) 226-2400
Grade Span: KG-12; **Agency Type:** 1
Schools: 6
4 Primary; 1 Middle; 1 High; 0 Other Level
6 Regular; 0 Special Education; 0 Vocational; 0 Alternative
0 Magnet; 0 Charter; 5 Title I Eligible; 2 School-wide Title I
Students: 2,811 (n/a% male; n/a% female)
Individual Education Program: 457 (16.3%);
English Language Learner: n/a; Migrant: 0 (0.0%)
Eligible for Free Lunch Program: 851 (30.3%)
Eligible for Reduced-Price Lunch Program: 309 (11.0%)
Teachers: 207.0 (13.6 to 1)
Librarians/Media Specialists: 3.0 (937.0 to 1)
Guidance Counselors: 6.0 (468.5 to 1)
Current Spending: ($ per student per year):
Total: $7,674; Instruction: $4,732; Support Services: $2,607
Enrollment, Drop-out Rates and Diploma Recipients by Race/Ethnicity

Category	Total	White	Black	Asian	AIAN	Hisp.
Enrollment (%)	100.0	91.8	6.9	0.6	0.2	0.4
Drop-out Rate (%)	2.7	2.2	15.8	0.0	0.0	0.0
H.S. Diplomas (#)	209	197	8	2	1	1

Keystone Oaks SD

1000 Kelton Ave • Pittsburgh, PA 15216-2421
(412) 571-6000 • http://www.kosd.org
Grade Span: KG-12; **Agency Type:** 1
Schools: 5
3 Primary; 1 Middle; 1 High; 0 Other Level
5 Regular; 0 Special Education; 0 Vocational; 0 Alternative
0 Magnet; 0 Charter; 3 Title I Eligible; 0 School-wide Title I
Students: 2,586 (n/a% male; n/a% female)
Individual Education Program: 297 (11.5%);
English Language Learner: n/a; Migrant: 0 (0.0%)
Eligible for Free Lunch Program: 348 (13.5%)
Eligible for Reduced-Price Lunch Program: 206 (8.0%)
Teachers: 172.7 (15.0 to 1)
Librarians/Media Specialists: 3.0 (862.0 to 1)
Guidance Counselors: 6.0 (431.0 to 1)
Current Spending: ($ per student per year):
Total: $8,589; Instruction: $5,291; Support Services: $2,999
Enrollment, Drop-out Rates and Diploma Recipients by Race/Ethnicity

Category	Total	White	Black	Asian	AIAN	Hisp.
Enrollment (%)	100.0	96.4	1.8	1.2	0.0	0.6
Drop-out Rate (%)	3.4	3.3	0.0	20.0	0.0	0.0
H.S. Diplomas (#)	198	190	3	3	1	1

Mckeesport Area SD

2225 5th Ave • Mc Keesport, PA 15132-1145
(412) 664-3610
Grade Span: KG-12; **Agency Type:** 1
Schools: 7
3 Primary; 3 Middle; 1 High; 0 Other Level
7 Regular; 0 Special Education; 0 Vocational; 0 Alternative
0 Magnet; 0 Charter; 7 Title I Eligible; 3 School-wide Title I
Students: 4,862 (n/a% male; n/a% female)
Individual Education Program: 766 (15.8%);
English Language Learner: n/a; Migrant: 0 (0.0%)
Eligible for Free Lunch Program: 2,139 (44.0%)
Eligible for Reduced-Price Lunch Program: 323 (6.6%)
Teachers: 294.6 (16.5 to 1)
Librarians/Media Specialists: 6.0 (810.3 to 1)
Guidance Counselors: 10.0 (486.2 to 1)
Current Spending: ($ per student per year):
Total: $7,647; Instruction: $4,987; Support Services: $2,403
Enrollment, Drop-out Rates and Diploma Recipients by Race/Ethnicity

Category	Total	White	Black	Asian	AIAN	Hisp.
Enrollment (%)	100.0	60.2	38.2	0.2	0.5	0.9
Drop-out Rate (%)	3.1	2.2	5.6	0.0	0.0	0.0
H.S. Diplomas (#)	292	220	69	1	1	1

Montour SD

223 Clever Rd • Mc Kees Rocks, PA 15136-4012
(412) 490-6500
Grade Span: KG-12; **Agency Type:** 1
Schools: 5
3 Primary; 1 Middle; 1 High; 0 Other Level
5 Regular; 0 Special Education; 0 Vocational; 0 Alternative
0 Magnet; 0 Charter; 5 Title I Eligible; 0 School-wide Title I
Students: 3,334 (n/a% male; n/a% female)
Individual Education Program: 367 (11.0%);
English Language Learner: n/a; Migrant: 0 (0.0%)
Eligible for Free Lunch Program: 166 (5.0%)
Eligible for Reduced-Price Lunch Program: 47 (1.4%)
Teachers: 202.5 (16.5 to 1)
Librarians/Media Specialists: 5.0 (666.8 to 1)
Guidance Counselors: 11.0 (303.1 to 1)
Current Spending: ($ per student per year):
Total: $7,932; Instruction: $5,070; Support Services: $2,666
Enrollment, Drop-out Rates and Diploma Recipients by Race/Ethnicity

Category	Total	White	Black	Asian	AIAN	Hisp.
Enrollment (%)	100.0	96.0	2.1	1.0	0.4	0.4
Drop-out Rate (%)	1.7	1.8	0.0	0.0	0.0	0.0
H.S. Diplomas (#)	256	250	3	3	0	0

Moon Area SD

1407 Beers School Rd • Moon Township, PA 15108-2509
(412) 264-9440 • http://www.masd.k12.pa.us
Grade Span: KG-12; **Agency Type:** 1
Schools: 6
4 Primary; 1 Middle; 1 High; 0 Other Level
6 Regular; 0 Special Education; 0 Vocational; 0 Alternative
0 Magnet; 0 Charter; 4 Title I Eligible; 0 School-wide Title I
Students: 3,663 (n/a% male; n/a% female)
Individual Education Program: 511 (14.0%);
English Language Learner: n/a; Migrant: 0 (0.0%)
Eligible for Free Lunch Program: 205 (5.6%)
Eligible for Reduced-Price Lunch Program: 78 (2.1%)
Teachers: 254.0 (14.4 to 1)
Librarians/Media Specialists: 5.0 (732.6 to 1)
Guidance Counselors: 6.0 (610.5 to 1)
Current Spending: ($ per student per year):
Total: $8,751; Instruction: $5,579; Support Services: $2,939
Enrollment, Drop-out Rates and Diploma Recipients by Race/Ethnicity

Category	Total	White	Black	Asian	AIAN	Hisp.
Enrollment (%)	100.0	92.3	5.1	1.9	0.0	0.8
Drop-out Rate (%)	1.4	1.5	0.0	0.0	n/a	0.0
H.S. Diplomas (#)	220	202	7	7	0	4

Mount Lebanon SD

7 Horsman Dr • Pittsburgh, PA 15228-1107
(412) 344-2077 • http://www.mtlebanon.k12.pa.us
Grade Span: KG-12; **Agency Type:** 1
Schools: 10
7 Primary; 2 Middle; 1 High; 0 Other Level
10 Regular; 0 Special Education; 0 Vocational; 0 Alternative
0 Magnet; 0 Charter; 5 Title I Eligible; 0 School-wide Title I
Students: 5,610 (n/a% male; n/a% female)
Individual Education Program: 597 (10.6%);
English Language Learner: n/a; Migrant: 0 (0.0%)
Eligible for Free Lunch Program: 14 (0.2%)
Eligible for Reduced-Price Lunch Program: 24 (0.4%)
Teachers: 373.0 (15.0 to 1)
Librarians/Media Specialists: 10.0 (561.0 to 1)
Guidance Counselors: 12.0 (467.5 to 1)
Current Spending: ($ per student per year):
Total: $8,343; Instruction: $5,407; Support Services: $2,758

Enrollment, Drop-out Rates and Diploma Recipients by Race/Ethnicity

Category	Total	White	Black	Asian	AIAN	Hisp.
Enrollment (%)	100.0	94.3	1.4	3.4	0.1	0.9
Drop-out Rate (%)	0.9	0.8	9.1	0.0	n/a	0.0
H.S. Diplomas (#)	452	426	5	19	0	2

North Allegheny SD

200 Hillvue Ln • Pittsburgh, PA 15237-5344
(412) 366-2100 • http://NAllegheny.k12.pa.us
Grade Span: KG-12; **Agency Type:** 1
Schools: 12
7 Primary; 3 Middle; 1 High; 1 Other Level
12 Regular; 0 Special Education; 0 Vocational; 0 Alternative
0 Magnet; 0 Charter; 0 Title I Eligible; 0 School-wide Title I
Students: 8,212 (n/a% male; n/a% female)
Individual Education Program: 802 (9.8%);
English Language Learner: n/a; Migrant: 0 (0.0%)
Eligible for Free Lunch Program: 128 (1.6%)
Eligible for Reduced-Price Lunch Program: 88 (1.1%)
Teachers: 544.1 (15.1 to 1)
Librarians/Media Specialists: 14.0 (586.6 to 1)
Guidance Counselors: 21.0 (391.0 to 1)
Current Spending: ($ per student per year):
Total: $8,760; Instruction: $5,700; Support Services: $2,850
Enrollment, Drop-out Rates and Diploma Recipients by Race/Ethnicity

Category	Total	White	Black	Asian	AIAN	Hisp.
Enrollment (%)	100.0	93.5	1.2	4.5	0.1	0.6
Drop-out Rate (%)	1.4	1.4	2.7	0.0	0.0	0.0
H.S. Diplomas (#)	685	661	8	15	0	1

North Hills SD

135 6th Ave • Pittsburgh, PA 15229-1291
(412) 318-1000 • http://www.nhsd.k12.pa.us
Grade Span: KG-12; **Agency Type:** 1
Schools: 9
7 Primary; 1 Middle; 1 High; 0 Other Level
9 Regular; 0 Special Education; 0 Vocational; 0 Alternative
0 Magnet; 0 Charter; 2 Title I Eligible; 0 School-wide Title I
Students: 4,902 (n/a% male; n/a% female)
Individual Education Program: 586 (12.0%);
English Language Learner: n/a; Migrant: 0 (0.0%)
Eligible for Free Lunch Program: 325 (6.6%)
Eligible for Reduced-Price Lunch Program: 296 (6.0%)
Teachers: 330.5 (14.8 to 1)
Librarians/Media Specialists: 10.0 (490.2 to 1)
Guidance Counselors: 12.5 (392.2 to 1)
Current Spending: ($ per student per year):
Total: $9,069; Instruction: $5,793; Support Services: $2,987
Enrollment, Drop-out Rates and Diploma Recipients by Race/Ethnicity

Category	Total	White	Black	Asian	AIAN	Hisp.
Enrollment (%)	100.0	96.2	1.8	1.4	0.0	0.5
Drop-out Rate (%)	1.2	1.2	3.1	0.0	0.0	0.0
H.S. Diplomas (#)	385	368	10	2	0	5

Northgate SD

591 Union Ave • Pittsburgh, PA 15202-2958
(412) 734-8001 • http://www.northgate.k12.pa.us
Grade Span: KG-12; **Agency Type:** 1
Schools: 3
2 Primary; 0 Middle; 1 High; 0 Other Level
3 Regular; 0 Special Education; 0 Vocational; 0 Alternative
0 Magnet; 0 Charter; 3 Title I Eligible; 0 School-wide Title I
Students: 1,568 (n/a% male; n/a% female)
Individual Education Program: 173 (11.0%);
English Language Learner: n/a; Migrant: 0 (0.0%)
Eligible for Free Lunch Program: 400 (25.5%)
Eligible for Reduced-Price Lunch Program: 134 (8.5%)
Teachers: 107.5 (14.6 to 1)
Librarians/Media Specialists: 2.0 (784.0 to 1)
Guidance Counselors: 4.0 (392.0 to 1)
Current Spending: ($ per student per year):
Total: $7,341; Instruction: $4,692; Support Services: $2,376
Enrollment, Drop-out Rates and Diploma Recipients by Race/Ethnicity

Category	Total	White	Black	Asian	AIAN	Hisp.
Enrollment (%)	100.0	88.6	10.3	0.8	0.0	0.3
Drop-out Rate (%)	1.5	1.7	0.0	0.0	n/a	0.0
H.S. Diplomas (#)	99	86	12	1	0	0

Penn Hills SD

309 Collins Dr • Pittsburgh, PA 15235-3839
(412) 793-7000 • http://www.phsd.k12.pa.us
Grade Span: KG-12; **Agency Type:** 1
Schools: 8
6 Primary; 1 Middle; 1 High; 0 Other Level
8 Regular; 0 Special Education; 0 Vocational; 0 Alternative
0 Magnet; 0 Charter; 7 Title I Eligible; 0 School-wide Title I
Students: 6,005 (n/a% male; n/a% female)
Individual Education Program: 772 (12.9%);
English Language Learner: n/a; Migrant: 0 (0.0%)
Eligible for Free Lunch Program: 1,555 (25.9%)
Eligible for Reduced-Price Lunch Program: 495 (8.2%)
Teachers: 410.5 (14.6 to 1)
Librarians/Media Specialists: 5.0 (1,201.0 to 1)
Guidance Counselors: 13.0 (461.9 to 1)
Current Spending: ($ per student per year):
Total: $7,902; Instruction: $4,934; Support Services: $2,679
Enrollment, Drop-out Rates and Diploma Recipients by Race/Ethnicity

Category	Total	White	Black	Asian	AIAN	Hisp.
Enrollment (%)	100.0	52.6	46.3	0.6	0.0	0.4
Drop-out Rate (%)	3.1	2.6	4.0	12.5	n/a	0.0
H.S. Diplomas (#)	411	261	149	1	0	0

Pine-Richland SD

702 Warrendale Rd • Gibsonia, PA 15044-9534
(724) 625-7773 • http://www.prsd.k12.pa.us
Grade Span: KG-12; **Agency Type:** 1
Schools: 5
3 Primary; 1 Middle; 1 High; 0 Other Level
5 Regular; 0 Special Education; 0 Vocational; 0 Alternative
0 Magnet; 0 Charter; 1 Title I Eligible; 0 School-wide Title I
Students: 3,733 (n/a% male; n/a% female)
Individual Education Program: 351 (9.4%);
English Language Learner: n/a; Migrant: 0 (0.0%)
Eligible for Free Lunch Program: 93 (2.5%)
Eligible for Reduced-Price Lunch Program: 44 (1.2%)
Teachers: 258.7 (14.4 to 1)
Librarians/Media Specialists: 5.0 (746.6 to 1)
Guidance Counselors: 8.0 (466.6 to 1)
Current Spending: ($ per student per year):
Total: $7,503; Instruction: $4,860; Support Services: $2,433
Enrollment, Drop-out Rates and Diploma Recipients by Race/Ethnicity

Category	Total	White	Black	Asian	AIAN	Hisp.
Enrollment (%)	100.0	97.1	1.0	1.0	0.2	0.6
Drop-out Rate (%)	1.5	1.5	0.0	0.0	n/a	0.0
H.S. Diplomas (#)	261	258	1	2	0	0

Pittsburgh SD

341 S Bellefield Ave • Pittsburgh, PA 15213-3552
(412) 622-3500 • http://www.pps.pgh.pa.us
Grade Span: KG-12; **Agency Type:** 1
Schools: 93
57 Primary; 19 Middle; 12 High; 5 Other Level
90 Regular; 3 Special Education; 0 Vocational; 0 Alternative
0 Magnet; 0 Charter; 83 Title I Eligible; 60 School-wide Title I
Students: 35,146 (n/a% male; n/a% female)
Individual Education Program: 6,083 (17.3%);
English Language Learner: n/a; Migrant: 0 (0.0%)
Eligible for Free Lunch Program: 18,520 (52.7%)
Eligible for Reduced-Price Lunch Program: 2,402 (6.8%)
Teachers: 2,709.7 (13.0 to 1)
Librarians/Media Specialists: 58.7 (598.7 to 1)
Guidance Counselors: 68.0 (516.9 to 1)
Current Spending: ($ per student per year):
Total: $9,240; Instruction: $5,122; Support Services: $3,792
Enrollment, Drop-out Rates and Diploma Recipients by Race/Ethnicity

Category	Total	White	Black	Asian	AIAN	Hisp.
Enrollment (%)	100.0	39.6	58.2	1.5	0.1	0.6
Drop-out Rate (%)	6.7	6.4	7.2	2.4	0.0	4.5
H.S. Diplomas (#)	1,899	1,031	828	26	3	11

Plum Borough SD

200 School Rd • Plum, PA 15239-1453
(412) 795-0100 • http://www.pbsd.k12.pa.us
Grade Span: KG-12; **Agency Type:** 1
Schools: 7
5 Primary; 1 Middle; 1 High; 0 Other Level
7 Regular; 0 Special Education; 0 Vocational; 0 Alternative
0 Magnet; 0 Charter; 4 Title I Eligible; 0 School-wide Title I
Students: 4,374 (n/a% male; n/a% female)
Individual Education Program: 313 (7.2%);
English Language Learner: n/a; Migrant: 0 (0.0%)
Eligible for Free Lunch Program: 297 (6.8%)
Eligible for Reduced-Price Lunch Program: 144 (3.3%)
Teachers: 256.0 (17.1 to 1)
Librarians/Media Specialists: 4.0 (1,093.5 to 1)
Guidance Counselors: 7.0 (624.9 to 1)
Current Spending: ($ per student per year):
Total: $6,942; Instruction: $4,592; Support Services: $2,060

Enrollment, Drop-out Rates and Diploma Recipients by Race/Ethnicity

Category	Total	White	Black	Asian	AIAN	Hisp.
Enrollment (%)	100.0	95.1	3.2	1.2	0.2	0.4
Drop-out Rate (%)	1.1	1.1	0.0	0.0	0.0	0.0
H.S. Diplomas (#)	324	306	8	5	3	2

Quaker Valley SD

203 Graham St • Sewickley, PA 15143-1813
(412) 749-3600 • http://www.qvsd.org
Grade Span: KG-12; **Agency Type:** 1
Schools: 4
2 Primary; 1 Middle; 1 High; 0 Other Level
4 Regular; 0 Special Education; 0 Vocational; 0 Alternative
0 Magnet; 0 Charter; 2 Title I Eligible; 0 School-wide Title I
Students: 1,978 (n/a% male; n/a% female)
Individual Education Program: 242 (12.2%);
English Language Learner: n/a; Migrant: 0 (0.0%)
Eligible for Free Lunch Program: 194 (9.8%)
Eligible for Reduced-Price Lunch Program: 54 (2.7%)
Teachers: 133.5 (14.8 to 1)
Librarians/Media Specialists: 4.0 (494.5 to 1)
Guidance Counselors: 6.0 (329.7 to 1)
Current Spending: ($ per student per year):
Total: $10,619; Instruction: $6,140; Support Services: $4,217
Enrollment, Drop-out Rates and Diploma Recipients by Race/Ethnicity

Category	Total	White	Black	Asian	AIAN	Hisp.
Enrollment (%)	100.0	88.8	8.1	1.7	0.2	1.2
Drop-out Rate (%)	0.9	0.8	2.2	0.0	0.0	0.0
H.S. Diplomas (#)	146	137	8	1	0	0

Shaler Area SD

1800 Mount Royal Blvd • Glenshaw, PA 15116-2117
(412) 492-1200 • http://sasd.k12.pa.us
Grade Span: KG-12; **Agency Type:** 1
Schools: 8
5 Primary; 1 Middle; 1 High; 1 Other Level
8 Regular; 0 Special Education; 0 Vocational; 0 Alternative
0 Magnet; 0 Charter; 5 Title I Eligible; 0 School-wide Title I
Students: 5,557 (n/a% male; n/a% female)
Individual Education Program: 959 (17.3%);
English Language Learner: n/a; Migrant: 0 (0.0%)
Eligible for Free Lunch Program: 522 (9.4%)
Eligible for Reduced-Price Lunch Program: 308 (5.5%)
Teachers: 377.9 (14.7 to 1)
Librarians/Media Specialists: 8.0 (694.6 to 1)
Guidance Counselors: 9.0 (617.4 to 1)
Current Spending: ($ per student per year):
Total: $8,006; Instruction: $5,090; Support Services: $2,659
Enrollment, Drop-out Rates and Diploma Recipients by Race/Ethnicity

Category	Total	White	Black	Asian	AIAN	Hisp.
Enrollment (%)	100.0	98.0	0.8	0.7	0.4	0.1
Drop-out Rate (%)	1.1	1.1	0.0	0.0	0.0	0.0
H.S. Diplomas (#)	418	417	0	0	1	0

South Allegheny SD

2743 Washington Blvd • Mc Keesport, PA 15133-2017
(412) 675-3070
Grade Span: KG-12; **Agency Type:** 1
Schools: 5
2 Primary; 1 Middle; 1 High; 0 Other Level
4 Regular; 0 Special Education; 0 Vocational; 0 Alternative
0 Magnet; 0 Charter; 4 Title I Eligible; 0 School-wide Title I
Students: 1,815 (n/a% male; n/a% female)
Individual Education Program: 224 (12.3%);
English Language Learner: n/a; Migrant: 0 (0.0%)
Eligible for Free Lunch Program: 387 (21.3%)
Eligible for Reduced-Price Lunch Program: 188 (10.4%)
Teachers: 113.5 (16.0 to 1)
Librarians/Media Specialists: 2.0 (907.5 to 1)
Guidance Counselors: 5.0 (363.0 to 1)
Current Spending: ($ per student per year):
Total: $6,597; Instruction: $4,101; Support Services: $2,244
Enrollment, Drop-out Rates and Diploma Recipients by Race/Ethnicity

Category	Total	White	Black	Asian	AIAN	Hisp.
Enrollment (%)	100.0	97.9	1.5	0.2	0.2	0.2
Drop-out Rate (%)	1.8	1.8	0.0	n/a	0.0	0.0
H.S. Diplomas (#)	123	123	0	0	0	0

South Fayette Township SD

2250 Old Oakdale Rd • Mc Donald, PA 15057-2580
(412) 221-4542
Grade Span: KG-12; **Agency Type:** 1
Schools: 3
1 Primary; 1 Middle; 1 High; 0 Other Level
3 Regular; 0 Special Education; 0 Vocational; 0 Alternative
0 Magnet; 0 Charter; 3 Title I Eligible; 0 School-wide Title I
Students: 1,794 (n/a% male; n/a% female)
Individual Education Program: 158 (8.8%);
English Language Learner: n/a; Migrant: 0 (0.0%)
Eligible for Free Lunch Program: 112 (6.2%)
Eligible for Reduced-Price Lunch Program: 65 (3.6%)
Teachers: 119.0 (15.1 to 1)
Librarians/Media Specialists: 3.0 (598.0 to 1)
Guidance Counselors: 4.0 (448.5 to 1)
Current Spending: ($ per student per year):
Total: $8,010; Instruction: $5,230; Support Services: $2,559
Enrollment, Drop-out Rates and Diploma Recipients by Race/Ethnicity

Category	Total	White	Black	Asian	AIAN	Hisp.
Enrollment (%)	100.0	93.4	4.2	1.7	0.2	0.5
Drop-out Rate (%)	0.8	0.9	0.0	0.0	n/a	0.0
H.S. Diplomas (#)	94	90	3	1	0	0

South Park SD

2178 Ridge Rd • South Park, PA 15129-8885
(412) 655-3111
Grade Span: KG-12; **Agency Type:** 1
Schools: 3
1 Primary; 1 Middle; 1 High; 0 Other Level
3 Regular; 0 Special Education; 0 Vocational; 0 Alternative
0 Magnet; 0 Charter; 3 Title I Eligible; 0 School-wide Title I
Students: 2,296 (n/a% male; n/a% female)
Individual Education Program: 204 (8.9%);
English Language Learner: n/a; Migrant: 0 (0.0%)
Eligible for Free Lunch Program: 180 (7.8%)
Eligible for Reduced-Price Lunch Program: 83 (3.6%)
Teachers: 119.5 (19.2 to 1)
Librarians/Media Specialists: 3.0 (765.3 to 1)
Guidance Counselors: 5.0 (459.2 to 1)
Current Spending: ($ per student per year):
Total: $6,884; Instruction: $4,359; Support Services: $2,320
Enrollment, Drop-out Rates and Diploma Recipients by Race/Ethnicity

Category	Total	White	Black	Asian	AIAN	Hisp.
Enrollment (%)	100.0	95.0	3.9	0.6	0.4	0.0
Drop-out Rate (%)	1.6	1.4	8.0	0.0	n/a	n/a
H.S. Diplomas (#)	168	164	4	0	0	0

Steel Valley SD

220 E Oliver Rd • Munhall, PA 15120-2759
(412) 464-3650
Grade Span: KG-12; **Agency Type:** 1
Schools: 5
3 Primary; 1 Middle; 1 High; 0 Other Level
5 Regular; 0 Special Education; 0 Vocational; 0 Alternative
0 Magnet; 0 Charter; 3 Title I Eligible; 1 School-wide Title I
Students: 2,273 (n/a% male; n/a% female)
Individual Education Program: 299 (13.2%);
English Language Learner: n/a; Migrant: 0 (0.0%)
Eligible for Free Lunch Program: 838 (36.9%)
Eligible for Reduced-Price Lunch Program: 143 (6.3%)
Teachers: 138.0 (16.5 to 1)
Librarians/Media Specialists: 4.0 (568.3 to 1)
Guidance Counselors: 5.0 (454.6 to 1)
Current Spending: ($ per student per year):
Total: $7,152; Instruction: $4,867; Support Services: $2,030
Enrollment, Drop-out Rates and Diploma Recipients by Race/Ethnicity

Category	Total	White	Black	Asian	AIAN	Hisp.
Enrollment (%)	100.0	69.3	27.9	2.6	0.0	0.2
Drop-out Rate (%)	2.3	1.5	6.2	0.0	0.0	0.0
H.S. Diplomas (#)	160	124	26	8	0	2

Sto-Rox SD

19 May Avenue, Ste 205 • Mckees Rocks, PA 15136-3615
(412) 778-8871
Grade Span: KG-12; **Agency Type:** 1
Schools: 4
2 Primary; 1 Middle; 1 High; 0 Other Level
4 Regular; 0 Special Education; 0 Vocational; 0 Alternative
0 Magnet; 0 Charter; 4 Title I Eligible; 0 School-wide Title I
Students: 1,614 (n/a% male; n/a% female)
Individual Education Program: 386 (23.9%);
English Language Learner: n/a; Migrant: 0 (0.0%)
Eligible for Free Lunch Program: 932 (57.7%)
Eligible for Reduced-Price Lunch Program: 151 (9.4%)
Teachers: 115.0 (14.0 to 1)
Librarians/Media Specialists: 3.0 (538.0 to 1)
Guidance Counselors: 4.0 (403.5 to 1)
Current Spending: ($ per student per year):
Total: $10,209; Instruction: $6,402; Support Services: $3,372

Enrollment, Drop-out Rates and Diploma Recipients by Race/Ethnicity

Category	Total	White	Black	Asian	AIAN	Hisp.
Enrollment (%)	100.0	62.7	35.7	0.7	0.1	0.8
Drop-out Rate (%)	4.9	3.2	10.8	0.0	0.0	0.0
H.S. Diplomas (#)	74	59	14	0	0	1

Upper Saint Clair SD

1820 Mclughln Rn Rd Upr St Clr • Pittsburgh, PA 15241-2396
(412) 833-1600 • http://www.uscsd.k12.pa.us
Grade Span: KG-12; **Agency Type:** 1
Schools: 6
3 Primary; 2 Middle; 1 High; 0 Other Level
6 Regular; 0 Special Education; 0 Vocational; 0 Alternative
0 Magnet; 0 Charter; 4 Title I Eligible; 0 School-wide Title I
Students: 4,174 (n/a% male; n/a% female)
Individual Education Program: 410 (9.8%);
English Language Learner: n/a; Migrant: 0 (0.0%)
Eligible for Free Lunch Program: 35 (0.8%)
Eligible for Reduced-Price Lunch Program: 33 (0.8%)
Teachers: 255.6 (16.3 to 1)
Librarians/Media Specialists: 6.0 (695.7 to 1)
Guidance Counselors: 13.0 (321.1 to 1)
Current Spending: ($ per student per year):
Total: $8,889; Instruction: $5,529; Support Services: $3,056

Enrollment, Drop-out Rates and Diploma Recipients by Race/Ethnicity

Category	Total	White	Black	Asian	AIAN	Hisp.
Enrollment (%)	100.0	93.3	0.9	5.0	0.0	0.7
Drop-out Rate (%)	0.0	0.0	0.0	0.0	n/a	0.0
H.S. Diplomas (#)	308	284	5	17	0	2

West Allegheny SD

PO Box 55 • Imperial, PA 15126-0055
(724) 695-3422 • http://www.westallegheny.k12.pa.us
Grade Span: KG-12; **Agency Type:** 1
Schools: 5
2 Primary; 1 Middle; 1 High; 0 Other Level
4 Regular; 0 Special Education; 0 Vocational; 0 Alternative
0 Magnet; 0 Charter; 3 Title I Eligible; 0 School-wide Title I
Students: 3,229 (n/a% male; n/a% female)
Individual Education Program: 417 (12.9%);
English Language Learner: n/a; Migrant: 0 (0.0%)
Eligible for Free Lunch Program: 294 (9.1%)
Eligible for Reduced-Price Lunch Program: 106 (3.3%)
Teachers: 213.0 (15.2 to 1)
Librarians/Media Specialists: 4.0 (807.3 to 1)
Guidance Counselors: 7.0 (461.3 to 1)
Current Spending: ($ per student per year):
Total: $8,504; Instruction: $5,194; Support Services: $3,040

Enrollment, Drop-out Rates and Diploma Recipients by Race/Ethnicity

Category	Total	White	Black	Asian	AIAN	Hisp.
Enrollment (%)	100.0	95.0	3.1	1.3	0.1	0.6
Drop-out Rate (%)	1.7	1.7	0.0	0.0	n/a	0.0
H.S. Diplomas (#)	206	195	10	1	0	0

West Jefferson Hills SD

835 Old Clairton Rd • Jefferson Hills, PA 15025-3131
(412) 655-8450
Grade Span: KG-12; **Agency Type:** 1
Schools: 5
3 Primary; 1 Middle; 1 High; 0 Other Level
5 Regular; 0 Special Education; 0 Vocational; 0 Alternative
0 Magnet; 0 Charter; 3 Title I Eligible; 0 School-wide Title I
Students: 2,957 (n/a% male; n/a% female)
Individual Education Program: 307 (10.4%);
English Language Learner: n/a; Migrant: 0 (0.0%)
Eligible for Free Lunch Program: 154 (5.2%)
Eligible for Reduced-Price Lunch Program: 86 (2.9%)
Teachers: 158.0 (18.7 to 1)
Librarians/Media Specialists: 5.0 (591.4 to 1)
Guidance Counselors: 4.0 (739.3 to 1)
Current Spending: ($ per student per year):
Total: $7,249; Instruction: $4,511; Support Services: $2,494

Enrollment, Drop-out Rates and Diploma Recipients by Race/Ethnicity

Category	Total	White	Black	Asian	AIAN	Hisp.
Enrollment (%)	100.0	96.2	2.5	1.0	0.1	0.2
Drop-out Rate (%)	1.3	1.2	7.1	0.0	0.0	0.0
H.S. Diplomas (#)	212	208	2	2	0	0

West Mifflin Area SD

515 Camp Hollow Rd • West Mifflin, PA 15122-2697
(412) 466-9131 • http://www.wmasd.org
Grade Span: KG-12; **Agency Type:** 1
Schools: 6
4 Primary; 1 Middle; 1 High; 0 Other Level
6 Regular; 0 Special Education; 0 Vocational; 0 Alternative
0 Magnet; 0 Charter; 4 Title I Eligible; 0 School-wide Title I
Students: 3,377 (n/a% male; n/a% female)
Individual Education Program: 421 (12.5%);
English Language Learner: n/a; Migrant: 0 (0.0%)
Eligible for Free Lunch Program: 654 (19.4%)
Eligible for Reduced-Price Lunch Program: 208 (6.2%)
Teachers: 173.5 (19.5 to 1)
Librarians/Media Specialists: 5.0 (675.4 to 1)
Guidance Counselors: 5.0 (675.4 to 1)
Current Spending: ($ per student per year):
Total: $7,759; Instruction: $4,612; Support Services: $2,881

Enrollment, Drop-out Rates and Diploma Recipients by Race/Ethnicity

Category	Total	White	Black	Asian	AIAN	Hisp.
Enrollment (%)	100.0	81.3	18.0	0.3	0.0	0.4
Drop-out Rate (%)	1.0	0.8	2.5	0.0	n/a	0.0
H.S. Diplomas (#)	208	185	22	1	0	0

Wilkinsburg Borough SD

718 Wallace Ave • Wilkinsburg, PA 15221-2215
(412) 371-9667
Grade Span: PK-12; **Agency Type:** 1
Schools: 5
3 Primary; 1 Middle; 1 High; 0 Other Level
5 Regular; 0 Special Education; 0 Vocational; 0 Alternative
0 Magnet; 0 Charter; 3 Title I Eligible; 3 School-wide Title I
Students: 1,781 (n/a% male; n/a% female)
Individual Education Program: 336 (18.9%);
English Language Learner: n/a; Migrant: 0 (0.0%)
Eligible for Free Lunch Program: 1,140 (64.0%)
Eligible for Reduced-Price Lunch Program: 155 (8.7%)
Teachers: 140.0 (12.7 to 1)
Librarians/Media Specialists: 1.0 (1,781.0 to 1)
Guidance Counselors: 5.0 (356.2 to 1)
Current Spending: ($ per student per year):
Total: $9,767; Instruction: $6,112; Support Services: $3,137

Enrollment, Drop-out Rates and Diploma Recipients by Race/Ethnicity

Category	Total	White	Black	Asian	AIAN	Hisp.
Enrollment (%)	100.0	1.8	97.9	0.1	0.1	0.2
Drop-out Rate (%)	13.0	16.7	12.9	n/a	n/a	n/a
H.S. Diplomas (#)	74	5	69	0	0	0

Woodland Hills SD

2430 Greensburg Pike • Pittsburgh, PA 15221-3611
(412) 731-1300 • http://www.whsd.k12.pa.us
Grade Span: KG-12; **Agency Type:** 1
Schools: 9
3 Primary; 5 Middle; 1 High; 0 Other Level
9 Regular; 0 Special Education; 0 Vocational; 0 Alternative
0 Magnet; 0 Charter; 8 Title I Eligible; 6 School-wide Title I
Students: 5,894 (n/a% male; n/a% female)
Individual Education Program: 883 (15.0%);
English Language Learner: n/a; Migrant: 0 (0.0%)
Eligible for Free Lunch Program: 2,359 (40.0%)
Eligible for Reduced-Price Lunch Program: 510 (8.7%)
Teachers: 388.2 (15.2 to 1)
Librarians/Media Specialists: 9.5 (620.4 to 1)
Guidance Counselors: 15.0 (392.9 to 1)
Current Spending: ($ per student per year):
Total: $8,939; Instruction: $5,296; Support Services: $3,305

Enrollment, Drop-out Rates and Diploma Recipients by Race/Ethnicity

Category	Total	White	Black	Asian	AIAN	Hisp.
Enrollment (%)	100.0	45.2	53.3	1.0	0.1	0.4
Drop-out Rate (%)	4.3	3.5	5.6	0.0	n/a	11.1
H.S. Diplomas (#)	359	247	108	4	0	0

Armstrong County

Apollo-Ridge SD

PO Box 219 • Spring Church, PA 15686-0219
(724) 478-1141
Grade Span: KG-12; **Agency Type:** 1
Schools: 6
4 Primary; 1 Middle; 1 High; 0 Other Level
6 Regular; 0 Special Education; 0 Vocational; 0 Alternative
0 Magnet; 0 Charter; 6 Title I Eligible; 0 School-wide Title I
Students: 1,645 (n/a% male; n/a% female)
Individual Education Program: 242 (14.7%);
English Language Learner: n/a; Migrant: 0 (0.0%)
Eligible for Free Lunch Program: 467 (28.4%)
Eligible for Reduced-Price Lunch Program: 173 (10.5%)
Teachers: 100.0 (16.5 to 1)
Librarians/Media Specialists: 3.0 (548.3 to 1)
Guidance Counselors: 4.0 (411.3 to 1)
Current Spending: ($ per student per year):
Total: $7,188; Instruction: $4,342; Support Services: $2,463

Enrollment, Drop-out Rates and Diploma Recipients by Race/Ethnicity

Category	Total	White	Black	Asian	AIAN	Hisp.
Enrollment (%)	100.0	97.2	2.3	0.2	0.1	0.2
Drop-out Rate (%)	4.4	4.5	0.0	0.0	0.0	0.0
H.S. Diplomas (#)	89	88	1	0	0	0

Armstrong SD

410 Main St • Ford City, PA 16226-1613
(724) 763-7151 • http://www.asd.k12.pa.us
Grade Span: KG-12; **Agency Type:** 1
Schools: 13
8 Primary; 1 Middle; 4 High; 0 Other Level
13 Regular; 0 Special Education; 0 Vocational; 0 Alternative
0 Magnet; 0 Charter; 9 Title I Eligible; 0 School-wide Title I
Students: 6,539 (n/a% male; n/a% female)
Individual Education Program: 970 (14.8%);
English Language Learner: n/a; Migrant: 0 (0.0%)
Eligible for Free Lunch Program: 1,516 (23.2%)
Eligible for Reduced-Price Lunch Program: 709 (10.8%)
Teachers: 427.5 (15.3 to 1)
Librarians/Media Specialists: 10.0 (653.9 to 1)
Guidance Counselors: 9.0 (726.6 to 1)
Current Spending: ($ per student per year):
Total: $8,414; Instruction: $5,211; Support Services: $2,910

Enrollment, Drop-out Rates and Diploma Recipients by Race/Ethnicity

Category	Total	White	Black	Asian	AIAN	Hisp.
Enrollment (%)	100.0	98.6	1.0	0.1	0.0	0.2
Drop-out Rate (%)	2.5	2.6	0.0	0.0	0.0	0.0
H.S. Diplomas (#)	388	380	7	0	1	0

Freeport Area SD

PO Box C • Freeport, PA 16229-0303
(724) 295-5141 • http://www.freeport.k12.pa.us
Grade Span: KG-12; **Agency Type:** 1
Schools: 5
3 Primary; 1 Middle; 1 High; 0 Other Level
5 Regular; 0 Special Education; 0 Vocational; 0 Alternative
0 Magnet; 0 Charter; 3 Title I Eligible; 0 School-wide Title I
Students: 1,952 (n/a% male; n/a% female)
Individual Education Program: 216 (11.1%);
English Language Learner: n/a; Migrant: 0 (0.0%)
Eligible for Free Lunch Program: 237 (12.1%)
Eligible for Reduced-Price Lunch Program: 173 (8.9%)
Teachers: 125.0 (15.6 to 1)
Librarians/Media Specialists: 3.0 (650.7 to 1)
Guidance Counselors: 4.0 (488.0 to 1)
Current Spending: ($ per student per year):
Total: $7,756; Instruction: $4,857; Support Services: $2,487

Enrollment, Drop-out Rates and Diploma Recipients by Race/Ethnicity

Category	Total	White	Black	Asian	AIAN	Hisp.
Enrollment (%)	100.0	98.7	1.1	0.1	0.0	0.1
Drop-out Rate (%)	2.0	2.0	0.0	n/a	n/a	0.0
H.S. Diplomas (#)	117	117	0	0	0	0

Beaver County

Ambridge Area SD

740 Park Rd • Ambridge, PA 15003-2474
(724) 266-8870 • http://www.ambridge.k12.pa.us
Grade Span: KG-12; **Agency Type:** 1
Schools: 5
3 Primary; 1 Middle; 1 High; 0 Other Level
5 Regular; 0 Special Education; 0 Vocational; 0 Alternative
0 Magnet; 0 Charter; 3 Title I Eligible; 0 School-wide Title I
Students: 3,132 (n/a% male; n/a% female)
Individual Education Program: 601 (19.2%);
English Language Learner: n/a; Migrant: 0 (0.0%)
Eligible for Free Lunch Program: 610 (19.5%)
Eligible for Reduced-Price Lunch Program: 223 (7.1%)
Teachers: 189.5 (16.5 to 1)
Librarians/Media Specialists: 4.0 (783.0 to 1)
Guidance Counselors: 4.0 (783.0 to 1)
Current Spending: ($ per student per year):
Total: $7,463; Instruction: $4,632; Support Services: $2,512

Enrollment, Drop-out Rates and Diploma Recipients by Race/Ethnicity

Category	Total	White	Black	Asian	AIAN	Hisp.
Enrollment (%)	100.0	89.9	9.1	0.4	0.2	0.5
Drop-out Rate (%)	1.3	1.1	4.3	0.0	n/a	0.0
H.S. Diplomas (#)	234	221	13	0	0	0

Beaver Area SD

855 2nd St • Beaver, PA 15009-2600
(724) 774-4010 • http://www.basd.k12.pa.us
Grade Span: KG-12; **Agency Type:** 1
Schools: 4
2 Primary; 1 Middle; 1 High; 0 Other Level
4 Regular; 0 Special Education; 0 Vocational; 0 Alternative
0 Magnet; 0 Charter; 2 Title I Eligible; 0 School-wide Title I
Students: 2,090 (n/a% male; n/a% female)
Individual Education Program: 182 (8.7%);
English Language Learner: n/a; Migrant: 0 (0.0%)
Eligible for Free Lunch Program: 110 (5.3%)
Eligible for Reduced-Price Lunch Program: 40 (1.9%)
Teachers: 121.5 (17.2 to 1)
Librarians/Media Specialists: 2.0 (1,045.0 to 1)
Guidance Counselors: 7.0 (298.6 to 1)
Current Spending: ($ per student per year):
Total: $6,760; Instruction: $4,228; Support Services: $2,373

Enrollment, Drop-out Rates and Diploma Recipients by Race/Ethnicity

Category	Total	White	Black	Asian	AIAN	Hisp.
Enrollment (%)	100.0	97.8	1.4	0.4	0.0	0.4
Drop-out Rate (%)	0.7	0.7	0.0	0.0	n/a	n/a
H.S. Diplomas (#)	153	152	1	0	0	0

Big Beaver Falls Area SD

820 16th St • Beaver Falls, PA 15010-4065
(724) 843-3470 • http://www.tigerweb.org
Grade Span: KG-12; **Agency Type:** 1
Schools: 5
3 Primary; 1 Middle; 1 High; 0 Other Level
5 Regular; 0 Special Education; 0 Vocational; 0 Alternative
0 Magnet; 0 Charter; 4 Title I Eligible; 0 School-wide Title I
Students: 1,991 (n/a% male; n/a% female)
Individual Education Program: 261 (13.1%);
English Language Learner: n/a; Migrant: 0 (0.0%)
Eligible for Free Lunch Program: 786 (39.5%)
Eligible for Reduced-Price Lunch Program: 208 (10.4%)
Teachers: 141.0 (14.1 to 1)
Librarians/Media Specialists: 3.0 (663.7 to 1)
Guidance Counselors: 7.0 (284.4 to 1)
Current Spending: ($ per student per year):
Total: $8,035; Instruction: $4,762; Support Services: $2,875

Enrollment, Drop-out Rates and Diploma Recipients by Race/Ethnicity

Category	Total	White	Black	Asian	AIAN	Hisp.
Enrollment (%)	100.0	71.7	27.3	0.4	0.1	0.6
Drop-out Rate (%)	9.0	7.3	16.3	n/a	n/a	0.0
H.S. Diplomas (#)	119	84	35	0	0	0

Blackhawk SD

500 Blackhawk Rd • Beaver Falls, PA 15010-1410
(724) 846-6600 • http://www.ccia.com/~bhhs2/bhs1.html
Grade Span: KG-12; **Agency Type:** 1
Schools: 5
3 Primary; 1 Middle; 1 High; 0 Other Level
5 Regular; 0 Special Education; 0 Vocational; 0 Alternative
0 Magnet; 0 Charter; 3 Title I Eligible; 0 School-wide Title I
Students: 2,834 (n/a% male; n/a% female)
Individual Education Program: 251 (8.9%);
English Language Learner: n/a; Migrant: 0 (0.0%)
Eligible for Free Lunch Program: 280 (9.9%)
Eligible for Reduced-Price Lunch Program: 93 (3.3%)
Teachers: 166.5 (17.0 to 1)
Librarians/Media Specialists: 3.0 (944.7 to 1)
Guidance Counselors: 6.0 (472.3 to 1)
Current Spending: ($ per student per year):
Total: $6,916; Instruction: $4,408; Support Services: $2,239

Enrollment, Drop-out Rates and Diploma Recipients by Race/Ethnicity

Category	Total	White	Black	Asian	AIAN	Hisp.
Enrollment (%)	100.0	97.2	1.9	0.7	0.2	0.0
Drop-out Rate (%)	2.2	2.2	0.0	0.0	0.0	0.0
H.S. Diplomas (#)	221	216	3	2	0	0

Center Area SD

160 Baker Rd Ext • Monaca, PA 15061-2571
(724) 775-5600
Grade Span: KG-12; **Agency Type:** 1
Schools: 3
1 Primary; 1 Middle; 1 High; 0 Other Level
3 Regular; 0 Special Education; 0 Vocational; 0 Alternative
0 Magnet; 0 Charter; 2 Title I Eligible; 0 School-wide Title I
Students: 2,017 (n/a% male; n/a% female)
Individual Education Program: 205 (10.2%);
English Language Learner: n/a; Migrant: 0 (0.0%)
Eligible for Free Lunch Program: 128 (6.3%)
Eligible for Reduced-Price Lunch Program: 47 (2.3%)
Teachers: 127.4 (15.8 to 1)
Librarians/Media Specialists: 3.0 (672.3 to 1)
Guidance Counselors: 4.0 (504.3 to 1)
Current Spending: ($ per student per year):
Total: $6,718; Instruction: $4,365; Support Services: $2,100

Enrollment, Drop-out Rates and Diploma Recipients by Race/Ethnicity

Category	Total	White	Black	Asian	AIAN	Hisp.
Enrollment (%)	100.0	94.9	3.8	0.7	0.3	0.3
Drop-out Rate (%)	0.7	0.7	0.0	0.0	0.0	0.0
H.S. Diplomas (#)	137	130	6	0	0	1

Freedom Area SD

1701 8th Ave • Freedom, PA 15042-2000
(724) 775-7644 • http://www.freedom.k12.pa.us
Grade Span: KG-12; **Agency Type:** 1
Schools: 4
2 Primary; 1 Middle; 1 High; 0 Other Level
4 Regular; 0 Special Education; 0 Vocational; 0 Alternative
0 Magnet; 0 Charter; 3 Title I Eligible; 0 School-wide Title I
Students: 1,808 (n/a% male; n/a% female)
Individual Education Program: 224 (12.4%);
English Language Learner: n/a; Migrant: 0 (0.0%)
Eligible for Free Lunch Program: 315 (17.4%)
Eligible for Reduced-Price Lunch Program: 150 (8.3%)
Teachers: 106.0 (17.1 to 1)
Librarians/Media Specialists: 3.0 (602.7 to 1)
Guidance Counselors: 3.0 (602.7 to 1)
Current Spending: ($ per student per year):
Total: $7,010; Instruction: $4,405; Support Services: $2,275
Enrollment, Drop-out Rates and Diploma Recipients by Race/Ethnicity

Category	Total	White	Black	Asian	AIAN	Hisp.
Enrollment (%)	100.0	96.6	2.8	0.4	0.1	0.2
Drop-out Rate (%)	1.2	1.2	0.0	n/a	0.0	0.0
H.S. Diplomas (#)	129	126	3	0	0	0

Hopewell Area SD

2354 Brodhead Rd • Aliquippa, PA 15001-4501
(724) 375-6691 • http://www.hopewell.k12.pa.us
Grade Span: KG-12; **Agency Type:** 1
Schools: 6
4 Primary; 1 Middle; 1 High; 0 Other Level
6 Regular; 0 Special Education; 0 Vocational; 0 Alternative
0 Magnet; 0 Charter; 5 Title I Eligible; 0 School-wide Title I
Students: 2,970 (n/a% male; n/a% female)
Individual Education Program: 360 (12.1%);
English Language Learner: n/a; Migrant: 0 (0.0%)
Eligible for Free Lunch Program: 347 (11.7%)
Eligible for Reduced-Price Lunch Program: 144 (4.8%)
Teachers: 183.2 (16.2 to 1)
Librarians/Media Specialists: 4.0 (742.5 to 1)
Guidance Counselors: 6.0 (495.0 to 1)
Current Spending: ($ per student per year):
Total: $7,292; Instruction: $4,675; Support Services: $2,363
Enrollment, Drop-out Rates and Diploma Recipients by Race/Ethnicity

Category	Total	White	Black	Asian	AIAN	Hisp.
Enrollment (%)	100.0	96.9	2.6	0.3	0.0	0.3
Drop-out Rate (%)	2.1	2.2	0.0	0.0	0.0	0.0
H.S. Diplomas (#)	228	218	4	2	3	1

New Brighton Area SD

3225 43rd St • New Brighton, PA 15066-2655
(724) 843-1795 • http://nbsd.k12.pa.us
Grade Span: KG-12; **Agency Type:** 1
Schools: 3
1 Primary; 1 Middle; 1 High; 0 Other Level
3 Regular; 0 Special Education; 0 Vocational; 0 Alternative
0 Magnet; 0 Charter; 3 Title I Eligible; 0 School-wide Title I
Students: 1,980 (n/a% male; n/a% female)
Individual Education Program: 185 (9.3%);
English Language Learner: n/a; Migrant: 0 (0.0%)
Eligible for Free Lunch Program: 523 (26.4%)
Eligible for Reduced-Price Lunch Program: 191 (9.6%)
Teachers: 119.5 (16.6 to 1)
Librarians/Media Specialists: 2.0 (990.0 to 1)
Guidance Counselors: 4.0 (495.0 to 1)
Current Spending: ($ per student per year):
Total: $6,749; Instruction: $4,252; Support Services: $2,124
Enrollment, Drop-out Rates and Diploma Recipients by Race/Ethnicity

Category	Total	White	Black	Asian	AIAN	Hisp.
Enrollment (%)	100.0	87.4	11.8	0.2	0.2	0.5
Drop-out Rate (%)	3.6	3.5	5.8	0.0	0.0	n/a
H.S. Diplomas (#)	123	111	11	1	0	0

Riverside Beaver County SD

318 Country Club Dr • Ellwood City, PA 16117-4910
(724) 758-7512 • http://www.riverside.k12.pa.us
Grade Span: KG-12; **Agency Type:** 1
Schools: 4
2 Primary; 1 Middle; 1 High; 0 Other Level
4 Regular; 0 Special Education; 0 Vocational; 0 Alternative
0 Magnet; 0 Charter; 3 Title I Eligible; 0 School-wide Title I
Students: 1,979 (n/a% male; n/a% female)
Individual Education Program: 262 (13.2%);
English Language Learner: n/a; Migrant: 0 (0.0%)
Eligible for Free Lunch Program: 375 (18.9%)
Eligible for Reduced-Price Lunch Program: 201 (10.2%)
Teachers: 121.0 (16.4 to 1)
Librarians/Media Specialists: 3.0 (659.7 to 1)
Guidance Counselors: 3.5 (565.4 to 1)
Current Spending: ($ per student per year):
Total: $6,814; Instruction: $4,115; Support Services: $2,367
Enrollment, Drop-out Rates and Diploma Recipients by Race/Ethnicity

Category	Total	White	Black	Asian	AIAN	Hisp.
Enrollment (%)	100.0	99.0	0.9	0.1	0.0	0.0
Drop-out Rate (%)	2.9	2.9	0.0	0.0	n/a	n/a
H.S. Diplomas (#)	133	132	0	0	0	1

Bedford County

Bedford Area SD

330 E John St • Bedford, PA 15522-1427
(814) 623-4290 • http://www.bedford.k12.pa.us
Grade Span: KG-12; **Agency Type:** 1
Schools: 5
2 Primary; 1 Middle; 1 High; 1 Other Level
5 Regular; 0 Special Education; 0 Vocational; 0 Alternative
0 Magnet; 0 Charter; 3 Title I Eligible; 0 School-wide Title I
Students: 2,344 (n/a% male; n/a% female)
Individual Education Program: 334 (14.2%);
English Language Learner: n/a; Migrant: 7 (0.3%)
Eligible for Free Lunch Program: 497 (21.2%)
Eligible for Reduced-Price Lunch Program: 258 (11.0%)
Teachers: 145.6 (16.1 to 1)
Librarians/Media Specialists: 4.0 (586.0 to 1)
Guidance Counselors: 5.0 (468.8 to 1)
Current Spending: ($ per student per year):
Total: $6,681; Instruction: $4,015; Support Services: $2,332
Enrollment, Drop-out Rates and Diploma Recipients by Race/Ethnicity

Category	Total	White	Black	Asian	AIAN	Hisp.
Enrollment (%)	100.0	98.2	1.0	0.5	0.0	0.3
Drop-out Rate (%)	3.2	3.1	12.5	0.0	n/a	0.0
H.S. Diplomas (#)	136	136	0	0	0	0

Chestnut Ridge SD

PO Box 80 • Fishertown, PA 15539-0080
(814) 839-4195 • http://lion.crsd.k12.pa.us
Grade Span: KG-12; **Agency Type:** 1
Schools: 4
2 Primary; 1 Middle; 1 High; 0 Other Level
4 Regular; 0 Special Education; 0 Vocational; 0 Alternative
0 Magnet; 0 Charter; 3 Title I Eligible; 0 School-wide Title I
Students: 1,820 (n/a% male; n/a% female)
Individual Education Program: 287 (15.8%);
English Language Learner: n/a; Migrant: 1 (0.1%)
Eligible for Free Lunch Program: 391 (21.5%)
Eligible for Reduced-Price Lunch Program: 233 (12.8%)
Teachers: 108.4 (16.8 to 1)
Librarians/Media Specialists: 3.0 (606.7 to 1)
Guidance Counselors: 4.0 (455.0 to 1)
Current Spending: ($ per student per year):
Total: $6,433; Instruction: $3,947; Support Services: $2,114
Enrollment, Drop-out Rates and Diploma Recipients by Race/Ethnicity

Category	Total	White	Black	Asian	AIAN	Hisp.
Enrollment (%)	100.0	98.6	0.5	0.5	0.0	0.3
Drop-out Rate (%)	4.4	4.3	33.3	0.0	0.0	0.0
H.S. Diplomas (#)	138	135	0	3	0	0

Everett Area SD

427 E S St • Everett, PA 15537-1295
(814) 652-9114 • http://www.everett.k12.pa.us/
Grade Span: KG-12; **Agency Type:** 1
Schools: 5
4 Primary; 0 Middle; 1 High; 0 Other Level
5 Regular; 0 Special Education; 0 Vocational; 0 Alternative
0 Magnet; 0 Charter; 5 Title I Eligible; 0 School-wide Title I
Students: 1,519 (n/a% male; n/a% female)
Individual Education Program: 253 (16.7%);
English Language Learner: n/a; Migrant: 0 (0.0%)
Eligible for Free Lunch Program: 402 (26.5%)
Eligible for Reduced-Price Lunch Program: 232 (15.3%)
Teachers: 97.0 (15.7 to 1)
Librarians/Media Specialists: 2.0 (759.5 to 1)
Guidance Counselors: 3.0 (506.3 to 1)
Current Spending: ($ per student per year):
Total: $7,318; Instruction: $4,472; Support Services: $2,503

Enrollment, Drop-out Rates and Diploma Recipients by Race/Ethnicity

Category	Total	White	Black	Asian	AIAN	Hisp.
Enrollment (%)	100.0	99.0	0.7	0.2	0.0	0.1
Drop-out Rate (%)	4.3	4.4	0.0	n/a	n/a	0.0
H.S. Diplomas (#)	114	112	1	0	0	1

Berks County

Boyertown Area SD

911 Montgomery Ave • Boyertown, PA 19512-9607
(610) 367-6031 • http://www.netjunction.com/basd/index.html
Grade Span: KG-12; **Agency Type:** 1
Schools: 10
7 Primary; 2 Middle; 1 High; 0 Other Level
10 Regular; 0 Special Education; 0 Vocational; 0 Alternative
0 Magnet; 0 Charter; 7 Title I Eligible; 0 School-wide Title I
Students: 6,806 (n/a% male; n/a% female)
Individual Education Program: 793 (11.7%);
English Language Learner: n/a; Migrant: 0 (0.0%)
Eligible for Free Lunch Program: 306 (4.5%)
Eligible for Reduced-Price Lunch Program: 174 (2.6%)
Teachers: 392.4 (17.3 to 1)
Librarians/Media Specialists: 9.5 (716.4 to 1)
Guidance Counselors: 13.0 (523.5 to 1)
Current Spending: ($ per student per year):
Total: $6,833; Instruction: $4,212; Support Services: $2,358
Enrollment, Drop-out Rates and Diploma Recipients by Race/Ethnicity

Category	Total	White	Black	Asian	AIAN	Hisp.
Enrollment (%)	100.0	97.2	1.3	0.7	0.2	0.5
Drop-out Rate (%)	2.2	2.2	8.3	0.0	0.0	0.0
H.S. Diplomas (#)	464	458	1	4	0	1

Brandywine Heights Area SD

200 W Weis St • Topton, PA 19562-1532
(610) 682-5100 • http://www.bhasd.k12.pa.us
Grade Span: KG-12; **Agency Type:** 1
Schools: 5
3 Primary; 1 Middle; 1 High; 0 Other Level
5 Regular; 0 Special Education; 0 Vocational; 0 Alternative
0 Magnet; 0 Charter; 3 Title I Eligible; 0 School-wide Title I
Students: 1,984 (n/a% male; n/a% female)
Individual Education Program: 323 (16.3%);
English Language Learner: n/a; Migrant: 3 (0.2%)
Eligible for Free Lunch Program: 170 (8.6%)
Eligible for Reduced-Price Lunch Program: 40 (2.0%)
Teachers: 134.4 (14.8 to 1)
Librarians/Media Specialists: 3.6 (551.1 to 1)
Guidance Counselors: 6.0 (330.7 to 1)
Current Spending: ($ per student per year):
Total: $7,386; Instruction: $4,635; Support Services: $2,516
Enrollment, Drop-out Rates and Diploma Recipients by Race/Ethnicity

Category	Total	White	Black	Asian	AIAN	Hisp.
Enrollment (%)	100.0	98.7	0.5	0.3	0.1	0.6
Drop-out Rate (%)	3.0	3.0	0.0	0.0	n/a	0.0
H.S. Diplomas (#)	135	134	0	0	0	1

Conrad Weiser Area SD

44 Big Spring Rd • Robesonia, PA 19551-8948
(610) 693-8545
Grade Span: KG-12; **Agency Type:** 1
Schools: 4
2 Primary; 1 Middle; 1 High; 0 Other Level
4 Regular; 0 Special Education; 0 Vocational; 0 Alternative
0 Magnet; 0 Charter; 3 Title I Eligible; 0 School-wide Title I
Students: 2,748 (n/a% male; n/a% female)
Individual Education Program: 371 (13.5%);
English Language Learner: n/a; Migrant: 8 (0.3%)
Eligible for Free Lunch Program: 233 (8.5%)
Eligible for Reduced-Price Lunch Program: 114 (4.1%)
Teachers: 187.5 (14.7 to 1)
Librarians/Media Specialists: 4.0 (687.0 to 1)
Guidance Counselors: 8.0 (343.5 to 1)
Current Spending: ($ per student per year):
Total: $7,539; Instruction: $4,974; Support Services: $2,243
Enrollment, Drop-out Rates and Diploma Recipients by Race/Ethnicity

Category	Total	White	Black	Asian	AIAN	Hisp.
Enrollment (%)	100.0	94.3	2.6	0.4	0.1	2.7
Drop-out Rate (%)	1.9	1.9	3.8	0.0	n/a	0.0
H.S. Diplomas (#)	175	166	4	0	0	5

Daniel Boone Area SD

PO Box 186 • Douglassville, PA 19518-0186
(610) 582-6140 • http://www.dboone.k12.pa.us
Grade Span: KG-12; **Agency Type:** 1
Schools: 6
4 Primary; 1 Middle; 1 High; 0 Other Level
6 Regular; 0 Special Education; 0 Vocational; 0 Alternative
0 Magnet; 0 Charter; 0 Title I Eligible; 0 School-wide Title I
Students: 3,297 (n/a% male; n/a% female)
Individual Education Program: 407 (12.3%);
English Language Learner: n/a; Migrant: 0 (0.0%)
Eligible for Free Lunch Program: 205 (6.2%)
Eligible for Reduced-Price Lunch Program: 156 (4.7%)
Teachers: 197.8 (16.7 to 1)
Librarians/Media Specialists: 5.0 (659.4 to 1)
Guidance Counselors: 7.0 (471.0 to 1)
Current Spending: ($ per student per year):
Total: $6,505; Instruction: $3,953; Support Services: $2,255
Enrollment, Drop-out Rates and Diploma Recipients by Race/Ethnicity

Category	Total	White	Black	Asian	AIAN	Hisp.
Enrollment (%)	100.0	94.7	2.6	0.8	0.0	1.9
Drop-out Rate (%)	4.3	4.3	0.0	0.0	0.0	10.0
H.S. Diplomas (#)	166	166	0	0	0	0

Exeter Township SD

3650 Perkiomen Ave • Reading, PA 19606-2713
(610) 779-0700 • http://www.exeter.k12.pa.us
Grade Span: KG-12; **Agency Type:** 1
Schools: 6
3 Primary; 1 Middle; 1 High; 0 Other Level
5 Regular; 0 Special Education; 0 Vocational; 0 Alternative
0 Magnet; 0 Charter; 3 Title I Eligible; 0 School-wide Title I
Students: 3,982 (n/a% male; n/a% female)
Individual Education Program: 514 (12.9%);
English Language Learner: n/a; Migrant: 5 (0.1%)
Eligible for Free Lunch Program: 286 (7.2%)
Eligible for Reduced-Price Lunch Program: 150 (3.8%)
Teachers: 235.3 (16.9 to 1)
Librarians/Media Specialists: 5.0 (796.4 to 1)
Guidance Counselors: 10.0 (398.2 to 1)
Current Spending: ($ per student per year):
Total: $6,590; Instruction: $4,357; Support Services: $1,941
Enrollment, Drop-out Rates and Diploma Recipients by Race/Ethnicity

Category	Total	White	Black	Asian	AIAN	Hisp.
Enrollment (%)	100.0	93.5	2.9	1.4	0.3	1.9
Drop-out Rate (%)	2.1	2.2	0.0	0.0	0.0	0.0
H.S. Diplomas (#)	268	249	3	12	0	4

Fleetwood Area SD

801 N Richmond St • Fleetwood, PA 19522-1031
(610) 944-9598
Grade Span: KG-12; **Agency Type:** 1
Schools: 5
3 Primary; 1 Middle; 1 High; 0 Other Level
5 Regular; 0 Special Education; 0 Vocational; 0 Alternative
0 Magnet; 0 Charter; 4 Title I Eligible; 0 School-wide Title I
Students: 2,531 (n/a% male; n/a% female)
Individual Education Program: 287 (11.3%);
English Language Learner: n/a; Migrant: 5 (0.2%)
Eligible for Free Lunch Program: 177 (7.0%)
Eligible for Reduced-Price Lunch Program: 95 (3.8%)
Teachers: 165.0 (15.3 to 1)
Librarians/Media Specialists: 3.0 (843.7 to 1)
Guidance Counselors: 6.0 (421.8 to 1)
Current Spending: ($ per student per year):
Total: $7,042; Instruction: $4,123; Support Services: $2,623
Enrollment, Drop-out Rates and Diploma Recipients by Race/Ethnicity

Category	Total	White	Black	Asian	AIAN	Hisp.
Enrollment (%)	100.0	95.3	0.9	1.0	0.0	2.7
Drop-out Rate (%)	2.7	2.8	0.0	0.0	n/a	0.0
H.S. Diplomas (#)	158	151	2	2	0	3

Governor Mifflin SD

10 S Waverly St • Shillington, PA 19607-2642
(610) 775-1461 • http://www.gmsd.k12.pa.us
Grade Span: KG-12; **Agency Type:** 1
Schools: 5
2 Primary; 2 Middle; 1 High; 0 Other Level
5 Regular; 0 Special Education; 0 Vocational; 0 Alternative
0 Magnet; 0 Charter; 4 Title I Eligible; 0 School-wide Title I
Students: 4,196 (n/a% male; n/a% female)
Individual Education Program: 479 (11.4%);
English Language Learner: n/a; Migrant: 0 (0.0%)
Eligible for Free Lunch Program: 261 (6.2%)
Eligible for Reduced-Price Lunch Program: 140 (3.3%)
Teachers: 257.5 (16.3 to 1)
Librarians/Media Specialists: 5.0 (839.2 to 1)
Guidance Counselors: 11.0 (381.5 to 1)
Current Spending: ($ per student per year):
Total: $7,111; Instruction: $4,564; Support Services: $2,226

Enrollment, Drop-out Rates and Diploma Recipients by Race/Ethnicity

Category	Total	White	Black	Asian	AIAN	Hisp.
Enrollment (%)	100.0	91.5	2.6	1.9	0.0	3.9
Drop-out Rate (%)	2.4	2.0	5.6	3.6	n/a	14.3
H.S. Diplomas (#)	316	298	3	8	0	7

Hamburg Area SD

Windsor St • Hamburg, PA 19526-0401
(610) 562-2241
Grade Span: KG-12; **Agency Type:** 1
Schools: 7
5 Primary; 1 Middle; 1 High; 0 Other Level
7 Regular; 0 Special Education; 0 Vocational; 0 Alternative
0 Magnet; 0 Charter; 4 Title I Eligible; 0 School-wide Title I
Students: 2,766 (n/a% male; n/a% female)
Individual Education Program: 322 (11.6%);
English Language Learner: n/a; Migrant: 0 (0.0%)
Eligible for Free Lunch Program: 221 (8.0%)
Eligible for Reduced-Price Lunch Program: 79 (2.9%)
Teachers: 154.0 (18.0 to 1)
Librarians/Media Specialists: 4.0 (691.5 to 1)
Guidance Counselors: 6.0 (461.0 to 1)
Current Spending: ($ per student per year):
Total: $6,526; Instruction: $4,261; Support Services: $1,959

Enrollment, Drop-out Rates and Diploma Recipients by Race/Ethnicity

Category	Total	White	Black	Asian	AIAN	Hisp.
Enrollment (%)	100.0	97.9	0.3	0.3	0.0	1.4
Drop-out Rate (%)	3.0	3.1	0.0	0.0	n/a	0.0
H.S. Diplomas (#)	180	176	1	2	0	1

Kutztown Area SD

50 Trexler Ave • Kutztown, PA 19530-9722
(610) 683-7361 • http://www.kasd.org
Grade Span: KG-12; **Agency Type:** 1
Schools: 6
4 Primary; 1 Middle; 1 High; 0 Other Level
6 Regular; 0 Special Education; 0 Vocational; 0 Alternative
0 Magnet; 0 Charter; 5 Title I Eligible; 0 School-wide Title I
Students: 1,830 (n/a% male; n/a% female)
Individual Education Program: 292 (16.0%);
English Language Learner: n/a; Migrant: 0 (0.0%)
Eligible for Free Lunch Program: 127 (6.9%)
Eligible for Reduced-Price Lunch Program: 54 (3.0%)
Teachers: 132.7 (13.8 to 1)
Librarians/Media Specialists: 4.0 (457.5 to 1)
Guidance Counselors: 5.0 (366.0 to 1)
Current Spending: ($ per student per year):
Total: $8,396; Instruction: $5,229; Support Services: $2,833

Enrollment, Drop-out Rates and Diploma Recipients by Race/Ethnicity

Category	Total	White	Black	Asian	AIAN	Hisp.
Enrollment (%)	100.0	98.0	0.6	0.7	0.0	0.8
Drop-out Rate (%)	1.0	1.1	n/a	0.0	n/a	0.0
H.S. Diplomas (#)	133	132	0	1	0	0

Muhlenberg SD

801 Bellevue Ave Laureldale • Reading, PA 19605-1799
(610) 921-8070 • http://www.muhlsd.berksiu.k12.pa.us
Grade Span: KG-12; **Agency Type:** 1
Schools: 3
1 Primary; 1 Middle; 1 High; 0 Other Level
3 Regular; 0 Special Education; 0 Vocational; 0 Alternative
0 Magnet; 0 Charter; 3 Title I Eligible; 0 School-wide Title I
Students: 3,005 (n/a% male; n/a% female)
Individual Education Program: 367 (12.2%);
English Language Learner: n/a; Migrant: 17 (0.6%)
Eligible for Free Lunch Program: 308 (10.2%)
Eligible for Reduced-Price Lunch Program: 162 (5.4%)
Teachers: 198.5 (15.1 to 1)
Librarians/Media Specialists: 3.0 (1,001.7 to 1)
Guidance Counselors: 10.0 (300.5 to 1)
Current Spending: ($ per student per year):
Total: $7,762; Instruction: $5,011; Support Services: $2,453

Enrollment, Drop-out Rates and Diploma Recipients by Race/Ethnicity

Category	Total	White	Black	Asian	AIAN	Hisp.
Enrollment (%)	100.0	88.9	2.0	1.1	0.0	8.1
Drop-out Rate (%)	2.7	2.5	11.8	0.0	0.0	4.3
H.S. Diplomas (#)	199	181	1	4	0	13

Oley Valley SD

17 Jefferson St • Oley, PA 19547-8774
(610) 987-4100 • http://www.oleysd.k12.pa.us
Grade Span: KG-12; **Agency Type:** 1
Schools: 3
1 Primary; 1 Middle; 1 High; 0 Other Level
3 Regular; 0 Special Education; 0 Vocational; 0 Alternative
0 Magnet; 0 Charter; 3 Title I Eligible; 0 School-wide Title I
Students: 2,199 (n/a% male; n/a% female)
Individual Education Program: 273 (12.4%);
English Language Learner: n/a; Migrant: 0 (0.0%)
Eligible for Free Lunch Program: 74 (3.4%)
Eligible for Reduced-Price Lunch Program: 27 (1.2%)
Teachers: 140.6 (15.6 to 1)
Librarians/Media Specialists: 3.0 (733.0 to 1)
Guidance Counselors: 6.0 (366.5 to 1)
Current Spending: ($ per student per year):
Total: $6,594; Instruction: $4,207; Support Services: $2,131

Enrollment, Drop-out Rates and Diploma Recipients by Race/Ethnicity

Category	Total	White	Black	Asian	AIAN	Hisp.
Enrollment (%)	100.0	98.3	0.5	0.6	0.0	0.6
Drop-out Rate (%)	2.2	2.2	0.0	0.0	0.0	0.0
H.S. Diplomas (#)	127	123	2	0	0	2

Reading SD

800 Washington St • Reading, PA 19601-3616
(610) 371-5611
Grade Span: PK-12; **Agency Type:** 1
Schools: 19
14 Primary; 4 Middle; 1 High; 0 Other Level
19 Regular; 0 Special Education; 0 Vocational; 0 Alternative
0 Magnet; 0 Charter; 11 Title I Eligible; 11 School-wide Title I
Students: 16,128 (n/a% male; n/a% female)
Individual Education Program: 1,897 (11.8%);
English Language Learner: n/a; Migrant: 1,022 (6.3%)
Eligible for Free Lunch Program: 9,142 (56.7%)
Eligible for Reduced-Price Lunch Program: 1,704 (10.6%)
Teachers: 894.0 (18.0 to 1)
Librarians/Media Specialists: 18.0 (896.0 to 1)
Guidance Counselors: 36.0 (448.0 to 1)
Current Spending: ($ per student per year):
Total: $6,266; Instruction: $4,043; Support Services: $1,844

Enrollment, Drop-out Rates and Diploma Recipients by Race/Ethnicity

Category	Total	White	Black	Asian	AIAN	Hisp.
Enrollment (%)	100.0	21.6	15.3	1.0	0.1	62.1
Drop-out Rate (%)	13.0	9.2	12.7	10.9	100.0	15.5
H.S. Diplomas (#)	570	195	115	11	0	249

Schuylkill Valley SD

929 Lakeshore Dr • Leesport, PA 19533-8631
(610) 916-0957
Grade Span: KG-12; **Agency Type:** 1
Schools: 3
1 Primary; 1 Middle; 1 High; 0 Other Level
3 Regular; 0 Special Education; 0 Vocational; 0 Alternative
0 Magnet; 0 Charter; 2 Title I Eligible; 0 School-wide Title I
Students: 1,928 (n/a% male; n/a% female)
Individual Education Program: 223 (11.6%);
English Language Learner: n/a; Migrant: 0 (0.0%)
Eligible for Free Lunch Program: 120 (6.2%)
Eligible for Reduced-Price Lunch Program: 98 (5.1%)
Teachers: 125.1 (15.4 to 1)
Librarians/Media Specialists: 3.0 (642.7 to 1)
Guidance Counselors: 5.0 (385.6 to 1)
Current Spending: ($ per student per year):
Total: $8,113; Instruction: $5,419; Support Services: $2,374

Enrollment, Drop-out Rates and Diploma Recipients by Race/Ethnicity

Category	Total	White	Black	Asian	AIAN	Hisp.
Enrollment (%)	100.0	95.4	1.2	0.4	0.0	3.1
Drop-out Rate (%)	1.3	1.4	0.0	0.0	n/a	0.0
H.S. Diplomas (#)	141	138	2	0	0	1

Tulpehocken Area SD

428 New Schaefferstown Rd • Bernville, PA 19506-8939
(610) 488-6286
Grade Span: KG-12; **Agency Type:** 1
Schools: 3
2 Primary; 0 Middle; 1 High; 0 Other Level
3 Regular; 0 Special Education; 0 Vocational; 0 Alternative
0 Magnet; 0 Charter; 2 Title I Eligible; 0 School-wide Title I
Students: 1,727 (n/a% male; n/a% female)
Individual Education Program: 263 (15.2%);
English Language Learner: n/a; Migrant: 25 (1.4%)
Eligible for Free Lunch Program: 157 (9.1%)
Eligible for Reduced-Price Lunch Program: 116 (6.7%)
Teachers: 113.8 (15.2 to 1)
Librarians/Media Specialists: 3.0 (575.7 to 1)
Guidance Counselors: 5.2 (332.1 to 1)
Current Spending: ($ per student per year):
Total: $7,773; Instruction: $4,734; Support Services: $2,723

Enrollment, Drop-out Rates and Diploma Recipients by Race/Ethnicity

Category	Total	White	Black	Asian	AIAN	Hisp.
Enrollment (%)	100.0	95.9	0.8	0.2	0.3	2.9
Drop-out Rate (%)	3.2	3.4	0.0	0.0	n/a	0.0
H.S. Diplomas (#)	119	113	0	4	0	2

Twin Valley SD

4851 N Twin Valley Rd • Elverson, PA 19520-8995
(610) 286-8611
Grade Span: KG-12; **Agency Type:** 1
Schools: 5
3 Primary; 1 Middle; 1 High; 0 Other Level
5 Regular; 0 Special Education; 0 Vocational; 0 Alternative
0 Magnet; 0 Charter; 3 Title I Eligible; 0 School-wide Title I
Students: 3,111 (n/a% male; n/a% female)
Individual Education Program: 428 (13.8%);
English Language Learner: n/a; Migrant: 0 (0.0%)
Eligible for Free Lunch Program: 188 (6.0%)
Eligible for Reduced-Price Lunch Program: 156 (5.0%)
Teachers: 204.7 (15.2 to 1)
Librarians/Media Specialists: 5.0 (622.2 to 1)
Guidance Counselors: 8.0 (388.9 to 1)
Current Spending: ($ per student per year):
Total: $7,617; Instruction: $4,951; Support Services: $2,424
Enrollment, Drop-out Rates and Diploma Recipients by Race/Ethnicity

Category	Total	White	Black	Asian	AIAN	Hisp.
Enrollment (%)	100.0	97.6	1.4	0.5	0.0	0.5
Drop-out Rate (%)	2.4	2.4	8.3	0.0	0.0	0.0
H.S. Diplomas (#)	190	186	0	3	0	1

Wilson SD

2601 Grandview Blvd • West Lawn, PA 19609-1324
(610) 670-0180 • http://www.wilson.k12.pa.us
Grade Span: KG-12; **Agency Type:** 1
Schools: 10
7 Primary; 2 Middle; 1 High; 0 Other Level
10 Regular; 0 Special Education; 0 Vocational; 0 Alternative
0 Magnet; 0 Charter; 5 Title I Eligible; 0 School-wide Title I
Students: 5,103 (n/a% male; n/a% female)
Individual Education Program: 633 (12.4%);
English Language Learner: n/a; Migrant: 8 (0.2%)
Eligible for Free Lunch Program: 349 (6.8%)
Eligible for Reduced-Price Lunch Program: 170 (3.3%)
Teachers: 311.5 (16.4 to 1)
Librarians/Media Specialists: 8.0 (637.9 to 1)
Guidance Counselors: 13.0 (392.5 to 1)
Current Spending: ($ per student per year):
Total: $7,729; Instruction: $4,886; Support Services: $2,389
Enrollment, Drop-out Rates and Diploma Recipients by Race/Ethnicity

Category	Total	White	Black	Asian	AIAN	Hisp.
Enrollment (%)	100.0	87.2	4.9	2.9	0.2	4.8
Drop-out Rate (%)	2.0	1.9	7.1	2.1	0.0	4.2
H.S. Diplomas (#)	362	344	10	5	0	3

Wyomissing Area SD

630 Evans Ave • Wyomissing, PA 19610-2636
(610) 374-4031 • http://www.wyoarea.k12.pa.us
Grade Span: KG-12; **Agency Type:** 1
Schools: 3
1 Primary; 1 Middle; 1 High; 0 Other Level
3 Regular; 0 Special Education; 0 Vocational; 0 Alternative
0 Magnet; 0 Charter; 0 Title I Eligible; 0 School-wide Title I
Students: 1,822 (n/a% male; n/a% female)
Individual Education Program: 164 (9.0%);
English Language Learner: n/a; Migrant: 1 (0.1%)
Eligible for Free Lunch Program: 130 (7.1%)
Eligible for Reduced-Price Lunch Program: 59 (3.2%)
Teachers: 126.6 (14.4 to 1)
Librarians/Media Specialists: 3.0 (607.3 to 1)
Guidance Counselors: 7.0 (260.3 to 1)
Current Spending: ($ per student per year):
Total: $8,096; Instruction: $5,119; Support Services: $2,669
Enrollment, Drop-out Rates and Diploma Recipients by Race/Ethnicity

Category	Total	White	Black	Asian	AIAN	Hisp.
Enrollment (%)	100.0	90.5	2.1	2.5	0.1	4.7
Drop-out Rate (%)	2.5	2.6	0.0	0.0	n/a	5.3
H.S. Diplomas (#)	123	116	0	0	0	7

Blair County

Altoona Area SD

1415 6th Ave • Altoona, PA 16602-2427
(814) 946-8211 • http://www.aasdcat.com/aasd
Grade Span: KG-12; **Agency Type:** 1
Schools: 14
10 Primary; 2 Middle; 2 High; 0 Other Level
14 Regular; 0 Special Education; 0 Vocational; 0 Alternative
0 Magnet; 0 Charter; 10 Title I Eligible; 6 School-wide Title I
Students: 8,521 (n/a% male; n/a% female)
Individual Education Program: 1,384 (16.2%);
English Language Learner: n/a; Migrant: 0 (0.0%)
Eligible for Free Lunch Program: 2,975 (34.9%)
Eligible for Reduced-Price Lunch Program: 885 (10.4%)
Teachers: 519.0 (16.4 to 1)
Librarians/Media Specialists: 6.0 (1,420.2 to 1)
Guidance Counselors: 18.0 (473.4 to 1)
Current Spending: ($ per student per year):
Total: $6,675; Instruction: $4,294; Support Services: $2,094
Enrollment, Drop-out Rates and Diploma Recipients by Race/Ethnicity

Category	Total	White	Black	Asian	AIAN	Hisp.
Enrollment (%)	100.0	94.3	4.8	0.3	0.0	0.6
Drop-out Rate (%)	5.2	5.2	5.2	8.3	0.0	11.1
H.S. Diplomas (#)	567	549	13	4	0	1

Hollidaysburg Area SD

201 Jackson St • Hollidaysburg, PA 16648-1615
(814) 695-8702 • http://www.tigerwires.com
Grade Span: KG-12; **Agency Type:** 1
Schools: 6
4 Primary; 1 Middle; 1 High; 0 Other Level
6 Regular; 0 Special Education; 0 Vocational; 0 Alternative
0 Magnet; 0 Charter; 4 Title I Eligible; 0 School-wide Title I
Students: 3,817 (n/a% male; n/a% female)
Individual Education Program: 462 (12.1%);
English Language Learner: n/a; Migrant: 0 (0.0%)
Eligible for Free Lunch Program: 646 (16.9%)
Eligible for Reduced-Price Lunch Program: 243 (6.4%)
Teachers: 248.0 (15.4 to 1)
Librarians/Media Specialists: 4.0 (954.3 to 1)
Guidance Counselors: 10.0 (381.7 to 1)
Current Spending: ($ per student per year):
Total: $6,921; Instruction: $4,488; Support Services: $2,116
Enrollment, Drop-out Rates and Diploma Recipients by Race/Ethnicity

Category	Total	White	Black	Asian	AIAN	Hisp.
Enrollment (%)	100.0	98.5	0.5	0.8	0.1	0.2
Drop-out Rate (%)	2.3	2.4	0.0	0.0	0.0	0.0
H.S. Diplomas (#)	326	319	4	2	1	0

Spring Cove SD

1100 E Main St • Roaring Spring, PA 16673-1633
(814) 224-5124
Grade Span: KG-12; **Agency Type:** 1
Schools: 5
3 Primary; 1 Middle; 1 High; 0 Other Level
5 Regular; 0 Special Education; 0 Vocational; 0 Alternative
0 Magnet; 0 Charter; 4 Title I Eligible; 0 School-wide Title I
Students: 1,987 (n/a% male; n/a% female)
Individual Education Program: 292 (14.7%);
English Language Learner: n/a; Migrant: 5 (0.3%)
Eligible for Free Lunch Program: 410 (20.6%)
Eligible for Reduced-Price Lunch Program: 173 (8.7%)
Teachers: 128.0 (15.5 to 1)
Librarians/Media Specialists: 3.0 (662.3 to 1)
Guidance Counselors: 5.0 (397.4 to 1)
Current Spending: ($ per student per year):
Total: $6,851; Instruction: $4,056; Support Services: $2,449
Enrollment, Drop-out Rates and Diploma Recipients by Race/Ethnicity

Category	Total	White	Black	Asian	AIAN	Hisp.
Enrollment (%)	100.0	98.9	0.5	0.5	0.0	0.2
Drop-out Rate (%)	2.0	1.9	100.0	0.0	n/a	0.0
H.S. Diplomas (#)	159	158	0	1	0	0

Tyrone Area SD

701 Clay Ave • Tyrone, PA 16686-1415
(814) 684-0710 • http://www.tyrone.k12.pa.us
Grade Span: KG-12; **Agency Type:** 1
Schools: 3
1 Primary; 1 Middle; 1 High; 0 Other Level
3 Regular; 0 Special Education; 0 Vocational; 0 Alternative
0 Magnet; 0 Charter; 2 Title I Eligible; 0 School-wide Title I
Students: 1,993 (n/a% male; n/a% female)
Individual Education Program: 386 (19.4%);
English Language Learner: n/a; Migrant: 1 (0.1%)
Eligible for Free Lunch Program: 505 (25.3%)
Eligible for Reduced-Price Lunch Program: 245 (12.3%)
Teachers: 132.5 (15.0 to 1)
Librarians/Media Specialists: 2.0 (996.5 to 1)
Guidance Counselors: 7.0 (284.7 to 1)
Current Spending: ($ per student per year):
Total: $6,881; Instruction: $3,813; Support Services: $2,729

Enrollment, Drop-out Rates and Diploma Recipients by Race/Ethnicity

Category	Total	White	Black	Asian	AIAN	Hisp.
Enrollment (%)	100.0	98.2	1.0	0.5	0.1	0.3
Drop-out Rate (%)	4.5	4.5	0.0	0.0	n/a	0.0
H.S. Diplomas (#)	122	120	1	1	0	0

Bradford County

Athens Area SD

204 Willow St • Athens, PA 18810-1213
(570) 888-7766 • http://www.athensasd.k12.pa.us
Grade Span: KG-12; **Agency Type:** 1
Schools: 7
4 Primary; 1 Middle; 1 High; 1 Other Level
7 Regular; 0 Special Education; 0 Vocational; 0 Alternative
0 Magnet; 0 Charter; 4 Title I Eligible; 1 School-wide Title I
Students: 2,490 (n/a% male; n/a% female)
Individual Education Program: 435 (17.5%);
English Language Learner: n/a; Migrant: 16 (0.6%)
Eligible for Free Lunch Program: 465 (18.7%)
Eligible for Reduced-Price Lunch Program: 226 (9.1%)
Teachers: 184.5 (13.5 to 1)
Librarians/Media Specialists: 6.0 (415.0 to 1)
Guidance Counselors: 4.0 (622.5 to 1)
Current Spending: ($ per student per year):
Total: $7,807; Instruction: $5,031; Support Services: $2,463
Enrollment, Drop-out Rates and Diploma Recipients by Race/Ethnicity

Category	Total	White	Black	Asian	AIAN	Hisp.
Enrollment (%)	100.0	97.5	1.0	0.6	0.3	0.5
Drop-out Rate (%)	4.1	3.9	0.0	0.0	25.0	50.0
H.S. Diplomas (#)	162	155	0	5	1	1

Towanda Area SD

101 N 4th St • Towanda, PA 18848-1319
(570) 265-9894 • http://www.tsd.k12.pa.us
Grade Span: PK-12; **Agency Type:** 1
Schools: 6
4 Primary; 1 Middle; 1 High; 0 Other Level
6 Regular; 0 Special Education; 0 Vocational; 0 Alternative
0 Magnet; 0 Charter; 5 Title I Eligible; 0 School-wide Title I
Students: 1,835 (n/a% male; n/a% female)
Individual Education Program: 270 (14.7%);
English Language Learner: n/a; Migrant: 18 (1.0%)
Eligible for Free Lunch Program: 490 (26.7%)
Eligible for Reduced-Price Lunch Program: 233 (12.7%)
Teachers: 117.1 (15.7 to 1)
Librarians/Media Specialists: 3.0 (611.7 to 1)
Guidance Counselors: 4.0 (458.8 to 1)
Current Spending: ($ per student per year):
Total: $7,793; Instruction: $4,737; Support Services: $2,652
Enrollment, Drop-out Rates and Diploma Recipients by Race/Ethnicity

Category	Total	White	Black	Asian	AIAN	Hisp.
Enrollment (%)	100.0	99.3	0.5	0.0	0.0	0.2
Drop-out Rate (%)	3.3	3.2	0.0	20.0	n/a	0.0
H.S. Diplomas (#)	126	121	1	1	0	3

Troy Area SD

PO Box 67 • Troy, PA 16947-0067
(570) 297-2750 • http://www.troyschoolspa.org
Grade Span: KG-12; **Agency Type:** 1
Schools: 6
4 Primary; 1 Middle; 1 High; 0 Other Level
6 Regular; 0 Special Education; 0 Vocational; 0 Alternative
0 Magnet; 0 Charter; 5 Title I Eligible; 0 School-wide Title I
Students: 1,945 (n/a% male; n/a% female)
Individual Education Program: 268 (13.8%);
English Language Learner: n/a; Migrant: 44 (2.3%)
Eligible for Free Lunch Program: 474 (24.4%)
Eligible for Reduced-Price Lunch Program: 193 (9.9%)
Teachers: 120.0 (16.2 to 1)
Librarians/Media Specialists: 4.0 (486.3 to 1)
Guidance Counselors: 4.0 (486.3 to 1)
Current Spending: ($ per student per year):
Total: $7,374; Instruction: $4,698; Support Services: $2,353
Enrollment, Drop-out Rates and Diploma Recipients by Race/Ethnicity

Category	Total	White	Black	Asian	AIAN	Hisp.
Enrollment (%)	100.0	96.8	1.6	0.3	0.6	0.7
Drop-out Rate (%)	2.1	2.2	0.0	0.0	0.0	0.0
H.S. Diplomas (#)	119	119	0	0	0	0

Wyalusing Area SD

PO Box 157 • Wyalusing, PA 18853-0157
(570) 746-1605
Grade Span: KG-12; **Agency Type:** 1
Schools: 5
4 Primary; 0 Middle; 1 High; 0 Other Level
5 Regular; 0 Special Education; 0 Vocational; 0 Alternative
0 Magnet; 0 Charter; 5 Title I Eligible; 0 School-wide Title I
Students: 1,512 (n/a% male; n/a% female)
Individual Education Program: 151 (10.0%);
English Language Learner: n/a; Migrant: 19 (1.3%)
Eligible for Free Lunch Program: 334 (22.1%)
Eligible for Reduced-Price Lunch Program: 120 (7.9%)
Teachers: 97.0 (15.6 to 1)
Librarians/Media Specialists: 2.0 (756.0 to 1)
Guidance Counselors: 3.0 (504.0 to 1)
Current Spending: ($ per student per year):
Total: $7,317; Instruction: $4,579; Support Services: $2,427
Enrollment, Drop-out Rates and Diploma Recipients by Race/Ethnicity

Category	Total	White	Black	Asian	AIAN	Hisp.
Enrollment (%)	100.0	96.0	1.5	0.7	0.1	1.6
Drop-out Rate (%)	3.1	3.1	11.1	0.0	0.0	0.0
H.S. Diplomas (#)	99	95	1	2	0	1

Bucks County

Bensalem Township SD

3000 Donallen Dr • Bensalem, PA 19020-1898
(215) 750-2800 • http://www.bensalemschools.org
Grade Span: KG-12; **Agency Type:** 1
Schools: 10
6 Primary; 3 Middle; 1 High; 0 Other Level
10 Regular; 0 Special Education; 0 Vocational; 0 Alternative
0 Magnet; 0 Charter; 6 Title I Eligible; 1 School-wide Title I
Students: 6,599 (n/a% male; n/a% female)
Individual Education Program: 1,041 (15.8%);
English Language Learner: n/a; Migrant: 0 (0.0%)
Eligible for Free Lunch Program: 1,258 (19.1%)
Eligible for Reduced-Price Lunch Program: 469 (7.1%)
Teachers: 390.4 (16.9 to 1)
Librarians/Media Specialists: 9.0 (733.2 to 1)
Guidance Counselors: 18.0 (366.6 to 1)
Current Spending: ($ per student per year):
Total: $9,430; Instruction: $5,749; Support Services: $3,384
Enrollment, Drop-out Rates and Diploma Recipients by Race/Ethnicity

Category	Total	White	Black	Asian	AIAN	Hisp.
Enrollment (%)	100.0	71.7	12.2	10.2	0.2	5.8
Drop-out Rate (%)	2.8	2.6	3.0	1.0	n/a	11.3
H.S. Diplomas (#)	500	394	37	48	0	21

Bristol Township SD

6401 Mill Creek Rd • Levittown, PA 19057-4014
(215) 943-3200 • http://www.bciu.k12.pa.us/btsd
Grade Span: KG-12; **Agency Type:** 1
Schools: 13
9 Primary; 3 Middle; 1 High; 0 Other Level
13 Regular; 0 Special Education; 0 Vocational; 0 Alternative
0 Magnet; 0 Charter; 11 Title I Eligible; 0 School-wide Title I
Students: 6,897 (n/a% male; n/a% female)
Individual Education Program: 1,390 (20.2%);
English Language Learner: n/a; Migrant: 0 (0.0%)
Eligible for Free Lunch Program: 1,915 (27.8%)
Eligible for Reduced-Price Lunch Program: 580 (8.4%)
Teachers: 460.0 (15.0 to 1)
Librarians/Media Specialists: 13.0 (530.5 to 1)
Guidance Counselors: 11.0 (627.0 to 1)
Current Spending: ($ per student per year):
Total: $9,324; Instruction: $5,869; Support Services: $3,147
Enrollment, Drop-out Rates and Diploma Recipients by Race/Ethnicity

Category	Total	White	Black	Asian	AIAN	Hisp.
Enrollment (%)	100.0	74.5	16.9	2.8	0.5	5.3
Drop-out Rate (%)	2.8	2.8	4.4	0.0	0.0	1.3
H.S. Diplomas (#)	426	319	59	28	3	17

Centennial SD

433 Centennial Rd • Warminster, PA 18974-5448
(215) 441-6000 • http://www.centennialsd.org
Grade Span: KG-12; **Agency Type:** 1
Schools: 9
6 Primary; 2 Middle; 1 High; 0 Other Level
9 Regular; 0 Special Education; 0 Vocational; 0 Alternative
0 Magnet; 0 Charter; 6 Title I Eligible; 0 School-wide Title I
Students: 6,344 (n/a% male; n/a% female)
Individual Education Program: 1,084 (17.1%);
English Language Learner: n/a; Migrant: 0 (0.0%)
Eligible for Free Lunch Program: 537 (8.5%)
Eligible for Reduced-Price Lunch Program: 385 (6.1%)
Teachers: 383.0 (16.6 to 1)
Librarians/Media Specialists: 8.0 (793.0 to 1)
Guidance Counselors: 15.0 (422.9 to 1)

Current Spending: ($ per student per year):
Total: $7,838; Instruction: $4,899; Support Services: $2,699
Enrollment, Drop-out Rates and Diploma Recipients by Race/Ethnicity

Category	Total	White	Black	Asian	AIAN	Hisp.
Enrollment (%)	100.0	88.1	4.4	2.5	0.2	4.9
Drop-out Rate (%)	1.2	1.2	2.6	1.5	0.0	0.0
H.S. Diplomas (#)	456	417	9	15	0	15

Central Bucks SD
16 Welden Dr • Doylestown, PA 18901-2359
(215) 345-1400 • http://www.cbsd.org
Grade Span: KG-12; **Agency Type:** 1
Schools: 21
14 Primary; 5 Middle; 2 High; 0 Other Level
21 Regular; 0 Special Education; 0 Vocational; 0 Alternative
0 Magnet; 0 Charter; 9 Title I Eligible; 0 School-wide Title I
Students: 18,549 (n/a% male; n/a% female)
Individual Education Program: 1,961 (10.6%);
English Language Learner: n/a; Migrant: 6 (<0.1%)
Eligible for Free Lunch Program: 198 (1.1%)
Eligible for Reduced-Price Lunch Program: 112 (0.6%)
Teachers: 1,034.3 (17.9 to 1)
Librarians/Media Specialists: 23.6 (786.0 to 1)
Guidance Counselors: 45.0 (412.2 to 1)
Current Spending: ($ per student per year):
Total: $7,445; Instruction: $4,852; Support Services: $2,379
Enrollment, Drop-out Rates and Diploma Recipients by Race/Ethnicity

Category	Total	White	Black	Asian	AIAN	Hisp.
Enrollment (%)	100.0	95.1	1.5	2.3	0.0	1.1
Drop-out Rate (%)	1.4	1.4	1.2	0.9	n/a	0.0
H.S. Diplomas (#)	1,082	1,023	23	27	0	9

Council Rock SD
251 Twining Ford Rd • Richboro, PA 18954-1843
(215) 355-9901 • http://www.crsd.org
Grade Span: KG-12; **Agency Type:** 1
Schools: 15
10 Primary; 3 Middle; 2 High; 0 Other Level
15 Regular; 0 Special Education; 0 Vocational; 0 Alternative
0 Magnet; 0 Charter; 9 Title I Eligible; 0 School-wide Title I
Students: 12,362 (n/a% male; n/a% female)
Individual Education Program: 1,645 (13.3%);
English Language Learner: n/a; Migrant: 0 (0.0%)
Eligible for Free Lunch Program: 81 (0.7%)
Eligible for Reduced-Price Lunch Program: 63 (0.5%)
Teachers: 789.5 (15.7 to 1)
Librarians/Media Specialists: 18.7 (661.1 to 1)
Guidance Counselors: 22.0 (561.9 to 1)
Current Spending: ($ per student per year):
Total: $9,451; Instruction: $6,472; Support Services: $2,746
Enrollment, Drop-out Rates and Diploma Recipients by Race/Ethnicity

Category	Total	White	Black	Asian	AIAN	Hisp.
Enrollment (%)	100.0	95.4	0.9	3.3	0.0	0.4
Drop-out Rate (%)	0.3	0.3	0.0	0.0	0.0	0.0
H.S. Diplomas (#)	912	872	6	28	0	6

Neshaminy SD
2001 Old Lincoln Hwy • Langhorne, PA 19047-3295
(215) 752-6300 • http://www.neshaminy.k12.pa.us
Grade Span: KG-12; **Agency Type:** 1
Schools: 14
8 Primary; 4 Middle; 2 High; 0 Other Level
14 Regular; 0 Special Education; 0 Vocational; 0 Alternative
0 Magnet; 0 Charter; 9 Title I Eligible; 0 School-wide Title I
Students: 9,629 (n/a% male; n/a% female)
Individual Education Program: 1,539 (16.0%);
English Language Learner: n/a; Migrant: 0 (0.0%)
Eligible for Free Lunch Program: 784 (8.1%)
Eligible for Reduced-Price Lunch Program: 374 (3.9%)
Teachers: 544.0 (17.7 to 1)
Librarians/Media Specialists: 13.0 (740.7 to 1)
Guidance Counselors: 22.0 (437.7 to 1)
Current Spending: ($ per student per year):
Total: $10,156; Instruction: $6,739; Support Services: $3,144
Enrollment, Drop-out Rates and Diploma Recipients by Race/Ethnicity

Category	Total	White	Black	Asian	AIAN	Hisp.
Enrollment (%)	100.0	93.9	3.0	2.0	0.1	1.1
Drop-out Rate (%)	1.8	1.6	4.9	4.2	0.0	0.0
H.S. Diplomas (#)	796	755	20	20	0	1

Palisades SD
39 Thomas Free Dr • Kintnersville, PA 18930-9657
(610) 847-5131 • http://www.palisadessd.org
Grade Span: KG-12; **Agency Type:** 1
Schools: 5
3 Primary; 1 Middle; 1 High; 0 Other Level
5 Regular; 0 Special Education; 0 Vocational; 0 Alternative
0 Magnet; 0 Charter; 2 Title I Eligible; 0 School-wide Title I
Students: 2,148 (n/a% male; n/a% female)
Individual Education Program: 361 (16.8%);
English Language Learner: n/a; Migrant: 0 (0.0%)
Eligible for Free Lunch Program: 81 (3.8%)
Eligible for Reduced-Price Lunch Program: 55 (2.6%)
Teachers: 143.4 (15.0 to 1)
Librarians/Media Specialists: 3.0 (716.0 to 1)
Guidance Counselors: 7.0 (306.9 to 1)
Current Spending: ($ per student per year):
Total: $9,247; Instruction: $5,306; Support Services: $3,676
Enrollment, Drop-out Rates and Diploma Recipients by Race/Ethnicity

Category	Total	White	Black	Asian	AIAN	Hisp.
Enrollment (%)	100.0	98.1	0.7	0.6	0.0	0.6
Drop-out Rate (%)	1.6	1.7	0.0	0.0	0.0	0.0
H.S. Diplomas (#)	161	160	0	1	0	0

Pennridge SD
1506 N 5th St • Perkasie, PA 18944-2207
(215) 257-5011 • http://www.bciu.k12.pa.us/pennridge/psd/psd.htm
Grade Span: KG-12; **Agency Type:** 1
Schools: 10
7 Primary; 2 Middle; 1 High; 0 Other Level
10 Regular; 0 Special Education; 0 Vocational; 0 Alternative
0 Magnet; 0 Charter; 8 Title I Eligible; 0 School-wide Title I
Students: 6,923 (n/a% male; n/a% female)
Individual Education Program: 907 (13.1%);
English Language Learner: n/a; Migrant: 7 (0.1%)
Eligible for Free Lunch Program: 378 (5.5%)
Eligible for Reduced-Price Lunch Program: 244 (3.5%)
Teachers: 396.4 (17.5 to 1)
Librarians/Media Specialists: 10.0 (692.3 to 1)
Guidance Counselors: 17.0 (407.2 to 1)
Current Spending: ($ per student per year):
Total: $7,696; Instruction: $4,808; Support Services: $2,612
Enrollment, Drop-out Rates and Diploma Recipients by Race/Ethnicity

Category	Total	White	Black	Asian	AIAN	Hisp.
Enrollment (%)	100.0	96.7	1.2	0.7	0.0	1.3
Drop-out Rate (%)	2.6	2.5	4.5	4.3	0.0	3.3
H.S. Diplomas (#)	477	451	6	6	4	10

Pennsbury SD
134 Yardley Ave • Fallsington, PA 19058-0338
(215) 428-4100 • http://www.pennsbury.k12.pa.us
Grade Span: KG-12; **Agency Type:** 1
Schools: 16
11 Primary; 3 Middle; 1 High; 1 Other Level
16 Regular; 0 Special Education; 0 Vocational; 0 Alternative
0 Magnet; 0 Charter; 8 Title I Eligible; 0 School-wide Title I
Students: 11,050 (n/a% male; n/a% female)
Individual Education Program: 1,415 (12.8%);
English Language Learner: n/a; Migrant: 0 (0.0%)
Eligible for Free Lunch Program: 491 (4.4%)
Eligible for Reduced-Price Lunch Program: 261 (2.4%)
Teachers: 680.9 (16.2 to 1)
Librarians/Media Specialists: 15.0 (736.7 to 1)
Guidance Counselors: 30.0 (368.3 to 1)
Current Spending: ($ per student per year):
Total: $9,284; Instruction: $6,284; Support Services: $2,765
Enrollment, Drop-out Rates and Diploma Recipients by Race/Ethnicity

Category	Total	White	Black	Asian	AIAN	Hisp.
Enrollment (%)	100.0	88.5	4.6	4.5	0.4	2.0
Drop-out Rate (%)	1.6	1.6	2.6	1.2	3.3	0.0
H.S. Diplomas (#)	737	681	21	22	4	9

Quakertown Community SD
600 Park Ave • Quakertown, PA 18951-1588
(215) 529-2000 • http://www.qcsd.org
Grade Span: KG-12; **Agency Type:** 1
Schools: 9
6 Primary; 2 Middle; 1 High; 0 Other Level
9 Regular; 0 Special Education; 0 Vocational; 0 Alternative
0 Magnet; 0 Charter; 4 Title I Eligible; 0 School-wide Title I
Students: 5,229 (n/a% male; n/a% female)
Individual Education Program: 648 (12.4%);
English Language Learner: n/a; Migrant: 0 (0.0%)
Eligible for Free Lunch Program: 454 (8.7%)
Eligible for Reduced-Price Lunch Program: 294 (5.6%)
Teachers: 281.4 (18.6 to 1)
Librarians/Media Specialists: 8.0 (653.6 to 1)
Guidance Counselors: 11.6 (450.8 to 1)
Current Spending: ($ per student per year):
Total: $7,608; Instruction: $4,815; Support Services: $2,541

Enrollment, Drop-out Rates and Diploma Recipients by Race/Ethnicity

Category	Total	White	Black	Asian	AIAN	Hisp.
Enrollment (%)	100.0	95.9	1.5	0.7	0.2	1.7
Drop-out Rate (%)	2.5	2.6	0.0	0.0	n/a	0.0
H.S. Diplomas (#)	334	326	4	1	0	3

Butler County

Butler Area SD

110 Campus Ln • Butler, PA 16001-2662
(724) 287-8721 • http://www.butler.k12.pa.us
Grade Span: KG-12; **Agency Type:** 1
Schools: 14
11 Primary; 1 Middle; 1 High; 1 Other Level
14 Regular; 0 Special Education; 0 Vocational; 0 Alternative
0 Magnet; 0 Charter; 8 Title I Eligible; 0 School-wide Title I
Students: 8,349 (n/a% male; n/a% female)
Individual Education Program: 1,263 (15.1%);
English Language Learner: n/a; Migrant: 1 (<0.1%)
Eligible for Free Lunch Program: 1,419 (17.0%)
Eligible for Reduced-Price Lunch Program: 527 (6.3%)
Teachers: 495.6 (16.8 to 1)
Librarians/Media Specialists: 9.2 (907.5 to 1)
Guidance Counselors: 13.0 (642.2 to 1)
Current Spending: ($ per student per year):
Total: $6,890; Instruction: $4,492; Support Services: $2,146
Enrollment, Drop-out Rates and Diploma Recipients by Race/Ethnicity

Category	Total	White	Black	Asian	AIAN	Hisp.
Enrollment (%)	100.0	96.7	1.7	0.6	0.2	0.9
Drop-out Rate (%)	3.3	3.3	2.9	0.0	0.0	0.0
H.S. Diplomas (#)	558	546	3	2	1	6

Karns City Area SD

1446 Kittanning Pike • Karns City, PA 16041-1818
(724) 756-2030 • http://www.karnscity.k12.pa.us
Grade Span: KG-12; **Agency Type:** 1
Schools: 4
3 Primary; 0 Middle; 1 High; 0 Other Level
4 Regular; 0 Special Education; 0 Vocational; 0 Alternative
0 Magnet; 0 Charter; 0 Title I Eligible; 0 School-wide Title I
Students: 1,841 (n/a% male; n/a% female)
Individual Education Program: 214 (11.6%);
English Language Learner: n/a; Migrant: 0 (0.0%)
Eligible for Free Lunch Program: 382 (20.7%)
Eligible for Reduced-Price Lunch Program: 193 (10.5%)
Teachers: 117.0 (15.7 to 1)
Librarians/Media Specialists: 2.0 (920.5 to 1)
Guidance Counselors: 4.0 (460.3 to 1)
Current Spending: ($ per student per year):
Total: $6,983; Instruction: $4,299; Support Services: $2,331
Enrollment, Drop-out Rates and Diploma Recipients by Race/Ethnicity

Category	Total	White	Black	Asian	AIAN	Hisp.
Enrollment (%)	100.0	99.7	0.3	0.0	0.0	0.0
Drop-out Rate (%)	2.7	2.7	0.0	0.0	n/a	n/a
H.S. Diplomas (#)	130	129	1	0	0	0

Mars Area SD

545 Route 228 • Mars, PA 16046-3123
(724) 625-1518
Grade Span: KG-12; **Agency Type:** 1
Schools: 5
3 Primary; 1 Middle; 1 High; 0 Other Level
5 Regular; 0 Special Education; 0 Vocational; 0 Alternative
0 Magnet; 0 Charter; 0 Title I Eligible; 0 School-wide Title I
Students: 2,703 (n/a% male; n/a% female)
Individual Education Program: 154 (5.7%);
English Language Learner: n/a; Migrant: 0 (0.0%)
Eligible for Free Lunch Program: 141 (5.2%)
Eligible for Reduced-Price Lunch Program: 97 (3.6%)
Teachers: 171.0 (15.8 to 1)
Librarians/Media Specialists: 4.0 (675.8 to 1)
Guidance Counselors: 6.0 (450.5 to 1)
Current Spending: ($ per student per year):
Total: $6,678; Instruction: $4,196; Support Services: $2,294
Enrollment, Drop-out Rates and Diploma Recipients by Race/Ethnicity

Category	Total	White	Black	Asian	AIAN	Hisp.
Enrollment (%)	100.0	99.3	0.3	0.1	0.1	0.1
Drop-out Rate (%)	1.2	1.2	0.0	0.0	0.0	0.0
H.S. Diplomas (#)	207	202	2	2	0	1

Moniteau SD

1810 W Sunbury Rd • West Sunbury, PA 16061-1220
(724) 637-2117 • http://www.moniteau.k12.pa.us
Grade Span: KG-12; **Agency Type:** 1
Schools: 3
2 Primary; 0 Middle; 1 High; 0 Other Level
3 Regular; 0 Special Education; 0 Vocational; 0 Alternative
0 Magnet; 0 Charter; 0 Title I Eligible; 0 School-wide Title I
Students: 1,725 (n/a% male; n/a% female)
Individual Education Program: 248 (14.4%);
English Language Learner: n/a; Migrant: 0 (0.0%)
Eligible for Free Lunch Program: 409 (23.7%)
Eligible for Reduced-Price Lunch Program: 166 (9.6%)
Teachers: 93.0 (18.5 to 1)
Librarians/Media Specialists: 2.0 (862.5 to 1)
Guidance Counselors: 3.0 (575.0 to 1)
Current Spending: ($ per student per year):
Total: $6,507; Instruction: $3,890; Support Services: $2,271
Enrollment, Drop-out Rates and Diploma Recipients by Race/Ethnicity

Category	Total	White	Black	Asian	AIAN	Hisp.
Enrollment (%)	100.0	98.7	0.5	0.3	0.1	0.5
Drop-out Rate (%)	3.0	3.0	0.0	n/a	0.0	n/a
H.S. Diplomas (#)	103	102	0	1	0	0

Seneca Valley SD

124 Seneca School Rd • Harmony, PA 16037-9101
(724) 452-6040 • http://www.seneca.k12.pa.us
Grade Span: KG-12; **Agency Type:** 1
Schools: 9
4 Primary; 3 Middle; 1 High; 1 Other Level
9 Regular; 0 Special Education; 0 Vocational; 0 Alternative
0 Magnet; 0 Charter; 5 Title I Eligible; 0 School-wide Title I
Students: 7,621 (n/a% male; n/a% female)
Individual Education Program: 985 (12.9%);
English Language Learner: n/a; Migrant: 0 (0.0%)
Eligible for Free Lunch Program: 422 (5.5%)
Eligible for Reduced-Price Lunch Program: 175 (2.3%)
Teachers: 483.1 (15.8 to 1)
Librarians/Media Specialists: 8.0 (952.6 to 1)
Guidance Counselors: 15.5 (491.7 to 1)
Current Spending: ($ per student per year):
Total: $6,415; Instruction: $4,366; Support Services: $1,782
Enrollment, Drop-out Rates and Diploma Recipients by Race/Ethnicity

Category	Total	White	Black	Asian	AIAN	Hisp.
Enrollment (%)	100.0	97.0	1.3	1.1	0.1	0.5
Drop-out Rate (%)	2.6	2.7	0.0	0.0	0.0	0.0
H.S. Diplomas (#)	497	485	3	6	0	3

Slippery Rock Area SD

201 Kiester Rd • Slippery Rock, PA 16057-1601
(724) 794-2960
Grade Span: KG-12; **Agency Type:** 1
Schools: 5
3 Primary; 1 Middle; 1 High; 0 Other Level
5 Regular; 0 Special Education; 0 Vocational; 0 Alternative
0 Magnet; 0 Charter; 0 Title I Eligible; 0 School-wide Title I
Students: 2,553 (n/a% male; n/a% female)
Individual Education Program: 349 (13.7%);
English Language Learner: n/a; Migrant: 0 (0.0%)
Eligible for Free Lunch Program: 369 (14.5%)
Eligible for Reduced-Price Lunch Program: 205 (8.0%)
Teachers: 149.3 (17.1 to 1)
Librarians/Media Specialists: 3.0 (851.0 to 1)
Guidance Counselors: 5.0 (510.6 to 1)
Current Spending: ($ per student per year):
Total: $6,189; Instruction: $3,875; Support Services: $2,055
Enrollment, Drop-out Rates and Diploma Recipients by Race/Ethnicity

Category	Total	White	Black	Asian	AIAN	Hisp.
Enrollment (%)	100.0	98.5	0.7	0.5	0.2	0.1
Drop-out Rate (%)	3.5	3.5	0.0	0.0	n/a	n/a
H.S. Diplomas (#)	151	151	0	0	0	0

South Butler County SD

328 Knoch Rd • Saxonburg, PA 16056-0657
(724) 352-1700 • http://southbutler.k12.pa.us
Grade Span: KG-12; **Agency Type:** 1
Schools: 4
1 Primary; 2 Middle; 1 High; 0 Other Level
4 Regular; 0 Special Education; 0 Vocational; 0 Alternative
0 Magnet; 0 Charter; 2 Title I Eligible; 0 School-wide Title I
Students: 2,954 (n/a% male; n/a% female)
Individual Education Program: 261 (8.8%);
English Language Learner: n/a; Migrant: 0 (0.0%)
Eligible for Free Lunch Program: 260 (8.8%)
Eligible for Reduced-Price Lunch Program: 128 (4.3%)
Teachers: 169.5 (17.4 to 1)
Librarians/Media Specialists: 4.0 (738.5 to 1)
Guidance Counselors: 5.0 (590.8 to 1)
Current Spending: ($ per student per year):
Total: $6,404; Instruction: $3,891; Support Services: $2,280

Enrollment, Drop-out Rates and Diploma Recipients by Race/Ethnicity

Category	Total	White	Black	Asian	AIAN	Hisp.
Enrollment (%)	100.0	99.3	0.5	0.0	0.1	0.1
Drop-out Rate (%)	2.5	2.4	0.0	n/a	n/a	50.0
H.S. Diplomas (#)	220	220	0	0	0	0

Cambria County

Cambria Heights SD

PO Box 66 • Patton, PA 16668-0066
(814) 674-3626 • http://www.chsd.k12.pa.us
Grade Span: KG-12; **Agency Type:** 1
Schools: 3
1 Primary; 1 Middle; 1 High; 0 Other Level
3 Regular; 0 Special Education; 0 Vocational; 0 Alternative
0 Magnet; 0 Charter; 2 Title I Eligible; 0 School-wide Title I
Students: 1,612 (n/a% male; n/a% female)
Individual Education Program: 203 (12.6%);
English Language Learner: n/a; Migrant: 0 (0.0%)
Eligible for Free Lunch Program: 378 (23.4%)
Eligible for Reduced-Price Lunch Program: 161 (10.0%)
Teachers: 117.2 (13.8 to 1)
Librarians/Media Specialists: 3.0 (537.3 to 1)
Guidance Counselors: 5.0 (322.4 to 1)
Current Spending: ($ per student per year):
Total: $7,255; Instruction: $4,543; Support Services: $2,434
Enrollment, Drop-out Rates and Diploma Recipients by Race/Ethnicity

Category	Total	White	Black	Asian	AIAN	Hisp.
Enrollment (%)	100.0	99.1	0.4	0.0	0.1	0.4
Drop-out Rate (%)	2.1	2.1	0.0	n/a	n/a	0.0
H.S. Diplomas (#)	147	147	0	0	0	0

Central Cambria SD

208 Schoolhouse Rd • Ebensburg, PA 15931-7617
(814) 472-8870 • http://www.cchs.k12.pa.us
Grade Span: KG-12; **Agency Type:** 1
Schools: 4
2 Primary; 1 Middle; 1 High; 0 Other Level
4 Regular; 0 Special Education; 0 Vocational; 0 Alternative
0 Magnet; 0 Charter; 2 Title I Eligible; 0 School-wide Title I
Students: 1,909 (n/a% male; n/a% female)
Individual Education Program: 287 (15.0%);
English Language Learner: n/a; Migrant: 0 (0.0%)
Eligible for Free Lunch Program: 321 (16.8%)
Eligible for Reduced-Price Lunch Program: 212 (11.1%)
Teachers: 124.0 (15.4 to 1)
Librarians/Media Specialists: 3.0 (636.3 to 1)
Guidance Counselors: 5.0 (381.8 to 1)
Current Spending: ($ per student per year):
Total: $7,037; Instruction: $4,285; Support Services: $2,428
Enrollment, Drop-out Rates and Diploma Recipients by Race/Ethnicity

Category	Total	White	Black	Asian	AIAN	Hisp.
Enrollment (%)	100.0	98.6	0.6	0.7	0.0	0.1
Drop-out Rate (%)	2.3	2.4	0.0	0.0	n/a	0.0
H.S. Diplomas (#)	180	179	0	1	0	0

Forest Hills SD

PO Box 158 • Sidman, PA 15955-0158
(814) 487-7613 • http://www.fhsd.k12.pa.us
Grade Span: KG-12; **Agency Type:** 1
Schools: 3
1 Primary; 1 Middle; 1 High; 0 Other Level
3 Regular; 0 Special Education; 0 Vocational; 0 Alternative
0 Magnet; 0 Charter; 2 Title I Eligible; 0 School-wide Title I
Students: 2,308 (n/a% male; n/a% female)
Individual Education Program: 261 (11.3%);
English Language Learner: n/a; Migrant: 0 (0.0%)
Eligible for Free Lunch Program: 513 (22.2%)
Eligible for Reduced-Price Lunch Program: 289 (12.5%)
Teachers: 140.0 (16.5 to 1)
Librarians/Media Specialists: 4.0 (577.0 to 1)
Guidance Counselors: 5.0 (461.6 to 1)
Current Spending: ($ per student per year):
Total: $6,275; Instruction: $3,978; Support Services: $1,982
Enrollment, Drop-out Rates and Diploma Recipients by Race/Ethnicity

Category	Total	White	Black	Asian	AIAN	Hisp.
Enrollment (%)	100.0	99.3	0.6	0.0	0.0	0.1
Drop-out Rate (%)	0.4	0.4	0.0	n/a	n/a	n/a
H.S. Diplomas (#)	157	157	0	0	0	0

Greater Johnstown SD

1091 Broad St • Johnstown, PA 15906-2437
(814) 533-5651 • http://trojan.gjsd.k12.pa.us
Grade Span: PK-12; **Agency Type:** 1
Schools: 4
2 Primary; 0 Middle; 1 High; 1 Other Level
4 Regular; 0 Special Education; 0 Vocational; 0 Alternative
0 Magnet; 0 Charter; 4 Title I Eligible; 2 School-wide Title I
Students: 3,388 (n/a% male; n/a% female)
Individual Education Program: 558 (16.5%);
English Language Learner: n/a; Migrant: 0 (0.0%)
Eligible for Free Lunch Program: 2,074 (61.2%)
Eligible for Reduced-Price Lunch Program: 423 (12.5%)
Teachers: 234.5 (14.4 to 1)
Librarians/Media Specialists: 4.0 (847.0 to 1)
Guidance Counselors: 6.0 (564.7 to 1)
Current Spending: ($ per student per year):
Total: $7,987; Instruction: $5,230; Support Services: $2,364
Enrollment, Drop-out Rates and Diploma Recipients by Race/Ethnicity

Category	Total	White	Black	Asian	AIAN	Hisp.
Enrollment (%)	100.0	73.3	24.9	0.2	0.2	1.5
Drop-out Rate (%)	3.9	3.9	3.9	0.0	n/a	6.3
H.S. Diplomas (#)	177	135	36	2	0	4

Penn Cambria SD

201 6th St • Cresson, PA 16630-1363
(814) 886-8121
Grade Span: KG-12; **Agency Type:** 1
Schools: 5
2 Primary; 2 Middle; 0 High; 1 Other Level
5 Regular; 0 Special Education; 0 Vocational; 0 Alternative
0 Magnet; 0 Charter; 5 Title I Eligible; 0 School-wide Title I
Students: 1,906 (n/a% male; n/a% female)
Individual Education Program: 278 (14.6%);
English Language Learner: n/a; Migrant: 0 (0.0%)
Eligible for Free Lunch Program: 426 (22.4%)
Eligible for Reduced-Price Lunch Program: 225 (11.8%)
Teachers: 128.0 (14.9 to 1)
Librarians/Media Specialists: 4.0 (476.5 to 1)
Guidance Counselors: 6.0 (317.7 to 1)
Current Spending: ($ per student per year):
Total: $7,581; Instruction: $4,699; Support Services: $2,467
Enrollment, Drop-out Rates and Diploma Recipients by Race/Ethnicity

Category	Total	White	Black	Asian	AIAN	Hisp.
Enrollment (%)	100.0	98.8	0.5	0.0	0.3	0.4
Drop-out Rate (%)	1.0	1.0	0.0	0.0	0.0	0.0
H.S. Diplomas (#)	173	171	2	0	0	0

Richland SD

PO Box 5370 • Johnstown, PA 15904-5370
(814) 266-6063
Grade Span: KG-12; **Agency Type:** 1
Schools: 3
1 Primary; 1 Middle; 1 High; 0 Other Level
3 Regular; 0 Special Education; 0 Vocational; 0 Alternative
0 Magnet; 0 Charter; 2 Title I Eligible; 0 School-wide Title I
Students: 1,586 (n/a% male; n/a% female)
Individual Education Program: 154 (9.7%);
English Language Learner: n/a; Migrant: 0 (0.0%)
Eligible for Free Lunch Program: 111 (7.0%)
Eligible for Reduced-Price Lunch Program: 65 (4.1%)
Teachers: 94.0 (16.9 to 1)
Librarians/Media Specialists: 3.0 (528.7 to 1)
Guidance Counselors: 3.0 (528.7 to 1)
Current Spending: ($ per student per year):
Total: $7,279; Instruction: $4,417; Support Services: $2,577
Enrollment, Drop-out Rates and Diploma Recipients by Race/Ethnicity

Category	Total	White	Black	Asian	AIAN	Hisp.
Enrollment (%)	100.0	96.3	1.1	1.9	0.1	0.6
Drop-out Rate (%)	1.0	1.0	0.0	0.0	n/a	0.0
H.S. Diplomas (#)	136	133	1	2	0	0

Westmont Hilltop SD

827 Diamond Blvd • Johnstown, PA 15905-2348
(814) 255-6751 • http://westy.jtwn.k12.pa.us
Grade Span: KG-12; **Agency Type:** 1
Schools: 3
1 Primary; 1 Middle; 1 High; 0 Other Level
3 Regular; 0 Special Education; 0 Vocational; 0 Alternative
0 Magnet; 0 Charter; 3 Title I Eligible; 0 School-wide Title I
Students: 1,674 (n/a% male; n/a% female)
Individual Education Program: 163 (9.7%);
English Language Learner: n/a; Migrant: 0 (0.0%)
Eligible for Free Lunch Program: 159 (9.5%)
Eligible for Reduced-Price Lunch Program: 102 (6.1%)
Teachers: 100.1 (16.7 to 1)
Librarians/Media Specialists: 3.0 (558.0 to 1)
Guidance Counselors: 5.0 (334.8 to 1)
Current Spending: ($ per student per year):
Total: $7,057; Instruction: $4,405; Support Services: $2,397

Enrollment, Drop-out Rates and Diploma Recipients by Race/Ethnicity

Category	Total	White	Black	Asian	AIAN	Hisp.
Enrollment (%)	100.0	96.7	1.0	1.2	0.4	0.8
Drop-out Rate (%)	0.9	0.7	0.0	0.0	n/a	11.1
H.S. Diplomas (#)	139	134	2	1	0	2

Carbon County

Jim Thorpe Area SD

140 W 10th St • Jim Thorpe, PA 18229-1702
(570) 325-3691 • http://www.jtasd.k12.pa.us/index.html
Grade Span: KG-12; **Agency Type:** 1
Schools: 3
1 Primary; 1 Middle; 1 High; 0 Other Level
3 Regular; 0 Special Education; 0 Vocational; 0 Alternative
0 Magnet; 0 Charter; 3 Title I Eligible; 0 School-wide Title I
Students: 1,774 (n/a% male; n/a% female)
Individual Education Program: 259 (14.6%);
English Language Learner: n/a; Migrant: 0 (0.0%)
Eligible for Free Lunch Program: 332 (18.7%)
Eligible for Reduced-Price Lunch Program: 164 (9.2%)
Teachers: 97.6 (18.2 to 1)
Librarians/Media Specialists: 3.0 (591.3 to 1)
Guidance Counselors: 3.0 (591.3 to 1)
Current Spending: ($ per student per year):
Total: $8,319; Instruction: $4,813; Support Services: $3,195
Enrollment, Drop-out Rates and Diploma Recipients by Race/Ethnicity

Category	Total	White	Black	Asian	AIAN	Hisp.
Enrollment (%)	100.0	89.5	5.0	0.8	0.2	4.5
Drop-out Rate (%)	0.7	0.8	0.0	0.0	0.0	0.0
H.S. Diplomas (#)	96	81	10	2	0	3

Lehighton Area SD

1000 Union St • Lehighton, PA 18235-1700
(610) 377-4490
Grade Span: KG-12; **Agency Type:** 1
Schools: 6
4 Primary; 1 Middle; 1 High; 0 Other Level
6 Regular; 0 Special Education; 0 Vocational; 0 Alternative
0 Magnet; 0 Charter; 5 Title I Eligible; 0 School-wide Title I
Students: 2,469 (n/a% male; n/a% female)
Individual Education Program: 282 (11.4%);
English Language Learner: n/a; Migrant: 0 (0.0%)
Eligible for Free Lunch Program: 334 (13.5%)
Eligible for Reduced-Price Lunch Program: 165 (6.7%)
Teachers: 169.0 (14.6 to 1)
Librarians/Media Specialists: 4.0 (617.3 to 1)
Guidance Counselors: 6.0 (411.5 to 1)
Current Spending: ($ per student per year):
Total: $7,374; Instruction: $4,763; Support Services: $2,338
Enrollment, Drop-out Rates and Diploma Recipients by Race/Ethnicity

Category	Total	White	Black	Asian	AIAN	Hisp.
Enrollment (%)	100.0	97.7	0.8	0.8	0.1	0.7
Drop-out Rate (%)	4.9	4.6	50.0	25.0	0.0	0.0
H.S. Diplomas (#)	172	169	1	1	0	1

Palmerton Area SD

PO Box 350 • Palmerton, PA 18071-0350
(610) 826-2364 • http://www.palmerton.k12.pa.us/
Grade Span: KG-12; **Agency Type:** 1
Schools: 4
2 Primary; 1 Middle; 1 High; 0 Other Level
4 Regular; 0 Special Education; 0 Vocational; 0 Alternative
0 Magnet; 0 Charter; 4 Title I Eligible; 0 School-wide Title I
Students: 1,987 (n/a% male; n/a% female)
Individual Education Program: 284 (14.3%);
English Language Learner: n/a; Migrant: 0 (0.0%)
Eligible for Free Lunch Program: 220 (11.1%)
Eligible for Reduced-Price Lunch Program: 149 (7.5%)
Teachers: 109.2 (18.2 to 1)
Librarians/Media Specialists: 2.0 (993.5 to 1)
Guidance Counselors: 5.0 (397.4 to 1)
Current Spending: ($ per student per year):
Total: $6,587; Instruction: $4,209; Support Services: $2,063
Enrollment, Drop-out Rates and Diploma Recipients by Race/Ethnicity

Category	Total	White	Black	Asian	AIAN	Hisp.
Enrollment (%)	100.0	98.0	0.3	0.7	0.1	1.0
Drop-out Rate (%)	2.4	2.3	n/a	0.0	n/a	0.0
H.S. Diplomas (#)	129	128	0	0	0	1

Centre County

Bald Eagle Area SD

751 S Eaglevalley Rd • Wingate, PA 16823-4740
(814) 355-4860 • http://www.beasd.k12.pa.us
Grade Span: KG-12; **Agency Type:** 1
Schools: 5
4 Primary; 0 Middle; 1 High; 0 Other Level
5 Regular; 0 Special Education; 0 Vocational; 0 Alternative
0 Magnet; 0 Charter; 3 Title I Eligible; 0 School-wide Title I
Students: 2,081 (n/a% male; n/a% female)
Individual Education Program: 261 (12.5%);
English Language Learner: n/a; Migrant: 0 (0.0%)
Eligible for Free Lunch Program: 336 (16.1%)
Eligible for Reduced-Price Lunch Program: 267 (12.8%)
Teachers: 140.0 (14.9 to 1)
Librarians/Media Specialists: 2.0 (1,040.5 to 1)
Guidance Counselors: 5.0 (416.2 to 1)
Current Spending: ($ per student per year):
Total: $7,146; Instruction: $4,372; Support Services: $2,401
Enrollment, Drop-out Rates and Diploma Recipients by Race/Ethnicity

Category	Total	White	Black	Asian	AIAN	Hisp.
Enrollment (%)	100.0	99.4	0.2	0.1	0.0	0.3
Drop-out Rate (%)	2.8	2.8	0.0	n/a	0.0	n/a
H.S. Diplomas (#)	186	184	0	2	0	0

Bellefonte Area SD

318 N Allegheny St • Bellefonte, PA 16823-1613
(814) 355-4814 • http://www.basd.net
Grade Span: KG-12; **Agency Type:** 1
Schools: 6
4 Primary; 1 Middle; 1 High; 0 Other Level
6 Regular; 0 Special Education; 0 Vocational; 0 Alternative
0 Magnet; 0 Charter; 6 Title I Eligible; 0 School-wide Title I
Students: 2,988 (n/a% male; n/a% female)
Individual Education Program: 470 (15.7%);
English Language Learner: n/a; Migrant: 1 (<0.1%)
Eligible for Free Lunch Program: 501 (16.8%)
Eligible for Reduced-Price Lunch Program: 267 (8.9%)
Teachers: 195.0 (15.3 to 1)
Librarians/Media Specialists: 4.0 (747.0 to 1)
Guidance Counselors: 8.0 (373.5 to 1)
Current Spending: ($ per student per year):
Total: $7,123; Instruction: $4,484; Support Services: $2,349
Enrollment, Drop-out Rates and Diploma Recipients by Race/Ethnicity

Category	Total	White	Black	Asian	AIAN	Hisp.
Enrollment (%)	100.0	97.9	1.5	0.3	0.0	0.2
Drop-out Rate (%)	3.0	3.0	0.0	0.0	n/a	0.0
H.S. Diplomas (#)	218	216	2	0	0	0

Penns Valley Area SD

4528 Penns Valley Rd • Spring Mills, PA 16875-9403
(814) 422-8814 • http://www.pennsvalley.org
Grade Span: KG-12; **Agency Type:** 1
Schools: 5
4 Primary; 0 Middle; 1 High; 0 Other Level
5 Regular; 0 Special Education; 0 Vocational; 0 Alternative
0 Magnet; 0 Charter; 4 Title I Eligible; 0 School-wide Title I
Students: 1,636 (n/a% male; n/a% female)
Individual Education Program: 269 (16.4%);
English Language Learner: n/a; Migrant: 0 (0.0%)
Eligible for Free Lunch Program: 186 (11.4%)
Eligible for Reduced-Price Lunch Program: 128 (7.8%)
Teachers: 111.5 (14.7 to 1)
Librarians/Media Specialists: 2.0 (818.0 to 1)
Guidance Counselors: 4.0 (409.0 to 1)
Current Spending: ($ per student per year):
Total: $8,167; Instruction: $5,054; Support Services: $2,819
Enrollment, Drop-out Rates and Diploma Recipients by Race/Ethnicity

Category	Total	White	Black	Asian	AIAN	Hisp.
Enrollment (%)	100.0	98.5	0.2	0.8	0.1	0.4
Drop-out Rate (%)	1.1	1.2	0.0	0.0	n/a	n/a
H.S. Diplomas (#)	103	103	0	0	0	0

State College Area SD

131 W Nittany Ave • State College, PA 16801-4812
(814) 231-1011 • http://www.scasd.k12.pa.us
Grade Span: KG-12; **Agency Type:** 1
Schools: 11
8 Primary; 2 Middle; 1 High; 0 Other Level
11 Regular; 0 Special Education; 0 Vocational; 0 Alternative
0 Magnet; 0 Charter; 5 Title I Eligible; 0 School-wide Title I
Students: 7,451 (n/a% male; n/a% female)
Individual Education Program: 849 (11.4%);
English Language Learner: n/a; Migrant: 1 (<0.1%)

Eligible for Free Lunch Program: 663 (8.9%)
Eligible for Reduced-Price Lunch Program: 307 (4.1%)
Teachers: 508.5 (14.7 to 1)
Librarians/Media Specialists: 11.0 (677.4 to 1)
Guidance Counselors: 21.6 (345.0 to 1)
Current Spending: ($ per student per year):
Total: $8,361; Instruction: $5,203; Support Services: $2,844
Enrollment, Drop-out Rates and Diploma Recipients by Race/Ethnicity

Category	Total	White	Black	Asian	AIAN	Hisp.
Enrollment (%)	100.0	86.4	3.0	6.5	1.0	3.0
Drop-out Rate (%)	1.4	1.3	3.4	0.0	0.0	2.5
H.S. Diplomas (#)	610	592	9	6	0	3

Chester County

Avon Grove SD
375 S Jennersville Rd • West Grove, PA 19390-8401
(610) 869-2441 • http://www.avongrove.org
Grade Span: KG-12; **Agency Type:** 1
Schools: 4
2 Primary; 1 Middle; 1 High; 0 Other Level
4 Regular; 0 Special Education; 0 Vocational; 0 Alternative
0 Magnet; 0 Charter; 2 Title I Eligible; 0 School-wide Title I
Students: 4,700 (n/a% male; n/a% female)
Individual Education Program: 616 (13.1%);
English Language Learner: n/a; Migrant: 237 (5.0%)
Eligible for Free Lunch Program: 345 (7.3%)
Eligible for Reduced-Price Lunch Program: 157 (3.3%)
Teachers: 279.5 (16.8 to 1)
Librarians/Media Specialists: 5.0 (940.0 to 1)
Guidance Counselors: 15.0 (313.3 to 1)
Current Spending: ($ per student per year):
Total: $6,590; Instruction: $3,796; Support Services: $2,583
Enrollment, Drop-out Rates and Diploma Recipients by Race/Ethnicity

Category	Total	White	Black	Asian	AIAN	Hisp.
Enrollment (%)	100.0	83.9	3.6	0.6	0.0	12.0
Drop-out Rate (%)	3.5	2.3	15.2	0.0	n/a	11.4
H.S. Diplomas (#)	272	245	6	1	0	20

Coatesville Area SD
1515 E Lincoln Hwy • Coatesville, PA 19320-2447
(610) 383-7900 • http://www.coatesville.k12.pa.us
Grade Span: KG-12; **Agency Type:** 1
Schools: 12
7 Primary; 3 Middle; 1 High; 1 Other Level
12 Regular; 0 Special Education; 0 Vocational; 0 Alternative
0 Magnet; 0 Charter; 8 Title I Eligible; 0 School-wide Title I
Students: 7,548 (n/a% male; n/a% female)
Individual Education Program: 1,012 (13.4%);
English Language Learner: n/a; Migrant: 50 (0.7%)
Eligible for Free Lunch Program: 1,925 (25.5%)
Eligible for Reduced-Price Lunch Program: 546 (7.2%)
Teachers: 483.5 (15.6 to 1)
Librarians/Media Specialists: 10.0 (754.8 to 1)
Guidance Counselors: 22.0 (343.1 to 1)
Current Spending: ($ per student per year):
Total: $8,315; Instruction: $4,876; Support Services: $3,181
Enrollment, Drop-out Rates and Diploma Recipients by Race/Ethnicity

Category	Total	White	Black	Asian	AIAN	Hisp.
Enrollment (%)	100.0	60.2	31.8	1.0	0.1	7.0
Drop-out Rate (%)	4.4	3.3	6.1	3.7	n/a	10.3
H.S. Diplomas (#)	526	353	146	9	0	18

Downingtown Area SD
122 Wallace Ave • Downingtown, PA 19335-2643
(610) 269-8460 • http://www.dasd-adm.org/
Grade Span: KG-12; **Agency Type:** 1
Schools: 14
9 Primary; 2 Middle; 1 High; 1 Other Level
13 Regular; 0 Special Education; 0 Vocational; 0 Alternative
0 Magnet; 0 Charter; 6 Title I Eligible; 0 School-wide Title I
Students: 10,430 (n/a% male; n/a% female)
Individual Education Program: 1,460 (14.0%);
English Language Learner: n/a; Migrant: 2 (<0.1%)
Eligible for Free Lunch Program: 171 (1.6%)
Eligible for Reduced-Price Lunch Program: 98 (0.9%)
Teachers: 660.6 (15.8 to 1)
Librarians/Media Specialists: 13.4 (778.4 to 1)
Guidance Counselors: 26.0 (401.2 to 1)
Current Spending: ($ per student per year):
Total: $7,961; Instruction: $4,907; Support Services: $2,863
Enrollment, Drop-out Rates and Diploma Recipients by Race/Ethnicity

Category	Total	White	Black	Asian	AIAN	Hisp.
Enrollment (%)	100.0	92.2	4.1	2.5	0.1	1.1
Drop-out Rate (%)	1.1	0.9	6.0	0.0	0.0	4.5
H.S. Diplomas (#)	610	570	21	17	0	2

Great Valley SD
47 Church Rd • Malvern, PA 19355-1539
(610) 889-2100 • http://www.great-valley.k12.pa.us
Grade Span: KG-12; **Agency Type:** 1
Schools: 5
3 Primary; 1 Middle; 1 High; 0 Other Level
5 Regular; 0 Special Education; 0 Vocational; 0 Alternative
0 Magnet; 0 Charter; 4 Title I Eligible; 0 School-wide Title I
Students: 3,647 (n/a% male; n/a% female)
Individual Education Program: 558 (15.3%);
English Language Learner: n/a; Migrant: 0 (0.0%)
Eligible for Free Lunch Program: 96 (2.6%)
Eligible for Reduced-Price Lunch Program: 71 (1.9%)
Teachers: 240.9 (15.1 to 1)
Librarians/Media Specialists: 5.0 (729.4 to 1)
Guidance Counselors: 12.0 (303.9 to 1)
Current Spending: ($ per student per year):
Total: $10,457; Instruction: $6,291; Support Services: $3,874
Enrollment, Drop-out Rates and Diploma Recipients by Race/Ethnicity

Category	Total	White	Black	Asian	AIAN	Hisp.
Enrollment (%)	100.0	90.7	3.0	4.8	0.1	1.5
Drop-out Rate (%)	0.3	0.3	0.0	0.0	0.0	0.0
H.S. Diplomas (#)	232	207	10	12	1	2

Kennett Consolidated SD
300 E S St • Kennett Square, PA 19348-3655
(610) 444-6600 • http://www.kennett.k12.pa.us
Grade Span: KG-12; **Agency Type:** 1
Schools: 5
3 Primary; 1 Middle; 1 High; 0 Other Level
5 Regular; 0 Special Education; 0 Vocational; 0 Alternative
0 Magnet; 0 Charter; 2 Title I Eligible; 0 School-wide Title I
Students: 3,865 (n/a% male; n/a% female)
Individual Education Program: 449 (11.6%);
English Language Learner: n/a; Migrant: 544 (14.1%)
Eligible for Free Lunch Program: 685 (17.7%)
Eligible for Reduced-Price Lunch Program: 163 (4.2%)
Teachers: 238.7 (16.2 to 1)
Librarians/Media Specialists: 5.0 (773.0 to 1)
Guidance Counselors: 8.5 (454.7 to 1)
Current Spending: ($ per student per year):
Total: $7,973; Instruction: $4,878; Support Services: $2,849
Enrollment, Drop-out Rates and Diploma Recipients by Race/Ethnicity

Category	Total	White	Black	Asian	AIAN	Hisp.
Enrollment (%)	100.0	65.5	4.2	1.8	0.0	28.6
Drop-out Rate (%)	2.1	1.3	0.0	0.0	n/a	5.5
H.S. Diplomas (#)	189	137	19	5	0	28

Octorara Area SD
PO Box 500 • Atglen, PA 19310-0500
(610) 593-8213 • http://www.octorara.k12.pa.us/
Grade Span: KG-12; **Agency Type:** 1
Schools: 4
2 Primary; 1 Middle; 1 High; 0 Other Level
4 Regular; 0 Special Education; 0 Vocational; 0 Alternative
0 Magnet; 0 Charter; 4 Title I Eligible; 0 School-wide Title I
Students: 2,650 (n/a% male; n/a% female)
Individual Education Program: 364 (13.7%);
English Language Learner: n/a; Migrant: 30 (1.1%)
Eligible for Free Lunch Program: 283 (10.7%)
Eligible for Reduced-Price Lunch Program: 104 (3.9%)
Teachers: 179.0 (14.8 to 1)
Librarians/Media Specialists: 3.0 (883.3 to 1)
Guidance Counselors: 8.0 (331.3 to 1)
Current Spending: ($ per student per year):
Total: $7,949; Instruction: $5,061; Support Services: $2,668
Enrollment, Drop-out Rates and Diploma Recipients by Race/Ethnicity

Category	Total	White	Black	Asian	AIAN	Hisp.
Enrollment (%)	100.0	89.4	5.9	0.2	0.0	4.5
Drop-out Rate (%)	3.8	3.1	10.7	0.0	n/a	50.0
H.S. Diplomas (#)	141	127	8	2	0	4

Owen J Roberts SD
901 Ridge Rd • Pottstown, PA 19465-8402
(610) 469-5100 • http://www.ojr.k12.pa.us
Grade Span: KG-12; **Agency Type:** 1
Schools: 6
4 Primary; 1 Middle; 1 High; 0 Other Level
6 Regular; 0 Special Education; 0 Vocational; 0 Alternative

0 Magnet; 0 Charter; 2 Title I Eligible; 0 School-wide Title I
Students: 4,093 (n/a% male; n/a% female)
Individual Education Program: 531 (13.0%);
English Language Learner: n/a; Migrant: 0 (0.0%)
Eligible for Free Lunch Program: 222 (5.4%)
Eligible for Reduced-Price Lunch Program: 143 (3.5%)
Teachers: 256.6 (16.0 to 1)
Librarians/Media Specialists: 4.0 (1,023.3 to 1)
Guidance Counselors: 10.0 (409.3 to 1)
Current Spending: ($ per student per year):
Total: $8,770; Instruction: $4,811; Support Services: $3,664
Enrollment, Drop-out Rates and Diploma Recipients by Race/Ethnicity

Category	Total	White	Black	Asian	AIAN	Hisp.
Enrollment (%)	100.0	97.0	2.1	0.3	0.1	0.5
Drop-out Rate (%)	0.6	0.6	6.7	0.0	0.0	0.0
H.S. Diplomas (#)	261	258	2	0	0	1

Oxford Area SD
119 S 5th St • Oxford, PA 19363-1770
(610) 932-6600 • http://www.oxford.k12.pa.us
Grade Span: KG-12; **Agency Type:** 1
Schools: 5
2 Primary; 2 Middle; 1 High; 0 Other Level
5 Regular; 0 Special Education; 0 Vocational; 0 Alternative
0 Magnet; 0 Charter; 5 Title I Eligible; 0 School-wide Title I
Students: 3,247 (n/a% male; n/a% female)
Individual Education Program: 396 (12.2%);
English Language Learner: n/a; Migrant: 101 (3.1%)
Eligible for Free Lunch Program: 595 (18.3%)
Eligible for Reduced-Price Lunch Program: 207 (6.4%)
Teachers: 210.5 (15.4 to 1)
Librarians/Media Specialists: 4.5 (721.6 to 1)
Guidance Counselors: 6.5 (499.5 to 1)
Current Spending: ($ per student per year):
Total: $6,051; Instruction: $3,847; Support Services: $1,955
Enrollment, Drop-out Rates and Diploma Recipients by Race/Ethnicity

Category	Total	White	Black	Asian	AIAN	Hisp.
Enrollment (%)	100.0	79.4	6.6	0.5	0.1	13.4
Drop-out Rate (%)	3.2	3.1	2.6	0.0	n/a	5.5
H.S. Diplomas (#)	162	136	16	3	0	7

Phoenixville Area SD
1120 Gay St • Phoenixville, PA 19460-4417
(610) 933-8861 • http://www.pasd.com
Grade Span: KG-12; **Agency Type:** 1
Schools: 6
4 Primary; 1 Middle; 1 High; 0 Other Level
6 Regular; 0 Special Education; 0 Vocational; 0 Alternative
0 Magnet; 0 Charter; 2 Title I Eligible; 0 School-wide Title I
Students: 3,232 (n/a% male; n/a% female)
Individual Education Program: 493 (15.3%);
English Language Learner: n/a; Migrant: 0 (0.0%)
Eligible for Free Lunch Program: 315 (9.7%)
Eligible for Reduced-Price Lunch Program: 147 (4.5%)
Teachers: 234.6 (13.8 to 1)
Librarians/Media Specialists: 5.6 (577.1 to 1)
Guidance Counselors: 10.6 (304.9 to 1)
Current Spending: ($ per student per year):
Total: $10,070; Instruction: $6,248; Support Services: $3,545
Enrollment, Drop-out Rates and Diploma Recipients by Race/Ethnicity

Category	Total	White	Black	Asian	AIAN	Hisp.
Enrollment (%)	100.0	84.0	10.2	2.6	0.1	3.1
Drop-out Rate (%)	2.0	1.8	5.9	0.0	0.0	0.0
H.S. Diplomas (#)	184	165	14	3	0	2

Tredyffrin-Easttown SD
738 First Ave • Berwyn, PA 19312-1779
(610) 240-1900 • http://www.tesd.k12.pa.us
Grade Span: KG-12; **Agency Type:** 1
Schools: 8
5 Primary; 2 Middle; 1 High; 0 Other Level
8 Regular; 0 Special Education; 0 Vocational; 0 Alternative
0 Magnet; 0 Charter; 0 Title I Eligible; 0 School-wide Title I
Students: 5,633 (n/a% male; n/a% female)
Individual Education Program: 662 (11.8%);
English Language Learner: n/a; Migrant: 0 (0.0%)
Eligible for Free Lunch Program: 81 (1.4%)
Eligible for Reduced-Price Lunch Program: 31 (0.6%)
Teachers: 394.1 (14.3 to 1)
Librarians/Media Specialists: 9.0 (625.9 to 1)
Guidance Counselors: 21.0 (268.2 to 1)
Current Spending: ($ per student per year):
Total: $10,631; Instruction: $6,463; Support Services: $3,913

Enrollment, Drop-out Rates and Diploma Recipients by Race/Ethnicity

Category	Total	White	Black	Asian	AIAN	Hisp.
Enrollment (%)	100.0	88.9	3.0	7.0	0.1	1.0
Drop-out Rate (%)	0.1	0.1	0.0	0.0	0.0	0.0
H.S. Diplomas (#)	372	331	9	29	0	3

Unionville-Chadds Ford SD
740 Unionville Rd • Kennett Square, PA 19348-1531
(610) 347-0970 • http://www.ucf.k12.pa.us
Grade Span: KG-12; **Agency Type:** 1
Schools: 5
3 Primary; 1 Middle; 1 High; 0 Other Level
5 Regular; 0 Special Education; 0 Vocational; 0 Alternative
0 Magnet; 0 Charter; 0 Title I Eligible; 0 School-wide Title I
Students: 3,838 (n/a% male; n/a% female)
Individual Education Program: 483 (12.6%);
English Language Learner: n/a; Migrant: 7 (0.2%)
Eligible for Free Lunch Program: 46 (1.2%)
Eligible for Reduced-Price Lunch Program: 29 (0.8%)
Teachers: 252.4 (15.2 to 1)
Librarians/Media Specialists: 5.7 (673.3 to 1)
Guidance Counselors: 13.0 (295.2 to 1)
Current Spending: ($ per student per year):
Total: $8,847; Instruction: $5,335; Support Services: $3,227
Enrollment, Drop-out Rates and Diploma Recipients by Race/Ethnicity

Category	Total	White	Black	Asian	AIAN	Hisp.
Enrollment (%)	100.0	94.3	0.5	3.3	0.1	1.8
Drop-out Rate (%)	0.4	0.5	0.0	0.0	n/a	0.0
H.S. Diplomas (#)	279	264	0	11	1	3

West Chester Area SD
829 Paoli Pike • West Chester, PA 19380-4551
(610) 436-7000 • http://www.wcasd.k12.pa.us
Grade Span: KG-12; **Agency Type:** 1
Schools: 15
10 Primary; 3 Middle; 2 High; 0 Other Level
15 Regular; 0 Special Education; 0 Vocational; 0 Alternative
0 Magnet; 0 Charter; 12 Title I Eligible; 0 School-wide Title I
Students: 11,590 (n/a% male; n/a% female)
Individual Education Program: 1,449 (12.5%);
English Language Learner: n/a; Migrant: 12 (0.1%)
Eligible for Free Lunch Program: 478 (4.1%)
Eligible for Reduced-Price Lunch Program: 162 (1.4%)
Teachers: 698.6 (16.6 to 1)
Librarians/Media Specialists: 14.0 (827.9 to 1)
Guidance Counselors: 35.0 (331.1 to 1)
Current Spending: ($ per student per year):
Total: $8,628; Instruction: $5,464; Support Services: $2,983
Enrollment, Drop-out Rates and Diploma Recipients by Race/Ethnicity

Category	Total	White	Black	Asian	AIAN	Hisp.
Enrollment (%)	100.0	84.3	8.2	4.2	0.1	3.2
Drop-out Rate (%)	1.5	1.1	3.8	0.0	33.3	6.5
H.S. Diplomas (#)	876	744	76	34	0	22

Clearfield County

Clearfield Area SD
PO Box 710 • Clearfield, PA 16830-0710
(814) 765-5511 • http://www.clearfield.org
Grade Span: KG-12; **Agency Type:** 1
Schools: 8
5 Primary; 1 Middle; 1 High; 0 Other Level
7 Regular; 0 Special Education; 0 Vocational; 0 Alternative
0 Magnet; 0 Charter; 7 Title I Eligible; 2 School-wide Title I
Students: 3,047 (n/a% male; n/a% female)
Individual Education Program: 423 (13.9%);
English Language Learner: n/a; Migrant: 0 (0.0%)
Eligible for Free Lunch Program: 1,383 (45.4%)
Eligible for Reduced-Price Lunch Program: 337 (11.1%)
Teachers: 188.5 (16.2 to 1)
Librarians/Media Specialists: 4.0 (761.8 to 1)
Guidance Counselors: 6.0 (507.8 to 1)
Current Spending: ($ per student per year):
Total: $6,911; Instruction: $4,329; Support Services: $2,228
Enrollment, Drop-out Rates and Diploma Recipients by Race/Ethnicity

Category	Total	White	Black	Asian	AIAN	Hisp.
Enrollment (%)	100.0	98.0	1.1	0.5	0.1	0.3
Drop-out Rate (%)	3.9	3.9	16.7	0.0	0.0	0.0
H.S. Diplomas (#)	193	187	1	4	0	1

Dubois Area SD
500 Liberty Blvd • Du Bois, PA 15801-2437
(814) 371-2700 • http://www.dasd.k12.pa.us
Grade Span: KG-12; **Agency Type:** 1
Schools: 10

8 Primary; 1 Middle; 1 High; 0 Other Level
10 Regular; 0 Special Education; 0 Vocational; 0 Alternative
0 Magnet; 0 Charter; 8 Title I Eligible; 0 School-wide Title I
Students: 4,618 (n/a% male; n/a% female)
Individual Education Program: 618 (13.4%);
English Language Learner: n/a; Migrant: 0 (0.0%)
Eligible for Free Lunch Program: 1,287 (27.9%)
Eligible for Reduced-Price Lunch Program: 392 (8.5%)
Teachers: 284.6 (16.2 to 1)
Librarians/Media Specialists: 3.0 (1,539.3 to 1)
Guidance Counselors: 11.0 (419.8 to 1)
Current Spending: ($ per student per year):
Total: $6,548; Instruction: $4,352; Support Services: $1,941
Enrollment, Drop-out Rates and Diploma Recipients by Race/Ethnicity

Category	Total	White	Black	Asian	AIAN	Hisp.
Enrollment (%)	100.0	99.0	0.3	0.4	0.1	0.2
Drop-out Rate (%)	3.8	3.7	0.0	0.0	0.0	100.0
H.S. Diplomas (#)	246	243	1	0	0	2

Philipsburg-Osceola Area SD
200 Short St • Philipsburg, PA 16866-2640
(814) 342-1050 • http://www.poasd.org
Grade Span: KG-12; **Agency Type:** 1
Schools: 6
4 Primary; 1 Middle; 1 High; 0 Other Level
6 Regular; 0 Special Education; 0 Vocational; 0 Alternative
0 Magnet; 0 Charter; 5 Title I Eligible; 0 School-wide Title I
Students: 2,228 (n/a% male; n/a% female)
Individual Education Program: 270 (12.1%);
English Language Learner: n/a; Migrant: 0 (0.0%)
Eligible for Free Lunch Program: 496 (22.3%)
Eligible for Reduced-Price Lunch Program: 248 (11.1%)
Teachers: 157.5 (14.1 to 1)
Librarians/Media Specialists: 5.0 (445.6 to 1)
Guidance Counselors: 7.0 (318.3 to 1)
Current Spending: ($ per student per year):
Total: $7,058; Instruction: $4,342; Support Services: $2,375
Enrollment, Drop-out Rates and Diploma Recipients by Race/Ethnicity

Category	Total	White	Black	Asian	AIAN	Hisp.
Enrollment (%)	100.0	98.6	0.6	0.4	0.0	0.4
Drop-out Rate (%)	2.9	2.9	0.0	0.0	n/a	0.0
H.S. Diplomas (#)	148	147	1	0	0	0

Clinton County

Keystone Central SD
95 W 4th St • Lock Haven, PA 17745-1100
(570) 893-4900 • http://oak.kcsd.k12.pa.us
Grade Span: KG-12; **Agency Type:** 1
Schools: 12
9 Primary; 1 Middle; 1 High; 1 Other Level
12 Regular; 0 Special Education; 0 Vocational; 0 Alternative
0 Magnet; 0 Charter; 10 Title I Eligible; 0 School-wide Title I
Students: 4,768 (n/a% male; n/a% female)
Individual Education Program: 830 (17.4%);
English Language Learner: n/a; Migrant: 2 (<0.1%)
Eligible for Free Lunch Program: 1,335 (28.0%)
Eligible for Reduced-Price Lunch Program: 514 (10.8%)
Teachers: 360.5 (13.2 to 1)
Librarians/Media Specialists: 6.0 (794.7 to 1)
Guidance Counselors: 12.0 (397.3 to 1)
Current Spending: ($ per student per year):
Total: $8,745; Instruction: $5,657; Support Services: $2,779
Enrollment, Drop-out Rates and Diploma Recipients by Race/Ethnicity

Category	Total	White	Black	Asian	AIAN	Hisp.
Enrollment (%)	100.0	97.6	1.0	0.9	0.1	0.4
Drop-out Rate (%)	3.0	3.0	0.0	0.0	0.0	0.0
H.S. Diplomas (#)	369	365	2	0	1	1

Columbia County

Berwick Area SD
500 Line St • Berwick, PA 18603-3300
(570) 759-6400 • http://www.berwicksd.org
Grade Span: KG-12; **Agency Type:** 1
Schools: 7
5 Primary; 1 Middle; 1 High; 0 Other Level
7 Regular; 0 Special Education; 0 Vocational; 0 Alternative
0 Magnet; 0 Charter; 0 Title I Eligible; 0 School-wide Title I
Students: 3,455 (n/a% male; n/a% female)
Individual Education Program: 620 (17.9%);
English Language Learner: n/a; Migrant: 0 (0.0%)
Eligible for Free Lunch Program: 873 (25.3%)
Eligible for Reduced-Price Lunch Program: 365 (10.6%)
Teachers: 241.0 (14.3 to 1)
Librarians/Media Specialists: 3.0 (1,151.7 to 1)
Guidance Counselors: 5.0 (691.0 to 1)
Current Spending: ($ per student per year):
Total: $7,203; Instruction: $4,819; Support Services: $2,055
Enrollment, Drop-out Rates and Diploma Recipients by Race/Ethnicity

Category	Total	White	Black	Asian	AIAN	Hisp.
Enrollment (%)	100.0	96.6	1.3	0.3	0.0	1.8
Drop-out Rate (%)	4.1	4.2	0.0	0.0	n/a	0.0
H.S. Diplomas (#)	208	205	1	1	0	1

Bloomsburg Area SD
728 E 5th St • Bloomsburg, PA 17815-2305
(570) 784-5000
Grade Span: KG-12; **Agency Type:** 1
Schools: 5
3 Primary; 1 Middle; 1 High; 0 Other Level
5 Regular; 0 Special Education; 0 Vocational; 0 Alternative
0 Magnet; 0 Charter; 3 Title I Eligible; 0 School-wide Title I
Students: 1,776 (n/a% male; n/a% female)
Individual Education Program: 273 (15.4%);
English Language Learner: n/a; Migrant: 0 (0.0%)
Eligible for Free Lunch Program: 369 (20.8%)
Eligible for Reduced-Price Lunch Program: 193 (10.9%)
Teachers: 125.5 (14.2 to 1)
Librarians/Media Specialists: 3.0 (592.0 to 1)
Guidance Counselors: 4.0 (444.0 to 1)
Current Spending: ($ per student per year):
Total: $7,171; Instruction: $4,612; Support Services: $2,281
Enrollment, Drop-out Rates and Diploma Recipients by Race/Ethnicity

Category	Total	White	Black	Asian	AIAN	Hisp.
Enrollment (%)	100.0	93.8	2.8	1.7	0.0	1.7
Drop-out Rate (%)	3.2	3.2	8.3	0.0	n/a	0.0
H.S. Diplomas (#)	100	97	1	1	0	1

Central Columbia SD
4777 Old Berwick Rd • Bloomsburg, PA 17815-3515
(570) 784-2850 • http://www.centralcolumbia.k12.pa.us
Grade Span: KG-12; **Agency Type:** 1
Schools: 3
1 Primary; 1 Middle; 1 High; 0 Other Level
3 Regular; 0 Special Education; 0 Vocational; 0 Alternative
0 Magnet; 0 Charter; 3 Title I Eligible; 0 School-wide Title I
Students: 2,224 (n/a% male; n/a% female)
Individual Education Program: 224 (10.1%);
English Language Learner: n/a; Migrant: 0 (0.0%)
Eligible for Free Lunch Program: 216 (9.7%)
Eligible for Reduced-Price Lunch Program: 146 (6.6%)
Teachers: 134.0 (16.6 to 1)
Librarians/Media Specialists: 3.0 (741.3 to 1)
Guidance Counselors: 4.0 (556.0 to 1)
Current Spending: ($ per student per year):
Total: $6,660; Instruction: $4,096; Support Services: $2,307
Enrollment, Drop-out Rates and Diploma Recipients by Race/Ethnicity

Category	Total	White	Black	Asian	AIAN	Hisp.
Enrollment (%)	100.0	96.4	0.9	1.7	0.1	0.9
Drop-out Rate (%)	1.7	1.7	0.0	0.0	0.0	0.0
H.S. Diplomas (#)	146	139	1	6	0	0

Crawford County

Conneaut SD
219 W School Dr • Linesville, PA 16424-8609
(814) 683-5900 • http://connwww.iu5.org
Grade Span: KG-12; **Agency Type:** 1
Schools: 7
4 Primary; 0 Middle; 3 High; 0 Other Level
7 Regular; 0 Special Education; 0 Vocational; 0 Alternative
0 Magnet; 0 Charter; 0 Title I Eligible; 0 School-wide Title I
Students: 2,968 (n/a% male; n/a% female)
Individual Education Program: 447 (15.1%);
English Language Learner: n/a; Migrant: 1 (<0.1%)
Eligible for Free Lunch Program: 822 (27.7%)
Eligible for Reduced-Price Lunch Program: 321 (10.8%)
Teachers: 189.8 (15.6 to 1)
Librarians/Media Specialists: 6.0 (494.7 to 1)
Guidance Counselors: 6.0 (494.7 to 1)
Current Spending: ($ per student per year):
Total: $6,395; Instruction: $3,878; Support Services: $2,244
Enrollment, Drop-out Rates and Diploma Recipients by Race/Ethnicity

Category	Total	White	Black	Asian	AIAN	Hisp.
Enrollment (%)	100.0	98.2	1.0	0.5	0.0	0.3
Drop-out Rate (%)	3.9	4.0	0.0	0.0	0.0	0.0
H.S. Diplomas (#)	223	219	1	1	0	2

Crawford Central SD

11280 Mercer Pike • Meadville, PA 16335-9504
(814) 724-3960 • http://craw.org
Grade Span: KG-12; **Agency Type:** 1
Schools: 9
6 Primary; 1 Middle; 2 High; 0 Other Level
9 Regular; 0 Special Education; 0 Vocational; 0 Alternative
0 Magnet; 0 Charter; 6 Title I Eligible; 1 School-wide Title I
Students: 4,301 (n/a% male; n/a% female)
Individual Education Program: 716 (16.6%);
English Language Learner: n/a; Migrant: 0 (0.0%)
Eligible for Free Lunch Program: 1,129 (26.2%)
Eligible for Reduced-Price Lunch Program: 268 (6.2%)
Teachers: 302.1 (14.2 to 1)
Librarians/Media Specialists: 6.0 (716.8 to 1)
Guidance Counselors: 14.0 (307.2 to 1)
Current Spending: ($ per student per year):
Total: $7,732; Instruction: $4,991; Support Services: $2,514
Enrollment, Drop-out Rates and Diploma Recipients by Race/Ethnicity

Category	Total	White	Black	Asian	AIAN	Hisp.
Enrollment (%)	100.0	90.1	7.1	1.0	0.9	0.9
Drop-out Rate (%)	3.8	3.3	15.5	0.0	0.0	0.0
H.S. Diplomas (#)	343	327	10	1	0	5

Penncrest SD

PO Box 808 • Saegertown, PA 16433-0808
(814) 763-2323 • http://penncrest.iu5.org
Grade Span: KG-12; **Agency Type:** 1
Schools: 7
4 Primary; 0 Middle; 3 High; 0 Other Level
7 Regular; 0 Special Education; 0 Vocational; 0 Alternative
0 Magnet; 0 Charter; 0 Title I Eligible; 0 School-wide Title I
Students: 3,982 (n/a% male; n/a% female)
Individual Education Program: 533 (13.4%);
English Language Learner: n/a; Migrant: 0 (0.0%)
Eligible for Free Lunch Program: 862 (21.6%)
Eligible for Reduced-Price Lunch Program: 351 (8.8%)
Teachers: 252.5 (15.8 to 1)
Librarians/Media Specialists: 6.5 (612.6 to 1)
Guidance Counselors: 9.0 (442.4 to 1)
Current Spending: ($ per student per year):
Total: $7,462; Instruction: $4,620; Support Services: $2,572
Enrollment, Drop-out Rates and Diploma Recipients by Race/Ethnicity

Category	Total	White	Black	Asian	AIAN	Hisp.
Enrollment (%)	100.0	99.3	0.4	0.1	0.0	0.2
Drop-out Rate (%)	1.7	1.7	0.0	0.0	n/a	0.0
H.S. Diplomas (#)	299	295	4	0	0	0

Cumberland County

Big Spring SD

45 Mount Rock Rd • Newville, PA 17241-9412
(717) 776-2000 • http://www.bigspring.k12.pa.us/
Grade Span: KG-12; **Agency Type:** 1
Schools: 7
5 Primary; 1 Middle; 1 High; 0 Other Level
7 Regular; 0 Special Education; 0 Vocational; 0 Alternative
0 Magnet; 0 Charter; 5 Title I Eligible; 0 School-wide Title I
Students: 3,203 (n/a% male; n/a% female)
Individual Education Program: 521 (16.3%);
English Language Learner: n/a; Migrant: 6 (0.2%)
Eligible for Free Lunch Program: 283 (8.8%)
Eligible for Reduced-Price Lunch Program: 228 (7.1%)
Teachers: 226.8 (14.1 to 1)
Librarians/Media Specialists: 4.0 (800.8 to 1)
Guidance Counselors: 7.0 (457.6 to 1)
Current Spending: ($ per student per year):
Total: $6,446; Instruction: $4,080; Support Services: $2,092
Enrollment, Drop-out Rates and Diploma Recipients by Race/Ethnicity

Category	Total	White	Black	Asian	AIAN	Hisp.
Enrollment (%)	100.0	97.7	1.0	0.3	0.3	0.7
Drop-out Rate (%)	3.1	3.1	0.0	0.0	n/a	25.0
H.S. Diplomas (#)	209	204	3	2	0	0

Carlisle Area SD

623 W Penn St • Carlisle, PA 17013-2239
(717) 240-6800 • http://www.carlisleschools.org
Grade Span: KG-12; **Agency Type:** 1
Schools: 10
7 Primary; 2 Middle; 1 High; 0 Other Level
10 Regular; 0 Special Education; 0 Vocational; 0 Alternative
0 Magnet; 0 Charter; 5 Title I Eligible; 0 School-wide Title I
Students: 4,751 (n/a% male; n/a% female)
Individual Education Program: 718 (15.1%);
English Language Learner: n/a; Migrant: 35 (0.7%)
Eligible for Free Lunch Program: 550 (11.6%)
Eligible for Reduced-Price Lunch Program: 202 (4.3%)
Teachers: 335.2 (14.2 to 1)
Librarians/Media Specialists: 5.2 (913.7 to 1)
Guidance Counselors: 16.5 (287.9 to 1)
Current Spending: ($ per student per year):
Total: $7,229; Instruction: $4,587; Support Services: $2,360
Enrollment, Drop-out Rates and Diploma Recipients by Race/Ethnicity

Category	Total	White	Black	Asian	AIAN	Hisp.
Enrollment (%)	100.0	87.1	8.6	1.8	0.4	2.1
Drop-out Rate (%)	3.5	3.4	2.7	2.7	n/a	10.0
H.S. Diplomas (#)	319	272	22	12	2	11

Cumberland Valley SD

6746 Carlisle Pike • Mechanicsburg, PA 17050-1711
(717) 697-8261 • http://www.cvschools.org/
Grade Span: KG-12; **Agency Type:** 1
Schools: 10
7 Primary; 2 Middle; 1 High; 0 Other Level
10 Regular; 0 Special Education; 0 Vocational; 0 Alternative
0 Magnet; 0 Charter; 5 Title I Eligible; 0 School-wide Title I
Students: 7,667 (n/a% male; n/a% female)
Individual Education Program: 911 (11.9%);
English Language Learner: n/a; Migrant: 0 (0.0%)
Eligible for Free Lunch Program: 246 (3.2%)
Eligible for Reduced-Price Lunch Program: 164 (2.1%)
Teachers: 477.8 (16.0 to 1)
Librarians/Media Specialists: 5.0 (1,533.4 to 1)
Guidance Counselors: 21.0 (365.1 to 1)
Current Spending: ($ per student per year):
Total: $6,794; Instruction: $4,281; Support Services: $2,256
Enrollment, Drop-out Rates and Diploma Recipients by Race/Ethnicity

Category	Total	White	Black	Asian	AIAN	Hisp.
Enrollment (%)	100.0	93.2	1.3	4.4	0.2	0.9
Drop-out Rate (%)	2.1	2.2	3.3	1.0	0.0	0.0
H.S. Diplomas (#)	545	512	4	20	1	8

East Pennsboro Area SD

890 Valley St • Enola, PA 17025-1541
(717) 732-3601 • http://www.epasd.k12.pa.us
Grade Span: KG-12; **Agency Type:** 1
Schools: 4
2 Primary; 1 Middle; 1 High; 0 Other Level
4 Regular; 0 Special Education; 0 Vocational; 0 Alternative
0 Magnet; 0 Charter; 2 Title I Eligible; 0 School-wide Title I
Students: 2,723 (n/a% male; n/a% female)
Individual Education Program: 372 (13.7%);
English Language Learner: n/a; Migrant: 8 (0.3%)
Eligible for Free Lunch Program: 221 (8.1%)
Eligible for Reduced-Price Lunch Program: 163 (6.0%)
Teachers: 185.6 (14.7 to 1)
Librarians/Media Specialists: 4.0 (680.8 to 1)
Guidance Counselors: 7.0 (389.0 to 1)
Current Spending: ($ per student per year):
Total: $6,612; Instruction: $4,348; Support Services: $2,027
Enrollment, Drop-out Rates and Diploma Recipients by Race/Ethnicity

Category	Total	White	Black	Asian	AIAN	Hisp.
Enrollment (%)	100.0	92.3	2.1	3.7	0.3	1.6
Drop-out Rate (%)	3.8	4.0	0.0	3.4	0.0	0.0
H.S. Diplomas (#)	149	139	2	5	0	3

Mechanicsburg Area SD

500 S Broad St • Mechanicsburg, PA 17050
(717) 691-4500 • http://www.mbgsd.k12.pa.us/
Grade Span: KG-12; **Agency Type:** 1
Schools: 8
6 Primary; 1 Middle; 1 High; 0 Other Level
8 Regular; 0 Special Education; 0 Vocational; 0 Alternative
0 Magnet; 0 Charter; 5 Title I Eligible; 0 School-wide Title I
Students: 3,549 (n/a% male; n/a% female)
Individual Education Program: 402 (11.3%);
English Language Learner: n/a; Migrant: 20 (0.6%)
Eligible for Free Lunch Program: 336 (9.5%)
Eligible for Reduced-Price Lunch Program: 148 (4.2%)
Teachers: 243.3 (14.6 to 1)
Librarians/Media Specialists: 4.0 (887.3 to 1)
Guidance Counselors: 10.0 (354.9 to 1)
Current Spending: ($ per student per year):
Total: $7,226; Instruction: $4,774; Support Services: $2,137
Enrollment, Drop-out Rates and Diploma Recipients by Race/Ethnicity

Category	Total	White	Black	Asian	AIAN	Hisp.
Enrollment (%)	100.0	94.8	2.3	1.3	0.1	1.5
Drop-out Rate (%)	1.5	1.2	14.3	0.0	0.0	33.3
H.S. Diplomas (#)	230	219	4	5	0	2

Shippensburg Area SD

317 N Morris St • Shippensburg, PA 17257-1654
(717) 530-2700 • http://www.ship.k12.pa.us
Grade Span: KG-12; **Agency Type:** 1
Schools: 5
3 Primary; 1 Middle; 1 High; 0 Other Level
5 Regular; 0 Special Education; 0 Vocational; 0 Alternative
0 Magnet; 0 Charter; 3 Title I Eligible; 0 School-wide Title I
Students: 3,270 (n/a% male; n/a% female)
Individual Education Program: 445 (13.6%);
English Language Learner: n/a; Migrant: 1 (<0.1%)
Eligible for Free Lunch Program: 406 (12.4%)
Eligible for Reduced-Price Lunch Program: 267 (8.2%)
Teachers: 187.4 (17.4 to 1)
Librarians/Media Specialists: 4.0 (817.5 to 1)
Guidance Counselors: 7.0 (467.1 to 1)
Current Spending: ($ per student per year):
Total: $6,218; Instruction: $4,017; Support Services: $1,930
Enrollment, Drop-out Rates and Diploma Recipients by Race/Ethnicity

Category	Total	White	Black	Asian	AIAN	Hisp.
Enrollment (%)	100.0	95.0	3.1	0.9	0.1	1.0
Drop-out Rate (%)	2.2	2.3	0.0	0.0	0.0	0.0
H.S. Diplomas (#)	208	199	4	1	0	4

South Middleton SD

4 Forge Rd • Boiling Springs, PA 17007-9523
(717) 258-6484 • http://www.bubblers.k12.pa.us
Grade Span: KG-12; **Agency Type:** 1
Schools: 4
1 Primary; 2 Middle; 1 High; 0 Other Level
4 Regular; 0 Special Education; 0 Vocational; 0 Alternative
0 Magnet; 0 Charter; 0 Title I Eligible; 0 School-wide Title I
Students: 2,154 (n/a% male; n/a% female)
Individual Education Program: 273 (12.7%);
English Language Learner: n/a; Migrant: 0 (0.0%)
Eligible for Free Lunch Program: 78 (3.6%)
Eligible for Reduced-Price Lunch Program: 40 (1.9%)
Teachers: 150.0 (14.4 to 1)
Librarians/Media Specialists: 4.0 (538.5 to 1)
Guidance Counselors: 7.0 (307.7 to 1)
Current Spending: ($ per student per year):
Total: $7,001; Instruction: $4,494; Support Services: $2,256
Enrollment, Drop-out Rates and Diploma Recipients by Race/Ethnicity

Category	Total	White	Black	Asian	AIAN	Hisp.
Enrollment (%)	100.0	97.4	0.8	0.9	0.3	0.5
Drop-out Rate (%)	4.4	4.5	0.0	0.0	0.0	0.0
H.S. Diplomas (#)	154	152	0	1	1	0

Dauphin County

Central Dauphin SD

600 Rutherford Rd • Harrisburg, PA 17109-5227
(717) 545-4703 • http://www.cdsd.k12.pa.us/
Grade Span: KG-12; **Agency Type:** 1
Schools: 19
14 Primary; 3 Middle; 2 High; 0 Other Level
19 Regular; 0 Special Education; 0 Vocational; 0 Alternative
0 Magnet; 0 Charter; 9 Title I Eligible; 0 School-wide Title I
Students: 11,018 (n/a% male; n/a% female)
Individual Education Program: 1,380 (12.5%);
English Language Learner: n/a; Migrant: 133 (1.2%)
Eligible for Free Lunch Program: 1,823 (16.5%)
Eligible for Reduced-Price Lunch Program: 642 (5.8%)
Teachers: 740.1 (14.9 to 1)
Librarians/Media Specialists: 17.0 (648.1 to 1)
Guidance Counselors: 27.5 (400.7 to 1)
Current Spending: ($ per student per year):
Total: $7,064; Instruction: $4,526; Support Services: $2,266
Enrollment, Drop-out Rates and Diploma Recipients by Race/Ethnicity

Category	Total	White	Black	Asian	AIAN	Hisp.
Enrollment (%)	100.0	73.1	18.4	3.5	0.2	4.8
Drop-out Rate (%)	2.6	2.6	0.8	2.8	0.0	9.5
H.S. Diplomas (#)	706	569	82	28	1	26

Derry Township SD

PO Box 898 • Hershey, PA 17033-0898
(717) 534-2501 • http://www.hershey.k12.pa.us
Grade Span: KG-12; **Agency Type:** 1
Schools: 5
2 Primary; 2 Middle; 1 High; 0 Other Level
5 Regular; 0 Special Education; 0 Vocational; 0 Alternative
0 Magnet; 0 Charter; 0 Title I Eligible; 0 School-wide Title I
Students: 3,405 (n/a% male; n/a% female)
Individual Education Program: 331 (9.7%);
English Language Learner: n/a; Migrant: 3 (0.1%)
Eligible for Free Lunch Program: 125 (3.7%)
Eligible for Reduced-Price Lunch Program: 91 (2.7%)
Teachers: 213.1 (16.0 to 1)
Librarians/Media Specialists: 5.0 (681.0 to 1)
Guidance Counselors: 9.0 (378.3 to 1)
Current Spending: ($ per student per year):
Total: $7,206; Instruction: $4,427; Support Services: $2,450
Enrollment, Drop-out Rates and Diploma Recipients by Race/Ethnicity

Category	Total	White	Black	Asian	AIAN	Hisp.
Enrollment (%)	100.0	92.1	1.8	4.8	0.2	1.1
Drop-out Rate (%)	0.8	0.7	7.7	0.0	0.0	0.0
H.S. Diplomas (#)	247	239	1	3	2	2

Harrisburg City SD

1201 N Sixth St • Harrisburg, PA 17102-1406
(717) 703-4000 • http://www.hbgsd.k12.pa.us
Grade Span: KG-12; **Agency Type:** 1
Schools: 16
12 Primary; 0 Middle; 1 High; 2 Other Level
15 Regular; 0 Special Education; 0 Vocational; 0 Alternative
0 Magnet; 0 Charter; 14 Title I Eligible; 14 School-wide Title I
Students: 7,492 (n/a% male; n/a% female)
Individual Education Program: 1,309 (17.5%);
English Language Learner: n/a; Migrant: 243 (3.2%)
Eligible for Free Lunch Program: 4,106 (54.8%)
Eligible for Reduced-Price Lunch Program: 385 (5.1%)
Teachers: 579.0 (12.9 to 1)
Librarians/Media Specialists: 6.0 (1,248.7 to 1)
Guidance Counselors: 22.0 (340.5 to 1)
Current Spending: ($ per student per year):
Total: $10,202; Instruction: $6,268; Support Services: $3,498
Enrollment, Drop-out Rates and Diploma Recipients by Race/Ethnicity

Category	Total	White	Black	Asian	AIAN	Hisp.
Enrollment (%)	100.0	6.2	77.7	2.0	0.1	14.1
Drop-out Rate (%)	12.8	18.1	11.7	8.3	0.0	18.5
H.S. Diplomas (#)	199	20	153	14	0	12

Lower Dauphin SD

291 E Main St • Hummelstown, PA 17036-1799
(717) 566-5300 • http://www.ldsd.org
Grade Span: KG-12; **Agency Type:** 1
Schools: 7
5 Primary; 1 Middle; 1 High; 0 Other Level
7 Regular; 0 Special Education; 0 Vocational; 0 Alternative
0 Magnet; 0 Charter; 3 Title I Eligible; 0 School-wide Title I
Students: 3,913 (n/a% male; n/a% female)
Individual Education Program: 618 (15.8%);
English Language Learner: n/a; Migrant: 1 (<0.1%)
Eligible for Free Lunch Program: 302 (7.7%)
Eligible for Reduced-Price Lunch Program: 204 (5.2%)
Teachers: 260.0 (15.1 to 1)
Librarians/Media Specialists: 4.0 (978.3 to 1)
Guidance Counselors: 12.0 (326.1 to 1)
Current Spending: ($ per student per year):
Total: $7,035; Instruction: $4,474; Support Services: $2,282
Enrollment, Drop-out Rates and Diploma Recipients by Race/Ethnicity

Category	Total	White	Black	Asian	AIAN	Hisp.
Enrollment (%)	100.0	95.9	1.8	0.8	0.2	1.3
Drop-out Rate (%)	2.1	1.3	0.0	10.0	n/a	9.1
H.S. Diplomas (#)	254	248	1	0	0	5

Middletown Area SD

55 W Water St • Middletown, PA 17057-1448
(717) 948-3300 • http://www.middletownschools.com/
Grade Span: KG-12; **Agency Type:** 1
Schools: 6
2 Primary; 2 Middle; 1 High; 0 Other Level
5 Regular; 0 Special Education; 0 Vocational; 0 Alternative
0 Magnet; 0 Charter; 2 Title I Eligible; 0 School-wide Title I
Students: 2,675 (n/a% male; n/a% female)
Individual Education Program: 450 (16.8%);
English Language Learner: n/a; Migrant: 0 (0.0%)
Eligible for Free Lunch Program: 394 (14.7%)
Eligible for Reduced-Price Lunch Program: 199 (7.4%)
Teachers: 192.0 (13.9 to 1)
Librarians/Media Specialists: 4.5 (594.4 to 1)
Guidance Counselors: 8.0 (334.4 to 1)
Current Spending: ($ per student per year):
Total: $7,058; Instruction: $4,420; Support Services: $2,384
Enrollment, Drop-out Rates and Diploma Recipients by Race/Ethnicity

Category	Total	White	Black	Asian	AIAN	Hisp.
Enrollment (%)	100.0	82.5	11.0	1.0	0.6	4.9
Drop-out Rate (%)	2.4	2.5	1.5	0.0	0.0	3.2
H.S. Diplomas (#)	173	153	9	3	0	8

PDE Division of Data Services

333market Street, 14th Floor • Harrisburg, PA 17126-0333
(717) 778-2644
Grade Span: KG-12; **Agency Type:** 5
Schools: 2
0 Primary; 0 Middle; 0 High; 2 Other Level
0 Regular; 2 Special Education; 0 Vocational; 0 Alternative
0 Magnet; 0 Charter; 0 Title I Eligible; 0 School-wide Title I
Students: 15,044 (n/a% male; n/a% female)
Individual Education Program: 0 (0.0%);
English Language Learner: n/a; Migrant: n/a
Eligible for Free Lunch Program: n/a
Eligible for Reduced-Price Lunch Program: n/a
Teachers: n/a
Librarians/Media Specialists: n/a
Guidance Counselors: n/a
Current Spending: ($ per student per year):
Total: n/a; Instruction: n/a; Support Services: n/a
Enrollment, Drop-out Rates and Diploma Recipients by Race/Ethnicity

Category	Total	White	Black	Asian	AIAN	Hisp.
Enrollment (%)	100.0	78.9	15.4	1.0	0.2	4.5
Drop-out Rate (%)	n/a	n/a	n/a	n/a	n/a	n/a
H.S. Diplomas (#)	0	0	0	0	0	0

Susquehanna Township SD

3550 Elmerton Ave • Harrisburg, PA 17109-1131
(717) 657-5100 • http://www.hannasd.org
Grade Span: KG-12; **Agency Type:** 1
Schools: 5
3 Primary; 1 Middle; 1 High; 0 Other Level
5 Regular; 0 Special Education; 0 Vocational; 0 Alternative
0 Magnet; 0 Charter; 4 Title I Eligible; 0 School-wide Title I
Students: 3,108 (n/a% male; n/a% female)
Individual Education Program: 487 (15.7%);
English Language Learner: n/a; Migrant: 14 (0.5%)
Eligible for Free Lunch Program: 334 (10.7%)
Eligible for Reduced-Price Lunch Program: 190 (6.1%)
Teachers: 194.3 (16.0 to 1)
Librarians/Media Specialists: 4.0 (777.0 to 1)
Guidance Counselors: 8.0 (388.5 to 1)
Current Spending: ($ per student per year):
Total: $6,834; Instruction: $4,353; Support Services: $2,160
Enrollment, Drop-out Rates and Diploma Recipients by Race/Ethnicity

Category	Total	White	Black	Asian	AIAN	Hisp.
Enrollment (%)	100.0	54.2	38.8	3.0	0.4	3.6
Drop-out Rate (%)	2.4	1.1	4.7	3.1	0.0	5.0
H.S. Diplomas (#)	190	116	59	9	0	6

Delaware County

Chester-Upland SD

1720 Melrose Ave • Chester, PA 19013-5837
(610) 447-3600
Grade Span: KG-12; **Agency Type:** 1
Schools: 10
6 Primary; 3 Middle; 1 High; 0 Other Level
10 Regular; 0 Special Education; 0 Vocational; 0 Alternative
0 Magnet; 0 Charter; 8 Title I Eligible; 6 School-wide Title I
Students: 5,289 (n/a% male; n/a% female)
Individual Education Program: 1,167 (22.1%);
English Language Learner: n/a; Migrant: 37 (0.7%)
Eligible for Free Lunch Program: 3,238 (61.2%)
Eligible for Reduced-Price Lunch Program: 253 (4.8%)
Teachers: 330.0 (16.0 to 1)
Librarians/Media Specialists: 6.0 (881.5 to 1)
Guidance Counselors: 11.0 (480.8 to 1)
Current Spending: ($ per student per year):
Total: $9,778; Instruction: $6,024; Support Services: $3,401
Enrollment, Drop-out Rates and Diploma Recipients by Race/Ethnicity

Category	Total	White	Black	Asian	AIAN	Hisp.
Enrollment (%)	100.0	3.4	89.6	0.0	0.0	7.0
Drop-out Rate (%)	2.0	0.0	2.0	n/a	0.0	3.3
H.S. Diplomas (#)	267	3	255	0	0	9

Chichester SD

PO Box 2100 • Boothwyn, PA 19061-2499
(610) 485-6881 • http://www.chichesterschools.net
Grade Span: PK-12; **Agency Type:** 1
Schools: 6
4 Primary; 1 Middle; 1 High; 0 Other Level
6 Regular; 0 Special Education; 0 Vocational; 0 Alternative
0 Magnet; 0 Charter; 2 Title I Eligible; 0 School-wide Title I
Students: 3,697 (n/a% male; n/a% female)
Individual Education Program: 612 (16.6%);
English Language Learner: n/a; Migrant: 0 (0.0%)
Eligible for Free Lunch Program: 869 (23.5%)
Eligible for Reduced-Price Lunch Program: 276 (7.5%)
Teachers: 234.0 (15.8 to 1)
Librarians/Media Specialists: 3.0 (1,232.3 to 1)
Guidance Counselors: 11.0 (336.1 to 1)
Current Spending: ($ per student per year):
Total: $8,573; Instruction: $5,553; Support Services: $2,733
Enrollment, Drop-out Rates and Diploma Recipients by Race/Ethnicity

Category	Total	White	Black	Asian	AIAN	Hisp.
Enrollment (%)	100.0	85.3	12.3	1.1	0.1	1.3
Drop-out Rate (%)	2.5	2.7	0.8	0.0	n/a	0.0
H.S. Diplomas (#)	285	242	31	6	0	6

Garnet Valley SD

80 Station Rd • Glen Mills, PA 19342-1558
(610) 579-7300
Grade Span: KG-12; **Agency Type:** 1
Schools: 5
3 Primary; 1 Middle; 1 High; 0 Other Level
5 Regular; 0 Special Education; 0 Vocational; 0 Alternative
0 Magnet; 0 Charter; 3 Title I Eligible; 0 School-wide Title I
Students: 3,824 (n/a% male; n/a% female)
Individual Education Program: 635 (16.6%);
English Language Learner: n/a; Migrant: 0 (0.0%)
Eligible for Free Lunch Program: 53 (1.4%)
Eligible for Reduced-Price Lunch Program: 30 (0.8%)
Teachers: 264.2 (14.5 to 1)
Librarians/Media Specialists: 5.0 (764.8 to 1)
Guidance Counselors: 10.4 (367.7 to 1)
Current Spending: ($ per student per year):
Total: $8,586; Instruction: $5,521; Support Services: $2,793
Enrollment, Drop-out Rates and Diploma Recipients by Race/Ethnicity

Category	Total	White	Black	Asian	AIAN	Hisp.
Enrollment (%)	100.0	94.2	1.3	3.9	0.0	0.6
Drop-out Rate (%)	0.8	0.8	0.0	0.0	n/a	0.0
H.S. Diplomas (#)	198	190	2	3	0	3

Haverford Township SD

1801 Darby Rd • Havertown, PA 19083-3729
(610) 853-5900 • http://www.haverford.k12.pa.us
Grade Span: KG-12; **Agency Type:** 1
Schools: 7
5 Primary; 1 Middle; 1 High; 0 Other Level
7 Regular; 0 Special Education; 0 Vocational; 0 Alternative
0 Magnet; 0 Charter; 6 Title I Eligible; 0 School-wide Title I
Students: 5,419 (n/a% male; n/a% female)
Individual Education Program: 859 (15.9%);
English Language Learner: n/a; Migrant: 0 (0.0%)
Eligible for Free Lunch Program: 109 (2.0%)
Eligible for Reduced-Price Lunch Program: 54 (1.0%)
Teachers: 335.8 (16.1 to 1)
Librarians/Media Specialists: 7.0 (774.1 to 1)
Guidance Counselors: 13.0 (416.8 to 1)
Current Spending: ($ per student per year):
Total: $8,060; Instruction: $4,991; Support Services: $2,868
Enrollment, Drop-out Rates and Diploma Recipients by Race/Ethnicity

Category	Total	White	Black	Asian	AIAN	Hisp.
Enrollment (%)	100.0	90.9	3.3	4.9	0.1	0.8
Drop-out Rate (%)	1.3	1.1	2.6	2.9	0.0	0.0
H.S. Diplomas (#)	420	379	13	23	0	5

Interboro SD

900 Washington Ave • Prospect Park, PA 19076-1412
(610) 461-6700 • http://www.interboro.k12.pa.us
Grade Span: KG-12; **Agency Type:** 1
Schools: 6
5 Primary; 0 Middle; 1 High; 0 Other Level
6 Regular; 0 Special Education; 0 Vocational; 0 Alternative
0 Magnet; 0 Charter; 4 Title I Eligible; 0 School-wide Title I
Students: 3,951 (n/a% male; n/a% female)
Individual Education Program: 555 (14.0%);
English Language Learner: n/a; Migrant: 0 (0.0%)
Eligible for Free Lunch Program: 491 (12.4%)
Eligible for Reduced-Price Lunch Program: 227 (5.7%)
Teachers: 255.3 (15.5 to 1)
Librarians/Media Specialists: 4.0 (987.8 to 1)
Guidance Counselors: 7.0 (564.4 to 1)
Current Spending: ($ per student per year):
Total: $8,756; Instruction: $5,618; Support Services: $2,906
Enrollment, Drop-out Rates and Diploma Recipients by Race/Ethnicity

Category	Total	White	Black	Asian	AIAN	Hisp.
Enrollment (%)	100.0	95.3	2.1	1.4	0.2	1.1
Drop-out Rate (%)	2.0	2.0	0.0	0.0	0.0	0.0
H.S. Diplomas (#)	283	280	1	2	0	0

Marple Newtown SD

40 Media Line Rd Ste 206 • Newtown Square, PA 19073-4614
(610) 359-4200 • http://www.marple.net/schools
Grade Span: KG-12; **Agency Type:** 1
Schools: 6
4 Primary; 1 Middle; 1 High; 0 Other Level
6 Regular; 0 Special Education; 0 Vocational; 0 Alternative
0 Magnet; 0 Charter; 4 Title I Eligible; 0 School-wide Title I
Students: 3,403 (n/a% male; n/a% female)
Individual Education Program: 583 (17.1%);
English Language Learner: n/a; Migrant: 0 (0.0%)
Eligible for Free Lunch Program: 84 (2.5%)
Eligible for Reduced-Price Lunch Program: 45 (1.3%)
Teachers: 250.6 (13.6 to 1)
Librarians/Media Specialists: 6.0 (567.2 to 1)
Guidance Counselors: 9.0 (378.1 to 1)
Current Spending: ($ per student per year):
Total: $9,916; Instruction: $6,618; Support Services: $3,155
Enrollment, Drop-out Rates and Diploma Recipients by Race/Ethnicity

Category	Total	White	Black	Asian	AIAN	Hisp.
Enrollment (%)	100.0	90.4	0.9	8.1	0.0	0.6
Drop-out Rate (%)	1.5	1.3	0.0	3.4	n/a	0.0
H.S. Diplomas (#)	277	254	3	19	0	1

Penn-Delco SD

95 Concord Rd • Aston, PA 19014-2907
(610) 497-6300 • http://www.pdsd.org
Grade Span: KG-12; **Agency Type:** 1
Schools: 6
4 Primary; 1 Middle; 1 High; 0 Other Level
6 Regular; 0 Special Education; 0 Vocational; 0 Alternative
0 Magnet; 0 Charter; 0 Title I Eligible; 0 School-wide Title I
Students: 3,333 (n/a% male; n/a% female)
Individual Education Program: 573 (17.2%);
English Language Learner: n/a; Migrant: 0 (0.0%)
Eligible for Free Lunch Program: 93 (2.8%)
Eligible for Reduced-Price Lunch Program: 65 (2.0%)
Teachers: 206.7 (16.1 to 1)
Librarians/Media Specialists: 4.0 (833.3 to 1)
Guidance Counselors: 9.0 (370.3 to 1)
Current Spending: ($ per student per year):
Total: $7,445; Instruction: $4,650; Support Services: $2,557
Enrollment, Drop-out Rates and Diploma Recipients by Race/Ethnicity

Category	Total	White	Black	Asian	AIAN	Hisp.
Enrollment (%)	100.0	96.8	2.0	0.6	0.3	0.4
Drop-out Rate (%)	3.0	2.9	10.5	0.0	0.0	0.0
H.S. Diplomas (#)	222	213	0	7	0	2

Radnor Township SD

135 S Wayne Ave • Wayne, PA 19087-4194
(610) 688-8100 • http://www.radnor.com/schools/schools.html
Grade Span: KG-12; **Agency Type:** 1
Schools: 5
3 Primary; 1 Middle; 1 High; 0 Other Level
5 Regular; 0 Special Education; 0 Vocational; 0 Alternative
0 Magnet; 0 Charter; 2 Title I Eligible; 0 School-wide Title I
Students: 3,247 (n/a% male; n/a% female)
Individual Education Program: 521 (16.0%);
English Language Learner: n/a; Migrant: 0 (0.0%)
Eligible for Free Lunch Program: 74 (2.3%)
Eligible for Reduced-Price Lunch Program: 25 (0.8%)
Teachers: 256.0 (12.7 to 1)
Librarians/Media Specialists: 5.0 (649.4 to 1)
Guidance Counselors: 12.0 (270.6 to 1)
Current Spending: ($ per student per year):
Total: $12,367; Instruction: $7,572; Support Services: $4,550
Enrollment, Drop-out Rates and Diploma Recipients by Race/Ethnicity

Category	Total	White	Black	Asian	AIAN	Hisp.
Enrollment (%)	100.0	83.8	3.7	10.8	0.1	1.6
Drop-out Rate (%)	0.3	0.4	0.0	0.0	n/a	0.0
H.S. Diplomas (#)	229	200	6	19	0	4

Ridley SD

1001 Morton Ave • Folsom, PA 19033-2934
(610) 534-1900 • http://www.ridleysd.k12.pa.us
Grade Span: KG-12; **Agency Type:** 1
Schools: 9
7 Primary; 1 Middle; 1 High; 0 Other Level
9 Regular; 0 Special Education; 0 Vocational; 0 Alternative
0 Magnet; 0 Charter; 2 Title I Eligible; 0 School-wide Title I
Students: 5,649 (n/a% male; n/a% female)
Individual Education Program: 989 (17.5%);
English Language Learner: n/a; Migrant: 1 (<0.1%)
Eligible for Free Lunch Program: 712 (12.6%)
Eligible for Reduced-Price Lunch Program: 318 (5.6%)
Teachers: 392.1 (14.4 to 1)
Librarians/Media Specialists: 2.0 (2,824.5 to 1)
Guidance Counselors: 9.0 (627.7 to 1)
Current Spending: ($ per student per year):
Total: $8,386; Instruction: $5,880; Support Services: $2,266
Enrollment, Drop-out Rates and Diploma Recipients by Race/Ethnicity

Category	Total	White	Black	Asian	AIAN	Hisp.
Enrollment (%)	100.0	91.5	6.1	1.4	0.3	0.7
Drop-out Rate (%)	2.0	2.1	1.8	0.0	n/a	0.0
H.S. Diplomas (#)	421	394	22	5	0	0

Rose Tree Media SD

308 N Olive St • Media, PA 19063-2403
(610) 627-6000 • http://www.rosetree.k12.pa.us/
Grade Span: KG-12; **Agency Type:** 1
Schools: 6
4 Primary; 1 Middle; 1 High; 0 Other Level
6 Regular; 0 Special Education; 0 Vocational; 0 Alternative
0 Magnet; 0 Charter; 2 Title I Eligible; 0 School-wide Title I
Students: 4,024 (n/a% male; n/a% female)
Individual Education Program: 614 (15.3%);
English Language Learner: n/a; Migrant: 0 (0.0%)
Eligible for Free Lunch Program: 133 (3.3%)
Eligible for Reduced-Price Lunch Program: 59 (1.5%)
Teachers: 288.1 (14.0 to 1)
Librarians/Media Specialists: 3.0 (1,341.3 to 1)
Guidance Counselors: 13.0 (309.5 to 1)
Current Spending: ($ per student per year):
Total: $9,937; Instruction: $5,899; Support Services: $3,756
Enrollment, Drop-out Rates and Diploma Recipients by Race/Ethnicity

Category	Total	White	Black	Asian	AIAN	Hisp.
Enrollment (%)	100.0	89.3	6.6	3.1	0.1	0.8
Drop-out Rate (%)	1.5	1.5	1.3	0.0	0.0	0.0
H.S. Diplomas (#)	294	256	23	9	1	5

Southeast Delco SD

1560 Delmar Dr • Folcroft, PA 19032-0328
(610) 522-4300
Grade Span: KG-12; **Agency Type:** 1
Schools: 7
4 Primary; 1 Middle; 2 High; 0 Other Level
7 Regular; 0 Special Education; 0 Vocational; 0 Alternative
0 Magnet; 0 Charter; 7 Title I Eligible; 0 School-wide Title I
Students: 3,911 (n/a% male; n/a% female)
Individual Education Program: 843 (21.6%);
English Language Learner: n/a; Migrant: 0 (0.0%)
Eligible for Free Lunch Program: 1,349 (34.5%)
Eligible for Reduced-Price Lunch Program: 483 (12.3%)
Teachers: 251.0 (15.6 to 1)
Librarians/Media Specialists: 2.0 (1,955.5 to 1)
Guidance Counselors: 10.0 (391.1 to 1)
Current Spending: ($ per student per year):
Total: $8,014; Instruction: $5,250; Support Services: $2,481
Enrollment, Drop-out Rates and Diploma Recipients by Race/Ethnicity

Category	Total	White	Black	Asian	AIAN	Hisp.
Enrollment (%)	100.0	56.7	40.5	1.2	0.0	1.6
Drop-out Rate (%)	4.6	5.4	2.4	0.0	n/a	30.0
H.S. Diplomas (#)	205	126	73	4	0	2

Springfield SD

111 W Leamy Ave • Springfield, PA 19064-2306
(610) 938-6004 • http://www.springfieldsd-delco.org
Grade Span: KG-12; **Agency Type:** 1
Schools: 4
2 Primary; 1 Middle; 1 High; 0 Other Level
4 Regular; 0 Special Education; 0 Vocational; 0 Alternative
0 Magnet; 0 Charter; 2 Title I Eligible; 0 School-wide Title I
Students: 3,293 (n/a% male; n/a% female)
Individual Education Program: 473 (14.4%);
English Language Learner: n/a; Migrant: 0 (0.0%)
Eligible for Free Lunch Program: 97 (2.9%)
Eligible for Reduced-Price Lunch Program: 22 (0.7%)
Teachers: 211.1 (15.6 to 1)
Librarians/Media Specialists: 4.0 (823.3 to 1)
Guidance Counselors: 9.0 (365.9 to 1)
Current Spending: ($ per student per year):
Total: $8,811; Instruction: $5,574; Support Services: $3,000
Enrollment, Drop-out Rates and Diploma Recipients by Race/Ethnicity

Category	Total	White	Black	Asian	AIAN	Hisp.
Enrollment (%)	100.0	92.0	5.3	2.2	0.0	0.4
Drop-out Rate (%)	1.0	0.9	3.2	0.0	0.0	0.0
H.S. Diplomas (#)	281	251	18	11	0	1

Upper Darby SD

4611 Bond Ave • Drexel Hill, PA 19026-4592
(610) 789-7200 • http://www.udsd.k12.pa.us
Grade Span: KG-12; **Agency Type:** 1
Schools: 12
9 Primary; 2 Middle; 1 High; 0 Other Level
12 Regular; 0 Special Education; 0 Vocational; 0 Alternative
0 Magnet; 0 Charter; 6 Title I Eligible; 0 School-wide Title I
Students: 12,040 (n/a% male; n/a% female)
Individual Education Program: 1,652 (13.7%);
English Language Learner: n/a; Migrant: 0 (0.0%)
Eligible for Free Lunch Program: 2,626 (21.8%)
Eligible for Reduced-Price Lunch Program: 661 (5.5%)
Teachers: 722.5 (16.7 to 1)
Librarians/Media Specialists: 12.5 (963.2 to 1)
Guidance Counselors: 21.0 (573.3 to 1)
Current Spending: ($ per student per year):
Total: $6,881; Instruction: $4,753; Support Services: $1,949
Enrollment, Drop-out Rates and Diploma Recipients by Race/Ethnicity

Category	Total	White	Black	Asian	AIAN	Hisp.
Enrollment (%)	100.0	61.1	25.5	12.0	0.0	1.4
Drop-out Rate (%)	4.5	4.7	4.6	3.0	n/a	5.0
H.S. Diplomas (#)	694	513	75	103	1	2

Wallingford-Swarthmore SD

200 S Providence Rd • Wallingford, PA 19086-6334
(610) 892-3413
Grade Span: KG-12; **Agency Type:** 1
Schools: 6
4 Primary; 1 Middle; 1 High; 0 Other Level
6 Regular; 0 Special Education; 0 Vocational; 0 Alternative
0 Magnet; 0 Charter; 4 Title I Eligible; 0 School-wide Title I
Students: 3,468 (n/a% male; n/a% female)
Individual Education Program: 613 (17.7%);
English Language Learner: n/a; Migrant: 0 (0.0%)
Eligible for Free Lunch Program: 116 (3.3%)
Eligible for Reduced-Price Lunch Program: 46 (1.3%)
Teachers: 249.4 (13.9 to 1)
Librarians/Media Specialists: 5.0 (693.6 to 1)
Guidance Counselors: 10.8 (321.1 to 1)
Current Spending: ($ per student per year):
Total: $9,496; Instruction: $6,232; Support Services: $3,020
Enrollment, Drop-out Rates and Diploma Recipients by Race/Ethnicity

Category	Total	White	Black	Asian	AIAN	Hisp.
Enrollment (%)	100.0	88.1	7.0	4.0	0.3	0.6
Drop-out Rate (%)	0.9	1.0	0.0	0.0	0.0	0.0
H.S. Diplomas (#)	289	253	20	9	0	7

William Penn SD

100 Green Ave Annex • Lansdowne, PA 19050-2095
(610) 284-8000 • http://www.wpsd.k12.pa.us
Grade Span: KG-12; **Agency Type:** 1
Schools: 10
7 Primary; 2 Middle; 1 High; 0 Other Level
10 Regular; 0 Special Education; 0 Vocational; 0 Alternative
2 Magnet; 0 Charter; 7 Title I Eligible; 0 School-wide Title I
Students: 5,576 (n/a% male; n/a% female)
Individual Education Program: 1,126 (20.2%);
English Language Learner: n/a; Migrant: 0 (0.0%)
Eligible for Free Lunch Program: 2,172 (39.0%)
Eligible for Reduced-Price Lunch Program: 414 (7.4%)
Teachers: 347.0 (16.1 to 1)
Librarians/Media Specialists: 7.5 (743.5 to 1)
Guidance Counselors: 11.0 (506.9 to 1)
Current Spending: ($ per student per year):
Total: $8,357; Instruction: $5,393; Support Services: $2,649
Enrollment, Drop-out Rates and Diploma Recipients by Race/Ethnicity

Category	Total	White	Black	Asian	AIAN	Hisp.
Enrollment (%)	100.0	13.9	82.6	1.4	0.8	1.3
Drop-out Rate (%)	3.1	4.2	2.9	0.0	0.0	0.0
H.S. Diplomas (#)	306	52	250	2	0	2

Elk County

Saint Marys Area SD

977 S Saint Marys Rd • Saint Marys, PA 15857-2832
(814) 834-7831 • http://www.smasd.org
Grade Span: KG-12; **Agency Type:** 1
Schools: 5
3 Primary; 1 Middle; 1 High; 0 Other Level
5 Regular; 0 Special Education; 0 Vocational; 0 Alternative
0 Magnet; 0 Charter; 0 Title I Eligible; 0 School-wide Title I
Students: 2,552 (n/a% male; n/a% female)
Individual Education Program: 328 (12.9%);
English Language Learner: n/a; Migrant: 0 (0.0%)
Eligible for Free Lunch Program: 342 (13.4%)
Eligible for Reduced-Price Lunch Program: 243 (9.5%)
Teachers: 149.0 (17.1 to 1)
Librarians/Media Specialists: 3.0 (850.7 to 1)
Guidance Counselors: 6.0 (425.3 to 1)
Current Spending: ($ per student per year):
Total: $6,532; Instruction: $4,098; Support Services: $2,160
Enrollment, Drop-out Rates and Diploma Recipients by Race/Ethnicity

Category	Total	White	Black	Asian	AIAN	Hisp.
Enrollment (%)	100.0	98.2	0.7	0.5	0.1	0.4
Drop-out Rate (%)	2.8	2.6	100.0	0.0	n/a	100.0
H.S. Diplomas (#)	207	205	0	2	0	0

Erie County

Corry Area SD

800 E S St • Corry, PA 16407-2054
(814) 664-4677 • http://corry.iu5.org
Grade Span: KG-12; **Agency Type:** 1
Schools: 6
5 Primary; 0 Middle; 1 High; 0 Other Level
6 Regular; 0 Special Education; 0 Vocational; 0 Alternative
0 Magnet; 0 Charter; 0 Title I Eligible; 0 School-wide Title I
Students: 2,556 (n/a% male; n/a% female)
Individual Education Program: 448 (17.5%);
English Language Learner: n/a; Migrant: 0 (0.0%)
Eligible for Free Lunch Program: 904 (35.4%)
Eligible for Reduced-Price Lunch Program: 257 (10.1%)
Teachers: 172.0 (14.9 to 1)
Librarians/Media Specialists: 3.0 (852.0 to 1)
Guidance Counselors: 6.0 (426.0 to 1)
Current Spending: ($ per student per year):
Total: $6,884; Instruction: $4,225; Support Services: $2,359
Enrollment, Drop-out Rates and Diploma Recipients by Race/Ethnicity

Category	Total	White	Black	Asian	AIAN	Hisp.
Enrollment (%)	100.0	99.2	0.3	0.2	0.0	0.2
Drop-out Rate (%)	2.9	2.9	0.0	0.0	n/a	0.0
H.S. Diplomas (#)	178	174	0	2	0	2

Erie City SD

148 W 21st St • Erie, PA 16502
(814) 874-6001 • http://esd.iu5.org
Grade Span: KG-12; **Agency Type:** 1
Schools: 21
14 Primary; 3 Middle; 4 High; 0 Other Level
21 Regular; 0 Special Education; 0 Vocational; 0 Alternative
2 Magnet; 0 Charter; 20 Title I Eligible; 1 School-wide Title I
Students: 12,908 (n/a% male; n/a% female)
Individual Education Program: 2,506 (19.4%);
English Language Learner: n/a; Migrant: 1,014 (7.9%)
Eligible for Free Lunch Program: 7,598 (58.9%)
Eligible for Reduced-Price Lunch Program: 1,092 (8.5%)
Teachers: 830.5 (15.5 to 1)
Librarians/Media Specialists: 8.0 (1,613.5 to 1)
Guidance Counselors: 29.0 (445.1 to 1)
Current Spending: ($ per student per year):
Total: $7,555; Instruction: $4,538; Support Services: $2,680
Enrollment, Drop-out Rates and Diploma Recipients by Race/Ethnicity

Category	Total	White	Black	Asian	AIAN	Hisp.
Enrollment (%)	100.0	56.1	33.2	1.6	0.1	9.0
Drop-out Rate (%)	4.3	3.8	5.6	3.5	0.0	5.1
H.S. Diplomas (#)	630	435	151	15	0	29

Fairview SD

7460 Mccray Rd • Fairview, PA 16415-2401
(814) 474-2600 • http://www.iu5.org/fsd/
Grade Span: KG-12; **Agency Type:** 1
Schools: 3
1 Primary; 1 Middle; 1 High; 0 Other Level
3 Regular; 0 Special Education; 0 Vocational; 0 Alternative
0 Magnet; 0 Charter; 0 Title I Eligible; 0 School-wide Title I
Students: 1,585 (n/a% male; n/a% female)
Individual Education Program: 170 (10.7%);
English Language Learner: n/a; Migrant: 0 (0.0%)
Eligible for Free Lunch Program: 129 (8.1%)
Eligible for Reduced-Price Lunch Program: 65 (4.1%)
Teachers: 102.0 (15.5 to 1)
Librarians/Media Specialists: 3.0 (528.3 to 1)
Guidance Counselors: 4.0 (396.3 to 1)
Current Spending: ($ per student per year):
Total: $7,745; Instruction: $4,604; Support Services: $2,892

Enrollment, Drop-out Rates and Diploma Recipients by Race/Ethnicity

Category	Total	White	Black	Asian	AIAN	Hisp.
Enrollment (%)	100.0	95.7	1.5	1.0	0.4	1.4
Drop-out Rate (%)	1.2	1.2	0.0	0.0	0.0	0.0
H.S. Diplomas (#)	114	111	2	1	0	0

Fort Leboeuf SD

PO Box 810 • Waterford, PA 16441-0810
(814) 796-2638
Grade Span: KG-12; **Agency Type:** 1
Schools: 5
3 Primary; 1 Middle; 1 High; 0 Other Level
5 Regular; 0 Special Education; 0 Vocational; 0 Alternative
0 Magnet; 0 Charter; 4 Title I Eligible; 0 School-wide Title I
Students: 2,348 (n/a% male; n/a% female)
Individual Education Program: 359 (15.3%);
English Language Learner: n/a; Migrant: 1 (<0.1%)
Eligible for Free Lunch Program: 424 (18.1%)
Eligible for Reduced-Price Lunch Program: 227 (9.7%)
Teachers: 133.5 (17.6 to 1)
Librarians/Media Specialists: 3.0 (782.7 to 1)
Guidance Counselors: 6.0 (391.3 to 1)
Current Spending: ($ per student per year):
Total: $5,855; Instruction: $3,586; Support Services: $2,000
Enrollment, Drop-out Rates and Diploma Recipients by Race/Ethnicity

Category	Total	White	Black	Asian	AIAN	Hisp.
Enrollment (%)	100.0	98.2	1.2	0.4	0.0	0.2
Drop-out Rate (%)	2.9	3.0	0.0	0.0	n/a	0.0
H.S. Diplomas (#)	174	173	1	0	0	0

General Mclane SD

11771 Edinboro Rd • Edinboro, PA 16412-1025
(814) 734-1033
Grade Span: KG-12; **Agency Type:** 1
Schools: 4
2 Primary; 1 Middle; 1 High; 0 Other Level
4 Regular; 0 Special Education; 0 Vocational; 0 Alternative
0 Magnet; 0 Charter; 3 Title I Eligible; 0 School-wide Title I
Students: 2,526 (n/a% male; n/a% female)
Individual Education Program: 297 (11.8%);
English Language Learner: n/a; Migrant: 0 (0.0%)
Eligible for Free Lunch Program: 315 (12.5%)
Eligible for Reduced-Price Lunch Program: 167 (6.6%)
Teachers: 156.0 (16.2 to 1)
Librarians/Media Specialists: 4.0 (631.5 to 1)
Guidance Counselors: 7.0 (360.9 to 1)
Current Spending: ($ per student per year):
Total: $6,503; Instruction: $4,173; Support Services: $2,106
Enrollment, Drop-out Rates and Diploma Recipients by Race/Ethnicity

Category	Total	White	Black	Asian	AIAN	Hisp.
Enrollment (%)	100.0	97.7	1.2	0.6	0.3	0.1
Drop-out Rate (%)	1.9	1.8	0.0	n/a	0.0	n/a
H.S. Diplomas (#)	258	253	3	1	0	1

Girard SD

1100 Rice Ave • Girard, PA 16417-1143
(814) 774-5666 • http://www.gsd.k12.pa.us
Grade Span: KG-12; **Agency Type:** 1
Schools: 3
1 Primary; 1 Middle; 1 High; 0 Other Level
3 Regular; 0 Special Education; 0 Vocational; 0 Alternative
0 Magnet; 0 Charter; 2 Title I Eligible; 0 School-wide Title I
Students: 2,029 (n/a% male; n/a% female)
Individual Education Program: 261 (12.9%);
English Language Learner: n/a; Migrant: 0 (0.0%)
Eligible for Free Lunch Program: 523 (25.8%)
Eligible for Reduced-Price Lunch Program: 272 (13.4%)
Teachers: 121.0 (16.8 to 1)
Librarians/Media Specialists: 2.0 (1,014.5 to 1)
Guidance Counselors: 3.0 (676.3 to 1)
Current Spending: ($ per student per year):
Total: $6,431; Instruction: $4,233; Support Services: $1,914
Enrollment, Drop-out Rates and Diploma Recipients by Race/Ethnicity

Category	Total	White	Black	Asian	AIAN	Hisp.
Enrollment (%)	100.0	98.4	1.3	0.0	0.0	0.2
Drop-out Rate (%)	3.2	3.2	0.0	0.0	n/a	0.0
H.S. Diplomas (#)	127	123	3	1	0	0

Harbor Creek SD

6375 Buffalo Rd • Harborcreek, PA 16421-1632
(814) 897-2100 • http://hcsd.iu5.org
Grade Span: KG-12; **Agency Type:** 1
Schools: 4
3 Primary; 0 Middle; 1 High; 0 Other Level
4 Regular; 0 Special Education; 0 Vocational; 0 Alternative
0 Magnet; 0 Charter; 3 Title I Eligible; 0 School-wide Title I
Students: 2,183 (n/a% male; n/a% female)
Individual Education Program: 242 (11.1%);
English Language Learner: n/a; Migrant: 0 (0.0%)
Eligible for Free Lunch Program: 291 (13.3%)
Eligible for Reduced-Price Lunch Program: 123 (5.6%)
Teachers: 146.9 (14.9 to 1)
Librarians/Media Specialists: 2.0 (1,091.5 to 1)
Guidance Counselors: 5.0 (436.6 to 1)
Current Spending: ($ per student per year):
Total: $6,806; Instruction: $4,389; Support Services: $2,124
Enrollment, Drop-out Rates and Diploma Recipients by Race/Ethnicity

Category	Total	White	Black	Asian	AIAN	Hisp.
Enrollment (%)	100.0	98.1	1.2	0.5	0.0	0.1
Drop-out Rate (%)	2.1	2.2	0.0	n/a	n/a	0.0
H.S. Diplomas (#)	219	217	2	0	0	0

Millcreek Township SD

3740 W 26th St • Erie, PA 16506-2039
(814) 835-5300 • http://www.mtsd.org/main/index.html
Grade Span: KG-12; **Agency Type:** 1
Schools: 13
7 Primary; 3 Middle; 2 High; 1 Other Level
13 Regular; 0 Special Education; 0 Vocational; 0 Alternative
0 Magnet; 0 Charter; 0 Title I Eligible; 0 School-wide Title I
Students: 7,112 (n/a% male; n/a% female)
Individual Education Program: 795 (11.2%);
English Language Learner: n/a; Migrant: 29 (0.4%)
Eligible for Free Lunch Program: 824 (11.6%)
Eligible for Reduced-Price Lunch Program: 499 (7.0%)
Teachers: 443.5 (16.0 to 1)
Librarians/Media Specialists: 5.5 (1,293.1 to 1)
Guidance Counselors: 14.0 (508.0 to 1)
Current Spending: ($ per student per year):
Total: $6,974; Instruction: $4,417; Support Services: $2,283
Enrollment, Drop-out Rates and Diploma Recipients by Race/Ethnicity

Category	Total	White	Black	Asian	AIAN	Hisp.
Enrollment (%)	100.0	94.4	1.9	1.9	0.2	1.5
Drop-out Rate (%)	3.7	3.7	2.9	2.8	0.0	4.2
H.S. Diplomas (#)	504	483	4	11	0	6

North East SD

50 E Division St • North East, PA 16428-1351
(814) 725-8671 • http://www.nesd1.k12.pa.us
Grade Span: KG-12; **Agency Type:** 1
Schools: 4
2 Primary; 1 Middle; 1 High; 0 Other Level
4 Regular; 0 Special Education; 0 Vocational; 0 Alternative
0 Magnet; 0 Charter; 2 Title I Eligible; 0 School-wide Title I
Students: 1,968 (n/a% male; n/a% female)
Individual Education Program: 202 (10.3%);
English Language Learner: n/a; Migrant: 3 (0.2%)
Eligible for Free Lunch Program: 348 (17.7%)
Eligible for Reduced-Price Lunch Program: 199 (10.1%)
Teachers: 112.5 (17.5 to 1)
Librarians/Media Specialists: 3.0 (656.0 to 1)
Guidance Counselors: 5.0 (393.6 to 1)
Current Spending: ($ per student per year):
Total: $5,952; Instruction: $3,640; Support Services: $2,070
Enrollment, Drop-out Rates and Diploma Recipients by Race/Ethnicity

Category	Total	White	Black	Asian	AIAN	Hisp.
Enrollment (%)	100.0	98.8	0.4	0.3	0.1	0.5
Drop-out Rate (%)	1.6	1.5	n/a	0.0	n/a	25.0
H.S. Diplomas (#)	157	155	2	0	0	0

Northwestern SD

100 Harthan Way • Albion, PA 16401-1368
(814) 756-4116
Grade Span: KG-12; **Agency Type:** 1
Schools: 4
2 Primary; 1 Middle; 1 High; 0 Other Level
4 Regular; 0 Special Education; 0 Vocational; 0 Alternative
0 Magnet; 0 Charter; 3 Title I Eligible; 0 School-wide Title I
Students: 1,915 (n/a% male; n/a% female)
Individual Education Program: 292 (15.2%);
English Language Learner: n/a; Migrant: 1 (0.1%)
Eligible for Free Lunch Program: 530 (27.7%)
Eligible for Reduced-Price Lunch Program: 182 (9.5%)
Teachers: 107.2 (17.9 to 1)
Librarians/Media Specialists: 3.0 (638.3 to 1)
Guidance Counselors: 4.0 (478.8 to 1)
Current Spending: ($ per student per year):
Total: $5,513; Instruction: $3,623; Support Services: $1,656

Enrollment, Drop-out Rates and Diploma Recipients by Race/Ethnicity

Category	Total	White	Black	Asian	AIAN	Hisp.
Enrollment (%)	100.0	98.3	0.9	0.2	0.1	0.5
Drop-out Rate (%)	5.3	5.2	14.3	0.0	0.0	0.0
H.S. Diplomas (#)	125	125	0	0	0	0

Wattsburg Area SD

10782 Wattsburg Rd • Erie, PA 16509
(814) 824-3400
Grade Span: KG-12; **Agency Type:** 1
Schools: 3
1 Primary; 1 Middle; 1 High; 0 Other Level
3 Regular; 0 Special Education; 0 Vocational; 0 Alternative
0 Magnet; 0 Charter; 0 Title I Eligible; 0 School-wide Title I
Students: 1,719 (n/a% male; n/a% female)
Individual Education Program: 236 (13.7%);
English Language Learner: n/a; Migrant: 0 (0.0%)
Eligible for Free Lunch Program: 262 (15.2%)
Eligible for Reduced-Price Lunch Program: 131 (7.6%)
Teachers: 88.0 (19.5 to 1)
Librarians/Media Specialists: 3.0 (573.0 to 1)
Guidance Counselors: 4.0 (429.8 to 1)
Current Spending: ($ per student per year):
Total: $6,327; Instruction: $3,682; Support Services: $2,409
Enrollment, Drop-out Rates and Diploma Recipients by Race/Ethnicity

Category	Total	White	Black	Asian	AIAN	Hisp.
Enrollment (%)	100.0	99.5	0.2	0.2	0.0	0.1
Drop-out Rate (%)	2.5	2.5	n/a	n/a	n/a	n/a
H.S. Diplomas (#)	147	147	0	0	0	0

Fayette County

Albert Gallatin Area SD

2625 Morgantown Rd • Uniontown, PA 15401-6703
(724) 564-7190
Grade Span: KG-12; **Agency Type:** 1
Schools: 9
6 Primary; 2 Middle; 1 High; 0 Other Level
9 Regular; 0 Special Education; 0 Vocational; 0 Alternative
0 Magnet; 0 Charter; 9 Title I Eligible; 8 School-wide Title I
Students: 4,149 (n/a% male; n/a% female)
Individual Education Program: 707 (17.0%);
English Language Learner: n/a; Migrant: 0 (0.0%)
Eligible for Free Lunch Program: 1,656 (39.9%)
Eligible for Reduced-Price Lunch Program: 359 (8.7%)
Teachers: 250.5 (16.6 to 1)
Librarians/Media Specialists: 6.0 (691.5 to 1)
Guidance Counselors: 7.0 (592.7 to 1)
Current Spending: ($ per student per year):
Total: $6,668; Instruction: $3,991; Support Services: $2,340
Enrollment, Drop-out Rates and Diploma Recipients by Race/Ethnicity

Category	Total	White	Black	Asian	AIAN	Hisp.
Enrollment (%)	100.0	95.2	4.6	0.1	0.1	0.0
Drop-out Rate (%)	3.7	3.7	2.0	0.0	0.0	n/a
H.S. Diplomas (#)	289	277	11	1	0	0

Brownsville Area SD

1025 Lewis St • Brownsville, PA 15417
(724) 785-2021
Grade Span: KG-12; **Agency Type:** 1
Schools: 5
3 Primary; 1 Middle; 1 High; 0 Other Level
5 Regular; 0 Special Education; 0 Vocational; 0 Alternative
0 Magnet; 0 Charter; 4 Title I Eligible; 3 School-wide Title I
Students: 2,087 (n/a% male; n/a% female)
Individual Education Program: 322 (15.4%);
English Language Learner: n/a; Migrant: 0 (0.0%)
Eligible for Free Lunch Program: 1,103 (52.9%)
Eligible for Reduced-Price Lunch Program: 192 (9.2%)
Teachers: 131.5 (15.9 to 1)
Librarians/Media Specialists: 5.0 (417.4 to 1)
Guidance Counselors: 5.0 (417.4 to 1)
Current Spending: ($ per student per year):
Total: $7,709; Instruction: $4,580; Support Services: $2,753
Enrollment, Drop-out Rates and Diploma Recipients by Race/Ethnicity

Category	Total	White	Black	Asian	AIAN	Hisp.
Enrollment (%)	100.0	85.9	13.7	0.1	0.1	0.2
Drop-out Rate (%)	6.0	5.4	11.0	n/a	n/a	0.0
H.S. Diplomas (#)	139	124	15	0	0	0

Connellsville Area SD

125 N 7th St • Connellsville, PA 15425-2556
(724) 628-3300 • http://www.casdfalcons.org/
Grade Span: KG-12; **Agency Type:** 1
Schools: 11
8 Primary; 2 Middle; 1 High; 0 Other Level
11 Regular; 0 Special Education; 0 Vocational; 0 Alternative
0 Magnet; 0 Charter; 11 Title I Eligible; 10 School-wide Title I
Students: 5,851 (n/a% male; n/a% female)
Individual Education Program: 1,094 (18.7%);
English Language Learner: n/a; Migrant: 0 (0.0%)
Eligible for Free Lunch Program: 2,429 (41.5%)
Eligible for Reduced-Price Lunch Program: 775 (13.2%)
Teachers: 356.5 (16.4 to 1)
Librarians/Media Specialists: 7.0 (835.9 to 1)
Guidance Counselors: 11.0 (531.9 to 1)
Current Spending: ($ per student per year):
Total: $6,791; Instruction: $4,099; Support Services: $2,343
Enrollment, Drop-out Rates and Diploma Recipients by Race/Ethnicity

Category	Total	White	Black	Asian	AIAN	Hisp.
Enrollment (%)	100.0	96.8	2.7	0.2	0.0	0.2
Drop-out Rate (%)	5.0	5.1	0.0	0.0	0.0	0.0
H.S. Diplomas (#)	375	368	7	0	0	0

Laurel Highlands SD

304 Bailey Ave • Uniontown, PA 15401-2461
(724) 437-2821 • http://www.hhs.net/lhsd/
Grade Span: KG-12; **Agency Type:** 1
Schools: 7
5 Primary; 1 Middle; 1 High; 0 Other Level
7 Regular; 0 Special Education; 0 Vocational; 0 Alternative
0 Magnet; 0 Charter; 6 Title I Eligible; 4 School-wide Title I
Students: 3,742 (n/a% male; n/a% female)
Individual Education Program: 430 (11.5%);
English Language Learner: n/a; Migrant: 0 (0.0%)
Eligible for Free Lunch Program: 1,274 (34.0%)
Eligible for Reduced-Price Lunch Program: 291 (7.8%)
Teachers: 205.0 (18.3 to 1)
Librarians/Media Specialists: 5.0 (748.4 to 1)
Guidance Counselors: 5.0 (748.4 to 1)
Current Spending: ($ per student per year):
Total: $7,197; Instruction: $4,638; Support Services: $2,265
Enrollment, Drop-out Rates and Diploma Recipients by Race/Ethnicity

Category	Total	White	Black	Asian	AIAN	Hisp.
Enrollment (%)	100.0	93.5	5.5	0.5	0.1	0.5
Drop-out Rate (%)	3.6	3.6	6.5	0.0	0.0	0.0
H.S. Diplomas (#)	244	236	6	1	1	0

Uniontown Area SD

23 E Church St • Uniontown, PA 15401-3510
(724) 438-4501
Grade Span: KG-12; **Agency Type:** 1
Schools: 8
6 Primary; 1 Middle; 1 High; 0 Other Level
8 Regular; 0 Special Education; 0 Vocational; 0 Alternative
0 Magnet; 0 Charter; 8 Title I Eligible; 7 School-wide Title I
Students: 3,538 (n/a% male; n/a% female)
Individual Education Program: 533 (15.1%);
English Language Learner: n/a; Migrant: 0 (0.0%)
Eligible for Free Lunch Program: 1,480 (41.8%)
Eligible for Reduced-Price Lunch Program: 267 (7.5%)
Teachers: 217.0 (16.3 to 1)
Librarians/Media Specialists: 6.0 (589.7 to 1)
Guidance Counselors: 10.0 (353.8 to 1)
Current Spending: ($ per student per year):
Total: $7,641; Instruction: $4,524; Support Services: $2,805
Enrollment, Drop-out Rates and Diploma Recipients by Race/Ethnicity

Category	Total	White	Black	Asian	AIAN	Hisp.
Enrollment (%)	100.0	81.7	17.8	0.2	0.1	0.1
Drop-out Rate (%)	1.9	1.8	2.7	0.0	n/a	0.0
H.S. Diplomas (#)	216	195	21	0	0	0

Franklin County

Chambersburg Area SD

435 Stanley Ave • Chambersburg, PA 17201-3405
(717) 263-9281 • http://www.chambersburg.k12.pa.us
Grade Span: KG-12; **Agency Type:** 1
Schools: 21
18 Primary; 1 Middle; 1 High; 1 Other Level
21 Regular; 0 Special Education; 0 Vocational; 0 Alternative
0 Magnet; 0 Charter; 12 Title I Eligible; 2 School-wide Title I
Students: 8,036 (n/a% male; n/a% female)
Individual Education Program: 1,253 (15.6%);
English Language Learner: n/a; Migrant: 214 (2.7%)
Eligible for Free Lunch Program: 1,402 (17.4%)
Eligible for Reduced-Price Lunch Program: 509 (6.3%)
Teachers: 456.4 (17.6 to 1)
Librarians/Media Specialists: 11.0 (730.5 to 1)
Guidance Counselors: 19.0 (422.9 to 1)

Current Spending: ($ per student per year):
Total: $6,363; Instruction: $4,088; Support Services: $1,985
Enrollment, Drop-out Rates and Diploma Recipients by Race/Ethnicity

Category	Total	White	Black	Asian	AIAN	Hisp.
Enrollment (%)	100.0	84.2	8.7	1.2	0.2	5.6
Drop-out Rate (%)	4.4	4.1	7.6	0.0	0.0	8.5
H.S. Diplomas (#)	502	451	25	10	0	16

Greencastle-Antrim SD
500 E Leitersburg St • Greencastle, PA 17225-1138
(717) 597-2187 • http://www.greencastle.k12.pa.us
Grade Span: KG-12; **Agency Type:** 1
Schools: 4
2 Primary; 1 Middle; 1 High; 0 Other Level
4 Regular; 0 Special Education; 0 Vocational; 0 Alternative
0 Magnet; 0 Charter; 4 Title I Eligible; 0 School-wide Title I
Students: 2,683 (n/a% male; n/a% female)
Individual Education Program: 324 (12.1%);
English Language Learner: n/a; Migrant: 0 (0.0%)
Eligible for Free Lunch Program: 258 (9.6%)
Eligible for Reduced-Price Lunch Program: 142 (5.3%)
Teachers: 143.6 (18.7 to 1)
Librarians/Media Specialists: 3.0 (894.3 to 1)
Guidance Counselors: 5.0 (536.6 to 1)
Current Spending: ($ per student per year):
Total: $6,091; Instruction: $3,955; Support Services: $1,867
Enrollment, Drop-out Rates and Diploma Recipients by Race/Ethnicity

Category	Total	White	Black	Asian	AIAN	Hisp.
Enrollment (%)	100.0	96.4	2.1	0.4	0.0	1.1
Drop-out Rate (%)	1.9	2.0	0.0	0.0	n/a	0.0
H.S. Diplomas (#)	169	168	0	1	0	0

Tuscarora SD
118 E Seminary St • Mercersburg, PA 17236-1606
(717) 328-3127
Grade Span: KG-12; **Agency Type:** 1
Schools: 6
4 Primary; 1 Middle; 1 High; 0 Other Level
6 Regular; 0 Special Education; 0 Vocational; 0 Alternative
0 Magnet; 0 Charter; 3 Title I Eligible; 0 School-wide Title I
Students: 2,590 (n/a% male; n/a% female)
Individual Education Program: 473 (18.3%);
English Language Learner: n/a; Migrant: 7 (0.3%)
Eligible for Free Lunch Program: 397 (15.3%)
Eligible for Reduced-Price Lunch Program: 272 (10.5%)
Teachers: 168.1 (15.4 to 1)
Librarians/Media Specialists: 3.0 (863.3 to 1)
Guidance Counselors: 5.0 (518.0 to 1)
Current Spending: ($ per student per year):
Total: $6,809; Instruction: $4,199; Support Services: $2,277
Enrollment, Drop-out Rates and Diploma Recipients by Race/Ethnicity

Category	Total	White	Black	Asian	AIAN	Hisp.
Enrollment (%)	100.0	96.3	2.4	0.2	0.1	1.0
Drop-out Rate (%)	2.2	2.3	0.0	0.0	0.0	0.0
H.S. Diplomas (#)	157	155	1	0	0	1

Waynesboro Area SD
210 Clayton Ave • Waynesboro, PA 17268-2066
(717) 762-1191
Grade Span: KG-12; **Agency Type:** 1
Schools: 6
4 Primary; 1 Middle; 1 High; 0 Other Level
6 Regular; 0 Special Education; 0 Vocational; 0 Alternative
0 Magnet; 0 Charter; 2 Title I Eligible; 0 School-wide Title I
Students: 4,072 (n/a% male; n/a% female)
Individual Education Program: 616 (15.1%);
English Language Learner: n/a; Migrant: 5 (0.1%)
Eligible for Free Lunch Program: 679 (16.7%)
Eligible for Reduced-Price Lunch Program: 429 (10.5%)
Teachers: 254.5 (16.0 to 1)
Librarians/Media Specialists: 7.0 (581.7 to 1)
Guidance Counselors: 8.0 (509.0 to 1)
Current Spending: ($ per student per year):
Total: $6,358; Instruction: $4,022; Support Services: $2,031
Enrollment, Drop-out Rates and Diploma Recipients by Race/Ethnicity

Category	Total	White	Black	Asian	AIAN	Hisp.
Enrollment (%)	100.0	95.0	3.0	0.7	0.2	1.0
Drop-out Rate (%)	2.9	3.0	0.0	0.0	0.0	16.7
H.S. Diplomas (#)	293	274	10	6	1	2

Greene County

Central Greene SD
PO Box 472 • Waynesburg, PA 15370-0472
(724) 627-8151 • http://gctc.grvt.org/~cg/
Grade Span: KG-12; **Agency Type:** 1
Schools: 4
2 Primary; 1 Middle; 1 High; 0 Other Level
4 Regular; 0 Special Education; 0 Vocational; 0 Alternative
0 Magnet; 0 Charter; 3 Title I Eligible; 2 School-wide Title I
Students: 2,268 (n/a% male; n/a% female)
Individual Education Program: 498 (22.0%);
English Language Learner: n/a; Migrant: 0 (0.0%)
Eligible for Free Lunch Program: 771 (34.0%)
Eligible for Reduced-Price Lunch Program: 223 (9.8%)
Teachers: 164.7 (13.8 to 1)
Librarians/Media Specialists: 2.0 (1,134.0 to 1)
Guidance Counselors: 5.0 (453.6 to 1)
Current Spending: ($ per student per year):
Total: $8,064; Instruction: $4,994; Support Services: $2,772
Enrollment, Drop-out Rates and Diploma Recipients by Race/Ethnicity

Category	Total	White	Black	Asian	AIAN	Hisp.
Enrollment (%)	100.0	98.0	0.8	0.7	0.0	0.5
Drop-out Rate (%)	2.3	2.3	0.0	0.0	n/a	0.0
H.S. Diplomas (#)	145	141	1	3	0	0

Huntingdon County

Huntingdon Area SD
2400 Cassady Ave Ste 2 • Huntingdon, PA 16652-2618
(814) 643-4140
Grade Span: KG-12; **Agency Type:** 1
Schools: 6
4 Primary; 1 Middle; 1 High; 0 Other Level
6 Regular; 0 Special Education; 0 Vocational; 0 Alternative
0 Magnet; 0 Charter; 5 Title I Eligible; 0 School-wide Title I
Students: 2,473 (n/a% male; n/a% female)
Individual Education Program: 397 (16.1%);
English Language Learner: n/a; Migrant: 0 (0.0%)
Eligible for Free Lunch Program: 598 (24.2%)
Eligible for Reduced-Price Lunch Program: 296 (12.0%)
Teachers: 173.5 (14.3 to 1)
Librarians/Media Specialists: 4.0 (618.3 to 1)
Guidance Counselors: 4.0 (618.3 to 1)
Current Spending: ($ per student per year):
Total: $6,342; Instruction: $3,802; Support Services: $2,228
Enrollment, Drop-out Rates and Diploma Recipients by Race/Ethnicity

Category	Total	White	Black	Asian	AIAN	Hisp.
Enrollment (%)	100.0	96.7	2.2	0.5	0.0	0.5
Drop-out Rate (%)	3.9	4.0	0.0	0.0	n/a	0.0
H.S. Diplomas (#)	156	154	0	0	0	2

Mount Union Area SD
28 W Market St • Mount Union, PA 17066-1232
(814) 542-8631
Grade Span: KG-12; **Agency Type:** 1
Schools: 4
3 Primary; 0 Middle; 1 High; 0 Other Level
4 Regular; 0 Special Education; 0 Vocational; 0 Alternative
0 Magnet; 0 Charter; 3 Title I Eligible; 0 School-wide Title I
Students: 1,565 (n/a% male; n/a% female)
Individual Education Program: 263 (16.8%);
English Language Learner: n/a; Migrant: 0 (0.0%)
Eligible for Free Lunch Program: 366 (23.4%)
Eligible for Reduced-Price Lunch Program: 161 (10.3%)
Teachers: 120.5 (13.0 to 1)
Librarians/Media Specialists: 2.0 (782.5 to 1)
Guidance Counselors: 3.0 (521.7 to 1)
Current Spending: ($ per student per year):
Total: $6,777; Instruction: $4,497; Support Services: $2,005
Enrollment, Drop-out Rates and Diploma Recipients by Race/Ethnicity

Category	Total	White	Black	Asian	AIAN	Hisp.
Enrollment (%)	100.0	93.0	5.9	0.2	0.0	0.8
Drop-out Rate (%)	3.9	3.5	6.9	0.0	n/a	50.0
H.S. Diplomas (#)	95	90	4	1	0	0

Indiana County

Blairsville-Saltsburg SD
102 School Ln • Blairsville, PA 15717-8709
(724) 459-5500 • http://www.ARIN.k12.pa.us/blarsalt.html
Grade Span: KG-12; **Agency Type:** 1
Schools: 5
2 Primary; 1 Middle; 1 High; 1 Other Level
5 Regular; 0 Special Education; 0 Vocational; 0 Alternative

0 Magnet; 0 Charter; 4 Title I Eligible; 0 School-wide Title I
Students: 2,257 (n/a% male; n/a% female)
Individual Education Program: 356 (15.8%);
English Language Learner: n/a; Migrant: 0 (0.0%)
Eligible for Free Lunch Program: 559 (24.8%)
Eligible for Reduced-Price Lunch Program: 247 (10.9%)
Teachers: 136.0 (16.6 to 1)
Librarians/Media Specialists: 4.0 (564.3 to 1)
Guidance Counselors: 6.0 (376.2 to 1)
Current Spending: ($ per student per year):
Total: $7,354; Instruction: $4,656; Support Services: $2,380
Enrollment, Drop-out Rates and Diploma Recipients by Race/Ethnicity

Category	Total	White	Black	Asian	AIAN	Hisp.
Enrollment (%)	100.0	97.0	2.7	0.1	0.0	0.2
Drop-out Rate (%)	2.6	2.6	0.0	0.0	n/a	0.0
H.S. Diplomas (#)	139	138	0	0	0	1

Indiana Area SD

501 E Pike • Indiana, PA 15701-2234
(724) 463-8713 • http://www.iasd.cc
Grade Span: KG-12; **Agency Type:** 1
Schools: 6
4 Primary; 1 Middle; 1 High; 0 Other Level
6 Regular; 0 Special Education; 0 Vocational; 0 Alternative
0 Magnet; 0 Charter; 1 Title I Eligible; 0 School-wide Title I
Students: 3,312 (n/a% male; n/a% female)
Individual Education Program: 376 (11.4%);
English Language Learner: n/a; Migrant: 0 (0.0%)
Eligible for Free Lunch Program: 567 (17.1%)
Eligible for Reduced-Price Lunch Program: 187 (5.6%)
Teachers: 238.8 (13.9 to 1)
Librarians/Media Specialists: 6.0 (552.0 to 1)
Guidance Counselors: 10.0 (331.2 to 1)
Current Spending: ($ per student per year):
Total: $8,759; Instruction: $5,879; Support Services: $2,614
Enrollment, Drop-out Rates and Diploma Recipients by Race/Ethnicity

Category	Total	White	Black	Asian	AIAN	Hisp.
Enrollment (%)	100.0	92.7	3.3	3.4	0.2	0.4
Drop-out Rate (%)	3.1	2.9	12.1	0.0	0.0	0.0
H.S. Diplomas (#)	264	248	9	6	0	1

Marion Center Area SD

PO Box 156 • Marion Center, PA 15759-0156
(724) 397-4911 • http://www.arin.k12.pa.us/marion/
Grade Span: PK-12; **Agency Type:** 1
Schools: 3
1 Primary; 1 Middle; 1 High; 0 Other Level
3 Regular; 0 Special Education; 0 Vocational; 0 Alternative
0 Magnet; 0 Charter; 5 Title I Eligible; 0 School-wide Title I
Students: 1,752 (n/a% male; n/a% female)
Individual Education Program: 224 (12.8%);
English Language Learner: n/a; Migrant: 1 (0.1%)
Eligible for Free Lunch Program: 445 (25.4%)
Eligible for Reduced-Price Lunch Program: 207 (11.8%)
Teachers: 121.5 (14.4 to 1)
Librarians/Media Specialists: 3.0 (584.0 to 1)
Guidance Counselors: 6.0 (292.0 to 1)
Current Spending: ($ per student per year):
Total: $7,257; Instruction: $4,286; Support Services: $2,635
Enrollment, Drop-out Rates and Diploma Recipients by Race/Ethnicity

Category	Total	White	Black	Asian	AIAN	Hisp.
Enrollment (%)	100.0	98.9	0.8	0.0	0.0	0.3
Drop-out Rate (%)	3.9	3.9	0.0	n/a	n/a	0.0
H.S. Diplomas (#)	159	158	1	0	0	0

Jefferson County

Brookville Area SD

PO Box 479 • Brookville, PA 15825-0479
(814) 849-8372 • http://www.brookville.k12.pa.us
Grade Span: KG-12; **Agency Type:** 1
Schools: 4
3 Primary; 0 Middle; 1 High; 0 Other Level
4 Regular; 0 Special Education; 0 Vocational; 0 Alternative
0 Magnet; 0 Charter; 4 Title I Eligible; 0 School-wide Title I
Students: 1,947 (n/a% male; n/a% female)
Individual Education Program: 315 (16.2%);
English Language Learner: n/a; Migrant: 0 (0.0%)
Eligible for Free Lunch Program: 368 (18.9%)
Eligible for Reduced-Price Lunch Program: 184 (9.5%)
Teachers: 126.0 (15.5 to 1)
Librarians/Media Specialists: 2.5 (778.8 to 1)
Guidance Counselors: 5.0 (389.4 to 1)
Current Spending: ($ per student per year):
Total: $7,243; Instruction: $4,561; Support Services: $2,388
Enrollment, Drop-out Rates and Diploma Recipients by Race/Ethnicity

Category	Total	White	Black	Asian	AIAN	Hisp.
Enrollment (%)	100.0	97.7	0.8	0.8	0.3	0.5
Drop-out Rate (%)	2.4	2.3	20.0	0.0	n/a	0.0
H.S. Diplomas (#)	122	121	0	1	0	0

Punxsutawney Area SD

600 N Findley St • Punxsutawney, PA 15767-1467
(814) 938-5151 • http://www.punxsy.k12.pa.us
Grade Span: KG-12; **Agency Type:** 1
Schools: 11
9 Primary; 1 Middle; 1 High; 0 Other Level
11 Regular; 0 Special Education; 0 Vocational; 0 Alternative
0 Magnet; 0 Charter; 10 Title I Eligible; 5 School-wide Title I
Students: 2,856 (n/a% male; n/a% female)
Individual Education Program: 456 (16.0%);
English Language Learner: n/a; Migrant: 0 (0.0%)
Eligible for Free Lunch Program: 599 (21.0%)
Eligible for Reduced-Price Lunch Program: 240 (8.4%)
Teachers: 209.8 (13.6 to 1)
Librarians/Media Specialists: 4.0 (714.0 to 1)
Guidance Counselors: 8.0 (357.0 to 1)
Current Spending: ($ per student per year):
Total: $8,020; Instruction: $5,135; Support Services: $2,511
Enrollment, Drop-out Rates and Diploma Recipients by Race/Ethnicity

Category	Total	White	Black	Asian	AIAN	Hisp.
Enrollment (%)	100.0	98.8	0.4	0.2	0.1	0.4
Drop-out Rate (%)	2.4	2.5	0.0	0.0	0.0	n/a
H.S. Diplomas (#)	202	200	1	1	0	0

Juniata County

Juniata County SD

Hcr-63 Box 7d S 7th St • Mifflintown, PA 17059-9806
(717) 436-2111
Grade Span: KG-12; **Agency Type:** 1
Schools: 12
9 Primary; 1 Middle; 2 High; 0 Other Level
12 Regular; 0 Special Education; 0 Vocational; 0 Alternative
0 Magnet; 0 Charter; 10 Title I Eligible; 0 School-wide Title I
Students: 3,260 (n/a% male; n/a% female)
Individual Education Program: 375 (11.5%);
English Language Learner: n/a; Migrant: 41 (1.3%)
Eligible for Free Lunch Program: 502 (15.4%)
Eligible for Reduced-Price Lunch Program: 313 (9.6%)
Teachers: 204.2 (16.0 to 1)
Librarians/Media Specialists: 4.5 (724.4 to 1)
Guidance Counselors: 7.0 (465.7 to 1)
Current Spending: ($ per student per year):
Total: $5,652; Instruction: $3,407; Support Services: $1,969
Enrollment, Drop-out Rates and Diploma Recipients by Race/Ethnicity

Category	Total	White	Black	Asian	AIAN	Hisp.
Enrollment (%)	100.0	95.7	0.7	0.8	0.0	2.8
Drop-out Rate (%)	2.2	2.2	0.0	0.0	0.0	0.0
H.S. Diplomas (#)	233	228	0	0	0	5

Lackawanna County

Abington Heights SD

200 E Grove St • Clarks Summit, PA 18411-1776
(570) 586-2511 • http://www.ahsd.org
Grade Span: KG-12; **Agency Type:** 1
Schools: 6
4 Primary; 1 Middle; 1 High; 0 Other Level
6 Regular; 0 Special Education; 0 Vocational; 0 Alternative
0 Magnet; 0 Charter; 3 Title I Eligible; 0 School-wide Title I
Students: 3,690 (n/a% male; n/a% female)
Individual Education Program: 472 (12.8%);
English Language Learner: n/a; Migrant: 6 (0.2%)
Eligible for Free Lunch Program: 170 (4.6%)
Eligible for Reduced-Price Lunch Program: 99 (2.7%)
Teachers: 222.6 (16.6 to 1)
Librarians/Media Specialists: 4.0 (922.5 to 1)
Guidance Counselors: 9.0 (410.0 to 1)
Current Spending: ($ per student per year):
Total: $7,541; Instruction: $4,883; Support Services: $2,423
Enrollment, Drop-out Rates and Diploma Recipients by Race/Ethnicity

Category	Total	White	Black	Asian	AIAN	Hisp.
Enrollment (%)	100.0	96.3	1.0	1.9	0.0	0.8
Drop-out Rate (%)	0.6	0.6	0.0	0.0	n/a	0.0
H.S. Diplomas (#)	278	276	1	1	0	0

Dunmore SD

300 W Warren St • Dunmore, PA 18512-1992
(570) 343-2110 • http://ns.neiu.k12.pa.us/WWW/DUN/dunmore.htm
Grade Span: KG-12; **Agency Type:** 1
Schools: 3
1 Primary; 1 Middle; 1 High; 0 Other Level
3 Regular; 0 Special Education; 0 Vocational; 0 Alternative
0 Magnet; 0 Charter; 1 Title I Eligible; 0 School-wide Title I
Students: 1,693 (n/a% male; n/a% female)
Individual Education Program: 207 (12.2%);
English Language Learner: n/a; Migrant: 0 (0.0%)
Eligible for Free Lunch Program: 259 (15.3%)
Eligible for Reduced-Price Lunch Program: 71 (4.2%)
Teachers: 95.0 (17.8 to 1)
Librarians/Media Specialists: 2.0 (846.5 to 1)
Guidance Counselors: 4.0 (423.3 to 1)
Current Spending: ($ per student per year):
Total: $6,439; Instruction: $4,300; Support Services: $1,887
Enrollment, Drop-out Rates and Diploma Recipients by Race/Ethnicity

Category	Total	White	Black	Asian	AIAN	Hisp.
Enrollment (%)	100.0	97.7	1.1	0.2	0.0	1.0
Drop-out Rate (%)	2.0	1.9	25.0	0.0	n/a	0.0
H.S. Diplomas (#)	122	121	1	0	0	0

Lakeland SD

1569 Lakeland Dr • Jermyn, PA 18433-9801
(570) 254-9485 • http://ns.neiu.k12.pa.us/WWW/LAKELAND/index.html
Grade Span: KG-12; **Agency Type:** 1
Schools: 3
2 Primary; 0 Middle; 1 High; 0 Other Level
3 Regular; 0 Special Education; 0 Vocational; 0 Alternative
0 Magnet; 0 Charter; 2 Title I Eligible; 0 School-wide Title I
Students: 1,694 (n/a% male; n/a% female)
Individual Education Program: 237 (14.0%);
English Language Learner: n/a; Migrant: 0 (0.0%)
Eligible for Free Lunch Program: 259 (15.3%)
Eligible for Reduced-Price Lunch Program: 119 (7.0%)
Teachers: 89.0 (19.0 to 1)
Librarians/Media Specialists: 2.0 (847.0 to 1)
Guidance Counselors: 4.0 (423.5 to 1)
Current Spending: ($ per student per year):
Total: $5,828; Instruction: $3,656; Support Services: $1,969
Enrollment, Drop-out Rates and Diploma Recipients by Race/Ethnicity

Category	Total	White	Black	Asian	AIAN	Hisp.
Enrollment (%)	100.0	98.0	0.9	0.5	0.2	0.5
Drop-out Rate (%)	1.6	1.7	0.0	0.0	0.0	0.0
H.S. Diplomas (#)	118	117	0	0	1	0

Mid Valley SD

52 Underwood Rd • Throop, PA 18512-1196
(570) 307-1119 • http://mvsd.neiu.k12.pa.us
Grade Span: KG-12; **Agency Type:** 1
Schools: 2
1 Primary; 0 Middle; 1 High; 0 Other Level
2 Regular; 0 Special Education; 0 Vocational; 0 Alternative
0 Magnet; 0 Charter; 1 Title I Eligible; 0 School-wide Title I
Students: 1,559 (n/a% male; n/a% female)
Individual Education Program: 269 (17.3%);
English Language Learner: n/a; Migrant: 0 (0.0%)
Eligible for Free Lunch Program: 259 (16.6%)
Eligible for Reduced-Price Lunch Program: 139 (8.9%)
Teachers: 98.7 (15.8 to 1)
Librarians/Media Specialists: 2.0 (779.5 to 1)
Guidance Counselors: 6.0 (259.8 to 1)
Current Spending: ($ per student per year):
Total: $6,540; Instruction: $4,329; Support Services: $1,968
Enrollment, Drop-out Rates and Diploma Recipients by Race/Ethnicity

Category	Total	White	Black	Asian	AIAN	Hisp.
Enrollment (%)	100.0	97.4	1.3	0.3	0.1	0.9
Drop-out Rate (%)	2.4	2.2	0.0	0.0	0.0	n/a
H.S. Diplomas (#)	118	118	0	0	0	0

North Pocono SD

701 Church St • Moscow, PA 18444-9391
(570) 842-7659 • http://ns.neiu.k12.pa.us./WWW/NP/
Grade Span: KG-12; **Agency Type:** 1
Schools: 5
3 Primary; 1 Middle; 1 High; 0 Other Level
5 Regular; 0 Special Education; 0 Vocational; 0 Alternative
0 Magnet; 0 Charter; 3 Title I Eligible; 0 School-wide Title I
Students: 3,253 (n/a% male; n/a% female)
Individual Education Program: 370 (11.4%);
English Language Learner: n/a; Migrant: 0 (0.0%)
Eligible for Free Lunch Program: 500 (15.4%)
Eligible for Reduced-Price Lunch Program: 213 (6.5%)
Teachers: 191.0 (17.0 to 1)
Librarians/Media Specialists: 3.0 (1,084.3 to 1)
Guidance Counselors: 9.0 (361.4 to 1)
Current Spending: ($ per student per year):
Total: $6,866; Instruction: $4,377; Support Services: $2,236
Enrollment, Drop-out Rates and Diploma Recipients by Race/Ethnicity

Category	Total	White	Black	Asian	AIAN	Hisp.
Enrollment (%)	100.0	96.7	1.2	0.6	0.4	1.1
Drop-out Rate (%)	2.5	2.6	0.0	0.0	0.0	0.0
H.S. Diplomas (#)	260	255	2	1	0	2

Scranton SD

425 N Washington Ave • Scranton, PA 18503-1305
(570) 348-3400 • http://www.scrsd.org/
Grade Span: KG-12; **Agency Type:** 1
Schools: 18
13 Primary; 3 Middle; 2 High; 0 Other Level
18 Regular; 0 Special Education; 0 Vocational; 0 Alternative
0 Magnet; 0 Charter; 17 Title I Eligible; 0 School-wide Title I
Students: 8,841 (n/a% male; n/a% female)
Individual Education Program: 1,569 (17.7%);
English Language Learner: n/a; Migrant: 228 (2.6%)
Eligible for Free Lunch Program: 3,320 (37.6%)
Eligible for Reduced-Price Lunch Program: 611 (6.9%)
Teachers: 616.6 (14.3 to 1)
Librarians/Media Specialists: 14.0 (631.5 to 1)
Guidance Counselors: 21.0 (421.0 to 1)
Current Spending: ($ per student per year):
Total: $8,940; Instruction: $6,428; Support Services: $2,296
Enrollment, Drop-out Rates and Diploma Recipients by Race/Ethnicity

Category	Total	White	Black	Asian	AIAN	Hisp.
Enrollment (%)	100.0	82.1	8.6	1.0	0.1	8.3
Drop-out Rate (%)	4.4	4.3	4.7	4.9	0.0	5.1
H.S. Diplomas (#)	525	477	24	9	1	14

Valley View SD

1 Columbus Dr • Archbald, PA 18403-1538
(570) 876-5080 • http://vvsd.neiu.k12.pa.us/vvsd/dist/vvsd.html
Grade Span: KG-12; **Agency Type:** 1
Schools: 4
2 Primary; 1 Middle; 1 High; 0 Other Level
4 Regular; 0 Special Education; 0 Vocational; 0 Alternative
0 Magnet; 0 Charter; 2 Title I Eligible; 0 School-wide Title I
Students: 2,640 (n/a% male; n/a% female)
Individual Education Program: 314 (11.9%);
English Language Learner: n/a; Migrant: 2 (0.1%)
Eligible for Free Lunch Program: 376 (14.2%)
Eligible for Reduced-Price Lunch Program: 153 (5.8%)
Teachers: 151.0 (17.5 to 1)
Librarians/Media Specialists: 3.0 (880.0 to 1)
Guidance Counselors: 7.0 (377.1 to 1)
Current Spending: ($ per student per year):
Total: $6,023; Instruction: $3,661; Support Services: $2,119
Enrollment, Drop-out Rates and Diploma Recipients by Race/Ethnicity

Category	Total	White	Black	Asian	AIAN	Hisp.
Enrollment (%)	100.0	97.2	0.8	0.7	0.0	1.2
Drop-out Rate (%)	0.4	0.4	0.0	0.0	n/a	0.0
H.S. Diplomas (#)	183	181	1	0	1	0

Lancaster County

Cocalico SD

800 S 4th St • Denver, PA 17517-1139
(717) 336-1413 • http://www.cocalico.k12.pa.us
Grade Span: KG-12; **Agency Type:** 1
Schools: 6
4 Primary; 1 Middle; 1 High; 0 Other Level
6 Regular; 0 Special Education; 0 Vocational; 0 Alternative
0 Magnet; 0 Charter; 5 Title I Eligible; 0 School-wide Title I
Students: 3,531 (n/a% male; n/a% female)
Individual Education Program: 498 (14.1%);
English Language Learner: n/a; Migrant: 3 (0.1%)
Eligible for Free Lunch Program: 298 (8.4%)
Eligible for Reduced-Price Lunch Program: 201 (5.7%)
Teachers: 208.5 (16.9 to 1)
Librarians/Media Specialists: 5.0 (706.2 to 1)
Guidance Counselors: 8.0 (441.4 to 1)
Current Spending: ($ per student per year):
Total: $6,162; Instruction: $3,902; Support Services: $1,943
Enrollment, Drop-out Rates and Diploma Recipients by Race/Ethnicity

Category	Total	White	Black	Asian	AIAN	Hisp.
Enrollment (%)	100.0	93.9	1.2	2.5	0.2	2.3
Drop-out Rate (%)	2.3	2.5	0.0	0.0	0.0	0.0
H.S. Diplomas (#)	203	196	1	3	0	3

Columbia Borough SD

98 S 6th St • Columbia, PA 17512-1572
(717) 684-2283
Grade Span: KG-12; **Agency Type:** 1
Schools: 3
2 Primary; 0 Middle; 1 High; 0 Other Level
3 Regular; 0 Special Education; 0 Vocational; 0 Alternative
0 Magnet; 0 Charter; 2 Title I Eligible; 0 School-wide Title I
Students: 1,536 (n/a% male; n/a% female)
Individual Education Program: 388 (25.3%);
English Language Learner: n/a; Migrant: 6 (0.4%)
Eligible for Free Lunch Program: 403 (26.2%)
Eligible for Reduced-Price Lunch Program: 154 (10.0%)
Teachers: 97.5 (15.8 to 1)
Librarians/Media Specialists: 2.0 (768.0 to 1)
Guidance Counselors: 3.0 (512.0 to 1)
Current Spending: ($ per student per year):
Total: $6,314; Instruction: $4,051; Support Services: $1,893
Enrollment, Drop-out Rates and Diploma Recipients by Race/Ethnicity

Category	Total	White	Black	Asian	AIAN	Hisp.
Enrollment (%)	100.0	79.4	10.3	1.0	0.1	9.2
Drop-out Rate (%)	4.2	4.4	2.7	0.0	0.0	5.0
H.S. Diplomas (#)	82	63	11	1	0	7

Conestoga Valley SD

2110 Horseshoe Rd • Lancaster, PA 17601-6099
(717) 397-2421 • http://www.cvsd.k12.pa.us
Grade Span: KG-12; **Agency Type:** 1
Schools: 7
5 Primary; 1 Middle; 1 High; 0 Other Level
7 Regular; 0 Special Education; 0 Vocational; 0 Alternative
0 Magnet; 0 Charter; 5 Title I Eligible; 0 School-wide Title I
Students: 3,834 (n/a% male; n/a% female)
Individual Education Program: 467 (12.2%);
English Language Learner: n/a; Migrant: 12 (0.3%)
Eligible for Free Lunch Program: 301 (7.9%)
Eligible for Reduced-Price Lunch Program: 302 (7.9%)
Teachers: 228.3 (16.8 to 1)
Librarians/Media Specialists: 6.0 (639.0 to 1)
Guidance Counselors: 10.5 (365.1 to 1)
Current Spending: ($ per student per year):
Total: $7,143; Instruction: $4,702; Support Services: $2,143
Enrollment, Drop-out Rates and Diploma Recipients by Race/Ethnicity

Category	Total	White	Black	Asian	AIAN	Hisp.
Enrollment (%)	100.0	85.5	3.2	5.2	0.0	6.1
Drop-out Rate (%)	3.1	2.6	0.0	5.7	n/a	2.0
H.S. Diplomas (#)	254	231	4	7	0	12

Donegal SD

366 S Market Ave • Mount Joy, PA 17552-2700
(717) 653-1447 • http://www.donegal.k12.pa.us
Grade Span: KG-12; **Agency Type:** 1
Schools: 6
4 Primary; 1 Middle; 1 High; 0 Other Level
6 Regular; 0 Special Education; 0 Vocational; 0 Alternative
0 Magnet; 0 Charter; 4 Title I Eligible; 0 School-wide Title I
Students: 2,538 (n/a% male; n/a% female)
Individual Education Program: 453 (17.8%);
English Language Learner: n/a; Migrant: 9 (0.4%)
Eligible for Free Lunch Program: 289 (11.4%)
Eligible for Reduced-Price Lunch Program: 151 (5.9%)
Teachers: 162.7 (15.6 to 1)
Librarians/Media Specialists: 4.0 (634.5 to 1)
Guidance Counselors: 6.0 (423.0 to 1)
Current Spending: ($ per student per year):
Total: $6,614; Instruction: $4,151; Support Services: $2,186
Enrollment, Drop-out Rates and Diploma Recipients by Race/Ethnicity

Category	Total	White	Black	Asian	AIAN	Hisp.
Enrollment (%)	100.0	93.3	1.7	1.1	0.2	3.6
Drop-out Rate (%)	3.4	3.6	0.0	0.0	n/a	0.0
H.S. Diplomas (#)	152	146	3	3	0	0

Eastern Lancaster County SD

PO Box 609 • New Holland, PA 17557-0609
(717) 354-1500 • http://www.elanco.k12.pa.us
Grade Span: KG-12; **Agency Type:** 1
Schools: 7
4 Primary; 2 Middle; 1 High; 0 Other Level
7 Regular; 0 Special Education; 0 Vocational; 0 Alternative
0 Magnet; 0 Charter; 5 Title I Eligible; 0 School-wide Title I
Students: 3,486 (n/a% male; n/a% female)
Individual Education Program: 388 (11.1%);
English Language Learner: n/a; Migrant: 8 (0.2%)
Eligible for Free Lunch Program: 391 (11.2%)
Eligible for Reduced-Price Lunch Program: 239 (6.9%)
Teachers: 215.4 (16.2 to 1)
Librarians/Media Specialists: 5.0 (697.2 to 1)
Guidance Counselors: 8.0 (435.8 to 1)
Current Spending: ($ per student per year):
Total: $6,559; Instruction: $4,002; Support Services: $2,293
Enrollment, Drop-out Rates and Diploma Recipients by Race/Ethnicity

Category	Total	White	Black	Asian	AIAN	Hisp.
Enrollment (%)	100.0	92.7	1.3	2.7	0.0	3.3
Drop-out Rate (%)	2.9	3.1	0.0	0.0	n/a	0.0
H.S. Diplomas (#)	234	224	2	7	0	1

Elizabethtown Area SD

600 E High St • Elizabethtown, PA 17022-1713
(717) 367-1521 • http://www.etown.k12.pa.us
Grade Span: KG-12; **Agency Type:** 1
Schools: 7
5 Primary; 1 Middle; 1 High; 0 Other Level
7 Regular; 0 Special Education; 0 Vocational; 0 Alternative
0 Magnet; 0 Charter; 4 Title I Eligible; 0 School-wide Title I
Students: 3,902 (n/a% male; n/a% female)
Individual Education Program: 577 (14.8%);
English Language Learner: n/a; Migrant: 10 (0.3%)
Eligible for Free Lunch Program: 216 (5.5%)
Eligible for Reduced-Price Lunch Program: 186 (4.8%)
Teachers: 225.2 (17.3 to 1)
Librarians/Media Specialists: 5.0 (780.4 to 1)
Guidance Counselors: 10.0 (390.2 to 1)
Current Spending: ($ per student per year):
Total: $5,856; Instruction: $3,666; Support Services: $1,926
Enrollment, Drop-out Rates and Diploma Recipients by Race/Ethnicity

Category	Total	White	Black	Asian	AIAN	Hisp.
Enrollment (%)	100.0	95.5	1.1	1.1	0.3	2.0
Drop-out Rate (%)	2.2	2.2	8.3	0.0	0.0	0.0
H.S. Diplomas (#)	244	232	1	8	0	3

Ephrata Area SD

803 Oak Blvd • Ephrata, PA 17522-1960
(717) 733-1513 • http://www.easd.k12.pa.us
Grade Span: PK-12; **Agency Type:** 1
Schools: 7
5 Primary; 1 Middle; 1 High; 0 Other Level
7 Regular; 0 Special Education; 0 Vocational; 0 Alternative
0 Magnet; 0 Charter; 5 Title I Eligible; 0 School-wide Title I
Students: 4,136 (n/a% male; n/a% female)
Individual Education Program: 548 (13.2%);
English Language Learner: n/a; Migrant: 15 (0.4%)
Eligible for Free Lunch Program: 459 (11.1%)
Eligible for Reduced-Price Lunch Program: 270 (6.5%)
Teachers: 250.1 (16.5 to 1)
Librarians/Media Specialists: 7.5 (551.5 to 1)
Guidance Counselors: 8.0 (517.0 to 1)
Current Spending: ($ per student per year):
Total: $6,266; Instruction: $4,033; Support Services: $1,917
Enrollment, Drop-out Rates and Diploma Recipients by Race/Ethnicity

Category	Total	White	Black	Asian	AIAN	Hisp.
Enrollment (%)	100.0	95.6	0.4	1.9	0.1	2.1
Drop-out Rate (%)	1.0	0.9	0.0	2.5	0.0	4.2
H.S. Diplomas (#)	269	262	1	5	0	1

Hempfield SD

200 Church St • Landisville, PA 17538-1300
(717) 898-5560 • http://www.hempfield.k12.pa.us
Grade Span: KG-12; **Agency Type:** 1
Schools: 10
7 Primary; 2 Middle; 1 High; 0 Other Level
10 Regular; 0 Special Education; 0 Vocational; 0 Alternative
0 Magnet; 0 Charter; 7 Title I Eligible; 0 School-wide Title I
Students: 7,218 (n/a% male; n/a% female)
Individual Education Program: 1,028 (14.2%);
English Language Learner: n/a; Migrant: 58 (0.8%)
Eligible for Free Lunch Program: 611 (8.5%)
Eligible for Reduced-Price Lunch Program: 307 (4.3%)
Teachers: 420.1 (17.2 to 1)
Librarians/Media Specialists: 10.0 (721.8 to 1)
Guidance Counselors: 11.0 (656.2 to 1)
Current Spending: ($ per student per year):
Total: $6,636; Instruction: $4,292; Support Services: $1,982
Enrollment, Drop-out Rates and Diploma Recipients by Race/Ethnicity

Category	Total	White	Black	Asian	AIAN	Hisp.
Enrollment (%)	100.0	88.6	2.7	2.7	0.3	5.7
Drop-out Rate (%)	2.7	2.5	11.6	4.3	0.0	3.4
H.S. Diplomas (#)	546	499	10	19	1	17

Lampeter-Strasburg SD

PO Box 428 • Lampeter, PA 17537-0428
(717) 464-3311 • http://www.lampstras.k12.pa.us
Grade Span: KG-12; **Agency Type:** 1
Schools: 5
3 Primary; 1 Middle; 1 High; 0 Other Level
5 Regular; 0 Special Education; 0 Vocational; 0 Alternative
0 Magnet; 0 Charter; 4 Title I Eligible; 0 School-wide Title I
Students: 3,178 (n/a% male; n/a% female)
Individual Education Program: 382 (12.0%);
English Language Learner: n/a; Migrant: 3 (0.1%)
Eligible for Free Lunch Program: 135 (4.2%)
Eligible for Reduced-Price Lunch Program: 87 (2.7%)
Teachers: 190.3 (16.7 to 1)
Librarians/Media Specialists: 3.0 (1,059.3 to 1)
Guidance Counselors: 7.0 (454.0 to 1)
Current Spending: ($ per student per year):
Total: $6,614; Instruction: $4,391; Support Services: $1,801
Enrollment, Drop-out Rates and Diploma Recipients by Race/Ethnicity

Category	Total	White	Black	Asian	AIAN	Hisp.
Enrollment (%)	100.0	95.1	1.6	1.1	0.1	2.1
Drop-out Rate (%)	1.8	1.2	22.2	0.0	n/a	30.8
H.S. Diplomas (#)	183	173	1	2	0	7

Lancaster SD

1020 Lehigh Ave • Lancaster, PA 17602-2452
(717) 291-6121 • http://www.lancaster.k12.pa.us/
Grade Span: PK-12; **Agency Type:** 1
Schools: 20
13 Primary; 4 Middle; 1 High; 2 Other Level
20 Regular; 0 Special Education; 0 Vocational; 0 Alternative
0 Magnet; 0 Charter; 20 Title I Eligible; 0 School-wide Title I
Students: 11,206 (n/a% male; n/a% female)
Individual Education Program: 2,482 (22.1%);
English Language Learner: n/a; Migrant: 1,053 (9.4%)
Eligible for Free Lunch Program: 6,275 (56.0%)
Eligible for Reduced-Price Lunch Program: 1,184 (10.6%)
Teachers: 696.5 (16.1 to 1)
Librarians/Media Specialists: 19.0 (589.8 to 1)
Guidance Counselors: 26.9 (416.6 to 1)
Current Spending: ($ per student per year):
Total: $7,509; Instruction: $4,837; Support Services: $2,330
Enrollment, Drop-out Rates and Diploma Recipients by Race/Ethnicity

Category	Total	White	Black	Asian	AIAN	Hisp.
Enrollment (%)	100.0	25.3	23.1	2.6	0.2	48.8
Drop-out Rate (%)	9.2	6.4	8.8	4.1	150.0	11.9
H.S. Diplomas (#)	461	172	110	28	0	151

Manheim Central SD

71 N Hazel St • Manheim, PA 17545-1511
(717) 665-3422 • http://www.mcsd.k12.pa.us
Grade Span: KG-12; **Agency Type:** 1
Schools: 8
6 Primary; 1 Middle; 1 High; 0 Other Level
8 Regular; 0 Special Education; 0 Vocational; 0 Alternative
0 Magnet; 0 Charter; 4 Title I Eligible; 0 School-wide Title I
Students: 3,075 (n/a% male; n/a% female)
Individual Education Program: 461 (15.0%);
English Language Learner: n/a; Migrant: 14 (0.5%)
Eligible for Free Lunch Program: 262 (8.5%)
Eligible for Reduced-Price Lunch Program: 232 (7.5%)
Teachers: 189.3 (16.2 to 1)
Librarians/Media Specialists: 4.6 (668.5 to 1)
Guidance Counselors: 7.0 (439.3 to 1)
Current Spending: ($ per student per year):
Total: $6,878; Instruction: $4,457; Support Services: $2,102
Enrollment, Drop-out Rates and Diploma Recipients by Race/Ethnicity

Category	Total	White	Black	Asian	AIAN	Hisp.
Enrollment (%)	100.0	95.4	1.5	1.1	0.2	1.7
Drop-out Rate (%)	2.9	3.0	0.0	0.0	n/a	0.0
H.S. Diplomas (#)	221	205	3	10	0	3

Manheim Township SD

PO Box 5134 • Lancaster, PA 17601-5134
(717) 569-8231 • http://www.mtwp.k12.pa.us
Grade Span: KG-12; **Agency Type:** 1
Schools: 9
5 Primary; 2 Middle; 1 High; 1 Other Level
9 Regular; 0 Special Education; 0 Vocational; 0 Alternative
0 Magnet; 0 Charter; 4 Title I Eligible; 0 School-wide Title I
Students: 5,316 (n/a% male; n/a% female)
Individual Education Program: 605 (11.4%);
English Language Learner: n/a; Migrant: 10 (0.2%)
Eligible for Free Lunch Program: 241 (4.5%)
Eligible for Reduced-Price Lunch Program: 152 (2.9%)
Teachers: 341.2 (15.6 to 1)
Librarians/Media Specialists: 9.5 (559.6 to 1)
Guidance Counselors: 14.0 (379.7 to 1)
Current Spending: ($ per student per year):
Total: $7,391; Instruction: $4,459; Support Services: $2,682
Enrollment, Drop-out Rates and Diploma Recipients by Race/Ethnicity

Category	Total	White	Black	Asian	AIAN	Hisp.
Enrollment (%)	100.0	85.0	3.6	5.3	0.1	5.9
Drop-out Rate (%)	2.2	1.8	2.6	4.3	0.0	7.9
H.S. Diplomas (#)	356	325	8	14	0	9

Penn Manor SD

PO Box 1001 • Millersville, PA 17551-0301
(717) 872-9500 • http://www.pmsd.k12.pa.us
Grade Span: KG-12; **Agency Type:** 1
Schools: 10
7 Primary; 2 Middle; 1 High; 0 Other Level
10 Regular; 0 Special Education; 0 Vocational; 0 Alternative
0 Magnet; 0 Charter; 5 Title I Eligible; 0 School-wide Title I
Students: 5,361 (n/a% male; n/a% female)
Individual Education Program: 761 (14.2%);
English Language Learner: n/a; Migrant: 4 (0.1%)
Eligible for Free Lunch Program: 461 (8.6%)
Eligible for Reduced-Price Lunch Program: 243 (4.5%)
Teachers: 312.8 (17.1 to 1)
Librarians/Media Specialists: 6.0 (893.5 to 1)
Guidance Counselors: 12.5 (428.9 to 1)
Current Spending: ($ per student per year):
Total: $6,282; Instruction: $4,039; Support Services: $1,920
Enrollment, Drop-out Rates and Diploma Recipients by Race/Ethnicity

Category	Total	White	Black	Asian	AIAN	Hisp.
Enrollment (%)	100.0	93.5	1.9	1.3	0.1	3.2
Drop-out Rate (%)	1.5	1.5	3.0	4.0	0.0	0.0
H.S. Diplomas (#)	350	332	7	4	1	6

Pequea Valley SD

PO Box 130 • Kinzers, PA 17535-0130
(717) 768-5530 • http://www.pvsd.k12.pa.us
Grade Span: KG-12; **Agency Type:** 1
Schools: 5
3 Primary; 1 Middle; 1 High; 0 Other Level
5 Regular; 0 Special Education; 0 Vocational; 0 Alternative
0 Magnet; 0 Charter; 3 Title I Eligible; 0 School-wide Title I
Students: 2,001 (n/a% male; n/a% female)
Individual Education Program: 271 (13.5%);
English Language Learner: n/a; Migrant: 1 (0.1%)
Eligible for Free Lunch Program: 253 (12.6%)
Eligible for Reduced-Price Lunch Program: 133 (6.6%)
Teachers: 129.5 (15.5 to 1)
Librarians/Media Specialists: 4.0 (500.3 to 1)
Guidance Counselors: 4.0 (500.3 to 1)
Current Spending: ($ per student per year):
Total: $7,901; Instruction: $4,756; Support Services: $2,816
Enrollment, Drop-out Rates and Diploma Recipients by Race/Ethnicity

Category	Total	White	Black	Asian	AIAN	Hisp.
Enrollment (%)	100.0	95.8	2.3	0.9	0.0	1.0
Drop-out Rate (%)	2.4	2.3	0.0	0.0	0.0	16.7
H.S. Diplomas (#)	108	100	2	3	0	3

Solanco SD

121 S Hess St • Quarryville, PA 17566-1225
(717) 786-8401 • http://www.solanco.k12.pa.us
Grade Span: KG-12; **Agency Type:** 1
Schools: 7
4 Primary; 2 Middle; 1 High; 0 Other Level
7 Regular; 0 Special Education; 0 Vocational; 0 Alternative
0 Magnet; 0 Charter; 5 Title I Eligible; 0 School-wide Title I
Students: 4,027 (n/a% male; n/a% female)
Individual Education Program: 359 (8.9%);
English Language Learner: n/a; Migrant: 5 (0.1%)
Eligible for Free Lunch Program: 334 (8.3%)
Eligible for Reduced-Price Lunch Program: 231 (5.7%)
Teachers: 209.6 (19.2 to 1)
Librarians/Media Specialists: 6.0 (671.2 to 1)
Guidance Counselors: 9.0 (447.4 to 1)
Current Spending: ($ per student per year):
Total: $5,769; Instruction: $3,452; Support Services: $2,029
Enrollment, Drop-out Rates and Diploma Recipients by Race/Ethnicity

Category	Total	White	Black	Asian	AIAN	Hisp.
Enrollment (%)	100.0	96.0	1.2	0.4	0.2	2.2
Drop-out Rate (%)	2.5	2.5	0.0	0.0	n/a	0.0
H.S. Diplomas (#)	305	302	2	0	0	1

Warwick SD

301 W Orange St • Lititz, PA 17543-1814
(717) 626-3734 • http://www.warwick.k12.pa.us
Grade Span: KG-12; **Agency Type:** 1
Schools: 6
4 Primary; 1 Middle; 1 High; 0 Other Level
6 Regular; 0 Special Education; 0 Vocational; 0 Alternative
0 Magnet; 0 Charter; 4 Title I Eligible; 0 School-wide Title I
Students: 4,705 (n/a% male; n/a% female)
Individual Education Program: 763 (16.2%);
English Language Learner: n/a; Migrant: 9 (0.2%)
Eligible for Free Lunch Program: 289 (6.1%)
Eligible for Reduced-Price Lunch Program: 193 (4.1%)
Teachers: 288.4 (16.3 to 1)
Librarians/Media Specialists: 6.0 (784.2 to 1)
Guidance Counselors: 6.8 (691.9 to 1)
Current Spending: ($ per student per year):
Total: $6,460; Instruction: $4,334; Support Services: $1,838
Enrollment, Drop-out Rates and Diploma Recipients by Race/Ethnicity

Category	Total	White	Black	Asian	AIAN	Hisp.
Enrollment (%)	100.0	94.9	1.4	1.3	0.1	2.2
Drop-out Rate (%)	3.6	3.5	4.2	3.6	0.0	7.7
H.S. Diplomas (#)	305	289	0	4	2	10

Lawrence County

Ellwood City Area SD

501 Crescent Ave • Ellwood City, PA 16117-1957
(724) 752-1591 • http://www.ellwood.k12.pa.us
Grade Span: KG-12; **Agency Type:** 1
Schools: 5
4 Primary; 0 Middle; 1 High; 0 Other Level
5 Regular; 0 Special Education; 0 Vocational; 0 Alternative
0 Magnet; 0 Charter; 0 Title I Eligible; 0 School-wide Title I
Students: 2,246 (n/a% male; n/a% female)
Individual Education Program: 306 (13.6%);
English Language Learner: n/a; Migrant: 0 (0.0%)
Eligible for Free Lunch Program: 558 (24.8%)
Eligible for Reduced-Price Lunch Program: 210 (9.4%)
Teachers: 133.0 (16.9 to 1)
Librarians/Media Specialists: 2.0 (1,123.0 to 1)
Guidance Counselors: 3.0 (748.7 to 1)
Current Spending: ($ per student per year):
Total: $6,512; Instruction: $4,272; Support Services: $1,970
Enrollment, Drop-out Rates and Diploma Recipients by Race/Ethnicity

Category	Total	White	Black	Asian	AIAN	Hisp.
Enrollment (%)	100.0	97.2	2.1	0.3	0.0	0.4
Drop-out Rate (%)	3.4	3.4	0.0	0.0	0.0	0.0
H.S. Diplomas (#)	155	151	2	1	0	1

Mohawk Area SD

PO Box 25 • Bessemer, PA 16112-0025
(724) 667-7723 • http://www.mohawk.k12.pa.us
Grade Span: KG-12; **Agency Type:** 1
Schools: 2
1 Primary; 0 Middle; 1 High; 0 Other Level
2 Regular; 0 Special Education; 0 Vocational; 0 Alternative
0 Magnet; 0 Charter; 0 Title I Eligible; 0 School-wide Title I
Students: 2,017 (n/a% male; n/a% female)
Individual Education Program: 225 (11.2%);
English Language Learner: n/a; Migrant: 0 (0.0%)
Eligible for Free Lunch Program: 371 (18.4%)
Eligible for Reduced-Price Lunch Program: 136 (6.7%)
Teachers: 126.0 (16.0 to 1)
Librarians/Media Specialists: 2.0 (1,008.5 to 1)
Guidance Counselors: 3.0 (672.3 to 1)
Current Spending: ($ per student per year):
Total: $6,115; Instruction: $4,193; Support Services: $1,623
Enrollment, Drop-out Rates and Diploma Recipients by Race/Ethnicity

Category	Total	White	Black	Asian	AIAN	Hisp.
Enrollment (%)	100.0	98.9	0.6	0.4	0.0	0.0
Drop-out Rate (%)	1.1	1.1	0.0	0.0	n/a	0.0
H.S. Diplomas (#)	109	109	0	0	0	0

New Castle Area SD

420 Fern St • New Castle, PA 16101-2596
(724) 656-4756 • http://www.newcastle.k12.pa.us
Grade Span: KG-12; **Agency Type:** 1
Schools: 8
5 Primary; 2 Middle; 1 High; 0 Other Level
8 Regular; 0 Special Education; 0 Vocational; 0 Alternative
0 Magnet; 0 Charter; 6 Title I Eligible; 5 School-wide Title I
Students: 3,816 (n/a% male; n/a% female)
Individual Education Program: 628 (16.5%);
English Language Learner: n/a; Migrant: 0 (0.0%)
Eligible for Free Lunch Program: 1,595 (41.8%)
Eligible for Reduced-Price Lunch Program: 195 (5.1%)
Teachers: 232.0 (16.4 to 1)
Librarians/Media Specialists: 6.0 (636.0 to 1)
Guidance Counselors: 3.0 (1,272.0 to 1)
Current Spending: ($ per student per year):
Total: $6,992; Instruction: $4,665; Support Services: $2,021
Enrollment, Drop-out Rates and Diploma Recipients by Race/Ethnicity

Category	Total	White	Black	Asian	AIAN	Hisp.
Enrollment (%)	100.0	73.4	25.4	0.4	0.2	0.6
Drop-out Rate (%)	2.7	2.5	3.9	n/a	0.0	0.0
H.S. Diplomas (#)	163	146	17	0	0	0

Wilmington Area SD

300 Wood St • New Wilmington, PA 16142-1016
(724) 656-8866
Grade Span: KG-12; **Agency Type:** 1
Schools: 5
3 Primary; 1 Middle; 1 High; 0 Other Level
5 Regular; 0 Special Education; 0 Vocational; 0 Alternative
0 Magnet; 0 Charter; 0 Title I Eligible; 0 School-wide Title I
Students: 1,599 (n/a% male; n/a% female)
Individual Education Program: 259 (16.2%);
English Language Learner: n/a; Migrant: 0 (0.0%)
Eligible for Free Lunch Program: 236 (14.8%)
Eligible for Reduced-Price Lunch Program: 108 (6.8%)
Teachers: 99.4 (16.1 to 1)
Librarians/Media Specialists: 1.0 (1,599.0 to 1)
Guidance Counselors: 3.0 (533.0 to 1)
Current Spending: ($ per student per year):
Total: $6,779; Instruction: $4,408; Support Services: $2,149
Enrollment, Drop-out Rates and Diploma Recipients by Race/Ethnicity

Category	Total	White	Black	Asian	AIAN	Hisp.
Enrollment (%)	100.0	98.3	1.1	0.4	0.0	0.3
Drop-out Rate (%)	2.5	2.2	100.0	0.0	n/a	0.0
H.S. Diplomas (#)	129	128	0	0	0	1

Lebanon County

Annville-Cleona SD

520 S White Oak St • Annville, PA 17003-2200
(717) 867-7600 • http://www.acsd.k12.pa.us
Grade Span: KG-12; **Agency Type:** 1
Schools: 4
2 Primary; 1 Middle; 1 High; 0 Other Level
4 Regular; 0 Special Education; 0 Vocational; 0 Alternative
0 Magnet; 0 Charter; 3 Title I Eligible; 0 School-wide Title I
Students: 1,655 (n/a% male; n/a% female)
Individual Education Program: 201 (12.1%);
English Language Learner: n/a; Migrant: 0 (0.0%)
Eligible for Free Lunch Program: 114 (6.9%)
Eligible for Reduced-Price Lunch Program: 54 (3.3%)
Teachers: 104.0 (15.9 to 1)
Librarians/Media Specialists: 3.0 (551.7 to 1)
Guidance Counselors: 5.0 (331.0 to 1)
Current Spending: ($ per student per year):
Total: $6,285; Instruction: $3,944; Support Services: $2,051
Enrollment, Drop-out Rates and Diploma Recipients by Race/Ethnicity

Category	Total	White	Black	Asian	AIAN	Hisp.
Enrollment (%)	100.0	96.0	0.9	1.1	0.0	2.0
Drop-out Rate (%)	1.1	1.2	0.0	0.0	n/a	0.0
H.S. Diplomas (#)	119	116	0	2	0	1

Cornwall-Lebanon SD

105 E Evergreen Rd • Lebanon, PA 17042-7595
(717) 272-2031 • http://www.clsd.k12.pa.us
Grade Span: KG-12; **Agency Type:** 1
Schools: 6
4 Primary; 1 Middle; 1 High; 0 Other Level
6 Regular; 0 Special Education; 0 Vocational; 0 Alternative
0 Magnet; 0 Charter; 4 Title I Eligible; 0 School-wide Title I
Students: 4,642 (n/a% male; n/a% female)
Individual Education Program: 511 (11.0%);
English Language Learner: n/a; Migrant: 72 (1.6%)
Eligible for Free Lunch Program: 680 (14.6%)
Eligible for Reduced-Price Lunch Program: 279 (6.0%)
Teachers: 291.7 (15.9 to 1)
Librarians/Media Specialists: 6.0 (773.7 to 1)
Guidance Counselors: 5.0 (928.4 to 1)
Current Spending: ($ per student per year):
Total: $6,778; Instruction: $4,371; Support Services: $2,120

Enrollment, Drop-out Rates and Diploma Recipients by Race/Ethnicity

Category	Total	White	Black	Asian	AIAN	Hisp.
Enrollment (%)	100.0	88.0	2.2	2.1	0.1	7.6
Drop-out Rate (%)	2.8	2.4	0.0	0.0	0.0	10.1
H.S. Diplomas (#)	322	292	3	4	0	23

Eastern Lebanon County SD

180 Elco Dr • Myerstown, PA 17067-2604
(717) 866-7117 • http://www.elco.k12.pa.us
Grade Span: KG-12; **Agency Type:** 1
Schools: 6
4 Primary; 1 Middle; 1 High; 0 Other Level
6 Regular; 0 Special Education; 0 Vocational; 0 Alternative
0 Magnet; 0 Charter; 5 Title I Eligible; 0 School-wide Title I
Students: 2,392 (n/a% male; n/a% female)
Individual Education Program: 321 (13.4%);
English Language Learner: n/a; Migrant: 0 (0.0%)
Eligible for Free Lunch Program: 183 (7.7%)
Eligible for Reduced-Price Lunch Program: 156 (6.5%)
Teachers: 144.0 (16.6 to 1)
Librarians/Media Specialists: 3.0 (797.3 to 1)
Guidance Counselors: 6.0 (398.7 to 1)
Current Spending: ($ per student per year):
Total: $7,207; Instruction: $4,403; Support Services: $2,478

Enrollment, Drop-out Rates and Diploma Recipients by Race/Ethnicity

Category	Total	White	Black	Asian	AIAN	Hisp.
Enrollment (%)	100.0	98.3	0.9	0.3	0.0	0.4
Drop-out Rate (%)	1.8	1.8	0.0	0.0	n/a	0.0
H.S. Diplomas (#)	164	162	0	1	0	1

Lebanon SD

1000 S 8th St • Lebanon, PA 17042-6726
(717) 273-9391 • http://www.lebanon.k12.pa.us
Grade Span: PK-12; **Agency Type:** 1
Schools: 7
5 Primary; 1 Middle; 1 High; 0 Other Level
7 Regular; 0 Special Education; 0 Vocational; 0 Alternative
0 Magnet; 0 Charter; 7 Title I Eligible; 6 School-wide Title I
Students: 4,236 (n/a% male; n/a% female)
Individual Education Program: 640 (15.1%);
English Language Learner: n/a; Migrant: 413 (9.7%)
Eligible for Free Lunch Program: 1,439 (34.0%)
Eligible for Reduced-Price Lunch Program: 416 (9.8%)
Teachers: 217.0 (19.5 to 1)
Librarians/Media Specialists: 4.0 (1,059.0 to 1)
Guidance Counselors: 11.0 (385.1 to 1)
Current Spending: ($ per student per year):
Total: $6,094; Instruction: $4,014; Support Services: $1,795

Enrollment, Drop-out Rates and Diploma Recipients by Race/Ethnicity

Category	Total	White	Black	Asian	AIAN	Hisp.
Enrollment (%)	100.0	58.3	5.0	1.2	0.0	35.4
Drop-out Rate (%)	6.4	6.5	2.9	0.0	n/a	6.8
H.S. Diplomas (#)	192	141	5	4	0	42

Northern Lebanon SD

PO Box 100 • Fredericksburg, PA 17026-0100
(717) 865-2117 • http://www.norleb.k12.pa.us
Grade Span: KG-12; **Agency Type:** 1
Schools: 6
4 Primary; 1 Middle; 1 High; 0 Other Level
6 Regular; 0 Special Education; 0 Vocational; 0 Alternative
0 Magnet; 0 Charter; 5 Title I Eligible; 0 School-wide Title I
Students: 2,448 (n/a% male; n/a% female)
Individual Education Program: 307 (12.5%);
English Language Learner: n/a; Migrant: 8 (0.3%)
Eligible for Free Lunch Program: 210 (8.6%)
Eligible for Reduced-Price Lunch Program: 132 (5.4%)
Teachers: 153.0 (16.0 to 1)
Librarians/Media Specialists: 2.0 (1,224.0 to 1)
Guidance Counselors: 6.0 (408.0 to 1)
Current Spending: ($ per student per year):
Total: $7,169; Instruction: $4,321; Support Services: $2,505

Enrollment, Drop-out Rates and Diploma Recipients by Race/Ethnicity

Category	Total	White	Black	Asian	AIAN	Hisp.
Enrollment (%)	100.0	96.9	0.7	0.5	0.0	2.0
Drop-out Rate (%)	5.5	5.6	0.0	0.0	n/a	0.0
H.S. Diplomas (#)	161	159	0	0	0	2

Palmyra Area SD

1125 Park Dr • Palmyra, PA 17078-3447
(717) 838-3144 • http://www.palmyra.k12.pa.us
Grade Span: KG-12; **Agency Type:** 1
Schools: 5
3 Primary; 1 Middle; 1 High; 0 Other Level
5 Regular; 0 Special Education; 0 Vocational; 0 Alternative
0 Magnet; 0 Charter; 3 Title I Eligible; 0 School-wide Title I
Students: 2,775 (n/a% male; n/a% female)
Individual Education Program: 341 (12.3%);
English Language Learner: n/a; Migrant: 0 (0.0%)
Eligible for Free Lunch Program: 118 (4.3%)
Eligible for Reduced-Price Lunch Program: 97 (3.5%)
Teachers: 167.5 (16.6 to 1)
Librarians/Media Specialists: 3.0 (925.0 to 1)
Guidance Counselors: 7.0 (396.4 to 1)
Current Spending: ($ per student per year):
Total: $5,866; Instruction: $3,860; Support Services: $1,714

Enrollment, Drop-out Rates and Diploma Recipients by Race/Ethnicity

Category	Total	White	Black	Asian	AIAN	Hisp.
Enrollment (%)	100.0	95.2	1.4	2.2	0.1	1.0
Drop-out Rate (%)	2.4	2.3	0.0	5.6	0.0	10.0
H.S. Diplomas (#)	191	186	1	1	0	3

Lehigh County

Allentown City SD

PO Box 328 • Allentown, PA 18105-0328
(484) 765-4000 • http://www.allentownsd.org/
Grade Span: KG-12; **Agency Type:** 1
Schools: 23
17 Primary; 4 Middle; 2 High; 0 Other Level
23 Regular; 0 Special Education; 0 Vocational; 0 Alternative
0 Magnet; 0 Charter; 15 Title I Eligible; 14 School-wide Title I
Students: 16,693 (n/a% male; n/a% female)
Individual Education Program: 1,951 (11.7%);
English Language Learner: n/a; Migrant: 378 (2.3%)
Eligible for Free Lunch Program: 8,398 (50.3%)
Eligible for Reduced-Price Lunch Program: 1,703 (10.2%)
Teachers: 886.4 (18.8 to 1)
Librarians/Media Specialists: 17.0 (981.9 to 1)
Guidance Counselors: 35.6 (468.9 to 1)
Current Spending: ($ per student per year):
Total: $6,407; Instruction: $4,352; Support Services: $1,803

Enrollment, Drop-out Rates and Diploma Recipients by Race/Ethnicity

Category	Total	White	Black	Asian	AIAN	Hisp.
Enrollment (%)	100.0	32.5	15.6	2.2	0.2	49.6
Drop-out Rate (%)	3.9	3.4	2.7	5.7	0.0	4.7
H.S. Diplomas (#)	686	371	74	20	0	221

Catasauqua Area SD

201 N 14th St • Catasauqua, PA 18032-1107
(610) 264-5571 • http://www.cattysd.org
Grade Span: KG-12; **Agency Type:** 1
Schools: 3
1 Primary; 1 Middle; 1 High; 0 Other Level
3 Regular; 0 Special Education; 0 Vocational; 0 Alternative
0 Magnet; 0 Charter; 2 Title I Eligible; 0 School-wide Title I
Students: 1,755 (n/a% male; n/a% female)
Individual Education Program: 269 (15.3%);
English Language Learner: n/a; Migrant: 0 (0.0%)
Eligible for Free Lunch Program: 239 (13.6%)
Eligible for Reduced-Price Lunch Program: 93 (5.3%)
Teachers: 116.6 (15.1 to 1)
Librarians/Media Specialists: 3.0 (585.0 to 1)
Guidance Counselors: 5.0 (351.0 to 1)
Current Spending: ($ per student per year):
Total: $7,245; Instruction: $4,792; Support Services: $2,170

Enrollment, Drop-out Rates and Diploma Recipients by Race/Ethnicity

Category	Total	White	Black	Asian	AIAN	Hisp.
Enrollment (%)	100.0	87.7	4.6	1.3	0.3	6.2
Drop-out Rate (%)	1.6	1.5	0.0	0.0	0.0	5.9
H.S. Diplomas (#)	96	84	4	2	0	6

East Penn SD

800 Pine St • Emmaus, PA 18049
(610) 966-8300 • http://www.eastpenn.k12.pa.us
Grade Span: KG-12; **Agency Type:** 1
Schools: 11
8 Primary; 2 Middle; 1 High; 0 Other Level
11 Regular; 0 Special Education; 0 Vocational; 0 Alternative
0 Magnet; 0 Charter; 8 Title I Eligible; 0 School-wide Title I
Students: 6,916 (n/a% male; n/a% female)
Individual Education Program: 684 (9.9%);
English Language Learner: n/a; Migrant: 0 (0.0%)
Eligible for Free Lunch Program: 351 (5.1%)
Eligible for Reduced-Price Lunch Program: 177 (2.6%)
Teachers: 412.1 (16.8 to 1)
Librarians/Media Specialists: 8.0 (864.5 to 1)
Guidance Counselors: 17.6 (393.0 to 1)
Current Spending: ($ per student per year):
Total: $7,440; Instruction: $4,551; Support Services: $2,637

Enrollment, Drop-out Rates and Diploma Recipients by Race/Ethnicity

Category	Total	White	Black	Asian	AIAN	Hisp.
Enrollment (%)	100.0	92.7	1.9	3.4	0.1	1.9
Drop-out Rate (%)	2.4	2.4	0.0	1.1	0.0	8.0
H.S. Diplomas (#)	490	455	3	27	0	5

Northern Lehigh SD

1201 Shadow Oaks Ln • Slatington, PA 18080-1237
(610) 767-9800 • http://www.nlsd.k12.pa.us
Grade Span: KG-12; **Agency Type:** 1
Schools: 4
2 Primary; 1 Middle; 1 High; 0 Other Level
4 Regular; 0 Special Education; 0 Vocational; 0 Alternative
0 Magnet; 0 Charter; 2 Title I Eligible; 0 School-wide Title I
Students: 2,113 (n/a% male; n/a% female)
Individual Education Program: 258 (12.2%);
English Language Learner: n/a; Migrant: 0 (0.0%)
Eligible for Free Lunch Program: 425 (20.1%)
Eligible for Reduced-Price Lunch Program: 77 (3.6%)
Teachers: 124.3 (17.0 to 1)
Librarians/Media Specialists: 3.0 (704.3 to 1)
Guidance Counselors: 5.0 (422.6 to 1)
Current Spending: ($ per student per year):
Total: $6,934; Instruction: $4,206; Support Services: $2,440
Enrollment, Drop-out Rates and Diploma Recipients by Race/Ethnicity

Category	Total	White	Black	Asian	AIAN	Hisp.
Enrollment (%)	100.0	96.5	1.2	0.2	0.0	2.1
Drop-out Rate (%)	2.9	3.0	0.0	0.0	n/a	0.0
H.S. Diplomas (#)	145	142	1	1	0	1

Northwestern Lehigh SD

6493 Route 309 • New Tripoli, PA 18066-2038
(610) 298-8661 • http://www.nwlehighsd.org
Grade Span: KG-12; **Agency Type:** 1
Schools: 4
2 Primary; 1 Middle; 1 High; 0 Other Level
4 Regular; 0 Special Education; 0 Vocational; 0 Alternative
0 Magnet; 0 Charter; 0 Title I Eligible; 0 School-wide Title I
Students: 2,332 (n/a% male; n/a% female)
Individual Education Program: 340 (14.6%);
English Language Learner: n/a; Migrant: 0 (0.0%)
Eligible for Free Lunch Program: 106 (4.5%)
Eligible for Reduced-Price Lunch Program: 80 (3.4%)
Teachers: 148.0 (15.8 to 1)
Librarians/Media Specialists: 3.8 (613.7 to 1)
Guidance Counselors: 6.0 (388.7 to 1)
Current Spending: ($ per student per year):
Total: $7,522; Instruction: $4,591; Support Services: $2,632
Enrollment, Drop-out Rates and Diploma Recipients by Race/Ethnicity

Category	Total	White	Black	Asian	AIAN	Hisp.
Enrollment (%)	100.0	96.4	0.9	0.9	0.1	1.7
Drop-out Rate (%)	2.2	2.3	0.0	0.0	n/a	0.0
H.S. Diplomas (#)	160	156	0	1	0	3

Parkland SD

1210 Springhouse Rd • Allentown, PA 18104-2119
(610) 351-5503
Grade Span: KG-12; **Agency Type:** 1
Schools: 10
7 Primary; 2 Middle; 1 High; 0 Other Level
10 Regular; 0 Special Education; 0 Vocational; 0 Alternative
0 Magnet; 0 Charter; 6 Title I Eligible; 0 School-wide Title I
Students: 8,462 (n/a% male; n/a% female)
Individual Education Program: 959 (11.3%);
English Language Learner: n/a; Migrant: 0 (0.0%)
Eligible for Free Lunch Program: 264 (3.1%)
Eligible for Reduced-Price Lunch Program: 153 (1.8%)
Teachers: 488.8 (17.3 to 1)
Librarians/Media Specialists: 10.7 (790.8 to 1)
Guidance Counselors: 22.0 (384.6 to 1)
Current Spending: ($ per student per year):
Total: $7,470; Instruction: $4,591; Support Services: $2,618
Enrollment, Drop-out Rates and Diploma Recipients by Race/Ethnicity

Category	Total	White	Black	Asian	AIAN	Hisp.
Enrollment (%)	100.0	90.7	1.8	5.5	0.1	1.9
Drop-out Rate (%)	0.9	1.0	0.0	0.0	0.0	0.0
H.S. Diplomas (#)	600	563	9	17	1	10

Salisbury Township SD

1140 Salisbury Rd • Allentown, PA 18103-4252
(610) 797-2062 • http://www.salisbury.k12.pa.us
Grade Span: KG-12; **Agency Type:** 1
Schools: 4
2 Primary; 1 Middle; 1 High; 0 Other Level
4 Regular; 0 Special Education; 0 Vocational; 0 Alternative
0 Magnet; 0 Charter; 2 Title I Eligible; 0 School-wide Title I
Students: 1,867 (n/a% male; n/a% female)
Individual Education Program: 260 (13.9%);
English Language Learner: n/a; Migrant: 0 (0.0%)
Eligible for Free Lunch Program: 125 (6.7%)
Eligible for Reduced-Price Lunch Program: 63 (3.4%)
Teachers: 115.0 (16.2 to 1)
Librarians/Media Specialists: 4.0 (466.8 to 1)
Guidance Counselors: 4.0 (466.8 to 1)
Current Spending: ($ per student per year):
Total: $10,745; Instruction: $5,276; Support Services: $5,193
Enrollment, Drop-out Rates and Diploma Recipients by Race/Ethnicity

Category	Total	White	Black	Asian	AIAN	Hisp.
Enrollment (%)	100.0	89.4	3.5	2.7	0.5	3.8
Drop-out Rate (%)	1.3	1.4	0.0	0.0	n/a	0.0
H.S. Diplomas (#)	131	118	4	4	0	5

Southern Lehigh SD

5775 Main St • Center Valley, PA 18034-9703
(610) 282-3121 • http://www.solehi.k12.pa.us
Grade Span: KG-12; **Agency Type:** 1
Schools: 5
3 Primary; 1 Middle; 1 High; 0 Other Level
5 Regular; 0 Special Education; 0 Vocational; 0 Alternative
0 Magnet; 0 Charter; 3 Title I Eligible; 0 School-wide Title I
Students: 2,911 (n/a% male; n/a% female)
Individual Education Program: 340 (11.7%);
English Language Learner: n/a; Migrant: 0 (0.0%)
Eligible for Free Lunch Program: 88 (3.0%)
Eligible for Reduced-Price Lunch Program: 44 (1.5%)
Teachers: 169.3 (17.2 to 1)
Librarians/Media Specialists: 4.8 (606.5 to 1)
Guidance Counselors: 5.0 (582.2 to 1)
Current Spending: ($ per student per year):
Total: $7,503; Instruction: $4,292; Support Services: $2,956
Enrollment, Drop-out Rates and Diploma Recipients by Race/Ethnicity

Category	Total	White	Black	Asian	AIAN	Hisp.
Enrollment (%)	100.0	94.8	0.9	2.4	0.0	1.9
Drop-out Rate (%)	0.9	0.7	0.0	0.0	n/a	50.0
H.S. Diplomas (#)	198	192	0	4	0	2

Whitehall-Coplay SD

2940 Macarthur Rd • Whitehall, PA 18052-3408
(610) 439-1431 • http://www.whitehallcoplay.org/
Grade Span: KG-12; **Agency Type:** 1
Schools: 4
2 Primary; 1 Middle; 1 High; 0 Other Level
4 Regular; 0 Special Education; 0 Vocational; 0 Alternative
0 Magnet; 0 Charter; 3 Title I Eligible; 0 School-wide Title I
Students: 3,886 (n/a% male; n/a% female)
Individual Education Program: 402 (10.3%);
English Language Learner: n/a; Migrant: 3 (0.1%)
Eligible for Free Lunch Program: 493 (12.7%)
Eligible for Reduced-Price Lunch Program: 263 (6.8%)
Teachers: 219.5 (17.7 to 1)
Librarians/Media Specialists: 4.0 (971.5 to 1)
Guidance Counselors: 9.0 (431.8 to 1)
Current Spending: ($ per student per year):
Total: $6,537; Instruction: $4,010; Support Services: $2,274
Enrollment, Drop-out Rates and Diploma Recipients by Race/Ethnicity

Category	Total	White	Black	Asian	AIAN	Hisp.
Enrollment (%)	100.0	83.2	5.8	3.5	0.3	7.2
Drop-out Rate (%)	1.9	1.9	1.8	2.3	0.0	0.0
H.S. Diplomas (#)	276	246	17	6	0	7

Luzerne County

Crestwood SD

281 S Mountain Blvd • Mountain Top, PA 18707-1913
(570) 474-6888 • http://www.crestwoodhigh.org
Grade Span: KG-12; **Agency Type:** 1
Schools: 4
2 Primary; 1 Middle; 1 High; 0 Other Level
4 Regular; 0 Special Education; 0 Vocational; 0 Alternative
0 Magnet; 0 Charter; 3 Title I Eligible; 0 School-wide Title I
Students: 2,885 (n/a% male; n/a% female)
Individual Education Program: 331 (11.5%);
English Language Learner: n/a; Migrant: 0 (0.0%)
Eligible for Free Lunch Program: 265 (9.2%)
Eligible for Reduced-Price Lunch Program: 121 (4.2%)
Teachers: 147.3 (19.6 to 1)
Librarians/Media Specialists: 3.0 (961.7 to 1)
Guidance Counselors: 5.0 (577.0 to 1)
Current Spending: ($ per student per year):
Total: $6,364; Instruction: $3,991; Support Services: $2,126

Enrollment, Drop-out Rates and Diploma Recipients by Race/Ethnicity

Category	Total	White	Black	Asian	AIAN	Hisp.
Enrollment (%)	100.0	96.3	0.9	2.1	0.2	0.5
Drop-out Rate (%)	1.6	1.6	0.0	0.0	0.0	0.0
H.S. Diplomas (#)	235	230	0	2	1	2

Dallas SD

PO Box 2000 • Dallas, PA 18612-0720
(570) 675-5201 • http://www.dallassd.com
Grade Span: KG-12; **Agency Type:** 1
Schools: 4
2 Primary; 1 Middle; 1 High; 0 Other Level
4 Regular; 0 Special Education; 0 Vocational; 0 Alternative
0 Magnet; 0 Charter; 3 Title I Eligible; 0 School-wide Title I
Students: 2,579 (n/a% male; n/a% female)
Individual Education Program: 298 (11.6%);
English Language Learner: n/a; Migrant: 0 (0.0%)
Eligible for Free Lunch Program: 169 (6.6%)
Eligible for Reduced-Price Lunch Program: 101 (3.9%)
Teachers: 145.5 (17.7 to 1)
Librarians/Media Specialists: 3.0 (859.7 to 1)
Guidance Counselors: 6.0 (429.8 to 1)
Current Spending: ($ per student per year):
Total: $7,318; Instruction: $4,531; Support Services: $2,571
Enrollment, Drop-out Rates and Diploma Recipients by Race/Ethnicity

Category	Total	White	Black	Asian	AIAN	Hisp.
Enrollment (%)	100.0	98.0	0.5	0.9	0.0	0.5
Drop-out Rate (%)	0.4	0.4	0.0	0.0	n/a	n/a
H.S. Diplomas (#)	176	173	1	2	0	0

Greater Nanticoke Area SD

427 Kosciuszko St • Nanticoke, PA 18634-2690
(570) 735-1270 • http://www.gnasd.com
Grade Span: KG-12; **Agency Type:** 1
Schools: 5
3 Primary; 1 Middle; 1 High; 0 Other Level
5 Regular; 0 Special Education; 0 Vocational; 0 Alternative
0 Magnet; 0 Charter; 4 Title I Eligible; 0 School-wide Title I
Students: 2,186 (n/a% male; n/a% female)
Individual Education Program: 348 (15.9%);
English Language Learner: n/a; Migrant: 0 (0.0%)
Eligible for Free Lunch Program: 504 (23.1%)
Eligible for Reduced-Price Lunch Program: 179 (8.2%)
Teachers: 111.5 (19.6 to 1)
Librarians/Media Specialists: 1.0 (2,186.0 to 1)
Guidance Counselors: 4.0 (546.5 to 1)
Current Spending: ($ per student per year):
Total: $6,780; Instruction: $4,389; Support Services: $2,207
Enrollment, Drop-out Rates and Diploma Recipients by Race/Ethnicity

Category	Total	White	Black	Asian	AIAN	Hisp.
Enrollment (%)	100.0	96.8	1.8	0.5	0.1	0.7
Drop-out Rate (%)	3.6	3.7	0.0	0.0	0.0	0.0
H.S. Diplomas (#)	139	137	2	0	0	0

Hanover Area SD

1600 Sans Souci Pkwy • Wilkes Barre, PA 18706
(570) 831-2313 • http://www.hanoverarea.org
Grade Span: KG-12; **Agency Type:** 1
Schools: 5
3 Primary; 1 Middle; 1 High; 0 Other Level
5 Regular; 0 Special Education; 0 Vocational; 0 Alternative
0 Magnet; 0 Charter; 4 Title I Eligible; 0 School-wide Title I
Students: 2,073 (n/a% male; n/a% female)
Individual Education Program: 376 (18.1%);
English Language Learner: n/a; Migrant: 0 (0.0%)
Eligible for Free Lunch Program: 600 (28.9%)
Eligible for Reduced-Price Lunch Program: 254 (12.3%)
Teachers: 124.0 (16.7 to 1)
Librarians/Media Specialists: 3.0 (691.0 to 1)
Guidance Counselors: 6.0 (345.5 to 1)
Current Spending: ($ per student per year):
Total: $7,575; Instruction: $4,656; Support Services: $2,619
Enrollment, Drop-out Rates and Diploma Recipients by Race/Ethnicity

Category	Total	White	Black	Asian	AIAN	Hisp.
Enrollment (%)	100.0	96.0	2.3	0.2	0.0	1.4
Drop-out Rate (%)	3.3	3.2	12.5	n/a	n/a	0.0
H.S. Diplomas (#)	145	145	0	0	0	0

Hazleton Area SD

1515 W 23rd St • Hazleton, PA 18202-1647
(570) 459-3111 • http://www.hasd.k12.pa.us/
Grade Span: KG-12; **Agency Type:** 1
Schools: 9
8 Primary; 0 Middle; 1 High; 0 Other Level
9 Regular; 0 Special Education; 0 Vocational; 0 Alternative
0 Magnet; 0 Charter; 6 Title I Eligible; 0 School-wide Title I
Students: 8,813 (n/a% male; n/a% female)
Individual Education Program: 852 (9.7%);
English Language Learner: n/a; Migrant: 91 (1.0%)
Eligible for Free Lunch Program: 1,299 (14.7%)
Eligible for Reduced-Price Lunch Program: 376 (4.3%)
Teachers: 456.0 (19.3 to 1)
Librarians/Media Specialists: 4.0 (2,203.3 to 1)
Guidance Counselors: 14.0 (629.5 to 1)
Current Spending: ($ per student per year):
Total: $7,073; Instruction: $4,696; Support Services: $2,101
Enrollment, Drop-out Rates and Diploma Recipients by Race/Ethnicity

Category	Total	White	Black	Asian	AIAN	Hisp.
Enrollment (%)	100.0	90.4	1.5	0.8	0.1	7.2
Drop-out Rate (%)	2.2	2.3	0.0	10.0	n/a	0.0
H.S. Diplomas (#)	535	513	2	3	0	17

Lake-Lehman SD

PO Box 38 • Lehman, PA 18627-0038
(570) 675-2165
Grade Span: KG-12; **Agency Type:** 1
Schools: 5
3 Primary; 1 Middle; 1 High; 0 Other Level
5 Regular; 0 Special Education; 0 Vocational; 0 Alternative
0 Magnet; 0 Charter; 3 Title I Eligible; 0 School-wide Title I
Students: 2,194 (n/a% male; n/a% female)
Individual Education Program: 254 (11.6%);
English Language Learner: n/a; Migrant: 4 (0.2%)
Eligible for Free Lunch Program: 363 (16.5%)
Eligible for Reduced-Price Lunch Program: 144 (6.6%)
Teachers: 129.5 (16.9 to 1)
Librarians/Media Specialists: 3.0 (731.3 to 1)
Guidance Counselors: 6.0 (365.7 to 1)
Current Spending: ($ per student per year):
Total: $6,830; Instruction: $4,196; Support Services: $2,348
Enrollment, Drop-out Rates and Diploma Recipients by Race/Ethnicity

Category	Total	White	Black	Asian	AIAN	Hisp.
Enrollment (%)	100.0	98.9	0.2	0.3	0.1	0.5
Drop-out Rate (%)	1.9	1.9	0.0	0.0	n/a	0.0
H.S. Diplomas (#)	145	144	0	1	0	0

Pittston Area SD

5 Stout St • Pittston, PA 18640-3391
(570) 654-2271 • http://www.pittstonarea.com
Grade Span: KG-12; **Agency Type:** 1
Schools: 5
3 Primary; 1 Middle; 1 High; 0 Other Level
5 Regular; 0 Special Education; 0 Vocational; 0 Alternative
0 Magnet; 0 Charter; 3 Title I Eligible; 0 School-wide Title I
Students: 3,107 (n/a% male; n/a% female)
Individual Education Program: 329 (10.6%);
English Language Learner: n/a; Migrant: 0 (0.0%)
Eligible for Free Lunch Program: 443 (14.3%)
Eligible for Reduced-Price Lunch Program: 208 (6.7%)
Teachers: 183.0 (17.0 to 1)
Librarians/Media Specialists: 4.0 (776.8 to 1)
Guidance Counselors: 5.0 (621.4 to 1)
Current Spending: ($ per student per year):
Total: $7,617; Instruction: $4,883; Support Services: $2,425
Enrollment, Drop-out Rates and Diploma Recipients by Race/Ethnicity

Category	Total	White	Black	Asian	AIAN	Hisp.
Enrollment (%)	100.0	98.7	0.6	0.5	0.1	0.1
Drop-out Rate (%)	4.1	4.1	0.0	0.0	0.0	0.0
H.S. Diplomas (#)	245	240	1	4	0	0

Wilkes-Barre Area SD

730 S Main St • Wilkes Barre, PA 18711-0376
(570) 826-7182 • http://www.wbasd.k12.pa.us
Grade Span: KG-12; **Agency Type:** 1
Schools: 9
5 Primary; 1 Middle; 3 High; 0 Other Level
9 Regular; 0 Special Education; 0 Vocational; 0 Alternative
0 Magnet; 0 Charter; 6 Title I Eligible; 0 School-wide Title I
Students: 6,976 (n/a% male; n/a% female)
Individual Education Program: 1,057 (15.2%);
English Language Learner: n/a; Migrant: 0 (0.0%)
Eligible for Free Lunch Program: 1,799 (25.8%)
Eligible for Reduced-Price Lunch Program: 497 (7.1%)
Teachers: 451.0 (15.5 to 1)
Librarians/Media Specialists: 7.0 (996.6 to 1)
Guidance Counselors: 13.0 (536.6 to 1)
Current Spending: ($ per student per year):
Total: $8,209; Instruction: $5,204; Support Services: $2,720

Enrollment, Drop-out Rates and Diploma Recipients by Race/Ethnicity

Category	Total	White	Black	Asian	AIAN	Hisp.
Enrollment (%)	100.0	83.3	11.1	1.1	0.3	4.2
Drop-out Rate (%)	2.9	2.7	6.3	0.0	12.5	0.0
H.S. Diplomas (#)	525	494	20	6	0	5

Wyoming Area SD

20 Memorial St • Exeter, PA 18643-2659
(570) 655-3733 • http://www.wyoarea.com
Grade Span: KG-12; **Agency Type:** 1
Schools: 5
4 Primary; 0 Middle; 1 High; 0 Other Level
5 Regular; 0 Special Education; 0 Vocational; 0 Alternative
0 Magnet; 0 Charter; 4 Title I Eligible; 0 School-wide Title I
Students: 2,590 (n/a% male; n/a% female)
Individual Education Program: 338 (13.1%);
English Language Learner: n/a; Migrant: 0 (0.0%)
Eligible for Free Lunch Program: 409 (15.8%)
Eligible for Reduced-Price Lunch Program: 198 (7.6%)
Teachers: 139.5 (18.6 to 1)
Librarians/Media Specialists: 2.0 (1,295.0 to 1)
Guidance Counselors: 5.0 (518.0 to 1)
Current Spending: ($ per student per year):
Total: $6,264; Instruction: $4,091; Support Services: $1,976

Enrollment, Drop-out Rates and Diploma Recipients by Race/Ethnicity

Category	Total	White	Black	Asian	AIAN	Hisp.
Enrollment (%)	100.0	97.5	1.7	0.3	0.1	0.4
Drop-out Rate (%)	3.5	3.2	40.0	0.0	n/a	100.0
H.S. Diplomas (#)	180	179	1	0	0	0

Wyoming Valley West SD

450 N Maple Ave • Kingston, PA 18704-3630
(570) 288-6551 • http://www.www.liu18.k12.pa.us
Grade Span: KG-12; **Agency Type:** 1
Schools: 9
7 Primary; 1 Middle; 1 High; 0 Other Level
9 Regular; 0 Special Education; 0 Vocational; 0 Alternative
0 Magnet; 0 Charter; 6 Title I Eligible; 0 School-wide Title I
Students: 5,162 (n/a% male; n/a% female)
Individual Education Program: 730 (14.1%);
English Language Learner: n/a; Migrant: 0 (0.0%)
Eligible for Free Lunch Program: 1,371 (26.6%)
Eligible for Reduced-Price Lunch Program: 435 (8.4%)
Teachers: 305.5 (16.9 to 1)
Librarians/Media Specialists: 6.0 (860.3 to 1)
Guidance Counselors: 9.0 (573.6 to 1)
Current Spending: ($ per student per year):
Total: $7,008; Instruction: $4,893; Support Services: $1,739

Enrollment, Drop-out Rates and Diploma Recipients by Race/Ethnicity

Category	Total	White	Black	Asian	AIAN	Hisp.
Enrollment (%)	100.0	94.8	2.9	0.8	0.2	1.3
Drop-out Rate (%)	3.6	3.3	62.5	0.0	0.0	0.0
H.S. Diplomas (#)	321	314	1	3	1	2

Lycoming County

East Lycoming SD

349 Cemetery St • Hughesville, PA 17737-1028
(570) 584-2131 • http://www.eastlycoming.net
Grade Span: KG-12; **Agency Type:** 1
Schools: 4
3 Primary; 0 Middle; 1 High; 0 Other Level
4 Regular; 0 Special Education; 0 Vocational; 0 Alternative
0 Magnet; 0 Charter; 3 Title I Eligible; 0 School-wide Title I
Students: 1,837 (n/a% male; n/a% female)
Individual Education Program: 225 (12.2%);
English Language Learner: n/a; Migrant: 0 (0.0%)
Eligible for Free Lunch Program: 325 (17.7%)
Eligible for Reduced-Price Lunch Program: 138 (7.5%)
Teachers: 129.0 (14.2 to 1)
Librarians/Media Specialists: 0.0 (0.0 to 1)
Guidance Counselors: 3.0 (612.3 to 1)
Current Spending: ($ per student per year):
Total: $7,004; Instruction: $4,514; Support Services: $2,147

Enrollment, Drop-out Rates and Diploma Recipients by Race/Ethnicity

Category	Total	White	Black	Asian	AIAN	Hisp.
Enrollment (%)	100.0	98.7	0.9	0.1	0.1	0.2
Drop-out Rate (%)	2.6	2.5	0.0	0.0	n/a	50.0
H.S. Diplomas (#)	141	141	0	0	0	0

Jersey Shore Area SD

175 A & P Dr • Jersey Shore, PA 17740-9268
(570) 398-1561 • http://www.jsasd.k12.pa.us
Grade Span: KG-12; **Agency Type:** 1
Schools: 6
4 Primary; 1 Middle; 1 High; 0 Other Level
6 Regular; 0 Special Education; 0 Vocational; 0 Alternative
0 Magnet; 0 Charter; 3 Title I Eligible; 0 School-wide Title I
Students: 3,083 (n/a% male; n/a% female)
Individual Education Program: 488 (15.8%);
English Language Learner: n/a; Migrant: 0 (0.0%)
Eligible for Free Lunch Program: 557 (18.1%)
Eligible for Reduced-Price Lunch Program: 298 (9.7%)
Teachers: 196.3 (15.7 to 1)
Librarians/Media Specialists: 5.0 (616.6 to 1)
Guidance Counselors: 6.0 (513.8 to 1)
Current Spending: ($ per student per year):
Total: $7,237; Instruction: $4,610; Support Services: $2,315

Enrollment, Drop-out Rates and Diploma Recipients by Race/Ethnicity

Category	Total	White	Black	Asian	AIAN	Hisp.
Enrollment (%)	100.0	98.1	0.8	1.0	0.1	0.1
Drop-out Rate (%)	4.0	4.0	n/a	0.0	0.0	n/a
H.S. Diplomas (#)	197	195	0	2	0	0

Montoursville Area SD

50 N Arch St • Montoursville, PA 17754-1902
(570) 368-2491 • http://www.montoursville.k12.pa.us
Grade Span: KG-12; **Agency Type:** 1
Schools: 4
2 Primary; 1 Middle; 1 High; 0 Other Level
4 Regular; 0 Special Education; 0 Vocational; 0 Alternative
0 Magnet; 0 Charter; 3 Title I Eligible; 0 School-wide Title I
Students: 2,211 (n/a% male; n/a% female)
Individual Education Program: 200 (9.0%);
English Language Learner: n/a; Migrant: 0 (0.0%)
Eligible for Free Lunch Program: 160 (7.2%)
Eligible for Reduced-Price Lunch Program: 76 (3.4%)
Teachers: 138.5 (16.0 to 1)
Librarians/Media Specialists: 2.0 (1,105.5 to 1)
Guidance Counselors: 6.0 (368.5 to 1)
Current Spending: ($ per student per year):
Total: $6,224; Instruction: $3,995; Support Services: $1,975

Enrollment, Drop-out Rates and Diploma Recipients by Race/Ethnicity

Category	Total	White	Black	Asian	AIAN	Hisp.
Enrollment (%)	100.0	98.6	0.6	0.5	0.0	0.2
Drop-out Rate (%)	5.1	5.0	n/a	0.0	n/a	100.0
H.S. Diplomas (#)	168	165	1	2	0	0

Williamsport Area SD

201 W 3rd St • Williamsport, PA 17701-6409
(570) 327-5500 • http://www.wasd.org
Grade Span: KG-12; **Agency Type:** 1
Schools: 11
6 Primary; 3 Middle; 2 High; 0 Other Level
11 Regular; 0 Special Education; 0 Vocational; 0 Alternative
0 Magnet; 0 Charter; 7 Title I Eligible; 6 School-wide Title I
Students: 6,113 (n/a% male; n/a% female)
Individual Education Program: 1,270 (20.8%);
English Language Learner: n/a; Migrant: 0 (0.0%)
Eligible for Free Lunch Program: 2,230 (36.5%)
Eligible for Reduced-Price Lunch Program: 648 (10.6%)
Teachers: 417.1 (14.7 to 1)
Librarians/Media Specialists: 5.0 (1,222.6 to 1)
Guidance Counselors: 18.0 (339.6 to 1)
Current Spending: ($ per student per year):
Total: $7,712; Instruction: $5,099; Support Services: $2,346

Enrollment, Drop-out Rates and Diploma Recipients by Race/Ethnicity

Category	Total	White	Black	Asian	AIAN	Hisp.
Enrollment (%)	100.0	77.6	20.7	1.0	0.0	0.7
Drop-out Rate (%)	4.0	4.1	3.4	0.0	n/a	0.0
H.S. Diplomas (#)	372	321	47	2	0	2

Mckean County

Bradford Area SD

PO Box 375 • Bradford, PA 16701-1831
(814) 362-3841 • http://www.bradfordareaschools.org
Grade Span: KG-12; **Agency Type:** 1
Schools: 4
2 Primary; 1 Middle; 1 High; 0 Other Level
4 Regular; 0 Special Education; 0 Vocational; 0 Alternative
0 Magnet; 0 Charter; 3 Title I Eligible; 0 School-wide Title I
Students: 3,040 (n/a% male; n/a% female)
Individual Education Program: 403 (13.3%);
English Language Learner: n/a; Migrant: 0 (0.0%)
Eligible for Free Lunch Program: 885 (29.1%)
Eligible for Reduced-Price Lunch Program: 192 (6.3%)
Teachers: 194.7 (15.6 to 1)
Librarians/Media Specialists: 7.0 (434.3 to 1)
Guidance Counselors: 6.0 (506.7 to 1)

Current Spending: ($ per student per year):
Total: $7,803; Instruction: $5,001; Support Services: $2,558
Enrollment, Drop-out Rates and Diploma Recipients by Race/Ethnicity

Category	Total	White	Black	Asian	AIAN	Hisp.
Enrollment (%)	100.0	95.2	1.3	1.1	1.2	1.2
Drop-out Rate (%)	3.9	3.9	0.0	0.0	0.0	28.6
H.S. Diplomas (#)	177	169	0	5	0	3

Mercer County

Greenville Area SD

9 Donation Rd • Greenville, PA 16125-1789
(724) 588-2500 • http://www.greenville.k12.pa.us
Grade Span: KG-12; **Agency Type:** 1
Schools: 3
1 Primary; 1 Middle; 1 High; 0 Other Level
3 Regular; 0 Special Education; 0 Vocational; 0 Alternative
0 Magnet; 0 Charter; 0 Title I Eligible; 0 School-wide Title I
Students: 1,663 (n/a% male; n/a% female)
Individual Education Program: 234 (14.1%);
English Language Learner: n/a; Migrant: 0 (0.0%)
Eligible for Free Lunch Program: 355 (21.3%)
Eligible for Reduced-Price Lunch Program: 80 (4.8%)
Teachers: 107.0 (15.5 to 1)
Librarians/Media Specialists: 1.0 (1,663.0 to 1)
Guidance Counselors: 3.0 (554.3 to 1)
Current Spending: ($ per student per year):
Total: $6,958; Instruction: $4,534; Support Services: $2,105
Enrollment, Drop-out Rates and Diploma Recipients by Race/Ethnicity

Category	Total	White	Black	Asian	AIAN	Hisp.
Enrollment (%)	100.0	98.0	0.7	0.8	0.0	0.4
Drop-out Rate (%)	3.4	3.4	0.0	0.0	n/a	n/a
H.S. Diplomas (#)	116	114	1	1	0	0

Grove City Area SD

511 Highland Ave • Grove City, PA 16127-1107
(724) 458-6733 • http://www.grovecity.k12.pa.us
Grade Span: KG-12; **Agency Type:** 1
Schools: 7
3 Primary; 2 Middle; 2 High; 0 Other Level
7 Regular; 0 Special Education; 0 Vocational; 0 Alternative
0 Magnet; 0 Charter; 0 Title I Eligible; 0 School-wide Title I
Students: 2,760 (n/a% male; n/a% female)
Individual Education Program: 307 (11.1%);
English Language Learner: n/a; Migrant: 0 (0.0%)
Eligible for Free Lunch Program: 302 (10.9%)
Eligible for Reduced-Price Lunch Program: 127 (4.6%)
Teachers: 172.0 (16.0 to 1)
Librarians/Media Specialists: 4.0 (690.0 to 1)
Guidance Counselors: 6.0 (460.0 to 1)
Current Spending: ($ per student per year):
Total: $6,554; Instruction: $4,490; Support Services: $1,851
Enrollment, Drop-out Rates and Diploma Recipients by Race/Ethnicity

Category	Total	White	Black	Asian	AIAN	Hisp.
Enrollment (%)	100.0	88.2	9.4	0.9	0.1	1.4
Drop-out Rate (%)	1.2	1.3	0.6	0.0	0.0	4.0
H.S. Diplomas (#)	187	161	18	4	0	4

Hermitage SD

411 N Hermitage Rd • Hermitage, PA 16148-3316
(724) 981-8750 • http://www.hermitage.k12.pa.us
Grade Span: KG-12; **Agency Type:** 1
Schools: 5
2 Primary; 2 Middle; 1 High; 0 Other Level
5 Regular; 0 Special Education; 0 Vocational; 0 Alternative
0 Magnet; 0 Charter; 0 Title I Eligible; 0 School-wide Title I
Students: 2,316 (n/a% male; n/a% female)
Individual Education Program: 278 (12.0%);
English Language Learner: n/a; Migrant: 0 (0.0%)
Eligible for Free Lunch Program: 410 (17.7%)
Eligible for Reduced-Price Lunch Program: 128 (5.5%)
Teachers: 137.5 (16.8 to 1)
Librarians/Media Specialists: 4.0 (579.0 to 1)
Guidance Counselors: 4.0 (579.0 to 1)
Current Spending: ($ per student per year):
Total: $7,197; Instruction: $4,718; Support Services: $2,199
Enrollment, Drop-out Rates and Diploma Recipients by Race/Ethnicity

Category	Total	White	Black	Asian	AIAN	Hisp.
Enrollment (%)	100.0	91.1	7.3	0.9	0.1	0.5
Drop-out Rate (%)	1.2	1.3	0.0	0.0	n/a	0.0
H.S. Diplomas (#)	164	158	4	2	0	0

Mercer Area SD

545 W Butler St • Mercer, PA 16137-0032
(724) 662-5100 • http://www.mercer.k12.pa.us
Grade Span: KG-12; **Agency Type:** 1
Schools: 2
1 Primary; 0 Middle; 1 High; 0 Other Level
2 Regular; 0 Special Education; 0 Vocational; 0 Alternative
0 Magnet; 0 Charter; 0 Title I Eligible; 0 School-wide Title I
Students: 1,560 (n/a% male; n/a% female)
Individual Education Program: 229 (14.7%);
English Language Learner: n/a; Migrant: 0 (0.0%)
Eligible for Free Lunch Program: 237 (15.2%)
Eligible for Reduced-Price Lunch Program: 110 (7.1%)
Teachers: 92.6 (16.8 to 1)
Librarians/Media Specialists: 2.0 (780.0 to 1)
Guidance Counselors: 3.0 (520.0 to 1)
Current Spending: ($ per student per year):
Total: $6,401; Instruction: $4,111; Support Services: $1,998
Enrollment, Drop-out Rates and Diploma Recipients by Race/Ethnicity

Category	Total	White	Black	Asian	AIAN	Hisp.
Enrollment (%)	100.0	96.9	1.5	1.0	0.0	0.6
Drop-out Rate (%)	2.0	2.0	0.0	0.0	n/a	0.0
H.S. Diplomas (#)	106	106	0	0	0	0

Reynolds SD

531 Reynolds Rd • Greenville, PA 16125-8804
(724) 646-3240 • http://www.reynoldssd.com
Grade Span: KG-12; **Agency Type:** 1
Schools: 2
1 Primary; 0 Middle; 1 High; 0 Other Level
2 Regular; 0 Special Education; 0 Vocational; 0 Alternative
0 Magnet; 0 Charter; 0 Title I Eligible; 0 School-wide Title I
Students: 1,563 (n/a% male; n/a% female)
Individual Education Program: 229 (14.7%);
English Language Learner: n/a; Migrant: 0 (0.0%)
Eligible for Free Lunch Program: 403 (25.8%)
Eligible for Reduced-Price Lunch Program: 160 (10.2%)
Teachers: 86.0 (18.2 to 1)
Librarians/Media Specialists: 2.0 (781.5 to 1)
Guidance Counselors: 3.0 (521.0 to 1)
Current Spending: ($ per student per year):
Total: $7,321; Instruction: $4,326; Support Services: $2,674
Enrollment, Drop-out Rates and Diploma Recipients by Race/Ethnicity

Category	Total	White	Black	Asian	AIAN	Hisp.
Enrollment (%)	100.0	97.8	1.8	0.1	0.1	0.3
Drop-out Rate (%)	1.4	1.4	0.0	0.0	n/a	n/a
H.S. Diplomas (#)	109	107	0	0	2	0

Sharon City SD

215 Forker Blvd • Sharon, PA 16146-3606
(724) 983-4000 • http://www.sharon.k12.pa.us
Grade Span: KG-12; **Agency Type:** 1
Schools: 4
3 Primary; 0 Middle; 1 High; 0 Other Level
4 Regular; 0 Special Education; 0 Vocational; 0 Alternative
0 Magnet; 0 Charter; 0 Title I Eligible; 0 School-wide Title I
Students: 2,374 (n/a% male; n/a% female)
Individual Education Program: 385 (16.2%);
English Language Learner: n/a; Migrant: 0 (0.0%)
Eligible for Free Lunch Program: 1,141 (48.1%)
Eligible for Reduced-Price Lunch Program: 206 (8.7%)
Teachers: 157.4 (15.1 to 1)
Librarians/Media Specialists: 2.0 (1,187.0 to 1)
Guidance Counselors: 5.0 (474.8 to 1)
Current Spending: ($ per student per year):
Total: $7,236; Instruction: $4,866; Support Services: $2,020
Enrollment, Drop-out Rates and Diploma Recipients by Race/Ethnicity

Category	Total	White	Black	Asian	AIAN	Hisp.
Enrollment (%)	100.0	75.0	23.1	0.5	0.5	0.8
Drop-out Rate (%)	6.3	7.1	3.2	0.0	n/a	0.0
H.S. Diplomas (#)	133	116	17	0	0	0

Mifflin County

Mifflin County SD

201 Eighth St - Highland Park • Lewistown, PA 17044-1197
(717) 248-0148 • http://www.mcsdk12.org
Grade Span: KG-12; **Agency Type:** 1
Schools: 14
9 Primary; 3 Middle; 2 High; 0 Other Level
14 Regular; 0 Special Education; 0 Vocational; 0 Alternative
0 Magnet; 0 Charter; 8 Title I Eligible; 0 School-wide Title I
Students: 6,166 (n/a% male; n/a% female)
Individual Education Program: 902 (14.6%);
English Language Learner: n/a; Migrant: 18 (0.3%)

Eligible for Free Lunch Program: 1,298 (21.1%)
Eligible for Reduced-Price Lunch Program: 534 (8.7%)
Teachers: 424.5 (14.5 to 1)
Librarians/Media Specialists: 7.0 (880.9 to 1)
Guidance Counselors: 12.0 (513.8 to 1)
Current Spending: ($ per student per year):
Total: $6,692; Instruction: $4,413; Support Services: $1,986
Enrollment, Drop-out Rates and Diploma Recipients by Race/Ethnicity

Category	Total	White	Black	Asian	AIAN	Hisp.
Enrollment (%)	100.0	96.1	1.9	0.8	0.2	0.9
Drop-out Rate (%)	4.8	4.7	11.1	0.0	33.3	0.0
H.S. Diplomas (#)	376	371	2	3	0	0

Monroe County

East Stroudsburg Area SD

PO Box 298 • East Stroudsburg, PA 18301-0298
(570) 424-8500 • http://www.cavalier.net/
Grade Span: KG-12; **Agency Type:** 1
Schools: 10
5 Primary; 3 Middle; 2 High; 0 Other Level
10 Regular; 0 Special Education; 0 Vocational; 0 Alternative
0 Magnet; 0 Charter; 10 Title I Eligible; 0 School-wide Title I
Students: 7,481 (n/a% male; n/a% female)
Individual Education Program: 1,262 (16.9%);
English Language Learner: n/a; Migrant: 0 (0.0%)
Eligible for Free Lunch Program: 1,152 (15.4%)
Eligible for Reduced-Price Lunch Program: 430 (5.7%)
Teachers: 497.9 (15.0 to 1)
Librarians/Media Specialists: 10.0 (748.1 to 1)
Guidance Counselors: 19.0 (393.7 to 1)
Current Spending: ($ per student per year):
Total: $7,496; Instruction: $4,665; Support Services: $2,516
Enrollment, Drop-out Rates and Diploma Recipients by Race/Ethnicity

Category	Total	White	Black	Asian	AIAN	Hisp.
Enrollment (%)	100.0	71.9	13.5	2.0	0.2	12.5
Drop-out Rate (%)	3.1	3.2	0.4	2.5	42.9	4.7
H.S. Diplomas (#)	436	324	53	10	2	47

Pleasant Valley SD

Route 115 • Brodheadsville, PA 18322-2002
(570) 402-1000 • http://www.pvbears.org
Grade Span: KG-12; **Agency Type:** 1
Schools: 7
4 Primary; 2 Middle; 1 High; 0 Other Level
7 Regular; 0 Special Education; 0 Vocational; 0 Alternative
0 Magnet; 0 Charter; 4 Title I Eligible; 0 School-wide Title I
Students: 6,664 (n/a% male; n/a% female)
Individual Education Program: 766 (11.5%);
English Language Learner: n/a; Migrant: 0 (0.0%)
Eligible for Free Lunch Program: 627 (9.4%)
Eligible for Reduced-Price Lunch Program: 231 (3.5%)
Teachers: 372.5 (17.9 to 1)
Librarians/Media Specialists: 7.0 (952.0 to 1)
Guidance Counselors: 14.0 (476.0 to 1)
Current Spending: ($ per student per year):
Total: $6,101; Instruction: $3,782; Support Services: $2,078
Enrollment, Drop-out Rates and Diploma Recipients by Race/Ethnicity

Category	Total	White	Black	Asian	AIAN	Hisp.
Enrollment (%)	100.0	86.3	6.0	1.0	0.2	6.6
Drop-out Rate (%)	3.2	3.3	2.1	5.9	25.0	2.0
H.S. Diplomas (#)	391	361	13	4	0	13

Pocono Mountain SD

PO Box 200 • Swiftwater, PA 18370-0200
(570) 839-7121 • http://www.pmsd.org/index.html
Grade Span: KG-12; **Agency Type:** 1
Schools: 11
7 Primary; 1 Middle; 1 High; 2 Other Level
11 Regular; 0 Special Education; 0 Vocational; 0 Alternative
0 Magnet; 0 Charter; 4 Title I Eligible; 0 School-wide Title I
Students: 11,166 (n/a% male; n/a% female)
Individual Education Program: 1,372 (12.3%);
English Language Learner: n/a; Migrant: 0 (0.0%)
Eligible for Free Lunch Program: 2,548 (22.8%)
Eligible for Reduced-Price Lunch Program: 995 (8.9%)
Teachers: 698.8 (16.0 to 1)
Librarians/Media Specialists: 10.0 (1,116.6 to 1)
Guidance Counselors: 32.0 (348.9 to 1)
Current Spending: ($ per student per year):
Total: $6,520; Instruction: $4,005; Support Services: $2,278
Enrollment, Drop-out Rates and Diploma Recipients by Race/Ethnicity

Category	Total	White	Black	Asian	AIAN	Hisp.
Enrollment (%)	100.0	68.1	16.4	1.6	0.2	13.7
Drop-out Rate (%)	2.1	1.7	3.3	0.0	0.0	3.0
H.S. Diplomas (#)	729	505	118	11	2	93

Stroudsburg Area SD

123 Linden St • Stroudsburg, PA 18360-1315
(570) 421-1990 • http://www.stroudsburg.k12.pa.us
Grade Span: KG-12; **Agency Type:** 1
Schools: 8
5 Primary; 2 Middle; 1 High; 0 Other Level
8 Regular; 0 Special Education; 0 Vocational; 0 Alternative
0 Magnet; 0 Charter; 6 Title I Eligible; 0 School-wide Title I
Students: 5,298 (n/a% male; n/a% female)
Individual Education Program: 602 (11.4%);
English Language Learner: n/a; Migrant: 0 (0.0%)
Eligible for Free Lunch Program: 685 (12.9%)
Eligible for Reduced-Price Lunch Program: 275 (5.2%)
Teachers: 336.2 (15.8 to 1)
Librarians/Media Specialists: 6.0 (883.0 to 1)
Guidance Counselors: 13.0 (407.5 to 1)
Current Spending: ($ per student per year):
Total: $7,831; Instruction: $5,044; Support Services: $2,541
Enrollment, Drop-out Rates and Diploma Recipients by Race/Ethnicity

Category	Total	White	Black	Asian	AIAN	Hisp.
Enrollment (%)	100.0	75.6	13.3	2.0	0.3	8.9
Drop-out Rate (%)	3.3	3.4	3.0	0.0	0.0	3.6
H.S. Diplomas (#)	298	219	35	13	0	31

Montgomery County

Abington SD

970 Highland Ave • Abington, PA 19001-4535
(215) 884-4700 • http://www.abington.k12.pa.us
Grade Span: KG-12; **Agency Type:** 1
Schools: 9
7 Primary; 1 Middle; 1 High; 0 Other Level
9 Regular; 0 Special Education; 0 Vocational; 0 Alternative
0 Magnet; 0 Charter; 6 Title I Eligible; 0 School-wide Title I
Students: 7,426 (n/a% male; n/a% female)
Individual Education Program: 867 (11.7%);
English Language Learner: n/a; Migrant: 0 (0.0%)
Eligible for Free Lunch Program: 468 (6.3%)
Eligible for Reduced-Price Lunch Program: 215 (2.9%)
Teachers: 448.1 (16.6 to 1)
Librarians/Media Specialists: 11.0 (675.1 to 1)
Guidance Counselors: 13.0 (571.2 to 1)
Current Spending: ($ per student per year):
Total: $9,267; Instruction: $5,545; Support Services: $3,478
Enrollment, Drop-out Rates and Diploma Recipients by Race/Ethnicity

Category	Total	White	Black	Asian	AIAN	Hisp.
Enrollment (%)	100.0	73.3	18.8	6.0	0.1	1.7
Drop-out Rate (%)	1.3	1.4	1.1	0.0	n/a	2.8
H.S. Diplomas (#)	556	418	100	30	0	8

Cheltenham Township SD

1000 Ashbourne Rd • Elkins Park, PA 19027-1031
(215) 886-9500 • http://www.cheltenham.org
Grade Span: KG-12; **Agency Type:** 1
Schools: 8
4 Primary; 3 Middle; 1 High; 0 Other Level
8 Regular; 0 Special Education; 0 Vocational; 0 Alternative
0 Magnet; 0 Charter; 6 Title I Eligible; 0 School-wide Title I
Students: 4,886 (n/a% male; n/a% female)
Individual Education Program: 617 (12.6%);
English Language Learner: n/a; Migrant: 0 (0.0%)
Eligible for Free Lunch Program: 77 (1.6%)
Eligible for Reduced-Price Lunch Program: 47 (1.0%)
Teachers: 345.4 (14.1 to 1)
Librarians/Media Specialists: 8.0 (610.8 to 1)
Guidance Counselors: 15.0 (325.7 to 1)
Current Spending: ($ per student per year):
Total: $10,341; Instruction: $6,591; Support Services: $3,511
Enrollment, Drop-out Rates and Diploma Recipients by Race/Ethnicity

Category	Total	White	Black	Asian	AIAN	Hisp.
Enrollment (%)	100.0	52.4	36.1	8.8	0.1	2.6
Drop-out Rate (%)	1.7	1.2	1.6	4.0	0.0	9.1
H.S. Diplomas (#)	383	238	110	26	1	8

Colonial SD

230 Flourtown Rd • Plymouth Meeting, PA 19462-1252
(610) 834-1670 • http://www.colonialsd.org
Grade Span: KG-12; **Agency Type:** 1
Schools: 7

4 Primary; 2 Middle; 1 High; 0 Other Level
7 Regular; 0 Special Education; 0 Vocational; 0 Alternative
0 Magnet; 0 Charter; 3 Title I Eligible; 1 School-wide Title I
Students: 4,678 (n/a% male; n/a% female)
Individual Education Program: 685 (14.6%);
English Language Learner: n/a; Migrant: 0 (0.0%)
Eligible for Free Lunch Program: 331 (7.1%)
Eligible for Reduced-Price Lunch Program: 115 (2.5%)
Teachers: 338.2 (13.8 to 1)
Librarians/Media Specialists: 6.4 (730.9 to 1)
Guidance Counselors: 13.5 (346.5 to 1)
Current Spending: ($ per student per year):
Total: $10,617; Instruction: $6,658; Support Services: $3,652
Enrollment, Drop-out Rates and Diploma Recipients by Race/Ethnicity

Category	Total	White	Black	Asian	AIAN	Hisp.
Enrollment (%)	100.0	86.0	8.2	4.3	0.3	1.2
Drop-out Rate (%)	1.9	1.3	5.4	6.7	n/a	9.1
H.S. Diplomas (#)	350	308	19	16	0	7

Hatboro-Horsham SD

229 Meetinghouse Rd • Horsham, PA 19044-2192
(215) 672-5660 • http://www.hatboro-horsham.org
Grade Span: KG-12; **Agency Type:** 1
Schools: 8
6 Primary; 1 Middle; 1 High; 0 Other Level
8 Regular; 0 Special Education; 0 Vocational; 0 Alternative
0 Magnet; 0 Charter; 5 Title I Eligible; 0 School-wide Title I
Students: 5,568 (n/a% male; n/a% female)
Individual Education Program: 609 (10.9%);
English Language Learner: n/a; Migrant: 0 (0.0%)
Eligible for Free Lunch Program: 165 (3.0%)
Eligible for Reduced-Price Lunch Program: 93 (1.7%)
Teachers: 355.3 (15.7 to 1)
Librarians/Media Specialists: 8.1 (687.4 to 1)
Guidance Counselors: 15.4 (361.6 to 1)
Current Spending: ($ per student per year):
Total: $9,167; Instruction: $5,950; Support Services: $2,999
Enrollment, Drop-out Rates and Diploma Recipients by Race/Ethnicity

Category	Total	White	Black	Asian	AIAN	Hisp.
Enrollment (%)	100.0	87.8	3.9	6.5	0.1	1.6
Drop-out Rate (%)	0.6	0.7	0.0	0.0	0.0	0.0
H.S. Diplomas (#)	355	314	15	18	1	7

Lower Merion SD

301 E Montgomery Ave • Ardmore, PA 19003-3399
(610) 645-1800 • http://www.lmsd.org
Grade Span: KG-12; **Agency Type:** 1
Schools: 10
6 Primary; 2 Middle; 2 High; 0 Other Level
10 Regular; 0 Special Education; 0 Vocational; 0 Alternative
0 Magnet; 0 Charter; 6 Title I Eligible; 0 School-wide Title I
Students: 6,581 (n/a% male; n/a% female)
Individual Education Program: 1,119 (17.0%);
English Language Learner: n/a; Migrant: 0 (0.0%)
Eligible for Free Lunch Program: 240 (3.6%)
Eligible for Reduced-Price Lunch Program: 80 (1.2%)
Teachers: 526.4 (12.5 to 1)
Librarians/Media Specialists: 10.0 (658.1 to 1)
Guidance Counselors: 23.4 (281.2 to 1)
Current Spending: ($ per student per year):
Total: $13,654; Instruction: $8,385; Support Services: $4,998
Enrollment, Drop-out Rates and Diploma Recipients by Race/Ethnicity

Category	Total	White	Black	Asian	AIAN	Hisp.
Enrollment (%)	100.0	86.1	7.2	5.0	0.4	1.3
Drop-out Rate (%)	0.5	0.3	1.9	1.2	0.0	0.0
H.S. Diplomas (#)	455	399	33	18	0	5

Lower Moreland Township SD

2551 Murray Ave • Huntingdon Valley, PA 19006-6208
(215) 938-0270 • http://www.lmtsd.org
Grade Span: KG-12; **Agency Type:** 1
Schools: 3
1 Primary; 1 Middle; 1 High; 0 Other Level
3 Regular; 0 Special Education; 0 Vocational; 0 Alternative
0 Magnet; 0 Charter; 3 Title I Eligible; 0 School-wide Title I
Students: 1,696 (n/a% male; n/a% female)
Individual Education Program: 192 (11.3%);
English Language Learner: n/a; Migrant: 0 (0.0%)
Eligible for Free Lunch Program: 11 (0.6%)
Eligible for Reduced-Price Lunch Program: 15 (0.9%)
Teachers: 113.0 (15.0 to 1)
Librarians/Media Specialists: 3.0 (565.3 to 1)
Guidance Counselors: 6.0 (282.7 to 1)
Current Spending: ($ per student per year):
Total: $10,092; Instruction: $6,420; Support Services: $3,434
Enrollment, Drop-out Rates and Diploma Recipients by Race/Ethnicity

Category	Total	White	Black	Asian	AIAN	Hisp.
Enrollment (%)	100.0	93.9	0.3	4.5	0.1	1.1
Drop-out Rate (%)	0.2	0.2	0.0	0.0	n/a	0.0
H.S. Diplomas (#)	126	115	0	10	0	1

Methacton SD

1000 Kriebel Mill Rd • Norristown, PA 19403-1047
(610) 489-5000 • http://www.methacton.org
Grade Span: KG-12; **Agency Type:** 1
Schools: 7
5 Primary; 1 Middle; 1 High; 0 Other Level
7 Regular; 0 Special Education; 0 Vocational; 0 Alternative
0 Magnet; 0 Charter; 5 Title I Eligible; 0 School-wide Title I
Students: 5,128 (n/a% male; n/a% female)
Individual Education Program: 554 (10.8%);
English Language Learner: n/a; Migrant: 2 (<0.1%)
Eligible for Free Lunch Program: 68 (1.3%)
Eligible for Reduced-Price Lunch Program: 36 (0.7%)
Teachers: 347.0 (14.8 to 1)
Librarians/Media Specialists: 7.0 (732.6 to 1)
Guidance Counselors: 14.0 (366.3 to 1)
Current Spending: ($ per student per year):
Total: $9,039; Instruction: $5,413; Support Services: $3,350
Enrollment, Drop-out Rates and Diploma Recipients by Race/Ethnicity

Category	Total	White	Black	Asian	AIAN	Hisp.
Enrollment (%)	100.0	88.0	3.0	7.7	0.1	1.2
Drop-out Rate (%)	1.8	1.8	2.6	0.0	0.0	10.0
H.S. Diplomas (#)	301	271	10	15	1	4

Norristown Area SD

401 N Whitehall Rd • Norristown, PA 19403-2745
(610) 630-5000 • http://www.nasd.k12.pa.us
Grade Span: KG-12; **Agency Type:** 1
Schools: 11
6 Primary; 2 Middle; 1 High; 2 Other Level
11 Regular; 0 Special Education; 0 Vocational; 0 Alternative
0 Magnet; 0 Charter; 11 Title I Eligible; 5 School-wide Title I
Students: 6,846 (n/a% male; n/a% female)
Individual Education Program: 1,138 (16.6%);
English Language Learner: n/a; Migrant: 11 (0.2%)
Eligible for Free Lunch Program: 2,796 (40.8%)
Eligible for Reduced-Price Lunch Program: 740 (10.8%)
Teachers: 510.8 (13.4 to 1)
Librarians/Media Specialists: 11.0 (622.4 to 1)
Guidance Counselors: 15.5 (441.7 to 1)
Current Spending: ($ per student per year):
Total: $9,824; Instruction: $6,074; Support Services: $3,414
Enrollment, Drop-out Rates and Diploma Recipients by Race/Ethnicity

Category	Total	White	Black	Asian	AIAN	Hisp.
Enrollment (%)	100.0	37.7	50.2	2.1	0.0	10.0
Drop-out Rate (%)	4.9	4.1	5.8	0.0	0.0	7.9
H.S. Diplomas (#)	396	211	144	14	1	26

North Penn SD

401 E Hancock St • Lansdale, PA 19446-3960
(215) 368-0400 • http://www.northpennschools.k12.pa.us
Grade Span: KG-12; **Agency Type:** 1
Schools: 17
13 Primary; 3 Middle; 1 High; 0 Other Level
17 Regular; 0 Special Education; 0 Vocational; 0 Alternative
0 Magnet; 0 Charter; 8 Title I Eligible; 0 School-wide Title I
Students: 13,574 (n/a% male; n/a% female)
Individual Education Program: 1,753 (12.9%);
English Language Learner: n/a; Migrant: 107 (0.8%)
Eligible for Free Lunch Program: 861 (6.3%)
Eligible for Reduced-Price Lunch Program: 472 (3.5%)
Teachers: 762.5 (17.8 to 1)
Librarians/Media Specialists: 18.0 (754.1 to 1)
Guidance Counselors: 29.6 (458.6 to 1)
Current Spending: ($ per student per year):
Total: $8,229; Instruction: $5,341; Support Services: $2,446
Enrollment, Drop-out Rates and Diploma Recipients by Race/Ethnicity

Category	Total	White	Black	Asian	AIAN	Hisp.
Enrollment (%)	100.0	79.8	5.4	12.5	0.0	2.2
Drop-out Rate (%)	1.6	1.7	1.6	1.1	0.0	0.0
H.S. Diplomas (#)	1,003	826	39	122	1	15

Pennsylvania Virtual CS

425 Swede St • Norristown, PA 19401
(610) 275-8501
Grade Span: KG-05; **Agency Type:** 7
Schools: 1
1 Primary; 0 Middle; 0 High; 0 Other Level
1 Regular; 0 Special Education; 0 Vocational; 0 Alternative

0 Magnet; 1 Charter; 0 Title I Eligible; 0 School-wide Title I
Students: 1,818 (n/a% male; n/a% female)
Individual Education Program: 63 (3.5%);
English Language Learner: n/a; Migrant: 0 (0.0%)
Eligible for Free Lunch Program: 0 (0.0%)
Eligible for Reduced-Price Lunch Program: 0 (0.0%)
Teachers: 45.0 (40.4 to 1)
Librarians/Media Specialists: 0.0 (0.0 to 1)
Guidance Counselors: 0.0 (0.0 to 1)
Current Spending: ($ per student per year):
Total: n/a; Instruction: n/a; Support Services: n/a
Enrollment, Drop-out Rates and Diploma Recipients by Race/Ethnicity

Category	Total	White	Black	Asian	AIAN	Hisp.
Enrollment (%)	100.0	88.5	7.8	0.7	0.4	2.6
Drop-out Rate (%)	n/a	n/a	n/a	n/a	n/a	n/a
H.S. Diplomas (#)	n/a	n/a	n/a	n/a	n/a	n/a

Perkiomen Valley SD
3 Iron Bridge Dr • Collegeville, PA 19426-2042
(610) 489-8506 • http://mciunix.mciu.k12.pa.us:80/~pvweb/
Grade Span: KG-12; **Agency Type:** 1
Schools: 5
3 Primary; 1 Middle; 1 High; 0 Other Level
5 Regular; 0 Special Education; 0 Vocational; 0 Alternative
0 Magnet; 0 Charter; 5 Title I Eligible; 0 School-wide Title I
Students: 4,833 (n/a% male; n/a% female)
Individual Education Program: 453 (9.4%);
English Language Learner: n/a; Migrant: 0 (0.0%)
Eligible for Free Lunch Program: 218 (4.5%)
Eligible for Reduced-Price Lunch Program: 159 (3.3%)
Teachers: 291.1 (16.6 to 1)
Librarians/Media Specialists: 5.0 (966.6 to 1)
Guidance Counselors: 10.0 (483.3 to 1)
Current Spending: ($ per student per year):
Total: $8,355; Instruction: $4,888; Support Services: $3,212
Enrollment, Drop-out Rates and Diploma Recipients by Race/Ethnicity

Category	Total	White	Black	Asian	AIAN	Hisp.
Enrollment (%)	100.0	92.0	3.6	2.9	0.1	1.3
Drop-out Rate (%)	1.9	2.0	0.0	0.0	0.0	0.0
H.S. Diplomas (#)	222	212	8	1	1	0

Pottsgrove SD
1301 Kauffman Rd • Pottstown, PA 19464-2303
(610) 327-2277 • http://pgsd.org
Grade Span: KG-12; **Agency Type:** 1
Schools: 5
3 Primary; 1 Middle; 1 High; 0 Other Level
5 Regular; 0 Special Education; 0 Vocational; 0 Alternative
0 Magnet; 0 Charter; 4 Title I Eligible; 0 School-wide Title I
Students: 3,201 (n/a% male; n/a% female)
Individual Education Program: 396 (12.4%);
English Language Learner: n/a; Migrant: 0 (0.0%)
Eligible for Free Lunch Program: 289 (9.0%)
Eligible for Reduced-Price Lunch Program: 84 (2.6%)
Teachers: 199.2 (16.1 to 1)
Librarians/Media Specialists: 5.0 (640.2 to 1)
Guidance Counselors: 8.5 (376.6 to 1)
Current Spending: ($ per student per year):
Total: $8,160; Instruction: $5,110; Support Services: $2,799
Enrollment, Drop-out Rates and Diploma Recipients by Race/Ethnicity

Category	Total	White	Black	Asian	AIAN	Hisp.
Enrollment (%)	100.0	84.3	13.4	1.0	0.3	1.1
Drop-out Rate (%)	2.5	2.5	2.4	0.0	0.0	0.0
H.S. Diplomas (#)	220	190	23	1	2	4

Pottstown SD
230 Beech St • Pottstown, PA 19464-5591
(610) 323-8200 • http://www.pottstownschools.com
Grade Span: PK-12; **Agency Type:** 1
Schools: 7
5 Primary; 1 Middle; 1 High; 0 Other Level
7 Regular; 0 Special Education; 0 Vocational; 0 Alternative
0 Magnet; 0 Charter; 6 Title I Eligible; 0 School-wide Title I
Students: 3,312 (n/a% male; n/a% female)
Individual Education Program: 634 (19.1%);
English Language Learner: n/a; Migrant: 0 (0.0%)
Eligible for Free Lunch Program: 1,034 (31.2%)
Eligible for Reduced-Price Lunch Program: 310 (9.4%)
Teachers: 209.4 (15.8 to 1)
Librarians/Media Specialists: 4.6 (720.0 to 1)
Guidance Counselors: 7.0 (473.1 to 1)
Current Spending: ($ per student per year):
Total: $8,433; Instruction: $5,129; Support Services: $3,029
Enrollment, Drop-out Rates and Diploma Recipients by Race/Ethnicity

Category	Total	White	Black	Asian	AIAN	Hisp.
Enrollment (%)	100.0	59.1	33.4	0.6	0.2	6.8
Drop-out Rate (%)	7.8	7.4	7.5	0.0	n/a	15.6
H.S. Diplomas (#)	143	96	41	0	0	6

Souderton Area SD
760 Lower Rd • Souderton, PA 18964-2311
(215) 723-6061 • http://www.soudertonsd.org
Grade Span: KG-12; **Agency Type:** 1
Schools: 10
6 Primary; 1 Middle; 1 High; 1 Other Level
9 Regular; 0 Special Education; 0 Vocational; 0 Alternative
0 Magnet; 0 Charter; 5 Title I Eligible; 0 School-wide Title I
Students: 6,551 (n/a% male; n/a% female)
Individual Education Program: 764 (11.7%);
English Language Learner: n/a; Migrant: 73 (1.1%)
Eligible for Free Lunch Program: 309 (4.7%)
Eligible for Reduced-Price Lunch Program: 161 (2.5%)
Teachers: 407.3 (16.1 to 1)
Librarians/Media Specialists: 9.0 (727.9 to 1)
Guidance Counselors: 15.0 (436.7 to 1)
Current Spending: ($ per student per year):
Total: $7,926; Instruction: $5,054; Support Services: $2,657
Enrollment, Drop-out Rates and Diploma Recipients by Race/Ethnicity

Category	Total	White	Black	Asian	AIAN	Hisp.
Enrollment (%)	100.0	90.1	3.2	4.0	0.1	2.5
Drop-out Rate (%)	1.9	1.9	4.1	0.0	0.0	2.1
H.S. Diplomas (#)	432	398	14	9	0	11

Spring-Ford Area SD
199 Bechtel Rd • Collegeville, PA 19426-2829
(610) 705-6000 • http://mciunix.mciu.k12.pa.us/~sfasdweb
Grade Span: KG-12; **Agency Type:** 1
Schools: 8
5 Primary; 2 Middle; 1 High; 0 Other Level
8 Regular; 0 Special Education; 0 Vocational; 0 Alternative
0 Magnet; 0 Charter; 5 Title I Eligible; 0 School-wide Title I
Students: 6,245 (n/a% male; n/a% female)
Individual Education Program: 850 (13.6%);
English Language Learner: n/a; Migrant: 0 (0.0%)
Eligible for Free Lunch Program: 255 (4.1%)
Eligible for Reduced-Price Lunch Program: 155 (2.5%)
Teachers: 376.3 (16.6 to 1)
Librarians/Media Specialists: 8.0 (780.6 to 1)
Guidance Counselors: 16.0 (390.3 to 1)
Current Spending: ($ per student per year):
Total: $8,405; Instruction: $5,048; Support Services: $3,071
Enrollment, Drop-out Rates and Diploma Recipients by Race/Ethnicity

Category	Total	White	Black	Asian	AIAN	Hisp.
Enrollment (%)	100.0	91.8	3.8	2.9	0.1	1.3
Drop-out Rate (%)	1.6	1.7	0.0	0.0	0.0	0.0
H.S. Diplomas (#)	359	331	17	5	0	6

Springfield Township SD
1901 E Paper Mill Rd • Oreland, PA 19075-2499
(215) 233-6000 • http://www.springfield.k12.pa.us
Grade Span: KG-12; **Agency Type:** 1
Schools: 4
2 Primary; 1 Middle; 1 High; 0 Other Level
4 Regular; 0 Special Education; 0 Vocational; 0 Alternative
0 Magnet; 0 Charter; 3 Title I Eligible; 0 School-wide Title I
Students: 2,086 (n/a% male; n/a% female)
Individual Education Program: 332 (15.9%);
English Language Learner: n/a; Migrant: 0 (0.0%)
Eligible for Free Lunch Program: 36 (1.7%)
Eligible for Reduced-Price Lunch Program: 19 (0.9%)
Teachers: 154.0 (13.5 to 1)
Librarians/Media Specialists: 4.0 (521.5 to 1)
Guidance Counselors: 7.0 (298.0 to 1)
Current Spending: ($ per student per year):
Total: $10,240; Instruction: $6,099; Support Services: $3,923
Enrollment, Drop-out Rates and Diploma Recipients by Race/Ethnicity

Category	Total	White	Black	Asian	AIAN	Hisp.
Enrollment (%)	100.0	83.6	12.4	2.8	0.0	1.2
Drop-out Rate (%)	1.4	1.5	1.3	0.0	n/a	0.0
H.S. Diplomas (#)	142	116	20	6	0	0

Upper Dublin SD
1580 Fort Washington Ave • Maple Glen, PA 19002
(215) 643-8800 • http://mciu.org/~udsdweb/
Grade Span: KG-12; **Agency Type:** 1
Schools: 6
4 Primary; 1 Middle; 1 High; 0 Other Level
6 Regular; 0 Special Education; 0 Vocational; 0 Alternative

0 Magnet; 0 Charter; 4 Title I Eligible; 0 School-wide Title I
Students: 4,366 (n/a% male; n/a% female)
Individual Education Program: 503 (11.5%);
English Language Learner: n/a; Migrant: 0 (0.0%)
Eligible for Free Lunch Program: 201 (4.6%)
Eligible for Reduced-Price Lunch Program: 57 (1.3%)
Teachers: 277.7 (15.7 to 1)
Librarians/Media Specialists: 6.0 (727.7 to 1)
Guidance Counselors: 12.0 (363.8 to 1)
Current Spending: ($ per student per year):
Total: $8,688; Instruction: $5,562; Support Services: $2,878
Enrollment, Drop-out Rates and Diploma Recipients by Race/Ethnicity

Category	Total	White	Black	Asian	AIAN	Hisp.
Enrollment (%)	100.0	82.2	7.7	9.5	0.1	0.6
Drop-out Rate (%)	0.2	0.1	0.0	0.8	0.0	11.1
H.S. Diplomas (#)	345	274	28	40	0	3

Upper Merion Area SD
435 Crossfield Rd • King Of Prussia, PA 19406-2363
(610) 337-6001
Grade Span: KG-12; **Agency Type:** 1
Schools: 6
4 Primary; 1 Middle; 1 High; 0 Other Level
6 Regular; 0 Special Education; 0 Vocational; 0 Alternative
0 Magnet; 0 Charter; 4 Title I Eligible; 0 School-wide Title I
Students: 3,397 (n/a% male; n/a% female)
Individual Education Program: 451 (13.3%);
English Language Learner: n/a; Migrant: 0 (0.0%)
Eligible for Free Lunch Program: 205 (6.0%)
Eligible for Reduced-Price Lunch Program: 134 (3.9%)
Teachers: 242.2 (14.0 to 1)
Librarians/Media Specialists: 7.5 (452.9 to 1)
Guidance Counselors: 11.0 (308.8 to 1)
Current Spending: ($ per student per year):
Total: $12,442; Instruction: $7,557; Support Services: $4,468
Enrollment, Drop-out Rates and Diploma Recipients by Race/Ethnicity

Category	Total	White	Black	Asian	AIAN	Hisp.
Enrollment (%)	100.0	80.2	7.3	10.2	0.1	2.2
Drop-out Rate (%)	1.6	1.6	1.4	1.1	n/a	7.7
H.S. Diplomas (#)	212	171	12	24	0	5

Upper Moreland Township SD
2900 Terwood Rd • Willow Grove, PA 19090-1431
(215) 659-6800 • http://www.umsd.k12.pa.us
Grade Span: KG-12; **Agency Type:** 1
Schools: 4
2 Primary; 1 Middle; 1 High; 0 Other Level
4 Regular; 0 Special Education; 0 Vocational; 0 Alternative
0 Magnet; 0 Charter; 3 Title I Eligible; 0 School-wide Title I
Students: 3,112 (n/a% male; n/a% female)
Individual Education Program: 318 (10.2%);
English Language Learner: n/a; Migrant: 3 (0.1%)
Eligible for Free Lunch Program: 184 (5.9%)
Eligible for Reduced-Price Lunch Program: 97 (3.1%)
Teachers: 193.6 (16.1 to 1)
Librarians/Media Specialists: 4.0 (778.0 to 1)
Guidance Counselors: 8.0 (389.0 to 1)
Current Spending: ($ per student per year):
Total: $8,481; Instruction: $5,186; Support Services: $3,010
Enrollment, Drop-out Rates and Diploma Recipients by Race/Ethnicity

Category	Total	White	Black	Asian	AIAN	Hisp.
Enrollment (%)	100.0	88.4	6.7	3.5	0.0	1.3
Drop-out Rate (%)	0.7	0.8	0.0	0.0	n/a	0.0
H.S. Diplomas (#)	239	221	10	2	0	6

Upper Perkiomen SD
201 W 5th St • East Greenville, PA 18041-1509
(215) 679-7961 • http://mciunix.mciu.k12.pa.us/~upsd/
Grade Span: KG-12; **Agency Type:** 1
Schools: 4
2 Primary; 1 Middle; 1 High; 0 Other Level
4 Regular; 0 Special Education; 0 Vocational; 0 Alternative
0 Magnet; 0 Charter; 3 Title I Eligible; 0 School-wide Title I
Students: 3,383 (n/a% male; n/a% female)
Individual Education Program: 383 (11.3%);
English Language Learner: n/a; Migrant: 2 (0.1%)
Eligible for Free Lunch Program: 303 (9.0%)
Eligible for Reduced-Price Lunch Program: 203 (6.0%)
Teachers: 188.6 (17.9 to 1)
Librarians/Media Specialists: 4.0 (845.8 to 1)
Guidance Counselors: 7.0 (483.3 to 1)
Current Spending: ($ per student per year):
Total: $7,522; Instruction: $4,728; Support Services: $2,476

Enrollment, Drop-out Rates and Diploma Recipients by Race/Ethnicity

Category	Total	White	Black	Asian	AIAN	Hisp.
Enrollment (%)	100.0	95.2	1.6	0.7	0.3	2.2
Drop-out Rate (%)	1.8	1.8	0.0	0.0	0.0	5.0
H.S. Diplomas (#)	266	260	1	2	0	3

Wissahickon SD
601 Knight Rd • Ambler, PA 19002-3441
(215) 619-8000 • http://mciunix.mciu.k12.pa.us:80/~wsdweb/
Grade Span: KG-12; **Agency Type:** 1
Schools: 7
5 Primary; 1 Middle; 1 High; 0 Other Level
7 Regular; 0 Special Education; 0 Vocational; 0 Alternative
0 Magnet; 0 Charter; 5 Title I Eligible; 0 School-wide Title I
Students: 4,596 (n/a% male; n/a% female)
Individual Education Program: 686 (14.9%);
English Language Learner: n/a; Migrant: 4 (0.1%)
Eligible for Free Lunch Program: 113 (2.5%)
Eligible for Reduced-Price Lunch Program: 40 (0.9%)
Teachers: 299.8 (15.3 to 1)
Librarians/Media Specialists: 6.5 (707.1 to 1)
Guidance Counselors: 14.8 (310.5 to 1)
Current Spending: ($ per student per year):
Total: $10,518; Instruction: $6,889; Support Services: $3,367
Enrollment, Drop-out Rates and Diploma Recipients by Race/Ethnicity

Category	Total	White	Black	Asian	AIAN	Hisp.
Enrollment (%)	100.0	72.6	13.5	11.7	0.1	2.0
Drop-out Rate (%)	1.5	1.2	3.8	0.6	0.0	5.6
H.S. Diplomas (#)	293	213	40	38	0	2

Montour County

Danville Area SD
600 Walnut St • Danville, PA 17821-9131
(570) 271-3268 • http://www.danville.k12.pa.us
Grade Span: KG-12; **Agency Type:** 1
Schools: 6
4 Primary; 1 Middle; 1 High; 0 Other Level
6 Regular; 0 Special Education; 0 Vocational; 0 Alternative
0 Magnet; 0 Charter; 3 Title I Eligible; 0 School-wide Title I
Students: 2,688 (n/a% male; n/a% female)
Individual Education Program: 299 (11.1%);
English Language Learner: n/a; Migrant: 0 (0.0%)
Eligible for Free Lunch Program: 475 (17.7%)
Eligible for Reduced-Price Lunch Program: 211 (7.8%)
Teachers: 190.0 (14.1 to 1)
Librarians/Media Specialists: 2.0 (1,344.0 to 1)
Guidance Counselors: 7.5 (358.4 to 1)
Current Spending: ($ per student per year):
Total: $7,005; Instruction: $4,503; Support Services: $2,201
Enrollment, Drop-out Rates and Diploma Recipients by Race/Ethnicity

Category	Total	White	Black	Asian	AIAN	Hisp.
Enrollment (%)	100.0	95.5	1.3	2.0	0.3	0.9
Drop-out Rate (%)	2.0	2.2	0.0	0.0	0.0	0.0
H.S. Diplomas (#)	201	187	3	8	0	3

Northampton County

Bangor Area SD
123 Five Points Richmond Rd • Bangor, PA 18013-5272
(610) 588-2163 • http://www.bangor.k12.pa.us/
Grade Span: KG-12; **Agency Type:** 1
Schools: 5
2 Primary; 2 Middle; 1 High; 0 Other Level
5 Regular; 0 Special Education; 0 Vocational; 0 Alternative
0 Magnet; 0 Charter; 4 Title I Eligible; 0 School-wide Title I
Students: 3,620 (n/a% male; n/a% female)
Individual Education Program: 583 (16.1%);
English Language Learner: n/a; Migrant: 0 (0.0%)
Eligible for Free Lunch Program: 417 (11.5%)
Eligible for Reduced-Price Lunch Program: 232 (6.4%)
Teachers: 207.2 (17.5 to 1)
Librarians/Media Specialists: 4.0 (905.0 to 1)
Guidance Counselors: 7.0 (517.1 to 1)
Current Spending: ($ per student per year):
Total: $6,555; Instruction: $3,779; Support Services: $2,480
Enrollment, Drop-out Rates and Diploma Recipients by Race/Ethnicity

Category	Total	White	Black	Asian	AIAN	Hisp.
Enrollment (%)	100.0	96.7	1.3	0.2	0.2	1.6
Drop-out Rate (%)	3.6	3.7	0.0	0.0	0.0	0.0
H.S. Diplomas (#)	220	213	2	3	0	2

Bethlehem Area SD

1516 Sycamore St • Bethlehem, PA 18017-6099
(610) 861-0500 • http://www.beth.k12.pa.us/
Grade Span: KG-12; **Agency Type:** 1
Schools: 22
16 Primary; 4 Middle; 2 High; 0 Other Level
22 Regular; 0 Special Education; 0 Vocational; 0 Alternative
0 Magnet; 0 Charter; 10 Title I Eligible; 5 School-wide Title I
Students: 14,615 (n/a% male; n/a% female)
Individual Education Program: 1,800 (12.3%);
English Language Learner: n/a; Migrant: 103 (0.7%)
Eligible for Free Lunch Program: 3,759 (25.7%)
Eligible for Reduced-Price Lunch Program: 1,102 (7.5%)
Teachers: 937.5 (15.6 to 1)
Librarians/Media Specialists: 14.4 (1,014.9 to 1)
Guidance Counselors: 47.0 (311.0 to 1)
Current Spending: ($ per student per year):
Total: $6,999; Instruction: $4,509; Support Services: $2,147
Enrollment, Drop-out Rates and Diploma Recipients by Race/Ethnicity

Category	Total	White	Black	Asian	AIAN	Hisp.
Enrollment (%)	100.0	64.3	6.2	1.9	0.1	27.5
Drop-out Rate (%)	4.1	2.5	3.3	0.0	0.0	9.2
H.S. Diplomas (#)	920	667	42	21	0	190

Easton Area SD

811 Northampton St • Easton, PA 18042-4298
(610) 250-2400 • http://easdnet1.eastonsd.org
Grade Span: KG-12; **Agency Type:** 1
Schools: 9
6 Primary; 2 Middle; 1 High; 0 Other Level
9 Regular; 0 Special Education; 0 Vocational; 0 Alternative
0 Magnet; 0 Charter; 6 Title I Eligible; 0 School-wide Title I
Students: 8,437 (n/a% male; n/a% female)
Individual Education Program: 1,006 (11.9%);
English Language Learner: n/a; Migrant: 10 (0.1%)
Eligible for Free Lunch Program: 1,441 (17.1%)
Eligible for Reduced-Price Lunch Program: 437 (5.2%)
Teachers: 541.7 (15.6 to 1)
Librarians/Media Specialists: 9.6 (878.9 to 1)
Guidance Counselors: 20.0 (421.9 to 1)
Current Spending: ($ per student per year):
Total: $6,875; Instruction: $4,479; Support Services: $2,222
Enrollment, Drop-out Rates and Diploma Recipients by Race/Ethnicity

Category	Total	White	Black	Asian	AIAN	Hisp.
Enrollment (%)	100.0	73.0	14.9	2.1	0.1	9.8
Drop-out Rate (%)	5.5	4.7	8.8	0.0	n/a	12.2
H.S. Diplomas (#)	502	411	56	9	0	26

Nazareth Area SD

One Education Plaza • Nazareth, PA 18064-2042
(610) 759-1170 • http://www.nazarethasd.k12.pa.us
Grade Span: KG-12; **Agency Type:** 1
Schools: 5
3 Primary; 1 Middle; 1 High; 0 Other Level
5 Regular; 0 Special Education; 0 Vocational; 0 Alternative
0 Magnet; 0 Charter; 2 Title I Eligible; 0 School-wide Title I
Students: 4,335 (n/a% male; n/a% female)
Individual Education Program: 461 (10.6%);
English Language Learner: n/a; Migrant: 0 (0.0%)
Eligible for Free Lunch Program: 176 (4.1%)
Eligible for Reduced-Price Lunch Program: 127 (2.9%)
Teachers: 257.0 (16.9 to 1)
Librarians/Media Specialists: 3.0 (1,445.0 to 1)
Guidance Counselors: 6.0 (722.5 to 1)
Current Spending: ($ per student per year):
Total: $7,088; Instruction: $4,429; Support Services: $2,412
Enrollment, Drop-out Rates and Diploma Recipients by Race/Ethnicity

Category	Total	White	Black	Asian	AIAN	Hisp.
Enrollment (%)	100.0	96.8	0.9	1.2	0.0	1.1
Drop-out Rate (%)	1.7	1.7	12.5	0.0	n/a	0.0
H.S. Diplomas (#)	254	248	1	3	0	2

Northampton Area SD

2014 Laubach Ave • Northampton, PA 18067-0118
(610) 262-7811 • http://www.northampton.k12.pa.us
Grade Span: KG-12; **Agency Type:** 1
Schools: 6
4 Primary; 1 Middle; 1 High; 0 Other Level
6 Regular; 0 Special Education; 0 Vocational; 0 Alternative
0 Magnet; 0 Charter; 4 Title I Eligible; 0 School-wide Title I
Students: 5,536 (n/a% male; n/a% female)
Individual Education Program: 755 (13.6%);
English Language Learner: n/a; Migrant: 0 (0.0%)
Eligible for Free Lunch Program: 273 (4.9%)
Eligible for Reduced-Price Lunch Program: 195 (3.5%)
Teachers: 341.0 (16.2 to 1)
Librarians/Media Specialists: 6.0 (922.7 to 1)
Guidance Counselors: 14.5 (381.8 to 1)
Current Spending: ($ per student per year):
Total: $7,435; Instruction: $4,555; Support Services: $2,590
Enrollment, Drop-out Rates and Diploma Recipients by Race/Ethnicity

Category	Total	White	Black	Asian	AIAN	Hisp.
Enrollment (%)	100.0	96.7	0.9	0.8	0.0	1.6
Drop-out Rate (%)	3.9	3.7	0.0	0.0	0.0	27.8
H.S. Diplomas (#)	339	334	0	3	0	2

Pen Argyl Area SD

1620 Teels Rd • Pen Argyl, PA 18072-9734
(610) 863-3191 • http://www.pahs.org
Grade Span: KG-12; **Agency Type:** 1
Schools: 3
1 Primary; 1 Middle; 1 High; 0 Other Level
3 Regular; 0 Special Education; 0 Vocational; 0 Alternative
0 Magnet; 0 Charter; 3 Title I Eligible; 0 School-wide Title I
Students: 2,010 (n/a% male; n/a% female)
Individual Education Program: 189 (9.4%);
English Language Learner: n/a; Migrant: 0 (0.0%)
Eligible for Free Lunch Program: 164 (8.2%)
Eligible for Reduced-Price Lunch Program: 104 (5.2%)
Teachers: 114.5 (17.6 to 1)
Librarians/Media Specialists: 2.0 (1,005.0 to 1)
Guidance Counselors: 5.0 (402.0 to 1)
Current Spending: ($ per student per year):
Total: $6,579; Instruction: $3,998; Support Services: $2,321
Enrollment, Drop-out Rates and Diploma Recipients by Race/Ethnicity

Category	Total	White	Black	Asian	AIAN	Hisp.
Enrollment (%)	100.0	94.5	1.0	1.8	0.2	2.5
Drop-out Rate (%)	3.3	3.3	0.0	0.0	0.0	12.5
H.S. Diplomas (#)	137	133	2	2	0	0

Saucon Valley SD

2097 Polk Valley Rd • Hellertown, PA 18055-2400
(610) 838-7026 • http://www.sauconvalley.k12.pa.us
Grade Span: KG-12; **Agency Type:** 1
Schools: 3
1 Primary; 1 Middle; 1 High; 0 Other Level
3 Regular; 0 Special Education; 0 Vocational; 0 Alternative
0 Magnet; 0 Charter; 3 Title I Eligible; 0 School-wide Title I
Students: 2,295 (n/a% male; n/a% female)
Individual Education Program: 234 (10.2%);
English Language Learner: n/a; Migrant: 2 (0.1%)
Eligible for Free Lunch Program: 173 (7.5%)
Eligible for Reduced-Price Lunch Program: 85 (3.7%)
Teachers: 151.8 (15.1 to 1)
Librarians/Media Specialists: 2.4 (956.3 to 1)
Guidance Counselors: 8.0 (286.9 to 1)
Current Spending: ($ per student per year):
Total: $7,692; Instruction: $4,660; Support Services: $2,757
Enrollment, Drop-out Rates and Diploma Recipients by Race/Ethnicity

Category	Total	White	Black	Asian	AIAN	Hisp.
Enrollment (%)	100.0	97.8	0.9	0.4	0.0	0.9
Drop-out Rate (%)	1.8	1.6	0.0	0.0	0.0	22.2
H.S. Diplomas (#)	174	167	1	1	1	4

Wilson Area SD

2040 Washington Blvd • Easton, PA 18042-3890
(484) 373-6000 • http://www.wilsonareasd.org
Grade Span: KG-12; **Agency Type:** 1
Schools: 5
3 Primary; 1 Middle; 1 High; 0 Other Level
5 Regular; 0 Special Education; 0 Vocational; 0 Alternative
0 Magnet; 0 Charter; 4 Title I Eligible; 0 School-wide Title I
Students: 2,247 (n/a% male; n/a% female)
Individual Education Program: 348 (15.5%);
English Language Learner: n/a; Migrant: 2 (0.1%)
Eligible for Free Lunch Program: 193 (8.6%)
Eligible for Reduced-Price Lunch Program: 140 (6.2%)
Teachers: 144.8 (15.5 to 1)
Librarians/Media Specialists: 3.5 (642.0 to 1)
Guidance Counselors: 7.0 (321.0 to 1)
Current Spending: ($ per student per year):
Total: $6,550; Instruction: $3,997; Support Services: $2,253
Enrollment, Drop-out Rates and Diploma Recipients by Race/Ethnicity

Category	Total	White	Black	Asian	AIAN	Hisp.
Enrollment (%)	100.0	90.3	3.9	1.9	0.0	3.8
Drop-out Rate (%)	5.0	4.7	12.0	0.0	0.0	9.1
H.S. Diplomas (#)	141	129	7	3	0	2

Northumberland County

Milton Area SD

700 Mahoning St • Milton, PA 17847-2231
(570) 742-7614 • http://www.milton.k12.pa.us
Grade Span: KG-12; **Agency Type:** 1
Schools: 5
3 Primary; 1 Middle; 1 High; 0 Other Level
5 Regular; 0 Special Education; 0 Vocational; 0 Alternative
0 Magnet; 0 Charter; 4 Title I Eligible; 0 School-wide Title I
Students: 2,532 (n/a% male; n/a% female)
Individual Education Program: 252 (10.0%);
English Language Learner: n/a; Migrant: 0 (0.0%)
Eligible for Free Lunch Program: 589 (23.3%)
Eligible for Reduced-Price Lunch Program: 264 (10.4%)
Teachers: 175.8 (14.4 to 1)
Librarians/Media Specialists: 3.0 (844.0 to 1)
Guidance Counselors: 7.0 (361.7 to 1)
Current Spending: ($ per student per year):
Total: $6,718; Instruction: $4,454; Support Services: $1,914
Enrollment, Drop-out Rates and Diploma Recipients by Race/Ethnicity

Category	Total	White	Black	Asian	AIAN	Hisp.
Enrollment (%)	100.0	92.8	3.8	0.5	0.0	2.9
Drop-out Rate (%)	3.2	3.4	0.0	0.0	n/a	0.0
H.S. Diplomas (#)	191	179	5	1	0	6

Mount Carmel Area SD

600 W 5th St • Mount Carmel, PA 17851-1897
(570) 339-3473 • http://www.mca.k12.pa.us
Grade Span: PK-12; **Agency Type:** 1
Schools: 2
1 Primary; 0 Middle; 1 High; 0 Other Level
2 Regular; 0 Special Education; 0 Vocational; 0 Alternative
0 Magnet; 0 Charter; 2 Title I Eligible; 0 School-wide Title I
Students: 1,762 (n/a% male; n/a% female)
Individual Education Program: 175 (9.9%);
English Language Learner: n/a; Migrant: 0 (0.0%)
Eligible for Free Lunch Program: 419 (23.8%)
Eligible for Reduced-Price Lunch Program: 199 (11.3%)
Teachers: 111.0 (15.9 to 1)
Librarians/Media Specialists: 2.0 (881.0 to 1)
Guidance Counselors: 3.0 (587.3 to 1)
Current Spending: ($ per student per year):
Total: $5,553; Instruction: $3,666; Support Services: $1,558
Enrollment, Drop-out Rates and Diploma Recipients by Race/Ethnicity

Category	Total	White	Black	Asian	AIAN	Hisp.
Enrollment (%)	100.0	99.3	0.1	0.2	0.1	0.4
Drop-out Rate (%)	1.8	1.8	n/a	n/a	n/a	0.0
H.S. Diplomas (#)	109	109	0	0	0	0

Shamokin Area SD

2000 W State St • Coal Township, PA 17866-2807
(570) 648-5752 • http://www.indians.k12.pa.us
Grade Span: PK-12; **Agency Type:** 1
Schools: 2
1 Primary; 0 Middle; 1 High; 0 Other Level
2 Regular; 0 Special Education; 0 Vocational; 0 Alternative
0 Magnet; 0 Charter; 2 Title I Eligible; 0 School-wide Title I
Students: 2,585 (n/a% male; n/a% female)
Individual Education Program: 380 (14.7%);
English Language Learner: n/a; Migrant: 0 (0.0%)
Eligible for Free Lunch Program: 888 (34.4%)
Eligible for Reduced-Price Lunch Program: 447 (17.3%)
Teachers: 143.0 (18.1 to 1)
Librarians/Media Specialists: 2.0 (1,292.5 to 1)
Guidance Counselors: 4.0 (646.3 to 1)
Current Spending: ($ per student per year):
Total: $5,949; Instruction: $4,034; Support Services: $1,606
Enrollment, Drop-out Rates and Diploma Recipients by Race/Ethnicity

Category	Total	White	Black	Asian	AIAN	Hisp.
Enrollment (%)	100.0	98.6	0.4	0.3	0.0	0.7
Drop-out Rate (%)	7.0	6.9	n/a	n/a	n/a	25.0
H.S. Diplomas (#)	174	170	0	2	0	2

Shikellamy SD

200 Island Blvd • Sunbury, PA 17801-1028
(570) 286-3720 • http://www.shikbraves.org/
Grade Span: KG-12; **Agency Type:** 1
Schools: 7
4 Primary; 2 Middle; 1 High; 0 Other Level
7 Regular; 0 Special Education; 0 Vocational; 0 Alternative
0 Magnet; 0 Charter; 4 Title I Eligible; 0 School-wide Title I
Students: 3,365 (n/a% male; n/a% female)
Individual Education Program: 314 (9.3%);
English Language Learner: n/a; Migrant: 5 (0.1%)
Eligible for Free Lunch Program: 796 (23.7%)
Eligible for Reduced-Price Lunch Program: 320 (9.5%)
Teachers: 201.5 (16.7 to 1)
Librarians/Media Specialists: 5.0 (673.0 to 1)
Guidance Counselors: 7.0 (480.7 to 1)
Current Spending: ($ per student per year):
Total: $6,526; Instruction: $4,418; Support Services: $1,811
Enrollment, Drop-out Rates and Diploma Recipients by Race/Ethnicity

Category	Total	White	Black	Asian	AIAN	Hisp.
Enrollment (%)	100.0	93.5	2.3	0.4	0.1	3.8
Drop-out Rate (%)	4.6	4.5	9.1	0.0	n/a	4.8
H.S. Diplomas (#)	241	233	3	1	0	4

Warrior Run SD

4800 Susquehanna Tr • Turbotville, PA 17772-9766
(570) 649-5138 • http://www.wrsd.org
Grade Span: KG-12; **Agency Type:** 1
Schools: 4
2 Primary; 1 Middle; 1 High; 0 Other Level
4 Regular; 0 Special Education; 0 Vocational; 0 Alternative
0 Magnet; 0 Charter; 3 Title I Eligible; 0 School-wide Title I
Students: 1,894 (n/a% male; n/a% female)
Individual Education Program: 236 (12.5%);
English Language Learner: n/a; Migrant: 0 (0.0%)
Eligible for Free Lunch Program: 214 (11.3%)
Eligible for Reduced-Price Lunch Program: 160 (8.4%)
Teachers: 135.2 (14.0 to 1)
Librarians/Media Specialists: 3.0 (631.3 to 1)
Guidance Counselors: 6.0 (315.7 to 1)
Current Spending: ($ per student per year):
Total: $6,285; Instruction: $3,871; Support Services: $2,118
Enrollment, Drop-out Rates and Diploma Recipients by Race/Ethnicity

Category	Total	White	Black	Asian	AIAN	Hisp.
Enrollment (%)	100.0	97.8	1.3	0.3	0.0	0.6
Drop-out Rate (%)	3.1	3.2	0.0	0.0	n/a	0.0
H.S. Diplomas (#)	148	146	0	2	0	0

Perry County

Susquenita SD

1725 Schoolhouse Rd • Duncannon, PA 17020-9582
(717) 957-2303 • http://www.susq.k12.pa.us
Grade Span: KG-12; **Agency Type:** 1
Schools: 3
1 Primary; 1 Middle; 1 High; 0 Other Level
3 Regular; 0 Special Education; 0 Vocational; 0 Alternative
0 Magnet; 0 Charter; 3 Title I Eligible; 0 School-wide Title I
Students: 2,393 (n/a% male; n/a% female)
Individual Education Program: 370 (15.5%);
English Language Learner: n/a; Migrant: 0 (0.0%)
Eligible for Free Lunch Program: 292 (12.2%)
Eligible for Reduced-Price Lunch Program: 165 (6.9%)
Teachers: 154.0 (15.5 to 1)
Librarians/Media Specialists: 2.0 (1,196.5 to 1)
Guidance Counselors: 5.0 (478.6 to 1)
Current Spending: ($ per student per year):
Total: $6,667; Instruction: $3,919; Support Services: $2,437
Enrollment, Drop-out Rates and Diploma Recipients by Race/Ethnicity

Category	Total	White	Black	Asian	AIAN	Hisp.
Enrollment (%)	100.0	98.9	0.5	0.1	0.2	0.4
Drop-out Rate (%)	3.9	3.9	0.0	0.0	0.0	0.0
H.S. Diplomas (#)	149	146	0	1	0	2

West Perry SD

2606 Shermans Valley Rd • Elliottsburg, PA 17024-9706
(717) 789-3934
Grade Span: KG-12; **Agency Type:** 1
Schools: 6
3 Primary; 1 Middle; 2 High; 0 Other Level
5 Regular; 1 Special Education; 0 Vocational; 0 Alternative
0 Magnet; 0 Charter; 4 Title I Eligible; 0 School-wide Title I
Students: 2,881 (n/a% male; n/a% female)
Individual Education Program: 514 (17.8%);
English Language Learner: n/a; Migrant: 0 (0.0%)
Eligible for Free Lunch Program: 465 (16.1%)
Eligible for Reduced-Price Lunch Program: 183 (6.4%)
Teachers: 205.1 (14.0 to 1)
Librarians/Media Specialists: 4.0 (720.3 to 1)
Guidance Counselors: 7.5 (384.1 to 1)
Current Spending: ($ per student per year):
Total: $6,795; Instruction: $4,223; Support Services: $2,289

Enrollment, Drop-out Rates and Diploma Recipients by Race/Ethnicity

Category	Total	White	Black	Asian	AIAN	Hisp.
Enrollment (%)	100.0	97.9	1.3	0.0	0.1	0.7
Drop-out Rate (%)	5.4	5.4	0.0	0.0	n/a	0.0
H.S. Diplomas (#)	173	171	0	1	0	1

Philadelphia County

Philadelphia City SD

Pkwy at 21st St • Philadelphia, PA 19103-1099
(215) 299-7000 • http://www.philsch.k12.pa.us
Grade Span: KG-12; **Agency Type:** 1
Schools: 262
175 Primary; 42 Middle; 36 High; 9 Other Level
252 Regular; 5 Special Education; 5 Vocational; 0 Alternative
10 Magnet; 0 Charter; 261 Title I Eligible; 261 School-wide Title I
Students: 192,683 (n/a% male; n/a% female)
Individual Education Program: 23,476 (12.2%);
English Language Learner: n/a; Migrant: 782 (0.4%)
Eligible for Free Lunch Program: 121,012 (62.8%)
Eligible for Reduced-Price Lunch Program: 12,695 (6.6%)
Teachers: 9,866.0 (19.5 to 1)
Librarians/Media Specialists: 111.0 (1,735.9 to 1)
Guidance Counselors: 363.0 (530.8 to 1)
Current Spending: ($ per student per year):
Total: $6,947; Instruction: $3,917; Support Services: $2,699
Enrollment, Drop-out Rates and Diploma Recipients by Race/Ethnicity

Category	Total	White	Black	Asian	AIAN	Hisp.
Enrollment (%)	100.0	15.2	65.3	5.2	0.2	14.2
Drop-out Rate (%)	9.2	8.2	9.4	6.2	4.4	11.3
H.S. Diplomas (#)	8,559	1,879	5,193	684	12	791

Pike County

Delaware Valley SD

236 Route 6 And 209 • Milford, PA 18337-9454
(570) 296-1800 • http://dvasdweb.dvasd.k12.pa.us
Grade Span: KG-12; **Agency Type:** 1
Schools: 7
4 Primary; 2 Middle; 1 High; 0 Other Level
7 Regular; 0 Special Education; 0 Vocational; 0 Alternative
0 Magnet; 0 Charter; 4 Title I Eligible; 0 School-wide Title I
Students: 5,182 (n/a% male; n/a% female)
Individual Education Program: 424 (8.2%);
English Language Learner: n/a; Migrant: 0 (0.0%)
Eligible for Free Lunch Program: 694 (13.4%)
Eligible for Reduced-Price Lunch Program: 279 (5.4%)
Teachers: 318.6 (16.3 to 1)
Librarians/Media Specialists: 6.0 (863.7 to 1)
Guidance Counselors: 11.0 (471.1 to 1)
Current Spending: ($ per student per year):
Total: $6,676; Instruction: $4,464; Support Services: $2,022
Enrollment, Drop-out Rates and Diploma Recipients by Race/Ethnicity

Category	Total	White	Black	Asian	AIAN	Hisp.
Enrollment (%)	100.0	92.4	2.9	0.8	0.3	3.7
Drop-out Rate (%)	2.7	2.5	5.3	0.0	n/a	8.8
H.S. Diplomas (#)	322	304	7	2	0	9

Schuylkill County

Blue Mountain SD

PO Box 188 • Orwigsburg, PA 17961-0279
(570) 366-0515
Grade Span: KG-12; **Agency Type:** 1
Schools: 5
3 Primary; 1 Middle; 1 High; 0 Other Level
5 Regular; 0 Special Education; 0 Vocational; 0 Alternative
0 Magnet; 0 Charter; 5 Title I Eligible; 0 School-wide Title I
Students: 2,963 (n/a% male; n/a% female)
Individual Education Program: 403 (13.6%);
English Language Learner: n/a; Migrant: 0 (0.0%)
Eligible for Free Lunch Program: 232 (7.8%)
Eligible for Reduced-Price Lunch Program: 153 (5.2%)
Teachers: 162.5 (18.2 to 1)
Librarians/Media Specialists: 4.0 (740.8 to 1)
Guidance Counselors: 7.0 (423.3 to 1)
Current Spending: ($ per student per year):
Total: $6,053; Instruction: $3,533; Support Services: $2,232
Enrollment, Drop-out Rates and Diploma Recipients by Race/Ethnicity

Category	Total	White	Black	Asian	AIAN	Hisp.
Enrollment (%)	100.0	96.3	1.2	1.6	0.0	1.0
Drop-out Rate (%)	2.9	3.0	0.0	0.0	n/a	0.0
H.S. Diplomas (#)	206	200	0	6	0	0

North Schuylkill SD

15 Academy Ln Route 61 • Ashland, PA 17921-9301
(570) 874-0466 • http://www.north-schuylkill.k12.pa.us
Grade Span: KG-12; **Agency Type:** 1
Schools: 4
3 Primary; 0 Middle; 1 High; 0 Other Level
4 Regular; 0 Special Education; 0 Vocational; 0 Alternative
0 Magnet; 0 Charter; 4 Title I Eligible; 0 School-wide Title I
Students: 2,012 (n/a% male; n/a% female)
Individual Education Program: 290 (14.4%);
English Language Learner: n/a; Migrant: 0 (0.0%)
Eligible for Free Lunch Program: 396 (19.7%)
Eligible for Reduced-Price Lunch Program: 208 (10.3%)
Teachers: 113.5 (17.7 to 1)
Librarians/Media Specialists: 2.0 (1,006.0 to 1)
Guidance Counselors: 4.0 (503.0 to 1)
Current Spending: ($ per student per year):
Total: $5,820; Instruction: $3,731; Support Services: $1,786
Enrollment, Drop-out Rates and Diploma Recipients by Race/Ethnicity

Category	Total	White	Black	Asian	AIAN	Hisp.
Enrollment (%)	100.0	98.9	0.4	0.2	0.0	0.3
Drop-out Rate (%)	3.4	3.3	33.3	0.0	n/a	0.0
H.S. Diplomas (#)	147	147	0	0	0	0

Pine Grove Area SD

103 School St • Pine Grove, PA 17963-1698
(570) 345-2731 • http://www.pgasd.com
Grade Span: KG-12; **Agency Type:** 1
Schools: 3
1 Primary; 1 Middle; 1 High; 0 Other Level
3 Regular; 0 Special Education; 0 Vocational; 0 Alternative
0 Magnet; 0 Charter; 2 Title I Eligible; 0 School-wide Title I
Students: 1,778 (n/a% male; n/a% female)
Individual Education Program: 194 (10.9%);
English Language Learner: n/a; Migrant: 2 (0.1%)
Eligible for Free Lunch Program: 247 (13.9%)
Eligible for Reduced-Price Lunch Program: 121 (6.8%)
Teachers: 101.0 (17.6 to 1)
Librarians/Media Specialists: 3.0 (592.7 to 1)
Guidance Counselors: 5.0 (355.6 to 1)
Current Spending: ($ per student per year):
Total: $6,343; Instruction: $3,705; Support Services: $2,293
Enrollment, Drop-out Rates and Diploma Recipients by Race/Ethnicity

Category	Total	White	Black	Asian	AIAN	Hisp.
Enrollment (%)	100.0	98.8	0.8	0.0	0.0	0.4
Drop-out Rate (%)	1.7	1.7	0.0	0.0	0.0	n/a
H.S. Diplomas (#)	138	136	1	1	0	0

Pottsville Area SD

1501 Laurel Blvd • Pottsville, PA 17901-1419
(570) 621-2900 • http://www.pottsville.k12.pa.us
Grade Span: KG-12; **Agency Type:** 1
Schools: 3
1 Primary; 1 Middle; 1 High; 0 Other Level
3 Regular; 0 Special Education; 0 Vocational; 0 Alternative
0 Magnet; 0 Charter; 2 Title I Eligible; 0 School-wide Title I
Students: 3,117 (n/a% male; n/a% female)
Individual Education Program: 445 (14.3%);
English Language Learner: n/a; Migrant: 0 (0.0%)
Eligible for Free Lunch Program: 799 (25.6%)
Eligible for Reduced-Price Lunch Program: 312 (10.0%)
Teachers: 154.0 (20.2 to 1)
Librarians/Media Specialists: 3.0 (1,039.0 to 1)
Guidance Counselors: 6.0 (519.5 to 1)
Current Spending: ($ per student per year):
Total: $6,143; Instruction: $3,771; Support Services: $2,022
Enrollment, Drop-out Rates and Diploma Recipients by Race/Ethnicity

Category	Total	White	Black	Asian	AIAN	Hisp.
Enrollment (%)	100.0	95.0	3.0	0.7	0.4	1.0
Drop-out Rate (%)	3.6	3.6	4.5	0.0	0.0	9.1
H.S. Diplomas (#)	261	246	6	2	1	6

Tamaqua Area SD

PO Box 112 • Tamaqua, PA 18252-0112
(570) 668-2570
Grade Span: KG-12; **Agency Type:** 1
Schools: 5
3 Primary; 1 Middle; 1 High; 0 Other Level
5 Regular; 0 Special Education; 0 Vocational; 0 Alternative
0 Magnet; 0 Charter; 2 Title I Eligible; 0 School-wide Title I
Students: 2,262 (n/a% male; n/a% female)
Individual Education Program: 310 (13.7%);
English Language Learner: n/a; Migrant: 0 (0.0%)
Eligible for Free Lunch Program: 407 (18.0%)
Eligible for Reduced-Price Lunch Program: 151 (6.7%)

Teachers: 125.4 (18.0 to 1)
Librarians/Media Specialists: 3.0 (754.0 to 1)
Guidance Counselors: 4.0 (565.5 to 1)
Current Spending: ($ per student per year):
Total: $6,254; Instruction: $3,750; Support Services: $2,221
Enrollment, Drop-out Rates and Diploma Recipients by Race/Ethnicity

Category	Total	White	Black	Asian	AIAN	Hisp.
Enrollment (%)	100.0	98.0	0.6	0.5	0.0	0.8
Drop-out Rate (%)	4.6	4.8	0.0	0.0	n/a	0.0
H.S. Diplomas (#)	132	129	2	1	0	0

Snyder County

Midd-West SD
568 E Main St • Middleburg, PA 17842-1295
(570) 837-0046 • http://www.midd-westsd.k12.pa.us
Grade Span: KG-12; **Agency Type:** 1
Schools: 7
5 Primary; 0 Middle; 2 High; 0 Other Level
7 Regular; 0 Special Education; 0 Vocational; 0 Alternative
0 Magnet; 0 Charter; 5 Title I Eligible; 0 School-wide Title I
Students: 2,545 (n/a% male; n/a% female)
Individual Education Program: 386 (15.2%);
English Language Learner: n/a; Migrant: 0 (0.0%)
Eligible for Free Lunch Program: 446 (17.5%)
Eligible for Reduced-Price Lunch Program: 243 (9.5%)
Teachers: 181.0 (14.1 to 1)
Librarians/Media Specialists: 4.0 (636.3 to 1)
Guidance Counselors: 7.0 (363.6 to 1)
Current Spending: ($ per student per year):
Total: $6,525; Instruction: $4,210; Support Services: $1,996
Enrollment, Drop-out Rates and Diploma Recipients by Race/Ethnicity

Category	Total	White	Black	Asian	AIAN	Hisp.
Enrollment (%)	100.0	98.7	0.7	0.1	0.2	0.3
Drop-out Rate (%)	3.6	3.7	0.0	0.0	n/a	0.0
H.S. Diplomas (#)	174	173	0	1	0	0

Selinsgrove Area SD
401 N 18th St • Selinsgrove, PA 17870-1153
(570) 374-1144 • http://www.selinsgroveasd.k12.pa.us
Grade Span: KG-12; **Agency Type:** 1
Schools: 5
3 Primary; 1 Middle; 1 High; 0 Other Level
5 Regular; 0 Special Education; 0 Vocational; 0 Alternative
0 Magnet; 0 Charter; 4 Title I Eligible; 0 School-wide Title I
Students: 2,906 (n/a% male; n/a% female)
Individual Education Program: 360 (12.4%);
English Language Learner: n/a; Migrant: 0 (0.0%)
Eligible for Free Lunch Program: 401 (13.8%)
Eligible for Reduced-Price Lunch Program: 234 (8.1%)
Teachers: 183.0 (15.9 to 1)
Librarians/Media Specialists: 4.0 (726.5 to 1)
Guidance Counselors: 8.0 (363.3 to 1)
Current Spending: ($ per student per year):
Total: $6,743; Instruction: $4,390; Support Services: $2,102
Enrollment, Drop-out Rates and Diploma Recipients by Race/Ethnicity

Category	Total	White	Black	Asian	AIAN	Hisp.
Enrollment (%)	100.0	94.5	2.3	1.2	0.2	1.7
Drop-out Rate (%)	2.3	2.3	0.0	0.0	n/a	8.3
H.S. Diplomas (#)	203	198	0	2	0	3

Somerset County

Somerset Area SD
645 S Columbia Ave Ste 110 • Somerset, PA 15501-2511
(814) 445-9714
Grade Span: KG-12; **Agency Type:** 1
Schools: 6
3 Primary; 2 Middle; 1 High; 0 Other Level
6 Regular; 0 Special Education; 0 Vocational; 0 Alternative
0 Magnet; 0 Charter; 4 Title I Eligible; 0 School-wide Title I
Students: 2,824 (n/a% male; n/a% female)
Individual Education Program: 392 (13.9%);
English Language Learner: n/a; Migrant: 0 (0.0%)
Eligible for Free Lunch Program: 574 (20.3%)
Eligible for Reduced-Price Lunch Program: 209 (7.4%)
Teachers: 173.4 (16.3 to 1)
Librarians/Media Specialists: 2.0 (1,412.0 to 1)
Guidance Counselors: 5.0 (564.8 to 1)
Current Spending: ($ per student per year):
Total: $6,548; Instruction: $4,356; Support Services: $1,927
Enrollment, Drop-out Rates and Diploma Recipients by Race/Ethnicity

Category	Total	White	Black	Asian	AIAN	Hisp.
Enrollment (%)	100.0	97.4	1.0	1.1	0.1	0.4
Drop-out Rate (%)	2.5	2.5	0.0	0.0	0.0	0.0
H.S. Diplomas (#)	212	209	1	2	0	0

Susquehanna County

Elk Lake SD
PO Box 100 • Dimock, PA 18816-0100
(570) 278-1106
Grade Span: KG-12; **Agency Type:** 1
Schools: 2
1 Primary; 0 Middle; 1 High; 0 Other Level
2 Regular; 0 Special Education; 0 Vocational; 0 Alternative
0 Magnet; 0 Charter; 2 Title I Eligible; 0 School-wide Title I
Students: 1,585 (n/a% male; n/a% female)
Individual Education Program: 244 (15.4%);
English Language Learner: n/a; Migrant: 7 (0.4%)
Eligible for Free Lunch Program: 331 (20.9%)
Eligible for Reduced-Price Lunch Program: 107 (6.8%)
Teachers: 104.4 (15.2 to 1)
Librarians/Media Specialists: 2.0 (792.5 to 1)
Guidance Counselors: 3.0 (528.3 to 1)
Current Spending: ($ per student per year):
Total: $6,704; Instruction: $4,246; Support Services: $2,113
Enrollment, Drop-out Rates and Diploma Recipients by Race/Ethnicity

Category	Total	White	Black	Asian	AIAN	Hisp.
Enrollment (%)	100.0	98.9	0.5	0.0	0.1	0.5
Drop-out Rate (%)	2.8	2.8	0.0	n/a	n/a	0.0
H.S. Diplomas (#)	93	93	0	0	0	0

Montrose Area SD
80 High School Rd • Montrose, PA 18801-9501
(570) 278-3731
Grade Span: KG-12; **Agency Type:** 1
Schools: 3
2 Primary; 0 Middle; 1 High; 0 Other Level
3 Regular; 0 Special Education; 0 Vocational; 0 Alternative
0 Magnet; 0 Charter; 3 Title I Eligible; 0 School-wide Title I
Students: 1,991 (n/a% male; n/a% female)
Individual Education Program: 356 (17.9%);
English Language Learner: n/a; Migrant: 5 (0.3%)
Eligible for Free Lunch Program: 309 (15.5%)
Eligible for Reduced-Price Lunch Program: 182 (9.1%)
Teachers: 128.0 (15.6 to 1)
Librarians/Media Specialists: 3.0 (663.7 to 1)
Guidance Counselors: 5.0 (398.2 to 1)
Current Spending: ($ per student per year):
Total: $7,446; Instruction: $4,533; Support Services: $2,612
Enrollment, Drop-out Rates and Diploma Recipients by Race/Ethnicity

Category	Total	White	Black	Asian	AIAN	Hisp.
Enrollment (%)	100.0	97.8	1.0	0.6	0.1	0.5
Drop-out Rate (%)	2.9	2.9	20.0	0.0	n/a	0.0
H.S. Diplomas (#)	121	119	1	1	0	0

Tioga County

Northern Tioga SD
117 Coates Ave • Elkland, PA 16920-1305
(814) 258-5642
Grade Span: KG-12; **Agency Type:** 1
Schools: 6
3 Primary; 0 Middle; 3 High; 0 Other Level
6 Regular; 0 Special Education; 0 Vocational; 0 Alternative
0 Magnet; 0 Charter; 6 Title I Eligible; 0 School-wide Title I
Students: 2,615 (n/a% male; n/a% female)
Individual Education Program: 313 (12.0%);
English Language Learner: n/a; Migrant: 17 (0.7%)
Eligible for Free Lunch Program: 861 (32.9%)
Eligible for Reduced-Price Lunch Program: 327 (12.5%)
Teachers: 200.0 (13.1 to 1)
Librarians/Media Specialists: 4.0 (653.8 to 1)
Guidance Counselors: 4.0 (653.8 to 1)
Current Spending: ($ per student per year):
Total: $7,146; Instruction: $4,596; Support Services: $2,176
Enrollment, Drop-out Rates and Diploma Recipients by Race/Ethnicity

Category	Total	White	Black	Asian	AIAN	Hisp.
Enrollment (%)	100.0	98.0	0.7	0.2	0.2	0.9
Drop-out Rate (%)	4.9	4.8	20.0	0.0	n/a	0.0
H.S. Diplomas (#)	158	155	1	1	0	1

Southern Tioga SD

241 Main St • Blossburg, PA 16912-1125
(570) 638-2183
Grade Span: KG-12; **Agency Type:** 1
Schools: 6
3 Primary; 0 Middle; 3 High; 0 Other Level
6 Regular; 0 Special Education; 0 Vocational; 0 Alternative
0 Magnet; 0 Charter; 4 Title I Eligible; 0 School-wide Title I
Students: 2,328 (n/a% male; n/a% female)
Individual Education Program: 257 (11.0%);
English Language Learner: n/a; Migrant: 17 (0.7%)
Eligible for Free Lunch Program: 537 (23.1%)
Eligible for Reduced-Price Lunch Program: 301 (12.9%)
Teachers: 153.7 (15.1 to 1)
Librarians/Media Specialists: 5.0 (465.6 to 1)
Guidance Counselors: 7.0 (332.6 to 1)
Current Spending: ($ per student per year):
Total: $7,458; Instruction: $4,695; Support Services: $2,447
Enrollment, Drop-out Rates and Diploma Recipients by Race/Ethnicity

Category	Total	White	Black	Asian	AIAN	Hisp.
Enrollment (%)	100.0	97.3	1.7	0.9	0.0	0.0
Drop-out Rate (%)	2.8	2.9	0.0	0.0	n/a	0.0
H.S. Diplomas (#)	174	174	0	0	0	0

Wellsboro Area SD

2 Charles St • Wellsboro, PA 16901-1401
(570) 724-4424 • http://www.wellsborosd.k12.pa.us
Grade Span: KG-12; **Agency Type:** 1
Schools: 4
2 Primary; 1 Middle; 1 High; 0 Other Level
4 Regular; 0 Special Education; 0 Vocational; 0 Alternative
0 Magnet; 0 Charter; 2 Title I Eligible; 0 School-wide Title I
Students: 1,716 (n/a% male; n/a% female)
Individual Education Program: 192 (11.2%);
English Language Learner: n/a; Migrant: 11 (0.6%)
Eligible for Free Lunch Program: 389 (22.7%)
Eligible for Reduced-Price Lunch Program: 157 (9.1%)
Teachers: 123.4 (13.9 to 1)
Librarians/Media Specialists: 3.0 (572.0 to 1)
Guidance Counselors: 4.0 (429.0 to 1)
Current Spending: ($ per student per year):
Total: $7,371; Instruction: $4,655; Support Services: $2,414
Enrollment, Drop-out Rates and Diploma Recipients by Race/Ethnicity

Category	Total	White	Black	Asian	AIAN	Hisp.
Enrollment (%)	100.0	97.1	0.8	1.3	0.1	0.8
Drop-out Rate (%)	2.1	2.1	0.0	0.0	n/a	0.0
H.S. Diplomas (#)	147	145	0	0	0	2

Union County

Lewisburg Area SD

PO Box 351 • Lewisburg, PA 17837-0351
(570) 523-3220 • http://www.dragon.k12.pa.us
Grade Span: KG-12; **Agency Type:** 1
Schools: 4
1 Primary; 2 Middle; 1 High; 0 Other Level
4 Regular; 0 Special Education; 0 Vocational; 0 Alternative
0 Magnet; 0 Charter; 3 Title I Eligible; 0 School-wide Title I
Students: 1,831 (n/a% male; n/a% female)
Individual Education Program: 152 (8.3%);
English Language Learner: n/a; Migrant: 0 (0.0%)
Eligible for Free Lunch Program: 189 (10.3%)
Eligible for Reduced-Price Lunch Program: 62 (3.4%)
Teachers: 118.7 (15.4 to 1)
Librarians/Media Specialists: 5.0 (366.2 to 1)
Guidance Counselors: 7.0 (261.6 to 1)
Current Spending: ($ per student per year):
Total: $7,485; Instruction: $4,510; Support Services: $2,727
Enrollment, Drop-out Rates and Diploma Recipients by Race/Ethnicity

Category	Total	White	Black	Asian	AIAN	Hisp.
Enrollment (%)	100.0	93.6	2.0	1.9	0.1	2.5
Drop-out Rate (%)	0.5	0.4	0.0	11.1	n/a	0.0
H.S. Diplomas (#)	154	148	3	2	0	1

Mifflinburg Area SD

PO Box 285 • Mifflinburg, PA 17844-0285
(570) 966-8200 • http://www.mifflinburg.org
Grade Span: KG-12; **Agency Type:** 1
Schools: 6
4 Primary; 1 Middle; 1 High; 0 Other Level
6 Regular; 0 Special Education; 0 Vocational; 0 Alternative
0 Magnet; 0 Charter; 4 Title I Eligible; 0 School-wide Title I
Students: 2,591 (n/a% male; n/a% female)
Individual Education Program: 259 (10.0%);
English Language Learner: n/a; Migrant: 0 (0.0%)
Eligible for Free Lunch Program: 338 (13.0%)
Eligible for Reduced-Price Lunch Program: 219 (8.5%)
Teachers: 151.1 (17.1 to 1)
Librarians/Media Specialists: 3.0 (863.7 to 1)
Guidance Counselors: 4.0 (647.8 to 1)
Current Spending: ($ per student per year):
Total: $5,784; Instruction: $3,724; Support Services: $1,778
Enrollment, Drop-out Rates and Diploma Recipients by Race/Ethnicity

Category	Total	White	Black	Asian	AIAN	Hisp.
Enrollment (%)	100.0	97.3	1.6	0.3	0.2	0.6
Drop-out Rate (%)	2.6	2.7	0.0	0.0	0.0	0.0
H.S. Diplomas (#)	174	173	0	1	0	0

Venango County

Cranberry Area SD

3 Education Dr • Seneca, PA 16346-9709
(814) 676-5628 • http://cranberry.iu6.k12.pa.us
Grade Span: KG-12; **Agency Type:** 1
Schools: 6
4 Primary; 1 Middle; 1 High; 0 Other Level
6 Regular; 0 Special Education; 0 Vocational; 0 Alternative
0 Magnet; 0 Charter; 5 Title I Eligible; 0 School-wide Title I
Students: 1,510 (n/a% male; n/a% female)
Individual Education Program: 257 (17.0%);
English Language Learner: n/a; Migrant: 0 (0.0%)
Eligible for Free Lunch Program: 370 (24.5%)
Eligible for Reduced-Price Lunch Program: 125 (8.3%)
Teachers: 100.5 (15.0 to 1)
Librarians/Media Specialists: 3.0 (503.3 to 1)
Guidance Counselors: 3.0 (503.3 to 1)
Current Spending: ($ per student per year):
Total: $7,259; Instruction: $4,410; Support Services: $2,566
Enrollment, Drop-out Rates and Diploma Recipients by Race/Ethnicity

Category	Total	White	Black	Asian	AIAN	Hisp.
Enrollment (%)	100.0	98.4	0.5	0.3	0.1	0.7
Drop-out Rate (%)	5.5	5.5	0.0	0.0	n/a	0.0
H.S. Diplomas (#)	92	92	0	0	0	0

Franklin Area SD

417 13th St • Franklin, PA 16323-1310
(814) 432-8917 • http://www.fasd.k12.pa.us
Grade Span: KG-12; **Agency Type:** 1
Schools: 8
6 Primary; 1 Middle; 1 High; 0 Other Level
8 Regular; 0 Special Education; 0 Vocational; 0 Alternative
0 Magnet; 0 Charter; 6 Title I Eligible; 0 School-wide Title I
Students: 2,399 (n/a% male; n/a% female)
Individual Education Program: 477 (19.9%);
English Language Learner: n/a; Migrant: 0 (0.0%)
Eligible for Free Lunch Program: 583 (24.3%)
Eligible for Reduced-Price Lunch Program: 178 (7.4%)
Teachers: 165.7 (14.5 to 1)
Librarians/Media Specialists: 2.8 (856.8 to 1)
Guidance Counselors: 4.0 (599.8 to 1)
Current Spending: ($ per student per year):
Total: $7,313; Instruction: $4,539; Support Services: $2,463
Enrollment, Drop-out Rates and Diploma Recipients by Race/Ethnicity

Category	Total	White	Black	Asian	AIAN	Hisp.
Enrollment (%)	100.0	93.8	5.3	0.7	0.0	0.2
Drop-out Rate (%)	4.7	4.8	0.0	0.0	n/a	0.0
H.S. Diplomas (#)	196	189	5	1	0	1

Oil City Area SD

825 Grandview Rd • Oil City, PA 16301-0929
(814) 676-1867 • http://www.oilcitysd@mail.ocasd.org
Grade Span: KG-12; **Agency Type:** 1
Schools: 6
4 Primary; 1 Middle; 1 High; 0 Other Level
6 Regular; 0 Special Education; 0 Vocational; 0 Alternative
0 Magnet; 0 Charter; 6 Title I Eligible; 1 School-wide Title I
Students: 2,573 (n/a% male; n/a% female)
Individual Education Program: 509 (19.8%);
English Language Learner: n/a; Migrant: 0 (0.0%)
Eligible for Free Lunch Program: 796 (30.9%)
Eligible for Reduced-Price Lunch Program: 212 (8.2%)
Teachers: 150.0 (17.2 to 1)
Librarians/Media Specialists: 3.0 (857.7 to 1)
Guidance Counselors: 4.0 (643.3 to 1)
Current Spending: ($ per student per year):
Total: $6,976; Instruction: $4,254; Support Services: $2,464

Enrollment, Drop-out Rates and Diploma Recipients by Race/Ethnicity

Category	Total	White	Black	Asian	AIAN	Hisp.
Enrollment (%)	100.0	96.7	1.7	0.5	0.3	0.9
Drop-out Rate (%)	4.0	4.0	0.0	0.0	0.0	20.0
H.S. Diplomas (#)	172	169	1	0	1	1

Titusville Area SD

221 N Washington St • Titusville, PA 16354-1785
(814) 827-2715 • http://www.gorockets.org
Grade Span: PK-12; **Agency Type:** 1
Schools: 7
5 Primary; 1 Middle; 1 High; 0 Other Level
7 Regular; 0 Special Education; 0 Vocational; 0 Alternative
0 Magnet; 0 Charter; 0 Title I Eligible; 0 School-wide Title I
Students: 2,529 (n/a% male; n/a% female)
Individual Education Program: 404 (16.0%);
English Language Learner: n/a; Migrant: 0 (0.0%)
Eligible for Free Lunch Program: 607 (24.0%)
Eligible for Reduced-Price Lunch Program: 233 (9.2%)
Teachers: 154.6 (16.4 to 1)
Librarians/Media Specialists: 3.0 (843.0 to 1)
Guidance Counselors: 4.0 (632.3 to 1)
Current Spending: ($ per student per year):
Total: $6,614; Instruction: $4,133; Support Services: $2,188
Enrollment, Drop-out Rates and Diploma Recipients by Race/Ethnicity

Category	Total	White	Black	Asian	AIAN	Hisp.
Enrollment (%)	100.0	98.5	0.6	0.2	0.2	0.5
Drop-out Rate (%)	4.8	4.9	0.0	0.0	n/a	0.0
H.S. Diplomas (#)	162	161	0	0	0	1

Warren County

Warren County SD

185 Hospital Dr • North Warren, PA 16365-4885
(814) 723-6900
Grade Span: KG-12; **Agency Type:** 1
Schools: 19
13 Primary; 1 Middle; 4 High; 1 Other Level
19 Regular; 0 Special Education; 0 Vocational; 0 Alternative
0 Magnet; 0 Charter; 13 Title I Eligible; 0 School-wide Title I
Students: 6,307 (n/a% male; n/a% female)
Individual Education Program: 1,140 (18.1%);
English Language Learner: n/a; Migrant: 0 (0.0%)
Eligible for Free Lunch Program: 1,293 (20.5%)
Eligible for Reduced-Price Lunch Program: 516 (8.2%)
Teachers: 418.0 (15.1 to 1)
Librarians/Media Specialists: 10.0 (630.7 to 1)
Guidance Counselors: 14.0 (450.5 to 1)
Current Spending: ($ per student per year):
Total: $6,890; Instruction: $4,264; Support Services: $2,392
Enrollment, Drop-out Rates and Diploma Recipients by Race/Ethnicity

Category	Total	White	Black	Asian	AIAN	Hisp.
Enrollment (%)	100.0	98.4	0.5	0.6	0.1	0.3
Drop-out Rate (%)	4.3	4.3	0.0	0.0	0.0	0.0
H.S. Diplomas (#)	499	489	0	4	3	3

Washington County

Burgettstown Area SD

100 Bavington Rd • Burgettstown, PA 15021-2727
(724) 947-3324 • http://www.burgettstown.k12.pa.us
Grade Span: KG-12; **Agency Type:** 1
Schools: 2
1 Primary; 0 Middle; 1 High; 0 Other Level
2 Regular; 0 Special Education; 0 Vocational; 0 Alternative
0 Magnet; 0 Charter; 1 Title I Eligible; 0 School-wide Title I
Students: 1,527 (n/a% male; n/a% female)
Individual Education Program: 235 (15.4%);
English Language Learner: n/a; Migrant: 0 (0.0%)
Eligible for Free Lunch Program: 291 (19.1%)
Eligible for Reduced-Price Lunch Program: 119 (7.8%)
Teachers: 101.0 (15.1 to 1)
Librarians/Media Specialists: 2.0 (763.5 to 1)
Guidance Counselors: 4.0 (381.8 to 1)
Current Spending: ($ per student per year):
Total: $6,162; Instruction: $4,080; Support Services: $1,773
Enrollment, Drop-out Rates and Diploma Recipients by Race/Ethnicity

Category	Total	White	Black	Asian	AIAN	Hisp.
Enrollment (%)	100.0	97.3	2.2	0.2	0.0	0.3
Drop-out Rate (%)	5.3	4.9	27.3	0.0	0.0	0.0
H.S. Diplomas (#)	88	86	2	0	0	0

Canon-Mcmillan SD

1 N Jefferson Ave • Canonsburg, PA 15317-1305
(724) 746-2940 • http://www.cmsd.k12.pa.us
Grade Span: KG-12; **Agency Type:** 1
Schools: 10
7 Primary; 2 Middle; 1 High; 0 Other Level
10 Regular; 0 Special Education; 0 Vocational; 0 Alternative
0 Magnet; 0 Charter; 4 Title I Eligible; 0 School-wide Title I
Students: 4,236 (n/a% male; n/a% female)
Individual Education Program: 454 (10.7%);
English Language Learner: n/a; Migrant: 5 (0.1%)
Eligible for Free Lunch Program: 490 (11.6%)
Eligible for Reduced-Price Lunch Program: 210 (5.0%)
Teachers: 265.0 (16.0 to 1)
Librarians/Media Specialists: 6.0 (706.0 to 1)
Guidance Counselors: 10.0 (423.6 to 1)
Current Spending: ($ per student per year):
Total: $7,738; Instruction: $4,824; Support Services: $2,603
Enrollment, Drop-out Rates and Diploma Recipients by Race/Ethnicity

Category	Total	White	Black	Asian	AIAN	Hisp.
Enrollment (%)	100.0	92.6	6.1	0.7	0.2	0.4
Drop-out Rate (%)	2.8	2.3	8.9	0.0	0.0	40.0
H.S. Diplomas (#)	244	230	12	2	0	0

Charleroi SD

125 Fecsen Dr • Charleroi, PA 15022-2279
(724) 483-3509
Grade Span: KG-12; **Agency Type:** 1
Schools: 3
1 Primary; 1 Middle; 1 High; 0 Other Level
3 Regular; 0 Special Education; 0 Vocational; 0 Alternative
0 Magnet; 0 Charter; 2 Title I Eligible; 0 School-wide Title I
Students: 1,693 (n/a% male; n/a% female)
Individual Education Program: 292 (17.2%);
English Language Learner: n/a; Migrant: 0 (0.0%)
Eligible for Free Lunch Program: 456 (26.9%)
Eligible for Reduced-Price Lunch Program: 131 (7.7%)
Teachers: 99.5 (17.0 to 1)
Librarians/Media Specialists: 2.0 (846.5 to 1)
Guidance Counselors: 5.0 (338.6 to 1)
Current Spending: ($ per student per year):
Total: $6,098; Instruction: $3,733; Support Services: $2,108
Enrollment, Drop-out Rates and Diploma Recipients by Race/Ethnicity

Category	Total	White	Black	Asian	AIAN	Hisp.
Enrollment (%)	100.0	95.5	4.3	0.1	0.1	0.0
Drop-out Rate (%)	1.8	1.7	7.1	0.0	n/a	n/a
H.S. Diplomas (#)	120	118	2	0	0	0

Mcguffey SD

PO Box 431 • Claysville, PA 15323-0431
(724) 663-7745
Grade Span: KG-12; **Agency Type:** 1
Schools: 4
2 Primary; 1 Middle; 1 High; 0 Other Level
4 Regular; 0 Special Education; 0 Vocational; 0 Alternative
0 Magnet; 0 Charter; 2 Title I Eligible; 0 School-wide Title I
Students: 2,432 (n/a% male; n/a% female)
Individual Education Program: 308 (12.7%);
English Language Learner: n/a; Migrant: 0 (0.0%)
Eligible for Free Lunch Program: 551 (22.7%)
Eligible for Reduced-Price Lunch Program: 132 (5.4%)
Teachers: 153.0 (15.9 to 1)
Librarians/Media Specialists: 3.0 (810.7 to 1)
Guidance Counselors: 5.0 (486.4 to 1)
Current Spending: ($ per student per year):
Total: $7,614; Instruction: $4,893; Support Services: $2,413
Enrollment, Drop-out Rates and Diploma Recipients by Race/Ethnicity

Category	Total	White	Black	Asian	AIAN	Hisp.
Enrollment (%)	100.0	99.2	0.3	0.3	0.0	0.1
Drop-out Rate (%)	1.8	1.9	0.0	n/a	n/a	0.0
H.S. Diplomas (#)	182	181	1	0	0	0

Peters Township SD

631 E Mcmurray Rd • Mcmurray, PA 15317-3430
(724) 941-6251
Grade Span: KG-12; **Agency Type:** 1
Schools: 5
2 Primary; 2 Middle; 1 High; 0 Other Level
5 Regular; 0 Special Education; 0 Vocational; 0 Alternative
0 Magnet; 0 Charter; 2 Title I Eligible; 0 School-wide Title I
Students: 3,769 (n/a% male; n/a% female)
Individual Education Program: 266 (7.1%);
English Language Learner: n/a; Migrant: 3 (0.1%)
Eligible for Free Lunch Program: 55 (1.5%)
Eligible for Reduced-Price Lunch Program: 22 (0.6%)

Teachers: 208.9 (18.0 to 1)
Librarians/Media Specialists: 5.0 (753.8 to 1)
Guidance Counselors: 8.0 (471.1 to 1)
Current Spending: ($ per student per year):
Total: $6,672; Instruction: $4,170; Support Services: $2,310
Enrollment, Drop-out Rates and Diploma Recipients by Race/Ethnicity

Category	Total	White	Black	Asian	AIAN	Hisp.
Enrollment (%)	100.0	97.5	0.7	1.0	0.1	0.7
Drop-out Rate (%)	0.5	0.5	0.0	0.0	0.0	0.0
H.S. Diplomas (#)	270	262	2	4	1	1

Ringgold SD
400 Main St • New Eagle, PA 15067-1108
(724) 258-9329
Grade Span: KG-12; **Agency Type:** 1
Schools: 6
3 Primary; 2 Middle; 1 High; 0 Other Level
6 Regular; 0 Special Education; 0 Vocational; 0 Alternative
0 Magnet; 0 Charter; 3 Title I Eligible; 0 School-wide Title I
Students: 3,763 (n/a% male; n/a% female)
Individual Education Program: 476 (12.6%);
English Language Learner: n/a; Migrant: 0 (0.0%)
Eligible for Free Lunch Program: 897 (23.8%)
Eligible for Reduced-Price Lunch Program: 273 (7.3%)
Teachers: 234.5 (16.0 to 1)
Librarians/Media Specialists: 5.0 (752.6 to 1)
Guidance Counselors: 7.0 (537.6 to 1)
Current Spending: ($ per student per year):
Total: $6,877; Instruction: $4,531; Support Services: $2,085
Enrollment, Drop-out Rates and Diploma Recipients by Race/Ethnicity

Category	Total	White	Black	Asian	AIAN	Hisp.
Enrollment (%)	100.0	90.2	8.6	0.5	0.2	0.7
Drop-out Rate (%)	2.4	2.3	3.0	50.0	0.0	0.0
H.S. Diplomas (#)	270	254	14	2	0	0

Trinity Area SD
231 Park Ave • Washington, PA 15301-5713
(724) 225-9880 • http://www.trinitypride.k12.pa.us
Grade Span: KG-12; **Agency Type:** 1
Schools: 6
4 Primary; 1 Middle; 1 High; 0 Other Level
6 Regular; 0 Special Education; 0 Vocational; 0 Alternative
0 Magnet; 0 Charter; 4 Title I Eligible; 0 School-wide Title I
Students: 3,782 (n/a% male; n/a% female)
Individual Education Program: 543 (14.4%);
English Language Learner: n/a; Migrant: 0 (0.0%)
Eligible for Free Lunch Program: 514 (13.6%)
Eligible for Reduced-Price Lunch Program: 191 (5.1%)
Teachers: 240.0 (15.8 to 1)
Librarians/Media Specialists: 6.0 (630.3 to 1)
Guidance Counselors: 7.0 (540.3 to 1)
Current Spending: ($ per student per year):
Total: $7,564; Instruction: $4,788; Support Services: $2,443
Enrollment, Drop-out Rates and Diploma Recipients by Race/Ethnicity

Category	Total	White	Black	Asian	AIAN	Hisp.
Enrollment (%)	100.0	95.4	3.6	0.3	0.1	0.5
Drop-out Rate (%)	2.1	2.1	4.0	0.0	n/a	n/a
H.S. Diplomas (#)	282	276	5	0	0	1

Washington SD
201 Allison Ave • Washington, PA 15301-4272
(724) 223-5010 • http://www.washington.k12.pa.us
Grade Span: KG-12; **Agency Type:** 1
Schools: 3
1 Primary; 1 Middle; 1 High; 0 Other Level
3 Regular; 0 Special Education; 0 Vocational; 0 Alternative
0 Magnet; 0 Charter; 3 Title I Eligible; 1 School-wide Title I
Students: 2,108 (n/a% male; n/a% female)
Individual Education Program: 381 (18.1%);
English Language Learner: n/a; Migrant: 0 (0.0%)
Eligible for Free Lunch Program: 220 (10.4%)
Eligible for Reduced-Price Lunch Program: 60 (2.8%)
Teachers: 152.0 (13.9 to 1)
Librarians/Media Specialists: 2.0 (1,054.0 to 1)
Guidance Counselors: 5.0 (421.6 to 1)
Current Spending: ($ per student per year):
Total: $7,160; Instruction: $4,603; Support Services: $2,201
Enrollment, Drop-out Rates and Diploma Recipients by Race/Ethnicity

Category	Total	White	Black	Asian	AIAN	Hisp.
Enrollment (%)	100.0	67.7	31.4	0.3	0.0	0.6
Drop-out Rate (%)	4.2	3.7	6.3	0.0	n/a	0.0
H.S. Diplomas (#)	127	102	25	0	0	0

Wayne County

Wallenpaupack Area SD
Hc 6 Box 6075 • Hawley, PA 18428-9007
(570) 226-4557 • http://www.paupack.ptd.net
Grade Span: KG-12; **Agency Type:** 1
Schools: 5
3 Primary; 1 Middle; 1 High; 0 Other Level
5 Regular; 0 Special Education; 0 Vocational; 0 Alternative
0 Magnet; 0 Charter; 5 Title I Eligible; 0 School-wide Title I
Students: 3,866 (n/a% male; n/a% female)
Individual Education Program: 626 (16.2%);
English Language Learner: n/a; Migrant: 0 (0.0%)
Eligible for Free Lunch Program: 901 (23.3%)
Eligible for Reduced-Price Lunch Program: 456 (11.8%)
Teachers: 274.5 (14.1 to 1)
Librarians/Media Specialists: 5.0 (773.2 to 1)
Guidance Counselors: 9.0 (429.6 to 1)
Current Spending: ($ per student per year):
Total: $8,068; Instruction: $5,192; Support Services: $2,522
Enrollment, Drop-out Rates and Diploma Recipients by Race/Ethnicity

Category	Total	White	Black	Asian	AIAN	Hisp.
Enrollment (%)	100.0	92.6	3.3	0.6	0.1	3.5
Drop-out Rate (%)	3.0	3.1	0.0	0.0	n/a	2.8
H.S. Diplomas (#)	266	240	8	1	0	17

Wayne Highlands SD
474 Grove St • Honesdale, PA 18431-1099
(570) 253-4661 • http://ns.neiu.k12.pa.us/WWW/WH/index.htm
Grade Span: KG-12; **Agency Type:** 1
Schools: 6
4 Primary; 1 Middle; 1 High; 0 Other Level
6 Regular; 0 Special Education; 0 Vocational; 0 Alternative
0 Magnet; 0 Charter; 6 Title I Eligible; 0 School-wide Title I
Students: 3,313 (n/a% male; n/a% female)
Individual Education Program: 470 (14.2%);
English Language Learner: n/a; Migrant: 2 (0.1%)
Eligible for Free Lunch Program: 732 (22.1%)
Eligible for Reduced-Price Lunch Program: 354 (10.7%)
Teachers: 212.8 (15.6 to 1)
Librarians/Media Specialists: 3.0 (1,104.3 to 1)
Guidance Counselors: 9.0 (368.1 to 1)
Current Spending: ($ per student per year):
Total: $7,759; Instruction: $4,874; Support Services: $2,580
Enrollment, Drop-out Rates and Diploma Recipients by Race/Ethnicity

Category	Total	White	Black	Asian	AIAN	Hisp.
Enrollment (%)	100.0	97.7	0.6	0.3	0.1	1.3
Drop-out Rate (%)	1.9	2.0	0.0	0.0	n/a	0.0
H.S. Diplomas (#)	206	197	2	5	0	2

Western Wayne SD
PO Box 500 • South Canaan, PA 18459-0158
(570) 937-4270 • http://westernwayne.org
Grade Span: PK-12; **Agency Type:** 1
Schools: 5
3 Primary; 1 Middle; 1 High; 0 Other Level
5 Regular; 0 Special Education; 0 Vocational; 0 Alternative
0 Magnet; 0 Charter; 5 Title I Eligible; 0 School-wide Title I
Students: 2,526 (n/a% male; n/a% female)
Individual Education Program: 326 (12.9%);
English Language Learner: n/a; Migrant: 0 (0.0%)
Eligible for Free Lunch Program: 661 (26.2%)
Eligible for Reduced-Price Lunch Program: 315 (12.5%)
Teachers: 157.3 (16.1 to 1)
Librarians/Media Specialists: 3.0 (842.0 to 1)
Guidance Counselors: 8.0 (315.8 to 1)
Current Spending: ($ per student per year):
Total: $8,241; Instruction: $5,012; Support Services: $2,895
Enrollment, Drop-out Rates and Diploma Recipients by Race/Ethnicity

Category	Total	White	Black	Asian	AIAN	Hisp.
Enrollment (%)	100.0	95.7	2.3	0.5	0.0	1.6
Drop-out Rate (%)	4.5	4.7	0.0	0.0	n/a	0.0
H.S. Diplomas (#)	150	146	2	0	0	2

Westmoreland County

Belle Vernon Area SD
270 Crest Ave • Belle Vernon, PA 15012-9625
(724) 929-5262 • http://wiu.k12.pa.us/bva/bva.html
Grade Span: KG-12; **Agency Type:** 1
Schools: 5
2 Primary; 2 Middle; 1 High; 0 Other Level
5 Regular; 0 Special Education; 0 Vocational; 0 Alternative
0 Magnet; 0 Charter; 4 Title I Eligible; 0 School-wide Title I
Students: 2,969 (n/a% male; n/a% female)

Individual Education Program: 376 (12.7%);
English Language Learner: n/a; Migrant: 0 (0.0%)
Eligible for Free Lunch Program: 521 (17.5%)
Eligible for Reduced-Price Lunch Program: 240 (8.1%)
Teachers: 154.0 (19.3 to 1)
Librarians/Media Specialists: 5.0 (593.8 to 1)
Guidance Counselors: 6.0 (494.8 to 1)
Current Spending: ($ per student per year):
Total: $6,252; Instruction: $3,823; Support Services: $2,130
Enrollment, Drop-out Rates and Diploma Recipients by Race/Ethnicity

Category	Total	White	Black	Asian	AIAN	Hisp.
Enrollment (%)	100.0	96.0	3.3	0.2	0.2	0.3
Drop-out Rate (%)	2.9	3.0	0.0	0.0	0.0	0.0
H.S. Diplomas (#)	190	185	3	1	0	1

Burrell SD
1021 Puckety Church Rd • Lower Burrell, PA 15068-9706
(724) 334-1406 • http://wiu.k12.pa.us/burrell/
Grade Span: KG-12; **Agency Type:** 1
Schools: 4
2 Primary; 1 Middle; 1 High; 0 Other Level
4 Regular; 0 Special Education; 0 Vocational; 0 Alternative
0 Magnet; 0 Charter; 2 Title I Eligible; 0 School-wide Title I
Students: 2,257 (n/a% male; n/a% female)
Individual Education Program: 266 (11.8%);
English Language Learner: n/a; Migrant: 0 (0.0%)
Eligible for Free Lunch Program: 296 (13.1%)
Eligible for Reduced-Price Lunch Program: 108 (4.8%)
Teachers: 126.0 (17.9 to 1)
Librarians/Media Specialists: 3.0 (752.3 to 1)
Guidance Counselors: 4.0 (564.3 to 1)
Current Spending: ($ per student per year):
Total: $6,825; Instruction: $4,149; Support Services: $2,424
Enrollment, Drop-out Rates and Diploma Recipients by Race/Ethnicity

Category	Total	White	Black	Asian	AIAN	Hisp.
Enrollment (%)	100.0	97.5	1.9	0.3	0.3	0.1
Drop-out Rate (%)	3.6	3.5	20.0	0.0	n/a	n/a
H.S. Diplomas (#)	164	163	1	0	0	0

Derry Area SD
982 N Chestnut St Ext • Derry, PA 15627-7600
(724) 694-1401 • http://wiu.k12.pa.us/derry/
Grade Span: PK-12; **Agency Type:** 1
Schools: 6
4 Primary; 1 Middle; 1 High; 0 Other Level
6 Regular; 0 Special Education; 0 Vocational; 0 Alternative
0 Magnet; 0 Charter; 5 Title I Eligible; 4 School-wide Title I
Students: 2,838 (n/a% male; n/a% female)
Individual Education Program: 248 (8.7%);
English Language Learner: n/a; Migrant: 0 (0.0%)
Eligible for Free Lunch Program: 670 (23.6%)
Eligible for Reduced-Price Lunch Program: 304 (10.7%)
Teachers: 172.0 (16.5 to 1)
Librarians/Media Specialists: 3.0 (946.0 to 1)
Guidance Counselors: 6.0 (473.0 to 1)
Current Spending: ($ per student per year):
Total: $6,739; Instruction: $4,099; Support Services: $2,344
Enrollment, Drop-out Rates and Diploma Recipients by Race/Ethnicity

Category	Total	White	Black	Asian	AIAN	Hisp.
Enrollment (%)	100.0	97.5	1.5	0.1	0.4	0.5
Drop-out Rate (%)	2.5	2.5	0.0	0.0	6.3	0.0
H.S. Diplomas (#)	179	178	1	0	0	0

Franklin Regional SD
3210 School Rd • Murrysville, PA 15668-1553
(724) 327-5456 • http://www.franklinregional.k12.pa.us
Grade Span: KG-12; **Agency Type:** 1
Schools: 5
3 Primary; 1 Middle; 1 High; 0 Other Level
5 Regular; 0 Special Education; 0 Vocational; 0 Alternative
0 Magnet; 0 Charter; 3 Title I Eligible; 0 School-wide Title I
Students: 3,817 (n/a% male; n/a% female)
Individual Education Program: 391 (10.2%);
English Language Learner: n/a; Migrant: 0 (0.0%)
Eligible for Free Lunch Program: 128 (3.4%)
Eligible for Reduced-Price Lunch Program: 44 (1.2%)
Teachers: 226.7 (16.8 to 1)
Librarians/Media Specialists: 5.0 (763.4 to 1)
Guidance Counselors: 10.0 (381.7 to 1)
Current Spending: ($ per student per year):
Total: $7,323; Instruction: $4,678; Support Services: $2,439
Enrollment, Drop-out Rates and Diploma Recipients by Race/Ethnicity

Category	Total	White	Black	Asian	AIAN	Hisp.
Enrollment (%)	100.0	95.7	0.5	3.0	0.4	0.3
Drop-out Rate (%)	1.0	1.0	0.0	0.0	0.0	0.0
H.S. Diplomas (#)	281	268	1	9	0	3

Greater Latrobe SD
410 Main St • Latrobe, PA 15650-1598
(724) 539-4200 • http://wiu.k12.pa.us/latrobe
Grade Span: KG-12; **Agency Type:** 1
Schools: 5
3 Primary; 1 Middle; 1 High; 0 Other Level
5 Regular; 0 Special Education; 0 Vocational; 0 Alternative
0 Magnet; 0 Charter; 3 Title I Eligible; 0 School-wide Title I
Students: 4,335 (n/a% male; n/a% female)
Individual Education Program: 410 (9.5%);
English Language Learner: n/a; Migrant: 0 (0.0%)
Eligible for Free Lunch Program: 536 (12.4%)
Eligible for Reduced-Price Lunch Program: 317 (7.3%)
Teachers: 242.8 (17.9 to 1)
Librarians/Media Specialists: 5.0 (867.0 to 1)
Guidance Counselors: 9.0 (481.7 to 1)
Current Spending: ($ per student per year):
Total: $6,030; Instruction: $3,811; Support Services: $1,943
Enrollment, Drop-out Rates and Diploma Recipients by Race/Ethnicity

Category	Total	White	Black	Asian	AIAN	Hisp.
Enrollment (%)	100.0	97.9	0.4	1.3	0.0	0.4
Drop-out Rate (%)	3.3	3.3	0.0	0.0	n/a	0.0
H.S. Diplomas (#)	284	281	1	2	0	0

Greensburg Salem SD
11 Park St • Greensburg, PA 15601-1839
(724) 832-2901
Grade Span: KG-12; **Agency Type:** 1
Schools: 5
3 Primary; 1 Middle; 1 High; 0 Other Level
5 Regular; 0 Special Education; 0 Vocational; 0 Alternative
0 Magnet; 0 Charter; 3 Title I Eligible; 0 School-wide Title I
Students: 3,583 (n/a% male; n/a% female)
Individual Education Program: 402 (11.2%);
English Language Learner: n/a; Migrant: 0 (0.0%)
Eligible for Free Lunch Program: 900 (25.1%)
Eligible for Reduced-Price Lunch Program: 284 (7.9%)
Teachers: 193.5 (18.5 to 1)
Librarians/Media Specialists: 4.0 (895.8 to 1)
Guidance Counselors: 7.0 (511.9 to 1)
Current Spending: ($ per student per year):
Total: $6,450; Instruction: $4,058; Support Services: $2,104
Enrollment, Drop-out Rates and Diploma Recipients by Race/Ethnicity

Category	Total	White	Black	Asian	AIAN	Hisp.
Enrollment (%)	100.0	92.0	7.0	0.6	0.1	0.3
Drop-out Rate (%)	2.0	1.9	4.2	0.0	n/a	0.0
H.S. Diplomas (#)	250	239	10	1	0	0

Hempfield Area SD
RR 6 Box 76 • Greensburg, PA 15601-9315
(724) 834-2590 • http://wiu.k12.pa.us/hempfield_area
Grade Span: KG-12; **Agency Type:** 1
Schools: 12
7 Primary; 3 Middle; 2 High; 0 Other Level
12 Regular; 0 Special Education; 0 Vocational; 0 Alternative
0 Magnet; 0 Charter; 7 Title I Eligible; 0 School-wide Title I
Students: 6,602 (n/a% male; n/a% female)
Individual Education Program: 699 (10.6%);
English Language Learner: n/a; Migrant: 0 (0.0%)
Eligible for Free Lunch Program: 652 (9.9%)
Eligible for Reduced-Price Lunch Program: 317 (4.8%)
Teachers: 418.5 (15.8 to 1)
Librarians/Media Specialists: 11.0 (600.2 to 1)
Guidance Counselors: 18.0 (366.8 to 1)
Current Spending: ($ per student per year):
Total: $7,501; Instruction: $4,980; Support Services: $2,270
Enrollment, Drop-out Rates and Diploma Recipients by Race/Ethnicity

Category	Total	White	Black	Asian	AIAN	Hisp.
Enrollment (%)	100.0	97.5	0.8	1.2	0.2	0.3
Drop-out Rate (%)	2.1	2.1	5.9	0.0	9.1	0.0
H.S. Diplomas (#)	491	480	5	5	1	0

Jeannette City SD
Park St Central Admin Bldg • Jeannette, PA 15644-0418
(724) 523-5497
Grade Span: KG-12; **Agency Type:** 1
Schools: 2
1 Primary; 0 Middle; 1 High; 0 Other Level
2 Regular; 0 Special Education; 0 Vocational; 0 Alternative

0 Magnet; 0 Charter; 1 Title I Eligible; 1 School-wide Title I
Students: 1,508 (n/a% male; n/a% female)
Individual Education Program: 231 (15.3%);
English Language Learner: n/a; Migrant: 0 (0.0%)
Eligible for Free Lunch Program: 569 (37.7%)
Eligible for Reduced-Price Lunch Program: 188 (12.5%)
Teachers: 85.0 (17.7 to 1)
Librarians/Media Specialists: 2.0 (754.0 to 1)
Guidance Counselors: 3.0 (502.7 to 1)
Current Spending: ($ per student per year):
Total: $6,036; Instruction: $3,616; Support Services: $2,025
Enrollment, Drop-out Rates and Diploma Recipients by Race/Ethnicity

Category	Total	White	Black	Asian	AIAN	Hisp.
Enrollment (%)	100.0	83.0	16.7	0.2	0.0	0.1
Drop-out Rate (%)	2.8	2.6	4.9	n/a	n/a	n/a
H.S. Diplomas (#)	92	86	6	0	0	0

Kiski Area SD

200 Poplar St • Vandergrift, PA 15690-1466
(724) 845-2022 • http://www.kiskiarea.com
Grade Span: KG-12; **Agency Type:** 1
Schools: 9
7 Primary; 1 Middle; 1 High; 0 Other Level
9 Regular; 0 Special Education; 0 Vocational; 0 Alternative
0 Magnet; 0 Charter; 6 Title I Eligible; 2 School-wide Title I
Students: 4,477 (n/a% male; n/a% female)
Individual Education Program: 608 (13.6%);
English Language Learner: n/a; Migrant: 0 (0.0%)
Eligible for Free Lunch Program: 752 (16.8%)
Eligible for Reduced-Price Lunch Program: 323 (7.2%)
Teachers: 234.0 (19.1 to 1)
Librarians/Media Specialists: 3.0 (1,492.3 to 1)
Guidance Counselors: 6.0 (746.2 to 1)
Current Spending: ($ per student per year):
Total: $6,674; Instruction: $3,839; Support Services: $2,556
Enrollment, Drop-out Rates and Diploma Recipients by Race/Ethnicity

Category	Total	White	Black	Asian	AIAN	Hisp.
Enrollment (%)	100.0	95.4	4.1	0.3	0.0	0.2
Drop-out Rate (%)	2.8	2.9	0.0	0.0	n/a	n/a
H.S. Diplomas (#)	340	323	14	3	0	0

Ligonier Valley SD

339 W Main St • Ligonier, PA 15658-1248
(724) 238-5696 • http://wiu.k12.pa.us/ligonier
Grade Span: KG-12; **Agency Type:** 1
Schools: 5
2 Primary; 1 Middle; 2 High; 0 Other Level
5 Regular; 0 Special Education; 0 Vocational; 0 Alternative
0 Magnet; 0 Charter; 2 Title I Eligible; 1 School-wide Title I
Students: 2,184 (n/a% male; n/a% female)
Individual Education Program: 301 (13.8%);
English Language Learner: n/a; Migrant: 0 (0.0%)
Eligible for Free Lunch Program: 471 (21.6%)
Eligible for Reduced-Price Lunch Program: 193 (8.8%)
Teachers: 124.5 (17.5 to 1)
Librarians/Media Specialists: 5.0 (436.8 to 1)
Guidance Counselors: 5.0 (436.8 to 1)
Current Spending: ($ per student per year):
Total: $7,527; Instruction: $4,296; Support Services: $2,851
Enrollment, Drop-out Rates and Diploma Recipients by Race/Ethnicity

Category	Total	White	Black	Asian	AIAN	Hisp.
Enrollment (%)	100.0	99.1	0.7	0.0	0.0	0.2
Drop-out Rate (%)	2.7	2.8	0.0	0.0	n/a	0.0
H.S. Diplomas (#)	147	146	0	1	0	0

Mount Pleasant Area SD

RR 4 Box 2222 • Mount Pleasant, PA 15666-9041
(724) 547-5706 • http://www.mpasd.net/
Grade Span: KG-12; **Agency Type:** 1
Schools: 5
4 Primary; 0 Middle; 1 High; 0 Other Level
5 Regular; 0 Special Education; 0 Vocational; 0 Alternative
0 Magnet; 0 Charter; 5 Title I Eligible; 0 School-wide Title I
Students: 2,587 (n/a% male; n/a% female)
Individual Education Program: 394 (15.2%);
English Language Learner: n/a; Migrant: 5 (0.2%)
Eligible for Free Lunch Program: 556 (21.5%)
Eligible for Reduced-Price Lunch Program: 203 (7.8%)
Teachers: 145.0 (17.8 to 1)
Librarians/Media Specialists: 3.0 (862.3 to 1)
Guidance Counselors: 7.0 (369.6 to 1)
Current Spending: ($ per student per year):
Total: $6,618; Instruction: $4,048; Support Services: $2,306
Enrollment, Drop-out Rates and Diploma Recipients by Race/Ethnicity

Category	Total	White	Black	Asian	AIAN	Hisp.
Enrollment (%)	100.0	97.5	1.7	0.3	0.0	0.4
Drop-out Rate (%)	3.8	3.8	0.0	0.0	0.0	n/a
H.S. Diplomas (#)	186	184	2	0	0	0

New Kensington-Arnold SD

701 Stevenson Blvd • New Kensington, PA 15068-5372
(724) 335-8581 • http://nkasd.wiu.k12.pa.us
Grade Span: PK-12; **Agency Type:** 1
Schools: 7
4 Primary; 2 Middle; 1 High; 0 Other Level
7 Regular; 0 Special Education; 0 Vocational; 0 Alternative
0 Magnet; 0 Charter; 6 Title I Eligible; 1 School-wide Title I
Students: 2,571 (n/a% male; n/a% female)
Individual Education Program: 453 (17.6%);
English Language Learner: n/a; Migrant: 0 (0.0%)
Eligible for Free Lunch Program: 986 (38.4%)
Eligible for Reduced-Price Lunch Program: 235 (9.1%)
Teachers: 153.0 (16.8 to 1)
Librarians/Media Specialists: 3.0 (857.0 to 1)
Guidance Counselors: 4.0 (642.8 to 1)
Current Spending: ($ per student per year):
Total: $6,557; Instruction: $4,178; Support Services: $2,062
Enrollment, Drop-out Rates and Diploma Recipients by Race/Ethnicity

Category	Total	White	Black	Asian	AIAN	Hisp.
Enrollment (%)	100.0	70.8	27.4	0.3	0.6	0.9
Drop-out Rate (%)	7.0	6.4	9.9	0.0	0.0	0.0
H.S. Diplomas (#)	143	113	29	0	0	1

Norwin SD

281 Mcmahon Dr • North Huntingdon, PA 15642-2403
(724) 863-5052 • http://wiu.k12.pa.us/norwin
Grade Span: KG-12; **Agency Type:** 1
Schools: 10
5 Primary; 2 Middle; 1 High; 0 Other Level
8 Regular; 0 Special Education; 0 Vocational; 0 Alternative
0 Magnet; 0 Charter; 5 Title I Eligible; 0 School-wide Title I
Students: 5,172 (n/a% male; n/a% female)
Individual Education Program: 594 (11.5%);
English Language Learner: n/a; Migrant: 0 (0.0%)
Eligible for Free Lunch Program: 540 (10.4%)
Eligible for Reduced-Price Lunch Program: 321 (6.2%)
Teachers: 277.5 (18.6 to 1)
Librarians/Media Specialists: 5.0 (1,034.4 to 1)
Guidance Counselors: 11.0 (470.2 to 1)
Current Spending: ($ per student per year):
Total: $6,490; Instruction: $4,041; Support Services: $2,119
Enrollment, Drop-out Rates and Diploma Recipients by Race/Ethnicity

Category	Total	White	Black	Asian	AIAN	Hisp.
Enrollment (%)	100.0	97.8	1.0	1.0	0.1	0.1
Drop-out Rate (%)	1.5	1.5	0.0	0.0	0.0	0.0
H.S. Diplomas (#)	373	370	3	0	0	0

Penn-Trafford SD

PO Box 530 • Harrison City, PA 15636-0530
(724) 744-4496 • http://penntrafford.org
Grade Span: KG-12; **Agency Type:** 1
Schools: 8
5 Primary; 2 Middle; 1 High; 0 Other Level
8 Regular; 0 Special Education; 0 Vocational; 0 Alternative
0 Magnet; 0 Charter; 4 Title I Eligible; 0 School-wide Title I
Students: 4,805 (n/a% male; n/a% female)
Individual Education Program: 493 (10.3%);
English Language Learner: n/a; Migrant: 0 (0.0%)
Eligible for Free Lunch Program: 280 (5.8%)
Eligible for Reduced-Price Lunch Program: 161 (3.4%)
Teachers: 246.5 (19.5 to 1)
Librarians/Media Specialists: 4.0 (1,201.3 to 1)
Guidance Counselors: 6.0 (800.8 to 1)
Current Spending: ($ per student per year):
Total: $5,743; Instruction: $3,626; Support Services: $1,897
Enrollment, Drop-out Rates and Diploma Recipients by Race/Ethnicity

Category	Total	White	Black	Asian	AIAN	Hisp.
Enrollment (%)	100.0	98.2	0.9	0.4	0.2	0.2
Drop-out Rate (%)	0.6	0.6	0.0	0.0	0.0	0.0
H.S. Diplomas (#)	355	348	2	4	1	0

Southmoreland SD

609 Parker Ave • Scottdale, PA 15683-1026
(724) 887-2000 • http://www.southmoreland.net/
Grade Span: KG-12; **Agency Type:** 1
Schools: 5
3 Primary; 1 Middle; 1 High; 0 Other Level
5 Regular; 0 Special Education; 0 Vocational; 0 Alternative

0 Magnet; 0 Charter; 4 Title I Eligible; 0 School-wide Title I
Students: 2,349 (n/a% male; n/a% female)
Individual Education Program: 424 (18.1%);
English Language Learner: n/a; Migrant: 0 (0.0%)
Eligible for Free Lunch Program: 610 (26.0%)
Eligible for Reduced-Price Lunch Program: 233 (9.9%)
Teachers: 138.0 (17.0 to 1)
Librarians/Media Specialists: 3.0 (783.0 to 1)
Guidance Counselors: 8.0 (293.6 to 1)
Current Spending: ($ per student per year):
Total: $7,052; Instruction: $4,539; Support Services: $2,173
Enrollment, Drop-out Rates and Diploma Recipients by Race/Ethnicity

Category	Total	White	Black	Asian	AIAN	Hisp.
Enrollment (%)	100.0	97.7	1.3	0.4	0.1	0.6
Drop-out Rate (%)	1.7	1.8	0.0	0.0	0.0	0.0
H.S. Diplomas (#)	153	150	3	0	0	0

Yough SD
99 Lowber Rd • Herminie, PA 15637-1219
(724) 446-7272 • http://www.yough.net
Grade Span: KG-12; **Agency Type:** 1
Schools: 5
3 Primary; 1 Middle; 1 High; 0 Other Level
5 Regular; 0 Special Education; 0 Vocational; 0 Alternative
0 Magnet; 0 Charter; 4 Title I Eligible; 0 School-wide Title I
Students: 2,609 (n/a% male; n/a% female)
Individual Education Program: 309 (11.8%);
English Language Learner: n/a; Migrant: 0 (0.0%)
Eligible for Free Lunch Program: 583 (22.3%)
Eligible for Reduced-Price Lunch Program: 228 (8.7%)
Teachers: 152.0 (17.2 to 1)
Librarians/Media Specialists: 5.0 (521.8 to 1)
Guidance Counselors: 6.0 (434.8 to 1)
Current Spending: ($ per student per year):
Total: $6,592; Instruction: $4,393; Support Services: $1,919
Enrollment, Drop-out Rates and Diploma Recipients by Race/Ethnicity

Category	Total	White	Black	Asian	AIAN	Hisp.
Enrollment (%)	100.0	97.9	1.8	0.3	0.0	0.0
Drop-out Rate (%)	1.7	1.7	0.0	n/a	0.0	n/a
H.S. Diplomas (#)	157	157	0	0	0	0

Wyoming County

Tunkhannock Area SD
41 Philadelphia Ave • Tunkhannock, PA 18657-1602
(570) 836-3111
Grade Span: KG-12; **Agency Type:** 1
Schools: 6
4 Primary; 1 Middle; 1 High; 0 Other Level
6 Regular; 0 Special Education; 0 Vocational; 0 Alternative
0 Magnet; 0 Charter; 5 Title I Eligible; 0 School-wide Title I
Students: 3,191 (n/a% male; n/a% female)
Individual Education Program: 360 (11.3%);
English Language Learner: n/a; Migrant: 15 (0.5%)
Eligible for Free Lunch Program: 692 (21.7%)
Eligible for Reduced-Price Lunch Program: 314 (9.8%)
Teachers: 223.3 (14.3 to 1)
Librarians/Media Specialists: 4.0 (797.8 to 1)
Guidance Counselors: 7.0 (455.9 to 1)
Current Spending: ($ per student per year):
Total: $7,412; Instruction: $4,651; Support Services: $2,444
Enrollment, Drop-out Rates and Diploma Recipients by Race/Ethnicity

Category	Total	White	Black	Asian	AIAN	Hisp.
Enrollment (%)	100.0	98.3	1.1	0.4	0.0	0.2
Drop-out Rate (%)	1.8	1.8	0.0	n/a	n/a	0.0
H.S. Diplomas (#)	241	237	0	1	0	3

York County

Central York SD
775 Marion Rd • York, PA 17402-1554
(717) 846-6789 • http://www.cysd.k12.pa.us
Grade Span: KG-12; **Agency Type:** 1
Schools: 7
5 Primary; 1 Middle; 1 High; 0 Other Level
7 Regular; 0 Special Education; 0 Vocational; 0 Alternative
0 Magnet; 0 Charter; 4 Title I Eligible; 0 School-wide Title I
Students: 4,540 (n/a% male; n/a% female)
Individual Education Program: 560 (12.3%);
English Language Learner: n/a; Migrant: 1 (<0.1%)
Eligible for Free Lunch Program: 437 (9.6%)
Eligible for Reduced-Price Lunch Program: 209 (4.6%)
Teachers: 268.2 (16.9 to 1)
Librarians/Media Specialists: 5.0 (908.0 to 1)
Guidance Counselors: 12.7 (357.5 to 1)
Current Spending: ($ per student per year):
Total: $6,183; Instruction: $3,703; Support Services: $2,164
Enrollment, Drop-out Rates and Diploma Recipients by Race/Ethnicity

Category	Total	White	Black	Asian	AIAN	Hisp.
Enrollment (%)	100.0	85.8	7.2	3.1	0.3	3.5
Drop-out Rate (%)	1.0	0.8	1.8	4.7	0.0	3.2
H.S. Diplomas (#)	264	241	11	9	1	2

Dallastown Area SD
700 New School Ln • Dallastown, PA 17313-9242
(717) 244-4021 • http://www.dallastown.k12.pa.us
Grade Span: KG-12; **Agency Type:** 1
Schools: 7
5 Primary; 1 Middle; 1 High; 0 Other Level
7 Regular; 0 Special Education; 0 Vocational; 0 Alternative
0 Magnet; 0 Charter; 5 Title I Eligible; 0 School-wide Title I
Students: 5,177 (n/a% male; n/a% female)
Individual Education Program: 597 (11.5%);
English Language Learner: n/a; Migrant: 4 (0.1%)
Eligible for Free Lunch Program: 294 (5.7%)
Eligible for Reduced-Price Lunch Program: 193 (3.7%)
Teachers: 331.0 (15.6 to 1)
Librarians/Media Specialists: 6.0 (862.8 to 1)
Guidance Counselors: 13.0 (398.2 to 1)
Current Spending: ($ per student per year):
Total: $7,261; Instruction: $4,913; Support Services: $2,048
Enrollment, Drop-out Rates and Diploma Recipients by Race/Ethnicity

Category	Total	White	Black	Asian	AIAN	Hisp.
Enrollment (%)	100.0	94.1	2.2	1.8	0.1	1.8
Drop-out Rate (%)	2.1	2.1	0.0	0.0	0.0	4.5
H.S. Diplomas (#)	382	365	8	8	0	1

Dover Area SD
2 School Ln • Dover, PA 17315-1498
(717) 292-3671 • http://www.dover.k12.pa.us
Grade Span: KG-12; **Agency Type:** 1
Schools: 7
4 Primary; 2 Middle; 1 High; 0 Other Level
7 Regular; 0 Special Education; 0 Vocational; 0 Alternative
0 Magnet; 0 Charter; 4 Title I Eligible; 0 School-wide Title I
Students: 3,718 (n/a% male; n/a% female)
Individual Education Program: 550 (14.8%);
English Language Learner: n/a; Migrant: 0 (0.0%)
Eligible for Free Lunch Program: 295 (7.9%)
Eligible for Reduced-Price Lunch Program: 270 (7.3%)
Teachers: 218.2 (17.0 to 1)
Librarians/Media Specialists: 4.0 (929.5 to 1)
Guidance Counselors: 10.0 (371.8 to 1)
Current Spending: ($ per student per year):
Total: $6,290; Instruction: $3,813; Support Services: $2,201
Enrollment, Drop-out Rates and Diploma Recipients by Race/Ethnicity

Category	Total	White	Black	Asian	AIAN	Hisp.
Enrollment (%)	100.0	96.0	2.4	0.6	0.0	1.0
Drop-out Rate (%)	3.6	3.7	0.0	0.0	n/a	0.0
H.S. Diplomas (#)	241	235	2	1	0	3

Eastern York SD
PO Box 150 • Wrightsville, PA 17368-0150
(717) 252-1555 • http://www.easternyork.com
Grade Span: KG-12; **Agency Type:** 1
Schools: 5
3 Primary; 1 Middle; 1 High; 0 Other Level
5 Regular; 0 Special Education; 0 Vocational; 0 Alternative
0 Magnet; 0 Charter; 3 Title I Eligible; 0 School-wide Title I
Students: 2,721 (n/a% male; n/a% female)
Individual Education Program: 517 (19.0%);
English Language Learner: n/a; Migrant: 4 (0.1%)
Eligible for Free Lunch Program: 307 (11.3%)
Eligible for Reduced-Price Lunch Program: 180 (6.6%)
Teachers: 195.0 (14.0 to 1)
Librarians/Media Specialists: 3.0 (907.0 to 1)
Guidance Counselors: 7.5 (362.8 to 1)
Current Spending: ($ per student per year):
Total: $6,634; Instruction: $4,259; Support Services: $2,077
Enrollment, Drop-out Rates and Diploma Recipients by Race/Ethnicity

Category	Total	White	Black	Asian	AIAN	Hisp.
Enrollment (%)	100.0	95.5	1.6	0.9	0.0	1.9
Drop-out Rate (%)	3.3	3.5	0.0	0.0	n/a	0.0
H.S. Diplomas (#)	176	171	2	3	0	0

Hanover Public SD
403 Moul Ave • Hanover, PA 17331-1541
(717) 637-9000 • http://www.hpsd.k12.pa.us
Grade Span: KG-12; **Agency Type:** 1
Schools: 5

3 Primary; 1 Middle; 1 High; 0 Other Level
5 Regular; 0 Special Education; 0 Vocational; 0 Alternative
0 Magnet; 0 Charter; 3 Title I Eligible; 0 School-wide Title I
Students: 1,734 (n/a% male; n/a% female)
Individual Education Program: 303 (17.5%);
English Language Learner: n/a; Migrant: 53 (3.1%)
Eligible for Free Lunch Program: 270 (15.6%)
Eligible for Reduced-Price Lunch Program: 127 (7.3%)
Teachers: 114.0 (15.2 to 1)
Librarians/Media Specialists: 3.0 (578.0 to 1)
Guidance Counselors: 4.0 (433.5 to 1)
Current Spending: ($ per student per year):
Total: $7,599; Instruction: $4,841; Support Services: $2,468
Enrollment, Drop-out Rates and Diploma Recipients by Race/Ethnicity

Category	Total	White	Black	Asian	AIAN	Hisp.
Enrollment (%)	100.0	90.8	2.0	2.0	0.1	5.1
Drop-out Rate (%)	3.0	3.2	0.0	0.0	n/a	0.0
H.S. Diplomas (#)	92	88	0	2	0	2

Northeastern York SD

41 Harding St • Manchester, PA 17345-1119
(717) 266-3667 • http://www.nesd.k12.pa.us
Grade Span: KG-12; **Agency Type:** 1
Schools: 7
4 Primary; 2 Middle; 1 High; 0 Other Level
7 Regular; 0 Special Education; 0 Vocational; 0 Alternative
0 Magnet; 0 Charter; 3 Title I Eligible; 0 School-wide Title I
Students: 3,007 (n/a% male; n/a% female)
Individual Education Program: 520 (17.3%);
English Language Learner: n/a; Migrant: 7 (0.2%)
Eligible for Free Lunch Program: 551 (18.3%)
Eligible for Reduced-Price Lunch Program: 339 (11.3%)
Teachers: 190.8 (15.8 to 1)
Librarians/Media Specialists: 6.0 (501.2 to 1)
Guidance Counselors: 8.0 (375.9 to 1)
Current Spending: ($ per student per year):
Total: $6,237; Instruction: $3,779; Support Services: $2,127
Enrollment, Drop-out Rates and Diploma Recipients by Race/Ethnicity

Category	Total	White	Black	Asian	AIAN	Hisp.
Enrollment (%)	100.0	96.9	1.2	0.1	0.1	1.8
Drop-out Rate (%)	2.8	2.9	0.0	0.0	n/a	0.0
H.S. Diplomas (#)	136	133	2	1	0	0

Northern York County SD

149 S Baltimore St • Dillsburg, PA 17019-1035
(717) 432-8691 • http://www.nycsd.k12.pa.us/
Grade Span: KG-12; **Agency Type:** 1
Schools: 6
4 Primary; 1 Middle; 1 High; 0 Other Level
6 Regular; 0 Special Education; 0 Vocational; 0 Alternative
0 Magnet; 0 Charter; 6 Title I Eligible; 0 School-wide Title I
Students: 3,169 (n/a% male; n/a% female)
Individual Education Program: 312 (9.8%);
English Language Learner: n/a; Migrant: 2 (0.1%)
Eligible for Free Lunch Program: 143 (4.5%)
Eligible for Reduced-Price Lunch Program: 103 (3.3%)
Teachers: 208.8 (15.2 to 1)
Librarians/Media Specialists: 4.0 (792.3 to 1)
Guidance Counselors: 7.0 (452.7 to 1)
Current Spending: ($ per student per year):
Total: $6,415; Instruction: $4,071; Support Services: $2,124
Enrollment, Drop-out Rates and Diploma Recipients by Race/Ethnicity

Category	Total	White	Black	Asian	AIAN	Hisp.
Enrollment (%)	100.0	96.6	0.7	1.3	0.3	1.1
Drop-out Rate (%)	3.3	3.3	0.0	8.3	0.0	0.0
H.S. Diplomas (#)	185	180	0	4	1	0

Red Lion Area SD

696 Delta Rd • Red Lion, PA 17356-9185
(717) 244-4518
Grade Span: KG-12; **Agency Type:** 1
Schools: 10
8 Primary; 1 Middle; 1 High; 0 Other Level
10 Regular; 0 Special Education; 0 Vocational; 0 Alternative
0 Magnet; 0 Charter; 7 Title I Eligible; 0 School-wide Title I
Students: 5,444 (n/a% male; n/a% female)
Individual Education Program: 789 (14.5%);
English Language Learner: n/a; Migrant: 0 (0.0%)
Eligible for Free Lunch Program: 438 (8.0%)
Eligible for Reduced-Price Lunch Program: 327 (6.0%)
Teachers: 314.0 (17.3 to 1)
Librarians/Media Specialists: 5.0 (1,088.8 to 1)
Guidance Counselors: 10.0 (544.4 to 1)
Current Spending: ($ per student per year):
Total: $6,034; Instruction: $3,797; Support Services: $1,926

Enrollment, Drop-out Rates and Diploma Recipients by Race/Ethnicity

Category	Total	White	Black	Asian	AIAN	Hisp.
Enrollment (%)	100.0	97.5	0.8	0.9	0.1	0.7
Drop-out Rate (%)	2.7	2.7	0.0	0.0	n/a	0.0
H.S. Diplomas (#)	306	297	1	8	0	0

South Eastern SD

104 E Main St • Fawn Grove, PA 17321-9545
(717) 382-4843 • http://sesd.k12.pa.us
Grade Span: KG-12; **Agency Type:** 1
Schools: 6
3 Primary; 1 Middle; 1 High; 1 Other Level
6 Regular; 0 Special Education; 0 Vocational; 0 Alternative
0 Magnet; 0 Charter; 4 Title I Eligible; 0 School-wide Title I
Students: 3,248 (n/a% male; n/a% female)
Individual Education Program: 479 (14.7%);
English Language Learner: n/a; Migrant: 0 (0.0%)
Eligible for Free Lunch Program: 159 (4.9%)
Eligible for Reduced-Price Lunch Program: 104 (3.2%)
Teachers: 195.2 (16.6 to 1)
Librarians/Media Specialists: 4.0 (812.0 to 1)
Guidance Counselors: 7.0 (464.0 to 1)
Current Spending: ($ per student per year):
Total: $5,612; Instruction: $3,594; Support Services: $1,803
Enrollment, Drop-out Rates and Diploma Recipients by Race/Ethnicity

Category	Total	White	Black	Asian	AIAN	Hisp.
Enrollment (%)	100.0	96.7	1.6	1.1	0.3	0.3
Drop-out Rate (%)	2.4	2.3	20.0	0.0	n/a	0.0
H.S. Diplomas (#)	184	180	2	2	0	0

South Western SD

225 Bowman Rd • Hanover, PA 17331-4213
(717) 632-2500 • http://www.swsd.k12.pa.us
Grade Span: KG-12; **Agency Type:** 1
Schools: 6
4 Primary; 1 Middle; 1 High; 0 Other Level
6 Regular; 0 Special Education; 0 Vocational; 0 Alternative
0 Magnet; 0 Charter; 3 Title I Eligible; 0 School-wide Title I
Students: 3,908 (n/a% male; n/a% female)
Individual Education Program: 422 (10.8%);
English Language Learner: n/a; Migrant: 10 (0.3%)
Eligible for Free Lunch Program: 244 (6.2%)
Eligible for Reduced-Price Lunch Program: 176 (4.5%)
Teachers: 234.1 (16.7 to 1)
Librarians/Media Specialists: 4.4 (888.2 to 1)
Guidance Counselors: 10.0 (390.8 to 1)
Current Spending: ($ per student per year):
Total: $6,282; Instruction: $3,898; Support Services: $2,105
Enrollment, Drop-out Rates and Diploma Recipients by Race/Ethnicity

Category	Total	White	Black	Asian	AIAN	Hisp.
Enrollment (%)	100.0	96.3	1.6	1.2	0.0	0.9
Drop-out Rate (%)	2.5	2.4	12.5	0.0	n/a	0.0
H.S. Diplomas (#)	276	273	2	1	0	0

Southern York County SD

PO Box 128 • Glen Rock, PA 17327-0128
(717) 235-4811 • http://www.syc.k12.pa.us/
Grade Span: KG-12; **Agency Type:** 1
Schools: 5
3 Primary; 1 Middle; 1 High; 0 Other Level
5 Regular; 0 Special Education; 0 Vocational; 0 Alternative
0 Magnet; 0 Charter; 4 Title I Eligible; 0 School-wide Title I
Students: 3,274 (n/a% male; n/a% female)
Individual Education Program: 520 (15.9%);
English Language Learner: n/a; Migrant: 0 (0.0%)
Eligible for Free Lunch Program: 178 (5.4%)
Eligible for Reduced-Price Lunch Program: 64 (2.0%)
Teachers: 207.8 (15.8 to 1)
Librarians/Media Specialists: 5.0 (654.8 to 1)
Guidance Counselors: 8.0 (409.3 to 1)
Current Spending: ($ per student per year):
Total: $6,776; Instruction: $4,378; Support Services: $2,123
Enrollment, Drop-out Rates and Diploma Recipients by Race/Ethnicity

Category	Total	White	Black	Asian	AIAN	Hisp.
Enrollment (%)	100.0	97.6	1.3	0.4	0.1	0.7
Drop-out Rate (%)	2.3	2.2	0.0	0.0	n/a	11.1
H.S. Diplomas (#)	210	206	2	2	0	0

Spring Grove Area SD

100 E College Ave • Spring Grove, PA 17362-1219
(717) 225-4731 • http://www.sgasd.org
Grade Span: KG-12; **Agency Type:** 1
Schools: 7
4 Primary; 2 Middle; 1 High; 0 Other Level
7 Regular; 0 Special Education; 0 Vocational; 0 Alternative

0 Magnet; 0 Charter; 5 Title I Eligible; 0 School-wide Title I
Students: 3,904 (n/a% male; n/a% female)
Individual Education Program: 642 (16.4%);
English Language Learner: n/a; Migrant: 4 (0.1%)
Eligible for Free Lunch Program: 300 (7.7%)
Eligible for Reduced-Price Lunch Program: 225 (5.8%)
Teachers: 237.0 (16.5 to 1)
Librarians/Media Specialists: 6.0 (650.7 to 1)
Guidance Counselors: 10.0 (390.4 to 1)
Current Spending: ($ per student per year):
Total: $6,016; Instruction: $3,656; Support Services: $2,057
Enrollment, Drop-out Rates and Diploma Recipients by Race/Ethnicity

Category	Total	White	Black	Asian	AIAN	Hisp.
Enrollment (%)	100.0	97.0	1.1	0.2	0.6	1.1
Drop-out Rate (%)	2.3	2.0	0.0	0.0	0.0	75.0
H.S. Diplomas (#)	201	198	2	1	0	0

West Shore SD
PO Box 803 • New Cumberland, PA 17070-0803
(717) 938-9577
Grade Span: KG-12; **Agency Type:** 1
Schools: 16
10 Primary; 4 Middle; 2 High; 0 Other Level
16 Regular; 0 Special Education; 0 Vocational; 0 Alternative
0 Magnet; 0 Charter; 13 Title I Eligible; 0 School-wide Title I
Students: 8,298 (n/a% male; n/a% female)
Individual Education Program: 1,216 (14.7%);
English Language Learner: n/a; Migrant: 30 (0.4%)
Eligible for Free Lunch Program: 747 (9.0%)
Eligible for Reduced-Price Lunch Program: 317 (3.8%)
Teachers: 503.5 (16.5 to 1)
Librarians/Media Specialists: 13.0 (638.3 to 1)
Guidance Counselors: 21.0 (395.1 to 1)
Current Spending: ($ per student per year):
Total: $6,521; Instruction: $4,264; Support Services: $1,967
Enrollment, Drop-out Rates and Diploma Recipients by Race/Ethnicity

Category	Total	White	Black	Asian	AIAN	Hisp.
Enrollment (%)	100.0	93.6	2.7	2.0	0.1	1.7
Drop-out Rate (%)	2.5	2.4	12.1	1.6	0.0	7.9
H.S. Diplomas (#)	556	527	6	14	1	8

West York Area SD
2605 W Market St • York, PA 17404-5529
(717) 792-3067 • http://www.wyasd.k12.pa.us
Grade Span: KG-12; **Agency Type:** 1
Schools: 6
4 Primary; 1 Middle; 1 High; 0 Other Level
6 Regular; 0 Special Education; 0 Vocational; 0 Alternative
0 Magnet; 0 Charter; 3 Title I Eligible; 0 School-wide Title I
Students: 3,043 (n/a% male; n/a% female)
Individual Education Program: 409 (13.4%);
English Language Learner: n/a; Migrant: 5 (0.2%)
Eligible for Free Lunch Program: 379 (12.5%)
Eligible for Reduced-Price Lunch Program: 185 (6.1%)
Teachers: 183.7 (16.6 to 1)
Librarians/Media Specialists: 4.0 (760.8 to 1)
Guidance Counselors: 8.0 (380.4 to 1)
Current Spending: ($ per student per year):
Total: $6,093; Instruction: $3,793; Support Services: $2,049
Enrollment, Drop-out Rates and Diploma Recipients by Race/Ethnicity

Category	Total	White	Black	Asian	AIAN	Hisp.
Enrollment (%)	100.0	91.2	4.5	1.3	0.1	2.9
Drop-out Rate (%)	1.7	1.5	10.0	10.0	0.0	n/a
H.S. Diplomas (#)	168	158	1	6	0	3

York City SD
PO Box 1927 • York, PA 17405-1927
(717) 845-3571 • http://www.ycs.k12.pa.us/default.html
Grade Span: KG-12; **Agency Type:** 1
Schools: 9
6 Primary; 2 Middle; 1 High; 0 Other Level
9 Regular; 0 Special Education; 0 Vocational; 0 Alternative
0 Magnet; 0 Charter; 9 Title I Eligible; 0 School-wide Title I
Students: 6,654 (n/a% male; n/a% female)
Individual Education Program: 1,171 (17.6%);
English Language Learner: n/a; Migrant: 200 (3.0%)
Eligible for Free Lunch Program: 4,187 (62.9%)
Eligible for Reduced-Price Lunch Program: 712 (10.7%)
Teachers: 416.0 (16.0 to 1)
Librarians/Media Specialists: 4.0 (1,663.5 to 1)
Guidance Counselors: 10.0 (665.4 to 1)
Current Spending: ($ per student per year):
Total: $7,440; Instruction: $4,852; Support Services: $2,167
Enrollment, Drop-out Rates and Diploma Recipients by Race/Ethnicity

Category	Total	White	Black	Asian	AIAN	Hisp.
Enrollment (%)	100.0	27.0	43.5	1.4	0.2	27.9
Drop-out Rate (%)	11.1	13.8	9.0	6.1	0.0	12.6
H.S. Diplomas (#)	279	75	119	15	0	70

York Suburban SD
1800 Hollywood Dr • York, PA 17403-4256
(717) 848-2814 • http://www.yshs.k12.pa.us
Grade Span: KG-12; **Agency Type:** 1
Schools: 5
3 Primary; 1 Middle; 1 High; 0 Other Level
5 Regular; 0 Special Education; 0 Vocational; 0 Alternative
0 Magnet; 0 Charter; 2 Title I Eligible; 0 School-wide Title I
Students: 2,647 (n/a% male; n/a% female)
Individual Education Program: 316 (11.9%);
English Language Learner: n/a; Migrant: 8 (0.3%)
Eligible for Free Lunch Program: 135 (5.1%)
Eligible for Reduced-Price Lunch Program: 132 (5.0%)
Teachers: 180.4 (14.7 to 1)
Librarians/Media Specialists: 4.0 (661.8 to 1)
Guidance Counselors: 8.6 (307.8 to 1)
Current Spending: ($ per student per year):
Total: $8,472; Instruction: $5,601; Support Services: $2,583
Enrollment, Drop-out Rates and Diploma Recipients by Race/Ethnicity

Category	Total	White	Black	Asian	AIAN	Hisp.
Enrollment (%)	100.0	89.1	4.7	2.8	0.1	3.3
Drop-out Rate (%)	0.7	0.7	0.0	0.0	0.0	0.0
H.S. Diplomas (#)	170	170	0	0	0	0

Number of Schools

Rank	Number	District Name	City
1	262	Philadelphia City SD	Philadelphia
2	93	Pittsburgh SD	Pittsburgh
3	23	Allentown City SD	Allentown
4	22	Bethlehem Area SD	Bethlehem
5	21	Central Bucks SD	Doylestown
5	21	Chambersburg Area SD	Chambersburg
5	21	Erie City SD	Erie
8	20	Lancaster SD	Lancaster
9	19	Central Dauphin SD	Harrisburg
9	19	Reading SD	Reading
9	19	Warren County SD	North Warren
12	18	Scranton SD	Scranton
13	17	North Penn SD	Lansdale
14	16	Harrisburg City SD	Harrisburg
14	16	Pennsbury SD	Fallsington
14	16	West Shore SD	New Cumberland
17	15	Council Rock SD	Richboro
17	15	West Chester Area SD	West Chester
19	14	Altoona Area SD	Altoona
19	14	Butler Area SD	Butler
19	14	Downingtown Area SD	Downingtown
19	14	Mifflin County SD	Lewistown
19	14	Neshaminy SD	Langhorne
24	13	Armstrong SD	Ford City
24	13	Bristol Township SD	Levittown
24	13	Millcreek Township SD	Erie
27	12	Coatesville Area SD	Coatesville
27	12	Hempfield Area SD	Greensburg
27	12	Juniata County SD	Mifflintown
27	12	Keystone Central SD	Lock Haven
27	12	North Allegheny SD	Pittsburgh
27	12	Upper Darby SD	Drexel Hill
33	11	Connellsville Area SD	Connellsville
33	11	East Penn SD	Emmaus
33	11	Norristown Area SD	Norristown
33	11	Pocono Mountain SD	Swiftwater
33	11	Punxsutawney Area SD	Punxsutawney
33	11	State College Area SD	State College
33	11	Williamsport Area SD	Williamsport
40	10	Bensalem Township SD	Bensalem
40	10	Boyertown Area SD	Boyertown
40	10	Canon-Mcmillan SD	Canonsburg
40	10	Carlisle Area SD	Carlisle
40	10	Chester-Upland SD	Chester
40	10	Cumberland Valley SD	Mechanicsburg
40	10	Dubois Area SD	Du Bois
40	10	East Stroudsburg Area SD	E Stroudsburg
40	10	Hempfield SD	Landisville
40	10	Lower Merion SD	Ardmore
40	10	Mount Lebanon SD	Pittsburgh
40	10	Norwin SD	N Huntingdon
40	10	Parkland SD	Allentown
40	10	Penn Manor SD	Millersville
40	10	Pennridge SD	Perkasie
40	10	Red Lion Area SD	Red Lion
40	10	Souderton Area SD	Souderton
40	10	William Penn SD	Lansdowne
40	10	Wilson SD	West Lawn
59	9	Abington SD	Abington
59	9	Albert Gallatin Area SD	Uniontown
59	9	Centennial SD	Warminster
59	9	Crawford Central SD	Meadville
59	9	Easton Area SD	Easton
59	9	Hazleton Area SD	Hazleton
59	9	Kiski Area SD	Vandergrift
59	9	Manheim Township SD	Lancaster
59	9	North Hills SD	Pittsburgh
59	9	Quakertown Community SD	Quakertown
59	9	Ridley SD	Folsom
59	9	Seneca Valley SD	Harmony
59	9	Wilkes-Barre Area SD	Wilkes Barre
59	9	Woodland Hills SD	Pittsburgh
59	9	Wyoming Valley West SD	Kingston
59	9	York City SD	York
75	8	Bethel Park SD	Bethel Park
75	8	Cheltenham Township SD	Elkins Park
75	8	Clearfield Area SD	Clearfield
75	8	Franklin Area SD	Franklin
75	8	Gateway SD	Monroeville
75	8	Hatboro-Horsham SD	Horsham
75	8	Manheim Central SD	Manheim
75	8	Mechanicsburg Area SD	Mechanicsburg
75	8	New Castle Area SD	New Castle
75	8	Penn Hills SD	Pittsburgh
75	8	Penn-Trafford SD	Harrison City
75	8	Shaler Area SD	Glenshaw
75	8	Spring-Ford Area SD	Collegeville
75	8	Stroudsburg Area SD	Stroudsburg
75	8	Tredyffrin-Easttown SD	Berwyn
75	8	Uniontown Area SD	Uniontown
91	7	Athens Area SD	Athens
91	7	Berwick Area SD	Berwick
91	7	Big Spring SD	Newville
91	7	Central York SD	York
91	7	Colonial SD	Plymouth Meeting
91	7	Conestoga Valley SD	Lancaster
91	7	Conneaut SD	Linesville
91	7	Dallastown Area SD	Dallastown
91	7	Delaware Valley SD	Milford
91	7	Dover Area SD	Dover
91	7	Eastern Lancaster County SD	New Holland
91	7	Elizabeth Forward SD	Elizabeth
91	7	Elizabethtown Area SD	Elizabethtown
91	7	Ephrata Area SD	Ephrata
91	7	Gettysburg Area SD	Gettysburg
91	7	Grove City Area SD	Grove City
91	7	Hamburg Area SD	Hamburg
91	7	Haverford Township SD	Havertown
91	7	Laurel Highlands SD	Uniontown
91	7	Lebanon SD	Lebanon
91	7	Lower Dauphin SD	Hummelstown
91	7	Mckeesport Area SD	Mc Keesport
91	7	Methacton SD	Norristown
91	7	Midd-West SD	Middleburg
91	7	New Kensington-Arnold SD	New Kensington
91	7	Northeastern York SD	Manchester
91	7	Penncrest SD	Saegertown
91	7	Pleasant Valley SD	Brodheadsville
91	7	Plum Borough SD	Plum
91	7	Pottstown SD	Pottstown
91	7	Shikellamy SD	Sunbury
91	7	Solanco SD	Quarryville
91	7	Southeast Delco SD	Folcroft
91	7	Spring Grove Area SD	Spring Grove
91	7	Titusville Area SD	Titusville
91	7	Wissahickon SD	Ambler
127	6	Abington Heights SD	Clarks Summit
127	6	Apollo-Ridge SD	Spring Church
127	6	Bellefonte Area SD	Bellefonte
127	6	Chichester SD	Boothwyn
127	6	Cocalico SD	Denver
127	6	Cornwall-Lebanon SD	Lebanon
127	6	Corry Area SD	Corry
127	6	Cranberry Area SD	Seneca
127	6	Daniel Boone Area SD	Douglassville
127	6	Danville Area SD	Danville
127	6	Derry Area SD	Derry
127	6	Donegal SD	Mount Joy
127	6	Eastern Lebanon County SD	Myerstown
127	6	Exeter Township SD	Reading
127	6	Fox Chapel Area SD	Pittsburgh
127	6	Highlands SD	Natrona Heights
127	6	Hollidaysburg Area SD	Hollidaysburg
127	6	Hopewell Area SD	Aliquippa
127	6	Huntingdon Area SD	Huntingdon
127	6	Indiana Area SD	Indiana
127	6	Interboro SD	Prospect Park
127	6	Jersey Shore Area SD	Jersey Shore
127	6	Kutztown Area SD	Kutztown
127	6	Lehighton Area SD	Lehighton
127	6	Marple Newtown SD	Newtown Square
127	6	Middletown Area SD	Middletown
127	6	Mifflinburg Area SD	Mifflinburg
127	6	Moon Area SD	Moon Township
127	6	Northampton Area SD	Northampton
127	6	Northern Lebanon SD	Fredericksburg
127	6	Northern Tioga SD	Elkland
127	6	Northern York County SD	Dillsburg
127	6	Oil City Area SD	Oil City
127	6	Owen J Roberts SD	Pottstown
127	6	Penn-Delco SD	Aston
127	6	Philipsburg-Osceola Area SD	Philipsburg
127	6	Phoenixville Area SD	Phoenixville
127	6	Ringgold SD	New Eagle
127	6	Rose Tree Media SD	Media
127	6	Somerset Area SD	Somerset
127	6	South Eastern SD	Fawn Grove
127	6	South Western SD	Hanover
127	6	Southern Tioga SD	Blossburg
127	6	Towanda Area SD	Towanda
127	6	Trinity Area SD	Washington
127	6	Troy Area SD	Troy
127	6	Tunkhannock Area SD	Tunkhannock
127	6	Tuscarora SD	Mercersburg
127	6	Upper Dublin SD	Maple Glen
127	6	Upper Merion Area SD	King Of Prussia
127	6	Upper Saint Clair SD	Pittsburgh
127	6	Wallingford-Swarthmore SD	Wallingford
127	6	Warwick SD	Lititz
127	6	Wayne Highlands SD	Honesdale
127	6	Waynesboro Area SD	Waynesboro
127	6	West Mifflin Area SD	West Mifflin
127	6	West Perry SD	Elliottsburg
127	6	West York Area SD	York
185	5	Ambridge Area SD	Ambridge
185	5	Bald Eagle Area SD	Wingate
185	5	Baldwin-Whitehall SD	Pittsburgh
185	5	Bangor Area SD	Bangor
185	5	Bedford Area SD	Bedford
185	5	Belle Vernon Area SD	Belle Vernon
185	5	Big Beaver Falls Area SD	Beaver Falls
185	5	Blackhawk SD	Beaver Falls
185	5	Blairsville-Saltsburg SD	Blairsville
185	5	Bloomsburg Area SD	Bloomsburg
185	5	Blue Mountain SD	Orwigsburg
185	5	Brandywine Heights Area SD	Topton
185	5	Brownsville Area SD	Brownsville
185	5	Derry Township SD	Hershey
185	5	Eastern York SD	Wrightsville
185	5	Ellwood City Area SD	Ellwood City
185	5	Everett Area SD	Everett
185	5	Fleetwood Area SD	Fleetwood
185	5	Fort Leboeuf SD	Waterford
185	5	Franklin Regional SD	Murrysville
185	5	Freeport Area SD	Freeport
185	5	Garnet Valley SD	Glen Mills
185	5	Governor Mifflin SD	Shillington
185	5	Great Valley SD	Malvern
185	5	Greater Latrobe SD	Latrobe
185	5	Greater Nanticoke Area SD	Nanticoke
185	5	Greensburg Salem SD	Greensburg
185	5	Hampton Township SD	Gibsonia
185	5	Hanover Area SD	Wilkes Barre
185	5	Hanover Public SD	Hanover
185	5	Hermitage SD	Hermitage
185	5	Kennett Consolidated SD	Kennett Square
185	5	Keystone Oaks SD	Pittsburgh
185	5	Lake-Lehman SD	Lehman
185	5	Lampeter-Strasburg SD	Lampeter
185	5	Ligonier Valley SD	Ligonier
185	5	Mars Area SD	Mars
185	5	Milton Area SD	Milton
185	5	Montour SD	Mc Kees Rocks
185	5	Mount Pleasant Area SD	Mount Pleasant
185	5	Nazareth Area SD	Nazareth
185	5	North Pocono SD	Moscow
185	5	Oxford Area SD	Oxford
185	5	Palisades SD	Kintnersville
185	5	Palmyra Area SD	Palmyra
185	5	Penn Cambria SD	Cresson
185	5	Penns Valley Area SD	Spring Mills
185	5	Pequea Valley SD	Kinzers
185	5	Perkiomen Valley SD	Collegeville
185	5	Peters Township SD	Mcmurray
185	5	Pine-Richland SD	Gibsonia
185	5	Pittston Area SD	Pittston
185	5	Pottsgrove SD	Pottstown
185	5	Radnor Township SD	Wayne
185	5	Saint Marys Area SD	Saint Marys
185	5	Selinsgrove Area SD	Selinsgrove
185	5	Shippensburg Area SD	Shippensburg
185	5	Slippery Rock Area SD	Slippery Rock
185	5	South Allegheny SD	Mc Keesport
185	5	Southern Lehigh SD	Center Valley
185	5	Southern York County SD	Glen Rock
185	5	Southmoreland SD	Scottdale
185	5	Spring Cove SD	Roaring Spring
185	5	Steel Valley SD	Munhall
185	5	Susquehanna Township SD	Harrisburg
185	5	Tamaqua Area SD	Tamaqua
185	5	Twin Valley SD	Elverson
185	5	Unionville-Chadds Ford SD	Kennett Square
185	5	Upper Adams SD	Biglerville
185	5	Wallenpaupack Area SD	Hawley
185	5	West Allegheny SD	Imperial
185	5	West Jefferson Hills SD	Jefferson Hls
185	5	Western Wayne SD	South Canaan
185	5	Wilkinsburg Borough SD	Wilkinsburg
185	5	Wilmington Area SD	New Wilmington
185	5	Wilson Area SD	Easton
185	5	Wyalusing Area SD	Wyalusing
185	5	Wyoming Area SD	Exeter
185	5	York Suburban SD	York
185	5	Yough SD	Herminie
265	4	Annville-Cleona SD	Annville
265	4	Avon Grove SD	West Grove
265	4	Beaver Area SD	Beaver
265	4	Bradford Area SD	Bradford
265	4	Brookville Area SD	Brookville
265	4	Burrell SD	Lower Burrell
265	4	Central Cambria SD	Ebensburg
265	4	Central Greene SD	Waynesburg
265	4	Chartiers Valley SD	Pittsburgh
265	4	Chestnut Ridge SD	Fishertown
265	4	Conewago Valley SD	New Oxford

265	4	Conrad Weiser Area SD	Robesonia
265	4	Crestwood SD	Mountain Top
265	4	Dallas SD	Dallas
265	4	Deer Lakes SD	Russellton
265	4	East Lycoming SD	Hughesville
265	4	East Pennsboro Area SD	Enola
265	4	Freedom Area SD	Freedom
265	4	General Mclane SD	Edinboro
265	4	Greater Johnstown SD	Johnstown
265	4	Greencastle-Antrim SD	Greencastle
265	4	Harbor Creek SD	Harborcreek
265	4	Karns City Area SD	Karns City
265	4	Lewisburg Area SD	Lewisburg
265	4	Mcguffey SD	Claysville
265	4	Montoursville Area SD	Montoursville
265	4	Mount Union Area SD	Mount Union
265	4	North East SD	North East
265	4	North Schuylkill SD	Ashland
265	4	Northern Lehigh SD	Slatington
265	4	Northwestern SD	Albion
265	4	Northwestern Lehigh SD	New Tripoli
265	4	Octorara Area SD	Atglen
265	4	Palmerton Area SD	Palmerton
265	4	Quaker Valley SD	Sewickley
265	4	Riverside Beaver County SD	Ellwood City
265	4	Salisbury Township SD	Allentown
265	4	Sharon City SD	Sharon
265	4	South Butler County SD	Saxonburg
265	4	South Middleton SD	Boiling Springs
265	4	Springfield SD	Springfield
265	4	Springfield Township SD	Oreland
265	4	Sto-Rox SD	Mckees Rocks
265	4	Upper Moreland Township SD	Willow Grove
265	4	Upper Perkiomen SD	East Greenville
265	4	Valley View SD	Archbald
265	4	Warrior Run SD	Turbotville
265	4	Wellsboro Area SD	Wellsboro
265	4	Whitehall-Coplay SD	Whitehall
314	3	Bermudian Springs SD	York Springs
314	3	Cambria Heights SD	Patton
314	3	Carlynton SD	Carnegie
314	3	Catasauqua Area SD	Catasauqua
314	3	Center Area SD	Monaca
314	3	Central Columbia SD	Bloomsburg
314	3	Charleroi SD	Charleroi
314	3	Columbia Borough SD	Columbia
314	3	Dunmore SD	Dunmore
314	3	East Allegheny SD	N Versailles
314	3	Fairview SD	Fairview
314	3	Forest Hills SD	Sidman
314	3	Girard SD	Girard
314	3	Greenville Area SD	Greenville
314	3	Jim Thorpe Area SD	Jim Thorpe
314	3	Lakeland SD	Jermyn
314	3	Littlestown Area SD	Littlestown
314	3	Lower Moreland Township SD	Huntingdon Vly
314	3	Marion Center Area SD	Marion Center
314	3	Moniteau SD	West Sunbury
314	3	Montrose Area SD	Montrose
314	3	Muhlenberg SD	Reading
314	3	New Brighton Area SD	New Brighton
314	3	Northgate SD	Pittsburgh
314	3	Oley Valley SD	Oley
314	3	Pen Argyl Area SD	Pen Argyl
314	3	Pine Grove Area SD	Pine Grove
314	3	Pottsville Area SD	Pottsville
314	3	Richland SD	Johnstown
314	3	Saucon Valley SD	Hellertown
314	3	Schuylkill Valley SD	Leesport
314	3	South Fayette Township SD	Mc Donald
314	3	South Park SD	South Park
314	3	Susquenita SD	Duncannon
314	3	Tulpehocken Area SD	Bernville
314	3	Tyrone Area SD	Tyrone
314	3	Washington SD	Washington
314	3	Wattsburg Area SD	Erie
314	3	Westmont Hilltop SD	Johnstown
314	3	Wyomissing Area SD	Wyomissing
354	2	Burgettstown Area SD	Burgettstown
354	2	Elk Lake SD	Dimock
354	2	Jeannette City SD	Jeannette
354	2	Mercer Area SD	Mercer
354	2	Mid Valley SD	Throop
354	2	Mohawk Area SD	Bessemer
354	2	Mount Carmel Area SD	Mount Carmel
354	2	PDE Division of Data Services	Harrisburg
354	2	Reynolds SD	Greenville
354	2	Shamokin Area SD	Coal Township
364	1	Pennsylvania Virtual CS	Norristown

Number of Teachers

Rank	Number	District Name	City
1	9,866	Philadelphia City SD	Philadelphia
2	2,709	Pittsburgh SD	Pittsburgh
3	1,034	Central Bucks SD	Doylestown
4	937	Bethlehem Area SD	Bethlehem
5	894	Reading SD	Reading
6	886	Allentown City SD	Allentown
7	830	Erie City SD	Erie
8	789	Council Rock SD	Richboro
9	762	North Penn SD	Lansdale
10	740	Central Dauphin SD	Harrisburg
11	722	Upper Darby SD	Drexel Hill
12	698	Pocono Mountain SD	Swiftwater
13	698	West Chester Area SD	West Chester
14	696	Lancaster SD	Lancaster
15	680	Pennsbury SD	Fallsington
16	660	Downingtown Area SD	Downingtown
17	616	Scranton SD	Scranton
18	579	Harrisburg City SD	Harrisburg
19	544	North Allegheny SD	Pittsburgh
20	544	Neshaminy SD	Langhorne
21	541	Easton Area SD	Easton
22	526	Lower Merion SD	Ardmore
23	519	Altoona Area SD	Altoona
24	510	Norristown Area SD	Norristown
25	508	State College Area SD	State College
26	503	West Shore SD	New Cumberland
27	497	East Stroudsburg Area SD	E Stroudsburg
28	495	Butler Area SD	Butler
29	488	Parkland SD	Allentown
30	483	Coatesville Area SD	Coatesville
31	483	Seneca Valley SD	Harmony
32	477	Cumberland Valley SD	Mechanicsburg
33	460	Bristol Township SD	Levittown
34	456	Chambersburg Area SD	Chambersburg
35	456	Hazleton Area SD	Hazleton
36	451	Wilkes-Barre Area SD	Wilkes Barre
37	448	Abington SD	Abington
38	443	Millcreek Township SD	Erie
39	427	Armstrong SD	Ford City
40	424	Mifflin County SD	Lewistown
41	420	Hempfield SD	Landisville
42	418	Hempfield Area SD	Greensburg
43	418	Warren County SD	North Warren
44	417	Williamsport Area SD	Williamsport
45	416	York City SD	York
46	412	East Penn SD	Emmaus
47	410	Penn Hills SD	Pittsburgh
48	407	Souderton Area SD	Souderton
49	396	Pennridge SD	Perkasie
50	394	Tredyffrin-Easttown SD	Berwyn
51	392	Boyertown Area SD	Boyertown
52	392	Ridley SD	Folsom
53	390	Bensalem Township SD	Bensalem
54	388	Woodland Hills SD	Pittsburgh
55	383	Centennial SD	Warminster
56	377	Shaler Area SD	Glenshaw
57	376	Spring-Ford Area SD	Collegeville
58	373	Mount Lebanon SD	Pittsburgh
59	372	Pleasant Valley SD	Brodheadsville
60	370	Fox Chapel Area SD	Pittsburgh
61	360	Keystone Central SD	Lock Haven
62	356	Connellsville Area SD	Connellsville
63	355	Hatboro-Horsham SD	Horsham
64	351	Bethel Park SD	Bethel Park
65	347	Methacton SD	Norristown
65	347	William Penn SD	Lansdowne
67	345	Cheltenham Township SD	Elkins Park
68	341	Manheim Township SD	Lancaster
69	341	Northampton Area SD	Northampton
70	338	Colonial SD	Plymouth Meeting
71	336	Stroudsburg Area SD	Stroudsburg
72	335	Haverford Township SD	Havertown
73	335	Carlisle Area SD	Carlisle
74	331	Dallastown Area SD	Dallastown
75	330	North Hills SD	Pittsburgh
76	330	Chester-Upland SD	Chester
77	318	Delaware Valley SD	Milford
78	314	Red Lion Area SD	Red Lion
79	312	Penn Manor SD	Millersville
80	311	Wilson SD	West Lawn
81	305	Wyoming Valley West SD	Kingston
82	304	Gateway SD	Monroeville
83	302	Crawford Central SD	Meadville
84	299	Wissahickon SD	Ambler
85	294	Mckeesport Area SD	Mc Keesport
86	291	Cornwall-Lebanon SD	Lebanon
87	291	Perkiomen Valley SD	Collegeville
88	288	Warwick SD	Lititz
89	288	Rose Tree Media SD	Media
90	284	Dubois Area SD	Du Bois
91	281	Quakertown Community SD	Quakertown
92	280	Baldwin-Whitehall SD	Pittsburgh
93	279	Avon Grove SD	West Grove
94	277	Upper Dublin SD	Maple Glen
95	277	Norwin SD	N Huntingdon
96	274	Wallenpaupack Area SD	Hawley
97	268	Central York SD	York
98	265	Canon-Mcmillan SD	Canonsburg
99	264	Garnet Valley SD	Glen Mills
100	260	Lower Dauphin SD	Hummelstown
101	258	Pine-Richland SD	Gibsonia
102	257	Governor Mifflin SD	Shillington
103	257	Nazareth Area SD	Nazareth
104	256	Owen J Roberts SD	Pottstown
105	256	Plum Borough SD	Plum
105	256	Radnor Township SD	Wayne
107	255	Upper Saint Clair SD	Pittsburgh
108	255	Interboro SD	Prospect Park
109	254	Waynesboro Area SD	Waynesboro
110	254	Moon Area SD	Moon Township
111	252	Penncrest SD	Saegertown
112	252	Unionville-Chadds Ford SD	Kennett Square
113	251	Southeast Delco SD	Folcroft
114	250	Marple Newtown SD	Newtown Square
115	250	Albert Gallatin Area SD	Uniontown
116	250	Ephrata Area SD	Ephrata
117	249	Wallingford-Swarthmore SD	Wallingford
118	248	Hollidaysburg Area SD	Hollidaysburg
119	246	Penn-Trafford SD	Harrison City
120	243	Mechanicsburg Area SD	Mechanicsburg
121	242	Greater Latrobe SD	Latrobe
122	242	Upper Merion Area SD	King Of Prussia
123	241	Berwick Area SD	Berwick
124	240	Great Valley SD	Malvern
125	240	Trinity Area SD	Washington
126	238	Indiana Area SD	Indiana
127	238	Kennett Consolidated SD	Kennett Square
128	237	Spring Grove Area SD	Spring Grove
129	235	Exeter Township SD	Reading
130	234	Phoenixville Area SD	Phoenixville
131	234	Greater Johnstown SD	Johnstown
131	234	Ringgold SD	New Eagle
133	234	South Western SD	Hanover
134	234	Chichester SD	Boothwyn
134	234	Kiski Area SD	Vandergrift
136	232	New Castle Area SD	New Castle
137	229	Gettysburg Area SD	Gettysburg
138	228	Conestoga Valley SD	Lancaster
139	226	Big Spring SD	Newville
140	226	Franklin Regional SD	Murrysville
141	226	Chartiers Valley SD	Pittsburgh
142	225	Elizabethtown Area SD	Elizabethtown
143	223	Tunkhannock Area SD	Tunkhannock
144	222	Abington Heights SD	Clarks Summit
145	219	Whitehall-Coplay SD	Whitehall
146	218	Dover Area SD	Dover
147	217	Lebanon SD	Lebanon
147	217	Uniontown Area SD	Uniontown
149	215	Eastern Lancaster County SD	New Holland
150	213	Derry Township SD	Hershey
151	213	West Allegheny SD	Imperial
152	212	Wayne Highlands SD	Honesdale
153	211	Springfield SD	Springfield
154	210	Oxford Area SD	Oxford
155	209	Punxsutawney Area SD	Punxsutawney
156	209	Solanco SD	Quarryville
157	209	Pottstown SD	Pottstown
158	208	Peters Township SD	Mcmurray
159	208	Northern York County SD	Dillsburg
160	208	Cocalico SD	Denver
161	207	Southern York County SD	Glen Rock
162	207	Bangor Area SD	Bangor
163	207	Highlands SD	Natrona Heights
164	206	Penn-Delco SD	Aston
165	205	West Perry SD	Elliottsburg
166	205	Laurel Highlands SD	Uniontown
167	204	Twin Valley SD	Elverson
168	204	Juniata County SD	Mifflintown
169	202	Montour SD	Mc Kees Rocks
170	201	Shikellamy SD	Sunbury
171	200	Northern Tioga SD	Elkland
172	199	Pottsgrove SD	Pottstown
173	198	Muhlenberg SD	Reading
174	197	Daniel Boone Area SD	Douglassville
175	196	Hampton Township SD	Gibsonia
176	196	Jersey Shore Area SD	Jersey Shore
177	195	South Eastern SD	Fawn Grove
178	195	Bellefonte Area SD	Bellefonte
178	195	Eastern York SD	Wrightsville
180	194	Conewago Valley SD	New Oxford
181	194	Bradford Area SD	Bradford
182	194	Susquehanna Township SD	Harrisburg
183	193	Upper Moreland Township SD	Willow Grove
184	193	Greensburg Salem SD	Greensburg
185	192	Middletown Area SD	Middletown

186	191	North Pocono SD	Moscow
187	190	Northeastern York SD	Manchester
188	190	Lampeter-Strasburg SD	Lampeter
189	190	Danville Area SD	Danville
190	189	Conneaut SD	Linesville
191	189	Ambridge Area SD	Ambridge
192	189	Manheim Central SD	Manheim
193	188	Upper Perkiomen SD	East Greenville
194	188	Clearfield Area SD	Clearfield
195	187	Conrad Weiser Area SD	Robesonia
196	187	Shippensburg Area SD	Shippensburg
197	185	East Pennsboro Area SD	Enola
198	185	Elizabeth Forward SD	Elizabeth
199	184	Athens Area SD	Athens
200	183	West York Area SD	York
201	183	Hopewell Area SD	Aliquippa
202	183	Pittston Area SD	Pittston
202	183	Selinsgrove Area SD	Selinsgrove
204	181	Midd-West SD	Middleburg
205	180	York Suburban SD	York
206	179	Octorara Area SD	Atglen
207	175	Milton Area SD	Milton
208	173	Huntingdon Area SD	Huntingdon
208	173	West Mifflin Area SD	West Mifflin
210	173	Somerset Area SD	Somerset
211	172	Keystone Oaks SD	Pittsburgh
212	172	Corry Area SD	Corry
212	172	Derry Area SD	Derry
212	172	Grove City Area SD	Grove City
215	171	Mars Area SD	Mars
216	169	South Butler County SD	Saxonburg
217	169	Southern Lehigh SD	Center Valley
218	169	Lehighton Area SD	Lehighton
219	168	Tuscarora SD	Mercersburg
220	167	Palmyra Area SD	Palmyra
221	166	Blackhawk SD	Beaver Falls
222	165	Franklin Area SD	Franklin
223	165	Fleetwood Area SD	Fleetwood
224	164	Central Greene SD	Waynesburg
225	162	Donegal SD	Mount Joy
226	162	Blue Mountain SD	Orwigsburg
227	158	West Jefferson Hills SD	Jefferson Hls
228	157	Philipsburg-Osceola Area SD	Philipsburg
229	157	Sharon City SD	Sharon
230	157	Western Wayne SD	South Canaan
231	156	General Mclane SD	Edinboro
232	154	Titusville Area SD	Titusville
233	154	Belle Vernon Area SD	Belle Vernon
233	154	Hamburg Area SD	Hamburg
233	154	Pottsville Area SD	Pottsville
233	154	Springfield Township SD	Oreland
233	154	Susquenita SD	Duncannon
238	153	Southern Tioga SD	Blossburg
239	153	Mcguffey SD	Claysville
239	153	New Kensington-Arnold SD	New Kensington
239	153	Northern Lebanon SD	Fredericksburg
242	152	Washington SD	Washington
242	152	Yough SD	Herminie
244	151	Saucon Valley SD	Hellertown
245	151	Mifflinburg Area SD	Mifflinburg
246	151	Valley View SD	Archbald
247	150	Oil City Area SD	Oil City
247	150	South Middleton SD	Boiling Springs
249	149	Slippery Rock Area SD	Slippery Rock
250	149	Saint Marys Area SD	Saint Marys
251	148	Northwestern Lehigh SD	New Tripoli
252	147	Crestwood SD	Mountain Top
253	146	Harbor Creek SD	Harborcreek
254	145	Bedford Area SD	Bedford
255	145	Dallas SD	Dallas
256	145	Mount Pleasant Area SD	Mount Pleasant
257	144	Wilson Area SD	Easton
258	144	Eastern Lebanon County SD	Myerstown
259	143	Greencastle-Antrim SD	Greencastle
260	143	Palisades SD	Kintnersville
261	143	Shamokin Area SD	Coal Township
262	141	Big Beaver Falls Area SD	Beaver Falls
263	140	Oley Valley SD	Oley
264	140	Bald Eagle Area SD	Wingate
264	140	Forest Hills SD	Sidman
264	140	Wilkinsburg Borough SD	Wilkinsburg
267	139	Wyoming Area SD	Exeter
268	138	Montoursville Area SD	Montoursville
269	138	Southmoreland SD	Scottdale
269	138	Steel Valley SD	Munhall
271	137	Hermitage SD	Hermitage
272	136	Blairsville-Saltsburg SD	Blairsville
273	135	Deer Lakes SD	Russellton
274	135	Warrior Run SD	Turbotville
275	134	Brandywine Heights Area SD	Topton
276	134	Central Columbia SD	Bloomsburg
277	133	Fort Leboeuf SD	Waterford
277	133	Quaker Valley SD	Sewickley
279	133	Ellwood City Area SD	Ellwood City
279	133	Littlestown Area SD	Littlestown
281	132	Kutztown Area SD	Kutztown
282	132	Tyrone Area SD	Tyrone
283	131	Brownsville Area SD	Brownsville
284	129	Lake-Lehman SD	Lehman
284	129	Pequea Valley SD	Kinzers
286	129	East Lycoming SD	Hughesville
287	128	Montrose Area SD	Montrose
287	128	Penn Cambria SD	Cresson
287	128	Spring Cove SD	Roaring Spring
290	127	Center Area SD	Monaca
291	126	Bermudian Springs SD	York Springs
292	126	Wyomissing Area SD	Wyomissing
293	126	Brookville Area SD	Brookville
293	126	Burrell SD	Lower Burrell
293	126	Mohawk Area SD	Bessemer
296	125	Bloomsburg Area SD	Bloomsburg
297	125	Tamaqua Area SD	Tamaqua
298	125	Schuylkill Valley SD	Leesport
299	125	Freeport Area SD	Freeport
300	124	Ligonier Valley SD	Ligonier
301	124	Northern Lehigh SD	Slatington
302	124	Central Cambria SD	Ebensburg
302	124	Hanover Area SD	Wilkes Barre
304	123	Wellsboro Area SD	Wellsboro
305	121	Beaver Area SD	Beaver
305	121	Marion Center Area SD	Marion Center
307	121	Girard SD	Girard
307	121	Riverside Beaver County SD	Ellwood City
309	120	Mount Union Area SD	Mount Union
310	120	Troy Area SD	Troy
311	119	New Brighton Area SD	New Brighton
311	119	South Park SD	South Park
313	119	South Fayette Township SD	Mc Donald
314	118	Lewisburg Area SD	Lewisburg
315	117	East Allegheny SD	N Versailles
316	117	Cambria Heights SD	Patton
317	117	Towanda Area SD	Towanda
318	117	Karns City Area SD	Karns City
319	116	Catasauqua Area SD	Catasauqua
320	115	Salisbury Township SD	Allentown
320	115	Sto-Rox SD	Mckees Rocks
322	114	Pen Argyl Area SD	Pen Argyl
323	114	Hanover Public SD	Hanover
324	113	Tulpehocken Area SD	Bernville
325	113	North Schuylkill SD	Ashland
325	113	South Allegheny SD	Mc Keesport
327	113	Lower Moreland Township SD	Huntingdon Vly
328	112	North East SD	North East
329	111	Greater Nanticoke Area SD	Nanticoke
329	111	Penns Valley Area SD	Spring Mills
331	111	Mount Carmel Area SD	Mount Carmel
332	109	Palmerton Area SD	Palmerton
333	108	Chestnut Ridge SD	Fishertown
334	108	Upper Adams SD	Biglerville
335	107	Northgate SD	Pittsburgh
336	107	Northwestern SD	Albion
337	107	Greenville Area SD	Greenville
338	106	Freedom Area SD	Freedom
339	104	Elk Lake SD	Dimock
340	104	Annville-Cleona SD	Annville
341	102	Fairview SD	Fairview
342	101	Burgettstown Area SD	Burgettstown
342	101	Carlynton SD	Carnegie
342	101	Pine Grove Area SD	Pine Grove
345	100	Cranberry Area SD	Seneca
346	100	Westmont Hilltop SD	Johnstown
347	100	Apollo-Ridge SD	Spring Church
348	99	Charleroi SD	Charleroi
349	99	Wilmington Area SD	New Wilmington
350	98	Mid Valley SD	Throop
351	97	Jim Thorpe Area SD	Jim Thorpe
352	97	Columbia Borough SD	Columbia
353	97	Everett Area SD	Everett
353	97	Wyalusing Area SD	Wyalusing
355	95	Dunmore SD	Dunmore
356	94	Richland SD	Johnstown
357	93	Moniteau SD	West Sunbury
358	92	Mercer Area SD	Mercer
359	89	Lakeland SD	Jermyn
360	88	Wattsburg Area SD	Erie
361	86	Reynolds SD	Greenville
362	85	Jeannette City SD	Jeannette
363	45	Pennsylvania Virtual CS	Norristown
364	n/a	PDE Division of Data Services	Harrisburg

Number of Students

Rank	Number	District Name	City
1	192,683	Philadelphia City SD	Philadelphia
2	35,146	Pittsburgh SD	Pittsburgh
3	18,549	Central Bucks SD	Doylestown
4	16,693	Allentown City SD	Allentown
5	16,128	Reading SD	Reading
6	15,044	PDE Division of Data Services	Harrisburg
7	14,615	Bethlehem Area SD	Bethlehem
8	13,574	North Penn SD	Lansdale
9	12,908	Erie City SD	Erie
10	12,362	Council Rock SD	Richboro
11	12,040	Upper Darby SD	Drexel Hill
12	11,590	West Chester Area SD	West Chester
13	11,206	Lancaster SD	Lancaster
14	11,166	Pocono Mountain SD	Swiftwater
15	11,050	Pennsbury SD	Fallsington
16	11,018	Central Dauphin SD	Harrisburg
17	10,430	Downingtown Area SD	Downingtown
18	9,629	Neshaminy SD	Langhorne
19	8,841	Scranton SD	Scranton
20	8,813	Hazleton Area SD	Hazleton
21	8,521	Altoona Area SD	Altoona
22	8,462	Parkland SD	Allentown
23	8,437	Easton Area SD	Easton
24	8,349	Butler Area SD	Butler
25	8,298	West Shore SD	New Cumberland
26	8,212	North Allegheny SD	Pittsburgh
27	8,036	Chambersburg Area SD	Chambersburg
28	7,667	Cumberland Valley SD	Mechanicsburg
29	7,621	Seneca Valley SD	Harmony
30	7,548	Coatesville Area SD	Coatesville
31	7,492	Harrisburg City SD	Harrisburg
32	7,481	East Stroudsburg Area SD	E Stroudsburg
33	7,451	State College Area SD	State College
34	7,426	Abington SD	Abington
35	7,218	Hempfield SD	Landisville
36	7,112	Millcreek Township SD	Erie
37	6,976	Wilkes-Barre Area SD	Wilkes Barre
38	6,923	Pennridge SD	Perkasie
39	6,916	East Penn SD	Emmaus
40	6,897	Bristol Township SD	Levittown
41	6,846	Norristown Area SD	Norristown
42	6,806	Boyertown Area SD	Boyertown
43	6,664	Pleasant Valley SD	Brodheadsville
44	6,654	York City SD	York
45	6,602	Hempfield Area SD	Greensburg
46	6,599	Bensalem Township SD	Bensalem
47	6,581	Lower Merion SD	Ardmore
48	6,551	Souderton Area SD	Souderton
49	6,539	Armstrong SD	Ford City
50	6,344	Centennial SD	Warminster
51	6,307	Warren County SD	North Warren
52	6,245	Spring-Ford Area SD	Collegeville
53	6,166	Mifflin County SD	Lewistown
54	6,113	Williamsport Area SD	Williamsport
55	6,005	Penn Hills SD	Pittsburgh
56	5,894	Woodland Hills SD	Pittsburgh
57	5,851	Connellsville Area SD	Connellsville
58	5,649	Ridley SD	Folsom
59	5,633	Tredyffrin-Easttown SD	Berwyn
60	5,610	Mount Lebanon SD	Pittsburgh
61	5,576	William Penn SD	Lansdowne
62	5,568	Hatboro-Horsham SD	Horsham
63	5,557	Shaler Area SD	Glenshaw
64	5,536	Northampton Area SD	Northampton
65	5,444	Red Lion Area SD	Red Lion
66	5,419	Haverford Township SD	Havertown
67	5,361	Penn Manor SD	Millersville
68	5,316	Manheim Township SD	Lancaster
69	5,298	Stroudsburg Area SD	Stroudsburg
70	5,289	Chester-Upland SD	Chester
71	5,277	Bethel Park SD	Bethel Park
72	5,229	Quakertown Community SD	Quakertown
73	5,182	Delaware Valley SD	Milford
74	5,177	Dallastown Area SD	Dallastown
75	5,172	Norwin SD	N Huntingdon
76	5,162	Wyoming Valley West SD	Kingston
77	5,128	Methacton SD	Norristown
78	5,103	Wilson SD	West Lawn
79	4,902	North Hills SD	Pittsburgh
80	4,886	Cheltenham Township SD	Elkins Park
81	4,862	Mckeesport Area SD	Mc Keesport
82	4,833	Perkiomen Valley SD	Collegeville
83	4,805	Penn-Trafford SD	Harrison City
84	4,768	Keystone Central SD	Lock Haven
85	4,751	Carlisle Area SD	Carlisle
86	4,741	Baldwin-Whitehall SD	Pittsburgh
87	4,705	Warwick SD	Lititz
88	4,700	Avon Grove SD	West Grove
89	4,678	Colonial SD	Plymouth Meeting
90	4,642	Cornwall-Lebanon SD	Lebanon
91	4,618	Dubois Area SD	Du Bois
92	4,598	Fox Chapel Area SD	Pittsburgh
93	4,596	Wissahickon SD	Ambler
94	4,540	Central York SD	York
95	4,477	Kiski Area SD	Vandergrift

96	4,397	Gateway SD	Monroeville
97	4,374	Plum Borough SD	Plum
98	4,366	Upper Dublin SD	Maple Glen
99	4,335	Greater Latrobe SD	Latrobe
99	4,335	Nazareth Area SD	Nazareth
101	4,301	Crawford Central SD	Meadville
102	4,236	Canon-Mcmillan SD	Canonsburg
102	4,236	Lebanon SD	Lebanon
104	4,196	Governor Mifflin SD	Shillington
105	4,174	Upper Saint Clair SD	Pittsburgh
106	4,149	Albert Gallatin Area SD	Uniontown
107	4,136	Ephrata Area SD	Ephrata
108	4,093	Owen J Roberts SD	Pottstown
109	4,072	Waynesboro Area SD	Waynesboro
110	4,027	Solanco SD	Quarryville
111	4,024	Rose Tree Media SD	Media
112	3,982	Exeter Township SD	Reading
112	3,982	Penncrest SD	Saegertown
114	3,951	Interboro SD	Prospect Park
115	3,913	Lower Dauphin SD	Hummelstown
116	3,911	Southeast Delco SD	Folcroft
117	3,908	South Western SD	Hanover
118	3,904	Spring Grove Area SD	Spring Grove
119	3,902	Elizabethtown Area SD	Elizabethtown
120	3,886	Whitehall-Coplay SD	Whitehall
121	3,866	Wallenpaupack Area SD	Hawley
122	3,865	Kennett Consolidated SD	Kennett Square
123	3,838	Unionville-Chadds Ford SD	Kennett Square
124	3,834	Conestoga Valley SD	Lancaster
125	3,824	Garnet Valley SD	Glen Mills
126	3,817	Franklin Regional SD	Murrysville
126	3,817	Hollidaysburg Area SD	Hollidaysburg
128	3,816	New Castle Area SD	New Castle
129	3,782	Trinity Area SD	Washington
130	3,769	Peters Township SD	Mcmurray
131	3,763	Ringgold SD	New Eagle
132	3,742	Laurel Highlands SD	Uniontown
133	3,733	Pine-Richland SD	Gibsonia
134	3,718	Dover Area SD	Dover
135	3,697	Chichester SD	Boothwyn
136	3,690	Abington Heights SD	Clarks Summit
137	3,682	Conewago Valley SD	New Oxford
138	3,663	Moon Area SD	Moon Township
139	3,647	Great Valley SD	Malvern
140	3,620	Bangor Area SD	Bangor
141	3,583	Greensburg Salem SD	Greensburg
142	3,549	Mechanicsburg Area SD	Mechanicsburg
143	3,538	Uniontown Area SD	Uniontown
144	3,531	Cocalico SD	Denver
145	3,501	Gettysburg Area SD	Gettysburg
146	3,486	Eastern Lancaster County SD	New Holland
147	3,468	Wallingford-Swarthmore SD	Wallingford
148	3,455	Berwick Area SD	Berwick
149	3,439	Chartiers Valley SD	Pittsburgh
150	3,405	Derry Township SD	Hershey
151	3,403	Marple Newtown SD	Newtown Square
152	3,397	Upper Merion Area SD	King Of Prussia
153	3,388	Greater Johnstown SD	Johnstown
154	3,383	Upper Perkiomen SD	East Greenville
155	3,377	West Mifflin Area SD	West Mifflin
156	3,365	Shikellamy SD	Sunbury
157	3,334	Montour SD	Mc Kees Rocks
158	3,333	Penn-Delco SD	Aston
159	3,313	Wayne Highlands SD	Honesdale
160	3,312	Indiana Area SD	Indiana
160	3,312	Pottstown SD	Pottstown
162	3,297	Daniel Boone Area SD	Douglassville
163	3,293	Springfield SD	Springfield
164	3,274	Southern York County SD	Glen Rock
165	3,270	Shippensburg Area SD	Shippensburg
166	3,260	Juniata County SD	Mifflintown
167	3,253	North Pocono SD	Moscow
168	3,248	South Eastern SD	Fawn Grove
169	3,247	Oxford Area SD	Oxford
169	3,247	Radnor Township SD	Wayne
171	3,232	Phoenixville Area SD	Phoenixville
172	3,229	Hampton Township SD	Gibsonia
172	3,229	West Allegheny SD	Imperial
174	3,203	Big Spring SD	Newville
175	3,201	Pottsgrove SD	Pottstown
176	3,191	Tunkhannock Area SD	Tunkhannock
177	3,178	Lampeter-Strasburg SD	Lampeter
178	3,169	Northern York County SD	Dillsburg
179	3,132	Ambridge Area SD	Ambridge
180	3,117	Pottsville Area SD	Pottsville
181	3,112	Upper Moreland Township SD	Willow Grove
182	3,111	Twin Valley SD	Elverson
183	3,108	Susquehanna Township SD	Harrisburg
184	3,107	Pittston Area SD	Pittston
185	3,083	Jersey Shore Area SD	Jersey Shore
186	3,075	Manheim Central SD	Manheim
187	3,047	Clearfield Area SD	Clearfield
188	3,043	West York Area SD	York
189	3,040	Bradford Area SD	Bradford
190	3,007	Northeastern York SD	Manchester
191	3,005	Muhlenberg SD	Reading
192	2,988	Bellefonte Area SD	Bellefonte
193	2,970	Hopewell Area SD	Aliquippa
194	2,969	Belle Vernon Area SD	Belle Vernon
195	2,968	Conneaut SD	Linesville
196	2,966	Elizabeth Forward SD	Elizabeth
197	2,963	Blue Mountain SD	Orwigsburg
198	2,957	West Jefferson Hills SD	Jefferson Hls
199	2,954	South Butler County SD	Saxonburg
200	2,911	Southern Lehigh SD	Center Valley
201	2,906	Selinsgrove Area SD	Selinsgrove
202	2,885	Crestwood SD	Mountain Top
203	2,881	West Perry SD	Elliottsburg
204	2,856	Punxsutawney Area SD	Punxsutawney
205	2,838	Derry Area SD	Derry
206	2,834	Blackhawk SD	Beaver Falls
207	2,824	Somerset Area SD	Somerset
208	2,811	Highlands SD	Natrona Heights
209	2,775	Palmyra Area SD	Palmyra
210	2,766	Hamburg Area SD	Hamburg
211	2,760	Grove City Area SD	Grove City
212	2,748	Conrad Weiser Area SD	Robesonia
213	2,723	East Pennsboro Area SD	Enola
214	2,721	Eastern York SD	Wrightsville
215	2,703	Mars Area SD	Mars
216	2,688	Danville Area SD	Danville
217	2,683	Greencastle-Antrim SD	Greencastle
218	2,675	Middletown Area SD	Middletown
219	2,650	Octorara Area SD	Atglen
220	2,647	York Suburban SD	York
221	2,640	Valley View SD	Archbald
222	2,615	Northern Tioga SD	Elkland
223	2,609	Yough SD	Herminie
224	2,591	Mifflinburg Area SD	Mifflinburg
225	2,590	Tuscarora SD	Mercersburg
225	2,590	Wyoming Area SD	Exeter
227	2,587	Mount Pleasant Area SD	Mount Pleasant
228	2,586	Keystone Oaks SD	Pittsburgh
229	2,585	Shamokin Area SD	Coal Township
230	2,579	Dallas SD	Dallas
231	2,573	Oil City Area SD	Oil City
232	2,571	New Kensington-Arnold SD	New Kensington
233	2,556	Corry Area SD	Corry
234	2,553	Slippery Rock Area SD	Slippery Rock
235	2,552	Saint Marys Area SD	Saint Marys
236	2,545	Midd-West SD	Middleburg
237	2,538	Donegal SD	Mount Joy
238	2,532	Milton Area SD	Milton
239	2,531	Fleetwood Area SD	Fleetwood
240	2,529	Titusville Area SD	Titusville
241	2,526	General Mclane SD	Edinboro
241	2,526	Western Wayne SD	South Canaan
243	2,490	Athens Area SD	Athens
244	2,473	Huntingdon Area SD	Huntingdon
245	2,469	Lehighton Area SD	Lehighton
246	2,448	Northern Lebanon SD	Fredericksburg
247	2,432	Mcguffey SD	Claysville
248	2,399	Franklin Area SD	Franklin
249	2,393	Susquenita SD	Duncannon
250	2,392	Eastern Lebanon County SD	Myerstown
251	2,374	Sharon City SD	Sharon
252	2,349	Southmoreland SD	Scottdale
253	2,348	Fort Leboeuf SD	Waterford
254	2,344	Bedford Area SD	Bedford
255	2,338	Littlestown Area SD	Littlestown
256	2,332	Northwestern Lehigh SD	New Tripoli
257	2,328	Southern Tioga SD	Blossburg
258	2,316	Hermitage SD	Hermitage
259	2,308	Forest Hills SD	Sidman
260	2,296	South Park SD	South Park
261	2,295	Saucon Valley SD	Hellertown
262	2,273	Steel Valley SD	Munhall
263	2,268	Central Greene SD	Waynesburg
264	2,262	Tamaqua Area SD	Tamaqua
265	2,257	Blairsville-Saltsburg SD	Blairsville
265	2,257	Burrell SD	Lower Burrell
267	2,247	Wilson Area SD	Easton
268	2,246	Ellwood City Area SD	Ellwood City
269	2,228	Philipsburg-Osceola Area SD	Philipsburg
270	2,224	Central Columbia SD	Bloomsburg
271	2,211	Montoursville Area SD	Montoursville
272	2,199	Oley Valley SD	Oley
273	2,194	Lake-Lehman SD	Lehman
274	2,186	Greater Nanticoke Area SD	Nanticoke
275	2,184	Ligonier Valley SD	Ligonier
276	2,183	Harbor Creek SD	Harborcreek
277	2,161	Bermudian Springs SD	York Springs
278	2,154	South Middleton SD	Boiling Springs
279	2,148	Palisades SD	Kintnersville
280	2,113	Northern Lehigh SD	Slatington
281	2,108	Washington SD	Washington
282	2,103	Deer Lakes SD	Russellton
283	2,090	Beaver Area SD	Beaver
284	2,087	Brownsville Area SD	Brownsville
285	2,086	Springfield Township SD	Oreland
286	2,081	Bald Eagle Area SD	Wingate
287	2,073	Hanover Area SD	Wilkes Barre
288	2,029	Girard SD	Girard
289	2,017	Center Area SD	Monaca
289	2,017	Mohawk Area SD	Bessemer
291	2,012	North Schuylkill SD	Ashland
292	2,010	Pen Argyl Area SD	Pen Argyl
293	2,002	East Allegheny SD	N Versailles
294	2,001	Pequea Valley SD	Kinzers
295	1,993	Tyrone Area SD	Tyrone
296	1,991	Big Beaver Falls Area SD	Beaver Falls
296	1,991	Montrose Area SD	Montrose
298	1,987	Palmerton Area SD	Palmerton
298	1,987	Spring Cove SD	Roaring Spring
300	1,984	Brandywine Heights Area SD	Topton
301	1,980	New Brighton Area SD	New Brighton
302	1,979	Riverside Beaver County SD	Ellwood City
303	1,978	Quaker Valley SD	Sewickley
304	1,968	North East SD	North East
305	1,952	Freeport Area SD	Freeport
306	1,947	Brookville Area SD	Brookville
307	1,945	Troy Area SD	Troy
308	1,928	Schuylkill Valley SD	Leesport
309	1,915	Northwestern SD	Albion
310	1,909	Central Cambria SD	Ebensburg
311	1,906	Penn Cambria SD	Cresson
312	1,894	Warrior Run SD	Turbotville
313	1,867	Salisbury Township SD	Allentown
314	1,841	Karns City Area SD	Karns City
315	1,837	East Lycoming SD	Hughesville
316	1,835	Towanda Area SD	Towanda
317	1,831	Lewisburg Area SD	Lewisburg
318	1,830	Kutztown Area SD	Kutztown
319	1,822	Wyomissing Area SD	Wyomissing
320	1,820	Chestnut Ridge SD	Fishertown
321	1,818	Pennsylvania Virtual CS	Norristown
322	1,815	South Allegheny SD	Mc Keesport
323	1,808	Freedom Area SD	Freedom
324	1,794	South Fayette Township SD	Mc Donald
325	1,781	Wilkinsburg Borough SD	Wilkinsburg
326	1,778	Pine Grove Area SD	Pine Grove
327	1,776	Bloomsburg Area SD	Bloomsburg
328	1,774	Jim Thorpe Area SD	Jim Thorpe
329	1,762	Mount Carmel Area SD	Mount Carmel
330	1,755	Catasauqua Area SD	Catasauqua
331	1,752	Marion Center Area SD	Marion Center
332	1,735	Upper Adams SD	Biglerville
333	1,734	Hanover Public SD	Hanover
334	1,727	Tulpehocken Area SD	Bernville
335	1,725	Moniteau SD	West Sunbury
336	1,719	Wattsburg Area SD	Erie
337	1,716	Wellsboro Area SD	Wellsboro
338	1,696	Lower Moreland Township SD	Huntingdon Vly
339	1,694	Lakeland SD	Jermyn
340	1,693	Charleroi SD	Charleroi
340	1,693	Dunmore SD	Dunmore
342	1,674	Westmont Hilltop SD	Johnstown
343	1,663	Greenville Area SD	Greenville
344	1,655	Annville-Cleona SD	Annville
345	1,650	Carlynton SD	Carnegie
346	1,645	Apollo-Ridge SD	Spring Church
347	1,636	Penns Valley Area SD	Spring Mills
348	1,614	Sto-Rox SD	Mckees Rocks
349	1,612	Cambria Heights SD	Patton
350	1,599	Wilmington Area SD	New Wilmington
351	1,586	Richland SD	Johnstown
352	1,585	Elk Lake SD	Dimock
352	1,585	Fairview SD	Fairview
354	1,568	Northgate SD	Pittsburgh
355	1,565	Mount Union Area SD	Mount Union
356	1,563	Reynolds SD	Greenville
357	1,560	Mercer Area SD	Mercer
358	1,559	Mid Valley SD	Throop
359	1,536	Columbia Borough SD	Columbia
360	1,527	Burgettstown Area SD	Burgettstown
361	1,519	Everett Area SD	Everett
362	1,512	Wyalusing Area SD	Wyalusing
363	1,510	Cranberry Area SD	Seneca
364	1,508	Jeannette City SD	Jeannette

Male Students

Rank	Percent	District Name	City
1	n/a	Abington Heights SD	Clarks Summit
1	n/a	Abington SD	Abington
1	n/a	Albert Gallatin Area SD	Uniontown
1	n/a	Allentown City SD	Allentown
1	n/a	Altoona Area SD	Altoona

1	n/a	Ambridge Area SD	Ambridge
1	n/a	Annville-Cleona SD	Annville
1	n/a	Apollo-Ridge SD	Spring Church
1	n/a	Armstrong SD	Ford City
1	n/a	Athens Area SD	Athens
1	n/a	Avon Grove SD	West Grove
1	n/a	Bald Eagle Area SD	Wingate
1	n/a	Baldwin-Whitehall SD	Pittsburgh
1	n/a	Bangor Area SD	Bangor
1	n/a	Beaver Area SD	Beaver
1	n/a	Bedford Area SD	Bedford
1	n/a	Belle Vernon Area SD	Belle Vernon
1	n/a	Bellefonte Area SD	Bellefonte
1	n/a	Bensalem Township SD	Bensalem
1	n/a	Bermudian Springs SD	York Springs
1	n/a	Berwick Area SD	Berwick
1	n/a	Bethel Park SD	Bethel Park
1	n/a	Bethlehem Area SD	Bethlehem
1	n/a	Big Beaver Falls Area SD	Beaver Falls
1	n/a	Big Spring SD	Newville
1	n/a	Blackhawk SD	Beaver Falls
1	n/a	Blairsville-Saltsburg SD	Blairsville
1	n/a	Bloomsburg Area SD	Bloomsburg
1	n/a	Blue Mountain SD	Orwigsburg
1	n/a	Boyertown Area SD	Boyertown
1	n/a	Bradford Area SD	Bradford
1	n/a	Brandywine Heights Area SD	Topton
1	n/a	Bristol Township SD	Levittown
1	n/a	Brookville Area SD	Brookville
1	n/a	Brownsville Area SD	Brownsville
1	n/a	Burgettstown Area SD	Burgettstown
1	n/a	Burrell SD	Lower Burrell
1	n/a	Butler Area SD	Butler
1	n/a	Cambria Heights SD	Patton
1	n/a	Canon-Mcmillan SD	Canonsburg
1	n/a	Carlisle Area SD	Carlisle
1	n/a	Carlynton SD	Carnegie
1	n/a	Catasauqua Area SD	Catasauqua
1	n/a	Centennial SD	Warminster
1	n/a	Center Area SD	Monaca
1	n/a	Central Bucks SD	Doylestown
1	n/a	Central Cambria SD	Ebensburg
1	n/a	Central Columbia SD	Bloomsburg
1	n/a	Central Dauphin SD	Harrisburg
1	n/a	Central Greene SD	Waynesburg
1	n/a	Central York SD	York
1	n/a	Chambersburg Area SD	Chambersburg
1	n/a	Charleroi SD	Charleroi
1	n/a	Chartiers Valley SD	Pittsburgh
1	n/a	Cheltenham Township SD	Elkins Park
1	n/a	Chester-Upland SD	Chester
1	n/a	Chestnut Ridge SD	Fishertown
1	n/a	Chichester SD	Boothwyn
1	n/a	Clearfield Area SD	Clearfield
1	n/a	Coatesville Area SD	Coatesville
1	n/a	Cocalico SD	Denver
1	n/a	Colonial SD	Plymouth Meeting
1	n/a	Columbia Borough SD	Columbia
1	n/a	Conestoga Valley SD	Lancaster
1	n/a	Conewago Valley SD	New Oxford
1	n/a	Conneaut SD	Linesville
1	n/a	Connellsville Area SD	Connellsville
1	n/a	Conrad Weiser Area SD	Robesonia
1	n/a	Cornwall-Lebanon SD	Lebanon
1	n/a	Corry Area SD	Corry
1	n/a	Council Rock SD	Richboro
1	n/a	Cranberry Area SD	Seneca
1	n/a	Crawford Central SD	Meadville
1	n/a	Crestwood SD	Mountain Top
1	n/a	Cumberland Valley SD	Mechanicsburg
1	n/a	Dallas SD	Dallas
1	n/a	Dallastown Area SD	Dallastown
1	n/a	Daniel Boone Area SD	Douglassville
1	n/a	Danville Area SD	Danville
1	n/a	Deer Lakes SD	Russellton
1	n/a	Delaware Valley SD	Milford
1	n/a	Derry Area SD	Derry
1	n/a	Derry Township SD	Hershey
1	n/a	Donegal SD	Mount Joy
1	n/a	Dover Area SD	Dover
1	n/a	Downingtown Area SD	Downingtown
1	n/a	Dubois Area SD	Du Bois
1	n/a	Dunmore SD	Dunmore
1	n/a	East Allegheny SD	N Versailles
1	n/a	East Lycoming SD	Hughesville
1	n/a	East Penn SD	Emmaus
1	n/a	East Pennsboro Area SD	Enola
1	n/a	East Stroudsburg Area SD	E Stroudsburg
1	n/a	Eastern Lancaster County SD	New Holland
1	n/a	Eastern Lebanon County SD	Myerstown
1	n/a	Eastern York SD	Wrightsville
1	n/a	Easton Area SD	Easton
1	n/a	Elizabeth Forward SD	Elizabeth
1	n/a	Elizabethtown Area SD	Elizabethtown
1	n/a	Elk Lake SD	Dimock
1	n/a	Ellwood City Area SD	Ellwood City
1	n/a	Ephrata Area SD	Ephrata
1	n/a	Erie City SD	Erie
1	n/a	Everett Area SD	Everett
1	n/a	Exeter Township SD	Reading
1	n/a	Fairview SD	Fairview
1	n/a	Fleetwood Area SD	Fleetwood
1	n/a	Forest Hills SD	Sidman
1	n/a	Fort Leboeuf SD	Waterford
1	n/a	Fox Chapel Area SD	Pittsburgh
1	n/a	Franklin Area SD	Franklin
1	n/a	Franklin Regional SD	Murrysville
1	n/a	Freedom Area SD	Freedom
1	n/a	Freeport Area SD	Freeport
1	n/a	Garnet Valley SD	Glen Mills
1	n/a	Gateway SD	Monroeville
1	n/a	General Mclane SD	Edinboro
1	n/a	Gettysburg Area SD	Gettysburg
1	n/a	Girard SD	Girard
1	n/a	Governor Mifflin SD	Shillington
1	n/a	Great Valley SD	Malvern
1	n/a	Greater Johnstown SD	Johnstown
1	n/a	Greater Latrobe SD	Latrobe
1	n/a	Greater Nanticoke Area SD	Nanticoke
1	n/a	Greencastle-Antrim SD	Greencastle
1	n/a	Greensburg Salem SD	Greensburg
1	n/a	Greenville Area SD	Greenville
1	n/a	Grove City Area SD	Grove City
1	n/a	Hamburg Area SD	Hamburg
1	n/a	Hampton Township SD	Gibsonia
1	n/a	Hanover Area SD	Wilkes Barre
1	n/a	Hanover Public SD	Hanover
1	n/a	Harbor Creek SD	Harborcreek
1	n/a	Harrisburg City SD	Harrisburg
1	n/a	Hatboro-Horsham SD	Horsham
1	n/a	Haverford Township SD	Havertown
1	n/a	Hazleton Area SD	Hazleton
1	n/a	Hempfield SD	Landisville
1	n/a	Hempfield Area SD	Greensburg
1	n/a	Hermitage SD	Hermitage
1	n/a	Highlands SD	Natrona Heights
1	n/a	Hollidaysburg Area SD	Hollidaysburg
1	n/a	Hopewell Area SD	Aliquippa
1	n/a	Huntingdon Area SD	Huntingdon
1	n/a	Indiana Area SD	Indiana
1	n/a	Interboro SD	Prospect Park
1	n/a	Jeannette City SD	Jeannette
1	n/a	Jersey Shore Area SD	Jersey Shore
1	n/a	Jim Thorpe Area SD	Jim Thorpe
1	n/a	Juniata County SD	Mifflintown
1	n/a	Karns City Area SD	Karns City
1	n/a	Kennett Consolidated SD	Kennett Square
1	n/a	Keystone Central SD	Lock Haven
1	n/a	Keystone Oaks SD	Pittsburgh
1	n/a	Kiski Area SD	Vandergrift
1	n/a	Kutztown Area SD	Kutztown
1	n/a	Lake-Lehman SD	Lehman
1	n/a	Lakeland SD	Jermyn
1	n/a	Lampeter-Strasburg SD	Lampeter
1	n/a	Lancaster SD	Lancaster
1	n/a	Laurel Highlands SD	Uniontown
1	n/a	Lebanon SD	Lebanon
1	n/a	Lehighton Area SD	Lehighton
1	n/a	Lewisburg Area SD	Lewisburg
1	n/a	Ligonier Valley SD	Ligonier
1	n/a	Littlestown Area SD	Littlestown
1	n/a	Lower Dauphin SD	Hummelstown
1	n/a	Lower Merion SD	Ardmore
1	n/a	Lower Moreland Township SD	Huntingdon Vly
1	n/a	Manheim Central SD	Manheim
1	n/a	Manheim Township SD	Lancaster
1	n/a	Marion Center Area SD	Marion Center
1	n/a	Marple Newtown SD	Newtown Square
1	n/a	Mars Area SD	Mars
1	n/a	Mcguffey SD	Claysville
1	n/a	Mckeesport Area SD	Mc Keesport
1	n/a	Mechanicsburg Area SD	Mechanicsburg
1	n/a	Mercer Area SD	Mercer
1	n/a	Methacton SD	Norristown
1	n/a	Mid Valley SD	Throop
1	n/a	Midd-West SD	Middleburg
1	n/a	Middletown Area SD	Middletown
1	n/a	Mifflin County SD	Lewistown
1	n/a	Mifflinburg Area SD	Mifflinburg
1	n/a	Millcreek Township SD	Erie
1	n/a	Milton Area SD	Milton
1	n/a	Mohawk Area SD	Bessemer
1	n/a	Moniteau SD	West Sunbury
1	n/a	Montour SD	Mc Kees Rocks
1	n/a	Montoursville Area SD	Montoursville
1	n/a	Montrose Area SD	Montrose
1	n/a	Moon Area SD	Moon Township
1	n/a	Mount Carmel Area SD	Mount Carmel
1	n/a	Mount Lebanon SD	Pittsburgh
1	n/a	Mount Pleasant Area SD	Mount Pleasant
1	n/a	Mount Union Area SD	Mount Union
1	n/a	Muhlenberg SD	Reading
1	n/a	Nazareth Area SD	Nazareth
1	n/a	Neshaminy SD	Langhorne
1	n/a	New Brighton Area SD	New Brighton
1	n/a	New Castle Area SD	New Castle
1	n/a	New Kensington-Arnold SD	New Kensington
1	n/a	Norristown Area SD	Norristown
1	n/a	North Allegheny SD	Pittsburgh
1	n/a	North East SD	North East
1	n/a	North Hills SD	Pittsburgh
1	n/a	North Penn SD	Lansdale
1	n/a	North Pocono SD	Moscow
1	n/a	North Schuylkill SD	Ashland
1	n/a	Northampton Area SD	Northampton
1	n/a	Northeastern York SD	Manchester
1	n/a	Northern Lebanon SD	Fredericksburg
1	n/a	Northern Lehigh SD	Slatington
1	n/a	Northern Tioga SD	Elkland
1	n/a	Northern York County SD	Dillsburg
1	n/a	Northgate SD	Pittsburgh
1	n/a	Northwestern SD	Albion
1	n/a	Northwestern Lehigh SD	New Tripoli
1	n/a	Norwin SD	N Huntingdon
1	n/a	Octorara Area SD	Atglen
1	n/a	Oil City Area SD	Oil City
1	n/a	Oley Valley SD	Oley
1	n/a	Owen J Roberts SD	Pottstown
1	n/a	Oxford Area SD	Oxford
1	n/a	PDE Division of Data Services	Harrisburg
1	n/a	Palisades SD	Kintnersville
1	n/a	Palmerton Area SD	Palmerton
1	n/a	Palmyra Area SD	Palmyra
1	n/a	Parkland SD	Allentown
1	n/a	Pen Argyl Area SD	Pen Argyl
1	n/a	Penn Cambria SD	Cresson
1	n/a	Penn Hills SD	Pittsburgh
1	n/a	Penn Manor SD	Millersville
1	n/a	Penn-Delco SD	Aston
1	n/a	Penn-Trafford SD	Harrison City
1	n/a	Penncrest SD	Saegertown
1	n/a	Pennridge SD	Perkasie
1	n/a	Penns Valley Area SD	Spring Mills
1	n/a	Pennsbury SD	Fallsington
1	n/a	Pennsylvania Virtual CS	Norristown
1	n/a	Pequea Valley SD	Kinzers
1	n/a	Perkiomen Valley SD	Collegeville
1	n/a	Peters Township SD	Mcmurray
1	n/a	Philadelphia City SD	Philadelphia
1	n/a	Philipsburg-Osceola Area SD	Philipsburg
1	n/a	Phoenixville Area SD	Phoenixville
1	n/a	Pine Grove Area SD	Pine Grove
1	n/a	Pine-Richland SD	Gibsonia
1	n/a	Pittsburgh SD	Pittsburgh
1	n/a	Pittston Area SD	Pittston
1	n/a	Pleasant Valley SD	Brodheadsville
1	n/a	Plum Borough SD	Plum
1	n/a	Pocono Mountain SD	Swiftwater
1	n/a	Pottsgrove SD	Pottstown
1	n/a	Pottstown SD	Pottstown
1	n/a	Pottsville Area SD	Pottsville
1	n/a	Punxsutawney Area SD	Punxsutawney
1	n/a	Quaker Valley SD	Sewickley
1	n/a	Quakertown Community SD	Quakertown
1	n/a	Radnor Township SD	Wayne
1	n/a	Reading SD	Reading
1	n/a	Red Lion Area SD	Red Lion
1	n/a	Reynolds SD	Greenville
1	n/a	Richland SD	Johnstown
1	n/a	Ridley SD	Folsom
1	n/a	Ringgold SD	New Eagle
1	n/a	Riverside Beaver County SD	Ellwood City
1	n/a	Rose Tree Media SD	Media
1	n/a	Saint Marys Area SD	Saint Marys
1	n/a	Salisbury Township SD	Allentown
1	n/a	Saucon Valley SD	Hellertown
1	n/a	Schuylkill Valley SD	Leesport
1	n/a	Scranton SD	Scranton
1	n/a	Selinsgrove Area SD	Selinsgrove
1	n/a	Seneca Valley SD	Harmony
1	n/a	Shaler Area SD	Glenshaw
1	n/a	Shamokin Area SD	Coal Township
1	n/a	Sharon City SD	Sharon
1	n/a	Shikellamy SD	Sunbury
1	n/a	Shippensburg Area SD	Shippensburg
1	n/a	Slippery Rock Area SD	Slippery Rock
1	n/a	Solanco SD	Quarryville

1	n/a	Somerset Area SD	Somerset
1	n/a	Souderton Area SD	Souderton
1	n/a	South Allegheny SD	Mc Keesport
1	n/a	South Butler County SD	Saxonburg
1	n/a	South Eastern SD	Fawn Grove
1	n/a	South Fayette Township SD	Mc Donald
1	n/a	South Middleton SD	Boiling Springs
1	n/a	South Park SD	South Park
1	n/a	South Western SD	Hanover
1	n/a	Southeast Delco SD	Folcroft
1	n/a	Southern Lehigh SD	Center Valley
1	n/a	Southern Tioga SD	Blossburg
1	n/a	Southern York County SD	Glen Rock
1	n/a	Southmoreland SD	Scottdale
1	n/a	Spring Cove SD	Roaring Spring
1	n/a	Spring Grove Area SD	Spring Grove
1	n/a	Spring-Ford Area SD	Collegeville
1	n/a	Springfield SD	Springfield
1	n/a	Springfield Township SD	Oreland
1	n/a	State College Area SD	State College
1	n/a	Steel Valley SD	Munhall
1	n/a	Sto-Rox SD	Mckees Rocks
1	n/a	Stroudsburg Area SD	Stroudsburg
1	n/a	Susquehanna Township SD	Harrisburg
1	n/a	Susquenita SD	Duncannon
1	n/a	Tamaqua Area SD	Tamaqua
1	n/a	Titusville Area SD	Titusville
1	n/a	Towanda Area SD	Towanda
1	n/a	Tredyffrin-Easttown SD	Berwyn
1	n/a	Trinity Area SD	Washington
1	n/a	Troy Area SD	Troy
1	n/a	Tulpehocken Area SD	Bernville
1	n/a	Tunkhannock Area SD	Tunkhannock
1	n/a	Tuscarora SD	Mercersburg
1	n/a	Twin Valley SD	Elverson
1	n/a	Tyrone Area SD	Tyrone
1	n/a	Uniontown Area SD	Uniontown
1	n/a	Unionville-Chadds Ford SD	Kennett Square
1	n/a	Upper Adams SD	Biglerville
1	n/a	Upper Darby SD	Drexel Hill
1	n/a	Upper Dublin SD	Maple Glen
1	n/a	Upper Merion Area SD	King Of Prussia
1	n/a	Upper Moreland Township SD	Willow Grove
1	n/a	Upper Perkiomen SD	East Greenville
1	n/a	Upper Saint Clair SD	Pittsburgh
1	n/a	Valley View SD	Archbald
1	n/a	Wallenpaupack Area SD	Hawley
1	n/a	Wallingford-Swarthmore SD	Wallingford
1	n/a	Warren County SD	North Warren
1	n/a	Warrior Run SD	Turbotville
1	n/a	Warwick SD	Lititz
1	n/a	Washington SD	Washington
1	n/a	Wattsburg Area SD	Erie
1	n/a	Wayne Highlands SD	Honesdale
1	n/a	Waynesboro Area SD	Waynesboro
1	n/a	Wellsboro Area SD	Wellsboro
1	n/a	West Allegheny SD	Imperial
1	n/a	West Chester Area SD	West Chester
1	n/a	West Jefferson Hills SD	Jefferson Hls
1	n/a	West Mifflin Area SD	West Mifflin
1	n/a	West Perry SD	Elliottsburg
1	n/a	West Shore SD	New Cumberland
1	n/a	West York Area SD	York
1	n/a	Western Wayne SD	South Canaan
1	n/a	Westmont Hilltop SD	Johnstown
1	n/a	Whitehall-Coplay SD	Whitehall
1	n/a	Wilkes-Barre Area SD	Wilkes Barre
1	n/a	Wilkinsburg Borough SD	Wilkinsburg
1	n/a	William Penn SD	Lansdowne
1	n/a	Williamsport Area SD	Williamsport
1	n/a	Wilmington Area SD	New Wilmington
1	n/a	Wilson SD	West Lawn
1	n/a	Wilson Area SD	Easton
1	n/a	Wissahickon SD	Ambler
1	n/a	Woodland Hills SD	Pittsburgh
1	n/a	Wyalusing Area SD	Wyalusing
1	n/a	Wyoming Area SD	Exeter
1	n/a	Wyoming Valley West SD	Kingston
1	n/a	Wyomissing Area SD	Wyomissing
1	n/a	York City SD	York
1	n/a	York Suburban SD	York
1	n/a	Yough SD	Herminie

Female Students

Rank	Percent	District Name	City
1	n/a	Abington Heights SD	Clarks Summit
1	n/a	Abington SD	Abington
1	n/a	Albert Gallatin Area SD	Uniontown
1	n/a	Allentown City SD	Allentown
1	n/a	Altoona Area SD	Altoona
1	n/a	Ambridge Area SD	Ambridge
1	n/a	Annville-Cleona SD	Annville
1	n/a	Apollo-Ridge SD	Spring Church
1	n/a	Armstrong SD	Ford City
1	n/a	Athens Area SD	Athens
1	n/a	Avon Grove SD	West Grove
1	n/a	Bald Eagle Area SD	Wingate
1	n/a	Baldwin-Whitehall SD	Pittsburgh
1	n/a	Bangor Area SD	Bangor
1	n/a	Beaver Area SD	Beaver
1	n/a	Bedford Area SD	Bedford
1	n/a	Belle Vernon Area SD	Belle Vernon
1	n/a	Bellefonte Area SD	Bellefonte
1	n/a	Bensalem Township SD	Bensalem
1	n/a	Bermudian Springs SD	York Springs
1	n/a	Berwick Area SD	Berwick
1	n/a	Bethel Park SD	Bethel Park
1	n/a	Bethlehem Area SD	Bethlehem
1	n/a	Big Beaver Falls Area SD	Beaver Falls
1	n/a	Big Spring SD	Newville
1	n/a	Blackhawk SD	Beaver Falls
1	n/a	Blairsville-Saltsburg SD	Blairsville
1	n/a	Bloomsburg Area SD	Bloomsburg
1	n/a	Blue Mountain SD	Orwigsburg
1	n/a	Boyertown Area SD	Boyertown
1	n/a	Bradford Area SD	Bradford
1	n/a	Brandywine Heights Area SD	Topton
1	n/a	Bristol Township SD	Levittown
1	n/a	Brookville Area SD	Brookville
1	n/a	Brownsville Area SD	Brownsville
1	n/a	Burgettstown Area SD	Burgettstown
1	n/a	Burrell SD	Lower Burrell
1	n/a	Butler Area SD	Butler
1	n/a	Cambria Heights SD	Patton
1	n/a	Canon-Mcmillan SD	Canonsburg
1	n/a	Carlisle Area SD	Carlisle
1	n/a	Carlynton SD	Carnegie
1	n/a	Catasauqua Area SD	Catasauqua
1	n/a	Centennial SD	Warminster
1	n/a	Center Area SD	Monaca
1	n/a	Central Bucks SD	Doylestown
1	n/a	Central Cambria SD	Ebensburg
1	n/a	Central Columbia SD	Bloomsburg
1	n/a	Central Dauphin SD	Harrisburg
1	n/a	Central Greene SD	Waynesburg
1	n/a	Central York SD	York
1	n/a	Chambersburg Area SD	Chambersburg
1	n/a	Charleroi SD	Charleroi
1	n/a	Chartiers Valley SD	Pittsburgh
1	n/a	Cheltenham Township SD	Elkins Park
1	n/a	Chester-Upland SD	Chester
1	n/a	Chestnut Ridge SD	Fishertown
1	n/a	Chichester SD	Boothwyn
1	n/a	Clearfield Area SD	Clearfield
1	n/a	Coatesville Area SD	Coatesville
1	n/a	Cocalico SD	Denver
1	n/a	Colonial SD	Plymouth Meeting
1	n/a	Columbia Borough SD	Columbia
1	n/a	Conestoga Valley SD	Lancaster
1	n/a	Conewago Valley SD	New Oxford
1	n/a	Conneaut SD	Linesville
1	n/a	Connellsville Area SD	Connellsville
1	n/a	Conrad Weiser Area SD	Robesonia
1	n/a	Cornwall-Lebanon SD	Lebanon
1	n/a	Corry Area SD	Corry
1	n/a	Council Rock SD	Richboro
1	n/a	Cranberry Area SD	Seneca
1	n/a	Crawford Central SD	Meadville
1	n/a	Crestwood SD	Mountain Top
1	n/a	Cumberland Valley SD	Mechanicsburg
1	n/a	Dallas SD	Dallas
1	n/a	Dallastown Area SD	Dallastown
1	n/a	Daniel Boone Area SD	Douglassville
1	n/a	Danville Area SD	Danville
1	n/a	Deer Lakes SD	Russellton
1	n/a	Delaware Valley SD	Milford
1	n/a	Derry Area SD	Derry
1	n/a	Derry Township SD	Hershey
1	n/a	Donegal SD	Mount Joy
1	n/a	Dover Area SD	Dover
1	n/a	Downingtown Area SD	Downingtown
1	n/a	Dubois Area SD	Du Bois
1	n/a	Dunmore SD	Dunmore
1	n/a	East Allegheny SD	N Versailles
1	n/a	East Lycoming SD	Hughesville
1	n/a	East Penn SD	Emmaus
1	n/a	East Pennsboro Area SD	Enola
1	n/a	East Stroudsburg Area SD	E Stroudsburg
1	n/a	Eastern Lancaster County SD	New Holland
1	n/a	Eastern Lebanon County SD	Myerstown
1	n/a	Eastern York SD	Wrightsville
1	n/a	Easton Area SD	Easton
1	n/a	Elizabeth Forward SD	Elizabeth
1	n/a	Elizabethtown Area SD	Elizabethtown
1	n/a	Elk Lake SD	Dimock
1	n/a	Ellwood City Area SD	Ellwood City
1	n/a	Ephrata Area SD	Ephrata
1	n/a	Erie City SD	Erie
1	n/a	Everett Area SD	Everett
1	n/a	Exeter Township SD	Reading
1	n/a	Fairview SD	Fairview
1	n/a	Fleetwood Area SD	Fleetwood
1	n/a	Forest Hills SD	Sidman
1	n/a	Fort Leboeuf SD	Waterford
1	n/a	Fox Chapel Area SD	Pittsburgh
1	n/a	Franklin Area SD	Franklin
1	n/a	Franklin Regional SD	Murrysville
1	n/a	Freedom Area SD	Freedom
1	n/a	Freeport Area SD	Freeport
1	n/a	Garnet Valley SD	Glen Mills
1	n/a	Gateway SD	Monroeville
1	n/a	General Mclane SD	Edinboro
1	n/a	Gettysburg Area SD	Gettysburg
1	n/a	Girard SD	Girard
1	n/a	Governor Mifflin SD	Shillington
1	n/a	Great Valley SD	Malvern
1	n/a	Greater Johnstown SD	Johnstown
1	n/a	Greater Latrobe SD	Latrobe
1	n/a	Greater Nanticoke Area SD	Nanticoke
1	n/a	Greencastle-Antrim SD	Greencastle
1	n/a	Greensburg Salem SD	Greensburg
1	n/a	Greenville Area SD	Greenville
1	n/a	Grove City Area SD	Grove City
1	n/a	Hamburg Area SD	Hamburg
1	n/a	Hampton Township SD	Gibsonia
1	n/a	Hanover Area SD	Wilkes Barre
1	n/a	Hanover Public SD	Hanover
1	n/a	Harbor Creek SD	Harborcreek
1	n/a	Harrisburg City SD	Harrisburg
1	n/a	Hatboro-Horsham SD	Horsham
1	n/a	Haverford Township SD	Havertown
1	n/a	Hazleton Area SD	Hazleton
1	n/a	Hempfield SD	Landisville
1	n/a	Hempfield Area SD	Greensburg
1	n/a	Hermitage SD	Hermitage
1	n/a	Highlands SD	Natrona Heights
1	n/a	Hollidaysburg Area SD	Hollidaysburg
1	n/a	Hopewell Area SD	Aliquippa
1	n/a	Huntingdon Area SD	Huntingdon
1	n/a	Indiana Area SD	Indiana
1	n/a	Interboro SD	Prospect Park
1	n/a	Jeannette City SD	Jeannette
1	n/a	Jersey Shore Area SD	Jersey Shore
1	n/a	Jim Thorpe Area SD	Jim Thorpe
1	n/a	Juniata County SD	Mifflintown
1	n/a	Karns City Area SD	Karns City
1	n/a	Kennett Consolidated SD	Kennett Square
1	n/a	Keystone Central SD	Lock Haven
1	n/a	Keystone Oaks SD	Pittsburgh
1	n/a	Kiski Area SD	Vandergrift
1	n/a	Kutztown Area SD	Kutztown
1	n/a	Lake-Lehman SD	Lehman
1	n/a	Lakeland SD	Jermyn
1	n/a	Lampeter-Strasburg SD	Lampeter
1	n/a	Lancaster SD	Lancaster
1	n/a	Laurel Highlands SD	Uniontown
1	n/a	Lebanon SD	Lebanon
1	n/a	Lehighton Area SD	Lehighton
1	n/a	Lewisburg Area SD	Lewisburg
1	n/a	Ligonier Valley SD	Ligonier
1	n/a	Littlestown Area SD	Littlestown
1	n/a	Lower Dauphin SD	Hummelstown
1	n/a	Lower Merion SD	Ardmore
1	n/a	Lower Moreland Township SD	Huntingdon Vly
1	n/a	Manheim Central SD	Manheim
1	n/a	Manheim Township SD	Lancaster
1	n/a	Marion Center Area SD	Marion Center
1	n/a	Marple Newtown SD	Newtown Square
1	n/a	Mars Area SD	Mars
1	n/a	Mcguffey SD	Claysville
1	n/a	Mckeesport Area SD	Mc Keesport
1	n/a	Mechanicsburg Area SD	Mechanicsburg
1	n/a	Mercer Area SD	Mercer
1	n/a	Methacton SD	Norristown
1	n/a	Mid Valley SD	Throop
1	n/a	Midd-West SD	Middleburg
1	n/a	Middletown Area SD	Middletown
1	n/a	Mifflin County SD	Lewistown
1	n/a	Mifflinburg Area SD	Mifflinburg
1	n/a	Millcreek Township SD	Erie
1	n/a	Milton Area SD	Milton
1	n/a	Mohawk Area SD	Bessemer
1	n/a	Moniteau SD	West Sunbury
1	n/a	Montour SD	Mc Kees Rocks
1	n/a	Montoursville Area SD	Montoursville
1	n/a	Montrose Area SD	Montrose
1	n/a	Moon Area SD	Moon Township

Rank	Percent	District Name	City
1	n/a	Mount Carmel Area SD	Mount Carmel
1	n/a	Mount Lebanon SD	Pittsburgh
1	n/a	Mount Pleasant Area SD	Mount Pleasant
1	n/a	Mount Union Area SD	Mount Union
1	n/a	Muhlenberg SD	Reading
1	n/a	Nazareth Area SD	Nazareth
1	n/a	Neshaminy SD	Langhorne
1	n/a	New Brighton Area SD	New Brighton
1	n/a	New Castle Area SD	New Castle
1	n/a	New Kensington-Arnold SD	New Kensington
1	n/a	Norristown Area SD	Norristown
1	n/a	North Allegheny SD	Pittsburgh
1	n/a	North East SD	North East
1	n/a	North Hills SD	Pittsburgh
1	n/a	North Penn SD	Lansdale
1	n/a	North Pocono SD	Moscow
1	n/a	North Schuylkill SD	Ashland
1	n/a	Northampton Area SD	Northampton
1	n/a	Northeastern York SD	Manchester
1	n/a	Northern Lebanon SD	Fredericksburg
1	n/a	Northern Lehigh SD	Slatington
1	n/a	Northern Tioga SD	Elkland
1	n/a	Northern York County SD	Dillsburg
1	n/a	Northgate SD	Pittsburgh
1	n/a	Northwestern SD	Albion
1	n/a	Northwestern Lehigh SD	New Tripoli
1	n/a	Norwin SD	N Huntingdon
1	n/a	Octorara Area SD	Atglen
1	n/a	Oil City Area SD	Oil City
1	n/a	Oley Valley SD	Oley
1	n/a	Owen J Roberts SD	Pottstown
1	n/a	Oxford Area SD	Oxford
1	n/a	PDE Division of Data Services	Harrisburg
1	n/a	Palisades SD	Kintnersville
1	n/a	Palmerton Area SD	Palmerton
1	n/a	Palmyra Area SD	Palmyra
1	n/a	Parkland SD	Allentown
1	n/a	Pen Argyl Area SD	Pen Argyl
1	n/a	Penn Cambria SD	Cresson
1	n/a	Penn Hills SD	Pittsburgh
1	n/a	Penn Manor SD	Millersville
1	n/a	Penn-Delco SD	Aston
1	n/a	Penn-Trafford SD	Harrison City
1	n/a	Penncrest SD	Saegertown
1	n/a	Pennridge SD	Perkasie
1	n/a	Penns Valley Area SD	Spring Mills
1	n/a	Pennsbury SD	Fallsington
1	n/a	Pennsylvania Virtual CS	Norristown
1	n/a	Pequea Valley SD	Kinzers
1	n/a	Perkiomen Valley SD	Collegeville
1	n/a	Peters Township SD	Mcmurray
1	n/a	Philadelphia City SD	Philadelphia
1	n/a	Philipsburg-Osceola Area SD	Philipsburg
1	n/a	Phoenixville Area SD	Phoenixville
1	n/a	Pine Grove Area SD	Pine Grove
1	n/a	Pine-Richland SD	Gibsonia
1	n/a	Pittsburgh SD	Pittsburgh
1	n/a	Pittston Area SD	Pittston
1	n/a	Pleasant Valley SD	Brodheadsville
1	n/a	Plum Borough SD	Plum
1	n/a	Pocono Mountain SD	Swiftwater
1	n/a	Pottsgrove SD	Pottstown
1	n/a	Pottstown SD	Pottstown
1	n/a	Pottsville Area SD	Pottsville
1	n/a	Punxsutawney Area SD	Punxsutawney
1	n/a	Quaker Valley SD	Sewickley
1	n/a	Quakertown Community SD	Quakertown
1	n/a	Radnor Township SD	Wayne
1	n/a	Reading SD	Reading
1	n/a	Red Lion Area SD	Red Lion
1	n/a	Reynolds SD	Greenville
1	n/a	Richland SD	Johnstown
1	n/a	Ridley SD	Folsom
1	n/a	Ringgold SD	New Eagle
1	n/a	Riverside Beaver County SD	Ellwood City
1	n/a	Rose Tree Media SD	Media
1	n/a	Saint Marys Area SD	Saint Marys
1	n/a	Salisbury Township SD	Allentown
1	n/a	Saucon Valley SD	Hellertown
1	n/a	Schuylkill Valley SD	Leesport
1	n/a	Scranton SD	Scranton
1	n/a	Selinsgrove Area SD	Selinsgrove
1	n/a	Seneca Valley SD	Harmony
1	n/a	Shaler Area SD	Glenshaw
1	n/a	Shamokin Area SD	Coal Township
1	n/a	Sharon City SD	Sharon
1	n/a	Shikellamy SD	Sunbury
1	n/a	Shippensburg Area SD	Shippensburg
1	n/a	Slippery Rock Area SD	Slippery Rock
1	n/a	Solanco SD	Quarryville
1	n/a	Somerset Area SD	Somerset
1	n/a	Souderton Area SD	Souderton
1	n/a	South Allegheny SD	Mc Keesport
1	n/a	South Butler County SD	Saxonburg
1	n/a	South Eastern SD	Fawn Grove
1	n/a	South Fayette Township SD	Mc Donald
1	n/a	South Middleton SD	Boiling Springs
1	n/a	South Park SD	South Park
1	n/a	South Western SD	Hanover
1	n/a	Southeast Delco SD	Folcroft
1	n/a	Southern Lehigh SD	Center Valley
1	n/a	Southern Tioga SD	Blossburg
1	n/a	Southern York County SD	Glen Rock
1	n/a	Southmoreland SD	Scottdale
1	n/a	Spring Cove SD	Roaring Spring
1	n/a	Spring Grove Area SD	Spring Grove
1	n/a	Spring-Ford Area SD	Collegeville
1	n/a	Springfield SD	Springfield
1	n/a	Springfield Township SD	Oreland
1	n/a	State College Area SD	State College
1	n/a	Steel Valley SD	Munhall
1	n/a	Sto-Rox SD	Mckees Rocks
1	n/a	Stroudsburg Area SD	Stroudsburg
1	n/a	Susquehanna Township SD	Harrisburg
1	n/a	Susquenita SD	Duncannon
1	n/a	Tamaqua Area SD	Tamaqua
1	n/a	Titusville Area SD	Titusville
1	n/a	Towanda Area SD	Towanda
1	n/a	Tredyffrin-Easttown SD	Berwyn
1	n/a	Trinity Area SD	Washington
1	n/a	Troy Area SD	Troy
1	n/a	Tulpehocken Area SD	Bernville
1	n/a	Tunkhannock Area SD	Tunkhannock
1	n/a	Tuscarora SD	Mercersburg
1	n/a	Twin Valley SD	Elverson
1	n/a	Tyrone Area SD	Tyrone
1	n/a	Uniontown Area SD	Uniontown
1	n/a	Unionville-Chadds Ford SD	Kennett Square
1	n/a	Upper Adams SD	Biglerville
1	n/a	Upper Darby SD	Drexel Hill
1	n/a	Upper Dublin SD	Maple Glen
1	n/a	Upper Merion Area SD	King Of Prussia
1	n/a	Upper Moreland Township SD	Willow Grove
1	n/a	Upper Perkiomen SD	East Greenville
1	n/a	Upper Saint Clair SD	Pittsburgh
1	n/a	Valley View SD	Archbald
1	n/a	Wallenpaupack Area SD	Hawley
1	n/a	Wallingford-Swarthmore SD	Wallingford
1	n/a	Warren County SD	North Warren
1	n/a	Warrior Run SD	Turbotville
1	n/a	Warwick SD	Lititz
1	n/a	Washington SD	Washington
1	n/a	Wattsburg Area SD	Erie
1	n/a	Wayne Highlands SD	Honesdale
1	n/a	Waynesboro Area SD	Waynesboro
1	n/a	Wellsboro Area SD	Wellsboro
1	n/a	West Allegheny SD	Imperial
1	n/a	West Chester Area SD	West Chester
1	n/a	West Jefferson Hills SD	Jefferson Hls
1	n/a	West Mifflin Area SD	West Mifflin
1	n/a	West Perry SD	Elliottsburg
1	n/a	West Shore SD	New Cumberland
1	n/a	West York Area SD	York
1	n/a	Western Wayne SD	South Canaan
1	n/a	Westmont Hilltop SD	Johnstown
1	n/a	Whitehall-Coplay SD	Whitehall
1	n/a	Wilkes-Barre Area SD	Wilkes Barre
1	n/a	Wilkinsburg Borough SD	Wilkinsburg
1	n/a	William Penn SD	Lansdowne
1	n/a	Williamsport Area SD	Williamsport
1	n/a	Wilmington Area SD	New Wilmington
1	n/a	Wilson SD	West Lawn
1	n/a	Wilson Area SD	Easton
1	n/a	Wissahickon SD	Ambler
1	n/a	Woodland Hills SD	Pittsburgh
1	n/a	Wyalusing Area SD	Wyalusing
1	n/a	Wyoming Area SD	Exeter
1	n/a	Wyoming Valley West SD	Kingston
1	n/a	Wyomissing Area SD	Wyomissing
1	n/a	York City SD	York
1	n/a	York Suburban SD	York
1	n/a	Yough SD	Herminie

Individual Education Program Students

Rank	Percent	District Name	City
1	25.3	Columbia Borough SD	Columbia
2	23.9	Sto-Rox SD	Mckees Rocks
3	22.1	Chester-Upland SD	Chester
3	22.1	Lancaster SD	Lancaster
5	22.0	Central Greene SD	Waynesburg
6	21.6	Southeast Delco SD	Folcroft
7	20.8	Williamsport Area SD	Williamsport
8	20.2	Bristol Township SD	Levittown
8	20.2	William Penn SD	Lansdowne
10	19.9	Franklin Area SD	Franklin
11	19.8	Oil City Area SD	Oil City
12	19.4	Erie City SD	Erie
12	19.4	Tyrone Area SD	Tyrone
14	19.2	Ambridge Area SD	Ambridge
15	19.1	Pottstown SD	Pottstown
16	19.0	Eastern York SD	Wrightsville
17	18.9	Wilkinsburg Borough SD	Wilkinsburg
18	18.7	Connellsville Area SD	Connellsville
19	18.3	Tuscarora SD	Mercersburg
20	18.1	Hanover Area SD	Wilkes Barre
20	18.1	Southmoreland SD	Scottdale
20	18.1	Warren County SD	North Warren
20	18.1	Washington SD	Washington
24	17.9	Berwick Area SD	Berwick
24	17.9	Montrose Area SD	Montrose
26	17.8	Donegal SD	Mount Joy
26	17.8	West Perry SD	Elliottsburg
28	17.7	Scranton SD	Scranton
28	17.7	Wallingford-Swarthmore SD	Wallingford
30	17.6	New Kensington-Arnold SD	New Kensington
30	17.6	York City SD	York
32	17.5	Athens Area SD	Athens
32	17.5	Corry Area SD	Corry
32	17.5	Hanover Public SD	Hanover
32	17.5	Harrisburg City SD	Harrisburg
32	17.5	Ridley SD	Folsom
37	17.4	Keystone Central SD	Lock Haven
38	17.3	Mid Valley SD	Throop
38	17.3	Northeastern York SD	Manchester
38	17.3	Pittsburgh SD	Pittsburgh
38	17.3	Shaler Area SD	Glenshaw
42	17.2	Charleroi SD	Charleroi
42	17.2	Penn-Delco SD	Aston
44	17.1	Centennial SD	Warminster
44	17.1	Marple Newtown SD	Newtown Square
46	17.0	Albert Gallatin Area SD	Uniontown
46	17.0	Cranberry Area SD	Seneca
46	17.0	Lower Merion SD	Ardmore
49	16.9	East Stroudsburg Area SD	E Stroudsburg
50	16.8	Middletown Area SD	Middletown
50	16.8	Mount Union Area SD	Mount Union
50	16.8	Palisades SD	Kintnersville
53	16.7	Everett Area SD	Everett
54	16.6	Chichester SD	Boothwyn
54	16.6	Crawford Central SD	Meadville
54	16.6	Garnet Valley SD	Glen Mills
54	16.6	Norristown Area SD	Norristown
58	16.5	Greater Johnstown SD	Johnstown
58	16.5	New Castle Area SD	New Castle
58	16.5	Upper Adams SD	Biglerville
61	16.4	Penns Valley Area SD	Spring Mills
61	16.4	Spring Grove Area SD	Spring Grove
63	16.3	Big Spring SD	Newville
63	16.3	Brandywine Heights Area SD	Topton
63	16.3	Highlands SD	Natrona Heights
66	16.2	Altoona Area SD	Altoona
66	16.2	Brookville Area SD	Brookville
66	16.2	Sharon City SD	Sharon
66	16.2	Wallenpaupack Area SD	Hawley
66	16.2	Warwick SD	Lititz
66	16.2	Wilmington Area SD	New Wilmington
72	16.1	Bangor Area SD	Bangor
72	16.1	Huntingdon Area SD	Huntingdon
74	16.0	Kutztown Area SD	Kutztown
74	16.0	Neshaminy SD	Langhorne
74	16.0	Punxsutawney Area SD	Punxsutawney
74	16.0	Radnor Township SD	Wayne
74	16.0	Titusville Area SD	Titusville
79	15.9	Greater Nanticoke Area SD	Nanticoke
79	15.9	Haverford Township SD	Havertown
79	15.9	Southern York County SD	Glen Rock
79	15.9	Springfield Township SD	Oreland
83	15.8	Bensalem Township SD	Bensalem
83	15.8	Blairsville-Saltsburg SD	Blairsville
83	15.8	Chestnut Ridge SD	Fishertown
83	15.8	Jersey Shore Area SD	Jersey Shore
83	15.8	Lower Dauphin SD	Hummelstown
83	15.8	Mckeesport Area SD	Mc Keesport
89	15.7	Bellefonte Area SD	Bellefonte
89	15.7	Susquehanna Township SD	Harrisburg
91	15.6	Chambersburg Area SD	Chambersburg
92	15.5	Susquenita SD	Duncannon
92	15.5	Wilson Area SD	Easton
94	15.4	Bloomsburg Area SD	Bloomsburg
94	15.4	Brownsville Area SD	Brownsville
94	15.4	Burgettstown Area SD	Burgettstown
94	15.4	Elk Lake SD	Dimock
98	15.3	Catasauqua Area SD	Catasauqua
98	15.3	Fort Leboeuf SD	Waterford
98	15.3	Great Valley SD	Malvern
98	15.3	Jeannette City SD	Jeannette
98	15.3	Phoenixville Area SD	Phoenixville

98	15.3	Rose Tree Media SD	Media
104	15.2	Midd-West SD	Middleburg
104	15.2	Mount Pleasant Area SD	Mount Pleasant
104	15.2	Northwestern SD	Albion
104	15.2	Tulpehocken Area SD	Bernville
104	15.2	Wilkes-Barre Area SD	Wilkes Barre
109	15.1	Butler Area SD	Butler
109	15.1	Carlisle Area SD	Carlisle
109	15.1	Conneaut SD	Linesville
109	15.1	East Allegheny SD	N Versailles
109	15.1	Lebanon SD	Lebanon
109	15.1	Uniontown Area SD	Uniontown
109	15.1	Waynesboro Area SD	Waynesboro
116	15.0	Central Cambria SD	Ebensburg
116	15.0	Manheim Central SD	Manheim
116	15.0	Woodland Hills SD	Pittsburgh
119	14.9	Wissahickon SD	Ambler
120	14.8	Armstrong SD	Ford City
120	14.8	Dover Area SD	Dover
120	14.8	Elizabethtown Area SD	Elizabethtown
123	14.7	Apollo-Ridge SD	Spring Church
123	14.7	Mercer Area SD	Mercer
123	14.7	Reynolds SD	Greenville
123	14.7	Shamokin Area SD	Coal Township
123	14.7	South Eastern SD	Fawn Grove
123	14.7	Spring Cove SD	Roaring Spring
123	14.7	Towanda Area SD	Towanda
123	14.7	West Shore SD	New Cumberland
131	14.6	Colonial SD	Plymouth Meeting
131	14.6	Gettysburg Area SD	Gettysburg
131	14.6	Jim Thorpe Area SD	Jim Thorpe
131	14.6	Mifflin County SD	Lewistown
131	14.6	Northwestern Lehigh SD	New Tripoli
131	14.6	Penn Cambria SD	Cresson
137	14.5	Red Lion Area SD	Red Lion
138	14.4	Moniteau SD	West Sunbury
138	14.4	North Schuylkill SD	Ashland
138	14.4	Springfield SD	Springfield
138	14.4	Trinity Area SD	Washington
142	14.3	Palmerton Area SD	Palmerton
142	14.3	Pottsville Area SD	Pottsville
144	14.2	Bedford Area SD	Bedford
144	14.2	Hempfield SD	Landisville
144	14.2	Penn Manor SD	Millersville
144	14.2	Wayne Highlands SD	Honesdale
148	14.1	Cocalico SD	Denver
148	14.1	Greenville Area SD	Greenville
148	14.1	Wyoming Valley West SD	Kingston
151	14.0	Deer Lakes SD	Russellton
151	14.0	Downingtown Area SD	Downingtown
151	14.0	Interboro SD	Prospect Park
151	14.0	Lakeland SD	Jermyn
151	14.0	Moon Area SD	Moon Township
156	13.9	Clearfield Area SD	Clearfield
156	13.9	Gateway SD	Monroeville
156	13.9	Salisbury Township SD	Allentown
156	13.9	Somerset Area SD	Somerset
160	13.8	Ligonier Valley SD	Ligonier
160	13.8	Troy Area SD	Troy
160	13.8	Twin Valley SD	Elverson
163	13.7	East Pennsboro Area SD	Enola
163	13.7	Octorara Area SD	Atglen
163	13.7	Slippery Rock Area SD	Slippery Rock
163	13.7	Tamaqua Area SD	Tamaqua
163	13.7	Upper Darby SD	Drexel Hill
163	13.7	Wattsburg Area SD	Erie
169	13.6	Blue Mountain SD	Orwigsburg
169	13.6	Ellwood City Area SD	Ellwood City
169	13.6	Kiski Area SD	Vandergrift
169	13.6	Northampton Area SD	Northampton
169	13.6	Shippensburg Area SD	Shippensburg
169	13.6	Spring-Ford Area SD	Collegeville
175	13.5	Conrad Weiser Area SD	Robesonia
175	13.5	Pequea Valley SD	Kinzers
177	13.4	Coatesville Area SD	Coatesville
177	13.4	Dubois Area SD	Du Bois
177	13.4	Eastern Lebanon County SD	Myerstown
177	13.4	Elizabeth Forward SD	Elizabeth
177	13.4	Penncrest SD	Saegertown
177	13.4	West York Area SD	York
183	13.3	Bradford Area SD	Bradford
183	13.3	Council Rock SD	Richboro
183	13.3	Upper Merion Area SD	King Of Prussia
186	13.2	Ephrata Area SD	Ephrata
186	13.2	Riverside Beaver County SD	Ellwood City
186	13.2	Steel Valley SD	Munhall
189	13.1	Avon Grove SD	West Grove
189	13.1	Big Beaver Falls Area SD	Beaver Falls
189	13.1	Conewago Valley SD	New Oxford
189	13.1	Pennridge SD	Perkasie
189	13.1	Wyoming Area SD	Exeter
194	13.0	Owen J Roberts SD	Pottstown
195	12.9	Exeter Township SD	Reading
195	12.9	Girard SD	Girard
195	12.9	North Penn SD	Lansdale
195	12.9	Penn Hills SD	Pittsburgh
195	12.9	Saint Marys Area SD	Saint Marys
195	12.9	Seneca Valley SD	Harmony
195	12.9	West Allegheny SD	Imperial
195	12.9	Western Wayne SD	South Canaan
203	12.8	Abington Heights SD	Clarks Summit
203	12.8	Marion Center Area SD	Marion Center
203	12.8	Pennsbury SD	Fallsington
206	12.7	Belle Vernon Area SD	Belle Vernon
206	12.7	Mcguffey SD	Claysville
206	12.7	South Middleton SD	Boiling Springs
209	12.6	Cambria Heights SD	Patton
209	12.6	Cheltenham Township SD	Elkins Park
209	12.6	Ringgold SD	New Eagle
209	12.6	Unionville-Chadds Ford SD	Kennett Square
213	12.5	Bald Eagle Area SD	Wingate
213	12.5	Central Dauphin SD	Harrisburg
213	12.5	Northern Lebanon SD	Fredericksburg
213	12.5	Warrior Run SD	Turbotville
213	12.5	West Chester Area SD	West Chester
213	12.5	West Mifflin Area SD	West Mifflin
219	12.4	Freedom Area SD	Freedom
219	12.4	Oley Valley SD	Oley
219	12.4	Pottsgrove SD	Pottstown
219	12.4	Quakertown Community SD	Quakertown
219	12.4	Selinsgrove Area SD	Selinsgrove
219	12.4	Wilson SD	West Lawn
225	12.3	Bethlehem Area SD	Bethlehem
225	12.3	Central York SD	York
225	12.3	Daniel Boone Area SD	Douglassville
225	12.3	Palmyra Area SD	Palmyra
225	12.3	Pocono Mountain SD	Swiftwater
225	12.3	South Allegheny SD	Mc Keesport
231	12.2	Carlynton SD	Carnegie
231	12.2	Conestoga Valley SD	Lancaster
231	12.2	Dunmore SD	Dunmore
231	12.2	East Lycoming SD	Hughesville
231	12.2	Muhlenberg SD	Reading
231	12.2	Northern Lehigh SD	Slatington
231	12.2	Oxford Area SD	Oxford
231	12.2	Philadelphia City SD	Philadelphia
231	12.2	Quaker Valley SD	Sewickley
240	12.1	Annville-Cleona SD	Annville
240	12.1	Greencastle-Antrim SD	Greencastle
240	12.1	Hollidaysburg Area SD	Hollidaysburg
240	12.1	Hopewell Area SD	Aliquippa
240	12.1	Littlestown Area SD	Littlestown
240	12.1	Philipsburg-Osceola Area SD	Philipsburg
246	12.0	Hermitage SD	Hermitage
246	12.0	Lampeter-Strasburg SD	Lampeter
246	12.0	North Hills SD	Pittsburgh
246	12.0	Northern Tioga SD	Elkland
250	11.9	Cumberland Valley SD	Mechanicsburg
250	11.9	Easton Area SD	Easton
250	11.9	Valley View SD	Archbald
250	11.9	York Suburban SD	York
254	11.8	Burrell SD	Lower Burrell
254	11.8	General Mclane SD	Edinboro
254	11.8	Reading SD	Reading
254	11.8	Tredyffrin-Easttown SD	Berwyn
254	11.8	Yough SD	Herminie
259	11.7	Abington SD	Abington
259	11.7	Allentown City SD	Allentown
259	11.7	Boyertown Area SD	Boyertown
259	11.7	Souderton Area SD	Souderton
259	11.7	Southern Lehigh SD	Center Valley
264	11.6	Dallas SD	Dallas
264	11.6	Hamburg Area SD	Hamburg
264	11.6	Karns City Area SD	Karns City
264	11.6	Kennett Consolidated SD	Kennett Square
264	11.6	Lake-Lehman SD	Lehman
264	11.6	Schuylkill Valley SD	Leesport
270	11.5	Baldwin-Whitehall SD	Pittsburgh
270	11.5	Crestwood SD	Mountain Top
270	11.5	Dallastown Area SD	Dallastown
270	11.5	Juniata County SD	Mifflintown
270	11.5	Keystone Oaks SD	Pittsburgh
270	11.5	Laurel Highlands SD	Uniontown
270	11.5	Norwin SD	N Huntingdon
270	11.5	Pleasant Valley SD	Brodheadsville
270	11.5	Upper Dublin SD	Maple Glen
279	11.4	Fox Chapel Area SD	Pittsburgh
279	11.4	Governor Mifflin SD	Shillington
279	11.4	Indiana Area SD	Indiana
279	11.4	Lehighton Area SD	Lehighton
279	11.4	Manheim Township SD	Lancaster
279	11.4	North Pocono SD	Moscow
279	11.4	State College Area SD	State College
279	11.4	Stroudsburg Area SD	Stroudsburg
287	11.3	Bethel Park SD	Bethel Park
287	11.3	Fleetwood Area SD	Fleetwood
287	11.3	Forest Hills SD	Sidman
287	11.3	Lower Moreland Township SD	Huntingdon Vly
287	11.3	Mechanicsburg Area SD	Mechanicsburg
287	11.3	Parkland SD	Allentown
287	11.3	Tunkhannock Area SD	Tunkhannock
287	11.3	Upper Perkiomen SD	East Greenville
295	11.2	Greensburg Salem SD	Greensburg
295	11.2	Millcreek Township SD	Erie
295	11.2	Mohawk Area SD	Bessemer
295	11.2	Wellsboro Area SD	Wellsboro
299	11.1	Danville Area SD	Danville
299	11.1	Eastern Lancaster County SD	New Holland
299	11.1	Freeport Area SD	Freeport
299	11.1	Grove City Area SD	Grove City
299	11.1	Harbor Creek SD	Harborcreek
304	11.0	Cornwall-Lebanon SD	Lebanon
304	11.0	Montour SD	Mc Kees Rocks
304	11.0	Northgate SD	Pittsburgh
304	11.0	Southern Tioga SD	Blossburg
308	10.9	Hatboro-Horsham SD	Horsham
308	10.9	Pine Grove Area SD	Pine Grove
310	10.8	Methacton SD	Norristown
310	10.8	South Western SD	Hanover
312	10.7	Canon-Mcmillan SD	Canonsburg
312	10.7	Fairview SD	Fairview
314	10.6	Central Bucks SD	Doylestown
314	10.6	Hempfield Area SD	Greensburg
314	10.6	Mount Lebanon SD	Pittsburgh
314	10.6	Nazareth Area SD	Nazareth
314	10.6	Pittston Area SD	Pittston
319	10.4	West Jefferson Hills SD	Jefferson Hls
320	10.3	Hampton Township SD	Gibsonia
320	10.3	North East SD	North East
320	10.3	Penn-Trafford SD	Harrison City
320	10.3	Whitehall-Coplay SD	Whitehall
324	10.2	Center Area SD	Monaca
324	10.2	Chartiers Valley SD	Pittsburgh
324	10.2	Franklin Regional SD	Murrysville
324	10.2	Saucon Valley SD	Hellertown
324	10.2	Upper Moreland Township SD	Willow Grove
329	10.1	Central Columbia SD	Bloomsburg
330	10.0	Mifflinburg Area SD	Mifflinburg
330	10.0	Milton Area SD	Milton
330	10.0	Wyalusing Area SD	Wyalusing
333	9.9	East Penn SD	Emmaus
333	9.9	Mount Carmel Area SD	Mount Carmel
335	9.8	North Allegheny SD	Pittsburgh
335	9.8	Northern York County SD	Dillsburg
335	9.8	Upper Saint Clair SD	Pittsburgh
338	9.7	Derry Township SD	Hershey
338	9.7	Hazleton Area SD	Hazleton
338	9.7	Richland SD	Johnstown
338	9.7	Westmont Hilltop SD	Johnstown
342	9.5	Greater Latrobe SD	Latrobe
343	9.4	Pen Argyl Area SD	Pen Argyl
343	9.4	Perkiomen Valley SD	Collegeville
343	9.4	Pine-Richland SD	Gibsonia
346	9.3	New Brighton Area SD	New Brighton
346	9.3	Shikellamy SD	Sunbury
348	9.0	Montoursville Area SD	Montoursville
348	9.0	Wyomissing Area SD	Wyomissing
350	8.9	Blackhawk SD	Beaver Falls
350	8.9	Solanco SD	Quarryville
350	8.9	South Park SD	South Park
353	8.8	South Butler County SD	Saxonburg
353	8.8	South Fayette Township SD	Mc Donald
355	8.7	Beaver Area SD	Beaver
355	8.7	Derry Area SD	Derry
357	8.3	Lewisburg Area SD	Lewisburg
358	8.2	Delaware Valley SD	Milford
359	7.8	Bermudian Springs SD	York Springs
360	7.2	Plum Borough SD	Plum
361	7.1	Peters Township SD	Mcmurray
362	5.7	Mars Area SD	Mars
363	3.5	Pennsylvania Virtual CS	Norristown
364	0.0	PDE Division of Data Services	Harrisburg

English Language Learner Students

Rank	Percent	District Name	City
1	n/a	Abington Heights SD	Clarks Summit
1	n/a	Abington SD	Abington
1	n/a	Albert Gallatin Area SD	Uniontown
1	n/a	Allentown City SD	Allentown
1	n/a	Altoona Area SD	Altoona
1	n/a	Ambridge Area SD	Ambridge
1	n/a	Annville-Cleona SD	Annville
1	n/a	Apollo-Ridge SD	Spring Church
1	n/a	Armstrong SD	Ford City
1	n/a	Athens Area SD	Athens
1	n/a	Avon Grove SD	West Grove
1	n/a	Bald Eagle Area SD	Wingate

Rank	%	District	City
1	n/a	Baldwin-Whitehall SD	Pittsburgh
1	n/a	Bangor Area SD	Bangor
1	n/a	Beaver Area SD	Beaver
1	n/a	Bedford Area SD	Bedford
1	n/a	Belle Vernon Area SD	Belle Vernon
1	n/a	Bellefonte Area SD	Bellefonte
1	n/a	Bensalem Township SD	Bensalem
1	n/a	Bermudian Springs SD	York Springs
1	n/a	Berwick Area SD	Berwick
1	n/a	Bethel Park SD	Bethel Park
1	n/a	Bethlehem Area SD	Bethlehem
1	n/a	Big Beaver Falls Area SD	Beaver Falls
1	n/a	Big Spring SD	Newville
1	n/a	Blackhawk SD	Beaver Falls
1	n/a	Blairsville-Saltsburg SD	Blairsville
1	n/a	Bloomsburg Area SD	Bloomsburg
1	n/a	Blue Mountain SD	Orwigsburg
1	n/a	Boyertown Area SD	Boyertown
1	n/a	Bradford Area SD	Bradford
1	n/a	Brandywine Heights Area SD	Topton
1	n/a	Bristol Township SD	Levittown
1	n/a	Brookville Area SD	Brookville
1	n/a	Brownsville Area SD	Brownsville
1	n/a	Burgettstown Area SD	Burgettstown
1	n/a	Burrell SD	Lower Burrell
1	n/a	Butler Area SD	Butler
1	n/a	Cambria Heights SD	Patton
1	n/a	Canon-Mcmillan SD	Canonsburg
1	n/a	Carlisle Area SD	Carlisle
1	n/a	Carlynton SD	Carnegie
1	n/a	Catasauqua Area SD	Catasauqua
1	n/a	Centennial SD	Warminster
1	n/a	Center Area SD	Monaca
1	n/a	Central Bucks SD	Doylestown
1	n/a	Central Cambria SD	Ebensburg
1	n/a	Central Columbia SD	Bloomsburg
1	n/a	Central Dauphin SD	Harrisburg
1	n/a	Central Greene SD	Waynesburg
1	n/a	Central York SD	York
1	n/a	Chambersburg Area SD	Chambersburg
1	n/a	Charleroi SD	Charleroi
1	n/a	Chartiers Valley SD	Pittsburgh
1	n/a	Cheltenham Township SD	Elkins Park
1	n/a	Chester-Upland SD	Chester
1	n/a	Chestnut Ridge SD	Fishertown
1	n/a	Chichester SD	Boothwyn
1	n/a	Clearfield Area SD	Clearfield
1	n/a	Coatesville Area SD	Coatesville
1	n/a	Cocalico SD	Denver
1	n/a	Colonial SD	Plymouth Meeting
1	n/a	Columbia Borough SD	Columbia
1	n/a	Conestoga Valley SD	Lancaster
1	n/a	Conewago Valley SD	New Oxford
1	n/a	Conneaut SD	Linesville
1	n/a	Connellsville Area SD	Connellsville
1	n/a	Conrad Weiser Area SD	Robesonia
1	n/a	Cornwall-Lebanon SD	Lebanon
1	n/a	Corry Area SD	Corry
1	n/a	Council Rock SD	Richboro
1	n/a	Cranberry Area SD	Seneca
1	n/a	Crawford Central SD	Meadville
1	n/a	Crestwood SD	Mountain Top
1	n/a	Cumberland Valley SD	Mechanicsburg
1	n/a	Dallas SD	Dallas
1	n/a	Dallastown Area SD	Dallastown
1	n/a	Daniel Boone Area SD	Douglassville
1	n/a	Danville Area SD	Danville
1	n/a	Deer Lakes SD	Russellton
1	n/a	Delaware Valley SD	Milford
1	n/a	Derry Area SD	Derry
1	n/a	Derry Township SD	Hershey
1	n/a	Donegal SD	Mount Joy
1	n/a	Dover Area SD	Dover
1	n/a	Downingtown Area SD	Downingtown
1	n/a	Dubois Area SD	Du Bois
1	n/a	Dunmore SD	Dunmore
1	n/a	East Allegheny SD	N Versailles
1	n/a	East Lycoming SD	Hughesville
1	n/a	East Penn SD	Emmaus
1	n/a	East Pennsboro Area SD	Enola
1	n/a	East Stroudsburg Area SD	E Stroudsburg
1	n/a	Eastern Lancaster County SD	New Holland
1	n/a	Eastern Lebanon County SD	Myerstown
1	n/a	Eastern York SD	Wrightsville
1	n/a	Easton Area SD	Easton
1	n/a	Elizabeth Forward SD	Elizabeth
1	n/a	Elizabethtown Area SD	Elizabethtown
1	n/a	Elk Lake SD	Dimock
1	n/a	Ellwood City Area SD	Ellwood City
1	n/a	Ephrata Area SD	Ephrata
1	n/a	Erie City SD	Erie
1	n/a	Everett Area SD	Everett

Rank	%	District	City
1	n/a	Exeter Township SD	Reading
1	n/a	Fairview SD	Fairview
1	n/a	Fleetwood Area SD	Fleetwood
1	n/a	Forest Hills SD	Sidman
1	n/a	Fort Leboeuf SD	Waterford
1	n/a	Fox Chapel Area SD	Pittsburgh
1	n/a	Franklin Area SD	Franklin
1	n/a	Franklin Regional SD	Murrysville
1	n/a	Freedom Area SD	Freedom
1	n/a	Freeport Area SD	Freeport
1	n/a	Garnet Valley SD	Glen Mills
1	n/a	Gateway SD	Monroeville
1	n/a	General Mclane SD	Edinboro
1	n/a	Gettysburg Area SD	Gettysburg
1	n/a	Girard SD	Girard
1	n/a	Governor Mifflin SD	Shillington
1	n/a	Great Valley SD	Malvern
1	n/a	Greater Johnstown SD	Johnstown
1	n/a	Greater Latrobe SD	Latrobe
1	n/a	Greater Nanticoke Area SD	Nanticoke
1	n/a	Greencastle-Antrim SD	Greencastle
1	n/a	Greensburg Salem SD	Greensburg
1	n/a	Greenville Area SD	Greenville
1	n/a	Grove City Area SD	Grove City
1	n/a	Hamburg Area SD	Hamburg
1	n/a	Hampton Township SD	Gibsonia
1	n/a	Hanover Area SD	Wilkes Barre
1	n/a	Hanover Public SD	Hanover
1	n/a	Harbor Creek SD	Harborcreek
1	n/a	Harrisburg City SD	Harrisburg
1	n/a	Hatboro-Horsham SD	Horsham
1	n/a	Haverford Township SD	Havertown
1	n/a	Hazleton Area SD	Hazleton
1	n/a	Hempfield SD	Landisville
1	n/a	Hempfield Area SD	Greensburg
1	n/a	Hermitage SD	Hermitage
1	n/a	Highlands SD	Natrona Heights
1	n/a	Hollidaysburg Area SD	Hollidaysburg
1	n/a	Hopewell Area SD	Aliquippa
1	n/a	Huntingdon Area SD	Huntingdon
1	n/a	Indiana Area SD	Indiana
1	n/a	Interboro SD	Prospect Park
1	n/a	Jeannette City SD	Jeannette
1	n/a	Jersey Shore Area SD	Jersey Shore
1	n/a	Jim Thorpe Area SD	Jim Thorpe
1	n/a	Juniata County SD	Mifflintown
1	n/a	Karns City Area SD	Karns City
1	n/a	Kennett Consolidated SD	Kennett Square
1	n/a	Keystone Central SD	Lock Haven
1	n/a	Keystone Oaks SD	Pittsburgh
1	n/a	Kiski Area SD	Vandergrift
1	n/a	Kutztown Area SD	Kutztown
1	n/a	Lake-Lehman SD	Lehman
1	n/a	Lakeland SD	Jermyn
1	n/a	Lampeter-Strasburg SD	Lampeter
1	n/a	Lancaster SD	Lancaster
1	n/a	Laurel Highlands SD	Uniontown
1	n/a	Lebanon SD	Lebanon
1	n/a	Lehighton Area SD	Lehighton
1	n/a	Lewisburg Area SD	Lewisburg
1	n/a	Ligonier Valley SD	Ligonier
1	n/a	Littlestown Area SD	Littlestown
1	n/a	Lower Dauphin SD	Hummelstown
1	n/a	Lower Merion SD	Ardmore
1	n/a	Lower Moreland Township SD	Huntingdon Vly
1	n/a	Manheim Central SD	Manheim
1	n/a	Manheim Township SD	Lancaster
1	n/a	Marion Center Area SD	Marion Center
1	n/a	Marple Newtown SD	Newtown Square
1	n/a	Mars Area SD	Mars
1	n/a	Mcguffey SD	Claysville
1	n/a	Mckeesport Area SD	Mc Keesport
1	n/a	Mechanicsburg Area SD	Mechanicsburg
1	n/a	Mercer Area SD	Mercer
1	n/a	Methacton SD	Norristown
1	n/a	Mid Valley SD	Throop
1	n/a	Midd-West SD	Middleburg
1	n/a	Middletown Area SD	Middletown
1	n/a	Mifflin County SD	Lewistown
1	n/a	Mifflinburg Area SD	Mifflinburg
1	n/a	Millcreek Township SD	Erie
1	n/a	Milton Area SD	Milton
1	n/a	Mohawk Area SD	Bessemer
1	n/a	Moniteau SD	West Sunbury
1	n/a	Montour SD	Mc Kees Rocks
1	n/a	Montoursville Area SD	Montoursville
1	n/a	Montrose Area SD	Montrose
1	n/a	Moon Area SD	Moon Township
1	n/a	Mount Carmel Area SD	Mount Carmel
1	n/a	Mount Lebanon SD	Pittsburgh
1	n/a	Mount Pleasant Area SD	Mount Pleasant
1	n/a	Mount Union Area SD	Mount Union
1	n/a	Muhlenberg SD	Reading

Rank	%	District	City
1	n/a	Nazareth Area SD	Nazareth
1	n/a	Neshaminy SD	Langhorne
1	n/a	New Brighton Area SD	New Brighton
1	n/a	New Castle Area SD	New Castle
1	n/a	New Kensington-Arnold SD	New Kensington
1	n/a	Norristown Area SD	Norristown
1	n/a	North Allegheny SD	Pittsburgh
1	n/a	North East SD	North East
1	n/a	North Hills SD	Pittsburgh
1	n/a	North Penn SD	Lansdale
1	n/a	North Pocono SD	Moscow
1	n/a	North Schuylkill SD	Ashland
1	n/a	Northampton Area SD	Northampton
1	n/a	Northeastern York SD	Manchester
1	n/a	Northern Lebanon SD	Fredericksburg
1	n/a	Northern Lehigh SD	Slatington
1	n/a	Northern Tioga SD	Elkland
1	n/a	Northern York County SD	Dillsburg
1	n/a	Northgate SD	Pittsburgh
1	n/a	Northwestern SD	Albion
1	n/a	Northwestern Lehigh SD	New Tripoli
1	n/a	Norwin SD	N Huntingdon
1	n/a	Octorara Area SD	Atglen
1	n/a	Oil City Area SD	Oil City
1	n/a	Oley Valley SD	Oley
1	n/a	Owen J Roberts SD	Pottstown
1	n/a	Oxford Area SD	Oxford
1	n/a	PDE Division of Data Services	Harrisburg
1	n/a	Palisades SD	Kintnersville
1	n/a	Palmerton Area SD	Palmerton
1	n/a	Palmyra Area SD	Palmyra
1	n/a	Parkland SD	Allentown
1	n/a	Pen Argyl Area SD	Pen Argyl
1	n/a	Penn Cambria SD	Cresson
1	n/a	Penn Hills SD	Pittsburgh
1	n/a	Penn Manor SD	Millersville
1	n/a	Penn-Delco SD	Aston
1	n/a	Penn-Trafford SD	Harrison City
1	n/a	Penncrest SD	Saegertown
1	n/a	Pennridge SD	Perkasie
1	n/a	Penns Valley Area SD	Spring Mills
1	n/a	Pennsbury SD	Fallsington
1	n/a	Pennsylvania Virtual CS	Norristown
1	n/a	Pequea Valley SD	Kinzers
1	n/a	Perkiomen Valley SD	Collegeville
1	n/a	Peters Township SD	Mcmurray
1	n/a	Philadelphia City SD	Philadelphia
1	n/a	Philipsburg-Osceola Area SD	Philipsburg
1	n/a	Phoenixville Area SD	Phoenixville
1	n/a	Pine Grove Area SD	Pine Grove
1	n/a	Pine-Richland SD	Gibsonia
1	n/a	Pittsburgh SD	Pittsburgh
1	n/a	Pittston Area SD	Pittston
1	n/a	Pleasant Valley SD	Brodheadsville
1	n/a	Plum Borough SD	Plum
1	n/a	Pocono Mountain SD	Swiftwater
1	n/a	Pottsgrove SD	Pottstown
1	n/a	Pottstown SD	Pottstown
1	n/a	Pottsville Area SD	Pottsville
1	n/a	Punxsutawney Area SD	Punxsutawney
1	n/a	Quaker Valley SD	Sewickley
1	n/a	Quakertown Community SD	Quakertown
1	n/a	Radnor Township SD	Wayne
1	n/a	Reading SD	Reading
1	n/a	Red Lion Area SD	Red Lion
1	n/a	Reynolds SD	Greenville
1	n/a	Richland SD	Johnstown
1	n/a	Ridley SD	Folsom
1	n/a	Ringgold SD	New Eagle
1	n/a	Riverside Beaver County SD	Ellwood City
1	n/a	Rose Tree Media SD	Media
1	n/a	Saint Marys Area SD	Saint Marys
1	n/a	Salisbury Township SD	Allentown
1	n/a	Saucon Valley SD	Hellertown
1	n/a	Schuylkill Valley SD	Leesport
1	n/a	Scranton SD	Scranton
1	n/a	Selinsgrove Area SD	Selinsgrove
1	n/a	Seneca Valley SD	Harmony
1	n/a	Shaler Area SD	Glenshaw
1	n/a	Shamokin Area SD	Coal Township
1	n/a	Sharon City SD	Sharon
1	n/a	Shikellamy SD	Sunbury
1	n/a	Shippensburg Area SD	Shippensburg
1	n/a	Slippery Rock Area SD	Slippery Rock
1	n/a	Solanco SD	Quarryville
1	n/a	Somerset Area SD	Somerset
1	n/a	Souderton Area SD	Souderton
1	n/a	South Allegheny SD	Mc Keesport
1	n/a	South Butler County SD	Saxonburg
1	n/a	South Eastern SD	Fawn Grove
1	n/a	South Fayette Township SD	Mc Donald
1	n/a	South Middleton SD	Boiling Springs

1	n/a	South Park SD	South Park
1	n/a	South Western SD	Hanover
1	n/a	Southeast Delco SD	Folcroft
1	n/a	Southern Lehigh SD	Center Valley
1	n/a	Southern Tioga SD	Blossburg
1	n/a	Southern York County SD	Glen Rock
1	n/a	Southmoreland SD	Scottdale
1	n/a	Spring Cove SD	Roaring Spring
1	n/a	Spring Grove Area SD	Spring Grove
1	n/a	Spring-Ford Area SD	Collegeville
1	n/a	Springfield SD	Springfield
1	n/a	Springfield Township SD	Oreland
1	n/a	State College Area SD	State College
1	n/a	Steel Valley SD	Munhall
1	n/a	Sto-Rox SD	Mckees Rocks
1	n/a	Stroudsburg Area SD	Stroudsburg
1	n/a	Susquehanna Township SD	Harrisburg
1	n/a	Susquenita SD	Duncannon
1	n/a	Tamaqua Area SD	Tamaqua
1	n/a	Titusville Area SD	Titusville
1	n/a	Towanda Area SD	Towanda
1	n/a	Tredyffrin-Easttown SD	Berwyn
1	n/a	Trinity Area SD	Washington
1	n/a	Troy Area SD	Troy
1	n/a	Tulpehocken Area SD	Bernville
1	n/a	Tunkhannock Area SD	Tunkhannock
1	n/a	Tuscarora SD	Mercersburg
1	n/a	Twin Valley SD	Elverson
1	n/a	Tyrone Area SD	Tyrone
1	n/a	Uniontown Area SD	Uniontown
1	n/a	Unionville-Chadds Ford SD	Kennett Square
1	n/a	Upper Adams SD	Biglerville
1	n/a	Upper Darby SD	Drexel Hill
1	n/a	Upper Dublin SD	Maple Glen
1	n/a	Upper Merion Area SD	King Of Prussia
1	n/a	Upper Moreland Township SD	Willow Grove
1	n/a	Upper Perkiomen SD	East Greenville
1	n/a	Upper Saint Clair SD	Pittsburgh
1	n/a	Valley View SD	Archbald
1	n/a	Wallenpaupack Area SD	Hawley
1	n/a	Wallingford-Swarthmore SD	Wallingford
1	n/a	Warren County SD	North Warren
1	n/a	Warrior Run SD	Turbotville
1	n/a	Warwick SD	Lititz
1	n/a	Washington SD	Washington
1	n/a	Wattsburg Area SD	Erie
1	n/a	Wayne Highlands SD	Honesdale
1	n/a	Waynesboro Area SD	Waynesboro
1	n/a	Wellsboro Area SD	Wellsboro
1	n/a	West Allegheny SD	Imperial
1	n/a	West Chester Area SD	West Chester
1	n/a	West Jefferson Hills SD	Jefferson Hls
1	n/a	West Mifflin Area SD	West Mifflin
1	n/a	West Perry SD	Elliottsburg
1	n/a	West Shore SD	New Cumberland
1	n/a	West York Area SD	York
1	n/a	Western Wayne SD	South Canaan
1	n/a	Westmont Hilltop SD	Johnstown
1	n/a	Whitehall-Coplay SD	Whitehall
1	n/a	Wilkes-Barre Area SD	Wilkes Barre
1	n/a	Wilkinsburg Borough SD	Wilkinsburg
1	n/a	William Penn SD	Lansdowne
1	n/a	Williamsport Area SD	Williamsport
1	n/a	Wilmington Area SD	New Wilmington
1	n/a	Wilson SD	West Lawn
1	n/a	Wilson Area SD	Easton
1	n/a	Wissahickon SD	Ambler
1	n/a	Woodland Hills SD	Pittsburgh
1	n/a	Wyalusing Area SD	Wyalusing
1	n/a	Wyoming Area SD	Exeter
1	n/a	Wyoming Valley West SD	Kingston
1	n/a	Wyomissing Area SD	Wyomissing
1	n/a	York City SD	York
1	n/a	York Suburban SD	York
1	n/a	Yough SD	Herminie

Migrant Students

Rank	Percent	District Name	City
1	14.1	Kennett Consolidated SD	Kennett Square
2	11.9	Upper Adams SD	Biglerville
3	9.7	Lebanon SD	Lebanon
4	9.4	Lancaster SD	Lancaster
5	7.9	Erie City SD	Erie
6	6.3	Reading SD	Reading
7	5.0	Avon Grove SD	West Grove
8	4.8	Gettysburg Area SD	Gettysburg
9	4.6	Bermudian Springs SD	York Springs
10	3.7	Conewago Valley SD	New Oxford
11	3.2	Harrisburg City SD	Harrisburg
12	3.1	Hanover Public SD	Hanover
12	3.1	Oxford Area SD	Oxford
14	3.0	York City SD	York
15	2.7	Chambersburg Area SD	Chambersburg
16	2.6	Scranton SD	Scranton
17	2.3	Allentown City SD	Allentown
17	2.3	Troy Area SD	Troy
19	1.6	Cornwall-Lebanon SD	Lebanon
20	1.4	Tulpehocken Area SD	Bernville
21	1.3	Juniata County SD	Mifflintown
21	1.3	Wyalusing Area SD	Wyalusing
23	1.2	Central Dauphin SD	Harrisburg
24	1.1	Octorara Area SD	Atglen
24	1.1	Souderton Area SD	Souderton
26	1.0	Hazleton Area SD	Hazleton
26	1.0	Towanda Area SD	Towanda
28	0.8	Hempfield SD	Landisville
28	0.8	North Penn SD	Lansdale
30	0.7	Bethlehem Area SD	Bethlehem
30	0.7	Carlisle Area SD	Carlisle
30	0.7	Chester-Upland SD	Chester
30	0.7	Coatesville Area SD	Coatesville
30	0.7	Northern Tioga SD	Elkland
30	0.7	Southern Tioga SD	Blossburg
36	0.6	Athens Area SD	Athens
36	0.6	Mechanicsburg Area SD	Mechanicsburg
36	0.6	Muhlenberg SD	Reading
36	0.6	Wellsboro Area SD	Wellsboro
40	0.5	Manheim Central SD	Manheim
40	0.5	Susquehanna Township SD	Harrisburg
40	0.5	Tunkhannock Area SD	Tunkhannock
43	0.4	Columbia Borough SD	Columbia
43	0.4	Donegal SD	Mount Joy
43	0.4	Elk Lake SD	Dimock
43	0.4	Ephrata Area SD	Ephrata
43	0.4	Millcreek Township SD	Erie
43	0.4	Philadelphia City SD	Philadelphia
43	0.4	West Shore SD	New Cumberland
50	0.3	Bedford Area SD	Bedford
50	0.3	Conestoga Valley SD	Lancaster
50	0.3	Conrad Weiser Area SD	Robesonia
50	0.3	East Pennsboro Area SD	Enola
50	0.3	Elizabethtown Area SD	Elizabethtown
50	0.3	Mifflin County SD	Lewistown
50	0.3	Montrose Area SD	Montrose
50	0.3	Northern Lebanon SD	Fredericksburg
50	0.3	South Western SD	Hanover
50	0.3	Spring Cove SD	Roaring Spring
50	0.3	Tuscarora SD	Mercersburg
50	0.3	York Suburban SD	York
62	0.2	Abington Heights SD	Clarks Summit
62	0.2	Big Spring SD	Newville
62	0.2	Brandywine Heights Area SD	Topton
62	0.2	Eastern Lancaster County SD	New Holland
62	0.2	Fleetwood Area SD	Fleetwood
62	0.2	Lake-Lehman SD	Lehman
62	0.2	Manheim Township SD	Lancaster
62	0.2	Mount Pleasant Area SD	Mount Pleasant
62	0.2	Norristown Area SD	Norristown
62	0.2	North East SD	North East
62	0.2	Northeastern York SD	Manchester
62	0.2	Unionville-Chadds Ford SD	Kennett Square
62	0.2	Warwick SD	Lititz
62	0.2	West York Area SD	York
62	0.2	Wilson SD	West Lawn
77	0.1	Canon-Mcmillan SD	Canonsburg
77	0.1	Chestnut Ridge SD	Fishertown
77	0.1	Cocalico SD	Denver
77	0.1	Dallastown Area SD	Dallastown
77	0.1	Derry Township SD	Hershey
77	0.1	Eastern York SD	Wrightsville
77	0.1	Easton Area SD	Easton
77	0.1	Exeter Township SD	Reading
77	0.1	Lampeter-Strasburg SD	Lampeter
77	0.1	Littlestown Area SD	Littlestown
77	0.1	Marion Center Area SD	Marion Center
77	0.1	Northern York County SD	Dillsburg
77	0.1	Northwestern SD	Albion
77	0.1	Penn Manor SD	Millersville
77	0.1	Pennridge SD	Perkasie
77	0.1	Pequea Valley SD	Kinzers
77	0.1	Peters Township SD	Mcmurray
77	0.1	Pine Grove Area SD	Pine Grove
77	0.1	Saucon Valley SD	Hellertown
77	0.1	Shikellamy SD	Sunbury
77	0.1	Solanco SD	Quarryville
77	0.1	Spring Grove Area SD	Spring Grove
77	0.1	Tyrone Area SD	Tyrone
77	0.1	Upper Moreland Township SD	Willow Grove
77	0.1	Upper Perkiomen SD	East Greenville
77	0.1	Valley View SD	Archbald
77	0.1	Wayne Highlands SD	Honesdale
77	0.1	Waynesboro Area SD	Waynesboro
77	0.1	West Chester Area SD	West Chester
77	0.1	Whitehall-Coplay SD	Whitehall
77	0.1	Wilson Area SD	Easton
77	0.1	Wissahickon SD	Ambler
77	0.1	Wyomissing Area SD	Wyomissing
110	0.0	Bellefonte Area SD	Bellefonte
110	0.0	Butler Area SD	Butler
110	0.0	Central Bucks SD	Doylestown
110	0.0	Central York SD	York
110	0.0	Conneaut SD	Linesville
110	0.0	Downingtown Area SD	Downingtown
110	0.0	Fort Leboeuf SD	Waterford
110	0.0	Keystone Central SD	Lock Haven
110	0.0	Lower Dauphin SD	Hummelstown
110	0.0	Methacton SD	Norristown
110	0.0	Ridley SD	Folsom
110	0.0	Shippensburg Area SD	Shippensburg
110	0.0	State College Area SD	State College
123	0.0	Abington SD	Abington
123	0.0	Albert Gallatin Area SD	Uniontown
123	0.0	Altoona Area SD	Altoona
123	0.0	Ambridge Area SD	Ambridge
123	0.0	Annville-Cleona SD	Annville
123	0.0	Apollo-Ridge SD	Spring Church
123	0.0	Armstrong SD	Ford City
123	0.0	Bald Eagle Area SD	Wingate
123	0.0	Baldwin-Whitehall SD	Pittsburgh
123	0.0	Bangor Area SD	Bangor
123	0.0	Beaver Area SD	Beaver
123	0.0	Belle Vernon Area SD	Belle Vernon
123	0.0	Bensalem Township SD	Bensalem
123	0.0	Berwick Area SD	Berwick
123	0.0	Bethel Park SD	Bethel Park
123	0.0	Big Beaver Falls Area SD	Beaver Falls
123	0.0	Blackhawk SD	Beaver Falls
123	0.0	Blairsville-Saltsburg SD	Blairsville
123	0.0	Bloomsburg Area SD	Bloomsburg
123	0.0	Blue Mountain SD	Orwigsburg
123	0.0	Boyertown Area SD	Boyertown
123	0.0	Bradford Area SD	Bradford
123	0.0	Bristol Township SD	Levittown
123	0.0	Brookville Area SD	Brookville
123	0.0	Brownsville Area SD	Brownsville
123	0.0	Burgettstown Area SD	Burgettstown
123	0.0	Burrell SD	Lower Burrell
123	0.0	Cambria Heights SD	Patton
123	0.0	Carlynton SD	Carnegie
123	0.0	Catasauqua Area SD	Catasauqua
123	0.0	Centennial SD	Warminster
123	0.0	Center Area SD	Monaca
123	0.0	Central Cambria SD	Ebensburg
123	0.0	Central Columbia SD	Bloomsburg
123	0.0	Central Greene SD	Waynesburg
123	0.0	Charleroi SD	Charleroi
123	0.0	Chartiers Valley SD	Pittsburgh
123	0.0	Cheltenham Township SD	Elkins Park
123	0.0	Chichester SD	Boothwyn
123	0.0	Clearfield Area SD	Clearfield
123	0.0	Colonial SD	Plymouth Meeting
123	0.0	Connellsville Area SD	Connellsville
123	0.0	Corry Area SD	Corry
123	0.0	Council Rock SD	Richboro
123	0.0	Cranberry Area SD	Seneca
123	0.0	Crawford Central SD	Meadville
123	0.0	Crestwood SD	Mountain Top
123	0.0	Cumberland Valley SD	Mechanicsburg
123	0.0	Dallas SD	Dallas
123	0.0	Daniel Boone Area SD	Douglassville
123	0.0	Danville Area SD	Danville
123	0.0	Deer Lakes SD	Russellton
123	0.0	Delaware Valley SD	Milford
123	0.0	Derry Area SD	Derry
123	0.0	Dover Area SD	Dover
123	0.0	Dubois Area SD	Du Bois
123	0.0	Dunmore SD	Dunmore
123	0.0	East Allegheny SD	N Versailles
123	0.0	East Lycoming SD	Hughesville
123	0.0	East Penn SD	Emmaus
123	0.0	East Stroudsburg Area SD	E Stroudsburg
123	0.0	Eastern Lebanon County SD	Myerstown
123	0.0	Elizabeth Forward SD	Elizabeth
123	0.0	Ellwood City Area SD	Ellwood City
123	0.0	Everett Area SD	Everett
123	0.0	Fairview SD	Fairview
123	0.0	Forest Hills SD	Sidman
123	0.0	Fox Chapel Area SD	Pittsburgh
123	0.0	Franklin Area SD	Franklin
123	0.0	Franklin Regional SD	Murrysville
123	0.0	Freedom Area SD	Freedom
123	0.0	Freeport Area SD	Freeport
123	0.0	Garnet Valley SD	Glen Mills
123	0.0	Gateway SD	Monroeville
123	0.0	General Mclane SD	Edinboro
123	0.0	Girard SD	Girard
123	0.0	Governor Mifflin SD	Shillington

123	0.0	Great Valley SD	Malvern
123	0.0	Greater Johnstown SD	Johnstown
123	0.0	Greater Latrobe SD	Latrobe
123	0.0	Greater Nanticoke Area SD	Nanticoke
123	0.0	Greencastle-Antrim SD	Greencastle
123	0.0	Greensburg Salem SD	Greensburg
123	0.0	Greenville Area SD	Greenville
123	0.0	Grove City Area SD	Grove City
123	0.0	Hamburg Area SD	Hamburg
123	0.0	Hampton Township SD	Gibsonia
123	0.0	Hanover Area SD	Wilkes Barre
123	0.0	Harbor Creek SD	Harborcreek
123	0.0	Hatboro-Horsham SD	Horsham
123	0.0	Haverford Township SD	Havertown
123	0.0	Hempfield Area SD	Greensburg
123	0.0	Hermitage SD	Hermitage
123	0.0	Highlands SD	Natrona Heights
123	0.0	Hollidaysburg Area SD	Hollidaysburg
123	0.0	Hopewell Area SD	Aliquippa
123	0.0	Huntingdon Area SD	Huntingdon
123	0.0	Indiana Area SD	Indiana
123	0.0	Interboro SD	Prospect Park
123	0.0	Jeannette City SD	Jeannette
123	0.0	Jersey Shore Area SD	Jersey Shore
123	0.0	Jim Thorpe Area SD	Jim Thorpe
123	0.0	Karns City Area SD	Karns City
123	0.0	Keystone Oaks SD	Pittsburgh
123	0.0	Kiski Area SD	Vandergrift
123	0.0	Kutztown Area SD	Kutztown
123	0.0	Lakeland SD	Jermyn
123	0.0	Laurel Highlands SD	Uniontown
123	0.0	Lehighton Area SD	Lehighton
123	0.0	Lewisburg Area SD	Lewisburg
123	0.0	Ligonier Valley SD	Ligonier
123	0.0	Lower Merion SD	Ardmore
123	0.0	Lower Moreland Township SD	Huntingdon Vly
123	0.0	Marple Newtown SD	Newtown Square
123	0.0	Mars Area SD	Mars
123	0.0	Mcguffey SD	Claysville
123	0.0	Mckeesport Area SD	Mc Keesport
123	0.0	Mercer Area SD	Mercer
123	0.0	Mid Valley SD	Throop
123	0.0	Midd-West SD	Middleburg
123	0.0	Middletown Area SD	Middletown
123	0.0	Mifflinburg Area SD	Mifflinburg
123	0.0	Milton Area SD	Milton
123	0.0	Mohawk Area SD	Bessemer
123	0.0	Moniteau SD	West Sunbury
123	0.0	Montour SD	Mc Kees Rocks
123	0.0	Montoursville Area SD	Montoursville
123	0.0	Moon Area SD	Moon Township
123	0.0	Mount Carmel Area SD	Mount Carmel
123	0.0	Mount Lebanon SD	Pittsburgh
123	0.0	Mount Union Area SD	Mount Union
123	0.0	Nazareth Area SD	Nazareth
123	0.0	Neshaminy SD	Langhorne
123	0.0	New Brighton Area SD	New Brighton
123	0.0	New Castle Area SD	New Castle
123	0.0	New Kensington-Arnold SD	New Kensington
123	0.0	North Allegheny SD	Pittsburgh
123	0.0	North Hills SD	Pittsburgh
123	0.0	North Pocono SD	Moscow
123	0.0	North Schuylkill SD	Ashland
123	0.0	Northampton Area SD	Northampton
123	0.0	Northern Lehigh SD	Slatington
123	0.0	Northgate SD	Pittsburgh
123	0.0	Northwestern Lehigh SD	New Tripoli
123	0.0	Norwin SD	N Huntingdon
123	0.0	Oil City Area SD	Oil City
123	0.0	Oley Valley SD	Oley
123	0.0	Owen J Roberts SD	Pottstown
123	0.0	Palisades SD	Kintnersville
123	0.0	Palmerton Area SD	Palmerton
123	0.0	Palmyra Area SD	Palmyra
123	0.0	Parkland SD	Allentown
123	0.0	Pen Argyl Area SD	Pen Argyl
123	0.0	Penn Cambria SD	Cresson
123	0.0	Penn Hills SD	Pittsburgh
123	0.0	Penn-Delco SD	Aston
123	0.0	Penn-Trafford SD	Harrison City
123	0.0	Penncrest SD	Saegertown
123	0.0	Penns Valley Area SD	Spring Mills
123	0.0	Pennsbury SD	Fallsington
123	0.0	Pennsylvania Virtual CS	Norristown
123	0.0	Perkiomen Valley SD	Collegeville
123	0.0	Philipsburg-Osceola Area SD	Philipsburg
123	0.0	Phoenixville Area SD	Phoenixville
123	0.0	Pine-Richland SD	Gibsonia
123	0.0	Pittsburgh SD	Pittsburgh
123	0.0	Pittston Area SD	Pittston
123	0.0	Pleasant Valley SD	Brodheadsville
123	0.0	Plum Borough SD	Plum
123	0.0	Pocono Mountain SD	Swiftwater
123	0.0	Pottsgrove SD	Pottstown
123	0.0	Pottstown SD	Pottstown
123	0.0	Pottsville Area SD	Pottsville
123	0.0	Punxsutawney Area SD	Punxsutawney
123	0.0	Quaker Valley SD	Sewickley
123	0.0	Quakertown Community SD	Quakertown
123	0.0	Radnor Township SD	Wayne
123	0.0	Red Lion Area SD	Red Lion
123	0.0	Reynolds SD	Greenville
123	0.0	Richland SD	Johnstown
123	0.0	Ringgold SD	New Eagle
123	0.0	Riverside Beaver County SD	Ellwood City
123	0.0	Rose Tree Media SD	Media
123	0.0	Saint Marys Area SD	Saint Marys
123	0.0	Salisbury Township SD	Allentown
123	0.0	Schuylkill Valley SD	Leesport
123	0.0	Selinsgrove Area SD	Selinsgrove
123	0.0	Seneca Valley SD	Harmony
123	0.0	Shaler Area SD	Glenshaw
123	0.0	Shamokin Area SD	Coal Township
123	0.0	Sharon City SD	Sharon
123	0.0	Slippery Rock Area SD	Slippery Rock
123	0.0	Somerset Area SD	Somerset
123	0.0	South Allegheny SD	Mc Keesport
123	0.0	South Butler County SD	Saxonburg
123	0.0	South Eastern SD	Fawn Grove
123	0.0	South Fayette Township SD	Mc Donald
123	0.0	South Middleton SD	Boiling Springs
123	0.0	South Park SD	South Park
123	0.0	Southeast Delco SD	Folcroft
123	0.0	Southern Lehigh SD	Center Valley
123	0.0	Southern York County SD	Glen Rock
123	0.0	Southmoreland SD	Scottdale
123	0.0	Spring-Ford Area SD	Collegeville
123	0.0	Springfield SD	Springfield
123	0.0	Springfield Township SD	Oreland
123	0.0	Steel Valley SD	Munhall
123	0.0	Sto-Rox SD	Mckees Rocks
123	0.0	Stroudsburg Area SD	Stroudsburg
123	0.0	Susquenita SD	Duncannon
123	0.0	Tamaqua Area SD	Tamaqua
123	0.0	Titusville Area SD	Titusville
123	0.0	Tredyffrin-Easttown SD	Berwyn
123	0.0	Trinity Area SD	Washington
123	0.0	Twin Valley SD	Elverson
123	0.0	Uniontown Area SD	Uniontown
123	0.0	Upper Darby SD	Drexel Hill
123	0.0	Upper Dublin SD	Maple Glen
123	0.0	Upper Merion Area SD	King Of Prussia
123	0.0	Upper Saint Clair SD	Pittsburgh
123	0.0	Wallenpaupack Area SD	Hawley
123	0.0	Wallingford-Swarthmore SD	Wallingford
123	0.0	Warren County SD	North Warren
123	0.0	Warrior Run SD	Turbotville
123	0.0	Washington SD	Washington
123	0.0	Wattsburg Area SD	Erie
123	0.0	West Allegheny SD	Imperial
123	0.0	West Jefferson Hills SD	Jefferson Hls
123	0.0	West Mifflin Area SD	West Mifflin
123	0.0	West Perry SD	Elliottsburg
123	0.0	Western Wayne SD	South Canaan
123	0.0	Westmont Hilltop SD	Johnstown
123	0.0	Wilkes-Barre Area SD	Wilkes Barre
123	0.0	Wilkinsburg Borough SD	Wilkinsburg
123	0.0	William Penn SD	Lansdowne
123	0.0	Williamsport Area SD	Williamsport
123	0.0	Wilmington Area SD	New Wilmington
123	0.0	Woodland Hills SD	Pittsburgh
123	0.0	Wyoming Area SD	Exeter
123	0.0	Wyoming Valley West SD	Kingston
123	0.0	Yough SD	Herminie
364	n/a	PDE Division of Data Services	Harrisburg

Students Eligible for Free Lunch

Rank	Percent	District Name	City
1	64.0	Wilkinsburg Borough SD	Wilkinsburg
2	62.9	York City SD	York
3	62.8	Philadelphia City SD	Philadelphia
4	61.2	Chester-Upland SD	Chester
4	61.2	Greater Johnstown SD	Johnstown
6	58.9	Erie City SD	Erie
7	57.7	Sto-Rox SD	Mckees Rocks
8	56.7	Reading SD	Reading
9	56.0	Lancaster SD	Lancaster
10	54.8	Harrisburg City SD	Harrisburg
11	52.9	Brownsville Area SD	Brownsville
12	52.7	Pittsburgh SD	Pittsburgh
13	50.3	Allentown City SD	Allentown
14	48.1	Sharon City SD	Sharon
15	45.4	Clearfield Area SD	Clearfield
16	44.0	Mckeesport Area SD	Mc Keesport
17	41.8	New Castle Area SD	New Castle
17	41.8	Uniontown Area SD	Uniontown
19	41.5	Connellsville Area SD	Connellsville
20	40.8	Norristown Area SD	Norristown
21	40.0	Woodland Hills SD	Pittsburgh
22	39.9	Albert Gallatin Area SD	Uniontown
23	39.5	Big Beaver Falls Area SD	Beaver Falls
24	39.0	William Penn SD	Lansdowne
25	38.4	New Kensington-Arnold SD	New Kensington
26	37.7	Jeannette City SD	Jeannette
27	37.6	Scranton SD	Scranton
28	36.9	Steel Valley SD	Munhall
29	36.5	Williamsport Area SD	Williamsport
30	35.4	Corry Area SD	Corry
31	34.9	Altoona Area SD	Altoona
32	34.5	Southeast Delco SD	Folcroft
33	34.4	Shamokin Area SD	Coal Township
34	34.0	Central Greene SD	Waynesburg
34	34.0	Laurel Highlands SD	Uniontown
34	34.0	Lebanon SD	Lebanon
37	32.9	Northern Tioga SD	Elkland
38	31.2	Pottstown SD	Pottstown
39	30.9	Oil City Area SD	Oil City
40	30.3	Highlands SD	Natrona Heights
41	29.6	East Allegheny SD	N Versailles
42	29.1	Bradford Area SD	Bradford
43	28.9	Hanover Area SD	Wilkes Barre
44	28.4	Apollo-Ridge SD	Spring Church
45	28.0	Keystone Central SD	Lock Haven
46	27.9	Dubois Area SD	Du Bois
47	27.8	Bristol Township SD	Levittown
48	27.7	Conneaut SD	Linesville
48	27.7	Northwestern SD	Albion
50	26.9	Charleroi SD	Charleroi
51	26.7	Towanda Area SD	Towanda
52	26.6	Wyoming Valley West SD	Kingston
53	26.5	Everett Area SD	Everett
54	26.4	New Brighton Area SD	New Brighton
55	26.2	Columbia Borough SD	Columbia
55	26.2	Crawford Central SD	Meadville
55	26.2	Western Wayne SD	South Canaan
58	26.0	Southmoreland SD	Scottdale
59	25.9	Penn Hills SD	Pittsburgh
60	25.8	Girard SD	Girard
60	25.8	Reynolds SD	Greenville
60	25.8	Wilkes-Barre Area SD	Wilkes Barre
63	25.7	Bethlehem Area SD	Bethlehem
64	25.6	Pottsville Area SD	Pottsville
65	25.5	Coatesville Area SD	Coatesville
65	25.5	Northgate SD	Pittsburgh
67	25.4	Marion Center Area SD	Marion Center
68	25.3	Berwick Area SD	Berwick
68	25.3	Tyrone Area SD	Tyrone
70	25.1	Greensburg Salem SD	Greensburg
71	24.8	Blairsville-Saltsburg SD	Blairsville
71	24.8	Ellwood City Area SD	Ellwood City
73	24.5	Cranberry Area SD	Seneca
74	24.4	Troy Area SD	Troy
75	24.3	Franklin Area SD	Franklin
76	24.2	Huntingdon Area SD	Huntingdon
77	24.0	Titusville Area SD	Titusville
78	23.8	Mount Carmel Area SD	Mount Carmel
78	23.8	Ringgold SD	New Eagle
80	23.7	Moniteau SD	West Sunbury
80	23.7	Shikellamy SD	Sunbury
82	23.6	Derry Area SD	Derry
83	23.5	Chichester SD	Boothwyn
84	23.4	Cambria Heights SD	Patton
84	23.4	Mount Union Area SD	Mount Union
86	23.3	Milton Area SD	Milton
86	23.3	Wallenpaupack Area SD	Hawley
88	23.2	Armstrong SD	Ford City
89	23.1	Greater Nanticoke Area SD	Nanticoke
89	23.1	Southern Tioga SD	Blossburg
91	22.8	Pocono Mountain SD	Swiftwater
92	22.7	Mcguffey SD	Claysville
92	22.7	Wellsboro Area SD	Wellsboro
94	22.4	Penn Cambria SD	Cresson
95	22.3	Philipsburg-Osceola Area SD	Philipsburg
95	22.3	Yough SD	Herminie
97	22.2	Forest Hills SD	Sidman
98	22.1	Wayne Highlands SD	Honesdale
98	22.1	Wyalusing Area SD	Wyalusing
100	21.8	Upper Darby SD	Drexel Hill
101	21.7	Tunkhannock Area SD	Tunkhannock
102	21.6	Ligonier Valley SD	Ligonier
102	21.6	Penncrest SD	Saegertown
102	21.6	Upper Adams SD	Biglerville
105	21.5	Chestnut Ridge SD	Fishertown
105	21.5	Mount Pleasant Area SD	Mount Pleasant
107	21.3	Greenville Area SD	Greenville
107	21.3	South Allegheny SD	Mc Keesport
109	21.2	Bedford Area SD	Bedford

110	21.1	Mifflin County SD	Lewistown
111	21.0	Punxsutawney Area SD	Punxsutawney
112	20.9	Elk Lake SD	Dimock
113	20.8	Bloomsburg Area SD	Bloomsburg
114	20.7	Karns City Area SD	Karns City
115	20.6	Spring Cove SD	Roaring Spring
116	20.5	Warren County SD	North Warren
117	20.3	Somerset Area SD	Somerset
118	20.1	Northern Lehigh SD	Slatington
119	19.7	North Schuylkill SD	Ashland
120	19.5	Ambridge Area SD	Ambridge
121	19.4	West Mifflin Area SD	West Mifflin
122	19.1	Bensalem Township SD	Bensalem
122	19.1	Burgettstown Area SD	Burgettstown
122	19.1	Gettysburg Area SD	Gettysburg
125	18.9	Brookville Area SD	Brookville
125	18.9	Riverside Beaver County SD	Ellwood City
127	18.7	Athens Area SD	Athens
127	18.7	Jim Thorpe Area SD	Jim Thorpe
129	18.4	Mohawk Area SD	Bessemer
130	18.3	Northeastern York SD	Manchester
130	18.3	Oxford Area SD	Oxford
132	18.1	Fort Leboeuf SD	Waterford
132	18.1	Jersey Shore Area SD	Jersey Shore
134	18.0	Tamaqua Area SD	Tamaqua
135	17.7	Danville Area SD	Danville
135	17.7	East Lycoming SD	Hughesville
135	17.7	Hermitage SD	Hermitage
135	17.7	Kennett Consolidated SD	Kennett Square
135	17.7	North East SD	North East
140	17.5	Belle Vernon Area SD	Belle Vernon
140	17.5	Midd-West SD	Middleburg
142	17.4	Chambersburg Area SD	Chambersburg
142	17.4	Freedom Area SD	Freedom
144	17.1	Easton Area SD	Easton
144	17.1	Indiana Area SD	Indiana
146	17.0	Butler Area SD	Butler
147	16.9	Hollidaysburg Area SD	Hollidaysburg
148	16.8	Bellefonte Area SD	Bellefonte
148	16.8	Central Cambria SD	Ebensburg
148	16.8	Kiski Area SD	Vandergrift
151	16.7	Waynesboro Area SD	Waynesboro
152	16.6	Mid Valley SD	Throop
153	16.5	Central Dauphin SD	Harrisburg
153	16.5	Lake-Lehman SD	Lehman
155	16.1	Bald Eagle Area SD	Wingate
155	16.1	West Perry SD	Elliottsburg
157	15.8	Wyoming Area SD	Exeter
158	15.6	Hanover Public SD	Hanover
159	15.5	Carlynton SD	Carnegie
159	15.5	Montrose Area SD	Montrose
161	15.4	East Stroudsburg Area SD	E Stroudsburg
161	15.4	Juniata County SD	Mifflintown
161	15.4	North Pocono SD	Moscow
164	15.3	Dunmore SD	Dunmore
164	15.3	Lakeland SD	Jermyn
164	15.3	Tuscarora SD	Mercersburg
167	15.2	Mercer Area SD	Mercer
167	15.2	Wattsburg Area SD	Erie
169	14.8	Wilmington Area SD	New Wilmington
170	14.7	Hazleton Area SD	Hazleton
170	14.7	Middletown Area SD	Middletown
172	14.6	Cornwall-Lebanon SD	Lebanon
173	14.5	Slippery Rock Area SD	Slippery Rock
174	14.4	Conewago Valley SD	New Oxford
175	14.3	Pittston Area SD	Pittston
176	14.2	Valley View SD	Archbald
177	13.9	Pine Grove Area SD	Pine Grove
178	13.8	Gateway SD	Monroeville
178	13.8	Selinsgrove Area SD	Selinsgrove
180	13.6	Catasauqua Area SD	Catasauqua
180	13.6	Trinity Area SD	Washington
182	13.5	Keystone Oaks SD	Pittsburgh
182	13.5	Lehighton Area SD	Lehighton
184	13.4	Delaware Valley SD	Milford
184	13.4	Saint Marys Area SD	Saint Marys
186	13.3	Harbor Creek SD	Harborcreek
187	13.1	Burrell SD	Lower Burrell
188	13.0	Mifflinburg Area SD	Mifflinburg
189	12.9	Chartiers Valley SD	Pittsburgh
189	12.9	Stroudsburg Area SD	Stroudsburg
191	12.7	Whitehall-Coplay SD	Whitehall
192	12.6	Elizabeth Forward SD	Elizabeth
192	12.6	Pequea Valley SD	Kinzers
192	12.6	Ridley SD	Folsom
195	12.5	Baldwin-Whitehall SD	Pittsburgh
195	12.5	General Mclane SD	Edinboro
195	12.5	West York Area SD	York
198	12.4	Greater Latrobe SD	Latrobe
198	12.4	Interboro SD	Prospect Park
198	12.4	Shippensburg Area SD	Shippensburg
201	12.2	Susquenita SD	Duncannon
202	12.1	Freeport Area SD	Freeport
203	12.0	Littlestown Area SD	Littlestown
204	11.7	Hopewell Area SD	Aliquippa
205	11.6	Canon-Mcmillan SD	Canonsburg
205	11.6	Carlisle Area SD	Carlisle
205	11.6	Millcreek Township SD	Erie
208	11.5	Bangor Area SD	Bangor
209	11.4	Donegal SD	Mount Joy
209	11.4	Penns Valley Area SD	Spring Mills
211	11.3	Eastern York SD	Wrightsville
211	11.3	Warrior Run SD	Turbotville
213	11.2	Eastern Lancaster County SD	New Holland
214	11.1	Ephrata Area SD	Ephrata
214	11.1	Palmerton Area SD	Palmerton
216	10.9	Grove City Area SD	Grove City
217	10.7	Octorara Area SD	Atglen
217	10.7	Susquehanna Township SD	Harrisburg
219	10.4	Deer Lakes SD	Russellton
219	10.4	Norwin SD	N Huntingdon
219	10.4	Washington SD	Washington
222	10.3	Lewisburg Area SD	Lewisburg
223	10.2	Muhlenberg SD	Reading
224	9.9	Blackhawk SD	Beaver Falls
224	9.9	Hempfield Area SD	Greensburg
226	9.8	Bermudian Springs SD	York Springs
226	9.8	Quaker Valley SD	Sewickley
228	9.7	Central Columbia SD	Bloomsburg
228	9.7	Phoenixville Area SD	Phoenixville
230	9.6	Central York SD	York
230	9.6	Greencastle-Antrim SD	Greencastle
232	9.5	Mechanicsburg Area SD	Mechanicsburg
232	9.5	Westmont Hilltop SD	Johnstown
234	9.4	Pleasant Valley SD	Brodheadsville
234	9.4	Shaler Area SD	Glenshaw
236	9.2	Crestwood SD	Mountain Top
237	9.1	Tulpehocken Area SD	Bernville
237	9.1	West Allegheny SD	Imperial
239	9.0	Pottsgrove SD	Pottstown
239	9.0	Upper Perkiomen SD	East Greenville
239	9.0	West Shore SD	New Cumberland
242	8.9	State College Area SD	State College
243	8.8	Big Spring SD	Newville
243	8.8	South Butler County SD	Saxonburg
245	8.7	Quakertown Community SD	Quakertown
246	8.6	Brandywine Heights Area SD	Topton
246	8.6	Northern Lebanon SD	Fredericksburg
246	8.6	Penn Manor SD	Millersville
246	8.6	Wilson Area SD	Easton
250	8.5	Centennial SD	Warminster
250	8.5	Conrad Weiser Area SD	Robesonia
250	8.5	Hempfield SD	Landisville
250	8.5	Manheim Central SD	Manheim
254	8.4	Cocalico SD	Denver
255	8.3	Solanco SD	Quarryville
256	8.2	Pen Argyl Area SD	Pen Argyl
257	8.1	East Pennsboro Area SD	Enola
257	8.1	Fairview SD	Fairview
257	8.1	Neshaminy SD	Langhorne
260	8.0	Hamburg Area SD	Hamburg
260	8.0	Red Lion Area SD	Red Lion
262	7.9	Conestoga Valley SD	Lancaster
262	7.9	Dover Area SD	Dover
264	7.8	Blue Mountain SD	Orwigsburg
264	7.8	South Park SD	South Park
266	7.7	Eastern Lebanon County SD	Myerstown
266	7.7	Lower Dauphin SD	Hummelstown
266	7.7	Spring Grove Area SD	Spring Grove
269	7.5	Saucon Valley SD	Hellertown
270	7.3	Avon Grove SD	West Grove
271	7.2	Exeter Township SD	Reading
271	7.2	Montoursville Area SD	Montoursville
273	7.1	Colonial SD	Plymouth Meeting
273	7.1	Wyomissing Area SD	Wyomissing
275	7.0	Fleetwood Area SD	Fleetwood
275	7.0	Richland SD	Johnstown
277	6.9	Annville-Cleona SD	Annville
277	6.9	Kutztown Area SD	Kutztown
279	6.8	Plum Borough SD	Plum
279	6.8	Wilson SD	West Lawn
281	6.7	Fox Chapel Area SD	Pittsburgh
281	6.7	Salisbury Township SD	Allentown
283	6.6	Dallas SD	Dallas
283	6.6	North Hills SD	Pittsburgh
285	6.3	Abington SD	Abington
285	6.3	Center Area SD	Monaca
285	6.3	North Penn SD	Lansdale
288	6.2	Daniel Boone Area SD	Douglassville
288	6.2	Governor Mifflin SD	Shillington
288	6.2	Schuylkill Valley SD	Leesport
288	6.2	South Fayette Township SD	Mc Donald
288	6.2	South Western SD	Hanover
293	6.1	Warwick SD	Lititz
294	6.0	Twin Valley SD	Elverson
294	6.0	Upper Merion Area SD	King Of Prussia
296	5.9	Upper Moreland Township SD	Willow Grove
297	5.8	Penn-Trafford SD	Harrison City
298	5.7	Dallastown Area SD	Dallastown
299	5.6	Moon Area SD	Moon Township
300	5.5	Elizabethtown Area SD	Elizabethtown
300	5.5	Pennridge SD	Perkasie
300	5.5	Seneca Valley SD	Harmony
303	5.4	Owen J Roberts SD	Pottstown
303	5.4	Southern York County SD	Glen Rock
305	5.3	Beaver Area SD	Beaver
306	5.2	Mars Area SD	Mars
306	5.2	West Jefferson Hills SD	Jefferson Hls
308	5.1	East Penn SD	Emmaus
308	5.1	York Suburban SD	York
310	5.0	Montour SD	Mc Kees Rocks
311	4.9	Northampton Area SD	Northampton
311	4.9	South Eastern SD	Fawn Grove
313	4.7	Souderton Area SD	Souderton
314	4.6	Abington Heights SD	Clarks Summit
314	4.6	Upper Dublin SD	Maple Glen
316	4.5	Boyertown Area SD	Boyertown
316	4.5	Manheim Township SD	Lancaster
316	4.5	Northern York County SD	Dillsburg
316	4.5	Northwestern Lehigh SD	New Tripoli
316	4.5	Perkiomen Valley SD	Collegeville
321	4.4	Pennsbury SD	Fallsington
322	4.3	Palmyra Area SD	Palmyra
323	4.2	Lampeter-Strasburg SD	Lampeter
324	4.1	Nazareth Area SD	Nazareth
324	4.1	Spring-Ford Area SD	Collegeville
324	4.1	West Chester Area SD	West Chester
327	3.8	Palisades SD	Kintnersville
328	3.7	Derry Township SD	Hershey
329	3.6	Lower Merion SD	Ardmore
329	3.6	South Middleton SD	Boiling Springs
331	3.5	Hampton Township SD	Gibsonia
332	3.4	Bethel Park SD	Bethel Park
332	3.4	Franklin Regional SD	Murrysville
332	3.4	Oley Valley SD	Oley
335	3.3	Rose Tree Media SD	Media
335	3.3	Wallingford-Swarthmore SD	Wallingford
337	3.2	Cumberland Valley SD	Mechanicsburg
338	3.1	Parkland SD	Allentown
339	3.0	Hatboro-Horsham SD	Horsham
339	3.0	Southern Lehigh SD	Center Valley
341	2.9	Springfield SD	Springfield
342	2.8	Penn-Delco SD	Aston
343	2.6	Great Valley SD	Malvern
344	2.5	Marple Newtown SD	Newtown Square
344	2.5	Pine-Richland SD	Gibsonia
344	2.5	Wissahickon SD	Ambler
347	2.3	Radnor Township SD	Wayne
348	2.0	Haverford Township SD	Havertown
349	1.7	Springfield Township SD	Oreland
350	1.6	Cheltenham Township SD	Elkins Park
350	1.6	Downingtown Area SD	Downingtown
350	1.6	North Allegheny SD	Pittsburgh
353	1.5	Peters Township SD	Mcmurray
354	1.4	Garnet Valley SD	Glen Mills
354	1.4	Tredyffrin-Easttown SD	Berwyn
356	1.3	Methacton SD	Norristown
357	1.2	Unionville-Chadds Ford SD	Kennett Square
358	1.1	Central Bucks SD	Doylestown
359	0.8	Upper Saint Clair SD	Pittsburgh
360	0.7	Council Rock SD	Richboro
361	0.6	Lower Moreland Township SD	Huntingdon Vly
362	0.2	Mount Lebanon SD	Pittsburgh
363	0.0	Pennsylvania Virtual CS	Norristown
364	n/a	PDE Division of Data Services	Harrisburg

Students Eligible for Reduced-Price Lunch

Rank	Percent	District Name	City
1	17.3	Shamokin Area SD	Coal Township
2	15.3	Everett Area SD	Everett
3	13.4	Girard SD	Girard
4	13.2	Connellsville Area SD	Connellsville
5	12.9	Southern Tioga SD	Blossburg
6	12.8	Bald Eagle Area SD	Wingate
6	12.8	Chestnut Ridge SD	Fishertown
8	12.7	Towanda Area SD	Towanda
9	12.5	Forest Hills SD	Sidman
9	12.5	Greater Johnstown SD	Johnstown
9	12.5	Jeannette City SD	Jeannette
9	12.5	Northern Tioga SD	Elkland
9	12.5	Western Wayne SD	South Canaan
14	12.3	Hanover Area SD	Wilkes Barre
14	12.3	Southeast Delco SD	Folcroft
14	12.3	Tyrone Area SD	Tyrone
17	12.0	Huntingdon Area SD	Huntingdon

Rank	Value	District	City
18	11.8	Marion Center Area SD	Marion Center
18	11.8	Penn Cambria SD	Cresson
18	11.8	Wallenpaupack Area SD	Hawley
21	11.3	Mount Carmel Area SD	Mount Carmel
21	11.3	Northeastern York SD	Manchester
23	11.1	Central Cambria SD	Ebensburg
23	11.1	Clearfield Area SD	Clearfield
23	11.1	Philipsburg-Osceola Area SD	Philipsburg
26	11.0	Bedford Area SD	Bedford
26	11.0	Highlands SD	Natrona Heights
28	10.9	Blairsville-Saltsburg SD	Blairsville
28	10.9	Bloomsburg Area SD	Bloomsburg
30	10.8	Armstrong SD	Ford City
30	10.8	Conneaut SD	Linesville
30	10.8	Keystone Central SD	Lock Haven
30	10.8	Norristown Area SD	Norristown
34	10.7	Derry Area SD	Derry
34	10.7	Wayne Highlands SD	Honesdale
34	10.7	York City SD	York
37	10.6	Berwick Area SD	Berwick
37	10.6	Lancaster SD	Lancaster
37	10.6	Reading SD	Reading
37	10.6	Upper Adams SD	Biglerville
37	10.6	Williamsport Area SD	Williamsport
42	10.5	Apollo-Ridge SD	Spring Church
42	10.5	Karns City Area SD	Karns City
42	10.5	Tuscarora SD	Mercersburg
42	10.5	Waynesboro Area SD	Waynesboro
46	10.4	Altoona Area SD	Altoona
46	10.4	Big Beaver Falls Area SD	Beaver Falls
46	10.4	Milton Area SD	Milton
46	10.4	South Allegheny SD	Mc Keesport
50	10.3	Mount Union Area SD	Mount Union
50	10.3	North Schuylkill SD	Ashland
52	10.2	Allentown City SD	Allentown
52	10.2	Reynolds SD	Greenville
52	10.2	Riverside Beaver County SD	Ellwood City
55	10.1	Corry Area SD	Corry
55	10.1	North East SD	North East
57	10.0	Cambria Heights SD	Patton
57	10.0	Columbia Borough SD	Columbia
57	10.0	Pottsville Area SD	Pottsville
60	9.9	Southmoreland SD	Scottdale
60	9.9	Troy Area SD	Troy
62	9.8	Central Greene SD	Waynesburg
62	9.8	Lebanon SD	Lebanon
62	9.8	Tunkhannock Area SD	Tunkhannock
65	9.7	Fort Leboeuf SD	Waterford
65	9.7	Jersey Shore Area SD	Jersey Shore
67	9.6	Juniata County SD	Mifflintown
67	9.6	Moniteau SD	West Sunbury
67	9.6	New Brighton Area SD	New Brighton
70	9.5	Brookville Area SD	Brookville
70	9.5	Midd-West SD	Middleburg
70	9.5	Northwestern SD	Albion
70	9.5	Saint Marys Area SD	Saint Marys
70	9.5	Shikellamy SD	Sunbury
75	9.4	Ellwood City Area SD	Ellwood City
75	9.4	Pottstown SD	Pottstown
75	9.4	Sto-Rox SD	Mckees Rocks
78	9.2	Brownsville Area SD	Brownsville
78	9.2	Jim Thorpe Area SD	Jim Thorpe
78	9.2	Titusville Area SD	Titusville
81	9.1	Athens Area SD	Athens
81	9.1	Montrose Area SD	Montrose
81	9.1	New Kensington-Arnold SD	New Kensington
81	9.1	Wellsboro Area SD	Wellsboro
85	8.9	Bellefonte Area SD	Bellefonte
85	8.9	Freeport Area SD	Freeport
85	8.9	Mid Valley SD	Throop
85	8.9	Pocono Mountain SD	Swiftwater
89	8.8	Ligonier Valley SD	Ligonier
89	8.8	Penncrest SD	Saegertown
91	8.7	Albert Gallatin Area SD	Uniontown
91	8.7	Conewago Valley SD	New Oxford
91	8.7	Mifflin County SD	Lewistown
91	8.7	Sharon City SD	Sharon
91	8.7	Spring Cove SD	Roaring Spring
91	8.7	Wilkinsburg Borough SD	Wilkinsburg
91	8.7	Woodland Hills SD	Pittsburgh
91	8.7	Yough SD	Herminie
99	8.5	Dubois Area SD	Du Bois
99	8.5	Erie City SD	Erie
99	8.5	Mifflinburg Area SD	Mifflinburg
99	8.5	Northgate SD	Pittsburgh
103	8.4	Bermudian Springs SD	York Springs
103	8.4	Bristol Township SD	Levittown
103	8.4	Punxsutawney Area SD	Punxsutawney
103	8.4	Warrior Run SD	Turbotville
103	8.4	Wyoming Valley West SD	Kingston
108	8.3	Cranberry Area SD	Seneca
108	8.3	Freedom Area SD	Freedom
110	8.2	Greater Nanticoke Area SD	Nanticoke
110	8.2	Oil City Area SD	Oil City
110	8.2	Penn Hills SD	Pittsburgh
110	8.2	Shippensburg Area SD	Shippensburg
110	8.2	Warren County SD	North Warren
115	8.1	Belle Vernon Area SD	Belle Vernon
115	8.1	Selinsgrove Area SD	Selinsgrove
117	8.0	Keystone Oaks SD	Pittsburgh
117	8.0	Slippery Rock Area SD	Slippery Rock
119	7.9	Conestoga Valley SD	Lancaster
119	7.9	Greensburg Salem SD	Greensburg
119	7.9	Wyalusing Area SD	Wyalusing
122	7.8	Burgettstown Area SD	Burgettstown
122	7.8	Danville Area SD	Danville
122	7.8	East Allegheny SD	N Versailles
122	7.8	Laurel Highlands SD	Uniontown
122	7.8	Mount Pleasant Area SD	Mount Pleasant
122	7.8	Penns Valley Area SD	Spring Mills
128	7.7	Charleroi SD	Charleroi
129	7.6	Wattsburg Area SD	Erie
129	7.6	Wyoming Area SD	Exeter
131	7.5	Bethlehem Area SD	Bethlehem
131	7.5	Chichester SD	Boothwyn
131	7.5	East Lycoming SD	Hughesville
131	7.5	Manheim Central SD	Manheim
131	7.5	Palmerton Area SD	Palmerton
131	7.5	Uniontown Area SD	Uniontown
137	7.4	Franklin Area SD	Franklin
137	7.4	Middletown Area SD	Middletown
137	7.4	Somerset Area SD	Somerset
137	7.4	William Penn SD	Lansdowne
141	7.3	Dover Area SD	Dover
141	7.3	Greater Latrobe SD	Latrobe
141	7.3	Hanover Public SD	Hanover
141	7.3	Ringgold SD	New Eagle
145	7.2	Coatesville Area SD	Coatesville
145	7.2	Elizabeth Forward SD	Elizabeth
145	7.2	Gateway SD	Monroeville
145	7.2	Kiski Area SD	Vandergrift
149	7.1	Ambridge Area SD	Ambridge
149	7.1	Bensalem Township SD	Bensalem
149	7.1	Big Spring SD	Newville
149	7.1	Mercer Area SD	Mercer
149	7.1	Wilkes-Barre Area SD	Wilkes Barre
154	7.0	Gettysburg Area SD	Gettysburg
154	7.0	Lakeland SD	Jermyn
154	7.0	Millcreek Township SD	Erie
157	6.9	Eastern Lancaster County SD	New Holland
157	6.9	Scranton SD	Scranton
157	6.9	Susquenita SD	Duncannon
160	6.8	Elk Lake SD	Dimock
160	6.8	Pine Grove Area SD	Pine Grove
160	6.8	Pittsburgh SD	Pittsburgh
160	6.8	Whitehall-Coplay SD	Whitehall
160	6.8	Wilmington Area SD	New Wilmington
165	6.7	Lehighton Area SD	Lehighton
165	6.7	Mohawk Area SD	Bessemer
165	6.7	Pittston Area SD	Pittston
165	6.7	Tamaqua Area SD	Tamaqua
165	6.7	Tulpehocken Area SD	Bernville
170	6.6	Central Columbia SD	Bloomsburg
170	6.6	Eastern York SD	Wrightsville
170	6.6	General Mclane SD	Edinboro
170	6.6	Lake-Lehman SD	Lehman
170	6.6	Littlestown Area SD	Littlestown
170	6.6	Mckeesport Area SD	Mc Keesport
170	6.6	Pequea Valley SD	Kinzers
170	6.6	Philadelphia City SD	Philadelphia
178	6.5	Eastern Lebanon County SD	Myerstown
178	6.5	Ephrata Area SD	Ephrata
178	6.5	North Pocono SD	Moscow
181	6.4	Bangor Area SD	Bangor
181	6.4	Hollidaysburg Area SD	Hollidaysburg
181	6.4	Oxford Area SD	Oxford
181	6.4	West Perry SD	Elliottsburg
185	6.3	Bradford Area SD	Bradford
185	6.3	Butler Area SD	Butler
185	6.3	Chambersburg Area SD	Chambersburg
185	6.3	Steel Valley SD	Munhall
189	6.2	Crawford Central SD	Meadville
189	6.2	Norwin SD	N Huntingdon
189	6.2	West Mifflin Area SD	West Mifflin
189	6.2	Wilson Area SD	Easton
193	6.1	Centennial SD	Warminster
193	6.1	Deer Lakes SD	Russellton
193	6.1	Susquehanna Township SD	Harrisburg
193	6.1	West York Area SD	York
193	6.1	Westmont Hilltop SD	Johnstown
198	6.0	Cornwall-Lebanon SD	Lebanon
198	6.0	East Pennsboro Area SD	Enola
198	6.0	North Hills SD	Pittsburgh
198	6.0	Red Lion Area SD	Red Lion
198	6.0	Upper Perkiomen SD	East Greenville
203	5.9	Donegal SD	Mount Joy
204	5.8	Central Dauphin SD	Harrisburg
204	5.8	Spring Grove Area SD	Spring Grove
204	5.8	Valley View SD	Archbald
207	5.7	Cocalico SD	Denver
207	5.7	East Stroudsburg Area SD	E Stroudsburg
207	5.7	Interboro SD	Prospect Park
207	5.7	Solanco SD	Quarryville
211	5.6	Baldwin-Whitehall SD	Pittsburgh
211	5.6	Harbor Creek SD	Harborcreek
211	5.6	Indiana Area SD	Indiana
211	5.6	Quakertown Community SD	Quakertown
211	5.6	Ridley SD	Folsom
216	5.5	Hermitage SD	Hermitage
216	5.5	Shaler Area SD	Glenshaw
216	5.5	Upper Darby SD	Drexel Hill
219	5.4	Delaware Valley SD	Milford
219	5.4	Mcguffey SD	Claysville
219	5.4	Muhlenberg SD	Reading
219	5.4	Northern Lebanon SD	Fredericksburg
223	5.3	Catasauqua Area SD	Catasauqua
223	5.3	Greencastle-Antrim SD	Greencastle
225	5.2	Blue Mountain SD	Orwigsburg
225	5.2	Easton Area SD	Easton
225	5.2	Lower Dauphin SD	Hummelstown
225	5.2	Pen Argyl Area SD	Pen Argyl
225	5.2	Stroudsburg Area SD	Stroudsburg
230	5.1	Chartiers Valley SD	Pittsburgh
230	5.1	Harrisburg City SD	Harrisburg
230	5.1	New Castle Area SD	New Castle
230	5.1	Schuylkill Valley SD	Leesport
230	5.1	Trinity Area SD	Washington
235	5.0	Canon-Mcmillan SD	Canonsburg
235	5.0	Twin Valley SD	Elverson
235	5.0	York Suburban SD	York
238	4.8	Burrell SD	Lower Burrell
238	4.8	Chester-Upland SD	Chester
238	4.8	Elizabethtown Area SD	Elizabethtown
238	4.8	Greenville Area SD	Greenville
238	4.8	Hempfield Area SD	Greensburg
238	4.8	Hopewell Area SD	Aliquippa
244	4.7	Daniel Boone Area SD	Douglassville
245	4.6	Central York SD	York
245	4.6	Grove City Area SD	Grove City
247	4.5	Carlynton SD	Carnegie
247	4.5	Penn Manor SD	Millersville
247	4.5	Phoenixville Area SD	Phoenixville
247	4.5	South Western SD	Hanover
251	4.3	Carlisle Area SD	Carlisle
251	4.3	Hazleton Area SD	Hazleton
251	4.3	Hempfield SD	Landisville
251	4.3	South Butler County SD	Saxonburg
255	4.2	Crestwood SD	Mountain Top
255	4.2	Dunmore SD	Dunmore
255	4.2	Kennett Consolidated SD	Kennett Square
255	4.2	Mechanicsburg Area SD	Mechanicsburg
259	4.1	Conrad Weiser Area SD	Robesonia
259	4.1	Fairview SD	Fairview
259	4.1	Richland SD	Johnstown
259	4.1	State College Area SD	State College
259	4.1	Warwick SD	Lititz
264	3.9	Dallas SD	Dallas
264	3.9	Neshaminy SD	Langhorne
264	3.9	Octorara Area SD	Atglen
264	3.9	Upper Merion Area SD	King Of Prussia
268	3.8	Exeter Township SD	Reading
268	3.8	Fleetwood Area SD	Fleetwood
268	3.8	West Shore SD	New Cumberland
271	3.7	Dallastown Area SD	Dallastown
271	3.7	Saucon Valley SD	Hellertown
273	3.6	Mars Area SD	Mars
273	3.6	Northern Lehigh SD	Slatington
273	3.6	South Fayette Township SD	Mc Donald
273	3.6	South Park SD	South Park
277	3.5	North Penn SD	Lansdale
277	3.5	Northampton Area SD	Northampton
277	3.5	Owen J Roberts SD	Pottstown
277	3.5	Palmyra Area SD	Palmyra
277	3.5	Pennridge SD	Perkasie
277	3.5	Pleasant Valley SD	Brodheadsville
283	3.4	Lewisburg Area SD	Lewisburg
283	3.4	Montoursville Area SD	Montoursville
283	3.4	Northwestern Lehigh SD	New Tripoli
283	3.4	Penn-Trafford SD	Harrison City
283	3.4	Salisbury Township SD	Allentown
288	3.3	Annville-Cleona SD	Annville
288	3.3	Avon Grove SD	West Grove
288	3.3	Blackhawk SD	Beaver Falls
288	3.3	Governor Mifflin SD	Shillington
288	3.3	Northern York County SD	Dillsburg
288	3.3	Perkiomen Valley SD	Collegeville
288	3.3	Plum Borough SD	Plum

288	3.3	West Allegheny SD	Imperial
288	3.3	Wilson SD	West Lawn
297	3.2	South Eastern SD	Fawn Grove
297	3.2	Wyomissing Area SD	Wyomissing
299	3.1	Upper Moreland Township SD	Willow Grove
300	3.0	Kutztown Area SD	Kutztown
301	2.9	Abington SD	Abington
301	2.9	Hamburg Area SD	Hamburg
301	2.9	Manheim Township SD	Lancaster
301	2.9	Nazareth Area SD	Nazareth
301	2.9	West Jefferson Hills SD	Jefferson Hls
306	2.8	Fox Chapel Area SD	Pittsburgh
306	2.8	Washington SD	Washington
308	2.7	Abington Heights SD	Clarks Summit
308	2.7	Derry Township SD	Hershey
308	2.7	Lampeter-Strasburg SD	Lampeter
308	2.7	Quaker Valley SD	Sewickley
312	2.6	Bethel Park SD	Bethel Park
312	2.6	Boyertown Area SD	Boyertown
312	2.6	East Penn SD	Emmaus
312	2.6	Palisades SD	Kintnersville
312	2.6	Pottsgrove SD	Pottstown
317	2.5	Colonial SD	Plymouth Meeting
317	2.5	Souderton Area SD	Souderton
317	2.5	Spring-Ford Area SD	Collegeville
320	2.4	Pennsbury SD	Fallsington
321	2.3	Center Area SD	Monaca
321	2.3	Seneca Valley SD	Harmony
323	2.1	Cumberland Valley SD	Mechanicsburg
323	2.1	Hampton Township SD	Gibsonia
323	2.1	Moon Area SD	Moon Township
326	2.0	Brandywine Heights Area SD	Topton
326	2.0	Penn-Delco SD	Aston
326	2.0	Southern York County SD	Glen Rock
329	1.9	Beaver Area SD	Beaver
329	1.9	Great Valley SD	Malvern
329	1.9	South Middleton SD	Boiling Springs
332	1.8	Parkland SD	Allentown
333	1.7	Hatboro-Horsham SD	Horsham
334	1.5	Rose Tree Media SD	Media
334	1.5	Southern Lehigh SD	Center Valley
336	1.4	Montour SD	Mc Kees Rocks
336	1.4	West Chester Area SD	West Chester
338	1.3	Marple Newtown SD	Newtown Square
338	1.3	Upper Dublin SD	Maple Glen
338	1.3	Wallingford-Swarthmore SD	Wallingford
341	1.2	Franklin Regional SD	Murrysville
341	1.2	Lower Merion SD	Ardmore
341	1.2	Oley Valley SD	Oley
341	1.2	Pine-Richland SD	Gibsonia
345	1.1	North Allegheny SD	Pittsburgh
346	1.0	Cheltenham Township SD	Elkins Park
346	1.0	Haverford Township SD	Havertown
348	0.9	Downingtown Area SD	Downingtown
348	0.9	Lower Moreland Township SD	Huntingdon Vly
348	0.9	Springfield Township SD	Oreland
348	0.9	Wissahickon SD	Ambler
352	0.8	Garnet Valley SD	Glen Mills
352	0.8	Radnor Township SD	Wayne
352	0.8	Unionville-Chadds Ford SD	Kennett Square
352	0.8	Upper Saint Clair SD	Pittsburgh
356	0.7	Methacton SD	Norristown
356	0.7	Springfield SD	Springfield
358	0.6	Central Bucks SD	Doylestown
358	0.6	Peters Township SD	Mcmurray
358	0.6	Tredyffrin-Easttown SD	Berwyn
361	0.5	Council Rock SD	Richboro
362	0.4	Mount Lebanon SD	Pittsburgh
363	0.0	Pennsylvania Virtual CS	Norristown
364	n/a	PDE Division of Data Services	Harrisburg

Student/Teacher Ratio

Rank	Ratio	District Name	City
1	40.4	Pennsylvania Virtual CS	Norristown
2	20.2	Pottsville Area SD	Pottsville
3	19.6	Crestwood SD	Mountain Top
3	19.6	Greater Nanticoke Area SD	Nanticoke
5	19.5	Lebanon SD	Lebanon
5	19.5	Penn-Trafford SD	Harrison City
5	19.5	Philadelphia City SD	Philadelphia
5	19.5	Wattsburg Area SD	Erie
5	19.5	West Mifflin Area SD	West Mifflin
10	19.3	Belle Vernon Area SD	Belle Vernon
10	19.3	Hazleton Area SD	Hazleton
12	19.2	Solanco SD	Quarryville
12	19.2	South Park SD	South Park
14	19.1	Kiski Area SD	Vandergrift
15	19.0	Lakeland SD	Jermyn
16	18.9	Conewago Valley SD	New Oxford
17	18.8	Allentown City SD	Allentown
18	18.7	Greencastle-Antrim SD	Greencastle
18	18.7	West Jefferson Hills SD	Jefferson Hls
20	18.6	Norwin SD	N Huntingdon
20	18.6	Quakertown Community SD	Quakertown
20	18.6	Wyoming Area SD	Exeter
23	18.5	Greensburg Salem SD	Greensburg
23	18.5	Moniteau SD	West Sunbury
25	18.3	Laurel Highlands SD	Uniontown
26	18.2	Blue Mountain SD	Orwigsburg
26	18.2	Jim Thorpe Area SD	Jim Thorpe
26	18.2	Palmerton Area SD	Palmerton
26	18.2	Reynolds SD	Greenville
30	18.1	Shamokin Area SD	Coal Township
31	18.0	Hamburg Area SD	Hamburg
31	18.0	Peters Township SD	Mcmurray
31	18.0	Reading SD	Reading
31	18.0	Tamaqua Area SD	Tamaqua
35	17.9	Burrell SD	Lower Burrell
35	17.9	Central Bucks SD	Doylestown
35	17.9	Greater Latrobe SD	Latrobe
35	17.9	Northwestern SD	Albion
35	17.9	Pleasant Valley SD	Brodheadsville
35	17.9	Upper Perkiomen SD	East Greenville
41	17.8	Dunmore SD	Dunmore
41	17.8	Mount Pleasant Area SD	Mount Pleasant
41	17.8	North Penn SD	Lansdale
44	17.7	Dallas SD	Dallas
44	17.7	Jeannette City SD	Jeannette
44	17.7	Neshaminy SD	Langhorne
44	17.7	North Schuylkill SD	Ashland
44	17.7	Whitehall-Coplay SD	Whitehall
49	17.6	Chambersburg Area SD	Chambersburg
49	17.6	Fort Leboeuf SD	Waterford
49	17.6	Littlestown Area SD	Littlestown
49	17.6	Pen Argyl Area SD	Pen Argyl
49	17.6	Pine Grove Area SD	Pine Grove
54	17.5	Bangor Area SD	Bangor
54	17.5	Ligonier Valley SD	Ligonier
54	17.5	North East SD	North East
54	17.5	Pennridge SD	Perkasie
54	17.5	Valley View SD	Archbald
59	17.4	Shippensburg Area SD	Shippensburg
59	17.4	South Butler County SD	Saxonburg
61	17.3	Boyertown Area SD	Boyertown
61	17.3	Elizabethtown Area SD	Elizabethtown
61	17.3	Parkland SD	Allentown
61	17.3	Red Lion Area SD	Red Lion
65	17.2	Beaver Area SD	Beaver
65	17.2	Hempfield SD	Landisville
65	17.2	Oil City Area SD	Oil City
65	17.2	Southern Lehigh SD	Center Valley
65	17.2	Yough SD	Herminie
70	17.1	East Allegheny SD	N Versailles
70	17.1	Freedom Area SD	Freedom
70	17.1	Mifflinburg Area SD	Mifflinburg
70	17.1	Penn Manor SD	Millersville
70	17.1	Plum Borough SD	Plum
70	17.1	Saint Marys Area SD	Saint Marys
70	17.1	Slippery Rock Area SD	Slippery Rock
77	17.0	Bermudian Springs SD	York Springs
77	17.0	Blackhawk SD	Beaver Falls
77	17.0	Charleroi SD	Charleroi
77	17.0	Dover Area SD	Dover
77	17.0	North Pocono SD	Moscow
77	17.0	Northern Lehigh SD	Slatington
77	17.0	Pittston Area SD	Pittston
77	17.0	Southmoreland SD	Scottdale
85	16.9	Baldwin-Whitehall SD	Pittsburgh
85	16.9	Bensalem Township SD	Bensalem
85	16.9	Central York SD	York
85	16.9	Cocalico SD	Denver
85	16.9	Ellwood City Area SD	Ellwood City
85	16.9	Exeter Township SD	Reading
85	16.9	Lake-Lehman SD	Lehman
85	16.9	Nazareth Area SD	Nazareth
85	16.9	Richland SD	Johnstown
85	16.9	Wyoming Valley West SD	Kingston
95	16.8	Avon Grove SD	West Grove
95	16.8	Butler Area SD	Butler
95	16.8	Chestnut Ridge SD	Fishertown
95	16.8	Conestoga Valley SD	Lancaster
95	16.8	East Penn SD	Emmaus
95	16.8	Franklin Regional SD	Murrysville
95	16.8	Girard SD	Girard
95	16.8	Hermitage SD	Hermitage
95	16.8	Mercer Area SD	Mercer
95	16.8	New Kensington-Arnold SD	New Kensington
105	16.7	Daniel Boone Area SD	Douglassville
105	16.7	Hanover Area SD	Wilkes Barre
105	16.7	Lampeter-Strasburg SD	Lampeter
105	16.7	Shikellamy SD	Sunbury
105	16.7	South Western SD	Hanover
105	16.7	Upper Darby SD	Drexel Hill
105	16.7	Westmont Hilltop SD	Johnstown
112	16.6	Abington Heights SD	Clarks Summit
112	16.6	Abington SD	Abington
112	16.6	Albert Gallatin Area SD	Uniontown
112	16.6	Blairsville-Saltsburg SD	Blairsville
112	16.6	Centennial SD	Warminster
112	16.6	Central Columbia SD	Bloomsburg
112	16.6	Eastern Lebanon County SD	Myerstown
112	16.6	New Brighton Area SD	New Brighton
112	16.6	Palmyra Area SD	Palmyra
112	16.6	Perkiomen Valley SD	Collegeville
112	16.6	South Eastern SD	Fawn Grove
112	16.6	Spring-Ford Area SD	Collegeville
112	16.6	West Chester Area SD	West Chester
112	16.6	West York Area SD	York
126	16.5	Ambridge Area SD	Ambridge
126	16.5	Apollo-Ridge SD	Spring Church
126	16.5	Derry Area SD	Derry
126	16.5	Ephrata Area SD	Ephrata
126	16.5	Forest Hills SD	Sidman
126	16.5	Mckeesport Area SD	Mc Keesport
126	16.5	Montour SD	Mc Kees Rocks
126	16.5	Spring Grove Area SD	Spring Grove
126	16.5	Steel Valley SD	Munhall
126	16.5	West Shore SD	New Cumberland
136	16.4	Altoona Area SD	Altoona
136	16.4	Connellsville Area SD	Connellsville
136	16.4	Hampton Township SD	Gibsonia
136	16.4	New Castle Area SD	New Castle
136	16.4	Riverside Beaver County SD	Ellwood City
136	16.4	Titusville Area SD	Titusville
136	16.4	Wilson SD	West Lawn
143	16.3	Carlynton SD	Carnegie
143	16.3	Delaware Valley SD	Milford
143	16.3	Governor Mifflin SD	Shillington
143	16.3	Somerset Area SD	Somerset
143	16.3	Uniontown Area SD	Uniontown
143	16.3	Upper Saint Clair SD	Pittsburgh
143	16.3	Warwick SD	Lititz
150	16.2	Clearfield Area SD	Clearfield
150	16.2	Dubois Area SD	Du Bois
150	16.2	Eastern Lancaster County SD	New Holland
150	16.2	General Mclane SD	Edinboro
150	16.2	Hopewell Area SD	Aliquippa
150	16.2	Kennett Consolidated SD	Kennett Square
150	16.2	Manheim Central SD	Manheim
150	16.2	Northampton Area SD	Northampton
150	16.2	Pennsbury SD	Fallsington
150	16.2	Salisbury Township SD	Allentown
150	16.2	Troy Area SD	Troy
161	16.1	Bedford Area SD	Bedford
161	16.1	Haverford Township SD	Havertown
161	16.1	Lancaster SD	Lancaster
161	16.1	Penn-Delco SD	Aston
161	16.1	Pottsgrove SD	Pottstown
161	16.1	Souderton Area SD	Souderton
161	16.1	Upper Adams SD	Biglerville
161	16.1	Upper Moreland Township SD	Willow Grove
161	16.1	Western Wayne SD	South Canaan
161	16.1	William Penn SD	Lansdowne
161	16.1	Wilmington Area SD	New Wilmington
172	16.0	Canon-Mcmillan SD	Canonsburg
172	16.0	Chester-Upland SD	Chester
172	16.0	Cumberland Valley SD	Mechanicsburg
172	16.0	Derry Township SD	Hershey
172	16.0	Elizabeth Forward SD	Elizabeth
172	16.0	Grove City Area SD	Grove City
172	16.0	Juniata County SD	Mifflintown
172	16.0	Millcreek Township SD	Erie
172	16.0	Mohawk Area SD	Bessemer
172	16.0	Montoursville Area SD	Montoursville
172	16.0	Northern Lebanon SD	Fredericksburg
172	16.0	Owen J Roberts SD	Pottstown
172	16.0	Pocono Mountain SD	Swiftwater
172	16.0	Ringgold SD	New Eagle
172	16.0	South Allegheny SD	Mc Keesport
172	16.0	Susquehanna Township SD	Harrisburg
172	16.0	Waynesboro Area SD	Waynesboro
172	16.0	York City SD	York
190	15.9	Annville-Cleona SD	Annville
190	15.9	Brownsville Area SD	Brownsville
190	15.9	Cornwall-Lebanon SD	Lebanon
190	15.9	Mcguffey SD	Claysville
190	15.9	Mount Carmel Area SD	Mount Carmel
190	15.9	Selinsgrove Area SD	Selinsgrove
196	15.8	Center Area SD	Monaca
196	15.8	Chichester SD	Boothwyn
196	15.8	Columbia Borough SD	Columbia
196	15.8	Downingtown Area SD	Downingtown
196	15.8	Hempfield Area SD	Greensburg
196	15.8	Mars Area SD	Mars
196	15.8	Mid Valley SD	Throop
196	15.8	Northeastern York SD	Manchester
196	15.8	Northwestern Lehigh SD	New Tripoli

196	15.8	Penncrest SD	Saegertown
196	15.8	Pottstown SD	Pottstown
196	15.8	Seneca Valley SD	Harmony
196	15.8	Southern York County SD	Glen Rock
196	15.8	Stroudsburg Area SD	Stroudsburg
196	15.8	Trinity Area SD	Washington
211	15.7	Council Rock SD	Richboro
211	15.7	Everett Area SD	Everett
211	15.7	Hatboro-Horsham SD	Horsham
211	15.7	Jersey Shore Area SD	Jersey Shore
211	15.7	Karns City Area SD	Karns City
211	15.7	Towanda Area SD	Towanda
211	15.7	Upper Dublin SD	Maple Glen
218	15.6	Bethlehem Area SD	Bethlehem
218	15.6	Bradford Area SD	Bradford
218	15.6	Coatesville Area SD	Coatesville
218	15.6	Conneaut SD	Linesville
218	15.6	Dallastown Area SD	Dallastown
218	15.6	Donegal SD	Mount Joy
218	15.6	Easton Area SD	Easton
218	15.6	Freeport Area SD	Freeport
218	15.6	Manheim Township SD	Lancaster
218	15.6	Montrose Area SD	Montrose
218	15.6	Oley Valley SD	Oley
218	15.6	Southeast Delco SD	Folcroft
218	15.6	Springfield SD	Springfield
218	15.6	Wayne Highlands SD	Honesdale
218	15.6	Wyalusing Area SD	Wyalusing
233	15.5	Brookville Area SD	Brookville
233	15.5	Deer Lakes SD	Russellton
233	15.5	Erie City SD	Erie
233	15.5	Fairview SD	Fairview
233	15.5	Greenville Area SD	Greenville
233	15.5	Interboro SD	Prospect Park
233	15.5	Pequea Valley SD	Kinzers
233	15.5	Spring Cove SD	Roaring Spring
233	15.5	Susquenita SD	Duncannon
233	15.5	Wilkes-Barre Area SD	Wilkes Barre
233	15.5	Wilson Area SD	Easton
244	15.4	Central Cambria SD	Ebensburg
244	15.4	Hollidaysburg Area SD	Hollidaysburg
244	15.4	Lewisburg Area SD	Lewisburg
244	15.4	Oxford Area SD	Oxford
244	15.4	Schuylkill Valley SD	Leesport
244	15.4	Tuscarora SD	Mercersburg
250	15.3	Armstrong SD	Ford City
250	15.3	Bellefonte Area SD	Bellefonte
250	15.3	Fleetwood Area SD	Fleetwood
250	15.3	Wissahickon SD	Ambler
254	15.2	Chartiers Valley SD	Pittsburgh
254	15.2	Elk Lake SD	Dimock
254	15.2	Gettysburg Area SD	Gettysburg
254	15.2	Hanover Public SD	Hanover
254	15.2	Northern York County SD	Dillsburg
254	15.2	Tulpehocken Area SD	Bernville
254	15.2	Twin Valley SD	Elverson
254	15.2	Unionville-Chadds Ford SD	Kennett Square
254	15.2	West Allegheny SD	Imperial
254	15.2	Woodland Hills SD	Pittsburgh
264	15.1	Burgettstown Area SD	Burgettstown
264	15.1	Catasauqua Area SD	Catasauqua
264	15.1	Great Valley SD	Malvern
264	15.1	Lower Dauphin SD	Hummelstown
264	15.1	Muhlenberg SD	Reading
264	15.1	North Allegheny SD	Pittsburgh
264	15.1	Saucon Valley SD	Hellertown
264	15.1	Sharon City SD	Sharon
264	15.1	South Fayette Township SD	Mc Donald
264	15.1	Southern Tioga SD	Blossburg
264	15.1	Warren County SD	North Warren
275	15.0	Bethel Park SD	Bethel Park
275	15.0	Bristol Township SD	Levittown
275	15.0	Cranberry Area SD	Seneca
275	15.0	East Stroudsburg Area SD	E Stroudsburg
275	15.0	Keystone Oaks SD	Pittsburgh
275	15.0	Lower Moreland Township SD	Huntingdon Vly
275	15.0	Mount Lebanon SD	Pittsburgh
275	15.0	Palisades SD	Kintnersville
275	15.0	Tyrone Area SD	Tyrone
284	14.9	Bald Eagle Area SD	Wingate
284	14.9	Central Dauphin SD	Harrisburg
284	14.9	Corry Area SD	Corry
284	14.9	Harbor Creek SD	Harborcreek
284	14.9	Penn Cambria SD	Cresson
289	14.8	Brandywine Heights Area SD	Topton
289	14.8	Methacton SD	Norristown
289	14.8	North Hills SD	Pittsburgh
289	14.8	Octorara Area SD	Atglen
289	14.8	Quaker Valley SD	Sewickley
294	14.7	Conrad Weiser Area SD	Robesonia
294	14.7	East Pennsboro Area SD	Enola
294	14.7	Penns Valley Area SD	Spring Mills
294	14.7	Shaler Area SD	Glenshaw
294	14.7	State College Area SD	State College
294	14.7	Williamsport Area SD	Williamsport
294	14.7	York Suburban SD	York
301	14.6	Lehighton Area SD	Lehighton
301	14.6	Mechanicsburg Area SD	Mechanicsburg
301	14.6	Northgate SD	Pittsburgh
301	14.6	Penn Hills SD	Pittsburgh
305	14.5	Franklin Area SD	Franklin
305	14.5	Garnet Valley SD	Glen Mills
305	14.5	Gateway SD	Monroeville
305	14.5	Mifflin County SD	Lewistown
309	14.4	Greater Johnstown SD	Johnstown
309	14.4	Marion Center Area SD	Marion Center
309	14.4	Milton Area SD	Milton
309	14.4	Moon Area SD	Moon Township
309	14.4	Pine-Richland SD	Gibsonia
309	14.4	Ridley SD	Folsom
309	14.4	South Middleton SD	Boiling Springs
309	14.4	Wyomissing Area SD	Wyomissing
317	14.3	Berwick Area SD	Berwick
317	14.3	Huntingdon Area SD	Huntingdon
317	14.3	Scranton SD	Scranton
317	14.3	Tredyffrin-Easttown SD	Berwyn
317	14.3	Tunkhannock Area SD	Tunkhannock
322	14.2	Bloomsburg Area SD	Bloomsburg
322	14.2	Carlisle Area SD	Carlisle
322	14.2	Crawford Central SD	Meadville
322	14.2	East Lycoming SD	Hughesville
326	14.1	Big Beaver Falls Area SD	Beaver Falls
326	14.1	Big Spring SD	Newville
326	14.1	Cheltenham Township SD	Elkins Park
326	14.1	Danville Area SD	Danville
326	14.1	Midd-West SD	Middleburg
326	14.1	Philipsburg-Osceola Area SD	Philipsburg
326	14.1	Wallenpaupack Area SD	Hawley
333	14.0	Eastern York SD	Wrightsville
333	14.0	Rose Tree Media SD	Media
333	14.0	Sto-Rox SD	Mckees Rocks
333	14.0	Upper Merion Area SD	King Of Prussia
333	14.0	Warrior Run SD	Turbotville
333	14.0	West Perry SD	Elliottsburg
339	13.9	Indiana Area SD	Indiana
339	13.9	Middletown Area SD	Middletown
339	13.9	Wallingford-Swarthmore SD	Wallingford
339	13.9	Washington SD	Washington
339	13.9	Wellsboro Area SD	Wellsboro
344	13.8	Cambria Heights SD	Patton
344	13.8	Central Greene SD	Waynesburg
344	13.8	Colonial SD	Plymouth Meeting
344	13.8	Kutztown Area SD	Kutztown
344	13.8	Phoenixville Area SD	Phoenixville
349	13.6	Highlands SD	Natrona Heights
349	13.6	Marple Newtown SD	Newtown Square
349	13.6	Punxsutawney Area SD	Punxsutawney
352	13.5	Athens Area SD	Athens
352	13.5	Springfield Township SD	Oreland
354	13.4	Norristown Area SD	Norristown
355	13.2	Keystone Central SD	Lock Haven
356	13.1	Northern Tioga SD	Elkland
357	13.0	Mount Union Area SD	Mount Union
357	13.0	Pittsburgh SD	Pittsburgh
359	12.9	Harrisburg City SD	Harrisburg
360	12.7	Radnor Township SD	Wayne
360	12.7	Wilkinsburg Borough SD	Wilkinsburg
362	12.5	Lower Merion SD	Ardmore
363	12.4	Fox Chapel Area SD	Pittsburgh
364	n/a	PDE Division of Data Services	Harrisburg

Student/Librarian Ratio

Rank	Ratio	District Name	City
1	2,824.5	Ridley SD	Folsom
2	2,203.3	Hazleton Area SD	Hazleton
3	2,186.0	Greater Nanticoke Area SD	Nanticoke
4	1,955.5	Southeast Delco SD	Folcroft
5	1,781.0	Wilkinsburg Borough SD	Wilkinsburg
6	1,735.9	Philadelphia City SD	Philadelphia
7	1,663.5	York City SD	York
8	1,663.0	Greenville Area SD	Greenville
9	1,613.5	Erie City SD	Erie
10	1,599.0	Wilmington Area SD	New Wilmington
11	1,539.3	Dubois Area SD	Du Bois
12	1,533.4	Cumberland Valley SD	Mechanicsburg
13	1,492.3	Kiski Area SD	Vandergrift
14	1,445.0	Nazareth Area SD	Nazareth
15	1,420.2	Altoona Area SD	Altoona
16	1,412.0	Somerset Area SD	Somerset
17	1,344.0	Danville Area SD	Danville
18	1,341.3	Rose Tree Media SD	Media
19	1,295.0	Wyoming Area SD	Exeter
20	1,293.1	Millcreek Township SD	Erie
21	1,292.5	Shamokin Area SD	Coal Township
22	1,248.7	Harrisburg City SD	Harrisburg
23	1,232.3	Chichester SD	Boothwyn
24	1,224.0	Northern Lebanon SD	Fredericksburg
25	1,222.6	Williamsport Area SD	Williamsport
26	1,201.3	Penn-Trafford SD	Harrison City
27	1,201.0	Penn Hills SD	Pittsburgh
28	1,196.5	Susquenita SD	Duncannon
29	1,187.0	Sharon City SD	Sharon
30	1,151.7	Berwick Area SD	Berwick
31	1,134.0	Central Greene SD	Waynesburg
32	1,123.0	Ellwood City Area SD	Ellwood City
33	1,116.6	Pocono Mountain SD	Swiftwater
34	1,105.5	Montoursville Area SD	Montoursville
35	1,104.3	Wayne Highlands SD	Honesdale
36	1,093.5	Plum Borough SD	Plum
37	1,091.5	Harbor Creek SD	Harborcreek
38	1,088.8	Red Lion Area SD	Red Lion
39	1,084.3	North Pocono SD	Moscow
40	1,059.3	Lampeter-Strasburg SD	Lampeter
41	1,059.0	Lebanon SD	Lebanon
42	1,054.0	Washington SD	Washington
43	1,045.0	Beaver Area SD	Beaver
44	1,040.5	Bald Eagle Area SD	Wingate
45	1,039.0	Pottsville Area SD	Pottsville
46	1,034.4	Norwin SD	N Huntingdon
47	1,023.3	Owen J Roberts SD	Pottstown
48	1,014.9	Bethlehem Area SD	Bethlehem
49	1,014.5	Girard SD	Girard
50	1,008.5	Mohawk Area SD	Bessemer
51	1,006.0	North Schuylkill SD	Ashland
52	1,005.0	Pen Argyl Area SD	Pen Argyl
53	1,001.7	Muhlenberg SD	Reading
54	996.6	Wilkes-Barre Area SD	Wilkes Barre
55	996.5	Tyrone Area SD	Tyrone
56	993.5	Palmerton Area SD	Palmerton
57	990.0	New Brighton Area SD	New Brighton
58	988.7	Elizabeth Forward SD	Elizabeth
59	987.8	Interboro SD	Prospect Park
60	981.9	Allentown City SD	Allentown
61	978.3	Lower Dauphin SD	Hummelstown
62	971.5	Whitehall-Coplay SD	Whitehall
63	966.6	Perkiomen Valley SD	Collegeville
64	963.2	Upper Darby SD	Drexel Hill
65	961.7	Crestwood SD	Mountain Top
66	956.3	Saucon Valley SD	Hellertown
67	954.3	Hollidaysburg Area SD	Hollidaysburg
68	952.6	Seneca Valley SD	Harmony
69	952.0	Pleasant Valley SD	Brodheadsville
70	946.0	Derry Area SD	Derry
71	944.7	Blackhawk SD	Beaver Falls
72	940.0	Avon Grove SD	West Grove
73	937.0	Highlands SD	Natrona Heights
74	929.5	Dover Area SD	Dover
75	925.0	Palmyra Area SD	Palmyra
76	922.7	Northampton Area SD	Northampton
77	922.5	Abington Heights SD	Clarks Summit
78	920.5	Conewago Valley SD	New Oxford
78	920.5	Karns City Area SD	Karns City
80	913.7	Carlisle Area SD	Carlisle
81	908.0	Central York SD	York
82	907.5	Butler Area SD	Butler
82	907.5	South Allegheny SD	Mc Keesport
84	907.0	Eastern York SD	Wrightsville
85	905.0	Bangor Area SD	Bangor
86	896.0	Reading SD	Reading
87	895.8	Greensburg Salem SD	Greensburg
88	894.3	Greencastle-Antrim SD	Greencastle
89	893.5	Penn Manor SD	Millersville
90	888.2	South Western SD	Hanover
91	887.3	Mechanicsburg Area SD	Mechanicsburg
92	883.3	Octorara Area SD	Atglen
93	883.0	Stroudsburg Area SD	Stroudsburg
94	881.5	Chester-Upland SD	Chester
95	881.0	Mount Carmel Area SD	Mount Carmel
96	880.9	Mifflin County SD	Lewistown
97	880.0	Valley View SD	Archbald
98	879.4	Gateway SD	Monroeville
99	878.9	Easton Area SD	Easton
100	867.5	Upper Adams SD	Biglerville
101	867.0	Greater Latrobe SD	Latrobe
102	864.5	East Penn SD	Emmaus
103	863.7	Delaware Valley SD	Milford
103	863.7	Mifflinburg Area SD	Mifflinburg
105	863.3	Tuscarora SD	Mercersburg
106	862.8	Dallastown Area SD	Dallastown
107	862.5	Moniteau SD	West Sunbury
108	862.3	Mount Pleasant Area SD	Mount Pleasant
109	862.0	Baldwin-Whitehall SD	Pittsburgh
109	862.0	Keystone Oaks SD	Pittsburgh
111	860.3	Wyoming Valley West SD	Kingston
112	859.8	Chartiers Valley SD	Pittsburgh
113	859.7	Dallas SD	Dallas
114	857.7	Oil City Area SD	Oil City

115	857.0	New Kensington-Arnold SD	New Kensington
116	856.8	Franklin Area SD	Franklin
117	852.0	Corry Area SD	Corry
118	851.0	Slippery Rock Area SD	Slippery Rock
119	850.7	Saint Marys Area SD	Saint Marys
120	847.0	Greater Johnstown SD	Johnstown
120	847.0	Lakeland SD	Jermyn
122	846.5	Charleroi SD	Charleroi
122	846.5	Dunmore SD	Dunmore
124	845.8	Upper Perkiomen SD	East Greenville
125	844.0	Milton Area SD	Milton
126	843.7	Fleetwood Area SD	Fleetwood
127	843.0	Titusville Area SD	Titusville
128	842.0	Western Wayne SD	South Canaan
129	839.2	Governor Mifflin SD	Shillington
130	835.9	Connellsville Area SD	Connellsville
131	833.3	Penn-Delco SD	Aston
132	827.9	West Chester Area SD	West Chester
133	825.0	Carlynton SD	Carnegie
134	823.3	Springfield SD	Springfield
135	818.0	Penns Valley Area SD	Spring Mills
136	817.5	Shippensburg Area SD	Shippensburg
137	812.0	South Eastern SD	Fawn Grove
138	810.7	Mcguffey SD	Claysville
139	810.3	Mckeesport Area SD	Mc Keesport
140	807.3	West Allegheny SD	Imperial
141	800.8	Big Spring SD	Newville
141	800.8	East Allegheny SD	N Versailles
143	797.8	Tunkhannock Area SD	Tunkhannock
144	797.3	Eastern Lebanon County SD	Myerstown
145	796.4	Exeter Township SD	Reading
146	794.7	Keystone Central SD	Lock Haven
147	793.0	Centennial SD	Warminster
148	792.5	Elk Lake SD	Dimock
149	792.3	Northern York County SD	Dillsburg
150	790.8	Parkland SD	Allentown
151	786.0	Central Bucks SD	Doylestown
152	784.2	Warwick SD	Lititz
153	784.0	Northgate SD	Pittsburgh
154	783.0	Ambridge Area SD	Ambridge
154	783.0	Southmoreland SD	Scottdale
156	782.7	Fort Leboeuf SD	Waterford
157	782.5	Mount Union Area SD	Mount Union
158	781.5	Reynolds SD	Greenville
159	780.6	Spring-Ford Area SD	Collegeville
160	780.4	Elizabethtown Area SD	Elizabethtown
161	780.0	Mercer Area SD	Mercer
162	779.5	Mid Valley SD	Throop
163	779.3	Littlestown Area SD	Littlestown
164	778.8	Brookville Area SD	Brookville
165	778.4	Downingtown Area SD	Downingtown
166	778.0	Upper Moreland Township SD	Willow Grove
167	777.0	Susquehanna Township SD	Harrisburg
168	776.8	Pittston Area SD	Pittston
169	774.1	Haverford Township SD	Havertown
170	773.7	Cornwall-Lebanon SD	Lebanon
171	773.2	Wallenpaupack Area SD	Hawley
172	773.0	Kennett Consolidated SD	Kennett Square
173	768.0	Columbia Borough SD	Columbia
174	766.3	Fox Chapel Area SD	Pittsburgh
175	765.3	South Park SD	South Park
176	764.8	Garnet Valley SD	Glen Mills
177	763.5	Burgettstown Area SD	Burgettstown
178	763.4	Franklin Regional SD	Murrysville
179	761.8	Clearfield Area SD	Clearfield
180	760.8	West York Area SD	York
181	759.5	Everett Area SD	Everett
182	756.0	Wyalusing Area SD	Wyalusing
183	754.8	Coatesville Area SD	Coatesville
184	754.1	North Penn SD	Lansdale
185	754.0	Jeannette City SD	Jeannette
185	754.0	Tamaqua Area SD	Tamaqua
187	753.8	Peters Township SD	Mcmurray
188	752.6	Ringgold SD	New Eagle
189	752.3	Burrell SD	Lower Burrell
190	748.4	Laurel Highlands SD	Uniontown
191	748.1	East Stroudsburg Area SD	E Stroudsburg
192	747.0	Bellefonte Area SD	Bellefonte
193	746.6	Pine-Richland SD	Gibsonia
194	743.5	William Penn SD	Lansdowne
195	742.5	Hopewell Area SD	Aliquippa
196	741.3	Central Columbia SD	Bloomsburg
197	740.8	Blue Mountain SD	Orwigsburg
198	740.7	Neshaminy SD	Langhorne
199	738.5	South Butler County SD	Saxonburg
200	736.7	Pennsbury SD	Fallsington
201	733.2	Bensalem Township SD	Bensalem
202	733.0	Oley Valley SD	Oley
203	732.6	Methacton SD	Norristown
203	732.6	Moon Area SD	Moon Township
205	731.3	Lake-Lehman SD	Lehman
206	730.9	Colonial SD	Plymouth Meeting
207	730.5	Chambersburg Area SD	Chambersburg
208	729.4	Great Valley SD	Malvern
209	727.9	Souderton Area SD	Souderton
210	727.7	Upper Dublin SD	Maple Glen
211	726.5	Selinsgrove Area SD	Selinsgrove
212	724.4	Juniata County SD	Mifflintown
213	721.8	Hempfield SD	Landisville
214	721.6	Oxford Area SD	Oxford
215	720.3	Bermudian Springs SD	York Springs
215	720.3	West Perry SD	Elliottsburg
217	720.0	Pottstown SD	Pottstown
218	716.8	Crawford Central SD	Meadville
219	716.4	Boyertown Area SD	Boyertown
220	716.0	Palisades SD	Kintnersville
221	714.0	Punxsutawney Area SD	Punxsutawney
222	707.1	Wissahickon SD	Ambler
223	706.2	Cocalico SD	Denver
224	706.0	Canon-Mcmillan SD	Canonsburg
225	704.3	Northern Lehigh SD	Slatington
226	700.2	Gettysburg Area SD	Gettysburg
227	697.2	Eastern Lancaster County SD	New Holland
228	695.7	Upper Saint Clair SD	Pittsburgh
229	694.6	Shaler Area SD	Glenshaw
230	693.6	Wallingford-Swarthmore SD	Wallingford
231	692.3	Pennridge SD	Perkasie
232	691.5	Albert Gallatin Area SD	Uniontown
232	691.5	Hamburg Area SD	Hamburg
234	691.0	Hanover Area SD	Wilkes Barre
235	690.0	Grove City Area SD	Grove City
236	687.4	Hatboro-Horsham SD	Horsham
237	687.0	Conrad Weiser Area SD	Robesonia
238	681.0	Derry Township SD	Hershey
239	680.8	East Pennsboro Area SD	Enola
240	677.4	State College Area SD	State College
241	675.8	Mars Area SD	Mars
242	675.4	West Mifflin Area SD	West Mifflin
243	675.1	Abington SD	Abington
244	673.3	Unionville-Chadds Ford SD	Kennett Square
245	673.0	Shikellamy SD	Sunbury
246	672.3	Center Area SD	Monaca
247	671.2	Solanco SD	Quarryville
248	668.5	Manheim Central SD	Manheim
249	666.8	Montour SD	Mc Kees Rocks
250	663.7	Big Beaver Falls Area SD	Beaver Falls
250	663.7	Montrose Area SD	Montrose
252	662.3	Spring Cove SD	Roaring Spring
253	661.8	York Suburban SD	York
254	661.1	Council Rock SD	Richboro
255	659.7	Riverside Beaver County SD	Ellwood City
256	659.4	Daniel Boone Area SD	Douglassville
257	658.1	Lower Merion SD	Ardmore
258	656.0	North East SD	North East
259	654.8	Southern York County SD	Glen Rock
260	653.9	Armstrong SD	Ford City
261	653.8	Northern Tioga SD	Elkland
262	653.6	Quakertown Community SD	Quakertown
263	650.7	Freeport Area SD	Freeport
263	650.7	Spring Grove Area SD	Spring Grove
265	649.4	Radnor Township SD	Wayne
266	648.1	Central Dauphin SD	Harrisburg
267	645.8	Hampton Township SD	Gibsonia
268	642.7	Schuylkill Valley SD	Leesport
269	642.0	Wilson Area SD	Easton
270	640.2	Pottsgrove SD	Pottstown
271	639.0	Conestoga Valley SD	Lancaster
272	638.3	Northwestern SD	Albion
272	638.3	West Shore SD	New Cumberland
274	637.9	Wilson SD	West Lawn
275	636.3	Central Cambria SD	Ebensburg
275	636.3	Midd-West SD	Middleburg
277	636.0	New Castle Area SD	New Castle
278	634.5	Donegal SD	Mount Joy
279	631.5	General Mclane SD	Edinboro
279	631.5	Scranton SD	Scranton
281	631.3	Warrior Run SD	Turbotville
282	630.7	Warren County SD	North Warren
283	630.3	Trinity Area SD	Washington
284	625.9	Tredyffrin-Easttown SD	Berwyn
285	622.4	Norristown Area SD	Norristown
286	622.2	Twin Valley SD	Elverson
287	620.4	Woodland Hills SD	Pittsburgh
288	618.3	Huntingdon Area SD	Huntingdon
289	617.3	Lehighton Area SD	Lehighton
290	616.6	Jersey Shore Area SD	Jersey Shore
291	613.7	Northwestern Lehigh SD	New Tripoli
292	612.6	Penncrest SD	Saegertown
293	611.7	Towanda Area SD	Towanda
294	610.8	Cheltenham Township SD	Elkins Park
295	607.3	Wyomissing Area SD	Wyomissing
296	606.7	Chestnut Ridge SD	Fishertown
297	606.5	Southern Lehigh SD	Center Valley
298	602.7	Freedom Area SD	Freedom
299	600.2	Hempfield Area SD	Greensburg
300	598.7	Pittsburgh SD	Pittsburgh
301	598.0	South Fayette Township SD	Mc Donald
302	594.4	Middletown Area SD	Middletown
303	593.8	Belle Vernon Area SD	Belle Vernon
304	592.7	Pine Grove Area SD	Pine Grove
305	592.0	Bloomsburg Area SD	Bloomsburg
306	591.4	West Jefferson Hills SD	Jefferson Hls
307	591.3	Jim Thorpe Area SD	Jim Thorpe
308	589.8	Lancaster SD	Lancaster
309	589.7	Uniontown Area SD	Uniontown
310	586.6	North Allegheny SD	Pittsburgh
311	586.3	Bethel Park SD	Bethel Park
312	586.0	Bedford Area SD	Bedford
313	585.0	Catasauqua Area SD	Catasauqua
314	584.0	Marion Center Area SD	Marion Center
315	581.7	Waynesboro Area SD	Waynesboro
316	579.0	Hermitage SD	Hermitage
317	578.0	Hanover Public SD	Hanover
318	577.1	Phoenixville Area SD	Phoenixville
319	577.0	Forest Hills SD	Sidman
320	575.7	Tulpehocken Area SD	Bernville
321	573.0	Wattsburg Area SD	Erie
322	572.0	Wellsboro Area SD	Wellsboro
323	568.3	Steel Valley SD	Munhall
324	567.2	Marple Newtown SD	Newtown Square
325	565.3	Lower Moreland Township SD	Huntingdon Vly
326	564.3	Blairsville-Saltsburg SD	Blairsville
327	561.0	Mount Lebanon SD	Pittsburgh
328	559.6	Manheim Township SD	Lancaster
329	558.0	Westmont Hilltop SD	Johnstown
330	552.0	Indiana Area SD	Indiana
331	551.7	Annville-Cleona SD	Annville
332	551.5	Ephrata Area SD	Ephrata
333	551.1	Brandywine Heights Area SD	Topton
334	548.3	Apollo-Ridge SD	Spring Church
335	538.5	South Middleton SD	Boiling Springs
336	538.0	Sto-Rox SD	Mckees Rocks
337	537.3	Cambria Heights SD	Patton
338	530.5	Bristol Township SD	Levittown
339	528.7	Richland SD	Johnstown
340	528.3	Fairview SD	Fairview
341	525.8	Deer Lakes SD	Russellton
342	521.8	Yough SD	Herminie
343	521.5	Springfield Township SD	Oreland
344	503.3	Cranberry Area SD	Seneca
345	501.2	Northeastern York SD	Manchester
346	500.3	Pequea Valley SD	Kinzers
347	494.7	Conneaut SD	Linesville
348	494.5	Quaker Valley SD	Sewickley
349	490.2	North Hills SD	Pittsburgh
350	486.3	Troy Area SD	Troy
351	476.5	Penn Cambria SD	Cresson
352	466.8	Salisbury Township SD	Allentown
353	465.6	Southern Tioga SD	Blossburg
354	457.5	Kutztown Area SD	Kutztown
355	452.9	Upper Merion Area SD	King Of Prussia
356	445.6	Philipsburg-Osceola Area SD	Philipsburg
357	436.8	Ligonier Valley SD	Ligonier
358	434.3	Bradford Area SD	Bradford
359	417.4	Brownsville Area SD	Brownsville
360	415.0	Athens Area SD	Athens
361	366.2	Lewisburg Area SD	Lewisburg
362	0.0	East Lycoming SD	Hughesville
362	0.0	Pennsylvania Virtual CS	Norristown
364	n/a	PDE Division of Data Services	Harrisburg

Student/Counselor Ratio

Rank	Ratio	District Name	City
1	1,272.0	New Castle Area SD	New Castle
2	1,051.5	Deer Lakes SD	Russellton
3	988.7	Elizabeth Forward SD	Elizabeth
4	928.4	Cornwall-Lebanon SD	Lebanon
5	825.0	Carlynton SD	Carnegie
6	800.8	Penn-Trafford SD	Harrison City
7	783.0	Ambridge Area SD	Ambridge
8	748.7	Ellwood City Area SD	Ellwood City
9	748.4	Laurel Highlands SD	Uniontown
10	746.2	Kiski Area SD	Vandergrift
11	739.3	West Jefferson Hills SD	Jefferson Hls
12	726.6	Armstrong SD	Ford City
13	722.5	Nazareth Area SD	Nazareth
14	691.9	Warwick SD	Lititz
15	691.0	Berwick Area SD	Berwick
16	677.3	Baldwin-Whitehall SD	Pittsburgh
17	676.3	Girard SD	Girard
18	675.4	West Mifflin Area SD	West Mifflin
19	672.3	Mohawk Area SD	Bessemer
20	665.4	York City SD	York
21	656.2	Hempfield SD	Landisville
22	653.8	Northern Tioga SD	Elkland
23	647.8	Mifflinburg Area SD	Mifflinburg
24	646.3	Shamokin Area SD	Coal Township

Rank	Value	District	City
25	645.8	Hampton Township SD	Gibsonia
26	643.3	Oil City Area SD	Oil City
27	642.8	New Kensington-Arnold SD	New Kensington
28	642.2	Butler Area SD	Butler
29	632.3	Titusville Area SD	Titusville
30	629.5	Hazleton Area SD	Hazleton
31	627.7	Ridley SD	Folsom
32	627.0	Bristol Township SD	Levittown
33	624.9	Plum Borough SD	Plum
34	622.5	Athens Area SD	Athens
35	621.4	Pittston Area SD	Pittston
36	618.3	Huntingdon Area SD	Huntingdon
37	617.4	Shaler Area SD	Glenshaw
38	613.7	Conewago Valley SD	New Oxford
39	612.3	East Lycoming SD	Hughesville
40	610.5	Moon Area SD	Moon Township
41	602.7	Freedom Area SD	Freedom
42	599.8	Franklin Area SD	Franklin
43	592.7	Albert Gallatin Area SD	Uniontown
44	591.3	Jim Thorpe Area SD	Jim Thorpe
45	590.8	South Butler County SD	Saxonburg
46	587.3	Mount Carmel Area SD	Mount Carmel
47	584.5	Littlestown Area SD	Littlestown
48	582.2	Southern Lehigh SD	Center Valley
49	579.0	Hermitage SD	Hermitage
50	577.0	Crestwood SD	Mountain Top
51	575.0	Moniteau SD	West Sunbury
52	573.6	Wyoming Valley West SD	Kingston
53	573.3	Upper Darby SD	Drexel Hill
54	571.2	Abington SD	Abington
55	565.5	Tamaqua Area SD	Tamaqua
56	565.4	Riverside Beaver County SD	Ellwood City
57	564.8	Somerset Area SD	Somerset
58	564.7	Greater Johnstown SD	Johnstown
59	564.4	Interboro SD	Prospect Park
60	564.3	Burrell SD	Lower Burrell
61	561.9	Council Rock SD	Richboro
62	556.0	Central Columbia SD	Bloomsburg
63	554.3	Greenville Area SD	Greenville
64	546.5	Greater Nanticoke Area SD	Nanticoke
65	544.4	Red Lion Area SD	Red Lion
66	540.3	Bermudian Springs SD	York Springs
66	540.3	Trinity Area SD	Washington
68	537.6	Ringgold SD	New Eagle
69	536.6	Greencastle-Antrim SD	Greencastle
69	536.6	Wilkes-Barre Area SD	Wilkes Barre
71	533.0	Wilmington Area SD	New Wilmington
72	531.9	Connellsville Area SD	Connellsville
73	530.8	Philadelphia City SD	Philadelphia
74	528.7	Richland SD	Johnstown
75	528.3	Elk Lake SD	Dimock
76	527.7	Bethel Park SD	Bethel Park
77	523.5	Boyertown Area SD	Boyertown
78	521.7	Mount Union Area SD	Mount Union
79	521.0	Reynolds SD	Greenville
80	520.0	Mercer Area SD	Mercer
81	519.5	Pottsville Area SD	Pottsville
82	518.0	Tuscarora SD	Mercersburg
82	518.0	Wyoming Area SD	Exeter
84	517.1	Bangor Area SD	Bangor
85	517.0	Ephrata Area SD	Ephrata
86	516.9	Pittsburgh SD	Pittsburgh
87	513.8	Jersey Shore Area SD	Jersey Shore
87	513.8	Mifflin County SD	Lewistown
89	512.0	Columbia Borough SD	Columbia
90	511.9	Greensburg Salem SD	Greensburg
91	510.6	Slippery Rock Area SD	Slippery Rock
92	509.0	Waynesboro Area SD	Waynesboro
93	508.0	Millcreek Township SD	Erie
94	507.8	Clearfield Area SD	Clearfield
95	506.9	William Penn SD	Lansdowne
96	506.7	Bradford Area SD	Bradford
97	506.3	Everett Area SD	Everett
98	504.3	Center Area SD	Monaca
99	504.0	Wyalusing Area SD	Wyalusing
100	503.3	Cranberry Area SD	Seneca
101	503.0	North Schuylkill SD	Ashland
102	502.7	Jeannette City SD	Jeannette
103	500.5	East Allegheny SD	N Versailles
104	500.3	Pequea Valley SD	Kinzers
105	499.5	Oxford Area SD	Oxford
106	495.0	Hopewell Area SD	Aliquippa
106	495.0	New Brighton Area SD	New Brighton
108	494.8	Belle Vernon Area SD	Belle Vernon
109	494.7	Conneaut SD	Linesville
110	491.7	Seneca Valley SD	Harmony
111	488.0	Freeport Area SD	Freeport
112	486.4	Mcguffey SD	Claysville
113	486.3	Troy Area SD	Troy
114	486.2	Mckeesport Area SD	Mc Keesport
115	483.3	Perkiomen Valley SD	Collegeville
115	483.3	Upper Perkiomen SD	East Greenville
117	481.7	Greater Latrobe SD	Latrobe
118	480.8	Chester-Upland SD	Chester
119	480.7	Shikellamy SD	Sunbury
120	478.8	Northwestern SD	Albion
121	478.6	Susquenita SD	Duncannon
122	476.0	Pleasant Valley SD	Brodheadsville
123	474.8	Sharon City SD	Sharon
124	473.4	Altoona Area SD	Altoona
125	473.1	Pottstown SD	Pottstown
126	473.0	Derry Area SD	Derry
127	472.3	Blackhawk SD	Beaver Falls
128	471.1	Delaware Valley SD	Milford
128	471.1	Peters Township SD	Mcmurray
130	471.0	Daniel Boone Area SD	Douglassville
131	470.2	Norwin SD	N Huntingdon
132	468.9	Allentown City SD	Allentown
133	468.8	Bedford Area SD	Bedford
134	468.5	Highlands SD	Natrona Heights
135	467.5	Mount Lebanon SD	Pittsburgh
136	467.1	Shippensburg Area SD	Shippensburg
137	466.8	Salisbury Township SD	Allentown
138	466.6	Pine-Richland SD	Gibsonia
139	465.7	Juniata County SD	Mifflintown
140	464.0	South Eastern SD	Fawn Grove
141	461.9	Penn Hills SD	Pittsburgh
142	461.6	Forest Hills SD	Sidman
143	461.3	West Allegheny SD	Imperial
144	461.0	Hamburg Area SD	Hamburg
145	460.3	Karns City Area SD	Karns City
146	460.0	Grove City Area SD	Grove City
147	459.2	South Park SD	South Park
148	458.8	Towanda Area SD	Towanda
149	458.6	North Penn SD	Lansdale
150	457.6	Big Spring SD	Newville
151	455.9	Tunkhannock Area SD	Tunkhannock
152	455.0	Chestnut Ridge SD	Fishertown
153	454.7	Kennett Consolidated SD	Kennett Square
154	454.6	Steel Valley SD	Munhall
155	454.0	Lampeter-Strasburg SD	Lampeter
156	453.6	Central Greene SD	Waynesburg
157	452.7	Northern York County SD	Dillsburg
158	450.8	Quakertown Community SD	Quakertown
159	450.5	Mars Area SD	Mars
159	450.5	Warren County SD	North Warren
161	448.5	South Fayette Township SD	Mc Donald
162	448.0	Reading SD	Reading
163	447.4	Solanco SD	Quarryville
164	445.1	Erie City SD	Erie
165	444.0	Bloomsburg Area SD	Bloomsburg
166	442.4	Penncrest SD	Saegertown
167	441.7	Norristown Area SD	Norristown
168	441.4	Cocalico SD	Denver
169	439.3	Manheim Central SD	Manheim
170	437.7	Neshaminy SD	Langhorne
171	436.8	Ligonier Valley SD	Ligonier
172	436.7	Souderton Area SD	Souderton
173	436.6	Harbor Creek SD	Harborcreek
174	435.8	Eastern Lancaster County SD	New Holland
175	434.8	Yough SD	Herminie
176	433.8	Upper Adams SD	Biglerville
177	433.5	Hanover Public SD	Hanover
178	431.8	Whitehall-Coplay SD	Whitehall
179	431.0	Keystone Oaks SD	Pittsburgh
180	429.9	Chartiers Valley SD	Pittsburgh
181	429.8	Dallas SD	Dallas
181	429.8	Wattsburg Area SD	Erie
183	429.6	Wallenpaupack Area SD	Hawley
184	429.0	Wellsboro Area SD	Wellsboro
185	428.9	Penn Manor SD	Millersville
186	426.0	Corry Area SD	Corry
187	425.3	Saint Marys Area SD	Saint Marys
188	423.6	Canon-Mcmillan SD	Canonsburg
189	423.5	Lakeland SD	Jermyn
190	423.3	Blue Mountain SD	Orwigsburg
190	423.3	Dunmore SD	Dunmore
192	423.0	Donegal SD	Mount Joy
193	422.9	Centennial SD	Warminster
193	422.9	Chambersburg Area SD	Chambersburg
195	422.6	Northern Lehigh SD	Slatington
196	421.9	Easton Area SD	Easton
197	421.8	Fleetwood Area SD	Fleetwood
198	421.6	Washington SD	Washington
199	421.0	Scranton SD	Scranton
200	419.8	Dubois Area SD	Du Bois
201	417.4	Brownsville Area SD	Brownsville
202	416.8	Haverford Township SD	Havertown
203	416.6	Lancaster SD	Lancaster
204	416.2	Bald Eagle Area SD	Wingate
205	412.2	Central Bucks SD	Doylestown
206	411.5	Lehighton Area SD	Lehighton
207	411.3	Apollo-Ridge SD	Spring Church
208	410.0	Abington Heights SD	Clarks Summit
209	409.3	Owen J Roberts SD	Pottstown
209	409.3	Southern York County SD	Glen Rock
211	409.0	Penns Valley Area SD	Spring Mills
212	408.0	Northern Lebanon SD	Fredericksburg
213	407.5	Stroudsburg Area SD	Stroudsburg
214	407.2	Pennridge SD	Perkasie
215	403.5	Sto-Rox SD	Mckees Rocks
216	402.0	Pen Argyl Area SD	Pen Argyl
217	401.2	Downingtown Area SD	Downingtown
218	400.7	Central Dauphin SD	Harrisburg
219	399.7	Gateway SD	Monroeville
220	398.7	Eastern Lebanon County SD	Myerstown
221	398.2	Dallastown Area SD	Dallastown
221	398.2	Exeter Township SD	Reading
221	398.2	Montrose Area SD	Montrose
224	397.4	Palmerton Area SD	Palmerton
224	397.4	Spring Cove SD	Roaring Spring
226	397.3	Keystone Central SD	Lock Haven
227	396.4	Palmyra Area SD	Palmyra
228	396.3	Fairview SD	Fairview
229	395.1	West Shore SD	New Cumberland
230	393.7	East Stroudsburg Area SD	E Stroudsburg
231	393.6	North East SD	North East
232	393.0	East Penn SD	Emmaus
233	392.9	Woodland Hills SD	Pittsburgh
234	392.5	Wilson SD	West Lawn
235	392.2	North Hills SD	Pittsburgh
236	392.0	Northgate SD	Pittsburgh
237	391.3	Fort Leboeuf SD	Waterford
238	391.1	Southeast Delco SD	Folcroft
239	391.0	North Allegheny SD	Pittsburgh
240	390.8	South Western SD	Hanover
241	390.4	Spring Grove Area SD	Spring Grove
242	390.3	Spring-Ford Area SD	Collegeville
243	390.2	Elizabethtown Area SD	Elizabethtown
244	389.4	Brookville Area SD	Brookville
245	389.0	East Pennsboro Area SD	Enola
245	389.0	Upper Moreland Township SD	Willow Grove
247	388.9	Twin Valley SD	Elverson
248	388.7	Northwestern Lehigh SD	New Tripoli
249	388.5	Susquehanna Township SD	Harrisburg
250	385.6	Schuylkill Valley SD	Leesport
251	385.1	Lebanon SD	Lebanon
252	384.6	Parkland SD	Allentown
253	384.1	West Perry SD	Elliottsburg
254	383.2	Fox Chapel Area SD	Pittsburgh
255	381.8	Burgettstown Area SD	Burgettstown
255	381.8	Central Cambria SD	Ebensburg
255	381.8	Northampton Area SD	Northampton
258	381.7	Franklin Regional SD	Murrysville
258	381.7	Hollidaysburg Area SD	Hollidaysburg
260	381.5	Governor Mifflin SD	Shillington
261	380.4	West York Area SD	York
262	379.7	Manheim Township SD	Lancaster
263	378.3	Derry Township SD	Hershey
264	378.1	Marple Newtown SD	Newtown Square
265	377.1	Valley View SD	Archbald
266	376.6	Pottsgrove SD	Pottstown
267	376.2	Blairsville-Saltsburg SD	Blairsville
268	375.9	Northeastern York SD	Manchester
269	373.5	Bellefonte Area SD	Bellefonte
270	371.8	Dover Area SD	Dover
271	370.3	Penn-Delco SD	Aston
272	369.6	Mount Pleasant Area SD	Mount Pleasant
273	368.5	Montoursville Area SD	Montoursville
274	368.3	Pennsbury SD	Fallsington
275	368.1	Wayne Highlands SD	Honesdale
276	367.7	Garnet Valley SD	Glen Mills
277	366.8	Hempfield Area SD	Greensburg
278	366.6	Bensalem Township SD	Bensalem
279	366.5	Oley Valley SD	Oley
280	366.3	Methacton SD	Norristown
281	366.0	Kutztown Area SD	Kutztown
282	365.9	Springfield SD	Springfield
283	365.7	Lake-Lehman SD	Lehman
284	365.1	Conestoga Valley SD	Lancaster
284	365.1	Cumberland Valley SD	Mechanicsburg
286	363.8	Upper Dublin SD	Maple Glen
287	363.6	Midd-West SD	Middleburg
288	363.3	Selinsgrove Area SD	Selinsgrove
289	363.0	South Allegheny SD	Mc Keesport
290	362.8	Eastern York SD	Wrightsville
291	361.7	Milton Area SD	Milton
292	361.6	Hatboro-Horsham SD	Horsham
293	361.4	North Pocono SD	Moscow
294	360.9	General Mclane SD	Edinboro
295	358.4	Danville Area SD	Danville
296	357.5	Central York SD	York
297	357.0	Punxsutawney Area SD	Punxsutawney
298	356.2	Wilkinsburg Borough SD	Wilkinsburg
299	355.6	Pine Grove Area SD	Pine Grove
300	354.9	Mechanicsburg Area SD	Mechanicsburg
301	353.8	Uniontown Area SD	Uniontown

302	351.0	Catasauqua Area SD	Catasauqua
303	348.9	Pocono Mountain SD	Swiftwater
304	346.5	Colonial SD	Plymouth Meeting
305	345.5	Hanover Area SD	Wilkes Barre
306	345.0	State College Area SD	State College
307	343.5	Conrad Weiser Area SD	Robesonia
308	343.1	Coatesville Area SD	Coatesville
309	340.5	Harrisburg City SD	Harrisburg
310	339.6	Williamsport Area SD	Williamsport
311	338.6	Charleroi SD	Charleroi
312	336.1	Chichester SD	Boothwyn
313	334.8	Westmont Hilltop SD	Johnstown
314	334.4	Middletown Area SD	Middletown
315	332.6	Southern Tioga SD	Blossburg
316	332.1	Tulpehocken Area SD	Bernville
317	331.3	Octorara Area SD	Atglen
318	331.2	Indiana Area SD	Indiana
319	331.1	West Chester Area SD	West Chester
320	331.0	Annville-Cleona SD	Annville
321	330.7	Brandywine Heights Area SD	Topton
322	329.7	Quaker Valley SD	Sewickley
323	326.1	Lower Dauphin SD	Hummelstown
324	325.7	Cheltenham Township SD	Elkins Park
325	322.4	Cambria Heights SD	Patton
326	321.1	Upper Saint Clair SD	Pittsburgh
326	321.1	Wallingford-Swarthmore SD	Wallingford
328	321.0	Wilson Area SD	Easton
329	318.3	Gettysburg Area SD	Gettysburg
329	318.3	Philipsburg-Osceola Area SD	Philipsburg
331	317.7	Penn Cambria SD	Cresson
332	315.8	Western Wayne SD	South Canaan
333	315.7	Warrior Run SD	Turbotville
334	313.3	Avon Grove SD	West Grove
335	311.0	Bethlehem Area SD	Bethlehem
336	310.5	Wissahickon SD	Ambler
337	309.5	Rose Tree Media SD	Media
338	308.8	Upper Merion Area SD	King Of Prussia
339	307.8	York Suburban SD	York
340	307.7	South Middleton SD	Boiling Springs
341	307.2	Crawford Central SD	Meadville
342	306.9	Palisades SD	Kintnersville
343	304.9	Phoenixville Area SD	Phoenixville
344	303.9	Great Valley SD	Malvern
345	303.1	Montour SD	Mc Kees Rocks
346	300.5	Muhlenberg SD	Reading
347	298.6	Beaver Area SD	Beaver
348	298.0	Springfield Township SD	Oreland
349	295.2	Unionville-Chadds Ford SD	Kennett Square
350	293.6	Southmoreland SD	Scottdale
351	292.0	Marion Center Area SD	Marion Center
352	287.9	Carlisle Area SD	Carlisle
353	286.9	Saucon Valley SD	Hellertown
354	284.7	Tyrone Area SD	Tyrone
355	284.4	Big Beaver Falls Area SD	Beaver Falls
356	282.7	Lower Moreland Township SD	Huntingdon Vly
357	281.2	Lower Merion SD	Ardmore
358	270.6	Radnor Township SD	Wayne
359	268.2	Tredyffrin-Easttown SD	Berwyn
360	261.6	Lewisburg Area SD	Lewisburg
361	260.3	Wyomissing Area SD	Wyomissing
362	259.8	Mid Valley SD	Throop
363	0.0	Pennsylvania Virtual CS	Norristown
364	n/a	PDE Division of Data Services	Harrisburg

Current Spending per Student in FY2001

Rank	Dollars	District Name	City
1	13,654	Lower Merion SD	Ardmore
2	12,442	Upper Merion Area SD	King Of Prussia
3	12,367	Radnor Township SD	Wayne
4	10,745	Salisbury Township SD	Allentown
5	10,631	Tredyffrin-Easttown SD	Berwyn
6	10,619	Quaker Valley SD	Sewickley
7	10,617	Colonial SD	Plymouth Meeting
8	10,518	Wissahickon SD	Ambler
9	10,457	Great Valley SD	Malvern
10	10,341	Cheltenham Township SD	Elkins Park
11	10,240	Springfield Township SD	Oreland
12	10,209	Sto-Rox SD	Mckees Rocks
13	10,202	Harrisburg City SD	Harrisburg
14	10,156	Neshaminy SD	Langhorne
15	10,092	Lower Moreland Township SD	Huntingdon Vly
16	10,070	Phoenixville Area SD	Phoenixville
17	10,046	Gateway SD	Monroeville
18	9,937	Rose Tree Media SD	Media
19	9,916	Marple Newtown SD	Newtown Square
20	9,824	Norristown Area SD	Norristown
21	9,778	Chester-Upland SD	Chester
22	9,767	Wilkinsburg Borough SD	Wilkinsburg
23	9,631	Fox Chapel Area SD	Pittsburgh
24	9,496	Wallingford-Swarthmore SD	Wallingford
25	9,451	Council Rock SD	Richboro
26	9,430	Bensalem Township SD	Bensalem
27	9,324	Bristol Township SD	Levittown
28	9,284	Pennsbury SD	Fallsington
29	9,267	Abington SD	Abington
30	9,247	Palisades SD	Kintnersville
31	9,240	Pittsburgh SD	Pittsburgh
32	9,167	Hatboro-Horsham SD	Horsham
33	9,098	Carlynton SD	Carnegie
34	9,069	North Hills SD	Pittsburgh
35	9,039	Methacton SD	Norristown
36	8,940	Scranton SD	Scranton
37	8,939	Woodland Hills SD	Pittsburgh
38	8,889	Upper Saint Clair SD	Pittsburgh
39	8,847	Unionville-Chadds Ford SD	Kennett Square
40	8,811	Springfield SD	Springfield
41	8,770	Owen J Roberts SD	Pottstown
42	8,760	North Allegheny SD	Pittsburgh
43	8,759	Indiana Area SD	Indiana
44	8,756	Interboro SD	Prospect Park
45	8,751	Moon Area SD	Moon Township
46	8,745	Keystone Central SD	Lock Haven
47	8,688	Upper Dublin SD	Maple Glen
48	8,628	West Chester Area SD	West Chester
49	8,589	Keystone Oaks SD	Pittsburgh
50	8,586	Garnet Valley SD	Glen Mills
51	8,573	Chichester SD	Boothwyn
52	8,504	West Allegheny SD	Imperial
53	8,481	Upper Moreland Township SD	Willow Grove
54	8,472	York Suburban SD	York
55	8,433	Pottstown SD	Pottstown
56	8,414	Armstrong SD	Ford City
57	8,405	Spring-Ford Area SD	Collegeville
58	8,396	Kutztown Area SD	Kutztown
59	8,386	Ridley SD	Folsom
60	8,361	State College Area SD	State College
61	8,357	William Penn SD	Lansdowne
62	8,355	Perkiomen Valley SD	Collegeville
63	8,343	Mount Lebanon SD	Pittsburgh
64	8,319	Jim Thorpe Area SD	Jim Thorpe
65	8,315	Coatesville Area SD	Coatesville
66	8,241	Western Wayne SD	South Canaan
67	8,229	North Penn SD	Lansdale
68	8,214	Chartiers Valley SD	Pittsburgh
69	8,209	Wilkes-Barre Area SD	Wilkes Barre
70	8,167	Penns Valley Area SD	Spring Mills
71	8,160	Pottsgrove SD	Pottstown
72	8,113	Schuylkill Valley SD	Leesport
73	8,096	Wyomissing Area SD	Wyomissing
74	8,068	Wallenpaupack Area SD	Hawley
75	8,064	Central Greene SD	Waynesburg
76	8,060	Haverford Township SD	Havertown
77	8,035	Big Beaver Falls Area SD	Beaver Falls
78	8,020	Punxsutawney Area SD	Punxsutawney
79	8,014	Southeast Delco SD	Folcroft
80	8,010	Deer Lakes SD	Russellton
80	8,010	South Fayette Township SD	Mc Donald
82	8,006	Shaler Area SD	Glenshaw
83	7,987	Greater Johnstown SD	Johnstown
84	7,973	Kennett Consolidated SD	Kennett Square
85	7,961	Downingtown Area SD	Downingtown
86	7,949	Octorara Area SD	Atglen
87	7,941	Baldwin-Whitehall SD	Pittsburgh
88	7,932	Montour SD	Mc Kees Rocks
89	7,926	Souderton Area SD	Souderton
90	7,908	Bethel Park SD	Bethel Park
91	7,902	Penn Hills SD	Pittsburgh
92	7,901	Pequea Valley SD	Kinzers
93	7,838	Centennial SD	Warminster
94	7,831	Stroudsburg Area SD	Stroudsburg
95	7,807	Athens Area SD	Athens
96	7,803	Bradford Area SD	Bradford
97	7,793	Towanda Area SD	Towanda
98	7,773	Tulpehocken Area SD	Bernville
99	7,762	Muhlenberg SD	Reading
100	7,759	Wayne Highlands SD	Honesdale
100	7,759	West Mifflin Area SD	West Mifflin
102	7,756	Freeport Area SD	Freeport
103	7,745	Fairview SD	Fairview
104	7,738	Canon-Mcmillan SD	Canonsburg
105	7,732	Crawford Central SD	Meadville
106	7,729	Wilson SD	West Lawn
107	7,712	Williamsport Area SD	Williamsport
108	7,709	Brownsville Area SD	Brownsville
109	7,696	Pennridge SD	Perkasie
110	7,692	Saucon Valley SD	Hellertown
111	7,674	Highlands SD	Natrona Heights
112	7,673	East Allegheny SD	N Versailles
113	7,651	Hampton Township SD	Gibsonia
114	7,647	Mckeesport Area SD	Mc Keesport
115	7,641	Uniontown Area SD	Uniontown
116	7,617	Pittston Area SD	Pittston
116	7,617	Twin Valley SD	Elverson
118	7,614	Mcguffey SD	Claysville
119	7,608	Quakertown Community SD	Quakertown
120	7,599	Hanover Public SD	Hanover
121	7,581	Penn Cambria SD	Cresson
122	7,575	Hanover Area SD	Wilkes Barre
123	7,564	Trinity Area SD	Washington
124	7,555	Erie City SD	Erie
125	7,541	Abington Heights SD	Clarks Summit
126	7,539	Conrad Weiser Area SD	Robesonia
127	7,527	Ligonier Valley SD	Ligonier
128	7,522	Northwestern Lehigh SD	New Tripoli
128	7,522	Upper Perkiomen SD	East Greenville
130	7,509	Lancaster SD	Lancaster
131	7,503	Pine-Richland SD	Gibsonia
131	7,503	Southern Lehigh SD	Center Valley
133	7,501	Hempfield Area SD	Greensburg
134	7,496	East Stroudsburg Area SD	E Stroudsburg
135	7,485	Lewisburg Area SD	Lewisburg
136	7,470	Parkland SD	Allentown
137	7,463	Ambridge Area SD	Ambridge
138	7,462	Penncrest SD	Saegertown
139	7,458	Southern Tioga SD	Blossburg
140	7,453	Gettysburg Area SD	Gettysburg
141	7,446	Montrose Area SD	Montrose
142	7,445	Central Bucks SD	Doylestown
142	7,445	Penn-Delco SD	Aston
144	7,440	East Penn SD	Emmaus
144	7,440	York City SD	York
146	7,435	Northampton Area SD	Northampton
147	7,412	Tunkhannock Area SD	Tunkhannock
148	7,391	Manheim Township SD	Lancaster
149	7,386	Brandywine Heights Area SD	Topton
150	7,374	Lehighton Area SD	Lehighton
150	7,374	Troy Area SD	Troy
152	7,371	Wellsboro Area SD	Wellsboro
153	7,367	Elizabeth Forward SD	Elizabeth
154	7,354	Blairsville-Saltsburg SD	Blairsville
155	7,341	Northgate SD	Pittsburgh
156	7,323	Franklin Regional SD	Murrysville
157	7,321	Reynolds SD	Greenville
158	7,318	Dallas SD	Dallas
158	7,318	Everett Area SD	Everett
160	7,317	Wyalusing Area SD	Wyalusing
161	7,313	Franklin Area SD	Franklin
162	7,292	Hopewell Area SD	Aliquippa
163	7,279	Richland SD	Johnstown
164	7,261	Dallastown Area SD	Dallastown
165	7,259	Cranberry Area SD	Seneca
166	7,257	Marion Center Area SD	Marion Center
167	7,255	Cambria Heights SD	Patton
168	7,249	West Jefferson Hills SD	Jefferson Hls
169	7,245	Catasauqua Area SD	Catasauqua
170	7,243	Brookville Area SD	Brookville
171	7,237	Jersey Shore Area SD	Jersey Shore
172	7,236	Sharon City SD	Sharon
173	7,229	Carlisle Area SD	Carlisle
174	7,226	Mechanicsburg Area SD	Mechanicsburg
175	7,207	Eastern Lebanon County SD	Myerstown
176	7,206	Derry Township SD	Hershey
177	7,203	Berwick Area SD	Berwick
178	7,197	Hermitage SD	Hermitage
178	7,197	Laurel Highlands SD	Uniontown
180	7,188	Apollo-Ridge SD	Spring Church
181	7,171	Bloomsburg Area SD	Bloomsburg
182	7,169	Northern Lebanon SD	Fredericksburg
183	7,160	Washington SD	Washington
184	7,152	Steel Valley SD	Munhall
185	7,146	Bald Eagle Area SD	Wingate
185	7,146	Northern Tioga SD	Elkland
187	7,143	Conestoga Valley SD	Lancaster
188	7,123	Bellefonte Area SD	Bellefonte
189	7,111	Governor Mifflin SD	Shillington
190	7,088	Nazareth Area SD	Nazareth
191	7,073	Hazleton Area SD	Hazleton
192	7,064	Central Dauphin SD	Harrisburg
193	7,058	Middletown Area SD	Middletown
193	7,058	Philipsburg-Osceola Area SD	Philipsburg
195	7,057	Westmont Hilltop SD	Johnstown
196	7,052	Southmoreland SD	Scottdale
197	7,042	Fleetwood Area SD	Fleetwood
198	7,037	Central Cambria SD	Ebensburg
199	7,035	Lower Dauphin SD	Hummelstown
200	7,010	Freedom Area SD	Freedom
201	7,008	Wyoming Valley West SD	Kingston
202	7,005	Danville Area SD	Danville
203	7,004	East Lycoming SD	Hughesville
204	7,001	South Middleton SD	Boiling Springs
205	6,999	Bethlehem Area SD	Bethlehem
206	6,992	New Castle Area SD	New Castle
207	6,983	Karns City Area SD	Karns City
208	6,976	Oil City Area SD	Oil City
209	6,974	Millcreek Township SD	Erie
210	6,958	Greenville Area SD	Greenville
211	6,947	Philadelphia City SD	Philadelphia

212	6,942	Plum Borough SD	Plum
213	6,934	Northern Lehigh SD	Slatington
214	6,921	Hollidaysburg Area SD	Hollidaysburg
215	6,916	Blackhawk SD	Beaver Falls
216	6,911	Clearfield Area SD	Clearfield
217	6,890	Butler Area SD	Butler
217	6,890	Warren County SD	North Warren
219	6,884	Corry Area SD	Corry
219	6,884	South Park SD	South Park
221	6,881	Tyrone Area SD	Tyrone
221	6,881	Upper Darby SD	Drexel Hill
223	6,878	Manheim Central SD	Manheim
224	6,877	Ringgold SD	New Eagle
225	6,875	Easton Area SD	Easton
226	6,866	North Pocono SD	Moscow
227	6,851	Spring Cove SD	Roaring Spring
228	6,834	Susquehanna Township SD	Harrisburg
229	6,833	Boyertown Area SD	Boyertown
230	6,830	Lake-Lehman SD	Lehman
231	6,825	Burrell SD	Lower Burrell
232	6,814	Riverside Beaver County SD	Ellwood City
233	6,809	Tuscarora SD	Mercersburg
234	6,806	Harbor Creek SD	Harborcreek
235	6,795	West Perry SD	Elliottsburg
236	6,794	Cumberland Valley SD	Mechanicsburg
237	6,791	Connellsville Area SD	Connellsville
238	6,780	Greater Nanticoke Area SD	Nanticoke
239	6,779	Wilmington Area SD	New Wilmington
240	6,778	Cornwall-Lebanon SD	Lebanon
241	6,777	Mount Union Area SD	Mount Union
242	6,776	Southern York County SD	Glen Rock
243	6,760	Beaver Area SD	Beaver
244	6,749	New Brighton Area SD	New Brighton
245	6,743	Selinsgrove Area SD	Selinsgrove
246	6,739	Derry Area SD	Derry
247	6,718	Center Area SD	Monaca
247	6,718	Milton Area SD	Milton
249	6,704	Elk Lake SD	Dimock
250	6,692	Mifflin County SD	Lewistown
251	6,681	Bedford Area SD	Bedford
252	6,678	Mars Area SD	Mars
253	6,676	Delaware Valley SD	Milford
254	6,675	Altoona Area SD	Altoona
255	6,674	Kiski Area SD	Vandergrift
256	6,672	Peters Township SD	Mcmurray
257	6,668	Albert Gallatin Area SD	Uniontown
258	6,667	Susquenita SD	Duncannon
259	6,660	Central Columbia SD	Bloomsburg
260	6,636	Hempfield SD	Landisville
261	6,634	Eastern York SD	Wrightsville
262	6,618	Mount Pleasant Area SD	Mount Pleasant
263	6,614	Donegal SD	Mount Joy
263	6,614	Lampeter-Strasburg SD	Lampeter
263	6,614	Titusville Area SD	Titusville
266	6,612	East Pennsboro Area SD	Enola
267	6,597	South Allegheny SD	Mc Keesport
268	6,594	Oley Valley SD	Oley
269	6,592	Yough SD	Herminie
270	6,590	Avon Grove SD	West Grove
270	6,590	Exeter Township SD	Reading
272	6,587	Palmerton Area SD	Palmerton
273	6,579	Pen Argyl Area SD	Pen Argyl
274	6,559	Eastern Lancaster County SD	New Holland
275	6,557	New Kensington-Arnold SD	New Kensington
276	6,555	Bangor Area SD	Bangor
277	6,554	Grove City Area SD	Grove City
278	6,550	Wilson Area SD	Easton
279	6,548	Dubois Area SD	Du Bois
279	6,548	Somerset Area SD	Somerset
281	6,540	Mid Valley SD	Throop
282	6,537	Whitehall-Coplay SD	Whitehall
283	6,532	Saint Marys Area SD	Saint Marys
284	6,526	Hamburg Area SD	Hamburg
284	6,526	Shikellamy SD	Sunbury
286	6,525	Midd-West SD	Middleburg
287	6,521	West Shore SD	New Cumberland
288	6,520	Pocono Mountain SD	Swiftwater
289	6,512	Ellwood City Area SD	Ellwood City
290	6,507	Moniteau SD	West Sunbury
291	6,505	Daniel Boone Area SD	Douglassville
292	6,503	General Mclane SD	Edinboro
293	6,490	Norwin SD	N Huntingdon
294	6,460	Warwick SD	Lititz
295	6,450	Greensburg Salem SD	Greensburg
296	6,446	Big Spring SD	Newville
297	6,439	Dunmore SD	Dunmore
298	6,433	Chestnut Ridge SD	Fishertown
299	6,431	Girard SD	Girard
300	6,415	Northern York County SD	Dillsburg
300	6,415	Seneca Valley SD	Harmony
302	6,407	Allentown City SD	Allentown
303	6,404	South Butler County SD	Saxonburg
304	6,401	Mercer Area SD	Mercer
305	6,395	Conneaut SD	Linesville
306	6,364	Crestwood SD	Mountain Top
307	6,363	Chambersburg Area SD	Chambersburg
308	6,358	Waynesboro Area SD	Waynesboro
309	6,343	Pine Grove Area SD	Pine Grove
310	6,342	Huntingdon Area SD	Huntingdon
311	6,327	Wattsburg Area SD	Erie
312	6,314	Columbia Borough SD	Columbia
313	6,290	Dover Area SD	Dover
314	6,285	Annville-Cleona SD	Annville
314	6,285	Warrior Run SD	Turbotville
316	6,282	Penn Manor SD	Millersville
316	6,282	South Western SD	Hanover
318	6,275	Forest Hills SD	Sidman
319	6,266	Ephrata Area SD	Ephrata
319	6,266	Reading SD	Reading
321	6,264	Wyoming Area SD	Exeter
322	6,254	Tamaqua Area SD	Tamaqua
323	6,252	Belle Vernon Area SD	Belle Vernon
324	6,237	Northeastern York SD	Manchester
325	6,229	Upper Adams SD	Biglerville
326	6,224	Montoursville Area SD	Montoursville
327	6,218	Shippensburg Area SD	Shippensburg
328	6,189	Slippery Rock Area SD	Slippery Rock
329	6,183	Central York SD	York
330	6,162	Burgettstown Area SD	Burgettstown
330	6,162	Cocalico SD	Denver
332	6,143	Pottsville Area SD	Pottsville
333	6,115	Mohawk Area SD	Bessemer
334	6,101	Pleasant Valley SD	Brodheadsville
335	6,098	Charleroi SD	Charleroi
336	6,094	Lebanon SD	Lebanon
337	6,093	West York Area SD	York
338	6,091	Greencastle-Antrim SD	Greencastle
339	6,053	Blue Mountain SD	Orwigsburg
340	6,051	Oxford Area SD	Oxford
341	6,036	Jeannette City SD	Jeannette
342	6,034	Red Lion Area SD	Red Lion
343	6,030	Greater Latrobe SD	Latrobe
344	6,023	Valley View SD	Archbald
345	6,016	Spring Grove Area SD	Spring Grove
346	5,952	North East SD	North East
347	5,949	Shamokin Area SD	Coal Township
348	5,866	Palmyra Area SD	Palmyra
349	5,856	Elizabethtown Area SD	Elizabethtown
350	5,855	Fort Leboeuf SD	Waterford
351	5,845	Bermudian Springs SD	York Springs
352	5,828	Lakeland SD	Jermyn
353	5,820	North Schuylkill SD	Ashland
354	5,784	Mifflinburg Area SD	Mifflinburg
355	5,769	Solanco SD	Quarryville
356	5,743	Penn-Trafford SD	Harrison City
357	5,652	Juniata County SD	Mifflintown
358	5,612	South Eastern SD	Fawn Grove
359	5,553	Mount Carmel Area SD	Mount Carmel
360	5,531	Littlestown Area SD	Littlestown
361	5,513	Northwestern SD	Albion
362	5,347	Conewago Valley SD	New Oxford
363	n/a	PDE Division of Data Services	Harrisburg
363	n/a	Pennsylvania Virtual CS	Norristown

Number of Diploma Recipients

Rank	Number	District Name	City
1	8,559	Philadelphia City SD	Philadelphia
2	1,899	Pittsburgh SD	Pittsburgh
3	1,082	Central Bucks SD	Doylestown
4	1,003	North Penn SD	Lansdale
5	920	Bethlehem Area SD	Bethlehem
6	912	Council Rock SD	Richboro
7	876	West Chester Area SD	West Chester
8	796	Neshaminy SD	Langhorne
9	737	Pennsbury SD	Fallsington
10	729	Pocono Mountain SD	Swiftwater
11	706	Central Dauphin SD	Harrisburg
12	694	Upper Darby SD	Drexel Hill
13	686	Allentown City SD	Allentown
14	685	North Allegheny SD	Pittsburgh
15	630	Erie City SD	Erie
16	610	Downingtown Area SD	Downingtown
16	610	State College Area SD	State College
18	600	Parkland SD	Allentown
19	570	Reading SD	Reading
20	567	Altoona Area SD	Altoona
21	558	Butler Area SD	Butler
22	556	Abington SD	Abington
22	556	West Shore SD	New Cumberland
24	546	Hempfield SD	Landisville
25	545	Cumberland Valley SD	Mechanicsburg
26	535	Hazleton Area SD	Hazleton
27	526	Coatesville Area SD	Coatesville
28	525	Scranton SD	Scranton
28	525	Wilkes-Barre Area SD	Wilkes Barre
30	504	Millcreek Township SD	Erie
31	502	Chambersburg Area SD	Chambersburg
31	502	Easton Area SD	Easton
33	500	Bensalem Township SD	Bensalem
34	499	Warren County SD	North Warren
35	497	Seneca Valley SD	Harmony
36	491	Hempfield Area SD	Greensburg
37	490	East Penn SD	Emmaus
38	477	Pennridge SD	Perkasie
39	464	Boyertown Area SD	Boyertown
40	461	Lancaster SD	Lancaster
41	456	Centennial SD	Warminster
42	455	Lower Merion SD	Ardmore
43	452	Mount Lebanon SD	Pittsburgh
44	436	East Stroudsburg Area SD	E Stroudsburg
45	432	Souderton Area SD	Souderton
46	426	Bristol Township SD	Levittown
47	421	Ridley SD	Folsom
48	420	Haverford Township SD	Havertown
49	418	Shaler Area SD	Glenshaw
50	411	Penn Hills SD	Pittsburgh
51	402	Bethel Park SD	Bethel Park
52	396	Norristown Area SD	Norristown
53	395	Baldwin-Whitehall SD	Pittsburgh
54	391	Pleasant Valley SD	Brodheadsville
55	388	Armstrong SD	Ford City
56	385	North Hills SD	Pittsburgh
57	383	Cheltenham Township SD	Elkins Park
58	382	Dallastown Area SD	Dallastown
59	376	Mifflin County SD	Lewistown
60	375	Connellsville Area SD	Connellsville
61	373	Norwin SD	N Huntingdon
62	372	Tredyffrin-Easttown SD	Berwyn
62	372	Williamsport Area SD	Williamsport
64	369	Keystone Central SD	Lock Haven
65	362	Wilson SD	West Lawn
66	359	Spring-Ford Area SD	Collegeville
66	359	Woodland Hills SD	Pittsburgh
68	356	Manheim Township SD	Lancaster
69	355	Hatboro-Horsham SD	Horsham
69	355	Penn-Trafford SD	Harrison City
71	350	Colonial SD	Plymouth Meeting
71	350	Penn Manor SD	Millersville
73	345	Upper Dublin SD	Maple Glen
74	343	Crawford Central SD	Meadville
75	340	Gateway SD	Monroeville
75	340	Kiski Area SD	Vandergrift
77	339	Northampton Area SD	Northampton
78	334	Quakertown Community SD	Quakertown
79	326	Hollidaysburg Area SD	Hollidaysburg
80	324	Plum Borough SD	Plum
81	322	Cornwall-Lebanon SD	Lebanon
81	322	Delaware Valley SD	Milford
83	321	Wyoming Valley West SD	Kingston
84	319	Carlisle Area SD	Carlisle
85	318	Fox Chapel Area SD	Pittsburgh
86	316	Governor Mifflin SD	Shillington
87	308	Upper Saint Clair SD	Pittsburgh
88	306	Red Lion Area SD	Red Lion
88	306	William Penn SD	Lansdowne
90	305	Solanco SD	Quarryville
90	305	Warwick SD	Lititz
92	301	Methacton SD	Norristown
93	299	Penncrest SD	Saegertown
94	298	Stroudsburg Area SD	Stroudsburg
95	294	Rose Tree Media SD	Media
96	293	Waynesboro Area SD	Waynesboro
96	293	Wissahickon SD	Ambler
98	292	Mckeesport Area SD	Mc Keesport
99	289	Albert Gallatin Area SD	Uniontown
99	289	Wallingford-Swarthmore SD	Wallingford
101	285	Chichester SD	Boothwyn
102	284	Greater Latrobe SD	Latrobe
103	283	Interboro SD	Prospect Park
104	282	Trinity Area SD	Washington
105	281	Franklin Regional SD	Murrysville
105	281	Springfield SD	Springfield
107	279	Unionville-Chadds Ford SD	Kennett Square
107	279	York City SD	York
109	278	Abington Heights SD	Clarks Summit
110	277	Marple Newtown SD	Newtown Square
111	276	South Western SD	Hanover
111	276	Whitehall-Coplay SD	Whitehall
113	272	Avon Grove SD	West Grove
114	270	Peters Township SD	Mcmurray
114	270	Ringgold SD	New Eagle
116	269	Ephrata Area SD	Ephrata
117	268	Exeter Township SD	Reading
118	267	Chester-Upland SD	Chester
119	266	Upper Perkiomen SD	East Greenville
119	266	Wallenpaupack Area SD	Hawley
121	264	Central York SD	York

121	264	Indiana Area SD	Indiana
123	261	Owen J Roberts SD	Pottstown
123	261	Pine-Richland SD	Gibsonia
123	261	Pottsville Area SD	Pottsville
126	260	North Pocono SD	Moscow
127	258	General Mclane SD	Edinboro
128	256	Gettysburg Area SD	Gettysburg
128	256	Montour SD	Mc Kees Rocks
130	254	Conestoga Valley SD	Lancaster
130	254	Lower Dauphin SD	Hummelstown
130	254	Nazareth Area SD	Nazareth
133	252	Hampton Township SD	Gibsonia
134	250	Greensburg Salem SD	Greensburg
135	247	Derry Township SD	Hershey
136	246	Dubois Area SD	Du Bois
137	245	Pittston Area SD	Pittston
138	244	Canon-Mcmillan SD	Canonsburg
138	244	Elizabethtown Area SD	Elizabethtown
138	244	Laurel Highlands SD	Uniontown
141	241	Dover Area SD	Dover
141	241	Shikellamy SD	Sunbury
141	241	Tunkhannock Area SD	Tunkhannock
144	239	Upper Moreland Township SD	Willow Grove
145	235	Crestwood SD	Mountain Top
146	234	Ambridge Area SD	Ambridge
146	234	Chartiers Valley SD	Pittsburgh
146	234	Eastern Lancaster County SD	New Holland
149	233	Juniata County SD	Mifflintown
150	232	Great Valley SD	Malvern
151	230	Mechanicsburg Area SD	Mechanicsburg
152	229	Radnor Township SD	Wayne
153	228	Hopewell Area SD	Aliquippa
154	223	Conneaut SD	Linesville
155	222	Penn-Delco SD	Aston
155	222	Perkiomen Valley SD	Collegeville
157	221	Blackhawk SD	Beaver Falls
157	221	Manheim Central SD	Manheim
159	220	Bangor Area SD	Bangor
159	220	Moon Area SD	Moon Township
159	220	Pottsgrove SD	Pottstown
159	220	South Butler County SD	Saxonburg
163	219	Harbor Creek SD	Harborcreek
164	218	Bellefonte Area SD	Bellefonte
165	217	Conewago Valley SD	New Oxford
166	216	Uniontown Area SD	Uniontown
167	212	Somerset Area SD	Somerset
167	212	Upper Merion Area SD	King Of Prussia
167	212	West Jefferson Hills SD	Jefferson Hls
170	210	Southern York County SD	Glen Rock
171	209	Big Spring SD	Newville
171	209	Highlands SD	Natrona Heights
173	208	Berwick Area SD	Berwick
173	208	Shippensburg Area SD	Shippensburg
173	208	West Mifflin Area SD	West Mifflin
176	207	Mars Area SD	Mars
176	207	Saint Marys Area SD	Saint Marys
178	206	Blue Mountain SD	Orwigsburg
178	206	Wayne Highlands SD	Honesdale
178	206	West Allegheny SD	Imperial
181	205	Southeast Delco SD	Folcroft
182	203	Cocalico SD	Denver
182	203	Selinsgrove Area SD	Selinsgrove
184	202	Punxsutawney Area SD	Punxsutawney
185	201	Danville Area SD	Danville
185	201	Spring Grove Area SD	Spring Grove
187	199	Harrisburg City SD	Harrisburg
187	199	Muhlenberg SD	Reading
189	198	Garnet Valley SD	Glen Mills
189	198	Keystone Oaks SD	Pittsburgh
189	198	Southern Lehigh SD	Center Valley
192	197	Elizabeth Forward SD	Elizabeth
192	197	Jersey Shore Area SD	Jersey Shore
194	196	Franklin Area SD	Franklin
195	193	Clearfield Area SD	Clearfield
196	192	Lebanon SD	Lebanon
197	191	Milton Area SD	Milton
197	191	Palmyra Area SD	Palmyra
199	190	Belle Vernon Area SD	Belle Vernon
199	190	Susquehanna Township SD	Harrisburg
199	190	Twin Valley SD	Elverson
202	189	Kennett Consolidated SD	Kennett Square
203	187	Grove City Area SD	Grove City
204	186	Bald Eagle Area SD	Wingate
204	186	Mount Pleasant Area SD	Mount Pleasant
206	185	Northern York County SD	Dillsburg
207	184	Phoenixville Area SD	Phoenixville
207	184	South Eastern SD	Fawn Grove
209	183	Lampeter-Strasburg SD	Lampeter
209	183	Valley View SD	Archbald
211	182	Mcguffey SD	Claysville
212	180	Central Cambria SD	Ebensburg
212	180	Hamburg Area SD	Hamburg
212	180	Wyoming Area SD	Exeter
215	179	Derry Area SD	Derry
216	178	Corry Area SD	Corry
217	177	Bradford Area SD	Bradford
217	177	Greater Johnstown SD	Johnstown
219	176	Dallas SD	Dallas
219	176	Eastern York SD	Wrightsville
221	175	Conrad Weiser Area SD	Robesonia
222	174	Fort Leboeuf SD	Waterford
222	174	Midd-West SD	Middleburg
222	174	Mifflinburg Area SD	Mifflinburg
222	174	Saucon Valley SD	Hellertown
222	174	Shamokin Area SD	Coal Township
222	174	Southern Tioga SD	Blossburg
228	173	Middletown Area SD	Middletown
228	173	Penn Cambria SD	Cresson
228	173	West Perry SD	Elliottsburg
231	172	Lehighton Area SD	Lehighton
231	172	Oil City Area SD	Oil City
233	170	Deer Lakes SD	Russellton
233	170	York Suburban SD	York
235	169	Greencastle-Antrim SD	Greencastle
236	168	Montoursville Area SD	Montoursville
236	168	South Park SD	South Park
236	168	West York Area SD	York
239	166	Daniel Boone Area SD	Douglassville
240	164	Burrell SD	Lower Burrell
240	164	Eastern Lebanon County SD	Myerstown
240	164	Hermitage SD	Hermitage
243	163	New Castle Area SD	New Castle
244	162	Athens Area SD	Athens
244	162	Oxford Area SD	Oxford
244	162	Titusville Area SD	Titusville
247	161	Northern Lebanon SD	Fredericksburg
247	161	Palisades SD	Kintnersville
249	160	Northwestern Lehigh SD	New Tripoli
249	160	Steel Valley SD	Munhall
251	159	Marion Center Area SD	Marion Center
251	159	Spring Cove SD	Roaring Spring
253	158	Fleetwood Area SD	Fleetwood
253	158	Northern Tioga SD	Elkland
255	157	Forest Hills SD	Sidman
255	157	North East SD	North East
255	157	Tuscarora SD	Mercersburg
255	157	Yough SD	Herminie
259	156	Huntingdon Area SD	Huntingdon
260	155	Ellwood City Area SD	Ellwood City
261	154	Lewisburg Area SD	Lewisburg
261	154	South Middleton SD	Boiling Springs
263	153	Beaver Area SD	Beaver
263	153	Southmoreland SD	Scottdale
265	152	Donegal SD	Mount Joy
266	151	Slippery Rock Area SD	Slippery Rock
267	150	Western Wayne SD	South Canaan
268	149	East Pennsboro Area SD	Enola
268	149	Susquenita SD	Duncannon
270	148	Philipsburg-Osceola Area SD	Philipsburg
270	148	Warrior Run SD	Turbotville
272	147	Cambria Heights SD	Patton
272	147	Ligonier Valley SD	Ligonier
272	147	North Schuylkill SD	Ashland
272	147	Wattsburg Area SD	Erie
272	147	Wellsboro Area SD	Wellsboro
277	146	Central Columbia SD	Bloomsburg
277	146	Littlestown Area SD	Littlestown
277	146	Quaker Valley SD	Sewickley
280	145	Central Greene SD	Waynesburg
280	145	Hanover Area SD	Wilkes Barre
280	145	Lake-Lehman SD	Lehman
280	145	Northern Lehigh SD	Slatington
284	143	New Kensington-Arnold SD	New Kensington
284	143	Pottstown SD	Pottstown
286	142	Springfield Township SD	Oreland
287	141	East Lycoming SD	Hughesville
287	141	Octorara Area SD	Atglen
287	141	Schuylkill Valley SD	Leesport
287	141	Wilson Area SD	Easton
291	140	Bermudian Springs SD	York Springs
292	139	Blairsville-Saltsburg SD	Blairsville
292	139	Brownsville Area SD	Brownsville
292	139	Greater Nanticoke Area SD	Nanticoke
292	139	Westmont Hilltop SD	Johnstown
296	138	Chestnut Ridge SD	Fishertown
296	138	Pine Grove Area SD	Pine Grove
298	137	Center Area SD	Monaca
298	137	Pen Argyl Area SD	Pen Argyl
300	136	Bedford Area SD	Bedford
300	136	Northeastern York SD	Manchester
300	136	Richland SD	Johnstown
303	135	Brandywine Heights Area SD	Topton
304	133	Kutztown Area SD	Kutztown
304	133	Riverside Beaver County SD	Ellwood City
304	133	Sharon City SD	Sharon
307	132	Tamaqua Area SD	Tamaqua
308	131	Salisbury Township SD	Allentown
309	130	Karns City Area SD	Karns City
310	129	Freedom Area SD	Freedom
310	129	Palmerton Area SD	Palmerton
310	129	Wilmington Area SD	New Wilmington
313	127	Girard SD	Girard
313	127	Oley Valley SD	Oley
313	127	Washington SD	Washington
316	126	Lower Moreland Township SD	Huntingdon Vly
316	126	Towanda Area SD	Towanda
318	125	Northwestern SD	Albion
319	123	New Brighton Area SD	New Brighton
319	123	South Allegheny SD	Mc Keesport
319	123	Wyomissing Area SD	Wyomissing
322	122	Brookville Area SD	Brookville
322	122	Dunmore SD	Dunmore
322	122	Tyrone Area SD	Tyrone
325	121	Montrose Area SD	Montrose
326	120	Carlynton SD	Carnegie
326	120	Charleroi SD	Charleroi
328	119	Annville-Cleona SD	Annville
328	119	Big Beaver Falls Area SD	Beaver Falls
328	119	East Allegheny SD	N Versailles
328	119	Troy Area SD	Troy
328	119	Tulpehocken Area SD	Bernville
333	118	Lakeland SD	Jermyn
333	118	Mid Valley SD	Throop
335	117	Freeport Area SD	Freeport
336	116	Greenville Area SD	Greenville
337	114	Everett Area SD	Everett
337	114	Fairview SD	Fairview
337	114	Upper Adams SD	Biglerville
340	109	Mohawk Area SD	Bessemer
340	109	Mount Carmel Area SD	Mount Carmel
340	109	Reynolds SD	Greenville
343	108	Pequea Valley SD	Kinzers
344	106	Mercer Area SD	Mercer
345	103	Moniteau SD	West Sunbury
345	103	Penns Valley Area SD	Spring Mills
347	100	Bloomsburg Area SD	Bloomsburg
348	99	Northgate SD	Pittsburgh
348	99	Wyalusing Area SD	Wyalusing
350	96	Catasauqua Area SD	Catasauqua
350	96	Jim Thorpe Area SD	Jim Thorpe
352	95	Mount Union Area SD	Mount Union
353	94	South Fayette Township SD	Mc Donald
354	93	Elk Lake SD	Dimock
355	92	Cranberry Area SD	Seneca
355	92	Hanover Public SD	Hanover
355	92	Jeannette City SD	Jeannette
358	89	Apollo-Ridge SD	Spring Church
359	88	Burgettstown Area SD	Burgettstown
360	82	Columbia Borough SD	Columbia
361	74	Sto-Rox SD	Mckees Rocks
361	74	Wilkinsburg Borough SD	Wilkinsburg
363	0	PDE Division of Data Services	Harrisburg
364	n/a	Pennsylvania Virtual CS	Norristown

High School Drop-out Rate

Rank	Percent	District Name	City
1	13.0	Reading SD	Reading
1	13.0	Wilkinsburg Borough SD	Wilkinsburg
3	12.8	Harrisburg City SD	Harrisburg
4	11.1	York City SD	York
5	9.2	Lancaster SD	Lancaster
5	9.2	Philadelphia City SD	Philadelphia
7	9.0	Big Beaver Falls Area SD	Beaver Falls
8	7.8	Pottstown SD	Pottstown
9	7.0	New Kensington-Arnold SD	New Kensington
9	7.0	Shamokin Area SD	Coal Township
11	6.7	Pittsburgh SD	Pittsburgh
12	6.4	Lebanon SD	Lebanon
13	6.3	Sharon City SD	Sharon
14	6.0	Brownsville Area SD	Brownsville
15	5.8	Upper Adams SD	Biglerville
16	5.5	Cranberry Area SD	Seneca
16	5.5	Easton Area SD	Easton
16	5.5	Northern Lebanon SD	Fredericksburg
19	5.4	West Perry SD	Elliottsburg
20	5.3	Burgettstown Area SD	Burgettstown
20	5.3	Northwestern SD	Albion
22	5.2	Altoona Area SD	Altoona
23	5.1	Montoursville Area SD	Montoursville
24	5.0	Connellsville Area SD	Connellsville
24	5.0	Wilson Area SD	Easton
26	4.9	Lehighton Area SD	Lehighton
26	4.9	Littlestown Area SD	Littlestown
26	4.9	Norristown Area SD	Norristown
26	4.9	Northern Tioga SD	Elkland
26	4.9	Sto-Rox SD	Mckees Rocks
31	4.8	Mifflin County SD	Lewistown

Rank	Value	District	City
31	4.8	Titusville Area SD	Titusville
33	4.7	Franklin Area SD	Franklin
34	4.6	Shikellamy SD	Sunbury
34	4.6	Southeast Delco SD	Folcroft
34	4.6	Tamaqua Area SD	Tamaqua
37	4.5	Tyrone Area SD	Tyrone
37	4.5	Upper Darby SD	Drexel Hill
37	4.5	Western Wayne SD	South Canaan
40	4.4	Apollo-Ridge SD	Spring Church
40	4.4	Chambersburg Area SD	Chambersburg
40	4.4	Chestnut Ridge SD	Fishertown
40	4.4	Coatesville Area SD	Coatesville
40	4.4	Scranton SD	Scranton
40	4.4	South Middleton SD	Boiling Springs
46	4.3	Daniel Boone Area SD	Douglassville
46	4.3	East Allegheny SD	N Versailles
46	4.3	Erie City SD	Erie
46	4.3	Everett Area SD	Everett
46	4.3	Warren County SD	North Warren
46	4.3	Woodland Hills SD	Pittsburgh
52	4.2	Columbia Borough SD	Columbia
52	4.2	Washington SD	Washington
54	4.1	Athens Area SD	Athens
54	4.1	Berwick Area SD	Berwick
54	4.1	Bethlehem Area SD	Bethlehem
54	4.1	Pittston Area SD	Pittston
58	4.0	Jersey Shore Area SD	Jersey Shore
58	4.0	Oil City Area SD	Oil City
58	4.0	Williamsport Area SD	Williamsport
61	3.9	Allentown City SD	Allentown
61	3.9	Bradford Area SD	Bradford
61	3.9	Clearfield Area SD	Clearfield
61	3.9	Conneaut SD	Linesville
61	3.9	Greater Johnstown SD	Johnstown
61	3.9	Huntingdon Area SD	Huntingdon
61	3.9	Marion Center Area SD	Marion Center
61	3.9	Mount Union Area SD	Mount Union
61	3.9	Northampton Area SD	Northampton
61	3.9	Susquenita SD	Duncannon
71	3.8	Crawford Central SD	Meadville
71	3.8	Dubois Area SD	Du Bois
71	3.8	East Pennsboro Area SD	Enola
71	3.8	Mount Pleasant Area SD	Mount Pleasant
71	3.8	Octorara Area SD	Atglen
76	3.7	Albert Gallatin Area SD	Uniontown
76	3.7	Millcreek Township SD	Erie
78	3.6	Bangor Area SD	Bangor
78	3.6	Burrell SD	Lower Burrell
78	3.6	Dover Area SD	Dover
78	3.6	Greater Nanticoke Area SD	Nanticoke
78	3.6	Laurel Highlands SD	Uniontown
78	3.6	Midd-West SD	Middleburg
78	3.6	New Brighton Area SD	New Brighton
78	3.6	Pottsville Area SD	Pottsville
78	3.6	Warwick SD	Lititz
78	3.6	Wyoming Valley West SD	Kingston
88	3.5	Avon Grove SD	West Grove
88	3.5	Carlisle Area SD	Carlisle
88	3.5	Slippery Rock Area SD	Slippery Rock
88	3.5	Wyoming Area SD	Exeter
92	3.4	Donegal SD	Mount Joy
92	3.4	Ellwood City Area SD	Ellwood City
92	3.4	Greenville Area SD	Greenville
92	3.4	Keystone Oaks SD	Pittsburgh
92	3.4	North Schuylkill SD	Ashland
97	3.3	Butler Area SD	Butler
97	3.3	Eastern York SD	Wrightsville
97	3.3	Greater Latrobe SD	Latrobe
97	3.3	Hanover Area SD	Wilkes Barre
97	3.3	Northern York County SD	Dillsburg
97	3.3	Pen Argyl Area SD	Pen Argyl
97	3.3	Stroudsburg Area SD	Stroudsburg
97	3.3	Towanda Area SD	Towanda
105	3.2	Bedford Area SD	Bedford
105	3.2	Bloomsburg Area SD	Bloomsburg
105	3.2	Girard SD	Girard
105	3.2	Milton Area SD	Milton
105	3.2	Oxford Area SD	Oxford
105	3.2	Pleasant Valley SD	Brodheadsville
105	3.2	Tulpehocken Area SD	Bernville
112	3.1	Big Spring SD	Newville
112	3.1	Conestoga Valley SD	Lancaster
112	3.1	East Stroudsburg Area SD	E Stroudsburg
112	3.1	Gettysburg Area SD	Gettysburg
112	3.1	Indiana Area SD	Indiana
112	3.1	Mckeesport Area SD	Mc Keesport
112	3.1	Penn Hills SD	Pittsburgh
112	3.1	Warrior Run SD	Turbotville
112	3.1	William Penn SD	Lansdowne
112	3.1	Wyalusing Area SD	Wyalusing
122	3.0	Bellefonte Area SD	Bellefonte
122	3.0	Brandywine Heights Area SD	Topton
122	3.0	Hamburg Area SD	Hamburg
122	3.0	Hanover Public SD	Hanover
122	3.0	Keystone Central SD	Lock Haven
122	3.0	Moniteau SD	West Sunbury
122	3.0	Penn-Delco SD	Aston
122	3.0	Wallenpaupack Area SD	Hawley
130	2.9	Belle Vernon Area SD	Belle Vernon
130	2.9	Blue Mountain SD	Orwigsburg
130	2.9	Corry Area SD	Corry
130	2.9	Eastern Lancaster County SD	New Holland
130	2.9	Fort Leboeuf SD	Waterford
130	2.9	Manheim Central SD	Manheim
130	2.9	Montrose Area SD	Montrose
130	2.9	Northern Lehigh SD	Slatington
130	2.9	Philipsburg-Osceola Area SD	Philipsburg
130	2.9	Riverside Beaver County SD	Ellwood City
130	2.9	Waynesboro Area SD	Waynesboro
130	2.9	Wilkes-Barre Area SD	Wilkes Barre
142	2.8	Bald Eagle Area SD	Wingate
142	2.8	Bensalem Township SD	Bensalem
142	2.8	Bristol Township SD	Levittown
142	2.8	Canon-Mcmillan SD	Canonsburg
142	2.8	Cornwall-Lebanon SD	Lebanon
142	2.8	Elk Lake SD	Dimock
142	2.8	Jeannette City SD	Jeannette
142	2.8	Kiski Area SD	Vandergrift
142	2.8	Northeastern York SD	Manchester
142	2.8	Saint Marys Area SD	Saint Marys
142	2.8	Southern Tioga SD	Blossburg
153	2.7	Delaware Valley SD	Milford
153	2.7	Fleetwood Area SD	Fleetwood
153	2.7	Hempfield SD	Landisville
153	2.7	Highlands SD	Natrona Heights
153	2.7	Karns City Area SD	Karns City
153	2.7	Ligonier Valley SD	Ligonier
153	2.7	Muhlenberg SD	Reading
153	2.7	New Castle Area SD	New Castle
153	2.7	Red Lion Area SD	Red Lion
162	2.6	Blairsville-Saltsburg SD	Blairsville
162	2.6	Central Dauphin SD	Harrisburg
162	2.6	East Lycoming SD	Hughesville
162	2.6	Mifflinburg Area SD	Mifflinburg
162	2.6	Pennridge SD	Perkasie
162	2.6	Seneca Valley SD	Harmony
168	2.5	Armstrong SD	Ford City
168	2.5	Chichester SD	Boothwyn
168	2.5	Derry Area SD	Derry
168	2.5	North Pocono SD	Moscow
168	2.5	Pottsgrove SD	Pottstown
168	2.5	Quakertown Community SD	Quakertown
168	2.5	Solanco SD	Quarryville
168	2.5	Somerset Area SD	Somerset
168	2.5	South Butler County SD	Saxonburg
168	2.5	South Western SD	Hanover
168	2.5	Wattsburg Area SD	Erie
168	2.5	West Shore SD	New Cumberland
168	2.5	Wilmington Area SD	New Wilmington
168	2.5	Wyomissing Area SD	Wyomissing
182	2.4	Brookville Area SD	Brookville
182	2.4	East Penn SD	Emmaus
182	2.4	Elizabeth Forward SD	Elizabeth
182	2.4	Governor Mifflin SD	Shillington
182	2.4	Mid Valley SD	Throop
182	2.4	Middletown Area SD	Middletown
182	2.4	Palmerton Area SD	Palmerton
182	2.4	Palmyra Area SD	Palmyra
182	2.4	Pequea Valley SD	Kinzers
182	2.4	Punxsutawney Area SD	Punxsutawney
182	2.4	Ringgold SD	New Eagle
182	2.4	South Eastern SD	Fawn Grove
182	2.4	Susquehanna Township SD	Harrisburg
182	2.4	Twin Valley SD	Elverson
196	2.3	Central Cambria SD	Ebensburg
196	2.3	Central Greene SD	Waynesburg
196	2.3	Cocalico SD	Denver
196	2.3	Hollidaysburg Area SD	Hollidaysburg
196	2.3	Selinsgrove Area SD	Selinsgrove
196	2.3	Southern York County SD	Glen Rock
196	2.3	Spring Grove Area SD	Spring Grove
196	2.3	Steel Valley SD	Munhall
204	2.2	Blackhawk SD	Beaver Falls
204	2.2	Boyertown Area SD	Boyertown
204	2.2	Elizabethtown Area SD	Elizabethtown
204	2.2	Hazleton Area SD	Hazleton
204	2.2	Juniata County SD	Mifflintown
204	2.2	Manheim Township SD	Lancaster
204	2.2	Northwestern Lehigh SD	New Tripoli
204	2.2	Oley Valley SD	Oley
204	2.2	Shippensburg Area SD	Shippensburg
204	2.2	Tuscarora SD	Mercersburg
214	2.1	Cambria Heights SD	Patton
214	2.1	Cumberland Valley SD	Mechanicsburg
214	2.1	Dallastown Area SD	Dallastown
214	2.1	Exeter Township SD	Reading
214	2.1	Harbor Creek SD	Harborcreek
214	2.1	Hempfield Area SD	Greensburg
214	2.1	Hopewell Area SD	Aliquippa
214	2.1	Kennett Consolidated SD	Kennett Square
214	2.1	Lower Dauphin SD	Hummelstown
214	2.1	Pocono Mountain SD	Swiftwater
214	2.1	Trinity Area SD	Washington
214	2.1	Troy Area SD	Troy
214	2.1	Wellsboro Area SD	Wellsboro
227	2.0	Chartiers Valley SD	Pittsburgh
227	2.0	Chester-Upland SD	Chester
227	2.0	Danville Area SD	Danville
227	2.0	Dunmore SD	Dunmore
227	2.0	Freeport Area SD	Freeport
227	2.0	Greensburg Salem SD	Greensburg
227	2.0	Interboro SD	Prospect Park
227	2.0	Mercer Area SD	Mercer
227	2.0	Phoenixville Area SD	Phoenixville
227	2.0	Ridley SD	Folsom
227	2.0	Spring Cove SD	Roaring Spring
227	2.0	Wilson SD	West Lawn
239	1.9	Bermudian Springs SD	York Springs
239	1.9	Colonial SD	Plymouth Meeting
239	1.9	Conrad Weiser Area SD	Robesonia
239	1.9	General Mclane SD	Edinboro
239	1.9	Greencastle-Antrim SD	Greencastle
239	1.9	Lake-Lehman SD	Lehman
239	1.9	Perkiomen Valley SD	Collegeville
239	1.9	Souderton Area SD	Souderton
239	1.9	Uniontown Area SD	Uniontown
239	1.9	Wayne Highlands SD	Honesdale
239	1.9	Whitehall-Coplay SD	Whitehall
250	1.8	Carlynton SD	Carnegie
250	1.8	Charleroi SD	Charleroi
250	1.8	Eastern Lebanon County SD	Myerstown
250	1.8	Lampeter-Strasburg SD	Lampeter
250	1.8	Mcguffey SD	Claysville
250	1.8	Methacton SD	Norristown
250	1.8	Mount Carmel Area SD	Mount Carmel
250	1.8	Neshaminy SD	Langhorne
250	1.8	Saucon Valley SD	Hellertown
250	1.8	South Allegheny SD	Mc Keesport
250	1.8	Tunkhannock Area SD	Tunkhannock
250	1.8	Upper Perkiomen SD	East Greenville
262	1.7	Central Columbia SD	Bloomsburg
262	1.7	Cheltenham Township SD	Elkins Park
262	1.7	Gateway SD	Monroeville
262	1.7	Montour SD	Mc Kees Rocks
262	1.7	Nazareth Area SD	Nazareth
262	1.7	Penncrest SD	Saegertown
262	1.7	Pine Grove Area SD	Pine Grove
262	1.7	Southmoreland SD	Scottdale
262	1.7	West Allegheny SD	Imperial
262	1.7	West York Area SD	York
262	1.7	Yough SD	Herminie
273	1.6	Catasauqua Area SD	Catasauqua
273	1.6	Crestwood SD	Mountain Top
273	1.6	Lakeland SD	Jermyn
273	1.6	North East SD	North East
273	1.6	North Penn SD	Lansdale
273	1.6	Palisades SD	Kintnersville
273	1.6	Pennsbury SD	Fallsington
273	1.6	South Park SD	South Park
273	1.6	Spring-Ford Area SD	Collegeville
273	1.6	Upper Merion Area SD	King Of Prussia
283	1.5	Baldwin-Whitehall SD	Pittsburgh
283	1.5	Marple Newtown SD	Newtown Square
283	1.5	Mechanicsburg Area SD	Mechanicsburg
283	1.5	Northgate SD	Pittsburgh
283	1.5	Norwin SD	N Huntingdon
283	1.5	Penn Manor SD	Millersville
283	1.5	Pine-Richland SD	Gibsonia
283	1.5	Rose Tree Media SD	Media
283	1.5	West Chester Area SD	West Chester
283	1.5	Wissahickon SD	Ambler
293	1.4	Central Bucks SD	Doylestown
293	1.4	Moon Area SD	Moon Township
293	1.4	North Allegheny SD	Pittsburgh
293	1.4	Reynolds SD	Greenville
293	1.4	Springfield Township SD	Oreland
293	1.4	State College Area SD	State College
299	1.3	Abington SD	Abington
299	1.3	Ambridge Area SD	Ambridge
299	1.3	Deer Lakes SD	Russellton
299	1.3	Haverford Township SD	Havertown
299	1.3	Salisbury Township SD	Allentown
299	1.3	Schuylkill Valley SD	Leesport
299	1.3	West Jefferson Hills SD	Jefferson Hls
306	1.2	Centennial SD	Warminster
306	1.2	Conewago Valley SD	New Oxford
306	1.2	Fairview SD	Fairview

306	1.2	Freedom Area SD	Freedom
306	1.2	Grove City Area SD	Grove City
306	1.2	Hermitage SD	Hermitage
306	1.2	Mars Area SD	Mars
306	1.2	North Hills SD	Pittsburgh
314	1.1	Annville-Cleona SD	Annville
314	1.1	Downingtown Area SD	Downingtown
314	1.1	Mohawk Area SD	Bessemer
314	1.1	Penns Valley Area SD	Spring Mills
314	1.1	Plum Borough SD	Plum
314	1.1	Shaler Area SD	Glenshaw
320	1.0	Central York SD	York
320	1.0	Ephrata Area SD	Ephrata
320	1.0	Franklin Regional SD	Murrysville
320	1.0	Kutztown Area SD	Kutztown
320	1.0	Penn Cambria SD	Cresson
320	1.0	Richland SD	Johnstown
320	1.0	Springfield SD	Springfield
320	1.0	West Mifflin Area SD	West Mifflin
328	0.9	Fox Chapel Area SD	Pittsburgh
328	0.9	Mount Lebanon SD	Pittsburgh
328	0.9	Parkland SD	Allentown
328	0.9	Quaker Valley SD	Sewickley
328	0.9	Southern Lehigh SD	Center Valley
328	0.9	Wallingford-Swarthmore SD	Wallingford
328	0.9	Westmont Hilltop SD	Johnstown
335	0.8	Derry Township SD	Hershey
335	0.8	Garnet Valley SD	Glen Mills
335	0.8	Hampton Township SD	Gibsonia
335	0.8	South Fayette Township SD	Mc Donald
339	0.7	Beaver Area SD	Beaver
339	0.7	Bethel Park SD	Bethel Park
339	0.7	Center Area SD	Monaca
339	0.7	Jim Thorpe Area SD	Jim Thorpe
339	0.7	Upper Moreland Township SD	Willow Grove
339	0.7	York Suburban SD	York
345	0.6	Abington Heights SD	Clarks Summit
345	0.6	Hatboro-Horsham SD	Horsham
345	0.6	Owen J Roberts SD	Pottstown
345	0.6	Penn-Trafford SD	Harrison City
349	0.5	Lewisburg Area SD	Lewisburg
349	0.5	Lower Merion SD	Ardmore
349	0.5	Peters Township SD	Mcmurray
352	0.4	Dallas SD	Dallas
352	0.4	Forest Hills SD	Sidman
352	0.4	Unionville-Chadds Ford SD	Kennett Square
352	0.4	Valley View SD	Archbald
356	0.3	Council Rock SD	Richboro
356	0.3	Great Valley SD	Malvern
356	0.3	Radnor Township SD	Wayne
359	0.2	Lower Moreland Township SD	Huntingdon Vly
359	0.2	Upper Dublin SD	Maple Glen
361	0.1	Tredyffrin-Easttown SD	Berwyn
362	0.0	Upper Saint Clair SD	Pittsburgh
363	n/a	PDE Division of Data Services	Harrisburg
363	n/a	Pennsylvania Virtual CS	Norristown

Rhode Island

Rhode Island Public School Educational Profile

Category	Value	Category	Value
Schools *(2002-2003)*	335	**Diploma Recipients** *(2002-2003)*	9,006
Instructional Level		White, Non-Hispanic	7,132
Primary	216	Black, Non-Hispanic	657
Middle	57	Asian/Pacific Islander	317
High	54	American Indian/Alaskan Native	43
Other Level	8	Hispanic	857
Curriculum		**High School Drop-out Rate** (%) *(2000-2001)*	5.0
Regular	314	White, Non-Hispanic	3.9
Special Education	4	Black, Non-Hispanic	8.5
Vocational	12	Asian/Pacific Islander	5.8
Alternative	5	American Indian/Alaskan Native	8.4
Type		Hispanic	10.2
Magnet	17	**Staff** *(2002-2003)*	n/a
Charter	7	Teachers	n/a
Title I Eligible	149	Average Salary ($)	52,879
School-wide Title I	54	Librarians/Media Specialists	n/a
Students *(2002-2003)*	159,000	Guidance Counselors	n/a
Gender (%)		**Ratios** *(2002-2003)*	
Male	51.5	Student/Teacher Ratio	n/a
Female	48.5	Student/Librarian Ratio	n/a
Race/Ethnicity (%)		Student/Counselor Ratio	n/a
White, Non-Hispanic	72.2	**Current Spending** *($ per student in FY 2001)*	9,703
Black, Non-Hispanic	8.4	Instruction	6,260
Asian/Pacific Islander	3.3	Support Services	3,186
American Indian/Alaskan Native	0.5	**College Entrance Exam Scores** *(2003)*	
Hispanic	15.6	Scholastic Aptitude Test (SAT)	
Classification (%)		Participation Rate (%)	74
Individual Education Program (IEP)	20.4	Mean SAT I Verbal Score	502
Migrant	0.0	Mean SAT I Math Score	504
English Language Learner (ELL)	6.3	American College Testing Program (ACT)	
Eligible for Free Lunch Program	27.2	Participation Rate (%)	6
Eligible for Reduced-Price Lunch Program	6.1	Average Composite Score	21.7

***Note:** For an explanation of data, please refer to the User's Guide in the front of the book; n/a indicates data not available*

Rhode Island NAEP 2003 Test Scores

Reading			Mathematics		
Grade/Category	**Value**	**Rank**	**Grade/Category**	**Value**	**Rank**
4th Grade			**4th Grade**		
Average Proficiency	216.5 (1.3)	34/51	Average Proficiency	230.3 (1.0)	37/51
Proficiency by Gender/Race/Ethnicity			Proficiency by Gender/Race/Ethnicity		
Male	213.3 (1.5)	34/51	Male	231.5 (1.1)	37/51
Female	219.8 (1.5)	34/51	Female	229.1 (1.3)	39/51
White, Non-Hispanic	224.3 (1.3)	32/51	White, Non-Hispanic	238.8 (0.9)	37/51
Black, Non-Hispanic	196.1 (3.3)	27/42	Black, Non-Hispanic	210.2 (2.1)	36/42
Asian, Non-Hispanic	195.9 (2.7)	34/41	Asian, Non-Hispanic	207.3 (1.8)	42/43
American Indian, Non-Hispanic	220.6 (3.5)	17/25	American Indian, Non-Hispanic	224.7 (3.6)	24/26
Hispanic	n/a	n/a	Hispanic	n/a	n/a
Proficiency by Class Size			Proficiency by Class Size		
Less than 16 Students	*189.3 (7.7)*	36/45	Less than 16 Students	*219.9 (6.2)*	32/47
16 to 18 Students	220.1 (3.4)	17/48	16 to 18 Students	239.0 (2.9)	10/48
19 to 20 Students	221.6 (3.5)	17/50	19 to 20 Students	233.7 (2.9)	28/50
21 to 25 Students	221.2 (2.0)	24/51	21 to 25 Students	233.1 (1.7)	36/51
Greater than 25 Students	205.4 (2.7)	47/49	Greater than 25 Students	217.3 (3.1)	48/49
Percent Attaining Achievement Levels			Percent Attaining Achievement Levels		
Below Basic	37.8 (1.6)	19/51	Below Basic	28.5 (1.4)	12/51
Basic or Above	62.2 (1.6)	33/51	Basic or Above	71.5 (1.4)	40/51
Proficient or Above	29.2 (1.4)	34/51	Proficient or Above	28.1 (1.4)	36/51
Advanced or Above	6.7 (0.7)	27/51	Advanced or Above	2.9 (0.5)	31/51
8th Grade			**8th Grade**		
Average Proficiency	260.9 (0.7)	34/51	Average Proficiency	272.0 (0.7)	36/51
Proficiency by Gender/Race/Ethnicity			Proficiency by Gender/Race/Ethnicity		
Male	255.6 (1.3)	32/51	Male	272.6 (1.1)	37/51
Female	266.3 (0.9)	34/51	Female	271.4 (1.0)	37/51
White, Non-Hispanic	267.4 (0.8)	38/50	White, Non-Hispanic	279.8 (0.8)	41/50
Black, Non-Hispanic	241.3 (2.8)	30/41	Black, Non-Hispanic	244.0 (2.8)	36/41
Asian, Non-Hispanic	237.9 (1.9)	35/37	Asian, Non-Hispanic	244.8 (2.0)	37/37
American Indian, Non-Hispanic	251.6 (4.1)	22/23	American Indian, Non-Hispanic	265.1 (4.7)	22/23
Hispanic	n/a	n/a	Hispanic	n/a	n/a
Proficiency by Parents Highest Level of Ed.			Proficiency by Parents Highest Level of Ed.		
Did Not Finish High School	240.0 (3.8)	41/50	Did Not Finish High School	249.2 (3.1)	45/50
Graduated High School	253.1 (2.2)	31/50	Graduated High School	264.0 (1.8)	38/50
Some Education After High School	265.0 (1.5)	33/50	Some Education After High School	271.5 (2.2)	45/50
Graduated College	271.2 (1.1)	30/50	Graduated College	283.8 (1.0)	34/50
Percent Attaining Achievement Levels			Percent Attaining Achievement Levels		
Below Basic	28.9 (1.0)	18/51	Below Basic	37.4 (1.0)	15/51
Basic or Above	71.1 (1.0)	34/51	Basic or Above	62.6 (1.0)	37/51
Proficient or Above	29.9 (0.9)	32/51	Proficient or Above	23.8 (0.9)	35/51
Advanced or Above	2.7 (0.4)	21/51	Advanced or Above	3.1 (0.4)	39/51

***Note:** For an explanation of data, please refer to the User's Guide in the front of the book; values in italics indicate that the nature of the sample does not allow accurate determination of the variability of the statistic; n/a indicates data not available*

Bristol County

Barrington SD

283 County Rd • Barrington, RI 02806
Mailing Address: PO Box 95 • Barrington, RI 02806
(401) 245-5000 • http://www.barringtonschools.org/
Grade Span: PK-12; **Agency Type:** 1
Schools: 6
3 Primary; 2 Middle; 1 High; 0 Other Level
6 Regular; 0 Special Education; 0 Vocational; 0 Alternative
0 Magnet; 0 Charter; 1 Title I Eligible; 0 School-wide Title I
Students: 3,356 (53.1% male; 46.9% female)
Individual Education Program: 591 (17.6%);
English Language Learner: 10 (0.3%); Migrant: n/a
Eligible for Free Lunch Program: 62 (1.8%)
Eligible for Reduced-Price Lunch Program: 26 (0.8%)
Teachers: n/a
Librarians/Media Specialists: n/a
Guidance Counselors: n/a
Current Spending: ($ per student per year):
Total: $8,313; Instruction: $5,565; Support Services: $2,577
Enrollment, Drop-out Rates and Diploma Recipients by Race/Ethnicity

Category	Total	White	Black	Asian	AIAN	Hisp.
Enrollment (%)	100.0	96.3	0.6	2.4	0.2	0.5
Drop-out Rate (%)	2.2	2.2	0.0	0.0	n/a	20.0
H.S. Diplomas (#)	206	200	1	5	0	0

Bristol Warren RD

151 State St • Bristol, RI 02809
(401) 253-4000 • http://bw.k12.ri.us/
Grade Span: PK-12; **Agency Type:** 1
Schools: 9
5 Primary; 3 Middle; 1 High; 0 Other Level
9 Regular; 0 Special Education; 0 Vocational; 0 Alternative
1 Magnet; 0 Charter; 6 Title I Eligible; 0 School-wide Title I
Students: 3,824 (51.4% male; 48.6% female)
Individual Education Program: 857 (22.4%);
English Language Learner: 136 (3.6%); Migrant: n/a
Eligible for Free Lunch Program: 592 (15.5%)
Eligible for Reduced-Price Lunch Program: 263 (6.9%)
Teachers: n/a
Librarians/Media Specialists: n/a
Guidance Counselors: n/a
Current Spending: ($ per student per year):
Total: $10,021; Instruction: $6,847; Support Services: $2,928
Enrollment, Drop-out Rates and Diploma Recipients by Race/Ethnicity

Category	Total	White	Black	Asian	AIAN	Hisp.
Enrollment (%)	100.0	95.9	2.2	0.5	0.1	1.3
Drop-out Rate (%)	8.1	8.1	12.5	0.0	n/a	0.0
H.S. Diplomas (#)	205	201	1	3	0	0

Kent County

Coventry SD

222 Macarthur Blvd • Coventry, RI 02816
(401) 822-9400 • http://www.coventryschools.net/
Grade Span: PK-12; **Agency Type:** 1
Schools: 8
6 Primary; 1 Middle; 1 High; 0 Other Level
8 Regular; 0 Special Education; 0 Vocational; 0 Alternative
0 Magnet; 0 Charter; 3 Title I Eligible; 0 School-wide Title I
Students: 5,850 (51.5% male; 48.5% female)
Individual Education Program: 1,143 (19.5%);
English Language Learner: 9 (0.2%); Migrant: n/a
Eligible for Free Lunch Program: 459 (7.8%)
Eligible for Reduced-Price Lunch Program: 249 (4.3%)
Teachers: n/a
Librarians/Media Specialists: n/a
Guidance Counselors: n/a
Current Spending: ($ per student per year):
Total: $8,653; Instruction: $5,976; Support Services: $2,441
Enrollment, Drop-out Rates and Diploma Recipients by Race/Ethnicity

Category	Total	White	Black	Asian	AIAN	Hisp.
Enrollment (%)	100.0	96.4	1.5	0.9	0.1	1.1
Drop-out Rate (%)	1.8	1.9	0.0	0.0	n/a	0.0
H.S. Diplomas (#)	380	369	3	4	0	4

East Greenwich SD

111 Peirce St • East Greenwich, RI 02818
(401) 885-3300 • http://www.ri.net/schools/East_Greenwich/
Grade Span: PK-12; **Agency Type:** 1
Schools: 6
2 Primary; 3 Middle; 1 High; 0 Other Level
6 Regular; 0 Special Education; 0 Vocational; 0 Alternative
0 Magnet; 0 Charter; 1 Title I Eligible; 0 School-wide Title I
Students: 2,444 (49.6% male; 50.4% female)
Individual Education Program: 428 (17.5%);
English Language Learner: 33 (1.4%); Migrant: n/a
Eligible for Free Lunch Program: 116 (4.7%)
Eligible for Reduced-Price Lunch Program: 19 (0.8%)
Teachers: n/a
Librarians/Media Specialists: n/a
Guidance Counselors: n/a
Current Spending: ($ per student per year):
Total: $8,791; Instruction: $5,542; Support Services: $3,108
Enrollment, Drop-out Rates and Diploma Recipients by Race/Ethnicity

Category	Total	White	Black	Asian	AIAN	Hisp.
Enrollment (%)	100.0	95.2	1.0	2.7	0.2	1.0
Drop-out Rate (%)	2.6	2.8	0.0	0.0	0.0	0.0
H.S. Diplomas (#)	146	136	1	7	0	2

Exeter-W Greenwich RD

859 Nooseneck Hill Rd • West Greenwich, RI 02817
(401) 397-5125 • http://www.ewg.k12.ri.us/
Grade Span: PK-12; **Agency Type:** 1
Schools: 5
3 Primary; 1 Middle; 1 High; 0 Other Level
5 Regular; 0 Special Education; 0 Vocational; 0 Alternative
0 Magnet; 0 Charter; 2 Title I Eligible; 0 School-wide Title I
Students: 2,183 (49.8% male; 50.2% female)
Individual Education Program: 399 (18.3%);
English Language Learner: 7 (0.3%); Migrant: n/a
Eligible for Free Lunch Program: 165 (7.6%)
Eligible for Reduced-Price Lunch Program: 83 (3.8%)
Teachers: n/a
Librarians/Media Specialists: n/a
Guidance Counselors: n/a
Current Spending: ($ per student per year):
Total: $8,678; Instruction: $5,530; Support Services: $2,956
Enrollment, Drop-out Rates and Diploma Recipients by Race/Ethnicity

Category	Total	White	Black	Asian	AIAN	Hisp.
Enrollment (%)	100.0	96.3	0.7	0.7	0.7	1.5
Drop-out Rate (%)	0.7	0.7	n/a	0.0	0.0	0.0
H.S. Diplomas (#)	128	124	0	4	0	0

Warwick SD

34 Warwick Lake Ave • Warwick, RI 02889
(401) 734-3100 • http://www.warwickschools.org/
Grade Span: PK-12; **Agency Type:** 1
Schools: 27
20 Primary; 3 Middle; 4 High; 0 Other Level
26 Regular; 0 Special Education; 1 Vocational; 0 Alternative
0 Magnet; 0 Charter; 9 Title I Eligible; 0 School-wide Title I
Students: 12,085 (51.7% male; 48.3% female)
Individual Education Program: 2,647 (21.9%);
English Language Learner: 70 (0.6%); Migrant: n/a
Eligible for Free Lunch Program: 1,556 (12.9%)
Eligible for Reduced-Price Lunch Program: 745 (6.2%)
Teachers: n/a
Librarians/Media Specialists: n/a
Guidance Counselors: n/a
Current Spending: ($ per student per year):
Total: $10,084; Instruction: $6,633; Support Services: $3,237
Enrollment, Drop-out Rates and Diploma Recipients by Race/Ethnicity

Category	Total	White	Black	Asian	AIAN	Hisp.
Enrollment (%)	100.0	94.3	1.7	1.8	0.3	1.8
Drop-out Rate (%)	2.3	2.2	2.4	1.8	0.0	6.8
H.S. Diplomas (#)	782	752	5	8	4	13

West Warwick SD

10 Harris Ave • West Warwick, RI 02893
(401) 821-1180
Grade Span: PK-12; **Agency Type:** 1
Schools: 7
5 Primary; 1 Middle; 1 High; 0 Other Level
7 Regular; 0 Special Education; 0 Vocational; 0 Alternative
0 Magnet; 0 Charter; 2 Title I Eligible; 1 School-wide Title I
Students: 3,822 (51.2% male; 48.8% female)
Individual Education Program: 865 (22.6%);
English Language Learner: 91 (2.4%); Migrant: n/a
Eligible for Free Lunch Program: 950 (24.9%)
Eligible for Reduced-Price Lunch Program: 318 (8.3%)
Teachers: n/a
Librarians/Media Specialists: n/a
Guidance Counselors: n/a
Current Spending: ($ per student per year):
Total: $9,934; Instruction: $6,499; Support Services: $3,204

Enrollment, Drop-out Rates and Diploma Recipients by Race/Ethnicity

Category	Total	White	Black	Asian	AIAN	Hisp.
Enrollment (%)	100.0	88.1	3.2	1.7	0.9	6.0
Drop-out Rate (%)	7.9	8.1	1.9	0.0	20.0	7.3
H.S. Diplomas (#)	210	190	5	8	2	5

Newport County

Middletown SD

26 Oliphant Ln • Middletown, RI 02842
(401) 849-2122 • http://www.ri.net/middletown/
Grade Span: PK-12; **Agency Type:** 1
Schools: 6
4 Primary; 1 Middle; 1 High; 0 Other Level
6 Regular; 0 Special Education; 0 Vocational; 0 Alternative
0 Magnet; 0 Charter; 1 Title I Eligible; 0 School-wide Title I
Students: 2,838 (52.3% male; 47.7% female)
Individual Education Program: 580 (20.4%);
English Language Learner: 51 (1.8%); Migrant: n/a
Eligible for Free Lunch Program: 309 (10.9%)
Eligible for Reduced-Price Lunch Program: 170 (6.0%)
Teachers: n/a
Librarians/Media Specialists: n/a
Guidance Counselors: n/a
Current Spending: ($ per student per year):
Total: $9,580; Instruction: $6,251; Support Services: $3,084
Enrollment, Drop-out Rates and Diploma Recipients by Race/Ethnicity

Category	Total	White	Black	Asian	AIAN	Hisp.
Enrollment (%)	100.0	86.0	7.4	3.1	0.4	3.1
Drop-out Rate (%)	2.1	1.7	2.4	6.3	14.3	4.2
H.S. Diplomas (#)	169	150	6	7	0	6

Newport SD

437 Broadway • Newport, RI 02840
(401) 847-2100 • http://www.newportrischools.org/
Grade Span: PK-12; **Agency Type:** 1
Schools: 9
6 Primary; 1 Middle; 2 High; 0 Other Level
8 Regular; 0 Special Education; 1 Vocational; 0 Alternative
0 Magnet; 0 Charter; 6 Title I Eligible; 1 School-wide Title I
Students: 2,915 (50.0% male; 50.0% female)
Individual Education Program: 758 (26.0%);
English Language Learner: 119 (4.1%); Migrant: n/a
Eligible for Free Lunch Program: 1,190 (40.8%)
Eligible for Reduced-Price Lunch Program: 234 (8.0%)
Teachers: n/a
Librarians/Media Specialists: n/a
Guidance Counselors: n/a
Current Spending: ($ per student per year):
Total: $10,878; Instruction: $6,804; Support Services: $3,783
Enrollment, Drop-out Rates and Diploma Recipients by Race/Ethnicity

Category	Total	White	Black	Asian	AIAN	Hisp.
Enrollment (%)	100.0	59.8	23.0	1.7	2.5	13.0
Drop-out Rate (%)	6.3	5.7	11.9	0.0	0.0	5.7
H.S. Diplomas (#)	168	133	26	3	4	2

Portsmouth SD

29 Middle Rd • Portsmouth, RI 02871
(401) 683-1039 • http://portsmouthrischools.tripod.com/
Grade Span: PK-12; **Agency Type:** 1
Schools: 6
4 Primary; 1 Middle; 1 High; 0 Other Level
6 Regular; 0 Special Education; 0 Vocational; 0 Alternative
0 Magnet; 0 Charter; 2 Title I Eligible; 0 School-wide Title I
Students: 2,995 (52.7% male; 47.3% female)
Individual Education Program: 517 (17.3%);
English Language Learner: 7 (0.2%); Migrant: n/a
Eligible for Free Lunch Program: 123 (4.1%)
Eligible for Reduced-Price Lunch Program: 88 (2.9%)
Teachers: n/a
Librarians/Media Specialists: n/a
Guidance Counselors: n/a
Current Spending: ($ per student per year):
Total: $8,756; Instruction: $5,400; Support Services: $3,158
Enrollment, Drop-out Rates and Diploma Recipients by Race/Ethnicity

Category	Total	White	Black	Asian	AIAN	Hisp.
Enrollment (%)	100.0	95.9	1.7	1.9	0.0	0.5
Drop-out Rate (%)	1.3	1.3	9.1	0.0	0.0	0.0
H.S. Diplomas (#)	184	172	3	8	0	1

Tiverton SD

100 N Brayton Rd • Tiverton, RI 02878
(401) 624-8475 • http://www.tivschools.com/
Grade Span: PK-12; **Agency Type:** 1
Schools: 6
4 Primary; 1 Middle; 1 High; 0 Other Level
6 Regular; 0 Special Education; 0 Vocational; 0 Alternative
0 Magnet; 0 Charter; 2 Title I Eligible; 0 School-wide Title I
Students: 2,231 (51.4% male; 48.6% female)
Individual Education Program: 478 (21.4%);
English Language Learner: n/a; Migrant: n/a
Eligible for Free Lunch Program: 219 (9.8%)
Eligible for Reduced-Price Lunch Program: 107 (4.8%)
Teachers: n/a
Librarians/Media Specialists: n/a
Guidance Counselors: n/a
Current Spending: ($ per student per year):
Total: $8,056; Instruction: $5,303; Support Services: $2,491
Enrollment, Drop-out Rates and Diploma Recipients by Race/Ethnicity

Category	Total	White	Black	Asian	AIAN	Hisp.
Enrollment (%)	100.0	98.4	0.7	0.7	0.0	0.1
Drop-out Rate (%)	2.9	2.9	0.0	0.0	n/a	0.0
H.S. Diplomas (#)	136	134	1	0	0	1

Providence County

Burrillville SD

265 Sayles Ave • Pascoag, RI 02859
Mailing Address: 264 Sayles Ave • Pascoag, RI 02859
(401) 568-1301
Grade Span: PK-12; **Agency Type:** 1
Schools: 5
3 Primary; 1 Middle; 1 High; 0 Other Level
5 Regular; 0 Special Education; 0 Vocational; 0 Alternative
0 Magnet; 0 Charter; 3 Title I Eligible; 0 School-wide Title I
Students: 2,682 (51.2% male; 48.8% female)
Individual Education Program: 533 (19.9%);
English Language Learner: 3 (0.1%); Migrant: n/a
Eligible for Free Lunch Program: 311 (11.6%)
Eligible for Reduced-Price Lunch Program: 196 (7.3%)
Teachers: n/a
Librarians/Media Specialists: n/a
Guidance Counselors: n/a
Current Spending: ($ per student per year):
Total: $8,415; Instruction: $5,265; Support Services: $2,886
Enrollment, Drop-out Rates and Diploma Recipients by Race/Ethnicity

Category	Total	White	Black	Asian	AIAN	Hisp.
Enrollment (%)	100.0	98.0	0.8	0.4	0.1	0.6
Drop-out Rate (%)	6.1	6.1	0.0	n/a	n/a	0.0
H.S. Diplomas (#)	187	186	0	0	0	1

Central Falls SD

21 Hedley Ave • Central Falls, RI 02863
(401) 727-7700
Grade Span: PK-12; **Agency Type:** 1
Schools: 8
6 Primary; 1 Middle; 1 High; 0 Other Level
8 Regular; 0 Special Education; 0 Vocational; 0 Alternative
0 Magnet; 0 Charter; 7 Title I Eligible; 6 School-wide Title I
Students: 3,651 (51.8% male; 48.2% female)
Individual Education Program: 931 (25.5%);
English Language Learner: 1,039 (28.5%); Migrant: n/a
Eligible for Free Lunch Program: 2,435 (66.7%)
Eligible for Reduced-Price Lunch Program: 336 (9.2%)
Teachers: n/a
Librarians/Media Specialists: n/a
Guidance Counselors: n/a
Current Spending: ($ per student per year):
Total: $9,929; Instruction: $6,394; Support Services: $3,199
Enrollment, Drop-out Rates and Diploma Recipients by Race/Ethnicity

Category	Total	White	Black	Asian	AIAN	Hisp.
Enrollment (%)	100.0	22.5	10.8	0.4	0.3	66.1
Drop-out Rate (%)	9.3	5.7	25.7	0.0	0.0	8.8
H.S. Diplomas (#)	169	44	17	0	0	108

Cranston SD

845 Park Ave • Cranston, RI 02910
(401) 785-8170 • http://www.cpsed.net/
Grade Span: PK-12; **Agency Type:** 1
Schools: 25
18 Primary; 3 Middle; 3 High; 1 Other Level
24 Regular; 0 Special Education; 1 Vocational; 0 Alternative
0 Magnet; 1 Charter; 9 Title I Eligible; 2 School-wide Title I
Students: 11,269 (51.7% male; 48.3% female)
Individual Education Program: 2,274 (20.2%);
English Language Learner: 430 (3.8%); Migrant: n/a
Eligible for Free Lunch Program: 1,838 (16.3%)
Eligible for Reduced-Price Lunch Program: 518 (4.6%)
Teachers: n/a
Librarians/Media Specialists: n/a
Guidance Counselors: n/a

Current Spending: ($ per student per year):
Total: $8,646; Instruction: $5,572; Support Services: $2,882

Enrollment, Drop-out Rates and Diploma Recipients by Race/Ethnicity

Category	Total	White	Black	Asian	AIAN	Hisp.
Enrollment (%)	100.0	83.4	3.8	5.5	0.2	7.2
Drop-out Rate (%)	5.0	4.5	9.2	6.3	n/a	10.2
H.S. Diplomas (#)	707	591	28	48	1	39

Cumberland SD

2602 Mendon Rd • Cumberland, RI 02864
(401) 658-1600
Grade Span: PK-12; **Agency Type:** 1
Schools: 10
7 Primary; 2 Middle; 1 High; 0 Other Level
10 Regular; 0 Special Education; 0 Vocational; 0 Alternative
0 Magnet; 0 Charter; 2 Title I Eligible; 0 School-wide Title I
Students: 5,411 (51.5% male; 48.5% female)
Individual Education Program: 1,204 (22.3%);
English Language Learner: 121 (2.2%); Migrant: n/a
Eligible for Free Lunch Program: 445 (8.2%)
Eligible for Reduced-Price Lunch Program: 205 (3.8%)
Teachers: n/a
Librarians/Media Specialists: n/a
Guidance Counselors: n/a
Current Spending: ($ per student per year):
Total: $7,455; Instruction: $5,194; Support Services: $2,084

Enrollment, Drop-out Rates and Diploma Recipients by Race/Ethnicity

Category	Total	White	Black	Asian	AIAN	Hisp.
Enrollment (%)	100.0	93.3	1.7	1.3	0.2	3.6
Drop-out Rate (%)	1.6	1.5	0.0	0.0	0.0	4.4
H.S. Diplomas (#)	304	288	1	0	1	14

East Providence SD

80 Burnside Ave • East Providence, RI 02915
(401) 433-6222 • http://ep.k12.ri.us/
Grade Span: PK-12; **Agency Type:** 1
Schools: 15
10 Primary; 2 Middle; 3 High; 0 Other Level
13 Regular; 0 Special Education; 1 Vocational; 1 Alternative
0 Magnet; 0 Charter; 6 Title I Eligible; 1 School-wide Title I
Students: 6,442 (52.2% male; 47.8% female)
Individual Education Program: 1,379 (21.4%);
English Language Learner: 297 (4.6%); Migrant: n/a
Eligible for Free Lunch Program: 1,509 (23.4%)
Eligible for Reduced-Price Lunch Program: 621 (9.6%)
Teachers: n/a
Librarians/Media Specialists: n/a
Guidance Counselors: n/a
Current Spending: ($ per student per year):
Total: $9,393; Instruction: $6,265; Support Services: $2,899

Enrollment, Drop-out Rates and Diploma Recipients by Race/Ethnicity

Category	Total	White	Black	Asian	AIAN	Hisp.
Enrollment (%)	100.0	81.5	13.0	1.4	0.8	3.2
Drop-out Rate (%)	5.8	6.2	3.0	0.0	0.0	11.1
H.S. Diplomas (#)	419	343	64	6	0	6

Foster-Glocester RD

1145 Putnam Pike • Chepachet, RI 02814
Mailing Address: PO Box D • Chepachet, RI 02814
(401) 568-4175
Grade Span: 06-12; **Agency Type:** 1
Schools: 2
0 Primary; 1 Middle; 1 High; 0 Other Level
2 Regular; 0 Special Education; 0 Vocational; 0 Alternative
0 Magnet; 0 Charter; 1 Title I Eligible; 0 School-wide Title I
Students: 1,693 (51.4% male; 48.6% female)
Individual Education Program: 253 (14.9%);
English Language Learner: n/a; Migrant: n/a
Eligible for Free Lunch Program: 104 (6.1%)
Eligible for Reduced-Price Lunch Program: 34 (2.0%)
Teachers: n/a
Librarians/Media Specialists: n/a
Guidance Counselors: n/a
Current Spending: ($ per student per year):
Total: $8,073; Instruction: $5,490; Support Services: $2,378

Enrollment, Drop-out Rates and Diploma Recipients by Race/Ethnicity

Category	Total	White	Black	Asian	AIAN	Hisp.
Enrollment (%)	100.0	98.8	0.9	0.1	0.1	0.1
Drop-out Rate (%)	2.1	2.2	0.0	0.0	0.0	0.0
H.S. Diplomas (#)	186	182	2	1	0	1

Johnston SD

10 Memorial Ave • Johnston, RI 02919
(401) 233-1900 • http://www.ri.net/schools/Johnston/johnston/
Grade Span: PK-12; **Agency Type:** 1
Schools: 9
7 Primary; 1 Middle; 1 High; 0 Other Level
9 Regular; 0 Special Education; 0 Vocational; 0 Alternative
0 Magnet; 0 Charter; 4 Title I Eligible; 0 School-wide Title I
Students: 3,311 (52.0% male; 48.0% female)
Individual Education Program: 839 (25.3%);
English Language Learner: n/a; Migrant: n/a
Eligible for Free Lunch Program: 501 (15.1%)
Eligible for Reduced-Price Lunch Program: 136 (4.1%)
Teachers: n/a
Librarians/Media Specialists: n/a
Guidance Counselors: n/a
Current Spending: ($ per student per year):
Total: $8,800; Instruction: $5,766; Support Services: $2,849

Enrollment, Drop-out Rates and Diploma Recipients by Race/Ethnicity

Category	Total	White	Black	Asian	AIAN	Hisp.
Enrollment (%)	100.0	94.1	1.8	1.3	0.3	2.5
Drop-out Rate (%)	1.4	1.6	0.0	0.0	n/a	0.0
H.S. Diplomas (#)	142	142	0	0	0	0

Lincoln SD

1624 Lonsdale Ave • Lincoln, RI 02865
(401) 726-2150 • http://158.123.229.10/
Grade Span: PK-12; **Agency Type:** 1
Schools: 7
5 Primary; 1 Middle; 1 High; 0 Other Level
7 Regular; 0 Special Education; 0 Vocational; 0 Alternative
0 Magnet; 0 Charter; 3 Title I Eligible; 0 School-wide Title I
Students: 3,706 (52.0% male; 48.0% female)
Individual Education Program: 755 (20.4%);
English Language Learner: 35 (0.9%); Migrant: n/a
Eligible for Free Lunch Program: 239 (6.4%)
Eligible for Reduced-Price Lunch Program: 101 (2.7%)
Teachers: n/a
Librarians/Media Specialists: n/a
Guidance Counselors: n/a
Current Spending: ($ per student per year):
Total: $8,421; Instruction: $5,577; Support Services: $2,691

Enrollment, Drop-out Rates and Diploma Recipients by Race/Ethnicity

Category	Total	White	Black	Asian	AIAN	Hisp.
Enrollment (%)	100.0	93.3	1.5	2.7	0.2	2.4
Drop-out Rate (%)	2.4	2.3	10.0	0.0	0.0	5.0
H.S. Diplomas (#)	213	200	1	5	0	7

North Providence SD

9 George St • North Providence, RI 02911
(401) 233-1100
Grade Span: PK-12; **Agency Type:** 1
Schools: 9
6 Primary; 2 Middle; 1 High; 0 Other Level
9 Regular; 0 Special Education; 0 Vocational; 0 Alternative
0 Magnet; 0 Charter; 3 Title I Eligible; 0 School-wide Title I
Students: 3,445 (51.0% male; 49.0% female)
Individual Education Program: 700 (20.3%);
English Language Learner: n/a; Migrant: n/a
Eligible for Free Lunch Program: 491 (14.3%)
Eligible for Reduced-Price Lunch Program: 142 (4.1%)
Teachers: n/a
Librarians/Media Specialists: n/a
Guidance Counselors: n/a
Current Spending: ($ per student per year):
Total: $9,552; Instruction: $6,507; Support Services: $2,787

Enrollment, Drop-out Rates and Diploma Recipients by Race/Ethnicity

Category	Total	White	Black	Asian	AIAN	Hisp.
Enrollment (%)	100.0	84.2	4.8	2.0	0.1	8.8
Drop-out Rate (%)	2.6	2.3	3.1	0.0	0.0	6.9
H.S. Diplomas (#)	213	183	8	6	0	16

North Smithfield SD

450 Greenville Rd • North Smithfield, RI 02896
(401) 769-5492 • http://www.ri.net/schools/North_Smithfield/
Grade Span: PK-12; **Agency Type:** 1
Schools: 3
1 Primary; 1 Middle; 1 High; 0 Other Level
3 Regular; 0 Special Education; 0 Vocational; 0 Alternative
0 Magnet; 0 Charter; 0 Title I Eligible; 0 School-wide Title I
Students: 1,875 (49.9% male; 50.1% female)
Individual Education Program: 342 (18.2%);
English Language Learner: n/a; Migrant: n/a
Eligible for Free Lunch Program: 76 (4.1%)
Eligible for Reduced-Price Lunch Program: 69 (3.7%)

Teachers: n/a
Librarians/Media Specialists: n/a
Guidance Counselors: n/a
Current Spending: ($ per student per year):
Total: $7,986; Instruction: $5,183; Support Services: $2,603
Enrollment, Drop-out Rates and Diploma Recipients by Race/Ethnicity

Category	Total	White	Black	Asian	AIAN	Hisp.
Enrollment (%)	100.0	97.4	0.6	0.7	0.0	1.2
Drop-out Rate (%)	1.2	1.2	0.0	0.0	0.0	0.0
H.S. Diplomas (#)	130	129	0	1	0	0

Pawtucket SD

Park Place • Pawtucket, RI 02860
Mailing Address: PO Box 388 • Pawtucket, RI 02860
(401) 729-6315
Grade Span: PK-12; **Agency Type:** 1
Schools: 16
10 Primary; 4 Middle; 2 High; 0 Other Level
16 Regular; 0 Special Education; 0 Vocational; 0 Alternative
0 Magnet; 0 Charter; 10 Title I Eligible; 3 School-wide Title I
Students: 9,973 (51.8% male; 48.2% female)
Individual Education Program: 2,221 (22.3%);
English Language Learner: 1,052 (10.5%); Migrant: n/a
Eligible for Free Lunch Program: 4,983 (50.0%)
Eligible for Reduced-Price Lunch Program: 1,143 (11.5%)
Teachers: n/a
Librarians/Media Specialists: n/a
Guidance Counselors: n/a
Current Spending: ($ per student per year):
Total: $8,568; Instruction: $5,620; Support Services: $2,696
Enrollment, Drop-out Rates and Diploma Recipients by Race/Ethnicity

Category	Total	White	Black	Asian	AIAN	Hisp.
Enrollment (%)	100.0	51.4	20.1	1.3	0.6	26.6
Drop-out Rate (%)	11.0	11.2	9.3	5.0	22.2	12.0
H.S. Diplomas (#)	394	191	117	2	6	78

Providence SD

797 Westminster St • Providence, RI 02903
(401) 456-9211 • http://www.providenceschools.org/
Grade Span: PK-12; **Agency Type:** 1
Schools: 54
31 Primary; 9 Middle; 11 High; 3 Other Level
46 Regular; 2 Special Education; 2 Vocational; 4 Alternative
16 Magnet; 0 Charter; 33 Title I Eligible; 33 School-wide Title I
Students: 27,580 (50.9% male; 49.1% female)
Individual Education Program: 5,164 (18.7%);
English Language Learner: 6,002 (21.8%); Migrant: n/a
Eligible for Free Lunch Program: 18,710 (67.8%)
Eligible for Reduced-Price Lunch Program: 2,025 (7.3%)
Teachers: n/a
Librarians/Media Specialists: n/a
Guidance Counselors: n/a
Current Spending: ($ per student per year):
Total: $9,532; Instruction: $5,637; Support Services: $3,577
Enrollment, Drop-out Rates and Diploma Recipients by Race/Ethnicity

Category	Total	White	Black	Asian	AIAN	Hisp.
Enrollment (%)	100.0	15.3	22.4	8.3	0.8	53.3
Drop-out Rate (%)	10.3	8.9	9.9	9.6	6.1	11.4
H.S. Diplomas (#)	1,122	231	298	122	5	466

Scituate SD

197 Danielson Pike • North Scituate, RI 02857
Mailing Address: PO Box 188 • North Scituate, RI 02857
(401) 647-4100 • http://www.ScituateRI.net/
Grade Span: PK-12; **Agency Type:** 1
Schools: 5
3 Primary; 1 Middle; 1 High; 0 Other Level
5 Regular; 0 Special Education; 0 Vocational; 0 Alternative
0 Magnet; 0 Charter; 2 Title I Eligible; 0 School-wide Title I
Students: 1,782 (50.1% male; 49.9% female)
Individual Education Program: 311 (17.5%);
English Language Learner: n/a; Migrant: n/a
Eligible for Free Lunch Program: 94 (5.3%)
Eligible for Reduced-Price Lunch Program: 45 (2.5%)
Teachers: n/a
Librarians/Media Specialists: n/a
Guidance Counselors: n/a
Current Spending: ($ per student per year):
Total: $7,970; Instruction: $5,166; Support Services: $2,614
Enrollment, Drop-out Rates and Diploma Recipients by Race/Ethnicity

Category	Total	White	Black	Asian	AIAN	Hisp.
Enrollment (%)	100.0	97.1	0.4	1.6	0.1	0.7
Drop-out Rate (%)	1.8	1.8	0.0	0.0	n/a	n/a
H.S. Diplomas (#)	147	145	0	0	0	2

Smithfield SD

49 Farnum Pike • Esmond, RI 02917
(401) 231-6606 • http://shs.wsbe.org/
Grade Span: PK-12; **Agency Type:** 1
Schools: 6
4 Primary; 1 Middle; 1 High; 0 Other Level
6 Regular; 0 Special Education; 0 Vocational; 0 Alternative
0 Magnet; 0 Charter; 1 Title I Eligible; 0 School-wide Title I
Students: 2,703 (52.9% male; 47.1% female)
Individual Education Program: 490 (18.1%);
English Language Learner: n/a; Migrant: n/a
Eligible for Free Lunch Program: 107 (4.0%)
Eligible for Reduced-Price Lunch Program: 72 (2.7%)
Teachers: n/a
Librarians/Media Specialists: n/a
Guidance Counselors: n/a
Current Spending: ($ per student per year):
Total: $7,729; Instruction: $5,050; Support Services: $2,482
Enrollment, Drop-out Rates and Diploma Recipients by Race/Ethnicity

Category	Total	White	Black	Asian	AIAN	Hisp.
Enrollment (%)	100.0	98.0	0.6	0.7	0.0	0.7
Drop-out Rate (%)	2.3	2.4	0.0	0.0	n/a	0.0
H.S. Diplomas (#)	187	180	2	5	0	0

Woonsocket SD

108 High St • Woonsocket, RI 02895
(401) 767-4600 • http://woonsocketschools.com/
Grade Span: PK-12; **Agency Type:** 1
Schools: 13
10 Primary; 1 Middle; 2 High; 0 Other Level
12 Regular; 0 Special Education; 1 Vocational; 0 Alternative
0 Magnet; 0 Charter; 9 Title I Eligible; 7 School-wide Title I
Students: 6,839 (51.5% male; 48.5% female)
Individual Education Program: 1,633 (23.9%);
English Language Learner: 385 (5.6%); Migrant: n/a
Eligible for Free Lunch Program: 3,130 (45.8%)
Eligible for Reduced-Price Lunch Program: 817 (11.9%)
Teachers: n/a
Librarians/Media Specialists: n/a
Guidance Counselors: n/a
Current Spending: ($ per student per year):
Total: $8,077; Instruction: $5,706; Support Services: $2,067
Enrollment, Drop-out Rates and Diploma Recipients by Race/Ethnicity

Category	Total	White	Black	Asian	AIAN	Hisp.
Enrollment (%)	100.0	61.7	9.4	7.7	0.2	20.9
Drop-out Rate (%)	5.7	5.8	6.4	1.9	33.3	7.6
H.S. Diplomas (#)	339	237	29	32	0	41

Washington County

Chariho RD

Switch Rd 455a • Wood River Junction, RI 02894
(401) 364-7575
Grade Span: PK-12; **Agency Type:** 1
Schools: 7
4 Primary; 1 Middle; 2 High; 0 Other Level
6 Regular; 0 Special Education; 1 Vocational; 0 Alternative
0 Magnet; 0 Charter; 2 Title I Eligible; 0 School-wide Title I
Students: 3,861 (52.1% male; 47.9% female)
Individual Education Program: 716 (18.5%);
English Language Learner: 15 (0.4%); Migrant: n/a
Eligible for Free Lunch Program: 297 (7.7%)
Eligible for Reduced-Price Lunch Program: 213 (5.5%)
Teachers: n/a
Librarians/Media Specialists: n/a
Guidance Counselors: n/a
Current Spending: ($ per student per year):
Total: $9,251; Instruction: $6,231; Support Services: $2,801
Enrollment, Drop-out Rates and Diploma Recipients by Race/Ethnicity

Category	Total	White	Black	Asian	AIAN	Hisp.
Enrollment (%)	100.0	96.7	0.6	0.8	1.0	0.9
Drop-out Rate (%)	2.9	3.0	0.0	0.0	0.0	0.0
H.S. Diplomas (#)	280	271	1	2	5	1

Narragansett SD

25 Fifth Ave • Narragansett, RI 02882
(401) 792-9450 • http://www.narragansett.k12.ri.us/
Grade Span: PK-12; **Agency Type:** 1
Schools: 3
1 Primary; 1 Middle; 1 High; 0 Other Level
3 Regular; 0 Special Education; 0 Vocational; 0 Alternative
0 Magnet; 0 Charter; 1 Title I Eligible; 0 School-wide Title I
Students: 1,736 (51.3% male; 48.7% female)
Individual Education Program: 394 (22.7%);
English Language Learner: 8 (0.5%); Migrant: n/a

Eligible for Free Lunch Program: 137 (7.9%)
Eligible for Reduced-Price Lunch Program: 63 (3.6%)
Teachers: n/a
Librarians/Media Specialists: n/a
Guidance Counselors: n/a
Current Spending: ($ per student per year):
Total: $11,314; Instruction: $7,416; Support Services: $3,674
Enrollment, Drop-out Rates and Diploma Recipients by Race/Ethnicity

Category	Total	White	Black	Asian	AIAN	Hisp.
Enrollment (%)	100.0	94.2	2.5	1.2	1.4	0.7
Drop-out Rate (%)	0.9	1.0	0.0	0.0	0.0	0.0
H.S. Diplomas (#)	120	117	1	2	0	0

North Kingstown SD
100 Fairway • North Kingstown, RI 02852
(401) 268-6403 • http://www.nksd.net/
Grade Span: PK-12; **Agency Type:** 1
Schools: 10
7 Primary; 2 Middle; 1 High; 0 Other Level
10 Regular; 0 Special Education; 0 Vocational; 0 Alternative
0 Magnet; 0 Charter; 1 Title I Eligible; 0 School-wide Title I
Students: 4,647 (51.5% male; 48.5% female)
Individual Education Program: 746 (16.1%);
English Language Learner: 64 (1.4%); Migrant: n/a
Eligible for Free Lunch Program: 420 (9.0%)
Eligible for Reduced-Price Lunch Program: 138 (3.0%)
Teachers: n/a
Librarians/Media Specialists: n/a
Guidance Counselors: n/a
Current Spending: ($ per student per year):
Total: $9,326; Instruction: $5,891; Support Services: $3,187
Enrollment, Drop-out Rates and Diploma Recipients by Race/Ethnicity

Category	Total	White	Black	Asian	AIAN	Hisp.
Enrollment (%)	100.0	94.7	2.2	1.2	0.7	1.4
Drop-out Rate (%)	3.1	2.8	8.6	4.8	0.0	14.3
H.S. Diplomas (#)	316	302	5	4	0	5

South Kingstown SD
307 Curtis Corner Rd • Wakefield, RI 02879
(401) 792-9652 • http://www.skschools.net/
Grade Span: PK-12; **Agency Type:** 1
Schools: 10
6 Primary; 2 Middle; 1 High; 1 Other Level
9 Regular; 1 Special Education; 0 Vocational; 0 Alternative
0 Magnet; 0 Charter; 1 Title I Eligible; 0 School-wide Title I
Students: 4,238 (51.7% male; 48.3% female)
Individual Education Program: 877 (20.7%);
English Language Learner: n/a; Migrant: n/a
Eligible for Free Lunch Program: 370 (8.7%)
Eligible for Reduced-Price Lunch Program: 95 (2.2%)
Teachers: n/a
Librarians/Media Specialists: n/a
Guidance Counselors: n/a
Current Spending: ($ per student per year):
Total: $9,030; Instruction: $5,939; Support Services: $2,869
Enrollment, Drop-out Rates and Diploma Recipients by Race/Ethnicity

Category	Total	White	Black	Asian	AIAN	Hisp.
Enrollment (%)	100.0	88.0	3.8	3.5	2.6	2.0
Drop-out Rate (%)	4.1	3.4	16.7	2.4	15.7	3.8
H.S. Diplomas (#)	301	269	5	14	7	6

Westerly SD
44 Park Ave • Westerly, RI 02891
(401) 348-2700 • http://westerly.k12.ri.us/
Grade Span: PK-12; **Agency Type:** 1
Schools: 7
5 Primary; 1 Middle; 1 High; 0 Other Level
7 Regular; 0 Special Education; 0 Vocational; 0 Alternative
0 Magnet; 0 Charter; 4 Title I Eligible; 0 School-wide Title I
Students: 3,692 (50.4% male; 49.6% female)
Individual Education Program: 718 (19.4%);
English Language Learner: 52 (1.4%); Migrant: n/a
Eligible for Free Lunch Program: 564 (15.3%)
Eligible for Reduced-Price Lunch Program: 204 (5.5%)
Teachers: n/a
Librarians/Media Specialists: n/a
Guidance Counselors: n/a
Current Spending: ($ per student per year):
Total: $9,482; Instruction: $6,069; Support Services: $3,189
Enrollment, Drop-out Rates and Diploma Recipients by Race/Ethnicity

Category	Total	White	Black	Asian	AIAN	Hisp.
Enrollment (%)	100.0	91.8	1.9	3.7	1.2	1.4
Drop-out Rate (%)	2.5	2.0	9.1	0.0	0.0	71.4
H.S. Diplomas (#)	229	214	4	8	0	3

Number of Schools

Rank	Number	District Name	City
1	54	Providence SD	Providence
2	27	Warwick SD	Warwick
3	25	Cranston SD	Cranston
4	16	Pawtucket SD	Pawtucket
5	15	East Providence SD	E Providence
6	13	Woonsocket SD	Woonsocket
7	10	Cumberland SD	Cumberland
7	10	North Kingstown SD	N Kingstown
7	10	South Kingstown SD	Wakefield
10	9	Bristol Warren RD	Bristol
10	9	Johnston SD	Johnston
10	9	Newport SD	Newport
10	9	North Providence SD	N Providence
14	8	Central Falls SD	Central Falls
14	8	Coventry SD	Coventry
16	7	Chariho RD	Wood River Jct
16	7	Lincoln SD	Lincoln
16	7	West Warwick SD	West Warwick
16	7	Westerly SD	Westerly
20	6	Barrington SD	Barrington
20	6	East Greenwich SD	East Greenwich
20	6	Middletown SD	Middletown
20	6	Portsmouth SD	Portsmouth
20	6	Smithfield SD	Esmond
20	6	Tiverton SD	Tiverton
26	5	Burrillville SD	Pascoag
26	5	Exeter-W Greenwich RD	West Greenwich
26	5	Scituate SD	North Scituate
29	3	Narragansett SD	Narragansett
29	3	North Smithfield SD	N Smithfield
31	2	Foster-Glocester RD	Chepachet

Number of Teachers

Rank	Number	District Name	City
1	n/a	Barrington SD	Barrington
1	n/a	Bristol Warren RD	Bristol
1	n/a	Burrillville SD	Pascoag
1	n/a	Central Falls SD	Central Falls
1	n/a	Chariho RD	Wood River Jct
1	n/a	Coventry SD	Coventry
1	n/a	Cranston SD	Cranston
1	n/a	Cumberland SD	Cumberland
1	n/a	East Greenwich SD	East Greenwich
1	n/a	East Providence SD	E Providence
1	n/a	Exeter-W Greenwich RD	West Greenwich
1	n/a	Foster-Glocester RD	Chepachet
1	n/a	Johnston SD	Johnston
1	n/a	Lincoln SD	Lincoln
1	n/a	Middletown SD	Middletown
1	n/a	Narragansett SD	Narragansett
1	n/a	Newport SD	Newport
1	n/a	North Kingstown SD	N Kingstown
1	n/a	North Providence SD	N Providence
1	n/a	North Smithfield SD	N Smithfield
1	n/a	Pawtucket SD	Pawtucket
1	n/a	Portsmouth SD	Portsmouth
1	n/a	Providence SD	Providence
1	n/a	Scituate SD	North Scituate
1	n/a	Smithfield SD	Esmond
1	n/a	South Kingstown SD	Wakefield
1	n/a	Tiverton SD	Tiverton
1	n/a	Warwick SD	Warwick
1	n/a	West Warwick SD	West Warwick
1	n/a	Westerly SD	Westerly
1	n/a	Woonsocket SD	Woonsocket

Number of Students

Rank	Number	District Name	City
1	27,580	Providence SD	Providence
2	12,085	Warwick SD	Warwick
3	11,269	Cranston SD	Cranston
4	9,973	Pawtucket SD	Pawtucket
5	6,839	Woonsocket SD	Woonsocket
6	6,442	East Providence SD	E Providence
7	5,850	Coventry SD	Coventry
8	5,411	Cumberland SD	Cumberland
9	4,647	North Kingstown SD	N Kingstown
10	4,238	South Kingstown SD	Wakefield
11	3,861	Chariho RD	Wood River Jct
12	3,824	Bristol Warren RD	Bristol
13	3,822	West Warwick SD	West Warwick
14	3,706	Lincoln SD	Lincoln
15	3,692	Westerly SD	Westerly
16	3,651	Central Falls SD	Central Falls
17	3,445	North Providence SD	N Providence
18	3,356	Barrington SD	Barrington
19	3,311	Johnston SD	Johnston
20	2,995	Portsmouth SD	Portsmouth
21	2,915	Newport SD	Newport
22	2,838	Middletown SD	Middletown
23	2,703	Smithfield SD	Esmond
24	2,682	Burrillville SD	Pascoag
25	2,444	East Greenwich SD	East Greenwich
26	2,231	Tiverton SD	Tiverton
27	2,183	Exeter-W Greenwich RD	West Greenwich
28	1,875	North Smithfield SD	N Smithfield
29	1,782	Scituate SD	North Scituate
30	1,736	Narragansett SD	Narragansett
31	1,693	Foster-Glocester RD	Chepachet

Male Students

Rank	Percent	District Name	City
1	53.1	Barrington SD	Barrington
2	52.9	Smithfield SD	Esmond
3	52.7	Portsmouth SD	Portsmouth
4	52.3	Middletown SD	Middletown
5	52.2	East Providence SD	E Providence
6	52.1	Chariho RD	Wood River Jct
7	52.0	Johnston SD	Johnston
7	52.0	Lincoln SD	Lincoln
9	51.8	Central Falls SD	Central Falls
9	51.8	Pawtucket SD	Pawtucket
11	51.7	Cranston SD	Cranston
11	51.7	South Kingstown SD	Wakefield
11	51.7	Warwick SD	Warwick
14	51.5	Coventry SD	Coventry
14	51.5	Cumberland SD	Cumberland
14	51.5	North Kingstown SD	N Kingstown
14	51.5	Woonsocket SD	Woonsocket
18	51.4	Bristol Warren RD	Bristol
18	51.4	Foster-Glocester RD	Chepachet
18	51.4	Tiverton SD	Tiverton
21	51.3	Narragansett SD	Narragansett
22	51.2	Burrillville SD	Pascoag
22	51.2	West Warwick SD	West Warwick
24	51.0	North Providence SD	N Providence
25	50.9	Providence SD	Providence
26	50.4	Westerly SD	Westerly
27	50.1	Scituate SD	North Scituate
28	50.0	Newport SD	Newport
29	49.9	North Smithfield SD	N Smithfield
30	49.8	Exeter-W Greenwich RD	West Greenwich
31	49.6	East Greenwich SD	East Greenwich

Female Students

Rank	Percent	District Name	City
1	50.4	East Greenwich SD	East Greenwich
2	50.2	Exeter-W Greenwich RD	West Greenwich
3	50.1	North Smithfield SD	N Smithfield
4	50.0	Newport SD	Newport
5	49.9	Scituate SD	North Scituate
6	49.6	Westerly SD	Westerly
7	49.1	Providence SD	Providence
8	49.0	North Providence SD	N Providence
9	48.8	Burrillville SD	Pascoag
9	48.8	West Warwick SD	West Warwick
11	48.7	Narragansett SD	Narragansett
12	48.6	Bristol Warren RD	Bristol
12	48.6	Foster-Glocester RD	Chepachet
12	48.6	Tiverton SD	Tiverton
15	48.5	Coventry SD	Coventry
15	48.5	Cumberland SD	Cumberland
15	48.5	North Kingstown SD	N Kingstown
15	48.5	Woonsocket SD	Woonsocket
19	48.3	Cranston SD	Cranston
19	48.3	South Kingstown SD	Wakefield
19	48.3	Warwick SD	Warwick
22	48.2	Central Falls SD	Central Falls
22	48.2	Pawtucket SD	Pawtucket
24	48.0	Johnston SD	Johnston
24	48.0	Lincoln SD	Lincoln
26	47.9	Chariho RD	Wood River Jct
27	47.8	East Providence SD	E Providence
28	47.7	Middletown SD	Middletown
29	47.3	Portsmouth SD	Portsmouth
30	47.1	Smithfield SD	Esmond
31	46.9	Barrington SD	Barrington

Individual Education Program Students

Rank	Percent	District Name	City
1	26.0	Newport SD	Newport
2	25.5	Central Falls SD	Central Falls
3	25.3	Johnston SD	Johnston
4	23.9	Woonsocket SD	Woonsocket
5	22.7	Narragansett SD	Narragansett
6	22.6	West Warwick SD	West Warwick
7	22.4	Bristol Warren RD	Bristol
8	22.3	Cumberland SD	Cumberland
8	22.3	Pawtucket SD	Pawtucket
10	21.9	Warwick SD	Warwick
11	21.4	East Providence SD	E Providence
11	21.4	Tiverton SD	Tiverton
13	20.7	South Kingstown SD	Wakefield
14	20.4	Lincoln SD	Lincoln
14	20.4	Middletown SD	Middletown
16	20.3	North Providence SD	N Providence
17	20.2	Cranston SD	Cranston
18	19.9	Burrillville SD	Pascoag
19	19.5	Coventry SD	Coventry
20	19.4	Westerly SD	Westerly
21	18.7	Providence SD	Providence
22	18.5	Chariho RD	Wood River Jct
23	18.3	Exeter-W Greenwich RD	West Greenwich
24	18.2	North Smithfield SD	N Smithfield
25	18.1	Smithfield SD	Esmond
26	17.6	Barrington SD	Barrington
27	17.5	East Greenwich SD	East Greenwich
27	17.5	Scituate SD	North Scituate
29	17.3	Portsmouth SD	Portsmouth
30	16.1	North Kingstown SD	N Kingstown
31	14.9	Foster-Glocester RD	Chepachet

English Language Learner Students

Rank	Percent	District Name	City
1	28.5	Central Falls SD	Central Falls
2	21.8	Providence SD	Providence
3	10.5	Pawtucket SD	Pawtucket
4	5.6	Woonsocket SD	Woonsocket
5	4.6	East Providence SD	E Providence
6	4.1	Newport SD	Newport
7	3.8	Cranston SD	Cranston
8	3.6	Bristol Warren RD	Bristol
9	2.4	West Warwick SD	West Warwick
10	2.2	Cumberland SD	Cumberland
11	1.8	Middletown SD	Middletown
12	1.4	East Greenwich SD	East Greenwich
12	1.4	North Kingstown SD	N Kingstown
12	1.4	Westerly SD	Westerly
15	0.9	Lincoln SD	Lincoln
16	0.6	Warwick SD	Warwick
17	0.5	Narragansett SD	Narragansett
18	0.4	Chariho RD	Wood River Jct
19	0.3	Barrington SD	Barrington
19	0.3	Exeter-W Greenwich RD	West Greenwich
21	0.2	Coventry SD	Coventry
21	0.2	Portsmouth SD	Portsmouth
23	0.1	Burrillville SD	Pascoag
24	n/a	Foster-Glocester RD	Chepachet
24	n/a	Johnston SD	Johnston
24	n/a	North Providence SD	N Providence
24	n/a	North Smithfield SD	N Smithfield
24	n/a	Scituate SD	North Scituate
24	n/a	Smithfield SD	Esmond
24	n/a	South Kingstown SD	Wakefield
24	n/a	Tiverton SD	Tiverton

Migrant Students

Rank	Percent	District Name	City
1	n/a	Barrington SD	Barrington
1	n/a	Bristol Warren RD	Bristol
1	n/a	Burrillville SD	Pascoag
1	n/a	Central Falls SD	Central Falls
1	n/a	Chariho RD	Wood River Jct
1	n/a	Coventry SD	Coventry
1	n/a	Cranston SD	Cranston
1	n/a	Cumberland SD	Cumberland
1	n/a	East Greenwich SD	East Greenwich
1	n/a	East Providence SD	E Providence
1	n/a	Exeter-W Greenwich RD	West Greenwich
1	n/a	Foster-Glocester RD	Chepachet
1	n/a	Johnston SD	Johnston
1	n/a	Lincoln SD	Lincoln
1	n/a	Middletown SD	Middletown
1	n/a	Narragansett SD	Narragansett
1	n/a	Newport SD	Newport
1	n/a	North Kingstown SD	N Kingstown
1	n/a	North Providence SD	N Providence
1	n/a	North Smithfield SD	N Smithfield
1	n/a	Pawtucket SD	Pawtucket
1	n/a	Portsmouth SD	Portsmouth
1	n/a	Providence SD	Providence
1	n/a	Scituate SD	North Scituate
1	n/a	Smithfield SD	Esmond
1	n/a	South Kingstown SD	Wakefield
1	n/a	Tiverton SD	Tiverton
1	n/a	Warwick SD	Warwick
1	n/a	West Warwick SD	West Warwick
1	n/a	Westerly SD	Westerly
1	n/a	Woonsocket SD	Woonsocket

Students Eligible for Free Lunch

Rank	Percent	District Name	City
1	67.8	Providence SD	Providence
2	66.7	Central Falls SD	Central Falls
3	50.0	Pawtucket SD	Pawtucket
4	45.8	Woonsocket SD	Woonsocket
5	40.8	Newport SD	Newport
6	24.9	West Warwick SD	West Warwick
7	23.4	East Providence SD	E Providence
8	16.3	Cranston SD	Cranston
9	15.5	Bristol Warren RD	Bristol
10	15.3	Westerly SD	Westerly
11	15.1	Johnston SD	Johnston
12	14.3	North Providence SD	N Providence
13	12.9	Warwick SD	Warwick
14	11.6	Burrillville SD	Pascoag
15	10.9	Middletown SD	Middletown
16	9.8	Tiverton SD	Tiverton
17	9.0	North Kingstown SD	N Kingstown
18	8.7	South Kingstown SD	Wakefield
19	8.2	Cumberland SD	Cumberland
20	7.9	Narragansett SD	Narragansett
21	7.8	Coventry SD	Coventry
22	7.7	Chariho RD	Wood River Jct
23	7.6	Exeter-W Greenwich RD	West Greenwich
24	6.4	Lincoln SD	Lincoln
25	6.1	Foster-Glocester RD	Chepachet
26	5.3	Scituate SD	North Scituate
27	4.7	East Greenwich SD	East Greenwich
28	4.1	North Smithfield SD	N Smithfield
28	4.1	Portsmouth SD	Portsmouth
30	4.0	Smithfield SD	Esmond
31	1.8	Barrington SD	Barrington

Students Eligible for Reduced-Price Lunch

Rank	Percent	District Name	City
1	11.9	Woonsocket SD	Woonsocket
2	11.5	Pawtucket SD	Pawtucket
3	9.6	East Providence SD	E Providence
4	9.2	Central Falls SD	Central Falls
5	8.3	West Warwick SD	West Warwick
6	8.0	Newport SD	Newport
7	7.3	Burrillville SD	Pascoag
7	7.3	Providence SD	Providence
9	6.9	Bristol Warren RD	Bristol
10	6.2	Warwick SD	Warwick
11	6.0	Middletown SD	Middletown
12	5.5	Chariho RD	Wood River Jct
12	5.5	Westerly SD	Westerly
14	4.8	Tiverton SD	Tiverton
15	4.6	Cranston SD	Cranston
16	4.3	Coventry SD	Coventry
17	4.1	Johnston SD	Johnston
17	4.1	North Providence SD	N Providence
19	3.8	Cumberland SD	Cumberland
19	3.8	Exeter-W Greenwich RD	West Greenwich
21	3.7	North Smithfield SD	N Smithfield
22	3.6	Narragansett SD	Narragansett
23	3.0	North Kingstown SD	N Kingstown
24	2.9	Portsmouth SD	Portsmouth
25	2.7	Lincoln SD	Lincoln
25	2.7	Smithfield SD	Esmond
27	2.5	Scituate SD	North Scituate
28	2.2	South Kingstown SD	Wakefield
29	2.0	Foster-Glocester RD	Chepachet
30	0.8	Barrington SD	Barrington
30	0.8	East Greenwich SD	East Greenwich

Student/Teacher Ratio

Rank	Ratio	District Name	City
1	n/a	Barrington SD	Barrington
1	n/a	Bristol Warren RD	Bristol
1	n/a	Burrillville SD	Pascoag
1	n/a	Central Falls SD	Central Falls
1	n/a	Chariho RD	Wood River Jct
1	n/a	Coventry SD	Coventry
1	n/a	Cranston SD	Cranston
1	n/a	Cumberland SD	Cumberland
1	n/a	East Greenwich SD	East Greenwich
1	n/a	East Providence SD	E Providence
1	n/a	Exeter-W Greenwich RD	West Greenwich
1	n/a	Foster-Glocester RD	Chepachet
1	n/a	Johnston SD	Johnston
1	n/a	Lincoln SD	Lincoln
1	n/a	Middletown SD	Middletown
1	n/a	Narragansett SD	Narragansett
1	n/a	Newport SD	Newport
1	n/a	North Kingstown SD	N Kingstown
1	n/a	North Providence SD	N Providence
1	n/a	North Smithfield SD	N Smithfield
1	n/a	Pawtucket SD	Pawtucket
1	n/a	Portsmouth SD	Portsmouth
1	n/a	Providence SD	Providence
1	n/a	Scituate SD	North Scituate
1	n/a	Smithfield SD	Esmond
1	n/a	South Kingstown SD	Wakefield
1	n/a	Tiverton SD	Tiverton
1	n/a	Warwick SD	Warwick
1	n/a	West Warwick SD	West Warwick
1	n/a	Westerly SD	Westerly
1	n/a	Woonsocket SD	Woonsocket

Student/Librarian Ratio

Rank	Ratio	District Name	City
1	n/a	Barrington SD	Barrington
1	n/a	Bristol Warren RD	Bristol
1	n/a	Burrillville SD	Pascoag
1	n/a	Central Falls SD	Central Falls
1	n/a	Chariho RD	Wood River Jct
1	n/a	Coventry SD	Coventry
1	n/a	Cranston SD	Cranston
1	n/a	Cumberland SD	Cumberland
1	n/a	East Greenwich SD	East Greenwich
1	n/a	East Providence SD	E Providence
1	n/a	Exeter-W Greenwich RD	West Greenwich
1	n/a	Foster-Glocester RD	Chepachet
1	n/a	Johnston SD	Johnston
1	n/a	Lincoln SD	Lincoln
1	n/a	Middletown SD	Middletown
1	n/a	Narragansett SD	Narragansett
1	n/a	Newport SD	Newport
1	n/a	North Kingstown SD	N Kingstown
1	n/a	North Providence SD	N Providence
1	n/a	North Smithfield SD	N Smithfield
1	n/a	Pawtucket SD	Pawtucket
1	n/a	Portsmouth SD	Portsmouth
1	n/a	Providence SD	Providence
1	n/a	Scituate SD	North Scituate
1	n/a	Smithfield SD	Esmond
1	n/a	South Kingstown SD	Wakefield
1	n/a	Tiverton SD	Tiverton
1	n/a	Warwick SD	Warwick
1	n/a	West Warwick SD	West Warwick
1	n/a	Westerly SD	Westerly
1	n/a	Woonsocket SD	Woonsocket

Student/Counselor Ratio

Rank	Ratio	District Name	City
1	n/a	Barrington SD	Barrington
1	n/a	Bristol Warren RD	Bristol
1	n/a	Burrillville SD	Pascoag
1	n/a	Central Falls SD	Central Falls
1	n/a	Chariho RD	Wood River Jct
1	n/a	Coventry SD	Coventry
1	n/a	Cranston SD	Cranston
1	n/a	Cumberland SD	Cumberland
1	n/a	East Greenwich SD	East Greenwich
1	n/a	East Providence SD	E Providence
1	n/a	Exeter-W Greenwich RD	West Greenwich
1	n/a	Foster-Glocester RD	Chepachet
1	n/a	Johnston SD	Johnston
1	n/a	Lincoln SD	Lincoln
1	n/a	Middletown SD	Middletown
1	n/a	Narragansett SD	Narragansett
1	n/a	Newport SD	Newport
1	n/a	North Kingstown SD	N Kingstown
1	n/a	North Providence SD	N Providence
1	n/a	North Smithfield SD	N Smithfield
1	n/a	Pawtucket SD	Pawtucket
1	n/a	Portsmouth SD	Portsmouth
1	n/a	Providence SD	Providence
1	n/a	Scituate SD	North Scituate
1	n/a	Smithfield SD	Esmond
1	n/a	South Kingstown SD	Wakefield
1	n/a	Tiverton SD	Tiverton
1	n/a	Warwick SD	Warwick
1	n/a	West Warwick SD	West Warwick
1	n/a	Westerly SD	Westerly
1	n/a	Woonsocket SD	Woonsocket

Current Spending per Student in FY2001

Rank	Dollars	District Name	City
1	11,314	Narragansett SD	Narragansett
2	10,878	Newport SD	Newport
3	10,084	Warwick SD	Warwick
4	10,021	Bristol Warren RD	Bristol
5	9,934	West Warwick SD	West Warwick
6	9,929	Central Falls SD	Central Falls
7	9,580	Middletown SD	Middletown
8	9,552	North Providence SD	N Providence
9	9,532	Providence SD	Providence
10	9,482	Westerly SD	Westerly
11	9,393	East Providence SD	E Providence
12	9,326	North Kingstown SD	N Kingstown
13	9,251	Chariho RD	Wood River Jct
14	9,030	South Kingstown SD	Wakefield
15	8,800	Johnston SD	Johnston
16	8,791	East Greenwich SD	East Greenwich
17	8,756	Portsmouth SD	Portsmouth
18	8,678	Exeter-W Greenwich RD	West Greenwich
19	8,653	Coventry SD	Coventry
20	8,646	Cranston SD	Cranston
21	8,568	Pawtucket SD	Pawtucket
22	8,421	Lincoln SD	Lincoln
23	8,415	Burrillville SD	Pascoag
24	8,313	Barrington SD	Barrington
25	8,077	Woonsocket SD	Woonsocket
26	8,073	Foster-Glocester RD	Chepachet
27	8,056	Tiverton SD	Tiverton
28	7,986	North Smithfield SD	N Smithfield
29	7,970	Scituate SD	North Scituate
30	7,729	Smithfield SD	Esmond
31	7,455	Cumberland SD	Cumberland

Number of Diploma Recipients

Rank	Number	District Name	City
1	1,122	Providence SD	Providence
2	782	Warwick SD	Warwick
3	707	Cranston SD	Cranston
4	419	East Providence SD	E Providence
5	394	Pawtucket SD	Pawtucket
6	380	Coventry SD	Coventry
7	339	Woonsocket SD	Woonsocket
8	316	North Kingstown SD	N Kingstown
9	304	Cumberland SD	Cumberland
10	301	South Kingstown SD	Wakefield
11	280	Chariho RD	Wood River Jct
12	229	Westerly SD	Westerly
13	213	Lincoln SD	Lincoln
13	213	North Providence SD	N Providence
15	210	West Warwick SD	West Warwick
16	206	Barrington SD	Barrington
17	205	Bristol Warren RD	Bristol
18	187	Burrillville SD	Pascoag
18	187	Smithfield SD	Esmond
20	186	Foster-Glocester RD	Chepachet
21	184	Portsmouth SD	Portsmouth
22	169	Central Falls SD	Central Falls
22	169	Middletown SD	Middletown
24	168	Newport SD	Newport
25	147	Scituate SD	North Scituate
26	146	East Greenwich SD	East Greenwich
27	142	Johnston SD	Johnston
28	136	Tiverton SD	Tiverton
29	130	North Smithfield SD	N Smithfield
30	128	Exeter-W Greenwich RD	West Greenwich
31	120	Narragansett SD	Narragansett

High School Drop-out Rate

Rank	Percent	District Name	City
1	11.0	Pawtucket SD	Pawtucket
2	10.3	Providence SD	Providence
3	9.3	Central Falls SD	Central Falls
4	8.1	Bristol Warren RD	Bristol
5	7.9	West Warwick SD	West Warwick
6	6.3	Newport SD	Newport
7	6.1	Burrillville SD	Pascoag
8	5.8	East Providence SD	E Providence
9	5.7	Woonsocket SD	Woonsocket
10	5.0	Cranston SD	Cranston
11	4.1	South Kingstown SD	Wakefield
12	3.1	North Kingstown SD	N Kingstown
13	2.9	Chariho RD	Wood River Jct
13	2.9	Tiverton SD	Tiverton
15	2.6	East Greenwich SD	East Greenwich
15	2.6	North Providence SD	N Providence
17	2.5	Westerly SD	Westerly
18	2.4	Lincoln SD	Lincoln
19	2.3	Smithfield SD	Esmond
19	2.3	Warwick SD	Warwick
21	2.2	Barrington SD	Barrington
22	2.1	Foster-Glocester RD	Chepachet
22	2.1	Middletown SD	Middletown
24	1.8	Coventry SD	Coventry
24	1.8	Scituate SD	North Scituate
26	1.6	Cumberland SD	Cumberland
27	1.4	Johnston SD	Johnston
28	1.3	Portsmouth SD	Portsmouth
29	1.2	North Smithfield SD	N Smithfield
30	0.9	Narragansett SD	Narragansett
31	0.7	Exeter-W Greenwich RD	West Greenwich

South Carolina

South Carolina Public School Educational Profile

Category	Value	Category	Value
Schools *(2002-2003)*	1,156	**Diploma Recipients** *(2002-2003)*	31,302
Instructional Level		White, Non-Hispanic	0
Primary	631	Black, Non-Hispanic	0
Middle	251	Asian/Pacific Islander	0
High	248	American Indian/Alaskan Native	0
Other Level	26	Hispanic	0
Curriculum		**High School Drop-out Rate** (%) *(2000-2001)*	3.3
Regular	1,089	White, Non-Hispanic	3.0
Special Education	7	Black, Non-Hispanic	3.8
Vocational	40	Asian/Pacific Islander	1.2
Alternative	20	American Indian/Alaskan Native	6.4
Type		Hispanic	3.8
Magnet	25	**Staff** *(2002-2003)*	57,322.0
Charter	13	Teachers	46,567.8
Title I Eligible	529	Average Salary ($)	40,362
School-wide Title I	472	Librarians/Media Specialists	1,131.0
Students *(2002-2003)*	694,584	Guidance Counselors	1,717.2
Gender (%)		**Ratios** *(2002-2003)*	
Male	51.2	Student/Teacher Ratio	14.9 to 1
Female	48.8	Student/Librarian Ratio	614.1 to 1
Race/Ethnicity (%)		Student/Counselor Ratio	404.5 to 1
White, Non-Hispanic	54.2	**Current Spending** *($ per student in FY 2001)*	6,866
Black, Non-Hispanic	41.3	Instruction	4,134
Asian/Pacific Islander	1.1	Support Services	2,359
American Indian/Alaskan Native	0.3	**College Entrance Exam Scores** *(2003)*	
Hispanic	2.7	Scholastic Aptitude Test (SAT)	
Classification (%)		Participation Rate (%)	59
Individual Education Program (IEP)	15.8	Mean SAT I Verbal Score	493
Migrant	0.1	Mean SAT I Math Score	496
English Language Learner (ELL)	1.1	American College Testing Program (ACT)	
Eligible for Free Lunch Program	41.8	Participation Rate (%)	34
Eligible for Reduced-Price Lunch Program	7.8	Average Composite Score	19.2

Note: *For an explanation of data, please refer to the User's Guide in the front of the book; n/a indicates data not available*

South Carolina NAEP 2003 Test Scores

Reading			Mathematics		
Grade/Category	**Value**	**Rank**	**Grade/Category**	**Value**	**Rank**
4th Grade			**4th Grade**		
Average Proficiency	214.8 (1.3)	36/51	Average Proficiency	235.8 (0.9)	25/51
Proficiency by Gender/Race/Ethnicity			Proficiency by Gender/Race/Ethnicity		
Male	210.5 (1.3)	37/51	Male	237.4 (1.0)	23/51
Female	219.0 (1.6)	35/51	Female	234.1 (1.0)	26/51
White, Non-Hispanic	226.4 (1.5)	22/51	White, Non-Hispanic	245.5 (1.0)	11/51
Black, Non-Hispanic	199.4 (1.4)	22/42	Black, Non-Hispanic	222.3 (1.0)	7/42
Asian, Non-Hispanic	205.1 (5.7)	19/41	Asian, Non-Hispanic	232.4 (3.8)	3/43
American Indian, Non-Hispanic	n/a	n/a	American Indian, Non-Hispanic	n/a	n/a
Hispanic	n/a	n/a	Hispanic	n/a	n/a
Proficiency by Class Size			Proficiency by Class Size		
Less than 16 Students	*197.2 (4.0)*	32/45	Less than 16 Students	*227.9 (5.3)*	15/47
16 to 18 Students	*210.4 (3.2)*	33/48	16 to 18 Students	*235.5 (3.0)*	19/48
19 to 20 Students	213.2 (3.7)	36/50	19 to 20 Students	233.9 (2.6)	27/50
21 to 25 Students	216.9 (1.9)	40/51	21 to 25 Students	236.8 (1.3)	28/51
Greater than 25 Students	*217.7 (2.3)*	30/49	Greater than 25 Students	*237.8 (3.0)*	15/49
Percent Attaining Achievement Levels			Percent Attaining Achievement Levels		
Below Basic	40.5 (1.6)	14/51	Below Basic	20.8 (1.2)	28/51
Basic or Above	59.5 (1.6)	38/51	Basic or Above	79.2 (1.2)	24/51
Proficient or Above	25.7 (1.3)	42/51	Proficient or Above	31.8 (1.5)	26/51
Advanced or Above	5.4 (0.7)	41/51	Advanced or Above	3.9 (0.5)	18/51
8th Grade			**8th Grade**		
Average Proficiency	258.1 (1.3)	37/51	Average Proficiency	277.3 (1.3)	30/51
Proficiency by Gender/Race/Ethnicity			Proficiency by Gender/Race/Ethnicity		
Male	253.2 (1.5)	38/51	Male	280.1 (1.6)	28/51
Female	262.7 (1.6)	41/51	Female	274.4 (1.4)	34/51
White, Non-Hispanic	269.3 (1.1)	25/50	White, Non-Hispanic	290.9 (1.1)	8/50
Black, Non-Hispanic	243.8 (1.7)	22/41	Black, Non-Hispanic	258.1 (1.6)	9/41
Asian, Non-Hispanic	n/a	n/a	Asian, Non-Hispanic	n/a	n/a
American Indian, Non-Hispanic	n/a	n/a	American Indian, Non-Hispanic	n/a	n/a
Hispanic	n/a	n/a	Hispanic	n/a	n/a
Proficiency by Parents Highest Level of Ed.			Proficiency by Parents Highest Level of Ed.		
Did Not Finish High School	250.9 (2.8)	8/50	Did Not Finish High School	268.7 (2.2)	2/50
Graduated High School	248.5 (1.9)	43/50	Graduated High School	266.8 (1.9)	31/50
Some Education After High School	264.5 (1.5)	38/50	Some Education After High School	283.0 (1.5)	13/50
Graduated College	263.6 (1.8)	44/50	Graduated College	284.2 (1.5)	33/50
Percent Attaining Achievement Levels			Percent Attaining Achievement Levels		
Below Basic	30.6 (1.7)	13/51	Below Basic	32.2 (1.5)	20/51
Basic or Above	69.4 (1.7)	38/51	Basic or Above	67.8 (1.5)	31/51
Proficient or Above	24.2 (1.5)	43/51	Proficient or Above	26.3 (1.3)	32/51
Advanced or Above	1.7 (0.5)	42/51	Advanced or Above	4.8 (0.5)	27/51

Note: *For an explanation of data, please refer to the User's Guide in the front of the book; values in italics indicate that the nature of the sample does not allow accurate determination of the variability of the statistic; n/a indicates data not available*

Abbeville County

Abbeville County SD

400 Greenville St • Abbeville, SC 29620-1556
(864) 459-5427 • http://www.acsd.k12.sc.us
Grade Span: PK-12; **Agency Type:** 1
Schools: 11
5 Primary; 1 Middle; 3 High; 2 Other Level
10 Regular; 0 Special Education; 1 Vocational; 0 Alternative
0 Magnet; 1 Charter; 7 Title I Eligible; 7 School-wide Title I
Students: 3,839 (51.7% male; 48.3% female)
Individual Education Program: 672 (17.5%);
English Language Learner: 22 (0.6%); Migrant: 0 (0.0%)
Eligible for Free Lunch Program: 1,963 (51.1%)
Eligible for Reduced-Price Lunch Program: 317 (8.3%)
Teachers: 269.1 (14.3 to 1)
Librarians/Media Specialists: 9.0 (426.6 to 1)
Guidance Counselors: 9.3 (412.8 to 1)
Current Spending: ($ per student per year):
Total: $6,696; Instruction: $4,026; Support Services: $2,228
Enrollment, Drop-out Rates and Diploma Recipients by Race/Ethnicity

Category	Total	White	Black	Asian	AIAN	Hisp.
Enrollment (%)	100.0	56.1	42.4	0.4	0.0	1.0
Drop-out Rate (%)	5.9	5.2	6.8	0.0	n/a	0.0
H.S. Diplomas (#)	171	n/a	n/a	n/a	n/a	n/a

Aiken County

Aiken County SD

1000 Brookhaven Dr • Aiken, SC 29803-1137
(803) 641-2700 • http://www.aiken.k12.sc.us
Grade Span: PK-12; **Agency Type:** 1
Schools: 39
20 Primary; 11 Middle; 8 High; 0 Other Level
38 Regular; 0 Special Education; 1 Vocational; 0 Alternative
0 Magnet; 2 Charter; 24 Title I Eligible; 24 School-wide Title I
Students: 25,358 (51.2% male; 48.8% female)
Individual Education Program: 3,492 (13.8%);
English Language Learner: 220 (0.9%); Migrant: 10 (<0.1%)
Eligible for Free Lunch Program: 10,793 (42.6%)
Eligible for Reduced-Price Lunch Program: 1,655 (6.5%)
Teachers: 1,580.3 (16.0 to 1)
Librarians/Media Specialists: 40.1 (632.4 to 1)
Guidance Counselors: 52.4 (483.9 to 1)
Current Spending: ($ per student per year):
Total: $5,609; Instruction: $3,507; Support Services: $1,805
Enrollment, Drop-out Rates and Diploma Recipients by Race/Ethnicity

Category	Total	White	Black	Asian	AIAN	Hisp.
Enrollment (%)	100.0	60.1	35.7	0.7	0.2	3.0
Drop-out Rate (%)	3.1	2.8	3.5	0.0	0.0	7.8
H.S. Diplomas (#)	1,218	n/a	n/a	n/a	n/a	n/a

Allendale County

Allendale County SD

PO Box 458 • Allendale, SC 29810-0458
(803) 584-4603 • http://www.acs.k12.sc.us/
Grade Span: PK-12; **Agency Type:** 1
Schools: 4
2 Primary; 1 Middle; 1 High; 0 Other Level
4 Regular; 0 Special Education; 0 Vocational; 0 Alternative
0 Magnet; 0 Charter; 3 Title I Eligible; 3 School-wide Title I
Students: 1,918 (51.2% male; 48.8% female)
Individual Education Program: 407 (21.2%);
English Language Learner: 9 (0.5%); Migrant: 0 (0.0%)
Eligible for Free Lunch Program: 1,620 (84.5%)
Eligible for Reduced-Price Lunch Program: 99 (5.2%)
Teachers: 153.0 (12.5 to 1)
Librarians/Media Specialists: 4.0 (479.5 to 1)
Guidance Counselors: 6.0 (319.7 to 1)
Current Spending: ($ per student per year):
Total: $9,342; Instruction: $5,204; Support Services: $3,509
Enrollment, Drop-out Rates and Diploma Recipients by Race/Ethnicity

Category	Total	White	Black	Asian	AIAN	Hisp.
Enrollment (%)	100.0	3.6	94.8	0.3	0.0	1.2
Drop-out Rate (%)	3.3	3.0	3.3	0.0	n/a	0.0
H.S. Diplomas (#)	78	n/a	n/a	n/a	n/a	n/a

Anderson County

Anderson County SD 01

Box 99 • Williamston, SC 29697-0099
(864) 847-7344 • http://www.anderson1.k12.sc.us
Grade Span: PK-12; **Agency Type:** 1
Schools: 15
10 Primary; 3 Middle; 2 High; 0 Other Level
15 Regular; 0 Special Education; 0 Vocational; 0 Alternative
0 Magnet; 0 Charter; 2 Title I Eligible; 1 School-wide Title I
Students: 7,939 (51.6% male; 48.4% female)
Individual Education Program: 1,183 (14.9%);
English Language Learner: 54 (0.7%); Migrant: 1 (<0.1%)
Eligible for Free Lunch Program: 1,740 (21.9%)
Eligible for Reduced-Price Lunch Program: 630 (7.9%)
Teachers: 453.3 (17.5 to 1)
Librarians/Media Specialists: 14.5 (547.5 to 1)
Guidance Counselors: 17.5 (453.7 to 1)
Current Spending: ($ per student per year):
Total: $5,410; Instruction: $3,412; Support Services: $1,708
Enrollment, Drop-out Rates and Diploma Recipients by Race/Ethnicity

Category	Total	White	Black	Asian	AIAN	Hisp.
Enrollment (%)	100.0	89.9	7.5	0.5	0.2	1.8
Drop-out Rate (%)	1.8	1.7	2.2	0.0	0.0	6.7
H.S. Diplomas (#)	380	n/a	n/a	n/a	n/a	n/a

Anderson County SD 02

PO Box 266 • Honea Path, SC 29654-0266
(843) 369-7364 • http://www.anderson2.k12.sc.us
Grade Span: PK-12; **Agency Type:** 1
Schools: 7
3 Primary; 3 Middle; 1 High; 0 Other Level
7 Regular; 0 Special Education; 0 Vocational; 0 Alternative
0 Magnet; 0 Charter; 6 Title I Eligible; 0 School-wide Title I
Students: 3,772 (51.0% male; 49.0% female)
Individual Education Program: 791 (21.0%);
English Language Learner: 10 (0.3%); Migrant: 0 (0.0%)
Eligible for Free Lunch Program: 1,223 (32.4%)
Eligible for Reduced-Price Lunch Program: 278 (7.4%)
Teachers: 215.1 (17.5 to 1)
Librarians/Media Specialists: 6.0 (628.7 to 1)
Guidance Counselors: 9.0 (419.1 to 1)
Current Spending: ($ per student per year):
Total: $6,014; Instruction: $3,696; Support Services: $1,986
Enrollment, Drop-out Rates and Diploma Recipients by Race/Ethnicity

Category	Total	White	Black	Asian	AIAN	Hisp.
Enrollment (%)	100.0	77.7	20.4	0.4	0.1	1.4
Drop-out Rate (%)	8.2	9.4	4.3	0.0	n/a	0.0
H.S. Diplomas (#)	177	n/a	n/a	n/a	n/a	n/a

Anderson County SD 03

Box 118 • Iva, SC 29655-0118
(864) 348-6196 • http://www.anderson3.k12.sc.us
Grade Span: PK-12; **Agency Type:** 1
Schools: 4
2 Primary; 1 Middle; 1 High; 0 Other Level
4 Regular; 0 Special Education; 0 Vocational; 0 Alternative
0 Magnet; 0 Charter; 2 Title I Eligible; 2 School-wide Title I
Students: 2,662 (52.3% male; 47.7% female)
Individual Education Program: 548 (20.6%);
English Language Learner: 3 (0.1%); Migrant: 0 (0.0%)
Eligible for Free Lunch Program: 1,065 (40.0%)
Eligible for Reduced-Price Lunch Program: 284 (10.7%)
Teachers: 165.9 (16.0 to 1)
Librarians/Media Specialists: 4.0 (665.5 to 1)
Guidance Counselors: 5.0 (532.4 to 1)
Current Spending: ($ per student per year):
Total: $5,909; Instruction: $3,449; Support Services: $2,008
Enrollment, Drop-out Rates and Diploma Recipients by Race/Ethnicity

Category	Total	White	Black	Asian	AIAN	Hisp.
Enrollment (%)	100.0	86.0	13.0	0.2	0.2	0.5
Drop-out Rate (%)	2.4	2.2	3.3	0.0	0.0	n/a
H.S. Diplomas (#)	106	n/a	n/a	n/a	n/a	n/a

Anderson County SD 04

Box 545 • Pendleton, SC 29670-0545
(864) 646-8000 • http://www.anderson4.k12.sc.us
Grade Span: PK-12; **Agency Type:** 1
Schools: 5
3 Primary; 1 Middle; 1 High; 0 Other Level
5 Regular; 0 Special Education; 0 Vocational; 0 Alternative
0 Magnet; 0 Charter; 2 Title I Eligible; 2 School-wide Title I
Students: 2,834 (51.1% male; 48.9% female)
Individual Education Program: 418 (14.7%);
English Language Learner: 8 (0.3%); Migrant: 0 (0.0%)
Eligible for Free Lunch Program: 848 (29.9%)
Eligible for Reduced-Price Lunch Program: 271 (9.6%)
Teachers: 174.3 (16.3 to 1)
Librarians/Media Specialists: 5.0 (566.8 to 1)
Guidance Counselors: 8.0 (354.3 to 1)
Current Spending: ($ per student per year):
Total: $6,989; Instruction: $4,014; Support Services: $2,543

Enrollment, Drop-out Rates and Diploma Recipients by Race/Ethnicity

Category	Total	White	Black	Asian	AIAN	Hisp.
Enrollment (%)	100.0	76.9	21.9	0.3	0.0	0.7
Drop-out Rate (%)	0.9	1.2	0.0	0.0	n/a	0.0
H.S. Diplomas (#)	99	n/a	n/a	n/a	n/a	n/a

Anderson County SD 05

Box 439 • Anderson, SC 29622-0439
(864) 260-5000 • http://www.anderson5.net
Grade Span: PK-12; **Agency Type:** 1
Schools: 17
10 Primary; 3 Middle; 2 High; 2 Other Level
17 Regular; 0 Special Education; 0 Vocational; 0 Alternative
0 Magnet; 0 Charter; 4 Title I Eligible; 4 School-wide Title I
Students: 11,792 (50.9% male; 49.1% female)
Individual Education Program: 1,810 (15.3%);
English Language Learner: 50 (0.4%); Migrant: 2 (<0.1%)
Eligible for Free Lunch Program: 4,391 (37.2%)
Eligible for Reduced-Price Lunch Program: 745 (6.3%)
Teachers: 788.6 (15.0 to 1)
Librarians/Media Specialists: 16.0 (737.0 to 1)
Guidance Counselors: 37.0 (318.7 to 1)
Current Spending: ($ per student per year):
Total: $6,655; Instruction: $3,914; Support Services: $2,414
Enrollment, Drop-out Rates and Diploma Recipients by Race/Ethnicity

Category	Total	White	Black	Asian	AIAN	Hisp.
Enrollment (%)	100.0	61.1	36.6	0.9	0.1	1.3
Drop-out Rate (%)	5.1	4.5	7.0	0.0	0.0	0.0
H.S. Diplomas (#)	542	n/a	n/a	n/a	n/a	n/a

Bamberg County

Bamberg County SD 01

Box 526 • Bamberg, SC 29003-0526
(803) 245-3053
Grade Span: PK-12; **Agency Type:** 1
Schools: 5
2 Primary; 2 Middle; 1 High; 0 Other Level
5 Regular; 0 Special Education; 0 Vocational; 0 Alternative
0 Magnet; 0 Charter; 4 Title I Eligible; 4 School-wide Title I
Students: 1,704 (52.1% male; 47.9% female)
Individual Education Program: 374 (21.9%);
English Language Learner: 0 (0.0%); Migrant: 0 (0.0%)
Eligible for Free Lunch Program: 965 (56.6%)
Eligible for Reduced-Price Lunch Program: 136 (8.0%)
Teachers: 120.3 (14.2 to 1)
Librarians/Media Specialists: 4.0 (426.0 to 1)
Guidance Counselors: 5.7 (298.9 to 1)
Current Spending: ($ per student per year):
Total: $6,949; Instruction: $4,127; Support Services: $2,360
Enrollment, Drop-out Rates and Diploma Recipients by Race/Ethnicity

Category	Total	White	Black	Asian	AIAN	Hisp.
Enrollment (%)	100.0	39.8	59.3	0.4	0.1	0.4
Drop-out Rate (%)	2.5	1.5	3.1	0.0	n/a	n/a
H.S. Diplomas (#)	95	n/a	n/a	n/a	n/a	n/a

Barnwell County

Barnwell County SD 45

2008 Hagood Ave • Barnwell, SC 29812
(803) 541-1300 • http://www.barnwellweb.com/bsd45
Grade Span: PK-12; **Agency Type:** 1
Schools: 3
1 Primary; 1 Middle; 1 High; 0 Other Level
3 Regular; 0 Special Education; 0 Vocational; 0 Alternative
0 Magnet; 0 Charter; 1 Title I Eligible; 1 School-wide Title I
Students: 2,806 (52.7% male; 47.3% female)
Individual Education Program: 512 (18.2%);
English Language Learner: 4 (0.1%); Migrant: 0 (0.0%)
Eligible for Free Lunch Program: 1,326 (47.3%)
Eligible for Reduced-Price Lunch Program: 232 (8.3%)
Teachers: 183.3 (15.3 to 1)
Librarians/Media Specialists: 3.0 (935.3 to 1)
Guidance Counselors: 6.0 (467.7 to 1)
Current Spending: ($ per student per year):
Total: $6,175; Instruction: $3,933; Support Services: $1,847
Enrollment, Drop-out Rates and Diploma Recipients by Race/Ethnicity

Category	Total	White	Black	Asian	AIAN	Hisp.
Enrollment (%)	100.0	54.3	43.5	0.5	0.3	1.2
Drop-out Rate (%)	3.1	2.7	3.0	n/a	n/a	18.2
H.S. Diplomas (#)	125	n/a	n/a	n/a	n/a	n/a

Beaufort County

Beaufort County SD

PO Box 309 • Beaufort, SC 29902-0309
(843) 525-4200 • http://beaufort.schoolnet.com
Grade Span: PK-12; **Agency Type:** 1
Schools: 25
16 Primary; 6 Middle; 3 High; 0 Other Level
25 Regular; 0 Special Education; 0 Vocational; 0 Alternative
0 Magnet; 0 Charter; 10 Title I Eligible; 10 School-wide Title I
Students: 18,133 (51.0% male; 49.0% female)
Individual Education Program: 2,326 (12.8%);
English Language Learner: 940 (5.2%); Migrant: 0 (0.0%)
Eligible for Free Lunch Program: 7,031 (38.8%)
Eligible for Reduced-Price Lunch Program: 1,505 (8.3%)
Teachers: 1,251.9 (14.5 to 1)
Librarians/Media Specialists: 25.0 (725.3 to 1)
Guidance Counselors: 46.0 (394.2 to 1)
Current Spending: ($ per student per year):
Total: $7,286; Instruction: $4,160; Support Services: $2,713
Enrollment, Drop-out Rates and Diploma Recipients by Race/Ethnicity

Category	Total	White	Black	Asian	AIAN	Hisp.
Enrollment (%)	100.0	46.4	42.0	1.0	0.1	10.4
Drop-out Rate (%)	3.4	3.3	3.1	5.9	0.0	6.5
H.S. Diplomas (#)	759	n/a	n/a	n/a	n/a	n/a

Berkeley County

Berkeley County SD

PO Box 608 • Moncks Corner, SC 29461-0608
(843) 761-8600 • http://WWW.BERKELEY.K12.SC.US
Grade Span: PK-12; **Agency Type:** 1
Schools: 36
21 Primary; 9 Middle; 6 High; 0 Other Level
36 Regular; 0 Special Education; 0 Vocational; 0 Alternative
0 Magnet; 0 Charter; 26 Title I Eligible; 26 School-wide Title I
Students: 28,585 (51.8% male; 48.2% female)
Individual Education Program: 4,410 (15.4%);
English Language Learner: 380 (1.3%); Migrant: 1 (<0.1%)
Eligible for Free Lunch Program: 11,406 (39.9%)
Eligible for Reduced-Price Lunch Program: 3,230 (11.3%)
Teachers: 1,748.0 (16.4 to 1)
Librarians/Media Specialists: 38.0 (752.2 to 1)
Guidance Counselors: 63.0 (453.7 to 1)
Current Spending: ($ per student per year):
Total: $6,247; Instruction: $3,682; Support Services: $2,238
Enrollment, Drop-out Rates and Diploma Recipients by Race/Ethnicity

Category	Total	White	Black	Asian	AIAN	Hisp.
Enrollment (%)	100.0	58.5	36.2	1.8	0.4	3.0
Drop-out Rate (%)	4.0	4.4	3.7	1.9	4.0	3.1
H.S. Diplomas (#)	1,302	n/a	n/a	n/a	n/a	n/a

Calhoun County

Calhoun County SD

101 Richland Ave • Saint Matthews, SC 29135-0215
(803) 655-7310 • http://www.calhoun.k12.sc.us/
Grade Span: PK-12; **Agency Type:** 1
Schools: 4
2 Primary; 1 Middle; 1 High; 0 Other Level
4 Regular; 0 Special Education; 0 Vocational; 0 Alternative
0 Magnet; 0 Charter; 3 Title I Eligible; 3 School-wide Title I
Students: 1,961 (49.7% male; 50.3% female)
Individual Education Program: 391 (19.9%);
English Language Learner: 26 (1.3%); Migrant: 1 (0.1%)
Eligible for Free Lunch Program: 1,399 (71.3%)
Eligible for Reduced-Price Lunch Program: 186 (9.5%)
Teachers: 154.5 (12.7 to 1)
Librarians/Media Specialists: 4.0 (490.3 to 1)
Guidance Counselors: 4.6 (426.3 to 1)
Current Spending: ($ per student per year):
Total: $7,367; Instruction: $4,199; Support Services: $2,745
Enrollment, Drop-out Rates and Diploma Recipients by Race/Ethnicity

Category	Total	White	Black	Asian	AIAN	Hisp.
Enrollment (%)	100.0	22.4	75.4	0.0	0.0	2.0
Drop-out Rate (%)	1.4	0.0	1.7	n/a	n/a	0.0
H.S. Diplomas (#)	75	n/a	n/a	n/a	n/a	n/a

Charleston County

Charleston County SD

75 Calhoun St • Charleston, SC 29401-6413
(843) 724-7716 • http://www.charleston.k12.sc.us
Grade Span: PK-12; **Agency Type:** 1
Schools: 80

49 Primary; 16 Middle; 13 High; 2 Other Level
80 Regular; 0 Special Education; 0 Vocational; 0 Alternative
10 Magnet; 0 Charter; 41 Title I Eligible; 41 School-wide Title I
Students: 44,008 (51.1% male; 48.9% female)
Individual Education Program: 6,335 (14.4%);
English Language Learner: 410 (0.9%); Migrant: 12 (<0.1%)
Eligible for Free Lunch Program: 20,320 (46.2%)
Eligible for Reduced-Price Lunch Program: 3,011 (6.8%)
Teachers: 3,101.4 (14.2 to 1)
Librarians/Media Specialists: 80.0 (550.1 to 1)
Guidance Counselors: 107.1 (410.9 to 1)
Current Spending: ($ per student per year):
Total: $6,169; Instruction: $3,846; Support Services: $1,977
Enrollment, Drop-out Rates and Diploma Recipients by Race/Ethnicity

Category	Total	White	Black	Asian	AIAN	Hisp.
Enrollment (%)	100.0	39.4	56.4	1.3	0.2	2.6
Drop-out Rate (%)	2.8	1.8	3.5	0.7	0.0	1.6
H.S. Diplomas (#)	1,666	n/a	n/a	n/a	n/a	n/a

Cherokee County

Cherokee County SD
Box 460 • Gaffney, SC 29342-0460
(864) 489-0261 • http://www.cherokee1.k12.sc.us/
Grade Span: PK-12; **Agency Type:** 1
Schools: 19
12 Primary; 4 Middle; 3 High; 0 Other Level
18 Regular; 0 Special Education; 1 Vocational; 0 Alternative
0 Magnet; 0 Charter; 7 Title I Eligible; 7 School-wide Title I
Students: 9,298 (50.2% male; 49.8% female)
Individual Education Program: 1,077 (11.6%);
English Language Learner: 159 (1.7%); Migrant: 0 (0.0%)
Eligible for Free Lunch Program: 4,183 (45.0%)
Eligible for Reduced-Price Lunch Program: 820 (8.8%)
Teachers: 621.7 (15.0 to 1)
Librarians/Media Specialists: 18.5 (502.6 to 1)
Guidance Counselors: 24.0 (387.4 to 1)
Current Spending: ($ per student per year):
Total: $6,390; Instruction: $3,856; Support Services: $2,179
Enrollment, Drop-out Rates and Diploma Recipients by Race/Ethnicity

Category	Total	White	Black	Asian	AIAN	Hisp.
Enrollment (%)	100.0	68.1	28.7	0.5	0.1	2.5
Drop-out Rate (%)	3.1	2.7	3.8	6.3	0.0	3.8
H.S. Diplomas (#)	380	n/a	n/a	n/a	n/a	n/a

Chester County

Chester County SD
109 Hinton St • Chester, SC 29706-2022
(803) 385-6122 • http://www.chester.k12.sc.us
Grade Span: PK-12; **Agency Type:** 1
Schools: 10
3 Primary; 3 Middle; 3 High; 1 Other Level
9 Regular; 0 Special Education; 1 Vocational; 0 Alternative
0 Magnet; 0 Charter; 3 Title I Eligible; 3 School-wide Title I
Students: 6,489 (52.1% male; 47.9% female)
Individual Education Program: 1,033 (15.9%);
English Language Learner: 17 (0.3%); Migrant: 0 (0.0%)
Eligible for Free Lunch Program: 3,053 (47.0%)
Eligible for Reduced-Price Lunch Program: 457 (7.0%)
Teachers: 463.6 (14.0 to 1)
Librarians/Media Specialists: 8.0 (811.1 to 1)
Guidance Counselors: 16.0 (405.6 to 1)
Current Spending: ($ per student per year):
Total: $6,386; Instruction: $3,918; Support Services: $2,202
Enrollment, Drop-out Rates and Diploma Recipients by Race/Ethnicity

Category	Total	White	Black	Asian	AIAN	Hisp.
Enrollment (%)	100.0	48.3	50.4	0.4	0.2	0.7
Drop-out Rate (%)	5.3	5.3	5.2	25.0	0.0	0.0
H.S. Diplomas (#)	231	n/a	n/a	n/a	n/a	n/a

Chesterfield County SD
401 W Blvd • Chesterfield, SC 29709-1534
(843) 623-2175 • http://www.chesterfield.k12.sc.us
Grade Span: PK-12; **Agency Type:** 1
Schools: 16
9 Primary; 3 Middle; 4 High; 0 Other Level
16 Regular; 0 Special Education; 0 Vocational; 0 Alternative
0 Magnet; 0 Charter; 8 Title I Eligible; 8 School-wide Title I
Students: 8,292 (50.5% male; 49.5% female)
Individual Education Program: 1,420 (17.1%);
English Language Learner: 92 (1.1%); Migrant: 0 (0.0%)
Eligible for Free Lunch Program: 4,163 (50.2%)
Eligible for Reduced-Price Lunch Program: 801 (9.7%)
Teachers: 552.9 (15.0 to 1)
Librarians/Media Specialists: 14.5 (571.9 to 1)
Guidance Counselors: 17.0 (487.8 to 1)
Current Spending: ($ per student per year):
Total: $6,294; Instruction: $3,776; Support Services: $2,191
Enrollment, Drop-out Rates and Diploma Recipients by Race/Ethnicity

Category	Total	White	Black	Asian	AIAN	Hisp.
Enrollment (%)	100.0	55.6	42.1	0.3	0.2	1.8
Drop-out Rate (%)	4.8	4.3	5.6	12.5	0.0	0.0
H.S. Diplomas (#)	367	n/a	n/a	n/a	n/a	n/a

Clarendon County

Clarendon County SD 02
PO Box 1252 • Manning, SC 29102-1252
(803) 435-4435
Grade Span: PK-12; **Agency Type:** 1
Schools: 6
2 Primary; 2 Middle; 2 High; 0 Other Level
6 Regular; 0 Special Education; 0 Vocational; 0 Alternative
0 Magnet; 1 Charter; 3 Title I Eligible; 3 School-wide Title I
Students: 3,584 (49.1% male; 50.9% female)
Individual Education Program: 663 (18.5%);
English Language Learner: 22 (0.6%); Migrant: 2 (0.1%)
Eligible for Free Lunch Program: 2,378 (66.4%)
Eligible for Reduced-Price Lunch Program: 260 (7.3%)
Teachers: 203.9 (17.6 to 1)
Librarians/Media Specialists: 6.0 (597.3 to 1)
Guidance Counselors: 5.0 (716.8 to 1)
Current Spending: ($ per student per year):
Total: $5,781; Instruction: $3,601; Support Services: $1,727
Enrollment, Drop-out Rates and Diploma Recipients by Race/Ethnicity

Category	Total	White	Black	Asian	AIAN	Hisp.
Enrollment (%)	100.0	30.2	67.4	0.3	0.2	1.8
Drop-out Rate (%)	3.9	4.5	3.5	0.0	n/a	12.5
H.S. Diplomas (#)	167	n/a	n/a	n/a	n/a	n/a

Colleton County

Colleton County SD
PO Box 290 • Walterboro, SC 29488-0290
(843) 549-5715 • http://www.colleton.k12.sc.us
Grade Span: PK-12; **Agency Type:** 1
Schools: 12
7 Primary; 3 Middle; 2 High; 0 Other Level
11 Regular; 0 Special Education; 1 Vocational; 0 Alternative
0 Magnet; 0 Charter; 9 Title I Eligible; 9 School-wide Title I
Students: 6,850 (50.9% male; 49.1% female)
Individual Education Program: 964 (14.1%);
English Language Learner: 16 (0.2%); Migrant: 0 (0.0%)
Eligible for Free Lunch Program: 4,339 (63.3%)
Eligible for Reduced-Price Lunch Program: 492 (7.2%)
Teachers: 444.8 (15.4 to 1)
Librarians/Media Specialists: 12.0 (570.8 to 1)
Guidance Counselors: 19.0 (360.5 to 1)
Current Spending: ($ per student per year):
Total: $6,590; Instruction: $3,843; Support Services: $2,383
Enrollment, Drop-out Rates and Diploma Recipients by Race/Ethnicity

Category	Total	White	Black	Asian	AIAN	Hisp.
Enrollment (%)	100.0	40.0	57.8	0.3	0.7	1.0
Drop-out Rate (%)	6.8	8.7	5.5	0.0	0.0	0.0
H.S. Diplomas (#)	266	n/a	n/a	n/a	n/a	n/a

Darlington County

Darlington County SD
PO Box 117 • Darlington, SC 29532-0493
(843) 398-5200 • http://www.darlington.k12.sc.us
Grade Span: PK-12; **Agency Type:** 1
Schools: 22
10 Primary; 7 Middle; 5 High; 0 Other Level
22 Regular; 0 Special Education; 0 Vocational; 0 Alternative
3 Magnet; 1 Charter; 14 Title I Eligible; 14 School-wide Title I
Students: 11,767 (51.8% male; 48.2% female)
Individual Education Program: 2,132 (18.1%);
English Language Learner: 36 (0.3%); Migrant: 0 (0.0%)
Eligible for Free Lunch Program: 6,606 (56.1%)
Eligible for Reduced-Price Lunch Program: 915 (7.8%)
Teachers: 821.8 (14.3 to 1)
Librarians/Media Specialists: 24.0 (490.3 to 1)
Guidance Counselors: 33.0 (356.6 to 1)
Current Spending: ($ per student per year):
Total: $6,709; Instruction: $3,892; Support Services: $2,430

Enrollment, Drop-out Rates and Diploma Recipients by Race/Ethnicity

Category	Total	White	Black	Asian	AIAN	Hisp.
Enrollment (%)	100.0	41.2	57.6	0.3	0.1	0.8
Drop-out Rate (%)	2.9	2.4	3.5	0.0	0.0	0.0
H.S. Diplomas (#)	483	n/a	n/a	n/a	n/a	n/a

Dillon County

Dillon County SD 02

405 W Washington St • Dillon, SC 29536-2855
(843) 774-1200 • http://www.dillon2.k12.sc.us/
Grade Span: PK-12; **Agency Type:** 1
Schools: 6
3 Primary; 2 Middle; 1 High; 0 Other Level
6 Regular; 0 Special Education; 0 Vocational; 0 Alternative
0 Magnet; 0 Charter; 5 Title I Eligible; 5 School-wide Title I
Students: 3,874 (52.4% male; 47.6% female)
Individual Education Program: 498 (12.9%);
English Language Learner: 48 (1.2%); Migrant: 0 (0.0%)
Eligible for Free Lunch Program: 2,803 (72.4%)
Eligible for Reduced-Price Lunch Program: 335 (8.6%)
Teachers: 223.4 (17.3 to 1)
Librarians/Media Specialists: 6.0 (645.7 to 1)
Guidance Counselors: 10.0 (387.4 to 1)
Current Spending: ($ per student per year):
Total: $5,642; Instruction: $3,178; Support Services: $2,103

Enrollment, Drop-out Rates and Diploma Recipients by Race/Ethnicity

Category	Total	White	Black	Asian	AIAN	Hisp.
Enrollment (%)	100.0	28.1	66.6	0.4	3.0	1.7
Drop-out Rate (%)	6.9	4.2	7.5	0.0	27.8	33.3
H.S. Diplomas (#)	165	n/a	n/a	n/a	n/a	n/a

Dillon County SD 03

502 N Richardson St • Latta, SC 29565-1415
(843) 752-7101 • http://www.dillon3.k12.sc.us
Grade Span: PK-12; **Agency Type:** 1
Schools: 3
1 Primary; 1 Middle; 1 High; 0 Other Level
3 Regular; 0 Special Education; 0 Vocational; 0 Alternative
0 Magnet; 0 Charter; 0 Title I Eligible; 0 School-wide Title I
Students: 1,551 (51.5% male; 48.5% female)
Individual Education Program: 253 (16.3%);
English Language Learner: 0 (0.0%); Migrant: 12 (0.8%)
Eligible for Free Lunch Program: 916 (59.1%)
Eligible for Reduced-Price Lunch Program: 111 (7.2%)
Teachers: 96.3 (16.1 to 1)
Librarians/Media Specialists: 3.0 (517.0 to 1)
Guidance Counselors: 3.0 (517.0 to 1)
Current Spending: ($ per student per year):
Total: $5,776; Instruction: $3,291; Support Services: $2,022

Enrollment, Drop-out Rates and Diploma Recipients by Race/Ethnicity

Category	Total	White	Black	Asian	AIAN	Hisp.
Enrollment (%)	100.0	51.9	46.0	0.1	1.1	0.8
Drop-out Rate (%)	3.4	3.3	3.1	n/a	33.3	0.0
H.S. Diplomas (#)	77	n/a	n/a	n/a	n/a	n/a

Dorchester County

Dorchester County SD 02

102 Greenwave Blvd • Summerville, SC 29483-2455
(843) 873-2901
Grade Span: PK-12; **Agency Type:** 1
Schools: 16
9 Primary; 5 Middle; 2 High; 0 Other Level
16 Regular; 0 Special Education; 0 Vocational; 0 Alternative
0 Magnet; 0 Charter; 6 Title I Eligible; 0 School-wide Title I
Students: 17,765 (51.3% male; 48.7% female)
Individual Education Program: 2,370 (13.3%);
English Language Learner: 85 (0.5%); Migrant: 1 (<0.1%)
Eligible for Free Lunch Program: 3,924 (22.1%)
Eligible for Reduced-Price Lunch Program: 1,120 (6.3%)
Teachers: 1,108.5 (16.0 to 1)
Librarians/Media Specialists: 20.0 (888.3 to 1)
Guidance Counselors: 49.0 (362.6 to 1)
Current Spending: ($ per student per year):
Total: $5,900; Instruction: $3,675; Support Services: $1,985

Enrollment, Drop-out Rates and Diploma Recipients by Race/Ethnicity

Category	Total	White	Black	Asian	AIAN	Hisp.
Enrollment (%)	100.0	67.9	28.2	1.4	0.5	1.9
Drop-out Rate (%)	3.5	3.1	4.2	0.0	16.7	4.8
H.S. Diplomas (#)	883	n/a	n/a	n/a	n/a	n/a

Dorchester County SD 04

500 Ridge St • Saint George, SC 29477-2452
(843) 563-4535 • http://www.dorchester4.k12.sc.us
Grade Span: PK-12; **Agency Type:** 1
Schools: 4
2 Primary; 1 Middle; 1 High; 0 Other Level
4 Regular; 0 Special Education; 0 Vocational; 0 Alternative
0 Magnet; 0 Charter; 3 Title I Eligible; 3 School-wide Title I
Students: 2,514 (53.6% male; 46.4% female)
Individual Education Program: 413 (16.4%);
English Language Learner: 8 (0.3%); Migrant: 0 (0.0%)
Eligible for Free Lunch Program: 1,586 (63.1%)
Eligible for Reduced-Price Lunch Program: 264 (10.5%)
Teachers: 185.8 (13.5 to 1)
Librarians/Media Specialists: 3.0 (838.0 to 1)
Guidance Counselors: 6.0 (419.0 to 1)
Current Spending: ($ per student per year):
Total: $7,528; Instruction: $4,209; Support Services: $2,812

Enrollment, Drop-out Rates and Diploma Recipients by Race/Ethnicity

Category	Total	White	Black	Asian	AIAN	Hisp.
Enrollment (%)	100.0	27.6	68.9	0.4	2.1	1.0
Drop-out Rate (%)	3.9	5.8	3.3	0.0	12.5	0.0
H.S. Diplomas (#)	116	n/a	n/a	n/a	n/a	n/a

Edgefield County

Edgefield County SD

PO Box 608 • Edgefield, SC 29824-0608
(803) 275-4601 • http://www.edgefield.k12.sc.us
Grade Span: PK-12; **Agency Type:** 1
Schools: 8
4 Primary; 2 Middle; 2 High; 0 Other Level
7 Regular; 0 Special Education; 1 Vocational; 0 Alternative
0 Magnet; 0 Charter; 4 Title I Eligible; 4 School-wide Title I
Students: 4,088 (52.3% male; 47.7% female)
Individual Education Program: 708 (17.3%);
English Language Learner: 3 (0.1%); Migrant: 0 (0.0%)
Eligible for Free Lunch Program: 1,977 (48.4%)
Eligible for Reduced-Price Lunch Program: 346 (8.5%)
Teachers: 288.5 (14.2 to 1)
Librarians/Media Specialists: 8.0 (511.0 to 1)
Guidance Counselors: 9.0 (454.2 to 1)
Current Spending: ($ per student per year):
Total: $6,730; Instruction: $3,904; Support Services: $2,424

Enrollment, Drop-out Rates and Diploma Recipients by Race/Ethnicity

Category	Total	White	Black	Asian	AIAN	Hisp.
Enrollment (%)	100.0	48.3	49.8	0.2	0.0	1.7
Drop-out Rate (%)	3.7	3.1	4.4	0.0	0.0	0.0
H.S. Diplomas (#)	177	n/a	n/a	n/a	n/a	n/a

Fairfield County

Fairfield County SD

Drawer 622 • Winnsboro, SC 29180-0622
(803) 635-4607 • http://www.fairfield.k12.sc.us
Grade Span: PK-12; **Agency Type:** 1
Schools: 9
5 Primary; 2 Middle; 2 High; 0 Other Level
8 Regular; 0 Special Education; 1 Vocational; 0 Alternative
0 Magnet; 0 Charter; 5 Title I Eligible; 5 School-wide Title I
Students: 3,610 (49.5% male; 50.5% female)
Individual Education Program: 763 (21.1%);
English Language Learner: 3 (0.1%); Migrant: 30 (0.8%)
Eligible for Free Lunch Program: 2,380 (65.9%)
Eligible for Reduced-Price Lunch Program: 434 (12.0%)
Teachers: 285.4 (12.6 to 1)
Librarians/Media Specialists: 9.0 (401.1 to 1)
Guidance Counselors: 13.0 (277.7 to 1)
Current Spending: ($ per student per year):
Total: $8,702; Instruction: $4,696; Support Services: $3,548

Enrollment, Drop-out Rates and Diploma Recipients by Race/Ethnicity

Category	Total	White	Black	Asian	AIAN	Hisp.
Enrollment (%)	100.0	12.5	86.0	0.2	0.0	1.2
Drop-out Rate (%)	3.0	6.3	2.6	0.0	0.0	0.0
H.S. Diplomas (#)	159	n/a	n/a	n/a	n/a	n/a

Florence County

Florence County SD 01

319 S Dargan St • Florence, SC 29506-2538
(843) 669-4141 • http://www.fsd1.org
Grade Span: PK-12; **Agency Type:** 1
Schools: 20
12 Primary; 4 Middle; 4 High; 0 Other Level
19 Regular; 0 Special Education; 1 Vocational; 0 Alternative

0 Magnet; 0 Charter; 12 Title I Eligible; 12 School-wide Title I
Students: 14,783 (50.7% male; 49.3% female)
Individual Education Program: 2,342 (15.8%);
English Language Learner: 69 (0.5%); Migrant: 1 (<0.1%)
Eligible for Free Lunch Program: 6,368 (43.1%)
Eligible for Reduced-Price Lunch Program: 1,054 (7.1%)
Teachers: 947.0 (15.6 to 1)
Librarians/Media Specialists: 22.0 (672.0 to 1)
Guidance Counselors: 30.0 (492.8 to 1)
Current Spending: ($ per student per year):
Total: $6,213; Instruction: $3,812; Support Services: $2,063
Enrollment, Drop-out Rates and Diploma Recipients by Race/Ethnicity

Category	Total	White	Black	Asian	AIAN	Hisp.
Enrollment (%)	100.0	45.7	51.9	1.2	0.1	0.9
Drop-out Rate (%)	3.9	2.9	5.0	0.0	12.5	3.4
H.S. Diplomas (#)	721	n/a	n/a	n/a	n/a	n/a

Florence County SD 03
Drawer 1389 • Lake City, SC 29560-1389
(843) 394-8652 • http://www.florence3.k12.sc.us
Grade Span: PK-12; **Agency Type:** 1
Schools: 8
5 Primary; 2 Middle; 1 High; 0 Other Level
8 Regular; 0 Special Education; 0 Vocational; 0 Alternative
0 Magnet; 0 Charter; 7 Title I Eligible; 7 School-wide Title I
Students: 4,138 (52.4% male; 47.6% female)
Individual Education Program: 893 (21.6%);
English Language Learner: 15 (0.4%); Migrant: 8 (0.2%)
Eligible for Free Lunch Program: 2,945 (71.2%)
Eligible for Reduced-Price Lunch Program: 207 (5.0%)
Teachers: 286.2 (14.5 to 1)
Librarians/Media Specialists: 7.0 (591.1 to 1)
Guidance Counselors: 9.0 (459.8 to 1)
Current Spending: ($ per student per year):
Total: $6,478; Instruction: $3,553; Support Services: $2,474
Enrollment, Drop-out Rates and Diploma Recipients by Race/Ethnicity

Category	Total	White	Black	Asian	AIAN	Hisp.
Enrollment (%)	100.0	32.6	66.2	0.2	0.0	0.8
Drop-out Rate (%)	1.3	1.0	1.5	n/a	n/a	0.0
H.S. Diplomas (#)	193	n/a	n/a	n/a	n/a	n/a

Florence County SD 05
PO Box 98 • Johnsonville, SC 29555-0098
(843) 386-2358
Grade Span: PK-12; **Agency Type:** 1
Schools: 3
1 Primary; 1 Middle; 1 High; 0 Other Level
3 Regular; 0 Special Education; 0 Vocational; 0 Alternative
0 Magnet; 0 Charter; 2 Title I Eligible; 2 School-wide Title I
Students: 1,541 (51.8% male; 48.2% female)
Individual Education Program: 337 (21.9%);
English Language Learner: 6 (0.4%); Migrant: 0 (0.0%)
Eligible for Free Lunch Program: 702 (45.6%)
Eligible for Reduced-Price Lunch Program: 101 (6.6%)
Teachers: 101.7 (15.2 to 1)
Librarians/Media Specialists: 3.0 (513.7 to 1)
Guidance Counselors: 3.0 (513.7 to 1)
Current Spending: ($ per student per year):
Total: $6,488; Instruction: $3,781; Support Services: $2,297
Enrollment, Drop-out Rates and Diploma Recipients by Race/Ethnicity

Category	Total	White	Black	Asian	AIAN	Hisp.
Enrollment (%)	100.0	68.0	31.0	0.3	0.0	0.7
Drop-out Rate (%)	6.8	4.9	11.5	n/a	n/a	100.0
H.S. Diplomas (#)	62	n/a	n/a	n/a	n/a	n/a

Georgetown County

Georgetown County SD
624 Front St • Georgetown, SC 29440-3624
(843) 546-2561 • http://www.gcsd.k12.sc.us
Grade Span: PK-12; **Agency Type:** 1
Schools: 17
9 Primary; 4 Middle; 4 High; 0 Other Level
17 Regular; 0 Special Education; 0 Vocational; 0 Alternative
0 Magnet; 0 Charter; 9 Title I Eligible; 9 School-wide Title I
Students: 10,418 (51.3% male; 48.7% female)
Individual Education Program: 1,821 (17.5%);
English Language Learner: 95 (0.9%); Migrant: 0 (0.0%)
Eligible for Free Lunch Program: 5,490 (52.7%)
Eligible for Reduced-Price Lunch Program: 843 (8.1%)
Teachers: 773.8 (13.5 to 1)
Librarians/Media Specialists: 18.0 (578.8 to 1)
Guidance Counselors: 26.4 (394.6 to 1)
Current Spending: ($ per student per year):
Total: $7,364; Instruction: $4,172; Support Services: $2,802
Enrollment, Drop-out Rates and Diploma Recipients by Race/Ethnicity

Category	Total	White	Black	Asian	AIAN	Hisp.
Enrollment (%)	100.0	42.6	55.6	0.4	0.1	1.2
Drop-out Rate (%)	1.5	1.9	1.2	0.0	n/a	5.6
H.S. Diplomas (#)	486	n/a	n/a	n/a	n/a	n/a

Greenville County

Greenville County SD
Box 2848 301 Camperdown Way • Greenville, SC 29602-2848
(864) 241-3457 • http://www.greenville.k12.sc.us
Grade Span: PK-12; **Agency Type:** 1
Schools: 94
54 Primary; 18 Middle; 19 High; 3 Other Level
88 Regular; 2 Special Education; 4 Vocational; 0 Alternative
12 Magnet; 3 Charter; 16 Title I Eligible; 15 School-wide Title I
Students: 63,270 (51.2% male; 48.8% female)
Individual Education Program: 10,363 (16.4%);
English Language Learner: 246 (0.4%); Migrant: 16 (<0.1%)
Eligible for Free Lunch Program: 18,790 (29.7%)
Eligible for Reduced-Price Lunch Program: 4,047 (6.4%)
Teachers: 4,058.1 (15.6 to 1)
Librarians/Media Specialists: 97.0 (652.3 to 1)
Guidance Counselors: 138.7 (456.2 to 1)
Current Spending: ($ per student per year):
Total: $6,030; Instruction: $3,658; Support Services: $1,990
Enrollment, Drop-out Rates and Diploma Recipients by Race/Ethnicity

Category	Total	White	Black	Asian	AIAN	Hisp.
Enrollment (%)	100.0	64.7	28.2	1.6	0.1	5.2
Drop-out Rate (%)	2.2	2.0	2.9	0.7	0.0	2.0
H.S. Diplomas (#)	2,934	n/a	n/a	n/a	n/a	n/a

Greenwood County

Greenwood 50 County SD
Box 248 • Greenwood, SC 29648-0248
(864) 223-4348 • http://www.gwd50.k12.sc.us
Grade Span: PK-12; **Agency Type:** 1
Schools: 15
10 Primary; 3 Middle; 2 High; 0 Other Level
15 Regular; 0 Special Education; 0 Vocational; 0 Alternative
0 Magnet; 0 Charter; 9 Title I Eligible; 9 School-wide Title I
Students: 9,478 (50.1% male; 49.9% female)
Individual Education Program: 1,686 (17.8%);
English Language Learner: 310 (3.3%); Migrant: 33 (0.3%)
Eligible for Free Lunch Program: 3,873 (40.9%)
Eligible for Reduced-Price Lunch Program: 680 (7.2%)
Teachers: 638.7 (14.8 to 1)
Librarians/Media Specialists: 15.0 (631.9 to 1)
Guidance Counselors: 23.0 (412.1 to 1)
Current Spending: ($ per student per year):
Total: $5,998; Instruction: $3,736; Support Services: $1,932
Enrollment, Drop-out Rates and Diploma Recipients by Race/Ethnicity

Category	Total	White	Black	Asian	AIAN	Hisp.
Enrollment (%)	100.0	50.1	44.1	1.1	0.0	4.6
Drop-out Rate (%)	4.2	2.5	6.2	0.0	0.0	6.8
H.S. Diplomas (#)	427	n/a	n/a	n/a	n/a	n/a

Greenwood 52 County SD
605 Johnston Rd • Ninety Six, SC 29666-1149
(843) 543-3100 • http://www.ninetysix.k12.sc.us
Grade Span: PK-12; **Agency Type:** 1
Schools: 4
2 Primary; 1 Middle; 1 High; 0 Other Level
4 Regular; 0 Special Education; 0 Vocational; 0 Alternative
0 Magnet; 0 Charter; 1 Title I Eligible; 0 School-wide Title I
Students: 1,720 (51.2% male; 48.8% female)
Individual Education Program: 234 (13.6%);
English Language Learner: 0 (0.0%); Migrant: 0 (0.0%)
Eligible for Free Lunch Program: 479 (27.8%)
Eligible for Reduced-Price Lunch Program: 154 (9.0%)
Teachers: 110.6 (15.6 to 1)
Librarians/Media Specialists: 4.0 (430.0 to 1)
Guidance Counselors: 4.0 (430.0 to 1)
Current Spending: ($ per student per year):
Total: $5,571; Instruction: $3,509; Support Services: $1,754
Enrollment, Drop-out Rates and Diploma Recipients by Race/Ethnicity

Category	Total	White	Black	Asian	AIAN	Hisp.
Enrollment (%)	100.0	74.3	24.9	0.3	0.2	0.3
Drop-out Rate (%)	1.5	1.8	0.7	n/a	n/a	0.0
H.S. Diplomas (#)	91	n/a	n/a	n/a	n/a	n/a

Hampton County

Hampton 1 County SD

Box 177 • Hampton, SC 29924-0177
(803) 943-4576
Grade Span: PK-12; **Agency Type:** 1
Schools: 7
5 Primary; 1 Middle; 1 High; 0 Other Level
7 Regular; 0 Special Education; 0 Vocational; 0 Alternative
0 Magnet; 0 Charter; 5 Title I Eligible; 5 School-wide Title I
Students: 2,829 (51.7% male; 48.3% female)
Individual Education Program: 394 (13.9%);
English Language Learner: 1 (<0.1%); Migrant: 0 (0.0%)
Eligible for Free Lunch Program: 1,431 (50.6%)
Eligible for Reduced-Price Lunch Program: 371 (13.1%)
Teachers: 180.2 (15.7 to 1)
Librarians/Media Specialists: 5.5 (514.4 to 1)
Guidance Counselors: 7.5 (377.2 to 1)
Current Spending: ($ per student per year):
Total: $6,039; Instruction: $3,708; Support Services: $1,916
Enrollment, Drop-out Rates and Diploma Recipients by Race/Ethnicity

Category	Total	White	Black	Asian	AIAN	Hisp.
Enrollment (%)	100.0	42.6	56.7	0.4	0.0	0.3
Drop-out Rate (%)	5.4	4.1	6.1	n/a	n/a	50.0
H.S. Diplomas (#)	104	n/a	n/a	n/a	n/a	n/a

Hampton 2 County SD

Box 1028 • Estill, SC 29918-1028
(803) 625-2875 • http://www.hampton2.k12.sc.us
Grade Span: PK-12; **Agency Type:** 1
Schools: 3
1 Primary; 1 Middle; 1 High; 0 Other Level
3 Regular; 0 Special Education; 0 Vocational; 0 Alternative
0 Magnet; 0 Charter; 3 Title I Eligible; 3 School-wide Title I
Students: 1,512 (51.1% male; 48.9% female)
Individual Education Program: 271 (17.9%);
English Language Learner: 18 (1.2%); Migrant: 6 (0.4%)
Eligible for Free Lunch Program: 1,207 (79.8%)
Eligible for Reduced-Price Lunch Program: 117 (7.7%)
Teachers: 105.0 (14.4 to 1)
Librarians/Media Specialists: 3.0 (504.0 to 1)
Guidance Counselors: 4.4 (343.6 to 1)
Current Spending: ($ per student per year):
Total: $7,453; Instruction: $3,760; Support Services: $3,186
Enrollment, Drop-out Rates and Diploma Recipients by Race/Ethnicity

Category	Total	White	Black	Asian	AIAN	Hisp.
Enrollment (%)	100.0	2.1	95.2	0.1	0.0	2.5
Drop-out Rate (%)	3.9	16.7	3.7	n/a	n/a	n/a
H.S. Diplomas (#)	68	n/a	n/a	n/a	n/a	n/a

Horry County

Horry County SD

1600 Horry St • Conway, SC 29527-4100
(843) 248-2206 • http://www.hcs.k12.sc.us
Grade Span: PK-12; **Agency Type:** 1
Schools: 46
23 Primary; 11 Middle; 12 High; 0 Other Level
43 Regular; 0 Special Education; 3 Vocational; 0 Alternative
0 Magnet; 0 Charter; 25 Title I Eligible; 25 School-wide Title I
Students: 30,826 (51.3% male; 48.7% female)
Individual Education Program: 5,247 (17.0%);
English Language Learner: 493 (1.6%); Migrant: 9 (<0.1%)
Eligible for Free Lunch Program: 14,884 (48.3%)
Eligible for Reduced-Price Lunch Program: 2,053 (6.7%)
Teachers: 2,024.8 (15.2 to 1)
Librarians/Media Specialists: 44.0 (700.6 to 1)
Guidance Counselors: 74.0 (416.6 to 1)
Current Spending: ($ per student per year):
Total: $6,829; Instruction: $4,045; Support Services: $2,397
Enrollment, Drop-out Rates and Diploma Recipients by Race/Ethnicity

Category	Total	White	Black	Asian	AIAN	Hisp.
Enrollment (%)	100.0	69.0	26.3	1.0	0.3	3.1
Drop-out Rate (%)	1.9	1.8	2.2	0.0	0.0	3.5
H.S. Diplomas (#)	1,335	n/a	n/a	n/a	n/a	n/a

Jasper County

Jasper County SD

Box 848 • Ridgeland, SC 29936-0848
(843) 726-7200
Grade Span: PK-12; **Agency Type:** 1
Schools: 4
2 Primary; 1 Middle; 1 High; 0 Other Level
4 Regular; 0 Special Education; 0 Vocational; 0 Alternative
0 Magnet; 0 Charter; 3 Title I Eligible; 3 School-wide Title I
Students: 3,147 (52.4% male; 47.6% female)
Individual Education Program: 398 (12.6%);
English Language Learner: 193 (6.1%); Migrant: 11 (0.3%)
Eligible for Free Lunch Program: 1,867 (59.3%)
Eligible for Reduced-Price Lunch Program: 302 (9.6%)
Teachers: 200.5 (15.7 to 1)
Librarians/Media Specialists: 4.0 (786.8 to 1)
Guidance Counselors: 7.5 (419.6 to 1)
Current Spending: ($ per student per year):
Total: $6,484; Instruction: $3,607; Support Services: $2,453
Enrollment, Drop-out Rates and Diploma Recipients by Race/Ethnicity

Category	Total	White	Black	Asian	AIAN	Hisp.
Enrollment (%)	100.0	13.2	76.3	0.2	0.0	10.2
Drop-out Rate (%)	0.6	1.5	0.5	0.0	0.0	0.0
H.S. Diplomas (#)	85	n/a	n/a	n/a	n/a	n/a

Kershaw County

Kershaw County SD

1301 Dubose Court • Camden, SC 29020-3799
(803) 432-8416 • http://www.kershaw.k12.sc.us
Grade Span: PK-12; **Agency Type:** 1
Schools: 19
12 Primary; 3 Middle; 4 High; 0 Other Level
18 Regular; 0 Special Education; 1 Vocational; 0 Alternative
0 Magnet; 0 Charter; 8 Title I Eligible; 8 School-wide Title I
Students: 10,079 (51.6% male; 48.4% female)
Individual Education Program: 1,342 (13.3%);
English Language Learner: 63 (0.6%); Migrant: 0 (0.0%)
Eligible for Free Lunch Program: 3,873 (38.4%)
Eligible for Reduced-Price Lunch Program: 932 (9.2%)
Teachers: 642.5 (15.7 to 1)
Librarians/Media Specialists: 19.5 (516.9 to 1)
Guidance Counselors: 25.0 (403.2 to 1)
Current Spending: ($ per student per year):
Total: $6,521; Instruction: $3,749; Support Services: $2,353
Enrollment, Drop-out Rates and Diploma Recipients by Race/Ethnicity

Category	Total	White	Black	Asian	AIAN	Hisp.
Enrollment (%)	100.0	64.5	33.0	0.3	0.1	2.0
Drop-out Rate (%)	3.8	4.0	3.6	0.0	0.0	0.0
H.S. Diplomas (#)	525	n/a	n/a	n/a	n/a	n/a

Lancaster County

Lancaster County SD

300 S Catawba St • Lancaster, SC 29721-0130
(803) 286-6972
Grade Span: PK-12; **Agency Type:** 1
Schools: 20
11 Primary; 4 Middle; 5 High; 0 Other Level
19 Regular; 0 Special Education; 1 Vocational; 0 Alternative
0 Magnet; 1 Charter; 9 Title I Eligible; 9 School-wide Title I
Students: 11,352 (52.1% male; 47.9% female)
Individual Education Program: 1,597 (14.1%);
English Language Learner: 105 (0.9%); Migrant: 0 (0.0%)
Eligible for Free Lunch Program: 4,488 (39.5%)
Eligible for Reduced-Price Lunch Program: 924 (8.1%)
Teachers: 724.2 (15.7 to 1)
Librarians/Media Specialists: 18.0 (630.7 to 1)
Guidance Counselors: 24.0 (473.0 to 1)
Current Spending: ($ per student per year):
Total: $6,133; Instruction: $3,750; Support Services: $2,042
Enrollment, Drop-out Rates and Diploma Recipients by Race/Ethnicity

Category	Total	White	Black	Asian	AIAN	Hisp.
Enrollment (%)	100.0	62.8	35.1	0.2	0.2	1.7
Drop-out Rate (%)	8.0	6.9	9.8	8.3	25.0	18.2
H.S. Diplomas (#)	503	n/a	n/a	n/a	n/a	n/a

Laurens County

Laurens County SD 55

1029 W Main St • Laurens, SC 29360-2654
(864) 984-3568 • http://www.laurens55.k12.sc.us
Grade Span: PK-12; **Agency Type:** 1
Schools: 11
7 Primary; 3 Middle; 1 High; 0 Other Level
11 Regular; 0 Special Education; 0 Vocational; 0 Alternative
0 Magnet; 0 Charter; 5 Title I Eligible; 5 School-wide Title I
Students: 6,242 (51.7% male; 48.3% female)
Individual Education Program: 1,259 (20.2%);
English Language Learner: 114 (1.8%); Migrant: 18 (0.3%)
Eligible for Free Lunch Program: 2,821 (45.2%)
Eligible for Reduced-Price Lunch Program: 524 (8.4%)
Teachers: 384.5 (16.2 to 1)

Librarians/Media Specialists: 11.0 (567.5 to 1)
Guidance Counselors: 15.0 (416.1 to 1)
Current Spending: ($ per student per year):
Total: $5,895; Instruction: $3,467; Support Services: $2,120
Enrollment, Drop-out Rates and Diploma Recipients by Race/Ethnicity

Category	Total	White	Black	Asian	AIAN	Hisp.
Enrollment (%)	100.0	61.3	35.1	0.1	0.0	3.2
Drop-out Rate (%)	3.8	3.7	4.1	n/a	n/a	0.0
H.S. Diplomas (#)	229	n/a	n/a	n/a	n/a	n/a

Laurens County SD 56

600 E Florida St • Clinton, SC 29325-2603
(843) 833-0800 • http://www.laurens56.k12.sc.us
Grade Span: PK-12; **Agency Type:** 1
Schools: 7
4 Primary; 2 Middle; 1 High; 0 Other Level
7 Regular; 0 Special Education; 0 Vocational; 0 Alternative
0 Magnet; 0 Charter; 5 Title I Eligible; 5 School-wide Title I
Students: 3,481 (51.6% male; 48.4% female)
Individual Education Program: 750 (21.5%);
English Language Learner: 26 (0.7%); Migrant: 0 (0.0%)
Eligible for Free Lunch Program: 1,818 (52.2%)
Eligible for Reduced-Price Lunch Program: 345 (9.9%)
Teachers: 226.3 (15.4 to 1)
Librarians/Media Specialists: 7.0 (497.3 to 1)
Guidance Counselors: 8.0 (435.1 to 1)
Current Spending: ($ per student per year):
Total: $6,122; Instruction: $3,564; Support Services: $2,162
Enrollment, Drop-out Rates and Diploma Recipients by Race/Ethnicity

Category	Total	White	Black	Asian	AIAN	Hisp.
Enrollment (%)	100.0	55.5	43.0	0.3	0.1	1.0
Drop-out Rate (%)	3.1	2.6	3.8	0.0	n/a	0.0
H.S. Diplomas (#)	175	n/a	n/a	n/a	n/a	n/a

Lee County

Lee County SD

PO Box 507 • Bishopville, SC 29010-0507
(803) 484-5327 • http://www.lee.k12.sc.us
Grade Span: PK-12; **Agency Type:** 1
Schools: 7
3 Primary; 2 Middle; 2 High; 0 Other Level
6 Regular; 0 Special Education; 1 Vocational; 0 Alternative
0 Magnet; 0 Charter; 5 Title I Eligible; 5 School-wide Title I
Students: 2,952 (50.8% male; 49.2% female)
Individual Education Program: 452 (15.3%);
English Language Learner: 11 (0.4%); Migrant: 0 (0.0%)
Eligible for Free Lunch Program: 2,201 (74.6%)
Eligible for Reduced-Price Lunch Program: 227 (7.7%)
Teachers: 230.5 (12.8 to 1)
Librarians/Media Specialists: 6.0 (492.0 to 1)
Guidance Counselors: 9.5 (310.7 to 1)
Current Spending: ($ per student per year):
Total: $7,475; Instruction: $4,328; Support Services: $2,593
Enrollment, Drop-out Rates and Diploma Recipients by Race/Ethnicity

Category	Total	White	Black	Asian	AIAN	Hisp.
Enrollment (%)	100.0	5.8	93.1	0.1	0.0	0.9
Drop-out Rate (%)	8.6	14.0	8.3	n/a	n/a	0.0
H.S. Diplomas (#)	119	n/a	n/a	n/a	n/a	n/a

Lexington County

Lexington County SD 01

PO Box 1869 • Lexington, SC 29072-1869
(803) 359-4178 • http://www.lexington1.net
Grade Span: PK-12; **Agency Type:** 1
Schools: 20
10 Primary; 5 Middle; 5 High; 0 Other Level
19 Regular; 0 Special Education; 1 Vocational; 0 Alternative
0 Magnet; 0 Charter; 5 Title I Eligible; 1 School-wide Title I
Students: 18,748 (51.6% male; 48.4% female)
Individual Education Program: 2,840 (15.1%);
English Language Learner: 122 (0.7%); Migrant: 0 (0.0%)
Eligible for Free Lunch Program: 3,980 (21.2%)
Eligible for Reduced-Price Lunch Program: 1,295 (6.9%)
Teachers: 1,293.4 (14.5 to 1)
Librarians/Media Specialists: 23.0 (815.1 to 1)
Guidance Counselors: 41.0 (457.3 to 1)
Current Spending: ($ per student per year):
Total: $6,684; Instruction: $4,139; Support Services: $2,260
Enrollment, Drop-out Rates and Diploma Recipients by Race/Ethnicity

Category	Total	White	Black	Asian	AIAN	Hisp.
Enrollment (%)	100.0	88.1	7.9	1.3	0.4	2.0
Drop-out Rate (%)	1.8	1.8	2.0	0.0	0.0	0.0
H.S. Diplomas (#)	906	n/a	n/a	n/a	n/a	n/a

Lexington County SD 02

715 Ninth St • W Columbia, SC 29169-7169
(803) 739-4017
Grade Span: PK-12; **Agency Type:** 1
Schools: 16
10 Primary; 4 Middle; 2 High; 0 Other Level
16 Regular; 0 Special Education; 0 Vocational; 0 Alternative
0 Magnet; 0 Charter; 8 Title I Eligible; 8 School-wide Title I
Students: 9,171 (51.0% male; 49.0% female)
Individual Education Program: 1,376 (15.0%);
English Language Learner: 131 (1.4%); Migrant: 1 (<0.1%)
Eligible for Free Lunch Program: 3,393 (37.0%)
Eligible for Reduced-Price Lunch Program: 748 (8.2%)
Teachers: 650.0 (14.1 to 1)
Librarians/Media Specialists: 18.0 (509.5 to 1)
Guidance Counselors: 23.5 (390.3 to 1)
Current Spending: ($ per student per year):
Total: $7,194; Instruction: $4,386; Support Services: $2,464
Enrollment, Drop-out Rates and Diploma Recipients by Race/Ethnicity

Category	Total	White	Black	Asian	AIAN	Hisp.
Enrollment (%)	100.0	62.6	32.7	1.2	0.2	2.9
Drop-out Rate (%)	2.9	3.3	1.9	2.9	n/a	3.4
H.S. Diplomas (#)	459	n/a	n/a	n/a	n/a	n/a

Lexington County SD 03

121 W Columbia Ave • Batesburg, SC 29006-2124
(803) 532-4423 • http://www.lex3.k12.sc.us
Grade Span: PK-12; **Agency Type:** 1
Schools: 4
2 Primary; 1 Middle; 1 High; 0 Other Level
4 Regular; 0 Special Education; 0 Vocational; 0 Alternative
0 Magnet; 0 Charter; 3 Title I Eligible; 3 School-wide Title I
Students: 2,392 (52.1% male; 47.9% female)
Individual Education Program: 407 (17.0%);
English Language Learner: 6 (0.3%); Migrant: 0 (0.0%)
Eligible for Free Lunch Program: 1,075 (44.9%)
Eligible for Reduced-Price Lunch Program: 204 (8.5%)
Teachers: 154.9 (15.4 to 1)
Librarians/Media Specialists: 4.0 (598.0 to 1)
Guidance Counselors: 4.3 (556.3 to 1)
Current Spending: ($ per student per year):
Total: $7,606; Instruction: $4,282; Support Services: $2,878
Enrollment, Drop-out Rates and Diploma Recipients by Race/Ethnicity

Category	Total	White	Black	Asian	AIAN	Hisp.
Enrollment (%)	100.0	54.3	43.8	0.3	0.1	1.3
Drop-out Rate (%)	2.9	1.9	4.8	n/a	0.0	0.0
H.S. Diplomas (#)	125	n/a	n/a	n/a	n/a	n/a

Lexington County SD 04

Box 569 • Swansea, SC 29160-0569
(803) 568-3886 • http://www.lex4.k12.sc.us
Grade Span: PK-12; **Agency Type:** 1
Schools: 6
3 Primary; 2 Middle; 1 High; 0 Other Level
6 Regular; 0 Special Education; 0 Vocational; 0 Alternative
0 Magnet; 0 Charter; 4 Title I Eligible; 0 School-wide Title I
Students: 3,671 (52.6% male; 47.4% female)
Individual Education Program: 669 (18.2%);
English Language Learner: 6 (0.2%); Migrant: 0 (0.0%)
Eligible for Free Lunch Program: 1,932 (52.6%)
Eligible for Reduced-Price Lunch Program: 337 (9.2%)
Teachers: 224.7 (16.3 to 1)
Librarians/Media Specialists: 5.0 (734.2 to 1)
Guidance Counselors: 8.0 (458.9 to 1)
Current Spending: ($ per student per year):
Total: $6,165; Instruction: $3,510; Support Services: $2,281
Enrollment, Drop-out Rates and Diploma Recipients by Race/Ethnicity

Category	Total	White	Black	Asian	AIAN	Hisp.
Enrollment (%)	100.0	76.9	20.8	0.3	0.0	2.0
Drop-out Rate (%)	6.4	6.8	5.6	0.0	0.0	0.0
H.S. Diplomas (#)	108	n/a	n/a	n/a	n/a	n/a

Lexington County SD 05

Box 938 • Ballentine, SC 29002-0938
(803) 732-8000 • http://www.lex5.k12.sc.us
Grade Span: PK-12; **Agency Type:** 1
Schools: 18
11 Primary; 4 Middle; 3 High; 0 Other Level
18 Regular; 0 Special Education; 0 Vocational; 0 Alternative
0 Magnet; 0 Charter; 4 Title I Eligible; 0 School-wide Title I
Students: 15,531 (51.7% male; 48.3% female)
Individual Education Program: 2,052 (13.2%);
English Language Learner: 139 (0.9%); Migrant: 0 (0.0%)
Eligible for Free Lunch Program: 2,220 (14.3%)
Eligible for Reduced-Price Lunch Program: 699 (4.5%)

Teachers: 1,094.0 (14.2 to 1)
Librarians/Media Specialists: 21.0 (739.6 to 1)
Guidance Counselors: 37.0 (419.8 to 1)
Current Spending: ($ per student per year):
Total: $6,920; Instruction: $4,140; Support Services: $2,464
Enrollment, Drop-out Rates and Diploma Recipients by Race/Ethnicity

Category	Total	White	Black	Asian	AIAN	Hisp.
Enrollment (%)	100.0	71.2	24.9	2.0	0.1	1.3
Drop-out Rate (%)	2.1	1.8	3.2	0.8	0.0	2.9
H.S. Diplomas (#)	1,002	n/a	n/a	n/a	n/a	n/a

Marion County

Marion County SD 01

616 Northside Ave • Marion, SC 29571-2399
(843) 423-1811 • http://www.marion1.k12.sc.us
Grade Span: PK-12; **Agency Type:** 1
Schools: 4
2 Primary; 1 Middle; 1 High; 0 Other Level
4 Regular; 0 Special Education; 0 Vocational; 0 Alternative
0 Magnet; 0 Charter; 4 Title I Eligible; 4 School-wide Title I
Students: 3,254 (52.0% male; 48.0% female)
Individual Education Program: 628 (19.3%);
English Language Learner: 0 (0.0%); Migrant: 0 (0.0%)
Eligible for Free Lunch Program: 2,171 (66.7%)
Eligible for Reduced-Price Lunch Program: 225 (6.9%)
Teachers: 201.2 (16.2 to 1)
Librarians/Media Specialists: 5.0 (650.8 to 1)
Guidance Counselors: 8.0 (406.8 to 1)
Current Spending: ($ per student per year):
Total: $6,086; Instruction: $3,811; Support Services: $1,855
Enrollment, Drop-out Rates and Diploma Recipients by Race/Ethnicity

Category	Total	White	Black	Asian	AIAN	Hisp.
Enrollment (%)	100.0	26.5	72.5	0.3	0.2	0.5
Drop-out Rate (%)	2.9	2.2	3.3	0.0	0.0	n/a
H.S. Diplomas (#)	170	n/a	n/a	n/a	n/a	n/a

Marion County SD 02

Box 689 • Mullins, SC 29574-0689
(843) 464-3700 • http://www.marion2.k12.sc.us
Grade Span: PK-12; **Agency Type:** 1
Schools: 5
2 Primary; 2 Middle; 1 High; 0 Other Level
5 Regular; 0 Special Education; 0 Vocational; 0 Alternative
0 Magnet; 0 Charter; 3 Title I Eligible; 3 School-wide Title I
Students: 2,299 (50.9% male; 49.1% female)
Individual Education Program: 518 (22.5%);
English Language Learner: 5 (0.2%); Migrant: 0 (0.0%)
Eligible for Free Lunch Program: 1,385 (60.2%)
Eligible for Reduced-Price Lunch Program: 165 (7.2%)
Teachers: 139.0 (16.5 to 1)
Librarians/Media Specialists: 4.0 (574.8 to 1)
Guidance Counselors: 7.0 (328.4 to 1)
Current Spending: ($ per student per year):
Total: $6,324; Instruction: $3,782; Support Services: $2,006
Enrollment, Drop-out Rates and Diploma Recipients by Race/Ethnicity

Category	Total	White	Black	Asian	AIAN	Hisp.
Enrollment (%)	100.0	26.3	72.7	0.0	0.0	0.8
Drop-out Rate (%)	3.5	3.6	3.4	0.0	0.0	0.0
H.S. Diplomas (#)	117	n/a	n/a	n/a	n/a	n/a

Marlboro County

Marlboro County SD

PO Box 947 • Bennettsville, SC 29512-4002
(843) 479-4016
Grade Span: PK-12; **Agency Type:** 1
Schools: 9
6 Primary; 2 Middle; 1 High; 0 Other Level
9 Regular; 0 Special Education; 0 Vocational; 0 Alternative
0 Magnet; 0 Charter; 7 Title I Eligible; 7 School-wide Title I
Students: 5,159 (51.6% male; 48.4% female)
Individual Education Program: 767 (14.9%);
English Language Learner: 0 (0.0%); Migrant: 0 (0.0%)
Eligible for Free Lunch Program: 3,395 (65.8%)
Eligible for Reduced-Price Lunch Program: 629 (12.2%)
Teachers: 335.0 (15.4 to 1)
Librarians/Media Specialists: 9.0 (573.2 to 1)
Guidance Counselors: 11.0 (469.0 to 1)
Current Spending: ($ per student per year):
Total: $5,612; Instruction: $3,233; Support Services: $1,990
Enrollment, Drop-out Rates and Diploma Recipients by Race/Ethnicity

Category	Total	White	Black	Asian	AIAN	Hisp.
Enrollment (%)	100.0	33.2	62.9	0.2	3.3	0.4
Drop-out Rate (%)	9.0	12.0	7.0	0.0	15.6	100.0
H.S. Diplomas (#)	207	n/a	n/a	n/a	n/a	n/a

Newberry County

Newberry County SD

Box 718 • Newberry, SC 29108-0718
(803) 321-2600 • http://www.newberry.k12.sc.us
Grade Span: PK-12; **Agency Type:** 1
Schools: 14
7 Primary; 3 Middle; 4 High; 0 Other Level
13 Regular; 0 Special Education; 1 Vocational; 0 Alternative
0 Magnet; 0 Charter; 7 Title I Eligible; 7 School-wide Title I
Students: 5,922 (52.0% male; 48.0% female)
Individual Education Program: 1,160 (19.6%);
English Language Learner: 214 (3.6%); Migrant: 102 (1.7%)
Eligible for Free Lunch Program: 2,922 (49.3%)
Eligible for Reduced-Price Lunch Program: 606 (10.2%)
Teachers: 451.8 (13.1 to 1)
Librarians/Media Specialists: 14.0 (423.0 to 1)
Guidance Counselors: 19.5 (303.7 to 1)
Current Spending: ($ per student per year):
Total: $7,154; Instruction: $4,152; Support Services: $2,598
Enrollment, Drop-out Rates and Diploma Recipients by Race/Ethnicity

Category	Total	White	Black	Asian	AIAN	Hisp.
Enrollment (%)	100.0	46.4	47.9	0.1	0.0	5.6
Drop-out Rate (%)	4.1	3.5	4.7	0.0	0.0	6.9
H.S. Diplomas (#)	268	n/a	n/a	n/a	n/a	n/a

Oconee County

Oconee County SD

PO Box 649 • Walhalla, SC 29691-0006
(843) 638-4029 • http://www.oconee.k12.sc.us
Grade Span: PK-12; **Agency Type:** 1
Schools: 21
11 Primary; 5 Middle; 5 High; 0 Other Level
20 Regular; 0 Special Education; 1 Vocational; 0 Alternative
0 Magnet; 0 Charter; 6 Title I Eligible; 6 School-wide Title I
Students: 10,684 (52.1% male; 47.9% female)
Individual Education Program: 2,162 (20.2%);
English Language Learner: 192 (1.8%); Migrant: 0 (0.0%)
Eligible for Free Lunch Program: 3,902 (36.5%)
Eligible for Reduced-Price Lunch Program: 1,066 (10.0%)
Teachers: 787.5 (13.6 to 1)
Librarians/Media Specialists: 20.0 (534.2 to 1)
Guidance Counselors: 26.5 (403.2 to 1)
Current Spending: ($ per student per year):
Total: $6,908; Instruction: $4,105; Support Services: $2,411
Enrollment, Drop-out Rates and Diploma Recipients by Race/Ethnicity

Category	Total	White	Black	Asian	AIAN	Hisp.
Enrollment (%)	100.0	81.4	13.0	0.5	0.2	4.9
Drop-out Rate (%)	1.9	1.8	1.8	3.6	0.0	5.2
H.S. Diplomas (#)	496	n/a	n/a	n/a	n/a	n/a

Orangeburg County

Orangeburg County SD 03

1515 Brant Avenue • Holly Hill, SC 29059
Mailing Address: PO Box 98 • Holly Hill, SC 29059
(803) 496-3288 • http://www.obg3.k12.sc.us
Grade Span: PK-12; **Agency Type:** 1
Schools: 7
4 Primary; 1 Middle; 2 High; 0 Other Level
7 Regular; 0 Special Education; 0 Vocational; 0 Alternative
0 Magnet; 0 Charter; 6 Title I Eligible; 6 School-wide Title I
Students: 3,800 (50.1% male; 49.9% female)
Individual Education Program: 695 (18.3%);
English Language Learner: 23 (0.6%); Migrant: 0 (0.0%)
Eligible for Free Lunch Program: 2,993 (78.8%)
Eligible for Reduced-Price Lunch Program: 320 (8.4%)
Teachers: 266.3 (14.3 to 1)
Librarians/Media Specialists: 7.0 (542.9 to 1)
Guidance Counselors: 12.0 (316.7 to 1)
Current Spending: ($ per student per year):
Total: $7,517; Instruction: $4,266; Support Services: $2,827
Enrollment, Drop-out Rates and Diploma Recipients by Race/Ethnicity

Category	Total	White	Black	Asian	AIAN	Hisp.
Enrollment (%)	100.0	10.1	88.8	0.1	0.1	1.1
Drop-out Rate (%)	9.3	18.8	8.4	0.0	0.0	0.0
H.S. Diplomas (#)	154	n/a	n/a	n/a	n/a	n/a

Orangeburg County SD 04

PO Box 69 • Cordova, SC 29039-0006
(803) 534-7420 • http://www.orangeburg4.com
Grade Span: PK-12; **Agency Type:** 1
Schools: 8
4 Primary; 1 Middle; 3 High; 0 Other Level
8 Regular; 0 Special Education; 0 Vocational; 0 Alternative
0 Magnet; 0 Charter; 7 Title I Eligible; 7 School-wide Title I
Students: 4,436 (50.6% male; 49.4% female)
Individual Education Program: 688 (15.5%);
English Language Learner: 3 (0.1%); Migrant: 3 (0.1%)
Eligible for Free Lunch Program: 2,511 (56.6%)
Eligible for Reduced-Price Lunch Program: 512 (11.5%)
Teachers: 286.9 (15.5 to 1)
Librarians/Media Specialists: 7.0 (633.7 to 1)
Guidance Counselors: 11.0 (403.3 to 1)
Current Spending: ($ per student per year):
Total: $6,841; Instruction: $4,121; Support Services: $2,233
Enrollment, Drop-out Rates and Diploma Recipients by Race/Ethnicity

Category	Total	White	Black	Asian	AIAN	Hisp.
Enrollment (%)	100.0	46.0	53.0	0.2	0.2	0.6
Drop-out Rate (%)	4.4	5.3	3.5	0.0	0.0	0.0
H.S. Diplomas (#)	193	n/a	n/a	n/a	n/a	n/a

Orangeburg County SD 05

578 Ellis Ave • Orangeburg, SC 29115-5022
(803) 534-5454 • http://www.orangeburg5.k12.sc.us
Grade Span: PK-12; **Agency Type:** 1
Schools: 14
8 Primary; 2 Middle; 2 High; 2 Other Level
13 Regular; 0 Special Education; 1 Vocational; 0 Alternative
0 Magnet; 0 Charter; 8 Title I Eligible; 8 School-wide Title I
Students: 7,909 (50.5% male; 49.5% female)
Individual Education Program: 1,356 (17.1%);
English Language Learner: 0 (0.0%); Migrant: 0 (0.0%)
Eligible for Free Lunch Program: 5,498 (69.5%)
Eligible for Reduced-Price Lunch Program: 737 (9.3%)
Teachers: 581.5 (13.6 to 1)
Librarians/Media Specialists: 15.0 (527.3 to 1)
Guidance Counselors: 21.0 (376.6 to 1)
Current Spending: ($ per student per year):
Total: $7,106; Instruction: $4,033; Support Services: $2,634
Enrollment, Drop-out Rates and Diploma Recipients by Race/Ethnicity

Category	Total	White	Black	Asian	AIAN	Hisp.
Enrollment (%)	100.0	9.7	89.0	0.6	0.0	0.6
Drop-out Rate (%)	3.3	1.8	3.6	0.0	0.0	0.0
H.S. Diplomas (#)	399	n/a	n/a	n/a	n/a	n/a

Pickens County

Pickens County SD

1348 Griffin Mill Rd • Easley, SC 29640-9808
(864) 855-8150 • http://www.pickens.k12.sc.us
Grade Span: PK-12; **Agency Type:** 1
Schools: 25
15 Primary; 5 Middle; 5 High; 0 Other Level
24 Regular; 0 Special Education; 1 Vocational; 0 Alternative
0 Magnet; 0 Charter; 8 Title I Eligible; 0 School-wide Title I
Students: 16,471 (50.7% male; 49.3% female)
Individual Education Program: 2,375 (14.4%);
English Language Learner: 170 (1.0%); Migrant: 1 (<0.1%)
Eligible for Free Lunch Program: 4,537 (27.5%)
Eligible for Reduced-Price Lunch Program: 1,376 (8.4%)
Teachers: 1,054.7 (15.6 to 1)
Librarians/Media Specialists: 27.0 (610.0 to 1)
Guidance Counselors: 36.2 (455.0 to 1)
Current Spending: ($ per student per year):
Total: $6,053; Instruction: $3,701; Support Services: $1,994
Enrollment, Drop-out Rates and Diploma Recipients by Race/Ethnicity

Category	Total	White	Black	Asian	AIAN	Hisp.
Enrollment (%)	100.0	88.0	9.1	0.8	0.1	1.9
Drop-out Rate (%)	4.7	4.8	5.1	0.0	0.0	2.2
H.S. Diplomas (#)	755	n/a	n/a	n/a	n/a	n/a

Richland County

Richland County SD 01

1616 Richland St • Columbia, SC 29201-2657
(803) 733-6041 • http://www.richlandone.org/
Grade Span: PK-12; **Agency Type:** 1
Schools: 48
28 Primary; 9 Middle; 8 High; 3 Other Level
44 Regular; 3 Special Education; 1 Vocational; 0 Alternative
0 Magnet; 0 Charter; 22 Title I Eligible; 22 School-wide Title I
Students: 27,393 (50.7% male; 49.3% female)
Individual Education Program: 3,976 (14.5%);
English Language Learner: 282 (1.0%); Migrant: 3 (<0.1%)
Eligible for Free Lunch Program: 14,473 (52.8%)
Eligible for Reduced-Price Lunch Program: 2,000 (7.3%)
Teachers: 2,040.1 (13.4 to 1)
Librarians/Media Specialists: 54.0 (507.3 to 1)
Guidance Counselors: 86.0 (318.5 to 1)
Current Spending: ($ per student per year):
Total: $8,223; Instruction: $4,810; Support Services: $3,064
Enrollment, Drop-out Rates and Diploma Recipients by Race/Ethnicity

Category	Total	White	Black	Asian	AIAN	Hisp.
Enrollment (%)	100.0	18.8	78.4	0.7	0.1	1.8
Drop-out Rate (%)	4.3	2.7	4.7	0.0	0.0	6.9
H.S. Diplomas (#)	1,178	n/a	n/a	n/a	n/a	n/a

Richland County SD 02

6831 Brookfield Rd • Columbia, SC 29206-2205
(803) 787-1910 • http://www.richland2.org/
Grade Span: PK-12; **Agency Type:** 1
Schools: 23
16 Primary; 2 Middle; 3 High; 0 Other Level
21 Regular; 0 Special Education; 0 Vocational; 0 Alternative
0 Magnet; 0 Charter; 7 Title I Eligible; 5 School-wide Title I
Students: 19,349 (50.4% male; 49.6% female)
Individual Education Program: 2,428 (12.5%);
English Language Learner: 202 (1.0%); Migrant: 0 (0.0%)
Eligible for Free Lunch Program: 4,935 (25.5%)
Eligible for Reduced-Price Lunch Program: 1,477 (7.6%)
Teachers: 1,274.8 (15.2 to 1)
Librarians/Media Specialists: 22.0 (879.5 to 1)
Guidance Counselors: 43.0 (450.0 to 1)
Current Spending: ($ per student per year):
Total: $6,768; Instruction: $4,158; Support Services: $2,341
Enrollment, Drop-out Rates and Diploma Recipients by Race/Ethnicity

Category	Total	White	Black	Asian	AIAN	Hisp.
Enrollment (%)	100.0	39.7	54.0	2.6	0.2	3.3
Drop-out Rate (%)	3.7	3.3	4.0	3.2	0.0	3.3
H.S. Diplomas (#)	958	n/a	n/a	n/a	n/a	n/a

Saluda County

Saluda County SD

404 N Wise Rd • Saluda, SC 29138-1024
(843) 445-8441 • http://www.saludak-12.org/
Grade Span: PK-12; **Agency Type:** 1
Schools: 5
3 Primary; 1 Middle; 1 High; 0 Other Level
5 Regular; 0 Special Education; 0 Vocational; 0 Alternative
0 Magnet; 0 Charter; 2 Title I Eligible; 2 School-wide Title I
Students: 2,196 (51.1% male; 48.9% female)
Individual Education Program: 422 (19.2%);
English Language Learner: 170 (7.7%); Migrant: 102 (4.6%)
Eligible for Free Lunch Program: 1,105 (50.3%)
Eligible for Reduced-Price Lunch Program: 192 (8.7%)
Teachers: 162.4 (13.5 to 1)
Librarians/Media Specialists: 4.0 (549.0 to 1)
Guidance Counselors: 8.0 (274.5 to 1)
Current Spending: ($ per student per year):
Total: $6,784; Instruction: $3,847; Support Services: $2,495
Enrollment, Drop-out Rates and Diploma Recipients by Race/Ethnicity

Category	Total	White	Black	Asian	AIAN	Hisp.
Enrollment (%)	100.0	49.8	39.3	0.0	0.0	10.9
Drop-out Rate (%)	3.6	2.9	4.3	n/a	n/a	6.7
H.S. Diplomas (#)	79	n/a	n/a	n/a	n/a	n/a

Spartanburg County

Spartanburg County SD 01

Box 218 • Campobello, SC 29322-0218
(864) 468-4542 • http://www.spartanburg1.k12.sc.us/
Grade Span: PK-12; **Agency Type:** 1
Schools: 9
5 Primary; 2 Middle; 2 High; 0 Other Level
9 Regular; 0 Special Education; 0 Vocational; 0 Alternative
0 Magnet; 0 Charter; 5 Title I Eligible; 0 School-wide Title I
Students: 4,529 (51.3% male; 48.7% female)
Individual Education Program: 817 (18.0%);
English Language Learner: 57 (1.3%); Migrant: 10 (0.2%)
Eligible for Free Lunch Program: 1,385 (30.6%)
Eligible for Reduced-Price Lunch Program: 421 (9.3%)
Teachers: 323.3 (14.0 to 1)
Librarians/Media Specialists: 8.0 (566.1 to 1)
Guidance Counselors: 13.5 (335.5 to 1)
Current Spending: ($ per student per year):
Total: $6,567; Instruction: $4,012; Support Services: $2,199

Enrollment, Drop-out Rates and Diploma Recipients by Race/Ethnicity

Category	Total	White	Black	Asian	AIAN	Hisp.
Enrollment (%)	100.0	83.4	12.4	1.6	0.2	2.3
Drop-out Rate (%)	1.4	1.7	0.0	0.0	n/a	0.0
H.S. Diplomas (#)	211	n/a	n/a	n/a	n/a	n/a

Spartanburg County SD 02

4606parris Bridge Rd • Spartanburg, SC 29316-6021
(843) 578-0128 • http://www.spartanburg2.k12.sc.us
Grade Span: PK-12; **Agency Type:** 1
Schools: 13
7 Primary; 3 Middle; 2 High; 1 Other Level
13 Regular; 0 Special Education; 0 Vocational; 0 Alternative
0 Magnet; 0 Charter; 4 Title I Eligible; 4 School-wide Title I
Students: 8,580 (51.4% male; 48.6% female)
Individual Education Program: 1,031 (12.0%);
English Language Learner: 313 (3.6%); Migrant: 82 (1.0%)
Eligible for Free Lunch Program: 2,343 (27.3%)
Eligible for Reduced-Price Lunch Program: 769 (9.0%)
Teachers: 476.4 (18.0 to 1)
Librarians/Media Specialists: 14.0 (612.9 to 1)
Guidance Counselors: 17.0 (504.7 to 1)
Current Spending: ($ per student per year):
Total: $5,481; Instruction: $3,338; Support Services: $1,830

Enrollment, Drop-out Rates and Diploma Recipients by Race/Ethnicity

Category	Total	White	Black	Asian	AIAN	Hisp.
Enrollment (%)	100.0	81.4	11.5	2.9	0.0	3.8
Drop-out Rate (%)	2.2	2.3	2.0	0.0	0.0	8.7
H.S. Diplomas (#)	409	n/a	n/a	n/a	n/a	n/a

Spartanburg County SD 03

Box 267 • Glendale, SC 29346-0267
(843) 579-8000 • http://www.spa3.K12.sc.us
Grade Span: PK-12; **Agency Type:** 1
Schools: 7
4 Primary; 2 Middle; 1 High; 0 Other Level
7 Regular; 0 Special Education; 0 Vocational; 0 Alternative
0 Magnet; 0 Charter; 4 Title I Eligible; 0 School-wide Title I
Students: 3,231 (50.1% male; 49.9% female)
Individual Education Program: 530 (16.4%);
English Language Learner: 64 (2.0%); Migrant: 0 (0.0%)
Eligible for Free Lunch Program: 1,267 (39.2%)
Eligible for Reduced-Price Lunch Program: 321 (9.9%)
Teachers: 233.0 (13.9 to 1)
Librarians/Media Specialists: 7.0 (461.6 to 1)
Guidance Counselors: 12.0 (269.3 to 1)
Current Spending: ($ per student per year):
Total: $8,584; Instruction: $4,344; Support Services: $3,861

Enrollment, Drop-out Rates and Diploma Recipients by Race/Ethnicity

Category	Total	White	Black	Asian	AIAN	Hisp.
Enrollment (%)	100.0	75.1	21.2	1.2	0.2	2.3
Drop-out Rate (%)	0.6	0.7	0.0	0.0	0.0	0.0
H.S. Diplomas (#)	161	n/a	n/a	n/a	n/a	n/a

Spartanburg County SD 04

118 Mcedco Rd • Woodruff, SC 29388-0669
(864) 476-3186
Grade Span: PK-12; **Agency Type:** 1
Schools: 4
2 Primary; 1 Middle; 1 High; 0 Other Level
4 Regular; 0 Special Education; 0 Vocational; 0 Alternative
0 Magnet; 0 Charter; 2 Title I Eligible; 0 School-wide Title I
Students: 2,980 (51.1% male; 48.9% female)
Individual Education Program: 336 (11.3%);
English Language Learner: 10 (0.3%); Migrant: 0 (0.0%)
Eligible for Free Lunch Program: 1,064 (35.7%)
Eligible for Reduced-Price Lunch Program: 261 (8.8%)
Teachers: 174.0 (17.1 to 1)
Librarians/Media Specialists: 4.0 (745.0 to 1)
Guidance Counselors: 5.0 (596.0 to 1)
Current Spending: ($ per student per year):
Total: $5,754; Instruction: $3,432; Support Services: $1,971

Enrollment, Drop-out Rates and Diploma Recipients by Race/Ethnicity

Category	Total	White	Black	Asian	AIAN	Hisp.
Enrollment (%)	100.0	75.4	21.4	0.1	0.1	2.9
Drop-out Rate (%)	0.9	0.7	1.5	0.0	n/a	0.0
H.S. Diplomas (#)	101	n/a	n/a	n/a	n/a	n/a

Spartanburg County SD 05

PO Box 307 • Duncan, SC 29334-0307
(864) 949-2350 • http://www.spart5.k12.sc.us
Grade Span: PK-12; **Agency Type:** 1
Schools: 8
4 Primary; 3 Middle; 1 High; 0 Other Level
8 Regular; 0 Special Education; 0 Vocational; 0 Alternative
0 Magnet; 0 Charter; 2 Title I Eligible; 2 School-wide Title I
Students: 6,208 (52.2% male; 47.8% female)
Individual Education Program: 1,161 (18.7%);
English Language Learner: 125 (2.0%); Migrant: 0 (0.0%)
Eligible for Free Lunch Program: 1,906 (30.7%)
Eligible for Reduced-Price Lunch Program: 504 (8.1%)
Teachers: 437.7 (14.2 to 1)
Librarians/Media Specialists: 8.0 (776.0 to 1)
Guidance Counselors: 14.0 (443.4 to 1)
Current Spending: ($ per student per year):
Total: $6,639; Instruction: $4,259; Support Services: $2,038

Enrollment, Drop-out Rates and Diploma Recipients by Race/Ethnicity

Category	Total	White	Black	Asian	AIAN	Hisp.
Enrollment (%)	100.0	71.3	22.8	2.0	0.1	3.7
Drop-out Rate (%)	3.0	2.7	4.2	0.0	n/a	6.7
H.S. Diplomas (#)	268	n/a	n/a	n/a	n/a	n/a

Spartanburg County SD 06

1493 W O Ezell Blvd • Spartanburg, SC 29301-2615
(843) 576-4212 • http://www.Spartanburg6.k12.sc.us
Grade Span: PK-12; **Agency Type:** 1
Schools: 14
9 Primary; 3 Middle; 1 High; 1 Other Level
14 Regular; 0 Special Education; 0 Vocational; 0 Alternative
0 Magnet; 0 Charter; 6 Title I Eligible; 3 School-wide Title I
Students: 9,534 (51.2% male; 48.8% female)
Individual Education Program: 1,278 (13.4%);
English Language Learner: 214 (2.2%); Migrant: 0 (0.0%)
Eligible for Free Lunch Program: 3,165 (33.2%)
Eligible for Reduced-Price Lunch Program: 663 (7.0%)
Teachers: 625.0 (15.3 to 1)
Librarians/Media Specialists: 14.0 (681.0 to 1)
Guidance Counselors: 25.0 (381.4 to 1)
Current Spending: ($ per student per year):
Total: $5,711; Instruction: $3,675; Support Services: $1,656

Enrollment, Drop-out Rates and Diploma Recipients by Race/Ethnicity

Category	Total	White	Black	Asian	AIAN	Hisp.
Enrollment (%)	100.0	60.6	29.4	3.5	0.4	5.9
Drop-out Rate (%)	1.4	1.0	2.5	0.0	0.0	0.0
H.S. Diplomas (#)	498	n/a	n/a	n/a	n/a	n/a

Spartanburg County SD 07

610 Dupre • Spartanburg, SC 29304-0970
Mailing Address: PO Box 970 • Spartanburg, SC 29304-0970
(864) 594-4400 • http://www.spart7.k12.sc.us
Grade Span: PK-12; **Agency Type:** 1
Schools: 14
9 Primary; 3 Middle; 1 High; 1 Other Level
13 Regular; 1 Special Education; 0 Vocational; 0 Alternative
0 Magnet; 0 Charter; 4 Title I Eligible; 4 School-wide Title I
Students: 8,843 (51.2% male; 48.8% female)
Individual Education Program: 1,717 (19.4%);
English Language Learner: 88 (1.0%); Migrant: 17 (0.2%)
Eligible for Free Lunch Program: 4,768 (53.9%)
Eligible for Reduced-Price Lunch Program: 647 (7.3%)
Teachers: 677.2 (13.1 to 1)
Librarians/Media Specialists: 15.0 (589.5 to 1)
Guidance Counselors: 21.5 (411.3 to 1)
Current Spending: ($ per student per year):
Total: $8,875; Instruction: $5,265; Support Services: $3,186

Enrollment, Drop-out Rates and Diploma Recipients by Race/Ethnicity

Category	Total	White	Black	Asian	AIAN	Hisp.
Enrollment (%)	100.0	34.2	61.0	2.7	0.1	1.8
Drop-out Rate (%)	3.8	2.0	5.3	5.1	0.0	7.9
H.S. Diplomas (#)	372	n/a	n/a	n/a	n/a	n/a

Sumter County

Sumter County SD 02

1345 Wilson Hall Rd • Sumter, SC 29150-0002
(803) 469-6900 • http://myschoolonline.com/sc/sumter2
Grade Span: PK-12; **Agency Type:** 1
Schools: 15
8 Primary; 5 Middle; 2 High; 0 Other Level
15 Regular; 0 Special Education; 0 Vocational; 0 Alternative
0 Magnet; 0 Charter; 10 Title I Eligible; 10 School-wide Title I
Students: 9,856 (51.2% male; 48.8% female)
Individual Education Program: 1,634 (16.6%);
English Language Learner: 7 (0.1%); Migrant: 0 (0.0%)
Eligible for Free Lunch Program: 5,440 (55.2%)
Eligible for Reduced-Price Lunch Program: 1,408 (14.3%)
Teachers: 610.3 (16.1 to 1)
Librarians/Media Specialists: 16.0 (616.0 to 1)
Guidance Counselors: 33.0 (298.7 to 1)
Current Spending: ($ per student per year):
Total: $6,064; Instruction: $3,447; Support Services: $2,218

Enrollment, Drop-out Rates and Diploma Recipients by Race/Ethnicity

Category	Total	White	Black	Asian	AIAN	Hisp.
Enrollment (%)	100.0	38.2	59.1	0.9	0.3	1.4
Drop-out Rate (%)	2.9	3.2	2.8	0.0	0.0	0.0
H.S. Diplomas (#)	356	n/a	n/a	n/a	n/a	n/a

Sumter County SD 17

PO Box 1180 • Sumter, SC 29150-1180
(803) 469-8536 • http://www.sumter17.k12.sc.us
Grade Span: PK-12; **Agency Type:** 1
Schools: 11
7 Primary; 3 Middle; 1 High; 0 Other Level
11 Regular; 0 Special Education; 0 Vocational; 0 Alternative
0 Magnet; 0 Charter; 8 Title I Eligible; 8 School-wide Title I
Students: 9,200 (50.7% male; 49.3% female)
Individual Education Program: 1,412 (15.3%);
English Language Learner: 26 (0.3%); Migrant: 0 (0.0%)
Eligible for Free Lunch Program: 4,683 (50.9%)
Eligible for Reduced-Price Lunch Program: 903 (9.8%)
Teachers: 607.8 (15.1 to 1)
Librarians/Media Specialists: 11.0 (836.4 to 1)
Guidance Counselors: 20.0 (460.0 to 1)
Current Spending: ($ per student per year):
Total: $6,318; Instruction: $3,853; Support Services: $1,966

Enrollment, Drop-out Rates and Diploma Recipients by Race/Ethnicity

Category	Total	White	Black	Asian	AIAN	Hisp.
Enrollment (%)	100.0	33.0	64.7	1.0	0.2	1.0
Drop-out Rate (%)	2.9	2.4	3.3	0.0	0.0	0.0
H.S. Diplomas (#)	416	n/a	n/a	n/a	n/a	n/a

Union County

Union County SD

Box 907 • Union, SC 29379-0907
(864) 429-1740 • http://www.union.k12.sc.us
Grade Span: PK-12; **Agency Type:** 1
Schools: 9
4 Primary; 2 Middle; 2 High; 1 Other Level
9 Regular; 0 Special Education; 0 Vocational; 0 Alternative
0 Magnet; 0 Charter; 4 Title I Eligible; 4 School-wide Title I
Students: 5,264 (50.3% male; 49.7% female)
Individual Education Program: 1,095 (20.8%);
English Language Learner: 5 (0.1%); Migrant: 0 (0.0%)
Eligible for Free Lunch Program: 2,438 (46.3%)
Eligible for Reduced-Price Lunch Program: 516 (9.8%)
Teachers: 377.1 (14.0 to 1)
Librarians/Media Specialists: 8.0 (658.0 to 1)
Guidance Counselors: 13.0 (404.9 to 1)
Current Spending: ($ per student per year):
Total: $6,637; Instruction: $4,112; Support Services: $2,147

Enrollment, Drop-out Rates and Diploma Recipients by Race/Ethnicity

Category	Total	White	Black	Asian	AIAN	Hisp.
Enrollment (%)	100.0	58.0	41.2	0.3	0.1	0.3
Drop-out Rate (%)	4.4	4.3	4.6	0.0	n/a	0.0
H.S. Diplomas (#)	234	n/a	n/a	n/a	n/a	n/a

Williamsburg County

Williamsburg County SD

Box 1067 • Kingstree, SC 29556-1067
(843) 354-5571 • http://www.wcsd.k12.sc.us
Grade Span: PK-12; **Agency Type:** 1
Schools: 14
7 Primary; 2 Middle; 5 High; 0 Other Level
13 Regular; 0 Special Education; 1 Vocational; 0 Alternative
0 Magnet; 1 Charter; 10 Title I Eligible; 10 School-wide Title I
Students: 6,121 (51.4% male; 48.6% female)
Individual Education Program: 1,295 (21.2%);
English Language Learner: 34 (0.6%); Migrant: 1 (<0.1%)
Eligible for Free Lunch Program: 4,556 (74.4%)
Eligible for Reduced-Price Lunch Program: 356 (5.8%)
Teachers: 386.0 (15.9 to 1)
Librarians/Media Specialists: 12.5 (489.7 to 1)
Guidance Counselors: 18.0 (340.1 to 1)
Current Spending: ($ per student per year):
Total: $6,657; Instruction: $3,765; Support Services: $2,422

Enrollment, Drop-out Rates and Diploma Recipients by Race/Ethnicity

Category	Total	White	Black	Asian	AIAN	Hisp.
Enrollment (%)	100.0	8.2	91.3	0.0	0.0	0.4
Drop-out Rate (%)	2.1	5.9	1.8	0.0	n/a	0.0
H.S. Diplomas (#)	271	n/a	n/a	n/a	n/a	n/a

York County

York County SD 01

Box 770 • York, SC 29745-0770
(803) 684-9916 • http://www.york.k12.sc.us
Grade Span: PK-12; **Agency Type:** 1
Schools: 8
4 Primary; 1 Middle; 2 High; 1 Other Level
7 Regular; 0 Special Education; 1 Vocational; 0 Alternative
0 Magnet; 0 Charter; 4 Title I Eligible; 3 School-wide Title I
Students: 5,242 (51.5% male; 48.5% female)
Individual Education Program: 830 (15.8%);
English Language Learner: 43 (0.8%); Migrant: 0 (0.0%)
Eligible for Free Lunch Program: 1,830 (34.9%)
Eligible for Reduced-Price Lunch Program: 520 (9.9%)
Teachers: 337.5 (15.5 to 1)
Librarians/Media Specialists: 8.0 (655.3 to 1)
Guidance Counselors: 11.6 (451.9 to 1)
Current Spending: ($ per student per year):
Total: $6,307; Instruction: $3,891; Support Services: $2,041

Enrollment, Drop-out Rates and Diploma Recipients by Race/Ethnicity

Category	Total	White	Black	Asian	AIAN	Hisp.
Enrollment (%)	100.0	73.5	22.3	0.8	0.8	2.3
Drop-out Rate (%)	5.6	5.2	6.4	0.0	0.0	12.5
H.S. Diplomas (#)	242	n/a	n/a	n/a	n/a	n/a

York County SD 02

PO Box 99 • Clover, SC 29710-0099
(803) 222-7191 • http://www.clover.k12.sc.us
Grade Span: PK-12; **Agency Type:** 1
Schools: 8
6 Primary; 1 Middle; 1 High; 0 Other Level
8 Regular; 0 Special Education; 0 Vocational; 0 Alternative
0 Magnet; 0 Charter; 3 Title I Eligible; 0 School-wide Title I
Students: 5,216 (52.7% male; 47.3% female)
Individual Education Program: 656 (12.6%);
English Language Learner: 67 (1.3%); Migrant: 0 (0.0%)
Eligible for Free Lunch Program: 1,225 (23.5%)
Eligible for Reduced-Price Lunch Program: 393 (7.5%)
Teachers: 372.6 (14.0 to 1)
Librarians/Media Specialists: 10.0 (521.6 to 1)
Guidance Counselors: 14.0 (372.6 to 1)
Current Spending: ($ per student per year):
Total: $8,446; Instruction: $5,021; Support Services: $3,058

Enrollment, Drop-out Rates and Diploma Recipients by Race/Ethnicity

Category	Total	White	Black	Asian	AIAN	Hisp.
Enrollment (%)	100.0	83.6	12.4	1.8	0.1	2.0
Drop-out Rate (%)	5.7	5.6	5.6	7.7	n/a	11.8
H.S. Diplomas (#)	198	n/a	n/a	n/a	n/a	n/a

York County SD 03

PO Drawer 10072 • Rock Hill, SC 29731-0072
(803) 324-5360 • http://www.rock-hill.k12.sc.us
Grade Span: PK-12; **Agency Type:** 1
Schools: 23
16 Primary; 4 Middle; 3 High; 0 Other Level
22 Regular; 0 Special Education; 1 Vocational; 0 Alternative
0 Magnet; 1 Charter; 7 Title I Eligible; 7 School-wide Title I
Students: 15,530 (51.0% male; 49.0% female)
Individual Education Program: 1,906 (12.3%);
English Language Learner: 244 (1.6%); Migrant: 14 (0.1%)
Eligible for Free Lunch Program: 4,427 (28.5%)
Eligible for Reduced-Price Lunch Program: 1,039 (6.7%)
Teachers: 969.2 (16.0 to 1)
Librarians/Media Specialists: 23.0 (675.2 to 1)
Guidance Counselors: 40.0 (388.3 to 1)
Current Spending: ($ per student per year):
Total: $6,478; Instruction: $3,954; Support Services: $2,237

Enrollment, Drop-out Rates and Diploma Recipients by Race/Ethnicity

Category	Total	White	Black	Asian	AIAN	Hisp.
Enrollment (%)	100.0	58.1	35.4	1.7	1.7	3.0
Drop-out Rate (%)	1.6	1.5	1.8	0.0	3.6	2.0
H.S. Diplomas (#)	755	n/a	n/a	n/a	n/a	n/a

York County SD 04

120 E Elliott St • Fort Mill, SC 29715-0369
(803) 548-2527 • http://www.fort-mill.k12.sc.us
Grade Span: PK-12; **Agency Type:** 1
Schools: 8
5 Primary; 1 Middle; 1 High; 1 Other Level
8 Regular; 0 Special Education; 0 Vocational; 0 Alternative
0 Magnet; 0 Charter; 2 Title I Eligible; 0 School-wide Title I
Students: 5,941 (51.9% male; 48.1% female)
Individual Education Program: 619 (10.4%);
English Language Learner: 51 (0.9%); Migrant: 0 (0.0%)

Eligible for Free Lunch Program: 610 (10.3%)
Eligible for Reduced-Price Lunch Program: 193 (3.2%)

Teachers: 378.2 (15.7 to 1)

Librarians/Media Specialists: 9.0 (660.1 to 1)

Guidance Counselors: 13.0 (457.0 to 1)

Current Spending: ($ per student per year):
Total: $6,467; Instruction: $3,952; Support Services: $2,241

Enrollment, Drop-out Rates and Diploma Recipients by Race/Ethnicity

Category	Total	White	Black	Asian	AIAN	Hisp.
Enrollment (%)	100.0	87.1	9.1	1.4	0.1	2.1
Drop-out Rate (%)	2.0	2.0	3.2	0.0	0.0	0.0
H.S. Diplomas (#)	299	n/a	n/a	n/a	n/a	n/a

Number of Schools

Rank	Number	District Name	City
1	94	Greenville County SD	Greenville
2	80	Charleston County SD	Charleston
3	48	Richland County SD 01	Columbia
4	46	Horry County SD	Conway
5	39	Aiken County SD	Aiken
6	36	Berkeley County SD	Moncks Corner
7	25	Beaufort County SD	Beaufort
7	25	Pickens County SD	Easley
9	23	Richland County SD 02	Columbia
9	23	York County SD 03	Rock Hill
11	22	Darlington County SD	Darlington
12	21	Oconee County SD	Walhalla
13	20	Florence County SD 01	Florence
13	20	Lancaster County SD	Lancaster
13	20	Lexington County SD 01	Lexington
16	19	Cherokee County SD	Gaffney
16	19	Kershaw County SD	Camden
18	18	Lexington County SD 05	Ballentine
19	17	Anderson County SD 05	Anderson
19	17	Georgetown County SD	Georgetown
21	16	Chesterfield County SD	Chesterfield
21	16	Dorchester County SD 02	Summerville
21	16	Lexington County SD 02	W Columbia
24	15	Anderson County SD 01	Williamston
24	15	Greenwood 50 County SD	Greenwood
24	15	Sumter County SD 02	Sumter
27	14	Newberry County SD	Newberry
27	14	Orangeburg County SD 05	Orangeburg
27	14	Spartanburg County SD 06	Spartanburg
27	14	Spartanburg County SD 07	Spartanburg
27	14	Williamsburg County SD	Kingstree
32	13	Spartanburg County SD 02	Spartanburg
33	12	Colleton County SD	Walterboro
34	11	Abbeville County SD	Abbeville
34	11	Laurens County SD 55	Laurens
34	11	Sumter County SD 17	Sumter
37	10	Chester County SD	Chester
38	9	Fairfield County SD	Winnsboro
38	9	Marlboro County SD	Bennettsville
38	9	Spartanburg County SD 01	Campobello
38	9	Union County SD	Union
42	8	Edgefield County SD	Edgefield
42	8	Florence County SD 03	Lake City
42	8	Orangeburg County SD 04	Cordova
42	8	Spartanburg County SD 05	Duncan
42	8	York County SD 01	York
42	8	York County SD 02	Clover
42	8	York County SD 04	Fort Mill
49	7	Anderson County SD 02	Honea Path
49	7	Hampton 1 County SD	Hampton
49	7	Laurens County SD 56	Clinton
49	7	Lee County SD	Bishopville
49	7	Orangeburg County SD 03	Holly Hill
49	7	Spartanburg County SD 03	Glendale
55	6	Clarendon County SD 02	Manning
55	6	Dillon County SD 02	Dillon
55	6	Lexington County SD 04	Swansea
58	5	Anderson County SD 04	Pendleton
58	5	Bamberg County SD 01	Bamberg
58	5	Marion County SD 02	Mullins
58	5	Saluda County SD	Saluda
62	4	Allendale County SD	Allendale
62	4	Anderson County SD 03	Iva
62	4	Calhoun County SD	Saint Matthews
62	4	Dorchester County SD 04	Saint George
62	4	Greenwood 52 County SD	Ninety Six
62	4	Jasper County SD	Ridgeland
62	4	Lexington County SD 03	Batesburg
62	4	Marion County SD 01	Marion
62	4	Spartanburg County SD 04	Woodruff
71	3	Barnwell County SD 45	Barnwell
71	3	Dillon County SD 03	Latta
71	3	Florence County SD 05	Johnsonville
71	3	Hampton 2 County SD	Estill

Number of Teachers

Rank	Number	District Name	City
1	4,058	Greenville County SD	Greenville
2	3,101	Charleston County SD	Charleston
3	2,040	Richland County SD 01	Columbia
4	2,024	Horry County SD	Conway
5	1,748	Berkeley County SD	Moncks Corner
6	1,580	Aiken County SD	Aiken
7	1,293	Lexington County SD 01	Lexington
8	1,274	Richland County SD 02	Columbia
9	1,251	Beaufort County SD	Beaufort
10	1,108	Dorchester County SD 02	Summerville
11	1,094	Lexington County SD 05	Ballentine
12	1,054	Pickens County SD	Easley
13	969	York County SD 03	Rock Hill
14	947	Florence County SD 01	Florence
15	821	Darlington County SD	Darlington
16	788	Anderson County SD 05	Anderson
17	787	Oconee County SD	Walhalla
18	773	Georgetown County SD	Georgetown
19	724	Lancaster County SD	Lancaster
20	677	Spartanburg County SD 07	Spartanburg
21	650	Lexington County SD 02	W Columbia
22	642	Kershaw County SD	Camden
23	638	Greenwood 50 County SD	Greenwood
24	625	Spartanburg County SD 06	Spartanburg
25	621	Cherokee County SD	Gaffney
26	610	Sumter County SD 02	Sumter
27	607	Sumter County SD 17	Sumter
28	581	Orangeburg County SD 05	Orangeburg
29	552	Chesterfield County SD	Chesterfield
30	476	Spartanburg County SD 02	Spartanburg
31	463	Chester County SD	Chester
32	453	Anderson County SD 01	Williamston
33	451	Newberry County SD	Newberry
34	444	Colleton County SD	Walterboro
35	437	Spartanburg County SD 05	Duncan
36	386	Williamsburg County SD	Kingstree
37	384	Laurens County SD 55	Laurens
38	378	York County SD 04	Fort Mill
39	377	Union County SD	Union
40	372	York County SD 02	Clover
41	337	York County SD 01	York
42	335	Marlboro County SD	Bennettsville
43	323	Spartanburg County SD 01	Campobello
44	288	Edgefield County SD	Edgefield
45	286	Orangeburg County SD 04	Cordova
46	286	Florence County SD 03	Lake City
47	285	Fairfield County SD	Winnsboro
48	269	Abbeville County SD	Abbeville
49	266	Orangeburg County SD 03	Holly Hill
50	233	Spartanburg County SD 03	Glendale
51	230	Lee County SD	Bishopville
52	226	Laurens County SD 56	Clinton
53	224	Lexington County SD 04	Swansea
54	223	Dillon County SD 02	Dillon
55	215	Anderson County SD 02	Honea Path
56	203	Clarendon County SD 02	Manning
57	201	Marion County SD 01	Marion
58	200	Jasper County SD	Ridgeland
59	185	Dorchester County SD 04	Saint George
60	183	Barnwell County SD 45	Barnwell
61	180	Hampton 1 County SD	Hampton
62	174	Anderson County SD 04	Pendleton
63	174	Spartanburg County SD 04	Woodruff
64	165	Anderson County SD 03	Iva
65	162	Saluda County SD	Saluda
66	154	Lexington County SD 03	Batesburg
67	154	Calhoun County SD	Saint Matthews
68	153	Allendale County SD	Allendale
69	139	Marion County SD 02	Mullins
70	120	Bamberg County SD 01	Bamberg
71	110	Greenwood 52 County SD	Ninety Six
72	105	Hampton 2 County SD	Estill
73	101	Florence County SD 05	Johnsonville
74	96	Dillon County SD 03	Latta

Number of Students

Rank	Number	District Name	City
1	63,270	Greenville County SD	Greenville
2	44,008	Charleston County SD	Charleston
3	30,826	Horry County SD	Conway
4	28,585	Berkeley County SD	Moncks Corner
5	27,393	Richland County SD 01	Columbia
6	25,358	Aiken County SD	Aiken
7	19,349	Richland County SD 02	Columbia
8	18,748	Lexington County SD 01	Lexington
9	18,133	Beaufort County SD	Beaufort
10	17,765	Dorchester County SD 02	Summerville
11	16,471	Pickens County SD	Easley
12	15,531	Lexington County SD 05	Ballentine
13	15,530	York County SD 03	Rock Hill
14	14,783	Florence County SD 01	Florence
15	11,792	Anderson County SD 05	Anderson
16	11,767	Darlington County SD	Darlington
17	11,352	Lancaster County SD	Lancaster
18	10,684	Oconee County SD	Walhalla
19	10,418	Georgetown County SD	Georgetown
20	10,079	Kershaw County SD	Camden
21	9,856	Sumter County SD 02	Sumter
22	9,534	Spartanburg County SD 06	Spartanburg
23	9,478	Greenwood 50 County SD	Greenwood
24	9,298	Cherokee County SD	Gaffney
25	9,200	Sumter County SD 17	Sumter
26	9,171	Lexington County SD 02	W Columbia
27	8,843	Spartanburg County SD 07	Spartanburg
28	8,580	Spartanburg County SD 02	Spartanburg
29	8,292	Chesterfield County SD	Chesterfield
30	7,939	Anderson County SD 01	Williamston
31	7,909	Orangeburg County SD 05	Orangeburg
32	6,850	Colleton County SD	Walterboro
33	6,489	Chester County SD	Chester
34	6,242	Laurens County SD 55	Laurens
35	6,208	Spartanburg County SD 05	Duncan
36	6,121	Williamsburg County SD	Kingstree
37	5,941	York County SD 04	Fort Mill
38	5,922	Newberry County SD	Newberry
39	5,264	Union County SD	Union
40	5,242	York County SD 01	York
41	5,216	York County SD 02	Clover
42	5,159	Marlboro County SD	Bennettsville
43	4,529	Spartanburg County SD 01	Campobello
44	4,436	Orangeburg County SD 04	Cordova
45	4,138	Florence County SD 03	Lake City
46	4,088	Edgefield County SD	Edgefield
47	3,874	Dillon County SD 02	Dillon
48	3,839	Abbeville County SD	Abbeville
49	3,800	Orangeburg County SD 03	Holly Hill
50	3,772	Anderson County SD 02	Honea Path
51	3,671	Lexington County SD 04	Swansea
52	3,610	Fairfield County SD	Winnsboro
53	3,584	Clarendon County SD 02	Manning
54	3,481	Laurens County SD 56	Clinton
55	3,254	Marion County SD 01	Marion
56	3,231	Spartanburg County SD 03	Glendale
57	3,147	Jasper County SD	Ridgeland
58	2,980	Spartanburg County SD 04	Woodruff
59	2,952	Lee County SD	Bishopville
60	2,834	Anderson County SD 04	Pendleton
61	2,829	Hampton 1 County SD	Hampton
62	2,806	Barnwell County SD 45	Barnwell
63	2,662	Anderson County SD 03	Iva
64	2,514	Dorchester County SD 04	Saint George
65	2,392	Lexington County SD 03	Batesburg
66	2,299	Marion County SD 02	Mullins
67	2,196	Saluda County SD	Saluda
68	1,961	Calhoun County SD	Saint Matthews
69	1,918	Allendale County SD	Allendale
70	1,720	Greenwood 52 County SD	Ninety Six
71	1,704	Bamberg County SD 01	Bamberg
72	1,551	Dillon County SD 03	Latta
73	1,541	Florence County SD 05	Johnsonville
74	1,512	Hampton 2 County SD	Estill

Male Students

Rank	Percent	District Name	City
1	53.6	Dorchester County SD 04	Saint George
2	52.7	Barnwell County SD 45	Barnwell
2	52.7	York County SD 02	Clover
4	52.6	Lexington County SD 04	Swansea
5	52.4	Dillon County SD 02	Dillon
5	52.4	Florence County SD 03	Lake City
5	52.4	Jasper County SD	Ridgeland
8	52.3	Anderson County SD 03	Iva
8	52.3	Edgefield County SD	Edgefield
10	52.2	Spartanburg County SD 05	Duncan
11	52.1	Bamberg County SD 01	Bamberg
11	52.1	Chester County SD	Chester
11	52.1	Lancaster County SD	Lancaster
11	52.1	Lexington County SD 03	Batesburg
11	52.1	Oconee County SD	Walhalla
16	52.0	Marion County SD 01	Marion
16	52.0	Newberry County SD	Newberry
18	51.9	York County SD 04	Fort Mill
19	51.8	Berkeley County SD	Moncks Corner
19	51.8	Darlington County SD	Darlington
19	51.8	Florence County SD 05	Johnsonville
22	51.7	Abbeville County SD	Abbeville
22	51.7	Hampton 1 County SD	Hampton
22	51.7	Laurens County SD 55	Laurens
22	51.7	Lexington County SD 05	Ballentine
26	51.6	Anderson County SD 01	Williamston
26	51.6	Kershaw County SD	Camden
26	51.6	Laurens County SD 56	Clinton
26	51.6	Lexington County SD 01	Lexington
26	51.6	Marlboro County SD	Bennettsville
31	51.5	Dillon County SD 03	Latta
31	51.5	York County SD 01	York
33	51.4	Spartanburg County SD 02	Spartanburg
33	51.4	Williamsburg County SD	Kingstree
35	51.3	Dorchester County SD 02	Summerville
35	51.3	Georgetown County SD	Georgetown
35	51.3	Horry County SD	Conway
35	51.3	Spartanburg County SD 01	Campobello
39	51.2	Aiken County SD	Aiken
39	51.2	Allendale County SD	Allendale
39	51.2	Greenville County SD	Greenville
39	51.2	Greenwood 52 County SD	Ninety Six

Rank	Percent	District Name	City
39	51.2	Spartanburg County SD 06	Spartanburg
39	51.2	Spartanburg County SD 07	Spartanburg
39	51.2	Sumter County SD 02	Sumter
46	51.1	Anderson County SD 04	Pendleton
46	51.1	Charleston County SD	Charleston
46	51.1	Hampton 2 County SD	Estill
46	51.1	Saluda County SD	Saluda
46	51.1	Spartanburg County SD 04	Woodruff
51	51.0	Anderson County SD 02	Honea Path
51	51.0	Beaufort County SD	Beaufort
51	51.0	Lexington County SD 02	W Columbia
51	51.0	York County SD 03	Rock Hill
55	50.9	Anderson County SD 05	Anderson
55	50.9	Colleton County SD	Walterboro
55	50.9	Marion County SD 02	Mullins
58	50.8	Lee County SD	Bishopville
59	50.7	Florence County SD 01	Florence
59	50.7	Pickens County SD	Easley
59	50.7	Richland County SD 01	Columbia
59	50.7	Sumter County SD 17	Sumter
63	50.6	Orangeburg County SD 04	Cordova
64	50.5	Chesterfield County SD	Chesterfield
64	50.5	Orangeburg County SD 05	Orangeburg
66	50.4	Richland County SD 02	Columbia
67	50.3	Union County SD	Union
68	50.2	Cherokee County SD	Gaffney
69	50.1	Greenwood 50 County SD	Greenwood
69	50.1	Orangeburg County SD 03	Holly Hill
69	50.1	Spartanburg County SD 03	Glendale
72	49.7	Calhoun County SD	Saint Matthews
73	49.5	Fairfield County SD	Winnsboro
74	49.1	Clarendon County SD 02	Manning

Female Students

Rank	Percent	District Name	City
1	50.9	Clarendon County SD 02	Manning
2	50.5	Fairfield County SD	Winnsboro
3	50.3	Calhoun County SD	Saint Matthews
4	49.9	Greenwood 50 County SD	Greenwood
4	49.9	Orangeburg County SD 03	Holly Hill
4	49.9	Spartanburg County SD 03	Glendale
7	49.8	Cherokee County SD	Gaffney
8	49.7	Union County SD	Union
9	49.6	Richland County SD 02	Columbia
10	49.5	Chesterfield County SD	Chesterfield
10	49.5	Orangeburg County SD 05	Orangeburg
12	49.4	Orangeburg County SD 04	Cordova
13	49.3	Florence County SD 01	Florence
13	49.3	Pickens County SD	Easley
13	49.3	Richland County SD 01	Columbia
13	49.3	Sumter County SD 17	Sumter
17	49.2	Lee County SD	Bishopville
18	49.1	Anderson County SD 05	Anderson
18	49.1	Colleton County SD	Walterboro
18	49.1	Marion County SD 02	Mullins
21	49.0	Anderson County SD 02	Honea Path
21	49.0	Beaufort County SD	Beaufort
21	49.0	Lexington County SD 02	W Columbia
21	49.0	York County SD 03	Rock Hill
25	48.9	Anderson County SD 04	Pendleton
25	48.9	Charleston County SD	Charleston
25	48.9	Hampton 2 County SD	Estill
25	48.9	Saluda County SD	Saluda
25	48.9	Spartanburg County SD 04	Woodruff
30	48.8	Aiken County SD	Aiken
30	48.8	Allendale County SD	Allendale
30	48.8	Greenville County SD	Greenville
30	48.8	Greenwood 52 County SD	Ninety Six
30	48.8	Spartanburg County SD 06	Spartanburg
30	48.8	Spartanburg County SD 07	Spartanburg
30	48.8	Sumter County SD 02	Sumter
37	48.7	Dorchester County SD 02	Summerville
37	48.7	Georgetown County SD	Georgetown
37	48.7	Horry County SD	Conway
37	48.7	Spartanburg County SD 01	Campobello
41	48.6	Spartanburg County SD 02	Spartanburg
41	48.6	Williamsburg County SD	Kingstree
43	48.5	Dillon County SD 03	Latta
43	48.5	York County SD 01	York
45	48.4	Anderson County SD 01	Williamston
45	48.4	Kershaw County SD	Camden
45	48.4	Laurens County SD 56	Clinton
45	48.4	Lexington County SD 01	Lexington
45	48.4	Marlboro County SD	Bennettsville
50	48.3	Abbeville County SD	Abbeville
50	48.3	Hampton 1 County SD	Hampton
50	48.3	Laurens County SD 55	Laurens
50	48.3	Lexington County SD 05	Ballentine
54	48.2	Berkeley County SD	Moncks Corner
54	48.2	Darlington County SD	Darlington
54	48.2	Florence County SD 05	Johnsonville
57	48.1	York County SD 04	Fort Mill
58	48.0	Marion County SD 01	Marion
58	48.0	Newberry County SD	Newberry
60	47.9	Bamberg County SD 01	Bamberg
60	47.9	Chester County SD	Chester
60	47.9	Lancaster County SD	Lancaster
60	47.9	Lexington County SD 03	Batesburg
60	47.9	Oconee County SD	Walhalla
65	47.8	Spartanburg County SD 05	Duncan
66	47.7	Anderson County SD 03	Iva
66	47.7	Edgefield County SD	Edgefield
68	47.6	Dillon County SD 02	Dillon
68	47.6	Florence County SD 03	Lake City
68	47.6	Jasper County SD	Ridgeland
71	47.4	Lexington County SD 04	Swansea
72	47.3	Barnwell County SD 45	Barnwell
72	47.3	York County SD 02	Clover
74	46.4	Dorchester County SD 04	Saint George

Individual Education Program Students

Rank	Percent	District Name	City
1	22.5	Marion County SD 02	Mullins
2	21.9	Bamberg County SD 01	Bamberg
2	21.9	Florence County SD 05	Johnsonville
4	21.6	Florence County SD 03	Lake City
5	21.5	Laurens County SD 56	Clinton
6	21.2	Allendale County SD	Allendale
6	21.2	Williamsburg County SD	Kingstree
8	21.1	Fairfield County SD	Winnsboro
9	21.0	Anderson County SD 02	Honea Path
10	20.8	Union County SD	Union
11	20.6	Anderson County SD 03	Iva
12	20.2	Laurens County SD 55	Laurens
12	20.2	Oconee County SD	Walhalla
14	19.9	Calhoun County SD	Saint Matthews
15	19.6	Newberry County SD	Newberry
16	19.4	Spartanburg County SD 07	Spartanburg
17	19.3	Marion County SD 01	Marion
18	19.2	Saluda County SD	Saluda
19	18.7	Spartanburg County SD 05	Duncan
20	18.5	Clarendon County SD 02	Manning
21	18.3	Orangeburg County SD 03	Holly Hill
22	18.2	Barnwell County SD 45	Barnwell
22	18.2	Lexington County SD 04	Swansea
24	18.1	Darlington County SD	Darlington
25	18.0	Spartanburg County SD 01	Campobello
26	17.9	Hampton 2 County SD	Estill
27	17.8	Greenwood 50 County SD	Greenwood
28	17.5	Abbeville County SD	Abbeville
28	17.5	Georgetown County SD	Georgetown
30	17.3	Edgefield County SD	Edgefield
31	17.1	Chesterfield County SD	Chesterfield
31	17.1	Orangeburg County SD 05	Orangeburg
33	17.0	Horry County SD	Conway
33	17.0	Lexington County SD 03	Batesburg
35	16.6	Sumter County SD 02	Sumter
36	16.4	Dorchester County SD 04	Saint George
36	16.4	Greenville County SD	Greenville
36	16.4	Spartanburg County SD 03	Glendale
39	16.3	Dillon County SD 03	Latta
40	15.9	Chester County SD	Chester
41	15.8	Florence County SD 01	Florence
41	15.8	York County SD 01	York
43	15.5	Orangeburg County SD 04	Cordova
44	15.4	Berkeley County SD	Moncks Corner
45	15.3	Anderson County SD 05	Anderson
45	15.3	Lee County SD	Bishopville
45	15.3	Sumter County SD 17	Sumter
48	15.1	Lexington County SD 01	Lexington
49	15.0	Lexington County SD 02	W Columbia
50	14.9	Anderson County SD 01	Williamston
50	14.9	Marlboro County SD	Bennettsville
52	14.7	Anderson County SD 04	Pendleton
53	14.5	Richland County SD 01	Columbia
54	14.4	Charleston County SD	Charleston
54	14.4	Pickens County SD	Easley
56	14.1	Colleton County SD	Walterboro
56	14.1	Lancaster County SD	Lancaster
58	13.9	Hampton 1 County SD	Hampton
59	13.8	Aiken County SD	Aiken
60	13.6	Greenwood 52 County SD	Ninety Six
61	13.4	Spartanburg County SD 06	Spartanburg
62	13.3	Dorchester County SD 02	Summerville
62	13.3	Kershaw County SD	Camden
64	13.2	Lexington County SD 05	Ballentine
65	12.9	Dillon County SD 02	Dillon
66	12.8	Beaufort County SD	Beaufort
67	12.6	Jasper County SD	Ridgeland
67	12.6	York County SD 02	Clover
69	12.5	Richland County SD 02	Columbia
70	12.3	York County SD 03	Rock Hill
71	12.0	Spartanburg County SD 02	Spartanburg
72	11.6	Cherokee County SD	Gaffney
73	11.3	Spartanburg County SD 04	Woodruff
74	10.4	York County SD 04	Fort Mill

English Language Learner Students

Rank	Percent	District Name	City
1	7.7	Saluda County SD	Saluda
2	6.1	Jasper County SD	Ridgeland
3	5.2	Beaufort County SD	Beaufort
4	3.6	Newberry County SD	Newberry
4	3.6	Spartanburg County SD 02	Spartanburg
6	3.3	Greenwood 50 County SD	Greenwood
7	2.2	Spartanburg County SD 06	Spartanburg
8	2.0	Spartanburg County SD 03	Glendale
8	2.0	Spartanburg County SD 05	Duncan
10	1.8	Laurens County SD 55	Laurens
10	1.8	Oconee County SD	Walhalla
12	1.7	Cherokee County SD	Gaffney
13	1.6	Horry County SD	Conway
13	1.6	York County SD 03	Rock Hill
15	1.4	Lexington County SD 02	W Columbia
16	1.3	Berkeley County SD	Moncks Corner
16	1.3	Calhoun County SD	Saint Matthews
16	1.3	Spartanburg County SD 01	Campobello
16	1.3	York County SD 02	Clover
20	1.2	Dillon County SD 02	Dillon
20	1.2	Hampton 2 County SD	Estill
22	1.1	Chesterfield County SD	Chesterfield
23	1.0	Pickens County SD	Easley
23	1.0	Richland County SD 01	Columbia
23	1.0	Richland County SD 02	Columbia
23	1.0	Spartanburg County SD 07	Spartanburg
27	0.9	Aiken County SD	Aiken
27	0.9	Charleston County SD	Charleston
27	0.9	Georgetown County SD	Georgetown
27	0.9	Lancaster County SD	Lancaster
27	0.9	Lexington County SD 05	Ballentine
27	0.9	York County SD 04	Fort Mill
33	0.8	York County SD 01	York
34	0.7	Anderson County SD 01	Williamston
34	0.7	Laurens County SD 56	Clinton
34	0.7	Lexington County SD 01	Lexington
37	0.6	Abbeville County SD	Abbeville
37	0.6	Clarendon County SD 02	Manning
37	0.6	Kershaw County SD	Camden
37	0.6	Orangeburg County SD 03	Holly Hill
37	0.6	Williamsburg County SD	Kingstree
42	0.5	Allendale County SD	Allendale
42	0.5	Dorchester County SD 02	Summerville
42	0.5	Florence County SD 01	Florence
45	0.4	Anderson County SD 05	Anderson
45	0.4	Florence County SD 03	Lake City
45	0.4	Florence County SD 05	Johnsonville
45	0.4	Greenville County SD	Greenville
45	0.4	Lee County SD	Bishopville
50	0.3	Anderson County SD 02	Honea Path
50	0.3	Anderson County SD 04	Pendleton
50	0.3	Chester County SD	Chester
50	0.3	Darlington County SD	Darlington
50	0.3	Dorchester County SD 04	Saint George
50	0.3	Lexington County SD 03	Batesburg
50	0.3	Spartanburg County SD 04	Woodruff
50	0.3	Sumter County SD 17	Sumter
58	0.2	Colleton County SD	Walterboro
58	0.2	Lexington County SD 04	Swansea
58	0.2	Marion County SD 02	Mullins
61	0.1	Anderson County SD 03	Iva
61	0.1	Barnwell County SD 45	Barnwell
61	0.1	Edgefield County SD	Edgefield
61	0.1	Fairfield County SD	Winnsboro
61	0.1	Orangeburg County SD 04	Cordova
61	0.1	Sumter County SD 02	Sumter
61	0.1	Union County SD	Union
68	0.0	Hampton 1 County SD	Hampton
69	0.0	Bamberg County SD 01	Bamberg
69	0.0	Dillon County SD 03	Latta
69	0.0	Greenwood 52 County SD	Ninety Six
69	0.0	Marion County SD 01	Marion
69	0.0	Marlboro County SD	Bennettsville
69	0.0	Orangeburg County SD 05	Orangeburg

Migrant Students

Rank	Percent	District Name	City
1	4.6	Saluda County SD	Saluda
2	1.7	Newberry County SD	Newberry
3	1.0	Spartanburg County SD 02	Spartanburg
4	0.8	Dillon County SD 03	Latta
4	0.8	Fairfield County SD	Winnsboro
6	0.4	Hampton 2 County SD	Estill
7	0.3	Greenwood 50 County SD	Greenwood
7	0.3	Jasper County SD	Ridgeland
7	0.3	Laurens County SD 55	Laurens

10	0.2	Florence County SD 03	Lake City
10	0.2	Spartanburg County SD 01	Campobello
10	0.2	Spartanburg County SD 07	Spartanburg
13	0.1	Calhoun County SD	Saint Matthews
13	0.1	Clarendon County SD 02	Manning
13	0.1	Orangeburg County SD 04	Cordova
13	0.1	York County SD 03	Rock Hill
17	0.0	Aiken County SD	Aiken
17	0.0	Anderson County SD 01	Williamston
17	0.0	Anderson County SD 05	Anderson
17	0.0	Berkeley County SD	Moncks Corner
17	0.0	Charleston County SD	Charleston
17	0.0	Dorchester County SD 02	Summerville
17	0.0	Florence County SD 01	Florence
17	0.0	Greenville County SD	Greenville
17	0.0	Horry County SD	Conway
17	0.0	Lexington County SD 02	W Columbia
17	0.0	Pickens County SD	Easley
17	0.0	Richland County SD 01	Columbia
17	0.0	Williamsburg County SD	Kingstree
30	0.0	Abbeville County SD	Abbeville
30	0.0	Allendale County SD	Allendale
30	0.0	Anderson County SD 02	Honea Path
30	0.0	Anderson County SD 03	Iva
30	0.0	Anderson County SD 04	Pendleton
30	0.0	Bamberg County SD 01	Bamberg
30	0.0	Barnwell County SD 45	Barnwell
30	0.0	Beaufort County SD	Beaufort
30	0.0	Cherokee County SD	Gaffney
30	0.0	Chester County SD	Chester
30	0.0	Chesterfield County SD	Chesterfield
30	0.0	Colleton County SD	Walterboro
30	0.0	Darlington County SD	Darlington
30	0.0	Dillon County SD 02	Dillon
30	0.0	Dorchester County SD 04	Saint George
30	0.0	Edgefield County SD	Edgefield
30	0.0	Florence County SD 05	Johnsonville
30	0.0	Georgetown County SD	Georgetown
30	0.0	Greenwood 52 County SD	Ninety Six
30	0.0	Hampton 1 County SD	Hampton
30	0.0	Kershaw County SD	Camden
30	0.0	Lancaster County SD	Lancaster
30	0.0	Laurens County SD 56	Clinton
30	0.0	Lee County SD	Bishopville
30	0.0	Lexington County SD 01	Lexington
30	0.0	Lexington County SD 03	Batesburg
30	0.0	Lexington County SD 04	Swansea
30	0.0	Lexington County SD 05	Ballentine
30	0.0	Marion County SD 01	Marion
30	0.0	Marion County SD 02	Mullins
30	0.0	Marlboro County SD	Bennettsville
30	0.0	Oconee County SD	Walhalla
30	0.0	Orangeburg County SD 03	Holly Hill
30	0.0	Orangeburg County SD 05	Orangeburg
30	0.0	Richland County SD 02	Columbia
30	0.0	Spartanburg County SD 03	Glendale
30	0.0	Spartanburg County SD 04	Woodruff
30	0.0	Spartanburg County SD 05	Duncan
30	0.0	Spartanburg County SD 06	Spartanburg
30	0.0	Sumter County SD 02	Sumter
30	0.0	Sumter County SD 17	Sumter
30	0.0	Union County SD	Union
30	0.0	York County SD 01	York
30	0.0	York County SD 02	Clover
30	0.0	York County SD 04	Fort Mill

Students Eligible for Free Lunch

Rank	Percent	District Name	City
1	84.5	Allendale County SD	Allendale
2	79.8	Hampton 2 County SD	Estill
3	78.8	Orangeburg County SD 03	Holly Hill
4	74.6	Lee County SD	Bishopville
5	74.4	Williamsburg County SD	Kingstree
6	72.4	Dillon County SD 02	Dillon
7	71.3	Calhoun County SD	Saint Matthews
8	71.2	Florence County SD 03	Lake City
9	69.5	Orangeburg County SD 05	Orangeburg
10	66.7	Marion County SD 01	Marion
11	66.4	Clarendon County SD 02	Manning
12	65.9	Fairfield County SD	Winnsboro
13	65.8	Marlboro County SD	Bennettsville
14	63.3	Colleton County SD	Walterboro
15	63.1	Dorchester County SD 04	Saint George
16	60.2	Marion County SD 02	Mullins
17	59.3	Jasper County SD	Ridgeland
18	59.1	Dillon County SD 03	Latta
19	56.6	Bamberg County SD 01	Bamberg
19	56.6	Orangeburg County SD 04	Cordova
21	56.1	Darlington County SD	Darlington
22	55.2	Sumter County SD 02	Sumter
23	53.9	Spartanburg County SD 07	Spartanburg
24	52.8	Richland County SD 01	Columbia
25	52.7	Georgetown County SD	Georgetown
26	52.6	Lexington County SD 04	Swansea
27	52.2	Laurens County SD 56	Clinton
28	51.1	Abbeville County SD	Abbeville
29	50.9	Sumter County SD 17	Sumter
30	50.6	Hampton 1 County SD	Hampton
31	50.3	Saluda County SD	Saluda
32	50.2	Chesterfield County SD	Chesterfield
33	49.3	Newberry County SD	Newberry
34	48.4	Edgefield County SD	Edgefield
35	48.3	Horry County SD	Conway
36	47.3	Barnwell County SD 45	Barnwell
37	47.0	Chester County SD	Chester
38	46.3	Union County SD	Union
39	46.2	Charleston County SD	Charleston
40	45.6	Florence County SD 05	Johnsonville
41	45.2	Laurens County SD 55	Laurens
42	45.0	Cherokee County SD	Gaffney
43	44.9	Lexington County SD 03	Batesburg
44	43.1	Florence County SD 01	Florence
45	42.6	Aiken County SD	Aiken
46	40.9	Greenwood 50 County SD	Greenwood
47	40.0	Anderson County SD 03	Iva
48	39.9	Berkeley County SD	Moncks Corner
49	39.5	Lancaster County SD	Lancaster
50	39.2	Spartanburg County SD 03	Glendale
51	38.8	Beaufort County SD	Beaufort
52	38.4	Kershaw County SD	Camden
53	37.2	Anderson County SD 05	Anderson
54	37.0	Lexington County SD 02	W Columbia
55	36.5	Oconee County SD	Walhalla
56	35.7	Spartanburg County SD 04	Woodruff
57	34.9	York County SD 01	York
58	33.2	Spartanburg County SD 06	Spartanburg
59	32.4	Anderson County SD 02	Honea Path
60	30.7	Spartanburg County SD 05	Duncan
61	30.6	Spartanburg County SD 01	Campobello
62	29.9	Anderson County SD 04	Pendleton
63	29.7	Greenville County SD	Greenville
64	28.5	York County SD 03	Rock Hill
65	27.8	Greenwood 52 County SD	Ninety Six
66	27.5	Pickens County SD	Easley
67	27.3	Spartanburg County SD 02	Spartanburg
68	25.5	Richland County SD 02	Columbia
69	23.5	York County SD 02	Clover
70	22.1	Dorchester County SD 02	Summerville
71	21.9	Anderson County SD 01	Williamston
72	21.2	Lexington County SD 01	Lexington
73	14.3	Lexington County SD 05	Ballentine
74	10.3	York County SD 04	Fort Mill

Students Eligible for Reduced-Price Lunch

Rank	Percent	District Name	City
1	14.3	Sumter County SD 02	Sumter
2	13.1	Hampton 1 County SD	Hampton
3	12.2	Marlboro County SD	Bennettsville
4	12.0	Fairfield County SD	Winnsboro
5	11.5	Orangeburg County SD 04	Cordova
6	11.3	Berkeley County SD	Moncks Corner
7	10.7	Anderson County SD 03	Iva
8	10.5	Dorchester County SD 04	Saint George
9	10.2	Newberry County SD	Newberry
10	10.0	Oconee County SD	Walhalla
11	9.9	Laurens County SD 56	Clinton
11	9.9	Spartanburg County SD 03	Glendale
11	9.9	York County SD 01	York
14	9.8	Sumter County SD 17	Sumter
14	9.8	Union County SD	Union
16	9.7	Chesterfield County SD	Chesterfield
17	9.6	Anderson County SD 04	Pendleton
17	9.6	Jasper County SD	Ridgeland
19	9.5	Calhoun County SD	Saint Matthews
20	9.3	Orangeburg County SD 05	Orangeburg
20	9.3	Spartanburg County SD 01	Campobello
22	9.2	Kershaw County SD	Camden
22	9.2	Lexington County SD 04	Swansea
24	9.0	Greenwood 52 County SD	Ninety Six
24	9.0	Spartanburg County SD 02	Spartanburg
26	8.8	Cherokee County SD	Gaffney
26	8.8	Spartanburg County SD 04	Woodruff
28	8.7	Saluda County SD	Saluda
29	8.6	Dillon County SD 02	Dillon
30	8.5	Edgefield County SD	Edgefield
30	8.5	Lexington County SD 03	Batesburg
32	8.4	Laurens County SD 55	Laurens
32	8.4	Orangeburg County SD 03	Holly Hill
32	8.4	Pickens County SD	Easley
35	8.3	Abbeville County SD	Abbeville
35	8.3	Barnwell County SD 45	Barnwell
35	8.3	Beaufort County SD	Beaufort
38	8.2	Lexington County SD 02	W Columbia
39	8.1	Georgetown County SD	Georgetown
39	8.1	Lancaster County SD	Lancaster
39	8.1	Spartanburg County SD 05	Duncan
42	8.0	Bamberg County SD 01	Bamberg
43	7.9	Anderson County SD 01	Williamston
44	7.8	Darlington County SD	Darlington
45	7.7	Hampton 2 County SD	Estill
45	7.7	Lee County SD	Bishopville
47	7.6	Richland County SD 02	Columbia
48	7.5	York County SD 02	Clover
49	7.4	Anderson County SD 02	Honea Path
50	7.3	Clarendon County SD 02	Manning
50	7.3	Richland County SD 01	Columbia
50	7.3	Spartanburg County SD 07	Spartanburg
53	7.2	Colleton County SD	Walterboro
53	7.2	Dillon County SD 03	Latta
53	7.2	Greenwood 50 County SD	Greenwood
53	7.2	Marion County SD 02	Mullins
57	7.1	Florence County SD 01	Florence
58	7.0	Chester County SD	Chester
58	7.0	Spartanburg County SD 06	Spartanburg
60	6.9	Lexington County SD 01	Lexington
60	6.9	Marion County SD 01	Marion
62	6.8	Charleston County SD	Charleston
63	6.7	Horry County SD	Conway
63	6.7	York County SD 03	Rock Hill
65	6.6	Florence County SD 05	Johnsonville
66	6.5	Aiken County SD	Aiken
67	6.4	Greenville County SD	Greenville
68	6.3	Anderson County SD 05	Anderson
68	6.3	Dorchester County SD 02	Summerville
70	5.8	Williamsburg County SD	Kingstree
71	5.2	Allendale County SD	Allendale
72	5.0	Florence County SD 03	Lake City
73	4.5	Lexington County SD 05	Ballentine
74	3.2	York County SD 04	Fort Mill

Student/Teacher Ratio

Rank	Ratio	District Name	City
1	18.0	Spartanburg County SD 02	Spartanburg
2	17.6	Clarendon County SD 02	Manning
3	17.5	Anderson County SD 01	Williamston
3	17.5	Anderson County SD 02	Honea Path
5	17.3	Dillon County SD 02	Dillon
6	17.1	Spartanburg County SD 04	Woodruff
7	16.5	Marion County SD 02	Mullins
8	16.4	Berkeley County SD	Moncks Corner
9	16.3	Anderson County SD 04	Pendleton
9	16.3	Lexington County SD 04	Swansea
11	16.2	Laurens County SD 55	Laurens
11	16.2	Marion County SD 01	Marion
13	16.1	Dillon County SD 03	Latta
13	16.1	Sumter County SD 02	Sumter
15	16.0	Aiken County SD	Aiken
15	16.0	Anderson County SD 03	Iva
15	16.0	Dorchester County SD 02	Summerville
15	16.0	York County SD 03	Rock Hill
19	15.9	Williamsburg County SD	Kingstree
20	15.7	Hampton 1 County SD	Hampton
20	15.7	Jasper County SD	Ridgeland
20	15.7	Kershaw County SD	Camden
20	15.7	Lancaster County SD	Lancaster
20	15.7	York County SD 04	Fort Mill
25	15.6	Florence County SD 01	Florence
25	15.6	Greenville County SD	Greenville
25	15.6	Greenwood 52 County SD	Ninety Six
25	15.6	Pickens County SD	Easley
29	15.5	Orangeburg County SD 04	Cordova
29	15.5	York County SD 01	York
31	15.4	Colleton County SD	Walterboro
31	15.4	Laurens County SD 56	Clinton
31	15.4	Lexington County SD 03	Batesburg
31	15.4	Marlboro County SD	Bennettsville
35	15.3	Barnwell County SD 45	Barnwell
35	15.3	Spartanburg County SD 06	Spartanburg
37	15.2	Florence County SD 05	Johnsonville
37	15.2	Horry County SD	Conway
37	15.2	Richland County SD 02	Columbia
40	15.1	Sumter County SD 17	Sumter
41	15.0	Anderson County SD 05	Anderson
41	15.0	Cherokee County SD	Gaffney
41	15.0	Chesterfield County SD	Chesterfield
44	14.8	Greenwood 50 County SD	Greenwood
45	14.5	Beaufort County SD	Beaufort
45	14.5	Florence County SD 03	Lake City
45	14.5	Lexington County SD 01	Lexington
48	14.4	Hampton 2 County SD	Estill
49	14.3	Abbeville County SD	Abbeville
49	14.3	Darlington County SD	Darlington
49	14.3	Orangeburg County SD 03	Holly Hill
52	14.2	Bamberg County SD 01	Bamberg

52	14.2	Charleston County SD	Charleston
52	14.2	Edgefield County SD	Edgefield
52	14.2	Lexington County SD 05	Ballentine
52	14.2	Spartanburg County SD 05	Duncan
57	14.1	Lexington County SD 02	W Columbia
58	14.0	Chester County SD	Chester
58	14.0	Spartanburg County SD 01	Campobello
58	14.0	Union County SD	Union
58	14.0	York County SD 02	Clover
62	13.9	Spartanburg County SD 03	Glendale
63	13.6	Oconee County SD	Walhalla
63	13.6	Orangeburg County SD 05	Orangeburg
65	13.5	Dorchester County SD 04	Saint George
65	13.5	Georgetown County SD	Georgetown
65	13.5	Saluda County SD	Saluda
68	13.4	Richland County SD 01	Columbia
69	13.1	Newberry County SD	Newberry
69	13.1	Spartanburg County SD 07	Spartanburg
71	12.8	Lee County SD	Bishopville
72	12.7	Calhoun County SD	Saint Matthews
73	12.6	Fairfield County SD	Winnsboro
74	12.5	Allendale County SD	Allendale

Student/Librarian Ratio

Rank	Ratio	District Name	City
1	935.3	Barnwell County SD 45	Barnwell
2	888.3	Dorchester County SD 02	Summerville
3	879.5	Richland County SD 02	Columbia
4	838.0	Dorchester County SD 04	Saint George
5	836.4	Sumter County SD 17	Sumter
6	815.1	Lexington County SD 01	Lexington
7	811.1	Chester County SD	Chester
8	786.8	Jasper County SD	Ridgeland
9	776.0	Spartanburg County SD 05	Duncan
10	752.2	Berkeley County SD	Moncks Corner
11	745.0	Spartanburg County SD 04	Woodruff
12	739.6	Lexington County SD 05	Ballentine
13	737.0	Anderson County SD 05	Anderson
14	734.2	Lexington County SD 04	Swansea
15	725.3	Beaufort County SD	Beaufort
16	700.6	Horry County SD	Conway
17	681.0	Spartanburg County SD 06	Spartanburg
18	675.2	York County SD 03	Rock Hill
19	672.0	Florence County SD 01	Florence
20	665.5	Anderson County SD 03	Iva
21	660.1	York County SD 04	Fort Mill
22	658.0	Union County SD	Union
23	655.3	York County SD 01	York
24	652.3	Greenville County SD	Greenville
25	650.8	Marion County SD 01	Marion
26	645.7	Dillon County SD 02	Dillon
27	633.7	Orangeburg County SD 04	Cordova
28	632.4	Aiken County SD	Aiken
29	631.9	Greenwood 50 County SD	Greenwood
30	630.7	Lancaster County SD	Lancaster
31	628.7	Anderson County SD 02	Honea Path
32	616.0	Sumter County SD 02	Sumter
33	612.9	Spartanburg County SD 02	Spartanburg
34	610.0	Pickens County SD	Easley
35	598.0	Lexington County SD 03	Batesburg
36	597.3	Clarendon County SD 02	Manning
37	591.1	Florence County SD 03	Lake City
38	589.5	Spartanburg County SD 07	Spartanburg
39	578.8	Georgetown County SD	Georgetown
40	574.8	Marion County SD 02	Mullins
41	573.2	Marlboro County SD	Bennettsville
42	571.9	Chesterfield County SD	Chesterfield
43	570.8	Colleton County SD	Walterboro
44	567.5	Laurens County SD 55	Laurens
45	566.8	Anderson County SD 04	Pendleton
46	566.1	Spartanburg County SD 01	Campobello
47	550.1	Charleston County SD	Charleston
48	549.0	Saluda County SD	Saluda
49	547.5	Anderson County SD 01	Williamston
50	542.9	Orangeburg County SD 03	Holly Hill
51	534.2	Oconee County SD	Walhalla
52	527.3	Orangeburg County SD 05	Orangeburg
53	521.6	York County SD 02	Clover
54	517.0	Dillon County SD 03	Latta
55	516.9	Kershaw County SD	Camden
56	514.4	Hampton 1 County SD	Hampton
57	513.7	Florence County SD 05	Johnsonville
58	511.0	Edgefield County SD	Edgefield
59	509.5	Lexington County SD 02	W Columbia
60	507.3	Richland County SD 01	Columbia
61	504.0	Hampton 2 County SD	Estill
62	502.6	Cherokee County SD	Gaffney
63	497.3	Laurens County SD 56	Clinton
64	492.0	Lee County SD	Bishopville
65	490.3	Calhoun County SD	Saint Matthews
65	490.3	Darlington County SD	Darlington
67	489.7	Williamsburg County SD	Kingstree
68	479.5	Allendale County SD	Allendale
69	461.6	Spartanburg County SD 03	Glendale
70	430.0	Greenwood 52 County SD	Ninety Six
71	426.6	Abbeville County SD	Abbeville
72	426.0	Bamberg County SD 01	Bamberg
73	423.0	Newberry County SD	Newberry
74	401.1	Fairfield County SD	Winnsboro

Student/Counselor Ratio

Rank	Ratio	District Name	City
1	716.8	Clarendon County SD 02	Manning
2	596.0	Spartanburg County SD 04	Woodruff
3	556.3	Lexington County SD 03	Batesburg
4	532.4	Anderson County SD 03	Iva
5	517.0	Dillon County SD 03	Latta
6	513.7	Florence County SD 05	Johnsonville
7	504.7	Spartanburg County SD 02	Spartanburg
8	492.8	Florence County SD 01	Florence
9	487.8	Chesterfield County SD	Chesterfield
10	483.9	Aiken County SD	Aiken
11	473.0	Lancaster County SD	Lancaster
12	469.0	Marlboro County SD	Bennettsville
13	467.7	Barnwell County SD 45	Barnwell
14	460.0	Sumter County SD 17	Sumter
15	459.8	Florence County SD 03	Lake City
16	458.9	Lexington County SD 04	Swansea
17	457.3	Lexington County SD 01	Lexington
18	457.0	York County SD 04	Fort Mill
19	456.2	Greenville County SD	Greenville
20	455.0	Pickens County SD	Easley
21	454.2	Edgefield County SD	Edgefield
22	453.7	Anderson County SD 01	Williamston
22	453.7	Berkeley County SD	Moncks Corner
24	451.9	York County SD 01	York
25	450.0	Richland County SD 02	Columbia
26	443.4	Spartanburg County SD 05	Duncan
27	435.1	Laurens County SD 56	Clinton
28	430.0	Greenwood 52 County SD	Ninety Six
29	426.3	Calhoun County SD	Saint Matthews
30	419.8	Lexington County SD 05	Ballentine
31	419.6	Jasper County SD	Ridgeland
32	419.1	Anderson County SD 02	Honea Path
33	419.0	Dorchester County SD 04	Saint George
34	416.6	Horry County SD	Conway
35	416.1	Laurens County SD 55	Laurens
36	412.8	Abbeville County SD	Abbeville
37	412.1	Greenwood 50 County SD	Greenwood
38	411.3	Spartanburg County SD 07	Spartanburg
39	410.9	Charleston County SD	Charleston
40	406.8	Marion County SD 01	Marion
41	405.6	Chester County SD	Chester
42	404.9	Union County SD	Union
43	403.3	Orangeburg County SD 04	Cordova
44	403.2	Kershaw County SD	Camden
44	403.2	Oconee County SD	Walhalla
46	394.6	Georgetown County SD	Georgetown
47	394.2	Beaufort County SD	Beaufort
48	390.3	Lexington County SD 02	W Columbia
49	388.3	York County SD 03	Rock Hill
50	387.4	Cherokee County SD	Gaffney
50	387.4	Dillon County SD 02	Dillon
52	381.4	Spartanburg County SD 06	Spartanburg
53	377.2	Hampton 1 County SD	Hampton
54	376.6	Orangeburg County SD 05	Orangeburg
55	372.6	York County SD 02	Clover
56	362.6	Dorchester County SD 02	Summerville
57	360.5	Colleton County SD	Walterboro
58	356.6	Darlington County SD	Darlington
59	354.3	Anderson County SD 04	Pendleton
60	343.6	Hampton 2 County SD	Estill
61	340.1	Williamsburg County SD	Kingstree
62	335.5	Spartanburg County SD 01	Campobello
63	328.4	Marion County SD 02	Mullins
64	319.7	Allendale County SD	Allendale
65	318.7	Anderson County SD 05	Anderson
66	318.5	Richland County SD 01	Columbia
67	316.7	Orangeburg County SD 03	Holly Hill
68	310.7	Lee County SD	Bishopville
69	303.7	Newberry County SD	Newberry
70	298.9	Bamberg County SD 01	Bamberg
71	298.7	Sumter County SD 02	Sumter
72	277.7	Fairfield County SD	Winnsboro
73	274.5	Saluda County SD	Saluda
74	269.3	Spartanburg County SD 03	Glendale

Current Spending per Student in FY2001

Rank	Dollars	District Name	City
1	9,342	Allendale County SD	Allendale
2	8,875	Spartanburg County SD 07	Spartanburg
3	8,702	Fairfield County SD	Winnsboro
4	8,584	Spartanburg County SD 03	Glendale
5	8,446	York County SD 02	Clover
6	8,223	Richland County SD 01	Columbia
7	7,606	Lexington County SD 03	Batesburg
8	7,528	Dorchester County SD 04	Saint George
9	7,517	Orangeburg County SD 03	Holly Hill
10	7,475	Lee County SD	Bishopville
11	7,453	Hampton 2 County SD	Estill
12	7,367	Calhoun County SD	Saint Matthews
13	7,364	Georgetown County SD	Georgetown
14	7,286	Beaufort County SD	Beaufort
15	7,194	Lexington County SD 02	W Columbia
16	7,154	Newberry County SD	Newberry
17	7,106	Orangeburg County SD 05	Orangeburg
18	6,989	Anderson County SD 04	Pendleton
19	6,949	Bamberg County SD 01	Bamberg
20	6,920	Lexington County SD 05	Ballentine
21	6,908	Oconee County SD	Walhalla
22	6,841	Orangeburg County SD 04	Cordova
23	6,829	Horry County SD	Conway
24	6,784	Saluda County SD	Saluda
25	6,768	Richland County SD 02	Columbia
26	6,730	Edgefield County SD	Edgefield
27	6,709	Darlington County SD	Darlington
28	6,696	Abbeville County SD	Abbeville
29	6,684	Lexington County SD 01	Lexington
30	6,657	Williamsburg County SD	Kingstree
31	6,655	Anderson County SD 05	Anderson
32	6,639	Spartanburg County SD 05	Duncan
33	6,637	Union County SD	Union
34	6,590	Colleton County SD	Walterboro
35	6,567	Spartanburg County SD 01	Campobello
36	6,521	Kershaw County SD	Camden
37	6,488	Florence County SD 05	Johnsonville
38	6,484	Jasper County SD	Ridgeland
39	6,478	Florence County SD 03	Lake City
39	6,478	York County SD 03	Rock Hill
41	6,467	York County SD 04	Fort Mill
42	6,390	Cherokee County SD	Gaffney
43	6,386	Chester County SD	Chester
44	6,324	Marion County SD 02	Mullins
45	6,318	Sumter County SD 17	Sumter
46	6,307	York County SD 01	York
47	6,294	Chesterfield County SD	Chesterfield
48	6,247	Berkeley County SD	Moncks Corner
49	6,213	Florence County SD 01	Florence
50	6,175	Barnwell County SD 45	Barnwell
51	6,169	Charleston County SD	Charleston
52	6,165	Lexington County SD 04	Swansea
53	6,133	Lancaster County SD	Lancaster
54	6,122	Laurens County SD 56	Clinton
55	6,086	Marion County SD 01	Marion
56	6,064	Sumter County SD 02	Sumter
57	6,053	Pickens County SD	Easley
58	6,039	Hampton 1 County SD	Hampton
59	6,030	Greenville County SD	Greenville
60	6,014	Anderson County SD 02	Honea Path
61	5,998	Greenwood 50 County SD	Greenwood
62	5,909	Anderson County SD 03	Iva
63	5,900	Dorchester County SD 02	Summerville
64	5,895	Laurens County SD 55	Laurens
65	5,781	Clarendon County SD 02	Manning
66	5,776	Dillon County SD 03	Latta
67	5,754	Spartanburg County SD 04	Woodruff
68	5,711	Spartanburg County SD 06	Spartanburg
69	5,642	Dillon County SD 02	Dillon
70	5,612	Marlboro County SD	Bennettsville
71	5,609	Aiken County SD	Aiken
72	5,571	Greenwood 52 County SD	Ninety Six
73	5,481	Spartanburg County SD 02	Spartanburg
74	5,410	Anderson County SD 01	Williamston

Number of Diploma Recipients

Rank	Number	District Name	City
1	2,934	Greenville County SD	Greenville
2	1,666	Charleston County SD	Charleston
3	1,335	Horry County SD	Conway
4	1,302	Berkeley County SD	Moncks Corner
5	1,218	Aiken County SD	Aiken
6	1,178	Richland County SD 01	Columbia
7	1,002	Lexington County SD 05	Ballentine
8	958	Richland County SD 02	Columbia
9	906	Lexington County SD 01	Lexington
10	883	Dorchester County SD 02	Summerville
11	759	Beaufort County SD	Beaufort
12	755	Pickens County SD	Easley
12	755	York County SD 03	Rock Hill
14	721	Florence County SD 01	Florence
15	542	Anderson County SD 05	Anderson
16	525	Kershaw County SD	Camden
17	503	Lancaster County SD	Lancaster
18	498	Spartanburg County SD 06	Spartanburg
19	496	Oconee County SD	Walhalla

20	486	Georgetown County SD	Georgetown
21	483	Darlington County SD	Darlington
22	459	Lexington County SD 02	W Columbia
23	427	Greenwood 50 County SD	Greenwood
24	416	Sumter County SD 17	Sumter
25	409	Spartanburg County SD 02	Spartanburg
26	399	Orangeburg County SD 05	Orangeburg
27	380	Anderson County SD 01	Williamston
27	380	Cherokee County SD	Gaffney
29	372	Spartanburg County SD 07	Spartanburg
30	367	Chesterfield County SD	Chesterfield
31	356	Sumter County SD 02	Sumter
32	299	York County SD 04	Fort Mill
33	271	Williamsburg County SD	Kingstree
34	268	Newberry County SD	Newberry
34	268	Spartanburg County SD 05	Duncan
36	266	Colleton County SD	Walterboro
37	242	York County SD 01	York
38	234	Union County SD	Union
39	231	Chester County SD	Chester
40	229	Laurens County SD 55	Laurens
41	211	Spartanburg County SD 01	Campobello
42	207	Marlboro County SD	Bennettsville
43	198	York County SD 02	Clover
44	193	Florence County SD 03	Lake City
44	193	Orangeburg County SD 04	Cordova
46	177	Anderson County SD 02	Honea Path
46	177	Edgefield County SD	Edgefield
48	175	Laurens County SD 56	Clinton
49	171	Abbeville County SD	Abbeville
50	170	Marion County SD 01	Marion
51	167	Clarendon County SD 02	Manning
52	165	Dillon County SD 02	Dillon
53	161	Spartanburg County SD 03	Glendale
54	159	Fairfield County SD	Winnsboro
55	154	Orangeburg County SD 03	Holly Hill
56	125	Barnwell County SD 45	Barnwell
56	125	Lexington County SD 03	Batesburg
58	119	Lee County SD	Bishopville
59	117	Marion County SD 02	Mullins
60	116	Dorchester County SD 04	Saint George
61	108	Lexington County SD 04	Swansea
62	106	Anderson County SD 03	Iva
63	104	Hampton 1 County SD	Hampton
64	101	Spartanburg County SD 04	Woodruff
65	99	Anderson County SD 04	Pendleton
66	95	Bamberg County SD 01	Bamberg
67	91	Greenwood 52 County SD	Ninety Six
68	85	Jasper County SD	Ridgeland
69	79	Saluda County SD	Saluda
70	78	Allendale County SD	Allendale
71	77	Dillon County SD 03	Latta
72	75	Calhoun County SD	Saint Matthews
73	68	Hampton 2 County SD	Estill
74	62	Florence County SD 05	Johnsonville

High School Drop-out Rate

Rank	Percent	District Name	City
1	9.3	Orangeburg County SD 03	Holly Hill
2	9.0	Marlboro County SD	Bennettsville
3	8.6	Lee County SD	Bishopville
4	8.2	Anderson County SD 02	Honea Path
5	8.0	Lancaster County SD	Lancaster
6	6.9	Dillon County SD 02	Dillon
7	6.8	Colleton County SD	Walterboro
7	6.8	Florence County SD 05	Johnsonville
9	6.4	Lexington County SD 04	Swansea
10	5.9	Abbeville County SD	Abbeville
11	5.7	York County SD 02	Clover
12	5.6	York County SD 01	York
13	5.4	Hampton 1 County SD	Hampton
14	5.3	Chester County SD	Chester
15	5.1	Anderson County SD 05	Anderson
16	4.8	Chesterfield County SD	Chesterfield
17	4.7	Pickens County SD	Easley
18	4.4	Orangeburg County SD 04	Cordova
18	4.4	Union County SD	Union
20	4.3	Richland County SD 01	Columbia
21	4.2	Greenwood 50 County SD	Greenwood
22	4.1	Newberry County SD	Newberry
23	4.0	Berkeley County SD	Moncks Corner
24	3.9	Clarendon County SD 02	Manning
24	3.9	Dorchester County SD 04	Saint George
24	3.9	Florence County SD 01	Florence
24	3.9	Hampton 2 County SD	Estill
28	3.8	Kershaw County SD	Camden
28	3.8	Laurens County SD 55	Laurens
28	3.8	Spartanburg County SD 07	Spartanburg
31	3.7	Edgefield County SD	Edgefield
31	3.7	Richland County SD 02	Columbia
33	3.6	Saluda County SD	Saluda
34	3.5	Dorchester County SD 02	Summerville
34	3.5	Marion County SD 02	Mullins
36	3.4	Beaufort County SD	Beaufort
36	3.4	Dillon County SD 03	Latta
38	3.3	Allendale County SD	Allendale
38	3.3	Orangeburg County SD 05	Orangeburg
40	3.1	Aiken County SD	Aiken
40	3.1	Barnwell County SD 45	Barnwell
40	3.1	Cherokee County SD	Gaffney
40	3.1	Laurens County SD 56	Clinton
44	3.0	Fairfield County SD	Winnsboro
44	3.0	Spartanburg County SD 05	Duncan
46	2.9	Darlington County SD	Darlington
46	2.9	Lexington County SD 02	W Columbia
46	2.9	Lexington County SD 03	Batesburg
46	2.9	Marion County SD 01	Marion
46	2.9	Sumter County SD 02	Sumter
46	2.9	Sumter County SD 17	Sumter
52	2.8	Charleston County SD	Charleston
53	2.5	Bamberg County SD 01	Bamberg
54	2.4	Anderson County SD 03	Iva
55	2.2	Greenville County SD	Greenville
55	2.2	Spartanburg County SD 02	Spartanburg
57	2.1	Lexington County SD 05	Ballentine
57	2.1	Williamsburg County SD	Kingstree
59	2.0	York County SD 04	Fort Mill
60	1.9	Horry County SD	Conway
60	1.9	Oconee County SD	Walhalla
62	1.8	Anderson County SD 01	Williamston
62	1.8	Lexington County SD 01	Lexington
64	1.6	York County SD 03	Rock Hill
65	1.5	Georgetown County SD	Georgetown
65	1.5	Greenwood 52 County SD	Ninety Six
67	1.4	Calhoun County SD	Saint Matthews
67	1.4	Spartanburg County SD 01	Campobello
67	1.4	Spartanburg County SD 06	Spartanburg
70	1.3	Florence County SD 03	Lake City
71	0.9	Anderson County SD 04	Pendleton
71	0.9	Spartanburg County SD 04	Woodruff
73	0.6	Jasper County SD	Ridgeland
73	0.6	Spartanburg County SD 03	Glendale

South Dakota

South Dakota Public School Educational Profile

Category	Value	Category	Value
Schools *(2002-2003)*	773	**Diploma Recipients** *(2002-2003)*	8,796
Instructional Level		White, Non-Hispanic	8,232
Primary	377	Black, Non-Hispanic	49
Middle	172	Asian/Pacific Islander	99
High	185	American Indian/Alaskan Native	354
Other Level	39	Hispanic	62
Curriculum		**High School Drop-out Rate** (%) *(2000-2001)*	3.9
Regular	744	White, Non-Hispanic	2.6
Special Education	7	Black, Non-Hispanic	6.3
Vocational	0	Asian/Pacific Islander	3.9
Alternative	22	American Indian/Alaskan Native	20.6
Type		Hispanic	8.7
Magnet	0	**Staff** *(2002-2003)*	19,033.6
Charter	0	Teachers	9,256.4
Title I Eligible	367	Average Salary ($)	32,414
School-wide Title I	139	Librarians/Media Specialists	162.3
Students *(2002-2003)*	128,049	Guidance Counselors	320.1
Gender (%)		**Ratios** *(2002-2003)*	
Male	51.8	Student/Teacher Ratio	13.8 to 1
Female	48.2	Student/Librarian Ratio	789.0 to 1
Race/Ethnicity (%)		Student/Counselor Ratio	400.0 to 1
White, Non-Hispanic	85.3	**Current Spending** *($ per student in FY 2001)*	6,424
Black, Non-Hispanic	1.5	Instruction	3,803
Asian/Pacific Islander	1.0	Support Services	2,273
American Indian/Alaskan Native	10.6	**College Entrance Exam Scores** *(2003)*	
Hispanic	1.6	Scholastic Aptitude Test (SAT)	
Classification (%)		Participation Rate (%)	4
Individual Education Program (IEP)	13.5	Mean SAT I Verbal Score	588
Migrant	1.8	Mean SAT I Math Score	588
English Language Learner (ELL)	3.5	American College Testing Program (ACT)	
Eligible for Free Lunch Program	21.3	Participation Rate (%)	70
Eligible for Reduced-Price Lunch Program	9.0	Average Composite Score	21.4

Note: *For an explanation of data, please refer to the User's Guide in the front of the book; n/a indicates data not available*

South Dakota NAEP 2003 Test Scores

Reading			Mathematics		
Grade/Category	Value	Rank	Grade/Category	Value	Rank
4th Grade			**4th Grade**		
Average Proficiency	222.3 (1.2)	13/51	Average Proficiency	237.3 (0.7)	17/51
Proficiency by Gender/Race/Ethnicity			Proficiency by Gender/Race/Ethnicity		
Male	219.5 (1.5)	10/51	Male	239.0 (0.8)	15/51
Female	225.1 (1.3)	21/51	Female	235.5 (1.0)	17/51
White, Non-Hispanic	226.5 (0.9)	20/51	White, Non-Hispanic	240.9 (0.6)	31/51
Black, Non-Hispanic	n/a	n/a	Black, Non-Hispanic	n/a	n/a
Asian, Non-Hispanic	n/a	n/a	Asian, Non-Hispanic	222.8 (3.7)	18/43
American Indian, Non-Hispanic	n/a	n/a	American Indian, Non-Hispanic	n/a	n/a
Hispanic	196.6 (3.4)	6/12	Hispanic	216.5 (2.1)	8/12
Proficiency by Class Size			Proficiency by Class Size		
Less than 16 Students	221.8 (3.2)	3/45	Less than 16 Students	231.2 (2.7)	9/47
16 to 18 Students	217.8 (3.3)	20/48	16 to 18 Students	235.2 (2.1)	20/48
19 to 20 Students	220.3 (4.1)	24/50	19 to 20 Students	237.8 (1.6)	13/50
21 to 25 Students	225.6 (1.7)	13/51	21 to 25 Students	238.9 (1.0)	20/51
Greater than 25 Students	220.4 (2.5)	22/49	Greater than 25 Students	240.1 (2.4)	11/49
Percent Attaining Achievement Levels			Percent Attaining Achievement Levels		
Below Basic	31.2 (1.4)	41/51	Below Basic	17.8 (1.0)	37/51
Basic or Above	68.8 (1.4)	11/51	Basic or Above	82.2 (1.0)	15/51
Proficient or Above	33.5 (1.3)	16/51	Proficient or Above	33.7 (1.3)	21/51
Advanced or Above	7.3 (0.7)	23/51	Advanced or Above	2.9 (0.4)	31/51
8th Grade			**8th Grade**		
Average Proficiency	270.0 (0.8)	4/51	Average Proficiency	284.9 (0.8)	7/51
Proficiency by Gender/Race/Ethnicity			Proficiency by Gender/Race/Ethnicity		
Male	264.6 (1.2)	4/51	Male	285.9 (0.9)	5/51
Female	275.2 (1.1)	5/51	Female	283.8 (1.1)	7/51
White, Non-Hispanic	272.8 (0.8)	8/50	White, Non-Hispanic	288.2 (0.6)	18/50
Black, Non-Hispanic	n/a	n/a	Black, Non-Hispanic	n/a	n/a
Asian, Non-Hispanic	n/a	n/a	Asian, Non-Hispanic	n/a	n/a
American Indian, Non-Hispanic	n/a	n/a	American Indian, Non-Hispanic	n/a	n/a
Hispanic	246.0 (3.2)	4/10	Hispanic	254.9 (3.5)	9/11
Proficiency by Parents Highest Level of Ed.			Proficiency by Parents Highest Level of Ed.		
Did Not Finish High School	249.8 (3.4)	12/50	Did Not Finish High School	266.6 (3.7)	3/50
Graduated High School	264.2 (1.6)	1/50	Graduated High School	276.6 (1.7)	5/50
Some Education After High School	272.4 (1.5)	3/50	Some Education After High School	284.7 (1.7)	9/50
Graduated College	276.5 (0.9)	7/50	Graduated College	293.2 (0.8)	9/50
Percent Attaining Achievement Levels			Percent Attaining Achievement Levels		
Below Basic	18.5 (0.9)	49/51	Below Basic	21.8 (1.3)	47/51
Basic or Above	81.5 (0.9)	2/51	Basic or Above	78.2 (1.3)	5/51
Proficient or Above	38.6 (1.2)	3/51	Proficient or Above	34.7 (1.1)	8/51
Advanced or Above	2.9 (0.5)	20/51	Advanced or Above	4.8 (0.5)	27/51

Note: *For an explanation of data, please refer to the User's Guide in the front of the book; values in italics indicate that the nature of the sample does not allow accurate determination of the variability of the statistic; n/a indicates data not available*

Beadle County

Huron SD 02-2

88 3rd St SE • Huron, SD 57350-0949
Mailing Address: PO Box 949 • Huron, SD 57350-0949
(605) 353-6990
Grade Span: PK-12; **Agency Type:** 1
Schools: 11
7 Primary; 1 Middle; 3 High; 0 Other Level
9 Regular; 0 Special Education; 0 Vocational; 2 Alternative
0 Magnet; 0 Charter; 3 Title I Eligible; 3 School-wide Title I
Students: 2,195 (51.3% male; 48.7% female)
Individual Education Program: 289 (13.2%);
English Language Learner: 54 (2.5%); Migrant: 95 (4.3%)
Eligible for Free Lunch Program: 432 (19.7%)
Eligible for Reduced-Price Lunch Program: 229 (10.4%)
Teachers: 141.4 (15.5 to 1)
Librarians/Media Specialists: 2.0 (1,097.5 to 1)
Guidance Counselors: 4.0 (548.8 to 1)
Current Spending: ($ per student per year):
Total: $5,812; Instruction: $3,448; Support Services: $1,965
Enrollment, Drop-out Rates and Diploma Recipients by Race/Ethnicity

Category	Total	White	Black	Asian	AIAN	Hisp.
Enrollment (%)	100.0	92.8	2.5	0.8	2.6	1.4
Drop-out Rate (%)	3.9	3.9	0.0	0.0	9.5	0.0
H.S. Diplomas (#)	157	154	0	3	0	0

Brookings County

Brookings SD 05-1

2130 8th St S • Brookings, SD 57006-3507
(605) 696-4703 • http://www.bpsce.org/bsshp.htm
Grade Span: PK-12; **Agency Type:** 1
Schools: 5
3 Primary; 1 Middle; 1 High; 0 Other Level
5 Regular; 0 Special Education; 0 Vocational; 0 Alternative
0 Magnet; 0 Charter; 3 Title I Eligible; 0 School-wide Title I
Students: 2,693 (52.6% male; 47.4% female)
Individual Education Program: 340 (12.6%);
English Language Learner: 0 (0.0%); Migrant: 2 (0.1%)
Eligible for Free Lunch Program: 298 (11.1%)
Eligible for Reduced-Price Lunch Program: 152 (5.6%)
Teachers: 178.2 (15.1 to 1)
Librarians/Media Specialists: 4.5 (598.4 to 1)
Guidance Counselors: 7.5 (359.1 to 1)
Current Spending: ($ per student per year):
Total: $5,223; Instruction: $3,419; Support Services: $1,605
Enrollment, Drop-out Rates and Diploma Recipients by Race/Ethnicity

Category	Total	White	Black	Asian	AIAN	Hisp.
Enrollment (%)	100.0	91.2	1.2	3.2	2.9	1.5
Drop-out Rate (%)	1.3	1.2	0.0	0.0	7.7	0.0
H.S. Diplomas (#)	231	220	0	7	2	2

Brown County

Aberdeen SD 06-1

314 S Main St • Aberdeen, SD 57401-4146
(605) 725-7100 • http://www.aberdeen.k12.sd.us/
Grade Span: PK-12; **Agency Type:** 1
Schools: 9
5 Primary; 2 Middle; 1 High; 1 Other Level
8 Regular; 0 Special Education; 0 Vocational; 1 Alternative
0 Magnet; 0 Charter; 4 Title I Eligible; 0 School-wide Title I
Students: 3,797 (50.9% male; 49.1% female)
Individual Education Program: 540 (14.2%);
English Language Learner: 0 (0.0%); Migrant: 2 (0.1%)
Eligible for Free Lunch Program: 564 (14.9%)
Eligible for Reduced-Price Lunch Program: 261 (6.9%)
Teachers: 227.2 (16.7 to 1)
Librarians/Media Specialists: 4.0 (949.3 to 1)
Guidance Counselors: 10.7 (354.9 to 1)
Current Spending: ($ per student per year):
Total: $5,620; Instruction: $3,269; Support Services: $2,081
Enrollment, Drop-out Rates and Diploma Recipients by Race/Ethnicity

Category	Total	White	Black	Asian	AIAN	Hisp.
Enrollment (%)	100.0	89.9	0.6	0.9	7.8	0.8
Drop-out Rate (%)	4.3	3.6	12.5	0.0	16.4	0.0
H.S. Diplomas (#)	289	273	1	6	9	0

Codington County

Watertown SD 14-4

200 NE 9th St • Watertown, SD 57201-0730
Mailing Address: PO Box 730 • Watertown, SD 57201-0730
(605) 882-6312
Grade Span: PK-12; **Agency Type:** 1
Schools: 8
5 Primary; 1 Middle; 1 High; 1 Other Level
7 Regular; 0 Special Education; 0 Vocational; 1 Alternative
0 Magnet; 0 Charter; 4 Title I Eligible; 0 School-wide Title I
Students: 3,952 (50.9% male; 49.1% female)
Individual Education Program: 485 (12.3%);
English Language Learner: 0 (0.0%); Migrant: 31 (0.8%)
Eligible for Free Lunch Program: 580 (14.7%)
Eligible for Reduced-Price Lunch Program: 333 (8.4%)
Teachers: 238.7 (16.6 to 1)
Librarians/Media Specialists: 2.0 (1,976.0 to 1)
Guidance Counselors: 7.0 (564.6 to 1)
Current Spending: ($ per student per year):
Total: $5,186; Instruction: $3,419; Support Services: $1,527
Enrollment, Drop-out Rates and Diploma Recipients by Race/Ethnicity

Category	Total	White	Black	Asian	AIAN	Hisp.
Enrollment (%)	100.0	94.7	0.2	0.9	3.2	1.1
Drop-out Rate (%)	3.1	2.6	0.0	0.0	17.6	25.0
H.S. Diplomas (#)	1	1	0	0	0	0

Davison County

Mitchell SD 17-2

800 W 10th Ave • Mitchell, SD 57301-7760
Mailing Address: PO Box 7760 • Mitchell, SD 57301-7760
(605) 995-3010 • http://www.mitchell.k12.sd.us/
Grade Span: PK-12; **Agency Type:** 1
Schools: 8
5 Primary; 1 Middle; 2 High; 0 Other Level
8 Regular; 0 Special Education; 0 Vocational; 0 Alternative
0 Magnet; 0 Charter; 5 Title I Eligible; 0 School-wide Title I
Students: 2,611 (51.4% male; 48.6% female)
Individual Education Program: 407 (15.6%);
English Language Learner: 0 (0.0%); Migrant: 64 (2.5%)
Eligible for Free Lunch Program: 581 (22.3%)
Eligible for Reduced-Price Lunch Program: 199 (7.6%)
Teachers: 175.7 (14.9 to 1)
Librarians/Media Specialists: 1.0 (2,611.0 to 1)
Guidance Counselors: 6.9 (378.4 to 1)
Current Spending: ($ per student per year):
Total: $5,688; Instruction: $3,481; Support Services: $1,961
Enrollment, Drop-out Rates and Diploma Recipients by Race/Ethnicity

Category	Total	White	Black	Asian	AIAN	Hisp.
Enrollment (%)	100.0	92.1	0.8	0.9	4.6	1.6
Drop-out Rate (%)	0.2	0.1	0.0	0.0	6.3	0.0
H.S. Diplomas (#)	224	218	0	3	2	1

Dewey County

Cheyenne River

PO Box 2020 • Eagle Butte, SD 57625
(605) 964-8722
Grade Span: KG-12; **Agency Type:** 6
Schools: 4
1 Primary; 0 Middle; 0 High; 3 Other Level
4 Regular; 0 Special Education; 0 Vocational; 0 Alternative
0 Magnet; 0 Charter; 4 Title I Eligible; 4 School-wide Title I
Students: 1,575 (n/a% male; n/a% female)
Individual Education Program: n/a;
English Language Learner: n/a; Migrant: n/a
Eligible for Free Lunch Program: n/a
Eligible for Reduced-Price Lunch Program: n/a
Teachers: n/a
Librarians/Media Specialists: n/a
Guidance Counselors: n/a
Current Spending: ($ per student per year):
Total: n/a; Instruction: n/a; Support Services: n/a
Enrollment, Drop-out Rates and Diploma Recipients by Race/Ethnicity

Category	Total	White	Black	Asian	AIAN	Hisp.
Enrollment (%)	100.0	0.0	0.0	0.0	100.0	0.0
Drop-out Rate (%)	n/a	n/a	n/a	n/a	n/a	n/a
H.S. Diplomas (#)	n/a	n/a	n/a	n/a	n/a	n/a

Hughes County

Pierre SD 32-2

211 S Poplar Ave • Pierre, SD 57501-1845
(605) 773-7300
Grade Span: PK-12; **Agency Type:** 1
Schools: 7
5 Primary; 1 Middle; 1 High; 0 Other Level
7 Regular; 0 Special Education; 0 Vocational; 0 Alternative
0 Magnet; 0 Charter; 3 Title I Eligible; 0 School-wide Title I
Students: 2,864 (51.6% male; 48.4% female)
Individual Education Program: 346 (12.1%);
English Language Learner: 0 (0.0%); Migrant: 12 (0.4%)
Eligible for Free Lunch Program: 413 (14.4%)
Eligible for Reduced-Price Lunch Program: 135 (4.7%)
Teachers: 158.9 (18.0 to 1)
Librarians/Media Specialists: 2.0 (1,432.0 to 1)
Guidance Counselors: 8.0 (358.0 to 1)
Current Spending: ($ per student per year):
Total: $5,499; Instruction: $3,562; Support Services: $1,693
Enrollment, Drop-out Rates and Diploma Recipients by Race/Ethnicity

Category	Total	White	Black	Asian	AIAN	Hisp.
Enrollment (%)	100.0	84.6	0.2	0.9	12.9	1.4
Drop-out Rate (%)	5.9	3.8	0.0	0.0	40.0	0.0
H.S. Diplomas (#)	225	214	2	3	4	2

Lawrence County

Spearfish SD 40-2

525 E Illinois St • Spearfish, SD 57783-2521
(605) 717-1229 • http://spearfish.k12.sd.us/
Grade Span: PK-12; **Agency Type:** 1
Schools: 4
2 Primary; 1 Middle; 1 High; 0 Other Level
4 Regular; 0 Special Education; 0 Vocational; 0 Alternative
0 Magnet; 0 Charter; 2 Title I Eligible; 1 School-wide Title I
Students: 2,075 (52.8% male; 47.2% female)
Individual Education Program: 286 (13.8%);
English Language Learner: 4 (0.2%); Migrant: 17 (0.8%)
Eligible for Free Lunch Program: 288 (13.9%)
Eligible for Reduced-Price Lunch Program: 144 (6.9%)
Teachers: 130.7 (15.9 to 1)
Librarians/Media Specialists: 2.9 (715.5 to 1)
Guidance Counselors: 4.5 (461.1 to 1)
Current Spending: ($ per student per year):
Total: $5,715; Instruction: $3,673; Support Services: $1,809
Enrollment, Drop-out Rates and Diploma Recipients by Race/Ethnicity

Category	Total	White	Black	Asian	AIAN	Hisp.
Enrollment (%)	100.0	92.4	0.8	1.0	3.6	2.2
Drop-out Rate (%)	3.1	2.5	0.0	0.0	21.7	6.3
H.S. Diplomas (#)	174	164	1	1	6	2

Lincoln County

Lennox SD 41-4

201 S Elm St • Lennox, SD 57039-0038
Mailing Address: PO Box 38 • Lennox, SD 57039-0038
(605) 647-2202
Grade Span: PK-12; **Agency Type:** 1
Schools: 7
4 Primary; 2 Middle; 1 High; 0 Other Level
7 Regular; 0 Special Education; 0 Vocational; 0 Alternative
0 Magnet; 0 Charter; 4 Title I Eligible; 0 School-wide Title I
Students: 1,676 (52.0% male; 48.0% female)
Individual Education Program: 250 (14.9%);
English Language Learner: 0 (0.0%); Migrant: 8 (0.5%)
Eligible for Free Lunch Program: 153 (9.1%)
Eligible for Reduced-Price Lunch Program: 101 (6.0%)
Teachers: 108.7 (15.4 to 1)
Librarians/Media Specialists: 1.0 (1,676.0 to 1)
Guidance Counselors: 4.5 (372.4 to 1)
Current Spending: ($ per student per year):
Total: $5,131; Instruction: $2,951; Support Services: $1,917
Enrollment, Drop-out Rates and Diploma Recipients by Race/Ethnicity

Category	Total	White	Black	Asian	AIAN	Hisp.
Enrollment (%)	100.0	97.9	1.1	0.2	0.4	0.5
Drop-out Rate (%)	1.0	1.0	0.0	n/a	0.0	0.0
H.S. Diplomas (#)	84	83	1	0	0	0

Meade County

Meade SD 46-1

1230 Douglas St • Sturgis, SD 57785-1869
(605) 347-2523 • http://meade.k12.sd.us/
Grade Span: PK-12; **Agency Type:** 1
Schools: 14
11 Primary; 1 Middle; 2 High; 0 Other Level
13 Regular; 0 Special Education; 0 Vocational; 1 Alternative
0 Magnet; 0 Charter; 4 Title I Eligible; 0 School-wide Title I
Students: 2,765 (52.6% male; 47.4% female)
Individual Education Program: 313 (11.3%);
English Language Learner: 0 (0.0%); Migrant: 72 (2.6%)
Eligible for Free Lunch Program: 484 (17.5%)
Eligible for Reduced-Price Lunch Program: 236 (8.5%)
Teachers: 193.6 (14.3 to 1)
Librarians/Media Specialists: 2.0 (1,382.5 to 1)
Guidance Counselors: 8.0 (345.6 to 1)
Current Spending: ($ per student per year):
Total: $5,641; Instruction: $3,554; Support Services: $1,831
Enrollment, Drop-out Rates and Diploma Recipients by Race/Ethnicity

Category	Total	White	Black	Asian	AIAN	Hisp.
Enrollment (%)	100.0	93.3	1.0	1.0	3.2	1.4
Drop-out Rate (%)	2.6	2.6	0.0	0.0	4.2	0.0
H.S. Diplomas (#)	188	178	3	1	5	1

Minnehaha County

Brandon Valley SD 49-2

301 S Splitrock Blvd • Brandon, SD 57005-1651
(605) 582-2049 • http://www.splitrocktel.net/~bvsdco/
Grade Span: PK-12; **Agency Type:** 1
Schools: 4
2 Primary; 1 Middle; 1 High; 0 Other Level
4 Regular; 0 Special Education; 0 Vocational; 0 Alternative
0 Magnet; 0 Charter; 2 Title I Eligible; 0 School-wide Title I
Students: 2,635 (51.0% male; 49.0% female)
Individual Education Program: 257 (9.8%);
English Language Learner: 0 (0.0%); Migrant: 17 (0.6%)
Eligible for Free Lunch Program: 116 (4.4%)
Eligible for Reduced-Price Lunch Program: 101 (3.8%)
Teachers: 138.4 (19.0 to 1)
Librarians/Media Specialists: 2.9 (908.6 to 1)
Guidance Counselors: 5.0 (527.0 to 1)
Current Spending: ($ per student per year):
Total: $4,991; Instruction: $2,870; Support Services: $1,812
Enrollment, Drop-out Rates and Diploma Recipients by Race/Ethnicity

Category	Total	White	Black	Asian	AIAN	Hisp.
Enrollment (%)	100.0	97.4	0.6	0.9	0.6	0.5
Drop-out Rate (%)	0.5	0.5	0.0	0.0	0.0	0.0
H.S. Diplomas (#)	195	191	1	2	0	1

Sioux Falls SD 49-5

201 E 38th St • Sioux Falls, SD 57105-5898
(605) 367-7920 • http://www.sf.k12.sd.us/
Grade Span: PK-12; **Agency Type:** 1
Schools: 43
25 Primary; 5 Middle; 3 High; 10 Other Level
34 Regular; 4 Special Education; 0 Vocational; 5 Alternative
0 Magnet; 0 Charter; 7 Title I Eligible; 7 School-wide Title I
Students: 20,072 (51.7% male; 48.3% female)
Individual Education Program: 2,716 (13.5%);
English Language Learner: 754 (3.8%); Migrant: 694 (3.5%)
Eligible for Free Lunch Program: 3,509 (17.5%)
Eligible for Reduced-Price Lunch Program: 1,573 (7.8%)
Teachers: 1,212.3 (16.6 to 1)
Librarians/Media Specialists: 19.2 (1,045.4 to 1)
Guidance Counselors: 44.1 (455.1 to 1)
Current Spending: ($ per student per year):
Total: $5,778; Instruction: $3,554; Support Services: $1,955
Enrollment, Drop-out Rates and Diploma Recipients by Race/Ethnicity

Category	Total	White	Black	Asian	AIAN	Hisp.
Enrollment (%)	100.0	85.0	5.0	2.3	3.7	4.1
Drop-out Rate (%)	4.8	3.9	5.2	7.5	26.6	10.6
H.S. Diplomas (#)	1,131	1,051	24	23	15	18

Pennington County

Douglas SD 51-1

400 Patriot Dr • Box Elder, SD 57719-2218
(605) 923-0000 • http://www.dsdk12.net/
Grade Span: PK-12; **Agency Type:** 1
Schools: 6
3 Primary; 2 Middle; 1 High; 0 Other Level
6 Regular; 0 Special Education; 0 Vocational; 0 Alternative

0 Magnet; 0 Charter; 1 Title I Eligible; 0 School-wide Title I
Students: 2,535 (51.3% male; 48.7% female)
Individual Education Program: 447 (17.6%);
English Language Learner: 0 (0.0%); Migrant: 0 (0.0%)
Eligible for Free Lunch Program: 477 (18.8%)
Eligible for Reduced-Price Lunch Program: 393 (15.5%)
Teachers: 199.4 (12.7 to 1)
Librarians/Media Specialists: 3.0 (845.0 to 1)
Guidance Counselors: 7.0 (362.1 to 1)
Current Spending: ($ per student per year):
Total: $6,916; Instruction: $4,404; Support Services: $2,279
Enrollment, Drop-out Rates and Diploma Recipients by Race/Ethnicity

Category	Total	White	Black	Asian	AIAN	Hisp.
Enrollment (%)	100.0	84.1	4.6	1.8	6.1	3.4
Drop-out Rate (%)	5.9	5.9	3.8	4.8	11.8	0.0
H.S. Diplomas (#)	96	79	4	5	5	3

Rapid City Area SD 51-4

300 6th St • Rapid City, SD 57701-2724
(605) 394-4031
Grade Span: PK-12; **Agency Type:** 1
Schools: 25
16 Primary; 5 Middle; 3 High; 1 Other Level
24 Regular; 0 Special Education; 0 Vocational; 1 Alternative
0 Magnet; 0 Charter; 10 Title I Eligible; 6 School-wide Title I
Students: 13,820 (51.9% male; 48.1% female)
Individual Education Program: 1,673 (12.1%);
English Language Learner: 51 (0.4%); Migrant: 149 (1.1%)
Eligible for Free Lunch Program: 2,778 (20.1%)
Eligible for Reduced-Price Lunch Program: 814 (5.9%)
Teachers: 805.7 (17.2 to 1)
Librarians/Media Specialists: 19.0 (727.4 to 1)
Guidance Counselors: 23.0 (600.9 to 1)
Current Spending: ($ per student per year):
Total: $5,402; Instruction: $3,352; Support Services: $1,845
Enrollment, Drop-out Rates and Diploma Recipients by Race/Ethnicity

Category	Total	White	Black	Asian	AIAN	Hisp.
Enrollment (%)	100.0	78.7	1.5	1.3	16.6	1.9
Drop-out Rate (%)	7.0	4.6	19.1	7.0	23.1	12.3
H.S. Diplomas (#)	1,186	1,069	5	15	87	10

Shannon County

Pine Ridge Agency

PO Box 333 • Pine Ridge, SD 57770
(605) 867-1306
Grade Span: KG-12; **Agency Type:** 6
Schools: 7
3 Primary; 0 Middle; 0 High; 4 Other Level
7 Regular; 0 Special Education; 0 Vocational; 0 Alternative
0 Magnet; 0 Charter; 7 Title I Eligible; 7 School-wide Title I
Students: 3,179 (n/a% male; n/a% female)
Individual Education Program: n/a;
English Language Learner: n/a; Migrant: n/a
Eligible for Free Lunch Program: n/a
Eligible for Reduced-Price Lunch Program: n/a
Teachers: n/a
Librarians/Media Specialists: n/a
Guidance Counselors: n/a
Current Spending: ($ per student per year):
Total: n/a; Instruction: n/a; Support Services: n/a
Enrollment, Drop-out Rates and Diploma Recipients by Race/Ethnicity

Category	Total	White	Black	Asian	AIAN	Hisp.
Enrollment (%)	100.0	0.0	0.0	0.0	100.0	0.0
Drop-out Rate (%)	n/a	n/a	n/a	n/a	n/a	n/a
H.S. Diplomas (#)	n/a	n/a	n/a	n/a	n/a	n/a

Todd County

Todd County SD 66-1

E Denver Dr • Mission, SD 57555-0087
Mailing Address: PO Box 87 • Mission, SD 57555-0087
(605) 856-4457 • http://www.tcsdk12.org/
Grade Span: PK-12; **Agency Type:** 1
Schools: 12
9 Primary; 2 Middle; 1 High; 0 Other Level
12 Regular; 0 Special Education; 0 Vocational; 0 Alternative
0 Magnet; 0 Charter; 12 Title I Eligible; 12 School-wide Title I
Students: 2,072 (52.5% male; 47.5% female)
Individual Education Program: 331 (16.0%);
English Language Learner: 1,656 (79.9%); Migrant: 3 (0.1%)
Eligible for Free Lunch Program: 1,528 (73.7%)
Eligible for Reduced-Price Lunch Program: 144 (6.9%)
Teachers: 193.5 (10.7 to 1)
Librarians/Media Specialists: 2.0 (1,036.0 to 1)
Guidance Counselors: 12.0 (172.7 to 1)
Current Spending: ($ per student per year):
Total: $9,527; Instruction: $5,479; Support Services: $3,670
Enrollment, Drop-out Rates and Diploma Recipients by Race/Ethnicity

Category	Total	White	Black	Asian	AIAN	Hisp.
Enrollment (%)	100.0	4.8	0.3	0.0	94.8	0.0
Drop-out Rate (%)	29.7	7.7	0.0	n/a	31.5	0.0
H.S. Diplomas (#)	54	6	0	0	48	0

Yankton County

Yankton SD 63-3

1900 Ferdig • Yankton, SD 57078-0738
Mailing Address: PO Box 738 • Yankton, SD 57078-0738
(605) 665-3998 • http://www.ysd.k12.sd.us/
Grade Span: PK-12; **Agency Type:** 1
Schools: 6
4 Primary; 1 Middle; 1 High; 0 Other Level
6 Regular; 0 Special Education; 0 Vocational; 0 Alternative
0 Magnet; 0 Charter; 3 Title I Eligible; 0 School-wide Title I
Students: 3,140 (51.5% male; 48.5% female)
Individual Education Program: 454 (14.5%);
English Language Learner: 1 (<0.1%); Migrant: 21 (0.7%)
Eligible for Free Lunch Program: 569 (18.1%)
Eligible for Reduced-Price Lunch Program: 261 (8.3%)
Teachers: 184.1 (17.1 to 1)
Librarians/Media Specialists: 1.9 (1,652.6 to 1)
Guidance Counselors: 8.0 (392.5 to 1)
Current Spending: ($ per student per year):
Total: $5,216; Instruction: $3,118; Support Services: $1,816
Enrollment, Drop-out Rates and Diploma Recipients by Race/Ethnicity

Category	Total	White	Black	Asian	AIAN	Hisp.
Enrollment (%)	100.0	93.6	1.0	0.7	2.6	2.1
Drop-out Rate (%)	4.8	4.4	25.0	0.0	25.0	0.0
H.S. Diplomas (#)	229	224	1	2	2	0

Number of Schools

Rank	Number	District Name	City
1	43	Sioux Falls SD 49-5	Sioux Falls
2	25	Rapid City Area SD 51-4	Rapid City
3	14	Meade SD 46-1	Sturgis
4	12	Todd County SD 66-1	Mission
5	11	Huron SD 02-2	Huron
6	9	Aberdeen SD 06-1	Aberdeen
7	8	Mitchell SD 17-2	Mitchell
7	8	Watertown SD 14-4	Watertown
9	7	Lennox SD 41-4	Lennox
9	7	Pierre SD 32-2	Pierre
9	7	Pine Ridge Agency	Pine Ridge
12	6	Douglas SD 51-1	Box Elder
12	6	Yankton SD 63-3	Yankton
14	5	Brookings SD 05-1	Brookings
15	4	Brandon Valley SD 49-2	Brandon
15	4	Cheyenne River	Eagle Butte
15	4	Spearfish SD 40-2	Spearfish

Number of Teachers

Rank	Number	District Name	City
1	1,212	Sioux Falls SD 49-5	Sioux Falls
2	805	Rapid City Area SD 51-4	Rapid City
3	238	Watertown SD 14-4	Watertown
4	227	Aberdeen SD 06-1	Aberdeen
5	199	Douglas SD 51-1	Box Elder
6	193	Meade SD 46-1	Sturgis
7	193	Todd County SD 66-1	Mission
8	184	Yankton SD 63-3	Yankton
9	178	Brookings SD 05-1	Brookings
10	175	Mitchell SD 17-2	Mitchell
11	158	Pierre SD 32-2	Pierre
12	141	Huron SD 02-2	Huron
13	138	Brandon Valley SD 49-2	Brandon
14	130	Spearfish SD 40-2	Spearfish
15	108	Lennox SD 41-4	Lennox
16	n/a	Cheyenne River	Eagle Butte
16	n/a	Pine Ridge Agency	Pine Ridge

Number of Students

Rank	Number	District Name	City
1	20,072	Sioux Falls SD 49-5	Sioux Falls
2	13,820	Rapid City Area SD 51-4	Rapid City
3	3,952	Watertown SD 14-4	Watertown
4	3,797	Aberdeen SD 06-1	Aberdeen
5	3,179	Pine Ridge Agency	Pine Ridge
6	3,140	Yankton SD 63-3	Yankton
7	2,864	Pierre SD 32-2	Pierre
8	2,765	Meade SD 46-1	Sturgis
9	2,693	Brookings SD 05-1	Brookings
10	2,635	Brandon Valley SD 49-2	Brandon
11	2,611	Mitchell SD 17-2	Mitchell
12	2,535	Douglas SD 51-1	Box Elder
13	2,195	Huron SD 02-2	Huron
14	2,075	Spearfish SD 40-2	Spearfish
15	2,072	Todd County SD 66-1	Mission
16	1,676	Lennox SD 41-4	Lennox
17	1,575	Cheyenne River	Eagle Butte

Male Students

Rank	Percent	District Name	City
1	52.8	Spearfish SD 40-2	Spearfish
2	52.6	Brookings SD 05-1	Brookings
2	52.6	Meade SD 46-1	Sturgis
4	52.5	Todd County SD 66-1	Mission
5	52.0	Lennox SD 41-4	Lennox
6	51.9	Rapid City Area SD 51-4	Rapid City
7	51.7	Sioux Falls SD 49-5	Sioux Falls
8	51.6	Pierre SD 32-2	Pierre
9	51.5	Yankton SD 63-3	Yankton
10	51.4	Mitchell SD 17-2	Mitchell
11	51.3	Douglas SD 51-1	Box Elder
11	51.3	Huron SD 02-2	Huron
13	51.0	Brandon Valley SD 49-2	Brandon
14	50.9	Aberdeen SD 06-1	Aberdeen
14	50.9	Watertown SD 14-4	Watertown
16	n/a	Cheyenne River	Eagle Butte
16	n/a	Pine Ridge Agency	Pine Ridge

Female Students

Rank	Percent	District Name	City
1	49.1	Aberdeen SD 06-1	Aberdeen
1	49.1	Watertown SD 14-4	Watertown
3	49.0	Brandon Valley SD 49-2	Brandon
4	48.7	Douglas SD 51-1	Box Elder
4	48.7	Huron SD 02-2	Huron
6	48.6	Mitchell SD 17-2	Mitchell
7	48.5	Yankton SD 63-3	Yankton
8	48.4	Pierre SD 32-2	Pierre
9	48.3	Sioux Falls SD 49-5	Sioux Falls
10	48.1	Rapid City Area SD 51-4	Rapid City
11	48.0	Lennox SD 41-4	Lennox
12	47.5	Todd County SD 66-1	Mission
13	47.4	Brookings SD 05-1	Brookings
13	47.4	Meade SD 46-1	Sturgis
15	47.2	Spearfish SD 40-2	Spearfish
16	n/a	Cheyenne River	Eagle Butte
16	n/a	Pine Ridge Agency	Pine Ridge

Individual Education Program Students

Rank	Percent	District Name	City
1	17.6	Douglas SD 51-1	Box Elder
2	16.0	Todd County SD 66-1	Mission
3	15.6	Mitchell SD 17-2	Mitchell
4	14.9	Lennox SD 41-4	Lennox
5	14.5	Yankton SD 63-3	Yankton
6	14.2	Aberdeen SD 06-1	Aberdeen
7	13.8	Spearfish SD 40-2	Spearfish
8	13.5	Sioux Falls SD 49-5	Sioux Falls
9	13.2	Huron SD 02-2	Huron
10	12.6	Brookings SD 05-1	Brookings
11	12.3	Watertown SD 14-4	Watertown
12	12.1	Pierre SD 32-2	Pierre
12	12.1	Rapid City Area SD 51-4	Rapid City
14	11.3	Meade SD 46-1	Sturgis
15	9.8	Brandon Valley SD 49-2	Brandon
16	n/a	Cheyenne River	Eagle Butte
16	n/a	Pine Ridge Agency	Pine Ridge

English Language Learner Students

Rank	Percent	District Name	City
1	79.9	Todd County SD 66-1	Mission
2	3.8	Sioux Falls SD 49-5	Sioux Falls
3	2.5	Huron SD 02-2	Huron
4	0.4	Rapid City Area SD 51-4	Rapid City
5	0.2	Spearfish SD 40-2	Spearfish
6	0.0	Yankton SD 63-3	Yankton
7	0.0	Aberdeen SD 06-1	Aberdeen
7	0.0	Brandon Valley SD 49-2	Brandon
7	0.0	Brookings SD 05-1	Brookings
7	0.0	Douglas SD 51-1	Box Elder
7	0.0	Lennox SD 41-4	Lennox
7	0.0	Meade SD 46-1	Sturgis
7	0.0	Mitchell SD 17-2	Mitchell
7	0.0	Pierre SD 32-2	Pierre
7	0.0	Watertown SD 14-4	Watertown
16	n/a	Cheyenne River	Eagle Butte
16	n/a	Pine Ridge Agency	Pine Ridge

Migrant Students

Rank	Percent	District Name	City
1	4.3	Huron SD 02-2	Huron
2	3.5	Sioux Falls SD 49-5	Sioux Falls
3	2.6	Meade SD 46-1	Sturgis
4	2.5	Mitchell SD 17-2	Mitchell
5	1.1	Rapid City Area SD 51-4	Rapid City
6	0.8	Spearfish SD 40-2	Spearfish
6	0.8	Watertown SD 14-4	Watertown
8	0.7	Yankton SD 63-3	Yankton
9	0.6	Brandon Valley SD 49-2	Brandon
10	0.5	Lennox SD 41-4	Lennox
11	0.4	Pierre SD 32-2	Pierre
12	0.1	Aberdeen SD 06-1	Aberdeen
12	0.1	Brookings SD 05-1	Brookings
12	0.1	Todd County SD 66-1	Mission
15	0.0	Douglas SD 51-1	Box Elder
16	n/a	Cheyenne River	Eagle Butte
16	n/a	Pine Ridge Agency	Pine Ridge

Students Eligible for Free Lunch

Rank	Percent	District Name	City
1	73.7	Todd County SD 66-1	Mission
2	22.3	Mitchell SD 17-2	Mitchell
3	20.1	Rapid City Area SD 51-4	Rapid City
4	19.7	Huron SD 02-2	Huron
5	18.8	Douglas SD 51-1	Box Elder
6	18.1	Yankton SD 63-3	Yankton
7	17.5	Meade SD 46-1	Sturgis
7	17.5	Sioux Falls SD 49-5	Sioux Falls
9	14.9	Aberdeen SD 06-1	Aberdeen
10	14.7	Watertown SD 14-4	Watertown
11	14.4	Pierre SD 32-2	Pierre
12	13.9	Spearfish SD 40-2	Spearfish
13	11.1	Brookings SD 05-1	Brookings
14	9.1	Lennox SD 41-4	Lennox
15	4.4	Brandon Valley SD 49-2	Brandon
16	n/a	Cheyenne River	Eagle Butte
16	n/a	Pine Ridge Agency	Pine Ridge

Students Eligible for Reduced-Price Lunch

Rank	Percent	District Name	City
1	15.5	Douglas SD 51-1	Box Elder
2	10.4	Huron SD 02-2	Huron
3	8.5	Meade SD 46-1	Sturgis
4	8.4	Watertown SD 14-4	Watertown
5	8.3	Yankton SD 63-3	Yankton
6	7.8	Sioux Falls SD 49-5	Sioux Falls
7	7.6	Mitchell SD 17-2	Mitchell
8	6.9	Aberdeen SD 06-1	Aberdeen
8	6.9	Spearfish SD 40-2	Spearfish
8	6.9	Todd County SD 66-1	Mission
11	6.0	Lennox SD 41-4	Lennox
12	5.9	Rapid City Area SD 51-4	Rapid City
13	5.6	Brookings SD 05-1	Brookings
14	4.7	Pierre SD 32-2	Pierre
15	3.8	Brandon Valley SD 49-2	Brandon
16	n/a	Cheyenne River	Eagle Butte
16	n/a	Pine Ridge Agency	Pine Ridge

Student/Teacher Ratio

Rank	Ratio	District Name	City
1	19.0	Brandon Valley SD 49-2	Brandon
2	18.0	Pierre SD 32-2	Pierre
3	17.2	Rapid City Area SD 51-4	Rapid City
4	17.1	Yankton SD 63-3	Yankton
5	16.7	Aberdeen SD 06-1	Aberdeen
6	16.6	Sioux Falls SD 49-5	Sioux Falls
6	16.6	Watertown SD 14-4	Watertown
8	15.9	Spearfish SD 40-2	Spearfish
9	15.5	Huron SD 02-2	Huron
10	15.4	Lennox SD 41-4	Lennox
11	15.1	Brookings SD 05-1	Brookings
12	14.9	Mitchell SD 17-2	Mitchell
13	14.3	Meade SD 46-1	Sturgis
14	12.7	Douglas SD 51-1	Box Elder
15	10.7	Todd County SD 66-1	Mission
16	n/a	Cheyenne River	Eagle Butte
16	n/a	Pine Ridge Agency	Pine Ridge

Student/Librarian Ratio

Rank	Ratio	District Name	City
1	2,611.0	Mitchell SD 17-2	Mitchell
2	1,976.0	Watertown SD 14-4	Watertown
3	1,676.0	Lennox SD 41-4	Lennox
4	1,652.6	Yankton SD 63-3	Yankton
5	1,432.0	Pierre SD 32-2	Pierre
6	1,382.5	Meade SD 46-1	Sturgis
7	1,097.5	Huron SD 02-2	Huron
8	1,045.4	Sioux Falls SD 49-5	Sioux Falls
9	1,036.0	Todd County SD 66-1	Mission
10	949.3	Aberdeen SD 06-1	Aberdeen
11	908.6	Brandon Valley SD 49-2	Brandon
12	845.0	Douglas SD 51-1	Box Elder
13	727.4	Rapid City Area SD 51-4	Rapid City
14	715.5	Spearfish SD 40-2	Spearfish
15	598.4	Brookings SD 05-1	Brookings
16	n/a	Cheyenne River	Eagle Butte
16	n/a	Pine Ridge Agency	Pine Ridge

Student/Counselor Ratio

Rank	Ratio	District Name	City
1	600.9	Rapid City Area SD 51-4	Rapid City
2	564.6	Watertown SD 14-4	Watertown
3	548.8	Huron SD 02-2	Huron
4	527.0	Brandon Valley SD 49-2	Brandon
5	461.1	Spearfish SD 40-2	Spearfish
6	455.1	Sioux Falls SD 49-5	Sioux Falls
7	392.5	Yankton SD 63-3	Yankton
8	378.4	Mitchell SD 17-2	Mitchell
9	372.4	Lennox SD 41-4	Lennox
10	362.1	Douglas SD 51-1	Box Elder
11	359.1	Brookings SD 05-1	Brookings
12	358.0	Pierre SD 32-2	Pierre
13	354.9	Aberdeen SD 06-1	Aberdeen
14	345.6	Meade SD 46-1	Sturgis
15	172.7	Todd County SD 66-1	Mission
16	n/a	Cheyenne River	Eagle Butte
16	n/a	Pine Ridge Agency	Pine Ridge

Current Spending per Student in FY2001

Rank	Dollars	District Name	City
1	9,527	Todd County SD 66-1	Mission
2	6,916	Douglas SD 51-1	Box Elder

Rank	Number	District Name	City
3	5,812	Huron SD 02-2	Huron
4	5,778	Sioux Falls SD 49-5	Sioux Falls
5	5,715	Spearfish SD 40-2	Spearfish
6	5,688	Mitchell SD 17-2	Mitchell
7	5,641	Meade SD 46-1	Sturgis
8	5,620	Aberdeen SD 06-1	Aberdeen
9	5,499	Pierre SD 32-2	Pierre
10	5,402	Rapid City Area SD 51-4	Rapid City
11	5,223	Brookings SD 05-1	Brookings
12	5,216	Yankton SD 63-3	Yankton
13	5,186	Watertown SD 14-4	Watertown
14	5,131	Lennox SD 41-4	Lennox
15	4,991	Brandon Valley SD 49-2	Brandon
16	n/a	Cheyenne River	Eagle Butte
16	n/a	Pine Ridge Agency	Pine Ridge

Number of Diploma Recipients

Rank	Number	District Name	City
1	1,186	Rapid City Area SD 51-4	Rapid City
2	1,131	Sioux Falls SD 49-5	Sioux Falls
3	289	Aberdeen SD 06-1	Aberdeen
4	231	Brookings SD 05-1	Brookings
5	229	Yankton SD 63-3	Yankton
6	225	Pierre SD 32-2	Pierre
7	224	Mitchell SD 17-2	Mitchell
8	195	Brandon Valley SD 49-2	Brandon
9	188	Meade SD 46-1	Sturgis
10	174	Spearfish SD 40-2	Spearfish
11	157	Huron SD 02-2	Huron
12	96	Douglas SD 51-1	Box Elder
13	84	Lennox SD 41-4	Lennox
14	54	Todd County SD 66-1	Mission
15	1	Watertown SD 14-4	Watertown
16	n/a	Cheyenne River	Eagle Butte
16	n/a	Pine Ridge Agency	Pine Ridge

High School Drop-out Rate

Rank	Percent	District Name	City
1	29.7	Todd County SD 66-1	Mission
2	7.0	Rapid City Area SD 51-4	Rapid City
3	5.9	Douglas SD 51-1	Box Elder
3	5.9	Pierre SD 32-2	Pierre
5	4.8	Sioux Falls SD 49-5	Sioux Falls
5	4.8	Yankton SD 63-3	Yankton
7	4.3	Aberdeen SD 06-1	Aberdeen
8	3.9	Huron SD 02-2	Huron
9	3.1	Spearfish SD 40-2	Spearfish
9	3.1	Watertown SD 14-4	Watertown
11	2.6	Meade SD 46-1	Sturgis
12	1.3	Brookings SD 05-1	Brookings
13	1.0	Lennox SD 41-4	Lennox
14	0.5	Brandon Valley SD 49-2	Brandon
15	0.2	Mitchell SD 17-2	Mitchell
16	n/a	Cheyenne River	Eagle Butte
16	n/a	Pine Ridge Agency	Pine Ridge

Tennessee

Tennessee Public School Educational Profile

Category	Value	Category	Value
Schools *(2002-2003)*	1,659	**Diploma Recipients** *(2002-2003)*	40,894
Instructional Level		White, Non-Hispanic	0
Primary	977	Black, Non-Hispanic	0
Middle	295	Asian/Pacific Islander	0
High	311	American Indian/Alaskan Native	0
Other Level	76	Hispanic	0
Curriculum		**High School Drop-out Rate** (%) *(2000-2001)*	4.3
Regular	1,592	White, Non-Hispanic	n/a
Special Education	18	Black, Non-Hispanic	n/a
Vocational	24	Asian/Pacific Islander	n/a
Alternative	25	American Indian/Alaskan Native	n/a
Type		Hispanic	n/a
Magnet	23	**Staff** *(2002-2003)*	114,364.0
Charter	0	Teachers	58,652.5
Title I Eligible	817	Average Salary ($)	39,186
School-wide Title I	609	Librarians/Media Specialists	1,522.5
Students *(2002-2003)*	905,059	Guidance Counselors	1,879.1
Gender (%)		**Ratios** *(2002-2003)*	
Male	n/a	Student/Teacher Ratio	15.4 to 1
Female	n/a	Student/Librarian Ratio	594.5 to 1
Race/Ethnicity (%)		Student/Counselor Ratio	481.6 to 1
White, Non-Hispanic	0.0	**Current Spending** *($ per student in FY 2001)*	5,958
Black, Non-Hispanic	0.0	Instruction	3,877
Asian/Pacific Islander	0.0	Support Services	1,789
American Indian/Alaskan Native	0.0	**College Entrance Exam Scores** *(2003)*	
Hispanic	0.0	Scholastic Aptitude Test (SAT)	
Classification (%)		Participation Rate (%)	14
Individual Education Program (IEP)	15.8	Mean SAT I Verbal Score	568
Migrant	0.0	Mean SAT I Math Score	560
English Language Learner (ELL)	0.0	American College Testing Program (ACT)	
Eligible for Free Lunch Program	0.0	Participation Rate (%)	74
Eligible for Reduced-Price Lunch Program	0.0	Average Composite Score	20.4

Note: *For an explanation of data, please refer to the User's Guide in the front of the book; n/a indicates data not available*

Tennessee NAEP 2003 Test Scores

Reading			Mathematics		
Grade/Category	**Value**	**Rank**	**Grade/Category**	**Value**	**Rank**
4th Grade			**4th Grade**		
Average Proficiency	211.9 (1.6)	41/51	Average Proficiency	227.8 (1.0)	43/51
Proficiency by Gender/Race/Ethnicity			Proficiency by Gender/Race/Ethnicity		
Male	207.6 (1.7)	41/51	Male	227.8 (1.3)	45/51
Female	216.5 (2.0)	42/51	Female	227.7 (1.0)	41/51
White, Non-Hispanic	220.2 (1.4)	48/51	White, Non-Hispanic	235.0 (0.9)	47/51
Black, Non-Hispanic	188.2 (2.7)	40/42	Black, Non-Hispanic	207.6 (2.0)	40/42
Asian, Non-Hispanic	206.4 (5.6)	15/41	Asian, Non-Hispanic	*218.1 (4.8)*	31/43
American Indian, Non-Hispanic	n/a	n/a	American Indian, Non-Hispanic	n/a	n/a
Hispanic	n/a	n/a	Hispanic	n/a	n/a
Proficiency by Class Size			Proficiency by Class Size		
Less than 16 Students	*202.5 (6.3)*	27/45	Less than 16 Students	*226.3 (4.2)*	21/47
16 to 18 Students	*217.2 (4.5)*	22/48	16 to 18 Students	228.5 (3.1)	32/48
19 to 20 Students	209.6 (4.2)	41/50	19 to 20 Students	228.5 (3.3)	38/50
21 to 25 Students	212.9 (2.1)	42/51	21 to 25 Students	228.5 (1.6)	44/51
Greater than 25 Students	*205.3 (7.9)*	48/49	Greater than 25 Students	*223.3 (4.8)*	44/49
Percent Attaining Achievement Levels			Percent Attaining Achievement Levels		
Below Basic	42.8 (1.8)	10/51	Below Basic	30.4 (1.6)	9/51
Basic or Above	57.2 (1.8)	42/51	Basic or Above	69.6 (1.6)	43/51
Proficient or Above	26.2 (1.5)	40/51	Proficient or Above	23.7 (1.1)	42/51
Advanced or Above	6.1 (0.7)	35/51	Advanced or Above	2.4 (0.4)	36/51
8th Grade			**8th Grade**		
Average Proficiency	258.1 (1.2)	37/51	Average Proficiency	268.2 (1.8)	42/51
Proficiency by Gender/Race/Ethnicity			Proficiency by Gender/Race/Ethnicity		
Male	252.0 (1.5)	40/51	Male	268.0 (2.1)	43/51
Female	264.7 (1.3)	36/51	Female	268.3 (1.8)	42/51
White, Non-Hispanic	264.6 (1.0)	46/50	White, Non-Hispanic	276.8 (1.0)	44/50
Black, Non-Hispanic	238.8 (2.0)	35/41	Black, Non-Hispanic	241.7 (2.5)	37/41
Asian, Non-Hispanic	n/a	n/a	Asian, Non-Hispanic	n/a	n/a
American Indian, Non-Hispanic	n/a	n/a	American Indian, Non-Hispanic	n/a	n/a
Hispanic	n/a	n/a	Hispanic	n/a	n/a
Proficiency by Parents Highest Level of Ed.			Proficiency by Parents Highest Level of Ed.		
Did Not Finish High School	242.6 (2.8)	38/50	Did Not Finish High School	252.9 (2.4)	41/50
Graduated High School	250.8 (1.9)	35/50	Graduated High School	258.0 (2.3)	44/50
Some Education After High School	263.2 (2.0)	41/50	Some Education After High School	274.4 (2.1)	43/50
Graduated College	266.5 (1.6)	39/50	Graduated College	279.5 (2.0)	41/50
Percent Attaining Achievement Levels			Percent Attaining Achievement Levels		
Below Basic	31.1 (1.4)	12/51	Below Basic	41.4 (2.1)	9/51
Basic or Above	68.9 (1.4)	40/51	Basic or Above	58.6 (2.1)	43/51
Proficient or Above	26.0 (1.7)	39/51	Proficient or Above	21.0 (1.5)	40/51
Advanced or Above	1.8 (0.4)	41/51	Advanced or Above	2.9 (0.5)	40/51

***Note:** For an explanation of data, please refer to the User's Guide in the front of the book; values in italics indicate that the nature of the sample does not allow accurate determination of the variability of the statistic; n/a indicates data not available*

Anderson County

Anderson County SD

Ste 500, 101 S Main • Clinton, TN 37716-3619
(865) 463-8631 • http://www.acorns.k12.tn.us/
Grade Span: KG-12; **Agency Type:** 1
Schools: 17
9 Primary; 4 Middle; 3 High; 1 Other Level
15 Regular; 0 Special Education; 1 Vocational; 1 Alternative
0 Magnet; 0 Charter; 8 Title I Eligible; 8 School-wide Title I
Students: 6,933 (n/a% male; n/a% female)
Individual Education Program: 1,161 (16.7%);
English Language Learner: n/a; Migrant: n/a
Eligible for Free Lunch Program: n/a
Eligible for Reduced-Price Lunch Program: n/a
Teachers: 498.2 (13.9 to 1)
Librarians/Media Specialists: 13.9 (498.8 to 1)
Guidance Counselors: 17.0 (407.8 to 1)
Current Spending: ($ per student per year):
Total: $6,005; Instruction: $3,884; Support Services: $1,800
Enrollment, Drop-out Rates and Diploma Recipients by Race/Ethnicity

Category	Total	White	Black	Asian	AIAN	Hisp.
Enrollment (%)	100.0	0.0	0.0	0.0	0.0	0.0
Drop-out Rate (%)	2.6	n/a	n/a	n/a	n/a	n/a
H.S. Diplomas (#)	431	n/a	n/a	n/a	n/a	n/a

Oak Ridge City SD

New York Avenue • Oak Ridge, TN 37831-3221
Mailing Address: PO Box 6588 • Oak Ridge, TN 37831-3221
(865) 482-6320 • http://www.ortn.edu/
Grade Span: PK-12; **Agency Type:** 1
Schools: 8
5 Primary; 2 Middle; 1 High; 0 Other Level
8 Regular; 0 Special Education; 0 Vocational; 0 Alternative
0 Magnet; 0 Charter; 0 Title I Eligible; 0 School-wide Title I
Students: 4,349 (n/a% male; n/a% female)
Individual Education Program: 957 (22.0%);
English Language Learner: n/a; Migrant: n/a
Eligible for Free Lunch Program: n/a
Eligible for Reduced-Price Lunch Program: n/a
Teachers: 233.5 (18.6 to 1)
Librarians/Media Specialists: 8.0 (543.6 to 1)
Guidance Counselors: 15.0 (289.9 to 1)
Current Spending: ($ per student per year):
Total: $7,938; Instruction: $5,023; Support Services: $2,594
Enrollment, Drop-out Rates and Diploma Recipients by Race/Ethnicity

Category	Total	White	Black	Asian	AIAN	Hisp.
Enrollment (%)	100.0	0.0	0.0	0.0	0.0	0.0
Drop-out Rate (%)	3.8	n/a	n/a	n/a	n/a	n/a
H.S. Diplomas (#)	281	n/a	n/a	n/a	n/a	n/a

Arlington County

South and Eastern States Agency

51 Ventury Blvd, Ste 340 • Arlington, TN 37214
(703) 235-3233
Grade Span: PK-12; **Agency Type:** 6
Schools: 17
11 Primary; 1 Middle; 2 High; 3 Other Level
17 Regular; 0 Special Education; 0 Vocational; 0 Alternative
0 Magnet; 0 Charter; 17 Title I Eligible; 17 School-wide Title I
Students: 3,514 (n/a% male; n/a% female)
Individual Education Program: n/a;
English Language Learner: n/a; Migrant: n/a
Eligible for Free Lunch Program: n/a
Eligible for Reduced-Price Lunch Program: n/a
Teachers: n/a
Librarians/Media Specialists: n/a
Guidance Counselors: n/a
Current Spending: ($ per student per year):
Total: n/a; Instruction: n/a; Support Services: n/a
Enrollment, Drop-out Rates and Diploma Recipients by Race/Ethnicity

Category	Total	White	Black	Asian	AIAN	Hisp.
Enrollment (%)	100.0	0.0	0.0	0.0	100.0	0.0
Drop-out Rate (%)	n/a	n/a	n/a	n/a	n/a	n/a
H.S. Diplomas (#)	n/a	n/a	n/a	n/a	n/a	n/a

Bedford County

Bedford County SD

500 Madison St • Shelbyville, TN 37160-3341
(931) 684-3284 • http://www.bedfordk12tn.com/
Grade Span: KG-12; **Agency Type:** 1
Schools: 12
6 Primary; 2 Middle; 3 High; 1 Other Level
12 Regular; 0 Special Education; 0 Vocational; 0 Alternative
0 Magnet; 0 Charter; 6 Title I Eligible; 2 School-wide Title I
Students: 6,555 (n/a% male; n/a% female)
Individual Education Program: 997 (15.2%);
English Language Learner: n/a; Migrant: n/a
Eligible for Free Lunch Program: n/a
Eligible for Reduced-Price Lunch Program: n/a
Teachers: 410.3 (16.0 to 1)
Librarians/Media Specialists: 11.0 (595.9 to 1)
Guidance Counselors: 14.0 (468.2 to 1)
Current Spending: ($ per student per year):
Total: $4,828; Instruction: $3,091; Support Services: $1,451
Enrollment, Drop-out Rates and Diploma Recipients by Race/Ethnicity

Category	Total	White	Black	Asian	AIAN	Hisp.
Enrollment (%)	100.0	0.0	0.0	0.0	0.0	0.0
Drop-out Rate (%)	3.4	n/a	n/a	n/a	n/a	n/a
H.S. Diplomas (#)	272	n/a	n/a	n/a	n/a	n/a

Benton County

Benton County SD

197 Briarwood St • Camden, TN 38320-1381
(731) 584-6111 • http://www.benton-lea.benton.k12.tn.us/
Grade Span: KG-12; **Agency Type:** 1
Schools: 8
3 Primary; 1 Middle; 3 High; 1 Other Level
7 Regular; 0 Special Education; 1 Vocational; 0 Alternative
0 Magnet; 0 Charter; 5 Title I Eligible; 5 School-wide Title I
Students: 2,464 (n/a% male; n/a% female)
Individual Education Program: 424 (17.2%);
English Language Learner: n/a; Migrant: n/a
Eligible for Free Lunch Program: n/a
Eligible for Reduced-Price Lunch Program: n/a
Teachers: 177.2 (13.9 to 1)
Librarians/Media Specialists: 5.0 (492.8 to 1)
Guidance Counselors: 6.5 (379.1 to 1)
Current Spending: ($ per student per year):
Total: $5,405; Instruction: $3,556; Support Services: $1,603
Enrollment, Drop-out Rates and Diploma Recipients by Race/Ethnicity

Category	Total	White	Black	Asian	AIAN	Hisp.
Enrollment (%)	100.0	0.0	0.0	0.0	0.0	0.0
Drop-out Rate (%)	1.8	n/a	n/a	n/a	n/a	n/a
H.S. Diplomas (#)	95	n/a	n/a	n/a	n/a	n/a

Bledsoe County

Bledsoe County SD

PO Box 369 • Pikeville, TN 37367-0369
(423) 447-2914 • http://WWW.BLEDSOE.K12.TN.US/
Grade Span: KG-12; **Agency Type:** 1
Schools: 6
3 Primary; 1 Middle; 2 High; 0 Other Level
5 Regular; 0 Special Education; 1 Vocational; 0 Alternative
0 Magnet; 0 Charter; 3 Title I Eligible; 1 School-wide Title I
Students: 1,764 (n/a% male; n/a% female)
Individual Education Program: 405 (23.0%);
English Language Learner: n/a; Migrant: n/a
Eligible for Free Lunch Program: n/a
Eligible for Reduced-Price Lunch Program: n/a
Teachers: 121.0 (14.6 to 1)
Librarians/Media Specialists: 3.0 (588.0 to 1)
Guidance Counselors: 3.0 (588.0 to 1)
Current Spending: ($ per student per year):
Total: $5,536; Instruction: $3,223; Support Services: $1,905
Enrollment, Drop-out Rates and Diploma Recipients by Race/Ethnicity

Category	Total	White	Black	Asian	AIAN	Hisp.
Enrollment (%)	100.0	0.0	0.0	0.0	0.0	0.0
Drop-out Rate (%)	3.4	n/a	n/a	n/a	n/a	n/a
H.S. Diplomas (#)	55	n/a	n/a	n/a	n/a	n/a

Blount County

Blount County SD

831 Grandview Dr • Maryville, TN 37803-5312
(865) 984-1212 • http://www.blountk12.org/
Grade Span: KG-12; **Agency Type:** 1
Schools: 19
11 Primary; 4 Middle; 3 High; 1 Other Level
18 Regular; 1 Special Education; 0 Vocational; 0 Alternative
0 Magnet; 0 Charter; 7 Title I Eligible; 0 School-wide Title I
Students: 10,845 (n/a% male; n/a% female)
Individual Education Program: 1,798 (16.6%);
English Language Learner: n/a; Migrant: n/a
Eligible for Free Lunch Program: n/a
Eligible for Reduced-Price Lunch Program: n/a

Teachers: 650.2 (16.7 to 1)
Librarians/Media Specialists: 18.5 (586.2 to 1)
Guidance Counselors: 24.1 (450.0 to 1)
Current Spending: ($ per student per year):
Total: $5,446; Instruction: $3,569; Support Services: $1,548
Enrollment, Drop-out Rates and Diploma Recipients by Race/Ethnicity

Category	Total	White	Black	Asian	AIAN	Hisp.
Enrollment (%)	100.0	0.0	0.0	0.0	0.0	0.0
Drop-out Rate (%)	5.3	n/a	n/a	n/a	n/a	n/a
H.S. Diplomas (#)	509	n/a	n/a	n/a	n/a	n/a

Maryville City SD
833 Lawrence Ave • Maryville, TN 37801-4857
(865) 982-7122 • http://www.ci.maryville.tn.us/schools/
Grade Span: KG-12; **Agency Type:** 1
Schools: 7
4 Primary; 2 Middle; 1 High; 0 Other Level
7 Regular; 0 Special Education; 0 Vocational; 0 Alternative
0 Magnet; 0 Charter; 4 Title I Eligible; 0 School-wide Title I
Students: 4,359 (n/a% male; n/a% female)
Individual Education Program: 640 (14.7%);
English Language Learner: n/a; Migrant: n/a
Eligible for Free Lunch Program: n/a
Eligible for Reduced-Price Lunch Program: n/a
Teachers: 283.6 (15.4 to 1)
Librarians/Media Specialists: 7.0 (622.7 to 1)
Guidance Counselors: 10.0 (435.9 to 1)
Current Spending: ($ per student per year):
Total: $7,001; Instruction: $4,824; Support Services: $1,805
Enrollment, Drop-out Rates and Diploma Recipients by Race/Ethnicity

Category	Total	White	Black	Asian	AIAN	Hisp.
Enrollment (%)	100.0	0.0	0.0	0.0	0.0	0.0
Drop-out Rate (%)	0.6	n/a	n/a	n/a	n/a	n/a
H.S. Diplomas (#)	230	n/a	n/a	n/a	n/a	n/a

Bradley County

Bradley County SD
800 S Lee Hwy • Cleveland, TN 37311-5853
(423) 476-0620 • http://www.bradleyschools.org/
Grade Span: KG-12; **Agency Type:** 1
Schools: 16
11 Primary; 2 Middle; 2 High; 1 Other Level
15 Regular; 0 Special Education; 0 Vocational; 1 Alternative
0 Magnet; 0 Charter; 9 Title I Eligible; 9 School-wide Title I
Students: 9,177 (n/a% male; n/a% female)
Individual Education Program: 993 (10.8%);
English Language Learner: n/a; Migrant: n/a
Eligible for Free Lunch Program: n/a
Eligible for Reduced-Price Lunch Program: n/a
Teachers: 547.6 (16.8 to 1)
Librarians/Media Specialists: 17.0 (539.8 to 1)
Guidance Counselors: 20.0 (458.9 to 1)
Current Spending: ($ per student per year):
Total: $5,130; Instruction: $3,365; Support Services: $1,386
Enrollment, Drop-out Rates and Diploma Recipients by Race/Ethnicity

Category	Total	White	Black	Asian	AIAN	Hisp.
Enrollment (%)	100.0	0.0	0.0	0.0	0.0	0.0
Drop-out Rate (%)	4.7	n/a	n/a	n/a	n/a	n/a
H.S. Diplomas (#)	401	n/a	n/a	n/a	n/a	n/a

Cleveland City SD
4300 Mouse Creek Road, NW • Cleveland, TN 37312-3303
(423) 472-9571 • http://www.clevelandschools.org
Grade Span: KG-12; **Agency Type:** 1
Schools: 8
6 Primary; 1 Middle; 1 High; 0 Other Level
8 Regular; 0 Special Education; 0 Vocational; 0 Alternative
0 Magnet; 0 Charter; 3 Title I Eligible; 3 School-wide Title I
Students: 4,332 (n/a% male; n/a% female)
Individual Education Program: 664 (15.3%);
English Language Learner: n/a; Migrant: n/a
Eligible for Free Lunch Program: n/a
Eligible for Reduced-Price Lunch Program: n/a
Teachers: 297.2 (14.6 to 1)
Librarians/Media Specialists: 9.7 (446.6 to 1)
Guidance Counselors: 13.0 (333.2 to 1)
Current Spending: ($ per student per year):
Total: $5,928; Instruction: $3,926; Support Services: $1,695
Enrollment, Drop-out Rates and Diploma Recipients by Race/Ethnicity

Category	Total	White	Black	Asian	AIAN	Hisp.
Enrollment (%)	100.0	0.0	0.0	0.0	0.0	0.0
Drop-out Rate (%)	1.6	n/a	n/a	n/a	n/a	n/a
H.S. Diplomas (#)	185	n/a	n/a	n/a	n/a	n/a

Campbell County

Campbell County SD
522 Main Street • Jacksboro, TN 37757-0445
Mailing Address: PO Box 445 • Jacksboro, TN 37757-0445
(423) 562-8377 • http://www.campbell.k12.tn.us/
Grade Span: KG-12; **Agency Type:** 1
Schools: 16
10 Primary; 2 Middle; 3 High; 1 Other Level
16 Regular; 0 Special Education; 0 Vocational; 0 Alternative
0 Magnet; 0 Charter; 12 Title I Eligible; 12 School-wide Title I
Students: 5,923 (n/a% male; n/a% female)
Individual Education Program: 819 (13.8%);
English Language Learner: n/a; Migrant: n/a
Eligible for Free Lunch Program: n/a
Eligible for Reduced-Price Lunch Program: n/a
Teachers: 406.2 (14.6 to 1)
Librarians/Media Specialists: 12.0 (493.6 to 1)
Guidance Counselors: 10.1 (586.4 to 1)
Current Spending: ($ per student per year):
Total: $5,167; Instruction: $3,385; Support Services: $1,386
Enrollment, Drop-out Rates and Diploma Recipients by Race/Ethnicity

Category	Total	White	Black	Asian	AIAN	Hisp.
Enrollment (%)	100.0	0.0	0.0	0.0	0.0	0.0
Drop-out Rate (%)	3.3	n/a	n/a	n/a	n/a	n/a
H.S. Diplomas (#)	255	n/a	n/a	n/a	n/a	n/a

Cannon County

Cannon County SD
301 W Main St • Woodbury, TN 37190-1100
(615) 563-5752
Grade Span: KG-12; **Agency Type:** 1
Schools: 7
6 Primary; 0 Middle; 1 High; 0 Other Level
7 Regular; 0 Special Education; 0 Vocational; 0 Alternative
0 Magnet; 0 Charter; 4 Title I Eligible; 1 School-wide Title I
Students: 2,104 (n/a% male; n/a% female)
Individual Education Program: 347 (16.5%);
English Language Learner: n/a; Migrant: n/a
Eligible for Free Lunch Program: n/a
Eligible for Reduced-Price Lunch Program: n/a
Teachers: 149.5 (14.1 to 1)
Librarians/Media Specialists: 2.0 (1,052.0 to 1)
Guidance Counselors: 5.0 (420.8 to 1)
Current Spending: ($ per student per year):
Total: $4,967; Instruction: $3,327; Support Services: $1,300
Enrollment, Drop-out Rates and Diploma Recipients by Race/Ethnicity

Category	Total	White	Black	Asian	AIAN	Hisp.
Enrollment (%)	100.0	0.0	0.0	0.0	0.0	0.0
Drop-out Rate (%)	3.1	n/a	n/a	n/a	n/a	n/a
H.S. Diplomas (#)	99	n/a	n/a	n/a	n/a	n/a

Carter County

Carter County SD
305 Academy St • Elizabethton, TN 37643-2208
(423) 547-4000 • http://www.elizabethton-lea.carter.k12.tn.us/Carter/
Grade Span: KG-12; **Agency Type:** 1
Schools: 17
10 Primary; 1 Middle; 5 High; 1 Other Level
16 Regular; 0 Special Education; 0 Vocational; 1 Alternative
0 Magnet; 0 Charter; 11 Title I Eligible; 11 School-wide Title I
Students: 5,903 (n/a% male; n/a% female)
Individual Education Program: 881 (14.9%);
English Language Learner: n/a; Migrant: n/a
Eligible for Free Lunch Program: n/a
Eligible for Reduced-Price Lunch Program: n/a
Teachers: 445.8 (13.2 to 1)
Librarians/Media Specialists: 12.0 (491.9 to 1)
Guidance Counselors: 12.0 (491.9 to 1)
Current Spending: ($ per student per year):
Total: $5,541; Instruction: $3,575; Support Services: $1,628
Enrollment, Drop-out Rates and Diploma Recipients by Race/Ethnicity

Category	Total	White	Black	Asian	AIAN	Hisp.
Enrollment (%)	100.0	0.0	0.0	0.0	0.0	0.0
Drop-out Rate (%)	2.6	n/a	n/a	n/a	n/a	n/a
H.S. Diplomas (#)	149	n/a	n/a	n/a	n/a	n/a

Elizabethton City SD
804 S Watauga Ave • Elizabethton, TN 37643-4207
(423) 547-8000 • http://ecschools.net/
Grade Span: KG-12; **Agency Type:** 1
Schools: 5
3 Primary; 1 Middle; 1 High; 0 Other Level

5 Regular; 0 Special Education; 0 Vocational; 0 Alternative
0 Magnet; 0 Charter; 2 Title I Eligible; 2 School-wide Title I
Students: 2,187 (n/a% male; n/a% female)
Individual Education Program: 337 (15.4%);
English Language Learner: n/a; Migrant: n/a
Eligible for Free Lunch Program: n/a
Eligible for Reduced-Price Lunch Program: n/a
Teachers: 155.3 (14.1 to 1)
Librarians/Media Specialists: 6.0 (364.5 to 1)
Guidance Counselors: 6.0 (364.5 to 1)
Current Spending: ($ per student per year):
Total: $5,950; Instruction: $3,960; Support Services: $1,683
Enrollment, Drop-out Rates and Diploma Recipients by Race/Ethnicity

Category	Total	White	Black	Asian	AIAN	Hisp.
Enrollment (%)	100.0	0.0	0.0	0.0	0.0	0.0
Drop-out Rate (%)	2.4	n/a	n/a	n/a	n/a	n/a
H.S. Diplomas (#)	168	n/a	n/a	n/a	n/a	n/a

Cheatham County

Cheatham County SD
102 Elizabeth St • Ashland City, TN 37015-1101
(615) 792-5664 • http://www.cheatham-lea.k12.tn.us/
Grade Span: KG-12; **Agency Type:** 1
Schools: 14
7 Primary; 3 Middle; 4 High; 0 Other Level
14 Regular; 0 Special Education; 0 Vocational; 0 Alternative
0 Magnet; 0 Charter; 4 Title I Eligible; 0 School-wide Title I
Students: 6,875 (n/a% male; n/a% female)
Individual Education Program: 830 (12.1%);
English Language Learner: n/a; Migrant: n/a
Eligible for Free Lunch Program: n/a
Eligible for Reduced-Price Lunch Program: n/a
Teachers: 437.4 (15.7 to 1)
Librarians/Media Specialists: 13.0 (528.8 to 1)
Guidance Counselors: 19.1 (359.9 to 1)
Current Spending: ($ per student per year):
Total: $5,058; Instruction: $3,295; Support Services: $1,467
Enrollment, Drop-out Rates and Diploma Recipients by Race/Ethnicity

Category	Total	White	Black	Asian	AIAN	Hisp.
Enrollment (%)	100.0	0.0	0.0	0.0	0.0	0.0
Drop-out Rate (%)	0.5	n/a	n/a	n/a	n/a	n/a
H.S. Diplomas (#)	329	n/a	n/a	n/a	n/a	n/a

Chester County

Chester County SD
PO Box 327 • Henderson, TN 38340-0327
(731) 989-5134
Grade Span: KG-12; **Agency Type:** 1
Schools: 6
3 Primary; 2 Middle; 1 High; 0 Other Level
6 Regular; 0 Special Education; 0 Vocational; 0 Alternative
0 Magnet; 0 Charter; 4 Title I Eligible; 4 School-wide Title I
Students: 2,438 (n/a% male; n/a% female)
Individual Education Program: 248 (10.2%);
English Language Learner: n/a; Migrant: n/a
Eligible for Free Lunch Program: n/a
Eligible for Reduced-Price Lunch Program: n/a
Teachers: 139.3 (17.5 to 1)
Librarians/Media Specialists: 4.0 (609.5 to 1)
Guidance Counselors: 4.0 (609.5 to 1)
Current Spending: ($ per student per year):
Total: $4,585; Instruction: $2,965; Support Services: $1,307
Enrollment, Drop-out Rates and Diploma Recipients by Race/Ethnicity

Category	Total	White	Black	Asian	AIAN	Hisp.
Enrollment (%)	100.0	0.0	0.0	0.0	0.0	0.0
Drop-out Rate (%)	2.1	n/a	n/a	n/a	n/a	n/a
H.S. Diplomas (#)	105	n/a	n/a	n/a	n/a	n/a

Claiborne County

Claiborne County SD
PO Box 179 • Tazewell, TN 37879-0179
(423) 626-3543
Grade Span: PK-12; **Agency Type:** 1
Schools: 13
7 Primary; 2 Middle; 3 High; 1 Other Level
13 Regular; 0 Special Education; 0 Vocational; 0 Alternative
0 Magnet; 0 Charter; 9 Title I Eligible; 8 School-wide Title I
Students: 4,580 (n/a% male; n/a% female)
Individual Education Program: 855 (18.7%);
English Language Learner: n/a; Migrant: n/a
Eligible for Free Lunch Program: n/a
Eligible for Reduced-Price Lunch Program: n/a
Teachers: 350.7 (13.1 to 1)
Librarians/Media Specialists: 7.5 (610.7 to 1)
Guidance Counselors: 11.8 (388.1 to 1)
Current Spending: ($ per student per year):
Total: $5,686; Instruction: $3,777; Support Services: $1,469
Enrollment, Drop-out Rates and Diploma Recipients by Race/Ethnicity

Category	Total	White	Black	Asian	AIAN	Hisp.
Enrollment (%)	100.0	0.0	0.0	0.0	0.0	0.0
Drop-out Rate (%)	2.1	n/a	n/a	n/a	n/a	n/a
H.S. Diplomas (#)	172	n/a	n/a	n/a	n/a	n/a

Cocke County

Cocke County SD
305 Hedrick Dr • Newport, TN 37821-2908
(423) 623-7821 • http://www.cocke-lea.cocke.k12.tn.us/
Grade Span: KG-12; **Agency Type:** 1
Schools: 12
9 Primary; 0 Middle; 3 High; 0 Other Level
12 Regular; 0 Special Education; 0 Vocational; 0 Alternative
0 Magnet; 0 Charter; 9 Title I Eligible; 9 School-wide Title I
Students: 4,693 (n/a% male; n/a% female)
Individual Education Program: 861 (18.3%);
English Language Learner: n/a; Migrant: n/a
Eligible for Free Lunch Program: n/a
Eligible for Reduced-Price Lunch Program: n/a
Teachers: 311.3 (15.1 to 1)
Librarians/Media Specialists: 9.5 (494.0 to 1)
Guidance Counselors: 10.0 (469.3 to 1)
Current Spending: ($ per student per year):
Total: $5,180; Instruction: $3,284; Support Services: $1,448
Enrollment, Drop-out Rates and Diploma Recipients by Race/Ethnicity

Category	Total	White	Black	Asian	AIAN	Hisp.
Enrollment (%)	100.0	0.0	0.0	0.0	0.0	0.0
Drop-out Rate (%)	2.1	n/a	n/a	n/a	n/a	n/a
H.S. Diplomas (#)	277	n/a	n/a	n/a	n/a	n/a

Coffee County

Coffee County SD
1343 Mcarthur St • Manchester, TN 37355-1785
(931) 723-5150 • http://www.coffeecountyschools.com/
Grade Span: KG-12; **Agency Type:** 1
Schools: 8
5 Primary; 1 Middle; 1 High; 1 Other Level
7 Regular; 0 Special Education; 0 Vocational; 1 Alternative
0 Magnet; 0 Charter; 5 Title I Eligible; 5 School-wide Title I
Students: 4,150 (n/a% male; n/a% female)
Individual Education Program: 698 (16.8%);
English Language Learner: n/a; Migrant: n/a
Eligible for Free Lunch Program: n/a
Eligible for Reduced-Price Lunch Program: n/a
Teachers: 279.5 (14.8 to 1)
Librarians/Media Specialists: 7.7 (539.0 to 1)
Guidance Counselors: 10.0 (415.0 to 1)
Current Spending: ($ per student per year):
Total: $5,173; Instruction: $3,336; Support Services: $1,497
Enrollment, Drop-out Rates and Diploma Recipients by Race/Ethnicity

Category	Total	White	Black	Asian	AIAN	Hisp.
Enrollment (%)	100.0	0.0	0.0	0.0	0.0	0.0
Drop-out Rate (%)	2.6	n/a	n/a	n/a	n/a	n/a
H.S. Diplomas (#)	254	n/a	n/a	n/a	n/a	n/a

Tullahoma City SD
510 S Jackson St • Tullahoma, TN 37388-3468
(931) 454-2600 • http://www.tullahomacityschools.net/
Grade Span: KG-12; **Agency Type:** 1
Schools: 7
4 Primary; 2 Middle; 1 High; 0 Other Level
7 Regular; 0 Special Education; 0 Vocational; 0 Alternative
0 Magnet; 0 Charter; 3 Title I Eligible; 2 School-wide Title I
Students: 3,621 (n/a% male; n/a% female)
Individual Education Program: 698 (19.3%);
English Language Learner: n/a; Migrant: n/a
Eligible for Free Lunch Program: n/a
Eligible for Reduced-Price Lunch Program: n/a
Teachers: 223.4 (16.2 to 1)
Librarians/Media Specialists: 8.0 (452.6 to 1)
Guidance Counselors: 9.0 (402.3 to 1)
Current Spending: ($ per student per year):
Total: $5,650; Instruction: $3,793; Support Services: $1,532

Enrollment, Drop-out Rates and Diploma Recipients by Race/Ethnicity

Category	Total	White	Black	Asian	AIAN	Hisp.
Enrollment (%)	100.0	0.0	0.0	0.0	0.0	0.0
Drop-out Rate (%)	1.7	n/a	n/a	n/a	n/a	n/a
H.S. Diplomas (#)	236	n/a	n/a	n/a	n/a	n/a

Crockett County

Crockett County SD

102 Hwy 412 N • Alamo, TN 38001-9699
(731) 696-2604 • http://www.ccetc.org/
Grade Span: KG-12; **Agency Type:** 1
Schools: 5
3 Primary; 1 Middle; 1 High; 0 Other Level
5 Regular; 0 Special Education; 0 Vocational; 0 Alternative
0 Magnet; 0 Charter; 3 Title I Eligible; 0 School-wide Title I
Students: 1,730 (n/a% male; n/a% female)
Individual Education Program: 264 (15.3%);
English Language Learner: n/a; Migrant: n/a
Eligible for Free Lunch Program: n/a
Eligible for Reduced-Price Lunch Program: n/a
Teachers: 111.4 (15.5 to 1)
Librarians/Media Specialists: 2.0 (865.0 to 1)
Guidance Counselors: 5.0 (346.0 to 1)
Current Spending: ($ per student per year):
Total: $4,884; Instruction: $2,842; Support Services: $1,706
Enrollment, Drop-out Rates and Diploma Recipients by Race/Ethnicity

Category	Total	White	Black	Asian	AIAN	Hisp.
Enrollment (%)	100.0	0.0	0.0	0.0	0.0	0.0
Drop-out Rate (%)	1.1	n/a	n/a	n/a	n/a	n/a
H.S. Diplomas (#)	141	n/a	n/a	n/a	n/a	n/a

Cumberland County

Cumberland County SD

756 Stanley St • Crossville, TN 38555-4790
(931) 484-6135 • http://cumberland-lea.k12tn.net/
Grade Span: KG-12; **Agency Type:** 1
Schools: 10
9 Primary; 0 Middle; 1 High; 0 Other Level
10 Regular; 0 Special Education; 0 Vocational; 0 Alternative
0 Magnet; 0 Charter; 8 Title I Eligible; 8 School-wide Title I
Students: 6,759 (n/a% male; n/a% female)
Individual Education Program: 1,101 (16.3%);
English Language Learner: n/a; Migrant: n/a
Eligible for Free Lunch Program: n/a
Eligible for Reduced-Price Lunch Program: n/a
Teachers: 406.9 (16.6 to 1)
Librarians/Media Specialists: 8.3 (814.3 to 1)
Guidance Counselors: 10.3 (656.2 to 1)
Current Spending: ($ per student per year):
Total: $4,900; Instruction: $3,186; Support Services: $1,363
Enrollment, Drop-out Rates and Diploma Recipients by Race/Ethnicity

Category	Total	White	Black	Asian	AIAN	Hisp.
Enrollment (%)	100.0	0.0	0.0	0.0	0.0	0.0
Drop-out Rate (%)	2.6	n/a	n/a	n/a	n/a	n/a
H.S. Diplomas (#)	301	n/a	n/a	n/a	n/a	n/a

Davidson County

Nashville-Davidson County SD

2601 Bransford Ave • Nashville, TN 37204-2811
(615) 259-8419
Grade Span: KG-12; **Agency Type:** 1
Schools: 123
71 Primary; 31 Middle; 17 High; 4 Other Level
115 Regular; 4 Special Education; 0 Vocational; 4 Alternative
10 Magnet; 0 Charter; 51 Title I Eligible; 51 School-wide Title I
Students: 67,954 (n/a% male; n/a% female)
Individual Education Program: 10,676 (15.7%);
English Language Learner: n/a; Migrant: n/a
Eligible for Free Lunch Program: n/a
Eligible for Reduced-Price Lunch Program: n/a
Teachers: 4,614.3 (14.7 to 1)
Librarians/Media Specialists: 113.9 (596.6 to 1)
Guidance Counselors: 142.3 (477.5 to 1)
Current Spending: ($ per student per year):
Total: $6,648; Instruction: $4,320; Support Services: $2,015
Enrollment, Drop-out Rates and Diploma Recipients by Race/Ethnicity

Category	Total	White	Black	Asian	AIAN	Hisp.
Enrollment (%)	100.0	0.0	0.0	0.0	0.0	0.0
Drop-out Rate (%)	8.8	n/a	n/a	n/a	n/a	n/a
H.S. Diplomas (#)	2,609	n/a	n/a	n/a	n/a	n/a

De Kalb County

Dekalb County SD

110 S Public Square • Smithville, TN 37166-1723
(615) 597-4084 • http://www.dekalbschools.com
Grade Span: KG-12; **Agency Type:** 1
Schools: 5
3 Primary; 1 Middle; 1 High; 0 Other Level
5 Regular; 0 Special Education; 0 Vocational; 0 Alternative
0 Magnet; 0 Charter; 4 Title I Eligible; 3 School-wide Title I
Students: 2,594 (n/a% male; n/a% female)
Individual Education Program: 509 (19.6%);
English Language Learner: n/a; Migrant: n/a
Eligible for Free Lunch Program: n/a
Eligible for Reduced-Price Lunch Program: n/a
Teachers: 179.6 (14.4 to 1)
Librarians/Media Specialists: 5.0 (518.8 to 1)
Guidance Counselors: 5.0 (518.8 to 1)
Current Spending: ($ per student per year):
Total: $6,082; Instruction: $3,896; Support Services: $1,783
Enrollment, Drop-out Rates and Diploma Recipients by Race/Ethnicity

Category	Total	White	Black	Asian	AIAN	Hisp.
Enrollment (%)	100.0	0.0	0.0	0.0	0.0	0.0
Drop-out Rate (%)	4.6	n/a	n/a	n/a	n/a	n/a
H.S. Diplomas (#)	108	n/a	n/a	n/a	n/a	n/a

Dickson County

Dickson County SD

817 N Charlotte St • Dickson, TN 37055-1008
(615) 446-7571
Grade Span: KG-12; **Agency Type:** 1
Schools: 14
8 Primary; 3 Middle; 2 High; 1 Other Level
13 Regular; 0 Special Education; 0 Vocational; 1 Alternative
0 Magnet; 0 Charter; 7 Title I Eligible; 4 School-wide Title I
Students: 8,039 (n/a% male; n/a% female)
Individual Education Program: 1,549 (19.3%);
English Language Learner: n/a; Migrant: n/a
Eligible for Free Lunch Program: n/a
Eligible for Reduced-Price Lunch Program: n/a
Teachers: 523.7 (15.4 to 1)
Librarians/Media Specialists: 14.0 (574.2 to 1)
Guidance Counselors: 16.6 (484.3 to 1)
Current Spending: ($ per student per year):
Total: $5,277; Instruction: $3,365; Support Services: $1,576
Enrollment, Drop-out Rates and Diploma Recipients by Race/Ethnicity

Category	Total	White	Black	Asian	AIAN	Hisp.
Enrollment (%)	100.0	0.0	0.0	0.0	0.0	0.0
Drop-out Rate (%)	4.4	n/a	n/a	n/a	n/a	n/a
H.S. Diplomas (#)	396	n/a	n/a	n/a	n/a	n/a

Dyer County

Dyer County SD

159 Everett Ave • Dyersburg, TN 38024-5119
(731) 285-6712 • http://www.dyer-lea.dyer.k12.tn.us/
Grade Span: KG-12; **Agency Type:** 1
Schools: 7
5 Primary; 1 Middle; 1 High; 0 Other Level
7 Regular; 0 Special Education; 0 Vocational; 0 Alternative
0 Magnet; 0 Charter; 5 Title I Eligible; 1 School-wide Title I
Students: 3,163 (n/a% male; n/a% female)
Individual Education Program: 676 (21.4%);
English Language Learner: n/a; Migrant: n/a
Eligible for Free Lunch Program: n/a
Eligible for Reduced-Price Lunch Program: n/a
Teachers: 201.0 (15.7 to 1)
Librarians/Media Specialists: 3.0 (1,054.3 to 1)
Guidance Counselors: 5.0 (632.6 to 1)
Current Spending: ($ per student per year):
Total: $6,021; Instruction: $3,566; Support Services: $2,065
Enrollment, Drop-out Rates and Diploma Recipients by Race/Ethnicity

Category	Total	White	Black	Asian	AIAN	Hisp.
Enrollment (%)	100.0	0.0	0.0	0.0	0.0	0.0
Drop-out Rate (%)	1.3	n/a	n/a	n/a	n/a	n/a
H.S. Diplomas (#)	194	n/a	n/a	n/a	n/a	n/a

Dyersburg City SD

PO Box 1507 • Dyersburg, TN 38025-1507
(731) 286-3600 • http://www.dyersburg-lea.dyer.k12.tn.us/
Grade Span: KG-12; **Agency Type:** 1
Schools: 4
2 Primary; 1 Middle; 1 High; 0 Other Level
4 Regular; 0 Special Education; 0 Vocational; 0 Alternative

0 Magnet; 0 Charter; 3 Title I Eligible; 3 School-wide Title I
Students: 3,490 (n/a% male; n/a% female)
Individual Education Program: 553 (15.8%);
English Language Learner: n/a; Migrant: n/a
Eligible for Free Lunch Program: n/a
Eligible for Reduced-Price Lunch Program: n/a
Teachers: 216.9 (16.1 to 1)
Librarians/Media Specialists: 5.0 (698.0 to 1)
Guidance Counselors: 7.0 (498.6 to 1)
Current Spending: ($ per student per year):
Total: $5,717; Instruction: $3,895; Support Services: $1,480
Enrollment, Drop-out Rates and Diploma Recipients by Race/Ethnicity

Category	Total	White	Black	Asian	AIAN	Hisp.
Enrollment (%)	100.0	0.0	0.0	0.0	0.0	0.0
Drop-out Rate (%)	3.6	n/a	n/a	n/a	n/a	n/a
H.S. Diplomas (#)	197	n/a	n/a	n/a	n/a	n/a

Fayette County

Fayette County SD
126 W Market St • Somerville, TN 38068-0009
(901) 465-5260
Grade Span: KG-12; **Agency Type:** 1
Schools: 10
7 Primary; 2 Middle; 1 High; 0 Other Level
10 Regular; 0 Special Education; 0 Vocational; 0 Alternative
0 Magnet; 0 Charter; 10 Title I Eligible; 10 School-wide Title I
Students: 3,176 (n/a% male; n/a% female)
Individual Education Program: 466 (14.7%);
English Language Learner: n/a; Migrant: n/a
Eligible for Free Lunch Program: n/a
Eligible for Reduced-Price Lunch Program: n/a
Teachers: 245.5 (12.9 to 1)
Librarians/Media Specialists: 8.0 (397.0 to 1)
Guidance Counselors: 6.8 (467.1 to 1)
Current Spending: ($ per student per year):
Total: $5,635; Instruction: $3,340; Support Services: $1,826
Enrollment, Drop-out Rates and Diploma Recipients by Race/Ethnicity

Category	Total	White	Black	Asian	AIAN	Hisp.
Enrollment (%)	100.0	0.0	0.0	0.0	0.0	0.0
Drop-out Rate (%)	7.4	n/a	n/a	n/a	n/a	n/a
H.S. Diplomas (#)	138	n/a	n/a	n/a	n/a	n/a

Fentress County

Fentress County SD
PO Box 963 • Jamestown, TN 38556-0963
(931) 879-9218
Grade Span: KG-12; **Agency Type:** 1
Schools: 7
5 Primary; 0 Middle; 2 High; 0 Other Level
7 Regular; 0 Special Education; 0 Vocational; 0 Alternative
0 Magnet; 0 Charter; 6 Title I Eligible; 6 School-wide Title I
Students: 2,285 (n/a% male; n/a% female)
Individual Education Program: 317 (13.9%);
English Language Learner: n/a; Migrant: n/a
Eligible for Free Lunch Program: n/a
Eligible for Reduced-Price Lunch Program: n/a
Teachers: 163.3 (14.0 to 1)
Librarians/Media Specialists: 4.0 (571.3 to 1)
Guidance Counselors: 4.0 (571.3 to 1)
Current Spending: ($ per student per year):
Total: $5,103; Instruction: $3,400; Support Services: $1,346
Enrollment, Drop-out Rates and Diploma Recipients by Race/Ethnicity

Category	Total	White	Black	Asian	AIAN	Hisp.
Enrollment (%)	100.0	0.0	0.0	0.0	0.0	0.0
Drop-out Rate (%)	0.7	n/a	n/a	n/a	n/a	n/a
H.S. Diplomas (#)	150	n/a	n/a	n/a	n/a	n/a

Franklin County

Franklin County SD
215 S College St • Winchester, TN 37398-1519
(931) 967-0626 • http://www.fssd.org/
Grade Span: KG-12; **Agency Type:** 1
Schools: 12
8 Primary; 2 Middle; 1 High; 1 Other Level
12 Regular; 0 Special Education; 0 Vocational; 0 Alternative
0 Magnet; 0 Charter; 4 Title I Eligible; 4 School-wide Title I
Students: 5,845 (n/a% male; n/a% female)
Individual Education Program: 940 (16.1%);
English Language Learner: n/a; Migrant: n/a
Eligible for Free Lunch Program: n/a
Eligible for Reduced-Price Lunch Program: n/a
Teachers: 371.5 (15.7 to 1)
Librarians/Media Specialists: 12.0 (487.1 to 1)
Guidance Counselors: 12.5 (467.6 to 1)
Current Spending: ($ per student per year):
Total: $5,499; Instruction: $3,832; Support Services: $1,383
Enrollment, Drop-out Rates and Diploma Recipients by Race/Ethnicity

Category	Total	White	Black	Asian	AIAN	Hisp.
Enrollment (%)	100.0	0.0	0.0	0.0	0.0	0.0
Drop-out Rate (%)	4.0	n/a	n/a	n/a	n/a	n/a
H.S. Diplomas (#)	306	n/a	n/a	n/a	n/a	n/a

Gibson County

Gibson Special District
135 Hwy 45 W Box D • Dyer, TN 38330
(731) 692-3803 • http://volweb.utk.edu/school/gibson/gcsd99.html
Grade Span: KG-12; **Agency Type:** 1
Schools: 7
5 Primary; 1 Middle; 1 High; 0 Other Level
7 Regular; 0 Special Education; 0 Vocational; 0 Alternative
0 Magnet; 0 Charter; 4 Title I Eligible; 0 School-wide Title I
Students: 2,655 (n/a% male; n/a% female)
Individual Education Program: 389 (14.7%);
English Language Learner: n/a; Migrant: n/a
Eligible for Free Lunch Program: n/a
Eligible for Reduced-Price Lunch Program: n/a
Teachers: 157.0 (16.9 to 1)
Librarians/Media Specialists: 6.0 (442.5 to 1)
Guidance Counselors: 4.0 (663.8 to 1)
Current Spending: ($ per student per year):
Total: $4,837; Instruction: $3,136; Support Services: $1,342
Enrollment, Drop-out Rates and Diploma Recipients by Race/Ethnicity

Category	Total	White	Black	Asian	AIAN	Hisp.
Enrollment (%)	100.0	0.0	0.0	0.0	0.0	0.0
Drop-out Rate (%)	4.3	n/a	n/a	n/a	n/a	n/a
H.S. Diplomas (#)	126	n/a	n/a	n/a	n/a	n/a

Humboldt City SD
1421 Osborne St • Humboldt, TN 38343-2869
(731) 784-2652
Grade Span: KG-12; **Agency Type:** 1
Schools: 5
2 Primary; 2 Middle; 1 High; 0 Other Level
5 Regular; 0 Special Education; 0 Vocational; 0 Alternative
0 Magnet; 0 Charter; 3 Title I Eligible; 3 School-wide Title I
Students: 1,534 (n/a% male; n/a% female)
Individual Education Program: 282 (18.4%);
English Language Learner: n/a; Migrant: n/a
Eligible for Free Lunch Program: n/a
Eligible for Reduced-Price Lunch Program: n/a
Teachers: 106.2 (14.4 to 1)
Librarians/Media Specialists: 4.0 (383.5 to 1)
Guidance Counselors: 4.0 (383.5 to 1)
Current Spending: ($ per student per year):
Total: $5,567; Instruction: $3,545; Support Services: $1,633
Enrollment, Drop-out Rates and Diploma Recipients by Race/Ethnicity

Category	Total	White	Black	Asian	AIAN	Hisp.
Enrollment (%)	100.0	0.0	0.0	0.0	0.0	0.0
Drop-out Rate (%)	6.6	n/a	n/a	n/a	n/a	n/a
H.S. Diplomas (#)	94	n/a	n/a	n/a	n/a	n/a

Milan City Special SD
2048 S First • Milan, TN 38358-0528
Mailing Address: PO Box 528 • Milan, TN 38358-0528
(731) 686-0844 • http://www.milanssd.org/
Grade Span: KG-12; **Agency Type:** 1
Schools: 3
1 Primary; 1 Middle; 1 High; 0 Other Level
3 Regular; 0 Special Education; 0 Vocational; 0 Alternative
0 Magnet; 0 Charter; 1 Title I Eligible; 0 School-wide Title I
Students: 1,997 (n/a% male; n/a% female)
Individual Education Program: 276 (13.8%);
English Language Learner: n/a; Migrant: n/a
Eligible for Free Lunch Program: n/a
Eligible for Reduced-Price Lunch Program: n/a
Teachers: 137.3 (14.5 to 1)
Librarians/Media Specialists: 4.0 (499.3 to 1)
Guidance Counselors: 5.0 (399.4 to 1)
Current Spending: ($ per student per year):
Total: $5,144; Instruction: $3,392; Support Services: $1,434
Enrollment, Drop-out Rates and Diploma Recipients by Race/Ethnicity

Category	Total	White	Black	Asian	AIAN	Hisp.
Enrollment (%)	100.0	0.0	0.0	0.0	0.0	0.0
Drop-out Rate (%)	1.1	n/a	n/a	n/a	n/a	n/a
H.S. Diplomas (#)	123	n/a	n/a	n/a	n/a	n/a

Giles County

Giles County SD

270 Richland Dr • Pulaski, TN 38478-2609
(931) 363-4558 • http://www.giles-lea.giles.k12.tn.us
Grade Span: KG-12; **Agency Type:** 1
Schools: 8
5 Primary; 1 Middle; 1 High; 1 Other Level
8 Regular; 0 Special Education; 0 Vocational; 0 Alternative
0 Magnet; 0 Charter; 6 Title I Eligible; 0 School-wide Title I
Students: 4,504 (n/a% male; n/a% female)
Individual Education Program: 634 (14.1%);
English Language Learner: n/a; Migrant: n/a
Eligible for Free Lunch Program: n/a
Eligible for Reduced-Price Lunch Program: n/a
Teachers: 297.0 (15.2 to 1)
Librarians/Media Specialists: 10.0 (450.4 to 1)
Guidance Counselors: 11.0 (409.5 to 1)
Current Spending: ($ per student per year):
Total: $5,424; Instruction: $3,517; Support Services: $1,581
Enrollment, Drop-out Rates and Diploma Recipients by Race/Ethnicity

Category	Total	White	Black	Asian	AIAN	Hisp.
Enrollment (%)	100.0	0.0	0.0	0.0	0.0	0.0
Drop-out Rate (%)	4.8	n/a	n/a	n/a	n/a	n/a
H.S. Diplomas (#)	233	n/a	n/a	n/a	n/a	n/a

Grainger County

Grainger County SD

PO Box 38 • Rutledge, TN 37861-0038
(865) 828-3611 • http://www.grainger.k12.tn.us
Grade Span: KG-12; **Agency Type:** 1
Schools: 6
3 Primary; 0 Middle; 2 High; 1 Other Level
6 Regular; 0 Special Education; 0 Vocational; 0 Alternative
0 Magnet; 0 Charter; 4 Title I Eligible; 4 School-wide Title I
Students: 3,308 (n/a% male; n/a% female)
Individual Education Program: 559 (16.9%);
English Language Learner: n/a; Migrant: n/a
Eligible for Free Lunch Program: n/a
Eligible for Reduced-Price Lunch Program: n/a
Teachers: 203.0 (16.3 to 1)
Librarians/Media Specialists: 5.0 (661.6 to 1)
Guidance Counselors: 5.0 (661.6 to 1)
Current Spending: ($ per student per year):
Total: $4,666; Instruction: $3,198; Support Services: $1,153
Enrollment, Drop-out Rates and Diploma Recipients by Race/Ethnicity

Category	Total	White	Black	Asian	AIAN	Hisp.
Enrollment (%)	100.0	0.0	0.0	0.0	0.0	0.0
Drop-out Rate (%)	1.2	n/a	n/a	n/a	n/a	n/a
H.S. Diplomas (#)	170	n/a	n/a	n/a	n/a	n/a

Greene County

Greene County SD

910 W Summer St • Greeneville, TN 37743-3016
(423) 639-4194 • http://www.greene.xtn.net/~gcs/
Grade Span: KG-12; **Agency Type:** 1
Schools: 15
11 Primary; 0 Middle; 4 High; 0 Other Level
15 Regular; 0 Special Education; 0 Vocational; 0 Alternative
0 Magnet; 0 Charter; 11 Title I Eligible; 11 School-wide Title I
Students: 6,887 (n/a% male; n/a% female)
Individual Education Program: 1,393 (20.2%);
English Language Learner: n/a; Migrant: n/a
Eligible for Free Lunch Program: n/a
Eligible for Reduced-Price Lunch Program: n/a
Teachers: 442.9 (15.5 to 1)
Librarians/Media Specialists: 9.0 (765.2 to 1)
Guidance Counselors: 13.0 (529.8 to 1)
Current Spending: ($ per student per year):
Total: $4,985; Instruction: $3,204; Support Services: $1,440
Enrollment, Drop-out Rates and Diploma Recipients by Race/Ethnicity

Category	Total	White	Black	Asian	AIAN	Hisp.
Enrollment (%)	100.0	0.0	0.0	0.0	0.0	0.0
Drop-out Rate (%)	2.0	n/a	n/a	n/a	n/a	n/a
H.S. Diplomas (#)	339	n/a	n/a	n/a	n/a	n/a

Greeneville City SD

PO Box 1420 • Greeneville, TN 37744-1420
(423) 787-8000 • http://www.gcschools.net/
Grade Span: KG-12; **Agency Type:** 1
Schools: 7
4 Primary; 1 Middle; 2 High; 0 Other Level
6 Regular; 0 Special Education; 1 Vocational; 0 Alternative
0 Magnet; 0 Charter; 3 Title I Eligible; 0 School-wide Title I
Students: 2,626 (n/a% male; n/a% female)
Individual Education Program: 626 (23.8%);
English Language Learner: n/a; Migrant: n/a
Eligible for Free Lunch Program: n/a
Eligible for Reduced-Price Lunch Program: n/a
Teachers: 193.7 (13.6 to 1)
Librarians/Media Specialists: 6.0 (437.7 to 1)
Guidance Counselors: 10.0 (262.6 to 1)
Current Spending: ($ per student per year):
Total: $7,160; Instruction: $4,635; Support Services: $2,257
Enrollment, Drop-out Rates and Diploma Recipients by Race/Ethnicity

Category	Total	White	Black	Asian	AIAN	Hisp.
Enrollment (%)	100.0	0.0	0.0	0.0	0.0	0.0
Drop-out Rate (%)	0.5	n/a	n/a	n/a	n/a	n/a
H.S. Diplomas (#)	121	n/a	n/a	n/a	n/a	n/a

Grundy County

Grundy County SD

PO Box 97 • Altamont, TN 37301-0097
(931) 692-3467 •
http://volweb.utk.edu/Schools/grundyco/grundy.index.html
Grade Span: KG-12; **Agency Type:** 1
Schools: 7
6 Primary; 0 Middle; 1 High; 0 Other Level
7 Regular; 0 Special Education; 0 Vocational; 0 Alternative
0 Magnet; 0 Charter; 6 Title I Eligible; 6 School-wide Title I
Students: 2,264 (n/a% male; n/a% female)
Individual Education Program: 603 (26.6%);
English Language Learner: n/a; Migrant: n/a
Eligible for Free Lunch Program: n/a
Eligible for Reduced-Price Lunch Program: n/a
Teachers: 179.0 (12.6 to 1)
Librarians/Media Specialists: 2.0 (1,132.0 to 1)
Guidance Counselors: 4.0 (566.0 to 1)
Current Spending: ($ per student per year):
Total: $5,175; Instruction: $3,391; Support Services: $1,399
Enrollment, Drop-out Rates and Diploma Recipients by Race/Ethnicity

Category	Total	White	Black	Asian	AIAN	Hisp.
Enrollment (%)	100.0	0.0	0.0	0.0	0.0	0.0
Drop-out Rate (%)	5.5	n/a	n/a	n/a	n/a	n/a
H.S. Diplomas (#)	123	n/a	n/a	n/a	n/a	n/a

Hamblen County

Hamblen County SD

210 E Morris Blvd • Morristown, TN 37813-2341
(423) 586-7700 • http://www.hcboe.net
Grade Span: PK-12; **Agency Type:** 1
Schools: 20
12 Primary; 4 Middle; 3 High; 1 Other Level
18 Regular; 1 Special Education; 0 Vocational; 1 Alternative
0 Magnet; 0 Charter; 8 Title I Eligible; 8 School-wide Title I
Students: 8,982 (n/a% male; n/a% female)
Individual Education Program: 1,197 (13.3%);
English Language Learner: n/a; Migrant: n/a
Eligible for Free Lunch Program: n/a
Eligible for Reduced-Price Lunch Program: n/a
Teachers: 597.2 (15.0 to 1)
Librarians/Media Specialists: 19.0 (472.7 to 1)
Guidance Counselors: 18.4 (488.2 to 1)
Current Spending: ($ per student per year):
Total: $5,394; Instruction: $3,644; Support Services: $1,283
Enrollment, Drop-out Rates and Diploma Recipients by Race/Ethnicity

Category	Total	White	Black	Asian	AIAN	Hisp.
Enrollment (%)	100.0	0.0	0.0	0.0	0.0	0.0
Drop-out Rate (%)	1.7	n/a	n/a	n/a	n/a	n/a
H.S. Diplomas (#)	434	n/a	n/a	n/a	n/a	n/a

Hamilton County

Hamilton County SD

6703 Bonny Oaks Dr • Chattanooga, TN 37402-1092
(423) 209-8400 • http://www.hcde.org/
Grade Span: KG-12; **Agency Type:** 1
Schools: 81
48 Primary; 15 Middle; 13 High; 5 Other Level
76 Regular; 1 Special Education; 3 Vocational; 1 Alternative
3 Magnet; 0 Charter; 28 Title I Eligible; 28 School-wide Title I
Students: 40,564 (n/a% male; n/a% female)
Individual Education Program: 6,922 (17.1%);
English Language Learner: n/a; Migrant: n/a
Eligible for Free Lunch Program: n/a
Eligible for Reduced-Price Lunch Program: n/a

Teachers: 2,675.8 (15.2 to 1)
Librarians/Media Specialists: 80.9 (501.4 to 1)
Guidance Counselors: 82.7 (490.5 to 1)
Current Spending: ($ per student per year):
Total: $6,505; Instruction: $4,202; Support Services: $1,988
Enrollment, Drop-out Rates and Diploma Recipients by Race/Ethnicity

Category	Total	White	Black	Asian	AIAN	Hisp.
Enrollment (%)	100.0	0.0	0.0	0.0	0.0	0.0
Drop-out Rate (%)	6.4	n/a	n/a	n/a	n/a	n/a
H.S. Diplomas (#)	1,715	n/a	n/a	n/a	n/a	n/a

Hardeman County

Hardeman County SD
PO Box 112 • Bolivar, TN 38008-0112
(731) 658-2508
Grade Span: KG-12; **Agency Type:** 1
Schools: 9
6 Primary; 1 Middle; 2 High; 0 Other Level
9 Regular; 0 Special Education; 0 Vocational; 0 Alternative
0 Magnet; 0 Charter; 7 Title I Eligible; 7 School-wide Title I
Students: 4,513 (n/a% male; n/a% female)
Individual Education Program: 802 (17.8%);
English Language Learner: n/a; Migrant: n/a
Eligible for Free Lunch Program: n/a
Eligible for Reduced-Price Lunch Program: n/a
Teachers: 327.4 (13.8 to 1)
Librarians/Media Specialists: 8.0 (564.1 to 1)
Guidance Counselors: 11.0 (410.3 to 1)
Current Spending: ($ per student per year):
Total: $5,081; Instruction: $3,363; Support Services: $1,421
Enrollment, Drop-out Rates and Diploma Recipients by Race/Ethnicity

Category	Total	White	Black	Asian	AIAN	Hisp.
Enrollment (%)	100.0	0.0	0.0	0.0	0.0	0.0
Drop-out Rate (%)	4.9	n/a	n/a	n/a	n/a	n/a
H.S. Diplomas (#)	179	n/a	n/a	n/a	n/a	n/a

Hardin County

Hardin County SD
116 N Guinn St • Savannah, TN 38372-2026
(731) 925-3943 • http://www.hardin.k12.tn.us/
Grade Span: KG-12; **Agency Type:** 1
Schools: 10
8 Primary; 1 Middle; 1 High; 0 Other Level
10 Regular; 0 Special Education; 0 Vocational; 0 Alternative
0 Magnet; 0 Charter; 7 Title I Eligible; 6 School-wide Title I
Students: 3,798 (n/a% male; n/a% female)
Individual Education Program: 633 (16.7%);
English Language Learner: n/a; Migrant: n/a
Eligible for Free Lunch Program: n/a
Eligible for Reduced-Price Lunch Program: n/a
Teachers: 265.6 (14.3 to 1)
Librarians/Media Specialists: 8.0 (474.8 to 1)
Guidance Counselors: 11.0 (345.3 to 1)
Current Spending: ($ per student per year):
Total: $5,446; Instruction: $3,518; Support Services: $1,510
Enrollment, Drop-out Rates and Diploma Recipients by Race/Ethnicity

Category	Total	White	Black	Asian	AIAN	Hisp.
Enrollment (%)	100.0	0.0	0.0	0.0	0.0	0.0
Drop-out Rate (%)	4.7	n/a	n/a	n/a	n/a	n/a
H.S. Diplomas (#)	217	n/a	n/a	n/a	n/a	n/a

Hawkins County

Hawkins County SD
200 N Depot St • Rogersville, TN 37857-2639
(423) 272-7629 • http://www.hawkins.k12.tn.us/central/
Grade Span: KG-12; **Agency Type:** 1
Schools: 17
11 Primary; 3 Middle; 2 High; 1 Other Level
17 Regular; 0 Special Education; 0 Vocational; 0 Alternative
0 Magnet; 0 Charter; 12 Title I Eligible; 12 School-wide Title I
Students: 7,237 (n/a% male; n/a% female)
Individual Education Program: 1,453 (20.1%);
English Language Learner: n/a; Migrant: n/a
Eligible for Free Lunch Program: n/a
Eligible for Reduced-Price Lunch Program: n/a
Teachers: 506.4 (14.3 to 1)
Librarians/Media Specialists: 16.0 (452.3 to 1)
Guidance Counselors: 15.6 (463.9 to 1)
Current Spending: ($ per student per year):
Total: $5,342; Instruction: $3,535; Support Services: $1,477
Enrollment, Drop-out Rates and Diploma Recipients by Race/Ethnicity

Category	Total	White	Black	Asian	AIAN	Hisp.
Enrollment (%)	100.0	0.0	0.0	0.0	0.0	0.0
Drop-out Rate (%)	6.3	n/a	n/a	n/a	n/a	n/a
H.S. Diplomas (#)	323	n/a	n/a	n/a	n/a	n/a

Haywood County

Haywood County SD
900 E Main Str • Brownsville, TN 38012-2647
(731) 772-9613
Grade Span: KG-12; **Agency Type:** 1
Schools: 7
3 Primary; 2 Middle; 1 High; 1 Other Level
5 Regular; 1 Special Education; 0 Vocational; 1 Alternative
0 Magnet; 0 Charter; 4 Title I Eligible; 4 School-wide Title I
Students: 3,533 (n/a% male; n/a% female)
Individual Education Program: 554 (15.7%);
English Language Learner: n/a; Migrant: n/a
Eligible for Free Lunch Program: n/a
Eligible for Reduced-Price Lunch Program: n/a
Teachers: 245.8 (14.4 to 1)
Librarians/Media Specialists: 7.0 (504.7 to 1)
Guidance Counselors: 7.0 (504.7 to 1)
Current Spending: ($ per student per year):
Total: $5,698; Instruction: $3,648; Support Services: $1,558
Enrollment, Drop-out Rates and Diploma Recipients by Race/Ethnicity

Category	Total	White	Black	Asian	AIAN	Hisp.
Enrollment (%)	100.0	0.0	0.0	0.0	0.0	0.0
Drop-out Rate (%)	5.7	n/a	n/a	n/a	n/a	n/a
H.S. Diplomas (#)	162	n/a	n/a	n/a	n/a	n/a

Henderson County

Henderson County SD
35 Wilson St • Lexington, TN 38351
Mailing Address: PO Box 190 • Lexington, TN 38351
(731) 968-3661 • http://www.henderson-lea.henderson.k12.tn.us/
Grade Span: KG-12; **Agency Type:** 1
Schools: 10
7 Primary; 0 Middle; 2 High; 1 Other Level
9 Regular; 0 Special Education; 0 Vocational; 1 Alternative
0 Magnet; 0 Charter; 7 Title I Eligible; 0 School-wide Title I
Students: 3,438 (n/a% male; n/a% female)
Individual Education Program: 529 (15.4%);
English Language Learner: n/a; Migrant: n/a
Eligible for Free Lunch Program: n/a
Eligible for Reduced-Price Lunch Program: n/a
Teachers: 239.5 (14.4 to 1)
Librarians/Media Specialists: 9.0 (382.0 to 1)
Guidance Counselors: 9.0 (382.0 to 1)
Current Spending: ($ per student per year):
Total: $4,966; Instruction: $3,355; Support Services: $1,447
Enrollment, Drop-out Rates and Diploma Recipients by Race/Ethnicity

Category	Total	White	Black	Asian	AIAN	Hisp.
Enrollment (%)	100.0	0.0	0.0	0.0	0.0	0.0
Drop-out Rate (%)	2.8	n/a	n/a	n/a	n/a	n/a
H.S. Diplomas (#)	55	n/a	n/a	n/a	n/a	n/a

Henry County

Henry County SD
217 Grove Blvd • Paris, TN 38242-4711
(731) 642-9733 • http://www.henry.k12.tn.us/
Grade Span: KG-12; **Agency Type:** 1
Schools: 6
4 Primary; 0 Middle; 1 High; 1 Other Level
6 Regular; 0 Special Education; 0 Vocational; 0 Alternative
0 Magnet; 0 Charter; 5 Title I Eligible; 5 School-wide Title I
Students: 3,143 (n/a% male; n/a% female)
Individual Education Program: 484 (15.4%);
English Language Learner: n/a; Migrant: n/a
Eligible for Free Lunch Program: n/a
Eligible for Reduced-Price Lunch Program: n/a
Teachers: 198.8 (15.8 to 1)
Librarians/Media Specialists: 5.0 (628.6 to 1)
Guidance Counselors: 9.0 (349.2 to 1)
Current Spending: ($ per student per year):
Total: $5,600; Instruction: $3,461; Support Services: $1,778
Enrollment, Drop-out Rates and Diploma Recipients by Race/Ethnicity

Category	Total	White	Black	Asian	AIAN	Hisp.
Enrollment (%)	100.0	0.0	0.0	0.0	0.0	0.0
Drop-out Rate (%)	3.8	n/a	n/a	n/a	n/a	n/a
H.S. Diplomas (#)	221	n/a	n/a	n/a	n/a	n/a

Hickman County

Hickman County SD

115 Murphree Ave • Centerville, TN 37033-1430
(931) 729-3391 • http://www.hickman.k12.tn.us/
Grade Span: KG-12; **Agency Type:** 1
Schools: 7
4 Primary; 2 Middle; 1 High; 0 Other Level
7 Regular; 0 Special Education; 0 Vocational; 0 Alternative
0 Magnet; 0 Charter; 4 Title I Eligible; 0 School-wide Title I
Students: 3,838 (n/a% male; n/a% female)
Individual Education Program: 660 (17.2%);
English Language Learner: n/a; Migrant: n/a
Eligible for Free Lunch Program: n/a
Eligible for Reduced-Price Lunch Program: n/a
Teachers: 238.6 (16.1 to 1)
Librarians/Media Specialists: 7.0 (548.3 to 1)
Guidance Counselors: 8.0 (479.8 to 1)
Current Spending: ($ per student per year):
Total: $5,094; Instruction: $3,292; Support Services: $1,506
Enrollment, Drop-out Rates and Diploma Recipients by Race/Ethnicity

Category	Total	White	Black	Asian	AIAN	Hisp.
Enrollment (%)	100.0	0.0	0.0	0.0	0.0	0.0
Drop-out Rate (%)	2.7	n/a	n/a	n/a	n/a	n/a
H.S. Diplomas (#)	175	n/a	n/a	n/a	n/a	n/a

Humphreys County

Humphreys County SD

2443 Hwy 70 E • Waverly, TN 37185-2223
(931) 296-2568
Grade Span: KG-12; **Agency Type:** 1
Schools: 7
3 Primary; 2 Middle; 2 High; 0 Other Level
7 Regular; 0 Special Education; 0 Vocational; 0 Alternative
0 Magnet; 0 Charter; 2 Title I Eligible; 2 School-wide Title I
Students: 3,020 (n/a% male; n/a% female)
Individual Education Program: 401 (13.3%);
English Language Learner: n/a; Migrant: n/a
Eligible for Free Lunch Program: n/a
Eligible for Reduced-Price Lunch Program: n/a
Teachers: 198.5 (15.2 to 1)
Librarians/Media Specialists: 6.0 (503.3 to 1)
Guidance Counselors: 6.0 (503.3 to 1)
Current Spending: ($ per student per year):
Total: $5,262; Instruction: $3,385; Support Services: $1,480
Enrollment, Drop-out Rates and Diploma Recipients by Race/Ethnicity

Category	Total	White	Black	Asian	AIAN	Hisp.
Enrollment (%)	100.0	0.0	0.0	0.0	0.0	0.0
Drop-out Rate (%)	1.6	n/a	n/a	n/a	n/a	n/a
H.S. Diplomas (#)	159	n/a	n/a	n/a	n/a	n/a

Jackson County

Jackson County SD

205 W Gibson Ave • Gainsboro, TN 38562-9399
(931) 268-0268 • http://volweb.utk.edu/school/jackson/
Grade Span: KG-12; **Agency Type:** 1
Schools: 5
2 Primary; 1 Middle; 2 High; 0 Other Level
4 Regular; 0 Special Education; 1 Vocational; 0 Alternative
0 Magnet; 0 Charter; 2 Title I Eligible; 2 School-wide Title I
Students: 1,638 (n/a% male; n/a% female)
Individual Education Program: 297 (18.1%);
English Language Learner: n/a; Migrant: n/a
Eligible for Free Lunch Program: n/a
Eligible for Reduced-Price Lunch Program: n/a
Teachers: 119.7 (13.7 to 1)
Librarians/Media Specialists: 3.0 (546.0 to 1)
Guidance Counselors: 3.0 (546.0 to 1)
Current Spending: ($ per student per year):
Total: $4,890; Instruction: $3,120; Support Services: $1,409
Enrollment, Drop-out Rates and Diploma Recipients by Race/Ethnicity

Category	Total	White	Black	Asian	AIAN	Hisp.
Enrollment (%)	100.0	0.0	0.0	0.0	0.0	0.0
Drop-out Rate (%)	1.3	n/a	n/a	n/a	n/a	n/a
H.S. Diplomas (#)	76	n/a	n/a	n/a	n/a	n/a

Jefferson County

Jefferson County SD

PO Box 190 • Dandridge, TN 37725-0190
(865) 397-3194 • http://208.183.128.3/
Grade Span: KG-12; **Agency Type:** 1
Schools: 11
7 Primary; 2 Middle; 1 High; 1 Other Level
10 Regular; 0 Special Education; 0 Vocational; 1 Alternative
0 Magnet; 0 Charter; 7 Title I Eligible; 7 School-wide Title I
Students: 6,878 (n/a% male; n/a% female)
Individual Education Program: 1,176 (17.1%);
English Language Learner: n/a; Migrant: n/a
Eligible for Free Lunch Program: n/a
Eligible for Reduced-Price Lunch Program: n/a
Teachers: 440.5 (15.6 to 1)
Librarians/Media Specialists: 11.3 (608.7 to 1)
Guidance Counselors: 17.0 (404.6 to 1)
Current Spending: ($ per student per year):
Total: $5,157; Instruction: $3,290; Support Services: $1,571
Enrollment, Drop-out Rates and Diploma Recipients by Race/Ethnicity

Category	Total	White	Black	Asian	AIAN	Hisp.
Enrollment (%)	100.0	0.0	0.0	0.0	0.0	0.0
Drop-out Rate (%)	1.6	n/a	n/a	n/a	n/a	n/a
H.S. Diplomas (#)	374	n/a	n/a	n/a	n/a	n/a

Johnson County

Johnson County SD

211 N Church St • Mountain City, TN 37683-1325
(423) 727-2640 • http://www.jocoed@k12tn.net
Grade Span: KG-12; **Agency Type:** 1
Schools: 7
5 Primary; 1 Middle; 1 High; 0 Other Level
7 Regular; 0 Special Education; 0 Vocational; 0 Alternative
0 Magnet; 0 Charter; 5 Title I Eligible; 5 School-wide Title I
Students: 2,287 (n/a% male; n/a% female)
Individual Education Program: 415 (18.1%);
English Language Learner: n/a; Migrant: n/a
Eligible for Free Lunch Program: n/a
Eligible for Reduced-Price Lunch Program: n/a
Teachers: 154.6 (14.8 to 1)
Librarians/Media Specialists: 5.0 (457.4 to 1)
Guidance Counselors: 4.0 (571.8 to 1)
Current Spending: ($ per student per year):
Total: $5,963; Instruction: $3,770; Support Services: $1,820
Enrollment, Drop-out Rates and Diploma Recipients by Race/Ethnicity

Category	Total	White	Black	Asian	AIAN	Hisp.
Enrollment (%)	100.0	0.0	0.0	0.0	0.0	0.0
Drop-out Rate (%)	5.0	n/a	n/a	n/a	n/a	n/a
H.S. Diplomas (#)	125	n/a	n/a	n/a	n/a	n/a

Knox County

Knox County SD

912 S Gay St • Knoxville, TN 37902-2188
Mailing Address: PO Box 2188 • Knoxville, TN 37902-2188
(865) 594-1801 • http://www.korrnet.org/kcschool/
Grade Span: KG-12; **Agency Type:** 1
Schools: 88
51 Primary; 14 Middle; 17 High; 6 Other Level
79 Regular; 4 Special Education; 2 Vocational; 3 Alternative
5 Magnet; 0 Charter; 12 Title I Eligible; 12 School-wide Title I
Students: 53,411 (n/a% male; n/a% female)
Individual Education Program: 6,898 (12.9%);
English Language Learner: n/a; Migrant: n/a
Eligible for Free Lunch Program: n/a
Eligible for Reduced-Price Lunch Program: n/a
Teachers: 3,588.4 (14.9 to 1)
Librarians/Media Specialists: 89.8 (594.8 to 1)
Guidance Counselors: 89.6 (596.1 to 1)
Current Spending: ($ per student per year):
Total: $5,701; Instruction: $3,550; Support Services: $1,845
Enrollment, Drop-out Rates and Diploma Recipients by Race/Ethnicity

Category	Total	White	Black	Asian	AIAN	Hisp.
Enrollment (%)	100.0	0.0	0.0	0.0	0.0	0.0
Drop-out Rate (%)	2.4	n/a	n/a	n/a	n/a	n/a
H.S. Diplomas (#)	2,553	n/a	n/a	n/a	n/a	n/a

Lauderdale County

Lauderdale County SD

402 S Washington St • Ripley, TN 38063-0350
(731) 635-2941 • http://www.lced.net/
Grade Span: KG-12; **Agency Type:** 1
Schools: 7
3 Primary; 2 Middle; 2 High; 0 Other Level
7 Regular; 0 Special Education; 0 Vocational; 0 Alternative
0 Magnet; 0 Charter; 5 Title I Eligible; 5 School-wide Title I
Students: 4,578 (n/a% male; n/a% female)
Individual Education Program: 975 (21.3%);
English Language Learner: n/a; Migrant: n/a

Eligible for Free Lunch Program: n/a
Eligible for Reduced-Price Lunch Program: n/a
Teachers: 297.8 (15.4 to 1)
Librarians/Media Specialists: 8.0 (572.3 to 1)
Guidance Counselors: 10.0 (457.8 to 1)
Current Spending: ($ per student per year):
Total: $5,249; Instruction: $3,306; Support Services: $1,529
Enrollment, Drop-out Rates and Diploma Recipients by Race/Ethnicity

Category	Total	White	Black	Asian	AIAN	Hisp.
Enrollment (%)	100.0	0.0	0.0	0.0	0.0	0.0
Drop-out Rate (%)	5.1	n/a	n/a	n/a	n/a	n/a
H.S. Diplomas (#)	193	n/a	n/a	n/a	n/a	n/a

Lawrence County

Lawrence County SD
410 W Gaines St • Lawrenceburg, TN 38464-3110
(931) 762-3581
Grade Span: KG-12; **Agency Type:** 1
Schools: 13
8 Primary; 1 Middle; 4 High; 0 Other Level
13 Regular; 0 Special Education; 0 Vocational; 0 Alternative
0 Magnet; 0 Charter; 6 Title I Eligible; 1 School-wide Title I
Students: 6,700 (n/a% male; n/a% female)
Individual Education Program: 1,210 (18.1%);
English Language Learner: n/a; Migrant: n/a
Eligible for Free Lunch Program: n/a
Eligible for Reduced-Price Lunch Program: n/a
Teachers: 455.9 (14.7 to 1)
Librarians/Media Specialists: 13.0 (515.4 to 1)
Guidance Counselors: 12.9 (519.4 to 1)
Current Spending: ($ per student per year):
Total: $5,165; Instruction: $3,405; Support Services: $1,365
Enrollment, Drop-out Rates and Diploma Recipients by Race/Ethnicity

Category	Total	White	Black	Asian	AIAN	Hisp.
Enrollment (%)	100.0	0.0	0.0	0.0	0.0	0.0
Drop-out Rate (%)	2.7	n/a	n/a	n/a	n/a	n/a
H.S. Diplomas (#)	383	n/a	n/a	n/a	n/a	n/a

Lewis County

Lewis County SD
206 S Court St • Hohenwald, TN 38462-1736
(931) 796-3264 • http://volweb.utk.edu/Schools/lewisco/lewisco
Grade Span: KG-12; **Agency Type:** 1
Schools: 4
2 Primary; 1 Middle; 1 High; 0 Other Level
4 Regular; 0 Special Education; 0 Vocational; 0 Alternative
0 Magnet; 0 Charter; 3 Title I Eligible; 0 School-wide Title I
Students: 1,964 (n/a% male; n/a% female)
Individual Education Program: 294 (15.0%);
English Language Learner: n/a; Migrant: n/a
Eligible for Free Lunch Program: n/a
Eligible for Reduced-Price Lunch Program: n/a
Teachers: 130.1 (15.1 to 1)
Librarians/Media Specialists: 3.8 (516.8 to 1)
Guidance Counselors: 2.9 (677.2 to 1)
Current Spending: ($ per student per year):
Total: $4,569; Instruction: $2,901; Support Services: $1,349
Enrollment, Drop-out Rates and Diploma Recipients by Race/Ethnicity

Category	Total	White	Black	Asian	AIAN	Hisp.
Enrollment (%)	100.0	0.0	0.0	0.0	0.0	0.0
Drop-out Rate (%)	1.6	n/a	n/a	n/a	n/a	n/a
H.S. Diplomas (#)	93	n/a	n/a	n/a	n/a	n/a

Lincoln County

Lincoln County SD
206 E Davidson Dr • Fayetteville, TN 37334-3581
(931) 433-3565 • http://www.lcdoe.org/
Grade Span: KG-12; **Agency Type:** 1
Schools: 8
6 Primary; 0 Middle; 1 High; 1 Other Level
8 Regular; 0 Special Education; 0 Vocational; 0 Alternative
0 Magnet; 0 Charter; 4 Title I Eligible; 2 School-wide Title I
Students: 3,964 (n/a% male; n/a% female)
Individual Education Program: 451 (11.4%);
English Language Learner: n/a; Migrant: n/a
Eligible for Free Lunch Program: n/a
Eligible for Reduced-Price Lunch Program: n/a
Teachers: 264.3 (15.0 to 1)
Librarians/Media Specialists: 9.5 (417.3 to 1)
Guidance Counselors: 8.0 (495.5 to 1)
Current Spending: ($ per student per year):
Total: $5,037; Instruction: $3,454; Support Services: $1,433
Enrollment, Drop-out Rates and Diploma Recipients by Race/Ethnicity

Category	Total	White	Black	Asian	AIAN	Hisp.
Enrollment (%)	100.0	0.0	0.0	0.0	0.0	0.0
Drop-out Rate (%)	6.1	n/a	n/a	n/a	n/a	n/a
H.S. Diplomas (#)	266	n/a	n/a	n/a	n/a	n/a

Loudon County

Lenoir City SD
2145 Harrison Ave • Lenoir City, TN 37771-6623
(865) 986-8058
Grade Span: KG-12; **Agency Type:** 1
Schools: 3
1 Primary; 1 Middle; 1 High; 0 Other Level
3 Regular; 0 Special Education; 0 Vocational; 0 Alternative
0 Magnet; 0 Charter; 1 Title I Eligible; 1 School-wide Title I
Students: 2,015 (n/a% male; n/a% female)
Individual Education Program: 233 (11.6%);
English Language Learner: n/a; Migrant: n/a
Eligible for Free Lunch Program: n/a
Eligible for Reduced-Price Lunch Program: n/a
Teachers: 126.0 (16.0 to 1)
Librarians/Media Specialists: 3.0 (671.7 to 1)
Guidance Counselors: 7.0 (287.9 to 1)
Current Spending: ($ per student per year):
Total: $5,734; Instruction: $3,766; Support Services: $1,788
Enrollment, Drop-out Rates and Diploma Recipients by Race/Ethnicity

Category	Total	White	Black	Asian	AIAN	Hisp.
Enrollment (%)	100.0	0.0	0.0	0.0	0.0	0.0
Drop-out Rate (%)	3.6	n/a	n/a	n/a	n/a	n/a
H.S. Diplomas (#)	201	n/a	n/a	n/a	n/a	n/a

Loudon County SD
100 River Rd Box 113 • Loudon, TN 37774-1042
(865) 458-5411 • http://k12.loudoncounty.org
Grade Span: KG-12; **Agency Type:** 1
Schools: 9
5 Primary; 2 Middle; 1 High; 1 Other Level
9 Regular; 0 Special Education; 0 Vocational; 0 Alternative
0 Magnet; 0 Charter; 5 Title I Eligible; 4 School-wide Title I
Students: 4,817 (n/a% male; n/a% female)
Individual Education Program: 525 (10.9%);
English Language Learner: n/a; Migrant: n/a
Eligible for Free Lunch Program: n/a
Eligible for Reduced-Price Lunch Program: n/a
Teachers: 273.5 (17.6 to 1)
Librarians/Media Specialists: 9.0 (535.2 to 1)
Guidance Counselors: 8.0 (602.1 to 1)
Current Spending: ($ per student per year):
Total: $5,366; Instruction: $3,789; Support Services: $1,272
Enrollment, Drop-out Rates and Diploma Recipients by Race/Ethnicity

Category	Total	White	Black	Asian	AIAN	Hisp.
Enrollment (%)	100.0	0.0	0.0	0.0	0.0	0.0
Drop-out Rate (%)	2.8	n/a	n/a	n/a	n/a	n/a
H.S. Diplomas (#)	160	n/a	n/a	n/a	n/a	n/a

Macon County

Macon County SD
501 College St • Lafayette, TN 37083-1706
(615) 666-2125 • http://maconcountyschools.com
Grade Span: KG-12; **Agency Type:** 1
Schools: 7
3 Primary; 2 Middle; 1 High; 1 Other Level
7 Regular; 0 Special Education; 0 Vocational; 0 Alternative
0 Magnet; 0 Charter; 5 Title I Eligible; 2 School-wide Title I
Students: 3,538 (n/a% male; n/a% female)
Individual Education Program: 475 (13.4%);
English Language Learner: n/a; Migrant: n/a
Eligible for Free Lunch Program: n/a
Eligible for Reduced-Price Lunch Program: n/a
Teachers: 219.3 (16.1 to 1)
Librarians/Media Specialists: 7.0 (505.4 to 1)
Guidance Counselors: 6.0 (589.7 to 1)
Current Spending: ($ per student per year):
Total: $4,723; Instruction: $3,117; Support Services: $1,452
Enrollment, Drop-out Rates and Diploma Recipients by Race/Ethnicity

Category	Total	White	Black	Asian	AIAN	Hisp.
Enrollment (%)	100.0	0.0	0.0	0.0	0.0	0.0
Drop-out Rate (%)	2.6	n/a	n/a	n/a	n/a	n/a
H.S. Diplomas (#)	188	n/a	n/a	n/a	n/a	n/a

Madison County

Jackson-Madison Consolidated

310 N Pkwy • Jackson, TN 38305-2712
(731) 664-2500
Grade Span: KG-12; **Agency Type:** 1
Schools: 26
14 Primary; 8 Middle; 4 High; 0 Other Level
24 Regular; 0 Special Education; 0 Vocational; 2 Alternative
2 Magnet; 0 Charter; 7 Title I Eligible; 5 School-wide Title I
Students: 13,525 (n/a% male; n/a% female)
Individual Education Program: 2,934 (21.7%);
English Language Learner: n/a; Migrant: n/a
Eligible for Free Lunch Program: n/a
Eligible for Reduced-Price Lunch Program: n/a
Teachers: 932.6 (14.5 to 1)
Librarians/Media Specialists: 26.7 (506.6 to 1)
Guidance Counselors: 35.0 (386.4 to 1)
Current Spending: ($ per student per year):
Total: $6,209; Instruction: $4,105; Support Services: $1,773
Enrollment, Drop-out Rates and Diploma Recipients by Race/Ethnicity

Category	Total	White	Black	Asian	AIAN	Hisp.
Enrollment (%)	100.0	0.0	0.0	0.0	0.0	0.0
Drop-out Rate (%)	3.7	n/a	n/a	n/a	n/a	n/a
H.S. Diplomas (#)	683	n/a	n/a	n/a	n/a	n/a

Marion County

Marion County SD

204 Betsy Pack Dr • Jasper, TN 37347-3024
(423) 942-3434
Grade Span: KG-12; **Agency Type:** 1
Schools: 9
4 Primary; 2 Middle; 3 High; 0 Other Level
9 Regular; 0 Special Education; 0 Vocational; 0 Alternative
0 Magnet; 0 Charter; 4 Title I Eligible; 4 School-wide Title I
Students: 4,066 (n/a% male; n/a% female)
Individual Education Program: 558 (13.7%);
English Language Learner: n/a; Migrant: n/a
Eligible for Free Lunch Program: n/a
Eligible for Reduced-Price Lunch Program: n/a
Teachers: 262.5 (15.5 to 1)
Librarians/Media Specialists: 8.5 (478.4 to 1)
Guidance Counselors: 9.1 (446.8 to 1)
Current Spending: ($ per student per year):
Total: $5,333; Instruction: $3,482; Support Services: $1,471
Enrollment, Drop-out Rates and Diploma Recipients by Race/Ethnicity

Category	Total	White	Black	Asian	AIAN	Hisp.
Enrollment (%)	100.0	0.0	0.0	0.0	0.0	0.0
Drop-out Rate (%)	3.2	n/a	n/a	n/a	n/a	n/a
H.S. Diplomas (#)	188	n/a	n/a	n/a	n/a	n/a

Marshall County

Marshall County SD

700 Jones Circle • Lewisburg, TN 37091-2427
(931) 359-1581 • http://www.mcs.k12.tn.us/
Grade Span: KG-12; **Agency Type:** 1
Schools: 9
5 Primary; 1 Middle; 1 High; 2 Other Level
9 Regular; 0 Special Education; 0 Vocational; 0 Alternative
0 Magnet; 0 Charter; 3 Title I Eligible; 0 School-wide Title I
Students: 4,821 (n/a% male; n/a% female)
Individual Education Program: 833 (17.3%);
English Language Learner: n/a; Migrant: n/a
Eligible for Free Lunch Program: n/a
Eligible for Reduced-Price Lunch Program: n/a
Teachers: 296.1 (16.3 to 1)
Librarians/Media Specialists: 9.0 (535.7 to 1)
Guidance Counselors: 9.0 (535.7 to 1)
Current Spending: ($ per student per year):
Total: $5,489; Instruction: $3,460; Support Services: $1,703
Enrollment, Drop-out Rates and Diploma Recipients by Race/Ethnicity

Category	Total	White	Black	Asian	AIAN	Hisp.
Enrollment (%)	100.0	0.0	0.0	0.0	0.0	0.0
Drop-out Rate (%)	2.2	n/a	n/a	n/a	n/a	n/a
H.S. Diplomas (#)	246	n/a	n/a	n/a	n/a	n/a

Maury County

Maury County SD

501 W Eight St • Columbia, TN 38401-3191
(931) 388-8403
Grade Span: KG-12; **Agency Type:** 1
Schools: 18
9 Primary; 3 Middle; 3 High; 3 Other Level
18 Regular; 0 Special Education; 0 Vocational; 0 Alternative
0 Magnet; 0 Charter; 6 Title I Eligible; 3 School-wide Title I
Students: 10,990 (n/a% male; n/a% female)
Individual Education Program: 1,989 (18.1%);
English Language Learner: n/a; Migrant: n/a
Eligible for Free Lunch Program: n/a
Eligible for Reduced-Price Lunch Program: n/a
Teachers: 749.4 (14.7 to 1)
Librarians/Media Specialists: 19.4 (566.5 to 1)
Guidance Counselors: 24.0 (457.9 to 1)
Current Spending: ($ per student per year):
Total: $5,799; Instruction: $3,830; Support Services: $1,627
Enrollment, Drop-out Rates and Diploma Recipients by Race/Ethnicity

Category	Total	White	Black	Asian	AIAN	Hisp.
Enrollment (%)	100.0	0.0	0.0	0.0	0.0	0.0
Drop-out Rate (%)	3.2	n/a	n/a	n/a	n/a	n/a
H.S. Diplomas (#)	490	n/a	n/a	n/a	n/a	n/a

Mcminn County

Athens City Elementary SD

943 Crestway Dr • Athens, TN 37303-4130
(423) 745-2863 • http://www.athens-lea.mcminn.k12.tn.us/
Grade Span: KG-09; **Agency Type:** 1
Schools: 5
2 Primary; 3 Middle; 0 High; 0 Other Level
5 Regular; 0 Special Education; 0 Vocational; 0 Alternative
0 Magnet; 0 Charter; 5 Title I Eligible; 0 School-wide Title I
Students: 1,684 (n/a% male; n/a% female)
Individual Education Program: 314 (18.6%);
English Language Learner: n/a; Migrant: n/a
Eligible for Free Lunch Program: n/a
Eligible for Reduced-Price Lunch Program: n/a
Teachers: 106.3 (15.8 to 1)
Librarians/Media Specialists: 5.0 (336.8 to 1)
Guidance Counselors: 4.0 (421.0 to 1)
Current Spending: ($ per student per year):
Total: $5,668; Instruction: $3,565; Support Services: $1,741
Enrollment, Drop-out Rates and Diploma Recipients by Race/Ethnicity

Category	Total	White	Black	Asian	AIAN	Hisp.
Enrollment (%)	100.0	0.0	0.0	0.0	0.0	0.0
Drop-out Rate (%)	0.0	n/a	n/a	n/a	n/a	n/a
H.S. Diplomas (#)	n/a	n/a	n/a	n/a	n/a	n/a

Mcminn County SD

216 N Jackson • Athens, TN 37303-3640
(423) 745-1612 • http://www.mcminn-lea.mcminn.k12.tn.us/
Grade Span: KG-12; **Agency Type:** 1
Schools: 9
7 Primary; 0 Middle; 2 High; 0 Other Level
9 Regular; 0 Special Education; 0 Vocational; 0 Alternative
0 Magnet; 0 Charter; 7 Title I Eligible; 7 School-wide Title I
Students: 5,861 (n/a% male; n/a% female)
Individual Education Program: 1,066 (18.2%);
English Language Learner: n/a; Migrant: n/a
Eligible for Free Lunch Program: n/a
Eligible for Reduced-Price Lunch Program: n/a
Teachers: 342.2 (17.1 to 1)
Librarians/Media Specialists: 10.0 (586.1 to 1)
Guidance Counselors: 10.0 (586.1 to 1)
Current Spending: ($ per student per year):
Total: $5,022; Instruction: $3,309; Support Services: $1,424
Enrollment, Drop-out Rates and Diploma Recipients by Race/Ethnicity

Category	Total	White	Black	Asian	AIAN	Hisp.
Enrollment (%)	100.0	0.0	0.0	0.0	0.0	0.0
Drop-out Rate (%)	2.5	n/a	n/a	n/a	n/a	n/a
H.S. Diplomas (#)	351	n/a	n/a	n/a	n/a	n/a

Mcnairy County

Mcnairy County SD

170 W Court Ave • Selmer, TN 38375
(731) 645-3267 • http://www.mcnairy.org
Grade Span: KG-12; **Agency Type:** 1
Schools: 8
5 Primary; 1 Middle; 2 High; 0 Other Level
8 Regular; 0 Special Education; 0 Vocational; 0 Alternative
0 Magnet; 0 Charter; 5 Title I Eligible; 5 School-wide Title I
Students: 4,145 (n/a% male; n/a% female)
Individual Education Program: 518 (12.5%);
English Language Learner: n/a; Migrant: n/a
Eligible for Free Lunch Program: n/a
Eligible for Reduced-Price Lunch Program: n/a
Teachers: 283.5 (14.6 to 1)

Librarians/Media Specialists: 8.0 (518.1 to 1)
Guidance Counselors: 7.0 (592.1 to 1)
Current Spending: ($ per student per year):
Total: $5,054; Instruction: $3,455; Support Services: $1,254
Enrollment, Drop-out Rates and Diploma Recipients by Race/Ethnicity

Category	Total	White	Black	Asian	AIAN	Hisp.
Enrollment (%)	100.0	0.0	0.0	0.0	0.0	0.0
Drop-out Rate (%)	2.3	n/a	n/a	n/a	n/a	n/a
H.S. Diplomas (#)	181	n/a	n/a	n/a	n/a	n/a

Meigs County

Meigs County SD

PO Box 1039 • Decatur, TN 37322-1039
(423) 334-5793
Grade Span: KG-12; **Agency Type:** 1
Schools: 4
2 Primary; 1 Middle; 1 High; 0 Other Level
4 Regular; 0 Special Education; 0 Vocational; 0 Alternative
0 Magnet; 0 Charter; 3 Title I Eligible; 2 School-wide Title I
Students: 1,851 (n/a% male; n/a% female)
Individual Education Program: 288 (15.6%);
English Language Learner: n/a; Migrant: n/a
Eligible for Free Lunch Program: n/a
Eligible for Reduced-Price Lunch Program: n/a
Teachers: 117.0 (15.8 to 1)
Librarians/Media Specialists: 2.0 (925.5 to 1)
Guidance Counselors: 4.0 (462.8 to 1)
Current Spending: ($ per student per year):
Total: $5,069; Instruction: $3,409; Support Services: $1,290
Enrollment, Drop-out Rates and Diploma Recipients by Race/Ethnicity

Category	Total	White	Black	Asian	AIAN	Hisp.
Enrollment (%)	100.0	0.0	0.0	0.0	0.0	0.0
Drop-out Rate (%)	1.1	n/a	n/a	n/a	n/a	n/a
H.S. Diplomas (#)	98	n/a	n/a	n/a	n/a	n/a

Monroe County

Monroe County SD

205 Oak Grove Rd • Madisonville, TN 37354-5930
(423) 442-2373 • http://www.monroe.k12.tn.us
Grade Span: KG-12; **Agency Type:** 1
Schools: 11
6 Primary; 2 Middle; 3 High; 0 Other Level
11 Regular; 0 Special Education; 0 Vocational; 0 Alternative
0 Magnet; 0 Charter; 6 Title I Eligible; 5 School-wide Title I
Students: 5,093 (n/a% male; n/a% female)
Individual Education Program: 684 (13.4%);
English Language Learner: n/a; Migrant: n/a
Eligible for Free Lunch Program: n/a
Eligible for Reduced-Price Lunch Program: n/a
Teachers: 306.6 (16.6 to 1)
Librarians/Media Specialists: 9.3 (547.6 to 1)
Guidance Counselors: 8.0 (636.6 to 1)
Current Spending: ($ per student per year):
Total: $5,126; Instruction: $3,205; Support Services: $1,549
Enrollment, Drop-out Rates and Diploma Recipients by Race/Ethnicity

Category	Total	White	Black	Asian	AIAN	Hisp.
Enrollment (%)	100.0	0.0	0.0	0.0	0.0	0.0
Drop-out Rate (%)	3.4	n/a	n/a	n/a	n/a	n/a
H.S. Diplomas (#)	84	n/a	n/a	n/a	n/a	n/a

Montgomery County

Montgomery County Schools

621 Gracey Ave • Clarksville, TN 37040
(931) 648-5600 • http://www.cmcss.org/
Grade Span: KG-12; **Agency Type:** 1
Schools: 30
17 Primary; 7 Middle; 6 High; 0 Other Level
30 Regular; 0 Special Education; 0 Vocational; 0 Alternative
0 Magnet; 0 Charter; 11 Title I Eligible; 3 School-wide Title I
Students: 24,578 (n/a% male; n/a% female)
Individual Education Program: 3,320 (13.5%);
English Language Learner: n/a; Migrant: n/a
Eligible for Free Lunch Program: n/a
Eligible for Reduced-Price Lunch Program: n/a
Teachers: 1,511.0 (16.3 to 1)
Librarians/Media Specialists: 34.0 (722.9 to 1)
Guidance Counselors: 51.5 (477.2 to 1)
Current Spending: ($ per student per year):
Total: $5,134; Instruction: $3,077; Support Services: $1,790
Enrollment, Drop-out Rates and Diploma Recipients by Race/Ethnicity

Category	Total	White	Black	Asian	AIAN	Hisp.
Enrollment (%)	100.0	0.0	0.0	0.0	0.0	0.0
Drop-out Rate (%)	3.5	n/a	n/a	n/a	n/a	n/a
H.S. Diplomas (#)	1,063	n/a	n/a	n/a	n/a	n/a

Morgan County

Morgan County SD

710 Main St • Wartburg, TN 37887-0348
Mailing Address: PO Box 348 • Wartburg, TN 37887-0348
(423) 346-6214
Grade Span: KG-12; **Agency Type:** 1
Schools: 8
2 Primary; 1 Middle; 2 High; 3 Other Level
7 Regular; 0 Special Education; 1 Vocational; 0 Alternative
0 Magnet; 0 Charter; 6 Title I Eligible; 6 School-wide Title I
Students: 3,133 (n/a% male; n/a% female)
Individual Education Program: 537 (17.1%);
English Language Learner: n/a; Migrant: n/a
Eligible for Free Lunch Program: n/a
Eligible for Reduced-Price Lunch Program: n/a
Teachers: 226.0 (13.9 to 1)
Librarians/Media Specialists: 5.0 (626.6 to 1)
Guidance Counselors: 6.0 (522.2 to 1)
Current Spending: ($ per student per year):
Total: $5,108; Instruction: $3,295; Support Services: $1,485
Enrollment, Drop-out Rates and Diploma Recipients by Race/Ethnicity

Category	Total	White	Black	Asian	AIAN	Hisp.
Enrollment (%)	100.0	0.0	0.0	0.0	0.0	0.0
Drop-out Rate (%)	2.3	n/a	n/a	n/a	n/a	n/a
H.S. Diplomas (#)	186	n/a	n/a	n/a	n/a	n/a

Obion County

Obion County SD

316 S Third St • Union City, TN 38261-3724
(731) 885-9743 • http://www.obioncountyschools.com
Grade Span: KG-12; **Agency Type:** 1
Schools: 8
5 Primary; 0 Middle; 2 High; 1 Other Level
7 Regular; 0 Special Education; 1 Vocational; 0 Alternative
0 Magnet; 0 Charter; 5 Title I Eligible; 1 School-wide Title I
Students: 4,015 (n/a% male; n/a% female)
Individual Education Program: 675 (16.8%);
English Language Learner: n/a; Migrant: n/a
Eligible for Free Lunch Program: n/a
Eligible for Reduced-Price Lunch Program: n/a
Teachers: 257.0 (15.6 to 1)
Librarians/Media Specialists: 7.0 (573.6 to 1)
Guidance Counselors: 9.0 (446.1 to 1)
Current Spending: ($ per student per year):
Total: $5,274; Instruction: $3,493; Support Services: $1,448
Enrollment, Drop-out Rates and Diploma Recipients by Race/Ethnicity

Category	Total	White	Black	Asian	AIAN	Hisp.
Enrollment (%)	100.0	0.0	0.0	0.0	0.0	0.0
Drop-out Rate (%)	3.9	n/a	n/a	n/a	n/a	n/a
H.S. Diplomas (#)	206	n/a	n/a	n/a	n/a	n/a

Overton County

Overton County SD

112 Bussell St • Livingston, TN 38570
(931) 823-1287
Grade Span: KG-12; **Agency Type:** 1
Schools: 9
5 Primary; 1 Middle; 3 High; 0 Other Level
9 Regular; 0 Special Education; 0 Vocational; 0 Alternative
0 Magnet; 0 Charter; 5 Title I Eligible; 5 School-wide Title I
Students: 3,210 (n/a% male; n/a% female)
Individual Education Program: 687 (21.4%);
English Language Learner: n/a; Migrant: n/a
Eligible for Free Lunch Program: n/a
Eligible for Reduced-Price Lunch Program: n/a
Teachers: 224.0 (14.3 to 1)
Librarians/Media Specialists: 5.0 (642.0 to 1)
Guidance Counselors: 8.0 (401.3 to 1)
Current Spending: ($ per student per year):
Total: $4,973; Instruction: $3,260; Support Services: $1,339
Enrollment, Drop-out Rates and Diploma Recipients by Race/Ethnicity

Category	Total	White	Black	Asian	AIAN	Hisp.
Enrollment (%)	100.0	0.0	0.0	0.0	0.0	0.0
Drop-out Rate (%)	1.9	n/a	n/a	n/a	n/a	n/a
H.S. Diplomas (#)	181	n/a	n/a	n/a	n/a	n/a

Polk County

Polk County SD

PO Box A • Benton, TN 37307-1001
(423) 338-4506
Grade Span: KG-12; **Agency Type:** 1
Schools: 8
5 Primary; 1 Middle; 2 High; 0 Other Level
8 Regular; 0 Special Education; 0 Vocational; 0 Alternative
0 Magnet; 0 Charter; 5 Title I Eligible; 4 School-wide Title I
Students: 2,508 (n/a% male; n/a% female)
Individual Education Program: 286 (11.4%);
English Language Learner: n/a; Migrant: n/a
Eligible for Free Lunch Program: n/a
Eligible for Reduced-Price Lunch Program: n/a
Teachers: 156.1 (16.1 to 1)
Librarians/Media Specialists: 3.0 (836.0 to 1)
Guidance Counselors: 3.0 (836.0 to 1)
Current Spending: ($ per student per year):
Total: $5,342; Instruction: $3,649; Support Services: $1,523
Enrollment, Drop-out Rates and Diploma Recipients by Race/Ethnicity

Category	Total	White	Black	Asian	AIAN	Hisp.
Enrollment (%)	100.0	0.0	0.0	0.0	0.0	0.0
Drop-out Rate (%)	0.9	n/a	n/a	n/a	n/a	n/a
H.S. Diplomas (#)	91	n/a	n/a	n/a	n/a	n/a

Putnam County

Putnam County SD

1400 E Spring St • Cookeville, TN 38506-4313
(931) 526-9777 • http://www.putnam.k12.tn.us/
Grade Span: KG-12; **Agency Type:** 1
Schools: 17
8 Primary; 4 Middle; 4 High; 1 Other Level
16 Regular; 0 Special Education; 0 Vocational; 1 Alternative
0 Magnet; 0 Charter; 6 Title I Eligible; 0 School-wide Title I
Students: 9,560 (n/a% male; n/a% female)
Individual Education Program: 1,847 (19.3%);
English Language Learner: n/a; Migrant: n/a
Eligible for Free Lunch Program: n/a
Eligible for Reduced-Price Lunch Program: n/a
Teachers: 585.6 (16.3 to 1)
Librarians/Media Specialists: 18.0 (531.1 to 1)
Guidance Counselors: 24.1 (396.7 to 1)
Current Spending: ($ per student per year):
Total: $5,062; Instruction: $3,308; Support Services: $1,467
Enrollment, Drop-out Rates and Diploma Recipients by Race/Ethnicity

Category	Total	White	Black	Asian	AIAN	Hisp.
Enrollment (%)	100.0	0.0	0.0	0.0	0.0	0.0
Drop-out Rate (%)	1.7	n/a	n/a	n/a	n/a	n/a
H.S. Diplomas (#)	425	n/a	n/a	n/a	n/a	n/a

Rhea County

Rhea County SD

305 California Ave • Dayton, TN 37321-1409
(423) 775-7813 • http://www.rhea.k12.tn.us/
Grade Span: KG-12; **Agency Type:** 1
Schools: 5
4 Primary; 0 Middle; 1 High; 0 Other Level
5 Regular; 0 Special Education; 0 Vocational; 0 Alternative
0 Magnet; 0 Charter; 3 Title I Eligible; 3 School-wide Title I
Students: 3,856 (n/a% male; n/a% female)
Individual Education Program: 423 (11.0%);
English Language Learner: n/a; Migrant: n/a
Eligible for Free Lunch Program: n/a
Eligible for Reduced-Price Lunch Program: n/a
Teachers: 243.7 (15.8 to 1)
Librarians/Media Specialists: 4.0 (964.0 to 1)
Guidance Counselors: 6.0 (642.7 to 1)
Current Spending: ($ per student per year):
Total: $5,259; Instruction: $3,262; Support Services: $1,663
Enrollment, Drop-out Rates and Diploma Recipients by Race/Ethnicity

Category	Total	White	Black	Asian	AIAN	Hisp.
Enrollment (%)	100.0	0.0	0.0	0.0	0.0	0.0
Drop-out Rate (%)	7.4	n/a	n/a	n/a	n/a	n/a
H.S. Diplomas (#)	243	n/a	n/a	n/a	n/a	n/a

Roane County

Roane County SD

105 Bluff Rd • Kingston, TN 37763-7209
(865) 376-5592 • http://www.roane-lea.roane.k12.tn.us/
Grade Span: KG-12; **Agency Type:** 1
Schools: 13
6 Primary; 2 Middle; 4 High; 1 Other Level
12 Regular; 0 Special Education; 1 Vocational; 0 Alternative
0 Magnet; 0 Charter; 5 Title I Eligible; 5 School-wide Title I
Students: 5,936 (n/a% male; n/a% female)
Individual Education Program: 1,009 (17.0%);
English Language Learner: n/a; Migrant: n/a
Eligible for Free Lunch Program: n/a
Eligible for Reduced-Price Lunch Program: n/a
Teachers: 381.2 (15.6 to 1)
Librarians/Media Specialists: 11.0 (539.6 to 1)
Guidance Counselors: 8.0 (742.0 to 1)
Current Spending: ($ per student per year):
Total: $5,677; Instruction: $3,708; Support Services: $1,621
Enrollment, Drop-out Rates and Diploma Recipients by Race/Ethnicity

Category	Total	White	Black	Asian	AIAN	Hisp.
Enrollment (%)	100.0	0.0	0.0	0.0	0.0	0.0
Drop-out Rate (%)	3.1	n/a	n/a	n/a	n/a	n/a
H.S. Diplomas (#)	332	n/a	n/a	n/a	n/a	n/a

Robertson County

Robertson County SD

2121 Woodland St • Springfield, TN 37172-3736
Mailing Address: PO Box 130 • Springfield, TN 37172-3736
(615) 384-5588 • http://www.robcoschools.k12.tn.us/
Grade Span: KG-12; **Agency Type:** 1
Schools: 16
9 Primary; 2 Middle; 3 High; 2 Other Level
16 Regular; 0 Special Education; 0 Vocational; 0 Alternative
0 Magnet; 0 Charter; 4 Title I Eligible; 2 School-wide Title I
Students: 9,146 (n/a% male; n/a% female)
Individual Education Program: 1,686 (18.4%);
English Language Learner: n/a; Migrant: n/a
Eligible for Free Lunch Program: n/a
Eligible for Reduced-Price Lunch Program: n/a
Teachers: 613.6 (14.9 to 1)
Librarians/Media Specialists: 12.0 (762.2 to 1)
Guidance Counselors: 18.1 (505.3 to 1)
Current Spending: ($ per student per year):
Total: $4,775; Instruction: $3,375; Support Services: $1,279
Enrollment, Drop-out Rates and Diploma Recipients by Race/Ethnicity

Category	Total	White	Black	Asian	AIAN	Hisp.
Enrollment (%)	100.0	0.0	0.0	0.0	0.0	0.0
Drop-out Rate (%)	3.6	n/a	n/a	n/a	n/a	n/a
H.S. Diplomas (#)	410	n/a	n/a	n/a	n/a	n/a

Rutherford County

Murfreesboro City Elem SD

2552 S Church St • Murfreesboro, TN 37127-6342
(615) 893-2313 • http://www.cityschools.net/
Grade Span: KG-06; **Agency Type:** 1
Schools: 10
10 Primary; 0 Middle; 0 High; 0 Other Level
10 Regular; 0 Special Education; 0 Vocational; 0 Alternative
0 Magnet; 0 Charter; 4 Title I Eligible; 4 School-wide Title I
Students: 5,837 (n/a% male; n/a% female)
Individual Education Program: 717 (12.3%);
English Language Learner: n/a; Migrant: n/a
Eligible for Free Lunch Program: n/a
Eligible for Reduced-Price Lunch Program: n/a
Teachers: 390.4 (15.0 to 1)
Librarians/Media Specialists: 10.0 (583.7 to 1)
Guidance Counselors: 11.9 (490.5 to 1)
Current Spending: ($ per student per year):
Total: $5,811; Instruction: $3,888; Support Services: $1,728
Enrollment, Drop-out Rates and Diploma Recipients by Race/Ethnicity

Category	Total	White	Black	Asian	AIAN	Hisp.
Enrollment (%)	100.0	0.0	0.0	0.0	0.0	0.0
Drop-out Rate (%)	n/a	n/a	n/a	n/a	n/a	n/a
H.S. Diplomas (#)	n/a	n/a	n/a	n/a	n/a	n/a

Rutherford County SD

2240 S Park Blvd • Murfreesboro, TN 37128
(615) 893-5812 • http://www.rcs.k12.tn.us/
Grade Span: KG-12; **Agency Type:** 1
Schools: 36
20 Primary; 6 Middle; 7 High; 3 Other Level
35 Regular; 1 Special Education; 0 Vocational; 0 Alternative
2 Magnet; 0 Charter; 10 Title I Eligible; 4 School-wide Title I
Students: 28,069 (n/a% male; n/a% female)
Individual Education Program: 4,216 (15.0%);
English Language Learner: n/a; Migrant: n/a
Eligible for Free Lunch Program: n/a
Eligible for Reduced-Price Lunch Program: n/a

Teachers: 1,734.4 (16.2 to 1)
Librarians/Media Specialists: 36.7 (764.8 to 1)
Guidance Counselors: 58.9 (476.6 to 1)
Current Spending: ($ per student per year):
Total: $5,343; Instruction: $3,639; Support Services: $1,594

Enrollment, Drop-out Rates and Diploma Recipients by Race/Ethnicity

Category	Total	White	Black	Asian	AIAN	Hisp.
Enrollment (%)	100.0	0.0	0.0	0.0	0.0	0.0
Drop-out Rate (%)	3.1	n/a	n/a	n/a	n/a	n/a
H.S. Diplomas (#)	1,506	n/a	n/a	n/a	n/a	n/a

Scott County

Scott County SD

208 Court St • Huntsville, TN 37756-0037
Mailing Address: PO Box 37 • Huntsville, TN 37756-0037
(423) 663-2159 • http://www.scottcounty.net/
Grade Span: KG-12; **Agency Type:** 1
Schools: 7
5 Primary; 1 Middle; 1 High; 0 Other Level
7 Regular; 0 Special Education; 0 Vocational; 0 Alternative
0 Magnet; 0 Charter; 7 Title I Eligible; 6 School-wide Title I
Students: 2,619 (n/a% male; n/a% female)
Individual Education Program: 405 (15.5%);
English Language Learner: n/a; Migrant: n/a
Eligible for Free Lunch Program: n/a
Eligible for Reduced-Price Lunch Program: n/a
Teachers: 204.7 (12.8 to 1)
Librarians/Media Specialists: 5.0 (523.8 to 1)
Guidance Counselors: 4.0 (654.8 to 1)
Current Spending: ($ per student per year):
Total: $5,577; Instruction: $3,736; Support Services: $1,423

Enrollment, Drop-out Rates and Diploma Recipients by Race/Ethnicity

Category	Total	White	Black	Asian	AIAN	Hisp.
Enrollment (%)	100.0	0.0	0.0	0.0	0.0	0.0
Drop-out Rate (%)	9.1	n/a	n/a	n/a	n/a	n/a
H.S. Diplomas (#)	97	n/a	n/a	n/a	n/a	n/a

Sequatchie County

Sequatchie County SD

24 Spring St • Dunlap, TN 37327-0488
Mailing Address: PO Box 488 • Dunlap, TN 37327-0488
(423) 949-3617
Grade Span: KG-12; **Agency Type:** 1
Schools: 3
1 Primary; 1 Middle; 1 High; 0 Other Level
3 Regular; 0 Special Education; 0 Vocational; 0 Alternative
0 Magnet; 0 Charter; 2 Title I Eligible; 2 School-wide Title I
Students: 1,923 (n/a% male; n/a% female)
Individual Education Program: 348 (18.1%);
English Language Learner: n/a; Migrant: n/a
Eligible for Free Lunch Program: n/a
Eligible for Reduced-Price Lunch Program: n/a
Teachers: 128.0 (15.0 to 1)
Librarians/Media Specialists: 3.0 (641.0 to 1)
Guidance Counselors: 3.0 (641.0 to 1)
Current Spending: ($ per student per year):
Total: $4,634; Instruction: $3,015; Support Services: $1,325

Enrollment, Drop-out Rates and Diploma Recipients by Race/Ethnicity

Category	Total	White	Black	Asian	AIAN	Hisp.
Enrollment (%)	100.0	0.0	0.0	0.0	0.0	0.0
Drop-out Rate (%)	4.2	n/a	n/a	n/a	n/a	n/a
H.S. Diplomas (#)	80	n/a	n/a	n/a	n/a	n/a

Sevier County

Sevier County SD

226 Cedar St • Sevierville, TN 37862-3803
(865) 453-4671 • http://www.sevier.org/
Grade Span: KG-12; **Agency Type:** 1
Schools: 24
13 Primary; 4 Middle; 6 High; 1 Other Level
22 Regular; 1 Special Education; 0 Vocational; 1 Alternative
0 Magnet; 0 Charter; 12 Title I Eligible; 12 School-wide Title I
Students: 12,680 (n/a% male; n/a% female)
Individual Education Program: 1,921 (15.1%);
English Language Learner: n/a; Migrant: n/a
Eligible for Free Lunch Program: n/a
Eligible for Reduced-Price Lunch Program: n/a
Teachers: 830.1 (15.3 to 1)
Librarians/Media Specialists: 20.4 (621.6 to 1)
Guidance Counselors: 27.5 (461.1 to 1)
Current Spending: ($ per student per year):
Total: $5,573; Instruction: $3,521; Support Services: $1,718

Enrollment, Drop-out Rates and Diploma Recipients by Race/Ethnicity

Category	Total	White	Black	Asian	AIAN	Hisp.
Enrollment (%)	100.0	0.0	0.0	0.0	0.0	0.0
Drop-out Rate (%)	2.8	n/a	n/a	n/a	n/a	n/a
H.S. Diplomas (#)	614	n/a	n/a	n/a	n/a	n/a

Shelby County

Memphis City SD

2597 Avery Ave • Memphis, TN 38112-4818
(901) 325-5300 • http://www.memphis-schools.k12.tn.us/
Grade Span: KG-12; **Agency Type:** 1
Schools: 178
111 Primary; 28 Middle; 36 High; 3 Other Level
171 Regular; 1 Special Education; 6 Vocational; 0 Alternative
1 Magnet; 0 Charter; 133 Title I Eligible; 129 School-wide Title I
Students: 118,039 (n/a% male; n/a% female)
Individual Education Program: 14,515 (12.3%);
English Language Learner: n/a; Migrant: n/a
Eligible for Free Lunch Program: n/a
Eligible for Reduced-Price Lunch Program: n/a
Teachers: 7,203.7 (16.4 to 1)
Librarians/Media Specialists: 161.6 (730.4 to 1)
Guidance Counselors: 222.6 (530.3 to 1)
Current Spending: ($ per student per year):
Total: $6,326; Instruction: $3,811; Support Services: $2,179

Enrollment, Drop-out Rates and Diploma Recipients by Race/Ethnicity

Category	Total	White	Black	Asian	AIAN	Hisp.
Enrollment (%)	100.0	0.0	0.0	0.0	0.0	0.0
Drop-out Rate (%)	9.2	n/a	n/a	n/a	n/a	n/a
H.S. Diplomas (#)	3,933	n/a	n/a	n/a	n/a	n/a

Shelby County SD

160 S Hollywood • Memphis, TN 38112-4801
(901) 325-7900 • http://www.scs.k12.tn.us
Grade Span: KG-12; **Agency Type:** 1
Schools: 48
28 Primary; 13 Middle; 7 High; 0 Other Level
48 Regular; 0 Special Education; 0 Vocational; 0 Alternative
0 Magnet; 0 Charter; 7 Title I Eligible; 7 School-wide Title I
Students: 45,439 (n/a% male; n/a% female)
Individual Education Program: 9,068 (20.0%);
English Language Learner: n/a; Migrant: n/a
Eligible for Free Lunch Program: n/a
Eligible for Reduced-Price Lunch Program: n/a
Teachers: 2,593.6 (17.5 to 1)
Librarians/Media Specialists: 56.0 (811.4 to 1)
Guidance Counselors: 92.5 (491.2 to 1)
Current Spending: ($ per student per year):
Total: $5,051; Instruction: $3,359; Support Services: $1,501

Enrollment, Drop-out Rates and Diploma Recipients by Race/Ethnicity

Category	Total	White	Black	Asian	AIAN	Hisp.
Enrollment (%)	100.0	0.0	0.0	0.0	0.0	0.0
Drop-out Rate (%)	2.0	n/a	n/a	n/a	n/a	n/a
H.S. Diplomas (#)	2,550	n/a	n/a	n/a	n/a	n/a

Smith County

Smith County SD

207 N Main Str B • Carthage, TN 37030-0155
Mailing Address: PO Box 155 • Carthage, TN 37030-0155
(615) 735-9625 • http://boe.smithcounty.com/
Grade Span: KG-12; **Agency Type:** 1
Schools: 10
6 Primary; 1 Middle; 1 High; 2 Other Level
9 Regular; 0 Special Education; 1 Vocational; 0 Alternative
0 Magnet; 0 Charter; 5 Title I Eligible; 0 School-wide Title I
Students: 3,137 (n/a% male; n/a% female)
Individual Education Program: 451 (14.4%);
English Language Learner: n/a; Migrant: n/a
Eligible for Free Lunch Program: n/a
Eligible for Reduced-Price Lunch Program: n/a
Teachers: 195.0 (16.1 to 1)
Librarians/Media Specialists: 4.0 (784.3 to 1)
Guidance Counselors: 4.0 (784.3 to 1)
Current Spending: ($ per student per year):
Total: $4,389; Instruction: $2,957; Support Services: $1,096

Enrollment, Drop-out Rates and Diploma Recipients by Race/Ethnicity

Category	Total	White	Black	Asian	AIAN	Hisp.
Enrollment (%)	100.0	0.0	0.0	0.0	0.0	0.0
Drop-out Rate (%)	3.1	n/a	n/a	n/a	n/a	n/a
H.S. Diplomas (#)	160	n/a	n/a	n/a	n/a	n/a

Stewart County

Stewart County SD

1031 Spring Street • Dover, TN 37058-0433
Mailing Address: PO Box 433 • Dover, TN 37058-0433
(931) 232-5176
Grade Span: KG-12; **Agency Type:** 1
Schools: 3
2 Primary; 0 Middle; 1 High; 0 Other Level
3 Regular; 0 Special Education; 0 Vocational; 0 Alternative
0 Magnet; 0 Charter; 2 Title I Eligible; 2 School-wide Title I
Students: 2,091 (n/a% male; n/a% female)
Individual Education Program: 387 (18.5%);
English Language Learner: n/a; Migrant: n/a
Eligible for Free Lunch Program: n/a
Eligible for Reduced-Price Lunch Program: n/a
Teachers: 124.0 (16.9 to 1)
Librarians/Media Specialists: 3.0 (697.0 to 1)
Guidance Counselors: 3.0 (697.0 to 1)
Current Spending: ($ per student per year):
Total: $4,783; Instruction: $2,883; Support Services: $1,567
Enrollment, Drop-out Rates and Diploma Recipients by Race/Ethnicity

Category	Total	White	Black	Asian	AIAN	Hisp.
Enrollment (%)	100.0	0.0	0.0	0.0	0.0	0.0
Drop-out Rate (%)	3.1	n/a	n/a	n/a	n/a	n/a
H.S. Diplomas (#)	111	n/a	n/a	n/a	n/a	n/a

Sullivan County

Bristol City SD

615 Edgemont Ave • Bristol, TN 37620-2315
(423) 652-9451 • http://www.btcs.org/
Grade Span: KG-12; **Agency Type:** 1
Schools: 8
6 Primary; 1 Middle; 1 High; 0 Other Level
8 Regular; 0 Special Education; 0 Vocational; 0 Alternative
0 Magnet; 0 Charter; 3 Title I Eligible; 3 School-wide Title I
Students: 3,603 (n/a% male; n/a% female)
Individual Education Program: 548 (15.2%);
English Language Learner: n/a; Migrant: n/a
Eligible for Free Lunch Program: n/a
Eligible for Reduced-Price Lunch Program: n/a
Teachers: 246.5 (14.6 to 1)
Librarians/Media Specialists: 9.0 (400.3 to 1)
Guidance Counselors: 11.0 (327.5 to 1)
Current Spending: ($ per student per year):
Total: $6,618; Instruction: $4,194; Support Services: $2,118
Enrollment, Drop-out Rates and Diploma Recipients by Race/Ethnicity

Category	Total	White	Black	Asian	AIAN	Hisp.
Enrollment (%)	100.0	0.0	0.0	0.0	0.0	0.0
Drop-out Rate (%)	2.0	n/a	n/a	n/a	n/a	n/a
H.S. Diplomas (#)	205	n/a	n/a	n/a	n/a	n/a

Kingsport City SD

1701 E Center St • Kingsport, TN 37664-2608
(423) 378-2100 • http://www.kpt.k12.tn.us
Grade Span: PK-12; **Agency Type:** 1
Schools: 11
8 Primary; 2 Middle; 1 High; 0 Other Level
10 Regular; 1 Special Education; 0 Vocational; 0 Alternative
0 Magnet; 0 Charter; 5 Title I Eligible; 5 School-wide Title I
Students: 6,387 (n/a% male; n/a% female)
Individual Education Program: 1,152 (18.0%);
English Language Learner: n/a; Migrant: n/a
Eligible for Free Lunch Program: n/a
Eligible for Reduced-Price Lunch Program: n/a
Teachers: 437.6 (14.6 to 1)
Librarians/Media Specialists: 12.0 (532.3 to 1)
Guidance Counselors: 13.0 (491.3 to 1)
Current Spending: ($ per student per year):
Total: $6,588; Instruction: $4,263; Support Services: $1,993
Enrollment, Drop-out Rates and Diploma Recipients by Race/Ethnicity

Category	Total	White	Black	Asian	AIAN	Hisp.
Enrollment (%)	100.0	0.0	0.0	0.0	0.0	0.0
Drop-out Rate (%)	1.6	n/a	n/a	n/a	n/a	n/a
H.S. Diplomas (#)	297	n/a	n/a	n/a	n/a	n/a

Sullivan County SD

PO Box 306 • Blountville, TN 37617-0306
(423) 279-2300 • http://www.scde.k12.tn.us
Grade Span: KG-12; **Agency Type:** 1
Schools: 30
17 Primary; 8 Middle; 4 High; 1 Other Level
29 Regular; 1 Special Education; 0 Vocational; 0 Alternative
0 Magnet; 0 Charter; 13 Title I Eligible; 1 School-wide Title I
Students: 12,611 (n/a% male; n/a% female)
Individual Education Program: 2,445 (19.4%);
English Language Learner: n/a; Migrant: n/a
Eligible for Free Lunch Program: n/a
Eligible for Reduced-Price Lunch Program: n/a
Teachers: 888.8 (14.2 to 1)
Librarians/Media Specialists: 29.0 (434.9 to 1)
Guidance Counselors: 32.0 (394.1 to 1)
Current Spending: ($ per student per year):
Total: $7,061; Instruction: $4,093; Support Services: $2,600
Enrollment, Drop-out Rates and Diploma Recipients by Race/Ethnicity

Category	Total	White	Black	Asian	AIAN	Hisp.
Enrollment (%)	100.0	0.0	0.0	0.0	0.0	0.0
Drop-out Rate (%)	3.2	n/a	n/a	n/a	n/a	n/a
H.S. Diplomas (#)	610	n/a	n/a	n/a	n/a	n/a

Sumner County

Sumner County SD

225 E Main St • Gallatin, TN 37066-2908
(615) 451-5200 • http://www.sumnerschools.org
Grade Span: KG-12; **Agency Type:** 1
Schools: 41
23 Primary; 9 Middle; 8 High; 1 Other Level
40 Regular; 0 Special Education; 0 Vocational; 1 Alternative
0 Magnet; 0 Charter; 9 Title I Eligible; 0 School-wide Title I
Students: 23,299 (n/a% male; n/a% female)
Individual Education Program: 4,283 (18.4%);
English Language Learner: n/a; Migrant: n/a
Eligible for Free Lunch Program: n/a
Eligible for Reduced-Price Lunch Program: n/a
Teachers: 1,565.5 (14.9 to 1)
Librarians/Media Specialists: 38.0 (613.1 to 1)
Guidance Counselors: 47.5 (490.5 to 1)
Current Spending: ($ per student per year):
Total: $5,405; Instruction: $3,641; Support Services: $1,478
Enrollment, Drop-out Rates and Diploma Recipients by Race/Ethnicity

Category	Total	White	Black	Asian	AIAN	Hisp.
Enrollment (%)	100.0	0.0	0.0	0.0	0.0	0.0
Drop-out Rate (%)	5.0	n/a	n/a	n/a	n/a	n/a
H.S. Diplomas (#)	1,477	n/a	n/a	n/a	n/a	n/a

Tipton County

Tipton County SD

PO Box 486 • Covington, TN 38019-0486
(901) 476-7148 • http://www.tipton-county.com/
Grade Span: KG-12; **Agency Type:** 1
Schools: 11
4 Primary; 3 Middle; 3 High; 1 Other Level
10 Regular; 0 Special Education; 0 Vocational; 1 Alternative
0 Magnet; 0 Charter; 4 Title I Eligible; 1 School-wide Title I
Students: 10,094 (n/a% male; n/a% female)
Individual Education Program: 1,764 (17.5%);
English Language Learner: n/a; Migrant: n/a
Eligible for Free Lunch Program: n/a
Eligible for Reduced-Price Lunch Program: n/a
Teachers: 601.8 (16.8 to 1)
Librarians/Media Specialists: 10.0 (1,009.4 to 1)
Guidance Counselors: 18.0 (560.8 to 1)
Current Spending: ($ per student per year):
Total: $4,917; Instruction: $3,313; Support Services: $1,272
Enrollment, Drop-out Rates and Diploma Recipients by Race/Ethnicity

Category	Total	White	Black	Asian	AIAN	Hisp.
Enrollment (%)	100.0	0.0	0.0	0.0	0.0	0.0
Drop-out Rate (%)	3.6	n/a	n/a	n/a	n/a	n/a
H.S. Diplomas (#)	522	n/a	n/a	n/a	n/a	n/a

Unicoi County

Unicoi SD

600 N Elm Ave • Erwin, TN 37650-1310
(423) 743-1600
Grade Span: KG-12; **Agency Type:** 1
Schools: 6
4 Primary; 1 Middle; 1 High; 0 Other Level
6 Regular; 0 Special Education; 0 Vocational; 0 Alternative
0 Magnet; 0 Charter; 4 Title I Eligible; 4 School-wide Title I
Students: 2,501 (n/a% male; n/a% female)
Individual Education Program: 567 (22.7%);
English Language Learner: n/a; Migrant: n/a
Eligible for Free Lunch Program: n/a
Eligible for Reduced-Price Lunch Program: n/a
Teachers: 152.7 (16.4 to 1)
Librarians/Media Specialists: 5.0 (500.2 to 1)

Guidance Counselors: 4.0 (625.3 to 1)
Current Spending: ($ per student per year):
Total: $5,763; Instruction: $3,722; Support Services: $1,754
Enrollment, Drop-out Rates and Diploma Recipients by Race/Ethnicity

Category	Total	White	Black	Asian	AIAN	Hisp.
Enrollment (%)	100.0	0.0	0.0	0.0	0.0	0.0
Drop-out Rate (%)	1.3	n/a	n/a	n/a	n/a	n/a
H.S. Diplomas (#)	161	n/a	n/a	n/a	n/a	n/a

Union County

Union County SD

Box 10, 635 Main St • Maynardville, TN 37807-0010
(865) 992-5466 • http://www.union-city-hs.obion.k12.tn.us/
Grade Span: KG-12; **Agency Type:** 1
Schools: 7
4 Primary; 1 Middle; 1 High; 1 Other Level
6 Regular; 0 Special Education; 0 Vocational; 1 Alternative
0 Magnet; 0 Charter; 5 Title I Eligible; 4 School-wide Title I
Students: 3,116 (n/a% male; n/a% female)
Individual Education Program: 593 (19.0%);
English Language Learner: n/a; Migrant: n/a
Eligible for Free Lunch Program: n/a
Eligible for Reduced-Price Lunch Program: n/a
Teachers: 217.4 (14.3 to 1)
Librarians/Media Specialists: 3.0 (1,038.7 to 1)
Guidance Counselors: 4.0 (779.0 to 1)
Current Spending: ($ per student per year):
Total: $5,803; Instruction: $3,870; Support Services: $1,553
Enrollment, Drop-out Rates and Diploma Recipients by Race/Ethnicity

Category	Total	White	Black	Asian	AIAN	Hisp.
Enrollment (%)	100.0	0.0	0.0	0.0	0.0	0.0
Drop-out Rate (%)	3.3	n/a	n/a	n/a	n/a	n/a
H.S. Diplomas (#)	105	n/a	n/a	n/a	n/a	n/a

Warren County

Warren County SD

2548 Morrison St • Mcminnville, TN 37110-2545
(931) 668-4022
Grade Span: KG-12; **Agency Type:** 1
Schools: 11
8 Primary; 1 Middle; 1 High; 1 Other Level
10 Regular; 0 Special Education; 0 Vocational; 1 Alternative
0 Magnet; 0 Charter; 9 Title I Eligible; 4 School-wide Title I
Students: 6,144 (n/a% male; n/a% female)
Individual Education Program: 1,234 (20.1%);
English Language Learner: n/a; Migrant: n/a
Eligible for Free Lunch Program: n/a
Eligible for Reduced-Price Lunch Program: n/a
Teachers: 413.4 (14.9 to 1)
Librarians/Media Specialists: 11.0 (558.5 to 1)
Guidance Counselors: 14.0 (438.9 to 1)
Current Spending: ($ per student per year):
Total: $5,142; Instruction: $3,308; Support Services: $1,543
Enrollment, Drop-out Rates and Diploma Recipients by Race/Ethnicity

Category	Total	White	Black	Asian	AIAN	Hisp.
Enrollment (%)	100.0	0.0	0.0	0.0	0.0	0.0
Drop-out Rate (%)	2.3	n/a	n/a	n/a	n/a	n/a
H.S. Diplomas (#)	341	n/a	n/a	n/a	n/a	n/a

Washington County

Johnson City SD

PO Box 1517 • Johnson City, TN 37605-1517
(423) 434-5200 • http://www.jcschools.org
Grade Span: KG-12; **Agency Type:** 1
Schools: 10
8 Primary; 1 Middle; 1 High; 0 Other Level
10 Regular; 0 Special Education; 0 Vocational; 0 Alternative
0 Magnet; 0 Charter; 5 Title I Eligible; 5 School-wide Title I
Students: 6,859 (n/a% male; n/a% female)
Individual Education Program: 1,123 (16.4%);
English Language Learner: n/a; Migrant: n/a
Eligible for Free Lunch Program: n/a
Eligible for Reduced-Price Lunch Program: n/a
Teachers: 444.2 (15.4 to 1)
Librarians/Media Specialists: 9.0 (762.1 to 1)
Guidance Counselors: 15.0 (457.3 to 1)
Current Spending: ($ per student per year):
Total: $6,416; Instruction: $4,227; Support Services: $1,934
Enrollment, Drop-out Rates and Diploma Recipients by Race/Ethnicity

Category	Total	White	Black	Asian	AIAN	Hisp.
Enrollment (%)	100.0	0.0	0.0	0.0	0.0	0.0
Drop-out Rate (%)	0.3	n/a	n/a	n/a	n/a	n/a
H.S. Diplomas (#)	340	n/a	n/a	n/a	n/a	n/a

Washington County SD

405 W College St • Jonesborough, TN 37659-1009
(423) 753-1100 • http://www.wcde.org/
Grade Span: KG-12; **Agency Type:** 1
Schools: 13
8 Primary; 2 Middle; 2 High; 1 Other Level
13 Regular; 0 Special Education; 0 Vocational; 0 Alternative
0 Magnet; 0 Charter; 9 Title I Eligible; 0 School-wide Title I
Students: 8,596 (n/a% male; n/a% female)
Individual Education Program: 1,116 (13.0%);
English Language Learner: n/a; Migrant: n/a
Eligible for Free Lunch Program: n/a
Eligible for Reduced-Price Lunch Program: n/a
Teachers: 517.5 (16.6 to 1)
Librarians/Media Specialists: 15.5 (554.6 to 1)
Guidance Counselors: 17.0 (505.6 to 1)
Current Spending: ($ per student per year):
Total: $5,280; Instruction: $3,633; Support Services: $1,519
Enrollment, Drop-out Rates and Diploma Recipients by Race/Ethnicity

Category	Total	White	Black	Asian	AIAN	Hisp.
Enrollment (%)	100.0	0.0	0.0	0.0	0.0	0.0
Drop-out Rate (%)	5.2	n/a	n/a	n/a	n/a	n/a
H.S. Diplomas (#)	387	n/a	n/a	n/a	n/a	n/a

Wayne County

Wayne County SD

PO Box 658 • Waynesboro, TN 38485-0658
(931) 722-3548 • http://www.wayne-lea.wayne.k12.tn.us/
Grade Span: KG-12; **Agency Type:** 1
Schools: 8
2 Primary; 2 Middle; 3 High; 1 Other Level
7 Regular; 0 Special Education; 1 Vocational; 0 Alternative
0 Magnet; 0 Charter; 5 Title I Eligible; 5 School-wide Title I
Students: 2,706 (n/a% male; n/a% female)
Individual Education Program: 479 (17.7%);
English Language Learner: n/a; Migrant: n/a
Eligible for Free Lunch Program: n/a
Eligible for Reduced-Price Lunch Program: n/a
Teachers: 194.3 (13.9 to 1)
Librarians/Media Specialists: 6.0 (451.0 to 1)
Guidance Counselors: 5.0 (541.2 to 1)
Current Spending: ($ per student per year):
Total: $5,256; Instruction: $3,586; Support Services: $1,433
Enrollment, Drop-out Rates and Diploma Recipients by Race/Ethnicity

Category	Total	White	Black	Asian	AIAN	Hisp.
Enrollment (%)	100.0	0.0	0.0	0.0	0.0	0.0
Drop-out Rate (%)	4.6	n/a	n/a	n/a	n/a	n/a
H.S. Diplomas (#)	143	n/a	n/a	n/a	n/a	n/a

Weakley County

Weakley County SD

8319 Hwy 22, Ste A • Dresden, TN 38225
(731) 364-2247 • http://www.weakley-lea.weakley.k12.tn.us/
Grade Span: KG-12; **Agency Type:** 1
Schools: 12
5 Primary; 2 Middle; 3 High; 2 Other Level
12 Regular; 0 Special Education; 0 Vocational; 0 Alternative
0 Magnet; 0 Charter; 0 Title I Eligible; 0 School-wide Title I
Students: 4,874 (n/a% male; n/a% female)
Individual Education Program: 738 (15.1%);
English Language Learner: n/a; Migrant: n/a
Eligible for Free Lunch Program: n/a
Eligible for Reduced-Price Lunch Program: n/a
Teachers: 318.4 (15.3 to 1)
Librarians/Media Specialists: 8.9 (547.6 to 1)
Guidance Counselors: 11.4 (427.5 to 1)
Current Spending: ($ per student per year):
Total: $4,934; Instruction: $3,262; Support Services: $1,348
Enrollment, Drop-out Rates and Diploma Recipients by Race/Ethnicity

Category	Total	White	Black	Asian	AIAN	Hisp.
Enrollment (%)	100.0	0.0	0.0	0.0	0.0	0.0
Drop-out Rate (%)	2.3	n/a	n/a	n/a	n/a	n/a
H.S. Diplomas (#)	270	n/a	n/a	n/a	n/a	n/a

White County

White County SD

136 Baker St • Sparta, TN 38583-1700
(931) 836-2229
Grade Span: KG-12; **Agency Type:** 1
Schools: 9
7 Primary; 1 Middle; 1 High; 0 Other Level
9 Regular; 0 Special Education; 0 Vocational; 0 Alternative
0 Magnet; 0 Charter; 7 Title I Eligible; 7 School-wide Title I
Students: 3,847 (n/a% male; n/a% female)
Individual Education Program: 618 (16.1%);
English Language Learner: n/a; Migrant: n/a
Eligible for Free Lunch Program: n/a
Eligible for Reduced-Price Lunch Program: n/a
Teachers: 245.1 (15.7 to 1)
Librarians/Media Specialists: 7.0 (549.6 to 1)
Guidance Counselors: 9.0 (427.4 to 1)
Current Spending: ($ per student per year):
Total: $4,564; Instruction: $3,013; Support Services: $1,227
Enrollment, Drop-out Rates and Diploma Recipients by Race/Ethnicity

Category	Total	White	Black	Asian	AIAN	Hisp.
Enrollment (%)	100.0	0.0	0.0	0.0	0.0	0.0
Drop-out Rate (%)	3.0	n/a	n/a	n/a	n/a	n/a
H.S. Diplomas (#)	202	n/a	n/a	n/a	n/a	n/a

Williamson County

Franklin City Elementary SD

507 New Hwy 96 W • Franklin, TN 37064-2470
(615) 794-6624
Grade Span: KG-08; **Agency Type:** 1
Schools: 8
5 Primary; 3 Middle; 0 High; 0 Other Level
8 Regular; 0 Special Education; 0 Vocational; 0 Alternative
0 Magnet; 0 Charter; 2 Title I Eligible; 0 School-wide Title I
Students: 3,759 (n/a% male; n/a% female)
Individual Education Program: 547 (14.6%);
English Language Learner: n/a; Migrant: n/a
Eligible for Free Lunch Program: n/a
Eligible for Reduced-Price Lunch Program: n/a
Teachers: 294.2 (12.8 to 1)
Librarians/Media Specialists: 7.0 (537.0 to 1)
Guidance Counselors: 10.0 (375.9 to 1)
Current Spending: ($ per student per year):
Total: $7,584; Instruction: $4,847; Support Services: $2,435
Enrollment, Drop-out Rates and Diploma Recipients by Race/Ethnicity

Category	Total	White	Black	Asian	AIAN	Hisp.
Enrollment (%)	100.0	0.0	0.0	0.0	0.0	0.0
Drop-out Rate (%)	n/a	n/a	n/a	n/a	n/a	n/a
H.S. Diplomas (#)	n/a	n/a	n/a	n/a	n/a	n/a

Williamson County SD

1320 W Main, Ste 202 • Franklin, TN 37064-3736
(615) 595-4700 • http://www.wcs.edu
Grade Span: KG-12; **Agency Type:** 1
Schools: 32
19 Primary; 6 Middle; 6 High; 1 Other Level
32 Regular; 0 Special Education; 0 Vocational; 0 Alternative
0 Magnet; 0 Charter; 7 Title I Eligible; 0 School-wide Title I
Students: 20,988 (n/a% male; n/a% female)
Individual Education Program: 2,972 (14.2%);
English Language Learner: n/a; Migrant: n/a
Eligible for Free Lunch Program: n/a
Eligible for Reduced-Price Lunch Program: n/a
Teachers: 1,293.0 (16.2 to 1)
Librarians/Media Specialists: 34.5 (608.3 to 1)
Guidance Counselors: 49.2 (426.6 to 1)
Current Spending: ($ per student per year):
Total: $6,182; Instruction: $3,958; Support Services: $1,945
Enrollment, Drop-out Rates and Diploma Recipients by Race/Ethnicity

Category	Total	White	Black	Asian	AIAN	Hisp.
Enrollment (%)	100.0	0.0	0.0	0.0	0.0	0.0
Drop-out Rate (%)	1.4	n/a	n/a	n/a	n/a	n/a
H.S. Diplomas (#)	745	n/a	n/a	n/a	n/a	n/a

Wilson County

Lebanon City Elementary SD

701 Coles Ferry Pike • Lebanon, TN 37087-5631
(615) 449-6060
Grade Span: KG-08; **Agency Type:** 1
Schools: 5
3 Primary; 2 Middle; 0 High; 0 Other Level
5 Regular; 0 Special Education; 0 Vocational; 0 Alternative
0 Magnet; 0 Charter; 2 Title I Eligible; 1 School-wide Title I
Students: 2,951 (n/a% male; n/a% female)
Individual Education Program: 461 (15.6%);
English Language Learner: n/a; Migrant: n/a
Eligible for Free Lunch Program: n/a
Eligible for Reduced-Price Lunch Program: n/a
Teachers: 194.9 (15.1 to 1)
Librarians/Media Specialists: 5.0 (590.2 to 1)
Guidance Counselors: 5.0 (590.2 to 1)
Current Spending: ($ per student per year):
Total: $5,609; Instruction: $3,586; Support Services: $1,697
Enrollment, Drop-out Rates and Diploma Recipients by Race/Ethnicity

Category	Total	White	Black	Asian	AIAN	Hisp.
Enrollment (%)	100.0	0.0	0.0	0.0	0.0	0.0
Drop-out Rate (%)	n/a	n/a	n/a	n/a	n/a	n/a
H.S. Diplomas (#)	n/a	n/a	n/a	n/a	n/a	n/a

Wilson County SD

351 Stumpy Ln • Lebanon, TN 37090
(615) 444-3282 • http://www.wcschools.com/
Grade Span: KG-12; **Agency Type:** 1
Schools: 19
11 Primary; 2 Middle; 6 High; 0 Other Level
18 Regular; 0 Special Education; 1 Vocational; 0 Alternative
0 Magnet; 0 Charter; 4 Title I Eligible; 0 School-wide Title I
Students: 12,130 (n/a% male; n/a% female)
Individual Education Program: 1,552 (12.8%);
English Language Learner: n/a; Migrant: n/a
Eligible for Free Lunch Program: n/a
Eligible for Reduced-Price Lunch Program: n/a
Teachers: 718.0 (16.9 to 1)
Librarians/Media Specialists: 16.0 (758.1 to 1)
Guidance Counselors: 30.0 (404.3 to 1)
Current Spending: ($ per student per year):
Total: $5,459; Instruction: $3,241; Support Services: $1,978
Enrollment, Drop-out Rates and Diploma Recipients by Race/Ethnicity

Category	Total	White	Black	Asian	AIAN	Hisp.
Enrollment (%)	100.0	0.0	0.0	0.0	0.0	0.0
Drop-out Rate (%)	5.0	n/a	n/a	n/a	n/a	n/a
H.S. Diplomas (#)	648	n/a	n/a	n/a	n/a	n/a

Number of Schools

Rank	Number	District Name	City
1	178	Memphis City SD	Memphis
2	123	Nashville-Davidson County SD	Nashville
3	88	Knox County SD	Knoxville
4	81	Hamilton County SD	Chattanooga
5	48	Shelby County SD	Memphis
6	41	Sumner County SD	Gallatin
7	36	Rutherford County SD	Murfreesboro
8	32	Williamson County SD	Franklin
9	30	Montgomery County Schools	Clarksville
9	30	Sullivan County SD	Blountville
11	26	Jackson-Madison Consolidated	Jackson
12	24	Sevier County SD	Sevierville
13	20	Hamblen County SD	Morristown
14	19	Blount County SD	Maryville
14	19	Wilson County SD	Lebanon
16	18	Maury County SD	Columbia
17	17	Anderson County SD	Clinton
17	17	Carter County SD	Elizabethton
17	17	Hawkins County SD	Rogersville
17	17	Putnam County SD	Cookeville
17	17	South and Eastern States Agency	Arlington
22	16	Bradley County SD	Cleveland
22	16	Campbell County SD	Jacksboro
22	16	Robertson County SD	Springfield
25	15	Greene County SD	Greeneville
26	14	Cheatham County SD	Ashland City
26	14	Dickson County SD	Dickson
28	13	Claiborne County SD	Tazewell
28	13	Lawrence County SD	Lawrenceburg
28	13	Roane County SD	Kingston
28	13	Washington County SD	Jonesborough
32	12	Bedford County SD	Shelbyville
32	12	Cocke County SD	Newport
32	12	Franklin County SD	Winchester
32	12	Weakley County SD	Dresden
36	11	Jefferson County SD	Dandridge
36	11	Kingsport City SD	Kingsport
36	11	Monroe County SD	Madisonville
36	11	Tipton County SD	Covington
36	11	Warren County SD	Mcminnville
41	10	Cumberland County SD	Crossville
41	10	Fayette County SD	Somerville
41	10	Hardin County SD	Savannah
41	10	Henderson County SD	Lexington
41	10	Johnson City SD	Johnson City
41	10	Murfreesboro City Elem SD	Murfreesboro
41	10	Smith County SD	Carthage
48	9	Hardeman County SD	Bolivar
48	9	Loudon County SD	Loudon
48	9	Marion County SD	Jasper
48	9	Marshall County SD	Lewisburg
48	9	Mcminn County SD	Athens
48	9	Overton County SD	Livingston
48	9	White County SD	Sparta
55	8	Benton County SD	Camden
55	8	Bristol City SD	Bristol
55	8	Cleveland City SD	Cleveland
55	8	Coffee County SD	Manchester
55	8	Franklin City Elementary SD	Franklin
55	8	Giles County SD	Pulaski
55	8	Lincoln County SD	Fayetteville
55	8	Mcnairy County SD	Selmer
55	8	Morgan County SD	Wartburg
55	8	Oak Ridge City SD	Oak Ridge
55	8	Obion County SD	Union City
55	8	Polk County SD	Benton
55	8	Wayne County SD	Waynesboro
68	7	Cannon County SD	Woodbury
68	7	Dyer County SD	Dyersburg
68	7	Fentress County SD	Jamestown
68	7	Gibson Special District	Dyer
68	7	Greeneville City SD	Greeneville
68	7	Grundy County SD	Altamont
68	7	Haywood County SD	Brownsville
68	7	Hickman County SD	Centerville
68	7	Humphreys County SD	Waverly
68	7	Johnson County SD	Mountain City
68	7	Lauderdale County SD	Ripley
68	7	Macon County SD	Lafayette
68	7	Maryville City SD	Maryville
68	7	Scott County SD	Huntsville
68	7	Tullahoma City SD	Tullahoma
68	7	Union County SD	Maynardville
84	6	Bledsoe County SD	Pikeville
84	6	Chester County SD	Henderson
84	6	Grainger County SD	Rutledge
84	6	Henry County SD	Paris
84	6	Unicoi SD	Erwin
89	5	Athens City Elementary SD	Athens
89	5	Crockett County SD	Alamo
89	5	Dekalb County SD	Smithville
89	5	Elizabethton City SD	Elizabethton
89	5	Humboldt City SD	Humboldt
89	5	Jackson County SD	Gainsboro
89	5	Lebanon City Elementary SD	Lebanon
89	5	Rhea County SD	Dayton
97	4	Dyersburg City SD	Dyersburg
97	4	Lewis County SD	Hohenwald
97	4	Meigs County SD	Decatur
100	3	Lenoir City SD	Lenoir City
100	3	Milan City Special SD	Milan
100	3	Sequatchie County SD	Dunlap
100	3	Stewart County SD	Dover

Number of Teachers

Rank	Number	District Name	City
1	7,203	Memphis City SD	Memphis
2	4,614	Nashville-Davidson County SD	Nashville
3	3,588	Knox County SD	Knoxville
4	2,675	Hamilton County SD	Chattanooga
5	2,593	Shelby County SD	Memphis
6	1,734	Rutherford County SD	Murfreesboro
7	1,565	Sumner County SD	Gallatin
8	1,511	Montgomery County Schools	Clarksville
9	1,293	Williamson County SD	Franklin
10	932	Jackson-Madison Consolidated	Jackson
11	888	Sullivan County SD	Blountville
12	830	Sevier County SD	Sevierville
13	749	Maury County SD	Columbia
14	718	Wilson County SD	Lebanon
15	650	Blount County SD	Maryville
16	613	Robertson County SD	Springfield
17	601	Tipton County SD	Covington
18	597	Hamblen County SD	Morristown
19	585	Putnam County SD	Cookeville
20	547	Bradley County SD	Cleveland
21	523	Dickson County SD	Dickson
22	517	Washington County SD	Jonesborough
23	506	Hawkins County SD	Rogersville
24	498	Anderson County SD	Clinton
25	455	Lawrence County SD	Lawrenceburg
26	445	Carter County SD	Elizabethton
27	444	Johnson City SD	Johnson City
28	442	Greene County SD	Greeneville
29	440	Jefferson County SD	Dandridge
30	437	Kingsport City SD	Kingsport
31	437	Cheatham County SD	Ashland City
32	413	Warren County SD	Mcminnville
33	410	Bedford County SD	Shelbyville
34	406	Cumberland County SD	Crossville
35	406	Campbell County SD	Jacksboro
36	390	Murfreesboro City Elem SD	Murfreesboro
37	381	Roane County SD	Kingston
38	371	Franklin County SD	Winchester
39	350	Claiborne County SD	Tazewell
40	342	Mcminn County SD	Athens
41	327	Hardeman County SD	Bolivar
42	318	Weakley County SD	Dresden
43	311	Cocke County SD	Newport
44	306	Monroe County SD	Madisonville
45	297	Lauderdale County SD	Ripley
46	297	Cleveland City SD	Cleveland
47	297	Giles County SD	Pulaski
48	296	Marshall County SD	Lewisburg
49	294	Franklin City Elementary SD	Franklin
50	283	Maryville City SD	Maryville
51	283	Mcnairy County SD	Selmer
52	279	Coffee County SD	Manchester
53	273	Loudon County SD	Loudon
54	265	Hardin County SD	Savannah
55	264	Lincoln County SD	Fayetteville
56	262	Marion County SD	Jasper
57	257	Obion County SD	Union City
58	246	Bristol City SD	Bristol
59	245	Haywood County SD	Brownsville
60	245	Fayette County SD	Somerville
61	245	White County SD	Sparta
62	243	Rhea County SD	Dayton
63	239	Henderson County SD	Lexington
64	238	Hickman County SD	Centerville
65	233	Oak Ridge City SD	Oak Ridge
66	226	Morgan County SD	Wartburg
67	224	Overton County SD	Livingston
68	223	Tullahoma City SD	Tullahoma
69	219	Macon County SD	Lafayette
70	217	Union County SD	Maynardville
71	216	Dyersburg City SD	Dyersburg
72	204	Scott County SD	Huntsville
73	203	Grainger County SD	Rutledge
74	201	Dyer County SD	Dyersburg
75	198	Henry County SD	Paris
76	198	Humphreys County SD	Waverly
77	195	Smith County SD	Carthage
78	194	Lebanon City Elementary SD	Lebanon
79	194	Wayne County SD	Waynesboro
80	193	Greeneville City SD	Greeneville
81	179	Dekalb County SD	Smithville
82	179	Grundy County SD	Altamont
83	177	Benton County SD	Camden
84	163	Fentress County SD	Jamestown
85	157	Gibson Special District	Dyer
86	156	Polk County SD	Benton
87	155	Elizabethton City SD	Elizabethton
88	154	Johnson County SD	Mountain City
89	152	Unicoi SD	Erwin
90	149	Cannon County SD	Woodbury
91	139	Chester County SD	Henderson
92	137	Milan City Special SD	Milan
93	130	Lewis County SD	Hohenwald
94	128	Sequatchie County SD	Dunlap
95	126	Lenoir City SD	Lenoir City
96	124	Stewart County SD	Dover
97	121	Bledsoe County SD	Pikeville
98	119	Jackson County SD	Gainsboro
99	117	Meigs County SD	Decatur
100	111	Crockett County SD	Alamo
101	106	Athens City Elementary SD	Athens
102	106	Humboldt City SD	Humboldt
103	n/a	South and Eastern States Agency	Arlington

Number of Students

Rank	Number	District Name	City
1	118,039	Memphis City SD	Memphis
2	67,954	Nashville-Davidson County SD	Nashville
3	53,411	Knox County SD	Knoxville
4	45,439	Shelby County SD	Memphis
5	40,564	Hamilton County SD	Chattanooga
6	28,069	Rutherford County SD	Murfreesboro
7	24,578	Montgomery County Schools	Clarksville
8	23,299	Sumner County SD	Gallatin
9	20,988	Williamson County SD	Franklin
10	13,525	Jackson-Madison Consolidated	Jackson
11	12,680	Sevier County SD	Sevierville
12	12,611	Sullivan County SD	Blountville
13	12,130	Wilson County SD	Lebanon
14	10,990	Maury County SD	Columbia
15	10,845	Blount County SD	Maryville
16	10,094	Tipton County SD	Covington
17	9,560	Putnam County SD	Cookeville
18	9,177	Bradley County SD	Cleveland
19	9,146	Robertson County SD	Springfield
20	8,982	Hamblen County SD	Morristown
21	8,596	Washington County SD	Jonesborough
22	8,039	Dickson County SD	Dickson
23	7,237	Hawkins County SD	Rogersville
24	6,933	Anderson County SD	Clinton
25	6,887	Greene County SD	Greeneville
26	6,878	Jefferson County SD	Dandridge
27	6,875	Cheatham County SD	Ashland City
28	6,859	Johnson City SD	Johnson City
29	6,759	Cumberland County SD	Crossville
30	6,700	Lawrence County SD	Lawrenceburg
31	6,555	Bedford County SD	Shelbyville
32	6,387	Kingsport City SD	Kingsport
33	6,144	Warren County SD	Mcminnville
34	5,936	Roane County SD	Kingston
35	5,923	Campbell County SD	Jacksboro
36	5,903	Carter County SD	Elizabethton
37	5,861	Mcminn County SD	Athens
38	5,845	Franklin County SD	Winchester
39	5,837	Murfreesboro City Elem SD	Murfreesboro
40	5,093	Monroe County SD	Madisonville
41	4,874	Weakley County SD	Dresden
42	4,821	Marshall County SD	Lewisburg
43	4,817	Loudon County SD	Loudon
44	4,693	Cocke County SD	Newport
45	4,580	Claiborne County SD	Tazewell
46	4,578	Lauderdale County SD	Ripley
47	4,513	Hardeman County SD	Bolivar
48	4,504	Giles County SD	Pulaski
49	4,359	Maryville City SD	Maryville
50	4,349	Oak Ridge City SD	Oak Ridge
51	4,332	Cleveland City SD	Cleveland
52	4,150	Coffee County SD	Manchester
53	4,145	Mcnairy County SD	Selmer
54	4,066	Marion County SD	Jasper
55	4,015	Obion County SD	Union City
56	3,964	Lincoln County SD	Fayetteville
57	3,856	Rhea County SD	Dayton
58	3,847	White County SD	Sparta
59	3,838	Hickman County SD	Centerville
60	3,798	Hardin County SD	Savannah
61	3,759	Franklin City Elementary SD	Franklin
62	3,621	Tullahoma City SD	Tullahoma

63	3,603	Bristol City SD	Bristol
64	3,538	Macon County SD	Lafayette
65	3,533	Haywood County SD	Brownsville
66	3,514	South and Eastern States Agency	Arlington
67	3,490	Dyersburg City SD	Dyersburg
68	3,438	Henderson County SD	Lexington
69	3,308	Grainger County SD	Rutledge
70	3,210	Overton County SD	Livingston
71	3,176	Fayette County SD	Somerville
72	3,163	Dyer County SD	Dyersburg
73	3,143	Henry County SD	Paris
74	3,137	Smith County SD	Carthage
75	3,133	Morgan County SD	Wartburg
76	3,116	Union County SD	Maynardville
77	3,020	Humphreys County SD	Waverly
78	2,951	Lebanon City Elementary SD	Lebanon
79	2,706	Wayne County SD	Waynesboro
80	2,655	Gibson Special District	Dyer
81	2,626	Greeneville City SD	Greeneville
82	2,619	Scott County SD	Huntsville
83	2,594	Dekalb County SD	Smithville
84	2,508	Polk County SD	Benton
85	2,501	Unicoi SD	Erwin
86	2,464	Benton County SD	Camden
87	2,438	Chester County SD	Henderson
88	2,287	Johnson County SD	Mountain City
89	2,285	Fentress County SD	Jamestown
90	2,264	Grundy County SD	Altamont
91	2,187	Elizabethton City SD	Elizabethton
92	2,104	Cannon County SD	Woodbury
93	2,091	Stewart County SD	Dover
94	2,015	Lenoir City SD	Lenoir City
95	1,997	Milan City Special SD	Milan
96	1,964	Lewis County SD	Hohenwald
97	1,923	Sequatchie County SD	Dunlap
98	1,851	Meigs County SD	Decatur
99	1,764	Bledsoe County SD	Pikeville
100	1,730	Crockett County SD	Alamo
101	1,684	Athens City Elementary SD	Athens
102	1,638	Jackson County SD	Gainsboro
103	1,534	Humboldt City SD	Humboldt

Male Students

Rank	Percent	District Name	City
1	n/a	Anderson County SD	Clinton
1	n/a	Athens City Elementary SD	Athens
1	n/a	Bedford County SD	Shelbyville
1	n/a	Benton County SD	Camden
1	n/a	Bledsoe County SD	Pikeville
1	n/a	Blount County SD	Maryville
1	n/a	Bradley County SD	Cleveland
1	n/a	Bristol City SD	Bristol
1	n/a	Campbell County SD	Jacksboro
1	n/a	Cannon County SD	Woodbury
1	n/a	Carter County SD	Elizabethton
1	n/a	Cheatham County SD	Ashland City
1	n/a	Chester County SD	Henderson
1	n/a	Claiborne County SD	Tazewell
1	n/a	Cleveland City SD	Cleveland
1	n/a	Cocke County SD	Newport
1	n/a	Coffee County SD	Manchester
1	n/a	Crockett County SD	Alamo
1	n/a	Cumberland County SD	Crossville
1	n/a	Dekalb County SD	Smithville
1	n/a	Dickson County SD	Dickson
1	n/a	Dyer County SD	Dyersburg
1	n/a	Dyersburg City SD	Dyersburg
1	n/a	Elizabethton City SD	Elizabethton
1	n/a	Fayette County SD	Somerville
1	n/a	Fentress County SD	Jamestown
1	n/a	Franklin City Elementary SD	Franklin
1	n/a	Franklin County SD	Winchester
1	n/a	Gibson Special District	Dyer
1	n/a	Giles County SD	Pulaski
1	n/a	Grainger County SD	Rutledge
1	n/a	Greene County SD	Greeneville
1	n/a	Greeneville City SD	Greeneville
1	n/a	Grundy County SD	Altamont
1	n/a	Hamblen County SD	Morristown
1	n/a	Hamilton County SD	Chattanooga
1	n/a	Hardeman County SD	Bolivar
1	n/a	Hardin County SD	Savannah
1	n/a	Hawkins County SD	Rogersville
1	n/a	Haywood County SD	Brownsville
1	n/a	Henderson County SD	Lexington
1	n/a	Henry County SD	Paris
1	n/a	Hickman County SD	Centerville
1	n/a	Humboldt City SD	Humboldt
1	n/a	Humphreys County SD	Waverly
1	n/a	Jackson County SD	Gainsboro
1	n/a	Jackson-Madison Consolidated	Jackson
1	n/a	Jefferson County SD	Dandridge
1	n/a	Johnson City SD	Johnson City
1	n/a	Johnson County SD	Mountain City
1	n/a	Kingsport City SD	Kingsport
1	n/a	Knox County SD	Knoxville
1	n/a	Lauderdale County SD	Ripley
1	n/a	Lawrence County SD	Lawrenceburg
1	n/a	Lebanon City Elementary SD	Lebanon
1	n/a	Lenoir City SD	Lenoir City
1	n/a	Lewis County SD	Hohenwald
1	n/a	Lincoln County SD	Fayetteville
1	n/a	Loudon County SD	Loudon
1	n/a	Macon County SD	Lafayette
1	n/a	Marion County SD	Jasper
1	n/a	Marshall County SD	Lewisburg
1	n/a	Maryville City SD	Maryville
1	n/a	Maury County SD	Columbia
1	n/a	Mcminn County SD	Athens
1	n/a	Mcnairy County SD	Selmer
1	n/a	Meigs County SD	Decatur
1	n/a	Memphis City SD	Memphis
1	n/a	Milan City Special SD	Milan
1	n/a	Monroe County SD	Madisonville
1	n/a	Montgomery County Schools	Clarksville
1	n/a	Morgan County SD	Wartburg
1	n/a	Murfreesboro City Elem SD	Murfreesboro
1	n/a	Nashville-Davidson County SD	Nashville
1	n/a	Oak Ridge City SD	Oak Ridge
1	n/a	Obion County SD	Union City
1	n/a	Overton County SD	Livingston
1	n/a	Polk County SD	Benton
1	n/a	Putnam County SD	Cookeville
1	n/a	Rhea County SD	Dayton
1	n/a	Roane County SD	Kingston
1	n/a	Robertson County SD	Springfield
1	n/a	Rutherford County SD	Murfreesboro
1	n/a	Scott County SD	Huntsville
1	n/a	Sequatchie County SD	Dunlap
1	n/a	Sevier County SD	Sevierville
1	n/a	Shelby County SD	Memphis
1	n/a	Smith County SD	Carthage
1	n/a	South and Eastern States Agency	Arlington
1	n/a	Stewart County SD	Dover
1	n/a	Sullivan County SD	Blountville
1	n/a	Sumner County SD	Gallatin
1	n/a	Tipton County SD	Covington
1	n/a	Tullahoma City SD	Tullahoma
1	n/a	Unicoi SD	Erwin
1	n/a	Union County SD	Maynardville
1	n/a	Warren County SD	Mcminnville
1	n/a	Washington County SD	Jonesborough
1	n/a	Wayne County SD	Waynesboro
1	n/a	Weakley County SD	Dresden
1	n/a	White County SD	Sparta
1	n/a	Williamson County SD	Franklin
1	n/a	Wilson County SD	Lebanon

Female Students

Rank	Percent	District Name	City
1	n/a	Anderson County SD	Clinton
1	n/a	Athens City Elementary SD	Athens
1	n/a	Bedford County SD	Shelbyville
1	n/a	Benton County SD	Camden
1	n/a	Bledsoe County SD	Pikeville
1	n/a	Blount County SD	Maryville
1	n/a	Bradley County SD	Cleveland
1	n/a	Bristol City SD	Bristol
1	n/a	Campbell County SD	Jacksboro
1	n/a	Cannon County SD	Woodbury
1	n/a	Carter County SD	Elizabethton
1	n/a	Cheatham County SD	Ashland City
1	n/a	Chester County SD	Henderson
1	n/a	Claiborne County SD	Tazewell
1	n/a	Cleveland City SD	Cleveland
1	n/a	Cocke County SD	Newport
1	n/a	Coffee County SD	Manchester
1	n/a	Crockett County SD	Alamo
1	n/a	Cumberland County SD	Crossville
1	n/a	Dekalb County SD	Smithville
1	n/a	Dickson County SD	Dickson
1	n/a	Dyer County SD	Dyersburg
1	n/a	Dyersburg City SD	Dyersburg
1	n/a	Elizabethton City SD	Elizabethton
1	n/a	Fayette County SD	Somerville
1	n/a	Fentress County SD	Jamestown
1	n/a	Franklin City Elementary SD	Franklin
1	n/a	Franklin County SD	Winchester
1	n/a	Gibson Special District	Dyer
1	n/a	Giles County SD	Pulaski
1	n/a	Grainger County SD	Rutledge
1	n/a	Greene County SD	Greeneville
1	n/a	Greeneville City SD	Greeneville
1	n/a	Grundy County SD	Altamont
1	n/a	Hamblen County SD	Morristown
1	n/a	Hamilton County SD	Chattanooga
1	n/a	Hardeman County SD	Bolivar
1	n/a	Hardin County SD	Savannah
1	n/a	Hawkins County SD	Rogersville
1	n/a	Haywood County SD	Brownsville
1	n/a	Henderson County SD	Lexington
1	n/a	Henry County SD	Paris
1	n/a	Hickman County SD	Centerville
1	n/a	Humboldt City SD	Humboldt
1	n/a	Humphreys County SD	Waverly
1	n/a	Jackson County SD	Gainsboro
1	n/a	Jackson-Madison Consolidated	Jackson
1	n/a	Jefferson County SD	Dandridge
1	n/a	Johnson City SD	Johnson City
1	n/a	Johnson County SD	Mountain City
1	n/a	Kingsport City SD	Kingsport
1	n/a	Knox County SD	Knoxville
1	n/a	Lauderdale County SD	Ripley
1	n/a	Lawrence County SD	Lawrenceburg
1	n/a	Lebanon City Elementary SD	Lebanon
1	n/a	Lenoir City SD	Lenoir City
1	n/a	Lewis County SD	Hohenwald
1	n/a	Lincoln County SD	Fayetteville
1	n/a	Loudon County SD	Loudon
1	n/a	Macon County SD	Lafayette
1	n/a	Marion County SD	Jasper
1	n/a	Marshall County SD	Lewisburg
1	n/a	Maryville City SD	Maryville
1	n/a	Maury County SD	Columbia
1	n/a	Mcminn County SD	Athens
1	n/a	Mcnairy County SD	Selmer
1	n/a	Meigs County SD	Decatur
1	n/a	Memphis City SD	Memphis
1	n/a	Milan City Special SD	Milan
1	n/a	Monroe County SD	Madisonville
1	n/a	Montgomery County Schools	Clarksville
1	n/a	Morgan County SD	Wartburg
1	n/a	Murfreesboro City Elem SD	Murfreesboro
1	n/a	Nashville-Davidson County SD	Nashville
1	n/a	Oak Ridge City SD	Oak Ridge
1	n/a	Obion County SD	Union City
1	n/a	Overton County SD	Livingston
1	n/a	Polk County SD	Benton
1	n/a	Putnam County SD	Cookeville
1	n/a	Rhea County SD	Dayton
1	n/a	Roane County SD	Kingston
1	n/a	Robertson County SD	Springfield
1	n/a	Rutherford County SD	Murfreesboro
1	n/a	Scott County SD	Huntsville
1	n/a	Sequatchie County SD	Dunlap
1	n/a	Sevier County SD	Sevierville
1	n/a	Shelby County SD	Memphis
1	n/a	Smith County SD	Carthage
1	n/a	South and Eastern States Agency	Arlington
1	n/a	Stewart County SD	Dover
1	n/a	Sullivan County SD	Blountville
1	n/a	Sumner County SD	Gallatin
1	n/a	Tipton County SD	Covington
1	n/a	Tullahoma City SD	Tullahoma
1	n/a	Unicoi SD	Erwin
1	n/a	Union County SD	Maynardville
1	n/a	Warren County SD	Mcminnville
1	n/a	Washington County SD	Jonesborough
1	n/a	Wayne County SD	Waynesboro
1	n/a	Weakley County SD	Dresden
1	n/a	White County SD	Sparta
1	n/a	Williamson County SD	Franklin
1	n/a	Wilson County SD	Lebanon

Individual Education Program Students

Rank	Percent	District Name	City
1	26.6	Grundy County SD	Altamont
2	23.8	Greeneville City SD	Greeneville
3	23.0	Bledsoe County SD	Pikeville
4	22.7	Unicoi SD	Erwin
5	22.0	Oak Ridge City SD	Oak Ridge
6	21.7	Jackson-Madison Consolidated	Jackson
7	21.4	Dyer County SD	Dyersburg
7	21.4	Overton County SD	Livingston
9	21.3	Lauderdale County SD	Ripley
10	20.2	Greene County SD	Greeneville
11	20.1	Hawkins County SD	Rogersville
11	20.1	Warren County SD	Mcminnville
13	20.0	Shelby County SD	Memphis
14	19.6	Dekalb County SD	Smithville
15	19.4	Sullivan County SD	Blountville
16	19.3	Dickson County SD	Dickson
16	19.3	Putnam County SD	Cookeville
16	19.3	Tullahoma City SD	Tullahoma
19	19.0	Union County SD	Maynardville
20	18.7	Claiborne County SD	Tazewell

Rank	Percent	District Name	City
21	18.6	Athens City Elementary SD	Athens
22	18.5	Stewart County SD	Dover
23	18.4	Humboldt City SD	Humboldt
23	18.4	Robertson County SD	Springfield
23	18.4	Sumner County SD	Gallatin
26	18.3	Cocke County SD	Newport
27	18.2	Mcminn County SD	Athens
28	18.1	Jackson County SD	Gainsboro
28	18.1	Johnson County SD	Mountain City
28	18.1	Lawrence County SD	Lawrenceburg
28	18.1	Maury County SD	Columbia
28	18.1	Sequatchie County SD	Dunlap
33	18.0	Kingsport City SD	Kingsport
34	17.8	Hardeman County SD	Bolivar
35	17.7	Wayne County SD	Waynesboro
36	17.5	Tipton County SD	Covington
37	17.3	Marshall County SD	Lewisburg
38	17.2	Benton County SD	Camden
38	17.2	Hickman County SD	Centerville
40	17.1	Hamilton County SD	Chattanooga
40	17.1	Jefferson County SD	Dandridge
40	17.1	Morgan County SD	Wartburg
43	17.0	Roane County SD	Kingston
44	16.9	Grainger County SD	Rutledge
45	16.8	Coffee County SD	Manchester
45	16.8	Obion County SD	Union City
47	16.7	Anderson County SD	Clinton
47	16.7	Hardin County SD	Savannah
49	16.6	Blount County SD	Maryville
50	16.5	Cannon County SD	Woodbury
51	16.4	Johnson City SD	Johnson City
52	16.3	Cumberland County SD	Crossville
53	16.1	Franklin County SD	Winchester
53	16.1	White County SD	Sparta
55	15.8	Dyersburg City SD	Dyersburg
56	15.7	Haywood County SD	Brownsville
56	15.7	Nashville-Davidson County SD	Nashville
58	15.6	Lebanon City Elementary SD	Lebanon
58	15.6	Meigs County SD	Decatur
60	15.5	Scott County SD	Huntsville
61	15.4	Elizabethton City SD	Elizabethton
61	15.4	Henderson County SD	Lexington
61	15.4	Henry County SD	Paris
64	15.3	Cleveland City SD	Cleveland
64	15.3	Crockett County SD	Alamo
66	15.2	Bedford County SD	Shelbyville
66	15.2	Bristol City SD	Bristol
68	15.1	Sevier County SD	Sevierville
68	15.1	Weakley County SD	Dresden
70	15.0	Lewis County SD	Hohenwald
70	15.0	Rutherford County SD	Murfreesboro
72	14.9	Carter County SD	Elizabethton
73	14.7	Fayette County SD	Somerville
73	14.7	Gibson Special District	Dyer
73	14.7	Maryville City SD	Maryville
76	14.6	Franklin City Elementary SD	Franklin
77	14.4	Smith County SD	Carthage
78	14.2	Williamson County SD	Franklin
79	14.1	Giles County SD	Pulaski
80	13.9	Fentress County SD	Jamestown
81	13.8	Campbell County SD	Jacksboro
81	13.8	Milan City Special SD	Milan
83	13.7	Marion County SD	Jasper
84	13.5	Montgomery County Schools	Clarksville
85	13.4	Macon County SD	Lafayette
85	13.4	Monroe County SD	Madisonville
87	13.3	Hamblen County SD	Morristown
87	13.3	Humphreys County SD	Waverly
89	13.0	Washington County SD	Jonesborough
90	12.9	Knox County SD	Knoxville
91	12.8	Wilson County SD	Lebanon
92	12.5	Mcnairy County SD	Selmer
93	12.3	Memphis City SD	Memphis
93	12.3	Murfreesboro City Elem SD	Murfreesboro
95	12.1	Cheatham County SD	Ashland City
96	11.6	Lenoir City SD	Lenoir City
97	11.4	Lincoln County SD	Fayetteville
97	11.4	Polk County SD	Benton
99	11.0	Rhea County SD	Dayton
100	10.9	Loudon County SD	Loudon
101	10.8	Bradley County SD	Cleveland
102	10.2	Chester County SD	Henderson
103	n/a	South and Eastern States Agency	Arlington

English Language Learner Students

Rank	Percent	District Name	City
1	n/a	Anderson County SD	Clinton
1	n/a	Athens City Elementary SD	Athens
1	n/a	Bedford County SD	Shelbyville
1	n/a	Benton County SD	Camden
1	n/a	Bledsoe County SD	Pikeville
1	n/a	Blount County SD	Maryville
1	n/a	Bradley County SD	Cleveland
1	n/a	Bristol City SD	Bristol
1	n/a	Campbell County SD	Jacksboro
1	n/a	Cannon County SD	Woodbury
1	n/a	Carter County SD	Elizabethton
1	n/a	Cheatham County SD	Ashland City
1	n/a	Chester County SD	Henderson
1	n/a	Claiborne County SD	Tazewell
1	n/a	Cleveland City SD	Cleveland
1	n/a	Cocke County SD	Newport
1	n/a	Coffee County SD	Manchester
1	n/a	Crockett County SD	Alamo
1	n/a	Cumberland County SD	Crossville
1	n/a	Dekalb County SD	Smithville
1	n/a	Dickson County SD	Dickson
1	n/a	Dyer County SD	Dyersburg
1	n/a	Dyersburg City SD	Dyersburg
1	n/a	Elizabethton City SD	Elizabethton
1	n/a	Fayette County SD	Somerville
1	n/a	Fentress County SD	Jamestown
1	n/a	Franklin City Elementary SD	Franklin
1	n/a	Franklin County SD	Winchester
1	n/a	Gibson Special District	Dyer
1	n/a	Giles County SD	Pulaski
1	n/a	Grainger County SD	Rutledge
1	n/a	Greene County SD	Greeneville
1	n/a	Greeneville City SD	Greeneville
1	n/a	Grundy County SD	Altamont
1	n/a	Hamblen County SD	Morristown
1	n/a	Hamilton County SD	Chattanooga
1	n/a	Hardeman County SD	Bolivar
1	n/a	Hardin County SD	Savannah
1	n/a	Hawkins County SD	Rogersville
1	n/a	Haywood County SD	Brownsville
1	n/a	Henderson County SD	Lexington
1	n/a	Henry County SD	Paris
1	n/a	Hickman County SD	Centerville
1	n/a	Humboldt City SD	Humboldt
1	n/a	Humphreys County SD	Waverly
1	n/a	Jackson County SD	Gainsboro
1	n/a	Jackson-Madison Consolidated	Jackson
1	n/a	Jefferson County SD	Dandridge
1	n/a	Johnson City SD	Johnson City
1	n/a	Johnson County SD	Mountain City
1	n/a	Kingsport City SD	Kingsport
1	n/a	Knox County SD	Knoxville
1	n/a	Lauderdale County SD	Ripley
1	n/a	Lawrence County SD	Lawrenceburg
1	n/a	Lebanon City Elementary SD	Lebanon
1	n/a	Lenoir City SD	Lenoir City
1	n/a	Lewis County SD	Hohenwald
1	n/a	Lincoln County SD	Fayetteville
1	n/a	Loudon County SD	Loudon
1	n/a	Macon County SD	Lafayette
1	n/a	Marion County SD	Jasper
1	n/a	Marshall County SD	Lewisburg
1	n/a	Maryville City SD	Maryville
1	n/a	Maury County SD	Columbia
1	n/a	Mcminn County SD	Athens
1	n/a	Mcnairy County SD	Selmer
1	n/a	Meigs County SD	Decatur
1	n/a	Memphis City SD	Memphis
1	n/a	Milan City Special SD	Milan
1	n/a	Monroe County SD	Madisonville
1	n/a	Montgomery County Schools	Clarksville
1	n/a	Morgan County SD	Wartburg
1	n/a	Murfreesboro City Elem SD	Murfreesboro
1	n/a	Nashville-Davidson County SD	Nashville
1	n/a	Oak Ridge City SD	Oak Ridge
1	n/a	Obion County SD	Union City
1	n/a	Overton County SD	Livingston
1	n/a	Polk County SD	Benton
1	n/a	Putnam County SD	Cookeville
1	n/a	Rhea County SD	Dayton
1	n/a	Roane County SD	Kingston
1	n/a	Robertson County SD	Springfield
1	n/a	Rutherford County SD	Murfreesboro
1	n/a	Scott County SD	Huntsville
1	n/a	Sequatchie County SD	Dunlap
1	n/a	Sevier County SD	Sevierville
1	n/a	Shelby County SD	Memphis
1	n/a	Smith County SD	Carthage
1	n/a	South and Eastern States Agency	Arlington
1	n/a	Stewart County SD	Dover
1	n/a	Sullivan County SD	Blountville
1	n/a	Sumner County SD	Gallatin
1	n/a	Tipton County SD	Covington
1	n/a	Tullahoma City SD	Tullahoma
1	n/a	Unicoi SD	Erwin
1	n/a	Union County SD	Maynardville
1	n/a	Warren County SD	Mcminnville
1	n/a	Washington County SD	Jonesborough
1	n/a	Wayne County SD	Waynesboro
1	n/a	Weakley County SD	Dresden
1	n/a	White County SD	Sparta
1	n/a	Williamson County SD	Franklin
1	n/a	Wilson County SD	Lebanon

Migrant Students

Rank	Percent	District Name	City
1	n/a	Anderson County SD	Clinton
1	n/a	Athens City Elementary SD	Athens
1	n/a	Bedford County SD	Shelbyville
1	n/a	Benton County SD	Camden
1	n/a	Bledsoe County SD	Pikeville
1	n/a	Blount County SD	Maryville
1	n/a	Bradley County SD	Cleveland
1	n/a	Bristol City SD	Bristol
1	n/a	Campbell County SD	Jacksboro
1	n/a	Cannon County SD	Woodbury
1	n/a	Carter County SD	Elizabethton
1	n/a	Cheatham County SD	Ashland City
1	n/a	Chester County SD	Henderson
1	n/a	Claiborne County SD	Tazewell
1	n/a	Cleveland City SD	Cleveland
1	n/a	Cocke County SD	Newport
1	n/a	Coffee County SD	Manchester
1	n/a	Crockett County SD	Alamo
1	n/a	Cumberland County SD	Crossville
1	n/a	Dekalb County SD	Smithville
1	n/a	Dickson County SD	Dickson
1	n/a	Dyer County SD	Dyersburg
1	n/a	Dyersburg City SD	Dyersburg
1	n/a	Elizabethton City SD	Elizabethton
1	n/a	Fayette County SD	Somerville
1	n/a	Fentress County SD	Jamestown
1	n/a	Franklin City Elementary SD	Franklin
1	n/a	Franklin County SD	Winchester
1	n/a	Gibson Special District	Dyer
1	n/a	Giles County SD	Pulaski
1	n/a	Grainger County SD	Rutledge
1	n/a	Greene County SD	Greeneville
1	n/a	Greeneville City SD	Greeneville
1	n/a	Grundy County SD	Altamont
1	n/a	Hamblen County SD	Morristown
1	n/a	Hamilton County SD	Chattanooga
1	n/a	Hardeman County SD	Bolivar
1	n/a	Hardin County SD	Savannah
1	n/a	Hawkins County SD	Rogersville
1	n/a	Haywood County SD	Brownsville
1	n/a	Henderson County SD	Lexington
1	n/a	Henry County SD	Paris
1	n/a	Hickman County SD	Centerville
1	n/a	Humboldt City SD	Humboldt
1	n/a	Humphreys County SD	Waverly
1	n/a	Jackson County SD	Gainsboro
1	n/a	Jackson-Madison Consolidated	Jackson
1	n/a	Jefferson County SD	Dandridge
1	n/a	Johnson City SD	Johnson City
1	n/a	Johnson County SD	Mountain City
1	n/a	Kingsport City SD	Kingsport
1	n/a	Knox County SD	Knoxville
1	n/a	Lauderdale County SD	Ripley
1	n/a	Lawrence County SD	Lawrenceburg
1	n/a	Lebanon City Elementary SD	Lebanon
1	n/a	Lenoir City SD	Lenoir City
1	n/a	Lewis County SD	Hohenwald
1	n/a	Lincoln County SD	Fayetteville
1	n/a	Loudon County SD	Loudon
1	n/a	Macon County SD	Lafayette
1	n/a	Marion County SD	Jasper
1	n/a	Marshall County SD	Lewisburg
1	n/a	Maryville City SD	Maryville
1	n/a	Maury County SD	Columbia
1	n/a	Mcminn County SD	Athens
1	n/a	Mcnairy County SD	Selmer
1	n/a	Meigs County SD	Decatur
1	n/a	Memphis City SD	Memphis
1	n/a	Milan City Special SD	Milan
1	n/a	Monroe County SD	Madisonville
1	n/a	Montgomery County Schools	Clarksville
1	n/a	Morgan County SD	Wartburg
1	n/a	Murfreesboro City Elem SD	Murfreesboro
1	n/a	Nashville-Davidson County SD	Nashville
1	n/a	Oak Ridge City SD	Oak Ridge
1	n/a	Obion County SD	Union City
1	n/a	Overton County SD	Livingston
1	n/a	Polk County SD	Benton
1	n/a	Putnam County SD	Cookeville
1	n/a	Rhea County SD	Dayton
1	n/a	Roane County SD	Kingston
1	n/a	Robertson County SD	Springfield
1	n/a	Rutherford County SD	Murfreesboro
1	n/a	Scott County SD	Huntsville

1	n/a	Sequatchie County SD	Dunlap
1	n/a	Sevier County SD	Sevierville
1	n/a	Shelby County SD	Memphis
1	n/a	Smith County SD	Carthage
1	n/a	South and Eastern States Agency	Arlington
1	n/a	Stewart County SD	Dover
1	n/a	Sullivan County SD	Blountville
1	n/a	Sumner County SD	Gallatin
1	n/a	Tipton County SD	Covington
1	n/a	Tullahoma City SD	Tullahoma
1	n/a	Unicoi SD	Erwin
1	n/a	Union County SD	Maynardville
1	n/a	Warren County SD	Mcminnville
1	n/a	Washington County SD	Jonesborough
1	n/a	Wayne County SD	Waynesboro
1	n/a	Weakley County SD	Dresden
1	n/a	White County SD	Sparta
1	n/a	Williamson County SD	Franklin
1	n/a	Wilson County SD	Lebanon

Students Eligible for Free Lunch

Rank	Percent	District Name	City
1	n/a	Anderson County SD	Clinton
1	n/a	Athens City Elementary SD	Athens
1	n/a	Bedford County SD	Shelbyville
1	n/a	Benton County SD	Camden
1	n/a	Bledsoe County SD	Pikeville
1	n/a	Blount County SD	Maryville
1	n/a	Bradley County SD	Cleveland
1	n/a	Bristol City SD	Bristol
1	n/a	Campbell County SD	Jacksboro
1	n/a	Cannon County SD	Woodbury
1	n/a	Carter County SD	Elizabethton
1	n/a	Cheatham County SD	Ashland City
1	n/a	Chester County SD	Henderson
1	n/a	Claiborne County SD	Tazewell
1	n/a	Cleveland City SD	Cleveland
1	n/a	Cocke County SD	Newport
1	n/a	Coffee County SD	Manchester
1	n/a	Crockett County SD	Alamo
1	n/a	Cumberland County SD	Crossville
1	n/a	Dekalb County SD	Smithville
1	n/a	Dickson County SD	Dickson
1	n/a	Dyer County SD	Dyersburg
1	n/a	Dyersburg City SD	Dyersburg
1	n/a	Elizabethton City SD	Elizabethton
1	n/a	Fayette County SD	Somerville
1	n/a	Fentress County SD	Jamestown
1	n/a	Franklin City Elementary SD	Franklin
1	n/a	Franklin County SD	Winchester
1	n/a	Gibson Special District	Dyer
1	n/a	Giles County SD	Pulaski
1	n/a	Grainger County SD	Rutledge
1	n/a	Greene County SD	Greeneville
1	n/a	Greeneville City SD	Greeneville
1	n/a	Grundy County SD	Altamont
1	n/a	Hamblen County SD	Morristown
1	n/a	Hamilton County SD	Chattanooga
1	n/a	Hardeman County SD	Bolivar
1	n/a	Hardin County SD	Savannah
1	n/a	Hawkins County SD	Rogersville
1	n/a	Haywood County SD	Brownsville
1	n/a	Henderson County SD	Lexington
1	n/a	Henry County SD	Paris
1	n/a	Hickman County SD	Centerville
1	n/a	Humboldt City SD	Humboldt
1	n/a	Humphreys County SD	Waverly
1	n/a	Jackson County SD	Gainsboro
1	n/a	Jackson-Madison Consolidated	Jackson
1	n/a	Jefferson County SD	Dandridge
1	n/a	Johnson City SD	Johnson City
1	n/a	Johnson County SD	Mountain City
1	n/a	Kingsport City SD	Kingsport
1	n/a	Knox County SD	Knoxville
1	n/a	Lauderdale County SD	Ripley
1	n/a	Lawrence County SD	Lawrenceburg
1	n/a	Lebanon City Elementary SD	Lebanon
1	n/a	Lenoir City SD	Lenoir City
1	n/a	Lewis County SD	Hohenwald
1	n/a	Lincoln County SD	Fayetteville
1	n/a	Loudon County SD	Loudon
1	n/a	Macon County SD	Lafayette
1	n/a	Marion County SD	Jasper
1	n/a	Marshall County SD	Lewisburg
1	n/a	Maryville City SD	Maryville
1	n/a	Maury County SD	Columbia
1	n/a	Mcminn County SD	Athens
1	n/a	Mcnairy County SD	Selmer
1	n/a	Meigs County SD	Decatur
1	n/a	Memphis City SD	Memphis
1	n/a	Milan City Special SD	Milan
1	n/a	Monroe County SD	Madisonville
1	n/a	Montgomery County Schools	Clarksville
1	n/a	Morgan County SD	Wartburg
1	n/a	Murfreesboro City Elem SD	Murfreesboro
1	n/a	Nashville-Davidson County SD	Nashville
1	n/a	Oak Ridge City SD	Oak Ridge
1	n/a	Obion County SD	Union City
1	n/a	Overton County SD	Livingston
1	n/a	Polk County SD	Benton
1	n/a	Putnam County SD	Cookeville
1	n/a	Rhea County SD	Dayton
1	n/a	Roane County SD	Kingston
1	n/a	Robertson County SD	Springfield
1	n/a	Rutherford County SD	Murfreesboro
1	n/a	Scott County SD	Huntsville
1	n/a	Sequatchie County SD	Dunlap
1	n/a	Sevier County SD	Sevierville
1	n/a	Shelby County SD	Memphis
1	n/a	Smith County SD	Carthage
1	n/a	South and Eastern States Agency	Arlington
1	n/a	Stewart County SD	Dover
1	n/a	Sullivan County SD	Blountville
1	n/a	Sumner County SD	Gallatin
1	n/a	Tipton County SD	Covington
1	n/a	Tullahoma City SD	Tullahoma
1	n/a	Unicoi SD	Erwin
1	n/a	Union County SD	Maynardville
1	n/a	Warren County SD	Mcminnville
1	n/a	Washington County SD	Jonesborough
1	n/a	Wayne County SD	Waynesboro
1	n/a	Weakley County SD	Dresden
1	n/a	White County SD	Sparta
1	n/a	Williamson County SD	Franklin
1	n/a	Wilson County SD	Lebanon

Students Eligible for Reduced-Price Lunch

Rank	Percent	District Name	City
1	n/a	Anderson County SD	Clinton
1	n/a	Athens City Elementary SD	Athens
1	n/a	Bedford County SD	Shelbyville
1	n/a	Benton County SD	Camden
1	n/a	Bledsoe County SD	Pikeville
1	n/a	Blount County SD	Maryville
1	n/a	Bradley County SD	Cleveland
1	n/a	Bristol City SD	Bristol
1	n/a	Campbell County SD	Jacksboro
1	n/a	Cannon County SD	Woodbury
1	n/a	Carter County SD	Elizabethton
1	n/a	Cheatham County SD	Ashland City
1	n/a	Chester County SD	Henderson
1	n/a	Claiborne County SD	Tazewell
1	n/a	Cleveland City SD	Cleveland
1	n/a	Cocke County SD	Newport
1	n/a	Coffee County SD	Manchester
1	n/a	Crockett County SD	Alamo
1	n/a	Cumberland County SD	Crossville
1	n/a	Dekalb County SD	Smithville
1	n/a	Dickson County SD	Dickson
1	n/a	Dyer County SD	Dyersburg
1	n/a	Dyersburg City SD	Dyersburg
1	n/a	Elizabethton City SD	Elizabethton
1	n/a	Fayette County SD	Somerville
1	n/a	Fentress County SD	Jamestown
1	n/a	Franklin City Elementary SD	Franklin
1	n/a	Franklin County SD	Winchester
1	n/a	Gibson Special District	Dyer
1	n/a	Giles County SD	Pulaski
1	n/a	Grainger County SD	Rutledge
1	n/a	Greene County SD	Greeneville
1	n/a	Greeneville City SD	Greeneville
1	n/a	Grundy County SD	Altamont
1	n/a	Hamblen County SD	Morristown
1	n/a	Hamilton County SD	Chattanooga
1	n/a	Hardeman County SD	Bolivar
1	n/a	Hardin County SD	Savannah
1	n/a	Hawkins County SD	Rogersville
1	n/a	Haywood County SD	Brownsville
1	n/a	Henderson County SD	Lexington
1	n/a	Henry County SD	Paris
1	n/a	Hickman County SD	Centerville
1	n/a	Humboldt City SD	Humboldt
1	n/a	Humphreys County SD	Waverly
1	n/a	Jackson County SD	Gainsboro
1	n/a	Jackson-Madison Consolidated	Jackson
1	n/a	Jefferson County SD	Dandridge
1	n/a	Johnson City SD	Johnson City
1	n/a	Johnson County SD	Mountain City
1	n/a	Kingsport City SD	Kingsport
1	n/a	Knox County SD	Knoxville
1	n/a	Lauderdale County SD	Ripley
1	n/a	Lawrence County SD	Lawrenceburg
1	n/a	Lebanon City Elementary SD	Lebanon
1	n/a	Lenoir City SD	Lenoir City
1	n/a	Lewis County SD	Hohenwald
1	n/a	Lincoln County SD	Fayetteville
1	n/a	Loudon County SD	Loudon
1	n/a	Macon County SD	Lafayette
1	n/a	Marion County SD	Jasper
1	n/a	Marshall County SD	Lewisburg
1	n/a	Maryville City SD	Maryville
1	n/a	Maury County SD	Columbia
1	n/a	Mcminn County SD	Athens
1	n/a	Mcnairy County SD	Selmer
1	n/a	Meigs County SD	Decatur
1	n/a	Memphis City SD	Memphis
1	n/a	Milan City Special SD	Milan
1	n/a	Monroe County SD	Madisonville
1	n/a	Montgomery County Schools	Clarksville
1	n/a	Morgan County SD	Wartburg
1	n/a	Murfreesboro City Elem SD	Murfreesboro
1	n/a	Nashville-Davidson County SD	Nashville
1	n/a	Oak Ridge City SD	Oak Ridge
1	n/a	Obion County SD	Union City
1	n/a	Overton County SD	Livingston
1	n/a	Polk County SD	Benton
1	n/a	Putnam County SD	Cookeville
1	n/a	Rhea County SD	Dayton
1	n/a	Roane County SD	Kingston
1	n/a	Robertson County SD	Springfield
1	n/a	Rutherford County SD	Murfreesboro
1	n/a	Scott County SD	Huntsville
1	n/a	Sequatchie County SD	Dunlap
1	n/a	Sevier County SD	Sevierville
1	n/a	Shelby County SD	Memphis
1	n/a	Smith County SD	Carthage
1	n/a	South and Eastern States Agency	Arlington
1	n/a	Stewart County SD	Dover
1	n/a	Sullivan County SD	Blountville
1	n/a	Sumner County SD	Gallatin
1	n/a	Tipton County SD	Covington
1	n/a	Tullahoma City SD	Tullahoma
1	n/a	Unicoi SD	Erwin
1	n/a	Union County SD	Maynardville
1	n/a	Warren County SD	Mcminnville
1	n/a	Washington County SD	Jonesborough
1	n/a	Wayne County SD	Waynesboro
1	n/a	Weakley County SD	Dresden
1	n/a	White County SD	Sparta
1	n/a	Williamson County SD	Franklin
1	n/a	Wilson County SD	Lebanon

Student/Teacher Ratio

Rank	Ratio	District Name	City
1	18.6	Oak Ridge City SD	Oak Ridge
2	17.6	Loudon County SD	Loudon
3	17.5	Chester County SD	Henderson
3	17.5	Shelby County SD	Memphis
5	17.1	Mcminn County SD	Athens
6	16.9	Gibson Special District	Dyer
6	16.9	Stewart County SD	Dover
6	16.9	Wilson County SD	Lebanon
9	16.8	Bradley County SD	Cleveland
9	16.8	Tipton County SD	Covington
11	16.7	Blount County SD	Maryville
12	16.6	Cumberland County SD	Crossville
12	16.6	Monroe County SD	Madisonville
12	16.6	Washington County SD	Jonesborough
15	16.4	Memphis City SD	Memphis
15	16.4	Unicoi SD	Erwin
17	16.3	Grainger County SD	Rutledge
17	16.3	Marshall County SD	Lewisburg
17	16.3	Montgomery County Schools	Clarksville
17	16.3	Putnam County SD	Cookeville
21	16.2	Rutherford County SD	Murfreesboro
21	16.2	Tullahoma City SD	Tullahoma
21	16.2	Williamson County SD	Franklin
24	16.1	Dyersburg City SD	Dyersburg
24	16.1	Hickman County SD	Centerville
24	16.1	Macon County SD	Lafayette
24	16.1	Polk County SD	Benton
24	16.1	Smith County SD	Carthage
29	16.0	Bedford County SD	Shelbyville
29	16.0	Lenoir City SD	Lenoir City
31	15.8	Athens City Elementary SD	Athens
31	15.8	Henry County SD	Paris
31	15.8	Meigs County SD	Decatur
31	15.8	Rhea County SD	Dayton
35	15.7	Cheatham County SD	Ashland City
35	15.7	Dyer County SD	Dyersburg
35	15.7	Franklin County SD	Winchester
35	15.7	White County SD	Sparta
39	15.6	Jefferson County SD	Dandridge
39	15.6	Obion County SD	Union City

Rank	Ratio	District Name	City
39	15.6	Roane County SD	Kingston
42	15.5	Crockett County SD	Alamo
42	15.5	Greene County SD	Greeneville
42	15.5	Marion County SD	Jasper
45	15.4	Dickson County SD	Dickson
45	15.4	Johnson City SD	Johnson City
45	15.4	Lauderdale County SD	Ripley
45	15.4	Maryville City SD	Maryville
49	15.3	Sevier County SD	Sevierville
49	15.3	Weakley County SD	Dresden
51	15.2	Giles County SD	Pulaski
51	15.2	Hamilton County SD	Chattanooga
51	15.2	Humphreys County SD	Waverly
54	15.1	Cocke County SD	Newport
54	15.1	Lebanon City Elementary SD	Lebanon
54	15.1	Lewis County SD	Hohenwald
57	15.0	Hamblen County SD	Morristown
57	15.0	Lincoln County SD	Fayetteville
57	15.0	Murfreesboro City Elem SD	Murfreesboro
57	15.0	Sequatchie County SD	Dunlap
61	14.9	Knox County SD	Knoxville
61	14.9	Robertson County SD	Springfield
61	14.9	Sumner County SD	Gallatin
61	14.9	Warren County SD	Mcminnville
65	14.8	Coffee County SD	Manchester
65	14.8	Johnson County SD	Mountain City
67	14.7	Lawrence County SD	Lawrenceburg
67	14.7	Maury County SD	Columbia
67	14.7	Nashville-Davidson County SD	Nashville
70	14.6	Bledsoe County SD	Pikeville
70	14.6	Bristol City SD	Bristol
70	14.6	Campbell County SD	Jacksboro
70	14.6	Cleveland City SD	Cleveland
70	14.6	Kingsport City SD	Kingsport
70	14.6	Mcnairy County SD	Selmer
76	14.5	Jackson-Madison Consolidated	Jackson
76	14.5	Milan City Special SD	Milan
78	14.4	Dekalb County SD	Smithville
78	14.4	Haywood County SD	Brownsville
78	14.4	Henderson County SD	Lexington
78	14.4	Humboldt City SD	Humboldt
82	14.3	Hardin County SD	Savannah
82	14.3	Hawkins County SD	Rogersville
82	14.3	Overton County SD	Livingston
82	14.3	Union County SD	Maynardville
86	14.2	Sullivan County SD	Blountville
87	14.1	Cannon County SD	Woodbury
87	14.1	Elizabethton City SD	Elizabethton
89	14.0	Fentress County SD	Jamestown
90	13.9	Anderson County SD	Clinton
90	13.9	Benton County SD	Camden
90	13.9	Morgan County SD	Wartburg
90	13.9	Wayne County SD	Waynesboro
94	13.8	Hardeman County SD	Bolivar
95	13.7	Jackson County SD	Gainsboro
96	13.6	Greeneville City SD	Greeneville
97	13.2	Carter County SD	Elizabethton
98	13.1	Claiborne County SD	Tazewell
99	12.9	Fayette County SD	Somerville
100	12.8	Franklin City Elementary SD	Franklin
100	12.8	Scott County SD	Huntsville
102	12.6	Grundy County SD	Altamont
103	n/a	South and Eastern States Agency	Arlington

Student/Librarian Ratio

Rank	Ratio	District Name	City
1	1,132.0	Grundy County SD	Altamont
2	1,054.3	Dyer County SD	Dyersburg
3	1,052.0	Cannon County SD	Woodbury
4	1,038.7	Union County SD	Maynardville
5	1,009.4	Tipton County SD	Covington
6	964.0	Rhea County SD	Dayton
7	925.5	Meigs County SD	Decatur
8	865.0	Crockett County SD	Alamo
9	836.0	Polk County SD	Benton
10	814.3	Cumberland County SD	Crossville
11	811.4	Shelby County SD	Memphis
12	784.3	Smith County SD	Carthage
13	765.2	Greene County SD	Greeneville
14	764.8	Rutherford County SD	Murfreesboro
15	762.2	Robertson County SD	Springfield
16	762.1	Johnson City SD	Johnson City
17	758.1	Wilson County SD	Lebanon
18	730.4	Memphis City SD	Memphis
19	722.9	Montgomery County Schools	Clarksville
20	698.0	Dyersburg City SD	Dyersburg
21	697.0	Stewart County SD	Dover
22	671.7	Lenoir City SD	Lenoir City
23	661.6	Grainger County SD	Rutledge
24	642.0	Overton County SD	Livingston
25	641.0	Sequatchie County SD	Dunlap
26	628.6	Henry County SD	Paris
27	626.6	Morgan County SD	Wartburg
28	622.7	Maryville City SD	Maryville
29	621.6	Sevier County SD	Sevierville
30	613.1	Sumner County SD	Gallatin
31	610.7	Claiborne County SD	Tazewell
32	609.5	Chester County SD	Henderson
33	608.7	Jefferson County SD	Dandridge
34	608.3	Williamson County SD	Franklin
35	596.6	Nashville-Davidson County SD	Nashville
36	595.9	Bedford County SD	Shelbyville
37	594.8	Knox County SD	Knoxville
38	590.2	Lebanon City Elementary SD	Lebanon
39	588.0	Bledsoe County SD	Pikeville
40	586.2	Blount County SD	Maryville
41	586.1	Mcminn County SD	Athens
42	583.7	Murfreesboro City Elem SD	Murfreesboro
43	574.2	Dickson County SD	Dickson
44	573.6	Obion County SD	Union City
45	572.3	Lauderdale County SD	Ripley
46	571.3	Fentress County SD	Jamestown
47	566.5	Maury County SD	Columbia
48	564.1	Hardeman County SD	Bolivar
49	558.5	Warren County SD	Mcminnville
50	554.6	Washington County SD	Jonesborough
51	549.6	White County SD	Sparta
52	548.3	Hickman County SD	Centerville
53	547.6	Monroe County SD	Madisonville
53	547.6	Weakley County SD	Dresden
55	546.0	Jackson County SD	Gainsboro
56	543.6	Oak Ridge City SD	Oak Ridge
57	539.8	Bradley County SD	Cleveland
58	539.6	Roane County SD	Kingston
59	539.0	Coffee County SD	Manchester
60	537.0	Franklin City Elementary SD	Franklin
61	535.7	Marshall County SD	Lewisburg
62	535.2	Loudon County SD	Loudon
63	532.3	Kingsport City SD	Kingsport
64	531.1	Putnam County SD	Cookeville
65	528.8	Cheatham County SD	Ashland City
66	523.8	Scott County SD	Huntsville
67	518.8	Dekalb County SD	Smithville
68	518.1	Mcnairy County SD	Selmer
69	516.8	Lewis County SD	Hohenwald
70	515.4	Lawrence County SD	Lawrenceburg
71	506.6	Jackson-Madison Consolidated	Jackson
72	505.4	Macon County SD	Lafayette
73	504.7	Haywood County SD	Brownsville
74	503.3	Humphreys County SD	Waverly
75	501.4	Hamilton County SD	Chattanooga
76	500.2	Unicoi SD	Erwin
77	499.3	Milan City Special SD	Milan
78	498.8	Anderson County SD	Clinton
79	494.0	Cocke County SD	Newport
80	493.6	Campbell County SD	Jacksboro
81	492.8	Benton County SD	Camden
82	491.9	Carter County SD	Elizabethton
83	487.1	Franklin County SD	Winchester
84	478.4	Marion County SD	Jasper
85	474.8	Hardin County SD	Savannah
86	472.7	Hamblen County SD	Morristown
87	457.4	Johnson County SD	Mountain City
88	452.6	Tullahoma City SD	Tullahoma
89	452.3	Hawkins County SD	Rogersville
90	451.0	Wayne County SD	Waynesboro
91	450.4	Giles County SD	Pulaski
92	446.6	Cleveland City SD	Cleveland
93	442.5	Gibson Special District	Dyer
94	437.7	Greeneville City SD	Greeneville
95	434.9	Sullivan County SD	Blountville
96	417.3	Lincoln County SD	Fayetteville
97	400.3	Bristol City SD	Bristol
98	397.0	Fayette County SD	Somerville
99	383.5	Humboldt City SD	Humboldt
100	382.0	Henderson County SD	Lexington
101	364.5	Elizabethton City SD	Elizabethton
102	336.8	Athens City Elementary SD	Athens
103	n/a	South and Eastern States Agency	Arlington

Student/Counselor Ratio

Rank	Ratio	District Name	City
1	836.0	Polk County SD	Benton
2	784.3	Smith County SD	Carthage
3	779.0	Union County SD	Maynardville
4	742.0	Roane County SD	Kingston
5	697.0	Stewart County SD	Dover
6	677.2	Lewis County SD	Hohenwald
7	663.8	Gibson Special District	Dyer
8	661.6	Grainger County SD	Rutledge
9	656.2	Cumberland County SD	Crossville
10	654.8	Scott County SD	Huntsville
11	642.7	Rhea County SD	Dayton
12	641.0	Sequatchie County SD	Dunlap
13	636.6	Monroe County SD	Madisonville
14	632.6	Dyer County SD	Dyersburg
15	625.3	Unicoi SD	Erwin
16	609.5	Chester County SD	Henderson
17	602.1	Loudon County SD	Loudon
18	596.1	Knox County SD	Knoxville
19	592.1	Mcnairy County SD	Selmer
20	590.2	Lebanon City Elementary SD	Lebanon
21	589.7	Macon County SD	Lafayette
22	588.0	Bledsoe County SD	Pikeville
23	586.4	Campbell County SD	Jacksboro
24	586.1	Mcminn County SD	Athens
25	571.8	Johnson County SD	Mountain City
26	571.3	Fentress County SD	Jamestown
27	566.0	Grundy County SD	Altamont
28	560.8	Tipton County SD	Covington
29	546.0	Jackson County SD	Gainsboro
30	541.2	Wayne County SD	Waynesboro
31	535.7	Marshall County SD	Lewisburg
32	530.3	Memphis City SD	Memphis
33	529.8	Greene County SD	Greeneville
34	522.2	Morgan County SD	Wartburg
35	519.4	Lawrence County SD	Lawrenceburg
36	518.8	Dekalb County SD	Smithville
37	505.6	Washington County SD	Jonesborough
38	505.3	Robertson County SD	Springfield
39	504.7	Haywood County SD	Brownsville
40	503.3	Humphreys County SD	Waverly
41	498.6	Dyersburg City SD	Dyersburg
42	495.5	Lincoln County SD	Fayetteville
43	491.9	Carter County SD	Elizabethton
44	491.3	Kingsport City SD	Kingsport
45	491.2	Shelby County SD	Memphis
46	490.5	Hamilton County SD	Chattanooga
46	490.5	Murfreesboro City Elem SD	Murfreesboro
46	490.5	Sumner County SD	Gallatin
49	488.2	Hamblen County SD	Morristown
50	484.3	Dickson County SD	Dickson
51	479.8	Hickman County SD	Centerville
52	477.5	Nashville-Davidson County SD	Nashville
53	477.2	Montgomery County Schools	Clarksville
54	476.6	Rutherford County SD	Murfreesboro
55	469.3	Cocke County SD	Newport
56	468.2	Bedford County SD	Shelbyville
57	467.6	Franklin County SD	Winchester
58	467.1	Fayette County SD	Somerville
59	463.9	Hawkins County SD	Rogersville
60	462.8	Meigs County SD	Decatur
61	461.1	Sevier County SD	Sevierville
62	458.9	Bradley County SD	Cleveland
63	457.9	Maury County SD	Columbia
64	457.8	Lauderdale County SD	Ripley
65	457.3	Johnson City SD	Johnson City
66	450.0	Blount County SD	Maryville
67	446.8	Marion County SD	Jasper
68	446.1	Obion County SD	Union City
69	438.9	Warren County SD	Mcminnville
70	435.9	Maryville City SD	Maryville
71	427.5	Weakley County SD	Dresden
72	427.4	White County SD	Sparta
73	426.6	Williamson County SD	Franklin
74	421.0	Athens City Elementary SD	Athens
75	420.8	Cannon County SD	Woodbury
76	415.0	Coffee County SD	Manchester
77	410.3	Hardeman County SD	Bolivar
78	409.5	Giles County SD	Pulaski
79	407.8	Anderson County SD	Clinton
80	404.6	Jefferson County SD	Dandridge
81	404.3	Wilson County SD	Lebanon
82	402.3	Tullahoma City SD	Tullahoma
83	401.3	Overton County SD	Livingston
84	399.4	Milan City Special SD	Milan
85	396.7	Putnam County SD	Cookeville
86	394.1	Sullivan County SD	Blountville
87	388.1	Claiborne County SD	Tazewell
88	386.4	Jackson-Madison Consolidated	Jackson
89	383.5	Humboldt City SD	Humboldt
90	382.0	Henderson County SD	Lexington
91	379.1	Benton County SD	Camden
92	375.9	Franklin City Elementary SD	Franklin
93	364.5	Elizabethton City SD	Elizabethton
94	359.9	Cheatham County SD	Ashland City
95	349.2	Henry County SD	Paris
96	346.0	Crockett County SD	Alamo
97	345.3	Hardin County SD	Savannah
98	333.2	Cleveland City SD	Cleveland
99	327.5	Bristol City SD	Bristol
100	289.9	Oak Ridge City SD	Oak Ridge
101	287.9	Lenoir City SD	Lenoir City
102	262.6	Greeneville City SD	Greeneville
103	n/a	South and Eastern States Agency	Arlington

Current Spending per Student in FY2001

Rank	Dollars	District Name	City
1	7,938	Oak Ridge City SD	Oak Ridge
2	7,584	Franklin City Elementary SD	Franklin
3	7,160	Greeneville City SD	Greeneville
4	7,061	Sullivan County SD	Blountville
5	7,001	Maryville City SD	Maryville
6	6,648	Nashville-Davidson County SD	Nashville
7	6,618	Bristol City SD	Bristol
8	6,588	Kingsport City SD	Kingsport
9	6,505	Hamilton County SD	Chattanooga
10	6,416	Johnson City SD	Johnson City
11	6,326	Memphis City SD	Memphis
12	6,209	Jackson-Madison Consolidated	Jackson
13	6,182	Williamson County SD	Franklin
14	6,082	Dekalb County SD	Smithville
15	6,021	Dyer County SD	Dyersburg
16	6,005	Anderson County SD	Clinton
17	5,963	Johnson County SD	Mountain City
18	5,950	Elizabethton City SD	Elizabethton
19	5,928	Cleveland City SD	Cleveland
20	5,811	Murfreesboro City Elem SD	Murfreesboro
21	5,803	Union County SD	Maynardville
22	5,799	Maury County SD	Columbia
23	5,763	Unicoi SD	Erwin
24	5,734	Lenoir City SD	Lenoir City
25	5,717	Dyersburg City SD	Dyersburg
26	5,701	Knox County SD	Knoxville
27	5,698	Haywood County SD	Brownsville
28	5,686	Claiborne County SD	Tazewell
29	5,677	Roane County SD	Kingston
30	5,668	Athens City Elementary SD	Athens
31	5,650	Tullahoma City SD	Tullahoma
32	5,635	Fayette County SD	Somerville
33	5,609	Lebanon City Elementary SD	Lebanon
34	5,600	Henry County SD	Paris
35	5,577	Scott County SD	Huntsville
36	5,573	Sevier County SD	Sevierville
37	5,567	Humboldt City SD	Humboldt
38	5,541	Carter County SD	Elizabethton
39	5,536	Bledsoe County SD	Pikeville
40	5,499	Franklin County SD	Winchester
41	5,489	Marshall County SD	Lewisburg
42	5,459	Wilson County SD	Lebanon
43	5,446	Blount County SD	Maryville
43	5,446	Hardin County SD	Savannah
45	5,424	Giles County SD	Pulaski
46	5,405	Benton County SD	Camden
46	5,405	Sumner County SD	Gallatin
48	5,394	Hamblen County SD	Morristown
49	5,366	Loudon County SD	Loudon
50	5,343	Rutherford County SD	Murfreesboro
51	5,342	Hawkins County SD	Rogersville
51	5,342	Polk County SD	Benton
53	5,333	Marion County SD	Jasper
54	5,280	Washington County SD	Jonesborough
55	5,277	Dickson County SD	Dickson
56	5,274	Obion County SD	Union City
57	5,262	Humphreys County SD	Waverly
58	5,259	Rhea County SD	Dayton
59	5,256	Wayne County SD	Waynesboro
60	5,249	Lauderdale County SD	Ripley
61	5,180	Cocke County SD	Newport
62	5,175	Grundy County SD	Altamont
63	5,173	Coffee County SD	Manchester
64	5,167	Campbell County SD	Jacksboro
65	5,165	Lawrence County SD	Lawrenceburg
66	5,157	Jefferson County SD	Dandridge
67	5,144	Milan City Special SD	Milan
68	5,142	Warren County SD	Mcminnville
69	5,134	Montgomery County Schools	Clarksville
70	5,130	Bradley County SD	Cleveland
71	5,126	Monroe County SD	Madisonville
72	5,108	Morgan County SD	Wartburg
73	5,103	Fentress County SD	Jamestown
74	5,094	Hickman County SD	Centerville
75	5,081	Hardeman County SD	Bolivar
76	5,069	Meigs County SD	Decatur
77	5,062	Putnam County SD	Cookeville
78	5,058	Cheatham County SD	Ashland City
79	5,054	Mcnairy County SD	Selmer
80	5,051	Shelby County SD	Memphis
81	5,037	Lincoln County SD	Fayetteville
82	5,022	Mcminn County SD	Athens
83	4,985	Greene County SD	Greeneville
84	4,973	Overton County SD	Livingston
85	4,967	Cannon County SD	Woodbury
86	4,966	Henderson County SD	Lexington
87	4,934	Weakley County SD	Dresden
88	4,917	Tipton County SD	Covington
89	4,900	Cumberland County SD	Crossville
90	4,890	Jackson County SD	Gainsboro
91	4,884	Crockett County SD	Alamo
92	4,837	Gibson Special District	Dyer
93	4,828	Bedford County SD	Shelbyville
94	4,783	Stewart County SD	Dover
95	4,775	Robertson County SD	Springfield
96	4,723	Macon County SD	Lafayette
97	4,666	Grainger County SD	Rutledge
98	4,634	Sequatchie County SD	Dunlap
99	4,585	Chester County SD	Henderson
100	4,569	Lewis County SD	Hohenwald
101	4,564	White County SD	Sparta
102	4,389	Smith County SD	Carthage
103	n/a	South and Eastern States Agency	Arlington

Number of Diploma Recipients

Rank	Number	District Name	City
1	3,933	Memphis City SD	Memphis
2	2,609	Nashville-Davidson County SD	Nashville
3	2,553	Knox County SD	Knoxville
4	2,550	Shelby County SD	Memphis
5	1,715	Hamilton County SD	Chattanooga
6	1,506	Rutherford County SD	Murfreesboro
7	1,477	Sumner County SD	Gallatin
8	1,063	Montgomery County Schools	Clarksville
9	745	Williamson County SD	Franklin
10	683	Jackson-Madison Consolidated	Jackson
11	648	Wilson County SD	Lebanon
12	614	Sevier County SD	Sevierville
13	610	Sullivan County SD	Blountville
14	522	Tipton County SD	Covington
15	509	Blount County SD	Maryville
16	490	Maury County SD	Columbia
17	434	Hamblen County SD	Morristown
18	431	Anderson County SD	Clinton
19	425	Putnam County SD	Cookeville
20	410	Robertson County SD	Springfield
21	401	Bradley County SD	Cleveland
22	396	Dickson County SD	Dickson
23	387	Washington County SD	Jonesborough
24	383	Lawrence County SD	Lawrenceburg
25	374	Jefferson County SD	Dandridge
26	351	Mcminn County SD	Athens
27	341	Warren County SD	Mcminnville
28	340	Johnson City SD	Johnson City
29	339	Greene County SD	Greeneville
30	332	Roane County SD	Kingston
31	329	Cheatham County SD	Ashland City
32	323	Hawkins County SD	Rogersville
33	306	Franklin County SD	Winchester
34	301	Cumberland County SD	Crossville
35	297	Kingsport City SD	Kingsport
36	281	Oak Ridge City SD	Oak Ridge
37	277	Cocke County SD	Newport
38	272	Bedford County SD	Shelbyville
39	270	Weakley County SD	Dresden
40	266	Lincoln County SD	Fayetteville
41	255	Campbell County SD	Jacksboro
42	254	Coffee County SD	Manchester
43	246	Marshall County SD	Lewisburg
44	243	Rhea County SD	Dayton
45	236	Tullahoma City SD	Tullahoma
46	233	Giles County SD	Pulaski
47	230	Maryville City SD	Maryville
48	221	Henry County SD	Paris
49	217	Hardin County SD	Savannah
50	206	Obion County SD	Union City
51	205	Bristol City SD	Bristol
52	202	White County SD	Sparta
53	201	Lenoir City SD	Lenoir City
54	197	Dyersburg City SD	Dyersburg
55	194	Dyer County SD	Dyersburg
56	193	Lauderdale County SD	Ripley
57	188	Macon County SD	Lafayette
57	188	Marion County SD	Jasper
59	186	Morgan County SD	Wartburg
60	185	Cleveland City SD	Cleveland
61	181	Mcnairy County SD	Selmer
61	181	Overton County SD	Livingston
63	179	Hardeman County SD	Bolivar
64	175	Hickman County SD	Centerville
65	172	Claiborne County SD	Tazewell
66	170	Grainger County SD	Rutledge
67	168	Elizabethton City SD	Elizabethton
68	162	Haywood County SD	Brownsville
69	161	Unicoi SD	Erwin
70	160	Loudon County SD	Loudon
70	160	Smith County SD	Carthage
72	159	Humphreys County SD	Waverly
73	150	Fentress County SD	Jamestown
74	149	Carter County SD	Elizabethton
75	143	Wayne County SD	Waynesboro
76	141	Crockett County SD	Alamo
77	138	Fayette County SD	Somerville
78	126	Gibson Special District	Dyer
79	125	Johnson County SD	Mountain City
80	123	Grundy County SD	Altamont
80	123	Milan City Special SD	Milan
82	121	Greeneville City SD	Greeneville
83	111	Stewart County SD	Dover
84	108	Dekalb County SD	Smithville
85	105	Chester County SD	Henderson
85	105	Union County SD	Maynardville
87	99	Cannon County SD	Woodbury
88	98	Meigs County SD	Decatur
89	97	Scott County SD	Huntsville
90	95	Benton County SD	Camden
91	94	Humboldt City SD	Humboldt
92	93	Lewis County SD	Hohenwald
93	91	Polk County SD	Benton
94	84	Monroe County SD	Madisonville
95	80	Sequatchie County SD	Dunlap
96	76	Jackson County SD	Gainsboro
97	55	Bledsoe County SD	Pikeville
97	55	Henderson County SD	Lexington
99	n/a	Athens City Elementary SD	Athens
99	n/a	Franklin City Elementary SD	Franklin
99	n/a	Lebanon City Elementary SD	Lebanon
99	n/a	Murfreesboro City Elem SD	Murfreesboro
99	n/a	South and Eastern States Agency	Arlington

High School Drop-out Rate

Rank	Percent	District Name	City
1	9.2	Memphis City SD	Memphis
2	9.1	Scott County SD	Huntsville
3	8.8	Nashville-Davidson County SD	Nashville
4	7.4	Fayette County SD	Somerville
4	7.4	Rhea County SD	Dayton
6	6.6	Humboldt City SD	Humboldt
7	6.4	Hamilton County SD	Chattanooga
8	6.3	Hawkins County SD	Rogersville
9	6.1	Lincoln County SD	Fayetteville
10	5.7	Haywood County SD	Brownsville
11	5.5	Grundy County SD	Altamont
12	5.3	Blount County SD	Maryville
13	5.2	Washington County SD	Jonesborough
14	5.1	Lauderdale County SD	Ripley
15	5.0	Johnson County SD	Mountain City
15	5.0	Sumner County SD	Gallatin
15	5.0	Wilson County SD	Lebanon
18	4.9	Hardeman County SD	Bolivar
19	4.8	Giles County SD	Pulaski
20	4.7	Bradley County SD	Cleveland
20	4.7	Hardin County SD	Savannah
22	4.6	Dekalb County SD	Smithville
22	4.6	Wayne County SD	Waynesboro
24	4.4	Dickson County SD	Dickson
25	4.3	Gibson Special District	Dyer
26	4.2	Sequatchie County SD	Dunlap
27	4.0	Franklin County SD	Winchester
28	3.9	Obion County SD	Union City
29	3.8	Henry County SD	Paris
29	3.8	Oak Ridge City SD	Oak Ridge
31	3.7	Jackson-Madison Consolidated	Jackson
32	3.6	Dyersburg City SD	Dyersburg
32	3.6	Lenoir City SD	Lenoir City
32	3.6	Robertson County SD	Springfield
32	3.6	Tipton County SD	Covington
36	3.5	Montgomery County Schools	Clarksville
37	3.4	Bedford County SD	Shelbyville
37	3.4	Bledsoe County SD	Pikeville
37	3.4	Monroe County SD	Madisonville
40	3.3	Campbell County SD	Jacksboro
40	3.3	Union County SD	Maynardville
42	3.2	Marion County SD	Jasper
42	3.2	Maury County SD	Columbia
42	3.2	Sullivan County SD	Blountville
45	3.1	Cannon County SD	Woodbury
45	3.1	Roane County SD	Kingston
45	3.1	Rutherford County SD	Murfreesboro
45	3.1	Smith County SD	Carthage
45	3.1	Stewart County SD	Dover
50	3.0	White County SD	Sparta
51	2.8	Henderson County SD	Lexington
51	2.8	Loudon County SD	Loudon
51	2.8	Sevier County SD	Sevierville
54	2.7	Hickman County SD	Centerville
54	2.7	Lawrence County SD	Lawrenceburg
56	2.6	Anderson County SD	Clinton
56	2.6	Carter County SD	Elizabethton
56	2.6	Coffee County SD	Manchester
56	2.6	Cumberland County SD	Crossville
56	2.6	Macon County SD	Lafayette
61	2.5	Mcminn County SD	Athens
62	2.4	Elizabethton City SD	Elizabethton

62	2.4	Knox County SD	Knoxville
64	2.3	Mcnairy County SD	Selmer
64	2.3	Morgan County SD	Wartburg
64	2.3	Warren County SD	Mcminnville
64	2.3	Weakley County SD	Dresden
68	2.2	Marshall County SD	Lewisburg
69	2.1	Chester County SD	Henderson
69	2.1	Claiborne County SD	Tazewell
69	2.1	Cocke County SD	Newport
72	2.0	Bristol City SD	Bristol
72	2.0	Greene County SD	Greeneville
72	2.0	Shelby County SD	Memphis
75	1.9	Overton County SD	Livingston
76	1.8	Benton County SD	Camden
77	1.7	Hamblen County SD	Morristown
77	1.7	Putnam County SD	Cookeville
77	1.7	Tullahoma City SD	Tullahoma
80	1.6	Cleveland City SD	Cleveland
80	1.6	Humphreys County SD	Waverly
80	1.6	Jefferson County SD	Dandridge
80	1.6	Kingsport City SD	Kingsport
80	1.6	Lewis County SD	Hohenwald
85	1.4	Williamson County SD	Franklin
86	1.3	Dyer County SD	Dyersburg
86	1.3	Jackson County SD	Gainsboro
86	1.3	Unicoi SD	Erwin
89	1.2	Grainger County SD	Rutledge
90	1.1	Crockett County SD	Alamo
90	1.1	Meigs County SD	Decatur
90	1.1	Milan City Special SD	Milan
93	0.9	Polk County SD	Benton
94	0.7	Fentress County SD	Jamestown
95	0.6	Maryville City SD	Maryville
96	0.5	Cheatham County SD	Ashland City
96	0.5	Greeneville City SD	Greeneville
98	0.3	Johnson City SD	Johnson City
99	0.0	Athens City Elementary SD	Athens
100	n/a	Franklin City Elementary SD	Franklin
100	n/a	Lebanon City Elementary SD	Lebanon
100	n/a	Murfreesboro City Elem SD	Murfreesboro
100	n/a	South and Eastern States Agency	Arlington

Texas

Texas Public School Educational Profile

Category	Value	Category	Value
Schools *(2002-2003)*	7,888	**Diploma Recipients** *(2002-2003)*	225,167
Instructional Level		White, Non-Hispanic	112,386
Primary	3,949	Black, Non-Hispanic	30,030
Middle	1,572	Asian/Pacific Islander	7,707
High	1,435	American Indian/Alaskan Native	578
Other Level	932	Hispanic	74,466
Curriculum		**High School Drop-out Rate** (%) *(2000-2001)*	4.2
Regular	6,819	White, Non-Hispanic	2.5
Special Education	125	Black, Non-Hispanic	5.4
Vocational	29	Asian/Pacific Islander	2.2
Alternative	915	American Indian/Alaskan Native	5.0
Type		Hispanic	6.1
Magnet	0	**Staff** *(2002-2003)*	594,014.0
Charter	263	Teachers	288,656.0
Title I Eligible	4,799	Average Salary ($)	39,972
School-wide Title I	4,236	Librarians/Media Specialists	4,876.1
Students *(2002-2003)*	4,259,823	Guidance Counselors	9,924.8
Gender (%)		**Ratios** *(2002-2003)*	
Male	51.4	Student/Teacher Ratio	14.8 to 1
Female	48.6	Student/Librarian Ratio	873.6 to 1
Race/Ethnicity (%)		Student/Counselor Ratio	429.2 to 1
White, Non-Hispanic	39.8	**Current Spending** *($ per student in FY 2001)*	6,771
Black, Non-Hispanic	14.3	Instruction	4,089
Asian/Pacific Islander	2.9	Support Services	2,343
American Indian/Alaskan Native	0.3	**College Entrance Exam Scores** *(2003)*	
Hispanic	42.7	Scholastic Aptitude Test (SAT)	
Classification (%)		Participation Rate (%)	57
Individual Education Program (IEP)	11.8	Mean SAT I Verbal Score	493
Migrant	2.6	Mean SAT I Math Score	500
English Language Learner (ELL)	14.8	American College Testing Program (ACT)	
Eligible for Free Lunch Program	39.0	Participation Rate (%)	33
Eligible for Reduced-Price Lunch Program	7.2	Average Composite Score	20.1

Note: *For an explanation of data, please refer to the User's Guide in the front of the book; n/a indicates data not available*

Texas NAEP 2003 Test Scores

Reading			Mathematics		
Grade/Category	**Value**	**Rank**	**Grade/Category**	**Value**	**Rank**
4th Grade			**4th Grade**		
Average Proficiency	214.8 (1.0)	36/51	Average Proficiency	237.3 (0.9)	17/51
Proficiency by Gender/Race/Ethnicity			Proficiency by Gender/Race/Ethnicity		
Male	212.1 (1.4)	36/51	Male	238.8 (1.0)	16/51
Female	217.6 (1.2)	39/51	Female	235.8 (1.0)	16/51
White, Non-Hispanic	227.4 (1.6)	16/51	White, Non-Hispanic	247.6 (1.2)	4/51
Black, Non-Hispanic	202.3 (1.9)	13/42	Black, Non-Hispanic	226.0 (1.6)	1/42
Asian, Non-Hispanic	205.3 (1.3)	18/41	Asian, Non-Hispanic	230.0 (1.1)	7/43
American Indian, Non-Hispanic	*228.6 (4.3)*	12/25	American Indian, Non-Hispanic	257.9 (2.6)	1/26
Hispanic	n/a	n/a	Hispanic	n/a	n/a
Proficiency by Class Size			Proficiency by Class Size		
Less than 16 Students	*204.3 (2.9)*	23/45	Less than 16 Students	*228.0 (2.7)*	14/47
16 to 18 Students	213.1 (3.1)	28/48	16 to 18 Students	236.6 (2.0)	18/48
19 to 20 Students	213.0 (1.7)	38/50	19 to 20 Students	236.6 (1.8)	18/50
21 to 25 Students	217.4 (1.9)	38/51	21 to 25 Students	240.4 (1.7)	13/51
Greater than 25 Students	*207.8 (5.3)*	44/49	Greater than 25 Students	*222.9 (5.0)*	45/49
Percent Attaining Achievement Levels			Percent Attaining Achievement Levels		
Below Basic	41.0 (1.1)	13/51	Below Basic	17.7 (1.2)	38/51
Basic or Above	59.0 (1.1)	39/51	Basic or Above	82.3 (1.2)	14/51
Proficient or Above	26.5 (1.1)	39/51	Proficient or Above	32.9 (1.4)	24/51
Advanced or Above	5.6 (0.5)	40/51	Advanced or Above	3.5 (0.5)	24/51
8th Grade			**8th Grade**		
Average Proficiency	258.8 (1.1)	36/51	Average Proficiency	277.1 (1.1)	33/51
Proficiency by Gender/Race/Ethnicity			Proficiency by Gender/Race/Ethnicity		
Male	253.3 (1.4)	37/51	Male	278.1 (1.4)	32/51
Female	264.7 (1.3)	36/51	Female	276.0 (1.1)	30/51
White, Non-Hispanic	271.9 (1.3)	13/50	White, Non-Hispanic	290.2 (1.3)	10/50
Black, Non-Hispanic	246.5 (2.2)	13/41	Black, Non-Hispanic	259.8 (2.2)	7/41
Asian, Non-Hispanic	247.4 (1.3)	15/37	Asian, Non-Hispanic	266.9 (1.2)	3/37
American Indian, Non-Hispanic	*272.4 (4.4)*	9/23	American Indian, Non-Hispanic	*302.9 (5.4)*	3/23
Hispanic	n/a	n/a	Hispanic	n/a	n/a
Proficiency by Parents Highest Level of Ed.			Proficiency by Parents Highest Level of Ed.		
Did Not Finish High School	247.3 (2.0)	20/50	Did Not Finish High School	264.5 (1.8)	6/50
Graduated High School	250.9 (1.7)	34/50	Graduated High School	271.3 (2.1)	16/50
Some Education After High School	264.9 (1.5)	35/50	Some Education After High School	282.5 (1.5)	18/50
Graduated College	269.9 (1.5)	33/50	Graduated College	286.4 (1.6)	30/50
Percent Attaining Achievement Levels			Percent Attaining Achievement Levels		
Below Basic	29.5 (1.3)	16/51	Below Basic	31.4 (1.4)	23/51
Basic or Above	70.5 (1.3)	36/51	Basic or Above	68.6 (1.4)	29/51
Proficient or Above	25.9 (1.4)	40/51	Proficient or Above	24.9 (1.4)	34/51
Advanced or Above	1.9 (0.4)	38/51	Advanced or Above	4.1 (0.6)	35/51

Note: *For an explanation of data, please refer to the User's Guide in the front of the book; values in italics indicate that the nature of the sample does not allow accurate determination of the variability of the statistic; n/a indicates data not available*

Anderson County

Palestine ISD

1600 S Loop 256 • Palestine, TX 75801-5847
(903) 731-8001
Grade Span: PK-12; **Agency Type:** 1
Schools: 7
4 Primary; 2 Middle; 1 High; 0 Other Level
7 Regular; 0 Special Education; 0 Vocational; 0 Alternative
0 Magnet; 0 Charter; 7 Title I Eligible; 7 School-wide Title I
Students: 3,385 (51.5% male; 48.5% female)
Individual Education Program: 316 (9.3%);
English Language Learner: 277 (8.2%); Migrant: 4 (0.1%)
Eligible for Free Lunch Program: 1,816 (53.6%)
Eligible for Reduced-Price Lunch Program: 153 (4.5%)
Teachers: 258.0 (13.1 to 1)
Librarians/Media Specialists: 4.0 (846.3 to 1)
Guidance Counselors: 9.0 (376.1 to 1)
Current Spending: ($ per student per year):
Total: $6,456; Instruction: $3,994; Support Services: $2,102
Enrollment, Drop-out Rates and Diploma Recipients by Race/Ethnicity

Category	Total	White	Black	Asian	AIAN	Hisp.
Enrollment (%)	100.0	42.9	32.0	0.8	0.1	24.2
Drop-out Rate (%)	4.3	3.3	4.8	0.0	n/a	6.4
H.S. Diplomas (#)	201	112	63	3	0	23

Westwood ISD

4524 W Oak • Palestine, TX 75801-5453
Mailing Address: PO Box 260 • Palestine, TX 75802-0260
(903) 729-1776
Grade Span: PK-12; **Agency Type:** 1
Schools: 4
2 Primary; 1 Middle; 1 High; 0 Other Level
4 Regular; 0 Special Education; 0 Vocational; 0 Alternative
0 Magnet; 0 Charter; 2 Title I Eligible; 2 School-wide Title I
Students: 1,830 (50.8% male; 49.2% female)
Individual Education Program: 273 (14.9%);
English Language Learner: 29 (1.6%); Migrant: 0 (0.0%)
Eligible for Free Lunch Program: 606 (33.1%)
Eligible for Reduced-Price Lunch Program: 189 (10.3%)
Teachers: 120.8 (15.1 to 1)
Librarians/Media Specialists: 1.0 (1,830.0 to 1)
Guidance Counselors: 3.0 (610.0 to 1)
Current Spending: ($ per student per year):
Total: $5,201; Instruction: $3,241; Support Services: $1,639
Enrollment, Drop-out Rates and Diploma Recipients by Race/Ethnicity

Category	Total	White	Black	Asian	AIAN	Hisp.
Enrollment (%)	100.0	72.7	16.8	0.5	0.2	9.8
Drop-out Rate (%)	4.2	3.2	4.9	33.3	0.0	11.4
H.S. Diplomas (#)	91	75	11	0	1	4

Andrews County

Andrews ISD

405 NW 3rd St • Andrews, TX 79714-5098
(915) 523-3640 • http://andrews.esc18.net/
Grade Span: PK-12; **Agency Type:** 1
Schools: 7
4 Primary; 1 Middle; 1 High; 1 Other Level
6 Regular; 0 Special Education; 0 Vocational; 1 Alternative
0 Magnet; 0 Charter; 6 Title I Eligible; 0 School-wide Title I
Students: 3,040 (51.2% male; 48.8% female)
Individual Education Program: 560 (18.4%);
English Language Learner: 325 (10.7%); Migrant: 33 (1.1%)
Eligible for Free Lunch Program: 879 (28.9%)
Eligible for Reduced-Price Lunch Program: 281 (9.2%)
Teachers: 229.3 (13.3 to 1)
Librarians/Media Specialists: 4.8 (633.3 to 1)
Guidance Counselors: 5.5 (552.7 to 1)
Current Spending: ($ per student per year):
Total: $8,194; Instruction: $5,083; Support Services: $2,683
Enrollment, Drop-out Rates and Diploma Recipients by Race/Ethnicity

Category	Total	White	Black	Asian	AIAN	Hisp.
Enrollment (%)	100.0	43.2	1.8	0.6	0.2	54.2
Drop-out Rate (%)	2.1	1.8	5.3	0.0	0.0	2.2
H.S. Diplomas (#)	221	117	2	2	0	100

Angelina County

Central ISD

7622 US Hwy 69 N • Pollok, TX 75969-9710
(936) 853-2216
Grade Span: PK-12; **Agency Type:** 1
Schools: 5
2 Primary; 1 Middle; 2 High; 0 Other Level
4 Regular; 0 Special Education; 0 Vocational; 1 Alternative
0 Magnet; 0 Charter; 3 Title I Eligible; 3 School-wide Title I
Students: 1,621 (50.8% male; 49.2% female)
Individual Education Program: 267 (16.5%);
English Language Learner: 46 (2.8%); Migrant: 0 (0.0%)
Eligible for Free Lunch Program: 483 (29.8%)
Eligible for Reduced-Price Lunch Program: 172 (10.6%)
Teachers: 117.7 (13.8 to 1)
Librarians/Media Specialists: 2.0 (810.5 to 1)
Guidance Counselors: 4.0 (405.3 to 1)
Current Spending: ($ per student per year):
Total: $5,399; Instruction: $3,388; Support Services: $1,687
Enrollment, Drop-out Rates and Diploma Recipients by Race/Ethnicity

Category	Total	White	Black	Asian	AIAN	Hisp.
Enrollment (%)	100.0	85.7	3.3	0.4	0.2	10.4
Drop-out Rate (%)	1.2	1.3	0.0	0.0	n/a	0.0
H.S. Diplomas (#)	107	99	2	1	0	5

Diboll ISD

401 Dennis • Diboll, TX 75941-0550
Mailing Address: PO Box 550 • Diboll, TX 75941-0550
(936) 829-4718
Grade Span: PK-12; **Agency Type:** 1
Schools: 5
2 Primary; 0 Middle; 2 High; 1 Other Level
4 Regular; 0 Special Education; 0 Vocational; 1 Alternative
0 Magnet; 0 Charter; 4 Title I Eligible; 4 School-wide Title I
Students: 1,920 (53.8% male; 46.2% female)
Individual Education Program: 234 (12.2%);
English Language Learner: 337 (17.6%); Migrant: 0 (0.0%)
Eligible for Free Lunch Program: 993 (51.7%)
Eligible for Reduced-Price Lunch Program: 252 (13.1%)
Teachers: 148.1 (13.0 to 1)
Librarians/Media Specialists: 2.3 (834.8 to 1)
Guidance Counselors: 5.0 (384.0 to 1)
Current Spending: ($ per student per year):
Total: $7,031; Instruction: $4,388; Support Services: $2,252
Enrollment, Drop-out Rates and Diploma Recipients by Race/Ethnicity

Category	Total	White	Black	Asian	AIAN	Hisp.
Enrollment (%)	100.0	42.1	14.6	0.2	0.2	43.0
Drop-out Rate (%)	4.0	3.5	6.1	0.0	n/a	3.7
H.S. Diplomas (#)	104	41	22	0	0	41

Hudson ISD

State Hwy 94 W • Lufkin, TX 75904-8600
Mailing Address: 6735 Ted Trout Dr • Lufkin, TX 75904-8600
(936) 875-3351
Grade Span: PK-12; **Agency Type:** 1
Schools: 5
2 Primary; 1 Middle; 2 High; 0 Other Level
4 Regular; 0 Special Education; 0 Vocational; 1 Alternative
0 Magnet; 0 Charter; 5 Title I Eligible; 5 School-wide Title I
Students: 2,338 (50.5% male; 49.5% female)
Individual Education Program: 234 (10.0%);
English Language Learner: 141 (6.0%); Migrant: 0 (0.0%)
Eligible for Free Lunch Program: 966 (41.3%)
Eligible for Reduced-Price Lunch Program: 207 (8.9%)
Teachers: 160.0 (14.6 to 1)
Librarians/Media Specialists: 2.0 (1,169.0 to 1)
Guidance Counselors: 6.0 (389.7 to 1)
Current Spending: ($ per student per year):
Total: $5,564; Instruction: $3,319; Support Services: $1,890
Enrollment, Drop-out Rates and Diploma Recipients by Race/Ethnicity

Category	Total	White	Black	Asian	AIAN	Hisp.
Enrollment (%)	100.0	75.0	4.5	0.2	0.4	19.9
Drop-out Rate (%)	2.4	1.4	0.0	n/a	0.0	8.2
H.S. Diplomas (#)	131	111	4	0	0	16

Huntington ISD

908 Main St • Huntington, TX 75949-0328
Mailing Address: PO Box 328 • Huntington, TX 75949-0328
(936) 876-4287
Grade Span: PK-12; **Agency Type:** 1
Schools: 5
1 Primary; 2 Middle; 2 High; 0 Other Level
4 Regular; 0 Special Education; 0 Vocational; 1 Alternative
0 Magnet; 0 Charter; 4 Title I Eligible; 4 School-wide Title I
Students: 1,673 (52.5% male; 47.5% female)
Individual Education Program: 308 (18.4%);
English Language Learner: 17 (1.0%); Migrant: 7 (0.4%)
Eligible for Free Lunch Program: 580 (34.7%)
Eligible for Reduced-Price Lunch Program: 152 (9.1%)
Teachers: 123.5 (13.5 to 1)
Librarians/Media Specialists: 2.0 (836.5 to 1)
Guidance Counselors: 2.1 (796.7 to 1)

Current Spending: ($ per student per year):
Total: $5,869; Instruction: $3,655; Support Services: $1,892

Enrollment, Drop-out Rates and Diploma Recipients by Race/Ethnicity

Category	Total	White	Black	Asian	AIAN	Hisp.
Enrollment (%)	100.0	93.4	3.6	0.2	0.1	2.7
Drop-out Rate (%)	2.6	2.9	0.0	0.0	0.0	0.0
H.S. Diplomas (#)	108	97	8	0	0	3

Lufkin ISD

101 Cotton Sq • Lufkin, TX 75904
Mailing Address: PO Box 1407 • Lufkin, TX 75902-1407
(936) 634-6696 • http://www.lufkinisd.org/
Grade Span: PK-12; **Agency Type:** 1
Schools: 18
11 Primary; 1 Middle; 2 High; 4 Other Level
13 Regular; 2 Special Education; 0 Vocational; 3 Alternative
0 Magnet; 0 Charter; 11 Title I Eligible; 11 School-wide Title I
Students: 8,257 (50.3% male; 49.7% female)
Individual Education Program: 1,126 (13.6%);
English Language Learner: 916 (11.1%); Migrant: 123 (1.5%)
Eligible for Free Lunch Program: 4,357 (52.8%)
Eligible for Reduced-Price Lunch Program: 538 (6.5%)
Teachers: 605.4 (13.6 to 1)
Librarians/Media Specialists: 9.1 (907.4 to 1)
Guidance Counselors: 20.1 (410.8 to 1)
Current Spending: ($ per student per year):
Total: $6,024; Instruction: $3,671; Support Services: $1,992

Enrollment, Drop-out Rates and Diploma Recipients by Race/Ethnicity

Category	Total	White	Black	Asian	AIAN	Hisp.
Enrollment (%)	100.0	40.6	31.7	0.9	0.2	26.6
Drop-out Rate (%)	4.7	3.9	4.7	0.0	0.0	7.8
H.S. Diplomas (#)	476	240	161	4	1	70

Aransas County

Aransas County ISD

1700 Omohundro St • Rockport, TX 78382
Mailing Address: PO Box 907 • Rockport, TX 78381-0907
(361) 790-2212 • http://www.acisd.org/
Grade Span: PK-12; **Agency Type:** 1
Schools: 6
2 Primary; 2 Middle; 1 High; 0 Other Level
5 Regular; 0 Special Education; 0 Vocational; 0 Alternative
0 Magnet; 0 Charter; 5 Title I Eligible; 5 School-wide Title I
Students: 3,374 (52.9% male; 47.1% female)
Individual Education Program: 515 (15.3%);
English Language Learner: 151 (4.5%); Migrant: 0 (0.0%)
Eligible for Free Lunch Program: 1,536 (45.5%)
Eligible for Reduced-Price Lunch Program: 240 (7.1%)
Teachers: 244.3 (13.8 to 1)
Librarians/Media Specialists: 2.3 (1,467.0 to 1)
Guidance Counselors: 10.3 (327.6 to 1)
Current Spending: ($ per student per year):
Total: $7,247; Instruction: $4,335; Support Services: $2,572

Enrollment, Drop-out Rates and Diploma Recipients by Race/Ethnicity

Category	Total	White	Black	Asian	AIAN	Hisp.
Enrollment (%)	100.0	60.4	2.5	4.5	0.0	32.5
Drop-out Rate (%)	2.1	1.9	0.0	0.0	n/a	3.4
H.S. Diplomas (#)	210	140	4	14	0	52

Atascosa County

Lytle ISD

15437 Cottage St • Lytle, TX 78052-0745
Mailing Address: PO Box 745 • Lytle, TX 78052-0745
(830) 709-5100
Grade Span: PK-12; **Agency Type:** 1
Schools: 6
2 Primary; 2 Middle; 1 High; 1 Other Level
5 Regular; 0 Special Education; 0 Vocational; 1 Alternative
0 Magnet; 0 Charter; 2 Title I Eligible; 2 School-wide Title I
Students: 1,541 (51.5% male; 48.5% female)
Individual Education Program: 189 (12.3%);
English Language Learner: 156 (10.1%); Migrant: 84 (5.5%)
Eligible for Free Lunch Program: 832 (54.0%)
Eligible for Reduced-Price Lunch Program: 180 (11.7%)
Teachers: 111.0 (13.9 to 1)
Librarians/Media Specialists: 0.0 (0.0 to 1)
Guidance Counselors: 4.0 (385.3 to 1)
Current Spending: ($ per student per year):
Total: $6,292; Instruction: $3,960; Support Services: $1,978

Enrollment, Drop-out Rates and Diploma Recipients by Race/Ethnicity

Category	Total	White	Black	Asian	AIAN	Hisp.
Enrollment (%)	100.0	28.7	0.3	0.2	0.2	70.6
Drop-out Rate (%)	4.1	1.9	0.0	0.0	0.0	5.4
H.S. Diplomas (#)	90	42	0	1	0	47

Pleasanton ISD

831 Stadium Dr • Pleasanton, TX 78064-2499
(830) 569-1200
Grade Span: PK-12; **Agency Type:** 1
Schools: 8
3 Primary; 2 Middle; 2 High; 1 Other Level
6 Regular; 1 Special Education; 0 Vocational; 1 Alternative
0 Magnet; 0 Charter; 6 Title I Eligible; 6 School-wide Title I
Students: 3,489 (51.3% male; 48.7% female)
Individual Education Program: 594 (17.0%);
English Language Learner: 95 (2.7%); Migrant: 33 (0.9%)
Eligible for Free Lunch Program: 1,764 (50.6%)
Eligible for Reduced-Price Lunch Program: 361 (10.3%)
Teachers: 256.7 (13.6 to 1)
Librarians/Media Specialists: 3.0 (1,163.0 to 1)
Guidance Counselors: 11.0 (317.2 to 1)
Current Spending: ($ per student per year):
Total: $6,645; Instruction: $3,902; Support Services: $2,377

Enrollment, Drop-out Rates and Diploma Recipients by Race/Ethnicity

Category	Total	White	Black	Asian	AIAN	Hisp.
Enrollment (%)	100.0	35.4	0.8	0.5	0.0	63.3
Drop-out Rate (%)	3.6	1.9	0.0	0.0	n/a	4.9
H.S. Diplomas (#)	215	97	2	0	1	115

Poteet ISD

1100 School Dr • Poteet, TX 78065-0138
Mailing Address: PO Box 138 • Poteet, TX 78065-0138
(830) 742-3567
Grade Span: PK-12; **Agency Type:** 1
Schools: 4
1 Primary; 1 Middle; 1 High; 1 Other Level
3 Regular; 0 Special Education; 0 Vocational; 1 Alternative
0 Magnet; 0 Charter; 2 Title I Eligible; 2 School-wide Title I
Students: 1,651 (49.1% male; 50.9% female)
Individual Education Program: 254 (15.4%);
English Language Learner: 102 (6.2%); Migrant: 15 (0.9%)
Eligible for Free Lunch Program: 987 (59.8%)
Eligible for Reduced-Price Lunch Program: 238 (14.4%)
Teachers: 128.6 (12.8 to 1)
Librarians/Media Specialists: 3.0 (550.3 to 1)
Guidance Counselors: 3.7 (446.2 to 1)
Current Spending: ($ per student per year):
Total: $7,344; Instruction: $4,449; Support Services: $2,474

Enrollment, Drop-out Rates and Diploma Recipients by Race/Ethnicity

Category	Total	White	Black	Asian	AIAN	Hisp.
Enrollment (%)	100.0	15.7	0.4	0.2	0.1	83.5
Drop-out Rate (%)	2.6	1.1	n/a	0.0	n/a	3.0
H.S. Diplomas (#)	99	22	0	0	0	77

Austin County

Bellville ISD

404 E Main St • Bellville, TX 77418-1599
(979) 865-3133 • http://www.bellville.k12.tx.us/
Grade Span: PK-12; **Agency Type:** 1
Schools: 6
3 Primary; 1 Middle; 1 High; 1 Other Level
5 Regular; 0 Special Education; 0 Vocational; 1 Alternative
0 Magnet; 0 Charter; 2 Title I Eligible; 2 School-wide Title I
Students: 2,138 (51.3% male; 48.7% female)
Individual Education Program: 293 (13.7%);
English Language Learner: 124 (5.8%); Migrant: 2 (0.1%)
Eligible for Free Lunch Program: 493 (23.1%)
Eligible for Reduced-Price Lunch Program: 91 (4.3%)
Teachers: 156.1 (13.7 to 1)
Librarians/Media Specialists: 2.5 (855.2 to 1)
Guidance Counselors: 6.3 (339.4 to 1)
Current Spending: ($ per student per year):
Total: $5,739; Instruction: $3,472; Support Services: $1,990

Enrollment, Drop-out Rates and Diploma Recipients by Race/Ethnicity

Category	Total	White	Black	Asian	AIAN	Hisp.
Enrollment (%)	100.0	68.4	14.3	0.2	0.2	16.9
Drop-out Rate (%)	0.3	0.2	1.2	0.0	0.0	0.0
H.S. Diplomas (#)	147	117	17	0	1	12

Sealy ISD

939 W St • Sealy, TX 77474-3211
Mailing Address: 939 Tiger Ln • Sealy, TX 77474-3211
(979) 885-3516
Grade Span: PK-12; **Agency Type:** 1
Schools: 4
1 Primary; 2 Middle; 1 High; 0 Other Level
4 Regular; 0 Special Education; 0 Vocational; 0 Alternative
0 Magnet; 0 Charter; 2 Title I Eligible; 2 School-wide Title I
Students: 2,344 (51.1% male; 48.9% female)
Individual Education Program: 330 (14.1%);
English Language Learner: 172 (7.3%); Migrant: 19 (0.8%)
Eligible for Free Lunch Program: 842 (35.9%)
Eligible for Reduced-Price Lunch Program: 159 (6.8%)
Teachers: 164.6 (14.2 to 1)
Librarians/Media Specialists: 2.0 (1,172.0 to 1)
Guidance Counselors: 10.0 (234.4 to 1)
Current Spending: ($ per student per year):
Total: $6,374; Instruction: $4,192; Support Services: $1,852
Enrollment, Drop-out Rates and Diploma Recipients by Race/Ethnicity

Category	Total	White	Black	Asian	AIAN	Hisp.
Enrollment (%)	100.0	52.1	15.3	0.8	0.2	31.6
Drop-out Rate (%)	2.9	2.7	2.2	0.0	0.0	3.8
H.S. Diplomas (#)	128	89	11	1	0	27

Bandera County

Bandera ISD

2303 State Hwy 16 S • Bandera, TX 78003-0727
Mailing Address: PO Box 727 • Bandera, TX 78003-0727
(830) 796-3313
Grade Span: PK-12; **Agency Type:** 1
Schools: 5
2 Primary; 1 Middle; 1 High; 0 Other Level
4 Regular; 0 Special Education; 0 Vocational; 0 Alternative
0 Magnet; 0 Charter; 1 Title I Eligible; 1 School-wide Title I
Students: 2,625 (51.9% male; 48.1% female)
Individual Education Program: 402 (15.3%);
English Language Learner: 67 (2.6%); Migrant: 0 (0.0%)
Eligible for Free Lunch Program: 833 (31.7%)
Eligible for Reduced-Price Lunch Program: 207 (7.9%)
Teachers: 204.3 (12.8 to 1)
Librarians/Media Specialists: 3.5 (750.0 to 1)
Guidance Counselors: 8.0 (328.1 to 1)
Current Spending: ($ per student per year):
Total: $6,622; Instruction: $4,175; Support Services: $2,098
Enrollment, Drop-out Rates and Diploma Recipients by Race/Ethnicity

Category	Total	White	Black	Asian	AIAN	Hisp.
Enrollment (%)	100.0	78.6	0.8	0.3	0.6	19.5
Drop-out Rate (%)	4.7	5.2	0.0	n/a	0.0	2.5
H.S. Diplomas (#)	146	127	0	0	1	18

Bastrop County

Bastrop ISD

906 Farm St • Bastrop, TX 78602-3717
(512) 321-2292 • http://www.bastrop.isd.tenet.edu/
Grade Span: PK-12; **Agency Type:** 1
Schools: 11
4 Primary; 3 Middle; 2 High; 2 Other Level
8 Regular; 0 Special Education; 0 Vocational; 3 Alternative
0 Magnet; 0 Charter; 6 Title I Eligible; 0 School-wide Title I
Students: 7,254 (51.6% male; 48.4% female)
Individual Education Program: 929 (12.8%);
English Language Learner: 532 (7.3%); Migrant: 269 (3.7%)
Eligible for Free Lunch Program: 2,787 (38.4%)
Eligible for Reduced-Price Lunch Program: 641 (8.8%)
Teachers: 517.8 (14.0 to 1)
Librarians/Media Specialists: 9.0 (806.0 to 1)
Guidance Counselors: 23.8 (304.8 to 1)
Current Spending: ($ per student per year):
Total: $6,847; Instruction: $4,021; Support Services: $2,474
Enrollment, Drop-out Rates and Diploma Recipients by Race/Ethnicity

Category	Total	White	Black	Asian	AIAN	Hisp.
Enrollment (%)	100.0	55.9	10.4	0.6	0.4	32.7
Drop-out Rate (%)	5.9	5.4	9.4	0.0	0.0	5.8
H.S. Diplomas (#)	340	228	34	2	3	73

Elgin ISD

900 W 2nd St • Elgin, TX 78621-2515
Mailing Address: PO Box 351 • Elgin, TX 78621-0351
(512) 281-3434 • http://www.elginisd.net/
Grade Span: PK-12; **Agency Type:** 1
Schools: 5
2 Primary; 1 Middle; 2 High; 0 Other Level
4 Regular; 0 Special Education; 0 Vocational; 1 Alternative
0 Magnet; 0 Charter; 4 Title I Eligible; 4 School-wide Title I
Students: 3,070 (50.3% male; 49.7% female)
Individual Education Program: 393 (12.8%);
English Language Learner: 426 (13.9%); Migrant: 97 (3.2%)
Eligible for Free Lunch Program: 1,339 (43.6%)
Eligible for Reduced-Price Lunch Program: 273 (8.9%)
Teachers: 222.5 (13.8 to 1)
Librarians/Media Specialists: 1.9 (1,615.8 to 1)
Guidance Counselors: 9.0 (341.1 to 1)
Current Spending: ($ per student per year):
Total: $6,745; Instruction: $4,141; Support Services: $2,223
Enrollment, Drop-out Rates and Diploma Recipients by Race/Ethnicity

Category	Total	White	Black	Asian	AIAN	Hisp.
Enrollment (%)	100.0	42.6	13.3	0.5	0.3	43.3
Drop-out Rate (%)	3.1	2.6	2.6	0.0	n/a	4.2
H.S. Diplomas (#)	164	82	25	1	0	56

Smithville ISD

901 NE 6th St • Smithville, TX 78957-0479
Mailing Address: PO Box 479 • Smithville, TX 78957-0479
(512) 237-2487
Grade Span: PK-12; **Agency Type:** 1
Schools: 5
1 Primary; 2 Middle; 1 High; 1 Other Level
4 Regular; 0 Special Education; 0 Vocational; 1 Alternative
0 Magnet; 0 Charter; 3 Title I Eligible; 2 School-wide Title I
Students: 1,872 (52.8% male; 47.2% female)
Individual Education Program: 290 (15.5%);
English Language Learner: 52 (2.8%); Migrant: 57 (3.0%)
Eligible for Free Lunch Program: 659 (35.2%)
Eligible for Reduced-Price Lunch Program: 179 (9.6%)
Teachers: 140.5 (13.3 to 1)
Librarians/Media Specialists: 4.0 (468.0 to 1)
Guidance Counselors: 5.0 (374.4 to 1)
Current Spending: ($ per student per year):
Total: $6,478; Instruction: $4,091; Support Services: $2,031
Enrollment, Drop-out Rates and Diploma Recipients by Race/Ethnicity

Category	Total	White	Black	Asian	AIAN	Hisp.
Enrollment (%)	100.0	71.2	11.5	0.3	0.2	16.9
Drop-out Rate (%)	4.1	2.6	10.0	0.0	0.0	6.8
H.S. Diplomas (#)	103	76	10	0	0	17

Bee County

Beeville ISD

2400 N Saint Mary's St • Beeville, TX 78102-2494
(361) 358-7111 • http://www.beevilleisd.esc2.net/
Grade Span: PK-12; **Agency Type:** 1
Schools: 8
4 Primary; 2 Middle; 2 High; 0 Other Level
7 Regular; 0 Special Education; 0 Vocational; 1 Alternative
0 Magnet; 0 Charter; 8 Title I Eligible; 8 School-wide Title I
Students: 3,816 (51.1% male; 48.9% female)
Individual Education Program: 426 (11.2%);
English Language Learner: 83 (2.2%); Migrant: 18 (0.5%)
Eligible for Free Lunch Program: 2,105 (55.2%)
Eligible for Reduced-Price Lunch Program: 408 (10.7%)
Teachers: 255.0 (15.0 to 1)
Librarians/Media Specialists: 3.0 (1,272.0 to 1)
Guidance Counselors: 13.0 (293.5 to 1)
Current Spending: ($ per student per year):
Total: $6,497; Instruction: $3,962; Support Services: $2,190
Enrollment, Drop-out Rates and Diploma Recipients by Race/Ethnicity

Category	Total	White	Black	Asian	AIAN	Hisp.
Enrollment (%)	100.0	22.7	3.5	0.5	0.1	73.2
Drop-out Rate (%)	2.8	0.8	5.1	0.0	0.0	3.7
H.S. Diplomas (#)	223	81	8	4	0	130

Bell County

Belton ISD

616 E 6th Ave • Belton, TX 76513-2707
Mailing Address: PO Box 269 • Belton, TX 76513-0269
(254) 939-1881 • http://www.bisd.net/
Grade Span: PK-12; **Agency Type:** 1
Schools: 13
6 Primary; 3 Middle; 2 High; 1 Other Level
10 Regular; 0 Special Education; 0 Vocational; 2 Alternative
0 Magnet; 0 Charter; 6 Title I Eligible; 6 School-wide Title I
Students: 6,959 (51.7% male; 48.3% female)
Individual Education Program: 1,150 (16.5%);
English Language Learner: 386 (5.5%); Migrant: 31 (0.4%)
Eligible for Free Lunch Program: 2,402 (34.5%)
Eligible for Reduced-Price Lunch Program: 564 (8.1%)

Teachers: 459.6 (15.1 to 1)
Librarians/Media Specialists: 5.1 (1,364.5 to 1)
Guidance Counselors: 17.0 (409.4 to 1)
Current Spending: ($ per student per year):
Total: $6,108; Instruction: $3,627; Support Services: $2,143
Enrollment, Drop-out Rates and Diploma Recipients by Race/Ethnicity

Category	Total	White	Black	Asian	AIAN	Hisp.
Enrollment (%)	100.0	66.5	5.9	0.8	0.7	26.1
Drop-out Rate (%)	1.7	1.6	5.4	0.0	0.0	1.4
H.S. Diplomas (#)	463	345	23	8	6	81

Killeen ISD

200 NW S Young Dr • Killeen, TX 76543-4025
Mailing Address: PO Box 967 • Killeen, TX 76540-0967
(254) 501-0006 • http://www.killeenisd.org/
Grade Span: PK-12; **Agency Type:** 1
Schools: 47
25 Primary; 11 Middle; 7 High; 4 Other Level
42 Regular; 0 Special Education; 0 Vocational; 5 Alternative
0 Magnet; 0 Charter; 22 Title I Eligible; 17 School-wide Title I
Students: 31,258 (51.3% male; 48.7% female)
Individual Education Program: 4,152 (13.3%);
English Language Learner: 1,624 (5.2%); Migrant: 31 (0.1%)
Eligible for Free Lunch Program: 10,101 (32.3%)
Eligible for Reduced-Price Lunch Program: 5,087 (16.3%)
Teachers: 2,196.0 (14.2 to 1)
Librarians/Media Specialists: 39.6 (789.3 to 1)
Guidance Counselors: 67.9 (460.4 to 1)
Current Spending: ($ per student per year):
Total: $6,295; Instruction: $3,765; Support Services: $2,276
Enrollment, Drop-out Rates and Diploma Recipients by Race/Ethnicity

Category	Total	White	Black	Asian	AIAN	Hisp.
Enrollment (%)	100.0	35.9	40.9	4.3	0.7	18.2
Drop-out Rate (%)	3.2	3.0	3.5	1.5	2.6	3.8
H.S. Diplomas (#)	1,358	442	551	92	4	269

Temple ISD

200 N 23rd St • Temple, TX 76504-2486
Mailing Address: PO Box 788 • Temple, TX 76503-0788
(254) 778-6721
Grade Span: PK-12; **Agency Type:** 1
Schools: 17
10 Primary; 3 Middle; 1 High; 2 Other Level
14 Regular; 0 Special Education; 0 Vocational; 2 Alternative
0 Magnet; 0 Charter; 13 Title I Eligible; 13 School-wide Title I
Students: 8,429 (50.4% male; 49.6% female)
Individual Education Program: 1,417 (16.8%);
English Language Learner: 547 (6.5%); Migrant: 48 (0.6%)
Eligible for Free Lunch Program: 3,832 (45.5%)
Eligible for Reduced-Price Lunch Program: 690 (8.2%)
Teachers: 621.3 (13.6 to 1)
Librarians/Media Specialists: 12.7 (663.7 to 1)
Guidance Counselors: 18.0 (468.3 to 1)
Current Spending: ($ per student per year):
Total: $6,565; Instruction: $3,969; Support Services: $2,253
Enrollment, Drop-out Rates and Diploma Recipients by Race/Ethnicity

Category	Total	White	Black	Asian	AIAN	Hisp.
Enrollment (%)	100.0	42.7	28.9	1.6	0.3	26.5
Drop-out Rate (%)	3.2	1.6	5.3	2.3	0.0	4.4
H.S. Diplomas (#)	441	226	121	8	0	86

Bexar County

Alamo Heights ISD

7101 Broadway St • San Antonio, TX 78209-3797
(210) 824-2483 • http://www.ahisd.net/
Grade Span: PK-12; **Agency Type:** 1
Schools: 6
3 Primary; 1 Middle; 1 High; 1 Other Level
5 Regular; 0 Special Education; 0 Vocational; 1 Alternative
0 Magnet; 0 Charter; 3 Title I Eligible; 0 School-wide Title I
Students: 4,421 (51.9% male; 48.1% female)
Individual Education Program: 474 (10.7%);
English Language Learner: 211 (4.8%); Migrant: 0 (0.0%)
Eligible for Free Lunch Program: 667 (15.1%)
Eligible for Reduced-Price Lunch Program: 177 (4.0%)
Teachers: 320.0 (13.8 to 1)
Librarians/Media Specialists: 3.3 (1,339.7 to 1)
Guidance Counselors: 10.8 (409.4 to 1)
Current Spending: ($ per student per year):
Total: $7,327; Instruction: $4,739; Support Services: $2,293
Enrollment, Drop-out Rates and Diploma Recipients by Race/Ethnicity

Category	Total	White	Black	Asian	AIAN	Hisp.
Enrollment (%)	100.0	68.2	2.1	1.3	0.1	28.4
Drop-out Rate (%)	0.8	0.4	4.5	0.0	n/a	1.6
H.S. Diplomas (#)	347	243	5	2	0	97

East Central ISD

6634 New Sulphur Springs Rd • San Antonio, TX 78263-9701
(210) 648-7861 • http://www.ecisd.net/
Grade Span: PK-12; **Agency Type:** 1
Schools: 13
6 Primary; 3 Middle; 1 High; 3 Other Level
10 Regular; 0 Special Education; 0 Vocational; 3 Alternative
0 Magnet; 0 Charter; 6 Title I Eligible; 6 School-wide Title I
Students: 7,945 (51.6% male; 48.4% female)
Individual Education Program: 1,021 (12.9%);
English Language Learner: 316 (4.0%); Migrant: 35 (0.4%)
Eligible for Free Lunch Program: 3,077 (38.7%)
Eligible for Reduced-Price Lunch Program: 964 (12.1%)
Teachers: 517.8 (15.3 to 1)
Librarians/Media Specialists: 8.7 (913.2 to 1)
Guidance Counselors: 18.5 (429.5 to 1)
Current Spending: ($ per student per year):
Total: $6,282; Instruction: $3,812; Support Services: $2,181
Enrollment, Drop-out Rates and Diploma Recipients by Race/Ethnicity

Category	Total	White	Black	Asian	AIAN	Hisp.
Enrollment (%)	100.0	38.6	11.5	0.4	0.2	49.3
Drop-out Rate (%)	2.7	1.8	2.0	8.3	0.0	3.9
H.S. Diplomas (#)	492	228	58	3	1	202

Edgewood ISD

5358 W Commerce St • San Antonio, TX 78237-1354
(210) 444-4500 • http://www.edgewood.esc7.net/
Grade Span: PK-12; **Agency Type:** 1
Schools: 26
13 Primary; 4 Middle; 3 High; 3 Other Level
20 Regular; 0 Special Education; 0 Vocational; 3 Alternative
0 Magnet; 0 Charter; 21 Title I Eligible; 21 School-wide Title I
Students: 13,164 (50.9% male; 49.1% female)
Individual Education Program: 1,927 (14.6%);
English Language Learner: 2,927 (22.2%); Migrant: 334 (2.5%)
Eligible for Free Lunch Program: 1,458 (11.1%)
Eligible for Reduced-Price Lunch Program: 98 (0.7%)
Teachers: 806.6 (16.3 to 1)
Librarians/Media Specialists: 16.0 (822.8 to 1)
Guidance Counselors: 24.6 (535.1 to 1)
Current Spending: ($ per student per year):
Total: $6,931; Instruction: $4,029; Support Services: $2,501
Enrollment, Drop-out Rates and Diploma Recipients by Race/Ethnicity

Category	Total	White	Black	Asian	AIAN	Hisp.
Enrollment (%)	100.0	1.1	1.6	0.1	0.0	97.1
Drop-out Rate (%)	6.1	2.7	3.7	0.0	0.0	6.2
H.S. Diplomas (#)	622	10	13	2	2	595

Harlandale ISD

102 Genevieve St • San Antonio, TX 78214-2997
(210) 921-4300
Grade Span: PK-12; **Agency Type:** 1
Schools: 30
16 Primary; 7 Middle; 6 High; 1 Other Level
20 Regular; 4 Special Education; 0 Vocational; 6 Alternative
0 Magnet; 0 Charter; 22 Title I Eligible; 21 School-wide Title I
Students: 14,422 (51.8% male; 48.2% female)
Individual Education Program: 2,235 (15.5%);
English Language Learner: 1,854 (12.9%); Migrant: 170 (1.2%)
Eligible for Free Lunch Program: 3,866 (26.8%)
Eligible for Reduced-Price Lunch Program: 614 (4.3%)
Teachers: 983.5 (14.7 to 1)
Librarians/Media Specialists: 21.0 (686.8 to 1)
Guidance Counselors: 36.0 (400.6 to 1)
Current Spending: ($ per student per year):
Total: $7,623; Instruction: $4,376; Support Services: $2,786
Enrollment, Drop-out Rates and Diploma Recipients by Race/Ethnicity

Category	Total	White	Black	Asian	AIAN	Hisp.
Enrollment (%)	100.0	4.7	0.6	0.1	0.1	94.6
Drop-out Rate (%)	4.3	3.0	0.0	0.0	0.0	4.4
H.S. Diplomas (#)	800	62	1	0	0	737

Judson ISD

8012 Shin Oak • San Antonio, TX 78233-2457
(210) 659-9600 •
http://www.judsonisd.org/education/district/district.php?sectionid=1
Grade Span: PK-12; **Agency Type:** 1
Schools: 21
13 Primary; 3 Middle; 2 High; 3 Other Level

18 Regular; 0 Special Education; 0 Vocational; 3 Alternative
0 Magnet; 0 Charter; 12 Title I Eligible; 10 School-wide Title I

Students: 17,627 (52.3% male; 47.7% female)
Individual Education Program: 1,992 (11.3%);
English Language Learner: 665 (3.8%); Migrant: 8 (<0.1%)
Eligible for Free Lunch Program: 6,504 (36.9%)
Eligible for Reduced-Price Lunch Program: 2,245 (12.7%)

Teachers: 1,196.2 (14.7 to 1)
Librarians/Media Specialists: 16.6 (1,061.9 to 1)
Guidance Counselors: 35.0 (503.6 to 1)
Current Spending: ($ per student per year):
Total: $6,215; Instruction: $3,959; Support Services: $1,983

Enrollment, Drop-out Rates and Diploma Recipients by Race/Ethnicity

Category	Total	White	Black	Asian	AIAN	Hisp.
Enrollment (%)	100.0	31.1	25.2	2.8	0.3	40.6
Drop-out Rate (%)	3.8	2.8	2.9	3.5	0.0	5.6
H.S. Diplomas (#)	842	348	191	24	3	276

North East ISD

8961 Tesoro Dr • San Antonio, TX 78217-6225
(210) 804-7000 • http://www.neisd.net/index.html
Grade Span: PK-12; **Agency Type:** 1
Schools: 69
39 Primary; 13 Middle; 10 High; 7 Other Level
56 Regular; 5 Special Education; 0 Vocational; 8 Alternative
0 Magnet; 0 Charter; 20 Title I Eligible; 20 School-wide Title I

Students: 55,053 (50.8% male; 49.2% female)
Individual Education Program: 8,818 (16.0%);
English Language Learner: 2,412 (4.4%); Migrant: 26 (<0.1%)
Eligible for Free Lunch Program: 14,634 (26.6%)
Eligible for Reduced-Price Lunch Program: 3,874 (7.0%)

Teachers: 3,716.8 (14.8 to 1)
Librarians/Media Specialists: 60.9 (904.0 to 1)
Guidance Counselors: 152.0 (362.2 to 1)
Current Spending: ($ per student per year):
Total: $6,356; Instruction: $3,989; Support Services: $2,107

Enrollment, Drop-out Rates and Diploma Recipients by Race/Ethnicity

Category	Total	White	Black	Asian	AIAN	Hisp.
Enrollment (%)	100.0	46.8	9.5	2.7	0.2	40.8
Drop-out Rate (%)	2.0	1.5	2.3	0.9	0.0	2.8
H.S. Diplomas (#)	3,208	1,705	266	102	6	1,129

Northside ISD

5900 Evers Rd • San Antonio, TX 78238-1699
(210) 706-8770 • http://www.nisd.net/
Grade Span: PK-12; **Agency Type:** 1
Schools: 89
51 Primary; 14 Middle; 12 High; 12 Other Level
67 Regular; 7 Special Education; 0 Vocational; 15 Alternative
0 Magnet; 0 Charter; 30 Title I Eligible; 30 School-wide Title I

Students: 69,409 (51.7% male; 48.3% female)
Individual Education Program: 10,544 (15.2%);
English Language Learner: 4,313 (6.2%); Migrant: 268 (0.4%)
Eligible for Free Lunch Program: 23,954 (34.5%)
Eligible for Reduced-Price Lunch Program: 7,126 (10.3%)

Teachers: 4,573.8 (15.2 to 1)
Librarians/Media Specialists: 68.0 (1,020.7 to 1)
Guidance Counselors: 209.0 (332.1 to 1)
Current Spending: ($ per student per year):
Total: $6,238; Instruction: $3,861; Support Services: $2,086

Enrollment, Drop-out Rates and Diploma Recipients by Race/Ethnicity

Category	Total	White	Black	Asian	AIAN	Hisp.
Enrollment (%)	100.0	32.8	6.9	2.4	0.2	57.6
Drop-out Rate (%)	3.3	2.3	2.4	1.5	8.3	4.3
H.S. Diplomas (#)	3,928	1,583	296	110	12	1,927

San Antonio ISD

141 Lavaca St • San Antonio, TX 78210-1039
(210) 299-5500
Grade Span: PK-12; **Agency Type:** 1
Schools: 107
67 Primary; 19 Middle; 12 High; 8 Other Level
89 Regular; 6 Special Education; 0 Vocational; 11 Alternative
0 Magnet; 0 Charter; 92 Title I Eligible; 92 School-wide Title I

Students: 57,120 (51.1% male; 48.9% female)
Individual Education Program: 7,342 (12.9%);
English Language Learner: 10,864 (19.0%); Migrant: 2,615 (4.6%)
Eligible for Free Lunch Program: 19,907 (34.9%)
Eligible for Reduced-Price Lunch Program: 1,667 (2.9%)

Teachers: 3,635.8 (15.7 to 1)
Librarians/Media Specialists: 73.1 (781.4 to 1)
Guidance Counselors: 152.6 (374.3 to 1)
Current Spending: ($ per student per year):
Total: $6,933; Instruction: $4,281; Support Services: $2,242

Enrollment, Drop-out Rates and Diploma Recipients by Race/Ethnicity

Category	Total	White	Black	Asian	AIAN	Hisp.
Enrollment (%)	100.0	3.8	9.3	0.2	0.1	86.5
Drop-out Rate (%)	7.6	5.9	7.6	8.1	0.0	7.7
H.S. Diplomas (#)	2,727	124	258	14	0	2,331

Somerset ISD

19644 Somerset Rd • Somerset, TX 78069-0279
Mailing Address: PO Box 279 • Somerset, TX 78069-0279
(866) 852-9858
Grade Span: PK-12; **Agency Type:** 1
Schools: 8
3 Primary; 2 Middle; 1 High; 1 Other Level
6 Regular; 0 Special Education; 1 Vocational; 0 Alternative
0 Magnet; 0 Charter; 5 Title I Eligible; 5 School-wide Title I

Students: 3,154 (52.5% male; 47.5% female)
Individual Education Program: 431 (13.7%);
English Language Learner: 227 (7.2%); Migrant: 104 (3.3%)
Eligible for Free Lunch Program: 2,130 (67.5%)
Eligible for Reduced-Price Lunch Program: 417 (13.2%)

Teachers: 216.4 (14.6 to 1)
Librarians/Media Specialists: 4.0 (788.5 to 1)
Guidance Counselors: 8.0 (394.3 to 1)
Current Spending: ($ per student per year):
Total: $6,765; Instruction: $4,096; Support Services: $2,261

Enrollment, Drop-out Rates and Diploma Recipients by Race/Ethnicity

Category	Total	White	Black	Asian	AIAN	Hisp.
Enrollment (%)	100.0	18.7	1.3	0.1	0.1	79.7
Drop-out Rate (%)	4.3	3.3	0.0	0.0	0.0	4.7
H.S. Diplomas (#)	127	33	0	1	1	92

South San Antonio ISD

2515 Bobcat Ln • San Antonio, TX 78224-1268
(210) 977-7000
Grade Span: PK-12; **Agency Type:** 1
Schools: 20
10 Primary; 3 Middle; 4 High; 2 Other Level
15 Regular; 0 Special Education; 0 Vocational; 4 Alternative
0 Magnet; 0 Charter; 17 Title I Eligible; 17 School-wide Title I

Students: 10,040 (51.9% male; 48.1% female)
Individual Education Program: 1,122 (11.2%);
English Language Learner: 1,726 (17.2%); Migrant: 336 (3.3%)
Eligible for Free Lunch Program: 7,993 (79.6%)
Eligible for Reduced-Price Lunch Program: 1,091 (10.9%)

Teachers: 672.7 (14.9 to 1)
Librarians/Media Specialists: 12.0 (836.7 to 1)
Guidance Counselors: 23.0 (436.5 to 1)
Current Spending: ($ per student per year):
Total: $6,699; Instruction: $4,269; Support Services: $2,033

Enrollment, Drop-out Rates and Diploma Recipients by Race/Ethnicity

Category	Total	White	Black	Asian	AIAN	Hisp.
Enrollment (%)	100.0	3.0	1.7	0.3	0.2	94.8
Drop-out Rate (%)	7.5	5.8	4.7	0.0	n/a	7.6
H.S. Diplomas (#)	474	16	5	1	0	452

Southside ISD

1460 Martinez Losoya Rd • San Antonio, TX 78221-9613
(210) 626-0600
Grade Span: PK-12; **Agency Type:** 1
Schools: 8
2 Primary; 2 Middle; 1 High; 2 Other Level
5 Regular; 0 Special Education; 0 Vocational; 2 Alternative
0 Magnet; 0 Charter; 5 Title I Eligible; 5 School-wide Title I

Students: 4,720 (51.6% male; 48.4% female)
Individual Education Program: 681 (14.4%);
English Language Learner: 411 (8.7%); Migrant: 159 (3.4%)
Eligible for Free Lunch Program: 3,243 (68.7%)
Eligible for Reduced-Price Lunch Program: 517 (11.0%)

Teachers: 301.9 (15.6 to 1)
Librarians/Media Specialists: 5.0 (944.0 to 1)
Guidance Counselors: 12.0 (393.3 to 1)
Current Spending: ($ per student per year):
Total: $5,894; Instruction: $3,527; Support Services: $2,005

Enrollment, Drop-out Rates and Diploma Recipients by Race/Ethnicity

Category	Total	White	Black	Asian	AIAN	Hisp.
Enrollment (%)	100.0	16.2	1.6	0.9	0.1	81.2
Drop-out Rate (%)	5.2	5.7	5.9	0.0	0.0	5.2
H.S. Diplomas (#)	264	36	2	7	1	218

Southwest ISD

11914 Dragon Ln • San Antonio, TX 78252-2647
(210) 622-4300
Grade Span: PK-12; **Agency Type:** 1
Schools: 15
9 Primary; 3 Middle; 1 High; 1 Other Level

13 Regular; 0 Special Education; 0 Vocational; 1 Alternative
0 Magnet; 0 Charter; 13 Title I Eligible; 13 School-wide Title I
Students: 9,640 (51.0% male; 49.0% female)
Individual Education Program: 1,274 (13.2%);
English Language Learner: 1,063 (11.0%); Migrant: 236 (2.4%)
Eligible for Free Lunch Program: 6,392 (66.3%)
Eligible for Reduced-Price Lunch Program: 1,142 (11.8%)
Teachers: 647.0 (14.9 to 1)
Librarians/Media Specialists: 6.0 (1,606.7 to 1)
Guidance Counselors: 24.0 (401.7 to 1)
Current Spending: ($ per student per year):
Total: $6,008; Instruction: $3,768; Support Services: $1,922
Enrollment, Drop-out Rates and Diploma Recipients by Race/Ethnicity

Category	Total	White	Black	Asian	AIAN	Hisp.
Enrollment (%)	100.0	10.4	4.0	0.3	0.2	85.1
Drop-out Rate (%)	5.0	2.5	0.8	0.0	0.0	5.7
H.S. Diplomas (#)	476	72	25	3	0	376

Bowie County

Liberty-Eylau ISD

2901 Leopard Dr • Texarkana, TX 75501-7817
(903) 832-1535
Grade Span: PK-12; **Agency Type:** 1
Schools: 7
3 Primary; 1 Middle; 2 High; 1 Other Level
5 Regular; 0 Special Education; 0 Vocational; 2 Alternative
0 Magnet; 0 Charter; 3 Title I Eligible; 3 School-wide Title I
Students: 2,677 (51.4% male; 48.6% female)
Individual Education Program: 436 (16.3%);
English Language Learner: 12 (0.4%); Migrant: 8 (0.3%)
Eligible for Free Lunch Program: 1,556 (58.1%)
Eligible for Reduced-Price Lunch Program: 180 (6.7%)
Teachers: 211.4 (12.7 to 1)
Librarians/Media Specialists: 4.0 (669.3 to 1)
Guidance Counselors: 7.4 (361.8 to 1)
Current Spending: ($ per student per year):
Total: $7,178; Instruction: $4,650; Support Services: $2,175
Enrollment, Drop-out Rates and Diploma Recipients by Race/Ethnicity

Category	Total	White	Black	Asian	AIAN	Hisp.
Enrollment (%)	100.0	51.2	46.8	0.2	0.1	1.6
Drop-out Rate (%)	3.1	3.1	3.0	n/a	0.0	2.3
H.S. Diplomas (#)	164	80	77	0	1	6

Pleasant Grove ISD

5605 Cooks Ln • Texarkana, TX 75503-1599
Mailing Address: 8500 N Kings Hwy • Texarkana, TX 75503-4893
(903) 831-4086
Grade Span: PK-12; **Agency Type:** 1
Schools: 3
1 Primary; 1 Middle; 1 High; 0 Other Level
3 Regular; 0 Special Education; 0 Vocational; 0 Alternative
0 Magnet; 0 Charter; 1 Title I Eligible; 0 School-wide Title I
Students: 1,918 (50.7% male; 49.3% female)
Individual Education Program: 171 (8.9%);
English Language Learner: 23 (1.2%); Migrant: 1 (0.1%)
Eligible for Free Lunch Program: 181 (9.4%)
Eligible for Reduced-Price Lunch Program: 65 (3.4%)
Teachers: 134.5 (14.3 to 1)
Librarians/Media Specialists: 3.0 (639.3 to 1)
Guidance Counselors: 4.0 (479.5 to 1)
Current Spending: ($ per student per year):
Total: $5,360; Instruction: $3,407; Support Services: $1,741
Enrollment, Drop-out Rates and Diploma Recipients by Race/Ethnicity

Category	Total	White	Black	Asian	AIAN	Hisp.
Enrollment (%)	100.0	88.6	7.0	2.1	0.3	1.9
Drop-out Rate (%)	1.3	1.0	5.7	0.0	n/a	0.0
H.S. Diplomas (#)	130	116	10	2	0	2

Texarkana ISD

4241 Summerhill Rd • Texarkana, TX 75503-2733
(903) 794-3651
Grade Span: PK-12; **Agency Type:** 1
Schools: 11
7 Primary; 1 Middle; 2 High; 1 Other Level
9 Regular; 0 Special Education; 0 Vocational; 2 Alternative
0 Magnet; 0 Charter; 7 Title I Eligible; 7 School-wide Title I
Students: 5,635 (50.4% male; 49.6% female)
Individual Education Program: 887 (15.7%);
English Language Learner: 90 (1.6%); Migrant: 2 (<0.1%)
Eligible for Free Lunch Program: 3,174 (56.3%)
Eligible for Reduced-Price Lunch Program: 365 (6.5%)
Teachers: 376.6 (15.0 to 1)
Librarians/Media Specialists: 1.9 (2,965.8 to 1)
Guidance Counselors: 16.8 (335.4 to 1)
Current Spending: ($ per student per year):
Total: $6,056; Instruction: $3,683; Support Services: $2,031
Enrollment, Drop-out Rates and Diploma Recipients by Race/Ethnicity

Category	Total	White	Black	Asian	AIAN	Hisp.
Enrollment (%)	100.0	44.9	49.9	0.7	0.3	4.2
Drop-out Rate (%)	5.2	3.3	7.2	7.7	50.0	8.1
H.S. Diplomas (#)	276	162	107	4	0	3

Brazoria County

Alvin ISD

301 E House St • Alvin, TX 77511-3581
(281) 388-1130 • http://www.alvin.isd.tenet.edu/
Grade Span: PK-12; **Agency Type:** 1
Schools: 17
7 Primary; 7 Middle; 1 High; 2 Other Level
14 Regular; 1 Special Education; 0 Vocational; 2 Alternative
0 Magnet; 0 Charter; 15 Title I Eligible; 15 School-wide Title I
Students: 11,756 (52.2% male; 47.8% female)
Individual Education Program: 1,479 (12.6%);
English Language Learner: 1,117 (9.5%); Migrant: 82 (0.7%)
Eligible for Free Lunch Program: 4,575 (38.9%)
Eligible for Reduced-Price Lunch Program: 1,054 (9.0%)
Teachers: 778.2 (15.1 to 1)
Librarians/Media Specialists: 14.0 (839.7 to 1)
Guidance Counselors: 22.0 (534.4 to 1)
Current Spending: ($ per student per year):
Total: $6,356; Instruction: $3,906; Support Services: $2,120
Enrollment, Drop-out Rates and Diploma Recipients by Race/Ethnicity

Category	Total	White	Black	Asian	AIAN	Hisp.
Enrollment (%)	100.0	56.0	3.3	2.0	0.2	38.4
Drop-out Rate (%)	4.7	4.0	7.2	1.8	0.0	6.2
H.S. Diplomas (#)	509	355	19	9	0	126

Angleton ISD

1900 N Downing Rd • Angleton, TX 77515-3799
(979) 849-8594 • http://www.aisd.net/
Grade Span: PK-12; **Agency Type:** 1
Schools: 15
5 Primary; 2 Middle; 2 High; 4 Other Level
9 Regular; 0 Special Education; 0 Vocational; 4 Alternative
0 Magnet; 0 Charter; 8 Title I Eligible; 1 School-wide Title I
Students: 6,503 (51.6% male; 48.4% female)
Individual Education Program: 926 (14.2%);
English Language Learner: 358 (5.5%); Migrant: 15 (0.2%)
Eligible for Free Lunch Program: 2,127 (32.7%)
Eligible for Reduced-Price Lunch Program: 504 (7.8%)
Teachers: 420.3 (15.5 to 1)
Librarians/Media Specialists: 8.0 (812.9 to 1)
Guidance Counselors: 14.0 (464.5 to 1)
Current Spending: ($ per student per year):
Total: $5,832; Instruction: $3,662; Support Services: $1,873
Enrollment, Drop-out Rates and Diploma Recipients by Race/Ethnicity

Category	Total	White	Black	Asian	AIAN	Hisp.
Enrollment (%)	100.0	51.8	15.4	0.8	0.2	31.8
Drop-out Rate (%)	1.7	1.6	3.0	0.0	20.0	1.0
H.S. Diplomas (#)	318	187	51	4	1	75

Brazosport ISD

301 W Brazoswood Dr • Clute, TX 77531-3598
Mailing Address: PO Drawer Z • Freeport, TX 77541-1926
(979) 265-6181 • http://www.brazosport.isd.tenet.edu/
Grade Span: PK-12; **Agency Type:** 1
Schools: 21
11 Primary; 5 Middle; 2 High; 3 Other Level
18 Regular; 0 Special Education; 0 Vocational; 3 Alternative
0 Magnet; 0 Charter; 8 Title I Eligible; 8 School-wide Title I
Students: 13,198 (51.5% male; 48.5% female)
Individual Education Program: 1,805 (13.7%);
English Language Learner: 981 (7.4%); Migrant: 513 (3.9%)
Eligible for Free Lunch Program: 4,814 (36.5%)
Eligible for Reduced-Price Lunch Program: 907 (6.9%)
Teachers: 814.8 (16.2 to 1)
Librarians/Media Specialists: 19.5 (676.8 to 1)
Guidance Counselors: 33.7 (391.6 to 1)
Current Spending: ($ per student per year):
Total: $6,108; Instruction: $3,724; Support Services: $2,050
Enrollment, Drop-out Rates and Diploma Recipients by Race/Ethnicity

Category	Total	White	Black	Asian	AIAN	Hisp.
Enrollment (%)	100.0	51.2	9.8	1.4	0.2	37.5
Drop-out Rate (%)	4.1	3.0	4.5	5.0	0.0	6.2
H.S. Diplomas (#)	733	449	53	14	3	214

Columbia-Brazoria ISD
521 S 16th St • West Columbia, TX 77486-0158
Mailing Address: PO Box 158 • West Columbia, TX 77486-0158
(979) 345-5147 • http://www.columbia-brazoria.isd.tenet.edu/
Grade Span: PK-12; **Agency Type:** 1
Schools: 9
3 Primary; 2 Middle; 1 High; 1 Other Level
6 Regular; 0 Special Education; 0 Vocational; 1 Alternative
0 Magnet; 0 Charter; 4 Title I Eligible; 4 School-wide Title I
Students: 3,119 (50.4% male; 49.6% female)
Individual Education Program: 351 (11.3%);
English Language Learner: 112 (3.6%); Migrant: 1 (<0.1%)
Eligible for Free Lunch Program: 1,042 (33.4%)
Eligible for Reduced-Price Lunch Program: 185 (5.9%)
Teachers: 207.7 (15.0 to 1)
Librarians/Media Specialists: 3.8 (820.8 to 1)
Guidance Counselors: 5.3 (588.5 to 1)
Current Spending: ($ per student per year):
Total: $5,900; Instruction: $3,525; Support Services: $2,037
Enrollment, Drop-out Rates and Diploma Recipients by Race/Ethnicity

Category	Total	White	Black	Asian	AIAN	Hisp.
Enrollment (%)	100.0	64.5	16.0	0.6	0.4	18.5
Drop-out Rate (%)	3.9	3.3	6.2	0.0	0.0	4.2
H.S. Diplomas (#)	185	123	39	1	0	22

Pearland ISD
2337 N Galveston Ave • Pearland, TX 77581-4245
Mailing Address: PO Box 7 • Pearland, TX 77581-4209
(281) 485-3203
Grade Span: PK-12; **Agency Type:** 1
Schools: 16
8 Primary; 6 Middle; 1 High; 1 Other Level
14 Regular; 0 Special Education; 0 Vocational; 2 Alternative
0 Magnet; 0 Charter; 4 Title I Eligible; 0 School-wide Title I
Students: 12,235 (51.0% male; 49.0% female)
Individual Education Program: 1,220 (10.0%);
English Language Learner: 660 (5.4%); Migrant: 7 (0.1%)
Eligible for Free Lunch Program: 1,572 (12.8%)
Eligible for Reduced-Price Lunch Program: 488 (4.0%)
Teachers: 775.5 (15.8 to 1)
Librarians/Media Specialists: 14.5 (843.8 to 1)
Guidance Counselors: 24.3 (503.5 to 1)
Current Spending: ($ per student per year):
Total: $5,632; Instruction: $3,341; Support Services: $2,055
Enrollment, Drop-out Rates and Diploma Recipients by Race/Ethnicity

Category	Total	White	Black	Asian	AIAN	Hisp.
Enrollment (%)	100.0	59.1	11.1	7.5	0.1	22.1
Drop-out Rate (%)	2.7	3.0	0.0	1.4	0.0	3.2
H.S. Diplomas (#)	628	426	54	29	2	117

Sweeny ISD
1310 N Elm St • Sweeny, TX 77480-1399
(979) 491-8000
Grade Span: PK-12; **Agency Type:** 1
Schools: 4
1 Primary; 1 Middle; 1 High; 1 Other Level
3 Regular; 0 Special Education; 0 Vocational; 1 Alternative
0 Magnet; 0 Charter; 3 Title I Eligible; 3 School-wide Title I
Students: 2,200 (53.1% male; 46.9% female)
Individual Education Program: 266 (12.1%);
English Language Learner: 57 (2.6%); Migrant: 0 (0.0%)
Eligible for Free Lunch Program: 585 (26.6%)
Eligible for Reduced-Price Lunch Program: 149 (6.8%)
Teachers: 150.1 (14.7 to 1)
Librarians/Media Specialists: 3.0 (733.3 to 1)
Guidance Counselors: 6.0 (366.7 to 1)
Current Spending: ($ per student per year):
Total: $7,117; Instruction: $4,291; Support Services: $2,517
Enrollment, Drop-out Rates and Diploma Recipients by Race/Ethnicity

Category	Total	White	Black	Asian	AIAN	Hisp.
Enrollment (%)	100.0	67.6	17.1	0.1	0.3	14.9
Drop-out Rate (%)	0.7	1.0	0.0	0.0	0.0	0.0
H.S. Diplomas (#)	156	107	31	2	1	15

Brazos County

Bryan ISD
101 N Texas Ave • Bryan, TX 77803-5398
(979) 361-5200 • http://www.bryanisd.org/
Grade Span: PK-12; **Agency Type:** 1
Schools: 24
16 Primary; 3 Middle; 3 High; 2 Other Level
21 Regular; 1 Special Education; 0 Vocational; 2 Alternative
0 Magnet; 0 Charter; 15 Title I Eligible; 14 School-wide Title I
Students: 14,006 (51.6% male; 48.4% female)
Individual Education Program: 1,704 (12.2%);
English Language Learner: 1,506 (10.8%); Migrant: 304 (2.2%)
Eligible for Free Lunch Program: 7,565 (54.0%)
Eligible for Reduced-Price Lunch Program: 858 (6.1%)
Teachers: 967.4 (14.5 to 1)
Librarians/Media Specialists: 19.9 (703.8 to 1)
Guidance Counselors: 33.1 (423.1 to 1)
Current Spending: ($ per student per year):
Total: $6,382; Instruction: $3,874; Support Services: $2,141
Enrollment, Drop-out Rates and Diploma Recipients by Race/Ethnicity

Category	Total	White	Black	Asian	AIAN	Hisp.
Enrollment (%)	100.0	37.8	24.7	0.6	0.1	36.7
Drop-out Rate (%)	4.5	2.0	8.4	0.0	0.0	5.4
H.S. Diplomas (#)	699	365	143	5	1	185

College Station ISD
1812 Welsh Ave • College Station, TX 77840-4851
(979) 764-5400
Grade Span: PK-12; **Agency Type:** 1
Schools: 11
5 Primary; 4 Middle; 2 High; 0 Other Level
10 Regular; 0 Special Education; 0 Vocational; 1 Alternative
0 Magnet; 0 Charter; 3 Title I Eligible; 3 School-wide Title I
Students: 7,689 (52.7% male; 47.3% female)
Individual Education Program: 678 (8.8%);
English Language Learner: 377 (4.9%); Migrant: 0 (0.0%)
Eligible for Free Lunch Program: 1,085 (14.1%)
Eligible for Reduced-Price Lunch Program: 350 (4.6%)
Teachers: 526.9 (14.6 to 1)
Librarians/Media Specialists: 9.1 (844.9 to 1)
Guidance Counselors: 12.5 (615.1 to 1)
Current Spending: ($ per student per year):
Total: $6,515; Instruction: $4,016; Support Services: $2,210
Enrollment, Drop-out Rates and Diploma Recipients by Race/Ethnicity

Category	Total	White	Black	Asian	AIAN	Hisp.
Enrollment (%)	100.0	66.8	12.0	8.6	0.1	12.6
Drop-out Rate (%)	1.9	1.2	3.9	0.8	0.0	7.0
H.S. Diplomas (#)	512	401	44	33	0	34

Brooks County

Brooks County ISD
221 S Henry St • Falfurrias, TX 78355-4321
Mailing Address: PO Box 589 • Falfurrias, TX 78355-0589
(361) 325-5681
Grade Span: PK-12; **Agency Type:** 1
Schools: 4
2 Primary; 1 Middle; 1 High; 0 Other Level
4 Regular; 0 Special Education; 0 Vocational; 0 Alternative
0 Magnet; 0 Charter; 4 Title I Eligible; 4 School-wide Title I
Students: 1,719 (52.3% male; 47.7% female)
Individual Education Program: 246 (14.3%);
English Language Learner: 76 (4.4%); Migrant: 190 (11.1%)
Eligible for Free Lunch Program: 1,303 (75.8%)
Eligible for Reduced-Price Lunch Program: 77 (4.5%)
Teachers: 133.4 (12.9 to 1)
Librarians/Media Specialists: 1.0 (1,719.0 to 1)
Guidance Counselors: 4.0 (429.8 to 1)
Current Spending: ($ per student per year):
Total: $7,423; Instruction: $4,561; Support Services: $2,421
Enrollment, Drop-out Rates and Diploma Recipients by Race/Ethnicity

Category	Total	White	Black	Asian	AIAN	Hisp.
Enrollment (%)	100.0	4.2	0.2	0.1	0.1	95.5
Drop-out Rate (%)	4.8	6.5	0.0	0.0	n/a	4.7
H.S. Diplomas (#)	111	3	1	0	0	107

Brown County

Brownwood ISD
2707 Southside • Brownwood, TX 76801-6148
Mailing Address: PO Box 730 • Brownwood, TX 76804-0730
(915) 643-5644 • http://www.brownwoodisd.com/
Grade Span: PK-12; **Agency Type:** 1
Schools: 10
3 Primary; 3 Middle; 2 High; 1 Other Level
7 Regular; 0 Special Education; 0 Vocational; 2 Alternative
0 Magnet; 0 Charter; 6 Title I Eligible; 6 School-wide Title I
Students: 3,765 (51.5% male; 48.5% female)
Individual Education Program: 467 (12.4%);
English Language Learner: 124 (3.3%); Migrant: 18 (0.5%)
Eligible for Free Lunch Program: 1,766 (46.9%)
Eligible for Reduced-Price Lunch Program: 366 (9.7%)
Teachers: 278.3 (13.5 to 1)
Librarians/Media Specialists: 1.0 (3,765.0 to 1)
Guidance Counselors: 8.0 (470.6 to 1)

Current Spending: ($ per student per year):
Total: $6,183; Instruction: $4,019; Support Services: $1,884
Enrollment, Drop-out Rates and Diploma Recipients by Race/Ethnicity

Category	Total	White	Black	Asian	AIAN	Hisp.
Enrollment (%)	100.0	60.0	7.1	0.2	0.1	32.6
Drop-out Rate (%)	5.4	4.7	9.5	33.3	0.0	5.5
H.S. Diplomas (#)	250	162	20	1	0	67

Burleson County

Caldwell ISD

203 N Gray St • Caldwell, TX 77836-1549
(979) 567-9559
Grade Span: PK-12; **Agency Type:** 1
Schools: 5
2 Primary; 1 Middle; 1 High; 1 Other Level
4 Regular; 0 Special Education; 0 Vocational; 1 Alternative
0 Magnet; 0 Charter; 4 Title I Eligible; 3 School-wide Title I
Students: 1,914 (53.1% male; 46.9% female)
Individual Education Program: 247 (12.9%);
English Language Learner: 112 (5.9%); Migrant: 0 (0.0%)
Eligible for Free Lunch Program: 710 (37.1%)
Eligible for Reduced-Price Lunch Program: 143 (7.5%)
Teachers: 143.8 (13.3 to 1)
Librarians/Media Specialists: 1.0 (1,914.0 to 1)
Guidance Counselors: 7.0 (273.4 to 1)
Current Spending: ($ per student per year):
Total: $6,782; Instruction: $3,863; Support Services: $2,627
Enrollment, Drop-out Rates and Diploma Recipients by Race/Ethnicity

Category	Total	White	Black	Asian	AIAN	Hisp.
Enrollment (%)	100.0	63.4	14.4	0.2	0.1	21.9
Drop-out Rate (%)	3.6	2.4	6.5	0.0	0.0	6.8
H.S. Diplomas (#)	124	94	17	0	0	13

Burnet County

Burnet Cons ISD

208 E Brier Ln • Burnet, TX 78611-0180
(512) 756-2124 • http://www.burnet.txed.net/
Grade Span: PK-12; **Agency Type:** 1
Schools: 6
2 Primary; 2 Middle; 2 High; 0 Other Level
5 Regular; 0 Special Education; 0 Vocational; 1 Alternative
0 Magnet; 0 Charter; 4 Title I Eligible; 4 School-wide Title I
Students: 3,075 (50.6% male; 49.4% female)
Individual Education Program: 469 (15.3%);
English Language Learner: 136 (4.4%); Migrant: 27 (0.9%)
Eligible for Free Lunch Program: 990 (32.2%)
Eligible for Reduced-Price Lunch Program: 334 (10.9%)
Teachers: 221.3 (13.9 to 1)
Librarians/Media Specialists: 2.5 (1,230.0 to 1)
Guidance Counselors: 7.5 (410.0 to 1)
Current Spending: ($ per student per year):
Total: $6,548; Instruction: $4,067; Support Services: $2,174
Enrollment, Drop-out Rates and Diploma Recipients by Race/Ethnicity

Category	Total	White	Black	Asian	AIAN	Hisp.
Enrollment (%)	100.0	78.8	1.3	0.6	0.2	19.2
Drop-out Rate (%)	2.2	1.7	0.0	0.0	0.0	4.7
H.S. Diplomas (#)	169	139	4	0	0	26

Marble Falls ISD

2001 Broadway St • Marble Falls, TX 78654-4803
(830) 693-4357
Grade Span: PK-12; **Agency Type:** 1
Schools: 5
3 Primary; 1 Middle; 1 High; 0 Other Level
5 Regular; 0 Special Education; 0 Vocational; 0 Alternative
0 Magnet; 0 Charter; 5 Title I Eligible; 5 School-wide Title I
Students: 3,655 (50.0% male; 50.0% female)
Individual Education Program: 423 (11.6%);
English Language Learner: 332 (9.1%); Migrant: 71 (1.9%)
Eligible for Free Lunch Program: 1,352 (37.0%)
Eligible for Reduced-Price Lunch Program: 310 (8.5%)
Teachers: 260.6 (14.0 to 1)
Librarians/Media Specialists: 4.0 (913.8 to 1)
Guidance Counselors: 8.5 (430.0 to 1)
Current Spending: ($ per student per year):
Total: $6,788; Instruction: $3,775; Support Services: $2,687
Enrollment, Drop-out Rates and Diploma Recipients by Race/Ethnicity

Category	Total	White	Black	Asian	AIAN	Hisp.
Enrollment (%)	100.0	67.0	1.9	0.4	0.5	30.2
Drop-out Rate (%)	3.5	2.6	0.0	0.0	0.0	7.0
H.S. Diplomas (#)	193	155	2	1	2	33

Caldwell County

Lockhart ISD

105 S Colorado • Lockhart, TX 78644-2730
Mailing Address: PO Box 120 • Lockhart, TX 78644-0120
(512) 398-0000 • http://www.lockhart.k12.tx.us/
Grade Span: PK-12; **Agency Type:** 1
Schools: 9
4 Primary; 1 Middle; 2 High; 1 Other Level
7 Regular; 0 Special Education; 0 Vocational; 1 Alternative
0 Magnet; 0 Charter; 4 Title I Eligible; 4 School-wide Title I
Students: 4,469 (51.5% male; 48.5% female)
Individual Education Program: 675 (15.1%);
English Language Learner: 147 (3.3%); Migrant: 39 (0.9%)
Eligible for Free Lunch Program: 1,692 (37.9%)
Eligible for Reduced-Price Lunch Program: 545 (12.2%)
Teachers: 303.6 (14.7 to 1)
Librarians/Media Specialists: 7.0 (638.4 to 1)
Guidance Counselors: 11.0 (406.3 to 1)
Current Spending: ($ per student per year):
Total: $6,341; Instruction: $3,851; Support Services: $2,179
Enrollment, Drop-out Rates and Diploma Recipients by Race/Ethnicity

Category	Total	White	Black	Asian	AIAN	Hisp.
Enrollment (%)	100.0	40.0	8.2	0.5	0.2	51.1
Drop-out Rate (%)	4.2	2.7	3.4	7.7	0.0	6.1
H.S. Diplomas (#)	285	141	31	2	0	111

Luling ISD

212 E Bowie St • Luling, TX 78648-2904
(830) 875-3191
Grade Span: PK-12; **Agency Type:** 1
Schools: 5
3 Primary; 1 Middle; 1 High; 0 Other Level
5 Regular; 0 Special Education; 0 Vocational; 0 Alternative
0 Magnet; 0 Charter; 5 Title I Eligible; 5 School-wide Title I
Students: 1,594 (50.3% male; 49.7% female)
Individual Education Program: 181 (11.4%);
English Language Learner: 109 (6.8%); Migrant: 82 (5.1%)
Eligible for Free Lunch Program: 867 (54.4%)
Eligible for Reduced-Price Lunch Program: 161 (10.1%)
Teachers: 110.6 (14.4 to 1)
Librarians/Media Specialists: 1.0 (1,594.0 to 1)
Guidance Counselors: 4.0 (398.5 to 1)
Current Spending: ($ per student per year):
Total: $5,524; Instruction: $3,725; Support Services: $1,450
Enrollment, Drop-out Rates and Diploma Recipients by Race/Ethnicity

Category	Total	White	Black	Asian	AIAN	Hisp.
Enrollment (%)	100.0	39.5	9.0	0.3	0.1	51.1
Drop-out Rate (%)	5.3	3.3	2.3	0.0	n/a	8.0
H.S. Diplomas (#)	86	44	6	0	0	36

Calhoun County

Calhoun County ISD

525 N Commerce St • Port Lavaca, TX 77979-3034
(361) 552-9728
Grade Span: PK-12; **Agency Type:** 1
Schools: 9
5 Primary; 1 Middle; 2 High; 1 Other Level
7 Regular; 0 Special Education; 0 Vocational; 2 Alternative
0 Magnet; 0 Charter; 4 Title I Eligible; 4 School-wide Title I
Students: 4,216 (51.4% male; 48.6% female)
Individual Education Program: 526 (12.5%);
English Language Learner: 291 (6.9%); Migrant: 25 (0.6%)
Eligible for Free Lunch Program: 1,944 (46.1%)
Eligible for Reduced-Price Lunch Program: 383 (9.1%)
Teachers: 286.4 (14.7 to 1)
Librarians/Media Specialists: 3.0 (1,405.3 to 1)
Guidance Counselors: 10.0 (421.6 to 1)
Current Spending: ($ per student per year):
Total: $7,118; Instruction: $4,192; Support Services: $2,573
Enrollment, Drop-out Rates and Diploma Recipients by Race/Ethnicity

Category	Total	White	Black	Asian	AIAN	Hisp.
Enrollment (%)	100.0	40.2	2.3	4.0	0.0	53.4
Drop-out Rate (%)	9.4	4.6	5.9	0.0	n/a	16.1
H.S. Diplomas (#)	225	112	7	15	0	91

Cameron County

Brownsville ISD

1900 Price Rd • Brownsville, TX 78521-2417
(956) 548-8000
Grade Span: PK-12; **Agency Type:** 1
Schools: 52
32 Primary; 10 Middle; 6 High; 4 Other Level

47 Regular; 0 Special Education; 0 Vocational; 5 Alternative
0 Magnet; 0 Charter; 49 Title I Eligible; 49 School-wide Title I
Students: 44,340 (51.2% male; 48.8% female)
Individual Education Program: 5,372 (12.1%);
English Language Learner: 20,896 (47.1%); Migrant: 4,797 (10.8%)
Eligible for Free Lunch Program: 3,692 (8.3%)
Eligible for Reduced-Price Lunch Program: 404 (0.9%)
Teachers: 3,023.0 (14.7 to 1)
Librarians/Media Specialists: 50.8 (872.8 to 1)
Guidance Counselors: 135.9 (326.3 to 1)
Current Spending: ($ per student per year):
Total: $6,788; Instruction: $4,066; Support Services: $2,299
Enrollment, Drop-out Rates and Diploma Recipients by Race/Ethnicity

Category	Total	White	Black	Asian	AIAN	Hisp.
Enrollment (%)	100.0	1.9	0.1	0.3	0.0	97.7
Drop-out Rate (%)	3.7	1.3	0.0	3.3	0.0	3.8
H.S. Diplomas (#)	1,854	63	5	5	0	1,781

Harlingen Cons ISD
1409 E Harrison St • Harlingen, TX 78550-7129
(956) 427-3400 • http://www.harlingen.isd.tenet.edu/
Grade Span: PK-12; **Agency Type:** 1
Schools: 26
16 Primary; 4 Middle; 3 High; 3 Other Level
22 Regular; 0 Special Education; 0 Vocational; 4 Alternative
0 Magnet; 0 Charter; 21 Title I Eligible; 21 School-wide Title I
Students: 16,497 (51.8% male; 48.2% female)
Individual Education Program: 1,739 (10.5%);
English Language Learner: 2,176 (13.2%); Migrant: 1,949 (11.8%)
Eligible for Free Lunch Program: 10,633 (64.5%)
Eligible for Reduced-Price Lunch Program: 921 (5.6%)
Teachers: 1,032.3 (16.0 to 1)
Librarians/Media Specialists: 13.0 (1,269.0 to 1)
Guidance Counselors: 41.9 (393.7 to 1)
Current Spending: ($ per student per year):
Total: $6,215; Instruction: $3,905; Support Services: $1,967
Enrollment, Drop-out Rates and Diploma Recipients by Race/Ethnicity

Category	Total	White	Black	Asian	AIAN	Hisp.
Enrollment (%)	100.0	11.4	0.7	0.7	0.0	87.1
Drop-out Rate (%)	4.9	1.6	0.0	0.0	50.0	5.5
H.S. Diplomas (#)	807	140	7	6	0	654

La Feria ISD
203 E Oleander • La Feria, TX 78559-1159
Mailing Address: PO Box 1159 • La Feria, TX 78559-1159
(956) 797-2612
Grade Span: PK-12; **Agency Type:** 1
Schools: 8
3 Primary; 2 Middle; 1 High; 2 Other Level
6 Regular; 0 Special Education; 0 Vocational; 2 Alternative
0 Magnet; 0 Charter; 6 Title I Eligible; 6 School-wide Title I
Students: 2,840 (50.9% male; 49.1% female)
Individual Education Program: 268 (9.4%);
English Language Learner: 391 (13.8%); Migrant: 203 (7.1%)
Eligible for Free Lunch Program: 1,606 (56.5%)
Eligible for Reduced-Price Lunch Program: 196 (6.9%)
Teachers: 201.7 (14.1 to 1)
Librarians/Media Specialists: 3.0 (946.7 to 1)
Guidance Counselors: 7.0 (405.7 to 1)
Current Spending: ($ per student per year):
Total: $6,312; Instruction: $4,263; Support Services: $1,713
Enrollment, Drop-out Rates and Diploma Recipients by Race/Ethnicity

Category	Total	White	Black	Asian	AIAN	Hisp.
Enrollment (%)	100.0	9.5	0.2	0.1	0.0	90.1
Drop-out Rate (%)	2.2	1.1	33.3	n/a	n/a	2.2
H.S. Diplomas (#)	167	20	1	0	0	146

Los Fresnos CISD
600 N Mesquite St • Los Fresnos, TX 78566-3634
Mailing Address: PO Box 309 • Los Fresnos, TX 78566-0309
(956) 233-4407
Grade Span: PK-12; **Agency Type:** 1
Schools: 9
6 Primary; 2 Middle; 1 High; 0 Other Level
9 Regular; 0 Special Education; 0 Vocational; 0 Alternative
0 Magnet; 0 Charter; 9 Title I Eligible; 9 School-wide Title I
Students: 7,246 (51.7% male; 48.3% female)
Individual Education Program: 940 (13.0%);
English Language Learner: 1,969 (27.2%); Migrant: 610 (8.4%)
Eligible for Free Lunch Program: 2,776 (38.3%)
Eligible for Reduced-Price Lunch Program: 333 (4.6%)
Teachers: 470.1 (15.4 to 1)
Librarians/Media Specialists: 10.8 (670.9 to 1)
Guidance Counselors: 16.6 (436.5 to 1)
Current Spending: ($ per student per year):
Total: $6,924; Instruction: $4,127; Support Services: $2,396

Enrollment, Drop-out Rates and Diploma Recipients by Race/Ethnicity

Category	Total	White	Black	Asian	AIAN	Hisp.
Enrollment (%)	100.0	6.5	0.3	0.2	0.1	92.8
Drop-out Rate (%)	2.8	0.6	0.0	0.0	0.0	3.1
H.S. Diplomas (#)	369	36	2	0	1	330

Point Isabel ISD
202 Port Rd • Port Isabel, TX 78578-2433
Mailing Address: Drawer A H • Port Isabel, TX 78578-2433
(956) 943-0000
Grade Span: PK-12; **Agency Type:** 1
Schools: 4
2 Primary; 1 Middle; 1 High; 0 Other Level
4 Regular; 0 Special Education; 0 Vocational; 0 Alternative
0 Magnet; 0 Charter; 4 Title I Eligible; 4 School-wide Title I
Students: 2,433 (50.7% male; 49.3% female)
Individual Education Program: 266 (10.9%);
English Language Learner: 666 (27.4%); Migrant: 174 (7.2%)
Eligible for Free Lunch Program: 1,424 (58.5%)
Eligible for Reduced-Price Lunch Program: 135 (5.5%)
Teachers: 160.9 (15.1 to 1)
Librarians/Media Specialists: 4.5 (540.7 to 1)
Guidance Counselors: 7.5 (324.4 to 1)
Current Spending: ($ per student per year):
Total: $6,512; Instruction: $3,837; Support Services: $2,268
Enrollment, Drop-out Rates and Diploma Recipients by Race/Ethnicity

Category	Total	White	Black	Asian	AIAN	Hisp.
Enrollment (%)	100.0	14.5	0.3	0.2	0.0	84.9
Drop-out Rate (%)	4.3	6.6	0.0	0.0	0.0	4.0
H.S. Diplomas (#)	149	30	1	1	0	117

Rio Hondo ISD
215 W Colorado • Rio Hondo, TX 78583-0220
Mailing Address: PO Box 220 • Rio Hondo, TX 78583-0220
(956) 748-4400
Grade Span: PK-12; **Agency Type:** 1
Schools: 5
1 Primary; 2 Middle; 1 High; 0 Other Level
4 Regular; 0 Special Education; 0 Vocational; 0 Alternative
0 Magnet; 0 Charter; 4 Title I Eligible; 4 School-wide Title I
Students: 2,107 (52.2% male; 47.8% female)
Individual Education Program: 324 (15.4%);
English Language Learner: 254 (12.1%); Migrant: 180 (8.5%)
Eligible for Free Lunch Program: 952 (45.2%)
Eligible for Reduced-Price Lunch Program: 154 (7.3%)
Teachers: 126.5 (16.7 to 1)
Librarians/Media Specialists: 1.0 (2,107.0 to 1)
Guidance Counselors: 5.0 (421.4 to 1)
Current Spending: ($ per student per year):
Total: $7,502; Instruction: $4,378; Support Services: $2,674
Enrollment, Drop-out Rates and Diploma Recipients by Race/Ethnicity

Category	Total	White	Black	Asian	AIAN	Hisp.
Enrollment (%)	100.0	4.9	0.0	0.0	0.0	95.1
Drop-out Rate (%)	4.1	0.0	n/a	n/a	n/a	4.4
H.S. Diplomas (#)	109	6	0	0	0	103

San Benito Cons ISD
240 N Crockett St • San Benito, TX 78586-4608
(956) 361-6110
Grade Span: PK-12; **Agency Type:** 1
Schools: 18
10 Primary; 2 Middle; 1 High; 5 Other Level
14 Regular; 0 Special Education; 0 Vocational; 4 Alternative
0 Magnet; 0 Charter; 15 Title I Eligible; 15 School-wide Title I
Students: 9,610 (51.9% male; 48.1% female)
Individual Education Program: 1,151 (12.0%);
English Language Learner: 2,294 (23.9%); Migrant: 1,367 (14.2%)
Eligible for Free Lunch Program: 2,215 (23.0%)
Eligible for Reduced-Price Lunch Program: 260 (2.7%)
Teachers: 557.1 (17.3 to 1)
Librarians/Media Specialists: 11.7 (821.4 to 1)
Guidance Counselors: 25.5 (376.9 to 1)
Current Spending: ($ per student per year):
Total: $6,913; Instruction: $4,038; Support Services: $2,458
Enrollment, Drop-out Rates and Diploma Recipients by Race/Ethnicity

Category	Total	White	Black	Asian	AIAN	Hisp.
Enrollment (%)	100.0	2.2	0.1	0.1	0.0	97.6
Drop-out Rate (%)	7.1	0.0	0.0	0.0	n/a	7.4
H.S. Diplomas (#)	399	8	1	0	0	390

South Texas ISD
100 Med High Dr • Mercedes, TX 78570-9702
(956) 565-2454
Grade Span: 01-12; **Agency Type:** 1
Schools: 6

0 Primary; 0 Middle; 3 High; 1 Other Level
3 Regular; 1 Special Education; 0 Vocational; 0 Alternative
0 Magnet; 0 Charter; 3 Title I Eligible; 3 School-wide Title I
Students: 2,007 (48.1% male; 51.9% female)
Individual Education Program: 185 (9.2%);
English Language Learner: 110 (5.5%); Migrant: 80 (4.0%)
Eligible for Free Lunch Program: 798 (39.8%)
Eligible for Reduced-Price Lunch Program: 202 (10.1%)
Teachers: 171.5 (11.7 to 1)
Librarians/Media Specialists: 5.0 (401.4 to 1)
Guidance Counselors: 10.0 (200.7 to 1)
Current Spending: ($ per student per year):
Total: $9,210; Instruction: $5,213; Support Services: $3,726
Enrollment, Drop-out Rates and Diploma Recipients by Race/Ethnicity

Category	Total	White	Black	Asian	AIAN	Hisp.
Enrollment (%)	100.0	17.5	0.5	6.3	0.2	75.5
Drop-out Rate (%)	0.5	0.3	0.0	0.0	0.0	0.7
H.S. Diplomas (#)	353	70	1	23	0	259

Camp County

Pittsburg ISD

402 Broach St • Pittsburg, TX 75686-1039
Mailing Address: PO Box 1189 • Pittsburg, TX 75686-0621
(903) 856-3628
Grade Span: PK-12; **Agency Type:** 1
Schools: 5
2 Primary; 2 Middle; 1 High; 0 Other Level
5 Regular; 0 Special Education; 0 Vocational; 0 Alternative
0 Magnet; 0 Charter; 5 Title I Eligible; 5 School-wide Title I
Students: 2,298 (52.7% male; 47.3% female)
Individual Education Program: 375 (16.3%);
English Language Learner: 242 (10.5%); Migrant: 244 (10.6%)
Eligible for Free Lunch Program: 1,269 (55.2%)
Eligible for Reduced-Price Lunch Program: 185 (8.1%)
Teachers: 165.1 (13.9 to 1)
Librarians/Media Specialists: 4.0 (574.5 to 1)
Guidance Counselors: 5.0 (459.6 to 1)
Current Spending: ($ per student per year):
Total: $5,945; Instruction: $4,103; Support Services: $1,543
Enrollment, Drop-out Rates and Diploma Recipients by Race/Ethnicity

Category	Total	White	Black	Asian	AIAN	Hisp.
Enrollment (%)	100.0	52.2	22.6	0.2	0.1	24.9
Drop-out Rate (%)	2.5	3.0	1.2	0.0	0.0	3.4
H.S. Diplomas (#)	105	63	30	1	0	11

Cass County

Atlanta ISD

315 Buckner St • Atlanta, TX 75551-2211
(903) 796-4194
Grade Span: PK-12; **Agency Type:** 1
Schools: 5
2 Primary; 1 Middle; 1 High; 1 Other Level
4 Regular; 0 Special Education; 0 Vocational; 1 Alternative
0 Magnet; 0 Charter; 4 Title I Eligible; 4 School-wide Title I
Students: 1,928 (51.8% male; 48.2% female)
Individual Education Program: 363 (18.8%);
English Language Learner: 13 (0.7%); Migrant: 68 (3.5%)
Eligible for Free Lunch Program: 901 (46.7%)
Eligible for Reduced-Price Lunch Program: 186 (9.6%)
Teachers: 152.7 (12.6 to 1)
Librarians/Media Specialists: 3.6 (535.6 to 1)
Guidance Counselors: 4.9 (393.5 to 1)
Current Spending: ($ per student per year):
Total: $6,765; Instruction: $4,222; Support Services: $2,193
Enrollment, Drop-out Rates and Diploma Recipients by Race/Ethnicity

Category	Total	White	Black	Asian	AIAN	Hisp.
Enrollment (%)	100.0	61.6	35.8	0.1	0.1	2.4
Drop-out Rate (%)	0.5	0.6	0.5	0.0	0.0	0.0
H.S. Diplomas (#)	135	81	53	0	0	1

Chambers County

Barbers Hill ISD

9600 Eagle Dr • Mount Belvieu, TX 77580-1108
Mailing Address: PO Box 1108 • Mount Belvieu, TX 77580-1108
(281) 576-2221
Grade Span: PK-12; **Agency Type:** 1
Schools: 8
2 Primary; 2 Middle; 2 High; 2 Other Level
5 Regular; 1 Special Education; 0 Vocational; 2 Alternative
0 Magnet; 0 Charter; 1 Title I Eligible; 1 School-wide Title I
Students: 2,945 (51.0% male; 49.0% female)
Individual Education Program: 256 (8.7%);
English Language Learner: 72 (2.4%); Migrant: 1 (<0.1%)
Eligible for Free Lunch Program: 410 (13.9%)
Eligible for Reduced-Price Lunch Program: 136 (4.6%)
Teachers: 203.5 (14.5 to 1)
Librarians/Media Specialists: 5.0 (589.0 to 1)
Guidance Counselors: 6.0 (490.8 to 1)
Current Spending: ($ per student per year):
Total: $6,973; Instruction: $4,222; Support Services: $2,444
Enrollment, Drop-out Rates and Diploma Recipients by Race/Ethnicity

Category	Total	White	Black	Asian	AIAN	Hisp.
Enrollment (%)	100.0	84.9	2.8	0.3	0.3	11.7
Drop-out Rate (%)	2.2	2.0	0.0	n/a	0.0	3.8
H.S. Diplomas (#)	143	127	3	0	0	13

Cherokee County

Jacksonville ISD

1547 E Pine St • Jacksonville, TX 75766-5408
Mailing Address: PO Box 631 • Jacksonville, TX 75766-0631
(903) 586-6511
Grade Span: PK-12; **Agency Type:** 1
Schools: 8
4 Primary; 2 Middle; 1 High; 1 Other Level
7 Regular; 0 Special Education; 0 Vocational; 1 Alternative
0 Magnet; 0 Charter; 8 Title I Eligible; 8 School-wide Title I
Students: 4,725 (51.5% male; 48.5% female)
Individual Education Program: 607 (12.8%);
English Language Learner: 791 (16.7%); Migrant: 6 (0.1%)
Eligible for Free Lunch Program: 2,696 (57.1%)
Eligible for Reduced-Price Lunch Program: 310 (6.6%)
Teachers: 350.4 (13.5 to 1)
Librarians/Media Specialists: 5.4 (875.0 to 1)
Guidance Counselors: 10.0 (472.5 to 1)
Current Spending: ($ per student per year):
Total: $6,122; Instruction: $3,698; Support Services: $2,041
Enrollment, Drop-out Rates and Diploma Recipients by Race/Ethnicity

Category	Total	White	Black	Asian	AIAN	Hisp.
Enrollment (%)	100.0	47.2	22.4	0.4	0.2	29.7
Drop-out Rate (%)	1.8	1.4	1.6	25.0	0.0	2.8
H.S. Diplomas (#)	239	148	49	2	0	40

Rusk ISD

203 E 7th St • Rusk, TX 75785-1122
(903) 683-5592
Grade Span: PK-12; **Agency Type:** 1
Schools: 4
2 Primary; 1 Middle; 1 High; 0 Other Level
4 Regular; 0 Special Education; 0 Vocational; 0 Alternative
0 Magnet; 0 Charter; 3 Title I Eligible; 3 School-wide Title I
Students: 1,923 (51.5% male; 48.5% female)
Individual Education Program: 279 (14.5%);
English Language Learner: 75 (3.9%); Migrant: 14 (0.7%)
Eligible for Free Lunch Program: 829 (43.1%)
Eligible for Reduced-Price Lunch Program: 156 (8.1%)
Teachers: 157.6 (12.2 to 1)
Librarians/Media Specialists: 1.0 (1,923.0 to 1)
Guidance Counselors: 5.0 (384.6 to 1)
Current Spending: ($ per student per year):
Total: $6,212; Instruction: $3,868; Support Services: $2,009
Enrollment, Drop-out Rates and Diploma Recipients by Race/Ethnicity

Category	Total	White	Black	Asian	AIAN	Hisp.
Enrollment (%)	100.0	73.5	16.0	0.4	0.3	9.8
Drop-out Rate (%)	2.9	2.7	3.5	0.0	0.0	3.1
H.S. Diplomas (#)	104	72	21	2	1	8

Collin County

Allen ISD

601 E Main St • Allen, TX 75002-2837
Mailing Address: PO Box 13 • Allen, TX 75013-0013
(972) 727-0511 • http://www.allenisd.org/
Grade Span: PK-12; **Agency Type:** 1
Schools: 16
10 Primary; 2 Middle; 1 High; 2 Other Level
14 Regular; 0 Special Education; 0 Vocational; 1 Alternative
0 Magnet; 0 Charter; 3 Title I Eligible; 0 School-wide Title I
Students: 12,585 (51.1% male; 48.9% female)
Individual Education Program: 1,418 (11.3%);
English Language Learner: 479 (3.8%); Migrant: 4 (<0.1%)
Eligible for Free Lunch Program: 604 (4.8%)
Eligible for Reduced-Price Lunch Program: 196 (1.6%)
Teachers: 778.4 (16.2 to 1)
Librarians/Media Specialists: 13.4 (939.2 to 1)
Guidance Counselors: 21.5 (585.3 to 1)

Current Spending: ($ per student per year):
Total: $5,992; Instruction: $3,641; Support Services: $2,128
Enrollment, Drop-out Rates and Diploma Recipients by Race/Ethnicity

Category	Total	White	Black	Asian	AIAN	Hisp.
Enrollment (%)	100.0	78.5	7.2	5.1	0.7	8.5
Drop-out Rate (%)	1.1	0.8	1.4	1.4	4.0	3.7
H.S. Diplomas (#)	739	636	35	20	4	44

Frisco ISD
6942 W Maple • Frisco, TX 75034-3401
Mailing Address: PO Box 910 • Frisco, TX 75034-0910
(469) 633-6000 • http://www.friscoisd.org/
Grade Span: PK-12; **Agency Type:** 1
Schools: 20
13 Primary; 4 Middle; 1 High; 1 Other Level
17 Regular; 0 Special Education; 0 Vocational; 2 Alternative
0 Magnet; 0 Charter; 5 Title I Eligible; 0 School-wide Title I
Students: 11,145 (50.3% male; 49.7% female)
Individual Education Program: 1,201 (10.8%);
English Language Learner: 483 (4.3%); Migrant: 0 (0.0%)
Eligible for Free Lunch Program: 725 (6.5%)
Eligible for Reduced-Price Lunch Program: 316 (2.8%)
Teachers: 825.3 (13.5 to 1)
Librarians/Media Specialists: 18.0 (619.2 to 1)
Guidance Counselors: 26.1 (427.0 to 1)
Current Spending: ($ per student per year):
Total: $6,190; Instruction: $3,795; Support Services: $2,101
Enrollment, Drop-out Rates and Diploma Recipients by Race/Ethnicity

Category	Total	White	Black	Asian	AIAN	Hisp.
Enrollment (%)	100.0	72.6	7.8	5.7	0.8	13.2
Drop-out Rate (%)	2.4	2.1	2.7	0.0	12.5	3.3
H.S. Diplomas (#)	334	256	14	8	3	53

Mckinney ISD
#1 Duvall St • Mckinney, TX 75069-3211
(469) 742-4070
Grade Span: PK-12; **Agency Type:** 1
Schools: 25
15 Primary; 3 Middle; 3 High; 4 Other Level
21 Regular; 0 Special Education; 0 Vocational; 4 Alternative
0 Magnet; 0 Charter; 5 Title I Eligible; 5 School-wide Title I
Students: 15,279 (51.9% male; 48.1% female)
Individual Education Program: 1,688 (11.0%);
English Language Learner: 1,273 (8.3%); Migrant: 9 (0.1%)
Eligible for Free Lunch Program: 2,888 (18.9%)
Eligible for Reduced-Price Lunch Program: 525 (3.4%)
Teachers: 1,073.3 (14.2 to 1)
Librarians/Media Specialists: 20.0 (764.0 to 1)
Guidance Counselors: 33.1 (461.6 to 1)
Current Spending: ($ per student per year):
Total: $6,229; Instruction: $3,777; Support Services: $2,195
Enrollment, Drop-out Rates and Diploma Recipients by Race/Ethnicity

Category	Total	White	Black	Asian	AIAN	Hisp.
Enrollment (%)	100.0	67.5	8.9	2.0	0.5	21.1
Drop-out Rate (%)	3.2	1.8	9.7	0.0	13.3	6.2
H.S. Diplomas (#)	604	460	47	8	4	85

Plano ISD
2700 W 15th • Plano, TX 75075-5898
(469) 752-8100
Grade Span: PK-12; **Agency Type:** 1
Schools: 72
45 Primary; 11 Middle; 3 High; 9 Other Level
62 Regular; 0 Special Education; 0 Vocational; 6 Alternative
0 Magnet; 0 Charter; 17 Title I Eligible; 4 School-wide Title I
Students: 51,039 (51.2% male; 48.8% female)
Individual Education Program: 5,762 (11.3%);
English Language Learner: 4,740 (9.3%); Migrant: 2 (<0.1%)
Eligible for Free Lunch Program: 5,442 (10.7%)
Eligible for Reduced-Price Lunch Program: 1,400 (2.7%)
Teachers: 3,623.8 (14.1 to 1)
Librarians/Media Specialists: 64.6 (790.1 to 1)
Guidance Counselors: 129.5 (394.1 to 1)
Current Spending: ($ per student per year):
Total: $6,687; Instruction: $4,303; Support Services: $2,129
Enrollment, Drop-out Rates and Diploma Recipients by Race/Ethnicity

Category	Total	White	Black	Asian	AIAN	Hisp.
Enrollment (%)	100.0	64.5	8.2	15.1	0.4	11.8
Drop-out Rate (%)	0.8	0.7	1.1	0.3	2.7	2.4
H.S. Diplomas (#)	2,795	2,010	192	418	5	170

Princeton ISD
321 Panther Pkwy • Princeton, TX 75407-1002
(972) 736-3503
Grade Span: PK-12; **Agency Type:** 1
Schools: 5
1 Primary; 2 Middle; 1 High; 0 Other Level
4 Regular; 0 Special Education; 0 Vocational; 0 Alternative
0 Magnet; 0 Charter; 2 Title I Eligible; 2 School-wide Title I
Students: 2,247 (53.5% male; 46.5% female)
Individual Education Program: 338 (15.0%);
English Language Learner: 125 (5.6%); Migrant: 8 (0.4%)
Eligible for Free Lunch Program: 665 (29.6%)
Eligible for Reduced-Price Lunch Program: 184 (8.2%)
Teachers: 150.7 (14.9 to 1)
Librarians/Media Specialists: 3.1 (724.8 to 1)
Guidance Counselors: 4.9 (458.6 to 1)
Current Spending: ($ per student per year):
Total: $5,565; Instruction: $3,307; Support Services: $1,924
Enrollment, Drop-out Rates and Diploma Recipients by Race/Ethnicity

Category	Total	White	Black	Asian	AIAN	Hisp.
Enrollment (%)	100.0	78.9	1.7	0.2	0.6	18.6
Drop-out Rate (%)	1.7	1.9	0.0	0.0	0.0	1.4
H.S. Diplomas (#)	97	85	3	0	1	8

Wylie ISD
951 S Ballard • Wylie, TX 75098-4175
Mailing Address: PO Box 490 • Wylie, TX 75098-0490
(972) 442-5444
Grade Span: PK-12; **Agency Type:** 1
Schools: 10
5 Primary; 2 Middle; 1 High; 1 Other Level
8 Regular; 0 Special Education; 0 Vocational; 1 Alternative
0 Magnet; 0 Charter; 5 Title I Eligible; 0 School-wide Title I
Students: 5,710 (51.2% male; 48.8% female)
Individual Education Program: 653 (11.4%);
English Language Learner: 243 (4.3%); Migrant: 11 (0.2%)
Eligible for Free Lunch Program: 737 (12.9%)
Eligible for Reduced-Price Lunch Program: 249 (4.4%)
Teachers: 399.9 (14.3 to 1)
Librarians/Media Specialists: 3.0 (1,903.3 to 1)
Guidance Counselors: 12.3 (464.2 to 1)
Current Spending: ($ per student per year):
Total: $7,081; Instruction: $4,107; Support Services: $2,671
Enrollment, Drop-out Rates and Diploma Recipients by Race/Ethnicity

Category	Total	White	Black	Asian	AIAN	Hisp.
Enrollment (%)	100.0	76.8	6.1	2.2	1.0	13.7
Drop-out Rate (%)	2.6	2.8	0.0	0.0	14.3	1.8
H.S. Diplomas (#)	235	206	11	2	1	15

Colorado County

Columbus ISD
105 Cardinal Ln • Columbus, TX 78934-0578
(979) 732-5704
Grade Span: PK-12; **Agency Type:** 1
Schools: 3
1 Primary; 1 Middle; 1 High; 0 Other Level
3 Regular; 0 Special Education; 0 Vocational; 0 Alternative
0 Magnet; 0 Charter; 1 Title I Eligible; 1 School-wide Title I
Students: 1,614 (51.1% male; 48.9% female)
Individual Education Program: 232 (14.4%);
English Language Learner: 106 (6.6%); Migrant: 0 (0.0%)
Eligible for Free Lunch Program: 496 (30.7%)
Eligible for Reduced-Price Lunch Program: 143 (8.9%)
Teachers: 113.3 (14.2 to 1)
Librarians/Media Specialists: 3.0 (538.0 to 1)
Guidance Counselors: 4.0 (403.5 to 1)
Current Spending: ($ per student per year):
Total: $6,018; Instruction: $3,889; Support Services: $1,832
Enrollment, Drop-out Rates and Diploma Recipients by Race/Ethnicity

Category	Total	White	Black	Asian	AIAN	Hisp.
Enrollment (%)	100.0	65.8	12.9	0.2	0.1	21.0
Drop-out Rate (%)	1.5	0.3	3.3	0.0	n/a	5.8
H.S. Diplomas (#)	98	77	9	0	0	12

Comal County

Comal ISD
1421 N Business 35 • New Braunfels, TX 78130-3240
(830) 221-2000 • http://www.comalisd.org/
Grade Span: PK-12; **Agency Type:** 1
Schools: 21
10 Primary; 6 Middle; 3 High; 1 Other Level
19 Regular; 0 Special Education; 0 Vocational; 1 Alternative
0 Magnet; 0 Charter; 8 Title I Eligible; 0 School-wide Title I

Students: 11,305 (52.9% male; 47.1% female)
Individual Education Program: 1,578 (14.0%);
English Language Learner: 326 (2.9%); Migrant: 87 (0.8%)
Eligible for Free Lunch Program: 2,721 (24.1%)
Eligible for Reduced-Price Lunch Program: 733 (6.5%)
Teachers: 764.1 (14.8 to 1)
Librarians/Media Specialists: 16.9 (668.9 to 1)
Guidance Counselors: 25.7 (439.9 to 1)
Current Spending: ($ per student per year):
Total: $6,173; Instruction: $3,796; Support Services: $2,102
Enrollment, Drop-out Rates and Diploma Recipients by Race/Ethnicity

Category	Total	White	Black	Asian	AIAN	Hisp.
Enrollment (%)	100.0	75.4	1.2	0.5	0.2	22.8
Drop-out Rate (%)	3.1	2.7	6.1	0.0	0.0	4.7
H.S. Diplomas (#)	681	553	9	3	0	116

New Braunfels ISD

430 W Mill • New Braunfels, TX 78130-7993
Mailing Address: Box 311688 • New Braunfels, TX 78131-1688
(830) 643-5700 • http://www.newbraunfels.txed.net/
Grade Span: PK-12; **Agency Type:** 1
Schools: 12
7 Primary; 2 Middle; 1 High; 2 Other Level
10 Regular; 0 Special Education; 0 Vocational; 2 Alternative
0 Magnet; 0 Charter; 9 Title I Eligible; 7 School-wide Title I
Students: 6,285 (50.5% male; 49.5% female)
Individual Education Program: 739 (11.8%);
English Language Learner: 519 (8.3%); Migrant: 108 (1.7%)
Eligible for Free Lunch Program: 1,681 (26.7%)
Eligible for Reduced-Price Lunch Program: 486 (7.7%)
Teachers: 408.3 (15.4 to 1)
Librarians/Media Specialists: 6.3 (997.6 to 1)
Guidance Counselors: 13.8 (455.4 to 1)
Current Spending: ($ per student per year):
Total: $5,902; Instruction: $3,646; Support Services: $1,960
Enrollment, Drop-out Rates and Diploma Recipients by Race/Ethnicity

Category	Total	White	Black	Asian	AIAN	Hisp.
Enrollment (%)	100.0	54.0	1.8	0.6	0.1	43.4
Drop-out Rate (%)	4.0	2.1	3.8	0.0	0.0	7.1
H.S. Diplomas (#)	413	265	6	1	0	141

Cooke County

Gainesville ISD

1201 Lindsay St • Gainesville, TX 76240-5621
(940) 665-4362
Grade Span: PK-12; **Agency Type:** 1
Schools: 8
3 Primary; 2 Middle; 1 High; 1 Other Level
6 Regular; 0 Special Education; 0 Vocational; 1 Alternative
0 Magnet; 0 Charter; 4 Title I Eligible; 4 School-wide Title I
Students: 2,975 (50.1% male; 49.9% female)
Individual Education Program: 433 (14.6%);
English Language Learner: 396 (13.3%); Migrant: 54 (1.8%)
Eligible for Free Lunch Program: 1,372 (46.1%)
Eligible for Reduced-Price Lunch Program: 238 (8.0%)
Teachers: 213.3 (13.9 to 1)
Librarians/Media Specialists: 3.0 (991.7 to 1)
Guidance Counselors: 8.0 (371.9 to 1)
Current Spending: ($ per student per year):
Total: $6,174; Instruction: $3,913; Support Services: $1,945
Enrollment, Drop-out Rates and Diploma Recipients by Race/Ethnicity

Category	Total	White	Black	Asian	AIAN	Hisp.
Enrollment (%)	100.0	59.6	9.2	0.5	0.8	29.8
Drop-out Rate (%)	4.6	3.3	5.2	0.0	0.0	9.0
H.S. Diplomas (#)	146	102	18	1	2	23

Coryell County

Copperas Cove ISD

703 W Ave D • Copperas Cove, TX 76522-0580
Mailing Address: PO Box 580 • Copperas Cove, TX 76522-0580
(254) 547-1227 • http://www.ccisd.com/
Grade Span: PK-12; **Agency Type:** 1
Schools: 13
6 Primary; 4 Middle; 2 High; 1 Other Level
12 Regular; 0 Special Education; 0 Vocational; 1 Alternative
0 Magnet; 0 Charter; 7 Title I Eligible; 7 School-wide Title I
Students: 7,599 (51.1% male; 48.9% female)
Individual Education Program: 988 (13.0%);
English Language Learner: 76 (1.0%); Migrant: 13 (0.2%)
Eligible for Free Lunch Program: 2,059 (27.1%)
Eligible for Reduced-Price Lunch Program: 846 (11.1%)
Teachers: 541.3 (14.0 to 1)
Librarians/Media Specialists: 13.0 (584.5 to 1)
Guidance Counselors: 17.8 (426.9 to 1)
Current Spending: ($ per student per year):
Total: $6,643; Instruction: $4,054; Support Services: $2,283
Enrollment, Drop-out Rates and Diploma Recipients by Race/Ethnicity

Category	Total	White	Black	Asian	AIAN	Hisp.
Enrollment (%)	100.0	57.1	25.8	3.1	1.0	13.0
Drop-out Rate (%)	3.9	4.1	3.2	2.9	0.0	5.0
H.S. Diplomas (#)	449	248	121	32	2	46

Gatesville ISD

311 S Lovers Ln • Gatesville, TX 76528-0759
(254) 865-7251
Grade Span: PK-12; **Agency Type:** 1
Schools: 5
2 Primary; 2 Middle; 1 High; 0 Other Level
5 Regular; 0 Special Education; 0 Vocational; 0 Alternative
0 Magnet; 0 Charter; 2 Title I Eligible; 2 School-wide Title I
Students: 2,594 (53.1% male; 46.9% female)
Individual Education Program: 437 (16.8%);
English Language Learner: 35 (1.3%); Migrant: 9 (0.3%)
Eligible for Free Lunch Program: 663 (25.6%)
Eligible for Reduced-Price Lunch Program: 220 (8.5%)
Teachers: 176.1 (14.7 to 1)
Librarians/Media Specialists: 3.9 (665.1 to 1)
Guidance Counselors: 6.0 (432.3 to 1)
Current Spending: ($ per student per year):
Total: $5,279; Instruction: $3,257; Support Services: $1,723
Enrollment, Drop-out Rates and Diploma Recipients by Race/Ethnicity

Category	Total	White	Black	Asian	AIAN	Hisp.
Enrollment (%)	100.0	82.0	4.4	0.8	0.4	12.3
Drop-out Rate (%)	4.1	3.9	10.3	0.0	0.0	3.3
H.S. Diplomas (#)	157	134	4	1	2	16

Dallam County

Dalhart ISD

315 Rock Is Ave • Dalhart, TX 79022-2639
(806) 244-7810 • http://www.dalhart.k12.tx.us/
Grade Span: PK-12; **Agency Type:** 1
Schools: 5
1 Primary; 2 Middle; 2 High; 0 Other Level
4 Regular; 0 Special Education; 0 Vocational; 1 Alternative
0 Magnet; 0 Charter; 5 Title I Eligible; 5 School-wide Title I
Students: 1,587 (51.8% male; 48.2% female)
Individual Education Program: 210 (13.2%);
English Language Learner: 122 (7.7%); Migrant: 178 (11.2%)
Eligible for Free Lunch Program: 652 (41.1%)
Eligible for Reduced-Price Lunch Program: 205 (12.9%)
Teachers: 126.0 (12.6 to 1)
Librarians/Media Specialists: 1.0 (1,587.0 to 1)
Guidance Counselors: 3.0 (529.0 to 1)
Current Spending: ($ per student per year):
Total: $6,384; Instruction: $3,982; Support Services: $2,090
Enrollment, Drop-out Rates and Diploma Recipients by Race/Ethnicity

Category	Total	White	Black	Asian	AIAN	Hisp.
Enrollment (%)	100.0	61.9	2.4	0.6	0.3	34.8
Drop-out Rate (%)	3.5	3.9	0.0	0.0	0.0	3.1
H.S. Diplomas (#)	67	53	2	0	0	12

Dallas County

Carrollton-Farmers Branch ISD

1445 N Perry Rd • Carrollton, TX 75006-6134
Mailing Address: PO Box 115186 • Carrollton, TX 75011-5186
(972) 466-6100 • http://www.cfbisd.edu/
Grade Span: PK-12; **Agency Type:** 1
Schools: 42
26 Primary; 6 Middle; 4 High; 4 Other Level
36 Regular; 0 Special Education; 0 Vocational; 4 Alternative
0 Magnet; 0 Charter; 17 Title I Eligible; 15 School-wide Title I
Students: 25,548 (51.1% male; 48.9% female)
Individual Education Program: 2,438 (9.5%);
English Language Learner: 5,581 (21.8%); Migrant: 40 (0.2%)
Eligible for Free Lunch Program: 8,083 (31.6%)
Eligible for Reduced-Price Lunch Program: 2,045 (8.0%)
Teachers: 1,712.4 (14.9 to 1)
Librarians/Media Specialists: 36.9 (692.4 to 1)
Guidance Counselors: 48.6 (525.7 to 1)
Current Spending: ($ per student per year):
Total: $6,539; Instruction: $3,941; Support Services: $2,357
Enrollment, Drop-out Rates and Diploma Recipients by Race/Ethnicity

Category	Total	White	Black	Asian	AIAN	Hisp.
Enrollment (%)	100.0	35.8	12.3	12.8	0.6	38.5
Drop-out Rate (%)	3.6	2.4	3.2	3.6	2.7	5.8
H.S. Diplomas (#)	1,277	695	123	201	1	257

Cedar Hill ISD

270 S Hwy 67 • Cedar Hill, TX 75104-0248
(972) 291-1581 • http://www.chisd.com/
Grade Span: PK-12; **Agency Type:** 1
Schools: 12
6 Primary; 4 Middle; 1 High; 1 Other Level
11 Regular; 0 Special Education; 0 Vocational; 1 Alternative
0 Magnet; 0 Charter; 4 Title I Eligible; 0 School-wide Title I
Students: 7,400 (51.9% male; 48.1% female)
Individual Education Program: 721 (9.7%);
English Language Learner: 275 (3.7%); Migrant: 3 (<0.1%)
Eligible for Free Lunch Program: 1,399 (18.9%)
Eligible for Reduced-Price Lunch Program: 478 (6.5%)
Teachers: 466.4 (15.9 to 1)
Librarians/Media Specialists: 11.0 (672.7 to 1)
Guidance Counselors: 18.0 (411.1 to 1)
Current Spending: ($ per student per year):
Total: $5,943; Instruction: $3,840; Support Services: $1,824
Enrollment, Drop-out Rates and Diploma Recipients by Race/Ethnicity

Category	Total	White	Black	Asian	AIAN	Hisp.
Enrollment (%)	100.0	29.8	51.6	1.9	0.5	16.3
Drop-out Rate (%)	2.4	1.4	3.0	3.3	12.5	3.2
H.S. Diplomas (#)	382	177	136	9	1	59

Coppell ISD

200 S Denton Tap Rd • Coppell, TX 75019-3205
(214) 496-6000 • http://www.coppellisd.com/
Grade Span: PK-12; **Agency Type:** 1
Schools: 16
10 Primary; 3 Middle; 1 High; 1 Other Level
14 Regular; 0 Special Education; 0 Vocational; 1 Alternative
0 Magnet; 0 Charter; 0 Title I Eligible; 0 School-wide Title I
Students: 9,937 (51.4% male; 48.6% female)
Individual Education Program: 804 (8.1%);
English Language Learner: 561 (5.6%); Migrant: 0 (0.0%)
Eligible for Free Lunch Program: 252 (2.5%)
Eligible for Reduced-Price Lunch Program: 149 (1.5%)
Teachers: 686.7 (14.5 to 1)
Librarians/Media Specialists: 12.8 (776.3 to 1)
Guidance Counselors: 24.4 (407.3 to 1)
Current Spending: ($ per student per year):
Total: $6,491; Instruction: $4,110; Support Services: $2,053
Enrollment, Drop-out Rates and Diploma Recipients by Race/Ethnicity

Category	Total	White	Black	Asian	AIAN	Hisp.
Enrollment (%)	100.0	73.3	3.9	14.5	0.3	7.9
Drop-out Rate (%)	0.8	0.7	1.4	0.3	0.0	2.8
H.S. Diplomas (#)	542	396	17	86	3	40

Dallas ISD

3700 Ross Ave • Dallas, TX 75204-5491
(972) 925-3700 • http://www.dallasisd.org/
Grade Span: PK-12; **Agency Type:** 1
Schools: 228
148 Primary; 39 Middle; 37 High; 2 Other Level
215 Regular; 1 Special Education; 0 Vocational; 10 Alternative
0 Magnet; 0 Charter; 185 Title I Eligible; 185 School-wide Title I
Students: 163,347 (50.7% male; 49.3% female)
Individual Education Program: 12,903 (7.9%);
English Language Learner: 52,269 (32.0%); Migrant: 1,241 (0.8%)
Eligible for Free Lunch Program: 111,418 (68.2%)
Eligible for Reduced-Price Lunch Program: 12,494 (7.6%)
Teachers: 10,940.7 (14.9 to 1)
Librarians/Media Specialists: 206.0 (792.9 to 1)
Guidance Counselors: 392.6 (416.1 to 1)
Current Spending: ($ per student per year):
Total: $6,572; Instruction: $4,006; Support Services: $2,259
Enrollment, Drop-out Rates and Diploma Recipients by Race/Ethnicity

Category	Total	White	Black	Asian	AIAN	Hisp.
Enrollment (%)	100.0	6.7	32.9	1.2	0.3	58.9
Drop-out Rate (%)	5.4	3.8	6.1	2.6	6.3	5.3
H.S. Diplomas (#)	6,532	710	2,764	159	23	2,876

Desoto ISD

200 E Belt Line Rd • Desoto, TX 75115-5795
(972) 223-6666 • http://www.desotoisd.org/disd/home.nsf/home?open
Grade Span: PK-12; **Agency Type:** 1
Schools: 12
5 Primary; 4 Middle; 1 High; 2 Other Level
11 Regular; 0 Special Education; 0 Vocational; 1 Alternative
0 Magnet; 0 Charter; 2 Title I Eligible; 2 School-wide Title I
Students: 7,592 (50.1% male; 49.9% female)
Individual Education Program: 930 (12.2%);
English Language Learner: 270 (3.6%); Migrant: 4 (0.1%)
Eligible for Free Lunch Program: 1,977 (26.0%)
Eligible for Reduced-Price Lunch Program: 597 (7.9%)
Teachers: 514.4 (14.8 to 1)
Librarians/Media Specialists: 10.1 (751.7 to 1)
Guidance Counselors: 15.1 (502.8 to 1)
Current Spending: ($ per student per year):
Total: $5,634; Instruction: $3,470; Support Services: $1,896
Enrollment, Drop-out Rates and Diploma Recipients by Race/Ethnicity

Category	Total	White	Black	Asian	AIAN	Hisp.
Enrollment (%)	100.0	20.2	66.2	1.1	0.2	12.3
Drop-out Rate (%)	1.7	2.9	0.9	0.0	33.3	1.8
H.S. Diplomas (#)	386	149	205	3	2	27

Duncanville ISD

802 S Main St • Duncanville, TX 75137-2316
(972) 708-2000 • http://www.duncanvilleisd.org/
Grade Span: PK-12; **Agency Type:** 1
Schools: 18
7 Primary; 5 Middle; 2 High; 3 Other Level
14 Regular; 0 Special Education; 0 Vocational; 3 Alternative
0 Magnet; 0 Charter; 6 Title I Eligible; 6 School-wide Title I
Students: 10,956 (51.4% male; 48.6% female)
Individual Education Program: 1,270 (11.6%);
English Language Learner: 1,056 (9.6%); Migrant: 7 (0.1%)
Eligible for Free Lunch Program: 3,764 (34.4%)
Eligible for Reduced-Price Lunch Program: 1,212 (11.1%)
Teachers: 701.8 (15.6 to 1)
Librarians/Media Specialists: 12.1 (905.5 to 1)
Guidance Counselors: 33.0 (332.0 to 1)
Current Spending: ($ per student per year):
Total: $6,069; Instruction: $3,505; Support Services: $2,173
Enrollment, Drop-out Rates and Diploma Recipients by Race/Ethnicity

Category	Total	White	Black	Asian	AIAN	Hisp.
Enrollment (%)	100.0	25.3	43.4	2.6	0.2	28.5
Drop-out Rate (%)	1.1	1.0	0.5	2.3	0.0	2.8
H.S. Diplomas (#)	707	298	278	16	1	114

Garland ISD

720 Stadium Dr • Garland, TX 75040-4616
(972) 494-8201 • http://www.garlandisd.net/
Grade Span: PK-12; **Agency Type:** 1
Schools: 70
46 Primary; 13 Middle; 7 High; 4 Other Level
64 Regular; 2 Special Education; 0 Vocational; 4 Alternative
0 Magnet; 0 Charter; 29 Title I Eligible; 0 School-wide Title I
Students: 54,007 (51.5% male; 48.5% female)
Individual Education Program: 6,703 (12.4%);
English Language Learner: 10,762 (19.9%); Migrant: 200 (0.4%)
Eligible for Free Lunch Program: 16,671 (30.9%)
Eligible for Reduced-Price Lunch Program: 3,822 (7.1%)
Teachers: 3,405.2 (15.9 to 1)
Librarians/Media Specialists: 72.9 (740.8 to 1)
Guidance Counselors: 121.1 (446.0 to 1)
Current Spending: ($ per student per year):
Total: $5,354; Instruction: $3,359; Support Services: $1,746
Enrollment, Drop-out Rates and Diploma Recipients by Race/Ethnicity

Category	Total	White	Black	Asian	AIAN	Hisp.
Enrollment (%)	100.0	42.0	17.4	6.8	0.6	33.1
Drop-out Rate (%)	2.0	1.7	1.7	1.7	3.2	3.0
H.S. Diplomas (#)	2,689	1,489	448	201	20	531

Grand Prairie ISD

2602 S Belt Line Rd • Grand Prairie, TX 75052-5344
Mailing Address: Box 531170 • Grand Prairie, TX 75053-1170
(972) 264-6141 • http://www.gpisd.org/
Grade Span: PK-12; **Agency Type:** 1
Schools: 33
21 Primary; 6 Middle; 2 High; 4 Other Level
29 Regular; 0 Special Education; 0 Vocational; 4 Alternative
0 Magnet; 0 Charter; 13 Title I Eligible; 13 School-wide Title I
Students: 21,582 (51.0% male; 49.0% female)
Individual Education Program: 2,855 (13.2%);
English Language Learner: 3,643 (16.9%); Migrant: 69 (0.3%)
Eligible for Free Lunch Program: 9,868 (45.7%)
Eligible for Reduced-Price Lunch Program: 2,623 (12.2%)
Teachers: 1,489.6 (14.5 to 1)
Librarians/Media Specialists: 30.0 (719.4 to 1)
Guidance Counselors: 48.0 (449.6 to 1)
Current Spending: ($ per student per year):
Total: $5,864; Instruction: $3,646; Support Services: $1,904
Enrollment, Drop-out Rates and Diploma Recipients by Race/Ethnicity

Category	Total	White	Black	Asian	AIAN	Hisp.
Enrollment (%)	100.0	27.8	14.9	4.1	0.8	52.4
Drop-out Rate (%)	4.1	3.2	3.5	2.9	16.1	5.1
H.S. Diplomas (#)	1,035	400	158	63	9	405

Highland Park ISD

7015 Westchester Dr • Dallas, TX 75205-1061
(214) 780-3000 • http://www.hpisd.org/
Grade Span: PK-12; **Agency Type:** 1
Schools: 7
4 Primary; 2 Middle; 1 High; 0 Other Level
7 Regular; 0 Special Education; 0 Vocational; 0 Alternative
0 Magnet; 0 Charter; 0 Title I Eligible; 0 School-wide Title I
Students: 5,986 (49.6% male; 50.4% female)
Individual Education Program: 565 (9.4%);
English Language Learner: 30 (0.5%); Migrant: 0 (0.0%)
Eligible for Free Lunch Program: 0 (0.0%)
Eligible for Reduced-Price Lunch Program: 0 (0.0%)
Teachers: 387.1 (15.5 to 1)
Librarians/Media Specialists: 7.1 (843.1 to 1)
Guidance Counselors: 15.4 (388.7 to 1)
Current Spending: ($ per student per year):
Total: $6,737; Instruction: $4,533; Support Services: $2,197
Enrollment, Drop-out Rates and Diploma Recipients by Race/Ethnicity

Category	Total	White	Black	Asian	AIAN	Hisp.
Enrollment (%)	100.0	96.4	0.2	1.6	0.1	1.7
Drop-out Rate (%)	0.7	0.6	0.0	0.0	0.0	4.5
H.S. Diplomas (#)	414	402	0	6	1	5

Honors Academy

4300 Macarthur Ave Ste 160 • Dallas, TX 75209
(214) 521-6365
Grade Span: PK-12; **Agency Type:** 7
Schools: 12
2 Primary; 0 Middle; 4 High; 4 Other Level
1 Regular; 0 Special Education; 0 Vocational; 9 Alternative
0 Magnet; 10 Charter; 1 Title I Eligible; 1 School-wide Title I
Students: 1,929 (51.3% male; 48.7% female)
Individual Education Program: 159 (8.2%);
English Language Learner: 17 (0.9%); Migrant: 4 (0.2%)
Eligible for Free Lunch Program: 501 (26.0%)
Eligible for Reduced-Price Lunch Program: 159 (8.2%)
Teachers: 110.2 (17.5 to 1)
Librarians/Media Specialists: 0.0 (0.0 to 1)
Guidance Counselors: 3.0 (643.0 to 1)
Current Spending: ($ per student per year):
Total: $6,014; Instruction: $3,264; Support Services: $2,648
Enrollment, Drop-out Rates and Diploma Recipients by Race/Ethnicity

Category	Total	White	Black	Asian	AIAN	Hisp.
Enrollment (%)	100.0	35.0	48.2	1.2	0.3	15.3
Drop-out Rate (%)	17.3	12.2	18.7	22.2	33.3	25.3
H.S. Diplomas (#)	225	131	63	6	0	25

Irving ISD

901 N O'connor Rd • Irving, TX 75061-4596
Mailing Address: PO Box 152637 • Irving, TX 75015-2637
(972) 273-6000
Grade Span: PK-12; **Agency Type:** 1
Schools: 39
23 Primary; 7 Middle; 4 High; 5 Other Level
33 Regular; 2 Special Education; 0 Vocational; 4 Alternative
0 Magnet; 0 Charter; 33 Title I Eligible; 33 School-wide Title I
Students: 30,860 (51.8% male; 48.2% female)
Individual Education Program: 2,950 (9.6%);
English Language Learner: 10,289 (33.3%); Migrant: 221 (0.7%)
Eligible for Free Lunch Program: 15,015 (48.7%)
Eligible for Reduced-Price Lunch Program: 3,265 (10.6%)
Teachers: 2,208.5 (14.0 to 1)
Librarians/Media Specialists: 34.1 (905.0 to 1)
Guidance Counselors: 83.0 (371.8 to 1)
Current Spending: ($ per student per year):
Total: $6,259; Instruction: $4,124; Support Services: $1,854
Enrollment, Drop-out Rates and Diploma Recipients by Race/Ethnicity

Category	Total	White	Black	Asian	AIAN	Hisp.
Enrollment (%)	100.0	26.6	12.9	4.9	0.5	55.0
Drop-out Rate (%)	4.2	3.1	3.2	3.1	0.0	5.8
H.S. Diplomas (#)	1,308	581	202	100	3	422

Lancaster ISD

1201 N Dallas Ave • Lancaster, TX 75146-1621
Mailing Address: PO Box 400 • Lancaster, TX 75146-0400
(972) 227-4141 • http://www.lancasterisd.org/home.htm
Grade Span: PK-12; **Agency Type:** 1
Schools: 10
5 Primary; 2 Middle; 1 High; 2 Other Level
8 Regular; 0 Special Education; 0 Vocational; 2 Alternative
0 Magnet; 0 Charter; 5 Title I Eligible; 5 School-wide Title I
Students: 4,318 (50.6% male; 49.4% female)
Individual Education Program: 510 (11.8%);
English Language Learner: 253 (5.9%); Migrant: 16 (0.4%)
Eligible for Free Lunch Program: 1,753 (40.6%)
Eligible for Reduced-Price Lunch Program: 466 (10.8%)
Teachers: 306.2 (14.1 to 1)
Librarians/Media Specialists: 9.0 (479.8 to 1)
Guidance Counselors: 11.5 (375.5 to 1)
Current Spending: ($ per student per year):
Total: $6,087; Instruction: $3,468; Support Services: $2,342
Enrollment, Drop-out Rates and Diploma Recipients by Race/Ethnicity

Category	Total	White	Black	Asian	AIAN	Hisp.
Enrollment (%)	100.0	11.4	73.2	0.3	0.2	14.9
Drop-out Rate (%)	1.5	2.2	1.3	0.0	0.0	1.6
H.S. Diplomas (#)	252	59	169	2	0	22

Mesquite ISD

405 E Davis St • Mesquite, TX 75149-4701
(972) 288-6411 • http://www.mesquiteisd.org/misdweb/index.html
Grade Span: PK-12; **Agency Type:** 1
Schools: 43
29 Primary; 7 Middle; 5 High; 2 Other Level
41 Regular; 0 Special Education; 0 Vocational; 2 Alternative
0 Magnet; 0 Charter; 11 Title I Eligible; 11 School-wide Title I
Students: 33,833 (51.1% male; 48.9% female)
Individual Education Program: 4,735 (14.0%);
English Language Learner: 3,034 (9.0%); Migrant: 49 (0.1%)
Eligible for Free Lunch Program: 9,112 (26.9%)
Eligible for Reduced-Price Lunch Program: 2,657 (7.9%)
Teachers: 2,125.7 (15.9 to 1)
Librarians/Media Specialists: 42.9 (788.6 to 1)
Guidance Counselors: 70.0 (483.3 to 1)
Current Spending: ($ per student per year):
Total: $5,627; Instruction: $3,334; Support Services: $2,013
Enrollment, Drop-out Rates and Diploma Recipients by Race/Ethnicity

Category	Total	White	Black	Asian	AIAN	Hisp.
Enrollment (%)	100.0	49.7	19.9	3.8	0.7	25.8
Drop-out Rate (%)	3.7	3.8	3.7	0.8	3.6	4.3
H.S. Diplomas (#)	1,956	1,226	324	99	14	293

Richardson ISD

400 S Greenville Ave • Richardson, TX 75081-4198
(469) 593-0000
Grade Span: PK-12; **Agency Type:** 1
Schools: 56
39 Primary; 9 Middle; 4 High; 3 Other Level
53 Regular; 0 Special Education; 0 Vocational; 2 Alternative
0 Magnet; 0 Charter; 22 Title I Eligible; 15 School-wide Title I
Students: 35,052 (51.5% male; 48.5% female)
Individual Education Program: 4,075 (11.6%);
English Language Learner: 6,468 (18.5%); Migrant: 32 (0.1%)
Eligible for Free Lunch Program: 11,308 (32.3%)
Eligible for Reduced-Price Lunch Program: 2,453 (7.0%)
Teachers: 2,285.4 (15.3 to 1)
Librarians/Media Specialists: 55.0 (637.3 to 1)
Guidance Counselors: 99.0 (354.1 to 1)
Current Spending: ($ per student per year):
Total: $6,382; Instruction: $3,869; Support Services: $2,268
Enrollment, Drop-out Rates and Diploma Recipients by Race/Ethnicity

Category	Total	White	Black	Asian	AIAN	Hisp.
Enrollment (%)	100.0	42.4	24.3	8.9	0.4	24.0
Drop-out Rate (%)	2.3	1.2	2.8	3.3	7.7	5.5
H.S. Diplomas (#)	1,891	1,263	276	202	8	142

Wilmer-Hutchins ISD

3820 E Illinois Ave • Dallas, TX 75216-4140
(214) 376-7311
Grade Span: PK-12; **Agency Type:** 1
Schools: 7
4 Primary; 1 Middle; 1 High; 1 Other Level
6 Regular; 0 Special Education; 0 Vocational; 1 Alternative
0 Magnet; 0 Charter; 7 Title I Eligible; 7 School-wide Title I
Students: 2,906 (51.4% male; 48.6% female)
Individual Education Program: 220 (7.6%);
English Language Learner: 369 (12.7%); Migrant: 12 (0.4%)
Eligible for Free Lunch Program: 1,382 (47.6%)
Eligible for Reduced-Price Lunch Program: 165 (5.7%)
Teachers: 208.2 (14.0 to 1)
Librarians/Media Specialists: 2.0 (1,453.0 to 1)
Guidance Counselors: 7.0 (415.1 to 1)
Current Spending: ($ per student per year):
Total: $6,576; Instruction: $3,449; Support Services: $2,778
Enrollment, Drop-out Rates and Diploma Recipients by Race/Ethnicity

Category	Total	White	Black	Asian	AIAN	Hisp.
Enrollment (%)	100.0	3.9	70.4	0.1	0.2	25.4
Drop-out Rate (%)	6.7	3.2	6.2	n/a	150.0	8.1
H.S. Diplomas (#)	102	1	90	0	0	11

Dawson County

Lamesa ISD

212 N Houston • Lamesa, TX 79331-5442
Mailing Address: PO Box 261 • Lamesa, TX 79331-0261
(806) 872-5461 • http://lamesa.esc17.net/
Grade Span: PK-12; **Agency Type:** 1
Schools: 4
2 Primary; 1 Middle; 1 High; 0 Other Level
4 Regular; 0 Special Education; 0 Vocational; 0 Alternative
0 Magnet; 0 Charter; 4 Title I Eligible; 4 School-wide Title I
Students: 2,164 (51.9% male; 48.1% female)
Individual Education Program: 258 (11.9%);
English Language Learner: 177 (8.2%); Migrant: 174 (8.0%)
Eligible for Free Lunch Program: 1,211 (56.0%)
Eligible for Reduced-Price Lunch Program: 123 (5.7%)
Teachers: 155.4 (13.9 to 1)
Librarians/Media Specialists: 2.0 (1,082.0 to 1)
Guidance Counselors: 4.0 (541.0 to 1)
Current Spending: ($ per student per year):
Total: $6,225; Instruction: $4,077; Support Services: $1,824
Enrollment, Drop-out Rates and Diploma Recipients by Race/Ethnicity

Category	Total	White	Black	Asian	AIAN	Hisp.
Enrollment (%)	100.0	24.2	4.4	0.2	0.0	71.2
Drop-out Rate (%)	4.7	2.1	5.9	0.0	n/a	5.9
H.S. Diplomas (#)	171	68	7	0	0	96

De Witt County

Cuero ISD

405 Park Hts Dr • Cuero, TX 77954-2132
(361) 275-3832
Grade Span: PK-12; **Agency Type:** 1
Schools: 6
2 Primary; 1 Middle; 1 High; 2 Other Level
4 Regular; 0 Special Education; 0 Vocational; 2 Alternative
0 Magnet; 0 Charter; 2 Title I Eligible; 2 School-wide Title I
Students: 1,994 (51.7% male; 48.3% female)
Individual Education Program: 251 (12.6%);
English Language Learner: 20 (1.0%); Migrant: 13 (0.7%)
Eligible for Free Lunch Program: 745 (37.4%)
Eligible for Reduced-Price Lunch Program: 171 (8.6%)
Teachers: 149.9 (13.3 to 1)
Librarians/Media Specialists: 2.1 (949.5 to 1)
Guidance Counselors: 6.0 (332.3 to 1)
Current Spending: ($ per student per year):
Total: $7,899; Instruction: $4,906; Support Services: $2,639
Enrollment, Drop-out Rates and Diploma Recipients by Race/Ethnicity

Category	Total	White	Black	Asian	AIAN	Hisp.
Enrollment (%)	100.0	51.3	13.1	0.4	0.2	35.0
Drop-out Rate (%)	3.2	1.8	5.7	0.0	0.0	5.3
H.S. Diplomas (#)	158	109	14	0	1	34

Yoakum ISD

102 Mc Kinnon St • Yoakum, TX 77995-1623
Mailing Address: PO Box 737 • Yoakum, TX 77995-0737
(361) 293-3162
Grade Span: PK-12; **Agency Type:** 1
Schools: 5
2 Primary; 1 Middle; 1 High; 0 Other Level
4 Regular; 0 Special Education; 0 Vocational; 0 Alternative
0 Magnet; 0 Charter; 2 Title I Eligible; 2 School-wide Title I
Students: 1,547 (51.0% male; 49.0% female)
Individual Education Program: 206 (13.3%);
English Language Learner: 100 (6.5%); Migrant: 2 (0.1%)
Eligible for Free Lunch Program: 646 (41.8%)
Eligible for Reduced-Price Lunch Program: 145 (9.4%)
Teachers: 123.8 (12.5 to 1)
Librarians/Media Specialists: 1.2 (1,289.2 to 1)
Guidance Counselors: 3.5 (442.0 to 1)
Current Spending: ($ per student per year):
Total: $6,784; Instruction: $4,673; Support Services: $1,772
Enrollment, Drop-out Rates and Diploma Recipients by Race/Ethnicity

Category	Total	White	Black	Asian	AIAN	Hisp.
Enrollment (%)	100.0	49.6	12.0	0.3	0.0	38.1
Drop-out Rate (%)	2.5	0.6	0.0	n/a	n/a	8.4
H.S. Diplomas (#)	88	63	10	0	0	15

Deaf Smith County

Hereford ISD

601 N 25 Mile Ave • Hereford, TX 79045-4406
(806) 364-0606 • http://www.hisd.net/
Grade Span: PK-12; **Agency Type:** 1
Schools: 8
4 Primary; 2 Middle; 1 High; 1 Other Level
8 Regular; 0 Special Education; 0 Vocational; 0 Alternative
0 Magnet; 0 Charter; 8 Title I Eligible; 8 School-wide Title I
Students: 3,989 (52.3% male; 47.7% female)
Individual Education Program: 516 (12.9%);
English Language Learner: 460 (11.5%); Migrant: 1,771 (44.4%)
Eligible for Free Lunch Program: 2,346 (58.8%)
Eligible for Reduced-Price Lunch Program: 361 (9.0%)
Teachers: 279.6 (14.3 to 1)
Librarians/Media Specialists: 8.0 (498.6 to 1)
Guidance Counselors: 11.0 (362.6 to 1)
Current Spending: ($ per student per year):
Total: $6,337; Instruction: $4,029; Support Services: $1,983
Enrollment, Drop-out Rates and Diploma Recipients by Race/Ethnicity

Category	Total	White	Black	Asian	AIAN	Hisp.
Enrollment (%)	100.0	19.4	1.3	0.1	0.1	79.1
Drop-out Rate (%)	3.3	1.1	0.0	0.0	0.0	4.5
H.S. Diplomas (#)	268	92	4	0	0	172

Denton County

Denton ISD

1307 N Locust St • Denton, TX 76201-3037
Mailing Address: PO Box 2387 • Denton, TX 76202-2387
(940) 369-0000 • http://www.dentonisd.org/index.htm
Grade Span: PK-12; **Agency Type:** 1
Schools: 25
13 Primary; 4 Middle; 3 High; 4 Other Level
19 Regular; 0 Special Education; 0 Vocational; 5 Alternative
0 Magnet; 0 Charter; 9 Title I Eligible; 7 School-wide Title I
Students: 15,149 (51.0% male; 49.0% female)
Individual Education Program: 2,053 (13.6%);
English Language Learner: 2,057 (13.6%); Migrant: 95 (0.6%)
Eligible for Free Lunch Program: 4,645 (30.7%)
Eligible for Reduced-Price Lunch Program: 808 (5.3%)
Teachers: 1,098.4 (13.8 to 1)
Librarians/Media Specialists: 19.6 (772.9 to 1)
Guidance Counselors: 37.0 (409.4 to 1)
Current Spending: ($ per student per year):
Total: $6,610; Instruction: $3,937; Support Services: $2,405
Enrollment, Drop-out Rates and Diploma Recipients by Race/Ethnicity

Category	Total	White	Black	Asian	AIAN	Hisp.
Enrollment (%)	100.0	59.6	11.7	2.0	0.6	26.1
Drop-out Rate (%)	4.5	3.6	7.1	1.6	14.3	6.7
H.S. Diplomas (#)	720	548	66	13	1	92

Lake Dallas ISD

315 E Hundley Dr • Lake Dallas, TX 75065-2629
Mailing Address: PO Box 548 • Lake Dallas, TX 75065-0548
(940) 497-4039 • http://www.ldisd.net/
Grade Span: PK-12; **Agency Type:** 1
Schools: 7
3 Primary; 2 Middle; 1 High; 1 Other Level
6 Regular; 0 Special Education; 0 Vocational; 1 Alternative
0 Magnet; 0 Charter; 1 Title I Eligible; 0 School-wide Title I
Students: 3,460 (53.1% male; 46.9% female)
Individual Education Program: 471 (13.6%);
English Language Learner: 127 (3.7%); Migrant: 7 (0.2%)
Eligible for Free Lunch Program: 519 (15.0%)
Eligible for Reduced-Price Lunch Program: 109 (3.2%)
Teachers: 271.0 (12.8 to 1)
Librarians/Media Specialists: 6.0 (576.7 to 1)
Guidance Counselors: 6.8 (508.8 to 1)
Current Spending: ($ per student per year):
Total: $6,176; Instruction: $3,851; Support Services: $2,080
Enrollment, Drop-out Rates and Diploma Recipients by Race/Ethnicity

Category	Total	White	Black	Asian	AIAN	Hisp.
Enrollment (%)	100.0	79.6	6.2	2.1	0.9	11.2
Drop-out Rate (%)	1.0	1.2	0.0	0.0	0.0	0.0
H.S. Diplomas (#)	168	137	5	4	2	20

Lewisville ISD

1800 Timber Creek Rd • Flower Mound, TX 75028-1198
Mailing Address: PO Box 217 • Lewisville, TX 75067-0217
(972) 539-1551
Grade Span: PK-12; **Agency Type:** 1
Schools: 56
34 Primary; 13 Middle; 6 High; 3 Other Level
53 Regular; 0 Special Education; 0 Vocational; 3 Alternative
0 Magnet; 0 Charter; 12 Title I Eligible; 1 School-wide Title I
Students: 43,122 (51.0% male; 49.0% female)
Individual Education Program: 4,936 (11.4%);
English Language Learner: 3,474 (8.1%); Migrant: 7 (<0.1%)
Eligible for Free Lunch Program: 4,482 (10.4%)
Eligible for Reduced-Price Lunch Program: 1,347 (3.1%)
Teachers: 2,990.6 (14.4 to 1)

Librarians/Media Specialists: 56.0 (770.0 to 1)
Guidance Counselors: 122.5 (352.0 to 1)
Current Spending: ($ per student per year):
Total: $6,130; Instruction: $3,973; Support Services: $1,879
Enrollment, Drop-out Rates and Diploma Recipients by Race/Ethnicity

Category	Total	White	Black	Asian	AIAN	Hisp.
Enrollment (%)	100.0	70.7	7.8	6.1	0.5	14.9
Drop-out Rate (%)	1.4	1.1	1.6	1.6	2.9	2.8
H.S. Diplomas (#)	2,267	1,785	164	88	8	222

Little Elm ISD

500 Lobo Ln • Little Elm, TX 75068-5220
(972) 292-1847 •
http://www.arlington.k12.tx.us/schools/elementary/little/jblittle.htm
Grade Span: PK-12; **Agency Type:** 1
Schools: 7
3 Primary; 2 Middle; 1 High; 0 Other Level
6 Regular; 0 Special Education; 0 Vocational; 0 Alternative
0 Magnet; 0 Charter; 4 Title I Eligible; 4 School-wide Title I
Students: 2,989 (51.6% male; 48.4% female)
Individual Education Program: 377 (12.6%);
English Language Learner: 392 (13.1%); Migrant: 236 (7.9%)
Eligible for Free Lunch Program: 857 (28.7%)
Eligible for Reduced-Price Lunch Program: 196 (6.6%)
Teachers: 211.4 (14.1 to 1)
Librarians/Media Specialists: 4.0 (747.3 to 1)
Guidance Counselors: 6.0 (498.2 to 1)
Current Spending: ($ per student per year):
Total: $7,013; Instruction: $3,968; Support Services: $2,623
Enrollment, Drop-out Rates and Diploma Recipients by Race/Ethnicity

Category	Total	White	Black	Asian	AIAN	Hisp.
Enrollment (%)	100.0	62.2	6.4	1.0	0.7	29.7
Drop-out Rate (%)	1.6	1.8	0.0	0.0	0.0	1.0
H.S. Diplomas (#)	104	78	2	2	0	22

Northwest ISD

1800 Hwy 114 • Fort Worth, TX 76177-0070
Mailing Address: PO Box 77070 • Fort Worth, TX 76177-0070
(817) 490-6473
Grade Span: PK-12; **Agency Type:** 1
Schools: 16
8 Primary; 3 Middle; 3 High; 0 Other Level
12 Regular; 0 Special Education; 0 Vocational; 2 Alternative
0 Magnet; 0 Charter; 4 Title I Eligible; 4 School-wide Title I
Students: 6,211 (52.0% male; 48.0% female)
Individual Education Program: 746 (12.0%);
English Language Learner: 199 (3.2%); Migrant: 4 (0.1%)
Eligible for Free Lunch Program: 885 (14.2%)
Eligible for Reduced-Price Lunch Program: 312 (5.0%)
Teachers: 444.1 (14.0 to 1)
Librarians/Media Specialists: 10.1 (615.0 to 1)
Guidance Counselors: 14.9 (416.8 to 1)
Current Spending: ($ per student per year):
Total: $8,109; Instruction: $4,683; Support Services: $3,157
Enrollment, Drop-out Rates and Diploma Recipients by Race/Ethnicity

Category	Total	White	Black	Asian	AIAN	Hisp.
Enrollment (%)	100.0	84.6	1.7	1.6	0.6	11.5
Drop-out Rate (%)	4.0	4.1	0.0	0.0	0.0	4.8
H.S. Diplomas (#)	285	257	1	6	2	19

Sanger ISD

601 Elm St • Sanger, TX 76266-9635
Mailing Address: PO Box 2399 • Sanger, TX 76266-0188
(940) 458-7438
Grade Span: PK-12; **Agency Type:** 1
Schools: 6
2 Primary; 2 Middle; 1 High; 1 Other Level
5 Regular; 0 Special Education; 0 Vocational; 1 Alternative
0 Magnet; 0 Charter; 5 Title I Eligible; 5 School-wide Title I
Students: 2,163 (53.5% male; 46.5% female)
Individual Education Program: 363 (16.8%);
English Language Learner: 89 (4.1%); Migrant: 18 (0.8%)
Eligible for Free Lunch Program: 433 (20.0%)
Eligible for Reduced-Price Lunch Program: 132 (6.1%)
Teachers: 169.8 (12.7 to 1)
Librarians/Media Specialists: 2.0 (1,081.5 to 1)
Guidance Counselors: 7.4 (292.3 to 1)
Current Spending: ($ per student per year):
Total: $7,449; Instruction: $4,437; Support Services: $2,726
Enrollment, Drop-out Rates and Diploma Recipients by Race/Ethnicity

Category	Total	White	Black	Asian	AIAN	Hisp.
Enrollment (%)	100.0	82.2	2.4	0.6	0.7	14.2
Drop-out Rate (%)	3.3	3.3	4.8	0.0	12.5	1.7
H.S. Diplomas (#)	155	138	3	1	2	11

Dimmit County

Carrizo Springs CISD

102 N 5th St • Carrizo Springs, TX 78834-3102
(830) 876-3503
Grade Span: PK-12; **Agency Type:** 1
Schools: 7
4 Primary; 2 Middle; 1 High; 0 Other Level
7 Regular; 0 Special Education; 0 Vocational; 0 Alternative
0 Magnet; 0 Charter; 7 Title I Eligible; 7 School-wide Title I
Students: 2,487 (52.2% male; 47.8% female)
Individual Education Program: 264 (10.6%);
English Language Learner: 279 (11.2%); Migrant: 433 (17.4%)
Eligible for Free Lunch Program: 884 (35.5%)
Eligible for Reduced-Price Lunch Program: 148 (6.0%)
Teachers: 185.9 (13.4 to 1)
Librarians/Media Specialists: 1.0 (2,487.0 to 1)
Guidance Counselors: 10.9 (228.2 to 1)
Current Spending: ($ per student per year):
Total: $7,453; Instruction: $4,444; Support Services: $2,478
Enrollment, Drop-out Rates and Diploma Recipients by Race/Ethnicity

Category	Total	White	Black	Asian	AIAN	Hisp.
Enrollment (%)	100.0	8.3	1.0	0.3	0.1	90.3
Drop-out Rate (%)	8.1	3.2	0.0	0.0	0.0	8.7
H.S. Diplomas (#)	135	11	0	0	0	124

Duval County

San Diego ISD

609 W Labbe St • San Diego, TX 78384-3499
(361) 279-3382
Grade Span: PK-12; **Agency Type:** 1
Schools: 4
2 Primary; 1 Middle; 1 High; 0 Other Level
4 Regular; 0 Special Education; 0 Vocational; 0 Alternative
0 Magnet; 0 Charter; 4 Title I Eligible; 4 School-wide Title I
Students: 1,581 (48.8% male; 51.2% female)
Individual Education Program: 160 (10.1%);
English Language Learner: 190 (12.0%); Migrant: 107 (6.8%)
Eligible for Free Lunch Program: 1,232 (77.9%)
Eligible for Reduced-Price Lunch Program: 103 (6.5%)
Teachers: 120.0 (13.2 to 1)
Librarians/Media Specialists: 1.0 (1,581.0 to 1)
Guidance Counselors: 3.0 (527.0 to 1)
Current Spending: ($ per student per year):
Total: $6,438; Instruction: $3,802; Support Services: $2,262
Enrollment, Drop-out Rates and Diploma Recipients by Race/Ethnicity

Category	Total	White	Black	Asian	AIAN	Hisp.
Enrollment (%)	100.0	0.6	0.0	0.0	0.0	99.4
Drop-out Rate (%)	3.0	0.0	n/a	n/a	0.0	3.0
H.S. Diplomas (#)	91	1	0	0	0	90

Ector County

Ector County ISD

802 N Sam Houston • Odessa, TX 79760-3912
Mailing Address: PO Box 3912 • Odessa, TX 79760-3912
(915) 332-9151
Grade Span: PK-12; **Agency Type:** 1
Schools: 42
28 Primary; 5 Middle; 7 High; 2 Other Level
37 Regular; 1 Special Education; 0 Vocational; 4 Alternative
0 Magnet; 0 Charter; 26 Title I Eligible; 26 School-wide Title I
Students: 26,594 (51.0% male; 49.0% female)
Individual Education Program: 2,979 (11.2%);
English Language Learner: 3,531 (13.3%); Migrant: 504 (1.9%)
Eligible for Free Lunch Program: 13,510 (50.8%)
Eligible for Reduced-Price Lunch Program: 2,217 (8.3%)
Teachers: 1,753.4 (15.2 to 1)
Librarians/Media Specialists: 34.0 (782.2 to 1)
Guidance Counselors: 65.0 (409.1 to 1)
Current Spending: ($ per student per year):
Total: $6,126; Instruction: $3,641; Support Services: $2,188
Enrollment, Drop-out Rates and Diploma Recipients by Race/Ethnicity

Category	Total	White	Black	Asian	AIAN	Hisp.
Enrollment (%)	100.0	36.1	5.4	0.7	0.5	57.3
Drop-out Rate (%)	6.2	4.4	7.1	1.7	2.3	7.7
H.S. Diplomas (#)	1,478	702	73	7	8	688

El Paso County

Canutillo ISD

7965 Artcraft • El Paso, TX 79932
Mailing Address: PO Box 100 • Canutillo, TX 79835-0100
(915) 877-7400
Grade Span: PK-12; **Agency Type:** 1
Schools: 6
4 Primary; 1 Middle; 1 High; 0 Other Level
6 Regular; 0 Special Education; 0 Vocational; 0 Alternative
0 Magnet; 0 Charter; 6 Title I Eligible; 6 School-wide Title I
Students: 4,715 (53.2% male; 46.8% female)
Individual Education Program: 495 (10.5%);
English Language Learner: 1,928 (40.9%); Migrant: 317 (6.7%)
Eligible for Free Lunch Program: 3,501 (74.3%)
Eligible for Reduced-Price Lunch Program: 476 (10.1%)
Teachers: 350.0 (13.5 to 1)
Librarians/Media Specialists: 6.0 (785.8 to 1)
Guidance Counselors: 9.0 (523.9 to 1)
Current Spending: ($ per student per year):
Total: $6,750; Instruction: $3,946; Support Services: $2,362
Enrollment, Drop-out Rates and Diploma Recipients by Race/Ethnicity

Category	Total	White	Black	Asian	AIAN	Hisp.
Enrollment (%)	100.0	4.4	0.2	0.0	0.0	95.3
Drop-out Rate (%)	7.6	5.9	66.7	0.0	0.0	7.6
H.S. Diplomas (#)	233	13	0	0	1	219

Clint ISD

125 Brown St • Clint, TX 79836-0779
Mailing Address: PO Box 779 • Clint, TX 79836-0779
(915) 851-2877 • http://www.clintweb.net/index.cfm
Grade Span: PK-12; **Agency Type:** 1
Schools: 11
5 Primary; 4 Middle; 2 High; 0 Other Level
11 Regular; 0 Special Education; 0 Vocational; 0 Alternative
0 Magnet; 0 Charter; 11 Title I Eligible; 10 School-wide Title I
Students: 8,216 (51.0% male; 49.0% female)
Individual Education Program: 723 (8.8%);
English Language Learner: 3,686 (44.9%); Migrant: 221 (2.7%)
Eligible for Free Lunch Program: 6,716 (81.7%)
Eligible for Reduced-Price Lunch Program: 699 (8.5%)
Teachers: 510.2 (16.1 to 1)
Librarians/Media Specialists: 6.4 (1,283.8 to 1)
Guidance Counselors: 18.9 (434.7 to 1)
Current Spending: ($ per student per year):
Total: $6,335; Instruction: $3,726; Support Services: $2,216
Enrollment, Drop-out Rates and Diploma Recipients by Race/Ethnicity

Category	Total	White	Black	Asian	AIAN	Hisp.
Enrollment (%)	100.0	4.3	0.3	0.1	0.1	95.2
Drop-out Rate (%)	3.7	2.2	0.0	0.0	0.0	3.8
H.S. Diplomas (#)	406	19	4	0	0	383

El Paso ISD

6531 Boeing Dr • El Paso, TX 79925
Mailing Address: PO Box 20100 • El Paso, TX 79998-0100
(915) 779-3781
Grade Span: PK-12; **Agency Type:** 1
Schools: 94
56 Primary; 16 Middle; 17 High; 4 Other Level
84 Regular; 2 Special Education; 1 Vocational; 6 Alternative
0 Magnet; 0 Charter; 74 Title I Eligible; 74 School-wide Title I
Students: 63,185 (51.2% male; 48.8% female)
Individual Education Program: 5,709 (9.0%);
English Language Learner: 19,207 (30.4%); Migrant: 2,206 (3.5%)
Eligible for Free Lunch Program: 37,299 (59.0%)
Eligible for Reduced-Price Lunch Program: 5,204 (8.2%)
Teachers: 4,433.9 (14.3 to 1)
Librarians/Media Specialists: 91.6 (689.8 to 1)
Guidance Counselors: 142.8 (442.5 to 1)
Current Spending: ($ per student per year):
Total: $6,197; Instruction: $3,870; Support Services: $2,014
Enrollment, Drop-out Rates and Diploma Recipients by Race/Ethnicity

Category	Total	White	Black	Asian	AIAN	Hisp.
Enrollment (%)	100.0	14.0	4.5	1.3	0.3	79.9
Drop-out Rate (%)	4.9	2.6	3.9	2.4	9.5	5.5
H.S. Diplomas (#)	3,353	687	133	53	1	2,479

Fabens ISD

821 NE Ave G • Fabens, TX 79838-0697
Mailing Address: PO Box 697 • Fabens, TX 79838-0697
(915) 764-2025
Grade Span: PK-12; **Agency Type:** 1
Schools: 6
3 Primary; 1 Middle; 2 High; 0 Other Level
5 Regular; 0 Special Education; 0 Vocational; 1 Alternative
0 Magnet; 0 Charter; 6 Title I Eligible; 6 School-wide Title I
Students: 2,812 (50.8% male; 49.2% female)
Individual Education Program: 185 (6.6%);
English Language Learner: 1,384 (49.2%); Migrant: 346 (12.3%)
Eligible for Free Lunch Program: 1,293 (46.0%)
Eligible for Reduced-Price Lunch Program: 227 (8.1%)
Teachers: 188.1 (14.9 to 1)
Librarians/Media Specialists: 1.1 (2,556.4 to 1)
Guidance Counselors: 6.0 (468.7 to 1)
Current Spending: ($ per student per year):
Total: $6,741; Instruction: $4,277; Support Services: $2,121
Enrollment, Drop-out Rates and Diploma Recipients by Race/Ethnicity

Category	Total	White	Black	Asian	AIAN	Hisp.
Enrollment (%)	100.0	2.0	0.1	0.1	0.2	97.6
Drop-out Rate (%)	5.9	0.0	0.0	n/a	n/a	6.0
H.S. Diplomas (#)	163	2	1	0	0	160

San Elizario ISD

1050 Chicken Ranch Rd • San Elizario, TX 79849-0920
Mailing Address: PO Box 920 • San Elizario, TX 79849-0920
(915) 872-3900
Grade Span: PK-12; **Agency Type:** 1
Schools: 7
4 Primary; 1 Middle; 1 High; 1 Other Level
6 Regular; 0 Special Education; 0 Vocational; 1 Alternative
0 Magnet; 0 Charter; 6 Title I Eligible; 6 School-wide Title I
Students: 3,690 (52.5% male; 47.5% female)
Individual Education Program: 475 (12.9%);
English Language Learner: 1,960 (53.1%); Migrant: 574 (15.6%)
Eligible for Free Lunch Program: 858 (23.3%)
Eligible for Reduced-Price Lunch Program: 0 (0.0%)
Teachers: 247.4 (14.9 to 1)
Librarians/Media Specialists: 6.0 (615.0 to 1)
Guidance Counselors: 11.0 (335.5 to 1)
Current Spending: ($ per student per year):
Total: $6,997; Instruction: $3,726; Support Services: $2,782
Enrollment, Drop-out Rates and Diploma Recipients by Race/Ethnicity

Category	Total	White	Black	Asian	AIAN	Hisp.
Enrollment (%)	100.0	0.7	0.2	0.0	0.0	99.1
Drop-out Rate (%)	6.7	14.3	n/a	0.0	n/a	6.7
H.S. Diplomas (#)	157	1	0	0	0	156

Socorro ISD

12300 Eastlake Dr • El Paso, TX 79928-5400
Mailing Address: PO Box 292800 • El Paso, TX 79929-2800
(915) 937-0000
Grade Span: PK-12; **Agency Type:** 1
Schools: 31
20 Primary; 7 Middle; 3 High; 1 Other Level
29 Regular; 0 Special Education; 0 Vocational; 2 Alternative
0 Magnet; 0 Charter; 30 Title I Eligible; 30 School-wide Title I
Students: 30,078 (51.3% male; 48.7% female)
Individual Education Program: 3,122 (10.4%);
English Language Learner: 9,026 (30.0%); Migrant: 722 (2.4%)
Eligible for Free Lunch Program: 17,980 (59.8%)
Eligible for Reduced-Price Lunch Program: 3,458 (11.5%)
Teachers: 1,758.6 (17.1 to 1)
Librarians/Media Specialists: 32.0 (939.9 to 1)
Guidance Counselors: 71.8 (418.9 to 1)
Current Spending: ($ per student per year):
Total: $5,559; Instruction: $3,290; Support Services: $2,018
Enrollment, Drop-out Rates and Diploma Recipients by Race/Ethnicity

Category	Total	White	Black	Asian	AIAN	Hisp.
Enrollment (%)	100.0	5.7	1.3	0.3	0.3	92.4
Drop-out Rate (%)	3.2	2.8	3.7	0.0	14.3	3.2
H.S. Diplomas (#)	1,533	120	16	13	1	1,383

Ysleta ISD

9600 Sims Dr • El Paso, TX 79925-7225
(915) 434-0000
Grade Span: PK-12; **Agency Type:** 1
Schools: 63
36 Primary; 12 Middle; 11 High; 2 Other Level
53 Regular; 0 Special Education; 0 Vocational; 8 Alternative
0 Magnet; 0 Charter; 56 Title I Eligible; 56 School-wide Title I
Students: 46,745 (50.9% male; 49.1% female)
Individual Education Program: 5,078 (10.9%);
English Language Learner: 11,104 (23.8%); Migrant: 513 (1.1%)
Eligible for Free Lunch Program: 20,361 (43.6%)
Eligible for Reduced-Price Lunch Program: 4,990 (10.7%)
Teachers: 2,939.3 (15.9 to 1)
Librarians/Media Specialists: 49.0 (954.0 to 1)
Guidance Counselors: 80.0 (584.3 to 1)
Current Spending: ($ per student per year):
Total: $6,067; Instruction: $3,793; Support Services: $2,015

Enrollment, Drop-out Rates and Diploma Recipients by Race/Ethnicity

Category	Total	White	Black	Asian	AIAN	Hisp.
Enrollment (%)	100.0	7.4	2.3	0.4	0.5	89.4
Drop-out Rate (%)	6.0	3.5	5.5	1.2	3.7	6.4
H.S. Diplomas (#)	2,842	285	78	15	18	2,446

Ellis County

Ennis ISD

303 W Knox • Ennis, TX 75119-3957
Mailing Address: PO Box 1420 • Ennis, TX 75120-1420
(972) 875-9027 • http://districtweb1.ednet10.net/ennis/home/index.html
Grade Span: PK-12; **Agency Type:** 1
Schools: 9
5 Primary; 3 Middle; 1 High; 0 Other Level
9 Regular; 0 Special Education; 0 Vocational; 0 Alternative
0 Magnet; 0 Charter; 9 Title I Eligible; 2 School-wide Title I
Students: 5,296 (51.5% male; 48.5% female)
Individual Education Program: 823 (15.5%);
English Language Learner: 788 (14.9%); Migrant: 29 (0.5%)
Eligible for Free Lunch Program: 2,300 (43.4%)
Eligible for Reduced-Price Lunch Program: 456 (8.6%)
Teachers: 353.6 (15.0 to 1)
Librarians/Media Specialists: 5.0 (1,059.2 to 1)
Guidance Counselors: 18.0 (294.2 to 1)
Current Spending: ($ per student per year):
Total: $6,117; Instruction: $3,955; Support Services: $1,842
Enrollment, Drop-out Rates and Diploma Recipients by Race/Ethnicity

Category	Total	White	Black	Asian	AIAN	Hisp.
Enrollment (%)	100.0	44.1	14.9	0.2	0.1	40.8
Drop-out Rate (%)	4.7	3.0	4.5	0.0	n/a	7.8
H.S. Diplomas (#)	260	142	52	0	0	66

Ferris ISD

303 E 5th St • Ferris, TX 75125-2225
Mailing Address: PO Box 459 • Ferris, TX 75125-0459
(972) 544-3858 • http://ferris.ednet10.net/
Grade Span: PK-12; **Agency Type:** 1
Schools: 5
2 Primary; 2 Middle; 1 High; 0 Other Level
5 Regular; 0 Special Education; 0 Vocational; 0 Alternative
0 Magnet; 0 Charter; 4 Title I Eligible; 4 School-wide Title I
Students: 2,184 (50.6% male; 49.4% female)
Individual Education Program: 367 (16.8%);
English Language Learner: 113 (5.2%); Migrant: 25 (1.1%)
Eligible for Free Lunch Program: 969 (44.4%)
Eligible for Reduced-Price Lunch Program: 276 (12.6%)
Teachers: 148.6 (14.7 to 1)
Librarians/Media Specialists: 2.0 (1,092.0 to 1)
Guidance Counselors: 5.0 (436.8 to 1)
Current Spending: ($ per student per year):
Total: $6,246; Instruction: $3,815; Support Services: $2,136
Enrollment, Drop-out Rates and Diploma Recipients by Race/Ethnicity

Category	Total	White	Black	Asian	AIAN	Hisp.
Enrollment (%)	100.0	45.2	10.9	0.2	0.3	43.5
Drop-out Rate (%)	2.4	2.3	1.1	n/a	0.0	3.4
H.S. Diplomas (#)	98	48	20	0	0	30

Midlothian ISD

100 Walter Stephenson Rd • Midlothian, TX 76065-3418
(972) 775-8296
Grade Span: PK-12; **Agency Type:** 1
Schools: 8
4 Primary; 2 Middle; 1 High; 1 Other Level
8 Regular; 0 Special Education; 0 Vocational; 0 Alternative
0 Magnet; 0 Charter; 2 Title I Eligible; 0 School-wide Title I
Students: 5,090 (51.4% male; 48.6% female)
Individual Education Program: 686 (13.5%);
English Language Learner: 167 (3.3%); Migrant: 21 (0.4%)
Eligible for Free Lunch Program: 560 (11.0%)
Eligible for Reduced-Price Lunch Program: 264 (5.2%)
Teachers: 373.7 (13.6 to 1)
Librarians/Media Specialists: 4.0 (1,272.5 to 1)
Guidance Counselors: 12.0 (424.2 to 1)
Current Spending: ($ per student per year):
Total: $5,860; Instruction: $3,771; Support Services: $1,871
Enrollment, Drop-out Rates and Diploma Recipients by Race/Ethnicity

Category	Total	White	Black	Asian	AIAN	Hisp.
Enrollment (%)	100.0	83.7	2.7	0.8	0.5	12.4
Drop-out Rate (%)	2.1	1.9	0.0	0.0	0.0	5.2
H.S. Diplomas (#)	258	229	7	2	1	19

Red Oak ISD

156 Louise Ritter Blvd • Red Oak, TX 75154-9000
Mailing Address: PO Box 9000 • Red Oak, TX 75154-9000
(972) 617-2941
Grade Span: PK-12; **Agency Type:** 1
Schools: 8
4 Primary; 2 Middle; 1 High; 1 Other Level
7 Regular; 0 Special Education; 0 Vocational; 1 Alternative
0 Magnet; 0 Charter; 1 Title I Eligible; 0 School-wide Title I
Students: 4,811 (50.6% male; 49.4% female)
Individual Education Program: 724 (15.0%);
English Language Learner: 191 (4.0%); Migrant: 1 (<0.1%)
Eligible for Free Lunch Program: 696 (14.5%)
Eligible for Reduced-Price Lunch Program: 151 (3.1%)
Teachers: 305.6 (15.7 to 1)
Librarians/Media Specialists: 5.4 (890.9 to 1)
Guidance Counselors: 15.0 (320.7 to 1)
Current Spending: ($ per student per year):
Total: $5,668; Instruction: $3,463; Support Services: $1,938
Enrollment, Drop-out Rates and Diploma Recipients by Race/Ethnicity

Category	Total	White	Black	Asian	AIAN	Hisp.
Enrollment (%)	100.0	75.2	6.1	0.6	0.7	17.4
Drop-out Rate (%)	4.0	3.8	1.3	0.0	16.7	5.8
H.S. Diplomas (#)	249	205	16	1	1	26

Waxahachie ISD

411 N Gibson St • Waxahachie, TX 75165-3007
(972) 923-4631
Grade Span: PK-12; **Agency Type:** 1
Schools: 10
5 Primary; 2 Middle; 2 High; 1 Other Level
9 Regular; 0 Special Education; 0 Vocational; 1 Alternative
0 Magnet; 0 Charter; 6 Title I Eligible; 0 School-wide Title I
Students: 5,812 (51.0% male; 49.0% female)
Individual Education Program: 891 (15.3%);
English Language Learner: 381 (6.6%); Migrant: 62 (1.1%)
Eligible for Free Lunch Program: 1,782 (30.7%)
Eligible for Reduced-Price Lunch Program: 383 (6.6%)
Teachers: 389.1 (14.9 to 1)
Librarians/Media Specialists: 2.0 (2,906.0 to 1)
Guidance Counselors: 7.8 (745.1 to 1)
Current Spending: ($ per student per year):
Total: $6,165; Instruction: $3,700; Support Services: $2,189
Enrollment, Drop-out Rates and Diploma Recipients by Race/Ethnicity

Category	Total	White	Black	Asian	AIAN	Hisp.
Enrollment (%)	100.0	58.4	15.4	0.3	0.4	25.4
Drop-out Rate (%)	2.2	1.8	3.0	0.0	0.0	3.0
H.S. Diplomas (#)	390	251	68	2	2	67

Erath County

Stephenville ISD

2655 W Overhill • Stephenville, TX 76401-3003
(254) 968-7990
Grade Span: PK-12; **Agency Type:** 1
Schools: 6
3 Primary; 2 Middle; 1 High; 0 Other Level
6 Regular; 0 Special Education; 0 Vocational; 0 Alternative
0 Magnet; 0 Charter; 5 Title I Eligible; 5 School-wide Title I
Students: 3,447 (52.5% male; 47.5% female)
Individual Education Program: 395 (11.5%);
English Language Learner: 183 (5.3%); Migrant: 5 (0.1%)
Eligible for Free Lunch Program: 943 (27.4%)
Eligible for Reduced-Price Lunch Program: 234 (6.8%)
Teachers: 222.2 (15.5 to 1)
Librarians/Media Specialists: 4.0 (861.8 to 1)
Guidance Counselors: 8.0 (430.9 to 1)
Current Spending: ($ per student per year):
Total: $5,595; Instruction: $3,755; Support Services: $1,576
Enrollment, Drop-out Rates and Diploma Recipients by Race/Ethnicity

Category	Total	White	Black	Asian	AIAN	Hisp.
Enrollment (%)	100.0	77.5	1.2	0.7	0.6	20.0
Drop-out Rate (%)	0.8	0.7	0.0	0.0	0.0	1.4
H.S. Diplomas (#)	224	197	1	3	0	23

Falls County

Marlin ISD

130 Coleman St • Marlin, TX 76661-2899
(254) 883-3585 • http://marlinisd.esc12.net/
Grade Span: PK-12; **Agency Type:** 1
Schools: 5
1 Primary; 1 Middle; 2 High; 1 Other Level
3 Regular; 0 Special Education; 0 Vocational; 2 Alternative
0 Magnet; 0 Charter; 3 Title I Eligible; 3 School-wide Title I

Students: 1,526 (54.5% male; 45.5% female)
Individual Education Program: 248 (16.3%);
English Language Learner: 95 (6.2%); Migrant: 15 (1.0%)
Eligible for Free Lunch Program: 979 (64.2%)
Eligible for Reduced-Price Lunch Program: 145 (9.5%)
Teachers: 124.3 (12.3 to 1)
Librarians/Media Specialists: 2.0 (763.0 to 1)
Guidance Counselors: 3.0 (508.7 to 1)
Current Spending: ($ per student per year):
Total: $6,912; Instruction: $4,197; Support Services: $2,434
Enrollment, Drop-out Rates and Diploma Recipients by Race/Ethnicity

Category	Total	White	Black	Asian	AIAN	Hisp.
Enrollment (%)	100.0	17.8	58.3	0.3	0.0	23.6
Drop-out Rate (%)	3.9	4.8	3.2	0.0	n/a	3.8
H.S. Diplomas (#)	92	41	34	1	0	16

Fannin County

Bonham ISD
220 W 11th • Bonham, TX 75418-3028
Mailing Address: PO Box 490 • Bonham, TX 75418-0490
(903) 583-5526
Grade Span: PK-12; **Agency Type:** 1
Schools: 7
2 Primary; 2 Middle; 1 High; 1 Other Level
6 Regular; 0 Special Education; 0 Vocational; 0 Alternative
0 Magnet; 0 Charter; 4 Title I Eligible; 0 School-wide Title I
Students: 2,010 (50.9% male; 49.1% female)
Individual Education Program: 313 (15.6%);
English Language Learner: 90 (4.5%); Migrant: 19 (0.9%)
Eligible for Free Lunch Program: 636 (31.6%)
Eligible for Reduced-Price Lunch Program: 157 (7.8%)
Teachers: 141.9 (14.2 to 1)
Librarians/Media Specialists: 2.4 (837.5 to 1)
Guidance Counselors: 7.0 (287.1 to 1)
Current Spending: ($ per student per year):
Total: $6,581; Instruction: $4,100; Support Services: $2,145
Enrollment, Drop-out Rates and Diploma Recipients by Race/Ethnicity

Category	Total	White	Black	Asian	AIAN	Hisp.
Enrollment (%)	100.0	80.6	8.2	1.0	1.5	8.8
Drop-out Rate (%)	3.2	2.8	3.9	0.0	0.0	13.3
H.S. Diplomas (#)	106	91	13	2	0	0

Fayette County

La Grange ISD
641 E Milam • La Grange, TX 78945-2819
Mailing Address: PO Box 100 • La Grange, TX 78945-0100
(979) 968-7000 •
http://lagrange.fais.net/New_City_site/schools/schools.htm
Grade Span: PK-12; **Agency Type:** 1
Schools: 4
1 Primary; 2 Middle; 1 High; 0 Other Level
4 Regular; 0 Special Education; 0 Vocational; 0 Alternative
0 Magnet; 0 Charter; 3 Title I Eligible; 3 School-wide Title I
Students: 1,933 (51.4% male; 48.6% female)
Individual Education Program: 227 (11.7%);
English Language Learner: 142 (7.3%); Migrant: 0 (0.0%)
Eligible for Free Lunch Program: 595 (30.8%)
Eligible for Reduced-Price Lunch Program: 162 (8.4%)
Teachers: 137.2 (14.1 to 1)
Librarians/Media Specialists: 2.0 (966.5 to 1)
Guidance Counselors: 4.0 (483.3 to 1)
Current Spending: ($ per student per year):
Total: $6,080; Instruction: $3,825; Support Services: $1,926
Enrollment, Drop-out Rates and Diploma Recipients by Race/Ethnicity

Category	Total	White	Black	Asian	AIAN	Hisp.
Enrollment (%)	100.0	66.3	10.2	0.4	0.5	22.7
Drop-out Rate (%)	2.5	1.5	9.6	0.0	n/a	3.8
H.S. Diplomas (#)	130	103	11	0	0	16

Fort Bend County

Fort Bend ISD
16431 Lexington Blvd • Sugar Land, TX 77479-2308
(281) 634-1000 • http://www.fortbend.k12.tx.us/
Grade Span: PK-12; **Agency Type:** 1
Schools: 60
36 Primary; 11 Middle; 10 High; 3 Other Level
56 Regular; 0 Special Education; 0 Vocational; 4 Alternative
0 Magnet; 0 Charter; 14 Title I Eligible; 11 School-wide Title I
Students: 59,489 (51.6% male; 48.4% female)
Individual Education Program: 5,966 (10.0%);
English Language Learner: 5,686 (9.6%); Migrant: 5 (<0.1%)
Eligible for Free Lunch Program: 11,400 (19.2%)
Eligible for Reduced-Price Lunch Program: 2,658 (4.5%)
Teachers: 3,585.4 (16.6 to 1)
Librarians/Media Specialists: 65.1 (913.8 to 1)
Guidance Counselors: 124.7 (477.1 to 1)
Current Spending: ($ per student per year):
Total: $5,932; Instruction: $3,675; Support Services: $2,049
Enrollment, Drop-out Rates and Diploma Recipients by Race/Ethnicity

Category	Total	White	Black	Asian	AIAN	Hisp.
Enrollment (%)	100.0	33.6	29.3	17.7	0.2	19.3
Drop-out Rate (%)	3.1	2.4	3.1	2.1	0.0	6.3
H.S. Diplomas (#)	3,630	1,457	971	743	0	459

Lamar CISD
3911 Ave I • Rosenberg, TX 77471-3960
(281) 341-3100 • http://www.lcisd.org/
Grade Span: PK-12; **Agency Type:** 1
Schools: 31
16 Primary; 5 Middle; 3 High; 4 Other Level
25 Regular; 1 Special Education; 0 Vocational; 2 Alternative
0 Magnet; 0 Charter; 16 Title I Eligible; 15 School-wide Title I
Students: 17,063 (50.6% male; 49.4% female)
Individual Education Program: 1,986 (11.6%);
English Language Learner: 1,755 (10.3%); Migrant: 11 (0.1%)
Eligible for Free Lunch Program: 6,687 (39.2%)
Eligible for Reduced-Price Lunch Program: 1,166 (6.8%)
Teachers: 1,096.0 (15.6 to 1)
Librarians/Media Specialists: 23.0 (741.9 to 1)
Guidance Counselors: 48.7 (350.4 to 1)
Current Spending: ($ per student per year):
Total: $6,734; Instruction: $4,072; Support Services: $2,308
Enrollment, Drop-out Rates and Diploma Recipients by Race/Ethnicity

Category	Total	White	Black	Asian	AIAN	Hisp.
Enrollment (%)	100.0	36.8	13.5	2.3	0.1	47.3
Drop-out Rate (%)	4.6	2.2	4.4	3.4	0.0	6.9
H.S. Diplomas (#)	796	366	98	9	2	321

Needville ISD
16227 Hwy 36 • Needville, TX 77461-0412
Mailing Address: PO Box 412 • Needville, TX 77461-0412
(979) 793-4308
Grade Span: PK-12; **Agency Type:** 1
Schools: 5
2 Primary; 2 Middle; 1 High; 0 Other Level
5 Regular; 0 Special Education; 0 Vocational; 0 Alternative
0 Magnet; 0 Charter; 3 Title I Eligible; 0 School-wide Title I
Students: 2,437 (51.6% male; 48.4% female)
Individual Education Program: 317 (13.0%);
English Language Learner: 93 (3.8%); Migrant: 0 (0.0%)
Eligible for Free Lunch Program: 509 (20.9%)
Eligible for Reduced-Price Lunch Program: 120 (4.9%)
Teachers: 162.0 (15.0 to 1)
Librarians/Media Specialists: 3.0 (812.3 to 1)
Guidance Counselors: 7.0 (348.1 to 1)
Current Spending: ($ per student per year):
Total: $5,715; Instruction: $3,638; Support Services: $1,800
Enrollment, Drop-out Rates and Diploma Recipients by Race/Ethnicity

Category	Total	White	Black	Asian	AIAN	Hisp.
Enrollment (%)	100.0	63.7	5.9	0.3	0.2	29.8
Drop-out Rate (%)	2.2	1.4	7.5	0.0	0.0	3.6
H.S. Diplomas (#)	170	121	11	0	1	37

Stafford Municipal School
1625 Staffordshire Rd • Stafford, TX 77477-6326
(281) 261-9200
Grade Span: PK-12; **Agency Type:** 1
Schools: 6
2 Primary; 2 Middle; 1 High; 1 Other Level
5 Regular; 0 Special Education; 0 Vocational; 1 Alternative
0 Magnet; 0 Charter; 4 Title I Eligible; 0 School-wide Title I
Students: 2,812 (52.8% male; 47.2% female)
Individual Education Program: 274 (9.7%);
English Language Learner: 377 (13.4%); Migrant: 0 (0.0%)
Eligible for Free Lunch Program: 682 (24.3%)
Eligible for Reduced-Price Lunch Program: 218 (7.8%)
Teachers: 203.2 (13.8 to 1)
Librarians/Media Specialists: 3.0 (937.3 to 1)
Guidance Counselors: 8.0 (351.5 to 1)
Current Spending: ($ per student per year):
Total: $6,163; Instruction: $3,934; Support Services: $1,930
Enrollment, Drop-out Rates and Diploma Recipients by Race/Ethnicity

Category	Total	White	Black	Asian	AIAN	Hisp.
Enrollment (%)	100.0	18.2	27.9	20.6	0.2	33.0
Drop-out Rate (%)	0.5	0.5	0.0	0.7	n/a	0.8
H.S. Diplomas (#)	179	41	45	44	0	49

Freestone County

Fairfield ISD

615 Post Oak Rd • Fairfield, TX 75840-2005
(903) 389-2532 • http://www.fairfield.k12.tx.us/
Grade Span: PK-12; **Agency Type:** 1
Schools: 4
1 Primary; 1 Middle; 1 High; 1 Other Level
3 Regular; 0 Special Education; 0 Vocational; 1 Alternative
0 Magnet; 0 Charter; 2 Title I Eligible; 2 School-wide Title I
Students: 1,630 (51.1% male; 48.9% female)
Individual Education Program: 223 (13.7%);
English Language Learner: 86 (5.3%); Migrant: 3 (0.2%)
Eligible for Free Lunch Program: 532 (32.6%)
Eligible for Reduced-Price Lunch Program: 111 (6.8%)
Teachers: 123.0 (13.3 to 1)
Librarians/Media Specialists: 2.0 (815.0 to 1)
Guidance Counselors: 8.0 (203.8 to 1)
Current Spending: ($ per student per year):
Total: $7,530; Instruction: $4,597; Support Services: $2,621
Enrollment, Drop-out Rates and Diploma Recipients by Race/Ethnicity

Category	Total	White	Black	Asian	AIAN	Hisp.
Enrollment (%)	100.0	63.7	22.5	1.1	0.9	11.7
Drop-out Rate (%)	1.6	1.4	1.9	0.0	0.0	2.5
H.S. Diplomas (#)	104	79	22	0	1	2

Frio County

Pearsall ISD

522 E Florida St • Pearsall, TX 78061-3315
(830) 334-8001
Grade Span: PK-12; **Agency Type:** 1
Schools: 6
2 Primary; 1 Middle; 1 High; 1 Other Level
4 Regular; 0 Special Education; 0 Vocational; 1 Alternative
0 Magnet; 0 Charter; 4 Title I Eligible; 4 School-wide Title I
Students: 2,279 (50.0% male; 50.0% female)
Individual Education Program: 232 (10.2%);
English Language Learner: 321 (14.1%); Migrant: 348 (15.3%)
Eligible for Free Lunch Program: 1,636 (71.8%)
Eligible for Reduced-Price Lunch Program: 220 (9.7%)
Teachers: 161.0 (14.2 to 1)
Librarians/Media Specialists: 0.0 (0.0 to 1)
Guidance Counselors: 8.0 (284.9 to 1)
Current Spending: ($ per student per year):
Total: $7,016; Instruction: $4,204; Support Services: $2,477
Enrollment, Drop-out Rates and Diploma Recipients by Race/Ethnicity

Category	Total	White	Black	Asian	AIAN	Hisp.
Enrollment (%)	100.0	10.8	0.8	0.3	0.0	88.1
Drop-out Rate (%)	5.4	2.5	0.0	0.0	n/a	5.8
H.S. Diplomas (#)	120	20	1	0	0	99

Gaines County

Seminole ISD

207 SW 6th St • Seminole, TX 79360-4305
(915) 758-3662
Grade Span: PK-12; **Agency Type:** 1
Schools: 6
2 Primary; 2 Middle; 1 High; 1 Other Level
5 Regular; 0 Special Education; 0 Vocational; 1 Alternative
0 Magnet; 0 Charter; 6 Title I Eligible; 6 School-wide Title I
Students: 2,180 (51.8% male; 48.2% female)
Individual Education Program: 355 (16.3%);
English Language Learner: 301 (13.8%); Migrant: 14 (0.6%)
Eligible for Free Lunch Program: 1,098 (50.4%)
Eligible for Reduced-Price Lunch Program: 146 (6.7%)
Teachers: 170.6 (12.8 to 1)
Librarians/Media Specialists: 3.0 (726.7 to 1)
Guidance Counselors: 5.9 (369.5 to 1)
Current Spending: ($ per student per year):
Total: $8,989; Instruction: $5,249; Support Services: $3,252
Enrollment, Drop-out Rates and Diploma Recipients by Race/Ethnicity

Category	Total	White	Black	Asian	AIAN	Hisp.
Enrollment (%)	100.0	57.8	2.0	0.1	0.2	39.8
Drop-out Rate (%)	2.8	0.5	7.1	n/a	0.0	5.6
H.S. Diplomas (#)	128	66	7	0	0	55

Galveston County

Clear Creek ISD

2425 E Main St • League City, TX 77573-2799
Mailing Address: PO Box 799 • League City, TX 77574-0799
(281) 332-2828 • http://www.ccisd.net/
Grade Span: PK-12; **Agency Type:** 1
Schools: 37
22 Primary; 8 Middle; 3 High; 2 Other Level
33 Regular; 0 Special Education; 0 Vocational; 2 Alternative
0 Magnet; 0 Charter; 6 Title I Eligible; 6 School-wide Title I
Students: 31,926 (51.4% male; 48.6% female)
Individual Education Program: 2,737 (8.6%);
English Language Learner: 2,085 (6.5%); Migrant: 1 (<0.1%)
Eligible for Free Lunch Program: 3,331 (10.4%)
Eligible for Reduced-Price Lunch Program: 1,088 (3.4%)
Teachers: 2,034.2 (15.7 to 1)
Librarians/Media Specialists: 36.0 (886.8 to 1)
Guidance Counselors: 65.8 (485.2 to 1)
Current Spending: ($ per student per year):
Total: $5,650; Instruction: $3,614; Support Services: $1,786
Enrollment, Drop-out Rates and Diploma Recipients by Race/Ethnicity

Category	Total	White	Black	Asian	AIAN	Hisp.
Enrollment (%)	100.0	68.5	7.1	9.4	0.3	14.8
Drop-out Rate (%)	2.4	2.2	3.1	0.8	7.1	4.8
H.S. Diplomas (#)	1,844	1,292	134	231	3	184

Dickinson ISD

4512 Hwy 3 • Dickinson, TX 77539-2026
Mailing Address: PO Box Z • Dickinson, TX 77539-2026
(281) 534-3581
Grade Span: PK-12; **Agency Type:** 1
Schools: 10
4 Primary; 2 Middle; 1 High; 3 Other Level
7 Regular; 0 Special Education; 0 Vocational; 3 Alternative
0 Magnet; 0 Charter; 5 Title I Eligible; 5 School-wide Title I
Students: 6,295 (51.8% male; 48.2% female)
Individual Education Program: 669 (10.6%);
English Language Learner: 926 (14.7%); Migrant: 46 (0.7%)
Eligible for Free Lunch Program: 3,006 (47.8%)
Eligible for Reduced-Price Lunch Program: 437 (6.9%)
Teachers: 396.1 (15.9 to 1)
Librarians/Media Specialists: 7.0 (899.3 to 1)
Guidance Counselors: 9.3 (676.9 to 1)
Current Spending: ($ per student per year):
Total: $6,222; Instruction: $3,825; Support Services: $2,079
Enrollment, Drop-out Rates and Diploma Recipients by Race/Ethnicity

Category	Total	White	Black	Asian	AIAN	Hisp.
Enrollment (%)	100.0	48.0	12.6	3.7	0.3	35.4
Drop-out Rate (%)	8.8	7.7	8.0	4.6	0.0	12.5
H.S. Diplomas (#)	247	149	27	13	0	58

Friendswood ISD

302 Laurel Dr • Friendswood, TX 77546-3923
(281) 482-1267 • http://www.friendswood.isd.tenet.edu/
Grade Span: PK-12; **Agency Type:** 1
Schools: 7
2 Primary; 3 Middle; 1 High; 1 Other Level
6 Regular; 0 Special Education; 1 Vocational; 0 Alternative
0 Magnet; 0 Charter; 2 Title I Eligible; 0 School-wide Title I
Students: 5,391 (51.5% male; 48.5% female)
Individual Education Program: 476 (8.8%);
English Language Learner: 32 (0.6%); Migrant: 0 (0.0%)
Eligible for Free Lunch Program: 108 (2.0%)
Eligible for Reduced-Price Lunch Program: 34 (0.6%)
Teachers: 324.6 (16.6 to 1)
Librarians/Media Specialists: 5.0 (1,078.2 to 1)
Guidance Counselors: 9.5 (567.5 to 1)
Current Spending: ($ per student per year):
Total: $5,708; Instruction: $3,556; Support Services: $1,928
Enrollment, Drop-out Rates and Diploma Recipients by Race/Ethnicity

Category	Total	White	Black	Asian	AIAN	Hisp.
Enrollment (%)	100.0	87.6	2.0	3.3	0.3	6.9
Drop-out Rate (%)	1.1	1.1	0.0	0.0	0.0	2.2
H.S. Diplomas (#)	381	336	8	10	1	26

Galveston ISD

3904 Ave T • Galveston, TX 77550-8643
Mailing Address: PO Box 660 • Galveston, TX 77553-0660
(409) 766-5100 • http://www.Galveston-Schools.org/
Grade Span: PK-12; **Agency Type:** 1
Schools: 17
10 Primary; 3 Middle; 1 High; 3 Other Level
13 Regular; 1 Special Education; 0 Vocational; 3 Alternative
0 Magnet; 0 Charter; 13 Title I Eligible; 11 School-wide Title I

Students: 9,192 (51.6% male; 48.4% female)
Individual Education Program: 1,055 (11.5%);
English Language Learner: 1,065 (11.6%); Migrant: 0 (0.0%)
Eligible for Free Lunch Program: 5,108 (55.6%)
Eligible for Reduced-Price Lunch Program: 694 (7.6%)
Teachers: 634.7 (14.5 to 1)
Librarians/Media Specialists: 11.1 (828.1 to 1)
Guidance Counselors: 12.0 (766.0 to 1)
Current Spending: ($ per student per year):
Total: $6,549; Instruction: $3,856; Support Services: $2,372
Enrollment, Drop-out Rates and Diploma Recipients by Race/Ethnicity

Category	Total	White	Black	Asian	AIAN	Hisp.
Enrollment (%)	100.0	26.7	33.0	2.8	0.3	37.2
Drop-out Rate (%)	9.4	7.3	10.5	0.0	0.0	11.1
H.S. Diplomas (#)	419	145	149	10	1	114

La Marque ISD

1727 Bayou Rd • La Marque, TX 77568-5209
Mailing Address: PO Box 7 • La Marque, TX 77568-0007
(409) 938-4251 • http://www.la-marque.isd.tenet.edu/
Grade Span: PK-12; **Agency Type:** 1
Schools: 9
6 Primary; 1 Middle; 1 High; 1 Other Level
8 Regular; 0 Special Education; 0 Vocational; 1 Alternative
0 Magnet; 0 Charter; 8 Title I Eligible; 8 School-wide Title I
Students: 3,883 (50.2% male; 49.8% female)
Individual Education Program: 467 (12.0%);
English Language Learner: 69 (1.8%); Migrant: 2 (0.1%)
Eligible for Free Lunch Program: 2,016 (51.9%)
Eligible for Reduced-Price Lunch Program: 266 (6.9%)
Teachers: 257.4 (15.1 to 1)
Librarians/Media Specialists: 7.0 (554.7 to 1)
Guidance Counselors: 9.0 (431.4 to 1)
Current Spending: ($ per student per year):
Total: $6,571; Instruction: $3,715; Support Services: $2,464
Enrollment, Drop-out Rates and Diploma Recipients by Race/Ethnicity

Category	Total	White	Black	Asian	AIAN	Hisp.
Enrollment (%)	100.0	17.8	67.0	0.3	0.3	14.6
Drop-out Rate (%)	5.2	6.1	5.0	9.1	0.0	3.6
H.S. Diplomas (#)	241	41	181	2	0	17

Santa Fe ISD

13304 Hwy 6 • Santa Fe, TX 77510-0370
Mailing Address: PO Box 370 • Santa Fe, TX 77510-0370
(409) 925-3526
Grade Span: PK-12; **Agency Type:** 1
Schools: 7
2 Primary; 3 Middle; 1 High; 1 Other Level
6 Regular; 0 Special Education; 0 Vocational; 1 Alternative
0 Magnet; 0 Charter; 4 Title I Eligible; 0 School-wide Title I
Students: 4,473 (52.9% male; 47.1% female)
Individual Education Program: 460 (10.3%);
English Language Learner: 86 (1.9%); Migrant: 0 (0.0%)
Eligible for Free Lunch Program: 785 (17.5%)
Eligible for Reduced-Price Lunch Program: 191 (4.3%)
Teachers: 264.0 (16.9 to 1)
Librarians/Media Specialists: 4.0 (1,118.3 to 1)
Guidance Counselors: 9.0 (497.0 to 1)
Current Spending: ($ per student per year):
Total: $5,622; Instruction: $3,367; Support Services: $2,009
Enrollment, Drop-out Rates and Diploma Recipients by Race/Ethnicity

Category	Total	White	Black	Asian	AIAN	Hisp.
Enrollment (%)	100.0	88.8	0.3	0.2	0.2	10.5
Drop-out Rate (%)	5.3	4.8	n/a	0.0	0.0	9.8
H.S. Diplomas (#)	241	220	0	1	0	20

Texas City ISD

1401 9th Ave N • Texas City, TX 77590-5495
Mailing Address: PO Box 1150 • Texas City, TX 77592-1150
(409) 942-2713
Grade Span: PK-12; **Agency Type:** 1
Schools: 10
5 Primary; 2 Middle; 1 High; 2 Other Level
7 Regular; 0 Special Education; 0 Vocational; 3 Alternative
0 Magnet; 0 Charter; 4 Title I Eligible; 4 School-wide Title I
Students: 5,842 (50.9% male; 49.1% female)
Individual Education Program: 616 (10.5%);
English Language Learner: 329 (5.6%); Migrant: 0 (0.0%)
Eligible for Free Lunch Program: 2,612 (44.7%)
Eligible for Reduced-Price Lunch Program: 380 (6.5%)
Teachers: 363.5 (16.1 to 1)
Librarians/Media Specialists: 7.1 (822.8 to 1)
Guidance Counselors: 13.0 (449.4 to 1)
Current Spending: ($ per student per year):
Total: $7,014; Instruction: $4,143; Support Services: $2,472

Enrollment, Drop-out Rates and Diploma Recipients by Race/Ethnicity

Category	Total	White	Black	Asian	AIAN	Hisp.
Enrollment (%)	100.0	49.2	19.4	0.7	0.2	30.4
Drop-out Rate (%)	6.8	5.4	6.2	0.0	0.0	10.4
H.S. Diplomas (#)	264	151	47	5	0	61

Gillespie County

Fredericksburg ISD

300-B W Main St • Fredericksburg, TX 78624-3853
(830) 997-9551 • http://www.fisd.org/
Grade Span: PK-12; **Agency Type:** 1
Schools: 6
3 Primary; 1 Middle; 2 High; 0 Other Level
5 Regular; 0 Special Education; 0 Vocational; 1 Alternative
0 Magnet; 0 Charter; 3 Title I Eligible; 2 School-wide Title I
Students: 2,838 (50.4% male; 49.6% female)
Individual Education Program: 334 (11.8%);
English Language Learner: 227 (8.0%); Migrant: 50 (1.8%)
Eligible for Free Lunch Program: 896 (31.6%)
Eligible for Reduced-Price Lunch Program: 240 (8.5%)
Teachers: 206.0 (13.8 to 1)
Librarians/Media Specialists: 2.4 (1,182.5 to 1)
Guidance Counselors: 6.2 (457.7 to 1)
Current Spending: ($ per student per year):
Total: $6,514; Instruction: $3,986; Support Services: $2,261
Enrollment, Drop-out Rates and Diploma Recipients by Race/Ethnicity

Category	Total	White	Black	Asian	AIAN	Hisp.
Enrollment (%)	100.0	63.9	0.6	0.4	0.4	34.8
Drop-out Rate (%)	2.0	1.1	20.0	0.0	0.0	4.7
H.S. Diplomas (#)	219	178	1	1	0	39

Gonzales County

Gonzales ISD

926 St Lawrence • Gonzales, TX 78629-4151
(830) 672-9551
Grade Span: PK-12; **Agency Type:** 1
Schools: 6
2 Primary; 2 Middle; 2 High; 0 Other Level
5 Regular; 0 Special Education; 0 Vocational; 1 Alternative
0 Magnet; 0 Charter; 5 Title I Eligible; 5 School-wide Title I
Students: 2,655 (51.6% male; 48.4% female)
Individual Education Program: 330 (12.4%);
English Language Learner: 225 (8.5%); Migrant: 65 (2.4%)
Eligible for Free Lunch Program: 1,435 (54.0%)
Eligible for Reduced-Price Lunch Program: 216 (8.1%)
Teachers: 192.8 (13.8 to 1)
Librarians/Media Specialists: 2.0 (1,327.5 to 1)
Guidance Counselors: 5.3 (500.9 to 1)
Current Spending: ($ per student per year):
Total: $6,293; Instruction: $4,003; Support Services: $2,013
Enrollment, Drop-out Rates and Diploma Recipients by Race/Ethnicity

Category	Total	White	Black	Asian	AIAN	Hisp.
Enrollment (%)	100.0	39.5	11.7	0.3	0.0	48.6
Drop-out Rate (%)	2.6	1.8	4.4	0.0	0.0	2.8
H.S. Diplomas (#)	147	67	28	1	1	50

Gray County

Pampa ISD

321 W Albert St • Pampa, TX 79065-7801
(806) 669-4700 • http://www.pampaisd.net/
Grade Span: PK-12; **Agency Type:** 1
Schools: 7
4 Primary; 1 Middle; 2 High; 0 Other Level
6 Regular; 0 Special Education; 0 Vocational; 1 Alternative
0 Magnet; 0 Charter; 3 Title I Eligible; 3 School-wide Title I
Students: 3,445 (49.6% male; 50.4% female)
Individual Education Program: 416 (12.1%);
English Language Learner: 184 (5.3%); Migrant: 17 (0.5%)
Eligible for Free Lunch Program: 1,208 (35.1%)
Eligible for Reduced-Price Lunch Program: 279 (8.1%)
Teachers: 255.6 (13.5 to 1)
Librarians/Media Specialists: 1.2 (2,870.8 to 1)
Guidance Counselors: 10.1 (341.1 to 1)
Current Spending: ($ per student per year):
Total: $5,884; Instruction: $3,743; Support Services: $1,860
Enrollment, Drop-out Rates and Diploma Recipients by Race/Ethnicity

Category	Total	White	Black	Asian	AIAN	Hisp.
Enrollment (%)	100.0	70.5	4.3	0.6	0.6	24.1
Drop-out Rate (%)	3.5	3.1	0.0	0.0	16.7	5.4
H.S. Diplomas (#)	253	207	9	4	4	29

Denison ISD

1201 S Rusk Ave • Denison, TX 75020-6340
(903) 462-7000 • http://www.denisonisd.net/
Grade Span: PK-12; **Agency Type:** 1
Schools: 11
7 Primary; 1 Middle; 2 High; 1 Other Level
9 Regular; 0 Special Education; 0 Vocational; 2 Alternative
0 Magnet; 0 Charter; 6 Title I Eligible; 6 School-wide Title I
Students: 4,544 (51.8% male; 48.2% female)
Individual Education Program: 845 (18.6%);
English Language Learner: 133 (2.9%); Migrant: 2 (<0.1%)
Eligible for Free Lunch Program: 1,745 (38.4%)
Eligible for Reduced-Price Lunch Program: 453 (10.0%)
Teachers: 302.7 (15.0 to 1)
Librarians/Media Specialists: 1.2 (3,786.7 to 1)
Guidance Counselors: 14.1 (322.3 to 1)
Current Spending: ($ per student per year):
Total: $6,032; Instruction: $3,738; Support Services: $1,962
Enrollment, Drop-out Rates and Diploma Recipients by Race/Ethnicity

Category	Total	White	Black	Asian	AIAN	Hisp.
Enrollment (%)	100.0	78.0	11.7	0.8	2.4	7.0
Drop-out Rate (%)	3.6	2.8	7.7	28.6	5.3	3.4
H.S. Diplomas (#)	226	188	24	2	2	10

Sherman ISD

120 W King St • Sherman, TX 75090-7133
Mailing Address: PO Box 1176 • Sherman, TX 75091-1176
(903) 891-6400
Grade Span: PK-12; **Agency Type:** 1
Schools: 14
6 Primary; 2 Middle; 2 High; 3 Other Level
10 Regular; 0 Special Education; 0 Vocational; 3 Alternative
0 Magnet; 0 Charter; 8 Title I Eligible; 5 School-wide Title I
Students: 6,244 (51.4% male; 48.6% female)
Individual Education Program: 1,042 (16.7%);
English Language Learner: 558 (8.9%); Migrant: 12 (0.2%)
Eligible for Free Lunch Program: 2,511 (40.2%)
Eligible for Reduced-Price Lunch Program: 416 (6.7%)
Teachers: 448.4 (13.9 to 1)
Librarians/Media Specialists: 4.1 (1,522.9 to 1)
Guidance Counselors: 11.7 (533.7 to 1)
Current Spending: ($ per student per year):
Total: $5,976; Instruction: $3,724; Support Services: $1,944
Enrollment, Drop-out Rates and Diploma Recipients by Race/Ethnicity

Category	Total	White	Black	Asian	AIAN	Hisp.
Enrollment (%)	100.0	62.8	16.4	1.1	1.2	18.4
Drop-out Rate (%)	3.8	3.5	4.8	0.0	0.0	4.8
H.S. Diplomas (#)	300	231	45	2	3	19

Whitesboro ISD

115 Fourth St • Whitesboro, TX 76273-0130
(903) 564-4200
Grade Span: PK-12; **Agency Type:** 1
Schools: 3
1 Primary; 1 Middle; 1 High; 0 Other Level
3 Regular; 0 Special Education; 0 Vocational; 0 Alternative
0 Magnet; 0 Charter; 1 Title I Eligible; 1 School-wide Title I
Students: 1,551 (52.4% male; 47.6% female)
Individual Education Program: 238 (15.3%);
English Language Learner: 29 (1.9%); Migrant: 1 (0.1%)
Eligible for Free Lunch Program: 402 (25.9%)
Eligible for Reduced-Price Lunch Program: 135 (8.7%)
Teachers: 111.1 (14.0 to 1)
Librarians/Media Specialists: 0.9 (1,723.3 to 1)
Guidance Counselors: 3.6 (430.8 to 1)
Current Spending: ($ per student per year):
Total: $5,883; Instruction: $3,845; Support Services: $1,721
Enrollment, Drop-out Rates and Diploma Recipients by Race/Ethnicity

Category	Total	White	Black	Asian	AIAN	Hisp.
Enrollment (%)	100.0	91.6	0.3	0.8	1.9	5.4
Drop-out Rate (%)	1.8	1.4	n/a	0.0	22.2	0.0
H.S. Diplomas (#)	88	86	0	0	1	1

Gregg County

Gladewater ISD

500 W Quitman • Gladewater, TX 75647-2011
(903) 845-6991 • http://gladewaterisd.com/
Grade Span: PK-12; **Agency Type:** 1
Schools: 6
2 Primary; 2 Middle; 1 High; 1 Other Level
6 Regular; 0 Special Education; 0 Vocational; 0 Alternative
0 Magnet; 0 Charter; 5 Title I Eligible; 5 School-wide Title I
Students: 2,225 (52.4% male; 47.6% female)
Individual Education Program: 432 (19.4%);
English Language Learner: 43 (1.9%); Migrant: 2 (0.1%)
Eligible for Free Lunch Program: 972 (43.7%)
Eligible for Reduced-Price Lunch Program: 186 (8.4%)
Teachers: 155.2 (14.3 to 1)
Librarians/Media Specialists: 4.0 (556.3 to 1)
Guidance Counselors: 6.0 (370.8 to 1)
Current Spending: ($ per student per year):
Total: $6,275; Instruction: $3,954; Support Services: $1,970
Enrollment, Drop-out Rates and Diploma Recipients by Race/Ethnicity

Category	Total	White	Black	Asian	AIAN	Hisp.
Enrollment (%)	100.0	71.8	20.6	0.7	0.4	6.5
Drop-out Rate (%)	3.6	4.4	0.8	0.0	n/a	0.0
H.S. Diplomas (#)	133	108	21	0	0	4

Kilgore ISD

301 N Kilgore St • Kilgore, TX 75662-5499
(903) 984-2073 • http://www.kisd.org/
Grade Span: PK-12; **Agency Type:** 1
Schools: 7
2 Primary; 2 Middle; 2 High; 1 Other Level
5 Regular; 0 Special Education; 0 Vocational; 2 Alternative
0 Magnet; 0 Charter; 4 Title I Eligible; 0 School-wide Title I
Students: 3,648 (49.5% male; 50.5% female)
Individual Education Program: 488 (13.4%);
English Language Learner: 242 (6.6%); Migrant: 2 (0.1%)
Eligible for Free Lunch Program: 1,644 (45.1%)
Eligible for Reduced-Price Lunch Program: 223 (6.1%)
Teachers: 273.8 (13.3 to 1)
Librarians/Media Specialists: 1.0 (3,648.0 to 1)
Guidance Counselors: 2.5 (1,459.2 to 1)
Current Spending: ($ per student per year):
Total: $5,475; Instruction: $3,513; Support Services: $1,677
Enrollment, Drop-out Rates and Diploma Recipients by Race/Ethnicity

Category	Total	White	Black	Asian	AIAN	Hisp.
Enrollment (%)	100.0	64.7	20.6	0.8	0.2	13.7
Drop-out Rate (%)	5.0	4.2	7.5	0.0	n/a	6.5
H.S. Diplomas (#)	227	166	42	0	0	19

Longview ISD

1301 E Young St • Longview, TX 75602
Mailing Address: PO Box 3268 • Longview, TX 75606-3268
(903) 381-2200 • http://www.lisd.org/www2/Main/default.asp
Grade Span: PK-12; **Agency Type:** 1
Schools: 18
11 Primary; 3 Middle; 1 High; 3 Other Level
15 Regular; 1 Special Education; 0 Vocational; 2 Alternative
0 Magnet; 0 Charter; 10 Title I Eligible; 10 School-wide Title I
Students: 8,330 (51.4% male; 48.6% female)
Individual Education Program: 1,224 (14.7%);
English Language Learner: 838 (10.1%); Migrant: 0 (0.0%)
Eligible for Free Lunch Program: 4,435 (53.2%)
Eligible for Reduced-Price Lunch Program: 603 (7.2%)
Teachers: 593.7 (14.0 to 1)
Librarians/Media Specialists: 16.0 (520.6 to 1)
Guidance Counselors: 20.0 (416.5 to 1)
Current Spending: ($ per student per year):
Total: $6,711; Instruction: $3,903; Support Services: $2,452
Enrollment, Drop-out Rates and Diploma Recipients by Race/Ethnicity

Category	Total	White	Black	Asian	AIAN	Hisp.
Enrollment (%)	100.0	30.0	49.7	0.7	0.3	19.3
Drop-out Rate (%)	4.2	2.4	4.5	0.0	0.0	10.7
H.S. Diplomas (#)	406	175	203	5	0	23

Pine Tree ISD

1001 W Fairmont St • Longview, TX 75604-3511
Mailing Address: PO Box 5878 • Longview, TX 75608-5878
(903) 295-5000
Grade Span: PK-12; **Agency Type:** 1
Schools: 7
3 Primary; 2 Middle; 1 High; 1 Other Level
7 Regular; 0 Special Education; 0 Vocational; 0 Alternative
0 Magnet; 0 Charter; 3 Title I Eligible; 3 School-wide Title I
Students: 4,641 (51.8% male; 48.2% female)
Individual Education Program: 508 (10.9%);
English Language Learner: 249 (5.4%); Migrant: 5 (0.1%)
Eligible for Free Lunch Program: 1,310 (28.2%)
Eligible for Reduced-Price Lunch Program: 272 (5.9%)
Teachers: 324.1 (14.3 to 1)
Librarians/Media Specialists: 6.1 (760.8 to 1)
Guidance Counselors: 9.7 (478.5 to 1)
Current Spending: ($ per student per year):
Total: $5,335; Instruction: $3,475; Support Services: $1,598

Enrollment, Drop-out Rates and Diploma Recipients by Race/Ethnicity

Category	Total	White	Black	Asian	AIAN	Hisp.
Enrollment (%)	100.0	70.5	11.9	2.0	0.4	15.3
Drop-out Rate (%)	1.1	0.9	1.0	0.0	33.3	2.2
H.S. Diplomas (#)	300	253	16	8	3	20

Spring Hill ISD

3101 Spring Hill Rd • Longview, TX 75605-2822
(903) 759-4404
Grade Span: PK-12; **Agency Type:** 1
Schools: 5
2 Primary; 2 Middle; 1 High; 0 Other Level
5 Regular; 0 Special Education; 0 Vocational; 0 Alternative
0 Magnet; 0 Charter; 2 Title I Eligible; 0 School-wide Title I
Students: 1,684 (50.5% male; 49.5% female)
Individual Education Program: 137 (8.1%);
English Language Learner: 21 (1.2%); Migrant: 0 (0.0%)
Eligible for Free Lunch Program: 255 (15.1%)
Eligible for Reduced-Price Lunch Program: 56 (3.3%)
Teachers: 117.4 (14.3 to 1)
Librarians/Media Specialists: 3.0 (561.3 to 1)
Guidance Counselors: 3.0 (561.3 to 1)
Current Spending: ($ per student per year):
Total: $5,915; Instruction: $3,800; Support Services: $1,833

Enrollment, Drop-out Rates and Diploma Recipients by Race/Ethnicity

Category	Total	White	Black	Asian	AIAN	Hisp.
Enrollment (%)	100.0	88.3	4.2	2.3	0.2	5.0
Drop-out Rate (%)	1.4	1.3	6.7	0.0	n/a	0.0
H.S. Diplomas (#)	109	100	2	1	0	6

Grimes County

Navasota ISD

705 E Washington Ave • Navasota, TX 77868-3005
Mailing Address: PO Box 511 • Navasota, TX 77868-0511
(936) 825-4200 • http://www.navasota.k12.tx.us/
Grade Span: PK-12; **Agency Type:** 1
Schools: 7
2 Primary; 2 Middle; 2 High; 1 Other Level
5 Regular; 0 Special Education; 0 Vocational; 2 Alternative
0 Magnet; 0 Charter; 3 Title I Eligible; 3 School-wide Title I
Students: 3,024 (50.4% male; 49.6% female)
Individual Education Program: 327 (10.8%);
English Language Learner: 263 (8.7%); Migrant: 30 (1.0%)
Eligible for Free Lunch Program: 1,514 (50.1%)
Eligible for Reduced-Price Lunch Program: 281 (9.3%)
Teachers: 213.8 (14.1 to 1)
Librarians/Media Specialists: 2.1 (1,440.0 to 1)
Guidance Counselors: 7.0 (432.0 to 1)
Current Spending: ($ per student per year):
Total: $6,055; Instruction: $3,531; Support Services: $2,165

Enrollment, Drop-out Rates and Diploma Recipients by Race/Ethnicity

Category	Total	White	Black	Asian	AIAN	Hisp.
Enrollment (%)	100.0	40.5	28.7	0.4	0.2	30.2
Drop-out Rate (%)	3.6	2.3	6.4	0.0	0.0	3.1
H.S. Diplomas (#)	197	98	57	1	0	41

Guadalupe County

Schertz-Cibolo-Universal City ISD

1060 Elbel Rd • Schertz, TX 78154-2099
(210) 945-6200
Grade Span: PK-12; **Agency Type:** 1
Schools: 12
5 Primary; 4 Middle; 2 High; 0 Other Level
10 Regular; 0 Special Education; 0 Vocational; 1 Alternative
0 Magnet; 0 Charter; 5 Title I Eligible; 4 School-wide Title I
Students: 6,718 (51.9% male; 48.1% female)
Individual Education Program: 796 (11.8%);
English Language Learner: 150 (2.2%); Migrant: 15 (0.2%)
Eligible for Free Lunch Program: 1,278 (19.0%)
Eligible for Reduced-Price Lunch Program: 442 (6.6%)
Teachers: 437.9 (15.3 to 1)
Librarians/Media Specialists: 10.0 (671.8 to 1)
Guidance Counselors: 16.0 (419.9 to 1)
Current Spending: ($ per student per year):
Total: $5,668; Instruction: $3,480; Support Services: $1,981

Enrollment, Drop-out Rates and Diploma Recipients by Race/Ethnicity

Category	Total	White	Black	Asian	AIAN	Hisp.
Enrollment (%)	100.0	63.4	9.7	1.8	0.3	24.9
Drop-out Rate (%)	2.5	2.1	2.8	0.0	0.0	4.1
H.S. Diplomas (#)	467	312	48	10	2	95

Seguin ISD

1221 E Kingsbury • Seguin, TX 78155
(830) 372-5771
Grade Span: PK-12; **Agency Type:** 1
Schools: 16
8 Primary; 3 Middle; 3 High; 2 Other Level
13 Regular; 0 Special Education; 0 Vocational; 3 Alternative
0 Magnet; 0 Charter; 12 Title I Eligible; 12 School-wide Title I
Students: 7,681 (51.6% male; 48.4% female)
Individual Education Program: 1,035 (13.5%);
English Language Learner: 712 (9.3%); Migrant: 478 (6.2%)
Eligible for Free Lunch Program: 3,716 (48.4%)
Eligible for Reduced-Price Lunch Program: 674 (8.8%)
Teachers: 569.1 (13.5 to 1)
Librarians/Media Specialists: 8.1 (948.3 to 1)
Guidance Counselors: 20.2 (380.2 to 1)
Current Spending: ($ per student per year):
Total: $6,279; Instruction: $3,951; Support Services: $1,997

Enrollment, Drop-out Rates and Diploma Recipients by Race/Ethnicity

Category	Total	White	Black	Asian	AIAN	Hisp.
Enrollment (%)	100.0	31.8	7.4	0.7	0.2	59.8
Drop-out Rate (%)	4.0	2.2	6.6	0.0	0.0	5.0
H.S. Diplomas (#)	384	169	36	8	0	171

Hale County

Plainview ISD

912 Portland St • Plainview, TX 79072-7060
Mailing Address: PO Box 1540 • Plainview, TX 79073-1540
(806) 296-6392
Grade Span: PK-12; **Agency Type:** 1
Schools: 13
6 Primary; 3 Middle; 1 High; 3 Other Level
11 Regular; 0 Special Education; 0 Vocational; 2 Alternative
0 Magnet; 0 Charter; 10 Title I Eligible; 10 School-wide Title I
Students: 5,864 (50.6% male; 49.4% female)
Individual Education Program: 865 (14.8%);
English Language Learner: 547 (9.3%); Migrant: 607 (10.4%)
Eligible for Free Lunch Program: 3,052 (52.0%)
Eligible for Reduced-Price Lunch Program: 341 (5.8%)
Teachers: 402.7 (14.6 to 1)
Librarians/Media Specialists: 8.1 (724.0 to 1)
Guidance Counselors: 16.0 (366.5 to 1)
Current Spending: ($ per student per year):
Total: $5,927; Instruction: $3,772; Support Services: $1,887

Enrollment, Drop-out Rates and Diploma Recipients by Race/Ethnicity

Category	Total	White	Black	Asian	AIAN	Hisp.
Enrollment (%)	100.0	27.0	5.7	0.6	0.3	66.5
Drop-out Rate (%)	6.2	2.9	2.7	0.0	0.0	8.6
H.S. Diplomas (#)	374	132	32	2	2	206

Hardin County

Hardin-Jefferson ISD

520 W Herring • Sour Lake, TX 77659-0490
Mailing Address: PO Box 490 • Sour Lake, TX 77659-0490
(409) 981-6400 • http://www.esc05.k12.tx.us/hjisd/index.htm
Grade Span: PK-12; **Agency Type:** 1
Schools: 7
2 Primary; 1 Middle; 2 High; 2 Other Level
4 Regular; 0 Special Education; 0 Vocational; 3 Alternative
0 Magnet; 0 Charter; 2 Title I Eligible; 2 School-wide Title I
Students: 2,099 (53.7% male; 46.3% female)
Individual Education Program: 295 (14.1%);
English Language Learner: 25 (1.2%); Migrant: 3 (0.1%)
Eligible for Free Lunch Program: 504 (24.0%)
Eligible for Reduced-Price Lunch Program: 121 (5.8%)
Teachers: 147.4 (14.2 to 1)
Librarians/Media Specialists: 1.0 (2,099.0 to 1)
Guidance Counselors: 5.9 (355.8 to 1)
Current Spending: ($ per student per year):
Total: $6,510; Instruction: $3,981; Support Services: $2,189

Enrollment, Drop-out Rates and Diploma Recipients by Race/Ethnicity

Category	Total	White	Black	Asian	AIAN	Hisp.
Enrollment (%)	100.0	83.8	12.5	0.2	0.2	3.2
Drop-out Rate (%)	2.9	3.0	1.2	n/a	0.0	4.8
H.S. Diplomas (#)	139	122	12	1	0	4

Lumberton ISD

121 S Main • Lumberton, TX 77657-0123
Mailing Address: PO Box 8123 • Lumberton, TX 77657-0123
(409) 755-4993
Grade Span: PK-12; **Agency Type:** 1
Schools: 6
2 Primary; 2 Middle; 1 High; 1 Other Level

5 Regular; 1 Special Education; 0 Vocational; 0 Alternative
0 Magnet; 0 Charter; 2 Title I Eligible; 0 School-wide Title I
Students: 3,352 (51.2% male; 48.8% female)
Individual Education Program: 415 (12.4%);
English Language Learner: 17 (0.5%); Migrant: 0 (0.0%)
Eligible for Free Lunch Program: 533 (15.9%)
Eligible for Reduced-Price Lunch Program: 253 (7.5%)
Teachers: 225.8 (14.8 to 1)
Librarians/Media Specialists: 4.0 (838.0 to 1)
Guidance Counselors: 7.1 (472.1 to 1)
Current Spending: ($ per student per year):
Total: $5,986; Instruction: $3,443; Support Services: $2,212
Enrollment, Drop-out Rates and Diploma Recipients by Race/Ethnicity

Category	Total	White	Black	Asian	AIAN	Hisp.
Enrollment (%)	100.0	97.4	0.1	0.4	0.2	1.9
Drop-out Rate (%)	1.4	1.3	0.0	25.0	0.0	4.0
H.S. Diplomas (#)	222	217	0	1	0	4

Silsbee ISD
415 W Ave N • Silsbee, TX 77656-4799
(409) 385-5286
Grade Span: PK-12; **Agency Type:** 1
Schools: 7
3 Primary; 2 Middle; 1 High; 0 Other Level
6 Regular; 0 Special Education; 0 Vocational; 0 Alternative
0 Magnet; 0 Charter; 5 Title I Eligible; 5 School-wide Title I
Students: 3,270 (52.9% male; 47.1% female)
Individual Education Program: 625 (19.1%);
English Language Learner: 20 (0.6%); Migrant: 6 (0.2%)
Eligible for Free Lunch Program: 1,033 (31.6%)
Eligible for Reduced-Price Lunch Program: 196 (6.0%)
Teachers: 234.4 (14.0 to 1)
Librarians/Media Specialists: 1.5 (2,180.0 to 1)
Guidance Counselors: 8.3 (394.0 to 1)
Current Spending: ($ per student per year):
Total: $7,147; Instruction: $4,466; Support Services: $2,380
Enrollment, Drop-out Rates and Diploma Recipients by Race/Ethnicity

Category	Total	White	Black	Asian	AIAN	Hisp.
Enrollment (%)	100.0	77.7	19.5	0.4	0.0	2.4
Drop-out Rate (%)	3.7	4.1	2.5	0.0	0.0	0.0
H.S. Diplomas (#)	208	155	50	1	0	2

Harris County

Aldine ISD
14910 Aldine Westfield Rd • Houston, TX 77032-3099
(281) 449-1011 • http://www.aldine.k12.tx.us/
Grade Span: PK-12; **Agency Type:** 1
Schools: 67
32 Primary; 17 Middle; 6 High; 9 Other Level
59 Regular; 1 Special Education; 0 Vocational; 4 Alternative
0 Magnet; 0 Charter; 63 Title I Eligible; 63 School-wide Title I
Students: 55,367 (51.5% male; 48.5% female)
Individual Education Program: 5,434 (9.8%);
English Language Learner: 12,966 (23.4%); Migrant: 32 (0.1%)
Eligible for Free Lunch Program: 35,564 (64.2%)
Eligible for Reduced-Price Lunch Program: 5,307 (9.6%)
Teachers: 3,722.5 (14.9 to 1)
Librarians/Media Specialists: 55.0 (1,006.7 to 1)
Guidance Counselors: 134.0 (413.2 to 1)
Current Spending: ($ per student per year):
Total: $6,835; Instruction: $4,268; Support Services: $2,206
Enrollment, Drop-out Rates and Diploma Recipients by Race/Ethnicity

Category	Total	White	Black	Asian	AIAN	Hisp.
Enrollment (%)	100.0	7.6	33.4	2.6	0.1	56.3
Drop-out Rate (%)	5.1	4.1	4.3	1.5	0.0	6.2
H.S. Diplomas (#)	2,149	286	834	74	0	955

Alief ISD
12302 High Star • Houston, TX 77072-1124
Mailing Address: PO Box 68 • Alief, TX 77411-0068
(281) 498-8110 • http://www.aliefisd.net/
Grade Span: PK-12; **Agency Type:** 1
Schools: 40
22 Primary; 11 Middle; 3 High; 4 Other Level
37 Regular; 1 Special Education; 0 Vocational; 2 Alternative
0 Magnet; 0 Charter; 20 Title I Eligible; 20 School-wide Title I
Students: 44,661 (51.3% male; 48.7% female)
Individual Education Program: 5,219 (11.7%);
English Language Learner: 12,996 (29.1%); Migrant: 0 (0.0%)
Eligible for Free Lunch Program: 21,775 (48.8%)
Eligible for Reduced-Price Lunch Program: 3,993 (8.9%)
Teachers: 2,947.1 (15.2 to 1)
Librarians/Media Specialists: 38.9 (1,148.1 to 1)
Guidance Counselors: 91.3 (489.2 to 1)
Current Spending: ($ per student per year):
Total: $5,987; Instruction: $3,826; Support Services: $1,841
Enrollment, Drop-out Rates and Diploma Recipients by Race/Ethnicity

Category	Total	White	Black	Asian	AIAN	Hisp.
Enrollment (%)	100.0	7.6	36.9	14.0	0.1	41.4
Drop-out Rate (%)	4.0	2.6	3.6	2.8	0.0	5.8
H.S. Diplomas (#)	1,960	279	626	485	0	570

Channelview ISD
1403 Sheldon Rd • Channelview, TX 77530-2603
(281) 452-8008 • http://www.channelview.isd.esc4.net/
Grade Span: PK-12; **Agency Type:** 1
Schools: 11
5 Primary; 2 Middle; 1 High; 3 Other Level
8 Regular; 0 Special Education; 0 Vocational; 3 Alternative
0 Magnet; 0 Charter; 9 Title I Eligible; 7 School-wide Title I
Students: 7,263 (52.1% male; 47.9% female)
Individual Education Program: 873 (12.0%);
English Language Learner: 1,380 (19.0%); Migrant: 23 (0.3%)
Eligible for Free Lunch Program: 3,098 (42.7%)
Eligible for Reduced-Price Lunch Program: 647 (8.9%)
Teachers: 436.9 (16.6 to 1)
Librarians/Media Specialists: 5.0 (1,452.6 to 1)
Guidance Counselors: 17.0 (427.2 to 1)
Current Spending: ($ per student per year):
Total: $6,012; Instruction: $3,751; Support Services: $1,929
Enrollment, Drop-out Rates and Diploma Recipients by Race/Ethnicity

Category	Total	White	Black	Asian	AIAN	Hisp.
Enrollment (%)	100.0	31.6	15.2	1.6	0.1	51.5
Drop-out Rate (%)	3.9	4.4	4.5	0.0	0.0	3.4
H.S. Diplomas (#)	301	133	48	6	0	114

Crosby ISD
706 Runneburg • Crosby, TX 77532-8009
Mailing Address: PO Box 2009 • Crosby, TX 77532-8009
(281) 328-9200 • http://www.crosby.isd.esc4.net/
Grade Span: PK-12; **Agency Type:** 1
Schools: 6
3 Primary; 2 Middle; 1 High; 0 Other Level
6 Regular; 0 Special Education; 0 Vocational; 0 Alternative
0 Magnet; 0 Charter; 4 Title I Eligible; 1 School-wide Title I
Students: 4,120 (51.9% male; 48.1% female)
Individual Education Program: 538 (13.1%);
English Language Learner: 174 (4.2%); Migrant: 0 (0.0%)
Eligible for Free Lunch Program: 1,226 (29.8%)
Eligible for Reduced-Price Lunch Program: 250 (6.1%)
Teachers: 263.6 (15.6 to 1)
Librarians/Media Specialists: 5.0 (824.0 to 1)
Guidance Counselors: 7.0 (588.6 to 1)
Current Spending: ($ per student per year):
Total: $6,415; Instruction: $3,892; Support Services: $2,205
Enrollment, Drop-out Rates and Diploma Recipients by Race/Ethnicity

Category	Total	White	Black	Asian	AIAN	Hisp.
Enrollment (%)	100.0	61.6	23.9	0.6	0.1	13.9
Drop-out Rate (%)	3.7	2.9	5.4	0.0	0.0	5.8
H.S. Diplomas (#)	219	146	49	4	0	20

Cypress-Fairbanks ISD
10300 Jones Rd • Houston, TX 77065-4208
Mailing Address: PO Box 692003 • Houston, TX 77269-2003
(281) 897-4000 • http://www.cfisd.net/
Grade Span: PK-12; **Agency Type:** 1
Schools: 59
35 Primary; 12 Middle; 8 High; 4 Other Level
54 Regular; 2 Special Education; 0 Vocational; 3 Alternative
0 Magnet; 0 Charter; 10 Title I Eligible; 10 School-wide Title I
Students: 71,165 (51.4% male; 48.6% female)
Individual Education Program: 6,905 (9.7%);
English Language Learner: 8,640 (12.1%); Migrant: 2 (<0.1%)
Eligible for Free Lunch Program: 13,459 (18.9%)
Eligible for Reduced-Price Lunch Program: 3,677 (5.2%)
Teachers: 4,603.4 (15.5 to 1)
Librarians/Media Specialists: 65.5 (1,086.5 to 1)
Guidance Counselors: 151.9 (468.5 to 1)
Current Spending: ($ per student per year):
Total: $6,357; Instruction: $3,986; Support Services: $2,085
Enrollment, Drop-out Rates and Diploma Recipients by Race/Ethnicity

Category	Total	White	Black	Asian	AIAN	Hisp.
Enrollment (%)	100.0	54.1	10.6	8.2	0.2	26.9
Drop-out Rate (%)	1.0	0.9	1.5	0.3	3.2	1.4
H.S. Diplomas (#)	3,938	2,490	388	353	6	701

Deer Park ISD

203 Ivy • Deer Park, TX 77536-2747
(832) 668-7000
Grade Span: PK-12; **Agency Type:** 1
Schools: 14
7 Primary; 4 Middle; 2 High; 1 Other Level
12 Regular; 0 Special Education; 0 Vocational; 2 Alternative
0 Magnet; 0 Charter; 3 Title I Eligible; 3 School-wide Title I
Students: 11,490 (51.3% male; 48.7% female)
Individual Education Program: 1,186 (10.3%);
English Language Learner: 1,037 (9.0%); Migrant: 0 (0.0%)
Eligible for Free Lunch Program: 2,311 (20.1%)
Eligible for Reduced-Price Lunch Program: 647 (5.6%)
Teachers: 732.1 (15.7 to 1)
Librarians/Media Specialists: 13.0 (883.8 to 1)
Guidance Counselors: 26.5 (433.6 to 1)
Current Spending: ($ per student per year):
Total: $6,694; Instruction: $4,003; Support Services: $2,396
Enrollment, Drop-out Rates and Diploma Recipients by Race/Ethnicity

Category	Total	White	Black	Asian	AIAN	Hisp.
Enrollment (%)	100.0	64.8	1.5	2.1	0.2	31.4
Drop-out Rate (%)	1.2	1.0	2.3	0.0	0.0	1.9
H.S. Diplomas (#)	678	523	2	18	1	134

Galena Park ISD

14705 Woodforest Blvd • Houston, TX 77015
Mailing Address: PO Box 565 • Galena Park, TX 77547-0565
(832) 386-1000
Grade Span: PK-12; **Agency Type:** 1
Schools: 23
12 Primary; 5 Middle; 3 High; 3 Other Level
20 Regular; 0 Special Education; 0 Vocational; 3 Alternative
0 Magnet; 0 Charter; 20 Title I Eligible; 20 School-wide Title I
Students: 20,013 (51.3% male; 48.7% female)
Individual Education Program: 2,381 (11.9%);
English Language Learner: 4,706 (23.5%); Migrant: 214 (1.1%)
Eligible for Free Lunch Program: 11,400 (57.0%)
Eligible for Reduced-Price Lunch Program: 1,605 (8.0%)
Teachers: 1,379.3 (14.5 to 1)
Librarians/Media Specialists: 17.6 (1,137.1 to 1)
Guidance Counselors: 37.1 (539.4 to 1)
Current Spending: ($ per student per year):
Total: $6,168; Instruction: $3,694; Support Services: $2,137
Enrollment, Drop-out Rates and Diploma Recipients by Race/Ethnicity

Category	Total	White	Black	Asian	AIAN	Hisp.
Enrollment (%)	100.0	12.4	21.4	1.7	0.1	64.4
Drop-out Rate (%)	4.3	3.0	2.4	3.1	0.0	5.5
H.S. Diplomas (#)	1,077	175	273	28	0	601

Goose Creek CISD

4544 Interstate 10 E • Baytown, TX 77521
Mailing Address: PO Box 30 • Baytown, TX 77522-0030
(281) 420-4800 • http://www.goosecreek.cisd.esc4.net/right.htm
Grade Span: PK-12; **Agency Type:** 1
Schools: 27
14 Primary; 5 Middle; 4 High; 2 Other Level
21 Regular; 1 Special Education; 0 Vocational; 3 Alternative
0 Magnet; 0 Charter; 14 Title I Eligible; 14 School-wide Title I
Students: 18,832 (51.0% male; 49.0% female)
Individual Education Program: 1,882 (10.0%);
English Language Learner: 2,697 (14.3%); Migrant: 958 (5.1%)
Eligible for Free Lunch Program: 9,210 (48.9%)
Eligible for Reduced-Price Lunch Program: 1,682 (8.9%)
Teachers: 1,166.5 (16.1 to 1)
Librarians/Media Specialists: 22.0 (856.0 to 1)
Guidance Counselors: 39.0 (482.9 to 1)
Current Spending: ($ per student per year):
Total: $6,838; Instruction: $4,016; Support Services: $2,429
Enrollment, Drop-out Rates and Diploma Recipients by Race/Ethnicity

Category	Total	White	Black	Asian	AIAN	Hisp.
Enrollment (%)	100.0	37.0	17.4	1.1	0.2	44.3
Drop-out Rate (%)	5.3	3.7	5.9	2.0	0.0	7.1
H.S. Diplomas (#)	899	476	151	12	1	259

Gulf Shores Academy

11300 S Post Oak #1 • Houston, TX 77035
(713) 723-3494
Grade Span: 07-12; **Agency Type:** 7
Schools: 5
0 Primary; 0 Middle; 5 High; 0 Other Level
0 Regular; 0 Special Education; 0 Vocational; 5 Alternative
0 Magnet; 5 Charter; 5 Title I Eligible; 5 School-wide Title I
Students: 2,031 (58.1% male; 41.9% female)
Individual Education Program: 73 (3.6%);
English Language Learner: 28 (1.4%); Migrant: 0 (0.0%)
Eligible for Free Lunch Program: 557 (27.4%)
Eligible for Reduced-Price Lunch Program: 141 (6.9%)
Teachers: 56.4 (36.0 to 1)
Librarians/Media Specialists: 2.0 (1,015.5 to 1)
Guidance Counselors: 4.0 (507.8 to 1)
Current Spending: ($ per student per year):
Total: $5,063; Instruction: $2,355; Support Services: $2,325
Enrollment, Drop-out Rates and Diploma Recipients by Race/Ethnicity

Category	Total	White	Black	Asian	AIAN	Hisp.
Enrollment (%)	100.0	2.7	73.2	0.9	0.0	23.2
Drop-out Rate (%)	8.0	12.5	8.3	n/a	n/a	6.4
H.S. Diplomas (#)	194	7	147	2	0	38

Houston ISD

3830 Richmond Ave • Houston, TX 77027-5838
(713) 892-6000 • http://www.houstonisd.org/
Grade Span: PK-12; **Agency Type:** 1
Schools: 308
208 Primary; 48 Middle; 36 High; 12 Other Level
283 Regular; 2 Special Education; 1 Vocational; 18 Alternative
0 Magnet; 0 Charter; 211 Title I Eligible; 211 School-wide Title I
Students: 212,099 (50.9% male; 49.1% female)
Individual Education Program: 20,931 (9.9%);
English Language Learner: 60,466 (28.5%); Migrant: 1,760 (0.8%)
Eligible for Free Lunch Program: 135,739 (64.0%)
Eligible for Reduced-Price Lunch Program: 18,033 (8.5%)
Teachers: 12,385.7 (17.1 to 1)
Librarians/Media Specialists: 258.0 (822.1 to 1)
Guidance Counselors: 280.7 (755.6 to 1)
Current Spending: ($ per student per year):
Total: $6,724; Instruction: $3,902; Support Services: $2,504
Enrollment, Drop-out Rates and Diploma Recipients by Race/Ethnicity

Category	Total	White	Black	Asian	AIAN	Hisp.
Enrollment (%)	100.0	9.3	30.5	3.0	0.1	57.1
Drop-out Rate (%)	8.0	3.4	7.9	3.2	15.8	9.6
H.S. Diplomas (#)	7,945	1,255	2,754	380	5	3,551

Huffman ISD

24302 F M 2100 • Huffman, TX 77336-2390
Mailing Address: PO Box 2390 • Huffman, TX 77336-2390
(281) 324-1871
Grade Span: PK-12; **Agency Type:** 1
Schools: 5
1 Primary; 2 Middle; 1 High; 1 Other Level
4 Regular; 0 Special Education; 0 Vocational; 1 Alternative
0 Magnet; 0 Charter; 2 Title I Eligible; 1 School-wide Title I
Students: 2,758 (53.7% male; 46.3% female)
Individual Education Program: 311 (11.3%);
English Language Learner: 42 (1.5%); Migrant: 0 (0.0%)
Eligible for Free Lunch Program: 491 (17.8%)
Eligible for Reduced-Price Lunch Program: 148 (5.4%)
Teachers: 167.0 (16.5 to 1)
Librarians/Media Specialists: 4.0 (689.5 to 1)
Guidance Counselors: 6.0 (459.7 to 1)
Current Spending: ($ per student per year):
Total: $6,385; Instruction: $3,555; Support Services: $2,556
Enrollment, Drop-out Rates and Diploma Recipients by Race/Ethnicity

Category	Total	White	Black	Asian	AIAN	Hisp.
Enrollment (%)	100.0	90.2	0.9	0.6	0.3	8.0
Drop-out Rate (%)	3.4	3.3	0.0	0.0	0.0	5.0
H.S. Diplomas (#)	182	170	0	1	1	10

Humble ISD

20200 Eastway Village Dr • Humble, TX 77347-2000
Mailing Address: PO Box 2000 • Humble, TX 77347-2000
(281) 641-1000 • http://www.humble.k12.tx.us/
Grade Span: PK-12; **Agency Type:** 1
Schools: 30
20 Primary; 6 Middle; 3 High; 0 Other Level
28 Regular; 0 Special Education; 0 Vocational; 1 Alternative
0 Magnet; 0 Charter; 4 Title I Eligible; 4 School-wide Title I
Students: 26,025 (51.3% male; 48.7% female)
Individual Education Program: 2,616 (10.1%);
English Language Learner: 1,451 (5.6%); Migrant: 3 (<0.1%)
Eligible for Free Lunch Program: 3,669 (14.1%)
Eligible for Reduced-Price Lunch Program: 1,225 (4.7%)
Teachers: 1,705.4 (15.3 to 1)
Librarians/Media Specialists: 28.5 (913.2 to 1)
Guidance Counselors: 59.8 (435.2 to 1)
Current Spending: ($ per student per year):
Total: $6,155; Instruction: $3,893; Support Services: $2,034

Enrollment, Drop-out Rates and Diploma Recipients by Race/Ethnicity

Category	Total	White	Black	Asian	AIAN	Hisp.
Enrollment (%)	100.0	68.5	11.2	3.4	0.3	16.7
Drop-out Rate (%)	2.0	1.5	3.0	1.5	6.3	4.5
H.S. Diplomas (#)	1,653	1,253	149	63	3	185

Katy ISD

6301 S Stadium Ln • Katy, TX 77494-1057
Mailing Address: PO Box 159 • Katy, TX 77492-0159
(281) 396-6000 • http://www.katy.isd.tenet.edu/
Grade Span: PK-12; **Agency Type:** 1
Schools: 39
22 Primary; 7 Middle; 5 High; 5 Other Level
35 Regular; 1 Special Education; 0 Vocational; 3 Alternative
0 Magnet; 0 Charter; 15 Title I Eligible; 2 School-wide Title I
Students: 39,864 (51.2% male; 48.8% female)
Individual Education Program: 4,020 (10.1%);
English Language Learner: 3,192 (8.0%); Migrant: 0 (0.0%)
Eligible for Free Lunch Program: 4,549 (11.4%)
Eligible for Reduced-Price Lunch Program: 1,360 (3.4%)
Teachers: 2,697.2 (14.8 to 1)
Librarians/Media Specialists: 38.0 (1,049.1 to 1)
Guidance Counselors: 74.6 (534.4 to 1)
Current Spending: ($ per student per year):
Total: $6,121; Instruction: $3,859; Support Services: $2,022

Enrollment, Drop-out Rates and Diploma Recipients by Race/Ethnicity

Category	Total	White	Black	Asian	AIAN	Hisp.
Enrollment (%)	100.0	66.9	6.2	6.7	0.2	20.0
Drop-out Rate (%)	1.2	0.8	0.2	0.3	0.0	3.5
H.S. Diplomas (#)	2,112	1,602	111	139	4	256

Klein ISD

7200 Spring-Cypress Rd • Klein, TX 77379-3299
(832) 249-4000
Grade Span: PK-12; **Agency Type:** 1
Schools: 34
20 Primary; 7 Middle; 3 High; 4 Other Level
31 Regular; 0 Special Education; 0 Vocational; 3 Alternative
0 Magnet; 0 Charter; 5 Title I Eligible; 5 School-wide Title I
Students: 35,355 (51.9% male; 48.1% female)
Individual Education Program: 4,304 (12.2%);
English Language Learner: 3,183 (9.0%); Migrant: 4 (<0.1%)
Eligible for Free Lunch Program: 6,286 (17.8%)
Eligible for Reduced-Price Lunch Program: 1,545 (4.4%)
Teachers: 2,171.2 (16.3 to 1)
Librarians/Media Specialists: 41.2 (858.1 to 1)
Guidance Counselors: 76.5 (462.2 to 1)
Current Spending: ($ per student per year):
Total: $6,258; Instruction: $3,887; Support Services: $2,078

Enrollment, Drop-out Rates and Diploma Recipients by Race/Ethnicity

Category	Total	White	Black	Asian	AIAN	Hisp.
Enrollment (%)	100.0	56.2	13.4	7.7	0.3	22.3
Drop-out Rate (%)	2.7	2.4	2.6	1.3	6.3	4.9
H.S. Diplomas (#)	2,112	1,374	259	190	10	279

La Porte ISD

1002 San Jacinto St • La Porte, TX 77571-6496
Mailing Address: 301 E Fairmont Pkwy • La Porte, TX 77571-6496
(281) 604-7015 • http://www.laporte.isd.esc4.net/
Grade Span: PK-12; **Agency Type:** 1
Schools: 13
6 Primary; 3 Middle; 1 High; 2 Other Level
10 Regular; 0 Special Education; 0 Vocational; 2 Alternative
0 Magnet; 0 Charter; 3 Title I Eligible; 3 School-wide Title I
Students: 7,761 (52.5% male; 47.5% female)
Individual Education Program: 761 (9.8%);
English Language Learner: 317 (4.1%); Migrant: 1 (<0.1%)
Eligible for Free Lunch Program: 1,690 (21.8%)
Eligible for Reduced-Price Lunch Program: 591 (7.6%)
Teachers: 477.8 (16.2 to 1)
Librarians/Media Specialists: 9.0 (862.3 to 1)
Guidance Counselors: 13.0 (597.0 to 1)
Current Spending: ($ per student per year):
Total: $6,616; Instruction: $3,991; Support Services: $2,334

Enrollment, Drop-out Rates and Diploma Recipients by Race/Ethnicity

Category	Total	White	Black	Asian	AIAN	Hisp.
Enrollment (%)	100.0	63.3	8.7	1.1	0.3	26.6
Drop-out Rate (%)	3.5	3.0	3.2	4.5	33.3	4.8
H.S. Diplomas (#)	472	324	41	6	2	99

North Forest ISD

7201 Langley • Houston, TX 77016
Mailing Address: PO Box 23278 • Houston, TX 77228-3278
(713) 633-1600
Grade Span: PK-12; **Agency Type:** 1
Schools: 18
8 Primary; 4 Middle; 3 High; 3 Other Level
14 Regular; 0 Special Education; 0 Vocational; 4 Alternative
0 Magnet; 0 Charter; 14 Title I Eligible; 12 School-wide Title I
Students: 11,182 (51.2% male; 48.8% female)
Individual Education Program: 781 (7.0%);
English Language Learner: 1,253 (11.2%); Migrant: 0 (0.0%)
Eligible for Free Lunch Program: 5,910 (52.9%)
Eligible for Reduced-Price Lunch Program: 403 (3.6%)
Teachers: 707.7 (15.8 to 1)
Librarians/Media Specialists: 13.5 (828.3 to 1)
Guidance Counselors: 33.0 (338.8 to 1)
Current Spending: ($ per student per year):
Total: $6,899; Instruction: $3,350; Support Services: $3,132

Enrollment, Drop-out Rates and Diploma Recipients by Race/Ethnicity

Category	Total	White	Black	Asian	AIAN	Hisp.
Enrollment (%)	100.0	0.6	76.8	0.0	0.0	22.6
Drop-out Rate (%)	6.3	23.1	5.4	50.0	n/a	11.2
H.S. Diplomas (#)	505	1	455	1	0	48

Pasadena ISD

1515 Cherrybrook • Pasadena, TX 77502-4099
(713) 920-6800 • http://www.pasadenaisd.org/
Grade Span: PK-12; **Agency Type:** 1
Schools: 56
33 Primary; 13 Middle; 7 High; 2 Other Level
48 Regular; 0 Special Education; 0 Vocational; 7 Alternative
0 Magnet; 0 Charter; 38 Title I Eligible; 37 School-wide Title I
Students: 44,836 (51.3% male; 48.7% female)
Individual Education Program: 3,281 (7.3%);
English Language Learner: 11,072 (24.7%); Migrant: 303 (0.7%)
Eligible for Free Lunch Program: 22,892 (51.1%)
Eligible for Reduced-Price Lunch Program: 4,965 (11.1%)
Teachers: 2,758.4 (16.3 to 1)
Librarians/Media Specialists: 42.0 (1,067.5 to 1)
Guidance Counselors: 82.1 (546.1 to 1)
Current Spending: ($ per student per year):
Total: $5,811; Instruction: $3,579; Support Services: $1,902

Enrollment, Drop-out Rates and Diploma Recipients by Race/Ethnicity

Category	Total	White	Black	Asian	AIAN	Hisp.
Enrollment (%)	100.0	21.6	5.9	3.3	0.2	69.0
Drop-out Rate (%)	6.4	4.7	5.6	3.2	3.4	7.6
H.S. Diplomas (#)	2,028	693	103	110	8	1,114

Sheldon ISD

8550 C E King Pkwy • Houston, TX 77044-2002
Mailing Address: 11411 C E King Pkwy • Houston, TX 77044-2002
(281) 727-2000
Grade Span: PK-12; **Agency Type:** 1
Schools: 8
4 Primary; 2 Middle; 2 High; 0 Other Level
7 Regular; 0 Special Education; 0 Vocational; 1 Alternative
0 Magnet; 0 Charter; 6 Title I Eligible; 6 School-wide Title I
Students: 4,183 (50.7% male; 49.3% female)
Individual Education Program: 480 (11.5%);
English Language Learner: 600 (14.3%); Migrant: 0 (0.0%)
Eligible for Free Lunch Program: 2,225 (53.2%)
Eligible for Reduced-Price Lunch Program: 423 (10.1%)
Teachers: 282.4 (14.8 to 1)
Librarians/Media Specialists: 7.0 (597.6 to 1)
Guidance Counselors: 10.0 (418.3 to 1)
Current Spending: ($ per student per year):
Total: $7,547; Instruction: $4,163; Support Services: $3,060

Enrollment, Drop-out Rates and Diploma Recipients by Race/Ethnicity

Category	Total	White	Black	Asian	AIAN	Hisp.
Enrollment (%)	100.0	34.0	22.4	0.6	0.2	42.7
Drop-out Rate (%)	4.6	4.1	3.8	0.0	0.0	6.5
H.S. Diplomas (#)	199	82	52	2	0	63

Spring Branch ISD

955 Campbell Rd • Houston, TX 77024-2803
(713) 464-1511
Grade Span: PK-12; **Agency Type:** 1
Schools: 50
33 Primary; 8 Middle; 4 High; 4 Other Level
45 Regular; 1 Special Education; 0 Vocational; 3 Alternative
0 Magnet; 0 Charter; 30 Title I Eligible; 30 School-wide Title I
Students: 32,993 (51.3% male; 48.7% female)
Individual Education Program: 3,622 (11.0%);
English Language Learner: 9,846 (29.8%); Migrant: 17 (0.1%)

Eligible for Free Lunch Program: 15,206 (46.1%)
Eligible for Reduced-Price Lunch Program: 2,084 (6.3%)
Teachers: 2,270.4 (14.5 to 1)
Librarians/Media Specialists: 32.3 (1,021.5 to 1)
Guidance Counselors: 70.6 (467.3 to 1)
Current Spending: ($ per student per year):
Total: $6,881; Instruction: $4,229; Support Services: $2,376
Enrollment, Drop-out Rates and Diploma Recipients by Race/Ethnicity

Category	Total	White	Black	Asian	AIAN	Hisp.
Enrollment (%)	100.0	35.3	6.5	6.6	0.1	51.6
Drop-out Rate (%)	3.3	1.8	3.9	1.6	0.0	5.3
H.S. Diplomas (#)	1,751	866	95	175	4	611

Spring ISD
16717 Ella Blvd • Houston, TX 77090-4299
(281) 586-1100
Grade Span: PK-12; **Agency Type:** 1
Schools: 26
15 Primary; 4 Middle; 2 High; 5 Other Level
22 Regular; 0 Special Education; 0 Vocational; 4 Alternative
0 Magnet; 0 Charter; 10 Title I Eligible; 10 School-wide Title I
Students: 25,492 (51.0% male; 49.0% female)
Individual Education Program: 2,631 (10.3%);
English Language Learner: 3,164 (12.4%); Migrant: 0 (0.0%)
Eligible for Free Lunch Program: 8,776 (34.4%)
Eligible for Reduced-Price Lunch Program: 2,375 (9.3%)
Teachers: 1,702.1 (15.0 to 1)
Librarians/Media Specialists: 25.5 (999.7 to 1)
Guidance Counselors: 62.7 (406.6 to 1)
Current Spending: ($ per student per year):
Total: $6,143; Instruction: $3,818; Support Services: $2,029
Enrollment, Drop-out Rates and Diploma Recipients by Race/Ethnicity

Category	Total	White	Black	Asian	AIAN	Hisp.
Enrollment (%)	100.0	34.7	29.7	6.0	0.2	29.5
Drop-out Rate (%)	3.2	3.0	3.2	0.9	0.0	4.4
H.S. Diplomas (#)	1,334	622	354	95	3	260

Tomball ISD
221 W Main St • Tomball, TX 77375-5529
(281) 357-3100
Grade Span: PK-12; **Agency Type:** 1
Schools: 10
4 Primary; 3 Middle; 1 High; 2 Other Level
8 Regular; 0 Special Education; 0 Vocational; 2 Alternative
0 Magnet; 0 Charter; 4 Title I Eligible; 4 School-wide Title I
Students: 8,106 (51.5% male; 48.5% female)
Individual Education Program: 753 (9.3%);
English Language Learner: 518 (6.4%); Migrant: 8 (0.1%)
Eligible for Free Lunch Program: 1,135 (14.0%)
Eligible for Reduced-Price Lunch Program: 219 (2.7%)
Teachers: 527.0 (15.4 to 1)
Librarians/Media Specialists: 7.1 (1,141.7 to 1)
Guidance Counselors: 13.7 (591.7 to 1)
Current Spending: ($ per student per year):
Total: $6,192; Instruction: $3,660; Support Services: $2,334
Enrollment, Drop-out Rates and Diploma Recipients by Race/Ethnicity

Category	Total	White	Black	Asian	AIAN	Hisp.
Enrollment (%)	100.0	77.9	5.3	2.1	0.3	14.4
Drop-out Rate (%)	1.7	1.5	3.1	4.2	0.0	3.2
H.S. Diplomas (#)	435	373	20	9	3	30

Hallsville ISD
Green St • Hallsville, TX 75650-0810
Mailing Address: PO Box 810 • Hallsville, TX 75650-0810
(903) 668-5990
Grade Span: PK-12; **Agency Type:** 1
Schools: 7
3 Primary; 2 Middle; 1 High; 1 Other Level
6 Regular; 0 Special Education; 0 Vocational; 1 Alternative
0 Magnet; 0 Charter; 4 Title I Eligible; 2 School-wide Title I
Students: 3,762 (52.6% male; 47.4% female)
Individual Education Program: 396 (10.5%);
English Language Learner: 60 (1.6%); Migrant: 0 (0.0%)
Eligible for Free Lunch Program: 884 (23.5%)
Eligible for Reduced-Price Lunch Program: 284 (7.5%)
Teachers: 262.0 (14.4 to 1)
Librarians/Media Specialists: 2.3 (1,635.7 to 1)
Guidance Counselors: 9.5 (396.0 to 1)
Current Spending: ($ per student per year):
Total: $6,309; Instruction: $3,768; Support Services: $2,227
Enrollment, Drop-out Rates and Diploma Recipients by Race/Ethnicity

Category	Total	White	Black	Asian	AIAN	Hisp.
Enrollment (%)	100.0	88.0	7.0	0.4	0.2	4.3
Drop-out Rate (%)	1.4	1.6	0.0	0.0	0.0	0.0
H.S. Diplomas (#)	237	210	21	4	0	2

Marshall ISD
1305 E Pinecrest Dr • Marshall, TX 75670-7349
Mailing Address: PO Box 879 • Marshall, TX 75671-0879
(903) 927-8701
Grade Span: PK-12; **Agency Type:** 1
Schools: 13
7 Primary; 3 Middle; 1 High; 2 Other Level
11 Regular; 0 Special Education; 0 Vocational; 2 Alternative
0 Magnet; 0 Charter; 13 Title I Eligible; 13 School-wide Title I
Students: 6,011 (51.5% male; 48.5% female)
Individual Education Program: 885 (14.7%);
English Language Learner: 498 (8.3%); Migrant: 0 (0.0%)
Eligible for Free Lunch Program: 3,047 (50.7%)
Eligible for Reduced-Price Lunch Program: 391 (6.5%)
Teachers: 422.0 (14.2 to 1)
Librarians/Media Specialists: 4.6 (1,306.7 to 1)
Guidance Counselors: 12.9 (466.0 to 1)
Current Spending: ($ per student per year):
Total: $5,575; Instruction: $3,573; Support Services: $1,686
Enrollment, Drop-out Rates and Diploma Recipients by Race/Ethnicity

Category	Total	White	Black	Asian	AIAN	Hisp.
Enrollment (%)	100.0	42.9	42.6	0.4	0.2	14.0
Drop-out Rate (%)	5.0	4.2	6.1	0.0	0.0	3.5
H.S. Diplomas (#)	374	188	162	1	1	22

Hays County

Dripping Springs ISD
510 Mercer • Dripping Springs, TX 78620-3867
Mailing Address: PO Box 479 • Dripping Springs, TX 78620-0479
(512) 858-4905 • http://www.dripping-springs.k12.tx.us/
Grade Span: PK-12; **Agency Type:** 1
Schools: 4
1 Primary; 2 Middle; 1 High; 0 Other Level
4 Regular; 0 Special Education; 0 Vocational; 0 Alternative
0 Magnet; 0 Charter; 3 Title I Eligible; 3 School-wide Title I
Students: 3,307 (51.6% male; 48.4% female)
Individual Education Program: 427 (12.9%);
English Language Learner: 72 (2.2%); Migrant: 16 (0.5%)
Eligible for Free Lunch Program: 196 (5.9%)
Eligible for Reduced-Price Lunch Program: 67 (2.0%)
Teachers: 214.7 (15.4 to 1)
Librarians/Media Specialists: 4.0 (826.8 to 1)
Guidance Counselors: 10.8 (306.2 to 1)
Current Spending: ($ per student per year):
Total: $6,431; Instruction: $3,884; Support Services: $2,214
Enrollment, Drop-out Rates and Diploma Recipients by Race/Ethnicity

Category	Total	White	Black	Asian	AIAN	Hisp.
Enrollment (%)	100.0	86.8	0.8	0.6	0.5	11.4
Drop-out Rate (%)	1.3	1.4	0.0	0.0	0.0	0.0
H.S. Diplomas (#)	230	207	1	2	2	18

Hays Cons ISD
21003 Ih 35 • Kyle, TX 78640-9530
(512) 268-2141
Grade Span: PK-12; **Agency Type:** 1
Schools: 15
7 Primary; 2 Middle; 1 High; 4 Other Level
11 Regular; 0 Special Education; 0 Vocational; 3 Alternative
0 Magnet; 0 Charter; 5 Title I Eligible; 5 School-wide Title I
Students: 8,663 (52.5% male; 47.5% female)
Individual Education Program: 1,078 (12.4%);
English Language Learner: 728 (8.4%); Migrant: 6 (0.1%)
Eligible for Free Lunch Program: 2,586 (29.9%)
Eligible for Reduced-Price Lunch Program: 845 (9.8%)
Teachers: 565.3 (15.3 to 1)
Librarians/Media Specialists: 12.0 (721.9 to 1)
Guidance Counselors: 22.0 (393.8 to 1)
Current Spending: ($ per student per year):
Total: $6,168; Instruction: $3,461; Support Services: $2,426
Enrollment, Drop-out Rates and Diploma Recipients by Race/Ethnicity

Category	Total	White	Black	Asian	AIAN	Hisp.
Enrollment (%)	100.0	43.8	4.2	0.5	0.2	51.3
Drop-out Rate (%)	2.7	1.4	1.5	0.0	0.0	4.4
H.S. Diplomas (#)	485	258	20	1	2	204

San Marcos CISD
501 S Lbj Dr • San Marcos, TX 78666-6821
Mailing Address: PO Box 1087 • San Marcos, TX 78667-1087
(512) 393-6700
Grade Span: PK-12; **Agency Type:** 1
Schools: 12
5 Primary; 3 Middle; 2 High; 1 Other Level
9 Regular; 0 Special Education; 0 Vocational; 2 Alternative
0 Magnet; 0 Charter; 6 Title I Eligible; 6 School-wide Title I

Students: 7,064 (51.2% male; 48.8% female)
Individual Education Program: 871 (12.3%);
English Language Learner: 426 (6.0%); Migrant: 46 (0.7%)
Eligible for Free Lunch Program: 3,364 (47.6%)
Eligible for Reduced-Price Lunch Program: 789 (11.2%)
Teachers: 467.4 (15.1 to 1)
Librarians/Media Specialists: 9.9 (713.5 to 1)
Guidance Counselors: 18.1 (390.3 to 1)
Current Spending: ($ per student per year):
Total: $6,767; Instruction: $4,184; Support Services: $2,274
Enrollment, Drop-out Rates and Diploma Recipients by Race/Ethnicity

Category	Total	White	Black	Asian	AIAN	Hisp.
Enrollment (%)	100.0	27.7	4.8	0.8	0.1	66.7
Drop-out Rate (%)	4.4	2.6	2.7	0.0	0.0	5.6
H.S. Diplomas (#)	407	150	22	6	0	229

Wimberley ISD
14401 Ranch Rd 12 • Wimberley, TX 78676-6216
(512) 847-2414
Grade Span: PK-12; **Agency Type:** 1
Schools: 4
2 Primary; 1 Middle; 1 High; 0 Other Level
4 Regular; 0 Special Education; 0 Vocational; 0 Alternative
0 Magnet; 0 Charter; 3 Title I Eligible; 0 School-wide Title I
Students: 1,812 (52.6% male; 47.4% female)
Individual Education Program: 232 (12.8%);
English Language Learner: 60 (3.3%); Migrant: 0 (0.0%)
Eligible for Free Lunch Program: 247 (13.6%)
Eligible for Reduced-Price Lunch Program: 65 (3.6%)
Teachers: 136.3 (13.3 to 1)
Librarians/Media Specialists: 2.0 (906.0 to 1)
Guidance Counselors: 3.9 (464.6 to 1)
Current Spending: ($ per student per year):
Total: $6,619; Instruction: $3,962; Support Services: $2,372
Enrollment, Drop-out Rates and Diploma Recipients by Race/Ethnicity

Category	Total	White	Black	Asian	AIAN	Hisp.
Enrollment (%)	100.0	87.0	1.1	0.3	0.7	10.8
Drop-out Rate (%)	0.3	0.2	25.0	0.0	0.0	0.0
H.S. Diplomas (#)	147	136	1	1	1	8

Henderson County

Athens ISD
104 Hawn St • Athens, TX 75751-2423
(903) 677-6900
Grade Span: PK-12; **Agency Type:** 1
Schools: 8
3 Primary; 3 Middle; 2 High; 0 Other Level
7 Regular; 0 Special Education; 0 Vocational; 1 Alternative
0 Magnet; 0 Charter; 6 Title I Eligible; 6 School-wide Title I
Students: 3,450 (51.6% male; 48.4% female)
Individual Education Program: 420 (12.2%);
English Language Learner: 534 (15.5%); Migrant: 2 (0.1%)
Eligible for Free Lunch Program: 1,472 (42.7%)
Eligible for Reduced-Price Lunch Program: 210 (6.1%)
Teachers: 245.3 (14.1 to 1)
Librarians/Media Specialists: 4.0 (862.5 to 1)
Guidance Counselors: 7.0 (492.9 to 1)
Current Spending: ($ per student per year):
Total: $6,197; Instruction: $3,973; Support Services: $1,920
Enrollment, Drop-out Rates and Diploma Recipients by Race/Ethnicity

Category	Total	White	Black	Asian	AIAN	Hisp.
Enrollment (%)	100.0	55.9	16.6	0.4	0.1	27.0
Drop-out Rate (%)	5.7	5.2	9.8	0.0	0.0	4.5
H.S. Diplomas (#)	192	129	26	2	1	34

Brownsboro ISD
Hwy 31 W • Brownsboro, TX 75756-0465
Mailing Address: PO Box 465 • Brownsboro, TX 75756-0465
(903) 852-3701 • http://www.brownsboro.k12.tx.us/
Grade Span: PK-12; **Agency Type:** 1
Schools: 7
3 Primary; 2 Middle; 2 High; 0 Other Level
6 Regular; 0 Special Education; 0 Vocational; 1 Alternative
0 Magnet; 0 Charter; 4 Title I Eligible; 4 School-wide Title I
Students: 2,620 (52.9% male; 47.1% female)
Individual Education Program: 319 (12.2%);
English Language Learner: 83 (3.2%); Migrant: 3 (0.1%)
Eligible for Free Lunch Program: 890 (34.0%)
Eligible for Reduced-Price Lunch Program: 232 (8.9%)
Teachers: 174.2 (15.0 to 1)
Librarians/Media Specialists: 1.0 (2,620.0 to 1)
Guidance Counselors: 11.0 (238.2 to 1)
Current Spending: ($ per student per year):
Total: $6,079; Instruction: $3,778; Support Services: $2,000
Enrollment, Drop-out Rates and Diploma Recipients by Race/Ethnicity

Category	Total	White	Black	Asian	AIAN	Hisp.
Enrollment (%)	100.0	81.8	8.9	0.4	0.3	8.6
Drop-out Rate (%)	2.6	3.0	0.0	0.0	0.0	2.3
H.S. Diplomas (#)	143	123	17	0	0	3

Eustace ISD
316 S Fm 316 • Eustace, TX 75124-0188
Mailing Address: PO Box 188 • Eustace, TX 75124-0188
(903) 425-5101
Grade Span: PK-12; **Agency Type:** 1
Schools: 4
2 Primary; 1 Middle; 1 High; 0 Other Level
4 Regular; 0 Special Education; 0 Vocational; 0 Alternative
0 Magnet; 0 Charter; 4 Title I Eligible; 4 School-wide Title I
Students: 1,576 (50.9% male; 49.1% female)
Individual Education Program: 332 (21.1%);
English Language Learner: 14 (0.9%); Migrant: 0 (0.0%)
Eligible for Free Lunch Program: 745 (47.3%)
Eligible for Reduced-Price Lunch Program: 135 (8.6%)
Teachers: 109.7 (14.4 to 1)
Librarians/Media Specialists: 2.0 (788.0 to 1)
Guidance Counselors: 4.0 (394.0 to 1)
Current Spending: ($ per student per year):
Total: $5,379; Instruction: $3,307; Support Services: $1,711
Enrollment, Drop-out Rates and Diploma Recipients by Race/Ethnicity

Category	Total	White	Black	Asian	AIAN	Hisp.
Enrollment (%)	100.0	91.2	1.6	0.1	0.6	6.3
Drop-out Rate (%)	7.1	7.0	16.7	0.0	0.0	7.7
H.S. Diplomas (#)	75	70	1	0	1	3

Hidalgo County

Donna ISD
116 N 10th St • Donna, TX 78537-2799
(956) 464-1600
Grade Span: PK-12; **Agency Type:** 1
Schools: 17
11 Primary; 2 Middle; 1 High; 2 Other Level
15 Regular; 0 Special Education; 0 Vocational; 1 Alternative
0 Magnet; 0 Charter; 15 Title I Eligible; 15 School-wide Title I
Students: 10,945 (51.2% male; 48.8% female)
Individual Education Program: 1,039 (9.5%);
English Language Learner: 5,608 (51.2%); Migrant: 3,283 (30.0%)
Eligible for Free Lunch Program: 6,603 (60.3%)
Eligible for Reduced-Price Lunch Program: 586 (5.4%)
Teachers: 744.2 (14.7 to 1)
Librarians/Media Specialists: 15.0 (729.7 to 1)
Guidance Counselors: 35.0 (312.7 to 1)
Current Spending: ($ per student per year):
Total: $6,842; Instruction: $3,887; Support Services: $2,530
Enrollment, Drop-out Rates and Diploma Recipients by Race/Ethnicity

Category	Total	White	Black	Asian	AIAN	Hisp.
Enrollment (%)	100.0	1.1	0.1	0.1	0.0	98.7
Drop-out Rate (%)	5.7	4.2	20.0	0.0	n/a	5.7
H.S. Diplomas (#)	429	5	0	1	0	423

Edcouch-Elsa ISD
920 Santa Rosa • Edcouch, TX 78538-0127
Mailing Address: PO Box 127 • Edcouch, TX 78538-0127
(956) 262-6000
Grade Span: PK-12; **Agency Type:** 1
Schools: 8
5 Primary; 1 Middle; 1 High; 1 Other Level
7 Regular; 0 Special Education; 0 Vocational; 1 Alternative
0 Magnet; 0 Charter; 7 Title I Eligible; 7 School-wide Title I
Students: 5,194 (51.0% male; 49.0% female)
Individual Education Program: 474 (9.1%);
English Language Learner: 2,097 (40.4%); Migrant: 1,616 (31.1%)
Eligible for Free Lunch Program: 1,046 (20.1%)
Eligible for Reduced-Price Lunch Program: 78 (1.5%)
Teachers: 317.0 (16.4 to 1)
Librarians/Media Specialists: 5.0 (1,038.8 to 1)
Guidance Counselors: 16.0 (324.6 to 1)
Current Spending: ($ per student per year):
Total: $7,109; Instruction: $4,154; Support Services: $2,432
Enrollment, Drop-out Rates and Diploma Recipients by Race/Ethnicity

Category	Total	White	Black	Asian	AIAN	Hisp.
Enrollment (%)	100.0	0.4	0.2	0.0	0.0	99.4
Drop-out Rate (%)	5.3	0.0	n/a	n/a	n/a	5.4
H.S. Diplomas (#)	279	3	0	0	0	276

Edinburg CISD

101 N 8th St • Edinburg, TX 78539-3303
Mailing Address: PO Box 990 • Edinburg, TX 78540-0990
(956) 316-7200
Grade Span: PK-12; **Agency Type:** 1
Schools: 34
24 Primary; 4 Middle; 3 High; 3 Other Level
31 Regular; 0 Special Education; 0 Vocational; 3 Alternative
0 Magnet; 0 Charter; 31 Title I Eligible; 31 School-wide Title I
Students: 24,100 (51.3% male; 48.7% female)
Individual Education Program: 2,093 (8.7%);
English Language Learner: 7,483 (31.0%); Migrant: 4,197 (17.4%)
Eligible for Free Lunch Program: 7,691 (31.9%)
Eligible for Reduced-Price Lunch Program: 745 (3.1%)
Teachers: 1,547.8 (15.6 to 1)
Librarians/Media Specialists: 33.0 (730.3 to 1)
Guidance Counselors: 63.0 (382.5 to 1)
Current Spending: ($ per student per year):
Total: $6,635; Instruction: $4,080; Support Services: $2,109
Enrollment, Drop-out Rates and Diploma Recipients by Race/Ethnicity

Category	Total	White	Black	Asian	AIAN	Hisp.
Enrollment (%)	100.0	2.6	0.2	0.3	0.0	96.8
Drop-out Rate (%)	5.8	1.6	0.0	0.0	100.0	6.0
H.S. Diplomas (#)	1,038	64	1	5	1	967

Hidalgo ISD

324 E Flora St • Hidalgo, TX 78557-3004
Mailing Address: PO Drawer D • Hidalgo, TX 78557-3004
(956) 843-3100
Grade Span: PK-12; **Agency Type:** 1
Schools: 6
3 Primary; 1 Middle; 2 High; 0 Other Level
5 Regular; 0 Special Education; 0 Vocational; 1 Alternative
0 Magnet; 0 Charter; 6 Title I Eligible; 6 School-wide Title I
Students: 3,036 (51.3% male; 48.7% female)
Individual Education Program: 218 (7.2%);
English Language Learner: 1,596 (52.6%); Migrant: 486 (16.0%)
Eligible for Free Lunch Program: 528 (17.4%)
Eligible for Reduced-Price Lunch Program: 14 (0.5%)
Teachers: 222.9 (13.6 to 1)
Librarians/Media Specialists: 5.0 (607.2 to 1)
Guidance Counselors: 10.0 (303.6 to 1)
Current Spending: ($ per student per year):
Total: $7,971; Instruction: $4,541; Support Services: $2,849
Enrollment, Drop-out Rates and Diploma Recipients by Race/Ethnicity

Category	Total	White	Black	Asian	AIAN	Hisp.
Enrollment (%)	100.0	0.2	0.0	0.2	0.0	99.5
Drop-out Rate (%)	4.2	0.0	0.0	n/a	n/a	4.2
H.S. Diplomas (#)	150	2	0	0	0	148

La Joya ISD

201 E Expy 83 • La Joya, TX 78560-2009
(956) 580-5441
Grade Span: PK-12; **Agency Type:** 1
Schools: 24
14 Primary; 4 Middle; 1 High; 4 Other Level
22 Regular; 0 Special Education; 0 Vocational; 1 Alternative
0 Magnet; 0 Charter; 23 Title I Eligible; 23 School-wide Title I
Students: 20,368 (51.6% male; 48.4% female)
Individual Education Program: 2,070 (10.2%);
English Language Learner: 10,052 (49.4%); Migrant: 5,819 (28.6%)
Eligible for Free Lunch Program: 12,378 (60.8%)
Eligible for Reduced-Price Lunch Program: 716 (3.5%)
Teachers: 1,290.2 (15.8 to 1)
Librarians/Media Specialists: 21.9 (930.0 to 1)
Guidance Counselors: 68.5 (297.3 to 1)
Current Spending: ($ per student per year):
Total: $6,338; Instruction: $3,782; Support Services: $2,151
Enrollment, Drop-out Rates and Diploma Recipients by Race/Ethnicity

Category	Total	White	Black	Asian	AIAN	Hisp.
Enrollment (%)	100.0	0.3	0.0	0.0	0.0	99.6
Drop-out Rate (%)	8.6	18.8	0.0	0.0	0.0	8.5
H.S. Diplomas (#)	765	6	0	1	0	758

Mcallen ISD

2000 N 23rd St • Mcallen, TX 78501-6126
(956) 618-6000
Grade Span: PK-12; **Agency Type:** 1
Schools: 33
20 Primary; 6 Middle; 4 High; 2 Other Level
29 Regular; 0 Special Education; 0 Vocational; 3 Alternative
0 Magnet; 0 Charter; 28 Title I Eligible; 26 School-wide Title I
Students: 23,376 (51.0% male; 49.0% female)
Individual Education Program: 2,203 (9.4%);
English Language Learner: 8,227 (35.2%); Migrant: 2,259 (9.7%)
Eligible for Free Lunch Program: 10,963 (46.9%)
Eligible for Reduced-Price Lunch Program: 2,017 (8.6%)
Teachers: 1,531.3 (15.3 to 1)
Librarians/Media Specialists: 29.1 (803.3 to 1)
Guidance Counselors: 93.0 (251.4 to 1)
Current Spending: ($ per student per year):
Total: $7,017; Instruction: $4,254; Support Services: $2,409
Enrollment, Drop-out Rates and Diploma Recipients by Race/Ethnicity

Category	Total	White	Black	Asian	AIAN	Hisp.
Enrollment (%)	100.0	8.6	0.5	1.8	0.0	89.0
Drop-out Rate (%)	5.9	1.6	11.1	1.2	0.0	6.6
H.S. Diplomas (#)	1,270	174	7	20	1	1,068

Mercedes ISD

206 E 6th St • Mercedes, TX 78570-3504
Mailing Address: PO Box 419 • Mercedes, TX 78570-0419
(956) 514-2000
Grade Span: PK-12; **Agency Type:** 1
Schools: 11
4 Primary; 2 Middle; 2 High; 2 Other Level
7 Regular; 0 Special Education; 0 Vocational; 3 Alternative
0 Magnet; 0 Charter; 8 Title I Eligible; 8 School-wide Title I
Students: 5,261 (50.8% male; 49.2% female)
Individual Education Program: 438 (8.3%);
English Language Learner: 1,692 (32.2%); Migrant: 1,096 (20.8%)
Eligible for Free Lunch Program: 1,110 (21.1%)
Eligible for Reduced-Price Lunch Program: 105 (2.0%)
Teachers: 337.7 (15.6 to 1)
Librarians/Media Specialists: 8.0 (657.6 to 1)
Guidance Counselors: 15.0 (350.7 to 1)
Current Spending: ($ per student per year):
Total: $7,628; Instruction: $4,367; Support Services: $2,787
Enrollment, Drop-out Rates and Diploma Recipients by Race/Ethnicity

Category	Total	White	Black	Asian	AIAN	Hisp.
Enrollment (%)	100.0	0.7	0.3	0.0	0.0	98.9
Drop-out Rate (%)	6.4	0.0	0.0	n/a	n/a	6.5
H.S. Diplomas (#)	256	6	1	0	0	249

Mission Cons ISD

1201 Bryce Dr • Mission, TX 78572-4399
(956) 580-5500
Grade Span: PK-12; **Agency Type:** 1
Schools: 17
11 Primary; 2 Middle; 2 High; 2 Other Level
15 Regular; 0 Special Education; 0 Vocational; 2 Alternative
0 Magnet; 0 Charter; 15 Title I Eligible; 15 School-wide Title I
Students: 13,802 (51.1% male; 48.9% female)
Individual Education Program: 864 (6.3%);
English Language Learner: 3,458 (25.1%); Migrant: 2,292 (16.6%)
Eligible for Free Lunch Program: 1,124 (8.1%)
Eligible for Reduced-Price Lunch Program: 94 (0.7%)
Teachers: 903.4 (15.3 to 1)
Librarians/Media Specialists: 17.9 (771.1 to 1)
Guidance Counselors: 42.7 (323.2 to 1)
Current Spending: ($ per student per year):
Total: $6,991; Instruction: $4,363; Support Services: $2,285
Enrollment, Drop-out Rates and Diploma Recipients by Race/Ethnicity

Category	Total	White	Black	Asian	AIAN	Hisp.
Enrollment (%)	100.0	2.4	0.1	0.1	0.0	97.4
Drop-out Rate (%)	7.2	3.7	0.0	0.0	n/a	7.3
H.S. Diplomas (#)	569	27	0	0	0	542

Pharr-San Juan-Alamo ISD

804 E Hwy 83 • Pharr, TX 78577-1225
Mailing Address: PO Box Y • Pharr, TX 78577-1225
(956) 702-5600
Grade Span: PK-12; **Agency Type:** 1
Schools: 38
25 Primary; 5 Middle; 5 High; 1 Other Level
33 Regular; 0 Special Education; 0 Vocational; 3 Alternative
0 Magnet; 0 Charter; 35 Title I Eligible; 35 School-wide Title I
Students: 25,210 (50.9% male; 49.1% female)
Individual Education Program: 2,172 (8.6%);
English Language Learner: 9,432 (37.4%); Migrant: 4,069 (16.1%)
Eligible for Free Lunch Program: 5,213 (20.7%)
Eligible for Reduced-Price Lunch Program: 477 (1.9%)
Teachers: 1,601.6 (15.7 to 1)
Librarians/Media Specialists: 29.4 (857.5 to 1)
Guidance Counselors: 61.9 (407.3 to 1)
Current Spending: ($ per student per year):
Total: $6,620; Instruction: $4,042; Support Services: $2,217

Enrollment, Drop-out Rates and Diploma Recipients by Race/Ethnicity

Category	Total	White	Black	Asian	AIAN	Hisp.
Enrollment (%)	100.0	1.2	0.1	0.1	0.0	98.6
Drop-out Rate (%)	6.7	4.4	0.0	0.0	n/a	6.7
H.S. Diplomas (#)	1,045	12	2	1	0	1,030

Progreso ISD

F M Rd 1015 • Progreso, TX 78579-0610
Mailing Address: PO Box 610 • Progreso, TX 78579-0610
(956) 565-6203
Grade Span: PK-12; **Agency Type:** 1
Schools: 5
2 Primary; 1 Middle; 1 High; 1 Other Level
4 Regular; 0 Special Education; 0 Vocational; 1 Alternative
0 Magnet; 0 Charter; 5 Title I Eligible; 5 School-wide Title I
Students: 2,128 (52.9% male; 47.1% female)
Individual Education Program: 133 (6.3%);
English Language Learner: 1,016 (47.7%); Migrant: 707 (33.2%)
Eligible for Free Lunch Program: 1,217 (57.2%)
Eligible for Reduced-Price Lunch Program: 39 (1.8%)
Teachers: 154.9 (13.7 to 1)
Librarians/Media Specialists: 4.0 (532.0 to 1)
Guidance Counselors: 5.5 (386.9 to 1)
Current Spending: ($ per student per year):
Total: $7,268; Instruction: $4,388; Support Services: $2,433
Enrollment, Drop-out Rates and Diploma Recipients by Race/Ethnicity

Category	Total	White	Black	Asian	AIAN	Hisp.
Enrollment (%)	100.0	0.3	0.0	0.0	0.0	99.7
Drop-out Rate (%)	3.9	0.0	n/a	n/a	n/a	4.0
H.S. Diplomas (#)	91	0	0	0	0	91

Sharyland ISD

1106 N Shary Rd • Mission, TX 78572-4652
(956) 580-5200
Grade Span: PK-12; **Agency Type:** 1
Schools: 8
5 Primary; 1 Middle; 2 High; 0 Other Level
6 Regular; 1 Special Education; 0 Vocational; 1 Alternative
0 Magnet; 0 Charter; 6 Title I Eligible; 6 School-wide Title I
Students: 6,236 (51.7% male; 48.3% female)
Individual Education Program: 513 (8.2%);
English Language Learner: 1,499 (24.0%); Migrant: 148 (2.4%)
Eligible for Free Lunch Program: 2,993 (48.0%)
Eligible for Reduced-Price Lunch Program: 573 (9.2%)
Teachers: 365.8 (17.0 to 1)
Librarians/Media Specialists: 6.0 (1,039.3 to 1)
Guidance Counselors: 18.7 (333.5 to 1)
Current Spending: ($ per student per year):
Total: $5,815; Instruction: $3,617; Support Services: $1,866
Enrollment, Drop-out Rates and Diploma Recipients by Race/Ethnicity

Category	Total	White	Black	Asian	AIAN	Hisp.
Enrollment (%)	100.0	14.6	0.6	1.4	0.1	83.3
Drop-out Rate (%)	1.0	0.3	0.0	0.0	0.0	1.3
H.S. Diplomas (#)	257	64	0	4	0	189

Valley View ISD

61/2 Mi S Jackson Rd • Pharr, TX 78577-9999
Mailing Address: Rt 1 Box 122 • Pharr, TX 78577-9705
(956) 843-8825
Grade Span: PK-12; **Agency Type:** 1
Schools: 5
3 Primary; 1 Middle; 1 High; 0 Other Level
5 Regular; 0 Special Education; 0 Vocational; 0 Alternative
0 Magnet; 0 Charter; 5 Title I Eligible; 5 School-wide Title I
Students: 2,695 (50.6% male; 49.4% female)
Individual Education Program: 259 (9.6%);
English Language Learner: 1,412 (52.4%); Migrant: 352 (13.1%)
Eligible for Free Lunch Program: 374 (13.9%)
Eligible for Reduced-Price Lunch Program: 35 (1.3%)
Teachers: 166.9 (16.1 to 1)
Librarians/Media Specialists: 3.0 (898.3 to 1)
Guidance Counselors: 8.0 (336.9 to 1)
Current Spending: ($ per student per year):
Total: $6,875; Instruction: $4,031; Support Services: $2,319
Enrollment, Drop-out Rates and Diploma Recipients by Race/Ethnicity

Category	Total	White	Black	Asian	AIAN	Hisp.
Enrollment (%)	100.0	0.1	0.0	0.0	0.0	99.9
Drop-out Rate (%)	4.5	n/a	n/a	n/a	n/a	4.5
H.S. Diplomas (#)	91	0	0	0	0	91

Weslaco ISD

319 W 4th St • Weslaco, TX 78596-6047
Mailing Address: PO Box 266 • Weslaco, TX 78599-0266
(956) 969-6500
Grade Span: PK-12; **Agency Type:** 1
Schools: 22
10 Primary; 4 Middle; 2 High; 4 Other Level
16 Regular; 0 Special Education; 1 Vocational; 3 Alternative
0 Magnet; 0 Charter; 16 Title I Eligible; 16 School-wide Title I
Students: 14,623 (51.3% male; 48.7% female)
Individual Education Program: 1,277 (8.7%);
English Language Learner: 4,216 (28.8%); Migrant: 4,786 (32.7%)
Eligible for Free Lunch Program: 6,038 (41.3%)
Eligible for Reduced-Price Lunch Program: 397 (2.7%)
Teachers: 950.7 (15.4 to 1)
Librarians/Media Specialists: 18.3 (799.1 to 1)
Guidance Counselors: 42.3 (345.7 to 1)
Current Spending: ($ per student per year):
Total: $7,060; Instruction: $4,099; Support Services: $2,519
Enrollment, Drop-out Rates and Diploma Recipients by Race/Ethnicity

Category	Total	White	Black	Asian	AIAN	Hisp.
Enrollment (%)	100.0	2.3	0.2	0.3	0.0	97.2
Drop-out Rate (%)	5.3	2.6	25.0	0.0	0.0	5.4
H.S. Diplomas (#)	611	28	0	3	0	580

Hill County

Hillsboro ISD

121 E Franklin St • Hillsboro, TX 76645-2137
Mailing Address: PO Box 459 • Hillsboro, TX 76645-0459
(254) 582-8585
Grade Span: PK-12; **Agency Type:** 1
Schools: 7
2 Primary; 2 Middle; 1 High; 2 Other Level
5 Regular; 0 Special Education; 0 Vocational; 2 Alternative
0 Magnet; 0 Charter; 5 Title I Eligible; 5 School-wide Title I
Students: 1,791 (51.6% male; 48.4% female)
Individual Education Program: 278 (15.5%);
English Language Learner: 247 (13.8%); Migrant: 18 (1.0%)
Eligible for Free Lunch Program: 994 (55.5%)
Eligible for Reduced-Price Lunch Program: 147 (8.2%)
Teachers: 144.2 (12.4 to 1)
Librarians/Media Specialists: 3.0 (597.0 to 1)
Guidance Counselors: 6.0 (298.5 to 1)
Current Spending: ($ per student per year):
Total: $7,754; Instruction: $4,559; Support Services: $2,806
Enrollment, Drop-out Rates and Diploma Recipients by Race/Ethnicity

Category	Total	White	Black	Asian	AIAN	Hisp.
Enrollment (%)	100.0	38.1	20.8	0.8	0.2	40.1
Drop-out Rate (%)	3.8	3.4	1.7	n/a	n/a	6.3
H.S. Diplomas (#)	113	59	23	1	0	30

Whitney ISD

305 S San Jacinto St • Whitney, TX 76692-2391
Mailing Address: PO Box 518 • Whitney, TX 76692-0518
(254) 694-2254
Grade Span: PK-12; **Agency Type:** 1
Schools: 4
2 Primary; 1 Middle; 1 High; 0 Other Level
4 Regular; 0 Special Education; 0 Vocational; 0 Alternative
0 Magnet; 0 Charter; 1 Title I Eligible; 1 School-wide Title I
Students: 1,546 (51.0% male; 49.0% female)
Individual Education Program: 206 (13.3%);
English Language Learner: 40 (2.6%); Migrant: 6 (0.4%)
Eligible for Free Lunch Program: 555 (35.9%)
Eligible for Reduced-Price Lunch Program: 102 (6.6%)
Teachers: 115.5 (13.4 to 1)
Librarians/Media Specialists: 3.0 (515.3 to 1)
Guidance Counselors: 3.5 (441.7 to 1)
Current Spending: ($ per student per year):
Total: $5,694; Instruction: $3,710; Support Services: $1,673
Enrollment, Drop-out Rates and Diploma Recipients by Race/Ethnicity

Category	Total	White	Black	Asian	AIAN	Hisp.
Enrollment (%)	100.0	85.6	3.3	0.2	0.2	10.7
Drop-out Rate (%)	3.7	2.8	11.1	n/a	0.0	9.3
H.S. Diplomas (#)	100	83	5	0	3	9

Hockley County

Levelland ISD

704 11th St • Levelland, TX 79336-5424
(806) 894-9628
Grade Span: PK-12; **Agency Type:** 1
Schools: 7
4 Primary; 0 Middle; 1 High; 2 Other Level

7 Regular; 0 Special Education; 0 Vocational; 0 Alternative
0 Magnet; 0 Charter; 7 Title I Eligible; 7 School-wide Title I
Students: 3,061 (52.0% male; 48.0% female)
Individual Education Program: 450 (14.7%);
English Language Learner: 115 (3.8%); Migrant: 455 (14.9%)
Eligible for Free Lunch Program: 1,537 (50.2%)
Eligible for Reduced-Price Lunch Program: 251 (8.2%)
Teachers: 246.0 (12.4 to 1)
Librarians/Media Specialists: 7.0 (437.3 to 1)
Guidance Counselors: 11.0 (278.3 to 1)
Current Spending: ($ per student per year):
Total: $7,263; Instruction: $4,628; Support Services: $2,350
Enrollment, Drop-out Rates and Diploma Recipients by Race/Ethnicity

Category	Total	White	Black	Asian	AIAN	Hisp.
Enrollment (%)	100.0	38.2	5.4	0.2	0.2	56.1
Drop-out Rate (%)	4.3	1.3	3.2	0.0	100.0	7.3
H.S. Diplomas (#)	199	109	12	0	0	78

Hood County

Granbury ISD
600 W Pearl St • Granbury, TX 76048-2046
(817) 408-4000 • http://www.granbury.k12.tx.us/
Grade Span: PK-12; **Agency Type:** 1
Schools: 13
4 Primary; 5 Middle; 2 High; 2 Other Level
10 Regular; 0 Special Education; 0 Vocational; 3 Alternative
0 Magnet; 0 Charter; 8 Title I Eligible; 7 School-wide Title I
Students: 6,563 (50.8% male; 49.2% female)
Individual Education Program: 857 (13.1%);
English Language Learner: 304 (4.6%); Migrant: 64 (1.0%)
Eligible for Free Lunch Program: 1,802 (27.5%)
Eligible for Reduced-Price Lunch Program: 405 (6.2%)
Teachers: 451.9 (14.5 to 1)
Librarians/Media Specialists: 8.9 (737.4 to 1)
Guidance Counselors: 15.9 (412.8 to 1)
Current Spending: ($ per student per year):
Total: $5,878; Instruction: $3,573; Support Services: $2,036
Enrollment, Drop-out Rates and Diploma Recipients by Race/Ethnicity

Category	Total	White	Black	Asian	AIAN	Hisp.
Enrollment (%)	100.0	85.8	0.9	0.7	0.6	12.0
Drop-out Rate (%)	3.6	3.5	0.0	0.0	0.0	4.7
H.S. Diplomas (#)	346	313	3	2	1	27

Hopkins County

Sulphur Springs ISD
631 Connally St • Sulphur Springs, TX 75482-2401
(903) 885-2153
Grade Span: PK-12; **Agency Type:** 1
Schools: 8
5 Primary; 2 Middle; 1 High; 0 Other Level
8 Regular; 0 Special Education; 0 Vocational; 0 Alternative
0 Magnet; 0 Charter; 6 Title I Eligible; 6 School-wide Title I
Students: 4,059 (50.6% male; 49.4% female)
Individual Education Program: 563 (13.9%);
English Language Learner: 208 (5.1%); Migrant: 126 (3.1%)
Eligible for Free Lunch Program: 1,377 (33.9%)
Eligible for Reduced-Price Lunch Program: 305 (7.5%)
Teachers: 296.8 (13.7 to 1)
Librarians/Media Specialists: 1.4 (2,899.3 to 1)
Guidance Counselors: 8.0 (507.4 to 1)
Current Spending: ($ per student per year):
Total: $6,253; Instruction: $4,008; Support Services: $1,904
Enrollment, Drop-out Rates and Diploma Recipients by Race/Ethnicity

Category	Total	White	Black	Asian	AIAN	Hisp.
Enrollment (%)	100.0	71.7	13.1	0.5	0.1	14.6
Drop-out Rate (%)	5.0	5.3	5.4	0.0	0.0	1.9
H.S. Diplomas (#)	254	193	40	1	0	20

Houston County

Crockett ISD
704 Burnet Ave • Crockett, TX 75835-2111
(936) 544-2125 • http://www.crockettisd.net/
Grade Span: PK-12; **Agency Type:** 1
Schools: 6
2 Primary; 2 Middle; 1 High; 1 Other Level
5 Regular; 0 Special Education; 0 Vocational; 1 Alternative
0 Magnet; 0 Charter; 4 Title I Eligible; 4 School-wide Title I
Students: 1,730 (51.5% male; 48.5% female)
Individual Education Program: 243 (14.0%);
English Language Learner: 79 (4.6%); Migrant: 62 (3.6%)
Eligible for Free Lunch Program: 1,087 (62.8%)
Eligible for Reduced-Price Lunch Program: 125 (7.2%)
Teachers: 138.6 (12.5 to 1)
Librarians/Media Specialists: 2.0 (865.0 to 1)
Guidance Counselors: 2.6 (665.4 to 1)
Current Spending: ($ per student per year):
Total: $6,975; Instruction: $4,460; Support Services: $2,110
Enrollment, Drop-out Rates and Diploma Recipients by Race/Ethnicity

Category	Total	White	Black	Asian	AIAN	Hisp.
Enrollment (%)	100.0	28.4	56.9	0.2	0.3	14.1
Drop-out Rate (%)	6.6	5.9	7.4	0.0	0.0	4.7
H.S. Diplomas (#)	116	32	69	3	0	12

Howard County

Big Spring ISD
708 E 11th Pl • Big Spring, TX 79720-4696
(915) 264-3600 • http://bsisd.esc18.net/
Grade Span: PK-12; **Agency Type:** 1
Schools: 11
5 Primary; 2 Middle; 1 High; 2 Other Level
9 Regular; 0 Special Education; 0 Vocational; 1 Alternative
0 Magnet; 0 Charter; 8 Title I Eligible; 8 School-wide Title I
Students: 3,967 (51.5% male; 48.5% female)
Individual Education Program: 463 (11.7%);
English Language Learner: 78 (2.0%); Migrant: 32 (0.8%)
Eligible for Free Lunch Program: 1,863 (47.0%)
Eligible for Reduced-Price Lunch Program: 362 (9.1%)
Teachers: 289.8 (13.7 to 1)
Librarians/Media Specialists: 0.8 (4,958.8 to 1)
Guidance Counselors: 6.7 (592.1 to 1)
Current Spending: ($ per student per year):
Total: $6,441; Instruction: $4,013; Support Services: $2,052
Enrollment, Drop-out Rates and Diploma Recipients by Race/Ethnicity

Category	Total	White	Black	Asian	AIAN	Hisp.
Enrollment (%)	100.0	41.8	6.7	0.7	0.5	50.2
Drop-out Rate (%)	2.9	2.2	2.6	0.0	0.0	3.9
H.S. Diplomas (#)	227	135	12	3	0	77

Hunt County

Commerce ISD
604 Culver • Commerce, TX 75428-3608
Mailing Address: PO Box 1251 • Commerce, TX 75429-1251
(903) 886-3755 • http://commerce.ednet10.net/
Grade Span: PK-12; **Agency Type:** 1
Schools: 5
2 Primary; 1 Middle; 2 High; 0 Other Level
4 Regular; 0 Special Education; 0 Vocational; 1 Alternative
0 Magnet; 0 Charter; 2 Title I Eligible; 2 School-wide Title I
Students: 1,834 (51.5% male; 48.5% female)
Individual Education Program: 305 (16.6%);
English Language Learner: 99 (5.4%); Migrant: 4 (0.2%)
Eligible for Free Lunch Program: 910 (49.6%)
Eligible for Reduced-Price Lunch Program: 127 (6.9%)
Teachers: 130.7 (14.0 to 1)
Librarians/Media Specialists: 2.2 (833.6 to 1)
Guidance Counselors: 7.0 (262.0 to 1)
Current Spending: ($ per student per year):
Total: $6,833; Instruction: $3,868; Support Services: $2,603
Enrollment, Drop-out Rates and Diploma Recipients by Race/Ethnicity

Category	Total	White	Black	Asian	AIAN	Hisp.
Enrollment (%)	100.0	62.8	24.9	1.7	0.8	9.9
Drop-out Rate (%)	3.0	3.3	2.8	0.0	0.0	0.0
H.S. Diplomas (#)	117	86	22	0	0	9

Greenville ISD
3504 King St • Greenville, TX 75401-5103
Mailing Address: PO Box 1022 • Greenville, TX 75403-1022
(903) 457-2500 • http://districtweb1.ednet10.net/greenville/
Grade Span: PK-12; **Agency Type:** 1
Schools: 14
6 Primary; 2 Middle; 2 High; 2 Other Level
9 Regular; 0 Special Education; 0 Vocational; 3 Alternative
0 Magnet; 0 Charter; 7 Title I Eligible; 7 School-wide Title I
Students: 5,220 (51.4% male; 48.6% female)
Individual Education Program: 596 (11.4%);
English Language Learner: 509 (9.8%); Migrant: 2 (<0.1%)
Eligible for Free Lunch Program: 2,366 (45.3%)
Eligible for Reduced-Price Lunch Program: 349 (6.7%)
Teachers: 377.4 (13.8 to 1)
Librarians/Media Specialists: 4.9 (1,065.3 to 1)
Guidance Counselors: 13.5 (386.7 to 1)
Current Spending: ($ per student per year):
Total: $5,979; Instruction: $3,828; Support Services: $1,841

Enrollment, Drop-out Rates and Diploma Recipients by Race/Ethnicity

Category	Total	White	Black	Asian	AIAN	Hisp.
Enrollment (%)	100.0	51.7	25.1	0.9	0.5	21.8
Drop-out Rate (%)	4.6	4.1	4.8	0.0	0.0	6.9
H.S. Diplomas (#)	289	193	64	2	0	30

Quinlan ISD

301 E Main St • Quinlan, TX 75474-9690
(903) 356-3293
Grade Span: PK-12; **Agency Type:** 1
Schools: 6
2 Primary; 2 Middle; 1 High; 1 Other Level
5 Regular; 0 Special Education; 0 Vocational; 1 Alternative
0 Magnet; 0 Charter; 5 Title I Eligible; 5 School-wide Title I
Students: 2,934 (51.7% male; 48.3% female)
Individual Education Program: 524 (17.9%);
English Language Learner: 54 (1.8%); Migrant: 1 (<0.1%)
Eligible for Free Lunch Program: 1,100 (37.5%)
Eligible for Reduced-Price Lunch Program: 226 (7.7%)
Teachers: 204.3 (14.4 to 1)
Librarians/Media Specialists: 3.0 (978.0 to 1)
Guidance Counselors: 6.0 (489.0 to 1)
Current Spending: ($ per student per year):
Total: $5,880; Instruction: $3,411; Support Services: $2,120

Enrollment, Drop-out Rates and Diploma Recipients by Race/Ethnicity

Category	Total	White	Black	Asian	AIAN	Hisp.
Enrollment (%)	100.0	90.9	0.9	0.3	1.2	6.6
Drop-out Rate (%)	5.0	4.9	0.0	0.0	0.0	8.2
H.S. Diplomas (#)	162	143	1	0	3	15

Hutchinson County

Borger ISD

200 E 9th St • Borger, TX 79007-3612
(806) 273-6481 • http://www.borgerisd.net/
Grade Span: PK-12; **Agency Type:** 1
Schools: 6
3 Primary; 1 Middle; 2 High; 0 Other Level
5 Regular; 0 Special Education; 0 Vocational; 1 Alternative
0 Magnet; 0 Charter; 4 Title I Eligible; 4 School-wide Title I
Students: 2,956 (51.7% male; 48.3% female)
Individual Education Program: 414 (14.0%);
English Language Learner: 190 (6.4%); Migrant: 26 (0.9%)
Eligible for Free Lunch Program: 1,061 (35.9%)
Eligible for Reduced-Price Lunch Program: 183 (6.2%)
Teachers: 208.8 (14.2 to 1)
Librarians/Media Specialists: 4.0 (739.0 to 1)
Guidance Counselors: 5.0 (591.2 to 1)
Current Spending: ($ per student per year):
Total: $5,895; Instruction: $3,974; Support Services: $1,677

Enrollment, Drop-out Rates and Diploma Recipients by Race/Ethnicity

Category	Total	White	Black	Asian	AIAN	Hisp.
Enrollment (%)	100.0	63.8	4.5	0.5	0.5	30.8
Drop-out Rate (%)	2.6	2.1	5.4	0.0	0.0	3.8
H.S. Diplomas (#)	201	149	12	1	1	38

Jackson County

Edna ISD

1307 W Gayle St • Edna, TX 77957-1504
Mailing Address: PO Box 919 • Edna, TX 77957-0919
(361) 782-3573
Grade Span: PK-12; **Agency Type:** 1
Schools: 5
2 Primary; 1 Middle; 1 High; 1 Other Level
4 Regular; 0 Special Education; 0 Vocational; 1 Alternative
0 Magnet; 0 Charter; 5 Title I Eligible; 5 School-wide Title I
Students: 1,611 (51.0% male; 49.0% female)
Individual Education Program: 199 (12.4%);
English Language Learner: 88 (5.5%); Migrant: 2 (0.1%)
Eligible for Free Lunch Program: 693 (43.0%)
Eligible for Reduced-Price Lunch Program: 73 (4.5%)
Teachers: 115.5 (13.9 to 1)
Librarians/Media Specialists: 1.0 (1,611.0 to 1)
Guidance Counselors: 3.0 (537.0 to 1)
Current Spending: ($ per student per year):
Total: $6,546; Instruction: $4,186; Support Services: $2,085

Enrollment, Drop-out Rates and Diploma Recipients by Race/Ethnicity

Category	Total	White	Black	Asian	AIAN	Hisp.
Enrollment (%)	100.0	51.2	13.5	0.2	0.1	34.9
Drop-out Rate (%)	3.0	2.7	3.4	0.0	0.0	3.3
H.S. Diplomas (#)	108	64	12	0	0	32

Jasper County

Buna ISD

Hwy 62 & 253 • Buna, TX 77612-1087
Mailing Address: PO Box 1087 • Buna, TX 77612-1087
(409) 994-5101
Grade Span: PK-12; **Agency Type:** 1
Schools: 3
1 Primary; 1 Middle; 1 High; 0 Other Level
3 Regular; 0 Special Education; 0 Vocational; 0 Alternative
0 Magnet; 0 Charter; 1 Title I Eligible; 1 School-wide Title I
Students: 1,631 (50.5% male; 49.5% female)
Individual Education Program: 267 (16.4%);
English Language Learner: 3 (0.2%); Migrant: 3 (0.2%)
Eligible for Free Lunch Program: 399 (24.5%)
Eligible for Reduced-Price Lunch Program: 130 (8.0%)
Teachers: 127.7 (12.8 to 1)
Librarians/Media Specialists: 0.3 (5,436.7 to 1)
Guidance Counselors: 3.4 (479.7 to 1)
Current Spending: ($ per student per year):
Total: $6,969; Instruction: $4,346; Support Services: $2,415

Enrollment, Drop-out Rates and Diploma Recipients by Race/Ethnicity

Category	Total	White	Black	Asian	AIAN	Hisp.
Enrollment (%)	100.0	93.4	3.8	0.3	1.0	1.5
Drop-out Rate (%)	1.8	1.5	2.6	n/a	0.0	8.3
H.S. Diplomas (#)	96	82	10	0	1	3

Jasper ISD

128 Park St • Jasper, TX 75951-3466
(409) 384-2401 • http://www.jasperisd.net/jasper.htm
Grade Span: PK-12; **Agency Type:** 1
Schools: 5
2 Primary; 2 Middle; 1 High; 0 Other Level
5 Regular; 0 Special Education; 0 Vocational; 0 Alternative
0 Magnet; 0 Charter; 4 Title I Eligible; 1 School-wide Title I
Students: 3,182 (51.7% male; 48.3% female)
Individual Education Program: 403 (12.7%);
English Language Learner: 119 (3.7%); Migrant: 0 (0.0%)
Eligible for Free Lunch Program: 1,716 (53.9%)
Eligible for Reduced-Price Lunch Program: 248 (7.8%)
Teachers: 227.1 (14.0 to 1)
Librarians/Media Specialists: 2.1 (1,515.2 to 1)
Guidance Counselors: 6.0 (530.3 to 1)
Current Spending: ($ per student per year):
Total: $7,055; Instruction: $4,235; Support Services: $2,401

Enrollment, Drop-out Rates and Diploma Recipients by Race/Ethnicity

Category	Total	White	Black	Asian	AIAN	Hisp.
Enrollment (%)	100.0	50.0	42.2	0.7	0.3	6.9
Drop-out Rate (%)	2.1	1.7	2.4	0.0	0.0	3.5
H.S. Diplomas (#)	192	111	67	1	1	12

Kirbyville CISD

206 E Main St • Kirbyville, TX 75956-2128
(409) 423-2284
Grade Span: PK-12; **Agency Type:** 1
Schools: 3
1 Primary; 1 Middle; 1 High; 0 Other Level
3 Regular; 0 Special Education; 0 Vocational; 0 Alternative
0 Magnet; 0 Charter; 1 Title I Eligible; 1 School-wide Title I
Students: 1,596 (51.3% male; 48.7% female)
Individual Education Program: 233 (14.6%);
English Language Learner: 14 (0.9%); Migrant: 10 (0.6%)
Eligible for Free Lunch Program: 595 (37.3%)
Eligible for Reduced-Price Lunch Program: 137 (8.6%)
Teachers: 111.8 (14.3 to 1)
Librarians/Media Specialists: 2.0 (798.0 to 1)
Guidance Counselors: 4.1 (389.3 to 1)
Current Spending: ($ per student per year):
Total: $5,716; Instruction: $3,659; Support Services: $1,801

Enrollment, Drop-out Rates and Diploma Recipients by Race/Ethnicity

Category	Total	White	Black	Asian	AIAN	Hisp.
Enrollment (%)	100.0	81.8	15.9	0.0	0.2	2.2
Drop-out Rate (%)	1.8	2.1	1.1	0.0	0.0	0.0
H.S. Diplomas (#)	119	87	28	0	1	3

Jefferson County

Beaumont ISD

3395 Harrison Ave • Beaumont, TX 77706-5009
(409) 899-9972 • http://www.beaumont.k12.tx.us/
Grade Span: PK-12; **Agency Type:** 1
Schools: 36
21 Primary; 7 Middle; 5 High; 3 Other Level
30 Regular; 1 Special Education; 0 Vocational; 5 Alternative
0 Magnet; 0 Charter; 21 Title I Eligible; 14 School-wide Title I

Students: 20,612 (50.3% male; 49.7% female)
Individual Education Program: 2,428 (11.8%);
English Language Learner: 1,050 (5.1%); Migrant: 0 (0.0%)
Eligible for Free Lunch Program: 11,555 (56.1%)
Eligible for Reduced-Price Lunch Program: 1,144 (5.6%)
Teachers: 1,478.2 (13.9 to 1)
Librarians/Media Specialists: 6.7 (3,076.4 to 1)
Guidance Counselors: 42.7 (482.7 to 1)
Current Spending: ($ per student per year):
Total: $6,699; Instruction: $4,067; Support Services: $2,232
Enrollment, Drop-out Rates and Diploma Recipients by Race/Ethnicity

Category	Total	White	Black	Asian	AIAN	Hisp.
Enrollment (%)	100.0	23.0	63.7	2.8	0.2	10.2
Drop-out Rate (%)	6.7	4.2	7.7	1.9	0.0	9.2
H.S. Diplomas (#)	1,153	338	713	40	1	61

Hamshire-Fannett ISD
12702 Second St • Hamshire, TX 77622-0223
Mailing Address: PO Box 223 • Hamshire, TX 77622-0223
(409) 243-2517 • http://www.hfisd.net/
Grade Span: PK-12; **Agency Type:** 1
Schools: 5
1 Primary; 2 Middle; 1 High; 1 Other Level
4 Regular; 0 Special Education; 0 Vocational; 1 Alternative
0 Magnet; 0 Charter; 2 Title I Eligible; 0 School-wide Title I
Students: 1,779 (51.8% male; 48.2% female)
Individual Education Program: 232 (13.0%);
English Language Learner: 34 (1.9%); Migrant: 0 (0.0%)
Eligible for Free Lunch Program: 330 (18.5%)
Eligible for Reduced-Price Lunch Program: 66 (3.7%)
Teachers: 124.2 (14.3 to 1)
Librarians/Media Specialists: 4.0 (444.8 to 1)
Guidance Counselors: 4.0 (444.8 to 1)
Current Spending: ($ per student per year):
Total: $6,044; Instruction: $3,715; Support Services: $2,025
Enrollment, Drop-out Rates and Diploma Recipients by Race/Ethnicity

Category	Total	White	Black	Asian	AIAN	Hisp.
Enrollment (%)	100.0	85.8	5.8	0.6	0.0	7.9
Drop-out Rate (%)	2.6	2.4	3.1	0.0	n/a	7.1
H.S. Diplomas (#)	120	110	3	2	0	5

Nederland ISD
220 N 17th St • Nederland, TX 77627-5029
(409) 724-2391 • http://www.nederland.k12.tx.us/
Grade Span: PK-12; **Agency Type:** 1
Schools: 9
4 Primary; 2 Middle; 1 High; 2 Other Level
7 Regular; 0 Special Education; 0 Vocational; 2 Alternative
0 Magnet; 0 Charter; 5 Title I Eligible; 1 School-wide Title I
Students: 5,101 (51.6% male; 48.4% female)
Individual Education Program: 799 (15.7%);
English Language Learner: 129 (2.5%); Migrant: 0 (0.0%)
Eligible for Free Lunch Program: 874 (17.1%)
Eligible for Reduced-Price Lunch Program: 290 (5.7%)
Teachers: 340.5 (15.0 to 1)
Librarians/Media Specialists: 5.3 (962.5 to 1)
Guidance Counselors: 9.5 (536.9 to 1)
Current Spending: ($ per student per year):
Total: $5,832; Instruction: $3,563; Support Services: $1,957
Enrollment, Drop-out Rates and Diploma Recipients by Race/Ethnicity

Category	Total	White	Black	Asian	AIAN	Hisp.
Enrollment (%)	100.0	86.7	2.8	5.1	0.1	5.3
Drop-out Rate (%)	2.7	2.7	0.0	3.0	0.0	3.1
H.S. Diplomas (#)	326	295	3	13	0	15

Port Arthur ISD
733 5th St • Port Arthur, TX 77640-6599
Mailing Address: PO Box 1388 • Port Arthur, TX 77641-1388
(409) 989-6244
Grade Span: PK-12; **Agency Type:** 1
Schools: 23
9 Primary; 2 Middle; 3 High; 4 Other Level
13 Regular; 1 Special Education; 0 Vocational; 4 Alternative
0 Magnet; 0 Charter; 10 Title I Eligible; 9 School-wide Title I
Students: 10,657 (50.2% male; 49.8% female)
Individual Education Program: 934 (8.8%);
English Language Learner: 1,442 (13.5%); Migrant: 58 (0.5%)
Eligible for Free Lunch Program: 7,669 (72.0%)
Eligible for Reduced-Price Lunch Program: 544 (5.1%)
Teachers: 664.0 (16.0 to 1)
Librarians/Media Specialists: 14.0 (761.2 to 1)
Guidance Counselors: 29.1 (366.2 to 1)
Current Spending: ($ per student per year):
Total: $7,240; Instruction: $4,324; Support Services: $2,552

Enrollment, Drop-out Rates and Diploma Recipients by Race/Ethnicity

Category	Total	White	Black	Asian	AIAN	Hisp.
Enrollment (%)	100.0	8.2	56.9	7.6	0.1	27.2
Drop-out Rate (%)	6.0	4.7	5.6	6.9	0.0	7.7
H.S. Diplomas (#)	547	79	350	47	0	71

Port Neches-Groves ISD
620 Ave C • Port Neches, TX 77651-3092
(409) 722-4244
Grade Span: PK-12; **Agency Type:** 1
Schools: 12
5 Primary; 4 Middle; 1 High; 2 Other Level
10 Regular; 0 Special Education; 0 Vocational; 2 Alternative
0 Magnet; 0 Charter; 7 Title I Eligible; 1 School-wide Title I
Students: 4,799 (50.1% male; 49.9% female)
Individual Education Program: 546 (11.4%);
English Language Learner: 76 (1.6%); Migrant: 2 (<0.1%)
Eligible for Free Lunch Program: 715 (14.9%)
Eligible for Reduced-Price Lunch Program: 201 (4.2%)
Teachers: 339.5 (14.1 to 1)
Librarians/Media Specialists: 11.0 (436.3 to 1)
Guidance Counselors: 13.0 (369.2 to 1)
Current Spending: ($ per student per year):
Total: $6,395; Instruction: $4,010; Support Services: $2,080
Enrollment, Drop-out Rates and Diploma Recipients by Race/Ethnicity

Category	Total	White	Black	Asian	AIAN	Hisp.
Enrollment (%)	100.0	87.5	1.0	3.1	0.4	8.0
Drop-out Rate (%)	2.1	2.2	0.0	0.0	0.0	2.6
H.S. Diplomas (#)	374	342	1	9	0	22

Jim Wells County

Alice ISD
1801 E Main St • Alice, TX 78332-4140
(361) 664-0981
Grade Span: PK-12; **Agency Type:** 1
Schools: 11
7 Primary; 3 Middle; 1 High; 0 Other Level
11 Regular; 0 Special Education; 0 Vocational; 0 Alternative
0 Magnet; 0 Charter; 11 Title I Eligible; 11 School-wide Title I
Students: 5,669 (51.7% male; 48.3% female)
Individual Education Program: 634 (11.2%);
English Language Learner: 248 (4.4%); Migrant: 413 (7.3%)
Eligible for Free Lunch Program: 3,336 (58.8%)
Eligible for Reduced-Price Lunch Program: 458 (8.1%)
Teachers: 381.7 (14.9 to 1)
Librarians/Media Specialists: 12.0 (472.4 to 1)
Guidance Counselors: 17.0 (333.5 to 1)
Current Spending: ($ per student per year):
Total: $6,224; Instruction: $3,767; Support Services: $2,127
Enrollment, Drop-out Rates and Diploma Recipients by Race/Ethnicity

Category	Total	White	Black	Asian	AIAN	Hisp.
Enrollment (%)	100.0	9.6	0.5	0.7	0.1	89.1
Drop-out Rate (%)	7.0	4.5	12.5	0.0	n/a	7.4
H.S. Diplomas (#)	269	41	3	2	0	223

Orange Grove ISD
504 S Dibrell • Orange Grove, TX 78372-0534
Mailing Address: PO Box 534 • Orange Grove, TX 78372-0534
(361) 384-2495
Grade Span: PK-12; **Agency Type:** 1
Schools: 4
2 Primary; 1 Middle; 1 High; 0 Other Level
4 Regular; 0 Special Education; 0 Vocational; 0 Alternative
0 Magnet; 0 Charter; 3 Title I Eligible; 3 School-wide Title I
Students: 1,572 (48.7% male; 51.3% female)
Individual Education Program: 192 (12.2%);
English Language Learner: 48 (3.1%); Migrant: 112 (7.1%)
Eligible for Free Lunch Program: 812 (51.7%)
Eligible for Reduced-Price Lunch Program: 169 (10.8%)
Teachers: 103.8 (15.1 to 1)
Librarians/Media Specialists: 1.0 (1,572.0 to 1)
Guidance Counselors: 3.0 (524.0 to 1)
Current Spending: ($ per student per year):
Total: $6,174; Instruction: $3,796; Support Services: $1,985
Enrollment, Drop-out Rates and Diploma Recipients by Race/Ethnicity

Category	Total	White	Black	Asian	AIAN	Hisp.
Enrollment (%)	100.0	42.0	0.6	0.1	0.1	57.1
Drop-out Rate (%)	1.7	1.4	n/a	0.0	0.0	2.0
H.S. Diplomas (#)	96	41	1	0	1	53

Johnson County

Alvarado ISD

110 N Bill Jackson Dr • Alvarado, TX 76009-4206
Mailing Address: PO Box 387 • Alvarado, TX 76009-0387
(817) 783-6800 • http://www.alvarado.isd.tenet.edu/
Grade Span: PK-12; **Agency Type:** 1
Schools: 7
3 Primary; 2 Middle; 1 High; 1 Other Level
6 Regular; 0 Special Education; 0 Vocational; 1 Alternative
0 Magnet; 0 Charter; 5 Title I Eligible; 5 School-wide Title I
Students: 3,538 (52.1% male; 47.9% female)
Individual Education Program: 463 (13.1%);
English Language Learner: 162 (4.6%); Migrant: 3 (0.1%)
Eligible for Free Lunch Program: 1,305 (36.9%)
Eligible for Reduced-Price Lunch Program: 384 (10.9%)
Teachers: 214.1 (16.5 to 1)
Librarians/Media Specialists: 1.0 (3,538.0 to 1)
Guidance Counselors: 4.5 (786.2 to 1)
Current Spending: ($ per student per year):
Total: $5,856; Instruction: $3,540; Support Services: $2,024
Enrollment, Drop-out Rates and Diploma Recipients by Race/Ethnicity

Category	Total	White	Black	Asian	AIAN	Hisp.
Enrollment (%)	100.0	76.5	4.3	0.3	0.3	18.7
Drop-out Rate (%)	3.8	3.6	5.3	0.0	0.0	5.1
H.S. Diplomas (#)	196	170	10	0	1	15

Burleson ISD

1160 SW Wilshire Blvd • Burleson, TX 76028-5719
(817) 447-5730 • http://www.burlesonisd.net/
Grade Span: PK-12; **Agency Type:** 1
Schools: 11
7 Primary; 2 Middle; 2 High; 0 Other Level
10 Regular; 0 Special Education; 0 Vocational; 1 Alternative
0 Magnet; 0 Charter; 5 Title I Eligible; 5 School-wide Title I
Students: 6,863 (53.5% male; 46.5% female)
Individual Education Program: 575 (8.4%);
English Language Learner: 46 (0.7%); Migrant: 0 (0.0%)
Eligible for Free Lunch Program: 907 (13.2%)
Eligible for Reduced-Price Lunch Program: 401 (5.8%)
Teachers: 449.9 (15.3 to 1)
Librarians/Media Specialists: 6.0 (1,143.8 to 1)
Guidance Counselors: 14.0 (490.2 to 1)
Current Spending: ($ per student per year):
Total: $5,642; Instruction: $3,549; Support Services: $1,813
Enrollment, Drop-out Rates and Diploma Recipients by Race/Ethnicity

Category	Total	White	Black	Asian	AIAN	Hisp.
Enrollment (%)	100.0	91.5	0.8	0.5	0.5	6.7
Drop-out Rate (%)	3.4	3.4	0.0	0.0	0.0	4.3
H.S. Diplomas (#)	413	387	1	3	1	21

Cleburne ISD

103 S Walnut St • Cleburne, TX 76033-5422
(817) 202-1100
Grade Span: PK-12; **Agency Type:** 1
Schools: 14
7 Primary; 2 Middle; 2 High; 1 Other Level
10 Regular; 0 Special Education; 0 Vocational; 2 Alternative
0 Magnet; 0 Charter; 9 Title I Eligible; 4 School-wide Title I
Students: 6,380 (50.4% male; 49.6% female)
Individual Education Program: 791 (12.4%);
English Language Learner: 627 (9.8%); Migrant: 4 (0.1%)
Eligible for Free Lunch Program: 2,267 (35.5%)
Eligible for Reduced-Price Lunch Program: 511 (8.0%)
Teachers: 412.7 (15.5 to 1)
Librarians/Media Specialists: 4.0 (1,595.0 to 1)
Guidance Counselors: 16.0 (398.8 to 1)
Current Spending: ($ per student per year):
Total: $5,502; Instruction: $3,590; Support Services: $1,633
Enrollment, Drop-out Rates and Diploma Recipients by Race/Ethnicity

Category	Total	White	Black	Asian	AIAN	Hisp.
Enrollment (%)	100.0	66.4	5.1	0.9	0.2	27.5
Drop-out Rate (%)	5.4	5.2	10.5	7.7	0.0	4.5
H.S. Diplomas (#)	311	235	15	2	0	59

Joshua ISD

310 E 18th St • Joshua, TX 76058-3110
Mailing Address: PO Box 40 • Joshua, TX 76058-0040
(817) 558-3703
Grade Span: PK-12; **Agency Type:** 1
Schools: 7
3 Primary; 2 Middle; 2 High; 0 Other Level
6 Regular; 0 Special Education; 0 Vocational; 1 Alternative
0 Magnet; 0 Charter; 3 Title I Eligible; 3 School-wide Title I
Students: 4,425 (51.7% male; 48.3% female)
Individual Education Program: 532 (12.0%);
English Language Learner: 140 (3.2%); Migrant: 19 (0.4%)
Eligible for Free Lunch Program: 1,392 (31.5%)
Eligible for Reduced-Price Lunch Program: 412 (9.3%)
Teachers: 305.7 (14.5 to 1)
Librarians/Media Specialists: 5.0 (885.0 to 1)
Guidance Counselors: 9.0 (491.7 to 1)
Current Spending: ($ per student per year):
Total: $5,931; Instruction: $3,798; Support Services: $1,835
Enrollment, Drop-out Rates and Diploma Recipients by Race/Ethnicity

Category	Total	White	Black	Asian	AIAN	Hisp.
Enrollment (%)	100.0	87.2	1.1	0.4	0.2	11.1
Drop-out Rate (%)	5.3	5.2	0.0	0.0	0.0	8.3
H.S. Diplomas (#)	249	214	4	5	1	25

Venus ISD

401 S Hickory St • Venus, TX 76084-0364
Mailing Address: PO Box 364 • Venus, TX 76084-0364
(972) 366-3448
Grade Span: PK-12; **Agency Type:** 1
Schools: 5
2 Primary; 1 Middle; 2 High; 0 Other Level
4 Regular; 0 Special Education; 0 Vocational; 1 Alternative
0 Magnet; 0 Charter; 4 Title I Eligible; 4 School-wide Title I
Students: 1,871 (53.7% male; 46.3% female)
Individual Education Program: 480 (25.7%);
English Language Learner: 187 (10.0%); Migrant: 187 (10.0%)
Eligible for Free Lunch Program: 899 (48.0%)
Eligible for Reduced-Price Lunch Program: 266 (14.2%)
Teachers: 129.0 (14.5 to 1)
Librarians/Media Specialists: 2.0 (935.5 to 1)
Guidance Counselors: 3.0 (623.7 to 1)
Current Spending: ($ per student per year):
Total: $5,488; Instruction: $3,539; Support Services: $1,550
Enrollment, Drop-out Rates and Diploma Recipients by Race/Ethnicity

Category	Total	White	Black	Asian	AIAN	Hisp.
Enrollment (%)	100.0	61.1	2.6	2.7	0.6	32.9
Drop-out Rate (%)	2.3	2.7	0.0	0.0	50.0	0.8
H.S. Diplomas (#)	100	61	3	5	1	30

Kaufman County

Crandall ISD

300 W Lewis St • Crandall, TX 75114-0128
Mailing Address: PO Box 128 • Crandall, TX 75114-0128
(972) 427-8004 • http://www.crandall-isd.net/
Grade Span: PK-12; **Agency Type:** 1
Schools: 5
2 Primary; 1 Middle; 1 High; 1 Other Level
4 Regular; 0 Special Education; 0 Vocational; 1 Alternative
0 Magnet; 0 Charter; 2 Title I Eligible; 2 School-wide Title I
Students: 2,048 (52.6% male; 47.4% female)
Individual Education Program: 271 (13.2%);
English Language Learner: 66 (3.2%); Migrant: 0 (0.0%)
Eligible for Free Lunch Program: 297 (14.5%)
Eligible for Reduced-Price Lunch Program: 103 (5.0%)
Teachers: 141.3 (14.5 to 1)
Librarians/Media Specialists: 3.0 (682.7 to 1)
Guidance Counselors: 3.0 (682.7 to 1)
Current Spending: ($ per student per year):
Total: $5,895; Instruction: $3,410; Support Services: $2,232
Enrollment, Drop-out Rates and Diploma Recipients by Race/Ethnicity

Category	Total	White	Black	Asian	AIAN	Hisp.
Enrollment (%)	100.0	84.5	4.8	0.4	0.8	9.4
Drop-out Rate (%)	1.1	1.2	0.0	0.0	0.0	0.0
H.S. Diplomas (#)	122	112	4	1	0	5

Forney ISD

600 S Bois D'arc St • Forney, TX 75126-9682
(972) 564-4055 • http://forney.ednet10.net/prod_site/index.html
Grade Span: PK-12; **Agency Type:** 1
Schools: 6
3 Primary; 1 Middle; 1 High; 1 Other Level
5 Regular; 0 Special Education; 0 Vocational; 1 Alternative
0 Magnet; 0 Charter; 4 Title I Eligible; 0 School-wide Title I
Students: 3,350 (52.5% male; 47.5% female)
Individual Education Program: 419 (12.5%);
English Language Learner: 64 (1.9%); Migrant: 13 (0.4%)
Eligible for Free Lunch Program: 300 (9.0%)
Eligible for Reduced-Price Lunch Program: 102 (3.0%)
Teachers: 220.8 (15.2 to 1)
Librarians/Media Specialists: 2.5 (1,340.0 to 1)
Guidance Counselors: 6.1 (549.2 to 1)
Current Spending: ($ per student per year):
Total: $5,854; Instruction: $3,487; Support Services: $2,082

Enrollment, Drop-out Rates and Diploma Recipients by Race/Ethnicity

Category	Total	White	Black	Asian	AIAN	Hisp.
Enrollment (%)	100.0	83.2	5.3	0.5	0.5	10.5
Drop-out Rate (%)	1.2	1.4	0.0	0.0	0.0	0.0
H.S. Diplomas (#)	176	158	10	0	0	8

Kaufman ISD

1000 S Houston St • Kaufman, TX 75142-2298
(972) 932-2622 • http://kaufman.ednet10.net/
Grade Span: PK-12; **Agency Type:** 1
Schools: 6
2 Primary; 2 Middle; 2 High; 0 Other Level
5 Regular; 0 Special Education; 0 Vocational; 1 Alternative
0 Magnet; 0 Charter; 3 Title I Eligible; 2 School-wide Title I
Students: 3,372 (50.6% male; 49.4% female)
Individual Education Program: 418 (12.4%);
English Language Learner: 390 (11.6%); Migrant: 16 (0.5%)
Eligible for Free Lunch Program: 1,260 (37.4%)
Eligible for Reduced-Price Lunch Program: 286 (8.5%)
Teachers: 218.9 (15.4 to 1)
Librarians/Media Specialists: 2.0 (1,686.0 to 1)
Guidance Counselors: 6.0 (562.0 to 1)
Current Spending: ($ per student per year):
Total: $5,993; Instruction: $3,685; Support Services: $2,071
Enrollment, Drop-out Rates and Diploma Recipients by Race/Ethnicity

Category	Total	White	Black	Asian	AIAN	Hisp.
Enrollment (%)	100.0	63.3	7.5	0.6	0.5	28.1
Drop-out Rate (%)	1.3	0.9	3.1	0.0	0.0	1.9
H.S. Diplomas (#)	155	109	16	2	0	28

Kemp ISD

905 S Main • Kemp, TX 75143-9155
Mailing Address: 202 W 17th St • Kemp, TX 75143-9155
(903) 498-1314
Grade Span: PK-12; **Agency Type:** 1
Schools: 4
2 Primary; 1 Middle; 1 High; 0 Other Level
4 Regular; 0 Special Education; 0 Vocational; 0 Alternative
0 Magnet; 0 Charter; 3 Title I Eligible; 3 School-wide Title I
Students: 1,678 (52.9% male; 47.1% female)
Individual Education Program: 265 (15.8%);
English Language Learner: 21 (1.3%); Migrant: 0 (0.0%)
Eligible for Free Lunch Program: 548 (32.7%)
Eligible for Reduced-Price Lunch Program: 103 (6.1%)
Teachers: 117.6 (14.3 to 1)
Librarians/Media Specialists: 2.0 (839.0 to 1)
Guidance Counselors: 4.0 (419.5 to 1)
Current Spending: ($ per student per year):
Total: $5,937; Instruction: $3,379; Support Services: $2,232
Enrollment, Drop-out Rates and Diploma Recipients by Race/Ethnicity

Category	Total	White	Black	Asian	AIAN	Hisp.
Enrollment (%)	100.0	89.9	4.2	0.2	0.8	4.8
Drop-out Rate (%)	4.1	3.9	8.3	0.0	33.3	0.0
H.S. Diplomas (#)	82	74	4	0	0	4

Mabank ISD

124 E Market St • Mabank, TX 75147-8377
(903) 887-9311
Grade Span: PK-12; **Agency Type:** 1
Schools: 6
3 Primary; 1 Middle; 1 High; 0 Other Level
5 Regular; 0 Special Education; 0 Vocational; 0 Alternative
0 Magnet; 0 Charter; 3 Title I Eligible; 3 School-wide Title I
Students: 3,266 (52.7% male; 47.3% female)
Individual Education Program: 592 (18.1%);
English Language Learner: 56 (1.7%); Migrant: 2 (0.1%)
Eligible for Free Lunch Program: 1,281 (39.2%)
Eligible for Reduced-Price Lunch Program: 309 (9.5%)
Teachers: 225.2 (14.5 to 1)
Librarians/Media Specialists: 4.0 (816.5 to 1)
Guidance Counselors: 9.0 (362.9 to 1)
Current Spending: ($ per student per year):
Total: $6,229; Instruction: $3,839; Support Services: $2,045
Enrollment, Drop-out Rates and Diploma Recipients by Race/Ethnicity

Category	Total	White	Black	Asian	AIAN	Hisp.
Enrollment (%)	100.0	89.1	2.6	0.6	0.5	7.2
Drop-out Rate (%)	2.0	2.0	0.0	0.0	0.0	4.1
H.S. Diplomas (#)	177	160	5	0	2	10

Terrell ISD

212 W High St • Terrell, TX 75160-2659
(972) 563-7504
Grade Span: PK-12; **Agency Type:** 1
Schools: 8
3 Primary; 3 Middle; 1 High; 1 Other Level
7 Regular; 1 Special Education; 0 Vocational; 0 Alternative
0 Magnet; 0 Charter; 7 Title I Eligible; 3 School-wide Title I
Students: 4,237 (53.4% male; 46.6% female)
Individual Education Program: 721 (17.0%);
English Language Learner: 483 (11.4%); Migrant: 18 (0.4%)
Eligible for Free Lunch Program: 2,091 (49.4%)
Eligible for Reduced-Price Lunch Program: 250 (5.9%)
Teachers: 307.0 (13.8 to 1)
Librarians/Media Specialists: 5.1 (830.8 to 1)
Guidance Counselors: 10.0 (423.7 to 1)
Current Spending: ($ per student per year):
Total: $6,450; Instruction: $3,881; Support Services: $2,257
Enrollment, Drop-out Rates and Diploma Recipients by Race/Ethnicity

Category	Total	White	Black	Asian	AIAN	Hisp.
Enrollment (%)	100.0	43.4	32.1	1.3	0.2	23.0
Drop-out Rate (%)	5.1	4.5	4.5	10.0	0.0	8.4
H.S. Diplomas (#)	208	102	80	0	0	26

Kendall County

Boerne ISD

123 W John's Rd • Boerne, TX 78006-2023
(830) 249-5000
Grade Span: PK-12; **Agency Type:** 1
Schools: 9
4 Primary; 2 Middle; 1 High; 1 Other Level
7 Regular; 0 Special Education; 0 Vocational; 1 Alternative
0 Magnet; 0 Charter; 3 Title I Eligible; 0 School-wide Title I
Students: 5,172 (51.9% male; 48.1% female)
Individual Education Program: 672 (13.0%);
English Language Learner: 177 (3.4%); Migrant: 13 (0.3%)
Eligible for Free Lunch Program: 649 (12.5%)
Eligible for Reduced-Price Lunch Program: 208 (4.0%)
Teachers: 376.0 (13.8 to 1)
Librarians/Media Specialists: 6.0 (862.0 to 1)
Guidance Counselors: 10.8 (478.9 to 1)
Current Spending: ($ per student per year):
Total: $6,060; Instruction: $3,740; Support Services: $2,104
Enrollment, Drop-out Rates and Diploma Recipients by Race/Ethnicity

Category	Total	White	Black	Asian	AIAN	Hisp.
Enrollment (%)	100.0	80.2	0.5	0.6	0.3	18.4
Drop-out Rate (%)	0.7	0.6	0.0	0.0	0.0	0.8
H.S. Diplomas (#)	353	285	2	0	0	66

Kerr County

Ingram ISD

510 College St • Ingram, TX 78025-4100
(830) 367-5517
Grade Span: PK-12; **Agency Type:** 1
Schools: 3
1 Primary; 1 Middle; 1 High; 0 Other Level
3 Regular; 0 Special Education; 0 Vocational; 0 Alternative
0 Magnet; 0 Charter; 3 Title I Eligible; 3 School-wide Title I
Students: 1,510 (51.7% male; 48.3% female)
Individual Education Program: 182 (12.1%);
English Language Learner: 79 (5.2%); Migrant: 3 (0.2%)
Eligible for Free Lunch Program: 642 (42.5%)
Eligible for Reduced-Price Lunch Program: 159 (10.5%)
Teachers: 125.9 (12.0 to 1)
Librarians/Media Specialists: 1.4 (1,078.6 to 1)
Guidance Counselors: 3.4 (444.1 to 1)
Current Spending: ($ per student per year):
Total: $7,621; Instruction: $4,752; Support Services: $2,486
Enrollment, Drop-out Rates and Diploma Recipients by Race/Ethnicity

Category	Total	White	Black	Asian	AIAN	Hisp.
Enrollment (%)	100.0	70.5	1.5	1.0	0.8	26.3
Drop-out Rate (%)	2.1	1.9	0.0	0.0	0.0	2.7
H.S. Diplomas (#)	87	73	0	0	0	14

Kerrville ISD

1009 Barnett St • Kerrville, TX 78028-4614
(830) 257-2200 • http://www.kerrvilleisd.net/
Grade Span: PK-12; **Agency Type:** 1
Schools: 11
5 Primary; 2 Middle; 1 High; 3 Other Level
8 Regular; 0 Special Education; 0 Vocational; 3 Alternative
0 Magnet; 0 Charter; 6 Title I Eligible; 6 School-wide Title I
Students: 4,768 (52.0% male; 48.0% female)
Individual Education Program: 664 (13.9%);
English Language Learner: 198 (4.2%); Migrant: 9 (0.2%)
Eligible for Free Lunch Program: 1,645 (34.5%)
Eligible for Reduced-Price Lunch Program: 403 (8.5%)
Teachers: 323.0 (14.8 to 1)
Librarians/Media Specialists: 2.0 (2,384.0 to 1)

Guidance Counselors: 13.4 (355.8 to 1)
Current Spending: ($ per student per year):
Total: $6,107; Instruction: $4,063; Support Services: $1,773
Enrollment, Drop-out Rates and Diploma Recipients by Race/Ethnicity

Category	Total	White	Black	Asian	AIAN	Hisp.
Enrollment (%)	100.0	58.5	3.8	0.9	0.4	36.4
Drop-out Rate (%)	5.9	3.2	7.1	14.3	0.0	11.8
H.S. Diplomas (#)	302	221	6	4	2	69

Kleberg County

Kingsville ISD
207 N Third St • Kingsville, TX 78363-4401
Mailing Address: PO Box 871 • Kingsville, TX 78364-0871
(361) 592-3387 • http://www.kvisd.esc2.net/
Grade Span: PK-12; **Agency Type:** 1
Schools: 15
7 Primary; 2 Middle; 3 High; 2 Other Level
10 Regular; 1 Special Education; 0 Vocational; 3 Alternative
0 Magnet; 0 Charter; 7 Title I Eligible; 7 School-wide Title I
Students: 4,623 (52.2% male; 47.8% female)
Individual Education Program: 715 (15.5%);
English Language Learner: 492 (10.6%); Migrant: 171 (3.7%)
Eligible for Free Lunch Program: 2,539 (54.9%)
Eligible for Reduced-Price Lunch Program: 453 (9.8%)
Teachers: 320.5 (14.4 to 1)
Librarians/Media Specialists: 6.0 (770.5 to 1)
Guidance Counselors: 18.0 (256.8 to 1)
Current Spending: ($ per student per year):
Total: $6,930; Instruction: $4,146; Support Services: $2,438
Enrollment, Drop-out Rates and Diploma Recipients by Race/Ethnicity

Category	Total	White	Black	Asian	AIAN	Hisp.
Enrollment (%)	100.0	14.6	4.2	0.8	0.3	80.1
Drop-out Rate (%)	4.9	1.7	6.7	0.0	0.0	5.7
H.S. Diplomas (#)	358	77	12	4	0	265

Lamar County

North Lamar ISD
3201 Lewis Ln • Paris, TX 75462-2092
(903) 737-2000 • http://www.northlamar.net/
Grade Span: PK-12; **Agency Type:** 1
Schools: 7
3 Primary; 2 Middle; 1 High; 0 Other Level
6 Regular; 0 Special Education; 0 Vocational; 0 Alternative
0 Magnet; 0 Charter; 4 Title I Eligible; 4 School-wide Title I
Students: 3,204 (51.9% male; 48.1% female)
Individual Education Program: 452 (14.1%);
English Language Learner: 24 (0.7%); Migrant: 37 (1.2%)
Eligible for Free Lunch Program: 767 (23.9%)
Eligible for Reduced-Price Lunch Program: 224 (7.0%)
Teachers: 228.4 (14.0 to 1)
Librarians/Media Specialists: 3.0 (1,068.0 to 1)
Guidance Counselors: 6.5 (492.9 to 1)
Current Spending: ($ per student per year):
Total: $5,584; Instruction: $3,708; Support Services: $1,556
Enrollment, Drop-out Rates and Diploma Recipients by Race/Ethnicity

Category	Total	White	Black	Asian	AIAN	Hisp.
Enrollment (%)	100.0	90.3	4.9	0.5	1.5	2.9
Drop-out Rate (%)	2.1	2.2	2.4	0.0	0.0	0.0
H.S. Diplomas (#)	203	183	10	2	3	5

Paris ISD
1920 Clarksville • Paris, TX 75460-1159
(903) 737-7473 • http://www.parisisd.net/
Grade Span: PK-12; **Agency Type:** 1
Schools: 9
3 Primary; 1 Middle; 2 High; 3 Other Level
7 Regular; 0 Special Education; 1 Vocational; 1 Alternative
0 Magnet; 0 Charter; 3 Title I Eligible; 3 School-wide Title I
Students: 3,888 (51.5% male; 48.5% female)
Individual Education Program: 622 (16.0%);
English Language Learner: 89 (2.3%); Migrant: 60 (1.5%)
Eligible for Free Lunch Program: 2,169 (55.8%)
Eligible for Reduced-Price Lunch Program: 246 (6.3%)
Teachers: 305.3 (12.7 to 1)
Librarians/Media Specialists: 4.0 (972.0 to 1)
Guidance Counselors: 9.8 (396.7 to 1)
Current Spending: ($ per student per year):
Total: $7,150; Instruction: $4,555; Support Services: $2,220
Enrollment, Drop-out Rates and Diploma Recipients by Race/Ethnicity

Category	Total	White	Black	Asian	AIAN	Hisp.
Enrollment (%)	100.0	50.8	41.9	0.8	1.3	5.3
Drop-out Rate (%)	4.3	4.7	3.9	0.0	25.0	0.0
H.S. Diplomas (#)	175	85	87	1	0	2

Lamb County

Littlefield ISD
1500 E Delano Ave • Littlefield, TX 79339-4207
(806) 385-3844
Grade Span: PK-12; **Agency Type:** 1
Schools: 5
2 Primary; 1 Middle; 1 High; 1 Other Level
4 Regular; 0 Special Education; 0 Vocational; 1 Alternative
0 Magnet; 0 Charter; 4 Title I Eligible; 4 School-wide Title I
Students: 1,592 (55.3% male; 44.7% female)
Individual Education Program: 267 (16.8%);
English Language Learner: 66 (4.1%); Migrant: 125 (7.9%)
Eligible for Free Lunch Program: 837 (52.6%)
Eligible for Reduced-Price Lunch Program: 148 (9.3%)
Teachers: 102.4 (15.5 to 1)
Librarians/Media Specialists: 1.9 (837.9 to 1)
Guidance Counselors: 2.0 (796.0 to 1)
Current Spending: ($ per student per year):
Total: $6,363; Instruction: $4,177; Support Services: $1,876
Enrollment, Drop-out Rates and Diploma Recipients by Race/Ethnicity

Category	Total	White	Black	Asian	AIAN	Hisp.
Enrollment (%)	100.0	35.8	6.7	0.3	0.1	57.2
Drop-out Rate (%)	4.1	1.2	2.9	n/a	n/a	6.7
H.S. Diplomas (#)	78	35	7	0	0	36

Lampasas County

Lampasas ISD
207 W 8th St • Lampasas, TX 76550-3125
(512) 556-6224 • http://www.lampasas.k12.tx.us/
Grade Span: PK-12; **Agency Type:** 1
Schools: 6
2 Primary; 0 Middle; 2 High; 1 Other Level
4 Regular; 0 Special Education; 0 Vocational; 1 Alternative
0 Magnet; 0 Charter; 3 Title I Eligible; 3 School-wide Title I
Students: 3,261 (52.3% male; 47.7% female)
Individual Education Program: 474 (14.5%);
English Language Learner: 88 (2.7%); Migrant: 111 (3.4%)
Eligible for Free Lunch Program: 1,134 (34.8%)
Eligible for Reduced-Price Lunch Program: 322 (9.9%)
Teachers: 214.1 (15.2 to 1)
Librarians/Media Specialists: 3.0 (1,087.0 to 1)
Guidance Counselors: 5.0 (652.2 to 1)
Current Spending: ($ per student per year):
Total: $5,708; Instruction: $3,543; Support Services: $1,907
Enrollment, Drop-out Rates and Diploma Recipients by Race/Ethnicity

Category	Total	White	Black	Asian	AIAN	Hisp.
Enrollment (%)	100.0	75.7	3.7	0.7	0.7	19.2
Drop-out Rate (%)	3.6	3.3	0.0	0.0	40.0	5.2
H.S. Diplomas (#)	212	163	11	4	2	32

Lee County

Giddings ISD
2249 N Main • Giddings, TX 78942-0389
Mailing Address: PO Box 389 • Giddings, TX 78942-0389
(979) 542-2854 • http://www.giddings.txed.net/
Grade Span: PK-12; **Agency Type:** 1
Schools: 5
1 Primary; 2 Middle; 2 High; 0 Other Level
4 Regular; 0 Special Education; 0 Vocational; 1 Alternative
0 Magnet; 0 Charter; 5 Title I Eligible; 5 School-wide Title I
Students: 1,813 (51.1% male; 48.9% female)
Individual Education Program: 197 (10.9%);
English Language Learner: 211 (11.6%); Migrant: 29 (1.6%)
Eligible for Free Lunch Program: 754 (41.6%)
Eligible for Reduced-Price Lunch Program: 136 (7.5%)
Teachers: 139.0 (13.0 to 1)
Librarians/Media Specialists: 3.0 (604.3 to 1)
Guidance Counselors: 6.0 (302.2 to 1)
Current Spending: ($ per student per year):
Total: $6,283; Instruction: $3,815; Support Services: $2,093
Enrollment, Drop-out Rates and Diploma Recipients by Race/Ethnicity

Category	Total	White	Black	Asian	AIAN	Hisp.
Enrollment (%)	100.0	45.1	14.3	0.3	0.3	40.0
Drop-out Rate (%)	1.9	0.9	4.8	0.0	n/a	2.3
H.S. Diplomas (#)	123	75	15	2	0	31

Liberty County

Cleveland ISD
103 Charles Barker Ave • Cleveland, TX 77327-4709
(281) 592-8717
Grade Span: PK-12; **Agency Type:** 1
Schools: 8
3 Primary; 2 Middle; 2 High; 1 Other Level
6 Regular; 0 Special Education; 0 Vocational; 2 Alternative
0 Magnet; 0 Charter; 6 Title I Eligible; 6 School-wide Title I
Students: 3,286 (50.5% male; 49.5% female)
Individual Education Program: 347 (10.6%);
English Language Learner: 360 (11.0%); Migrant: 14 (0.4%)
Eligible for Free Lunch Program: 1,644 (50.0%)
Eligible for Reduced-Price Lunch Program: 316 (9.6%)
Teachers: 210.7 (15.6 to 1)
Librarians/Media Specialists: 5.0 (657.2 to 1)
Guidance Counselors: 6.0 (547.7 to 1)
Current Spending: ($ per student per year):
Total: $5,864; Instruction: $3,440; Support Services: $2,123
Enrollment, Drop-out Rates and Diploma Recipients by Race/Ethnicity

Category	Total	White	Black	Asian	AIAN	Hisp.
Enrollment (%)	100.0	56.4	16.9	0.7	0.3	25.8
Drop-out Rate (%)	4.1	4.6	3.7	50.0	0.0	2.0
H.S. Diplomas (#)	162	97	37	1	3	24

Dayton ISD
209 W Hwy 90 • Dayton, TX 77535-2639
Mailing Address: PO Box 248 • Dayton, TX 77535-0248
(936) 258-2667 • http://www.dayton.isd.esc4.net/
Grade Span: PK-12; **Agency Type:** 1
Schools: 8
2 Primary; 3 Middle; 2 High; 1 Other Level
6 Regular; 0 Special Education; 0 Vocational; 2 Alternative
0 Magnet; 0 Charter; 5 Title I Eligible; 5 School-wide Title I
Students: 5,154 (52.1% male; 47.9% female)
Individual Education Program: 587 (11.4%);
English Language Learner: 257 (5.0%); Migrant: 0 (0.0%)
Eligible for Free Lunch Program: 1,665 (32.3%)
Eligible for Reduced-Price Lunch Program: 416 (8.1%)
Teachers: 302.3 (17.0 to 1)
Librarians/Media Specialists: 5.5 (937.1 to 1)
Guidance Counselors: 8.0 (644.3 to 1)
Current Spending: ($ per student per year):
Total: $5,436; Instruction: $3,294; Support Services: $1,856
Enrollment, Drop-out Rates and Diploma Recipients by Race/Ethnicity

Category	Total	White	Black	Asian	AIAN	Hisp.
Enrollment (%)	100.0	75.5	10.2	0.5	0.2	13.6
Drop-out Rate (%)	4.6	4.1	2.9	0.0	0.0	12.1
H.S. Diplomas (#)	247	202	26	2	0	17

Liberty ISD
1600 Grand Ave • Liberty, TX 77575-4725
(936) 336-7213 • http://www.liberty.isd.esc4.net/
Grade Span: PK-12; **Agency Type:** 1
Schools: 7
2 Primary; 1 Middle; 1 High; 2 Other Level
4 Regular; 0 Special Education; 0 Vocational; 2 Alternative
0 Magnet; 0 Charter; 4 Title I Eligible; 4 School-wide Title I
Students: 2,361 (50.5% male; 49.5% female)
Individual Education Program: 278 (11.8%);
English Language Learner: 182 (7.7%); Migrant: 0 (0.0%)
Eligible for Free Lunch Program: 979 (41.5%)
Eligible for Reduced-Price Lunch Program: 138 (5.8%)
Teachers: 169.6 (13.9 to 1)
Librarians/Media Specialists: 2.0 (1,180.5 to 1)
Guidance Counselors: 6.0 (393.5 to 1)
Current Spending: ($ per student per year):
Total: $7,364; Instruction: $4,532; Support Services: $2,505
Enrollment, Drop-out Rates and Diploma Recipients by Race/Ethnicity

Category	Total	White	Black	Asian	AIAN	Hisp.
Enrollment (%)	100.0	59.6	21.0	0.8	0.1	18.6
Drop-out Rate (%)	2.2	1.6	1.3	0.0	0.0	6.0
H.S. Diplomas (#)	153	93	34	1	1	24

Tarkington ISD
F M 163 • Cleveland, TX 77327-8811
Mailing Address: Rt 6 Box 130 • Cleveland, TX 77327-8811
(281) 592-8781
Grade Span: PK-12; **Agency Type:** 1
Schools: 4
2 Primary; 1 Middle; 1 High; 0 Other Level
4 Regular; 0 Special Education; 0 Vocational; 0 Alternative
0 Magnet; 0 Charter; 2 Title I Eligible; 2 School-wide Title I
Students: 1,824 (50.9% male; 49.1% female)
Individual Education Program: 193 (10.6%);
English Language Learner: 7 (0.4%); Migrant: 0 (0.0%)
Eligible for Free Lunch Program: 409 (22.4%)
Eligible for Reduced-Price Lunch Program: 110 (6.0%)
Teachers: 129.3 (14.1 to 1)
Librarians/Media Specialists: 2.0 (912.0 to 1)
Guidance Counselors: 4.0 (456.0 to 1)
Current Spending: ($ per student per year):
Total: $5,059; Instruction: $3,174; Support Services: $1,594
Enrollment, Drop-out Rates and Diploma Recipients by Race/Ethnicity

Category	Total	White	Black	Asian	AIAN	Hisp.
Enrollment (%)	100.0	95.7	0.9	0.0	0.4	3.0
Drop-out Rate (%)	1.9	1.8	0.0	0.0	n/a	11.1
H.S. Diplomas (#)	120	118	1	0	0	1

Limestone County

Groesbeck ISD
1202 N Ellis • Groesbeck, TX 76642-0559
Mailing Address: PO Box 559 • Groesbeck, TX 76642-0559
(254) 729-4100
Grade Span: PK-12; **Agency Type:** 1
Schools: 4
1 Primary; 1 Middle; 2 High; 0 Other Level
3 Regular; 0 Special Education; 0 Vocational; 1 Alternative
0 Magnet; 0 Charter; 1 Title I Eligible; 1 School-wide Title I
Students: 1,606 (51.7% male; 48.3% female)
Individual Education Program: 231 (14.4%);
English Language Learner: 57 (3.5%); Migrant: 1 (0.1%)
Eligible for Free Lunch Program: 656 (40.8%)
Eligible for Reduced-Price Lunch Program: 139 (8.7%)
Teachers: 130.4 (12.3 to 1)
Librarians/Media Specialists: 3.0 (535.3 to 1)
Guidance Counselors: 3.0 (535.3 to 1)
Current Spending: ($ per student per year):
Total: $7,571; Instruction: $4,470; Support Services: $2,763
Enrollment, Drop-out Rates and Diploma Recipients by Race/Ethnicity

Category	Total	White	Black	Asian	AIAN	Hisp.
Enrollment (%)	100.0	71.1	12.6	0.3	0.4	15.6
Drop-out Rate (%)	2.0	1.7	1.4	n/a	0.0	5.5
H.S. Diplomas (#)	113	85	14	0	1	13

Mexia ISD
405 E Milam • Mexia, TX 76667-2452
Mailing Address: PO Box 2000 • Mexia, TX 76667-2452
(254) 562-2888
Grade Span: PK-12; **Agency Type:** 1
Schools: 7
2 Primary; 0 Middle; 2 High; 2 Other Level
4 Regular; 0 Special Education; 0 Vocational; 2 Alternative
0 Magnet; 0 Charter; 3 Title I Eligible; 3 School-wide Title I
Students: 2,299 (53.2% male; 46.8% female)
Individual Education Program: 378 (16.4%);
English Language Learner: 163 (7.1%); Migrant: 14 (0.6%)
Eligible for Free Lunch Program: 1,159 (50.4%)
Eligible for Reduced-Price Lunch Program: 195 (8.5%)
Teachers: 164.9 (13.9 to 1)
Librarians/Media Specialists: 2.0 (1,149.5 to 1)
Guidance Counselors: 5.0 (459.8 to 1)
Current Spending: ($ per student per year):
Total: $7,218; Instruction: $4,469; Support Services: $2,406
Enrollment, Drop-out Rates and Diploma Recipients by Race/Ethnicity

Category	Total	White	Black	Asian	AIAN	Hisp.
Enrollment (%)	100.0	43.8	34.4	0.3	0.2	21.2
Drop-out Rate (%)	4.4	4.8	2.5	0.0	0.0	7.0
H.S. Diplomas (#)	124	64	47	0	0	13

Llano County

Llano ISD
200 E Lampasas • Llano, TX 78643-2734
(915) 247-4747 • http://www.llano.k12.tx.us/
Grade Span: PK-12; **Agency Type:** 1
Schools: 5
2 Primary; 2 Middle; 1 High; 0 Other Level
5 Regular; 0 Special Education; 0 Vocational; 0 Alternative
0 Magnet; 0 Charter; 2 Title I Eligible; 1 School-wide Title I
Students: 1,890 (53.4% male; 46.6% female)
Individual Education Program: 353 (18.7%);
English Language Learner: 53 (2.8%); Migrant: 8 (0.4%)
Eligible for Free Lunch Program: 579 (30.6%)
Eligible for Reduced-Price Lunch Program: 204 (10.8%)
Teachers: 173.2 (10.9 to 1)
Librarians/Media Specialists: 3.4 (555.9 to 1)
Guidance Counselors: 5.6 (337.5 to 1)

Current Spending: ($ per student per year):
Total: $8,211; Instruction: $4,901; Support Services: $2,908
Enrollment, Drop-out Rates and Diploma Recipients by Race/Ethnicity

Category	Total	White	Black	Asian	AIAN	Hisp.
Enrollment (%)	100.0	84.8	0.5	0.4	1.0	13.4
Drop-out Rate (%)	2.6	2.6	0.0	0.0	0.0	2.2
H.S. Diplomas (#)	92	81	1	0	0	10

Lubbock County

Frenship ISD

300 Main St • Wolfforth, TX 79382-0100
Mailing Address: PO Box 100 • Wolfforth, TX 79382-0100
(806) 866-9541 • http://www.frenship.k12.tx.us/
Grade Span: PK-12; **Agency Type:** 1
Schools: 9
4 Primary; 2 Middle; 2 High; 1 Other Level
7 Regular; 0 Special Education; 0 Vocational; 2 Alternative
0 Magnet; 0 Charter; 4 Title I Eligible; 4 School-wide Title I
Students: 5,484 (51.3% male; 48.7% female)
Individual Education Program: 637 (11.6%);
English Language Learner: 101 (1.8%); Migrant: 14 (0.3%)
Eligible for Free Lunch Program: 1,402 (25.6%)
Eligible for Reduced-Price Lunch Program: 460 (8.4%)
Teachers: 344.9 (15.9 to 1)
Librarians/Media Specialists: 4.0 (1,371.0 to 1)
Guidance Counselors: 11.0 (498.5 to 1)
Current Spending: ($ per student per year):
Total: $5,532; Instruction: $3,568; Support Services: $1,746
Enrollment, Drop-out Rates and Diploma Recipients by Race/Ethnicity

Category	Total	White	Black	Asian	AIAN	Hisp.
Enrollment (%)	100.0	65.8	4.6	1.3	0.5	27.7
Drop-out Rate (%)	2.2	1.5	3.6	0.0	0.0	4.4
H.S. Diplomas (#)	334	240	18	3	1	72

Lubbock ISD

1628 19th St • Lubbock, TX 79401-4895
(806) 766-1000 • http://www.lubbock.k12.tx.us/lbb/
Grade Span: PK-12; **Agency Type:** 1
Schools: 58
39 Primary; 10 Middle; 5 High; 4 Other Level
52 Regular; 1 Special Education; 0 Vocational; 5 Alternative
0 Magnet; 0 Charter; 27 Title I Eligible; 27 School-wide Title I
Students: 29,472 (51.0% male; 49.0% female)
Individual Education Program: 4,733 (16.1%);
English Language Learner: 727 (2.5%); Migrant: 638 (2.2%)
Eligible for Free Lunch Program: 13,330 (45.2%)
Eligible for Reduced-Price Lunch Program: 2,391 (8.1%)
Teachers: 2,101.3 (14.0 to 1)
Librarians/Media Specialists: 33.6 (877.1 to 1)
Guidance Counselors: 74.0 (398.3 to 1)
Current Spending: ($ per student per year):
Total: $6,483; Instruction: $4,057; Support Services: $2,158
Enrollment, Drop-out Rates and Diploma Recipients by Race/Ethnicity

Category	Total	White	Black	Asian	AIAN	Hisp.
Enrollment (%)	100.0	39.2	14.9	1.4	0.2	44.3
Drop-out Rate (%)	3.8	1.3	5.7	0.0	0.0	6.3
H.S. Diplomas (#)	1,737	894	232	26	2	583

Lubbock-Cooper ISD

Hwy 87 & Woodrow Rd • Lubbock, TX 79423-9530
Mailing Address: 16302 Loop 493 • Lubbock, TX 79423-9530
(806) 863-2282
Grade Span: PK-12; **Agency Type:** 1
Schools: 6
2 Primary; 2 Middle; 1 High; 0 Other Level
5 Regular; 0 Special Education; 0 Vocational; 0 Alternative
0 Magnet; 0 Charter; 3 Title I Eligible; 3 School-wide Title I
Students: 2,294 (53.4% male; 46.6% female)
Individual Education Program: 425 (18.5%);
English Language Learner: 70 (3.1%); Migrant: 9 (0.4%)
Eligible for Free Lunch Program: 749 (32.7%)
Eligible for Reduced-Price Lunch Program: 209 (9.1%)
Teachers: 154.2 (14.9 to 1)
Librarians/Media Specialists: 4.0 (573.5 to 1)
Guidance Counselors: 7.0 (327.7 to 1)
Current Spending: ($ per student per year):
Total: $6,092; Instruction: $3,694; Support Services: $1,974
Enrollment, Drop-out Rates and Diploma Recipients by Race/Ethnicity

Category	Total	White	Black	Asian	AIAN	Hisp.
Enrollment (%)	100.0	66.8	1.6	0.1	0.3	31.2
Drop-out Rate (%)	1.5	1.1	0.0	n/a	n/a	2.4
H.S. Diplomas (#)	111	88	0	0	0	23

Madison County

Madisonville CISD

718 Bacon St • Madisonville, TX 77864-2540
Mailing Address: PO Box 879 • Madisonville, TX 77864-0879
(936) 348-2797 • http://www.madisonvillecisd.org/
Grade Span: PK-12; **Agency Type:** 1
Schools: 4
2 Primary; 1 Middle; 1 High; 0 Other Level
4 Regular; 0 Special Education; 0 Vocational; 0 Alternative
0 Magnet; 0 Charter; 3 Title I Eligible; 3 School-wide Title I
Students: 2,115 (51.9% male; 48.1% female)
Individual Education Program: 248 (11.7%);
English Language Learner: 204 (9.6%); Migrant: 10 (0.5%)
Eligible for Free Lunch Program: 1,106 (52.3%)
Eligible for Reduced-Price Lunch Program: 176 (8.3%)
Teachers: 155.1 (13.6 to 1)
Librarians/Media Specialists: 1.0 (2,115.0 to 1)
Guidance Counselors: 4.3 (491.9 to 1)
Current Spending: ($ per student per year):
Total: $6,471; Instruction: $3,810; Support Services: $2,235
Enrollment, Drop-out Rates and Diploma Recipients by Race/Ethnicity

Category	Total	White	Black	Asian	AIAN	Hisp.
Enrollment (%)	100.0	56.5	23.1	0.3	0.3	19.8
Drop-out Rate (%)	5.6	4.5	6.6	0.0	0.0	10.1
H.S. Diplomas (#)	115	65	35	0	1	14

Matagorda County

Bay City ISD

520 7th St • Bay City, TX 77414-3610
(979) 245-5766
Grade Span: PK-12; **Agency Type:** 1
Schools: 9
3 Primary; 3 Middle; 1 High; 1 Other Level
7 Regular; 0 Special Education; 0 Vocational; 1 Alternative
0 Magnet; 0 Charter; 7 Title I Eligible; 6 School-wide Title I
Students: 4,321 (51.5% male; 48.5% female)
Individual Education Program: 566 (13.1%);
English Language Learner: 307 (7.1%); Migrant: 13 (0.3%)
Eligible for Free Lunch Program: 2,518 (58.3%)
Eligible for Reduced-Price Lunch Program: 403 (9.3%)
Teachers: 279.3 (15.5 to 1)
Librarians/Media Specialists: 6.0 (720.2 to 1)
Guidance Counselors: 12.0 (360.1 to 1)
Current Spending: ($ per student per year):
Total: $6,182; Instruction: $3,864; Support Services: $2,026
Enrollment, Drop-out Rates and Diploma Recipients by Race/Ethnicity

Category	Total	White	Black	Asian	AIAN	Hisp.
Enrollment (%)	100.0	36.7	18.4	0.9	0.1	43.8
Drop-out Rate (%)	2.5	0.9	4.9	0.0	0.0	3.3
H.S. Diplomas (#)	271	122	66	3	0	80

Palacios ISD

1209 12th St • Palacios, TX 77465-3799
(361) 972-5491 • http://www.palacios.k12.tx.us/
Grade Span: PK-12; **Agency Type:** 1
Schools: 5
1 Primary; 2 Middle; 1 High; 0 Other Level
4 Regular; 0 Special Education; 0 Vocational; 0 Alternative
0 Magnet; 0 Charter; 4 Title I Eligible; 4 School-wide Title I
Students: 1,679 (52.1% male; 47.9% female)
Individual Education Program: 180 (10.7%);
English Language Learner: 217 (12.9%); Migrant: 13 (0.8%)
Eligible for Free Lunch Program: 939 (55.9%)
Eligible for Reduced-Price Lunch Program: 134 (8.0%)
Teachers: 131.0 (12.8 to 1)
Librarians/Media Specialists: 2.6 (645.8 to 1)
Guidance Counselors: 3.2 (524.7 to 1)
Current Spending: ($ per student per year):
Total: $7,627; Instruction: $4,824; Support Services: $2,426
Enrollment, Drop-out Rates and Diploma Recipients by Race/Ethnicity

Category	Total	White	Black	Asian	AIAN	Hisp.
Enrollment (%)	100.0	28.5	4.2	13.7	0.3	53.3
Drop-out Rate (%)	4.1	1.8	0.0	3.5	n/a	6.5
H.S. Diplomas (#)	113	41	4	25	0	43

Maverick County

Eagle Pass ISD

1420 Eidson Rd • Eagle Pass, TX 78852-5604
(830) 773-5126 • http://www.eagle-pass.k12.tx.us/
Grade Span: PK-12; **Agency Type:** 1
Schools: 24
18 Primary; 2 Middle; 3 High; 1 Other Level

22 Regular; 0 Special Education; 0 Vocational; 2 Alternative
0 Magnet; 0 Charter; 24 Title I Eligible; 24 School-wide Title I
Students: 13,011 (51.2% male; 48.8% female)
Individual Education Program: 1,056 (8.1%);
English Language Learner: 4,638 (35.6%); Migrant: 2,250 (17.3%)
Eligible for Free Lunch Program: 9,546 (73.4%)
Eligible for Reduced-Price Lunch Program: 1,016 (7.8%)
Teachers: 761.2 (17.1 to 1)
Librarians/Media Specialists: 3.3 (3,942.7 to 1)
Guidance Counselors: 29.8 (436.6 to 1)
Current Spending: ($ per student per year):
Total: $6,102; Instruction: $3,740; Support Services: $1,924
Enrollment, Drop-out Rates and Diploma Recipients by Race/Ethnicity

Category	Total	White	Black	Asian	AIAN	Hisp.
Enrollment (%)	100.0	1.2	0.0	0.2	1.4	97.1
Drop-out Rate (%)	3.6	1.7	n/a	0.0	17.9	3.6
H.S. Diplomas (#)	582	12	0	2	1	567

Mclennan County

China Spring ISD
6301 Sylvia St • Waco, TX 76708-5817
Mailing Address: PO Box 250 • China Spring, TX 76633-0250
(254) 836-1115
Grade Span: PK-12; **Agency Type:** 1
Schools: 8
1 Primary; 2 Middle; 4 High; 1 Other Level
4 Regular; 2 Special Education; 0 Vocational; 2 Alternative
0 Magnet; 0 Charter; 2 Title I Eligible; 2 School-wide Title I
Students: 1,758 (47.2% male; 52.8% female)
Individual Education Program: 315 (17.9%);
English Language Learner: 15 (0.9%); Migrant: 0 (0.0%)
Eligible for Free Lunch Program: 203 (11.5%)
Eligible for Reduced-Price Lunch Program: 127 (7.2%)
Teachers: 107.2 (16.4 to 1)
Librarians/Media Specialists: 2.0 (879.0 to 1)
Guidance Counselors: 4.0 (439.5 to 1)
Current Spending: ($ per student per year):
Total: $6,061; Instruction: $4,104; Support Services: $1,668
Enrollment, Drop-out Rates and Diploma Recipients by Race/Ethnicity

Category	Total	White	Black	Asian	AIAN	Hisp.
Enrollment (%)	100.0	87.8	1.0	0.4	1.5	9.3
Drop-out Rate (%)	0.8	0.8	0.0	0.0	0.0	0.0
H.S. Diplomas (#)	123	115	1	0	0	7

Connally ISD
715 N Rita St • Waco, TX 76705-1199
(254) 799-2426 • http://www.connally.org/
Grade Span: PK-12; **Agency Type:** 1
Schools: 8
3 Primary; 2 Middle; 1 High; 2 Other Level
6 Regular; 0 Special Education; 0 Vocational; 2 Alternative
0 Magnet; 0 Charter; 6 Title I Eligible; 6 School-wide Title I
Students: 2,560 (54.0% male; 46.0% female)
Individual Education Program: 403 (15.7%);
English Language Learner: 58 (2.3%); Migrant: 5 (0.2%)
Eligible for Free Lunch Program: 1,115 (43.6%)
Eligible for Reduced-Price Lunch Program: 275 (10.7%)
Teachers: 187.2 (13.7 to 1)
Librarians/Media Specialists: 2.0 (1,280.0 to 1)
Guidance Counselors: 6.4 (400.0 to 1)
Current Spending: ($ per student per year):
Total: $6,460; Instruction: $4,026; Support Services: $2,102
Enrollment, Drop-out Rates and Diploma Recipients by Race/Ethnicity

Category	Total	White	Black	Asian	AIAN	Hisp.
Enrollment (%)	100.0	58.8	20.7	0.9	0.6	18.9
Drop-out Rate (%)	3.6	3.0	3.4	0.0	0.0	6.5
H.S. Diplomas (#)	147	92	26	2	1	26

La Vega ISD
3100 Bellmead Dr • Waco, TX 76705-3096
(254) 799-4963 • http://www.lavegaisd.org/
Grade Span: PK-12; **Agency Type:** 1
Schools: 8
2 Primary; 2 Middle; 2 High; 2 Other Level
5 Regular; 0 Special Education; 0 Vocational; 3 Alternative
0 Magnet; 0 Charter; 4 Title I Eligible; 4 School-wide Title I
Students: 2,529 (50.7% male; 49.3% female)
Individual Education Program: 376 (14.9%);
English Language Learner: 176 (7.0%); Migrant: 51 (2.0%)
Eligible for Free Lunch Program: 1,496 (59.2%)
Eligible for Reduced-Price Lunch Program: 304 (12.0%)
Teachers: 184.8 (13.7 to 1)
Librarians/Media Specialists: 4.0 (632.3 to 1)
Guidance Counselors: 7.0 (361.3 to 1)
Current Spending: ($ per student per year):
Total: $7,167; Instruction: $4,114; Support Services: $2,623
Enrollment, Drop-out Rates and Diploma Recipients by Race/Ethnicity

Category	Total	White	Black	Asian	AIAN	Hisp.
Enrollment (%)	100.0	42.6	23.6	1.1	0.2	32.5
Drop-out Rate (%)	9.0	10.6	8.4	0.0	100.0	6.2
H.S. Diplomas (#)	127	57	41	2	0	27

Lorena ISD
Lorena Isd • Lorena, TX 76655-9656
Mailing Address: PO Box 97 • Lorena, TX 76655-0097
(254) 857-3239
Grade Span: PK-12; **Agency Type:** 1
Schools: 4
1 Primary; 1 Middle; 2 High; 0 Other Level
3 Regular; 0 Special Education; 0 Vocational; 1 Alternative
0 Magnet; 0 Charter; 1 Title I Eligible; 0 School-wide Title I
Students: 1,591 (54.4% male; 45.6% female)
Individual Education Program: 274 (17.2%);
English Language Learner: 9 (0.6%); Migrant: 0 (0.0%)
Eligible for Free Lunch Program: 184 (11.6%)
Eligible for Reduced-Price Lunch Program: 68 (4.3%)
Teachers: 91.7 (17.4 to 1)
Librarians/Media Specialists: 2.0 (795.5 to 1)
Guidance Counselors: 2.5 (636.4 to 1)
Current Spending: ($ per student per year):
Total: $4,846; Instruction: $3,144; Support Services: $1,416
Enrollment, Drop-out Rates and Diploma Recipients by Race/Ethnicity

Category	Total	White	Black	Asian	AIAN	Hisp.
Enrollment (%)	100.0	89.9	1.0	0.3	0.3	8.5
Drop-out Rate (%)	1.0	0.7	0.0	0.0	0.0	6.5
H.S. Diplomas (#)	101	87	1	0	1	12

Midway ISD
901 Old Hewitt Rd • Hewitt, TX 76643-2967
Mailing Address: 1205 Foundation Dr • Waco, TX 76712-6899
(254) 761-5610
Grade Span: PK-12; **Agency Type:** 1
Schools: 9
5 Primary; 1 Middle; 1 High; 2 Other Level
8 Regular; 0 Special Education; 0 Vocational; 1 Alternative
0 Magnet; 0 Charter; 4 Title I Eligible; 1 School-wide Title I
Students: 5,786 (51.5% male; 48.5% female)
Individual Education Program: 571 (9.9%);
English Language Learner: 90 (1.6%); Migrant: 0 (0.0%)
Eligible for Free Lunch Program: 572 (9.9%)
Eligible for Reduced-Price Lunch Program: 299 (5.2%)
Teachers: 354.9 (16.3 to 1)
Librarians/Media Specialists: 8.9 (650.1 to 1)
Guidance Counselors: 14.1 (410.4 to 1)
Current Spending: ($ per student per year):
Total: $5,384; Instruction: $3,493; Support Services: $1,670
Enrollment, Drop-out Rates and Diploma Recipients by Race/Ethnicity

Category	Total	White	Black	Asian	AIAN	Hisp.
Enrollment (%)	100.0	77.3	8.0	3.3	0.3	11.2
Drop-out Rate (%)	2.2	2.2	2.0	0.0	25.0	2.7
H.S. Diplomas (#)	382	310	20	13	1	38

Robinson ISD
500 W Lyndale Ave • Robinson, TX 76706-5505
(254) 662-0194
Grade Span: PK-12; **Agency Type:** 1
Schools: 7
2 Primary; 2 Middle; 2 High; 1 Other Level
5 Regular; 0 Special Education; 0 Vocational; 2 Alternative
0 Magnet; 0 Charter; 5 Title I Eligible; 5 School-wide Title I
Students: 2,026 (53.1% male; 46.9% female)
Individual Education Program: 331 (16.3%);
English Language Learner: 15 (0.7%); Migrant: 5 (0.2%)
Eligible for Free Lunch Program: 261 (12.9%)
Eligible for Reduced-Price Lunch Program: 145 (7.2%)
Teachers: 156.0 (13.0 to 1)
Librarians/Media Specialists: 1.1 (1,841.8 to 1)
Guidance Counselors: 6.1 (332.1 to 1)
Current Spending: ($ per student per year):
Total: $5,976; Instruction: $3,842; Support Services: $1,893
Enrollment, Drop-out Rates and Diploma Recipients by Race/Ethnicity

Category	Total	White	Black	Asian	AIAN	Hisp.
Enrollment (%)	100.0	83.4	3.8	0.3	0.1	12.4
Drop-out Rate (%)	2.3	2.0	7.1	n/a	n/a	2.5
H.S. Diplomas (#)	153	119	8	0	0	26

Waco ISD
501 Franklin • Waco, TX 76701-0027
Mailing Address: PO Box 27 • Waco, TX 76703-0027
(254) 755-9420
Grade Span: PK-12; **Agency Type:** 1
Schools: 36
20 Primary; 7 Middle; 3 High; 5 Other Level
31 Regular; 0 Special Education; 0 Vocational; 4 Alternative
0 Magnet; 0 Charter; 32 Title I Eligible; 30 School-wide Title I
Students: 15,758 (50.9% male; 49.1% female)
Individual Education Program: 2,320 (14.7%);
English Language Learner: 1,721 (10.9%); Migrant: 0 (0.0%)
Eligible for Free Lunch Program: 11,064 (70.2%)
Eligible for Reduced-Price Lunch Program: 1,453 (9.2%)
Teachers: 1,063.1 (14.8 to 1)
Librarians/Media Specialists: 17.0 (926.9 to 1)
Guidance Counselors: 42.4 (371.7 to 1)
Current Spending: ($ per student per year):
Total: $6,267; Instruction: $3,674; Support Services: $2,195
Enrollment, Drop-out Rates and Diploma Recipients by Race/Ethnicity

Category	Total	White	Black	Asian	AIAN	Hisp.
Enrollment (%)	100.0	17.7	37.7	0.4	0.1	44.1
Drop-out Rate (%)	8.9	6.6	10.1	4.3	0.0	9.1
H.S. Diplomas (#)	588	120	232	2	1	233

West ISD
801 N Reagan • West, TX 76691-1198
(254) 826-7500
Grade Span: PK-12; **Agency Type:** 1
Schools: 8
1 Primary; 2 Middle; 2 High; 3 Other Level
4 Regular; 0 Special Education; 0 Vocational; 4 Alternative
0 Magnet; 0 Charter; 2 Title I Eligible; 2 School-wide Title I
Students: 1,540 (55.6% male; 44.4% female)
Individual Education Program: 358 (23.2%);
English Language Learner: 36 (2.3%); Migrant: 24 (1.6%)
Eligible for Free Lunch Program: 414 (26.9%)
Eligible for Reduced-Price Lunch Program: 105 (6.8%)
Teachers: 96.5 (16.0 to 1)
Librarians/Media Specialists: 3.0 (513.3 to 1)
Guidance Counselors: 2.0 (770.0 to 1)
Current Spending: ($ per student per year):
Total: $5,412; Instruction: $3,265; Support Services: $1,810
Enrollment, Drop-out Rates and Diploma Recipients by Race/Ethnicity

Category	Total	White	Black	Asian	AIAN	Hisp.
Enrollment (%)	100.0	86.6	3.1	0.0	0.5	9.8
Drop-out Rate (%)	0.7	0.8	0.0	n/a	0.0	0.0
H.S. Diplomas (#)	140	131	3	0	0	6

Medina County

Devine ISD
205 W College • Devine, TX 78016-6080
(830) 663-3611
Grade Span: PK-12; **Agency Type:** 1
Schools: 5
2 Primary; 1 Middle; 1 High; 1 Other Level
4 Regular; 0 Special Education; 0 Vocational; 1 Alternative
0 Magnet; 0 Charter; 3 Title I Eligible; 3 School-wide Title I
Students: 1,899 (51.7% male; 48.3% female)
Individual Education Program: 226 (11.9%);
English Language Learner: 54 (2.8%); Migrant: 4 (0.2%)
Eligible for Free Lunch Program: 800 (42.1%)
Eligible for Reduced-Price Lunch Program: 199 (10.5%)
Teachers: 135.4 (14.0 to 1)
Librarians/Media Specialists: 2.0 (949.5 to 1)
Guidance Counselors: 5.0 (379.8 to 1)
Current Spending: ($ per student per year):
Total: $6,224; Instruction: $4,078; Support Services: $1,880
Enrollment, Drop-out Rates and Diploma Recipients by Race/Ethnicity

Category	Total	White	Black	Asian	AIAN	Hisp.
Enrollment (%)	100.0	47.7	0.7	0.0	0.3	51.3
Drop-out Rate (%)	3.3	4.0	0.0	0.0	0.0	2.7
H.S. Diplomas (#)	139	75	2	1	3	58

Hondo ISD
2604 Ave E • Hondo, TX 78861-3137
Mailing Address: PO Box 308 • Hondo, TX 78861-0308
(830) 426-3027
Grade Span: PK-12; **Agency Type:** 1
Schools: 5
2 Primary; 1 Middle; 1 High; 1 Other Level
4 Regular; 0 Special Education; 0 Vocational; 1 Alternative
0 Magnet; 0 Charter; 4 Title I Eligible; 4 School-wide Title I
Students: 2,181 (52.2% male; 47.8% female)
Individual Education Program: 252 (11.6%);
English Language Learner: 94 (4.3%); Migrant: 10 (0.5%)
Eligible for Free Lunch Program: 665 (30.5%)
Eligible for Reduced-Price Lunch Program: 218 (10.0%)
Teachers: 176.8 (12.3 to 1)
Librarians/Media Specialists: 3.0 (727.0 to 1)
Guidance Counselors: 5.9 (369.7 to 1)
Current Spending: ($ per student per year):
Total: $6,381; Instruction: $4,165; Support Services: $1,954
Enrollment, Drop-out Rates and Diploma Recipients by Race/Ethnicity

Category	Total	White	Black	Asian	AIAN	Hisp.
Enrollment (%)	100.0	35.1	1.9	0.4	0.1	62.4
Drop-out Rate (%)	2.1	0.4	20.0	0.0	n/a	3.1
H.S. Diplomas (#)	125	61	1	1	0	62

Medina Valley ISD
8449 F M 471 S • Castroville, TX 78009-9531
(830) 931-2243
Grade Span: PK-12; **Agency Type:** 1
Schools: 6
3 Primary; 1 Middle; 1 High; 1 Other Level
5 Regular; 0 Special Education; 0 Vocational; 1 Alternative
0 Magnet; 0 Charter; 3 Title I Eligible; 3 School-wide Title I
Students: 3,018 (53.6% male; 46.4% female)
Individual Education Program: 396 (13.1%);
English Language Learner: 142 (4.7%); Migrant: 84 (2.8%)
Eligible for Free Lunch Program: 1,086 (36.0%)
Eligible for Reduced-Price Lunch Program: 275 (9.1%)
Teachers: 183.7 (16.4 to 1)
Librarians/Media Specialists: 1.0 (3,018.0 to 1)
Guidance Counselors: 7.0 (431.1 to 1)
Current Spending: ($ per student per year):
Total: $6,192; Instruction: $3,545; Support Services: $2,262
Enrollment, Drop-out Rates and Diploma Recipients by Race/Ethnicity

Category	Total	White	Black	Asian	AIAN	Hisp.
Enrollment (%)	100.0	47.8	1.4	0.6	0.6	49.6
Drop-out Rate (%)	1.9	2.1	0.0	0.0	0.0	1.8
H.S. Diplomas (#)	202	116	1	0	2	83

Midland County

Greenwood ISD
2700 Fm 1379 • Midland, TX 79706-5330
(915) 685-7800
Grade Span: PK-12; **Agency Type:** 1
Schools: 4
1 Primary; 2 Middle; 1 High; 0 Other Level
4 Regular; 0 Special Education; 0 Vocational; 0 Alternative
0 Magnet; 0 Charter; 3 Title I Eligible; 0 School-wide Title I
Students: 1,535 (52.2% male; 47.8% female)
Individual Education Program: 187 (12.2%);
English Language Learner: 71 (4.6%); Migrant: 1 (0.1%)
Eligible for Free Lunch Program: 299 (19.5%)
Eligible for Reduced-Price Lunch Program: 102 (6.6%)
Teachers: 100.6 (15.3 to 1)
Librarians/Media Specialists: 2.0 (767.5 to 1)
Guidance Counselors: 3.0 (511.7 to 1)
Current Spending: ($ per student per year):
Total: $5,466; Instruction: $3,688; Support Services: $1,546
Enrollment, Drop-out Rates and Diploma Recipients by Race/Ethnicity

Category	Total	White	Black	Asian	AIAN	Hisp.
Enrollment (%)	100.0	73.0	0.7	0.5	0.2	25.6
Drop-out Rate (%)	1.7	1.6	0.0	0.0	n/a	2.4
H.S. Diplomas (#)	133	115	0	0	0	18

Midland ISD
615 W Missouri Ave • Midland, TX 79701-5017
(915) 689-1000
Grade Span: PK-12; **Agency Type:** 1
Schools: 36
25 Primary; 5 Middle; 4 High; 2 Other Level
34 Regular; 0 Special Education; 0 Vocational; 2 Alternative
0 Magnet; 0 Charter; 16 Title I Eligible; 16 School-wide Title I
Students: 20,777 (50.5% male; 49.5% female)
Individual Education Program: 2,133 (10.3%);
English Language Learner: 1,804 (8.7%); Migrant: 369 (1.8%)
Eligible for Free Lunch Program: 8,536 (41.1%)
Eligible for Reduced-Price Lunch Program: 1,383 (6.7%)
Teachers: 1,402.0 (14.8 to 1)
Librarians/Media Specialists: 36.2 (574.0 to 1)
Guidance Counselors: 62.5 (332.4 to 1)
Current Spending: ($ per student per year):
Total: $6,286; Instruction: $3,897; Support Services: $2,061

Enrollment, Drop-out Rates and Diploma Recipients by Race/Ethnicity

Category	Total	White	Black	Asian	AIAN	Hisp.
Enrollment (%)	100.0	44.5	9.8	0.9	0.4	44.4
Drop-out Rate (%)	5.5	3.4	9.0	4.4	11.8	7.9
H.S. Diplomas (#)	1,207	716	97	10	9	375

Milam County

Cameron ISD

304 E 12th • Cameron, TX 76520-2751
Mailing Address: Box 712 • Cameron, TX 76520-0712
(254) 697-3512
Grade Span: PK-12; **Agency Type:** 1
Schools: 4
2 Primary; 1 Middle; 1 High; 0 Other Level
4 Regular; 0 Special Education; 0 Vocational; 0 Alternative
0 Magnet; 0 Charter; 4 Title I Eligible; 4 School-wide Title I
Students: 1,662 (53.4% male; 46.6% female)
Individual Education Program: 214 (12.9%);
English Language Learner: 111 (6.7%); Migrant: 24 (1.4%)
Eligible for Free Lunch Program: 893 (53.7%)
Eligible for Reduced-Price Lunch Program: 131 (7.9%)
Teachers: 134.8 (12.3 to 1)
Librarians/Media Specialists: 3.1 (536.1 to 1)
Guidance Counselors: 4.6 (361.3 to 1)
Current Spending: ($ per student per year):
Total: $6,245; Instruction: $4,176; Support Services: $1,764

Enrollment, Drop-out Rates and Diploma Recipients by Race/Ethnicity

Category	Total	White	Black	Asian	AIAN	Hisp.
Enrollment (%)	100.0	43.9	20.4	0.1	0.0	35.6
Drop-out Rate (%)	2.1	1.5	0.0	0.0	n/a	4.5
H.S. Diplomas (#)	119	67	14	1	0	37

Rockdale ISD

520 Davilla • Rockdale, TX 76567-0632
Mailing Address: PO Box 632 • Rockdale, TX 76567-0632
(512) 430-6000
Grade Span: PK-12; **Agency Type:** 1
Schools: 4
1 Primary; 1 Middle; 1 High; 0 Other Level
3 Regular; 0 Special Education; 0 Vocational; 0 Alternative
0 Magnet; 0 Charter; 1 Title I Eligible; 1 School-wide Title I
Students: 1,895 (52.1% male; 47.9% female)
Individual Education Program: 323 (17.0%);
English Language Learner: 90 (4.7%); Migrant: 0 (0.0%)
Eligible for Free Lunch Program: 818 (43.2%)
Eligible for Reduced-Price Lunch Program: 118 (6.2%)
Teachers: 120.9 (15.7 to 1)
Librarians/Media Specialists: 1.0 (1,895.0 to 1)
Guidance Counselors: 4.0 (473.8 to 1)
Current Spending: ($ per student per year):
Total: $6,375; Instruction: $3,810; Support Services: $2,291

Enrollment, Drop-out Rates and Diploma Recipients by Race/Ethnicity

Category	Total	White	Black	Asian	AIAN	Hisp.
Enrollment (%)	100.0	57.4	14.5	0.3	0.1	27.7
Drop-out Rate (%)	3.3	2.6	4.4	0.0	0.0	4.1
H.S. Diplomas (#)	96	58	14	0	0	24

Montague County

Bowie ISD

100 W Wichita St • Bowie, TX 76230-1168
Mailing Address: PO Box 1168 • Bowie, TX 76230-1168
(940) 872-1151 • http://www.esc9.net/bowie/
Grade Span: PK-12; **Agency Type:** 1
Schools: 4
2 Primary; 1 Middle; 1 High; 0 Other Level
4 Regular; 0 Special Education; 0 Vocational; 0 Alternative
0 Magnet; 0 Charter; 3 Title I Eligible; 3 School-wide Title I
Students: 1,679 (51.2% male; 48.8% female)
Individual Education Program: 217 (12.9%);
English Language Learner: 41 (2.4%); Migrant: 89 (5.3%)
Eligible for Free Lunch Program: 513 (30.6%)
Eligible for Reduced-Price Lunch Program: 142 (8.5%)
Teachers: 119.6 (14.0 to 1)
Librarians/Media Specialists: 3.0 (559.7 to 1)
Guidance Counselors: 4.0 (419.8 to 1)
Current Spending: ($ per student per year):
Total: $6,630; Instruction: $3,921; Support Services: $2,483

Enrollment, Drop-out Rates and Diploma Recipients by Race/Ethnicity

Category	Total	White	Black	Asian	AIAN	Hisp.
Enrollment (%)	100.0	90.1	0.1	0.2	0.8	8.8
Drop-out Rate (%)	1.7	1.4	n/a	n/a	n/a	8.0
H.S. Diplomas (#)	97	93	0	0	0	4

Montgomery County

Conroe ISD

3205 W Davis • Conroe, TX 77304
(936) 756-7751 • http://www.conroe.isd.tenet.edu/
Grade Span: PK-12; **Agency Type:** 1
Schools: 45
23 Primary; 13 Middle; 5 High; 4 Other Level
42 Regular; 1 Special Education; 0 Vocational; 2 Alternative
0 Magnet; 0 Charter; 14 Title I Eligible; 12 School-wide Title I
Students: 38,016 (51.4% male; 48.6% female)
Individual Education Program: 4,019 (10.6%);
English Language Learner: 3,528 (9.3%); Migrant: 27 (0.1%)
Eligible for Free Lunch Program: 8,726 (23.0%)
Eligible for Reduced-Price Lunch Program: 1,496 (3.9%)
Teachers: 2,512.0 (15.1 to 1)
Librarians/Media Specialists: 46.7 (814.0 to 1)
Guidance Counselors: 84.3 (451.0 to 1)
Current Spending: ($ per student per year):
Total: $5,883; Instruction: $3,599; Support Services: $2,104

Enrollment, Drop-out Rates and Diploma Recipients by Race/Ethnicity

Category	Total	White	Black	Asian	AIAN	Hisp.
Enrollment (%)	100.0	72.4	5.3	2.2	0.5	19.6
Drop-out Rate (%)	2.5	1.9	5.0	1.0	3.7	5.7
H.S. Diplomas (#)	2,202	1,753	99	65	6	279

Magnolia ISD

829 S Magnolia St • Magnolia, TX 77355-8547
Mailing Address: PO Box 88 • Magnolia, TX 77353-0088
(281) 356-3571 • http://www.magnoliaisd.org/
Grade Span: PK-12; **Agency Type:** 1
Schools: 14
6 Primary; 4 Middle; 2 High; 2 Other Level
11 Regular; 0 Special Education; 0 Vocational; 3 Alternative
0 Magnet; 0 Charter; 4 Title I Eligible; 4 School-wide Title I
Students: 8,557 (52.5% male; 47.5% female)
Individual Education Program: 978 (11.4%);
English Language Learner: 579 (6.8%); Migrant: 0 (0.0%)
Eligible for Free Lunch Program: 2,159 (25.2%)
Eligible for Reduced-Price Lunch Program: 476 (5.6%)
Teachers: 579.9 (14.8 to 1)
Librarians/Media Specialists: 8.2 (1,043.5 to 1)
Guidance Counselors: 17.1 (500.4 to 1)
Current Spending: ($ per student per year):
Total: $6,080; Instruction: $3,633; Support Services: $2,168

Enrollment, Drop-out Rates and Diploma Recipients by Race/Ethnicity

Category	Total	White	Black	Asian	AIAN	Hisp.
Enrollment (%)	100.0	81.3	3.0	0.4	0.3	15.0
Drop-out Rate (%)	2.4	2.2	5.7	12.5	0.0	3.1
H.S. Diplomas (#)	428	370	6	4	1	47

Montgomery ISD

13159 Walden Rd • Montgomery, TX 77356-1475
Mailing Address: PO Box 1475 • Montgomery, TX 77356-1475
(936) 582-1333
Grade Span: PK-12; **Agency Type:** 1
Schools: 7
1 Primary; 2 Middle; 1 High; 2 Other Level
5 Regular; 0 Special Education; 0 Vocational; 1 Alternative
0 Magnet; 0 Charter; 3 Title I Eligible; 0 School-wide Title I
Students: 4,178 (51.5% male; 48.5% female)
Individual Education Program: 487 (11.7%);
English Language Learner: 97 (2.3%); Migrant: 0 (0.0%)
Eligible for Free Lunch Program: 817 (19.6%)
Eligible for Reduced-Price Lunch Program: 189 (4.5%)
Teachers: 277.0 (15.1 to 1)
Librarians/Media Specialists: 5.0 (835.6 to 1)
Guidance Counselors: 7.0 (596.9 to 1)
Current Spending: ($ per student per year):
Total: $6,752; Instruction: $4,083; Support Services: $2,308

Enrollment, Drop-out Rates and Diploma Recipients by Race/Ethnicity

Category	Total	White	Black	Asian	AIAN	Hisp.
Enrollment (%)	100.0	85.5	6.8	0.8	0.2	6.6
Drop-out Rate (%)	2.5	2.7	1.4	0.0	0.0	0.0
H.S. Diplomas (#)	204	186	14	1	0	3

New Caney ISD

21580 Loop 494 • New Caney, TX 77357-9115
(281) 354-1166
Grade Span: PK-12; **Agency Type:** 1
Schools: 11
4 Primary; 2 Middle; 1 High; 4 Other Level
9 Regular; 0 Special Education; 0 Vocational; 2 Alternative
0 Magnet; 0 Charter; 7 Title I Eligible; 7 School-wide Title I
Students: 7,035 (51.8% male; 48.2% female)

Individual Education Program: 981 (13.9%);
English Language Learner: 518 (7.4%); Migrant: 19 (0.3%)
Eligible for Free Lunch Program: 2,467 (35.1%)
Eligible for Reduced-Price Lunch Program: 631 (9.0%)
Teachers: 465.8 (15.1 to 1)
Librarians/Media Specialists: 8.0 (879.4 to 1)
Guidance Counselors: 15.3 (459.8 to 1)
Current Spending: ($ per student per year):
Total: $5,731; Instruction: $3,304; Support Services: $2,069
Enrollment, Drop-out Rates and Diploma Recipients by Race/Ethnicity

Category	Total	White	Black	Asian	AIAN	Hisp.
Enrollment (%)	100.0	75.5	2.5	0.6	0.3	21.1
Drop-out Rate (%)	3.8	4.0	2.6	0.0	0.0	3.1
H.S. Diplomas (#)	277	238	7	1	1	30

Splendora ISD
23419 Fm 2090 • Splendora, TX 77372-6210
(281) 689-3129
Grade Span: PK-12; **Agency Type:** 1
Schools: 5
2 Primary; 1 Middle; 1 High; 0 Other Level
4 Regular; 0 Special Education; 0 Vocational; 0 Alternative
0 Magnet; 0 Charter; 4 Title I Eligible; 4 School-wide Title I
Students: 3,022 (51.5% male; 48.5% female)
Individual Education Program: 255 (8.4%);
English Language Learner: 110 (3.6%); Migrant: 4 (0.1%)
Eligible for Free Lunch Program: 1,102 (36.5%)
Eligible for Reduced-Price Lunch Program: 331 (11.0%)
Teachers: 204.2 (14.8 to 1)
Librarians/Media Specialists: 4.0 (755.5 to 1)
Guidance Counselors: 8.0 (377.8 to 1)
Current Spending: ($ per student per year):
Total: $6,153; Instruction: $3,868; Support Services: $1,950
Enrollment, Drop-out Rates and Diploma Recipients by Race/Ethnicity

Category	Total	White	Black	Asian	AIAN	Hisp.
Enrollment (%)	100.0	87.4	0.7	0.2	0.3	11.4
Drop-out Rate (%)	5.0	5.2	0.0	n/a	n/a	3.0
H.S. Diplomas (#)	125	110	1	0	0	14

Willis ISD
204 W Rogers St • Willis, TX 77378-9239
(936) 856-1200
Grade Span: PK-12; **Agency Type:** 1
Schools: 9
4 Primary; 2 Middle; 3 High; 0 Other Level
7 Regular; 0 Special Education; 0 Vocational; 2 Alternative
0 Magnet; 0 Charter; 5 Title I Eligible; 5 School-wide Title I
Students: 4,640 (51.3% male; 48.7% female)
Individual Education Program: 550 (11.9%);
English Language Learner: 407 (8.8%); Migrant: 5 (0.1%)
Eligible for Free Lunch Program: 1,648 (35.5%)
Eligible for Reduced-Price Lunch Program: 401 (8.6%)
Teachers: 292.7 (15.9 to 1)
Librarians/Media Specialists: 6.0 (773.3 to 1)
Guidance Counselors: 11.3 (410.6 to 1)
Current Spending: ($ per student per year):
Total: $5,990; Instruction: $3,231; Support Services: $2,464
Enrollment, Drop-out Rates and Diploma Recipients by Race/Ethnicity

Category	Total	White	Black	Asian	AIAN	Hisp.
Enrollment (%)	100.0	71.0	7.7	0.3	0.6	20.4
Drop-out Rate (%)	3.0	2.4	5.6	0.0	0.0	5.6
H.S. Diplomas (#)	259	205	23	1	0	30

Moore County

Dumas ISD
421 W 4th St • Dumas, TX 79029-0615
Mailing Address: PO Box 615 • Dumas, TX 79029-0615
(806) 935-6461 • http://www.dumas-k12.net/
Grade Span: PK-12; **Agency Type:** 1
Schools: 8
5 Primary; 1 Middle; 2 High; 0 Other Level
7 Regular; 0 Special Education; 0 Vocational; 1 Alternative
0 Magnet; 0 Charter; 6 Title I Eligible; 6 School-wide Title I
Students: 4,124 (51.9% male; 48.1% female)
Individual Education Program: 421 (10.2%);
English Language Learner: 1,062 (25.8%); Migrant: 2,001 (48.5%)
Eligible for Free Lunch Program: 1,889 (45.8%)
Eligible for Reduced-Price Lunch Program: 335 (8.1%)
Teachers: 289.7 (14.2 to 1)
Librarians/Media Specialists: 7.0 (589.1 to 1)
Guidance Counselors: 8.0 (515.5 to 1)
Current Spending: ($ per student per year):
Total: $5,621; Instruction: $3,669; Support Services: $1,700

Enrollment, Drop-out Rates and Diploma Recipients by Race/Ethnicity

Category	Total	White	Black	Asian	AIAN	Hisp.
Enrollment (%)	100.0	31.9	0.8	1.1	0.4	65.8
Drop-out Rate (%)	1.4	0.6	9.1	0.0	0.0	2.0
H.S. Diplomas (#)	243	111	2	3	0	127

Morris County

Daingerfield-Lone Star ISD
200 Tiger Dr • Daingerfield, TX 75638-0851
(903) 645-2239
Grade Span: PK-12; **Agency Type:** 1
Schools: 5
3 Primary; 1 Middle; 1 High; 0 Other Level
5 Regular; 0 Special Education; 0 Vocational; 0 Alternative
0 Magnet; 0 Charter; 5 Title I Eligible; 5 School-wide Title I
Students: 1,595 (53.0% male; 47.0% female)
Individual Education Program: 220 (13.8%);
English Language Learner: 43 (2.7%); Migrant: 76 (4.8%)
Eligible for Free Lunch Program: 808 (50.7%)
Eligible for Reduced-Price Lunch Program: 140 (8.8%)
Teachers: 131.1 (12.2 to 1)
Librarians/Media Specialists: 3.2 (498.4 to 1)
Guidance Counselors: 5.0 (319.0 to 1)
Current Spending: ($ per student per year):
Total: $7,665; Instruction: $4,691; Support Services: $2,585
Enrollment, Drop-out Rates and Diploma Recipients by Race/Ethnicity

Category	Total	White	Black	Asian	AIAN	Hisp.
Enrollment (%)	100.0	51.5	40.9	0.2	0.3	7.1
Drop-out Rate (%)	5.6	5.1	5.6	n/a	0.0	13.6
H.S. Diplomas (#)	89	53	29	0	1	6

Nacogdoches County

Nacogdoches ISD
511 S University Dr • Nacogdoches, TX 75961-5199
Mailing Address: PO Drawer 631521 • Nacogdoches, TX 75963-1521
(936) 569-5000 • http://www.nacogdoches.k12.tx.us/
Grade Span: PK-12; **Agency Type:** 1
Schools: 11
6 Primary; 2 Middle; 0 High; 2 Other Level
9 Regular; 0 Special Education; 0 Vocational; 1 Alternative
0 Magnet; 0 Charter; 7 Title I Eligible; 7 School-wide Title I
Students: 6,313 (51.3% male; 48.7% female)
Individual Education Program: 563 (8.9%);
English Language Learner: 1,005 (15.9%); Migrant: 160 (2.5%)
Eligible for Free Lunch Program: 3,601 (57.0%)
Eligible for Reduced-Price Lunch Program: 435 (6.9%)
Teachers: 428.1 (14.7 to 1)
Librarians/Media Specialists: 6.0 (1,052.2 to 1)
Guidance Counselors: 13.4 (471.1 to 1)
Current Spending: ($ per student per year):
Total: $6,065; Instruction: $3,509; Support Services: $2,183
Enrollment, Drop-out Rates and Diploma Recipients by Race/Ethnicity

Category	Total	White	Black	Asian	AIAN	Hisp.
Enrollment (%)	100.0	37.5	31.6	1.0	0.1	29.8
Drop-out Rate (%)	4.7	2.6	6.1	4.3	0.0	9.0
H.S. Diplomas (#)	399	240	95	8	0	56

Navarro County

Corsicana ISD
601 N 13th St • Corsicana, TX 75110-3298
(903) 874-7441
Grade Span: PK-12; **Agency Type:** 1
Schools: 9
4 Primary; 2 Middle; 1 High; 1 Other Level
8 Regular; 0 Special Education; 0 Vocational; 0 Alternative
0 Magnet; 0 Charter; 6 Title I Eligible; 6 School-wide Title I
Students: 5,476 (50.9% male; 49.1% female)
Individual Education Program: 726 (13.3%);
English Language Learner: 649 (11.9%); Migrant: 183 (3.3%)
Eligible for Free Lunch Program: 2,665 (48.7%)
Eligible for Reduced-Price Lunch Program: 384 (7.0%)
Teachers: 375.8 (14.6 to 1)
Librarians/Media Specialists: 4.0 (1,369.0 to 1)
Guidance Counselors: 14.0 (391.1 to 1)
Current Spending: ($ per student per year):
Total: $6,182; Instruction: $3,801; Support Services: $2,010
Enrollment, Drop-out Rates and Diploma Recipients by Race/Ethnicity

Category	Total	White	Black	Asian	AIAN	Hisp.
Enrollment (%)	100.0	41.5	25.8	1.3	0.3	31.1
Drop-out Rate (%)	4.8	3.7	4.6	0.0	0.0	8.0
H.S. Diplomas (#)	270	137	85	4	0	44

Nolan County

Sweetwater ISD

207 Musgrove St • Sweetwater, TX 79556-5321
(915) 235-8601
Grade Span: PK-12; **Agency Type:** 1
Schools: 7
3 Primary; 2 Middle; 2 High; 0 Other Level
6 Regular; 0 Special Education; 1 Vocational; 0 Alternative
0 Magnet; 0 Charter; 3 Title I Eligible; 3 School-wide Title I
Students: 2,311 (51.6% male; 48.4% female)
Individual Education Program: 380 (16.4%);
English Language Learner: 21 (0.9%); Migrant: 45 (1.9%)
Eligible for Free Lunch Program: 1,102 (47.7%)
Eligible for Reduced-Price Lunch Program: 191 (8.3%)
Teachers: 188.9 (12.2 to 1)
Librarians/Media Specialists: 1.0 (2,311.0 to 1)
Guidance Counselors: 5.0 (462.2 to 1)
Current Spending: ($ per student per year):
Total: $7,054; Instruction: $4,393; Support Services: $2,267
Enrollment, Drop-out Rates and Diploma Recipients by Race/Ethnicity

Category	Total	White	Black	Asian	AIAN	Hisp.
Enrollment (%)	100.0	52.6	8.6	0.0	0.0	38.8
Drop-out Rate (%)	4.8	3.1	11.3	0.0	100.0	5.6
H.S. Diplomas (#)	150	101	7	0	0	42

Nueces County

Calallen ISD

4205 Wildcat Dr • Corpus Christi, TX 78410-5198
(361) 242-5600 • http://www.calallen.k12.tx.us/
Grade Span: PK-12; **Agency Type:** 1
Schools: 7
4 Primary; 1 Middle; 1 High; 1 Other Level
6 Regular; 0 Special Education; 0 Vocational; 1 Alternative
0 Magnet; 0 Charter; 3 Title I Eligible; 3 School-wide Title I
Students: 4,061 (51.3% male; 48.7% female)
Individual Education Program: 495 (12.2%);
English Language Learner: 69 (1.7%); Migrant: 0 (0.0%)
Eligible for Free Lunch Program: 1,084 (26.7%)
Eligible for Reduced-Price Lunch Program: 241 (5.9%)
Teachers: 263.3 (15.4 to 1)
Librarians/Media Specialists: 4.0 (1,015.3 to 1)
Guidance Counselors: 11.0 (369.2 to 1)
Current Spending: ($ per student per year):
Total: $5,868; Instruction: $3,638; Support Services: $1,890
Enrollment, Drop-out Rates and Diploma Recipients by Race/Ethnicity

Category	Total	White	Black	Asian	AIAN	Hisp.
Enrollment (%)	100.0	56.5	1.9	0.5	0.3	40.9
Drop-out Rate (%)	2.5	2.3	5.3	0.0	0.0	3.1
H.S. Diplomas (#)	321	229	4	4	2	82

Corpus Christi ISD

801 Leopard St • Corpus Christi, TX 78401-2421
Mailing Address: PO Box 110 • Corpus Christi, TX 78403-0110
(361) 886-9002 • http://corpuschristiisd.org/
Grade Span: PK-12; **Agency Type:** 1
Schools: 64
41 Primary; 12 Middle; 6 High; 4 Other Level
59 Regular; 0 Special Education; 0 Vocational; 4 Alternative
0 Magnet; 0 Charter; 31 Title I Eligible; 31 School-wide Title I
Students: 39,355 (51.8% male; 48.2% female)
Individual Education Program: 5,644 (14.3%);
English Language Learner: 3,198 (8.1%); Migrant: 729 (1.9%)
Eligible for Free Lunch Program: 18,734 (47.6%)
Eligible for Reduced-Price Lunch Program: 3,516 (8.9%)
Teachers: 2,500.9 (15.7 to 1)
Librarians/Media Specialists: 41.5 (948.3 to 1)
Guidance Counselors: 110.6 (355.8 to 1)
Current Spending: ($ per student per year):
Total: $6,184; Instruction: $3,868; Support Services: $2,057
Enrollment, Drop-out Rates and Diploma Recipients by Race/Ethnicity

Category	Total	White	Black	Asian	AIAN	Hisp.
Enrollment (%)	100.0	20.8	5.6	1.3	0.3	71.9
Drop-out Rate (%)	6.5	3.1	8.1	6.6	0.0	7.8
H.S. Diplomas (#)	2,119	605	130	24	6	1,354

Flour Bluff ISD

2505 Waldron Rd • Corpus Christi, TX 78418-4798
(361) 694-9200 • http://www.flourbluffschools.net/
Grade Span: PK-12; **Agency Type:** 1
Schools: 7
3 Primary; 2 Middle; 1 High; 1 Other Level
6 Regular; 0 Special Education; 0 Vocational; 1 Alternative
0 Magnet; 0 Charter; 4 Title I Eligible; 4 School-wide Title I
Students: 4,991 (50.8% male; 49.2% female)
Individual Education Program: 649 (13.0%);
English Language Learner: 114 (2.3%); Migrant: 5 (0.1%)
Eligible for Free Lunch Program: 1,770 (35.5%)
Eligible for Reduced-Price Lunch Program: 510 (10.2%)
Teachers: 330.9 (15.1 to 1)
Librarians/Media Specialists: 5.0 (998.2 to 1)
Guidance Counselors: 13.1 (381.0 to 1)
Current Spending: ($ per student per year):
Total: $6,001; Instruction: $3,640; Support Services: $2,021
Enrollment, Drop-out Rates and Diploma Recipients by Race/Ethnicity

Category	Total	White	Black	Asian	AIAN	Hisp.
Enrollment (%)	100.0	62.7	6.2	3.5	1.1	26.5
Drop-out Rate (%)	2.7	2.5	5.2	0.0	5.3	3.4
H.S. Diplomas (#)	324	231	15	16	2	60

Robstown ISD

801 N 1st St • Robstown, TX 78380-2608
(361) 767-6600
Grade Span: PK-12; **Agency Type:** 1
Schools: 10
4 Primary; 2 Middle; 2 High; 2 Other Level
7 Regular; 0 Special Education; 0 Vocational; 3 Alternative
0 Magnet; 0 Charter; 8 Title I Eligible; 8 School-wide Title I
Students: 3,996 (52.0% male; 48.0% female)
Individual Education Program: 606 (15.2%);
English Language Learner: 208 (5.2%); Migrant: 3,496 (87.5%)
Eligible for Free Lunch Program: 3,235 (81.0%)
Eligible for Reduced-Price Lunch Program: 264 (6.6%)
Teachers: 284.0 (14.1 to 1)
Librarians/Media Specialists: 5.0 (799.2 to 1)
Guidance Counselors: 15.0 (266.4 to 1)
Current Spending: ($ per student per year):
Total: $6,600; Instruction: $3,882; Support Services: $2,268
Enrollment, Drop-out Rates and Diploma Recipients by Race/Ethnicity

Category	Total	White	Black	Asian	AIAN	Hisp.
Enrollment (%)	100.0	1.3	0.5	0.1	0.1	98.0
Drop-out Rate (%)	5.8	5.3	0.0	n/a	n/a	5.8
H.S. Diplomas (#)	199	3	2	0	0	194

Tuloso-Midway ISD

9760 La Branch • Corpus Christi, TX 78460-0900
Mailing Address: PO Box 10900 • Corpus Christi, TX 78460-0900
(361) 241-3286
Grade Span: PK-12; **Agency Type:** 1
Schools: 6
2 Primary; 1 Middle; 2 High; 1 Other Level
4 Regular; 0 Special Education; 0 Vocational; 2 Alternative
0 Magnet; 0 Charter; 5 Title I Eligible; 0 School-wide Title I
Students: 3,225 (50.0% male; 50.0% female)
Individual Education Program: 370 (11.5%);
English Language Learner: 138 (4.3%); Migrant: 0 (0.0%)
Eligible for Free Lunch Program: 1,308 (40.6%)
Eligible for Reduced-Price Lunch Program: 208 (6.4%)
Teachers: 203.4 (15.9 to 1)
Librarians/Media Specialists: 2.0 (1,612.5 to 1)
Guidance Counselors: 7.7 (418.8 to 1)
Current Spending: ($ per student per year):
Total: $6,090; Instruction: $3,656; Support Services: $2,138
Enrollment, Drop-out Rates and Diploma Recipients by Race/Ethnicity

Category	Total	White	Black	Asian	AIAN	Hisp.
Enrollment (%)	100.0	40.2	1.8	0.5	0.1	57.4
Drop-out Rate (%)	1.7	1.1	0.0	0.0	n/a	2.4
H.S. Diplomas (#)	223	113	9	1	1	99

West Oso ISD

5050 Rockford Dr • Corpus Christi, TX 78416-2530
(361) 855-3321
Grade Span: PK-12; **Agency Type:** 1
Schools: 6
2 Primary; 1 Middle; 1 High; 1 Other Level
4 Regular; 0 Special Education; 0 Vocational; 1 Alternative
0 Magnet; 0 Charter; 4 Title I Eligible; 4 School-wide Title I
Students: 1,872 (51.8% male; 48.2% female)
Individual Education Program: 237 (12.7%);
English Language Learner: 173 (9.2%); Migrant: 41 (2.2%)
Eligible for Free Lunch Program: 942 (50.3%)
Eligible for Reduced-Price Lunch Program: 150 (8.0%)
Teachers: 120.2 (15.6 to 1)
Librarians/Media Specialists: 3.0 (624.0 to 1)
Guidance Counselors: 5.0 (374.4 to 1)
Current Spending: ($ per student per year):
Total: $7,261; Instruction: $4,261; Support Services: $2,629

Enrollment, Drop-out Rates and Diploma Recipients by Race/Ethnicity

Category	Total	White	Black	Asian	AIAN	Hisp.
Enrollment (%)	100.0	2.6	14.5	0.1	0.0	82.7
Drop-out Rate (%)	8.6	6.3	5.6	n/a	0.0	9.5
H.S. Diplomas (#)	56	1	7	0	0	48

Ochiltree County

Perryton ISD

821 SW 17th Ave • Perryton, TX 79070-1048
Mailing Address: PO Box 1048 • Perryton, TX 79070-1048
(806) 435-5478
Grade Span: PK-12; **Agency Type:** 1
Schools: 6
2 Primary; 2 Middle; 2 High; 0 Other Level
5 Regular; 0 Special Education; 0 Vocational; 1 Alternative
0 Magnet; 0 Charter; 5 Title I Eligible; 5 School-wide Title I
Students: 1,976 (51.3% male; 48.7% female)
Individual Education Program: 183 (9.3%);
English Language Learner: 346 (17.5%); Migrant: 324 (16.4%)
Eligible for Free Lunch Program: 885 (44.8%)
Eligible for Reduced-Price Lunch Program: 210 (10.6%)
Teachers: 153.2 (12.9 to 1)
Librarians/Media Specialists: 1.3 (1,520.0 to 1)
Guidance Counselors: 3.2 (617.5 to 1)
Current Spending: ($ per student per year):
Total: $6,220; Instruction: $4,205; Support Services: $1,726
Enrollment, Drop-out Rates and Diploma Recipients by Race/Ethnicity

Category	Total	White	Black	Asian	AIAN	Hisp.
Enrollment (%)	100.0	51.4	0.3	0.5	0.4	47.4
Drop-out Rate (%)	2.5	1.6	n/a	0.0	100.0	4.0
H.S. Diplomas (#)	128	99	0	0	0	29

Orange County

Bridge City ISD

1031 W Roundbunch Rd • Bridge City, TX 77611-0847
(409) 735-1602
Grade Span: PK-12; **Agency Type:** 1
Schools: 5
2 Primary; 2 Middle; 1 High; 0 Other Level
5 Regular; 0 Special Education; 0 Vocational; 0 Alternative
0 Magnet; 0 Charter; 3 Title I Eligible; 0 School-wide Title I
Students: 2,674 (51.8% male; 48.2% female)
Individual Education Program: 341 (12.8%);
English Language Learner: 96 (3.6%); Migrant: 8 (0.3%)
Eligible for Free Lunch Program: 683 (25.5%)
Eligible for Reduced-Price Lunch Program: 143 (5.3%)
Teachers: 188.3 (14.2 to 1)
Librarians/Media Specialists: 4.2 (636.7 to 1)
Guidance Counselors: 6.1 (438.4 to 1)
Current Spending: ($ per student per year):
Total: $5,673; Instruction: $3,562; Support Services: $1,875
Enrollment, Drop-out Rates and Diploma Recipients by Race/Ethnicity

Category	Total	White	Black	Asian	AIAN	Hisp.
Enrollment (%)	100.0	90.5	0.4	2.7	0.6	5.9
Drop-out Rate (%)	2.3	2.3	0.0	0.0	25.0	0.0
H.S. Diplomas (#)	198	185	0	5	1	7

Little Cypress-Mauriceville CISD

7565 N Hwy 87 • Orange, TX 77632-0708
(409) 883-2232 • http://www.lcmcisd.org/
Grade Span: PK-12; **Agency Type:** 1
Schools: 6
2 Primary; 3 Middle; 1 High; 0 Other Level
6 Regular; 0 Special Education; 0 Vocational; 0 Alternative
0 Magnet; 0 Charter; 5 Title I Eligible; 5 School-wide Title I
Students: 3,664 (51.5% male; 48.5% female)
Individual Education Program: 609 (16.6%);
English Language Learner: 50 (1.4%); Migrant: 0 (0.0%)
Eligible for Free Lunch Program: 750 (20.5%)
Eligible for Reduced-Price Lunch Program: 142 (3.9%)
Teachers: 242.5 (15.1 to 1)
Librarians/Media Specialists: 5.0 (732.8 to 1)
Guidance Counselors: 7.0 (523.4 to 1)
Current Spending: ($ per student per year):
Total: $6,053; Instruction: $3,567; Support Services: $2,158
Enrollment, Drop-out Rates and Diploma Recipients by Race/Ethnicity

Category	Total	White	Black	Asian	AIAN	Hisp.
Enrollment (%)	100.0	89.8	4.4	0.9	0.4	4.5
Drop-out Rate (%)	1.4	1.6	0.0	0.0	0.0	0.0
H.S. Diplomas (#)	273	246	16	5	1	5

Orangefield ISD

9974 Fm 105 • Orangefield, TX 77639-0228
Mailing Address: PO Box 228 • Orangefield, TX 77639-0228
(409) 735-5337
Grade Span: PK-12; **Agency Type:** 1
Schools: 3
1 Primary; 1 Middle; 1 High; 0 Other Level
3 Regular; 0 Special Education; 0 Vocational; 0 Alternative
0 Magnet; 0 Charter; 1 Title I Eligible; 0 School-wide Title I
Students: 1,634 (52.5% male; 47.5% female)
Individual Education Program: 221 (13.5%);
English Language Learner: 20 (1.2%); Migrant: 0 (0.0%)
Eligible for Free Lunch Program: 219 (13.4%)
Eligible for Reduced-Price Lunch Program: 96 (5.9%)
Teachers: 111.6 (14.6 to 1)
Librarians/Media Specialists: 1.9 (860.0 to 1)
Guidance Counselors: 4.0 (408.5 to 1)
Current Spending: ($ per student per year):
Total: $5,657; Instruction: $3,413; Support Services: $1,929
Enrollment, Drop-out Rates and Diploma Recipients by Race/Ethnicity

Category	Total	White	Black	Asian	AIAN	Hisp.
Enrollment (%)	100.0	94.0	0.4	1.8	0.5	3.4
Drop-out Rate (%)	3.0	3.0	n/a	12.5	0.0	0.0
H.S. Diplomas (#)	100	93	0	1	1	5

Vidor ISD

120 E Bolivar St • Vidor, TX 77662-4907
(409) 769-2143
Grade Span: PK-12; **Agency Type:** 1
Schools: 7
3 Primary; 2 Middle; 2 High; 0 Other Level
6 Regular; 0 Special Education; 0 Vocational; 1 Alternative
0 Magnet; 0 Charter; 4 Title I Eligible; 0 School-wide Title I
Students: 5,185 (50.9% male; 49.1% female)
Individual Education Program: 954 (18.4%);
English Language Learner: 20 (0.4%); Migrant: 2 (<0.1%)
Eligible for Free Lunch Program: 1,920 (37.0%)
Eligible for Reduced-Price Lunch Program: 553 (10.7%)
Teachers: 364.5 (14.2 to 1)
Librarians/Media Specialists: 6.0 (864.2 to 1)
Guidance Counselors: 13.4 (386.9 to 1)
Current Spending: ($ per student per year):
Total: $5,968; Instruction: $3,848; Support Services: $1,818
Enrollment, Drop-out Rates and Diploma Recipients by Race/Ethnicity

Category	Total	White	Black	Asian	AIAN	Hisp.
Enrollment (%)	100.0	96.7	0.1	0.5	0.1	2.6
Drop-out Rate (%)	2.8	2.8	n/a	14.3	0.0	0.0
H.S. Diplomas (#)	337	327	0	2	0	8

West Orange-Cove CISD

505 N 15th St • Orange, TX 77631-1107
Mailing Address: PO Box 1107 • Orange, TX 77631-1107
(409) 882-5500
Grade Span: PK-12; **Agency Type:** 1
Schools: 9
4 Primary; 2 Middle; 3 High; 0 Other Level
8 Regular; 0 Special Education; 0 Vocational; 1 Alternative
0 Magnet; 0 Charter; 7 Title I Eligible; 7 School-wide Title I
Students: 3,334 (52.4% male; 47.6% female)
Individual Education Program: 554 (16.6%);
English Language Learner: 49 (1.5%); Migrant: 0 (0.0%)
Eligible for Free Lunch Program: 2,234 (67.0%)
Eligible for Reduced-Price Lunch Program: 182 (5.5%)
Teachers: 255.1 (13.1 to 1)
Librarians/Media Specialists: 6.4 (520.9 to 1)
Guidance Counselors: 11.0 (303.1 to 1)
Current Spending: ($ per student per year):
Total: $8,341; Instruction: $4,792; Support Services: $3,196
Enrollment, Drop-out Rates and Diploma Recipients by Race/Ethnicity

Category	Total	White	Black	Asian	AIAN	Hisp.
Enrollment (%)	100.0	36.9	57.3	0.7	0.3	4.8
Drop-out Rate (%)	4.6	3.9	5.0	12.5	0.0	8.3
H.S. Diplomas (#)	181	86	90	0	0	5

Palo Pinto County

Mineral Wells ISD

906 SW 5th Ave • Mineral Wells, TX 76067-4895
(940) 325-6404 • http://www.mwisd.esc11.net/
Grade Span: PK-12; **Agency Type:** 1
Schools: 6
2 Primary; 2 Middle; 2 High; 0 Other Level
5 Regular; 0 Special Education; 0 Vocational; 1 Alternative
0 Magnet; 0 Charter; 4 Title I Eligible; 4 School-wide Title I
Students: 3,670 (52.2% male; 47.8% female)

Individual Education Program: 680 (18.5%);
English Language Learner: 235 (6.4%); Migrant: 9 (0.2%)
Eligible for Free Lunch Program: 1,570 (42.8%)
Eligible for Reduced-Price Lunch Program: 296 (8.1%)
Teachers: 271.0 (13.5 to 1)
Librarians/Media Specialists: 3.1 (1,183.9 to 1)
Guidance Counselors: 9.2 (398.9 to 1)
Current Spending: ($ per student per year):
Total: $6,496; Instruction: $4,094; Support Services: $2,072
Enrollment, Drop-out Rates and Diploma Recipients by Race/Ethnicity

Category	Total	White	Black	Asian	AIAN	Hisp.
Enrollment (%)	100.0	69.6	4.7	0.7	0.7	24.3
Drop-out Rate (%)	2.1	1.6	4.8	0.0	0.0	3.6
H.S. Diplomas (#)	190	153	10	1	0	26

Panola County

Carthage ISD
#1 Bulldog Dr • Carthage, TX 75633-2370
(903) 693-3806
Grade Span: PK-12; **Agency Type:** 1
Schools: 5
2 Primary; 2 Middle; 1 High; 0 Other Level
5 Regular; 0 Special Education; 0 Vocational; 0 Alternative
0 Magnet; 0 Charter; 4 Title I Eligible; 4 School-wide Title I
Students: 3,007 (52.9% male; 47.1% female)
Individual Education Program: 446 (14.8%);
English Language Learner: 59 (2.0%); Migrant: 0 (0.0%)
Eligible for Free Lunch Program: 1,099 (36.5%)
Eligible for Reduced-Price Lunch Program: 173 (5.8%)
Teachers: 212.1 (14.2 to 1)
Librarians/Media Specialists: 5.0 (601.4 to 1)
Guidance Counselors: 6.0 (501.2 to 1)
Current Spending: ($ per student per year):
Total: $7,463; Instruction: $4,570; Support Services: $2,566
Enrollment, Drop-out Rates and Diploma Recipients by Race/Ethnicity

Category	Total	White	Black	Asian	AIAN	Hisp.
Enrollment (%)	100.0	66.0	27.0	0.4	0.3	6.2
Drop-out Rate (%)	2.2	2.6	0.5	0.0	0.0	4.9
H.S. Diplomas (#)	196	149	36	1	0	10

Parker County

Aledo ISD
1008 Bailey Ranch Rd • Aledo, TX 76008-4407
(817) 441-8327 • http://www.aledo.k12.tx.us/aisdweb/index.htm
Grade Span: PK-12; **Agency Type:** 1
Schools: 6
3 Primary; 1 Middle; 1 High; 1 Other Level
5 Regular; 0 Special Education; 0 Vocational; 1 Alternative
0 Magnet; 0 Charter; 3 Title I Eligible; 3 School-wide Title I
Students: 3,412 (52.3% male; 47.7% female)
Individual Education Program: 322 (9.4%);
English Language Learner: 41 (1.2%); Migrant: 10 (0.3%)
Eligible for Free Lunch Program: 191 (5.6%)
Eligible for Reduced-Price Lunch Program: 62 (1.8%)
Teachers: 238.3 (14.3 to 1)
Librarians/Media Specialists: 4.0 (853.0 to 1)
Guidance Counselors: 8.0 (426.5 to 1)
Current Spending: ($ per student per year):
Total: $6,125; Instruction: $3,962; Support Services: $1,870
Enrollment, Drop-out Rates and Diploma Recipients by Race/Ethnicity

Category	Total	White	Black	Asian	AIAN	Hisp.
Enrollment (%)	100.0	93.2	0.5	0.7	0.4	5.2
Drop-out Rate (%)	3.1	3.1	0.0	14.3	0.0	2.9
H.S. Diplomas (#)	218	207	0	3	0	8

Springtown ISD
101 E Second St • Springtown, TX 76082-2566
(817) 220-7243
Grade Span: PK-12; **Agency Type:** 1
Schools: 9
4 Primary; 2 Middle; 2 High; 1 Other Level
7 Regular; 0 Special Education; 0 Vocational; 2 Alternative
0 Magnet; 0 Charter; 5 Title I Eligible; 5 School-wide Title I
Students: 3,616 (52.8% male; 47.2% female)
Individual Education Program: 539 (14.9%);
English Language Learner: 59 (1.6%); Migrant: 3 (0.1%)
Eligible for Free Lunch Program: 1,040 (28.8%)
Eligible for Reduced-Price Lunch Program: 357 (9.9%)
Teachers: 263.1 (13.7 to 1)
Librarians/Media Specialists: 6.0 (602.7 to 1)
Guidance Counselors: 12.0 (301.3 to 1)
Current Spending: ($ per student per year):
Total: $6,652; Instruction: $4,014; Support Services: $2,383

Enrollment, Drop-out Rates and Diploma Recipients by Race/Ethnicity

Category	Total	White	Black	Asian	AIAN	Hisp.
Enrollment (%)	100.0	90.2	1.1	0.3	0.9	7.5
Drop-out Rate (%)	4.0	3.7	0.0	0.0	7.1	7.7
H.S. Diplomas (#)	174	162	0	0	2	10

Weatherford ISD
1100 Longhorn Dr • Weatherford, TX 76086-9999
(817) 598-2800
Grade Span: PK-12; **Agency Type:** 1
Schools: 14
7 Primary; 2 Middle; 2 High; 0 Other Level
10 Regular; 0 Special Education; 0 Vocational; 1 Alternative
0 Magnet; 0 Charter; 4 Title I Eligible; 4 School-wide Title I
Students: 7,104 (53.4% male; 46.6% female)
Individual Education Program: 994 (14.0%);
English Language Learner: 300 (4.2%); Migrant: 13 (0.2%)
Eligible for Free Lunch Program: 1,917 (27.0%)
Eligible for Reduced-Price Lunch Program: 459 (6.5%)
Teachers: 463.1 (15.3 to 1)
Librarians/Media Specialists: 8.9 (798.2 to 1)
Guidance Counselors: 19.6 (362.4 to 1)
Current Spending: ($ per student per year):
Total: $5,772; Instruction: $3,663; Support Services: $1,877
Enrollment, Drop-out Rates and Diploma Recipients by Race/Ethnicity

Category	Total	White	Black	Asian	AIAN	Hisp.
Enrollment (%)	100.0	82.1	1.6	0.8	0.6	14.8
Drop-out Rate (%)	4.3	3.7	6.1	8.3	8.3	9.4
H.S. Diplomas (#)	410	379	4	5	0	22

Pecos County

Fort Stockton ISD
101 W Division St • Fort Stockton, TX 79735-7107
(915) 336-4000 • http://www.fort-stockton.k12.tx.us/
Grade Span: PK-12; **Agency Type:** 1
Schools: 6
2 Primary; 2 Middle; 2 High; 0 Other Level
5 Regular; 0 Special Education; 0 Vocational; 1 Alternative
0 Magnet; 0 Charter; 5 Title I Eligible; 5 School-wide Title I
Students: 2,397 (51.2% male; 48.8% female)
Individual Education Program: 277 (11.6%);
English Language Learner: 317 (13.2%); Migrant: 186 (7.8%)
Eligible for Free Lunch Program: 1,227 (51.2%)
Eligible for Reduced-Price Lunch Program: 267 (11.1%)
Teachers: 177.9 (13.5 to 1)
Librarians/Media Specialists: 4.0 (599.3 to 1)
Guidance Counselors: 6.0 (399.5 to 1)
Current Spending: ($ per student per year):
Total: $8,196; Instruction: $4,922; Support Services: $2,823
Enrollment, Drop-out Rates and Diploma Recipients by Race/Ethnicity

Category	Total	White	Black	Asian	AIAN	Hisp.
Enrollment (%)	100.0	19.8	0.5	0.3	0.0	79.3
Drop-out Rate (%)	7.3	2.9	0.0	25.0	n/a	8.9
H.S. Diplomas (#)	172	42	0	2	0	128

Polk County

Livingston ISD
1412 S Houston • Livingston, TX 77351-1297
Mailing Address: PO Box 1297 • Livingston, TX 77351-1297
(936) 328-2100 • http://www.lioncountry.org/
Grade Span: PK-12; **Agency Type:** 1
Schools: 5
2 Primary; 2 Middle; 1 High; 0 Other Level
5 Regular; 0 Special Education; 0 Vocational; 0 Alternative
0 Magnet; 0 Charter; 3 Title I Eligible; 3 School-wide Title I
Students: 4,111 (51.0% male; 49.0% female)
Individual Education Program: 733 (17.8%);
English Language Learner: 160 (3.9%); Migrant: 10 (0.2%)
Eligible for Free Lunch Program: 1,731 (42.1%)
Eligible for Reduced-Price Lunch Program: 282 (6.9%)
Teachers: 265.4 (15.5 to 1)
Librarians/Media Specialists: 3.0 (1,370.3 to 1)
Guidance Counselors: 16.1 (255.3 to 1)
Current Spending: ($ per student per year):
Total: $6,284; Instruction: $3,898; Support Services: $2,052
Enrollment, Drop-out Rates and Diploma Recipients by Race/Ethnicity

Category	Total	White	Black	Asian	AIAN	Hisp.
Enrollment (%)	100.0	73.6	12.7	0.9	0.6	12.2
Drop-out Rate (%)	4.7	4.2	1.6	0.0	10.0	11.9
H.S. Diplomas (#)	250	208	20	3	2	17

Potter County

Amarillo ISD
7200 I-40 W • Amarillo, TX 79106-2598
(806) 354-4200 • http://www.amaisd.org/
Grade Span: PK-12; **Agency Type:** 1
Schools: 52
36 Primary; 8 Middle; 6 High; 1 Other Level
49 Regular; 0 Special Education; 1 Vocational; 1 Alternative
0 Magnet; 0 Charter; 33 Title I Eligible; 25 School-wide Title I
Students: 29,244 (51.2% male; 48.8% female)
Individual Education Program: 3,699 (12.6%);
English Language Learner: 2,535 (8.7%); Migrant: 1,997 (6.8%)
Eligible for Free Lunch Program: 14,072 (48.1%)
Eligible for Reduced-Price Lunch Program: 2,586 (8.8%)
Teachers: 2,005.5 (14.6 to 1)
Librarians/Media Specialists: 34.6 (845.2 to 1)
Guidance Counselors: 80.7 (362.4 to 1)
Current Spending: ($ per student per year):
Total: $5,982; Instruction: $3,808; Support Services: $1,889
Enrollment, Drop-out Rates and Diploma Recipients by Race/Ethnicity

Category	Total	White	Black	Asian	AIAN	Hisp.
Enrollment (%)	100.0	49.8	10.6	2.5	0.2	36.8
Drop-out Rate (%)	4.2	3.1	5.1	3.3	6.3	6.4
H.S. Diplomas (#)	1,544	1,013	134	60	2	335

Rains County

Rains ISD
1759 W US Hwy 69 • Emory, TX 75440-0247
Mailing Address: PO Box 247 • Emory, TX 75440-0247
(903) 473-2222
Grade Span: PK-12; **Agency Type:** 1
Schools: 3
1 Primary; 0 Middle; 1 High; 1 Other Level
3 Regular; 0 Special Education; 0 Vocational; 0 Alternative
0 Magnet; 0 Charter; 3 Title I Eligible; 0 School-wide Title I
Students: 1,512 (51.2% male; 48.8% female)
Individual Education Program: 233 (15.4%);
English Language Learner: 61 (4.0%); Migrant: 2 (0.1%)
Eligible for Free Lunch Program: 550 (36.4%)
Eligible for Reduced-Price Lunch Program: 106 (7.0%)
Teachers: 115.3 (13.1 to 1)
Librarians/Media Specialists: 2.0 (756.0 to 1)
Guidance Counselors: 3.0 (504.0 to 1)
Current Spending: ($ per student per year):
Total: $5,809; Instruction: $3,672; Support Services: $1,814
Enrollment, Drop-out Rates and Diploma Recipients by Race/Ethnicity

Category	Total	White	Black	Asian	AIAN	Hisp.
Enrollment (%)	100.0	87.2	3.4	0.7	1.0	7.7
Drop-out Rate (%)	2.8	3.1	0.0	0.0	0.0	0.0
H.S. Diplomas (#)	93	83	7	0	1	2

Randall County

Canyon ISD
508 16th St • Canyon, TX 79015-0899
Mailing Address: PO Box 899 • Canyon, TX 79015-0899
(806) 656-6100 • http://www.canyonisd.net/
Grade Span: PK-12; **Agency Type:** 1
Schools: 13
7 Primary; 2 Middle; 2 High; 2 Other Level
12 Regular; 0 Special Education; 0 Vocational; 1 Alternative
0 Magnet; 0 Charter; 4 Title I Eligible; 4 School-wide Title I
Students: 7,629 (51.5% male; 48.5% female)
Individual Education Program: 934 (12.2%);
English Language Learner: 29 (0.4%); Migrant: 3 (<0.1%)
Eligible for Free Lunch Program: 1,246 (16.3%)
Eligible for Reduced-Price Lunch Program: 394 (5.2%)
Teachers: 477.1 (16.0 to 1)
Librarians/Media Specialists: 12.0 (635.8 to 1)
Guidance Counselors: 16.3 (468.0 to 1)
Current Spending: ($ per student per year):
Total: $4,991; Instruction: $3,219; Support Services: $1,551
Enrollment, Drop-out Rates and Diploma Recipients by Race/Ethnicity

Category	Total	White	Black	Asian	AIAN	Hisp.
Enrollment (%)	100.0	83.9	1.8	1.0	0.6	12.8
Drop-out Rate (%)	2.6	2.2	5.0	0.0	0.0	5.9
H.S. Diplomas (#)	497	434	6	2	4	51

Reeves County

Pecos-Barstow-Toyah ISD
1302 S Park St • Pecos, TX 79772-5718
Mailing Address: PO Box 869 • Pecos, TX 79772-0869
(915) 447-7201
Grade Span: PK-12; **Agency Type:** 1
Schools: 7
2 Primary; 3 Middle; 1 High; 1 Other Level
6 Regular; 0 Special Education; 0 Vocational; 1 Alternative
0 Magnet; 0 Charter; 6 Title I Eligible; 6 School-wide Title I
Students: 2,467 (52.5% male; 47.5% female)
Individual Education Program: 289 (11.7%);
English Language Learner: 251 (10.2%); Migrant: 23 (0.9%)
Eligible for Free Lunch Program: 1,406 (57.0%)
Eligible for Reduced-Price Lunch Program: 257 (10.4%)
Teachers: 171.7 (14.4 to 1)
Librarians/Media Specialists: 4.0 (616.8 to 1)
Guidance Counselors: 6.0 (411.2 to 1)
Current Spending: ($ per student per year):
Total: $6,138; Instruction: $3,715; Support Services: $2,036
Enrollment, Drop-out Rates and Diploma Recipients by Race/Ethnicity

Category	Total	White	Black	Asian	AIAN	Hisp.
Enrollment (%)	100.0	10.0	2.1	0.3	0.1	87.5
Drop-out Rate (%)	2.6	0.0	0.0	0.0	0.0	3.0
H.S. Diplomas (#)	183	16	1	0	1	165

Rockwall County

Rockwall ISD
801 E Washington St • Rockwall, TX 75087-3832
(972) 771-0605
Grade Span: PK-12; **Agency Type:** 1
Schools: 14
9 Primary; 2 Middle; 2 High; 1 Other Level
13 Regular; 0 Special Education; 0 Vocational; 1 Alternative
0 Magnet; 0 Charter; 3 Title I Eligible; 1 School-wide Title I
Students: 9,616 (51.9% male; 48.1% female)
Individual Education Program: 965 (10.0%);
English Language Learner: 473 (4.9%); Migrant: 11 (0.1%)
Eligible for Free Lunch Program: 1,097 (11.4%)
Eligible for Reduced-Price Lunch Program: 235 (2.4%)
Teachers: 569.9 (16.9 to 1)
Librarians/Media Specialists: 10.9 (882.2 to 1)
Guidance Counselors: 21.4 (449.3 to 1)
Current Spending: ($ per student per year):
Total: $5,761; Instruction: $3,387; Support Services: $2,149
Enrollment, Drop-out Rates and Diploma Recipients by Race/Ethnicity

Category	Total	White	Black	Asian	AIAN	Hisp.
Enrollment (%)	100.0	79.8	4.9	1.8	0.3	13.2
Drop-out Rate (%)	4.8	4.2	8.1	2.2	0.0	9.7
H.S. Diplomas (#)	492	428	15	15	1	33

Royse City ISD
115 E I-30 • Royse City, TX 75189-0479
Mailing Address: PO Box 479 • Royse City, TX 75189-0479
(972) 636-2413
Grade Span: PK-12; **Agency Type:** 1
Schools: 6
3 Primary; 1 Middle; 1 High; 1 Other Level
5 Regular; 0 Special Education; 0 Vocational; 1 Alternative
0 Magnet; 0 Charter; 2 Title I Eligible; 0 School-wide Title I
Students: 2,494 (53.1% male; 46.9% female)
Individual Education Program: 362 (14.5%);
English Language Learner: 166 (6.7%); Migrant: 2 (0.1%)
Eligible for Free Lunch Program: 676 (27.1%)
Eligible for Reduced-Price Lunch Program: 183 (7.3%)
Teachers: 172.6 (14.4 to 1)
Librarians/Media Specialists: 4.9 (509.0 to 1)
Guidance Counselors: 5.0 (498.8 to 1)
Current Spending: ($ per student per year):
Total: $6,217; Instruction: $3,765; Support Services: $2,102
Enrollment, Drop-out Rates and Diploma Recipients by Race/Ethnicity

Category	Total	White	Black	Asian	AIAN	Hisp.
Enrollment (%)	100.0	70.4	5.7	0.5	0.3	23.1
Drop-out Rate (%)	5.6	5.7	8.0	0.0	0.0	5.2
H.S. Diplomas (#)	127	87	9	3	0	28

Rusk County

Henderson ISD

200 N High St • Henderson, TX 75652-3103
Mailing Address: PO Box 728 • Henderson, TX 75653-0728
(903) 657-8511 • http://www.hen.sprnet.org/
Grade Span: PK-12; **Agency Type:** 1
Schools: 8
4 Primary; 2 Middle; 1 High; 0 Other Level
7 Regular; 0 Special Education; 0 Vocational; 0 Alternative
0 Magnet; 0 Charter; 6 Title I Eligible; 6 School-wide Title I
Students: 3,521 (52.5% male; 47.5% female)
Individual Education Program: 547 (15.5%);
English Language Learner: 306 (8.7%); Migrant: 3 (0.1%)
Eligible for Free Lunch Program: 1,473 (41.8%)
Eligible for Reduced-Price Lunch Program: 266 (7.6%)
Teachers: 259.1 (13.6 to 1)
Librarians/Media Specialists: 4.9 (718.6 to 1)
Guidance Counselors: 8.6 (409.4 to 1)
Current Spending: ($ per student per year):
Total: $6,391; Instruction: $4,109; Support Services: $1,906
Enrollment, Drop-out Rates and Diploma Recipients by Race/Ethnicity

Category	Total	White	Black	Asian	AIAN	Hisp.
Enrollment (%)	100.0	58.7	24.8	0.5	0.1	16.0
Drop-out Rate (%)	2.9	2.1	3.5	0.0	n/a	7.2
H.S. Diplomas (#)	230	143	63	1	0	23

San Jacinto County

Coldspring-Oakhurst CISD

121 Commercial Ave • Coldspring, TX 77331-0039
Mailing Address: PO Box 39 • Coldspring, TX 77331-0039
(936) 653-1115
Grade Span: PK-12; **Agency Type:** 1
Schools: 4
2 Primary; 1 Middle; 1 High; 0 Other Level
4 Regular; 0 Special Education; 0 Vocational; 0 Alternative
0 Magnet; 0 Charter; 4 Title I Eligible; 4 School-wide Title I
Students: 1,778 (53.8% male; 46.2% female)
Individual Education Program: 192 (10.8%);
English Language Learner: 7 (0.4%); Migrant: 0 (0.0%)
Eligible for Free Lunch Program: 876 (49.3%)
Eligible for Reduced-Price Lunch Program: 114 (6.4%)
Teachers: 127.7 (13.9 to 1)
Librarians/Media Specialists: 0.8 (2,222.5 to 1)
Guidance Counselors: 4.0 (444.5 to 1)
Current Spending: ($ per student per year):
Total: $6,200; Instruction: $3,655; Support Services: $2,237
Enrollment, Drop-out Rates and Diploma Recipients by Race/Ethnicity

Category	Total	White	Black	Asian	AIAN	Hisp.
Enrollment (%)	100.0	68.5	26.6	0.3	0.7	3.9
Drop-out Rate (%)	4.2	5.1	2.2	n/a	n/a	8.3
H.S. Diplomas (#)	91	54	36	0	0	1

Shepherd ISD

1401 S Byrd Ave • Shepherd, TX 77371-0429
(936) 628-3396
Grade Span: PK-12; **Agency Type:** 1
Schools: 4
2 Primary; 1 Middle; 1 High; 0 Other Level
4 Regular; 0 Special Education; 0 Vocational; 0 Alternative
0 Magnet; 0 Charter; 3 Title I Eligible; 3 School-wide Title I
Students: 1,806 (54.0% male; 46.0% female)
Individual Education Program: 274 (15.2%);
English Language Learner: 76 (4.2%); Migrant: 5 (0.3%)
Eligible for Free Lunch Program: 871 (48.2%)
Eligible for Reduced-Price Lunch Program: 139 (7.7%)
Teachers: 137.3 (13.2 to 1)
Librarians/Media Specialists: 1.0 (1,806.0 to 1)
Guidance Counselors: 1.7 (1,062.4 to 1)
Current Spending: ($ per student per year):
Total: $5,840; Instruction: $3,556; Support Services: $1,936
Enrollment, Drop-out Rates and Diploma Recipients by Race/Ethnicity

Category	Total	White	Black	Asian	AIAN	Hisp.
Enrollment (%)	100.0	76.5	11.0	0.8	0.3	11.4
Drop-out Rate (%)	2.2	2.5	0.0	0.0	0.0	3.1
H.S. Diplomas (#)	94	75	12	1	0	6

San Patricio County

Aransas Pass ISD

244 W Harrison Blvd • Aransas Pass, TX 78336-2442
(361) 758-3466 • http://www.aransas-pass.k12.tx.us/
Grade Span: PK-12; **Agency Type:** 1
Schools: 5
2 Primary; 2 Middle; 1 High; 0 Other Level
5 Regular; 0 Special Education; 0 Vocational; 0 Alternative
0 Magnet; 0 Charter; 5 Title I Eligible; 5 School-wide Title I
Students: 2,109 (52.6% male; 47.4% female)
Individual Education Program: 339 (16.1%);
English Language Learner: 133 (6.3%); Migrant: 0 (0.0%)
Eligible for Free Lunch Program: 1,115 (52.9%)
Eligible for Reduced-Price Lunch Program: 219 (10.4%)
Teachers: 158.8 (13.3 to 1)
Librarians/Media Specialists: 2.0 (1,054.5 to 1)
Guidance Counselors: 5.1 (413.5 to 1)
Current Spending: ($ per student per year):
Total: $6,632; Instruction: $4,061; Support Services: $2,265
Enrollment, Drop-out Rates and Diploma Recipients by Race/Ethnicity

Category	Total	White	Black	Asian	AIAN	Hisp.
Enrollment (%)	100.0	49.4	4.2	0.6	0.3	45.5
Drop-out Rate (%)	4.3	4.5	0.0	0.0	0.0	4.5
H.S. Diplomas (#)	131	71	3	1	1	55

Gregory-Portland ISD

308 N Gregory Ave • Gregory, TX 78359-0338
Mailing Address: PO Box 338 • Gregory, TX 78359-0338
(361) 643-6566 • http://www.gpisd.esc2.net/
Grade Span: PK-12; **Agency Type:** 1
Schools: 8
4 Primary; 2 Middle; 1 High; 0 Other Level
7 Regular; 0 Special Education; 0 Vocational; 0 Alternative
0 Magnet; 0 Charter; 4 Title I Eligible; 1 School-wide Title I
Students: 4,291 (52.6% male; 47.4% female)
Individual Education Program: 509 (11.9%);
English Language Learner: 79 (1.8%); Migrant: 5 (0.1%)
Eligible for Free Lunch Program: 978 (22.8%)
Eligible for Reduced-Price Lunch Program: 409 (9.5%)
Teachers: 253.3 (16.9 to 1)
Librarians/Media Specialists: 2.5 (1,716.4 to 1)
Guidance Counselors: 9.0 (476.8 to 1)
Current Spending: ($ per student per year):
Total: $5,922; Instruction: $3,316; Support Services: $2,309
Enrollment, Drop-out Rates and Diploma Recipients by Race/Ethnicity

Category	Total	White	Black	Asian	AIAN	Hisp.
Enrollment (%)	100.0	54.3	4.2	1.3	0.3	39.9
Drop-out Rate (%)	2.5	1.7	5.3	0.0	0.0	3.6
H.S. Diplomas (#)	274	173	7	6	2	86

Ingleside ISD

2807 Mustang Dr • Ingleside, TX 78362-1313
Mailing Address: PO Box 1320 • Ingleside, TX 78362-1313
(361) 776-7631 • http://www.inglesideisd.esc2.net/
Grade Span: PK-12; **Agency Type:** 1
Schools: 5
2 Primary; 2 Middle; 1 High; 0 Other Level
5 Regular; 0 Special Education; 0 Vocational; 0 Alternative
0 Magnet; 0 Charter; 3 Title I Eligible; 3 School-wide Title I
Students: 2,263 (51.6% male; 48.4% female)
Individual Education Program: 253 (11.2%);
English Language Learner: 69 (3.0%); Migrant: 1 (<0.1%)
Eligible for Free Lunch Program: 609 (26.9%)
Eligible for Reduced-Price Lunch Program: 286 (12.6%)
Teachers: 145.9 (15.5 to 1)
Librarians/Media Specialists: 2.0 (1,131.5 to 1)
Guidance Counselors: 6.0 (377.2 to 1)
Current Spending: ($ per student per year):
Total: $6,445; Instruction: $4,244; Support Services: $1,951
Enrollment, Drop-out Rates and Diploma Recipients by Race/Ethnicity

Category	Total	White	Black	Asian	AIAN	Hisp.
Enrollment (%)	100.0	58.9	3.8	2.3	0.8	34.1
Drop-out Rate (%)	6.4	6.6	16.7	0.0	0.0	4.8
H.S. Diplomas (#)	126	80	7	3	1	35

Mathis ISD

602 E San Patricio Ave • Mathis, TX 78368-2429
Mailing Address: PO Box 1179 • Mathis, TX 78368-1179
(361) 547-3378 • http://www.mathisisd.esc2.net/
Grade Span: PK-12; **Agency Type:** 1
Schools: 4
1 Primary; 2 Middle; 1 High; 0 Other Level
4 Regular; 0 Special Education; 0 Vocational; 0 Alternative
0 Magnet; 0 Charter; 4 Title I Eligible; 4 School-wide Title I
Students: 2,025 (50.2% male; 49.8% female)
Individual Education Program: 225 (11.1%);
English Language Learner: 133 (6.6%); Migrant: 842 (41.6%)
Eligible for Free Lunch Program: 1,356 (67.0%)
Eligible for Reduced-Price Lunch Program: 188 (9.3%)
Teachers: 137.0 (14.8 to 1)
Librarians/Media Specialists: 3.0 (675.0 to 1)
Guidance Counselors: 8.0 (253.1 to 1)

Current Spending: ($ per student per year):
Total: $7,855; Instruction: $4,909; Support Services: $2,420
Enrollment, Drop-out Rates and Diploma Recipients by Race/Ethnicity

Category	Total	White	Black	Asian	AIAN	Hisp.
Enrollment (%)	100.0	11.8	0.9	0.0	0.0	87.3
Drop-out Rate (%)	7.5	6.4	0.0	n/a	n/a	8.0
H.S. Diplomas (#)	125	23	2	0	0	100

Sinton ISD

322 S Archer • Sinton, TX 78387-1337
(361) 364-6801
Grade Span: PK-12; **Agency Type:** 1
Schools: 7
2 Primary; 2 Middle; 1 High; 2 Other Level
5 Regular; 0 Special Education; 0 Vocational; 2 Alternative
0 Magnet; 0 Charter; 5 Title I Eligible; 5 School-wide Title I
Students: 2,132 (53.9% male; 46.1% female)
Individual Education Program: 269 (12.6%);
English Language Learner: 61 (2.9%); Migrant: 208 (9.8%)
Eligible for Free Lunch Program: 1,225 (57.5%)
Eligible for Reduced-Price Lunch Program: 179 (8.4%)
Teachers: 155.5 (13.7 to 1)
Librarians/Media Specialists: 1.0 (2,132.0 to 1)
Guidance Counselors: 7.5 (284.3 to 1)
Current Spending: ($ per student per year):
Total: $6,929; Instruction: $4,158; Support Services: $2,375
Enrollment, Drop-out Rates and Diploma Recipients by Race/Ethnicity

Category	Total	White	Black	Asian	AIAN	Hisp.
Enrollment (%)	100.0	21.2	1.7	0.2	0.1	76.8
Drop-out Rate (%)	3.1	1.2	0.0	0.0	0.0	3.8
H.S. Diplomas (#)	111	23	4	0	0	84

Scurry County

Snyder ISD

2901 37th St • Snyder, TX 79549-5226
(915) 573-5401
Grade Span: PK-12; **Agency Type:** 1
Schools: 8
5 Primary; 1 Middle; 2 High; 0 Other Level
7 Regular; 0 Special Education; 0 Vocational; 1 Alternative
0 Magnet; 0 Charter; 5 Title I Eligible; 5 School-wide Title I
Students: 2,657 (51.2% male; 48.8% female)
Individual Education Program: 468 (17.6%);
English Language Learner: 107 (4.0%); Migrant: 61 (2.3%)
Eligible for Free Lunch Program: 1,138 (42.8%)
Eligible for Reduced-Price Lunch Program: 162 (6.1%)
Teachers: 198.6 (13.4 to 1)
Librarians/Media Specialists: 2.0 (1,328.5 to 1)
Guidance Counselors: 5.0 (531.4 to 1)
Current Spending: ($ per student per year):
Total: $7,663; Instruction: $4,506; Support Services: $2,848
Enrollment, Drop-out Rates and Diploma Recipients by Race/Ethnicity

Category	Total	White	Black	Asian	AIAN	Hisp.
Enrollment (%)	100.0	50.2	4.7	0.3	0.5	44.3
Drop-out Rate (%)	3.4	1.6	4.5	100.0	0.0	5.8
H.S. Diplomas (#)	172	107	4	1	0	60

Shelby County

Center ISD

404 Mosby St • Center, TX 75935-3864
(936) 598-5642 • http://www.centerisd.org/
Grade Span: PK-12; **Agency Type:** 1
Schools: 5
2 Primary; 2 Middle; 1 High; 0 Other Level
5 Regular; 0 Special Education; 0 Vocational; 0 Alternative
0 Magnet; 0 Charter; 4 Title I Eligible; 4 School-wide Title I
Students: 2,457 (50.0% male; 50.0% female)
Individual Education Program: 289 (11.8%);
English Language Learner: 401 (16.3%); Migrant: 185 (7.5%)
Eligible for Free Lunch Program: 1,264 (51.4%)
Eligible for Reduced-Price Lunch Program: 168 (6.8%)
Teachers: 170.5 (14.4 to 1)
Librarians/Media Specialists: 3.0 (819.0 to 1)
Guidance Counselors: 5.0 (491.4 to 1)
Current Spending: ($ per student per year):
Total: $5,670; Instruction: $3,625; Support Services: $1,711
Enrollment, Drop-out Rates and Diploma Recipients by Race/Ethnicity

Category	Total	White	Black	Asian	AIAN	Hisp.
Enrollment (%)	100.0	49.0	27.7	0.3	0.2	22.8
Drop-out Rate (%)	3.9	2.9	6.3	0.0	0.0	2.7
H.S. Diplomas (#)	129	68	49	0	0	12

Smith County

Bullard ISD

218 Schoolhouse Rd • Bullard, TX 75757-0250
Mailing Address: PO Box 250 • Bullard, TX 75757-0250
(903) 894-6639
Grade Span: PK-12; **Agency Type:** 1
Schools: 6
1 Primary; 2 Middle; 1 High; 1 Other Level
4 Regular; 1 Special Education; 0 Vocational; 0 Alternative
0 Magnet; 0 Charter; 1 Title I Eligible; 0 School-wide Title I
Students: 1,501 (52.0% male; 48.0% female)
Individual Education Program: 179 (11.9%);
English Language Learner: 23 (1.5%); Migrant: 0 (0.0%)
Eligible for Free Lunch Program: 397 (26.4%)
Eligible for Reduced-Price Lunch Program: 111 (7.4%)
Teachers: 102.1 (14.7 to 1)
Librarians/Media Specialists: 0.0 (0.0 to 1)
Guidance Counselors: 4.0 (375.3 to 1)
Current Spending: ($ per student per year):
Total: $4,928; Instruction: $3,294; Support Services: $1,381
Enrollment, Drop-out Rates and Diploma Recipients by Race/Ethnicity

Category	Total	White	Black	Asian	AIAN	Hisp.
Enrollment (%)	100.0	89.3	6.0	0.2	0.5	4.0
Drop-out Rate (%)	3.0	3.4	0.0	0.0	0.0	0.0
H.S. Diplomas (#)	81	69	6	0	0	6

Chapel Hill ISD

11134 Cr 2249 • Tyler, TX 75707-9752
(903) 566-2441
Grade Span: PK-12; **Agency Type:** 1
Schools: 8
3 Primary; 1 Middle; 1 High; 3 Other Level
5 Regular; 2 Special Education; 0 Vocational; 1 Alternative
0 Magnet; 0 Charter; 5 Title I Eligible; 5 School-wide Title I
Students: 3,012 (52.3% male; 47.7% female)
Individual Education Program: 262 (8.7%);
English Language Learner: 258 (8.6%); Migrant: 0 (0.0%)
Eligible for Free Lunch Program: 1,365 (45.3%)
Eligible for Reduced-Price Lunch Program: 225 (7.5%)
Teachers: 215.1 (14.0 to 1)
Librarians/Media Specialists: 2.2 (1,369.1 to 1)
Guidance Counselors: 6.9 (436.5 to 1)
Current Spending: ($ per student per year):
Total: $6,295; Instruction: $3,797; Support Services: $2,202
Enrollment, Drop-out Rates and Diploma Recipients by Race/Ethnicity

Category	Total	White	Black	Asian	AIAN	Hisp.
Enrollment (%)	100.0	51.1	26.9	0.4	0.2	21.5
Drop-out Rate (%)	4.1	3.0	5.2	0.0	0.0	7.5
H.S. Diplomas (#)	202	131	43	1	0	27

Lindale ISD

505 Pierce St • Lindale, TX 75771-3336
Mailing Address: PO Box 370 • Lindale, TX 75771-0370
(903) 882-6157 • http://www.lind.sprnet.org/
Grade Span: PK-12; **Agency Type:** 1
Schools: 7
3 Primary; 2 Middle; 1 High; 1 Other Level
6 Regular; 1 Special Education; 0 Vocational; 0 Alternative
0 Magnet; 0 Charter; 4 Title I Eligible; 4 School-wide Title I
Students: 3,042 (50.9% male; 49.1% female)
Individual Education Program: 356 (11.7%);
English Language Learner: 82 (2.7%); Migrant: 6 (0.2%)
Eligible for Free Lunch Program: 703 (23.1%)
Eligible for Reduced-Price Lunch Program: 233 (7.7%)
Teachers: 214.6 (14.2 to 1)
Librarians/Media Specialists: 4.0 (760.5 to 1)
Guidance Counselors: 7.0 (434.6 to 1)
Current Spending: ($ per student per year):
Total: $5,712; Instruction: $3,640; Support Services: $1,806
Enrollment, Drop-out Rates and Diploma Recipients by Race/Ethnicity

Category	Total	White	Black	Asian	AIAN	Hisp.
Enrollment (%)	100.0	83.7	8.0	1.1	0.8	6.4
Drop-out Rate (%)	0.3	0.3	0.0	0.0	0.0	0.0
H.S. Diplomas (#)	172	152	12	2	4	2

Tyler ISD

1319 W Eighth St • Tyler, TX 75701-3800
Mailing Address: PO Box 2035 • Tyler, TX 75710-2035
(903) 531-3500
Grade Span: PK-12; **Agency Type:** 1
Schools: 30
17 Primary; 6 Middle; 2 High; 4 Other Level
24 Regular; 1 Special Education; 0 Vocational; 4 Alternative
0 Magnet; 0 Charter; 17 Title I Eligible; 17 School-wide Title I

Students: 17,096 (51.1% male; 48.9% female)
Individual Education Program: 2,181 (12.8%);
English Language Learner: 2,766 (16.2%); Migrant: 0 (0.0%)
Eligible for Free Lunch Program: 8,286 (48.5%)
Eligible for Reduced-Price Lunch Program: 1,153 (6.7%)
Teachers: 1,215.2 (14.1 to 1)
Librarians/Media Specialists: 21.0 (814.1 to 1)
Guidance Counselors: 37.9 (451.1 to 1)
Current Spending: ($ per student per year):
Total: $5,965; Instruction: $3,751; Support Services: $1,918
Enrollment, Drop-out Rates and Diploma Recipients by Race/Ethnicity

Category	Total	White	Black	Asian	AIAN	Hisp.
Enrollment (%)	100.0	33.5	35.5	1.0	0.3	29.7
Drop-out Rate (%)	4.6	2.9	5.6	2.1	0.0	6.4
H.S. Diplomas (#)	901	427	316	8	1	149

Whitehouse ISD

106 W Wildcat Dr • Whitehouse, TX 75791-3130
(903) 839-5500
Grade Span: PK-12; **Agency Type:** 1
Schools: 8
3 Primary; 2 Middle; 1 High; 2 Other Level
6 Regular; 0 Special Education; 0 Vocational; 2 Alternative
0 Magnet; 0 Charter; 3 Title I Eligible; 3 School-wide Title I
Students: 4,045 (51.6% male; 48.4% female)
Individual Education Program: 334 (8.3%);
English Language Learner: 70 (1.7%); Migrant: 0 (0.0%)
Eligible for Free Lunch Program: 778 (19.2%)
Eligible for Reduced-Price Lunch Program: 253 (6.3%)
Teachers: 252.7 (16.0 to 1)
Librarians/Media Specialists: 3.3 (1,225.8 to 1)
Guidance Counselors: 9.0 (449.4 to 1)
Current Spending: ($ per student per year):
Total: $4,990; Instruction: $3,220; Support Services: $1,546
Enrollment, Drop-out Rates and Diploma Recipients by Race/Ethnicity

Category	Total	White	Black	Asian	AIAN	Hisp.
Enrollment (%)	100.0	84.7	9.0	1.6	0.2	4.6
Drop-out Rate (%)	1.8	1.9	0.9	0.0	0.0	2.2
H.S. Diplomas (#)	264	222	25	5	1	11

Somervell County

Glen Rose ISD

1102 Stadium Dr • Glen Rose, TX 76043-2129
Mailing Address: PO Box 2129 • Glen Rose, TX 76043-2129
(254) 897-2517 • http://www.grisd.net/
Grade Span: PK-12; **Agency Type:** 1
Schools: 5
1 Primary; 2 Middle; 1 High; 0 Other Level
4 Regular; 0 Special Education; 0 Vocational; 0 Alternative
0 Magnet; 0 Charter; 1 Title I Eligible; 1 School-wide Title I
Students: 1,678 (51.7% male; 48.3% female)
Individual Education Program: 210 (12.5%);
English Language Learner: 151 (9.0%); Migrant: 6 (0.4%)
Eligible for Free Lunch Program: 525 (31.3%)
Eligible for Reduced-Price Lunch Program: 144 (8.6%)
Teachers: 140.0 (12.0 to 1)
Librarians/Media Specialists: 1.6 (1,048.8 to 1)
Guidance Counselors: 3.4 (493.5 to 1)
Current Spending: ($ per student per year):
Total: $10,154; Instruction: $5,967; Support Services: $3,732
Enrollment, Drop-out Rates and Diploma Recipients by Race/Ethnicity

Category	Total	White	Black	Asian	AIAN	Hisp.
Enrollment (%)	100.0	77.1	0.2	0.4	1.2	21.1
Drop-out Rate (%)	1.0	0.5	0.0	0.0	0.0	3.4
H.S. Diplomas (#)	103	83	1	0	0	19

Starr County

Rio Grande City CISD

Fort Ringgold • Rio Grande City, TX 78582-4799
(956) 716-6700
Grade Span: PK-12; **Agency Type:** 1
Schools: 12
9 Primary; 2 Middle; 1 High; 0 Other Level
12 Regular; 0 Special Education; 0 Vocational; 0 Alternative
0 Magnet; 0 Charter; 11 Title I Eligible; 11 School-wide Title I
Students: 9,206 (51.2% male; 48.8% female)
Individual Education Program: 1,228 (13.3%);
English Language Learner: 4,571 (49.7%); Migrant: 2,964 (32.2%)
Eligible for Free Lunch Program: 7,244 (78.7%)
Eligible for Reduced-Price Lunch Program: 281 (3.1%)
Teachers: 615.7 (15.0 to 1)
Librarians/Media Specialists: 8.0 (1,150.8 to 1)
Guidance Counselors: 30.9 (297.9 to 1)
Current Spending: ($ per student per year):
Total: $7,250; Instruction: $4,105; Support Services: $2,695
Enrollment, Drop-out Rates and Diploma Recipients by Race/Ethnicity

Category	Total	White	Black	Asian	AIAN	Hisp.
Enrollment (%)	100.0	0.2	0.0	0.2	0.0	99.6
Drop-out Rate (%)	10.1	0.0	0.0	0.0	0.0	10.2
H.S. Diplomas (#)	420	2	2	0	0	416

Roma ISD

703 N Gladiator Blvd • Roma, TX 78584-0187
Mailing Address: PO Box 187 • Roma, TX 78584-0187
(956) 849-1377
Grade Span: PK-12; **Agency Type:** 1
Schools: 10
5 Primary; 2 Middle; 2 High; 1 Other Level
8 Regular; 0 Special Education; 1 Vocational; 1 Alternative
0 Magnet; 0 Charter; 10 Title I Eligible; 10 School-wide Title I
Students: 6,171 (50.7% male; 49.3% female)
Individual Education Program: 518 (8.4%);
English Language Learner: 3,076 (49.8%); Migrant: 1,335 (21.6%)
Eligible for Free Lunch Program: 714 (11.6%)
Eligible for Reduced-Price Lunch Program: 55 (0.9%)
Teachers: 417.7 (14.8 to 1)
Librarians/Media Specialists: 8.1 (761.9 to 1)
Guidance Counselors: 14.0 (440.8 to 1)
Current Spending: ($ per student per year):
Total: $6,023; Instruction: $3,676; Support Services: $1,926
Enrollment, Drop-out Rates and Diploma Recipients by Race/Ethnicity

Category	Total	White	Black	Asian	AIAN	Hisp.
Enrollment (%)	100.0	0.3	0.0	0.0	0.0	99.7
Drop-out Rate (%)	6.9	0.0	n/a	n/a	n/a	6.8
H.S. Diplomas (#)	291	2	0	0	0	289

Stephens County

Breckenridge ISD

208 N Miller • Breckenridge, TX 76424-3492
Mailing Address: PO Box 1738 • Breckenridge, TX 76424-1738
(254) 559-2278
Grade Span: PK-12; **Agency Type:** 1
Schools: 6
2 Primary; 2 Middle; 1 High; 1 Other Level
5 Regular; 0 Special Education; 0 Vocational; 1 Alternative
0 Magnet; 0 Charter; 3 Title I Eligible; 3 School-wide Title I
Students: 1,653 (51.9% male; 48.1% female)
Individual Education Program: 220 (13.3%);
English Language Learner: 102 (6.2%); Migrant: 0 (0.0%)
Eligible for Free Lunch Program: 681 (41.2%)
Eligible for Reduced-Price Lunch Program: 98 (5.9%)
Teachers: 122.7 (13.5 to 1)
Librarians/Media Specialists: 3.0 (551.0 to 1)
Guidance Counselors: 4.0 (413.3 to 1)
Current Spending: ($ per student per year):
Total: $5,910; Instruction: $3,636; Support Services: $1,910
Enrollment, Drop-out Rates and Diploma Recipients by Race/Ethnicity

Category	Total	White	Black	Asian	AIAN	Hisp.
Enrollment (%)	100.0	70.6	2.4	0.5	0.7	25.8
Drop-out Rate (%)	3.3	3.7	0.0	0.0	0.0	1.9
H.S. Diplomas (#)	119	93	0	0	1	25

Tarrant County

Arlington ISD

1203 W Pioneer Pkwy • Arlington, TX 76013-6246
(817) 460-4611 • http://www.arlington.k12.tx.us/
Grade Span: PK-12; **Agency Type:** 1
Schools: 76
52 Primary; 13 Middle; 8 High; 3 Other Level
70 Regular; 0 Special Education; 0 Vocational; 6 Alternative
0 Magnet; 0 Charter; 31 Title I Eligible; 28 School-wide Title I
Students: 61,928 (51.0% male; 49.0% female)
Individual Education Program: 6,072 (9.8%);
English Language Learner: 9,728 (15.7%); Migrant: 17 (<0.1%)
Eligible for Free Lunch Program: 23,091 (37.3%)
Eligible for Reduced-Price Lunch Program: 3,667 (5.9%)
Teachers: 3,941.0 (15.7 to 1)
Librarians/Media Specialists: 65.2 (949.8 to 1)
Guidance Counselors: 127.4 (486.1 to 1)
Current Spending: ($ per student per year):
Total: $5,739; Instruction: $3,693; Support Services: $1,781
Enrollment, Drop-out Rates and Diploma Recipients by Race/Ethnicity

Category	Total	White	Black	Asian	AIAN	Hisp.
Enrollment (%)	100.0	41.9	22.2	6.9	0.5	28.5
Drop-out Rate (%)	7.6	5.5	9.4	5.6	9.7	13.2
H.S. Diplomas (#)	2,875	1,661	533	281	12	388

Azle ISD

300 Roe St • Azle, TX 76020-3194
(817) 444-3235 • http://www.azle.esc11.net/
Grade Span: PK-12; **Agency Type:** 1
Schools: 11
5 Primary; 4 Middle; 1 High; 1 Other Level
10 Regular; 0 Special Education; 0 Vocational; 1 Alternative
0 Magnet; 0 Charter; 7 Title I Eligible; 7 School-wide Title I
Students: 5,841 (52.8% male; 47.2% female)
Individual Education Program: 740 (12.7%);
English Language Learner: 51 (0.9%); Migrant: 3 (0.1%)
Eligible for Free Lunch Program: 1,320 (22.6%)
Eligible for Reduced-Price Lunch Program: 421 (7.2%)
Teachers: 390.9 (14.9 to 1)
Librarians/Media Specialists: 4.0 (1,460.3 to 1)
Guidance Counselors: 13.1 (445.9 to 1)
Current Spending: ($ per student per year):
Total: $5,863; Instruction: $3,705; Support Services: $1,802
Enrollment, Drop-out Rates and Diploma Recipients by Race/Ethnicity

Category	Total	White	Black	Asian	AIAN	Hisp.
Enrollment (%)	100.0	90.4	0.8	0.7	0.8	7.4
Drop-out Rate (%)	3.1	3.0	25.0	0.0	0.0	4.8
H.S. Diplomas (#)	355	319	3	2	3	28

Birdville ISD

6125 E Belknap St • Haltom City, TX 76117-4204
(817) 547-5700 • http://www.birdville.k12.tx.us/
Grade Span: PK-12; **Agency Type:** 1
Schools: 34
20 Primary; 7 Middle; 5 High; 2 Other Level
30 Regular; 1 Special Education; 0 Vocational; 3 Alternative
0 Magnet; 0 Charter; 9 Title I Eligible; 9 School-wide Title I
Students: 22,301 (52.0% male; 48.0% female)
Individual Education Program: 3,091 (13.9%);
English Language Learner: 1,605 (7.2%); Migrant: 14 (0.1%)
Eligible for Free Lunch Program: 5,526 (24.8%)
Eligible for Reduced-Price Lunch Program: 1,931 (8.7%)
Teachers: 1,419.0 (15.7 to 1)
Librarians/Media Specialists: 33.1 (673.7 to 1)
Guidance Counselors: 52.7 (423.2 to 1)
Current Spending: ($ per student per year):
Total: $6,043; Instruction: $3,958; Support Services: $1,772
Enrollment, Drop-out Rates and Diploma Recipients by Race/Ethnicity

Category	Total	White	Black	Asian	AIAN	Hisp.
Enrollment (%)	100.0	67.8	5.5	5.8	0.5	20.5
Drop-out Rate (%)	1.4	1.4	0.5	1.1	10.5	1.8
H.S. Diplomas (#)	1,164	902	37	78	1	146

Carroll ISD

1201 N Carroll Ave • Southlake, TX 76092-9405
(817) 949-8222 • http://www.southlakecarroll.edu/
Grade Span: PK-12; **Agency Type:** 1
Schools: 13
5 Primary; 5 Middle; 1 High; 1 Other Level
12 Regular; 0 Special Education; 0 Vocational; 0 Alternative
0 Magnet; 0 Charter; 0 Title I Eligible; 0 School-wide Title I
Students: 7,227 (52.1% male; 47.9% female)
Individual Education Program: 680 (9.4%);
English Language Learner: 17 (0.2%); Migrant: 0 (0.0%)
Eligible for Free Lunch Program: 76 (1.1%)
Eligible for Reduced-Price Lunch Program: 18 (0.2%)
Teachers: 498.7 (14.5 to 1)
Librarians/Media Specialists: 12.0 (602.3 to 1)
Guidance Counselors: 17.5 (413.0 to 1)
Current Spending: ($ per student per year):
Total: $6,789; Instruction: $4,181; Support Services: $2,329
Enrollment, Drop-out Rates and Diploma Recipients by Race/Ethnicity

Category	Total	White	Black	Asian	AIAN	Hisp.
Enrollment (%)	100.0	91.8	1.8	3.3	0.2	2.8
Drop-out Rate (%)	0.3	0.3	0.0	2.2	0.0	0.0
H.S. Diplomas (#)	439	408	4	14	1	12

Castleberry ISD

315 Churchill Rd • Fort Worth, TX 76114-3729
(817) 252-2000 • http://www.castleberryisd.net/
Grade Span: PK-12; **Agency Type:** 1
Schools: 8
2 Primary; 2 Middle; 2 High; 2 Other Level
5 Regular; 0 Special Education; 0 Vocational; 3 Alternative
0 Magnet; 0 Charter; 4 Title I Eligible; 4 School-wide Title I
Students: 3,252 (50.8% male; 49.2% female)
Individual Education Program: 336 (10.3%);
English Language Learner: 439 (13.5%); Migrant: 11 (0.3%)
Eligible for Free Lunch Program: 1,525 (46.9%)
Eligible for Reduced-Price Lunch Program: 251 (7.7%)
Teachers: 202.9 (16.0 to 1)
Librarians/Media Specialists: 4.0 (813.0 to 1)
Guidance Counselors: 10.0 (325.2 to 1)
Current Spending: ($ per student per year):
Total: $5,996; Instruction: $3,457; Support Services: $2,176
Enrollment, Drop-out Rates and Diploma Recipients by Race/Ethnicity

Category	Total	White	Black	Asian	AIAN	Hisp.
Enrollment (%)	100.0	50.5	1.5	0.6	0.2	47.1
Drop-out Rate (%)	5.4	5.0	0.0	0.0	0.0	6.4
H.S. Diplomas (#)	178	118	2	1	0	57

Crowley ISD

1008 Hwy 1187 • Crowley, TX 76036-0688
Mailing Address: PO Box 688 • Crowley, TX 76036-0688
(817) 297-5800 • http://www.crowley.k12.tx.us/
Grade Span: PK-12; **Agency Type:** 1
Schools: 13
8 Primary; 2 Middle; 2 High; 1 Other Level
12 Regular; 0 Special Education; 0 Vocational; 1 Alternative
0 Magnet; 0 Charter; 5 Title I Eligible; 4 School-wide Title I
Students: 10,818 (52.0% male; 48.0% female)
Individual Education Program: 1,414 (13.1%);
English Language Learner: 527 (4.9%); Migrant: 9 (0.1%)
Eligible for Free Lunch Program: 1,703 (15.7%)
Eligible for Reduced-Price Lunch Program: 758 (7.0%)
Teachers: 750.8 (14.4 to 1)
Librarians/Media Specialists: 13.5 (801.3 to 1)
Guidance Counselors: 21.2 (510.3 to 1)
Current Spending: ($ per student per year):
Total: $6,080; Instruction: $4,153; Support Services: $1,690
Enrollment, Drop-out Rates and Diploma Recipients by Race/Ethnicity

Category	Total	White	Black	Asian	AIAN	Hisp.
Enrollment (%)	100.0	54.5	24.5	4.3	0.7	16.0
Drop-out Rate (%)	1.6	1.5	1.3	0.0	0.0	3.2
H.S. Diplomas (#)	603	396	129	26	1	51

Eagle Mt-Saginaw ISD

1200 Old Decatur Rd • Fort Worth, TX 76179-4300
Mailing Address: PO Box 79160 • Fort Worth, TX 76179-9160
(817) 232-0880 • http://www.emsisd.com/index.html
Grade Span: PK-12; **Agency Type:** 1
Schools: 12
6 Primary; 2 Middle; 2 High; 2 Other Level
9 Regular; 0 Special Education; 0 Vocational; 3 Alternative
0 Magnet; 0 Charter; 4 Title I Eligible; 0 School-wide Title I
Students: 7,809 (51.6% male; 48.4% female)
Individual Education Program: 674 (8.6%);
English Language Learner: 289 (3.7%); Migrant: 0 (0.0%)
Eligible for Free Lunch Program: 1,145 (14.7%)
Eligible for Reduced-Price Lunch Program: 427 (5.5%)
Teachers: 453.7 (17.2 to 1)
Librarians/Media Specialists: 9.0 (867.7 to 1)
Guidance Counselors: 20.1 (388.5 to 1)
Current Spending: ($ per student per year):
Total: $5,721; Instruction: $3,695; Support Services: $1,774
Enrollment, Drop-out Rates and Diploma Recipients by Race/Ethnicity

Category	Total	White	Black	Asian	AIAN	Hisp.
Enrollment (%)	100.0	70.6	3.4	4.9	0.3	20.7
Drop-out Rate (%)	4.2	3.6	4.2	7.9	66.7	5.5
H.S. Diplomas (#)	406	323	11	15	0	57

Everman ISD

608 Townley Dr • Everman, TX 76140-5206
(817) 568-3500 • http://www.eisd.org/
Grade Span: PK-12; **Agency Type:** 1
Schools: 7
4 Primary; 1 Middle; 2 High; 0 Other Level
6 Regular; 0 Special Education; 0 Vocational; 1 Alternative
0 Magnet; 0 Charter; 5 Title I Eligible; 0 School-wide Title I
Students: 3,845 (51.4% male; 48.6% female)
Individual Education Program: 607 (15.8%);
English Language Learner: 466 (12.1%); Migrant: 6 (0.2%)
Eligible for Free Lunch Program: 2,163 (56.3%)
Eligible for Reduced-Price Lunch Program: 496 (12.9%)
Teachers: 241.8 (15.9 to 1)
Librarians/Media Specialists: 4.0 (961.3 to 1)
Guidance Counselors: 8.0 (480.6 to 1)
Current Spending: ($ per student per year):
Total: $6,169; Instruction: $3,919; Support Services: $1,892
Enrollment, Drop-out Rates and Diploma Recipients by Race/Ethnicity

Category	Total	White	Black	Asian	AIAN	Hisp.
Enrollment (%)	100.0	16.5	52.4	1.5	0.2	29.5
Drop-out Rate (%)	3.4	3.8	3.2	0.0	0.0	4.0
H.S. Diplomas (#)	127	28	75	1	0	23

Fort Worth ISD

100 N University Dr • Fort Worth, TX 76107-3010
(817) 871-2000 • http://www.fortworthisd.org/
Grade Span: PK-12; **Agency Type:** 1
Schools: 146
80 Primary; 30 Middle; 19 High; 14 Other Level
114 Regular; 1 Special Education; 1 Vocational; 27 Alternative
0 Magnet; 0 Charter; 76 Title I Eligible; 76 School-wide Title I
Students: 81,081 (50.9% male; 49.1% female)
Individual Education Program: 7,977 (9.8%);
English Language Learner: 20,744 (25.6%); Migrant: 126 (0.2%)
Eligible for Free Lunch Program: 47,358 (58.4%)
Eligible for Reduced-Price Lunch Program: 4,736 (5.8%)
Teachers: 4,967.3 (16.3 to 1)
Librarians/Media Specialists: 110.0 (737.1 to 1)
Guidance Counselors: 200.4 (404.6 to 1)
Current Spending: ($ per student per year):
Total: $6,365; Instruction: $3,650; Support Services: $2,418
Enrollment, Drop-out Rates and Diploma Recipients by Race/Ethnicity

Category	Total	White	Black	Asian	AIAN	Hisp.
Enrollment (%)	100.0	18.8	29.0	1.8	0.2	50.1
Drop-out Rate (%)	6.9	5.2	7.3	6.0	10.3	7.8
H.S. Diplomas (#)	3,222	909	1,053	112	3	1,145

Grapevine-Colleyville ISD

3051 Ira E Woods Ave • Grapevine, TX 76051-3897
(817) 488-9588 • http://www.gcisd-k12.org/
Grade Span: PK-12; **Agency Type:** 1
Schools: 19
11 Primary; 4 Middle; 3 High; 1 Other Level
17 Regular; 0 Special Education; 0 Vocational; 2 Alternative
0 Magnet; 0 Charter; 8 Title I Eligible; 0 School-wide Title I
Students: 13,834 (49.7% male; 50.3% female)
Individual Education Program: 1,036 (7.5%);
English Language Learner: 548 (4.0%); Migrant: 0 (0.0%)
Eligible for Free Lunch Program: 967 (7.0%)
Eligible for Reduced-Price Lunch Program: 187 (1.4%)
Teachers: 922.9 (15.0 to 1)
Librarians/Media Specialists: 11.1 (1,246.3 to 1)
Guidance Counselors: 31.3 (442.0 to 1)
Current Spending: ($ per student per year):
Total: $6,679; Instruction: $4,107; Support Services: $2,317
Enrollment, Drop-out Rates and Diploma Recipients by Race/Ethnicity

Category	Total	White	Black	Asian	AIAN	Hisp.
Enrollment (%)	100.0	81.5	3.2	5.3	0.5	9.5
Drop-out Rate (%)	1.5	1.4	5.9	0.7	0.0	2.6
H.S. Diplomas (#)	956	842	25	37	3	49

Hurst-Euless-Bedford ISD

1849a Central Dr • Bedford, TX 76022-6096
(817) 283-4461 • http://www.hebisd.edu/
Grade Span: PK-12; **Agency Type:** 1
Schools: 33
19 Primary; 5 Middle; 5 High; 3 Other Level
26 Regular; 1 Special Education; 0 Vocational; 5 Alternative
0 Magnet; 0 Charter; 13 Title I Eligible; 3 School-wide Title I
Students: 19,720 (51.3% male; 48.7% female)
Individual Education Program: 2,031 (10.3%);
English Language Learner: 1,906 (9.7%); Migrant: 15 (0.1%)
Eligible for Free Lunch Program: 5,306 (26.9%)
Eligible for Reduced-Price Lunch Program: 1,566 (7.9%)
Teachers: 1,263.3 (15.6 to 1)
Librarians/Media Specialists: 24.5 (804.9 to 1)
Guidance Counselors: 39.5 (499.2 to 1)
Current Spending: ($ per student per year):
Total: $6,147; Instruction: $3,777; Support Services: $2,092
Enrollment, Drop-out Rates and Diploma Recipients by Race/Ethnicity

Category	Total	White	Black	Asian	AIAN	Hisp.
Enrollment (%)	100.0	61.8	10.5	9.5	0.9	17.3
Drop-out Rate (%)	2.6	2.2	2.5	4.4	4.0	4.2
H.S. Diplomas (#)	1,227	900	96	109	7	115

Keller ISD

350 Keller Pkwy • Keller, TX 76248-3447
(817) 337-7500 • http://www.kellerisd.com/
Grade Span: PK-12; **Agency Type:** 1
Schools: 26
13 Primary; 8 Middle; 3 High; 1 Other Level
23 Regular; 0 Special Education; 0 Vocational; 2 Alternative
0 Magnet; 0 Charter; 7 Title I Eligible; 0 School-wide Title I
Students: 20,109 (51.7% male; 48.3% female)
Individual Education Program: 1,487 (7.4%);
English Language Learner: 645 (3.2%); Migrant: 9 (<0.1%)
Eligible for Free Lunch Program: 1,374 (6.8%)
Eligible for Reduced-Price Lunch Program: 594 (3.0%)
Teachers: 1,118.3 (18.0 to 1)
Librarians/Media Specialists: 18.6 (1,081.1 to 1)
Guidance Counselors: 31.7 (634.4 to 1)
Current Spending: ($ per student per year):
Total: $5,365; Instruction: $3,196; Support Services: $1,916
Enrollment, Drop-out Rates and Diploma Recipients by Race/Ethnicity

Category	Total	White	Black	Asian	AIAN	Hisp.
Enrollment (%)	100.0	78.9	4.6	5.8	0.4	10.3
Drop-out Rate (%)	2.6	2.6	2.0	2.4	0.0	2.7
H.S. Diplomas (#)	1,013	821	43	67	1	81

Kennedale ISD

120 W Mansfield Hwy • Kennedale, TX 76060-0467
Mailing Address: PO Box 467 • Kennedale, TX 76060-0467
(817) 483-3600 • http://www.kennedale.net/
Grade Span: PK-12; **Agency Type:** 1
Schools: 7
2 Primary; 2 Middle; 1 High; 0 Other Level
5 Regular; 0 Special Education; 0 Vocational; 0 Alternative
0 Magnet; 0 Charter; 3 Title I Eligible; 0 School-wide Title I
Students: 2,847 (51.7% male; 48.3% female)
Individual Education Program: 291 (10.2%);
English Language Learner: 93 (3.3%); Migrant: 0 (0.0%)
Eligible for Free Lunch Program: 454 (15.9%)
Eligible for Reduced-Price Lunch Program: 147 (5.2%)
Teachers: 185.8 (15.3 to 1)
Librarians/Media Specialists: 3.0 (949.0 to 1)
Guidance Counselors: 6.0 (474.5 to 1)
Current Spending: ($ per student per year):
Total: $5,707; Instruction: $3,723; Support Services: $1,775
Enrollment, Drop-out Rates and Diploma Recipients by Race/Ethnicity

Category	Total	White	Black	Asian	AIAN	Hisp.
Enrollment (%)	100.0	70.7	12.1	2.6	0.4	14.3
Drop-out Rate (%)	3.8	3.9	2.1	0.0	0.0	5.6
H.S. Diplomas (#)	134	105	14	2	0	13

Lake Worth ISD

6800 Telephone Rd • Lake Worth, TX 76135-2899
(817) 237-1491 •
http://www.lake-worth.k12.tx.us/education/district/district.php?sectionid=1
Grade Span: PK-12; **Agency Type:** 1
Schools: 8
3 Primary; 1 Middle; 3 High; 0 Other Level
4 Regular; 0 Special Education; 0 Vocational; 3 Alternative
0 Magnet; 0 Charter; 5 Title I Eligible; 5 School-wide Title I
Students: 2,156 (52.9% male; 47.1% female)
Individual Education Program: 197 (9.1%);
English Language Learner: 272 (12.6%); Migrant: 0 (0.0%)
Eligible for Free Lunch Program: 1,542 (71.5%)
Eligible for Reduced-Price Lunch Program: 180 (8.3%)
Teachers: 165.0 (13.1 to 1)
Librarians/Media Specialists: 3.0 (718.7 to 1)
Guidance Counselors: 3.0 (718.7 to 1)
Current Spending: ($ per student per year):
Total: $6,770; Instruction: $4,035; Support Services: $2,307
Enrollment, Drop-out Rates and Diploma Recipients by Race/Ethnicity

Category	Total	White	Black	Asian	AIAN	Hisp.
Enrollment (%)	100.0	48.7	6.6	1.2	0.9	42.6
Drop-out Rate (%)	4.6	5.6	0.0	0.0	n/a	3.0
H.S. Diplomas (#)	117	69	8	0	1	39

Mansfield ISD

605 E Broad St • Mansfield, TX 76063-1794
(817) 473-5600 • http://www.mansfieldisd.org/
Grade Span: PK-12; **Agency Type:** 1
Schools: 21
10 Primary; 6 Middle; 3 High; 1 Other Level
18 Regular; 0 Special Education; 0 Vocational; 2 Alternative
0 Magnet; 0 Charter; 3 Title I Eligible; 2 School-wide Title I
Students: 19,162 (51.5% male; 48.5% female)
Individual Education Program: 2,150 (11.2%);
English Language Learner: 1,148 (6.0%); Migrant: 3 (<0.1%)
Eligible for Free Lunch Program: 3,301 (17.2%)
Eligible for Reduced-Price Lunch Program: 979 (5.1%)
Teachers: 1,252.2 (15.3 to 1)
Librarians/Media Specialists: 14.5 (1,321.5 to 1)
Guidance Counselors: 39.8 (481.5 to 1)
Current Spending: ($ per student per year):
Total: $5,731; Instruction: $3,654; Support Services: $1,854
Enrollment, Drop-out Rates and Diploma Recipients by Race/Ethnicity

Category	Total	White	Black	Asian	AIAN	Hisp.
Enrollment (%)	100.0	62.7	18.0	4.1	0.4	14.7
Drop-out Rate (%)	2.6	2.4	2.6	1.8	14.3	3.9
H.S. Diplomas (#)	791	566	110	38	2	75

White Settlement ISD
401 S Cherry Ln • White Settlement, TX 76108-2521
(817) 367-1350
Grade Span: PK-12; **Agency Type:** 1
Schools: 9
4 Primary; 2 Middle; 1 High; 2 Other Level
7 Regular; 1 Special Education; 0 Vocational; 1 Alternative
0 Magnet; 0 Charter; 5 Title I Eligible; 5 School-wide Title I
Students: 4,787 (51.5% male; 48.5% female)
Individual Education Program: 598 (12.5%);
English Language Learner: 184 (3.8%); Migrant: 0 (0.0%)
Eligible for Free Lunch Program: 1,512 (31.6%)
Eligible for Reduced-Price Lunch Program: 288 (6.0%)
Teachers: 311.0 (15.4 to 1)
Librarians/Media Specialists: 3.5 (1,367.7 to 1)
Guidance Counselors: 10.0 (478.7 to 1)
Current Spending: ($ per student per year):
Total: $6,225; Instruction: $3,797; Support Services: $2,136
Enrollment, Drop-out Rates and Diploma Recipients by Race/Ethnicity

Category	Total	White	Black	Asian	AIAN	Hisp.
Enrollment (%)	100.0	69.5	7.5	2.4	0.6	20.0
Drop-out Rate (%)	4.5	4.9	0.0	11.4	18.2	2.4
H.S. Diplomas (#)	283	215	26	8	3	31

Taylor County

Abilene ISD
842 N Mockingbird • Abilene, TX 79603-5729
Mailing Address: PO Box 981 • Abilene, TX 79604-0981
(915) 677-1444
Grade Span: PK-12; **Agency Type:** 1
Schools: 43
20 Primary; 7 Middle; 4 High; 10 Other Level
26 Regular; 4 Special Education; 0 Vocational; 11 Alternative
0 Magnet; 0 Charter; 8 Title I Eligible; 8 School-wide Title I
Students: 17,466 (50.8% male; 49.2% female)
Individual Education Program: 3,125 (17.9%);
English Language Learner: 357 (2.0%); Migrant: 0 (0.0%)
Eligible for Free Lunch Program: 7,736 (44.3%)
Eligible for Reduced-Price Lunch Program: 1,732 (9.9%)
Teachers: 1,279.2 (13.7 to 1)
Librarians/Media Specialists: 22.0 (793.9 to 1)
Guidance Counselors: 48.0 (363.9 to 1)
Current Spending: ($ per student per year):
Total: $6,672; Instruction: $4,388; Support Services: $1,972
Enrollment, Drop-out Rates and Diploma Recipients by Race/Ethnicity

Category	Total	White	Black	Asian	AIAN	Hisp.
Enrollment (%)	100.0	54.9	12.5	1.2	0.4	31.0
Drop-out Rate (%)	5.2	3.4	7.2	3.8	10.0	8.9
H.S. Diplomas (#)	1,032	688	109	21	1	213

Wylie ISD
7049 Buffalo Gap Rd • Abilene, TX 79606-5448
(915) 692-4353
Grade Span: PK-12; **Agency Type:** 1
Schools: 7
3 Primary; 2 Middle; 1 High; 1 Other Level
6 Regular; 0 Special Education; 0 Vocational; 1 Alternative
0 Magnet; 0 Charter; 4 Title I Eligible; 0 School-wide Title I
Students: 2,774 (49.4% male; 50.6% female)
Individual Education Program: 343 (12.4%);
English Language Learner: 9 (0.3%); Migrant: 0 (0.0%)
Eligible for Free Lunch Program: 118 (4.3%)
Eligible for Reduced-Price Lunch Program: 87 (3.1%)
Teachers: 172.5 (16.1 to 1)
Librarians/Media Specialists: 2.0 (1,387.0 to 1)
Guidance Counselors: 6.4 (433.4 to 1)
Current Spending: ($ per student per year):
Total: $4,531; Instruction: $3,005; Support Services: $1,338
Enrollment, Drop-out Rates and Diploma Recipients by Race/Ethnicity

Category	Total	White	Black	Asian	AIAN	Hisp.
Enrollment (%)	100.0	88.9	2.2	1.6	0.5	6.7
Drop-out Rate (%)	1.5	1.3	6.3	10.0	0.0	2.6
H.S. Diplomas (#)	194	175	7	4	1	7

Terry County

Brownfield ISD
601 Tahoka Rd • Brownfield, TX 79316-3631
(806) 637-2591 • http://www.brownfield.k12.tx.us/
Grade Span: PK-12; **Agency Type:** 1
Schools: 5
2 Primary; 1 Middle; 1 High; 0 Other Level
4 Regular; 0 Special Education; 0 Vocational; 0 Alternative
0 Magnet; 0 Charter; 3 Title I Eligible; 2 School-wide Title I
Students: 1,984 (51.8% male; 48.2% female)
Individual Education Program: 288 (14.5%);
English Language Learner: 100 (5.0%); Migrant: 252 (12.7%)
Eligible for Free Lunch Program: 1,144 (57.7%)
Eligible for Reduced-Price Lunch Program: 165 (8.3%)
Teachers: 155.8 (12.7 to 1)
Librarians/Media Specialists: 3.9 (508.7 to 1)
Guidance Counselors: 5.9 (336.3 to 1)
Current Spending: ($ per student per year):
Total: $6,970; Instruction: $4,431; Support Services: $2,222
Enrollment, Drop-out Rates and Diploma Recipients by Race/Ethnicity

Category	Total	White	Black	Asian	AIAN	Hisp.
Enrollment (%)	100.0	31.8	4.7	0.4	0.4	62.8
Drop-out Rate (%)	4.2	1.7	2.9	0.0	0.0	6.0
H.S. Diplomas (#)	163	68	8	3	0	84

Titus County

Mount Pleasant ISD
105 N Riddle • Mount Pleasant, TX 75455
Mailing Address: PO Box 1117 • Mount Pleasant, TX 75456-1117
(903) 575-2000 • http://www.mpisd.net/
Grade Span: PK-12; **Agency Type:** 1
Schools: 10
5 Primary; 2 Middle; 3 High; 0 Other Level
8 Regular; 0 Special Education; 0 Vocational; 2 Alternative
0 Magnet; 0 Charter; 6 Title I Eligible; 6 School-wide Title I
Students: 4,977 (51.6% male; 48.4% female)
Individual Education Program: 683 (13.7%);
English Language Learner: 1,691 (34.0%); Migrant: 1,165 (23.4%)
Eligible for Free Lunch Program: 2,968 (59.6%)
Eligible for Reduced-Price Lunch Program: 495 (9.9%)
Teachers: 382.9 (13.0 to 1)
Librarians/Media Specialists: 2.0 (2,488.5 to 1)
Guidance Counselors: 13.0 (382.8 to 1)
Current Spending: ($ per student per year):
Total: $6,923; Instruction: $4,231; Support Services: $2,350
Enrollment, Drop-out Rates and Diploma Recipients by Race/Ethnicity

Category	Total	White	Black	Asian	AIAN	Hisp.
Enrollment (%)	100.0	32.3	16.2	0.5	0.3	50.8
Drop-out Rate (%)	3.7	3.5	6.0	0.0	0.0	3.2
H.S. Diplomas (#)	270	151	39	2	0	78

Tom Green County

San Angelo ISD
1621 University Ave • San Angelo, TX 76904-5164
(915) 947-3700
Grade Span: PK-12; **Agency Type:** 1
Schools: 28
19 Primary; 4 Middle; 2 High; 2 Other Level
25 Regular; 0 Special Education; 0 Vocational; 2 Alternative
0 Magnet; 0 Charter; 16 Title I Eligible; 16 School-wide Title I
Students: 15,280 (51.1% male; 48.9% female)
Individual Education Program: 1,973 (12.9%);
English Language Learner: 766 (5.0%); Migrant: 372 (2.4%)
Eligible for Free Lunch Program: 6,031 (39.5%)
Eligible for Reduced-Price Lunch Program: 1,527 (10.0%)
Teachers: 1,001.0 (15.3 to 1)
Librarians/Media Specialists: 19.0 (804.2 to 1)
Guidance Counselors: 35.0 (436.6 to 1)
Current Spending: ($ per student per year):
Total: $5,742; Instruction: $3,484; Support Services: $1,989
Enrollment, Drop-out Rates and Diploma Recipients by Race/Ethnicity

Category	Total	White	Black	Asian	AIAN	Hisp.
Enrollment (%)	100.0	45.0	6.3	1.1	0.2	47.4
Drop-out Rate (%)	4.1	2.7	2.7	0.0	0.0	6.3
H.S. Diplomas (#)	960	527	55	17	2	359

Travis County

Austin ISD
1111 W 6th St • Austin, TX 78703-5399
(512) 414-1700 • http://www.austin.isd.tenet.edu/
Grade Span: PK-12; **Agency Type:** 1
Schools: 111
75 Primary; 17 Middle; 13 High; 6 Other Level
104 Regular; 0 Special Education; 0 Vocational; 7 Alternative
0 Magnet; 0 Charter; 66 Title I Eligible; 66 School-wide Title I
Students: 78,608 (51.5% male; 48.5% female)
Individual Education Program: 9,486 (12.1%);
English Language Learner: 16,284 (20.7%); Migrant: 64 (0.1%)
Eligible for Free Lunch Program: 35,240 (44.8%)
Eligible for Reduced-Price Lunch Program: 6,378 (8.1%)
Teachers: 5,382.2 (14.6 to 1)

Librarians/Media Specialists: 103.5 (759.5 to 1)
Guidance Counselors: 167.5 (469.3 to 1)
Current Spending: ($ per student per year):
Total: $6,964; Instruction: $4,047; Support Services: $2,616
Enrollment, Drop-out Rates and Diploma Recipients by Race/Ethnicity

Category	Total	White	Black	Asian	AIAN	Hisp.
Enrollment (%)	100.0	31.2	14.4	2.7	0.3	51.5
Drop-out Rate (%)	5.6	2.8	7.2	2.8	3.9	7.9
H.S. Diplomas (#)	3,705	1,755	562	117	8	1,263

Del Valle ISD
5301 Ross Rd • Del Valle, TX 78617-9404
(512) 386-3000 • http://www.del-valle.k12.tx.us/
Grade Span: PK-12; **Agency Type:** 1
Schools: 10
6 Primary; 1 Middle; 2 High; 1 Other Level
8 Regular; 0 Special Education; 0 Vocational; 2 Alternative
0 Magnet; 0 Charter; 9 Title I Eligible; 9 School-wide Title I
Students: 7,326 (51.3% male; 48.7% female)
Individual Education Program: 1,022 (14.0%);
English Language Learner: 1,281 (17.5%); Migrant: 9 (0.1%)
Eligible for Free Lunch Program: 4,220 (57.6%)
Eligible for Reduced-Price Lunch Program: 1,021 (13.9%)
Teachers: 530.8 (13.8 to 1)
Librarians/Media Specialists: 7.0 (1,046.6 to 1)
Guidance Counselors: 17.0 (430.9 to 1)
Current Spending: ($ per student per year):
Total: $6,933; Instruction: $4,146; Support Services: $2,402
Enrollment, Drop-out Rates and Diploma Recipients by Race/Ethnicity

Category	Total	White	Black	Asian	AIAN	Hisp.
Enrollment (%)	100.0	16.9	14.5	1.3	0.5	66.9
Drop-out Rate (%)	4.7	3.7	5.8	0.0	0.0	4.9
H.S. Diplomas (#)	302	66	67	7	5	157

Eanes ISD
601 Camp Craft Rd • Austin, TX 78746-6511
(512) 329-3626 •
http://www.eanes.k12.tx.us/education/district/district.php?sectionid=1
Grade Span: PK-12; **Agency Type:** 1
Schools: 11
6 Primary; 2 Middle; 2 High; 0 Other Level
9 Regular; 0 Special Education; 0 Vocational; 1 Alternative
0 Magnet; 0 Charter; 4 Title I Eligible; 0 School-wide Title I
Students: 7,132 (52.2% male; 47.8% female)
Individual Education Program: 753 (10.6%);
English Language Learner: 107 (1.5%); Migrant: 0 (0.0%)
Eligible for Free Lunch Program: 110 (1.5%)
Eligible for Reduced-Price Lunch Program: 36 (0.5%)
Teachers: 539.8 (13.2 to 1)
Librarians/Media Specialists: 10.0 (713.2 to 1)
Guidance Counselors: 22.5 (317.0 to 1)
Current Spending: ($ per student per year):
Total: $6,969; Instruction: $4,456; Support Services: $2,215
Enrollment, Drop-out Rates and Diploma Recipients by Race/Ethnicity

Category	Total	White	Black	Asian	AIAN	Hisp.
Enrollment (%)	100.0	88.0	0.4	6.2	0.2	5.1
Drop-out Rate (%)	1.4	1.4	14.3	0.7	0.0	2.0
H.S. Diplomas (#)	528	466	2	33	2	25

Lake Travis ISD
3322 Ranch Rd 620 S • Austin, TX 78738-6801
(512) 533-6000
Grade Span: PK-12; **Agency Type:** 1
Schools: 8
4 Primary; 2 Middle; 1 High; 0 Other Level
7 Regular; 0 Special Education; 0 Vocational; 0 Alternative
0 Magnet; 0 Charter; 1 Title I Eligible; 0 School-wide Title I
Students: 4,671 (53.2% male; 46.8% female)
Individual Education Program: 504 (10.8%);
English Language Learner: 189 (4.0%); Migrant: 1 (<0.1%)
Eligible for Free Lunch Program: 390 (8.3%)
Eligible for Reduced-Price Lunch Program: 92 (2.0%)
Teachers: 311.2 (15.0 to 1)
Librarians/Media Specialists: 7.0 (667.3 to 1)
Guidance Counselors: 12.8 (364.9 to 1)
Current Spending: ($ per student per year):
Total: $6,609; Instruction: $4,208; Support Services: $2,157
Enrollment, Drop-out Rates and Diploma Recipients by Race/Ethnicity

Category	Total	White	Black	Asian	AIAN	Hisp.
Enrollment (%)	100.0	84.3	1.1	2.1	0.4	12.1
Drop-out Rate (%)	1.9	2.0	0.0	0.0	0.0	1.5
H.S. Diplomas (#)	269	234	0	3	0	32

Manor ISD
312 Murray Ave • Manor, TX 78653-0679
Mailing Address: PO Box 359 • Manor, TX 78653-0359
(512) 278-4000 • http://mustang.manor.isd.tenet.edu/
Grade Span: PK-12; **Agency Type:** 1
Schools: 7
3 Primary; 1 Middle; 1 High; 2 Other Level
5 Regular; 0 Special Education; 0 Vocational; 2 Alternative
0 Magnet; 0 Charter; 6 Title I Eligible; 6 School-wide Title I
Students: 3,020 (50.3% male; 49.7% female)
Individual Education Program: 401 (13.3%);
English Language Learner: 571 (18.9%); Migrant: 39 (1.3%)
Eligible for Free Lunch Program: 1,519 (50.3%)
Eligible for Reduced-Price Lunch Program: 316 (10.5%)
Teachers: 219.7 (13.7 to 1)
Librarians/Media Specialists: 5.0 (604.0 to 1)
Guidance Counselors: 8.0 (377.5 to 1)
Current Spending: ($ per student per year):
Total: $7,482; Instruction: $4,079; Support Services: $2,955
Enrollment, Drop-out Rates and Diploma Recipients by Race/Ethnicity

Category	Total	White	Black	Asian	AIAN	Hisp.
Enrollment (%)	100.0	30.2	20.2	1.6	0.1	47.8
Drop-out Rate (%)	3.9	2.8	2.7	0.0	0.0	5.7
H.S. Diplomas (#)	141	54	39	2	1	45

Pflugerville ISD
1401 W Pecan St • Pflugerville, TX 78660-2518
(512) 594-0000
Grade Span: PK-12; **Agency Type:** 1
Schools: 23
14 Primary; 5 Middle; 3 High; 0 Other Level
20 Regular; 0 Special Education; 0 Vocational; 2 Alternative
0 Magnet; 0 Charter; 9 Title I Eligible; 0 School-wide Title I
Students: 15,875 (52.1% male; 47.9% female)
Individual Education Program: 1,870 (11.8%);
English Language Learner: 1,421 (9.0%); Migrant: 14 (0.1%)
Eligible for Free Lunch Program: 3,266 (20.6%)
Eligible for Reduced-Price Lunch Program: 1,286 (8.1%)
Teachers: 1,018.9 (15.6 to 1)
Librarians/Media Specialists: 18.0 (881.9 to 1)
Guidance Counselors: 32.1 (494.5 to 1)
Current Spending: ($ per student per year):
Total: $5,654; Instruction: $3,591; Support Services: $1,814
Enrollment, Drop-out Rates and Diploma Recipients by Race/Ethnicity

Category	Total	White	Black	Asian	AIAN	Hisp.
Enrollment (%)	100.0	44.1	19.3	8.2	0.5	27.9
Drop-out Rate (%)	1.9	1.4	1.9	2.8	0.0	2.4
H.S. Diplomas (#)	864	463	138	78	2	183

Upshur County

Gilmer ISD
500 So Trinity • Gilmer, TX 75644-0040
(903) 843-2525
Grade Span: PK-12; **Agency Type:** 1
Schools: 4
2 Primary; 1 Middle; 1 High; 0 Other Level
4 Regular; 0 Special Education; 0 Vocational; 0 Alternative
0 Magnet; 0 Charter; 4 Title I Eligible; 4 School-wide Title I
Students: 2,346 (51.9% male; 48.1% female)
Individual Education Program: 349 (14.9%);
English Language Learner: 76 (3.2%); Migrant: 5 (0.2%)
Eligible for Free Lunch Program: 822 (35.0%)
Eligible for Reduced-Price Lunch Program: 184 (7.8%)
Teachers: 182.9 (12.8 to 1)
Librarians/Media Specialists: 4.0 (586.5 to 1)
Guidance Counselors: 5.0 (469.2 to 1)
Current Spending: ($ per student per year):
Total: $6,350; Instruction: $4,216; Support Services: $1,866
Enrollment, Drop-out Rates and Diploma Recipients by Race/Ethnicity

Category	Total	White	Black	Asian	AIAN	Hisp.
Enrollment (%)	100.0	73.2	19.2	0.2	0.8	6.6
Drop-out Rate (%)	3.8	3.2	6.4	n/a	0.0	3.3
H.S. Diplomas (#)	166	131	27	0	1	7

Uvalde County

Uvalde CISD
1000 N Getty • Uvalde, TX 78801-4206
Mailing Address: PO Box 1909 • Uvalde, TX 78802-1909
(830) 278-6655
Grade Span: PK-12; **Agency Type:** 1
Schools: 10
5 Primary; 3 Middle; 2 High; 0 Other Level
9 Regular; 0 Special Education; 0 Vocational; 1 Alternative

0 Magnet; 0 Charter; 10 Title I Eligible; 9 School-wide Title I
Students: 5,264 (52.0% male; 48.0% female)
Individual Education Program: 634 (12.0%);
English Language Learner: 550 (10.4%); Migrant: 906 (17.2%)
Eligible for Free Lunch Program: 3,425 (65.1%)
Eligible for Reduced-Price Lunch Program: 448 (8.5%)
Teachers: 371.4 (14.2 to 1)
Librarians/Media Specialists: 6.0 (877.3 to 1)
Guidance Counselors: 18.0 (292.4 to 1)
Current Spending: ($ per student per year):
Total: $6,573; Instruction: $3,943; Support Services: $2,281
Enrollment, Drop-out Rates and Diploma Recipients by Race/Ethnicity

Category	Total	White	Black	Asian	AIAN	Hisp.
Enrollment (%)	100.0	14.1	0.5	0.4	0.0	84.9
Drop-out Rate (%)	6.5	3.2	n/a	n/a	0.0	7.5
H.S. Diplomas (#)	273	66	0	1	0	206

Val Verde County

San Felipe-Del Rio CISD
205 Memorial Dr • Del Rio, TX 78842-0128
Mailing Address: PO Box 420128 • Del Rio, TX 78842-0128
(830) 778-4007
Grade Span: PK-12; **Agency Type:** 1
Schools: 14
8 Primary; 1 Middle; 1 High; 4 Other Level
14 Regular; 0 Special Education; 0 Vocational; 0 Alternative
0 Magnet; 0 Charter; 14 Title I Eligible; 14 School-wide Title I
Students: 10,320 (50.9% male; 49.1% female)
Individual Education Program: 1,213 (11.8%);
English Language Learner: 1,800 (17.4%); Migrant: 3,460 (33.5%)
Eligible for Free Lunch Program: 6,482 (62.8%)
Eligible for Reduced-Price Lunch Program: 1,078 (10.4%)
Teachers: 576.2 (17.9 to 1)
Librarians/Media Specialists: 11.0 (938.2 to 1)
Guidance Counselors: 25.0 (412.8 to 1)
Current Spending: ($ per student per year):
Total: $6,281; Instruction: $3,749; Support Services: $2,199
Enrollment, Drop-out Rates and Diploma Recipients by Race/Ethnicity

Category	Total	White	Black	Asian	AIAN	Hisp.
Enrollment (%)	100.0	9.9	1.4	0.4	0.1	88.2
Drop-out Rate (%)	3.7	2.1	0.0	0.0	0.0	4.0
H.S. Diplomas (#)	482	52	6	1	1	422

Van Zandt County

Canton ISD
225 W Elm St • Canton, TX 75103-1799
(903) 567-4179
Grade Span: PK-12; **Agency Type:** 1
Schools: 4
2 Primary; 1 Middle; 1 High; 0 Other Level
4 Regular; 0 Special Education; 0 Vocational; 0 Alternative
0 Magnet; 0 Charter; 4 Title I Eligible; 0 School-wide Title I
Students: 1,729 (50.9% male; 49.1% female)
Individual Education Program: 182 (10.5%);
English Language Learner: 28 (1.6%); Migrant: 1 (0.1%)
Eligible for Free Lunch Program: 474 (27.4%)
Eligible for Reduced-Price Lunch Program: 94 (5.4%)
Teachers: 121.5 (14.2 to 1)
Librarians/Media Specialists: 2.0 (864.5 to 1)
Guidance Counselors: 3.0 (576.3 to 1)
Current Spending: ($ per student per year):
Total: $5,812; Instruction: $3,901; Support Services: $1,611
Enrollment, Drop-out Rates and Diploma Recipients by Race/Ethnicity

Category	Total	White	Black	Asian	AIAN	Hisp.
Enrollment (%)	100.0	89.4	3.3	1.0	0.3	6.0
Drop-out Rate (%)	0.6	0.6	0.0	0.0	0.0	0.0
H.S. Diplomas (#)	105	93	7	2	0	3

Van ISD
549 E Texas St • Van, TX 75790-0697
Mailing Address: PO Box 697 • Van, TX 75790-0697
(903) 963-8328
Grade Span: PK-12; **Agency Type:** 1
Schools: 4
2 Primary; 1 Middle; 1 High; 0 Other Level
4 Regular; 0 Special Education; 0 Vocational; 0 Alternative
0 Magnet; 0 Charter; 2 Title I Eligible; 2 School-wide Title I
Students: 2,198 (52.0% male; 48.0% female)
Individual Education Program: 285 (13.0%);
English Language Learner: 105 (4.8%); Migrant: 0 (0.0%)
Eligible for Free Lunch Program: 749 (34.1%)
Eligible for Reduced-Price Lunch Program: 153 (7.0%)
Teachers: 155.6 (14.1 to 1)
Librarians/Media Specialists: 2.0 (1,099.0 to 1)
Guidance Counselors: 6.0 (366.3 to 1)
Current Spending: ($ per student per year):
Total: $5,898; Instruction: $3,645; Support Services: $1,933
Enrollment, Drop-out Rates and Diploma Recipients by Race/Ethnicity

Category	Total	White	Black	Asian	AIAN	Hisp.
Enrollment (%)	100.0	86.1	3.2	0.5	0.2	10.1
Drop-out Rate (%)	2.6	2.2	0.0	0.0	200.0	4.3
H.S. Diplomas (#)	121	111	4	0	0	6

Wills Point ISD
338 W N Commerce St • Wills Point, TX 75169-2504
(903) 873-3161
Grade Span: PK-12; **Agency Type:** 1
Schools: 5
2 Primary; 2 Middle; 1 High; 0 Other Level
5 Regular; 0 Special Education; 0 Vocational; 0 Alternative
0 Magnet; 0 Charter; 5 Title I Eligible; 5 School-wide Title I
Students: 2,653 (50.1% male; 49.9% female)
Individual Education Program: 334 (12.6%);
English Language Learner: 108 (4.1%); Migrant: 16 (0.6%)
Eligible for Free Lunch Program: 993 (37.4%)
Eligible for Reduced-Price Lunch Program: 229 (8.6%)
Teachers: 173.2 (15.3 to 1)
Librarians/Media Specialists: 3.0 (884.3 to 1)
Guidance Counselors: 5.0 (530.6 to 1)
Current Spending: ($ per student per year):
Total: $5,641; Instruction: $3,457; Support Services: $1,885
Enrollment, Drop-out Rates and Diploma Recipients by Race/Ethnicity

Category	Total	White	Black	Asian	AIAN	Hisp.
Enrollment (%)	100.0	81.4	8.0	0.3	0.3	10.0
Drop-out Rate (%)	2.0	1.7	2.7	n/a	0.0	4.3
H.S. Diplomas (#)	159	123	27	0	1	8

Victoria County

Victoria ISD
102 Profit Dr • Victoria, TX 77901-7346
Mailing Address: PO Box 1759 • Victoria, TX 77902-1759
(361) 576-3131
Grade Span: PK-12; **Agency Type:** 1
Schools: 28
16 Primary; 3 Middle; 3 High; 4 Other Level
20 Regular; 0 Special Education; 0 Vocational; 6 Alternative
0 Magnet; 0 Charter; 11 Title I Eligible; 11 School-wide Title I
Students: 14,556 (51.7% male; 48.3% female)
Individual Education Program: 1,757 (12.1%);
English Language Learner: 442 (3.0%); Migrant: 26 (0.2%)
Eligible for Free Lunch Program: 5,562 (38.2%)
Eligible for Reduced-Price Lunch Program: 1,085 (7.5%)
Teachers: 976.1 (14.9 to 1)
Librarians/Media Specialists: 16.4 (887.6 to 1)
Guidance Counselors: 39.8 (365.7 to 1)
Current Spending: ($ per student per year):
Total: $6,674; Instruction: $4,107; Support Services: $2,262
Enrollment, Drop-out Rates and Diploma Recipients by Race/Ethnicity

Category	Total	White	Black	Asian	AIAN	Hisp.
Enrollment (%)	100.0	38.6	8.6	0.9	0.3	51.6
Drop-out Rate (%)	6.0	2.8	5.3	0.0	0.0	9.4
H.S. Diplomas (#)	867	448	67	12	1	339

Walker County

Huntsville ISD
441 Fm 2821 E • Huntsville, TX 77320-9298
(936) 295-3421
Grade Span: PK-12; **Agency Type:** 1
Schools: 10
5 Primary; 2 Middle; 3 High; 0 Other Level
8 Regular; 0 Special Education; 0 Vocational; 2 Alternative
0 Magnet; 0 Charter; 7 Title I Eligible; 7 School-wide Title I
Students: 6,756 (50.9% male; 49.1% female)
Individual Education Program: 802 (11.9%);
English Language Learner: 438 (6.5%); Migrant: 52 (0.8%)
Eligible for Free Lunch Program: 2,083 (30.8%)
Eligible for Reduced-Price Lunch Program: 700 (10.4%)
Teachers: 452.4 (14.9 to 1)
Librarians/Media Specialists: 8.9 (759.1 to 1)
Guidance Counselors: 14.0 (482.6 to 1)
Current Spending: ($ per student per year):
Total: $5,726; Instruction: $3,329; Support Services: $2,081

Enrollment, Drop-out Rates and Diploma Recipients by Race/Ethnicity

Category	Total	White	Black	Asian	AIAN	Hisp.
Enrollment (%)	100.0	50.2	29.4	1.2	0.3	18.9
Drop-out Rate (%)	3.1	2.0	5.4	0.0	0.0	3.3
H.S. Diplomas (#)	357	221	87	2	1	46

Waller County

Royal ISD

2520 Durkin Rd • Brookshire, TX 77423-9418
Mailing Address: PO Box 489 • Pattison, TX 77466-0489
(281) 934-2248
Grade Span: PK-12; **Agency Type:** 1
Schools: 6
1 Primary; 1 Middle; 1 High; 0 Other Level
3 Regular; 0 Special Education; 0 Vocational; 0 Alternative
0 Magnet; 0 Charter; 3 Title I Eligible; 3 School-wide Title I
Students: 1,597 (50.9% male; 49.1% female)
Individual Education Program: 198 (12.4%);
English Language Learner: 258 (16.2%); Migrant: 3 (0.2%)
Eligible for Free Lunch Program: 1,038 (65.0%)
Eligible for Reduced-Price Lunch Program: 106 (6.6%)
Teachers: 115.4 (13.8 to 1)
Librarians/Media Specialists: 3.0 (532.3 to 1)
Guidance Counselors: 3.0 (532.3 to 1)
Current Spending: ($ per student per year):
Total: $6,948; Instruction: $3,940; Support Services: $2,624

Enrollment, Drop-out Rates and Diploma Recipients by Race/Ethnicity

Category	Total	White	Black	Asian	AIAN	Hisp.
Enrollment (%)	100.0	19.2	33.2	0.6	0.0	47.0
Drop-out Rate (%)	3.3	3.1	3.5	0.0	n/a	3.3
H.S. Diplomas (#)	70	15	26	1	0	28

Waller ISD

2214 Waller St • Waller, TX 77484-1918
(936) 931-3685
Grade Span: PK-12; **Agency Type:** 1
Schools: 8
4 Primary; 2 Middle; 1 High; 1 Other Level
7 Regular; 0 Special Education; 0 Vocational; 1 Alternative
0 Magnet; 0 Charter; 7 Title I Eligible; 7 School-wide Title I
Students: 4,651 (52.0% male; 48.0% female)
Individual Education Program: 473 (10.2%);
English Language Learner: 560 (12.0%); Migrant: 0 (0.0%)
Eligible for Free Lunch Program: 1,689 (36.3%)
Eligible for Reduced-Price Lunch Program: 342 (7.4%)
Teachers: 304.5 (15.3 to 1)
Librarians/Media Specialists: 5.0 (930.2 to 1)
Guidance Counselors: 10.2 (456.0 to 1)
Current Spending: ($ per student per year):
Total: $6,281; Instruction: $3,651; Support Services: $2,351

Enrollment, Drop-out Rates and Diploma Recipients by Race/Ethnicity

Category	Total	White	Black	Asian	AIAN	Hisp.
Enrollment (%)	100.0	55.0	16.9	1.0	0.6	26.6
Drop-out Rate (%)	3.5	3.5	1.8	0.0	20.0	4.5
H.S. Diplomas (#)	281	174	52	3	0	52

Ward County

Monahans-Wickett-Pyote ISD

606 S Betty Ave • Monahans, TX 79756-5018
(915) 943-6711
Grade Span: PK-12; **Agency Type:** 1
Schools: 7
3 Primary; 2 Middle; 2 High; 0 Other Level
6 Regular; 0 Special Education; 0 Vocational; 1 Alternative
0 Magnet; 0 Charter; 7 Title I Eligible; 7 School-wide Title I
Students: 1,977 (51.5% male; 48.5% female)
Individual Education Program: 284 (14.4%);
English Language Learner: 86 (4.4%); Migrant: 0 (0.0%)
Eligible for Free Lunch Program: 573 (29.0%)
Eligible for Reduced-Price Lunch Program: 174 (8.8%)
Teachers: 140.3 (14.1 to 1)
Librarians/Media Specialists: 0.4 (4,942.5 to 1)
Guidance Counselors: 2.2 (898.6 to 1)
Current Spending: ($ per student per year):
Total: $7,212; Instruction: $4,604; Support Services: $2,205

Enrollment, Drop-out Rates and Diploma Recipients by Race/Ethnicity

Category	Total	White	Black	Asian	AIAN	Hisp.
Enrollment (%)	100.0	44.6	6.8	0.4	0.2	48.0
Drop-out Rate (%)	5.7	4.0	9.1	0.0	n/a	7.3
H.S. Diplomas (#)	139	70	7	2	0	60

Washington County

Brenham ISD

711 Mansfield • Brenham, TX 77833-4732
Mailing Address: PO Box 1147 • Brenham, TX 77834-1147
(979) 277-6500
Grade Span: PK-12; **Agency Type:** 1
Schools: 8
3 Primary; 2 Middle; 1 High; 2 Other Level
7 Regular; 0 Special Education; 0 Vocational; 1 Alternative
0 Magnet; 0 Charter; 5 Title I Eligible; 0 School-wide Title I
Students: 4,735 (50.7% male; 49.3% female)
Individual Education Program: 525 (11.1%);
English Language Learner: 252 (5.3%); Migrant: 0 (0.0%)
Eligible for Free Lunch Program: 1,725 (36.4%)
Eligible for Reduced-Price Lunch Program: 308 (6.5%)
Teachers: 364.7 (13.0 to 1)
Librarians/Media Specialists: 3.5 (1,352.9 to 1)
Guidance Counselors: 12.1 (391.3 to 1)
Current Spending: ($ per student per year):
Total: $6,298; Instruction: $3,842; Support Services: $2,079

Enrollment, Drop-out Rates and Diploma Recipients by Race/Ethnicity

Category	Total	White	Black	Asian	AIAN	Hisp.
Enrollment (%)	100.0	54.7	29.0	1.4	0.1	14.8
Drop-out Rate (%)	3.5	1.7	6.9	10.3	0.0	5.1
H.S. Diplomas (#)	338	230	74	7	1	26

Webb County

Laredo ISD

1702 Houston St • Laredo, TX 78040-4906
(956) 795-3200
Grade Span: PK-12; **Agency Type:** 1
Schools: 29
20 Primary; 4 Middle; 3 High; 2 Other Level
27 Regular; 0 Special Education; 0 Vocational; 2 Alternative
0 Magnet; 0 Charter; 27 Title I Eligible; 27 School-wide Title I
Students: 24,279 (50.8% male; 49.2% female)
Individual Education Program: 3,477 (14.3%);
English Language Learner: 14,323 (59.0%); Migrant: 444 (1.8%)
Eligible for Free Lunch Program: 11,797 (48.6%)
Eligible for Reduced-Price Lunch Program: 817 (3.4%)
Teachers: 1,515.1 (16.0 to 1)
Librarians/Media Specialists: 27.6 (879.7 to 1)
Guidance Counselors: 55.8 (435.1 to 1)
Current Spending: ($ per student per year):
Total: $6,271; Instruction: $3,963; Support Services: $2,009

Enrollment, Drop-out Rates and Diploma Recipients by Race/Ethnicity

Category	Total	White	Black	Asian	AIAN	Hisp.
Enrollment (%)	100.0	0.7	0.1	0.1	0.0	99.2
Drop-out Rate (%)	6.1	10.4	50.0	0.0	0.0	6.0
H.S. Diplomas (#)	1,080	11	1	0	0	1,068

United ISD

201 Lindenwood Rd • Laredo, TX 78045-2499
(956) 717-6201
Grade Span: PK-12; **Agency Type:** 1
Schools: 37
22 Primary; 8 Middle; 4 High; 3 Other Level
35 Regular; 0 Special Education; 0 Vocational; 2 Alternative
0 Magnet; 0 Charter; 35 Title I Eligible; 33 School-wide Title I
Students: 30,725 (51.4% male; 48.6% female)
Individual Education Program: 3,673 (12.0%);
English Language Learner: 14,405 (46.9%); Migrant: 371 (1.2%)
Eligible for Free Lunch Program: 19,253 (62.7%)
Eligible for Reduced-Price Lunch Program: 3,089 (10.1%)
Teachers: 1,943.6 (15.8 to 1)
Librarians/Media Specialists: 34.0 (903.7 to 1)
Guidance Counselors: 67.8 (453.2 to 1)
Current Spending: ($ per student per year):
Total: $5,833; Instruction: $3,537; Support Services: $1,978

Enrollment, Drop-out Rates and Diploma Recipients by Race/Ethnicity

Category	Total	White	Black	Asian	AIAN	Hisp.
Enrollment (%)	100.0	2.3	0.2	0.5	0.0	97.0
Drop-out Rate (%)	2.6	1.5	16.7	0.0	0.0	2.7
H.S. Diplomas (#)	1,360	59	2	11	0	1,288

Wharton County

El Campo ISD

700 W Norris St • El Campo, TX 77437-2499
(979) 543-6771 • http://www.ecisd.org/
Grade Span: PK-12; **Agency Type:** 1
Schools: 5
2 Primary; 2 Middle; 1 High; 0 Other Level

5 Regular; 0 Special Education; 0 Vocational; 0 Alternative
0 Magnet; 0 Charter; 3 Title I Eligible; 3 School-wide Title I
Students: 3,573 (52.2% male; 47.8% female)
Individual Education Program: 449 (12.6%);
English Language Learner: 279 (7.8%); Migrant: 208 (5.8%)
Eligible for Free Lunch Program: 1,755 (49.1%)
Eligible for Reduced-Price Lunch Program: 324 (9.1%)
Teachers: 246.3 (14.5 to 1)
Librarians/Media Specialists: 3.0 (1,191.0 to 1)
Guidance Counselors: 10.0 (357.3 to 1)
Current Spending: ($ per student per year):
Total: $6,682; Instruction: $4,265; Support Services: $2,097
Enrollment, Drop-out Rates and Diploma Recipients by Race/Ethnicity

Category	Total	White	Black	Asian	AIAN	Hisp.
Enrollment (%)	100.0	36.7	13.9	0.3	0.1	49.1
Drop-out Rate (%)	1.8	0.7	2.5	0.0	0.0	3.0
H.S. Diplomas (#)	239	136	30	3	0	70

Wharton ISD

2100 N Fulton St • Wharton, TX 77488-3146
(979) 532-6201
Grade Span: PK-12; **Agency Type:** 1
Schools: 5
2 Primary; 1 Middle; 2 High; 0 Other Level
5 Regular; 0 Special Education; 0 Vocational; 0 Alternative
0 Magnet; 0 Charter; 5 Title I Eligible; 5 School-wide Title I
Students: 2,546 (50.9% male; 49.1% female)
Individual Education Program: 348 (13.7%);
English Language Learner: 141 (5.5%); Migrant: 8 (0.3%)
Eligible for Free Lunch Program: 1,213 (47.6%)
Eligible for Reduced-Price Lunch Program: 213 (8.4%)
Teachers: 187.2 (13.6 to 1)
Librarians/Media Specialists: 4.0 (636.5 to 1)
Guidance Counselors: 6.0 (424.3 to 1)
Current Spending: ($ per student per year):
Total: $6,614; Instruction: $4,297; Support Services: $2,019
Enrollment, Drop-out Rates and Diploma Recipients by Race/Ethnicity

Category	Total	White	Black	Asian	AIAN	Hisp.
Enrollment (%)	100.0	28.8	30.0	0.8	0.0	40.4
Drop-out Rate (%)	1.9	0.3	3.2	0.0	n/a	2.5
H.S. Diplomas (#)	179	67	65	1	0	46

Wichita County

Burkburnett ISD

416 Glendale St • Burkburnett, TX 76354-2499
(940) 569-3326
Grade Span: PK-12; **Agency Type:** 1
Schools: 6
3 Primary; 1 Middle; 2 High; 0 Other Level
5 Regular; 0 Special Education; 0 Vocational; 1 Alternative
0 Magnet; 0 Charter; 2 Title I Eligible; 2 School-wide Title I
Students: 3,706 (52.6% male; 47.4% female)
Individual Education Program: 455 (12.3%);
English Language Learner: 20 (0.5%); Migrant: 0 (0.0%)
Eligible for Free Lunch Program: 879 (23.7%)
Eligible for Reduced-Price Lunch Program: 439 (11.8%)
Teachers: 288.5 (12.8 to 1)
Librarians/Media Specialists: 5.0 (741.2 to 1)
Guidance Counselors: 8.0 (463.3 to 1)
Current Spending: ($ per student per year):
Total: $5,833; Instruction: $3,888; Support Services: $1,679
Enrollment, Drop-out Rates and Diploma Recipients by Race/Ethnicity

Category	Total	White	Black	Asian	AIAN	Hisp.
Enrollment (%)	100.0	80.8	7.0	2.3	1.8	8.1
Drop-out Rate (%)	4.8	5.2	1.2	0.0	14.3	5.3
H.S. Diplomas (#)	230	187	18	6	2	17

Iowa Park CISD

413 E Cash • Iowa Park, TX 76367-2014
Mailing Address: PO Box 898 • Iowa Park, TX 76367-0898
(940) 592-4193 • http://www.ipcisd.net/
Grade Span: PK-12; **Agency Type:** 1
Schools: 4
2 Primary; 1 Middle; 1 High; 0 Other Level
4 Regular; 0 Special Education; 0 Vocational; 0 Alternative
0 Magnet; 0 Charter; 2 Title I Eligible; 2 School-wide Title I
Students: 1,824 (50.9% male; 49.1% female)
Individual Education Program: 154 (8.4%);
English Language Learner: 2 (0.1%); Migrant: 0 (0.0%)
Eligible for Free Lunch Program: 345 (18.9%)
Eligible for Reduced-Price Lunch Program: 232 (12.7%)
Teachers: 125.6 (14.5 to 1)
Librarians/Media Specialists: 2.9 (629.0 to 1)
Guidance Counselors: 4.0 (456.0 to 1)
Current Spending: ($ per student per year):
Total: $5,242; Instruction: $3,448; Support Services: $1,524
Enrollment, Drop-out Rates and Diploma Recipients by Race/Ethnicity

Category	Total	White	Black	Asian	AIAN	Hisp.
Enrollment (%)	100.0	93.1	0.3	0.3	1.8	4.6
Drop-out Rate (%)	2.1	2.0	n/a	n/a	0.0	3.2
H.S. Diplomas (#)	136	134	0	1	0	1

Wichita Falls ISD

1104 Broad St • Wichita Falls, TX 76301-4412
Mailing Address: PO Box 97533 • Wichita Falls, TX 76307-2570
(940) 720-3303
Grade Span: PK-12; **Agency Type:** 1
Schools: 37
23 Primary; 4 Middle; 5 High; 4 Other Level
32 Regular; 1 Special Education; 0 Vocational; 3 Alternative
0 Magnet; 0 Charter; 21 Title I Eligible; 21 School-wide Title I
Students: 14,999 (51.1% male; 48.9% female)
Individual Education Program: 2,056 (13.7%);
English Language Learner: 634 (4.2%); Migrant: 62 (0.4%)
Eligible for Free Lunch Program: 6,036 (40.2%)
Eligible for Reduced-Price Lunch Program: 1,338 (8.9%)
Teachers: 1,114.1 (13.5 to 1)
Librarians/Media Specialists: 19.9 (753.7 to 1)
Guidance Counselors: 26.5 (566.0 to 1)
Current Spending: ($ per student per year):
Total: $6,484; Instruction: $4,037; Support Services: $2,129
Enrollment, Drop-out Rates and Diploma Recipients by Race/Ethnicity

Category	Total	White	Black	Asian	AIAN	Hisp.
Enrollment (%)	100.0	58.3	17.6	2.4	0.8	20.8
Drop-out Rate (%)	2.6	1.8	4.3	0.7	6.3	4.6
H.S. Diplomas (#)	1,071	736	141	33	6	155

Wilbarger County

Vernon ISD

1713 Wilbarger St #203 • Vernon, TX 76384-4741
(940) 553-1900
Grade Span: PK-12; **Agency Type:** 1
Schools: 6
2 Primary; 2 Middle; 1 High; 1 Other Level
5 Regular; 0 Special Education; 0 Vocational; 1 Alternative
0 Magnet; 0 Charter; 4 Title I Eligible; 4 School-wide Title I
Students: 2,358 (51.1% male; 48.9% female)
Individual Education Program: 397 (16.8%);
English Language Learner: 105 (4.5%); Migrant: 140 (5.9%)
Eligible for Free Lunch Program: 1,001 (42.5%)
Eligible for Reduced-Price Lunch Program: 261 (11.1%)
Teachers: 181.7 (13.0 to 1)
Librarians/Media Specialists: 3.0 (786.0 to 1)
Guidance Counselors: 6.5 (362.8 to 1)
Current Spending: ($ per student per year):
Total: $6,417; Instruction: $4,283; Support Services: $1,863
Enrollment, Drop-out Rates and Diploma Recipients by Race/Ethnicity

Category	Total	White	Black	Asian	AIAN	Hisp.
Enrollment (%)	100.0	53.8	9.7	0.6	0.4	35.5
Drop-out Rate (%)	2.0	1.3	2.9	0.0	0.0	3.2
H.S. Diplomas (#)	158	105	14	1	3	35

Willacy County

Lyford CISD

Simon Gomez Blvd • Lyford, TX 78569-9999
Mailing Address: PO Box 220 • Lyford, TX 78569-0220
(956) 347-3521
Grade Span: PK-12; **Agency Type:** 1
Schools: 4
2 Primary; 1 Middle; 1 High; 0 Other Level
4 Regular; 0 Special Education; 0 Vocational; 0 Alternative
0 Magnet; 0 Charter; 4 Title I Eligible; 4 School-wide Title I
Students: 1,505 (51.9% male; 48.1% female)
Individual Education Program: 156 (10.4%);
English Language Learner: 278 (18.5%); Migrant: 396 (26.3%)
Eligible for Free Lunch Program: 65 (4.3%)
Eligible for Reduced-Price Lunch Program: 4 (0.3%)
Teachers: 113.4 (13.3 to 1)
Librarians/Media Specialists: 1.0 (1,505.0 to 1)
Guidance Counselors: 5.0 (301.0 to 1)
Current Spending: ($ per student per year):
Total: $7,609; Instruction: $4,491; Support Services: $2,670
Enrollment, Drop-out Rates and Diploma Recipients by Race/Ethnicity

Category	Total	White	Black	Asian	AIAN	Hisp.
Enrollment (%)	100.0	3.5	0.4	0.0	0.0	96.1
Drop-out Rate (%)	7.3	8.3	0.0	0.0	n/a	7.3
H.S. Diplomas (#)	117	6	1	0	0	110

Raymondville ISD

One Bearkat Blvd • Raymondville, TX 78580-3351
(956) 689-2471
Grade Span: PK-12; **Agency Type:** 1
Schools: 4
2 Primary; 1 Middle; 1 High; 0 Other Level
4 Regular; 0 Special Education; 0 Vocational; 0 Alternative
0 Magnet; 0 Charter; 4 Title I Eligible; 4 School-wide Title I
Students: 2,674 (52.1% male; 47.9% female)
Individual Education Program: 298 (11.1%);
English Language Learner: 316 (11.8%); Migrant: 1,006 (37.6%)
Eligible for Free Lunch Program: 1,480 (55.3%)
Eligible for Reduced-Price Lunch Program: 107 (4.0%)
Teachers: 176.1 (15.2 to 1)
Librarians/Media Specialists: 4.0 (668.5 to 1)
Guidance Counselors: 8.0 (334.3 to 1)
Current Spending: ($ per student per year):
Total: $6,994; Instruction: $4,069; Support Services: $2,474
Enrollment, Drop-out Rates and Diploma Recipients by Race/Ethnicity

Category	Total	White	Black	Asian	AIAN	Hisp.
Enrollment (%)	100.0	3.1	0.2	0.2	0.0	96.4
Drop-out Rate (%)	8.0	10.5	0.0	n/a	n/a	7.9
H.S. Diplomas (#)	164	7	1	0	0	156

Williamson County

Georgetown ISD

603 Lakeway Dr • Georgetown, TX 78628-2843
(512) 943-5000 • http://www.georgetown.txed.net/
Grade Span: PK-12; **Agency Type:** 1
Schools: 17
8 Primary; 3 Middle; 2 High; 4 Other Level
13 Regular; 0 Special Education; 0 Vocational; 4 Alternative
0 Magnet; 0 Charter; 9 Title I Eligible; 4 School-wide Title I
Students: 8,602 (52.1% male; 47.9% female)
Individual Education Program: 836 (9.7%);
English Language Learner: 545 (6.3%); Migrant: 109 (1.3%)
Eligible for Free Lunch Program: 2,028 (23.6%)
Eligible for Reduced-Price Lunch Program: 686 (8.0%)
Teachers: 675.8 (12.7 to 1)
Librarians/Media Specialists: 11.2 (768.0 to 1)
Guidance Counselors: 19.8 (434.4 to 1)
Current Spending: ($ per student per year):
Total: $6,618; Instruction: $4,133; Support Services: $2,133
Enrollment, Drop-out Rates and Diploma Recipients by Race/Ethnicity

Category	Total	White	Black	Asian	AIAN	Hisp.
Enrollment (%)	100.0	68.7	3.8	0.7	0.2	26.5
Drop-out Rate (%)	2.9	2.0	11.0	0.0	16.7	5.2
H.S. Diplomas (#)	530	450	13	2	2	63

Hutto ISD

302 College • Hutto, TX 78634-0430
Mailing Address: PO Box 430 • Hutto, TX 78634-0430
(512) 759-3771
Grade Span: PK-12; **Agency Type:** 1
Schools: 3
1 Primary; 1 Middle; 1 High; 0 Other Level
3 Regular; 0 Special Education; 0 Vocational; 0 Alternative
0 Magnet; 0 Charter; 1 Title I Eligible; 0 School-wide Title I
Students: 1,640 (49.8% male; 50.2% female)
Individual Education Program: 180 (11.0%);
English Language Learner: 85 (5.2%); Migrant: 12 (0.7%)
Eligible for Free Lunch Program: 251 (15.3%)
Eligible for Reduced-Price Lunch Program: 145 (8.8%)
Teachers: 115.3 (14.2 to 1)
Librarians/Media Specialists: 3.0 (546.7 to 1)
Guidance Counselors: 3.0 (546.7 to 1)
Current Spending: ($ per student per year):
Total: $6,803; Instruction: $3,941; Support Services: $2,478
Enrollment, Drop-out Rates and Diploma Recipients by Race/Ethnicity

Category	Total	White	Black	Asian	AIAN	Hisp.
Enrollment (%)	100.0	66.3	8.0	0.9	0.2	24.6
Drop-out Rate (%)	3.0	2.2	0.0	0.0	0.0	9.3
H.S. Diplomas (#)	70	62	1	0	0	7

Leander ISD

204 W S St • Leander, TX 78641-1806
Mailing Address: PO Box 218 • Leander, TX 78646-0218
(512) 434-5000 • http://www.leanderisd.org/
Grade Span: PK-12; **Agency Type:** 1
Schools: 22
11 Primary; 4 Middle; 3 High; 2 Other Level
17 Regular; 0 Special Education; 0 Vocational; 3 Alternative
0 Magnet; 0 Charter; 8 Title I Eligible; 0 School-wide Title I
Students: 16,814 (51.8% male; 48.2% female)
Individual Education Program: 2,002 (11.9%);
English Language Learner: 609 (3.6%); Migrant: 15 (0.1%)
Eligible for Free Lunch Program: 2,038 (12.1%)
Eligible for Reduced-Price Lunch Program: 927 (5.5%)
Teachers: 1,157.6 (14.5 to 1)
Librarians/Media Specialists: 17.0 (989.1 to 1)
Guidance Counselors: 36.0 (467.1 to 1)
Current Spending: ($ per student per year):
Total: $5,955; Instruction: $3,537; Support Services: $2,109
Enrollment, Drop-out Rates and Diploma Recipients by Race/Ethnicity

Category	Total	White	Black	Asian	AIAN	Hisp.
Enrollment (%)	100.0	75.8	4.5	3.2	0.6	16.0
Drop-out Rate (%)	2.6	2.2	4.8	2.4	4.3	4.6
H.S. Diplomas (#)	765	609	35	18	4	99

Liberty Hill ISD

14001 W Hwy 29 • Liberty Hill, TX 78642-0068
Mailing Address: PO Box 68 • Liberty Hill, TX 78642-0068
(512) 260-5580
Grade Span: PK-12; **Agency Type:** 1
Schools: 5
2 Primary; 1 Middle; 1 High; 1 Other Level
4 Regular; 0 Special Education; 0 Vocational; 1 Alternative
0 Magnet; 0 Charter; 1 Title I Eligible; 0 School-wide Title I
Students: 1,770 (52.1% male; 47.9% female)
Individual Education Program: 209 (11.8%);
English Language Learner: 61 (3.4%); Migrant: 21 (1.2%)
Eligible for Free Lunch Program: 314 (17.7%)
Eligible for Reduced-Price Lunch Program: 141 (8.0%)
Teachers: 139.0 (12.7 to 1)
Librarians/Media Specialists: 0.2 (8,850.0 to 1)
Guidance Counselors: 3.0 (590.0 to 1)
Current Spending: ($ per student per year):
Total: $7,295; Instruction: $4,510; Support Services: $2,438
Enrollment, Drop-out Rates and Diploma Recipients by Race/Ethnicity

Category	Total	White	Black	Asian	AIAN	Hisp.
Enrollment (%)	100.0	81.5	1.1	0.8	0.5	16.2
Drop-out Rate (%)	1.4	0.8	0.0	0.0	n/a	4.5
H.S. Diplomas (#)	83	69	2	1	0	11

Round Rock ISD

1311 Round Rock Ave • Round Rock, TX 78681-4999
(512) 464-5000
Grade Span: PK-12; **Agency Type:** 1
Schools: 45
27 Primary; 8 Middle; 5 High; 4 Other Level
40 Regular; 0 Special Education; 0 Vocational; 4 Alternative
0 Magnet; 0 Charter; 7 Title I Eligible; 4 School-wide Title I
Students: 34,102 (51.3% male; 48.7% female)
Individual Education Program: 3,528 (10.3%);
English Language Learner: 1,989 (5.8%); Migrant: 89 (0.3%)
Eligible for Free Lunch Program: 4,518 (13.2%)
Eligible for Reduced-Price Lunch Program: 1,696 (5.0%)
Teachers: 2,320.7 (14.7 to 1)
Librarians/Media Specialists: 38.0 (897.4 to 1)
Guidance Counselors: 78.2 (436.1 to 1)
Current Spending: ($ per student per year):
Total: $6,410; Instruction: $4,023; Support Services: $2,119
Enrollment, Drop-out Rates and Diploma Recipients by Race/Ethnicity

Category	Total	White	Black	Asian	AIAN	Hisp.
Enrollment (%)	100.0	62.3	9.0	8.2	0.3	20.2
Drop-out Rate (%)	2.0	1.8	2.2	0.6	0.0	4.0
H.S. Diplomas (#)	1,977	1,421	157	123	8	268

Taylor ISD

602 W 12th St • Taylor, TX 76574-2998
(512) 352-6361
Grade Span: PK-12; **Agency Type:** 1
Schools: 8
3 Primary; 2 Middle; 1 High; 2 Other Level
6 Regular; 0 Special Education; 0 Vocational; 2 Alternative
0 Magnet; 0 Charter; 4 Title I Eligible; 4 School-wide Title I
Students: 3,160 (52.4% male; 47.6% female)
Individual Education Program: 419 (13.3%);
English Language Learner: 252 (8.0%); Migrant: 193 (6.1%)
Eligible for Free Lunch Program: 1,454 (46.0%)
Eligible for Reduced-Price Lunch Program: 271 (8.6%)
Teachers: 221.5 (14.3 to 1)
Librarians/Media Specialists: 4.0 (790.0 to 1)
Guidance Counselors: 7.0 (451.4 to 1)
Current Spending: ($ per student per year):
Total: $6,693; Instruction: $4,241; Support Services: $2,213

Enrollment, Drop-out Rates and Diploma Recipients by Race/Ethnicity

Category	Total	White	Black	Asian	AIAN	Hisp.
Enrollment (%)	100.0	35.3	15.1	0.2	0.6	48.8
Drop-out Rate (%)	2.4	1.5	3.8	0.0	0.0	2.9
H.S. Diplomas (#)	174	89	28	1	0	56

Wilson County

Floresville ISD

908 10th St • Floresville, TX 78114-1852
(830) 393-5300 • http://www.floresville.isd.tenet.edu/
Grade Span: PK-12; **Agency Type:** 1
Schools: 8
3 Primary; 1 Middle; 2 High; 2 Other Level
5 Regular; 0 Special Education; 0 Vocational; 3 Alternative
0 Magnet; 0 Charter; 4 Title I Eligible; 4 School-wide Title I
Students: 3,415 (51.0% male; 49.0% female)
Individual Education Program: 430 (12.6%);
English Language Learner: 116 (3.4%); Migrant: 21 (0.6%)
Eligible for Free Lunch Program: 1,287 (37.7%)
Eligible for Reduced-Price Lunch Program: 415 (12.2%)
Teachers: 245.4 (13.9 to 1)
Librarians/Media Specialists: 2.2 (1,552.3 to 1)
Guidance Counselors: 10.0 (341.5 to 1)
Current Spending: ($ per student per year):
Total: $6,732; Instruction: $4,122; Support Services: $2,304

Enrollment, Drop-out Rates and Diploma Recipients by Race/Ethnicity

Category	Total	White	Black	Asian	AIAN	Hisp.
Enrollment (%)	100.0	40.8	1.9	0.4	0.1	56.8
Drop-out Rate (%)	7.7	4.9	11.1	75.0	n/a	9.5
H.S. Diplomas (#)	207	95	7	2	0	103

La Vernia ISD

13600 US Hwy 87 W • La Vernia, TX 78121-9554
(830) 779-2181
Grade Span: PK-12; **Agency Type:** 1
Schools: 7
2 Primary; 1 Middle; 2 High; 2 Other Level
5 Regular; 0 Special Education; 0 Vocational; 2 Alternative
0 Magnet; 0 Charter; 1 Title I Eligible; 0 School-wide Title I
Students: 2,301 (52.5% male; 47.5% female)
Individual Education Program: 353 (15.3%);
English Language Learner: 71 (3.1%); Migrant: 5 (0.2%)
Eligible for Free Lunch Program: 460 (20.0%)
Eligible for Reduced-Price Lunch Program: 156 (6.8%)
Teachers: 149.8 (15.4 to 1)
Librarians/Media Specialists: 4.0 (575.3 to 1)
Guidance Counselors: 5.9 (390.0 to 1)
Current Spending: ($ per student per year):
Total: $5,436; Instruction: $3,469; Support Services: $1,692

Enrollment, Drop-out Rates and Diploma Recipients by Race/Ethnicity

Category	Total	White	Black	Asian	AIAN	Hisp.
Enrollment (%)	100.0	79.5	0.9	0.3	0.0	19.3
Drop-out Rate (%)	1.7	1.7	0.0	0.0	0.0	1.4
H.S. Diplomas (#)	141	126	2	0	0	13

Wise County

Bridgeport ISD

2107 15th St • Bridgeport, TX 76426-0036
(940) 683-5124
Grade Span: PK-12; **Agency Type:** 1
Schools: 6
2 Primary; 1 Middle; 2 High; 1 Other Level
4 Regular; 0 Special Education; 0 Vocational; 2 Alternative
0 Magnet; 0 Charter; 3 Title I Eligible; 3 School-wide Title I
Students: 2,201 (52.0% male; 48.0% female)
Individual Education Program: 314 (14.3%);
English Language Learner: 170 (7.7%); Migrant: 53 (2.4%)
Eligible for Free Lunch Program: 585 (26.6%)
Eligible for Reduced-Price Lunch Program: 153 (7.0%)
Teachers: 151.0 (14.6 to 1)
Librarians/Media Specialists: 3.0 (733.7 to 1)
Guidance Counselors: 8.0 (275.1 to 1)
Current Spending: ($ per student per year):
Total: $6,832; Instruction: $4,166; Support Services: $2,355

Enrollment, Drop-out Rates and Diploma Recipients by Race/Ethnicity

Category	Total	White	Black	Asian	AIAN	Hisp.
Enrollment (%)	100.0	73.6	0.5	0.2	0.6	25.2
Drop-out Rate (%)	2.8	2.1	0.0	0.0	0.0	6.0
H.S. Diplomas (#)	137	111	1	0	0	25

Decatur ISD

501 E Collins • Decatur, TX 76234-2360
(940) 627-3215 • http://www.decatur.esc11.net/
Grade Span: PK-12; **Agency Type:** 1
Schools: 6
3 Primary; 1 Middle; 2 High; 0 Other Level
5 Regular; 0 Special Education; 0 Vocational; 1 Alternative
0 Magnet; 0 Charter; 3 Title I Eligible; 3 School-wide Title I
Students: 2,729 (50.9% male; 49.1% female)
Individual Education Program: 311 (11.4%);
English Language Learner: 264 (9.7%); Migrant: 23 (0.8%)
Eligible for Free Lunch Program: 723 (26.5%)
Eligible for Reduced-Price Lunch Program: 186 (6.8%)
Teachers: 188.9 (14.4 to 1)
Librarians/Media Specialists: 2.4 (1,137.1 to 1)
Guidance Counselors: 5.4 (505.4 to 1)
Current Spending: ($ per student per year):
Total: $5,806; Instruction: $3,688; Support Services: $1,784

Enrollment, Drop-out Rates and Diploma Recipients by Race/Ethnicity

Category	Total	White	Black	Asian	AIAN	Hisp.
Enrollment (%)	100.0	71.6	1.5	0.8	0.6	25.4
Drop-out Rate (%)	0.6	0.3	0.0	0.0	0.0	2.1
H.S. Diplomas (#)	178	145	3	3	3	24

Wood County

Mineola ISD

1000 W Loop • Mineola, TX 75773-1617
(903) 569-2448
Grade Span: PK-12; **Agency Type:** 1
Schools: 4
2 Primary; 1 Middle; 1 High; 0 Other Level
4 Regular; 0 Special Education; 0 Vocational; 0 Alternative
0 Magnet; 0 Charter; 3 Title I Eligible; 3 School-wide Title I
Students: 1,562 (50.6% male; 49.4% female)
Individual Education Program: 207 (13.3%);
English Language Learner: 105 (6.7%); Migrant: 2 (0.1%)
Eligible for Free Lunch Program: 688 (44.0%)
Eligible for Reduced-Price Lunch Program: 119 (7.6%)
Teachers: 112.9 (13.8 to 1)
Librarians/Media Specialists: 2.0 (781.0 to 1)
Guidance Counselors: 3.0 (520.7 to 1)
Current Spending: ($ per student per year):
Total: $5,778; Instruction: $3,799; Support Services: $1,673

Enrollment, Drop-out Rates and Diploma Recipients by Race/Ethnicity

Category	Total	White	Black	Asian	AIAN	Hisp.
Enrollment (%)	100.0	71.2	9.7	0.3	0.5	18.3
Drop-out Rate (%)	6.4	5.9	6.9	0.0	40.0	5.9
H.S. Diplomas (#)	94	67	17	0	1	9

Winnsboro ISD

207 E Pine St • Winnsboro, TX 75494-2628
(903) 342-3737
Grade Span: PK-12; **Agency Type:** 1
Schools: 3
1 Primary; 1 Middle; 1 High; 0 Other Level
3 Regular; 0 Special Education; 0 Vocational; 0 Alternative
0 Magnet; 0 Charter; 3 Title I Eligible; 3 School-wide Title I
Students: 1,508 (53.3% male; 46.7% female)
Individual Education Program: 209 (13.9%);
English Language Learner: 69 (4.6%); Migrant: 41 (2.7%)
Eligible for Free Lunch Program: 509 (33.8%)
Eligible for Reduced-Price Lunch Program: 85 (5.6%)
Teachers: 102.3 (14.7 to 1)
Librarians/Media Specialists: 1.0 (1,508.0 to 1)
Guidance Counselors: 2.0 (754.0 to 1)
Current Spending: ($ per student per year):
Total: $5,675; Instruction: $3,615; Support Services: $1,752

Enrollment, Drop-out Rates and Diploma Recipients by Race/Ethnicity

Category	Total	White	Black	Asian	AIAN	Hisp.
Enrollment (%)	100.0	86.5	3.8	0.8	0.8	8.1
Drop-out Rate (%)	3.3	3.6	0.0	0.0	0.0	0.0
H.S. Diplomas (#)	89	78	4	2	0	5

Young County

Graham ISD

400 3rd St • Graham, TX 76450-3011
(940) 549-0595
Grade Span: PK-12; **Agency Type:** 1
Schools: 6
2 Primary; 2 Middle; 2 High; 0 Other Level
5 Regular; 0 Special Education; 0 Vocational; 1 Alternative
0 Magnet; 0 Charter; 5 Title I Eligible; 5 School-wide Title I
Students: 2,454 (51.6% male; 48.4% female)

Individual Education Program: 304 (12.4%);
English Language Learner: 123 (5.0%); Migrant: 30 (1.2%)
Eligible for Free Lunch Program: 728 (29.7%)
Eligible for Reduced-Price Lunch Program: 187 (7.6%)
Teachers: 167.1 (14.7 to 1)
Librarians/Media Specialists: 1.0 (2,454.0 to 1)
Guidance Counselors: 5.0 (490.8 to 1)
Current Spending: ($ per student per year):
Total: $5,750; Instruction: $3,680; Support Services: $1,763
Enrollment, Drop-out Rates and Diploma Recipients by Race/Ethnicity

Category	Total	White	Black	Asian	AIAN	Hisp.
Enrollment (%)	100.0	79.5	1.7	0.5	0.2	18.0
Drop-out Rate (%)	0.7	0.7	0.0	0.0	0.0	1.0
H.S. Diplomas (#)	153	134	2	0	1	16

Zapata County

Zapata County ISD
17th & Carla St • Zapata, TX 78076-0158
Mailing Address: PO Box 158 • Zapata, TX 78076-0158
(956) 765-6546
Grade Span: PK-12; **Agency Type:** 1
Schools: 9
4 Primary; 1 Middle; 1 High; 0 Other Level
6 Regular; 0 Special Education; 0 Vocational; 0 Alternative
0 Magnet; 0 Charter; 6 Title I Eligible; 6 School-wide Title I
Students: 3,130 (51.9% male; 48.1% female)
Individual Education Program: 304 (9.7%);
English Language Learner: 1,162 (37.1%); Migrant: 98 (3.1%)
Eligible for Free Lunch Program: 1,577 (50.4%)
Eligible for Reduced-Price Lunch Program: 168 (5.4%)
Teachers: 240.0 (13.0 to 1)
Librarians/Media Specialists: 5.8 (539.7 to 1)
Guidance Counselors: 9.8 (319.4 to 1)
Current Spending: ($ per student per year):
Total: $6,507; Instruction: $3,851; Support Services: $2,353
Enrollment, Drop-out Rates and Diploma Recipients by Race/Ethnicity

Category	Total	White	Black	Asian	AIAN	Hisp.
Enrollment (%)	100.0	2.8	0.0	0.1	0.0	97.1
Drop-out Rate (%)	4.6	4.7	n/a	n/a	n/a	4.6
H.S. Diplomas (#)	184	13	0	0	0	171

Zavala County

Crystal City ISD
805 E Crockett St • Crystal City, TX 78839-2799
(830) 374-2367 • http://www.crystal-city.k12.tx.us/
Grade Span: PK-12; **Agency Type:** 1
Schools: 4
1 Primary; 2 Middle; 1 High; 0 Other Level
4 Regular; 0 Special Education; 0 Vocational; 0 Alternative
0 Magnet; 0 Charter; 4 Title I Eligible; 4 School-wide Title I
Students: 2,096 (50.7% male; 49.3% female)
Individual Education Program: 221 (10.5%);
English Language Learner: 438 (20.9%); Migrant: 538 (25.7%)
Eligible for Free Lunch Program: 1,451 (69.2%)
Eligible for Reduced-Price Lunch Program: 98 (4.7%)
Teachers: 145.0 (14.5 to 1)
Librarians/Media Specialists: 2.0 (1,048.0 to 1)
Guidance Counselors: 7.0 (299.4 to 1)
Current Spending: ($ per student per year):
Total: $7,427; Instruction: $4,188; Support Services: $2,785
Enrollment, Drop-out Rates and Diploma Recipients by Race/Ethnicity

Category	Total	White	Black	Asian	AIAN	Hisp.
Enrollment (%)	100.0	1.1	0.9	0.0	0.0	98.0
Drop-out Rate (%)	9.1	42.9	0.0	n/a	0.0	8.6
H.S. Diplomas (#)	87	1	0	0	0	86

Number of Schools

Rank	Number	District Name	City
1	308	Houston ISD	Houston
2	228	Dallas ISD	Dallas
3	146	Fort Worth ISD	Fort Worth
4	111	Austin ISD	Austin
5	107	San Antonio ISD	San Antonio
6	94	El Paso ISD	El Paso
7	89	Northside ISD	San Antonio
8	76	Arlington ISD	Arlington
9	72	Plano ISD	Plano
10	70	Garland ISD	Garland
11	69	North East ISD	San Antonio
12	67	Aldine ISD	Houston
13	64	Corpus Christi ISD	Corpus Christi
14	63	Ysleta ISD	El Paso
15	60	Fort Bend ISD	Sugar Land
16	59	Cypress-Fairbanks ISD	Houston
17	58	Lubbock ISD	Lubbock
18	56	Lewisville ISD	Flower Mound
18	56	Pasadena ISD	Pasadena
18	56	Richardson ISD	Richardson
21	52	Amarillo ISD	Amarillo
21	52	Brownsville ISD	Brownsville
23	50	Spring Branch ISD	Houston
24	47	Killeen ISD	Killeen
25	45	Conroe ISD	Conroe
25	45	Round Rock ISD	Round Rock
27	43	Abilene ISD	Abilene
27	43	Mesquite ISD	Mesquite
29	42	Carrollton-Farmers Branch ISD	Carrollton
29	42	Ector County ISD	Odessa
31	40	Alief ISD	Houston
32	39	Irving ISD	Irving
32	39	Katy ISD	Katy
34	38	Pharr-San Juan-Alamo ISD	Pharr
35	37	Clear Creek ISD	League City
35	37	United ISD	Laredo
35	37	Wichita Falls ISD	Wichita Falls
38	36	Beaumont ISD	Beaumont
38	36	Midland ISD	Midland
38	36	Waco ISD	Waco
41	34	Birdville ISD	Haltom City
41	34	Edinburg CISD	Edinburg
41	34	Klein ISD	Klein
44	33	Grand Prairie ISD	Grand Prairie
44	33	Hurst-Euless-Bedford ISD	Bedford
44	33	Mcallen ISD	Mcallen
47	31	Lamar CISD	Rosenberg
47	31	Socorro ISD	El Paso
49	30	Harlandale ISD	San Antonio
49	30	Humble ISD	Humble
49	30	Tyler ISD	Tyler
52	29	Laredo ISD	Laredo
53	28	San Angelo ISD	San Angelo
53	28	Victoria ISD	Victoria
55	27	Goose Creek CISD	Baytown
56	26	Edgewood ISD	San Antonio
56	26	Harlingen Cons ISD	Harlingen
56	26	Keller ISD	Keller
56	26	Spring ISD	Houston
60	25	Denton ISD	Denton
60	25	Mckinney ISD	Mckinney
62	24	Bryan ISD	Bryan
62	24	Eagle Pass ISD	Eagle Pass
62	24	La Joya ISD	La Joya
65	23	Galena Park ISD	Houston
65	23	Pflugerville ISD	Pflugerville
65	23	Port Arthur ISD	Port Arthur
68	22	Leander ISD	Leander
68	22	Weslaco ISD	Weslaco
70	21	Brazosport ISD	Clute
70	21	Comal ISD	New Braunfels
70	21	Judson ISD	San Antonio
70	21	Mansfield ISD	Mansfield
74	20	Frisco ISD	Frisco
74	20	South San Antonio ISD	San Antonio
76	19	Grapevine-Colleyville ISD	Grapevine
77	18	Duncanville ISD	Duncanville
77	18	Longview ISD	Longview
77	18	Lufkin ISD	Lufkin
77	18	North Forest ISD	Houston
77	18	San Benito Cons ISD	San Benito
82	17	Alvin ISD	Alvin
82	17	Donna ISD	Donna
82	17	Galveston ISD	Galveston
82	17	Georgetown ISD	Georgetown
82	17	Mission Cons ISD	Mission
82	17	Temple ISD	Temple
88	16	Allen ISD	Allen
88	16	Coppell ISD	Coppell
88	16	Northwest ISD	Fort Worth
88	16	Pearland ISD	Pearland
88	16	Seguin ISD	Seguin
93	15	Angleton ISD	Angleton
93	15	Hays Cons ISD	Kyle
93	15	Kingsville ISD	Kingsville
93	15	Southwest ISD	San Antonio
97	14	Cleburne ISD	Cleburne
97	14	Deer Park ISD	Deer Park
97	14	Greenville ISD	Greenville
97	14	Magnolia ISD	Magnolia
97	14	Rockwall ISD	Rockwall
97	14	San Felipe-Del Rio CISD	Del Rio
97	14	Sherman ISD	Sherman
97	14	Weatherford ISD	Weatherford
105	13	Belton ISD	Belton
105	13	Canyon ISD	Canyon
105	13	Carroll ISD	Southlake
105	13	Copperas Cove ISD	Copperas Cove
105	13	Crowley ISD	Crowley
105	13	East Central ISD	San Antonio
105	13	Granbury ISD	Granbury
105	13	La Porte ISD	La Porte
105	13	Marshall ISD	Marshall
105	13	Plainview ISD	Plainview
115	12	Cedar Hill ISD	Cedar Hill
115	12	Desoto ISD	Desoto
115	12	Eagle Mt-Saginaw ISD	Fort Worth
115	12	Honors Academy	Dallas
115	12	New Braunfels ISD	New Braunfels
115	12	Port Neches-Groves ISD	Port Neches
115	12	Rio Grande City CISD	Rio Grande City
115	12	San Marcos CISD	San Marcos
115	12	Schertz-Cibolo-Universal City ISD	Schertz
124	11	Alice ISD	Alice
124	11	Azle ISD	Azle
124	11	Bastrop ISD	Bastrop
124	11	Big Spring ISD	Big Spring
124	11	Burleson ISD	Burleson
124	11	Channelview ISD	Channelview
124	11	Clint ISD	Clint
124	11	College Station ISD	College Station
124	11	Denison ISD	Denison
124	11	Eanes ISD	Austin
124	11	Kerrville ISD	Kerrville
124	11	Mercedes ISD	Mercedes
124	11	Nacogdoches ISD	Nacogdoches
124	11	New Caney ISD	New Caney
124	11	Texarkana ISD	Texarkana
139	10	Brownwood ISD	Brownwood
139	10	Del Valle ISD	Del Valle
139	10	Dickinson ISD	Dickinson
139	10	Huntsville ISD	Huntsville
139	10	Lancaster ISD	Lancaster
139	10	Mount Pleasant ISD	Mt Pleasant
139	10	Robstown ISD	Robstown
139	10	Roma ISD	Roma
139	10	Texas City ISD	Texas City
139	10	Tomball ISD	Tomball
139	10	Uvalde CISD	Uvalde
139	10	Waxahachie ISD	Waxahachie
139	10	Wylie ISD	Wylie
152	9	Bay City ISD	Bay City
152	9	Boerne ISD	Boerne
152	9	Calhoun County ISD	Port Lavaca
152	9	Columbia-Brazoria ISD	West Columbia
152	9	Corsicana ISD	Corsicana
152	9	Ennis ISD	Ennis
152	9	Frenship ISD	Wolfforth
152	9	La Marque ISD	La Marque
152	9	Lockhart ISD	Lockhart
152	9	Los Fresnos CISD	Los Fresnos
152	9	Midway ISD	Hewitt
152	9	Nederland ISD	Nederland
152	9	Paris ISD	Paris
152	9	Springtown ISD	Springtown
152	9	West Orange-Cove CISD	Orange
152	9	White Settlement ISD	White Settlement
152	9	Willis ISD	Willis
152	9	Zapata County ISD	Zapata
170	8	Athens ISD	Athens
170	8	Barbers Hill ISD	Mount Belvieu
170	8	Beeville ISD	Beeville
170	8	Brenham ISD	Brenham
170	8	Castleberry ISD	Fort Worth
170	8	Chapel Hill ISD	Tyler
170	8	China Spring ISD	Waco
170	8	Cleveland ISD	Cleveland
170	8	Connally ISD	Waco
170	8	Dayton ISD	Dayton
170	8	Dumas ISD	Dumas
170	8	Edcouch-Elsa ISD	Edcouch
170	8	Floresville ISD	Floresville
170	8	Gainesville ISD	Gainesville
170	8	Gregory-Portland ISD	Gregory
170	8	Henderson ISD	Henderson
170	8	Hereford ISD	Hereford
170	8	Jacksonville ISD	Jacksonville
170	8	La Feria ISD	La Feria
170	8	La Vega ISD	Waco
170	8	Lake Travis ISD	Austin
170	8	Lake Worth ISD	Lake Worth
170	8	Midlothian ISD	Midlothian
170	8	Pleasanton ISD	Pleasanton
170	8	Red Oak ISD	Red Oak
170	8	Sharyland ISD	Mission
170	8	Sheldon ISD	Houston
170	8	Snyder ISD	Snyder
170	8	Somerset ISD	Somerset
170	8	Southside ISD	San Antonio
170	8	Sulphur Springs ISD	Sulphur Springs
170	8	Taylor ISD	Taylor
170	8	Terrell ISD	Terrell
170	8	Waller ISD	Waller
170	8	West ISD	West
170	8	Whitehouse ISD	Whitehouse
206	7	Alvarado ISD	Alvarado
206	7	Andrews ISD	Andrews
206	7	Bonham ISD	Bonham
206	7	Brownsboro ISD	Brownsboro
206	7	Calallen ISD	Corpus Christi
206	7	Carrizo Springs CISD	Carrizo Springs
206	7	Everman ISD	Everman
206	7	Flour Bluff ISD	Corpus Christi
206	7	Friendswood ISD	Friendswood
206	7	Hallsville ISD	Hallsville
206	7	Hardin-Jefferson ISD	Sour Lake
206	7	Highland Park ISD	Dallas
206	7	Hillsboro ISD	Hillsboro
206	7	Joshua ISD	Joshua
206	7	Kennedale ISD	Kennedale
206	7	Kilgore ISD	Kilgore
206	7	La Vernia ISD	La Vernia
206	7	Lake Dallas ISD	Lake Dallas
206	7	Levelland ISD	Levelland
206	7	Liberty ISD	Liberty
206	7	Liberty-Eylau ISD	Texarkana
206	7	Lindale ISD	Lindale
206	7	Little Elm ISD	Little Elm
206	7	Manor ISD	Manor
206	7	Mexia ISD	Mexia
206	7	Monahans-Wickett-Pyote ISD	Monahans
206	7	Montgomery ISD	Montgomery
206	7	Navasota ISD	Navasota
206	7	North Lamar ISD	Paris
206	7	Palestine ISD	Palestine
206	7	Pampa ISD	Pampa
206	7	Pecos-Barstow-Toyah ISD	Pecos
206	7	Pine Tree ISD	Longview
206	7	Robinson ISD	Robinson
206	7	San Elizario ISD	San Elizario
206	7	Santa Fe ISD	Santa Fe
206	7	Silsbee ISD	Silsbee
206	7	Sinton ISD	Sinton
206	7	Sweetwater ISD	Sweetwater
206	7	Vidor ISD	Vidor
206	7	Wilmer-Hutchins ISD	Dallas
206	7	Wylie ISD	Abilene
248	6	Alamo Heights ISD	San Antonio
248	6	Aledo ISD	Aledo
248	6	Aransas County ISD	Rockport
248	6	Bellville ISD	Bellville
248	6	Borger ISD	Borger
248	6	Breckenridge ISD	Breckenridge
248	6	Bridgeport ISD	Bridgeport
248	6	Bullard ISD	Bullard
248	6	Burkburnett ISD	Burkburnett
248	6	Burnet Cons ISD	Burnet
248	6	Canutillo ISD	El Paso
248	6	Crockett ISD	Crockett
248	6	Crosby ISD	Crosby
248	6	Cuero ISD	Cuero
248	6	Decatur ISD	Decatur
248	6	Fabens ISD	Fabens
248	6	Forney ISD	Forney
248	6	Fort Stockton ISD	Fort Stockton
248	6	Fredericksburg ISD	Fredericksburg
248	6	Gladewater ISD	Gladewater
248	6	Gonzales ISD	Gonzales
248	6	Graham ISD	Graham
248	6	Hidalgo ISD	Hidalgo
248	6	Kaufman ISD	Kaufman
248	6	Lampasas ISD	Lampasas
248	6	Little Cypress-Mauriceville CISD	Orange
248	6	Lubbock-Cooper ISD	Lubbock
248	6	Lumberton ISD	Lumberton

248	6	Lytle ISD	Lytle
248	6	Mabank ISD	Mabank
248	6	Medina Valley ISD	Castroville
248	6	Mineral Wells ISD	Mineral Wells
248	6	Pearsall ISD	Pearsall
248	6	Perryton ISD	Perryton
248	6	Quinlan ISD	Quinlan
248	6	Royal ISD	Brookshire
248	6	Royse City ISD	Royse City
248	6	Sanger ISD	Sanger
248	6	Seminole ISD	Seminole
248	6	South Texas ISD	Mercedes
248	6	Stafford Municipal School	Stafford
248	6	Stephenville ISD	Stephenville
248	6	Tuloso-Midway ISD	Corpus Christi
248	6	Vernon ISD	Vernon
248	6	West Oso ISD	Corpus Christi
293	5	Aransas Pass ISD	Aransas Pass
293	5	Atlanta ISD	Atlanta
293	5	Bandera ISD	Bandera
293	5	Bridge City ISD	Bridge City
293	5	Brownfield ISD	Brownfield
293	5	Caldwell ISD	Caldwell
293	5	Carthage ISD	Carthage
293	5	Center ISD	Center
293	5	Central ISD	Pollok
293	5	Commerce ISD	Commerce
293	5	Crandall ISD	Crandall
293	5	Daingerfield-Lone Star ISD	Daingerfield
293	5	Dalhart ISD	Dalhart
293	5	Devine ISD	Devine
293	5	Diboll ISD	Diboll
293	5	Edna ISD	Edna
293	5	El Campo ISD	El Campo
293	5	Elgin ISD	Elgin
293	5	Ferris ISD	Ferris
293	5	Gatesville ISD	Gatesville
293	5	Giddings ISD	Giddings
293	5	Glen Rose ISD	Glen Rose
293	5	Gulf Shores Academy	Houston
293	5	Hamshire-Fannett ISD	Hamshire
293	5	Hondo ISD	Hondo
293	5	Hudson ISD	Lufkin
293	5	Huffman ISD	Huffman
293	5	Huntington ISD	Huntington
293	5	Ingleside ISD	Ingleside
293	5	Jasper ISD	Jasper
293	5	Liberty Hill ISD	Liberty Hill
293	5	Littlefield ISD	Littlefield
293	5	Livingston ISD	Livingston
293	5	Llano ISD	Llano
293	5	Luling ISD	Luling
293	5	Marble Falls ISD	Marble Falls
293	5	Marlin ISD	Marlin
293	5	Needville ISD	Needville
293	5	Palacios ISD	Palacios
293	5	Pittsburg ISD	Pittsburg
293	5	Princeton ISD	Princeton
293	5	Progreso ISD	Progreso
293	5	Rio Hondo ISD	Rio Hondo
293	5	Smithville ISD	Smithville
293	5	Splendora ISD	Splendora
293	5	Spring Hill ISD	Longview
293	5	Valley View ISD	Pharr
293	5	Venus ISD	Venus
293	5	Wharton ISD	Wharton
293	5	Wills Point ISD	Wills Point
293	5	Yoakum ISD	Yoakum
344	4	Bowie ISD	Bowie
344	4	Brooks County ISD	Falfurrias
344	4	Cameron ISD	Cameron
344	4	Canton ISD	Canton
344	4	Coldspring-Oakhurst CISD	Coldspring
344	4	Crystal City ISD	Crystal City
344	4	Dripping Springs ISD	Dripping Spgs
344	4	Eustace ISD	Eustace
344	4	Fairfield ISD	Fairfield
344	4	Gilmer ISD	Gilmer
344	4	Greenwood ISD	Midland
344	4	Groesbeck ISD	Groesbeck
344	4	Iowa Park CISD	Iowa Park
344	4	Kemp ISD	Kemp
344	4	La Grange ISD	La Grange
344	4	Lamesa ISD	Lamesa
344	4	Lorena ISD	Lorena
344	4	Lyford CISD	Lyford
344	4	Madisonville CISD	Madisonville
344	4	Mathis ISD	Mathis
344	4	Mineola ISD	Mineola
344	4	Orange Grove ISD	Orange Grove
344	4	Point Isabel ISD	Port Isabel
344	4	Poteet ISD	Poteet
344	4	Raymondville ISD	Raymondville
344	4	Rockdale ISD	Rockdale
344	4	Rusk ISD	Rusk
344	4	San Diego ISD	San Diego
344	4	Sealy ISD	Sealy
344	4	Shepherd ISD	Shepherd
344	4	Sweeny ISD	Sweeny
344	4	Tarkington ISD	Cleveland
344	4	Van ISD	Van
344	4	Westwood ISD	Palestine
344	4	Whitney ISD	Whitney
344	4	Wimberley ISD	Wimberley
380	3	Buna ISD	Buna
380	3	Columbus ISD	Columbus
380	3	Hutto ISD	Hutto
380	3	Ingram ISD	Ingram
380	3	Kirbyville CISD	Kirbyville
380	3	Orangefield ISD	Orangefield
380	3	Pleasant Grove ISD	Texarkana
380	3	Rains ISD	Emory
380	3	Whitesboro ISD	Whitesboro
380	3	Winnsboro ISD	Winnsboro

Number of Teachers

Rank	Number	District Name	City
1	12,385	Houston ISD	Houston
2	10,940	Dallas ISD	Dallas
3	5,382	Austin ISD	Austin
4	4,967	Fort Worth ISD	Fort Worth
5	4,603	Cypress-Fairbanks ISD	Houston
6	4,573	Northside ISD	San Antonio
7	4,433	El Paso ISD	El Paso
8	3,941	Arlington ISD	Arlington
9	3,722	Aldine ISD	Houston
10	3,716	North East ISD	San Antonio
11	3,635	San Antonio ISD	San Antonio
12	3,623	Plano ISD	Plano
13	3,585	Fort Bend ISD	Sugar Land
14	3,405	Garland ISD	Garland
15	3,023	Brownsville ISD	Brownsville
16	2,990	Lewisville ISD	Flower Mound
17	2,947	Alief ISD	Houston
18	2,939	Ysleta ISD	El Paso
19	2,758	Pasadena ISD	Pasadena
20	2,697	Katy ISD	Katy
21	2,512	Conroe ISD	Conroe
22	2,500	Corpus Christi ISD	Corpus Christi
23	2,320	Round Rock ISD	Round Rock
24	2,285	Richardson ISD	Richardson
25	2,270	Spring Branch ISD	Houston
26	2,208	Irving ISD	Irving
27	2,196	Killeen ISD	Killeen
28	2,171	Klein ISD	Klein
29	2,125	Mesquite ISD	Mesquite
30	2,101	Lubbock ISD	Lubbock
31	2,034	Clear Creek ISD	League City
32	2,005	Amarillo ISD	Amarillo
33	1,943	United ISD	Laredo
34	1,758	Socorro ISD	El Paso
35	1,753	Ector County ISD	Odessa
36	1,712	Carrollton-Farmers Branch ISD	Carrollton
37	1,705	Humble ISD	Humble
38	1,702	Spring ISD	Houston
39	1,601	Pharr-San Juan-Alamo ISD	Pharr
40	1,547	Edinburg CISD	Edinburg
41	1,531	Mcallen ISD	Mcallen
42	1,515	Laredo ISD	Laredo
43	1,489	Grand Prairie ISD	Grand Prairie
44	1,478	Beaumont ISD	Beaumont
45	1,419	Birdville ISD	Haltom City
46	1,402	Midland ISD	Midland
47	1,379	Galena Park ISD	Houston
48	1,290	La Joya ISD	La Joya
49	1,279	Abilene ISD	Abilene
50	1,263	Hurst-Euless-Bedford ISD	Bedford
51	1,252	Mansfield ISD	Mansfield
52	1,215	Tyler ISD	Tyler
53	1,196	Judson ISD	San Antonio
54	1,166	Goose Creek CISD	Baytown
55	1,157	Leander ISD	Leander
56	1,118	Keller ISD	Keller
57	1,114	Wichita Falls ISD	Wichita Falls
58	1,098	Denton ISD	Denton
59	1,096	Lamar CISD	Rosenberg
60	1,073	Mckinney ISD	Mckinney
61	1,063	Waco ISD	Waco
62	1,032	Harlingen Cons ISD	Harlingen
63	1,018	Pflugerville ISD	Pflugerville
64	1,001	San Angelo ISD	San Angelo
65	983	Harlandale ISD	San Antonio
66	976	Victoria ISD	Victoria
67	967	Bryan ISD	Bryan
68	950	Weslaco ISD	Weslaco
69	922	Grapevine-Colleyville ISD	Grapevine
70	903	Mission Cons ISD	Mission
71	825	Frisco ISD	Frisco
72	814	Brazosport ISD	Clute
73	806	Edgewood ISD	San Antonio
74	778	Allen ISD	Allen
75	778	Alvin ISD	Alvin
76	775	Pearland ISD	Pearland
77	764	Comal ISD	New Braunfels
78	761	Eagle Pass ISD	Eagle Pass
79	750	Crowley ISD	Crowley
80	744	Donna ISD	Donna
81	732	Deer Park ISD	Deer Park
82	707	North Forest ISD	Houston
83	701	Duncanville ISD	Duncanville
84	686	Coppell ISD	Coppell
85	675	Georgetown ISD	Georgetown
86	672	South San Antonio ISD	San Antonio
87	664	Port Arthur ISD	Port Arthur
88	647	Southwest ISD	San Antonio
89	634	Galveston ISD	Galveston
90	621	Temple ISD	Temple
91	615	Rio Grande City CISD	Rio Grande City
92	605	Lufkin ISD	Lufkin
93	593	Longview ISD	Longview
94	579	Magnolia ISD	Magnolia
95	576	San Felipe-Del Rio CISD	Del Rio
96	569	Rockwall ISD	Rockwall
97	569	Seguin ISD	Seguin
98	565	Hays Cons ISD	Kyle
99	557	San Benito Cons ISD	San Benito
100	541	Copperas Cove ISD	Copperas Cove
101	539	Eanes ISD	Austin
102	530	Del Valle ISD	Del Valle
103	527	Tomball ISD	Tomball
104	526	College Station ISD	College Station
105	517	Bastrop ISD	Bastrop
105	517	East Central ISD	San Antonio
107	514	Desoto ISD	Desoto
108	510	Clint ISD	Clint
109	498	Carroll ISD	Southlake
110	477	La Porte ISD	La Porte
111	477	Canyon ISD	Canyon
112	470	Los Fresnos CISD	Los Fresnos
113	467	San Marcos CISD	San Marcos
114	466	Cedar Hill ISD	Cedar Hill
115	465	New Caney ISD	New Caney
116	463	Weatherford ISD	Weatherford
117	459	Belton ISD	Belton
118	453	Eagle Mt-Saginaw ISD	Fort Worth
119	452	Huntsville ISD	Huntsville
120	451	Granbury ISD	Granbury
121	449	Burleson ISD	Burleson
122	448	Sherman ISD	Sherman
123	444	Northwest ISD	Fort Worth
124	437	Schertz-Cibolo-Universal City ISD	Schertz
125	436	Channelview ISD	Channelview
126	428	Nacogdoches ISD	Nacogdoches
127	422	Marshall ISD	Marshall
128	420	Angleton ISD	Angleton
129	417	Roma ISD	Roma
130	412	Cleburne ISD	Cleburne
131	408	New Braunfels ISD	New Braunfels
132	402	Plainview ISD	Plainview
133	399	Wylie ISD	Wylie
134	396	Dickinson ISD	Dickinson
135	390	Azle ISD	Azle
136	389	Waxahachie ISD	Waxahachie
137	387	Highland Park ISD	Dallas
138	382	Mount Pleasant ISD	Mt Pleasant
139	381	Alice ISD	Alice
140	377	Greenville ISD	Greenville
141	376	Texarkana ISD	Texarkana
142	376	Boerne ISD	Boerne
143	375	Corsicana ISD	Corsicana
144	373	Midlothian ISD	Midlothian
145	371	Uvalde CISD	Uvalde
146	365	Sharyland ISD	Mission
147	364	Brenham ISD	Brenham
148	364	Vidor ISD	Vidor
149	363	Texas City ISD	Texas City
150	354	Midway ISD	Hewitt
151	353	Ennis ISD	Ennis
152	350	Jacksonville ISD	Jacksonville
153	350	Canutillo ISD	El Paso
154	344	Frenship ISD	Wolfforth
155	340	Nederland ISD	Nederland
156	339	Port Neches-Groves ISD	Port Neches
157	337	Mercedes ISD	Mercedes
158	330	Flour Bluff ISD	Corpus Christi
159	324	Friendswood ISD	Friendswood
160	324	Pine Tree ISD	Longview

161	323	Kerrville ISD	Kerrville
162	320	Kingsville ISD	Kingsville
163	320	Alamo Heights ISD	San Antonio
164	317	Edcouch-Elsa ISD	Edcouch
165	311	Lake Travis ISD	Austin
166	311	White Settlement ISD	White Settlement
167	307	Terrell ISD	Terrell
168	306	Lancaster ISD	Lancaster
169	305	Joshua ISD	Joshua
170	305	Red Oak ISD	Red Oak
171	305	Paris ISD	Paris
172	304	Waller ISD	Waller
173	303	Lockhart ISD	Lockhart
174	302	Denison ISD	Denison
175	302	Dayton ISD	Dayton
176	301	Southside ISD	San Antonio
177	296	Sulphur Springs ISD	Sulphur Springs
178	292	Willis ISD	Willis
179	289	Big Spring ISD	Big Spring
180	289	Dumas ISD	Dumas
181	288	Burkburnett ISD	Burkburnett
182	286	Calhoun County ISD	Port Lavaca
183	284	Robstown ISD	Robstown
184	282	Sheldon ISD	Houston
185	279	Hereford ISD	Hereford
186	279	Bay City ISD	Bay City
187	278	Brownwood ISD	Brownwood
188	277	Montgomery ISD	Montgomery
189	273	Kilgore ISD	Kilgore
190	271	Lake Dallas ISD	Lake Dallas
190	271	Mineral Wells ISD	Mineral Wells
192	265	Livingston ISD	Livingston
193	264	Santa Fe ISD	Santa Fe
194	263	Crosby ISD	Crosby
195	263	Calallen ISD	Corpus Christi
196	263	Springtown ISD	Springtown
197	262	Hallsville ISD	Hallsville
198	260	Marble Falls ISD	Marble Falls
199	259	Henderson ISD	Henderson
200	258	Palestine ISD	Palestine
201	257	La Marque ISD	La Marque
202	256	Pleasanton ISD	Pleasanton
203	255	Pampa ISD	Pampa
204	255	West Orange-Cove CISD	Orange
205	255	Beeville ISD	Beeville
206	253	Gregory-Portland ISD	Gregory
207	252	Whitehouse ISD	Whitehouse
208	247	San Elizario ISD	San Elizario
209	246	El Campo ISD	El Campo
210	246	Levelland ISD	Levelland
211	245	Floresville ISD	Floresville
212	245	Athens ISD	Athens
213	244	Aransas County ISD	Rockport
214	242	Little Cypress-Mauriceville CISD	Orange
215	241	Everman ISD	Everman
216	240	Zapata County ISD	Zapata
217	238	Aledo ISD	Aledo
218	234	Silsbee ISD	Silsbee
219	229	Andrews ISD	Andrews
220	228	North Lamar ISD	Paris
221	227	Jasper ISD	Jasper
222	225	Lumberton ISD	Lumberton
223	225	Mabank ISD	Mabank
224	222	Hidalgo ISD	Hidalgo
225	222	Elgin ISD	Elgin
226	222	Stephenville ISD	Stephenville
227	221	Taylor ISD	Taylor
228	221	Burnet Cons ISD	Burnet
229	220	Forney ISD	Forney
230	219	Manor ISD	Manor
231	218	Kaufman ISD	Kaufman
232	216	Somerset ISD	Somerset
233	215	Chapel Hill ISD	Tyler
234	214	Dripping Springs ISD	Dripping Spgs
235	214	Lindale ISD	Lindale
236	214	Alvarado ISD	Alvarado
236	214	Lampasas ISD	Lampasas
238	213	Navasota ISD	Navasota
239	213	Gainesville ISD	Gainesville
240	212	Carthage ISD	Carthage
241	211	Liberty-Eylau ISD	Texarkana
241	211	Little Elm ISD	Little Elm
243	210	Cleveland ISD	Cleveland
244	208	Borger ISD	Borger
245	208	Wilmer-Hutchins ISD	Dallas
246	207	Columbia-Brazoria ISD	West Columbia
247	206	Fredericksburg ISD	Fredericksburg
248	204	Bandera ISD	Bandera
248	204	Quinlan ISD	Quinlan
250	204	Splendora ISD	Splendora
251	203	Barbers Hill ISD	Mount Belvieu
252	203	Tuloso-Midway ISD	Corpus Christi
253	203	Stafford Municipal School	Stafford
254	202	Castleberry ISD	Fort Worth
255	201	La Feria ISD	La Feria
256	198	Snyder ISD	Snyder
257	192	Gonzales ISD	Gonzales
258	188	Decatur ISD	Decatur
258	188	Sweetwater ISD	Sweetwater
260	188	Bridge City ISD	Bridge City
261	188	Fabens ISD	Fabens
262	187	Connally ISD	Waco
262	187	Wharton ISD	Wharton
264	185	Carrizo Springs CISD	Carrizo Springs
265	185	Kennedale ISD	Kennedale
266	184	La Vega ISD	Waco
267	183	Medina Valley ISD	Castroville
268	182	Gilmer ISD	Gilmer
269	181	Vernon ISD	Vernon
270	177	Fort Stockton ISD	Fort Stockton
271	176	Hondo ISD	Hondo
272	176	Gatesville ISD	Gatesville
272	176	Raymondville ISD	Raymondville
274	174	Brownsboro ISD	Brownsboro
275	173	Llano ISD	Llano
275	173	Wills Point ISD	Wills Point
277	172	Royse City ISD	Royse City
278	172	Wylie ISD	Abilene
279	171	Pecos-Barstow-Toyah ISD	Pecos
280	171	South Texas ISD	Mercedes
281	170	Seminole ISD	Seminole
282	170	Center ISD	Center
283	169	Sanger ISD	Sanger
284	169	Liberty ISD	Liberty
285	167	Graham ISD	Graham
286	167	Huffman ISD	Huffman
287	166	Valley View ISD	Pharr
288	165	Pittsburg ISD	Pittsburg
289	165	Lake Worth ISD	Lake Worth
290	164	Mexia ISD	Mexia
291	164	Sealy ISD	Sealy
292	162	Needville ISD	Needville
293	161	Pearsall ISD	Pearsall
294	160	Point Isabel ISD	Port Isabel
295	160	Hudson ISD	Lufkin
296	158	Aransas Pass ISD	Aransas Pass
297	157	Rusk ISD	Rusk
298	156	Bellville ISD	Bellville
299	156	Robinson ISD	Robinson
300	155	Brownfield ISD	Brownfield
301	155	Van ISD	Van
302	155	Sinton ISD	Sinton
303	155	Lamesa ISD	Lamesa
304	155	Gladewater ISD	Gladewater
305	155	Madisonville CISD	Madisonville
306	154	Progreso ISD	Progreso
307	154	Lubbock-Cooper ISD	Lubbock
308	153	Perryton ISD	Perryton
309	152	Atlanta ISD	Atlanta
310	151	Bridgeport ISD	Bridgeport
311	150	Princeton ISD	Princeton
312	150	Sweeny ISD	Sweeny
313	149	Cuero ISD	Cuero
314	149	La Vernia ISD	La Vernia
315	148	Ferris ISD	Ferris
316	148	Diboll ISD	Diboll
317	147	Hardin-Jefferson ISD	Sour Lake
318	145	Ingleside ISD	Ingleside
319	145	Crystal City ISD	Crystal City
320	144	Hillsboro ISD	Hillsboro
321	143	Caldwell ISD	Caldwell
322	141	Bonham ISD	Bonham
323	141	Crandall ISD	Crandall
324	140	Smithville ISD	Smithville
325	140	Monahans-Wickett-Pyote ISD	Monahans
326	140	Glen Rose ISD	Glen Rose
327	139	Giddings ISD	Giddings
327	139	Liberty Hill ISD	Liberty Hill
329	138	Crockett ISD	Crockett
330	137	Shepherd ISD	Shepherd
331	137	La Grange ISD	La Grange
332	137	Mathis ISD	Mathis
333	136	Wimberley ISD	Wimberley
334	135	Devine ISD	Devine
335	134	Cameron ISD	Cameron
336	134	Pleasant Grove ISD	Texarkana
337	133	Brooks County ISD	Falfurrias
338	131	Daingerfield-Lone Star ISD	Daingerfield
339	131	Palacios ISD	Palacios
340	130	Commerce ISD	Commerce
341	130	Groesbeck ISD	Groesbeck
342	129	Tarkington ISD	Cleveland
343	129	Venus ISD	Venus
344	128	Poteet ISD	Poteet
345	127	Buna ISD	Buna
345	127	Coldspring-Oakhurst CISD	Coldspring
347	126	Rio Hondo ISD	Rio Hondo
348	126	Dalhart ISD	Dalhart
349	125	Ingram ISD	Ingram
350	125	Iowa Park CISD	Iowa Park
351	124	Marlin ISD	Marlin
352	124	Hamshire-Fannett ISD	Hamshire
353	123	Yoakum ISD	Yoakum
354	123	Huntington ISD	Huntington
355	123	Fairfield ISD	Fairfield
356	122	Breckenridge ISD	Breckenridge
357	121	Canton ISD	Canton
358	120	Rockdale ISD	Rockdale
359	120	Westwood ISD	Palestine
360	120	West Oso ISD	Corpus Christi
361	120	San Diego ISD	San Diego
362	119	Bowie ISD	Bowie
363	117	Central ISD	Pollok
364	117	Kemp ISD	Kemp
365	117	Spring Hill ISD	Longview
366	115	Edna ISD	Edna
366	115	Whitney ISD	Whitney
368	115	Royal ISD	Brookshire
369	115	Hutto ISD	Hutto
369	115	Rains ISD	Emory
371	113	Lyford CISD	Lyford
372	113	Columbus ISD	Columbus
373	112	Mineola ISD	Mineola
374	111	Kirbyville CISD	Kirbyville
375	111	Orangefield ISD	Orangefield
376	111	Whitesboro ISD	Whitesboro
377	111	Lytle ISD	Lytle
378	110	Luling ISD	Luling
379	110	Honors Academy	Dallas
380	109	Eustace ISD	Eustace
381	107	China Spring ISD	Waco
382	103	Orange Grove ISD	Orange Grove
383	102	Littlefield ISD	Littlefield
384	102	Winnsboro ISD	Winnsboro
385	102	Bullard ISD	Bullard
386	100	Greenwood ISD	Midland
387	96	West ISD	West
388	91	Lorena ISD	Lorena
389	56	Gulf Shores Academy	Houston

Number of Students

Rank	Number	District Name	City
1	212,099	Houston ISD	Houston
2	163,347	Dallas ISD	Dallas
3	81,081	Fort Worth ISD	Fort Worth
4	78,608	Austin ISD	Austin
5	71,165	Cypress-Fairbanks ISD	Houston
6	69,409	Northside ISD	San Antonio
7	63,185	El Paso ISD	El Paso
8	61,928	Arlington ISD	Arlington
9	59,489	Fort Bend ISD	Sugar Land
10	57,120	San Antonio ISD	San Antonio
11	55,367	Aldine ISD	Houston
12	55,053	North East ISD	San Antonio
13	54,007	Garland ISD	Garland
14	51,039	Plano ISD	Plano
15	46,745	Ysleta ISD	El Paso
16	44,836	Pasadena ISD	Pasadena
17	44,661	Alief ISD	Houston
18	44,340	Brownsville ISD	Brownsville
19	43,122	Lewisville ISD	Flower Mound
20	39,864	Katy ISD	Katy
21	39,355	Corpus Christi ISD	Corpus Christi
22	38,016	Conroe ISD	Conroe
23	35,355	Klein ISD	Klein
24	35,052	Richardson ISD	Richardson
25	34,102	Round Rock ISD	Round Rock
26	33,833	Mesquite ISD	Mesquite
27	32,993	Spring Branch ISD	Houston
28	31,926	Clear Creek ISD	League City
29	31,258	Killeen ISD	Killeen
30	30,860	Irving ISD	Irving
31	30,725	United ISD	Laredo
32	30,078	Socorro ISD	El Paso
33	29,472	Lubbock ISD	Lubbock
34	29,244	Amarillo ISD	Amarillo
35	26,594	Ector County ISD	Odessa
36	26,025	Humble ISD	Humble
37	25,548	Carrollton-Farmers Branch ISD	Carrollton
38	25,492	Spring ISD	Houston
39	25,210	Pharr-San Juan-Alamo ISD	Pharr
40	24,279	Laredo ISD	Laredo
41	24,100	Edinburg CISD	Edinburg
42	23,376	Mcallen ISD	Mcallen
43	22,301	Birdville ISD	Haltom City
44	21,582	Grand Prairie ISD	Grand Prairie

Rank	Number	District	City
45	20,777	Midland ISD	Midland
46	20,612	Beaumont ISD	Beaumont
47	20,368	La Joya ISD	La Joya
48	20,109	Keller ISD	Keller
49	20,013	Galena Park ISD	Houston
50	19,720	Hurst-Euless-Bedford ISD	Bedford
51	19,162	Mansfield ISD	Mansfield
52	18,832	Goose Creek CISD	Baytown
53	17,627	Judson ISD	San Antonio
54	17,466	Abilene ISD	Abilene
55	17,096	Tyler ISD	Tyler
56	17,063	Lamar CISD	Rosenberg
57	16,814	Leander ISD	Leander
58	16,497	Harlingen Cons ISD	Harlingen
59	15,875	Pflugerville ISD	Pflugerville
60	15,758	Waco ISD	Waco
61	15,280	San Angelo ISD	San Angelo
62	15,279	Mckinney ISD	Mckinney
63	15,149	Denton ISD	Denton
64	14,999	Wichita Falls ISD	Wichita Falls
65	14,623	Weslaco ISD	Weslaco
66	14,556	Victoria ISD	Victoria
67	14,422	Harlandale ISD	San Antonio
68	14,006	Bryan ISD	Bryan
69	13,834	Grapevine-Colleyville ISD	Grapevine
70	13,802	Mission Cons ISD	Mission
71	13,198	Brazosport ISD	Clute
72	13,164	Edgewood ISD	San Antonio
73	13,011	Eagle Pass ISD	Eagle Pass
74	12,585	Allen ISD	Allen
75	12,235	Pearland ISD	Pearland
76	11,756	Alvin ISD	Alvin
77	11,490	Deer Park ISD	Deer Park
78	11,305	Comal ISD	New Braunfels
79	11,182	North Forest ISD	Houston
80	11,145	Frisco ISD	Frisco
81	10,956	Duncanville ISD	Duncanville
82	10,945	Donna ISD	Donna
83	10,818	Crowley ISD	Crowley
84	10,657	Port Arthur ISD	Port Arthur
85	10,320	San Felipe-Del Rio CISD	Del Rio
86	10,040	South San Antonio ISD	San Antonio
87	9,937	Coppell ISD	Coppell
88	9,640	Southwest ISD	San Antonio
89	9,616	Rockwall ISD	Rockwall
90	9,610	San Benito Cons ISD	San Benito
91	9,206	Rio Grande City CISD	Rio Grande City
92	9,192	Galveston ISD	Galveston
93	8,663	Hays Cons ISD	Kyle
94	8,602	Georgetown ISD	Georgetown
95	8,557	Magnolia ISD	Magnolia
96	8,429	Temple ISD	Temple
97	8,330	Longview ISD	Longview
98	8,257	Lufkin ISD	Lufkin
99	8,216	Clint ISD	Clint
100	8,106	Tomball ISD	Tomball
101	7,945	East Central ISD	San Antonio
102	7,809	Eagle Mt-Saginaw ISD	Fort Worth
103	7,761	La Porte ISD	La Porte
104	7,689	College Station ISD	College Station
105	7,681	Seguin ISD	Seguin
106	7,629	Canyon ISD	Canyon
107	7,599	Copperas Cove ISD	Copperas Cove
108	7,592	Desoto ISD	Desoto
109	7,400	Cedar Hill ISD	Cedar Hill
110	7,326	Del Valle ISD	Del Valle
111	7,263	Channelview ISD	Channelview
112	7,254	Bastrop ISD	Bastrop
113	7,246	Los Fresnos CISD	Los Fresnos
114	7,227	Carroll ISD	Southlake
115	7,132	Eanes ISD	Austin
116	7,104	Weatherford ISD	Weatherford
117	7,064	San Marcos CISD	San Marcos
118	7,035	New Caney ISD	New Caney
119	6,959	Belton ISD	Belton
120	6,863	Burleson ISD	Burleson
121	6,756	Huntsville ISD	Huntsville
122	6,718	Schertz-Cibolo-Universal City ISD	Schertz
123	6,563	Granbury ISD	Granbury
124	6,503	Angleton ISD	Angleton
125	6,380	Cleburne ISD	Cleburne
126	6,313	Nacogdoches ISD	Nacogdoches
127	6,295	Dickinson ISD	Dickinson
128	6,285	New Braunfels ISD	New Braunfels
129	6,244	Sherman ISD	Sherman
130	6,236	Sharyland ISD	Mission
131	6,211	Northwest ISD	Fort Worth
132	6,171	Roma ISD	Roma
133	6,011	Marshall ISD	Marshall
134	5,986	Highland Park ISD	Dallas
135	5,864	Plainview ISD	Plainview
136	5,842	Texas City ISD	Texas City
137	5,841	Azle ISD	Azle
138	5,812	Waxahachie ISD	Waxahachie
139	5,786	Midway ISD	Hewitt
140	5,710	Wylie ISD	Wylie
141	5,669	Alice ISD	Alice
142	5,635	Texarkana ISD	Texarkana
143	5,484	Frenship ISD	Wolfforth
144	5,476	Corsicana ISD	Corsicana
145	5,391	Friendswood ISD	Friendswood
146	5,296	Ennis ISD	Ennis
147	5,264	Uvalde CISD	Uvalde
148	5,261	Mercedes ISD	Mercedes
149	5,220	Greenville ISD	Greenville
150	5,194	Edcouch-Elsa ISD	Edcouch
151	5,185	Vidor ISD	Vidor
152	5,172	Boerne ISD	Boerne
153	5,154	Dayton ISD	Dayton
154	5,101	Nederland ISD	Nederland
155	5,090	Midlothian ISD	Midlothian
156	4,991	Flour Bluff ISD	Corpus Christi
157	4,977	Mount Pleasant ISD	Mt Pleasant
158	4,811	Red Oak ISD	Red Oak
159	4,799	Port Neches-Groves ISD	Port Neches
160	4,787	White Settlement ISD	White Settlement
161	4,768	Kerrville ISD	Kerrville
162	4,735	Brenham ISD	Brenham
163	4,725	Jacksonville ISD	Jacksonville
164	4,720	Southside ISD	San Antonio
165	4,715	Canutillo ISD	El Paso
166	4,671	Lake Travis ISD	Austin
167	4,651	Waller ISD	Waller
168	4,641	Pine Tree ISD	Longview
169	4,640	Willis ISD	Willis
170	4,623	Kingsville ISD	Kingsville
171	4,544	Denison ISD	Denison
172	4,473	Santa Fe ISD	Santa Fe
173	4,469	Lockhart ISD	Lockhart
174	4,425	Joshua ISD	Joshua
175	4,421	Alamo Heights ISD	San Antonio
176	4,321	Bay City ISD	Bay City
177	4,318	Lancaster ISD	Lancaster
178	4,291	Gregory-Portland ISD	Gregory
179	4,237	Terrell ISD	Terrell
180	4,216	Calhoun County ISD	Port Lavaca
181	4,183	Sheldon ISD	Houston
182	4,178	Montgomery ISD	Montgomery
183	4,124	Dumas ISD	Dumas
184	4,120	Crosby ISD	Crosby
185	4,111	Livingston ISD	Livingston
186	4,061	Calallen ISD	Corpus Christi
187	4,059	Sulphur Springs ISD	Sulphur Springs
188	4,045	Whitehouse ISD	Whitehouse
189	3,996	Robstown ISD	Robstown
190	3,989	Hereford ISD	Hereford
191	3,967	Big Spring ISD	Big Spring
192	3,888	Paris ISD	Paris
193	3,883	La Marque ISD	La Marque
194	3,845	Everman ISD	Everman
195	3,816	Beeville ISD	Beeville
196	3,765	Brownwood ISD	Brownwood
197	3,762	Hallsville ISD	Hallsville
198	3,706	Burkburnett ISD	Burkburnett
199	3,690	San Elizario ISD	San Elizario
200	3,670	Mineral Wells ISD	Mineral Wells
201	3,664	Little Cypress-Mauriceville CISD	Orange
202	3,655	Marble Falls ISD	Marble Falls
203	3,648	Kilgore ISD	Kilgore
204	3,616	Springtown ISD	Springtown
205	3,573	El Campo ISD	El Campo
206	3,538	Alvarado ISD	Alvarado
207	3,521	Henderson ISD	Henderson
208	3,489	Pleasanton ISD	Pleasanton
209	3,460	Lake Dallas ISD	Lake Dallas
210	3,450	Athens ISD	Athens
211	3,447	Stephenville ISD	Stephenville
212	3,445	Pampa ISD	Pampa
213	3,415	Floresville ISD	Floresville
214	3,412	Aledo ISD	Aledo
215	3,385	Palestine ISD	Palestine
216	3,374	Aransas County ISD	Rockport
217	3,372	Kaufman ISD	Kaufman
218	3,352	Lumberton ISD	Lumberton
219	3,350	Forney ISD	Forney
220	3,334	West Orange-Cove CISD	Orange
221	3,307	Dripping Springs ISD	Dripping Spgs
222	3,286	Cleveland ISD	Cleveland
223	3,270	Silsbee ISD	Silsbee
224	3,266	Mabank ISD	Mabank
225	3,261	Lampasas ISD	Lampasas
226	3,252	Castleberry ISD	Fort Worth
227	3,225	Tuloso-Midway ISD	Corpus Christi
228	3,204	North Lamar ISD	Paris
229	3,182	Jasper ISD	Jasper
230	3,160	Taylor ISD	Taylor
231	3,154	Somerset ISD	Somerset
232	3,130	Zapata County ISD	Zapata
233	3,119	Columbia-Brazoria ISD	West Columbia
234	3,075	Burnet Cons ISD	Burnet
235	3,070	Elgin ISD	Elgin
236	3,061	Levelland ISD	Levelland
237	3,042	Lindale ISD	Lindale
238	3,040	Andrews ISD	Andrews
239	3,036	Hidalgo ISD	Hidalgo
240	3,024	Navasota ISD	Navasota
241	3,022	Splendora ISD	Splendora
242	3,020	Manor ISD	Manor
243	3,018	Medina Valley ISD	Castroville
244	3,012	Chapel Hill ISD	Tyler
245	3,007	Carthage ISD	Carthage
246	2,989	Little Elm ISD	Little Elm
247	2,975	Gainesville ISD	Gainesville
248	2,956	Borger ISD	Borger
249	2,945	Barbers Hill ISD	Mount Belvieu
250	2,934	Quinlan ISD	Quinlan
251	2,906	Wilmer-Hutchins ISD	Dallas
252	2,847	Kennedale ISD	Kennedale
253	2,840	La Feria ISD	La Feria
254	2,838	Fredericksburg ISD	Fredericksburg
255	2,812	Fabens ISD	Fabens
255	2,812	Stafford Municipal School	Stafford
257	2,774	Wylie ISD	Abilene
258	2,758	Huffman ISD	Huffman
259	2,729	Decatur ISD	Decatur
260	2,695	Valley View ISD	Pharr
261	2,677	Liberty-Eylau ISD	Texarkana
262	2,674	Bridge City ISD	Bridge City
262	2,674	Raymondville ISD	Raymondville
264	2,657	Snyder ISD	Snyder
265	2,655	Gonzales ISD	Gonzales
266	2,653	Wills Point ISD	Wills Point
267	2,625	Bandera ISD	Bandera
268	2,620	Brownsboro ISD	Brownsboro
269	2,594	Gatesville ISD	Gatesville
270	2,560	Connally ISD	Waco
271	2,546	Wharton ISD	Wharton
272	2,529	La Vega ISD	Waco
273	2,494	Royse City ISD	Royse City
274	2,487	Carrizo Springs CISD	Carrizo Springs
275	2,467	Pecos-Barstow-Toyah ISD	Pecos
276	2,457	Center ISD	Center
277	2,454	Graham ISD	Graham
278	2,437	Needville ISD	Needville
279	2,433	Point Isabel ISD	Port Isabel
280	2,397	Fort Stockton ISD	Fort Stockton
281	2,361	Liberty ISD	Liberty
282	2,358	Vernon ISD	Vernon
283	2,346	Gilmer ISD	Gilmer
284	2,344	Sealy ISD	Sealy
285	2,338	Hudson ISD	Lufkin
286	2,311	Sweetwater ISD	Sweetwater
287	2,301	La Vernia ISD	La Vernia
288	2,299	Mexia ISD	Mexia
289	2,298	Pittsburg ISD	Pittsburg
290	2,294	Lubbock-Cooper ISD	Lubbock
291	2,279	Pearsall ISD	Pearsall
292	2,263	Ingleside ISD	Ingleside
293	2,247	Princeton ISD	Princeton
294	2,225	Gladewater ISD	Gladewater
295	2,201	Bridgeport ISD	Bridgeport
296	2,200	Sweeny ISD	Sweeny
297	2,198	Van ISD	Van
298	2,184	Ferris ISD	Ferris
299	2,181	Hondo ISD	Hondo
300	2,180	Seminole ISD	Seminole
301	2,164	Lamesa ISD	Lamesa
302	2,163	Sanger ISD	Sanger
303	2,156	Lake Worth ISD	Lake Worth
304	2,138	Bellville ISD	Bellville
305	2,132	Sinton ISD	Sinton
306	2,128	Progreso ISD	Progreso
307	2,115	Madisonville CISD	Madisonville
308	2,109	Aransas Pass ISD	Aransas Pass
309	2,107	Rio Hondo ISD	Rio Hondo
310	2,099	Hardin-Jefferson ISD	Sour Lake
311	2,096	Crystal City ISD	Crystal City
312	2,048	Crandall ISD	Crandall
313	2,031	Gulf Shores Academy	Houston
314	2,026	Robinson ISD	Robinson
315	2,025	Mathis ISD	Mathis
316	2,010	Bonham ISD	Bonham
317	2,007	South Texas ISD	Mercedes
318	1,994	Cuero ISD	Cuero
319	1,984	Brownfield ISD	Brownfield
320	1,977	Monahans-Wickett-Pyote ISD	Monahans
321	1,976	Perryton ISD	Perryton
322	1,933	La Grange ISD	La Grange

323	1,929	Honors Academy	Dallas
324	1,928	Atlanta ISD	Atlanta
325	1,923	Rusk ISD	Rusk
326	1,920	Diboll ISD	Diboll
327	1,918	Pleasant Grove ISD	Texarkana
328	1,914	Caldwell ISD	Caldwell
329	1,899	Devine ISD	Devine
330	1,895	Rockdale ISD	Rockdale
331	1,890	Llano ISD	Llano
332	1,872	Smithville ISD	Smithville
332	1,872	West Oso ISD	Corpus Christi
334	1,871	Venus ISD	Venus
335	1,834	Commerce ISD	Commerce
336	1,830	Westwood ISD	Palestine
337	1,824	Iowa Park CISD	Iowa Park
337	1,824	Tarkington ISD	Cleveland
339	1,813	Giddings ISD	Giddings
340	1,812	Wimberley ISD	Wimberley
341	1,806	Shepherd ISD	Shepherd
342	1,791	Hillsboro ISD	Hillsboro
343	1,779	Hamshire-Fannett ISD	Hamshire
344	1,778	Coldspring-Oakhurst CISD	Coldspring
345	1,770	Liberty Hill ISD	Liberty Hill
346	1,758	China Spring ISD	Waco
347	1,730	Crockett ISD	Crockett
348	1,729	Canton ISD	Canton
349	1,719	Brooks County ISD	Falfurrias
350	1,684	Spring Hill ISD	Longview
351	1,679	Bowie ISD	Bowie
351	1,679	Palacios ISD	Palacios
353	1,678	Glen Rose ISD	Glen Rose
353	1,678	Kemp ISD	Kemp
355	1,673	Huntington ISD	Huntington
356	1,662	Cameron ISD	Cameron
357	1,653	Breckenridge ISD	Breckenridge
358	1,651	Poteet ISD	Poteet
359	1,640	Hutto ISD	Hutto
360	1,634	Orangefield ISD	Orangefield
361	1,631	Buna ISD	Buna
362	1,630	Fairfield ISD	Fairfield
363	1,621	Central ISD	Pollok
364	1,614	Columbus ISD	Columbus
365	1,611	Edna ISD	Edna
366	1,606	Groesbeck ISD	Groesbeck
367	1,597	Royal ISD	Brookshire
368	1,596	Kirbyville CISD	Kirbyville
369	1,595	Daingerfield-Lone Star ISD	Daingerfield
370	1,594	Luling ISD	Luling
371	1,592	Littlefield ISD	Littlefield
372	1,591	Lorena ISD	Lorena
373	1,587	Dalhart ISD	Dalhart
374	1,581	San Diego ISD	San Diego
375	1,576	Eustace ISD	Eustace
376	1,572	Orange Grove ISD	Orange Grove
377	1,562	Mineola ISD	Mineola
378	1,551	Whitesboro ISD	Whitesboro
379	1,547	Yoakum ISD	Yoakum
380	1,546	Whitney ISD	Whitney
381	1,541	Lytle ISD	Lytle
382	1,540	West ISD	West
383	1,535	Greenwood ISD	Midland
384	1,526	Marlin ISD	Marlin
385	1,512	Rains ISD	Emory
386	1,510	Ingram ISD	Ingram
387	1,508	Winnsboro ISD	Winnsboro
388	1,505	Lyford CISD	Lyford
389	1,501	Bullard ISD	Bullard

Male Students

Rank	Percent	District Name	City
1	58.1	Gulf Shores Academy	Houston
2	55.6	West ISD	West
3	55.3	Littlefield ISD	Littlefield
4	54.5	Marlin ISD	Marlin
5	54.4	Lorena ISD	Lorena
6	54.0	Connally ISD	Waco
6	54.0	Shepherd ISD	Shepherd
8	53.9	Sinton ISD	Sinton
9	53.8	Coldspring-Oakhurst CISD	Coldspring
9	53.8	Diboll ISD	Diboll
11	53.7	Hardin-Jefferson ISD	Sour Lake
11	53.7	Huffman ISD	Huffman
11	53.7	Venus ISD	Venus
14	53.6	Medina Valley ISD	Castroville
15	53.5	Burleson ISD	Burleson
15	53.5	Princeton ISD	Princeton
15	53.5	Sanger ISD	Sanger
18	53.4	Cameron ISD	Cameron
18	53.4	Llano ISD	Llano
18	53.4	Lubbock-Cooper ISD	Lubbock
18	53.4	Terrell ISD	Terrell
18	53.4	Weatherford ISD	Weatherford
23	53.3	Winnsboro ISD	Winnsboro
24	53.2	Canutillo ISD	El Paso
24	53.2	Lake Travis ISD	Austin
24	53.2	Mexia ISD	Mexia
27	53.1	Caldwell ISD	Caldwell
27	53.1	Gatesville ISD	Gatesville
27	53.1	Lake Dallas ISD	Lake Dallas
27	53.1	Robinson ISD	Robinson
27	53.1	Royse City ISD	Royse City
27	53.1	Sweeny ISD	Sweeny
33	53.0	Daingerfield-Lone Star ISD	Daingerfield
34	52.9	Aransas County ISD	Rockport
34	52.9	Brownsboro ISD	Brownsboro
34	52.9	Carthage ISD	Carthage
34	52.9	Comal ISD	New Braunfels
34	52.9	Kemp ISD	Kemp
34	52.9	Lake Worth ISD	Lake Worth
34	52.9	Progreso ISD	Progreso
34	52.9	Santa Fe ISD	Santa Fe
34	52.9	Silsbee ISD	Silsbee
43	52.8	Azle ISD	Azle
43	52.8	Smithville ISD	Smithville
43	52.8	Springtown ISD	Springtown
43	52.8	Stafford Municipal School	Stafford
47	52.7	College Station ISD	College Station
47	52.7	Mabank ISD	Mabank
47	52.7	Pittsburg ISD	Pittsburg
50	52.6	Aransas Pass ISD	Aransas Pass
50	52.6	Burkburnett ISD	Burkburnett
50	52.6	Crandall ISD	Crandall
50	52.6	Gregory-Portland ISD	Gregory
50	52.6	Hallsville ISD	Hallsville
50	52.6	Wimberley ISD	Wimberley
56	52.5	Forney ISD	Forney
56	52.5	Hays Cons ISD	Kyle
56	52.5	Henderson ISD	Henderson
56	52.5	Huntington ISD	Huntington
56	52.5	La Porte ISD	La Porte
56	52.5	La Vernia ISD	La Vernia
56	52.5	Magnolia ISD	Magnolia
56	52.5	Orangefield ISD	Orangefield
56	52.5	Pecos-Barstow-Toyah ISD	Pecos
56	52.5	San Elizario ISD	San Elizario
56	52.5	Somerset ISD	Somerset
56	52.5	Stephenville ISD	Stephenville
68	52.4	Gladewater ISD	Gladewater
68	52.4	Taylor ISD	Taylor
68	52.4	West Orange-Cove CISD	Orange
68	52.4	Whitesboro ISD	Whitesboro
72	52.3	Aledo ISD	Aledo
72	52.3	Brooks County ISD	Falfurrias
72	52.3	Chapel Hill ISD	Tyler
72	52.3	Hereford ISD	Hereford
72	52.3	Judson ISD	San Antonio
72	52.3	Lampasas ISD	Lampasas
78	52.2	Alvin ISD	Alvin
78	52.2	Carrizo Springs CISD	Carrizo Springs
78	52.2	Eanes ISD	Austin
78	52.2	El Campo ISD	El Campo
78	52.2	Greenwood ISD	Midland
78	52.2	Hondo ISD	Hondo
78	52.2	Kingsville ISD	Kingsville
78	52.2	Mineral Wells ISD	Mineral Wells
78	52.2	Rio Hondo ISD	Rio Hondo
87	52.1	Alvarado ISD	Alvarado
87	52.1	Carroll ISD	Southlake
87	52.1	Channelview ISD	Channelview
87	52.1	Dayton ISD	Dayton
87	52.1	Georgetown ISD	Georgetown
87	52.1	Liberty Hill ISD	Liberty Hill
87	52.1	Palacios ISD	Palacios
87	52.1	Pflugerville ISD	Pflugerville
87	52.1	Raymondville ISD	Raymondville
87	52.1	Rockdale ISD	Rockdale
97	52.0	Birdville ISD	Haltom City
97	52.0	Bridgeport ISD	Bridgeport
97	52.0	Bullard ISD	Bullard
97	52.0	Crowley ISD	Crowley
97	52.0	Kerrville ISD	Kerrville
97	52.0	Levelland ISD	Levelland
97	52.0	Northwest ISD	Fort Worth
97	52.0	Robstown ISD	Robstown
97	52.0	Uvalde CISD	Uvalde
97	52.0	Van ISD	Van
97	52.0	Waller ISD	Waller
108	51.9	Alamo Heights ISD	San Antonio
108	51.9	Bandera ISD	Bandera
108	51.9	Boerne ISD	Boerne
108	51.9	Breckenridge ISD	Breckenridge
108	51.9	Cedar Hill ISD	Cedar Hill
108	51.9	Crosby ISD	Crosby
108	51.9	Dumas ISD	Dumas
108	51.9	Gilmer ISD	Gilmer
108	51.9	Klein ISD	Klein
108	51.9	Lamesa ISD	Lamesa
108	51.9	Lyford CISD	Lyford
108	51.9	Madisonville CISD	Madisonville
108	51.9	Mckinney ISD	Mckinney
108	51.9	North Lamar ISD	Paris
108	51.9	Rockwall ISD	Rockwall
108	51.9	San Benito Cons ISD	San Benito
108	51.9	Schertz-Cibolo-Universal City ISD	Schertz
108	51.9	South San Antonio ISD	San Antonio
108	51.9	Zapata County ISD	Zapata
127	51.8	Atlanta ISD	Atlanta
127	51.8	Bridge City ISD	Bridge City
127	51.8	Brownfield ISD	Brownfield
127	51.8	Corpus Christi ISD	Corpus Christi
127	51.8	Dalhart ISD	Dalhart
127	51.8	Denison ISD	Denison
127	51.8	Dickinson ISD	Dickinson
127	51.8	Hamshire-Fannett ISD	Hamshire
127	51.8	Harlandale ISD	San Antonio
127	51.8	Harlingen Cons ISD	Harlingen
127	51.8	Irving ISD	Irving
127	51.8	Leander ISD	Leander
127	51.8	New Caney ISD	New Caney
127	51.8	Pine Tree ISD	Longview
127	51.8	Seminole ISD	Seminole
127	51.8	West Oso ISD	Corpus Christi
143	51.7	Alice ISD	Alice
143	51.7	Belton ISD	Belton
143	51.7	Borger ISD	Borger
143	51.7	Cuero ISD	Cuero
143	51.7	Devine ISD	Devine
143	51.7	Glen Rose ISD	Glen Rose
143	51.7	Groesbeck ISD	Groesbeck
143	51.7	Ingram ISD	Ingram
143	51.7	Jasper ISD	Jasper
143	51.7	Joshua ISD	Joshua
143	51.7	Keller ISD	Keller
143	51.7	Kennedale ISD	Kennedale
143	51.7	Los Fresnos CISD	Los Fresnos
143	51.7	Northside ISD	San Antonio
143	51.7	Quinlan ISD	Quinlan
143	51.7	Sharyland ISD	Mission
143	51.7	Victoria ISD	Victoria
160	51.6	Angleton ISD	Angleton
160	51.6	Athens ISD	Athens
160	51.6	Bastrop ISD	Bastrop
160	51.6	Bryan ISD	Bryan
160	51.6	Dripping Springs ISD	Dripping Spgs
160	51.6	Eagle Mt-Saginaw ISD	Fort Worth
160	51.6	East Central ISD	San Antonio
160	51.6	Fort Bend ISD	Sugar Land
160	51.6	Galveston ISD	Galveston
160	51.6	Gonzales ISD	Gonzales
160	51.6	Graham ISD	Graham
160	51.6	Hillsboro ISD	Hillsboro
160	51.6	Ingleside ISD	Ingleside
160	51.6	La Joya ISD	La Joya
160	51.6	Little Elm ISD	Little Elm
160	51.6	Mount Pleasant ISD	Mt Pleasant
160	51.6	Nederland ISD	Nederland
160	51.6	Needville ISD	Needville
160	51.6	Seguin ISD	Seguin
160	51.6	Southside ISD	San Antonio
160	51.6	Sweetwater ISD	Sweetwater
160	51.6	Whitehouse ISD	Whitehouse
182	51.5	Aldine ISD	Houston
182	51.5	Austin ISD	Austin
182	51.5	Bay City ISD	Bay City
182	51.5	Big Spring ISD	Big Spring
182	51.5	Brazosport ISD	Clute
182	51.5	Brownwood ISD	Brownwood
182	51.5	Canyon ISD	Canyon
182	51.5	Commerce ISD	Commerce
182	51.5	Crockett ISD	Crockett
182	51.5	Ennis ISD	Ennis
182	51.5	Friendswood ISD	Friendswood
182	51.5	Garland ISD	Garland
182	51.5	Jacksonville ISD	Jacksonville
182	51.5	Little Cypress-Mauriceville CISD	Orange
182	51.5	Lockhart ISD	Lockhart
182	51.5	Lytle ISD	Lytle
182	51.5	Mansfield ISD	Mansfield
182	51.5	Marshall ISD	Marshall
182	51.5	Midway ISD	Hewitt
182	51.5	Monahans-Wickett-Pyote ISD	Monahans
182	51.5	Montgomery ISD	Montgomery
182	51.5	Palestine ISD	Palestine
182	51.5	Paris ISD	Paris
182	51.5	Richardson ISD	Richardson
182	51.5	Rusk ISD	Rusk

182	51.5	Splendora ISD	Splendora
182	51.5	Tomball ISD	Tomball
182	51.5	White Settlement ISD	White Settlement
210	51.4	Calhoun County ISD	Port Lavaca
210	51.4	Clear Creek ISD	League City
210	51.4	Conroe ISD	Conroe
210	51.4	Coppell ISD	Coppell
210	51.4	Cypress-Fairbanks ISD	Houston
210	51.4	Duncanville ISD	Duncanville
210	51.4	Everman ISD	Everman
210	51.4	Greenville ISD	Greenville
210	51.4	La Grange ISD	La Grange
210	51.4	Liberty-Eylau ISD	Texarkana
210	51.4	Longview ISD	Longview
210	51.4	Midlothian ISD	Midlothian
210	51.4	Sherman ISD	Sherman
210	51.4	United ISD	Laredo
210	51.4	Wilmer-Hutchins ISD	Dallas
225	51.3	Alief ISD	Houston
225	51.3	Bellville ISD	Bellville
225	51.3	Calallen ISD	Corpus Christi
225	51.3	Deer Park ISD	Deer Park
225	51.3	Del Valle ISD	Del Valle
225	51.3	Edinburg CISD	Edinburg
225	51.3	Frenship ISD	Wolfforth
225	51.3	Galena Park ISD	Houston
225	51.3	Hidalgo ISD	Hidalgo
225	51.3	Honors Academy	Dallas
225	51.3	Humble ISD	Humble
225	51.3	Hurst-Euless-Bedford ISD	Bedford
225	51.3	Killeen ISD	Killeen
225	51.3	Kirbyville CISD	Kirbyville
225	51.3	Nacogdoches ISD	Nacogdoches
225	51.3	Pasadena ISD	Pasadena
225	51.3	Perryton ISD	Perryton
225	51.3	Pleasanton ISD	Pleasanton
225	51.3	Round Rock ISD	Round Rock
225	51.3	Socorro ISD	El Paso
225	51.3	Spring Branch ISD	Houston
225	51.3	Weslaco ISD	Weslaco
225	51.3	Willis ISD	Willis
248	51.2	Amarillo ISD	Amarillo
248	51.2	Andrews ISD	Andrews
248	51.2	Bowie ISD	Bowie
248	51.2	Brownsville ISD	Brownsville
248	51.2	Donna ISD	Donna
248	51.2	Eagle Pass ISD	Eagle Pass
248	51.2	El Paso ISD	El Paso
248	51.2	Fort Stockton ISD	Fort Stockton
248	51.2	Katy ISD	Katy
248	51.2	Lumberton ISD	Lumberton
248	51.2	North Forest ISD	Houston
248	51.2	Plano ISD	Plano
248	51.2	Rains ISD	Emory
248	51.2	Rio Grande City CISD	Rio Grande City
248	51.2	San Marcos CISD	San Marcos
248	51.2	Snyder ISD	Snyder
248	51.2	Wylie ISD	Wylie
265	51.1	Allen ISD	Allen
265	51.1	Beeville ISD	Beeville
265	51.1	Carrollton-Farmers Branch ISD	Carrollton
265	51.1	Columbus ISD	Columbus
265	51.1	Copperas Cove ISD	Copperas Cove
265	51.1	Fairfield ISD	Fairfield
265	51.1	Giddings ISD	Giddings
265	51.1	Mesquite ISD	Mesquite
265	51.1	Mission Cons ISD	Mission
265	51.1	San Angelo ISD	San Angelo
265	51.1	San Antonio ISD	San Antonio
265	51.1	Sealy ISD	Sealy
265	51.1	Tyler ISD	Tyler
265	51.1	Vernon ISD	Vernon
265	51.1	Wichita Falls ISD	Wichita Falls
280	51.0	Arlington ISD	Arlington
280	51.0	Barbers Hill ISD	Mount Belvieu
280	51.0	Clint ISD	Clint
280	51.0	Denton ISD	Denton
280	51.0	Ector County ISD	Odessa
280	51.0	Edcouch-Elsa ISD	Edcouch
280	51.0	Edna ISD	Edna
280	51.0	Floresville ISD	Floresville
280	51.0	Goose Creek CISD	Baytown
280	51.0	Grand Prairie ISD	Grand Prairie
280	51.0	Lewisville ISD	Flower Mound
280	51.0	Livingston ISD	Livingston
280	51.0	Lubbock ISD	Lubbock
280	51.0	Mcallen ISD	Mcallen
280	51.0	Pearland ISD	Pearland
280	51.0	Southwest ISD	San Antonio
280	51.0	Spring ISD	Houston
280	51.0	Waxahachie ISD	Waxahachie
280	51.0	Whitney ISD	Whitney
280	51.0	Yoakum ISD	Yoakum
300	50.9	Bonham ISD	Bonham
300	50.9	Canton ISD	Canton
300	50.9	Corsicana ISD	Corsicana
300	50.9	Decatur ISD	Decatur
300	50.9	Edgewood ISD	San Antonio
300	50.9	Eustace ISD	Eustace
300	50.9	Fort Worth ISD	Fort Worth
300	50.9	Houston ISD	Houston
300	50.9	Huntsville ISD	Huntsville
300	50.9	Iowa Park CISD	Iowa Park
300	50.9	La Feria ISD	La Feria
300	50.9	Lindale ISD	Lindale
300	50.9	Pharr-San Juan-Alamo ISD	Pharr
300	50.9	Royal ISD	Brookshire
300	50.9	San Felipe-Del Rio CISD	Del Rio
300	50.9	Tarkington ISD	Cleveland
300	50.9	Texas City ISD	Texas City
300	50.9	Vidor ISD	Vidor
300	50.9	Waco ISD	Waco
300	50.9	Wharton ISD	Wharton
300	50.9	Ysleta ISD	El Paso
321	50.8	Abilene ISD	Abilene
321	50.8	Castleberry ISD	Fort Worth
321	50.8	Central ISD	Pollok
321	50.8	Fabens ISD	Fabens
321	50.8	Flour Bluff ISD	Corpus Christi
321	50.8	Granbury ISD	Granbury
321	50.8	Laredo ISD	Laredo
321	50.8	Mercedes ISD	Mercedes
321	50.8	North East ISD	San Antonio
321	50.8	Westwood ISD	Palestine
331	50.7	Brenham ISD	Brenham
331	50.7	Crystal City ISD	Crystal City
331	50.7	Dallas ISD	Dallas
331	50.7	La Vega ISD	Waco
331	50.7	Pleasant Grove ISD	Texarkana
331	50.7	Point Isabel ISD	Port Isabel
331	50.7	Roma ISD	Roma
331	50.7	Sheldon ISD	Houston
339	50.6	Burnet Cons ISD	Burnet
339	50.6	Ferris ISD	Ferris
339	50.6	Kaufman ISD	Kaufman
339	50.6	Lamar CISD	Rosenberg
339	50.6	Lancaster ISD	Lancaster
339	50.6	Mineola ISD	Mineola
339	50.6	Plainview ISD	Plainview
339	50.6	Red Oak ISD	Red Oak
339	50.6	Sulphur Springs ISD	Sulphur Springs
339	50.6	Valley View ISD	Pharr
349	50.5	Buna ISD	Buna
349	50.5	Cleveland ISD	Cleveland
349	50.5	Hudson ISD	Lufkin
349	50.5	Liberty ISD	Liberty
349	50.5	Midland ISD	Midland
349	50.5	New Braunfels ISD	New Braunfels
349	50.5	Spring Hill ISD	Longview
356	50.4	Cleburne ISD	Cleburne
356	50.4	Columbia-Brazoria ISD	West Columbia
356	50.4	Fredericksburg ISD	Fredericksburg
356	50.4	Navasota ISD	Navasota
356	50.4	Temple ISD	Temple
356	50.4	Texarkana ISD	Texarkana
362	50.3	Beaumont ISD	Beaumont
362	50.3	Elgin ISD	Elgin
362	50.3	Frisco ISD	Frisco
362	50.3	Lufkin ISD	Lufkin
362	50.3	Luling ISD	Luling
362	50.3	Manor ISD	Manor
368	50.2	La Marque ISD	La Marque
368	50.2	Mathis ISD	Mathis
368	50.2	Port Arthur ISD	Port Arthur
371	50.1	Desoto ISD	Desoto
371	50.1	Gainesville ISD	Gainesville
371	50.1	Port Neches-Groves ISD	Port Neches
371	50.1	Wills Point ISD	Wills Point
375	50.0	Center ISD	Center
375	50.0	Marble Falls ISD	Marble Falls
375	50.0	Pearsall ISD	Pearsall
375	50.0	Tuloso-Midway ISD	Corpus Christi
379	49.8	Hutto ISD	Hutto
380	49.7	Grapevine-Colleyville ISD	Grapevine
381	49.6	Highland Park ISD	Dallas
381	49.6	Pampa ISD	Pampa
383	49.5	Kilgore ISD	Kilgore
384	49.4	Wylie ISD	Abilene
385	49.1	Poteet ISD	Poteet
386	48.8	San Diego ISD	San Diego
387	48.7	Orange Grove ISD	Orange Grove
388	48.1	South Texas ISD	Mercedes
389	47.2	China Spring ISD	Waco

Female Students

Rank	Percent	District Name	City
1	52.8	China Spring ISD	Waco
2	51.9	South Texas ISD	Mercedes
3	51.3	Orange Grove ISD	Orange Grove
4	51.2	San Diego ISD	San Diego
5	50.9	Poteet ISD	Poteet
6	50.6	Wylie ISD	Abilene
7	50.5	Kilgore ISD	Kilgore
8	50.4	Highland Park ISD	Dallas
8	50.4	Pampa ISD	Pampa
10	50.3	Grapevine-Colleyville ISD	Grapevine
11	50.2	Hutto ISD	Hutto
12	50.0	Center ISD	Center
12	50.0	Marble Falls ISD	Marble Falls
12	50.0	Pearsall ISD	Pearsall
12	50.0	Tuloso-Midway ISD	Corpus Christi
16	49.9	Desoto ISD	Desoto
16	49.9	Gainesville ISD	Gainesville
16	49.9	Port Neches-Groves ISD	Port Neches
16	49.9	Wills Point ISD	Wills Point
20	49.8	La Marque ISD	La Marque
20	49.8	Mathis ISD	Mathis
20	49.8	Port Arthur ISD	Port Arthur
23	49.7	Beaumont ISD	Beaumont
23	49.7	Elgin ISD	Elgin
23	49.7	Frisco ISD	Frisco
23	49.7	Lufkin ISD	Lufkin
23	49.7	Luling ISD	Luling
23	49.7	Manor ISD	Manor
29	49.6	Cleburne ISD	Cleburne
29	49.6	Columbia-Brazoria ISD	West Columbia
29	49.6	Fredericksburg ISD	Fredericksburg
29	49.6	Navasota ISD	Navasota
29	49.6	Temple ISD	Temple
29	49.6	Texarkana ISD	Texarkana
35	49.5	Buna ISD	Buna
35	49.5	Cleveland ISD	Cleveland
35	49.5	Hudson ISD	Lufkin
35	49.5	Liberty ISD	Liberty
35	49.5	Midland ISD	Midland
35	49.5	New Braunfels ISD	New Braunfels
35	49.5	Spring Hill ISD	Longview
42	49.4	Burnet Cons ISD	Burnet
42	49.4	Ferris ISD	Ferris
42	49.4	Kaufman ISD	Kaufman
42	49.4	Lamar CISD	Rosenberg
42	49.4	Lancaster ISD	Lancaster
42	49.4	Mineola ISD	Mineola
42	49.4	Plainview ISD	Plainview
42	49.4	Red Oak ISD	Red Oak
42	49.4	Sulphur Springs ISD	Sulphur Springs
42	49.4	Valley View ISD	Pharr
52	49.3	Brenham ISD	Brenham
52	49.3	Crystal City ISD	Crystal City
52	49.3	Dallas ISD	Dallas
52	49.3	La Vega ISD	Waco
52	49.3	Pleasant Grove ISD	Texarkana
52	49.3	Point Isabel ISD	Port Isabel
52	49.3	Roma ISD	Roma
52	49.3	Sheldon ISD	Houston
60	49.2	Abilene ISD	Abilene
60	49.2	Castleberry ISD	Fort Worth
60	49.2	Central ISD	Pollok
60	49.2	Fabens ISD	Fabens
60	49.2	Flour Bluff ISD	Corpus Christi
60	49.2	Granbury ISD	Granbury
60	49.2	Laredo ISD	Laredo
60	49.2	Mercedes ISD	Mercedes
60	49.2	North East ISD	San Antonio
60	49.2	Westwood ISD	Palestine
70	49.1	Bonham ISD	Bonham
70	49.1	Canton ISD	Canton
70	49.1	Corsicana ISD	Corsicana
70	49.1	Decatur ISD	Decatur
70	49.1	Edgewood ISD	San Antonio
70	49.1	Eustace ISD	Eustace
70	49.1	Fort Worth ISD	Fort Worth
70	49.1	Houston ISD	Houston
70	49.1	Huntsville ISD	Huntsville
70	49.1	Iowa Park CISD	Iowa Park
70	49.1	La Feria ISD	La Feria
70	49.1	Lindale ISD	Lindale
70	49.1	Pharr-San Juan-Alamo ISD	Pharr
70	49.1	Royal ISD	Brookshire
70	49.1	San Felipe-Del Rio CISD	Del Rio
70	49.1	Tarkington ISD	Cleveland
70	49.1	Texas City ISD	Texas City
70	49.1	Vidor ISD	Vidor
70	49.1	Waco ISD	Waco
70	49.1	Wharton ISD	Wharton
70	49.1	Ysleta ISD	El Paso

91	49.0	Arlington ISD	Arlington
91	49.0	Barbers Hill ISD	Mount Belvieu
91	49.0	Clint ISD	Clint
91	49.0	Denton ISD	Denton
91	49.0	Ector County ISD	Odessa
91	49.0	Edcouch-Elsa ISD	Edcouch
91	49.0	Edna ISD	Edna
91	49.0	Floresville ISD	Floresville
91	49.0	Goose Creek CISD	Baytown
91	49.0	Grand Prairie ISD	Grand Prairie
91	49.0	Lewisville ISD	Flower Mound
91	49.0	Livingston ISD	Livingston
91	49.0	Lubbock ISD	Lubbock
91	49.0	Mcallen ISD	Mcallen
91	49.0	Pearland ISD	Pearland
91	49.0	Southwest ISD	San Antonio
91	49.0	Spring ISD	Houston
91	49.0	Waxahachie ISD	Waxahachie
91	49.0	Whitney ISD	Whitney
91	49.0	Yoakum ISD	Yoakum
111	48.9	Allen ISD	Allen
111	48.9	Beeville ISD	Beeville
111	48.9	Carrollton-Farmers Branch ISD	Carrollton
111	48.9	Columbus ISD	Columbus
111	48.9	Copperas Cove ISD	Copperas Cove
111	48.9	Fairfield ISD	Fairfield
111	48.9	Giddings ISD	Giddings
111	48.9	Mesquite ISD	Mesquite
111	48.9	Mission Cons ISD	Mission
111	48.9	San Angelo ISD	San Angelo
111	48.9	San Antonio ISD	San Antonio
111	48.9	Sealy ISD	Sealy
111	48.9	Tyler ISD	Tyler
111	48.9	Vernon ISD	Vernon
111	48.9	Wichita Falls ISD	Wichita Falls
126	48.8	Amarillo ISD	Amarillo
126	48.8	Andrews ISD	Andrews
126	48.8	Bowie ISD	Bowie
126	48.8	Brownsville ISD	Brownsville
126	48.8	Donna ISD	Donna
126	48.8	Eagle Pass ISD	Eagle Pass
126	48.8	El Paso ISD	El Paso
126	48.8	Fort Stockton ISD	Fort Stockton
126	48.8	Katy ISD	Katy
126	48.8	Lumberton ISD	Lumberton
126	48.8	North Forest ISD	Houston
126	48.8	Plano ISD	Plano
126	48.8	Rains ISD	Emory
126	48.8	Rio Grande City CISD	Rio Grande City
126	48.8	San Marcos CISD	San Marcos
126	48.8	Snyder ISD	Snyder
126	48.8	Wylie ISD	Wylie
143	48.7	Alief ISD	Houston
143	48.7	Bellville ISD	Bellville
143	48.7	Calallen ISD	Corpus Christi
143	48.7	Deer Park ISD	Deer Park
143	48.7	Del Valle ISD	Del Valle
143	48.7	Edinburg CISD	Edinburg
143	48.7	Frenship ISD	Wolfforth
143	48.7	Galena Park ISD	Houston
143	48.7	Hidalgo ISD	Hidalgo
143	48.7	Honors Academy	Dallas
143	48.7	Humble ISD	Humble
143	48.7	Hurst-Euless-Bedford ISD	Bedford
143	48.7	Killeen ISD	Killeen
143	48.7	Kirbyville CISD	Kirbyville
143	48.7	Nacogdoches ISD	Nacogdoches
143	48.7	Pasadena ISD	Pasadena
143	48.7	Perryton ISD	Perryton
143	48.7	Pleasanton ISD	Pleasanton
143	48.7	Round Rock ISD	Round Rock
143	48.7	Socorro ISD	El Paso
143	48.7	Spring Branch ISD	Houston
143	48.7	Weslaco ISD	Weslaco
143	48.7	Willis ISD	Willis
166	48.6	Calhoun County ISD	Port Lavaca
166	48.6	Clear Creek ISD	League City
166	48.6	Conroe ISD	Conroe
166	48.6	Coppell ISD	Coppell
166	48.6	Cypress-Fairbanks ISD	Houston
166	48.6	Duncanville ISD	Duncanville
166	48.6	Everman ISD	Everman
166	48.6	Greenville ISD	Greenville
166	48.6	La Grange ISD	La Grange
166	48.6	Liberty-Eylau ISD	Texarkana
166	48.6	Longview ISD	Longview
166	48.6	Midlothian ISD	Midlothian
166	48.6	Sherman ISD	Sherman
166	48.6	United ISD	Laredo
166	48.6	Wilmer-Hutchins ISD	Dallas
181	48.5	Aldine ISD	Houston
181	48.5	Austin ISD	Austin
181	48.5	Bay City ISD	Bay City
181	48.5	Big Spring ISD	Big Spring
181	48.5	Brazosport ISD	Clute
181	48.5	Brownwood ISD	Brownwood
181	48.5	Canyon ISD	Canyon
181	48.5	Commerce ISD	Commerce
181	48.5	Crockett ISD	Crockett
181	48.5	Ennis ISD	Ennis
181	48.5	Friendswood ISD	Friendswood
181	48.5	Garland ISD	Garland
181	48.5	Jacksonville ISD	Jacksonville
181	48.5	Little Cypress-Mauriceville CISD	Orange
181	48.5	Lockhart ISD	Lockhart
181	48.5	Lytle ISD	Lytle
181	48.5	Mansfield ISD	Mansfield
181	48.5	Marshall ISD	Marshall
181	48.5	Midway ISD	Hewitt
181	48.5	Monahans-Wickett-Pyote ISD	Monahans
181	48.5	Montgomery ISD	Montgomery
181	48.5	Palestine ISD	Palestine
181	48.5	Paris ISD	Paris
181	48.5	Richardson ISD	Richardson
181	48.5	Rusk ISD	Rusk
181	48.5	Splendora ISD	Splendora
181	48.5	Tomball ISD	Tomball
181	48.5	White Settlement ISD	White Settlement
209	48.4	Angleton ISD	Angleton
209	48.4	Athens ISD	Athens
209	48.4	Bastrop ISD	Bastrop
209	48.4	Bryan ISD	Bryan
209	48.4	Dripping Springs ISD	Dripping Spgs
209	48.4	Eagle Mt-Saginaw ISD	Fort Worth
209	48.4	East Central ISD	San Antonio
209	48.4	Fort Bend ISD	Sugar Land
209	48.4	Galveston ISD	Galveston
209	48.4	Gonzales ISD	Gonzales
209	48.4	Graham ISD	Graham
209	48.4	Hillsboro ISD	Hillsboro
209	48.4	Ingleside ISD	Ingleside
209	48.4	La Joya ISD	La Joya
209	48.4	Little Elm ISD	Little Elm
209	48.4	Mount Pleasant ISD	Mt Pleasant
209	48.4	Nederland ISD	Nederland
209	48.4	Needville ISD	Needville
209	48.4	Seguin ISD	Seguin
209	48.4	Southside ISD	San Antonio
209	48.4	Sweetwater ISD	Sweetwater
209	48.4	Whitehouse ISD	Whitehouse
231	48.3	Alice ISD	Alice
231	48.3	Belton ISD	Belton
231	48.3	Borger ISD	Borger
231	48.3	Cuero ISD	Cuero
231	48.3	Devine ISD	Devine
231	48.3	Glen Rose ISD	Glen Rose
231	48.3	Groesbeck ISD	Groesbeck
231	48.3	Ingram ISD	Ingram
231	48.3	Jasper ISD	Jasper
231	48.3	Joshua ISD	Joshua
231	48.3	Keller ISD	Keller
231	48.3	Kennedale ISD	Kennedale
231	48.3	Los Fresnos CISD	Los Fresnos
231	48.3	Northside ISD	San Antonio
231	48.3	Quinlan ISD	Quinlan
231	48.3	Sharyland ISD	Mission
231	48.3	Victoria ISD	Victoria
248	48.2	Atlanta ISD	Atlanta
248	48.2	Bridge City ISD	Bridge City
248	48.2	Brownfield ISD	Brownfield
248	48.2	Corpus Christi ISD	Corpus Christi
248	48.2	Dalhart ISD	Dalhart
248	48.2	Denison ISD	Denison
248	48.2	Dickinson ISD	Dickinson
248	48.2	Hamshire-Fannett ISD	Hamshire
248	48.2	Harlandale ISD	San Antonio
248	48.2	Harlingen Cons ISD	Harlingen
248	48.2	Irving ISD	Irving
248	48.2	Leander ISD	Leander
248	48.2	New Caney ISD	New Caney
248	48.2	Pine Tree ISD	Longview
248	48.2	Seminole ISD	Seminole
248	48.2	West Oso ISD	Corpus Christi
264	48.1	Alamo Heights ISD	San Antonio
264	48.1	Bandera ISD	Bandera
264	48.1	Boerne ISD	Boerne
264	48.1	Breckenridge ISD	Breckenridge
264	48.1	Cedar Hill ISD	Cedar Hill
264	48.1	Crosby ISD	Crosby
264	48.1	Dumas ISD	Dumas
264	48.1	Gilmer ISD	Gilmer
264	48.1	Klein ISD	Klein
264	48.1	Lamesa ISD	Lamesa
264	48.1	Lyford CISD	Lyford
264	48.1	Madisonville CISD	Madisonville
264	48.1	Mckinney ISD	Mckinney
264	48.1	North Lamar ISD	Paris
264	48.1	Rockwall ISD	Rockwall
264	48.1	San Benito Cons ISD	San Benito
264	48.1	Schertz-Cibolo-Universal City ISD	Schertz
264	48.1	South San Antonio ISD	San Antonio
264	48.1	Zapata County ISD	Zapata
283	48.0	Birdville ISD	Haltom City
283	48.0	Bridgeport ISD	Bridgeport
283	48.0	Bullard ISD	Bullard
283	48.0	Crowley ISD	Crowley
283	48.0	Kerrville ISD	Kerrville
283	48.0	Levelland ISD	Levelland
283	48.0	Northwest ISD	Fort Worth
283	48.0	Robstown ISD	Robstown
283	48.0	Uvalde CISD	Uvalde
283	48.0	Van ISD	Van
283	48.0	Waller ISD	Waller
294	47.9	Alvarado ISD	Alvarado
294	47.9	Carroll ISD	Southlake
294	47.9	Channelview ISD	Channelview
294	47.9	Dayton ISD	Dayton
294	47.9	Georgetown ISD	Georgetown
294	47.9	Liberty Hill ISD	Liberty Hill
294	47.9	Palacios ISD	Palacios
294	47.9	Pflugerville ISD	Pflugerville
294	47.9	Raymondville ISD	Raymondville
294	47.9	Rockdale ISD	Rockdale
304	47.8	Alvin ISD	Alvin
304	47.8	Carrizo Springs CISD	Carrizo Springs
304	47.8	Eanes ISD	Austin
304	47.8	El Campo ISD	El Campo
304	47.8	Greenwood ISD	Midland
304	47.8	Hondo ISD	Hondo
304	47.8	Kingsville ISD	Kingsville
304	47.8	Mineral Wells ISD	Mineral Wells
304	47.8	Rio Hondo ISD	Rio Hondo
313	47.7	Aledo ISD	Aledo
313	47.7	Brooks County ISD	Falfurrias
313	47.7	Chapel Hill ISD	Tyler
313	47.7	Hereford ISD	Hereford
313	47.7	Judson ISD	San Antonio
313	47.7	Lampasas ISD	Lampasas
319	47.6	Gladewater ISD	Gladewater
319	47.6	Taylor ISD	Taylor
319	47.6	West Orange-Cove CISD	Orange
319	47.6	Whitesboro ISD	Whitesboro
323	47.5	Forney ISD	Forney
323	47.5	Hays Cons ISD	Kyle
323	47.5	Henderson ISD	Henderson
323	47.5	Huntington ISD	Huntington
323	47.5	La Porte ISD	La Porte
323	47.5	La Vernia ISD	La Vernia
323	47.5	Magnolia ISD	Magnolia
323	47.5	Orangefield ISD	Orangefield
323	47.5	Pecos-Barstow-Toyah ISD	Pecos
323	47.5	San Elizario ISD	San Elizario
323	47.5	Somerset ISD	Somerset
323	47.5	Stephenville ISD	Stephenville
335	47.4	Aransas Pass ISD	Aransas Pass
335	47.4	Burkburnett ISD	Burkburnett
335	47.4	Crandall ISD	Crandall
335	47.4	Gregory-Portland ISD	Gregory
335	47.4	Hallsville ISD	Hallsville
335	47.4	Wimberley ISD	Wimberley
341	47.3	College Station ISD	College Station
341	47.3	Mabank ISD	Mabank
341	47.3	Pittsburg ISD	Pittsburg
344	47.2	Azle ISD	Azle
344	47.2	Smithville ISD	Smithville
344	47.2	Springtown ISD	Springtown
344	47.2	Stafford Municipal School	Stafford
348	47.1	Aransas County ISD	Rockport
348	47.1	Brownsboro ISD	Brownsboro
348	47.1	Carthage ISD	Carthage
348	47.1	Comal ISD	New Braunfels
348	47.1	Kemp ISD	Kemp
348	47.1	Lake Worth ISD	Lake Worth
348	47.1	Progreso ISD	Progreso
348	47.1	Santa Fe ISD	Santa Fe
348	47.1	Silsbee ISD	Silsbee
357	47.0	Daingerfield-Lone Star ISD	Daingerfield
358	46.9	Caldwell ISD	Caldwell
358	46.9	Gatesville ISD	Gatesville
358	46.9	Lake Dallas ISD	Lake Dallas
358	46.9	Robinson ISD	Robinson
358	46.9	Royse City ISD	Royse City
358	46.9	Sweeny ISD	Sweeny
364	46.8	Canutillo ISD	El Paso
364	46.8	Lake Travis ISD	Austin
364	46.8	Mexia ISD	Mexia
367	46.7	Winnsboro ISD	Winnsboro

Rank	Percent	District Name	City
368	46.6	Cameron ISD	Cameron
368	46.6	Llano ISD	Llano
368	46.6	Lubbock-Cooper ISD	Lubbock
368	46.6	Terrell ISD	Terrell
368	46.6	Weatherford ISD	Weatherford
373	46.5	Burleson ISD	Burleson
373	46.5	Princeton ISD	Princeton
373	46.5	Sanger ISD	Sanger
376	46.4	Medina Valley ISD	Castroville
377	46.3	Hardin-Jefferson ISD	Sour Lake
377	46.3	Huffman ISD	Huffman
377	46.3	Venus ISD	Venus
380	46.2	Coldspring-Oakhurst CISD	Coldspring
380	46.2	Diboll ISD	Diboll
382	46.1	Sinton ISD	Sinton
383	46.0	Connally ISD	Waco
383	46.0	Shepherd ISD	Shepherd
385	45.6	Lorena ISD	Lorena
386	45.5	Marlin ISD	Marlin
387	44.7	Littlefield ISD	Littlefield
388	44.4	West ISD	West
389	41.9	Gulf Shores Academy	Houston

Individual Education Program Students

Rank	Percent	District Name	City
1	25.7	Venus ISD	Venus
2	23.2	West ISD	West
3	21.1	Eustace ISD	Eustace
4	19.4	Gladewater ISD	Gladewater
5	19.1	Silsbee ISD	Silsbee
6	18.8	Atlanta ISD	Atlanta
7	18.7	Llano ISD	Llano
8	18.6	Denison ISD	Denison
9	18.5	Lubbock-Cooper ISD	Lubbock
9	18.5	Mineral Wells ISD	Mineral Wells
11	18.4	Andrews ISD	Andrews
11	18.4	Huntington ISD	Huntington
11	18.4	Vidor ISD	Vidor
14	18.1	Mabank ISD	Mabank
15	17.9	Abilene ISD	Abilene
15	17.9	China Spring ISD	Waco
15	17.9	Quinlan ISD	Quinlan
18	17.8	Livingston ISD	Livingston
19	17.6	Snyder ISD	Snyder
20	17.2	Lorena ISD	Lorena
21	17.0	Pleasanton ISD	Pleasanton
21	17.0	Rockdale ISD	Rockdale
21	17.0	Terrell ISD	Terrell
24	16.8	Ferris ISD	Ferris
24	16.8	Gatesville ISD	Gatesville
24	16.8	Littlefield ISD	Littlefield
24	16.8	Sanger ISD	Sanger
24	16.8	Temple ISD	Temple
24	16.8	Vernon ISD	Vernon
30	16.7	Sherman ISD	Sherman
31	16.6	Commerce ISD	Commerce
31	16.6	Little Cypress-Mauriceville CISD	Orange
31	16.6	West Orange-Cove CISD	Orange
34	16.5	Belton ISD	Belton
34	16.5	Central ISD	Pollok
36	16.4	Buna ISD	Buna
36	16.4	Mexia ISD	Mexia
36	16.4	Sweetwater ISD	Sweetwater
39	16.3	Liberty-Eylau ISD	Texarkana
39	16.3	Marlin ISD	Marlin
39	16.3	Pittsburg ISD	Pittsburg
39	16.3	Robinson ISD	Robinson
39	16.3	Seminole ISD	Seminole
44	16.1	Aransas Pass ISD	Aransas Pass
44	16.1	Lubbock ISD	Lubbock
46	16.0	North East ISD	San Antonio
46	16.0	Paris ISD	Paris
48	15.8	Everman ISD	Everman
48	15.8	Kemp ISD	Kemp
50	15.7	Connally ISD	Waco
50	15.7	Nederland ISD	Nederland
50	15.7	Texarkana ISD	Texarkana
53	15.6	Bonham ISD	Bonham
54	15.5	Ennis ISD	Ennis
54	15.5	Harlandale ISD	San Antonio
54	15.5	Henderson ISD	Henderson
54	15.5	Hillsboro ISD	Hillsboro
54	15.5	Kingsville ISD	Kingsville
54	15.5	Smithville ISD	Smithville
60	15.4	Poteet ISD	Poteet
60	15.4	Rains ISD	Emory
60	15.4	Rio Hondo ISD	Rio Hondo
63	15.3	Aransas County ISD	Rockport
63	15.3	Bandera ISD	Bandera
63	15.3	Burnet Cons ISD	Burnet
63	15.3	La Vernia ISD	La Vernia
63	15.3	Waxahachie ISD	Waxahachie
63	15.3	Whitesboro ISD	Whitesboro
69	15.2	Northside ISD	San Antonio
69	15.2	Robstown ISD	Robstown
69	15.2	Shepherd ISD	Shepherd
72	15.1	Lockhart ISD	Lockhart
73	15.0	Princeton ISD	Princeton
73	15.0	Red Oak ISD	Red Oak
75	14.9	Gilmer ISD	Gilmer
75	14.9	La Vega ISD	Waco
75	14.9	Springtown ISD	Springtown
75	14.9	Westwood ISD	Palestine
79	14.8	Carthage ISD	Carthage
79	14.8	Plainview ISD	Plainview
81	14.7	Levelland ISD	Levelland
81	14.7	Longview ISD	Longview
81	14.7	Marshall ISD	Marshall
81	14.7	Waco ISD	Waco
85	14.6	Edgewood ISD	San Antonio
85	14.6	Gainesville ISD	Gainesville
85	14.6	Kirbyville CISD	Kirbyville
88	14.5	Brownfield ISD	Brownfield
88	14.5	Lampasas ISD	Lampasas
88	14.5	Royse City ISD	Royse City
88	14.5	Rusk ISD	Rusk
92	14.4	Columbus ISD	Columbus
92	14.4	Groesbeck ISD	Groesbeck
92	14.4	Monahans-Wickett-Pyote ISD	Monahans
92	14.4	Southside ISD	San Antonio
96	14.3	Bridgeport ISD	Bridgeport
96	14.3	Brooks County ISD	Falfurrias
96	14.3	Corpus Christi ISD	Corpus Christi
96	14.3	Laredo ISD	Laredo
100	14.2	Angleton ISD	Angleton
101	14.1	Hardin-Jefferson ISD	Sour Lake
101	14.1	North Lamar ISD	Paris
101	14.1	Sealy ISD	Sealy
104	14.0	Borger ISD	Borger
104	14.0	Comal ISD	New Braunfels
104	14.0	Crockett ISD	Crockett
104	14.0	Del Valle ISD	Del Valle
104	14.0	Mesquite ISD	Mesquite
104	14.0	Weatherford ISD	Weatherford
110	13.9	Birdville ISD	Haltom City
110	13.9	Kerrville ISD	Kerrville
110	13.9	New Caney ISD	New Caney
110	13.9	Sulphur Springs ISD	Sulphur Springs
110	13.9	Winnsboro ISD	Winnsboro
115	13.8	Daingerfield-Lone Star ISD	Daingerfield
116	13.7	Bellville ISD	Bellville
116	13.7	Brazosport ISD	Clute
116	13.7	Fairfield ISD	Fairfield
116	13.7	Mount Pleasant ISD	Mt Pleasant
116	13.7	Somerset ISD	Somerset
116	13.7	Wharton ISD	Wharton
116	13.7	Wichita Falls ISD	Wichita Falls
123	13.6	Denton ISD	Denton
123	13.6	Lake Dallas ISD	Lake Dallas
123	13.6	Lufkin ISD	Lufkin
126	13.5	Midlothian ISD	Midlothian
126	13.5	Orangefield ISD	Orangefield
126	13.5	Seguin ISD	Seguin
129	13.4	Kilgore ISD	Kilgore
130	13.3	Breckenridge ISD	Breckenridge
130	13.3	Corsicana ISD	Corsicana
130	13.3	Killeen ISD	Killeen
130	13.3	Manor ISD	Manor
130	13.3	Mineola ISD	Mineola
130	13.3	Rio Grande City CISD	Rio Grande City
130	13.3	Taylor ISD	Taylor
130	13.3	Whitney ISD	Whitney
130	13.3	Yoakum ISD	Yoakum
139	13.2	Crandall ISD	Crandall
139	13.2	Dalhart ISD	Dalhart
139	13.2	Grand Prairie ISD	Grand Prairie
139	13.2	Southwest ISD	San Antonio
143	13.1	Alvarado ISD	Alvarado
143	13.1	Bay City ISD	Bay City
143	13.1	Crosby ISD	Crosby
143	13.1	Crowley ISD	Crowley
143	13.1	Granbury ISD	Granbury
143	13.1	Medina Valley ISD	Castroville
149	13.0	Boerne ISD	Boerne
149	13.0	Copperas Cove ISD	Copperas Cove
149	13.0	Flour Bluff ISD	Corpus Christi
149	13.0	Hamshire-Fannett ISD	Hamshire
149	13.0	Los Fresnos CISD	Los Fresnos
149	13.0	Needville ISD	Needville
149	13.0	Van ISD	Van
156	12.9	Bowie ISD	Bowie
156	12.9	Caldwell ISD	Caldwell
156	12.9	Cameron ISD	Cameron
156	12.9	Dripping Springs ISD	Dripping Spgs
156	12.9	East Central ISD	San Antonio
156	12.9	Hereford ISD	Hereford
156	12.9	San Angelo ISD	San Angelo
156	12.9	San Antonio ISD	San Antonio
156	12.9	San Elizario ISD	San Elizario
165	12.8	Bastrop ISD	Bastrop
165	12.8	Bridge City ISD	Bridge City
165	12.8	Elgin ISD	Elgin
165	12.8	Jacksonville ISD	Jacksonville
165	12.8	Tyler ISD	Tyler
165	12.8	Wimberley ISD	Wimberley
171	12.7	Azle ISD	Azle
171	12.7	Jasper ISD	Jasper
171	12.7	West Oso ISD	Corpus Christi
174	12.6	Alvin ISD	Alvin
174	12.6	Amarillo ISD	Amarillo
174	12.6	Cuero ISD	Cuero
174	12.6	El Campo ISD	El Campo
174	12.6	Floresville ISD	Floresville
174	12.6	Little Elm ISD	Little Elm
174	12.6	Sinton ISD	Sinton
174	12.6	Wills Point ISD	Wills Point
182	12.5	Calhoun County ISD	Port Lavaca
182	12.5	Forney ISD	Forney
182	12.5	Glen Rose ISD	Glen Rose
182	12.5	White Settlement ISD	White Settlement
186	12.4	Brownwood ISD	Brownwood
186	12.4	Cleburne ISD	Cleburne
186	12.4	Edna ISD	Edna
186	12.4	Garland ISD	Garland
186	12.4	Gonzales ISD	Gonzales
186	12.4	Graham ISD	Graham
186	12.4	Hays Cons ISD	Kyle
186	12.4	Kaufman ISD	Kaufman
186	12.4	Lumberton ISD	Lumberton
186	12.4	Royal ISD	Brookshire
186	12.4	Wylie ISD	Abilene
197	12.3	Burkburnett ISD	Burkburnett
197	12.3	Lytle ISD	Lytle
197	12.3	San Marcos CISD	San Marcos
200	12.2	Athens ISD	Athens
200	12.2	Brownsboro ISD	Brownsboro
200	12.2	Bryan ISD	Bryan
200	12.2	Calallen ISD	Corpus Christi
200	12.2	Canyon ISD	Canyon
200	12.2	Desoto ISD	Desoto
200	12.2	Diboll ISD	Diboll
200	12.2	Greenwood ISD	Midland
200	12.2	Klein ISD	Klein
200	12.2	Orange Grove ISD	Orange Grove
210	12.1	Austin ISD	Austin
210	12.1	Brownsville ISD	Brownsville
210	12.1	Ingram ISD	Ingram
210	12.1	Pampa ISD	Pampa
210	12.1	Sweeny ISD	Sweeny
210	12.1	Victoria ISD	Victoria
216	12.0	Channelview ISD	Channelview
216	12.0	Joshua ISD	Joshua
216	12.0	La Marque ISD	La Marque
216	12.0	Northwest ISD	Fort Worth
216	12.0	San Benito Cons ISD	San Benito
216	12.0	United ISD	Laredo
216	12.0	Uvalde CISD	Uvalde
223	11.9	Bullard ISD	Bullard
223	11.9	Devine ISD	Devine
223	11.9	Galena Park ISD	Houston
223	11.9	Gregory-Portland ISD	Gregory
223	11.9	Huntsville ISD	Huntsville
223	11.9	Lamesa ISD	Lamesa
223	11.9	Leander ISD	Leander
223	11.9	Willis ISD	Willis
231	11.8	Beaumont ISD	Beaumont
231	11.8	Center ISD	Center
231	11.8	Fredericksburg ISD	Fredericksburg
231	11.8	Lancaster ISD	Lancaster
231	11.8	Liberty Hill ISD	Liberty Hill
231	11.8	Liberty ISD	Liberty
231	11.8	New Braunfels ISD	New Braunfels
231	11.8	Pflugerville ISD	Pflugerville
231	11.8	San Felipe-Del Rio CISD	Del Rio
231	11.8	Schertz-Cibolo-Universal City ISD	Schertz
241	11.7	Alief ISD	Houston
241	11.7	Big Spring ISD	Big Spring
241	11.7	La Grange ISD	La Grange
241	11.7	Lindale ISD	Lindale
241	11.7	Madisonville CISD	Madisonville
241	11.7	Montgomery ISD	Montgomery
241	11.7	Pecos-Barstow-Toyah ISD	Pecos
248	11.6	Duncanville ISD	Duncanville
248	11.6	Fort Stockton ISD	Fort Stockton
248	11.6	Frenship ISD	Wolfforth
248	11.6	Hondo ISD	Hondo
248	11.6	Lamar CISD	Rosenberg

Rank	Percent	District Name	City
248	11.6	Marble Falls ISD	Marble Falls
248	11.6	Richardson ISD	Richardson
255	11.5	Galveston ISD	Galveston
255	11.5	Sheldon ISD	Houston
255	11.5	Stephenville ISD	Stephenville
255	11.5	Tuloso-Midway ISD	Corpus Christi
259	11.4	Dayton ISD	Dayton
259	11.4	Decatur ISD	Decatur
259	11.4	Greenville ISD	Greenville
259	11.4	Lewisville ISD	Flower Mound
259	11.4	Luling ISD	Luling
259	11.4	Magnolia ISD	Magnolia
259	11.4	Port Neches-Groves ISD	Port Neches
259	11.4	Wylie ISD	Wylie
267	11.3	Allen ISD	Allen
267	11.3	Columbia-Brazoria ISD	West Columbia
267	11.3	Huffman ISD	Huffman
267	11.3	Judson ISD	San Antonio
267	11.3	Plano ISD	Plano
272	11.2	Alice ISD	Alice
272	11.2	Beeville ISD	Beeville
272	11.2	Ector County ISD	Odessa
272	11.2	Ingleside ISD	Ingleside
272	11.2	Mansfield ISD	Mansfield
272	11.2	South San Antonio ISD	San Antonio
278	11.1	Brenham ISD	Brenham
278	11.1	Mathis ISD	Mathis
278	11.1	Raymondville ISD	Raymondville
281	11.0	Hutto ISD	Hutto
281	11.0	Mckinney ISD	Mckinney
281	11.0	Spring Branch ISD	Houston
284	10.9	Giddings ISD	Giddings
284	10.9	Pine Tree ISD	Longview
284	10.9	Point Isabel ISD	Port Isabel
284	10.9	Ysleta ISD	El Paso
288	10.8	Coldspring-Oakhurst CISD	Coldspring
288	10.8	Frisco ISD	Frisco
288	10.8	Lake Travis ISD	Austin
288	10.8	Navasota ISD	Navasota
292	10.7	Alamo Heights ISD	San Antonio
292	10.7	Palacios ISD	Palacios
294	10.6	Carrizo Springs CISD	Carrizo Springs
294	10.6	Cleveland ISD	Cleveland
294	10.6	Conroe ISD	Conroe
294	10.6	Dickinson ISD	Dickinson
294	10.6	Eanes ISD	Austin
294	10.6	Tarkington ISD	Cleveland
300	10.5	Canton ISD	Canton
300	10.5	Canutillo ISD	El Paso
300	10.5	Crystal City ISD	Crystal City
300	10.5	Hallsville ISD	Hallsville
300	10.5	Harlingen Cons ISD	Harlingen
300	10.5	Texas City ISD	Texas City
306	10.4	Lyford CISD	Lyford
306	10.4	Socorro ISD	El Paso
308	10.3	Castleberry ISD	Fort Worth
308	10.3	Deer Park ISD	Deer Park
308	10.3	Hurst-Euless-Bedford ISD	Bedford
308	10.3	Midland ISD	Midland
308	10.3	Round Rock ISD	Round Rock
308	10.3	Santa Fe ISD	Santa Fe
308	10.3	Spring ISD	Houston
315	10.2	Dumas ISD	Dumas
315	10.2	Kennedale ISD	Kennedale
315	10.2	La Joya ISD	La Joya
315	10.2	Pearsall ISD	Pearsall
315	10.2	Waller ISD	Waller
320	10.1	Humble ISD	Humble
320	10.1	Katy ISD	Katy
320	10.1	San Diego ISD	San Diego
323	10.0	Fort Bend ISD	Sugar Land
323	10.0	Goose Creek CISD	Baytown
323	10.0	Hudson ISD	Lufkin
323	10.0	Pearland ISD	Pearland
323	10.0	Rockwall ISD	Rockwall
328	9.9	Houston ISD	Houston
328	9.9	Midway ISD	Hewitt
330	9.8	Aldine ISD	Houston
330	9.8	Arlington ISD	Arlington
330	9.8	Fort Worth ISD	Fort Worth
330	9.8	La Porte ISD	La Porte
334	9.7	Cedar Hill ISD	Cedar Hill
334	9.7	Cypress-Fairbanks ISD	Houston
334	9.7	Georgetown ISD	Georgetown
334	9.7	Stafford Municipal School	Stafford
334	9.7	Zapata County ISD	Zapata
339	9.6	Irving ISD	Irving
339	9.6	Valley View ISD	Pharr
341	9.5	Carrollton-Farmers Branch ISD	Carrollton
341	9.5	Donna ISD	Donna
343	9.4	Aledo ISD	Aledo
343	9.4	Carroll ISD	Southlake
343	9.4	Highland Park ISD	Dallas
343	9.4	La Feria ISD	La Feria
343	9.4	Mcallen ISD	Mcallen
348	9.3	Palestine ISD	Palestine
348	9.3	Perryton ISD	Perryton
348	9.3	Tomball ISD	Tomball
351	9.2	South Texas ISD	Mercedes
352	9.1	Edcouch-Elsa ISD	Edcouch
352	9.1	Lake Worth ISD	Lake Worth
354	9.0	El Paso ISD	El Paso
355	8.9	Nacogdoches ISD	Nacogdoches
355	8.9	Pleasant Grove ISD	Texarkana
357	8.8	Clint ISD	Clint
357	8.8	College Station ISD	College Station
357	8.8	Friendswood ISD	Friendswood
357	8.8	Port Arthur ISD	Port Arthur
361	8.7	Barbers Hill ISD	Mount Belvieu
361	8.7	Chapel Hill ISD	Tyler
361	8.7	Edinburg CISD	Edinburg
361	8.7	Weslaco ISD	Weslaco
365	8.6	Clear Creek ISD	League City
365	8.6	Eagle Mt-Saginaw ISD	Fort Worth
365	8.6	Pharr-San Juan-Alamo ISD	Pharr
368	8.4	Burleson ISD	Burleson
368	8.4	Iowa Park CISD	Iowa Park
368	8.4	Roma ISD	Roma
368	8.4	Splendora ISD	Splendora
372	8.3	Mercedes ISD	Mercedes
372	8.3	Whitehouse ISD	Whitehouse
374	8.2	Honors Academy	Dallas
374	8.2	Sharyland ISD	Mission
376	8.1	Coppell ISD	Coppell
376	8.1	Eagle Pass ISD	Eagle Pass
376	8.1	Spring Hill ISD	Longview
379	7.9	Dallas ISD	Dallas
380	7.6	Wilmer-Hutchins ISD	Dallas
381	7.5	Grapevine-Colleyville ISD	Grapevine
382	7.4	Keller ISD	Keller
383	7.3	Pasadena ISD	Pasadena
384	7.2	Hidalgo ISD	Hidalgo
385	7.0	North Forest ISD	Houston
386	6.6	Fabens ISD	Fabens
387	6.3	Mission Cons ISD	Mission
387	6.3	Progreso ISD	Progreso
389	3.6	Gulf Shores Academy	Houston

English Language Learner Students

Rank	Percent	District Name	City
1	59.0	Laredo ISD	Laredo
2	53.1	San Elizario ISD	San Elizario
3	52.6	Hidalgo ISD	Hidalgo
4	52.4	Valley View ISD	Pharr
5	51.2	Donna ISD	Donna
6	49.8	Roma ISD	Roma
7	49.7	Rio Grande City CISD	Rio Grande City
8	49.4	La Joya ISD	La Joya
9	49.2	Fabens ISD	Fabens
10	47.7	Progreso ISD	Progreso
11	47.1	Brownsville ISD	Brownsville
12	46.9	United ISD	Laredo
13	44.9	Clint ISD	Clint
14	40.9	Canutillo ISD	El Paso
15	40.4	Edcouch-Elsa ISD	Edcouch
16	37.4	Pharr-San Juan-Alamo ISD	Pharr
17	37.1	Zapata County ISD	Zapata
18	35.6	Eagle Pass ISD	Eagle Pass
19	35.2	Mcallen ISD	Mcallen
20	34.0	Mount Pleasant ISD	Mt Pleasant
21	33.3	Irving ISD	Irving
22	32.2	Mercedes ISD	Mercedes
23	32.0	Dallas ISD	Dallas
24	31.0	Edinburg CISD	Edinburg
25	30.4	El Paso ISD	El Paso
26	30.0	Socorro ISD	El Paso
27	29.8	Spring Branch ISD	Houston
28	29.1	Alief ISD	Houston
29	28.8	Weslaco ISD	Weslaco
30	28.5	Houston ISD	Houston
31	27.4	Point Isabel ISD	Port Isabel
32	27.2	Los Fresnos CISD	Los Fresnos
33	25.8	Dumas ISD	Dumas
34	25.6	Fort Worth ISD	Fort Worth
35	25.1	Mission Cons ISD	Mission
36	24.7	Pasadena ISD	Pasadena
37	24.0	Sharyland ISD	Mission
38	23.9	San Benito Cons ISD	San Benito
39	23.8	Ysleta ISD	El Paso
40	23.5	Galena Park ISD	Houston
41	23.4	Aldine ISD	Houston
42	22.2	Edgewood ISD	San Antonio
43	21.8	Carrollton-Farmers Branch ISD	Carrollton
44	20.9	Crystal City ISD	Crystal City
45	20.7	Austin ISD	Austin
46	19.9	Garland ISD	Garland
47	19.0	Channelview ISD	Channelview
47	19.0	San Antonio ISD	San Antonio
49	18.9	Manor ISD	Manor
50	18.5	Lyford CISD	Lyford
50	18.5	Richardson ISD	Richardson
52	17.6	Diboll ISD	Diboll
53	17.5	Del Valle ISD	Del Valle
53	17.5	Perryton ISD	Perryton
55	17.4	San Felipe-Del Rio CISD	Del Rio
56	17.2	South San Antonio ISD	San Antonio
57	16.9	Grand Prairie ISD	Grand Prairie
58	16.7	Jacksonville ISD	Jacksonville
59	16.3	Center ISD	Center
60	16.2	Royal ISD	Brookshire
60	16.2	Tyler ISD	Tyler
62	15.9	Nacogdoches ISD	Nacogdoches
63	15.7	Arlington ISD	Arlington
64	15.5	Athens ISD	Athens
65	14.9	Ennis ISD	Ennis
66	14.7	Dickinson ISD	Dickinson
67	14.3	Goose Creek CISD	Baytown
67	14.3	Sheldon ISD	Houston
69	14.1	Pearsall ISD	Pearsall
70	13.9	Elgin ISD	Elgin
71	13.8	Hillsboro ISD	Hillsboro
71	13.8	La Feria ISD	La Feria
71	13.8	Seminole ISD	Seminole
74	13.6	Denton ISD	Denton
75	13.5	Castleberry ISD	Fort Worth
75	13.5	Port Arthur ISD	Port Arthur
77	13.4	Stafford Municipal School	Stafford
78	13.3	Ector County ISD	Odessa
78	13.3	Gainesville ISD	Gainesville
80	13.2	Fort Stockton ISD	Fort Stockton
80	13.2	Harlingen Cons ISD	Harlingen
82	13.1	Little Elm ISD	Little Elm
83	12.9	Harlandale ISD	San Antonio
83	12.9	Palacios ISD	Palacios
85	12.7	Wilmer-Hutchins ISD	Dallas
86	12.6	Lake Worth ISD	Lake Worth
87	12.4	Spring ISD	Houston
88	12.1	Cypress-Fairbanks ISD	Houston
88	12.1	Everman ISD	Everman
88	12.1	Rio Hondo ISD	Rio Hondo
91	12.0	San Diego ISD	San Diego
91	12.0	Waller ISD	Waller
93	11.9	Corsicana ISD	Corsicana
94	11.8	Raymondville ISD	Raymondville
95	11.6	Galveston ISD	Galveston
95	11.6	Giddings ISD	Giddings
95	11.6	Kaufman ISD	Kaufman
98	11.5	Hereford ISD	Hereford
99	11.4	Terrell ISD	Terrell
100	11.2	Carrizo Springs CISD	Carrizo Springs
100	11.2	North Forest ISD	Houston
102	11.1	Lufkin ISD	Lufkin
103	11.0	Cleveland ISD	Cleveland
103	11.0	Southwest ISD	San Antonio
105	10.9	Waco ISD	Waco
106	10.8	Bryan ISD	Bryan
107	10.7	Andrews ISD	Andrews
108	10.6	Kingsville ISD	Kingsville
109	10.5	Pittsburg ISD	Pittsburg
110	10.4	Uvalde CISD	Uvalde
111	10.3	Lamar CISD	Rosenberg
112	10.2	Pecos-Barstow-Toyah ISD	Pecos
113	10.1	Longview ISD	Longview
113	10.1	Lytle ISD	Lytle
115	10.0	Venus ISD	Venus
116	9.8	Cleburne ISD	Cleburne
116	9.8	Greenville ISD	Greenville
118	9.7	Decatur ISD	Decatur
118	9.7	Hurst-Euless-Bedford ISD	Bedford
120	9.6	Duncanville ISD	Duncanville
120	9.6	Fort Bend ISD	Sugar Land
120	9.6	Madisonville CISD	Madisonville
123	9.5	Alvin ISD	Alvin
124	9.3	Conroe ISD	Conroe
124	9.3	Plainview ISD	Plainview
124	9.3	Plano ISD	Plano
124	9.3	Seguin ISD	Seguin
128	9.2	West Oso ISD	Corpus Christi
129	9.1	Marble Falls ISD	Marble Falls
130	9.0	Deer Park ISD	Deer Park
130	9.0	Glen Rose ISD	Glen Rose
130	9.0	Klein ISD	Klein
130	9.0	Mesquite ISD	Mesquite
130	9.0	Pflugerville ISD	Pflugerville
135	8.9	Sherman ISD	Sherman
136	8.8	Willis ISD	Willis
137	8.7	Amarillo ISD	Amarillo

137	8.7	Henderson ISD	Henderson
137	8.7	Midland ISD	Midland
137	8.7	Navasota ISD	Navasota
137	8.7	Southside ISD	San Antonio
142	8.6	Chapel Hill ISD	Tyler
143	8.5	Gonzales ISD	Gonzales
144	8.4	Hays Cons ISD	Kyle
145	8.3	Marshall ISD	Marshall
145	8.3	Mckinney ISD	Mckinney
145	8.3	New Braunfels ISD	New Braunfels
148	8.2	Lamesa ISD	Lamesa
148	8.2	Palestine ISD	Palestine
150	8.1	Corpus Christi ISD	Corpus Christi
150	8.1	Lewisville ISD	Flower Mound
152	8.0	Fredericksburg ISD	Fredericksburg
152	8.0	Katy ISD	Katy
152	8.0	Taylor ISD	Taylor
155	7.8	El Campo ISD	El Campo
156	7.7	Bridgeport ISD	Bridgeport
156	7.7	Dalhart ISD	Dalhart
156	7.7	Liberty ISD	Liberty
159	7.4	Brazosport ISD	Clute
159	7.4	New Caney ISD	New Caney
161	7.3	Bastrop ISD	Bastrop
161	7.3	La Grange ISD	La Grange
161	7.3	Sealy ISD	Sealy
164	7.2	Birdville ISD	Haltom City
164	7.2	Somerset ISD	Somerset
166	7.1	Bay City ISD	Bay City
166	7.1	Mexia ISD	Mexia
168	7.0	La Vega ISD	Waco
169	6.9	Calhoun County ISD	Port Lavaca
170	6.8	Luling ISD	Luling
170	6.8	Magnolia ISD	Magnolia
172	6.7	Cameron ISD	Cameron
172	6.7	Mineola ISD	Mineola
172	6.7	Royse City ISD	Royse City
175	6.6	Columbus ISD	Columbus
175	6.6	Kilgore ISD	Kilgore
175	6.6	Mathis ISD	Mathis
175	6.6	Waxahachie ISD	Waxahachie
179	6.5	Clear Creek ISD	League City
179	6.5	Huntsville ISD	Huntsville
179	6.5	Temple ISD	Temple
179	6.5	Yoakum ISD	Yoakum
183	6.4	Borger ISD	Borger
183	6.4	Mineral Wells ISD	Mineral Wells
183	6.4	Tomball ISD	Tomball
186	6.3	Aransas Pass ISD	Aransas Pass
186	6.3	Georgetown ISD	Georgetown
188	6.2	Breckenridge ISD	Breckenridge
188	6.2	Marlin ISD	Marlin
188	6.2	Northside ISD	San Antonio
188	6.2	Poteet ISD	Poteet
192	6.0	Hudson ISD	Lufkin
192	6.0	Mansfield ISD	Mansfield
192	6.0	San Marcos CISD	San Marcos
195	5.9	Caldwell ISD	Caldwell
195	5.9	Lancaster ISD	Lancaster
197	5.8	Bellville ISD	Bellville
197	5.8	Round Rock ISD	Round Rock
199	5.6	Coppell ISD	Coppell
199	5.6	Humble ISD	Humble
199	5.6	Princeton ISD	Princeton
199	5.6	Texas City ISD	Texas City
203	5.5	Angleton ISD	Angleton
203	5.5	Belton ISD	Belton
203	5.5	Edna ISD	Edna
203	5.5	South Texas ISD	Mercedes
203	5.5	Wharton ISD	Wharton
208	5.4	Commerce ISD	Commerce
208	5.4	Pearland ISD	Pearland
208	5.4	Pine Tree ISD	Longview
211	5.3	Brenham ISD	Brenham
211	5.3	Fairfield ISD	Fairfield
211	5.3	Pampa ISD	Pampa
211	5.3	Stephenville ISD	Stephenville
215	5.2	Ferris ISD	Ferris
215	5.2	Hutto ISD	Hutto
215	5.2	Ingram ISD	Ingram
215	5.2	Killeen ISD	Killeen
215	5.2	Robstown ISD	Robstown
220	5.1	Beaumont ISD	Beaumont
220	5.1	Sulphur Springs ISD	Sulphur Springs
222	5.0	Brownfield ISD	Brownfield
222	5.0	Dayton ISD	Dayton
222	5.0	Graham ISD	Graham
222	5.0	San Angelo ISD	San Angelo
226	4.9	College Station ISD	College Station
226	4.9	Crowley ISD	Crowley
226	4.9	Rockwall ISD	Rockwall
229	4.8	Alamo Heights ISD	San Antonio
229	4.8	Van ISD	Van
231	4.7	Medina Valley ISD	Castroville
231	4.7	Rockdale ISD	Rockdale
233	4.6	Alvarado ISD	Alvarado
233	4.6	Crockett ISD	Crockett
233	4.6	Granbury ISD	Granbury
233	4.6	Greenwood ISD	Midland
233	4.6	Winnsboro ISD	Winnsboro
238	4.5	Aransas County ISD	Rockport
238	4.5	Bonham ISD	Bonham
238	4.5	Vernon ISD	Vernon
241	4.4	Alice ISD	Alice
241	4.4	Brooks County ISD	Falfurrias
241	4.4	Burnet Cons ISD	Burnet
241	4.4	Monahans-Wickett-Pyote ISD	Monahans
241	4.4	North East ISD	San Antonio
246	4.3	Frisco ISD	Frisco
246	4.3	Hondo ISD	Hondo
246	4.3	Tuloso-Midway ISD	Corpus Christi
246	4.3	Wylie ISD	Wylie
250	4.2	Crosby ISD	Crosby
250	4.2	Kerrville ISD	Kerrville
250	4.2	Shepherd ISD	Shepherd
250	4.2	Weatherford ISD	Weatherford
250	4.2	Wichita Falls ISD	Wichita Falls
255	4.1	La Porte ISD	La Porte
255	4.1	Littlefield ISD	Littlefield
255	4.1	Sanger ISD	Sanger
255	4.1	Wills Point ISD	Wills Point
259	4.0	East Central ISD	San Antonio
259	4.0	Grapevine-Colleyville ISD	Grapevine
259	4.0	Lake Travis ISD	Austin
259	4.0	Rains ISD	Emory
259	4.0	Red Oak ISD	Red Oak
259	4.0	Snyder ISD	Snyder
265	3.9	Livingston ISD	Livingston
265	3.9	Rusk ISD	Rusk
267	3.8	Allen ISD	Allen
267	3.8	Judson ISD	San Antonio
267	3.8	Levelland ISD	Levelland
267	3.8	Needville ISD	Needville
267	3.8	White Settlement ISD	White Settlement
272	3.7	Cedar Hill ISD	Cedar Hill
272	3.7	Eagle Mt-Saginaw ISD	Fort Worth
272	3.7	Jasper ISD	Jasper
272	3.7	Lake Dallas ISD	Lake Dallas
276	3.6	Bridge City ISD	Bridge City
276	3.6	Columbia-Brazoria ISD	West Columbia
276	3.6	Desoto ISD	Desoto
276	3.6	Leander ISD	Leander
276	3.6	Splendora ISD	Splendora
281	3.5	Groesbeck ISD	Groesbeck
282	3.4	Boerne ISD	Boerne
282	3.4	Floresville ISD	Floresville
282	3.4	Liberty Hill ISD	Liberty Hill
285	3.3	Brownwood ISD	Brownwood
285	3.3	Kennedale ISD	Kennedale
285	3.3	Lockhart ISD	Lockhart
285	3.3	Midlothian ISD	Midlothian
285	3.3	Wimberley ISD	Wimberley
290	3.2	Brownsboro ISD	Brownsboro
290	3.2	Crandall ISD	Crandall
290	3.2	Gilmer ISD	Gilmer
290	3.2	Joshua ISD	Joshua
290	3.2	Keller ISD	Keller
290	3.2	Northwest ISD	Fort Worth
296	3.1	La Vernia ISD	La Vernia
296	3.1	Lubbock-Cooper ISD	Lubbock
296	3.1	Orange Grove ISD	Orange Grove
299	3.0	Ingleside ISD	Ingleside
299	3.0	Victoria ISD	Victoria
301	2.9	Comal ISD	New Braunfels
301	2.9	Denison ISD	Denison
301	2.9	Sinton ISD	Sinton
304	2.8	Central ISD	Pollok
304	2.8	Devine ISD	Devine
304	2.8	Llano ISD	Llano
304	2.8	Smithville ISD	Smithville
308	2.7	Daingerfield-Lone Star ISD	Daingerfield
308	2.7	Lampasas ISD	Lampasas
308	2.7	Lindale ISD	Lindale
308	2.7	Pleasanton ISD	Pleasanton
312	2.6	Bandera ISD	Bandera
312	2.6	Sweeny ISD	Sweeny
312	2.6	Whitney ISD	Whitney
315	2.5	Lubbock ISD	Lubbock
315	2.5	Nederland ISD	Nederland
317	2.4	Barbers Hill ISD	Mount Belvieu
317	2.4	Bowie ISD	Bowie
319	2.3	Connally ISD	Waco
319	2.3	Flour Bluff ISD	Corpus Christi
319	2.3	Montgomery ISD	Montgomery
319	2.3	Paris ISD	Paris
319	2.3	West ISD	West
324	2.2	Beeville ISD	Beeville
324	2.2	Dripping Springs ISD	Dripping Spgs
324	2.2	Schertz-Cibolo-Universal City ISD	Schertz
327	2.0	Abilene ISD	Abilene
327	2.0	Big Spring ISD	Big Spring
327	2.0	Carthage ISD	Carthage
330	1.9	Forney ISD	Forney
330	1.9	Gladewater ISD	Gladewater
330	1.9	Hamshire-Fannett ISD	Hamshire
330	1.9	Santa Fe ISD	Santa Fe
330	1.9	Whitesboro ISD	Whitesboro
335	1.8	Frenship ISD	Wolfforth
335	1.8	Gregory-Portland ISD	Gregory
335	1.8	La Marque ISD	La Marque
335	1.8	Quinlan ISD	Quinlan
339	1.7	Calallen ISD	Corpus Christi
339	1.7	Mabank ISD	Mabank
339	1.7	Whitehouse ISD	Whitehouse
342	1.6	Canton ISD	Canton
342	1.6	Hallsville ISD	Hallsville
342	1.6	Midway ISD	Hewitt
342	1.6	Port Neches-Groves ISD	Port Neches
342	1.6	Springtown ISD	Springtown
342	1.6	Texarkana ISD	Texarkana
342	1.6	Westwood ISD	Palestine
349	1.5	Bullard ISD	Bullard
349	1.5	Eanes ISD	Austin
349	1.5	Huffman ISD	Huffman
349	1.5	West Orange-Cove CISD	Orange
353	1.4	Gulf Shores Academy	Houston
353	1.4	Little Cypress-Mauriceville CISD	Orange
355	1.3	Gatesville ISD	Gatesville
355	1.3	Kemp ISD	Kemp
357	1.2	Aledo ISD	Aledo
357	1.2	Hardin-Jefferson ISD	Sour Lake
357	1.2	Orangefield ISD	Orangefield
357	1.2	Pleasant Grove ISD	Texarkana
357	1.2	Spring Hill ISD	Longview
362	1.0	Copperas Cove ISD	Copperas Cove
362	1.0	Cuero ISD	Cuero
362	1.0	Huntington ISD	Huntington
365	0.9	Azle ISD	Azle
365	0.9	China Spring ISD	Waco
365	0.9	Eustace ISD	Eustace
365	0.9	Honors Academy	Dallas
365	0.9	Kirbyville CISD	Kirbyville
365	0.9	Sweetwater ISD	Sweetwater
371	0.7	Atlanta ISD	Atlanta
371	0.7	Burleson ISD	Burleson
371	0.7	North Lamar ISD	Paris
371	0.7	Robinson ISD	Robinson
375	0.6	Friendswood ISD	Friendswood
375	0.6	Lorena ISD	Lorena
375	0.6	Silsbee ISD	Silsbee
378	0.5	Burkburnett ISD	Burkburnett
378	0.5	Highland Park ISD	Dallas
378	0.5	Lumberton ISD	Lumberton
381	0.4	Canyon ISD	Canyon
381	0.4	Coldspring-Oakhurst CISD	Coldspring
381	0.4	Liberty-Eylau ISD	Texarkana
381	0.4	Tarkington ISD	Cleveland
381	0.4	Vidor ISD	Vidor
386	0.3	Wylie ISD	Abilene
387	0.2	Buna ISD	Buna
387	0.2	Carroll ISD	Southlake
389	0.1	Iowa Park CISD	Iowa Park

Migrant Students

Rank	Percent	District Name	City
1	87.5	Robstown ISD	Robstown
2	48.5	Dumas ISD	Dumas
3	44.4	Hereford ISD	Hereford
4	41.6	Mathis ISD	Mathis
5	37.6	Raymondville ISD	Raymondville
6	33.5	San Felipe-Del Rio CISD	Del Rio
7	33.2	Progreso ISD	Progreso
8	32.7	Weslaco ISD	Weslaco
9	32.2	Rio Grande City CISD	Rio Grande City
10	31.1	Edcouch-Elsa ISD	Edcouch
11	30.0	Donna ISD	Donna
12	28.6	La Joya ISD	La Joya
13	26.3	Lyford CISD	Lyford
14	25.7	Crystal City ISD	Crystal City
15	23.4	Mount Pleasant ISD	Mt Pleasant
16	21.6	Roma ISD	Roma
17	20.8	Mercedes ISD	Mercedes
18	17.4	Carrizo Springs CISD	Carrizo Springs
18	17.4	Edinburg CISD	Edinburg
20	17.3	Eagle Pass ISD	Eagle Pass
21	17.2	Uvalde CISD	Uvalde
22	16.6	Mission Cons ISD	Mission

Rank	Value	District	City
23	16.4	Perryton ISD	Perryton
24	16.1	Pharr-San Juan-Alamo ISD	Pharr
25	16.0	Hidalgo ISD	Hidalgo
26	15.6	San Elizario ISD	San Elizario
27	15.3	Pearsall ISD	Pearsall
28	14.9	Levelland ISD	Levelland
29	14.2	San Benito Cons ISD	San Benito
30	13.1	Valley View ISD	Pharr
31	12.7	Brownfield ISD	Brownfield
32	12.3	Fabens ISD	Fabens
33	11.8	Harlingen Cons ISD	Harlingen
34	11.2	Dalhart ISD	Dalhart
35	11.1	Brooks County ISD	Falfurrias
36	10.8	Brownsville ISD	Brownsville
37	10.6	Pittsburg ISD	Pittsburg
38	10.4	Plainview ISD	Plainview
39	10.0	Venus ISD	Venus
40	9.8	Sinton ISD	Sinton
41	9.7	Mcallen ISD	Mcallen
42	8.5	Rio Hondo ISD	Rio Hondo
43	8.4	Los Fresnos CISD	Los Fresnos
44	8.0	Lamesa ISD	Lamesa
45	7.9	Little Elm ISD	Little Elm
45	7.9	Littlefield ISD	Littlefield
47	7.8	Fort Stockton ISD	Fort Stockton
48	7.5	Center ISD	Center
49	7.3	Alice ISD	Alice
50	7.2	Point Isabel ISD	Port Isabel
51	7.1	La Feria ISD	La Feria
51	7.1	Orange Grove ISD	Orange Grove
53	6.8	Amarillo ISD	Amarillo
53	6.8	San Diego ISD	San Diego
55	6.7	Canutillo ISD	El Paso
56	6.2	Seguin ISD	Seguin
57	6.1	Taylor ISD	Taylor
58	5.9	Vernon ISD	Vernon
59	5.8	El Campo ISD	El Campo
60	5.5	Lytle ISD	Lytle
61	5.3	Bowie ISD	Bowie
62	5.1	Goose Creek CISD	Baytown
62	5.1	Luling ISD	Luling
64	4.8	Daingerfield-Lone Star ISD	Daingerfield
65	4.6	San Antonio ISD	San Antonio
66	4.0	South Texas ISD	Mercedes
67	3.9	Brazosport ISD	Clute
68	3.7	Bastrop ISD	Bastrop
68	3.7	Kingsville ISD	Kingsville
70	3.6	Crockett ISD	Crockett
71	3.5	Atlanta ISD	Atlanta
71	3.5	El Paso ISD	El Paso
73	3.4	Lampasas ISD	Lampasas
73	3.4	Southside ISD	San Antonio
75	3.3	Corsicana ISD	Corsicana
75	3.3	Somerset ISD	Somerset
75	3.3	South San Antonio ISD	San Antonio
78	3.2	Elgin ISD	Elgin
79	3.1	Sulphur Springs ISD	Sulphur Springs
79	3.1	Zapata County ISD	Zapata
81	3.0	Smithville ISD	Smithville
82	2.8	Medina Valley ISD	Castroville
83	2.7	Clint ISD	Clint
83	2.7	Winnsboro ISD	Winnsboro
85	2.5	Edgewood ISD	San Antonio
85	2.5	Nacogdoches ISD	Nacogdoches
87	2.4	Bridgeport ISD	Bridgeport
87	2.4	Gonzales ISD	Gonzales
87	2.4	San Angelo ISD	San Angelo
87	2.4	Sharyland ISD	Mission
87	2.4	Socorro ISD	El Paso
87	2.4	Southwest ISD	San Antonio
93	2.3	Snyder ISD	Snyder
94	2.2	Bryan ISD	Bryan
94	2.2	Lubbock ISD	Lubbock
94	2.2	West Oso ISD	Corpus Christi
97	2.0	La Vega ISD	Waco
98	1.9	Corpus Christi ISD	Corpus Christi
98	1.9	Ector County ISD	Odessa
98	1.9	Marble Falls ISD	Marble Falls
98	1.9	Sweetwater ISD	Sweetwater
102	1.8	Fredericksburg ISD	Fredericksburg
102	1.8	Gainesville ISD	Gainesville
102	1.8	Laredo ISD	Laredo
102	1.8	Midland ISD	Midland
106	1.7	New Braunfels ISD	New Braunfels
107	1.6	Giddings ISD	Giddings
107	1.6	West ISD	West
109	1.5	Lufkin ISD	Lufkin
109	1.5	Paris ISD	Paris
111	1.4	Cameron ISD	Cameron
112	1.3	Georgetown ISD	Georgetown
112	1.3	Manor ISD	Manor
114	1.2	Graham ISD	Graham
114	1.2	Harlandale ISD	San Antonio
114	1.2	Liberty Hill ISD	Liberty Hill
114	1.2	North Lamar ISD	Paris
114	1.2	United ISD	Laredo
119	1.1	Andrews ISD	Andrews
119	1.1	Ferris ISD	Ferris
119	1.1	Galena Park ISD	Houston
119	1.1	Waxahachie ISD	Waxahachie
119	1.1	Ysleta ISD	El Paso
124	1.0	Granbury ISD	Granbury
124	1.0	Hillsboro ISD	Hillsboro
124	1.0	Marlin ISD	Marlin
124	1.0	Navasota ISD	Navasota
128	0.9	Bonham ISD	Bonham
128	0.9	Borger ISD	Borger
128	0.9	Burnet Cons ISD	Burnet
128	0.9	Lockhart ISD	Lockhart
128	0.9	Pecos-Barstow-Toyah ISD	Pecos
128	0.9	Pleasanton ISD	Pleasanton
128	0.9	Poteet ISD	Poteet
135	0.8	Big Spring ISD	Big Spring
135	0.8	Comal ISD	New Braunfels
135	0.8	Dallas ISD	Dallas
135	0.8	Decatur ISD	Decatur
135	0.8	Houston ISD	Houston
135	0.8	Huntsville ISD	Huntsville
135	0.8	Palacios ISD	Palacios
135	0.8	Sanger ISD	Sanger
135	0.8	Sealy ISD	Sealy
144	0.7	Alvin ISD	Alvin
144	0.7	Cuero ISD	Cuero
144	0.7	Dickinson ISD	Dickinson
144	0.7	Hutto ISD	Hutto
144	0.7	Irving ISD	Irving
144	0.7	Pasadena ISD	Pasadena
144	0.7	Rusk ISD	Rusk
144	0.7	San Marcos CISD	San Marcos
152	0.6	Calhoun County ISD	Port Lavaca
152	0.6	Denton ISD	Denton
152	0.6	Floresville ISD	Floresville
152	0.6	Kirbyville CISD	Kirbyville
152	0.6	Mexia ISD	Mexia
152	0.6	Seminole ISD	Seminole
152	0.6	Temple ISD	Temple
152	0.6	Wills Point ISD	Wills Point
160	0.5	Beeville ISD	Beeville
160	0.5	Brownwood ISD	Brownwood
160	0.5	Dripping Springs ISD	Dripping Spgs
160	0.5	Ennis ISD	Ennis
160	0.5	Hondo ISD	Hondo
160	0.5	Kaufman ISD	Kaufman
160	0.5	Madisonville CISD	Madisonville
160	0.5	Pampa ISD	Pampa
160	0.5	Port Arthur ISD	Port Arthur
169	0.4	Belton ISD	Belton
169	0.4	Cleveland ISD	Cleveland
169	0.4	East Central ISD	San Antonio
169	0.4	Forney ISD	Forney
169	0.4	Garland ISD	Garland
169	0.4	Glen Rose ISD	Glen Rose
169	0.4	Huntington ISD	Huntington
169	0.4	Joshua ISD	Joshua
169	0.4	Lancaster ISD	Lancaster
169	0.4	Llano ISD	Llano
169	0.4	Lubbock-Cooper ISD	Lubbock
169	0.4	Midlothian ISD	Midlothian
169	0.4	Northside ISD	San Antonio
169	0.4	Princeton ISD	Princeton
169	0.4	Terrell ISD	Terrell
169	0.4	Whitney ISD	Whitney
169	0.4	Wichita Falls ISD	Wichita Falls
169	0.4	Wilmer-Hutchins ISD	Dallas
187	0.3	Aledo ISD	Aledo
187	0.3	Bay City ISD	Bay City
187	0.3	Boerne ISD	Boerne
187	0.3	Bridge City ISD	Bridge City
187	0.3	Castleberry ISD	Fort Worth
187	0.3	Channelview ISD	Channelview
187	0.3	Frenship ISD	Wolfforth
187	0.3	Gatesville ISD	Gatesville
187	0.3	Grand Prairie ISD	Grand Prairie
187	0.3	Liberty-Eylau ISD	Texarkana
187	0.3	New Caney ISD	New Caney
187	0.3	Round Rock ISD	Round Rock
187	0.3	Shepherd ISD	Shepherd
187	0.3	Wharton ISD	Wharton
201	0.2	Angleton ISD	Angleton
201	0.2	Buna ISD	Buna
201	0.2	Carrollton-Farmers Branch ISD	Carrollton
201	0.2	Commerce ISD	Commerce
201	0.2	Connally ISD	Waco
201	0.2	Copperas Cove ISD	Copperas Cove
201	0.2	Devine ISD	Devine
201	0.2	Everman ISD	Everman
201	0.2	Fairfield ISD	Fairfield
201	0.2	Fort Worth ISD	Fort Worth
201	0.2	Gilmer ISD	Gilmer
201	0.2	Honors Academy	Dallas
201	0.2	Ingram ISD	Ingram
201	0.2	Kerrville ISD	Kerrville
201	0.2	La Vernia ISD	La Vernia
201	0.2	Lake Dallas ISD	Lake Dallas
201	0.2	Lindale ISD	Lindale
201	0.2	Livingston ISD	Livingston
201	0.2	Mineral Wells ISD	Mineral Wells
201	0.2	Robinson ISD	Robinson
201	0.2	Royal ISD	Brookshire
201	0.2	Schertz-Cibolo-Universal City ISD	Schertz
201	0.2	Sherman ISD	Sherman
201	0.2	Silsbee ISD	Silsbee
201	0.2	Victoria ISD	Victoria
201	0.2	Weatherford ISD	Weatherford
201	0.2	Wylie ISD	Wylie
228	0.1	Aldine ISD	Houston
228	0.1	Alvarado ISD	Alvarado
228	0.1	Athens ISD	Athens
228	0.1	Austin ISD	Austin
228	0.1	Azle ISD	Azle
228	0.1	Bellville ISD	Bellville
228	0.1	Birdville ISD	Haltom City
228	0.1	Brownsboro ISD	Brownsboro
228	0.1	Canton ISD	Canton
228	0.1	Cleburne ISD	Cleburne
228	0.1	Conroe ISD	Conroe
228	0.1	Crowley ISD	Crowley
228	0.1	Del Valle ISD	Del Valle
228	0.1	Desoto ISD	Desoto
228	0.1	Duncanville ISD	Duncanville
228	0.1	Edna ISD	Edna
228	0.1	Flour Bluff ISD	Corpus Christi
228	0.1	Gladewater ISD	Gladewater
228	0.1	Greenwood ISD	Midland
228	0.1	Gregory-Portland ISD	Gregory
228	0.1	Groesbeck ISD	Groesbeck
228	0.1	Hardin-Jefferson ISD	Sour Lake
228	0.1	Hays Cons ISD	Kyle
228	0.1	Henderson ISD	Henderson
228	0.1	Hurst-Euless-Bedford ISD	Bedford
228	0.1	Jacksonville ISD	Jacksonville
228	0.1	Kilgore ISD	Kilgore
228	0.1	Killeen ISD	Killeen
228	0.1	La Marque ISD	La Marque
228	0.1	Lamar CISD	Rosenberg
228	0.1	Leander ISD	Leander
228	0.1	Mabank ISD	Mabank
228	0.1	Mckinney ISD	Mckinney
228	0.1	Mesquite ISD	Mesquite
228	0.1	Mineola ISD	Mineola
228	0.1	Northwest ISD	Fort Worth
228	0.1	Palestine ISD	Palestine
228	0.1	Pearland ISD	Pearland
228	0.1	Pflugerville ISD	Pflugerville
228	0.1	Pine Tree ISD	Longview
228	0.1	Pleasant Grove ISD	Texarkana
228	0.1	Rains ISD	Emory
228	0.1	Richardson ISD	Richardson
228	0.1	Rockwall ISD	Rockwall
228	0.1	Royse City ISD	Royse City
228	0.1	Splendora ISD	Splendora
228	0.1	Spring Branch ISD	Houston
228	0.1	Springtown ISD	Springtown
228	0.1	Stephenville ISD	Stephenville
228	0.1	Tomball ISD	Tomball
228	0.1	Whitesboro ISD	Whitesboro
228	0.1	Willis ISD	Willis
228	0.1	Yoakum ISD	Yoakum
281	0.0	Allen ISD	Allen
281	0.0	Arlington ISD	Arlington
281	0.0	Barbers Hill ISD	Mount Belvieu
281	0.0	Canyon ISD	Canyon
281	0.0	Cedar Hill ISD	Cedar Hill
281	0.0	Clear Creek ISD	League City
281	0.0	Columbia-Brazoria ISD	West Columbia
281	0.0	Cypress-Fairbanks ISD	Houston
281	0.0	Denison ISD	Denison
281	0.0	Fort Bend ISD	Sugar Land
281	0.0	Greenville ISD	Greenville
281	0.0	Humble ISD	Humble
281	0.0	Ingleside ISD	Ingleside
281	0.0	Judson ISD	San Antonio
281	0.0	Keller ISD	Keller
281	0.0	Klein ISD	Klein
281	0.0	La Porte ISD	La Porte
281	0.0	Lake Travis ISD	Austin
281	0.0	Lewisville ISD	Flower Mound

Rank	Percent	District Name	City
281	0.0	Mansfield ISD	Mansfield
281	0.0	North East ISD	San Antonio
281	0.0	Plano ISD	Plano
281	0.0	Port Neches-Groves ISD	Port Neches
281	0.0	Quinlan ISD	Quinlan
281	0.0	Red Oak ISD	Red Oak
281	0.0	Texarkana ISD	Texarkana
281	0.0	Vidor ISD	Vidor
308	0.0	Abilene ISD	Abilene
308	0.0	Alamo Heights ISD	San Antonio
308	0.0	Alief ISD	Houston
308	0.0	Aransas County ISD	Rockport
308	0.0	Aransas Pass ISD	Aransas Pass
308	0.0	Bandera ISD	Bandera
308	0.0	Beaumont ISD	Beaumont
308	0.0	Breckenridge ISD	Breckenridge
308	0.0	Brenham ISD	Brenham
308	0.0	Bullard ISD	Bullard
308	0.0	Burkburnett ISD	Burkburnett
308	0.0	Burleson ISD	Burleson
308	0.0	Calallen ISD	Corpus Christi
308	0.0	Caldwell ISD	Caldwell
308	0.0	Carroll ISD	Southlake
308	0.0	Carthage ISD	Carthage
308	0.0	Central ISD	Pollok
308	0.0	Chapel Hill ISD	Tyler
308	0.0	China Spring ISD	Waco
308	0.0	Coldspring-Oakhurst CISD	Coldspring
308	0.0	College Station ISD	College Station
308	0.0	Columbus ISD	Columbus
308	0.0	Coppell ISD	Coppell
308	0.0	Crandall ISD	Crandall
308	0.0	Crosby ISD	Crosby
308	0.0	Dayton ISD	Dayton
308	0.0	Deer Park ISD	Deer Park
308	0.0	Diboll ISD	Diboll
308	0.0	Eagle Mt-Saginaw ISD	Fort Worth
308	0.0	Eanes ISD	Austin
308	0.0	Eustace ISD	Eustace
308	0.0	Friendswood ISD	Friendswood
308	0.0	Frisco ISD	Frisco
308	0.0	Galveston ISD	Galveston
308	0.0	Grapevine-Colleyville ISD	Grapevine
308	0.0	Gulf Shores Academy	Houston
308	0.0	Hallsville ISD	Hallsville
308	0.0	Hamshire-Fannett ISD	Hamshire
308	0.0	Highland Park ISD	Dallas
308	0.0	Hudson ISD	Lufkin
308	0.0	Huffman ISD	Huffman
308	0.0	Iowa Park CISD	Iowa Park
308	0.0	Jasper ISD	Jasper
308	0.0	Katy ISD	Katy
308	0.0	Kemp ISD	Kemp
308	0.0	Kennedale ISD	Kennedale
308	0.0	La Grange ISD	La Grange
308	0.0	Lake Worth ISD	Lake Worth
308	0.0	Liberty ISD	Liberty
308	0.0	Little Cypress-Mauriceville CISD	Orange
308	0.0	Longview ISD	Longview
308	0.0	Lorena ISD	Lorena
308	0.0	Lumberton ISD	Lumberton
308	0.0	Magnolia ISD	Magnolia
308	0.0	Marshall ISD	Marshall
308	0.0	Midway ISD	Hewitt
308	0.0	Monahans-Wickett-Pyote ISD	Monahans
308	0.0	Montgomery ISD	Montgomery
308	0.0	Nederland ISD	Nederland
308	0.0	Needville ISD	Needville
308	0.0	North Forest ISD	Houston
308	0.0	Orangefield ISD	Orangefield
308	0.0	Rockdale ISD	Rockdale
308	0.0	Santa Fe ISD	Santa Fe
308	0.0	Sheldon ISD	Houston
308	0.0	Spring Hill ISD	Longview
308	0.0	Spring ISD	Houston
308	0.0	Stafford Municipal School	Stafford
308	0.0	Sweeny ISD	Sweeny
308	0.0	Tarkington ISD	Cleveland
308	0.0	Texas City ISD	Texas City
308	0.0	Tuloso-Midway ISD	Corpus Christi
308	0.0	Tyler ISD	Tyler
308	0.0	Van ISD	Van
308	0.0	Waco ISD	Waco
308	0.0	Waller ISD	Waller
308	0.0	West Orange-Cove CISD	Orange
308	0.0	Westwood ISD	Palestine
308	0.0	White Settlement ISD	White Settlement
308	0.0	Whitehouse ISD	Whitehouse
308	0.0	Wimberley ISD	Wimberley
308	0.0	Wylie ISD	Abilene

Students Eligible for Free Lunch

Rank	Percent	District Name	City
1	81.7	Clint ISD	Clint
2	81.0	Robstown ISD	Robstown
3	79.6	South San Antonio ISD	San Antonio
4	78.7	Rio Grande City CISD	Rio Grande City
5	77.9	San Diego ISD	San Diego
6	75.8	Brooks County ISD	Falfurrias
7	74.3	Canutillo ISD	El Paso
8	73.4	Eagle Pass ISD	Eagle Pass
9	72.0	Port Arthur ISD	Port Arthur
10	71.8	Pearsall ISD	Pearsall
11	71.5	Lake Worth ISD	Lake Worth
12	70.2	Waco ISD	Waco
13	69.2	Crystal City ISD	Crystal City
14	68.7	Southside ISD	San Antonio
15	68.2	Dallas ISD	Dallas
16	67.5	Somerset ISD	Somerset
17	67.0	Mathis ISD	Mathis
17	67.0	West Orange-Cove CISD	Orange
19	66.3	Southwest ISD	San Antonio
20	65.1	Uvalde CISD	Uvalde
21	65.0	Royal ISD	Brookshire
22	64.5	Harlingen Cons ISD	Harlingen
23	64.2	Aldine ISD	Houston
23	64.2	Marlin ISD	Marlin
25	64.0	Houston ISD	Houston
26	62.8	Crockett ISD	Crockett
26	62.8	San Felipe-Del Rio CISD	Del Rio
28	62.7	United ISD	Laredo
29	60.8	La Joya ISD	La Joya
30	60.3	Donna ISD	Donna
31	59.8	Poteet ISD	Poteet
31	59.8	Socorro ISD	El Paso
33	59.6	Mount Pleasant ISD	Mt Pleasant
34	59.2	La Vega ISD	Waco
35	59.0	El Paso ISD	El Paso
36	58.8	Alice ISD	Alice
36	58.8	Hereford ISD	Hereford
38	58.5	Point Isabel ISD	Port Isabel
39	58.4	Fort Worth ISD	Fort Worth
40	58.3	Bay City ISD	Bay City
41	58.1	Liberty-Eylau ISD	Texarkana
42	57.7	Brownfield ISD	Brownfield
43	57.6	Del Valle ISD	Del Valle
44	57.5	Sinton ISD	Sinton
45	57.2	Progreso ISD	Progreso
46	57.1	Jacksonville ISD	Jacksonville
47	57.0	Galena Park ISD	Houston
47	57.0	Nacogdoches ISD	Nacogdoches
47	57.0	Pecos-Barstow-Toyah ISD	Pecos
50	56.5	La Feria ISD	La Feria
51	56.3	Everman ISD	Everman
51	56.3	Texarkana ISD	Texarkana
53	56.1	Beaumont ISD	Beaumont
54	56.0	Lamesa ISD	Lamesa
55	55.9	Palacios ISD	Palacios
56	55.8	Paris ISD	Paris
57	55.6	Galveston ISD	Galveston
58	55.5	Hillsboro ISD	Hillsboro
59	55.3	Raymondville ISD	Raymondville
60	55.2	Beeville ISD	Beeville
60	55.2	Pittsburg ISD	Pittsburg
62	54.9	Kingsville ISD	Kingsville
63	54.4	Luling ISD	Luling
64	54.0	Bryan ISD	Bryan
64	54.0	Gonzales ISD	Gonzales
64	54.0	Lytle ISD	Lytle
67	53.9	Jasper ISD	Jasper
68	53.7	Cameron ISD	Cameron
69	53.6	Palestine ISD	Palestine
70	53.2	Longview ISD	Longview
70	53.2	Sheldon ISD	Houston
72	52.9	Aransas Pass ISD	Aransas Pass
72	52.9	North Forest ISD	Houston
74	52.8	Lufkin ISD	Lufkin
75	52.6	Littlefield ISD	Littlefield
76	52.3	Madisonville CISD	Madisonville
77	52.0	Plainview ISD	Plainview
78	51.9	La Marque ISD	La Marque
79	51.7	Diboll ISD	Diboll
79	51.7	Orange Grove ISD	Orange Grove
81	51.4	Center ISD	Center
82	51.2	Fort Stockton ISD	Fort Stockton
83	51.1	Pasadena ISD	Pasadena
84	50.8	Ector County ISD	Odessa
85	50.7	Daingerfield-Lone Star ISD	Daingerfield
85	50.7	Marshall ISD	Marshall
87	50.6	Pleasanton ISD	Pleasanton
88	50.4	Mexia ISD	Mexia
88	50.4	Seminole ISD	Seminole
88	50.4	Zapata County ISD	Zapata
91	50.3	Manor ISD	Manor
91	50.3	West Oso ISD	Corpus Christi
93	50.2	Levelland ISD	Levelland
94	50.1	Navasota ISD	Navasota
95	50.0	Cleveland ISD	Cleveland
96	49.6	Commerce ISD	Commerce
97	49.4	Terrell ISD	Terrell
98	49.3	Coldspring-Oakhurst CISD	Coldspring
99	49.1	El Campo ISD	El Campo
100	48.9	Goose Creek CISD	Baytown
101	48.8	Alief ISD	Houston
102	48.7	Corsicana ISD	Corsicana
102	48.7	Irving ISD	Irving
104	48.6	Laredo ISD	Laredo
105	48.5	Tyler ISD	Tyler
106	48.4	Seguin ISD	Seguin
107	48.2	Shepherd ISD	Shepherd
108	48.1	Amarillo ISD	Amarillo
109	48.0	Sharyland ISD	Mission
109	48.0	Venus ISD	Venus
111	47.8	Dickinson ISD	Dickinson
112	47.7	Sweetwater ISD	Sweetwater
113	47.6	Corpus Christi ISD	Corpus Christi
113	47.6	San Marcos CISD	San Marcos
113	47.6	Wharton ISD	Wharton
113	47.6	Wilmer-Hutchins ISD	Dallas
117	47.3	Eustace ISD	Eustace
118	47.0	Big Spring ISD	Big Spring
119	46.9	Brownwood ISD	Brownwood
119	46.9	Castleberry ISD	Fort Worth
119	46.9	Mcallen ISD	Mcallen
122	46.7	Atlanta ISD	Atlanta
123	46.1	Calhoun County ISD	Port Lavaca
123	46.1	Gainesville ISD	Gainesville
123	46.1	Spring Branch ISD	Houston
126	46.0	Fabens ISD	Fabens
126	46.0	Taylor ISD	Taylor
128	45.8	Dumas ISD	Dumas
129	45.7	Grand Prairie ISD	Grand Prairie
130	45.5	Aransas County ISD	Rockport
130	45.5	Temple ISD	Temple
132	45.3	Chapel Hill ISD	Tyler
132	45.3	Greenville ISD	Greenville
134	45.2	Lubbock ISD	Lubbock
134	45.2	Rio Hondo ISD	Rio Hondo
136	45.1	Kilgore ISD	Kilgore
137	44.8	Austin ISD	Austin
137	44.8	Perryton ISD	Perryton
139	44.7	Texas City ISD	Texas City
140	44.4	Ferris ISD	Ferris
141	44.3	Abilene ISD	Abilene
142	44.0	Mineola ISD	Mineola
143	43.7	Gladewater ISD	Gladewater
144	43.6	Connally ISD	Waco
144	43.6	Elgin ISD	Elgin
144	43.6	Ysleta ISD	El Paso
147	43.4	Ennis ISD	Ennis
148	43.2	Rockdale ISD	Rockdale
149	43.1	Rusk ISD	Rusk
150	43.0	Edna ISD	Edna
151	42.8	Mineral Wells ISD	Mineral Wells
151	42.8	Snyder ISD	Snyder
153	42.7	Athens ISD	Athens
153	42.7	Channelview ISD	Channelview
155	42.5	Ingram ISD	Ingram
155	42.5	Vernon ISD	Vernon
157	42.1	Devine ISD	Devine
157	42.1	Livingston ISD	Livingston
159	41.8	Henderson ISD	Henderson
159	41.8	Yoakum ISD	Yoakum
161	41.6	Giddings ISD	Giddings
162	41.5	Liberty ISD	Liberty
163	41.3	Hudson ISD	Lufkin
163	41.3	Weslaco ISD	Weslaco
165	41.2	Breckenridge ISD	Breckenridge
166	41.1	Dalhart ISD	Dalhart
166	41.1	Midland ISD	Midland
168	40.8	Groesbeck ISD	Groesbeck
169	40.6	Lancaster ISD	Lancaster
169	40.6	Tuloso-Midway ISD	Corpus Christi
171	40.2	Sherman ISD	Sherman
171	40.2	Wichita Falls ISD	Wichita Falls
173	39.8	South Texas ISD	Mercedes
174	39.5	San Angelo ISD	San Angelo
175	39.2	Lamar CISD	Rosenberg
175	39.2	Mabank ISD	Mabank
177	38.9	Alvin ISD	Alvin
178	38.7	East Central ISD	San Antonio
179	38.4	Bastrop ISD	Bastrop
179	38.4	Denison ISD	Denison
181	38.3	Los Fresnos CISD	Los Fresnos
182	38.2	Victoria ISD	Victoria

183	37.9	Lockhart ISD	Lockhart
184	37.7	Floresville ISD	Floresville
185	37.5	Quinlan ISD	Quinlan
186	37.4	Cuero ISD	Cuero
186	37.4	Kaufman ISD	Kaufman
186	37.4	Wills Point ISD	Wills Point
189	37.3	Arlington ISD	Arlington
189	37.3	Kirbyville CISD	Kirbyville
191	37.1	Caldwell ISD	Caldwell
192	37.0	Marble Falls ISD	Marble Falls
192	37.0	Vidor ISD	Vidor
194	36.9	Alvarado ISD	Alvarado
194	36.9	Judson ISD	San Antonio
196	36.5	Brazosport ISD	Clute
196	36.5	Carthage ISD	Carthage
196	36.5	Splendora ISD	Splendora
199	36.4	Brenham ISD	Brenham
199	36.4	Rains ISD	Emory
201	36.3	Waller ISD	Waller
202	36.0	Medina Valley ISD	Castroville
203	35.9	Borger ISD	Borger
203	35.9	Sealy ISD	Sealy
203	35.9	Whitney ISD	Whitney
206	35.5	Carrizo Springs CISD	Carrizo Springs
206	35.5	Cleburne ISD	Cleburne
206	35.5	Flour Bluff ISD	Corpus Christi
206	35.5	Willis ISD	Willis
210	35.2	Smithville ISD	Smithville
211	35.1	New Caney ISD	New Caney
211	35.1	Pampa ISD	Pampa
213	35.0	Gilmer ISD	Gilmer
214	34.9	San Antonio ISD	San Antonio
215	34.8	Lampasas ISD	Lampasas
216	34.7	Huntington ISD	Huntington
217	34.5	Belton ISD	Belton
217	34.5	Kerrville ISD	Kerrville
217	34.5	Northside ISD	San Antonio
220	34.4	Duncanville ISD	Duncanville
220	34.4	Spring ISD	Houston
222	34.1	Van ISD	Van
223	34.0	Brownsboro ISD	Brownsboro
224	33.9	Sulphur Springs ISD	Sulphur Springs
225	33.8	Winnsboro ISD	Winnsboro
226	33.4	Columbia-Brazoria ISD	West Columbia
227	33.1	Westwood ISD	Palestine
228	32.7	Angleton ISD	Angleton
228	32.7	Kemp ISD	Kemp
228	32.7	Lubbock-Cooper ISD	Lubbock
231	32.6	Fairfield ISD	Fairfield
232	32.3	Dayton ISD	Dayton
232	32.3	Killeen ISD	Killeen
232	32.3	Richardson ISD	Richardson
235	32.2	Burnet Cons ISD	Burnet
236	31.9	Edinburg CISD	Edinburg
237	31.7	Bandera ISD	Bandera
238	31.6	Bonham ISD	Bonham
238	31.6	Carrollton-Farmers Branch ISD	Carrollton
238	31.6	Fredericksburg ISD	Fredericksburg
238	31.6	Silsbee ISD	Silsbee
238	31.6	White Settlement ISD	White Settlement
243	31.5	Joshua ISD	Joshua
244	31.3	Glen Rose ISD	Glen Rose
245	30.9	Garland ISD	Garland
246	30.8	Huntsville ISD	Huntsville
246	30.8	La Grange ISD	La Grange
248	30.7	Columbus ISD	Columbus
248	30.7	Denton ISD	Denton
248	30.7	Waxahachie ISD	Waxahachie
251	30.6	Bowie ISD	Bowie
251	30.6	Llano ISD	Llano
253	30.5	Hondo ISD	Hondo
254	29.9	Hays Cons ISD	Kyle
255	29.8	Central ISD	Pollok
255	29.8	Crosby ISD	Crosby
257	29.7	Graham ISD	Graham
258	29.6	Princeton ISD	Princeton
259	29.0	Monahans-Wickett-Pyote ISD	Monahans
260	28.9	Andrews ISD	Andrews
261	28.8	Springtown ISD	Springtown
262	28.7	Little Elm ISD	Little Elm
263	28.2	Pine Tree ISD	Longview
264	27.5	Granbury ISD	Granbury
265	27.4	Canton ISD	Canton
265	27.4	Gulf Shores Academy	Houston
265	27.4	Stephenville ISD	Stephenville
268	27.1	Copperas Cove ISD	Copperas Cove
268	27.1	Royse City ISD	Royse City
270	27.0	Weatherford ISD	Weatherford
271	26.9	Hurst-Euless-Bedford ISD	Bedford
271	26.9	Ingleside ISD	Ingleside
271	26.9	Mesquite ISD	Mesquite
271	26.9	West ISD	West
275	26.8	Harlandale ISD	San Antonio
276	26.7	Calallen ISD	Corpus Christi
276	26.7	New Braunfels ISD	New Braunfels
278	26.6	Bridgeport ISD	Bridgeport
278	26.6	North East ISD	San Antonio
278	26.6	Sweeny ISD	Sweeny
281	26.5	Decatur ISD	Decatur
282	26.4	Bullard ISD	Bullard
283	26.0	Desoto ISD	Desoto
283	26.0	Honors Academy	Dallas
285	25.9	Whitesboro ISD	Whitesboro
286	25.6	Frenship ISD	Wolfforth
286	25.6	Gatesville ISD	Gatesville
288	25.5	Bridge City ISD	Bridge City
289	25.2	Magnolia ISD	Magnolia
290	24.8	Birdville ISD	Haltom City
291	24.5	Buna ISD	Buna
292	24.3	Stafford Municipal School	Stafford
293	24.1	Comal ISD	New Braunfels
294	24.0	Hardin-Jefferson ISD	Sour Lake
295	23.9	North Lamar ISD	Paris
296	23.7	Burkburnett ISD	Burkburnett
297	23.6	Georgetown ISD	Georgetown
298	23.5	Hallsville ISD	Hallsville
299	23.3	San Elizario ISD	San Elizario
300	23.1	Bellville ISD	Bellville
300	23.1	Lindale ISD	Lindale
302	23.0	Conroe ISD	Conroe
302	23.0	San Benito Cons ISD	San Benito
304	22.8	Gregory-Portland ISD	Gregory
305	22.6	Azle ISD	Azle
306	22.4	Tarkington ISD	Cleveland
307	21.8	La Porte ISD	La Porte
308	21.1	Mercedes ISD	Mercedes
309	20.9	Needville ISD	Needville
310	20.7	Pharr-San Juan-Alamo ISD	Pharr
311	20.6	Pflugerville ISD	Pflugerville
312	20.5	Little Cypress-Mauriceville CISD	Orange
313	20.1	Deer Park ISD	Deer Park
313	20.1	Edcouch-Elsa ISD	Edcouch
315	20.0	La Vernia ISD	La Vernia
315	20.0	Sanger ISD	Sanger
317	19.6	Montgomery ISD	Montgomery
318	19.5	Greenwood ISD	Midland
319	19.2	Fort Bend ISD	Sugar Land
319	19.2	Whitehouse ISD	Whitehouse
321	19.0	Schertz-Cibolo-Universal City ISD	Schertz
322	18.9	Cedar Hill ISD	Cedar Hill
322	18.9	Cypress-Fairbanks ISD	Houston
322	18.9	Iowa Park CISD	Iowa Park
322	18.9	Mckinney ISD	Mckinney
326	18.5	Hamshire-Fannett ISD	Hamshire
327	17.8	Huffman ISD	Huffman
327	17.8	Klein ISD	Klein
329	17.7	Liberty Hill ISD	Liberty Hill
330	17.5	Santa Fe ISD	Santa Fe
331	17.4	Hidalgo ISD	Hidalgo
332	17.2	Mansfield ISD	Mansfield
333	17.1	Nederland ISD	Nederland
334	16.3	Canyon ISD	Canyon
335	15.9	Kennedale ISD	Kennedale
335	15.9	Lumberton ISD	Lumberton
337	15.7	Crowley ISD	Crowley
338	15.3	Hutto ISD	Hutto
339	15.1	Alamo Heights ISD	San Antonio
339	15.1	Spring Hill ISD	Longview
341	15.0	Lake Dallas ISD	Lake Dallas
342	14.9	Port Neches-Groves ISD	Port Neches
343	14.7	Eagle Mt-Saginaw ISD	Fort Worth
344	14.5	Crandall ISD	Crandall
344	14.5	Red Oak ISD	Red Oak
346	14.2	Northwest ISD	Fort Worth
347	14.1	College Station ISD	College Station
347	14.1	Humble ISD	Humble
349	14.0	Tomball ISD	Tomball
350	13.9	Barbers Hill ISD	Mount Belvieu
350	13.9	Valley View ISD	Pharr
352	13.6	Wimberley ISD	Wimberley
353	13.4	Orangefield ISD	Orangefield
354	13.2	Burleson ISD	Burleson
354	13.2	Round Rock ISD	Round Rock
356	12.9	Robinson ISD	Robinson
356	12.9	Wylie ISD	Wylie
358	12.8	Pearland ISD	Pearland
359	12.5	Boerne ISD	Boerne
360	12.1	Leander ISD	Leander
361	11.6	Lorena ISD	Lorena
361	11.6	Roma ISD	Roma
363	11.5	China Spring ISD	Waco
364	11.4	Katy ISD	Katy
364	11.4	Rockwall ISD	Rockwall
366	11.1	Edgewood ISD	San Antonio
367	11.0	Midlothian ISD	Midlothian
368	10.7	Plano ISD	Plano
369	10.4	Clear Creek ISD	League City
369	10.4	Lewisville ISD	Flower Mound
371	9.9	Midway ISD	Hewitt
372	9.4	Pleasant Grove ISD	Texarkana
373	9.0	Forney ISD	Forney
374	8.3	Brownsville ISD	Brownsville
374	8.3	Lake Travis ISD	Austin
376	8.1	Mission Cons ISD	Mission
377	7.0	Grapevine-Colleyville ISD	Grapevine
378	6.8	Keller ISD	Keller
379	6.5	Frisco ISD	Frisco
380	5.9	Dripping Springs ISD	Dripping Spgs
381	5.6	Aledo ISD	Aledo
382	4.8	Allen ISD	Allen
383	4.3	Lyford CISD	Lyford
383	4.3	Wylie ISD	Abilene
385	2.5	Coppell ISD	Coppell
386	2.0	Friendswood ISD	Friendswood
387	1.5	Eanes ISD	Austin
388	1.1	Carroll ISD	Southlake
389	0.0	Highland Park ISD	Dallas

Students Eligible for Reduced-Price Lunch

Rank	Percent	District Name	City
1	16.3	Killeen ISD	Killeen
2	14.4	Poteet ISD	Poteet
3	14.2	Venus ISD	Venus
4	13.9	Del Valle ISD	Del Valle
5	13.2	Somerset ISD	Somerset
6	13.1	Diboll ISD	Diboll
7	12.9	Dalhart ISD	Dalhart
7	12.9	Everman ISD	Everman
9	12.7	Iowa Park CISD	Iowa Park
9	12.7	Judson ISD	San Antonio
11	12.6	Ferris ISD	Ferris
11	12.6	Ingleside ISD	Ingleside
13	12.2	Floresville ISD	Floresville
13	12.2	Grand Prairie ISD	Grand Prairie
13	12.2	Lockhart ISD	Lockhart
16	12.1	East Central ISD	San Antonio
17	12.0	La Vega ISD	Waco
18	11.8	Burkburnett ISD	Burkburnett
18	11.8	Southwest ISD	San Antonio
20	11.7	Lytle ISD	Lytle
21	11.5	Socorro ISD	El Paso
22	11.2	San Marcos CISD	San Marcos
23	11.1	Copperas Cove ISD	Copperas Cove
23	11.1	Duncanville ISD	Duncanville
23	11.1	Fort Stockton ISD	Fort Stockton
23	11.1	Pasadena ISD	Pasadena
23	11.1	Vernon ISD	Vernon
28	11.0	Southside ISD	San Antonio
28	11.0	Splendora ISD	Splendora
30	10.9	Alvarado ISD	Alvarado
30	10.9	Burnet Cons ISD	Burnet
30	10.9	South San Antonio ISD	San Antonio
33	10.8	Lancaster ISD	Lancaster
33	10.8	Llano ISD	Llano
33	10.8	Orange Grove ISD	Orange Grove
36	10.7	Beeville ISD	Beeville
36	10.7	Connally ISD	Waco
36	10.7	Vidor ISD	Vidor
36	10.7	Ysleta ISD	El Paso
40	10.6	Central ISD	Pollok
40	10.6	Irving ISD	Irving
40	10.6	Perryton ISD	Perryton
43	10.5	Devine ISD	Devine
43	10.5	Ingram ISD	Ingram
43	10.5	Manor ISD	Manor
46	10.4	Aransas Pass ISD	Aransas Pass
46	10.4	Huntsville ISD	Huntsville
46	10.4	Pecos-Barstow-Toyah ISD	Pecos
46	10.4	San Felipe-Del Rio CISD	Del Rio
50	10.3	Northside ISD	San Antonio
50	10.3	Pleasanton ISD	Pleasanton
50	10.3	Westwood ISD	Palestine
53	10.2	Flour Bluff ISD	Corpus Christi
54	10.1	Canutillo ISD	El Paso
54	10.1	Luling ISD	Luling
54	10.1	Sheldon ISD	Houston
54	10.1	South Texas ISD	Mercedes
54	10.1	United ISD	Laredo
59	10.0	Denison ISD	Denison
59	10.0	Hondo ISD	Hondo
59	10.0	San Angelo ISD	San Angelo
62	9.9	Abilene ISD	Abilene
62	9.9	Lampasas ISD	Lampasas
62	9.9	Mount Pleasant ISD	Mt Pleasant
62	9.9	Springtown ISD	Springtown
66	9.8	Hays Cons ISD	Kyle

66	9.8	Kingsville ISD	Kingsville
68	9.7	Brownwood ISD	Brownwood
68	9.7	Pearsall ISD	Pearsall
70	9.6	Aldine ISD	Houston
70	9.6	Atlanta ISD	Atlanta
70	9.6	Cleveland ISD	Cleveland
70	9.6	Smithville ISD	Smithville
74	9.5	Gregory-Portland ISD	Gregory
74	9.5	Mabank ISD	Mabank
74	9.5	Marlin ISD	Marlin
77	9.4	Yoakum ISD	Yoakum
78	9.3	Bay City ISD	Bay City
78	9.3	Joshua ISD	Joshua
78	9.3	Littlefield ISD	Littlefield
78	9.3	Mathis ISD	Mathis
78	9.3	Navasota ISD	Navasota
78	9.3	Spring ISD	Houston
84	9.2	Andrews ISD	Andrews
84	9.2	Sharyland ISD	Mission
84	9.2	Waco ISD	Waco
87	9.1	Big Spring ISD	Big Spring
87	9.1	Calhoun County ISD	Port Lavaca
87	9.1	El Campo ISD	El Campo
87	9.1	Huntington ISD	Huntington
87	9.1	Lubbock-Cooper ISD	Lubbock
87	9.1	Medina Valley ISD	Castroville
93	9.0	Alvin ISD	Alvin
93	9.0	Hereford ISD	Hereford
93	9.0	New Caney ISD	New Caney
96	8.9	Alief ISD	Houston
96	8.9	Brownsboro ISD	Brownsboro
96	8.9	Channelview ISD	Channelview
96	8.9	Columbus ISD	Columbus
96	8.9	Corpus Christi ISD	Corpus Christi
96	8.9	Elgin ISD	Elgin
96	8.9	Goose Creek CISD	Baytown
96	8.9	Hudson ISD	Lufkin
96	8.9	Wichita Falls ISD	Wichita Falls
105	8.8	Amarillo ISD	Amarillo
105	8.8	Bastrop ISD	Bastrop
105	8.8	Daingerfield-Lone Star ISD	Daingerfield
105	8.8	Hutto ISD	Hutto
105	8.8	Monahans-Wickett-Pyote ISD	Monahans
105	8.8	Seguin ISD	Seguin
111	8.7	Birdville ISD	Haltom City
111	8.7	Groesbeck ISD	Groesbeck
111	8.7	Whitesboro ISD	Whitesboro
114	8.6	Cuero ISD	Cuero
114	8.6	Ennis ISD	Ennis
114	8.6	Eustace ISD	Eustace
114	8.6	Glen Rose ISD	Glen Rose
114	8.6	Kirbyville CISD	Kirbyville
114	8.6	Mcallen ISD	Mcallen
114	8.6	Taylor ISD	Taylor
114	8.6	Willis ISD	Willis
114	8.6	Wills Point ISD	Wills Point
123	8.5	Bowie ISD	Bowie
123	8.5	Clint ISD	Clint
123	8.5	Fredericksburg ISD	Fredericksburg
123	8.5	Gatesville ISD	Gatesville
123	8.5	Houston ISD	Houston
123	8.5	Kaufman ISD	Kaufman
123	8.5	Kerrville ISD	Kerrville
123	8.5	Marble Falls ISD	Marble Falls
123	8.5	Mexia ISD	Mexia
123	8.5	Uvalde CISD	Uvalde
133	8.4	Frenship ISD	Wolfforth
133	8.4	Gladewater ISD	Gladewater
133	8.4	La Grange ISD	La Grange
133	8.4	Sinton ISD	Sinton
133	8.4	Wharton ISD	Wharton
138	8.3	Brownfield ISD	Brownfield
138	8.3	Ector County ISD	Odessa
138	8.3	Lake Worth ISD	Lake Worth
138	8.3	Madisonville CISD	Madisonville
138	8.3	Sweetwater ISD	Sweetwater
143	8.2	El Paso ISD	El Paso
143	8.2	Hillsboro ISD	Hillsboro
143	8.2	Honors Academy	Dallas
143	8.2	Levelland ISD	Levelland
143	8.2	Princeton ISD	Princeton
143	8.2	Temple ISD	Temple
149	8.1	Alice ISD	Alice
149	8.1	Austin ISD	Austin
149	8.1	Belton ISD	Belton
149	8.1	Dayton ISD	Dayton
149	8.1	Dumas ISD	Dumas
149	8.1	Fabens ISD	Fabens
149	8.1	Gonzales ISD	Gonzales
149	8.1	Lubbock ISD	Lubbock
149	8.1	Mineral Wells ISD	Mineral Wells
149	8.1	Pampa ISD	Pampa
149	8.1	Pflugerville ISD	Pflugerville
149	8.1	Pittsburg ISD	Pittsburg
149	8.1	Rusk ISD	Rusk
162	8.0	Buna ISD	Buna
162	8.0	Carrollton-Farmers Branch ISD	Carrollton
162	8.0	Cleburne ISD	Cleburne
162	8.0	Gainesville ISD	Gainesville
162	8.0	Galena Park ISD	Houston
162	8.0	Georgetown ISD	Georgetown
162	8.0	Liberty Hill ISD	Liberty Hill
162	8.0	Palacios ISD	Palacios
162	8.0	West Oso ISD	Corpus Christi
171	7.9	Bandera ISD	Bandera
171	7.9	Cameron ISD	Cameron
171	7.9	Desoto ISD	Desoto
171	7.9	Hurst-Euless-Bedford ISD	Bedford
171	7.9	Mesquite ISD	Mesquite
176	7.8	Angleton ISD	Angleton
176	7.8	Bonham ISD	Bonham
176	7.8	Eagle Pass ISD	Eagle Pass
176	7.8	Gilmer ISD	Gilmer
176	7.8	Jasper ISD	Jasper
176	7.8	Stafford Municipal School	Stafford
182	7.7	Castleberry ISD	Fort Worth
182	7.7	Lindale ISD	Lindale
182	7.7	New Braunfels ISD	New Braunfels
182	7.7	Quinlan ISD	Quinlan
182	7.7	Shepherd ISD	Shepherd
187	7.6	Dallas ISD	Dallas
187	7.6	Galveston ISD	Galveston
187	7.6	Graham ISD	Graham
187	7.6	Henderson ISD	Henderson
187	7.6	La Porte ISD	La Porte
187	7.6	Mineola ISD	Mineola
193	7.5	Caldwell ISD	Caldwell
193	7.5	Chapel Hill ISD	Tyler
193	7.5	Giddings ISD	Giddings
193	7.5	Hallsville ISD	Hallsville
193	7.5	Lumberton ISD	Lumberton
193	7.5	Sulphur Springs ISD	Sulphur Springs
193	7.5	Victoria ISD	Victoria
200	7.4	Bullard ISD	Bullard
200	7.4	Waller ISD	Waller
202	7.3	Rio Hondo ISD	Rio Hondo
202	7.3	Royse City ISD	Royse City
204	7.2	Azle ISD	Azle
204	7.2	China Spring ISD	Waco
204	7.2	Crockett ISD	Crockett
204	7.2	Longview ISD	Longview
204	7.2	Robinson ISD	Robinson
209	7.1	Aransas County ISD	Rockport
209	7.1	Garland ISD	Garland
211	7.0	Bridgeport ISD	Bridgeport
211	7.0	Corsicana ISD	Corsicana
211	7.0	Crowley ISD	Crowley
211	7.0	North East ISD	San Antonio
211	7.0	North Lamar ISD	Paris
211	7.0	Rains ISD	Emory
211	7.0	Richardson ISD	Richardson
211	7.0	Van ISD	Van
219	6.9	Brazosport ISD	Clute
219	6.9	Commerce ISD	Commerce
219	6.9	Dickinson ISD	Dickinson
219	6.9	Gulf Shores Academy	Houston
219	6.9	La Feria ISD	La Feria
219	6.9	La Marque ISD	La Marque
219	6.9	Livingston ISD	Livingston
219	6.9	Nacogdoches ISD	Nacogdoches
227	6.8	Center ISD	Center
227	6.8	Decatur ISD	Decatur
227	6.8	Fairfield ISD	Fairfield
227	6.8	La Vernia ISD	La Vernia
227	6.8	Lamar CISD	Rosenberg
227	6.8	Sealy ISD	Sealy
227	6.8	Stephenville ISD	Stephenville
227	6.8	Sweeny ISD	Sweeny
227	6.8	West ISD	West
236	6.7	Greenville ISD	Greenville
236	6.7	Liberty-Eylau ISD	Texarkana
236	6.7	Midland ISD	Midland
236	6.7	Seminole ISD	Seminole
236	6.7	Sherman ISD	Sherman
236	6.7	Tyler ISD	Tyler
242	6.6	Greenwood ISD	Midland
242	6.6	Jacksonville ISD	Jacksonville
242	6.6	Little Elm ISD	Little Elm
242	6.6	Robstown ISD	Robstown
242	6.6	Royal ISD	Brookshire
242	6.6	Schertz-Cibolo-Universal City ISD	Schertz
242	6.6	Waxahachie ISD	Waxahachie
242	6.6	Whitney ISD	Whitney
250	6.5	Brenham ISD	Brenham
250	6.5	Cedar Hill ISD	Cedar Hill
250	6.5	Comal ISD	New Braunfels
250	6.5	Lufkin ISD	Lufkin
250	6.5	Marshall ISD	Marshall
250	6.5	San Diego ISD	San Diego
250	6.5	Texarkana ISD	Texarkana
250	6.5	Texas City ISD	Texas City
250	6.5	Weatherford ISD	Weatherford
259	6.4	Coldspring-Oakhurst CISD	Coldspring
259	6.4	Tuloso-Midway ISD	Corpus Christi
261	6.3	Paris ISD	Paris
261	6.3	Spring Branch ISD	Houston
261	6.3	Whitehouse ISD	Whitehouse
264	6.2	Borger ISD	Borger
264	6.2	Granbury ISD	Granbury
264	6.2	Rockdale ISD	Rockdale
267	6.1	Athens ISD	Athens
267	6.1	Bryan ISD	Bryan
267	6.1	Crosby ISD	Crosby
267	6.1	Kemp ISD	Kemp
267	6.1	Kilgore ISD	Kilgore
267	6.1	Sanger ISD	Sanger
267	6.1	Snyder ISD	Snyder
274	6.0	Carrizo Springs CISD	Carrizo Springs
274	6.0	Silsbee ISD	Silsbee
274	6.0	Tarkington ISD	Cleveland
274	6.0	White Settlement ISD	White Settlement
278	5.9	Arlington ISD	Arlington
278	5.9	Breckenridge ISD	Breckenridge
278	5.9	Calallen ISD	Corpus Christi
278	5.9	Columbia-Brazoria ISD	West Columbia
278	5.9	Orangefield ISD	Orangefield
278	5.9	Pine Tree ISD	Longview
278	5.9	Terrell ISD	Terrell
285	5.8	Burleson ISD	Burleson
285	5.8	Carthage ISD	Carthage
285	5.8	Fort Worth ISD	Fort Worth
285	5.8	Hardin-Jefferson ISD	Sour Lake
285	5.8	Liberty ISD	Liberty
285	5.8	Plainview ISD	Plainview
291	5.7	Lamesa ISD	Lamesa
291	5.7	Nederland ISD	Nederland
291	5.7	Wilmer-Hutchins ISD	Dallas
294	5.6	Beaumont ISD	Beaumont
294	5.6	Deer Park ISD	Deer Park
294	5.6	Harlingen Cons ISD	Harlingen
294	5.6	Magnolia ISD	Magnolia
294	5.6	Winnsboro ISD	Winnsboro
299	5.5	Eagle Mt-Saginaw ISD	Fort Worth
299	5.5	Leander ISD	Leander
299	5.5	Point Isabel ISD	Port Isabel
299	5.5	West Orange-Cove CISD	Orange
303	5.4	Canton ISD	Canton
303	5.4	Donna ISD	Donna
303	5.4	Huffman ISD	Huffman
303	5.4	Zapata County ISD	Zapata
307	5.3	Bridge City ISD	Bridge City
307	5.3	Denton ISD	Denton
309	5.2	Canyon ISD	Canyon
309	5.2	Cypress-Fairbanks ISD	Houston
309	5.2	Kennedale ISD	Kennedale
309	5.2	Midlothian ISD	Midlothian
309	5.2	Midway ISD	Hewitt
314	5.1	Mansfield ISD	Mansfield
314	5.1	Port Arthur ISD	Port Arthur
316	5.0	Crandall ISD	Crandall
316	5.0	Northwest ISD	Fort Worth
316	5.0	Round Rock ISD	Round Rock
319	4.9	Needville ISD	Needville
320	4.7	Crystal City ISD	Crystal City
320	4.7	Humble ISD	Humble
322	4.6	Barbers Hill ISD	Mount Belvieu
322	4.6	College Station ISD	College Station
322	4.6	Los Fresnos CISD	Los Fresnos
325	4.5	Brooks County ISD	Falfurrias
325	4.5	Edna ISD	Edna
325	4.5	Fort Bend ISD	Sugar Land
325	4.5	Montgomery ISD	Montgomery
325	4.5	Palestine ISD	Palestine
330	4.4	Klein ISD	Klein
330	4.4	Wylie ISD	Wylie
332	4.3	Bellville ISD	Bellville
332	4.3	Harlandale ISD	San Antonio
332	4.3	Lorena ISD	Lorena
332	4.3	Santa Fe ISD	Santa Fe
336	4.2	Port Neches-Groves ISD	Port Neches
337	4.0	Alamo Heights ISD	San Antonio
337	4.0	Boerne ISD	Boerne
337	4.0	Pearland ISD	Pearland
337	4.0	Raymondville ISD	Raymondville
341	3.9	Conroe ISD	Conroe
341	3.9	Little Cypress-Mauriceville CISD	Orange
343	3.7	Hamshire-Fannett ISD	Hamshire

344	3.6	North Forest ISD	Houston
344	3.6	Wimberley ISD	Wimberley
346	3.5	La Joya ISD	La Joya
347	3.4	Clear Creek ISD	League City
347	3.4	Katy ISD	Katy
347	3.4	Laredo ISD	Laredo
347	3.4	Mckinney ISD	Mckinney
347	3.4	Pleasant Grove ISD	Texarkana
352	3.3	Spring Hill ISD	Longview
353	3.2	Lake Dallas ISD	Lake Dallas
354	3.1	Edinburg CISD	Edinburg
354	3.1	Lewisville ISD	Flower Mound
354	3.1	Red Oak ISD	Red Oak
354	3.1	Rio Grande City CISD	Rio Grande City
354	3.1	Wylie ISD	Abilene
359	3.0	Forney ISD	Forney
359	3.0	Keller ISD	Keller
361	2.9	San Antonio ISD	San Antonio
362	2.8	Frisco ISD	Frisco
363	2.7	Plano ISD	Plano
363	2.7	San Benito Cons ISD	San Benito
363	2.7	Tomball ISD	Tomball
363	2.7	Weslaco ISD	Weslaco
367	2.4	Rockwall ISD	Rockwall
368	2.0	Dripping Springs ISD	Dripping Spgs
368	2.0	Lake Travis ISD	Austin
368	2.0	Mercedes ISD	Mercedes
371	1.9	Pharr-San Juan-Alamo ISD	Pharr
372	1.8	Aledo ISD	Aledo
372	1.8	Progreso ISD	Progreso
374	1.6	Allen ISD	Allen
375	1.5	Coppell ISD	Coppell
375	1.5	Edcouch-Elsa ISD	Edcouch
377	1.4	Grapevine-Colleyville ISD	Grapevine
378	1.3	Valley View ISD	Pharr
379	0.9	Brownsville ISD	Brownsville
379	0.9	Roma ISD	Roma
381	0.7	Edgewood ISD	San Antonio
381	0.7	Mission Cons ISD	Mission
383	0.6	Friendswood ISD	Friendswood
384	0.5	Eanes ISD	Austin
384	0.5	Hidalgo ISD	Hidalgo
386	0.3	Lyford CISD	Lyford
387	0.2	Carroll ISD	Southlake
388	0.0	Highland Park ISD	Dallas
388	0.0	San Elizario ISD	San Elizario

Student/Teacher Ratio

Rank	Ratio	District Name	City
1	36.0	Gulf Shores Academy	Houston
2	18.0	Keller ISD	Keller
3	17.9	San Felipe-Del Rio CISD	Del Rio
4	17.5	Honors Academy	Dallas
5	17.4	Lorena ISD	Lorena
6	17.3	San Benito Cons ISD	San Benito
7	17.2	Eagle Mt-Saginaw ISD	Fort Worth
8	17.1	Eagle Pass ISD	Eagle Pass
8	17.1	Houston ISD	Houston
8	17.1	Socorro ISD	El Paso
11	17.0	Dayton ISD	Dayton
11	17.0	Sharyland ISD	Mission
13	16.9	Gregory-Portland ISD	Gregory
13	16.9	Rockwall ISD	Rockwall
13	16.9	Santa Fe ISD	Santa Fe
16	16.7	Rio Hondo ISD	Rio Hondo
17	16.6	Channelview ISD	Channelview
17	16.6	Fort Bend ISD	Sugar Land
17	16.6	Friendswood ISD	Friendswood
20	16.5	Alvarado ISD	Alvarado
20	16.5	Huffman ISD	Huffman
22	16.4	China Spring ISD	Waco
22	16.4	Edcouch-Elsa ISD	Edcouch
22	16.4	Medina Valley ISD	Castroville
25	16.3	Edgewood ISD	San Antonio
25	16.3	Fort Worth ISD	Fort Worth
25	16.3	Klein ISD	Klein
25	16.3	Midway ISD	Hewitt
25	16.3	Pasadena ISD	Pasadena
30	16.2	Allen ISD	Allen
30	16.2	Brazosport ISD	Clute
30	16.2	La Porte ISD	La Porte
33	16.1	Clint ISD	Clint
33	16.1	Goose Creek CISD	Baytown
33	16.1	Texas City ISD	Texas City
33	16.1	Valley View ISD	Pharr
33	16.1	Wylie ISD	Abilene
38	16.0	Canyon ISD	Canyon
38	16.0	Castleberry ISD	Fort Worth
38	16.0	Harlingen Cons ISD	Harlingen
38	16.0	Laredo ISD	Laredo
38	16.0	Port Arthur ISD	Port Arthur
38	16.0	West ISD	West
38	16.0	Whitehouse ISD	Whitehouse
45	15.9	Cedar Hill ISD	Cedar Hill
45	15.9	Dickinson ISD	Dickinson
45	15.9	Everman ISD	Everman
45	15.9	Frenship ISD	Wolfforth
45	15.9	Garland ISD	Garland
45	15.9	Mesquite ISD	Mesquite
45	15.9	Tuloso-Midway ISD	Corpus Christi
45	15.9	Willis ISD	Willis
45	15.9	Ysleta ISD	El Paso
54	15.8	La Joya ISD	La Joya
54	15.8	North Forest ISD	Houston
54	15.8	Pearland ISD	Pearland
54	15.8	United ISD	Laredo
58	15.7	Arlington ISD	Arlington
58	15.7	Birdville ISD	Haltom City
58	15.7	Clear Creek ISD	League City
58	15.7	Corpus Christi ISD	Corpus Christi
58	15.7	Deer Park ISD	Deer Park
58	15.7	Pharr-San Juan-Alamo ISD	Pharr
58	15.7	Red Oak ISD	Red Oak
58	15.7	Rockdale ISD	Rockdale
58	15.7	San Antonio ISD	San Antonio
67	15.6	Cleveland ISD	Cleveland
67	15.6	Crosby ISD	Crosby
67	15.6	Duncanville ISD	Duncanville
67	15.6	Edinburg CISD	Edinburg
67	15.6	Hurst-Euless-Bedford ISD	Bedford
67	15.6	Lamar CISD	Rosenberg
67	15.6	Mercedes ISD	Mercedes
67	15.6	Pflugerville ISD	Pflugerville
67	15.6	Southside ISD	San Antonio
67	15.6	West Oso ISD	Corpus Christi
77	15.5	Angleton ISD	Angleton
77	15.5	Bay City ISD	Bay City
77	15.5	Cleburne ISD	Cleburne
77	15.5	Cypress-Fairbanks ISD	Houston
77	15.5	Highland Park ISD	Dallas
77	15.5	Ingleside ISD	Ingleside
77	15.5	Littlefield ISD	Littlefield
77	15.5	Livingston ISD	Livingston
77	15.5	Stephenville ISD	Stephenville
86	15.4	Calallen ISD	Corpus Christi
86	15.4	Dripping Springs ISD	Dripping Spgs
86	15.4	Kaufman ISD	Kaufman
86	15.4	La Vernia ISD	La Vernia
86	15.4	Los Fresnos CISD	Los Fresnos
86	15.4	New Braunfels ISD	New Braunfels
86	15.4	Tomball ISD	Tomball
86	15.4	Weslaco ISD	Weslaco
86	15.4	White Settlement ISD	White Settlement
95	15.3	Burleson ISD	Burleson
95	15.3	East Central ISD	San Antonio
95	15.3	Greenwood ISD	Midland
95	15.3	Hays Cons ISD	Kyle
95	15.3	Humble ISD	Humble
95	15.3	Kennedale ISD	Kennedale
95	15.3	Mansfield ISD	Mansfield
95	15.3	Mcallen ISD	Mcallen
95	15.3	Mission Cons ISD	Mission
95	15.3	Richardson ISD	Richardson
95	15.3	San Angelo ISD	San Angelo
95	15.3	Schertz-Cibolo-Universal City ISD	Schertz
95	15.3	Waller ISD	Waller
95	15.3	Weatherford ISD	Weatherford
95	15.3	Wills Point ISD	Wills Point
110	15.2	Alief ISD	Houston
110	15.2	Ector County ISD	Odessa
110	15.2	Forney ISD	Forney
110	15.2	Lampasas ISD	Lampasas
110	15.2	Northside ISD	San Antonio
110	15.2	Raymondville ISD	Raymondville
116	15.1	Alvin ISD	Alvin
116	15.1	Belton ISD	Belton
116	15.1	Conroe ISD	Conroe
116	15.1	Flour Bluff ISD	Corpus Christi
116	15.1	La Marque ISD	La Marque
116	15.1	Little Cypress-Mauriceville CISD	Orange
116	15.1	Montgomery ISD	Montgomery
116	15.1	New Caney ISD	New Caney
116	15.1	Orange Grove ISD	Orange Grove
116	15.1	Point Isabel ISD	Port Isabel
116	15.1	San Marcos CISD	San Marcos
116	15.1	Westwood ISD	Palestine
128	15.0	Beeville ISD	Beeville
128	15.0	Brownsboro ISD	Brownsboro
128	15.0	Columbia-Brazoria ISD	West Columbia
128	15.0	Denison ISD	Denison
128	15.0	Ennis ISD	Ennis
128	15.0	Grapevine-Colleyville ISD	Grapevine
128	15.0	Lake Travis ISD	Austin
128	15.0	Nederland ISD	Nederland
128	15.0	Needville ISD	Needville
128	15.0	Rio Grande City CISD	Rio Grande City
128	15.0	Spring ISD	Houston
128	15.0	Texarkana ISD	Texarkana
140	14.9	Aldine ISD	Houston
140	14.9	Alice ISD	Alice
140	14.9	Azle ISD	Azle
140	14.9	Carrollton-Farmers Branch ISD	Carrollton
140	14.9	Dallas ISD	Dallas
140	14.9	Fabens ISD	Fabens
140	14.9	Huntsville ISD	Huntsville
140	14.9	Lubbock-Cooper ISD	Lubbock
140	14.9	Princeton ISD	Princeton
140	14.9	San Elizario ISD	San Elizario
140	14.9	South San Antonio ISD	San Antonio
140	14.9	Southwest ISD	San Antonio
140	14.9	Victoria ISD	Victoria
140	14.9	Waxahachie ISD	Waxahachie
154	14.8	Comal ISD	New Braunfels
154	14.8	Desoto ISD	Desoto
154	14.8	Katy ISD	Katy
154	14.8	Kerrville ISD	Kerrville
154	14.8	Lumberton ISD	Lumberton
154	14.8	Magnolia ISD	Magnolia
154	14.8	Mathis ISD	Mathis
154	14.8	Midland ISD	Midland
154	14.8	North East ISD	San Antonio
154	14.8	Roma ISD	Roma
154	14.8	Sheldon ISD	Houston
154	14.8	Splendora ISD	Splendora
154	14.8	Waco ISD	Waco
167	14.7	Brownsville ISD	Brownsville
167	14.7	Bullard ISD	Bullard
167	14.7	Calhoun County ISD	Port Lavaca
167	14.7	Donna ISD	Donna
167	14.7	Ferris ISD	Ferris
167	14.7	Gatesville ISD	Gatesville
167	14.7	Graham ISD	Graham
167	14.7	Harlandale ISD	San Antonio
167	14.7	Judson ISD	San Antonio
167	14.7	Lockhart ISD	Lockhart
167	14.7	Nacogdoches ISD	Nacogdoches
167	14.7	Round Rock ISD	Round Rock
167	14.7	Sweeny ISD	Sweeny
167	14.7	Winnsboro ISD	Winnsboro
181	14.6	Amarillo ISD	Amarillo
181	14.6	Austin ISD	Austin
181	14.6	Bridgeport ISD	Bridgeport
181	14.6	College Station ISD	College Station
181	14.6	Corsicana ISD	Corsicana
181	14.6	Hudson ISD	Lufkin
181	14.6	Orangefield ISD	Orangefield
181	14.6	Plainview ISD	Plainview
181	14.6	Somerset ISD	Somerset
190	14.5	Barbers Hill ISD	Mount Belvieu
190	14.5	Bryan ISD	Bryan
190	14.5	Carroll ISD	Southlake
190	14.5	Coppell ISD	Coppell
190	14.5	Crandall ISD	Crandall
190	14.5	Crystal City ISD	Crystal City
190	14.5	El Campo ISD	El Campo
190	14.5	Galena Park ISD	Houston
190	14.5	Galveston ISD	Galveston
190	14.5	Granbury ISD	Granbury
190	14.5	Grand Prairie ISD	Grand Prairie
190	14.5	Iowa Park CISD	Iowa Park
190	14.5	Joshua ISD	Joshua
190	14.5	Leander ISD	Leander
190	14.5	Mabank ISD	Mabank
190	14.5	Spring Branch ISD	Houston
190	14.5	Venus ISD	Venus
207	14.4	Center ISD	Center
207	14.4	Crowley ISD	Crowley
207	14.4	Decatur ISD	Decatur
207	14.4	Eustace ISD	Eustace
207	14.4	Hallsville ISD	Hallsville
207	14.4	Kingsville ISD	Kingsville
207	14.4	Lewisville ISD	Flower Mound
207	14.4	Luling ISD	Luling
207	14.4	Pecos-Barstow-Toyah ISD	Pecos
207	14.4	Quinlan ISD	Quinlan
207	14.4	Royse City ISD	Royse City
218	14.3	Aledo ISD	Aledo
218	14.3	El Paso ISD	El Paso
218	14.3	Gladewater ISD	Gladewater
218	14.3	Hamshire-Fannett ISD	Hamshire
218	14.3	Hereford ISD	Hereford
218	14.3	Kemp ISD	Kemp
218	14.3	Kirbyville CISD	Kirbyville
218	14.3	Pine Tree ISD	Longview
218	14.3	Pleasant Grove ISD	Texarkana
218	14.3	Spring Hill ISD	Longview
218	14.3	Taylor ISD	Taylor

218	14.3	Wylie ISD	Wylie
230	14.2	Bonham ISD	Bonham
230	14.2	Borger ISD	Borger
230	14.2	Bridge City ISD	Bridge City
230	14.2	Canton ISD	Canton
230	14.2	Carthage ISD	Carthage
230	14.2	Columbus ISD	Columbus
230	14.2	Dumas ISD	Dumas
230	14.2	Hardin-Jefferson ISD	Sour Lake
230	14.2	Hutto ISD	Hutto
230	14.2	Killeen ISD	Killeen
230	14.2	Lindale ISD	Lindale
230	14.2	Marshall ISD	Marshall
230	14.2	Mckinney ISD	Mckinney
230	14.2	Pearsall ISD	Pearsall
230	14.2	Sealy ISD	Sealy
230	14.2	Uvalde CISD	Uvalde
230	14.2	Vidor ISD	Vidor
247	14.1	Athens ISD	Athens
247	14.1	La Feria ISD	La Feria
247	14.1	La Grange ISD	La Grange
247	14.1	Lancaster ISD	Lancaster
247	14.1	Little Elm ISD	Little Elm
247	14.1	Monahans-Wickett-Pyote ISD	Monahans
247	14.1	Navasota ISD	Navasota
247	14.1	Plano ISD	Plano
247	14.1	Port Neches-Groves ISD	Port Neches
247	14.1	Robstown ISD	Robstown
247	14.1	Tarkington ISD	Cleveland
247	14.1	Tyler ISD	Tyler
247	14.1	Van ISD	Van
260	14.0	Bastrop ISD	Bastrop
260	14.0	Bowie ISD	Bowie
260	14.0	Chapel Hill ISD	Tyler
260	14.0	Commerce ISD	Commerce
260	14.0	Copperas Cove ISD	Copperas Cove
260	14.0	Devine ISD	Devine
260	14.0	Irving ISD	Irving
260	14.0	Jasper ISD	Jasper
260	14.0	Longview ISD	Longview
260	14.0	Lubbock ISD	Lubbock
260	14.0	Marble Falls ISD	Marble Falls
260	14.0	North Lamar ISD	Paris
260	14.0	Northwest ISD	Fort Worth
260	14.0	Silsbee ISD	Silsbee
260	14.0	Whitesboro ISD	Whitesboro
260	14.0	Wilmer-Hutchins ISD	Dallas
276	13.9	Beaumont ISD	Beaumont
276	13.9	Burnet Cons ISD	Burnet
276	13.9	Coldspring-Oakhurst CISD	Coldspring
276	13.9	Edna ISD	Edna
276	13.9	Floresville ISD	Floresville
276	13.9	Gainesville ISD	Gainesville
276	13.9	Lamesa ISD	Lamesa
276	13.9	Liberty ISD	Liberty
276	13.9	Lytle ISD	Lytle
276	13.9	Mexia ISD	Mexia
276	13.9	Pittsburg ISD	Pittsburg
276	13.9	Sherman ISD	Sherman
288	13.8	Alamo Heights ISD	San Antonio
288	13.8	Aransas County ISD	Rockport
288	13.8	Boerne ISD	Boerne
288	13.8	Central ISD	Pollok
288	13.8	Del Valle ISD	Del Valle
288	13.8	Denton ISD	Denton
288	13.8	Elgin ISD	Elgin
288	13.8	Fredericksburg ISD	Fredericksburg
288	13.8	Gonzales ISD	Gonzales
288	13.8	Greenville ISD	Greenville
288	13.8	Mineola ISD	Mineola
288	13.8	Royal ISD	Brookshire
288	13.8	Stafford Municipal School	Stafford
288	13.8	Terrell ISD	Terrell
302	13.7	Abilene ISD	Abilene
302	13.7	Bellville ISD	Bellville
302	13.7	Big Spring ISD	Big Spring
302	13.7	Connally ISD	Waco
302	13.7	La Vega ISD	Waco
302	13.7	Manor ISD	Manor
302	13.7	Progreso ISD	Progreso
302	13.7	Sinton ISD	Sinton
302	13.7	Springtown ISD	Springtown
302	13.7	Sulphur Springs ISD	Sulphur Springs
312	13.6	Henderson ISD	Henderson
312	13.6	Hidalgo ISD	Hidalgo
312	13.6	Lufkin ISD	Lufkin
312	13.6	Madisonville CISD	Madisonville
312	13.6	Midlothian ISD	Midlothian
312	13.6	Pleasanton ISD	Pleasanton
312	13.6	Temple ISD	Temple
312	13.6	Wharton ISD	Wharton
320	13.5	Breckenridge ISD	Breckenridge
320	13.5	Brownwood ISD	Brownwood
320	13.5	Canutillo ISD	El Paso
320	13.5	Fort Stockton ISD	Fort Stockton
320	13.5	Frisco ISD	Frisco
320	13.5	Huntington ISD	Huntington
320	13.5	Jacksonville ISD	Jacksonville
320	13.5	Mineral Wells ISD	Mineral Wells
320	13.5	Pampa ISD	Pampa
320	13.5	Seguin ISD	Seguin
320	13.5	Wichita Falls ISD	Wichita Falls
331	13.4	Carrizo Springs CISD	Carrizo Springs
331	13.4	Snyder ISD	Snyder
331	13.4	Whitney ISD	Whitney
334	13.3	Andrews ISD	Andrews
334	13.3	Aransas Pass ISD	Aransas Pass
334	13.3	Caldwell ISD	Caldwell
334	13.3	Cuero ISD	Cuero
334	13.3	Fairfield ISD	Fairfield
334	13.3	Kilgore ISD	Kilgore
334	13.3	Lyford CISD	Lyford
334	13.3	Smithville ISD	Smithville
334	13.3	Wimberley ISD	Wimberley
343	13.2	Eanes ISD	Austin
343	13.2	San Diego ISD	San Diego
343	13.2	Shepherd ISD	Shepherd
346	13.1	Lake Worth ISD	Lake Worth
346	13.1	Palestine ISD	Palestine
346	13.1	Rains ISD	Emory
346	13.1	West Orange-Cove CISD	Orange
350	13.0	Brenham ISD	Brenham
350	13.0	Diboll ISD	Diboll
350	13.0	Giddings ISD	Giddings
350	13.0	Mount Pleasant ISD	Mt Pleasant
350	13.0	Robinson ISD	Robinson
350	13.0	Vernon ISD	Vernon
350	13.0	Zapata County ISD	Zapata
357	12.9	Brooks County ISD	Falfurrias
357	12.9	Perryton ISD	Perryton
359	12.8	Bandera ISD	Bandera
359	12.8	Buna ISD	Buna
359	12.8	Burkburnett ISD	Burkburnett
359	12.8	Gilmer ISD	Gilmer
359	12.8	Lake Dallas ISD	Lake Dallas
359	12.8	Palacios ISD	Palacios
359	12.8	Poteet ISD	Poteet
359	12.8	Seminole ISD	Seminole
367	12.7	Brownfield ISD	Brownfield
367	12.7	Georgetown ISD	Georgetown
367	12.7	Liberty Hill ISD	Liberty Hill
367	12.7	Liberty-Eylau ISD	Texarkana
367	12.7	Paris ISD	Paris
367	12.7	Sanger ISD	Sanger
373	12.6	Atlanta ISD	Atlanta
373	12.6	Dalhart ISD	Dalhart
375	12.5	Crockett ISD	Crockett
375	12.5	Yoakum ISD	Yoakum
377	12.4	Hillsboro ISD	Hillsboro
377	12.4	Levelland ISD	Levelland
379	12.3	Cameron ISD	Cameron
379	12.3	Groesbeck ISD	Groesbeck
379	12.3	Hondo ISD	Hondo
379	12.3	Marlin ISD	Marlin
383	12.2	Daingerfield-Lone Star ISD	Daingerfield
383	12.2	Rusk ISD	Rusk
383	12.2	Sweetwater ISD	Sweetwater
386	12.0	Glen Rose ISD	Glen Rose
386	12.0	Ingram ISD	Ingram
388	11.7	South Texas ISD	Mercedes
389	10.9	Llano ISD	Llano

Student/Librarian Ratio

Rank	Ratio	District Name	City
1	8,850.0	Liberty Hill ISD	Liberty Hill
2	5,436.7	Buna ISD	Buna
3	4,958.8	Big Spring ISD	Big Spring
4	4,942.5	Monahans-Wickett-Pyote ISD	Monahans
5	3,942.7	Eagle Pass ISD	Eagle Pass
6	3,786.7	Denison ISD	Denison
7	3,765.0	Brownwood ISD	Brownwood
8	3,648.0	Kilgore ISD	Kilgore
9	3,538.0	Alvarado ISD	Alvarado
10	3,076.4	Beaumont ISD	Beaumont
11	3,018.0	Medina Valley ISD	Castroville
12	2,965.8	Texarkana ISD	Texarkana
13	2,906.0	Waxahachie ISD	Waxahachie
14	2,899.3	Sulphur Springs ISD	Sulphur Springs
15	2,870.8	Pampa ISD	Pampa
16	2,620.0	Brownsboro ISD	Brownsboro
17	2,556.4	Fabens ISD	Fabens
18	2,488.5	Mount Pleasant ISD	Mt Pleasant
19	2,487.0	Carrizo Springs CISD	Carrizo Springs
20	2,454.0	Graham ISD	Graham
21	2,384.0	Kerrville ISD	Kerrville
22	2,311.0	Sweetwater ISD	Sweetwater
23	2,222.5	Coldspring-Oakhurst CISD	Coldspring
24	2,180.0	Silsbee ISD	Silsbee
25	2,132.0	Sinton ISD	Sinton
26	2,115.0	Madisonville CISD	Madisonville
27	2,107.0	Rio Hondo ISD	Rio Hondo
28	2,099.0	Hardin-Jefferson ISD	Sour Lake
29	1,923.0	Rusk ISD	Rusk
30	1,914.0	Caldwell ISD	Caldwell
31	1,903.3	Wylie ISD	Wylie
32	1,895.0	Rockdale ISD	Rockdale
33	1,841.8	Robinson ISD	Robinson
34	1,830.0	Westwood ISD	Palestine
35	1,806.0	Shepherd ISD	Shepherd
36	1,723.3	Whitesboro ISD	Whitesboro
37	1,719.0	Brooks County ISD	Falfurrias
38	1,716.4	Gregory-Portland ISD	Gregory
39	1,686.0	Kaufman ISD	Kaufman
40	1,635.7	Hallsville ISD	Hallsville
41	1,615.8	Elgin ISD	Elgin
42	1,612.5	Tuloso-Midway ISD	Corpus Christi
43	1,611.0	Edna ISD	Edna
44	1,606.7	Southwest ISD	San Antonio
45	1,595.0	Cleburne ISD	Cleburne
46	1,594.0	Luling ISD	Luling
47	1,587.0	Dalhart ISD	Dalhart
48	1,581.0	San Diego ISD	San Diego
49	1,572.0	Orange Grove ISD	Orange Grove
50	1,552.3	Floresville ISD	Floresville
51	1,522.9	Sherman ISD	Sherman
52	1,520.0	Perryton ISD	Perryton
53	1,515.2	Jasper ISD	Jasper
54	1,508.0	Winnsboro ISD	Winnsboro
55	1,505.0	Lyford CISD	Lyford
56	1,467.0	Aransas County ISD	Rockport
57	1,460.3	Azle ISD	Azle
58	1,453.0	Wilmer-Hutchins ISD	Dallas
59	1,452.6	Channelview ISD	Channelview
60	1,440.0	Navasota ISD	Navasota
61	1,405.3	Calhoun County ISD	Port Lavaca
62	1,387.0	Wylie ISD	Abilene
63	1,371.0	Frenship ISD	Wolfforth
64	1,370.3	Livingston ISD	Livingston
65	1,369.1	Chapel Hill ISD	Tyler
66	1,369.0	Corsicana ISD	Corsicana
67	1,367.7	White Settlement ISD	White Settlement
68	1,364.5	Belton ISD	Belton
69	1,352.9	Brenham ISD	Brenham
70	1,340.0	Forney ISD	Forney
71	1,339.7	Alamo Heights ISD	San Antonio
72	1,328.5	Snyder ISD	Snyder
73	1,327.5	Gonzales ISD	Gonzales
74	1,321.5	Mansfield ISD	Mansfield
75	1,306.7	Marshall ISD	Marshall
76	1,289.2	Yoakum ISD	Yoakum
77	1,283.8	Clint ISD	Clint
78	1,280.0	Connally ISD	Waco
79	1,272.5	Midlothian ISD	Midlothian
80	1,272.0	Beeville ISD	Beeville
81	1,269.0	Harlingen Cons ISD	Harlingen
82	1,246.3	Grapevine-Colleyville ISD	Grapevine
83	1,230.0	Burnet Cons ISD	Burnet
84	1,225.8	Whitehouse ISD	Whitehouse
85	1,191.0	El Campo ISD	El Campo
86	1,183.9	Mineral Wells ISD	Mineral Wells
87	1,182.5	Fredericksburg ISD	Fredericksburg
88	1,180.5	Liberty ISD	Liberty
89	1,172.0	Sealy ISD	Sealy
90	1,169.0	Hudson ISD	Lufkin
91	1,163.0	Pleasanton ISD	Pleasanton
92	1,150.8	Rio Grande City CISD	Rio Grande City
93	1,149.5	Mexia ISD	Mexia
94	1,148.1	Alief ISD	Houston
95	1,143.8	Burleson ISD	Burleson
96	1,141.7	Tomball ISD	Tomball
97	1,137.1	Decatur ISD	Decatur
97	1,137.1	Galena Park ISD	Houston
99	1,131.5	Ingleside ISD	Ingleside
100	1,118.3	Santa Fe ISD	Santa Fe
101	1,099.0	Van ISD	Van
102	1,092.0	Ferris ISD	Ferris
103	1,087.0	Lampasas ISD	Lampasas
104	1,086.5	Cypress-Fairbanks ISD	Houston
105	1,082.0	Lamesa ISD	Lamesa
106	1,081.5	Sanger ISD	Sanger
107	1,081.1	Keller ISD	Keller
108	1,078.6	Ingram ISD	Ingram
109	1,078.2	Friendswood ISD	Friendswood
110	1,068.0	North Lamar ISD	Paris
111	1,067.5	Pasadena ISD	Pasadena
112	1,065.3	Greenville ISD	Greenville
113	1,061.9	Judson ISD	San Antonio

Rank	Value	District	City
114	1,059.2	Ennis ISD	Ennis
115	1,054.5	Aransas Pass ISD	Aransas Pass
116	1,052.2	Nacogdoches ISD	Nacogdoches
117	1,049.1	Katy ISD	Katy
118	1,048.8	Glen Rose ISD	Glen Rose
119	1,048.0	Crystal City ISD	Crystal City
120	1,046.6	Del Valle ISD	Del Valle
121	1,043.5	Magnolia ISD	Magnolia
122	1,039.3	Sharyland ISD	Mission
123	1,038.8	Edcouch-Elsa ISD	Edcouch
124	1,021.5	Spring Branch ISD	Houston
125	1,020.7	Northside ISD	San Antonio
126	1,015.5	Gulf Shores Academy	Houston
127	1,015.3	Calallen ISD	Corpus Christi
128	1,006.7	Aldine ISD	Houston
129	999.7	Spring ISD	Houston
130	998.2	Flour Bluff ISD	Corpus Christi
131	997.6	New Braunfels ISD	New Braunfels
132	991.7	Gainesville ISD	Gainesville
133	989.1	Leander ISD	Leander
134	978.0	Quinlan ISD	Quinlan
135	972.0	Paris ISD	Paris
136	966.5	La Grange ISD	La Grange
137	962.5	Nederland ISD	Nederland
138	961.3	Everman ISD	Everman
139	954.0	Ysleta ISD	El Paso
140	949.8	Arlington ISD	Arlington
141	949.5	Cuero ISD	Cuero
141	949.5	Devine ISD	Devine
143	949.0	Kennedale ISD	Kennedale
144	948.3	Corpus Christi ISD	Corpus Christi
144	948.3	Seguin ISD	Seguin
146	946.7	La Feria ISD	La Feria
147	944.0	Southside ISD	San Antonio
148	939.9	Socorro ISD	El Paso
149	939.2	Allen ISD	Allen
150	938.2	San Felipe-Del Rio CISD	Del Rio
151	937.3	Stafford Municipal School	Stafford
152	937.1	Dayton ISD	Dayton
153	935.5	Venus ISD	Venus
154	930.2	Waller ISD	Waller
155	930.0	La Joya ISD	La Joya
156	926.9	Waco ISD	Waco
157	913.8	Fort Bend ISD	Sugar Land
157	913.8	Marble Falls ISD	Marble Falls
159	913.2	East Central ISD	San Antonio
159	913.2	Humble ISD	Humble
161	912.0	Tarkington ISD	Cleveland
162	907.4	Lufkin ISD	Lufkin
163	906.0	Wimberley ISD	Wimberley
164	905.5	Duncanville ISD	Duncanville
165	905.0	Irving ISD	Irving
166	904.0	North East ISD	San Antonio
167	903.7	United ISD	Laredo
168	899.3	Dickinson ISD	Dickinson
169	898.3	Valley View ISD	Pharr
170	897.4	Round Rock ISD	Round Rock
171	890.9	Red Oak ISD	Red Oak
172	887.6	Victoria ISD	Victoria
173	886.8	Clear Creek ISD	League City
174	885.0	Joshua ISD	Joshua
175	884.3	Wills Point ISD	Wills Point
176	883.8	Deer Park ISD	Deer Park
177	882.2	Rockwall ISD	Rockwall
178	881.9	Pflugerville ISD	Pflugerville
179	879.7	Laredo ISD	Laredo
180	879.4	New Caney ISD	New Caney
181	879.0	China Spring ISD	Waco
182	877.3	Uvalde CISD	Uvalde
183	877.1	Lubbock ISD	Lubbock
184	875.0	Jacksonville ISD	Jacksonville
185	872.8	Brownsville ISD	Brownsville
186	867.7	Eagle Mt-Saginaw ISD	Fort Worth
187	865.0	Crockett ISD	Crockett
188	864.5	Canton ISD	Canton
189	864.2	Vidor ISD	Vidor
190	862.5	Athens ISD	Athens
191	862.3	La Porte ISD	La Porte
192	862.0	Boerne ISD	Boerne
193	861.8	Stephenville ISD	Stephenville
194	860.0	Orangefield ISD	Orangefield
195	858.1	Klein ISD	Klein
196	857.5	Pharr-San Juan-Alamo ISD	Pharr
197	856.0	Goose Creek CISD	Baytown
198	855.2	Bellville ISD	Bellville
199	853.0	Aledo ISD	Aledo
200	846.3	Palestine ISD	Palestine
201	845.2	Amarillo ISD	Amarillo
202	844.9	College Station ISD	College Station
203	843.8	Pearland ISD	Pearland
204	843.1	Highland Park ISD	Dallas
205	839.7	Alvin ISD	Alvin
206	839.0	Kemp ISD	Kemp
207	838.0	Lumberton ISD	Lumberton
208	837.9	Littlefield ISD	Littlefield
209	837.5	Bonham ISD	Bonham
210	836.7	South San Antonio ISD	San Antonio
211	836.5	Huntington ISD	Huntington
212	835.6	Montgomery ISD	Montgomery
213	834.8	Diboll ISD	Diboll
214	833.6	Commerce ISD	Commerce
215	830.8	Terrell ISD	Terrell
216	828.3	North Forest ISD	Houston
217	828.1	Galveston ISD	Galveston
218	826.8	Dripping Springs ISD	Dripping Spgs
219	824.0	Crosby ISD	Crosby
220	822.8	Edgewood ISD	San Antonio
220	822.8	Texas City ISD	Texas City
222	822.1	Houston ISD	Houston
223	821.4	San Benito Cons ISD	San Benito
224	820.8	Columbia-Brazoria ISD	West Columbia
225	819.0	Center ISD	Center
226	816.5	Mabank ISD	Mabank
227	815.0	Fairfield ISD	Fairfield
228	814.1	Tyler ISD	Tyler
229	814.0	Conroe ISD	Conroe
230	813.0	Castleberry ISD	Fort Worth
231	812.9	Angleton ISD	Angleton
232	812.3	Needville ISD	Needville
233	810.5	Central ISD	Pollok
234	806.0	Bastrop ISD	Bastrop
235	804.9	Hurst-Euless-Bedford ISD	Bedford
236	804.2	San Angelo ISD	San Angelo
237	803.3	Mcallen ISD	Mcallen
238	801.3	Crowley ISD	Crowley
239	799.2	Robstown ISD	Robstown
240	799.1	Weslaco ISD	Weslaco
241	798.2	Weatherford ISD	Weatherford
242	798.0	Kirbyville CISD	Kirbyville
243	795.5	Lorena ISD	Lorena
244	793.9	Abilene ISD	Abilene
245	792.9	Dallas ISD	Dallas
246	790.1	Plano ISD	Plano
247	790.0	Taylor ISD	Taylor
248	789.3	Killeen ISD	Killeen
249	788.6	Mesquite ISD	Mesquite
250	788.5	Somerset ISD	Somerset
251	788.0	Eustace ISD	Eustace
252	786.0	Vernon ISD	Vernon
253	785.8	Canutillo ISD	El Paso
254	782.2	Ector County ISD	Odessa
255	781.4	San Antonio ISD	San Antonio
256	781.0	Mineola ISD	Mineola
257	776.3	Coppell ISD	Coppell
258	773.3	Willis ISD	Willis
259	772.9	Denton ISD	Denton
260	771.1	Mission Cons ISD	Mission
261	770.5	Kingsville ISD	Kingsville
262	770.0	Lewisville ISD	Flower Mound
263	768.0	Georgetown ISD	Georgetown
264	767.5	Greenwood ISD	Midland
265	764.0	Mckinney ISD	Mckinney
266	763.0	Marlin ISD	Marlin
267	761.9	Roma ISD	Roma
268	761.2	Port Arthur ISD	Port Arthur
269	760.8	Pine Tree ISD	Longview
270	760.5	Lindale ISD	Lindale
271	759.5	Austin ISD	Austin
272	759.1	Huntsville ISD	Huntsville
273	756.0	Rains ISD	Emory
274	755.5	Splendora ISD	Splendora
275	753.7	Wichita Falls ISD	Wichita Falls
276	751.7	Desoto ISD	Desoto
277	750.0	Bandera ISD	Bandera
278	747.3	Little Elm ISD	Little Elm
279	741.9	Lamar CISD	Rosenberg
280	741.2	Burkburnett ISD	Burkburnett
281	740.8	Garland ISD	Garland
282	739.0	Borger ISD	Borger
283	737.4	Granbury ISD	Granbury
284	737.1	Fort Worth ISD	Fort Worth
285	733.7	Bridgeport ISD	Bridgeport
286	733.3	Sweeny ISD	Sweeny
287	732.8	Little Cypress-Mauriceville CISD	Orange
288	730.3	Edinburg CISD	Edinburg
289	729.7	Donna ISD	Donna
290	727.0	Hondo ISD	Hondo
291	726.7	Seminole ISD	Seminole
292	724.8	Princeton ISD	Princeton
293	724.0	Plainview ISD	Plainview
294	721.9	Hays Cons ISD	Kyle
295	720.2	Bay City ISD	Bay City
296	719.4	Grand Prairie ISD	Grand Prairie
297	718.7	Lake Worth ISD	Lake Worth
298	718.6	Henderson ISD	Henderson
299	713.5	San Marcos CISD	San Marcos
300	713.2	Eanes ISD	Austin
301	703.8	Bryan ISD	Bryan
302	692.4	Carrollton-Farmers Branch ISD	Carrollton
303	689.8	El Paso ISD	El Paso
304	689.5	Huffman ISD	Huffman
305	686.8	Harlandale ISD	San Antonio
306	682.7	Crandall ISD	Crandall
307	676.8	Brazosport ISD	Clute
308	675.0	Mathis ISD	Mathis
309	673.7	Birdville ISD	Haltom City
310	672.7	Cedar Hill ISD	Cedar Hill
311	671.8	Schertz-Cibolo-Universal City ISD	Schertz
312	670.9	Los Fresnos CISD	Los Fresnos
313	669.3	Liberty-Eylau ISD	Texarkana
314	668.9	Comal ISD	New Braunfels
315	668.5	Raymondville ISD	Raymondville
316	667.3	Lake Travis ISD	Austin
317	665.1	Gatesville ISD	Gatesville
318	663.7	Temple ISD	Temple
319	657.6	Mercedes ISD	Mercedes
320	657.2	Cleveland ISD	Cleveland
321	650.1	Midway ISD	Hewitt
322	645.8	Palacios ISD	Palacios
323	639.3	Pleasant Grove ISD	Texarkana
324	638.4	Lockhart ISD	Lockhart
325	637.3	Richardson ISD	Richardson
326	636.7	Bridge City ISD	Bridge City
327	636.5	Wharton ISD	Wharton
328	635.8	Canyon ISD	Canyon
329	633.3	Andrews ISD	Andrews
330	632.3	La Vega ISD	Waco
331	629.0	Iowa Park CISD	Iowa Park
332	624.0	West Oso ISD	Corpus Christi
333	619.2	Frisco ISD	Frisco
334	616.8	Pecos-Barstow-Toyah ISD	Pecos
335	615.0	Northwest ISD	Fort Worth
335	615.0	San Elizario ISD	San Elizario
337	607.2	Hidalgo ISD	Hidalgo
338	604.3	Giddings ISD	Giddings
339	604.0	Manor ISD	Manor
340	602.7	Springtown ISD	Springtown
341	602.3	Carroll ISD	Southlake
342	601.4	Carthage ISD	Carthage
343	599.3	Fort Stockton ISD	Fort Stockton
344	597.6	Sheldon ISD	Houston
345	597.0	Hillsboro ISD	Hillsboro
346	589.1	Dumas ISD	Dumas
347	589.0	Barbers Hill ISD	Mount Belvieu
348	586.5	Gilmer ISD	Gilmer
349	584.5	Copperas Cove ISD	Copperas Cove
350	576.7	Lake Dallas ISD	Lake Dallas
351	575.3	La Vernia ISD	La Vernia
352	574.5	Pittsburg ISD	Pittsburg
353	574.0	Midland ISD	Midland
354	573.5	Lubbock-Cooper ISD	Lubbock
355	561.3	Spring Hill ISD	Longview
356	559.7	Bowie ISD	Bowie
357	556.3	Gladewater ISD	Gladewater
358	555.9	Llano ISD	Llano
359	554.7	La Marque ISD	La Marque
360	551.0	Breckenridge ISD	Breckenridge
361	550.3	Poteet ISD	Poteet
362	546.7	Hutto ISD	Hutto
363	540.7	Point Isabel ISD	Port Isabel
364	539.7	Zapata County ISD	Zapata
365	538.0	Columbus ISD	Columbus
366	536.1	Cameron ISD	Cameron
367	535.6	Atlanta ISD	Atlanta
368	535.3	Groesbeck ISD	Groesbeck
369	532.3	Royal ISD	Brookshire
370	532.0	Progreso ISD	Progreso
371	520.9	West Orange-Cove CISD	Orange
372	520.6	Longview ISD	Longview
373	515.3	Whitney ISD	Whitney
374	513.3	West ISD	West
375	509.0	Royse City ISD	Royse City
376	508.7	Brownfield ISD	Brownfield
377	498.6	Hereford ISD	Hereford
378	498.4	Daingerfield-Lone Star ISD	Daingerfield
379	479.8	Lancaster ISD	Lancaster
380	472.4	Alice ISD	Alice
381	468.0	Smithville ISD	Smithville
382	444.8	Hamshire-Fannett ISD	Hamshire
383	437.3	Levelland ISD	Levelland
384	436.3	Port Neches-Groves ISD	Port Neches
385	401.4	South Texas ISD	Mercedes
386	0.0	Bullard ISD	Bullard
386	0.0	Honors Academy	Dallas
386	0.0	Lytle ISD	Lytle
386	0.0	Pearsall ISD	Pearsall

Student/Counselor Ratio

Rank	Ratio	District Name	City
1	1,459.2	Kilgore ISD	Kilgore
2	1,062.4	Shepherd ISD	Shepherd
3	898.6	Monahans-Wickett-Pyote ISD	Monahans
4	796.7	Huntington ISD	Huntington
5	796.0	Littlefield ISD	Littlefield
6	786.2	Alvarado ISD	Alvarado
7	770.0	West ISD	West
8	766.0	Galveston ISD	Galveston
9	755.6	Houston ISD	Houston
10	754.0	Winnsboro ISD	Winnsboro
11	745.1	Waxahachie ISD	Waxahachie
12	718.7	Lake Worth ISD	Lake Worth
13	682.7	Crandall ISD	Crandall
14	676.9	Dickinson ISD	Dickinson
15	665.4	Crockett ISD	Crockett
16	652.2	Lampasas ISD	Lampasas
17	644.3	Dayton ISD	Dayton
18	643.0	Honors Academy	Dallas
19	636.4	Lorena ISD	Lorena
20	634.4	Keller ISD	Keller
21	623.7	Venus ISD	Venus
22	617.5	Perryton ISD	Perryton
23	615.1	College Station ISD	College Station
24	610.0	Westwood ISD	Palestine
25	597.0	La Porte ISD	La Porte
26	596.9	Montgomery ISD	Montgomery
27	592.1	Big Spring ISD	Big Spring
28	591.7	Tomball ISD	Tomball
29	591.2	Borger ISD	Borger
30	590.0	Liberty Hill ISD	Liberty Hill
31	588.6	Crosby ISD	Crosby
32	588.5	Columbia-Brazoria ISD	West Columbia
33	585.3	Allen ISD	Allen
34	584.3	Ysleta ISD	El Paso
35	576.3	Canton ISD	Canton
36	567.5	Friendswood ISD	Friendswood
37	566.0	Wichita Falls ISD	Wichita Falls
38	562.0	Kaufman ISD	Kaufman
39	561.3	Spring Hill ISD	Longview
40	552.7	Andrews ISD	Andrews
41	549.2	Forney ISD	Forney
42	547.7	Cleveland ISD	Cleveland
43	546.7	Hutto ISD	Hutto
44	546.1	Pasadena ISD	Pasadena
45	541.0	Lamesa ISD	Lamesa
46	539.4	Galena Park ISD	Houston
47	537.0	Edna ISD	Edna
48	536.9	Nederland ISD	Nederland
49	535.3	Groesbeck ISD	Groesbeck
50	535.1	Edgewood ISD	San Antonio
51	534.4	Alvin ISD	Alvin
51	534.4	Katy ISD	Katy
53	533.7	Sherman ISD	Sherman
54	532.3	Royal ISD	Brookshire
55	531.4	Snyder ISD	Snyder
56	530.6	Wills Point ISD	Wills Point
57	530.3	Jasper ISD	Jasper
58	529.0	Dalhart ISD	Dalhart
59	527.0	San Diego ISD	San Diego
60	525.7	Carrollton-Farmers Branch ISD	Carrollton
61	524.7	Palacios ISD	Palacios
62	524.0	Orange Grove ISD	Orange Grove
63	523.9	Canutillo ISD	El Paso
64	523.4	Little Cypress-Mauriceville CISD	Orange
65	520.7	Mineola ISD	Mineola
66	515.5	Dumas ISD	Dumas
67	511.7	Greenwood ISD	Midland
68	510.3	Crowley ISD	Crowley
69	508.8	Lake Dallas ISD	Lake Dallas
70	508.7	Marlin ISD	Marlin
71	507.8	Gulf Shores Academy	Houston
72	507.4	Sulphur Springs ISD	Sulphur Springs
73	505.4	Decatur ISD	Decatur
74	504.0	Rains ISD	Emory
75	503.6	Judson ISD	San Antonio
76	503.5	Pearland ISD	Pearland
77	502.8	Desoto ISD	Desoto
78	501.2	Carthage ISD	Carthage
79	500.9	Gonzales ISD	Gonzales
80	500.4	Magnolia ISD	Magnolia
81	499.2	Hurst-Euless-Bedford ISD	Bedford
82	498.8	Royse City ISD	Royse City
83	498.5	Frenship ISD	Wolfforth
84	498.2	Little Elm ISD	Little Elm
85	497.0	Santa Fe ISD	Santa Fe
86	494.5	Pflugerville ISD	Pflugerville
87	493.5	Glen Rose ISD	Glen Rose
88	492.9	Athens ISD	Athens
88	492.9	North Lamar ISD	Paris
90	491.9	Madisonville CISD	Madisonville
91	491.7	Joshua ISD	Joshua
92	491.4	Center ISD	Center
93	490.8	Barbers Hill ISD	Mount Belvieu
93	490.8	Graham ISD	Graham
95	490.2	Burleson ISD	Burleson
96	489.2	Alief ISD	Houston
97	489.0	Quinlan ISD	Quinlan
98	486.1	Arlington ISD	Arlington
99	485.2	Clear Creek ISD	League City
100	483.3	La Grange ISD	La Grange
100	483.3	Mesquite ISD	Mesquite
102	482.9	Goose Creek CISD	Baytown
103	482.7	Beaumont ISD	Beaumont
104	482.6	Huntsville ISD	Huntsville
105	481.5	Mansfield ISD	Mansfield
106	480.6	Everman ISD	Everman
107	479.7	Buna ISD	Buna
108	479.5	Pleasant Grove ISD	Texarkana
109	478.9	Boerne ISD	Boerne
110	478.7	White Settlement ISD	White Settlement
111	478.5	Pine Tree ISD	Longview
112	477.1	Fort Bend ISD	Sugar Land
113	476.8	Gregory-Portland ISD	Gregory
114	474.5	Kennedale ISD	Kennedale
115	473.8	Rockdale ISD	Rockdale
116	472.5	Jacksonville ISD	Jacksonville
117	472.1	Lumberton ISD	Lumberton
118	471.1	Nacogdoches ISD	Nacogdoches
119	470.6	Brownwood ISD	Brownwood
120	469.3	Austin ISD	Austin
121	469.2	Gilmer ISD	Gilmer
122	468.7	Fabens ISD	Fabens
123	468.5	Cypress-Fairbanks ISD	Houston
124	468.3	Temple ISD	Temple
125	468.0	Canyon ISD	Canyon
126	467.3	Spring Branch ISD	Houston
127	467.1	Leander ISD	Leander
128	466.0	Marshall ISD	Marshall
129	464.6	Wimberley ISD	Wimberley
130	464.5	Angleton ISD	Angleton
131	464.2	Wylie ISD	Wylie
132	463.3	Burkburnett ISD	Burkburnett
133	462.2	Klein ISD	Klein
133	462.2	Sweetwater ISD	Sweetwater
135	461.6	Mckinney ISD	Mckinney
136	460.4	Killeen ISD	Killeen
137	459.8	Mexia ISD	Mexia
137	459.8	New Caney ISD	New Caney
139	459.7	Huffman ISD	Huffman
140	459.6	Pittsburg ISD	Pittsburg
141	458.6	Princeton ISD	Princeton
142	457.7	Fredericksburg ISD	Fredericksburg
143	456.0	Iowa Park CISD	Iowa Park
143	456.0	Tarkington ISD	Cleveland
143	456.0	Waller ISD	Waller
146	455.4	New Braunfels ISD	New Braunfels
147	453.2	United ISD	Laredo
148	451.4	Taylor ISD	Taylor
149	451.1	Tyler ISD	Tyler
150	451.0	Conroe ISD	Conroe
151	449.6	Grand Prairie ISD	Grand Prairie
152	449.4	Texas City ISD	Texas City
152	449.4	Whitehouse ISD	Whitehouse
154	449.3	Rockwall ISD	Rockwall
155	446.2	Poteet ISD	Poteet
156	446.0	Garland ISD	Garland
157	445.9	Azle ISD	Azle
158	444.8	Hamshire-Fannett ISD	Hamshire
159	444.5	Coldspring-Oakhurst CISD	Coldspring
160	444.1	Ingram ISD	Ingram
161	442.5	El Paso ISD	El Paso
162	442.0	Grapevine-Colleyville ISD	Grapevine
162	442.0	Yoakum ISD	Yoakum
164	441.7	Whitney ISD	Whitney
165	440.8	Roma ISD	Roma
166	439.9	Comal ISD	New Braunfels
167	439.5	China Spring ISD	Waco
168	438.4	Bridge City ISD	Bridge City
169	436.8	Ferris ISD	Ferris
170	436.6	Eagle Pass ISD	Eagle Pass
170	436.6	San Angelo ISD	San Angelo
172	436.5	Chapel Hill ISD	Tyler
172	436.5	Los Fresnos CISD	Los Fresnos
172	436.5	South San Antonio ISD	San Antonio
175	436.1	Round Rock ISD	Round Rock
176	435.2	Humble ISD	Humble
177	435.1	Laredo ISD	Laredo
178	434.7	Clint ISD	Clint
179	434.6	Lindale ISD	Lindale
180	434.4	Georgetown ISD	Georgetown
181	433.6	Deer Park ISD	Deer Park
182	433.4	Wylie ISD	Abilene
183	432.3	Gatesville ISD	Gatesville
184	432.0	Navasota ISD	Navasota
185	431.4	La Marque ISD	La Marque
186	431.1	Medina Valley ISD	Castroville
187	430.9	Del Valle ISD	Del Valle
187	430.9	Stephenville ISD	Stephenville
189	430.8	Whitesboro ISD	Whitesboro
190	430.0	Marble Falls ISD	Marble Falls
191	429.8	Brooks County ISD	Falfurrias
192	429.5	East Central ISD	San Antonio
193	427.2	Channelview ISD	Channelview
194	427.0	Frisco ISD	Frisco
195	426.9	Copperas Cove ISD	Copperas Cove
196	426.5	Aledo ISD	Aledo
197	424.3	Wharton ISD	Wharton
198	424.2	Midlothian ISD	Midlothian
199	423.7	Terrell ISD	Terrell
200	423.2	Birdville ISD	Haltom City
201	423.1	Bryan ISD	Bryan
202	421.6	Calhoun County ISD	Port Lavaca
203	421.4	Rio Hondo ISD	Rio Hondo
204	419.9	Schertz-Cibolo-Universal City ISD	Schertz
205	419.8	Bowie ISD	Bowie
206	419.5	Kemp ISD	Kemp
207	418.9	Socorro ISD	El Paso
208	418.8	Tuloso-Midway ISD	Corpus Christi
209	418.3	Sheldon ISD	Houston
210	416.8	Northwest ISD	Fort Worth
211	416.5	Longview ISD	Longview
212	416.1	Dallas ISD	Dallas
213	415.1	Wilmer-Hutchins ISD	Dallas
214	413.5	Aransas Pass ISD	Aransas Pass
215	413.3	Breckenridge ISD	Breckenridge
216	413.2	Aldine ISD	Houston
217	413.0	Carroll ISD	Southlake
218	412.8	Granbury ISD	Granbury
218	412.8	San Felipe-Del Rio CISD	Del Rio
220	411.2	Pecos-Barstow-Toyah ISD	Pecos
221	411.1	Cedar Hill ISD	Cedar Hill
222	410.8	Lufkin ISD	Lufkin
223	410.6	Willis ISD	Willis
224	410.4	Midway ISD	Hewitt
225	410.0	Burnet Cons ISD	Burnet
226	409.4	Alamo Heights ISD	San Antonio
226	409.4	Belton ISD	Belton
226	409.4	Denton ISD	Denton
226	409.4	Henderson ISD	Henderson
230	409.1	Ector County ISD	Odessa
231	408.5	Orangefield ISD	Orangefield
232	407.3	Coppell ISD	Coppell
232	407.3	Pharr-San Juan-Alamo ISD	Pharr
234	406.6	Spring ISD	Houston
235	406.3	Lockhart ISD	Lockhart
236	405.7	La Feria ISD	La Feria
237	405.3	Central ISD	Pollok
238	404.6	Fort Worth ISD	Fort Worth
239	403.5	Columbus ISD	Columbus
240	401.7	Southwest ISD	San Antonio
241	400.6	Harlandale ISD	San Antonio
242	400.0	Connally ISD	Waco
243	399.5	Fort Stockton ISD	Fort Stockton
244	398.9	Mineral Wells ISD	Mineral Wells
245	398.8	Cleburne ISD	Cleburne
246	398.5	Luling ISD	Luling
247	398.3	Lubbock ISD	Lubbock
248	396.7	Paris ISD	Paris
249	396.0	Hallsville ISD	Hallsville
250	394.3	Somerset ISD	Somerset
251	394.1	Plano ISD	Plano
252	394.0	Eustace ISD	Eustace
252	394.0	Silsbee ISD	Silsbee
254	393.8	Hays Cons ISD	Kyle
255	393.7	Harlingen Cons ISD	Harlingen
256	393.5	Atlanta ISD	Atlanta
256	393.5	Liberty ISD	Liberty
258	393.3	Southside ISD	San Antonio
259	391.6	Brazosport ISD	Clute
260	391.3	Brenham ISD	Brenham
261	391.1	Corsicana ISD	Corsicana
262	390.3	San Marcos CISD	San Marcos
263	390.0	La Vernia ISD	La Vernia
264	389.7	Hudson ISD	Lufkin
265	389.3	Kirbyville CISD	Kirbyville
266	388.7	Highland Park ISD	Dallas
267	388.5	Eagle Mt-Saginaw ISD	Fort Worth
268	386.9	Progreso ISD	Progreso
268	386.9	Vidor ISD	Vidor
270	386.7	Greenville ISD	Greenville
271	385.3	Lytle ISD	Lytle
272	384.6	Rusk ISD	Rusk
273	384.0	Diboll ISD	Diboll
274	382.8	Mount Pleasant ISD	Mt Pleasant
275	382.5	Edinburg CISD	Edinburg

Rank	Value	District Name	City
276	381.0	Flour Bluff ISD	Corpus Christi
277	380.2	Seguin ISD	Seguin
278	379.8	Devine ISD	Devine
279	377.8	Splendora ISD	Splendora
280	377.5	Manor ISD	Manor
281	377.2	Ingleside ISD	Ingleside
282	376.9	San Benito Cons ISD	San Benito
283	376.1	Palestine ISD	Palestine
284	375.5	Lancaster ISD	Lancaster
285	375.3	Bullard ISD	Bullard
286	374.4	Smithville ISD	Smithville
286	374.4	West Oso ISD	Corpus Christi
288	374.3	San Antonio ISD	San Antonio
289	371.9	Gainesville ISD	Gainesville
290	371.8	Irving ISD	Irving
291	371.7	Waco ISD	Waco
292	370.8	Gladewater ISD	Gladewater
293	369.7	Hondo ISD	Hondo
294	369.5	Seminole ISD	Seminole
295	369.2	Calallen ISD	Corpus Christi
295	369.2	Port Neches-Groves ISD	Port Neches
297	366.7	Sweeny ISD	Sweeny
298	366.5	Plainview ISD	Plainview
299	366.3	Van ISD	Van
300	366.2	Port Arthur ISD	Port Arthur
301	365.7	Victoria ISD	Victoria
302	364.9	Lake Travis ISD	Austin
303	363.9	Abilene ISD	Abilene
304	362.9	Mabank ISD	Mabank
305	362.8	Vernon ISD	Vernon
306	362.6	Hereford ISD	Hereford
307	362.4	Amarillo ISD	Amarillo
307	362.4	Weatherford ISD	Weatherford
309	362.2	North East ISD	San Antonio
310	361.8	Liberty-Eylau ISD	Texarkana
311	361.3	Cameron ISD	Cameron
311	361.3	La Vega ISD	Waco
313	360.1	Bay City ISD	Bay City
314	357.3	El Campo ISD	El Campo
315	355.8	Corpus Christi ISD	Corpus Christi
315	355.8	Hardin-Jefferson ISD	Sour Lake
315	355.8	Kerrville ISD	Kerrville
318	354.1	Richardson ISD	Richardson
319	352.0	Lewisville ISD	Flower Mound
320	351.5	Stafford Municipal School	Stafford
321	350.7	Mercedes ISD	Mercedes
322	350.4	Lamar CISD	Rosenberg
323	348.1	Needville ISD	Needville
324	345.7	Weslaco ISD	Weslaco
325	341.5	Floresville ISD	Floresville
326	341.1	Elgin ISD	Elgin
326	341.1	Pampa ISD	Pampa
328	339.4	Bellville ISD	Bellville
329	338.8	North Forest ISD	Houston
330	337.5	Llano ISD	Llano
331	336.9	Valley View ISD	Pharr
332	336.3	Brownfield ISD	Brownfield
333	335.5	San Elizario ISD	San Elizario
334	335.4	Texarkana ISD	Texarkana
335	334.3	Raymondville ISD	Raymondville
336	333.5	Alice ISD	Alice
336	333.5	Sharyland ISD	Mission
338	332.4	Midland ISD	Midland
339	332.3	Cuero ISD	Cuero
340	332.1	Northside ISD	San Antonio
340	332.1	Robinson ISD	Robinson
342	332.0	Duncanville ISD	Duncanville
343	328.1	Bandera ISD	Bandera
344	327.7	Lubbock-Cooper ISD	Lubbock
345	327.6	Aransas County ISD	Rockport
346	326.3	Brownsville ISD	Brownsville
347	325.2	Castleberry ISD	Fort Worth
348	324.6	Edcouch-Elsa ISD	Edcouch
349	324.4	Point Isabel ISD	Port Isabel
350	323.2	Mission Cons ISD	Mission
351	322.3	Denison ISD	Denison
352	320.7	Red Oak ISD	Red Oak
353	319.4	Zapata County ISD	Zapata
354	319.0	Daingerfield-Lone Star ISD	Daingerfield
355	317.2	Pleasanton ISD	Pleasanton
356	317.0	Eanes ISD	Austin
357	312.7	Donna ISD	Donna
358	306.2	Dripping Springs ISD	Dripping Spgs
359	304.8	Bastrop ISD	Bastrop
360	303.6	Hidalgo ISD	Hidalgo
361	303.1	West Orange-Cove CISD	Orange
362	302.2	Giddings ISD	Giddings
363	301.3	Springtown ISD	Springtown
364	301.0	Lyford CISD	Lyford
365	299.4	Crystal City ISD	Crystal City
366	298.5	Hillsboro ISD	Hillsboro
367	297.9	Rio Grande City CISD	Rio Grande City
368	297.3	La Joya ISD	La Joya
369	294.2	Ennis ISD	Ennis
370	293.5	Beeville ISD	Beeville
371	292.4	Uvalde CISD	Uvalde
372	292.3	Sanger ISD	Sanger
373	287.1	Bonham ISD	Bonham
374	284.9	Pearsall ISD	Pearsall
375	284.3	Sinton ISD	Sinton
376	278.3	Levelland ISD	Levelland
377	275.1	Bridgeport ISD	Bridgeport
378	273.4	Caldwell ISD	Caldwell
379	266.4	Robstown ISD	Robstown
380	262.0	Commerce ISD	Commerce
381	256.8	Kingsville ISD	Kingsville
382	255.3	Livingston ISD	Livingston
383	253.1	Mathis ISD	Mathis
384	251.4	Mcallen ISD	Mcallen
385	238.2	Brownsboro ISD	Brownsboro
386	234.4	Sealy ISD	Sealy
387	228.2	Carrizo Springs CISD	Carrizo Springs
388	203.8	Fairfield ISD	Fairfield
389	200.7	South Texas ISD	Mercedes

Current Spending per Student in FY2001

Rank	Dollars	District Name	City
1	10,154	Glen Rose ISD	Glen Rose
2	9,210	South Texas ISD	Mercedes
3	8,989	Seminole ISD	Seminole
4	8,341	West Orange-Cove CISD	Orange
5	8,211	Llano ISD	Llano
6	8,196	Fort Stockton ISD	Fort Stockton
7	8,194	Andrews ISD	Andrews
8	8,109	Northwest ISD	Fort Worth
9	7,971	Hidalgo ISD	Hidalgo
10	7,899	Cuero ISD	Cuero
11	7,855	Mathis ISD	Mathis
12	7,754	Hillsboro ISD	Hillsboro
13	7,665	Daingerfield-Lone Star ISD	Daingerfield
14	7,663	Snyder ISD	Snyder
15	7,628	Mercedes ISD	Mercedes
16	7,627	Palacios ISD	Palacios
17	7,623	Harlandale ISD	San Antonio
18	7,621	Ingram ISD	Ingram
19	7,609	Lyford CISD	Lyford
20	7,571	Groesbeck ISD	Groesbeck
21	7,547	Sheldon ISD	Houston
22	7,530	Fairfield ISD	Fairfield
23	7,502	Rio Hondo ISD	Rio Hondo
24	7,482	Manor ISD	Manor
25	7,463	Carthage ISD	Carthage
26	7,453	Carrizo Springs CISD	Carrizo Springs
27	7,449	Sanger ISD	Sanger
28	7,427	Crystal City ISD	Crystal City
29	7,423	Brooks County ISD	Falfurrias
30	7,364	Liberty ISD	Liberty
31	7,344	Poteet ISD	Poteet
32	7,327	Alamo Heights ISD	San Antonio
33	7,295	Liberty Hill ISD	Liberty Hill
34	7,268	Progreso ISD	Progreso
35	7,263	Levelland ISD	Levelland
36	7,261	West Oso ISD	Corpus Christi
37	7,250	Rio Grande City CISD	Rio Grande City
38	7,247	Aransas County ISD	Rockport
39	7,240	Port Arthur ISD	Port Arthur
40	7,218	Mexia ISD	Mexia
41	7,212	Monahans-Wickett-Pyote ISD	Monahans
42	7,178	Liberty-Eylau ISD	Texarkana
43	7,167	La Vega ISD	Waco
44	7,150	Paris ISD	Paris
45	7,147	Silsbee ISD	Silsbee
46	7,118	Calhoun County ISD	Port Lavaca
47	7,117	Sweeny ISD	Sweeny
48	7,109	Edcouch-Elsa ISD	Edcouch
49	7,081	Wylie ISD	Wylie
50	7,060	Weslaco ISD	Weslaco
51	7,055	Jasper ISD	Jasper
52	7,054	Sweetwater ISD	Sweetwater
53	7,031	Diboll ISD	Diboll
54	7,017	Mcallen ISD	Mcallen
55	7,016	Pearsall ISD	Pearsall
56	7,014	Texas City ISD	Texas City
57	7,013	Little Elm ISD	Little Elm
58	6,997	San Elizario ISD	San Elizario
59	6,994	Raymondville ISD	Raymondville
60	6,991	Mission Cons ISD	Mission
61	6,975	Crockett ISD	Crockett
62	6,973	Barbers Hill ISD	Mount Belvieu
63	6,970	Brownfield ISD	Brownfield
64	6,969	Buna ISD	Buna
64	6,969	Eanes ISD	Austin
66	6,964	Austin ISD	Austin
67	6,948	Royal ISD	Brookshire
68	6,933	Del Valle ISD	Del Valle
68	6,933	San Antonio ISD	San Antonio
70	6,931	Edgewood ISD	San Antonio
71	6,930	Kingsville ISD	Kingsville
72	6,929	Sinton ISD	Sinton
73	6,924	Los Fresnos CISD	Los Fresnos
74	6,923	Mount Pleasant ISD	Mt Pleasant
75	6,913	San Benito Cons ISD	San Benito
76	6,912	Marlin ISD	Marlin
77	6,899	North Forest ISD	Houston
78	6,881	Spring Branch ISD	Houston
79	6,875	Valley View ISD	Pharr
80	6,847	Bastrop ISD	Bastrop
81	6,842	Donna ISD	Donna
82	6,838	Goose Creek CISD	Baytown
83	6,835	Aldine ISD	Houston
84	6,833	Commerce ISD	Commerce
85	6,832	Bridgeport ISD	Bridgeport
86	6,803	Hutto ISD	Hutto
87	6,789	Carroll ISD	Southlake
88	6,788	Brownsville ISD	Brownsville
88	6,788	Marble Falls ISD	Marble Falls
90	6,784	Yoakum ISD	Yoakum
91	6,782	Caldwell ISD	Caldwell
92	6,770	Lake Worth ISD	Lake Worth
93	6,767	San Marcos CISD	San Marcos
94	6,765	Atlanta ISD	Atlanta
94	6,765	Somerset ISD	Somerset
96	6,752	Montgomery ISD	Montgomery
97	6,750	Canutillo ISD	El Paso
98	6,745	Elgin ISD	Elgin
99	6,741	Fabens ISD	Fabens
100	6,737	Highland Park ISD	Dallas
101	6,734	Lamar CISD	Rosenberg
102	6,732	Floresville ISD	Floresville
103	6,724	Houston ISD	Houston
104	6,711	Longview ISD	Longview
105	6,699	Beaumont ISD	Beaumont
105	6,699	South San Antonio ISD	San Antonio
107	6,694	Deer Park ISD	Deer Park
108	6,693	Taylor ISD	Taylor
109	6,687	Plano ISD	Plano
110	6,682	El Campo ISD	El Campo
111	6,679	Grapevine-Colleyville ISD	Grapevine
112	6,674	Victoria ISD	Victoria
113	6,672	Abilene ISD	Abilene
114	6,652	Springtown ISD	Springtown
115	6,645	Pleasanton ISD	Pleasanton
116	6,643	Copperas Cove ISD	Copperas Cove
117	6,635	Edinburg CISD	Edinburg
118	6,632	Aransas Pass ISD	Aransas Pass
119	6,630	Bowie ISD	Bowie
120	6,622	Bandera ISD	Bandera
121	6,620	Pharr-San Juan-Alamo ISD	Pharr
122	6,619	Wimberley ISD	Wimberley
123	6,618	Georgetown ISD	Georgetown
124	6,616	La Porte ISD	La Porte
125	6,614	Wharton ISD	Wharton
126	6,610	Denton ISD	Denton
127	6,609	Lake Travis ISD	Austin
128	6,600	Robstown ISD	Robstown
129	6,581	Bonham ISD	Bonham
130	6,576	Wilmer-Hutchins ISD	Dallas
131	6,573	Uvalde CISD	Uvalde
132	6,572	Dallas ISD	Dallas
133	6,571	La Marque ISD	La Marque
134	6,565	Temple ISD	Temple
135	6,549	Galveston ISD	Galveston
136	6,548	Burnet Cons ISD	Burnet
137	6,546	Edna ISD	Edna
138	6,539	Carrollton-Farmers Branch ISD	Carrollton
139	6,515	College Station ISD	College Station
140	6,514	Fredericksburg ISD	Fredericksburg
141	6,512	Point Isabel ISD	Port Isabel
142	6,510	Hardin-Jefferson ISD	Sour Lake
143	6,507	Zapata County ISD	Zapata
144	6,497	Beeville ISD	Beeville
145	6,496	Mineral Wells ISD	Mineral Wells
146	6,491	Coppell ISD	Coppell
147	6,484	Wichita Falls ISD	Wichita Falls
148	6,483	Lubbock ISD	Lubbock
149	6,478	Smithville ISD	Smithville
150	6,471	Madisonville CISD	Madisonville
151	6,460	Connally ISD	Waco
152	6,456	Palestine ISD	Palestine
153	6,450	Terrell ISD	Terrell
154	6,445	Ingleside ISD	Ingleside
155	6,441	Big Spring ISD	Big Spring
156	6,438	San Diego ISD	San Diego
157	6,431	Dripping Springs ISD	Dripping Spgs
158	6,417	Vernon ISD	Vernon
159	6,415	Crosby ISD	Crosby
160	6,410	Round Rock ISD	Round Rock

161	6,395	Port Neches-Groves ISD	Port Neches
162	6,391	Henderson ISD	Henderson
163	6,385	Huffman ISD	Huffman
164	6,384	Dalhart ISD	Dalhart
165	6,382	Bryan ISD	Bryan
165	6,382	Richardson ISD	Richardson
167	6,381	Hondo ISD	Hondo
168	6,375	Rockdale ISD	Rockdale
169	6,374	Sealy ISD	Sealy
170	6,365	Fort Worth ISD	Fort Worth
171	6,363	Littlefield ISD	Littlefield
172	6,357	Cypress-Fairbanks ISD	Houston
173	6,356	Alvin ISD	Alvin
173	6,356	North East ISD	San Antonio
175	6,350	Gilmer ISD	Gilmer
176	6,341	Lockhart ISD	Lockhart
177	6,338	La Joya ISD	La Joya
178	6,337	Hereford ISD	Hereford
179	6,335	Clint ISD	Clint
180	6,312	La Feria ISD	La Feria
181	6,309	Hallsville ISD	Hallsville
182	6,298	Brenham ISD	Brenham
183	6,295	Chapel Hill ISD	Tyler
183	6,295	Killeen ISD	Killeen
185	6,293	Gonzales ISD	Gonzales
186	6,292	Lytle ISD	Lytle
187	6,286	Midland ISD	Midland
188	6,284	Livingston ISD	Livingston
189	6,283	Giddings ISD	Giddings
190	6,282	East Central ISD	San Antonio
191	6,281	San Felipe-Del Rio CISD	Del Rio
191	6,281	Waller ISD	Waller
193	6,279	Seguin ISD	Seguin
194	6,275	Gladewater ISD	Gladewater
195	6,271	Laredo ISD	Laredo
196	6,267	Waco ISD	Waco
197	6,259	Irving ISD	Irving
198	6,258	Klein ISD	Klein
199	6,253	Sulphur Springs ISD	Sulphur Springs
200	6,246	Ferris ISD	Ferris
201	6,245	Cameron ISD	Cameron
202	6,238	Northside ISD	San Antonio
203	6,229	Mabank ISD	Mabank
203	6,229	Mckinney ISD	Mckinney
205	6,225	Lamesa ISD	Lamesa
205	6,225	White Settlement ISD	White Settlement
207	6,224	Alice ISD	Alice
207	6,224	Devine ISD	Devine
209	6,222	Dickinson ISD	Dickinson
210	6,220	Perryton ISD	Perryton
211	6,217	Royse City ISD	Royse City
212	6,215	Harlingen Cons ISD	Harlingen
212	6,215	Judson ISD	San Antonio
214	6,212	Rusk ISD	Rusk
215	6,200	Coldspring-Oakhurst CISD	Coldspring
216	6,197	Athens ISD	Athens
216	6,197	El Paso ISD	El Paso
218	6,192	Medina Valley ISD	Castroville
218	6,192	Tomball ISD	Tomball
220	6,190	Frisco ISD	Frisco
221	6,184	Corpus Christi ISD	Corpus Christi
222	6,183	Brownwood ISD	Brownwood
223	6,182	Bay City ISD	Bay City
223	6,182	Corsicana ISD	Corsicana
225	6,176	Lake Dallas ISD	Lake Dallas
226	6,174	Gainesville ISD	Gainesville
226	6,174	Orange Grove ISD	Orange Grove
228	6,173	Comal ISD	New Braunfels
229	6,169	Everman ISD	Everman
230	6,168	Galena Park ISD	Houston
230	6,168	Hays Cons ISD	Kyle
232	6,165	Waxahachie ISD	Waxahachie
233	6,163	Stafford Municipal School	Stafford
234	6,155	Humble ISD	Humble
235	6,153	Splendora ISD	Splendora
236	6,147	Hurst-Euless-Bedford ISD	Bedford
237	6,143	Spring ISD	Houston
238	6,138	Pecos-Barstow-Toyah ISD	Pecos
239	6,130	Lewisville ISD	Flower Mound
240	6,126	Ector County ISD	Odessa
241	6,125	Aledo ISD	Aledo
242	6,122	Jacksonville ISD	Jacksonville
243	6,121	Katy ISD	Katy
244	6,117	Ennis ISD	Ennis
245	6,108	Belton ISD	Belton
245	6,108	Brazosport ISD	Clute
247	6,107	Kerrville ISD	Kerrville
248	6,102	Eagle Pass ISD	Eagle Pass
249	6,092	Lubbock-Cooper ISD	Lubbock
250	6,090	Tuloso-Midway ISD	Corpus Christi
251	6,087	Lancaster ISD	Lancaster
252	6,080	Crowley ISD	Crowley
252	6,080	La Grange ISD	La Grange
252	6,080	Magnolia ISD	Magnolia
255	6,079	Brownsboro ISD	Brownsboro
256	6,069	Duncanville ISD	Duncanville
257	6,067	Ysleta ISD	El Paso
258	6,065	Nacogdoches ISD	Nacogdoches
259	6,061	China Spring ISD	Waco
260	6,060	Boerne ISD	Boerne
261	6,056	Texarkana ISD	Texarkana
262	6,055	Navasota ISD	Navasota
263	6,053	Little Cypress-Mauriceville CISD	Orange
264	6,044	Hamshire-Fannett ISD	Hamshire
265	6,043	Birdville ISD	Haltom City
266	6,032	Denison ISD	Denison
267	6,024	Lufkin ISD	Lufkin
268	6,023	Roma ISD	Roma
269	6,018	Columbus ISD	Columbus
270	6,014	Honors Academy	Dallas
271	6,012	Channelview ISD	Channelview
272	6,008	Southwest ISD	San Antonio
273	6,001	Flour Bluff ISD	Corpus Christi
274	5,996	Castleberry ISD	Fort Worth
275	5,993	Kaufman ISD	Kaufman
276	5,992	Allen ISD	Allen
277	5,990	Willis ISD	Willis
278	5,987	Alief ISD	Houston
279	5,986	Lumberton ISD	Lumberton
280	5,982	Amarillo ISD	Amarillo
281	5,979	Greenville ISD	Greenville
282	5,976	Robinson ISD	Robinson
282	5,976	Sherman ISD	Sherman
284	5,968	Vidor ISD	Vidor
285	5,965	Tyler ISD	Tyler
286	5,955	Leander ISD	Leander
287	5,945	Pittsburg ISD	Pittsburg
288	5,943	Cedar Hill ISD	Cedar Hill
289	5,937	Kemp ISD	Kemp
290	5,932	Fort Bend ISD	Sugar Land
291	5,931	Joshua ISD	Joshua
292	5,927	Plainview ISD	Plainview
293	5,922	Gregory-Portland ISD	Gregory
294	5,915	Spring Hill ISD	Longview
295	5,910	Breckenridge ISD	Breckenridge
296	5,902	New Braunfels ISD	New Braunfels
297	5,900	Columbia-Brazoria ISD	West Columbia
298	5,898	Van ISD	Van
299	5,895	Borger ISD	Borger
299	5,895	Crandall ISD	Crandall
301	5,894	Southside ISD	San Antonio
302	5,884	Pampa ISD	Pampa
303	5,883	Conroe ISD	Conroe
303	5,883	Whitesboro ISD	Whitesboro
305	5,880	Quinlan ISD	Quinlan
306	5,878	Granbury ISD	Granbury
307	5,869	Huntington ISD	Huntington
308	5,868	Calallen ISD	Corpus Christi
309	5,864	Cleveland ISD	Cleveland
309	5,864	Grand Prairie ISD	Grand Prairie
311	5,863	Azle ISD	Azle
312	5,860	Midlothian ISD	Midlothian
313	5,856	Alvarado ISD	Alvarado
314	5,854	Forney ISD	Forney
315	5,840	Shepherd ISD	Shepherd
316	5,833	Burkburnett ISD	Burkburnett
316	5,833	United ISD	Laredo
318	5,832	Angleton ISD	Angleton
318	5,832	Nederland ISD	Nederland
320	5,815	Sharyland ISD	Mission
321	5,812	Canton ISD	Canton
322	5,811	Pasadena ISD	Pasadena
323	5,809	Rains ISD	Emory
324	5,806	Decatur ISD	Decatur
325	5,778	Mineola ISD	Mineola
326	5,772	Weatherford ISD	Weatherford
327	5,761	Rockwall ISD	Rockwall
328	5,750	Graham ISD	Graham
329	5,742	San Angelo ISD	San Angelo
330	5,739	Arlington ISD	Arlington
330	5,739	Bellville ISD	Bellville
332	5,731	Mansfield ISD	Mansfield
332	5,731	New Caney ISD	New Caney
334	5,726	Huntsville ISD	Huntsville
335	5,721	Eagle Mt-Saginaw ISD	Fort Worth
336	5,716	Kirbyville CISD	Kirbyville
337	5,715	Needville ISD	Needville
338	5,712	Lindale ISD	Lindale
339	5,708	Friendswood ISD	Friendswood
339	5,708	Lampasas ISD	Lampasas
341	5,707	Kennedale ISD	Kennedale
342	5,694	Whitney ISD	Whitney
343	5,675	Winnsboro ISD	Winnsboro
344	5,673	Bridge City ISD	Bridge City
345	5,670	Center ISD	Center
346	5,668	Red Oak ISD	Red Oak
346	5,668	Schertz-Cibolo-Universal City ISD	Schertz
348	5,657	Orangefield ISD	Orangefield
349	5,654	Pflugerville ISD	Pflugerville
350	5,650	Clear Creek ISD	League City
351	5,642	Burleson ISD	Burleson
352	5,641	Wills Point ISD	Wills Point
353	5,634	Desoto ISD	Desoto
354	5,632	Pearland ISD	Pearland
355	5,627	Mesquite ISD	Mesquite
356	5,622	Santa Fe ISD	Santa Fe
357	5,621	Dumas ISD	Dumas
358	5,595	Stephenville ISD	Stephenville
359	5,584	North Lamar ISD	Paris
360	5,575	Marshall ISD	Marshall
361	5,565	Princeton ISD	Princeton
362	5,564	Hudson ISD	Lufkin
363	5,559	Socorro ISD	El Paso
364	5,532	Frenship ISD	Wolfforth
365	5,524	Luling ISD	Luling
366	5,502	Cleburne ISD	Cleburne
367	5,488	Venus ISD	Venus
368	5,475	Kilgore ISD	Kilgore
369	5,466	Greenwood ISD	Midland
370	5,436	Dayton ISD	Dayton
370	5,436	La Vernia ISD	La Vernia
372	5,412	West ISD	West
373	5,399	Central ISD	Pollok
374	5,384	Midway ISD	Hewitt
375	5,379	Eustace ISD	Eustace
376	5,365	Keller ISD	Keller
377	5,360	Pleasant Grove ISD	Texarkana
378	5,354	Garland ISD	Garland
379	5,335	Pine Tree ISD	Longview
380	5,279	Gatesville ISD	Gatesville
381	5,242	Iowa Park CISD	Iowa Park
382	5,201	Westwood ISD	Palestine
383	5,063	Gulf Shores Academy	Houston
384	5,059	Tarkington ISD	Cleveland
385	4,991	Canyon ISD	Canyon
386	4,990	Whitehouse ISD	Whitehouse
387	4,928	Bullard ISD	Bullard
388	4,846	Lorena ISD	Lorena
389	4,531	Wylie ISD	Abilene

Number of Diploma Recipients

Rank	Number	District Name	City
1	7,945	Houston ISD	Houston
2	6,532	Dallas ISD	Dallas
3	3,938	Cypress-Fairbanks ISD	Houston
4	3,928	Northside ISD	San Antonio
5	3,705	Austin ISD	Austin
6	3,630	Fort Bend ISD	Sugar Land
7	3,353	El Paso ISD	El Paso
8	3,222	Fort Worth ISD	Fort Worth
9	3,208	North East ISD	San Antonio
10	2,875	Arlington ISD	Arlington
11	2,842	Ysleta ISD	El Paso
12	2,795	Plano ISD	Plano
13	2,727	San Antonio ISD	San Antonio
14	2,689	Garland ISD	Garland
15	2,267	Lewisville ISD	Flower Mound
16	2,202	Conroe ISD	Conroe
17	2,149	Aldine ISD	Houston
18	2,119	Corpus Christi ISD	Corpus Christi
19	2,112	Katy ISD	Katy
19	2,112	Klein ISD	Klein
21	2,028	Pasadena ISD	Pasadena
22	1,977	Round Rock ISD	Round Rock
23	1,960	Alief ISD	Houston
24	1,956	Mesquite ISD	Mesquite
25	1,891	Richardson ISD	Richardson
26	1,854	Brownsville ISD	Brownsville
27	1,844	Clear Creek ISD	League City
28	1,751	Spring Branch ISD	Houston
29	1,737	Lubbock ISD	Lubbock
30	1,653	Humble ISD	Humble
31	1,544	Amarillo ISD	Amarillo
32	1,533	Socorro ISD	El Paso
33	1,478	Ector County ISD	Odessa
34	1,360	United ISD	Laredo
35	1,358	Killeen ISD	Killeen
36	1,334	Spring ISD	Houston
37	1,308	Irving ISD	Irving
38	1,277	Carrollton-Farmers Branch ISD	Carrollton
39	1,270	Mcallen ISD	Mcallen
40	1,227	Hurst-Euless-Bedford ISD	Bedford
41	1,207	Midland ISD	Midland
42	1,164	Birdville ISD	Haltom City
43	1,153	Beaumont ISD	Beaumont
44	1,080	Laredo ISD	Laredo

Rank	Number	District	City
45	1,077	Galena Park ISD	Houston
46	1,071	Wichita Falls ISD	Wichita Falls
47	1,045	Pharr-San Juan-Alamo ISD	Pharr
48	1,038	Edinburg CISD	Edinburg
49	1,035	Grand Prairie ISD	Grand Prairie
50	1,032	Abilene ISD	Abilene
51	1,013	Keller ISD	Keller
52	960	San Angelo ISD	San Angelo
53	956	Grapevine-Colleyville ISD	Grapevine
54	901	Tyler ISD	Tyler
55	899	Goose Creek CISD	Baytown
56	867	Victoria ISD	Victoria
57	864	Pflugerville ISD	Pflugerville
58	842	Judson ISD	San Antonio
59	807	Harlingen Cons ISD	Harlingen
60	800	Harlandale ISD	San Antonio
61	796	Lamar CISD	Rosenberg
62	791	Mansfield ISD	Mansfield
63	765	La Joya ISD	La Joya
63	765	Leander ISD	Leander
65	739	Allen ISD	Allen
66	733	Brazosport ISD	Clute
67	720	Denton ISD	Denton
68	707	Duncanville ISD	Duncanville
69	699	Bryan ISD	Bryan
70	681	Comal ISD	New Braunfels
71	678	Deer Park ISD	Deer Park
72	628	Pearland ISD	Pearland
73	622	Edgewood ISD	San Antonio
74	611	Weslaco ISD	Weslaco
75	604	Mckinney ISD	Mckinney
76	603	Crowley ISD	Crowley
77	588	Waco ISD	Waco
78	582	Eagle Pass ISD	Eagle Pass
79	569	Mission Cons ISD	Mission
80	547	Port Arthur ISD	Port Arthur
81	542	Coppell ISD	Coppell
82	530	Georgetown ISD	Georgetown
83	528	Eanes ISD	Austin
84	512	College Station ISD	College Station
85	509	Alvin ISD	Alvin
86	505	North Forest ISD	Houston
87	497	Canyon ISD	Canyon
88	492	East Central ISD	San Antonio
88	492	Rockwall ISD	Rockwall
90	485	Hays Cons ISD	Kyle
91	482	San Felipe-Del Rio CISD	Del Rio
92	476	Lufkin ISD	Lufkin
92	476	Southwest ISD	San Antonio
94	474	South San Antonio ISD	San Antonio
95	472	La Porte ISD	La Porte
96	467	Schertz-Cibolo-Universal City ISD	Schertz
97	463	Belton ISD	Belton
98	449	Copperas Cove ISD	Copperas Cove
99	441	Temple ISD	Temple
100	439	Carroll ISD	Southlake
101	435	Tomball ISD	Tomball
102	429	Donna ISD	Donna
103	428	Magnolia ISD	Magnolia
104	420	Rio Grande City CISD	Rio Grande City
105	419	Galveston ISD	Galveston
106	414	Highland Park ISD	Dallas
107	413	Burleson ISD	Burleson
107	413	New Braunfels ISD	New Braunfels
109	410	Weatherford ISD	Weatherford
110	407	San Marcos CISD	San Marcos
111	406	Clint ISD	Clint
111	406	Eagle Mt-Saginaw ISD	Fort Worth
111	406	Longview ISD	Longview
114	399	Nacogdoches ISD	Nacogdoches
114	399	San Benito Cons ISD	San Benito
116	390	Waxahachie ISD	Waxahachie
117	386	Desoto ISD	Desoto
118	384	Seguin ISD	Seguin
119	382	Cedar Hill ISD	Cedar Hill
119	382	Midway ISD	Hewitt
121	381	Friendswood ISD	Friendswood
122	374	Marshall ISD	Marshall
122	374	Plainview ISD	Plainview
122	374	Port Neches-Groves ISD	Port Neches
125	369	Los Fresnos CISD	Los Fresnos
126	358	Kingsville ISD	Kingsville
127	357	Huntsville ISD	Huntsville
128	355	Azle ISD	Azle
129	353	Boerne ISD	Boerne
129	353	South Texas ISD	Mercedes
131	347	Alamo Heights ISD	San Antonio
132	346	Granbury ISD	Granbury
133	340	Bastrop ISD	Bastrop
134	338	Brenham ISD	Brenham
135	337	Vidor ISD	Vidor
136	334	Frenship ISD	Wolfforth
136	334	Frisco ISD	Frisco
138	326	Nederland ISD	Nederland
139	324	Flour Bluff ISD	Corpus Christi
140	321	Calallen ISD	Corpus Christi
141	318	Angleton ISD	Angleton
142	311	Cleburne ISD	Cleburne
143	302	Del Valle ISD	Del Valle
143	302	Kerrville ISD	Kerrville
145	301	Channelview ISD	Channelview
146	300	Pine Tree ISD	Longview
146	300	Sherman ISD	Sherman
148	291	Roma ISD	Roma
149	289	Greenville ISD	Greenville
150	285	Lockhart ISD	Lockhart
150	285	Northwest ISD	Fort Worth
152	283	White Settlement ISD	White Settlement
153	281	Waller ISD	Waller
154	279	Edcouch-Elsa ISD	Edcouch
155	277	New Caney ISD	New Caney
156	276	Texarkana ISD	Texarkana
157	274	Gregory-Portland ISD	Gregory
158	273	Little Cypress-Mauriceville CISD	Orange
158	273	Uvalde CISD	Uvalde
160	271	Bay City ISD	Bay City
161	270	Corsicana ISD	Corsicana
161	270	Mount Pleasant ISD	Mt Pleasant
163	269	Alice ISD	Alice
163	269	Lake Travis ISD	Austin
165	268	Hereford ISD	Hereford
166	264	Southside ISD	San Antonio
166	264	Texas City ISD	Texas City
166	264	Whitehouse ISD	Whitehouse
169	260	Ennis ISD	Ennis
170	259	Willis ISD	Willis
171	258	Midlothian ISD	Midlothian
172	257	Sharyland ISD	Mission
173	256	Mercedes ISD	Mercedes
174	254	Sulphur Springs ISD	Sulphur Springs
175	253	Pampa ISD	Pampa
176	252	Lancaster ISD	Lancaster
177	250	Brownwood ISD	Brownwood
177	250	Livingston ISD	Livingston
179	249	Joshua ISD	Joshua
179	249	Red Oak ISD	Red Oak
181	247	Dayton ISD	Dayton
181	247	Dickinson ISD	Dickinson
183	243	Dumas ISD	Dumas
184	241	La Marque ISD	La Marque
184	241	Santa Fe ISD	Santa Fe
186	239	El Campo ISD	El Campo
186	239	Jacksonville ISD	Jacksonville
188	237	Hallsville ISD	Hallsville
189	235	Wylie ISD	Wylie
190	233	Canutillo ISD	El Paso
191	230	Burkburnett ISD	Burkburnett
191	230	Dripping Springs ISD	Dripping Spgs
191	230	Henderson ISD	Henderson
194	227	Big Spring ISD	Big Spring
194	227	Kilgore ISD	Kilgore
196	226	Denison ISD	Denison
197	225	Calhoun County ISD	Port Lavaca
197	225	Honors Academy	Dallas
199	224	Stephenville ISD	Stephenville
200	223	Beeville ISD	Beeville
200	223	Tuloso-Midway ISD	Corpus Christi
202	222	Lumberton ISD	Lumberton
203	221	Andrews ISD	Andrews
204	219	Crosby ISD	Crosby
204	219	Fredericksburg ISD	Fredericksburg
206	218	Aledo ISD	Aledo
207	215	Pleasanton ISD	Pleasanton
208	212	Lampasas ISD	Lampasas
209	210	Aransas County ISD	Rockport
210	208	Silsbee ISD	Silsbee
210	208	Terrell ISD	Terrell
212	207	Floresville ISD	Floresville
213	204	Montgomery ISD	Montgomery
214	203	North Lamar ISD	Paris
215	202	Chapel Hill ISD	Tyler
215	202	Medina Valley ISD	Castroville
217	201	Borger ISD	Borger
217	201	Palestine ISD	Palestine
219	199	Levelland ISD	Levelland
219	199	Robstown ISD	Robstown
219	199	Sheldon ISD	Houston
222	198	Bridge City ISD	Bridge City
223	197	Navasota ISD	Navasota
224	196	Alvarado ISD	Alvarado
224	196	Carthage ISD	Carthage
226	194	Gulf Shores Academy	Houston
226	194	Wylie ISD	Abilene
228	193	Marble Falls ISD	Marble Falls
229	192	Athens ISD	Athens
229	192	Jasper ISD	Jasper
231	190	Mineral Wells ISD	Mineral Wells
232	185	Columbia-Brazoria ISD	West Columbia
233	184	Zapata County ISD	Zapata
234	183	Pecos-Barstow-Toyah ISD	Pecos
235	182	Huffman ISD	Huffman
236	181	West Orange-Cove CISD	Orange
237	179	Stafford Municipal School	Stafford
237	179	Wharton ISD	Wharton
239	178	Castleberry ISD	Fort Worth
239	178	Decatur ISD	Decatur
241	177	Mabank ISD	Mabank
242	176	Forney ISD	Forney
243	175	Paris ISD	Paris
244	174	Springtown ISD	Springtown
244	174	Taylor ISD	Taylor
246	172	Fort Stockton ISD	Fort Stockton
246	172	Lindale ISD	Lindale
246	172	Snyder ISD	Snyder
249	171	Lamesa ISD	Lamesa
250	170	Needville ISD	Needville
251	169	Burnet Cons ISD	Burnet
252	168	Lake Dallas ISD	Lake Dallas
253	167	La Feria ISD	La Feria
254	166	Gilmer ISD	Gilmer
255	164	Elgin ISD	Elgin
255	164	Liberty-Eylau ISD	Texarkana
255	164	Raymondville ISD	Raymondville
258	163	Brownfield ISD	Brownfield
258	163	Fabens ISD	Fabens
260	162	Cleveland ISD	Cleveland
260	162	Quinlan ISD	Quinlan
262	159	Wills Point ISD	Wills Point
263	158	Cuero ISD	Cuero
263	158	Vernon ISD	Vernon
265	157	Gatesville ISD	Gatesville
265	157	San Elizario ISD	San Elizario
267	156	Sweeny ISD	Sweeny
268	155	Kaufman ISD	Kaufman
268	155	Sanger ISD	Sanger
270	153	Graham ISD	Graham
270	153	Liberty ISD	Liberty
270	153	Robinson ISD	Robinson
273	150	Hidalgo ISD	Hidalgo
273	150	Sweetwater ISD	Sweetwater
275	149	Point Isabel ISD	Port Isabel
276	147	Bellville ISD	Bellville
276	147	Connally ISD	Waco
276	147	Gonzales ISD	Gonzales
276	147	Wimberley ISD	Wimberley
280	146	Bandera ISD	Bandera
280	146	Gainesville ISD	Gainesville
282	143	Barbers Hill ISD	Mount Belvieu
282	143	Brownsboro ISD	Brownsboro
284	141	La Vernia ISD	La Vernia
284	141	Manor ISD	Manor
286	140	West ISD	West
287	139	Devine ISD	Devine
287	139	Hardin-Jefferson ISD	Sour Lake
287	139	Monahans-Wickett-Pyote ISD	Monahans
290	137	Bridgeport ISD	Bridgeport
291	136	Iowa Park CISD	Iowa Park
292	135	Atlanta ISD	Atlanta
292	135	Carrizo Springs CISD	Carrizo Springs
294	134	Kennedale ISD	Kennedale
295	133	Gladewater ISD	Gladewater
295	133	Greenwood ISD	Midland
297	131	Aransas Pass ISD	Aransas Pass
297	131	Hudson ISD	Lufkin
299	130	La Grange ISD	La Grange
299	130	Pleasant Grove ISD	Texarkana
301	129	Center ISD	Center
302	128	Perryton ISD	Perryton
302	128	Sealy ISD	Sealy
302	128	Seminole ISD	Seminole
305	127	Everman ISD	Everman
305	127	La Vega ISD	Waco
305	127	Royse City ISD	Royse City
305	127	Somerset ISD	Somerset
309	126	Ingleside ISD	Ingleside
310	125	Hondo ISD	Hondo
310	125	Mathis ISD	Mathis
310	125	Splendora ISD	Splendora
313	124	Caldwell ISD	Caldwell
313	124	Mexia ISD	Mexia
315	123	China Spring ISD	Waco
315	123	Giddings ISD	Giddings
317	122	Crandall ISD	Crandall
318	121	Van ISD	Van
319	120	Hamshire-Fannett ISD	Hamshire
319	120	Pearsall ISD	Pearsall
319	120	Tarkington ISD	Cleveland
322	119	Breckenridge ISD	Breckenridge

322	119	Cameron ISD	Cameron
322	119	Kirbyville CISD	Kirbyville
325	117	Commerce ISD	Commerce
325	117	Lake Worth ISD	Lake Worth
325	117	Lyford CISD	Lyford
328	116	Crockett ISD	Crockett
329	115	Madisonville CISD	Madisonville
330	113	Groesbeck ISD	Groesbeck
330	113	Hillsboro ISD	Hillsboro
330	113	Palacios ISD	Palacios
333	111	Brooks County ISD	Falfurrias
333	111	Lubbock-Cooper ISD	Lubbock
333	111	Sinton ISD	Sinton
336	109	Rio Hondo ISD	Rio Hondo
336	109	Spring Hill ISD	Longview
338	108	Edna ISD	Edna
338	108	Huntington ISD	Huntington
340	107	Central ISD	Pollok
341	106	Bonham ISD	Bonham
342	105	Canton ISD	Canton
342	105	Pittsburg ISD	Pittsburg
344	104	Diboll ISD	Diboll
344	104	Fairfield ISD	Fairfield
344	104	Little Elm ISD	Little Elm
344	104	Rusk ISD	Rusk
348	103	Glen Rose ISD	Glen Rose
348	103	Smithville ISD	Smithville
350	102	Wilmer-Hutchins ISD	Dallas
351	101	Lorena ISD	Lorena
352	100	Orangefield ISD	Orangefield
352	100	Venus ISD	Venus
352	100	Whitney ISD	Whitney
355	99	Poteet ISD	Poteet
356	98	Columbus ISD	Columbus
356	98	Ferris ISD	Ferris
358	97	Bowie ISD	Bowie
358	97	Princeton ISD	Princeton
360	96	Buna ISD	Buna
360	96	Orange Grove ISD	Orange Grove
360	96	Rockdale ISD	Rockdale
363	94	Mineola ISD	Mineola
363	94	Shepherd ISD	Shepherd
365	93	Rains ISD	Emory
366	92	Llano ISD	Llano
366	92	Marlin ISD	Marlin
368	91	Coldspring-Oakhurst CISD	Coldspring
368	91	Progreso ISD	Progreso
368	91	San Diego ISD	San Diego
368	91	Valley View ISD	Pharr
368	91	Westwood ISD	Palestine
373	90	Lytle ISD	Lytle
374	89	Daingerfield-Lone Star ISD	Daingerfield
374	89	Winnsboro ISD	Winnsboro
376	88	Whitesboro ISD	Whitesboro
376	88	Yoakum ISD	Yoakum
378	87	Crystal City ISD	Crystal City
378	87	Ingram ISD	Ingram
380	86	Luling ISD	Luling
381	83	Liberty Hill ISD	Liberty Hill
382	82	Kemp ISD	Kemp
383	81	Bullard ISD	Bullard
384	78	Littlefield ISD	Littlefield
385	75	Eustace ISD	Eustace
386	70	Hutto ISD	Hutto
386	70	Royal ISD	Brookshire
388	67	Dalhart ISD	Dalhart
389	56	West Oso ISD	Corpus Christi

High School Drop-out Rate

Rank	Percent	District Name	City
1	17.3	Honors Academy	Dallas
2	10.1	Rio Grande City CISD	Rio Grande City
3	9.4	Calhoun County ISD	Port Lavaca
3	9.4	Galveston ISD	Galveston
5	9.1	Crystal City ISD	Crystal City
6	9.0	La Vega ISD	Waco
7	8.9	Waco ISD	Waco
8	8.8	Dickinson ISD	Dickinson
9	8.6	La Joya ISD	La Joya
9	8.6	West Oso ISD	Corpus Christi
11	8.1	Carrizo Springs CISD	Carrizo Springs
12	8.0	Gulf Shores Academy	Houston
12	8.0	Houston ISD	Houston
12	8.0	Raymondville ISD	Raymondville
15	7.7	Floresville ISD	Floresville
16	7.6	Arlington ISD	Arlington
16	7.6	Canutillo ISD	El Paso
16	7.6	San Antonio ISD	San Antonio
19	7.5	Mathis ISD	Mathis
19	7.5	South San Antonio ISD	San Antonio
21	7.3	Fort Stockton ISD	Fort Stockton
21	7.3	Lyford CISD	Lyford
23	7.2	Mission Cons ISD	Mission
24	7.1	Eustace ISD	Eustace
24	7.1	San Benito Cons ISD	San Benito
26	7.0	Alice ISD	Alice
27	6.9	Fort Worth ISD	Fort Worth
27	6.9	Roma ISD	Roma
29	6.8	Texas City ISD	Texas City
30	6.7	Beaumont ISD	Beaumont
30	6.7	Pharr-San Juan-Alamo ISD	Pharr
30	6.7	San Elizario ISD	San Elizario
30	6.7	Wilmer-Hutchins ISD	Dallas
34	6.6	Crockett ISD	Crockett
35	6.5	Corpus Christi ISD	Corpus Christi
35	6.5	Uvalde CISD	Uvalde
37	6.4	Ingleside ISD	Ingleside
37	6.4	Mercedes ISD	Mercedes
37	6.4	Mineola ISD	Mineola
37	6.4	Pasadena ISD	Pasadena
41	6.3	North Forest ISD	Houston
42	6.2	Ector County ISD	Odessa
42	6.2	Plainview ISD	Plainview
44	6.1	Edgewood ISD	San Antonio
44	6.1	Laredo ISD	Laredo
46	6.0	Port Arthur ISD	Port Arthur
46	6.0	Victoria ISD	Victoria
46	6.0	Ysleta ISD	El Paso
49	5.9	Bastrop ISD	Bastrop
49	5.9	Fabens ISD	Fabens
49	5.9	Kerrville ISD	Kerrville
49	5.9	Mcallen ISD	Mcallen
53	5.8	Edinburg CISD	Edinburg
53	5.8	Robstown ISD	Robstown
55	5.7	Athens ISD	Athens
55	5.7	Donna ISD	Donna
55	5.7	Monahans-Wickett-Pyote ISD	Monahans
58	5.6	Austin ISD	Austin
58	5.6	Daingerfield-Lone Star ISD	Daingerfield
58	5.6	Madisonville CISD	Madisonville
58	5.6	Royse City ISD	Royse City
62	5.5	Midland ISD	Midland
63	5.4	Brownwood ISD	Brownwood
63	5.4	Castleberry ISD	Fort Worth
63	5.4	Cleburne ISD	Cleburne
63	5.4	Dallas ISD	Dallas
63	5.4	Pearsall ISD	Pearsall
68	5.3	Edcouch-Elsa ISD	Edcouch
68	5.3	Goose Creek CISD	Baytown
68	5.3	Joshua ISD	Joshua
68	5.3	Luling ISD	Luling
68	5.3	Santa Fe ISD	Santa Fe
68	5.3	Weslaco ISD	Weslaco
74	5.2	Abilene ISD	Abilene
74	5.2	La Marque ISD	La Marque
74	5.2	Southside ISD	San Antonio
74	5.2	Texarkana ISD	Texarkana
78	5.1	Aldine ISD	Houston
78	5.1	Terrell ISD	Terrell
80	5.0	Kilgore ISD	Kilgore
80	5.0	Marshall ISD	Marshall
80	5.0	Quinlan ISD	Quinlan
80	5.0	Southwest ISD	San Antonio
80	5.0	Splendora ISD	Splendora
80	5.0	Sulphur Springs ISD	Sulphur Springs
86	4.9	El Paso ISD	El Paso
86	4.9	Harlingen Cons ISD	Harlingen
86	4.9	Kingsville ISD	Kingsville
89	4.8	Brooks County ISD	Falfurrias
89	4.8	Burkburnett ISD	Burkburnett
89	4.8	Corsicana ISD	Corsicana
89	4.8	Rockwall ISD	Rockwall
89	4.8	Sweetwater ISD	Sweetwater
94	4.7	Alvin ISD	Alvin
94	4.7	Bandera ISD	Bandera
94	4.7	Del Valle ISD	Del Valle
94	4.7	Ennis ISD	Ennis
94	4.7	Lamesa ISD	Lamesa
94	4.7	Livingston ISD	Livingston
94	4.7	Lufkin ISD	Lufkin
94	4.7	Nacogdoches ISD	Nacogdoches
102	4.6	Dayton ISD	Dayton
102	4.6	Gainesville ISD	Gainesville
102	4.6	Greenville ISD	Greenville
102	4.6	Lake Worth ISD	Lake Worth
102	4.6	Lamar CISD	Rosenberg
102	4.6	Sheldon ISD	Houston
102	4.6	Tyler ISD	Tyler
102	4.6	West Orange-Cove CISD	Orange
102	4.6	Zapata County ISD	Zapata
111	4.5	Bryan ISD	Bryan
111	4.5	Denton ISD	Denton
111	4.5	Valley View ISD	Pharr
111	4.5	White Settlement ISD	White Settlement
115	4.4	Mexia ISD	Mexia
115	4.4	San Marcos CISD	San Marcos
117	4.3	Aransas Pass ISD	Aransas Pass
117	4.3	Galena Park ISD	Houston
117	4.3	Harlandale ISD	San Antonio
117	4.3	Levelland ISD	Levelland
117	4.3	Palestine ISD	Palestine
117	4.3	Paris ISD	Paris
117	4.3	Point Isabel ISD	Port Isabel
117	4.3	Somerset ISD	Somerset
117	4.3	Weatherford ISD	Weatherford
126	4.2	Amarillo ISD	Amarillo
126	4.2	Brownfield ISD	Brownfield
126	4.2	Coldspring-Oakhurst CISD	Coldspring
126	4.2	Eagle Mt-Saginaw ISD	Fort Worth
126	4.2	Hidalgo ISD	Hidalgo
126	4.2	Irving ISD	Irving
126	4.2	Lockhart ISD	Lockhart
126	4.2	Longview ISD	Longview
126	4.2	Westwood ISD	Palestine
135	4.1	Brazosport ISD	Clute
135	4.1	Chapel Hill ISD	Tyler
135	4.1	Cleveland ISD	Cleveland
135	4.1	Gatesville ISD	Gatesville
135	4.1	Grand Prairie ISD	Grand Prairie
135	4.1	Kemp ISD	Kemp
135	4.1	Littlefield ISD	Littlefield
135	4.1	Lytle ISD	Lytle
135	4.1	Palacios ISD	Palacios
135	4.1	Rio Hondo ISD	Rio Hondo
135	4.1	San Angelo ISD	San Angelo
135	4.1	Smithville ISD	Smithville
147	4.0	Alief ISD	Houston
147	4.0	Diboll ISD	Diboll
147	4.0	New Braunfels ISD	New Braunfels
147	4.0	Northwest ISD	Fort Worth
147	4.0	Red Oak ISD	Red Oak
147	4.0	Seguin ISD	Seguin
147	4.0	Springtown ISD	Springtown
154	3.9	Center ISD	Center
154	3.9	Channelview ISD	Channelview
154	3.9	Columbia-Brazoria ISD	West Columbia
154	3.9	Copperas Cove ISD	Copperas Cove
154	3.9	Manor ISD	Manor
154	3.9	Marlin ISD	Marlin
154	3.9	Progreso ISD	Progreso
161	3.8	Alvarado ISD	Alvarado
161	3.8	Gilmer ISD	Gilmer
161	3.8	Hillsboro ISD	Hillsboro
161	3.8	Judson ISD	San Antonio
161	3.8	Kennedale ISD	Kennedale
161	3.8	Lubbock ISD	Lubbock
161	3.8	New Caney ISD	New Caney
161	3.8	Sherman ISD	Sherman
169	3.7	Brownsville ISD	Brownsville
169	3.7	Clint ISD	Clint
169	3.7	Crosby ISD	Crosby
169	3.7	Mesquite ISD	Mesquite
169	3.7	Mount Pleasant ISD	Mt Pleasant
169	3.7	San Felipe-Del Rio CISD	Del Rio
169	3.7	Silsbee ISD	Silsbee
169	3.7	Whitney ISD	Whitney
177	3.6	Caldwell ISD	Caldwell
177	3.6	Carrollton-Farmers Branch ISD	Carrollton
177	3.6	Connally ISD	Waco
177	3.6	Denison ISD	Denison
177	3.6	Eagle Pass ISD	Eagle Pass
177	3.6	Gladewater ISD	Gladewater
177	3.6	Granbury ISD	Granbury
177	3.6	Lampasas ISD	Lampasas
177	3.6	Navasota ISD	Navasota
177	3.6	Pleasanton ISD	Pleasanton
187	3.5	Brenham ISD	Brenham
187	3.5	Dalhart ISD	Dalhart
187	3.5	La Porte ISD	La Porte
187	3.5	Marble Falls ISD	Marble Falls
187	3.5	Pampa ISD	Pampa
187	3.5	Waller ISD	Waller
193	3.4	Burleson ISD	Burleson
193	3.4	Everman ISD	Everman
193	3.4	Huffman ISD	Huffman
193	3.4	Snyder ISD	Snyder
197	3.3	Breckenridge ISD	Breckenridge
197	3.3	Devine ISD	Devine
197	3.3	Hereford ISD	Hereford
197	3.3	Northside ISD	San Antonio
197	3.3	Rockdale ISD	Rockdale
197	3.3	Royal ISD	Brookshire
197	3.3	Sanger ISD	Sanger
197	3.3	Spring Branch ISD	Houston
197	3.3	Winnsboro ISD	Winnsboro
206	3.2	Bonham ISD	Bonham

206	3.2	Cuero ISD	Cuero
206	3.2	Killeen ISD	Killeen
206	3.2	Mckinney ISD	Mckinney
206	3.2	Socorro ISD	El Paso
206	3.2	Spring ISD	Houston
206	3.2	Temple ISD	Temple
213	3.1	Aledo ISD	Aledo
213	3.1	Azle ISD	Azle
213	3.1	Comal ISD	New Braunfels
213	3.1	Elgin ISD	Elgin
213	3.1	Fort Bend ISD	Sugar Land
213	3.1	Huntsville ISD	Huntsville
213	3.1	Liberty-Eylau ISD	Texarkana
213	3.1	Sinton ISD	Sinton
221	3.0	Bullard ISD	Bullard
221	3.0	Commerce ISD	Commerce
221	3.0	Edna ISD	Edna
221	3.0	Hutto ISD	Hutto
221	3.0	Orangefield ISD	Orangefield
221	3.0	San Diego ISD	San Diego
221	3.0	Willis ISD	Willis
228	2.9	Big Spring ISD	Big Spring
228	2.9	Georgetown ISD	Georgetown
228	2.9	Hardin-Jefferson ISD	Sour Lake
228	2.9	Henderson ISD	Henderson
228	2.9	Rusk ISD	Rusk
228	2.9	Sealy ISD	Sealy
234	2.8	Beeville ISD	Beeville
234	2.8	Bridgeport ISD	Bridgeport
234	2.8	Los Fresnos CISD	Los Fresnos
234	2.8	Rains ISD	Emory
234	2.8	Seminole ISD	Seminole
234	2.8	Vidor ISD	Vidor
240	2.7	East Central ISD	San Antonio
240	2.7	Flour Bluff ISD	Corpus Christi
240	2.7	Hays Cons ISD	Kyle
240	2.7	Klein ISD	Klein
240	2.7	Nederland ISD	Nederland
240	2.7	Pearland ISD	Pearland
246	2.6	Borger ISD	Borger
246	2.6	Brownsboro ISD	Brownsboro
246	2.6	Canyon ISD	Canyon
246	2.6	Gonzales ISD	Gonzales
246	2.6	Hamshire-Fannett ISD	Hamshire
246	2.6	Huntington ISD	Huntington
246	2.6	Hurst-Euless-Bedford ISD	Bedford
246	2.6	Keller ISD	Keller
246	2.6	Leander ISD	Leander
246	2.6	Llano ISD	Llano
246	2.6	Mansfield ISD	Mansfield
246	2.6	Pecos-Barstow-Toyah ISD	Pecos
246	2.6	Poteet ISD	Poteet
246	2.6	United ISD	Laredo
246	2.6	Van ISD	Van
246	2.6	Wichita Falls ISD	Wichita Falls
246	2.6	Wylie ISD	Wylie
263	2.5	Bay City ISD	Bay City
263	2.5	Calallen ISD	Corpus Christi
263	2.5	Conroe ISD	Conroe
263	2.5	Gregory-Portland ISD	Gregory
263	2.5	La Grange ISD	La Grange
263	2.5	Montgomery ISD	Montgomery
263	2.5	Perryton ISD	Perryton
263	2.5	Pittsburg ISD	Pittsburg
263	2.5	Schertz-Cibolo-Universal City ISD	Schertz
263	2.5	Yoakum ISD	Yoakum
273	2.4	Cedar Hill ISD	Cedar Hill
273	2.4	Clear Creek ISD	League City
273	2.4	Ferris ISD	Ferris
273	2.4	Frisco ISD	Frisco
273	2.4	Hudson ISD	Lufkin
273	2.4	Magnolia ISD	Magnolia
273	2.4	Taylor ISD	Taylor
280	2.3	Bridge City ISD	Bridge City
280	2.3	Richardson ISD	Richardson
280	2.3	Robinson ISD	Robinson
280	2.3	Venus ISD	Venus
284	2.2	Barbers Hill ISD	Mount Belvieu
284	2.2	Burnet Cons ISD	Burnet
284	2.2	Carthage ISD	Carthage
284	2.2	Frenship ISD	Wolfforth
284	2.2	La Feria ISD	La Feria
284	2.2	Liberty ISD	Liberty
284	2.2	Midway ISD	Hewitt
284	2.2	Needville ISD	Needville
284	2.2	Shepherd ISD	Shepherd
284	2.2	Waxahachie ISD	Waxahachie
294	2.1	Andrews ISD	Andrews
294	2.1	Aransas County ISD	Rockport
294	2.1	Cameron ISD	Cameron
294	2.1	Hondo ISD	Hondo
294	2.1	Ingram ISD	Ingram
294	2.1	Iowa Park CISD	Iowa Park
294	2.1	Jasper ISD	Jasper
294	2.1	Midlothian ISD	Midlothian
294	2.1	Mineral Wells ISD	Mineral Wells
294	2.1	North Lamar ISD	Paris
294	2.1	Port Neches-Groves ISD	Port Neches
305	2.0	Fredericksburg ISD	Fredericksburg
305	2.0	Garland ISD	Garland
305	2.0	Groesbeck ISD	Groesbeck
305	2.0	Humble ISD	Humble
305	2.0	Mabank ISD	Mabank
305	2.0	North East ISD	San Antonio
305	2.0	Round Rock ISD	Round Rock
305	2.0	Vernon ISD	Vernon
305	2.0	Wills Point ISD	Wills Point
314	1.9	College Station ISD	College Station
314	1.9	Giddings ISD	Giddings
314	1.9	Lake Travis ISD	Austin
314	1.9	Medina Valley ISD	Castroville
314	1.9	Pflugerville ISD	Pflugerville
314	1.9	Tarkington ISD	Cleveland
314	1.9	Wharton ISD	Wharton
321	1.8	Buna ISD	Buna
321	1.8	El Campo ISD	El Campo
321	1.8	Jacksonville ISD	Jacksonville
321	1.8	Kirbyville CISD	Kirbyville
321	1.8	Whitehouse ISD	Whitehouse
321	1.8	Whitesboro ISD	Whitesboro
327	1.7	Angleton ISD	Angleton
327	1.7	Belton ISD	Belton
327	1.7	Bowie ISD	Bowie
327	1.7	Desoto ISD	Desoto
327	1.7	Greenwood ISD	Midland
327	1.7	La Vernia ISD	La Vernia
327	1.7	Orange Grove ISD	Orange Grove
327	1.7	Princeton ISD	Princeton
327	1.7	Tomball ISD	Tomball
327	1.7	Tuloso-Midway ISD	Corpus Christi
337	1.6	Crowley ISD	Crowley
337	1.6	Fairfield ISD	Fairfield
337	1.6	Little Elm ISD	Little Elm
340	1.5	Columbus ISD	Columbus
340	1.5	Grapevine-Colleyville ISD	Grapevine
340	1.5	Lancaster ISD	Lancaster
340	1.5	Lubbock-Cooper ISD	Lubbock
340	1.5	Wylie ISD	Abilene
345	1.4	Birdville ISD	Haltom City
345	1.4	Dumas ISD	Dumas
345	1.4	Eanes ISD	Austin
345	1.4	Hallsville ISD	Hallsville
345	1.4	Lewisville ISD	Flower Mound
345	1.4	Liberty Hill ISD	Liberty Hill
345	1.4	Little Cypress-Mauriceville CISD	Orange
345	1.4	Lumberton ISD	Lumberton
345	1.4	Spring Hill ISD	Longview
354	1.3	Dripping Springs ISD	Dripping Spgs
354	1.3	Kaufman ISD	Kaufman
354	1.3	Pleasant Grove ISD	Texarkana
357	1.2	Central ISD	Pollok
357	1.2	Deer Park ISD	Deer Park
357	1.2	Forney ISD	Forney
357	1.2	Katy ISD	Katy
361	1.1	Allen ISD	Allen
361	1.1	Crandall ISD	Crandall
361	1.1	Duncanville ISD	Duncanville
361	1.1	Friendswood ISD	Friendswood
361	1.1	Pine Tree ISD	Longview
366	1.0	Cypress-Fairbanks ISD	Houston
366	1.0	Glen Rose ISD	Glen Rose
366	1.0	Lake Dallas ISD	Lake Dallas
366	1.0	Lorena ISD	Lorena
366	1.0	Sharyland ISD	Mission
371	0.8	Alamo Heights ISD	San Antonio
371	0.8	China Spring ISD	Waco
371	0.8	Coppell ISD	Coppell
371	0.8	Plano ISD	Plano
371	0.8	Stephenville ISD	Stephenville
376	0.7	Boerne ISD	Boerne
376	0.7	Graham ISD	Graham
376	0.7	Highland Park ISD	Dallas
376	0.7	Sweeny ISD	Sweeny
376	0.7	West ISD	West
381	0.6	Canton ISD	Canton
381	0.6	Decatur ISD	Decatur
383	0.5	Atlanta ISD	Atlanta
383	0.5	South Texas ISD	Mercedes
383	0.5	Stafford Municipal School	Stafford
386	0.3	Bellville ISD	Bellville
386	0.3	Carroll ISD	Southlake
386	0.3	Lindale ISD	Lindale
386	0.3	Wimberley ISD	Wimberley

Utah

Utah Public School Educational Profile

Category	Value	Category	Value
Schools *(2002-2003)*	806	**Diploma Recipients** *(2002-2003)*	30,183
Instructional Level		White, Non-Hispanic	27,307
Primary	483	Black, Non-Hispanic	172
Middle	125	Asian/Pacific Islander	817
High	166	American Indian/Alaskan Native	313
Other Level	32	Hispanic	1,574
Curriculum		**High School Drop-out Rate** (%) *(2000-2001)*	3.7
Regular	729	White, Non-Hispanic	3.2
Special Education	21	Black, Non-Hispanic	7.9
Vocational	0	Asian/Pacific Islander	4.9
Alternative	56	American Indian/Alaskan Native	8.3
Type		Hispanic	9.0
Magnet	1	**Staff** *(2002-2003)*	41,740.8
Charter	12	Teachers	22,569.4
Title I Eligible	221	Average Salary ($)	38,268
School-wide Title I	135	Librarians/Media Specialists	282.0
Students *(2002-2003)*	484,983	Guidance Counselors	683.2
Gender (%)		**Ratios** *(2002-2003)*	
Male	51.5	Student/Teacher Ratio	21.5 to 1
Female	48.5	Student/Librarian Ratio	1,719.8 to 1
Race/Ethnicity (%)		Student/Counselor Ratio	709.9 to 1
White, Non-Hispanic	84.1	**Current Spending** *($ per student in FY 2001)*	4,900
Black, Non-Hispanic	1.1	Instruction	3,197
Asian/Pacific Islander	2.9	Support Services	1,435
American Indian/Alaskan Native	1.5	**College Entrance Exam Scores** *(2003)*	
Hispanic	10.4	Scholastic Aptitude Test (SAT)	
Classification (%)		Participation Rate (%)	7
Individual Education Program (IEP)	11.6	Mean SAT I Verbal Score	566
Migrant	0.8	Mean SAT I Math Score	559
English Language Learner (ELL)	8.9	American College Testing Program (ACT)	
Eligible for Free Lunch Program	21.7	Participation Rate (%)	67
Eligible for Reduced-Price Lunch Program	9.2	Average Composite Score	21.3

Note: *For an explanation of data, please refer to the User's Guide in the front of the book; n/a indicates data not available*

Utah NAEP 2003 Test Scores

Reading			Mathematics		
Grade/Category	**Value**	**Rank**	**Grade/Category**	**Value**	**Rank**
4th Grade			**4th Grade**		
Average Proficiency	219.3 (1.0)	25/51	Average Proficiency	234.8 (0.8)	30/51
Proficiency by Gender/Race/Ethnicity			Proficiency by Gender/Race/Ethnicity		
Male	214.9 (1.3)	31/51	Male	236.0 (1.0)	30/51
Female	223.8 (1.1)	24/51	Female	233.4 (0.9)	28/51
White, Non-Hispanic	223.3 (1.0)	37/51	White, Non-Hispanic	238.2 (0.8)	38/51
Black, Non-Hispanic	n/a	n/a	Black, Non-Hispanic	n/a	n/a
Asian, Non-Hispanic	194.0 (2.7)	38/41	Asian, Non-Hispanic	215.8 (1.8)	38/43
American Indian, Non-Hispanic	211.7 (5.1)	22/25	American Indian, Non-Hispanic	223.9 (2.2)	26/26
Hispanic	n/a	n/a	Hispanic	n/a	n/a
Proficiency by Class Size			Proficiency by Class Size		
Less than 16 Students	n/a	n/a	Less than 16 Students	n/a	n/a
16 to 18 Students	*209.1 (8.1)*	34/48	16 to 18 Students	*232.5 (4.9)*	27/48
19 to 20 Students	*230.8 (4.6)*	2/50	19 to 20 Students	*231.3 (5.9)*	35/50
21 to 25 Students	219.3 (2.1)	32/51	21 to 25 Students	235.4 (1.2)	33/51
Greater than 25 Students	220.5 (1.3)	21/49	Greater than 25 Students	235.2 (1.2)	27/49
Percent Attaining Achievement Levels			Percent Attaining Achievement Levels		
Below Basic	33.9 (1.3)	30/51	Below Basic	21.0 (1.1)	26/51
Basic or Above	66.1 (1.3)	22/51	Basic or Above	79.0 (1.1)	26/51
Proficient or Above	31.7 (1.2)	28/51	Proficient or Above	31.3 (1.3)	28/51
Advanced or Above	6.6 (0.7)	28/51	Advanced or Above	2.4 (0.4)	36/51
8th Grade			**8th Grade**		
Average Proficiency	264.3 (0.8)	28/51	Average Proficiency	280.6 (1.0)	23/51
Proficiency by Gender/Race/Ethnicity			Proficiency by Gender/Race/Ethnicity		
Male	259.0 (1.1)	25/51	Male	281.7 (1.3)	21/51
Female	269.4 (1.1)	29/51	Female	279.6 (1.2)	23/51
White, Non-Hispanic	267.7 (0.8)	37/50	White, Non-Hispanic	284.9 (1.0)	29/50
Black, Non-Hispanic	n/a	n/a	Black, Non-Hispanic	n/a	n/a
Asian, Non-Hispanic	241.0 (2.9)	30/37	Asian, Non-Hispanic	248.8 (3.0)	34/37
American Indian, Non-Hispanic	262.3 (4.2)	17/23	American Indian, Non-Hispanic	275.0 (3.7)	20/23
Hispanic	n/a	n/a	Hispanic	n/a	n/a
Proficiency by Parents Highest Level of Ed.			Proficiency by Parents Highest Level of Ed.		
Did Not Finish High School	238.3 (3.9)	44/50	Did Not Finish High School	253.3 (3.7)	38/50
Graduated High School	249.1 (2.1)	42/50	Graduated High School	265.1 (1.7)	35/50
Some Education After High School	262.3 (1.7)	44/50	Some Education After High School	281.2 (1.5)	24/50
Graduated College	272.8 (1.0)	26/50	Graduated College	291.7 (1.1)	15/50
Percent Attaining Achievement Levels			Percent Attaining Achievement Levels		
Below Basic	23.6 (1.0)	27/51	Below Basic	28.3 (1.1)	29/51
Basic or Above	76.4 (1.0)	25/51	Basic or Above	71.7 (1.1)	21/51
Proficient or Above	32.4 (1.4)	26/51	Proficient or Above	31.0 (1.5)	21/51
Advanced or Above	2.0 (0.4)	35/51	Advanced or Above	5.7 (0.7)	17/51

***Note:** For an explanation of data, please refer to the User's Guide in the front of the book; values in italics indicate that the nature of the sample does not allow accurate determination of the variability of the statistic; n/a indicates data not available*

Box Elder County

Box Elder SD

960 S Main • Brigham City, UT 84302-2598
(435) 734-4800 • http://www.boxelder.k12.ut.us
Grade Span: PK-12; **Agency Type:** 1
Schools: 25
15 Primary; 2 Middle; 4 High; 4 Other Level
23 Regular; 1 Special Education; 0 Vocational; 1 Alternative
0 Magnet; 0 Charter; 6 Title I Eligible; 0 School-wide Title I
Students: 10,663 (52.2% male; 47.8% female)
Individual Education Program: 1,454 (13.6%);
English Language Learner: 239 (2.2%); Migrant: 322 (3.0%)
Eligible for Free Lunch Program: 2,156 (20.2%)
Eligible for Reduced-Price Lunch Program: 1,336 (12.5%)
Teachers: 519.3 (20.5 to 1)
Librarians/Media Specialists: 6.0 (1,777.2 to 1)
Guidance Counselors: 18.0 (592.4 to 1)
Current Spending: ($ per student per year):
Total: $4,485; Instruction: $2,907; Support Services: $1,329
Enrollment, Drop-out Rates and Diploma Recipients by Race/Ethnicity

Category	Total	White	Black	Asian	AIAN	Hisp.
Enrollment (%)	100.0	90.2	0.4	1.0	0.8	7.6
Drop-out Rate (%)	4.4	3.7	0.0	2.1	23.1	14.7
H.S. Diplomas (#)	805	762	2	10	3	28

Cache County

Cache SD

2063 N 1200 E • Logan, UT 84341-2099
(435) 752-3925 • http://www.cache.k12.ut.us
Grade Span: KG-12; **Agency Type:** 1
Schools: 22
12 Primary; 4 Middle; 4 High; 2 Other Level
20 Regular; 0 Special Education; 0 Vocational; 2 Alternative
0 Magnet; 0 Charter; 7 Title I Eligible; 1 School-wide Title I
Students: 12,934 (51.3% male; 48.7% female)
Individual Education Program: 1,595 (12.3%);
English Language Learner: 665 (5.1%); Migrant: 229 (1.8%)
Eligible for Free Lunch Program: 2,050 (15.8%)
Eligible for Reduced-Price Lunch Program: 1,615 (12.5%)
Teachers: 585.3 (22.1 to 1)
Librarians/Media Specialists: 19.0 (680.7 to 1)
Guidance Counselors: 18.6 (695.4 to 1)
Current Spending: ($ per student per year):
Total: $4,530; Instruction: $2,885; Support Services: $1,369
Enrollment, Drop-out Rates and Diploma Recipients by Race/Ethnicity

Category	Total	White	Black	Asian	AIAN	Hisp.
Enrollment (%)	100.0	93.1	0.3	0.9	0.3	5.5
Drop-out Rate (%)	2.9	2.5	0.0	14.7	9.1	11.2
H.S. Diplomas (#)	895	859	0	5	0	31

Logan SD

101 W Center • Logan, UT 84321-4563
(435) 755-2300 • http://www.lcsd.logan.k12.ut.us
Grade Span: KG-12; **Agency Type:** 1
Schools: 9
6 Primary; 1 Middle; 2 High; 0 Other Level
8 Regular; 0 Special Education; 0 Vocational; 1 Alternative
0 Magnet; 0 Charter; 4 Title I Eligible; 3 School-wide Title I
Students: 6,016 (50.5% male; 49.5% female)
Individual Education Program: 649 (10.8%);
English Language Learner: 728 (12.1%); Migrant: 3 (<0.1%)
Eligible for Free Lunch Program: 1,695 (28.2%)
Eligible for Reduced-Price Lunch Program: 648 (10.8%)
Teachers: 293.9 (20.5 to 1)
Librarians/Media Specialists: 4.1 (1,467.3 to 1)
Guidance Counselors: 7.0 (859.4 to 1)
Current Spending: ($ per student per year):
Total: $4,363; Instruction: $3,126; Support Services: $974
Enrollment, Drop-out Rates and Diploma Recipients by Race/Ethnicity

Category	Total	White	Black	Asian	AIAN	Hisp.
Enrollment (%)	100.0	77.9	1.1	4.6	1.3	15.2
Drop-out Rate (%)	5.1	4.3	8.3	3.5	17.6	14.2
H.S. Diplomas (#)	405	345	6	22	3	29

Carbon County

Carbon SD

251 W 400 N • Price, UT 84501-1438
Mailing Address: PO Box 1438 • Price, UT 84501-1438
(435) 637-1732 • http://www.carbon.k12.ut.us
Grade Span: KG-12; **Agency Type:** 1
Schools: 11
6 Primary; 2 Middle; 3 High; 0 Other Level
9 Regular; 1 Special Education; 0 Vocational; 1 Alternative
0 Magnet; 0 Charter; 6 Title I Eligible; 3 School-wide Title I
Students: 3,827 (51.4% male; 48.6% female)
Individual Education Program: 653 (17.1%);
English Language Learner: 25 (0.7%); Migrant: 0 (0.0%)
Eligible for Free Lunch Program: 1,256 (32.8%)
Eligible for Reduced-Price Lunch Program: 427 (11.2%)
Teachers: 222.3 (17.2 to 1)
Librarians/Media Specialists: 2.3 (1,663.9 to 1)
Guidance Counselors: 9.8 (390.5 to 1)
Current Spending: ($ per student per year):
Total: $6,263; Instruction: $4,119; Support Services: $1,812
Enrollment, Drop-out Rates and Diploma Recipients by Race/Ethnicity

Category	Total	White	Black	Asian	AIAN	Hisp.
Enrollment (%)	100.0	86.8	0.3	0.5	1.3	11.0
Drop-out Rate (%)	2.8	2.5	0.0	0.0	18.2	4.9
H.S. Diplomas (#)	273	240	0	2	3	28

Davis County

Davis SD

45 E State St • Farmington, UT 84025-2344
(801) 402-5261 • http://www.davis.k12.ut.us
Grade Span: PK-12; **Agency Type:** 1
Schools: 85
53 Primary; 14 Middle; 17 High; 1 Other Level
73 Regular; 2 Special Education; 0 Vocational; 10 Alternative
0 Magnet; 0 Charter; 13 Title I Eligible; 2 School-wide Title I
Students: 60,367 (51.4% male; 48.6% female)
Individual Education Program: 5,587 (9.3%);
English Language Learner: 2,899 (4.8%); Migrant: 129 (0.2%)
Eligible for Free Lunch Program: 8,511 (14.1%)
Eligible for Reduced-Price Lunch Program: 4,832 (8.0%)
Teachers: 2,657.9 (22.7 to 1)
Librarians/Media Specialists: 19.5 (3,095.7 to 1)
Guidance Counselors: 107.2 (563.1 to 1)
Current Spending: ($ per student per year):
Total: $4,536; Instruction: $2,843; Support Services: $1,319
Enrollment, Drop-out Rates and Diploma Recipients by Race/Ethnicity

Category	Total	White	Black	Asian	AIAN	Hisp.
Enrollment (%)	100.0	90.6	1.3	2.0	0.6	5.5
Drop-out Rate (%)	1.8	1.7	3.1	1.7	1.1	3.7
H.S. Diplomas (#)	3,765	3,524	24	91	14	112

Duchesne County

Duchesne SD

90 E 100 S • Duchesne, UT 84021-0446
Mailing Address: PO Box 446 • Duchesne, UT 84021-0446
(435) 738-2411
Grade Span: KG-12; **Agency Type:** 1
Schools: 15
6 Primary; 2 Middle; 5 High; 2 Other Level
12 Regular; 2 Special Education; 0 Vocational; 1 Alternative
0 Magnet; 0 Charter; 6 Title I Eligible; 0 School-wide Title I
Students: 3,993 (50.5% male; 49.5% female)
Individual Education Program: 635 (15.9%);
English Language Learner: 104 (2.6%); Migrant: 0 (0.0%)
Eligible for Free Lunch Program: 1,189 (29.8%)
Eligible for Reduced-Price Lunch Program: 568 (14.2%)
Teachers: 214.2 (18.6 to 1)
Librarians/Media Specialists: 6.5 (614.3 to 1)
Guidance Counselors: 6.1 (654.6 to 1)
Current Spending: ($ per student per year):
Total: $5,245; Instruction: $3,157; Support Services: $1,824
Enrollment, Drop-out Rates and Diploma Recipients by Race/Ethnicity

Category	Total	White	Black	Asian	AIAN	Hisp.
Enrollment (%)	100.0	87.9	0.2	0.5	8.6	2.8
Drop-out Rate (%)	3.6	3.2	n/a	0.0	10.0	0.0
H.S. Diplomas (#)	303	289	0	1	8	5

Emery County

Emery SD

130 N Main • Huntington, UT 84528
Mailing Address: PO Box 120 • Huntington, UT 84528
(435) 687-9846 • http://www.emery.k12.ut.us
Grade Span: PK-12; **Agency Type:** 1
Schools: 10
6 Primary; 2 Middle; 2 High; 0 Other Level
10 Regular; 0 Special Education; 0 Vocational; 0 Alternative
0 Magnet; 0 Charter; 4 Title I Eligible; 2 School-wide Title I
Students: 2,455 (52.4% male; 47.6% female)
Individual Education Program: 469 (19.1%);
English Language Learner: 77 (3.1%); Migrant: 0 (0.0%)

Eligible for Free Lunch Program: 684 (27.9%)
Eligible for Reduced-Price Lunch Program: 434 (17.7%)
Teachers: 138.2 (17.8 to 1)
Librarians/Media Specialists: 1.5 (1,636.7 to 1)
Guidance Counselors: 2.0 (1,227.5 to 1)
Current Spending: ($ per student per year):
Total: $5,594; Instruction: $3,732; Support Services: $1,567
Enrollment, Drop-out Rates and Diploma Recipients by Race/Ethnicity

Category	Total	White	Black	Asian	AIAN	Hisp.
Enrollment (%)	100.0	93.2	0.6	0.8	0.4	5.1
Drop-out Rate (%)	1.7	1.8	n/a	0.0	0.0	0.0
H.S. Diplomas (#)	219	212	0	1	1	5

Iron County

Iron SD
2077 W Royal Hunte Dr • Cedar City, UT 84720-2566
(435) 586-2804 • http://www.iron.k12.ut.us
Grade Span: PK-12; **Agency Type:** 1
Schools: 14
7 Primary; 2 Middle; 4 High; 1 Other Level
12 Regular; 0 Special Education; 0 Vocational; 2 Alternative
0 Magnet; 0 Charter; 5 Title I Eligible; 3 School-wide Title I
Students: 7,269 (52.1% male; 47.9% female)
Individual Education Program: 959 (13.2%);
English Language Learner: 396 (5.4%); Migrant: 0 (0.0%)
Eligible for Free Lunch Program: 2,004 (27.6%)
Eligible for Reduced-Price Lunch Program: 892 (12.3%)
Teachers: 346.5 (21.0 to 1)
Librarians/Media Specialists: 3.0 (2,423.0 to 1)
Guidance Counselors: 8.2 (886.5 to 1)
Current Spending: ($ per student per year):
Total: $5,185; Instruction: $3,414; Support Services: $1,508
Enrollment, Drop-out Rates and Diploma Recipients by Race/Ethnicity

Category	Total	White	Black	Asian	AIAN	Hisp.
Enrollment (%)	100.0	89.4	0.7	0.9	3.5	5.4
Drop-out Rate (%)	2.1	2.2	0.0	0.0	1.4	0.0
H.S. Diplomas (#)	482	445	3	5	12	17

Juab County

Juab SD
42 E 200 N • Nephi, UT 84648-1531
(435) 623-1940 • http://utahreach.usu.edu/juab/schools/district.htm
Grade Span: KG-12; **Agency Type:** 1
Schools: 4
2 Primary; 1 Middle; 1 High; 0 Other Level
4 Regular; 0 Special Education; 0 Vocational; 0 Alternative
0 Magnet; 0 Charter; 2 Title I Eligible; 1 School-wide Title I
Students: 1,872 (50.9% male; 49.1% female)
Individual Education Program: 263 (14.0%);
English Language Learner: 3 (0.2%); Migrant: 0 (0.0%)
Eligible for Free Lunch Program: 345 (18.4%)
Eligible for Reduced-Price Lunch Program: 284 (15.2%)
Teachers: 82.2 (22.8 to 1)
Librarians/Media Specialists: 0.3 (6,240.0 to 1)
Guidance Counselors: 2.5 (748.8 to 1)
Current Spending: ($ per student per year):
Total: $4,492; Instruction: $2,846; Support Services: $1,353
Enrollment, Drop-out Rates and Diploma Recipients by Race/Ethnicity

Category	Total	White	Black	Asian	AIAN	Hisp.
Enrollment (%)	100.0	96.3	0.4	0.9	0.4	2.0
Drop-out Rate (%)	0.9	0.9	n/a	0.0	0.0	0.0
H.S. Diplomas (#)	124	121	0	1	1	1

Millard County

Millard SD
160 W Main • Delta, UT 84624-0666
Mailing Address: PO Box 666 • Delta, UT 84624-0666
(435) 864-5600 • http://www.millard.k12.ut.us
Grade Span: KG-12; **Agency Type:** 1
Schools: 9
4 Primary; 2 Middle; 3 High; 0 Other Level
9 Regular; 0 Special Education; 0 Vocational; 0 Alternative
0 Magnet; 0 Charter; 5 Title I Eligible; 2 School-wide Title I
Students: 3,142 (53.0% male; 47.0% female)
Individual Education Program: 443 (14.1%);
English Language Learner: 278 (8.8%); Migrant: 182 (5.8%)
Eligible for Free Lunch Program: 887 (28.2%)
Eligible for Reduced-Price Lunch Program: 507 (16.1%)
Teachers: 178.0 (17.7 to 1)
Librarians/Media Specialists: 6.3 (498.7 to 1)
Guidance Counselors: 4.0 (785.5 to 1)
Current Spending: ($ per student per year):
Total: $6,014; Instruction: $3,833; Support Services: $1,842
Enrollment, Drop-out Rates and Diploma Recipients by Race/Ethnicity

Category	Total	White	Black	Asian	AIAN	Hisp.
Enrollment (%)	100.0	87.5	0.2	1.1	1.5	9.7
Drop-out Rate (%)	2.6	2.2	n/a	7.7	0.0	9.4
H.S. Diplomas (#)	263	247	0	1	2	13

Morgan County

Morgan SD
240 E Young St • Morgan, UT 84050-0530
Mailing Address: PO Box 530 • Morgan, UT 84050-0530
(801) 829-3411 • http://www.morgan.k12.ut.us
Grade Span: PK-12; **Agency Type:** 1
Schools: 3
1 Primary; 1 Middle; 1 High; 0 Other Level
3 Regular; 0 Special Education; 0 Vocational; 0 Alternative
0 Magnet; 0 Charter; 1 Title I Eligible; 0 School-wide Title I
Students: 2,016 (51.2% male; 48.8% female)
Individual Education Program: 144 (7.1%);
English Language Learner: 7 (0.3%); Migrant: 0 (0.0%)
Eligible for Free Lunch Program: 154 (7.6%)
Eligible for Reduced-Price Lunch Program: 187 (9.3%)
Teachers: 99.2 (20.3 to 1)
Librarians/Media Specialists: 1.3 (1,550.8 to 1)
Guidance Counselors: 2.9 (695.2 to 1)
Current Spending: ($ per student per year):
Total: $4,682; Instruction: $3,044; Support Services: $1,327
Enrollment, Drop-out Rates and Diploma Recipients by Race/Ethnicity

Category	Total	White	Black	Asian	AIAN	Hisp.
Enrollment (%)	100.0	97.8	0.1	0.6	0.1	1.4
Drop-out Rate (%)	1.4	1.4	0.0	0.0	n/a	0.0
H.S. Diplomas (#)	174	170	0	1	0	3

Salt Lake County

Granite SD
340 E 3545 S • Salt Lake City, UT 84115-4697
(801) 685-5000 • http://www.granite.k12.ut.us
Grade Span: PK-12; **Agency Type:** 1
Schools: 96
61 Primary; 16 Middle; 17 High; 2 Other Level
86 Regular; 3 Special Education; 0 Vocational; 7 Alternative
0 Magnet; 0 Charter; 16 Title I Eligible; 16 School-wide Title I
Students: 71,181 (51.5% male; 48.5% female)
Individual Education Program: 8,218 (11.5%);
English Language Learner: 11,894 (16.7%); Migrant: 0 (0.0%)
Eligible for Free Lunch Program: 19,389 (27.2%)
Eligible for Reduced-Price Lunch Program: 6,707 (9.4%)
Teachers: 3,438.3 (20.7 to 1)
Librarians/Media Specialists: 25.7 (2,769.7 to 1)
Guidance Counselors: 105.1 (677.3 to 1)
Current Spending: ($ per student per year):
Total: $4,451; Instruction: $2,958; Support Services: $1,276
Enrollment, Drop-out Rates and Diploma Recipients by Race/Ethnicity

Category	Total	White	Black	Asian	AIAN	Hisp.
Enrollment (%)	100.0	73.1	1.5	6.4	1.2	17.7
Drop-out Rate (%)	7.1	6.6	14.9	6.2	14.2	10.0
H.S. Diplomas (#)	4,170	3,464	28	273	27	378

Jordan SD
9361 S 300 E • Sandy, UT 84070-2998
(801) 567-8100 • http://www.jordandistrict.org
Grade Span: KG-12; **Agency Type:** 1
Schools: 80
53 Primary; 15 Middle; 12 High; 0 Other Level
76 Regular; 3 Special Education; 0 Vocational; 1 Alternative
0 Magnet; 0 Charter; 10 Title I Eligible; 6 School-wide Title I
Students: 73,808 (51.5% male; 48.5% female)
Individual Education Program: 7,825 (10.6%);
English Language Learner: 3,187 (4.3%); Migrant: 165 (0.2%)
Eligible for Free Lunch Program: 9,558 (12.9%)
Eligible for Reduced-Price Lunch Program: 4,898 (6.6%)
Teachers: 3,119.9 (23.7 to 1)
Librarians/Media Specialists: 27.1 (2,723.5 to 1)
Guidance Counselors: 70.4 (1,048.4 to 1)
Current Spending: ($ per student per year):
Total: $4,308; Instruction: $2,819; Support Services: $1,248
Enrollment, Drop-out Rates and Diploma Recipients by Race/Ethnicity

Category	Total	White	Black	Asian	AIAN	Hisp.
Enrollment (%)	100.0	91.1	0.6	2.2	0.5	5.6
Drop-out Rate (%)	4.4	3.9	9.2	6.3	10.9	12.5
H.S. Diplomas (#)	4,916	4,662	13	80	14	147

Murray SD

147 E 5065 S • Murray, UT 84107-4898
(801) 264-7400 • http://www.mury.k12.ut.us
Grade Span: KG-12; **Agency Type:** 1
Schools: 12
7 Primary; 2 Middle; 2 High; 1 Other Level
10 Regular; 0 Special Education; 0 Vocational; 2 Alternative
0 Magnet; 0 Charter; 4 Title I Eligible; 0 School-wide Title I
Students: 6,336 (50.8% male; 49.2% female)
Individual Education Program: 551 (8.7%);
English Language Learner: 381 (6.0%); Migrant: 0 (0.0%)
Eligible for Free Lunch Program: 1,002 (15.8%)
Eligible for Reduced-Price Lunch Program: 427 (6.7%)
Teachers: 307.2 (20.6 to 1)
Librarians/Media Specialists: 4.0 (1,584.0 to 1)
Guidance Counselors: 8.1 (782.2 to 1)
Current Spending: ($ per student per year):
Total: $4,689; Instruction: $2,907; Support Services: $1,528
Enrollment, Drop-out Rates and Diploma Recipients by Race/Ethnicity

Category	Total	White	Black	Asian	AIAN	Hisp.
Enrollment (%)	100.0	84.0	1.8	3.3	0.9	9.9
Drop-out Rate (%)	2.7	2.7	0.0	0.0	3.2	3.7
H.S. Diplomas (#)	480	434	2	14	3	27

Salt Lake City SD

440 E 100 S • Salt Lake City, UT 84111-1898
(801) 578-8599 • http://www.slc.k12.ut.us
Grade Span: PK-12; **Agency Type:** 1
Schools: 42
31 Primary; 5 Middle; 4 High; 2 Other Level
39 Regular; 2 Special Education; 0 Vocational; 1 Alternative
0 Magnet; 0 Charter; 19 Title I Eligible; 18 School-wide Title I
Students: 24,850 (51.3% male; 48.7% female)
Individual Education Program: 3,155 (12.7%);
English Language Learner: 8,693 (35.0%); Migrant: 0 (0.0%)
Eligible for Free Lunch Program: 11,394 (45.9%)
Eligible for Reduced-Price Lunch Program: 2,480 (10.0%)
Teachers: 1,287.2 (19.3 to 1)
Librarians/Media Specialists: 38.4 (647.1 to 1)
Guidance Counselors: 36.4 (682.7 to 1)
Current Spending: ($ per student per year):
Total: $5,440; Instruction: $3,461; Support Services: $1,650
Enrollment, Drop-out Rates and Diploma Recipients by Race/Ethnicity

Category	Total	White	Black	Asian	AIAN	Hisp.
Enrollment (%)	100.0	52.1	4.0	10.1	1.9	31.9
Drop-out Rate (%)	9.0	6.5	12.0	8.2	23.0	15.3
H.S. Diplomas (#)	1,202	849	41	113	17	182

San Juan County

San Juan SD

200 N Main St • Blanding, UT 84511-3600
(435) 678-1200 • http://www.sanjuan.k12.ut.us
Grade Span: PK-12; **Agency Type:** 1
Schools: 13
7 Primary; 1 Middle; 5 High; 0 Other Level
13 Regular; 0 Special Education; 0 Vocational; 0 Alternative
0 Magnet; 0 Charter; 8 Title I Eligible; 8 School-wide Title I
Students: 2,989 (51.7% male; 48.3% female)
Individual Education Program: 352 (11.8%);
English Language Learner: 2,006 (67.1%); Migrant: 0 (0.0%)
Eligible for Free Lunch Program: 1,740 (58.2%)
Eligible for Reduced-Price Lunch Program: 357 (11.9%)
Teachers: 205.9 (14.5 to 1)
Librarians/Media Specialists: 8.9 (335.8 to 1)
Guidance Counselors: 4.8 (622.7 to 1)
Current Spending: ($ per student per year):
Total: $8,774; Instruction: $4,792; Support Services: $3,571
Enrollment, Drop-out Rates and Diploma Recipients by Race/Ethnicity

Category	Total	White	Black	Asian	AIAN	Hisp.
Enrollment (%)	100.0	41.1	0.2	0.5	55.4	2.8
Drop-out Rate (%)	3.1	0.9	n/a	0.0	4.8	3.2
H.S. Diplomas (#)	199	99	0	0	93	7

Sanpete County

North Sanpete SD

220 E 700 S • Mount Pleasant, UT 84647-1327
(435) 462-2485 • http://www.nsanpete.k12.ut.us
Grade Span: PK-12; **Agency Type:** 1
Schools: 7
5 Primary; 1 Middle; 1 High; 0 Other Level
7 Regular; 0 Special Education; 0 Vocational; 0 Alternative
0 Magnet; 0 Charter; 5 Title I Eligible; 4 School-wide Title I
Students: 2,450 (49.7% male; 50.3% female)
Individual Education Program: 326 (13.3%);
English Language Learner: 159 (6.5%); Migrant: 372 (15.2%)
Eligible for Free Lunch Program: 799 (32.6%)
Eligible for Reduced-Price Lunch Program: 398 (16.2%)
Teachers: 118.4 (20.7 to 1)
Librarians/Media Specialists: 1.0 (2,450.0 to 1)
Guidance Counselors: 2.0 (1,225.0 to 1)
Current Spending: ($ per student per year):
Total: $5,205; Instruction: $3,237; Support Services: $1,643
Enrollment, Drop-out Rates and Diploma Recipients by Race/Ethnicity

Category	Total	White	Black	Asian	AIAN	Hisp.
Enrollment (%)	100.0	88.4	0.4	0.9	0.9	9.4
Drop-out Rate (%)	4.8	4.5	0.0	0.0	n/a	10.6
H.S. Diplomas (#)	175	161	0	1	0	13

South Sanpete SD

39 S Main • Manti, UT 84642-1398
(435) 835-2261 • http://www.ssanpete.k12.ut.us
Grade Span: PK-12; **Agency Type:** 1
Schools: 7
3 Primary; 2 Middle; 2 High; 0 Other Level
7 Regular; 0 Special Education; 0 Vocational; 0 Alternative
0 Magnet; 0 Charter; 3 Title I Eligible; 3 School-wide Title I
Students: 2,818 (53.2% male; 46.8% female)
Individual Education Program: 498 (17.7%);
English Language Learner: 151 (5.4%); Migrant: 6 (0.2%)
Eligible for Free Lunch Program: 838 (29.7%)
Eligible for Reduced-Price Lunch Program: 435 (15.4%)
Teachers: 152.3 (18.5 to 1)
Librarians/Media Specialists: 0.0 (0.0 to 1)
Guidance Counselors: 3.5 (805.1 to 1)
Current Spending: ($ per student per year):
Total: $5,311; Instruction: $3,635; Support Services: $1,363
Enrollment, Drop-out Rates and Diploma Recipients by Race/Ethnicity

Category	Total	White	Black	Asian	AIAN	Hisp.
Enrollment (%)	100.0	90.2	0.3	1.5	1.3	6.6
Drop-out Rate (%)	1.5	1.3	0.0	0.0	0.0	6.7
H.S. Diplomas (#)	226	211	0	5	3	7

Sevier County

Sevier SD

195 E 500 N • Richfield, UT 84701-1899
(435) 896-8214
Grade Span: PK-12; **Agency Type:** 1
Schools: 15
5 Primary; 4 Middle; 6 High; 0 Other Level
12 Regular; 0 Special Education; 0 Vocational; 3 Alternative
0 Magnet; 0 Charter; 3 Title I Eligible; 0 School-wide Title I
Students: 4,406 (51.8% male; 48.2% female)
Individual Education Program: 571 (13.0%);
English Language Learner: 25 (0.6%); Migrant: 0 (0.0%)
Eligible for Free Lunch Program: 1,298 (29.5%)
Eligible for Reduced-Price Lunch Program: 638 (14.5%)
Teachers: 221.4 (19.9 to 1)
Librarians/Media Specialists: 0.0 (0.0 to 1)
Guidance Counselors: 3.9 (1,129.7 to 1)
Current Spending: ($ per student per year):
Total: $5,087; Instruction: $3,254; Support Services: $1,557
Enrollment, Drop-out Rates and Diploma Recipients by Race/Ethnicity

Category	Total	White	Black	Asian	AIAN	Hisp.
Enrollment (%)	100.0	94.4	0.1	0.5	2.2	2.7
Drop-out Rate (%)	4.2	4.0	0.0	0.0	14.7	5.6
H.S. Diplomas (#)	305	296	0	3	3	3

Summit County

Park City SD

2700 Kearns Blvd • Park City, UT 84060-7476
(435) 645-5600 • http://www.parkcity.k12.ut.us
Grade Span: PK-12; **Agency Type:** 1
Schools: 8
4 Primary; 2 Middle; 2 High; 0 Other Level
7 Regular; 0 Special Education; 0 Vocational; 1 Alternative
0 Magnet; 1 Charter; 2 Title I Eligible; 0 School-wide Title I
Students: 4,009 (52.7% male; 47.3% female)
Individual Education Program: 397 (9.9%);
English Language Learner: 363 (9.1%); Migrant: 0 (0.0%)
Eligible for Free Lunch Program: 310 (7.7%)
Eligible for Reduced-Price Lunch Program: 75 (1.9%)
Teachers: 216.0 (18.6 to 1)
Librarians/Media Specialists: 5.0 (801.8 to 1)
Guidance Counselors: 8.7 (460.8 to 1)
Current Spending: ($ per student per year):
Total: $5,799; Instruction: $3,547; Support Services: $2,028

Enrollment, Drop-out Rates and Diploma Recipients by Race/Ethnicity

Category	Total	White	Black	Asian	AIAN	Hisp.
Enrollment (%)	100.0	88.4	0.4	1.3	0.1	9.8
Drop-out Rate (%)	2.7	1.3	0.0	0.0	0.0	23.1
H.S. Diplomas (#)	282	263	0	4	1	14

Tooele County

Tooele SD

66 W Vine • Tooele, UT 84074-2035
(435) 833-1900 • http://tcsd.tooele.k12.ut.us
Grade Span: KG-12; **Agency Type:** 1
Schools: 20
13 Primary; 2 Middle; 5 High; 0 Other Level
19 Regular; 0 Special Education; 0 Vocational; 1 Alternative
0 Magnet; 0 Charter; 6 Title I Eligible; 2 School-wide Title I
Students: 10,034 (51.0% male; 49.0% female)
Individual Education Program: 1,273 (12.7%);
English Language Learner: 343 (3.4%); Migrant: 0 (0.0%)
Eligible for Free Lunch Program: 2,320 (23.1%)
Eligible for Reduced-Price Lunch Program: 1,090 (10.9%)
Teachers: 439.3 (22.8 to 1)
Librarians/Media Specialists: 5.0 (2,006.8 to 1)
Guidance Counselors: 12.3 (815.8 to 1)
Current Spending: ($ per student per year):
Total: $4,270; Instruction: $2,728; Support Services: $1,264
Enrollment, Drop-out Rates and Diploma Recipients by Race/Ethnicity

Category	Total	White	Black	Asian	AIAN	Hisp.
Enrollment (%)	100.0	85.9	0.8	1.1	1.9	10.3
Drop-out Rate (%)	1.7	1.6	0.0	0.0	0.0	3.1
H.S. Diplomas (#)	513	430	5	10	9	59

Uintah County

Uintah SD

635 W 200 S • Vernal, UT 84078-3099
(435) 781-3100 • http://server1.do.uintah.k12.ut.us
Grade Span: KG-12; **Agency Type:** 1
Schools: 12
6 Primary; 3 Middle; 1 High; 2 Other Level
11 Regular; 0 Special Education; 0 Vocational; 1 Alternative
0 Magnet; 0 Charter; 6 Title I Eligible; 5 School-wide Title I
Students: 5,682 (52.4% male; 47.6% female)
Individual Education Program: 918 (16.2%);
English Language Learner: 586 (10.3%); Migrant: 0 (0.0%)
Eligible for Free Lunch Program: 1,717 (30.2%)
Eligible for Reduced-Price Lunch Program: 799 (14.1%)
Teachers: 313.5 (18.1 to 1)
Librarians/Media Specialists: 2.0 (2,841.0 to 1)
Guidance Counselors: 8.5 (668.5 to 1)
Current Spending: ($ per student per year):
Total: $5,278; Instruction: $3,407; Support Services: $1,558
Enrollment, Drop-out Rates and Diploma Recipients by Race/Ethnicity

Category	Total	White	Black	Asian	AIAN	Hisp.
Enrollment (%)	100.0	84.6	0.1	0.7	11.9	2.7
Drop-out Rate (%)	5.5	4.9	20.0	0.0	11.2	11.5
H.S. Diplomas (#)	393	368	1	3	8	13

Utah County

Alpine SD

575 N 100 E • American Fork, UT 84003-1700
(801) 756-8400 • http://www.alpine.k12.ut.us
Grade Span: KG-12; **Agency Type:** 1
Schools: 59
40 Primary; 8 Middle; 9 High; 2 Other Level
55 Regular; 2 Special Education; 0 Vocational; 2 Alternative
0 Magnet; 0 Charter; 8 Title I Eligible; 5 School-wide Title I
Students: 49,159 (51.4% male; 48.6% female)
Individual Education Program: 4,912 (10.0%);
English Language Learner: 2,319 (4.7%); Migrant: 895 (1.8%)
Eligible for Free Lunch Program: 7,781 (15.8%)
Eligible for Reduced-Price Lunch Program: 3,692 (7.5%)
Teachers: 2,061.6 (23.8 to 1)
Librarians/Media Specialists: 14.1 (3,486.5 to 1)
Guidance Counselors: 56.9 (864.0 to 1)
Current Spending: ($ per student per year):
Total: $4,119; Instruction: $2,765; Support Services: $1,156
Enrollment, Drop-out Rates and Diploma Recipients by Race/Ethnicity

Category	Total	White	Black	Asian	AIAN	Hisp.
Enrollment (%)	100.0	90.6	0.6	1.9	0.6	6.4
Drop-out Rate (%)	2.0	1.8	3.3	3.4	6.3	5.6
H.S. Diplomas (#)	2,726	2,598	1	41	15	71

Nebo SD

350 S Main • Spanish Fork, UT 84660-2499
(801) 354-7400 • http://www.nebo.edu
Grade Span: PK-12; **Agency Type:** 1
Schools: 32
20 Primary; 3 Middle; 5 High; 3 Other Level
29 Regular; 0 Special Education; 0 Vocational; 2 Alternative
0 Magnet; 0 Charter; 8 Title I Eligible; 2 School-wide Title I
Students: 23,197 (52.1% male; 47.9% female)
Individual Education Program: 2,870 (12.4%);
English Language Learner: 892 (3.8%); Migrant: 483 (2.1%)
Eligible for Free Lunch Program: 3,816 (16.5%)
Eligible for Reduced-Price Lunch Program: 2,189 (9.4%)
Teachers: 958.6 (24.2 to 1)
Librarians/Media Specialists: 10.1 (2,296.7 to 1)
Guidance Counselors: 28.7 (808.3 to 1)
Current Spending: ($ per student per year):
Total: $4,480; Instruction: $2,654; Support Services: $1,225
Enrollment, Drop-out Rates and Diploma Recipients by Race/Ethnicity

Category	Total	White	Black	Asian	AIAN	Hisp.
Enrollment (%)	100.0	91.9	0.4	1.1	0.9	5.8
Drop-out Rate (%)	1.4	1.4	0.0	0.0	0.0	2.2
H.S. Diplomas (#)	1,303	1,237	3	14	9	40

Provo SD

280 W 940 N • Provo, UT 84604-3394
(801) 374-4800 • http://www.provo.k12.ut.us
Grade Span: KG-12; **Agency Type:** 1
Schools: 25
13 Primary; 3 Middle; 7 High; 2 Other Level
18 Regular; 1 Special Education; 0 Vocational; 6 Alternative
0 Magnet; 0 Charter; 3 Title I Eligible; 3 School-wide Title I
Students: 13,227 (51.4% male; 48.6% female)
Individual Education Program: 1,515 (11.5%);
English Language Learner: 2,197 (16.6%); Migrant: 143 (1.1%)
Eligible for Free Lunch Program: 4,137 (31.3%)
Eligible for Reduced-Price Lunch Program: 1,249 (9.4%)
Teachers: 687.0 (19.3 to 1)
Librarians/Media Specialists: 17.8 (743.1 to 1)
Guidance Counselors: 14.8 (893.7 to 1)
Current Spending: ($ per student per year):
Total: $5,395; Instruction: $3,755; Support Services: $1,384
Enrollment, Drop-out Rates and Diploma Recipients by Race/Ethnicity

Category	Total	White	Black	Asian	AIAN	Hisp.
Enrollment (%)	100.0	74.7	0.8	4.5	1.4	18.6
Drop-out Rate (%)	0.8	0.8	0.0	0.0	0.0	1.2
H.S. Diplomas (#)	763	647	4	34	7	71

Wasatch County

Wasatch SD

301 S Main • Heber City, UT 84032-1799
(435) 654-0280 • http://www.wasatch.k12.ut.us
Grade Span: KG-12; **Agency Type:** 1
Schools: 7
3 Primary; 1 Middle; 2 High; 1 Other Level
6 Regular; 0 Special Education; 0 Vocational; 1 Alternative
0 Magnet; 0 Charter; 3 Title I Eligible; 0 School-wide Title I
Students: 3,916 (51.8% male; 48.2% female)
Individual Education Program: 567 (14.5%);
English Language Learner: 205 (5.2%); Migrant: 0 (0.0%)
Eligible for Free Lunch Program: 605 (15.4%)
Eligible for Reduced-Price Lunch Program: 270 (6.9%)
Teachers: 195.9 (20.0 to 1)
Librarians/Media Specialists: 3.0 (1,305.3 to 1)
Guidance Counselors: 6.2 (631.6 to 1)
Current Spending: ($ per student per year):
Total: $4,849; Instruction: $3,285; Support Services: $1,374
Enrollment, Drop-out Rates and Diploma Recipients by Race/Ethnicity

Category	Total	White	Black	Asian	AIAN	Hisp.
Enrollment (%)	100.0	89.6	0.5	0.5	0.4	9.0
Drop-out Rate (%)	1.8	1.9	0.0	0.0	0.0	2.5
H.S. Diplomas (#)	277	265	0	1	1	10

Washington County

Washington SD

121 W Tabernacle • Saint George, UT 84770-3390
(435) 673-3553 • http://www.wash.k12.ut.us
Grade Span: PK-12; **Agency Type:** 1
Schools: 32
19 Primary; 4 Middle; 7 High; 2 Other Level
30 Regular; 0 Special Education; 0 Vocational; 2 Alternative
0 Magnet; 0 Charter; 12 Title I Eligible; 8 School-wide Title I
Students: 19,697 (51.5% male; 48.5% female)

Individual Education Program: 2,197 (11.2%);
English Language Learner: 1,153 (5.9%); Migrant: 0 (0.0%)
Eligible for Free Lunch Program: 4,052 (20.6%)
Eligible for Reduced-Price Lunch Program: 2,077 (10.5%)
Teachers: 862.7 (22.8 to 1)
Librarians/Media Specialists: 10.0 (1,969.7 to 1)
Guidance Counselors: 30.7 (641.6 to 1)
Current Spending: ($ per student per year):
Total: $4,467; Instruction: $2,928; Support Services: $1,333
Enrollment, Drop-out Rates and Diploma Recipients by Race/Ethnicity

Category	Total	White	Black	Asian	AIAN	Hisp.
Enrollment (%)	100.0	89.4	0.5	1.5	2.1	6.5
Drop-out Rate (%)	2.5	2.4	0.0	1.2	9.3	3.4
H.S. Diplomas (#)	1,214	1,132	0	31	13	38

Weber County

Ogden SD

1950 Monroe Blvd • Ogden, UT 84401-0619
(801) 625-8700 • http://www.ogden.k12.ut.us
Grade Span: KG-12; **Agency Type:** 1
Schools: 25
15 Primary; 4 Middle; 6 High; 0 Other Level
21 Regular; 0 Special Education; 0 Vocational; 4 Alternative
0 Magnet; 0 Charter; 11 Title I Eligible; 11 School-wide Title I
Students: 13,331 (51.7% male; 48.3% female)
Individual Education Program: 1,498 (11.2%);
English Language Learner: 2,587 (19.4%); Migrant: 1,176 (8.8%)
Eligible for Free Lunch Program: 7,119 (53.4%)
Eligible for Reduced-Price Lunch Program: 1,281 (9.6%)
Teachers: 652.7 (20.4 to 1)
Librarians/Media Specialists: 19.7 (676.7 to 1)
Guidance Counselors: 29.6 (450.4 to 1)
Current Spending: ($ per student per year):
Total: $5,450; Instruction: $3,159; Support Services: $1,908
Enrollment, Drop-out Rates and Diploma Recipients by Race/Ethnicity

Category	Total	White	Black	Asian	AIAN	Hisp.
Enrollment (%)	100.0	56.0	3.1	1.9	1.5	37.6
Drop-out Rate (%)	6.7	5.2	2.7	7.5	17.0	10.6
H.S. Diplomas (#)	656	479	21	15	8	133

Weber SD

5320 S Adams Ave Pkwy • Ogden, UT 84405-6913
(801) 476-7800 • http://www.weber.k12.ut.us
Grade Span: KG-12; **Agency Type:** 1
Schools: 41
27 Primary; 8 Middle; 5 High; 1 Other Level
39 Regular; 1 Special Education; 0 Vocational; 1 Alternative
0 Magnet; 0 Charter; 3 Title I Eligible; 3 School-wide Title I
Students: 28,125 (52.0% male; 48.0% female)
Individual Education Program: 3,754 (13.3%);
English Language Learner: 344 (1.2%); Migrant: 0 (0.0%)
Eligible for Free Lunch Program: 3,732 (13.3%)
Eligible for Reduced-Price Lunch Program: 2,454 (8.7%)
Teachers: 1,236.2 (22.8 to 1)
Librarians/Media Specialists: 11.9 (2,363.4 to 1)
Guidance Counselors: 49.5 (568.2 to 1)
Current Spending: ($ per student per year):
Total: $4,413; Instruction: $2,919; Support Services: $1,205
Enrollment, Drop-out Rates and Diploma Recipients by Race/Ethnicity

Category	Total	White	Black	Asian	AIAN	Hisp.
Enrollment (%)	100.0	91.3	1.0	1.4	0.5	5.9
Drop-out Rate (%)	1.7	1.5	2.3	1.5	2.1	4.9
H.S. Diplomas (#)	1,898	1,771	17	31	12	67

Number of Schools

Rank	Number	District Name	City
1	96	Granite SD	Salt Lake City
2	85	Davis SD	Farmington
3	80	Jordan SD	Sandy
4	59	Alpine SD	American Fork
5	42	Salt Lake City SD	Salt Lake City
6	41	Weber SD	Ogden
7	32	Nebo SD	Spanish Fork
7	32	Washington SD	Saint George
9	25	Box Elder SD	Brigham City
9	25	Ogden SD	Ogden
9	25	Provo SD	Provo
12	22	Cache SD	Logan
13	20	Tooele SD	Tooele
14	15	Duchesne SD	Duchesne
14	15	Sevier SD	Richfield
16	14	Iron SD	Cedar City
17	13	San Juan SD	Blanding
18	12	Murray SD	Murray
18	12	Uintah SD	Vernal
20	11	Carbon SD	Price
21	10	Emery SD	Huntington
22	9	Logan SD	Logan
22	9	Millard SD	Delta
24	8	Park City SD	Park City
25	7	North Sanpete SD	Mount Pleasant
25	7	South Sanpete SD	Manti
25	7	Wasatch SD	Heber City
28	4	Juab SD	Nephi
29	3	Morgan SD	Morgan

Number of Teachers

Rank	Number	District Name	City
1	3,438	Granite SD	Salt Lake City
2	3,119	Jordan SD	Sandy
3	2,657	Davis SD	Farmington
4	2,061	Alpine SD	American Fork
5	1,287	Salt Lake City SD	Salt Lake City
6	1,236	Weber SD	Ogden
7	958	Nebo SD	Spanish Fork
8	862	Washington SD	Saint George
9	687	Provo SD	Provo
10	652	Ogden SD	Ogden
11	585	Cache SD	Logan
12	519	Box Elder SD	Brigham City
13	439	Tooele SD	Tooele
14	346	Iron SD	Cedar City
15	313	Uintah SD	Vernal
16	307	Murray SD	Murray
17	293	Logan SD	Logan
18	222	Carbon SD	Price
19	221	Sevier SD	Richfield
20	216	Park City SD	Park City
21	214	Duchesne SD	Duchesne
22	205	San Juan SD	Blanding
23	195	Wasatch SD	Heber City
24	178	Millard SD	Delta
25	152	South Sanpete SD	Manti
26	138	Emery SD	Huntington
27	118	North Sanpete SD	Mount Pleasant
28	99	Morgan SD	Morgan
29	82	Juab SD	Nephi

Number of Students

Rank	Number	District Name	City
1	73,808	Jordan SD	Sandy
2	71,181	Granite SD	Salt Lake City
3	60,367	Davis SD	Farmington
4	49,159	Alpine SD	American Fork
5	28,125	Weber SD	Ogden
6	24,850	Salt Lake City SD	Salt Lake City
7	23,197	Nebo SD	Spanish Fork
8	19,697	Washington SD	Saint George
9	13,331	Ogden SD	Ogden
10	13,227	Provo SD	Provo
11	12,934	Cache SD	Logan
12	10,663	Box Elder SD	Brigham City
13	10,034	Tooele SD	Tooele
14	7,269	Iron SD	Cedar City
15	6,336	Murray SD	Murray
16	6,016	Logan SD	Logan
17	5,682	Uintah SD	Vernal
18	4,406	Sevier SD	Richfield
19	4,009	Park City SD	Park City
20	3,993	Duchesne SD	Duchesne
21	3,916	Wasatch SD	Heber City
22	3,827	Carbon SD	Price
23	3,142	Millard SD	Delta
24	2,989	San Juan SD	Blanding
25	2,818	South Sanpete SD	Manti
26	2,455	Emery SD	Huntington
27	2,450	North Sanpete SD	Mount Pleasant
28	2,016	Morgan SD	Morgan
29	1,872	Juab SD	Nephi

Male Students

Rank	Percent	District Name	City
1	53.2	South Sanpete SD	Manti
2	53.0	Millard SD	Delta
3	52.7	Park City SD	Park City
4	52.4	Emery SD	Huntington
4	52.4	Uintah SD	Vernal
6	52.2	Box Elder SD	Brigham City
7	52.1	Iron SD	Cedar City
7	52.1	Nebo SD	Spanish Fork
9	52.0	Weber SD	Ogden
10	51.8	Sevier SD	Richfield
10	51.8	Wasatch SD	Heber City
12	51.7	Ogden SD	Ogden
12	51.7	San Juan SD	Blanding
14	51.5	Granite SD	Salt Lake City
14	51.5	Jordan SD	Sandy
14	51.5	Washington SD	Saint George
17	51.4	Alpine SD	American Fork
17	51.4	Carbon SD	Price
17	51.4	Davis SD	Farmington
17	51.4	Provo SD	Provo
21	51.3	Cache SD	Logan
21	51.3	Salt Lake City SD	Salt Lake City
23	51.2	Morgan SD	Morgan
24	51.0	Tooele SD	Tooele
25	50.9	Juab SD	Nephi
26	50.8	Murray SD	Murray
27	50.5	Duchesne SD	Duchesne
27	50.5	Logan SD	Logan
29	49.7	North Sanpete SD	Mount Pleasant

Female Students

Rank	Percent	District Name	City
1	50.3	North Sanpete SD	Mount Pleasant
2	49.5	Duchesne SD	Duchesne
2	49.5	Logan SD	Logan
4	49.2	Murray SD	Murray
5	49.1	Juab SD	Nephi
6	49.0	Tooele SD	Tooele
7	48.8	Morgan SD	Morgan
8	48.7	Cache SD	Logan
8	48.7	Salt Lake City SD	Salt Lake City
10	48.6	Alpine SD	American Fork
10	48.6	Carbon SD	Price
10	48.6	Davis SD	Farmington
10	48.6	Provo SD	Provo
14	48.5	Granite SD	Salt Lake City
14	48.5	Jordan SD	Sandy
14	48.5	Washington SD	Saint George
17	48.3	Ogden SD	Ogden
17	48.3	San Juan SD	Blanding
19	48.2	Sevier SD	Richfield
19	48.2	Wasatch SD	Heber City
21	48.0	Weber SD	Ogden
22	47.9	Iron SD	Cedar City
22	47.9	Nebo SD	Spanish Fork
24	47.8	Box Elder SD	Brigham City
25	47.6	Emery SD	Huntington
25	47.6	Uintah SD	Vernal
27	47.3	Park City SD	Park City
28	47.0	Millard SD	Delta
29	46.8	South Sanpete SD	Manti

Individual Education Program Students

Rank	Percent	District Name	City
1	19.1	Emery SD	Huntington
2	17.7	South Sanpete SD	Manti
3	17.1	Carbon SD	Price
4	16.2	Uintah SD	Vernal
5	15.9	Duchesne SD	Duchesne
6	14.5	Wasatch SD	Heber City
7	14.1	Millard SD	Delta
8	14.0	Juab SD	Nephi
9	13.6	Box Elder SD	Brigham City
10	13.3	North Sanpete SD	Mount Pleasant
10	13.3	Weber SD	Ogden
12	13.2	Iron SD	Cedar City
13	13.0	Sevier SD	Richfield
14	12.7	Salt Lake City SD	Salt Lake City
14	12.7	Tooele SD	Tooele
16	12.4	Nebo SD	Spanish Fork
17	12.3	Cache SD	Logan
18	11.8	San Juan SD	Blanding
19	11.5	Granite SD	Salt Lake City
19	11.5	Provo SD	Provo
21	11.2	Ogden SD	Ogden
21	11.2	Washington SD	Saint George
23	10.8	Logan SD	Logan
24	10.6	Jordan SD	Sandy
25	10.0	Alpine SD	American Fork
26	9.9	Park City SD	Park City
27	9.3	Davis SD	Farmington
28	8.7	Murray SD	Murray
29	7.1	Morgan SD	Morgan

English Language Learner Students

Rank	Percent	District Name	City
1	67.1	San Juan SD	Blanding
2	35.0	Salt Lake City SD	Salt Lake City
3	19.4	Ogden SD	Ogden
4	16.7	Granite SD	Salt Lake City
5	16.6	Provo SD	Provo
6	12.1	Logan SD	Logan
7	10.3	Uintah SD	Vernal
8	9.1	Park City SD	Park City
9	8.8	Millard SD	Delta
10	6.5	North Sanpete SD	Mount Pleasant
11	6.0	Murray SD	Murray
12	5.9	Washington SD	Saint George
13	5.4	Iron SD	Cedar City
13	5.4	South Sanpete SD	Manti
15	5.2	Wasatch SD	Heber City
16	5.1	Cache SD	Logan
17	4.8	Davis SD	Farmington
18	4.7	Alpine SD	American Fork
19	4.3	Jordan SD	Sandy
20	3.8	Nebo SD	Spanish Fork
21	3.4	Tooele SD	Tooele
22	3.1	Emery SD	Huntington
23	2.6	Duchesne SD	Duchesne
24	2.2	Box Elder SD	Brigham City
25	1.2	Weber SD	Ogden
26	0.7	Carbon SD	Price
27	0.6	Sevier SD	Richfield
28	0.3	Morgan SD	Morgan
29	0.2	Juab SD	Nephi

Migrant Students

Rank	Percent	District Name	City
1	15.2	North Sanpete SD	Mount Pleasant
2	8.8	Ogden SD	Ogden
3	5.8	Millard SD	Delta
4	3.0	Box Elder SD	Brigham City
5	2.1	Nebo SD	Spanish Fork
6	1.8	Alpine SD	American Fork
6	1.8	Cache SD	Logan
8	1.1	Provo SD	Provo
9	0.2	Davis SD	Farmington
9	0.2	Jordan SD	Sandy
9	0.2	South Sanpete SD	Manti
12	0.0	Logan SD	Logan
13	0.0	Carbon SD	Price
13	0.0	Duchesne SD	Duchesne
13	0.0	Emery SD	Huntington
13	0.0	Granite SD	Salt Lake City
13	0.0	Iron SD	Cedar City
13	0.0	Juab SD	Nephi
13	0.0	Morgan SD	Morgan
13	0.0	Murray SD	Murray
13	0.0	Park City SD	Park City
13	0.0	Salt Lake City SD	Salt Lake City
13	0.0	San Juan SD	Blanding
13	0.0	Sevier SD	Richfield
13	0.0	Tooele SD	Tooele
13	0.0	Uintah SD	Vernal
13	0.0	Wasatch SD	Heber City
13	0.0	Washington SD	Saint George
13	0.0	Weber SD	Ogden

Students Eligible for Free Lunch

Rank	Percent	District Name	City
1	58.2	San Juan SD	Blanding
2	53.4	Ogden SD	Ogden
3	45.9	Salt Lake City SD	Salt Lake City
4	32.8	Carbon SD	Price
5	32.6	North Sanpete SD	Mount Pleasant
6	31.3	Provo SD	Provo
7	30.2	Uintah SD	Vernal
8	29.8	Duchesne SD	Duchesne
9	29.7	South Sanpete SD	Manti
10	29.5	Sevier SD	Richfield
11	28.2	Logan SD	Logan
11	28.2	Millard SD	Delta

13	27.9	Emery SD	Huntington
14	27.6	Iron SD	Cedar City
15	27.2	Granite SD	Salt Lake City
16	23.1	Tooele SD	Tooele
17	20.6	Washington SD	Saint George
18	20.2	Box Elder SD	Brigham City
19	18.4	Juab SD	Nephi
20	16.5	Nebo SD	Spanish Fork
21	15.8	Alpine SD	American Fork
21	15.8	Cache SD	Logan
21	15.8	Murray SD	Murray
24	15.4	Wasatch SD	Heber City
25	14.1	Davis SD	Farmington
26	13.3	Weber SD	Ogden
27	12.9	Jordan SD	Sandy
28	7.7	Park City SD	Park City
29	7.6	Morgan SD	Morgan

Students Eligible for Reduced-Price Lunch

Rank	Percent	District Name	City
1	17.7	Emery SD	Huntington
2	16.2	North Sanpete SD	Mount Pleasant
3	16.1	Millard SD	Delta
4	15.4	South Sanpete SD	Manti
5	15.2	Juab SD	Nephi
6	14.5	Sevier SD	Richfield
7	14.2	Duchesne SD	Duchesne
8	14.1	Uintah SD	Vernal
9	12.5	Box Elder SD	Brigham City
9	12.5	Cache SD	Logan
11	12.3	Iron SD	Cedar City
12	11.9	San Juan SD	Blanding
13	11.2	Carbon SD	Price
14	10.9	Tooele SD	Tooele
15	10.8	Logan SD	Logan
16	10.5	Washington SD	Saint George
17	10.0	Salt Lake City SD	Salt Lake City
18	9.6	Ogden SD	Ogden
19	9.4	Granite SD	Salt Lake City
19	9.4	Nebo SD	Spanish Fork
19	9.4	Provo SD	Provo
22	9.3	Morgan SD	Morgan
23	8.7	Weber SD	Ogden
24	8.0	Davis SD	Farmington
25	7.5	Alpine SD	American Fork
26	6.9	Wasatch SD	Heber City
27	6.7	Murray SD	Murray
28	6.6	Jordan SD	Sandy
29	1.9	Park City SD	Park City

Student/Teacher Ratio

Rank	Ratio	District Name	City
1	24.2	Nebo SD	Spanish Fork
2	23.8	Alpine SD	American Fork
3	23.7	Jordan SD	Sandy
4	22.8	Juab SD	Nephi
4	22.8	Tooele SD	Tooele
4	22.8	Washington SD	Saint George
4	22.8	Weber SD	Ogden
8	22.7	Davis SD	Farmington
9	22.1	Cache SD	Logan
10	21.0	Iron SD	Cedar City
11	20.7	Granite SD	Salt Lake City
11	20.7	North Sanpete SD	Mount Pleasant
13	20.6	Murray SD	Murray
14	20.5	Box Elder SD	Brigham City
14	20.5	Logan SD	Logan
16	20.4	Ogden SD	Ogden
17	20.3	Morgan SD	Morgan
18	20.0	Wasatch SD	Heber City
19	19.9	Sevier SD	Richfield
20	19.3	Provo SD	Provo
20	19.3	Salt Lake City SD	Salt Lake City
22	18.6	Duchesne SD	Duchesne
22	18.6	Park City SD	Park City
24	18.5	South Sanpete SD	Manti
25	18.1	Uintah SD	Vernal
26	17.8	Emery SD	Huntington
27	17.7	Millard SD	Delta
28	17.2	Carbon SD	Price
29	14.5	San Juan SD	Blanding

Student/Librarian Ratio

Rank	Ratio	District Name	City
1	6,240.0	Juab SD	Nephi
2	3,486.5	Alpine SD	American Fork
3	3,095.7	Davis SD	Farmington
4	2,841.0	Uintah SD	Vernal
5	2,769.7	Granite SD	Salt Lake City
6	2,723.5	Jordan SD	Sandy
7	2,450.0	North Sanpete SD	Mount Pleasant
8	2,423.0	Iron SD	Cedar City
9	2,363.4	Weber SD	Ogden
10	2,296.7	Nebo SD	Spanish Fork
11	2,006.8	Tooele SD	Tooele
12	1,969.7	Washington SD	Saint George
13	1,777.2	Box Elder SD	Brigham City
14	1,663.9	Carbon SD	Price
15	1,636.7	Emery SD	Huntington
16	1,584.0	Murray SD	Murray
17	1,550.8	Morgan SD	Morgan
18	1,467.3	Logan SD	Logan
19	1,305.3	Wasatch SD	Heber City
20	801.8	Park City SD	Park City
21	743.1	Provo SD	Provo
22	680.7	Cache SD	Logan
23	676.7	Ogden SD	Ogden
24	647.1	Salt Lake City SD	Salt Lake City
25	614.3	Duchesne SD	Duchesne
26	498.7	Millard SD	Delta
27	335.8	San Juan SD	Blanding
28	0.0	Sevier SD	Richfield
28	0.0	South Sanpete SD	Manti

Student/Counselor Ratio

Rank	Ratio	District Name	City
1	1,227.5	Emery SD	Huntington
2	1,225.0	North Sanpete SD	Mount Pleasant
3	1,129.7	Sevier SD	Richfield
4	1,048.4	Jordan SD	Sandy
5	893.7	Provo SD	Provo
6	886.5	Iron SD	Cedar City
7	864.0	Alpine SD	American Fork
8	859.4	Logan SD	Logan
9	815.8	Tooele SD	Tooele
10	808.3	Nebo SD	Spanish Fork
11	805.1	South Sanpete SD	Manti
12	785.5	Millard SD	Delta
13	782.2	Murray SD	Murray
14	748.8	Juab SD	Nephi
15	695.4	Cache SD	Logan
16	695.2	Morgan SD	Morgan
17	682.7	Salt Lake City SD	Salt Lake City
18	677.3	Granite SD	Salt Lake City
19	668.5	Uintah SD	Vernal
20	654.6	Duchesne SD	Duchesne
21	641.6	Washington SD	Saint George
22	631.6	Wasatch SD	Heber City
23	622.7	San Juan SD	Blanding
24	592.4	Box Elder SD	Brigham City
25	568.2	Weber SD	Ogden
26	563.1	Davis SD	Farmington
27	460.8	Park City SD	Park City
28	450.4	Ogden SD	Ogden
29	390.5	Carbon SD	Price

Current Spending per Student in FY2001

Rank	Dollars	District Name	City
1	8,774	San Juan SD	Blanding
2	6,263	Carbon SD	Price
3	6,014	Millard SD	Delta
4	5,799	Park City SD	Park City
5	5,594	Emery SD	Huntington
6	5,450	Ogden SD	Ogden
7	5,440	Salt Lake City SD	Salt Lake City
8	5,395	Provo SD	Provo
9	5,311	South Sanpete SD	Manti
10	5,278	Uintah SD	Vernal
11	5,245	Duchesne SD	Duchesne
12	5,205	North Sanpete SD	Mount Pleasant
13	5,185	Iron SD	Cedar City
14	5,087	Sevier SD	Richfield
15	4,849	Wasatch SD	Heber City
16	4,689	Murray SD	Murray
17	4,682	Morgan SD	Morgan
18	4,536	Davis SD	Farmington
19	4,530	Cache SD	Logan
20	4,492	Juab SD	Nephi
21	4,485	Box Elder SD	Brigham City
22	4,480	Nebo SD	Spanish Fork
23	4,467	Washington SD	Saint George
24	4,451	Granite SD	Salt Lake City
25	4,413	Weber SD	Ogden
26	4,363	Logan SD	Logan
27	4,308	Jordan SD	Sandy
28	4,270	Tooele SD	Tooele
29	4,119	Alpine SD	American Fork

Number of Diploma Recipients

Rank	Number	District Name	City
1	4,916	Jordan SD	Sandy
2	4,170	Granite SD	Salt Lake City
3	3,765	Davis SD	Farmington
4	2,726	Alpine SD	American Fork
5	1,898	Weber SD	Ogden
6	1,303	Nebo SD	Spanish Fork
7	1,214	Washington SD	Saint George
8	1,202	Salt Lake City SD	Salt Lake City
9	895	Cache SD	Logan
10	805	Box Elder SD	Brigham City
11	763	Provo SD	Provo
12	656	Ogden SD	Ogden
13	513	Tooele SD	Tooele
14	482	Iron SD	Cedar City
15	480	Murray SD	Murray
16	405	Logan SD	Logan
17	393	Uintah SD	Vernal
18	305	Sevier SD	Richfield
19	303	Duchesne SD	Duchesne
20	282	Park City SD	Park City
21	277	Wasatch SD	Heber City
22	273	Carbon SD	Price
23	263	Millard SD	Delta
24	226	South Sanpete SD	Manti
25	219	Emery SD	Huntington
26	199	San Juan SD	Blanding
27	175	North Sanpete SD	Mount Pleasant
28	174	Morgan SD	Morgan
29	124	Juab SD	Nephi

High School Drop-out Rate

Rank	Percent	District Name	City
1	9.0	Salt Lake City SD	Salt Lake City
2	7.1	Granite SD	Salt Lake City
3	6.7	Ogden SD	Ogden
4	5.5	Uintah SD	Vernal
5	5.1	Logan SD	Logan
6	4.8	North Sanpete SD	Mount Pleasant
7	4.4	Box Elder SD	Brigham City
7	4.4	Jordan SD	Sandy
9	4.2	Sevier SD	Richfield
10	3.6	Duchesne SD	Duchesne
11	3.1	San Juan SD	Blanding
12	2.9	Cache SD	Logan
13	2.8	Carbon SD	Price
14	2.7	Murray SD	Murray
14	2.7	Park City SD	Park City
16	2.6	Millard SD	Delta
17	2.5	Washington SD	Saint George
18	2.1	Iron SD	Cedar City
19	2.0	Alpine SD	American Fork
20	1.8	Davis SD	Farmington
20	1.8	Wasatch SD	Heber City
22	1.7	Emery SD	Huntington
22	1.7	Tooele SD	Tooele
22	1.7	Weber SD	Ogden
25	1.5	South Sanpete SD	Manti
26	1.4	Morgan SD	Morgan
26	1.4	Nebo SD	Spanish Fork
28	0.9	Juab SD	Nephi
29	0.8	Provo SD	Provo

Vermont

Vermont Public School Educational Profile

Category	Value	Category	Value
Schools *(2002-2003)*	391	**Diploma Recipients** *(2002-2003)*	7,083
Instructional Level		White, Non-Hispanic	0
Primary	259	Black, Non-Hispanic	0
Middle	24	Asian/Pacific Islander	0
High	61	American Indian/Alaskan Native	0
Other Level	47	Hispanic	0
Curriculum		**High School Drop-out Rate** (%) *(2000-2001)*	4.7
Regular	314	White, Non-Hispanic	4.7
Special Education	61	Black, Non-Hispanic	7.0
Vocational	14	Asian/Pacific Islander	2.5
Alternative	2	American Indian/Alaskan Native	7.0
Type		Hispanic	7.5
Magnet	0	**Staff** *(2002-2003)*	18,386.2
Charter	0	Teachers	8,542.6
Title I Eligible	215	Average Salary ($)	42,038
School-wide Title I	94	Librarians/Media Specialists	234.4
Students *(2002-2003)*	99,978	Guidance Counselors	417.8
Gender (%)		**Ratios** *(2002-2003)*	
Male	51.6	Student/Teacher Ratio	11.7 to 1
Female	48.4	Student/Librarian Ratio	426.5 to 1
Race/Ethnicity (%)		Student/Counselor Ratio	239.3 to 1
White, Non-Hispanic	95.8	**Current Spending** *($ per student in FY 2001)*	9,806
Black, Non-Hispanic	1.3	Instruction	6,314
Asian/Pacific Islander	1.6	Support Services	3,217
American Indian/Alaskan Native	0.6	**College Entrance Exam Scores** *(2003)*	
Hispanic	0.7	Scholastic Aptitude Test (SAT)	
Classification (%)		Participation Rate (%)	70
Individual Education Program (IEP)	13.8	Mean SAT I Verbal Score	515
Migrant	0.9	Mean SAT I Math Score	512
English Language Learner (ELL)	1.1	American College Testing Program (ACT)	
Eligible for Free Lunch Program	18.5	Participation Rate (%)	11
Eligible for Reduced-Price Lunch Program	7.0	Average Composite Score	22.5

Note: *For an explanation of data, please refer to the User's Guide in the front of the book; n/a indicates data not available*

Vermont NAEP 2003 Test Scores

Reading			Mathematics		
Grade/Category	**Value**	**Rank**	**Grade/Category**	**Value**	**Rank**
4th Grade			**4th Grade**		
Average Proficiency	226.1 (0.9)	4/51	Average Proficiency	241.9 (0.8)	3/51
Proficiency by Gender/Race/Ethnicity			Proficiency by Gender/Race/Ethnicity		
Male	223.5 (1.1)	4/51	Male	243.7 (0.9)	3/51
Female	228.9 (1.2)	5/51	Female	240.2 (1.0)	3/51
White, Non-Hispanic	226.0 (0.9)	25/51	White, Non-Hispanic	242.2 (0.8)	24/51
Black, Non-Hispanic	n/a	n/a	Black, Non-Hispanic	n/a	n/a
Asian, Non-Hispanic	n/a	n/a	Asian, Non-Hispanic	n/a	n/a
American Indian, Non-Hispanic	n/a	n/a	American Indian, Non-Hispanic	n/a	n/a
Hispanic	n/a	n/a	Hispanic	n/a	n/a
Proficiency by Class Size			Proficiency by Class Size		
Less than 16 Students	222.3 (2.1)	2/45	Less than 16 Students	240.6 (1.6)	1/47
16 to 18 Students	226.4 (2.0)	4/48	16 to 18 Students	239.9 (1.5)	8/48
19 to 20 Students	227.4 (1.8)	5/50	19 to 20 Students	244.6 (1.5)	1/50
21 to 25 Students	228.3 (1.9)	4/51	21 to 25 Students	242.2 (1.9)	9/51
Greater than 25 Students	n/a	n/a	Greater than 25 Students	n/a	n/a
Percent Attaining Achievement Levels			Percent Attaining Achievement Levels		
Below Basic	26.6 (1.5)	49/51	Below Basic	15.2 (1.1)	47/51
Basic or Above	73.4 (1.5)	3/51	Basic or Above	84.8 (1.1)	4/51
Proficient or Above	36.8 (1.1)	6/51	Proficient or Above	41.9 (1.2)	2/51
Advanced or Above	8.1 (0.8)	11/51	Advanced or Above	5.5 (0.5)	6/51
8th Grade			**8th Grade**		
Average Proficiency	270.5 (0.8)	3/51	Average Proficiency	285.6 (0.8)	6/51
Proficiency by Gender/Race/Ethnicity			Proficiency by Gender/Race/Ethnicity		
Male	264.8 (1.2)	3/51	Male	285.7 (1.1)	7/51
Female	276.2 (1.1)	2/51	Female	285.6 (0.8)	4/51
White, Non-Hispanic	271.0 (0.8)	19/50	White, Non-Hispanic	286.0 (0.8)	26/50
Black, Non-Hispanic	n/a	n/a	Black, Non-Hispanic	n/a	n/a
Asian, Non-Hispanic	n/a	n/a	Asian, Non-Hispanic	n/a	n/a
American Indian, Non-Hispanic	n/a	n/a	American Indian, Non-Hispanic	n/a	n/a
Hispanic	n/a	n/a	Hispanic	n/a	n/a
Proficiency by Parents Highest Level of Ed.			Proficiency by Parents Highest Level of Ed.		
Did Not Finish High School	247.8 (4.1)	17/50	Did Not Finish High School	262.2 (2.8)	10/50
Graduated High School	261.1 (1.5)	6/50	Graduated High School	276.2 (1.4)	6/50
Some Education After High School	270.0 (1.8)	18/50	Some Education After High School	285.6 (1.3)	8/50
Graduated College	279.7 (1.0)	2/50	Graduated College	294.3 (1.0)	6/50
Percent Attaining Achievement Levels			Percent Attaining Achievement Levels		
Below Basic	18.7 (1.1)	47/51	Below Basic	22.8 (0.9)	46/51
Basic or Above	81.3 (1.1)	5/51	Basic or Above	77.2 (0.9)	6/51
Proficient or Above	38.5 (1.2)	4/51	Proficient or Above	35.0 (1.1)	6/51
Advanced or Above	4.0 (0.5)	4/51	Advanced or Above	6.8 (0.7)	6/51

Note: *For an explanation of data, please refer to the User's Guide in the front of the book; values in italics indicate that the nature of the sample does not allow accurate determination of the variability of the statistic; n/a indicates data not available*

Bennington County

Mount Anthony UHSD 14

301 Park St Ext • Bennington, VT 05201-5011
(802) 447-7511
Grade Span: 07-12; **Agency Type:** 2
Schools: 3
0 Primary; 1 Middle; 2 High; 0 Other Level
2 Regular; 0 Special Education; 1 Vocational; 0 Alternative
0 Magnet; 0 Charter; 2 Title I Eligible; 0 School-wide Title I
Students: 1,836 (51.3% male; 48.7% female)
Individual Education Program: 0 (0.0%);
English Language Learner: 0 (0.0%); Migrant: 1 (0.1%)
Eligible for Free Lunch Program: 333 (18.1%)
Eligible for Reduced-Price Lunch Program: 39 (2.1%)
Teachers: 115.4 (15.9 to 1)
Librarians/Media Specialists: 2.0 (918.0 to 1)
Guidance Counselors: 14.0 (131.1 to 1)
Current Spending: ($ per student per year):
Total: $6,627; Instruction: $4,055; Support Services: $2,570
Enrollment, Drop-out Rates and Diploma Recipients by Race/Ethnicity

Category	Total	White	Black	Asian	AIAN	Hisp.
Enrollment (%)	100.0	97.8	0.7	0.9	0.2	0.4
Drop-out Rate (%)	7.2	7.3	0.0	0.0	0.0	14.3
H.S. Diplomas (#)	285	n/a	n/a	n/a	n/a	n/a

Chittenden County

Burlington SD

150 Colchester Ave • Burlington, VT 05401
(802) 864-8461 • http://burlington.k12.vt.us/
Grade Span: PK-12; **Agency Type:** 2
Schools: 12
7 Primary; 2 Middle; 2 High; 1 Other Level
9 Regular; 1 Special Education; 1 Vocational; 1 Alternative
0 Magnet; 0 Charter; 8 Title I Eligible; 3 School-wide Title I
Students: 3,648 (52.2% male; 47.8% female)
Individual Education Program: 542 (14.9%);
English Language Learner: 356 (9.8%); Migrant: 11 (0.3%)
Eligible for Free Lunch Program: 1,358 (37.2%)
Eligible for Reduced-Price Lunch Program: 307 (8.4%)
Teachers: 292.9 (12.5 to 1)
Librarians/Media Specialists: 9.0 (405.3 to 1)
Guidance Counselors: 14.6 (249.9 to 1)
Current Spending: ($ per student per year):
Total: $9,669; Instruction: $6,130; Support Services: $3,188
Enrollment, Drop-out Rates and Diploma Recipients by Race/Ethnicity

Category	Total	White	Black	Asian	AIAN	Hisp.
Enrollment (%)	100.0	84.5	6.5	6.4	0.4	2.2
Drop-out Rate (%)	6.9	7.0	9.1	1.4	50.0	11.1
H.S. Diplomas (#)	199	n/a	n/a	n/a	n/a	n/a

Colchester SD

125 Laker Ln • Colchester, VT 05446-0055
Mailing Address: Box 27 • Colchester, VT 05446-0055
(802) 658-4047 • http://www.colchestersd.k12.vt.us/
Grade Span: PK-12; **Agency Type:** 2
Schools: 5
3 Primary; 1 Middle; 1 High; 0 Other Level
5 Regular; 0 Special Education; 0 Vocational; 0 Alternative
0 Magnet; 0 Charter; 3 Title I Eligible; 0 School-wide Title I
Students: 2,517 (52.0% male; 48.0% female)
Individual Education Program: 267 (10.6%);
English Language Learner: 42 (1.7%); Migrant: 1 (<0.1%)
Eligible for Free Lunch Program: 212 (8.4%)
Eligible for Reduced-Price Lunch Program: 87 (3.5%)
Teachers: 164.4 (15.3 to 1)
Librarians/Media Specialists: 5.0 (503.4 to 1)
Guidance Counselors: 9.8 (256.8 to 1)
Current Spending: ($ per student per year):
Total: $7,636; Instruction: $4,594; Support Services: $2,784
Enrollment, Drop-out Rates and Diploma Recipients by Race/Ethnicity

Category	Total	White	Black	Asian	AIAN	Hisp.
Enrollment (%)	100.0	96.5	1.4	1.2	0.1	0.8
Drop-out Rate (%)	1.4	1.1	16.7	14.3	0.0	0.0
H.S. Diplomas (#)	159	n/a	n/a	n/a	n/a	n/a

Essex Community Education Ctr

2 Educational Dr • Essex Junction, VT 05452-3167
(802) 879-5500
Grade Span: 09-12; **Agency Type:** 2
Schools: 2
0 Primary; 0 Middle; 2 High; 0 Other Level
1 Regular; 0 Special Education; 1 Vocational; 0 Alternative
0 Magnet; 0 Charter; 0 Title I Eligible; 0 School-wide Title I
Students: 1,568 (52.4% male; 47.6% female)
Individual Education Program: 0 (0.0%);
English Language Learner: 0 (0.0%); Migrant: 0 (0.0%)
Eligible for Free Lunch Program: 67 (4.3%)
Eligible for Reduced-Price Lunch Program: 50 (3.2%)
Teachers: 117.9 (13.3 to 1)
Librarians/Media Specialists: 1.0 (1,568.0 to 1)
Guidance Counselors: 8.7 (180.2 to 1)
Current Spending: ($ per student per year):
Total: $10,972; Instruction: $7,355; Support Services: $3,024
Enrollment, Drop-out Rates and Diploma Recipients by Race/Ethnicity

Category	Total	White	Black	Asian	AIAN	Hisp.
Enrollment (%)	100.0	94.8	1.1	2.9	0.3	0.9
Drop-out Rate (%)	2.2	2.2	0.0	0.0	0.0	7.7
H.S. Diplomas (#)	337	n/a	n/a	n/a	n/a	n/a

Milton Id SD

42 Herrick Ave • Milton, VT 05468-0018
(802) 893-3210
Grade Span: PK-12; **Agency Type:** 2
Schools: 3
1 Primary; 1 Middle; 1 High; 0 Other Level
3 Regular; 0 Special Education; 0 Vocational; 0 Alternative
0 Magnet; 0 Charter; 2 Title I Eligible; 2 School-wide Title I
Students: 1,860 (52.5% male; 47.5% female)
Individual Education Program: 279 (15.0%);
English Language Learner: 6 (0.3%); Migrant: 4 (0.2%)
Eligible for Free Lunch Program: 205 (11.0%)
Eligible for Reduced-Price Lunch Program: 122 (6.6%)
Teachers: 141.5 (13.1 to 1)
Librarians/Media Specialists: 3.0 (620.0 to 1)
Guidance Counselors: 7.5 (248.0 to 1)
Current Spending: ($ per student per year):
Total: $7,463; Instruction: $4,398; Support Services: $2,884
Enrollment, Drop-out Rates and Diploma Recipients by Race/Ethnicity

Category	Total	White	Black	Asian	AIAN	Hisp.
Enrollment (%)	100.0	98.1	0.5	0.5	0.3	0.6
Drop-out Rate (%)	6.8	6.9	0.0	0.0	n/a	0.0
H.S. Diplomas (#)	114	n/a	n/a	n/a	n/a	n/a

Mount Mansfield USD 17

211 Browns Trace Rd • Jericho, VT 05465-9498
(802) 899-4690
Grade Span: 05-12; **Agency Type:** 2
Schools: 3
0 Primary; 2 Middle; 1 High; 0 Other Level
3 Regular; 0 Special Education; 0 Vocational; 0 Alternative
0 Magnet; 0 Charter; 1 Title I Eligible; 0 School-wide Title I
Students: 1,957 (52.7% male; 47.3% female)
Individual Education Program: 0 (0.0%);
English Language Learner: 0 (0.0%); Migrant: 0 (0.0%)
Eligible for Free Lunch Program: 108 (5.5%)
Eligible for Reduced-Price Lunch Program: 54 (2.8%)
Teachers: 129.1 (15.2 to 1)
Librarians/Media Specialists: 3.0 (652.3 to 1)
Guidance Counselors: 8.0 (244.6 to 1)
Current Spending: ($ per student per year):
Total: $5,922; Instruction: $4,086; Support Services: $1,545
Enrollment, Drop-out Rates and Diploma Recipients by Race/Ethnicity

Category	Total	White	Black	Asian	AIAN	Hisp.
Enrollment (%)	100.0	97.9	1.0	0.6	0.2	0.4
Drop-out Rate (%)	1.7	1.5	22.2	0.0	0.0	n/a
H.S. Diplomas (#)	247	n/a	n/a	n/a	n/a	n/a

South Burlington SD

550 Dorset St • South Burlington, VT 05403-6296
(802) 652-7250
Grade Span: KG-12; **Agency Type:** 2
Schools: 5
3 Primary; 1 Middle; 1 High; 0 Other Level
5 Regular; 0 Special Education; 0 Vocational; 0 Alternative
0 Magnet; 0 Charter; 1 Title I Eligible; 0 School-wide Title I
Students: 2,617 (51.1% male; 48.9% female)
Individual Education Program: 270 (10.3%);
English Language Learner: 100 (3.8%); Migrant: 1 (<0.1%)
Eligible for Free Lunch Program: 193 (7.4%)
Eligible for Reduced-Price Lunch Program: 119 (4.5%)
Teachers: 203.5 (12.9 to 1)
Librarians/Media Specialists: 5.0 (523.4 to 1)
Guidance Counselors: 10.0 (261.7 to 1)
Current Spending: ($ per student per year):
Total: $9,689; Instruction: $6,200; Support Services: $3,233

Enrollment, Drop-out Rates and Diploma Recipients by Race/Ethnicity

Category	Total	White	Black	Asian	AIAN	Hisp.
Enrollment (%)	100.0	90.8	1.7	6.3	0.0	1.1
Drop-out Rate (%)	3.2	3.3	0.0	0.0	0.0	0.0
H.S. Diplomas (#)	195	n/a	n/a	n/a	n/a	n/a

Rutland County

Rutland City SD

6 Church St • Rutland, VT 05701-0969
(802) 773-1900
Grade Span: KG-12; **Agency Type:** 2
Schools: 6
3 Primary; 1 Middle; 2 High; 0 Other Level
5 Regular; 0 Special Education; 1 Vocational; 0 Alternative
0 Magnet; 0 Charter; 4 Title I Eligible; 4 School-wide Title I
Students: 2,806 (50.2% male; 49.8% female)
Individual Education Program: 317 (11.3%);
English Language Learner: 3 (0.1%); Migrant: 1 (<0.1%)
Eligible for Free Lunch Program: 817 (29.1%)
Eligible for Reduced-Price Lunch Program: 191 (6.8%)
Teachers: 211.1 (13.3 to 1)
Librarians/Media Specialists: 2.0 (1,403.0 to 1)
Guidance Counselors: 12.0 (233.8 to 1)
Current Spending: ($ per student per year):
Total: $8,930; Instruction: $6,422; Support Services: $2,180

Enrollment, Drop-out Rates and Diploma Recipients by Race/Ethnicity

Category	Total	White	Black	Asian	AIAN	Hisp.
Enrollment (%)	100.0	96.4	1.4	1.4	0.2	0.7
Drop-out Rate (%)	6.1	6.3	7.7	0.0	0.0	0.0
H.S. Diplomas (#)	238	n/a	n/a	n/a	n/a	n/a

Windsor County

Hartford SD

73 Highland Ave • White River Junction, VT 05001-8018
(802) 295-8600
Grade Span: PK-12; **Agency Type:** 2
Schools: 6
3 Primary; 1 Middle; 2 High; 0 Other Level
5 Regular; 0 Special Education; 1 Vocational; 0 Alternative
0 Magnet; 0 Charter; 3 Title I Eligible; 0 School-wide Title I
Students: 1,962 (50.1% male; 49.9% female)
Individual Education Program: 239 (12.2%);
English Language Learner: 6 (0.3%); Migrant: 1 (0.1%)
Eligible for Free Lunch Program: 192 (9.8%)
Eligible for Reduced-Price Lunch Program: 51 (2.6%)
Teachers: 163.1 (12.0 to 1)
Librarians/Media Specialists: 5.0 (392.4 to 1)
Guidance Counselors: 10.0 (196.2 to 1)
Current Spending: ($ per student per year):
Total: $8,400; Instruction: $5,241; Support Services: $2,958

Enrollment, Drop-out Rates and Diploma Recipients by Race/Ethnicity

Category	Total	White	Black	Asian	AIAN	Hisp.
Enrollment (%)	100.0	97.0	1.4	1.1	0.1	0.4
Drop-out Rate (%)	4.3	4.1	100.0	0.0	0.0	0.0
H.S. Diplomas (#)	181	n/a	n/a	n/a	n/a	n/a

Number of Schools

Rank	Number	District Name	City
1	12	Burlington SD	Burlington
2	6	Hartford SD	White River Jct
2	6	Rutland City SD	Rutland
4	5	Colchester SD	Colchester
4	5	South Burlington SD	S Burlington
6	3	Milton Id SD	Milton
6	3	Mount Anthony UHSD 14	Bennington
6	3	Mount Mansfield USD 17	Jericho
9	2	Essex Community Education Ctr	Essex Junction

Number of Teachers

Rank	Number	District Name	City
1	292	Burlington SD	Burlington
2	211	Rutland City SD	Rutland
3	203	South Burlington SD	S Burlington
4	164	Colchester SD	Colchester
5	163	Hartford SD	White River Jct
6	141	Milton Id SD	Milton
7	129	Mount Mansfield USD 17	Jericho
8	117	Essex Community Education Ctr	Essex Junction
9	115	Mount Anthony UHSD 14	Bennington

Number of Students

Rank	Number	District Name	City
1	3,648	Burlington SD	Burlington
2	2,806	Rutland City SD	Rutland
3	2,617	South Burlington SD	S Burlington
4	2,517	Colchester SD	Colchester
5	1,962	Hartford SD	White River Jct
6	1,957	Mount Mansfield USD 17	Jericho
7	1,860	Milton Id SD	Milton
8	1,836	Mount Anthony UHSD 14	Bennington
9	1,568	Essex Community Education Ctr	Essex Junction

Male Students

Rank	Percent	District Name	City
1	52.7	Mount Mansfield USD 17	Jericho
2	52.5	Milton Id SD	Milton
3	52.4	Essex Community Education Ctr	Essex Junction
4	52.2	Burlington SD	Burlington
5	52.0	Colchester SD	Colchester
6	51.3	Mount Anthony UHSD 14	Bennington
7	51.1	South Burlington SD	S Burlington
8	50.2	Rutland City SD	Rutland
9	50.1	Hartford SD	White River Jct

Female Students

Rank	Percent	District Name	City
1	49.9	Hartford SD	White River Jct
2	49.8	Rutland City SD	Rutland
3	48.9	South Burlington SD	S Burlington
4	48.7	Mount Anthony UHSD 14	Bennington
5	48.0	Colchester SD	Colchester
6	47.8	Burlington SD	Burlington
7	47.6	Essex Community Education Ctr	Essex Junction
8	47.5	Milton Id SD	Milton
9	47.3	Mount Mansfield USD 17	Jericho

Individual Education Program Students

Rank	Percent	District Name	City
1	15.0	Milton Id SD	Milton
2	14.9	Burlington SD	Burlington
3	12.2	Hartford SD	White River Jct
4	11.3	Rutland City SD	Rutland
5	10.6	Colchester SD	Colchester
6	10.3	South Burlington SD	S Burlington
7	0.0	Essex Community Education Ctr	Essex Junction
7	0.0	Mount Anthony UHSD 14	Bennington
7	0.0	Mount Mansfield USD 17	Jericho

English Language Learner Students

Rank	Percent	District Name	City
1	9.8	Burlington SD	Burlington
2	3.8	South Burlington SD	S Burlington
3	1.7	Colchester SD	Colchester
4	0.3	Hartford SD	White River Jct
4	0.3	Milton Id SD	Milton
6	0.1	Rutland City SD	Rutland
7	0.0	Essex Community Education Ctr	Essex Junction
7	0.0	Mount Anthony UHSD 14	Bennington
7	0.0	Mount Mansfield USD 17	Jericho

Migrant Students

Rank	Percent	District Name	City
1	0.3	Burlington SD	Burlington
2	0.2	Milton Id SD	Milton
3	0.1	Hartford SD	White River Jct
3	0.1	Mount Anthony UHSD 14	Bennington
5	0.0	Colchester SD	Colchester
5	0.0	Rutland City SD	Rutland
5	0.0	South Burlington SD	S Burlington
8	0.0	Essex Community Education Ctr	Essex Junction
8	0.0	Mount Mansfield USD 17	Jericho

Students Eligible for Free Lunch

Rank	Percent	District Name	City
1	37.2	Burlington SD	Burlington
2	29.1	Rutland City SD	Rutland
3	18.1	Mount Anthony UHSD 14	Bennington
4	11.0	Milton Id SD	Milton
5	9.8	Hartford SD	White River Jct
6	8.4	Colchester SD	Colchester
7	7.4	South Burlington SD	S Burlington
8	5.5	Mount Mansfield USD 17	Jericho
9	4.3	Essex Community Education Ctr	Essex Junction

Students Eligible for Reduced-Price Lunch

Rank	Percent	District Name	City
1	8.4	Burlington SD	Burlington
2	6.8	Rutland City SD	Rutland
3	6.6	Milton Id SD	Milton
4	4.5	South Burlington SD	S Burlington
5	3.5	Colchester SD	Colchester
6	3.2	Essex Community Education Ctr	Essex Junction
7	2.8	Mount Mansfield USD 17	Jericho
8	2.6	Hartford SD	White River Jct
9	2.1	Mount Anthony UHSD 14	Bennington

Student/Teacher Ratio

Rank	Ratio	District Name	City
1	15.9	Mount Anthony UHSD 14	Bennington
2	15.3	Colchester SD	Colchester
3	15.2	Mount Mansfield USD 17	Jericho
4	13.3	Essex Community Education Ctr	Essex Junction
4	13.3	Rutland City SD	Rutland
6	13.1	Milton Id SD	Milton
7	12.9	South Burlington SD	S Burlington
8	12.5	Burlington SD	Burlington
9	12.0	Hartford SD	White River Jct

Student/Librarian Ratio

Rank	Ratio	District Name	City
1	1,568.0	Essex Community Education Ctr	Essex Junction
2	1,403.0	Rutland City SD	Rutland
3	918.0	Mount Anthony UHSD 14	Bennington
4	652.3	Mount Mansfield USD 17	Jericho
5	620.0	Milton Id SD	Milton
6	523.4	South Burlington SD	S Burlington
7	503.4	Colchester SD	Colchester
8	405.3	Burlington SD	Burlington
9	392.4	Hartford SD	White River Jct

Student/Counselor Ratio

Rank	Ratio	District Name	City
1	261.7	South Burlington SD	S Burlington
2	256.8	Colchester SD	Colchester
3	249.9	Burlington SD	Burlington
4	248.0	Milton Id SD	Milton
5	244.6	Mount Mansfield USD 17	Jericho
6	233.8	Rutland City SD	Rutland
7	196.2	Hartford SD	White River Jct
8	180.2	Essex Community Education Ctr	Essex Junction
9	131.1	Mount Anthony UHSD 14	Bennington

Current Spending per Student in FY2001

Rank	Dollars	District Name	City
1	10,972	Essex Community Education Ctr	Essex Junction
2	9,689	South Burlington SD	S Burlington
3	9,669	Burlington SD	Burlington
4	8,930	Rutland City SD	Rutland
5	8,400	Hartford SD	White River Jct
6	7,636	Colchester SD	Colchester
7	7,463	Milton Id SD	Milton
8	6,627	Mount Anthony UHSD 14	Bennington
9	5,922	Mount Mansfield USD 17	Jericho

Number of Diploma Recipients

Rank	Number	District Name	City
1	337	Essex Community Education Ctr	Essex Junction
2	285	Mount Anthony UHSD 14	Bennington
3	247	Mount Mansfield USD 17	Jericho
4	238	Rutland City SD	Rutland
5	199	Burlington SD	Burlington
6	195	South Burlington SD	S Burlington
7	181	Hartford SD	White River Jct
8	159	Colchester SD	Colchester
9	114	Milton Id SD	Milton

High School Drop-out Rate

Rank	Percent	District Name	City
1	7.2	Mount Anthony UHSD 14	Bennington
2	6.9	Burlington SD	Burlington
3	6.8	Milton Id SD	Milton
4	6.1	Rutland City SD	Rutland
5	4.3	Hartford SD	White River Jct
6	3.2	South Burlington SD	S Burlington
7	2.2	Essex Community Education Ctr	Essex Junction
8	1.7	Mount Mansfield USD 17	Jericho
9	1.4	Colchester SD	Colchester

Virginia

Virginia Public School Educational Profile

Category	Value	Category	Value
Schools *(2002-2003)*	2,059	**Diploma Recipients** *(2002-2003)*	66,519
Instructional Level		White, Non-Hispanic	45,485
Primary	1,163	Black, Non-Hispanic	15,084
Middle	342	Asian/Pacific Islander	3,353
High	315	American Indian/Alaskan Native	143
Other Level	239	Hispanic	2,454
Curriculum		**High School Drop-out Rate** (%) *(2000-2001)*	3.5
Regular	1,825	White, Non-Hispanic	2.8
Special Education	56	Black, Non-Hispanic	4.9
Vocational	47	Asian/Pacific Islander	2.4
Alternative	131	American Indian/Alaskan Native	6.3
Type		Hispanic	6.4
Magnet	178	**Staff** *(2002-2003)*	158,887.0
Charter	7	Teachers	99,918.4
Title I Eligible	780	Average Salary ($)	42,778
School-wide Title I	287	Librarians/Media Specialists	1,851.1
Students *(2002-2003)*	1,176,559	Guidance Counselors	2,362.2
Gender (%)		**Ratios** *(2002-2003)*	
Male	51.3	Student/Teacher Ratio	11.8 to 1
Female	48.7	Student/Librarian Ratio	635.6 to 1
Race/Ethnicity (%)		Student/Counselor Ratio	498.1 to 1
White, Non-Hispanic	61.3	**Current Spending** *($ per student in FY 2001)*	7,496
Black, Non-Hispanic	27.0	Instruction	4,620
Asian/Pacific Islander	4.5	Support Services	2,583
American Indian/Alaskan Native	0.3	**College Entrance Exam Scores** *(2003)*	
Hispanic	6.1	Scholastic Aptitude Test (SAT)	
Classification (%)		Participation Rate (%)	71
Individual Education Program (IEP)	14.4	Mean SAT I Verbal Score	514
Migrant	0.1	Mean SAT I Math Score	510
English Language Learner (ELL)	4.2	American College Testing Program (ACT)	
Eligible for Free Lunch Program	23.2	Participation Rate (%)	12
Eligible for Reduced-Price Lunch Program	7.0	Average Composite Score	20.6

Note: *For an explanation of data, please refer to the User's Guide in the front of the book; n/a indicates data not available*

Virginia NAEP 2003 Test Scores

Reading			Mathematics		
Grade/Category	Value	Rank	Grade/Category	Value	Rank
4th Grade			**4th Grade**		
Average Proficiency	223.3 (1.5)	9/51	Average Proficiency	239.2 (1.1)	9/51
Proficiency by Gender/Race/Ethnicity			Proficiency by Gender/Race/Ethnicity		
Male	219.2 (1.8)	11/51	Male	239.8 (1.3)	12/51
Female	227.6 (1.6)	7/51	Female	238.6 (1.0)	8/51
White, Non-Hispanic	231.1 (2.0)	9/51	White, Non-Hispanic	245.9 (1.4)	9/51
Black, Non-Hispanic	206.0 (2.1)	7/42	Black, Non-Hispanic	223.0 (0.9)	3/42
Asian, Non-Hispanic	210.1 (3.0)	7/41	Asian, Non-Hispanic	230.3 (2.2)	6/43
American Indian, Non-Hispanic	235.3 (4.5)	3/25	American Indian, Non-Hispanic	254.7 (3.9)	4/26
Hispanic	n/a	n/a	Hispanic	n/a	n/a
Proficiency by Class Size			Proficiency by Class Size		
Less than 16 Students	207.5 (5.8)	17/45	Less than 16 Students	228.2 (6.3)	13/47
16 to 18 Students	*221.3 (3.5)*	12/48	16 to 18 Students	*231.2 (3.5)*	28/48
19 to 20 Students	221.7 (4.2)	16/50	19 to 20 Students	234.3 (2.6)	26/50
21 to 25 Students	221.2 (1.7)	24/51	21 to 25 Students	240.8 (1.7)	12/51
Greater than 25 Students	232.0 (4.2)	1/49	Greater than 25 Students	243.0 (2.3)	6/49
Percent Attaining Achievement Levels			Percent Attaining Achievement Levels		
Below Basic	31.3 (1.6)	38/51	Below Basic	17.2 (1.2)	42/51
Basic or Above	68.7 (1.6)	12/51	Basic or Above	82.8 (1.2)	10/51
Proficient or Above	35.1 (1.8)	9/51	Proficient or Above	36.1 (1.8)	11/51
Advanced or Above	8.8 (1.0)	8/51	Advanced or Above	5.1 (0.8)	10/51
8th Grade			**8th Grade**		
Average Proficiency	268.0 (1.1)	8/51	Average Proficiency	281.7 (1.3)	16/51
Proficiency by Gender/Race/Ethnicity			Proficiency by Gender/Race/Ethnicity		
Male	263.4 (1.1)	9/51	Male	283.3 (1.2)	15/51
Female	272.4 (1.5)	13/51	Female	280.1 (1.8)	20/51
White, Non-Hispanic	274.9 (1.4)	6/50	White, Non-Hispanic	290.0 (1.9)	11/50
Black, Non-Hispanic	250.3 (1.4)	4/41	Black, Non-Hispanic	261.9 (1.1)	4/41
Asian, Non-Hispanic	265.6 (3.2)	2/37	Asian, Non-Hispanic	268.4 (4.0)	2/37
American Indian, Non-Hispanic	273.8 (2.8)	8/23	American Indian, Non-Hispanic	297.0 (2.9)	7/23
Hispanic	n/a	n/a	Hispanic	n/a	n/a
Proficiency by Parents Highest Level of Ed.			Proficiency by Parents Highest Level of Ed.		
Did Not Finish High School	252.3 (4.2)	3/50	Did Not Finish High School	261.9 (2.3)	11/50
Graduated High School	257.0 (1.4)	21/50	Graduated High School	271.1 (1.5)	18/50
Some Education After High School	271.3 (1.6)	10/50	Some Education After High School	281.8 (1.8)	20/50
Graduated College	275.8 (1.5)	10/50	Graduated College	290.8 (1.5)	22/50
Percent Attaining Achievement Levels			Percent Attaining Achievement Levels		
Below Basic	21.2 (1.2)	41/51	Below Basic	27.5 (1.5)	33/51
Basic or Above	78.8 (1.2)	11/51	Basic or Above	72.5 (1.5)	19/51
Proficient or Above	35.8 (1.5)	13/51	Proficient or Above	31.1 (1.6)	20/51
Advanced or Above	3.4 (0.5)	10/51	Advanced or Above	5.9 (0.8)	14/51

Note: *For an explanation of data, please refer to the User's Guide in the front of the book; values in italics indicate that the nature of the sample does not allow accurate determination of the variability of the statistic; n/a indicates data not available*

Accomack County

Accomack County Public Schools

23296 Courthouse Ave • Accomac, VA 23301-0330
Mailing Address: PO Box 330 • Accomac, VA 23301-0330
(757) 787-5754 • http://www.sbo.accomack.k12.va.us/public/
Grade Span: PK-12; **Agency Type:** 1
Schools: 15
5 Primary; 3 Middle; 2 High; 5 Other Level
12 Regular; 0 Special Education; 2 Vocational; 1 Alternative
0 Magnet; 0 Charter; 4 Title I Eligible; 4 School-wide Title I
Students: 5,445 (52.0% male; 48.0% female)
Individual Education Program: 678 (12.5%);
English Language Learner: 373 (6.9%); Migrant: 170 (3.1%)
Eligible for Free Lunch Program: 2,659 (48.8%)
Eligible for Reduced-Price Lunch Program: 546 (10.0%)
Teachers: 479.0 (11.4 to 1)
Librarians/Media Specialists: 11.0 (495.0 to 1)
Guidance Counselors: 11.0 (495.0 to 1)
Current Spending: ($ per student per year):
Total: $6,846; Instruction: $4,182; Support Services: $2,299
Enrollment, Drop-out Rates and Diploma Recipients by Race/Ethnicity

Category	Total	White	Black	Asian	AIAN	Hisp.
Enrollment (%)	100.0	43.0	46.9	0.6	0.1	9.4
Drop-out Rate (%)	8.5	6.9	10.5	0.0	0.0	4.3
H.S. Diplomas (#)	255	125	121	0	2	7

Albemarle County

Albemarle County Public Schools

401 Mcintire Rd • Charlottesville, VA 22902-4596
(434) 296-5826 • http://k12.albemarle.org/
Grade Span: PK-12; **Agency Type:** 1
Schools: 25
16 Primary; 5 Middle; 4 High; 0 Other Level
25 Regular; 0 Special Education; 0 Vocational; 0 Alternative
0 Magnet; 1 Charter; 13 Title I Eligible; 0 School-wide Title I
Students: 12,253 (51.1% male; 48.9% female)
Individual Education Program: 2,021 (16.5%);
English Language Learner: 618 (5.0%); Migrant: 50 (0.4%)
Eligible for Free Lunch Program: 1,631 (13.3%)
Eligible for Reduced-Price Lunch Program: 596 (4.9%)
Teachers: 1,174.0 (10.4 to 1)
Librarians/Media Specialists: 24.0 (510.5 to 1)
Guidance Counselors: 25.9 (473.1 to 1)
Current Spending: ($ per student per year):
Total: $7,693; Instruction: $4,615; Support Services: $2,805
Enrollment, Drop-out Rates and Diploma Recipients by Race/Ethnicity

Category	Total	White	Black	Asian	AIAN	Hisp.
Enrollment (%)	100.0	79.7	13.0	3.4	0.1	3.7
Drop-out Rate (%)	1.9	1.7	2.9	0.0	50.0	3.9
H.S. Diplomas (#)	762	649	78	23	0	12

Alexandria City

Alexandria City Public Schools

2000 N Beauregard St • Alexandria, VA 22311-1712
(703) 824-6610 • http://www.acps.k12.va.us/
Grade Span: PK-12; **Agency Type:** 1
Schools: 16
13 Primary; 2 Middle; 1 High; 0 Other Level
16 Regular; 0 Special Education; 0 Vocational; 0 Alternative
3 Magnet; 0 Charter; 10 Title I Eligible; 0 School-wide Title I
Students: 10,971 (50.9% male; 49.1% female)
Individual Education Program: 1,926 (17.6%);
English Language Learner: 2,412 (22.0%); Migrant: 0 (0.0%)
Eligible for Free Lunch Program: 4,172 (38.0%)
Eligible for Reduced-Price Lunch Program: 1,112 (10.1%)
Teachers: 1,214.3 (9.0 to 1)
Librarians/Media Specialists: 23.0 (477.0 to 1)
Guidance Counselors: 31.0 (353.9 to 1)
Current Spending: ($ per student per year):
Total: $11,305; Instruction: $6,795; Support Services: $4,185
Enrollment, Drop-out Rates and Diploma Recipients by Race/Ethnicity

Category	Total	White	Black	Asian	AIAN	Hisp.
Enrollment (%)	100.0	22.9	43.6	6.4	0.3	26.8
Drop-out Rate (%)	5.2	2.3	6.0	3.9	0.0	7.4
H.S. Diplomas (#)	533	191	224	38	1	79

Alleghany County

Alleghany County Public Schools

110 Rosedale Ave • Covington, VA 24426-1296
(540) 965-1800 • http://www.alleghany.k12.va.us/
Grade Span: PK-12; **Agency Type:** 1
Schools: 7
5 Primary; 1 Middle; 1 High; 0 Other Level
7 Regular; 0 Special Education; 0 Vocational; 0 Alternative
0 Magnet; 0 Charter; 4 Title I Eligible; 0 School-wide Title I
Students: 2,929 (52.4% male; 47.6% female)
Individual Education Program: 482 (16.5%);
English Language Learner: 6 (0.2%); Migrant: 0 (0.0%)
Eligible for Free Lunch Program: 740 (25.3%)
Eligible for Reduced-Price Lunch Program: 230 (7.9%)
Teachers: 268.8 (10.9 to 1)
Librarians/Media Specialists: 7.0 (418.4 to 1)
Guidance Counselors: 7.0 (418.4 to 1)
Current Spending: ($ per student per year):
Total: $7,131; Instruction: $4,232; Support Services: $2,636
Enrollment, Drop-out Rates and Diploma Recipients by Race/Ethnicity

Category	Total	White	Black	Asian	AIAN	Hisp.
Enrollment (%)	100.0	92.9	6.6	0.1	0.1	0.2
Drop-out Rate (%)	2.3	2.5	0.0	0.0	n/a	n/a
H.S. Diplomas (#)	173	163	10	0	0	0

Amelia County

Amelia County Public Schools

16410 Dunn St • Amelia, VA 23002
(804) 561-2621 • http://eclipse.achs.amelia.k12.va.us/public
Grade Span: PK-12; **Agency Type:** 1
Schools: 3
1 Primary; 1 Middle; 1 High; 0 Other Level
3 Regular; 0 Special Education; 0 Vocational; 0 Alternative
0 Magnet; 0 Charter; 1 Title I Eligible; 0 School-wide Title I
Students: 1,726 (52.7% male; 47.3% female)
Individual Education Program: 295 (17.1%);
English Language Learner: 1 (0.1%); Migrant: 0 (0.0%)
Eligible for Free Lunch Program: 432 (25.0%)
Eligible for Reduced-Price Lunch Program: 158 (9.2%)
Teachers: 144.0 (12.0 to 1)
Librarians/Media Specialists: 3.0 (575.3 to 1)
Guidance Counselors: 3.0 (575.3 to 1)
Current Spending: ($ per student per year):
Total: $6,333; Instruction: $3,753; Support Services: $2,332
Enrollment, Drop-out Rates and Diploma Recipients by Race/Ethnicity

Category	Total	White	Black	Asian	AIAN	Hisp.
Enrollment (%)	100.0	63.8	35.3	0.1	0.2	0.5
Drop-out Rate (%)	4.6	5.5	3.2	0.0	n/a	0.0
H.S. Diplomas (#)	109	55	53	1	0	0

Amherst County

Amherst County Public Schools

153 Washington St • Amherst, VA 24521-1257
Mailing Address: PO Box 1257 • Amherst, VA 24521-1257
(434) 946-9387 • http://www.amherst.k12.va.us/
Grade Span: PK-12; **Agency Type:** 1
Schools: 10
7 Primary; 2 Middle; 1 High; 0 Other Level
10 Regular; 0 Special Education; 0 Vocational; 0 Alternative
0 Magnet; 0 Charter; 6 Title I Eligible; 0 School-wide Title I
Students: 4,645 (52.0% male; 48.0% female)
Individual Education Program: 562 (12.1%);
English Language Learner: 11 (0.2%); Migrant: 0 (0.0%)
Eligible for Free Lunch Program: 1,219 (26.2%)
Eligible for Reduced-Price Lunch Program: 309 (6.7%)
Teachers: 430.7 (10.8 to 1)
Librarians/Media Specialists: 10.0 (464.5 to 1)
Guidance Counselors: 9.5 (488.9 to 1)
Current Spending: ($ per student per year):
Total: $6,081; Instruction: $3,919; Support Services: $1,889
Enrollment, Drop-out Rates and Diploma Recipients by Race/Ethnicity

Category	Total	White	Black	Asian	AIAN	Hisp.
Enrollment (%)	100.0	70.7	27.2	0.5	0.8	0.9
Drop-out Rate (%)	3.5	4.0	2.1	0.0	10.0	0.0
H.S. Diplomas (#)	266	193	66	1	6	0

Appomattox County

Appomattox County Public Schools

124 Court St • Appomattox, VA 24522-0548
Mailing Address: PO Box 548 • Appomattox, VA 24522-0548
(434) 352-8251 • http://www.appomattox.k12.va.us/acps/index.aspx
Grade Span: PK-12; **Agency Type:** 1
Schools: 4
2 Primary; 1 Middle; 1 High; 0 Other Level
4 Regular; 0 Special Education; 0 Vocational; 0 Alternative
0 Magnet; 0 Charter; 2 Title I Eligible; 0 School-wide Title I
Students: 2,364 (52.2% male; 47.8% female)
Individual Education Program: 367 (15.5%);
English Language Learner: 4 (0.2%); Migrant: 0 (0.0%)
Eligible for Free Lunch Program: 686 (29.0%)
Eligible for Reduced-Price Lunch Program: 175 (7.4%)
Teachers: 206.5 (11.4 to 1)
Librarians/Media Specialists: 4.0 (591.0 to 1)
Guidance Counselors: 4.0 (591.0 to 1)
Current Spending: ($ per student per year):
Total: $6,130; Instruction: $4,022; Support Services: $1,814

Enrollment, Drop-out Rates and Diploma Recipients by Race/Ethnicity

Category	Total	White	Black	Asian	AIAN	Hisp.
Enrollment (%)	100.0	68.5	31.1	0.1	0.0	0.3
Drop-out Rate (%)	2.1	1.5	4.0	0.0	n/a	0.0
H.S. Diplomas (#)	140	107	32	0	0	1

Arlington County

Arlington County Public Schools

1426 N Quincy St • Arlington, VA 22207-3646
(703) 228-6010 • http://www.arlington.k12.va.us/
Grade Span: PK-12; **Agency Type:** 1
Schools: 31
21 Primary; 5 Middle; 3 High; 2 Other Level
29 Regular; 1 Special Education; 1 Vocational; 0 Alternative
7 Magnet; 0 Charter; 15 Title I Eligible; 3 School-wide Title I
Students: 19,135 (51.1% male; 48.9% female)
Individual Education Program: 3,222 (16.8%);
English Language Learner: 4,988 (26.1%); Migrant: 0 (0.0%)
Eligible for Free Lunch Program: 5,493 (28.7%)
Eligible for Reduced-Price Lunch Program: 1,665 (8.7%)
Teachers: 2,144.6 (8.9 to 1)
Librarians/Media Specialists: 37.8 (506.2 to 1)
Guidance Counselors: 65.0 (294.4 to 1)
Current Spending: ($ per student per year):
Total: $11,388; Instruction: $6,806; Support Services: $4,309

Enrollment, Drop-out Rates and Diploma Recipients by Race/Ethnicity

Category	Total	White	Black	Asian	AIAN	Hisp.
Enrollment (%)	100.0	41.6	14.2	10.0	0.1	34.1
Drop-out Rate (%)	2.6	1.2	3.3	2.3	0.0	4.1
H.S. Diplomas (#)	923	460	133	111	1	218

Augusta County

Augusta County Public Schools

6 John Lewis Rd • Fishersville, VA 22939-9610
(540) 245-5100 • http://www.augusta.k12.va.us/
Grade Span: PK-12; **Agency Type:** 1
Schools: 20
12 Primary; 3 Middle; 5 High; 0 Other Level
20 Regular; 0 Special Education; 0 Vocational; 0 Alternative
0 Magnet; 0 Charter; 9 Title I Eligible; 0 School-wide Title I
Students: 10,674 (51.4% male; 48.6% female)
Individual Education Program: 1,546 (14.5%);
English Language Learner: 91 (0.9%); Migrant: 11 (0.1%)
Eligible for Free Lunch Program: 1,853 (17.4%)
Eligible for Reduced-Price Lunch Program: 782 (7.3%)
Teachers: 882.0 (12.1 to 1)
Librarians/Media Specialists: 15.0 (711.6 to 1)
Guidance Counselors: 17.0 (627.9 to 1)
Current Spending: ($ per student per year):
Total: $6,380; Instruction: $4,214; Support Services: $1,933

Enrollment, Drop-out Rates and Diploma Recipients by Race/Ethnicity

Category	Total	White	Black	Asian	AIAN	Hisp.
Enrollment (%)	100.0	95.2	2.9	0.4	0.1	1.4
Drop-out Rate (%)	2.1	2.1	3.1	0.0	0.0	0.0
H.S. Diplomas (#)	713	679	25	3	0	6

Bedford County

Bedford County Public Schools

310 S Bridge St • Bedford, VA 24523-0748
Mailing Address: PO Box 748 • Bedford, VA 24523-0748
(540) 586-1045 • http://www.bedford.k12.va.us/
Grade Span: PK-12; **Agency Type:** 1
Schools: 22
15 Primary; 3 Middle; 3 High; 1 Other Level
21 Regular; 0 Special Education; 1 Vocational; 0 Alternative
0 Magnet; 0 Charter; 10 Title I Eligible; 0 School-wide Title I
Students: 10,942 (52.0% male; 48.0% female)
Individual Education Program: 1,432 (13.1%);
English Language Learner: 24 (0.2%); Migrant: 0 (0.0%)
Eligible for Free Lunch Program: 2,096 (19.2%)
Eligible for Reduced-Price Lunch Program: 819 (7.5%)
Teachers: 922.0 (11.9 to 1)
Librarians/Media Specialists: 21.0 (521.0 to 1)
Guidance Counselors: 21.0 (521.0 to 1)
Current Spending: ($ per student per year):
Total: $5,411; Instruction: $3,390; Support Services: $1,716

Enrollment, Drop-out Rates and Diploma Recipients by Race/Ethnicity

Category	Total	White	Black	Asian	AIAN	Hisp.
Enrollment (%)	100.0	87.9	10.5	0.6	0.3	0.8
Drop-out Rate (%)	2.0	2.0	2.3	0.0	100.0	0.0
H.S. Diplomas (#)	669	600	62	5	0	2

Botetourt County

Botetourt County Public Schools

143 Poor Farm Rd • Fincastle, VA 24090-0309
(540) 473-8263 • http://www.bcps.k12.va.us/
Grade Span: PK-12; **Agency Type:** 1
Schools: 12
7 Primary; 2 Middle; 2 High; 1 Other Level
11 Regular; 0 Special Education; 1 Vocational; 0 Alternative
0 Magnet; 0 Charter; 4 Title I Eligible; 0 School-wide Title I
Students: 4,733 (51.6% male; 48.4% female)
Individual Education Program: 842 (17.8%);
English Language Learner: 11 (0.2%); Migrant: 0 (0.0%)
Eligible for Free Lunch Program: 441 (9.3%)
Eligible for Reduced-Price Lunch Program: 156 (3.3%)
Teachers: 425.4 (11.1 to 1)
Librarians/Media Specialists: 11.0 (430.3 to 1)
Guidance Counselors: 12.0 (394.4 to 1)
Current Spending: ($ per student per year):
Total: $6,887; Instruction: $4,451; Support Services: $2,209

Enrollment, Drop-out Rates and Diploma Recipients by Race/Ethnicity

Category	Total	White	Black	Asian	AIAN	Hisp.
Enrollment (%)	100.0	95.6	3.2	0.6	0.3	0.3
Drop-out Rate (%)	3.1	2.8	8.2	0.0	0.0	12.5
H.S. Diplomas (#)	313	300	9	1	1	2

Bristol City

Bristol City Public Schools

222 Oak St • Bristol, VA 24201-4198
(276) 821-5600 • http://www.bristolvaschools.org/
Grade Span: PK-12; **Agency Type:** 1
Schools: 7
4 Primary; 1 Middle; 1 High; 1 Other Level
6 Regular; 1 Special Education; 0 Vocational; 0 Alternative
0 Magnet; 0 Charter; 4 Title I Eligible; 0 School-wide Title I
Students: 2,332 (50.8% male; 49.2% female)
Individual Education Program: 428 (18.4%);
English Language Learner: 16 (0.7%); Migrant: 0 (0.0%)
Eligible for Free Lunch Program: 953 (40.9%)
Eligible for Reduced-Price Lunch Program: 154 (6.6%)
Teachers: 223.8 (10.4 to 1)
Librarians/Media Specialists: 6.0 (388.7 to 1)
Guidance Counselors: 6.0 (388.7 to 1)
Current Spending: ($ per student per year):
Total: $7,360; Instruction: $4,858; Support Services: $2,198

Enrollment, Drop-out Rates and Diploma Recipients by Race/Ethnicity

Category	Total	White	Black	Asian	AIAN	Hisp.
Enrollment (%)	100.0	88.3	9.6	0.8	0.0	1.3
Drop-out Rate (%)	2.8	2.9	0.0	0.0	n/a	16.7
H.S. Diplomas (#)	123	112	10	0	0	1

Brunswick County

Brunswick County Public Schools

219 N Main St • Lawrenceville, VA 23868-0309
Mailing Address: PO Box 309 • Lawrenceville, VA 23868-0309
(434) 848-3138 • http://www.brun.k12.va.us/
Grade Span: PK-12; **Agency Type:** 1
Schools: 6
4 Primary; 1 Middle; 1 High; 0 Other Level
6 Regular; 0 Special Education; 0 Vocational; 0 Alternative
0 Magnet; 0 Charter; 4 Title I Eligible; 0 School-wide Title I
Students: 2,477 (52.4% male; 47.6% female)
Individual Education Program: 304 (12.3%);
English Language Learner: 3 (0.1%); Migrant: 0 (0.0%)
Eligible for Free Lunch Program: 1,324 (53.5%)
Eligible for Reduced-Price Lunch Program: 270 (10.9%)
Teachers: 235.8 (10.5 to 1)
Librarians/Media Specialists: 6.0 (412.8 to 1)
Guidance Counselors: 4.0 (619.3 to 1)
Current Spending: ($ per student per year):
Total: $7,847; Instruction: $4,069; Support Services: $3,307
Enrollment, Drop-out Rates and Diploma Recipients by Race/Ethnicity

Category	Total	White	Black	Asian	AIAN	Hisp.
Enrollment (%)	100.0	20.1	79.1	0.2	0.0	0.6
Drop-out Rate (%)	6.5	7.3	6.3	0.0	0.0	0.0
H.S. Diplomas (#)	154	36	117	0	0	1

Buchanan County

Buchanan County Public Schools

Rt 83 Slate Creek Rd • Grundy, VA 24614-0833
(276) 935-4551 • http://www.buc.k12.va.us/
Grade Span: PK-12; **Agency Type:** 1
Schools: 11
6 Primary; 0 Middle; 4 High; 1 Other Level
10 Regular; 0 Special Education; 1 Vocational; 0 Alternative
0 Magnet; 0 Charter; 6 Title I Eligible; 2 School-wide Title I
Students: 4,029 (47.9% male; 52.1% female)
Individual Education Program: 723 (17.9%);
English Language Learner: n/a; Migrant: 0 (0.0%)
Eligible for Free Lunch Program: 2,018 (50.1%)
Eligible for Reduced-Price Lunch Program: 592 (14.7%)
Teachers: 396.0 (10.2 to 1)
Librarians/Media Specialists: 10.3 (391.2 to 1)
Guidance Counselors: 11.0 (366.3 to 1)
Current Spending: ($ per student per year):
Total: $7,320; Instruction: $4,442; Support Services: $2,482
Enrollment, Drop-out Rates and Diploma Recipients by Race/Ethnicity

Category	Total	White	Black	Asian	AIAN	Hisp.
Enrollment (%)	100.0	99.9	0.0	0.0	0.0	0.0
Drop-out Rate (%)	2.9	2.9	0.0	n/a	n/a	n/a
H.S. Diplomas (#)	260	258	2	0	0	0

Buckingham County

Buckingham County Public Schools

Rte 60 • Buckingham, VA 23921-0024
Mailing Address: PO Box 24 • Buckingham, VA 23921-0024
(434) 969-6100 • http://www.bchs.k12.va.us/
Grade Span: PK-12; **Agency Type:** 1
Schools: 6
3 Primary; 2 Middle; 1 High; 0 Other Level
6 Regular; 0 Special Education; 0 Vocational; 0 Alternative
0 Magnet; 0 Charter; 3 Title I Eligible; 3 School-wide Title I
Students: 2,210 (52.0% male; 48.0% female)
Individual Education Program: 334 (15.1%);
English Language Learner: 8 (0.4%); Migrant: 0 (0.0%)
Eligible for Free Lunch Program: 928 (42.0%)
Eligible for Reduced-Price Lunch Program: 250 (11.3%)
Teachers: 203.4 (10.9 to 1)
Librarians/Media Specialists: 6.0 (368.3 to 1)
Guidance Counselors: 3.0 (736.7 to 1)
Current Spending: ($ per student per year):
Total: $6,769; Instruction: $4,222; Support Services: $2,238
Enrollment, Drop-out Rates and Diploma Recipients by Race/Ethnicity

Category	Total	White	Black	Asian	AIAN	Hisp.
Enrollment (%)	100.0	50.1	48.7	0.3	0.2	0.7
Drop-out Rate (%)	6.5	4.6	9.2	0.0	0.0	0.0
H.S. Diplomas (#)	111	74	35	0	0	2

Campbell County

Campbell County Public Schools

684 Village Hwy • Rustburg, VA 24588-0099
Mailing Address: PO Box 99 • Rustburg, VA 24588-0099
(434) 332-8201 • http://www.campbell.k12.va.us/
Grade Span: PK-12; **Agency Type:** 1
Schools: 16
8 Primary; 2 Middle; 2 High; 4 Other Level
14 Regular; 0 Special Education; 1 Vocational; 1 Alternative
0 Magnet; 0 Charter; 6 Title I Eligible; 0 School-wide Title I
Students: 8,861 (51.1% male; 48.9% female)
Individual Education Program: 1,056 (11.9%);
English Language Learner: 28 (0.3%); Migrant: 0 (0.0%)
Eligible for Free Lunch Program: 2,003 (22.6%)
Eligible for Reduced-Price Lunch Program: 679 (7.7%)
Teachers: 759.8 (11.7 to 1)
Librarians/Media Specialists: 13.0 (681.6 to 1)
Guidance Counselors: 12.8 (692.3 to 1)
Current Spending: ($ per student per year):
Total: $6,188; Instruction: $3,773; Support Services: $2,134
Enrollment, Drop-out Rates and Diploma Recipients by Race/Ethnicity

Category	Total	White	Black	Asian	AIAN	Hisp.
Enrollment (%)	100.0	79.1	19.2	1.0	0.0	0.6
Drop-out Rate (%)	2.7	2.0	5.7	0.0	0.0	0.0
H.S. Diplomas (#)	486	405	75	6	0	0

Caroline County

Caroline County Public Schools

16221 Richmond Turnpike • Bowling Green, VA 22427-2203
(804) 633-5088 • http://www.caroline.k12.va.us/
Grade Span: PK-12; **Agency Type:** 1
Schools: 6
4 Primary; 1 Middle; 1 High; 0 Other Level
6 Regular; 0 Special Education; 0 Vocational; 0 Alternative
0 Magnet; 0 Charter; 2 Title I Eligible; 1 School-wide Title I
Students: 3,765 (51.8% male; 48.2% female)
Individual Education Program: 477 (12.7%);
English Language Learner: 16 (0.4%); Migrant: 0 (0.0%)
Eligible for Free Lunch Program: 1,079 (28.7%)
Eligible for Reduced-Price Lunch Program: 327 (8.7%)
Teachers: 291.0 (12.9 to 1)
Librarians/Media Specialists: 6.0 (627.5 to 1)
Guidance Counselors: 9.0 (418.3 to 1)
Current Spending: ($ per student per year):
Total: $6,075; Instruction: $3,650; Support Services: $2,114
Enrollment, Drop-out Rates and Diploma Recipients by Race/Ethnicity

Category	Total	White	Black	Asian	AIAN	Hisp.
Enrollment (%)	100.0	54.5	42.7	0.5	0.4	1.2
Drop-out Rate (%)	1.2	1.2	1.2	0.0	0.0	0.0
H.S. Diplomas (#)	200	117	82	1	0	0

Carroll County

Carroll County Public Schools

605-9 N Pine St • Hillsville, VA 24343-1453
(276) 728-3191 • http://www.ccpsd.k12.va.us/
Grade Span: PK-12; **Agency Type:** 1
Schools: 10
8 Primary; 0 Middle; 1 High; 1 Other Level
10 Regular; 0 Special Education; 0 Vocational; 0 Alternative
0 Magnet; 0 Charter; 8 Title I Eligible; 1 School-wide Title I
Students: 4,061 (53.5% male; 46.5% female)
Individual Education Program: 757 (18.6%);
English Language Learner: 40 (1.0%); Migrant: 45 (1.1%)
Eligible for Free Lunch Program: 1,384 (34.1%)
Eligible for Reduced-Price Lunch Program: 526 (13.0%)
Teachers: 432.8 (9.4 to 1)
Librarians/Media Specialists: 10.0 (406.1 to 1)
Guidance Counselors: 8.5 (477.8 to 1)
Current Spending: ($ per student per year):
Total: $6,781; Instruction: $4,159; Support Services: $2,273
Enrollment, Drop-out Rates and Diploma Recipients by Race/Ethnicity

Category	Total	White	Black	Asian	AIAN	Hisp.
Enrollment (%)	100.0	96.2	0.6	0.2	0.0	2.9
Drop-out Rate (%)	3.1	3.1	0.0	0.0	n/a	5.6
H.S. Diplomas (#)	211	208	0	1	0	2

Charlotte County

Charlotte County Public Schools

250 Legrande Ave, Ste E • Charlotte Ct House, VA 23923-0790
Mailing Address: PO Box 790 • Charlotte Ct House, VA 23923-0790
(434) 542-5151
Grade Span: PK-12; **Agency Type:** 1
Schools: 7
5 Primary; 1 Middle; 1 High; 0 Other Level
7 Regular; 0 Special Education; 0 Vocational; 0 Alternative
0 Magnet; 0 Charter; 2 Title I Eligible; 0 School-wide Title I
Students: 2,289 (50.2% male; 49.8% female)
Individual Education Program: 309 (13.5%);
English Language Learner: 4 (0.2%); Migrant: 0 (0.0%)
Eligible for Free Lunch Program: 843 (36.8%)
Eligible for Reduced-Price Lunch Program: 285 (12.5%)
Teachers: 189.5 (12.1 to 1)
Librarians/Media Specialists: 5.0 (457.8 to 1)
Guidance Counselors: 3.0 (763.0 to 1)
Current Spending: ($ per student per year):
Total: $6,641; Instruction: $4,124; Support Services: $2,156
Enrollment, Drop-out Rates and Diploma Recipients by Race/Ethnicity

Category	Total	White	Black	Asian	AIAN	Hisp.
Enrollment (%)	100.0	59.0	39.1	0.3	0.3	1.3
Drop-out Rate (%)	2.1	2.1	2.1	n/a	0.0	0.0
H.S. Diplomas (#)	135	76	58	1	0	0

Charlottesville City Pub Schools

1562 Dairy Rd • Charlottesville, VA 22903-1304
(434) 245-2400 • http://www.ccs.k12.va.us/
Grade Span: PK-12; **Agency Type:** 1
Schools: 10
6 Primary; 2 Middle; 1 High; 1 Other Level
9 Regular; 0 Special Education; 0 Vocational; 1 Alternative
0 Magnet; 0 Charter; 7 Title I Eligible; 3 School-wide Title I
Students: 4,420 (51.1% male; 48.9% female)
Individual Education Program: 800 (18.1%);
English Language Learner: 151 (3.4%); Migrant: 4 (0.1%)
Eligible for Free Lunch Program: 1,717 (38.8%)
Eligible for Reduced-Price Lunch Program: 333 (7.5%)
Teachers: 461.5 (9.6 to 1)
Librarians/Media Specialists: 10.5 (421.0 to 1)
Guidance Counselors: 13.0 (340.0 to 1)
Current Spending: ($ per student per year):
Total: $9,962; Instruction: $5,998; Support Services: $3,702
Enrollment, Drop-out Rates and Diploma Recipients by Race/Ethnicity

Category	Total	White	Black	Asian	AIAN	Hisp.
Enrollment (%)	100.0	44.2	48.1	1.8	0.2	2.5
Drop-out Rate (%)	3.0	2.1	4.2	0.0	n/a	11.1
H.S. Diplomas (#)	194	108	82	1	0	3

Chesapeake City

Chesapeake City Public Schools

312 Cedar Rd • Chesapeake, VA 23322
Mailing Address: PO Box 16496 • Chesapeake, VA 23328-5204
(757) 547-0165 • http://eclipse.cps.k12.va.us/
Grade Span: PK-12; **Agency Type:** 1
Schools: 46
26 Primary; 12 Middle; 6 High; 2 Other Level
44 Regular; 0 Special Education; 0 Vocational; 2 Alternative
0 Magnet; 0 Charter; 11 Title I Eligible; 6 School-wide Title I
Students: 39,380 (51.4% male; 48.6% female)
Individual Education Program: 6,828 (17.3%);
English Language Learner: 220 (0.6%); Migrant: 0 (0.0%)
Eligible for Free Lunch Program: 7,417 (18.8%)
Eligible for Reduced-Price Lunch Program: 2,125 (5.4%)
Teachers: 2,895.0 (13.6 to 1)
Librarians/Media Specialists: 143.0 (275.4 to 1)
Guidance Counselors: 80.0 (492.3 to 1)
Current Spending: ($ per student per year):
Total: $6,842; Instruction: $4,327; Support Services: $2,295
Enrollment, Drop-out Rates and Diploma Recipients by Race/Ethnicity

Category	Total	White	Black	Asian	AIAN	Hisp.
Enrollment (%)	100.0	59.9	35.1	2.1	0.4	1.7
Drop-out Rate (%)	3.4	2.7	4.5	4.1	0.0	3.3
H.S. Diplomas (#)	2,298	1,464	739	56	7	32

Chesterfield County

Chesterfield County Public Schools

9900 Krause Rd • Chesterfield, VA 23832-0001
Mailing Address: PO Box 10 • Chesterfield, VA 23832-0001
(804) 748-1411 • http://chesterfield.k12.va.us/
Grade Span: PK-12; **Agency Type:** 1
Schools: 59
36 Primary; 12 Middle; 10 High; 1 Other Level
56 Regular; 0 Special Education; 1 Vocational; 2 Alternative
1 Magnet; 0 Charter; 12 Title I Eligible; 7 School-wide Title I
Students: 53,621 (51.4% male; 48.6% female)
Individual Education Program: 7,895 (14.7%);
English Language Learner: 1,222 (2.3%); Migrant: 0 (0.0%)
Eligible for Free Lunch Program: 5,763 (10.7%)
Eligible for Reduced-Price Lunch Program: 2,075 (3.9%)
Teachers: 4,011.3 (13.4 to 1)
Librarians/Media Specialists: 63.8 (840.5 to 1)
Guidance Counselors: 102.5 (523.1 to 1)
Current Spending: ($ per student per year):
Total: $6,243; Instruction: $3,956; Support Services: $2,033
Enrollment, Drop-out Rates and Diploma Recipients by Race/Ethnicity

Category	Total	White	Black	Asian	AIAN	Hisp.
Enrollment (%)	100.0	69.2	23.9	2.8	0.5	3.7
Drop-out Rate (%)	4.5	4.1	5.6	3.9	4.7	8.3
H.S. Diplomas (#)	3,292	2,392	725	103	14	58

Clarke County

Clarke County Public Schools

309 W Main St • Berryville, VA 22611-1230
(540) 955-6100 • http://www.clarke.k12.va.us/
Grade Span: PK-12; **Agency Type:** 1
Schools: 5
3 Primary; 1 Middle; 1 High; 0 Other Level
5 Regular; 0 Special Education; 0 Vocational; 0 Alternative
0 Magnet; 0 Charter; 3 Title I Eligible; 0 School-wide Title I
Students: 2,063 (51.7% male; 48.3% female)
Individual Education Program: 216 (10.5%);
English Language Learner: 16 (0.8%); Migrant: 2 (0.1%)
Eligible for Free Lunch Program: 217 (10.5%)
Eligible for Reduced-Price Lunch Program: 58 (2.8%)
Teachers: 196.7 (10.5 to 1)
Librarians/Media Specialists: 5.0 (412.6 to 1)
Guidance Counselors: 3.0 (687.7 to 1)
Current Spending: ($ per student per year):
Total: $7,385; Instruction: $4,641; Support Services: $2,488
Enrollment, Drop-out Rates and Diploma Recipients by Race/Ethnicity

Category	Total	White	Black	Asian	AIAN	Hisp.
Enrollment (%)	100.0	91.4	6.2	0.6	0.2	1.6
Drop-out Rate (%)	1.8	1.8	0.0	0.0	0.0	9.1
H.S. Diplomas (#)	144	134	10	0	0	0

Colonial Heights County

Colonial Heights City Pub Schools

512 Blvd • Colonial Heights, VA 23834-3798
(804) 524-3400 • http://www.colonialhts.net/
Grade Span: PK-12; **Agency Type:** 1
Schools: 5
3 Primary; 1 Middle; 1 High; 0 Other Level
5 Regular; 0 Special Education; 0 Vocational; 0 Alternative
0 Magnet; 0 Charter; 3 Title I Eligible; 0 School-wide Title I
Students: 2,774 (52.9% male; 47.1% female)
Individual Education Program: 415 (15.0%);
English Language Learner: 48 (1.7%); Migrant: 0 (0.0%)
Eligible for Free Lunch Program: 272 (9.8%)
Eligible for Reduced-Price Lunch Program: 122 (4.4%)
Teachers: 264.4 (10.5 to 1)
Librarians/Media Specialists: 5.0 (554.8 to 1)
Guidance Counselors: 6.0 (462.3 to 1)
Current Spending: ($ per student per year):
Total: $7,572; Instruction: $4,985; Support Services: $2,330
Enrollment, Drop-out Rates and Diploma Recipients by Race/Ethnicity

Category	Total	White	Black	Asian	AIAN	Hisp.
Enrollment (%)	100.0	85.7	9.1	3.7	0.0	1.5
Drop-out Rate (%)	5.4	5.1	9.5	5.4	n/a	7.1
H.S. Diplomas (#)	166	147	11	7	0	1

Culpeper County

Culpeper County Public Schools

450 Radio Ln • Culpeper, VA 22701-1542
(540) 825-3677 • http://culpeperschools.org/
Grade Span: PK-12; **Agency Type:** 1
Schools: 9
6 Primary; 2 Middle; 1 High; 0 Other Level
9 Regular; 0 Special Education; 0 Vocational; 0 Alternative
0 Magnet; 0 Charter; 4 Title I Eligible; 0 School-wide Title I
Students: 6,037 (50.5% male; 49.5% female)
Individual Education Program: 697 (11.5%);
English Language Learner: 72 (1.2%); Migrant: 3 (<0.1%)
Eligible for Free Lunch Program: 878 (14.5%)
Eligible for Reduced-Price Lunch Program: 316 (5.2%)
Teachers: 524.0 (11.5 to 1)
Librarians/Media Specialists: 8.0 (754.6 to 1)
Guidance Counselors: 17.0 (355.1 to 1)
Current Spending: ($ per student per year):
Total: $6,624; Instruction: $4,334; Support Services: $1,998
Enrollment, Drop-out Rates and Diploma Recipients by Race/Ethnicity

Category	Total	White	Black	Asian	AIAN	Hisp.
Enrollment (%)	100.0	75.2	20.8	0.8	0.1	3.1
Drop-out Rate (%)	4.3	3.6	7.4	0.0	0.0	3.3
H.S. Diplomas (#)	309	257	44	2	0	6

Danville City

Danville City Public Schools

313 Municipal Bldg • Danville, VA 24541
(434) 799-6400 • http://web.dps.k12.va.us/dps/default.htm
Grade Span: PK-12; **Agency Type:** 1
Schools: 17
10 Primary; 3 Middle; 1 High; 3 Other Level
15 Regular; 0 Special Education; 0 Vocational; 2 Alternative
11 Magnet; 0 Charter; 10 Title I Eligible; 9 School-wide Title I
Students: 7,585 (51.4% male; 48.6% female)
Individual Education Program: 972 (12.8%);
English Language Learner: 179 (2.4%); Migrant: 0 (0.0%)
Eligible for Free Lunch Program: 3,735 (49.2%)
Eligible for Reduced-Price Lunch Program: 490 (6.5%)
Teachers: 703.9 (10.8 to 1)
Librarians/Media Specialists: 16.5 (459.7 to 1)
Guidance Counselors: 15.0 (505.7 to 1)
Current Spending: ($ per student per year):
Total: $6,812; Instruction: $4,380; Support Services: $2,202
Enrollment, Drop-out Rates and Diploma Recipients by Race/Ethnicity

Category	Total	White	Black	Asian	AIAN	Hisp.
Enrollment (%)	100.0	28.1	67.5	0.4	0.1	1.9
Drop-out Rate (%)	5.7	3.5	7.3	0.0	n/a	6.7
H.S. Diplomas (#)	397	191	202	3	0	1

Dickenson County

Dickenson County Public Schools

Volunteer St • Clintwood, VA 24228-1127
Mailing Address: PO Box 1127 • Clintwood, VA 24228-1127
(276) 926-4643 • http://www.dickenson.k12.va.us/
Grade Span: PK-12; **Agency Type:** 1
Schools: 9
5 Primary; 0 Middle; 3 High; 1 Other Level
8 Regular; 0 Special Education; 1 Vocational; 0 Alternative
0 Magnet; 0 Charter; 5 Title I Eligible; 4 School-wide Title I
Students: 2,719 (51.7% male; 48.3% female)
Individual Education Program: 426 (15.7%);
English Language Learner: n/a; Migrant: 0 (0.0%)
Eligible for Free Lunch Program: 1,164 (42.8%)
Eligible for Reduced-Price Lunch Program: 382 (14.0%)
Teachers: 327.3 (8.3 to 1)
Librarians/Media Specialists: 8.0 (339.9 to 1)
Guidance Counselors: 7.0 (388.4 to 1)
Current Spending: ($ per student per year):
Total: $7,199; Instruction: $4,225; Support Services: $2,486
Enrollment, Drop-out Rates and Diploma Recipients by Race/Ethnicity

Category	Total	White	Black	Asian	AIAN	Hisp.
Enrollment (%)	100.0	99.3	0.6	0.0	0.0	0.1
Drop-out Rate (%)	3.3	3.3	0.0	n/a	n/a	n/a
H.S. Diplomas (#)	189	189	0	0	0	0

Dinwiddie County

Dinwiddie County Public Schools

14016 Boydton Plank Rd • Dinwiddie, VA 23841-0007
Mailing Address: PO Box 7 • Dinwiddie, VA 23841-0007
(804) 469-4190 • http://www.dinwiddie.k12.va.us/
Grade Span: PK-12; **Agency Type:** 1
Schools: 7
5 Primary; 1 Middle; 1 High; 0 Other Level
7 Regular; 0 Special Education; 0 Vocational; 0 Alternative
0 Magnet; 0 Charter; 3 Title I Eligible; 0 School-wide Title I
Students: 4,423 (52.2% male; 47.8% female)
Individual Education Program: 567 (12.8%);
English Language Learner: 35 (0.8%); Migrant: 0 (0.0%)
Eligible for Free Lunch Program: 1,193 (27.0%)
Eligible for Reduced-Price Lunch Program: 352 (8.0%)
Teachers: 372.0 (11.9 to 1)
Librarians/Media Specialists: 9.0 (491.4 to 1)
Guidance Counselors: 9.0 (491.4 to 1)
Current Spending: ($ per student per year):
Total: $6,287; Instruction: $3,898; Support Services: $2,120
Enrollment, Drop-out Rates and Diploma Recipients by Race/Ethnicity

Category	Total	White	Black	Asian	AIAN	Hisp.
Enrollment (%)	100.0	57.2	40.5	0.4	0.2	1.8
Drop-out Rate (%)	5.3	5.1	5.3	0.0	0.0	21.4
H.S. Diplomas (#)	203	124	78	1	0	0

Essex County

Essex County Public Schools

109 N Cross St • Tappahannock, VA 22560-0756
Mailing Address: PO Box 756 • Tappahannock, VA 22560-0756
(804) 443-4366 • http://www.essex.k12.va.us/
Grade Span: PK-12; **Agency Type:** 1
Schools: 3
1 Primary; 1 Middle; 1 High; 0 Other Level
3 Regular; 0 Special Education; 0 Vocational; 0 Alternative
0 Magnet; 0 Charter; 2 Title I Eligible; 0 School-wide Title I
Students: 1,626 (48.9% male; 51.1% female)
Individual Education Program: 317 (19.5%);
English Language Learner: n/a; Migrant: 0 (0.0%)
Eligible for Free Lunch Program: 563 (34.6%)
Eligible for Reduced-Price Lunch Program: 180 (11.1%)
Teachers: 157.0 (10.4 to 1)
Librarians/Media Specialists: 3.0 (542.0 to 1)
Guidance Counselors: 3.0 (542.0 to 1)
Current Spending: ($ per student per year):
Total: $6,730; Instruction: $4,450; Support Services: $1,982
Enrollment, Drop-out Rates and Diploma Recipients by Race/Ethnicity

Category	Total	White	Black	Asian	AIAN	Hisp.
Enrollment (%)	100.0	43.7	55.4	0.7	0.1	0.2
Drop-out Rate (%)	3.0	2.8	3.2	n/a	n/a	0.0
H.S. Diplomas (#)	105	48	56	1	0	0

Fairfax County

Fairfax County Public Schools

10700 Page Ave • Fairfax, VA 22030-4006
(703) 246-2631 • http://www.fcps.k12.va.us/
Grade Span: PK-12; **Agency Type:** 1
Schools: 202
132 Primary; 23 Middle; 28 High; 15 Other Level
179 Regular; 8 Special Education; 1 Vocational; 10 Alternative
67 Magnet; 0 Charter; 36 Title I Eligible; 27 School-wide Title I
Students: 162,585 (51.8% male; 48.2% female)
Individual Education Program: 23,078 (14.2%);
English Language Learner: 20,974 (12.9%); Migrant: 0 (0.0%)
Eligible for Free Lunch Program: 20,611 (12.7%)
Eligible for Reduced-Price Lunch Program: 9,347 (5.7%)
Teachers: 13,946.8 (11.7 to 1)
Librarians/Media Specialists: 226.7 (717.2 to 1)
Guidance Counselors: 419.9 (387.2 to 1)
Current Spending: ($ per student per year):
Total: $9,038; Instruction: $5,552; Support Services: $3,175
Enrollment, Drop-out Rates and Diploma Recipients by Race/Ethnicity

Category	Total	White	Black	Asian	AIAN	Hisp.
Enrollment (%)	100.0	54.1	10.5	16.6	0.4	14.6
Drop-out Rate (%)	2.8	1.6	5.1	2.2	3.3	7.9
H.S. Diplomas (#)	10,450	6,715	1,055	1,757	16	907

Falls Church City

Falls Church City Public Schools

803 W Broad St Ste 300 • Falls Church, VA 22046-3432
(703) 248-5601 • http://www.fccps.k12.va.us/
Grade Span: PK-12; **Agency Type:** 1
Schools: 4
2 Primary; 1 Middle; 1 High; 0 Other Level
4 Regular; 0 Special Education; 0 Vocational; 0 Alternative
0 Magnet; 0 Charter; 1 Title I Eligible; 0 School-wide Title I
Students: 1,833 (51.7% male; 48.3% female)
Individual Education Program: 296 (16.1%);
English Language Learner: 120 (6.5%); Migrant: 0 (0.0%)
Eligible for Free Lunch Program: 93 (5.1%)
Eligible for Reduced-Price Lunch Program: 62 (3.4%)
Teachers: 189.9 (9.7 to 1)
Librarians/Media Specialists: 4.0 (458.3 to 1)
Guidance Counselors: 4.6 (398.5 to 1)
Current Spending: ($ per student per year):
Total: $11,207; Instruction: $6,412; Support Services: $4,224
Enrollment, Drop-out Rates and Diploma Recipients by Race/Ethnicity

Category	Total	White	Black	Asian	AIAN	Hisp.
Enrollment (%)	100.0	77.6	4.2	8.9	0.2	9.1
Drop-out Rate (%)	0.4	0.5	0.0	0.0	n/a	0.0
H.S. Diplomas (#)	117	93	7	8	0	9

Fauquier County

Fauquier County Public Schools

320 Hospital Dr • Warrenton, VA 20186-3037
(540) 351-1000 • http://www.fcps1.org/
Grade Span: PK-12; **Agency Type:** 1
Schools: 17
10 Primary; 4 Middle; 2 High; 1 Other Level
16 Regular; 0 Special Education; 0 Vocational; 1 Alternative
0 Magnet; 0 Charter; 8 Title I Eligible; 2 School-wide Title I
Students: 10,040 (50.7% male; 49.3% female)
Individual Education Program: 1,342 (13.4%);
English Language Learner: 139 (1.4%); Migrant: 0 (0.0%)
Eligible for Free Lunch Program: 1,129 (11.2%)
Eligible for Reduced-Price Lunch Program: 340 (3.4%)
Teachers: 892.4 (11.3 to 1)
Librarians/Media Specialists: 17.5 (573.7 to 1)
Guidance Counselors: 20.0 (502.0 to 1)
Current Spending: ($ per student per year):
Total: $7,019; Instruction: $4,362; Support Services: $2,381
Enrollment, Drop-out Rates and Diploma Recipients by Race/Ethnicity

Category	Total	White	Black	Asian	AIAN	Hisp.
Enrollment (%)	100.0	86.7	9.8	0.7	0.2	2.6
Drop-out Rate (%)	5.6	4.7	11.9	6.5	0.0	17.1
H.S. Diplomas (#)	651	586	52	9	0	4

Floyd County

Floyd County Public Schools

140 Harris Hart Rd NE • Floyd, VA 24091-9710
(540) 745-9400 • http://www.floyd.k12.va.us/
Grade Span: PK-12; **Agency Type:** 1
Schools: 5
4 Primary; 0 Middle; 1 High; 0 Other Level
5 Regular; 0 Special Education; 0 Vocational; 0 Alternative
0 Magnet; 0 Charter; 4 Title I Eligible; 0 School-wide Title I
Students: 2,030 (49.1% male; 50.9% female)
Individual Education Program: 380 (18.7%);
English Language Learner: 35 (1.7%); Migrant: 8 (0.4%)
Eligible for Free Lunch Program: 480 (23.6%)
Eligible for Reduced-Price Lunch Program: 203 (10.0%)
Teachers: 159.0 (12.8 to 1)
Librarians/Media Specialists: 0.0 (0.0 to 1)
Guidance Counselors: 0.0 (0.0 to 1)
Current Spending: ($ per student per year):
Total: $6,447; Instruction: $4,073; Support Services: $2,243
Enrollment, Drop-out Rates and Diploma Recipients by Race/Ethnicity

Category	Total	White	Black	Asian	AIAN	Hisp.
Enrollment (%)	100.0	94.3	3.3	0.2	0.0	2.2
Drop-out Rate (%)	2.1	2.2	0.0	n/a	n/a	0.0
H.S. Diplomas (#)	115	114	1	0	0	0

Fluvanna County

Fluvanna County Public Schools

14455 James Madison Hwy • Palmyra, VA 22963-0419
Mailing Address: PO Box 419 • Palmyra, VA 22963-0419
(434) 589-8208 • http://www.fluco.org/
Grade Span: PK-12; **Agency Type:** 1
Schools: 5
3 Primary; 1 Middle; 1 High; 0 Other Level
5 Regular; 0 Special Education; 0 Vocational; 0 Alternative
0 Magnet; 0 Charter; 2 Title I Eligible; 0 School-wide Title I
Students: 3,287 (51.0% male; 49.0% female)
Individual Education Program: 480 (14.6%);
English Language Learner: 10 (0.3%); Migrant: 0 (0.0%)
Eligible for Free Lunch Program: 404 (12.3%)
Eligible for Reduced-Price Lunch Program: 150 (4.6%)
Teachers: 292.2 (11.2 to 1)
Librarians/Media Specialists: 6.0 (547.8 to 1)
Guidance Counselors: 5.8 (566.7 to 1)
Current Spending: ($ per student per year):
Total: $6,381; Instruction: $4,115; Support Services: $2,195
Enrollment, Drop-out Rates and Diploma Recipients by Race/Ethnicity

Category	Total	White	Black	Asian	AIAN	Hisp.
Enrollment (%)	100.0	77.0	21.2	0.5	0.0	1.2
Drop-out Rate (%)	4.3	3.9	5.7	0.0	0.0	12.5
H.S. Diplomas (#)	183	148	34	0	0	1

Franklin County

Franklin County Public Schools

25 Bernard Rd • Rocky Mount, VA 24151-6614
(540) 483-5138 • http://www.franklincity.k12.va.us/
Grade Span: PK-12; **Agency Type:** 1
Schools: 16
11 Primary; 3 Middle; 1 High; 1 Other Level
16 Regular; 0 Special Education; 0 Vocational; 0 Alternative
0 Magnet; 1 Charter; 8 Title I Eligible; 7 School-wide Title I
Students: 7,244 (50.9% male; 49.1% female)
Individual Education Program: 1,321 (18.2%);
English Language Learner: 48 (0.7%); Migrant: 0 (0.0%)
Eligible for Free Lunch Program: 2,062 (28.5%)
Eligible for Reduced-Price Lunch Program: 558 (7.7%)
Teachers: 620.8 (11.7 to 1)
Librarians/Media Specialists: 15.0 (482.9 to 1)
Guidance Counselors: 16.0 (452.8 to 1)
Current Spending: ($ per student per year):
Total: $6,390; Instruction: $3,842; Support Services: $2,232
Enrollment, Drop-out Rates and Diploma Recipients by Race/Ethnicity

Category	Total	White	Black	Asian	AIAN	Hisp.
Enrollment (%)	100.0	84.9	12.7	0.6	0.1	1.7
Drop-out Rate (%)	4.5	4.5	4.6	0.0	0.0	16.7
H.S. Diplomas (#)	418	362	49	4	0	3

Frederick County

Frederick County Public Schools

1415 Amherst St • Winchester, VA 22601
Mailing Address: PO Box 3508 • Winchester, VA 22604-2546
(540) 662-3888
Grade Span: PK-12; **Agency Type:** 1
Schools: 16
10 Primary; 3 Middle; 2 High; 0 Other Level
15 Regular; 0 Special Education; 0 Vocational; 0 Alternative
0 Magnet; 0 Charter; 8 Title I Eligible; 0 School-wide Title I
Students: 10,969 (51.3% male; 48.7% female)
Individual Education Program: 1,680 (15.3%);
English Language Learner: 233 (2.1%); Migrant: 62 (0.6%)
Eligible for Free Lunch Program: 1,244 (11.3%)
Eligible for Reduced-Price Lunch Program: 499 (4.5%)
Teachers: 932.3 (11.8 to 1)
Librarians/Media Specialists: 17.0 (645.2 to 1)
Guidance Counselors: 23.0 (476.9 to 1)
Current Spending: ($ per student per year):
Total: $6,876; Instruction: $4,339; Support Services: $2,294
Enrollment, Drop-out Rates and Diploma Recipients by Race/Ethnicity

Category	Total	White	Black	Asian	AIAN	Hisp.
Enrollment (%)	100.0	84.3	3.9	1.3	0.3	10.3
Drop-out Rate (%)	3.8	3.7	7.0	0.0	0.0	8.5
H.S. Diplomas (#)	548	510	20	6	1	11

Fredericksburg City Public Schools

817 Princess Anne St • Fredericksburg, VA 22401-5819
(540) 372-1130 • http://www.cityschools.com/
Grade Span: PK-12; **Agency Type:** 1
Schools: 4

2 Primary; 1 Middle; 1 High; 0 Other Level
3 Regular; 1 Special Education; 0 Vocational; 0 Alternative
0 Magnet; 0 Charter; 2 Title I Eligible; 2 School-wide Title I
Students: 2,417 (50.1% male; 49.9% female)
Individual Education Program: 357 (14.8%);
English Language Learner: 92 (3.8%); Migrant: 0 (0.0%)
Eligible for Free Lunch Program: 1,056 (43.7%)
Eligible for Reduced-Price Lunch Program: 165 (6.8%)
Teachers: 222.8 (10.8 to 1)
Librarians/Media Specialists: 3.0 (805.7 to 1)
Guidance Counselors: 5.0 (483.4 to 1)
Current Spending: ($ per student per year):
Total: $9,414; Instruction: $6,179; Support Services: $2,857
Enrollment, Drop-out Rates and Diploma Recipients by Race/Ethnicity

Category	Total	White	Black	Asian	AIAN	Hisp.
Enrollment (%)	100.0	46.5	42.7	2.2	0.1	8.5
Drop-out Rate (%)	2.1	1.5	3.4	0.0	n/a	0.0
H.S. Diplomas (#)	114	72	35	4	0	3

Giles County

Giles County Public Schools
151 School Rd • Pearisburg, VA 24134-9725
(540) 921-1421 • http://sbo.gilesk12.org/
Grade Span: PK-12; **Agency Type:** 1
Schools: 6
3 Primary; 0 Middle; 2 High; 1 Other Level
5 Regular; 0 Special Education; 1 Vocational; 0 Alternative
0 Magnet; 0 Charter; 2 Title I Eligible; 0 School-wide Title I
Students: 2,562 (50.9% male; 49.1% female)
Individual Education Program: 315 (12.3%);
English Language Learner: 4 (0.2%); Migrant: 0 (0.0%)
Eligible for Free Lunch Program: 552 (21.5%)
Eligible for Reduced-Price Lunch Program: 222 (8.7%)
Teachers: 215.5 (11.9 to 1)
Librarians/Media Specialists: 5.0 (512.4 to 1)
Guidance Counselors: 6.0 (427.0 to 1)
Current Spending: ($ per student per year):
Total: $6,766; Instruction: $4,338; Support Services: $2,309
Enrollment, Drop-out Rates and Diploma Recipients by Race/Ethnicity

Category	Total	White	Black	Asian	AIAN	Hisp.
Enrollment (%)	100.0	97.4	1.5	0.7	0.0	0.4
Drop-out Rate (%)	3.5	3.3	12.5	n/a	0.0	0.0
H.S. Diplomas (#)	149	144	4	0	0	1

Gloucester County

Gloucester County Public Schools
6506 Main St • Gloucester, VA 23061-2320
Mailing Address: PO Box 2320 • Gloucester, VA 23061-2320
(804) 693-1425 • http://gets.gc.k12.va.us/
Grade Span: PK-12; **Agency Type:** 1
Schools: 10
6 Primary; 2 Middle; 2 High; 0 Other Level
10 Regular; 0 Special Education; 0 Vocational; 0 Alternative
0 Magnet; 1 Charter; 6 Title I Eligible; 0 School-wide Title I
Students: 6,333 (51.4% male; 48.6% female)
Individual Education Program: 766 (12.1%);
English Language Learner: n/a; Migrant: 0 (0.0%)
Eligible for Free Lunch Program: 820 (12.9%)
Eligible for Reduced-Price Lunch Program: 309 (4.9%)
Teachers: 517.5 (12.2 to 1)
Librarians/Media Specialists: 10.0 (633.3 to 1)
Guidance Counselors: 11.0 (575.7 to 1)
Current Spending: ($ per student per year):
Total: $6,418; Instruction: $3,969; Support Services: $2,194
Enrollment, Drop-out Rates and Diploma Recipients by Race/Ethnicity

Category	Total	White	Black	Asian	AIAN	Hisp.
Enrollment (%)	100.0	85.4	12.0	0.9	0.3	1.4
Drop-out Rate (%)	3.2	3.1	4.4	3.7	0.0	0.0
H.S. Diplomas (#)	374	322	40	5	1	6

Goochland County

Goochland County Public Schools
2938 River Rd W • Goochland, VA 23063-0169
Mailing Address: PO Box 169 • Goochland, VA 23063-0169
(804) 556-5601 • http://www.glnd.k12.va.us/
Grade Span: PK-12; **Agency Type:** 1
Schools: 5
3 Primary; 1 Middle; 1 High; 0 Other Level
5 Regular; 0 Special Education; 0 Vocational; 0 Alternative
0 Magnet; 0 Charter; 2 Title I Eligible; 0 School-wide Title I
Students: 2,066 (52.5% male; 47.5% female)
Individual Education Program: 385 (18.6%);
English Language Learner: 0 (0.0%); Migrant: 0 (0.0%)
Eligible for Free Lunch Program: 278 (13.5%)
Eligible for Reduced-Price Lunch Program: 141 (6.8%)
Teachers: 208.1 (9.9 to 1)
Librarians/Media Specialists: 5.0 (413.2 to 1)
Guidance Counselors: 5.0 (413.2 to 1)
Current Spending: ($ per student per year):
Total: $7,656; Instruction: $4,471; Support Services: $3,097
Enrollment, Drop-out Rates and Diploma Recipients by Race/Ethnicity

Category	Total	White	Black	Asian	AIAN	Hisp.
Enrollment (%)	100.0	66.7	31.8	0.4	0.0	1.1
Drop-out Rate (%)	1.2	0.8	2.0	0.0	n/a	0.0
H.S. Diplomas (#)	130	76	53	1	0	0

Grayson County

Grayson County Public Schools
412 E Main St • Independence, VA 24348-0888
Mailing Address: PO Box 888 • Independence, VA 24348-0888
(276) 773-2832 • http://www.grayson.k12.va.us/
Grade Span: PK-12; **Agency Type:** 1
Schools: 11
6 Primary; 2 Middle; 1 High; 2 Other Level
10 Regular; 0 Special Education; 1 Vocational; 0 Alternative
0 Magnet; 0 Charter; 4 Title I Eligible; 3 School-wide Title I
Students: 2,281 (50.2% male; 49.8% female)
Individual Education Program: 319 (14.0%);
English Language Learner: 6 (0.3%); Migrant: 8 (0.4%)
Eligible for Free Lunch Program: 871 (38.2%)
Eligible for Reduced-Price Lunch Program: 318 (13.9%)
Teachers: 229.4 (9.9 to 1)
Librarians/Media Specialists: 8.0 (285.1 to 1)
Guidance Counselors: 4.0 (570.3 to 1)
Current Spending: ($ per student per year):
Total: $6,998; Instruction: $4,179; Support Services: $2,586
Enrollment, Drop-out Rates and Diploma Recipients by Race/Ethnicity

Category	Total	White	Black	Asian	AIAN	Hisp.
Enrollment (%)	100.0	94.9	3.1	0.1	0.1	1.8
Drop-out Rate (%)	2.4	2.3	6.7	n/a	n/a	0.0
H.S. Diplomas (#)	115	113	2	0	0	0

Greene County

Greene County Public Schools
40 Celt Rd • Standardsville, VA 22973-1140
Mailing Address: PO Box 1140 • Standardsville, VA 22973-1140
(434) 985-5254 • http://www.greenecountyschools.com/
Grade Span: PK-12; **Agency Type:** 1
Schools: 7
3 Primary; 1 Middle; 1 High; 2 Other Level
6 Regular; 0 Special Education; 1 Vocational; 0 Alternative
0 Magnet; 1 Charter; 3 Title I Eligible; 0 School-wide Title I
Students: 2,705 (52.0% male; 48.0% female)
Individual Education Program: 532 (19.7%);
English Language Learner: 20 (0.7%); Migrant: 0 (0.0%)
Eligible for Free Lunch Program: 471 (17.4%)
Eligible for Reduced-Price Lunch Program: 189 (7.0%)
Teachers: 116.0 (23.3 to 1)
Librarians/Media Specialists: 2.0 (1,352.5 to 1)
Guidance Counselors: 4.0 (676.3 to 1)
Current Spending: ($ per student per year):
Total: $7,171; Instruction: $4,677; Support Services: $2,406
Enrollment, Drop-out Rates and Diploma Recipients by Race/Ethnicity

Category	Total	White	Black	Asian	AIAN	Hisp.
Enrollment (%)	100.0	87.2	9.9	0.4	0.4	2.0
Drop-out Rate (%)	2.9	2.7	4.2	0.0	0.0	0.0
H.S. Diplomas (#)	144	125	16	0	0	3

Greensville County

Greensville County Public Schools
105 Ruffin St • Emporia, VA 23847-1156
Mailing Address: PO Box 1156 • Emporia, VA 23847-1156
(434) 634-3748 • http://www.greensville.k12.va.us/
Grade Span: PK-12; **Agency Type:** 3
Schools: 5
1 Primary; 2 Middle; 2 High; 0 Other Level
4 Regular; 0 Special Education; 0 Vocational; 1 Alternative
0 Magnet; 0 Charter; 3 Title I Eligible; 3 School-wide Title I
Students: 2,770 (52.3% male; 47.7% female)
Individual Education Program: 472 (17.0%);
English Language Learner: 12 (0.4%); Migrant: 0 (0.0%)
Eligible for Free Lunch Program: 1,248 (45.1%)
Eligible for Reduced-Price Lunch Program: 252 (9.1%)
Teachers: 247.0 (11.2 to 1)

Librarians/Media Specialists: 5.0 (554.0 to 1)
Guidance Counselors: 6.0 (461.7 to 1)
Current Spending: ($ per student per year):
Total: $6,748; Instruction: $4,239; Support Services: $2,209
Enrollment, Drop-out Rates and Diploma Recipients by Race/Ethnicity

Category	Total	White	Black	Asian	AIAN	Hisp.
Enrollment (%)	100.0	25.6	73.3	0.1	0.1	0.9
Drop-out Rate (%)	2.4	3.5	2.0	n/a	n/a	0.0
H.S. Diplomas (#)	152	45	107	0	0	0

Halifax County

Halifax County Public Schools
Mary Bethune Ofc Complex • Halifax, VA 24558-1849
Mailing Address: PO Box 1849 • Halifax, VA 24558-1849
(434) 476-2171 • http://www.halifax.k12.va.us/
Grade Span: PK-12; **Agency Type:** 1
Schools: 16
12 Primary; 2 Middle; 2 High; 0 Other Level
15 Regular; 0 Special Education; 0 Vocational; 1 Alternative
0 Magnet; 0 Charter; 11 Title I Eligible; 0 School-wide Title I
Students: 5,912 (51.0% male; 49.0% female)
Individual Education Program: 1,209 (20.4%);
English Language Learner: 15 (0.3%); Migrant: 0 (0.0%)
Eligible for Free Lunch Program: 2,735 (46.3%)
Eligible for Reduced-Price Lunch Program: 639 (10.8%)
Teachers: 580.4 (10.2 to 1)
Librarians/Media Specialists: 14.0 (422.3 to 1)
Guidance Counselors: 16.0 (369.5 to 1)
Current Spending: ($ per student per year):
Total: $6,826; Instruction: $4,158; Support Services: $2,304
Enrollment, Drop-out Rates and Diploma Recipients by Race/Ethnicity

Category	Total	White	Black	Asian	AIAN	Hisp.
Enrollment (%)	100.0	49.4	49.1	0.2	0.1	1.2
Drop-out Rate (%)	2.4	1.5	3.4	0.0	0.0	8.3
H.S. Diplomas (#)	347	183	160	1	1	2

Hampton City

Hampton City Public Schools
1 Franklin St • Hampton, VA 23669-3570
(757) 727-2000 • http://www.sbo.hampton.k12.va.us/
Grade Span: PK-12; **Agency Type:** 1
Schools: 37
24 Primary; 6 Middle; 4 High; 2 Other Level
35 Regular; 0 Special Education; 0 Vocational; 1 Alternative
2 Magnet; 1 Charter; 15 Title I Eligible; 10 School-wide Title I
Students: 22,996 (51.2% male; 48.8% female)
Individual Education Program: 3,150 (13.7%);
English Language Learner: 272 (1.2%); Migrant: 0 (0.0%)
Eligible for Free Lunch Program: 7,244 (31.5%)
Eligible for Reduced-Price Lunch Program: 2,073 (9.0%)
Teachers: 2,004.5 (11.5 to 1)
Librarians/Media Specialists: 44.0 (522.6 to 1)
Guidance Counselors: 54.0 (425.9 to 1)
Current Spending: ($ per student per year):
Total: $6,670; Instruction: $4,134; Support Services: $2,197
Enrollment, Drop-out Rates and Diploma Recipients by Race/Ethnicity

Category	Total	White	Black	Asian	AIAN	Hisp.
Enrollment (%)	100.0	35.4	60.0	1.8	0.4	2.4
Drop-out Rate (%)	2.7	2.7	2.7	3.1	4.8	2.1
H.S. Diplomas (#)	1,279	540	692	22	4	21

Hanover County

Hanover County Public Schools
200 Berkley St • Ashland, VA 23005-1399
(804) 365-4500 • http://hcps2.hanover.k12.va.us/
Grade Span: PK-12; **Agency Type:** 1
Schools: 21
13 Primary; 4 Middle; 3 High; 0 Other Level
20 Regular; 0 Special Education; 0 Vocational; 0 Alternative
0 Magnet; 0 Charter; 5 Title I Eligible; 0 School-wide Title I
Students: 17,563 (51.2% male; 48.8% female)
Individual Education Program: 2,591 (14.8%);
English Language Learner: 99 (0.6%); Migrant: 0 (0.0%)
Eligible for Free Lunch Program: 1,079 (6.1%)
Eligible for Reduced-Price Lunch Program: 336 (1.9%)
Teachers: 1,498.0 (11.7 to 1)
Librarians/Media Specialists: 26.0 (675.5 to 1)
Guidance Counselors: 30.0 (585.4 to 1)
Current Spending: ($ per student per year):
Total: $5,955; Instruction: $3,949; Support Services: $1,732

Enrollment, Drop-out Rates and Diploma Recipients by Race/Ethnicity

Category	Total	White	Black	Asian	AIAN	Hisp.
Enrollment (%)	100.0	87.8	9.9	1.2	0.2	0.8
Drop-out Rate (%)	0.4	0.3	1.2	0.0	0.0	0.0
H.S. Diplomas (#)	1,060	956	90	5	3	6

Harrisonburg City

Harrisonburg City Public Schools
317 S Main St • Harrisonburg, VA 22801-3606
(540) 434-9916 • http://www.harrisonburg.k12.va.us/
Grade Span: PK-12; **Agency Type:** 1
Schools: 6
4 Primary; 1 Middle; 1 High; 0 Other Level
6 Regular; 0 Special Education; 0 Vocational; 0 Alternative
0 Magnet; 0 Charter; 4 Title I Eligible; 0 School-wide Title I
Students: 3,999 (51.3% male; 48.7% female)
Individual Education Program: 683 (17.1%);
English Language Learner: 1,195 (29.9%); Migrant: 106 (2.7%)
Eligible for Free Lunch Program: 1,473 (36.8%)
Eligible for Reduced-Price Lunch Program: 322 (8.1%)
Teachers: 410.6 (9.7 to 1)
Librarians/Media Specialists: 7.0 (571.3 to 1)
Guidance Counselors: 7.5 (533.2 to 1)
Current Spending: ($ per student per year):
Total: $8,017; Instruction: $5,063; Support Services: $2,489
Enrollment, Drop-out Rates and Diploma Recipients by Race/Ethnicity

Category	Total	White	Black	Asian	AIAN	Hisp.
Enrollment (%)	100.0	62.6	11.6	4.3	0.0	21.5
Drop-out Rate (%)	1.9	1.3	1.9	5.3	n/a	4.5
H.S. Diplomas (#)	244	186	23	8	0	27

Henrico County

Henrico County Public Schools
3820 Nine Mile Rd • Richmond, VA 23233-0420
(804) 652-3717 • http://www.henrico.k12.va.us/
Grade Span: PK-12; **Agency Type:** 1
Schools: 65
42 Primary; 10 Middle; 8 High; 5 Other Level
60 Regular; 1 Special Education; 2 Vocational; 2 Alternative
7 Magnet; 0 Charter; 13 Title I Eligible; 5 School-wide Title I
Students: 43,698 (51.3% male; 48.7% female)
Individual Education Program: 6,062 (13.9%);
English Language Learner: 1,363 (3.1%); Migrant: 0 (0.0%)
Eligible for Free Lunch Program: 5,801 (13.3%)
Eligible for Reduced-Price Lunch Program: 1,768 (4.0%)
Teachers: 3,371.4 (13.0 to 1)
Librarians/Media Specialists: 74.0 (590.5 to 1)
Guidance Counselors: 86.1 (507.5 to 1)
Current Spending: ($ per student per year):
Total: $6,414; Instruction: $3,950; Support Services: $2,210
Enrollment, Drop-out Rates and Diploma Recipients by Race/Ethnicity

Category	Total	White	Black	Asian	AIAN	Hisp.
Enrollment (%)	100.0	57.2	35.0	4.2	0.2	2.5
Drop-out Rate (%)	2.3	1.8	3.1	2.3	0.0	4.4
H.S. Diplomas (#)	2,400	1,515	713	119	3	50

Henry County

Henry County Public Schools
3300 Kings Mountain Rd • Collinsville, VA 24078-8958
Mailing Address: PO Box 8958 • Collinsville, VA 24078-8958
(276) 634-4712 •
http://henryva.schoolwires.com/henrycounty/site/default.asp
Grade Span: PK-12; **Agency Type:** 1
Schools: 20
12 Primary; 4 Middle; 4 High; 0 Other Level
20 Regular; 0 Special Education; 0 Vocational; 0 Alternative
0 Magnet; 0 Charter; 10 Title I Eligible; 10 School-wide Title I
Students: 8,526 (50.4% male; 49.6% female)
Individual Education Program: 1,597 (18.7%);
English Language Learner: 278 (3.3%); Migrant: 0 (0.0%)
Eligible for Free Lunch Program: 2,787 (32.7%)
Eligible for Reduced-Price Lunch Program: 572 (6.7%)
Teachers: 800.0 (10.7 to 1)
Librarians/Media Specialists: 20.0 (426.3 to 1)
Guidance Counselors: 20.0 (426.3 to 1)
Current Spending: ($ per student per year):
Total: $6,658; Instruction: $4,166; Support Services: $2,166

Enrollment, Drop-out Rates and Diploma Recipients by Race/Ethnicity

Category	Total	White	Black	Asian	AIAN	Hisp.
Enrollment (%)	100.0	66.5	28.8	0.6	0.0	4.0
Drop-out Rate (%)	4.2	4.2	4.3	0.0	n/a	9.4
H.S. Diplomas (#)	512	349	154	4	0	5

Hopewell City

Hopewell City Public Schools

103 N 12th Ave • Hopewell, VA 23860-3758
(804) 541-6400 • http://www.hopewell.k12.va.us/
Grade Span: PK-12; **Agency Type:** 1
Schools: 7
4 Primary; 1 Middle; 1 High; 1 Other Level
6 Regular; 0 Special Education; 0 Vocational; 1 Alternative
0 Magnet; 0 Charter; 3 Title I Eligible; 3 School-wide Title I
Students: 3,913 (51.7% male; 48.3% female)
Individual Education Program: 717 (18.3%);
English Language Learner: 30 (0.8%); Migrant: 0 (0.0%)
Eligible for Free Lunch Program: 1,866 (47.7%)
Eligible for Reduced-Price Lunch Program: 412 (10.5%)
Teachers: 376.5 (10.4 to 1)
Librarians/Media Specialists: 5.0 (782.6 to 1)
Guidance Counselors: 7.0 (559.0 to 1)
Current Spending: ($ per student per year):
Total: $7,225; Instruction: $4,583; Support Services: $2,308
Enrollment, Drop-out Rates and Diploma Recipients by Race/Ethnicity

Category	Total	White	Black	Asian	AIAN	Hisp.
Enrollment (%)	100.0	42.7	53.6	0.5	0.1	3.1
Drop-out Rate (%)	5.4	4.6	6.2	9.1	0.0	4.2
H.S. Diplomas (#)	217	123	88	1	0	5

Isle Of Wight County

Isle of Wight County Pub Schools

17124 Monument Circle • Isle Of Wight, VA 23397-0078
Mailing Address: PO Box 78 • Isle Of Wight, VA 23397-0078
(757) 357-0449 • http://www.iwcs.k12.va.us/
Grade Span: PK-12; **Agency Type:** 1
Schools: 8
4 Primary; 2 Middle; 2 High; 0 Other Level
8 Regular; 0 Special Education; 0 Vocational; 0 Alternative
0 Magnet; 0 Charter; 4 Title I Eligible; 0 School-wide Title I
Students: 5,040 (52.3% male; 47.7% female)
Individual Education Program: 688 (13.7%);
English Language Learner: 10 (0.2%); Migrant: 0 (0.0%)
Eligible for Free Lunch Program: 1,316 (26.1%)
Eligible for Reduced-Price Lunch Program: 291 (5.8%)
Teachers: 386.5 (13.0 to 1)
Librarians/Media Specialists: 1.0 (5,040.0 to 1)
Guidance Counselors: 0.0 (0.0 to 1)
Current Spending: ($ per student per year):
Total: $6,832; Instruction: $4,346; Support Services: $2,181
Enrollment, Drop-out Rates and Diploma Recipients by Race/Ethnicity

Category	Total	White	Black	Asian	AIAN	Hisp.
Enrollment (%)	100.0	63.6	34.6	0.4	0.6	0.7
Drop-out Rate (%)	1.5	1.4	2.0	0.0	0.0	0.0
H.S. Diplomas (#)	273	200	69	2	1	1

King George County

King George County Public Schools

9100 St Anthony's Rd • King George, VA 22485-0021
Mailing Address: PO Box 1239 • King George, VA 22485-0021
(540) 775-5833 • http://www.kgcs.k12.va.us/
Grade Span: PK-12; **Agency Type:** 1
Schools: 4
2 Primary; 1 Middle; 1 High; 0 Other Level
4 Regular; 0 Special Education; 0 Vocational; 0 Alternative
0 Magnet; 0 Charter; 2 Title I Eligible; 0 School-wide Title I
Students: 3,048 (52.2% male; 47.8% female)
Individual Education Program: 474 (15.6%);
English Language Learner: 1 (<0.1%); Migrant: 0 (0.0%)
Eligible for Free Lunch Program: 550 (18.0%)
Eligible for Reduced-Price Lunch Program: 126 (4.1%)
Teachers: 224.5 (13.6 to 1)
Librarians/Media Specialists: 2.0 (1,524.0 to 1)
Guidance Counselors: 1.0 (3,048.0 to 1)
Current Spending: ($ per student per year):
Total: $6,710; Instruction: $4,049; Support Services: $2,436

Enrollment, Drop-out Rates and Diploma Recipients by Race/Ethnicity

Category	Total	White	Black	Asian	AIAN	Hisp.
Enrollment (%)	100.0	69.1	21.8	1.1	0.3	1.3
Drop-out Rate (%)	2.2	1.5	4.7	0.0	0.0	0.0
H.S. Diplomas (#)	216	160	48	4	1	3

King William County

King William County Public Schools

18548 King William Rd • King William, VA 23086-0185
Mailing Address: PO Box 185 • King William, VA 23086-0185
(804) 769-3434 • http://www.kwcps.k12.va.us/
Grade Span: PK-12; **Agency Type:** 1
Schools: 4
1 Primary; 1 Middle; 1 High; 0 Other Level
3 Regular; 0 Special Education; 0 Vocational; 0 Alternative
0 Magnet; 0 Charter; 2 Title I Eligible; 0 School-wide Title I
Students: 1,957 (52.5% male; 47.5% female)
Individual Education Program: 347 (17.7%);
English Language Learner: 2 (0.1%); Migrant: 0 (0.0%)
Eligible for Free Lunch Program: 357 (18.2%)
Eligible for Reduced-Price Lunch Program: 123 (6.3%)
Teachers: 179.0 (10.9 to 1)
Librarians/Media Specialists: 3.0 (652.3 to 1)
Guidance Counselors: 5.0 (391.4 to 1)
Current Spending: ($ per student per year):
Total: $7,174; Instruction: $4,249; Support Services: $2,437
Enrollment, Drop-out Rates and Diploma Recipients by Race/Ethnicity

Category	Total	White	Black	Asian	AIAN	Hisp.
Enrollment (%)	100.0	68.5	28.6	0.2	2.2	0.6
Drop-out Rate (%)	0.2	0.0	0.5	0.0	0.0	n/a
H.S. Diplomas (#)	110	62	46	0	2	0

Lancaster County

Lancaster County Public Schools

2330 Irvington Rd • Kilmarnock, VA 22482-2000
(804) 435-3183 • http://www.lcs.k12.va.us/
Grade Span: PK-12; **Agency Type:** 1
Schools: 3
1 Primary; 1 Middle; 1 High; 0 Other Level
3 Regular; 0 Special Education; 0 Vocational; 0 Alternative
0 Magnet; 0 Charter; 1 Title I Eligible; 1 School-wide Title I
Students: 1,517 (53.7% male; 46.3% female)
Individual Education Program: 176 (11.6%);
English Language Learner: n/a; Migrant: 0 (0.0%)
Eligible for Free Lunch Program: 621 (40.9%)
Eligible for Reduced-Price Lunch Program: 131 (8.6%)
Teachers: 147.0 (10.3 to 1)
Librarians/Media Specialists: 3.0 (505.7 to 1)
Guidance Counselors: 3.0 (505.7 to 1)
Current Spending: ($ per student per year):
Total: $7,055; Instruction: $4,420; Support Services: $2,245
Enrollment, Drop-out Rates and Diploma Recipients by Race/Ethnicity

Category	Total	White	Black	Asian	AIAN	Hisp.
Enrollment (%)	100.0	46.2	52.5	0.3	0.1	0.8
Drop-out Rate (%)	3.5	2.4	4.7	n/a	n/a	0.0
H.S. Diplomas (#)	93	41	52	0	0	0

Lee County

Lee County Public Schools

5 Park St • Jonesville, VA 24263-1201
(276) 346-2107 • http://www.leectysch.com/
Grade Span: PK-12; **Agency Type:** 1
Schools: 14
9 Primary; 2 Middle; 2 High; 1 Other Level
13 Regular; 0 Special Education; 1 Vocational; 0 Alternative
0 Magnet; 0 Charter; 11 Title I Eligible; 10 School-wide Title I
Students: 3,806 (51.6% male; 48.4% female)
Individual Education Program: 770 (20.2%);
English Language Learner: 5 (0.1%); Migrant: 0 (0.0%)
Eligible for Free Lunch Program: 1,885 (49.5%)
Eligible for Reduced-Price Lunch Program: 406 (10.7%)
Teachers: 423.0 (9.0 to 1)
Librarians/Media Specialists: 10.0 (380.6 to 1)
Guidance Counselors: 8.0 (475.8 to 1)
Current Spending: ($ per student per year):
Total: $7,246; Instruction: $4,795; Support Services: $2,109
Enrollment, Drop-out Rates and Diploma Recipients by Race/Ethnicity

Category	Total	White	Black	Asian	AIAN	Hisp.
Enrollment (%)	100.0	99.0	0.4	0.0	0.2	0.3
Drop-out Rate (%)	1.0	1.0	0.0	0.0	0.0	n/a
H.S. Diplomas (#)	184	183	1	0	0	0

Loudoun County

Loudoun County Public Schools

102 N St NW • Leesburg, VA 20176-2203
(703) 771-6400 • http://www.loudoun.k12.va.us/
Grade Span: PK-12; **Agency Type:** 1
Schools: 56
38 Primary; 8 Middle; 6 High; 4 Other Level
54 Regular; 0 Special Education; 1 Vocational; 1 Alternative
0 Magnet; 0 Charter; 18 Title I Eligible; 0 School-wide Title I
Students: 37,532 (51.2% male; 48.8% female)
Individual Education Program: 4,128 (11.0%);
English Language Learner: 1,778 (4.7%); Migrant: 0 (0.0%)
Eligible for Free Lunch Program: 2,475 (6.6%)
Eligible for Reduced-Price Lunch Program: 1,368 (3.6%)
Teachers: 3,199.0 (11.7 to 1)
Librarians/Media Specialists: 63.0 (595.7 to 1)
Guidance Counselors: 106.5 (352.4 to 1)
Current Spending: ($ per student per year):
Total: $7,822; Instruction: $5,006; Support Services: $2,576

Enrollment, Drop-out Rates and Diploma Recipients by Race/Ethnicity

Category	Total	White	Black	Asian	AIAN	Hisp.
Enrollment (%)	100.0	74.5	8.5	7.8	0.3	9.0
Drop-out Rate (%)	1.8	1.5	3.4	1.5	0.0	3.6
H.S. Diplomas (#)	1,766	1,385	134	136	2	109

Louisa County

Louisa County Public Schools

953 Davis Hwy • Mineral, VA 23117-0007
Mailing Address: PO Box 7 • Mineral, VA 23117-0007
(540) 894-5115 • http://www.lcps.k12.va.us/
Grade Span: PK-12; **Agency Type:** 1
Schools: 5
3 Primary; 1 Middle; 1 High; 0 Other Level
5 Regular; 0 Special Education; 0 Vocational; 0 Alternative
0 Magnet; 0 Charter; 2 Title I Eligible; 1 School-wide Title I
Students: 4,282 (52.8% male; 47.2% female)
Individual Education Program: 592 (13.8%);
English Language Learner: 10 (0.2%); Migrant: 0 (0.0%)
Eligible for Free Lunch Program: 1,079 (25.2%)
Eligible for Reduced-Price Lunch Program: 386 (9.0%)
Teachers: 358.0 (12.0 to 1)
Librarians/Media Specialists: 7.0 (611.7 to 1)
Guidance Counselors: 8.0 (535.3 to 1)
Current Spending: ($ per student per year):
Total: $6,490; Instruction: $3,787; Support Services: $2,408

Enrollment, Drop-out Rates and Diploma Recipients by Race/Ethnicity

Category	Total	White	Black	Asian	AIAN	Hisp.
Enrollment (%)	100.0	71.3	27.4	0.2	0.4	0.8
Drop-out Rate (%)	4.7	4.8	4.6	0.0	0.0	0.0
H.S. Diplomas (#)	303	232	67	2	0	2

Lunenburg County

Lunenburg County Public Schools

1615 Eighth St • Victoria, VA 23974-0649
Mailing Address: PO Box X • Victoria, VA 23974-0649
(434) 696-2116 • http://www.ssvawebs.com/lunweb/index.htm
Grade Span: PK-12; **Agency Type:** 1
Schools: 4
2 Primary; 1 Middle; 1 High; 0 Other Level
4 Regular; 0 Special Education; 0 Vocational; 0 Alternative
0 Magnet; 0 Charter; 2 Title I Eligible; 0 School-wide Title I
Students: 1,773 (48.3% male; 51.7% female)
Individual Education Program: 323 (18.2%);
English Language Learner: 5 (0.3%); Migrant: 3 (0.2%)
Eligible for Free Lunch Program: 937 (52.8%)
Eligible for Reduced-Price Lunch Program: 185 (10.4%)
Teachers: 173.6 (10.2 to 1)
Librarians/Media Specialists: 4.0 (443.3 to 1)
Guidance Counselors: 4.0 (443.3 to 1)
Current Spending: ($ per student per year):
Total: $7,076; Instruction: $4,278; Support Services: $2,410

Enrollment, Drop-out Rates and Diploma Recipients by Race/Ethnicity

Category	Total	White	Black	Asian	AIAN	Hisp.
Enrollment (%)	100.0	49.6	48.7	0.2	0.4	1.1
Drop-out Rate (%)	4.7	5.5	4.0	0.0	n/a	0.0
H.S. Diplomas (#)	116	61	55	0	0	0

Lynchburg City

Lynchburg City Public Schools

915 Court St • Lynchburg, VA 24504
Mailing Address: PO Box 1599 • Lynchburg, VA 24505-1599
(434) 522-3700 • http://www.lynchburg.org/
Grade Span: PK-12; **Agency Type:** 1
Schools: 17
11 Primary; 3 Middle; 2 High; 1 Other Level
16 Regular; 0 Special Education; 0 Vocational; 1 Alternative
3 Magnet; 0 Charter; 14 Title I Eligible; 11 School-wide Title I
Students: 8,955 (50.8% male; 49.2% female)
Individual Education Program: 1,369 (15.3%);
English Language Learner: 64 (0.7%); Migrant: 0 (0.0%)
Eligible for Free Lunch Program: 3,668 (41.0%)
Eligible for Reduced-Price Lunch Program: 427 (4.8%)
Teachers: 806.4 (11.1 to 1)
Librarians/Media Specialists: 19.0 (471.3 to 1)
Guidance Counselors: 21.0 (426.4 to 1)
Current Spending: ($ per student per year):
Total: $7,160; Instruction: $4,439; Support Services: $2,453

Enrollment, Drop-out Rates and Diploma Recipients by Race/Ethnicity

Category	Total	White	Black	Asian	AIAN	Hisp.
Enrollment (%)	100.0	45.7	50.6	1.3	0.2	1.0
Drop-out Rate (%)	1.3	1.1	1.6	0.0	0.0	0.0
H.S. Diplomas (#)	504	289	199	12	0	4

Madison County

Madison County Public Schools

Route 687 • Madison, VA 22727-0647
Mailing Address: PO Box 647 • Madison, VA 22727-0647
(540) 948-6836 • http://www.madisonschools.k12.va.us/
Grade Span: PK-12; **Agency Type:** 1
Schools: 5
3 Primary; 1 Middle; 1 High; 0 Other Level
5 Regular; 0 Special Education; 0 Vocational; 0 Alternative
0 Magnet; 0 Charter; 3 Title I Eligible; 0 School-wide Title I
Students: 1,830 (50.0% male; 50.0% female)
Individual Education Program: 290 (15.8%);
English Language Learner: 4 (0.2%); Migrant: 7 (0.4%)
Eligible for Free Lunch Program: 309 (16.9%)
Eligible for Reduced-Price Lunch Program: 77 (4.2%)
Teachers: 176.0 (10.4 to 1)
Librarians/Media Specialists: 4.0 (457.5 to 1)
Guidance Counselors: 4.0 (457.5 to 1)
Current Spending: ($ per student per year):
Total: $6,887; Instruction: $4,067; Support Services: $2,587

Enrollment, Drop-out Rates and Diploma Recipients by Race/Ethnicity

Category	Total	White	Black	Asian	AIAN	Hisp.
Enrollment (%)	100.0	82.8	16.3	0.3	0.1	0.4
Drop-out Rate (%)	2.7	2.9	1.9	0.0	0.0	0.0
H.S. Diplomas (#)	146	123	20	1	1	1

Manassas City

Manassas City Public Schools

9000 Tudor Ln • Manassas, VA 20110-5700
(703) 257-8808 • http://www.manassas.k12.va.us/
Grade Span: PK-12; **Agency Type:** 1
Schools: 8
5 Primary; 1 Middle; 1 High; 1 Other Level
7 Regular; 0 Special Education; 0 Vocational; 1 Alternative
0 Magnet; 0 Charter; 2 Title I Eligible; 0 School-wide Title I
Students: 6,673 (51.8% male; 48.2% female)
Individual Education Program: 782 (11.7%);
English Language Learner: 1,184 (17.7%); Migrant: 0 (0.0%)
Eligible for Free Lunch Program: 947 (14.2%)
Eligible for Reduced-Price Lunch Program: 399 (6.0%)
Teachers: 554.1 (12.0 to 1)
Librarians/Media Specialists: 9.5 (702.4 to 1)
Guidance Counselors: 10.0 (667.3 to 1)
Current Spending: ($ per student per year):
Total: $7,296; Instruction: $4,599; Support Services: $2,469

Enrollment, Drop-out Rates and Diploma Recipients by Race/Ethnicity

Category	Total	White	Black	Asian	AIAN	Hisp.
Enrollment (%)	100.0	54.4	16.8	4.5	0.3	24.1
Drop-out Rate (%)	2.2	1.4	3.7	2.4	0.0	4.6
H.S. Diplomas (#)	355	269	39	16	0	31

Manassas Park City

Manassas Park City Public Schools

One Park Center Ct Ste A • Manassas Park, VA 20111-2395
(703) 335-8850 • http://www.mpark.net/
Grade Span: PK-12; **Agency Type:** 1
Schools: 4
1 Primary; 2 Middle; 1 High; 0 Other Level
4 Regular; 0 Special Education; 0 Vocational; 0 Alternative
0 Magnet; 0 Charter; 2 Title I Eligible; 0 School-wide Title I
Students: 2,327 (51.7% male; 48.3% female)
Individual Education Program: 315 (13.5%);
English Language Learner: 494 (21.2%); Migrant: 0 (0.0%)
Eligible for Free Lunch Program: 516 (22.2%)
Eligible for Reduced-Price Lunch Program: 204 (8.8%)
Teachers: 209.1 (11.1 to 1)
Librarians/Media Specialists: 3.0 (775.7 to 1)
Guidance Counselors: 4.0 (581.8 to 1)
Current Spending: ($ per student per year):
Total: $7,319; Instruction: $4,293; Support Services: $2,754
Enrollment, Drop-out Rates and Diploma Recipients by Race/Ethnicity

Category	Total	White	Black	Asian	AIAN	Hisp.
Enrollment (%)	100.0	50.7	14.3	7.0	0.3	27.8
Drop-out Rate (%)	2.1	2.4	1.3	3.8	0.0	1.1
H.S. Diplomas (#)	91	46	14	4	1	26

Martinsville City

Martinsville City Public Schools

202 Cleveland Ave • Martinsville, VA 24115-5548
(276) 632-6313 • http://www.martinsville.k12.va.us/
Grade Span: PK-12; **Agency Type:** 1
Schools: 6
4 Primary; 1 Middle; 1 High; 0 Other Level
6 Regular; 0 Special Education; 0 Vocational; 0 Alternative
0 Magnet; 0 Charter; 3 Title I Eligible; 3 School-wide Title I
Students: 2,694 (50.0% male; 50.0% female)
Individual Education Program: 395 (14.7%);
English Language Learner: 73 (2.7%); Migrant: 0 (0.0%)
Eligible for Free Lunch Program: 1,189 (44.1%)
Eligible for Reduced-Price Lunch Program: 214 (7.9%)
Teachers: 254.2 (10.6 to 1)
Librarians/Media Specialists: 6.0 (449.0 to 1)
Guidance Counselors: 8.0 (336.8 to 1)
Current Spending: ($ per student per year):
Total: $7,520; Instruction: $4,633; Support Services: $2,549
Enrollment, Drop-out Rates and Diploma Recipients by Race/Ethnicity

Category	Total	White	Black	Asian	AIAN	Hisp.
Enrollment (%)	100.0	38.6	57.1	1.1	0.0	1.7
Drop-out Rate (%)	2.0	0.8	3.0	0.0	n/a	0.0
H.S. Diplomas (#)	158	71	86	0	0	1

Mecklenburg County

Mecklenburg County Public Schools

939 Jefferson St • Boydton, VA 23917-0190
(434) 738-6111 • http://www.meck.k12.va.us/
Grade Span: PK-12; **Agency Type:** 1
Schools: 11
7 Primary; 2 Middle; 2 High; 0 Other Level
11 Regular; 0 Special Education; 0 Vocational; 0 Alternative
0 Magnet; 0 Charter; 7 Title I Eligible; 3 School-wide Title I
Students: 4,879 (51.9% male; 48.1% female)
Individual Education Program: 774 (15.9%);
English Language Learner: 28 (0.6%); Migrant: 0 (0.0%)
Eligible for Free Lunch Program: 2,204 (45.2%)
Eligible for Reduced-Price Lunch Program: 542 (11.1%)
Teachers: 387.1 (12.6 to 1)
Librarians/Media Specialists: 8.5 (574.0 to 1)
Guidance Counselors: 8.0 (609.9 to 1)
Current Spending: ($ per student per year):
Total: $6,273; Instruction: $4,037; Support Services: $1,901
Enrollment, Drop-out Rates and Diploma Recipients by Race/Ethnicity

Category	Total	White	Black	Asian	AIAN	Hisp.
Enrollment (%)	100.0	50.9	47.4	0.3	0.1	1.4
Drop-out Rate (%)	4.7	4.1	5.4	0.0	n/a	0.0
H.S. Diplomas (#)	279	164	112	0	0	3

Montgomery County

Montgomery County Public Schools

200 Junkin St • Christiansburg, VA 24073-3098
(540) 382-5100 • http://www.mcps.org/
Grade Span: PK-12; **Agency Type:** 1
Schools: 21
12 Primary; 4 Middle; 4 High; 1 Other Level
20 Regular; 0 Special Education; 0 Vocational; 1 Alternative
0 Magnet; 0 Charter; 10 Title I Eligible; 3 School-wide Title I
Students: 9,313 (51.2% male; 48.8% female)
Individual Education Program: 1,253 (13.5%);
English Language Learner: 144 (1.5%); Migrant: 0 (0.0%)
Eligible for Free Lunch Program: 2,162 (23.2%)
Eligible for Reduced-Price Lunch Program: 731 (7.8%)
Teachers: 922.9 (10.1 to 1)
Librarians/Media Specialists: 21.0 (443.5 to 1)
Guidance Counselors: 26.0 (358.2 to 1)
Current Spending: ($ per student per year):
Total: $7,162; Instruction: $4,224; Support Services: $2,631
Enrollment, Drop-out Rates and Diploma Recipients by Race/Ethnicity

Category	Total	White	Black	Asian	AIAN	Hisp.
Enrollment (%)	100.0	89.7	5.6	2.9	0.4	1.4
Drop-out Rate (%)	4.2	4.4	2.0	0.0	0.0	9.5
H.S. Diplomas (#)	563	520	22	15	0	6

Nelson County

Nelson County Public Schools

84 Courthouse Square • Lovingston, VA 22949-0276
Mailing Address: PO Box 276 • Lovingston, VA 22949-0276
(434) 263-8311 • http://www.nelson.k12.va.us/
Grade Span: PK-12; **Agency Type:** 1
Schools: 4
2 Primary; 1 Middle; 1 High; 0 Other Level
4 Regular; 0 Special Education; 0 Vocational; 0 Alternative
0 Magnet; 0 Charter; 2 Title I Eligible; 0 School-wide Title I
Students: 2,030 (52.0% male; 48.0% female)
Individual Education Program: 346 (17.0%);
English Language Learner: 39 (1.9%); Migrant: 10 (0.5%)
Eligible for Free Lunch Program: 564 (27.8%)
Eligible for Reduced-Price Lunch Program: 168 (8.3%)
Teachers: 192.8 (10.5 to 1)
Librarians/Media Specialists: 4.0 (507.5 to 1)
Guidance Counselors: 4.0 (507.5 to 1)
Current Spending: ($ per student per year):
Total: $7,401; Instruction: $4,269; Support Services: $2,796
Enrollment, Drop-out Rates and Diploma Recipients by Race/Ethnicity

Category	Total	White	Black	Asian	AIAN	Hisp.
Enrollment (%)	100.0	77.8	19.8	0.2	0.1	2.1
Drop-out Rate (%)	2.7	3.0	1.5	0.0	0.0	0.0
H.S. Diplomas (#)	129	97	30	0	0	2

New Kent County

New Kent County Public Schools

12007 Courthouse Cir • New Kent, VA 23124-0110
Mailing Address: PO Box 110 • New Kent, VA 23124-0110
(804) 966-9650 • http://www.newkentschools.org/
Grade Span: PK-12; **Agency Type:** 1
Schools: 4
2 Primary; 1 Middle; 1 High; 0 Other Level
4 Regular; 0 Special Education; 0 Vocational; 0 Alternative
0 Magnet; 0 Charter; 1 Title I Eligible; 0 School-wide Title I
Students: 2,455 (51.4% male; 48.6% female)
Individual Education Program: 456 (18.6%);
English Language Learner: 7 (0.3%); Migrant: 0 (0.0%)
Eligible for Free Lunch Program: 272 (11.1%)
Eligible for Reduced-Price Lunch Program: 73 (3.0%)
Teachers: 220.5 (11.1 to 1)
Librarians/Media Specialists: 4.0 (613.8 to 1)
Guidance Counselors: 5.0 (491.0 to 1)
Current Spending: ($ per student per year):
Total: $6,199; Instruction: $3,868; Support Services: $2,169
Enrollment, Drop-out Rates and Diploma Recipients by Race/Ethnicity

Category	Total	White	Black	Asian	AIAN	Hisp.
Enrollment (%)	100.0	81.0	15.8	0.5	1.3	1.4
Drop-out Rate (%)	3.3	3.1	3.6	0.0	33.3	0.0
H.S. Diplomas (#)	144	113	26	3	1	1

Newport News City

Newport News City Public Schools

12465 Warwick Blvd • Newport News, VA 23606-3041
(757) 591-4545 • http://www.sbo.nn.k12.va.us/
Grade Span: PK-12; **Agency Type:** 1
Schools: 48
30 Primary; 9 Middle; 5 High; 4 Other Level
44 Regular; 0 Special Education; 0 Vocational; 4 Alternative
10 Magnet; 0 Charter; 17 Title I Eligible; 0 School-wide Title I
Students: 32,887 (50.5% male; 49.5% female)
Individual Education Program: 4,271 (13.0%);

English Language Learner: 223 (0.7%); Migrant: 0 (0.0%)
Eligible for Free Lunch Program: 11,984 (36.4%)
Eligible for Reduced-Price Lunch Program: 3,213 (9.8%)
Teachers: 2,702.6 (12.2 to 1)
Librarians/Media Specialists: 31.0 (1,060.9 to 1)
Guidance Counselors: 77.5 (424.3 to 1)
Current Spending: ($ per student per year):
Total: $6,657; Instruction: $4,038; Support Services: $2,296
Enrollment, Drop-out Rates and Diploma Recipients by Race/Ethnicity

Category	Total	White	Black	Asian	AIAN	Hisp.
Enrollment (%)	100.0	35.9	56.1	2.5	0.9	4.6
Drop-out Rate (%)	4.1	3.1	4.9	4.3	1.5	5.6
H.S. Diplomas (#)	1,570	640	811	51	7	61

Norfolk City

Norfolk City Public Schools

800 E City Hall Ave • Norfolk, VA 23510
Mailing Address: PO Box 1357 • Norfolk, VA 23501
(757) 628-3830 • http://www.nps.k12.va.us/
Grade Span: PK-12; **Agency Type:** 1
Schools: 58
39 Primary; 8 Middle; 6 High; 5 Other Level
50 Regular; 2 Special Education; 2 Vocational; 4 Alternative
1 Magnet; 0 Charter; 20 Title I Eligible; 18 School-wide Title I
Students: 36,745 (50.6% male; 49.4% female)
Individual Education Program: 4,994 (13.6%);
English Language Learner: 82 (0.2%); Migrant: 0 (0.0%)
Eligible for Free Lunch Program: 17,580 (47.8%)
Eligible for Reduced-Price Lunch Program: 4,516 (12.3%)
Teachers: 3,363.0 (10.9 to 1)
Librarians/Media Specialists: 60.0 (612.4 to 1)
Guidance Counselors: 80.0 (459.3 to 1)
Current Spending: ($ per student per year):
Total: $7,141; Instruction: $4,358; Support Services: $2,477
Enrollment, Drop-out Rates and Diploma Recipients by Race/Ethnicity

Category	Total	White	Black	Asian	AIAN	Hisp.
Enrollment (%)	100.0	27.2	67.8	2.1	0.2	2.6
Drop-out Rate (%)	5.3	3.8	6.1	2.5	31.6	3.3
H.S. Diplomas (#)	1,348	503	759	49	2	35

Northampton County

Northampton County Public Schools

7207 Young St • Machipongo, VA 23405-0360
(757) 678-5151 • http://www.ncps.k12.va.us/
Grade Span: PK-12; **Agency Type:** 1
Schools: 5
2 Primary; 1 Middle; 1 High; 1 Other Level
4 Regular; 0 Special Education; 0 Vocational; 1 Alternative
0 Magnet; 0 Charter; 2 Title I Eligible; 2 School-wide Title I
Students: 2,079 (50.1% male; 49.9% female)
Individual Education Program: 296 (14.2%);
English Language Learner: 114 (5.5%); Migrant: 92 (4.4%)
Eligible for Free Lunch Program: 1,196 (57.5%)
Eligible for Reduced-Price Lunch Program: 185 (8.9%)
Teachers: 202.0 (10.3 to 1)
Librarians/Media Specialists: 4.0 (519.8 to 1)
Guidance Counselors: 5.0 (415.8 to 1)
Current Spending: ($ per student per year):
Total: $7,456; Instruction: $4,591; Support Services: $2,621
Enrollment, Drop-out Rates and Diploma Recipients by Race/Ethnicity

Category	Total	White	Black	Asian	AIAN	Hisp.
Enrollment (%)	100.0	38.5	54.5	0.3	0.0	6.6
Drop-out Rate (%)	3.5	3.2	3.7	0.0	n/a	5.3
H.S. Diplomas (#)	134	63	69	1	0	1

Nottoway County

Nottoway County Public Schools

Hwy 460 • Nottoway, VA 23955-0047
Mailing Address: PO Box 47 • Nottoway, VA 23955-0047
(434) 645-9596 • http://nottowaynt.k12.nottoway.state.va.us/
Grade Span: PK-12; **Agency Type:** 1
Schools: 7
3 Primary; 2 Middle; 1 High; 1 Other Level
6 Regular; 0 Special Education; 0 Vocational; 1 Alternative
0 Magnet; 0 Charter; 4 Title I Eligible; 4 School-wide Title I
Students: 2,491 (52.3% male; 47.7% female)
Individual Education Program: 459 (18.4%);
English Language Learner: 25 (1.0%); Migrant: 18 (0.7%)
Eligible for Free Lunch Program: 1,039 (41.7%)
Eligible for Reduced-Price Lunch Program: 255 (10.2%)
Teachers: 221.5 (11.2 to 1)
Librarians/Media Specialists: 4.0 (622.8 to 1)
Guidance Counselors: 4.0 (622.8 to 1)
Current Spending: ($ per student per year):
Total: $6,667; Instruction: $4,080; Support Services: $2,241
Enrollment, Drop-out Rates and Diploma Recipients by Race/Ethnicity

Category	Total	White	Black	Asian	AIAN	Hisp.
Enrollment (%)	100.0	51.4	46.6	0.1	0.1	1.8
Drop-out Rate (%)	6.0	5.6	6.6	0.0	n/a	0.0
H.S. Diplomas (#)	144	70	70	1	0	3

Orange County

Orange County Public Schools

437 Waugh Blvd • Orange, VA 22960-1859
(540) 661-4550 • http://www.ocss-va.org/
Grade Span: PK-12; **Agency Type:** 1
Schools: 8
4 Primary; 2 Middle; 1 High; 0 Other Level
7 Regular; 0 Special Education; 0 Vocational; 0 Alternative
0 Magnet; 0 Charter; 4 Title I Eligible; 3 School-wide Title I
Students: 3,996 (49.7% male; 50.3% female)
Individual Education Program: 585 (14.6%);
English Language Learner: 20 (0.5%); Migrant: 1 (<0.1%)
Eligible for Free Lunch Program: 837 (20.9%)
Eligible for Reduced-Price Lunch Program: 247 (6.2%)
Teachers: 370.1 (10.8 to 1)
Librarians/Media Specialists: 8.0 (499.5 to 1)
Guidance Counselors: 7.0 (570.9 to 1)
Current Spending: ($ per student per year):
Total: $6,990; Instruction: $4,467; Support Services: $2,271
Enrollment, Drop-out Rates and Diploma Recipients by Race/Ethnicity

Category	Total	White	Black	Asian	AIAN	Hisp.
Enrollment (%)	100.0	79.1	19.0	0.5	0.0	1.5
Drop-out Rate (%)	1.8	2.0	0.9	0.0	0.0	0.0
H.S. Diplomas (#)	256	201	51	0	1	3

Page County

Page County Public Schools

735 W Main St • Luray, VA 22835-1030
(540) 743-6533 • http://eclipse.pagecounty.k12.va.us/~pcps/index.html
Grade Span: PK-12; **Agency Type:** 1
Schools: 8
5 Primary; 0 Middle; 2 High; 1 Other Level
7 Regular; 0 Special Education; 1 Vocational; 0 Alternative
0 Magnet; 0 Charter; 5 Title I Eligible; 0 School-wide Title I
Students: 3,640 (50.2% male; 49.8% female)
Individual Education Program: 435 (12.0%);
English Language Learner: 19 (0.5%); Migrant: 19 (0.5%)
Eligible for Free Lunch Program: 964 (26.5%)
Eligible for Reduced-Price Lunch Program: 300 (8.2%)
Teachers: 314.0 (11.6 to 1)
Librarians/Media Specialists: 7.0 (520.0 to 1)
Guidance Counselors: 8.0 (455.0 to 1)
Current Spending: ($ per student per year):
Total: $6,130; Instruction: $4,158; Support Services: $1,678
Enrollment, Drop-out Rates and Diploma Recipients by Race/Ethnicity

Category	Total	White	Black	Asian	AIAN	Hisp.
Enrollment (%)	100.0	95.8	2.9	0.3	0.0	1.0
Drop-out Rate (%)	5.0	5.0	6.3	0.0	0.0	0.0
H.S. Diplomas (#)	206	196	6	2	0	2

Patrick County

Patrick County Public Schools

104 Ruckers St • Stuart, VA 24171-0346
Mailing Address: PO Box 346 • Stuart, VA 24171-0346
(276) 694-3163 • http://www.patrick-county.org/
Grade Span: PK-12; **Agency Type:** 1
Schools: 7
5 Primary; 1 Middle; 1 High; 0 Other Level
7 Regular; 0 Special Education; 0 Vocational; 0 Alternative
0 Magnet; 0 Charter; 6 Title I Eligible; 0 School-wide Title I
Students: 2,643 (51.4% male; 48.6% female)
Individual Education Program: 453 (17.1%);
English Language Learner: 79 (3.0%); Migrant: 7 (0.3%)
Eligible for Free Lunch Program: 883 (33.4%)
Eligible for Reduced-Price Lunch Program: 202 (7.6%)
Teachers: 229.5 (11.5 to 1)
Librarians/Media Specialists: 6.0 (440.5 to 1)
Guidance Counselors: 6.0 (440.5 to 1)
Current Spending: ($ per student per year):
Total: $6,428; Instruction: $4,095; Support Services: $1,993

Enrollment, Drop-out Rates and Diploma Recipients by Race/Ethnicity

Category	Total	White	Black	Asian	AIAN	Hisp.
Enrollment (%)	100.0	88.9	7.8	0.2	0.2	3.0
Drop-out Rate (%)	2.6	1.9	8.3	100.0	n/a	0.0
H.S. Diplomas (#)	170	155	15	0	0	0

Petersburg City

Petersburg City Public Schools

141 E Wythe St • Petersburg, VA 23803-4535
(804) 732-0510 • http://www.ppsk12.com/
Grade Span: PK-12; **Agency Type:** 1
Schools: 10
7 Primary; 2 Middle; 1 High; 0 Other Level
10 Regular; 0 Special Education; 0 Vocational; 0 Alternative
0 Magnet; 0 Charter; 9 Title I Eligible; 7 School-wide Title I
Students: 5,616 (50.4% male; 49.6% female)
Individual Education Program: 783 (13.9%);
English Language Learner: 36 (0.6%); Migrant: 0 (0.0%)
Eligible for Free Lunch Program: 3,421 (60.9%)
Eligible for Reduced-Price Lunch Program: 520 (9.3%)
Teachers: 467.0 (12.0 to 1)
Librarians/Media Specialists: 10.0 (561.6 to 1)
Guidance Counselors: 9.0 (624.0 to 1)
Current Spending: ($ per student per year):
Total: $7,301; Instruction: $4,348; Support Services: $2,552

Enrollment, Drop-out Rates and Diploma Recipients by Race/Ethnicity

Category	Total	White	Black	Asian	AIAN	Hisp.
Enrollment (%)	100.0	2.0	96.9	0.1	0.1	1.0
Drop-out Rate (%)	9.0	0.0	16.6	0.0	0.0	5.9
H.S. Diplomas (#)	237	2	235	0	0	0

Pittsylvania County

Pittsylvania County Public Schools

39 Bank St SE • Chatham, VA 24531-0232
(434) 432-2761
Grade Span: PK-12; **Agency Type:** 1
Schools: 20
9 Primary; 5 Middle; 4 High; 2 Other Level
18 Regular; 0 Special Education; 1 Vocational; 1 Alternative
0 Magnet; 0 Charter; 11 Title I Eligible; 7 School-wide Title I
Students: 9,036 (52.0% male; 48.0% female)
Individual Education Program: 1,192 (13.2%);
English Language Learner: 107 (1.2%); Migrant: 45 (0.5%)
Eligible for Free Lunch Program: 2,582 (28.6%)
Eligible for Reduced-Price Lunch Program: 662 (7.3%)
Teachers: 794.7 (11.4 to 1)
Librarians/Media Specialists: 18.0 (502.0 to 1)
Guidance Counselors: 25.0 (361.4 to 1)
Current Spending: ($ per student per year):
Total: $6,062; Instruction: $3,721; Support Services: $2,023

Enrollment, Drop-out Rates and Diploma Recipients by Race/Ethnicity

Category	Total	White	Black	Asian	AIAN	Hisp.
Enrollment (%)	100.0	67.5	30.6	0.2	0.0	1.7
Drop-out Rate (%)	3.6	3.7	3.4	0.0	n/a	0.0
H.S. Diplomas (#)	581	416	163	1	0	1

Poquoson City

Poquoson City Public Schools

500 City Hall Ave • Poquoson, VA 23662-0068
(757) 868-3055 • http://www.sbo.poquoson.k12.va.us/
Grade Span: PK-12; **Agency Type:** 1
Schools: 4
2 Primary; 1 Middle; 1 High; 0 Other Level
4 Regular; 0 Special Education; 0 Vocational; 0 Alternative
0 Magnet; 0 Charter; 2 Title I Eligible; 0 School-wide Title I
Students: 2,510 (52.9% male; 47.1% female)
Individual Education Program: 270 (10.8%);
English Language Learner: 3 (0.1%); Migrant: 0 (0.0%)
Eligible for Free Lunch Program: 74 (2.9%)
Eligible for Reduced-Price Lunch Program: 42 (1.7%)
Teachers: 210.0 (12.0 to 1)
Librarians/Media Specialists: 4.0 (627.5 to 1)
Guidance Counselors: 4.0 (627.5 to 1)
Current Spending: ($ per student per year):
Total: $5,993; Instruction: $3,697; Support Services: $2,203

Enrollment, Drop-out Rates and Diploma Recipients by Race/Ethnicity

Category	Total	White	Black	Asian	AIAN	Hisp.
Enrollment (%)	100.0	96.4	0.5	1.8	0.6	0.8
Drop-out Rate (%)	0.6	0.6	0.0	0.0	n/a	0.0
H.S. Diplomas (#)	180	171	1	8	0	0

Portsmouth City

Portsmouth City Public Schools

801 Crawford St • Portsmouth, VA 23704-3822
Mailing Address: PO Box 998 • Portsmouth, VA 23705-0998
(757) 393-8742 • http://pps.k12.va.us/
Grade Span: PK-12; **Agency Type:** 1
Schools: 27
16 Primary; 4 Middle; 4 High; 3 Other Level
23 Regular; 1 Special Education; 1 Vocational; 2 Alternative
6 Magnet; 0 Charter; 14 Title I Eligible; 14 School-wide Title I
Students: 15,977 (51.0% male; 49.0% female)
Individual Education Program: 2,264 (14.2%);
English Language Learner: 16 (0.1%); Migrant: 0 (0.0%)
Eligible for Free Lunch Program: 7,599 (47.6%)
Eligible for Reduced-Price Lunch Program: 1,404 (8.8%)
Teachers: 1,320.0 (12.1 to 1)
Librarians/Media Specialists: 29.0 (550.9 to 1)
Guidance Counselors: 30.0 (532.6 to 1)
Current Spending: ($ per student per year):
Total: $7,346; Instruction: $4,315; Support Services: $2,662

Enrollment, Drop-out Rates and Diploma Recipients by Race/Ethnicity

Category	Total	White	Black	Asian	AIAN	Hisp.
Enrollment (%)	100.0	27.6	70.4	0.8	0.1	1.1
Drop-out Rate (%)	6.8	3.9	8.2	0.0	0.0	9.5
H.S. Diplomas (#)	736	224	500	4	4	4

Powhatan County

Powhatan County Public Schools

2320 Skaggs Rd • Powhatan, VA 23139-5713
(804) 598-5700 • http://www.powhatan.k12.va.us/
Grade Span: PK-12; **Agency Type:** 1
Schools: 5
2 Primary; 1 Middle; 1 High; 1 Other Level
4 Regular; 0 Special Education; 1 Vocational; 0 Alternative
0 Magnet; 0 Charter; 2 Title I Eligible; 0 School-wide Title I
Students: 3,832 (51.1% male; 48.9% female)
Individual Education Program: 609 (15.9%);
English Language Learner: 3 (0.1%); Migrant: 0 (0.0%)
Eligible for Free Lunch Program: 330 (8.6%)
Eligible for Reduced-Price Lunch Program: 126 (3.3%)
Teachers: 352.6 (10.9 to 1)
Librarians/Media Specialists: 5.0 (766.4 to 1)
Guidance Counselors: 7.0 (547.4 to 1)
Current Spending: ($ per student per year):
Total: $6,859; Instruction: $4,303; Support Services: $2,342

Enrollment, Drop-out Rates and Diploma Recipients by Race/Ethnicity

Category	Total	White	Black	Asian	AIAN	Hisp.
Enrollment (%)	100.0	87.2	11.5	0.3	0.2	0.8
Drop-out Rate (%)	3.6	3.4	4.7	0.0	0.0	0.0
H.S. Diplomas (#)	207	183	21	0	1	2

Prince Edward County

Prince Edward County Pub Schools

35 Eagle Dr • Farmville, VA 23901-9011
(434) 392-2100 • http://www.pecps.k12.va.us/
Grade Span: PK-12; **Agency Type:** 1
Schools: 3
1 Primary; 1 Middle; 1 High; 0 Other Level
3 Regular; 0 Special Education; 0 Vocational; 0 Alternative
0 Magnet; 0 Charter; 3 Title I Eligible; 3 School-wide Title I
Students: 2,798 (51.6% male; 48.4% female)
Individual Education Program: 515 (18.4%);
English Language Learner: 3 (0.1%); Migrant: 2 (0.1%)
Eligible for Free Lunch Program: 1,356 (48.5%)
Eligible for Reduced-Price Lunch Program: 312 (11.2%)
Teachers: 242.7 (11.5 to 1)
Librarians/Media Specialists: 3.0 (932.7 to 1)
Guidance Counselors: 5.0 (559.6 to 1)
Current Spending: ($ per student per year):
Total: $6,416; Instruction: $3,990; Support Services: $2,198

Enrollment, Drop-out Rates and Diploma Recipients by Race/Ethnicity

Category	Total	White	Black	Asian	AIAN	Hisp.
Enrollment (%)	100.0	38.7	59.9	0.7	0.1	0.6
Drop-out Rate (%)	3.2	4.5	2.4	0.0	0.0	0.0
H.S. Diplomas (#)	131	64	64	1	0	2

Prince George County

Prince George County Pub Schools

6410 Courts Rd • Prince George, VA 23875
Mailing Address: PO Box 400 • Prince George, VA 23875
(804) 733-2700 • http://pgs.k12.va.us/
Grade Span: PK-12; **Agency Type:** 1
Schools: 10
7 Primary; 1 Middle; 1 High; 1 Other Level
10 Regular; 0 Special Education; 0 Vocational; 0 Alternative
0 Magnet; 0 Charter; 6 Title I Eligible; 0 School-wide Title I
Students: 6,035 (51.7% male; 48.3% female)
Individual Education Program: 658 (10.9%);
English Language Learner: 23 (0.4%); Migrant: 0 (0.0%)
Eligible for Free Lunch Program: 932 (15.4%)
Eligible for Reduced-Price Lunch Program: 441 (7.3%)
Teachers: 474.0 (12.7 to 1)
Librarians/Media Specialists: 11.0 (548.6 to 1)
Guidance Counselors: 14.0 (431.1 to 1)
Current Spending: ($ per student per year):
Total: $6,113; Instruction: $3,668; Support Services: $2,174
Enrollment, Drop-out Rates and Diploma Recipients by Race/Ethnicity

Category	Total	White	Black	Asian	AIAN	Hisp.
Enrollment (%)	100.0	56.1	37.1	1.5	0.1	3.4
Drop-out Rate (%)	3.8	4.0	2.9	0.0	0.0	12.8
H.S. Diplomas (#)	312	197	105	1	0	9

Prince William County

Prince William County Pub Schools

14800 Joplin Rd • Manassas, VA 20112
Mailing Address: PO Box 389 • Manassas, VA 20108-0389
(703) 791-8712 • http://www.pwcs.edu/
Grade Span: PK-12; **Agency Type:** 1
Schools: 75
48 Primary; 13 Middle; 8 High; 5 Other Level
68 Regular; 3 Special Education; 0 Vocational; 3 Alternative
24 Magnet; 0 Charter; 18 Title I Eligible; 1 School-wide Title I
Students: 60,541 (51.3% male; 48.7% female)
Individual Education Program: 7,280 (12.0%);
English Language Learner: 5,523 (9.1%); Migrant: 0 (0.0%)
Eligible for Free Lunch Program: 10,719 (17.7%)
Eligible for Reduced-Price Lunch Program: 4,029 (6.7%)
Teachers: 4,140.4 (14.6 to 1)
Librarians/Media Specialists: 62.0 (976.5 to 1)
Guidance Counselors: 73.8 (820.3 to 1)
Current Spending: ($ per student per year):
Total: $6,950; Instruction: $4,050; Support Services: $2,631
Enrollment, Drop-out Rates and Diploma Recipients by Race/Ethnicity

Category	Total	White	Black	Asian	AIAN	Hisp.
Enrollment (%)	100.0	52.1	23.7	5.1	0.4	15.4
Drop-out Rate (%)	5.1	4.4	6.4	4.3	5.9	7.3
H.S. Diplomas (#)	3,196	2,031	753	155	18	239

Virginia-New York District

3308 John Quick Road, Ste 201 • Quantico, VA 22134-1702
(703) 784-2319
Grade Span: PK-12; **Agency Type:** 6
Schools: 7
4 Primary; 2 Middle; 0 High; 1 Other Level
7 Regular; 0 Special Education; 0 Vocational; 0 Alternative
0 Magnet; 0 Charter; 0 Title I Eligible; 0 School-wide Title I
Students: 1,992 (n/a% male; n/a% female)
Individual Education Program: 180 (9.0%);
English Language Learner: 16 (0.8%); Migrant: n/a
Eligible for Free Lunch Program: n/a
Eligible for Reduced-Price Lunch Program: n/a
Teachers: 175.0 (11.4 to 1)
Librarians/Media Specialists: 7.0 (284.6 to 1)
Guidance Counselors: 8.0 (249.0 to 1)
Current Spending: ($ per student per year):
Total: n/a; Instruction: n/a; Support Services: n/a
Enrollment, Drop-out Rates and Diploma Recipients by Race/Ethnicity

Category	Total	White	Black	Asian	AIAN	Hisp.
Enrollment (%)	100.0	72.0	11.4	2.7	0.8	10.9
Drop-out Rate (%)	n/a	n/a	n/a	n/a	n/a	n/a
H.S. Diplomas (#)	38	18	9	2	0	1

Pulaski County

Pulaski County Public Schools

44 Third St NW • Pulaski, VA 24301-5008
(540) 643-0200 • http://admin.sbo.pulaski.k12.va.us/
Grade Span: PK-12; **Agency Type:** 1
Schools: 11
8 Primary; 2 Middle; 1 High; 0 Other Level
11 Regular; 0 Special Education; 0 Vocational; 0 Alternative
0 Magnet; 0 Charter; 4 Title I Eligible; 2 School-wide Title I
Students: 4,977 (51.8% male; 48.2% female)
Individual Education Program: 891 (17.9%);
English Language Learner: 37 (0.7%); Migrant: 3 (0.1%)
Eligible for Free Lunch Program: 1,444 (29.0%)
Eligible for Reduced-Price Lunch Program: 390 (7.8%)
Teachers: 444.5 (11.2 to 1)
Librarians/Media Specialists: 10.0 (497.7 to 1)
Guidance Counselors: 13.0 (382.8 to 1)
Current Spending: ($ per student per year):
Total: $6,604; Instruction: $4,015; Support Services: $2,256
Enrollment, Drop-out Rates and Diploma Recipients by Race/Ethnicity

Category	Total	White	Black	Asian	AIAN	Hisp.
Enrollment (%)	100.0	90.8	7.8	0.6	0.1	0.8
Drop-out Rate (%)	4.1	3.6	11.2	0.0	n/a	0.0
H.S. Diplomas (#)	329	301	23	5	0	0

Radford City

Radford City Public Schools

1612 Wadsworth St • Radford, VA 24143-3698
(540) 731-3647 • http://www.rcps.org/
Grade Span: PK-12; **Agency Type:** 1
Schools: 4
1 Primary; 2 Middle; 1 High; 0 Other Level
4 Regular; 0 Special Education; 0 Vocational; 0 Alternative
0 Magnet; 0 Charter; 2 Title I Eligible; 0 School-wide Title I
Students: 1,553 (50.8% male; 49.2% female)
Individual Education Program: 205 (13.2%);
English Language Learner: 17 (1.1%); Migrant: 0 (0.0%)
Eligible for Free Lunch Program: 303 (19.5%)
Eligible for Reduced-Price Lunch Program: 50 (3.2%)
Teachers: 133.7 (11.6 to 1)
Librarians/Media Specialists: 3.0 (517.7 to 1)
Guidance Counselors: 3.0 (517.7 to 1)
Current Spending: ($ per student per year):
Total: $6,566; Instruction: $4,159; Support Services: $2,149
Enrollment, Drop-out Rates and Diploma Recipients by Race/Ethnicity

Category	Total	White	Black	Asian	AIAN	Hisp.
Enrollment (%)	100.0	86.4	10.4	2.5	0.0	0.6
Drop-out Rate (%)	2.2	2.6	0.0	0.0	n/a	0.0
H.S. Diplomas (#)	102	86	14	2	0	0

Richmond City

Richmond City Public Schools

301 N 9th St • Richmond, VA 23219-3913
(804) 780-7700
Grade Span: PK-12; **Agency Type:** 1
Schools: 59
32 Primary; 10 Middle; 8 High; 9 Other Level
50 Regular; 4 Special Education; 1 Vocational; 4 Alternative
0 Magnet; 0 Charter; 40 Title I Eligible; 38 School-wide Title I
Students: 26,136 (50.1% male; 49.9% female)
Individual Education Program: 4,219 (16.1%);
English Language Learner: 409 (1.6%); Migrant: 0 (0.0%)
Eligible for Free Lunch Program: 15,290 (58.5%)
Eligible for Reduced-Price Lunch Program: 2,055 (7.9%)
Teachers: 2,360.5 (11.1 to 1)
Librarians/Media Specialists: 2.0 (13,068.0 to 1)
Guidance Counselors: 60.0 (435.6 to 1)
Current Spending: ($ per student per year):
Total: $9,008; Instruction: $5,390; Support Services: $3,265
Enrollment, Drop-out Rates and Diploma Recipients by Race/Ethnicity

Category	Total	White	Black	Asian	AIAN	Hisp.
Enrollment (%)	100.0	6.9	90.3	0.6	0.1	2.1
Drop-out Rate (%)	2.8	2.4	2.8	4.7	33.3	7.9
H.S. Diplomas (#)	1,058	46	998	7	0	7

Roanoke County

Roanoke County Public Schools

5937 Cove Rd NW • Roanoke, VA 24019-2403
(540) 562-3900 • http://www.rcs.k12.va.us/
Grade Span: PK-12; **Agency Type:** 1
Schools: 30
17 Primary; 5 Middle; 6 High; 2 Other Level
27 Regular; 0 Special Education; 1 Vocational; 2 Alternative
0 Magnet; 0 Charter; 8 Title I Eligible; 0 School-wide Title I
Students: 14,238 (51.1% male; 48.9% female)
Individual Education Program: 2,340 (16.4%);
English Language Learner: 156 (1.1%); Migrant: 0 (0.0%)
Eligible for Free Lunch Program: 1,211 (8.5%)

Eligible for Reduced-Price Lunch Program: 566 (4.0%)
Teachers: 1,375.9 (10.3 to 1)
Librarians/Media Specialists: 29.0 (491.0 to 1)
Guidance Counselors: 31.9 (446.3 to 1)
Current Spending: ($ per student per year):
Total: $6,958; Instruction: $4,465; Support Services: $2,244

Enrollment, Drop-out Rates and Diploma Recipients by Race/Ethnicity

Category	Total	White	Black	Asian	AIAN	Hisp.
Enrollment (%)	100.0	91.3	4.8	2.6	0.1	1.3
Drop-out Rate (%)	1.3	1.0	1.7	0.0	110.0	3.1
H.S. Diplomas (#)	929	859	47	16	0	7

Roanoke City Public Schools

40 Douglas Ave NW • Roanoke, VA 24012-4699
Mailing Address: PO Box 13145 • Roanoke, VA 24031
(540) 853-2381 • http://www.roanoke.k12.va.us/
Grade Span: PK-12; **Agency Type:** 1
Schools: 31
21 Primary; 6 Middle; 4 High; 0 Other Level
30 Regular; 0 Special Education; 0 Vocational; 1 Alternative
14 Magnet; 1 Charter; 15 Title I Eligible; 15 School-wide Title I
Students: 13,725 (50.6% male; 49.4% female)
Individual Education Program: 2,328 (17.0%);
English Language Learner: 414 (3.0%); Migrant: 0 (0.0%)
Eligible for Free Lunch Program: 6,927 (50.5%)
Eligible for Reduced-Price Lunch Program: 1,103 (8.0%)
Teachers: 1,351.3 (10.2 to 1)
Librarians/Media Specialists: 26.1 (525.9 to 1)
Guidance Counselors: 35.1 (391.0 to 1)
Current Spending: ($ per student per year):
Total: $7,675; Instruction: $4,855; Support Services: $2,515

Enrollment, Drop-out Rates and Diploma Recipients by Race/Ethnicity

Category	Total	White	Black	Asian	AIAN	Hisp.
Enrollment (%)	100.0	50.3	45.4	2.0	0.1	2.2
Drop-out Rate (%)	8.6	7.5	9.9	9.8	0.0	11.1
H.S. Diplomas (#)	498	267	214	12	1	4

Rockbridge County

Rockbridge County Public Schools

1972 Big Spring Dr • Lexington, VA 24450-2738
(540) 463-7386 • http://www.rcs.rang.k12.va.us/
Grade Span: PK-12; **Agency Type:** 1
Schools: 8
5 Primary; 2 Middle; 1 High; 0 Other Level
8 Regular; 0 Special Education; 0 Vocational; 0 Alternative
0 Magnet; 0 Charter; 4 Title I Eligible; 0 School-wide Title I
Students: 3,000 (52.4% male; 47.6% female)
Individual Education Program: 439 (14.6%);
English Language Learner: 9 (0.3%); Migrant: 2 (0.1%)
Eligible for Free Lunch Program: 642 (21.4%)
Eligible for Reduced-Price Lunch Program: 247 (8.2%)
Teachers: 302.1 (9.9 to 1)
Librarians/Media Specialists: 9.0 (333.3 to 1)
Guidance Counselors: 8.0 (375.0 to 1)
Current Spending: ($ per student per year):
Total: $7,002; Instruction: $4,458; Support Services: $2,271

Enrollment, Drop-out Rates and Diploma Recipients by Race/Ethnicity

Category	Total	White	Black	Asian	AIAN	Hisp.
Enrollment (%)	100.0	94.0	4.2	0.7	0.5	0.6
Drop-out Rate (%)	3.5	2.8	16.1	0.0	n/a	0.0
H.S. Diplomas (#)	210	198	9	2	0	1

Rockingham County

Rockingham County Public Schools

2 S Main St • Harrisonburg, VA 22801
(540) 564-3230 • http://www.rockingham.k12.va.us/
Grade Span: PK-12; **Agency Type:** 1
Schools: 21
13 Primary; 4 Middle; 3 High; 1 Other Level
20 Regular; 0 Special Education; 0 Vocational; 1 Alternative
0 Magnet; 0 Charter; 6 Title I Eligible; 0 School-wide Title I
Students: 11,126 (51.7% male; 48.3% female)
Individual Education Program: 1,429 (12.8%);
English Language Learner: 621 (5.6%); Migrant: 122 (1.1%)
Eligible for Free Lunch Program: 1,994 (17.9%)
Eligible for Reduced-Price Lunch Program: 893 (8.0%)
Teachers: 1,012.9 (11.0 to 1)
Librarians/Media Specialists: 22.0 (505.7 to 1)
Guidance Counselors: 23.0 (483.7 to 1)
Current Spending: ($ per student per year):
Total: $6,587; Instruction: $3,993; Support Services: $2,272

Enrollment, Drop-out Rates and Diploma Recipients by Race/Ethnicity

Category	Total	White	Black	Asian	AIAN	Hisp.
Enrollment (%)	100.0	91.8	2.1	0.5	0.0	5.5
Drop-out Rate (%)	3.4	3.1	5.3	0.0	0.0	14.7
H.S. Diplomas (#)	686	652	15	3	0	16

Russell County

Russell County Public Schools

1 School Board Dr • Lebanon, VA 24266-0008
(276) 889-6500 • http://www.russell.k12.va.us/
Grade Span: PK-12; **Agency Type:** 1
Schools: 13
8 Primary; 1 Middle; 3 High; 1 Other Level
12 Regular; 0 Special Education; 1 Vocational; 0 Alternative
0 Magnet; 0 Charter; 9 Title I Eligible; 6 School-wide Title I
Students: 4,156 (47.0% male; 53.0% female)
Individual Education Program: 707 (17.0%);
English Language Learner: n/a; Migrant: 1 (<0.1%)
Eligible for Free Lunch Program: 1,536 (37.0%)
Eligible for Reduced-Price Lunch Program: 387 (9.3%)
Teachers: 365.4 (11.4 to 1)
Librarians/Media Specialists: 7.0 (593.7 to 1)
Guidance Counselors: 12.0 (346.3 to 1)
Current Spending: ($ per student per year):
Total: $6,161; Instruction: $3,730; Support Services: $2,133

Enrollment, Drop-out Rates and Diploma Recipients by Race/Ethnicity

Category	Total	White	Black	Asian	AIAN	Hisp.
Enrollment (%)	100.0	93.6	0.5	0.0	0.0	0.2
Drop-out Rate (%)	2.1	2.1	10.0	0.0	n/a	0.0
H.S. Diplomas (#)	270	269	1	0	0	0

Salem City

Salem City Public Schools

510 S College Ave • Salem, VA 24153-5054
(540) 389-0130 • http://www.salem.k12.va.us/
Grade Span: PK-12; **Agency Type:** 1
Schools: 6
4 Primary; 1 Middle; 1 High; 0 Other Level
6 Regular; 0 Special Education; 0 Vocational; 0 Alternative
0 Magnet; 0 Charter; 3 Title I Eligible; 0 School-wide Title I
Students: 3,940 (51.2% male; 48.8% female)
Individual Education Program: 473 (12.0%);
English Language Learner: 21 (0.5%); Migrant: 0 (0.0%)
Eligible for Free Lunch Program: 504 (12.8%)
Eligible for Reduced-Price Lunch Program: 208 (5.3%)
Teachers: 333.3 (11.8 to 1)
Librarians/Media Specialists: 7.0 (562.9 to 1)
Guidance Counselors: 7.7 (511.7 to 1)
Current Spending: ($ per student per year):
Total: $6,878; Instruction: $4,632; Support Services: $1,982

Enrollment, Drop-out Rates and Diploma Recipients by Race/Ethnicity

Category	Total	White	Black	Asian	AIAN	Hisp.
Enrollment (%)	100.0	89.1	8.2	2.0	0.0	0.7
Drop-out Rate (%)	1.9	2.0	1.2	0.0	n/a	0.0
H.S. Diplomas (#)	267	235	17	11	0	4

Scott County

Scott County Public Schools

261 E Jackson St • Gate City, VA 24251-3422
(276) 386-6118 • http://scott.k12.va.us/
Grade Span: PK-12; **Agency Type:** 1
Schools: 14
7 Primary; 3 Middle; 3 High; 1 Other Level
13 Regular; 0 Special Education; 1 Vocational; 0 Alternative
0 Magnet; 0 Charter; 8 Title I Eligible; 4 School-wide Title I
Students: 3,705 (51.1% male; 48.9% female)
Individual Education Program: 642 (17.3%);
English Language Learner: 4 (0.1%); Migrant: 0 (0.0%)
Eligible for Free Lunch Program: 1,339 (36.1%)
Eligible for Reduced-Price Lunch Program: 397 (10.7%)
Teachers: 342.5 (10.8 to 1)
Librarians/Media Specialists: 11.0 (336.8 to 1)
Guidance Counselors: 7.0 (529.3 to 1)
Current Spending: ($ per student per year):
Total: $6,535; Instruction: $4,053; Support Services: $2,143

Enrollment, Drop-out Rates and Diploma Recipients by Race/Ethnicity

Category	Total	White	Black	Asian	AIAN	Hisp.
Enrollment (%)	100.0	98.4	0.7	0.2	0.1	0.6
Drop-out Rate (%)	1.7	1.7	0.0	0.0	n/a	0.0
H.S. Diplomas (#)	219	217	2	0	0	0

Shenandoah County

Shenandoah County Public Schools

600 N Main St #200 • Woodstock, VA 22664-1855
(540) 459-6222 • http://www.shenandoah.k12.va.us/
Grade Span: PK-12; **Agency Type:** 1
Schools: 10
3 Primary; 3 Middle; 3 High; 1 Other Level
9 Regular; 0 Special Education; 1 Vocational; 0 Alternative
0 Magnet; 0 Charter; 3 Title I Eligible; 0 School-wide Title I
Students: 5,681 (51.5% male; 48.5% female)
Individual Education Program: 794 (14.0%);
English Language Learner: 115 (2.0%); Migrant: 147 (2.6%)
Eligible for Free Lunch Program: 1,008 (17.7%)
Eligible for Reduced-Price Lunch Program: 378 (6.7%)
Teachers: 532.0 (10.7 to 1)
Librarians/Media Specialists: 10.0 (568.1 to 1)
Guidance Counselors: 12.0 (473.4 to 1)
Current Spending: ($ per student per year):
Total: $6,660; Instruction: $4,156; Support Services: $2,288
Enrollment, Drop-out Rates and Diploma Recipients by Race/Ethnicity

Category	Total	White	Black	Asian	AIAN	Hisp.
Enrollment (%)	100.0	91.6	1.8	0.5	0.1	6.1
Drop-out Rate (%)	4.0	3.8	3.8	0.0	n/a	10.0
H.S. Diplomas (#)	357	339	5	3	0	10

Smyth County

Smyth County Public Schools

121 Bagley Cir Ste 300 • Marion, VA 24354-3140
(276) 783-3791 • http://www.scsb.org/
Grade Span: PK-12; **Agency Type:** 1
Schools: 14
7 Primary; 3 Middle; 3 High; 1 Other Level
13 Regular; 0 Special Education; 1 Vocational; 0 Alternative
0 Magnet; 0 Charter; 7 Title I Eligible; 0 School-wide Title I
Students: 5,066 (51.6% male; 48.4% female)
Individual Education Program: 909 (17.9%);
English Language Learner: 27 (0.5%); Migrant: 0 (0.0%)
Eligible for Free Lunch Program: 1,725 (34.1%)
Eligible for Reduced-Price Lunch Program: 459 (9.1%)
Teachers: 542.5 (9.3 to 1)
Librarians/Media Specialists: 12.0 (422.2 to 1)
Guidance Counselors: 11.0 (460.5 to 1)
Current Spending: ($ per student per year):
Total: $6,347; Instruction: $4,336; Support Services: $1,844
Enrollment, Drop-out Rates and Diploma Recipients by Race/Ethnicity

Category	Total	White	Black	Asian	AIAN	Hisp.
Enrollment (%)	100.0	97.4	1.6	0.3	0.2	0.6
Drop-out Rate (%)	1.4	1.4	0.0	0.0	0.0	0.0
H.S. Diplomas (#)	302	296	3	0	1	2

Southampton County

Southampton County Public Schools

21308 Plank Rd • Courtland, VA 23837-0096
Mailing Address: PO Box 96 • Courtland, VA 23837-0096
(757) 653-2692 • http://www.southampton.k12.va.us/
Grade Span: PK-12; **Agency Type:** 1
Schools: 6
4 Primary; 1 Middle; 1 High; 0 Other Level
6 Regular; 0 Special Education; 0 Vocational; 0 Alternative
0 Magnet; 0 Charter; 4 Title I Eligible; 0 School-wide Title I
Students: 2,832 (53.0% male; 47.0% female)
Individual Education Program: 489 (17.3%);
English Language Learner: 2 (0.1%); Migrant: 0 (0.0%)
Eligible for Free Lunch Program: 927 (32.7%)
Eligible for Reduced-Price Lunch Program: 234 (8.3%)
Teachers: 236.0 (12.0 to 1)
Librarians/Media Specialists: 6.0 (472.0 to 1)
Guidance Counselors: 6.0 (472.0 to 1)
Current Spending: ($ per student per year):
Total: $6,893; Instruction: $4,147; Support Services: $2,388
Enrollment, Drop-out Rates and Diploma Recipients by Race/Ethnicity

Category	Total	White	Black	Asian	AIAN	Hisp.
Enrollment (%)	100.0	49.0	49.8	0.4	0.2	0.7
Drop-out Rate (%)	4.3	2.7	5.8	0.0	n/a	0.0
H.S. Diplomas (#)	152	89	61	1	0	1

Spotsylvania County

Spotsylvania County Public Schools

6717 Smith Station Rd • Spotsylvania, VA 22553-1803
(540) 898-6032 • http://205.174.118.254/index.htm
Grade Span: PK-12; **Agency Type:** 1
Schools: 29
16 Primary; 6 Middle; 6 High; 1 Other Level
26 Regular; 0 Special Education; 1 Vocational; 2 Alternative
0 Magnet; 0 Charter; 15 Title I Eligible; 0 School-wide Title I
Students: 21,391 (51.2% male; 48.8% female)
Individual Education Program: 3,141 (14.7%);
English Language Learner: 274 (1.3%); Migrant: 0 (0.0%)
Eligible for Free Lunch Program: 2,560 (12.0%)
Eligible for Reduced-Price Lunch Program: 985 (4.6%)
Teachers: 1,812.3 (11.8 to 1)
Librarians/Media Specialists: 30.0 (713.0 to 1)
Guidance Counselors: 34.0 (629.1 to 1)
Current Spending: ($ per student per year):
Total: $6,600; Instruction: $4,153; Support Services: $2,193
Enrollment, Drop-out Rates and Diploma Recipients by Race/Ethnicity

Category	Total	White	Black	Asian	AIAN	Hisp.
Enrollment (%)	100.0	76.5	17.6	1.9	0.3	3.6
Drop-out Rate (%)	3.1	2.9	4.3	3.4	0.0	3.0
H.S. Diplomas (#)	1,119	862	180	25	8	44

Stafford County

Stafford County Public Schools

31 Stafford Ave • Stafford, VA 22554-7213
(540) 658-6000 • http://www.pen.k12.va.us/Div/Stafford/
Grade Span: PK-12; **Agency Type:** 1
Schools: 24
14 Primary; 6 Middle; 4 High; 0 Other Level
24 Regular; 0 Special Education; 0 Vocational; 0 Alternative
0 Magnet; 0 Charter; 8 Title I Eligible; 0 School-wide Title I
Students: 24,003 (51.5% male; 48.5% female)
Individual Education Program: 2,571 (10.7%);
English Language Learner: 270 (1.1%); Migrant: 0 (0.0%)
Eligible for Free Lunch Program: 2,256 (9.4%)
Eligible for Reduced-Price Lunch Program: 851 (3.5%)
Teachers: 1,805.7 (13.3 to 1)
Librarians/Media Specialists: 31.0 (774.3 to 1)
Guidance Counselors: 37.5 (640.1 to 1)
Current Spending: ($ per student per year):
Total: $6,503; Instruction: $4,070; Support Services: $2,166
Enrollment, Drop-out Rates and Diploma Recipients by Race/Ethnicity

Category	Total	White	Black	Asian	AIAN	Hisp.
Enrollment (%)	100.0	74.3	18.6	2.3	0.4	3.9
Drop-out Rate (%)	2.4	2.5	2.4	0.0	4.5	1.0
H.S. Diplomas (#)	1,359	1,031	188	45	1	94

Staunton City

Staunton City Public Schools

116 W Beverly St • Staunton, VA 24401-4203
Mailing Address: PO Box 900 • Staunton, VA 24402-0900
(540) 332-3920 • http://www.staunton.k12.va.us/
Grade Span: PK-12; **Agency Type:** 1
Schools: 6
4 Primary; 1 Middle; 1 High; 0 Other Level
6 Regular; 0 Special Education; 0 Vocational; 0 Alternative
0 Magnet; 0 Charter; 4 Title I Eligible; 0 School-wide Title I
Students: 2,691 (50.7% male; 49.3% female)
Individual Education Program: 465 (17.3%);
English Language Learner: 11 (0.4%); Migrant: 0 (0.0%)
Eligible for Free Lunch Program: 881 (32.7%)
Eligible for Reduced-Price Lunch Program: 223 (8.3%)
Teachers: 288.4 (9.3 to 1)
Librarians/Media Specialists: 5.0 (538.2 to 1)
Guidance Counselors: 7.0 (384.4 to 1)
Current Spending: ($ per student per year):
Total: $7,995; Instruction: $5,309; Support Services: $2,382
Enrollment, Drop-out Rates and Diploma Recipients by Race/Ethnicity

Category	Total	White	Black	Asian	AIAN	Hisp.
Enrollment (%)	100.0	74.8	23.1	0.6	0.2	1.3
Drop-out Rate (%)	6.5	6.7	6.1	0.0	100.0	0.0
H.S. Diplomas (#)	169	129	37	1	0	2

Suffolk City

Suffolk City Public Schools

524 N Main St • Suffolk, VA 23434-1549
Mailing Address: PO Box 1549 • Suffolk, VA 23439-1549
(757) 925-5500 • http://www.sps.k12.va.us/
Grade Span: PK-12; **Agency Type:** 1
Schools: 20
12 Primary; 4 Middle; 2 High; 2 Other Level
18 Regular; 0 Special Education; 0 Vocational; 2 Alternative
0 Magnet; 0 Charter; 12 Title I Eligible; 0 School-wide Title I
Students: 12,685 (51.2% male; 48.8% female)
Individual Education Program: 1,558 (12.3%);
English Language Learner: 15 (0.1%); Migrant: 0 (0.0%)
Eligible for Free Lunch Program: 4,105 (32.4%)
Eligible for Reduced-Price Lunch Program: 1,017 (8.0%)
Teachers: 1,004.4 (12.6 to 1)
Librarians/Media Specialists: 21.0 (604.0 to 1)
Guidance Counselors: 23.0 (551.5 to 1)
Current Spending: ($ per student per year):
Total: $6,161; Instruction: $3,990; Support Services: $1,869
Enrollment, Drop-out Rates and Diploma Recipients by Race/Ethnicity

Category	Total	White	Black	Asian	AIAN	Hisp.
Enrollment (%)	100.0	40.7	57.3	0.8	0.2	1.0
Drop-out Rate (%)	4.0	3.3	4.6	12.0	0.0	0.0
H.S. Diplomas (#)	531	262	264	2	0	3

Tazewell County

Tazewell County Public Schools

209 W Fincastle • Tazewell, VA 24651-0927
(276) 988-5511 • http://www.tazewell.k12.va.us/web1/index.html
Grade Span: PK-12; **Agency Type:** 1
Schools: 17
9 Primary; 3 Middle; 3 High; 2 Other Level
16 Regular; 0 Special Education; 1 Vocational; 0 Alternative
0 Magnet; 0 Charter; 9 Title I Eligible; 1 School-wide Title I
Students: 7,002 (51.3% male; 48.7% female)
Individual Education Program: 1,054 (15.1%);
English Language Learner: 2 (<0.1%); Migrant: 0 (0.0%)
Eligible for Free Lunch Program: 2,701 (38.6%)
Eligible for Reduced-Price Lunch Program: 638 (9.1%)
Teachers: 630.1 (11.1 to 1)
Librarians/Media Specialists: 12.5 (560.2 to 1)
Guidance Counselors: 11.6 (603.6 to 1)
Current Spending: ($ per student per year):
Total: $6,424; Instruction: $4,104; Support Services: $1,981
Enrollment, Drop-out Rates and Diploma Recipients by Race/Ethnicity

Category	Total	White	Black	Asian	AIAN	Hisp.
Enrollment (%)	100.0	95.9	2.7	1.2	0.0	0.1
Drop-out Rate (%)	2.9	3.0	0.0	0.0	0.0	n/a
H.S. Diplomas (#)	447	429	15	2	1	0

Virginia Beach City

Virginia Beach City Public Schools

2512 George Mason Dr • Virginia Beach, VA 23456-6038
Mailing Address: PO Box 6038 • Virginia Beach, VA 23456-6038
(757) 427-4585 • http://www.vbschools.com/
Grade Span: PK-12; **Agency Type:** 1
Schools: 85
55 Primary; 15 Middle; 13 High; 2 Other Level
80 Regular; 0 Special Education; 1 Vocational; 4 Alternative
5 Magnet; 0 Charter; 13 Title I Eligible; 3 School-wide Title I
Students: 75,902 (51.1% male; 48.9% female)
Individual Education Program: 10,411 (13.7%);
English Language Learner: 849 (1.1%); Migrant: 0 (0.0%)
Eligible for Free Lunch Program: 14,569 (19.2%)
Eligible for Reduced-Price Lunch Program: 8,585 (11.3%)
Teachers: 5,339.3 (14.2 to 1)
Librarians/Media Specialists: 0.0 (0.0 to 1)
Guidance Counselors: 0.0 (0.0 to 1)
Current Spending: ($ per student per year):
Total: $6,647; Instruction: $4,070; Support Services: $2,328
Enrollment, Drop-out Rates and Diploma Recipients by Race/Ethnicity

Category	Total	White	Black	Asian	AIAN	Hisp.
Enrollment (%)	100.0	61.1	28.6	5.7	0.3	4.4
Drop-out Rate (%)	5.2	4.8	6.4	4.1	13.9	6.6
H.S. Diplomas (#)	4,455	2,914	1,042	340	16	143

Warren County

Warren County Public Schools

210 N Commerce Ave • Front Royal, VA 22630-4419
(540) 635-2171 • http://www.wcps.k12.va.us/
Grade Span: PK-12; **Agency Type:** 1
Schools: 8
5 Primary; 2 Middle; 1 High; 0 Other Level
8 Regular; 0 Special Education; 0 Vocational; 0 Alternative
0 Magnet; 0 Charter; 4 Title I Eligible; 0 School-wide Title I
Students: 5,104 (51.4% male; 48.6% female)
Individual Education Program: 765 (15.0%);
English Language Learner: 36 (0.7%); Migrant: 2 (<0.1%)
Eligible for Free Lunch Program: 927 (18.2%)
Eligible for Reduced-Price Lunch Program: 205 (4.0%)
Teachers: 389.0 (13.1 to 1)
Librarians/Media Specialists: 9.0 (567.1 to 1)
Guidance Counselors: 10.0 (510.4 to 1)
Current Spending: ($ per student per year):
Total: $5,871; Instruction: $3,429; Support Services: $2,164
Enrollment, Drop-out Rates and Diploma Recipients by Race/Ethnicity

Category	Total	White	Black	Asian	AIAN	Hisp.
Enrollment (%)	100.0	89.8	6.9	1.0	0.3	2.1
Drop-out Rate (%)	3.3	3.4	0.0	0.0	0.0	22.2
H.S. Diplomas (#)	261	239	17	2	0	3

Washington County

Washington County Public Schools

812 Thompson Dr • Abingdon, VA 24210-2354
(276) 628-1826 • http://www.wcs.k12.va.us/
Grade Span: PK-12; **Agency Type:** 1
Schools: 17
7 Primary; 4 Middle; 4 High; 2 Other Level
15 Regular; 0 Special Education; 2 Vocational; 0 Alternative
0 Magnet; 0 Charter; 6 Title I Eligible; 0 School-wide Title I
Students: 7,173 (50.5% male; 49.5% female)
Individual Education Program: 927 (12.9%);
English Language Learner: 4 (0.1%); Migrant: 0 (0.0%)
Eligible for Free Lunch Program: 2,054 (28.6%)
Eligible for Reduced-Price Lunch Program: 647 (9.0%)
Teachers: 538.7 (13.3 to 1)
Librarians/Media Specialists: 11.0 (652.1 to 1)
Guidance Counselors: 12.0 (597.8 to 1)
Current Spending: ($ per student per year):
Total: $6,696; Instruction: $4,285; Support Services: $2,069
Enrollment, Drop-out Rates and Diploma Recipients by Race/Ethnicity

Category	Total	White	Black	Asian	AIAN	Hisp.
Enrollment (%)	100.0	97.2	1.8	0.5	0.1	0.5
Drop-out Rate (%)	2.1	2.2	0.0	0.0	0.0	0.0
H.S. Diplomas (#)	494	481	6	4	0	3

Waynesboro City

Waynesboro City Public Schools

301 Pine Ave • Waynesboro, VA 22980-4761
(540) 946-4600 • http://www.waynesboro.k12.va.us/
Grade Span: PK-12; **Agency Type:** 1
Schools: 6
4 Primary; 1 Middle; 1 High; 0 Other Level
6 Regular; 0 Special Education; 0 Vocational; 0 Alternative
0 Magnet; 0 Charter; 2 Title I Eligible; 2 School-wide Title I
Students: 2,982 (51.3% male; 48.7% female)
Individual Education Program: 340 (11.4%);
English Language Learner: 64 (2.1%); Migrant: 27 (0.9%)
Eligible for Free Lunch Program: 990 (33.2%)
Eligible for Reduced-Price Lunch Program: 251 (8.4%)
Teachers: 253.8 (11.7 to 1)
Librarians/Media Specialists: 6.0 (497.0 to 1)
Guidance Counselors: 6.0 (497.0 to 1)
Current Spending: ($ per student per year):
Total: $7,181; Instruction: $4,634; Support Services: $2,274
Enrollment, Drop-out Rates and Diploma Recipients by Race/Ethnicity

Category	Total	White	Black	Asian	AIAN	Hisp.
Enrollment (%)	100.0	76.6	16.2	1.3	0.4	5.5
Drop-out Rate (%)	2.8	2.5	3.8	0.0	0.0	5.9
H.S. Diplomas (#)	162	142	14	1	0	5

Westmoreland County

Westmoreland County Public Schools

141 Opal Ln • Montross, VA 22520-1060
(804) 493-8018 • http://www.wmlcps.org/
Grade Span: PK-12; **Agency Type:** 1
Schools: 4

2 Primary; 1 Middle; 1 High; 0 Other Level
4 Regular; 0 Special Education; 0 Vocational; 0 Alternative
0 Magnet; 0 Charter; 2 Title I Eligible; 2 School-wide Title I
Students: 2,005 (51.8% male; 48.2% female)
Individual Education Program: 233 (11.6%);
English Language Learner: 55 (2.7%); Migrant: 120 (6.0%)
Eligible for Free Lunch Program: 861 (42.9%)
Eligible for Reduced-Price Lunch Program: 187 (9.3%)
Teachers: 176.0 (11.4 to 1)
Librarians/Media Specialists: 4.0 (501.3 to 1)
Guidance Counselors: 4.0 (501.3 to 1)
Current Spending: ($ per student per year):
Total: $6,303; Instruction: $3,682; Support Services: $2,247
Enrollment, Drop-out Rates and Diploma Recipients by Race/Ethnicity

Category	Total	White	Black	Asian	AIAN	Hisp.
Enrollment (%)	100.0	40.9	52.5	0.2	0.0	6.3
Drop-out Rate (%)	2.3	2.7	2.0	n/a	n/a	0.0
H.S. Diplomas (#)	135	57	74	0	0	4

Williamsburg City

Williamsburg-James City Co Pub Schls
101-D Mounts Bay Rd • Williamsburg, VA 23185-8783
Mailing Address: PO Box 8783 • Williamsburg, VA 23187-8783
(757) 253-6777 • http://www.wjcc.k12.va.us/
Grade Span: PK-12; **Agency Type:** 3
Schools: 12
7 Primary; 3 Middle; 2 High; 0 Other Level
12 Regular; 0 Special Education; 0 Vocational; 0 Alternative
0 Magnet; 0 Charter; 6 Title I Eligible; 0 School-wide Title I
Students: 8,553 (50.8% male; 49.2% female)
Individual Education Program: 1,100 (12.9%);
English Language Learner: 53 (0.6%); Migrant: 0 (0.0%)
Eligible for Free Lunch Program: 1,152 (13.5%)
Eligible for Reduced-Price Lunch Program: 372 (4.3%)
Teachers: 805.4 (10.6 to 1)
Librarians/Media Specialists: 14.0 (610.9 to 1)
Guidance Counselors: 15.0 (570.2 to 1)
Current Spending: ($ per student per year):
Total: $8,084; Instruction: $4,911; Support Services: $2,923
Enrollment, Drop-out Rates and Diploma Recipients by Race/Ethnicity

Category	Total	White	Black	Asian	AIAN	Hisp.
Enrollment (%)	100.0	71.5	22.9	2.4	0.8	2.5
Drop-out Rate (%)	1.4	1.0	3.1	0.0	0.0	0.0
H.S. Diplomas (#)	525	406	90	17	1	11

Winchester City

Winchester City Public Schools
12 N Washington St • Winchester, VA 22601
Mailing Address: PO Box 551 • Winchester, VA 22604-0551
(540) 667-4253 • http://www.wps.k12.va.us/
Grade Span: PK-12; **Agency Type:** 1
Schools: 6
4 Primary; 1 Middle; 1 High; 0 Other Level
6 Regular; 0 Special Education; 0 Vocational; 0 Alternative
0 Magnet; 0 Charter; 4 Title I Eligible; 0 School-wide Title I
Students: 3,540 (50.6% male; 49.4% female)
Individual Education Program: 680 (19.2%);
English Language Learner: 361 (10.2%); Migrant: 58 (1.6%)
Eligible for Free Lunch Program: 990 (28.0%)
Eligible for Reduced-Price Lunch Program: 283 (8.0%)
Teachers: 344.1 (10.3 to 1)
Librarians/Media Specialists: 5.0 (708.0 to 1)
Guidance Counselors: 7.0 (505.7 to 1)
Current Spending: ($ per student per year):
Total: $8,653; Instruction: $5,577; Support Services: $2,763
Enrollment, Drop-out Rates and Diploma Recipients by Race/Ethnicity

Category	Total	White	Black	Asian	AIAN	Hisp.
Enrollment (%)	100.0	69.6	17.8	2.1	0.5	10.0
Drop-out Rate (%)	4.4	4.2	5.2	4.0	0.0	6.5
H.S. Diplomas (#)	181	151	26	2	0	2

Wise County

Wise County Public Schools
628 Lake St • Wise, VA 24293-1217
Mailing Address: PO Box 1217 • Wise, VA 24293-1217
(276) 328-8017
Grade Span: PK-12; **Agency Type:** 1
Schools: 17
6 Primary; 3 Middle; 6 High; 2 Other Level
15 Regular; 0 Special Education; 1 Vocational; 1 Alternative
0 Magnet; 0 Charter; 6 Title I Eligible; 1 School-wide Title I
Students: 6,900 (51.4% male; 48.6% female)
Individual Education Program: 1,004 (14.6%);
English Language Learner: 18 (0.3%); Migrant: 0 (0.0%)
Eligible for Free Lunch Program: 2,752 (39.9%)
Eligible for Reduced-Price Lunch Program: 538 (7.8%)
Teachers: 674.9 (10.2 to 1)
Librarians/Media Specialists: 14.9 (463.1 to 1)
Guidance Counselors: 16.5 (418.2 to 1)
Current Spending: ($ per student per year):
Total: $6,696; Instruction: $4,256; Support Services: $2,156
Enrollment, Drop-out Rates and Diploma Recipients by Race/Ethnicity

Category	Total	White	Black	Asian	AIAN	Hisp.
Enrollment (%)	100.0	97.7	1.5	0.3	0.0	0.5
Drop-out Rate (%)	3.0	3.0	2.0	0.0	0.0	0.0
H.S. Diplomas (#)	463	446	14	1	0	2

Wythe County

Wythe County Public Schools
1570 W Reservoir St • Wytheville, VA 24382-1500
(276) 228-5411 • http://wcps.wythe.k12.va.us/public/
Grade Span: PK-12; **Agency Type:** 1
Schools: 13
6 Primary; 3 Middle; 3 High; 1 Other Level
12 Regular; 0 Special Education; 1 Vocational; 0 Alternative
3 Magnet; 0 Charter; 6 Title I Eligible; 0 School-wide Title I
Students: 4,302 (50.9% male; 49.1% female)
Individual Education Program: 514 (11.9%);
English Language Learner: 1 (<0.1%); Migrant: 0 (0.0%)
Eligible for Free Lunch Program: 1,241 (28.8%)
Eligible for Reduced-Price Lunch Program: 403 (9.4%)
Teachers: 374.4 (11.5 to 1)
Librarians/Media Specialists: 12.0 (358.5 to 1)
Guidance Counselors: 11.0 (391.1 to 1)
Current Spending: ($ per student per year):
Total: $6,057; Instruction: $3,896; Support Services: $1,900
Enrollment, Drop-out Rates and Diploma Recipients by Race/Ethnicity

Category	Total	White	Black	Asian	AIAN	Hisp.
Enrollment (%)	100.0	95.3	3.8	0.4	0.0	0.4
Drop-out Rate (%)	1.9	1.9	2.8	0.0	n/a	0.0
H.S. Diplomas (#)	273	266	5	1	0	1

York County

York County Public Schools
302 Dare Rd • Yorktown, VA 23692-2795
(757) 898-0300 • http://yorkcountyschools.org/
Grade Span: PK-12; **Agency Type:** 1
Schools: 19
10 Primary; 4 Middle; 4 High; 1 Other Level
19 Regular; 0 Special Education; 0 Vocational; 0 Alternative
1 Magnet; 1 Charter; 4 Title I Eligible; 0 School-wide Title I
Students: 11,921 (51.5% male; 48.5% female)
Individual Education Program: 1,134 (9.5%);
English Language Learner: 121 (1.0%); Migrant: 0 (0.0%)
Eligible for Free Lunch Program: 879 (7.4%)
Eligible for Reduced-Price Lunch Program: 743 (6.2%)
Teachers: 948.0 (12.6 to 1)
Librarians/Media Specialists: 18.0 (662.3 to 1)
Guidance Counselors: 22.0 (541.9 to 1)
Current Spending: ($ per student per year):
Total: $6,260; Instruction: $3,733; Support Services: $2,327
Enrollment, Drop-out Rates and Diploma Recipients by Race/Ethnicity

Category	Total	White	Black	Asian	AIAN	Hisp.
Enrollment (%)	100.0	75.7	15.8	4.7	0.6	3.2
Drop-out Rate (%)	1.1	0.9	2.0	0.0	0.0	7.1
H.S. Diplomas (#)	835	652	105	50	2	26

Number of Schools

Rank	Number	District Name	City
1	202	Fairfax County Public Schools	Fairfax
2	85	Virginia Beach City Public Schls	Virginia Beach
3	75	Prince William County Pub Schools	Manassas
4	65	Henrico County Public Schools	Richmond
5	59	Chesterfield County Public Schools	Chesterfield
5	59	Richmond City Public Schools	Richmond
7	58	Norfolk City Public Schools	Norfolk
8	56	Loudoun County Public Schools	Leesburg
9	48	Newport News City Public Schools	Newport News
10	46	Chesapeake City Public Schools	Chesapeake
11	37	Hampton City Public Schools	Hampton
12	31	Arlington County Public Schools	Arlington
12	31	Roanoke City Public Schools	Roanoke
14	30	Roanoke County Public Schools	Roanoke
15	29	Spotsylvania Co Public Schools	Spotsylvania
16	27	Portsmouth City Public Schools	Portsmouth
17	25	Albemarle County Public Schools	Charlottesville
18	24	Stafford County Public Schools	Stafford
19	22	Bedford County Public Schools	Bedford
20	21	Hanover County Public Schools	Ashland
20	21	Montgomery County Public Schools	Christiansburg
20	21	Rockingham County Public Schools	Harrisonburg
23	20	Augusta County Public Schools	Fishersville
23	20	Henry County Public Schools	Collinsville
23	20	Pittsylvania County Public Schools	Chatham
23	20	Suffolk City Public Schools	Suffolk
27	19	York County Public Schools	Yorktown
28	17	Danville City Public Schools	Danville
28	17	Fauquier County Public Schools	Warrenton
28	17	Lynchburg City Public Schools	Lynchburg
28	17	Tazewell County Public Schools	Tazewell
28	17	Washington County Public Schools	Abingdon
28	17	Wise County Public Schools	Wise
34	16	Alexandria City Public Schools	Alexandria
34	16	Campbell County Public Schools	Rustburg
34	16	Franklin County Public Schools	Rocky Mount
34	16	Frederick County Public Schools	Winchester
34	16	Halifax County Public Schools	Halifax
39	15	Accomack County Public Schools	Accomac
40	14	Lee County Public Schools	Jonesville
40	14	Scott County Public Schools	Gate City
40	14	Smyth County Public Schools	Marion
43	13	Russell County Public Schools	Lebanon
43	13	Wythe County Public Schools	Wytheville
45	12	Botetourt County Public Schools	Fincastle
45	12	Williamsburg-James City Co PS	Williamsburg
47	11	Buchanan County Public Schools	Grundy
47	11	Grayson County Public Schools	Independence
47	11	Mecklenburg County Public Schools	Boydton
47	11	Pulaski County Public Schools	Pulaski
51	10	Amherst County Public Schools	Amherst
51	10	Carroll County Public Schools	Hillsville
51	10	Charlottesville City Pub Schools	Charlottesville
51	10	Gloucester County Public Schools	Gloucester
51	10	Petersburg City Public Schools	Petersburg
51	10	Prince George County Pub Schools	Prince George
51	10	Shenandoah County Public Schools	Woodstock
58	9	Culpeper County Public Schools	Culpeper
58	9	Dickenson County Public Schools	Clintwood
60	8	Isle of Wight County Pub Schools	Isle Of Wight
60	8	Manassas City Public Schools	Manassas
60	8	Orange County Public Schools	Orange
60	8	Page County Public Schools	Luray
60	8	Rockbridge County Public Schools	Lexington
60	8	Warren County Public Schools	Front Royal
66	7	Alleghany County Public Schools	Covington
66	7	Bristol City Public Schools	Bristol
66	7	Charlotte County Public Schools	Charlotte Ct Hse
66	7	Dinwiddie County Public Schools	Dinwiddie
66	7	Greene County Public Schools	Standardsville
66	7	Hopewell City Public Schools	Hopewell
66	7	Nottoway County Public Schools	Nottoway
66	7	Patrick County Public Schools	Stuart
66	7	Virginia-New York District	Quantico
75	6	Brunswick County Public Schools	Lawrenceville
75	6	Buckingham County Public Schools	Buckingham
75	6	Caroline County Public Schools	Bowling Green
75	6	Giles County Public Schools	Pearisburg
75	6	Harrisonburg City Public Schools	Harrisonburg
75	6	Martinsville City Public Schools	Martinsville
75	6	Salem City Public Schools	Salem
75	6	Southampton County Public Schools	Courtland
75	6	Staunton City Public Schools	Staunton
75	6	Waynesboro City Public Schools	Waynesboro
75	6	Winchester City Public Schools	Winchester
86	5	Clarke County Public Schools	Berryville
86	5	Colonial Heights City Pub Schools	Colonial Hgts
86	5	Floyd County Public Schools	Floyd
86	5	Fluvanna County Public Schools	Palmyra
86	5	Goochland County Public Schools	Goochland
86	5	Greensville County Public Schools	Emporia
86	5	Louisa County Public Schools	Mineral
86	5	Madison County Public Schools	Madison
86	5	Northampton County Public Schools	Machipongo
86	5	Powhatan County Public Schools	Powhatan
96	4	Appomattox County Public Schools	Appomattox
96	4	Falls Church City Public Schools	Falls Church
96	4	Fredericksburg City Public Schools	Fredericksburg
96	4	King George County Public Schools	King George
96	4	King William County Public Schools	King William
96	4	Lunenburg County Public Schools	Victoria
96	4	Manassas Park City Public Schools	Manassas Park
96	4	Nelson County Public Schools	Lovingston
96	4	New Kent County Public Schools	New Kent
96	4	Poquoson City Public Schools	Poquoson
96	4	Radford City Public Schools	Radford
96	4	Westmoreland Co Public Schools	Montross
108	3	Amelia County Public Schools	Amelia
108	3	Essex County Public Schools	Tappahannock
108	3	Lancaster County Public Schools	Kilmarnock
108	3	Prince Edward County Pub Schools	Farmville

Number of Teachers

Rank	Number	District Name	City
1	13,946	Fairfax County Public Schools	Fairfax
2	5,339	Virginia Beach City Public Schls	Virginia Beach
3	4,140	Prince William County Pub Schools	Manassas
4	4,011	Chesterfield County Public Schools	Chesterfield
5	3,371	Henrico County Public Schools	Richmond
6	3,363	Norfolk City Public Schools	Norfolk
7	3,199	Loudoun County Public Schools	Leesburg
8	2,895	Chesapeake City Public Schools	Chesapeake
9	2,702	Newport News City Public Schools	Newport News
10	2,360	Richmond City Public Schools	Richmond
11	2,144	Arlington County Public Schools	Arlington
12	2,004	Hampton City Public Schools	Hampton
13	1,812	Spotsylvania Co Public Schools	Spotsylvania
14	1,805	Stafford County Public Schools	Stafford
15	1,498	Hanover County Public Schools	Ashland
16	1,375	Roanoke County Public Schools	Roanoke
17	1,351	Roanoke City Public Schools	Roanoke
18	1,320	Portsmouth City Public Schools	Portsmouth
19	1,214	Alexandria City Public Schools	Alexandria
20	1,174	Albemarle County Public Schools	Charlottesville
21	1,012	Rockingham County Public Schools	Harrisonburg
22	1,004	Suffolk City Public Schools	Suffolk
23	948	York County Public Schools	Yorktown
24	932	Frederick County Public Schools	Winchester
25	922	Montgomery County Public Schools	Christiansburg
26	922	Bedford County Public Schools	Bedford
27	892	Fauquier County Public Schools	Warrenton
28	882	Augusta County Public Schools	Fishersville
29	806	Lynchburg City Public Schools	Lynchburg
30	805	Williamsburg-James City Co PS	Williamsburg
31	800	Henry County Public Schools	Collinsville
32	794	Pittsylvania County Public Schools	Chatham
33	759	Campbell County Public Schools	Rustburg
34	703	Danville City Public Schools	Danville
35	674	Wise County Public Schools	Wise
36	630	Tazewell County Public Schools	Tazewell
37	620	Franklin County Public Schools	Rocky Mount
38	580	Halifax County Public Schools	Halifax
39	554	Manassas City Public Schools	Manassas
40	542	Smyth County Public Schools	Marion
41	538	Washington County Public Schools	Abingdon
42	532	Shenandoah County Public Schools	Woodstock
43	524	Culpeper County Public Schools	Culpeper
44	517	Gloucester County Public Schools	Gloucester
45	479	Accomack County Public Schools	Accomac
46	474	Prince George County Pub Schools	Prince George
47	467	Petersburg City Public Schools	Petersburg
48	461	Charlottesville City Pub Schools	Charlottesville
49	444	Pulaski County Public Schools	Pulaski
50	432	Carroll County Public Schools	Hillsville
51	430	Amherst County Public Schools	Amherst
52	425	Botetourt County Public Schools	Fincastle
53	423	Lee County Public Schools	Jonesville
54	410	Harrisonburg City Public Schools	Harrisonburg
55	396	Buchanan County Public Schools	Grundy
56	389	Warren County Public Schools	Front Royal
57	387	Mecklenburg County Public Schools	Boydton
58	386	Isle of Wight County Pub Schools	Isle Of Wight
59	376	Hopewell City Public Schools	Hopewell
60	374	Wythe County Public Schools	Wytheville
61	372	Dinwiddie County Public Schools	Dinwiddie
62	370	Orange County Public Schools	Orange
63	365	Russell County Public Schools	Lebanon
64	358	Louisa County Public Schools	Mineral
65	352	Powhatan County Public Schools	Powhatan
66	344	Winchester City Public Schools	Winchester
67	342	Scott County Public Schools	Gate City
68	333	Salem City Public Schools	Salem
69	327	Dickenson County Public Schools	Clintwood
70	314	Page County Public Schools	Luray
71	302	Rockbridge County Public Schools	Lexington
72	292	Fluvanna County Public Schools	Palmyra
73	291	Caroline County Public Schools	Bowling Green
74	288	Staunton City Public Schools	Staunton
75	268	Alleghany County Public Schools	Covington
76	264	Colonial Heights City Pub Schools	Colonial Hgts
77	254	Martinsville City Public Schools	Martinsville
78	253	Waynesboro City Public Schools	Waynesboro
79	247	Greensville County Public Schools	Emporia
80	242	Prince Edward County Pub Schools	Farmville
81	236	Southampton County Public Schools	Courtland
82	235	Brunswick County Public Schools	Lawrenceville
83	229	Patrick County Public Schools	Stuart
84	229	Grayson County Public Schools	Independence
85	224	King George County Public Schools	King George
86	223	Bristol City Public Schools	Bristol
87	222	Fredericksburg City Public Schools	Fredericksburg
88	221	Nottoway County Public Schools	Nottoway
89	220	New Kent County Public Schools	New Kent
90	215	Giles County Public Schools	Pearisburg
91	210	Poquoson City Public Schools	Poquoson
92	209	Manassas Park City Public Schools	Manassas Park
93	208	Goochland County Public Schools	Goochland
94	206	Appomattox County Public Schools	Appomattox
95	203	Buckingham County Public Schools	Buckingham
96	202	Northampton County Public Schools	Machipongo
97	196	Clarke County Public Schools	Berryville
98	192	Nelson County Public Schools	Lovingston
99	189	Falls Church City Public Schools	Falls Church
100	189	Charlotte County Public Schools	Charlotte Ct Hse
101	179	King William County Public Schools	King William
102	176	Madison County Public Schools	Madison
102	176	Westmoreland Co Public Schools	Montross
104	175	Virginia-New York District	Quantico
105	173	Lunenburg County Public Schools	Victoria
106	159	Floyd County Public Schools	Floyd
107	157	Essex County Public Schools	Tappahannock
108	147	Lancaster County Public Schools	Kilmarnock
109	144	Amelia County Public Schools	Amelia
110	133	Radford City Public Schools	Radford
111	116	Greene County Public Schools	Standardsville

Number of Students

Rank	Number	District Name	City
1	162,585	Fairfax County Public Schools	Fairfax
2	75,902	Virginia Beach City Public Schls	Virginia Beach
3	60,541	Prince William County Pub Schools	Manassas
4	53,621	Chesterfield County Public Schools	Chesterfield
5	43,698	Henrico County Public Schools	Richmond
6	39,380	Chesapeake City Public Schools	Chesapeake
7	37,532	Loudoun County Public Schools	Leesburg
8	36,745	Norfolk City Public Schools	Norfolk
9	32,887	Newport News City Public Schools	Newport News
10	26,136	Richmond City Public Schools	Richmond
11	24,003	Stafford County Public Schools	Stafford
12	22,996	Hampton City Public Schools	Hampton
13	21,391	Spotsylvania Co Public Schools	Spotsylvania
14	19,135	Arlington County Public Schools	Arlington
15	17,563	Hanover County Public Schools	Ashland
16	15,977	Portsmouth City Public Schools	Portsmouth
17	14,238	Roanoke County Public Schools	Roanoke
18	13,725	Roanoke City Public Schools	Roanoke
19	12,685	Suffolk City Public Schools	Suffolk
20	12,253	Albemarle County Public Schools	Charlottesville
21	11,921	York County Public Schools	Yorktown
22	11,126	Rockingham County Public Schools	Harrisonburg
23	10,971	Alexandria City Public Schools	Alexandria
24	10,969	Frederick County Public Schools	Winchester
25	10,942	Bedford County Public Schools	Bedford
26	10,674	Augusta County Public Schools	Fishersville
27	10,040	Fauquier County Public Schools	Warrenton
28	9,313	Montgomery County Public Schools	Christiansburg
29	9,036	Pittsylvania County Public Schools	Chatham
30	8,955	Lynchburg City Public Schools	Lynchburg
31	8,861	Campbell County Public Schools	Rustburg
32	8,553	Williamsburg-James City Co PS	Williamsburg
33	8,526	Henry County Public Schools	Collinsville
34	7,585	Danville City Public Schools	Danville
35	7,244	Franklin County Public Schools	Rocky Mount
36	7,173	Washington County Public Schools	Abingdon
37	7,002	Tazewell County Public Schools	Tazewell
38	6,900	Wise County Public Schools	Wise
39	6,673	Manassas City Public Schools	Manassas
40	6,333	Gloucester County Public Schools	Gloucester
41	6,037	Culpeper County Public Schools	Culpeper
42	6,035	Prince George County Pub Schools	Prince George
43	5,912	Halifax County Public Schools	Halifax
44	5,681	Shenandoah County Public Schools	Woodstock
45	5,616	Petersburg City Public Schools	Petersburg
46	5,445	Accomack County Public Schools	Accomac

47	5,104	Warren County Public Schools	Front Royal
48	5,066	Smyth County Public Schools	Marion
49	5,040	Isle of Wight County Pub Schools	Isle Of Wight
50	4,977	Pulaski County Public Schools	Pulaski
51	4,879	Mecklenburg County Public Schools	Boydton
52	4,733	Botetourt County Public Schools	Fincastle
53	4,645	Amherst County Public Schools	Amherst
54	4,423	Dinwiddie County Public Schools	Dinwiddie
55	4,420	Charlottesville City Pub Schools	Charlottesville
56	4,302	Wythe County Public Schools	Wytheville
57	4,282	Louisa County Public Schools	Mineral
58	4,156	Russell County Public Schools	Lebanon
59	4,061	Carroll County Public Schools	Hillsville
60	4,029	Buchanan County Public Schools	Grundy
61	3,999	Harrisonburg City Public Schools	Harrisonburg
62	3,996	Orange County Public Schools	Orange
63	3,940	Salem City Public Schools	Salem
64	3,913	Hopewell City Public Schools	Hopewell
65	3,832	Powhatan County Public Schools	Powhatan
66	3,806	Lee County Public Schools	Jonesville
67	3,765	Caroline County Public Schools	Bowling Green
68	3,705	Scott County Public Schools	Gate City
69	3,640	Page County Public Schools	Luray
70	3,540	Winchester City Public Schools	Winchester
71	3,287	Fluvanna County Public Schools	Palmyra
72	3,048	King George County Public Schools	King George
73	3,000	Rockbridge County Public Schools	Lexington
74	2,982	Waynesboro City Public Schools	Waynesboro
75	2,929	Alleghany County Public Schools	Covington
76	2,832	Southampton County Public Schools	Courtland
77	2,798	Prince Edward County Pub Schools	Farmville
78	2,774	Colonial Heights City Pub Schools	Colonial Hgts
79	2,770	Greensville County Public Schools	Emporia
80	2,719	Dickenson County Public Schools	Clintwood
81	2,705	Greene County Public Schools	Standardsville
82	2,694	Martinsville City Public Schools	Martinsville
83	2,691	Staunton City Public Schools	Staunton
84	2,643	Patrick County Public Schools	Stuart
85	2,562	Giles County Public Schools	Pearisburg
86	2,510	Poquoson City Public Schools	Poquoson
87	2,491	Nottoway County Public Schools	Nottoway
88	2,477	Brunswick County Public Schools	Lawrenceville
89	2,455	New Kent County Public Schools	New Kent
90	2,417	Fredericksburg City Public Schools	Fredericksburg
91	2,364	Appomattox County Public Schools	Appomattox
92	2,332	Bristol City Public Schools	Bristol
93	2,327	Manassas Park City Public Schools	Manassas Park
94	2,289	Charlotte County Public Schools	Charlotte Ct Hse
95	2,281	Grayson County Public Schools	Independence
96	2,210	Buckingham County Public Schools	Buckingham
97	2,079	Northampton County Public Schools	Machipongo
98	2,066	Goochland County Public Schools	Goochland
99	2,063	Clarke County Public Schools	Berryville
100	2,030	Floyd County Public Schools	Floyd
100	2,030	Nelson County Public Schools	Lovingston
102	2,005	Westmoreland Co Public Schools	Montross
103	1,992	Virginia-New York District	Quantico
104	1,957	King William County Public Schools	King William
105	1,833	Falls Church City Public Schools	Falls Church
106	1,830	Madison County Public Schools	Madison
107	1,773	Lunenburg County Public Schools	Victoria
108	1,726	Amelia County Public Schools	Amelia
109	1,626	Essex County Public Schools	Tappahannock
110	1,553	Radford City Public Schools	Radford
111	1,517	Lancaster County Public Schools	Kilmarnock

Male Students

Rank	Percent	District Name	City
1	53.7	Lancaster County Public Schools	Kilmarnock
2	53.5	Carroll County Public Schools	Hillsville
3	53.0	Southampton County Public Schools	Courtland
4	52.9	Colonial Heights City Pub Schools	Colonial Hgts
4	52.9	Poquoson City Public Schools	Poquoson
6	52.8	Louisa County Public Schools	Mineral
7	52.7	Amelia County Public Schools	Amelia
8	52.5	Goochland County Public Schools	Goochland
8	52.5	King William County Public Schools	King William
10	52.4	Alleghany County Public Schools	Covington
10	52.4	Brunswick County Public Schools	Lawrenceville
10	52.4	Rockbridge County Public Schools	Lexington
13	52.3	Greensville County Public Schools	Emporia
13	52.3	Isle of Wight County Pub Schools	Isle Of Wight
13	52.3	Nottoway County Public Schools	Nottoway
16	52.2	Appomattox County Public Schools	Appomattox
16	52.2	Dinwiddie County Public Schools	Dinwiddie
16	52.2	King George County Public Schools	King George
19	52.0	Accomack County Public Schools	Accomac
19	52.0	Amherst County Public Schools	Amherst
19	52.0	Bedford County Public Schools	Bedford
19	52.0	Buckingham County Public Schools	Buckingham
19	52.0	Greene County Public Schools	Standardsville
19	52.0	Nelson County Public Schools	Lovingston
19	52.0	Pittsylvania County Public Schools	Chatham
26	51.9	Mecklenburg County Public Schools	Boydton
27	51.8	Caroline County Public Schools	Bowling Green
27	51.8	Fairfax County Public Schools	Fairfax
27	51.8	Manassas City Public Schools	Manassas
27	51.8	Pulaski County Public Schools	Pulaski
27	51.8	Westmoreland Co Public Schools	Montross
32	51.7	Clarke County Public Schools	Berryville
32	51.7	Dickenson County Public Schools	Clintwood
32	51.7	Falls Church City Public Schools	Falls Church
32	51.7	Hopewell City Public Schools	Hopewell
32	51.7	Manassas Park City Public Schools	Manassas Park
32	51.7	Prince George County Pub Schools	Prince George
32	51.7	Rockingham County Public Schools	Harrisonburg
39	51.6	Botetourt County Public Schools	Fincastle
39	51.6	Lee County Public Schools	Jonesville
39	51.6	Prince Edward County Pub Schools	Farmville
39	51.6	Smyth County Public Schools	Marion
43	51.5	Shenandoah County Public Schools	Woodstock
43	51.5	Stafford County Public Schools	Stafford
43	51.5	York County Public Schools	Yorktown
46	51.4	Augusta County Public Schools	Fishersville
46	51.4	Chesapeake City Public Schools	Chesapeake
46	51.4	Chesterfield County Public Schools	Chesterfield
46	51.4	Danville City Public Schools	Danville
46	51.4	Gloucester County Public Schools	Gloucester
46	51.4	New Kent County Public Schools	New Kent
46	51.4	Patrick County Public Schools	Stuart
46	51.4	Warren County Public Schools	Front Royal
46	51.4	Wise County Public Schools	Wise
55	51.3	Frederick County Public Schools	Winchester
55	51.3	Harrisonburg City Public Schools	Harrisonburg
55	51.3	Henrico County Public Schools	Richmond
55	51.3	Prince William County Pub Schools	Manassas
55	51.3	Tazewell County Public Schools	Tazewell
55	51.3	Waynesboro City Public Schools	Waynesboro
61	51.2	Hampton City Public Schools	Hampton
61	51.2	Hanover County Public Schools	Ashland
61	51.2	Loudoun County Public Schools	Leesburg
61	51.2	Montgomery County Public Schools	Christiansburg
61	51.2	Salem City Public Schools	Salem
61	51.2	Spotsylvania Co Public Schools	Spotsylvania
61	51.2	Suffolk City Public Schools	Suffolk
68	51.1	Albemarle County Public Schools	Charlottesville
68	51.1	Arlington County Public Schools	Arlington
68	51.1	Campbell County Public Schools	Rustburg
68	51.1	Charlottesville City Pub Schools	Charlottesville
68	51.1	Powhatan County Public Schools	Powhatan
68	51.1	Roanoke County Public Schools	Roanoke
68	51.1	Scott County Public Schools	Gate City
68	51.1	Virginia Beach City Public Schls	Virginia Beach
76	51.0	Fluvanna County Public Schools	Palmyra
76	51.0	Halifax County Public Schools	Halifax
76	51.0	Portsmouth City Public Schools	Portsmouth
79	50.9	Alexandria City Public Schools	Alexandria
79	50.9	Franklin County Public Schools	Rocky Mount
79	50.9	Giles County Public Schools	Pearisburg
79	50.9	Wythe County Public Schools	Wytheville
83	50.8	Bristol City Public Schools	Bristol
83	50.8	Lynchburg City Public Schools	Lynchburg
83	50.8	Radford City Public Schools	Radford
83	50.8	Williamsburg-James City Co PS	Williamsburg
87	50.7	Fauquier County Public Schools	Warrenton
87	50.7	Staunton City Public Schools	Staunton
89	50.6	Norfolk City Public Schools	Norfolk
89	50.6	Roanoke City Public Schools	Roanoke
89	50.6	Winchester City Public Schools	Winchester
92	50.5	Culpeper County Public Schools	Culpeper
92	50.5	Newport News City Public Schools	Newport News
92	50.5	Washington County Public Schools	Abingdon
95	50.4	Henry County Public Schools	Collinsville
95	50.4	Petersburg City Public Schools	Petersburg
97	50.2	Charlotte County Public Schools	Charlotte Ct Hse
97	50.2	Grayson County Public Schools	Independence
97	50.2	Page County Public Schools	Luray
100	50.1	Fredericksburg City Public Schools	Fredericksburg
100	50.1	Northampton County Public Schools	Machipongo
100	50.1	Richmond City Public Schools	Richmond
103	50.0	Madison County Public Schools	Madison
103	50.0	Martinsville City Public Schools	Martinsville
105	49.7	Orange County Public Schools	Orange
106	49.1	Floyd County Public Schools	Floyd
107	48.9	Essex County Public Schools	Tappahannock
108	48.3	Lunenburg County Public Schools	Victoria
109	47.9	Buchanan County Public Schools	Grundy
110	47.0	Russell County Public Schools	Lebanon
111	n/a	Virginia-New York District	Quantico

Female Students

Rank	Percent	District Name	City
1	53.0	Russell County Public Schools	Lebanon
2	52.1	Buchanan County Public Schools	Grundy
3	51.7	Lunenburg County Public Schools	Victoria
4	51.1	Essex County Public Schools	Tappahannock
5	50.9	Floyd County Public Schools	Floyd
6	50.3	Orange County Public Schools	Orange
7	50.0	Madison County Public Schools	Madison
7	50.0	Martinsville City Public Schools	Martinsville
9	49.9	Fredericksburg City Public Schools	Fredericksburg
9	49.9	Northampton County Public Schools	Machipongo
9	49.9	Richmond City Public Schools	Richmond
12	49.8	Charlotte County Public Schools	Charlotte Ct Hse
12	49.8	Grayson County Public Schools	Independence
12	49.8	Page County Public Schools	Luray
15	49.6	Henry County Public Schools	Collinsville
15	49.6	Petersburg City Public Schools	Petersburg
17	49.5	Culpeper County Public Schools	Culpeper
17	49.5	Newport News City Public Schools	Newport News
17	49.5	Washington County Public Schools	Abingdon
20	49.4	Norfolk City Public Schools	Norfolk
20	49.4	Roanoke City Public Schools	Roanoke
20	49.4	Winchester City Public Schools	Winchester
23	49.3	Fauquier County Public Schools	Warrenton
23	49.3	Staunton City Public Schools	Staunton
25	49.2	Bristol City Public Schools	Bristol
25	49.2	Lynchburg City Public Schools	Lynchburg
25	49.2	Radford City Public Schools	Radford
25	49.2	Williamsburg-James City Co PS	Williamsburg
29	49.1	Alexandria City Public Schools	Alexandria
29	49.1	Franklin County Public Schools	Rocky Mount
29	49.1	Giles County Public Schools	Pearisburg
29	49.1	Wythe County Public Schools	Wytheville
33	49.0	Fluvanna County Public Schools	Palmyra
33	49.0	Halifax County Public Schools	Halifax
33	49.0	Portsmouth City Public Schools	Portsmouth
36	48.9	Albemarle County Public Schools	Charlottesville
36	48.9	Arlington County Public Schools	Arlington
36	48.9	Campbell County Public Schools	Rustburg
36	48.9	Charlottesville City Pub Schools	Charlottesville
36	48.9	Powhatan County Public Schools	Powhatan
36	48.9	Roanoke County Public Schools	Roanoke
36	48.9	Scott County Public Schools	Gate City
36	48.9	Virginia Beach City Public Schls	Virginia Beach
44	48.8	Hampton City Public Schools	Hampton
44	48.8	Hanover County Public Schools	Ashland
44	48.8	Loudoun County Public Schools	Leesburg
44	48.8	Montgomery County Public Schools	Christiansburg
44	48.8	Salem City Public Schools	Salem
44	48.8	Spotsylvania Co Public Schools	Spotsylvania
44	48.8	Suffolk City Public Schools	Suffolk
51	48.7	Frederick County Public Schools	Winchester
51	48.7	Harrisonburg City Public Schools	Harrisonburg
51	48.7	Henrico County Public Schools	Richmond
51	48.7	Prince William County Pub Schools	Manassas
51	48.7	Tazewell County Public Schools	Tazewell
51	48.7	Waynesboro City Public Schools	Waynesboro
57	48.6	Augusta County Public Schools	Fishersville
57	48.6	Chesapeake City Public Schools	Chesapeake
57	48.6	Chesterfield County Public Schools	Chesterfield
57	48.6	Danville City Public Schools	Danville
57	48.6	Gloucester County Public Schools	Gloucester
57	48.6	New Kent County Public Schools	New Kent
57	48.6	Patrick County Public Schools	Stuart
57	48.6	Warren County Public Schools	Front Royal
57	48.6	Wise County Public Schools	Wise
66	48.5	Shenandoah County Public Schools	Woodstock
66	48.5	Stafford County Public Schools	Stafford
66	48.5	York County Public Schools	Yorktown
69	48.4	Botetourt County Public Schools	Fincastle
69	48.4	Lee County Public Schools	Jonesville
69	48.4	Prince Edward County Pub Schools	Farmville
69	48.4	Smyth County Public Schools	Marion
73	48.3	Clarke County Public Schools	Berryville
73	48.3	Dickenson County Public Schools	Clintwood
73	48.3	Falls Church City Public Schools	Falls Church
73	48.3	Hopewell City Public Schools	Hopewell
73	48.3	Manassas Park City Public Schools	Manassas Park
73	48.3	Prince George County Pub Schools	Prince George
73	48.3	Rockingham County Public Schools	Harrisonburg
80	48.2	Caroline County Public Schools	Bowling Green
80	48.2	Fairfax County Public Schools	Fairfax
80	48.2	Manassas City Public Schools	Manassas
80	48.2	Pulaski County Public Schools	Pulaski
80	48.2	Westmoreland Co Public Schools	Montross
85	48.1	Mecklenburg County Public Schools	Boydton
86	48.0	Accomack County Public Schools	Accomac
86	48.0	Amherst County Public Schools	Amherst
86	48.0	Bedford County Public Schools	Bedford
86	48.0	Buckingham County Public Schools	Buckingham
86	48.0	Greene County Public Schools	Standardsville
86	48.0	Nelson County Public Schools	Lovingston
86	48.0	Pittsylvania County Public Schools	Chatham
93	47.8	Appomattox County Public Schools	Appomattox
93	47.8	Dinwiddie County Public Schools	Dinwiddie
93	47.8	King George County Public Schools	King George

Rank	Percent	District Name	City
96	47.7	Greensville County Public Schools	Emporia
96	47.7	Isle of Wight County Pub Schools	Isle Of Wight
96	47.7	Nottoway County Public Schools	Nottoway
99	47.6	Alleghany County Public Schools	Covington
99	47.6	Brunswick County Public Schools	Lawrenceville
99	47.6	Rockbridge County Public Schools	Lexington
102	47.5	Goochland County Public Schools	Goochland
102	47.5	King William County Public Schools	King William
104	47.3	Amelia County Public Schools	Amelia
105	47.2	Louisa County Public Schools	Mineral
106	47.1	Colonial Heights City Pub Schools	Colonial Hgts
106	47.1	Poquoson City Public Schools	Poquoson
108	47.0	Southampton County Public Schools	Courtland
109	46.5	Carroll County Public Schools	Hillsville
110	46.3	Lancaster County Public Schools	Kilmarnock
111	n/a	Virginia-New York District	Quantico

Individual Education Program Students

Rank	Percent	District Name	City
1	20.4	Halifax County Public Schools	Halifax
2	20.2	Lee County Public Schools	Jonesville
3	19.7	Greene County Public Schools	Standardsville
4	19.5	Essex County Public Schools	Tappahannock
5	19.2	Winchester City Public Schools	Winchester
6	18.7	Floyd County Public Schools	Floyd
6	18.7	Henry County Public Schools	Collinsville
8	18.6	Carroll County Public Schools	Hillsville
8	18.6	Goochland County Public Schools	Goochland
8	18.6	New Kent County Public Schools	New Kent
11	18.4	Bristol City Public Schools	Bristol
11	18.4	Nottoway County Public Schools	Nottoway
11	18.4	Prince Edward County Pub Schools	Farmville
14	18.3	Hopewell City Public Schools	Hopewell
15	18.2	Franklin County Public Schools	Rocky Mount
15	18.2	Lunenburg County Public Schools	Victoria
17	18.1	Charlottesville City Pub Schools	Charlottesville
18	17.9	Buchanan County Public Schools	Grundy
18	17.9	Pulaski County Public Schools	Pulaski
18	17.9	Smyth County Public Schools	Marion
21	17.8	Botetourt County Public Schools	Fincastle
22	17.7	King William County Public Schools	King William
23	17.6	Alexandria City Public Schools	Alexandria
24	17.3	Chesapeake City Public Schools	Chesapeake
24	17.3	Scott County Public Schools	Gate City
24	17.3	Southampton County Public Schools	Courtland
24	17.3	Staunton City Public Schools	Staunton
28	17.1	Amelia County Public Schools	Amelia
28	17.1	Harrisonburg City Public Schools	Harrisonburg
28	17.1	Patrick County Public Schools	Stuart
31	17.0	Greensville County Public Schools	Emporia
31	17.0	Nelson County Public Schools	Lovingston
31	17.0	Roanoke County Public Schools	Roanoke
31	17.0	Russell County Public Schools	Lebanon
35	16.8	Arlington County Public Schools	Arlington
36	16.5	Albemarle County Public Schools	Charlottesville
36	16.5	Alleghany County Public Schools	Covington
38	16.4	Roanoke City Public Schools	Roanoke
39	16.1	Falls Church City Public Schools	Falls Church
39	16.1	Richmond City Public Schools	Richmond
41	15.9	Mecklenburg County Public Schools	Boydton
41	15.9	Powhatan County Public Schools	Powhatan
43	15.8	Madison County Public Schools	Madison
44	15.7	Dickenson County Public Schools	Clintwood
45	15.6	King George County Public Schools	King George
46	15.5	Appomattox County Public Schools	Appomattox
47	15.3	Frederick County Public Schools	Winchester
47	15.3	Lynchburg City Public Schools	Lynchburg
49	15.1	Buckingham County Public Schools	Buckingham
49	15.1	Tazewell County Public Schools	Tazewell
51	15.0	Colonial Heights City Pub Schools	Colonial Hgts
51	15.0	Warren County Public Schools	Front Royal
53	14.8	Fredericksburg City Public Schools	Fredericksburg
53	14.8	Hanover County Public Schools	Ashland
55	14.7	Chesterfield County Public Schools	Chesterfield
55	14.7	Martinsville City Public Schools	Martinsville
55	14.7	Spotsylvania Co Public Schools	Spotsylvania
58	14.6	Fluvanna County Public Schools	Palmyra
58	14.6	Orange County Public Schools	Orange
58	14.6	Rockbridge County Public Schools	Lexington
58	14.6	Wise County Public Schools	Wise
62	14.5	Augusta County Public Schools	Fishersville
63	14.2	Fairfax County Public Schools	Fairfax
63	14.2	Northampton County Public Schools	Machipongo
63	14.2	Portsmouth City Public Schools	Portsmouth
66	14.0	Grayson County Public Schools	Independence
66	14.0	Shenandoah County Public Schools	Woodstock
68	13.9	Henrico County Public Schools	Richmond
68	13.9	Petersburg City Public Schools	Petersburg
70	13.8	Louisa County Public Schools	Mineral
71	13.7	Hampton City Public Schools	Hampton
71	13.7	Isle of Wight County Pub Schools	Isle Of Wight
71	13.7	Virginia Beach City Public Schls	Virginia Beach
74	13.6	Norfolk City Public Schools	Norfolk
75	13.5	Charlotte County Public Schools	Charlotte Ct Hse
75	13.5	Manassas Park City Public Schools	Manassas Park
75	13.5	Montgomery County Public Schools	Christiansburg
78	13.4	Fauquier County Public Schools	Warrenton
79	13.2	Pittsylvania County Public Schools	Chatham
79	13.2	Radford City Public Schools	Radford
81	13.1	Bedford County Public Schools	Bedford
82	13.0	Newport News City Public Schools	Newport News
83	12.9	Washington County Public Schools	Abingdon
83	12.9	Williamsburg-James City Co PS	Williamsburg
85	12.8	Danville City Public Schools	Danville
85	12.8	Dinwiddie County Public Schools	Dinwiddie
85	12.8	Rockingham County Public Schools	Harrisonburg
88	12.7	Caroline County Public Schools	Bowling Green
89	12.5	Accomack County Public Schools	Accomac
90	12.3	Brunswick County Public Schools	Lawrenceville
90	12.3	Giles County Public Schools	Pearisburg
90	12.3	Suffolk City Public Schools	Suffolk
93	12.1	Amherst County Public Schools	Amherst
93	12.1	Gloucester County Public Schools	Gloucester
95	12.0	Page County Public Schools	Luray
95	12.0	Prince William County Pub Schools	Manassas
95	12.0	Salem City Public Schools	Salem
98	11.9	Campbell County Public Schools	Rustburg
98	11.9	Wythe County Public Schools	Wytheville
100	11.7	Manassas City Public Schools	Manassas
101	11.6	Lancaster County Public Schools	Kilmarnock
101	11.6	Westmoreland Co Public Schools	Montross
103	11.5	Culpeper County Public Schools	Culpeper
104	11.4	Waynesboro City Public Schools	Waynesboro
105	11.0	Loudoun County Public Schools	Leesburg
106	10.9	Prince George County Pub Schools	Prince George
107	10.8	Poquoson City Public Schools	Poquoson
108	10.7	Stafford County Public Schools	Stafford
109	10.5	Clarke County Public Schools	Berryville
110	9.5	York County Public Schools	Yorktown
111	9.0	Virginia-New York District	Quantico

English Language Learner Students

Rank	Percent	District Name	City
1	29.9	Harrisonburg City Public Schools	Harrisonburg
2	26.1	Arlington County Public Schools	Arlington
3	22.0	Alexandria City Public Schools	Alexandria
4	21.2	Manassas Park City Public Schools	Manassas Park
5	17.7	Manassas City Public Schools	Manassas
6	12.9	Fairfax County Public Schools	Fairfax
7	10.2	Winchester City Public Schools	Winchester
8	9.1	Prince William County Pub Schools	Manassas
9	6.9	Accomack County Public Schools	Accomac
10	6.5	Falls Church City Public Schools	Falls Church
11	5.6	Rockingham County Public Schools	Harrisonburg
12	5.5	Northampton County Public Schools	Machipongo
13	5.0	Albemarle County Public Schools	Charlottesville
14	4.7	Loudoun County Public Schools	Leesburg
15	3.8	Fredericksburg City Public Schools	Fredericksburg
16	3.4	Charlottesville City Pub Schools	Charlottesville
17	3.3	Henry County Public Schools	Collinsville
18	3.1	Henrico County Public Schools	Richmond
19	3.0	Patrick County Public Schools	Stuart
19	3.0	Roanoke City Public Schools	Roanoke
21	2.7	Martinsville City Public Schools	Martinsville
21	2.7	Westmoreland Co Public Schools	Montross
23	2.4	Danville City Public Schools	Danville
24	2.3	Chesterfield County Public Schools	Chesterfield
25	2.1	Frederick County Public Schools	Winchester
25	2.1	Waynesboro City Public Schools	Waynesboro
27	2.0	Shenandoah County Public Schools	Woodstock
28	1.9	Nelson County Public Schools	Lovingston
29	1.7	Colonial Heights City Pub Schools	Colonial Hgts
29	1.7	Floyd County Public Schools	Floyd
31	1.6	Richmond City Public Schools	Richmond
32	1.5	Montgomery County Public Schools	Christiansburg
33	1.4	Fauquier County Public Schools	Warrenton
34	1.3	Spotsylvania Co Public Schools	Spotsylvania
35	1.2	Culpeper County Public Schools	Culpeper
35	1.2	Hampton City Public Schools	Hampton
35	1.2	Pittsylvania County Public Schools	Chatham
38	1.1	Radford City Public Schools	Radford
38	1.1	Roanoke County Public Schools	Roanoke
38	1.1	Stafford County Public Schools	Stafford
38	1.1	Virginia Beach City Public Schls	Virginia Beach
42	1.0	Carroll County Public Schools	Hillsville
42	1.0	Nottoway County Public Schools	Nottoway
42	1.0	York County Public Schools	Yorktown
45	0.9	Augusta County Public Schools	Fishersville
46	0.8	Clarke County Public Schools	Berryville
46	0.8	Dinwiddie County Public Schools	Dinwiddie
46	0.8	Hopewell City Public Schools	Hopewell
46	0.8	Virginia-New York District	Quantico
50	0.7	Bristol City Public Schools	Bristol
50	0.7	Franklin County Public Schools	Rocky Mount
50	0.7	Greene County Public Schools	Standardsville
50	0.7	Lynchburg City Public Schools	Lynchburg
50	0.7	Newport News City Public Schools	Newport News
50	0.7	Pulaski County Public Schools	Pulaski
50	0.7	Warren County Public Schools	Front Royal
57	0.6	Chesapeake City Public Schools	Chesapeake
57	0.6	Hanover County Public Schools	Ashland
57	0.6	Mecklenburg County Public Schools	Boydton
57	0.6	Petersburg City Public Schools	Petersburg
57	0.6	Williamsburg-James City Co PS	Williamsburg
62	0.5	Orange County Public Schools	Orange
62	0.5	Page County Public Schools	Luray
62	0.5	Salem City Public Schools	Salem
62	0.5	Smyth County Public Schools	Marion
66	0.4	Buckingham County Public Schools	Buckingham
66	0.4	Caroline County Public Schools	Bowling Green
66	0.4	Greensville County Public Schools	Emporia
66	0.4	Prince George County Pub Schools	Prince George
66	0.4	Staunton City Public Schools	Staunton
71	0.3	Campbell County Public Schools	Rustburg
71	0.3	Fluvanna County Public Schools	Palmyra
71	0.3	Grayson County Public Schools	Independence
71	0.3	Halifax County Public Schools	Halifax
71	0.3	Lunenburg County Public Schools	Victoria
71	0.3	New Kent County Public Schools	New Kent
71	0.3	Rockbridge County Public Schools	Lexington
71	0.3	Wise County Public Schools	Wise
79	0.2	Alleghany County Public Schools	Covington
79	0.2	Amherst County Public Schools	Amherst
79	0.2	Appomattox County Public Schools	Appomattox
79	0.2	Bedford County Public Schools	Bedford
79	0.2	Botetourt County Public Schools	Fincastle
79	0.2	Charlotte County Public Schools	Charlotte Ct Hse
79	0.2	Giles County Public Schools	Pearisburg
79	0.2	Isle of Wight County Pub Schools	Isle Of Wight
79	0.2	Louisa County Public Schools	Mineral
79	0.2	Madison County Public Schools	Madison
79	0.2	Norfolk City Public Schools	Norfolk
90	0.1	Amelia County Public Schools	Amelia
90	0.1	Brunswick County Public Schools	Lawrenceville
90	0.1	King William County Public Schools	King William
90	0.1	Lee County Public Schools	Jonesville
90	0.1	Poquoson City Public Schools	Poquoson
90	0.1	Portsmouth City Public Schools	Portsmouth
90	0.1	Powhatan County Public Schools	Powhatan
90	0.1	Prince Edward County Pub Schools	Farmville
90	0.1	Scott County Public Schools	Gate City
90	0.1	Southampton County Public Schools	Courtland
90	0.1	Suffolk City Public Schools	Suffolk
90	0.1	Washington County Public Schools	Abingdon
102	0.0	King George County Public Schools	King George
102	0.0	Tazewell County Public Schools	Tazewell
102	0.0	Wythe County Public Schools	Wytheville
105	0.0	Goochland County Public Schools	Goochland
106	n/a	Buchanan County Public Schools	Grundy
106	n/a	Dickenson County Public Schools	Clintwood
106	n/a	Essex County Public Schools	Tappahannock
106	n/a	Gloucester County Public Schools	Gloucester
106	n/a	Lancaster County Public Schools	Kilmarnock
106	n/a	Russell County Public Schools	Lebanon

Migrant Students

Rank	Percent	District Name	City
1	6.0	Westmoreland Co Public Schools	Montross
2	4.4	Northampton County Public Schools	Machipongo
3	3.1	Accomack County Public Schools	Accomac
4	2.7	Harrisonburg City Public Schools	Harrisonburg
5	2.6	Shenandoah County Public Schools	Woodstock
6	1.6	Winchester City Public Schools	Winchester
7	1.1	Carroll County Public Schools	Hillsville
7	1.1	Rockingham County Public Schools	Harrisonburg
9	0.9	Waynesboro City Public Schools	Waynesboro
10	0.7	Nottoway County Public Schools	Nottoway
11	0.6	Frederick County Public Schools	Winchester
12	0.5	Nelson County Public Schools	Lovingston
12	0.5	Page County Public Schools	Luray
12	0.5	Pittsylvania County Public Schools	Chatham
15	0.4	Albemarle County Public Schools	Charlottesville
15	0.4	Floyd County Public Schools	Floyd
15	0.4	Grayson County Public Schools	Independence
15	0.4	Madison County Public Schools	Madison
19	0.3	Patrick County Public Schools	Stuart
20	0.2	Lunenburg County Public Schools	Victoria
21	0.1	Augusta County Public Schools	Fishersville
21	0.1	Charlottesville City Pub Schools	Charlottesville
21	0.1	Clarke County Public Schools	Berryville
21	0.1	Prince Edward County Pub Schools	Farmville
21	0.1	Pulaski County Public Schools	Pulaski
21	0.1	Rockbridge County Public Schools	Lexington
27	0.0	Culpeper County Public Schools	Culpeper
27	0.0	Orange County Public Schools	Orange
27	0.0	Russell County Public Schools	Lebanon

Rank	Percent	District Name	City
27	0.0	Warren County Public Schools	Front Royal
31	0.0	Alexandria City Public Schools	Alexandria
31	0.0	Alleghany County Public Schools	Covington
31	0.0	Amelia County Public Schools	Amelia
31	0.0	Amherst County Public Schools	Amherst
31	0.0	Appomattox County Public Schools	Appomattox
31	0.0	Arlington County Public Schools	Arlington
31	0.0	Bedford County Public Schools	Bedford
31	0.0	Botetourt County Public Schools	Fincastle
31	0.0	Bristol City Public Schools	Bristol
31	0.0	Brunswick County Public Schools	Lawrenceville
31	0.0	Buchanan County Public Schools	Grundy
31	0.0	Buckingham County Public Schools	Buckingham
31	0.0	Campbell County Public Schools	Rustburg
31	0.0	Caroline County Public Schools	Bowling Green
31	0.0	Charlotte County Public Schools	Charlotte Ct Hse
31	0.0	Chesapeake City Public Schools	Chesapeake
31	0.0	Chesterfield County Public Schools	Chesterfield
31	0.0	Colonial Heights City Pub Schools	Colonial Hgts
31	0.0	Danville City Public Schools	Danville
31	0.0	Dickenson County Public Schools	Clintwood
31	0.0	Dinwiddie County Public Schools	Dinwiddie
31	0.0	Essex County Public Schools	Tappahannock
31	0.0	Fairfax County Public Schools	Fairfax
31	0.0	Falls Church City Public Schools	Falls Church
31	0.0	Fauquier County Public Schools	Warrenton
31	0.0	Fluvanna County Public Schools	Palmyra
31	0.0	Franklin County Public Schools	Rocky Mount
31	0.0	Fredericksburg City Public Schools	Fredericksburg
31	0.0	Giles County Public Schools	Pearisburg
31	0.0	Gloucester County Public Schools	Gloucester
31	0.0	Goochland County Public Schools	Goochland
31	0.0	Greene County Public Schools	Standardsville
31	0.0	Greensville County Public Schools	Emporia
31	0.0	Halifax County Public Schools	Halifax
31	0.0	Hampton City Public Schools	Hampton
31	0.0	Hanover County Public Schools	Ashland
31	0.0	Henrico County Public Schools	Richmond
31	0.0	Henry County Public Schools	Collinsville
31	0.0	Hopewell City Public Schools	Hopewell
31	0.0	Isle of Wight County Pub Schools	Isle Of Wight
31	0.0	King George County Public Schools	King George
31	0.0	King William County Public Schools	King William
31	0.0	Lancaster County Public Schools	Kilmarnock
31	0.0	Lee County Public Schools	Jonesville
31	0.0	Loudoun County Public Schools	Leesburg
31	0.0	Louisa County Public Schools	Mineral
31	0.0	Lynchburg City Public Schools	Lynchburg
31	0.0	Manassas City Public Schools	Manassas
31	0.0	Manassas Park City Public Schools	Manassas Park
31	0.0	Martinsville City Public Schools	Martinsville
31	0.0	Mecklenburg County Public Schools	Boydton
31	0.0	Montgomery County Public Schools	Christiansburg
31	0.0	New Kent County Public Schools	New Kent
31	0.0	Newport News City Public Schools	Newport News
31	0.0	Norfolk City Public Schools	Norfolk
31	0.0	Petersburg City Public Schools	Petersburg
31	0.0	Poquoson City Public Schools	Poquoson
31	0.0	Portsmouth City Public Schools	Portsmouth
31	0.0	Powhatan County Public Schools	Powhatan
31	0.0	Prince George County Pub Schools	Prince George
31	0.0	Prince William County Pub Schools	Manassas
31	0.0	Radford City Public Schools	Radford
31	0.0	Richmond City Public Schools	Richmond
31	0.0	Roanoke City Public Schools	Roanoke
31	0.0	Roanoke County Public Schools	Roanoke
31	0.0	Salem City Public Schools	Salem
31	0.0	Scott County Public Schools	Gate City
31	0.0	Smyth County Public Schools	Marion
31	0.0	Southampton County Public Schools	Courtland
31	0.0	Spotsylvania Co Public Schools	Spotsylvania
31	0.0	Stafford County Public Schools	Stafford
31	0.0	Staunton City Public Schools	Staunton
31	0.0	Suffolk City Public Schools	Suffolk
31	0.0	Tazewell County Public Schools	Tazewell
31	0.0	Virginia Beach City Public Schls	Virginia Beach
31	0.0	Washington County Public Schools	Abingdon
31	0.0	Williamsburg-James City Co PS	Williamsburg
31	0.0	Wise County Public Schools	Wise
31	0.0	Wythe County Public Schools	Wytheville
31	0.0	York County Public Schools	Yorktown
111	n/a	Virginia-New York District	Quantico

Students Eligible for Free Lunch

Rank	Percent	District Name	City
1	60.9	Petersburg City Public Schools	Petersburg
2	58.5	Richmond City Public Schools	Richmond
3	57.5	Northampton County Public Schools	Machipongo
4	53.5	Brunswick County Public Schools	Lawrenceville
5	52.8	Lunenburg County Public Schools	Victoria
6	50.5	Roanoke County Public Schools	Roanoke
7	50.1	Buchanan County Public Schools	Grundy
8	49.5	Lee County Public Schools	Jonesville
9	49.2	Danville City Public Schools	Danville
10	48.8	Accomack County Public Schools	Accomac
11	48.5	Prince Edward County Pub Schools	Farmville
12	47.8	Norfolk City Public Schools	Norfolk
13	47.7	Hopewell City Public Schools	Hopewell
14	47.6	Portsmouth City Public Schools	Portsmouth
15	46.3	Halifax County Public Schools	Halifax
16	45.2	Mecklenburg County Public Schools	Boydton
17	45.1	Greensville County Public Schools	Emporia
18	44.1	Martinsville City Public Schools	Martinsville
19	43.7	Fredericksburg City Public Schools	Fredericksburg
20	42.9	Westmoreland Co Public Schools	Montross
21	42.8	Dickenson County Public Schools	Clintwood
22	42.0	Buckingham County Public Schools	Buckingham
23	41.7	Nottoway County Public Schools	Nottoway
24	41.0	Lynchburg City Public Schools	Lynchburg
25	40.9	Bristol City Public Schools	Bristol
25	40.9	Lancaster County Public Schools	Kilmarnock
27	39.9	Wise County Public Schools	Wise
28	38.8	Charlottesville City Pub Schools	Charlottesville
29	38.6	Tazewell County Public Schools	Tazewell
30	38.2	Grayson County Public Schools	Independence
31	38.0	Alexandria City Public Schools	Alexandria
32	37.0	Russell County Public Schools	Lebanon
33	36.8	Charlotte County Public Schools	Charlotte Ct Hse
33	36.8	Harrisonburg City Public Schools	Harrisonburg
35	36.4	Newport News City Public Schools	Newport News
36	36.1	Scott County Public Schools	Gate City
37	34.6	Essex County Public Schools	Tappahannock
38	34.1	Carroll County Public Schools	Hillsville
38	34.1	Smyth County Public Schools	Marion
40	33.4	Patrick County Public Schools	Stuart
41	33.2	Waynesboro City Public Schools	Waynesboro
42	32.7	Henry County Public Schools	Collinsville
42	32.7	Southampton County Public Schools	Courtland
42	32.7	Staunton City Public Schools	Staunton
45	32.4	Suffolk City Public Schools	Suffolk
46	31.5	Hampton City Public Schools	Hampton
47	29.0	Appomattox County Public Schools	Appomattox
47	29.0	Pulaski County Public Schools	Pulaski
49	28.8	Wythe County Public Schools	Wytheville
50	28.7	Arlington County Public Schools	Arlington
50	28.7	Caroline County Public Schools	Bowling Green
52	28.6	Pittsylvania County Public Schools	Chatham
52	28.6	Washington County Public Schools	Abingdon
54	28.5	Franklin County Public Schools	Rocky Mount
55	28.0	Winchester City Public Schools	Winchester
56	27.8	Nelson County Public Schools	Lovingston
57	27.0	Dinwiddie County Public Schools	Dinwiddie
58	26.5	Page County Public Schools	Luray
59	26.2	Amherst County Public Schools	Amherst
60	26.1	Isle of Wight County Pub Schools	Isle Of Wight
61	25.3	Alleghany County Public Schools	Covington
62	25.2	Louisa County Public Schools	Mineral
63	25.0	Amelia County Public Schools	Amelia
64	23.6	Floyd County Public Schools	Floyd
65	23.2	Montgomery County Public Schools	Christiansburg
66	22.6	Campbell County Public Schools	Rustburg
67	22.2	Manassas Park City Public Schools	Manassas Park
68	21.5	Giles County Public Schools	Pearisburg
69	21.4	Rockbridge County Public Schools	Lexington
70	20.9	Orange County Public Schools	Orange
71	19.5	Radford City Public Schools	Radford
72	19.2	Bedford County Public Schools	Bedford
72	19.2	Virginia Beach City Public Schls	Virginia Beach
74	18.8	Chesapeake City Public Schools	Chesapeake
75	18.2	King William County Public Schools	King William
75	18.2	Warren County Public Schools	Front Royal
77	18.0	King George County Public Schools	King George
78	17.9	Rockingham County Public Schools	Harrisonburg
79	17.7	Prince William County Pub Schools	Manassas
79	17.7	Shenandoah County Public Schools	Woodstock
81	17.4	Augusta County Public Schools	Fishersville
81	17.4	Greene County Public Schools	Standardsville
83	16.9	Madison County Public Schools	Madison
84	15.4	Prince George County Pub Schools	Prince George
85	14.5	Culpeper County Public Schools	Culpeper
86	14.2	Manassas City Public Schools	Manassas
87	13.5	Goochland County Public Schools	Goochland
87	13.5	Williamsburg-James City Co PS	Williamsburg
89	13.3	Albemarle County Public Schools	Charlottesville
89	13.3	Henrico County Public Schools	Richmond
91	12.9	Gloucester County Public Schools	Gloucester
92	12.8	Salem City Public Schools	Salem
93	12.7	Fairfax County Public Schools	Fairfax
94	12.3	Fluvanna County Public Schools	Palmyra
95	12.0	Spotsylvania Co Public Schools	Spotsylvania
96	11.3	Frederick County Public Schools	Winchester
97	11.2	Fauquier County Public Schools	Warrenton
98	11.1	New Kent County Public Schools	New Kent
99	10.7	Chesterfield County Public Schools	Chesterfield
100	10.5	Clarke County Public Schools	Berryville
101	9.8	Colonial Heights City Pub Schools	Colonial Hgts
102	9.4	Stafford County Public Schools	Stafford
103	9.3	Botetourt County Public Schools	Fincastle
104	8.6	Powhatan County Public Schools	Powhatan
105	8.5	Roanoke County Public Schools	Roanoke
106	7.4	York County Public Schools	Yorktown
107	6.6	Loudoun County Public Schools	Leesburg
108	6.1	Hanover County Public Schools	Ashland
109	5.1	Falls Church City Public Schools	Falls Church
110	2.9	Poquoson City Public Schools	Poquoson
111	n/a	Virginia-New York District	Quantico

Students Eligible for Reduced-Price Lunch

Rank	Percent	District Name	City
1	14.7	Buchanan County Public Schools	Grundy
2	14.0	Dickenson County Public Schools	Clintwood
3	13.9	Grayson County Public Schools	Independence
4	13.0	Carroll County Public Schools	Hillsville
5	12.5	Charlotte County Public Schools	Charlotte Ct Hse
6	12.3	Norfolk City Public Schools	Norfolk
7	11.3	Buckingham County Public Schools	Buckingham
7	11.3	Virginia Beach City Public Schls	Virginia Beach
9	11.2	Prince Edward County Pub Schools	Farmville
10	11.1	Essex County Public Schools	Tappahannock
10	11.1	Mecklenburg County Public Schools	Boydton
12	10.9	Brunswick County Public Schools	Lawrenceville
13	10.8	Halifax County Public Schools	Halifax
14	10.7	Lee County Public Schools	Jonesville
14	10.7	Scott County Public Schools	Gate City
16	10.5	Hopewell City Public Schools	Hopewell
17	10.4	Lunenburg County Public Schools	Victoria
18	10.2	Nottoway County Public Schools	Nottoway
19	10.1	Alexandria City Public Schools	Alexandria
20	10.0	Accomack County Public Schools	Accomac
20	10.0	Floyd County Public Schools	Floyd
22	9.8	Newport News City Public Schools	Newport News
23	9.4	Wythe County Public Schools	Wytheville
24	9.3	Petersburg City Public Schools	Petersburg
24	9.3	Russell County Public Schools	Lebanon
24	9.3	Westmoreland Co Public Schools	Montross
27	9.2	Amelia County Public Schools	Amelia
28	9.1	Greensville County Public Schools	Emporia
28	9.1	Smyth County Public Schools	Marion
28	9.1	Tazewell County Public Schools	Tazewell
31	9.0	Hampton City Public Schools	Hampton
31	9.0	Louisa County Public Schools	Mineral
31	9.0	Washington County Public Schools	Abingdon
34	8.9	Northampton County Public Schools	Machipongo
35	8.8	Manassas Park City Public Schools	Manassas Park
35	8.8	Portsmouth City Public Schools	Portsmouth
37	8.7	Arlington County Public Schools	Arlington
37	8.7	Caroline County Public Schools	Bowling Green
37	8.7	Giles County Public Schools	Pearisburg
40	8.6	Lancaster County Public Schools	Kilmarnock
41	8.4	Waynesboro City Public Schools	Waynesboro
42	8.3	Nelson County Public Schools	Lovingston
42	8.3	Southampton County Public Schools	Courtland
42	8.3	Staunton City Public Schools	Staunton
45	8.2	Page County Public Schools	Luray
45	8.2	Rockbridge County Public Schools	Lexington
47	8.1	Harrisonburg City Public Schools	Harrisonburg
48	8.0	Dinwiddie County Public Schools	Dinwiddie
48	8.0	Roanoke City Public Schools	Roanoke
48	8.0	Rockingham County Public Schools	Harrisonburg
48	8.0	Suffolk City Public Schools	Suffolk
48	8.0	Winchester City Public Schools	Winchester
53	7.9	Alleghany County Public Schools	Covington
53	7.9	Martinsville City Public Schools	Martinsville
53	7.9	Richmond City Public Schools	Richmond
56	7.8	Montgomery County Public Schools	Christiansburg
56	7.8	Pulaski County Public Schools	Pulaski
56	7.8	Wise County Public Schools	Wise
59	7.7	Campbell County Public Schools	Rustburg
59	7.7	Franklin County Public Schools	Rocky Mount
61	7.6	Patrick County Public Schools	Stuart
62	7.5	Bedford County Public Schools	Bedford
62	7.5	Charlottesville City Pub Schools	Charlottesville
64	7.4	Appomattox County Public Schools	Appomattox
65	7.3	Augusta County Public Schools	Fishersville
65	7.3	Pittsylvania County Public Schools	Chatham
65	7.3	Prince George County Pub Schools	Prince George
68	7.0	Greene County Public Schools	Standardsville
69	6.8	Fredericksburg City Public Schools	Fredericksburg
69	6.8	Goochland County Public Schools	Goochland
71	6.7	Amherst County Public Schools	Amherst
71	6.7	Henry County Public Schools	Collinsville
71	6.7	Prince William County Pub Schools	Manassas
71	6.7	Shenandoah County Public Schools	Woodstock
75	6.6	Bristol City Public Schools	Bristol
76	6.5	Danville City Public Schools	Danville

Rank	Value	District Name	City
77	6.3	King William County Public Schools	King William
78	6.2	Orange County Public Schools	Orange
78	6.2	York County Public Schools	Yorktown
80	6.0	Manassas City Public Schools	Manassas
81	5.8	Isle of Wight County Pub Schools	Isle Of Wight
82	5.7	Fairfax County Public Schools	Fairfax
83	5.4	Chesapeake City Public Schools	Chesapeake
84	5.3	Salem City Public Schools	Salem
85	5.2	Culpeper County Public Schools	Culpeper
86	4.9	Albemarle County Public Schools	Charlottesville
86	4.9	Gloucester County Public Schools	Gloucester
88	4.8	Lynchburg City Public Schools	Lynchburg
89	4.6	Fluvanna County Public Schools	Palmyra
89	4.6	Spotsylvania Co Public Schools	Spotsylvania
91	4.5	Frederick County Public Schools	Winchester
92	4.4	Colonial Heights City Pub Schools	Colonial Hgts
93	4.3	Williamsburg-James City Co PS	Williamsburg
94	4.2	Madison County Public Schools	Madison
95	4.1	King George County Public Schools	King George
96	4.0	Henrico County Public Schools	Richmond
96	4.0	Roanoke County Public Schools	Roanoke
96	4.0	Warren County Public Schools	Front Royal
99	3.9	Chesterfield County Public Schools	Chesterfield
100	3.6	Loudoun County Public Schools	Leesburg
101	3.5	Stafford County Public Schools	Stafford
102	3.4	Falls Church City Public Schools	Falls Church
102	3.4	Fauquier County Public Schools	Warrenton
104	3.3	Botetourt County Public Schools	Fincastle
104	3.3	Powhatan County Public Schools	Powhatan
106	3.2	Radford City Public Schools	Radford
107	3.0	New Kent County Public Schools	New Kent
108	2.8	Clarke County Public Schools	Berryville
109	1.9	Hanover County Public Schools	Ashland
110	1.7	Poquoson City Public Schools	Poquoson
111	n/a	Virginia-New York District	Quantico

Student/Teacher Ratio

Rank	Ratio	District Name	City
1	23.3	Greene County Public Schools	Standardsville
2	14.6	Prince William County Pub Schools	Manassas
3	14.2	Virginia Beach City Public Schls	Virginia Beach
4	13.6	Chesapeake City Public Schools	Chesapeake
4	13.6	King George County Public Schools	King George
6	13.4	Chesterfield County Public Schools	Chesterfield
7	13.3	Stafford County Public Schools	Stafford
7	13.3	Washington County Public Schools	Abingdon
9	13.1	Warren County Public Schools	Front Royal
10	13.0	Henrico County Public Schools	Richmond
10	13.0	Isle of Wight County Pub Schools	Isle Of Wight
12	12.9	Caroline County Public Schools	Bowling Green
13	12.8	Floyd County Public Schools	Floyd
14	12.7	Prince George County Pub Schools	Prince George
15	12.6	Mecklenburg County Public Schools	Boydton
15	12.6	Suffolk City Public Schools	Suffolk
15	12.6	York County Public Schools	Yorktown
18	12.2	Gloucester County Public Schools	Gloucester
18	12.2	Newport News City Public Schools	Newport News
20	12.1	Augusta County Public Schools	Fishersville
20	12.1	Charlotte County Public Schools	Charlotte Ct Hse
20	12.1	Portsmouth City Public Schools	Portsmouth
23	12.0	Amelia County Public Schools	Amelia
23	12.0	Louisa County Public Schools	Mineral
23	12.0	Manassas City Public Schools	Manassas
23	12.0	Petersburg City Public Schools	Petersburg
23	12.0	Poquoson City Public Schools	Poquoson
23	12.0	Southampton County Public Schools	Courtland
29	11.9	Bedford County Public Schools	Bedford
29	11.9	Dinwiddie County Public Schools	Dinwiddie
29	11.9	Giles County Public Schools	Pearisburg
32	11.8	Frederick County Public Schools	Winchester
32	11.8	Salem City Public Schools	Salem
32	11.8	Spotsylvania Co Public Schools	Spotsylvania
35	11.7	Campbell County Public Schools	Rustburg
35	11.7	Fairfax County Public Schools	Fairfax
35	11.7	Franklin County Public Schools	Rocky Mount
35	11.7	Hanover County Public Schools	Ashland
35	11.7	Loudoun County Public Schools	Leesburg
35	11.7	Waynesboro City Public Schools	Waynesboro
41	11.6	Page County Public Schools	Luray
41	11.6	Radford City Public Schools	Radford
43	11.5	Culpeper County Public Schools	Culpeper
43	11.5	Hampton City Public Schools	Hampton
43	11.5	Patrick County Public Schools	Stuart
43	11.5	Prince Edward County Pub Schools	Farmville
43	11.5	Wythe County Public Schools	Wytheville
48	11.4	Accomack County Public Schools	Accomac
48	11.4	Appomattox County Public Schools	Appomattox
48	11.4	Pittsylvania County Public Schools	Chatham
48	11.4	Russell County Public Schools	Lebanon
48	11.4	Virginia-New York District	Quantico
48	11.4	Westmoreland Co Public Schools	Montross
54	11.3	Fauquier County Public Schools	Warrenton
55	11.2	Fluvanna County Public Schools	Palmyra
55	11.2	Greensville County Public Schools	Emporia
55	11.2	Nottoway County Public Schools	Nottoway
55	11.2	Pulaski County Public Schools	Pulaski
59	11.1	Botetourt County Public Schools	Fincastle
59	11.1	Lynchburg City Public Schools	Lynchburg
59	11.1	Manassas Park City Public Schools	Manassas Park
59	11.1	New Kent County Public Schools	New Kent
59	11.1	Richmond City Public Schools	Richmond
59	11.1	Tazewell County Public Schools	Tazewell
65	11.0	Rockingham County Public Schools	Harrisonburg
66	10.9	Alleghany County Public Schools	Covington
66	10.9	Buckingham County Public Schools	Buckingham
66	10.9	King William County Public Schools	King William
66	10.9	Norfolk City Public Schools	Norfolk
66	10.9	Powhatan County Public Schools	Powhatan
71	10.8	Amherst County Public Schools	Amherst
71	10.8	Danville City Public Schools	Danville
71	10.8	Fredericksburg City Public Schools	Fredericksburg
71	10.8	Orange County Public Schools	Orange
71	10.8	Scott County Public Schools	Gate City
76	10.7	Henry County Public Schools	Collinsville
76	10.7	Shenandoah County Public Schools	Woodstock
78	10.6	Martinsville City Public Schools	Martinsville
78	10.6	Williamsburg-James City Co PS	Williamsburg
80	10.5	Brunswick County Public Schools	Lawrenceville
80	10.5	Clarke County Public Schools	Berryville
80	10.5	Colonial Heights City Pub Schools	Colonial Hgts
80	10.5	Nelson County Public Schools	Lovingston
84	10.4	Albemarle County Public Schools	Charlottesville
84	10.4	Bristol City Public Schools	Bristol
84	10.4	Essex County Public Schools	Tappahannock
84	10.4	Hopewell City Public Schools	Hopewell
84	10.4	Madison County Public Schools	Madison
89	10.3	Lancaster County Public Schools	Kilmarnock
89	10.3	Northampton County Public Schools	Machipongo
89	10.3	Roanoke County Public Schools	Roanoke
89	10.3	Winchester City Public Schools	Winchester
93	10.2	Buchanan County Public Schools	Grundy
93	10.2	Halifax County Public Schools	Halifax
93	10.2	Lunenburg County Public Schools	Victoria
93	10.2	Roanoke City Public Schools	Roanoke
93	10.2	Wise County Public Schools	Wise
98	10.1	Montgomery County Public Schools	Christiansburg
99	9.9	Goochland County Public Schools	Goochland
99	9.9	Grayson County Public Schools	Independence
99	9.9	Rockbridge County Public Schools	Lexington
102	9.7	Falls Church City Public Schools	Falls Church
102	9.7	Harrisonburg City Public Schools	Harrisonburg
104	9.6	Charlottesville City Pub Schools	Charlottesville
105	9.4	Carroll County Public Schools	Hillsville
106	9.3	Smyth County Public Schools	Marion
106	9.3	Staunton City Public Schools	Staunton
108	9.0	Alexandria City Public Schools	Alexandria
108	9.0	Lee County Public Schools	Jonesville
110	8.9	Arlington County Public Schools	Arlington
111	8.3	Dickenson County Public Schools	Clintwood

Student/Librarian Ratio

Rank	Ratio	District Name	City
1	13,068.0	Richmond City Public Schools	Richmond
2	5,040.0	Isle of Wight County Pub Schools	Isle Of Wight
3	1,524.0	King George County Public Schools	King George
4	1,352.5	Greene County Public Schools	Standardsville
5	1,060.9	Newport News City Public Schools	Newport News
6	976.5	Prince William County Pub Schools	Manassas
7	932.7	Prince Edward County Pub Schools	Farmville
8	840.5	Chesterfield County Public Schools	Chesterfield
9	805.7	Fredericksburg City Public Schools	Fredericksburg
10	782.6	Hopewell City Public Schools	Hopewell
11	775.7	Manassas Park City Public Schools	Manassas Park
12	774.3	Stafford County Public Schools	Stafford
13	766.4	Powhatan County Public Schools	Powhatan
14	754.6	Culpeper County Public Schools	Culpeper
15	717.2	Fairfax County Public Schools	Fairfax
16	713.0	Spotsylvania Co Public Schools	Spotsylvania
17	711.6	Augusta County Public Schools	Fishersville
18	708.0	Winchester City Public Schools	Winchester
19	702.4	Manassas City Public Schools	Manassas
20	681.6	Campbell County Public Schools	Rustburg
21	675.5	Hanover County Public Schools	Ashland
22	662.3	York County Public Schools	Yorktown
23	652.3	King William County Public Schools	King William
24	652.1	Washington County Public Schools	Abingdon
25	645.2	Frederick County Public Schools	Winchester
26	633.3	Gloucester County Public Schools	Gloucester
27	627.5	Caroline County Public Schools	Bowling Green
27	627.5	Poquoson City Public Schools	Poquoson
29	622.8	Nottoway County Public Schools	Nottoway
30	613.8	New Kent County Public Schools	New Kent
31	612.4	Norfolk City Public Schools	Norfolk
32	611.7	Louisa County Public Schools	Mineral
33	610.9	Williamsburg-James City Co PS	Williamsburg
34	604.0	Suffolk City Public Schools	Suffolk
35	595.7	Loudoun County Public Schools	Leesburg
36	593.7	Russell County Public Schools	Lebanon
37	591.0	Appomattox County Public Schools	Appomattox
38	590.5	Henrico County Public Schools	Richmond
39	575.3	Amelia County Public Schools	Amelia
40	574.0	Mecklenburg County Public Schools	Boydton
41	573.7	Fauquier County Public Schools	Warrenton
42	571.3	Harrisonburg City Public Schools	Harrisonburg
43	568.1	Shenandoah County Public Schools	Woodstock
44	567.1	Warren County Public Schools	Front Royal
45	562.9	Salem City Public Schools	Salem
46	561.6	Petersburg City Public Schools	Petersburg
47	560.2	Tazewell County Public Schools	Tazewell
48	554.8	Colonial Heights City Pub Schools	Colonial Hgts
49	554.0	Greensville County Public Schools	Emporia
50	550.9	Portsmouth City Public Schools	Portsmouth
51	548.6	Prince George County Pub Schools	Prince George
52	547.8	Fluvanna County Public Schools	Palmyra
53	542.0	Essex County Public Schools	Tappahannock
54	538.2	Staunton City Public Schools	Staunton
55	525.9	Roanoke City Public Schools	Roanoke
56	522.6	Hampton City Public Schools	Hampton
57	521.0	Bedford County Public Schools	Bedford
58	520.0	Page County Public Schools	Luray
59	519.8	Northampton County Public Schools	Machipongo
60	517.7	Radford City Public Schools	Radford
61	512.4	Giles County Public Schools	Pearisburg
62	510.5	Albemarle County Public Schools	Charlottesville
63	507.5	Nelson County Public Schools	Lovingston
64	506.2	Arlington County Public Schools	Arlington
65	505.7	Lancaster County Public Schools	Kilmarnock
65	505.7	Rockingham County Public Schools	Harrisonburg
67	502.0	Pittsylvania County Public Schools	Chatham
68	501.3	Westmoreland Co Public Schools	Montross
69	499.5	Orange County Public Schools	Orange
70	497.7	Pulaski County Public Schools	Pulaski
71	497.0	Waynesboro City Public Schools	Waynesboro
72	495.0	Accomack County Public Schools	Accomac
73	491.4	Dinwiddie County Public Schools	Dinwiddie
74	491.0	Roanoke County Public Schools	Roanoke
75	482.9	Franklin County Public Schools	Rocky Mount
76	477.0	Alexandria City Public Schools	Alexandria
77	472.0	Southampton County Public Schools	Courtland
78	471.3	Lynchburg City Public Schools	Lynchburg
79	464.5	Amherst County Public Schools	Amherst
80	463.1	Wise County Public Schools	Wise
81	459.7	Danville City Public Schools	Danville
82	458.3	Falls Church City Public Schools	Falls Church
83	457.8	Charlotte County Public Schools	Charlotte Ct Hse
84	457.5	Madison County Public Schools	Madison
85	449.0	Martinsville City Public Schools	Martinsville
86	443.5	Montgomery County Public Schools	Christiansburg
87	443.3	Lunenburg County Public Schools	Victoria
88	440.5	Patrick County Public Schools	Stuart
89	430.3	Botetourt County Public Schools	Fincastle
90	426.3	Henry County Public Schools	Collinsville
91	422.3	Halifax County Public Schools	Halifax
92	422.2	Smyth County Public Schools	Marion
93	421.0	Charlottesville City Pub Schools	Charlottesville
94	418.4	Alleghany County Public Schools	Covington
95	413.2	Goochland County Public Schools	Goochland
96	412.8	Brunswick County Public Schools	Lawrenceville
97	412.6	Clarke County Public Schools	Berryville
98	406.1	Carroll County Public Schools	Hillsville
99	391.2	Buchanan County Public Schools	Grundy
100	388.7	Bristol City Public Schools	Bristol
101	380.6	Lee County Public Schools	Jonesville
102	368.3	Buckingham County Public Schools	Buckingham
103	358.5	Wythe County Public Schools	Wytheville
104	339.9	Dickenson County Public Schools	Clintwood
105	336.8	Scott County Public Schools	Gate City
106	333.3	Rockbridge County Public Schools	Lexington
107	285.1	Grayson County Public Schools	Independence
108	284.6	Virginia-New York District	Quantico
109	275.4	Chesapeake City Public Schools	Chesapeake
110	0.0	Floyd County Public Schools	Floyd
110	0.0	Virginia Beach City Public Schls	Virginia Beach

Student/Counselor Ratio

Rank	Ratio	District Name	City
1	3,048.0	King George County Public Schools	King George
2	820.3	Prince William County Pub Schools	Manassas
3	763.0	Charlotte County Public Schools	Charlotte Ct Hse
4	736.7	Buckingham County Public Schools	Buckingham
5	692.3	Campbell County Public Schools	Rustburg
6	687.7	Clarke County Public Schools	Berryville
7	676.3	Greene County Public Schools	Standardsville
8	667.3	Manassas City Public Schools	Manassas
9	640.1	Stafford County Public Schools	Stafford
10	629.1	Spotsylvania Co Public Schools	Spotsylvania

11	627.9	Augusta County Public Schools	Fishersville
12	627.5	Poquoson City Public Schools	Poquoson
13	624.0	Petersburg City Public Schools	Petersburg
14	622.8	Nottoway County Public Schools	Nottoway
15	619.3	Brunswick County Public Schools	Lawrenceville
16	609.9	Mecklenburg County Public Schools	Boydton
17	603.6	Tazewell County Public Schools	Tazewell
18	597.8	Washington County Public Schools	Abingdon
19	591.0	Appomattox County Public Schools	Appomattox
20	585.4	Hanover County Public Schools	Ashland
21	581.8	Manassas Park City Public Schools	Manassas Park
22	575.7	Gloucester County Public Schools	Gloucester
23	575.3	Amelia County Public Schools	Amelia
24	570.9	Orange County Public Schools	Orange
25	570.3	Grayson County Public Schools	Independence
26	570.2	Williamsburg-James City Co PS	Williamsburg
27	566.7	Fluvanna County Public Schools	Palmyra
28	559.6	Prince Edward County Pub Schools	Farmville
29	559.0	Hopewell City Public Schools	Hopewell
30	551.5	Suffolk City Public Schools	Suffolk
31	547.4	Powhatan County Public Schools	Powhatan
32	542.0	Essex County Public Schools	Tappahannock
33	541.9	York County Public Schools	Yorktown
34	535.3	Louisa County Public Schools	Mineral
35	533.2	Harrisonburg City Public Schools	Harrisonburg
36	532.6	Portsmouth City Public Schools	Portsmouth
37	529.3	Scott County Public Schools	Gate City
38	523.1	Chesterfield County Public Schools	Chesterfield
39	521.0	Bedford County Public Schools	Bedford
40	517.7	Radford City Public Schools	Radford
41	511.7	Salem City Public Schools	Salem
42	510.4	Warren County Public Schools	Front Royal
43	507.5	Henrico County Public Schools	Richmond
43	507.5	Nelson County Public Schools	Lovingston
45	505.7	Danville City Public Schools	Danville
45	505.7	Lancaster County Public Schools	Kilmarnock
45	505.7	Winchester City Public Schools	Winchester
48	502.0	Fauquier County Public Schools	Warrenton
49	501.3	Westmoreland Co Public Schools	Montross
50	497.0	Waynesboro City Public Schools	Waynesboro
51	495.0	Accomack County Public Schools	Accomac
52	492.3	Chesapeake City Public Schools	Chesapeake
53	491.4	Dinwiddie County Public Schools	Dinwiddie
54	491.0	New Kent County Public Schools	New Kent
55	488.9	Amherst County Public Schools	Amherst
56	483.7	Rockingham County Public Schools	Harrisonburg
57	483.4	Fredericksburg City Public Schools	Fredericksburg
58	477.8	Carroll County Public Schools	Hillsville
59	476.9	Frederick County Public Schools	Winchester
60	475.8	Lee County Public Schools	Jonesville
61	473.4	Shenandoah County Public Schools	Woodstock
62	473.1	Albemarle County Public Schools	Charlottesville
63	472.0	Southampton County Public Schools	Courtland
64	462.3	Colonial Heights City Pub Schools	Colonial Hgts
65	461.7	Greensville County Public Schools	Emporia
66	460.5	Smyth County Public Schools	Marion
67	459.3	Norfolk City Public Schools	Norfolk
68	457.5	Madison County Public Schools	Madison
69	455.0	Page County Public Schools	Luray
70	452.8	Franklin County Public Schools	Rocky Mount
71	446.3	Roanoke County Public Schools	Roanoke
72	443.3	Lunenburg County Public Schools	Victoria
73	440.5	Patrick County Public Schools	Stuart
74	435.6	Richmond City Public Schools	Richmond
75	431.1	Prince George County Pub Schools	Prince George
76	427.0	Giles County Public Schools	Pearisburg
77	426.4	Lynchburg City Public Schools	Lynchburg
78	426.3	Henry County Public Schools	Collinsville
79	425.9	Hampton City Public Schools	Hampton
80	424.3	Newport News City Public Schools	Newport News
81	418.4	Alleghany County Public Schools	Covington
82	418.3	Caroline County Public Schools	Bowling Green
83	418.2	Wise County Public Schools	Wise
84	415.8	Northampton County Public Schools	Machipongo
85	413.2	Goochland County Public Schools	Goochland
86	398.5	Falls Church City Public Schools	Falls Church
87	394.4	Botetourt County Public Schools	Fincastle
88	391.4	King William County Public Schools	King William
89	391.1	Wythe County Public Schools	Wytheville
90	391.0	Roanoke City Public Schools	Roanoke
91	388.7	Bristol City Public Schools	Bristol
92	388.4	Dickenson County Public Schools	Clintwood
93	387.2	Fairfax County Public Schools	Fairfax
94	384.4	Staunton City Public Schools	Staunton
95	382.8	Pulaski County Public Schools	Pulaski
96	375.0	Rockbridge County Public Schools	Lexington
97	369.5	Halifax County Public Schools	Halifax
98	366.3	Buchanan County Public Schools	Grundy
99	361.4	Pittsylvania County Public Schools	Chatham
100	358.2	Montgomery County Public Schools	Christiansburg
101	355.1	Culpeper County Public Schools	Culpeper
102	353.9	Alexandria City Public Schools	Alexandria
103	352.4	Loudoun County Public Schools	Leesburg
104	346.3	Russell County Public Schools	Lebanon
105	340.0	Charlottesville City Pub Schools	Charlottesville
106	336.8	Martinsville City Public Schools	Martinsville
107	294.4	Arlington County Public Schools	Arlington
108	249.0	Virginia-New York District	Quantico
109	0.0	Floyd County Public Schools	Floyd
109	0.0	Isle of Wight County Pub Schools	Isle Of Wight
109	0.0	Virginia Beach City Public Schls	Virginia Beach

Current Spending per Student in FY2001

Rank	Dollars	District Name	City
1	11,388	Arlington County Public Schools	Arlington
2	11,305	Alexandria City Public Schools	Alexandria
3	11,207	Falls Church City Public Schools	Falls Church
4	9,962	Charlottesville City Pub Schools	Charlottesville
5	9,414	Fredericksburg City Public Schools	Fredericksburg
6	9,038	Fairfax County Public Schools	Fairfax
7	9,008	Richmond City Public Schools	Richmond
8	8,653	Winchester City Public Schools	Winchester
9	8,084	Williamsburg-James City Co PS	Williamsburg
10	8,017	Harrisonburg City Public Schools	Harrisonburg
11	7,995	Staunton City Public Schools	Staunton
12	7,847	Brunswick County Public Schools	Lawrenceville
13	7,822	Loudoun County Public Schools	Leesburg
14	7,693	Albemarle County Public Schools	Charlottesville
15	7,675	Roanoke City Public Schools	Roanoke
16	7,656	Goochland County Public Schools	Goochland
17	7,572	Colonial Heights City Pub Schools	Colonial Hgts
18	7,520	Martinsville City Public Schools	Martinsville
19	7,456	Northampton County Public Schools	Machipongo
20	7,401	Nelson County Public Schools	Lovingston
21	7,385	Clarke County Public Schools	Berryville
22	7,360	Bristol City Public Schools	Bristol
23	7,346	Portsmouth City Public Schools	Portsmouth
24	7,320	Buchanan County Public Schools	Grundy
25	7,319	Manassas Park City Public Schools	Manassas Park
26	7,301	Petersburg City Public Schools	Petersburg
27	7,296	Manassas City Public Schools	Manassas
28	7,246	Lee County Public Schools	Jonesville
29	7,225	Hopewell City Public Schools	Hopewell
30	7,199	Dickenson County Public Schools	Clintwood
31	7,181	Waynesboro City Public Schools	Waynesboro
32	7,174	King William County Public Schools	King William
33	7,171	Greene County Public Schools	Standardsville
34	7,162	Montgomery County Public Schools	Christiansburg
35	7,160	Lynchburg City Public Schools	Lynchburg
36	7,141	Norfolk City Public Schools	Norfolk
37	7,131	Alleghany County Public Schools	Covington
38	7,076	Lunenburg County Public Schools	Victoria
39	7,055	Lancaster County Public Schools	Kilmarnock
40	7,019	Fauquier County Public Schools	Warrenton
41	7,002	Rockbridge County Public Schools	Lexington
42	6,998	Grayson County Public Schools	Independence
43	6,990	Orange County Public Schools	Orange
44	6,958	Roanoke County Public Schools	Roanoke
45	6,950	Prince William County Pub Schools	Manassas
46	6,893	Southampton County Public Schools	Courtland
47	6,887	Botetourt County Public Schools	Fincastle
47	6,887	Madison County Public Schools	Madison
49	6,878	Salem City Public Schools	Salem
50	6,876	Frederick County Public Schools	Winchester
51	6,859	Powhatan County Public Schools	Powhatan
52	6,846	Accomack County Public Schools	Accomac
53	6,842	Chesapeake City Public Schools	Chesapeake
54	6,832	Isle of Wight County Pub Schools	Isle Of Wight
55	6,826	Halifax County Public Schools	Halifax
56	6,812	Danville City Public Schools	Danville
57	6,781	Carroll County Public Schools	Hillsville
58	6,769	Buckingham County Public Schools	Buckingham
59	6,766	Giles County Public Schools	Pearisburg
60	6,748	Greensville County Public Schools	Emporia
61	6,730	Essex County Public Schools	Tappahannock
62	6,710	King George County Public Schools	King George
63	6,696	Washington County Public Schools	Abingdon
63	6,696	Wise County Public Schools	Wise
65	6,670	Hampton City Public Schools	Hampton
66	6,667	Nottoway County Public Schools	Nottoway
67	6,660	Shenandoah County Public Schools	Woodstock
68	6,658	Henry County Public Schools	Collinsville
69	6,657	Newport News City Public Schools	Newport News
70	6,647	Virginia Beach City Public Schls	Virginia Beach
71	6,641	Charlotte County Public Schools	Charlotte Ct Hse
72	6,624	Culpeper County Public Schools	Culpeper
73	6,604	Pulaski County Public Schools	Pulaski
74	6,600	Spotsylvania Co Public Schools	Spotsylvania
75	6,587	Rockingham County Public Schools	Harrisonburg
76	6,566	Radford City Public Schools	Radford
77	6,535	Scott County Public Schools	Gate City
78	6,503	Stafford County Public Schools	Stafford
79	6,490	Louisa County Public Schools	Mineral
80	6,447	Floyd County Public Schools	Floyd
81	6,428	Patrick County Public Schools	Stuart
82	6,424	Tazewell County Public Schools	Tazewell
83	6,418	Gloucester County Public Schools	Gloucester
84	6,416	Prince Edward County Pub Schools	Farmville
85	6,414	Henrico County Public Schools	Richmond
86	6,390	Franklin County Public Schools	Rocky Mount
87	6,381	Fluvanna County Public Schools	Palmyra
88	6,380	Augusta County Public Schools	Fishersville
89	6,347	Smyth County Public Schools	Marion
90	6,333	Amelia County Public Schools	Amelia
91	6,303	Westmoreland Co Public Schools	Montross
92	6,287	Dinwiddie County Public Schools	Dinwiddie
93	6,273	Mecklenburg County Public Schools	Boydton
94	6,260	York County Public Schools	Yorktown
95	6,243	Chesterfield County Public Schools	Chesterfield
96	6,199	New Kent County Public Schools	New Kent
97	6,188	Campbell County Public Schools	Rustburg
98	6,161	Russell County Public Schools	Lebanon
98	6,161	Suffolk City Public Schools	Suffolk
100	6,130	Appomattox County Public Schools	Appomattox
100	6,130	Page County Public Schools	Luray
102	6,113	Prince George County Pub Schools	Prince George
103	6,081	Amherst County Public Schools	Amherst
104	6,075	Caroline County Public Schools	Bowling Green
105	6,062	Pittsylvania County Public Schools	Chatham
106	6,057	Wythe County Public Schools	Wytheville
107	5,993	Poquoson City Public Schools	Poquoson
108	5,955	Hanover County Public Schools	Ashland
109	5,871	Warren County Public Schools	Front Royal
110	5,411	Bedford County Public Schools	Bedford
111	n/a	Virginia-New York District	Quantico

Number of Diploma Recipients

Rank	Number	District Name	City
1	10,450	Fairfax County Public Schools	Fairfax
2	4,455	Virginia Beach City Public Schls	Virginia Beach
3	3,292	Chesterfield County Public Schools	Chesterfield
4	3,196	Prince William County Pub Schools	Manassas
5	2,400	Henrico County Public Schools	Richmond
6	2,298	Chesapeake City Public Schools	Chesapeake
7	1,766	Loudoun County Public Schools	Leesburg
8	1,570	Newport News City Public Schools	Newport News
9	1,359	Stafford County Public Schools	Stafford
10	1,348	Norfolk City Public Schools	Norfolk
11	1,279	Hampton City Public Schools	Hampton
12	1,119	Spotsylvania Co Public Schools	Spotsylvania
13	1,060	Hanover County Public Schools	Ashland
14	1,058	Richmond City Public Schools	Richmond
15	929	Roanoke County Public Schools	Roanoke
16	923	Arlington County Public Schools	Arlington
17	835	York County Public Schools	Yorktown
18	762	Albemarle County Public Schools	Charlottesville
19	736	Portsmouth City Public Schools	Portsmouth
20	713	Augusta County Public Schools	Fishersville
21	686	Rockingham County Public Schools	Harrisonburg
22	669	Bedford County Public Schools	Bedford
23	651	Fauquier County Public Schools	Warrenton
24	581	Pittsylvania County Public Schools	Chatham
25	563	Montgomery County Public Schools	Christiansburg
26	548	Frederick County Public Schools	Winchester
27	533	Alexandria City Public Schools	Alexandria
28	531	Suffolk City Public Schools	Suffolk
29	525	Williamsburg-James City Co PS	Williamsburg
30	512	Henry County Public Schools	Collinsville
31	504	Lynchburg City Public Schools	Lynchburg
32	498	Roanoke City Public Schools	Roanoke
33	494	Washington County Public Schools	Abingdon
34	486	Campbell County Public Schools	Rustburg
35	463	Wise County Public Schools	Wise
36	447	Tazewell County Public Schools	Tazewell
37	418	Franklin County Public Schools	Rocky Mount
38	397	Danville City Public Schools	Danville
39	374	Gloucester County Public Schools	Gloucester
40	357	Shenandoah County Public Schools	Woodstock
41	355	Manassas City Public Schools	Manassas
42	347	Halifax County Public Schools	Halifax
43	329	Pulaski County Public Schools	Pulaski
44	313	Botetourt County Public Schools	Fincastle
45	312	Prince George County Pub Schools	Prince George
46	309	Culpeper County Public Schools	Culpeper
47	303	Louisa County Public Schools	Mineral
48	302	Smyth County Public Schools	Marion
49	279	Mecklenburg County Public Schools	Boydton
50	273	Isle of Wight County Pub Schools	Isle Of Wight
50	273	Wythe County Public Schools	Wytheville
52	270	Russell County Public Schools	Lebanon
53	267	Salem City Public Schools	Salem
54	266	Amherst County Public Schools	Amherst
55	261	Warren County Public Schools	Front Royal
56	260	Buchanan County Public Schools	Grundy
57	256	Orange County Public Schools	Orange
58	255	Accomack County Public Schools	Accomac

59	244	Harrisonburg City Public Schools	Harrisonburg
60	237	Petersburg City Public Schools	Petersburg
61	219	Scott County Public Schools	Gate City
62	217	Hopewell City Public Schools	Hopewell
63	216	King George County Public Schools	King George
64	211	Carroll County Public Schools	Hillsville
65	210	Rockbridge County Public Schools	Lexington
66	207	Powhatan County Public Schools	Powhatan
67	206	Page County Public Schools	Luray
68	203	Dinwiddie County Public Schools	Dinwiddie
69	200	Caroline County Public Schools	Bowling Green
70	194	Charlottesville City Pub Schools	Charlottesville
71	189	Dickenson County Public Schools	Clintwood
72	184	Lee County Public Schools	Jonesville
73	183	Fluvanna County Public Schools	Palmyra
74	181	Winchester City Public Schools	Winchester
75	180	Poquoson City Public Schools	Poquoson
76	173	Alleghany County Public Schools	Covington
77	170	Patrick County Public Schools	Stuart
78	169	Staunton City Public Schools	Staunton
79	166	Colonial Heights City Pub Schools	Colonial Hgts
80	162	Waynesboro City Public Schools	Waynesboro
81	158	Martinsville City Public Schools	Martinsville
82	154	Brunswick County Public Schools	Lawrenceville
83	152	Greensville County Public Schools	Emporia
83	152	Southampton County Public Schools	Courtland
85	149	Giles County Public Schools	Pearisburg
86	146	Madison County Public Schools	Madison
87	144	Clarke County Public Schools	Berryville
87	144	Greene County Public Schools	Standardsville
87	144	New Kent County Public Schools	New Kent
87	144	Nottoway County Public Schools	Nottoway
91	140	Appomattox County Public Schools	Appomattox
92	135	Charlotte County Public Schools	Charlotte Ct Hse
92	135	Westmoreland Co Public Schools	Montross
94	134	Northampton County Public Schools	Machipongo
95	131	Prince Edward County Pub Schools	Farmville
96	130	Goochland County Public Schools	Goochland
97	129	Nelson County Public Schools	Lovingston
98	123	Bristol City Public Schools	Bristol
99	117	Falls Church City Public Schools	Falls Church
100	116	Lunenburg County Public Schools	Victoria
101	115	Floyd County Public Schools	Floyd
101	115	Grayson County Public Schools	Independence
103	114	Fredericksburg City Public Schools	Fredericksburg
104	111	Buckingham County Public Schools	Buckingham
105	110	King William County Public Schools	King William
106	109	Amelia County Public Schools	Amelia
107	105	Essex County Public Schools	Tappahannock
108	102	Radford City Public Schools	Radford
109	93	Lancaster County Public Schools	Kilmarnock
110	91	Manassas Park City Public Schools	Manassas Park
111	38	Virginia-New York District	Quantico

High School Drop-out Rate

Rank	Percent	District Name	City
1	9.0	Petersburg City Public Schools	Petersburg
2	8.6	Roanoke City Public Schools	Roanoke
3	8.5	Accomack County Public Schools	Accomac
4	6.8	Portsmouth City Public Schools	Portsmouth
5	6.5	Brunswick County Public Schools	Lawrenceville
5	6.5	Buckingham County Public Schools	Buckingham
5	6.5	Staunton City Public Schools	Staunton
8	6.0	Nottoway County Public Schools	Nottoway
9	5.7	Danville City Public Schools	Danville
10	5.6	Fauquier County Public Schools	Warrenton
11	5.4	Colonial Heights City Pub Schools	Colonial Hgts
11	5.4	Hopewell City Public Schools	Hopewell
13	5.3	Dinwiddie County Public Schools	Dinwiddie
13	5.3	Norfolk City Public Schools	Norfolk
15	5.2	Alexandria City Public Schools	Alexandria
15	5.2	Virginia Beach City Public Schls	Virginia Beach
17	5.1	Prince William County Pub Schools	Manassas
18	5.0	Page County Public Schools	Luray
19	4.7	Louisa County Public Schools	Mineral
19	4.7	Lunenburg County Public Schools	Victoria
19	4.7	Mecklenburg County Public Schools	Boydton
22	4.6	Amelia County Public Schools	Amelia
23	4.5	Chesterfield County Public Schools	Chesterfield
23	4.5	Franklin County Public Schools	Rocky Mount
25	4.4	Winchester City Public Schools	Winchester
26	4.3	Culpeper County Public Schools	Culpeper
26	4.3	Fluvanna County Public Schools	Palmyra
26	4.3	Southampton County Public Schools	Courtland
29	4.2	Henry County Public Schools	Collinsville
29	4.2	Montgomery County Public Schools	Christiansburg
31	4.1	Newport News City Public Schools	Newport News
31	4.1	Pulaski County Public Schools	Pulaski
33	4.0	Shenandoah County Public Schools	Woodstock
33	4.0	Suffolk City Public Schools	Suffolk
35	3.8	Frederick County Public Schools	Winchester
35	3.8	Prince George County Pub Schools	Prince George
37	3.6	Pittsylvania County Public Schools	Chatham
37	3.6	Powhatan County Public Schools	Powhatan
39	3.5	Amherst County Public Schools	Amherst
39	3.5	Giles County Public Schools	Pearisburg
39	3.5	Lancaster County Public Schools	Kilmarnock
39	3.5	Northampton County Public Schools	Machipongo
39	3.5	Rockbridge County Public Schools	Lexington
44	3.4	Chesapeake City Public Schools	Chesapeake
44	3.4	Rockingham County Public Schools	Harrisonburg
46	3.3	Dickenson County Public Schools	Clintwood
46	3.3	New Kent County Public Schools	New Kent
46	3.3	Warren County Public Schools	Front Royal
49	3.2	Gloucester County Public Schools	Gloucester
49	3.2	Prince Edward County Pub Schools	Farmville
51	3.1	Botetourt County Public Schools	Fincastle
51	3.1	Carroll County Public Schools	Hillsville
51	3.1	Spotsylvania Co Public Schools	Spotsylvania
54	3.0	Charlottesville City Pub Schools	Charlottesville
54	3.0	Essex County Public Schools	Tappahannock
54	3.0	Wise County Public Schools	Wise
57	2.9	Buchanan County Public Schools	Grundy
57	2.9	Greene County Public Schools	Standardsville
57	2.9	Tazewell County Public Schools	Tazewell
60	2.8	Bristol City Public Schools	Bristol
60	2.8	Fairfax County Public Schools	Fairfax
60	2.8	Richmond City Public Schools	Richmond
60	2.8	Waynesboro City Public Schools	Waynesboro
64	2.7	Campbell County Public Schools	Rustburg
64	2.7	Hampton City Public Schools	Hampton
64	2.7	Madison County Public Schools	Madison
64	2.7	Nelson County Public Schools	Lovingston
68	2.6	Arlington County Public Schools	Arlington
68	2.6	Patrick County Public Schools	Stuart
70	2.4	Grayson County Public Schools	Independence
70	2.4	Greensville County Public Schools	Emporia
70	2.4	Halifax County Public Schools	Halifax
70	2.4	Stafford County Public Schools	Stafford
74	2.3	Alleghany County Public Schools	Covington
74	2.3	Henrico County Public Schools	Richmond
74	2.3	Westmoreland Co Public Schools	Montross
77	2.2	King George County Public Schools	King George
77	2.2	Manassas City Public Schools	Manassas
77	2.2	Radford City Public Schools	Radford
80	2.1	Appomattox County Public Schools	Appomattox
80	2.1	Augusta County Public Schools	Fishersville
80	2.1	Charlotte County Public Schools	Charlotte Ct Hse
80	2.1	Floyd County Public Schools	Floyd
80	2.1	Fredericksburg City Public Schools	Fredericksburg
80	2.1	Manassas Park City Public Schools	Manassas Park
80	2.1	Russell County Public Schools	Lebanon
80	2.1	Washington County Public Schools	Abingdon
88	2.0	Bedford County Public Schools	Bedford
88	2.0	Martinsville City Public Schools	Martinsville
90	1.9	Albemarle County Public Schools	Charlottesville
90	1.9	Harrisonburg City Public Schools	Harrisonburg
90	1.9	Salem City Public Schools	Salem
90	1.9	Wythe County Public Schools	Wytheville
94	1.8	Clarke County Public Schools	Berryville
94	1.8	Loudoun County Public Schools	Leesburg
94	1.8	Orange County Public Schools	Orange
97	1.7	Scott County Public Schools	Gate City
98	1.5	Isle of Wight County Pub Schools	Isle Of Wight
99	1.4	Smyth County Public Schools	Marion
99	1.4	Williamsburg-James City Co PS	Williamsburg
101	1.3	Lynchburg City Public Schools	Lynchburg
101	1.3	Roanoke County Public Schools	Roanoke
103	1.2	Caroline County Public Schools	Bowling Green
103	1.2	Goochland County Public Schools	Goochland
105	1.1	York County Public Schools	Yorktown
106	1.0	Lee County Public Schools	Jonesville
107	0.6	Poquoson City Public Schools	Poquoson
108	0.4	Falls Church City Public Schools	Falls Church
108	0.4	Hanover County Public Schools	Ashland
110	0.2	King William County Public Schools	King William
111	n/a	Virginia-New York District	Quantico

Washington

Washington Public School Educational Profile

Category	Value	Category	Value
Schools *(2002-2003)*	2,217	**Diploma Recipients** *(2002-2003)*	58,311
Instructional Level		White, Non-Hispanic	45,918
Primary	1,182	Black, Non-Hispanic	2,306
Middle	358	Asian/Pacific Islander	5,030
High	479	American Indian/Alaskan Native	1,120
Other Level	198	Hispanic	3,937
Curriculum		**High School Drop-out Rate** (%) *(2000-2001)*	n/a
Regular	1,871	White, Non-Hispanic	n/a
Special Education	82	Black, Non-Hispanic	n/a
Vocational	11	Asian/Pacific Islander	n/a
Alternative	253	American Indian/Alaskan Native	n/a
Type		Hispanic	n/a
Magnet	0	**Staff** *(2002-2003)*	112,737.0
Charter	0	Teachers	52,951.6
Title I Eligible	921	Average Salary ($)	44,961
School-wide Title I	366	Librarians/Media Specialists	1,324.7
Students *(2002-2003)*	1,014,798	Guidance Counselors	1,971.5
Gender (%)		**Ratios** *(2002-2003)*	
Male	51.6	Student/Teacher Ratio	19.2 to 1
Female	48.4	Student/Librarian Ratio	766.1 to 1
Race/Ethnicity (%)		Student/Counselor Ratio	514.7 to 1
White, Non-Hispanic	72.6	**Current Spending** *($ per student in FY 2001)*	7,039
Black, Non-Hispanic	5.6	Instruction	4,189
Asian/Pacific Islander	7.6	Support Services	2,508
American Indian/Alaskan Native	2.6	**College Entrance Exam Scores** *(2003)*	
Hispanic	11.6	Scholastic Aptitude Test (SAT)	
Classification (%)		Participation Rate (%)	56
Individual Education Program (IEP)	12.0	Mean SAT I Verbal Score	530
Migrant	0.0	Mean SAT I Math Score	532
English Language Learner (ELL)	6.9	American College Testing Program (ACT)	
Eligible for Free Lunch Program	25.6	Participation Rate (%)	16
Eligible for Reduced-Price Lunch Program	8.7	Average Composite Score	22.5

Note: *For an explanation of data, please refer to the User's Guide in the front of the book; n/a indicates data not available*

Washington NAEP 2003 Test Scores

Reading			Mathematics		
Grade/Category	Value	Rank	Grade/Category	Value	Rank
4th Grade			**4th Grade**		
Average Proficiency	221.1 (1.1)	20/51	Average Proficiency	238.3 (1.0)	12/51
Proficiency by Gender/Race/Ethnicity			Proficiency by Gender/Race/Ethnicity		
Male	216.3 (1.3)	20/51	Male	239.9 (1.1)	11/51
Female	225.9 (1.3)	15/51	Female	236.6 (1.0)	13/51
White, Non-Hispanic	226.2 (1.1)	24/51	White, Non-Hispanic	241.9 (0.9)	27/51
Black, Non-Hispanic	212.2 (2.4)	1/42	Black, Non-Hispanic	222.5 (2.5)	6/42
Asian, Non-Hispanic	201.4 (2.7)	27/41	Asian, Non-Hispanic	223.0 (2.1)	17/43
American Indian, Non-Hispanic	218.4 (2.9)	19/25	American Indian, Non-Hispanic	244.2 (2.3)	18/26
Hispanic	208.5 (4.9)	2/12	Hispanic	228.9 (3.6)	1/12
Proficiency by Class Size			Proficiency by Class Size		
Less than 16 Students	n/a	n/a	Less than 16 Students	*230.8 (5.3)*	10/47
16 to 18 Students	*212.2 (7.7)*	30/48	16 to 18 Students	*237.8 (5.7)*	13/48
19 to 20 Students	*221.3 (4.2)*	20/50	19 to 20 Students	*241.2 (3.6)*	7/50
21 to 25 Students	220.8 (1.7)	26/51	21 to 25 Students	239.1 (1.3)	18/51
Greater than 25 Students	223.2 (2.4)	13/49	Greater than 25 Students	236.7 (2.0)	21/49
Percent Attaining Achievement Levels			Percent Attaining Achievement Levels		
Below Basic	32.8 (1.3)	32/51	Below Basic	19.0 (1.1)	35/51
Basic or Above	67.2 (1.3)	19/51	Basic or Above	81.0 (1.1)	17/51
Proficient or Above	33.1 (1.3)	17/51	Proficient or Above	36.2 (1.5)	10/51
Advanced or Above	7.4 (0.8)	21/51	Advanced or Above	5.0 (0.6)	11/51
8th Grade			**8th Grade**		
Average Proficiency	264.5 (0.9)	24/51	Average Proficiency	281.2 (0.9)	19/51
Proficiency by Gender/Race/Ethnicity			Proficiency by Gender/Race/Ethnicity		
Male	258.4 (1.4)	29/51	Male	281.7 (1.1)	21/51
Female	270.9 (1.1)	21/51	Female	280.6 (1.2)	17/51
White, Non-Hispanic	268.0 (1.1)	34/50	White, Non-Hispanic	284.8 (1.1)	31/50
Black, Non-Hispanic	250.6 (3.3)	3/41	Black, Non-Hispanic	262.5 (3.1)	3/41
Asian, Non-Hispanic	246.1 (2.6)	20/37	Asian, Non-Hispanic	263.3 (3.0)	7/37
American Indian, Non-Hispanic	269.7 (2.6)	11/23	American Indian, Non-Hispanic	285.0 (3.9)	15/23
Hispanic	247.3 (7.1)	2/10	Hispanic	264.2 (5.3)	2/11
Proficiency by Parents Highest Level of Ed.			Proficiency by Parents Highest Level of Ed.		
Did Not Finish High School	248.1 (3.1)	15/50	Did Not Finish High School	262.9 (2.0)	9/50
Graduated High School	257.3 (1.7)	18/50	Graduated High School	271.1 (1.7)	18/50
Some Education After High School	271.4 (1.7)	9/50	Some Education After High School	282.9 (1.6)	14/50
Graduated College	271.9 (1.2)	28/50	Graduated College	291.7 (1.4)	15/50
Percent Attaining Achievement Levels			Percent Attaining Achievement Levels		
Below Basic	24.4 (1.1)	25/51	Below Basic	28.1 (1.2)	32/51
Basic or Above	75.6 (1.1)	27/51	Basic or Above	71.9 (1.2)	20/51
Proficient or Above	33.0 (1.1)	24/51	Proficient or Above	32.3 (1.3)	14/51
Advanced or Above	3.1 (0.5)	14/51	Advanced or Above	6.0 (0.8)	13/51

Note: *For an explanation of data, please refer to the User's Guide in the front of the book; values in italics indicate that the nature of the sample does not allow accurate determination of the variability of the statistic; n/a indicates data not available*

Adams County

Othello SD 147

615 E Juniper St • Othello, WA 99344-1463
(509) 488-2659 • http://www.othello.wednet.edu/
Grade Span: KG-12; **Agency Type:** 1
Schools: 5
3 Primary; 1 Middle; 1 High; 0 Other Level
5 Regular; 0 Special Education; 0 Vocational; 0 Alternative
0 Magnet; 0 Charter; 5 Title I Eligible; 5 School-wide Title I
Students: 3,111 (51.4% male; 48.6% female)
Individual Education Program: 345 (11.1%);
English Language Learner: 1,004 (32.3%); Migrant: n/a
Eligible for Free Lunch Program: 1,722 (55.4%)
Eligible for Reduced-Price Lunch Program: 463 (14.9%)
Teachers: 159.6 (19.5 to 1)
Librarians/Media Specialists: 5.0 (622.2 to 1)
Guidance Counselors: 5.0 (622.2 to 1)
Current Spending: ($ per student per year):
Total: $6,247; Instruction: $3,984; Support Services: $1,846
Enrollment, Drop-out Rates and Diploma Recipients by Race/Ethnicity

Category	Total	White	Black	Asian	AIAN	Hisp.
Enrollment (%)	100.0	25.3	0.4	0.5	0.1	73.8
Drop-out Rate (%)	n/a	n/a	n/a	n/a	n/a	n/a
H.S. Diplomas (#)	161	62	1	0	0	98

Asotin County

Clarkston SD 250

1294 Chestnut • Clarkston, WA 99403-2557
(509) 758-2531 • http://jawbone.clarkston.wednet.edu/
Grade Span: PK-12; **Agency Type:** 1
Schools: 8
4 Primary; 1 Middle; 2 High; 1 Other Level
6 Regular; 1 Special Education; 0 Vocational; 1 Alternative
0 Magnet; 0 Charter; 4 Title I Eligible; 3 School-wide Title I
Students: 2,814 (51.9% male; 48.1% female)
Individual Education Program: 398 (14.1%);
English Language Learner: 11 (0.4%); Migrant: n/a
Eligible for Free Lunch Program: 825 (29.3%)
Eligible for Reduced-Price Lunch Program: 262 (9.3%)
Teachers: 140.3 (20.1 to 1)
Librarians/Media Specialists: 4.0 (703.5 to 1)
Guidance Counselors: 3.7 (760.5 to 1)
Current Spending: ($ per student per year):
Total: $6,655; Instruction: $4,093; Support Services: $2,142
Enrollment, Drop-out Rates and Diploma Recipients by Race/Ethnicity

Category	Total	White	Black	Asian	AIAN	Hisp.
Enrollment (%)	100.0	93.4	0.7	0.6	2.3	2.9
Drop-out Rate (%)	n/a	n/a	n/a	n/a	n/a	n/a
H.S. Diplomas (#)	157	150	1	3	0	3

Benton County

Kennewick SD 17

524 S Auburn St • Kennewick, WA 99336-5601
(509) 585-3020 • http://www.ksd.org/ksd.org/htmls/index2.htm
Grade Span: PK-12; **Agency Type:** 1
Schools: 24
14 Primary; 4 Middle; 5 High; 1 Other Level
22 Regular; 0 Special Education; 1 Vocational; 1 Alternative
0 Magnet; 0 Charter; 5 Title I Eligible; 2 School-wide Title I
Students: 14,698 (51.5% male; 48.5% female)
Individual Education Program: 1,573 (10.7%);
English Language Learner: 1,508 (10.3%); Migrant: n/a
Eligible for Free Lunch Program: 4,298 (29.2%)
Eligible for Reduced-Price Lunch Program: 1,164 (7.9%)
Teachers: 712.5 (20.6 to 1)
Librarians/Media Specialists: 21.0 (699.9 to 1)
Guidance Counselors: 30.7 (478.8 to 1)
Current Spending: ($ per student per year):
Total: $6,764; Instruction: $4,291; Support Services: $2,155
Enrollment, Drop-out Rates and Diploma Recipients by Race/Ethnicity

Category	Total	White	Black	Asian	AIAN	Hisp.
Enrollment (%)	100.0	74.4	2.1	2.1	0.4	21.0
Drop-out Rate (%)	n/a	n/a	n/a	n/a	n/a	n/a
H.S. Diplomas (#)	977	824	12	25	2	114

Kiona-Benton SD 52

1107 Grace • Benton City, WA 99320-9704
(509) 588-3717 • http://www.owt.com/kibe/
Grade Span: PK-12; **Agency Type:** 1
Schools: 4
1 Primary; 2 Middle; 1 High; 0 Other Level
4 Regular; 0 Special Education; 0 Vocational; 0 Alternative
0 Magnet; 0 Charter; 2 Title I Eligible; 2 School-wide Title I
Students: 1,664 (51.3% male; 48.7% female)
Individual Education Program: 205 (12.3%);
English Language Learner: 150 (9.0%); Migrant: n/a
Eligible for Free Lunch Program: 598 (35.9%)
Eligible for Reduced-Price Lunch Program: 156 (9.4%)
Teachers: 84.1 (19.8 to 1)
Librarians/Media Specialists: 2.0 (832.0 to 1)
Guidance Counselors: 2.0 (832.0 to 1)
Current Spending: ($ per student per year):
Total: $6,238; Instruction: $3,680; Support Services: $2,224
Enrollment, Drop-out Rates and Diploma Recipients by Race/Ethnicity

Category	Total	White	Black	Asian	AIAN	Hisp.
Enrollment (%)	100.0	76.4	0.7	1.3	0.5	21.0
Drop-out Rate (%)	n/a	n/a	n/a	n/a	n/a	n/a
H.S. Diplomas (#)	99	87	0	0	1	11

Prosser SD 116

823 Park Ave • Prosser, WA 99350-1264
(509) 786-3323 • http://www.prosserschools.org/
Grade Span: PK-12; **Agency Type:** 1
Schools: 6
3 Primary; 1 Middle; 2 High; 0 Other Level
5 Regular; 0 Special Education; 0 Vocational; 1 Alternative
0 Magnet; 0 Charter; 4 Title I Eligible; 3 School-wide Title I
Students: 2,790 (50.5% male; 49.5% female)
Individual Education Program: 316 (11.3%);
English Language Learner: 639 (22.9%); Migrant: n/a
Eligible for Free Lunch Program: 1,201 (43.0%)
Eligible for Reduced-Price Lunch Program: 272 (9.7%)
Teachers: 143.7 (19.4 to 1)
Librarians/Media Specialists: 4.5 (620.0 to 1)
Guidance Counselors: 6.9 (404.3 to 1)
Current Spending: ($ per student per year):
Total: $6,614; Instruction: $3,775; Support Services: $2,434
Enrollment, Drop-out Rates and Diploma Recipients by Race/Ethnicity

Category	Total	White	Black	Asian	AIAN	Hisp.
Enrollment (%)	100.0	53.2	0.9	1.1	0.2	44.7
Drop-out Rate (%)	n/a	n/a	n/a	n/a	n/a	n/a
H.S. Diplomas (#)	165	103	0	0	0	62

Richland SD 400

615 Snow Ave • Richland, WA 99352-3899
(509) 942-2400 • http://www.rsd.edu/
Grade Span: PK-12; **Agency Type:** 1
Schools: 15
8 Primary; 3 Middle; 3 High; 1 Other Level
14 Regular; 0 Special Education; 0 Vocational; 1 Alternative
0 Magnet; 0 Charter; 5 Title I Eligible; 0 School-wide Title I
Students: 9,800 (51.2% male; 48.8% female)
Individual Education Program: 1,193 (12.2%);
English Language Learner: 316 (3.2%); Migrant: n/a
Eligible for Free Lunch Program: 1,484 (15.1%)
Eligible for Reduced-Price Lunch Program: 558 (5.7%)
Teachers: 491.4 (19.9 to 1)
Librarians/Media Specialists: 14.0 (700.0 to 1)
Guidance Counselors: 20.9 (468.9 to 1)
Current Spending: ($ per student per year):
Total: $6,102; Instruction: $3,662; Support Services: $2,113
Enrollment, Drop-out Rates and Diploma Recipients by Race/Ethnicity

Category	Total	White	Black	Asian	AIAN	Hisp.
Enrollment (%)	100.0	87.6	2.4	4.0	0.8	5.2
Drop-out Rate (%)	n/a	n/a	n/a	n/a	n/a	n/a
H.S. Diplomas (#)	743	671	10	40	3	19

Chelan County

Cashmere SD 222

210 S Division St • Cashmere, WA 98815-1133
(509) 782-3355 • http://www.cashmere.wednet.edu/
Grade Span: PK-12; **Agency Type:** 1
Schools: 3
1 Primary; 1 Middle; 1 High; 0 Other Level
3 Regular; 0 Special Education; 0 Vocational; 0 Alternative
0 Magnet; 0 Charter; 2 Title I Eligible; 0 School-wide Title I
Students: 1,509 (52.3% male; 47.7% female)
Individual Education Program: 145 (9.6%);
English Language Learner: 142 (9.4%); Migrant: n/a
Eligible for Free Lunch Program: 416 (27.6%)
Eligible for Reduced-Price Lunch Program: 161 (10.7%)
Teachers: 78.4 (19.2 to 1)
Librarians/Media Specialists: 1.6 (943.1 to 1)
Guidance Counselors: 2.5 (603.6 to 1)
Current Spending: ($ per student per year):
Total: $6,386; Instruction: $4,025; Support Services: $1,968

Enrollment, Drop-out Rates and Diploma Recipients by Race/Ethnicity

Category	Total	White	Black	Asian	AIAN	Hisp.
Enrollment (%)	100.0	71.0	0.6	0.7	0.8	27.0
Drop-out Rate (%)	n/a	n/a	n/a	n/a	n/a	n/a
H.S. Diplomas (#)	96	81	0	0	0	15

Wenatchee SD 246

235 Sunset Ave • Wenatchee, WA 98801-1999
(509) 663-8161 • http://home.wsd.wednet.edu/
Grade Span: PK-12; **Agency Type:** 1
Schools: 16
7 Primary; 3 Middle; 3 High; 3 Other Level
13 Regular; 1 Special Education; 0 Vocational; 2 Alternative
0 Magnet; 0 Charter; 6 Title I Eligible; 2 School-wide Title I
Students: 7,402 (51.1% male; 48.9% female)
Individual Education Program: 710 (9.6%);
English Language Learner: 1,530 (20.7%); Migrant: n/a
Eligible for Free Lunch Program: 2,658 (35.9%)
Eligible for Reduced-Price Lunch Program: 529 (7.1%)
Teachers: 369.5 (20.0 to 1)
Librarians/Media Specialists: 10.8 (685.4 to 1)
Guidance Counselors: 16.5 (448.6 to 1)
Current Spending: ($ per student per year):
Total: $6,140; Instruction: $3,780; Support Services: $2,042
Enrollment, Drop-out Rates and Diploma Recipients by Race/Ethnicity

Category	Total	White	Black	Asian	AIAN	Hisp.
Enrollment (%)	100.0	64.6	0.3	1.4	1.3	32.4
Drop-out Rate (%)	n/a	n/a	n/a	n/a	n/a	n/a
H.S. Diplomas (#)	432	320	0	10	5	97

Clallam County

Port Angeles SD 121

216 E 4th St • Port Angeles, WA 98362-3023
(360) 457-8575 • http://www.pasd.wednet.edu/
Grade Span: PK-12; **Agency Type:** 1
Schools: 12
6 Primary; 2 Middle; 3 High; 1 Other Level
9 Regular; 0 Special Education; 1 Vocational; 2 Alternative
0 Magnet; 0 Charter; 8 Title I Eligible; 4 School-wide Title I
Students: 4,749 (52.5% male; 47.5% female)
Individual Education Program: 715 (15.1%);
English Language Learner: 22 (0.5%); Migrant: n/a
Eligible for Free Lunch Program: 1,326 (27.9%)
Eligible for Reduced-Price Lunch Program: 457 (9.6%)
Teachers: 250.5 (19.0 to 1)
Librarians/Media Specialists: 3.0 (1,583.0 to 1)
Guidance Counselors: 2.9 (1,637.6 to 1)
Current Spending: ($ per student per year):
Total: $6,624; Instruction: $4,183; Support Services: $2,148
Enrollment, Drop-out Rates and Diploma Recipients by Race/Ethnicity

Category	Total	White	Black	Asian	AIAN	Hisp.
Enrollment (%)	100.0	86.2	1.5	2.1	8.1	2.1
Drop-out Rate (%)	n/a	n/a	n/a	n/a	n/a	n/a
H.S. Diplomas (#)	121	104	2	7	5	3

Sequim SD 323

503 N Sequim Ave • Sequim, WA 98382-3161
(360) 582-3260 • http://www.sequimschools.wednet.edu/
Grade Span: PK-12; **Agency Type:** 1
Schools: 5
2 Primary; 1 Middle; 1 High; 1 Other Level
4 Regular; 0 Special Education; 0 Vocational; 1 Alternative
0 Magnet; 0 Charter; 3 Title I Eligible; 0 School-wide Title I
Students: 2,884 (51.4% male; 48.6% female)
Individual Education Program: 263 (9.1%);
English Language Learner: 59 (2.0%); Migrant: n/a
Eligible for Free Lunch Program: 561 (19.5%)
Eligible for Reduced-Price Lunch Program: 248 (8.6%)
Teachers: 143.8 (20.1 to 1)
Librarians/Media Specialists: 4.0 (721.0 to 1)
Guidance Counselors: 6.0 (480.7 to 1)
Current Spending: ($ per student per year):
Total: $5,907; Instruction: $3,807; Support Services: $1,748
Enrollment, Drop-out Rates and Diploma Recipients by Race/Ethnicity

Category	Total	White	Black	Asian	AIAN	Hisp.
Enrollment (%)	100.0	87.2	0.9	3.1	3.9	4.9
Drop-out Rate (%)	n/a	n/a	n/a	n/a	n/a	n/a
H.S. Diplomas (#)	203	180	1	7	7	8

Clark County

Battle Ground SD 119

11104 NE 149th St • Brush Prairie, WA 98606-9565
(360) 885-5302 • http://www.bgsd.k12.wa.us/
Grade Span: PK-12; **Agency Type:** 1
Schools: 18
8 Primary; 5 Middle; 3 High; 2 Other Level
13 Regular; 1 Special Education; 0 Vocational; 4 Alternative
0 Magnet; 0 Charter; 2 Title I Eligible; 0 School-wide Title I
Students: 12,024 (51.8% male; 48.2% female)
Individual Education Program: 1,414 (11.8%);
English Language Learner: 198 (1.6%); Migrant: n/a
Eligible for Free Lunch Program: 1,509 (12.5%)
Eligible for Reduced-Price Lunch Program: 802 (6.7%)
Teachers: 555.9 (21.6 to 1)
Librarians/Media Specialists: 13.0 (924.9 to 1)
Guidance Counselors: 9.0 (1,336.0 to 1)
Current Spending: ($ per student per year):
Total: $5,908; Instruction: $3,473; Support Services: $2,138
Enrollment, Drop-out Rates and Diploma Recipients by Race/Ethnicity

Category	Total	White	Black	Asian	AIAN	Hisp.
Enrollment (%)	100.0	92.6	1.1	2.0	0.9	3.4
Drop-out Rate (%)	n/a	n/a	n/a	n/a	n/a	n/a
H.S. Diplomas (#)	843	793	3	17	6	24

Camas SD 117

1919 NE Ione St • Camas, WA 98607-1145
(360) 817-4400 • http://www.camas.wednet.edu/
Grade Span: PK-12; **Agency Type:** 1
Schools: 7
5 Primary; 1 Middle; 1 High; 0 Other Level
7 Regular; 0 Special Education; 0 Vocational; 0 Alternative
0 Magnet; 0 Charter; 2 Title I Eligible; 0 School-wide Title I
Students: 4,335 (52.0% male; 48.0% female)
Individual Education Program: 458 (10.6%);
English Language Learner: 42 (1.0%); Migrant: n/a
Eligible for Free Lunch Program: 463 (10.7%)
Eligible for Reduced-Price Lunch Program: 262 (6.0%)
Teachers: 216.2 (20.1 to 1)
Librarians/Media Specialists: 7.0 (619.3 to 1)
Guidance Counselors: 7.8 (555.8 to 1)
Current Spending: ($ per student per year):
Total: $6,189; Instruction: $3,635; Support Services: $2,236
Enrollment, Drop-out Rates and Diploma Recipients by Race/Ethnicity

Category	Total	White	Black	Asian	AIAN	Hisp.
Enrollment (%)	100.0	90.1	1.6	4.4	0.9	3.0
Drop-out Rate (%)	n/a	n/a	n/a	n/a	n/a	n/a
H.S. Diplomas (#)	203	190	1	5	1	6

Evergreen SD 114

13501 NE 28th St • Vancouver, WA 98668-8910
(360) 604-4005 • http://www.egreen.wednet.edu/
Grade Span: PK-12; **Agency Type:** 1
Schools: 33
19 Primary; 7 Middle; 7 High; 0 Other Level
27 Regular; 1 Special Education; 1 Vocational; 4 Alternative
0 Magnet; 0 Charter; 12 Title I Eligible; 0 School-wide Title I
Students: 23,369 (51.0% male; 49.0% female)
Individual Education Program: 2,665 (11.4%);
English Language Learner: 1,146 (4.9%); Migrant: n/a
Eligible for Free Lunch Program: 5,401 (23.1%)
Eligible for Reduced-Price Lunch Program: 2,493 (10.7%)
Teachers: 1,229.8 (19.0 to 1)
Librarians/Media Specialists: 28.8 (811.4 to 1)
Guidance Counselors: 49.1 (475.9 to 1)
Current Spending: ($ per student per year):
Total: $6,388; Instruction: $3,786; Support Services: $2,307
Enrollment, Drop-out Rates and Diploma Recipients by Race/Ethnicity

Category	Total	White	Black	Asian	AIAN	Hisp.
Enrollment (%)	100.0	82.5	4.2	7.3	1.0	5.1
Drop-out Rate (%)	n/a	n/a	n/a	n/a	n/a	n/a
H.S. Diplomas (#)	1,147	973	31	101	5	37

Hockinson SD 98

15916 NE 182nd Ave • Brush Prairie, WA 98606-9765
(360) 256-5270
Grade Span: KG-09; **Agency Type:** 1
Schools: 4
2 Primary; 1 Middle; 0 High; 1 Other Level
4 Regular; 0 Special Education; 0 Vocational; 0 Alternative
0 Magnet; 0 Charter; 0 Title I Eligible; 0 School-wide Title I
Students: 1,554 (53.0% male; 47.0% female)
Individual Education Program: 153 (9.8%);
English Language Learner: n/a; Migrant: n/a

Eligible for Free Lunch Program: 150 (9.7%)
Eligible for Reduced-Price Lunch Program: 65 (4.2%)
Teachers: 72.7 (21.4 to 1)
Librarians/Media Specialists: 2.0 (777.0 to 1)
Guidance Counselors: 1.0 (1,554.0 to 1)
Current Spending: ($ per student per year):
Total: $5,899; Instruction: $3,700; Support Services: $1,991
Enrollment, Drop-out Rates and Diploma Recipients by Race/Ethnicity

Category	Total	White	Black	Asian	AIAN	Hisp.
Enrollment (%)	100.0	96.3	0.5	1.0	0.2	2.1
Drop-out Rate (%)	n/a	n/a	n/a	n/a	n/a	n/a
H.S. Diplomas (#)	n/a	n/a	n/a	n/a	n/a	n/a

Ridgefield SD 122
2724 S Hillhurst Rd • Ridgefield, WA 98642-9088
(360) 887-0200 • http://www.ridge.k12.wa.us/
Grade Span: KG-12; **Agency Type:** 1
Schools: 4
2 Primary; 1 Middle; 1 High; 0 Other Level
4 Regular; 0 Special Education; 0 Vocational; 0 Alternative
0 Magnet; 0 Charter; 1 Title I Eligible; 0 School-wide Title I
Students: 1,824 (52.9% male; 47.1% female)
Individual Education Program: 193 (10.6%);
English Language Learner: 15 (0.8%); Migrant: n/a
Eligible for Free Lunch Program: 245 (13.4%)
Eligible for Reduced-Price Lunch Program: 111 (6.1%)
Teachers: 85.1 (21.4 to 1)
Librarians/Media Specialists: 1.0 (1,824.0 to 1)
Guidance Counselors: 2.0 (912.0 to 1)
Current Spending: ($ per student per year):
Total: $5,922; Instruction: $3,848; Support Services: $1,698
Enrollment, Drop-out Rates and Diploma Recipients by Race/Ethnicity

Category	Total	White	Black	Asian	AIAN	Hisp.
Enrollment (%)	100.0	90.6	0.9	3.1	1.7	3.7
Drop-out Rate (%)	n/a	n/a	n/a	n/a	n/a	n/a
H.S. Diplomas (#)	108	100	0	3	3	2

Vancouver SD 37
2901 Falk Rd • Vancouver, WA 98661-5683
(360) 313-1200 • http://www.vannet.k12.wa.us/
Grade Span: PK-12; **Agency Type:** 1
Schools: 37
21 Primary; 5 Middle; 7 High; 4 Other Level
34 Regular; 1 Special Education; 0 Vocational; 2 Alternative
0 Magnet; 0 Charter; 21 Title I Eligible; 18 School-wide Title I
Students: 22,166 (51.2% male; 48.8% female)
Individual Education Program: 2,761 (12.5%);
English Language Learner: 2,250 (10.2%); Migrant: n/a
Eligible for Free Lunch Program: 7,288 (32.9%)
Eligible for Reduced-Price Lunch Program: 1,868 (8.4%)
Teachers: 1,122.9 (19.7 to 1)
Librarians/Media Specialists: 29.0 (764.3 to 1)
Guidance Counselors: 49.7 (446.0 to 1)
Current Spending: ($ per student per year):
Total: $6,551; Instruction: $3,909; Support Services: $2,356
Enrollment, Drop-out Rates and Diploma Recipients by Race/Ethnicity

Category	Total	White	Black	Asian	AIAN	Hisp.
Enrollment (%)	100.0	78.9	4.7	4.7	2.1	9.6
Drop-out Rate (%)	n/a	n/a	n/a	n/a	n/a	n/a
H.S. Diplomas (#)	1,170	996	32	77	15	50

Washougal SD 112-6
2349 B St • Washougal, WA 98671-2497
(360) 954-3000 • http://www.washougal.k12.wa.us/
Grade Span: PK-12; **Agency Type:** 1
Schools: 8
4 Primary; 2 Middle; 2 High; 0 Other Level
7 Regular; 1 Special Education; 0 Vocational; 0 Alternative
0 Magnet; 0 Charter; 3 Title I Eligible; 0 School-wide Title I
Students: 2,666 (51.0% male; 49.0% female)
Individual Education Program: 305 (11.4%);
English Language Learner: 58 (2.2%); Migrant: n/a
Eligible for Free Lunch Program: 561 (21.0%)
Eligible for Reduced-Price Lunch Program: 217 (8.1%)
Teachers: 138.8 (19.2 to 1)
Librarians/Media Specialists: 1.0 (2,666.0 to 1)
Guidance Counselors: 3.5 (761.7 to 1)
Current Spending: ($ per student per year):
Total: $6,625; Instruction: $4,076; Support Services: $2,213
Enrollment, Drop-out Rates and Diploma Recipients by Race/Ethnicity

Category	Total	White	Black	Asian	AIAN	Hisp.
Enrollment (%)	100.0	92.3	1.1	2.1	1.4	3.1
Drop-out Rate (%)	n/a	n/a	n/a	n/a	n/a	n/a
H.S. Diplomas (#)	124	121	0	2	0	1

Cowlitz County

Kelso SD 458
601 Crawford St • Kelso, WA 98626-4398
(360) 501-1927 • http://www.kelso.wednet.edu/
Grade Span: PK-12; **Agency Type:** 1
Schools: 12
7 Primary; 2 Middle; 1 High; 2 Other Level
11 Regular; 1 Special Education; 0 Vocational; 0 Alternative
0 Magnet; 0 Charter; 3 Title I Eligible; 3 School-wide Title I
Students: 5,306 (51.6% male; 48.4% female)
Individual Education Program: 635 (12.0%);
English Language Learner: 154 (2.9%); Migrant: n/a
Eligible for Free Lunch Program: 1,705 (32.1%)
Eligible for Reduced-Price Lunch Program: 473 (8.9%)
Teachers: 267.6 (19.8 to 1)
Librarians/Media Specialists: 9.0 (589.6 to 1)
Guidance Counselors: 7.0 (758.0 to 1)
Current Spending: ($ per student per year):
Total: $6,542; Instruction: $3,885; Support Services: $2,267
Enrollment, Drop-out Rates and Diploma Recipients by Race/Ethnicity

Category	Total	White	Black	Asian	AIAN	Hisp.
Enrollment (%)	100.0	84.5	1.3	1.5	6.7	6.0
Drop-out Rate (%)	n/a	n/a	n/a	n/a	n/a	n/a
H.S. Diplomas (#)	283	248	2	3	22	8

Longview SD 122
2715 Lilac St • Longview, WA 98632-3596
(360) 575-7016 • http://www.longview.k12.wa.us/
Grade Span: PK-12; **Agency Type:** 1
Schools: 15
10 Primary; 2 Middle; 2 High; 1 Other Level
13 Regular; 2 Special Education; 0 Vocational; 0 Alternative
0 Magnet; 0 Charter; 5 Title I Eligible; 4 School-wide Title I
Students: 7,506 (51.4% male; 48.6% female)
Individual Education Program: 977 (13.0%);
English Language Learner: 285 (3.8%); Migrant: n/a
Eligible for Free Lunch Program: 2,452 (32.7%)
Eligible for Reduced-Price Lunch Program: 549 (7.3%)
Teachers: 376.6 (19.9 to 1)
Librarians/Media Specialists: 11.8 (636.1 to 1)
Guidance Counselors: 18.9 (397.1 to 1)
Current Spending: ($ per student per year):
Total: $6,469; Instruction: $3,870; Support Services: $2,282
Enrollment, Drop-out Rates and Diploma Recipients by Race/Ethnicity

Category	Total	White	Black	Asian	AIAN	Hisp.
Enrollment (%)	100.0	82.0	1.6	3.1	3.9	9.3
Drop-out Rate (%)	n/a	n/a	n/a	n/a	n/a	n/a
H.S. Diplomas (#)	360	319	2	23	4	12

Woodland SD 404
800 3rd St • Woodland, WA 98674-8467
(360) 225-9451 • http://www.woodland.wednet.edu/
Grade Span: PK-12; **Agency Type:** 1
Schools: 6
2 Primary; 2 Middle; 2 High; 0 Other Level
5 Regular; 0 Special Education; 0 Vocational; 1 Alternative
0 Magnet; 0 Charter; 2 Title I Eligible; 0 School-wide Title I
Students: 1,962 (53.8% male; 46.2% female)
Individual Education Program: 221 (11.3%);
English Language Learner: 58 (3.0%); Migrant: n/a
Eligible for Free Lunch Program: 406 (20.7%)
Eligible for Reduced-Price Lunch Program: 196 (10.0%)
Teachers: 94.9 (20.7 to 1)
Librarians/Media Specialists: 3.0 (654.0 to 1)
Guidance Counselors: 4.0 (490.5 to 1)
Current Spending: ($ per student per year):
Total: $6,460; Instruction: $3,638; Support Services: $2,460
Enrollment, Drop-out Rates and Diploma Recipients by Race/Ethnicity

Category	Total	White	Black	Asian	AIAN	Hisp.
Enrollment (%)	100.0	90.4	1.0	0.9	1.0	6.7
Drop-out Rate (%)	n/a	n/a	n/a	n/a	n/a	n/a
H.S. Diplomas (#)	102	97	0	2	0	3

Douglas County

Eastmont SD 206
460 9th St NE • East Wenatchee, WA 98802-4443
(509) 884-7169 • http://www.eastmont.wednet.edu/
Grade Span: KG-12; **Agency Type:** 1
Schools: 10
5 Primary; 1 Middle; 2 High; 2 Other Level
9 Regular; 0 Special Education; 1 Vocational; 0 Alternative
0 Magnet; 0 Charter; 6 Title I Eligible; 1 School-wide Title I
Students: 5,462 (51.7% male; 48.3% female)

Individual Education Program: 672 (12.3%);
English Language Learner: 585 (10.7%); Migrant: n/a
Eligible for Free Lunch Program: 1,605 (29.4%)
Eligible for Reduced-Price Lunch Program: 452 (8.3%)
Teachers: 268.4 (20.4 to 1)
Librarians/Media Specialists: 8.4 (650.2 to 1)
Guidance Counselors: 5.9 (925.8 to 1)
Current Spending: ($ per student per year):
Total: $6,055; Instruction: $3,962; Support Services: $1,792
Enrollment, Drop-out Rates and Diploma Recipients by Race/Ethnicity

Category	Total	White	Black	Asian	AIAN	Hisp.
Enrollment (%)	100.0	71.0	0.8	1.2	1.4	25.6
Drop-out Rate (%)	n/a	n/a	n/a	n/a	n/a	n/a
H.S. Diplomas (#)	343	271	0	3	5	64

Franklin County

North Franklin SD 51
1100 W Clark St • Connell, WA 99326-0829
(509) 234-2021 • http://www.nfsd.k12.wa.us/
Grade Span: PK-12; **Agency Type:** 1
Schools: 8
4 Primary; 1 Middle; 2 High; 1 Other Level
7 Regular; 1 Special Education; 0 Vocational; 0 Alternative
0 Magnet; 0 Charter; 5 Title I Eligible; 4 School-wide Title I
Students: 1,985 (51.2% male; 48.8% female)
Individual Education Program: 221 (11.1%);
English Language Learner: 598 (30.1%); Migrant: n/a
Eligible for Free Lunch Program: 1,223 (61.6%)
Eligible for Reduced-Price Lunch Program: 195 (9.8%)
Teachers: 108.7 (18.3 to 1)
Librarians/Media Specialists: 3.3 (601.5 to 1)
Guidance Counselors: 3.4 (583.8 to 1)
Current Spending: ($ per student per year):
Total: $7,150; Instruction: $4,295; Support Services: $2,519
Enrollment, Drop-out Rates and Diploma Recipients by Race/Ethnicity

Category	Total	White	Black	Asian	AIAN	Hisp.
Enrollment (%)	100.0	39.3	0.4	1.7	0.5	58.1
Drop-out Rate (%)	n/a	n/a	n/a	n/a	n/a	n/a
H.S. Diplomas (#)	112	60	0	1	0	51

Pasco SD 001
1215 W Lewis St • Pasco, WA 99301-5472
(509) 543-6700 • http://www.pasco.wednet.edu/
Grade Span: KG-12; **Agency Type:** 1
Schools: 14
9 Primary; 2 Middle; 2 High; 1 Other Level
13 Regular; 0 Special Education; 0 Vocational; 1 Alternative
0 Magnet; 0 Charter; 13 Title I Eligible; 12 School-wide Title I
Students: 9,785 (51.2% male; 48.8% female)
Individual Education Program: 1,028 (10.5%);
English Language Learner: 3,996 (40.8%); Migrant: n/a
Eligible for Free Lunch Program: 5,268 (53.8%)
Eligible for Reduced-Price Lunch Program: 905 (9.2%)
Teachers: 528.9 (18.5 to 1)
Librarians/Media Specialists: 9.4 (1,041.0 to 1)
Guidance Counselors: 17.7 (552.8 to 1)
Current Spending: ($ per student per year):
Total: $6,836; Instruction: $4,049; Support Services: $2,379
Enrollment, Drop-out Rates and Diploma Recipients by Race/Ethnicity

Category	Total	White	Black	Asian	AIAN	Hisp.
Enrollment (%)	100.0	27.6	2.9	1.6	0.4	67.5
Drop-out Rate (%)	n/a	n/a	n/a	n/a	n/a	n/a
H.S. Diplomas (#)	325	175	11	11	2	126

Grant County

Ephrata SD 165
499 C St NW • Ephrata, WA 98823-1690
(509) 754-2474 • http://www.esd165.org/
Grade Span: PK-12; **Agency Type:** 1
Schools: 7
3 Primary; 2 Middle; 1 High; 1 Other Level
6 Regular; 1 Special Education; 0 Vocational; 0 Alternative
0 Magnet; 0 Charter; 3 Title I Eligible; 0 School-wide Title I
Students: 2,317 (50.9% male; 49.1% female)
Individual Education Program: 221 (9.5%);
English Language Learner: 193 (8.3%); Migrant: n/a
Eligible for Free Lunch Program: 587 (25.3%)
Eligible for Reduced-Price Lunch Program: 274 (11.8%)
Teachers: 112.3 (20.6 to 1)
Librarians/Media Specialists: 3.0 (772.3 to 1)
Guidance Counselors: 5.8 (399.5 to 1)
Current Spending: ($ per student per year):
Total: $6,476; Instruction: $3,880; Support Services: $2,288
Enrollment, Drop-out Rates and Diploma Recipients by Race/Ethnicity

Category	Total	White	Black	Asian	AIAN	Hisp.
Enrollment (%)	100.0	80.1	0.6	1.4	0.7	17.3
Drop-out Rate (%)	n/a	n/a	n/a	n/a	n/a	n/a
H.S. Diplomas (#)	163	144	0	3	1	15

Moses Lake SD 161
920 W Ivy Ave • Moses Lake, WA 98837-2047
(509) 766-2650 • http://www.moseslakeschools.org/
Grade Span: PK-12; **Agency Type:** 1
Schools: 13
8 Primary; 3 Middle; 2 High; 0 Other Level
11 Regular; 0 Special Education; 0 Vocational; 2 Alternative
0 Magnet; 0 Charter; 10 Title I Eligible; 4 School-wide Title I
Students: 6,812 (51.5% male; 48.5% female)
Individual Education Program: 786 (11.5%);
English Language Learner: 571 (8.4%); Migrant: n/a
Eligible for Free Lunch Program: 2,785 (40.9%)
Eligible for Reduced-Price Lunch Program: 687 (10.1%)
Teachers: 338.8 (20.1 to 1)
Librarians/Media Specialists: 3.8 (1,792.6 to 1)
Guidance Counselors: 10.9 (625.0 to 1)
Current Spending: ($ per student per year):
Total: $6,276; Instruction: $3,942; Support Services: $1,994
Enrollment, Drop-out Rates and Diploma Recipients by Race/Ethnicity

Category	Total	White	Black	Asian	AIAN	Hisp.
Enrollment (%)	100.0	66.3	2.4	1.5	1.1	28.7
Drop-out Rate (%)	n/a	n/a	n/a	n/a	n/a	n/a
H.S. Diplomas (#)	353	273	2	11	1	66

Quincy SD 144
119 J St SW • Quincy, WA 98848-1330
(509) 787-4571 • http://www.qsd.wednet.edu/
Grade Span: PK-12; **Agency Type:** 1
Schools: 7
4 Primary; 2 Middle; 1 High; 0 Other Level
6 Regular; 1 Special Education; 0 Vocational; 0 Alternative
0 Magnet; 0 Charter; 4 Title I Eligible; 1 School-wide Title I
Students: 2,331 (53.7% male; 46.3% female)
Individual Education Program: 297 (12.7%);
English Language Learner: 685 (29.4%); Migrant: n/a
Eligible for Free Lunch Program: 1,199 (51.4%)
Eligible for Reduced-Price Lunch Program: 276 (11.8%)
Teachers: 133.6 (17.4 to 1)
Librarians/Media Specialists: 1.0 (2,331.0 to 1)
Guidance Counselors: 5.0 (466.2 to 1)
Current Spending: ($ per student per year):
Total: $6,391; Instruction: $3,983; Support Services: $2,035
Enrollment, Drop-out Rates and Diploma Recipients by Race/Ethnicity

Category	Total	White	Black	Asian	AIAN	Hisp.
Enrollment (%)	100.0	31.4	0.1	0.3	0.3	67.9
Drop-out Rate (%)	n/a	n/a	n/a	n/a	n/a	n/a
H.S. Diplomas (#)	117	67	0	0	0	50

Wahluke SD 73
411 E Saddle Mt Dr • Mattawa, WA 99349-0952
(509) 932-4565
Grade Span: PK-12; **Agency Type:** 1
Schools: 5
2 Primary; 1 Middle; 2 High; 0 Other Level
4 Regular; 0 Special Education; 0 Vocational; 1 Alternative
0 Magnet; 0 Charter; 3 Title I Eligible; 3 School-wide Title I
Students: 1,643 (52.2% male; 47.8% female)
Individual Education Program: 191 (11.6%);
English Language Learner: 955 (58.1%); Migrant: n/a
Eligible for Free Lunch Program: 1,206 (73.4%)
Eligible for Reduced-Price Lunch Program: 195 (11.9%)
Teachers: 99.9 (16.4 to 1)
Librarians/Media Specialists: 1.0 (1,643.0 to 1)
Guidance Counselors: 4.0 (410.8 to 1)
Current Spending: ($ per student per year):
Total: $6,627; Instruction: $3,901; Support Services: $2,305
Enrollment, Drop-out Rates and Diploma Recipients by Race/Ethnicity

Category	Total	White	Black	Asian	AIAN	Hisp.
Enrollment (%)	100.0	14.2	0.0	0.5	1.0	84.4
Drop-out Rate (%)	n/a	n/a	n/a	n/a	n/a	n/a
H.S. Diplomas (#)	72	31	0	0	0	41

Grays Harbor County

Aberdeen SD 5
216 N G St • Aberdeen, WA 98520-5297
(360) 538-2006 • http://www.asd5.org/
Grade Span: PK-12; **Agency Type:** 1
Schools: 13

7 Primary; 1 Middle; 3 High; 2 Other Level
11 Regular; 0 Special Education; 0 Vocational; 2 Alternative
0 Magnet; 0 Charter; 7 Title I Eligible; 6 School-wide Title I
Students: 4,178 (50.8% male; 49.2% female)
Individual Education Program: 559 (13.4%);
English Language Learner: 198 (4.7%); Migrant: n/a
Eligible for Free Lunch Program: 1,948 (46.6%)
Eligible for Reduced-Price Lunch Program: 397 (9.5%)
Teachers: 218.1 (19.2 to 1)
Librarians/Media Specialists: 2.0 (2,089.0 to 1)
Guidance Counselors: 8.0 (522.3 to 1)
Current Spending: ($ per student per year):
Total: $6,582; Instruction: $4,241; Support Services: $1,940
Enrollment, Drop-out Rates and Diploma Recipients by Race/Ethnicity

Category	Total	White	Black	Asian	AIAN	Hisp.
Enrollment (%)	100.0	76.3	1.1	4.6	7.8	10.2
Drop-out Rate (%)	n/a	n/a	n/a	n/a	n/a	n/a
H.S. Diplomas (#)	273	230	4	10	23	6

Elma SD 68
1235 Monte Elma Rd • Elma, WA 98541-9038
(360) 482-2822 • http://wonders.eburg.wednet.edu/
Grade Span: KG-12; **Agency Type:** 1
Schools: 4
1 Primary; 1 Middle; 2 High; 0 Other Level
3 Regular; 0 Special Education; 0 Vocational; 1 Alternative
0 Magnet; 0 Charter; 1 Title I Eligible; 1 School-wide Title I
Students: 2,001 (53.2% male; 46.8% female)
Individual Education Program: 262 (13.1%);
English Language Learner: 48 (2.4%); Migrant: n/a
Eligible for Free Lunch Program: 549 (27.4%)
Eligible for Reduced-Price Lunch Program: 179 (8.9%)
Teachers: 106.5 (18.8 to 1)
Librarians/Media Specialists: 0.0 (0.0 to 1)
Guidance Counselors: 4.0 (500.3 to 1)
Current Spending: ($ per student per year):
Total: $6,365; Instruction: $4,080; Support Services: $1,932
Enrollment, Drop-out Rates and Diploma Recipients by Race/Ethnicity

Category	Total	White	Black	Asian	AIAN	Hisp.
Enrollment (%)	100.0	88.6	1.2	1.3	3.8	4.9
Drop-out Rate (%)	n/a	n/a	n/a	n/a	n/a	n/a
H.S. Diplomas (#)	171	149	2	5	7	8

Hoquiam SD 28
305 Simpson Ave • Hoquiam, WA 98550-2419
(360) 538-8200 • http://www.hoquiam.k12.wa.us/
Grade Span: KG-12; **Agency Type:** 1
Schools: 6
4 Primary; 1 Middle; 1 High; 0 Other Level
6 Regular; 0 Special Education; 0 Vocational; 0 Alternative
0 Magnet; 0 Charter; 4 Title I Eligible; 3 School-wide Title I
Students: 2,100 (52.4% male; 47.6% female)
Individual Education Program: 257 (12.2%);
English Language Learner: 91 (4.3%); Migrant: n/a
Eligible for Free Lunch Program: 899 (42.8%)
Eligible for Reduced-Price Lunch Program: 276 (13.1%)
Teachers: 108.8 (19.3 to 1)
Librarians/Media Specialists: 1.0 (2,100.0 to 1)
Guidance Counselors: 3.0 (700.0 to 1)
Current Spending: ($ per student per year):
Total: $6,776; Instruction: $4,059; Support Services: $2,313
Enrollment, Drop-out Rates and Diploma Recipients by Race/Ethnicity

Category	Total	White	Black	Asian	AIAN	Hisp.
Enrollment (%)	100.0	80.9	1.5	2.5	6.7	8.4
Drop-out Rate (%)	n/a	n/a	n/a	n/a	n/a	n/a
H.S. Diplomas (#)	114	96	1	6	3	8

Island County

Oak Harbor SD 201
350 S Oak Harbor St • Oak Harbor, WA 98277-5015
(360) 279-5006 • http://www.ohsd.net/
Grade Span: PK-12; **Agency Type:** 1
Schools: 13
7 Primary; 2 Middle; 3 High; 1 Other Level
10 Regular; 2 Special Education; 0 Vocational; 1 Alternative
0 Magnet; 0 Charter; 4 Title I Eligible; 0 School-wide Title I
Students: 6,153 (51.9% male; 48.1% female)
Individual Education Program: 657 (10.7%);
English Language Learner: 166 (2.7%); Migrant: n/a
Eligible for Free Lunch Program: 971 (15.8%)
Eligible for Reduced-Price Lunch Program: 795 (12.9%)
Teachers: 310.0 (19.8 to 1)
Librarians/Media Specialists: 9.0 (683.7 to 1)
Guidance Counselors: 12.9 (477.0 to 1)
Current Spending: ($ per student per year):
Total: $5,739; Instruction: $3,679; Support Services: $1,921
Enrollment, Drop-out Rates and Diploma Recipients by Race/Ethnicity

Category	Total	White	Black	Asian	AIAN	Hisp.
Enrollment (%)	100.0	72.8	7.1	13.8	1.3	5.0
Drop-out Rate (%)	n/a	n/a	n/a	n/a	n/a	n/a
H.S. Diplomas (#)	378	284	8	64	3	19

South Whidbey SD 206
721 Camano Ave • Langley, WA 98260-9577
(360) 221-6100 • http://www.islandweb.org/schools/swsd.htm
Grade Span: PK-12; **Agency Type:** 1
Schools: 7
3 Primary; 1 Middle; 2 High; 1 Other Level
4 Regular; 1 Special Education; 0 Vocational; 2 Alternative
0 Magnet; 0 Charter; 2 Title I Eligible; 0 School-wide Title I
Students: 2,364 (50.4% male; 49.6% female)
Individual Education Program: 254 (10.7%);
English Language Learner: 10 (0.4%); Migrant: n/a
Eligible for Free Lunch Program: 224 (9.5%)
Eligible for Reduced-Price Lunch Program: 137 (5.8%)
Teachers: 120.7 (19.6 to 1)
Librarians/Media Specialists: 3.2 (738.8 to 1)
Guidance Counselors: 4.7 (503.0 to 1)
Current Spending: ($ per student per year):
Total: $6,405; Instruction: $3,870; Support Services: $2,279
Enrollment, Drop-out Rates and Diploma Recipients by Race/Ethnicity

Category	Total	White	Black	Asian	AIAN	Hisp.
Enrollment (%)	100.0	91.4	1.3	3.6	1.4	2.3
Drop-out Rate (%)	n/a	n/a	n/a	n/a	n/a	n/a
H.S. Diplomas (#)	168	162	1	4	0	1

Jefferson County

Port Townsend SD 50
450 Fir St Lincoln Bldg • Port Townsend, WA 98368-6441
(360) 379-4501 • http://www.ptsd.wednet.edu/
Grade Span: PK-12; **Agency Type:** 1
Schools: 5
2 Primary; 1 Middle; 1 High; 1 Other Level
4 Regular; 0 Special Education; 0 Vocational; 1 Alternative
0 Magnet; 0 Charter; 1 Title I Eligible; 0 School-wide Title I
Students: 1,741 (51.1% male; 48.9% female)
Individual Education Program: 220 (12.6%);
English Language Learner: 19 (1.1%); Migrant: n/a
Eligible for Free Lunch Program: 421 (24.2%)
Eligible for Reduced-Price Lunch Program: 223 (12.8%)
Teachers: 86.9 (20.0 to 1)
Librarians/Media Specialists: 2.8 (621.8 to 1)
Guidance Counselors: 4.2 (414.5 to 1)
Current Spending: ($ per student per year):
Total: $6,330; Instruction: $3,903; Support Services: $2,016
Enrollment, Drop-out Rates and Diploma Recipients by Race/Ethnicity

Category	Total	White	Black	Asian	AIAN	Hisp.
Enrollment (%)	100.0	89.7	2.1	3.3	2.7	2.1
Drop-out Rate (%)	n/a	n/a	n/a	n/a	n/a	n/a
H.S. Diplomas (#)	161	154	1	3	3	0

King County

Auburn SD 408
915 4th St NE • Auburn, WA 98002-4499
(253) 931-4914 • http://www.auburn.wednet.edu/
Grade Span: PK-12; **Agency Type:** 1
Schools: 20
12 Primary; 4 Middle; 3 High; 1 Other Level
18 Regular; 1 Special Education; 0 Vocational; 1 Alternative
0 Magnet; 0 Charter; 8 Title I Eligible; 1 School-wide Title I
Students: 13,621 (51.1% male; 48.9% female)
Individual Education Program: 1,385 (10.2%);
English Language Learner: 831 (6.1%); Migrant: n/a
Eligible for Free Lunch Program: 3,511 (25.8%)
Eligible for Reduced-Price Lunch Program: 1,259 (9.2%)
Teachers: 686.6 (19.8 to 1)
Librarians/Media Specialists: 18.0 (756.7 to 1)
Guidance Counselors: 32.0 (425.7 to 1)
Current Spending: ($ per student per year):
Total: $6,174; Instruction: $3,802; Support Services: $2,044
Enrollment, Drop-out Rates and Diploma Recipients by Race/Ethnicity

Category	Total	White	Black	Asian	AIAN	Hisp.
Enrollment (%)	100.0	74.3	5.0	7.1	4.3	9.3
Drop-out Rate (%)	n/a	n/a	n/a	n/a	n/a	n/a
H.S. Diplomas (#)	836	717	19	50	16	34

Bellevue SD 405

12111 NE 1st St • Bellevue, WA 98005-3183
(425) 456-4172 • http://belnet.bellevue.k12.wa.us/
Grade Span: PK-12; **Agency Type:** 1
Schools: 31
16 Primary; 6 Middle; 7 High; 2 Other Level
25 Regular; 1 Special Education; 0 Vocational; 5 Alternative
0 Magnet; 0 Charter; 9 Title I Eligible; 2 School-wide Title I
Students: 15,656 (51.9% male; 48.1% female)
Individual Education Program: 1,495 (9.5%);
English Language Learner: 1,801 (11.5%); Migrant: n/a
Eligible for Free Lunch Program: 1,929 (12.3%)
Eligible for Reduced-Price Lunch Program: 747 (4.8%)
Teachers: 863.2 (18.1 to 1)
Librarians/Media Specialists: 20.8 (752.7 to 1)
Guidance Counselors: 32.2 (486.2 to 1)
Current Spending: ($ per student per year):
Total: $6,847; Instruction: $4,071; Support Services: $2,470
Enrollment, Drop-out Rates and Diploma Recipients by Race/Ethnicity

Category	Total	White	Black	Asian	AIAN	Hisp.
Enrollment (%)	100.0	68.4	2.7	20.7	0.4	7.8
Drop-out Rate (%)	n/a	n/a	n/a	n/a	n/a	n/a
H.S. Diplomas (#)	1,090	773	33	253	1	30

Enumclaw SD 216

2929 Mcdougall Ave • Enumclaw, WA 98022-7499
(360) 802-7100 • http://www.enumclaw.wednet.edu/
Grade Span: PK-12; **Agency Type:** 1
Schools: 9
5 Primary; 3 Middle; 1 High; 0 Other Level
9 Regular; 0 Special Education; 0 Vocational; 0 Alternative
0 Magnet; 0 Charter; 1 Title I Eligible; 0 School-wide Title I
Students: 5,112 (50.9% male; 49.1% female)
Individual Education Program: 602 (11.8%);
English Language Learner: 49 (1.0%); Migrant: n/a
Eligible for Free Lunch Program: 571 (11.2%)
Eligible for Reduced-Price Lunch Program: 298 (5.8%)
Teachers: 244.3 (20.9 to 1)
Librarians/Media Specialists: 6.1 (838.0 to 1)
Guidance Counselors: 13.0 (393.2 to 1)
Current Spending: ($ per student per year):
Total: $6,447; Instruction: $3,831; Support Services: $2,297
Enrollment, Drop-out Rates and Diploma Recipients by Race/Ethnicity

Category	Total	White	Black	Asian	AIAN	Hisp.
Enrollment (%)	100.0	91.4	0.6	1.4	1.8	4.7
Drop-out Rate (%)	n/a	n/a	n/a	n/a	n/a	n/a
H.S. Diplomas (#)	316	299	3	5	2	7

Federal Way SD 210

31405 18th Ave S • Federal Way, WA 98003-5433
(253) 945-2000 • http://www.fwsd.wednet.edu/
Grade Span: PK-12; **Agency Type:** 1
Schools: 37
23 Primary; 7 Middle; 4 High; 3 Other Level
32 Regular; 2 Special Education; 0 Vocational; 3 Alternative
0 Magnet; 0 Charter; 8 Title I Eligible; 7 School-wide Title I
Students: 22,449 (51.6% male; 48.4% female)
Individual Education Program: 2,688 (12.0%);
English Language Learner: 2,071 (9.2%); Migrant: n/a
Eligible for Free Lunch Program: 5,304 (23.6%)
Eligible for Reduced-Price Lunch Program: 2,256 (10.0%)
Teachers: 1,147.7 (19.6 to 1)
Librarians/Media Specialists: 30.4 (738.5 to 1)
Guidance Counselors: 40.0 (561.2 to 1)
Current Spending: ($ per student per year):
Total: $5,935; Instruction: $3,686; Support Services: $1,950
Enrollment, Drop-out Rates and Diploma Recipients by Race/Ethnicity

Category	Total	White	Black	Asian	AIAN	Hisp.
Enrollment (%)	100.0	59.6	12.6	16.2	1.5	10.2
Drop-out Rate (%)	n/a	n/a	n/a	n/a	n/a	n/a
H.S. Diplomas (#)	1,151	805	100	188	11	47

Highline SD 401

15675 Ambaum Bldv SW • Seattle, WA 98166-0100
(206) 433-2217 • http://www.hsd401.org/
Grade Span: KG-12; **Agency Type:** 1
Schools: 32
21 Primary; 5 Middle; 6 High; 0 Other Level
30 Regular; 0 Special Education; 1 Vocational; 1 Alternative
0 Magnet; 0 Charter; 20 Title I Eligible; 14 School-wide Title I
Students: 17,735 (51.5% male; 48.5% female)
Individual Education Program: 2,071 (11.7%);
English Language Learner: 2,066 (11.6%); Migrant: n/a
Eligible for Free Lunch Program: 7,037 (39.7%)
Eligible for Reduced-Price Lunch Program: 1,882 (10.6%)
Teachers: 954.6 (18.6 to 1)
Librarians/Media Specialists: 31.8 (557.7 to 1)
Guidance Counselors: 42.7 (415.3 to 1)
Current Spending: ($ per student per year):
Total: $6,683; Instruction: $3,860; Support Services: $2,519
Enrollment, Drop-out Rates and Diploma Recipients by Race/Ethnicity

Category	Total	White	Black	Asian	AIAN	Hisp.
Enrollment (%)	100.0	45.9	13.3	20.7	2.1	17.9
Drop-out Rate (%)	n/a	n/a	n/a	n/a	n/a	n/a
H.S. Diplomas (#)	984	625	58	215	16	70

Issaquah SD 411

565 NW Holly St • Issaquah, WA 98027-2899
(425) 837-7002 • http://www.issaquah.wednet.edu/
Grade Span: PK-12; **Agency Type:** 1
Schools: 23
12 Primary; 4 Middle; 5 High; 2 Other Level
21 Regular; 1 Special Education; 0 Vocational; 1 Alternative
0 Magnet; 0 Charter; 6 Title I Eligible; 0 School-wide Title I
Students: 14,759 (52.1% male; 47.9% female)
Individual Education Program: 1,644 (11.1%);
English Language Learner: 227 (1.5%); Migrant: n/a
Eligible for Free Lunch Program: 564 (3.8%)
Eligible for Reduced-Price Lunch Program: 325 (2.2%)
Teachers: 730.4 (20.2 to 1)
Librarians/Media Specialists: 20.0 (738.0 to 1)
Guidance Counselors: 26.0 (567.7 to 1)
Current Spending: ($ per student per year):
Total: $6,204; Instruction: $3,645; Support Services: $2,221
Enrollment, Drop-out Rates and Diploma Recipients by Race/Ethnicity

Category	Total	White	Black	Asian	AIAN	Hisp.
Enrollment (%)	100.0	82.9	1.7	12.0	0.6	2.8
Drop-out Rate (%)	n/a	n/a	n/a	n/a	n/a	n/a
H.S. Diplomas (#)	896	769	11	97	3	16

Kent SD 415

12033 SE 256th St • Kent, WA 98031-6643
(253) 373-7200 • http://www.kent.wednet.edu/
Grade Span: PK-12; **Agency Type:** 1
Schools: 42
28 Primary; 7 Middle; 6 High; 1 Other Level
39 Regular; 0 Special Education; 0 Vocational; 3 Alternative
0 Magnet; 0 Charter; 15 Title I Eligible; 7 School-wide Title I
Students: 26,694 (51.8% male; 48.2% female)
Individual Education Program: 3,162 (11.8%);
English Language Learner: 3,066 (11.5%); Migrant: n/a
Eligible for Free Lunch Program: 5,948 (22.3%)
Eligible for Reduced-Price Lunch Program: 2,270 (8.5%)
Teachers: 1,435.6 (18.6 to 1)
Librarians/Media Specialists: 24.5 (1,089.6 to 1)
Guidance Counselors: 50.8 (525.5 to 1)
Current Spending: ($ per student per year):
Total: $6,296; Instruction: $3,839; Support Services: $2,147
Enrollment, Drop-out Rates and Diploma Recipients by Race/Ethnicity

Category	Total	White	Black	Asian	AIAN	Hisp.
Enrollment (%)	100.0	67.1	9.9	14.6	1.2	7.2
Drop-out Rate (%)	n/a	n/a	n/a	n/a	n/a	n/a
H.S. Diplomas (#)	1,535	1,122	114	228	13	58

Lake Washington SD 414

16250 NE 74th St • Redmond, WA 98052-7817
(425) 702-3257 • http://www.lkwash.wednet.edu/
Grade Span: PK-12; **Agency Type:** 1
Schools: 47
29 Primary; 9 Middle; 7 High; 2 Other Level
37 Regular; 1 Special Education; 0 Vocational; 9 Alternative
0 Magnet; 0 Charter; 11 Title I Eligible; 0 School-wide Title I
Students: 24,098 (51.9% male; 48.1% female)
Individual Education Program: 2,262 (9.4%);
English Language Learner: 1,292 (5.4%); Migrant: n/a
Eligible for Free Lunch Program: 1,814 (7.5%)
Eligible for Reduced-Price Lunch Program: 725 (3.0%)
Teachers: 1,180.6 (20.4 to 1)
Librarians/Media Specialists: 36.3 (663.9 to 1)
Guidance Counselors: 44.9 (536.7 to 1)
Current Spending: ($ per student per year):
Total: $6,356; Instruction: $3,882; Support Services: $2,167
Enrollment, Drop-out Rates and Diploma Recipients by Race/Ethnicity

Category	Total	White	Black	Asian	AIAN	Hisp.
Enrollment (%)	100.0	79.1	2.5	12.0	0.7	5.7
Drop-out Rate (%)	n/a	n/a	n/a	n/a	n/a	n/a
H.S. Diplomas (#)	1,651	1,386	32	171	9	53

Mercer Island SD 400

4160 86th Ave SE • Mercer Island, WA 98040-4196
(206) 236-3300 • http://www.misd.wednet.edu/
Grade Span: KG-12; **Agency Type:** 1
Schools: 6
4 Primary; 1 Middle; 1 High; 0 Other Level
5 Regular; 1 Special Education; 0 Vocational; 0 Alternative
0 Magnet; 0 Charter; 2 Title I Eligible; 0 School-wide Title I
Students: 4,133 (52.3% male; 47.7% female)
Individual Education Program: 374 (9.0%);
English Language Learner: 96 (2.3%); Migrant: n/a
Eligible for Free Lunch Program: 27 (0.7%)
Eligible for Reduced-Price Lunch Program: 32 (0.8%)
Teachers: 202.9 (20.4 to 1)
Librarians/Media Specialists: 5.0 (826.6 to 1)
Guidance Counselors: 7.7 (536.8 to 1)
Current Spending: ($ per student per year):
Total: $6,554; Instruction: $3,625; Support Services: $2,517
Enrollment, Drop-out Rates and Diploma Recipients by Race/Ethnicity

Category	Total	White	Black	Asian	AIAN	Hisp.
Enrollment (%)	100.0	79.5	1.4	17.3	0.2	1.5
Drop-out Rate (%)	n/a	n/a	n/a	n/a	n/a	n/a
H.S. Diplomas (#)	330	268	8	50	1	3

Northshore SD 417

18315 Bothell Way NE • Bothell, WA 98011-1983
(425) 489-6353 • http://www.nsd.org/
Grade Span: PK-12; **Agency Type:** 1
Schools: 35
21 Primary; 6 Middle; 5 High; 3 Other Level
31 Regular; 1 Special Education; 0 Vocational; 3 Alternative
0 Magnet; 0 Charter; 11 Title I Eligible; 0 School-wide Title I
Students: 20,181 (52.3% male; 47.7% female)
Individual Education Program: 2,442 (12.1%);
English Language Learner: 531 (2.6%); Migrant: n/a
Eligible for Free Lunch Program: 1,320 (6.5%)
Eligible for Reduced-Price Lunch Program: 633 (3.1%)
Teachers: 1,014.8 (19.9 to 1)
Librarians/Media Specialists: 31.9 (632.6 to 1)
Guidance Counselors: 29.7 (679.5 to 1)
Current Spending: ($ per student per year):
Total: $6,543; Instruction: $3,944; Support Services: $2,293
Enrollment, Drop-out Rates and Diploma Recipients by Race/Ethnicity

Category	Total	White	Black	Asian	AIAN	Hisp.
Enrollment (%)	100.0	81.8	2.3	9.4	1.1	5.4
Drop-out Rate (%)	n/a	n/a	n/a	n/a	n/a	n/a
H.S. Diplomas (#)	1,413	1,247	18	96	12	40

Renton SD 403

Kohlwes Educ Ctr, 300 SW 7th • Renton, WA 98055-2307
(425) 204-2340 • http://www.renton.wednet.edu/
Grade Span: PK-12; **Agency Type:** 1
Schools: 27
15 Primary; 3 Middle; 7 High; 2 Other Level
20 Regular; 4 Special Education; 0 Vocational; 3 Alternative
0 Magnet; 0 Charter; 8 Title I Eligible; 2 School-wide Title I
Students: 13,100 (52.2% male; 47.8% female)
Individual Education Program: 1,634 (12.5%);
English Language Learner: 1,090 (8.3%); Migrant: n/a
Eligible for Free Lunch Program: 3,451 (26.3%)
Eligible for Reduced-Price Lunch Program: 1,236 (9.4%)
Teachers: 641.8 (20.4 to 1)
Librarians/Media Specialists: 19.9 (658.3 to 1)
Guidance Counselors: 27.5 (476.4 to 1)
Current Spending: ($ per student per year):
Total: $6,398; Instruction: $3,756; Support Services: $2,357
Enrollment, Drop-out Rates and Diploma Recipients by Race/Ethnicity

Category	Total	White	Black	Asian	AIAN	Hisp.
Enrollment (%)	100.0	51.1	17.7	20.3	1.5	9.5
Drop-out Rate (%)	n/a	n/a	n/a	n/a	n/a	n/a
H.S. Diplomas (#)	651	357	101	148	15	30

Riverview Special Services

32240 NE 50th St • Carnation, WA 98014-6332
(425) 844-4504 • http://www.riverview.wednet.edu/
Grade Span: PK-12; **Agency Type:** 1
Schools: 8
4 Primary; 1 Middle; 2 High; 1 Other Level
6 Regular; 0 Special Education; 0 Vocational; 2 Alternative
0 Magnet; 0 Charter; 3 Title I Eligible; 0 School-wide Title I
Students: 2,912 (50.7% male; 49.3% female)
Individual Education Program: 328 (11.3%);
English Language Learner: 49 (1.7%); Migrant: n/a
Eligible for Free Lunch Program: 217 (7.5%)
Eligible for Reduced-Price Lunch Program: 128 (4.4%)
Teachers: 148.8 (19.6 to 1)
Librarians/Media Specialists: 5.0 (582.4 to 1)
Guidance Counselors: 5.5 (529.5 to 1)
Current Spending: ($ per student per year):
Total: $6,419; Instruction: $3,788; Support Services: $2,239
Enrollment, Drop-out Rates and Diploma Recipients by Race/Ethnicity

Category	Total	White	Black	Asian	AIAN	Hisp.
Enrollment (%)	100.0	90.5	0.4	2.9	1.1	5.0
Drop-out Rate (%)	n/a	n/a	n/a	n/a	n/a	n/a
H.S. Diplomas (#)	150	135	0	3	4	8

Seattle SD 1

815 4th Ave N • Seattle, WA 98109-3902
(206) 252-0100 • http://www.seattleschools.org/area/main/index.dxml
Grade Span: PK-12; **Agency Type:** 1
Schools: 132
74 Primary; 11 Middle; 34 High; 13 Other Level
88 Regular; 8 Special Education; 0 Vocational; 36 Alternative
0 Magnet; 0 Charter; 34 Title I Eligible; 34 School-wide Title I
Students: 47,853 (51.3% male; 48.7% female)
Individual Education Program: 5,991 (12.5%);
English Language Learner: 5,564 (11.6%); Migrant: n/a
Eligible for Free Lunch Program: 15,541 (32.5%)
Eligible for Reduced-Price Lunch Program: 3,659 (7.6%)
Teachers: 2,662.4 (18.0 to 1)
Librarians/Media Specialists: 76.4 (626.3 to 1)
Guidance Counselors: 95.9 (499.0 to 1)
Current Spending: ($ per student per year):
Total: $8,082; Instruction: $4,430; Support Services: $3,363
Enrollment, Drop-out Rates and Diploma Recipients by Race/Ethnicity

Category	Total	White	Black	Asian	AIAN	Hisp.
Enrollment (%)	100.0	40.1	23.0	23.3	2.6	11.0
Drop-out Rate (%)	n/a	n/a	n/a	n/a	n/a	n/a
H.S. Diplomas (#)	2,629	1,046	542	779	60	202

Shoreline SD 412

18560 1st Ave NE • Shoreline, WA 98155-2118
(206) 361-4203 • http://www.shorelineschools.org/
Grade Span: PK-12; **Agency Type:** 1
Schools: 20
12 Primary; 2 Middle; 4 High; 2 Other Level
16 Regular; 2 Special Education; 0 Vocational; 2 Alternative
0 Magnet; 0 Charter; 8 Title I Eligible; 0 School-wide Title I
Students: 10,099 (52.2% male; 47.8% female)
Individual Education Program: 1,270 (12.6%);
English Language Learner: 638 (6.3%); Migrant: n/a
Eligible for Free Lunch Program: 1,004 (9.9%)
Eligible for Reduced-Price Lunch Program: 499 (4.9%)
Teachers: 533.5 (18.9 to 1)
Librarians/Media Specialists: 15.0 (673.3 to 1)
Guidance Counselors: 13.5 (748.1 to 1)
Current Spending: ($ per student per year):
Total: $7,199; Instruction: $4,175; Support Services: $2,668
Enrollment, Drop-out Rates and Diploma Recipients by Race/Ethnicity

Category	Total	White	Black	Asian	AIAN	Hisp.
Enrollment (%)	100.0	69.5	5.8	18.3	1.3	5.0
Drop-out Rate (%)	n/a	n/a	n/a	n/a	n/a	n/a
H.S. Diplomas (#)	746	540	16	160	6	24

Snoqualmie SD 410

8001 Silva Ave SE • Snoqualmie, WA 98065-0400
(425) 831-8000 • http://www.snoqualmie.k12.wa.us/
Grade Span: PK-12; **Agency Type:** 1
Schools: 8
4 Primary; 2 Middle; 2 High; 0 Other Level
7 Regular; 0 Special Education; 0 Vocational; 1 Alternative
0 Magnet; 0 Charter; 4 Title I Eligible; 0 School-wide Title I
Students: 4,719 (52.0% male; 48.0% female)
Individual Education Program: 499 (10.6%);
English Language Learner: 25 (0.5%); Migrant: n/a
Eligible for Free Lunch Program: 402 (8.5%)
Eligible for Reduced-Price Lunch Program: 246 (5.2%)
Teachers: 229.5 (20.6 to 1)
Librarians/Media Specialists: 5.5 (858.0 to 1)
Guidance Counselors: 6.1 (773.6 to 1)
Current Spending: ($ per student per year):
Total: $6,341; Instruction: $3,694; Support Services: $2,266
Enrollment, Drop-out Rates and Diploma Recipients by Race/Ethnicity

Category	Total	White	Black	Asian	AIAN	Hisp.
Enrollment (%)	100.0	92.3	1.1	2.2	1.5	2.8
Drop-out Rate (%)	n/a	n/a	n/a	n/a	n/a	n/a
H.S. Diplomas (#)	240	221	0	4	2	13

Tahoma SD 409

25720 Maple Valley Blk Diam • Maple Valley, WA 98038-8313
(425) 413-3400 • http://www.tahoma.wednet.edu/
Grade Span: PK-12; **Agency Type:** 1
Schools: 10
4 Primary; 1 Middle; 3 High; 2 Other Level
8 Regular; 1 Special Education; 0 Vocational; 1 Alternative
0 Magnet; 0 Charter; 2 Title I Eligible; 0 School-wide Title I
Students: 6,272 (51.0% male; 49.0% female)
Individual Education Program: 819 (13.1%);
English Language Learner: 38 (0.6%); Migrant: n/a
Eligible for Free Lunch Program: 370 (5.9%)
Eligible for Reduced-Price Lunch Program: 205 (3.3%)
Teachers: 310.3 (20.2 to 1)
Librarians/Media Specialists: 4.0 (1,568.0 to 1)
Guidance Counselors: 8.6 (729.3 to 1)
Current Spending: ($ per student per year):
Total: $6,101; Instruction: $3,691; Support Services: $2,141
Enrollment, Drop-out Rates and Diploma Recipients by Race/Ethnicity

Category	Total	White	Black	Asian	AIAN	Hisp.
Enrollment (%)	100.0	91.2	1.8	2.7	1.1	3.3
Drop-out Rate (%)	n/a	n/a	n/a	n/a	n/a	n/a
H.S. Diplomas (#)	351	328	6	13	1	3

Tukwila SD 406

4640 S 144th St • Tukwila, WA 98168-4134
(206) 901-8000 • http://www.tukwila.wednet.edu/
Grade Span: PK-12; **Agency Type:** 1
Schools: 5
3 Primary; 1 Middle; 1 High; 0 Other Level
5 Regular; 0 Special Education; 0 Vocational; 0 Alternative
0 Magnet; 0 Charter; 4 Title I Eligible; 4 School-wide Title I
Students: 2,742 (51.8% male; 48.2% female)
Individual Education Program: 280 (10.2%);
English Language Learner: 781 (28.5%); Migrant: n/a
Eligible for Free Lunch Program: 1,381 (50.4%)
Eligible for Reduced-Price Lunch Program: 289 (10.5%)
Teachers: 135.5 (20.2 to 1)
Librarians/Media Specialists: 5.0 (548.4 to 1)
Guidance Counselors: 3.6 (761.7 to 1)
Current Spending: ($ per student per year):
Total: $7,233; Instruction: $4,188; Support Services: $2,726
Enrollment, Drop-out Rates and Diploma Recipients by Race/Ethnicity

Category	Total	White	Black	Asian	AIAN	Hisp.
Enrollment (%)	100.0	37.1	21.7	17.4	1.6	22.2
Drop-out Rate (%)	n/a	n/a	n/a	n/a	n/a	n/a
H.S. Diplomas (#)	139	78	15	30	5	11

Vashon Island SD 402

20414 Vashon Hwy SW • Vashon, WA 98070-6503
(206) 463-6000 • http://www.vashonsd.wednet.edu/
Grade Span: PK-12; **Agency Type:** 1
Schools: 4
1 Primary; 1 Middle; 1 High; 1 Other Level
3 Regular; 0 Special Education; 0 Vocational; 1 Alternative
0 Magnet; 0 Charter; 2 Title I Eligible; 0 School-wide Title I
Students: 1,606 (52.3% male; 47.7% female)
Individual Education Program: 179 (11.1%);
English Language Learner: 16 (1.0%); Migrant: n/a
Eligible for Free Lunch Program: 92 (5.7%)
Eligible for Reduced-Price Lunch Program: 33 (2.1%)
Teachers: 85.8 (18.7 to 1)
Librarians/Media Specialists: 3.0 (535.3 to 1)
Guidance Counselors: 3.7 (434.1 to 1)
Current Spending: ($ per student per year):
Total: $6,553; Instruction: $3,792; Support Services: $2,432
Enrollment, Drop-out Rates and Diploma Recipients by Race/Ethnicity

Category	Total	White	Black	Asian	AIAN	Hisp.
Enrollment (%)	100.0	91.5	1.6	3.1	0.8	3.0
Drop-out Rate (%)	n/a	n/a	n/a	n/a	n/a	n/a
H.S. Diplomas (#)	132	119	3	4	2	4

Kitsap County

Bainbridge Island SD 303

8489 Madison Ave NE • Bainbridge Isl, WA 98110-2999
(206) 780-1050 • http://www.bainbridge.wednet.edu/
Grade Span: PK-12; **Agency Type:** 1
Schools: 11
6 Primary; 2 Middle; 3 High; 0 Other Level
6 Regular; 1 Special Education; 0 Vocational; 4 Alternative
0 Magnet; 0 Charter; 2 Title I Eligible; 0 School-wide Title I
Students: 4,142 (51.2% male; 48.8% female)
Individual Education Program: 488 (11.8%);
English Language Learner: 26 (0.6%); Migrant: n/a
Eligible for Free Lunch Program: 129 (3.1%)
Eligible for Reduced-Price Lunch Program: 92 (2.2%)
Teachers: 197.4 (21.0 to 1)
Librarians/Media Specialists: 6.0 (690.3 to 1)
Guidance Counselors: 10.4 (398.3 to 1)
Current Spending: ($ per student per year):
Total: $6,176; Instruction: $3,621; Support Services: $2,294
Enrollment, Drop-out Rates and Diploma Recipients by Race/Ethnicity

Category	Total	White	Black	Asian	AIAN	Hisp.
Enrollment (%)	100.0	90.2	1.5	4.4	1.4	2.5
Drop-out Rate (%)	n/a	n/a	n/a	n/a	n/a	n/a
H.S. Diplomas (#)	294	268	5	18	1	2

Bremerton SD 100

1111 Carr Blvd • Bremerton, WA 98312-2212
(360) 478-5100 • http://bhs1.bremerton.wednet.edu/
Grade Span: KG-12; **Agency Type:** 1
Schools: 14
8 Primary; 1 Middle; 3 High; 2 Other Level
11 Regular; 0 Special Education; 1 Vocational; 2 Alternative
0 Magnet; 0 Charter; 9 Title I Eligible; 8 School-wide Title I
Students: 5,787 (50.6% male; 49.4% female)
Individual Education Program: 704 (12.2%);
English Language Learner: 61 (1.1%); Migrant: n/a
Eligible for Free Lunch Program: 2,127 (36.8%)
Eligible for Reduced-Price Lunch Program: 765 (13.2%)
Teachers: 336.7 (17.2 to 1)
Librarians/Media Specialists: 10.0 (578.7 to 1)
Guidance Counselors: 8.8 (657.6 to 1)
Current Spending: ($ per student per year):
Total: $6,927; Instruction: $4,195; Support Services: $2,413
Enrollment, Drop-out Rates and Diploma Recipients by Race/Ethnicity

Category	Total	White	Black	Asian	AIAN	Hisp.
Enrollment (%)	100.0	66.9	11.5	11.9	3.8	5.9
Drop-out Rate (%)	n/a	n/a	n/a	n/a	n/a	n/a
H.S. Diplomas (#)	265	197	32	19	5	12

Central Kitsap SD 401

9210 Silverdale Way NW • Silverdale, WA 98383-9197
(360) 692-3100 • http://www.cksd.wednet.edu/
Grade Span: PK-12; **Agency Type:** 1
Schools: 24
14 Primary; 3 Middle; 5 High; 2 Other Level
20 Regular; 0 Special Education; 0 Vocational; 4 Alternative
0 Magnet; 0 Charter; 10 Title I Eligible; 0 School-wide Title I
Students: 13,393 (51.4% male; 48.6% female)
Individual Education Program: 1,796 (13.4%);
English Language Learner: 237 (1.8%); Migrant: n/a
Eligible for Free Lunch Program: 1,622 (12.1%)
Eligible for Reduced-Price Lunch Program: 1,258 (9.4%)
Teachers: 694.2 (19.3 to 1)
Librarians/Media Specialists: 21.5 (622.9 to 1)
Guidance Counselors: 18.0 (744.1 to 1)
Current Spending: ($ per student per year):
Total: $6,655; Instruction: $4,069; Support Services: $2,261
Enrollment, Drop-out Rates and Diploma Recipients by Race/Ethnicity

Category	Total	White	Black	Asian	AIAN	Hisp.
Enrollment (%)	100.0	76.6	5.7	12.4	1.1	4.2
Drop-out Rate (%)	n/a	n/a	n/a	n/a	n/a	n/a
H.S. Diplomas (#)	972	787	23	148	14	0

North Kitsap SD 400

18360 Caldart Ave NE • Poulsbo, WA 98370-8775
(360) 779-8702 • http://www.nksd.wednet.edu/
Grade Span: PK-12; **Agency Type:** 1
Schools: 14
7 Primary; 3 Middle; 2 High; 2 Other Level
11 Regular; 1 Special Education; 0 Vocational; 2 Alternative
0 Magnet; 0 Charter; 6 Title I Eligible; 0 School-wide Title I
Students: 7,163 (52.5% male; 47.5% female)
Individual Education Program: 852 (11.9%);
English Language Learner: 94 (1.3%); Migrant: n/a
Eligible for Free Lunch Program: 946 (13.2%)
Eligible for Reduced-Price Lunch Program: 430 (6.0%)
Teachers: 366.2 (19.6 to 1)
Librarians/Media Specialists: 9.9 (723.5 to 1)
Guidance Counselors: 15.8 (453.4 to 1)
Current Spending: ($ per student per year):
Total: $6,502; Instruction: $3,856; Support Services: $2,357
Enrollment, Drop-out Rates and Diploma Recipients by Race/Ethnicity

Category	Total	White	Black	Asian	AIAN	Hisp.
Enrollment (%)	100.0	83.4	1.7	4.1	6.6	4.1
Drop-out Rate (%)	n/a	n/a	n/a	n/a	n/a	n/a
H.S. Diplomas (#)	401	342	8	26	13	12

South Kitsap SD 402

1962 Hoover Ave SE • Port Orchard, WA 98366-3098
(360) 874-7380 • http://www.skitsap.wednet.edu/
Grade Span: PK-12; **Agency Type:** 1
Schools: 17
10 Primary; 3 Middle; 2 High; 2 Other Level
14 Regular; 1 Special Education; 0 Vocational; 2 Alternative
0 Magnet; 0 Charter; 9 Title I Eligible; 0 School-wide Title I
Students: 11,169 (50.9% male; 49.1% female)
Individual Education Program: 1,497 (13.4%);
English Language Learner: 52 (0.5%); Migrant: n/a
Eligible for Free Lunch Program: 1,940 (17.4%)
Eligible for Reduced-Price Lunch Program: 897 (8.0%)
Teachers: 579.7 (19.3 to 1)
Librarians/Media Specialists: 9.0 (1,241.0 to 1)
Guidance Counselors: 19.5 (572.8 to 1)
Current Spending: ($ per student per year):
Total: $5,646; Instruction: $3,369; Support Services: $2,018
Enrollment, Drop-out Rates and Diploma Recipients by Race/Ethnicity

Category	Total	White	Black	Asian	AIAN	Hisp.
Enrollment (%)	100.0	83.3	3.3	6.7	3.0	3.6
Drop-out Rate (%)	n/a	n/a	n/a	n/a	n/a	n/a
H.S. Diplomas (#)	625	526	15	50	18	16

Kittitas County

Ellensburg SD 401

506 N Sprague St • Ellensburg, WA 98926-3195
(509) 925-8010 • http://wonders.eburg.wednet.edu/
Grade Span: KG-12; **Agency Type:** 1
Schools: 5
3 Primary; 1 Middle; 1 High; 0 Other Level
5 Regular; 0 Special Education; 0 Vocational; 0 Alternative
0 Magnet; 0 Charter; 4 Title I Eligible; 1 School-wide Title I
Students: 2,843 (52.4% male; 47.6% female)
Individual Education Program: 361 (12.7%);
English Language Learner: 117 (4.1%); Migrant: n/a
Eligible for Free Lunch Program: 675 (23.7%)
Eligible for Reduced-Price Lunch Program: 212 (7.5%)
Teachers: 146.1 (19.5 to 1)
Librarians/Media Specialists: 5.0 (568.6 to 1)
Guidance Counselors: 7.9 (359.9 to 1)
Current Spending: ($ per student per year):
Total: $6,326; Instruction: $3,781; Support Services: $2,186
Enrollment, Drop-out Rates and Diploma Recipients by Race/Ethnicity

Category	Total	White	Black	Asian	AIAN	Hisp.
Enrollment (%)	100.0	85.4	1.2	2.0	1.1	10.4
Drop-out Rate (%)	n/a	n/a	n/a	n/a	n/a	n/a
H.S. Diplomas (#)	227	207	2	3	2	13

Lewis County

Centralia SD 401

2320 Borst Ave • Centralia, WA 98531-1498
(360) 330-7600 • http://www.centralia1.wednet.edu/firstpage.htm
Grade Span: KG-12; **Agency Type:** 1
Schools: 7
3 Primary; 3 Middle; 1 High; 0 Other Level
7 Regular; 0 Special Education; 0 Vocational; 0 Alternative
0 Magnet; 0 Charter; 3 Title I Eligible; 3 School-wide Title I
Students: 3,376 (50.5% male; 49.5% female)
Individual Education Program: 475 (14.1%);
English Language Learner: 207 (6.1%); Migrant: n/a
Eligible for Free Lunch Program: 1,298 (38.4%)
Eligible for Reduced-Price Lunch Program: 360 (10.7%)
Teachers: 175.4 (19.2 to 1)
Librarians/Media Specialists: 2.0 (1,688.0 to 1)
Guidance Counselors: 9.5 (355.4 to 1)
Current Spending: ($ per student per year):
Total: $6,710; Instruction: $4,154; Support Services: $2,214
Enrollment, Drop-out Rates and Diploma Recipients by Race/Ethnicity

Category	Total	White	Black	Asian	AIAN	Hisp.
Enrollment (%)	100.0	81.5	0.7	2.3	0.9	14.6
Drop-out Rate (%)	n/a	n/a	n/a	n/a	n/a	n/a
H.S. Diplomas (#)	179	162	0	6	2	9

Chehalis SD 302

310 SW 16th St • Chehalis, WA 98532-3809
(360) 748-8681 • http://www.chehalis.k12.wa.us/
Grade Span: KG-12; **Agency Type:** 1
Schools: 7
3 Primary; 1 Middle; 2 High; 1 Other Level
7 Regular; 0 Special Education; 0 Vocational; 0 Alternative
0 Magnet; 0 Charter; 2 Title I Eligible; 0 School-wide Title I
Students: 3,038 (53.7% male; 46.3% female)
Individual Education Program: 349 (11.5%);
English Language Learner: 79 (2.6%); Migrant: n/a
Eligible for Free Lunch Program: 685 (22.5%)
Eligible for Reduced-Price Lunch Program: 227 (7.5%)
Teachers: 162.5 (18.7 to 1)
Librarians/Media Specialists: 4.5 (675.1 to 1)
Guidance Counselors: 4.0 (759.5 to 1)
Current Spending: ($ per student per year):
Total: $7,208; Instruction: $4,309; Support Services: $2,529
Enrollment, Drop-out Rates and Diploma Recipients by Race/Ethnicity

Category	Total	White	Black	Asian	AIAN	Hisp.
Enrollment (%)	100.0	86.0	3.2	1.4	1.3	8.0
Drop-out Rate (%)	n/a	n/a	n/a	n/a	n/a	n/a
H.S. Diplomas (#)	210	190	3	7	1	9

Mason County

North Mason SD 403

71 E Campus Dr • Belfair, WA 98528-8305
(360) 277-2300 • http://www.nmsd.wednet.edu/
Grade Span: KG-12; **Agency Type:** 1
Schools: 6
2 Primary; 1 Middle; 2 High; 1 Other Level
4 Regular; 0 Special Education; 0 Vocational; 2 Alternative
0 Magnet; 0 Charter; 2 Title I Eligible; 0 School-wide Title I
Students: 2,389 (51.6% male; 48.4% female)
Individual Education Program: 279 (11.7%);
English Language Learner: 23 (1.0%); Migrant: n/a
Eligible for Free Lunch Program: 554 (23.2%)
Eligible for Reduced-Price Lunch Program: 224 (9.4%)
Teachers: 125.5 (19.0 to 1)
Librarians/Media Specialists: 4.0 (597.3 to 1)
Guidance Counselors: 4.6 (519.3 to 1)
Current Spending: ($ per student per year):
Total: $6,306; Instruction: $3,707; Support Services: $2,239
Enrollment, Drop-out Rates and Diploma Recipients by Race/Ethnicity

Category	Total	White	Black	Asian	AIAN	Hisp.
Enrollment (%)	100.0	87.3	2.3	3.8	2.7	3.9
Drop-out Rate (%)	n/a	n/a	n/a	n/a	n/a	n/a
H.S. Diplomas (#)	166	156	1	7	1	1

Shelton SD 309

700 S 1st St • Shelton, WA 98584-3602
(360) 426-1687 • http://www.shelton.wednet.edu/
Grade Span: PK-12; **Agency Type:** 1
Schools: 8
3 Primary; 2 Middle; 3 High; 0 Other Level
6 Regular; 0 Special Education; 0 Vocational; 2 Alternative
0 Magnet; 0 Charter; 3 Title I Eligible; 3 School-wide Title I
Students: 4,133 (52.0% male; 48.0% female)
Individual Education Program: 560 (13.5%);
English Language Learner: 134 (3.2%); Migrant: n/a
Eligible for Free Lunch Program: 1,639 (39.7%)
Eligible for Reduced-Price Lunch Program: 372 (9.0%)
Teachers: 220.1 (18.8 to 1)
Librarians/Media Specialists: 3.3 (1,252.4 to 1)
Guidance Counselors: 9.4 (439.7 to 1)
Current Spending: ($ per student per year):
Total: $6,510; Instruction: $3,865; Support Services: $2,284
Enrollment, Drop-out Rates and Diploma Recipients by Race/Ethnicity

Category	Total	White	Black	Asian	AIAN	Hisp.
Enrollment (%)	100.0	78.2	0.8	2.5	9.4	9.1
Drop-out Rate (%)	n/a	n/a	n/a	n/a	n/a	n/a
H.S. Diplomas (#)	318	270	2	7	30	9

Okanogan County

Omak SD 19

619 W Bartlett Ave • Omak, WA 98841-9700
(509) 826-7681 • http://www.omaksd.wednet.edu/
Grade Span: PK-12; **Agency Type:** 1
Schools: 5
2 Primary; 1 Middle; 2 High; 0 Other Level
4 Regular; 0 Special Education; 0 Vocational; 1 Alternative
0 Magnet; 0 Charter; 1 Title I Eligible; 1 School-wide Title I
Students: 1,935 (51.2% male; 48.8% female)
Individual Education Program: 301 (15.6%);
English Language Learner: 82 (4.2%); Migrant: n/a
Eligible for Free Lunch Program: 737 (38.1%)
Eligible for Reduced-Price Lunch Program: 213 (11.0%)
Teachers: 102.3 (18.9 to 1)
Librarians/Media Specialists: 1.5 (1,290.0 to 1)
Guidance Counselors: 5.6 (345.5 to 1)
Current Spending: ($ per student per year):
Total: $6,802; Instruction: $4,159; Support Services: $2,313

Enrollment, Drop-out Rates and Diploma Recipients by Race/Ethnicity

Category	Total	White	Black	Asian	AIAN	Hisp.
Enrollment (%)	100.0	59.9	0.5	1.5	26.3	11.8
Drop-out Rate (%)	n/a	n/a	n/a	n/a	n/a	n/a
H.S. Diplomas (#)	109	76	1	1	23	8

Pierce County

Bethel SD 403

516 176th St E • Spanaway, WA 98387-8399
(253) 539-6024 • http://www.bethel.wednet.edu/
Grade Span: PK-12; **Agency Type:** 1
Schools: 23
16 Primary; 4 Middle; 3 High; 0 Other Level
22 Regular; 0 Special Education; 0 Vocational; 1 Alternative
0 Magnet; 0 Charter; 8 Title I Eligible; 3 School-wide Title I
Students: 16,641 (52.5% male; 47.5% female)
Individual Education Program: 2,263 (13.6%);
English Language Learner: 161 (1.0%); Migrant: n/a
Eligible for Free Lunch Program: 3,351 (20.1%)
Eligible for Reduced-Price Lunch Program: 1,688 (10.1%)
Teachers: 809.9 (20.5 to 1)
Librarians/Media Specialists: 21.0 (792.4 to 1)
Guidance Counselors: 17.5 (950.9 to 1)
Current Spending: ($ per student per year):
Total: $6,037; Instruction: $3,544; Support Services: $2,191
Enrollment, Drop-out Rates and Diploma Recipients by Race/Ethnicity

Category	Total	White	Black	Asian	AIAN	Hisp.
Enrollment (%)	100.0	72.8	9.6	9.3	2.9	5.5
Drop-out Rate (%)	n/a	n/a	n/a	n/a	n/a	n/a
H.S. Diplomas (#)	975	668	110	125	33	39

Clover Park SD 400

10903 Gravelly Lake Dr SW • Lakewood, WA 98499-1341
(253) 589-7500 • http://cpsd.cloverpark.k12.wa.us/
Grade Span: PK-12; **Agency Type:** 1
Schools: 32
20 Primary; 5 Middle; 3 High; 4 Other Level
27 Regular; 2 Special Education; 0 Vocational; 3 Alternative
0 Magnet; 0 Charter; 15 Title I Eligible; 15 School-wide Title I
Students: 13,501 (52.2% male; 47.8% female)
Individual Education Program: 1,833 (13.6%);
English Language Learner: 937 (6.9%); Migrant: n/a
Eligible for Free Lunch Program: 4,876 (36.1%)
Eligible for Reduced-Price Lunch Program: 2,040 (15.1%)
Teachers: 737.2 (18.3 to 1)
Librarians/Media Specialists: 23.8 (567.3 to 1)
Guidance Counselors: 32.8 (411.6 to 1)
Current Spending: ($ per student per year):
Total: $6,990; Instruction: $3,977; Support Services: $2,664
Enrollment, Drop-out Rates and Diploma Recipients by Race/Ethnicity

Category	Total	White	Black	Asian	AIAN	Hisp.
Enrollment (%)	100.0	53.6	22.5	10.2	1.7	12.0
Drop-out Rate (%)	n/a	n/a	n/a	n/a	n/a	n/a
H.S. Diplomas (#)	455	231	104	72	13	35

Eatonville SD 404

208 Lynch St • Eatonville, WA 98328-0698
(360) 879-1000 • http://cruiser.eatonville.wednet.edu/
Grade Span: KG-12; **Agency Type:** 1
Schools: 5
3 Primary; 1 Middle; 1 High; 0 Other Level
5 Regular; 0 Special Education; 0 Vocational; 0 Alternative
0 Magnet; 0 Charter; 2 Title I Eligible; 0 School-wide Title I
Students: 2,092 (52.7% male; 47.3% female)
Individual Education Program: 244 (11.7%);
English Language Learner: 21 (1.0%); Migrant: n/a
Eligible for Free Lunch Program: 436 (20.8%)
Eligible for Reduced-Price Lunch Program: 245 (11.7%)
Teachers: 111.6 (18.7 to 1)
Librarians/Media Specialists: 2.0 (1,046.0 to 1)
Guidance Counselors: 4.0 (523.0 to 1)
Current Spending: ($ per student per year):
Total: $6,075; Instruction: $3,450; Support Services: $2,322
Enrollment, Drop-out Rates and Diploma Recipients by Race/Ethnicity

Category	Total	White	Black	Asian	AIAN	Hisp.
Enrollment (%)	100.0	91.3	1.1	2.1	2.6	2.9
Drop-out Rate (%)	n/a	n/a	n/a	n/a	n/a	n/a
H.S. Diplomas (#)	126	120	0	2	0	4

Fife SD 417

5802 20th St E • Tacoma, WA 98424-2000
(253) 284-1000 • http://www.fifeschools.com/
Grade Span: KG-12; **Agency Type:** 1
Schools: 6
3 Primary; 1 Middle; 2 High; 0 Other Level
5 Regular; 0 Special Education; 0 Vocational; 1 Alternative
0 Magnet; 0 Charter; 0 Title I Eligible; 0 School-wide Title I
Students: 3,137 (51.5% male; 48.5% female)
Individual Education Program: 316 (10.1%);
English Language Learner: 90 (2.9%); Migrant: n/a
Eligible for Free Lunch Program: 578 (18.4%)
Eligible for Reduced-Price Lunch Program: 289 (9.2%)
Teachers: 160.2 (19.6 to 1)
Librarians/Media Specialists: 4.0 (784.3 to 1)
Guidance Counselors: 5.5 (570.4 to 1)
Current Spending: ($ per student per year):
Total: $6,587; Instruction: $3,912; Support Services: $2,322
Enrollment, Drop-out Rates and Diploma Recipients by Race/Ethnicity

Category	Total	White	Black	Asian	AIAN	Hisp.
Enrollment (%)	100.0	75.9	4.5	6.5	3.6	9.5
Drop-out Rate (%)	n/a	n/a	n/a	n/a	n/a	n/a
H.S. Diplomas (#)	202	176	5	5	8	8

Franklin Pierce SD 402

315 129th St S • Tacoma, WA 98444-5099
(253) 537-0211 • http://www.fp.k12.wa.us/
Grade Span: PK-12; **Agency Type:** 1
Schools: 14
7 Primary; 2 Middle; 5 High; 0 Other Level
11 Regular; 0 Special Education; 0 Vocational; 3 Alternative
0 Magnet; 0 Charter; 6 Title I Eligible; 6 School-wide Title I
Students: 7,758 (51.0% male; 49.0% female)
Individual Education Program: 941 (12.1%);
English Language Learner: 142 (1.8%); Migrant: n/a
Eligible for Free Lunch Program: 2,479 (32.0%)
Eligible for Reduced-Price Lunch Program: 1,004 (12.9%)
Teachers: 399.4 (19.4 to 1)
Librarians/Media Specialists: 5.5 (1,410.5 to 1)
Guidance Counselors: 16.3 (476.0 to 1)
Current Spending: ($ per student per year):
Total: $6,442; Instruction: $3,932; Support Services: $2,205
Enrollment, Drop-out Rates and Diploma Recipients by Race/Ethnicity

Category	Total	White	Black	Asian	AIAN	Hisp.
Enrollment (%)	100.0	63.6	14.9	11.2	2.1	8.1
Drop-out Rate (%)	n/a	n/a	n/a	n/a	n/a	n/a
H.S. Diplomas (#)	407	294	36	54	11	12

Orting SD 344

120 Washington Ave N • Orting, WA 98360-8403
(360) 893-6500 • http://www.orting.wednet.edu/
Grade Span: PK-12; **Agency Type:** 1
Schools: 4
2 Primary; 1 Middle; 1 High; 0 Other Level
4 Regular; 0 Special Education; 0 Vocational; 0 Alternative
0 Magnet; 0 Charter; 1 Title I Eligible; 0 School-wide Title I
Students: 1,858 (52.2% male; 47.8% female)
Individual Education Program: 258 (13.9%);
English Language Learner: 24 (1.3%); Migrant: n/a
Eligible for Free Lunch Program: 271 (14.6%)
Eligible for Reduced-Price Lunch Program: 180 (9.7%)
Teachers: 102.2 (18.2 to 1)
Librarians/Media Specialists: 2.0 (929.0 to 1)
Guidance Counselors: 1.9 (977.9 to 1)
Current Spending: ($ per student per year):
Total: $6,256; Instruction: $3,758; Support Services: $2,209
Enrollment, Drop-out Rates and Diploma Recipients by Race/Ethnicity

Category	Total	White	Black	Asian	AIAN	Hisp.
Enrollment (%)	100.0	93.1	0.9	2.4	0.8	2.9
Drop-out Rate (%)	n/a	n/a	n/a	n/a	n/a	n/a
H.S. Diplomas (#)	95	84	0	1	0	10

Peninsula SD 401

14015 62nd Ave NW • Gig Harbor, WA 98332-8698
(253) 857-3525 • http://www.peninsula.wednet.edu/
Grade Span: PK-12; **Agency Type:** 1
Schools: 16
8 Primary; 4 Middle; 3 High; 1 Other Level
14 Regular; 0 Special Education; 0 Vocational; 2 Alternative
0 Magnet; 0 Charter; 7 Title I Eligible; 1 School-wide Title I
Students: 9,595 (52.1% male; 47.9% female)
Individual Education Program: 1,180 (12.3%);
English Language Learner: 30 (0.3%); Migrant: n/a
Eligible for Free Lunch Program: 1,054 (11.0%)
Eligible for Reduced-Price Lunch Program: 535 (5.6%)
Teachers: 475.1 (20.2 to 1)
Librarians/Media Specialists: 5.0 (1,919.0 to 1)
Guidance Counselors: 27.5 (348.9 to 1)
Current Spending: ($ per student per year):
Total: $6,292; Instruction: $3,816; Support Services: $2,174

Enrollment, Drop-out Rates and Diploma Recipients by Race/Ethnicity

Category	Total	White	Black	Asian	AIAN	Hisp.
Enrollment (%)	100.0	88.9	1.5	3.2	3.4	2.9
Drop-out Rate (%)	n/a	n/a	n/a	n/a	n/a	n/a
H.S. Diplomas (#)	604	553	4	11	16	20

Puyallup SD 3

302 2nd St SE • Puyallup, WA 98372-3220
(253) 841-8769 • http://www.puyallup.k12.wa.us/
Grade Span: PK-12; **Agency Type:** 1
Schools: 33
22 Primary; 6 Middle; 4 High; 1 Other Level
31 Regular; 0 Special Education; 0 Vocational; 2 Alternative
0 Magnet; 0 Charter; 8 Title I Eligible; 1 School-wide Title I
Students: 19,819 (50.9% male; 49.1% female)
Individual Education Program: 2,325 (11.7%);
English Language Learner: 191 (1.0%); Migrant: n/a
Eligible for Free Lunch Program: 2,530 (12.8%)
Eligible for Reduced-Price Lunch Program: 1,519 (7.7%)
Teachers: 1,022.7 (19.4 to 1)
Librarians/Media Specialists: 26.8 (739.5 to 1)
Guidance Counselors: 44.6 (444.4 to 1)
Current Spending: ($ per student per year):
Total: $6,274; Instruction: $3,738; Support Services: $2,253
Enrollment, Drop-out Rates and Diploma Recipients by Race/Ethnicity

Category	Total	White	Black	Asian	AIAN	Hisp.
Enrollment (%)	100.0	83.1	4.0	6.0	1.8	5.1
Drop-out Rate (%)	n/a	n/a	n/a	n/a	n/a	n/a
H.S. Diplomas (#)	1,153	985	27	71	35	35

Steilacoom Historical SD

510 Chambers St • Steilacoom, WA 98388-3311
(253) 983-2200 • http://steilacoom.k12.wa.us/
Grade Span: PK-12; **Agency Type:** 1
Schools: 7
5 Primary; 1 Middle; 1 High; 0 Other Level
7 Regular; 0 Special Education; 0 Vocational; 0 Alternative
0 Magnet; 0 Charter; 2 Title I Eligible; 0 School-wide Title I
Students: 2,111 (52.3% male; 47.7% female)
Individual Education Program: 277 (13.1%);
English Language Learner: 66 (3.1%); Migrant: n/a
Eligible for Free Lunch Program: 279 (13.2%)
Eligible for Reduced-Price Lunch Program: 145 (6.9%)
Teachers: 108.4 (19.5 to 1)
Librarians/Media Specialists: 3.0 (703.7 to 1)
Guidance Counselors: 6.0 (351.8 to 1)
Current Spending: ($ per student per year):
Total: $6,405; Instruction: $3,577; Support Services: $2,504
Enrollment, Drop-out Rates and Diploma Recipients by Race/Ethnicity

Category	Total	White	Black	Asian	AIAN	Hisp.
Enrollment (%)	100.0	67.8	13.9	11.2	0.9	6.2
Drop-out Rate (%)	n/a	n/a	n/a	n/a	n/a	n/a
H.S. Diplomas (#)	125	87	13	15	2	8

Sumner SD 320

1202 Wood Ave • Sumner, WA 98390-1933
(253) 891-6080 • http://www.sumner.wednet.edu/
Grade Span: PK-12; **Agency Type:** 1
Schools: 13
9 Primary; 3 Middle; 1 High; 0 Other Level
12 Regular; 1 Special Education; 0 Vocational; 0 Alternative
0 Magnet; 0 Charter; 6 Title I Eligible; 0 School-wide Title I
Students: 7,984 (51.3% male; 48.7% female)
Individual Education Program: 967 (12.1%);
English Language Learner: 105 (1.3%); Migrant: n/a
Eligible for Free Lunch Program: 1,177 (14.7%)
Eligible for Reduced-Price Lunch Program: 578 (7.2%)
Teachers: 379.9 (21.0 to 1)
Librarians/Media Specialists: 9.5 (840.4 to 1)
Guidance Counselors: 11.7 (682.4 to 1)
Current Spending: ($ per student per year):
Total: $6,200; Instruction: $3,653; Support Services: $2,240
Enrollment, Drop-out Rates and Diploma Recipients by Race/Ethnicity

Category	Total	White	Black	Asian	AIAN	Hisp.
Enrollment (%)	100.0	87.9	1.6	2.9	2.1	5.5
Drop-out Rate (%)	n/a	n/a	n/a	n/a	n/a	n/a
H.S. Diplomas (#)	396	372	2	10	5	7

Tacoma SD 10

601 S 8th • Tacoma, WA 98405
(253) 571-1010 • http://www.tacoma.k12.wa.us/
Grade Span: PK-12; **Agency Type:** 1
Schools: 65
36 Primary; 10 Middle; 13 High; 6 Other Level
52 Regular; 2 Special Education; 0 Vocational; 11 Alternative
0 Magnet; 0 Charter; 24 Title I Eligible; 22 School-wide Title I
Students: 33,955 (51.3% male; 48.7% female)
Individual Education Program: 4,382 (12.9%);
English Language Learner: 2,355 (6.9%); Migrant: n/a
Eligible for Free Lunch Program: 14,103 (41.5%)
Eligible for Reduced-Price Lunch Program: 4,140 (12.2%)
Teachers: 1,786.3 (19.0 to 1)
Librarians/Media Specialists: 53.4 (635.9 to 1)
Guidance Counselors: 86.7 (391.6 to 1)
Current Spending: ($ per student per year):
Total: $7,045; Instruction: $4,056; Support Services: $2,668
Enrollment, Drop-out Rates and Diploma Recipients by Race/Ethnicity

Category	Total	White	Black	Asian	AIAN	Hisp.
Enrollment (%)	100.0	54.4	21.5	12.8	2.0	9.2
Drop-out Rate (%)	n/a	n/a	n/a	n/a	n/a	n/a
H.S. Diplomas (#)	1,462	876	268	221	23	74

University Place SD 83

3717 Grandview Dr W • University Place, WA 98466-2138
(253) 566-5600
Grade Span: PK-12; **Agency Type:** 1
Schools: 10
4 Primary; 2 Middle; 2 High; 2 Other Level
8 Regular; 1 Special Education; 0 Vocational; 1 Alternative
0 Magnet; 0 Charter; 3 Title I Eligible; 0 School-wide Title I
Students: 5,296 (51.2% male; 48.8% female)
Individual Education Program: 615 (11.6%);
English Language Learner: 110 (2.1%); Migrant: n/a
Eligible for Free Lunch Program: 786 (14.8%)
Eligible for Reduced-Price Lunch Program: 471 (8.9%)
Teachers: 287.5 (18.4 to 1)
Librarians/Media Specialists: 6.0 (882.7 to 1)
Guidance Counselors: 9.6 (551.7 to 1)
Current Spending: ($ per student per year):
Total: $6,393; Instruction: $3,706; Support Services: $2,292
Enrollment, Drop-out Rates and Diploma Recipients by Race/Ethnicity

Category	Total	White	Black	Asian	AIAN	Hisp.
Enrollment (%)	100.0	69.0	13.6	12.2	1.0	4.2
Drop-out Rate (%)	n/a	n/a	n/a	n/a	n/a	n/a
H.S. Diplomas (#)	410	285	45	63	3	14

White River SD 416

240 N A St • Buckley, WA 98321-2050
(360) 829-0600 • http://www.whiteriver.wednet.edu/index.shtml
Grade Span: PK-12; **Agency Type:** 1
Schools: 8
5 Primary; 1 Middle; 1 High; 1 Other Level
7 Regular; 0 Special Education; 0 Vocational; 1 Alternative
0 Magnet; 0 Charter; 3 Title I Eligible; 0 School-wide Title I
Students: 4,384 (50.5% male; 49.5% female)
Individual Education Program: 527 (12.0%);
English Language Learner: 13 (0.3%); Migrant: n/a
Eligible for Free Lunch Program: 604 (13.8%)
Eligible for Reduced-Price Lunch Program: 351 (8.0%)
Teachers: 222.8 (19.7 to 1)
Librarians/Media Specialists: 6.0 (730.7 to 1)
Guidance Counselors: 8.0 (548.0 to 1)
Current Spending: ($ per student per year):
Total: $6,250; Instruction: $3,769; Support Services: $2,130
Enrollment, Drop-out Rates and Diploma Recipients by Race/Ethnicity

Category	Total	White	Black	Asian	AIAN	Hisp.
Enrollment (%)	100.0	91.6	0.8	1.8	2.9	2.9
Drop-out Rate (%)	n/a	n/a	n/a	n/a	n/a	n/a
H.S. Diplomas (#)	232	219	0	6	5	2

Skagit County

Anacortes SD 103

2200 M Ave • Anacortes, WA 98221-3794
(360) 293-1200 • http://www.anacortes.k12.wa.us/
Grade Span: KG-12; **Agency Type:** 1
Schools: 11
4 Primary; 1 Middle; 3 High; 3 Other Level
6 Regular; 1 Special Education; 0 Vocational; 4 Alternative
0 Magnet; 0 Charter; 3 Title I Eligible; 1 School-wide Title I
Students: 3,137 (50.7% male; 49.3% female)
Individual Education Program: 396 (12.6%);
English Language Learner: 47 (1.5%); Migrant: n/a
Eligible for Free Lunch Program: 504 (16.1%)
Eligible for Reduced-Price Lunch Program: 218 (6.9%)
Teachers: 150.1 (20.9 to 1)
Librarians/Media Specialists: 5.5 (570.4 to 1)
Guidance Counselors: 7.2 (435.7 to 1)
Current Spending: ($ per student per year):
Total: $6,511; Instruction: $4,109; Support Services: $2,120

Enrollment, Drop-out Rates and Diploma Recipients by Race/Ethnicity

Category	Total	White	Black	Asian	AIAN	Hisp.
Enrollment (%)	100.0	89.0	1.0	3.8	1.6	4.6
Drop-out Rate (%)	n/a	n/a	n/a	n/a	n/a	n/a
H.S. Diplomas (#)	197	179	3	9	2	4

Burlington-Edison SD 100

927 E Fairhaven Ave • Burlington, WA 98233-1900
(360) 757-3311 • http://www.be.wednet.edu/
Grade Span: PK-12; **Agency Type:** 1
Schools: 7
6 Primary; 0 Middle; 1 High; 0 Other Level
6 Regular; 0 Special Education; 0 Vocational; 1 Alternative
0 Magnet; 0 Charter; 2 Title I Eligible; 2 School-wide Title I
Students: 3,648 (50.9% male; 49.1% female)
Individual Education Program: 445 (12.2%);
English Language Learner: 454 (12.4%); Migrant: n/a
Eligible for Free Lunch Program: 898 (24.6%)
Eligible for Reduced-Price Lunch Program: 252 (6.9%)
Teachers: 174.4 (20.9 to 1)
Librarians/Media Specialists: 6.0 (608.0 to 1)
Guidance Counselors: 7.6 (480.0 to 1)
Current Spending: ($ per student per year):
Total: $6,576; Instruction: $3,929; Support Services: $2,242

Enrollment, Drop-out Rates and Diploma Recipients by Race/Ethnicity

Category	Total	White	Black	Asian	AIAN	Hisp.
Enrollment (%)	100.0	75.0	0.6	2.5	0.9	20.9
Drop-out Rate (%)	n/a	n/a	n/a	n/a	n/a	n/a
H.S. Diplomas (#)	203	181	0	6	1	15

Mount Vernon SD 320

124 E Lawrence St • Mount Vernon, WA 98273-2999
(360) 428-6181 • http://www.mv.k12.wa.us/
Grade Span: KG-12; **Agency Type:** 1
Schools: 11
6 Primary; 2 Middle; 1 High; 2 Other Level
10 Regular; 1 Special Education; 0 Vocational; 0 Alternative
0 Magnet; 0 Charter; 7 Title I Eligible; 6 School-wide Title I
Students: 5,798 (51.2% male; 48.8% female)
Individual Education Program: 759 (13.1%);
English Language Learner: 1,606 (27.7%); Migrant: n/a
Eligible for Free Lunch Program: 2,502 (43.2%)
Eligible for Reduced-Price Lunch Program: 563 (9.7%)
Teachers: 301.7 (19.2 to 1)
Librarians/Media Specialists: 9.0 (644.2 to 1)
Guidance Counselors: 14.0 (414.1 to 1)
Current Spending: ($ per student per year):
Total: $6,851; Instruction: $4,219; Support Services: $2,201

Enrollment, Drop-out Rates and Diploma Recipients by Race/Ethnicity

Category	Total	White	Black	Asian	AIAN	Hisp.
Enrollment (%)	100.0	56.1	1.5	2.4	1.3	38.7
Drop-out Rate (%)	n/a	n/a	n/a	n/a	n/a	n/a
H.S. Diplomas (#)	293	239	1	7	2	44

Sedro-Woolley SD 101

801 Tr Rd • Sedro Woolley, WA 98284-9387
(360) 855-3500 • http://www.swsd.wednet.edu/
Grade Span: PK-12; **Agency Type:** 1
Schools: 11
6 Primary; 2 Middle; 1 High; 2 Other Level
9 Regular; 1 Special Education; 0 Vocational; 1 Alternative
0 Magnet; 0 Charter; 5 Title I Eligible; 1 School-wide Title I
Students: 4,587 (53.2% male; 46.8% female)
Individual Education Program: 636 (13.9%);
English Language Learner: 115 (2.5%); Migrant: n/a
Eligible for Free Lunch Program: 1,155 (25.2%)
Eligible for Reduced-Price Lunch Program: 429 (9.4%)
Teachers: 251.6 (18.2 to 1)
Librarians/Media Specialists: 6.3 (728.1 to 1)
Guidance Counselors: 9.6 (477.8 to 1)
Current Spending: ($ per student per year):
Total: $6,421; Instruction: $3,789; Support Services: $2,288

Enrollment, Drop-out Rates and Diploma Recipients by Race/Ethnicity

Category	Total	White	Black	Asian	AIAN	Hisp.
Enrollment (%)	100.0	85.0	1.3	1.4	3.2	9.0
Drop-out Rate (%)	n/a	n/a	n/a	n/a	n/a	n/a
H.S. Diplomas (#)	310	258	5	19	7	21

Snohomish County

Arlington SD 16

315 N French Ave • Arlington, WA 98223-1317
(360) 435-2156 • http://www.asd.wednet.edu/
Grade Span: KG-12; **Agency Type:** 1
Schools: 10
5 Primary; 1 Middle; 2 High; 2 Other Level
8 Regular; 0 Special Education; 0 Vocational; 2 Alternative
0 Magnet; 0 Charter; 2 Title I Eligible; 0 School-wide Title I
Students: 5,146 (50.8% male; 49.2% female)
Individual Education Program: 636 (12.4%);
English Language Learner: 71 (1.4%); Migrant: n/a
Eligible for Free Lunch Program: 669 (13.0%)
Eligible for Reduced-Price Lunch Program: 313 (6.1%)
Teachers: 260.2 (19.8 to 1)
Librarians/Media Specialists: 4.5 (1,143.6 to 1)
Guidance Counselors: 9.7 (530.5 to 1)
Current Spending: ($ per student per year):
Total: $5,987; Instruction: $3,817; Support Services: $1,903

Enrollment, Drop-out Rates and Diploma Recipients by Race/Ethnicity

Category	Total	White	Black	Asian	AIAN	Hisp.
Enrollment (%)	100.0	90.3	1.2	2.3	2.0	4.2
Drop-out Rate (%)	n/a	n/a	n/a	n/a	n/a	n/a
H.S. Diplomas (#)	270	248	0	8	4	10

Edmonds SD 15

20420 68th Ave W • Lynnwood, WA 98036-7400
(425) 670-7003 • http://www.edmonds.wednet.edu/
Grade Span: PK-12; **Agency Type:** 1
Schools: 42
26 Primary; 4 Middle; 8 High; 4 Other Level
31 Regular; 3 Special Education; 1 Vocational; 7 Alternative
0 Magnet; 0 Charter; 14 Title I Eligible; 2 School-wide Title I
Students: 21,998 (51.7% male; 48.3% female)
Individual Education Program: 2,717 (12.4%);
English Language Learner: 1,608 (7.3%); Migrant: n/a
Eligible for Free Lunch Program: 3,461 (15.7%)
Eligible for Reduced-Price Lunch Program: 1,653 (7.5%)
Teachers: 1,103.7 (19.9 to 1)
Librarians/Media Specialists: 34.4 (639.5 to 1)
Guidance Counselors: 34.6 (635.8 to 1)
Current Spending: ($ per student per year):
Total: $6,319; Instruction: $3,753; Support Services: $2,288

Enrollment, Drop-out Rates and Diploma Recipients by Race/Ethnicity

Category	Total	White	Black	Asian	AIAN	Hisp.
Enrollment (%)	100.0	73.5	5.0	13.4	1.6	6.5
Drop-out Rate (%)	n/a	n/a	n/a	n/a	n/a	n/a
H.S. Diplomas (#)	1,111	855	27	183	16	30

Everett SD 2

4730 Colby Ave • Everett, WA 98203-2999
(425) 339-4205 • http://www.everett.k12.wa.us/
Grade Span: PK-12; **Agency Type:** 1
Schools: 33
17 Primary; 5 Middle; 9 High; 2 Other Level
25 Regular; 4 Special Education; 0 Vocational; 4 Alternative
0 Magnet; 0 Charter; 7 Title I Eligible; 3 School-wide Title I
Students: 18,743 (52.1% male; 47.9% female)
Individual Education Program: 2,184 (11.7%);
English Language Learner: 1,107 (5.9%); Migrant: n/a
Eligible for Free Lunch Program: 3,537 (18.9%)
Eligible for Reduced-Price Lunch Program: 1,310 (7.0%)
Teachers: 887.0 (21.1 to 1)
Librarians/Media Specialists: 23.8 (787.5 to 1)
Guidance Counselors: 37.6 (498.5 to 1)
Current Spending: ($ per student per year):
Total: $6,395; Instruction: $3,827; Support Services: $2,278

Enrollment, Drop-out Rates and Diploma Recipients by Race/Ethnicity

Category	Total	White	Black	Asian	AIAN	Hisp.
Enrollment (%)	100.0	76.4	4.4	10.8	1.8	6.6
Drop-out Rate (%)	n/a	n/a	n/a	n/a	n/a	n/a
H.S. Diplomas (#)	885	718	18	105	9	35

Granite Falls SD 332

307 N Alder Ave • Granite Falls, WA 98252-8908
(360) 691-7717 • http://www.gfalls.wednet.edu/
Grade Span: KG-12; **Agency Type:** 1
Schools: 4
2 Primary; 1 Middle; 1 High; 0 Other Level
4 Regular; 0 Special Education; 0 Vocational; 0 Alternative
0 Magnet; 0 Charter; 1 Title I Eligible; 0 School-wide Title I
Students: 2,391 (51.5% male; 48.5% female)
Individual Education Program: 357 (14.9%);
English Language Learner: 9 (0.4%); Migrant: n/a
Eligible for Free Lunch Program: 461 (19.3%)
Eligible for Reduced-Price Lunch Program: 260 (10.9%)
Teachers: 112.5 (21.3 to 1)
Librarians/Media Specialists: 3.0 (797.0 to 1)
Guidance Counselors: 5.5 (434.7 to 1)
Current Spending: ($ per student per year):
Total: $5,864; Instruction: $3,374; Support Services: $2,180

Enrollment, Drop-out Rates and Diploma Recipients by Race/Ethnicity

Category	Total	White	Black	Asian	AIAN	Hisp.
Enrollment (%)	100.0	92.1	0.7	1.3	2.3	3.6
Drop-out Rate (%)	n/a	n/a	n/a	n/a	n/a	n/a
H.S. Diplomas (#)	104	93	0	4	4	3

Lake Stevens SD 4

12309 22nd St NE • Lake Stevens, WA 98258-9500
(425) 335-1553 • http://www.lkstevens.wednet.edu/
Grade Span: PK-12; **Agency Type:** 1
Schools: 11
6 Primary; 2 Middle; 2 High; 1 Other Level
9 Regular; 0 Special Education; 0 Vocational; 2 Alternative
0 Magnet; 0 Charter; 3 Title I Eligible; 0 School-wide Title I
Students: 7,290 (51.0% male; 49.0% female)
Individual Education Program: 833 (11.4%);
English Language Learner: 69 (0.9%); Migrant: n/a
Eligible for Free Lunch Program: 903 (12.4%)
Eligible for Reduced-Price Lunch Program: 517 (7.1%)
Teachers: 341.2 (21.4 to 1)
Librarians/Media Specialists: 9.0 (810.0 to 1)
Guidance Counselors: 14.9 (489.3 to 1)
Current Spending: ($ per student per year):
Total: $5,734; Instruction: $3,519; Support Services: $1,899

Enrollment, Drop-out Rates and Diploma Recipients by Race/Ethnicity

Category	Total	White	Black	Asian	AIAN	Hisp.
Enrollment (%)	100.0	89.3	1.6	3.5	1.2	4.4
Drop-out Rate (%)	n/a	n/a	n/a	n/a	n/a	n/a
H.S. Diplomas (#)	373	346	2	10	8	7

Lakewood SD 306

17110 16th Dr NE • North Lakewood, WA 98259-0220
(360) 652-4500 • http://www.lwsd.wednet.edu/
Grade Span: PK-12; **Agency Type:** 1
Schools: 4
2 Primary; 1 Middle; 1 High; 0 Other Level
4 Regular; 0 Special Education; 0 Vocational; 0 Alternative
0 Magnet; 0 Charter; 0 Title I Eligible; 0 School-wide Title I
Students: 2,582 (51.9% male; 48.1% female)
Individual Education Program: 314 (12.2%);
English Language Learner: 35 (1.4%); Migrant: n/a
Eligible for Free Lunch Program: 379 (14.7%)
Eligible for Reduced-Price Lunch Program: 276 (10.7%)
Teachers: 123.9 (20.8 to 1)
Librarians/Media Specialists: 3.0 (860.7 to 1)
Guidance Counselors: 5.9 (437.6 to 1)
Current Spending: ($ per student per year):
Total: $6,165; Instruction: $3,354; Support Services: $2,479

Enrollment, Drop-out Rates and Diploma Recipients by Race/Ethnicity

Category	Total	White	Black	Asian	AIAN	Hisp.
Enrollment (%)	100.0	86.7	3.4	3.8	1.2	4.8
Drop-out Rate (%)	n/a	n/a	n/a	n/a	n/a	n/a
H.S. Diplomas (#)	129	118	2	1	2	6

Marysville SD 25

4220 80th St NE • Marysville, WA 98270-3498
(360) 653-0800 • http://www.msvl.wednet.edu/
Grade Span: PK-12; **Agency Type:** 1
Schools: 20
11 Primary; 3 Middle; 2 High; 4 Other Level
15 Regular; 1 Special Education; 0 Vocational; 4 Alternative
0 Magnet; 0 Charter; 3 Title I Eligible; 2 School-wide Title I
Students: 12,009 (51.8% male; 48.2% female)
Individual Education Program: 1,588 (13.2%);
English Language Learner: 313 (2.6%); Migrant: n/a
Eligible for Free Lunch Program: 2,066 (17.2%)
Eligible for Reduced-Price Lunch Program: 1,035 (8.6%)
Teachers: 567.1 (21.2 to 1)
Librarians/Media Specialists: 12.8 (938.2 to 1)
Guidance Counselors: 23.9 (502.5 to 1)
Current Spending: ($ per student per year):
Total: $6,401; Instruction: $3,949; Support Services: $2,181

Enrollment, Drop-out Rates and Diploma Recipients by Race/Ethnicity

Category	Total	White	Black	Asian	AIAN	Hisp.
Enrollment (%)	100.0	79.1	2.1	5.8	7.9	5.2
Drop-out Rate (%)	n/a	n/a	n/a	n/a	n/a	n/a
H.S. Diplomas (#)	601	495	9	49	25	23

Monroe SD 103

200 E Fremont St • Monroe, WA 98272-2336
(360) 794-3000 • http://www.monroe.wednet.edu/
Grade Span: PK-12; **Agency Type:** 1
Schools: 15
5 Primary; 3 Middle; 3 High; 4 Other Level
9 Regular; 4 Special Education; 0 Vocational; 2 Alternative
0 Magnet; 0 Charter; 1 Title I Eligible; 0 School-wide Title I
Students: 6,226 (50.4% male; 49.6% female)
Individual Education Program: 664 (10.7%);
English Language Learner: 173 (2.8%); Migrant: n/a
Eligible for Free Lunch Program: 773 (12.4%)
Eligible for Reduced-Price Lunch Program: 410 (6.6%)
Teachers: 298.3 (20.9 to 1)
Librarians/Media Specialists: 7.1 (876.9 to 1)
Guidance Counselors: 14.3 (435.4 to 1)
Current Spending: ($ per student per year):
Total: $5,976; Instruction: $3,621; Support Services: $2,059

Enrollment, Drop-out Rates and Diploma Recipients by Race/Ethnicity

Category	Total	White	Black	Asian	AIAN	Hisp.
Enrollment (%)	100.0	85.6	1.2	3.5	0.9	8.8
Drop-out Rate (%)	n/a	n/a	n/a	n/a	n/a	n/a
H.S. Diplomas (#)	353	327	2	12	1	11

Mukilteo SD 6

9401 Sharon Dr • Everett, WA 98204-2699
(425) 356-1220 • http://www.mukilteo.wednet.edu/
Grade Span: PK-12; **Agency Type:** 1
Schools: 21
12 Primary; 4 Middle; 4 High; 1 Other Level
17 Regular; 1 Special Education; 1 Vocational; 2 Alternative
0 Magnet; 0 Charter; 6 Title I Eligible; 0 School-wide Title I
Students: 13,865 (51.7% male; 48.3% female)
Individual Education Program: 1,477 (10.7%);
English Language Learner: 1,116 (8.0%); Migrant: n/a
Eligible for Free Lunch Program: 3,417 (24.6%)
Eligible for Reduced-Price Lunch Program: 1,246 (9.0%)
Teachers: 716.3 (19.4 to 1)
Librarians/Media Specialists: 17.0 (815.6 to 1)
Guidance Counselors: 17.0 (815.6 to 1)
Current Spending: ($ per student per year):
Total: $6,312; Instruction: $3,914; Support Services: $2,068

Enrollment, Drop-out Rates and Diploma Recipients by Race/Ethnicity

Category	Total	White	Black	Asian	AIAN	Hisp.
Enrollment (%)	100.0	70.9	5.1	13.2	1.6	9.3
Drop-out Rate (%)	n/a	n/a	n/a	n/a	n/a	n/a
H.S. Diplomas (#)	745	530	28	132	10	45

Snohomish SD 201

1601 Ave D • Snohomish, WA 98290-1799
(360) 563-7280 • http://www.sno.wednet.edu/
Grade Span: KG-12; **Agency Type:** 1
Schools: 20
9 Primary; 4 Middle; 3 High; 4 Other Level
16 Regular; 1 Special Education; 0 Vocational; 3 Alternative
0 Magnet; 0 Charter; 5 Title I Eligible; 0 School-wide Title I
Students: 8,991 (52.1% male; 47.9% female)
Individual Education Program: 1,068 (11.9%);
English Language Learner: 81 (0.9%); Migrant: n/a
Eligible for Free Lunch Program: 569 (6.3%)
Eligible for Reduced-Price Lunch Program: 289 (3.2%)
Teachers: 406.6 (22.1 to 1)
Librarians/Media Specialists: 12.2 (737.0 to 1)
Guidance Counselors: 14.9 (603.4 to 1)
Current Spending: ($ per student per year):
Total: $5,792; Instruction: $3,555; Support Services: $1,993

Enrollment, Drop-out Rates and Diploma Recipients by Race/Ethnicity

Category	Total	White	Black	Asian	AIAN	Hisp.
Enrollment (%)	100.0	90.9	0.9	3.8	0.9	3.5
Drop-out Rate (%)	n/a	n/a	n/a	n/a	n/a	n/a
H.S. Diplomas (#)	557	526	7	15	0	9

Stanwood-Camano SD 401

9307 271st St NW • Stanwood, WA 98292-8072
(360) 629-1200 • http://www.stanwood.wednet.edu/
Grade Span: KG-12; **Agency Type:** 1
Schools: 9
5 Primary; 2 Middle; 2 High; 0 Other Level
8 Regular; 0 Special Education; 0 Vocational; 1 Alternative
0 Magnet; 0 Charter; 2 Title I Eligible; 0 School-wide Title I
Students: 5,559 (51.8% male; 48.2% female)
Individual Education Program: 681 (12.3%);
English Language Learner: 64 (1.2%); Migrant: n/a
Eligible for Free Lunch Program: 711 (12.8%)
Eligible for Reduced-Price Lunch Program: 375 (6.7%)
Teachers: 277.6 (20.0 to 1)
Librarians/Media Specialists: 8.0 (694.9 to 1)
Guidance Counselors: 8.2 (677.9 to 1)
Current Spending: ($ per student per year):
Total: $6,010; Instruction: $3,611; Support Services: $2,106

Enrollment, Drop-out Rates and Diploma Recipients by Race/Ethnicity

Category	Total	White	Black	Asian	AIAN	Hisp.
Enrollment (%)	100.0	92.2	0.8	1.9	1.2	3.9
Drop-out Rate (%)	n/a	n/a	n/a	n/a	n/a	n/a
H.S. Diplomas (#)	318	297	6	5	4	6

Sultan Home School

514 4th St • Sultan, WA 98294-0399
(360) 793-9804 • http://www.sultan.k12.wa.us/
Grade Span: PK-12; **Agency Type:** 1
Schools: 5
3 Primary; 1 Middle; 1 High; 0 Other Level
4 Regular; 1 Special Education; 0 Vocational; 0 Alternative
0 Magnet; 0 Charter; 2 Title I Eligible; 0 School-wide Title I
Students: 2,342 (52.7% male; 47.3% female)
Individual Education Program: 388 (16.6%);
English Language Learner: 27 (1.2%); Migrant: n/a
Eligible for Free Lunch Program: 548 (23.4%)
Eligible for Reduced-Price Lunch Program: 273 (11.7%)
Teachers: 113.9 (20.6 to 1)
Librarians/Media Specialists: 4.0 (585.5 to 1)
Guidance Counselors: 4.0 (585.5 to 1)
Current Spending: ($ per student per year):
Total: $6,061; Instruction: $3,680; Support Services: $2,069
Enrollment, Drop-out Rates and Diploma Recipients by Race/Ethnicity

Category	Total	White	Black	Asian	AIAN	Hisp.
Enrollment (%)	100.0	89.4	0.8	2.4	2.2	5.2
Drop-out Rate (%)	n/a	n/a	n/a	n/a	n/a	n/a
H.S. Diplomas (#)	85	77	1	1	0	6

Spokane County

Central Valley SD 356

19307 E Cataldo Ave • Greenacres, WA 99016-9404
(509) 228-5404 • http://www.cvsd.org/
Grade Span: PK-12; **Agency Type:** 1
Schools: 22
14 Primary; 5 Middle; 2 High; 1 Other Level
21 Regular; 0 Special Education; 0 Vocational; 1 Alternative
0 Magnet; 0 Charter; 10 Title I Eligible; 0 School-wide Title I
Students: 11,195 (51.3% male; 48.7% female)
Individual Education Program: 1,425 (12.7%);
English Language Learner: 124 (1.1%); Migrant: n/a
Eligible for Free Lunch Program: 2,169 (19.4%)
Eligible for Reduced-Price Lunch Program: 1,202 (10.7%)
Teachers: 624.7 (17.9 to 1)
Librarians/Media Specialists: 21.0 (533.1 to 1)
Guidance Counselors: 26.0 (430.6 to 1)
Current Spending: ($ per student per year):
Total: $6,465; Instruction: $4,007; Support Services: $2,150
Enrollment, Drop-out Rates and Diploma Recipients by Race/Ethnicity

Category	Total	White	Black	Asian	AIAN	Hisp.
Enrollment (%)	100.0	92.2	1.8	2.0	1.6	2.5
Drop-out Rate (%)	n/a	n/a	n/a	n/a	n/a	n/a
H.S. Diplomas (#)	756	713	9	18	9	7

Cheney SD 360

520 4th St • Cheney, WA 99004-1695
(509) 235-6205 • http://www.cheneysd.org/
Grade Span: PK-12; **Agency Type:** 1
Schools: 9
6 Primary; 1 Middle; 2 High; 0 Other Level
7 Regular; 1 Special Education; 0 Vocational; 1 Alternative
0 Magnet; 0 Charter; 6 Title I Eligible; 1 School-wide Title I
Students: 3,485 (49.6% male; 50.4% female)
Individual Education Program: 495 (14.2%);
English Language Learner: 13 (0.4%); Migrant: n/a
Eligible for Free Lunch Program: 958 (27.5%)
Eligible for Reduced-Price Lunch Program: 353 (10.1%)
Teachers: 197.5 (17.6 to 1)
Librarians/Media Specialists: 5.5 (633.6 to 1)
Guidance Counselors: 9.4 (370.7 to 1)
Current Spending: ($ per student per year):
Total: $6,777; Instruction: $4,052; Support Services: $2,448
Enrollment, Drop-out Rates and Diploma Recipients by Race/Ethnicity

Category	Total	White	Black	Asian	AIAN	Hisp.
Enrollment (%)	100.0	88.1	2.7	3.3	2.3	3.6
Drop-out Rate (%)	n/a	n/a	n/a	n/a	n/a	n/a
H.S. Diplomas (#)	4	4	0	0	0	0

Deer Park SD 414

908 E Crawford • Deer Park, WA 99006-0490
(509) 276-5051 • http://www.dpsd.org/
Grade Span: PK-12; **Agency Type:** 1
Schools: 5
2 Primary; 1 Middle; 1 High; 1 Other Level
4 Regular; 0 Special Education; 0 Vocational; 1 Alternative
0 Magnet; 0 Charter; 3 Title I Eligible; 0 School-wide Title I
Students: 2,123 (53.4% male; 46.6% female)
Individual Education Program: 294 (13.8%);
English Language Learner: n/a; Migrant: n/a
Eligible for Free Lunch Program: 808 (38.1%)
Eligible for Reduced-Price Lunch Program: 358 (16.9%)
Teachers: 99.2 (21.4 to 1)
Librarians/Media Specialists: 1.7 (1,248.8 to 1)
Guidance Counselors: 3.9 (544.4 to 1)
Current Spending: ($ per student per year):
Total: $6,538; Instruction: $3,983; Support Services: $2,188
Enrollment, Drop-out Rates and Diploma Recipients by Race/Ethnicity

Category	Total	White	Black	Asian	AIAN	Hisp.
Enrollment (%)	100.0	95.1	0.4	0.9	1.9	1.7
Drop-out Rate (%)	n/a	n/a	n/a	n/a	n/a	n/a
H.S. Diplomas (#)	133	128	2	0	1	2

East Valley SD 361

12325 E Grace Ave • Spokane, WA 99216-3716
(509) 924-1830 • http://www.evsd.org/
Grade Span: PK-12; **Agency Type:** 1
Schools: 11
6 Primary; 2 Middle; 3 High; 0 Other Level
8 Regular; 0 Special Education; 0 Vocational; 3 Alternative
0 Magnet; 0 Charter; 5 Title I Eligible; 1 School-wide Title I
Students: 4,627 (51.4% male; 48.6% female)
Individual Education Program: 538 (11.6%);
English Language Learner: 72 (1.6%); Migrant: n/a
Eligible for Free Lunch Program: 1,342 (29.0%)
Eligible for Reduced-Price Lunch Program: 609 (13.2%)
Teachers: 234.1 (19.8 to 1)
Librarians/Media Specialists: 6.6 (701.1 to 1)
Guidance Counselors: 10.9 (424.5 to 1)
Current Spending: ($ per student per year):
Total: $6,649; Instruction: $4,039; Support Services: $2,221
Enrollment, Drop-out Rates and Diploma Recipients by Race/Ethnicity

Category	Total	White	Black	Asian	AIAN	Hisp.
Enrollment (%)	100.0	91.5	1.6	2.6	2.4	1.9
Drop-out Rate (%)	n/a	n/a	n/a	n/a	n/a	n/a
H.S. Diplomas (#)	299	275	2	11	6	5

Mead SD 354

12828 N Newport Hwy • Mead, WA 99021-9600
(509) 465-6000 • http://coldfusion.mead.k12.wa.us/index.cfm
Grade Span: KG-12; **Agency Type:** 1
Schools: 13
7 Primary; 2 Middle; 3 High; 1 Other Level
11 Regular; 0 Special Education; 0 Vocational; 2 Alternative
0 Magnet; 0 Charter; 3 Title I Eligible; 0 School-wide Title I
Students: 8,510 (50.4% male; 49.6% female)
Individual Education Program: 965 (11.3%);
English Language Learner: 75 (0.9%); Migrant: n/a
Eligible for Free Lunch Program: 1,033 (12.1%)
Eligible for Reduced-Price Lunch Program: 753 (8.8%)
Teachers: 420.3 (20.2 to 1)
Librarians/Media Specialists: 11.0 (773.6 to 1)
Guidance Counselors: 10.8 (788.0 to 1)
Current Spending: ($ per student per year):
Total: $6,470; Instruction: $3,806; Support Services: $2,230
Enrollment, Drop-out Rates and Diploma Recipients by Race/Ethnicity

Category	Total	White	Black	Asian	AIAN	Hisp.
Enrollment (%)	100.0	93.3	1.5	2.3	1.0	1.9
Drop-out Rate (%)	n/a	n/a	n/a	n/a	n/a	n/a
H.S. Diplomas (#)	679	633	5	19	6	16

Medical Lake SD 326

116 W Third St • Medical Lake, WA 99022-0128
(509) 565-3100 • http://www.mlsd.org/mlsd/
Grade Span: PK-12; **Agency Type:** 1
Schools: 5
2 Primary; 2 Middle; 1 High; 0 Other Level
5 Regular; 0 Special Education; 0 Vocational; 0 Alternative
0 Magnet; 0 Charter; 2 Title I Eligible; 0 School-wide Title I
Students: 2,300 (54.0% male; 46.0% female)
Individual Education Program: 267 (11.6%);
English Language Learner: n/a; Migrant: n/a
Eligible for Free Lunch Program: 307 (13.3%)
Eligible for Reduced-Price Lunch Program: 287 (12.5%)
Teachers: 122.6 (18.8 to 1)
Librarians/Media Specialists: 3.5 (657.1 to 1)
Guidance Counselors: 4.0 (575.0 to 1)
Current Spending: ($ per student per year):
Total: $6,696; Instruction: $4,097; Support Services: $2,259

Enrollment, Drop-out Rates and Diploma Recipients by Race/Ethnicity

Category	Total	White	Black	Asian	AIAN	Hisp.
Enrollment (%)	100.0	86.9	4.9	3.5	1.2	3.5
Drop-out Rate (%)	n/a	n/a	n/a	n/a	n/a	n/a
H.S. Diplomas (#)	140	127	6	3	3	1

Nine Mile Falls SD 325/179

10110 W Charles Rd • Nine Mile Fall, WA 99026-8623
(509) 466-5512 • http://www.9mile.org/
Grade Span: PK-12; **Agency Type:** 1
Schools: 5
2 Primary; 1 Middle; 1 High; 1 Other Level
4 Regular; 0 Special Education; 0 Vocational; 1 Alternative
0 Magnet; 0 Charter; 3 Title I Eligible; 0 School-wide Title I
Students: 1,655 (52.7% male; 47.3% female)
Individual Education Program: 201 (12.1%);
English Language Learner: 4 (0.2%); Migrant: n/a
Eligible for Free Lunch Program: 258 (15.6%)
Eligible for Reduced-Price Lunch Program: 125 (7.6%)
Teachers: 83.7 (19.8 to 1)
Librarians/Media Specialists: 2.0 (827.5 to 1)
Guidance Counselors: 2.1 (788.1 to 1)
Current Spending: ($ per student per year):
Total: $6,552; Instruction: $3,793; Support Services: $2,321
Enrollment, Drop-out Rates and Diploma Recipients by Race/Ethnicity

Category	Total	White	Black	Asian	AIAN	Hisp.
Enrollment (%)	100.0	94.7	1.3	1.3	0.8	1.8
Drop-out Rate (%)	n/a	n/a	n/a	n/a	n/a	n/a
H.S. Diplomas (#)	132	130	1	1	0	0

Riverside SD 416

34515 N Newport Hwy • Chattaroy, WA 99003-7706
(509) 464-8201 • http://www.riversidesd.org/
Grade Span: PK-12; **Agency Type:** 1
Schools: 6
2 Primary; 1 Middle; 2 High; 1 Other Level
4 Regular; 0 Special Education; 0 Vocational; 2 Alternative
0 Magnet; 0 Charter; 3 Title I Eligible; 0 School-wide Title I
Students: 2,002 (51.3% male; 48.7% female)
Individual Education Program: 249 (12.4%);
English Language Learner: n/a; Migrant: n/a
Eligible for Free Lunch Program: 526 (26.3%)
Eligible for Reduced-Price Lunch Program: 221 (11.0%)
Teachers: 94.5 (21.2 to 1)
Librarians/Media Specialists: 1.0 (2,002.0 to 1)
Guidance Counselors: 5.0 (400.4 to 1)
Current Spending: ($ per student per year):
Total: $6,585; Instruction: $3,767; Support Services: $2,526
Enrollment, Drop-out Rates and Diploma Recipients by Race/Ethnicity

Category	Total	White	Black	Asian	AIAN	Hisp.
Enrollment (%)	100.0	95.1	0.5	0.5	2.6	1.2
Drop-out Rate (%)	n/a	n/a	n/a	n/a	n/a	n/a
H.S. Diplomas (#)	10	9	0	0	0	1

Spokane SD 81

200 N Bernard St • Spokane, WA 99201-0282
(509) 354-7364 • http://www.sd81.k12.wa.us/
Grade Span: PK-12; **Agency Type:** 1
Schools: 67
37 Primary; 6 Middle; 16 High; 8 Other Level
47 Regular; 5 Special Education; 1 Vocational; 14 Alternative
0 Magnet; 0 Charter; 15 Title I Eligible; 5 School-wide Title I
Students: 31,362 (51.0% male; 49.0% female)
Individual Education Program: 3,981 (12.7%);
English Language Learner: 928 (3.0%); Migrant: n/a
Eligible for Free Lunch Program: 10,584 (33.7%)
Eligible for Reduced-Price Lunch Program: 3,840 (12.2%)
Teachers: 1,750.1 (17.9 to 1)
Librarians/Media Specialists: 46.2 (678.8 to 1)
Guidance Counselors: 71.0 (441.7 to 1)
Current Spending: ($ per student per year):
Total: $7,082; Instruction: $4,289; Support Services: $2,463
Enrollment, Drop-out Rates and Diploma Recipients by Race/Ethnicity

Category	Total	White	Black	Asian	AIAN	Hisp.
Enrollment (%)	100.0	86.0	4.8	2.6	3.7	2.9
Drop-out Rate (%)	n/a	n/a	n/a	n/a	n/a	n/a
H.S. Diplomas (#)	1,793	1,584	58	83	31	37

West Valley SD 363

2805 N Argonne Rd • Spokane, WA 99212-2245
(509) 924-2150 • http://www.wvsd.com/
Grade Span: PK-12; **Agency Type:** 1
Schools: 12
5 Primary; 3 Middle; 4 High; 0 Other Level
8 Regular; 0 Special Education; 0 Vocational; 4 Alternative
0 Magnet; 0 Charter; 3 Title I Eligible; 2 School-wide Title I
Students: 3,607 (50.5% male; 49.5% female)
Individual Education Program: 430 (11.9%);
English Language Learner: 63 (1.7%); Migrant: n/a
Eligible for Free Lunch Program: 1,287 (35.7%)
Eligible for Reduced-Price Lunch Program: 457 (12.7%)
Teachers: 171.8 (21.0 to 1)
Librarians/Media Specialists: 4.0 (901.8 to 1)
Guidance Counselors: 8.5 (424.4 to 1)
Current Spending: ($ per student per year):
Total: $6,702; Instruction: $3,920; Support Services: $2,460
Enrollment, Drop-out Rates and Diploma Recipients by Race/Ethnicity

Category	Total	White	Black	Asian	AIAN	Hisp.
Enrollment (%)	100.0	88.7	2.5	1.2	3.2	4.4
Drop-out Rate (%)	n/a	n/a	n/a	n/a	n/a	n/a
H.S. Diplomas (#)	283	260	1	4	7	11

Stevens County

Colville SD 115

217 S Hofstetter St • Colville, WA 99114-3239
(509) 684-7850 • http://www.colsd.org/
Grade Span: KG-12; **Agency Type:** 1
Schools: 5
2 Primary; 2 Middle; 1 High; 0 Other Level
5 Regular; 0 Special Education; 0 Vocational; 0 Alternative
0 Magnet; 0 Charter; 4 Title I Eligible; 0 School-wide Title I
Students: 2,186 (51.0% male; 49.0% female)
Individual Education Program: 266 (12.2%);
English Language Learner: 36 (1.6%); Migrant: n/a
Eligible for Free Lunch Program: 876 (40.1%)
Eligible for Reduced-Price Lunch Program: 274 (12.5%)
Teachers: 111.2 (19.7 to 1)
Librarians/Media Specialists: 3.0 (728.7 to 1)
Guidance Counselors: 2.4 (910.8 to 1)
Current Spending: ($ per student per year):
Total: $6,182; Instruction: $3,614; Support Services: $2,203
Enrollment, Drop-out Rates and Diploma Recipients by Race/Ethnicity

Category	Total	White	Black	Asian	AIAN	Hisp.
Enrollment (%)	100.0	92.8	0.5	2.0	2.9	1.8
Drop-out Rate (%)	n/a	n/a	n/a	n/a	n/a	n/a
H.S. Diplomas (#)	170	165	0	3	2	0

Thurston County

North Thurston SD 3

305 College St NE • Lacey, WA 98516-5390
(360) 412-4413 • http://www.ntsd.wednet.edu/
Grade Span: PK-12; **Agency Type:** 1
Schools: 19
12 Primary; 3 Middle; 4 High; 0 Other Level
18 Regular; 0 Special Education; 0 Vocational; 1 Alternative
0 Magnet; 0 Charter; 7 Title I Eligible; 0 School-wide Title I
Students: 13,089 (50.6% male; 49.4% female)
Individual Education Program: 1,675 (12.8%);
English Language Learner: 200 (1.5%); Migrant: n/a
Eligible for Free Lunch Program: 2,905 (22.2%)
Eligible for Reduced-Price Lunch Program: 1,668 (12.7%)
Teachers: 725.4 (18.0 to 1)
Librarians/Media Specialists: 17.6 (743.7 to 1)
Guidance Counselors: 28.6 (457.7 to 1)
Current Spending: ($ per student per year):
Total: $6,584; Instruction: $4,135; Support Services: $2,129
Enrollment, Drop-out Rates and Diploma Recipients by Race/Ethnicity

Category	Total	White	Black	Asian	AIAN	Hisp.
Enrollment (%)	100.0	68.2	8.8	12.8	2.5	7.7
Drop-out Rate (%)	n/a	n/a	n/a	n/a	n/a	n/a
H.S. Diplomas (#)	822	578	81	117	11	35

Olympia SD 111

1113 Legion Way SE • Olympia, WA 98501-1697
(360) 753-8850 • http://kids.osd.wednet.edu/
Grade Span: KG-12; **Agency Type:** 1
Schools: 18
11 Primary; 4 Middle; 3 High; 0 Other Level
17 Regular; 0 Special Education; 0 Vocational; 1 Alternative
0 Magnet; 0 Charter; 8 Title I Eligible; 3 School-wide Title I
Students: 8,991 (52.2% male; 47.8% female)
Individual Education Program: 1,078 (12.0%);
English Language Learner: 144 (1.6%); Migrant: n/a
Eligible for Free Lunch Program: 1,313 (14.6%)
Eligible for Reduced-Price Lunch Program: 426 (4.7%)
Teachers: 468.2 (19.2 to 1)
Librarians/Media Specialists: 11.4 (788.7 to 1)
Guidance Counselors: 11.7 (768.5 to 1)

Current Spending: ($ per student per year):
Total: $6,537; Instruction: $4,054; Support Services: $2,119
Enrollment, Drop-out Rates and Diploma Recipients by Race/Ethnicity

Category	Total	White	Black	Asian	AIAN	Hisp.
Enrollment (%)	100.0	81.1	3.3	9.5	1.4	4.7
Drop-out Rate (%)	n/a	n/a	n/a	n/a	n/a	n/a
H.S. Diplomas (#)	681	583	9	61	2	26

Rochester SD 401

9917 Hwy 12 SW • Rochester, WA 98579-9601
(360) 273-5536
Grade Span: KG-12; **Agency Type:** 1
Schools: 6
2 Primary; 1 Middle; 3 High; 0 Other Level
5 Regular; 0 Special Education; 0 Vocational; 1 Alternative
0 Magnet; 0 Charter; 3 Title I Eligible; 0 School-wide Title I
Students: 2,161 (57.6% male; 42.4% female)
Individual Education Program: 371 (17.2%);
English Language Learner: 66 (3.1%); Migrant: n/a
Eligible for Free Lunch Program: 587 (27.2%)
Eligible for Reduced-Price Lunch Program: 222 (10.3%)
Teachers: 122.2 (17.7 to 1)
Librarians/Media Specialists: 1.0 (2,161.0 to 1)
Guidance Counselors: 6.0 (360.2 to 1)
Current Spending: ($ per student per year):
Total: $7,504; Instruction: $4,581; Support Services: $2,568
Enrollment, Drop-out Rates and Diploma Recipients by Race/Ethnicity

Category	Total	White	Black	Asian	AIAN	Hisp.
Enrollment (%)	100.0	79.6	2.8	1.8	4.5	11.3
Drop-out Rate (%)	n/a	n/a	n/a	n/a	n/a	n/a
H.S. Diplomas (#)	106	94	1	2	4	5

Tumwater SD 33

419 Linwood Ave SW • Tumwater, WA 98512-8499
(360) 709-7000 • http://www.tumwater.k12.wa.us/
Grade Span: KG-12; **Agency Type:** 1
Schools: 13
6 Primary; 2 Middle; 4 High; 1 Other Level
11 Regular; 0 Special Education; 1 Vocational; 1 Alternative
0 Magnet; 0 Charter; 4 Title I Eligible; 0 School-wide Title I
Students: 6,150 (51.2% male; 48.8% female)
Individual Education Program: 739 (12.0%);
English Language Learner: 42 (0.7%); Migrant: n/a
Eligible for Free Lunch Program: 1,130 (18.4%)
Eligible for Reduced-Price Lunch Program: 566 (9.2%)
Teachers: 319.5 (19.2 to 1)
Librarians/Media Specialists: 10.0 (615.0 to 1)
Guidance Counselors: 12.5 (492.0 to 1)
Current Spending: ($ per student per year):
Total: $6,741; Instruction: $3,907; Support Services: $2,475
Enrollment, Drop-out Rates and Diploma Recipients by Race/Ethnicity

Category	Total	White	Black	Asian	AIAN	Hisp.
Enrollment (%)	100.0	89.2	1.9	3.2	2.1	3.6
Drop-out Rate (%)	n/a	n/a	n/a	n/a	n/a	n/a
H.S. Diplomas (#)	341	316	4	7	4	10

Yelm Community Schools

404 Yelm Ave W • Yelm, WA 98597-7678
(360) 458-6114 • http://www.ycs.wednet.edu/
Grade Span: PK-12; **Agency Type:** 1
Schools: 8
4 Primary; 2 Middle; 1 High; 1 Other Level
7 Regular; 0 Special Education; 0 Vocational; 1 Alternative
0 Magnet; 0 Charter; 4 Title I Eligible; 0 School-wide Title I
Students: 4,671 (51.1% male; 48.9% female)
Individual Education Program: 605 (13.0%);
English Language Learner: 31 (0.7%); Migrant: n/a
Eligible for Free Lunch Program: 1,129 (24.2%)
Eligible for Reduced-Price Lunch Program: 631 (13.5%)
Teachers: 238.4 (19.6 to 1)
Librarians/Media Specialists: 5.7 (819.5 to 1)
Guidance Counselors: 11.5 (406.2 to 1)
Current Spending: ($ per student per year):
Total: $6,379; Instruction: $3,735; Support Services: $2,260
Enrollment, Drop-out Rates and Diploma Recipients by Race/Ethnicity

Category	Total	White	Black	Asian	AIAN	Hisp.
Enrollment (%)	100.0	87.2	2.3	3.0	2.6	4.8
Drop-out Rate (%)	n/a	n/a	n/a	n/a	n/a	n/a
H.S. Diplomas (#)	266	233	8	7	9	9

Walla Walla County

Walla Walla SD 140

364 S Park St • Walla Walla, WA 99362-3249
(509) 527-3000 • http://www.wwps.org/
Grade Span: PK-12; **Agency Type:** 1
Schools: 15
8 Primary; 2 Middle; 4 High; 1 Other Level
12 Regular; 0 Special Education; 0 Vocational; 3 Alternative
0 Magnet; 0 Charter; 6 Title I Eligible; 5 School-wide Title I
Students: 6,215 (51.7% male; 48.3% female)
Individual Education Program: 756 (12.2%);
English Language Learner: 626 (10.1%); Migrant: n/a
Eligible for Free Lunch Program: 2,154 (34.7%)
Eligible for Reduced-Price Lunch Program: 504 (8.1%)
Teachers: 329.8 (18.8 to 1)
Librarians/Media Specialists: 9.0 (690.6 to 1)
Guidance Counselors: 9.4 (661.2 to 1)
Current Spending: ($ per student per year):
Total: $6,561; Instruction: $4,148; Support Services: $2,028
Enrollment, Drop-out Rates and Diploma Recipients by Race/Ethnicity

Category	Total	White	Black	Asian	AIAN	Hisp.
Enrollment (%)	100.0	67.9	1.3	1.9	0.8	28.1
Drop-out Rate (%)	n/a	n/a	n/a	n/a	n/a	n/a
H.S. Diplomas (#)	457	366	6	10	2	73

Whatcom County

Bellingham SD 501

1306 Dupont St • Bellingham, WA 98225-3198
(360) 676-6501 • http://www.bham.wednet.edu/
Grade Span: PK-12; **Agency Type:** 1
Schools: 28
14 Primary; 4 Middle; 5 High; 5 Other Level
21 Regular; 2 Special Education; 0 Vocational; 5 Alternative
0 Magnet; 0 Charter; 6 Title I Eligible; 3 School-wide Title I
Students: 10,455 (51.0% male; 49.0% female)
Individual Education Program: 1,308 (12.5%);
English Language Learner: 423 (4.0%); Migrant: n/a
Eligible for Free Lunch Program: 2,183 (20.9%)
Eligible for Reduced-Price Lunch Program: 828 (7.9%)
Teachers: 543.5 (19.2 to 1)
Librarians/Media Specialists: 19.0 (550.3 to 1)
Guidance Counselors: 16.8 (622.3 to 1)
Current Spending: ($ per student per year):
Total: $6,518; Instruction: $3,988; Support Services: $2,215
Enrollment, Drop-out Rates and Diploma Recipients by Race/Ethnicity

Category	Total	White	Black	Asian	AIAN	Hisp.
Enrollment (%)	100.0	82.2	2.3	5.8	2.6	7.1
Drop-out Rate (%)	n/a	n/a	n/a	n/a	n/a	n/a
H.S. Diplomas (#)	710	628	12	42	5	23

Blaine SD 503

770 Mitchell Ave • Blaine, WA 98230-9149
(360) 332-5881 • http://www.blaine.wednet.edu/
Grade Span: PK-12; **Agency Type:** 1
Schools: 5
3 Primary; 1 Middle; 1 High; 0 Other Level
5 Regular; 0 Special Education; 0 Vocational; 0 Alternative
0 Magnet; 0 Charter; 1 Title I Eligible; 0 School-wide Title I
Students: 2,038 (51.5% male; 48.5% female)
Individual Education Program: 227 (11.1%);
English Language Learner: 108 (5.3%); Migrant: n/a
Eligible for Free Lunch Program: 580 (28.5%)
Eligible for Reduced-Price Lunch Program: 194 (9.5%)
Teachers: 101.2 (20.1 to 1)
Librarians/Media Specialists: 3.0 (679.3 to 1)
Guidance Counselors: 6.0 (339.7 to 1)
Current Spending: ($ per student per year):
Total: $6,779; Instruction: $4,054; Support Services: $2,322
Enrollment, Drop-out Rates and Diploma Recipients by Race/Ethnicity

Category	Total	White	Black	Asian	AIAN	Hisp.
Enrollment (%)	100.0	85.5	1.8	4.3	2.6	5.8
Drop-out Rate (%)	n/a	n/a	n/a	n/a	n/a	n/a
H.S. Diplomas (#)	107	92	3	8	1	3

Ferndale SD 502

6041 Vista Dr • Ferndale, WA 98248-9317
(360) 383-9207 • http://www.ferndale.wednet.edu/
Grade Span: PK-12; **Agency Type:** 1
Schools: 10
7 Primary; 2 Middle; 1 High; 0 Other Level
10 Regular; 0 Special Education; 0 Vocational; 0 Alternative
0 Magnet; 0 Charter; 7 Title I Eligible; 1 School-wide Title I
Students: 5,005 (51.2% male; 48.8% female)

Individual Education Program: 702 (14.0%);
English Language Learner: 211 (4.2%); Migrant: n/a
Eligible for Free Lunch Program: 1,584 (31.6%)
Eligible for Reduced-Price Lunch Program: 549 (11.0%)
Teachers: 285.1 (17.6 to 1)
Librarians/Media Specialists: 9.0 (556.1 to 1)
Guidance Counselors: 10.5 (476.7 to 1)
Current Spending: ($ per student per year):
Total: $6,203; Instruction: $3,805; Support Services: $2,095

Enrollment, Drop-out Rates and Diploma Recipients by Race/Ethnicity

Category	Total	White	Black	Asian	AIAN	Hisp.
Enrollment (%)	100.0	76.5	1.3	2.4	11.6	8.3
Drop-out Rate (%)	n/a	n/a	n/a	n/a	n/a	n/a
H.S. Diplomas (#)	259	217	1	1	24	16

Lynden SD 504

1203 Bradley Rd • Lynden, WA 98264-9514
(360) 354-4443 • http://www.lynden.wednet.edu/
Grade Span: PK-12; **Agency Type:** 1
Schools: 6
4 Primary; 1 Middle; 1 High; 0 Other Level
5 Regular; 1 Special Education; 0 Vocational; 0 Alternative
0 Magnet; 0 Charter; 3 Title I Eligible; 0 School-wide Title I
Students: 2,618 (51.4% male; 48.6% female)
Individual Education Program: 247 (9.4%);
English Language Learner: 260 (9.9%); Migrant: n/a
Eligible for Free Lunch Program: 696 (26.6%)
Eligible for Reduced-Price Lunch Program: 255 (9.7%)
Teachers: 127.3 (20.6 to 1)
Librarians/Media Specialists: 1.0 (2,618.0 to 1)
Guidance Counselors: 5.1 (513.3 to 1)
Current Spending: ($ per student per year):
Total: $6,090; Instruction: $3,790; Support Services: $1,922

Enrollment, Drop-out Rates and Diploma Recipients by Race/Ethnicity

Category	Total	White	Black	Asian	AIAN	Hisp.
Enrollment (%)	100.0	79.3	0.7	3.6	1.8	14.6
Drop-out Rate (%)	n/a	n/a	n/a	n/a	n/a	n/a
H.S. Diplomas (#)	158	132	0	6	1	19

Meridian SD 505

214 W Laurel Rd • Bellingham, WA 98226-9623
(360) 398-7111 • http://www.meridian.wednet.edu/
Grade Span: PK-12; **Agency Type:** 1
Schools: 5
2 Primary; 2 Middle; 1 High; 0 Other Level
5 Regular; 0 Special Education; 0 Vocational; 0 Alternative
0 Magnet; 0 Charter; 2 Title I Eligible; 0 School-wide Title I
Students: 1,582 (52.5% male; 47.5% female)
Individual Education Program: 219 (13.8%);
English Language Learner: 160 (10.1%); Migrant: n/a
Eligible for Free Lunch Program: 399 (25.2%)
Eligible for Reduced-Price Lunch Program: 181 (11.4%)
Teachers: 84.0 (18.8 to 1)
Librarians/Media Specialists: 1.0 (1,582.0 to 1)
Guidance Counselors: 3.2 (494.4 to 1)
Current Spending: ($ per student per year):
Total: $5,927; Instruction: $3,643; Support Services: $1,941

Enrollment, Drop-out Rates and Diploma Recipients by Race/Ethnicity

Category	Total	White	Black	Asian	AIAN	Hisp.
Enrollment (%)	100.0	85.9	0.9	3.2	1.7	8.2
Drop-out Rate (%)	n/a	n/a	n/a	n/a	n/a	n/a
H.S. Diplomas (#)	97	86	0	6	1	4

Mount Baker SD 507

4936 Deming Rd • Deming, WA 98244-0095
(360) 383-2000 • http://www.mtbaker.wednet.edu/
Grade Span: KG-12; **Agency Type:** 1
Schools: 6
3 Primary; 1 Middle; 2 High; 0 Other Level
5 Regular; 0 Special Education; 0 Vocational; 1 Alternative
0 Magnet; 0 Charter; 3 Title I Eligible; 1 School-wide Title I
Students: 2,431 (49.5% male; 50.5% female)
Individual Education Program: 327 (13.5%);
English Language Learner: 161 (6.6%); Migrant: n/a
Eligible for Free Lunch Program: 841 (34.6%)
Eligible for Reduced-Price Lunch Program: 280 (11.5%)
Teachers: 125.8 (19.3 to 1)
Librarians/Media Specialists: 2.0 (1,215.5 to 1)
Guidance Counselors: 4.4 (552.5 to 1)
Current Spending: ($ per student per year):
Total: $6,701; Instruction: $3,974; Support Services: $2,321

Enrollment, Drop-out Rates and Diploma Recipients by Race/Ethnicity

Category	Total	White	Black	Asian	AIAN	Hisp.
Enrollment (%)	100.0	84.7	0.8	1.5	7.8	5.1
Drop-out Rate (%)	n/a	n/a	n/a	n/a	n/a	n/a
H.S. Diplomas (#)	135	119	0	2	12	2

Nooksack Valley SD 506

3326 E Badger Rd • Everson, WA 98247-9232
(360) 988-4754 • http://www.nv.k12.wa.us/
Grade Span: PK-12; **Agency Type:** 1
Schools: 7
4 Primary; 1 Middle; 2 High; 0 Other Level
6 Regular; 1 Special Education; 0 Vocational; 0 Alternative
0 Magnet; 0 Charter; 3 Title I Eligible; 2 School-wide Title I
Students: 1,846 (49.2% male; 50.8% female)
Individual Education Program: 225 (12.2%);
English Language Learner: 119 (6.4%); Migrant: n/a
Eligible for Free Lunch Program: 516 (28.0%)
Eligible for Reduced-Price Lunch Program: 286 (15.5%)
Teachers: 102.7 (18.0 to 1)
Librarians/Media Specialists: 1.0 (1,846.0 to 1)
Guidance Counselors: 3.9 (473.3 to 1)
Current Spending: ($ per student per year):
Total: $6,560; Instruction: $3,926; Support Services: $2,221

Enrollment, Drop-out Rates and Diploma Recipients by Race/Ethnicity

Category	Total	White	Black	Asian	AIAN	Hisp.
Enrollment (%)	100.0	75.3	0.5	1.5	6.3	16.4
Drop-out Rate (%)	n/a	n/a	n/a	n/a	n/a	n/a
H.S. Diplomas (#)	117	98	1	4	5	9

Whitman County

Pullman SD 267

240 SE Dexter St • Pullman, WA 99163-3585
(509) 332-3581 • http://www.psd267.wednet.edu/
Grade Span: KG-12; **Agency Type:** 1
Schools: 5
3 Primary; 1 Middle; 1 High; 0 Other Level
5 Regular; 0 Special Education; 0 Vocational; 0 Alternative
0 Magnet; 0 Charter; 3 Title I Eligible; 0 School-wide Title I
Students: 2,241 (52.6% male; 47.4% female)
Individual Education Program: 256 (11.4%);
English Language Learner: 75 (3.3%); Migrant: n/a
Eligible for Free Lunch Program: 386 (17.2%)
Eligible for Reduced-Price Lunch Program: 131 (5.8%)
Teachers: 111.3 (20.1 to 1)
Librarians/Media Specialists: 2.0 (1,120.5 to 1)
Guidance Counselors: 4.0 (560.3 to 1)
Current Spending: ($ per student per year):
Total: $6,783; Instruction: $4,157; Support Services: $2,221

Enrollment, Drop-out Rates and Diploma Recipients by Race/Ethnicity

Category	Total	White	Black	Asian	AIAN	Hisp.
Enrollment (%)	100.0	79.7	3.8	11.2	1.4	3.9
Drop-out Rate (%)	n/a	n/a	n/a	n/a	n/a	n/a
H.S. Diplomas (#)	166	144	4	10	3	5

Yakima County

East Valley SD 90

2002 Beaudry Rd • Yakima, WA 98901-8012
(509) 573-7320 • http://www.ysd.wednet.edu/
Grade Span: KG-12; **Agency Type:** 1
Schools: 5
2 Primary; 2 Middle; 1 High; 0 Other Level
5 Regular; 0 Special Education; 0 Vocational; 0 Alternative
0 Magnet; 0 Charter; 1 Title I Eligible; 0 School-wide Title I
Students: 2,392 (51.2% male; 48.8% female)
Individual Education Program: 299 (12.5%);
English Language Learner: 162 (6.8%); Migrant: n/a
Eligible for Free Lunch Program: 688 (28.8%)
Eligible for Reduced-Price Lunch Program: 322 (13.5%)
Teachers: 125.8 (19.0 to 1)
Librarians/Media Specialists: 1.5 (1,594.7 to 1)
Guidance Counselors: 5.5 (434.9 to 1)
Current Spending: ($ per student per year):
Total: $6,093; Instruction: $3,852; Support Services: $1,878

Enrollment, Drop-out Rates and Diploma Recipients by Race/Ethnicity

Category	Total	White	Black	Asian	AIAN	Hisp.
Enrollment (%)	100.0	70.4	1.3	0.4	1.8	26.2
Drop-out Rate (%)	n/a	n/a	n/a	n/a	n/a	n/a
H.S. Diplomas (#)	121	96	0	2	0	23

Grandview SD 200

913 W 2nd St • Grandview, WA 98930-1202
(509) 882-2271 • http://www.grandview.wednet.edu/
Grade Span: PK-12; **Agency Type:** 1
Schools: 8
3 Primary; 0 Middle; 4 High; 1 Other Level
6 Regular; 0 Special Education; 0 Vocational; 2 Alternative
0 Magnet; 0 Charter; 4 Title I Eligible; 2 School-wide Title I
Students: 3,200 (51.4% male; 48.6% female)
Individual Education Program: 361 (11.3%);
English Language Learner: 524 (16.4%); Migrant: n/a
Eligible for Free Lunch Program: 2,065 (64.5%)
Eligible for Reduced-Price Lunch Program: 310 (9.7%)
Teachers: 160.5 (19.9 to 1)
Librarians/Media Specialists: 5.0 (640.0 to 1)
Guidance Counselors: 7.0 (457.1 to 1)
Current Spending: ($ per student per year):
Total: $6,187; Instruction: $4,021; Support Services: $1,807
Enrollment, Drop-out Rates and Diploma Recipients by Race/Ethnicity

Category	Total	White	Black	Asian	AIAN	Hisp.
Enrollment (%)	100.0	19.3	0.5	0.7	0.4	79.1
Drop-out Rate (%)	n/a	n/a	n/a	n/a	n/a	n/a
H.S. Diplomas (#)	182	44	0	4	2	132

Naches Valley SD 3

24 Shafer Ave • Naches, WA 98937-9744
(509) 653-2220 • http://www.esd105.wednet.edu/
Grade Span: KG-12; **Agency Type:** 1
Schools: 3
2 Primary; 0 Middle; 1 High; 0 Other Level
3 Regular; 0 Special Education; 0 Vocational; 0 Alternative
0 Magnet; 0 Charter; 2 Title I Eligible; 0 School-wide Title I
Students: 1,624 (53.9% male; 46.1% female)
Individual Education Program: 163 (10.0%);
English Language Learner: 96 (5.9%); Migrant: n/a
Eligible for Free Lunch Program: 359 (22.1%)
Eligible for Reduced-Price Lunch Program: 154 (9.5%)
Teachers: 81.0 (20.0 to 1)
Librarians/Media Specialists: 3.0 (541.3 to 1)
Guidance Counselors: 2.4 (676.7 to 1)
Current Spending: ($ per student per year):
Total: $5,928; Instruction: $3,524; Support Services: $2,122
Enrollment, Drop-out Rates and Diploma Recipients by Race/Ethnicity

Category	Total	White	Black	Asian	AIAN	Hisp.
Enrollment (%)	100.0	83.9	1.2	0.6	1.0	13.3
Drop-out Rate (%)	n/a	n/a	n/a	n/a	n/a	n/a
H.S. Diplomas (#)	90	83	0	0	0	7

Selah SD 119

105 W Bartlett Ave • Selah, WA 98942-1117
(509) 697-0706 • http://www.selah.k12.wa.us/Index.cfm
Grade Span: PK-12; **Agency Type:** 1
Schools: 8
3 Primary; 1 Middle; 3 High; 1 Other Level
6 Regular; 1 Special Education; 0 Vocational; 1 Alternative
0 Magnet; 0 Charter; 2 Title I Eligible; 0 School-wide Title I
Students: 3,539 (51.4% male; 48.6% female)
Individual Education Program: 447 (12.6%);
English Language Learner: 149 (4.2%); Migrant: n/a
Eligible for Free Lunch Program: 1,028 (29.0%)
Eligible for Reduced-Price Lunch Program: 385 (10.9%)
Teachers: 174.6 (20.3 to 1)
Librarians/Media Specialists: 5.0 (707.8 to 1)
Guidance Counselors: 7.1 (498.5 to 1)
Current Spending: ($ per student per year):
Total: $6,046; Instruction: $3,837; Support Services: $1,896
Enrollment, Drop-out Rates and Diploma Recipients by Race/Ethnicity

Category	Total	White	Black	Asian	AIAN	Hisp.
Enrollment (%)	100.0	80.8	1.1	1.0	1.6	15.5
Drop-out Rate (%)	n/a	n/a	n/a	n/a	n/a	n/a
H.S. Diplomas (#)	214	186	1	7	1	19

Sunnyside SD 201

1110 S 6th St • Sunnyside, WA 98944-2197
(509) 836-6532 • http://www.sunnyside.wednet.edu/
Grade Span: PK-12; **Agency Type:** 1
Schools: 8
4 Primary; 2 Middle; 2 High; 0 Other Level
6 Regular; 0 Special Education; 0 Vocational; 2 Alternative
0 Magnet; 0 Charter; 6 Title I Eligible; 4 School-wide Title I
Students: 5,657 (51.3% male; 48.7% female)
Individual Education Program: 637 (11.3%);
English Language Learner: 1,422 (25.1%); Migrant: n/a
Eligible for Free Lunch Program: 3,711 (65.6%)
Eligible for Reduced-Price Lunch Program: 416 (7.4%)
Teachers: 270.8 (20.9 to 1)
Librarians/Media Specialists: 6.0 (942.8 to 1)
Guidance Counselors: 17.0 (332.8 to 1)
Current Spending: ($ per student per year):
Total: $6,548; Instruction: $3,846; Support Services: $2,364
Enrollment, Drop-out Rates and Diploma Recipients by Race/Ethnicity

Category	Total	White	Black	Asian	AIAN	Hisp.
Enrollment (%)	100.0	17.9	0.2	0.5	0.2	81.2
Drop-out Rate (%)	n/a	n/a	n/a	n/a	n/a	n/a
H.S. Diplomas (#)	279	85	1	6	0	187

Toppenish SD 202

106 Franklin Ave • Toppenish, WA 98948-1248
(509) 865-4455 • http://www.toppenish.wednet.edu/
Grade Span: PK-12; **Agency Type:** 1
Schools: 8
5 Primary; 1 Middle; 2 High; 0 Other Level
6 Regular; 1 Special Education; 0 Vocational; 1 Alternative
0 Magnet; 0 Charter; 6 Title I Eligible; 4 School-wide Title I
Students: 3,413 (51.7% male; 48.3% female)
Individual Education Program: 402 (11.8%);
English Language Learner: 2,279 (66.8%); Migrant: n/a
Eligible for Free Lunch Program: 2,488 (72.9%)
Eligible for Reduced-Price Lunch Program: 425 (12.5%)
Teachers: 196.4 (17.4 to 1)
Librarians/Media Specialists: 6.0 (568.8 to 1)
Guidance Counselors: 8.9 (383.5 to 1)
Current Spending: ($ per student per year):
Total: $6,659; Instruction: $4,041; Support Services: $2,212
Enrollment, Drop-out Rates and Diploma Recipients by Race/Ethnicity

Category	Total	White	Black	Asian	AIAN	Hisp.
Enrollment (%)	100.0	6.5	0.1	0.4	15.2	77.8
Drop-out Rate (%)	n/a	n/a	n/a	n/a	n/a	n/a
H.S. Diplomas (#)	142	19	0	1	20	102

Wapato SD 207

212 W 3rd St • Wapato, WA 98951-1308
(509) 877-4181 • http://www.wapato.k12.wa.us/
Grade Span: KG-12; **Agency Type:** 1
Schools: 6
3 Primary; 1 Middle; 0 High; 2 Other Level
5 Regular; 0 Special Education; 0 Vocational; 1 Alternative
0 Magnet; 0 Charter; 6 Title I Eligible; 6 School-wide Title I
Students: 3,403 (51.4% male; 48.6% female)
Individual Education Program: 381 (11.2%);
English Language Learner: 982 (28.9%); Migrant: n/a
Eligible for Free Lunch Program: 2,614 (76.8%)
Eligible for Reduced-Price Lunch Program: 305 (9.0%)
Teachers: 172.0 (19.8 to 1)
Librarians/Media Specialists: 4.5 (756.2 to 1)
Guidance Counselors: 8.1 (420.1 to 1)
Current Spending: ($ per student per year):
Total: $6,770; Instruction: $3,743; Support Services: $2,571
Enrollment, Drop-out Rates and Diploma Recipients by Race/Ethnicity

Category	Total	White	Black	Asian	AIAN	Hisp.
Enrollment (%)	100.0	8.9	0.3	2.3	27.0	61.5
Drop-out Rate (%)	n/a	n/a	n/a	n/a	n/a	n/a
H.S. Diplomas (#)	147	27	1	2	20	97

West Valley SD 208

8902 Zier Rd • Yakima, WA 98908-9240
(509) 972-6000 • http://www.esd105.wednet.edu/WestValley/
Grade Span: KG-12; **Agency Type:** 1
Schools: 9
6 Primary; 2 Middle; 1 High; 0 Other Level
9 Regular; 0 Special Education; 0 Vocational; 0 Alternative
0 Magnet; 0 Charter; 4 Title I Eligible; 0 School-wide Title I
Students: 4,565 (52.0% male; 48.0% female)
Individual Education Program: 536 (11.7%);
English Language Learner: 76 (1.7%); Migrant: n/a
Eligible for Free Lunch Program: 862 (18.9%)
Eligible for Reduced-Price Lunch Program: 394 (8.6%)
Teachers: 218.6 (20.9 to 1)
Librarians/Media Specialists: 3.0 (1,521.7 to 1)
Guidance Counselors: 12.4 (368.1 to 1)
Current Spending: ($ per student per year):
Total: $5,967; Instruction: $3,606; Support Services: $2,059
Enrollment, Drop-out Rates and Diploma Recipients by Race/Ethnicity

Category	Total	White	Black	Asian	AIAN	Hisp.
Enrollment (%)	100.0	81.9	1.4	2.4	1.9	12.4
Drop-out Rate (%)	n/a	n/a	n/a	n/a	n/a	n/a
H.S. Diplomas (#)	332	288	1	12	1	30

Yakima SD 7

104 N 4th Ave • Yakima, WA 98902-2636
(509) 573-7001 • http://www.ysd.wednet.edu/

Grade Span: PK-12; **Agency Type:** 1
Schools: 25
14 Primary; 4 Middle; 4 High; 3 Other Level
22 Regular; 0 Special Education; 1 Vocational; 2 Alternative
0 Magnet; 0 Charter; 19 Title I Eligible; 11 School-wide Title I
Students: 14,313 (51.5% male; 48.5% female)
Individual Education Program: 1,781 (12.4%);
English Language Learner: 4,444 (31.0%); Migrant: n/a
Eligible for Free Lunch Program: 7,779 (54.3%)
Eligible for Reduced-Price Lunch Program: 1,214 (8.5%)
Teachers: 787.6 (18.2 to 1)
Librarians/Media Specialists: 19.4 (737.8 to 1)
Guidance Counselors: 32.7 (437.7 to 1)
Current Spending: ($ per student per year):
Total: $7,093; Instruction: $4,544; Support Services: $2,194

Enrollment, Drop-out Rates and Diploma Recipients by Race/Ethnicity

Category	Total	White	Black	Asian	AIAN	Hisp.
Enrollment (%)	100.0	39.6	3.2	1.2	2.2	53.8
Drop-out Rate (%)	n/a	n/a	n/a	n/a	n/a	n/a
H.S. Diplomas (#)	616	366	26	19	5	200

Number of Schools

Rank	Number	District Name	City
1	132	Seattle SD 1	Seattle
2	67	Spokane SD 81	Spokane
3	65	Tacoma SD 10	Tacoma
4	47	Lake Washington SD 414	Redmond
5	42	Edmonds SD 15	Lynnwood
5	42	Kent SD 415	Kent
7	37	Federal Way SD 210	Federal Way
7	37	Vancouver SD 37	Vancouver
9	35	Northshore SD 417	Bothell
10	33	Everett SD 2	Everett
10	33	Evergreen SD 114	Vancouver
10	33	Puyallup SD 3	Puyallup
13	32	Clover Park SD 400	Lakewood
13	32	Highline SD 401	Seattle
15	31	Bellevue SD 405	Bellevue
16	28	Bellingham SD 501	Bellingham
17	27	Renton SD 403	Renton
18	25	Yakima SD 7	Yakima
19	24	Central Kitsap SD 401	Silverdale
19	24	Kennewick SD 17	Kennewick
21	23	Bethel SD 403	Spanaway
21	23	Issaquah SD 411	Issaquah
23	22	Central Valley SD 356	Greenacres
24	21	Mukilteo SD 6	Everett
25	20	Auburn SD 408	Auburn
25	20	Marysville SD 25	Marysville
25	20	Shoreline SD 412	Shoreline
25	20	Snohomish SD 201	Snohomish
29	19	North Thurston SD 3	Lacey
30	18	Battle Ground SD 119	Brush Prairie
30	18	Olympia SD 111	Olympia
32	17	South Kitsap SD 402	Port Orchard
33	16	Peninsula SD 401	Gig Harbor
33	16	Wenatchee SD 246	Wenatchee
35	15	Longview SD 122	Longview
35	15	Monroe SD 103	Monroe
35	15	Richland SD 400	Richland
35	15	Walla Walla SD 140	Walla Walla
39	14	Bremerton SD 100	Bremerton
39	14	Franklin Pierce SD 402	Tacoma
39	14	North Kitsap SD 400	Poulsbo
39	14	Pasco SD 001	Pasco
43	13	Aberdeen SD 5	Aberdeen
43	13	Mead SD 354	Mead
43	13	Moses Lake SD 161	Moses Lake
43	13	Oak Harbor SD 201	Oak Harbor
43	13	Sumner SD 320	Sumner
43	13	Tumwater SD 33	Tumwater
49	12	Kelso SD 458	Kelso
49	12	Port Angeles SD 121	Port Angeles
49	12	West Valley SD 363	Spokane
52	11	Anacortes SD 103	Anacortes
52	11	Bainbridge Island SD 303	Bainbridge Isl
52	11	East Valley SD 361	Spokane
52	11	Lake Stevens SD 4	Lake Stevens
52	11	Mount Vernon SD 320	Mount Vernon
52	11	Sedro-Woolley SD 101	Sedro Woolley
58	10	Arlington SD 16	Arlington
58	10	Eastmont SD 206	East Wenatchee
58	10	Ferndale SD 502	Ferndale
58	10	Tahoma SD 409	Maple Valley
58	10	University Place SD 83	Univ Place
63	9	Cheney SD 360	Cheney
63	9	Enumclaw SD 216	Enumclaw
63	9	Stanwood-Camano SD 401	Stanwood
63	9	West Valley SD 208	Yakima
67	8	Clarkston SD 250	Clarkston
67	8	Grandview SD 200	Grandview
67	8	North Franklin SD 51	Connell
67	8	Riverview Special Services	Carnation
67	8	Selah SD 119	Selah
67	8	Shelton SD 309	Shelton
67	8	Snoqualmie SD 410	Snoqualmie
67	8	Sunnyside SD 201	Sunnyside
67	8	Toppenish SD 202	Toppenish
67	8	Washougal SD 112-6	Washougal
67	8	White River SD 416	Buckley
67	8	Yelm Community Schools	Yelm
79	7	Burlington-Edison SD 100	Burlington
79	7	Camas SD 117	Camas
79	7	Centralia SD 401	Centralia
79	7	Chehalis SD 302	Chehalis
79	7	Ephrata SD 165	Ephrata
79	7	Nooksack Valley SD 506	Everson
79	7	Quincy SD 144	Quincy
79	7	South Whidbey SD 206	Langley
79	7	Steilacoom Historical SD	Steilacoom
88	6	Fife SD 417	Tacoma
88	6	Hoquiam SD 28	Hoquiam
88	6	Lynden SD 504	Lynden
88	6	Mercer Island SD 400	Mercer Island
88	6	Mount Baker SD 507	Deming
88	6	North Mason SD 403	Belfair
88	6	Prosser SD 116	Prosser
88	6	Riverside SD 416	Chattaroy
88	6	Rochester SD 401	Rochester
88	6	Wapato SD 207	Wapato
88	6	Woodland SD 404	Woodland
99	5	Blaine SD 503	Blaine
99	5	Colville SD 115	Colville
99	5	Deer Park SD 414	Deer Park
99	5	East Valley SD 90	Yakima
99	5	Eatonville SD 404	Eatonville
99	5	Ellensburg SD 401	Ellensburg
99	5	Medical Lake SD 326	Medical Lake
99	5	Meridian SD 505	Bellingham
99	5	Nine Mile Falls SD 325/179	Nine Mile Fall
99	5	Omak SD 19	Omak
99	5	Othello SD 147	Othello
99	5	Port Townsend SD 50	Port Townsend
99	5	Pullman SD 267	Pullman
99	5	Sequim SD 323	Sequim
99	5	Sultan Home School	Sultan
99	5	Tukwila SD 406	Tukwila
99	5	Wahluke SD 73	Mattawa
116	4	Elma SD 68	Elma
116	4	Granite Falls SD 332	Granite Falls
116	4	Hockinson SD 98	Brush Prairie
116	4	Kiona-Benton SD 52	Benton City
116	4	Lakewood SD 306	North Lakewood
116	4	Orting SD 344	Orting
116	4	Ridgefield SD 122	Ridgefield
116	4	Vashon Island SD 402	Vashon
124	3	Cashmere SD 222	Cashmere
124	3	Naches Valley SD 3	Naches

Number of Teachers

Rank	Number	District Name	City
1	2,662	Seattle SD 1	Seattle
2	1,786	Tacoma SD 10	Tacoma
3	1,750	Spokane SD 81	Spokane
4	1,435	Kent SD 415	Kent
5	1,229	Evergreen SD 114	Vancouver
6	1,180	Lake Washington SD 414	Redmond
7	1,147	Federal Way SD 210	Federal Way
8	1,122	Vancouver SD 37	Vancouver
9	1,103	Edmonds SD 15	Lynnwood
10	1,022	Puyallup SD 3	Puyallup
11	1,014	Northshore SD 417	Bothell
12	954	Highline SD 401	Seattle
13	887	Everett SD 2	Everett
14	863	Bellevue SD 405	Bellevue
15	809	Bethel SD 403	Spanaway
16	787	Yakima SD 7	Yakima
17	737	Clover Park SD 400	Lakewood
18	730	Issaquah SD 411	Issaquah
19	725	North Thurston SD 3	Lacey
20	716	Mukilteo SD 6	Everett
21	712	Kennewick SD 17	Kennewick
22	694	Central Kitsap SD 401	Silverdale
23	686	Auburn SD 408	Auburn
24	641	Renton SD 403	Renton
25	624	Central Valley SD 356	Greenacres
26	579	South Kitsap SD 402	Port Orchard
27	567	Marysville SD 25	Marysville
28	555	Battle Ground SD 119	Brush Prairie
29	543	Bellingham SD 501	Bellingham
30	533	Shoreline SD 412	Shoreline
31	528	Pasco SD 001	Pasco
32	491	Richland SD 400	Richland
33	475	Peninsula SD 401	Gig Harbor
34	468	Olympia SD 111	Olympia
35	420	Mead SD 354	Mead
36	406	Snohomish SD 201	Snohomish
37	399	Franklin Pierce SD 402	Tacoma
38	379	Sumner SD 320	Sumner
39	376	Longview SD 122	Longview
40	369	Wenatchee SD 246	Wenatchee
41	366	North Kitsap SD 400	Poulsbo
42	341	Lake Stevens SD 4	Lake Stevens
43	338	Moses Lake SD 161	Moses Lake
44	336	Bremerton SD 100	Bremerton
45	329	Walla Walla SD 140	Walla Walla
46	319	Tumwater SD 33	Tumwater
47	310	Tahoma SD 409	Maple Valley
48	310	Oak Harbor SD 201	Oak Harbor
49	301	Mount Vernon SD 320	Mount Vernon
50	298	Monroe SD 103	Monroe
51	287	University Place SD 83	Univ Place
52	285	Ferndale SD 502	Ferndale
53	277	Stanwood-Camano SD 401	Stanwood
54	270	Sunnyside SD 201	Sunnyside
55	268	Eastmont SD 206	East Wenatchee
56	267	Kelso SD 458	Kelso
57	260	Arlington SD 16	Arlington
58	251	Sedro-Woolley SD 101	Sedro Woolley
59	250	Port Angeles SD 121	Port Angeles
60	244	Enumclaw SD 216	Enumclaw
61	238	Yelm Community Schools	Yelm
62	234	East Valley SD 361	Spokane
63	229	Snoqualmie SD 410	Snoqualmie
64	222	White River SD 416	Buckley
65	220	Shelton SD 309	Shelton
66	218	West Valley SD 208	Yakima
67	218	Aberdeen SD 5	Aberdeen
68	216	Camas SD 117	Camas
69	202	Mercer Island SD 400	Mercer Island
70	197	Cheney SD 360	Cheney
71	197	Bainbridge Island SD 303	Bainbridge Isl
72	196	Toppenish SD 202	Toppenish
73	175	Centralia SD 401	Centralia
74	174	Selah SD 119	Selah
75	174	Burlington-Edison SD 100	Burlington
76	172	Wapato SD 207	Wapato
77	171	West Valley SD 363	Spokane
78	162	Chehalis SD 302	Chehalis
79	160	Grandview SD 200	Grandview
80	160	Fife SD 417	Tacoma
81	159	Othello SD 147	Othello
82	150	Anacortes SD 103	Anacortes
83	148	Riverview Special Services	Carnation
84	146	Ellensburg SD 401	Ellensburg
85	143	Sequim SD 323	Sequim
86	143	Prosser SD 116	Prosser
87	140	Clarkston SD 250	Clarkston
88	138	Washougal SD 112-6	Washougal
89	135	Tukwila SD 406	Tukwila
90	133	Quincy SD 144	Quincy
91	127	Lynden SD 504	Lynden
92	125	East Valley SD 90	Yakima
92	125	Mount Baker SD 507	Deming
94	125	North Mason SD 403	Belfair
95	123	Lakewood SD 306	North Lakewood
96	122	Medical Lake SD 326	Medical Lake
97	122	Rochester SD 401	Rochester
98	120	South Whidbey SD 206	Langley
99	113	Sultan Home School	Sultan
100	112	Granite Falls SD 332	Granite Falls
101	112	Ephrata SD 165	Ephrata
102	111	Eatonville SD 404	Eatonville
103	111	Pullman SD 267	Pullman
104	111	Colville SD 115	Colville
105	108	Hoquiam SD 28	Hoquiam
106	108	North Franklin SD 51	Connell
107	108	Steilacoom Historical SD	Steilacoom
108	106	Elma SD 68	Elma
109	102	Nooksack Valley SD 506	Everson
110	102	Omak SD 19	Omak
111	102	Orting SD 344	Orting
112	101	Blaine SD 503	Blaine
113	99	Wahluke SD 73	Mattawa
114	99	Deer Park SD 414	Deer Park
115	94	Woodland SD 404	Woodland
116	94	Riverside SD 416	Chattaroy
117	86	Port Townsend SD 50	Port Townsend
118	85	Vashon Island SD 402	Vashon
119	85	Ridgefield SD 122	Ridgefield
120	84	Kiona-Benton SD 52	Benton City
121	84	Meridian SD 505	Bellingham
122	83	Nine Mile Falls SD 325/179	Nine Mile Fall
123	81	Naches Valley SD 3	Naches
124	78	Cashmere SD 222	Cashmere
125	72	Hockinson SD 98	Brush Prairie

Number of Students

Rank	Number	District Name	City
1	47,853	Seattle SD 1	Seattle
2	33,955	Tacoma SD 10	Tacoma
3	31,362	Spokane SD 81	Spokane
4	26,694	Kent SD 415	Kent
5	24,098	Lake Washington SD 414	Redmond
6	23,369	Evergreen SD 114	Vancouver
7	22,449	Federal Way SD 210	Federal Way
8	22,166	Vancouver SD 37	Vancouver
9	21,998	Edmonds SD 15	Lynnwood
10	20,181	Northshore SD 417	Bothell
11	19,819	Puyallup SD 3	Puyallup
12	18,743	Everett SD 2	Everett
13	17,735	Highline SD 401	Seattle
14	16,641	Bethel SD 403	Spanaway
15	15,656	Bellevue SD 405	Bellevue
16	14,759	Issaquah SD 411	Issaquah
17	14,698	Kennewick SD 17	Kennewick
18	14,313	Yakima SD 7	Yakima

19	13,865	Mukilteo SD 6	Everett
20	13,621	Auburn SD 408	Auburn
21	13,501	Clover Park SD 400	Lakewood
22	13,393	Central Kitsap SD 401	Silverdale
23	13,100	Renton SD 403	Renton
24	13,089	North Thurston SD 3	Lacey
25	12,024	Battle Ground SD 119	Brush Prairie
26	12,009	Marysville SD 25	Marysville
27	11,195	Central Valley SD 356	Greenacres
28	11,169	South Kitsap SD 402	Port Orchard
29	10,455	Bellingham SD 501	Bellingham
30	10,099	Shoreline SD 412	Shoreline
31	9,800	Richland SD 400	Richland
32	9,785	Pasco SD 001	Pasco
33	9,595	Peninsula SD 401	Gig Harbor
34	8,991	Olympia SD 111	Olympia
34	8,991	Snohomish SD 201	Snohomish
36	8,510	Mead SD 354	Mead
37	7,984	Sumner SD 320	Sumner
38	7,758	Franklin Pierce SD 402	Tacoma
39	7,506	Longview SD 122	Longview
40	7,402	Wenatchee SD 246	Wenatchee
41	7,290	Lake Stevens SD 4	Lake Stevens
42	7,163	North Kitsap SD 400	Poulsbo
43	6,812	Moses Lake SD 161	Moses Lake
44	6,272	Tahoma SD 409	Maple Valley
45	6,226	Monroe SD 103	Monroe
46	6,215	Walla Walla SD 140	Walla Walla
47	6,153	Oak Harbor SD 201	Oak Harbor
48	6,150	Tumwater SD 33	Tumwater
49	5,798	Mount Vernon SD 320	Mount Vernon
50	5,787	Bremerton SD 100	Bremerton
51	5,657	Sunnyside SD 201	Sunnyside
52	5,559	Stanwood-Camano SD 401	Stanwood
53	5,462	Eastmont SD 206	East Wenatchee
54	5,306	Kelso SD 458	Kelso
55	5,296	University Place SD 83	Univ Place
56	5,146	Arlington SD 16	Arlington
57	5,112	Enumclaw SD 216	Enumclaw
58	5,005	Ferndale SD 502	Ferndale
59	4,749	Port Angeles SD 121	Port Angeles
60	4,719	Snoqualmie SD 410	Snoqualmie
61	4,671	Yelm Community Schools	Yelm
62	4,627	East Valley SD 361	Spokane
63	4,587	Sedro-Woolley SD 101	Sedro Woolley
64	4,565	West Valley SD 208	Yakima
65	4,384	White River SD 416	Buckley
66	4,335	Camas SD 117	Camas
67	4,178	Aberdeen SD 5	Aberdeen
68	4,142	Bainbridge Island SD 303	Bainbridge Isl
69	4,133	Mercer Island SD 400	Mercer Island
69	4,133	Shelton SD 309	Shelton
71	3,648	Burlington-Edison SD 100	Burlington
72	3,607	West Valley SD 363	Spokane
73	3,539	Selah SD 119	Selah
74	3,485	Cheney SD 360	Cheney
75	3,413	Toppenish SD 202	Toppenish
76	3,403	Wapato SD 207	Wapato
77	3,376	Centralia SD 401	Centralia
78	3,200	Grandview SD 200	Grandview
79	3,137	Anacortes SD 103	Anacortes
79	3,137	Fife SD 417	Tacoma
81	3,111	Othello SD 147	Othello
82	3,038	Chehalis SD 302	Chehalis
83	2,912	Riverview Special Services	Carnation
84	2,884	Sequim SD 323	Sequim
85	2,843	Ellensburg SD 401	Ellensburg
86	2,814	Clarkston SD 250	Clarkston
87	2,790	Prosser SD 116	Prosser
88	2,742	Tukwila SD 406	Tukwila
89	2,666	Washougal SD 112-6	Washougal
90	2,618	Lynden SD 504	Lynden
91	2,582	Lakewood SD 306	North Lakewood
92	2,431	Mount Baker SD 507	Deming
93	2,392	East Valley SD 90	Yakima
94	2,391	Granite Falls SD 332	Granite Falls
95	2,389	North Mason SD 403	Belfair
96	2,364	South Whidbey SD 206	Langley
97	2,342	Sultan Home School	Sultan
98	2,331	Quincy SD 144	Quincy
99	2,317	Ephrata SD 165	Ephrata
100	2,300	Medical Lake SD 326	Medical Lake
101	2,241	Pullman SD 267	Pullman
102	2,186	Colville SD 115	Colville
103	2,161	Rochester SD 401	Rochester
104	2,123	Deer Park SD 414	Deer Park
105	2,111	Steilacoom Historical SD	Steilacoom
106	2,100	Hoquiam SD 28	Hoquiam
107	2,092	Eatonville SD 404	Eatonville
108	2,038	Blaine SD 503	Blaine
109	2,002	Riverside SD 416	Chattaroy
110	2,001	Elma SD 68	Elma
111	1,985	North Franklin SD 51	Connell
112	1,962	Woodland SD 404	Woodland
113	1,935	Omak SD 19	Omak
114	1,858	Orting SD 344	Orting
115	1,846	Nooksack Valley SD 506	Everson
116	1,824	Ridgefield SD 122	Ridgefield
117	1,741	Port Townsend SD 50	Port Townsend
118	1,664	Kiona-Benton SD 52	Benton City
119	1,655	Nine Mile Falls SD 325/179	Nine Mile Fall
120	1,643	Wahluke SD 73	Mattawa
121	1,624	Naches Valley SD 3	Naches
122	1,606	Vashon Island SD 402	Vashon
123	1,582	Meridian SD 505	Bellingham
124	1,554	Hockinson SD 98	Brush Prairie
125	1,509	Cashmere SD 222	Cashmere

Male Students

Rank	Percent	District Name	City
1	57.6	Rochester SD 401	Rochester
2	54.0	Medical Lake SD 326	Medical Lake
3	53.9	Naches Valley SD 3	Naches
4	53.8	Woodland SD 404	Woodland
5	53.7	Chehalis SD 302	Chehalis
5	53.7	Quincy SD 144	Quincy
7	53.4	Deer Park SD 414	Deer Park
8	53.2	Elma SD 68	Elma
8	53.2	Sedro-Woolley SD 101	Sedro Woolley
10	53.0	Hockinson SD 98	Brush Prairie
11	52.9	Ridgefield SD 122	Ridgefield
12	52.7	Eatonville SD 404	Eatonville
12	52.7	Nine Mile Falls SD 325/179	Nine Mile Fall
12	52.7	Sultan Home School	Sultan
15	52.6	Pullman SD 267	Pullman
16	52.5	Bethel SD 403	Spanaway
16	52.5	Meridian SD 505	Bellingham
16	52.5	North Kitsap SD 400	Poulsbo
16	52.5	Port Angeles SD 121	Port Angeles
20	52.4	Ellensburg SD 401	Ellensburg
20	52.4	Hoquiam SD 28	Hoquiam
22	52.3	Cashmere SD 222	Cashmere
22	52.3	Mercer Island SD 400	Mercer Island
22	52.3	Northshore SD 417	Bothell
22	52.3	Steilacoom Historical SD	Steilacoom
22	52.3	Vashon Island SD 402	Vashon
27	52.2	Clover Park SD 400	Lakewood
27	52.2	Olympia SD 111	Olympia
27	52.2	Orting SD 344	Orting
27	52.2	Renton SD 403	Renton
27	52.2	Shoreline SD 412	Shoreline
27	52.2	Wahluke SD 73	Mattawa
33	52.1	Everett SD 2	Everett
33	52.1	Issaquah SD 411	Issaquah
33	52.1	Peninsula SD 401	Gig Harbor
33	52.1	Snohomish SD 201	Snohomish
37	52.0	Camas SD 117	Camas
37	52.0	Shelton SD 309	Shelton
37	52.0	Snoqualmie SD 410	Snoqualmie
37	52.0	West Valley SD 208	Yakima
41	51.9	Bellevue SD 405	Bellevue
41	51.9	Clarkston SD 250	Clarkston
41	51.9	Lake Washington SD 414	Redmond
41	51.9	Lakewood SD 306	North Lakewood
41	51.9	Oak Harbor SD 201	Oak Harbor
46	51.8	Battle Ground SD 119	Brush Prairie
46	51.8	Kent SD 415	Kent
46	51.8	Marysville SD 25	Marysville
46	51.8	Stanwood-Camano SD 401	Stanwood
46	51.8	Tukwila SD 406	Tukwila
51	51.7	Eastmont SD 206	East Wenatchee
51	51.7	Edmonds SD 15	Lynnwood
51	51.7	Mukilteo SD 6	Everett
51	51.7	Toppenish SD 202	Toppenish
51	51.7	Walla Walla SD 140	Walla Walla
56	51.6	Federal Way SD 210	Federal Way
56	51.6	Kelso SD 458	Kelso
56	51.6	North Mason SD 403	Belfair
59	51.5	Blaine SD 503	Blaine
59	51.5	Fife SD 417	Tacoma
59	51.5	Granite Falls SD 332	Granite Falls
59	51.5	Highline SD 401	Seattle
59	51.5	Kennewick SD 17	Kennewick
59	51.5	Moses Lake SD 161	Moses Lake
59	51.5	Yakima SD 7	Yakima
66	51.4	Central Kitsap SD 401	Silverdale
66	51.4	East Valley SD 361	Spokane
66	51.4	Grandview SD 200	Grandview
66	51.4	Longview SD 122	Longview
66	51.4	Lynden SD 504	Lynden
66	51.4	Othello SD 147	Othello
66	51.4	Selah SD 119	Selah
66	51.4	Sequim SD 323	Sequim
66	51.4	Wapato SD 207	Wapato
75	51.3	Central Valley SD 356	Greenacres
75	51.3	Kiona-Benton SD 52	Benton City
75	51.3	Riverside SD 416	Chattaroy
75	51.3	Seattle SD 1	Seattle
75	51.3	Sumner SD 320	Sumner
75	51.3	Sunnyside SD 201	Sunnyside
75	51.3	Tacoma SD 10	Tacoma
82	51.2	Bainbridge Island SD 303	Bainbridge Isl
82	51.2	East Valley SD 90	Yakima
82	51.2	Ferndale SD 502	Ferndale
82	51.2	Mount Vernon SD 320	Mount Vernon
82	51.2	North Franklin SD 51	Connell
82	51.2	Omak SD 19	Omak
82	51.2	Pasco SD 001	Pasco
82	51.2	Richland SD 400	Richland
82	51.2	Tumwater SD 33	Tumwater
82	51.2	University Place SD 83	Univ Place
82	51.2	Vancouver SD 37	Vancouver
93	51.1	Auburn SD 408	Auburn
93	51.1	Port Townsend SD 50	Port Townsend
93	51.1	Wenatchee SD 246	Wenatchee
93	51.1	Yelm Community Schools	Yelm
97	51.0	Bellingham SD 501	Bellingham
97	51.0	Colville SD 115	Colville
97	51.0	Evergreen SD 114	Vancouver
97	51.0	Franklin Pierce SD 402	Tacoma
97	51.0	Lake Stevens SD 4	Lake Stevens
97	51.0	Spokane SD 81	Spokane
97	51.0	Tahoma SD 409	Maple Valley
97	51.0	Washougal SD 112-6	Washougal
105	50.9	Burlington-Edison SD 100	Burlington
105	50.9	Enumclaw SD 216	Enumclaw
105	50.9	Ephrata SD 165	Ephrata
105	50.9	Puyallup SD 3	Puyallup
105	50.9	South Kitsap SD 402	Port Orchard
110	50.8	Aberdeen SD 5	Aberdeen
110	50.8	Arlington SD 16	Arlington
112	50.7	Anacortes SD 103	Anacortes
112	50.7	Riverview Special Services	Carnation
114	50.6	Bremerton SD 100	Bremerton
114	50.6	North Thurston SD 3	Lacey
116	50.5	Centralia SD 401	Centralia
116	50.5	Prosser SD 116	Prosser
116	50.5	West Valley SD 363	Spokane
116	50.5	White River SD 416	Buckley
120	50.4	Mead SD 354	Mead
120	50.4	Monroe SD 103	Monroe
120	50.4	South Whidbey SD 206	Langley
123	49.6	Cheney SD 360	Cheney
124	49.5	Mount Baker SD 507	Deming
125	49.2	Nooksack Valley SD 506	Everson

Female Students

Rank	Percent	District Name	City
1	50.8	Nooksack Valley SD 506	Everson
2	50.5	Mount Baker SD 507	Deming
3	50.4	Cheney SD 360	Cheney
4	49.6	Mead SD 354	Mead
4	49.6	Monroe SD 103	Monroe
4	49.6	South Whidbey SD 206	Langley
7	49.5	Centralia SD 401	Centralia
7	49.5	Prosser SD 116	Prosser
7	49.5	West Valley SD 363	Spokane
7	49.5	White River SD 416	Buckley
11	49.4	Bremerton SD 100	Bremerton
11	49.4	North Thurston SD 3	Lacey
13	49.3	Anacortes SD 103	Anacortes
13	49.3	Riverview Special Services	Carnation
15	49.2	Aberdeen SD 5	Aberdeen
15	49.2	Arlington SD 16	Arlington
17	49.1	Burlington-Edison SD 100	Burlington
17	49.1	Enumclaw SD 216	Enumclaw
17	49.1	Ephrata SD 165	Ephrata
17	49.1	Puyallup SD 3	Puyallup
17	49.1	South Kitsap SD 402	Port Orchard
22	49.0	Bellingham SD 501	Bellingham
22	49.0	Colville SD 115	Colville
22	49.0	Evergreen SD 114	Vancouver
22	49.0	Franklin Pierce SD 402	Tacoma
22	49.0	Lake Stevens SD 4	Lake Stevens
22	49.0	Spokane SD 81	Spokane
22	49.0	Tahoma SD 409	Maple Valley
22	49.0	Washougal SD 112-6	Washougal
30	48.9	Auburn SD 408	Auburn
30	48.9	Port Townsend SD 50	Port Townsend
30	48.9	Wenatchee SD 246	Wenatchee
30	48.9	Yelm Community Schools	Yelm
34	48.8	Bainbridge Island SD 303	Bainbridge Isl
34	48.8	East Valley SD 90	Yakima
34	48.8	Ferndale SD 502	Ferndale
34	48.8	Mount Vernon SD 320	Mount Vernon
34	48.8	North Franklin SD 51	Connell

34	48.8	Omak SD 19	Omak
34	48.8	Pasco SD 001	Pasco
34	48.8	Richland SD 400	Richland
34	48.8	Tumwater SD 33	Tumwater
34	48.8	University Place SD 83	Univ Place
34	48.8	Vancouver SD 37	Vancouver
45	48.7	Central Valley SD 356	Greenacres
45	48.7	Kiona-Benton SD 52	Benton City
45	48.7	Riverside SD 416	Chattaroy
45	48.7	Seattle SD 1	Seattle
45	48.7	Sumner SD 320	Sumner
45	48.7	Sunnyside SD 201	Sunnyside
45	48.7	Tacoma SD 10	Tacoma
52	48.6	Central Kitsap SD 401	Silverdale
52	48.6	East Valley SD 361	Spokane
52	48.6	Grandview SD 200	Grandview
52	48.6	Longview SD 122	Longview
52	48.6	Lynden SD 504	Lynden
52	48.6	Othello SD 147	Othello
52	48.6	Selah SD 119	Selah
52	48.6	Sequim SD 323	Sequim
52	48.6	Wapato SD 207	Wapato
61	48.5	Blaine SD 503	Blaine
61	48.5	Fife SD 417	Tacoma
61	48.5	Granite Falls SD 332	Granite Falls
61	48.5	Highline SD 401	Seattle
61	48.5	Kennewick SD 17	Kennewick
61	48.5	Moses Lake SD 161	Moses Lake
61	48.5	Yakima SD 7	Yakima
68	48.4	Federal Way SD 210	Federal Way
68	48.4	Kelso SD 458	Kelso
68	48.4	North Mason SD 403	Belfair
71	48.3	Eastmont SD 206	East Wenatchee
71	48.3	Edmonds SD 15	Lynnwood
71	48.3	Mukilteo SD 6	Everett
71	48.3	Toppenish SD 202	Toppenish
71	48.3	Walla Walla SD 140	Walla Walla
76	48.2	Battle Ground SD 119	Brush Prairie
76	48.2	Kent SD 415	Kent
76	48.2	Marysville SD 25	Marysville
76	48.2	Stanwood-Camano SD 401	Stanwood
76	48.2	Tukwila SD 406	Tukwila
81	48.1	Bellevue SD 405	Bellevue
81	48.1	Clarkston SD 250	Clarkston
81	48.1	Lake Washington SD 414	Redmond
81	48.1	Lakewood SD 306	North Lakewood
81	48.1	Oak Harbor SD 201	Oak Harbor
86	48.0	Camas SD 117	Camas
86	48.0	Shelton SD 309	Shelton
86	48.0	Snoqualmie SD 410	Snoqualmie
86	48.0	West Valley SD 208	Yakima
90	47.9	Everett SD 2	Everett
90	47.9	Issaquah SD 411	Issaquah
90	47.9	Peninsula SD 401	Gig Harbor
90	47.9	Snohomish SD 201	Snohomish
94	47.8	Clover Park SD 400	Lakewood
94	47.8	Olympia SD 111	Olympia
94	47.8	Orting SD 344	Orting
94	47.8	Renton SD 403	Renton
94	47.8	Shoreline SD 412	Shoreline
94	47.8	Wahluke SD 73	Mattawa
100	47.7	Cashmere SD 222	Cashmere
100	47.7	Mercer Island SD 400	Mercer Island
100	47.7	Northshore SD 417	Bothell
100	47.7	Steilacoom Historical SD	Steilacoom
100	47.7	Vashon Island SD 402	Vashon
105	47.6	Ellensburg SD 401	Ellensburg
105	47.6	Hoquiam SD 28	Hoquiam
107	47.5	Bethel SD 403	Spanaway
107	47.5	Meridian SD 505	Bellingham
107	47.5	North Kitsap SD 400	Poulsbo
107	47.5	Port Angeles SD 121	Port Angeles
111	47.4	Pullman SD 267	Pullman
112	47.3	Eatonville SD 404	Eatonville
112	47.3	Nine Mile Falls SD 325/179	Nine Mile Fall
112	47.3	Sultan Home School	Sultan
115	47.1	Ridgefield SD 122	Ridgefield
116	47.0	Hockinson SD 98	Brush Prairie
117	46.8	Elma SD 68	Elma
117	46.8	Sedro-Woolley SD 101	Sedro Woolley
119	46.6	Deer Park SD 414	Deer Park
120	46.3	Chehalis SD 302	Chehalis
120	46.3	Quincy SD 144	Quincy
122	46.2	Woodland SD 404	Woodland
123	46.1	Naches Valley SD 3	Naches
124	46.0	Medical Lake SD 326	Medical Lake
125	42.4	Rochester SD 401	Rochester

Individual Education Program Students

Rank	Percent	District Name	City
1	17.2	Rochester SD 401	Rochester
2	16.6	Sultan Home School	Sultan
3	15.6	Omak SD 19	Omak
4	15.1	Port Angeles SD 121	Port Angeles
5	14.9	Granite Falls SD 332	Granite Falls
6	14.2	Cheney SD 360	Cheney
7	14.1	Centralia SD 401	Centralia
7	14.1	Clarkston SD 250	Clarkston
9	14.0	Ferndale SD 502	Ferndale
10	13.9	Orting SD 344	Orting
10	13.9	Sedro-Woolley SD 101	Sedro Woolley
12	13.8	Deer Park SD 414	Deer Park
12	13.8	Meridian SD 505	Bellingham
14	13.6	Bethel SD 403	Spanaway
14	13.6	Clover Park SD 400	Lakewood
16	13.5	Mount Baker SD 507	Deming
16	13.5	Shelton SD 309	Shelton
18	13.4	Aberdeen SD 5	Aberdeen
18	13.4	Central Kitsap SD 401	Silverdale
18	13.4	South Kitsap SD 402	Port Orchard
21	13.2	Marysville SD 25	Marysville
22	13.1	Elma SD 68	Elma
22	13.1	Mount Vernon SD 320	Mount Vernon
22	13.1	Steilacoom Historical SD	Steilacoom
22	13.1	Tahoma SD 409	Maple Valley
26	13.0	Longview SD 122	Longview
26	13.0	Yelm Community Schools	Yelm
28	12.9	Tacoma SD 10	Tacoma
29	12.8	North Thurston SD 3	Lacey
30	12.7	Central Valley SD 356	Greenacres
30	12.7	Ellensburg SD 401	Ellensburg
30	12.7	Quincy SD 144	Quincy
30	12.7	Spokane SD 81	Spokane
34	12.6	Anacortes SD 103	Anacortes
34	12.6	Port Townsend SD 50	Port Townsend
34	12.6	Selah SD 119	Selah
34	12.6	Shoreline SD 412	Shoreline
38	12.5	Bellingham SD 501	Bellingham
38	12.5	East Valley SD 90	Yakima
38	12.5	Renton SD 403	Renton
38	12.5	Seattle SD 1	Seattle
38	12.5	Vancouver SD 37	Vancouver
43	12.4	Arlington SD 16	Arlington
43	12.4	Edmonds SD 15	Lynnwood
43	12.4	Riverside SD 416	Chattaroy
43	12.4	Yakima SD 7	Yakima
47	12.3	Eastmont SD 206	East Wenatchee
47	12.3	Kiona-Benton SD 52	Benton City
47	12.3	Peninsula SD 401	Gig Harbor
47	12.3	Stanwood-Camano SD 401	Stanwood
51	12.2	Bremerton SD 100	Bremerton
51	12.2	Burlington-Edison SD 100	Burlington
51	12.2	Colville SD 115	Colville
51	12.2	Hoquiam SD 28	Hoquiam
51	12.2	Lakewood SD 306	North Lakewood
51	12.2	Nooksack Valley SD 506	Everson
51	12.2	Richland SD 400	Richland
51	12.2	Walla Walla SD 140	Walla Walla
59	12.1	Franklin Pierce SD 402	Tacoma
59	12.1	Nine Mile Falls SD 325/179	Nine Mile Fall
59	12.1	Northshore SD 417	Bothell
59	12.1	Sumner SD 320	Sumner
63	12.0	Federal Way SD 210	Federal Way
63	12.0	Kelso SD 458	Kelso
63	12.0	Olympia SD 111	Olympia
63	12.0	Tumwater SD 33	Tumwater
63	12.0	White River SD 416	Buckley
68	11.9	North Kitsap SD 400	Poulsbo
68	11.9	Snohomish SD 201	Snohomish
68	11.9	West Valley SD 363	Spokane
71	11.8	Bainbridge Island SD 303	Bainbridge Isl
71	11.8	Battle Ground SD 119	Brush Prairie
71	11.8	Enumclaw SD 216	Enumclaw
71	11.8	Kent SD 415	Kent
71	11.8	Toppenish SD 202	Toppenish
76	11.7	Eatonville SD 404	Eatonville
76	11.7	Everett SD 2	Everett
76	11.7	Highline SD 401	Seattle
76	11.7	North Mason SD 403	Belfair
76	11.7	Puyallup SD 3	Puyallup
76	11.7	West Valley SD 208	Yakima
82	11.6	East Valley SD 361	Spokane
82	11.6	Medical Lake SD 326	Medical Lake
82	11.6	University Place SD 83	Univ Place
82	11.6	Wahluke SD 73	Mattawa
86	11.5	Chehalis SD 302	Chehalis
86	11.5	Moses Lake SD 161	Moses Lake
88	11.4	Evergreen SD 114	Vancouver
88	11.4	Lake Stevens SD 4	Lake Stevens
88	11.4	Pullman SD 267	Pullman
88	11.4	Washougal SD 112-6	Washougal
92	11.3	Grandview SD 200	Grandview
92	11.3	Mead SD 354	Mead
92	11.3	Prosser SD 116	Prosser
92	11.3	Riverview Special Services	Carnation
92	11.3	Sunnyside SD 201	Sunnyside
92	11.3	Woodland SD 404	Woodland
98	11.2	Wapato SD 207	Wapato
99	11.1	Blaine SD 503	Blaine
99	11.1	Issaquah SD 411	Issaquah
99	11.1	North Franklin SD 51	Connell
99	11.1	Othello SD 147	Othello
99	11.1	Vashon Island SD 402	Vashon
104	10.7	Kennewick SD 17	Kennewick
104	10.7	Monroe SD 103	Monroe
104	10.7	Mukilteo SD 6	Everett
104	10.7	Oak Harbor SD 201	Oak Harbor
104	10.7	South Whidbey SD 206	Langley
109	10.6	Camas SD 117	Camas
109	10.6	Ridgefield SD 122	Ridgefield
109	10.6	Snoqualmie SD 410	Snoqualmie
112	10.5	Pasco SD 001	Pasco
113	10.2	Auburn SD 408	Auburn
113	10.2	Tukwila SD 406	Tukwila
115	10.1	Fife SD 417	Tacoma
116	10.0	Naches Valley SD 3	Naches
117	9.8	Hockinson SD 98	Brush Prairie
118	9.6	Cashmere SD 222	Cashmere
118	9.6	Wenatchee SD 246	Wenatchee
120	9.5	Bellevue SD 405	Bellevue
120	9.5	Ephrata SD 165	Ephrata
122	9.4	Lake Washington SD 414	Redmond
122	9.4	Lynden SD 504	Lynden
124	9.1	Sequim SD 323	Sequim
125	9.0	Mercer Island SD 400	Mercer Island

English Language Learner Students

Rank	Percent	District Name	City
1	66.8	Toppenish SD 202	Toppenish
2	58.1	Wahluke SD 73	Mattawa
3	40.8	Pasco SD 001	Pasco
4	32.3	Othello SD 147	Othello
5	31.0	Yakima SD 7	Yakima
6	30.1	North Franklin SD 51	Connell
7	29.4	Quincy SD 144	Quincy
8	28.9	Wapato SD 207	Wapato
9	28.5	Tukwila SD 406	Tukwila
10	27.7	Mount Vernon SD 320	Mount Vernon
11	25.1	Sunnyside SD 201	Sunnyside
12	22.9	Prosser SD 116	Prosser
13	20.7	Wenatchee SD 246	Wenatchee
14	16.4	Grandview SD 200	Grandview
15	12.4	Burlington-Edison SD 100	Burlington
16	11.6	Highline SD 401	Seattle
16	11.6	Seattle SD 1	Seattle
18	11.5	Bellevue SD 405	Bellevue
18	11.5	Kent SD 415	Kent
20	10.7	Eastmont SD 206	East Wenatchee
21	10.3	Kennewick SD 17	Kennewick
22	10.2	Vancouver SD 37	Vancouver
23	10.1	Meridian SD 505	Bellingham
23	10.1	Walla Walla SD 140	Walla Walla
25	9.9	Lynden SD 504	Lynden
26	9.4	Cashmere SD 222	Cashmere
27	9.2	Federal Way SD 210	Federal Way
28	9.0	Kiona-Benton SD 52	Benton City
29	8.4	Moses Lake SD 161	Moses Lake
30	8.3	Ephrata SD 165	Ephrata
30	8.3	Renton SD 403	Renton
32	8.0	Mukilteo SD 6	Everett
33	7.3	Edmonds SD 15	Lynnwood
34	6.9	Clover Park SD 400	Lakewood
34	6.9	Tacoma SD 10	Tacoma
36	6.8	East Valley SD 90	Yakima
37	6.6	Mount Baker SD 507	Deming
38	6.4	Nooksack Valley SD 506	Everson
39	6.3	Shoreline SD 412	Shoreline
40	6.1	Auburn SD 408	Auburn
40	6.1	Centralia SD 401	Centralia
42	5.9	Everett SD 2	Everett
42	5.9	Naches Valley SD 3	Naches
44	5.4	Lake Washington SD 414	Redmond
45	5.3	Blaine SD 503	Blaine
46	4.9	Evergreen SD 114	Vancouver
47	4.7	Aberdeen SD 5	Aberdeen
48	4.3	Hoquiam SD 28	Hoquiam
49	4.2	Ferndale SD 502	Ferndale
49	4.2	Omak SD 19	Omak
49	4.2	Selah SD 119	Selah
52	4.1	Ellensburg SD 401	Ellensburg
53	4.0	Bellingham SD 501	Bellingham
54	3.8	Longview SD 122	Longview
55	3.3	Pullman SD 267	Pullman
56	3.2	Richland SD 400	Richland
56	3.2	Shelton SD 309	Shelton
58	3.1	Rochester SD 401	Rochester
58	3.1	Steilacoom Historical SD	Steilacoom

Rank	Percent	District Name	City
60	3.0	Spokane SD 81	Spokane
60	3.0	Woodland SD 404	Woodland
62	2.9	Fife SD 417	Tacoma
62	2.9	Kelso SD 458	Kelso
64	2.8	Monroe SD 103	Monroe
65	2.7	Oak Harbor SD 201	Oak Harbor
66	2.6	Chehalis SD 302	Chehalis
66	2.6	Marysville SD 25	Marysville
66	2.6	Northshore SD 417	Bothell
69	2.5	Sedro-Woolley SD 101	Sedro Woolley
70	2.4	Elma SD 68	Elma
71	2.3	Mercer Island SD 400	Mercer Island
72	2.2	Washougal SD 112-6	Washougal
73	2.1	University Place SD 83	Univ Place
74	2.0	Sequim SD 323	Sequim
75	1.8	Central Kitsap SD 401	Silverdale
75	1.8	Franklin Pierce SD 402	Tacoma
77	1.7	Riverview Special Services	Carnation
77	1.7	West Valley SD 208	Yakima
77	1.7	West Valley SD 363	Spokane
80	1.6	Battle Ground SD 119	Brush Prairie
80	1.6	Colville SD 115	Colville
80	1.6	East Valley SD 361	Spokane
80	1.6	Olympia SD 111	Olympia
84	1.5	Anacortes SD 103	Anacortes
84	1.5	Issaquah SD 411	Issaquah
84	1.5	North Thurston SD 3	Lacey
87	1.4	Arlington SD 16	Arlington
87	1.4	Lakewood SD 306	North Lakewood
89	1.3	North Kitsap SD 400	Poulsbo
89	1.3	Orting SD 344	Orting
89	1.3	Sumner SD 320	Sumner
92	1.2	Stanwood-Camano SD 401	Stanwood
92	1.2	Sultan Home School	Sultan
94	1.1	Bremerton SD 100	Bremerton
94	1.1	Central Valley SD 356	Greenacres
94	1.1	Port Townsend SD 50	Port Townsend
97	1.0	Bethel SD 403	Spanaway
97	1.0	Camas SD 117	Camas
97	1.0	Eatonville SD 404	Eatonville
97	1.0	Enumclaw SD 216	Enumclaw
97	1.0	North Mason SD 403	Belfair
97	1.0	Puyallup SD 3	Puyallup
97	1.0	Vashon Island SD 402	Vashon
104	0.9	Lake Stevens SD 4	Lake Stevens
104	0.9	Mead SD 354	Mead
104	0.9	Snohomish SD 201	Snohomish
107	0.8	Ridgefield SD 122	Ridgefield
108	0.7	Tumwater SD 33	Tumwater
108	0.7	Yelm Community Schools	Yelm
110	0.6	Bainbridge Island SD 303	Bainbridge Isl
110	0.6	Tahoma SD 409	Maple Valley
112	0.5	Port Angeles SD 121	Port Angeles
112	0.5	Snoqualmie SD 410	Snoqualmie
112	0.5	South Kitsap SD 402	Port Orchard
115	0.4	Cheney SD 360	Cheney
115	0.4	Clarkston SD 250	Clarkston
115	0.4	Granite Falls SD 332	Granite Falls
115	0.4	South Whidbey SD 206	Langley
119	0.3	Peninsula SD 401	Gig Harbor
119	0.3	White River SD 416	Buckley
121	0.2	Nine Mile Falls SD 325/179	Nine Mile Fall
122	n/a	Deer Park SD 414	Deer Park
122	n/a	Hockinson SD 98	Brush Prairie
122	n/a	Medical Lake SD 326	Medical Lake
122	n/a	Riverside SD 416	Chattaroy

Migrant Students

Rank	Percent	District Name	City
1	n/a	Aberdeen SD 5	Aberdeen
1	n/a	Anacortes SD 103	Anacortes
1	n/a	Arlington SD 16	Arlington
1	n/a	Auburn SD 408	Auburn
1	n/a	Bainbridge Island SD 303	Bainbridge Isl
1	n/a	Battle Ground SD 119	Brush Prairie
1	n/a	Bellevue SD 405	Bellevue
1	n/a	Bellingham SD 501	Bellingham
1	n/a	Bethel SD 403	Spanaway
1	n/a	Blaine SD 503	Blaine
1	n/a	Bremerton SD 100	Bremerton
1	n/a	Burlington-Edison SD 100	Burlington
1	n/a	Camas SD 117	Camas
1	n/a	Cashmere SD 222	Cashmere
1	n/a	Central Kitsap SD 401	Silverdale
1	n/a	Central Valley SD 356	Greenacres
1	n/a	Centralia SD 401	Centralia
1	n/a	Chehalis SD 302	Chehalis
1	n/a	Cheney SD 360	Cheney
1	n/a	Clarkston SD 250	Clarkston
1	n/a	Clover Park SD 400	Lakewood
1	n/a	Colville SD 115	Colville
1	n/a	Deer Park SD 414	Deer Park
1	n/a	East Valley SD 361	Spokane
1	n/a	East Valley SD 90	Yakima
1	n/a	Eastmont SD 206	East Wenatchee
1	n/a	Eatonville SD 404	Eatonville
1	n/a	Edmonds SD 15	Lynnwood
1	n/a	Ellensburg SD 401	Ellensburg
1	n/a	Elma SD 68	Elma
1	n/a	Enumclaw SD 216	Enumclaw
1	n/a	Ephrata SD 165	Ephrata
1	n/a	Everett SD 2	Everett
1	n/a	Evergreen SD 114	Vancouver
1	n/a	Federal Way SD 210	Federal Way
1	n/a	Ferndale SD 502	Ferndale
1	n/a	Fife SD 417	Tacoma
1	n/a	Franklin Pierce SD 402	Tacoma
1	n/a	Grandview SD 200	Grandview
1	n/a	Granite Falls SD 332	Granite Falls
1	n/a	Highline SD 401	Seattle
1	n/a	Hockinson SD 98	Brush Prairie
1	n/a	Hoquiam SD 28	Hoquiam
1	n/a	Issaquah SD 411	Issaquah
1	n/a	Kelso SD 458	Kelso
1	n/a	Kennewick SD 17	Kennewick
1	n/a	Kent SD 415	Kent
1	n/a	Kiona-Benton SD 52	Benton City
1	n/a	Lake Stevens SD 4	Lake Stevens
1	n/a	Lake Washington SD 414	Redmond
1	n/a	Lakewood SD 306	North Lakewood
1	n/a	Longview SD 122	Longview
1	n/a	Lynden SD 504	Lynden
1	n/a	Marysville SD 25	Marysville
1	n/a	Mead SD 354	Mead
1	n/a	Medical Lake SD 326	Medical Lake
1	n/a	Mercer Island SD 400	Mercer Island
1	n/a	Meridian SD 505	Bellingham
1	n/a	Monroe SD 103	Monroe
1	n/a	Moses Lake SD 161	Moses Lake
1	n/a	Mount Baker SD 507	Deming
1	n/a	Mount Vernon SD 320	Mount Vernon
1	n/a	Mukilteo SD 6	Everett
1	n/a	Naches Valley SD 3	Naches
1	n/a	Nine Mile Falls SD 325/179	Nine Mile Fall
1	n/a	Nooksack Valley SD 506	Everson
1	n/a	North Franklin SD 51	Connell
1	n/a	North Kitsap SD 400	Poulsbo
1	n/a	North Mason SD 403	Belfair
1	n/a	North Thurston SD 3	Lacey
1	n/a	Northshore SD 417	Bothell
1	n/a	Oak Harbor SD 201	Oak Harbor
1	n/a	Olympia SD 111	Olympia
1	n/a	Omak SD 19	Omak
1	n/a	Orting SD 344	Orting
1	n/a	Othello SD 147	Othello
1	n/a	Pasco SD 001	Pasco
1	n/a	Peninsula SD 401	Gig Harbor
1	n/a	Port Angeles SD 121	Port Angeles
1	n/a	Port Townsend SD 50	Port Townsend
1	n/a	Prosser SD 116	Prosser
1	n/a	Pullman SD 267	Pullman
1	n/a	Puyallup SD 3	Puyallup
1	n/a	Quincy SD 144	Quincy
1	n/a	Renton SD 403	Renton
1	n/a	Richland SD 400	Richland
1	n/a	Ridgefield SD 122	Ridgefield
1	n/a	Riverside SD 416	Chattaroy
1	n/a	Riverview Special Services	Carnation
1	n/a	Rochester SD 401	Rochester
1	n/a	Seattle SD 1	Seattle
1	n/a	Sedro-Woolley SD 101	Sedro Woolley
1	n/a	Selah SD 119	Selah
1	n/a	Sequim SD 323	Sequim
1	n/a	Shelton SD 309	Shelton
1	n/a	Shoreline SD 412	Shoreline
1	n/a	Snohomish SD 201	Snohomish
1	n/a	Snoqualmie SD 410	Snoqualmie
1	n/a	South Kitsap SD 402	Port Orchard
1	n/a	South Whidbey SD 206	Langley
1	n/a	Spokane SD 81	Spokane
1	n/a	Stanwood-Camano SD 401	Stanwood
1	n/a	Steilacoom Historical SD	Steilacoom
1	n/a	Sultan Home School	Sultan
1	n/a	Sumner SD 320	Sumner
1	n/a	Sunnyside SD 201	Sunnyside
1	n/a	Tacoma SD 10	Tacoma
1	n/a	Tahoma SD 409	Maple Valley
1	n/a	Toppenish SD 202	Toppenish
1	n/a	Tukwila SD 406	Tukwila
1	n/a	Tumwater SD 33	Tumwater
1	n/a	University Place SD 83	Univ Place
1	n/a	Vancouver SD 37	Vancouver
1	n/a	Vashon Island SD 402	Vashon
1	n/a	Wahluke SD 73	Mattawa
1	n/a	Walla Walla SD 140	Walla Walla
1	n/a	Wapato SD 207	Wapato
1	n/a	Washougal SD 112-6	Washougal
1	n/a	Wenatchee SD 246	Wenatchee
1	n/a	West Valley SD 208	Yakima
1	n/a	West Valley SD 363	Spokane
1	n/a	White River SD 416	Buckley
1	n/a	Woodland SD 404	Woodland
1	n/a	Yakima SD 7	Yakima
1	n/a	Yelm Community Schools	Yelm

Students Eligible for Free Lunch

Rank	Percent	District Name	City
1	76.8	Wapato SD 207	Wapato
2	73.4	Wahluke SD 73	Mattawa
3	72.9	Toppenish SD 202	Toppenish
4	65.6	Sunnyside SD 201	Sunnyside
5	64.5	Grandview SD 200	Grandview
6	61.6	North Franklin SD 51	Connell
7	55.4	Othello SD 147	Othello
8	54.3	Yakima SD 7	Yakima
9	53.8	Pasco SD 001	Pasco
10	51.4	Quincy SD 144	Quincy
11	50.4	Tukwila SD 406	Tukwila
12	46.6	Aberdeen SD 5	Aberdeen
13	43.2	Mount Vernon SD 320	Mount Vernon
14	43.0	Prosser SD 116	Prosser
15	42.8	Hoquiam SD 28	Hoquiam
16	41.5	Tacoma SD 10	Tacoma
17	40.9	Moses Lake SD 161	Moses Lake
18	40.1	Colville SD 115	Colville
19	39.7	Highline SD 401	Seattle
19	39.7	Shelton SD 309	Shelton
21	38.4	Centralia SD 401	Centralia
22	38.1	Deer Park SD 414	Deer Park
22	38.1	Omak SD 19	Omak
24	36.8	Bremerton SD 100	Bremerton
25	36.1	Clover Park SD 400	Lakewood
26	35.9	Kiona-Benton SD 52	Benton City
26	35.9	Wenatchee SD 246	Wenatchee
28	35.7	West Valley SD 363	Spokane
29	34.7	Walla Walla SD 140	Walla Walla
30	34.6	Mount Baker SD 507	Deming
31	33.7	Spokane SD 81	Spokane
32	32.9	Vancouver SD 37	Vancouver
33	32.7	Longview SD 122	Longview
34	32.5	Seattle SD 1	Seattle
35	32.1	Kelso SD 458	Kelso
36	32.0	Franklin Pierce SD 402	Tacoma
37	31.6	Ferndale SD 502	Ferndale
38	29.4	Eastmont SD 206	East Wenatchee
39	29.3	Clarkston SD 250	Clarkston
40	29.2	Kennewick SD 17	Kennewick
41	29.0	East Valley SD 361	Spokane
41	29.0	Selah SD 119	Selah
43	28.8	East Valley SD 90	Yakima
44	28.5	Blaine SD 503	Blaine
45	28.0	Nooksack Valley SD 506	Everson
46	27.9	Port Angeles SD 121	Port Angeles
47	27.6	Cashmere SD 222	Cashmere
48	27.5	Cheney SD 360	Cheney
49	27.4	Elma SD 68	Elma
50	27.2	Rochester SD 401	Rochester
51	26.6	Lynden SD 504	Lynden
52	26.3	Renton SD 403	Renton
52	26.3	Riverside SD 416	Chattaroy
54	25.8	Auburn SD 408	Auburn
55	25.3	Ephrata SD 165	Ephrata
56	25.2	Meridian SD 505	Bellingham
56	25.2	Sedro-Woolley SD 101	Sedro Woolley
58	24.6	Burlington-Edison SD 100	Burlington
58	24.6	Mukilteo SD 6	Everett
60	24.2	Port Townsend SD 50	Port Townsend
60	24.2	Yelm Community Schools	Yelm
62	23.7	Ellensburg SD 401	Ellensburg
63	23.6	Federal Way SD 210	Federal Way
64	23.4	Sultan Home School	Sultan
65	23.2	North Mason SD 403	Belfair
66	23.1	Evergreen SD 114	Vancouver
67	22.5	Chehalis SD 302	Chehalis
68	22.3	Kent SD 415	Kent
69	22.2	North Thurston SD 3	Lacey
70	22.1	Naches Valley SD 3	Naches
71	21.0	Washougal SD 112-6	Washougal
72	20.9	Bellingham SD 501	Bellingham
73	20.8	Eatonville SD 404	Eatonville
74	20.7	Woodland SD 404	Woodland
75	20.1	Bethel SD 403	Spanaway
76	19.5	Sequim SD 323	Sequim
77	19.4	Central Valley SD 356	Greenacres
78	19.3	Granite Falls SD 332	Granite Falls
79	18.9	Everett SD 2	Everett

Rank	Percent	District Name	City
79	18.9	West Valley SD 208	Yakima
81	18.4	Fife SD 417	Tacoma
81	18.4	Tumwater SD 33	Tumwater
83	17.4	South Kitsap SD 402	Port Orchard
84	17.2	Marysville SD 25	Marysville
84	17.2	Pullman SD 267	Pullman
86	16.1	Anacortes SD 103	Anacortes
87	15.8	Oak Harbor SD 201	Oak Harbor
88	15.7	Edmonds SD 15	Lynnwood
89	15.6	Nine Mile Falls SD 325/179	Nine Mile Fall
90	15.1	Richland SD 400	Richland
91	14.8	University Place SD 83	Univ Place
92	14.7	Lakewood SD 306	North Lakewood
92	14.7	Sumner SD 320	Sumner
94	14.6	Olympia SD 111	Olympia
94	14.6	Orting SD 344	Orting
96	13.8	White River SD 416	Buckley
97	13.4	Ridgefield SD 122	Ridgefield
98	13.3	Medical Lake SD 326	Medical Lake
99	13.2	North Kitsap SD 400	Poulsbo
99	13.2	Steilacoom Historical SD	Steilacoom
101	13.0	Arlington SD 16	Arlington
102	12.8	Puyallup SD 3	Puyallup
102	12.8	Stanwood-Camano SD 401	Stanwood
104	12.5	Battle Ground SD 119	Brush Prairie
105	12.4	Lake Stevens SD 4	Lake Stevens
105	12.4	Monroe SD 103	Monroe
107	12.3	Bellevue SD 405	Bellevue
108	12.1	Central Kitsap SD 401	Silverdale
108	12.1	Mead SD 354	Mead
110	11.2	Enumclaw SD 216	Enumclaw
111	11.0	Peninsula SD 401	Gig Harbor
112	10.7	Camas SD 117	Camas
113	9.9	Shoreline SD 412	Shoreline
114	9.7	Hockinson SD 98	Brush Prairie
115	9.5	South Whidbey SD 206	Langley
116	8.5	Snoqualmie SD 410	Snoqualmie
117	7.5	Lake Washington SD 414	Redmond
117	7.5	Riverview Special Services	Carnation
119	6.5	Northshore SD 417	Bothell
120	6.3	Snohomish SD 201	Snohomish
121	5.9	Tahoma SD 409	Maple Valley
122	5.7	Vashon Island SD 402	Vashon
123	3.8	Issaquah SD 411	Issaquah
124	3.1	Bainbridge Island SD 303	Bainbridge Isl
125	0.7	Mercer Island SD 400	Mercer Island

Students Eligible for Reduced-Price Lunch

Rank	Percent	District Name	City
1	16.9	Deer Park SD 414	Deer Park
2	15.5	Nooksack Valley SD 506	Everson
3	15.1	Clover Park SD 400	Lakewood
4	14.9	Othello SD 147	Othello
5	13.5	East Valley SD 90	Yakima
5	13.5	Yelm Community Schools	Yelm
7	13.2	Bremerton SD 100	Bremerton
7	13.2	East Valley SD 361	Spokane
9	13.1	Hoquiam SD 28	Hoquiam
10	12.9	Franklin Pierce SD 402	Tacoma
10	12.9	Oak Harbor SD 201	Oak Harbor
12	12.8	Port Townsend SD 50	Port Townsend
13	12.7	North Thurston SD 3	Lacey
13	12.7	West Valley SD 363	Spokane
15	12.5	Colville SD 115	Colville
15	12.5	Medical Lake SD 326	Medical Lake
15	12.5	Toppenish SD 202	Toppenish
18	12.2	Spokane SD 81	Spokane
18	12.2	Tacoma SD 10	Tacoma
20	11.9	Wahluke SD 73	Mattawa
21	11.8	Ephrata SD 165	Ephrata
21	11.8	Quincy SD 144	Quincy
23	11.7	Eatonville SD 404	Eatonville
23	11.7	Sultan Home School	Sultan
25	11.5	Mount Baker SD 507	Deming
26	11.4	Meridian SD 505	Bellingham
27	11.0	Ferndale SD 502	Ferndale
27	11.0	Omak SD 19	Omak
27	11.0	Riverside SD 416	Chattaroy
30	10.9	Granite Falls SD 332	Granite Falls
30	10.9	Selah SD 119	Selah
32	10.7	Cashmere SD 222	Cashmere
32	10.7	Central Valley SD 356	Greenacres
32	10.7	Centralia SD 401	Centralia
32	10.7	Evergreen SD 114	Vancouver
32	10.7	Lakewood SD 306	North Lakewood
37	10.6	Highline SD 401	Seattle
38	10.5	Tukwila SD 406	Tukwila
39	10.3	Rochester SD 401	Rochester
40	10.1	Bethel SD 403	Spanaway
40	10.1	Cheney SD 360	Cheney
40	10.1	Moses Lake SD 161	Moses Lake
43	10.0	Federal Way SD 210	Federal Way
43	10.0	Woodland SD 404	Woodland
45	9.8	North Franklin SD 51	Connell
46	9.7	Grandview SD 200	Grandview
46	9.7	Lynden SD 504	Lynden
46	9.7	Mount Vernon SD 320	Mount Vernon
46	9.7	Orting SD 344	Orting
46	9.7	Prosser SD 116	Prosser
51	9.6	Port Angeles SD 121	Port Angeles
52	9.5	Aberdeen SD 5	Aberdeen
52	9.5	Blaine SD 503	Blaine
52	9.5	Naches Valley SD 3	Naches
55	9.4	Central Kitsap SD 401	Silverdale
55	9.4	Kiona-Benton SD 52	Benton City
55	9.4	North Mason SD 403	Belfair
55	9.4	Renton SD 403	Renton
55	9.4	Sedro-Woolley SD 101	Sedro Woolley
60	9.3	Clarkston SD 250	Clarkston
61	9.2	Auburn SD 408	Auburn
61	9.2	Fife SD 417	Tacoma
61	9.2	Pasco SD 001	Pasco
61	9.2	Tumwater SD 33	Tumwater
65	9.0	Mukilteo SD 6	Everett
65	9.0	Shelton SD 309	Shelton
65	9.0	Wapato SD 207	Wapato
68	8.9	Elma SD 68	Elma
68	8.9	Kelso SD 458	Kelso
68	8.9	University Place SD 83	Univ Place
71	8.8	Mead SD 354	Mead
72	8.6	Marysville SD 25	Marysville
72	8.6	Sequim SD 323	Sequim
72	8.6	West Valley SD 208	Yakima
75	8.5	Kent SD 415	Kent
75	8.5	Yakima SD 7	Yakima
77	8.4	Vancouver SD 37	Vancouver
78	8.3	Eastmont SD 206	East Wenatchee
79	8.1	Walla Walla SD 140	Walla Walla
79	8.1	Washougal SD 112-6	Washougal
81	8.0	South Kitsap SD 402	Port Orchard
81	8.0	White River SD 416	Buckley
83	7.9	Bellingham SD 501	Bellingham
83	7.9	Kennewick SD 17	Kennewick
85	7.7	Puyallup SD 3	Puyallup
86	7.6	Nine Mile Falls SD 325/179	Nine Mile Fall
86	7.6	Seattle SD 1	Seattle
88	7.5	Chehalis SD 302	Chehalis
88	7.5	Edmonds SD 15	Lynnwood
88	7.5	Ellensburg SD 401	Ellensburg
91	7.4	Sunnyside SD 201	Sunnyside
92	7.3	Longview SD 122	Longview
93	7.2	Sumner SD 320	Sumner
94	7.1	Lake Stevens SD 4	Lake Stevens
94	7.1	Wenatchee SD 246	Wenatchee
96	7.0	Everett SD 2	Everett
97	6.9	Anacortes SD 103	Anacortes
97	6.9	Burlington-Edison SD 100	Burlington
97	6.9	Steilacoom Historical SD	Steilacoom
100	6.7	Battle Ground SD 119	Brush Prairie
100	6.7	Stanwood-Camano SD 401	Stanwood
102	6.6	Monroe SD 103	Monroe
103	6.1	Arlington SD 16	Arlington
103	6.1	Ridgefield SD 122	Ridgefield
105	6.0	Camas SD 117	Camas
105	6.0	North Kitsap SD 400	Poulsbo
107	5.8	Enumclaw SD 216	Enumclaw
107	5.8	Pullman SD 267	Pullman
107	5.8	South Whidbey SD 206	Langley
110	5.7	Richland SD 400	Richland
111	5.6	Peninsula SD 401	Gig Harbor
112	5.2	Snoqualmie SD 410	Snoqualmie
113	4.9	Shoreline SD 412	Shoreline
114	4.8	Bellevue SD 405	Bellevue
115	4.7	Olympia SD 111	Olympia
116	4.4	Riverview Special Services	Carnation
117	4.2	Hockinson SD 98	Brush Prairie
118	3.3	Tahoma SD 409	Maple Valley
119	3.2	Snohomish SD 201	Snohomish
120	3.1	Northshore SD 417	Bothell
121	3.0	Lake Washington SD 414	Redmond
122	2.2	Bainbridge Island SD 303	Bainbridge Isl
122	2.2	Issaquah SD 411	Issaquah
124	2.1	Vashon Island SD 402	Vashon
125	0.8	Mercer Island SD 400	Mercer Island

Student/Teacher Ratio

Rank	Ratio	District Name	City
1	22.1	Snohomish SD 201	Snohomish
2	21.6	Battle Ground SD 119	Brush Prairie
3	21.4	Deer Park SD 414	Deer Park
3	21.4	Hockinson SD 98	Brush Prairie
3	21.4	Lake Stevens SD 4	Lake Stevens
3	21.4	Ridgefield SD 122	Ridgefield
7	21.3	Granite Falls SD 332	Granite Falls
8	21.2	Marysville SD 25	Marysville
8	21.2	Riverside SD 416	Chattaroy
10	21.1	Everett SD 2	Everett
11	21.0	Bainbridge Island SD 303	Bainbridge Isl
11	21.0	Sumner SD 320	Sumner
11	21.0	West Valley SD 363	Spokane
14	20.9	Anacortes SD 103	Anacortes
14	20.9	Burlington-Edison SD 100	Burlington
14	20.9	Enumclaw SD 216	Enumclaw
14	20.9	Monroe SD 103	Monroe
14	20.9	Sunnyside SD 201	Sunnyside
14	20.9	West Valley SD 208	Yakima
20	20.8	Lakewood SD 306	North Lakewood
21	20.7	Woodland SD 404	Woodland
22	20.6	Ephrata SD 165	Ephrata
22	20.6	Kennewick SD 17	Kennewick
22	20.6	Lynden SD 504	Lynden
22	20.6	Snoqualmie SD 410	Snoqualmie
22	20.6	Sultan Home School	Sultan
27	20.5	Bethel SD 403	Spanaway
28	20.4	Eastmont SD 206	East Wenatchee
28	20.4	Lake Washington SD 414	Redmond
28	20.4	Mercer Island SD 400	Mercer Island
28	20.4	Renton SD 403	Renton
32	20.3	Selah SD 119	Selah
33	20.2	Issaquah SD 411	Issaquah
33	20.2	Mead SD 354	Mead
33	20.2	Peninsula SD 401	Gig Harbor
33	20.2	Tahoma SD 409	Maple Valley
33	20.2	Tukwila SD 406	Tukwila
38	20.1	Blaine SD 503	Blaine
38	20.1	Camas SD 117	Camas
38	20.1	Clarkston SD 250	Clarkston
38	20.1	Moses Lake SD 161	Moses Lake
38	20.1	Pullman SD 267	Pullman
38	20.1	Sequim SD 323	Sequim
44	20.0	Naches Valley SD 3	Naches
44	20.0	Port Townsend SD 50	Port Townsend
44	20.0	Stanwood-Camano SD 401	Stanwood
44	20.0	Wenatchee SD 246	Wenatchee
48	19.9	Edmonds SD 15	Lynnwood
48	19.9	Grandview SD 200	Grandview
48	19.9	Longview SD 122	Longview
48	19.9	Northshore SD 417	Bothell
48	19.9	Richland SD 400	Richland
53	19.8	Arlington SD 16	Arlington
53	19.8	Auburn SD 408	Auburn
53	19.8	East Valley SD 361	Spokane
53	19.8	Kelso SD 458	Kelso
53	19.8	Kiona-Benton SD 52	Benton City
53	19.8	Nine Mile Falls SD 325/179	Nine Mile Fall
53	19.8	Oak Harbor SD 201	Oak Harbor
53	19.8	Wapato SD 207	Wapato
61	19.7	Colville SD 115	Colville
61	19.7	Vancouver SD 37	Vancouver
61	19.7	White River SD 416	Buckley
64	19.6	Federal Way SD 210	Federal Way
64	19.6	Fife SD 417	Tacoma
64	19.6	North Kitsap SD 400	Poulsbo
64	19.6	Riverview Special Services	Carnation
64	19.6	South Whidbey SD 206	Langley
64	19.6	Yelm Community Schools	Yelm
70	19.5	Ellensburg SD 401	Ellensburg
70	19.5	Othello SD 147	Othello
70	19.5	Steilacoom Historical SD	Steilacoom
73	19.4	Franklin Pierce SD 402	Tacoma
73	19.4	Mukilteo SD 6	Everett
73	19.4	Prosser SD 116	Prosser
73	19.4	Puyallup SD 3	Puyallup
77	19.3	Central Kitsap SD 401	Silverdale
77	19.3	Hoquiam SD 28	Hoquiam
77	19.3	Mount Baker SD 507	Deming
77	19.3	South Kitsap SD 402	Port Orchard
81	19.2	Aberdeen SD 5	Aberdeen
81	19.2	Bellingham SD 501	Bellingham
81	19.2	Cashmere SD 222	Cashmere
81	19.2	Centralia SD 401	Centralia
81	19.2	Mount Vernon SD 320	Mount Vernon
81	19.2	Olympia SD 111	Olympia
81	19.2	Tumwater SD 33	Tumwater
81	19.2	Washougal SD 112-6	Washougal
89	19.0	East Valley SD 90	Yakima
89	19.0	Evergreen SD 114	Vancouver
89	19.0	North Mason SD 403	Belfair
89	19.0	Port Angeles SD 121	Port Angeles
89	19.0	Tacoma SD 10	Tacoma
94	18.9	Omak SD 19	Omak
94	18.9	Shoreline SD 412	Shoreline
96	18.8	Elma SD 68	Elma
96	18.8	Medical Lake SD 326	Medical Lake
96	18.8	Meridian SD 505	Bellingham

96	18.8	Shelton SD 309	Shelton
96	18.8	Walla Walla SD 140	Walla Walla
101	18.7	Chehalis SD 302	Chehalis
101	18.7	Eatonville SD 404	Eatonville
101	18.7	Vashon Island SD 402	Vashon
104	18.6	Highline SD 401	Seattle
104	18.6	Kent SD 415	Kent
106	18.5	Pasco SD 001	Pasco
107	18.4	University Place SD 83	Univ Place
108	18.3	Clover Park SD 400	Lakewood
108	18.3	North Franklin SD 51	Connell
110	18.2	Orting SD 344	Orting
110	18.2	Sedro-Woolley SD 101	Sedro Woolley
110	18.2	Yakima SD 7	Yakima
113	18.1	Bellevue SD 405	Bellevue
114	18.0	Nooksack Valley SD 506	Everson
114	18.0	North Thurston SD 3	Lacey
114	18.0	Seattle SD 1	Seattle
117	17.9	Central Valley SD 356	Greenacres
117	17.9	Spokane SD 81	Spokane
119	17.7	Rochester SD 401	Rochester
120	17.6	Cheney SD 360	Cheney
120	17.6	Ferndale SD 502	Ferndale
122	17.4	Quincy SD 144	Quincy
122	17.4	Toppenish SD 202	Toppenish
124	17.2	Bremerton SD 100	Bremerton
125	16.4	Wahluke SD 73	Mattawa

Student/Librarian Ratio

Rank	Ratio	District Name	City
1	2,666.0	Washougal SD 112-6	Washougal
2	2,618.0	Lynden SD 504	Lynden
3	2,331.0	Quincy SD 144	Quincy
4	2,161.0	Rochester SD 401	Rochester
5	2,100.0	Hoquiam SD 28	Hoquiam
6	2,089.0	Aberdeen SD 5	Aberdeen
7	2,002.0	Riverside SD 416	Chattaroy
8	1,919.0	Peninsula SD 401	Gig Harbor
9	1,846.0	Nooksack Valley SD 506	Everson
10	1,824.0	Ridgefield SD 122	Ridgefield
11	1,792.6	Moses Lake SD 161	Moses Lake
12	1,688.0	Centralia SD 401	Centralia
13	1,643.0	Wahluke SD 73	Mattawa
14	1,594.7	East Valley SD 90	Yakima
15	1,583.0	Port Angeles SD 121	Port Angeles
16	1,582.0	Meridian SD 505	Bellingham
17	1,568.0	Tahoma SD 409	Maple Valley
18	1,521.7	West Valley SD 208	Yakima
19	1,410.5	Franklin Pierce SD 402	Tacoma
20	1,290.0	Omak SD 19	Omak
21	1,252.4	Shelton SD 309	Shelton
22	1,248.8	Deer Park SD 414	Deer Park
23	1,241.0	South Kitsap SD 402	Port Orchard
24	1,215.5	Mount Baker SD 507	Deming
25	1,143.6	Arlington SD 16	Arlington
26	1,120.5	Pullman SD 267	Pullman
27	1,089.6	Kent SD 415	Kent
28	1,046.0	Eatonville SD 404	Eatonville
29	1,041.0	Pasco SD 001	Pasco
30	943.1	Cashmere SD 222	Cashmere
31	942.8	Sunnyside SD 201	Sunnyside
32	938.2	Marysville SD 25	Marysville
33	929.0	Orting SD 344	Orting
34	924.9	Battle Ground SD 119	Brush Prairie
35	901.8	West Valley SD 363	Spokane
36	882.7	University Place SD 83	Univ Place
37	876.9	Monroe SD 103	Monroe
38	860.7	Lakewood SD 306	North Lakewood
39	858.0	Snoqualmie SD 410	Snoqualmie
40	840.4	Sumner SD 320	Sumner
41	838.0	Enumclaw SD 216	Enumclaw
42	832.0	Kiona-Benton SD 52	Benton City
43	827.5	Nine Mile Falls SD 325/179	Nine Mile Fall
44	826.6	Mercer Island SD 400	Mercer Island
45	819.5	Yelm Community Schools	Yelm
46	815.6	Mukilteo SD 6	Everett
47	811.4	Evergreen SD 114	Vancouver
48	810.0	Lake Stevens SD 4	Lake Stevens
49	797.0	Granite Falls SD 332	Granite Falls
50	792.4	Bethel SD 403	Spanaway
51	788.7	Olympia SD 111	Olympia
52	787.5	Everett SD 2	Everett
53	784.3	Fife SD 417	Tacoma
54	777.0	Hockinson SD 98	Brush Prairie
55	773.6	Mead SD 354	Mead
56	772.3	Ephrata SD 165	Ephrata
57	764.3	Vancouver SD 37	Vancouver
58	756.7	Auburn SD 408	Auburn
59	756.2	Wapato SD 207	Wapato
60	752.7	Bellevue SD 405	Bellevue
61	743.7	North Thurston SD 3	Lacey
62	739.5	Puyallup SD 3	Puyallup
63	738.8	South Whidbey SD 206	Langley
64	738.5	Federal Way SD 210	Federal Way
65	738.0	Issaquah SD 411	Issaquah
66	737.8	Yakima SD 7	Yakima
67	737.0	Snohomish SD 201	Snohomish
68	730.7	White River SD 416	Buckley
69	728.7	Colville SD 115	Colville
70	728.1	Sedro-Woolley SD 101	Sedro Woolley
71	723.5	North Kitsap SD 400	Poulsbo
72	721.0	Sequim SD 323	Sequim
73	707.8	Selah SD 119	Selah
74	703.7	Steilacoom Historical SD	Steilacoom
75	703.5	Clarkston SD 250	Clarkston
76	701.1	East Valley SD 361	Spokane
77	700.0	Richland SD 400	Richland
78	699.9	Kennewick SD 17	Kennewick
79	694.9	Stanwood-Camano SD 401	Stanwood
80	690.6	Walla Walla SD 140	Walla Walla
81	690.3	Bainbridge Island SD 303	Bainbridge Isl
82	685.4	Wenatchee SD 246	Wenatchee
83	683.7	Oak Harbor SD 201	Oak Harbor
84	679.3	Blaine SD 503	Blaine
85	678.8	Spokane SD 81	Spokane
86	675.1	Chehalis SD 302	Chehalis
87	673.3	Shoreline SD 412	Shoreline
88	663.9	Lake Washington SD 414	Redmond
89	658.3	Renton SD 403	Renton
90	657.1	Medical Lake SD 326	Medical Lake
91	654.0	Woodland SD 404	Woodland
92	650.2	Eastmont SD 206	East Wenatchee
93	644.2	Mount Vernon SD 320	Mount Vernon
94	640.0	Grandview SD 200	Grandview
95	639.5	Edmonds SD 15	Lynnwood
96	636.1	Longview SD 122	Longview
97	635.9	Tacoma SD 10	Tacoma
98	633.6	Cheney SD 360	Cheney
99	632.6	Northshore SD 417	Bothell
100	626.3	Seattle SD 1	Seattle
101	622.9	Central Kitsap SD 401	Silverdale
102	622.2	Othello SD 147	Othello
103	621.8	Port Townsend SD 50	Port Townsend
104	620.0	Prosser SD 116	Prosser
105	619.3	Camas SD 117	Camas
106	615.0	Tumwater SD 33	Tumwater
107	608.0	Burlington-Edison SD 100	Burlington
108	601.5	North Franklin SD 51	Connell
109	597.3	North Mason SD 403	Belfair
110	589.6	Kelso SD 458	Kelso
111	585.5	Sultan Home School	Sultan
112	582.4	Riverview Special Services	Carnation
113	578.7	Bremerton SD 100	Bremerton
114	570.4	Anacortes SD 103	Anacortes
115	568.8	Toppenish SD 202	Toppenish
116	568.6	Ellensburg SD 401	Ellensburg
117	567.3	Clover Park SD 400	Lakewood
118	557.7	Highline SD 401	Seattle
119	556.1	Ferndale SD 502	Ferndale
120	550.3	Bellingham SD 501	Bellingham
121	548.4	Tukwila SD 406	Tukwila
122	541.3	Naches Valley SD 3	Naches
123	535.3	Vashon Island SD 402	Vashon
124	533.1	Central Valley SD 356	Greenacres
125	0.0	Elma SD 68	Elma

Student/Counselor Ratio

Rank	Ratio	District Name	City
1	1,637.6	Port Angeles SD 121	Port Angeles
2	1,554.0	Hockinson SD 98	Brush Prairie
3	1,336.0	Battle Ground SD 119	Brush Prairie
4	977.9	Orting SD 344	Orting
5	950.9	Bethel SD 403	Spanaway
6	925.8	Eastmont SD 206	East Wenatchee
7	912.0	Ridgefield SD 122	Ridgefield
8	910.8	Colville SD 115	Colville
9	832.0	Kiona-Benton SD 52	Benton City
10	815.6	Mukilteo SD 6	Everett
11	788.1	Nine Mile Falls SD 325/179	Nine Mile Fall
12	788.0	Mead SD 354	Mead
13	773.6	Snoqualmie SD 410	Snoqualmie
14	768.5	Olympia SD 111	Olympia
15	761.7	Tukwila SD 406	Tukwila
15	761.7	Washougal SD 112-6	Washougal
17	760.5	Clarkston SD 250	Clarkston
18	759.5	Chehalis SD 302	Chehalis
19	758.0	Kelso SD 458	Kelso
20	748.1	Shoreline SD 412	Shoreline
21	744.1	Central Kitsap SD 401	Silverdale
22	729.3	Tahoma SD 409	Maple Valley
23	700.0	Hoquiam SD 28	Hoquiam
24	682.4	Sumner SD 320	Sumner
25	679.5	Northshore SD 417	Bothell
26	677.9	Stanwood-Camano SD 401	Stanwood
27	676.7	Naches Valley SD 3	Naches
28	661.2	Walla Walla SD 140	Walla Walla
29	657.6	Bremerton SD 100	Bremerton
30	635.8	Edmonds SD 15	Lynnwood
31	625.0	Moses Lake SD 161	Moses Lake
32	622.3	Bellingham SD 501	Bellingham
33	622.2	Othello SD 147	Othello
34	603.6	Cashmere SD 222	Cashmere
35	603.4	Snohomish SD 201	Snohomish
36	585.5	Sultan Home School	Sultan
37	583.8	North Franklin SD 51	Connell
38	575.0	Medical Lake SD 326	Medical Lake
39	572.8	South Kitsap SD 402	Port Orchard
40	570.4	Fife SD 417	Tacoma
41	567.7	Issaquah SD 411	Issaquah
42	561.2	Federal Way SD 210	Federal Way
43	560.3	Pullman SD 267	Pullman
44	555.8	Camas SD 117	Camas
45	552.8	Pasco SD 001	Pasco
46	552.5	Mount Baker SD 507	Deming
47	551.7	University Place SD 83	Univ Place
48	548.0	White River SD 416	Buckley
49	544.4	Deer Park SD 414	Deer Park
50	536.8	Mercer Island SD 400	Mercer Island
51	536.7	Lake Washington SD 414	Redmond
52	530.5	Arlington SD 16	Arlington
53	529.5	Riverview Special Services	Carnation
54	525.5	Kent SD 415	Kent
55	523.0	Eatonville SD 404	Eatonville
56	522.3	Aberdeen SD 5	Aberdeen
57	519.3	North Mason SD 403	Belfair
58	513.3	Lynden SD 504	Lynden
59	503.0	South Whidbey SD 206	Langley
60	502.5	Marysville SD 25	Marysville
61	500.3	Elma SD 68	Elma
62	499.0	Seattle SD 1	Seattle
63	498.5	Everett SD 2	Everett
63	498.5	Selah SD 119	Selah
65	494.4	Meridian SD 505	Bellingham
66	492.0	Tumwater SD 33	Tumwater
67	490.5	Woodland SD 404	Woodland
68	489.3	Lake Stevens SD 4	Lake Stevens
69	486.2	Bellevue SD 405	Bellevue
70	480.7	Sequim SD 323	Sequim
71	480.0	Burlington-Edison SD 100	Burlington
72	478.8	Kennewick SD 17	Kennewick
73	477.8	Sedro-Woolley SD 101	Sedro Woolley
74	477.0	Oak Harbor SD 201	Oak Harbor
75	476.7	Ferndale SD 502	Ferndale
76	476.4	Renton SD 403	Renton
77	476.0	Franklin Pierce SD 402	Tacoma
78	475.9	Evergreen SD 114	Vancouver
79	473.3	Nooksack Valley SD 506	Everson
80	468.9	Richland SD 400	Richland
81	466.2	Quincy SD 144	Quincy
82	457.7	North Thurston SD 3	Lacey
83	457.1	Grandview SD 200	Grandview
84	453.4	North Kitsap SD 400	Poulsbo
85	448.6	Wenatchee SD 246	Wenatchee
86	446.0	Vancouver SD 37	Vancouver
87	444.4	Puyallup SD 3	Puyallup
88	441.7	Spokane SD 81	Spokane
89	439.7	Shelton SD 309	Shelton
90	437.7	Yakima SD 7	Yakima
91	437.6	Lakewood SD 306	North Lakewood
92	435.7	Anacortes SD 103	Anacortes
93	435.4	Monroe SD 103	Monroe
94	434.9	East Valley SD 90	Yakima
95	434.7	Granite Falls SD 332	Granite Falls
96	434.1	Vashon Island SD 402	Vashon
97	430.6	Central Valley SD 356	Greenacres
98	425.7	Auburn SD 408	Auburn
99	424.5	East Valley SD 361	Spokane
100	424.4	West Valley SD 363	Spokane
101	420.1	Wapato SD 207	Wapato
102	415.3	Highline SD 401	Seattle
103	414.5	Port Townsend SD 50	Port Townsend
104	414.1	Mount Vernon SD 320	Mount Vernon
105	411.6	Clover Park SD 400	Lakewood
106	410.8	Wahluke SD 73	Mattawa
107	406.2	Yelm Community Schools	Yelm
108	404.3	Prosser SD 116	Prosser
109	400.4	Riverside SD 416	Chattaroy
110	399.5	Ephrata SD 165	Ephrata
111	398.3	Bainbridge Island SD 303	Bainbridge Isl
112	397.1	Longview SD 122	Longview
113	393.2	Enumclaw SD 216	Enumclaw
114	391.6	Tacoma SD 10	Tacoma
115	383.5	Toppenish SD 202	Toppenish
116	370.7	Cheney SD 360	Cheney
117	368.1	West Valley SD 208	Yakima
118	360.2	Rochester SD 401	Rochester
119	359.9	Ellensburg SD 401	Ellensburg

120	355.4	Centralia SD 401	Centralia
121	351.8	Steilacoom Historical SD	Steilacoom
122	348.9	Peninsula SD 401	Gig Harbor
123	345.5	Omak SD 19	Omak
124	339.7	Blaine SD 503	Blaine
125	332.8	Sunnyside SD 201	Sunnyside

Current Spending per Student in FY2001

Rank	Dollars	District Name	City
1	8,082	Seattle SD 1	Seattle
2	7,504	Rochester SD 401	Rochester
3	7,233	Tukwila SD 406	Tukwila
4	7,208	Chehalis SD 302	Chehalis
5	7,199	Shoreline SD 412	Shoreline
6	7,150	North Franklin SD 51	Connell
7	7,093	Yakima SD 7	Yakima
8	7,082	Spokane SD 81	Spokane
9	7,045	Tacoma SD 10	Tacoma
10	6,990	Clover Park SD 400	Lakewood
11	6,927	Bremerton SD 100	Bremerton
12	6,851	Mount Vernon SD 320	Mount Vernon
13	6,847	Bellevue SD 405	Bellevue
14	6,836	Pasco SD 001	Pasco
15	6,802	Omak SD 19	Omak
16	6,783	Pullman SD 267	Pullman
17	6,779	Blaine SD 503	Blaine
18	6,777	Cheney SD 360	Cheney
19	6,776	Hoquiam SD 28	Hoquiam
20	6,770	Wapato SD 207	Wapato
21	6,764	Kennewick SD 17	Kennewick
22	6,741	Tumwater SD 33	Tumwater
23	6,710	Centralia SD 401	Centralia
24	6,702	West Valley SD 363	Spokane
25	6,701	Mount Baker SD 507	Deming
26	6,696	Medical Lake SD 326	Medical Lake
27	6,683	Highline SD 401	Seattle
28	6,659	Toppenish SD 202	Toppenish
29	6,655	Central Kitsap SD 401	Silverdale
29	6,655	Clarkston SD 250	Clarkston
31	6,649	East Valley SD 361	Spokane
32	6,627	Wahluke SD 73	Mattawa
33	6,625	Washougal SD 112-6	Washougal
34	6,624	Port Angeles SD 121	Port Angeles
35	6,614	Prosser SD 116	Prosser
36	6,587	Fife SD 417	Tacoma
37	6,585	Riverside SD 416	Chattaroy
38	6,584	North Thurston SD 3	Lacey
39	6,582	Aberdeen SD 5	Aberdeen
40	6,576	Burlington-Edison SD 100	Burlington
41	6,561	Walla Walla SD 140	Walla Walla
42	6,560	Nooksack Valley SD 506	Everson
43	6,554	Mercer Island SD 400	Mercer Island
44	6,553	Vashon Island SD 402	Vashon
45	6,552	Nine Mile Falls SD 325/179	Nine Mile Fall
46	6,551	Vancouver SD 37	Vancouver
47	6,548	Sunnyside SD 201	Sunnyside
48	6,543	Northshore SD 417	Bothell
49	6,542	Kelso SD 458	Kelso
50	6,538	Deer Park SD 414	Deer Park
51	6,537	Olympia SD 111	Olympia
52	6,518	Bellingham SD 501	Bellingham
53	6,511	Anacortes SD 103	Anacortes
54	6,510	Shelton SD 309	Shelton
55	6,502	North Kitsap SD 400	Poulsbo
56	6,476	Ephrata SD 165	Ephrata
57	6,470	Mead SD 354	Mead
58	6,469	Longview SD 122	Longview
59	6,465	Central Valley SD 356	Greenacres
60	6,460	Woodland SD 404	Woodland
61	6,447	Enumclaw SD 216	Enumclaw
62	6,442	Franklin Pierce SD 402	Tacoma
63	6,421	Sedro-Woolley SD 101	Sedro Woolley
64	6,419	Riverview Special Services	Carnation
65	6,405	South Whidbey SD 206	Langley
65	6,405	Steilacoom Historical SD	Steilacoom
67	6,401	Marysville SD 25	Marysville
68	6,398	Renton SD 403	Renton
69	6,395	Everett SD 2	Everett
70	6,393	University Place SD 83	Univ Place
71	6,391	Quincy SD 144	Quincy
72	6,388	Evergreen SD 114	Vancouver
73	6,386	Cashmere SD 222	Cashmere
74	6,379	Yelm Community Schools	Yelm
75	6,365	Elma SD 68	Elma
76	6,356	Lake Washington SD 414	Redmond
77	6,341	Snoqualmie SD 410	Snoqualmie
78	6,330	Port Townsend SD 50	Port Townsend
79	6,326	Ellensburg SD 401	Ellensburg
80	6,319	Edmonds SD 15	Lynnwood
81	6,312	Mukilteo SD 6	Everett
82	6,306	North Mason SD 403	Belfair
83	6,296	Kent SD 415	Kent
84	6,292	Peninsula SD 401	Gig Harbor
85	6,276	Moses Lake SD 161	Moses Lake
86	6,274	Puyallup SD 3	Puyallup
87	6,256	Orting SD 344	Orting
88	6,250	White River SD 416	Buckley
89	6,247	Othello SD 147	Othello
90	6,238	Kiona-Benton SD 52	Benton City
91	6,204	Issaquah SD 411	Issaquah
92	6,203	Ferndale SD 502	Ferndale
93	6,200	Sumner SD 320	Sumner
94	6,189	Camas SD 117	Camas
95	6,187	Grandview SD 200	Grandview
96	6,182	Colville SD 115	Colville
97	6,176	Bainbridge Island SD 303	Bainbridge Isl
98	6,174	Auburn SD 408	Auburn
99	6,165	Lakewood SD 306	North Lakewood
100	6,140	Wenatchee SD 246	Wenatchee
101	6,102	Richland SD 400	Richland
102	6,101	Tahoma SD 409	Maple Valley
103	6,093	East Valley SD 90	Yakima
104	6,090	Lynden SD 504	Lynden
105	6,075	Eatonville SD 404	Eatonville
106	6,061	Sultan Home School	Sultan
107	6,055	Eastmont SD 206	East Wenatchee
108	6,046	Selah SD 119	Selah
109	6,037	Bethel SD 403	Spanaway
110	6,010	Stanwood-Camano SD 401	Stanwood
111	5,987	Arlington SD 16	Arlington
112	5,976	Monroe SD 103	Monroe
113	5,967	West Valley SD 208	Yakima
114	5,935	Federal Way SD 210	Federal Way
115	5,928	Naches Valley SD 3	Naches
116	5,927	Meridian SD 505	Bellingham
117	5,922	Ridgefield SD 122	Ridgefield
118	5,908	Battle Ground SD 119	Brush Prairie
119	5,907	Sequim SD 323	Sequim
120	5,899	Hockinson SD 98	Brush Prairie
121	5,864	Granite Falls SD 332	Granite Falls
122	5,792	Snohomish SD 201	Snohomish
123	5,739	Oak Harbor SD 201	Oak Harbor
124	5,734	Lake Stevens SD 4	Lake Stevens
125	5,646	South Kitsap SD 402	Port Orchard

Number of Diploma Recipients

Rank	Number	District Name	City
1	2,629	Seattle SD 1	Seattle
2	1,793	Spokane SD 81	Spokane
3	1,651	Lake Washington SD 414	Redmond
4	1,535	Kent SD 415	Kent
5	1,462	Tacoma SD 10	Tacoma
6	1,413	Northshore SD 417	Bothell
7	1,170	Vancouver SD 37	Vancouver
8	1,153	Puyallup SD 3	Puyallup
9	1,151	Federal Way SD 210	Federal Way
10	1,147	Evergreen SD 114	Vancouver
11	1,111	Edmonds SD 15	Lynnwood
12	1,090	Bellevue SD 405	Bellevue
13	984	Highline SD 401	Seattle
14	977	Kennewick SD 17	Kennewick
15	975	Bethel SD 403	Spanaway
16	972	Central Kitsap SD 401	Silverdale
17	896	Issaquah SD 411	Issaquah
18	885	Everett SD 2	Everett
19	843	Battle Ground SD 119	Brush Prairie
20	836	Auburn SD 408	Auburn
21	822	North Thurston SD 3	Lacey
22	756	Central Valley SD 356	Greenacres
23	746	Shoreline SD 412	Shoreline
24	745	Mukilteo SD 6	Everett
25	743	Richland SD 400	Richland
26	710	Bellingham SD 501	Bellingham
27	681	Olympia SD 111	Olympia
28	679	Mead SD 354	Mead
29	651	Renton SD 403	Renton
30	625	South Kitsap SD 402	Port Orchard
31	616	Yakima SD 7	Yakima
32	604	Peninsula SD 401	Gig Harbor
33	601	Marysville SD 25	Marysville
34	557	Snohomish SD 201	Snohomish
35	457	Walla Walla SD 140	Walla Walla
36	455	Clover Park SD 400	Lakewood
37	432	Wenatchee SD 246	Wenatchee
38	410	University Place SD 83	Univ Place
39	407	Franklin Pierce SD 402	Tacoma
40	401	North Kitsap SD 400	Poulsbo
41	396	Sumner SD 320	Sumner
42	378	Oak Harbor SD 201	Oak Harbor
43	373	Lake Stevens SD 4	Lake Stevens
44	360	Longview SD 122	Longview
45	353	Monroe SD 103	Monroe
45	353	Moses Lake SD 161	Moses Lake
47	351	Tahoma SD 409	Maple Valley
48	343	Eastmont SD 206	East Wenatchee
49	341	Tumwater SD 33	Tumwater
50	332	West Valley SD 208	Yakima
51	330	Mercer Island SD 400	Mercer Island
52	325	Pasco SD 001	Pasco
53	318	Shelton SD 309	Shelton
53	318	Stanwood-Camano SD 401	Stanwood
55	316	Enumclaw SD 216	Enumclaw
56	310	Sedro-Woolley SD 101	Sedro Woolley
57	299	East Valley SD 361	Spokane
58	294	Bainbridge Island SD 303	Bainbridge Isl
59	293	Mount Vernon SD 320	Mount Vernon
60	283	Kelso SD 458	Kelso
60	283	West Valley SD 363	Spokane
62	279	Sunnyside SD 201	Sunnyside
63	273	Aberdeen SD 5	Aberdeen
64	270	Arlington SD 16	Arlington
65	266	Yelm Community Schools	Yelm
66	265	Bremerton SD 100	Bremerton
67	259	Ferndale SD 502	Ferndale
68	240	Snoqualmie SD 410	Snoqualmie
69	232	White River SD 416	Buckley
70	227	Ellensburg SD 401	Ellensburg
71	214	Selah SD 119	Selah
72	210	Chehalis SD 302	Chehalis
73	203	Burlington-Edison SD 100	Burlington
73	203	Camas SD 117	Camas
73	203	Sequim SD 323	Sequim
76	202	Fife SD 417	Tacoma
77	197	Anacortes SD 103	Anacortes
78	182	Grandview SD 200	Grandview
79	179	Centralia SD 401	Centralia
80	171	Elma SD 68	Elma
81	170	Colville SD 115	Colville
82	168	South Whidbey SD 206	Langley
83	166	North Mason SD 403	Belfair
83	166	Pullman SD 267	Pullman
85	165	Prosser SD 116	Prosser
86	163	Ephrata SD 165	Ephrata
87	161	Othello SD 147	Othello
87	161	Port Townsend SD 50	Port Townsend
89	158	Lynden SD 504	Lynden
90	157	Clarkston SD 250	Clarkston
91	150	Riverview Special Services	Carnation
92	147	Wapato SD 207	Wapato
93	142	Toppenish SD 202	Toppenish
94	140	Medical Lake SD 326	Medical Lake
95	139	Tukwila SD 406	Tukwila
96	135	Mount Baker SD 507	Deming
97	133	Deer Park SD 414	Deer Park
98	132	Nine Mile Falls SD 325/179	Nine Mile Fall
98	132	Vashon Island SD 402	Vashon
100	129	Lakewood SD 306	North Lakewood
101	126	Eatonville SD 404	Eatonville
102	125	Steilacoom Historical SD	Steilacoom
103	124	Washougal SD 112-6	Washougal
104	121	East Valley SD 90	Yakima
104	121	Port Angeles SD 121	Port Angeles
106	117	Nooksack Valley SD 506	Everson
106	117	Quincy SD 144	Quincy
108	114	Hoquiam SD 28	Hoquiam
109	112	North Franklin SD 51	Connell
110	109	Omak SD 19	Omak
111	108	Ridgefield SD 122	Ridgefield
112	107	Blaine SD 503	Blaine
113	106	Rochester SD 401	Rochester
114	104	Granite Falls SD 332	Granite Falls
115	102	Woodland SD 404	Woodland
116	99	Kiona-Benton SD 52	Benton City
117	97	Meridian SD 505	Bellingham
118	96	Cashmere SD 222	Cashmere
119	95	Orting SD 344	Orting
120	90	Naches Valley SD 3	Naches
121	85	Sultan Home School	Sultan
122	72	Wahluke SD 73	Mattawa
123	10	Riverside SD 416	Chattaroy
124	4	Cheney SD 360	Cheney
125	n/a	Hockinson SD 98	Brush Prairie

High School Drop-out Rate

Rank	Percent	District Name	City
1	n/a	Aberdeen SD 5	Aberdeen
1	n/a	Anacortes SD 103	Anacortes
1	n/a	Arlington SD 16	Arlington
1	n/a	Auburn SD 408	Auburn
1	n/a	Bainbridge Island SD 303	Bainbridge Isl
1	n/a	Battle Ground SD 119	Brush Prairie
1	n/a	Bellevue SD 405	Bellevue
1	n/a	Bellingham SD 501	Bellingham
1	n/a	Bethel SD 403	Spanaway
1	n/a	Blaine SD 503	Blaine
1	n/a	Bremerton SD 100	Bremerton

1	n/a	Burlington-Edison SD 100	Burlington
1	n/a	Camas SD 117	Camas
1	n/a	Cashmere SD 222	Cashmere
1	n/a	Central Kitsap SD 401	Silverdale
1	n/a	Central Valley SD 356	Greenacres
1	n/a	Centralia SD 401	Centralia
1	n/a	Chehalis SD 302	Chehalis
1	n/a	Cheney SD 360	Cheney
1	n/a	Clarkston SD 250	Clarkston
1	n/a	Clover Park SD 400	Lakewood
1	n/a	Colville SD 115	Colville
1	n/a	Deer Park SD 414	Deer Park
1	n/a	East Valley SD 361	Spokane
1	n/a	East Valley SD 90	Yakima
1	n/a	Eastmont SD 206	East Wenatchee
1	n/a	Eatonville SD 404	Eatonville
1	n/a	Edmonds SD 15	Lynnwood
1	n/a	Ellensburg SD 401	Ellensburg
1	n/a	Elma SD 68	Elma
1	n/a	Enumclaw SD 216	Enumclaw
1	n/a	Ephrata SD 165	Ephrata
1	n/a	Everett SD 2	Everett
1	n/a	Evergreen SD 114	Vancouver
1	n/a	Federal Way SD 210	Federal Way
1	n/a	Ferndale SD 502	Ferndale
1	n/a	Fife SD 417	Tacoma
1	n/a	Franklin Pierce SD 402	Tacoma
1	n/a	Grandview SD 200	Grandview
1	n/a	Granite Falls SD 332	Granite Falls
1	n/a	Highline SD 401	Seattle
1	n/a	Hockinson SD 98	Brush Prairie
1	n/a	Hoquiam SD 28	Hoquiam
1	n/a	Issaquah SD 411	Issaquah
1	n/a	Kelso SD 458	Kelso
1	n/a	Kennewick SD 17	Kennewick
1	n/a	Kent SD 415	Kent
1	n/a	Kiona-Benton SD 52	Benton City
1	n/a	Lake Stevens SD 4	Lake Stevens
1	n/a	Lake Washington SD 414	Redmond
1	n/a	Lakewood SD 306	North Lakewood
1	n/a	Longview SD 122	Longview
1	n/a	Lynden SD 504	Lynden
1	n/a	Marysville SD 25	Marysville
1	n/a	Mead SD 354	Mead
1	n/a	Medical Lake SD 326	Medical Lake
1	n/a	Mercer Island SD 400	Mercer Island
1	n/a	Meridian SD 505	Bellingham
1	n/a	Monroe SD 103	Monroe
1	n/a	Moses Lake SD 161	Moses Lake
1	n/a	Mount Baker SD 507	Deming
1	n/a	Mount Vernon SD 320	Mount Vernon
1	n/a	Mukilteo SD 6	Everett
1	n/a	Naches Valley SD 3	Naches
1	n/a	Nine Mile Falls SD 325/179	Nine Mile Fall
1	n/a	Nooksack Valley SD 506	Everson
1	n/a	North Franklin SD 51	Connell
1	n/a	North Kitsap SD 400	Poulsbo
1	n/a	North Mason SD 403	Belfair
1	n/a	North Thurston SD 3	Lacey
1	n/a	Northshore SD 417	Bothell
1	n/a	Oak Harbor SD 201	Oak Harbor
1	n/a	Olympia SD 111	Olympia
1	n/a	Omak SD 19	Omak
1	n/a	Orting SD 344	Orting
1	n/a	Othello SD 147	Othello
1	n/a	Pasco SD 001	Pasco
1	n/a	Peninsula SD 401	Gig Harbor
1	n/a	Port Angeles SD 121	Port Angeles
1	n/a	Port Townsend SD 50	Port Townsend
1	n/a	Prosser SD 116	Prosser
1	n/a	Pullman SD 267	Pullman
1	n/a	Puyallup SD 3	Puyallup
1	n/a	Quincy SD 144	Quincy
1	n/a	Renton SD 403	Renton
1	n/a	Richland SD 400	Richland
1	n/a	Ridgefield SD 122	Ridgefield
1	n/a	Riverside SD 416	Chattaroy
1	n/a	Riverview Special Services	Carnation
1	n/a	Rochester SD 401	Rochester
1	n/a	Seattle SD 1	Seattle
1	n/a	Sedro-Woolley SD 101	Sedro Woolley
1	n/a	Selah SD 119	Selah
1	n/a	Sequim SD 323	Sequim
1	n/a	Shelton SD 309	Shelton
1	n/a	Shoreline SD 412	Shoreline
1	n/a	Snohomish SD 201	Snohomish
1	n/a	Snoqualmie SD 410	Snoqualmie
1	n/a	South Kitsap SD 402	Port Orchard
1	n/a	South Whidbey SD 206	Langley
1	n/a	Spokane SD 81	Spokane
1	n/a	Stanwood-Camano SD 401	Stanwood
1	n/a	Steilacoom Historical SD	Steilacoom
1	n/a	Sultan Home School	Sultan
1	n/a	Sumner SD 320	Sumner
1	n/a	Sunnyside SD 201	Sunnyside
1	n/a	Tacoma SD 10	Tacoma
1	n/a	Tahoma SD 409	Maple Valley
1	n/a	Toppenish SD 202	Toppenish
1	n/a	Tukwila SD 406	Tukwila
1	n/a	Tumwater SD 33	Tumwater
1	n/a	University Place SD 83	Univ Place
1	n/a	Vancouver SD 37	Vancouver
1	n/a	Vashon Island SD 402	Vashon
1	n/a	Wahluke SD 73	Mattawa
1	n/a	Walla Walla SD 140	Walla Walla
1	n/a	Wapato SD 207	Wapato
1	n/a	Washougal SD 112-6	Washougal
1	n/a	Wenatchee SD 246	Wenatchee
1	n/a	West Valley SD 208	Yakima
1	n/a	West Valley SD 363	Spokane
1	n/a	White River SD 416	Buckley
1	n/a	Woodland SD 404	Woodland
1	n/a	Yakima SD 7	Yakima
1	n/a	Yelm Community Schools	Yelm

West Virginia

West Virginia Public School Educational Profile

Category	Value	Category	Value
Schools *(2002-2003)*	804	**Diploma Recipients** *(2002-2003)*	17,128
Instructional Level		White, Non-Hispanic	16,281
Primary	485	Black, Non-Hispanic	600
Middle	132	Asian/Pacific Islander	148
High	163	American Indian/Alaskan Native	29
Other Level	24	Hispanic	70
Curriculum		**High School Drop-out Rate** (%) *(2000-2001)*	4.2
Regular	737	White, Non-Hispanic	4.2
Special Education	10	Black, Non-Hispanic	5.2
Vocational	34	Asian/Pacific Islander	0.6
Alternative	23	American Indian/Alaskan Native	14.3
Type		Hispanic	7.3
Magnet	0	**Staff** *(2002-2003)*	38,102.6
Charter	0	Teachers	20,091.3
Title I Eligible	427	Average Salary ($)	38,497
School-wide Title I	335	Librarians/Media Specialists	390.8
Students *(2002-2003)*	282,455	Guidance Counselors	659.0
Gender (%)		**Ratios** *(2002-2003)*	
Male	51.9	Student/Teacher Ratio	14.1 to 1
Female	48.1	Student/Librarian Ratio	722.8 to 1
Race/Ethnicity (%)		Student/Counselor Ratio	428.6 to 1
White, Non-Hispanic	94.4	**Current Spending** *($ per student in FY 2001)*	7,844
Black, Non-Hispanic	4.5	Instruction	4,838
Asian/Pacific Islander	0.6	Support Services	2,549
American Indian/Alaskan Native	0.1	**College Entrance Exam Scores** *(2003)*	
Hispanic	0.5	Scholastic Aptitude Test (SAT)	
Classification (%)		Participation Rate (%)	20
Individual Education Program (IEP)	17.8	Mean SAT I Verbal Score	522
Migrant	0.0	Mean SAT I Math Score	510
English Language Learner (ELL)	0.5	American College Testing Program (ACT)	
Eligible for Free Lunch Program	37.9	Participation Rate (%)	63
Eligible for Reduced-Price Lunch Program	10.4	Average Composite Score	20.3

Note: *For an explanation of data, please refer to the User's Guide in the front of the book; n/a indicates data not available*

West Virginia NAEP 2003 Test Scores

Reading			Mathematics		
Grade/Category	**Value**	**Rank**	**Grade/Category**	**Value**	**Rank**
4th Grade			**4th Grade**		
Average Proficiency	219.2 (1.0)	26/51	Average Proficiency	230.8 (0.8)	36/51
Proficiency by Gender/Race/Ethnicity			Proficiency by Gender/Race/Ethnicity		
Male	215.1 (1.2)	29/51	Male	231.8 (1.0)	36/51
Female	223.4 (1.4)	25/51	Female	229.7 (1.0)	36/51
White, Non-Hispanic	219.7 (1.0)	49/51	White, Non-Hispanic	231.0 (0.8)	50/51
Black, Non-Hispanic	202.9 (3.7)	10/42	Black, Non-Hispanic	221.1 (2.7)	11/42
Asian, Non-Hispanic	n/a	n/a	Asian, Non-Hispanic	n/a	n/a
American Indian, Non-Hispanic	n/a	n/a	American Indian, Non-Hispanic	n/a	n/a
Hispanic	n/a	n/a	Hispanic	n/a	n/a
Proficiency by Class Size			Proficiency by Class Size		
Less than 16 Students	*212.9 (4.3)*	10/45	Less than 16 Students	221.9 (2.6)	28/47
16 to 18 Students	*222.9 (2.7)*	10/48	16 to 18 Students	232.6 (1.6)	26/48
19 to 20 Students	222.2 (2.7)	15/50	19 to 20 Students	*232.9 (2.2)*	32/50
21 to 25 Students	217.8 (1.6)	36/51	21 to 25 Students	231.0 (1.1)	40/51
Greater than 25 Students	219.6 (2.5)	24/49	Greater than 25 Students	232.2 (1.9)	33/49
Percent Attaining Achievement Levels			Percent Attaining Achievement Levels		
Below Basic	35.1 (1.5)	25/51	Below Basic	24.7 (1.4)	19/51
Basic or Above	64.9 (1.5)	26/51	Basic or Above	75.3 (1.4)	33/51
Proficient or Above	28.7 (1.4)	35/51	Proficient or Above	23.9 (1.2)	41/51
Advanced or Above	5.7 (0.7)	39/51	Advanced or Above	1.6 (0.4)	43/51
8th Grade			**8th Grade**		
Average Proficiency	259.6 (1.0)	35/51	Average Proficiency	270.8 (1.2)	40/51
Proficiency by Gender/Race/Ethnicity			Proficiency by Gender/Race/Ethnicity		
Male	253.8 (1.5)	35/51	Male	270.8 (1.3)	40/51
Female	265.3 (1.1)	35/51	Female	270.7 (1.4)	39/51
White, Non-Hispanic	260.1 (1.0)	49/50	White, Non-Hispanic	271.3 (1.2)	50/50
Black, Non-Hispanic	248.3 (2.9)	9/41	Black, Non-Hispanic	253.1 (4.0)	18/41
Asian, Non-Hispanic	n/a	n/a	Asian, Non-Hispanic	n/a	n/a
American Indian, Non-Hispanic	n/a	n/a	American Indian, Non-Hispanic	n/a	n/a
Hispanic	n/a	n/a	Hispanic	n/a	n/a
Proficiency by Parents Highest Level of Ed.			Proficiency by Parents Highest Level of Ed.		
Did Not Finish High School	250.2 (1.9)	10/50	Did Not Finish High School	254.7 (3.0)	32/50
Graduated High School	254.3 (1.8)	29/50	Graduated High School	266.0 (1.8)	33/50
Some Education After High School	264.3 (1.7)	39/50	Some Education After High School	274.9 (1.6)	41/50
Graduated College	266.8 (1.4)	37/50	Graduated College	279.2 (1.4)	42/50
Percent Attaining Achievement Levels			Percent Attaining Achievement Levels		
Below Basic	28.3 (1.3)	19/51	Below Basic	37.5 (1.8)	14/51
Basic or Above	71.7 (1.3)	33/51	Basic or Above	62.5 (1.8)	38/51
Proficient or Above	24.9 (1.1)	41/51	Proficient or Above	19.6 (1.3)	44/51
Advanced or Above	1.7 (0.5)	42/51	Advanced or Above	1.8 (0.3)	47/51

Note: *For an explanation of data, please refer to the User's Guide in the front of the book; values in italics indicate that the nature of the sample does not allow accurate determination of the variability of the statistic; n/a indicates data not available*

Barbour County

Barbour County SD

105 S Railroad St • Philippi, WV 26416-1177
(304) 457-3030
Grade Span: PK-12; **Agency Type:** 1
Schools: 9
6 Primary; 2 Middle; 1 High; 0 Other Level
9 Regular; 0 Special Education; 0 Vocational; 0 Alternative
0 Magnet; 0 Charter; 8 Title I Eligible; 8 School-wide Title I
Students: 2,604 (53.1% male; 46.9% female)
Individual Education Program: 501 (19.2%);
English Language Learner: 2 (0.1%); Migrant: 0 (0.0%)
Eligible for Free Lunch Program: 1,328 (51.0%)
Eligible for Reduced-Price Lunch Program: 351 (13.5%)
Teachers: 185.9 (14.0 to 1)
Librarians/Media Specialists: 3.8 (685.3 to 1)
Guidance Counselors: 4.0 (651.0 to 1)
Current Spending: ($ per student per year):
Total: $6,818; Instruction: $4,268; Support Services: $2,135
Enrollment, Drop-out Rates and Diploma Recipients by Race/Ethnicity

Category	Total	White	Black	Asian	AIAN	Hisp.
Enrollment (%)	100.0	98.2	0.7	0.3	0.6	0.2
Drop-out Rate (%)	3.8	3.6	0.0	0.0	28.6	0.0
H.S. Diplomas (#)	161	156	2	2	1	0

Berkeley County

Berkeley County SD

401 S Queen St • Martinsburg, WV 25401-3285
(304) 267-3500 • http://boe.berk.k12.wv.us/
Grade Span: PK-12; **Agency Type:** 1
Schools: 30
17 Primary; 8 Middle; 4 High; 1 Other Level
26 Regular; 3 Special Education; 1 Vocational; 0 Alternative
0 Magnet; 0 Charter; 19 Title I Eligible; 2 School-wide Title I
Students: 13,772 (51.0% male; 49.0% female)
Individual Education Program: 2,337 (17.0%);
English Language Learner: 147 (1.1%); Migrant: 2 (<0.1%)
Eligible for Free Lunch Program: 3,515 (25.5%)
Eligible for Reduced-Price Lunch Program: 1,477 (10.7%)
Teachers: 997.2 (13.8 to 1)
Librarians/Media Specialists: 21.5 (640.6 to 1)
Guidance Counselors: 36.0 (382.6 to 1)
Current Spending: ($ per student per year):
Total: $7,148; Instruction: $4,316; Support Services: $2,374
Enrollment, Drop-out Rates and Diploma Recipients by Race/Ethnicity

Category	Total	White	Black	Asian	AIAN	Hisp.
Enrollment (%)	100.0	88.9	7.8	0.7	0.2	2.4
Drop-out Rate (%)	7.6	7.7	5.4	0.0	0.0	15.9
H.S. Diplomas (#)	710	636	43	16	1	14

Boone County

Boone County SD

69 Ave B • Madison, WV 25130-1162
(304) 369-3131 • http://www.boonecountyboe.org/
Grade Span: PK-12; **Agency Type:** 1
Schools: 19
11 Primary; 3 Middle; 4 High; 1 Other Level
17 Regular; 0 Special Education; 1 Vocational; 1 Alternative
0 Magnet; 0 Charter; 11 Title I Eligible; 10 School-wide Title I
Students: 4,531 (52.3% male; 47.7% female)
Individual Education Program: 904 (20.0%);
English Language Learner: 0 (0.0%); Migrant: 0 (0.0%)
Eligible for Free Lunch Program: 1,708 (37.7%)
Eligible for Reduced-Price Lunch Program: 399 (8.8%)
Teachers: 372.0 (12.2 to 1)
Librarians/Media Specialists: 4.0 (1,132.8 to 1)
Guidance Counselors: 9.0 (503.4 to 1)
Current Spending: ($ per student per year):
Total: $8,689; Instruction: $5,181; Support Services: $3,003
Enrollment, Drop-out Rates and Diploma Recipients by Race/Ethnicity

Category	Total	White	Black	Asian	AIAN	Hisp.
Enrollment (%)	100.0	98.6	1.1	0.1	0.1	0.2
Drop-out Rate (%)	5.3	5.3	5.3	0.0	0.0	0.0
H.S. Diplomas (#)	256	253	2	1	0	0

Braxton County

Braxton County SD

411 N Hill Rd • Sutton, WV 26601-1147
(304) 765-7101 • http://boe.brax.k12.wv.us/INDEX.HTM
Grade Span: PK-12; **Agency Type:** 1
Schools: 8
6 Primary; 1 Middle; 1 High; 0 Other Level
8 Regular; 0 Special Education; 0 Vocational; 0 Alternative
0 Magnet; 0 Charter; 8 Title I Eligible; 8 School-wide Title I
Students: 2,587 (50.1% male; 49.9% female)
Individual Education Program: 519 (20.1%);
English Language Learner: 0 (0.0%); Migrant: 0 (0.0%)
Eligible for Free Lunch Program: 1,221 (47.2%)
Eligible for Reduced-Price Lunch Program: 283 (10.9%)
Teachers: 194.5 (13.3 to 1)
Librarians/Media Specialists: 2.0 (1,293.5 to 1)
Guidance Counselors: 6.0 (431.2 to 1)
Current Spending: ($ per student per year):
Total: $7,036; Instruction: $4,337; Support Services: $2,320
Enrollment, Drop-out Rates and Diploma Recipients by Race/Ethnicity

Category	Total	White	Black	Asian	AIAN	Hisp.
Enrollment (%)	100.0	99.3	0.4	0.2	0.0	0.0
Drop-out Rate (%)	4.4	4.4	0.0	0.0	n/a	n/a
H.S. Diplomas (#)	148	147	1	0	0	0

Brooke County

Brooke County SD

1201 Pleasant Ave • Wellsburg, WV 26070-1497
(304) 737-3481
Grade Span: PK-12; **Agency Type:** 1
Schools: 12
9 Primary; 2 Middle; 1 High; 0 Other Level
12 Regular; 0 Special Education; 0 Vocational; 0 Alternative
0 Magnet; 0 Charter; 6 Title I Eligible; 5 School-wide Title I
Students: 3,637 (50.8% male; 49.2% female)
Individual Education Program: 706 (19.4%);
English Language Learner: 0 (0.0%); Migrant: 0 (0.0%)
Eligible for Free Lunch Program: 869 (23.9%)
Eligible for Reduced-Price Lunch Program: 327 (9.0%)
Teachers: 261.0 (13.9 to 1)
Librarians/Media Specialists: 4.0 (909.3 to 1)
Guidance Counselors: 7.0 (519.6 to 1)
Current Spending: ($ per student per year):
Total: $7,632; Instruction: $4,750; Support Services: $2,526
Enrollment, Drop-out Rates and Diploma Recipients by Race/Ethnicity

Category	Total	White	Black	Asian	AIAN	Hisp.
Enrollment (%)	100.0	97.6	1.6	0.4	0.1	0.3
Drop-out Rate (%)	2.6	2.7	0.0	0.0	0.0	0.0
H.S. Diplomas (#)	279	274	4	1	0	0

Cabell County

Cabell County SD

620 20th St • Huntington, WV 25703
(304) 528-5000 • http://boe.cabe.k12.wv.us/
Grade Span: PK-12; **Agency Type:** 1
Schools: 31
20 Primary; 7 Middle; 3 High; 1 Other Level
28 Regular; 0 Special Education; 1 Vocational; 2 Alternative
0 Magnet; 0 Charter; 14 Title I Eligible; 14 School-wide Title I
Students: 12,294 (51.7% male; 48.3% female)
Individual Education Program: 2,145 (17.4%);
English Language Learner: 65 (0.5%); Migrant: 0 (0.0%)
Eligible for Free Lunch Program: 4,632 (37.7%)
Eligible for Reduced-Price Lunch Program: 1,228 (10.0%)
Teachers: 846.2 (14.5 to 1)
Librarians/Media Specialists: 11.5 (1,069.0 to 1)
Guidance Counselors: 27.0 (455.3 to 1)
Current Spending: ($ per student per year):
Total: $7,593; Instruction: $4,569; Support Services: $2,564
Enrollment, Drop-out Rates and Diploma Recipients by Race/Ethnicity

Category	Total	White	Black	Asian	AIAN	Hisp.
Enrollment (%)	100.0	91.6	6.9	0.8	0.3	0.4
Drop-out Rate (%)	6.2	5.7	13.4	0.0	17.6	11.8
H.S. Diplomas (#)	688	635	37	6	6	4

Clay County

Clay County SD

1 Gump St • Clay, WV 25043-0120
Mailing Address: PO Box 120 • Clay, WV 25043-0120
(304) 587-4266
Grade Span: PK-12; **Agency Type:** 1
Schools: 7
5 Primary; 1 Middle; 1 High; 0 Other Level
7 Regular; 0 Special Education; 0 Vocational; 0 Alternative
0 Magnet; 0 Charter; 6 Title I Eligible; 6 School-wide Title I
Students: 2,144 (50.3% male; 49.7% female)
Individual Education Program: 401 (18.7%);
English Language Learner: 0 (0.0%); Migrant: 0 (0.0%)

Eligible for Free Lunch Program: 1,337 (62.4%)
Eligible for Reduced-Price Lunch Program: 283 (13.2%)
Teachers: 159.7 (13.4 to 1)
Librarians/Media Specialists: 2.0 (1,072.0 to 1)
Guidance Counselors: 3.0 (714.7 to 1)
Current Spending: ($ per student per year):
Total: $7,656; Instruction: $4,656; Support Services: $2,259
Enrollment, Drop-out Rates and Diploma Recipients by Race/Ethnicity

Category	Total	White	Black	Asian	AIAN	Hisp.
Enrollment (%)	100.0	99.5	0.3	0.0	0.0	0.1
Drop-out Rate (%)	3.4	3.4	0.0	n/a	n/a	n/a
H.S. Diplomas (#)	121	120	0	0	0	1

Fayette County

Fayette County SD
111 Fayette Ave • Fayetteville, WV 25840-1219
(304) 574-1176 • http://boe.faye.k12.wv.us/
Grade Span: PK-12; **Agency Type:** 1
Schools: 27
14 Primary; 5 Middle; 7 High; 1 Other Level
26 Regular; 0 Special Education; 1 Vocational; 0 Alternative
0 Magnet; 0 Charter; 15 Title I Eligible; 14 School-wide Title I
Students: 6,972 (53.5% male; 46.5% female)
Individual Education Program: 1,108 (15.9%);
English Language Learner: 7 (0.1%); Migrant: 0 (0.0%)
Eligible for Free Lunch Program: 3,269 (46.9%)
Eligible for Reduced-Price Lunch Program: 673 (9.7%)
Teachers: 541.0 (12.9 to 1)
Librarians/Media Specialists: 7.0 (996.0 to 1)
Guidance Counselors: 14.5 (480.8 to 1)
Current Spending: ($ per student per year):
Total: $7,660; Instruction: $4,991; Support Services: $2,250
Enrollment, Drop-out Rates and Diploma Recipients by Race/Ethnicity

Category	Total	White	Black	Asian	AIAN	Hisp.
Enrollment (%)	100.0	92.3	7.1	0.1	0.1	0.4
Drop-out Rate (%)	5.2	5.3	3.3	0.0	0.0	16.7
H.S. Diplomas (#)	442	405	36	0	0	1

Grant County

Grant County SD
204 Jefferson Ave • Petersburg, WV 26847-1628
(304) 257-1011
Grade Span: PK-12; **Agency Type:** 1
Schools: 6
3 Primary; 0 Middle; 2 High; 1 Other Level
5 Regular; 0 Special Education; 1 Vocational; 0 Alternative
0 Magnet; 0 Charter; 3 Title I Eligible; 0 School-wide Title I
Students: 1,978 (50.9% male; 49.1% female)
Individual Education Program: 404 (20.4%);
English Language Learner: 0 (0.0%); Migrant: 0 (0.0%)
Eligible for Free Lunch Program: 669 (33.8%)
Eligible for Reduced-Price Lunch Program: 309 (15.6%)
Teachers: 151.9 (13.0 to 1)
Librarians/Media Specialists: 3.0 (659.3 to 1)
Guidance Counselors: 5.0 (395.6 to 1)
Current Spending: ($ per student per year):
Total: $7,089; Instruction: $4,309; Support Services: $2,301
Enrollment, Drop-out Rates and Diploma Recipients by Race/Ethnicity

Category	Total	White	Black	Asian	AIAN	Hisp.
Enrollment (%)	100.0	98.4	1.2	0.2	0.1	0.2
Drop-out Rate (%)	5.6	5.7	0.0	0.0	0.0	0.0
H.S. Diplomas (#)	128	126	1	0	0	1

Greenbrier County

Greenbrier County SD
202 Chestnut St • Lewisburg, WV 24901-1108
(304) 647-6457 • http://boe.gree.k12.wv.us/
Grade Span: PK-12; **Agency Type:** 1
Schools: 14
10 Primary; 2 Middle; 2 High; 0 Other Level
14 Regular; 0 Special Education; 0 Vocational; 0 Alternative
0 Magnet; 0 Charter; 0 Title I Eligible; 0 School-wide Title I
Students: 5,359 (52.2% male; 47.8% female)
Individual Education Program: 1,124 (21.0%);
English Language Learner: 0 (0.0%); Migrant: 0 (0.0%)
Eligible for Free Lunch Program: 2,073 (38.7%)
Eligible for Reduced-Price Lunch Program: 783 (14.6%)
Teachers: 371.6 (14.4 to 1)
Librarians/Media Specialists: 5.0 (1,071.8 to 1)
Guidance Counselors: 15.0 (357.3 to 1)
Current Spending: ($ per student per year):
Total: $7,128; Instruction: $4,662; Support Services: $2,040

Enrollment, Drop-out Rates and Diploma Recipients by Race/Ethnicity

Category	Total	White	Black	Asian	AIAN	Hisp.
Enrollment (%)	100.0	95.6	3.7	0.2	0.0	0.5
Drop-out Rate (%)	2.0	2.1	0.0	0.0	33.3	0.0
H.S. Diplomas (#)	329	314	14	1	0	0

Hampshire County

Hampshire County SD
46 S High St • Romney, WV 26757-1812
(304) 822-3528
Grade Span: PK-12; **Agency Type:** 1
Schools: 11
7 Primary; 2 Middle; 2 High; 0 Other Level
10 Regular; 0 Special Education; 1 Vocational; 0 Alternative
0 Magnet; 0 Charter; 7 Title I Eligible; 1 School-wide Title I
Students: 3,560 (52.3% male; 47.7% female)
Individual Education Program: 676 (19.0%);
English Language Learner: 4 (0.1%); Migrant: 0 (0.0%)
Eligible for Free Lunch Program: 1,262 (35.4%)
Eligible for Reduced-Price Lunch Program: 558 (15.7%)
Teachers: 244.5 (14.6 to 1)
Librarians/Media Specialists: 2.5 (1,424.0 to 1)
Guidance Counselors: 9.0 (395.6 to 1)
Current Spending: ($ per student per year):
Total: $6,921; Instruction: $4,223; Support Services: $2,237
Enrollment, Drop-out Rates and Diploma Recipients by Race/Ethnicity

Category	Total	White	Black	Asian	AIAN	Hisp.
Enrollment (%)	100.0	97.9	1.1	0.4	0.0	0.5
Drop-out Rate (%)	4.0	4.1	0.0	0.0	n/a	0.0
H.S. Diplomas (#)	198	193	5	0	0	0

Hancock County

Hancock County SD
104 N Court St • New Cumberland, WV 26047-1300
Mailing Address: PO Box 1300 • New Cumberland, WV 26047-1300
(304) 564-3411 • http://boe.hanc.k12.wv.us/
Grade Span: PK-12; **Agency Type:** 1
Schools: 11
6 Primary; 2 Middle; 3 High; 0 Other Level
10 Regular; 0 Special Education; 1 Vocational; 0 Alternative
0 Magnet; 0 Charter; 4 Title I Eligible; 0 School-wide Title I
Students: 4,374 (52.1% male; 47.9% female)
Individual Education Program: 757 (17.3%);
English Language Learner: 0 (0.0%); Migrant: 0 (0.0%)
Eligible for Free Lunch Program: 1,029 (23.5%)
Eligible for Reduced-Price Lunch Program: 333 (7.6%)
Teachers: 299.7 (14.6 to 1)
Librarians/Media Specialists: 3.8 (1,151.1 to 1)
Guidance Counselors: 8.0 (546.8 to 1)
Current Spending: ($ per student per year):
Total: $7,325; Instruction: $4,617; Support Services: $2,417
Enrollment, Drop-out Rates and Diploma Recipients by Race/Ethnicity

Category	Total	White	Black	Asian	AIAN	Hisp.
Enrollment (%)	100.0	95.3	3.9	0.3	0.2	0.3
Drop-out Rate (%)	4.0	4.1	1.9	0.0	0.0	0.0
H.S. Diplomas (#)	274	263	9	1	0	1

Hardy County

Hardy County SD
510 Ashby St • Moorefield, WV 26836-1001
(304) 538-2348 • http://www.hardycountyschools.com/
Grade Span: PK-12; **Agency Type:** 1
Schools: 5
2 Primary; 1 Middle; 2 High; 0 Other Level
5 Regular; 0 Special Education; 0 Vocational; 0 Alternative
0 Magnet; 0 Charter; 3 Title I Eligible; 0 School-wide Title I
Students: 2,313 (51.2% male; 48.8% female)
Individual Education Program: 461 (19.9%);
English Language Learner: 8 (0.3%); Migrant: 29 (1.3%)
Eligible for Free Lunch Program: 829 (35.8%)
Eligible for Reduced-Price Lunch Program: 409 (17.7%)
Teachers: 159.2 (14.5 to 1)
Librarians/Media Specialists: 5.0 (462.6 to 1)
Guidance Counselors: 5.0 (462.6 to 1)
Current Spending: ($ per student per year):
Total: $6,065; Instruction: $3,737; Support Services: $1,880
Enrollment, Drop-out Rates and Diploma Recipients by Race/Ethnicity

Category	Total	White	Black	Asian	AIAN	Hisp.
Enrollment (%)	100.0	97.0	2.2	0.1	0.0	0.6
Drop-out Rate (%)	1.3	1.4	0.0	n/a	n/a	0.0
H.S. Diplomas (#)	121	116	5	0	0	0

Harrison County

Harrison County SD

408 EB Saunders Way • Clarksburg, WV 26301
Mailing Address: PO Box 1370 • Clarksburg, WV 26302-1370
(304) 624-3300
Grade Span: PK-12; **Agency Type:** 1
Schools: 30
14 Primary; 6 Middle; 7 High; 3 Other Level
25 Regular; 3 Special Education; 1 Vocational; 1 Alternative
0 Magnet; 0 Charter; 17 Title I Eligible; 12 School-wide Title I
Students: 11,580 (51.2% male; 48.8% female)
Individual Education Program: 1,963 (17.0%);
English Language Learner: 2 (<0.1%); Migrant: 0 (0.0%)
Eligible for Free Lunch Program: 4,423 (38.2%)
Eligible for Reduced-Price Lunch Program: 1,169 (10.1%)
Teachers: 766.1 (15.1 to 1)
Librarians/Media Specialists: 22.0 (526.4 to 1)
Guidance Counselors: 22.0 (526.4 to 1)
Current Spending: ($ per student per year):
Total: $7,249; Instruction: $4,456; Support Services: $2,396
Enrollment, Drop-out Rates and Diploma Recipients by Race/Ethnicity

Category	Total	White	Black	Asian	AIAN	Hisp.
Enrollment (%)	100.0	96.7	2.5	0.5	0.1	0.2
Drop-out Rate (%)	4.1	4.1	1.4	0.0	0.0	7.1
H.S. Diplomas (#)	709	683	15	6	0	5

Jackson County

Jackson County SD

#1 School St • Ripley, WV 25271-0770
Mailing Address: PO Box 770 • Ripley, WV 25271-0770
(304) 372-7300
Grade Span: PK-12; **Agency Type:** 1
Schools: 13
8 Primary; 2 Middle; 3 High; 0 Other Level
12 Regular; 0 Special Education; 1 Vocational; 0 Alternative
0 Magnet; 0 Charter; 8 Title I Eligible; 8 School-wide Title I
Students: 5,038 (52.7% male; 47.3% female)
Individual Education Program: 882 (17.5%);
English Language Learner: 17 (0.3%); Migrant: 0 (0.0%)
Eligible for Free Lunch Program: 1,745 (34.6%)
Eligible for Reduced-Price Lunch Program: 448 (8.9%)
Teachers: 347.7 (14.5 to 1)
Librarians/Media Specialists: 4.0 (1,259.5 to 1)
Guidance Counselors: 11.0 (458.0 to 1)
Current Spending: ($ per student per year):
Total: $7,173; Instruction: $4,377; Support Services: $2,468
Enrollment, Drop-out Rates and Diploma Recipients by Race/Ethnicity

Category	Total	White	Black	Asian	AIAN	Hisp.
Enrollment (%)	100.0	99.0	0.3	0.4	0.0	0.2
Drop-out Rate (%)	4.8	4.8	0.0	0.0	0.0	0.0
H.S. Diplomas (#)	309	293	1	12	1	2

Jefferson County

Jefferson County SD

110mordington Ave • Charles Town, WV 25414-0987
Mailing Address: PO Box 987 • Charles Town, WV 25414-0987
(304) 725-9741
Grade Span: PK-12; **Agency Type:** 1
Schools: 13
9 Primary; 3 Middle; 1 High; 0 Other Level
13 Regular; 0 Special Education; 0 Vocational; 0 Alternative
0 Magnet; 0 Charter; 4 Title I Eligible; 2 School-wide Title I
Students: 7,274 (51.7% male; 48.3% female)
Individual Education Program: 1,183 (16.3%);
English Language Learner: 102 (1.4%); Migrant: 11 (0.2%)
Eligible for Free Lunch Program: 1,607 (22.1%)
Eligible for Reduced-Price Lunch Program: 727 (10.0%)
Teachers: 487.5 (14.9 to 1)
Librarians/Media Specialists: 14.0 (519.6 to 1)
Guidance Counselors: 16.0 (454.6 to 1)
Current Spending: ($ per student per year):
Total: $7,328; Instruction: $4,635; Support Services: $2,286
Enrollment, Drop-out Rates and Diploma Recipients by Race/Ethnicity

Category	Total	White	Black	Asian	AIAN	Hisp.
Enrollment (%)	100.0	87.2	9.4	0.8	0.2	2.5
Drop-out Rate (%)	6.7	6.7	5.9	5.9	50.0	13.6
H.S. Diplomas (#)	418	378	34	3	1	2

Kanawha County

Kanawha County SD

200 Elizabeth St • Charleston, WV 25311-2119
(304) 348-7732 • http://kcs.kana.k12.wv.us/
Grade Span: PK-12; **Agency Type:** 1
Schools: 72
48 Primary; 13 Middle; 11 High; 0 Other Level
67 Regular; 1 Special Education; 2 Vocational; 2 Alternative
0 Magnet; 0 Charter; 27 Title I Eligible; 27 School-wide Title I
Students: 28,417 (51.8% male; 48.2% female)
Individual Education Program: 4,635 (16.3%);
English Language Learner: 314 (1.1%); Migrant: 0 (0.0%)
Eligible for Free Lunch Program: 9,977 (35.1%)
Eligible for Reduced-Price Lunch Program: 2,433 (8.6%)
Teachers: 1,928.5 (14.7 to 1)
Librarians/Media Specialists: 66.0 (430.6 to 1)
Guidance Counselors: 83.9 (338.7 to 1)
Current Spending: ($ per student per year):
Total: $7,629; Instruction: $4,558; Support Services: $2,545
Enrollment, Drop-out Rates and Diploma Recipients by Race/Ethnicity

Category	Total	White	Black	Asian	AIAN	Hisp.
Enrollment (%)	100.0	87.0	11.4	1.1	0.0	0.4
Drop-out Rate (%)	5.6	5.5	7.4	0.9	0.0	3.3
H.S. Diplomas (#)	1,630	1,458	134	25	4	9

Lewis County

Lewis County SD

322 E 3rd St • Weston, WV 26452-2002
(304) 269-8300 • http://boe.lewi.k12.wv.us/
Grade Span: PK-12; **Agency Type:** 1
Schools: 7
5 Primary; 1 Middle; 1 High; 0 Other Level
7 Regular; 0 Special Education; 0 Vocational; 0 Alternative
0 Magnet; 0 Charter; 6 Title I Eligible; 5 School-wide Title I
Students: 2,743 (52.3% male; 47.7% female)
Individual Education Program: 592 (21.6%);
English Language Learner: 2 (0.1%); Migrant: 1 (<0.1%)
Eligible for Free Lunch Program: 1,172 (42.7%)
Eligible for Reduced-Price Lunch Program: 336 (12.2%)
Teachers: 198.0 (13.9 to 1)
Librarians/Media Specialists: 3.5 (783.7 to 1)
Guidance Counselors: 6.0 (457.2 to 1)
Current Spending: ($ per student per year):
Total: $7,121; Instruction: $4,253; Support Services: $2,380
Enrollment, Drop-out Rates and Diploma Recipients by Race/Ethnicity

Category	Total	White	Black	Asian	AIAN	Hisp.
Enrollment (%)	100.0	98.8	0.5	0.1	0.2	0.3
Drop-out Rate (%)	1.2	1.2	0.0	0.0	0.0	n/a
H.S. Diplomas (#)	192	189	0	2	1	0

Lincoln County

Lincoln County SD

10 Marland Ave • Hamlin, WV 25523-1099
(304) 824-3033
Grade Span: PK-12; **Agency Type:** 1
Schools: 12
7 Primary; 0 Middle; 5 High; 0 Other Level
11 Regular; 0 Special Education; 1 Vocational; 0 Alternative
0 Magnet; 0 Charter; 7 Title I Eligible; 7 School-wide Title I
Students: 3,873 (52.5% male; 47.5% female)
Individual Education Program: 834 (21.5%);
English Language Learner: 0 (0.0%); Migrant: 0 (0.0%)
Eligible for Free Lunch Program: 2,064 (53.3%)
Eligible for Reduced-Price Lunch Program: 436 (11.3%)
Teachers: 292.0 (13.3 to 1)
Librarians/Media Specialists: 5.0 (774.6 to 1)
Guidance Counselors: 5.0 (774.6 to 1)
Current Spending: ($ per student per year):
Total: $7,935; Instruction: $4,791; Support Services: $2,435
Enrollment, Drop-out Rates and Diploma Recipients by Race/Ethnicity

Category	Total	White	Black	Asian	AIAN	Hisp.
Enrollment (%)	100.0	99.5	0.2	0.1	0.0	0.2
Drop-out Rate (%)	2.6	2.6	n/a	n/a	n/a	n/a
H.S. Diplomas (#)	231	231	0	0	0	0

Logan County

Logan County SD

506 Holly Ave • Logan, WV 25601-0477
Mailing Address: PO Box 477 • Logan, WV 25601-0477
(304) 792-2060 • http://lc2.boe.loga.k12.wv.us/
Grade Span: PK-12; **Agency Type:** 1
Schools: 18
11 Primary; 2 Middle; 4 High; 1 Other Level
16 Regular; 1 Special Education; 1 Vocational; 0 Alternative
0 Magnet; 0 Charter; 12 Title I Eligible; 12 School-wide Title I
Students: 6,087 (51.5% male; 48.5% female)
Individual Education Program: 1,023 (16.8%);
English Language Learner: 6 (0.1%); Migrant: 0 (0.0%)
Eligible for Free Lunch Program: 2,707 (44.5%)
Eligible for Reduced-Price Lunch Program: 580 (9.5%)
Teachers: 447.6 (13.6 to 1)
Librarians/Media Specialists: 6.0 (1,014.5 to 1)
Guidance Counselors: 11.0 (553.4 to 1)
Current Spending: ($ per student per year):
Total: $7,189; Instruction: $4,593; Support Services: $2,165
Enrollment, Drop-out Rates and Diploma Recipients by Race/Ethnicity

Category	Total	White	Black	Asian	AIAN	Hisp.
Enrollment (%)	100.0	96.0	3.3	0.4	0.0	0.3
Drop-out Rate (%)	4.5	4.7	0.0	0.0	0.0	0.0
H.S. Diplomas (#)	402	383	11	2	1	5

Marion County

Marion County SD

200 Gaston Ave • Fairmont, WV 26554-2739
(304) 367-2100
Grade Span: PK-12; **Agency Type:** 1
Schools: 23
12 Primary; 6 Middle; 5 High; 0 Other Level
21 Regular; 0 Special Education; 1 Vocational; 1 Alternative
0 Magnet; 0 Charter; 10 Title I Eligible; 9 School-wide Title I
Students: 8,254 (51.5% male; 48.5% female)
Individual Education Program: 1,311 (15.9%);
English Language Learner: 5 (0.1%); Migrant: 0 (0.0%)
Eligible for Free Lunch Program: 2,950 (35.7%)
Eligible for Reduced-Price Lunch Program: 694 (8.4%)
Teachers: 615.0 (13.4 to 1)
Librarians/Media Specialists: 18.0 (458.6 to 1)
Guidance Counselors: 22.0 (375.2 to 1)
Current Spending: ($ per student per year):
Total: $7,753; Instruction: $4,658; Support Services: $2,721
Enrollment, Drop-out Rates and Diploma Recipients by Race/Ethnicity

Category	Total	White	Black	Asian	AIAN	Hisp.
Enrollment (%)	100.0	93.8	5.4	0.3	0.1	0.3
Drop-out Rate (%)	1.9	1.9	0.8	0.0	200.0	0.0
H.S. Diplomas (#)	634	600	26	5	1	2

Marshall County

Marshall County SD

2700 E 4th St • Moundsville, WV 26041-0578
Mailing Address: PO Box 578 • Moundsville, WV 26041-0578
(304) 843-4400 • http://boe.mars.k12.wv.us/
Grade Span: PK-12; **Agency Type:** 1
Schools: 16
11 Primary; 3 Middle; 2 High; 0 Other Level
16 Regular; 0 Special Education; 0 Vocational; 0 Alternative
0 Magnet; 0 Charter; 8 Title I Eligible; 7 School-wide Title I
Students: 5,375 (51.6% male; 48.4% female)
Individual Education Program: 1,100 (20.5%);
English Language Learner: 0 (0.0%); Migrant: 0 (0.0%)
Eligible for Free Lunch Program: 1,876 (34.9%)
Eligible for Reduced-Price Lunch Program: 553 (10.3%)
Teachers: 365.0 (14.7 to 1)
Librarians/Media Specialists: 5.0 (1,075.0 to 1)
Guidance Counselors: 14.0 (383.9 to 1)
Current Spending: ($ per student per year):
Total: $8,050; Instruction: $5,069; Support Services: $2,601
Enrollment, Drop-out Rates and Diploma Recipients by Race/Ethnicity

Category	Total	White	Black	Asian	AIAN	Hisp.
Enrollment (%)	100.0	98.7	0.7	0.2	0.1	0.3
Drop-out Rate (%)	3.5	3.6	0.0	0.0	0.0	n/a
H.S. Diplomas (#)	411	403	1	4	1	2

Mason County

Mason County SD

307 8th St • Point Pleasant, WV 25550-1298
(304) 675-4540 • http://boe.maso.k12.wv.us/
Grade Span: PK-12; **Agency Type:** 1
Schools: 16
9 Primary; 1 Middle; 4 High; 0 Other Level
13 Regular; 0 Special Education; 1 Vocational; 0 Alternative
0 Magnet; 0 Charter; 8 Title I Eligible; 4 School-wide Title I
Students: 4,267 (53.3% male; 46.7% female)
Individual Education Program: 871 (20.4%);
English Language Learner: 2 (<0.1%); Migrant: 0 (0.0%)
Eligible for Free Lunch Program: 1,696 (39.7%)
Eligible for Reduced-Price Lunch Program: 469 (11.0%)
Teachers: 316.1 (13.5 to 1)
Librarians/Media Specialists: 4.0 (1,066.8 to 1)
Guidance Counselors: 11.0 (387.9 to 1)
Current Spending: ($ per student per year):
Total: $7,405; Instruction: $4,774; Support Services: $2,204
Enrollment, Drop-out Rates and Diploma Recipients by Race/Ethnicity

Category	Total	White	Black	Asian	AIAN	Hisp.
Enrollment (%)	100.0	98.5	1.2	0.1	0.0	0.1
Drop-out Rate (%)	3.6	3.6	0.0	0.0	n/a	n/a
H.S. Diplomas (#)	271	270	0	0	0	1

Mcdowell County

Mcdowell County SD

30 Central Ave • Welch, WV 24801-2008
(304) 436-8441 • http://boe.mcdo.k12.wv.us/
Grade Span: PK-12; **Agency Type:** 1
Schools: 18
11 Primary; 2 Middle; 5 High; 0 Other Level
16 Regular; 0 Special Education; 1 Vocational; 1 Alternative
0 Magnet; 0 Charter; 13 Title I Eligible; 13 School-wide Title I
Students: 4,469 (52.5% male; 47.5% female)
Individual Education Program: 889 (19.9%);
English Language Learner: 0 (0.0%); Migrant: 0 (0.0%)
Eligible for Free Lunch Program: 3,159 (70.7%)
Eligible for Reduced-Price Lunch Program: 485 (10.9%)
Teachers: 344.0 (13.0 to 1)
Librarians/Media Specialists: 3.0 (1,489.7 to 1)
Guidance Counselors: 12.0 (372.4 to 1)
Current Spending: ($ per student per year):
Total: $8,522; Instruction: $5,510; Support Services: $2,573
Enrollment, Drop-out Rates and Diploma Recipients by Race/Ethnicity

Category	Total	White	Black	Asian	AIAN	Hisp.
Enrollment (%)	100.0	86.7	13.1	0.1	0.0	0.1
Drop-out Rate (%)	4.0	4.1	3.4	n/a	n/a	n/a
H.S. Diplomas (#)	237	210	27	0	0	0

Mercer County

Mercer County SD

1403 Honaker Ave • Princeton, WV 24740-3065
(304) 487-1551 • http://boe.merc.k12.wv.us/
Grade Span: PK-12; **Agency Type:** 1
Schools: 27
19 Primary; 3 Middle; 5 High; 0 Other Level
25 Regular; 0 Special Education; 1 Vocational; 1 Alternative
0 Magnet; 0 Charter; 16 Title I Eligible; 12 School-wide Title I
Students: 9,567 (51.7% male; 48.3% female)
Individual Education Program: 1,604 (16.8%);
English Language Learner: 3 (<0.1%); Migrant: 0 (0.0%)
Eligible for Free Lunch Program: 4,249 (44.4%)
Eligible for Reduced-Price Lunch Program: 999 (10.4%)
Teachers: 685.5 (14.0 to 1)
Librarians/Media Specialists: 21.0 (455.6 to 1)
Guidance Counselors: 23.0 (416.0 to 1)
Current Spending: ($ per student per year):
Total: $7,468; Instruction: $4,624; Support Services: $2,317
Enrollment, Drop-out Rates and Diploma Recipients by Race/Ethnicity

Category	Total	White	Black	Asian	AIAN	Hisp.
Enrollment (%)	100.0	90.3	8.8	0.5	0.1	0.2
Drop-out Rate (%)	3.9	4.1	2.2	0.0	0.0	0.0
H.S. Diplomas (#)	527	482	36	7	1	1

Mineral County

Mineral County SD

1 Baker Pl • Keyser, WV 26726-2898
(304) 788-4200 • http://mctc.mine.tec.wv.us/
Grade Span: PK-12; **Agency Type:** 1
Schools: 14

9 Primary; 1 Middle; 3 High; 1 Other Level
12 Regular; 0 Special Education; 2 Vocational; 0 Alternative
0 Magnet; 0 Charter; 8 Title I Eligible; 2 School-wide Title I

Students: 4,609 (51.0% male; 49.0% female)
Individual Education Program: 801 (17.4%);
English Language Learner: 8 (0.2%); Migrant: 0 (0.0%)
Eligible for Free Lunch Program: 1,456 (31.6%)
Eligible for Reduced-Price Lunch Program: 586 (12.7%)

Teachers: 318.0 (14.5 to 1)
Librarians/Media Specialists: 5.5 (838.0 to 1)
Guidance Counselors: 11.0 (419.0 to 1)
Current Spending: ($ per student per year):
Total: $7,247; Instruction: $4,263; Support Services: $2,561

Enrollment, Drop-out Rates and Diploma Recipients by Race/Ethnicity

Category	Total	White	Black	Asian	AIAN	Hisp.
Enrollment (%)	100.0	95.4	4.1	0.1	0.0	0.4
Drop-out Rate (%)	2.8	3.0	0.0	0.0	n/a	0.0
H.S. Diplomas (#)	283	262	18	2	0	1

Mingo County

Mingo County SD

815 Alderson St • Williamson, WV 25661-9746
Mailing Address: Rt 2 Box 310 • Williamson, WV 25661-9746
(304) 235-3333
Grade Span: PK-12; **Agency Type:** 1
Schools: 18
8 Primary; 4 Middle; 6 High; 0 Other Level
17 Regular; 0 Special Education; 1 Vocational; 0 Alternative
0 Magnet; 0 Charter; 12 Title I Eligible; 12 School-wide Title I

Students: 4,775 (51.7% male; 48.3% female)
Individual Education Program: 911 (19.1%);
English Language Learner: 1 (<0.1%); Migrant: 0 (0.0%)
Eligible for Free Lunch Program: 2,683 (56.2%)
Eligible for Reduced-Price Lunch Program: 501 (10.5%)

Teachers: 344.9 (13.8 to 1)
Librarians/Media Specialists: 4.2 (1,136.9 to 1)
Guidance Counselors: 11.0 (434.1 to 1)
Current Spending: ($ per student per year):
Total: $8,322; Instruction: $5,239; Support Services: $2,697

Enrollment, Drop-out Rates and Diploma Recipients by Race/Ethnicity

Category	Total	White	Black	Asian	AIAN	Hisp.
Enrollment (%)	100.0	97.0	2.7	0.1	0.0	0.1
Drop-out Rate (%)	2.8	2.8	2.1	0.0	0.0	n/a
H.S. Diplomas (#)	320	311	6	1	1	1

Monongalia County

Monongalia SD

13 S High St • Morgantown, WV 26501-7546
(304) 291-9210 • http://boe.mono.k12.wv.us/
Grade Span: PK-12; **Agency Type:** 1
Schools: 25
17 Primary; 4 Middle; 4 High; 0 Other Level
24 Regular; 0 Special Education; 1 Vocational; 0 Alternative
0 Magnet; 0 Charter; 9 Title I Eligible; 8 School-wide Title I

Students: 10,280 (51.9% male; 48.1% female)
Individual Education Program: 1,559 (15.2%);
English Language Learner: 456 (4.4%); Migrant: 0 (0.0%)
Eligible for Free Lunch Program: 2,897 (28.2%)
Eligible for Reduced-Price Lunch Program: 863 (8.4%)

Teachers: 700.8 (14.7 to 1)
Librarians/Media Specialists: 19.0 (541.1 to 1)
Guidance Counselors: 22.5 (456.9 to 1)
Current Spending: ($ per student per year):
Total: $7,394; Instruction: $4,435; Support Services: $2,565

Enrollment, Drop-out Rates and Diploma Recipients by Race/Ethnicity

Category	Total	White	Black	Asian	AIAN	Hisp.
Enrollment (%)	100.0	91.3	4.7	3.1	0.2	0.7
Drop-out Rate (%)	3.8	3.8	4.3	0.0	25.0	4.8
H.S. Diplomas (#)	629	602	16	11	0	0

Monroe County

Monroe County SD

Willow Bend Rd • Union, WV 24983-0330
Mailing Address: PO Box 330 • Union, WV 24983-0330
(304) 772-3094 • http://www.monroecountyschoolswv.org/
Grade Span: PK-12; **Agency Type:** 1
Schools: 5
2 Primary; 1 Middle; 2 High; 0 Other Level
4 Regular; 0 Special Education; 1 Vocational; 0 Alternative
0 Magnet; 0 Charter; 2 Title I Eligible; 2 School-wide Title I

Students: 2,116 (51.5% male; 48.5% female)
Individual Education Program: 399 (18.9%);
English Language Learner: 0 (0.0%); Migrant: 0 (0.0%)
Eligible for Free Lunch Program: 794 (37.5%)
Eligible for Reduced-Price Lunch Program: 331 (15.6%)

Teachers: 150.0 (14.1 to 1)
Librarians/Media Specialists: 1.0 (2,116.0 to 1)
Guidance Counselors: 1.8 (1,175.6 to 1)
Current Spending: ($ per student per year):
Total: $7,038; Instruction: $4,249; Support Services: $2,417

Enrollment, Drop-out Rates and Diploma Recipients by Race/Ethnicity

Category	Total	White	Black	Asian	AIAN	Hisp.
Enrollment (%)	100.0	98.1	1.3	0.2	0.2	0.2
Drop-out Rate (%)	3.9	3.6	0.0	25.0	50.0	0.0
H.S. Diplomas (#)	96	95	1	0	0	0

Morgan County

Morgan County SD

714 S Washington St • Berkeley Springs, WV 25411-1099
(304) 258-2430
Grade Span: PK-12; **Agency Type:** 1
Schools: 9
6 Primary; 1 Middle; 2 High; 0 Other Level
9 Regular; 0 Special Education; 0 Vocational; 0 Alternative
0 Magnet; 0 Charter; 4 Title I Eligible; 3 School-wide Title I

Students: 2,557 (51.8% male; 48.2% female)
Individual Education Program: 421 (16.5%);
English Language Learner: 1 (<0.1%); Migrant: 92 (3.6%)
Eligible for Free Lunch Program: 722 (28.2%)
Eligible for Reduced-Price Lunch Program: 360 (14.1%)

Teachers: 172.7 (14.8 to 1)
Librarians/Media Specialists: 3.5 (730.6 to 1)
Guidance Counselors: 6.0 (426.2 to 1)
Current Spending: ($ per student per year):
Total: $6,585; Instruction: $3,843; Support Services: $2,390

Enrollment, Drop-out Rates and Diploma Recipients by Race/Ethnicity

Category	Total	White	Black	Asian	AIAN	Hisp.
Enrollment (%)	100.0	98.1	0.9	0.1	0.1	0.8
Drop-out Rate (%)	4.3	4.2	10.0	0.0	n/a	0.0
H.S. Diplomas (#)	137	131	2	3	1	0

Nicholas County

Nicholas County SD

400 Old Main Dr • Summersville, WV 26651-1360
(304) 872-3611 • http://boe.nich.k12.wv.us/
Grade Span: PK-12; **Agency Type:** 1
Schools: 16
11 Primary; 2 Middle; 3 High; 0 Other Level
15 Regular; 0 Special Education; 1 Vocational; 0 Alternative
0 Magnet; 0 Charter; 0 Title I Eligible; 0 School-wide Title I

Students: 4,331 (52.5% male; 47.5% female)
Individual Education Program: 900 (20.8%);
English Language Learner: 1 (<0.1%); Migrant: 0 (0.0%)
Eligible for Free Lunch Program: 2,043 (47.2%)
Eligible for Reduced-Price Lunch Program: 511 (11.8%)

Teachers: 330.5 (13.1 to 1)
Librarians/Media Specialists: 4.0 (1,082.8 to 1)
Guidance Counselors: 9.5 (455.9 to 1)
Current Spending: ($ per student per year):
Total: $7,643; Instruction: $4,591; Support Services: $2,523

Enrollment, Drop-out Rates and Diploma Recipients by Race/Ethnicity

Category	Total	White	Black	Asian	AIAN	Hisp.
Enrollment (%)	100.0	99.1	0.4	0.2	0.0	0.3
Drop-out Rate (%)	3.4	3.4	0.0	0.0	0.0	0.0
H.S. Diplomas (#)	276	274	0	1	0	1

Ohio County

Ohio County SD

2203 National Rd • Wheeling, WV 26003-5203
(304) 243-0300
Grade Span: PK-12; **Agency Type:** 1
Schools: 13
9 Primary; 3 Middle; 1 High; 0 Other Level
13 Regular; 0 Special Education; 0 Vocational; 0 Alternative
0 Magnet; 0 Charter; 7 Title I Eligible; 4 School-wide Title I

Students: 5,552 (51.9% male; 48.1% female)
Individual Education Program: 883 (15.9%);
English Language Learner: 21 (0.4%); Migrant: 0 (0.0%)
Eligible for Free Lunch Program: 1,909 (34.4%)
Eligible for Reduced-Price Lunch Program: 487 (8.8%)

Teachers: 386.0 (14.4 to 1)
Librarians/Media Specialists: 10.0 (555.2 to 1)
Guidance Counselors: 12.0 (462.7 to 1)

Current Spending: ($ per student per year):
Total: $7,790; Instruction: $4,586; Support Services: $2,705
Enrollment, Drop-out Rates and Diploma Recipients by Race/Ethnicity

Category	Total	White	Black	Asian	AIAN	Hisp.
Enrollment (%)	100.0	91.4	7.4	0.9	0.1	0.2
Drop-out Rate (%)	4.5	4.4	5.6	0.0	25.0	20.0
H.S. Diplomas (#)	341	317	19	3	2	0

Preston County

Preston County SD
300 Preston Dr • Kingwood, WV 26537-0566
Mailing Address: PO Box 566 • Kingwood, WV 26537-0566
(304) 329-0580 • http://www.prestonboe.com/
Grade Span: PK-12; **Agency Type:** 1
Schools: 12
8 Primary; 3 Middle; 1 High; 0 Other Level
12 Regular; 0 Special Education; 0 Vocational; 0 Alternative
0 Magnet; 0 Charter; 7 Title I Eligible; 6 School-wide Title I
Students: 4,830 (51.1% male; 48.9% female)
Individual Education Program: 937 (19.4%);
English Language Learner: 2 (<0.1%); Migrant: 0 (0.0%)
Eligible for Free Lunch Program: 1,932 (40.0%)
Eligible for Reduced-Price Lunch Program: 758 (15.7%)
Teachers: 330.3 (14.6 to 1)
Librarians/Media Specialists: 5.0 (966.0 to 1)
Guidance Counselors: 10.0 (483.0 to 1)
Current Spending: ($ per student per year):
Total: $6,695; Instruction: $4,208; Support Services: $2,103
Enrollment, Drop-out Rates and Diploma Recipients by Race/Ethnicity

Category	Total	White	Black	Asian	AIAN	Hisp.
Enrollment (%)	100.0	99.0	0.7	0.2	0.1	0.1
Drop-out Rate (%)	4.6	4.7	0.0	0.0	0.0	0.0
H.S. Diplomas (#)	311	306	2	2	0	1

Putnam County

Putnam County SD
9 Courthouse Dr • Winfield, WV 25213-9347
(304) 586-0500 • http://boe.putn.k12.wv.us/boe/index.html
Grade Span: PK-12; **Agency Type:** 1
Schools: 22
13 Primary; 4 Middle; 5 High; 0 Other Level
21 Regular; 0 Special Education; 1 Vocational; 0 Alternative
0 Magnet; 0 Charter; 9 Title I Eligible; 9 School-wide Title I
Students: 8,746 (52.2% male; 47.8% female)
Individual Education Program: 1,638 (18.7%);
English Language Learner: 12 (0.1%); Migrant: 0 (0.0%)
Eligible for Free Lunch Program: 2,011 (23.0%)
Eligible for Reduced-Price Lunch Program: 616 (7.0%)
Teachers: 594.5 (14.7 to 1)
Librarians/Media Specialists: 8.0 (1,093.3 to 1)
Guidance Counselors: 21.0 (416.5 to 1)
Current Spending: ($ per student per year):
Total: $7,131; Instruction: $4,472; Support Services: $2,201
Enrollment, Drop-out Rates and Diploma Recipients by Race/Ethnicity

Category	Total	White	Black	Asian	AIAN	Hisp.
Enrollment (%)	100.0	98.0	1.1	0.6	0.1	0.2
Drop-out Rate (%)	3.2	3.2	0.0	0.0	33.3	16.7
H.S. Diplomas (#)	495	488	1	3	2	1

Raleigh County

Raleigh County SD
105 Adair St • Beckley, WV 25801-3733
(304) 256-4500 • http://boe.rale.k12.wv.us/
Grade Span: PK-12; **Agency Type:** 1
Schools: 34
21 Primary; 5 Middle; 8 High; 0 Other Level
31 Regular; 0 Special Education; 2 Vocational; 1 Alternative
0 Magnet; 0 Charter; 18 Title I Eligible; 17 School-wide Title I
Students: 11,903 (52.0% male; 48.0% female)
Individual Education Program: 1,938 (16.3%);
English Language Learner: 41 (0.3%); Migrant: 0 (0.0%)
Eligible for Free Lunch Program: 4,693 (39.4%)
Eligible for Reduced-Price Lunch Program: 1,189 (10.0%)
Teachers: 837.0 (14.2 to 1)
Librarians/Media Specialists: 11.0 (1,082.1 to 1)
Guidance Counselors: 34.0 (350.1 to 1)
Current Spending: ($ per student per year):
Total: $7,679; Instruction: $4,477; Support Services: $2,752
Enrollment, Drop-out Rates and Diploma Recipients by Race/Ethnicity

Category	Total	White	Black	Asian	AIAN	Hisp.
Enrollment (%)	100.0	88.5	10.2	0.8	0.1	0.4
Drop-out Rate (%)	4.5	4.1	8.0	0.0	0.0	11.1
H.S. Diplomas (#)	728	653	66	6	2	1

Randolph County

Randolph County SD
40 11th St • Elkins, WV 26241-3512
(304) 636-9150
Grade Span: PK-12; **Agency Type:** 1
Schools: 16
9 Primary; 1 Middle; 2 High; 4 Other Level
14 Regular; 0 Special Education; 1 Vocational; 1 Alternative
0 Magnet; 0 Charter; 11 Title I Eligible; 5 School-wide Title I
Students: 4,591 (51.5% male; 48.5% female)
Individual Education Program: 745 (16.2%);
English Language Learner: 0 (0.0%); Migrant: 0 (0.0%)
Eligible for Free Lunch Program: 1,836 (40.0%)
Eligible for Reduced-Price Lunch Program: 758 (16.5%)
Teachers: 341.0 (13.5 to 1)
Librarians/Media Specialists: 3.0 (1,530.3 to 1)
Guidance Counselors: 13.0 (353.2 to 1)
Current Spending: ($ per student per year):
Total: $6,719; Instruction: $4,414; Support Services: $1,919
Enrollment, Drop-out Rates and Diploma Recipients by Race/Ethnicity

Category	Total	White	Black	Asian	AIAN	Hisp.
Enrollment (%)	100.0	99.0	0.5	0.4	0.1	0.1
Drop-out Rate (%)	2.5	2.6	0.0	0.0	0.0	0.0
H.S. Diplomas (#)	273	264	3	3	1	2

Ritchie County

Ritchie County SD
134 S Penn Ave • Harrisville, WV 26362-1370
(304) 643-2991
Grade Span: PK-12; **Agency Type:** 1
Schools: 6
4 Primary; 1 Middle; 1 High; 0 Other Level
6 Regular; 0 Special Education; 0 Vocational; 0 Alternative
0 Magnet; 0 Charter; 4 Title I Eligible; 3 School-wide Title I
Students: 1,687 (50.9% male; 49.1% female)
Individual Education Program: 321 (19.0%);
English Language Learner: 0 (0.0%); Migrant: 0 (0.0%)
Eligible for Free Lunch Program: 677 (40.1%)
Eligible for Reduced-Price Lunch Program: 237 (14.0%)
Teachers: 114.0 (14.8 to 1)
Librarians/Media Specialists: 1.0 (1,687.0 to 1)
Guidance Counselors: 2.0 (843.5 to 1)
Current Spending: ($ per student per year):
Total: $7,749; Instruction: $4,800; Support Services: $2,440
Enrollment, Drop-out Rates and Diploma Recipients by Race/Ethnicity

Category	Total	White	Black	Asian	AIAN	Hisp.
Enrollment (%)	100.0	98.7	0.2	0.2	0.1	0.9
Drop-out Rate (%)	3.8	3.8	n/a	0.0	n/a	0.0
H.S. Diplomas (#)	113	113	0	0	0	0

Roane County

Roane County SD
Bowman St • Spencer, WV 25276-0609
Mailing Address: PO Box 609 • Spencer, WV 25276-0609
(304) 927-6400 • http://boe.roan.k12.wv.us/
Grade Span: PK-12; **Agency Type:** 1
Schools: 6
4 Primary; 1 Middle; 1 High; 0 Other Level
6 Regular; 0 Special Education; 0 Vocational; 0 Alternative
0 Magnet; 0 Charter; 5 Title I Eligible; 5 School-wide Title I
Students: 2,604 (53.4% male; 46.6% female)
Individual Education Program: 582 (22.4%);
English Language Learner: 2 (0.1%); Migrant: 0 (0.0%)
Eligible for Free Lunch Program: 1,271 (48.8%)
Eligible for Reduced-Price Lunch Program: 388 (14.9%)
Teachers: 187.7 (13.9 to 1)
Librarians/Media Specialists: 2.0 (1,302.0 to 1)
Guidance Counselors: 4.5 (578.7 to 1)
Current Spending: ($ per student per year):
Total: $6,785; Instruction: $4,037; Support Services: $2,115
Enrollment, Drop-out Rates and Diploma Recipients by Race/Ethnicity

Category	Total	White	Black	Asian	AIAN	Hisp.
Enrollment (%)	100.0	98.5	0.6	0.4	0.0	0.5
Drop-out Rate (%)	5.2	5.3	n/a	0.0	0.0	0.0
H.S. Diplomas (#)	174	172	0	1	0	1

Summers County

Summers County SD

116 Main St • Hinton, WV 25951-2439
(304) 466-6000
Grade Span: PK-12; **Agency Type:** 1
Schools: 5
3 Primary; 1 Middle; 1 High; 0 Other Level
5 Regular; 0 Special Education; 0 Vocational; 0 Alternative
0 Magnet; 0 Charter; 3 Title I Eligible; 3 School-wide Title I
Students: 1,624 (49.5% male; 50.5% female)
Individual Education Program: 378 (23.3%);
English Language Learner: 0 (0.0%); Migrant: 0 (0.0%)
Eligible for Free Lunch Program: 853 (52.5%)
Eligible for Reduced-Price Lunch Program: 200 (12.3%)
Teachers: 107.5 (15.1 to 1)
Librarians/Media Specialists: 1.0 (1,624.0 to 1)
Guidance Counselors: 4.0 (406.0 to 1)
Current Spending: ($ per student per year):
Total: $7,187; Instruction: $4,359; Support Services: $2,376
Enrollment, Drop-out Rates and Diploma Recipients by Race/Ethnicity

Category	Total	White	Black	Asian	AIAN	Hisp.
Enrollment (%)	100.0	95.2	3.9	0.2	0.2	0.4
Drop-out Rate (%)	3.4	3.5	0.0	0.0	0.0	0.0
H.S. Diplomas (#)	97	92	5	0	0	0

Taylor County

Taylor County SD

306 Beech St • Grafton, WV 26354-1836
(304) 265-2497 • http://www.wvonline.com/taylorcounty/index.htm
Grade Span: PK-12; **Agency Type:** 1
Schools: 7
4 Primary; 1 Middle; 2 High; 0 Other Level
6 Regular; 0 Special Education; 1 Vocational; 0 Alternative
0 Magnet; 0 Charter; 4 Title I Eligible; 1 School-wide Title I
Students: 2,445 (51.7% male; 48.3% female)
Individual Education Program: 460 (18.8%);
English Language Learner: 0 (0.0%); Migrant: 0 (0.0%)
Eligible for Free Lunch Program: 1,005 (41.1%)
Eligible for Reduced-Price Lunch Program: 267 (10.9%)
Teachers: 161.5 (15.1 to 1)
Librarians/Media Specialists: 4.0 (611.3 to 1)
Guidance Counselors: 5.5 (444.5 to 1)
Current Spending: ($ per student per year):
Total: $7,295; Instruction: $4,331; Support Services: $2,585
Enrollment, Drop-out Rates and Diploma Recipients by Race/Ethnicity

Category	Total	White	Black	Asian	AIAN	Hisp.
Enrollment (%)	100.0	98.4	0.9	0.4	0.1	0.2
Drop-out Rate (%)	1.3	1.3	0.0	0.0	n/a	0.0
H.S. Diplomas (#)	143	139	1	3	0	0

Tyler County

Tyler County SD

1993 Silver Knight St • Sistersville, WV 26175-0025
Mailing Address: PO Box 25 • Middlebourne, WV 26149-0025
(304) 758-2145
Grade Span: PK-12; **Agency Type:** 1
Schools: 4
2 Primary; 1 Middle; 1 High; 0 Other Level
4 Regular; 0 Special Education; 0 Vocational; 0 Alternative
0 Magnet; 0 Charter; 3 Title I Eligible; 0 School-wide Title I
Students: 1,544 (49.7% male; 50.3% female)
Individual Education Program: 342 (22.2%);
English Language Learner: 0 (0.0%); Migrant: 0 (0.0%)
Eligible for Free Lunch Program: 631 (40.9%)
Eligible for Reduced-Price Lunch Program: 172 (11.1%)
Teachers: 116.0 (13.3 to 1)
Librarians/Media Specialists: 2.0 (772.0 to 1)
Guidance Counselors: 4.0 (386.0 to 1)
Current Spending: ($ per student per year):
Total: $7,810; Instruction: $4,578; Support Services: $2,621
Enrollment, Drop-out Rates and Diploma Recipients by Race/Ethnicity

Category	Total	White	Black	Asian	AIAN	Hisp.
Enrollment (%)	100.0	99.4	0.5	0.1	0.0	0.1
Drop-out Rate (%)	1.9	1.8	n/a	n/a	n/a	0.0
H.S. Diplomas (#)	100	98	0	0	0	2

Upshur County

Upshur County SD

102 Smithfield St • Buckhannon, WV 26201-2620
(304) 472-5480
Grade Span: PK-12; **Agency Type:** 1
Schools: 12
9 Primary; 1 Middle; 2 High; 0 Other Level
11 Regular; 0 Special Education; 1 Vocational; 0 Alternative
0 Magnet; 0 Charter; 7 Title I Eligible; 7 School-wide Title I
Students: 3,904 (51.2% male; 48.8% female)
Individual Education Program: 748 (19.2%);
English Language Learner: 0 (0.0%); Migrant: 0 (0.0%)
Eligible for Free Lunch Program: 1,578 (40.4%)
Eligible for Reduced-Price Lunch Program: 459 (11.8%)
Teachers: 288.0 (13.6 to 1)
Librarians/Media Specialists: 2.0 (1,952.0 to 1)
Guidance Counselors: 10.0 (390.4 to 1)
Current Spending: ($ per student per year):
Total: $7,266; Instruction: $4,445; Support Services: $2,400
Enrollment, Drop-out Rates and Diploma Recipients by Race/Ethnicity

Category	Total	White	Black	Asian	AIAN	Hisp.
Enrollment (%)	100.0	98.5	0.8	0.3	0.1	0.3
Drop-out Rate (%)	4.9	5.0	0.0	0.0	0.0	0.0
H.S. Diplomas (#)	244	241	1	2	0	0

Wayne County

Wayne County SD

212 N Court St • Wayne, WV 25570-0070
Mailing Address: PO Box 70 • Wayne, WV 25570-0070
(304) 272-5116
Grade Span: PK-12; **Agency Type:** 1
Schools: 22
12 Primary; 6 Middle; 4 High; 0 Other Level
21 Regular; 0 Special Education; 1 Vocational; 0 Alternative
0 Magnet; 0 Charter; 12 Title I Eligible; 11 School-wide Title I
Students: 7,409 (52.7% male; 47.3% female)
Individual Education Program: 1,455 (19.6%);
English Language Learner: 7 (0.1%); Migrant: 0 (0.0%)
Eligible for Free Lunch Program: 3,213 (43.4%)
Eligible for Reduced-Price Lunch Program: 781 (10.5%)
Teachers: 539.2 (13.7 to 1)
Librarians/Media Specialists: 9.0 (823.2 to 1)
Guidance Counselors: 12.8 (578.8 to 1)
Current Spending: ($ per student per year):
Total: $7,258; Instruction: $4,519; Support Services: $2,341
Enrollment, Drop-out Rates and Diploma Recipients by Race/Ethnicity

Category	Total	White	Black	Asian	AIAN	Hisp.
Enrollment (%)	100.0	99.2	0.3	0.3	0.1	0.2
Drop-out Rate (%)	4.2	4.3	0.0	0.0	n/a	0.0
H.S. Diplomas (#)	395	391	0	3	0	1

Webster County

Webster County SD

315 S Main St • Webster Springs, WV 26288-1187
(304) 847-5638 • http://glade.webs.k12.wv.us/WebsterBdOff.htm
Grade Span: PK-12; **Agency Type:** 1
Schools: 5
4 Primary; 0 Middle; 1 High; 0 Other Level
5 Regular; 0 Special Education; 0 Vocational; 0 Alternative
0 Magnet; 0 Charter; 3 Title I Eligible; 3 School-wide Title I
Students: 1,718 (51.5% male; 48.5% female)
Individual Education Program: 323 (18.8%);
English Language Learner: 0 (0.0%); Migrant: 0 (0.0%)
Eligible for Free Lunch Program: 1,005 (58.5%)
Eligible for Reduced-Price Lunch Program: 190 (11.1%)
Teachers: 131.8 (13.0 to 1)
Librarians/Media Specialists: 1.0 (1,718.0 to 1)
Guidance Counselors: 3.5 (490.9 to 1)
Current Spending: ($ per student per year):
Total: $7,377; Instruction: $4,674; Support Services: $2,298
Enrollment, Drop-out Rates and Diploma Recipients by Race/Ethnicity

Category	Total	White	Black	Asian	AIAN	Hisp.
Enrollment (%)	100.0	99.7	0.2	0.0	0.0	0.1
Drop-out Rate (%)	3.4	3.4	n/a	0.0	n/a	n/a
H.S. Diplomas (#)	115	115	0	0	0	0

Wetzel County

Wetzel County SD

333 Foundry St • New Martinsville, WV 26155-1141
(304) 455-2441
Grade Span: PK-12; **Agency Type:** 1
Schools: 9
5 Primary; 0 Middle; 4 High; 0 Other Level
9 Regular; 0 Special Education; 0 Vocational; 0 Alternative
0 Magnet; 0 Charter; 4 Title I Eligible; 3 School-wide Title I
Students: 3,415 (50.8% male; 49.2% female)
Individual Education Program: 670 (19.6%);
English Language Learner: 13 (0.4%); Migrant: 0 (0.0%)
Eligible for Free Lunch Program: 1,237 (36.2%)
Eligible for Reduced-Price Lunch Program: 289 (8.5%)
Teachers: 238.5 (14.3 to 1)
Librarians/Media Specialists: 4.5 (758.9 to 1)
Guidance Counselors: 8.0 (426.9 to 1)
Current Spending: ($ per student per year):
Total: $7,210; Instruction: $4,428; Support Services: $2,446

Enrollment, Drop-out Rates and Diploma Recipients by Race/Ethnicity

Category	Total	White	Black	Asian	AIAN	Hisp.
Enrollment (%)	100.0	98.4	0.7	0.7	0.0	0.1
Drop-out Rate (%)	2.9	2.9	n/a	0.0	n/a	n/a
H.S. Diplomas (#)	223	222	0	0	0	1

Wood County

Wood County SD

1210 13th St • Parkersburg, WV 26101-4144
(304) 420-9663 • http://www.netassoc.net/wcboe/
Grade Span: PK-12; **Agency Type:** 1
Schools: 29
19 Primary; 5 Middle; 4 High; 1 Other Level
27 Regular; 1 Special Education; 1 Vocational; 0 Alternative
0 Magnet; 0 Charter; 9 Title I Eligible; 9 School-wide Title I
Students: 13,753 (51.1% male; 48.9% female)
Individual Education Program: 2,035 (14.8%);
English Language Learner: 28 (0.2%); Migrant: 0 (0.0%)
Eligible for Free Lunch Program: 4,326 (31.5%)
Eligible for Reduced-Price Lunch Program: 997 (7.2%)
Teachers: 914.5 (15.0 to 1)
Librarians/Media Specialists: 25.0 (550.1 to 1)
Guidance Counselors: 24.0 (573.0 to 1)
Current Spending: ($ per student per year):
Total: $7,404; Instruction: $4,543; Support Services: $2,443

Enrollment, Drop-out Rates and Diploma Recipients by Race/Ethnicity

Category	Total	White	Black	Asian	AIAN	Hisp.
Enrollment (%)	100.0	97.2	1.8	0.6	0.1	0.3
Drop-out Rate (%)	4.0	4.1	0.0	0.0	0.0	12.5
H.S. Diplomas (#)	778	757	9	8	1	3

Wyoming County

Wyoming County SD

Main St • Pineville, WV 24874-0069
Mailing Address: PO Box 69 • Pineville, WV 24874-0069
(304) 732-6262
Grade Span: PK-12; **Agency Type:** 1
Schools: 14
8 Primary; 3 Middle; 3 High; 0 Other Level
13 Regular; 0 Special Education; 1 Vocational; 0 Alternative
0 Magnet; 0 Charter; 11 Title I Eligible; 6 School-wide Title I
Students: 4,261 (52.5% male; 47.5% female)
Individual Education Program: 747 (17.5%);
English Language Learner: 0 (0.0%); Migrant: 0 (0.0%)
Eligible for Free Lunch Program: 2,202 (51.7%)
Eligible for Reduced-Price Lunch Program: 515 (12.1%)
Teachers: 340.5 (12.5 to 1)
Librarians/Media Specialists: 2.0 (2,130.5 to 1)
Guidance Counselors: 7.0 (608.7 to 1)
Current Spending: ($ per student per year):
Total: $8,340; Instruction: $5,398; Support Services: $2,249

Enrollment, Drop-out Rates and Diploma Recipients by Race/Ethnicity

Category	Total	White	Black	Asian	AIAN	Hisp.
Enrollment (%)	100.0	98.3	1.3	0.1	0.1	0.2
Drop-out Rate (%)	3.9	4.0	0.0	0.0	n/a	0.0
H.S. Diplomas (#)	309	306	2	1	0	0

Number of Schools

Rank	Number	District Name	City
1	72	Kanawha County SD	Charleston
2	34	Raleigh County SD	Beckley
3	31	Cabell County SD	Huntington
4	30	Berkeley County SD	Martinsburg
4	30	Harrison County SD	Clarksburg
6	29	Wood County SD	Parkersburg
7	27	Fayette County SD	Fayetteville
7	27	Mercer County SD	Princeton
9	25	Monongalia SD	Morgantown
10	23	Marion County SD	Fairmont
11	22	Putnam County SD	Winfield
11	22	Wayne County SD	Wayne
13	19	Boone County SD	Madison
14	18	Logan County SD	Logan
14	18	Mcdowell County SD	Welch
14	18	Mingo County SD	Williamson
17	16	Marshall County SD	Moundsville
17	16	Mason County SD	Point Pleasant
17	16	Nicholas County SD	Summersville
17	16	Randolph County SD	Elkins
21	14	Greenbrier County SD	Lewisburg
21	14	Mineral County SD	Keyser
21	14	Wyoming County SD	Pineville
24	13	Jackson County SD	Ripley
24	13	Jefferson County SD	Charles Town
24	13	Ohio County SD	Wheeling
27	12	Brooke County SD	Wellsburg
27	12	Lincoln County SD	Hamlin
27	12	Preston County SD	Kingwood
27	12	Upshur County SD	Buckhannon
31	11	Hampshire County SD	Romney
31	11	Hancock County SD	New Cumberland
33	9	Barbour County SD	Philippi
33	9	Morgan County SD	Berkeley Spgs
33	9	Wetzel County SD	New Martinsville
36	8	Braxton County SD	Sutton
37	7	Clay County SD	Clay
37	7	Lewis County SD	Weston
37	7	Taylor County SD	Grafton
40	6	Grant County SD	Petersburg
40	6	Ritchie County SD	Harrisville
40	6	Roane County SD	Spencer
43	5	Hardy County SD	Moorefield
43	5	Monroe County SD	Union
43	5	Summers County SD	Hinton
43	5	Webster County SD	Webster Spgs
47	4	Tyler County SD	Sistersville

Number of Teachers

Rank	Number	District Name	City
1	1,928	Kanawha County SD	Charleston
2	997	Berkeley County SD	Martinsburg
3	914	Wood County SD	Parkersburg
4	846	Cabell County SD	Huntington
5	837	Raleigh County SD	Beckley
6	766	Harrison County SD	Clarksburg
7	700	Monongalia SD	Morgantown
8	685	Mercer County SD	Princeton
9	615	Marion County SD	Fairmont
10	594	Putnam County SD	Winfield
11	541	Fayette County SD	Fayetteville
12	539	Wayne County SD	Wayne
13	487	Jefferson County SD	Charles Town
14	447	Logan County SD	Logan
15	386	Ohio County SD	Wheeling
16	372	Boone County SD	Madison
17	371	Greenbrier County SD	Lewisburg
18	365	Marshall County SD	Moundsville
19	347	Jackson County SD	Ripley
20	344	Mingo County SD	Williamson
21	344	Mcdowell County SD	Welch
22	341	Randolph County SD	Elkins
23	340	Wyoming County SD	Pineville
24	330	Nicholas County SD	Summersville
25	330	Preston County SD	Kingwood
26	318	Mineral County SD	Keyser
27	316	Mason County SD	Point Pleasant
28	299	Hancock County SD	New Cumberland
29	292	Lincoln County SD	Hamlin
30	288	Upshur County SD	Buckhannon
31	261	Brooke County SD	Wellsburg
32	244	Hampshire County SD	Romney
33	238	Wetzel County SD	New Martinsville
34	198	Lewis County SD	Weston
35	194	Braxton County SD	Sutton
36	187	Roane County SD	Spencer
37	185	Barbour County SD	Philippi
38	172	Morgan County SD	Berkeley Spgs
39	161	Taylor County SD	Grafton
40	159	Clay County SD	Clay
41	159	Hardy County SD	Moorefield
42	151	Grant County SD	Petersburg
43	150	Monroe County SD	Union
44	131	Webster County SD	Webster Spgs
45	116	Tyler County SD	Sistersville
46	114	Ritchie County SD	Harrisville
47	107	Summers County SD	Hinton

Number of Students

Rank	Number	District Name	City
1	28,417	Kanawha County SD	Charleston
2	13,772	Berkeley County SD	Martinsburg
3	13,753	Wood County SD	Parkersburg
4	12,294	Cabell County SD	Huntington
5	11,903	Raleigh County SD	Beckley
6	11,580	Harrison County SD	Clarksburg
7	10,280	Monongalia SD	Morgantown
8	9,567	Mercer County SD	Princeton
9	8,746	Putnam County SD	Winfield
10	8,254	Marion County SD	Fairmont
11	7,409	Wayne County SD	Wayne
12	7,274	Jefferson County SD	Charles Town
13	6,972	Fayette County SD	Fayetteville
14	6,087	Logan County SD	Logan
15	5,552	Ohio County SD	Wheeling
16	5,375	Marshall County SD	Moundsville
17	5,359	Greenbrier County SD	Lewisburg
18	5,038	Jackson County SD	Ripley
19	4,830	Preston County SD	Kingwood
20	4,775	Mingo County SD	Williamson
21	4,609	Mineral County SD	Keyser
22	4,591	Randolph County SD	Elkins
23	4,531	Boone County SD	Madison
24	4,469	Mcdowell County SD	Welch
25	4,374	Hancock County SD	New Cumberland
26	4,331	Nicholas County SD	Summersville
27	4,267	Mason County SD	Point Pleasant
28	4,261	Wyoming County SD	Pineville
29	3,904	Upshur County SD	Buckhannon
30	3,873	Lincoln County SD	Hamlin
31	3,637	Brooke County SD	Wellsburg
32	3,560	Hampshire County SD	Romney
33	3,415	Wetzel County SD	New Martinsville
34	2,743	Lewis County SD	Weston
35	2,604	Barbour County SD	Philippi
35	2,604	Roane County SD	Spencer
37	2,587	Braxton County SD	Sutton
38	2,557	Morgan County SD	Berkeley Spgs
39	2,445	Taylor County SD	Grafton
40	2,313	Hardy County SD	Moorefield
41	2,144	Clay County SD	Clay
42	2,116	Monroe County SD	Union
43	1,978	Grant County SD	Petersburg
44	1,718	Webster County SD	Webster Spgs
45	1,687	Ritchie County SD	Harrisville
46	1,624	Summers County SD	Hinton
47	1,544	Tyler County SD	Sistersville

Male Students

Rank	Percent	District Name	City
1	53.5	Fayette County SD	Fayetteville
2	53.4	Roane County SD	Spencer
3	53.3	Mason County SD	Point Pleasant
4	53.1	Barbour County SD	Philippi
5	52.7	Jackson County SD	Ripley
5	52.7	Wayne County SD	Wayne
7	52.5	Lincoln County SD	Hamlin
7	52.5	Mcdowell County SD	Welch
7	52.5	Nicholas County SD	Summersville
7	52.5	Wyoming County SD	Pineville
11	52.3	Boone County SD	Madison
11	52.3	Hampshire County SD	Romney
11	52.3	Lewis County SD	Weston
14	52.2	Greenbrier County SD	Lewisburg
14	52.2	Putnam County SD	Winfield
16	52.1	Hancock County SD	New Cumberland
17	52.0	Raleigh County SD	Beckley
18	51.9	Monongalia SD	Morgantown
18	51.9	Ohio County SD	Wheeling
20	51.8	Kanawha County SD	Charleston
20	51.8	Morgan County SD	Berkeley Spgs
22	51.7	Cabell County SD	Huntington
22	51.7	Jefferson County SD	Charles Town
22	51.7	Mercer County SD	Princeton
22	51.7	Mingo County SD	Williamson
22	51.7	Taylor County SD	Grafton
27	51.6	Marshall County SD	Moundsville
28	51.5	Logan County SD	Logan
28	51.5	Marion County SD	Fairmont
28	51.5	Monroe County SD	Union
28	51.5	Randolph County SD	Elkins
28	51.5	Webster County SD	Webster Spgs
33	51.2	Hardy County SD	Moorefield
33	51.2	Harrison County SD	Clarksburg
33	51.2	Upshur County SD	Buckhannon
36	51.1	Preston County SD	Kingwood
36	51.1	Wood County SD	Parkersburg
38	51.0	Berkeley County SD	Martinsburg
38	51.0	Mineral County SD	Keyser
40	50.9	Grant County SD	Petersburg
40	50.9	Ritchie County SD	Harrisville
42	50.8	Brooke County SD	Wellsburg
42	50.8	Wetzel County SD	New Martinsville
44	50.3	Clay County SD	Clay
45	50.1	Braxton County SD	Sutton
46	49.7	Tyler County SD	Sistersville
47	49.5	Summers County SD	Hinton

Female Students

Rank	Percent	District Name	City
1	50.5	Summers County SD	Hinton
2	50.3	Tyler County SD	Sistersville
3	49.9	Braxton County SD	Sutton
4	49.7	Clay County SD	Clay
5	49.2	Brooke County SD	Wellsburg
5	49.2	Wetzel County SD	New Martinsville
7	49.1	Grant County SD	Petersburg
7	49.1	Ritchie County SD	Harrisville
9	49.0	Berkeley County SD	Martinsburg
9	49.0	Mineral County SD	Keyser
11	48.9	Preston County SD	Kingwood
11	48.9	Wood County SD	Parkersburg
13	48.8	Hardy County SD	Moorefield
13	48.8	Harrison County SD	Clarksburg
13	48.8	Upshur County SD	Buckhannon
16	48.5	Logan County SD	Logan
16	48.5	Marion County SD	Fairmont
16	48.5	Monroe County SD	Union
16	48.5	Randolph County SD	Elkins
16	48.5	Webster County SD	Webster Spgs
21	48.4	Marshall County SD	Moundsville
22	48.3	Cabell County SD	Huntington
22	48.3	Jefferson County SD	Charles Town
22	48.3	Mercer County SD	Princeton
22	48.3	Mingo County SD	Williamson
22	48.3	Taylor County SD	Grafton
27	48.2	Kanawha County SD	Charleston
27	48.2	Morgan County SD	Berkeley Spgs
29	48.1	Monongalia SD	Morgantown
29	48.1	Ohio County SD	Wheeling
31	48.0	Raleigh County SD	Beckley
32	47.9	Hancock County SD	New Cumberland
33	47.8	Greenbrier County SD	Lewisburg
33	47.8	Putnam County SD	Winfield
35	47.7	Boone County SD	Madison
35	47.7	Hampshire County SD	Romney
35	47.7	Lewis County SD	Weston
38	47.5	Lincoln County SD	Hamlin
38	47.5	Mcdowell County SD	Welch
38	47.5	Nicholas County SD	Summersville
38	47.5	Wyoming County SD	Pineville
42	47.3	Jackson County SD	Ripley
42	47.3	Wayne County SD	Wayne
44	46.9	Barbour County SD	Philippi
45	46.7	Mason County SD	Point Pleasant
46	46.6	Roane County SD	Spencer
47	46.5	Fayette County SD	Fayetteville

Individual Education Program Students

Rank	Percent	District Name	City
1	23.3	Summers County SD	Hinton
2	22.4	Roane County SD	Spencer
3	22.2	Tyler County SD	Sistersville
4	21.6	Lewis County SD	Weston
5	21.5	Lincoln County SD	Hamlin
6	21.0	Greenbrier County SD	Lewisburg
7	20.8	Nicholas County SD	Summersville
8	20.5	Marshall County SD	Moundsville
9	20.4	Grant County SD	Petersburg
9	20.4	Mason County SD	Point Pleasant
11	20.1	Braxton County SD	Sutton
12	20.0	Boone County SD	Madison
13	19.9	Hardy County SD	Moorefield
13	19.9	Mcdowell County SD	Welch
15	19.6	Wayne County SD	Wayne
15	19.6	Wetzel County SD	New Martinsville
17	19.4	Brooke County SD	Wellsburg
17	19.4	Preston County SD	Kingwood
19	19.2	Barbour County SD	Philippi
19	19.2	Upshur County SD	Buckhannon
21	19.1	Mingo County SD	Williamson

Rank	Percent	District Name	City
22	19.0	Hampshire County SD	Romney
22	19.0	Ritchie County SD	Harrisville
24	18.9	Monroe County SD	Union
25	18.8	Taylor County SD	Grafton
25	18.8	Webster County SD	Webster Spgs
27	18.7	Clay County SD	Clay
27	18.7	Putnam County SD	Winfield
29	17.5	Jackson County SD	Ripley
29	17.5	Wyoming County SD	Pineville
31	17.4	Cabell County SD	Huntington
31	17.4	Mineral County SD	Keyser
33	17.3	Hancock County SD	New Cumberland
34	17.0	Berkeley County SD	Martinsburg
34	17.0	Harrison County SD	Clarksburg
36	16.8	Logan County SD	Logan
36	16.8	Mercer County SD	Princeton
38	16.5	Morgan County SD	Berkeley Spgs
39	16.3	Jefferson County SD	Charles Town
39	16.3	Kanawha County SD	Charleston
39	16.3	Raleigh County SD	Beckley
42	16.2	Randolph County SD	Elkins
43	15.9	Fayette County SD	Fayetteville
43	15.9	Marion County SD	Fairmont
43	15.9	Ohio County SD	Wheeling
46	15.2	Monongalia SD	Morgantown
47	14.8	Wood County SD	Parkersburg

English Language Learner Students

Rank	Percent	District Name	City
1	4.4	Monongalia SD	Morgantown
2	1.4	Jefferson County SD	Charles Town
3	1.1	Berkeley County SD	Martinsburg
3	1.1	Kanawha County SD	Charleston
5	0.5	Cabell County SD	Huntington
6	0.4	Ohio County SD	Wheeling
6	0.4	Wetzel County SD	New Martinsville
8	0.3	Hardy County SD	Moorefield
8	0.3	Jackson County SD	Ripley
8	0.3	Raleigh County SD	Beckley
11	0.2	Mineral County SD	Keyser
11	0.2	Wood County SD	Parkersburg
13	0.1	Barbour County SD	Philippi
13	0.1	Fayette County SD	Fayetteville
13	0.1	Hampshire County SD	Romney
13	0.1	Lewis County SD	Weston
13	0.1	Logan County SD	Logan
13	0.1	Marion County SD	Fairmont
13	0.1	Putnam County SD	Winfield
13	0.1	Roane County SD	Spencer
13	0.1	Wayne County SD	Wayne
22	0.0	Harrison County SD	Clarksburg
22	0.0	Mason County SD	Point Pleasant
22	0.0	Mercer County SD	Princeton
22	0.0	Mingo County SD	Williamson
22	0.0	Morgan County SD	Berkeley Spgs
22	0.0	Nicholas County SD	Summersville
22	0.0	Preston County SD	Kingwood
29	0.0	Boone County SD	Madison
29	0.0	Braxton County SD	Sutton
29	0.0	Brooke County SD	Wellsburg
29	0.0	Clay County SD	Clay
29	0.0	Grant County SD	Petersburg
29	0.0	Greenbrier County SD	Lewisburg
29	0.0	Hancock County SD	New Cumberland
29	0.0	Lincoln County SD	Hamlin
29	0.0	Marshall County SD	Moundsville
29	0.0	Mcdowell County SD	Welch
29	0.0	Monroe County SD	Union
29	0.0	Randolph County SD	Elkins
29	0.0	Ritchie County SD	Harrisville
29	0.0	Summers County SD	Hinton
29	0.0	Taylor County SD	Grafton
29	0.0	Tyler County SD	Sistersville
29	0.0	Upshur County SD	Buckhannon
29	0.0	Webster County SD	Webster Spgs
29	0.0	Wyoming County SD	Pineville

Migrant Students

Rank	Percent	District Name	City
1	3.6	Morgan County SD	Berkeley Spgs
2	1.3	Hardy County SD	Moorefield
3	0.2	Jefferson County SD	Charles Town
4	0.0	Berkeley County SD	Martinsburg
4	0.0	Lewis County SD	Weston
6	0.0	Barbour County SD	Philippi
6	0.0	Boone County SD	Madison
6	0.0	Braxton County SD	Sutton
6	0.0	Brooke County SD	Wellsburg
6	0.0	Cabell County SD	Huntington
6	0.0	Clay County SD	Clay
6	0.0	Fayette County SD	Fayetteville
6	0.0	Grant County SD	Petersburg
6	0.0	Greenbrier County SD	Lewisburg
6	0.0	Hampshire County SD	Romney
6	0.0	Hancock County SD	New Cumberland
6	0.0	Harrison County SD	Clarksburg
6	0.0	Jackson County SD	Ripley
6	0.0	Kanawha County SD	Charleston
6	0.0	Lincoln County SD	Hamlin
6	0.0	Logan County SD	Logan
6	0.0	Marion County SD	Fairmont
6	0.0	Marshall County SD	Moundsville
6	0.0	Mason County SD	Point Pleasant
6	0.0	Mcdowell County SD	Welch
6	0.0	Mercer County SD	Princeton
6	0.0	Mineral County SD	Keyser
6	0.0	Mingo County SD	Williamson
6	0.0	Monongalia SD	Morgantown
6	0.0	Monroe County SD	Union
6	0.0	Nicholas County SD	Summersville
6	0.0	Ohio County SD	Wheeling
6	0.0	Preston County SD	Kingwood
6	0.0	Putnam County SD	Winfield
6	0.0	Raleigh County SD	Beckley
6	0.0	Randolph County SD	Elkins
6	0.0	Ritchie County SD	Harrisville
6	0.0	Roane County SD	Spencer
6	0.0	Summers County SD	Hinton
6	0.0	Taylor County SD	Grafton
6	0.0	Tyler County SD	Sistersville
6	0.0	Upshur County SD	Buckhannon
6	0.0	Wayne County SD	Wayne
6	0.0	Webster County SD	Webster Spgs
6	0.0	Wetzel County SD	New Martinsville
6	0.0	Wood County SD	Parkersburg
6	0.0	Wyoming County SD	Pineville

Students Eligible for Free Lunch

Rank	Percent	District Name	City
1	70.7	Mcdowell County SD	Welch
2	62.4	Clay County SD	Clay
3	58.5	Webster County SD	Webster Spgs
4	56.2	Mingo County SD	Williamson
5	53.3	Lincoln County SD	Hamlin
6	52.5	Summers County SD	Hinton
7	51.7	Wyoming County SD	Pineville
8	51.0	Barbour County SD	Philippi
9	48.8	Roane County SD	Spencer
10	47.2	Braxton County SD	Sutton
10	47.2	Nicholas County SD	Summersville
12	46.9	Fayette County SD	Fayetteville
13	44.5	Logan County SD	Logan
14	44.4	Mercer County SD	Princeton
15	43.4	Wayne County SD	Wayne
16	42.7	Lewis County SD	Weston
17	41.1	Taylor County SD	Grafton
18	40.9	Tyler County SD	Sistersville
19	40.4	Upshur County SD	Buckhannon
20	40.1	Ritchie County SD	Harrisville
21	40.0	Preston County SD	Kingwood
21	40.0	Randolph County SD	Elkins
23	39.7	Mason County SD	Point Pleasant
24	39.4	Raleigh County SD	Beckley
25	38.7	Greenbrier County SD	Lewisburg
26	38.2	Harrison County SD	Clarksburg
27	37.7	Boone County SD	Madison
27	37.7	Cabell County SD	Huntington
29	37.5	Monroe County SD	Union
30	36.2	Wetzel County SD	New Martinsville
31	35.8	Hardy County SD	Moorefield
32	35.7	Marion County SD	Fairmont
33	35.4	Hampshire County SD	Romney
34	35.1	Kanawha County SD	Charleston
35	34.9	Marshall County SD	Moundsville
36	34.6	Jackson County SD	Ripley
37	34.4	Ohio County SD	Wheeling
38	33.8	Grant County SD	Petersburg
39	31.6	Mineral County SD	Keyser
40	31.5	Wood County SD	Parkersburg
41	28.2	Monongalia SD	Morgantown
41	28.2	Morgan County SD	Berkeley Spgs
43	25.5	Berkeley County SD	Martinsburg
44	23.9	Brooke County SD	Wellsburg
45	23.5	Hancock County SD	New Cumberland
46	23.0	Putnam County SD	Winfield
47	22.1	Jefferson County SD	Charles Town

Students Eligible for Reduced-Price Lunch

Rank	Percent	District Name	City
1	17.7	Hardy County SD	Moorefield
2	16.5	Randolph County SD	Elkins
3	15.7	Hampshire County SD	Romney
3	15.7	Preston County SD	Kingwood
5	15.6	Grant County SD	Petersburg
5	15.6	Monroe County SD	Union
7	14.9	Roane County SD	Spencer
8	14.6	Greenbrier County SD	Lewisburg
9	14.1	Morgan County SD	Berkeley Spgs
10	14.0	Ritchie County SD	Harrisville
11	13.5	Barbour County SD	Philippi
12	13.2	Clay County SD	Clay
13	12.7	Mineral County SD	Keyser
14	12.3	Summers County SD	Hinton
15	12.2	Lewis County SD	Weston
16	12.1	Wyoming County SD	Pineville
17	11.8	Nicholas County SD	Summersville
17	11.8	Upshur County SD	Buckhannon
19	11.3	Lincoln County SD	Hamlin
20	11.1	Tyler County SD	Sistersville
20	11.1	Webster County SD	Webster Spgs
22	11.0	Mason County SD	Point Pleasant
23	10.9	Braxton County SD	Sutton
23	10.9	Mcdowell County SD	Welch
23	10.9	Taylor County SD	Grafton
26	10.7	Berkeley County SD	Martinsburg
27	10.5	Mingo County SD	Williamson
27	10.5	Wayne County SD	Wayne
29	10.4	Mercer County SD	Princeton
30	10.3	Marshall County SD	Moundsville
31	10.1	Harrison County SD	Clarksburg
32	10.0	Cabell County SD	Huntington
32	10.0	Jefferson County SD	Charles Town
32	10.0	Raleigh County SD	Beckley
35	9.7	Fayette County SD	Fayetteville
36	9.5	Logan County SD	Logan
37	9.0	Brooke County SD	Wellsburg
38	8.9	Jackson County SD	Ripley
39	8.8	Boone County SD	Madison
39	8.8	Ohio County SD	Wheeling
41	8.6	Kanawha County SD	Charleston
42	8.5	Wetzel County SD	New Martinsville
43	8.4	Marion County SD	Fairmont
43	8.4	Monongalia SD	Morgantown
45	7.6	Hancock County SD	New Cumberland
46	7.2	Wood County SD	Parkersburg
47	7.0	Putnam County SD	Winfield

Student/Teacher Ratio

Rank	Ratio	District Name	City
1	15.1	Harrison County SD	Clarksburg
1	15.1	Summers County SD	Hinton
1	15.1	Taylor County SD	Grafton
4	15.0	Wood County SD	Parkersburg
5	14.9	Jefferson County SD	Charles Town
6	14.8	Morgan County SD	Berkeley Spgs
6	14.8	Ritchie County SD	Harrisville
8	14.7	Kanawha County SD	Charleston
8	14.7	Marshall County SD	Moundsville
8	14.7	Monongalia SD	Morgantown
8	14.7	Putnam County SD	Winfield
12	14.6	Hampshire County SD	Romney
12	14.6	Hancock County SD	New Cumberland
12	14.6	Preston County SD	Kingwood
15	14.5	Cabell County SD	Huntington
15	14.5	Hardy County SD	Moorefield
15	14.5	Jackson County SD	Ripley
15	14.5	Mineral County SD	Keyser
19	14.4	Greenbrier County SD	Lewisburg
19	14.4	Ohio County SD	Wheeling
21	14.3	Wetzel County SD	New Martinsville
22	14.2	Raleigh County SD	Beckley
23	14.1	Monroe County SD	Union
24	14.0	Barbour County SD	Philippi
24	14.0	Mercer County SD	Princeton
26	13.9	Brooke County SD	Wellsburg
26	13.9	Lewis County SD	Weston
26	13.9	Roane County SD	Spencer
29	13.8	Berkeley County SD	Martinsburg
29	13.8	Mingo County SD	Williamson
31	13.7	Wayne County SD	Wayne
32	13.6	Logan County SD	Logan
32	13.6	Upshur County SD	Buckhannon
34	13.5	Mason County SD	Point Pleasant
34	13.5	Randolph County SD	Elkins
36	13.4	Clay County SD	Clay
36	13.4	Marion County SD	Fairmont
38	13.3	Braxton County SD	Sutton
38	13.3	Lincoln County SD	Hamlin
38	13.3	Tyler County SD	Sistersville
41	13.1	Nicholas County SD	Summersville
42	13.0	Grant County SD	Petersburg
42	13.0	Mcdowell County SD	Welch
42	13.0	Webster County SD	Webster Spgs

45	12.9	Fayette County SD	Fayetteville
46	12.5	Wyoming County SD	Pineville
47	12.2	Boone County SD	Madison

Student/Librarian Ratio

Rank	Ratio	District Name	City
1	2,130.5	Wyoming County SD	Pineville
2	2,116.0	Monroe County SD	Union
3	1,952.0	Upshur County SD	Buckhannon
4	1,718.0	Webster County SD	Webster Spgs
5	1,687.0	Ritchie County SD	Harrisville
6	1,624.0	Summers County SD	Hinton
7	1,530.3	Randolph County SD	Elkins
8	1,489.7	Mcdowell County SD	Welch
9	1,424.0	Hampshire County SD	Romney
10	1,302.0	Roane County SD	Spencer
11	1,293.5	Braxton County SD	Sutton
12	1,259.5	Jackson County SD	Ripley
13	1,151.1	Hancock County SD	New Cumberland
14	1,136.9	Mingo County SD	Williamson
15	1,132.8	Boone County SD	Madison
16	1,093.3	Putnam County SD	Winfield
17	1,082.8	Nicholas County SD	Summersville
18	1,082.1	Raleigh County SD	Beckley
19	1,075.0	Marshall County SD	Moundsville
20	1,072.0	Clay County SD	Clay
21	1,071.8	Greenbrier County SD	Lewisburg
22	1,069.0	Cabell County SD	Huntington
23	1,066.8	Mason County SD	Point Pleasant
24	1,014.5	Logan County SD	Logan
25	996.0	Fayette County SD	Fayetteville
26	966.0	Preston County SD	Kingwood
27	909.3	Brooke County SD	Wellsburg
28	838.0	Mineral County SD	Keyser
29	823.2	Wayne County SD	Wayne
30	783.7	Lewis County SD	Weston
31	774.6	Lincoln County SD	Hamlin
32	772.0	Tyler County SD	Sistersville
33	758.9	Wetzel County SD	New Martinsville
34	730.6	Morgan County SD	Berkeley Spgs
35	685.3	Barbour County SD	Philippi
36	659.3	Grant County SD	Petersburg
37	640.6	Berkeley County SD	Martinsburg
38	611.3	Taylor County SD	Grafton
39	555.2	Ohio County SD	Wheeling
40	550.1	Wood County SD	Parkersburg
41	541.1	Monongalia SD	Morgantown
42	526.4	Harrison County SD	Clarksburg
43	519.6	Jefferson County SD	Charles Town
44	462.6	Hardy County SD	Moorefield
45	458.6	Marion County SD	Fairmont
46	455.6	Mercer County SD	Princeton
47	430.6	Kanawha County SD	Charleston

Student/Counselor Ratio

Rank	Ratio	District Name	City
1	1,175.6	Monroe County SD	Union
2	843.5	Ritchie County SD	Harrisville
3	774.6	Lincoln County SD	Hamlin
4	714.7	Clay County SD	Clay
5	651.0	Barbour County SD	Philippi
6	608.7	Wyoming County SD	Pineville
7	578.8	Wayne County SD	Wayne
8	578.7	Roane County SD	Spencer
9	573.0	Wood County SD	Parkersburg
10	553.4	Logan County SD	Logan
11	546.8	Hancock County SD	New Cumberland
12	526.4	Harrison County SD	Clarksburg
13	519.6	Brooke County SD	Wellsburg
14	503.4	Boone County SD	Madison
15	490.9	Webster County SD	Webster Spgs
16	483.0	Preston County SD	Kingwood
17	480.8	Fayette County SD	Fayetteville
18	462.7	Ohio County SD	Wheeling
19	462.6	Hardy County SD	Moorefield
20	458.0	Jackson County SD	Ripley
21	457.2	Lewis County SD	Weston
22	456.9	Monongalia SD	Morgantown
23	455.9	Nicholas County SD	Summersville
24	455.3	Cabell County SD	Huntington
25	454.6	Jefferson County SD	Charles Town
26	444.5	Taylor County SD	Grafton
27	434.1	Mingo County SD	Williamson
28	431.2	Braxton County SD	Sutton
29	426.9	Wetzel County SD	New Martinsville
30	426.2	Morgan County SD	Berkeley Spgs
31	419.0	Mineral County SD	Keyser
32	416.5	Putnam County SD	Winfield
33	416.0	Mercer County SD	Princeton
34	406.0	Summers County SD	Hinton
35	395.6	Grant County SD	Petersburg
35	395.6	Hampshire County SD	Romney
37	390.4	Upshur County SD	Buckhannon
38	387.9	Mason County SD	Point Pleasant
39	386.0	Tyler County SD	Sistersville
40	383.9	Marshall County SD	Moundsville
41	382.6	Berkeley County SD	Martinsburg
42	375.2	Marion County SD	Fairmont
43	372.4	Mcdowell County SD	Welch
44	357.3	Greenbrier County SD	Lewisburg
45	353.2	Randolph County SD	Elkins
46	350.1	Raleigh County SD	Beckley
47	338.7	Kanawha County SD	Charleston

Current Spending per Student in FY2001

Rank	Dollars	District Name	City
1	8,689	Boone County SD	Madison
2	8,522	Mcdowell County SD	Welch
3	8,340	Wyoming County SD	Pineville
4	8,322	Mingo County SD	Williamson
5	8,050	Marshall County SD	Moundsville
6	7,935	Lincoln County SD	Hamlin
7	7,810	Tyler County SD	Sistersville
8	7,790	Ohio County SD	Wheeling
9	7,753	Marion County SD	Fairmont
10	7,749	Ritchie County SD	Harrisville
11	7,679	Raleigh County SD	Beckley
12	7,660	Fayette County SD	Fayetteville
13	7,656	Clay County SD	Clay
14	7,643	Nicholas County SD	Summersville
15	7,632	Brooke County SD	Wellsburg
16	7,629	Kanawha County SD	Charleston
17	7,593	Cabell County SD	Huntington
18	7,468	Mercer County SD	Princeton
19	7,405	Mason County SD	Point Pleasant
20	7,404	Wood County SD	Parkersburg
21	7,394	Monongalia SD	Morgantown
22	7,377	Webster County SD	Webster Spgs
23	7,328	Jefferson County SD	Charles Town
24	7,325	Hancock County SD	New Cumberland
25	7,295	Taylor County SD	Grafton
26	7,266	Upshur County SD	Buckhannon
27	7,258	Wayne County SD	Wayne
28	7,249	Harrison County SD	Clarksburg
29	7,247	Mineral County SD	Keyser
30	7,210	Wetzel County SD	New Martinsville
31	7,189	Logan County SD	Logan
32	7,187	Summers County SD	Hinton
33	7,173	Jackson County SD	Ripley
34	7,148	Berkeley County SD	Martinsburg
35	7,131	Putnam County SD	Winfield
36	7,128	Greenbrier County SD	Lewisburg
37	7,121	Lewis County SD	Weston
38	7,089	Grant County SD	Petersburg
39	7,038	Monroe County SD	Union
40	7,036	Braxton County SD	Sutton
41	6,921	Hampshire County SD	Romney
42	6,818	Barbour County SD	Philippi
43	6,785	Roane County SD	Spencer
44	6,719	Randolph County SD	Elkins
45	6,695	Preston County SD	Kingwood
46	6,585	Morgan County SD	Berkeley Spgs
47	6,065	Hardy County SD	Moorefield

Number of Diploma Recipients

Rank	Number	District Name	City
1	1,630	Kanawha County SD	Charleston
2	778	Wood County SD	Parkersburg
3	728	Raleigh County SD	Beckley
4	710	Berkeley County SD	Martinsburg
5	709	Harrison County SD	Clarksburg
6	688	Cabell County SD	Huntington
7	634	Marion County SD	Fairmont
8	629	Monongalia SD	Morgantown
9	527	Mercer County SD	Princeton
10	495	Putnam County SD	Winfield
11	442	Fayette County SD	Fayetteville
12	418	Jefferson County SD	Charles Town
13	411	Marshall County SD	Moundsville
14	402	Logan County SD	Logan
15	395	Wayne County SD	Wayne
16	341	Ohio County SD	Wheeling
17	329	Greenbrier County SD	Lewisburg
18	320	Mingo County SD	Williamson
19	311	Preston County SD	Kingwood
20	309	Jackson County SD	Ripley
20	309	Wyoming County SD	Pineville
22	283	Mineral County SD	Keyser
23	279	Brooke County SD	Wellsburg
24	276	Nicholas County SD	Summersville
25	274	Hancock County SD	New Cumberland
26	273	Randolph County SD	Elkins
27	271	Mason County SD	Point Pleasant
28	256	Boone County SD	Madison
29	244	Upshur County SD	Buckhannon
30	237	Mcdowell County SD	Welch
31	231	Lincoln County SD	Hamlin
32	223	Wetzel County SD	New Martinsville
33	198	Hampshire County SD	Romney
34	192	Lewis County SD	Weston
35	174	Roane County SD	Spencer
36	161	Barbour County SD	Philippi
37	148	Braxton County SD	Sutton
38	143	Taylor County SD	Grafton
39	137	Morgan County SD	Berkeley Spgs
40	128	Grant County SD	Petersburg
41	121	Clay County SD	Clay
41	121	Hardy County SD	Moorefield
43	115	Webster County SD	Webster Spgs
44	113	Ritchie County SD	Harrisville
45	100	Tyler County SD	Sistersville
46	97	Summers County SD	Hinton
47	96	Monroe County SD	Union

High School Drop-out Rate

Rank	Percent	District Name	City
1	7.6	Berkeley County SD	Martinsburg
2	6.7	Jefferson County SD	Charles Town
3	6.2	Cabell County SD	Huntington
4	5.6	Grant County SD	Petersburg
4	5.6	Kanawha County SD	Charleston
6	5.3	Boone County SD	Madison
7	5.2	Fayette County SD	Fayetteville
7	5.2	Roane County SD	Spencer
9	4.9	Upshur County SD	Buckhannon
10	4.8	Jackson County SD	Ripley
11	4.6	Preston County SD	Kingwood
12	4.5	Logan County SD	Logan
12	4.5	Ohio County SD	Wheeling
12	4.5	Raleigh County SD	Beckley
15	4.4	Braxton County SD	Sutton
16	4.3	Morgan County SD	Berkeley Spgs
17	4.2	Wayne County SD	Wayne
18	4.1	Harrison County SD	Clarksburg
19	4.0	Hampshire County SD	Romney
19	4.0	Hancock County SD	New Cumberland
19	4.0	Mcdowell County SD	Welch
19	4.0	Wood County SD	Parkersburg
23	3.9	Mercer County SD	Princeton
23	3.9	Monroe County SD	Union
23	3.9	Wyoming County SD	Pineville
26	3.8	Barbour County SD	Philippi
26	3.8	Monongalia SD	Morgantown
26	3.8	Ritchie County SD	Harrisville
29	3.6	Mason County SD	Point Pleasant
30	3.5	Marshall County SD	Moundsville
31	3.4	Clay County SD	Clay
31	3.4	Nicholas County SD	Summersville
31	3.4	Summers County SD	Hinton
31	3.4	Webster County SD	Webster Spgs
35	3.2	Putnam County SD	Winfield
36	2.9	Wetzel County SD	New Martinsville
37	2.8	Mineral County SD	Keyser
37	2.8	Mingo County SD	Williamson
39	2.6	Brooke County SD	Wellsburg
39	2.6	Lincoln County SD	Hamlin
41	2.5	Randolph County SD	Elkins
42	2.0	Greenbrier County SD	Lewisburg
43	1.9	Marion County SD	Fairmont
43	1.9	Tyler County SD	Sistersville
45	1.3	Hardy County SD	Moorefield
45	1.3	Taylor County SD	Grafton
47	1.2	Lewis County SD	Weston

Wisconsin

Wisconsin Public School Educational Profile

Category	Value	Category	Value
Schools *(2002-2003)*	2,237	**Diploma Recipients** *(2002-2003)*	60,575
Instructional Level		White, Non-Hispanic	53,255
Primary	1,252	Black, Non-Hispanic	3,148
Middle	391	Asian/Pacific Islander	1,757
High	512	American Indian/Alaskan Native	623
Other Level	82	Hispanic	1,792
Curriculum		**High School Drop-out Rate** (%) *(2000-2001)*	2.3
Regular	2,042	White, Non-Hispanic	1.4
Special Education	11	Black, Non-Hispanic	9.8
Vocational	1	Asian/Pacific Islander	2.4
Alternative	183	American Indian/Alaskan Native	5.7
Type		Hispanic	6.5
Magnet	0	**Staff** *(2002-2003)*	113,263.0
Charter	129	Teachers	61,588.5
Title I Eligible	1,086	Average Salary ($)	41,617
School-wide Title I	288	Librarians/Media Specialists	1,340.4
Students *(2002-2003)*	881,231	Guidance Counselors	2,034.3
Gender (%)		**Ratios** *(2002-2003)*	
Male	51.6	Student/Teacher Ratio	14.3 to 1
Female	48.4	Student/Librarian Ratio	657.4 to 1
Race/Ethnicity (%)		Student/Counselor Ratio	433.2 to 1
White, Non-Hispanic	79.5	**Current Spending** *($ per student in FY 2001)*	8,634
Black, Non-Hispanic	10.4	Instruction	5,351
Asian/Pacific Islander	3.3	Support Services	3,005
American Indian/Alaskan Native	1.5	**College Entrance Exam Scores** *(2003)*	
Hispanic	5.4	Scholastic Aptitude Test (SAT)	
Classification (%)		Participation Rate (%)	7
Individual Education Program (IEP)	14.3	Mean SAT I Verbal Score	585
Migrant	0.1	Mean SAT I Math Score	594
English Language Learner (ELL)	2.9	American College Testing Program (ACT)	
Eligible for Free Lunch Program	0.0	Participation Rate (%)	69
Eligible for Reduced-Price Lunch Program	0.0	Average Composite Score	22.2

Note: *For an explanation of data, please refer to the User's Guide in the front of the book; n/a indicates data not available*

Wisconsin NAEP 2003 Test Scores

Reading			Mathematics		
Grade/Category	Value	Rank	Grade/Category	Value	Rank
4th Grade			**4th Grade**		
Average Proficiency	220.8 (0.8)	21/51	Average Proficiency	236.8 (0.9)	19/51
Proficiency by Gender/Race/Ethnicity			Proficiency by Gender/Race/Ethnicity		
Male	216.5 (1.2)	19/51	Male	238.0 (1.0)	20/51
Female	225.3 (1.1)	18/51	Female	235.4 (1.0)	18/51
White, Non-Hispanic	225.0 (1.0)	28/51	White, Non-Hispanic	243.3 (0.7)	18/51
Black, Non-Hispanic	199.8 (2.5)	20/42	Black, Non-Hispanic	208.8 (2.0)	38/42
Asian, Non-Hispanic	*209.1 (3.5)*	11/41	Asian, Non-Hispanic	221.2 (2.8)	22/43
American Indian, Non-Hispanic	213.2 (4.6)	21/25	American Indian, Non-Hispanic	229.6 (3.9)	22/26
Hispanic	*210.6 (3.5)*	1/12	Hispanic	*223.6 (3.0)*	3/12
Proficiency by Class Size			Proficiency by Class Size		
Less than 16 Students	*202.9 (5.0)*	26/45	Less than 16 Students	226.7 (5.0)	18/47
16 to 18 Students	224.0 (2.8)	7/48	16 to 18 Students	236.9 (2.0)	15/48
19 to 20 Students	222.4 (2.3)	14/50	19 to 20 Students	241.8 (3.0)	5/50
21 to 25 Students	223.4 (1.3)	19/51	21 to 25 Students	240.2 (1.4)	14/51
Greater than 25 Students	217.5 (2.4)	31/49	Greater than 25 Students	229.7 (2.8)	36/49
Percent Attaining Achievement Levels			Percent Attaining Achievement Levels		
Below Basic	32.2 (1.1)	34/51	Below Basic	20.6 (1.3)	29/51
Basic or Above	67.8 (1.1)	18/51	Basic or Above	79.4 (1.3)	23/51
Proficient or Above	32.6 (1.2)	22/51	Proficient or Above	35.2 (1.3)	15/51
Advanced or Above	6.6 (0.5)	28/51	Advanced or Above	4.3 (0.5)	14/51
8th Grade			**8th Grade**		
Average Proficiency	266.5 (1.3)	17/51	Average Proficiency	283.9 (1.3)	10/51
Proficiency by Gender/Race/Ethnicity			Proficiency by Gender/Race/Ethnicity		
Male	259.5 (1.6)	22/51	Male	284.2 (1.5)	10/51
Female	274.1 (1.4)	9/51	Female	283.6 (1.5)	9/51
White, Non-Hispanic	271.5 (1.0)	17/50	White, Non-Hispanic	289.7 (1.1)	14/50
Black, Non-Hispanic	233.8 (4.4)	39/41	Black, Non-Hispanic	241.1 (4.0)	38/41
Asian, Non-Hispanic	243.9 (5.0)	25/37	Asian, Non-Hispanic	261.8 (4.0)	14/37
American Indian, Non-Hispanic	252.9 (5.8)	21/23	American Indian, Non-Hispanic	273.0 (4.2)	21/23
Hispanic	n/a	n/a	Hispanic	n/a	n/a
Proficiency by Parents Highest Level of Ed.			Proficiency by Parents Highest Level of Ed.		
Did Not Finish High School	237.1 (3.7)	47/50	Did Not Finish High School	255.4 (4.5)	29/50
Graduated High School	259.9 (2.0)	9/50	Graduated High School	275.9 (1.6)	8/50
Some Education After High School	271.2 (1.7)	13/50	Some Education After High School	285.9 (1.9)	7/50
Graduated College	274.2 (1.3)	19/50	Graduated College	292.6 (1.5)	10/50
Percent Attaining Achievement Levels			Percent Attaining Achievement Levels		
Below Basic	22.8 (1.5)	34/51	Below Basic	24.8 (1.4)	41/51
Basic or Above	77.2 (1.5)	18/51	Basic or Above	75.2 (1.4)	11/51
Proficient or Above	36.5 (1.8)	11/51	Proficient or Above	35.2 (1.4)	4/51
Advanced or Above	3.0 (0.5)	15/51	Advanced or Above	6.4 (0.6)	10/51

***Note:** For an explanation of data, please refer to the User's Guide in the front of the book; values in italics indicate that the nature of the sample does not allow accurate determination of the variability of the statistic; n/a indicates data not available*

Adams County

Adams-Friendship Area

201 W 6th St • Friendship, WI 53934-9135
(608) 339-3213 • http://www.af.k12.wi.us
Grade Span: PK-12; **Agency Type:** 1
Schools: 8
4 Primary; 1 Middle; 2 High; 1 Other Level
7 Regular; 0 Special Education; 0 Vocational; 1 Alternative
0 Magnet; 0 Charter; 5 Title I Eligible; 5 School-wide Title I
Students: 2,157 (53.0% male; 47.0% female)
Individual Education Program: 424 (19.7%);
English Language Learner: 0 (0.0%); Migrant: 2 (0.1%)
Eligible for Free Lunch Program: n/a
Eligible for Reduced-Price Lunch Program: n/a
Teachers: 162.1 (13.3 to 1)
Librarians/Media Specialists: 2.0 (1,078.5 to 1)
Guidance Counselors: 7.0 (308.1 to 1)
Current Spending: ($ per student per year):
Total: $8,582; Instruction: $5,234; Support Services: $2,981
Enrollment, Drop-out Rates and Diploma Recipients by Race/Ethnicity

Category	Total	White	Black	Asian	AIAN	Hisp.
Enrollment (%)	100.0	93.6	0.9	0.1	1.3	4.1
Drop-out Rate (%)	1.6	1.6	20.0	0.0	0.0	0.0
H.S. Diplomas (#)	162	160	0	1	0	1

Ashland County

Ashland

502 Main St W • Ashland, WI 54806-1512
(715) 682-7080 • http://www.ashland.k12.wi.us
Grade Span: PK-12; **Agency Type:** 1
Schools: 5
3 Primary; 1 Middle; 1 High; 0 Other Level
5 Regular; 0 Special Education; 0 Vocational; 0 Alternative
0 Magnet; 0 Charter; 3 Title I Eligible; 0 School-wide Title I
Students: 2,309 (52.5% male; 47.5% female)
Individual Education Program: 328 (14.2%);
English Language Learner: 0 (0.0%); Migrant: 0 (0.0%)
Eligible for Free Lunch Program: n/a
Eligible for Reduced-Price Lunch Program: n/a
Teachers: 171.3 (13.5 to 1)
Librarians/Media Specialists: 4.1 (563.2 to 1)
Guidance Counselors: 6.0 (384.8 to 1)
Current Spending: ($ per student per year):
Total: $9,041; Instruction: $5,263; Support Services: $3,449
Enrollment, Drop-out Rates and Diploma Recipients by Race/Ethnicity

Category	Total	White	Black	Asian	AIAN	Hisp.
Enrollment (%)	100.0	78.5	0.6	0.9	19.6	0.4
Drop-out Rate (%)	n/a	n/a	n/a	n/a	n/a	n/a
H.S. Diplomas (#)	172	156	0	0	16	0

Barron County

Rice Lake Area

700 Augusta St • Rice Lake, WI 54868-1996
(715) 234-9007 • http://www.ricelake.k12.wi.us
Grade Span: PK-12; **Agency Type:** 1
Schools: 13
9 Primary; 1 Middle; 2 High; 1 Other Level
11 Regular; 1 Special Education; 0 Vocational; 1 Alternative
0 Magnet; 1 Charter; 6 Title I Eligible; 0 School-wide Title I
Students: 2,668 (51.2% male; 48.8% female)
Individual Education Program: 372 (13.9%);
English Language Learner: 0 (0.0%); Migrant: 0 (0.0%)
Eligible for Free Lunch Program: n/a
Eligible for Reduced-Price Lunch Program: n/a
Teachers: 179.4 (14.9 to 1)
Librarians/Media Specialists: 3.9 (684.1 to 1)
Guidance Counselors: 8.0 (333.5 to 1)
Current Spending: ($ per student per year):
Total: $7,925; Instruction: $4,729; Support Services: $2,891
Enrollment, Drop-out Rates and Diploma Recipients by Race/Ethnicity

Category	Total	White	Black	Asian	AIAN	Hisp.
Enrollment (%)	100.0	96.1	0.5	1.4	0.6	1.5
Drop-out Rate (%)	2.0	2.0	0.0	0.0	3.4	0.0
H.S. Diplomas (#)	220	213	1	5	1	0

Brown County

Ashwaubenon

1055 Griffiths Ln • Green Bay, WI 54304-5599
(920) 492-2905 • http://www.ashwaubenon.k12.wi.us
Grade Span: PK-12; **Agency Type:** 1
Schools: 5
3 Primary; 1 Middle; 1 High; 0 Other Level
5 Regular; 0 Special Education; 0 Vocational; 0 Alternative
0 Magnet; 0 Charter; 2 Title I Eligible; 0 School-wide Title I
Students: 3,126 (52.2% male; 47.8% female)
Individual Education Program: 487 (15.6%);
English Language Learner: 0 (0.0%); Migrant: 0 (0.0%)
Eligible for Free Lunch Program: n/a
Eligible for Reduced-Price Lunch Program: n/a
Teachers: 219.1 (14.3 to 1)
Librarians/Media Specialists: 4.0 (781.5 to 1)
Guidance Counselors: 8.2 (381.2 to 1)
Current Spending: ($ per student per year):
Total: $7,903; Instruction: $5,151; Support Services: $2,444
Enrollment, Drop-out Rates and Diploma Recipients by Race/Ethnicity

Category	Total	White	Black	Asian	AIAN	Hisp.
Enrollment (%)	100.0	91.4	2.3	3.4	1.4	1.5
Drop-out Rate (%)	0.7	0.7	0.0	0.0	14.3	0.0
H.S. Diplomas (#)	260	251	3	4	1	1

De Pere

1700 Chicago St • De Pere, WI 54115-3499
(920) 337-1032 • http://www.depere.k12.wi.us
Grade Span: PK-12; **Agency Type:** 1
Schools: 5
2 Primary; 2 Middle; 1 High; 0 Other Level
5 Regular; 0 Special Education; 0 Vocational; 0 Alternative
0 Magnet; 0 Charter; 2 Title I Eligible; 0 School-wide Title I
Students: 3,124 (50.2% male; 49.8% female)
Individual Education Program: 327 (10.5%);
English Language Learner: 0 (0.0%); Migrant: 0 (0.0%)
Eligible for Free Lunch Program: n/a
Eligible for Reduced-Price Lunch Program: n/a
Teachers: 204.7 (15.3 to 1)
Librarians/Media Specialists: 5.1 (612.5 to 1)
Guidance Counselors: 8.1 (385.7 to 1)
Current Spending: ($ per student per year):
Total: $6,488; Instruction: $3,796; Support Services: $2,381
Enrollment, Drop-out Rates and Diploma Recipients by Race/Ethnicity

Category	Total	White	Black	Asian	AIAN	Hisp.
Enrollment (%)	100.0	95.9	1.1	1.3	0.9	0.8
Drop-out Rate (%)	0.8	0.7	0.0	0.0	50.0	0.0
H.S. Diplomas (#)	231	225	3	1	1	1

Denmark

450 N Wall St • Denmark, WI 54208-9416
(920) 863-2176 • http://www.denmark.k12.wi.us
Grade Span: PK-12; **Agency Type:** 1
Schools: 5
2 Primary; 1 Middle; 2 High; 0 Other Level
4 Regular; 0 Special Education; 0 Vocational; 1 Alternative
0 Magnet; 1 Charter; 2 Title I Eligible; 0 School-wide Title I
Students: 1,688 (52.9% male; 47.1% female)
Individual Education Program: 261 (15.5%);
English Language Learner: 0 (0.0%); Migrant: 0 (0.0%)
Eligible for Free Lunch Program: n/a
Eligible for Reduced-Price Lunch Program: n/a
Teachers: 108.9 (15.5 to 1)
Librarians/Media Specialists: 2.0 (844.0 to 1)
Guidance Counselors: 4.0 (422.0 to 1)
Current Spending: ($ per student per year):
Total: $6,922; Instruction: $4,466; Support Services: $2,198
Enrollment, Drop-out Rates and Diploma Recipients by Race/Ethnicity

Category	Total	White	Black	Asian	AIAN	Hisp.
Enrollment (%)	100.0	96.3	0.4	1.2	0.7	1.3
Drop-out Rate (%)	1.1	1.1	0.0	0.0	0.0	0.0
H.S. Diplomas (#)	131	130	0	1	0	0

Green Bay Area

200 S Broadway • Green Bay, WI 54303
Mailing Address: PO Box 23387 • Green Bay, WI 54305-3387
(920) 448-2100 • http://www.greenbay.k12.wi.us
Grade Span: PK-12; **Agency Type:** 1
Schools: 36
26 Primary; 4 Middle; 4 High; 2 Other Level
36 Regular; 0 Special Education; 0 Vocational; 0 Alternative
0 Magnet; 0 Charter; 12 Title I Eligible; 7 School-wide Title I
Students: 20,474 (51.5% male; 48.5% female)
Individual Education Program: 3,846 (18.8%);
English Language Learner: 2,108 (10.3%); Migrant: 149 (0.7%)
Eligible for Free Lunch Program: n/a
Eligible for Reduced-Price Lunch Program: n/a
Teachers: 1,435.8 (14.3 to 1)
Librarians/Media Specialists: 24.0 (853.1 to 1)
Guidance Counselors: 48.5 (422.1 to 1)
Current Spending: ($ per student per year):
Total: $8,090; Instruction: $5,248; Support Services: $2,580

Enrollment, Drop-out Rates and Diploma Recipients by Race/Ethnicity

Category	Total	White	Black	Asian	AIAN	Hisp.
Enrollment (%)	100.0	71.5	4.1	8.4	5.0	11.1
Drop-out Rate (%)	2.9	2.2	4.9	4.0	8.7	6.1
H.S. Diplomas (#)	1,131	952	12	93	33	41

Howard-Suamico

2700 Lineville Rd • Green Bay, WI 54313-7197
(920) 662-7878 • http://www.hssd.k12.wi.us
Grade Span: PK-12; **Agency Type:** 1
Schools: 7
4 Primary; 2 Middle; 1 High; 0 Other Level
7 Regular; 0 Special Education; 0 Vocational; 0 Alternative
0 Magnet; 0 Charter; 2 Title I Eligible; 0 School-wide Title I
Students: 4,599 (51.1% male; 48.9% female)
Individual Education Program: 566 (12.3%);
English Language Learner: 23 (0.5%); Migrant: 0 (0.0%)
Eligible for Free Lunch Program: n/a
Eligible for Reduced-Price Lunch Program: n/a
Teachers: 288.8 (15.9 to 1)
Librarians/Media Specialists: 7.0 (657.0 to 1)
Guidance Counselors: 11.3 (407.0 to 1)
Current Spending: ($ per student per year):
Total: $6,775; Instruction: $4,104; Support Services: $2,422
Enrollment, Drop-out Rates and Diploma Recipients by Race/Ethnicity

Category	Total	White	Black	Asian	AIAN	Hisp.
Enrollment (%)	100.0	95.5	1.1	1.3	1.2	0.9
Drop-out Rate (%)	1.7	1.8	0.0	0.0	0.0	0.0
H.S. Diplomas (#)	271	259	5	3	2	2

Pulaski Community

143 W Green Bay St • Pulaski, WI 54162-0036
Mailing Address: PO Box 36 • Pulaski, WI 54162-0036
(920) 822-6000 • http://www.pulaski.k12.wi.us
Grade Span: PK-12; **Agency Type:** 1
Schools: 7
5 Primary; 1 Middle; 1 High; 0 Other Level
7 Regular; 0 Special Education; 0 Vocational; 0 Alternative
0 Magnet; 0 Charter; 2 Title I Eligible; 0 School-wide Title I
Students: 3,493 (51.3% male; 48.7% female)
Individual Education Program: 506 (14.5%);
English Language Learner: 0 (0.0%); Migrant: 0 (0.0%)
Eligible for Free Lunch Program: n/a
Eligible for Reduced-Price Lunch Program: n/a
Teachers: 237.9 (14.7 to 1)
Librarians/Media Specialists: 3.0 (1,164.3 to 1)
Guidance Counselors: 6.0 (582.2 to 1)
Current Spending: ($ per student per year):
Total: $7,715; Instruction: $4,522; Support Services: $2,852
Enrollment, Drop-out Rates and Diploma Recipients by Race/Ethnicity

Category	Total	White	Black	Asian	AIAN	Hisp.
Enrollment (%)	100.0	94.5	0.8	1.0	3.0	0.7
Drop-out Rate (%)	0.2	0.1	0.0	0.0	2.6	0.0
H.S. Diplomas (#)	232	221	0	2	8	1

West De Pere

930 Oak St • De Pere, WI 54115-1014
(920) 337-1393 • http://www.netnet.net/wdpschools
Grade Span: PK-12; **Agency Type:** 1
Schools: 3
1 Primary; 1 Middle; 1 High; 0 Other Level
3 Regular; 0 Special Education; 0 Vocational; 0 Alternative
0 Magnet; 0 Charter; 1 Title I Eligible; 0 School-wide Title I
Students: 1,916 (54.5% male; 45.5% female)
Individual Education Program: 267 (13.9%);
English Language Learner: 0 (0.0%); Migrant: 0 (0.0%)
Eligible for Free Lunch Program: n/a
Eligible for Reduced-Price Lunch Program: n/a
Teachers: 131.6 (14.6 to 1)
Librarians/Media Specialists: 0.8 (2,395.0 to 1)
Guidance Counselors: 4.0 (479.0 to 1)
Current Spending: ($ per student per year):
Total: $7,668; Instruction: $4,841; Support Services: $2,579
Enrollment, Drop-out Rates and Diploma Recipients by Race/Ethnicity

Category	Total	White	Black	Asian	AIAN	Hisp.
Enrollment (%)	100.0	86.5	1.0	0.9	10.1	1.4
Drop-out Rate (%)	0.3	0.4	0.0	0.0	0.0	0.0
H.S. Diplomas (#)	134	119	2	0	13	0

Chippewa County

Chippewa Falls Area

1130 Miles St • Chippewa Falls, WI 54729-1923
(715) 726-2417 • http://cfsd.chipfalls.k12.wi.us
Grade Span: PK-12; **Agency Type:** 1
Schools: 9
6 Primary; 1 Middle; 2 High; 0 Other Level
8 Regular; 0 Special Education; 0 Vocational; 1 Alternative
0 Magnet; 0 Charter; 0 Title I Eligible; 0 School-wide Title I
Students: 4,465 (51.2% male; 48.8% female)
Individual Education Program: 620 (13.9%);
English Language Learner: 0 (0.0%); Migrant: 0 (0.0%)
Eligible for Free Lunch Program: n/a
Eligible for Reduced-Price Lunch Program: n/a
Teachers: 296.7 (15.0 to 1)
Librarians/Media Specialists: 5.0 (893.0 to 1)
Guidance Counselors: 13.5 (330.7 to 1)
Current Spending: ($ per student per year):
Total: $7,774; Instruction: $4,667; Support Services: $2,839
Enrollment, Drop-out Rates and Diploma Recipients by Race/Ethnicity

Category	Total	White	Black	Asian	AIAN	Hisp.
Enrollment (%)	100.0	96.0	0.8	1.9	0.6	0.7
Drop-out Rate (%)	2.5	2.5	0.0	0.0	0.0	0.0
H.S. Diplomas (#)	363	359	0	1	2	1

Columbia County

Lodi

115 School St • Lodi, WI 53555-1046
(608) 592-3851 • http://www.lodi.k12.wi.us/
Grade Span: PK-12; **Agency Type:** 1
Schools: 5
2 Primary; 1 Middle; 2 High; 0 Other Level
4 Regular; 0 Special Education; 0 Vocational; 1 Alternative
0 Magnet; 1 Charter; 1 Title I Eligible; 0 School-wide Title I
Students: 1,654 (51.5% male; 48.5% female)
Individual Education Program: 225 (13.6%);
English Language Learner: 0 (0.0%); Migrant: 0 (0.0%)
Eligible for Free Lunch Program: n/a
Eligible for Reduced-Price Lunch Program: n/a
Teachers: 119.6 (13.8 to 1)
Librarians/Media Specialists: 3.2 (516.9 to 1)
Guidance Counselors: 4.4 (375.9 to 1)
Current Spending: ($ per student per year):
Total: $7,727; Instruction: $4,519; Support Services: $2,931
Enrollment, Drop-out Rates and Diploma Recipients by Race/Ethnicity

Category	Total	White	Black	Asian	AIAN	Hisp.
Enrollment (%)	100.0	97.3	0.8	0.6	0.6	0.6
Drop-out Rate (%)	1.0	1.1	0.0	0.0	0.0	0.0
H.S. Diplomas (#)	114	114	0	0	0	0

Portage Community

904 De Witt St • Portage, WI 53901-1726
(608) 742-4879 • http://www.portage.k12.wi.us
Grade Span: PK-12; **Agency Type:** 1
Schools: 10
6 Primary; 2 Middle; 2 High; 0 Other Level
8 Regular; 0 Special Education; 0 Vocational; 2 Alternative
0 Magnet; 2 Charter; 2 Title I Eligible; 0 School-wide Title I
Students: 2,622 (52.6% male; 47.4% female)
Individual Education Program: 410 (15.6%);
English Language Learner: 0 (0.0%); Migrant: 7 (0.3%)
Eligible for Free Lunch Program: n/a
Eligible for Reduced-Price Lunch Program: n/a
Teachers: 159.1 (16.5 to 1)
Librarians/Media Specialists: 1.6 (1,638.8 to 1)
Guidance Counselors: 6.9 (380.0 to 1)
Current Spending: ($ per student per year):
Total: $7,485; Instruction: $4,477; Support Services: $2,687
Enrollment, Drop-out Rates and Diploma Recipients by Race/Ethnicity

Category	Total	White	Black	Asian	AIAN	Hisp.
Enrollment (%)	100.0	95.2	0.8	0.6	0.8	2.6
Drop-out Rate (%)	0.3	0.3	0.0	0.0	n/a	0.0
H.S. Diplomas (#)	170	167	0	1	0	2

Dane County

De Forest Area

520 E Holum St • De Forest, WI 53532-1395
(608) 842-6577 • http://www.deforest.k12.wi.us
Grade Span: PK-12; **Agency Type:** 1
Schools: 7
5 Primary; 1 Middle; 1 High; 0 Other Level
7 Regular; 0 Special Education; 0 Vocational; 0 Alternative

0 Magnet; 0 Charter; 1 Title I Eligible; 0 School-wide Title I
Students: 3,111 (50.2% male; 49.8% female)
Individual Education Program: 421 (13.5%);
English Language Learner: 35 (1.1%); Migrant: 0 (0.0%)
Eligible for Free Lunch Program: n/a
Eligible for Reduced-Price Lunch Program: n/a
Teachers: 209.8 (14.8 to 1)
Librarians/Media Specialists: 6.7 (464.3 to 1)
Guidance Counselors: 8.8 (353.5 to 1)
Current Spending: ($ per student per year):
Total: $7,944; Instruction: $4,955; Support Services: $2,706

Enrollment, Drop-out Rates and Diploma Recipients by Race/Ethnicity

Category	Total	White	Black	Asian	AIAN	Hisp.
Enrollment (%)	100.0	92.7	1.7	2.1	1.0	2.6
Drop-out Rate (%)	0.4	0.4	0.0	0.0	0.0	0.0
H.S. Diplomas (#)	200	196	0	2	1	1

Madison Metropolitan

545 W Dayton St • Madison, WI 53703-1967
(608) 663-1607 • http://www.madison.k12.wi.us
Grade Span: PK-12; **Agency Type:** 1
Schools: 52
31 Primary; 12 Middle; 8 High; 1 Other Level
45 Regular; 0 Special Education; 0 Vocational; 7 Alternative
0 Magnet; 4 Charter; 16 Title I Eligible; 11 School-wide Title I
Students: 24,966 (50.4% male; 49.6% female)
Individual Education Program: 4,502 (18.0%);
English Language Learner: 2,931 (11.7%); Migrant: 71 (0.3%)
Eligible for Free Lunch Program: n/a
Eligible for Reduced-Price Lunch Program: n/a
Teachers: 2,028.8 (12.3 to 1)
Librarians/Media Specialists: 49.8 (501.3 to 1)
Guidance Counselors: 50.7 (492.4 to 1)
Current Spending: ($ per student per year):
Total: $10,208; Instruction: $6,331; Support Services: $3,620

Enrollment, Drop-out Rates and Diploma Recipients by Race/Ethnicity

Category	Total	White	Black	Asian	AIAN	Hisp.
Enrollment (%)	100.0	60.8	19.1	10.1	0.7	9.3
Drop-out Rate (%)	3.5	2.5	6.6	3.3	5.9	8.4
H.S. Diplomas (#)	1,607	1,231	154	140	4	78

Mcfarland

5101 Farwell St • Mc Farland, WI 53558-9216
(608) 838-3169
Grade Span: PK-12; **Agency Type:** 1
Schools: 5
3 Primary; 1 Middle; 1 High; 0 Other Level
5 Regular; 0 Special Education; 0 Vocational; 0 Alternative
0 Magnet; 0 Charter; 2 Title I Eligible; 0 School-wide Title I
Students: 1,969 (49.9% male; 50.1% female)
Individual Education Program: 306 (15.5%);
English Language Learner: 0 (0.0%); Migrant: 0 (0.0%)
Eligible for Free Lunch Program: n/a
Eligible for Reduced-Price Lunch Program: n/a
Teachers: 137.9 (14.3 to 1)
Librarians/Media Specialists: 4.0 (492.3 to 1)
Guidance Counselors: 6.3 (312.5 to 1)
Current Spending: ($ per student per year):
Total: $8,159; Instruction: $5,045; Support Services: $2,742

Enrollment, Drop-out Rates and Diploma Recipients by Race/Ethnicity

Category	Total	White	Black	Asian	AIAN	Hisp.
Enrollment (%)	100.0	94.1	1.4	2.6	0.4	1.6
Drop-out Rate (%)	0.9	1.0	0.0	0.0	0.0	0.0
H.S. Diplomas (#)	153	145	0	4	0	4

Middleton-Cross Plains

7106 S Ave • Middleton, WI 53562-3263
(608) 829-9004 • http://www.mcpasd.k12.wi.us/home.cfm
Grade Span: PK-12; **Agency Type:** 1
Schools: 10
6 Primary; 2 Middle; 2 High; 0 Other Level
9 Regular; 0 Special Education; 0 Vocational; 1 Alternative
0 Magnet; 1 Charter; 2 Title I Eligible; 0 School-wide Title I
Students: 5,330 (50.3% male; 49.7% female)
Individual Education Program: 739 (13.9%);
English Language Learner: 0 (0.0%); Migrant: 0 (0.0%)
Eligible for Free Lunch Program: n/a
Eligible for Reduced-Price Lunch Program: n/a
Teachers: 396.6 (13.4 to 1)
Librarians/Media Specialists: 12.2 (436.9 to 1)
Guidance Counselors: 13.0 (410.0 to 1)
Current Spending: ($ per student per year):
Total: $8,055; Instruction: $5,135; Support Services: $2,613

Enrollment, Drop-out Rates and Diploma Recipients by Race/Ethnicity

Category	Total	White	Black	Asian	AIAN	Hisp.
Enrollment (%)	100.0	90.5	3.2	3.3	0.3	2.8
Drop-out Rate (%)	1.2	1.1	4.8	2.4	0.0	2.6
H.S. Diplomas (#)	385	360	5	12	0	8

Monona Grove

5301 Monona Dr • Monona, WI 53716-3126
(608) 221-7660 • http://www.mgsd.k12.wi.us
Grade Span: PK-12; **Agency Type:** 1
Schools: 7
4 Primary; 1 Middle; 2 High; 0 Other Level
6 Regular; 0 Special Education; 0 Vocational; 1 Alternative
0 Magnet; 1 Charter; 4 Title I Eligible; 0 School-wide Title I
Students: 2,819 (52.0% male; 48.0% female)
Individual Education Program: 365 (12.9%);
English Language Learner: 0 (0.0%); Migrant: 0 (0.0%)
Eligible for Free Lunch Program: n/a
Eligible for Reduced-Price Lunch Program: n/a
Teachers: 219.3 (12.9 to 1)
Librarians/Media Specialists: 6.0 (469.8 to 1)
Guidance Counselors: 5.5 (512.5 to 1)
Current Spending: ($ per student per year):
Total: $8,499; Instruction: $4,987; Support Services: $3,272

Enrollment, Drop-out Rates and Diploma Recipients by Race/Ethnicity

Category	Total	White	Black	Asian	AIAN	Hisp.
Enrollment (%)	100.0	90.5	4.2	2.0	0.3	3.1
Drop-out Rate (%)	0.7	0.8	0.0	0.0	0.0	0.0
H.S. Diplomas (#)	178	167	3	2	0	6

Mount Horeb Area

1304 E Lincoln St • Mount Horeb, WI 53572-0087
Mailing Address: PO Box 87 • Mount Horeb, WI 53572-0087
(608) 437-2400 • http://www.mhasd.k12.wi.us
Grade Span: PK-12; **Agency Type:** 1
Schools: 5
3 Primary; 1 Middle; 1 High; 0 Other Level
5 Regular; 0 Special Education; 0 Vocational; 0 Alternative
0 Magnet; 0 Charter; 2 Title I Eligible; 0 School-wide Title I
Students: 2,055 (50.5% male; 49.5% female)
Individual Education Program: 233 (11.3%);
English Language Learner: 0 (0.0%); Migrant: 0 (0.0%)
Eligible for Free Lunch Program: n/a
Eligible for Reduced-Price Lunch Program: n/a
Teachers: 143.6 (14.3 to 1)
Librarians/Media Specialists: 3.6 (570.8 to 1)
Guidance Counselors: 5.0 (411.0 to 1)
Current Spending: ($ per student per year):
Total: $7,090; Instruction: $4,210; Support Services: $2,606

Enrollment, Drop-out Rates and Diploma Recipients by Race/Ethnicity

Category	Total	White	Black	Asian	AIAN	Hisp.
Enrollment (%)	100.0	96.9	1.4	0.7	0.3	0.7
Drop-out Rate (%)	n/a	n/a	n/a	n/a	n/a	n/a
H.S. Diplomas (#)	126	123	2	0	0	1

Oregon

200 N Main St • Oregon, WI 53575-1447
(608) 835-4003 • http://www.oregon.k12.wi.us
Grade Span: PK-12; **Agency Type:** 1
Schools: 6
3 Primary; 2 Middle; 1 High; 0 Other Level
6 Regular; 0 Special Education; 0 Vocational; 0 Alternative
0 Magnet; 0 Charter; 3 Title I Eligible; 0 School-wide Title I
Students: 3,429 (51.4% male; 48.6% female)
Individual Education Program: 463 (13.5%);
English Language Learner: 0 (0.0%); Migrant: 0 (0.0%)
Eligible for Free Lunch Program: n/a
Eligible for Reduced-Price Lunch Program: n/a
Teachers: 257.2 (13.3 to 1)
Librarians/Media Specialists: 5.0 (685.8 to 1)
Guidance Counselors: 8.9 (385.3 to 1)
Current Spending: ($ per student per year):
Total: $8,309; Instruction: $4,883; Support Services: $3,134

Enrollment, Drop-out Rates and Diploma Recipients by Race/Ethnicity

Category	Total	White	Black	Asian	AIAN	Hisp.
Enrollment (%)	100.0	95.3	1.2	1.4	0.5	1.6
Drop-out Rate (%)	0.5	0.5	0.0	0.0	0.0	0.0
H.S. Diplomas (#)	228	222	2	2	1	1

Stoughton Area

320 N St • Stoughton, WI 53589-1733
(608) 877-5001 • http://www.stoughton.k12.wi.us
Grade Span: PK-12; **Agency Type:** 1
Schools: 6
3 Primary; 2 Middle; 1 High; 0 Other Level

6 Regular; 0 Special Education; 0 Vocational; 0 Alternative
0 Magnet; 0 Charter; 3 Title I Eligible; 0 School-wide Title I
Students: 3,663 (51.3% male; 48.7% female)
Individual Education Program: 689 (18.8%);
English Language Learner: 0 (0.0%); Migrant: 0 (0.0%)
Eligible for Free Lunch Program: n/a
Eligible for Reduced-Price Lunch Program: n/a
Teachers: 256.2 (14.3 to 1)
Librarians/Media Specialists: 6.0 (610.5 to 1)
Guidance Counselors: 6.1 (600.5 to 1)
Current Spending: ($ per student per year):
Total: $7,252; Instruction: $4,682; Support Services: $2,390
Enrollment, Drop-out Rates and Diploma Recipients by Race/Ethnicity

Category	Total	White	Black	Asian	AIAN	Hisp.
Enrollment (%)	100.0	93.3	3.1	1.4	0.5	1.6
Drop-out Rate (%)	0.5	0.5	0.0	0.0	0.0	0.0
H.S. Diplomas (#)	254	239	2	3	1	9

Sun Prairie Area
501 S Bird St • Sun Prairie, WI 53590-2803
(608) 834-6502 • http://www.spasd.k12.wi.us
Grade Span: PK-12; **Agency Type:** 1
Schools: 10
5 Primary; 2 Middle; 3 High; 0 Other Level
8 Regular; 0 Special Education; 0 Vocational; 2 Alternative
0 Magnet; 2 Charter; 3 Title I Eligible; 0 School-wide Title I
Students: 4,987 (51.5% male; 48.5% female)
Individual Education Program: 731 (14.7%);
English Language Learner: 115 (2.3%); Migrant: 1 (<0.1%)
Eligible for Free Lunch Program: n/a
Eligible for Reduced-Price Lunch Program: n/a
Teachers: 365.0 (13.7 to 1)
Librarians/Media Specialists: 8.0 (623.4 to 1)
Guidance Counselors: 11.0 (453.4 to 1)
Current Spending: ($ per student per year):
Total: $8,009; Instruction: $4,975; Support Services: $2,801
Enrollment, Drop-out Rates and Diploma Recipients by Race/Ethnicity

Category	Total	White	Black	Asian	AIAN	Hisp.
Enrollment (%)	100.0	86.3	7.0	3.3	0.5	3.0
Drop-out Rate (%)	1.5	1.0	10.4	2.9	0.0	6.9
H.S. Diplomas (#)	347	330	6	5	1	5

Verona Area
700 N Main St • Verona, WI 53593-1153
(608) 845-4310 • http://www.verona.k12.wi.us
Grade Span: PK-12; **Agency Type:** 1
Schools: 9
6 Primary; 2 Middle; 1 High; 0 Other Level
7 Regular; 0 Special Education; 0 Vocational; 2 Alternative
0 Magnet; 2 Charter; 3 Title I Eligible; 0 School-wide Title I
Students: 4,448 (52.3% male; 47.7% female)
Individual Education Program: 539 (12.1%);
English Language Learner: 0 (0.0%); Migrant: 1 (<0.1%)
Eligible for Free Lunch Program: n/a
Eligible for Reduced-Price Lunch Program: n/a
Teachers: 360.7 (12.3 to 1)
Librarians/Media Specialists: 6.0 (741.3 to 1)
Guidance Counselors: 12.6 (353.0 to 1)
Current Spending: ($ per student per year):
Total: $8,507; Instruction: $5,464; Support Services: $2,750
Enrollment, Drop-out Rates and Diploma Recipients by Race/Ethnicity

Category	Total	White	Black	Asian	AIAN	Hisp.
Enrollment (%)	100.0	81.5	9.8	3.8	0.6	4.3
Drop-out Rate (%)	n/a	n/a	n/a	n/a	n/a	n/a
H.S. Diplomas (#)	280	256	8	7	1	8

Waunakee Community
101 School Dr • Waunakee, WI 53597-1637
(608) 849-2000 • http://www.waunakee.k12.wi.us
Grade Span: PK-12; **Agency Type:** 1
Schools: 5
2 Primary; 2 Middle; 1 High; 0 Other Level
5 Regular; 0 Special Education; 0 Vocational; 0 Alternative
0 Magnet; 0 Charter; 2 Title I Eligible; 0 School-wide Title I
Students: 2,963 (52.3% male; 47.7% female)
Individual Education Program: 393 (13.3%);
English Language Learner: 0 (0.0%); Migrant: 0 (0.0%)
Eligible for Free Lunch Program: n/a
Eligible for Reduced-Price Lunch Program: n/a
Teachers: 208.0 (14.2 to 1)
Librarians/Media Specialists: 5.9 (502.2 to 1)
Guidance Counselors: 6.0 (493.8 to 1)
Current Spending: ($ per student per year):
Total: $7,349; Instruction: $4,373; Support Services: $2,737
Enrollment, Drop-out Rates and Diploma Recipients by Race/Ethnicity

Category	Total	White	Black	Asian	AIAN	Hisp.
Enrollment (%)	100.0	97.0	0.9	1.0	0.2	0.9
Drop-out Rate (%)	n/a	n/a	n/a	n/a	n/a	n/a
H.S. Diplomas (#)	188	183	3	1	0	1

Dodge County

Beaver Dam
705 Mckinley St • Beaver Dam, WI 53916-1941
(920) 885-7309 • http://www.beaverdam.k12.wi.us
Grade Span: PK-12; **Agency Type:** 1
Schools: 10
7 Primary; 1 Middle; 1 High; 1 Other Level
9 Regular; 0 Special Education; 0 Vocational; 1 Alternative
0 Magnet; 1 Charter; 7 Title I Eligible; 0 School-wide Title I
Students: 3,418 (52.4% male; 47.6% female)
Individual Education Program: 557 (16.3%);
English Language Learner: 83 (2.4%); Migrant: 37 (1.1%)
Eligible for Free Lunch Program: n/a
Eligible for Reduced-Price Lunch Program: n/a
Teachers: 238.9 (14.3 to 1)
Librarians/Media Specialists: 3.1 (1,102.6 to 1)
Guidance Counselors: 7.5 (455.7 to 1)
Current Spending: ($ per student per year):
Total: $8,262; Instruction: $5,105; Support Services: $2,905
Enrollment, Drop-out Rates and Diploma Recipients by Race/Ethnicity

Category	Total	White	Black	Asian	AIAN	Hisp.
Enrollment (%)	100.0	90.3	1.0	1.2	0.5	7.1
Drop-out Rate (%)	1.0	1.0	0.0	0.0	0.0	0.0
H.S. Diplomas (#)	299	290	0	2	2	5

Douglas County

Superior
3025 Tower Ave • Superior, WI 54880-5369
(715) 394-8710 • http://www.superior.k12.wi.us
Grade Span: PK-12; **Agency Type:** 1
Schools: 9
6 Primary; 2 Middle; 1 High; 0 Other Level
9 Regular; 0 Special Education; 0 Vocational; 0 Alternative
0 Magnet; 0 Charter; 8 Title I Eligible; 5 School-wide Title I
Students: 5,063 (52.7% male; 47.3% female)
Individual Education Program: 630 (12.4%);
English Language Learner: 17 (0.3%); Migrant: 0 (0.0%)
Eligible for Free Lunch Program: n/a
Eligible for Reduced-Price Lunch Program: n/a
Teachers: 323.1 (15.7 to 1)
Librarians/Media Specialists: 7.0 (723.3 to 1)
Guidance Counselors: 14.0 (361.6 to 1)
Current Spending: ($ per student per year):
Total: $7,998; Instruction: $4,887; Support Services: $2,850
Enrollment, Drop-out Rates and Diploma Recipients by Race/Ethnicity

Category	Total	White	Black	Asian	AIAN	Hisp.
Enrollment (%)	100.0	90.4	1.5	1.9	5.4	0.9
Drop-out Rate (%)	4.2	4.1	7.1	0.0	6.0	10.0
H.S. Diplomas (#)	338	312	2	1	21	2

Dunn County

Menomonie Area
215 Pine Ave NE • Menomonie, WI 54751-1511
(715) 232-1642 • http://msd.k12.wi.us
Grade Span: PK-12; **Agency Type:** 1
Schools: 8
5 Primary; 1 Middle; 2 High; 0 Other Level
7 Regular; 0 Special Education; 0 Vocational; 1 Alternative
0 Magnet; 1 Charter; 6 Title I Eligible; 2 School-wide Title I
Students: 3,348 (50.8% male; 49.2% female)
Individual Education Program: 455 (13.6%);
English Language Learner: 177 (5.3%); Migrant: 0 (0.0%)
Eligible for Free Lunch Program: n/a
Eligible for Reduced-Price Lunch Program: n/a
Teachers: 223.6 (15.0 to 1)
Librarians/Media Specialists: 4.0 (837.0 to 1)
Guidance Counselors: 10.0 (334.8 to 1)
Current Spending: ($ per student per year):
Total: $8,241; Instruction: $4,881; Support Services: $2,970
Enrollment, Drop-out Rates and Diploma Recipients by Race/Ethnicity

Category	Total	White	Black	Asian	AIAN	Hisp.
Enrollment (%)	100.0	86.6	1.5	10.5	0.7	0.8
Drop-out Rate (%)	2.5	2.5	25.0	2.1	0.0	0.0
H.S. Diplomas (#)	258	225	0	23	1	9

Eau Claire County

Eau Claire Area
500 Main St • Eau Claire, WI 54701-3770
(715) 833-3465 • http://www.ecasd.k12.wi.us
Grade Span: PK-12; **Agency Type:** 1
Schools: 25
17 Primary; 3 Middle; 5 High; 0 Other Level
20 Regular; 0 Special Education; 0 Vocational; 5 Alternative
0 Magnet; 4 Charter; 11 Title I Eligible; 4 School-wide Title I
Students: 10,835 (51.3% male; 48.7% female)
Individual Education Program: 1,468 (13.5%);
English Language Learner: 616 (5.7%); Migrant: 0 (0.0%)
Eligible for Free Lunch Program: n/a
Eligible for Reduced-Price Lunch Program: n/a
Teachers: 780.4 (13.9 to 1)
Librarians/Media Specialists: 17.1 (633.6 to 1)
Guidance Counselors: 32.3 (335.4 to 1)
Current Spending: ($ per student per year):
Total: $8,064; Instruction: $4,975; Support Services: $2,787
Enrollment, Drop-out Rates and Diploma Recipients by Race/Ethnicity

Category	Total	White	Black	Asian	AIAN	Hisp.
Enrollment (%)	100.0	86.7	1.5	9.5	1.1	1.2
Drop-out Rate (%)	0.6	0.6	0.0	0.7	0.0	0.0
H.S. Diplomas (#)	978	865	10	74	20	9

Fond Du Lac County

Campbellsport
114 W Sheboygan St • Campbellsport, WI 53010-2791
(920) 533-8381 • http://www.csd.k12.wi.us
Grade Span: PK-12; **Agency Type:** 1
Schools: 4
2 Primary; 1 Middle; 1 High; 0 Other Level
4 Regular; 0 Special Education; 0 Vocational; 0 Alternative
0 Magnet; 0 Charter; 2 Title I Eligible; 0 School-wide Title I
Students: 1,527 (51.7% male; 48.3% female)
Individual Education Program: 230 (15.1%);
English Language Learner: 0 (0.0%); Migrant: 0 (0.0%)
Eligible for Free Lunch Program: n/a
Eligible for Reduced-Price Lunch Program: n/a
Teachers: 105.0 (14.5 to 1)
Librarians/Media Specialists: 2.0 (763.5 to 1)
Guidance Counselors: 3.0 (509.0 to 1)
Current Spending: ($ per student per year):
Total: $7,049; Instruction: $4,469; Support Services: $2,341
Enrollment, Drop-out Rates and Diploma Recipients by Race/Ethnicity

Category	Total	White	Black	Asian	AIAN	Hisp.
Enrollment (%)	100.0	98.2	0.3	0.1	0.2	1.1
Drop-out Rate (%)	0.9	0.9	n/a	0.0	n/a	0.0
H.S. Diplomas (#)	130	129	0	1	0	0

Fond Du Lac
72 W 9th St • Fond Du Lac, WI 54935-4956
(920) 906-6502 • http://www.fonddulac.k12.wi.us
Grade Span: PK-12; **Agency Type:** 1
Schools: 14
10 Primary; 3 Middle; 1 High; 0 Other Level
13 Regular; 1 Special Education; 0 Vocational; 0 Alternative
0 Magnet; 0 Charter; 7 Title I Eligible; 0 School-wide Title I
Students: 7,245 (50.9% male; 49.1% female)
Individual Education Program: 1,118 (15.4%);
English Language Learner: 81 (1.1%); Migrant: 0 (0.0%)
Eligible for Free Lunch Program: n/a
Eligible for Reduced-Price Lunch Program: n/a
Teachers: 478.1 (15.2 to 1)
Librarians/Media Specialists: 15.5 (467.4 to 1)
Guidance Counselors: 15.0 (483.0 to 1)
Current Spending: ($ per student per year):
Total: $7,332; Instruction: $4,642; Support Services: $2,465
Enrollment, Drop-out Rates and Diploma Recipients by Race/Ethnicity

Category	Total	White	Black	Asian	AIAN	Hisp.
Enrollment (%)	100.0	91.2	1.5	2.8	0.5	3.9
Drop-out Rate (%)	2.0	2.0	4.8	0.0	0.0	3.6
H.S. Diplomas (#)	463	440	4	14	1	4

Ripon
1120 Metomen St • Ripon, WI 54971-0991
Mailing Address: PO Box 991 • Ripon, WI 54971-0991
(920) 748-4600 • http://www.ripon.k12.wi.us
Grade Span: PK-12; **Agency Type:** 1
Schools: 4
2 Primary; 1 Middle; 1 High; 0 Other Level
4 Regular; 0 Special Education; 0 Vocational; 0 Alternative
0 Magnet; 0 Charter; 2 Title I Eligible; 0 School-wide Title I
Students: 1,713 (52.2% male; 47.8% female)
Individual Education Program: 239 (14.0%);
English Language Learner: 0 (0.0%); Migrant: 0 (0.0%)
Eligible for Free Lunch Program: n/a
Eligible for Reduced-Price Lunch Program: n/a
Teachers: 117.4 (14.6 to 1)
Librarians/Media Specialists: 3.0 (571.0 to 1)
Guidance Counselors: 4.5 (380.7 to 1)
Current Spending: ($ per student per year):
Total: $7,871; Instruction: $4,593; Support Services: $2,987
Enrollment, Drop-out Rates and Diploma Recipients by Race/Ethnicity

Category	Total	White	Black	Asian	AIAN	Hisp.
Enrollment (%)	100.0	95.2	0.4	0.7	0.3	3.4
Drop-out Rate (%)	0.2	0.2	0.0	0.0	0.0	0.0
H.S. Diplomas (#)	132	126	0	2	0	4

Waupun
950 Wilcox St • Waupun, WI 53963-2242
(920) 324-9341 • http://www.waupun.k12.wi.us
Grade Span: PK-12; **Agency Type:** 1
Schools: 8
5 Primary; 1 Middle; 1 High; 1 Other Level
7 Regular; 0 Special Education; 0 Vocational; 1 Alternative
0 Magnet; 1 Charter; 3 Title I Eligible; 0 School-wide Title I
Students: 2,320 (53.2% male; 46.8% female)
Individual Education Program: 345 (14.9%);
English Language Learner: 0 (0.0%); Migrant: 6 (0.3%)
Eligible for Free Lunch Program: n/a
Eligible for Reduced-Price Lunch Program: n/a
Teachers: 186.3 (12.5 to 1)
Librarians/Media Specialists: 3.0 (773.3 to 1)
Guidance Counselors: 6.0 (386.7 to 1)
Current Spending: ($ per student per year):
Total: $8,003; Instruction: $5,184; Support Services: $2,552
Enrollment, Drop-out Rates and Diploma Recipients by Race/Ethnicity

Category	Total	White	Black	Asian	AIAN	Hisp.
Enrollment (%)	100.0	96.3	0.6	0.2	0.3	2.6
Drop-out Rate (%)	1.4	1.5	0.0	0.0	0.0	0.0
H.S. Diplomas (#)	184	180	0	1	0	3

Grant County

Platteville
780 N 2nd St • Platteville, WI 53818-1847
(608) 342-4000 • http://www.platteville.k12.wi.us
Grade Span: PK-12; **Agency Type:** 1
Schools: 5
3 Primary; 1 Middle; 1 High; 0 Other Level
5 Regular; 0 Special Education; 0 Vocational; 0 Alternative
0 Magnet; 0 Charter; 3 Title I Eligible; 0 School-wide Title I
Students: 1,627 (50.0% male; 50.0% female)
Individual Education Program: 242 (14.9%);
English Language Learner: 0 (0.0%); Migrant: 0 (0.0%)
Eligible for Free Lunch Program: n/a
Eligible for Reduced-Price Lunch Program: n/a
Teachers: 113.1 (14.4 to 1)
Librarians/Media Specialists: 1.5 (1,084.7 to 1)
Guidance Counselors: 2.6 (625.8 to 1)
Current Spending: ($ per student per year):
Total: $8,512; Instruction: $5,168; Support Services: $2,999
Enrollment, Drop-out Rates and Diploma Recipients by Race/Ethnicity

Category	Total	White	Black	Asian	AIAN	Hisp.
Enrollment (%)	100.0	94.2	2.4	2.3	0.4	0.8
Drop-out Rate (%)	0.7	0.7	0.0	0.0	0.0	0.0
H.S. Diplomas (#)	146	141	1	3	0	1

Green County

Monroe
925 16th Ave Ste 3 • Monroe, WI 53566-1763
(608) 328-7171 • http://www.monroeschools.com
Grade Span: PK-12; **Agency Type:** 1
Schools: 7
3 Primary; 1 Middle; 3 High; 0 Other Level
6 Regular; 0 Special Education; 0 Vocational; 1 Alternative
0 Magnet; 1 Charter; 3 Title I Eligible; 0 School-wide Title I
Students: 2,645 (49.7% male; 50.3% female)
Individual Education Program: 456 (17.2%);
English Language Learner: 0 (0.0%); Migrant: 0 (0.0%)
Eligible for Free Lunch Program: n/a
Eligible for Reduced-Price Lunch Program: n/a
Teachers: 219.8 (12.0 to 1)
Librarians/Media Specialists: 5.0 (529.0 to 1)
Guidance Counselors: 8.1 (326.5 to 1)

Current Spending: ($ per student per year):
Total: $8,548; Instruction: $5,548; Support Services: $2,735

Enrollment, Drop-out Rates and Diploma Recipients by Race/Ethnicity

Category	Total	White	Black	Asian	AIAN	Hisp.
Enrollment (%)	100.0	96.0	1.1	0.9	0.8	1.2
Drop-out Rate (%)	1.3	1.3	0.0	0.0	0.0	0.0
H.S. Diplomas (#)	190	186	1	2	1	0

Berlin Area

295 E Marquette St • Berlin, WI 54923-1272
(920) 361-2004 • http://www.berlin.k12.wi.us
Grade Span: PK-12; **Agency Type:** 1
Schools: 4
2 Primary; 1 Middle; 1 High; 0 Other Level
4 Regular; 0 Special Education; 0 Vocational; 0 Alternative
0 Magnet; 0 Charter; 1 Title I Eligible; 0 School-wide Title I
Students: 1,730 (52.2% male; 47.8% female)
Individual Education Program: 252 (14.6%);
English Language Learner: 0 (0.0%); Migrant: 86 (5.0%)
Eligible for Free Lunch Program: n/a
Eligible for Reduced-Price Lunch Program: n/a
Teachers: 124.2 (13.9 to 1)
Librarians/Media Specialists: 3.0 (576.7 to 1)
Guidance Counselors: 5.0 (346.0 to 1)
Current Spending: ($ per student per year):
Total: $6,903; Instruction: $4,166; Support Services: $2,503

Enrollment, Drop-out Rates and Diploma Recipients by Race/Ethnicity

Category	Total	White	Black	Asian	AIAN	Hisp.
Enrollment (%)	100.0	87.6	0.5	1.9	0.1	10.0
Drop-out Rate (%)	0.2	0.2	n/a	0.0	n/a	0.0
H.S. Diplomas (#)	143	139	0	2	0	2

Jackson County

Black River Falls

301 N 4th St • Black River Fls, WI 54615-1227
(715) 284-4357 • http://www.brf.org
Grade Span: PK-12; **Agency Type:** 1
Schools: 5
3 Primary; 1 Middle; 1 High; 0 Other Level
5 Regular; 0 Special Education; 0 Vocational; 0 Alternative
0 Magnet; 0 Charter; 2 Title I Eligible; 1 School-wide Title I
Students: 1,921 (51.5% male; 48.5% female)
Individual Education Program: 313 (16.3%);
English Language Learner: 0 (0.0%); Migrant: 0 (0.0%)
Eligible for Free Lunch Program: n/a
Eligible for Reduced-Price Lunch Program: n/a
Teachers: 146.1 (13.1 to 1)
Librarians/Media Specialists: 3.5 (548.9 to 1)
Guidance Counselors: 5.0 (384.2 to 1)
Current Spending: ($ per student per year):
Total: $7,165; Instruction: $4,415; Support Services: $2,440

Enrollment, Drop-out Rates and Diploma Recipients by Race/Ethnicity

Category	Total	White	Black	Asian	AIAN	Hisp.
Enrollment (%)	100.0	79.7	0.5	0.9	18.1	0.8
Drop-out Rate (%)	1.9	1.2	n/a	0.0	5.0	25.0
H.S. Diplomas (#)	149	128	0	0	19	2

Jefferson County

Fort Atkinson

201 Park St • Fort Atkinson, WI 53538-2155
(920) 563-7807 • http://www.fortschools.org
Grade Span: PK-12; **Agency Type:** 1
Schools: 7
4 Primary; 1 Middle; 2 High; 0 Other Level
6 Regular; 0 Special Education; 0 Vocational; 1 Alternative
0 Magnet; 0 Charter; 3 Title I Eligible; 0 School-wide Title I
Students: 2,641 (52.1% male; 47.9% female)
Individual Education Program: 390 (14.8%);
English Language Learner: 12 (0.5%); Migrant: 0 (0.0%)
Eligible for Free Lunch Program: n/a
Eligible for Reduced-Price Lunch Program: n/a
Teachers: 192.9 (13.7 to 1)
Librarians/Media Specialists: 5.0 (528.2 to 1)
Guidance Counselors: 5.0 (528.2 to 1)
Current Spending: ($ per student per year):
Total: $8,355; Instruction: $4,776; Support Services: $3,300

Enrollment, Drop-out Rates and Diploma Recipients by Race/Ethnicity

Category	Total	White	Black	Asian	AIAN	Hisp.
Enrollment (%)	100.0	94.0	0.5	0.9	0.4	4.2
Drop-out Rate (%)	2.3	2.1	50.0	0.0	0.0	8.3
H.S. Diplomas (#)	219	213	0	1	0	5

Jefferson

206 S Taft Ave • Jefferson, WI 53549-1453
(920) 675-1000 • http://www.jefferson.k12.wi.us
Grade Span: PK-12; **Agency Type:** 1
Schools: 6
3 Primary; 1 Middle; 2 High; 0 Other Level
5 Regular; 0 Special Education; 0 Vocational; 1 Alternative
0 Magnet; 1 Charter; 3 Title I Eligible; 0 School-wide Title I
Students: 1,693 (52.7% male; 47.3% female)
Individual Education Program: 285 (16.8%);
English Language Learner: 0 (0.0%); Migrant: 0 (0.0%)
Eligible for Free Lunch Program: n/a
Eligible for Reduced-Price Lunch Program: n/a
Teachers: 132.0 (12.8 to 1)
Librarians/Media Specialists: 3.5 (483.7 to 1)
Guidance Counselors: 4.6 (368.0 to 1)
Current Spending: ($ per student per year):
Total: $8,876; Instruction: $5,345; Support Services: $3,195

Enrollment, Drop-out Rates and Diploma Recipients by Race/Ethnicity

Category	Total	White	Black	Asian	AIAN	Hisp.
Enrollment (%)	100.0	90.7	0.5	0.1	1.4	7.3
Drop-out Rate (%)	2.0	2.0	n/a	n/a	100.0	0.0
H.S. Diplomas (#)	101	98	0	1	0	2

Watertown

111 Dodge St • Watertown, WI 53094-4470
(920) 262-1460 • http://www.watertown.k12.wi.us
Grade Span: PK-12; **Agency Type:** 1
Schools: 8
6 Primary; 1 Middle; 1 High; 0 Other Level
8 Regular; 0 Special Education; 0 Vocational; 0 Alternative
0 Magnet; 0 Charter; 4 Title I Eligible; 0 School-wide Title I
Students: 3,715 (51.9% male; 48.1% female)
Individual Education Program: 690 (18.6%);
English Language Learner: 0 (0.0%); Migrant: 32 (0.9%)
Eligible for Free Lunch Program: n/a
Eligible for Reduced-Price Lunch Program: n/a
Teachers: 231.9 (16.0 to 1)
Librarians/Media Specialists: 4.9 (758.2 to 1)
Guidance Counselors: 8.5 (437.1 to 1)
Current Spending: ($ per student per year):
Total: $8,205; Instruction: $5,041; Support Services: $2,790

Enrollment, Drop-out Rates and Diploma Recipients by Race/Ethnicity

Category	Total	White	Black	Asian	AIAN	Hisp.
Enrollment (%)	100.0	88.1	0.9	0.9	1.1	9.0
Drop-out Rate (%)	1.3	1.2	11.1	0.0	5.6	2.0
H.S. Diplomas (#)	288	273	1	4	2	8

Juneau County

Mauston

510 Grayside Ave • Mauston, WI 53948-1952
(608) 847-5451 • http://www.mauston.k12.wi.us
Grade Span: PK-12; **Agency Type:** 1
Schools: 6
3 Primary; 2 Middle; 1 High; 0 Other Level
5 Regular; 0 Special Education; 0 Vocational; 1 Alternative
0 Magnet; 1 Charter; 3 Title I Eligible; 1 School-wide Title I
Students: 1,607 (53.0% male; 47.0% female)
Individual Education Program: 257 (16.0%);
English Language Learner: 0 (0.0%); Migrant: 0 (0.0%)
Eligible for Free Lunch Program: n/a
Eligible for Reduced-Price Lunch Program: n/a
Teachers: 134.0 (12.0 to 1)
Librarians/Media Specialists: 3.9 (412.1 to 1)
Guidance Counselors: 4.0 (401.8 to 1)
Current Spending: ($ per student per year):
Total: $7,969; Instruction: $4,787; Support Services: $2,805

Enrollment, Drop-out Rates and Diploma Recipients by Race/Ethnicity

Category	Total	White	Black	Asian	AIAN	Hisp.
Enrollment (%)	100.0	93.3	1.7	1.2	2.1	1.7
Drop-out Rate (%)	4.1	4.4	0.0	0.0	0.0	0.0
H.S. Diplomas (#)	116	110	2	3	0	1

Kenosha County

Kenosha

3600 52nd St • Kenosha, WI 53144
Mailing Address: PO Box 340 • Kenosha, WI 53141-0340
(262) 653-6320 • http://www.kusd.edu
Grade Span: PK-12; **Agency Type:** 1
Schools: 41
27 Primary; 7 Middle; 6 High; 1 Other Level
36 Regular; 0 Special Education; 1 Vocational; 4 Alternative
0 Magnet; 3 Charter; 18 Title I Eligible; 11 School-wide Title I

Students: 21,088 (52.3% male; 47.7% female)
Individual Education Program: 2,971 (14.1%);
English Language Learner: 708 (3.4%); Migrant: 0 (0.0%)
Eligible for Free Lunch Program: n/a
Eligible for Reduced-Price Lunch Program: n/a
Teachers: 1,412.7 (14.9 to 1)
Librarians/Media Specialists: 44.7 (471.8 to 1)
Guidance Counselors: 52.0 (405.5 to 1)
Current Spending: ($ per student per year):
Total: $8,150; Instruction: $5,012; Support Services: $2,889
Enrollment, Drop-out Rates and Diploma Recipients by Race/Ethnicity

Category	Total	White	Black	Asian	AIAN	Hisp.
Enrollment (%)	100.0	70.5	13.9	1.7	0.5	13.5
Drop-out Rate (%)	2.1	1.8	4.1	2.4	8.7	2.7
H.S. Diplomas (#)	1,305	1,071	100	22	1	111

Kewaunee County

Luxemburg-Casco

318 N Main St • Luxemburg, WI 54217-0070
Mailing Address: PO Box 70 • Luxemburg, WI 54217-0070
(920) 845-2391 • http://www.luxcasco.k12.wi.us
Grade Span: PK-12; **Agency Type:** 1
Schools: 4
2 Primary; 1 Middle; 1 High; 0 Other Level
4 Regular; 0 Special Education; 0 Vocational; 0 Alternative
0 Magnet; 0 Charter; 2 Title I Eligible; 0 School-wide Title I
Students: 1,911 (53.0% male; 47.0% female)
Individual Education Program: 269 (14.1%);
English Language Learner: 0 (0.0%); Migrant: 0 (0.0%)
Eligible for Free Lunch Program: n/a
Eligible for Reduced-Price Lunch Program: n/a
Teachers: 122.6 (15.6 to 1)
Librarians/Media Specialists: 4.0 (477.8 to 1)
Guidance Counselors: 4.5 (424.7 to 1)
Current Spending: ($ per student per year):
Total: $6,436; Instruction: $3,916; Support Services: $2,266
Enrollment, Drop-out Rates and Diploma Recipients by Race/Ethnicity

Category	Total	White	Black	Asian	AIAN	Hisp.
Enrollment (%)	100.0	98.3	0.6	0.4	0.4	0.4
Drop-out Rate (%)	0.6	0.3	0.0	50.0	50.0	n/a
H.S. Diplomas (#)	165	163	0	1	1	0

La Crosse County

Holmen

502 N Main St • Holmen, WI 54636-0580
Mailing Address: PO Box 580 • Holmen, WI 54636-0580
(608) 526-1301 • http://www.holmen.k12.wi.us
Grade Span: PK-12; **Agency Type:** 1
Schools: 6
4 Primary; 0 Middle; 1 High; 1 Other Level
6 Regular; 0 Special Education; 0 Vocational; 0 Alternative
0 Magnet; 0 Charter; 2 Title I Eligible; 0 School-wide Title I
Students: 3,077 (51.3% male; 48.7% female)
Individual Education Program: 369 (12.0%);
English Language Learner: 147 (4.8%); Migrant: 0 (0.0%)
Eligible for Free Lunch Program: n/a
Eligible for Reduced-Price Lunch Program: n/a
Teachers: 219.5 (14.0 to 1)
Librarians/Media Specialists: 7.0 (439.6 to 1)
Guidance Counselors: 7.8 (394.5 to 1)
Current Spending: ($ per student per year):
Total: $7,650; Instruction: $4,477; Support Services: $2,797
Enrollment, Drop-out Rates and Diploma Recipients by Race/Ethnicity

Category	Total	White	Black	Asian	AIAN	Hisp.
Enrollment (%)	100.0	90.6	1.0	6.9	0.8	0.7
Drop-out Rate (%)	0.9	0.9	0.0	0.0	0.0	0.0
H.S. Diplomas (#)	228	211	2	13	2	0

La Crosse

Hogan Admin Center • La Crosse, WI 54601-4982
(608) 789-7628 • http://www.centuryinter.net/hogan
Grade Span: PK-12; **Agency Type:** 1
Schools: 24
14 Primary; 5 Middle; 5 High; 0 Other Level
19 Regular; 0 Special Education; 0 Vocational; 5 Alternative
0 Magnet; 5 Charter; 13 Title I Eligible; 6 School-wide Title I
Students: 7,640 (52.0% male; 48.0% female)
Individual Education Program: 1,150 (15.1%);
English Language Learner: 515 (6.7%); Migrant: 0 (0.0%)
Eligible for Free Lunch Program: n/a
Eligible for Reduced-Price Lunch Program: n/a
Teachers: 582.3 (13.1 to 1)
Librarians/Media Specialists: 19.2 (397.9 to 1)
Guidance Counselors: 20.0 (382.0 to 1)
Current Spending: ($ per student per year):
Total: $9,061; Instruction: $5,763; Support Services: $2,827
Enrollment, Drop-out Rates and Diploma Recipients by Race/Ethnicity

Category	Total	White	Black	Asian	AIAN	Hisp.
Enrollment (%)	100.0	81.2	4.0	12.7	1.1	0.9
Drop-out Rate (%)	1.3	1.0	4.1	1.9	0.0	4.8
H.S. Diplomas (#)	499	422	10	57	5	5

Onalaska

1821 E Main St • Onalaska, WI 54650-0429
Mailing Address: PO Box 429 • Onalaska, WI 54650-0429
(608) 781-9700 • http://www.onalaska.k12.wi.us
Grade Span: PK-12; **Agency Type:** 1
Schools: 6
4 Primary; 1 Middle; 1 High; 0 Other Level
6 Regular; 0 Special Education; 0 Vocational; 0 Alternative
0 Magnet; 0 Charter; 3 Title I Eligible; 0 School-wide Title I
Students: 2,764 (51.0% male; 49.0% female)
Individual Education Program: 279 (10.1%);
English Language Learner: 50 (1.8%); Migrant: 0 (0.0%)
Eligible for Free Lunch Program: n/a
Eligible for Reduced-Price Lunch Program: n/a
Teachers: 185.6 (14.9 to 1)
Librarians/Media Specialists: 5.3 (521.5 to 1)
Guidance Counselors: 8.0 (345.5 to 1)
Current Spending: ($ per student per year):
Total: $7,821; Instruction: $4,581; Support Services: $2,951
Enrollment, Drop-out Rates and Diploma Recipients by Race/Ethnicity

Category	Total	White	Black	Asian	AIAN	Hisp.
Enrollment (%)	100.0	88.5	2.0	8.0	0.2	1.3
Drop-out Rate (%)	1.3	1.2	12.5	0.0	0.0	14.3
H.S. Diplomas (#)	228	220	2	6	0	0

West Salem

450 N Mark St • West Salem, WI 54669-1224
(608) 786-0700 • http://www.cesa4.k12.wi.us/cesaschools/26districts/
Grade Span: PK-12; **Agency Type:** 1
Schools: 3
1 Primary; 1 Middle; 1 High; 0 Other Level
3 Regular; 0 Special Education; 0 Vocational; 0 Alternative
0 Magnet; 0 Charter; 1 Title I Eligible; 0 School-wide Title I
Students: 1,607 (51.6% male; 48.4% female)
Individual Education Program: 172 (10.7%);
English Language Learner: 0 (0.0%); Migrant: 0 (0.0%)
Eligible for Free Lunch Program: n/a
Eligible for Reduced-Price Lunch Program: n/a
Teachers: 113.6 (14.1 to 1)
Librarians/Media Specialists: 3.8 (422.9 to 1)
Guidance Counselors: 3.0 (535.7 to 1)
Current Spending: ($ per student per year):
Total: $7,653; Instruction: $4,739; Support Services: $2,561
Enrollment, Drop-out Rates and Diploma Recipients by Race/Ethnicity

Category	Total	White	Black	Asian	AIAN	Hisp.
Enrollment (%)	100.0	96.5	0.8	1.5	0.7	0.6
Drop-out Rate (%)	0.4	0.4	0.0	0.0	0.0	0.0
H.S. Diplomas (#)	110	105	0	3	0	2

Langlade County

Antigo

120 S Dorr St • Antigo, WI 54409-1220
(715) 627-4355 • http://www.antigoschools.k12.wi.us
Grade Span: PK-12; **Agency Type:** 1
Schools: 12
10 Primary; 1 Middle; 1 High; 0 Other Level
12 Regular; 0 Special Education; 0 Vocational; 0 Alternative
0 Magnet; 0 Charter; 7 Title I Eligible; 3 School-wide Title I
Students: 2,898 (52.3% male; 47.7% female)
Individual Education Program: 467 (16.1%);
English Language Learner: 0 (0.0%); Migrant: 0 (0.0%)
Eligible for Free Lunch Program: n/a
Eligible for Reduced-Price Lunch Program: n/a
Teachers: 225.9 (12.8 to 1)
Librarians/Media Specialists: 3.0 (966.0 to 1)
Guidance Counselors: 8.0 (362.3 to 1)
Current Spending: ($ per student per year):
Total: $8,608; Instruction: $4,883; Support Services: $3,319
Enrollment, Drop-out Rates and Diploma Recipients by Race/Ethnicity

Category	Total	White	Black	Asian	AIAN	Hisp.
Enrollment (%)	100.0	96.3	0.6	0.4	1.7	0.9
Drop-out Rate (%)	1.0	1.1	0.0	0.0	0.0	0.0
H.S. Diplomas (#)	307	295	2	3	6	1

Lincoln County

Merrill Area
1111 N Sales St • Merrill, WI 54452-3198
(715) 536-4581 • http://www.maps.k12.wi.us
Grade Span: PK-12; **Agency Type:** 1
Schools: 10
8 Primary; 1 Middle; 1 High; 0 Other Level
10 Regular; 0 Special Education; 0 Vocational; 0 Alternative
0 Magnet; 0 Charter; 6 Title I Eligible; 0 School-wide Title I
Students: 3,352 (52.2% male; 47.8% female)
Individual Education Program: 410 (12.2%);
English Language Learner: 0 (0.0%); Migrant: 0 (0.0%)
Eligible for Free Lunch Program: n/a
Eligible for Reduced-Price Lunch Program: n/a
Teachers: 232.6 (14.4 to 1)
Librarians/Media Specialists: 2.0 (1,676.0 to 1)
Guidance Counselors: 9.0 (372.4 to 1)
Current Spending: ($ per student per year):
Total: $7,721; Instruction: $4,864; Support Services: $2,545
Enrollment, Drop-out Rates and Diploma Recipients by Race/Ethnicity

Category	Total	White	Black	Asian	AIAN	Hisp.
Enrollment (%)	100.0	97.3	0.2	1.3	0.2	1.0
Drop-out Rate (%)	1.8	1.6	0.0	7.7	14.3	0.0
H.S. Diplomas (#)	258	251	0	1	4	2

Tomahawk
328 N 4th St • Tomahawk, WI 54487-1370
(715) 453-5551 • http://www.tomahawk.k12.wi.us/
Grade Span: PK-12; **Agency Type:** 1
Schools: 3
1 Primary; 1 Middle; 1 High; 0 Other Level
3 Regular; 0 Special Education; 0 Vocational; 0 Alternative
0 Magnet; 0 Charter; 1 Title I Eligible; 0 School-wide Title I
Students: 1,642 (51.5% male; 48.5% female)
Individual Education Program: 189 (11.5%);
English Language Learner: 0 (0.0%); Migrant: 0 (0.0%)
Eligible for Free Lunch Program: n/a
Eligible for Reduced-Price Lunch Program: n/a
Teachers: 118.0 (13.9 to 1)
Librarians/Media Specialists: 3.0 (547.3 to 1)
Guidance Counselors: 5.0 (328.4 to 1)
Current Spending: ($ per student per year):
Total: $7,833; Instruction: $4,384; Support Services: $3,136
Enrollment, Drop-out Rates and Diploma Recipients by Race/Ethnicity

Category	Total	White	Black	Asian	AIAN	Hisp.
Enrollment (%)	100.0	97.9	0.4	0.7	0.5	0.5
Drop-out Rate (%)	0.3	0.3	n/a	0.0	0.0	0.0
H.S. Diplomas (#)	136	132	0	2	1	1

Manitowoc County

Manitowoc
1820 S 30 St • Manitowoc, WI 54220
Mailing Address: PO Box 1657 • Manitowoc, WI 54221-1657
(920) 686-4781 • http://www.mpsd.k12.wi.us
Grade Span: PK-12; **Agency Type:** 1
Schools: 10
7 Primary; 2 Middle; 1 High; 0 Other Level
10 Regular; 0 Special Education; 0 Vocational; 0 Alternative
0 Magnet; 0 Charter; 6 Title I Eligible; 0 School-wide Title I
Students: 5,411 (50.6% male; 49.4% female)
Individual Education Program: 656 (12.1%);
English Language Learner: 363 (6.7%); Migrant: 0 (0.0%)
Eligible for Free Lunch Program: n/a
Eligible for Reduced-Price Lunch Program: n/a
Teachers: 363.3 (14.9 to 1)
Librarians/Media Specialists: 4.0 (1,352.8 to 1)
Guidance Counselors: 10.0 (541.1 to 1)
Current Spending: ($ per student per year):
Total: $6,804; Instruction: $4,366; Support Services: $2,411
Enrollment, Drop-out Rates and Diploma Recipients by Race/Ethnicity

Category	Total	White	Black	Asian	AIAN	Hisp.
Enrollment (%)	100.0	83.7	1.3	10.4	0.8	3.8
Drop-out Rate (%)	3.5	3.4	8.3	4.7	0.0	0.0
H.S. Diplomas (#)	377	345	2	21	3	6

Two Rivers
4519 Lincoln Ave • Two Rivers, WI 54241-2134
(920) 793-4560 • http://www.trschools.k12.wi.us
Grade Span: PK-12; **Agency Type:** 1
Schools: 5
3 Primary; 1 Middle; 1 High; 0 Other Level
5 Regular; 0 Special Education; 0 Vocational; 0 Alternative
0 Magnet; 0 Charter; 2 Title I Eligible; 0 School-wide Title I
Students: 2,119 (52.7% male; 47.3% female)
Individual Education Program: 302 (14.3%);
English Language Learner: 77 (3.6%); Migrant: 0 (0.0%)
Eligible for Free Lunch Program: n/a
Eligible for Reduced-Price Lunch Program: n/a
Teachers: 162.4 (13.0 to 1)
Librarians/Media Specialists: 2.0 (1,059.5 to 1)
Guidance Counselors: 7.0 (302.7 to 1)
Current Spending: ($ per student per year):
Total: $7,458; Instruction: $4,564; Support Services: $2,656
Enrollment, Drop-out Rates and Diploma Recipients by Race/Ethnicity

Category	Total	White	Black	Asian	AIAN	Hisp.
Enrollment (%)	100.0	92.4	0.2	5.6	0.5	1.3
Drop-out Rate (%)	1.4	1.3	0.0	0.0	33.3	0.0
H.S. Diplomas (#)	165	150	1	11	2	1

Marathon County

D C Everest Area
6300 Alderson St • Weston, WI 54476-3908
(715) 359-4221
Grade Span: PK-12; **Agency Type:** 1
Schools: 10
7 Primary; 1 Middle; 1 High; 1 Other Level
10 Regular; 0 Special Education; 0 Vocational; 0 Alternative
0 Magnet; 0 Charter; 3 Title I Eligible; 0 School-wide Title I
Students: 5,145 (51.4% male; 48.6% female)
Individual Education Program: 618 (12.0%);
English Language Learner: 329 (6.4%); Migrant: 0 (0.0%)
Eligible for Free Lunch Program: n/a
Eligible for Reduced-Price Lunch Program: n/a
Teachers: 341.8 (15.1 to 1)
Librarians/Media Specialists: 8.0 (643.1 to 1)
Guidance Counselors: 13.0 (395.8 to 1)
Current Spending: ($ per student per year):
Total: $7,158; Instruction: $4,536; Support Services: $2,385
Enrollment, Drop-out Rates and Diploma Recipients by Race/Ethnicity

Category	Total	White	Black	Asian	AIAN	Hisp.
Enrollment (%)	100.0	88.7	0.4	9.7	0.4	0.7
Drop-out Rate (%)	0.8	0.9	0.0	0.0	0.0	0.0
H.S. Diplomas (#)	390	352	2	34	2	0

Mosinee
591 W State Hwy 153 • Mosinee, WI 54455-7499
(715) 693-2530 • http://www.mosinee.k12.wi.us
Grade Span: PK-12; **Agency Type:** 1
Schools: 3
1 Primary; 1 Middle; 1 High; 0 Other Level
3 Regular; 0 Special Education; 0 Vocational; 0 Alternative
0 Magnet; 0 Charter; 2 Title I Eligible; 0 School-wide Title I
Students: 2,024 (53.1% male; 46.9% female)
Individual Education Program: 283 (14.0%);
English Language Learner: 0 (0.0%); Migrant: 0 (0.0%)
Eligible for Free Lunch Program: n/a
Eligible for Reduced-Price Lunch Program: n/a
Teachers: 130.5 (15.5 to 1)
Librarians/Media Specialists: 2.1 (963.8 to 1)
Guidance Counselors: 4.0 (506.0 to 1)
Current Spending: ($ per student per year):
Total: $8,126; Instruction: $4,899; Support Services: $2,947
Enrollment, Drop-out Rates and Diploma Recipients by Race/Ethnicity

Category	Total	White	Black	Asian	AIAN	Hisp.
Enrollment (%)	100.0	97.0	1.0	0.7	0.1	1.2
Drop-out Rate (%)	0.1	0.2	0.0	0.0	0.0	0.0
H.S. Diplomas (#)	158	155	0	1	1	1

Wausau
650 S 7th Ave • Wausau, WI 54401
Mailing Address: 415 Seymour St • Wausau, WI 54402-0359
(715) 261-2561 • http://www.wausau.k12.wi.us
Grade Span: PK-12; **Agency Type:** 1
Schools: 19
15 Primary; 1 Middle; 2 High; 1 Other Level
18 Regular; 0 Special Education; 0 Vocational; 1 Alternative
0 Magnet; 1 Charter; 7 Title I Eligible; 0 School-wide Title I
Students: 8,949 (52.4% male; 47.6% female)
Individual Education Program: 1,173 (13.1%);
English Language Learner: 1,583 (17.7%); Migrant: 0 (0.0%)
Eligible for Free Lunch Program: n/a
Eligible for Reduced-Price Lunch Program: n/a
Teachers: 633.1 (14.1 to 1)
Librarians/Media Specialists: 11.8 (758.4 to 1)
Guidance Counselors: 23.5 (380.8 to 1)
Current Spending: ($ per student per year):
Total: $8,506; Instruction: $5,492; Support Services: $2,698

Enrollment, Drop-out Rates and Diploma Recipients by Race/Ethnicity

Category	Total	White	Black	Asian	AIAN	Hisp.
Enrollment (%)	100.0	72.7	1.3	24.0	0.8	1.3
Drop-out Rate (%)	1.1	0.9	0.0	1.6	0.0	7.7
H.S. Diplomas (#)	586	484	2	94	2	4

Marinette County

Marinette

2139 Pierce Ave • Marinette, WI 54143-3998
(715) 732-7905 • http://www.marinette.k12.wi.us
Grade Span: PK-12; **Agency Type:** 1
Schools: 8
7 Primary; 0 Middle; 1 High; 0 Other Level
8 Regular; 0 Special Education; 0 Vocational; 0 Alternative
0 Magnet; 0 Charter; 4 Title I Eligible; 0 School-wide Title I
Students: 2,564 (51.7% male; 48.3% female)
Individual Education Program: 356 (13.9%);
English Language Learner: 0 (0.0%); Migrant: 0 (0.0%)
Eligible for Free Lunch Program: n/a
Eligible for Reduced-Price Lunch Program: n/a
Teachers: 167.4 (15.3 to 1)
Librarians/Media Specialists: 2.0 (1,282.0 to 1)
Guidance Counselors: 7.0 (366.3 to 1)
Current Spending: ($ per student per year):
Total: $7,865; Instruction: $4,956; Support Services: $2,641
Enrollment, Drop-out Rates and Diploma Recipients by Race/Ethnicity

Category	Total	White	Black	Asian	AIAN	Hisp.
Enrollment (%)	100.0	97.8	0.7	0.3	0.7	0.5
Drop-out Rate (%)	1.1	1.1	100.0	0.0	0.0	0.0
H.S. Diplomas (#)	214	210	0	2	0	2

Milwaukee County

Brown Deer

8200 N 60th St • Brown Deer, WI 53223-3598
(414) 371-6767 • http://www.bdsd.k12.wi.us
Grade Span: PK-12; **Agency Type:** 1
Schools: 4
2 Primary; 1 Middle; 1 High; 0 Other Level
4 Regular; 0 Special Education; 0 Vocational; 0 Alternative
0 Magnet; 0 Charter; 0 Title I Eligible; 0 School-wide Title I
Students: 1,802 (54.6% male; 45.4% female)
Individual Education Program: 173 (9.6%);
English Language Learner: 0 (0.0%); Migrant: 0 (0.0%)
Eligible for Free Lunch Program: n/a
Eligible for Reduced-Price Lunch Program: n/a
Teachers: 115.0 (15.7 to 1)
Librarians/Media Specialists: 2.0 (901.0 to 1)
Guidance Counselors: 5.0 (360.4 to 1)
Current Spending: ($ per student per year):
Total: $8,973; Instruction: $5,182; Support Services: $3,499
Enrollment, Drop-out Rates and Diploma Recipients by Race/Ethnicity

Category	Total	White	Black	Asian	AIAN	Hisp.
Enrollment (%)	100.0	60.7	30.1	4.8	0.6	3.8
Drop-out Rate (%)	n/a	n/a	n/a	n/a	n/a	n/a
H.S. Diplomas (#)	127	98	22	4	0	3

Cudahy

2915 E Ramsey Ave • Cudahy, WI 53110-2559
(414) 294-7402 • http://www.cudahy.k12.wi.us/
Grade Span: PK-12; **Agency Type:** 1
Schools: 7
5 Primary; 1 Middle; 1 High; 0 Other Level
7 Regular; 0 Special Education; 0 Vocational; 0 Alternative
0 Magnet; 0 Charter; 3 Title I Eligible; 0 School-wide Title I
Students: 2,885 (52.4% male; 47.6% female)
Individual Education Program: 454 (15.7%);
English Language Learner: 0 (0.0%); Migrant: 0 (0.0%)
Eligible for Free Lunch Program: n/a
Eligible for Reduced-Price Lunch Program: n/a
Teachers: 212.4 (13.6 to 1)
Librarians/Media Specialists: 4.0 (721.3 to 1)
Guidance Counselors: 9.0 (320.6 to 1)
Current Spending: ($ per student per year):
Total: $8,546; Instruction: $5,631; Support Services: $2,674
Enrollment, Drop-out Rates and Diploma Recipients by Race/Ethnicity

Category	Total	White	Black	Asian	AIAN	Hisp.
Enrollment (%)	100.0	82.5	4.1	3.5	1.7	8.2
Drop-out Rate (%)	1.4	1.6	0.0	2.1	0.0	0.0
H.S. Diplomas (#)	203	159	12	17	4	11

Franklin Public

8255 W Forest Hill Ave • Franklin, WI 53132-9705
(414) 529-8269 • http://www.franklin.k12.wi.us
Grade Span: PK-12; **Agency Type:** 1
Schools: 7
5 Primary; 1 Middle; 1 High; 0 Other Level
7 Regular; 0 Special Education; 0 Vocational; 0 Alternative
0 Magnet; 0 Charter; 0 Title I Eligible; 0 School-wide Title I
Students: 3,866 (51.3% male; 48.7% female)
Individual Education Program: 396 (10.2%);
English Language Learner: 174 (4.5%); Migrant: 0 (0.0%)
Eligible for Free Lunch Program: n/a
Eligible for Reduced-Price Lunch Program: n/a
Teachers: 276.7 (14.0 to 1)
Librarians/Media Specialists: 7.0 (552.3 to 1)
Guidance Counselors: 11.0 (351.5 to 1)
Current Spending: ($ per student per year):
Total: $8,919; Instruction: $5,569; Support Services: $3,066
Enrollment, Drop-out Rates and Diploma Recipients by Race/Ethnicity

Category	Total	White	Black	Asian	AIAN	Hisp.
Enrollment (%)	100.0	83.0	5.8	6.9	0.8	3.5
Drop-out Rate (%)	0.1	0.1	0.0	1.2	0.0	0.0
H.S. Diplomas (#)	329	287	9	25	0	8

Greendale

5900 S 51st St • Greendale, WI 53129-2699
(414) 423-2700 • http://www.greendale.k12.wi.us
Grade Span: PK-12; **Agency Type:** 1
Schools: 5
3 Primary; 1 Middle; 1 High; 0 Other Level
5 Regular; 0 Special Education; 0 Vocational; 0 Alternative
0 Magnet; 0 Charter; 3 Title I Eligible; 0 School-wide Title I
Students: 2,216 (51.1% male; 48.9% female)
Individual Education Program: 254 (11.5%);
English Language Learner: 0 (0.0%); Migrant: 0 (0.0%)
Eligible for Free Lunch Program: n/a
Eligible for Reduced-Price Lunch Program: n/a
Teachers: 148.5 (14.9 to 1)
Librarians/Media Specialists: 3.0 (738.7 to 1)
Guidance Counselors: 6.0 (369.3 to 1)
Current Spending: ($ per student per year):
Total: $9,365; Instruction: $5,374; Support Services: $3,742
Enrollment, Drop-out Rates and Diploma Recipients by Race/Ethnicity

Category	Total	White	Black	Asian	AIAN	Hisp.
Enrollment (%)	100.0	89.1	2.8	3.7	0.3	4.2
Drop-out Rate (%)	0.7	0.6	5.3	0.0	0.0	0.0
H.S. Diplomas (#)	180	161	7	9	0	3

Greenfield

8500 W Chapman Ave • Greenfield, WI 53228-2915
(414) 529-9090 • http://www.greenfield.k12.wi.us
Grade Span: PK-12; **Agency Type:** 1
Schools: 6
4 Primary; 1 Middle; 1 High; 0 Other Level
6 Regular; 0 Special Education; 0 Vocational; 0 Alternative
0 Magnet; 0 Charter; 4 Title I Eligible; 0 School-wide Title I
Students: 3,341 (51.4% male; 48.6% female)
Individual Education Program: 376 (11.3%);
English Language Learner: 0 (0.0%); Migrant: 0 (0.0%)
Eligible for Free Lunch Program: n/a
Eligible for Reduced-Price Lunch Program: n/a
Teachers: 217.6 (15.4 to 1)
Librarians/Media Specialists: 6.0 (556.8 to 1)
Guidance Counselors: 10.6 (315.2 to 1)
Current Spending: ($ per student per year):
Total: $8,438; Instruction: $5,136; Support Services: $3,009
Enrollment, Drop-out Rates and Diploma Recipients by Race/Ethnicity

Category	Total	White	Black	Asian	AIAN	Hisp.
Enrollment (%)	100.0	80.3	4.2	5.8	1.6	8.1
Drop-out Rate (%)	0.9	0.8	2.3	0.0	0.0	1.2
H.S. Diplomas (#)	234	200	4	5	0	25

Milwaukee

5225 W Vliet St • Milwaukee, WI 53208
Mailing Address: PO Box 2181 • Milwaukee, WI 53201-2181
(414) 475-8001 • http://www.milwaukee.k12.wi.us
Grade Span: PK-12; **Agency Type:** 1
Schools: 218
131 Primary; 31 Middle; 41 High; 15 Other Level
191 Regular; 1 Special Education; 0 Vocational; 26 Alternative
0 Magnet; 21 Charter; 163 Title I Eligible; 160 School-wide Title I
Students: 97,293 (51.0% male; 49.0% female)
Individual Education Program: 16,018 (16.5%);
English Language Learner: 6,288 (6.5%); Migrant: 40 (<0.1%)
Eligible for Free Lunch Program: n/a

Eligible for Reduced-Price Lunch Program: n/a
Teachers: 6,494.5 (15.0 to 1)
Librarians/Media Specialists: 83.6 (1,163.8 to 1)
Guidance Counselors: 114.6 (849.0 to 1)
Current Spending: ($ per student per year):
Total: $9,283; Instruction: $5,590; Support Services: $3,390
Enrollment, Drop-out Rates and Diploma Recipients by Race/Ethnicity

Category	Total	White	Black	Asian	AIAN	Hisp.
Enrollment (%)	100.0	17.9	59.7	4.3	0.9	17.1
Drop-out Rate (%)	10.5	7.0	12.1	5.8	11.5	10.8
H.S. Diplomas (#)	3,912	995	2,102	199	49	567

Oak Creek-Franklin

7630 S 10th St • Oak Creek, WI 53154-1912
(414) 768-5886 • http://www.oakcreek.k12.wi.us
Grade Span: PK-12; **Agency Type:** 1
Schools: 8
5 Primary; 2 Middle; 1 High; 0 Other Level
8 Regular; 0 Special Education; 0 Vocational; 0 Alternative
0 Magnet; 0 Charter; 0 Title I Eligible; 0 School-wide Title I
Students: 4,937 (52.3% male; 47.7% female)
Individual Education Program: 600 (12.2%);
English Language Learner: 0 (0.0%); Migrant: 0 (0.0%)
Eligible for Free Lunch Program: n/a
Eligible for Reduced-Price Lunch Program: n/a
Teachers: 299.9 (16.5 to 1)
Librarians/Media Specialists: 5.0 (987.4 to 1)
Guidance Counselors: 13.6 (363.0 to 1)
Current Spending: ($ per student per year):
Total: $8,060; Instruction: $4,538; Support Services: $3,253
Enrollment, Drop-out Rates and Diploma Recipients by Race/Ethnicity

Category	Total	White	Black	Asian	AIAN	Hisp.
Enrollment (%)	100.0	82.7	4.2	4.6	1.1	7.3
Drop-out Rate (%)	1.4	1.5	0.0	0.0	0.0	1.9
H.S. Diplomas (#)	382	335	12	14	3	18

Shorewood

1701 E Capitol Dr • Shorewood, WI 53211-1996
(414) 963-6901 • http://www.shorewoodschools.org
Grade Span: PK-12; **Agency Type:** 1
Schools: 4
2 Primary; 1 Middle; 1 High; 0 Other Level
4 Regular; 0 Special Education; 0 Vocational; 0 Alternative
0 Magnet; 0 Charter; 4 Title I Eligible; 0 School-wide Title I
Students: 2,172 (48.7% male; 51.3% female)
Individual Education Program: 188 (8.7%);
English Language Learner: 160 (7.4%); Migrant: 0 (0.0%)
Eligible for Free Lunch Program: n/a
Eligible for Reduced-Price Lunch Program: n/a
Teachers: 154.4 (14.1 to 1)
Librarians/Media Specialists: 4.0 (543.0 to 1)
Guidance Counselors: 5.5 (394.9 to 1)
Current Spending: ($ per student per year):
Total: $8,816; Instruction: $5,707; Support Services: $2,931
Enrollment, Drop-out Rates and Diploma Recipients by Race/Ethnicity

Category	Total	White	Black	Asian	AIAN	Hisp.
Enrollment (%)	100.0	74.1	15.7	5.1	0.6	4.5
Drop-out Rate (%)	n/a	n/a	n/a	n/a	n/a	n/a
H.S. Diplomas (#)	179	142	20	8	1	8

South Milwaukee

1225 Memorial Dr • South Milwaukee, WI 53172-1625
(414) 768-6300 • http://www.sdsm.k12.wi.us
Grade Span: PK-12; **Agency Type:** 1
Schools: 7
4 Primary; 1 Middle; 2 High; 0 Other Level
6 Regular; 0 Special Education; 0 Vocational; 1 Alternative
0 Magnet; 1 Charter; 4 Title I Eligible; 0 School-wide Title I
Students: 3,602 (52.4% male; 47.6% female)
Individual Education Program: 442 (12.3%);
English Language Learner: 0 (0.0%); Migrant: 0 (0.0%)
Eligible for Free Lunch Program: n/a
Eligible for Reduced-Price Lunch Program: n/a
Teachers: 250.9 (14.4 to 1)
Librarians/Media Specialists: 4.0 (900.5 to 1)
Guidance Counselors: 11.0 (327.5 to 1)
Current Spending: ($ per student per year):
Total: $7,685; Instruction: $4,819; Support Services: $2,631
Enrollment, Drop-out Rates and Diploma Recipients by Race/Ethnicity

Category	Total	White	Black	Asian	AIAN	Hisp.
Enrollment (%)	100.0	83.8	5.4	2.7	1.0	7.1
Drop-out Rate (%)	1.8	1.6	1.3	0.0	16.7	4.9
H.S. Diplomas (#)	252	217	11	9	0	15

Wauwatosa

12121 W N Ave • Wauwatosa, WI 53226-2096
(414) 773-1010 • http://www.wauwatosaschools.org
Grade Span: PK-12; **Agency Type:** 1
Schools: 17
9 Primary; 2 Middle; 2 High; 4 Other Level
13 Regular; 0 Special Education; 0 Vocational; 4 Alternative
0 Magnet; 0 Charter; 7 Title I Eligible; 0 School-wide Title I
Students: 7,080 (51.6% male; 48.4% female)
Individual Education Program: 709 (10.0%);
English Language Learner: 0 (0.0%); Migrant: 0 (0.0%)
Eligible for Free Lunch Program: n/a
Eligible for Reduced-Price Lunch Program: n/a
Teachers: 473.5 (15.0 to 1)
Librarians/Media Specialists: 14.0 (505.7 to 1)
Guidance Counselors: 14.0 (505.7 to 1)
Current Spending: ($ per student per year):
Total: $8,279; Instruction: $5,039; Support Services: $3,059
Enrollment, Drop-out Rates and Diploma Recipients by Race/Ethnicity

Category	Total	White	Black	Asian	AIAN	Hisp.
Enrollment (%)	100.0	77.8	13.1	5.0	0.7	3.4
Drop-out Rate (%)	0.3	0.3	0.6	0.0	0.0	0.0
H.S. Diplomas (#)	496	406	48	25	3	14

West Allis

9333 W Lincoln Ave • West Allis, WI 53227-2395
(414) 604-3005 • http://www.wawm.k12.wi.us
Grade Span: PK-12; **Agency Type:** 1
Schools: 18
11 Primary; 1 Middle; 4 High; 2 Other Level
16 Regular; 0 Special Education; 0 Vocational; 2 Alternative
0 Magnet; 1 Charter; 8 Title I Eligible; 0 School-wide Title I
Students: 8,842 (51.6% male; 48.4% female)
Individual Education Program: 1,340 (15.2%);
English Language Learner: 121 (1.4%); Migrant: 0 (0.0%)
Eligible for Free Lunch Program: n/a
Eligible for Reduced-Price Lunch Program: n/a
Teachers: 604.0 (14.6 to 1)
Librarians/Media Specialists: 15.0 (589.5 to 1)
Guidance Counselors: 12.0 (736.8 to 1)
Current Spending: ($ per student per year):
Total: $8,273; Instruction: $4,983; Support Services: $3,065
Enrollment, Drop-out Rates and Diploma Recipients by Race/Ethnicity

Category	Total	White	Black	Asian	AIAN	Hisp.
Enrollment (%)	100.0	84.8	4.9	2.5	1.5	6.4
Drop-out Rate (%)	1.4	1.3	2.3	0.0	2.3	3.2
H.S. Diplomas (#)	637	587	17	14	4	15

Whitefish Bay

1200 E Fairmount Ave • Whitefish Bay, WI 53217-6099
(414) 963-3921 • http://www.wfbschools.com
Grade Span: PK-12; **Agency Type:** 1
Schools: 4
2 Primary; 1 Middle; 1 High; 0 Other Level
4 Regular; 0 Special Education; 0 Vocational; 0 Alternative
0 Magnet; 0 Charter; 4 Title I Eligible; 0 School-wide Title I
Students: 2,971 (50.3% male; 49.7% female)
Individual Education Program: 197 (6.6%);
English Language Learner: 0 (0.0%); Migrant: 0 (0.0%)
Eligible for Free Lunch Program: n/a
Eligible for Reduced-Price Lunch Program: n/a
Teachers: 189.7 (15.7 to 1)
Librarians/Media Specialists: 3.0 (990.3 to 1)
Guidance Counselors: 10.3 (288.4 to 1)
Current Spending: ($ per student per year):
Total: $8,412; Instruction: $4,865; Support Services: $3,534
Enrollment, Drop-out Rates and Diploma Recipients by Race/Ethnicity

Category	Total	White	Black	Asian	AIAN	Hisp.
Enrollment (%)	100.0	81.4	11.2	4.7	0.0	2.7
Drop-out Rate (%)	0.2	0.1	1.0	0.0	0.0	0.0
H.S. Diplomas (#)	211	165	31	7	2	6

Whitnall

5000 S 116th St • Greenfield, WI 53228-3197
(414) 525-8402 • http://www.whitnall.com
Grade Span: PK-12; **Agency Type:** 1
Schools: 4
2 Primary; 1 Middle; 1 High; 0 Other Level
4 Regular; 0 Special Education; 0 Vocational; 0 Alternative
0 Magnet; 0 Charter; 0 Title I Eligible; 0 School-wide Title I
Students: 2,517 (51.4% male; 48.6% female)
Individual Education Program: 282 (11.2%);
English Language Learner: 75 (3.0%); Migrant: 0 (0.0%)
Eligible for Free Lunch Program: n/a
Eligible for Reduced-Price Lunch Program: n/a

Teachers: 156.4 (16.1 to 1)
Librarians/Media Specialists: 4.0 (629.3 to 1)
Guidance Counselors: 6.0 (419.5 to 1)
Current Spending: ($ per student per year):
Total: $8,559; Instruction: $4,756; Support Services: $3,519
Enrollment, Drop-out Rates and Diploma Recipients by Race/Ethnicity

Category	Total	White	Black	Asian	AIAN	Hisp.
Enrollment (%)	100.0	88.5	3.0	5.8	0.5	2.2
Drop-out Rate (%)	n/a	n/a	n/a	n/a	n/a	n/a
H.S. Diplomas (#)	206	191	5	8	1	1

Monroe County

Sparta Area
506 N Black River St • Sparta, WI 54656-1548
(608) 269-3151 • http://www.spartan.org/education.html
Grade Span: PK-12; **Agency Type:** 1
Schools: 12
7 Primary; 2 Middle; 3 High; 0 Other Level
9 Regular; 0 Special Education; 0 Vocational; 3 Alternative
0 Magnet; 2 Charter; 6 Title I Eligible; 0 School-wide Title I
Students: 2,694 (50.3% male; 49.7% female)
Individual Education Program: 386 (14.3%);
English Language Learner: 0 (0.0%); Migrant: 0 (0.0%)
Eligible for Free Lunch Program: n/a
Eligible for Reduced-Price Lunch Program: n/a
Teachers: 200.5 (13.4 to 1)
Librarians/Media Specialists: 5.0 (538.8 to 1)
Guidance Counselors: 7.9 (341.0 to 1)
Current Spending: ($ per student per year):
Total: $7,504; Instruction: $4,677; Support Services: $2,545
Enrollment, Drop-out Rates and Diploma Recipients by Race/Ethnicity

Category	Total	White	Black	Asian	AIAN	Hisp.
Enrollment (%)	100.0	95.8	1.2	0.9	0.6	1.5
Drop-out Rate (%)	1.7	1.8	0.0	0.0	n/a	0.0
H.S. Diplomas (#)	206	204	0	2	0	0

Tomah Area
129 W Clifton St • Tomah, WI 54660-2507
(608) 374-7210 • http://www.tomah.k12.wi.us/
Grade Span: PK-12; **Agency Type:** 1
Schools: 10
6 Primary; 2 Middle; 1 High; 1 Other Level
9 Regular; 0 Special Education; 0 Vocational; 1 Alternative
0 Magnet; 0 Charter; 7 Title I Eligible; 0 School-wide Title I
Students: 2,983 (52.3% male; 47.7% female)
Individual Education Program: 359 (12.0%);
English Language Learner: 0 (0.0%); Migrant: 0 (0.0%)
Eligible for Free Lunch Program: n/a
Eligible for Reduced-Price Lunch Program: n/a
Teachers: 216.5 (13.8 to 1)
Librarians/Media Specialists: 4.9 (608.8 to 1)
Guidance Counselors: 8.0 (372.9 to 1)
Current Spending: ($ per student per year):
Total: $6,969; Instruction: $4,214; Support Services: $2,480
Enrollment, Drop-out Rates and Diploma Recipients by Race/Ethnicity

Category	Total	White	Black	Asian	AIAN	Hisp.
Enrollment (%)	100.0	93.6	1.4	0.9	3.2	0.9
Drop-out Rate (%)	0.4	0.4	0.0	0.0	0.0	0.0
H.S. Diplomas (#)	225	210	1	2	10	2

Oconto County

Oconto Falls
200 N Farm Rd • Oconto Falls, WI 54154-1221
(920) 846-4471 • http://www.ocontofalls.k12.wi.us
Grade Span: PK-12; **Agency Type:** 1
Schools: 6
3 Primary; 1 Middle; 2 High; 0 Other Level
4 Regular; 0 Special Education; 0 Vocational; 2 Alternative
0 Magnet; 2 Charter; 2 Title I Eligible; 0 School-wide Title I
Students: 1,937 (50.9% male; 49.1% female)
Individual Education Program: 321 (16.6%);
English Language Learner: 0 (0.0%); Migrant: 0 (0.0%)
Eligible for Free Lunch Program: n/a
Eligible for Reduced-Price Lunch Program: n/a
Teachers: 142.7 (13.6 to 1)
Librarians/Media Specialists: 2.9 (667.9 to 1)
Guidance Counselors: 6.9 (280.7 to 1)
Current Spending: ($ per student per year):
Total: $6,933; Instruction: $4,288; Support Services: $2,379

Enrollment, Drop-out Rates and Diploma Recipients by Race/Ethnicity

Category	Total	White	Black	Asian	AIAN	Hisp.
Enrollment (%)	100.0	97.2	0.7	0.4	0.9	0.9
Drop-out Rate (%)	n/a	n/a	n/a	n/a	n/a	n/a
H.S. Diplomas (#)	136	135	0	0	1	0

Oneida County

Rhinelander
315 S Oneida Ave • Rhinelander, WI 54501-3422
(715) 365-9750 • http://www.rhinelander.k12.wi.us
Grade Span: PK-12; **Agency Type:** 1
Schools: 10
8 Primary; 1 Middle; 1 High; 0 Other Level
10 Regular; 0 Special Education; 0 Vocational; 0 Alternative
0 Magnet; 0 Charter; 7 Title I Eligible; 0 School-wide Title I
Students: 3,227 (51.1% male; 48.9% female)
Individual Education Program: 392 (12.1%);
English Language Learner: 0 (0.0%); Migrant: 0 (0.0%)
Eligible for Free Lunch Program: n/a
Eligible for Reduced-Price Lunch Program: n/a
Teachers: 219.0 (14.7 to 1)
Librarians/Media Specialists: 3.0 (1,075.7 to 1)
Guidance Counselors: 9.1 (354.6 to 1)
Current Spending: ($ per student per year):
Total: $8,469; Instruction: $4,896; Support Services: $3,308
Enrollment, Drop-out Rates and Diploma Recipients by Race/Ethnicity

Category	Total	White	Black	Asian	AIAN	Hisp.
Enrollment (%)	100.0	95.8	0.7	0.8	1.7	1.0
Drop-out Rate (%)	2.8	2.8	0.0	0.0	16.7	0.0
H.S. Diplomas (#)	234	231	0	2	1	0

Outagamie County

Appleton Area
10 College Ave Ste 214 • Appleton, WI 54911
Mailing Address: PO Box 2019 • Appleton, WI 54912-2019
(920) 832-6126 • http://www.aasd.k12.wi.us
Grade Span: PK-12; **Agency Type:** 1
Schools: 32
18 Primary; 7 Middle; 7 High; 0 Other Level
23 Regular; 0 Special Education; 0 Vocational; 9 Alternative
0 Magnet; 9 Charter; 7 Title I Eligible; 1 School-wide Title I
Students: 14,948 (51.9% male; 48.1% female)
Individual Education Program: 2,136 (14.3%);
English Language Learner: 1,277 (8.5%); Migrant: 0 (0.0%)
Eligible for Free Lunch Program: n/a
Eligible for Reduced-Price Lunch Program: n/a
Teachers: 975.2 (15.3 to 1)
Librarians/Media Specialists: 23.6 (633.4 to 1)
Guidance Counselors: 33.0 (453.0 to 1)
Current Spending: ($ per student per year):
Total: $7,621; Instruction: $4,816; Support Services: $2,600
Enrollment, Drop-out Rates and Diploma Recipients by Race/Ethnicity

Category	Total	White	Black	Asian	AIAN	Hisp.
Enrollment (%)	100.0	83.2	2.1	10.3	0.8	3.6
Drop-out Rate (%)	0.9	0.7	1.8	1.9	6.7	5.6
H.S. Diplomas (#)	1,109	990	8	88	4	19

Freedom Area
N4021 County Rd E • Freedom, WI 54131-1008
Mailing Address: PO Box 1008 • Freedom, WI 54131-1008
(920) 788-7944 • http://www.freedomschools.k12.wi.us
Grade Span: PK-12; **Agency Type:** 1
Schools: 3
1 Primary; 1 Middle; 1 High; 0 Other Level
3 Regular; 0 Special Education; 0 Vocational; 0 Alternative
0 Magnet; 0 Charter; 1 Title I Eligible; 0 School-wide Title I
Students: 1,566 (54.0% male; 46.0% female)
Individual Education Program: 201 (12.8%);
English Language Learner: 0 (0.0%); Migrant: 0 (0.0%)
Eligible for Free Lunch Program: n/a
Eligible for Reduced-Price Lunch Program: n/a
Teachers: 98.4 (15.9 to 1)
Librarians/Media Specialists: 2.0 (783.0 to 1)
Guidance Counselors: 3.5 (447.4 to 1)
Current Spending: ($ per student per year):
Total: $7,089; Instruction: $4,525; Support Services: $2,308
Enrollment, Drop-out Rates and Diploma Recipients by Race/Ethnicity

Category	Total	White	Black	Asian	AIAN	Hisp.
Enrollment (%)	100.0	93.2	0.5	0.1	5.3	0.9
Drop-out Rate (%)	0.6	0.2	n/a	0.0	7.7	0.0
H.S. Diplomas (#)	147	141	0	0	6	0

Hortonville

246 N Olk St • Hortonville, WI 54944-0070
Mailing Address: PO Box 70 • Hortonville, WI 54944-0070
(920) 779-7900 • http://www.hasd.org
Grade Span: PK-12; **Agency Type:** 1
Schools: 5
2 Primary; 2 Middle; 1 High; 0 Other Level
5 Regular; 0 Special Education; 0 Vocational; 0 Alternative
0 Magnet; 0 Charter; 1 Title I Eligible; 0 School-wide Title I
Students: 2,915 (52.5% male; 47.5% female)
Individual Education Program: 368 (12.6%);
English Language Learner: 0 (0.0%); Migrant: 0 (0.0%)
Eligible for Free Lunch Program: n/a
Eligible for Reduced-Price Lunch Program: n/a
Teachers: 199.5 (14.6 to 1)
Librarians/Media Specialists: 3.0 (971.7 to 1)
Guidance Counselors: 7.0 (416.4 to 1)
Current Spending: ($ per student per year):
Total: $6,657; Instruction: $4,287; Support Services: $2,124
Enrollment, Drop-out Rates and Diploma Recipients by Race/Ethnicity

Category	Total	White	Black	Asian	AIAN	Hisp.
Enrollment (%)	100.0	95.7	0.3	1.7	0.1	2.2
Drop-out Rate (%)	n/a	n/a	n/a	n/a	n/a	n/a
H.S. Diplomas (#)	177	173	0	2	0	2

Kaukauna Area

112 Main Ave • Kaukauna, WI 54130-2437
(920) 766-6100 • http://kaukauna.k12.wi.us
Grade Span: PK-12; **Agency Type:** 1
Schools: 7
5 Primary; 1 Middle; 1 High; 0 Other Level
7 Regular; 0 Special Education; 0 Vocational; 0 Alternative
0 Magnet; 0 Charter; 5 Title I Eligible; 0 School-wide Title I
Students: 3,740 (50.7% male; 49.3% female)
Individual Education Program: 527 (14.1%);
English Language Learner: 125 (3.3%); Migrant: 0 (0.0%)
Eligible for Free Lunch Program: n/a
Eligible for Reduced-Price Lunch Program: n/a
Teachers: 244.2 (15.3 to 1)
Librarians/Media Specialists: 4.0 (935.0 to 1)
Guidance Counselors: 7.8 (479.5 to 1)
Current Spending: ($ per student per year):
Total: $7,754; Instruction: $4,911; Support Services: $2,588
Enrollment, Drop-out Rates and Diploma Recipients by Race/Ethnicity

Category	Total	White	Black	Asian	AIAN	Hisp.
Enrollment (%)	100.0	93.6	0.9	2.9	1.0	1.5
Drop-out Rate (%)	1.3	1.3	0.0	0.0	0.0	12.5
H.S. Diplomas (#)	246	241	0	3	1	1

Kimberly Area

217 E Kimberly Ave • Kimberly, WI 54136-1404
(920) 788-7900 • http://www.kimberly.k12.wi.us
Grade Span: PK-12; **Agency Type:** 1
Schools: 6
4 Primary; 1 Middle; 1 High; 0 Other Level
6 Regular; 0 Special Education; 0 Vocational; 0 Alternative
0 Magnet; 0 Charter; 2 Title I Eligible; 0 School-wide Title I
Students: 3,572 (48.0% male; 52.0% female)
Individual Education Program: 390 (10.9%);
English Language Learner: 0 (0.0%); Migrant: 0 (0.0%)
Eligible for Free Lunch Program: n/a
Eligible for Reduced-Price Lunch Program: n/a
Teachers: 223.8 (16.0 to 1)
Librarians/Media Specialists: 2.8 (1,275.7 to 1)
Guidance Counselors: 8.8 (405.9 to 1)
Current Spending: ($ per student per year):
Total: $6,739; Instruction: $4,195; Support Services: $2,384
Enrollment, Drop-out Rates and Diploma Recipients by Race/Ethnicity

Category	Total	White	Black	Asian	AIAN	Hisp.
Enrollment (%)	100.0	95.5	0.4	2.1	0.5	1.5
Drop-out Rate (%)	0.2	0.2	0.0	0.0	0.0	0.0
H.S. Diplomas (#)	181	179	0	2	0	0

Little Chute Area

325 Meulemans St Ste A • Little Chute, WI 54140-3300
(920) 788-7605
Grade Span: PK-12; **Agency Type:** 1
Schools: 3
1 Primary; 1 Middle; 1 High; 0 Other Level
3 Regular; 0 Special Education; 0 Vocational; 0 Alternative
0 Magnet; 0 Charter; 1 Title I Eligible; 0 School-wide Title I
Students: 1,554 (54.6% male; 45.4% female)
Individual Education Program: 176 (11.3%);
English Language Learner: 0 (0.0%); Migrant: 0 (0.0%)
Eligible for Free Lunch Program: n/a
Eligible for Reduced-Price Lunch Program: n/a
Teachers: 98.6 (15.8 to 1)
Librarians/Media Specialists: 2.3 (675.7 to 1)
Guidance Counselors: 4.6 (337.8 to 1)
Current Spending: ($ per student per year):
Total: $6,922; Instruction: $4,398; Support Services: $2,315
Enrollment, Drop-out Rates and Diploma Recipients by Race/Ethnicity

Category	Total	White	Black	Asian	AIAN	Hisp.
Enrollment (%)	100.0	93.3	1.0	2.0	0.7	3.0
Drop-out Rate (%)	0.7	0.7	n/a	0.0	0.0	0.0
H.S. Diplomas (#)	127	124	0	1	0	2

Seymour Community

10 Circle Dr • Seymour, WI 54165-1678
(920) 833-2304 • http://www.seymour.k12.wi.us
Grade Span: PK-12; **Agency Type:** 1
Schools: 4
2 Primary; 1 Middle; 1 High; 0 Other Level
4 Regular; 0 Special Education; 0 Vocational; 0 Alternative
0 Magnet; 0 Charter; 2 Title I Eligible; 0 School-wide Title I
Students: 2,444 (51.5% male; 48.5% female)
Individual Education Program: 324 (13.3%);
English Language Learner: 0 (0.0%); Migrant: 0 (0.0%)
Eligible for Free Lunch Program: n/a
Eligible for Reduced-Price Lunch Program: n/a
Teachers: 153.1 (16.0 to 1)
Librarians/Media Specialists: 4.0 (611.0 to 1)
Guidance Counselors: 6.0 (407.3 to 1)
Current Spending: ($ per student per year):
Total: $6,897; Instruction: $4,243; Support Services: $2,402
Enrollment, Drop-out Rates and Diploma Recipients by Race/Ethnicity

Category	Total	White	Black	Asian	AIAN	Hisp.
Enrollment (%)	100.0	84.1	0.2	1.6	12.7	1.4
Drop-out Rate (%)	0.1	0.0	0.0	0.0	0.9	0.0
H.S. Diplomas (#)	190	171	0	1	17	1

Ozaukee County

Cedarburg

W68-N611 Evergreen Blvd • Cedarburg, WI 53012-1899
(262) 376-6112 • http://www.cedarburg.k12.wi.us
Grade Span: PK-12; **Agency Type:** 1
Schools: 5
3 Primary; 1 Middle; 1 High; 0 Other Level
5 Regular; 0 Special Education; 0 Vocational; 0 Alternative
0 Magnet; 0 Charter; 0 Title I Eligible; 0 School-wide Title I
Students: 2,952 (51.5% male; 48.5% female)
Individual Education Program: 320 (10.8%);
English Language Learner: 0 (0.0%); Migrant: 0 (0.0%)
Eligible for Free Lunch Program: n/a
Eligible for Reduced-Price Lunch Program: n/a
Teachers: 187.3 (15.8 to 1)
Librarians/Media Specialists: 5.0 (590.4 to 1)
Guidance Counselors: 9.6 (307.5 to 1)
Current Spending: ($ per student per year):
Total: $7,685; Instruction: $4,694; Support Services: $2,808
Enrollment, Drop-out Rates and Diploma Recipients by Race/Ethnicity

Category	Total	White	Black	Asian	AIAN	Hisp.
Enrollment (%)	100.0	97.8	0.6	1.0	0.1	0.6
Drop-out Rate (%)	0.3	0.3	0.0	0.0	0.0	0.0
H.S. Diplomas (#)	222	219	1	1	0	1

Grafton

1900 Washington St • Grafton, WI 53024-2198
(262) 376-5440 • http://www.grafton.k12.wi.us
Grade Span: PK-12; **Agency Type:** 1
Schools: 5
3 Primary; 1 Middle; 1 High; 0 Other Level
5 Regular; 0 Special Education; 0 Vocational; 0 Alternative
0 Magnet; 0 Charter; 3 Title I Eligible; 0 School-wide Title I
Students: 2,029 (52.9% male; 47.1% female)
Individual Education Program: 277 (13.7%);
English Language Learner: 0 (0.0%); Migrant: 0 (0.0%)
Eligible for Free Lunch Program: n/a
Eligible for Reduced-Price Lunch Program: n/a
Teachers: 140.3 (14.5 to 1)
Librarians/Media Specialists: 4.0 (507.3 to 1)
Guidance Counselors: 5.0 (405.8 to 1)
Current Spending: ($ per student per year):
Total: $8,293; Instruction: $5,250; Support Services: $2,858
Enrollment, Drop-out Rates and Diploma Recipients by Race/Ethnicity

Category	Total	White	Black	Asian	AIAN	Hisp.
Enrollment (%)	100.0	96.5	1.2	1.2	0.1	1.0
Drop-out Rate (%)	0.5	0.5	0.0	0.0	0.0	0.0
H.S. Diplomas (#)	185	178	0	1	0	6

Mequon-Thiensville

5000 W Mequon Rd • Mequon, WI 53092-2044
(262) 238-8503 • http://www.mtsd.k12.wi.us
Grade Span: PK-12; **Agency Type:** 1
Schools: 7
4 Primary; 2 Middle; 1 High; 0 Other Level
7 Regular; 0 Special Education; 0 Vocational; 0 Alternative
0 Magnet; 0 Charter; 5 Title I Eligible; 0 School-wide Title I
Students: 4,171 (52.9% male; 47.1% female)
Individual Education Program: 415 (9.9%);
English Language Learner: 0 (0.0%); Migrant: 0 (0.0%)
Eligible for Free Lunch Program: n/a
Eligible for Reduced-Price Lunch Program: n/a
Teachers: 260.8 (16.0 to 1)
Librarians/Media Specialists: 5.4 (772.4 to 1)
Guidance Counselors: 11.0 (379.2 to 1)
Current Spending: ($ per student per year):
Total: $8,737; Instruction: $5,527; Support Services: $2,928
Enrollment, Drop-out Rates and Diploma Recipients by Race/Ethnicity

Category	Total	White	Black	Asian	AIAN	Hisp.
Enrollment (%)	100.0	88.7	5.9	3.6	0.3	1.5
Drop-out Rate (%)	0.4	0.5	0.0	0.0	0.0	0.0
H.S. Diplomas (#)	356	326	7	18	1	4

Port Washington-Saukville

100 W Monroe St • Port Washington, WI 53074-1267
(262) 268-6005 • http://www.pwssd.k12.wi.us
Grade Span: PK-12; **Agency Type:** 1
Schools: 5
3 Primary; 1 Middle; 1 High; 0 Other Level
5 Regular; 0 Special Education; 0 Vocational; 0 Alternative
0 Magnet; 0 Charter; 3 Title I Eligible; 0 School-wide Title I
Students: 2,649 (53.2% male; 46.8% female)
Individual Education Program: 344 (13.0%);
English Language Learner: 0 (0.0%); Migrant: 0 (0.0%)
Eligible for Free Lunch Program: n/a
Eligible for Reduced-Price Lunch Program: n/a
Teachers: 170.6 (15.5 to 1)
Librarians/Media Specialists: 3.0 (883.0 to 1)
Guidance Counselors: 7.8 (339.6 to 1)
Current Spending: ($ per student per year):
Total: $9,174; Instruction: $5,704; Support Services: $3,193
Enrollment, Drop-out Rates and Diploma Recipients by Race/Ethnicity

Category	Total	White	Black	Asian	AIAN	Hisp.
Enrollment (%)	100.0	93.9	2.6	0.6	0.6	2.4
Drop-out Rate (%)	2.0	1.9	0.0	0.0	66.7	0.0
H.S. Diplomas (#)	186	184	1	1	0	0

Pierce County

Ellsworth Community

300 Hillcrest St • Ellsworth, WI 54011-1500
Mailing Address: PO Box 1500 • Ellsworth, WI 54011-1500
(715) 273-3900 • http://www.ellsworth.k12.wi.us
Grade Span: PK-12; **Agency Type:** 1
Schools: 6
4 Primary; 1 Middle; 1 High; 0 Other Level
6 Regular; 0 Special Education; 0 Vocational; 0 Alternative
0 Magnet; 0 Charter; 4 Title I Eligible; 0 School-wide Title I
Students: 1,786 (52.6% male; 47.4% female)
Individual Education Program: 219 (12.3%);
English Language Learner: 0 (0.0%); Migrant: 0 (0.0%)
Eligible for Free Lunch Program: n/a
Eligible for Reduced-Price Lunch Program: n/a
Teachers: 124.5 (14.3 to 1)
Librarians/Media Specialists: 3.0 (595.3 to 1)
Guidance Counselors: 5.0 (357.2 to 1)
Current Spending: ($ per student per year):
Total: $8,032; Instruction: $4,852; Support Services: $2,820
Enrollment, Drop-out Rates and Diploma Recipients by Race/Ethnicity

Category	Total	White	Black	Asian	AIAN	Hisp.
Enrollment (%)	100.0	96.9	0.3	1.0	0.8	1.0
Drop-out Rate (%)	0.1	0.2	0.0	0.0	0.0	0.0
H.S. Diplomas (#)	156	149	1	3	2	1

River Falls

852 E Division St • River Falls, WI 54022-2599
(715) 425-1800 • http://www.rfsd.k12.wi.us
Grade Span: PK-12; **Agency Type:** 1
Schools: 7
4 Primary; 1 Middle; 2 High; 0 Other Level
5 Regular; 0 Special Education; 0 Vocational; 2 Alternative
0 Magnet; 2 Charter; 3 Title I Eligible; 0 School-wide Title I
Students: 2,933 (51.0% male; 49.0% female)
Individual Education Program: 355 (12.1%);
English Language Learner: 0 (0.0%); Migrant: 0 (0.0%)
Eligible for Free Lunch Program: n/a
Eligible for Reduced-Price Lunch Program: n/a
Teachers: 189.9 (15.4 to 1)
Librarians/Media Specialists: 5.0 (586.6 to 1)
Guidance Counselors: 7.5 (391.1 to 1)
Current Spending: ($ per student per year):
Total: $7,754; Instruction: $5,205; Support Services: $2,264
Enrollment, Drop-out Rates and Diploma Recipients by Race/Ethnicity

Category	Total	White	Black	Asian	AIAN	Hisp.
Enrollment (%)	100.0	95.0	1.7	1.1	1.0	1.3
Drop-out Rate (%)	0.9	1.0	0.0	0.0	0.0	0.0
H.S. Diplomas (#)	217	208	4	3	0	2

Polk County

Amery

115 Birch Ter • Amery, WI 54001-1027
(715) 268-0272 • http://www.amerysd.k12.wi.us
Grade Span: PK-12; **Agency Type:** 1
Schools: 4
2 Primary; 1 Middle; 1 High; 0 Other Level
4 Regular; 0 Special Education; 0 Vocational; 0 Alternative
0 Magnet; 0 Charter; 2 Title I Eligible; 0 School-wide Title I
Students: 1,852 (49.8% male; 50.2% female)
Individual Education Program: 267 (14.4%);
English Language Learner: 0 (0.0%); Migrant: 0 (0.0%)
Eligible for Free Lunch Program: n/a
Eligible for Reduced-Price Lunch Program: n/a
Teachers: 125.8 (14.7 to 1)
Librarians/Media Specialists: 2.5 (740.8 to 1)
Guidance Counselors: 5.5 (336.7 to 1)
Current Spending: ($ per student per year):
Total: $7,406; Instruction: $4,559; Support Services: $2,488
Enrollment, Drop-out Rates and Diploma Recipients by Race/Ethnicity

Category	Total	White	Black	Asian	AIAN	Hisp.
Enrollment (%)	100.0	96.4	0.4	0.6	1.4	1.1
Drop-out Rate (%)	n/a	n/a	n/a	n/a	n/a	n/a
H.S. Diplomas (#)	147	141	0	0	4	2

Osceola

331 Middle School Dr • Osceola, WI 54020-0128
Mailing Address: PO Box 128 • Osceola, WI 54020-0128
(715) 294-4140 • http://www.osceola.k12.wi.us
Grade Span: PK-12; **Agency Type:** 1
Schools: 4
2 Primary; 1 Middle; 1 High; 0 Other Level
4 Regular; 0 Special Education; 0 Vocational; 0 Alternative
0 Magnet; 0 Charter; 2 Title I Eligible; 0 School-wide Title I
Students: 1,757 (49.0% male; 51.0% female)
Individual Education Program: 205 (11.7%);
English Language Learner: 0 (0.0%); Migrant: 0 (0.0%)
Eligible for Free Lunch Program: n/a
Eligible for Reduced-Price Lunch Program: n/a
Teachers: 105.8 (16.6 to 1)
Librarians/Media Specialists: 2.0 (878.5 to 1)
Guidance Counselors: 4.0 (439.3 to 1)
Current Spending: ($ per student per year):
Total: $7,145; Instruction: $4,213; Support Services: $2,559
Enrollment, Drop-out Rates and Diploma Recipients by Race/Ethnicity

Category	Total	White	Black	Asian	AIAN	Hisp.
Enrollment (%)	100.0	95.5	0.9	0.8	0.9	2.0
Drop-out Rate (%)	0.5	0.3	0.0	16.7	0.0	0.0
H.S. Diplomas (#)	139	138	0	1	0	0

Portage County

Stevens Point Area

1900 Polk St • Stevens Point, WI 54481-5875
(715) 345-5444 • http://www.wisp.k12.wi.us
Grade Span: PK-12; **Agency Type:** 1
Schools: 19
11 Primary; 3 Middle; 4 High; 0 Other Level
10 Regular; 1 Special Education; 0 Vocational; 7 Alternative
0 Magnet; 5 Charter; 6 Title I Eligible; 0 School-wide Title I
Students: 7,681 (51.7% male; 48.3% female)
Individual Education Program: 956 (12.4%);
English Language Learner: 343 (4.5%); Migrant: 0 (0.0%)
Eligible for Free Lunch Program: n/a
Eligible for Reduced-Price Lunch Program: n/a
Teachers: 516.2 (14.9 to 1)
Librarians/Media Specialists: 14.0 (548.6 to 1)
Guidance Counselors: 9.0 (853.4 to 1)
Current Spending: ($ per student per year):
Total: $8,114; Instruction: $5,312; Support Services: $2,564

Enrollment, Drop-out Rates and Diploma Recipients by Race/Ethnicity

Category	Total	White	Black	Asian	AIAN	Hisp.
Enrollment (%)	100.0	87.5	1.2	8.0	0.5	2.8
Drop-out Rate (%)	1.8	1.7	9.5	1.2	5.0	7.0
H.S. Diplomas (#)	676	626	6	33	5	6

Racine County

Burlington Area

100 N Kane St • Burlington, WI 53105-1896
(262) 763-0210 • http://basd.k12.wi.us
Grade Span: PK-12; **Agency Type:** 1
Schools: 8
5 Primary; 2 Middle; 1 High; 0 Other Level
8 Regular; 0 Special Education; 0 Vocational; 0 Alternative
0 Magnet; 0 Charter; 4 Title I Eligible; 0 School-wide Title I
Students: 3,647 (51.3% male; 48.7% female)
Individual Education Program: 507 (13.9%);
English Language Learner: 53 (1.5%); Migrant: 0 (0.0%)
Eligible for Free Lunch Program: n/a
Eligible for Reduced-Price Lunch Program: n/a
Teachers: 237.1 (15.4 to 1)
Librarians/Media Specialists: 4.0 (911.8 to 1)
Guidance Counselors: 9.4 (388.0 to 1)
Current Spending: ($ per student per year):
Total: $6,801; Instruction: $4,241; Support Services: $2,274

Enrollment, Drop-out Rates and Diploma Recipients by Race/Ethnicity

Category	Total	White	Black	Asian	AIAN	Hisp.
Enrollment (%)	100.0	92.9	0.9	0.9	0.1	5.1
Drop-out Rate (%)	1.2	1.1	0.0	16.7	0.0	2.3
H.S. Diplomas (#)	248	230	1	3	0	14

Racine

2220 Northwestern Ave • Racine, WI 53404-2597
(262) 631-7064 • http://www.racine.k12.wi.us
Grade Span: PK-12; **Agency Type:** 1
Schools: 35
22 Primary; 6 Middle; 4 High; 3 Other Level
29 Regular; 0 Special Education; 0 Vocational; 6 Alternative
0 Magnet; 2 Charter; 17 Title I Eligible; 2 School-wide Title I
Students: 21,565 (51.9% male; 48.1% female)
Individual Education Program: 3,541 (16.4%);
English Language Learner: 1,198 (5.6%); Migrant: 0 (0.0%)
Eligible for Free Lunch Program: n/a
Eligible for Reduced-Price Lunch Program: n/a
Teachers: 1,366.8 (15.8 to 1)
Librarians/Media Specialists: 33.7 (639.9 to 1)
Guidance Counselors: 45.5 (474.0 to 1)
Current Spending: ($ per student per year):
Total: $8,134; Instruction: $5,141; Support Services: $2,728

Enrollment, Drop-out Rates and Diploma Recipients by Race/Ethnicity

Category	Total	White	Black	Asian	AIAN	Hisp.
Enrollment (%)	100.0	57.6	26.0	1.2	0.3	15.0
Drop-out Rate (%)	4.9	3.2	8.7	5.4	0.0	9.1
H.S. Diplomas (#)	1,163	890	170	10	0	93

Richland County

Richland

125 S Central Ave • Richland Center, WI 53581-2399
(608) 647-6106 • http://www.richland.k12.wi.us
Grade Span: PK-12; **Agency Type:** 1
Schools: 8
5 Primary; 1 Middle; 2 High; 0 Other Level
7 Regular; 0 Special Education; 0 Vocational; 1 Alternative
0 Magnet; 1 Charter; 5 Title I Eligible; 0 School-wide Title I
Students: 1,521 (52.3% male; 47.7% female)
Individual Education Program: 317 (20.8%);
English Language Learner: 0 (0.0%); Migrant: 1 (0.1%)
Eligible for Free Lunch Program: n/a
Eligible for Reduced-Price Lunch Program: n/a
Teachers: 121.1 (12.6 to 1)
Librarians/Media Specialists: 3.0 (507.0 to 1)
Guidance Counselors: 6.0 (253.5 to 1)
Current Spending: ($ per student per year):
Total: $8,967; Instruction: $5,508; Support Services: $3,067

Enrollment, Drop-out Rates and Diploma Recipients by Race/Ethnicity

Category	Total	White	Black	Asian	AIAN	Hisp.
Enrollment (%)	100.0	96.8	1.5	0.5	0.1	1.1
Drop-out Rate (%)	0.3	0.4	0.0	0.0	n/a	0.0
H.S. Diplomas (#)	143	142	0	0	0	1

Rock County

Beloit

1633 Keeler Ave • Beloit, WI 53511-4799
(608) 361-4017 • http://www.sdb.k12.wi.us
Grade Span: PK-12; **Agency Type:** 1
Schools: 17
13 Primary; 2 Middle; 2 High; 0 Other Level
16 Regular; 0 Special Education; 0 Vocational; 1 Alternative
0 Magnet; 1 Charter; 9 Title I Eligible; 9 School-wide Title I
Students: 6,799 (50.6% male; 49.4% female)
Individual Education Program: 1,264 (18.6%);
English Language Learner: 490 (7.2%); Migrant: 0 (0.0%)
Eligible for Free Lunch Program: n/a
Eligible for Reduced-Price Lunch Program: n/a
Teachers: 482.8 (14.1 to 1)
Librarians/Media Specialists: 10.5 (647.5 to 1)
Guidance Counselors: 12.1 (561.9 to 1)
Current Spending: ($ per student per year):
Total: $8,685; Instruction: $5,665; Support Services: $2,725

Enrollment, Drop-out Rates and Diploma Recipients by Race/Ethnicity

Category	Total	White	Black	Asian	AIAN	Hisp.
Enrollment (%)	100.0	57.4	27.6	0.9	0.4	13.8
Drop-out Rate (%)	3.7	2.8	4.7	4.5	50.0	6.5
H.S. Diplomas (#)	357	237	90	9	0	21

Edgerton

200 Elm High Dr • Edgerton, WI 53534-1498
(608) 884-9402 • http://www.edgerton.k12.wi.us
Grade Span: PK-12; **Agency Type:** 1
Schools: 4
2 Primary; 1 Middle; 1 High; 0 Other Level
4 Regular; 0 Special Education; 0 Vocational; 0 Alternative
0 Magnet; 0 Charter; 2 Title I Eligible; 0 School-wide Title I
Students: 1,878 (51.7% male; 48.3% female)
Individual Education Program: 364 (19.4%);
English Language Learner: 0 (0.0%); Migrant: 0 (0.0%)
Eligible for Free Lunch Program: n/a
Eligible for Reduced-Price Lunch Program: n/a
Teachers: 134.4 (14.0 to 1)
Librarians/Media Specialists: 3.0 (626.0 to 1)
Guidance Counselors: 4.0 (469.5 to 1)
Current Spending: ($ per student per year):
Total: $7,904; Instruction: $4,676; Support Services: $3,034

Enrollment, Drop-out Rates and Diploma Recipients by Race/Ethnicity

Category	Total	White	Black	Asian	AIAN	Hisp.
Enrollment (%)	100.0	95.4	0.5	1.0	0.3	2.8
Drop-out Rate (%)	1.1	1.1	0.0	0.0	0.0	0.0
H.S. Diplomas (#)	137	135	0	1	0	1

Evansville Community

340 Fair St • Evansville, WI 53536-1299
(608) 882-5224 • http://evansvilleschools.org
Grade Span: PK-12; **Agency Type:** 1
Schools: 4
2 Primary; 1 Middle; 1 High; 0 Other Level
4 Regular; 0 Special Education; 0 Vocational; 0 Alternative
0 Magnet; 0 Charter; 2 Title I Eligible; 0 School-wide Title I
Students: 1,643 (50.5% male; 49.5% female)
Individual Education Program: 230 (14.0%);
English Language Learner: 0 (0.0%); Migrant: 0 (0.0%)
Eligible for Free Lunch Program: n/a
Eligible for Reduced-Price Lunch Program: n/a
Teachers: 117.6 (14.0 to 1)
Librarians/Media Specialists: 3.5 (469.4 to 1)
Guidance Counselors: 3.0 (547.7 to 1)
Current Spending: ($ per student per year):
Total: $7,494; Instruction: $5,060; Support Services: $2,214

Enrollment, Drop-out Rates and Diploma Recipients by Race/Ethnicity

Category	Total	White	Black	Asian	AIAN	Hisp.
Enrollment (%)	100.0	95.1	0.9	0.5	0.3	3.2
Drop-out Rate (%)	2.2	1.6	0.0	0.0	0.0	100.0
H.S. Diplomas (#)	94	91	0	1	1	1

Janesville

527 S Franklin St • Janesville, WI 53545-4823
(608) 743-5050 • http://www.inwave.com/schools/jps
Grade Span: PK-12; **Agency Type:** 1
Schools: 18
12 Primary; 3 Middle; 3 High; 0 Other Level
17 Regular; 0 Special Education; 0 Vocational; 1 Alternative
0 Magnet; 1 Charter; 9 Title I Eligible; 1 School-wide Title I
Students: 10,699 (51.3% male; 48.7% female)
Individual Education Program: 1,763 (16.5%);
English Language Learner: 232 (2.2%); Migrant: 0 (0.0%)

Eligible for Free Lunch Program: n/a
Eligible for Reduced-Price Lunch Program: n/a
Teachers: 775.4 (13.8 to 1)
Librarians/Media Specialists: 19.0 (563.1 to 1)
Guidance Counselors: 26.0 (411.5 to 1)
Current Spending: ($ per student per year):
Total: $7,915; Instruction: $5,174; Support Services: $2,545
Enrollment, Drop-out Rates and Diploma Recipients by Race/Ethnicity

Category	Total	White	Black	Asian	AIAN	Hisp.
Enrollment (%)	100.0	89.7	4.4	1.8	0.4	3.6
Drop-out Rate (%)	3.0	2.9	2.5	6.1	10.0	5.6
H.S. Diplomas (#)	673	646	6	9	2	10

Milton
430 E High St Ste 2 • Milton, WI 53563-1502
(608) 868-9200 • http://www.milton.k12.wi.us
Grade Span: PK-12; **Agency Type:** 1
Schools: 6
3 Primary; 1 Middle; 1 High; 1 Other Level
6 Regular; 0 Special Education; 0 Vocational; 0 Alternative
0 Magnet; 0 Charter; 4 Title I Eligible; 0 School-wide Title I
Students: 2,941 (50.6% male; 49.4% female)
Individual Education Program: 306 (10.4%);
English Language Learner: 0 (0.0%); Migrant: 0 (0.0%)
Eligible for Free Lunch Program: n/a
Eligible for Reduced-Price Lunch Program: n/a
Teachers: 185.5 (15.9 to 1)
Librarians/Media Specialists: 5.0 (588.2 to 1)
Guidance Counselors: 7.5 (392.1 to 1)
Current Spending: ($ per student per year):
Total: $7,309; Instruction: $4,700; Support Services: $2,334
Enrollment, Drop-out Rates and Diploma Recipients by Race/Ethnicity

Category	Total	White	Black	Asian	AIAN	Hisp.
Enrollment (%)	100.0	96.8	0.6	1.2	0.2	1.2
Drop-out Rate (%)	1.3	1.3	0.0	14.3	0.0	0.0
H.S. Diplomas (#)	199	195	1	3	0	0

Sauk County

Baraboo
101 2nd Ave • Baraboo, WI 53913-2494
(608) 355-3950 • http://www.baraboo.k12.wi.us
Grade Span: PK-12; **Agency Type:** 1
Schools: 8
6 Primary; 1 Middle; 1 High; 0 Other Level
8 Regular; 0 Special Education; 0 Vocational; 0 Alternative
0 Magnet; 0 Charter; 6 Title I Eligible; 0 School-wide Title I
Students: 3,053 (50.8% male; 49.2% female)
Individual Education Program: 442 (14.5%);
English Language Learner: 0 (0.0%); Migrant: 0 (0.0%)
Eligible for Free Lunch Program: n/a
Eligible for Reduced-Price Lunch Program: n/a
Teachers: 203.3 (15.0 to 1)
Librarians/Media Specialists: 3.0 (1,017.7 to 1)
Guidance Counselors: 7.6 (401.7 to 1)
Current Spending: ($ per student per year):
Total: $7,230; Instruction: $4,526; Support Services: $2,414
Enrollment, Drop-out Rates and Diploma Recipients by Race/Ethnicity

Category	Total	White	Black	Asian	AIAN	Hisp.
Enrollment (%)	100.0	92.3	1.5	1.3	2.8	2.1
Drop-out Rate (%)	4.1	3.9	0.0	0.0	7.4	14.3
H.S. Diplomas (#)	214	207	0	0	5	2

Reedsburg
710 N Webb Ave • Reedsburg, WI 53959-1198
(608) 524-2401 • http://www.rsd.k12.wi.us
Grade Span: PK-12; **Agency Type:** 1
Schools: 8
6 Primary; 1 Middle; 1 High; 0 Other Level
8 Regular; 0 Special Education; 0 Vocational; 0 Alternative
0 Magnet; 0 Charter; 5 Title I Eligible; 0 School-wide Title I
Students: 2,499 (50.8% male; 49.2% female)
Individual Education Program: 397 (15.9%);
English Language Learner: 0 (0.0%); Migrant: 0 (0.0%)
Eligible for Free Lunch Program: n/a
Eligible for Reduced-Price Lunch Program: n/a
Teachers: 177.3 (14.1 to 1)
Librarians/Media Specialists: 4.0 (624.8 to 1)
Guidance Counselors: 5.0 (499.8 to 1)
Current Spending: ($ per student per year):
Total: $7,595; Instruction: $4,671; Support Services: $2,522
Enrollment, Drop-out Rates and Diploma Recipients by Race/Ethnicity

Category	Total	White	Black	Asian	AIAN	Hisp.
Enrollment (%)	100.0	95.6	0.6	0.4	1.4	2.1
Drop-out Rate (%)	3.4	3.0	0.0	50.0	25.0	50.0
H.S. Diplomas (#)	173	171	0	1	0	1

Sauk Prairie
213 Maple St • Sauk City, WI 53583-1097
(608) 643-5981 • http://www.saukpr.k12.wi.us
Grade Span: PK-12; **Agency Type:** 1
Schools: 7
5 Primary; 1 Middle; 1 High; 0 Other Level
7 Regular; 0 Special Education; 0 Vocational; 0 Alternative
0 Magnet; 0 Charter; 5 Title I Eligible; 0 School-wide Title I
Students: 2,672 (51.5% male; 48.5% female)
Individual Education Program: 430 (16.1%);
English Language Learner: 87 (3.3%); Migrant: 0 (0.0%)
Eligible for Free Lunch Program: n/a
Eligible for Reduced-Price Lunch Program: n/a
Teachers: 198.4 (13.5 to 1)
Librarians/Media Specialists: 4.5 (593.8 to 1)
Guidance Counselors: 7.8 (342.6 to 1)
Current Spending: ($ per student per year):
Total: $8,126; Instruction: $5,017; Support Services: $2,768
Enrollment, Drop-out Rates and Diploma Recipients by Race/Ethnicity

Category	Total	White	Black	Asian	AIAN	Hisp.
Enrollment (%)	100.0	92.8	0.6	1.0	0.6	5.1
Drop-out Rate (%)	1.9	1.7	50.0	0.0	0.0	6.3
H.S. Diplomas (#)	159	156	1	1	1	0

Wisconsin Dells
811 County Rd H • Wisconsin Dells, WI 53965-9636
(608) 254-7769 • http://www.sdwd.k12.wi.us/
Grade Span: PK-12; **Agency Type:** 1
Schools: 6
3 Primary; 1 Middle; 2 High; 0 Other Level
5 Regular; 0 Special Education; 0 Vocational; 1 Alternative
0 Magnet; 1 Charter; 3 Title I Eligible; 0 School-wide Title I
Students: 1,777 (49.8% male; 50.2% female)
Individual Education Program: 227 (12.8%);
English Language Learner: 0 (0.0%); Migrant: 0 (0.0%)
Eligible for Free Lunch Program: n/a
Eligible for Reduced-Price Lunch Program: n/a
Teachers: 121.2 (14.7 to 1)
Librarians/Media Specialists: 1.0 (1,777.0 to 1)
Guidance Counselors: 5.0 (355.4 to 1)
Current Spending: ($ per student per year):
Total: $7,479; Instruction: $4,654; Support Services: $2,554
Enrollment, Drop-out Rates and Diploma Recipients by Race/Ethnicity

Category	Total	White	Black	Asian	AIAN	Hisp.
Enrollment (%)	100.0	87.0	1.1	0.4	8.4	3.1
Drop-out Rate (%)	0.8	0.9	0.0	0.0	0.0	0.0
H.S. Diplomas (#)	118	107	2	3	4	2

Sawyer County

Hayward Community
15930 W 5th St • Hayward, WI 54843-0860
Mailing Address: PO Box 860 • Hayward, WI 54843-0860
(715) 634-2619 • http://www.hayward.k12.wi.us
Grade Span: PK-12; **Agency Type:** 1
Schools: 7
4 Primary; 1 Middle; 1 High; 1 Other Level
5 Regular; 0 Special Education; 0 Vocational; 2 Alternative
0 Magnet; 1 Charter; 5 Title I Eligible; 4 School-wide Title I
Students: 2,029 (51.2% male; 48.8% female)
Individual Education Program: 294 (14.5%);
English Language Learner: 0 (0.0%); Migrant: 0 (0.0%)
Eligible for Free Lunch Program: n/a
Eligible for Reduced-Price Lunch Program: n/a
Teachers: 145.6 (13.9 to 1)
Librarians/Media Specialists: 2.9 (699.7 to 1)
Guidance Counselors: 5.3 (382.8 to 1)
Current Spending: ($ per student per year):
Total: $8,274; Instruction: $4,826; Support Services: $3,092
Enrollment, Drop-out Rates and Diploma Recipients by Race/Ethnicity

Category	Total	White	Black	Asian	AIAN	Hisp.
Enrollment (%)	100.0	73.8	0.2	0.5	25.1	0.4
Drop-out Rate (%)	1.5	0.9	n/a	0.0	4.1	0.0
H.S. Diplomas (#)	109	92	0	0	17	0

Shawano County

Shawano-Gresham

218 County Rd B • Shawano, WI 54166-7054
(715) 526-3194 • http://www.sgsd.k12.wi.us
Grade Span: PK-12; **Agency Type:** 1
Schools: 6
3 Primary; 1 Middle; 2 High; 0 Other Level
6 Regular; 0 Special Education; 0 Vocational; 0 Alternative
0 Magnet; 0 Charter; 3 Title I Eligible; 0 School-wide Title I
Students: 2,966 (51.7% male; 48.3% female)
Individual Education Program: 462 (15.6%);
English Language Learner: 0 (0.0%); Migrant: 0 (0.0%)
Eligible for Free Lunch Program: n/a
Eligible for Reduced-Price Lunch Program: n/a
Teachers: 198.1 (15.0 to 1)
Librarians/Media Specialists: 4.0 (741.5 to 1)
Guidance Counselors: 5.7 (520.4 to 1)
Current Spending: ($ per student per year):
Total: $7,282; Instruction: $4,666; Support Services: $2,329
Enrollment, Drop-out Rates and Diploma Recipients by Race/Ethnicity

Category	Total	White	Black	Asian	AIAN	Hisp.
Enrollment (%)	100.0	79.8	0.8	0.9	16.1	2.4
Drop-out Rate (%)	2.3	1.7	50.0	10.0	4.4	11.1
H.S. Diplomas (#)	187	160	0	1	24	2

Sheboygan County

Plymouth

125 S Highland Ave • Plymouth, WI 53073-2599
(920) 892-2661 • http://www.plymouth.k12.wi.us
Grade Span: PK-12; **Agency Type:** 1
Schools: 7
5 Primary; 1 Middle; 1 High; 0 Other Level
7 Regular; 0 Special Education; 0 Vocational; 0 Alternative
0 Magnet; 0 Charter; 4 Title I Eligible; 0 School-wide Title I
Students: 2,470 (50.7% male; 49.3% female)
Individual Education Program: 372 (15.1%);
English Language Learner: 0 (0.0%); Migrant: 0 (0.0%)
Eligible for Free Lunch Program: n/a
Eligible for Reduced-Price Lunch Program: n/a
Teachers: 165.5 (14.9 to 1)
Librarians/Media Specialists: 1.9 (1,300.0 to 1)
Guidance Counselors: 9.5 (260.0 to 1)
Current Spending: ($ per student per year):
Total: $7,375; Instruction: $4,498; Support Services: $2,608
Enrollment, Drop-out Rates and Diploma Recipients by Race/Ethnicity

Category	Total	White	Black	Asian	AIAN	Hisp.
Enrollment (%)	100.0	96.3	0.2	0.5	0.8	2.1
Drop-out Rate (%)	1.2	1.2	0.0	0.0	0.0	0.0
H.S. Diplomas (#)	202	195	0	3	2	2

Sheboygan Area

830 Virginia Ave • Sheboygan, WI 53081-4427
(920) 459-3511 • http://www.sheboygan.k12.wi.us
Grade Span: PK-12; **Agency Type:** 1
Schools: 18
13 Primary; 3 Middle; 2 High; 0 Other Level
18 Regular; 0 Special Education; 0 Vocational; 0 Alternative
0 Magnet; 0 Charter; 6 Title I Eligible; 4 School-wide Title I
Students: 10,377 (51.0% male; 49.0% female)
Individual Education Program: 1,627 (15.7%);
English Language Learner: 1,892 (18.2%); Migrant: 0 (0.0%)
Eligible for Free Lunch Program: n/a
Eligible for Reduced-Price Lunch Program: n/a
Teachers: 726.3 (14.3 to 1)
Librarians/Media Specialists: 14.7 (705.9 to 1)
Guidance Counselors: 26.2 (396.1 to 1)
Current Spending: ($ per student per year):
Total: $8,102; Instruction: $5,333; Support Services: $2,550
Enrollment, Drop-out Rates and Diploma Recipients by Race/Ethnicity

Category	Total	White	Black	Asian	AIAN	Hisp.
Enrollment (%)	100.0	70.5	2.1	17.2	0.6	9.6
Drop-out Rate (%)	3.8	3.5	5.4	3.2	9.5	8.7
H.S. Diplomas (#)	768	597	7	111	6	47

Sheboygan Falls

220 Amherst Ave • Sheboygan Falls, WI 53085-1799
(920) 467-7893 • http://www.sheboyganfalls.k12.wi.us
Grade Span: PK-12; **Agency Type:** 1
Schools: 3
1 Primary; 1 Middle; 1 High; 0 Other Level
3 Regular; 0 Special Education; 0 Vocational; 0 Alternative
0 Magnet; 0 Charter; 2 Title I Eligible; 0 School-wide Title I
Students: 1,729 (52.5% male; 47.5% female)
Individual Education Program: 229 (13.2%);
English Language Learner: 0 (0.0%); Migrant: 0 (0.0%)
Eligible for Free Lunch Program: n/a
Eligible for Reduced-Price Lunch Program: n/a
Teachers: 119.6 (14.5 to 1)
Librarians/Media Specialists: 3.0 (576.3 to 1)
Guidance Counselors: 4.8 (360.2 to 1)
Current Spending: ($ per student per year):
Total: $7,796; Instruction: $4,756; Support Services: $2,741
Enrollment, Drop-out Rates and Diploma Recipients by Race/Ethnicity

Category	Total	White	Black	Asian	AIAN	Hisp.
Enrollment (%)	100.0	96.5	0.9	0.5	0.7	1.4
Drop-out Rate (%)	1.1	1.1	0.0	0.0	0.0	0.0
H.S. Diplomas (#)	133	130	1	1	0	1

St. Croix County

Hudson

1401 Vine St • Hudson, WI 54016-1880
(715) 386-4901 • http://www.hudson.k12.wi.us
Grade Span: PK-12; **Agency Type:** 1
Schools: 7
5 Primary; 1 Middle; 1 High; 0 Other Level
7 Regular; 0 Special Education; 0 Vocational; 0 Alternative
0 Magnet; 0 Charter; 3 Title I Eligible; 0 School-wide Title I
Students: 4,426 (52.8% male; 47.2% female)
Individual Education Program: 661 (14.9%);
English Language Learner: 0 (0.0%); Migrant: 0 (0.0%)
Eligible for Free Lunch Program: n/a
Eligible for Reduced-Price Lunch Program: n/a
Teachers: 295.7 (15.0 to 1)
Librarians/Media Specialists: 7.0 (632.3 to 1)
Guidance Counselors: 12.4 (356.9 to 1)
Current Spending: ($ per student per year):
Total: $7,356; Instruction: $4,480; Support Services: $2,521
Enrollment, Drop-out Rates and Diploma Recipients by Race/Ethnicity

Category	Total	White	Black	Asian	AIAN	Hisp.
Enrollment (%)	100.0	95.4	1.0	1.9	0.5	1.2
Drop-out Rate (%)	0.2	0.2	0.0	0.0	0.0	0.0
H.S. Diplomas (#)	314	309	0	2	0	3

New Richmond

701 E 11th St • New Richmond, WI 54017-2355
(715) 243-7411 • http://www.newrichmond.k12.wi.us
Grade Span: PK-12; **Agency Type:** 1
Schools: 4
3 Primary; 0 Middle; 1 High; 0 Other Level
4 Regular; 0 Special Education; 0 Vocational; 0 Alternative
0 Magnet; 0 Charter; 2 Title I Eligible; 0 School-wide Title I
Students: 2,443 (50.5% male; 49.5% female)
Individual Education Program: 317 (13.0%);
English Language Learner: 0 (0.0%); Migrant: 0 (0.0%)
Eligible for Free Lunch Program: n/a
Eligible for Reduced-Price Lunch Program: n/a
Teachers: 151.3 (16.1 to 1)
Librarians/Media Specialists: 3.8 (642.9 to 1)
Guidance Counselors: 6.0 (407.2 to 1)
Current Spending: ($ per student per year):
Total: $7,713; Instruction: $4,532; Support Services: $2,867
Enrollment, Drop-out Rates and Diploma Recipients by Race/Ethnicity

Category	Total	White	Black	Asian	AIAN	Hisp.
Enrollment (%)	100.0	95.7	0.8	1.4	0.6	1.5
Drop-out Rate (%)	0.4	0.4	0.0	0.0	0.0	0.0
H.S. Diplomas (#)	189	183	2	3	0	1

Taylor County

Medford Area

124 W State St • Medford, WI 54451-1771
(715) 748-4620 • http://www.medford.k12.wi.us
Grade Span: PK-12; **Agency Type:** 1
Schools: 4
2 Primary; 1 Middle; 1 High; 0 Other Level
4 Regular; 0 Special Education; 0 Vocational; 0 Alternative
0 Magnet; 0 Charter; 2 Title I Eligible; 0 School-wide Title I
Students: 2,297 (52.2% male; 47.8% female)
Individual Education Program: 247 (10.8%);
English Language Learner: 0 (0.0%); Migrant: 13 (0.6%)
Eligible for Free Lunch Program: n/a
Eligible for Reduced-Price Lunch Program: n/a
Teachers: 151.5 (15.2 to 1)
Librarians/Media Specialists: 3.0 (765.7 to 1)
Guidance Counselors: 4.6 (499.3 to 1)
Current Spending: ($ per student per year):
Total: $7,134; Instruction: $4,231; Support Services: $2,531

Enrollment, Drop-out Rates and Diploma Recipients by Race/Ethnicity

Category	Total	White	Black	Asian	AIAN	Hisp.
Enrollment (%)	100.0	97.2	0.5	0.9	0.3	1.1
Drop-out Rate (%)	0.3	0.3	0.0	0.0	0.0	0.0
H.S. Diplomas (#)	219	218	0	1	0	0

Vilas County

Northland Pines

1780 Pleasure Island Rd • Eagle River, WI 54521-8927
(715) 479-6487 • http://www.fen.com/wi/npsd
Grade Span: PK-12; **Agency Type:** 1
Schools: 5
3 Primary; 1 Middle; 1 High; 0 Other Level
5 Regular; 0 Special Education; 0 Vocational; 0 Alternative
0 Magnet; 0 Charter; 2 Title I Eligible; 0 School-wide Title I
Students: 1,579 (52.9% male; 47.1% female)
Individual Education Program: 203 (12.9%);
English Language Learner: 0 (0.0%); Migrant: 0 (0.0%)
Eligible for Free Lunch Program: n/a
Eligible for Reduced-Price Lunch Program: n/a
Teachers: 119.5 (13.2 to 1)
Librarians/Media Specialists: 2.0 (789.5 to 1)
Guidance Counselors: 6.0 (263.2 to 1)
Current Spending: ($ per student per year):
Total: $8,844; Instruction: $5,284; Support Services: $3,264
Enrollment, Drop-out Rates and Diploma Recipients by Race/Ethnicity

Category	Total	White	Black	Asian	AIAN	Hisp.
Enrollment (%)	100.0	97.0	0.4	0.4	0.6	1.5
Drop-out Rate (%)	1.2	1.3	0.0	0.0	0.0	0.0
H.S. Diplomas (#)	116	114	0	1	1	0

Walworth County

Delavan-Darien

324 Beloit St • Delavan, WI 53115-1606
(262) 728-2642 • http://www.ddschools.org
Grade Span: PK-12; **Agency Type:** 1
Schools: 5
3 Primary; 1 Middle; 1 High; 0 Other Level
5 Regular; 0 Special Education; 0 Vocational; 0 Alternative
0 Magnet; 0 Charter; 2 Title I Eligible; 0 School-wide Title I
Students: 2,771 (51.7% male; 48.3% female)
Individual Education Program: 358 (12.9%);
English Language Learner: 322 (11.6%); Migrant: 0 (0.0%)
Eligible for Free Lunch Program: n/a
Eligible for Reduced-Price Lunch Program: n/a
Teachers: 169.5 (16.3 to 1)
Librarians/Media Specialists: 4.0 (692.8 to 1)
Guidance Counselors: 6.0 (461.8 to 1)
Current Spending: ($ per student per year):
Total: $6,831; Instruction: $3,973; Support Services: $2,574
Enrollment, Drop-out Rates and Diploma Recipients by Race/Ethnicity

Category	Total	White	Black	Asian	AIAN	Hisp.
Enrollment (%)	100.0	69.8	2.6	0.8	0.4	26.4
Drop-out Rate (%)	3.2	2.1	6.3	0.0	0.0	8.2
H.S. Diplomas (#)	207	171	2	2	1	31

East Troy Community

2043 Division St • East Troy, WI 53120-1238
(262) 642-6710 • http://www.easttroy.k12.wi.us
Grade Span: KG-12; **Agency Type:** 1
Schools: 5
3 Primary; 1 Middle; 1 High; 0 Other Level
5 Regular; 0 Special Education; 0 Vocational; 0 Alternative
0 Magnet; 0 Charter; 2 Title I Eligible; 0 School-wide Title I
Students: 1,667 (50.9% male; 49.1% female)
Individual Education Program: 159 (9.5%);
English Language Learner: 0 (0.0%); Migrant: 0 (0.0%)
Eligible for Free Lunch Program: n/a
Eligible for Reduced-Price Lunch Program: n/a
Teachers: 113.4 (14.7 to 1)
Librarians/Media Specialists: 3.0 (555.7 to 1)
Guidance Counselors: 3.0 (555.7 to 1)
Current Spending: ($ per student per year):
Total: $6,933; Instruction: $4,367; Support Services: $2,349
Enrollment, Drop-out Rates and Diploma Recipients by Race/Ethnicity

Category	Total	White	Black	Asian	AIAN	Hisp.
Enrollment (%)	100.0	96.6	0.8	0.2	0.2	2.2
Drop-out Rate (%)	1.3	1.3	0.0	0.0	n/a	0.0
H.S. Diplomas (#)	145	143	1	0	0	1

Elkhorn Area

3 N Jackson St • Elkhorn, WI 53121-1905
(262) 723-3160 • http://www.elkhorn.k12.wi.us
Grade Span: KG-12; **Agency Type:** 1
Schools: 6
2 Primary; 1 Middle; 2 High; 0 Other Level
4 Regular; 0 Special Education; 0 Vocational; 1 Alternative
0 Magnet; 1 Charter; 3 Title I Eligible; 0 School-wide Title I
Students: 2,577 (51.5% male; 48.5% female)
Individual Education Program: 286 (11.1%);
English Language Learner: 132 (5.1%); Migrant: 0 (0.0%)
Eligible for Free Lunch Program: n/a
Eligible for Reduced-Price Lunch Program: n/a
Teachers: 163.9 (15.7 to 1)
Librarians/Media Specialists: 3.0 (859.0 to 1)
Guidance Counselors: 7.0 (368.1 to 1)
Current Spending: ($ per student per year):
Total: $7,064; Instruction: $4,235; Support Services: $2,588
Enrollment, Drop-out Rates and Diploma Recipients by Race/Ethnicity

Category	Total	White	Black	Asian	AIAN	Hisp.
Enrollment (%)	100.0	90.6	0.9	1.2	0.4	6.9
Drop-out Rate (%)	1.3	1.3	0.0	0.0	0.0	0.0
H.S. Diplomas (#)	181	169	0	3	0	9

Lake Geneva J1

208 E S St • Lake Geneva, WI 53147-2436
(262) 348-1000 • http://lakegenevaschools.com/
Grade Span: KG-08; **Agency Type:** 1
Schools: 5
4 Primary; 1 Middle; 0 High; 0 Other Level
5 Regular; 0 Special Education; 0 Vocational; 0 Alternative
0 Magnet; 0 Charter; 3 Title I Eligible; 0 School-wide Title I
Students: 1,717 (51.6% male; 48.4% female)
Individual Education Program: 200 (11.6%);
English Language Learner: 190 (11.1%); Migrant: 0 (0.0%)
Eligible for Free Lunch Program: n/a
Eligible for Reduced-Price Lunch Program: n/a
Teachers: 117.4 (14.6 to 1)
Librarians/Media Specialists: 1.5 (1,144.7 to 1)
Guidance Counselors: 4.0 (429.3 to 1)
Current Spending: ($ per student per year):
Total: $7,264; Instruction: $4,528; Support Services: $2,431
Enrollment, Drop-out Rates and Diploma Recipients by Race/Ethnicity

Category	Total	White	Black	Asian	AIAN	Hisp.
Enrollment (%)	100.0	79.7	2.3	0.9	0.2	16.9
Drop-out Rate (%)	n/a	n/a	n/a	n/a	n/a	n/a
H.S. Diplomas (#)	n/a	n/a	n/a	n/a	n/a	n/a

Whitewater

419 S Elizabeth St • Whitewater, WI 53190-1632
(262) 472-8708 • http://www.whitewater.k12.wi.us
Grade Span: PK-12; **Agency Type:** 1
Schools: 5
3 Primary; 1 Middle; 1 High; 0 Other Level
5 Regular; 0 Special Education; 0 Vocational; 0 Alternative
0 Magnet; 0 Charter; 2 Title I Eligible; 0 School-wide Title I
Students: 2,092 (51.3% male; 48.7% female)
Individual Education Program: 282 (13.5%);
English Language Learner: 17 (0.8%); Migrant: 0 (0.0%)
Eligible for Free Lunch Program: n/a
Eligible for Reduced-Price Lunch Program: n/a
Teachers: 138.3 (15.1 to 1)
Librarians/Media Specialists: 3.8 (550.5 to 1)
Guidance Counselors: 5.0 (418.4 to 1)
Current Spending: ($ per student per year):
Total: $7,477; Instruction: $4,266; Support Services: $2,907
Enrollment, Drop-out Rates and Diploma Recipients by Race/Ethnicity

Category	Total	White	Black	Asian	AIAN	Hisp.
Enrollment (%)	100.0	83.5	1.4	1.1	0.6	13.5
Drop-out Rate (%)	2.6	1.6	0.0	0.0	12.5	11.9
H.S. Diplomas (#)	144	129	0	3	0	12

Washburn County

Spooner

500 College St • Spooner, WI 54801-1298
(715) 635-2171 • http://www.spooner.k12.wi.us
Grade Span: PK-12; **Agency Type:** 1
Schools: 3
1 Primary; 1 Middle; 1 High; 0 Other Level
3 Regular; 0 Special Education; 0 Vocational; 0 Alternative
0 Magnet; 0 Charter; 2 Title I Eligible; 0 School-wide Title I
Students: 1,550 (53.8% male; 46.2% female)
Individual Education Program: 220 (14.2%);
English Language Learner: 0 (0.0%); Migrant: 0 (0.0%)

Eligible for Free Lunch Program: n/a
Eligible for Reduced-Price Lunch Program: n/a
Teachers: 113.1 (13.7 to 1)
Librarians/Media Specialists: 3.6 (430.6 to 1)
Guidance Counselors: 3.6 (430.6 to 1)
Current Spending: ($ per student per year):
Total: $7,827; Instruction: $4,961; Support Services: $2,637
Enrollment, Drop-out Rates and Diploma Recipients by Race/Ethnicity

Category	Total	White	Black	Asian	AIAN	Hisp.
Enrollment (%)	100.0	95.9	0.8	0.8	1.9	0.6
Drop-out Rate (%)	1.6	1.5	25.0	0.0	0.0	0.0
H.S. Diplomas (#)	153	147	2	3	1	0

Washington County

Germantown

N104w13840 Donges Bay Rd • Germantown, WI 53022-4499
(262) 253-3904 • http://www.germantown.k12.wi.us
Grade Span: PK-12; **Agency Type:** 1
Schools: 6
4 Primary; 1 Middle; 1 High; 0 Other Level
6 Regular; 0 Special Education; 0 Vocational; 0 Alternative
0 Magnet; 0 Charter; 0 Title I Eligible; 0 School-wide Title I
Students: 3,679 (52.3% male; 47.7% female)
Individual Education Program: 431 (11.7%);
English Language Learner: 0 (0.0%); Migrant: 0 (0.0%)
Eligible for Free Lunch Program: n/a
Eligible for Reduced-Price Lunch Program: n/a
Teachers: 252.9 (14.5 to 1)
Librarians/Media Specialists: 4.8 (766.5 to 1)
Guidance Counselors: 9.4 (391.4 to 1)
Current Spending: ($ per student per year):
Total: $8,396; Instruction: $4,832; Support Services: $3,249
Enrollment, Drop-out Rates and Diploma Recipients by Race/Ethnicity

Category	Total	White	Black	Asian	AIAN	Hisp.
Enrollment (%)	100.0	94.0	1.8	2.4	0.5	1.3
Drop-out Rate (%)	0.8	0.9	0.0	0.0	0.0	0.0
H.S. Diplomas (#)	271	262	2	4	1	2

Hartford J1

675 E Rossman St • Hartford, WI 53027-2347
(262) 673-3155 • http://www.hartfordjt1.k12.wi.us
Grade Span: PK-08; **Agency Type:** 1
Schools: 3
2 Primary; 1 Middle; 0 High; 0 Other Level
3 Regular; 0 Special Education; 0 Vocational; 0 Alternative
0 Magnet; 0 Charter; 2 Title I Eligible; 0 School-wide Title I
Students: 1,575 (51.5% male; 48.5% female)
Individual Education Program: 283 (18.0%);
English Language Learner: 0 (0.0%); Migrant: 0 (0.0%)
Eligible for Free Lunch Program: n/a
Eligible for Reduced-Price Lunch Program: n/a
Teachers: 114.1 (13.8 to 1)
Librarians/Media Specialists: 3.0 (525.0 to 1)
Guidance Counselors: 3.0 (525.0 to 1)
Current Spending: ($ per student per year):
Total: $8,338; Instruction: $5,402; Support Services: $2,628
Enrollment, Drop-out Rates and Diploma Recipients by Race/Ethnicity

Category	Total	White	Black	Asian	AIAN	Hisp.
Enrollment (%)	100.0	93.7	0.5	0.8	0.8	4.1
Drop-out Rate (%)	n/a	n/a	n/a	n/a	n/a	n/a
H.S. Diplomas (#)	n/a	n/a	n/a	n/a	n/a	n/a

Hartford Uhs

805 Cedar St • Hartford, WI 53027-2399
(262) 673-8950 • http://www.huhs.org
Grade Span: 09-12; **Agency Type:** 1
Schools: 1
0 Primary; 0 Middle; 1 High; 0 Other Level
1 Regular; 0 Special Education; 0 Vocational; 0 Alternative
0 Magnet; 0 Charter; 1 Title I Eligible; 0 School-wide Title I
Students: 1,701 (53.7% male; 46.3% female)
Individual Education Program: 199 (11.7%);
English Language Learner: 0 (0.0%); Migrant: 0 (0.0%)
Eligible for Free Lunch Program: n/a
Eligible for Reduced-Price Lunch Program: n/a
Teachers: 110.4 (15.4 to 1)
Librarians/Media Specialists: 1.3 (1,308.5 to 1)
Guidance Counselors: 5.0 (340.2 to 1)
Current Spending: ($ per student per year):
Total: $8,573; Instruction: $5,111; Support Services: $3,160
Enrollment, Drop-out Rates and Diploma Recipients by Race/Ethnicity

Category	Total	White	Black	Asian	AIAN	Hisp.
Enrollment (%)	100.0	95.8	0.2	1.1	0.3	2.6
Drop-out Rate (%)	2.4	2.3	0.0	4.8	16.7	6.3
H.S. Diplomas (#)	379	366	1	4	0	8

Kewaskum

1455 School St • Kewaskum, WI 53040-0037
Mailing Address: PO Box 37 • Kewaskum, WI 53040-0037
(262) 626-8427 • http://www.ksd.k12.wi.us
Grade Span: PK-12; **Agency Type:** 1
Schools: 5
3 Primary; 1 Middle; 1 High; 0 Other Level
5 Regular; 0 Special Education; 0 Vocational; 0 Alternative
0 Magnet; 0 Charter; 1 Title I Eligible; 0 School-wide Title I
Students: 1,920 (49.5% male; 50.5% female)
Individual Education Program: 227 (11.8%);
English Language Learner: 0 (0.0%); Migrant: 0 (0.0%)
Eligible for Free Lunch Program: n/a
Eligible for Reduced-Price Lunch Program: n/a
Teachers: 127.2 (15.1 to 1)
Librarians/Media Specialists: 2.0 (960.0 to 1)
Guidance Counselors: 5.0 (384.0 to 1)
Current Spending: ($ per student per year):
Total: $7,629; Instruction: $4,728; Support Services: $2,599
Enrollment, Drop-out Rates and Diploma Recipients by Race/Ethnicity

Category	Total	White	Black	Asian	AIAN	Hisp.
Enrollment (%)	100.0	97.2	0.2	0.5	0.8	1.3
Drop-out Rate (%)	2.5	2.6	n/a	0.0	0.0	0.0
H.S. Diplomas (#)	144	141	0	0	1	2

Slinger

207 Polk St • Slinger, WI 53086-9585
(262) 644-9615 • http://www.slinger.k12.wi.us
Grade Span: PK-12; **Agency Type:** 1
Schools: 5
3 Primary; 1 Middle; 1 High; 0 Other Level
5 Regular; 0 Special Education; 0 Vocational; 0 Alternative
0 Magnet; 0 Charter; 3 Title I Eligible; 0 School-wide Title I
Students: 2,846 (51.3% male; 48.7% female)
Individual Education Program: 319 (11.2%);
English Language Learner: 0 (0.0%); Migrant: 0 (0.0%)
Eligible for Free Lunch Program: n/a
Eligible for Reduced-Price Lunch Program: n/a
Teachers: 164.8 (17.3 to 1)
Librarians/Media Specialists: 3.0 (948.7 to 1)
Guidance Counselors: 8.0 (355.8 to 1)
Current Spending: ($ per student per year):
Total: $6,949; Instruction: $4,331; Support Services: $2,353
Enrollment, Drop-out Rates and Diploma Recipients by Race/Ethnicity

Category	Total	White	Black	Asian	AIAN	Hisp.
Enrollment (%)	100.0	98.0	0.4	0.4	0.2	1.0
Drop-out Rate (%)	1.4	1.5	0.0	0.0	0.0	0.0
H.S. Diplomas (#)	189	185	0	1	0	3

West Bend

735 S Main • West Bend, WI 53095-3999
Mailing Address: PO Box 2000 • West Bend, WI 53095-7900
(262) 335-5435 • http://www.west-bend.k12.wi.us
Grade Span: PK-12; **Agency Type:** 1
Schools: 11
7 Primary; 2 Middle; 2 High; 0 Other Level
11 Regular; 0 Special Education; 0 Vocational; 0 Alternative
0 Magnet; 0 Charter; 5 Title I Eligible; 0 School-wide Title I
Students: 6,826 (53.0% male; 47.0% female)
Individual Education Program: 825 (12.1%);
English Language Learner: 0 (0.0%); Migrant: 0 (0.0%)
Eligible for Free Lunch Program: n/a
Eligible for Reduced-Price Lunch Program: n/a
Teachers: 426.4 (16.0 to 1)
Librarians/Media Specialists: 10.0 (682.6 to 1)
Guidance Counselors: 16.0 (426.6 to 1)
Current Spending: ($ per student per year):
Total: $7,380; Instruction: $4,788; Support Services: $2,346
Enrollment, Drop-out Rates and Diploma Recipients by Race/Ethnicity

Category	Total	White	Black	Asian	AIAN	Hisp.
Enrollment (%)	100.0	95.8	0.9	0.6	0.7	1.9
Drop-out Rate (%)	0.5	0.4	0.0	6.3	0.0	2.3
H.S. Diplomas (#)	603	589	1	6	1	6

Waukesha County

Arrowhead Uhs

700 N Ave • Hartland, WI 53029-9502
(262) 369-3611 • http://www.ahs.k12.wi.us
Grade Span: 09-12; **Agency Type:** 1
Schools: 1
0 Primary; 0 Middle; 1 High; 0 Other Level
1 Regular; 0 Special Education; 0 Vocational; 0 Alternative
0 Magnet; 0 Charter; 1 Title I Eligible; 0 School-wide Title I
Students: 2,124 (51.7% male; 48.3% female)
Individual Education Program: 149 (7.0%);
English Language Learner: 0 (0.0%); Migrant: 0 (0.0%)
Eligible for Free Lunch Program: n/a
Eligible for Reduced-Price Lunch Program: n/a
Teachers: 128.1 (16.6 to 1)
Librarians/Media Specialists: 2.0 (1,062.0 to 1)
Guidance Counselors: 6.0 (354.0 to 1)
Current Spending: ($ per student per year):
Total: $9,425; Instruction: $5,729; Support Services: $3,453
Enrollment, Drop-out Rates and Diploma Recipients by Race/Ethnicity

Category	Total	White	Black	Asian	AIAN	Hisp.
Enrollment (%)	100.0	98.7	0.2	0.4	0.1	0.6
Drop-out Rate (%)	0.5	0.5	0.0	0.0	0.0	0.0
H.S. Diplomas (#)	457	450	0	4	1	2

Elmbrook

13780 Hope St • Brookfield, WI 53005-1700
Mailing Address: PO Box 1830 • Brookfield, WI 53008-1830
(262) 781-3030 • http://www.elmbrook.k12.wi.us
Grade Span: PK-12; **Agency Type:** 1
Schools: 11
6 Primary; 2 Middle; 2 High; 1 Other Level
10 Regular; 1 Special Education; 0 Vocational; 0 Alternative
0 Magnet; 0 Charter; 0 Title I Eligible; 0 School-wide Title I
Students: 7,633 (51.0% male; 49.0% female)
Individual Education Program: 874 (11.5%);
English Language Learner: 0 (0.0%); Migrant: 0 (0.0%)
Eligible for Free Lunch Program: n/a
Eligible for Reduced-Price Lunch Program: n/a
Teachers: 516.4 (14.8 to 1)
Librarians/Media Specialists: 8.8 (867.4 to 1)
Guidance Counselors: 14.0 (545.2 to 1)
Current Spending: ($ per student per year):
Total: $9,510; Instruction: $5,898; Support Services: $3,350
Enrollment, Drop-out Rates and Diploma Recipients by Race/Ethnicity

Category	Total	White	Black	Asian	AIAN	Hisp.
Enrollment (%)	100.0	87.8	4.6	5.9	0.1	1.7
Drop-out Rate (%)	0.2	0.2	1.5	0.0	0.0	0.0
H.S. Diplomas (#)	589	526	25	27	0	11

Hamilton

W220-N6151 Town Line Rd • Sussex, WI 53089-3999
(262) 246-1973 • http://www.hamiltondist.k12.wi.us
Grade Span: PK-12; **Agency Type:** 1
Schools: 8
5 Primary; 2 Middle; 1 High; 0 Other Level
7 Regular; 0 Special Education; 0 Vocational; 1 Alternative
0 Magnet; 1 Charter; 4 Title I Eligible; 0 School-wide Title I
Students: 3,988 (51.2% male; 48.8% female)
Individual Education Program: 379 (9.5%);
English Language Learner: 0 (0.0%); Migrant: 0 (0.0%)
Eligible for Free Lunch Program: n/a
Eligible for Reduced-Price Lunch Program: n/a
Teachers: 257.4 (15.5 to 1)
Librarians/Media Specialists: 5.9 (675.9 to 1)
Guidance Counselors: 8.0 (498.5 to 1)
Current Spending: ($ per student per year):
Total: $7,576; Instruction: $4,573; Support Services: $2,797
Enrollment, Drop-out Rates and Diploma Recipients by Race/Ethnicity

Category	Total	White	Black	Asian	AIAN	Hisp.
Enrollment (%)	100.0	92.6	2.3	2.9	0.6	1.6
Drop-out Rate (%)	0.3	0.4	0.0	0.0	0.0	0.0
H.S. Diplomas (#)	280	252	6	14	3	5

Kettle Moraine

563 A J Allen Cir • Wales, WI 53183-0901
Mailing Address: PO Box 901 • Wales, WI 53183-0901
(262) 968-6330 • http://www.kmsd.edu
Grade Span: PK-12; **Agency Type:** 1
Schools: 6
4 Primary; 1 Middle; 1 High; 0 Other Level
6 Regular; 0 Special Education; 0 Vocational; 0 Alternative
0 Magnet; 0 Charter; 2 Title I Eligible; 0 School-wide Title I
Students: 4,373 (51.2% male; 48.8% female)
Individual Education Program: 568 (13.0%);
English Language Learner: 0 (0.0%); Migrant: 11 (0.3%)
Eligible for Free Lunch Program: n/a
Eligible for Reduced-Price Lunch Program: n/a
Teachers: 286.3 (15.3 to 1)
Librarians/Media Specialists: 6.0 (728.8 to 1)
Guidance Counselors: 10.7 (408.7 to 1)
Current Spending: ($ per student per year):
Total: $8,195; Instruction: $5,221; Support Services: $2,658
Enrollment, Drop-out Rates and Diploma Recipients by Race/Ethnicity

Category	Total	White	Black	Asian	AIAN	Hisp.
Enrollment (%)	100.0	97.1	0.5	0.9	0.2	1.3
Drop-out Rate (%)	0.3	0.3	n/a	0.0	0.0	0.0
H.S. Diplomas (#)	342	326	0	4	2	10

Menomonee Falls

N84-W16579 Menomonee Ave • Menomonee Falls, WI 53051-3040
(262) 255-8440 • http://www.sdmf.k12.wi.us
Grade Span: PK-12; **Agency Type:** 1
Schools: 7
4 Primary; 1 Middle; 1 High; 1 Other Level
7 Regular; 0 Special Education; 0 Vocational; 0 Alternative
0 Magnet; 0 Charter; 3 Title I Eligible; 0 School-wide Title I
Students: 4,405 (50.6% male; 49.4% female)
Individual Education Program: 533 (12.1%);
English Language Learner: 20 (0.5%); Migrant: 0 (0.0%)
Eligible for Free Lunch Program: n/a
Eligible for Reduced-Price Lunch Program: n/a
Teachers: 300.4 (14.7 to 1)
Librarians/Media Specialists: 8.0 (550.6 to 1)
Guidance Counselors: 11.6 (379.7 to 1)
Current Spending: ($ per student per year):
Total: $9,130; Instruction: $5,536; Support Services: $3,354
Enrollment, Drop-out Rates and Diploma Recipients by Race/Ethnicity

Category	Total	White	Black	Asian	AIAN	Hisp.
Enrollment (%)	100.0	84.8	8.4	3.6	0.5	2.6
Drop-out Rate (%)	0.1	0.0	1.0	0.0	0.0	0.0
H.S. Diplomas (#)	275	243	15	10	2	5

Mukwonago

423 Division St • Mukwonago, WI 53149-1294
(262) 363-6304 • http://www.mukwonago.k12.wi.us
Grade Span: PK-12; **Agency Type:** 1
Schools: 7
5 Primary; 1 Middle; 1 High; 0 Other Level
7 Regular; 0 Special Education; 0 Vocational; 0 Alternative
0 Magnet; 0 Charter; 5 Title I Eligible; 0 School-wide Title I
Students: 5,003 (51.3% male; 48.7% female)
Individual Education Program: 628 (12.6%);
English Language Learner: 0 (0.0%); Migrant: 0 (0.0%)
Eligible for Free Lunch Program: n/a
Eligible for Reduced-Price Lunch Program: n/a
Teachers: 320.0 (15.6 to 1)
Librarians/Media Specialists: 6.9 (725.1 to 1)
Guidance Counselors: 9.0 (555.9 to 1)
Current Spending: ($ per student per year):
Total: $7,419; Instruction: $4,759; Support Services: $2,381
Enrollment, Drop-out Rates and Diploma Recipients by Race/Ethnicity

Category	Total	White	Black	Asian	AIAN	Hisp.
Enrollment (%)	100.0	96.3	0.6	0.8	0.5	1.8
Drop-out Rate (%)	0.4	0.4	0.0	0.0	0.0	0.0
H.S. Diplomas (#)	415	401	1	2	2	9

Muskego-Norway

S87-W18763 Woods Rd • Muskego, WI 53150-9374
(262) 679-5400 • http://www.mnsd.k12.wi.us
Grade Span: PK-12; **Agency Type:** 1
Schools: 8
5 Primary; 2 Middle; 1 High; 0 Other Level
8 Regular; 0 Special Education; 0 Vocational; 0 Alternative
0 Magnet; 0 Charter; 4 Title I Eligible; 0 School-wide Title I
Students: 4,641 (50.6% male; 49.4% female)
Individual Education Program: 586 (12.6%);
English Language Learner: 0 (0.0%); Migrant: 0 (0.0%)
Eligible for Free Lunch Program: n/a
Eligible for Reduced-Price Lunch Program: n/a
Teachers: 292.5 (15.9 to 1)
Librarians/Media Specialists: 7.4 (627.2 to 1)
Guidance Counselors: 11.4 (407.1 to 1)
Current Spending: ($ per student per year):
Total: $7,789; Instruction: $4,946; Support Services: $2,631

Enrollment, Drop-out Rates and Diploma Recipients by Race/Ethnicity

Category	Total	White	Black	Asian	AIAN	Hisp.
Enrollment (%)	100.0	96.1	0.5	1.0	0.5	1.9
Drop-out Rate (%)	0.3	0.2	0.0	6.7	0.0	0.0
H.S. Diplomas (#)	299	289	2	3	0	5

New Berlin

4333 S Sunnyslope Rd • New Berlin, WI 53151-6844
(262) 789-6220 • http://www.nbps.k12.wi.us
Grade Span: PK-12; **Agency Type:** 1
Schools: 11
7 Primary; 2 Middle; 2 High; 0 Other Level
11 Regular; 0 Special Education; 0 Vocational; 0 Alternative
0 Magnet; 0 Charter; 0 Title I Eligible; 0 School-wide Title I
Students: 4,610 (51.2% male; 48.8% female)
Individual Education Program: 563 (12.2%);
English Language Learner: 54 (1.2%); Migrant: 0 (0.0%)
Eligible for Free Lunch Program: n/a
Eligible for Reduced-Price Lunch Program: n/a
Teachers: 306.5 (15.0 to 1)
Librarians/Media Specialists: 9.0 (512.2 to 1)
Guidance Counselors: 7.0 (658.6 to 1)
Current Spending: ($ per student per year):
Total: $9,837; Instruction: $5,990; Support Services: $3,627

Enrollment, Drop-out Rates and Diploma Recipients by Race/Ethnicity

Category	Total	White	Black	Asian	AIAN	Hisp.
Enrollment (%)	100.0	90.9	1.2	5.2	0.4	2.3
Drop-out Rate (%)	0.3	0.3	0.0	0.0	0.0	0.0
H.S. Diplomas (#)	382	356	5	15	1	5

Oconomowoc Area

W360-N7077 Brown St • Oconomowoc, WI 53066-1197
(262) 560-2111 • http://www.oasd.k12.wi.us
Grade Span: PK-12; **Agency Type:** 1
Schools: 7
5 Primary; 1 Middle; 1 High; 0 Other Level
7 Regular; 0 Special Education; 0 Vocational; 0 Alternative
0 Magnet; 0 Charter; 0 Title I Eligible; 0 School-wide Title I
Students: 4,074 (51.0% male; 49.0% female)
Individual Education Program: 645 (15.8%);
English Language Learner: 0 (0.0%); Migrant: 0 (0.0%)
Eligible for Free Lunch Program: n/a
Eligible for Reduced-Price Lunch Program: n/a
Teachers: 264.8 (15.4 to 1)
Librarians/Media Specialists: 6.5 (626.8 to 1)
Guidance Counselors: 8.2 (496.8 to 1)
Current Spending: ($ per student per year):
Total: $8,472; Instruction: $5,251; Support Services: $2,935

Enrollment, Drop-out Rates and Diploma Recipients by Race/Ethnicity

Category	Total	White	Black	Asian	AIAN	Hisp.
Enrollment (%)	100.0	96.8	0.7	0.8	0.3	1.4
Drop-out Rate (%)	0.7	0.7	0.0	0.0	0.0	0.0
H.S. Diplomas (#)	321	315	1	3	1	1

Pewaukee

404 Lake St • Pewaukee, WI 53072-3630
(262) 691-2100 • http://www.pewaukee.k12.wi.us
Grade Span: PK-12; **Agency Type:** 1
Schools: 4
1 Primary; 2 Middle; 1 High; 0 Other Level
4 Regular; 0 Special Education; 0 Vocational; 0 Alternative
0 Magnet; 0 Charter; 0 Title I Eligible; 0 School-wide Title I
Students: 2,147 (52.4% male; 47.6% female)
Individual Education Program: 268 (12.5%);
English Language Learner: 0 (0.0%); Migrant: 0 (0.0%)
Eligible for Free Lunch Program: n/a
Eligible for Reduced-Price Lunch Program: n/a
Teachers: 140.1 (15.3 to 1)
Librarians/Media Specialists: 4.0 (536.8 to 1)
Guidance Counselors: 5.0 (429.4 to 1)
Current Spending: ($ per student per year):
Total: $8,090; Instruction: $4,854; Support Services: $2,963

Enrollment, Drop-out Rates and Diploma Recipients by Race/Ethnicity

Category	Total	White	Black	Asian	AIAN	Hisp.
Enrollment (%)	100.0	92.3	1.6	0.8	3.0	2.2
Drop-out Rate (%)	0.6	0.7	0.0	0.0	0.0	0.0
H.S. Diplomas (#)	127	125	0	2	0	0

Waukesha

222 Maple Ave • Waukesha, WI 53186-4725
(262) 970-1012 • http://www.waukesha.k12.wi.us
Grade Span: PK-12; **Agency Type:** 1
Schools: 25
17 Primary; 3 Middle; 5 High; 0 Other Level
23 Regular; 0 Special Education; 0 Vocational; 2 Alternative
0 Magnet; 2 Charter; 9 Title I Eligible; 0 School-wide Title I
Students: 12,795 (50.9% male; 49.1% female)
Individual Education Program: 1,688 (13.2%);
English Language Learner: 818 (6.4%); Migrant: 0 (0.0%)
Eligible for Free Lunch Program: n/a
Eligible for Reduced-Price Lunch Program: n/a
Teachers: 876.7 (14.6 to 1)
Librarians/Media Specialists: 14.2 (901.1 to 1)
Guidance Counselors: 27.5 (465.3 to 1)
Current Spending: ($ per student per year):
Total: $8,059; Instruction: $5,103; Support Services: $2,740

Enrollment, Drop-out Rates and Diploma Recipients by Race/Ethnicity

Category	Total	White	Black	Asian	AIAN	Hisp.
Enrollment (%)	100.0	83.8	2.2	2.4	0.6	11.0
Drop-out Rate (%)	0.3	0.3	0.0	0.0	0.0	0.6
H.S. Diplomas (#)	1,043	911	18	12	7	95

Waupaca County

Clintonville

26 9th St • Clintonville, WI 54929-1595
(715) 823-7206 • http://www.clintonville.k12.wi.us
Grade Span: PK-12; **Agency Type:** 1
Schools: 5
3 Primary; 1 Middle; 1 High; 0 Other Level
5 Regular; 0 Special Education; 0 Vocational; 0 Alternative
0 Magnet; 0 Charter; 2 Title I Eligible; 0 School-wide Title I
Students: 1,617 (52.7% male; 47.3% female)
Individual Education Program: 211 (13.0%);
English Language Learner: 0 (0.0%); Migrant: 0 (0.0%)
Eligible for Free Lunch Program: n/a
Eligible for Reduced-Price Lunch Program: n/a
Teachers: 126.4 (12.8 to 1)
Librarians/Media Specialists: 3.0 (539.0 to 1)
Guidance Counselors: 4.0 (404.3 to 1)
Current Spending: ($ per student per year):
Total: $8,164; Instruction: $5,098; Support Services: $2,751

Enrollment, Drop-out Rates and Diploma Recipients by Race/Ethnicity

Category	Total	White	Black	Asian	AIAN	Hisp.
Enrollment (%)	100.0	93.6	0.8	1.1	0.7	3.8
Drop-out Rate (%)	1.0	1.1	0.0	0.0	0.0	0.0
H.S. Diplomas (#)	108	103	0	2	1	2

New London

901 W Washington St • New London, WI 54961-1698
(920) 982-8530 • http://www.newlondon.k12.wi.us
Grade Span: PK-12; **Agency Type:** 1
Schools: 7
4 Primary; 1 Middle; 2 High; 0 Other Level
6 Regular; 0 Special Education; 0 Vocational; 1 Alternative
0 Magnet; 1 Charter; 3 Title I Eligible; 0 School-wide Title I
Students: 2,558 (52.5% male; 47.5% female)
Individual Education Program: 312 (12.2%);
English Language Learner: 56 (2.2%); Migrant: 0 (0.0%)
Eligible for Free Lunch Program: n/a
Eligible for Reduced-Price Lunch Program: n/a
Teachers: 173.0 (14.8 to 1)
Librarians/Media Specialists: 4.0 (639.5 to 1)
Guidance Counselors: 7.0 (365.4 to 1)
Current Spending: ($ per student per year):
Total: $7,420; Instruction: $4,579; Support Services: $2,479

Enrollment, Drop-out Rates and Diploma Recipients by Race/Ethnicity

Category	Total	White	Black	Asian	AIAN	Hisp.
Enrollment (%)	100.0	94.6	0.7	0.6	0.3	3.8
Drop-out Rate (%)	n/a	n/a	n/a	n/a	n/a	n/a
H.S. Diplomas (#)	186	181	1	0	1	3

Waupaca

515 School St • Waupaca, WI 54981-1658
(715) 258-4121 • http://wsd.waupaca.k12.wi.us
Grade Span: PK-12; **Agency Type:** 1
Schools: 7
4 Primary; 1 Middle; 2 High; 0 Other Level
6 Regular; 0 Special Education; 0 Vocational; 1 Alternative
0 Magnet; 0 Charter; 4 Title I Eligible; 0 School-wide Title I
Students: 2,716 (52.4% male; 47.6% female)
Individual Education Program: 324 (11.9%);
English Language Learner: 0 (0.0%); Migrant: 0 (0.0%)
Eligible for Free Lunch Program: n/a
Eligible for Reduced-Price Lunch Program: n/a
Teachers: 197.1 (13.8 to 1)
Librarians/Media Specialists: 4.0 (679.0 to 1)
Guidance Counselors: 4.0 (679.0 to 1)
Current Spending: ($ per student per year):
Total: $6,882; Instruction: $4,127; Support Services: $2,441

Enrollment, Drop-out Rates and Diploma Recipients by Race/Ethnicity

Category	Total	White	Black	Asian	AIAN	Hisp.
Enrollment (%)	100.0	94.1	0.7	0.7	1.3	3.2
Drop-out Rate (%)	0.9	0.8	0.0	0.0	n/a	4.5
H.S. Diplomas (#)	183	176	1	2	0	4

Waushara County

Wautoma Area

556 S Cambridge St • Wautoma, WI 54982-0870
Mailing Address: PO Box 870 • Wautoma, WI 54982-0870
(920) 787-7112 • http://www.wautoma.k12.wi.us
Grade Span: PK-12; **Agency Type:** 1
Schools: 4
2 Primary; 1 Middle; 1 High; 0 Other Level
4 Regular; 0 Special Education; 0 Vocational; 0 Alternative
0 Magnet; 0 Charter; 3 Title I Eligible; 3 School-wide Title I
Students: 1,616 (54.1% male; 45.9% female)
Individual Education Program: 198 (12.3%);
English Language Learner: 197 (12.2%); Migrant: 86 (5.3%)
Eligible for Free Lunch Program: n/a
Eligible for Reduced-Price Lunch Program: n/a
Teachers: 118.6 (13.6 to 1)
Librarians/Media Specialists: 3.0 (538.7 to 1)
Guidance Counselors: 4.0 (404.0 to 1)
Current Spending: ($ per student per year):
Total: $6,719; Instruction: $4,161; Support Services: $2,251
Enrollment, Drop-out Rates and Diploma Recipients by Race/Ethnicity

Category	Total	White	Black	Asian	AIAN	Hisp.
Enrollment (%)	100.0	86.0	0.7	0.6	0.8	11.9
Drop-out Rate (%)	0.4	0.4	0.0	0.0	0.0	0.0
H.S. Diplomas (#)	120	110	0	2	0	8

Winnebago County

Menasha

328 Sixth St • Menasha, WI 54952-0360
Mailing Address: PO Box 360 • Menasha, WI 54952-0360
(920) 967-1401 • http://www.mjsd.k12.wi.us
Grade Span: PK-12; **Agency Type:** 1
Schools: 9
6 Primary; 2 Middle; 1 High; 0 Other Level
8 Regular; 0 Special Education; 0 Vocational; 1 Alternative
0 Magnet; 1 Charter; 5 Title I Eligible; 0 School-wide Title I
Students: 3,654 (50.9% male; 49.1% female)
Individual Education Program: 487 (13.3%);
English Language Learner: 373 (10.2%); Migrant: 0 (0.0%)
Eligible for Free Lunch Program: n/a
Eligible for Reduced-Price Lunch Program: n/a
Teachers: 247.7 (14.8 to 1)
Librarians/Media Specialists: 4.8 (761.3 to 1)
Guidance Counselors: 9.0 (406.0 to 1)
Current Spending: ($ per student per year):
Total: $7,420; Instruction: $4,802; Support Services: $2,395
Enrollment, Drop-out Rates and Diploma Recipients by Race/Ethnicity

Category	Total	White	Black	Asian	AIAN	Hisp.
Enrollment (%)	100.0	82.6	1.9	5.0	0.7	9.8
Drop-out Rate (%)	2.4	2.3	9.1	4.1	14.3	0.0
H.S. Diplomas (#)	236	213	3	7	1	12

Neenah

410 S Commercial St • Neenah, WI 54956-2593
(920) 751-6808 • http://neenah.k12.wi.us
Grade Span: PK-12; **Agency Type:** 1
Schools: 13
10 Primary; 2 Middle; 1 High; 0 Other Level
13 Regular; 0 Special Education; 0 Vocational; 0 Alternative
0 Magnet; 0 Charter; 6 Title I Eligible; 0 School-wide Title I
Students: 6,449 (51.4% male; 48.6% female)
Individual Education Program: 884 (13.7%);
English Language Learner: 124 (1.9%); Migrant: 0 (0.0%)
Eligible for Free Lunch Program: n/a
Eligible for Reduced-Price Lunch Program: n/a
Teachers: 411.5 (15.7 to 1)
Librarians/Media Specialists: 14.0 (460.6 to 1)
Guidance Counselors: 17.0 (379.4 to 1)
Current Spending: ($ per student per year):
Total: $7,684; Instruction: $5,285; Support Services: $2,214
Enrollment, Drop-out Rates and Diploma Recipients by Race/Ethnicity

Category	Total	White	Black	Asian	AIAN	Hisp.
Enrollment (%)	100.0	92.9	1.5	2.4	0.8	2.6
Drop-out Rate (%)	2.2	2.2	0.0	3.3	0.0	6.5
H.S. Diplomas (#)	439	426	3	5	2	3

Oshkosh Area

215 S Eagle St • Oshkosh, WI 54902
Mailing Address: PO Box 3048 • Oshkosh, WI 54903-3048
(920) 424-0160 • http://www.oshkosh.k12.wi.us
Grade Span: PK-12; **Agency Type:** 1
Schools: 25
18 Primary; 5 Middle; 2 High; 0 Other Level
24 Regular; 0 Special Education; 0 Vocational; 1 Alternative
0 Magnet; 1 Charter; 13 Title I Eligible; 1 School-wide Title I
Students: 10,541 (51.7% male; 48.3% female)
Individual Education Program: 1,552 (14.7%);
English Language Learner: 531 (5.0%); Migrant: 0 (0.0%)
Eligible for Free Lunch Program: n/a
Eligible for Reduced-Price Lunch Program: n/a
Teachers: 706.3 (14.9 to 1)
Librarians/Media Specialists: 16.8 (627.4 to 1)
Guidance Counselors: 21.8 (483.5 to 1)
Current Spending: ($ per student per year):
Total: $7,359; Instruction: $4,980; Support Services: $2,184
Enrollment, Drop-out Rates and Diploma Recipients by Race/Ethnicity

Category	Total	White	Black	Asian	AIAN	Hisp.
Enrollment (%)	100.0	87.4	2.3	8.1	0.3	1.9
Drop-out Rate (%)	1.1	1.1	0.0	0.0	5.9	3.7
H.S. Diplomas (#)	671	615	6	38	1	11

Winneconne Community

233 S 3rd Ave • Winneconne, WI 54986-5000
Mailing Address: PO Box 5000 • Winneconne, WI 54986-5000
(920) 582-5802 • http://www.winneconne.k12.wi.us/district/index.html
Grade Span: PK-12; **Agency Type:** 1
Schools: 4
2 Primary; 1 Middle; 1 High; 0 Other Level
4 Regular; 0 Special Education; 0 Vocational; 0 Alternative
0 Magnet; 0 Charter; 1 Title I Eligible; 0 School-wide Title I
Students: 1,610 (53.7% male; 46.3% female)
Individual Education Program: 234 (14.5%);
English Language Learner: 0 (0.0%); Migrant: 0 (0.0%)
Eligible for Free Lunch Program: n/a
Eligible for Reduced-Price Lunch Program: n/a
Teachers: 109.9 (14.6 to 1)
Librarians/Media Specialists: 2.8 (575.0 to 1)
Guidance Counselors: 5.0 (322.0 to 1)
Current Spending: ($ per student per year):
Total: $7,149; Instruction: $4,234; Support Services: $2,666
Enrollment, Drop-out Rates and Diploma Recipients by Race/Ethnicity

Category	Total	White	Black	Asian	AIAN	Hisp.
Enrollment (%)	100.0	98.1	0.1	0.6	0.6	0.6
Drop-out Rate (%)	0.9	0.7	0.0	0.0	25.0	0.0
H.S. Diplomas (#)	127	126	0	1	0	0

Wood County

Marshfield

1010 E 4th St • Marshfield, WI 54449-4538
(715) 387-1101 • http://marshfield.k12.wi.us
Grade Span: PK-12; **Agency Type:** 1
Schools: 7
5 Primary; 1 Middle; 1 High; 0 Other Level
7 Regular; 0 Special Education; 0 Vocational; 0 Alternative
0 Magnet; 0 Charter; 5 Title I Eligible; 0 School-wide Title I
Students: 4,060 (51.8% male; 48.2% female)
Individual Education Program: 562 (13.8%);
English Language Learner: 0 (0.0%); Migrant: 0 (0.0%)
Eligible for Free Lunch Program: n/a
Eligible for Reduced-Price Lunch Program: n/a
Teachers: 254.8 (15.9 to 1)
Librarians/Media Specialists: 5.8 (700.0 to 1)
Guidance Counselors: 7.0 (580.0 to 1)
Current Spending: ($ per student per year):
Total: $7,881; Instruction: $5,176; Support Services: $2,493
Enrollment, Drop-out Rates and Diploma Recipients by Race/Ethnicity

Category	Total	White	Black	Asian	AIAN	Hisp.
Enrollment (%)	100.0	95.5	1.0	2.2	0.4	1.0
Drop-out Rate (%)	0.8	0.8	0.0	0.0	0.0	0.0
H.S. Diplomas (#)	352	342	1	4	1	4

Nekoosa

600 S Section St • Nekoosa, WI 54457-1498
(715) 886-8000 • http://www.nekoosa.k12.wi.us
Grade Span: KG-12; **Agency Type:** 1
Schools: 3
1 Primary; 1 Middle; 1 High; 0 Other Level
3 Regular; 0 Special Education; 0 Vocational; 0 Alternative
0 Magnet; 0 Charter; 2 Title I Eligible; 0 School-wide Title I
Students: 1,528 (51.5% male; 48.5% female)

Individual Education Program: 216 (14.1%);
English Language Learner: 0 (0.0%); Migrant: 0 (0.0%)
Eligible for Free Lunch Program: n/a
Eligible for Reduced-Price Lunch Program: n/a
Teachers: 108.5 (14.1 to 1)
Librarians/Media Specialists: 2.9 (526.9 to 1)
Guidance Counselors: 4.0 (382.0 to 1)
Current Spending: ($ per student per year):
Total: $7,248; Instruction: $4,295; Support Services: $2,723
Enrollment, Drop-out Rates and Diploma Recipients by Race/Ethnicity

Category	Total	White	Black	Asian	AIAN	Hisp.
Enrollment (%)	100.0	91.9	1.3	0.6	2.8	3.5
Drop-out Rate (%)	1.6	1.5	0.0	0.0	0.0	6.7
H.S. Diplomas (#)	95	92	0	0	2	1

Wisconsin Rapids

2510 Industrial St • Wis Rapids, WI 54495-2292
Mailing Address: 510 Peach St • Wisconsin Rapids, WI 54494-4698
(715) 422-6003 • http://www.wrps.org
Grade Span: PK-12; **Agency Type:** 1
Schools: 14
10 Primary; 2 Middle; 2 High; 0 Other Level
13 Regular; 0 Special Education; 0 Vocational; 1 Alternative
0 Magnet; 1 Charter; 6 Title I Eligible; 0 School-wide Title I
Students: 5,787 (51.7% male; 48.3% female)
Individual Education Program: 861 (14.9%);
English Language Learner: 266 (4.6%); Migrant: 0 (0.0%)
Eligible for Free Lunch Program: n/a
Eligible for Reduced-Price Lunch Program: n/a
Teachers: 429.1 (13.5 to 1)
Librarians/Media Specialists: 11.9 (486.3 to 1)
Guidance Counselors: 16.0 (361.7 to 1)
Current Spending: ($ per student per year):
Total: $8,320; Instruction: $5,328; Support Services: $2,715
Enrollment, Drop-out Rates and Diploma Recipients by Race/Ethnicity

Category	Total	White	Black	Asian	AIAN	Hisp.
Enrollment (%)	100.0	91.0	0.6	5.5	1.4	1.5
Drop-out Rate (%)	0.8	0.5	16.7	3.7	0.0	6.3
H.S. Diplomas (#)	501	466	2	22	5	6

Number of Schools

Rank	Number	District Name	City
1	218	Milwaukee	Milwaukee
2	52	Madison Metropolitan	Madison
3	41	Kenosha	Kenosha
4	36	Green Bay Area	Green Bay
5	35	Racine	Racine
6	32	Appleton Area	Appleton
7	25	Eau Claire Area	Eau Claire
7	25	Oshkosh Area	Oshkosh
7	25	Waukesha	Waukesha
10	24	La Crosse	La Crosse
11	19	Stevens Point Area	Stevens Point
11	19	Wausau	Wausau
13	18	Janesville	Janesville
13	18	Sheboygan Area	Sheboygan
13	18	West Allis	West Allis
16	17	Beloit	Beloit
16	17	Wauwatosa	Wauwatosa
18	14	Fond Du Lac	Fond Du Lac
18	14	Wisconsin Rapids	Wis Rapids
20	13	Neenah	Neenah
20	13	Rice Lake Area	Rice Lake
22	12	Antigo	Antigo
22	12	Sparta Area	Sparta
24	11	Elmbrook	Brookfield
24	11	New Berlin	New Berlin
24	11	West Bend	West Bend
27	10	Beaver Dam	Beaver Dam
27	10	D C Everest Area	Weston
27	10	Manitowoc	Manitowoc
27	10	Merrill Area	Merrill
27	10	Middleton-Cross Plains	Middleton
27	10	Portage Community	Portage
27	10	Rhinelander	Rhinelander
27	10	Sun Prairie Area	Sun Prairie
27	10	Tomah Area	Tomah
36	9	Chippewa Falls Area	Chippewa Falls
36	9	Menasha	Menasha
36	9	Superior	Superior
36	9	Verona Area	Verona
40	8	Adams-Friendship Area	Friendship
40	8	Baraboo	Baraboo
40	8	Burlington Area	Burlington
40	8	Hamilton	Sussex
40	8	Marinette	Marinette
40	8	Menomonie Area	Menomonie
40	8	Muskego-Norway	Muskego
40	8	Oak Creek-Franklin	Oak Creek
40	8	Reedsburg	Reedsburg
40	8	Richland	Richland Ctr
40	8	Watertown	Watertown
40	8	Waupun	Waupun
52	7	Cudahy	Cudahy
52	7	De Forest Area	De Forest
52	7	Fort Atkinson	Fort Atkinson
52	7	Franklin Public	Franklin
52	7	Hayward Community	Hayward
52	7	Howard-Suamico	Green Bay
52	7	Hudson	Hudson
52	7	Kaukauna Area	Kaukauna
52	7	Marshfield	Marshfield
52	7	Menomonee Falls	Menomonee Fls
52	7	Mequon-Thiensville	Mequon
52	7	Monona Grove	Monona
52	7	Monroe	Monroe
52	7	Mukwonago	Mukwonago
52	7	New London	New London
52	7	Oconomowoc Area	Oconomowoc
52	7	Plymouth	Plymouth
52	7	Pulaski Community	Pulaski
52	7	River Falls	River Falls
52	7	Sauk Prairie	Sauk City
52	7	South Milwaukee	S Milwaukee
52	7	Waupaca	Waupaca
74	6	Elkhorn Area	Elkhorn
74	6	Ellsworth Community	Ellsworth
74	6	Germantown	Germantown
74	6	Greenfield	Greenfield
74	6	Holmen	Holmen
74	6	Jefferson	Jefferson
74	6	Kettle Moraine	Wales
74	6	Kimberly Area	Kimberly
74	6	Mauston	Mauston
74	6	Milton	Milton
74	6	Oconto Falls	Oconto Falls
74	6	Onalaska	Onalaska
74	6	Oregon	Oregon
74	6	Shawano-Gresham	Shawano
74	6	Stoughton Area	Stoughton
74	6	Wisconsin Dells	Wisconsin Dells
90	5	Ashland	Ashland
90	5	Ashwaubenon	Green Bay
90	5	Black River Falls	Black River Fls
90	5	Cedarburg	Cedarburg
90	5	Clintonville	Clintonville
90	5	De Pere	De Pere
90	5	Delavan-Darien	Delavan
90	5	Denmark	Denmark
90	5	East Troy Community	East Troy
90	5	Grafton	Grafton
90	5	Greendale	Greendale
90	5	Hortonville	Hortonville
90	5	Kewaskum	Kewaskum
90	5	Lake Geneva J1	Lake Geneva
90	5	Lodi	Lodi
90	5	Mcfarland	Mc Farland
90	5	Mount Horeb Area	Mount Horeb
90	5	Northland Pines	Eagle River
90	5	Platteville	Platteville
90	5	Port Washington-Saukville	Pt Washington
90	5	Slinger	Slinger
90	5	Two Rivers	Two Rivers
90	5	Waunakee Community	Waunakee
90	5	Whitewater	Whitewater
114	4	Amery	Amery
114	4	Berlin Area	Berlin
114	4	Brown Deer	Brown Deer
114	4	Campbellsport	Campbellsport
114	4	Edgerton	Edgerton
114	4	Evansville Community	Evansville
114	4	Luxemburg-Casco	Luxemburg
114	4	Medford Area	Medford
114	4	New Richmond	New Richmond
114	4	Osceola	Osceola
114	4	Pewaukee	Pewaukee
114	4	Ripon	Ripon
114	4	Seymour Community	Seymour
114	4	Shorewood	Shorewood
114	4	Wautoma Area	Wautoma
114	4	Whitefish Bay	Whitefish Bay
114	4	Whitnall	Greenfield
114	4	Winneconne Community	Winneconne
132	3	Freedom Area	Freedom
132	3	Hartford J1	Hartford
132	3	Little Chute Area	Little Chute
132	3	Mosinee	Mosinee
132	3	Nekoosa	Nekoosa
132	3	Sheboygan Falls	Sheboygan Fls
132	3	Spooner	Spooner
132	3	Tomahawk	Tomahawk
132	3	West De Pere	De Pere
132	3	West Salem	West Salem
142	1	Arrowhead Uhs	Hartland
142	1	Hartford Uhs	Hartford

Number of Teachers

Rank	Number	District Name	City
1	6,494	Milwaukee	Milwaukee
2	2,028	Madison Metropolitan	Madison
3	1,435	Green Bay Area	Green Bay
4	1,412	Kenosha	Kenosha
5	1,366	Racine	Racine
6	975	Appleton Area	Appleton
7	876	Waukesha	Waukesha
8	780	Eau Claire Area	Eau Claire
9	775	Janesville	Janesville
10	726	Sheboygan Area	Sheboygan
11	706	Oshkosh Area	Oshkosh
12	633	Wausau	Wausau
13	604	West Allis	West Allis
14	582	La Crosse	La Crosse
15	516	Elmbrook	Brookfield
16	516	Stevens Point Area	Stevens Point
17	482	Beloit	Beloit
18	478	Fond Du Lac	Fond Du Lac
19	473	Wauwatosa	Wauwatosa
20	429	Wisconsin Rapids	Wis Rapids
21	426	West Bend	West Bend
22	411	Neenah	Neenah
23	396	Middleton-Cross Plains	Middleton
24	365	Sun Prairie Area	Sun Prairie
25	363	Manitowoc	Manitowoc
26	360	Verona Area	Verona
27	341	D C Everest Area	Weston
28	323	Superior	Superior
29	320	Mukwonago	Mukwonago
30	306	New Berlin	New Berlin
31	300	Menomonee Falls	Menomonee Fls
32	299	Oak Creek-Franklin	Oak Creek
33	296	Chippewa Falls Area	Chippewa Falls
34	295	Hudson	Hudson
35	292	Muskego-Norway	Muskego
36	288	Howard-Suamico	Green Bay
37	286	Kettle Moraine	Wales
38	276	Franklin Public	Franklin
39	264	Oconomowoc Area	Oconomowoc
40	260	Mequon-Thiensville	Mequon
41	257	Hamilton	Sussex
42	257	Oregon	Oregon
43	256	Stoughton Area	Stoughton
44	254	Marshfield	Marshfield
45	252	Germantown	Germantown
46	250	South Milwaukee	S Milwaukee
47	247	Menasha	Menasha
48	244	Kaukauna Area	Kaukauna
49	238	Beaver Dam	Beaver Dam
50	237	Pulaski Community	Pulaski
51	237	Burlington Area	Burlington
52	232	Merrill Area	Merrill
53	231	Watertown	Watertown
54	225	Antigo	Antigo
55	223	Kimberly Area	Kimberly
56	223	Menomonie Area	Menomonie
57	219	Monroe	Monroe
58	219	Holmen	Holmen
59	219	Monona Grove	Monona
60	219	Ashwaubenon	Green Bay
61	219	Rhinelander	Rhinelander
62	217	Greenfield	Greenfield
63	216	Tomah Area	Tomah
64	212	Cudahy	Cudahy
65	209	De Forest Area	De Forest
66	208	Waunakee Community	Waunakee
67	204	De Pere	De Pere
68	203	Baraboo	Baraboo
69	200	Sparta Area	Sparta
70	199	Hortonville	Hortonville
71	198	Sauk Prairie	Sauk City
72	198	Shawano-Gresham	Shawano
73	197	Waupaca	Waupaca
74	192	Fort Atkinson	Fort Atkinson
75	189	River Falls	River Falls
76	189	Whitefish Bay	Whitefish Bay
77	187	Cedarburg	Cedarburg
78	186	Waupun	Waupun
79	185	Onalaska	Onalaska
80	185	Milton	Milton
81	179	Rice Lake Area	Rice Lake
82	177	Reedsburg	Reedsburg
83	173	New London	New London
84	171	Ashland	Ashland
85	170	Port Washington-Saukville	Pt Washington
86	169	Delavan-Darien	Delavan
87	167	Marinette	Marinette
88	165	Plymouth	Plymouth
89	164	Slinger	Slinger
90	163	Elkhorn Area	Elkhorn
91	162	Two Rivers	Two Rivers
92	162	Adams-Friendship Area	Friendship
93	159	Portage Community	Portage
94	156	Whitnall	Greenfield
95	154	Shorewood	Shorewood
96	153	Seymour Community	Seymour
97	151	Medford Area	Medford
98	151	New Richmond	New Richmond
99	148	Greendale	Greendale
100	146	Black River Falls	Black River Fls
101	145	Hayward Community	Hayward
102	143	Mount Horeb Area	Mount Horeb
103	142	Oconto Falls	Oconto Falls
104	140	Grafton	Grafton
105	140	Pewaukee	Pewaukee
106	138	Whitewater	Whitewater
107	137	Mcfarland	Mc Farland
108	134	Edgerton	Edgerton
109	134	Mauston	Mauston
110	132	Jefferson	Jefferson
111	131	West De Pere	De Pere
112	130	Mosinee	Mosinee
113	128	Arrowhead Uhs	Hartland
114	127	Kewaskum	Kewaskum
115	126	Clintonville	Clintonville
116	125	Amery	Amery
117	124	Ellsworth Community	Ellsworth
118	124	Berlin Area	Berlin
119	122	Luxemburg-Casco	Luxemburg
120	121	Wisconsin Dells	Wisconsin Dells
121	121	Richland	Richland Ctr
122	119	Lodi	Lodi
122	119	Sheboygan Falls	Sheboygan Fls
124	119	Northland Pines	Eagle River
125	118	Wautoma Area	Wautoma
126	118	Tomahawk	Tomahawk
127	117	Evansville Community	Evansville
128	117	Lake Geneva J1	Lake Geneva

128	117	Ripon	Ripon
130	115	Brown Deer	Brown Deer
131	114	Hartford J1	Hartford
132	113	West Salem	West Salem
133	113	East Troy Community	East Troy
134	113	Platteville	Platteville
134	113	Spooner	Spooner
136	110	Hartford Uhs	Hartford
137	109	Winneconne Community	Winneconne
138	108	Denmark	Denmark
139	108	Nekoosa	Nekoosa
140	105	Osceola	Osceola
141	105	Campbellsport	Campbellsport
142	98	Little Chute Area	Little Chute
143	98	Freedom Area	Freedom

Number of Students

Rank	Number	District Name	City
1	97,293	Milwaukee	Milwaukee
2	24,966	Madison Metropolitan	Madison
3	21,565	Racine	Racine
4	21,088	Kenosha	Kenosha
5	20,474	Green Bay Area	Green Bay
6	14,948	Appleton Area	Appleton
7	12,795	Waukesha	Waukesha
8	10,835	Eau Claire Area	Eau Claire
9	10,699	Janesville	Janesville
10	10,541	Oshkosh Area	Oshkosh
11	10,377	Sheboygan Area	Sheboygan
12	8,949	Wausau	Wausau
13	8,842	West Allis	West Allis
14	7,681	Stevens Point Area	Stevens Point
15	7,640	La Crosse	La Crosse
16	7,633	Elmbrook	Brookfield
17	7,245	Fond Du Lac	Fond Du Lac
18	7,080	Wauwatosa	Wauwatosa
19	6,826	West Bend	West Bend
20	6,799	Beloit	Beloit
21	6,449	Neenah	Neenah
22	5,787	Wisconsin Rapids	Wis Rapids
23	5,411	Manitowoc	Manitowoc
24	5,330	Middleton-Cross Plains	Middleton
25	5,145	D C Everest Area	Weston
26	5,063	Superior	Superior
27	5,003	Mukwonago	Mukwonago
28	4,987	Sun Prairie Area	Sun Prairie
29	4,937	Oak Creek-Franklin	Oak Creek
30	4,641	Muskego-Norway	Muskego
31	4,610	New Berlin	New Berlin
32	4,599	Howard-Suamico	Green Bay
33	4,465	Chippewa Falls Area	Chippewa Falls
34	4,448	Verona Area	Verona
35	4,426	Hudson	Hudson
36	4,405	Menomonee Falls	Menomonee Fls
37	4,373	Kettle Moraine	Wales
38	4,171	Mequon-Thiensville	Mequon
39	4,074	Oconomowoc Area	Oconomowoc
40	4,060	Marshfield	Marshfield
41	3,988	Hamilton	Sussex
42	3,866	Franklin Public	Franklin
43	3,740	Kaukauna Area	Kaukauna
44	3,715	Watertown	Watertown
45	3,679	Germantown	Germantown
46	3,663	Stoughton Area	Stoughton
47	3,654	Menasha	Menasha
48	3,647	Burlington Area	Burlington
49	3,602	South Milwaukee	S Milwaukee
50	3,572	Kimberly Area	Kimberly
51	3,493	Pulaski Community	Pulaski
52	3,429	Oregon	Oregon
53	3,418	Beaver Dam	Beaver Dam
54	3,352	Merrill Area	Merrill
55	3,348	Menomonie Area	Menomonie
56	3,341	Greenfield	Greenfield
57	3,227	Rhinelander	Rhinelander
58	3,126	Ashwaubenon	Green Bay
59	3,124	De Pere	De Pere
60	3,111	De Forest Area	De Forest
61	3,077	Holmen	Holmen
62	3,053	Baraboo	Baraboo
63	2,983	Tomah Area	Tomah
64	2,971	Whitefish Bay	Whitefish Bay
65	2,966	Shawano-Gresham	Shawano
66	2,963	Waunakee Community	Waunakee
67	2,952	Cedarburg	Cedarburg
68	2,941	Milton	Milton
69	2,933	River Falls	River Falls
70	2,915	Hortonville	Hortonville
71	2,898	Antigo	Antigo
72	2,885	Cudahy	Cudahy
73	2,846	Slinger	Slinger
74	2,819	Monona Grove	Monona
75	2,771	Delavan-Darien	Delavan
76	2,764	Onalaska	Onalaska
77	2,716	Waupaca	Waupaca
78	2,694	Sparta Area	Sparta
79	2,672	Sauk Prairie	Sauk City
80	2,668	Rice Lake Area	Rice Lake
81	2,649	Port Washington-Saukville	Pt Washington
82	2,645	Monroe	Monroe
83	2,641	Fort Atkinson	Fort Atkinson
84	2,622	Portage Community	Portage
85	2,577	Elkhorn Area	Elkhorn
86	2,564	Marinette	Marinette
87	2,558	New London	New London
88	2,517	Whitnall	Greenfield
89	2,499	Reedsburg	Reedsburg
90	2,470	Plymouth	Plymouth
91	2,444	Seymour Community	Seymour
92	2,443	New Richmond	New Richmond
93	2,320	Waupun	Waupun
94	2,309	Ashland	Ashland
95	2,297	Medford Area	Medford
96	2,216	Greendale	Greendale
97	2,172	Shorewood	Shorewood
98	2,157	Adams-Friendship Area	Friendship
99	2,147	Pewaukee	Pewaukee
100	2,124	Arrowhead Uhs	Hartland
101	2,119	Two Rivers	Two Rivers
102	2,092	Whitewater	Whitewater
103	2,055	Mount Horeb Area	Mount Horeb
104	2,029	Grafton	Grafton
104	2,029	Hayward Community	Hayward
106	2,024	Mosinee	Mosinee
107	1,969	Mcfarland	Mc Farland
108	1,937	Oconto Falls	Oconto Falls
109	1,921	Black River Falls	Black River Fls
110	1,920	Kewaskum	Kewaskum
111	1,916	West De Pere	De Pere
112	1,911	Luxemburg-Casco	Luxemburg
113	1,878	Edgerton	Edgerton
114	1,852	Amery	Amery
115	1,802	Brown Deer	Brown Deer
116	1,786	Ellsworth Community	Ellsworth
117	1,777	Wisconsin Dells	Wisconsin Dells
118	1,757	Osceola	Osceola
119	1,730	Berlin Area	Berlin
120	1,729	Sheboygan Falls	Sheboygan Fls
121	1,717	Lake Geneva J1	Lake Geneva
122	1,713	Ripon	Ripon
123	1,701	Hartford Uhs	Hartford
124	1,693	Jefferson	Jefferson
125	1,688	Denmark	Denmark
126	1,667	East Troy Community	East Troy
127	1,654	Lodi	Lodi
128	1,643	Evansville Community	Evansville
129	1,642	Tomahawk	Tomahawk
130	1,627	Platteville	Platteville
131	1,617	Clintonville	Clintonville
132	1,616	Wautoma Area	Wautoma
133	1,610	Winneconne Community	Winneconne
134	1,607	Mauston	Mauston
134	1,607	West Salem	West Salem
136	1,579	Northland Pines	Eagle River
137	1,575	Hartford J1	Hartford
138	1,566	Freedom Area	Freedom
139	1,554	Little Chute Area	Little Chute
140	1,550	Spooner	Spooner
141	1,528	Nekoosa	Nekoosa
142	1,527	Campbellsport	Campbellsport
143	1,521	Richland	Richland Ctr

Male Students

Rank	Percent	District Name	City
1	54.6	Brown Deer	Brown Deer
1	54.6	Little Chute Area	Little Chute
3	54.5	West De Pere	De Pere
4	54.1	Wautoma Area	Wautoma
5	54.0	Freedom Area	Freedom
6	53.8	Spooner	Spooner
7	53.7	Hartford Uhs	Hartford
7	53.7	Winneconne Community	Winneconne
9	53.2	Port Washington-Saukville	Pt Washington
9	53.2	Waupun	Waupun
11	53.1	Mosinee	Mosinee
12	53.0	Adams-Friendship Area	Friendship
12	53.0	Luxemburg-Casco	Luxemburg
12	53.0	Mauston	Mauston
12	53.0	West Bend	West Bend
16	52.9	Denmark	Denmark
16	52.9	Grafton	Grafton
16	52.9	Mequon-Thiensville	Mequon
16	52.9	Northland Pines	Eagle River
20	52.8	Hudson	Hudson
21	52.7	Clintonville	Clintonville
21	52.7	Jefferson	Jefferson
21	52.7	Superior	Superior
21	52.7	Two Rivers	Two Rivers
25	52.6	Ellsworth Community	Ellsworth
25	52.6	Portage Community	Portage
27	52.5	Ashland	Ashland
27	52.5	Hortonville	Hortonville
27	52.5	New London	New London
27	52.5	Sheboygan Falls	Sheboygan Fls
31	52.4	Beaver Dam	Beaver Dam
31	52.4	Cudahy	Cudahy
31	52.4	Pewaukee	Pewaukee
31	52.4	South Milwaukee	S Milwaukee
31	52.4	Waupaca	Waupaca
31	52.4	Wausau	Wausau
37	52.3	Antigo	Antigo
37	52.3	Germantown	Germantown
37	52.3	Kenosha	Kenosha
37	52.3	Oak Creek-Franklin	Oak Creek
37	52.3	Richland	Richland Ctr
37	52.3	Tomah Area	Tomah
37	52.3	Verona Area	Verona
37	52.3	Waunakee Community	Waunakee
45	52.2	Ashwaubenon	Green Bay
45	52.2	Berlin Area	Berlin
45	52.2	Medford Area	Medford
45	52.2	Merrill Area	Merrill
45	52.2	Ripon	Ripon
50	52.1	Fort Atkinson	Fort Atkinson
51	52.0	La Crosse	La Crosse
51	52.0	Monona Grove	Monona
53	51.9	Appleton Area	Appleton
53	51.9	Racine	Racine
53	51.9	Watertown	Watertown
56	51.8	Marshfield	Marshfield
57	51.7	Arrowhead Uhs	Hartland
57	51.7	Campbellsport	Campbellsport
57	51.7	Delavan-Darien	Delavan
57	51.7	Edgerton	Edgerton
57	51.7	Marinette	Marinette
57	51.7	Oshkosh Area	Oshkosh
57	51.7	Shawano-Gresham	Shawano
57	51.7	Stevens Point Area	Stevens Point
57	51.7	Wisconsin Rapids	Wis Rapids
66	51.6	Lake Geneva J1	Lake Geneva
66	51.6	Wauwatosa	Wauwatosa
66	51.6	West Allis	West Allis
66	51.6	West Salem	West Salem
70	51.5	Black River Falls	Black River Fls
70	51.5	Cedarburg	Cedarburg
70	51.5	Elkhorn Area	Elkhorn
70	51.5	Green Bay Area	Green Bay
70	51.5	Hartford J1	Hartford
70	51.5	Lodi	Lodi
70	51.5	Nekoosa	Nekoosa
70	51.5	Sauk Prairie	Sauk City
70	51.5	Seymour Community	Seymour
70	51.5	Sun Prairie Area	Sun Prairie
70	51.5	Tomahawk	Tomahawk
81	51.4	D C Everest Area	Weston
81	51.4	Greenfield	Greenfield
81	51.4	Neenah	Neenah
81	51.4	Oregon	Oregon
81	51.4	Whitnall	Greenfield
86	51.3	Burlington Area	Burlington
86	51.3	Eau Claire Area	Eau Claire
86	51.3	Franklin Public	Franklin
86	51.3	Holmen	Holmen
86	51.3	Janesville	Janesville
86	51.3	Mukwonago	Mukwonago
86	51.3	Pulaski Community	Pulaski
86	51.3	Slinger	Slinger
86	51.3	Stoughton Area	Stoughton
86	51.3	Whitewater	Whitewater
96	51.2	Chippewa Falls Area	Chippewa Falls
96	51.2	Hamilton	Sussex
96	51.2	Hayward Community	Hayward
96	51.2	Kettle Moraine	Wales
96	51.2	New Berlin	New Berlin
96	51.2	Rice Lake Area	Rice Lake
102	51.1	Greendale	Greendale
102	51.1	Howard-Suamico	Green Bay
102	51.1	Rhinelander	Rhinelander
105	51.0	Elmbrook	Brookfield
105	51.0	Milwaukee	Milwaukee
105	51.0	Oconomowoc Area	Oconomowoc
105	51.0	Onalaska	Onalaska
105	51.0	River Falls	River Falls
105	51.0	Sheboygan Area	Sheboygan
111	50.9	East Troy Community	East Troy
111	50.9	Fond Du Lac	Fond Du Lac
111	50.9	Menasha	Menasha

111	50.9	Oconto Falls	Oconto Falls
111	50.9	Waukesha	Waukesha
116	50.8	Baraboo	Baraboo
116	50.8	Menomonie Area	Menomonie
116	50.8	Reedsburg	Reedsburg
119	50.7	Kaukauna Area	Kaukauna
119	50.7	Plymouth	Plymouth
121	50.6	Beloit	Beloit
121	50.6	Manitowoc	Manitowoc
121	50.6	Menomonee Falls	Menomonee Fls
121	50.6	Milton	Milton
121	50.6	Muskego-Norway	Muskego
126	50.5	Evansville Community	Evansville
126	50.5	Mount Horeb Area	Mount Horeb
126	50.5	New Richmond	New Richmond
129	50.4	Madison Metropolitan	Madison
130	50.3	Middleton-Cross Plains	Middleton
130	50.3	Sparta Area	Sparta
130	50.3	Whitefish Bay	Whitefish Bay
133	50.2	De Forest Area	De Forest
133	50.2	De Pere	De Pere
135	50.0	Platteville	Platteville
136	49.9	Mcfarland	Mc Farland
137	49.8	Amery	Amery
137	49.8	Wisconsin Dells	Wisconsin Dells
139	49.7	Monroe	Monroe
140	49.5	Kewaskum	Kewaskum
141	49.0	Osceola	Osceola
142	48.7	Shorewood	Shorewood
143	48.0	Kimberly Area	Kimberly

Female Students

Rank	Percent	District Name	City
1	52.0	Kimberly Area	Kimberly
2	51.3	Shorewood	Shorewood
3	51.0	Osceola	Osceola
4	50.5	Kewaskum	Kewaskum
5	50.3	Monroe	Monroe
6	50.2	Amery	Amery
6	50.2	Wisconsin Dells	Wisconsin Dells
8	50.1	Mcfarland	Mc Farland
9	50.0	Platteville	Platteville
10	49.8	De Forest Area	De Forest
10	49.8	De Pere	De Pere
12	49.7	Middleton-Cross Plains	Middleton
12	49.7	Sparta Area	Sparta
12	49.7	Whitefish Bay	Whitefish Bay
15	49.6	Madison Metropolitan	Madison
16	49.5	Evansville Community	Evansville
16	49.5	Mount Horeb Area	Mount Horeb
16	49.5	New Richmond	New Richmond
19	49.4	Beloit	Beloit
19	49.4	Manitowoc	Manitowoc
19	49.4	Menomonee Falls	Menomonee Fls
19	49.4	Milton	Milton
19	49.4	Muskego-Norway	Muskego
24	49.3	Kaukauna Area	Kaukauna
24	49.3	Plymouth	Plymouth
26	49.2	Baraboo	Baraboo
26	49.2	Menomonie Area	Menomonie
26	49.2	Reedsburg	Reedsburg
29	49.1	East Troy Community	East Troy
29	49.1	Fond Du Lac	Fond Du Lac
29	49.1	Menasha	Menasha
29	49.1	Oconto Falls	Oconto Falls
29	49.1	Waukesha	Waukesha
34	49.0	Elmbrook	Brookfield
34	49.0	Milwaukee	Milwaukee
34	49.0	Oconomowoc Area	Oconomowoc
34	49.0	Onalaska	Onalaska
34	49.0	River Falls	River Falls
34	49.0	Sheboygan Area	Sheboygan
40	48.9	Greendale	Greendale
40	48.9	Howard-Suamico	Green Bay
40	48.9	Rhinelander	Rhinelander
43	48.8	Chippewa Falls Area	Chippewa Falls
43	48.8	Hamilton	Sussex
43	48.8	Hayward Community	Hayward
43	48.8	Kettle Moraine	Wales
43	48.8	New Berlin	New Berlin
43	48.8	Rice Lake Area	Rice Lake
49	48.7	Burlington Area	Burlington
49	48.7	Eau Claire Area	Eau Claire
49	48.7	Franklin Public	Franklin
49	48.7	Holmen	Holmen
49	48.7	Janesville	Janesville
49	48.7	Mukwonago	Mukwonago
49	48.7	Pulaski Community	Pulaski
49	48.7	Slinger	Slinger
49	48.7	Stoughton Area	Stoughton
49	48.7	Whitewater	Whitewater
59	48.6	D C Everest Area	Weston
59	48.6	Greenfield	Greenfield
59	48.6	Neenah	Neenah
59	48.6	Oregon	Oregon
59	48.6	Whitnall	Greenfield
64	48.5	Black River Falls	Black River Fls
64	48.5	Cedarburg	Cedarburg
64	48.5	Elkhorn Area	Elkhorn
64	48.5	Green Bay Area	Green Bay
64	48.5	Hartford J1	Hartford
64	48.5	Lodi	Lodi
64	48.5	Nekoosa	Nekoosa
64	48.5	Sauk Prairie	Sauk City
64	48.5	Seymour Community	Seymour
64	48.5	Sun Prairie Area	Sun Prairie
64	48.5	Tomahawk	Tomahawk
75	48.4	Lake Geneva J1	Lake Geneva
75	48.4	Wauwatosa	Wauwatosa
75	48.4	West Allis	West Allis
75	48.4	West Salem	West Salem
79	48.3	Arrowhead Uhs	Hartland
79	48.3	Campbellsport	Campbellsport
79	48.3	Delavan-Darien	Delavan
79	48.3	Edgerton	Edgerton
79	48.3	Marinette	Marinette
79	48.3	Oshkosh Area	Oshkosh
79	48.3	Shawano-Gresham	Shawano
79	48.3	Stevens Point Area	Stevens Point
79	48.3	Wisconsin Rapids	Wis Rapids
88	48.2	Marshfield	Marshfield
89	48.1	Appleton Area	Appleton
89	48.1	Racine	Racine
89	48.1	Watertown	Watertown
92	48.0	La Crosse	La Crosse
92	48.0	Monona Grove	Monona
94	47.9	Fort Atkinson	Fort Atkinson
95	47.8	Ashwaubenon	Green Bay
95	47.8	Berlin Area	Berlin
95	47.8	Medford Area	Medford
95	47.8	Merrill Area	Merrill
95	47.8	Ripon	Ripon
100	47.7	Antigo	Antigo
100	47.7	Germantown	Germantown
100	47.7	Kenosha	Kenosha
100	47.7	Oak Creek-Franklin	Oak Creek
100	47.7	Richland	Richland Ctr
100	47.7	Tomah Area	Tomah
100	47.7	Verona Area	Verona
100	47.7	Waunakee Community	Waunakee
108	47.6	Beaver Dam	Beaver Dam
108	47.6	Cudahy	Cudahy
108	47.6	Pewaukee	Pewaukee
108	47.6	South Milwaukee	S Milwaukee
108	47.6	Waupaca	Waupaca
108	47.6	Wausau	Wausau
114	47.5	Ashland	Ashland
114	47.5	Hortonville	Hortonville
114	47.5	New London	New London
114	47.5	Sheboygan Falls	Sheboygan Fls
118	47.4	Ellsworth Community	Ellsworth
118	47.4	Portage Community	Portage
120	47.3	Clintonville	Clintonville
120	47.3	Jefferson	Jefferson
120	47.3	Superior	Superior
120	47.3	Two Rivers	Two Rivers
124	47.2	Hudson	Hudson
125	47.1	Denmark	Denmark
125	47.1	Grafton	Grafton
125	47.1	Mequon-Thiensville	Mequon
125	47.1	Northland Pines	Eagle River
129	47.0	Adams-Friendship Area	Friendship
129	47.0	Luxemburg-Casco	Luxemburg
129	47.0	Mauston	Mauston
129	47.0	West Bend	West Bend
133	46.9	Mosinee	Mosinee
134	46.8	Port Washington-Saukville	Pt Washington
134	46.8	Waupun	Waupun
136	46.3	Hartford Uhs	Hartford
136	46.3	Winneconne Community	Winneconne
138	46.2	Spooner	Spooner
139	46.0	Freedom Area	Freedom
140	45.9	Wautoma Area	Wautoma
141	45.5	West De Pere	De Pere
142	45.4	Brown Deer	Brown Deer
142	45.4	Little Chute Area	Little Chute

Individual Education Program Students

Rank	Percent	District Name	City
1	20.8	Richland	Richland Ctr
2	19.7	Adams-Friendship Area	Friendship
3	19.4	Edgerton	Edgerton
4	18.8	Green Bay Area	Green Bay
4	18.8	Stoughton Area	Stoughton
6	18.6	Beloit	Beloit
6	18.6	Watertown	Watertown
8	18.0	Hartford J1	Hartford
8	18.0	Madison Metropolitan	Madison
10	17.2	Monroe	Monroe
11	16.8	Jefferson	Jefferson
12	16.6	Oconto Falls	Oconto Falls
13	16.5	Janesville	Janesville
13	16.5	Milwaukee	Milwaukee
15	16.4	Racine	Racine
16	16.3	Beaver Dam	Beaver Dam
16	16.3	Black River Falls	Black River Fls
18	16.1	Antigo	Antigo
18	16.1	Sauk Prairie	Sauk City
20	16.0	Mauston	Mauston
21	15.9	Reedsburg	Reedsburg
22	15.8	Oconomowoc Area	Oconomowoc
23	15.7	Cudahy	Cudahy
23	15.7	Sheboygan Area	Sheboygan
25	15.6	Ashwaubenon	Green Bay
25	15.6	Portage Community	Portage
25	15.6	Shawano-Gresham	Shawano
28	15.5	Denmark	Denmark
28	15.5	Mcfarland	Mc Farland
30	15.4	Fond Du Lac	Fond Du Lac
31	15.2	West Allis	West Allis
32	15.1	Campbellsport	Campbellsport
32	15.1	La Crosse	La Crosse
32	15.1	Plymouth	Plymouth
35	14.9	Hudson	Hudson
35	14.9	Platteville	Platteville
35	14.9	Waupun	Waupun
35	14.9	Wisconsin Rapids	Wis Rapids
39	14.8	Fort Atkinson	Fort Atkinson
40	14.7	Oshkosh Area	Oshkosh
40	14.7	Sun Prairie Area	Sun Prairie
42	14.6	Berlin Area	Berlin
43	14.5	Baraboo	Baraboo
43	14.5	Hayward Community	Hayward
43	14.5	Pulaski Community	Pulaski
43	14.5	Winneconne Community	Winneconne
47	14.4	Amery	Amery
48	14.3	Appleton Area	Appleton
48	14.3	Sparta Area	Sparta
48	14.3	Two Rivers	Two Rivers
51	14.2	Ashland	Ashland
51	14.2	Spooner	Spooner
53	14.1	Kaukauna Area	Kaukauna
53	14.1	Kenosha	Kenosha
53	14.1	Luxemburg-Casco	Luxemburg
53	14.1	Nekoosa	Nekoosa
57	14.0	Evansville Community	Evansville
57	14.0	Mosinee	Mosinee
57	14.0	Ripon	Ripon
60	13.9	Burlington Area	Burlington
60	13.9	Chippewa Falls Area	Chippewa Falls
60	13.9	Marinette	Marinette
60	13.9	Middleton-Cross Plains	Middleton
60	13.9	Rice Lake Area	Rice Lake
60	13.9	West De Pere	De Pere
66	13.8	Marshfield	Marshfield
67	13.7	Grafton	Grafton
67	13.7	Neenah	Neenah
69	13.6	Lodi	Lodi
69	13.6	Menomonie Area	Menomonie
71	13.5	De Forest Area	De Forest
71	13.5	Eau Claire Area	Eau Claire
71	13.5	Oregon	Oregon
71	13.5	Whitewater	Whitewater
75	13.3	Menasha	Menasha
75	13.3	Seymour Community	Seymour
75	13.3	Waunakee Community	Waunakee
78	13.2	Sheboygan Falls	Sheboygan Fls
78	13.2	Waukesha	Waukesha
80	13.1	Wausau	Wausau
81	13.0	Clintonville	Clintonville
81	13.0	Kettle Moraine	Wales
81	13.0	New Richmond	New Richmond
81	13.0	Port Washington-Saukville	Pt Washington
85	12.9	Delavan-Darien	Delavan
85	12.9	Monona Grove	Monona
85	12.9	Northland Pines	Eagle River
88	12.8	Freedom Area	Freedom
88	12.8	Wisconsin Dells	Wisconsin Dells
90	12.6	Hortonville	Hortonville
90	12.6	Mukwonago	Mukwonago
90	12.6	Muskego-Norway	Muskego
93	12.5	Pewaukee	Pewaukee
94	12.4	Stevens Point Area	Stevens Point
94	12.4	Superior	Superior
96	12.3	Ellsworth Community	Ellsworth
96	12.3	Howard-Suamico	Green Bay

Rank	Percent	District Name	City
96	12.3	South Milwaukee	S Milwaukee
96	12.3	Wautoma Area	Wautoma
100	12.2	Merrill Area	Merrill
100	12.2	New Berlin	New Berlin
100	12.2	New London	New London
100	12.2	Oak Creek-Franklin	Oak Creek
104	12.1	Manitowoc	Manitowoc
104	12.1	Menomonee Falls	Menomonee Fls
104	12.1	Rhinelander	Rhinelander
104	12.1	River Falls	River Falls
104	12.1	Verona Area	Verona
104	12.1	West Bend	West Bend
110	12.0	D C Everest Area	Weston
110	12.0	Holmen	Holmen
110	12.0	Tomah Area	Tomah
113	11.9	Waupaca	Waupaca
114	11.8	Kewaskum	Kewaskum
115	11.7	Germantown	Germantown
115	11.7	Hartford Uhs	Hartford
115	11.7	Osceola	Osceola
118	11.6	Lake Geneva J1	Lake Geneva
119	11.5	Elmbrook	Brookfield
119	11.5	Greendale	Greendale
119	11.5	Tomahawk	Tomahawk
122	11.3	Greenfield	Greenfield
122	11.3	Little Chute Area	Little Chute
122	11.3	Mount Horeb Area	Mount Horeb
125	11.2	Slinger	Slinger
125	11.2	Whitnall	Greenfield
127	11.1	Elkhorn Area	Elkhorn
128	10.9	Kimberly Area	Kimberly
129	10.8	Cedarburg	Cedarburg
129	10.8	Medford Area	Medford
131	10.7	West Salem	West Salem
132	10.5	De Pere	De Pere
133	10.4	Milton	Milton
134	10.2	Franklin Public	Franklin
135	10.1	Onalaska	Onalaska
136	10.0	Wauwatosa	Wauwatosa
137	9.9	Mequon-Thiensville	Mequon
138	9.6	Brown Deer	Brown Deer
139	9.5	East Troy Community	East Troy
139	9.5	Hamilton	Sussex
141	8.7	Shorewood	Shorewood
142	7.0	Arrowhead Uhs	Hartland
143	6.6	Whitefish Bay	Whitefish Bay

English Language Learner Students

Rank	Percent	District Name	City
1	18.2	Sheboygan Area	Sheboygan
2	17.7	Wausau	Wausau
3	12.2	Wautoma Area	Wautoma
4	11.7	Madison Metropolitan	Madison
5	11.6	Delavan-Darien	Delavan
6	11.1	Lake Geneva J1	Lake Geneva
7	10.3	Green Bay Area	Green Bay
8	10.2	Menasha	Menasha
9	8.5	Appleton Area	Appleton
10	7.4	Shorewood	Shorewood
11	7.2	Beloit	Beloit
12	6.7	La Crosse	La Crosse
12	6.7	Manitowoc	Manitowoc
14	6.5	Milwaukee	Milwaukee
15	6.4	D C Everest Area	Weston
15	6.4	Waukesha	Waukesha
17	5.7	Eau Claire Area	Eau Claire
18	5.6	Racine	Racine
19	5.3	Menomonie Area	Menomonie
20	5.1	Elkhorn Area	Elkhorn
21	5.0	Oshkosh Area	Oshkosh
22	4.8	Holmen	Holmen
23	4.6	Wisconsin Rapids	Wis Rapids
24	4.5	Franklin Public	Franklin
24	4.5	Stevens Point Area	Stevens Point
26	3.6	Two Rivers	Two Rivers
27	3.4	Kenosha	Kenosha
28	3.3	Kaukauna Area	Kaukauna
28	3.3	Sauk Prairie	Sauk City
30	3.0	Whitnall	Greenfield
31	2.4	Beaver Dam	Beaver Dam
32	2.3	Sun Prairie Area	Sun Prairie
33	2.2	Janesville	Janesville
33	2.2	New London	New London
35	1.9	Neenah	Neenah
36	1.8	Onalaska	Onalaska
37	1.5	Burlington Area	Burlington
38	1.4	West Allis	West Allis
39	1.2	New Berlin	New Berlin
40	1.1	De Forest Area	De Forest
40	1.1	Fond Du Lac	Fond Du Lac
42	0.8	Whitewater	Whitewater
43	0.5	Fort Atkinson	Fort Atkinson
43	0.5	Howard-Suamico	Green Bay
43	0.5	Menomonee Falls	Menomonee Fls
46	0.3	Superior	Superior
47	0.0	Adams-Friendship Area	Friendship
47	0.0	Amery	Amery
47	0.0	Antigo	Antigo
47	0.0	Arrowhead Uhs	Hartland
47	0.0	Ashland	Ashland
47	0.0	Ashwaubenon	Green Bay
47	0.0	Baraboo	Baraboo
47	0.0	Berlin Area	Berlin
47	0.0	Black River Falls	Black River Fls
47	0.0	Brown Deer	Brown Deer
47	0.0	Campbellsport	Campbellsport
47	0.0	Cedarburg	Cedarburg
47	0.0	Chippewa Falls Area	Chippewa Falls
47	0.0	Clintonville	Clintonville
47	0.0	Cudahy	Cudahy
47	0.0	De Pere	De Pere
47	0.0	Denmark	Denmark
47	0.0	East Troy Community	East Troy
47	0.0	Edgerton	Edgerton
47	0.0	Ellsworth Community	Ellsworth
47	0.0	Elmbrook	Brookfield
47	0.0	Evansville Community	Evansville
47	0.0	Freedom Area	Freedom
47	0.0	Germantown	Germantown
47	0.0	Grafton	Grafton
47	0.0	Greendale	Greendale
47	0.0	Greenfield	Greenfield
47	0.0	Hamilton	Sussex
47	0.0	Hartford J1	Hartford
47	0.0	Hartford Uhs	Hartford
47	0.0	Hayward Community	Hayward
47	0.0	Hortonville	Hortonville
47	0.0	Hudson	Hudson
47	0.0	Jefferson	Jefferson
47	0.0	Kettle Moraine	Wales
47	0.0	Kewaskum	Kewaskum
47	0.0	Kimberly Area	Kimberly
47	0.0	Little Chute Area	Little Chute
47	0.0	Lodi	Lodi
47	0.0	Luxemburg-Casco	Luxemburg
47	0.0	Marinette	Marinette
47	0.0	Marshfield	Marshfield
47	0.0	Mauston	Mauston
47	0.0	Mcfarland	Mc Farland
47	0.0	Medford Area	Medford
47	0.0	Mequon-Thiensville	Mequon
47	0.0	Merrill Area	Merrill
47	0.0	Middleton-Cross Plains	Middleton
47	0.0	Milton	Milton
47	0.0	Monona Grove	Monona
47	0.0	Monroe	Monroe
47	0.0	Mosinee	Mosinee
47	0.0	Mount Horeb Area	Mount Horeb
47	0.0	Mukwonago	Mukwonago
47	0.0	Muskego-Norway	Muskego
47	0.0	Nekoosa	Nekoosa
47	0.0	New Richmond	New Richmond
47	0.0	Northland Pines	Eagle River
47	0.0	Oak Creek-Franklin	Oak Creek
47	0.0	Oconomowoc Area	Oconomowoc
47	0.0	Oconto Falls	Oconto Falls
47	0.0	Oregon	Oregon
47	0.0	Osceola	Osceola
47	0.0	Pewaukee	Pewaukee
47	0.0	Platteville	Platteville
47	0.0	Plymouth	Plymouth
47	0.0	Port Washington-Saukville	Pt Washington
47	0.0	Portage Community	Portage
47	0.0	Pulaski Community	Pulaski
47	0.0	Reedsburg	Reedsburg
47	0.0	Rhinelander	Rhinelander
47	0.0	Rice Lake Area	Rice Lake
47	0.0	Richland	Richland Ctr
47	0.0	Ripon	Ripon
47	0.0	River Falls	River Falls
47	0.0	Seymour Community	Seymour
47	0.0	Shawano-Gresham	Shawano
47	0.0	Sheboygan Falls	Sheboygan Fls
47	0.0	Slinger	Slinger
47	0.0	South Milwaukee	S Milwaukee
47	0.0	Sparta Area	Sparta
47	0.0	Spooner	Spooner
47	0.0	Stoughton Area	Stoughton
47	0.0	Tomah Area	Tomah
47	0.0	Tomahawk	Tomahawk
47	0.0	Verona Area	Verona
47	0.0	Watertown	Watertown
47	0.0	Waunakee Community	Waunakee
47	0.0	Waupaca	Waupaca
47	0.0	Waupun	Waupun
47	0.0	Wauwatosa	Wauwatosa
47	0.0	West Bend	West Bend
47	0.0	West De Pere	De Pere
47	0.0	West Salem	West Salem
47	0.0	Whitefish Bay	Whitefish Bay
47	0.0	Winneconne Community	Winneconne
47	0.0	Wisconsin Dells	Wisconsin Dells

Migrant Students

Rank	Percent	District Name	City
1	5.3	Wautoma Area	Wautoma
2	5.0	Berlin Area	Berlin
3	1.1	Beaver Dam	Beaver Dam
4	0.9	Watertown	Watertown
5	0.7	Green Bay Area	Green Bay
6	0.6	Medford Area	Medford
7	0.3	Kettle Moraine	Wales
7	0.3	Madison Metropolitan	Madison
7	0.3	Portage Community	Portage
7	0.3	Waupun	Waupun
11	0.1	Adams-Friendship Area	Friendship
11	0.1	Richland	Richland Ctr
13	0.0	Milwaukee	Milwaukee
13	0.0	Sun Prairie Area	Sun Prairie
13	0.0	Verona Area	Verona
16	0.0	Amery	Amery
16	0.0	Antigo	Antigo
16	0.0	Appleton Area	Appleton
16	0.0	Arrowhead Uhs	Hartland
16	0.0	Ashland	Ashland
16	0.0	Ashwaubenon	Green Bay
16	0.0	Baraboo	Baraboo
16	0.0	Beloit	Beloit
16	0.0	Black River Falls	Black River Fls
16	0.0	Brown Deer	Brown Deer
16	0.0	Burlington Area	Burlington
16	0.0	Campbellsport	Campbellsport
16	0.0	Cedarburg	Cedarburg
16	0.0	Chippewa Falls Area	Chippewa Falls
16	0.0	Clintonville	Clintonville
16	0.0	Cudahy	Cudahy
16	0.0	D C Everest Area	Weston
16	0.0	De Forest Area	De Forest
16	0.0	De Pere	De Pere
16	0.0	Delavan-Darien	Delavan
16	0.0	Denmark	Denmark
16	0.0	East Troy Community	East Troy
16	0.0	Eau Claire Area	Eau Claire
16	0.0	Edgerton	Edgerton
16	0.0	Elkhorn Area	Elkhorn
16	0.0	Ellsworth Community	Ellsworth
16	0.0	Elmbrook	Brookfield
16	0.0	Evansville Community	Evansville
16	0.0	Fond Du Lac	Fond Du Lac
16	0.0	Fort Atkinson	Fort Atkinson
16	0.0	Franklin Public	Franklin
16	0.0	Freedom Area	Freedom
16	0.0	Germantown	Germantown
16	0.0	Grafton	Grafton
16	0.0	Greendale	Greendale
16	0.0	Greenfield	Greenfield
16	0.0	Hamilton	Sussex
16	0.0	Hartford J1	Hartford
16	0.0	Hartford Uhs	Hartford
16	0.0	Hayward Community	Hayward
16	0.0	Holmen	Holmen
16	0.0	Hortonville	Hortonville
16	0.0	Howard-Suamico	Green Bay
16	0.0	Hudson	Hudson
16	0.0	Janesville	Janesville
16	0.0	Jefferson	Jefferson
16	0.0	Kaukauna Area	Kaukauna
16	0.0	Kenosha	Kenosha
16	0.0	Kewaskum	Kewaskum
16	0.0	Kimberly Area	Kimberly
16	0.0	La Crosse	La Crosse
16	0.0	Lake Geneva J1	Lake Geneva
16	0.0	Little Chute Area	Little Chute
16	0.0	Lodi	Lodi
16	0.0	Luxemburg-Casco	Luxemburg
16	0.0	Manitowoc	Manitowoc
16	0.0	Marinette	Marinette
16	0.0	Marshfield	Marshfield
16	0.0	Mauston	Mauston
16	0.0	Mcfarland	Mc Farland
16	0.0	Menasha	Menasha
16	0.0	Menomonee Falls	Menomonee Fls
16	0.0	Menomonie Area	Menomonie
16	0.0	Mequon-Thiensville	Mequon
16	0.0	Merrill Area	Merrill
16	0.0	Middleton-Cross Plains	Middleton
16	0.0	Milton	Milton

Rank	Percent	District Name	City
16	0.0	Monona Grove	Monona
16	0.0	Monroe	Monroe
16	0.0	Mosinee	Mosinee
16	0.0	Mount Horeb Area	Mount Horeb
16	0.0	Mukwonago	Mukwonago
16	0.0	Muskego-Norway	Muskego
16	0.0	Neenah	Neenah
16	0.0	Nekoosa	Nekoosa
16	0.0	New Berlin	New Berlin
16	0.0	New London	New London
16	0.0	New Richmond	New Richmond
16	0.0	Northland Pines	Eagle River
16	0.0	Oak Creek-Franklin	Oak Creek
16	0.0	Oconomowoc Area	Oconomowoc
16	0.0	Oconto Falls	Oconto Falls
16	0.0	Onalaska	Onalaska
16	0.0	Oregon	Oregon
16	0.0	Osceola	Osceola
16	0.0	Oshkosh Area	Oshkosh
16	0.0	Pewaukee	Pewaukee
16	0.0	Platteville	Platteville
16	0.0	Plymouth	Plymouth
16	0.0	Port Washington-Saukville	Pt Washington
16	0.0	Pulaski Community	Pulaski
16	0.0	Racine	Racine
16	0.0	Reedsburg	Reedsburg
16	0.0	Rhinelander	Rhinelander
16	0.0	Rice Lake Area	Rice Lake
16	0.0	Ripon	Ripon
16	0.0	River Falls	River Falls
16	0.0	Sauk Prairie	Sauk City
16	0.0	Seymour Community	Seymour
16	0.0	Shawano-Gresham	Shawano
16	0.0	Sheboygan Area	Sheboygan
16	0.0	Sheboygan Falls	Sheboygan Fls
16	0.0	Shorewood	Shorewood
16	0.0	Slinger	Slinger
16	0.0	South Milwaukee	S Milwaukee
16	0.0	Sparta Area	Sparta
16	0.0	Spooner	Spooner
16	0.0	Stevens Point Area	Stevens Point
16	0.0	Stoughton Area	Stoughton
16	0.0	Superior	Superior
16	0.0	Tomah Area	Tomah
16	0.0	Tomahawk	Tomahawk
16	0.0	Two Rivers	Two Rivers
16	0.0	Waukesha	Waukesha
16	0.0	Waunakee Community	Waunakee
16	0.0	Waupaca	Waupaca
16	0.0	Wausau	Wausau
16	0.0	Wauwatosa	Wauwatosa
16	0.0	West Allis	West Allis
16	0.0	West Bend	West Bend
16	0.0	West De Pere	De Pere
16	0.0	West Salem	West Salem
16	0.0	Whitefish Bay	Whitefish Bay
16	0.0	Whitewater	Whitewater
16	0.0	Whitnall	Greenfield
16	0.0	Winneconne Community	Winneconne
16	0.0	Wisconsin Dells	Wisconsin Dells
16	0.0	Wisconsin Rapids	Wis Rapids

Students Eligible for Free Lunch

Rank	Percent	District Name	City
1	n/a	Adams-Friendship Area	Friendship
1	n/a	Amery	Amery
1	n/a	Antigo	Antigo
1	n/a	Appleton Area	Appleton
1	n/a	Arrowhead Uhs	Hartland
1	n/a	Ashland	Ashland
1	n/a	Ashwaubenon	Green Bay
1	n/a	Baraboo	Baraboo
1	n/a	Beaver Dam	Beaver Dam
1	n/a	Beloit	Beloit
1	n/a	Berlin Area	Berlin
1	n/a	Black River Falls	Black River Fls
1	n/a	Brown Deer	Brown Deer
1	n/a	Burlington Area	Burlington
1	n/a	Campbellsport	Campbellsport
1	n/a	Cedarburg	Cedarburg
1	n/a	Chippewa Falls Area	Chippewa Falls
1	n/a	Clintonville	Clintonville
1	n/a	Cudahy	Cudahy
1	n/a	D C Everest Area	Weston
1	n/a	De Forest Area	De Forest
1	n/a	De Pere	De Pere
1	n/a	Delavan-Darien	Delavan
1	n/a	Denmark	Denmark
1	n/a	East Troy Community	East Troy
1	n/a	Eau Claire Area	Eau Claire
1	n/a	Edgerton	Edgerton
1	n/a	Elkhorn Area	Elkhorn
1	n/a	Ellsworth Community	Ellsworth
1	n/a	Elmbrook	Brookfield
1	n/a	Evansville Community	Evansville
1	n/a	Fond Du Lac	Fond Du Lac
1	n/a	Fort Atkinson	Fort Atkinson
1	n/a	Franklin Public	Franklin
1	n/a	Freedom Area	Freedom
1	n/a	Germantown	Germantown
1	n/a	Grafton	Grafton
1	n/a	Green Bay Area	Green Bay
1	n/a	Greendale	Greendale
1	n/a	Greenfield	Greenfield
1	n/a	Hamilton	Sussex
1	n/a	Hartford J1	Hartford
1	n/a	Hartford Uhs	Hartford
1	n/a	Hayward Community	Hayward
1	n/a	Holmen	Holmen
1	n/a	Hortonville	Hortonville
1	n/a	Howard-Suamico	Green Bay
1	n/a	Hudson	Hudson
1	n/a	Janesville	Janesville
1	n/a	Jefferson	Jefferson
1	n/a	Kaukauna Area	Kaukauna
1	n/a	Kenosha	Kenosha
1	n/a	Kettle Moraine	Wales
1	n/a	Kewaskum	Kewaskum
1	n/a	Kimberly Area	Kimberly
1	n/a	La Crosse	La Crosse
1	n/a	Lake Geneva J1	Lake Geneva
1	n/a	Little Chute Area	Little Chute
1	n/a	Lodi	Lodi
1	n/a	Luxemburg-Casco	Luxemburg
1	n/a	Madison Metropolitan	Madison
1	n/a	Manitowoc	Manitowoc
1	n/a	Marinette	Marinette
1	n/a	Marshfield	Marshfield
1	n/a	Mauston	Mauston
1	n/a	Mcfarland	Mc Farland
1	n/a	Medford Area	Medford
1	n/a	Menasha	Menasha
1	n/a	Menomonee Falls	Menomonee Fls
1	n/a	Menomonie Area	Menomonie
1	n/a	Mequon-Thiensville	Mequon
1	n/a	Merrill Area	Merrill
1	n/a	Middleton-Cross Plains	Middleton
1	n/a	Milton	Milton
1	n/a	Milwaukee	Milwaukee
1	n/a	Monona Grove	Monona
1	n/a	Monroe	Monroe
1	n/a	Mosinee	Mosinee
1	n/a	Mount Horeb Area	Mount Horeb
1	n/a	Mukwonago	Mukwonago
1	n/a	Muskego-Norway	Muskego
1	n/a	Neenah	Neenah
1	n/a	Nekoosa	Nekoosa
1	n/a	New Berlin	New Berlin
1	n/a	New London	New London
1	n/a	New Richmond	New Richmond
1	n/a	Northland Pines	Eagle River
1	n/a	Oak Creek-Franklin	Oak Creek
1	n/a	Oconomowoc Area	Oconomowoc
1	n/a	Oconto Falls	Oconto Falls
1	n/a	Onalaska	Onalaska
1	n/a	Oregon	Oregon
1	n/a	Osceola	Osceola
1	n/a	Oshkosh Area	Oshkosh
1	n/a	Pewaukee	Pewaukee
1	n/a	Platteville	Platteville
1	n/a	Plymouth	Plymouth
1	n/a	Port Washington-Saukville	Pt Washington
1	n/a	Portage Community	Portage
1	n/a	Pulaski Community	Pulaski
1	n/a	Racine	Racine
1	n/a	Reedsburg	Reedsburg
1	n/a	Rhinelander	Rhinelander
1	n/a	Rice Lake Area	Rice Lake
1	n/a	Richland	Richland Ctr
1	n/a	Ripon	Ripon
1	n/a	River Falls	River Falls
1	n/a	Sauk Prairie	Sauk City
1	n/a	Seymour Community	Seymour
1	n/a	Shawano-Gresham	Shawano
1	n/a	Sheboygan Area	Sheboygan
1	n/a	Sheboygan Falls	Sheboygan Fls
1	n/a	Shorewood	Shorewood
1	n/a	Slinger	Slinger
1	n/a	South Milwaukee	S Milwaukee
1	n/a	Sparta Area	Sparta
1	n/a	Spooner	Spooner
1	n/a	Stevens Point Area	Stevens Point
1	n/a	Stoughton Area	Stoughton
1	n/a	Sun Prairie Area	Sun Prairie
1	n/a	Superior	Superior
1	n/a	Tomah Area	Tomah
1	n/a	Tomahawk	Tomahawk
1	n/a	Two Rivers	Two Rivers
1	n/a	Verona Area	Verona
1	n/a	Watertown	Watertown
1	n/a	Waukesha	Waukesha
1	n/a	Waunakee Community	Waunakee
1	n/a	Waupaca	Waupaca
1	n/a	Waupun	Waupun
1	n/a	Wausau	Wausau
1	n/a	Wautoma Area	Wautoma
1	n/a	Wauwatosa	Wauwatosa
1	n/a	West Allis	West Allis
1	n/a	West Bend	West Bend
1	n/a	West De Pere	De Pere
1	n/a	West Salem	West Salem
1	n/a	Whitefish Bay	Whitefish Bay
1	n/a	Whitewater	Whitewater
1	n/a	Whitnall	Greenfield
1	n/a	Winneconne Community	Winneconne
1	n/a	Wisconsin Dells	Wisconsin Dells
1	n/a	Wisconsin Rapids	Wis Rapids

Students Eligible for Reduced-Price Lunch

Rank	Percent	District Name	City
1	n/a	Adams-Friendship Area	Friendship
1	n/a	Amery	Amery
1	n/a	Antigo	Antigo
1	n/a	Appleton Area	Appleton
1	n/a	Arrowhead Uhs	Hartland
1	n/a	Ashland	Ashland
1	n/a	Ashwaubenon	Green Bay
1	n/a	Baraboo	Baraboo
1	n/a	Beaver Dam	Beaver Dam
1	n/a	Beloit	Beloit
1	n/a	Berlin Area	Berlin
1	n/a	Black River Falls	Black River Fls
1	n/a	Brown Deer	Brown Deer
1	n/a	Burlington Area	Burlington
1	n/a	Campbellsport	Campbellsport
1	n/a	Cedarburg	Cedarburg
1	n/a	Chippewa Falls Area	Chippewa Falls
1	n/a	Clintonville	Clintonville
1	n/a	Cudahy	Cudahy
1	n/a	D C Everest Area	Weston
1	n/a	De Forest Area	De Forest
1	n/a	De Pere	De Pere
1	n/a	Delavan-Darien	Delavan
1	n/a	Denmark	Denmark
1	n/a	East Troy Community	East Troy
1	n/a	Eau Claire Area	Eau Claire
1	n/a	Edgerton	Edgerton
1	n/a	Elkhorn Area	Elkhorn
1	n/a	Ellsworth Community	Ellsworth
1	n/a	Elmbrook	Brookfield
1	n/a	Evansville Community	Evansville
1	n/a	Fond Du Lac	Fond Du Lac
1	n/a	Fort Atkinson	Fort Atkinson
1	n/a	Franklin Public	Franklin
1	n/a	Freedom Area	Freedom
1	n/a	Germantown	Germantown
1	n/a	Grafton	Grafton
1	n/a	Green Bay Area	Green Bay
1	n/a	Greendale	Greendale
1	n/a	Greenfield	Greenfield
1	n/a	Hamilton	Sussex
1	n/a	Hartford J1	Hartford
1	n/a	Hartford Uhs	Hartford
1	n/a	Hayward Community	Hayward
1	n/a	Holmen	Holmen
1	n/a	Hortonville	Hortonville
1	n/a	Howard-Suamico	Green Bay
1	n/a	Hudson	Hudson
1	n/a	Janesville	Janesville
1	n/a	Jefferson	Jefferson
1	n/a	Kaukauna Area	Kaukauna
1	n/a	Kenosha	Kenosha
1	n/a	Kettle Moraine	Wales
1	n/a	Kewaskum	Kewaskum
1	n/a	Kimberly Area	Kimberly
1	n/a	La Crosse	La Crosse
1	n/a	Lake Geneva J1	Lake Geneva
1	n/a	Little Chute Area	Little Chute
1	n/a	Lodi	Lodi
1	n/a	Luxemburg-Casco	Luxemburg
1	n/a	Madison Metropolitan	Madison
1	n/a	Manitowoc	Manitowoc
1	n/a	Marinette	Marinette
1	n/a	Marshfield	Marshfield

1	n/a	Mauston	Mauston
1	n/a	Mcfarland	Mc Farland
1	n/a	Medford Area	Medford
1	n/a	Menasha	Menasha
1	n/a	Menomonee Falls	Menomonee Fls
1	n/a	Menomonie Area	Menomonie
1	n/a	Mequon-Thiensville	Mequon
1	n/a	Merrill Area	Merrill
1	n/a	Middleton-Cross Plains	Middleton
1	n/a	Milton	Milton
1	n/a	Milwaukee	Milwaukee
1	n/a	Monona Grove	Monona
1	n/a	Monroe	Monroe
1	n/a	Mosinee	Mosinee
1	n/a	Mount Horeb Area	Mount Horeb
1	n/a	Mukwonago	Mukwonago
1	n/a	Muskego-Norway	Muskego
1	n/a	Neenah	Neenah
1	n/a	Nekoosa	Nekoosa
1	n/a	New Berlin	New Berlin
1	n/a	New London	New London
1	n/a	New Richmond	New Richmond
1	n/a	Northland Pines	Eagle River
1	n/a	Oak Creek-Franklin	Oak Creek
1	n/a	Oconomowoc Area	Oconomowoc
1	n/a	Oconto Falls	Oconto Falls
1	n/a	Onalaska	Onalaska
1	n/a	Oregon	Oregon
1	n/a	Osceola	Osceola
1	n/a	Oshkosh Area	Oshkosh
1	n/a	Pewaukee	Pewaukee
1	n/a	Platteville	Platteville
1	n/a	Plymouth	Plymouth
1	n/a	Port Washington-Saukville	Pt Washington
1	n/a	Portage Community	Portage
1	n/a	Pulaski Community	Pulaski
1	n/a	Racine	Racine
1	n/a	Reedsburg	Reedsburg
1	n/a	Rhinelander	Rhinelander
1	n/a	Rice Lake Area	Rice Lake
1	n/a	Richland	Richland Ctr
1	n/a	Ripon	Ripon
1	n/a	River Falls	River Falls
1	n/a	Sauk Prairie	Sauk City
1	n/a	Seymour Community	Seymour
1	n/a	Shawano-Gresham	Shawano
1	n/a	Sheboygan Area	Sheboygan
1	n/a	Sheboygan Falls	Sheboygan Fls
1	n/a	Shorewood	Shorewood
1	n/a	Slinger	Slinger
1	n/a	South Milwaukee	S Milwaukee
1	n/a	Sparta Area	Sparta
1	n/a	Spooner	Spooner
1	n/a	Stevens Point Area	Stevens Point
1	n/a	Stoughton Area	Stoughton
1	n/a	Sun Prairie Area	Sun Prairie
1	n/a	Superior	Superior
1	n/a	Tomah Area	Tomah
1	n/a	Tomahawk	Tomahawk
1	n/a	Two Rivers	Two Rivers
1	n/a	Verona Area	Verona
1	n/a	Watertown	Watertown
1	n/a	Waukesha	Waukesha
1	n/a	Waunakee Community	Waunakee
1	n/a	Waupaca	Waupaca
1	n/a	Waupun	Waupun
1	n/a	Wausau	Wausau
1	n/a	Wautoma Area	Wautoma
1	n/a	Wauwatosa	Wauwatosa
1	n/a	West Allis	West Allis
1	n/a	West Bend	West Bend
1	n/a	West De Pere	De Pere
1	n/a	West Salem	West Salem
1	n/a	Whitefish Bay	Whitefish Bay
1	n/a	Whitewater	Whitewater
1	n/a	Whitnall	Greenfield
1	n/a	Winneconne Community	Winneconne
1	n/a	Wisconsin Dells	Wisconsin Dells
1	n/a	Wisconsin Rapids	Wis Rapids

Student/Teacher Ratio

Rank	Ratio	District Name	City
1	17.3	Slinger	Slinger
2	16.6	Arrowhead Uhs	Hartland
2	16.6	Osceola	Osceola
4	16.5	Oak Creek-Franklin	Oak Creek
4	16.5	Portage Community	Portage
6	16.3	Delavan-Darien	Delavan
7	16.1	New Richmond	New Richmond
7	16.1	Whitnall	Greenfield
9	16.0	Kimberly Area	Kimberly
9	16.0	Mequon-Thiensville	Mequon
9	16.0	Seymour Community	Seymour
9	16.0	Watertown	Watertown
9	16.0	West Bend	West Bend
14	15.9	Freedom Area	Freedom
14	15.9	Howard-Suamico	Green Bay
14	15.9	Marshfield	Marshfield
14	15.9	Milton	Milton
14	15.9	Muskego-Norway	Muskego
19	15.8	Cedarburg	Cedarburg
19	15.8	Little Chute Area	Little Chute
19	15.8	Racine	Racine
22	15.7	Brown Deer	Brown Deer
22	15.7	Elkhorn Area	Elkhorn
22	15.7	Neenah	Neenah
22	15.7	Superior	Superior
22	15.7	Whitefish Bay	Whitefish Bay
27	15.6	Luxemburg-Casco	Luxemburg
27	15.6	Mukwonago	Mukwonago
29	15.5	Denmark	Denmark
29	15.5	Hamilton	Sussex
29	15.5	Mosinee	Mosinee
29	15.5	Port Washington-Saukville	Pt Washington
33	15.4	Burlington Area	Burlington
33	15.4	Greenfield	Greenfield
33	15.4	Hartford Uhs	Hartford
33	15.4	Oconomowoc Area	Oconomowoc
33	15.4	River Falls	River Falls
38	15.3	Appleton Area	Appleton
38	15.3	De Pere	De Pere
38	15.3	Kaukauna Area	Kaukauna
38	15.3	Kettle Moraine	Wales
38	15.3	Marinette	Marinette
38	15.3	Pewaukee	Pewaukee
44	15.2	Fond Du Lac	Fond Du Lac
44	15.2	Medford Area	Medford
46	15.1	D C Everest Area	Weston
46	15.1	Kewaskum	Kewaskum
46	15.1	Whitewater	Whitewater
49	15.0	Baraboo	Baraboo
49	15.0	Chippewa Falls Area	Chippewa Falls
49	15.0	Hudson	Hudson
49	15.0	Menomonie Area	Menomonie
49	15.0	Milwaukee	Milwaukee
49	15.0	New Berlin	New Berlin
49	15.0	Shawano-Gresham	Shawano
49	15.0	Wauwatosa	Wauwatosa
57	14.9	Greendale	Greendale
57	14.9	Kenosha	Kenosha
57	14.9	Manitowoc	Manitowoc
57	14.9	Onalaska	Onalaska
57	14.9	Oshkosh Area	Oshkosh
57	14.9	Plymouth	Plymouth
57	14.9	Rice Lake Area	Rice Lake
57	14.9	Stevens Point Area	Stevens Point
65	14.8	De Forest Area	De Forest
65	14.8	Elmbrook	Brookfield
65	14.8	Menasha	Menasha
65	14.8	New London	New London
69	14.7	Amery	Amery
69	14.7	East Troy Community	East Troy
69	14.7	Menomonee Falls	Menomonee Fls
69	14.7	Pulaski Community	Pulaski
69	14.7	Rhinelander	Rhinelander
69	14.7	Wisconsin Dells	Wisconsin Dells
75	14.6	Hortonville	Hortonville
75	14.6	Lake Geneva J1	Lake Geneva
75	14.6	Ripon	Ripon
75	14.6	Waukesha	Waukesha
75	14.6	West Allis	West Allis
75	14.6	West De Pere	De Pere
75	14.6	Winneconne Community	Winneconne
82	14.5	Campbellsport	Campbellsport
82	14.5	Germantown	Germantown
82	14.5	Grafton	Grafton
82	14.5	Sheboygan Falls	Sheboygan Fls
86	14.4	Merrill Area	Merrill
86	14.4	Platteville	Platteville
86	14.4	South Milwaukee	S Milwaukee
89	14.3	Ashwaubenon	Green Bay
89	14.3	Beaver Dam	Beaver Dam
89	14.3	Ellsworth Community	Ellsworth
89	14.3	Green Bay Area	Green Bay
89	14.3	Mcfarland	Mc Farland
89	14.3	Mount Horeb Area	Mount Horeb
89	14.3	Sheboygan Area	Sheboygan
89	14.3	Stoughton Area	Stoughton
97	14.2	Waunakee Community	Waunakee
98	14.1	Beloit	Beloit
98	14.1	Nekoosa	Nekoosa
98	14.1	Reedsburg	Reedsburg
98	14.1	Shorewood	Shorewood
98	14.1	Wausau	Wausau
98	14.1	West Salem	West Salem
104	14.0	Edgerton	Edgerton
104	14.0	Evansville Community	Evansville
104	14.0	Franklin Public	Franklin
104	14.0	Holmen	Holmen
108	13.9	Berlin Area	Berlin
108	13.9	Eau Claire Area	Eau Claire
108	13.9	Hayward Community	Hayward
108	13.9	Tomahawk	Tomahawk
112	13.8	Hartford J1	Hartford
112	13.8	Janesville	Janesville
112	13.8	Lodi	Lodi
112	13.8	Tomah Area	Tomah
112	13.8	Waupaca	Waupaca
117	13.7	Fort Atkinson	Fort Atkinson
117	13.7	Spooner	Spooner
117	13.7	Sun Prairie Area	Sun Prairie
120	13.6	Cudahy	Cudahy
120	13.6	Oconto Falls	Oconto Falls
120	13.6	Wautoma Area	Wautoma
123	13.5	Ashland	Ashland
123	13.5	Sauk Prairie	Sauk City
123	13.5	Wisconsin Rapids	Wis Rapids
126	13.4	Middleton-Cross Plains	Middleton
126	13.4	Sparta Area	Sparta
128	13.3	Adams-Friendship Area	Friendship
128	13.3	Oregon	Oregon
130	13.2	Northland Pines	Eagle River
131	13.1	Black River Falls	Black River Fls
131	13.1	La Crosse	La Crosse
133	13.0	Two Rivers	Two Rivers
134	12.9	Monona Grove	Monona
135	12.8	Antigo	Antigo
135	12.8	Clintonville	Clintonville
135	12.8	Jefferson	Jefferson
138	12.6	Richland	Richland Ctr
139	12.5	Waupun	Waupun
140	12.3	Madison Metropolitan	Madison
140	12.3	Verona Area	Verona
142	12.0	Mauston	Mauston
142	12.0	Monroe	Monroe

Student/Librarian Ratio

Rank	Ratio	District Name	City
1	2,395.0	West De Pere	De Pere
2	1,777.0	Wisconsin Dells	Wisconsin Dells
3	1,676.0	Merrill Area	Merrill
4	1,638.8	Portage Community	Portage
5	1,352.8	Manitowoc	Manitowoc
6	1,308.5	Hartford Uhs	Hartford
7	1,300.0	Plymouth	Plymouth
8	1,282.0	Marinette	Marinette
9	1,275.7	Kimberly Area	Kimberly
10	1,164.3	Pulaski Community	Pulaski
11	1,163.8	Milwaukee	Milwaukee
12	1,144.7	Lake Geneva J1	Lake Geneva
13	1,102.6	Beaver Dam	Beaver Dam
14	1,084.7	Platteville	Platteville
15	1,078.5	Adams-Friendship Area	Friendship
16	1,075.7	Rhinelander	Rhinelander
17	1,062.0	Arrowhead Uhs	Hartland
18	1,059.5	Two Rivers	Two Rivers
19	1,017.7	Baraboo	Baraboo
20	990.3	Whitefish Bay	Whitefish Bay
21	987.4	Oak Creek-Franklin	Oak Creek
22	971.7	Hortonville	Hortonville
23	966.0	Antigo	Antigo
24	963.8	Mosinee	Mosinee
25	960.0	Kewaskum	Kewaskum
26	948.7	Slinger	Slinger
27	935.0	Kaukauna Area	Kaukauna
28	911.8	Burlington Area	Burlington
29	901.1	Waukesha	Waukesha
30	901.0	Brown Deer	Brown Deer
31	900.5	South Milwaukee	S Milwaukee
32	893.0	Chippewa Falls Area	Chippewa Falls
33	883.0	Port Washington-Saukville	Pt Washington
34	878.5	Osceola	Osceola
35	867.4	Elmbrook	Brookfield
36	859.0	Elkhorn Area	Elkhorn
37	853.1	Green Bay Area	Green Bay
38	844.0	Denmark	Denmark
39	837.0	Menomonie Area	Menomonie
40	789.5	Northland Pines	Eagle River
41	783.0	Freedom Area	Freedom
42	781.5	Ashwaubenon	Green Bay
43	773.3	Waupun	Waupun
44	772.4	Mequon-Thiensville	Mequon
45	766.5	Germantown	Germantown
46	765.7	Medford Area	Medford
47	763.5	Campbellsport	Campbellsport
48	761.3	Menasha	Menasha

49	758.4	Wausau	Wausau
50	758.2	Watertown	Watertown
51	741.5	Shawano-Gresham	Shawano
52	741.3	Verona Area	Verona
53	740.8	Amery	Amery
54	738.7	Greendale	Greendale
55	728.8	Kettle Moraine	Wales
56	725.1	Mukwonago	Mukwonago
57	723.3	Superior	Superior
58	721.3	Cudahy	Cudahy
59	705.9	Sheboygan Area	Sheboygan
60	700.0	Marshfield	Marshfield
61	699.7	Hayward Community	Hayward
62	692.8	Delavan-Darien	Delavan
63	685.8	Oregon	Oregon
64	684.1	Rice Lake Area	Rice Lake
65	682.6	West Bend	West Bend
66	679.0	Waupaca	Waupaca
67	675.9	Hamilton	Sussex
68	675.7	Little Chute Area	Little Chute
69	667.9	Oconto Falls	Oconto Falls
70	657.0	Howard-Suamico	Green Bay
71	647.5	Beloit	Beloit
72	643.1	D C Everest Area	Weston
73	642.9	New Richmond	New Richmond
74	639.9	Racine	Racine
75	639.5	New London	New London
76	633.6	Eau Claire Area	Eau Claire
77	633.4	Appleton Area	Appleton
78	632.3	Hudson	Hudson
79	629.3	Whitnall	Greenfield
80	627.4	Oshkosh Area	Oshkosh
81	627.2	Muskego-Norway	Muskego
82	626.8	Oconomowoc Area	Oconomowoc
83	626.0	Edgerton	Edgerton
84	624.8	Reedsburg	Reedsburg
85	623.4	Sun Prairie Area	Sun Prairie
86	612.5	De Pere	De Pere
87	611.0	Seymour Community	Seymour
88	610.5	Stoughton Area	Stoughton
89	608.8	Tomah Area	Tomah
90	595.3	Ellsworth Community	Ellsworth
91	593.8	Sauk Prairie	Sauk City
92	590.4	Cedarburg	Cedarburg
93	589.5	West Allis	West Allis
94	588.2	Milton	Milton
95	586.6	River Falls	River Falls
96	576.7	Berlin Area	Berlin
97	576.3	Sheboygan Falls	Sheboygan Fls
98	575.0	Winneconne Community	Winneconne
99	571.0	Ripon	Ripon
100	570.8	Mount Horeb Area	Mount Horeb
101	563.2	Ashland	Ashland
102	563.1	Janesville	Janesville
103	556.8	Greenfield	Greenfield
104	555.7	East Troy Community	East Troy
105	552.3	Franklin Public	Franklin
106	550.6	Menomonee Falls	Menomonee Fls
107	550.5	Whitewater	Whitewater
108	548.9	Black River Falls	Black River Fls
109	548.6	Stevens Point Area	Stevens Point
110	547.3	Tomahawk	Tomahawk
111	543.0	Shorewood	Shorewood
112	539.0	Clintonville	Clintonville
113	538.8	Sparta Area	Sparta
114	538.7	Wautoma Area	Wautoma
115	536.8	Pewaukee	Pewaukee
116	529.0	Monroe	Monroe
117	528.2	Fort Atkinson	Fort Atkinson
118	526.9	Nekoosa	Nekoosa
119	525.0	Hartford J1	Hartford
120	521.5	Onalaska	Onalaska
121	516.9	Lodi	Lodi
122	512.2	New Berlin	New Berlin
123	507.3	Grafton	Grafton
124	507.0	Richland	Richland Ctr
125	505.7	Wauwatosa	Wauwatosa
126	502.2	Waunakee Community	Waunakee
127	501.3	Madison Metropolitan	Madison
128	492.3	Mcfarland	Mc Farland
129	486.3	Wisconsin Rapids	Wis Rapids
130	483.7	Jefferson	Jefferson
131	477.8	Luxemburg-Casco	Luxemburg
132	471.8	Kenosha	Kenosha
133	469.8	Monona Grove	Monona
134	469.4	Evansville Community	Evansville
135	467.4	Fond Du Lac	Fond Du Lac
136	464.3	De Forest Area	De Forest
137	460.6	Neenah	Neenah
138	439.6	Holmen	Holmen
139	436.9	Middleton-Cross Plains	Middleton
140	430.6	Spooner	Spooner
141	422.9	West Salem	West Salem
142	412.1	Mauston	Mauston
143	397.9	La Crosse	La Crosse

Student/Counselor Ratio

Rank	Ratio	District Name	City
1	853.4	Stevens Point Area	Stevens Point
2	849.0	Milwaukee	Milwaukee
3	736.8	West Allis	West Allis
4	679.0	Waupaca	Waupaca
5	658.6	New Berlin	New Berlin
6	625.8	Platteville	Platteville
7	600.5	Stoughton Area	Stoughton
8	582.2	Pulaski Community	Pulaski
9	580.0	Marshfield	Marshfield
10	561.9	Beloit	Beloit
11	555.9	Mukwonago	Mukwonago
12	555.7	East Troy Community	East Troy
13	547.7	Evansville Community	Evansville
14	545.2	Elmbrook	Brookfield
15	541.1	Manitowoc	Manitowoc
16	535.7	West Salem	West Salem
17	528.2	Fort Atkinson	Fort Atkinson
18	525.0	Hartford J1	Hartford
19	520.4	Shawano-Gresham	Shawano
20	512.5	Monona Grove	Monona
21	509.0	Campbellsport	Campbellsport
22	506.0	Mosinee	Mosinee
23	505.7	Wauwatosa	Wauwatosa
24	499.8	Reedsburg	Reedsburg
25	499.3	Medford Area	Medford
26	498.5	Hamilton	Sussex
27	496.8	Oconomowoc Area	Oconomowoc
28	493.8	Waunakee Community	Waunakee
29	492.4	Madison Metropolitan	Madison
30	483.5	Oshkosh Area	Oshkosh
31	483.0	Fond Du Lac	Fond Du Lac
32	479.5	Kaukauna Area	Kaukauna
33	479.0	West De Pere	De Pere
34	474.0	Racine	Racine
35	469.5	Edgerton	Edgerton
36	465.3	Waukesha	Waukesha
37	461.8	Delavan-Darien	Delavan
38	455.7	Beaver Dam	Beaver Dam
39	453.4	Sun Prairie Area	Sun Prairie
40	453.0	Appleton Area	Appleton
41	447.4	Freedom Area	Freedom
42	439.3	Osceola	Osceola
43	437.1	Watertown	Watertown
44	430.6	Spooner	Spooner
45	429.4	Pewaukee	Pewaukee
46	429.3	Lake Geneva J1	Lake Geneva
47	426.6	West Bend	West Bend
48	424.7	Luxemburg-Casco	Luxemburg
49	422.1	Green Bay Area	Green Bay
50	422.0	Denmark	Denmark
51	419.5	Whitnall	Greenfield
52	418.4	Whitewater	Whitewater
53	416.4	Hortonville	Hortonville
54	411.5	Janesville	Janesville
55	411.0	Mount Horeb Area	Mount Horeb
56	410.0	Middleton-Cross Plains	Middleton
57	408.7	Kettle Moraine	Wales
58	407.3	Seymour Community	Seymour
59	407.2	New Richmond	New Richmond
60	407.1	Muskego-Norway	Muskego
61	407.0	Howard-Suamico	Green Bay
62	406.0	Menasha	Menasha
63	405.9	Kimberly Area	Kimberly
64	405.8	Grafton	Grafton
65	405.5	Kenosha	Kenosha
66	404.3	Clintonville	Clintonville
67	404.0	Wautoma Area	Wautoma
68	401.8	Mauston	Mauston
69	401.7	Baraboo	Baraboo
70	396.1	Sheboygan Area	Sheboygan
71	395.8	D C Everest Area	Weston
72	394.9	Shorewood	Shorewood
73	394.5	Holmen	Holmen
74	392.1	Milton	Milton
75	391.4	Germantown	Germantown
76	391.1	River Falls	River Falls
77	388.0	Burlington Area	Burlington
78	386.7	Waupun	Waupun
79	385.7	De Pere	De Pere
80	385.3	Oregon	Oregon
81	384.8	Ashland	Ashland
82	384.2	Black River Falls	Black River Fls
83	384.0	Kewaskum	Kewaskum
84	382.8	Hayward Community	Hayward
85	382.0	La Crosse	La Crosse
85	382.0	Nekoosa	Nekoosa
87	381.2	Ashwaubenon	Green Bay
88	380.8	Wausau	Wausau
89	380.7	Ripon	Ripon
90	380.0	Portage Community	Portage
91	379.7	Menomonee Falls	Menomonee Fls
92	379.4	Neenah	Neenah
93	379.2	Mequon-Thiensville	Mequon
94	375.9	Lodi	Lodi
95	372.9	Tomah Area	Tomah
96	372.4	Merrill Area	Merrill
97	369.3	Greendale	Greendale
98	368.1	Elkhorn Area	Elkhorn
99	368.0	Jefferson	Jefferson
100	366.3	Marinette	Marinette
101	365.4	New London	New London
102	363.0	Oak Creek-Franklin	Oak Creek
103	362.3	Antigo	Antigo
104	361.7	Wisconsin Rapids	Wis Rapids
105	361.6	Superior	Superior
106	360.4	Brown Deer	Brown Deer
107	360.2	Sheboygan Falls	Sheboygan Fls
108	357.2	Ellsworth Community	Ellsworth
109	356.9	Hudson	Hudson
110	355.8	Slinger	Slinger
111	355.4	Wisconsin Dells	Wisconsin Dells
112	354.6	Rhinelander	Rhinelander
113	354.0	Arrowhead Uhs	Hartland
114	353.5	De Forest Area	De Forest
115	353.0	Verona Area	Verona
116	351.5	Franklin Public	Franklin
117	346.0	Berlin Area	Berlin
118	345.5	Onalaska	Onalaska
119	342.6	Sauk Prairie	Sauk City
120	341.0	Sparta Area	Sparta
121	340.2	Hartford Uhs	Hartford
122	339.6	Port Washington-Saukville	Pt Washington
123	337.8	Little Chute Area	Little Chute
124	336.7	Amery	Amery
125	335.4	Eau Claire Area	Eau Claire
126	334.8	Menomonie Area	Menomonie
127	333.5	Rice Lake Area	Rice Lake
128	330.7	Chippewa Falls Area	Chippewa Falls
129	328.4	Tomahawk	Tomahawk
130	327.5	South Milwaukee	S Milwaukee
131	326.5	Monroe	Monroe
132	322.0	Winneconne Community	Winneconne
133	320.6	Cudahy	Cudahy
134	315.2	Greenfield	Greenfield
135	312.5	Mcfarland	Mc Farland
136	308.1	Adams-Friendship Area	Friendship
137	307.5	Cedarburg	Cedarburg
138	302.7	Two Rivers	Two Rivers
139	288.4	Whitefish Bay	Whitefish Bay
140	280.7	Oconto Falls	Oconto Falls
141	263.2	Northland Pines	Eagle River
142	260.0	Plymouth	Plymouth
143	253.5	Richland	Richland Ctr

Current Spending per Student in FY2001

Rank	Dollars	District Name	City
1	10,208	Madison Metropolitan	Madison
2	9,837	New Berlin	New Berlin
3	9,510	Elmbrook	Brookfield
4	9,425	Arrowhead Uhs	Hartland
5	9,365	Greendale	Greendale
6	9,283	Milwaukee	Milwaukee
7	9,174	Port Washington-Saukville	Pt Washington
8	9,130	Menomonee Falls	Menomonee Fls
9	9,061	La Crosse	La Crosse
10	9,041	Ashland	Ashland
11	8,973	Brown Deer	Brown Deer
12	8,967	Richland	Richland Ctr
13	8,919	Franklin Public	Franklin
14	8,876	Jefferson	Jefferson
15	8,844	Northland Pines	Eagle River
16	8,816	Shorewood	Shorewood
17	8,737	Mequon-Thiensville	Mequon
18	8,685	Beloit	Beloit
19	8,608	Antigo	Antigo
20	8,582	Adams-Friendship Area	Friendship
21	8,573	Hartford Uhs	Hartford
22	8,559	Whitnall	Greenfield
23	8,548	Monroe	Monroe
24	8,546	Cudahy	Cudahy
25	8,512	Platteville	Platteville
26	8,507	Verona Area	Verona
27	8,506	Wausau	Wausau
28	8,499	Monona Grove	Monona
29	8,472	Oconomowoc Area	Oconomowoc
30	8,469	Rhinelander	Rhinelander
31	8,438	Greenfield	Greenfield
32	8,412	Whitefish Bay	Whitefish Bay

33	8,396	Germantown	Germantown
34	8,355	Fort Atkinson	Fort Atkinson
35	8,338	Hartford J1	Hartford
36	8,320	Wisconsin Rapids	Wis Rapids
37	8,309	Oregon	Oregon
38	8,293	Grafton	Grafton
39	8,279	Wauwatosa	Wauwatosa
40	8,274	Hayward Community	Hayward
41	8,273	West Allis	West Allis
42	8,262	Beaver Dam	Beaver Dam
43	8,241	Menomonie Area	Menomonie
44	8,205	Watertown	Watertown
45	8,195	Kettle Moraine	Wales
46	8,164	Clintonville	Clintonville
47	8,159	Mcfarland	Mc Farland
48	8,150	Kenosha	Kenosha
49	8,134	Racine	Racine
50	8,126	Mosinee	Mosinee
50	8,126	Sauk Prairie	Sauk City
52	8,114	Stevens Point Area	Stevens Point
53	8,102	Sheboygan Area	Sheboygan
54	8,090	Green Bay Area	Green Bay
54	8,090	Pewaukee	Pewaukee
56	8,064	Eau Claire Area	Eau Claire
57	8,060	Oak Creek-Franklin	Oak Creek
58	8,059	Waukesha	Waukesha
59	8,055	Middleton-Cross Plains	Middleton
60	8,032	Ellsworth Community	Ellsworth
61	8,009	Sun Prairie Area	Sun Prairie
62	8,003	Waupun	Waupun
63	7,998	Superior	Superior
64	7,969	Mauston	Mauston
65	7,944	De Forest Area	De Forest
66	7,925	Rice Lake Area	Rice Lake
67	7,915	Janesville	Janesville
68	7,904	Edgerton	Edgerton
69	7,903	Ashwaubenon	Green Bay
70	7,881	Marshfield	Marshfield
71	7,871	Ripon	Ripon
72	7,865	Marinette	Marinette
73	7,833	Tomahawk	Tomahawk
74	7,827	Spooner	Spooner
75	7,821	Onalaska	Onalaska
76	7,796	Sheboygan Falls	Sheboygan Fls
77	7,789	Muskego-Norway	Muskego
78	7,774	Chippewa Falls Area	Chippewa Falls
79	7,754	Kaukauna Area	Kaukauna
79	7,754	River Falls	River Falls
81	7,727	Lodi	Lodi
82	7,721	Merrill Area	Merrill
83	7,715	Pulaski Community	Pulaski
84	7,713	New Richmond	New Richmond
85	7,685	Cedarburg	Cedarburg
85	7,685	South Milwaukee	S Milwaukee
87	7,684	Neenah	Neenah
88	7,668	West De Pere	De Pere
89	7,653	West Salem	West Salem
90	7,650	Holmen	Holmen
91	7,629	Kewaskum	Kewaskum
92	7,621	Appleton Area	Appleton
93	7,595	Reedsburg	Reedsburg
94	7,576	Hamilton	Sussex
95	7,504	Sparta Area	Sparta
96	7,494	Evansville Community	Evansville
97	7,485	Portage Community	Portage
98	7,479	Wisconsin Dells	Wisconsin Dells
99	7,477	Whitewater	Whitewater
100	7,458	Two Rivers	Two Rivers
101	7,420	Menasha	Menasha
101	7,420	New London	New London
103	7,419	Mukwonago	Mukwonago
104	7,406	Amery	Amery
105	7,380	West Bend	West Bend
106	7,375	Plymouth	Plymouth
107	7,359	Oshkosh Area	Oshkosh
108	7,356	Hudson	Hudson
109	7,349	Waunakee Community	Waunakee
110	7,332	Fond Du Lac	Fond Du Lac
111	7,309	Milton	Milton
112	7,282	Shawano-Gresham	Shawano
113	7,264	Lake Geneva J1	Lake Geneva
114	7,252	Stoughton Area	Stoughton
115	7,248	Nekoosa	Nekoosa
116	7,230	Baraboo	Baraboo
117	7,165	Black River Falls	Black River Fls
118	7,158	D C Everest Area	Weston
119	7,149	Winneconne Community	Winneconne
120	7,145	Osceola	Osceola
121	7,134	Medford Area	Medford
122	7,090	Mount Horeb Area	Mount Horeb
123	7,089	Freedom Area	Freedom
124	7,064	Elkhorn Area	Elkhorn
125	7,049	Campbellsport	Campbellsport
126	6,969	Tomah Area	Tomah
127	6,949	Slinger	Slinger
128	6,933	East Troy Community	East Troy
128	6,933	Oconto Falls	Oconto Falls
130	6,922	Denmark	Denmark
130	6,922	Little Chute Area	Little Chute
132	6,903	Berlin Area	Berlin
133	6,897	Seymour Community	Seymour
134	6,882	Waupaca	Waupaca
135	6,831	Delavan-Darien	Delavan
136	6,804	Manitowoc	Manitowoc
137	6,801	Burlington Area	Burlington
138	6,775	Howard-Suamico	Green Bay
139	6,739	Kimberly Area	Kimberly
140	6,719	Wautoma Area	Wautoma
141	6,657	Hortonville	Hortonville
142	6,488	De Pere	De Pere
143	6,436	Luxemburg-Casco	Luxemburg

Number of Diploma Recipients

Rank	Number	District Name	City
1	3,912	Milwaukee	Milwaukee
2	1,607	Madison Metropolitan	Madison
3	1,305	Kenosha	Kenosha
4	1,163	Racine	Racine
5	1,131	Green Bay Area	Green Bay
6	1,109	Appleton Area	Appleton
7	1,043	Waukesha	Waukesha
8	978	Eau Claire Area	Eau Claire
9	768	Sheboygan Area	Sheboygan
10	676	Stevens Point Area	Stevens Point
11	673	Janesville	Janesville
12	671	Oshkosh Area	Oshkosh
13	637	West Allis	West Allis
14	603	West Bend	West Bend
15	589	Elmbrook	Brookfield
16	586	Wausau	Wausau
17	501	Wisconsin Rapids	Wis Rapids
18	499	La Crosse	La Crosse
19	496	Wauwatosa	Wauwatosa
20	463	Fond Du Lac	Fond Du Lac
21	457	Arrowhead Uhs	Hartland
22	439	Neenah	Neenah
23	415	Mukwonago	Mukwonago
24	390	D C Everest Area	Weston
25	385	Middleton-Cross Plains	Middleton
26	382	New Berlin	New Berlin
26	382	Oak Creek-Franklin	Oak Creek
28	379	Hartford Uhs	Hartford
29	377	Manitowoc	Manitowoc
30	363	Chippewa Falls Area	Chippewa Falls
31	357	Beloit	Beloit
32	356	Mequon-Thiensville	Mequon
33	352	Marshfield	Marshfield
34	347	Sun Prairie Area	Sun Prairie
35	342	Kettle Moraine	Wales
36	338	Superior	Superior
37	329	Franklin Public	Franklin
38	321	Oconomowoc Area	Oconomowoc
39	314	Hudson	Hudson
40	307	Antigo	Antigo
41	299	Beaver Dam	Beaver Dam
41	299	Muskego-Norway	Muskego
43	288	Watertown	Watertown
44	280	Hamilton	Sussex
44	280	Verona Area	Verona
46	275	Menomonee Falls	Menomonee Fls
47	271	Germantown	Germantown
47	271	Howard-Suamico	Green Bay
49	260	Ashwaubenon	Green Bay
50	258	Menomonie Area	Menomonie
50	258	Merrill Area	Merrill
52	254	Stoughton Area	Stoughton
53	252	South Milwaukee	S Milwaukee
54	248	Burlington Area	Burlington
55	246	Kaukauna Area	Kaukauna
56	236	Menasha	Menasha
57	234	Greenfield	Greenfield
57	234	Rhinelander	Rhinelander
59	232	Pulaski Community	Pulaski
60	231	De Pere	De Pere
61	228	Holmen	Holmen
61	228	Onalaska	Onalaska
61	228	Oregon	Oregon
64	225	Tomah Area	Tomah
65	222	Cedarburg	Cedarburg
66	220	Rice Lake Area	Rice Lake
67	219	Fort Atkinson	Fort Atkinson
67	219	Medford Area	Medford
69	217	River Falls	River Falls
70	214	Baraboo	Baraboo
70	214	Marinette	Marinette
72	211	Whitefish Bay	Whitefish Bay
73	207	Delavan-Darien	Delavan
74	206	Sparta Area	Sparta
74	206	Whitnall	Greenfield
76	203	Cudahy	Cudahy
77	202	Plymouth	Plymouth
78	200	De Forest Area	De Forest
79	199	Milton	Milton
80	190	Monroe	Monroe
80	190	Seymour Community	Seymour
82	189	New Richmond	New Richmond
82	189	Slinger	Slinger
84	188	Waunakee Community	Waunakee
85	187	Shawano-Gresham	Shawano
86	186	New London	New London
86	186	Port Washington-Saukville	Pt Washington
88	185	Grafton	Grafton
89	184	Waupun	Waupun
90	183	Waupaca	Waupaca
91	181	Elkhorn Area	Elkhorn
91	181	Kimberly Area	Kimberly
93	180	Greendale	Greendale
94	179	Shorewood	Shorewood
95	178	Monona Grove	Monona
96	177	Hortonville	Hortonville
97	173	Reedsburg	Reedsburg
98	172	Ashland	Ashland
99	170	Portage Community	Portage
100	165	Luxemburg-Casco	Luxemburg
100	165	Two Rivers	Two Rivers
102	162	Adams-Friendship Area	Friendship
103	159	Sauk Prairie	Sauk City
104	158	Mosinee	Mosinee
105	156	Ellsworth Community	Ellsworth
106	153	Mcfarland	Mc Farland
106	153	Spooner	Spooner
108	149	Black River Falls	Black River Fls
109	147	Amery	Amery
109	147	Freedom Area	Freedom
111	146	Platteville	Platteville
112	145	East Troy Community	East Troy
113	144	Kewaskum	Kewaskum
113	144	Whitewater	Whitewater
115	143	Berlin Area	Berlin
115	143	Richland	Richland Ctr
117	139	Osceola	Osceola
118	137	Edgerton	Edgerton
119	136	Oconto Falls	Oconto Falls
119	136	Tomahawk	Tomahawk
121	134	West De Pere	De Pere
122	133	Sheboygan Falls	Sheboygan Fls
123	132	Ripon	Ripon
124	131	Denmark	Denmark
125	130	Campbellsport	Campbellsport
126	127	Brown Deer	Brown Deer
126	127	Little Chute Area	Little Chute
126	127	Pewaukee	Pewaukee
126	127	Winneconne Community	Winneconne
130	126	Mount Horeb Area	Mount Horeb
131	120	Wautoma Area	Wautoma
132	118	Wisconsin Dells	Wisconsin Dells
133	116	Mauston	Mauston
133	116	Northland Pines	Eagle River
135	114	Lodi	Lodi
136	110	West Salem	West Salem
137	109	Hayward Community	Hayward
138	108	Clintonville	Clintonville
139	101	Jefferson	Jefferson
140	95	Nekoosa	Nekoosa
141	94	Evansville Community	Evansville
142	n/a	Hartford J1	Hartford
142	n/a	Lake Geneva J1	Lake Geneva

High School Drop-out Rate

Rank	Percent	District Name	City
1	10.5	Milwaukee	Milwaukee
2	4.9	Racine	Racine
3	4.2	Superior	Superior
4	4.1	Baraboo	Baraboo
4	4.1	Mauston	Mauston
6	3.8	Sheboygan Area	Sheboygan
7	3.7	Beloit	Beloit
8	3.5	Madison Metropolitan	Madison
8	3.5	Manitowoc	Manitowoc
10	3.4	Reedsburg	Reedsburg
11	3.2	Delavan-Darien	Delavan
12	3.0	Janesville	Janesville
13	2.9	Green Bay Area	Green Bay
14	2.8	Rhinelander	Rhinelander
15	2.6	Whitewater	Whitewater
16	2.5	Chippewa Falls Area	Chippewa Falls
16	2.5	Kewaskum	Kewaskum

16	2.5	Menomonie Area	Menomonie
19	2.4	Hartford Uhs	Hartford
19	2.4	Menasha	Menasha
21	2.3	Fort Atkinson	Fort Atkinson
21	2.3	Shawano-Gresham	Shawano
23	2.2	Evansville Community	Evansville
23	2.2	Neenah	Neenah
25	2.1	Kenosha	Kenosha
26	2.0	Fond Du Lac	Fond Du Lac
26	2.0	Jefferson	Jefferson
26	2.0	Port Washington-Saukville	Pt Washington
26	2.0	Rice Lake Area	Rice Lake
30	1.9	Black River Falls	Black River Fls
30	1.9	Sauk Prairie	Sauk City
32	1.8	Merrill Area	Merrill
32	1.8	South Milwaukee	S Milwaukee
32	1.8	Stevens Point Area	Stevens Point
35	1.7	Howard-Suamico	Green Bay
35	1.7	Sparta Area	Sparta
37	1.6	Adams-Friendship Area	Friendship
37	1.6	Nekoosa	Nekoosa
37	1.6	Spooner	Spooner
40	1.5	Hayward Community	Hayward
40	1.5	Sun Prairie Area	Sun Prairie
42	1.4	Cudahy	Cudahy
42	1.4	Oak Creek-Franklin	Oak Creek
42	1.4	Slinger	Slinger
42	1.4	Two Rivers	Two Rivers
42	1.4	Waupun	Waupun
42	1.4	West Allis	West Allis
48	1.3	East Troy Community	East Troy
48	1.3	Elkhorn Area	Elkhorn
48	1.3	Kaukauna Area	Kaukauna
48	1.3	La Crosse	La Crosse
48	1.3	Milton	Milton
48	1.3	Monroe	Monroe
48	1.3	Onalaska	Onalaska
48	1.3	Watertown	Watertown
56	1.2	Burlington Area	Burlington
56	1.2	Middleton-Cross Plains	Middleton
56	1.2	Northland Pines	Eagle River
56	1.2	Plymouth	Plymouth
60	1.1	Denmark	Denmark
60	1.1	Edgerton	Edgerton
60	1.1	Marinette	Marinette
60	1.1	Oshkosh Area	Oshkosh
60	1.1	Sheboygan Falls	Sheboygan Fls
60	1.1	Wausau	Wausau
66	1.0	Antigo	Antigo
66	1.0	Beaver Dam	Beaver Dam
66	1.0	Clintonville	Clintonville
66	1.0	Lodi	Lodi
70	0.9	Appleton Area	Appleton
70	0.9	Campbellsport	Campbellsport
70	0.9	Greenfield	Greenfield
70	0.9	Holmen	Holmen
70	0.9	Mcfarland	Mc Farland
70	0.9	River Falls	River Falls
70	0.9	Waupaca	Waupaca
70	0.9	Winneconne Community	Winneconne
78	0.8	D C Everest Area	Weston
78	0.8	De Pere	De Pere
78	0.8	Germantown	Germantown
78	0.8	Marshfield	Marshfield
78	0.8	Wisconsin Dells	Wisconsin Dells
78	0.8	Wisconsin Rapids	Wis Rapids
84	0.7	Ashwaubenon	Green Bay
84	0.7	Greendale	Greendale
84	0.7	Little Chute Area	Little Chute
84	0.7	Monona Grove	Monona
84	0.7	Oconomowoc Area	Oconomowoc
84	0.7	Platteville	Platteville
90	0.6	Eau Claire Area	Eau Claire
90	0.6	Freedom Area	Freedom
90	0.6	Luxemburg-Casco	Luxemburg
90	0.6	Pewaukee	Pewaukee
94	0.5	Arrowhead Uhs	Hartland
94	0.5	Grafton	Grafton
94	0.5	Oregon	Oregon
94	0.5	Osceola	Osceola
94	0.5	Stoughton Area	Stoughton
94	0.5	West Bend	West Bend
100	0.4	De Forest Area	De Forest
100	0.4	Mequon-Thiensville	Mequon
100	0.4	Mukwonago	Mukwonago
100	0.4	New Richmond	New Richmond
100	0.4	Tomah Area	Tomah
100	0.4	Wautoma Area	Wautoma
100	0.4	West Salem	West Salem
107	0.3	Cedarburg	Cedarburg
107	0.3	Hamilton	Sussex
107	0.3	Kettle Moraine	Wales
107	0.3	Medford Area	Medford
107	0.3	Muskego-Norway	Muskego
107	0.3	New Berlin	New Berlin
107	0.3	Portage Community	Portage
107	0.3	Richland	Richland Ctr
107	0.3	Tomahawk	Tomahawk
107	0.3	Waukesha	Waukesha
107	0.3	Wauwatosa	Wauwatosa
107	0.3	West De Pere	De Pere
119	0.2	Berlin Area	Berlin
119	0.2	Elmbrook	Brookfield
119	0.2	Hudson	Hudson
119	0.2	Kimberly Area	Kimberly
119	0.2	Pulaski Community	Pulaski
119	0.2	Ripon	Ripon
119	0.2	Whitefish Bay	Whitefish Bay
126	0.1	Ellsworth Community	Ellsworth
126	0.1	Franklin Public	Franklin
126	0.1	Menomonee Falls	Menomonee Fls
126	0.1	Mosinee	Mosinee
126	0.1	Seymour Community	Seymour
131	n/a	Amery	Amery
131	n/a	Ashland	Ashland
131	n/a	Brown Deer	Brown Deer
131	n/a	Hartford J1	Hartford
131	n/a	Hortonville	Hortonville
131	n/a	Lake Geneva J1	Lake Geneva
131	n/a	Mount Horeb Area	Mount Horeb
131	n/a	New London	New London
131	n/a	Oconto Falls	Oconto Falls
131	n/a	Shorewood	Shorewood
131	n/a	Verona Area	Verona
131	n/a	Waunakee Community	Waunakee
131	n/a	Whitnall	Greenfield

Wyoming

Wyoming Public School Educational Profile

Category	Value	Category	Value
Schools *(2002-2003)*	389	**Diploma Recipients** *(2002-2003)*	6,106
Instructional Level		White, Non-Hispanic	5,569
Primary	216	Black, Non-Hispanic	60
Middle	78	Asian/Pacific Islander	51
High	77	American Indian/Alaskan Native	102
Other Level	18	Hispanic	324
Curriculum		**High School Drop-out Rate** (%) *(2000-2001)*	6.4
Regular	362	White, Non-Hispanic	5.8
Special Education	0	Black, Non-Hispanic	16.9
Vocational	0	Asian/Pacific Islander	5.4
Alternative	27	American Indian/Alaskan Native	14.1
Type		Hispanic	11.6
Magnet	0	**Staff** *(2002-2003)*	13,736.2
Charter	1	Teachers	6,693.7
Title I Eligible	183	Average Salary ($)	37,789
School-wide Title I	53	Librarians/Media Specialists	134.5
Students *(2002-2003)*	86,448	Guidance Counselors	398.5
Gender (%)		**Ratios** *(2002-2003)*	
Male	51.8	Student/Teacher Ratio	12.9 to 1
Female	48.2	Student/Librarian Ratio	642.7 to 1
Race/Ethnicity (%)		Student/Counselor Ratio	216.9 to 1
White, Non-Hispanic	86.7	**Current Spending** *($ per student in FY 2001)*	8,645
Black, Non-Hispanic	1.3	Instruction	5,263
Asian/Pacific Islander	0.9	Support Services	3,096
American Indian/Alaskan Native	3.3	**College Entrance Exam Scores** *(2003)*	
Hispanic	7.7	Scholastic Aptitude Test (SAT)	
Classification (%)		Participation Rate (%)	11
Individual Education Program (IEP)	13.4	Mean SAT I Verbal Score	548
Migrant	0.2	Mean SAT I Math Score	549
English Language Learner (ELL)	4.1	American College Testing Program (ACT)	
Eligible for Free Lunch Program	20.8	Participation Rate (%)	62
Eligible for Reduced-Price Lunch Program	9.2	Average Composite Score	21.4

Note: *For an explanation of data, please refer to the User's Guide in the front of the book; n/a indicates data not available*

Wyoming NAEP 2003 Test Scores

Reading			Mathematics		
Grade/Category	Value	Rank	Grade/Category	Value	Rank
4th Grade			**4th Grade**		
Average Proficiency	222.1 (0.8)	16/51	Average Proficiency	241.1 (0.6)	7/51
Proficiency by Gender/Race/Ethnicity			Proficiency by Gender/Race/Ethnicity		
Male	219.0 (1.3)	12/51	Male	242.4 (0.7)	8/51
Female	225.3 (1.0)	18/51	Female	239.7 (0.8)	6/51
White, Non-Hispanic	224.4 (0.8)	31/51	White, Non-Hispanic	243.2 (0.6)	19/51
Black, Non-Hispanic	n/a	n/a	Black, Non-Hispanic	n/a	n/a
Asian, Non-Hispanic	213.6 (2.5)	2/41	Asian, Non-Hispanic	229.2 (1.7)	8/43
American Indian, Non-Hispanic	n/a	n/a	American Indian, Non-Hispanic	n/a	n/a
Hispanic	189.0 (3.5)	9/12	Hispanic	221.2 (2.6)	4/12
Proficiency by Class Size			Proficiency by Class Size		
Less than 16 Students	222.9 (2.7)	1/45	Less than 16 Students	239.8 (1.3)	2/47
16 to 18 Students	220.7 (1.5)	15/48	16 to 18 Students	237.2 (1.1)	14/48
19 to 20 Students	222.7 (1.5)	12/50	19 to 20 Students	241.5 (1.0)	6/50
21 to 25 Students	222.0 (1.5)	22/51	21 to 25 Students	242.8 (0.8)	7/51
Greater than 25 Students	224.8 (4.1)	8/49	Greater than 25 Students	244.3 (3.4)	3/49
Percent Attaining Achievement Levels			Percent Attaining Achievement Levels		
Below Basic	31.4 (1.3)	36/51	Below Basic	12.9 (0.8)	50/51
Basic or Above	68.6 (1.3)	15/51	Basic or Above	87.1 (0.8)	2/51
Proficient or Above	33.7 (1.1)	15/51	Proficient or Above	38.8 (1.1)	8/51
Advanced or Above	7.5 (0.7)	20/51	Advanced or Above	3.5 (0.4)	24/51
8th Grade			**8th Grade**		
Average Proficiency	267.0 (0.5)	15/51	Average Proficiency	283.5 (0.7)	12/51
Proficiency by Gender/Race/Ethnicity			Proficiency by Gender/Race/Ethnicity		
Male	262.3 (1.0)	12/51	Male	283.8 (0.9)	12/51
Female	272.2 (0.9)	16/51	Female	283.1 (1.0)	10/51
White, Non-Hispanic	269.1 (0.5)	26/50	White, Non-Hispanic	285.8 (0.7)	27/50
Black, Non-Hispanic	n/a	n/a	Black, Non-Hispanic	n/a	n/a
Asian, Non-Hispanic	255.0 (2.7)	6/37	Asian, Non-Hispanic	265.3 (2.2)	5/37
American Indian, Non-Hispanic	n/a	n/a	American Indian, Non-Hispanic	n/a	n/a
Hispanic	242.4 (3.3)	6/10	Hispanic	261.1 (4.1)	4/11
Proficiency by Parents Highest Level of Ed.			Proficiency by Parents Highest Level of Ed.		
Did Not Finish High School	246.8 (3.5)	24/50	Did Not Finish High School	269.4 (2.6)	1/50
Graduated High School	259.7 (1.5)	11/50	Graduated High School	276.8 (1.5)	4/50
Some Education After High School	270.6 (1.4)	15/50	Some Education After High School	284.4 (1.2)	10/50
Graduated College	274.0 (1.0)	21/50	Graduated College	291.1 (1.0)	19/50
Percent Attaining Achievement Levels			Percent Attaining Achievement Levels		
Below Basic	20.8 (0.9)	42/51	Below Basic	23.3 (1.0)	45/51
Basic or Above	79.2 (0.9)	10/51	Basic or Above	76.7 (1.0)	7/51
Proficient or Above	33.7 (1.1)	21/51	Proficient or Above	32.3 (1.0)	14/51
Advanced or Above	2.1 (0.2)	33/51	Advanced or Above	4.4 (0.5)	30/51

Note: *For an explanation of data, please refer to the User's Guide in the front of the book; values in italics indicate that the nature of the sample does not allow accurate determination of the variability of the statistic; n/a indicates data not available*

Albany County

Albany County SD #1

1948 Grand Ave • Laramie, WY 82070-4317
(307) 721-4400 • http://sage.ac1.k12.wy.us
Grade Span: KG-12; **Agency Type:** 1
Schools: 20
14 Primary; 2 Middle; 3 High; 1 Other Level
19 Regular; 0 Special Education; 0 Vocational; 1 Alternative
0 Magnet; 1 Charter; 7 Title I Eligible; 1 School-wide Title I
Students: 3,659 (53.1% male; 46.9% female)
Individual Education Program: 590 (16.1%);
English Language Learner: 16 (0.4%); Migrant: 0 (0.0%)
Eligible for Free Lunch Program: 635 (17.4%)
Eligible for Reduced-Price Lunch Program: 305 (8.3%)
Teachers: 316.9 (11.5 to 1)
Librarians/Media Specialists: 6.1 (599.8 to 1)
Guidance Counselors: 22.4 (163.3 to 1)
Current Spending: ($ per student per year):
Total: $7,700; Instruction: $4,672; Support Services: $2,739

Enrollment, Drop-out Rates and Diploma Recipients by Race/Ethnicity

Category	Total	White	Black	Asian	AIAN	Hisp.
Enrollment (%)	100.0	83.0	2.3	2.1	1.4	11.2
Drop-out Rate (%)	6.5	5.8	10.0	0.0	26.7	12.0
H.S. Diplomas (#)	277	242	4	2	6	23

Campbell County

Campbell County SD #1

1000 W 8th St • Gillette, WY 82717-3033
Mailing Address: PO Box 3033 • Gillette, WY 82717-3033
(307) 682-5171 • http://www.ccsd.k12.wy.us
Grade Span: KG-12; **Agency Type:** 1
Schools: 20
15 Primary; 2 Middle; 3 High; 0 Other Level
19 Regular; 0 Special Education; 0 Vocational; 1 Alternative
0 Magnet; 0 Charter; 10 Title I Eligible; 1 School-wide Title I
Students: 7,368 (51.8% male; 48.2% female)
Individual Education Program: 747 (10.1%);
English Language Learner: 165 (2.2%); Migrant: 0 (0.0%)
Eligible for Free Lunch Program: 964 (13.1%)
Eligible for Reduced-Price Lunch Program: 567 (7.7%)
Teachers: 540.8 (13.6 to 1)
Librarians/Media Specialists: 12.0 (614.0 to 1)
Guidance Counselors: 31.0 (237.7 to 1)
Current Spending: ($ per student per year):
Total: $7,495; Instruction: $4,238; Support Services: $2,998

Enrollment, Drop-out Rates and Diploma Recipients by Race/Ethnicity

Category	Total	White	Black	Asian	AIAN	Hisp.
Enrollment (%)	100.0	93.7	0.3	0.6	1.6	3.7
Drop-out Rate (%)	5.1	4.9	100.0	12.5	0.0	11.6
H.S. Diplomas (#)	534	515	0	2	4	13

Carbon County

Carbon County SD #1

615 Rodeo St • Rawlins, WY 82301-0160
Mailing Address: PO Box 160 • Rawlins, WY 82301-0160
(307) 328-9200
Grade Span: KG-12; **Agency Type:** 1
Schools: 9
5 Primary; 1 Middle; 2 High; 1 Other Level
7 Regular; 0 Special Education; 0 Vocational; 2 Alternative
0 Magnet; 0 Charter; 4 Title I Eligible; 3 School-wide Title I
Students: 1,778 (51.3% male; 48.7% female)
Individual Education Program: 254 (14.3%);
English Language Learner: 17 (1.0%); Migrant: 0 (0.0%)
Eligible for Free Lunch Program: 366 (20.6%)
Eligible for Reduced-Price Lunch Program: 112 (6.3%)
Teachers: 132.3 (13.4 to 1)
Librarians/Media Specialists: 3.0 (592.7 to 1)
Guidance Counselors: 5.7 (311.9 to 1)
Current Spending: ($ per student per year):
Total: $8,863; Instruction: $5,553; Support Services: $3,058

Enrollment, Drop-out Rates and Diploma Recipients by Race/Ethnicity

Category	Total	White	Black	Asian	AIAN	Hisp.
Enrollment (%)	100.0	76.7	1.0	1.1	0.8	20.5
Drop-out Rate (%)	7.5	4.7	0.0	6.7	50.0	18.4
H.S. Diplomas (#)	164	126	0	7	1	30

Converse County

Converse County SD #1

615 Hamilton St • Douglas, WY 82633-2615
(307) 358-2942 • http://www.ccsd1.k12.wy.us/
Grade Span: KG-12; **Agency Type:** 1
Schools: 8
6 Primary; 1 Middle; 1 High; 0 Other Level
8 Regular; 0 Special Education; 0 Vocational; 0 Alternative
0 Magnet; 0 Charter; 4 Title I Eligible; 0 School-wide Title I
Students: 1,688 (51.8% male; 48.2% female)
Individual Education Program: 228 (13.5%);
English Language Learner: 19 (1.1%); Migrant: 0 (0.0%)
Eligible for Free Lunch Program: 327 (19.4%)
Eligible for Reduced-Price Lunch Program: 139 (8.2%)
Teachers: 130.5 (12.9 to 1)
Librarians/Media Specialists: 3.0 (562.7 to 1)
Guidance Counselors: 7.0 (241.1 to 1)
Current Spending: ($ per student per year):
Total: $7,807; Instruction: $5,020; Support Services: $2,487

Enrollment, Drop-out Rates and Diploma Recipients by Race/Ethnicity

Category	Total	White	Black	Asian	AIAN	Hisp.
Enrollment (%)	100.0	90.4	0.6	0.8	1.0	7.2
Drop-out Rate (%)	5.7	5.9	n/a	0.0	0.0	3.2
H.S. Diplomas (#)	118	110	1	0	1	6

Fremont County

Fremont County SD #1

400 Baldwin Creek Rd • Lander, WY 82520
(307) 332-4711 • http://www.fre1.k12.wy.us
Grade Span: KG-12; **Agency Type:** 1
Schools: 8
5 Primary; 1 Middle; 2 High; 0 Other Level
7 Regular; 0 Special Education; 0 Vocational; 1 Alternative
0 Magnet; 0 Charter; 3 Title I Eligible; 2 School-wide Title I
Students: 1,877 (52.7% male; 47.3% female)
Individual Education Program: 261 (13.9%);
English Language Learner: 297 (15.8%); Migrant: 0 (0.0%)
Eligible for Free Lunch Program: 428 (22.8%)
Eligible for Reduced-Price Lunch Program: 145 (7.7%)
Teachers: 111.5 (16.8 to 1)
Librarians/Media Specialists: 4.0 (469.3 to 1)
Guidance Counselors: 9.0 (208.6 to 1)
Current Spending: ($ per student per year):
Total: $7,173; Instruction: $4,692; Support Services: $2,334

Enrollment, Drop-out Rates and Diploma Recipients by Race/Ethnicity

Category	Total	White	Black	Asian	AIAN	Hisp.
Enrollment (%)	100.0	79.0	0.6	1.2	15.6	3.6
Drop-out Rate (%)	9.3	8.3	n/a	50.0	12.6	5.0
H.S. Diplomas (#)	144	117	0	0	25	2

Fremont County SD #25

121 N 5th St W • Riverton, WY 82501-9407
(307) 856-9407 • http://www.fremont25.k12.wy.us/
Grade Span: KG-12; **Agency Type:** 1
Schools: 6
3 Primary; 2 Middle; 1 High; 0 Other Level
6 Regular; 0 Special Education; 0 Vocational; 0 Alternative
0 Magnet; 0 Charter; 4 Title I Eligible; 1 School-wide Title I
Students: 2,471 (50.4% male; 49.6% female)
Individual Education Program: 386 (15.6%);
English Language Learner: 400 (16.2%); Migrant: 0 (0.0%)
Eligible for Free Lunch Program: 703 (28.5%)
Eligible for Reduced-Price Lunch Program: 271 (11.0%)
Teachers: 178.8 (13.8 to 1)
Librarians/Media Specialists: 2.0 (1,235.5 to 1)
Guidance Counselors: 14.0 (176.5 to 1)
Current Spending: ($ per student per year):
Total: $7,795; Instruction: $4,808; Support Services: $2,730

Enrollment, Drop-out Rates and Diploma Recipients by Race/Ethnicity

Category	Total	White	Black	Asian	AIAN	Hisp.
Enrollment (%)	100.0	79.3	0.6	0.4	13.4	6.3
Drop-out Rate (%)	7.0	5.6	n/a	25.0	17.7	3.2
H.S. Diplomas (#)	176	154	0	2	10	10

Goshen County

Goshen County SD #1

2602 W E St • Torrington, WY 82240-1821
(307) 532-2171 • http://www.goshen.k12.wy.us
Grade Span: KG-12; **Agency Type:** 1
Schools: 12
6 Primary; 3 Middle; 3 High; 0 Other Level
12 Regular; 0 Special Education; 0 Vocational; 0 Alternative

0 Magnet; 0 Charter; 5 Title I Eligible; 5 School-wide Title I

Students: 1,889 (51.0% male; 49.0% female)
Individual Education Program: 277 (14.7%);
English Language Learner: 65 (3.4%); Migrant: 119 (6.3%)
Eligible for Free Lunch Program: 616 (32.6%)
Eligible for Reduced-Price Lunch Program: 264 (14.0%)

Teachers: 169.5 (11.1 to 1)
Librarians/Media Specialists: 4.2 (449.8 to 1)
Guidance Counselors: 9.0 (209.9 to 1)
Current Spending: ($ per student per year):
Total: $8,115; Instruction: $5,059; Support Services: $2,819

Enrollment, Drop-out Rates and Diploma Recipients by Race/Ethnicity

Category	Total	White	Black	Asian	AIAN	Hisp.
Enrollment (%)	100.0	84.3	0.1	0.2	1.2	14.3
Drop-out Rate (%)	3.3	2.9	n/a	0.0	25.0	4.4
H.S. Diplomas (#)	138	123	1	2	1	11

Laramie County

Laramie County SD #1

2810 House Ave • Cheyenne, WY 82001-2860
(307) 771-2100 • http://www.laramie1.k12.wy.us
Grade Span: KG-12; **Agency Type:** 1
Schools: 32
25 Primary; 4 Middle; 3 High; 0 Other Level
31 Regular; 0 Special Education; 0 Vocational; 1 Alternative
0 Magnet; 0 Charter; 12 Title I Eligible; 11 School-wide Title I

Students: 13,101 (51.3% male; 48.7% female)
Individual Education Program: 1,521 (11.6%);
English Language Learner: 543 (4.1%); Migrant: 0 (0.0%)
Eligible for Free Lunch Program: 2,641 (20.2%)
Eligible for Reduced-Price Lunch Program: 1,233 (9.4%)

Teachers: 885.3 (14.8 to 1)
Librarians/Media Specialists: 10.0 (1,310.1 to 1)
Guidance Counselors: 53.6 (244.4 to 1)
Current Spending: ($ per student per year):
Total: $6,804; Instruction: $4,355; Support Services: $2,223

Enrollment, Drop-out Rates and Diploma Recipients by Race/Ethnicity

Category	Total	White	Black	Asian	AIAN	Hisp.
Enrollment (%)	100.0	78.6	4.4	1.7	1.3	14.0
Drop-out Rate (%)	5.2	4.8	15.9	3.4	5.4	5.2
H.S. Diplomas (#)	783	653	36	9	4	81

Lincoln County

Lincoln County SD #2

222 E 4th Ave • Afton, WY 83110-0219
Mailing Address: PO Box 219 • Afton, WY 83110-0219
(307) 885-3811 • http://www.lcsd2.org
Grade Span: KG-12; **Agency Type:** 1
Schools: 9
3 Primary; 3 Middle; 3 High; 0 Other Level
8 Regular; 0 Special Education; 0 Vocational; 1 Alternative
0 Magnet; 0 Charter; 5 Title I Eligible; 1 School-wide Title I

Students: 2,403 (50.9% male; 49.1% female)
Individual Education Program: 260 (10.8%);
English Language Learner: 13 (0.5%); Migrant: 0 (0.0%)
Eligible for Free Lunch Program: 397 (16.5%)
Eligible for Reduced-Price Lunch Program: 362 (15.1%)

Teachers: 154.6 (15.5 to 1)
Librarians/Media Specialists: 2.9 (828.6 to 1)
Guidance Counselors: 5.0 (480.6 to 1)
Current Spending: ($ per student per year):
Total: $6,817; Instruction: $4,263; Support Services: $2,288

Enrollment, Drop-out Rates and Diploma Recipients by Race/Ethnicity

Category	Total	White	Black	Asian	AIAN	Hisp.
Enrollment (%)	100.0	97.0	0.1	0.8	0.5	1.5
Drop-out Rate (%)	4.4	4.2	0.0	n/a	0.0	28.6
H.S. Diplomas (#)	179	175	0	2	0	2

Natrona County

Natrona County SD #1

970 N Glenn Rd • Casper, WY 82601-1635
(307) 577-0200 • http://www.trib.com/WYOMING/NCSD/
Grade Span: KG-12; **Agency Type:** 1
Schools: 38
29 Primary; 5 Middle; 3 High; 1 Other Level
38 Regular; 0 Special Education; 0 Vocational; 0 Alternative
0 Magnet; 0 Charter; 12 Title I Eligible; 12 School-wide Title I

Students: 11,652 (51.9% male; 48.1% female)
Individual Education Program: 1,672 (14.3%);
English Language Learner: 27 (0.2%); Migrant: 0 (0.0%)
Eligible for Free Lunch Program: 2,630 (22.6%)
Eligible for Reduced-Price Lunch Program: 1,017 (8.7%)

Teachers: 803.7 (14.5 to 1)
Librarians/Media Specialists: 8.0 (1,456.5 to 1)
Guidance Counselors: 48.0 (242.8 to 1)
Current Spending: ($ per student per year):
Total: $7,271; Instruction: $4,619; Support Services: $2,434

Enrollment, Drop-out Rates and Diploma Recipients by Race/Ethnicity

Category	Total	White	Black	Asian	AIAN	Hisp.
Enrollment (%)	100.0	91.0	1.7	0.8	1.1	5.4
Drop-out Rate (%)	10.9	10.3	15.4	13.0	16.1	21.1
H.S. Diplomas (#)	733	693	8	5	2	25

Park County

Park County SD #1

160 N Evarts • Powell, WY 82435-2730
(307) 754-2215
Grade Span: KG-12; **Agency Type:** 1
Schools: 7
4 Primary; 1 Middle; 2 High; 0 Other Level
6 Regular; 0 Special Education; 0 Vocational; 1 Alternative
0 Magnet; 0 Charter; 4 Title I Eligible; 0 School-wide Title I

Students: 1,608 (49.8% male; 50.2% female)
Individual Education Program: 164 (10.2%);
English Language Learner: 16 (1.0%); Migrant: 9 (0.6%)
Eligible for Free Lunch Program: 340 (21.1%)
Eligible for Reduced-Price Lunch Program: 162 (10.1%)

Teachers: 114.3 (14.1 to 1)
Librarians/Media Specialists: 3.0 (536.0 to 1)
Guidance Counselors: 7.0 (229.7 to 1)
Current Spending: ($ per student per year):
Total: $6,683; Instruction: $3,741; Support Services: $2,724

Enrollment, Drop-out Rates and Diploma Recipients by Race/Ethnicity

Category	Total	White	Black	Asian	AIAN	Hisp.
Enrollment (%)	100.0	90.2	0.2	0.6	0.3	8.6
Drop-out Rate (%)	3.5	3.4	n/a	14.3	n/a	2.6
H.S. Diplomas (#)	122	110	0	0	0	12

Park County SD #6

919 Cody Ave • Cody, WY 82414-4115
(307) 587-4253 • http://www.park6.org/
Grade Span: KG-12; **Agency Type:** 1
Schools: 7
5 Primary; 1 Middle; 1 High; 0 Other Level
7 Regular; 0 Special Education; 0 Vocational; 0 Alternative
0 Magnet; 0 Charter; 2 Title I Eligible; 0 School-wide Title I

Students: 2,305 (51.2% male; 48.8% female)
Individual Education Program: 228 (9.9%);
English Language Learner: 3 (0.1%); Migrant: 0 (0.0%)
Eligible for Free Lunch Program: 275 (11.9%)
Eligible for Reduced-Price Lunch Program: 144 (6.2%)

Teachers: 167.0 (13.8 to 1)
Librarians/Media Specialists: 5.0 (461.0 to 1)
Guidance Counselors: 11.0 (209.5 to 1)
Current Spending: ($ per student per year):
Total: $6,932; Instruction: $4,096; Support Services: $2,684

Enrollment, Drop-out Rates and Diploma Recipients by Race/Ethnicity

Category	Total	White	Black	Asian	AIAN	Hisp.
Enrollment (%)	100.0	95.7	0.3	1.0	0.3	2.7
Drop-out Rate (%)	3.0	2.9	100.0	0.0	0.0	6.7
H.S. Diplomas (#)	196	190	0	1	1	4

Sheridan County

Sheridan County SD #2

620 Adair Avenue, 3rd Floor • Sheridan, WY 82801-0919
Mailing Address: PO Box 919 • Sheridan, WY 82801-0919
(307) 674-7405 • http://web.sheridan2.k12.wy.us
Grade Span: KG-12; **Agency Type:** 1
Schools: 12
7 Primary; 2 Middle; 2 High; 1 Other Level
10 Regular; 0 Special Education; 0 Vocational; 2 Alternative
0 Magnet; 0 Charter; 7 Title I Eligible; 3 School-wide Title I

Students: 3,172 (50.9% male; 49.1% female)
Individual Education Program: 404 (12.7%);
English Language Learner: 10 (0.3%); Migrant: 0 (0.0%)
Eligible for Free Lunch Program: 658 (20.7%)
Eligible for Reduced-Price Lunch Program: 337 (10.6%)

Teachers: 267.8 (11.8 to 1)
Librarians/Media Specialists: 3.0 (1,057.3 to 1)
Guidance Counselors: 16.0 (198.3 to 1)
Current Spending: ($ per student per year):
Total: $7,428; Instruction: $4,775; Support Services: $2,418

Enrollment, Drop-out Rates and Diploma Recipients by Race/Ethnicity

Category	Total	White	Black	Asian	AIAN	Hisp.
Enrollment (%)	100.0	92.4	0.6	1.4	1.8	3.8
Drop-out Rate (%)	6.5	6.2	33.3	5.9	22.2	0.0
H.S. Diplomas (#)	232	216	3	6	5	2

Sweetwater County

Sweetwater County SD #1

3550 Foothill Blvd • Rock Springs, WY 82902-1089
Mailing Address: PO Box 1089 • Rock Springs, WY 82902-1089
(307) 352-3400 • http://www.sw1.k12.wy.us/
Grade Span: KG-12; **Agency Type:** 1
Schools: 20
12 Primary; 5 Middle; 3 High; 0 Other Level
18 Regular; 0 Special Education; 0 Vocational; 2 Alternative
0 Magnet; 0 Charter; 7 Title I Eligible; 0 School-wide Title I
Students: 4,264 (51.6% male; 48.4% female)
Individual Education Program: 657 (15.4%);
English Language Learner: 66 (1.5%); Migrant: 0 (0.0%)
Eligible for Free Lunch Program: 757 (17.8%)
Eligible for Reduced-Price Lunch Program: 314 (7.4%)
Teachers: 327.3 (13.0 to 1)
Librarians/Media Specialists: 7.0 (609.1 to 1)
Guidance Counselors: 31.0 (137.5 to 1)
Current Spending: ($ per student per year):
Total: $8,023; Instruction: $4,703; Support Services: $3,083

Enrollment, Drop-out Rates and Diploma Recipients by Race/Ethnicity

Category	Total	White	Black	Asian	AIAN	Hisp.
Enrollment (%)	100.0	85.2	2.1	0.7	0.8	11.2
Drop-out Rate (%)	8.2	8.2	15.0	6.7	0.0	7.5
H.S. Diplomas (#)	270	241	3	4	0	22

Sweetwater County SD #2

320 Monroe Ave • Green River, WY 82935-4223
(307) 872-5500 • http://www.sw2.k12.wy.us/
Grade Span: KG-12; **Agency Type:** 1
Schools: 11
7 Primary; 2 Middle; 2 High; 0 Other Level
10 Regular; 0 Special Education; 0 Vocational; 1 Alternative
0 Magnet; 0 Charter; 6 Title I Eligible; 0 School-wide Title I
Students: 2,688 (52.3% male; 47.7% female)
Individual Education Program: 416 (15.5%);
English Language Learner: 36 (1.3%); Migrant: 0 (0.0%)
Eligible for Free Lunch Program: 325 (12.1%)
Eligible for Reduced-Price Lunch Program: 180 (6.7%)
Teachers: 206.5 (13.0 to 1)
Librarians/Media Specialists: 4.0 (672.0 to 1)
Guidance Counselors: 13.0 (206.8 to 1)
Current Spending: ($ per student per year):
Total: $7,936; Instruction: $4,556; Support Services: $3,141

Enrollment, Drop-out Rates and Diploma Recipients by Race/Ethnicity

Category	Total	White	Black	Asian	AIAN	Hisp.
Enrollment (%)	100.0	88.3	0.4	0.4	1.0	9.9
Drop-out Rate (%)	6.3	6.2	0.0	0.0	0.0	8.7
H.S. Diplomas (#)	212	186	1	1	1	23

Teton County

Teton County SD #1

225 S Cache • Jackson, WY 83001-0568
Mailing Address: PO Box 568 • Jackson, WY 83001-0568
(307) 733-2704 • http://www.tcsd.org
Grade Span: KG-12; **Agency Type:** 1
Schools: 8
5 Primary; 1 Middle; 2 High; 0 Other Level
7 Regular; 0 Special Education; 0 Vocational; 1 Alternative
0 Magnet; 0 Charter; 2 Title I Eligible; 0 School-wide Title I
Students: 2,248 (53.4% male; 46.6% female)
Individual Education Program: 259 (11.5%);
English Language Learner: 201 (8.9%); Migrant: 0 (0.0%)
Eligible for Free Lunch Program: 176 (7.8%)
Eligible for Reduced-Price Lunch Program: 90 (4.0%)
Teachers: 160.2 (14.0 to 1)
Librarians/Media Specialists: 3.0 (749.3 to 1)
Guidance Counselors: 8.0 (281.0 to 1)
Current Spending: ($ per student per year):
Total: $7,670; Instruction: $4,582; Support Services: $2,837

Enrollment, Drop-out Rates and Diploma Recipients by Race/Ethnicity

Category	Total	White	Black	Asian	AIAN	Hisp.
Enrollment (%)	100.0	89.0	0.1	0.7	0.0	10.1
Drop-out Rate (%)	5.8	3.6	n/a	n/a	n/a	48.6
H.S. Diplomas (#)	152	149	0	0	0	3

Uinta County

Uinta County SD #1

537 Tenth St • Evanston, WY 82931-6002
Mailing Address: PO Box 6002 • Evanston, WY 82931-6002
(307) 789-7571 • http://www.uinta1.k12.wy.us
Grade Span: KG-12; **Agency Type:** 1
Schools: 7
4 Primary; 2 Middle; 1 High; 0 Other Level
7 Regular; 0 Special Education; 0 Vocational; 0 Alternative
0 Magnet; 0 Charter; 2 Title I Eligible; 2 School-wide Title I
Students: 3,137 (51.6% male; 48.4% female)
Individual Education Program: 452 (14.4%);
English Language Learner: 54 (1.7%); Migrant: 5 (0.2%)
Eligible for Free Lunch Program: 789 (25.2%)
Eligible for Reduced-Price Lunch Program: 423 (13.5%)
Teachers: 232.4 (13.5 to 1)
Librarians/Media Specialists: 8.0 (392.1 to 1)
Guidance Counselors: 11.0 (285.2 to 1)
Current Spending: ($ per student per year):
Total: $7,400; Instruction: $4,381; Support Services: $2,708

Enrollment, Drop-out Rates and Diploma Recipients by Race/Ethnicity

Category	Total	White	Black	Asian	AIAN	Hisp.
Enrollment (%)	100.0	90.4	0.5	0.9	0.7	7.5
Drop-out Rate (%)	9.0	8.5	0.0	9.1	25.0	19.0
H.S. Diplomas (#)	215	204	0	1	1	9

Number of Schools

Rank	Number	District Name	City
1	38	Natrona County SD #1	Casper
2	32	Laramie County SD #1	Cheyenne
3	20	Albany County SD #1	Laramie
3	20	Campbell County SD #1	Gillette
3	20	Sweetwater County SD #1	Rock Springs
6	12	Goshen County SD #1	Torrington
6	12	Sheridan County SD #2	Sheridan
8	11	Sweetwater County SD #2	Green River
9	9	Carbon County SD #1	Rawlins
9	9	Lincoln County SD #2	Afton
11	8	Converse County SD #1	Douglas
11	8	Fremont County SD #1	Lander
11	8	Teton County SD #1	Jackson
14	7	Park County SD #1	Powell
14	7	Park County SD #6	Cody
14	7	Uinta County SD #1	Evanston
17	6	Fremont County SD #25	Riverton

Number of Teachers

Rank	Number	District Name	City
1	885	Laramie County SD #1	Cheyenne
2	803	Natrona County SD #1	Casper
3	540	Campbell County SD #1	Gillette
4	327	Sweetwater County SD #1	Rock Springs
5	316	Albany County SD #1	Laramie
6	267	Sheridan County SD #2	Sheridan
7	232	Uinta County SD #1	Evanston
8	206	Sweetwater County SD #2	Green River
9	178	Fremont County SD #25	Riverton
10	169	Goshen County SD #1	Torrington
11	167	Park County SD #6	Cody
12	160	Teton County SD #1	Jackson
13	154	Lincoln County SD #2	Afton
14	132	Carbon County SD #1	Rawlins
15	130	Converse County SD #1	Douglas
16	114	Park County SD #1	Powell
17	111	Fremont County SD #1	Lander

Number of Students

Rank	Number	District Name	City
1	13,101	Laramie County SD #1	Cheyenne
2	11,652	Natrona County SD #1	Casper
3	7,368	Campbell County SD #1	Gillette
4	4,264	Sweetwater County SD #1	Rock Springs
5	3,659	Albany County SD #1	Laramie
6	3,172	Sheridan County SD #2	Sheridan
7	3,137	Uinta County SD #1	Evanston
8	2,688	Sweetwater County SD #2	Green River
9	2,471	Fremont County SD #25	Riverton
10	2,403	Lincoln County SD #2	Afton
11	2,305	Park County SD #6	Cody
12	2,248	Teton County SD #1	Jackson
13	1,889	Goshen County SD #1	Torrington
14	1,877	Fremont County SD #1	Lander
15	1,778	Carbon County SD #1	Rawlins
16	1,688	Converse County SD #1	Douglas
17	1,608	Park County SD #1	Powell

Male Students

Rank	Percent	District Name	City
1	53.4	Teton County SD #1	Jackson
2	53.1	Albany County SD #1	Laramie
3	52.7	Fremont County SD #1	Lander
4	52.3	Sweetwater County SD #2	Green River
5	51.9	Natrona County SD #1	Casper
6	51.8	Campbell County SD #1	Gillette
6	51.8	Converse County SD #1	Douglas
8	51.6	Sweetwater County SD #1	Rock Springs
8	51.6	Uinta County SD #1	Evanston
10	51.3	Carbon County SD #1	Rawlins
10	51.3	Laramie County SD #1	Cheyenne
12	51.2	Park County SD #6	Cody
13	51.0	Goshen County SD #1	Torrington
14	50.9	Lincoln County SD #2	Afton
14	50.9	Sheridan County SD #2	Sheridan
16	50.4	Fremont County SD #25	Riverton
17	49.8	Park County SD #1	Powell

Female Students

Rank	Percent	District Name	City
1	50.2	Park County SD #1	Powell
2	49.6	Fremont County SD #25	Riverton
3	49.1	Lincoln County SD #2	Afton
3	49.1	Sheridan County SD #2	Sheridan
5	49.0	Goshen County SD #1	Torrington
6	48.8	Park County SD #6	Cody
7	48.7	Carbon County SD #1	Rawlins
7	48.7	Laramie County SD #1	Cheyenne
9	48.4	Sweetwater County SD #1	Rock Springs
9	48.4	Uinta County SD #1	Evanston
11	48.2	Campbell County SD #1	Gillette
11	48.2	Converse County SD #1	Douglas
13	48.1	Natrona County SD #1	Casper
14	47.7	Sweetwater County SD #2	Green River
15	47.3	Fremont County SD #1	Lander
16	46.9	Albany County SD #1	Laramie
17	46.6	Teton County SD #1	Jackson

Individual Education Program Students

Rank	Percent	District Name	City
1	16.1	Albany County SD #1	Laramie
2	15.6	Fremont County SD #25	Riverton
3	15.5	Sweetwater County SD #2	Green River
4	15.4	Sweetwater County SD #1	Rock Springs
5	14.7	Goshen County SD #1	Torrington
6	14.4	Uinta County SD #1	Evanston
7	14.3	Carbon County SD #1	Rawlins
7	14.3	Natrona County SD #1	Casper
9	13.9	Fremont County SD #1	Lander
10	13.5	Converse County SD #1	Douglas
11	12.7	Sheridan County SD #2	Sheridan
12	11.6	Laramie County SD #1	Cheyenne
13	11.5	Teton County SD #1	Jackson
14	10.8	Lincoln County SD #2	Afton
15	10.2	Park County SD #1	Powell
16	10.1	Campbell County SD #1	Gillette
17	9.9	Park County SD #6	Cody

English Language Learner Students

Rank	Percent	District Name	City
1	16.2	Fremont County SD #25	Riverton
2	15.8	Fremont County SD #1	Lander
3	8.9	Teton County SD #1	Jackson
4	4.1	Laramie County SD #1	Cheyenne
5	3.4	Goshen County SD #1	Torrington
6	2.2	Campbell County SD #1	Gillette
7	1.7	Uinta County SD #1	Evanston
8	1.5	Sweetwater County SD #1	Rock Springs
9	1.3	Sweetwater County SD #2	Green River
10	1.1	Converse County SD #1	Douglas
11	1.0	Carbon County SD #1	Rawlins
11	1.0	Park County SD #1	Powell
13	0.5	Lincoln County SD #2	Afton
14	0.4	Albany County SD #1	Laramie
15	0.3	Sheridan County SD #2	Sheridan
16	0.2	Natrona County SD #1	Casper
17	0.1	Park County SD #6	Cody

Migrant Students

Rank	Percent	District Name	City
1	6.3	Goshen County SD #1	Torrington
2	0.6	Park County SD #1	Powell
3	0.2	Uinta County SD #1	Evanston
4	0.0	Albany County SD #1	Laramie
4	0.0	Campbell County SD #1	Gillette
4	0.0	Carbon County SD #1	Rawlins
4	0.0	Converse County SD #1	Douglas
4	0.0	Fremont County SD #1	Lander
4	0.0	Fremont County SD #25	Riverton
4	0.0	Laramie County SD #1	Cheyenne
4	0.0	Lincoln County SD #2	Afton
4	0.0	Natrona County SD #1	Casper
4	0.0	Park County SD #6	Cody
4	0.0	Sheridan County SD #2	Sheridan
4	0.0	Sweetwater County SD #1	Rock Springs
4	0.0	Sweetwater County SD #2	Green River
4	0.0	Teton County SD #1	Jackson

Students Eligible for Free Lunch

Rank	Percent	District Name	City
1	32.6	Goshen County SD #1	Torrington
2	28.5	Fremont County SD #25	Riverton
3	25.2	Uinta County SD #1	Evanston
4	22.8	Fremont County SD #1	Lander
5	22.6	Natrona County SD #1	Casper
6	21.1	Park County SD #1	Powell
7	20.7	Sheridan County SD #2	Sheridan
8	20.6	Carbon County SD #1	Rawlins
9	20.2	Laramie County SD #1	Cheyenne
10	19.4	Converse County SD #1	Douglas
11	17.8	Sweetwater County SD #1	Rock Springs
12	17.4	Albany County SD #1	Laramie
13	16.5	Lincoln County SD #2	Afton
14	13.1	Campbell County SD #1	Gillette
15	12.1	Sweetwater County SD #2	Green River
16	11.9	Park County SD #6	Cody
17	7.8	Teton County SD #1	Jackson

Students Eligible for Reduced-Price Lunch

Rank	Percent	District Name	City
1	15.1	Lincoln County SD #2	Afton
2	14.0	Goshen County SD #1	Torrington
3	13.5	Uinta County SD #1	Evanston
4	11.0	Fremont County SD #25	Riverton
5	10.6	Sheridan County SD #2	Sheridan
6	10.1	Park County SD #1	Powell
7	9.4	Laramie County SD #1	Cheyenne
8	8.7	Natrona County SD #1	Casper
9	8.3	Albany County SD #1	Laramie
10	8.2	Converse County SD #1	Douglas
11	7.7	Campbell County SD #1	Gillette
11	7.7	Fremont County SD #1	Lander
13	7.4	Sweetwater County SD #1	Rock Springs
14	6.7	Sweetwater County SD #2	Green River
15	6.3	Carbon County SD #1	Rawlins
16	6.2	Park County SD #6	Cody
17	4.0	Teton County SD #1	Jackson

Student/Teacher Ratio

Rank	Ratio	District Name	City
1	16.8	Fremont County SD #1	Lander
2	15.5	Lincoln County SD #2	Afton
3	14.8	Laramie County SD #1	Cheyenne
4	14.5	Natrona County SD #1	Casper
5	14.1	Park County SD #1	Powell
6	14.0	Teton County SD #1	Jackson
7	13.8	Fremont County SD #25	Riverton
7	13.8	Park County SD #6	Cody
9	13.6	Campbell County SD #1	Gillette
10	13.5	Uinta County SD #1	Evanston
11	13.4	Carbon County SD #1	Rawlins
12	13.0	Sweetwater County SD #1	Rock Springs
12	13.0	Sweetwater County SD #2	Green River
14	12.9	Converse County SD #1	Douglas
15	11.8	Sheridan County SD #2	Sheridan
16	11.5	Albany County SD #1	Laramie
17	11.1	Goshen County SD #1	Torrington

Student/Librarian Ratio

Rank	Ratio	District Name	City
1	1,456.5	Natrona County SD #1	Casper
2	1,310.1	Laramie County SD #1	Cheyenne
3	1,235.5	Fremont County SD #25	Riverton
4	1,057.3	Sheridan County SD #2	Sheridan
5	828.6	Lincoln County SD #2	Afton
6	749.3	Teton County SD #1	Jackson
7	672.0	Sweetwater County SD #2	Green River
8	614.0	Campbell County SD #1	Gillette
9	609.1	Sweetwater County SD #1	Rock Springs
10	599.8	Albany County SD #1	Laramie
11	592.7	Carbon County SD #1	Rawlins
12	562.7	Converse County SD #1	Douglas
13	536.0	Park County SD #1	Powell
14	469.3	Fremont County SD #1	Lander
15	461.0	Park County SD #6	Cody
16	449.8	Goshen County SD #1	Torrington
17	392.1	Uinta County SD #1	Evanston

Student/Counselor Ratio

Rank	Ratio	District Name	City
1	480.6	Lincoln County SD #2	Afton
2	311.9	Carbon County SD #1	Rawlins
3	285.2	Uinta County SD #1	Evanston
4	281.0	Teton County SD #1	Jackson
5	244.4	Laramie County SD #1	Cheyenne
6	242.8	Natrona County SD #1	Casper
7	241.1	Converse County SD #1	Douglas
8	237.7	Campbell County SD #1	Gillette
9	229.7	Park County SD #1	Powell
10	209.9	Goshen County SD #1	Torrington
11	209.5	Park County SD #6	Cody
12	208.6	Fremont County SD #1	Lander
13	206.8	Sweetwater County SD #2	Green River
14	198.3	Sheridan County SD #2	Sheridan
15	176.5	Fremont County SD #25	Riverton
16	163.3	Albany County SD #1	Laramie
17	137.5	Sweetwater County SD #1	Rock Springs

Current Spending per Student in FY2001

Rank	Dollars	District Name	City
1	8,863	Carbon County SD #1	Rawlins
2	8,115	Goshen County SD #1	Torrington

3	8,023	Sweetwater County SD #1	Rock Springs
4	7,936	Sweetwater County SD #2	Green River
5	7,807	Converse County SD #1	Douglas
6	7,795	Fremont County SD #25	Riverton
7	7,700	Albany County SD #1	Laramie
8	7,670	Teton County SD #1	Jackson
9	7,495	Campbell County SD #1	Gillette
10	7,428	Sheridan County SD #2	Sheridan
11	7,400	Uinta County SD #1	Evanston
12	7,271	Natrona County SD #1	Casper
13	7,173	Fremont County SD #1	Lander
14	6,932	Park County SD #6	Cody
15	6,817	Lincoln County SD #2	Afton
16	6,804	Laramie County SD #1	Cheyenne
17	6,683	Park County SD #1	Powell

Number of Diploma Recipients

Rank	Number	District Name	City
1	783	Laramie County SD #1	Cheyenne
2	733	Natrona County SD #1	Casper
3	534	Campbell County SD #1	Gillette
4	277	Albany County SD #1	Laramie
5	270	Sweetwater County SD #1	Rock Springs
6	232	Sheridan County SD #2	Sheridan
7	215	Uinta County SD #1	Evanston
8	212	Sweetwater County SD #2	Green River
9	196	Park County SD #6	Cody
10	179	Lincoln County SD #2	Afton
11	176	Fremont County SD #25	Riverton
12	164	Carbon County SD #1	Rawlins
13	152	Teton County SD #1	Jackson
14	144	Fremont County SD #1	Lander
15	138	Goshen County SD #1	Torrington
16	122	Park County SD #1	Powell
17	118	Converse County SD #1	Douglas

High School Drop-out Rate

Rank	Percent	District Name	City
1	10.9	Natrona County SD #1	Casper
2	9.3	Fremont County SD #1	Lander
3	9.0	Uinta County SD #1	Evanston
4	8.2	Sweetwater County SD #1	Rock Springs
5	7.5	Carbon County SD #1	Rawlins
6	7.0	Fremont County SD #25	Riverton
7	6.5	Albany County SD #1	Laramie
7	6.5	Sheridan County SD #2	Sheridan
9	6.3	Sweetwater County SD #2	Green River
10	5.8	Teton County SD #1	Jackson
11	5.7	Converse County SD #1	Douglas
12	5.2	Laramie County SD #1	Cheyenne
13	5.1	Campbell County SD #1	Gillette
14	4.4	Lincoln County SD #2	Afton
15	3.5	Park County SD #1	Powell
16	3.3	Goshen County SD #1	Torrington
17	3.0	Park County SD #6	Cody

NATIONAL

National Public School Educational Profile

Category	Value	Category	Value
Schools *(2002-2003)*	95,862	**Diploma Recipients** *(2002-2003)*	2,635,272
Instructional Level		White, Non-Hispanic	1,733,938
Primary	53,207	Black, Non-Hispanic	327,277
Middle	16,069	Asian/Pacific Islander	130,925
High	18,627	American Indian/Alaskan Native	24,910
Other Level	7,959	Hispanic	305,809
Curriculum		**High School Drop-out Rate** (%) *(2000-2001)*	
Regular	86,327	White, Non-Hispanic	n/a
Special Education	2,114	Black, Non-Hispanic	n/a
Vocational	1,093	Asian/Pacific Islander	n/a
Alternative	6,328	American Indian/Alaskan Native	n/a
Type		Hispanic	n/a
Magnet	2,004	**Staff** *(2002-2003)*	5,716,262.2
Charter	2,575	Teachers	3,015,290.3
Title I Eligible	50,715	Average Salary ($)	45,771
School-wide Title I	24,400	Librarians/Media Specialists	54,197.0
Students *(2002-2003)*	48,113,207	Guidance Counselors	100,550.1
Gender (%)		**Ratios** *(2002-2003)*	
Male	51.4	Student/Teacher Ratio	16.0
Female	48.6	Student/Librarian Ratio	887.7
Race/Ethnicity (%)		Student/Counselor Ratio	478.5
White, Non-Hispanic	58.0	**Current Spending** *($ per student in FY 2001)*	7,727
Black, Non-Hispanic	16.7	Instruction	4,751
Asian/Pacific Islander	4.3	Support Services	2,654
American Indian/Alaskan Native	1.2	**College Entrance Exam Scores** *(2003)*	
Hispanic	17.7	Scholastic Aptitude Test (SAT)	
Classification (%)		Participation Rate (%)	48
Individual Education Program (IEP)	13.4	Mean SAT I Verbal Score	507
Migrant	1.2	Mean SAT I Math Score	519
English Language Learner (ELL)	8.5	American College Testing Program (ACT)	
Eligible for Free Lunch Program	28.4	Participation Rate (%)	40
Eligible for Reduced-Price Lunch Program	6.9	Average Composite Score	20.8

Note: *For an explanation of data, please refer to the User's Guide in the front of the book; n/a indicates data not available*

National Public School NAEP 2003 Test Scores

Reading		Mathematics	
Grade/Category	**Value**	**Grade/Category**	**Value**
4th Grade		**4th Grade**	
Average Proficiency	216.5 (0.3)	Average Proficiency	234.0 (0.2)
Proficiency by Gender/Race/Ethnicity		Proficiency by Gender/Race/Ethnicity	
Male	212.7 (0.3)	Male	235.3 (0.3)
Female	220.2 (0.3)	Female	232.6 (0.2)
White, Non-Hispanic	227.1 (0.2)	White, Non-Hispanic	242.7 (0.2)
Black, Non-Hispanic	197.3 (0.4)	Black, Non-Hispanic	215.8 (0.4)
Asian, Non-Hispanic	199.4 (0.6)	Asian, Non-Hispanic	221.4 (0.4)
American Indian, Non-Hispanic	224.5 (1.3)	American Indian, Non-Hispanic	246.0 (1.2)
Hispanic	201.6 (1.4)	Hispanic	224.3 (1.1)
Proficiency by Class Size		Proficiency by Class Size	
Less than 16 Students	200.4 (1.2)	Less than 16 Students	223.1 (0.9)
16 to 18 Students	216.0 (1.1)	16 to 18 Students	233.7 (0.7)
19 to 20 Students	218.0 (0.6)	19 to 20 Students	235.0 (0.5)
21 to 25 Students	220.4 (0.5)	21 to 25 Students	237.0 (0.4)
Greater than 25 Students	214.2 (0.6)	Greater than 25 Students	232.2 (0.5)
Percent Attaining Achievement Levels		Percent Attaining Achievement Levels	
Below Basic	38.4 (0.3)	Below Basic	23.9 (0.3)
Basic or Above	61.6 (0.3)	Basic or Above	76.1 (0.3)
Proficient or Above	29.7 (0.3)	Proficient or Above	31.2 (0.3)
Advanced or Above	6.9 (0.1)	Advanced or Above	3.7 (0.1)
8th Grade		**8th Grade**	
Average Proficiency	261.3 (0.2)	Average Proficiency	276.1 (0.3)
Proficiency by Gender/Race/Ethnicity		Proficiency by Gender/Race/Ethnicity	
Male	256.1 (0.3)	Male	277.0 (0.3)
Female	266.6 (0.3)	Female	275.2 (0.3)
White, Non-Hispanic	270.4 (0.2)	White, Non-Hispanic	286.5 (0.3)
Black, Non-Hispanic	243.6 (0.5)	Black, Non-Hispanic	251.7 (0.5)
Asian, Non-Hispanic	243.8 (0.7)	Asian, Non-Hispanic	258.1 (0.6)
American Indian, Non-Hispanic	268.4 (1.2)	American Indian, Non-Hispanic	289.4 (1.3)
Hispanic	248.3 (1.7)	Hispanic	264.6 (1.2)
Proficiency by Parents Highest Level of Ed.		Proficiency by Parents Highest Level of Ed.	
Did Not Finish High School	244.7 (0.6)	Did Not Finish High School	256.3 (0.6)
Graduated High School	253.4 (0.4)	Graduated High School	266.9 (0.4)
Some Education After High School	266.1 (0.4)	Some Education After High School	279.7 (0.4)
Graduated College	271.0 (0.3)	Graduated College	286.8 (0.4)
Percent Attaining Achievement Levels		Percent Attaining Achievement Levels	
Below Basic	27.8 (0.3)	Below Basic	33.3 (0.3)
Basic or Above	72.2 (0.3)	Basic or Above	66.7 (0.3)
Proficient or Above	30.0 (0.3)	Proficient or Above	27.3 (0.3)
Advanced or Above	2.6 (0.1)	Advanced or Above	4.9 (0.1)

Note: *For an explanation of data, please refer to the User's Guide in the front of the book*

Number of Schools

School districts ranked in *descending* order

Rank	Number	District Name	City, State
1	1,429	New York City Public Schools	Brooklyn, NY
2	677	Los Angeles Unified	Los Angeles, CA
3	608	City of Chicago SD 299	Chicago, IL
4	370	Dade County SD	Miami, FL
5	308	Houston ISD	Houston, TX
6	284	Hawaii Department of Education	Honolulu, HI
7	282	Clark County SD	Las Vegas, NV
8	273	Detroit City SD	Detroit, MI
9	262	Philadelphia City SD	Philadelphia, PA
10	259	Broward County SD	Fort Lauderdale, FL
11	229	Hillsborough County SD	Tampa, FL
12	228	Dallas ISD	Dallas, TX
13	218	Milwaukee	Milwaukee, WI
14	208	Palm Beach County SD	W Palm Beach, FL
15	204	Prince Georges County Pub Schools	Upper Marlboro, MD
16	202	Fairfax County Public Schools	Fairfax, VA
17	194	Montgomery County Public Schls	Rockville, MD
18	188	Orange County SD	Orlando, FL
19	185	San Diego Unified	San Diego, CA
20	184	Baltimore City Public Schools Sys	Baltimore, MD
21	181	Duval County SD	Jacksonville, FL
22	178	Memphis City SD	Memphis, TN
23	175	Jefferson County	Louisville, KY
24	172	Pinellas County SD	Largo, FL
25	170	Baltimore County Public Schls	Towson, MD
25	170	District of Columbia Pub Schls	Washington, DC
27	169	Jefferson County R-1	Golden, CO
28	162	Intermediate SD 287	Plymouth, MN
29	151	Columbus City SD	Columbus, OH
30	148	Polk County SD	Bartow, FL
31	146	Fort Worth ISD	Fort Worth, TX
32	144	Albuquerque Public Schools	Albuquerque, NM
32	144	Denver County 1	Denver, CO
32	144	Minneapolis	Minneapolis, MN
35	139	Dekalb County	Decatur, GA
36	135	Boston	Boston, MA
37	134	Charlotte-Mecklenburg Schools	Charlotte, NC
38	132	Seattle SD 1	Seattle, WA
39	129	Cleveland Municipal SD	Cleveland, OH
40	128	Orleans Parish School Board	New Orleans, LA
41	125	Saint Paul	Saint Paul, MN
41	125	Tucson Unified District	Tucson, AZ
43	124	Saint Louis City	Saint Louis, MO
44	123	Nashville-Davidson County SD	Nashville, TN
44	123	Wake County Schools	Raleigh, NC
46	119	Anne Arundel County Pub Schls	Annapolis, MD
47	114	San Francisco Unified	San Francisco, CA
48	111	Austin ISD	Austin, TX
49	110	Brevard County SD	Viera, FL
49	110	Oakland Unified	Oakland, CA
51	107	East Baton Rouge Parish School Bd	Baton Rouge, LA
51	107	San Antonio ISD	San Antonio, TX
53	104	Portland SD 1J	Portland, OR
54	103	Fresno Unified	Fresno, CA
54	103	Mobile County SD	Mobile, AL
56	102	Atlanta City	Atlanta, GA
56	102	Cobb County	Marietta, GA
56	102	Guilford County Schools	Greensboro, NC
59	100	Washoe County SD	Reno, NV
60	98	Anchorage SD	Anchorage, AK
61	96	Granite SD	Salt Lake City, UT
62	94	El Paso ISD	El Paso, TX
62	94	Grand Rapids Public Schools	Grand Rapids, MI
62	94	Greenville County SD	Greenville, SC
62	94	Oklahoma City	Oklahoma City, OK
66	93	Indianapolis Public Schools	Indianapolis, IN
66	93	Pittsburgh SD	Pittsburgh, PA
68	92	Birmingham City SD	Birmingham, AL
68	92	Volusia County SD	Deland, FL
70	91	Mesa Unified District	Mesa, AZ
71	90	Kansas City 33	Kansas City, MO
71	90	Wichita	Wichita, KS
73	89	Gwinnett County	Lawrenceville, GA
73	89	Long Beach Unified	Long Beach, CA
73	89	Northside ISD	San Antonio, TX
76	88	Knox County SD	Knoxville, TN
77	86	Buffalo City SD	Buffalo, NY
77	86	Cincinnati City SD	Cincinnati, OH
77	86	Escambia County SD	Pensacola, FL
77	86	Tulsa	Tulsa, OK
81	85	Davis SD	Farmington, UT
81	85	Jefferson Parish School Board	Harvey, LA
81	85	Virginia Beach City Public Schools	Virginia Beach, VA
84	84	Cumberland County Schools	Fayetteville, NC
84	84	Omaha Public Schools	Omaha, NE
84	84	San Juan Unified	Carmichael, CA
87	81	Fulton County	Atlanta, GA
87	81	Hamilton County SD	Chattanooga, TN
89	80	Charleston County SD	Charleston, SC
89	80	Jordan SD	Sandy, UT
89	80	Sacramento City Unified	Sacramento, CA
92	79	Lee County SD	Fort Myers, FL
93	77	Newark City	Newark, NJ
94	76	Arlington ISD	Arlington, TX
95	75	Caddo Parish School Board	Shreveport, LA
95	75	Prince William County Pub Schools	Manassas, VA
95	75	Seminole County SD	Sanford, FL
98	73	Manatee County SD	Bradenton, FL
99	72	Kanawha County SD	Charleston, WV
99	72	Pasco County SD	Land O' Lakes, FL
99	72	Plano ISD	Plano, TX
102	70	Garland ISD	Garland, TX
103	69	Howard County Pub Schls System	Ellicott City, MD
103	69	North East ISD	San Antonio, TX
103	69	Rochester City SD	Rochester, NY
103	69	Toledo City SD	Toledo, OH
107	68	Forsyth County Schools	Winston Salem, NC
108	67	Aldine ISD	Houston, TX
108	67	Garden Grove Unified	Garden Grove, CA
108	67	Spokane SD 81	Spokane, WA
111	66	Salem-Keizer SD 24J	Salem, OR
112	65	Colorado Springs 11	Colorado Spgs, CO
112	65	Henrico County Public Schools	Richmond, VA
112	65	Lincoln Public Schools	Lincoln, NE
112	65	Marion County SD	Ocala, FL
112	65	San Bernardino City Unified	San Bernardino, CA
112	65	Tacoma SD 10	Tacoma, WA
118	64	Corpus Christi ISD	Corpus Christi, TX
118	64	Fayette County	Lexington, KY
118	64	Jefferson County SD	Birmingham, AL

This section ranks 120 school districts at both the "top" and "bottom" of each category for a total of 240 districts per category. The "top" list (descending order) appears first, followed by the "bottom" list (ascending order).

Number of Schools

School districts ranked in *ascending* order

Rank	Number	District Name	City, State
1	1	Adlai E Stevenson Dist 125	Lincolnshire, IL
1	1	Argo Community HSD 217	Summit, IL
1	1	Arrowhead Uhs	Hartland, WI
1	1	Boces Eastern Suffolk (Suffolk I)	Patchogue, NY
1	1	Boces Monroe 1	Fairport, NY
1	1	Boces Nassau	Garden City, NY
1	1	Bozeman HS	Bozeman, MT
1	1	Bradley Bourbonnais CHSD 307	Bradley, IL
1	1	Butte HS	Butte, MT
1	1	Community High SD 94	West Chicago, IL
1	1	Electronic Classroom of Tomorrow	Columbus, OH
1	1	Evanston Twp HSD 202	Evanston, IL
1	1	Fenton Community HSD 100	Bensenville, IL
1	1	Grayslake Community High SD 127	Grayslake, IL
1	1	Greater Lowell Voc Tec	Tyngsborough, MA
1	1	Greater New Bedford	New Bedford, MA
1	1	Hartford Uhs	Hartford, WI
1	1	Homewood Flossmoor CHSD 233	Flossmoor, IL
1	1	Hononegah Community HSD 207	Rockton, IL
1	1	Hunterdon Central Reg	Flemington, NJ
1	1	Lake Forest Community HSD 115	Lake Forest, IL
1	1	Lake Park Community HSD 108	Roselle, IL
1	1	Lockport Twp HSD 205	Lockport, IL
1	1	Lyons Twp HSD 204	La Grange, IL
1	1	Mainland Regional	Linwood, NJ
1	1	Mundelein Cons High SD 120	Mundelein, IL
1	1	Norwich Free Academy	Norwich, CT
1	1	O'Fallon Twp High SD 203	Ofallon, IL
1	1	Oak Lawn Community HSD 229	Oak Lawn, IL
1	1	Oak Park & River Forest Dist 200	Oak Park, IL
1	1	Ottawa Twp HSD 140	Ottawa, IL
1	1	Passaic County Vocational	Wayne, NJ
1	1	Pekin Community HSD 303	Pekin, IL
1	1	Pennsylvania Virtual CS	Norristown, PA
1	1	Pinkerton Academy SD	Derry, NH
1	1	Reavis Twp HSD 220	Burbank, IL
1	1	United Twp HS District 30	East Moline, IL
1	1	Warren Twp High SD 121	Gurnee, IL
1	1	Watchung Hills Regional	Warren, NJ
1	1	Zion-Benton Twp HSD 126	Zion, IL
41	2	Acton-Boxborough	Acton, MA
41	2	Amherst-Pelham	Amherst, MA
41	2	Brooklyn Center	Brooklyn Center, MN
41	2	Burgettstown Area SD	Burgettstown, PA
41	2	Burlington County Vocational	Westampton Twp, NJ
41	2	Camden County Vocational	Sicklerville, NJ
41	2	Central Regional	Bayville, NJ
41	2	Clearview Regional	Mullica Hill, NJ
41	2	Colorado River Union High SD	Fort Mojave, AZ
41	2	Community High SD 128	Libertyville, IL
41	2	Community High SD 99	Downers Grove, IL
41	2	Crete Public Schools	Crete, NE
41	2	Delsea Regional HS District	Franklinville, NJ
41	2	Detroit Academy of Arts and Sciences	Detroit, MI
41	2	Du Page High SD 88	Villa Park, IL
41	2	Eastern Camden County Reg	Voorhees, NJ
41	2	Elk Lake SD	Dimock, PA
41	2	Essex Community Education Ctr	Essex Junction, VT
41	2	Exeter Region Cooperative SD	Exeter, NH
41	2	Flathead HS	Kalispell, MT
41	2	Floral Park-Bellerose UFSD	Floral Park, NY
41	2	Foster-Glocester RD	Chepachet, RI
41	2	Freetown-Lakeville	Lakeville, MA
41	2	Fremont SD 79	Mundelein, IL
41	2	Galt Joint Union High	Galt, CA
41	2	Great Falls HS	Great Falls, MT
41	2	Greater Egg Harbor Reg	Mays Landing, NJ
41	2	Hampton Bays UFSD	Hampton Bays, NY
41	2	Hazlehurst City SD	Hazlehurst, MS
41	2	Helena HS	Helena, MT
41	2	Hinsdale Twp HSD 86	Hinsdale, IL
41	2	Jacksonville City SD	Jacksonville, AL
41	2	Jeannette City SD	Jeannette, PA
41	2	King Philip	Wrentham, MA
41	2	Kingsway Regional	Woolwich Twp, NJ
41	2	Leyden Community HSD 212	Franklin Park, IL
41	2	Lincoln Way Community HSD 210	New Lenox, IL
41	2	Little Egg Harbor Twp	Little Egg Hbr, NJ
41	2	Long County	Ludowici, GA
41	2	Los Gatos-Saratoga Joint Union High	Los Gatos, CA
41	2	Lower Cape May Regional	Cape May, NJ
41	2	Manasquan Boro	Manasquan, NJ
41	2	Masconomet	Topsfield, MA
41	2	Mattituck-Cutchogue UFSD	Cutchogue, NY
41	2	Mchenry Community HSD 156	Mc Henry, IL
41	2	Melrose	Melrose, MN
41	2	Mercer Area SD	Mercer, PA
41	2	Mid Valley SD	Throop, PA
41	2	Millstone Twp	Clarksburg, NJ
41	2	Mohawk Area SD	Bessemer, PA
41	2	Morris Hills Regional	Rockaway, NJ
41	2	Mount Carmel Area SD	Mount Carmel, PA
41	2	Nauset	Orleans, MA
41	2	New Trier Twp HSD 203	Winnetka, IL
41	2	Niles Twp Community High SD 219	Skokie, IL
41	2	North Hunt-Voorhees Regional	Annandale, NJ
41	2	Northern Burlington Reg	Columbus, NJ
41	2	Northern Valley Regional	Demarest, NJ
41	2	Oro Grande Elementary	Oro Grande, CA
41	2	PDE Division of Data Services	Harrisburg, PA
41	2	Paoli Community School Corp	Paoli, IN
41	2	Pascack Valley Regional	Montvale, NJ
41	2	Pinelands Regional	Tuckerton, NJ
41	2	Proviso Twp HSD 209	Maywood, IL
41	2	Ramapo-Indian Hill Reg	Franklin Lakes, NJ
41	2	Rancocas Valley Regional	Mount Holly, NJ
41	2	Reynolds SD	Greenville, PA
41	2	Romoland Elementary	Homeland, CA
41	2	San Benito High	Hollister, CA
41	2	Santa Paula Union High	Santa Paula, CA
41	2	Schuylerville CSD	Schuylerville, NY
41	2	Shamokin Area SD	Coal Township, PA
41	2	Silver Lake	Kingston, MA
41	2	Somers Point City	Somers Point, NJ
41	2	Southern Regional	Manahawkin, NJ
41	2	Southwestern-Jefferson County	Hanover, IN
41	2	Towns County	Hiawassee, GA
41	2	Township High SD 113	Highland Park, IL
41	2	Upper Freehold Regional	Allentown, NJ
41	2	Warren Hills Regional	Washington, NJ

This section ranks 120 school districts at both the "top" and "bottom" of each category for a total of 240 districts per category. The "top" list (descending order) appears first, followed by the "bottom" list (ascending order).

Number of Teachers

School districts ranked in *descending* order

Rank	Number	District Name	City, State
1	65,803	New York City Public Schools	Brooklyn, NY
2	35,483	Los Angeles Unified	Los Angeles, CA
3	24,584	City of Chicago SD 299	Chicago, IL
4	18,656	Dade County SD	Miami, FL
5	13,946	Fairfax County Public Schools	Fairfax, VA
6	13,264	Broward County SD	Fort Lauderdale, FL
7	13,069	Clark County SD	Las Vegas, NV
8	12,385	Houston ISD	Houston, TX
9	10,973	Hawaii Department of Education	Honolulu, HI
10	10,940	Dallas ISD	Dallas, TX
11	10,499	Hillsborough County SD	Tampa, FL
12	9,866	Philadelphia City SD	Philadelphia, PA
13	9,128	Orange County SD	Orlando, FL
14	9,015	Montgomery County Public Schls	Rockville, MD
15	8,826	Palm Beach County SD	West Palm Beach, FL
16	8,365	Prince Georges County Pub Schools	Upper Marlboro, MD
17	8,047	Gwinnett County	Lawrenceville, GA
18	7,494	San Diego Unified	San Diego, CA
19	7,262	Charlotte-Mecklenburg Schools	Charlotte, NC
20	7,203	Memphis City SD	Memphis, TN
21	7,078	Baltimore County Public Schls	Towson, MD
22	6,806	Cobb County	Marietta, GA
23	6,789	Wake County Schools	Raleigh, NC
24	6,670	Cleveland Municipal SD	Cleveland, OH
25	6,620	Duval County SD	Jacksonville, FL
26	6,595	Dekalb County	Decatur, GA
27	6,530	Baltimore City Public Schools Sys	Baltimore, MD
28	6,516	Pinellas County SD	Largo, FL
29	6,494	Milwaukee	Milwaukee, WI
30	5,968	Albuquerque Public Schools	Albuquerque, NM
31	5,683	Detroit City SD	Detroit, MI
32	5,382	Austin ISD	Austin, TX
33	5,339	Virginia Beach City Public Schools	Virginia Beach, VA
34	5,328	Jefferson County	Louisville, KY
35	5,005	District of Columbia Pub Schls	Washington, DC
36	4,967	Fort Worth ISD	Fort Worth, TX
37	4,860	Fulton County	Atlanta, GA
38	4,857	Jefferson County R-1	Golden, CO
39	4,801	Polk County SD	Bartow, FL
40	4,614	Nashville-Davidson County SD	Nashville, TN
41	4,603	Cypress-Fairbanks ISD	Houston, TX
42	4,573	Northside ISD	San Antonio, TX
43	4,520	Long Beach Unified	Long Beach, CA
44	4,517	Boston	Boston, MA
45	4,511	Anne Arundel County Pub Schls	Annapolis, MD
46	4,471	Denver County 1	Denver, CO
47	4,433	El Paso ISD	El Paso, TX
48	4,288	Columbus City SD	Columbus, OH
49	4,236	Orleans Parish School Board	New Orleans, LA
50	4,140	Prince William County Pub Schools	Manassas, VA
51	4,089	Guilford County Schools	Greensboro, NC
52	4,079	Brevard County SD	Viera, FL
53	4,058	Greenville County SD	Greenville, SC
54	4,050	Mobile County SD	Mobile, AL
55	4,011	Chesterfield County Public Schools	Chesterfield, VA
56	3,941	Arlington ISD	Arlington, TX
57	3,938	Fresno Unified	Fresno, CA
58	3,874	Atlanta City	Atlanta, GA
59	3,824	Volusia County SD	Deland, FL
60	3,788	Washoe County SD	Reno, NV
61	3,722	Aldine ISD	Houston, TX
62	3,716	North East ISD	San Antonio, TX
63	3,684	Newark City	Newark, NJ
64	3,682	Mesa Unified District	Mesa, AZ
65	3,635	San Antonio ISD	San Antonio, TX
66	3,623	Plano ISD	Plano, TX
67	3,588	Knox County SD	Knoxville, TN
68	3,585	Fort Bend ISD	Sugar Land, TX
69	3,554	East Baton Rouge Parish School Bd	Baton Rouge, LA
70	3,548	Cincinnati City SD	Cincinnati, OH
71	3,519	Saint Louis City	Saint Louis, MO
72	3,463	Tucson Unified District	Tucson, AZ
73	3,438	Granite SD	Salt Lake City, UT
74	3,411	Seminole County SD	Sanford, FL
75	3,405	Garland ISD	Garland, TX
76	3,372	Jefferson Parish School Board	Harvey, LA
77	3,371	Henrico County Public Schools	Richmond, VA
78	3,363	Norfolk City Public Schools	Norfolk, VA
79	3,362	San Francisco Unified	San Francisco, CA
80	3,284	Cumberland County Schools	Fayetteville, NC
81	3,229	Buffalo City SD	Buffalo, NY
82	3,205	Howard County Pub Schls System	Ellicott City, MD
83	3,200	Lee County SD	Fort Myers, FL
84	3,199	Loudoun County Public Schools	Leesburg, VA
85	3,186	Forsyth County Schools	Winston Salem, NC
86	3,142	Minneapolis	Minneapolis, MN
87	3,119	Jordan SD	Sandy, UT
88	3,111	Omaha Public Schools	Omaha, NE
89	3,101	Charleston County SD	Charleston, SC
90	3,052	Pasco County SD	Land O' Lakes, FL
91	3,041	Wichita	Wichita, KS
92	3,023	Brownsville ISD	Brownsville, TX
93	2,991	Caddo Parish School Board	Shreveport, LA
94	2,990	Lewisville ISD	Flower Mound, TX
95	2,955	Saint Paul	Saint Paul, MN
96	2,947	Alief ISD	Houston, TX
97	2,943	Rochester City SD	Rochester, NY
98	2,939	Ysleta ISD	El Paso, TX
99	2,938	Santa Ana Unified	Santa Ana, CA
100	2,895	Chesapeake City Public Schools	Chesapeake, VA
101	2,889	Anchorage SD	Anchorage, AK
102	2,888	Oakland Unified	Oakland, CA
103	2,789	Indianapolis Public Schools	Indianapolis, IN
104	2,760	Portland SD 1J	Portland, OR
105	2,758	Pasadena ISD	Pasadena, TX
106	2,751	Toledo City SD	Toledo, OH
107	2,735	Clayton County	Jonesboro, GA
108	2,715	Cherry Creek 5	Greenwood Vlg, CO
109	2,709	Pittsburgh SD	Pittsburgh, PA
110	2,702	Newport News City Public Schools	Newport News, VA
111	2,697	Katy ISD	Katy, TX
112	2,675	Hamilton County SD	Chattanooga, TN
113	2,669	Tulsa	Tulsa, OK
114	2,666	Jersey City	Jersey City, NJ
115	2,662	Seattle SD 1	Seattle, WA
116	2,657	Davis SD	Farmington, UT
117	2,645	San Bernardino City Unified	San Bernardino, CA
118	2,643	Kansas City 33	Kansas City, MO
119	2,600	Elk Grove Unified	Elk Grove, CA
120	2,593	Shelby County SD	Memphis, TN

This section ranks 120 school districts at both the "top" and "bottom" of each category for a total of 240 districts per category. The "top" list (descending order) appears first, followed by the "bottom" list (ascending order).

Number of Teachers

School districts ranked in *ascending* order

Rank	Number	District Name	City, State
1	14	Meridian Public Schools	Sanford, MI
2	17	Cedar Springs Public Schools	Cedar Springs, MI
3	19	Charlotte Public Schools	Charlotte, MI
4	24	Peach Springs Unified District	Peach Springs, AZ
5	28	Jenison Public Schools	Jenison, MI
6	30	Zeeland Public Schools	Zeeland, MI
7	34	Ovid-Elsie Area Schools	Elsie, MI
8	39	Dundee Community Schools	Dundee, MI
9	45	Pennsylvania Virtual CS	Norristown, PA
10	48	Butte County Joint District	Arco, ID
11	50	Colorado River Union High SD	Fort Mojave, AZ
12	52	Houghton Lake Community Schools	Houghton Lake, MI
13	56	Gulf Shores Academy	Houston, TX
14	59	Washtenaw ISD	Ann Arbor, MI
15	62	Santa Paula Union High	Santa Paula, CA
16	63	Montrose Community Schools	Montrose, MI
17	63	Galena City SD	Galena, AK
18	65	Gorman Elementary	Gorman, CA
19	66	Julian Union Elementary	Julian, CA
20	69	Bronson Community SD	Bronson, MI
21	72	Hockinson SD 98	Brush Prairie, WA
22	72	Channahon SD 17	Channahon, IL
23	73	Bishop Union Elementary	Bishop, CA
24	73	Sonora Union High	Sonora, CA
25	74	Jamul-Dulzura Union Elementary	Jamul, CA
26	76	Westwood Unified	Westwood, CA
27	76	Sutherlin SD 130	Sutherlin, OR
28	77	Hanover Community School Corp	Cedar Lake, IN
29	77	Jefferson Elementary	Tracy, CA
29	77	Mohave Valley Elementary District	Mohave Valley, AZ
31	78	Cass City Public Schools	Cass City, MI
31	78	Romoland Elementary	Homeland, CA
33	78	Cashmere SD 222	Cashmere, WA
34	78	Porter Township School Corp	Valparaiso, IN
35	79	Beecher Community SD	Flint, MI
35	79	Michigan Center SD	Michigan Center, MI
37	80	Posen-Robbins El SD 143-5	Posen, IL
38	80	Brawley Union High	Brawley, CA
38	80	Mark West Union Elementary	Santa Rosa, CA
40	80	Riverdale Joint Unified	Riverdale, CA
41	81	Minooka Community CSD 201	Minooka, IL
41	81	Naches Valley SD 3	Naches, WA
41	81	Woodlake Union Elementary	Woodlake, CA
44	81	Fremont SD 79	Mundelein, IL
44	81	Fruitland District	Fruitland, ID
46	81	Fern Ridge SD 28J	Elmira, OR
46	81	Switzerland County School Corp	Vevay, IN
48	82	Carterville CUSD 5	Carterville, IL
48	82	Saint Helena Unified	Saint Helena, CA
50	82	Juab SD	Nephi, UT
50	82	Roseau	Roseau, MN
52	82	Littleton Elementary District	Cashion, AZ
53	83	Chowchilla Elementary	Chowchilla, CA
53	83	Southeast Dubois County Sch Corp	Ferdinand, IN
55	83	Lake Local SD	Millbury, OH
56	83	Colusa Unified	Colusa, CA
57	83	Elk Rapids Schools	Elk Rapids, MI
58	83	South Spencer County Sch Corp	Rockport, IN
59	83	Julian Union High	Julian, CA
59	83	Nine Mile Falls SD 325/179	Nine Mile Fall, WA
61	84	Cascade Union Elementary	Anderson, CA
61	84	Meridian SD 505	Bellingham, WA
61	84	Zane Trace Local SD	Chillicothe, OH
64	84	Kiona-Benton SD 52	Benton City, WA
65	84	North West Hendricks Schools	Lizton, IN
66	84	Manchester Local SD	Akron, OH
67	84	Siuslaw SD 97J	Florence, OR
68	85	Brookville Local SD	Brookville, OH
68	85	Freeland Community SD	Freeland, MI
68	85	Jeannette City SD	Jeannette, PA
71	85	Ridgefield SD 122	Ridgefield, WA
72	85	Bonsall Union Elementary	Bonsall, CA
72	85	Electronic Classroom of Tomorrow	Columbus, OH
74	85	Mother Lode Union Elementary	Placerville, CA
75	85	Piner-Olivet Union Elementary	Santa Rosa, CA
76	85	Montague Area Public Schools	Montague, MI
77	85	Cloverdale Unified	Cloverdale, CA
78	85	Vashon Island SD 402	Vashon, WA
79	86	Circle	Towanda, KS
79	86	Reynolds SD	Greenville, PA
81	86	Wickenburg Unified District	Wickenburg, AZ
82	86	Beardsley Elementary	Bakersfield, CA
82	86	Tecumseh Public Schools	Tecumseh, MI
82	86	Trimble County	Bedford, KY
85	86	Bradley Bourbonnais CHSD 307	Bradley, IL
85	86	King City Joint Union High	King City, CA
85	86	Quincy Community SD	Quincy, MI
88	86	Bradley SD 61	Bradley, IL
89	86	Port Townsend SD 50	Port Townsend, WA
89	86	Thermalito Union Elementary	Oroville, CA
91	87	Bayless	Saint Louis, MO
92	87	North College Hill City SD	Cincinnati, OH
93	87	Willows Unified	Willows, CA
94	87	Almont Community Schools	Almont, MI
94	87	Meridian CUSD 223	Stillman Valley, IL
96	87	Ballard County	Barlow, KY
96	87	Clare Public Schools	Clare, MI
96	87	Saint Anthony-New Brighton	Saint Anthony, MN
99	88	Amanda-Clearcreek Local SD	Amanda, OH
99	88	Greater New Bedford	New Bedford, MA
99	88	MSD Bluffton-Harrison	Bluffton, IN
99	88	Wattsburg Area SD	Erie, PA
103	88	Clawson City SD	Clawson, MI
104	88	Laveen Elementary District	Laveen, AZ
104	88	North Judson-San Pierre Sch Corp	North Judson, IN
106	88	Clinton-Massie Local SD	Clarksville, OH
107	89	Acton-Agua Dulce Unified	Acton, CA
107	89	Lakeland SD	Jermyn, PA
107	89	Southwestern-Jefferson County	Hanover, IN
107	89	West Bonner County District	Sandpoint, ID
111	89	Newton Falls Ex Vill SD	Newton Falls, OH
112	89	Bangor Public Schools (Van Buren)	Bangor, MI
112	89	East Jackson Community Schools	Jackson, MI
114	89	Live Oak Unified	Live Oak, CA
114	89	Maricopa County Regional District	Phoenix, AZ
116	89	Union Township School Corp	Valparaiso, IN
117	90	East Washington School Corp	Pekin, IN
117	90	Greeneview Local SD	Jamestown, OH
117	90	Oak Lawn Community HSD 229	Oak Lawn, IL
117	90	Wilmington CUSD 209U	Wilmington, IL

This section ranks 120 school districts at both the "top" and "bottom" of each category for a total of 240 districts per category. The "top" list (descending order) appears first, followed by the "bottom" list (ascending order).

Number of Students

School districts ranked in *descending* order

Rank	Number	District Name	City, State
1	1,077,381	New York City Public Schools	Brooklyn, NY
2	746,852	Los Angeles Unified	Los Angeles, CA
3	436,048	City of Chicago SD 299	Chicago, IL
4	373,395	Dade County SD	Miami, FL
5	267,925	Broward County SD	Fort Lauderdale, FL
6	256,574	Clark County SD	Las Vegas, NV
7	212,099	Houston ISD	Houston, TX
8	192,683	Philadelphia City SD	Philadelphia, PA
9	183,829	Hawaii Department of Education	Honolulu, HI
10	175,454	Hillsborough County SD	Tampa, FL
11	173,742	Detroit City SD	Detroit, MI
12	164,896	Palm Beach County SD	West Palm Beach, FL
13	163,347	Dallas ISD	Dallas, TX
14	162,585	Fairfax County Public Schools	Fairfax, VA
15	158,718	Orange County SD	Orlando, FL
16	140,753	San Diego Unified	San Diego, CA
17	138,983	Montgomery County Public Schls	Rockville, MD
18	135,439	Prince Georges County Pub Schools	Upper Marlboro, MD
19	128,126	Duval County SD	Jacksonville, FL
20	122,570	Gwinnett County	Lawrenceville, GA
21	118,039	Memphis City SD	Memphis, TN
22	114,772	Pinellas County SD	Largo, FL
23	109,767	Charlotte-Mecklenburg Schools	Charlotte, NC
24	108,297	Baltimore County Public Schls	Towson, MD
25	104,836	Wake County Schools	Raleigh, NC
26	100,389	Cobb County	Marietta, GA
27	97,967	Dekalb County	Decatur, GA
28	97,293	Milwaukee	Milwaukee, WI
29	97,212	Long Beach Unified	Long Beach, CA
30	96,230	Baltimore City Public Schools Sys	Baltimore, MD
31	95,651	Jefferson County	Louisville, KY
32	88,120	Albuquerque Public Schools	Albuquerque, NM
33	87,925	Jefferson County R-1	Golden, CO
34	82,179	Polk County SD	Bartow, FL
35	81,222	Fresno Unified	Fresno, CA
36	81,081	Fort Worth ISD	Fort Worth, TX
37	78,608	Austin ISD	Austin, TX
38	75,902	Virginia Beach City Public Schools	Virginia Beach, VA
39	75,269	Mesa Unified District	Mesa, AZ
40	74,787	Anne Arundel County Pub Schls	Annapolis, MD
41	73,808	Jordan SD	Sandy, UT
42	72,601	Brevard County SD	Viera, FL
43	71,972	Denver County 1	Denver, CO
44	71,616	Cleveland Municipal SD	Cleveland, OH
45	71,372	Fulton County	Atlanta, GA
46	71,181	Granite SD	Salt Lake City, UT
47	71,165	Cypress-Fairbanks ISD	Houston, TX
48	70,246	Orleans Parish School Board	New Orleans, LA
49	69,409	Northside ISD	San Antonio, TX
50	67,954	Nashville-Davidson County SD	Nashville, TN
51	67,522	District of Columbia Pub Schls	Washington, DC
52	65,677	Guilford County Schools	Greensboro, NC
53	64,175	Columbus City SD	Columbus, OH
54	64,058	Mobile County SD	Mobile, AL
55	63,610	Santa Ana Unified	Santa Ana, CA
56	63,446	Seminole County SD	Sanford, FL
57	63,270	Greenville County SD	Greenville, SC
58	63,185	El Paso ISD	El Paso, TX
59	63,172	Lee County SD	Fort Myers, FL
60	63,000	Volusia County SD	Deland, FL
61	61,958	Tucson Unified District	Tucson, AZ
62	61,928	Arlington ISD	Arlington, TX
63	61,552	Boston	Boston, MA
64	60,541	Prince William County Pub Schools	Manassas, VA
65	60,384	Washoe County SD	Reno, NV
66	60,367	Davis SD	Farmington, UT
67	59,489	Fort Bend ISD	Sugar Land, TX
68	58,216	San Francisco Unified	San Francisco, CA
69	57,120	San Antonio ISD	San Antonio, TX
70	56,096	San Bernardino City Unified	San Bernardino, CA
71	55,367	Aldine ISD	Houston, TX
72	55,053	North East ISD	San Antonio, TX
73	54,957	Pasco County SD	Land O' Lakes, FL
74	54,946	Atlanta City	Atlanta, GA
75	54,007	Garland ISD	Garland, TX
76	53,621	Chesterfield County Public Schools	Chesterfield, VA
77	53,411	Knox County SD	Knoxville, TN
78	52,850	Sacramento City Unified	Sacramento, CA
79	52,501	Oakland Unified	Oakland, CA
80	52,434	East Baton Rouge Parish School Bd	Baton Rouge, LA
81	52,418	Elk Grove Unified	Elk Grove, CA
82	52,212	San Juan Unified	Carmichael, CA
83	52,094	Cumberland County Schools	Fayetteville, NC
84	51,654	Portland SD 1J	Portland, OR
85	51,501	Jefferson Parish School Board	Harvey, LA
86	51,039	Plano ISD	Plano, TX
87	50,066	Garden Grove Unified	Garden Grove, CA
88	50,055	Anchorage SD	Anchorage, AK
89	49,594	Clayton County	Jonesboro, GA
90	49,159	Alpine SD	American Fork, UT
91	48,913	Wichita	Wichita, KS
92	48,608	Capistrano Unified	San Juan Capis, CA
93	47,853	Seattle SD 1	Seattle, WA
94	47,197	Howard County Pub Schls System	Ellicott City, MD
95	46,806	Forsyth County Schools	Winston Salem, NC
96	46,745	Ysleta ISD	El Paso, TX
97	46,037	Minneapolis	Minneapolis, MN
98	45,986	Omaha Public Schools	Omaha, NE
99	45,738	Cherry Creek 5	Greenwood Vlg, CO
100	45,480	Saint Louis City	Saint Louis, MO
101	45,439	Shelby County SD	Memphis, TN
102	44,836	Pasadena ISD	Pasadena, TX
103	44,661	Alief ISD	Houston, TX
104	44,556	Caddo Parish School Board	Shreveport, LA
105	44,340	Brownsville ISD	Brownsville, TX
106	44,019	Escambia County SD	Pensacola, FL
107	44,008	Charleston County SD	Charleston, SC
108	43,923	Saint Paul	Saint Paul, MN
109	43,698	Henrico County Public Schools	Richmond, VA
110	43,474	Buffalo City SD	Buffalo, NY
111	43,122	Lewisville ISD	Flower Mound, TX
112	43,029	Tulsa	Tulsa, OK
113	42,715	Cincinnati City SD	Cincinnati, OH
114	42,395	Newark City	Newark, NJ
115	41,977	Corona-Norco Unified	Norco, CA
116	41,383	Anoka-Hennepin	Coon Rapids, MN
117	40,888	Riverside Unified	Riverside, CA
118	40,856	Oklahoma City	Oklahoma City, OK
119	40,731	Indianapolis Public Schools	Indianapolis, IN
120	40,564	Hamilton County SD	Chattanooga, TN

This section ranks 120 school districts at both the "top" and "bottom" of each category for a total of 240 districts per category. The "top" list (descending order) appears first, followed by the "bottom" list (ascending order).

Number of Students

School districts ranked in *ascending* order

Rank	Number	District Name	City, State
1	1,500	Byron	Byron, MN
1	1,500	Harwich	Harwich, MA
1	1,500	Manchester Local SD	Akron, OH
1	1,500	Saint Helena Unified	Saint Helena, CA
1	1,500	Southwestern-Jefferson County	Hanover, IN
1	1,500	Wilson CSD	Wilson, NY
7	1,501	Bullard ISD	Bullard, TX
7	1,501	Colts Neck Twp	Colts Neck, NJ
7	1,501	Redwood Falls Area Schools	Redwood Falls, MN
10	1,502	Bronson Community SD	Bronson, MI
10	1,502	Oyster Bay-East Norwich CSD	Oyster Bay, NY
12	1,503	Brookfield Local SD	Brookfield, OH
12	1,503	Wickenburg Unified District	Wickenburg, AZ
14	1,504	Boonville R-I	Boonville, MO
14	1,504	Staples-Motley	Staples, MN
16	1,505	Lyford CISD	Lyford, TX
16	1,505	Roseau	Roseau, MN
18	1,508	Jeannette City SD	Jeannette, PA
18	1,508	Wickliffe City SD	Wickliffe, OH
18	1,508	Winnsboro ISD	Winnsboro, TX
21	1,509	Ballard County	Barlow, KY
21	1,509	Cashmere SD 222	Cashmere, WA
21	1,509	East Newton County R-VI	Granby, MO
24	1,510	Bayless	Saint Louis, MO
24	1,510	Butte County Joint District	Arco, ID
24	1,510	Channahon SD 17	Channahon, IL
24	1,510	Clawson City SD	Clawson, MI
24	1,510	Cranberry Area SD	Seneca, PA
24	1,510	Ingram ISD	Ingram, TX
24	1,510	Jones County Schools	Trenton, NC
24	1,510	Seminole	Seminole, OK
24	1,510	Wells-Ogunquit CSD	Wells, ME
33	1,511	Chatham CSD	Chatham, NY
33	1,511	Monmouth Unit SD 38	Monmouth, IL
33	1,511	South Spencer County Sch Corp	Rockport, IN
36	1,512	Hampton 2 County SD	Estill, SC
36	1,512	Mascoma Valley Reg SD	Enfield, NH
36	1,512	Rains ISD	Emory, TX
36	1,512	Wabash City Schools	Wabash, IN
36	1,512	Wyalusing Area SD	Wyalusing, PA
41	1,513	Crosby-Ironton	Crosby, MN
41	1,513	Gowanda CSD	Gowanda, NY
41	1,513	Quaboag Regional	Warren, MA
44	1,514	Hatch Valley Public Schools	Hatch, NM
45	1,515	Minnewaska	Glenwood, MN
45	1,515	North Arlington Boro	North Arlington, NJ
47	1,516	Bishop Union Elementary	Bishop, CA
47	1,516	MSAD 05 - Rockland	Rockland, ME
47	1,516	Waldwick Boro	Waldwick, NJ
50	1,517	Carle Place UFSD	Carle Place, NY
50	1,517	Fremont SD 79	Mundelein, IL
50	1,517	Lancaster County Public Schools	Kilmarnock, VA
53	1,518	Carrollton SD	Saginaw, MI
53	1,518	Union Township School Corp	Valparaiso, IN
55	1,519	Berkshire Hills	Stockbridge, MA
55	1,519	Circle	Towanda, KS
55	1,519	Clearview Local SD	Lorain, OH
55	1,519	Everett Area SD	Everett, PA
59	1,520	Croton-Harmon UFSD	Croton-On-Hud, NY
59	1,520	Elk Rapids Schools	Elk Rapids, MI
59	1,520	Grangeville Joint District	Grangeville, ID
59	1,520	Jefferson Elementary	Tracy, CA
59	1,520	Star City SD	Star City, AR
64	1,521	Boces Monroe 1	Fairport, NY
64	1,521	Richland	Richland Ctr, WI
64	1,521	Salem R-80	Salem, MO
67	1,522	Crete Public Schools	Crete, NE
67	1,522	North Judson-San Pierre Sch Corp	North Judson, IN
67	1,522	Northeast School Corp	Hymera, IN
67	1,522	Zane Trace Local SD	Chillicothe, OH
71	1,523	Fenton Community HSD 100	Bensenville, IL
71	1,523	Taylor Community School Corp	Kokomo, IN
73	1,524	Amherst	Amherst, MA
73	1,524	Bangor Public Schools (Van Buren)	Bangor, MI
73	1,524	Fruitland District	Fruitland, ID
73	1,524	Valley Stream 30 UFSD	Valley Stream, NY
77	1,525	Jefferson City	Jefferson, GA
77	1,525	Paulsboro Boro	Paulsboro, NJ
79	1,526	Cloverdale Community Schools	Cloverdale, IN
79	1,526	Marlin ISD	Marlin, TX
81	1,527	Burgettstown Area SD	Burgettstown, PA
81	1,527	Campbellsport	Campbellsport, WI
81	1,527	MSD Bluffton-Harrison	Bluffton, IN
84	1,528	Montevideo	Montevideo, MN
84	1,528	Nekoosa	Nekoosa, WI
84	1,528	Saint Anthony-New Brighton	Saint Anthony, MN
84	1,528	Wilmington CUSD 209U	Wilmington, IL
88	1,529	Regional SD 08	Hebron, CT
88	1,529	Towns County	Hiawassee, GA
88	1,529	Woodbury City	Woodbury, NJ
91	1,530	Independence Community SD	Independence, IA
91	1,530	Union Local SD	Morristown, OH
93	1,531	Brush RE-2(J)	Brush, CO
93	1,531	Butte HS	Butte, MT
93	1,531	Cheektowaga-Sloan UFSD	Sloan, NY
93	1,531	Sutherlin SD 130	Sutherlin, OR
97	1,532	Bradley SD 61	Bradley, IL
98	1,533	Eaton RE-2	Eaton, CO
98	1,533	Melrose	Melrose, MN
98	1,533	West Bonner County District	Sandpoint, ID
101	1,534	Humboldt City SD	Humboldt, TN
101	1,534	Labrae Local SD	Leavittsburg, OH
103	1,535	Allamakee Community SD	Waukon, IA
103	1,535	Greenwood ISD	Midland, TX
103	1,535	Michigan Center SD	Michigan Center, MI
106	1,536	Columbia Borough SD	Columbia, PA
106	1,536	Iola	Iola, KS
106	1,536	Minooka Community CSD 201	Minooka, IL
106	1,536	Salmon River CSD	Ft Covington, NY
106	1,536	Seneca Falls CSD	Seneca Falls, NY
111	1,537	Newton Falls Ex Vill SD	Newton Falls, OH
111	1,537	Wilkinson County SD	Woodville, MS
113	1,538	Colusa Unified	Colusa, CA
113	1,538	Dollarway SD	Pine Bluff, AR
113	1,538	Warsaw R-IX	Warsaw, MO
116	1,539	Highland SD	Hardy, AR
117	1,540	West ISD	West, TX
118	1,541	Florence County SD 05	Johnsonville, SC
118	1,541	Lytle ISD	Lytle, TX
120	1,542	Aspen 1	Aspen, CO

This section ranks 120 school districts at both the "top" and "bottom" of each category for a total of 240 districts per category. The "top" list (descending order) appears first, followed by the "bottom" list (ascending order).

Male Students

School districts ranked in *descending* order

Rank	Percent	District Name	City, State
1	89.9	Department of Corrections SD 428	Springfield, IL
2	74.0	Boces Eastern Suffolk (Suffolk I)	Patchogue, NY
2	74.0	Boces Nassau	Garden City, NY
4	72.0	Boces Monroe 1	Fairport, NY
5	71.9	San Bernardino County Supt.	San Bernardino, CA
6	69.9	Macomb ISD	Clinton Twp, MI
7	69.1	Coxsackie-Athens CSD	Coxsackie, NY
8	69.0	Santa Clara County Office of Ed	San Jose, CA
9	68.0	Los Angeles County Office of Ed	Downey, CA
10	67.4	Fresno County Office of Ed	Fresno, CA
11	66.9	Kern County Office of Ed	Bakersfield, CA
12	63.8	San Joaquin County Office of Ed	Stockton, CA
13	63.7	State Voc-Tech Schools	Middletown, CT
14	61.6	Area Coop Educational Services	North Haven, CT
15	60.1	Orange County Office of Ed	Costa Mesa, CA
15	60.1	San Diego County Office of Ed	San Diego, CA
17	59.8	Middlesex County Vocational	E Brunswick, NJ
18	59.0	Riverside County Office of Ed	Riverside, CA
19	58.5	Vassar Public Schools	Vassar, MI
20	58.3	Intermediate SD 287	Plymouth, MN
21	58.1	Gulf Shores Academy	Houston, TX
22	57.6	Rochester SD 401	Rochester, WA
23	57.4	Broadalbin-Perth CSD	Broadalbin, NY
24	57.3	Maricopa County Regional District	Phoenix, AZ
25	57.2	East Valley Institute of Technology	Mesa, AZ
26	56.2	Hudson City SD	Hudson, NY
27	55.8	Bergen County Vocational	Paramus, NJ
27	55.8	Martin County	Inez, KY
27	55.8	Washtenaw ISD	Ann Arbor, MI
30	55.6	West ISD	West, TX
31	55.5	Greater New Bedford	New Bedford, MA
32	55.4	Cascade Union Elementary	Anderson, CA
33	55.3	Littlefield ISD	Littlefield, TX
33	55.3	Saint Marys City SD	Saint Marys, OH
33	55.3	West Bonner County District	Sandpoint, ID
36	55.0	Canton Local SD	Canton, OH
36	55.0	Danville Independent	Danville, KY
36	55.0	Lower Twp	Cape May, NJ
36	55.0	Orange City SD	Cleveland, OH
40	54.9	Highland CSD	Highland, NY
41	54.8	Camden County Vocational	Sicklerville, NJ
41	54.8	Colbert County SD	Tuscumbia, AL
41	54.8	El Dorado	El Dorado, KS
41	54.8	Madison County SD	Madison, FL
41	54.8	Wickliffe City SD	Wickliffe, OH
46	54.7	Caldwell Parish School Board	Columbia, LA
46	54.7	Fruitland District	Fruitland, ID
48	54.6	Bath CSD	Bath, NY
48	54.6	Berlin SD	Berlin, NH
48	54.6	Brown Deer	Brown Deer, WI
48	54.6	Little Chute Area	Little Chute, WI
48	54.6	Mason County Central Schools	Scottville, MI
53	54.5	Greene County R-VIII	Rogersville, MO
53	54.5	Marlin ISD	Marlin, TX
53	54.5	Melrose	Melrose, MN
53	54.5	Monroe County	Tompkinsville, KY
53	54.5	Mount Pleasant Elementary	San Jose, CA
53	54.5	Redford Union SD	Redford, MI
53	54.5	Tallmadge City SD	Tallmadge, OH
53	54.5	West De Pere	De Pere, WI
61	54.4	Lorena ISD	Lorena, TX
61	54.4	Pike County SD	Troy, AL
63	54.3	Alliance Public Schools	Alliance, NE
63	54.3	Breathitt County	Jackson, KY
63	54.3	Burlington County Vocational	Westampton Twp, NJ
63	54.3	Crenshaw County SD	Luverne, AL
63	54.3	Hamtramck Public Schools	Hamtramck, MI
68	54.2	Buchanan Community Schools	Buchanan, MI
68	54.2	Clark Twp	Clark, NJ
68	54.2	Dale County SD	Ozark, AL
68	54.2	Menlo Park City Elementary	Atherton, CA
68	54.2	Niles Community SD	Niles, MI
68	54.2	Westonka	Mound, MN
74	54.1	Attica CSD	Attica, NY
74	54.1	East Windsor SD	East Windsor, CT
74	54.1	Genoa Area Local SD	Genoa, OH
74	54.1	Glenwood Community SD	Glenwood, IA
74	54.1	Hornell City SD	Hornell, NY
74	54.1	Maumee City SD	Maumee, OH
74	54.1	Osceola SD	Osceola, AR
74	54.1	Preble Shawnee Local SD	Camden, OH
74	54.1	Rocori	Cold Spring, MN
74	54.1	Scott County	Georgetown, KY
74	54.1	Wautoma Area	Wautoma, WI
74	54.1	Windsor C-1	Imperial, MO
86	54.0	Connally ISD	Waco, TX
86	54.0	Freedom Area	Freedom, WI
86	54.0	Litchfield SD	Hudson, NH
86	54.0	Medical Lake SD 326	Medical Lake, WA
86	54.0	Orrville City SD	Orrville, OH
86	54.0	Ross Local SD	Hamilton, OH
86	54.0	Shepherd ISD	Shepherd, TX
86	54.0	Wabash City Schools	Wabash, IN
94	53.9	Antioch Community High SD 117	Lake Villa, IL
94	53.9	Cass City Public Schools	Cass City, MI
94	53.9	Dover UFSD	Dover Plains, NY
94	53.9	Naches Valley SD 3	Naches, WA
94	53.9	North Arlington Boro	North Arlington, NJ
94	53.9	Saint Clair County SD	Ashville, AL
94	53.9	Sinton ISD	Sinton, TX
94	53.9	Three Rivers Local SD	Cleves, OH
94	53.9	Union Local SD	Morristown, OH
103	53.8	Audubon Boro	Audubon, NJ
103	53.8	Beachwood City SD	Beachwood, OH
103	53.8	Coldspring-Oakhurst CISD	Coldspring, TX
103	53.8	Diboll ISD	Diboll, TX
103	53.8	Greene County Schools	Snow Hill, NC
103	53.8	Hart County	Hartwell, GA
103	53.8	Mayfield City SD	Highland Hgts, OH
103	53.8	New Milford Boro	New Milford, NJ
103	53.8	Page Unified District	Page, AZ
103	53.8	Spooner	Spooner, WI
103	53.8	Woodland SD 404	Woodland, WA
114	53.7	Black Oak Mine Unified	Georgetown, CA
114	53.7	Caledonia Community Schools	Caledonia, MI
114	53.7	Chehalis SD 302	Chehalis, WA
114	53.7	Cleveland Hill UFSD	Cheektowaga, NY
114	53.7	Daleville City SD	Daleville, AL
114	53.7	Hardin-Jefferson ISD	Sour Lake, TX
114	53.7	Hartford Uhs	Hartford, WI

This section ranks 120 school districts at both the "top" and "bottom" of each category for a total of 240 districts per category. The "top" list (descending order) appears first, followed by the "bottom" list (ascending order).

Male Students

School districts ranked in *ascending* order

Rank	Percent	District Name	City, State
1	42.9	Essex County Voc-Tech	West Orange, NJ
2	46.5	Norwich Free Academy	Norwich, CT
3	47.0	Russell County Public Schools	Lebanon, VA
4	47.1	Byng	Ada, OK
5	47.2	China Spring ISD	Waco, TX
6	47.5	Galion City SD	Galion, OH
7	47.6	Concord	Concord, MA
7	47.6	Quaboag Regional	Warren, MA
9	47.7	Ramapo-Indian Hill Reg	Franklin Lakes, NJ
10	47.8	Julian Union Elementary	Julian, CA
11	47.9	Buchanan County Public Schools	Grundy, VA
11	47.9	Johnstown City SD	Johnstown, NY
13	48.0	Detroit Academy of Arts and Sciences	Detroit, MI
13	48.0	Kimberly Area	Kimberly, WI
15	48.1	South Texas ISD	Mercedes, TX
16	48.3	Doniphan R-I	Doniphan, MO
16	48.3	Gorman Elementary	Gorman, CA
16	48.3	King Philip	Wrentham, MA
16	48.3	Littleton	Littleton, MA
16	48.3	Lunenburg County Public Schools	Victoria, VA
16	48.3	North Adams	North Adams, MA
22	48.4	Las Vegas City Public Schools	Las Vegas, NM
22	48.4	Prairie Heights Com Sch Corp	Lagrange, IN
22	48.4	Westbury UFSD	Old Westbury, NY
25	48.5	Amherst	Amherst, MA
25	48.5	Danvers	Danvers, MA
25	48.5	Masconomet	Topsfield, MA
25	48.5	Mount Sinai UFSD	Mount Sinai, NY
25	48.5	Northeastern Clinton CSD	Champlain, NY
25	48.5	Regional SD 14	Woodbury, CT
31	48.6	Canton Public SD	Canton, MS
31	48.6	Clinton Twp	Annandale, NJ
31	48.6	Pojoaque Valley Public Schools	Santa Fe, NM
31	48.6	Southeast Dubois County Sch Corp	Ferdinand, IN
35	48.7	Allamakee Community SD	Waukon, IA
35	48.7	Altmar-Parish-Williamstown CSD	Parish, NY
35	48.7	Bishop Union Elementary	Bishop, CA
35	48.7	Greenfield Union Elementary	Greenfield, CA
35	48.7	Marshall	Marshall, MN
35	48.7	Orange Grove ISD	Orange Grove, TX
35	48.7	Passaic County Vocational	Wayne, NJ
35	48.7	Pitman Boro	Pitman, NJ
35	48.7	Proctor	Proctor, MN
35	48.7	Shorewood	Shorewood, WI
45	48.8	Carroll Community SD	Carroll, IA
45	48.8	Clare Public Schools	Clare, MI
45	48.8	Dexter R-XI	Dexter, MO
45	48.8	East Carroll Parish School Board	Lake Providence, LA
45	48.8	Flat Rock Community Schools	Flat Rock, MI
45	48.8	Mchenry Community HSD 156	Mc Henry, IL
45	48.8	North Spencer County Sch Corp	Lincoln City, IN
45	48.8	O'Fallon Twp High SD 203	Ofallon, IL
45	48.8	San Diego ISD	San Diego, TX
45	48.8	Shrewsbury	Shrewsbury, MA
45	48.8	Stafford SD	Stafford Spgs, CT
45	48.8	Trenton City	Trenton, NJ
57	48.9	Essex County Public Schools	Tappahannock, VA
57	48.9	Highland Park City Schools	Highland Park, MI
57	48.9	MSAD 05 - Rockland	Rockland, ME
57	48.9	Mccomb SD	Mccomb, MS
57	48.9	North Shore CSD	Sea Cliff, NY
57	48.9	Salmon River CSD	Ft Covington, NY
57	48.9	Sheffield-Sheffield Lake City	Sheffield Vlg, OH
57	48.9	Sussex-Wantage Regional	Wantage, NJ
57	48.9	Tunica County SD	Tunica, MS
66	49.0	Akron CSD	Akron, NY
66	49.0	Brookhaven SD	Brookhaven, MS
66	49.0	Grady County	Cairo, GA
66	49.0	Honeoye Falls-Lima CSD	Honeoye Falls, NY
66	49.0	Independence Community SD	Independence, IA
66	49.0	Marlington Local SD	Alliance, OH
66	49.0	Meridian CUSD 223	Stillman Valley, IL
66	49.0	Osceola	Osceola, WI
74	49.1	Bayless	Saint Louis, MO
74	49.1	Brawley Union High	Brawley, CA
74	49.1	Clarendon County SD 02	Manning, SC
74	49.1	Columbia Heights	Columbia Hgts, MN
74	49.1	Farmersville Unified	Farmersville, CA
74	49.1	Floyd County Public Schools	Floyd, VA
74	49.1	Freehold Regional	Englishtown, NJ
74	49.1	Fulton City SD	Fulton, NY
74	49.1	Ledyard SD	Ledyard, CT
74	49.1	Poteet ISD	Poteet, TX
74	49.1	Reavis Twp HSD 220	Burbank, IL
74	49.1	Selma City SD	Selma, AL
86	49.2	Albany	Albany, MN
86	49.2	Brush RE-2(J)	Brush, CO
86	49.2	Carterville CUSD 5	Carterville, IL
86	49.2	Kennett 39	Kennett, MO
86	49.2	Mount Pleasant Community SD	Mount Pleasant, IA
86	49.2	Nooksack Valley SD 506	Everson, WA
86	49.2	Olean City SD	Olean, NY
86	49.2	Pennsville	Pennsville, NJ
86	49.2	Swan Valley SD	Saginaw, MI
86	49.2	Taconic Hills CSD	Craryville, NY
86	49.2	Warsaw R-IX	Warsaw, MO
97	49.3	Buckeye Local SD	Ashtabula, OH
97	49.3	Centerville Community SD	Centerville, IA
97	49.3	Central Community Unit SD 301	Burlington, IL
97	49.3	Central Montcalm Public Schools	Stanton, MI
97	49.3	Central R-III	Park Hills, MO
97	49.3	Clearview Local SD	Lorain, OH
97	49.3	Electronic Classroom of Tomorrow	Columbus, OH
97	49.3	Freetown-Lakeville	Lakeville, MA
97	49.3	Geneva City SD	Geneva, NY
97	49.3	Hamilton-Wenham	Wenham, MA
97	49.3	Hammonton Town	Hammonton, NJ
97	49.3	Hazlet Twp	Hazlet, NJ
97	49.3	Lee County SD	Marianna, AR
97	49.3	MSAD 60 - North Berwick	North Berwick, ME
97	49.3	Maysville Local SD	Zanesville, OH
97	49.3	Mount Vernon SD 80	Mount Vernon, IL
97	49.3	Noxubee County SD	Macon, MS
97	49.3	River Delta Joint Unified	Rio Vista, CA
97	49.3	Saddle Brook Twp	Saddle Brook, NJ
97	49.3	Southwestern-Jefferson County	Hanover, IN
97	49.3	Turlock Joint Union High	Turlock, CA
97	49.3	Winthrop	Winthrop, MA
97	49.3	Zane Trace Local SD	Chillicothe, OH
97	49.3	Zanesville City SD	Zanesville, OH

This section ranks 120 school districts at both the "top" and "bottom" of each category for a total of 240 districts per category. The "top" list (descending order) appears first, followed by the "bottom" list (ascending order).

Female Students

School districts ranked in *descending* order

Rank	Percent	District Name	City, State
1	57.1	Essex County Voc-Tech	West Orange, NJ
2	53.5	Norwich Free Academy	Norwich, CT
3	53.0	Russell County Public Schools	Lebanon, VA
4	52.9	Byng	Ada, OK
5	52.8	China Spring ISD	Waco, TX
6	52.5	Galion City SD	Galion, OH
7	52.4	Concord	Concord, MA
7	52.4	Quaboag Regional	Warren, MA
9	52.3	Ramapo-Indian Hill Reg	Franklin Lakes, NJ
10	52.2	Julian Union Elementary	Julian, CA
11	52.1	Buchanan County Public Schools	Grundy, VA
11	52.1	Johnstown City SD	Johnstown, NY
13	52.0	Detroit Academy of Arts and Sciences	Detroit, MI
13	52.0	Kimberly Area	Kimberly, WI
15	51.9	South Texas ISD	Mercedes, TX
16	51.7	Doniphan R-I	Doniphan, MO
16	51.7	Gorman Elementary	Gorman, CA
16	51.7	King Philip	Wrentham, MA
16	51.7	Littleton	Littleton, MA
16	51.7	Lunenburg County Public Schools	Victoria, VA
16	51.7	North Adams	North Adams, MA
22	51.6	Las Vegas City Public Schools	Las Vegas, NM
22	51.6	Prairie Heights Com Sch Corp	Lagrange, IN
22	51.6	Westbury UFSD	Old Westbury, NY
25	51.5	Amherst	Amherst, MA
25	51.5	Danvers	Danvers, MA
25	51.5	Masconomet	Topsfield, MA
25	51.5	Mount Sinai UFSD	Mount Sinai, NY
25	51.5	Northeastern Clinton CSD	Champlain, NY
25	51.5	Regional SD 14	Woodbury, CT
31	51.4	Canton Public SD	Canton, MS
31	51.4	Clinton Twp	Annandale, NJ
31	51.4	Pojoaque Valley Public Schools	Santa Fe, NM
31	51.4	Southeast Dubois County Sch Corp	Ferdinand, IN
35	51.3	Allamakee Community SD	Waukon, IA
35	51.3	Altmar-Parish-Williamstown CSD	Parish, NY
35	51.3	Bishop Union Elementary	Bishop, CA
35	51.3	Greenfield Union Elementary	Greenfield, CA
35	51.3	Marshall	Marshall, MN
35	51.3	Orange Grove ISD	Orange Grove, TX
35	51.3	Passaic County Vocational	Wayne, NJ
35	51.3	Pitman Boro	Pitman, NJ
35	51.3	Proctor	Proctor, MN
35	51.3	Shorewood	Shorewood, WI
45	51.2	Carroll Community SD	Carroll, IA
45	51.2	Clare Public Schools	Clare, MI
45	51.2	Dexter R-XI	Dexter, MO
45	51.2	East Carroll Parish School Board	Lake Providence, LA
45	51.2	Flat Rock Community Schools	Flat Rock, MI
45	51.2	Mchenry Community HSD 156	Mc Henry, IL
45	51.2	North Spencer County Sch Corp	Lincoln City, IN
45	51.2	O'Fallon Twp High SD 203	Ofallon, IL
45	51.2	San Diego ISD	San Diego, TX
45	51.2	Shrewsbury	Shrewsbury, MA
45	51.2	Stafford SD	Stafford Spgs, CT
45	51.2	Trenton City	Trenton, NJ
57	51.1	Essex County Public Schools	Tappahannock, VA
57	51.1	Highland Park City Schools	Highland Park, MI
57	51.1	MSAD 05 - Rockland	Rockland, ME
57	51.1	Mccomb SD	Mccomb, MS
57	51.1	North Shore CSD	Sea Cliff, NY
57	51.1	Salmon River CSD	Ft Covington, NY
57	51.1	Sheffield-Sheffield Lake City	Sheffield Vlg, OH
57	51.1	Sussex-Wantage Regional	Wantage, NJ
57	51.1	Tunica County SD	Tunica, MS
66	51.0	Akron CSD	Akron, NY
66	51.0	Brookhaven SD	Brookhaven, MS
66	51.0	Grady County	Cairo, GA
66	51.0	Honeoye Falls-Lima CSD	Honeoye Falls, NY
66	51.0	Independence Community SD	Independence, IA
66	51.0	Marlington Local SD	Alliance, OH
66	51.0	Meridian CUSD 223	Stillman Valley, IL
66	51.0	Osceola	Osceola, WI
74	50.9	Bayless	Saint Louis, MO
74	50.9	Brawley Union High	Brawley, CA
74	50.9	Clarendon County SD 02	Manning, SC
74	50.9	Columbia Heights	Columbia Hgts, MN
74	50.9	Farmersville Unified	Farmersville, CA
74	50.9	Floyd County Public Schools	Floyd, VA
74	50.9	Freehold Regional	Englishtown, NJ
74	50.9	Fulton City SD	Fulton, NY
74	50.9	Ledyard SD	Ledyard, CT
74	50.9	Poteet ISD	Poteet, TX
74	50.9	Reavis Twp HSD 220	Burbank, IL
74	50.9	Selma City SD	Selma, AL
86	50.8	Albany	Albany, MN
86	50.8	Brush RE-2(J)	Brush, CO
86	50.8	Carterville CUSD 5	Carterville, IL
86	50.8	Kennett 39	Kennett, MO
86	50.8	Mount Pleasant Community SD	Mount Pleasant, IA
86	50.8	Nooksack Valley SD 506	Everson, WA
86	50.8	Olean City SD	Olean, NY
86	50.8	Pennsville	Pennsville, NJ
86	50.8	Swan Valley SD	Saginaw, MI
86	50.8	Taconic Hills CSD	Craryville, NY
86	50.8	Warsaw R-IX	Warsaw, MO
97	50.7	Buckeye Local SD	Ashtabula, OH
97	50.7	Centerville Community SD	Centerville, IA
97	50.7	Central Community Unit SD 301	Burlington, IL
97	50.7	Central Montcalm Public Schools	Stanton, MI
97	50.7	Central R-III	Park Hills, MO
97	50.7	Clearview Local SD	Lorain, OH
97	50.7	Electronic Classroom of Tomorrow	Columbus, OH
97	50.7	Freetown-Lakeville	Lakeville, MA
97	50.7	Geneva City SD	Geneva, NY
97	50.7	Hamilton-Wenham	Wenham, MA
97	50.7	Hammonton Town	Hammonton, NJ
97	50.7	Hazlet Twp	Hazlet, NJ
97	50.7	Lee County SD	Marianna, AR
97	50.7	MSAD 60 - North Berwick	North Berwick, ME
97	50.7	Maysville Local SD	Zanesville, OH
97	50.7	Mount Vernon SD 80	Mount Vernon, IL
97	50.7	Noxubee County SD	Macon, MS
97	50.7	River Delta Joint Unified	Rio Vista, CA
97	50.7	Saddle Brook Twp	Saddle Brook, NJ
97	50.7	Southwestern-Jefferson County	Hanover, IN
97	50.7	Turlock Joint Union High	Turlock, CA
97	50.7	Winthrop	Winthrop, MA
97	50.7	Zane Trace Local SD	Chillicothe, OH
97	50.7	Zanesville City SD	Zanesville, OH

This section ranks 120 school districts at both the "top" and "bottom" of each category for a total of 240 districts per category. The "top" list (descending order) appears first, followed by the "bottom" list (ascending order).

Female Students

School districts ranked in *ascending* order

Rank	Percent	District Name	City, State
1	10.1	Department of Corrections SD 428	Springfield, IL
2	26.0	Boces Eastern Suffolk (Suffolk I)	Patchogue, NY
2	26.0	Boces Nassau	Garden City, NY
4	28.0	Boces Monroe 1	Fairport, NY
5	28.1	San Bernardino County Supt.	San Bernardino, CA
6	30.1	Macomb ISD	Clinton Twp, MI
7	30.9	Coxsackie-Athens CSD	Coxsackie, NY
8	31.0	Santa Clara County Office of Ed	San Jose, CA
9	32.0	Los Angeles County Office of Ed	Downey, CA
10	32.6	Fresno County Office of Ed	Fresno, CA
11	33.1	Kern County Office of Ed	Bakersfield, CA
12	36.2	San Joaquin County Office of Ed	Stockton, CA
13	36.3	State Voc-Tech Schools	Middletown, CT
14	38.4	Area Coop Educational Services	North Haven, CT
15	39.9	Orange County Office of Ed	Costa Mesa, CA
15	39.9	San Diego County Office of Ed	San Diego, CA
17	40.2	Middlesex County Vocational	E Brunswick, NJ
18	41.0	Riverside County Office of Ed	Riverside, CA
19	41.5	Vassar Public Schools	Vassar, MI
20	41.7	Intermediate SD 287	Plymouth, MN
21	41.9	Gulf Shores Academy	Houston, TX
22	42.4	Rochester SD 401	Rochester, WA
23	42.6	Broadalbin-Perth CSD	Broadalbin, NY
24	42.7	Maricopa County Regional District	Phoenix, AZ
25	42.8	East Valley Institute of Technology	Mesa, AZ
26	43.8	Hudson City SD	Hudson, NY
27	44.2	Bergen County Vocational	Paramus, NJ
27	44.2	Martin County	Inez, KY
27	44.2	Washtenaw ISD	Ann Arbor, MI
30	44.4	West ISD	West, TX
31	44.5	Greater New Bedford	New Bedford, MA
32	44.6	Cascade Union Elementary	Anderson, CA
33	44.7	Littlefield ISD	Littlefield, TX
33	44.7	Saint Marys City SD	Saint Marys, OH
33	44.7	West Bonner County District	Sandpoint, ID
36	45.0	Canton Local SD	Canton, OH
36	45.0	Danville Independent	Danville, KY
36	45.0	Lower Twp	Cape May, NJ
36	45.0	Orange City SD	Cleveland, OH
40	45.1	Highland CSD	Highland, NY
41	45.2	Camden County Vocational	Sicklerville, NJ
41	45.2	Colbert County SD	Tuscumbia, AL
41	45.2	El Dorado	El Dorado, KS
41	45.2	Madison County SD	Madison, FL
41	45.2	Wickliffe City SD	Wickliffe, OH
46	45.3	Caldwell Parish School Board	Columbia, LA
46	45.3	Fruitland District	Fruitland, ID
48	45.4	Bath CSD	Bath, NY
48	45.4	Berlin SD	Berlin, NH
48	45.4	Brown Deer	Brown Deer, WI
48	45.4	Little Chute Area	Little Chute, WI
48	45.4	Mason County Central Schools	Scottville, MI
53	45.5	Greene County R-VIII	Rogersville, MO
53	45.5	Marlin ISD	Marlin, TX
53	45.5	Melrose	Melrose, MN
53	45.5	Monroe County	Tompkinsville, KY
53	45.5	Mount Pleasant Elementary	San Jose, CA
53	45.5	Redford Union SD	Redford, MI
53	45.5	Tallmadge City SD	Tallmadge, OH
53	45.5	West De Pere	De Pere, WI
61	45.6	Lorena ISD	Lorena, TX
61	45.6	Pike County SD	Troy, AL
63	45.7	Alliance Public Schools	Alliance, NE
63	45.7	Breathitt County	Jackson, KY
63	45.7	Burlington County Vocational	Westampton Twp, NJ
63	45.7	Crenshaw County SD	Luverne, AL
63	45.7	Hamtramck Public Schools	Hamtramck, MI
68	45.8	Buchanan Community Schools	Buchanan, MI
68	45.8	Clark Twp	Clark, NJ
68	45.8	Dale County SD	Ozark, AL
68	45.8	Menlo Park City Elementary	Atherton, CA
68	45.8	Niles Community SD	Niles, MI
68	45.8	Westonka	Mound, MN
74	45.9	Attica CSD	Attica, NY
74	45.9	East Windsor SD	East Windsor, CT
74	45.9	Genoa Area Local SD	Genoa, OH
74	45.9	Glenwood Community SD	Glenwood, IA
74	45.9	Hornell City SD	Hornell, NY
74	45.9	Maumee City SD	Maumee, OH
74	45.9	Osceola SD	Osceola, AR
74	45.9	Preble Shawnee Local SD	Camden, OH
74	45.9	Rocori	Cold Spring, MN
74	45.9	Scott County	Georgetown, KY
74	45.9	Wautoma Area	Wautoma, WI
74	45.9	Windsor C-1	Imperial, MO
86	46.0	Connally ISD	Waco, TX
86	46.0	Freedom Area	Freedom, WI
86	46.0	Litchfield SD	Hudson, NH
86	46.0	Medical Lake SD 326	Medical Lake, WA
86	46.0	Orrville City SD	Orrville, OH
86	46.0	Ross Local SD	Hamilton, OH
86	46.0	Shepherd ISD	Shepherd, TX
86	46.0	Wabash City Schools	Wabash, IN
94	46.1	Antioch Community High SD 117	Lake Villa, IL
94	46.1	Cass City Public Schools	Cass City, MI
94	46.1	Dover UFSD	Dover Plains, NY
94	46.1	Naches Valley SD 3	Naches, WA
94	46.1	North Arlington Boro	North Arlington, NJ
94	46.1	Saint Clair County SD	Ashville, AL
94	46.1	Sinton ISD	Sinton, TX
94	46.1	Three Rivers Local SD	Cleves, OH
94	46.1	Union Local SD	Morristown, OH
103	46.2	Audubon Boro	Audubon, NJ
103	46.2	Beachwood City SD	Beachwood, OH
103	46.2	Coldspring-Oakhurst CISD	Coldspring, TX
103	46.2	Diboll ISD	Diboll, TX
103	46.2	Greene County Schools	Snow Hill, NC
103	46.2	Hart County	Hartwell, GA
103	46.2	Mayfield City SD	Highland Hgts, OH
103	46.2	New Milford Boro	New Milford, NJ
103	46.2	Page Unified District	Page, AZ
103	46.2	Spooner	Spooner, WI
103	46.2	Woodland SD 404	Woodland, WA
114	46.3	Black Oak Mine Unified	Georgetown, CA
114	46.3	Caledonia Community Schools	Caledonia, MI
114	46.3	Chehalis SD 302	Chehalis, WA
114	46.3	Cleveland Hill UFSD	Cheektowaga, NY
114	46.3	Daleville City SD	Daleville, AL
114	46.3	Hardin-Jefferson ISD	Sour Lake, TX
114	46.3	Hartford Uhs	Hartford, WI

This section ranks 120 school districts at both the "top" and "bottom" of each category for a total of 240 districts per category. The "top" list (descending order) appears first, followed by the "bottom" list (ascending order).

Individual Education Program Students

School districts ranked in *descending* order

Rank	Percent	District Name	City, State
1	100.0	Boces Eastern Suffolk (Suffolk I)	Patchogue, NY
2	93.5	Special SD - Saint Louis County	Town & Ctry, MO
3	91.4	Santa Clara County Office of Ed	San Jose, CA
4	85.8	Boces Nassau	Garden City, NY
5	83.1	Boces Monroe 1	Fairport, NY
6	70.9	Riverside County Office of Ed	Riverside, CA
7	70.3	Fresno County Office of Ed	Fresno, CA
8	69.1	Amphitheater Unified District	Tucson, AZ
9	62.8	Los Angeles County Office of Ed	Downey, CA
10	56.1	Kern County Office of Ed	Bakersfield, CA
11	50.1	Belmont-Redwood Shores Elementary	Belmont, CA
12	34.8	Intermediate SD 287	Plymouth, MN
13	32.0	Burlington County Vocational	Westampton Twp, NJ
14	31.6	Camden County Vocational	Sicklerville, NJ
15	30.3	Los Alamos Public Schools	Los Alamos, NM
16	30.1	Carrollton SD	Saginaw, MI
17	28.9	Middlesex County Vocational	E Brunswick, NJ
18	28.6	San Joaquin County Office of Ed	Stockton, CA
19	28.0	Harrison Hills City SD	Hopedale, OH
20	28.0	Rantoul City SD 137	Rantoul, IL
21	27.8	Keansburg Boro	Keansburg, NJ
22	27.2	Barnegat Twp	Barnegat, NJ
23	26.9	Carlsbad Municipal Schools	Carlsbad, NM
24	26.6	Grundy County SD	Altamont, TN
25	26.3	Lovington Public Schools	Lovington, NM
26	26.2	New Castle Community Sch Corp	New Castle, IN
27	26.0	Jefferson County SD	Monticello, FL
28	26.0	Newport SD	Newport, RI
29	25.8	Roswell Independent Schools	Roswell, NM
30	25.6	Venus ISD	Venus, TX
31	25.6	Madison Consolidated Schools	Madison, IN
32	25.6	North Putnam Community Schools	Bainbridge, IN
33	25.5	Grand Rapids Public Schools	Grand Rapids, MI
34	25.4	Central Falls SD	Central Falls, RI
35	25.3	Madison County SD	Madison, FL
36	25.3	Johnston SD	Johnston, RI
37	25.2	Benton Community School Corp	Fowler, IN
38	25.2	San Diego County Office of Ed	San Diego, CA
39	25.2	Columbia Borough SD	Columbia, PA
40	25.1	Meriwether County	Greenville, GA
41	25.1	Mount Vernon SD 80	Mount Vernon, IL
42	24.9	Las Cruces Public Schools	Las Cruces, NM
43	24.9	East Longmeadow	E Longmeadow, MA
44	24.8	Greater Lowell Voc Tec	Tyngsborough, MA
45	24.7	Pinelands Regional	Tuckerton, NJ
46	24.4	Prentiss County SD	Booneville, MS
47	24.4	Redford Union SD	Redford, MI
48	24.2	Lower Cape May Regional	Cape May, NJ
49	24.1	Charleston CUSD 1	Charleston, IL
50	23.9	Sto-Rox SD	Mckees Rocks, PA
51	23.8	Woonsocket SD	Woonsocket, RI
52	23.8	South Bend Community Sch Corp	South Bend, IN
53	23.8	Greeneville City SD	Greeneville, TN
54	23.7	Pemberton Twp	Pemberton, NJ
55	23.6	Richmond Community School Corp	Richmond, IN
56	23.6	Gilchrist County SD	Trenton, FL
57	23.6	Upper Twp	Petersburg, NJ
58	23.5	Maple Shade Twp	Maple Shade, NJ
59	23.4	Southwestern-Jefferson County	Hanover, IN
60	23.3	Lackawanna City SD	Lackawanna, NY
61	23.3	Bradford County SD	Starke, FL
62	23.3	Dixie County SD	Cross City, FL
63	23.3	Plattsmouth Community Schools	Plattsmouth, NE
64	23.2	Summers County SD	Hinton, WV
65	23.2	West ISD	West, TX
66	23.2	Bradley SD 61	Bradley, IL
67	23.2	Levy County SD	Bronson, FL
68	23.2	Union County	Morganfiel, KY
69	23.1	Zanesville City SD	Zanesville, OH
70	23.0	Herrin CUSD 4	Herrin, IL
71	23.0	Randolph Central School Corp	Winchester, IN
72	22.9	Bledsoe County SD	Pikeville, TN
73	22.9	Southwest School Corp	Sullivan, IN
74	22.9	Cobre Consolidated Schools	Bayard, NM
75	22.8	South Madison Com Sch Corp	Pendleton, IN
76	22.8	Muncie Community Schools	Muncie, IN
77	22.8	Kokomo-Center Twp Con Sch Corp	Kokomo, IN
78	22.8	Floyd County	Rome, GA
79	22.7	Bloomfield Municipal Schools	Bloomfield, NM
80	22.7	Augusta Dept of Public Schools	Augusta, ME
81	22.7	Moriarty Muncipal Schools	Moriarty, NM
82	22.6	Clay County	Manchester, KY
83	22.6	Narragansett SD	Narragansett, RI
84	22.6	Streator Elem SD 44	Streator, IL
85	22.6	Unicoi SD	Erwin, TN
86	22.6	Belen Consolidated Schools	Belen, NM
87	22.6	West Warwick SD	West Warwick, RI
88	22.5	Marion County SD 02	Mullins, SC
89	22.5	Hopatcong	Hopatcong, NJ
90	22.4	Peoria SD 150	Peoria, IL
91	22.4	Bristol Warren RD	Bristol, RI
92	22.4	Los Lunas Public Schools	Los Lunas, NM
93	22.3	Sussex-Wantage Regional	Wantage, NJ
94	22.3	Centerville Community SD	Centerville, IA
95	22.3	Roane County SD	Spencer, WV
96	22.3	Cloverdale Community Schools	Cloverdale, IN
97	22.2	Asbury Park City	Asbury Park, NJ
98	22.2	Pawtucket SD	Pawtucket, RI
99	22.2	Shelbyville Central Schools	Shelbyville, IN
100	22.2	Cumberland SD	Cumberland, RI
101	22.2	Mattoon CUSD 2	Mattoon, IL
102	22.2	Burlington Community SD	Burlington, IA
103	22.2	Frankfort Community Unit SD 168	West Frankfort, IL
104	22.2	Lafayette School Corporation	Lafayette, IN
105	22.1	Garden City SD	Garden City, MI
106	22.1	Hamilton Twp	Hamilton Square, NJ
107	22.1	Tyler County SD	Sistersville, WV
108	22.1	Lancaster SD	Lancaster, PA
109	22.1	Northeast School Corp	Hymera, IN
110	22.1	Cambridge	Cambridge, MA
111	22.1	Greater Clark County Schools	Jeffersonville, IN
112	22.0	Macomb Community Unit SD 185	Macomb, IL
113	22.0	Chester-Upland SD	Chester, PA
114	22.0	Atchison Public Schools	Atchison, KS
115	22.0	Lower Twp	Cape May, NJ
116	22.0	Oak Ridge City SD	Oak Ridge, TN
117	22.0	Belleville SD 118	Belleville, IL
118	21.9	Woodbury City	Woodbury, NJ
119	21.9	Westwood Regional	Westwood, NJ
120	21.9	Central Greene SD	Waynesburg, PA

This section ranks 120 school districts at both the "top" and "bottom" of each category for a total of 240 districts per category. The "top" list (descending order) appears first, followed by the "bottom" list (ascending order).

Individual Education Program Students

School districts ranked in *ascending* order

Rank	Percent	District Name	City, State
1	0.0	Area Coop Educational Services	North Haven, CT
1	0.0	Capitol Region Education Council	Hartford, CT
1	0.0	Central Arizona Valley Inst of Tech	Coolidge, AZ
1	0.0	Colusa Unified	Colusa, CA
1	0.0	East Valley Institute of Technology	Mesa, AZ
1	0.0	Essex Community Education Ctr	Essex Junction, VT
1	0.0	Mount Anthony UHSD 14	Bennington, VT
1	0.0	Mount Mansfield USD 17	Jericho, VT
1	0.0	North Little Rock SD	N Little Rock, AR
1	0.0	Norwich Free Academy	Norwich, CT
1	0.0	PDE Division of Data Services	Harrisburg, PA
1	0.0	Pinkerton Academy SD	Derry, NH
1	0.0	Saint Helena Unified	Saint Helena, CA
1	0.0	Westwood Unified	Westwood, CA
1	0.0	Willows Unified	Willows, CA
16	0.4	Oro Grande Elementary	Oro Grande, CA
17	0.6	Tamalpais Union High	Larkspur, CA
18	1.5	Billerica	Billerica, MA
19	2.6	Chowchilla Elementary	Chowchilla, CA
20	2.7	Galena City SD	Galena, AK
21	2.8	Cutler-Orosi Joint Unified	Orosi, CA
22	2.9	Sycamore Community City SD	Cincinnati, OH
23	3.2	Detroit Academy of Arts and Sciences	Detroit, MI
24	3.3	Julian Union High	Julian, CA
25	3.4	Golden Plains Unified	San Joaquin, CA
25	3.4	Mattawan Consolidated School	Mattawan, MI
27	3.5	Pennsylvania Virtual CS	Norristown, PA
28	3.6	Gulf Shores Academy	Houston, TX
29	3.8	Belcourt 7	Belcourt, ND
30	3.9	Lindsay Unified	Lindsay, CA
31	4.0	Lynwood Unified	Lynwood, CA
32	4.6	Bethel-Tate Local SD	Bethel, OH
33	4.7	Cheyenne Mountain 12	Colorado Spgs, CO
33	4.7	Compton Unified	Compton, CA
35	4.8	Gorman Elementary	Gorman, CA
35	4.8	Live Oak Unified	Live Oak, CA
35	4.8	Los Banos Unified	Los Banos, CA
38	4.9	Aspen 1	Aspen, CO
38	4.9	Burton Elementary	Porterville, CA
40	5.0	Bow SD	Bow, NH
40	5.0	Buckeye Union Elementary	Shingle Springs, CA
42	5.1	Earlimart Elementary	Earlimart, CA
42	5.1	Gadsden Elementary District	San Luis, AZ
42	5.1	Hillsboro City SD	Hillsboro, OH
45	5.3	West Covina Unified	West Covina, CA
46	5.4	Electronic Classroom of Tomorrow	Columbus, OH
46	5.4	Hanford Elementary	Hanford, CA
46	5.4	Woodlake Union Elementary	Woodlake, CA
49	5.5	Exeter Union Elementary	Exeter, CA
49	5.5	Porterville Unified	Porterville, CA
51	5.6	Wheatland Elementary	Wheatland, CA
52	5.7	Mars Area SD	Mars, PA
53	5.8	Muscle Shoals City SD	Muscle Shoals, AL
53	5.8	Riverdale Joint Unified	Riverdale, CA
53	5.8	Salinas City Elementary	Salinas, CA
56	6.0	Corning Union Elementary	Corning, CA
56	6.0	Farmersville Unified	Farmersville, CA
58	6.1	Mendota Unified	Mendota, CA
58	6.1	Rye City SD	Rye, NY
60	6.2	Corcoran Joint Unified	Corcoran, CA
60	6.2	Jefferson Elementary	Tracy, CA
60	6.2	Roaring Fork RE-1	Glenwood Spgs, CO
60	6.2	Templeton Unified	Templeton, CA
64	6.3	Mission Cons ISD	Mission, TX
64	6.3	Parlier Unified	Parlier, CA
64	6.3	Progreso ISD	Progreso, TX
67	6.4	Bellflower Unified	Bellflower, CA
67	6.4	MSAD 51 - Cumberland	Cumberland Ctr, ME
67	6.4	Soledad Unified	Soledad, CA
70	6.5	Healdsburg Unified	Healdsburg, CA
71	6.6	Cupertino Union School	Cupertino, CA
71	6.6	Fabens ISD	Fabens, TX
71	6.6	Manasquan Boro	Manasquan, NJ
71	6.6	Whitefish Bay	Whitefish Bay, WI
75	6.7	Alisal Union Elementary	Salinas, CA
75	6.7	Calexico Unified	Calexico, CA
75	6.7	Norris Elementary	Bakersfield, CA
75	6.7	Walnut Valley Unified	Walnut, CA
79	6.8	Butte County Joint District	Arco, ID
79	6.8	Fullerton Joint Union High	Fullerton, CA
79	6.8	Gainesville City	Gainesville, GA
79	6.8	Madera Unified	Madera, CA
83	6.9	Academy 20	Colorado Spgs, CO
83	6.9	Jefferson Union High	Daly City, CA
83	6.9	North Monterey County Unified	Moss Landing, CA
83	6.9	Santa Maria-Bonita Elementary	Santa Maria, CA
83	6.9	Worth County	Sylvester, GA
88	7.0	Arrowhead Uhs	Hartland, WI
88	7.0	East Aurora UFSD	East Aurora, NY
88	7.0	Mother Lode Union Elementary	Placerville, CA
88	7.0	North Forest ISD	Houston, TX
88	7.0	Oakwood City SD	Dayton, OH
88	7.0	Winton Elementary	Winton, CA
94	7.1	Hamtramck Public Schools	Hamtramck, MI
94	7.1	Lakeport Unified	Lakeport, CA
94	7.1	Morgan SD	Morgan, UT
94	7.1	Peters Township SD	Mcmurray, PA
98	7.2	Brookfield SD	Brookfield, CT
98	7.2	Hidalgo ISD	Hidalgo, TX
98	7.2	Indian Hill Ex Vill SD	Cincinnati, OH
98	7.2	Inglewood Unified	Inglewood, CA
98	7.2	Lompoc Unified	Lompoc, CA
98	7.2	Plum Borough SD	Plum, PA
98	7.2	Windsor Unified	Windsor, CA
105	7.3	Anthony Wayne Local SD	Whitehouse, OH
105	7.3	Bangor Public Schools (Van Buren)	Bangor, MI
105	7.3	Brawley Elementary	Brawley, CA
105	7.3	Flathead HS	Kalispell, MT
105	7.3	Pasadena ISD	Pasadena, TX
105	7.3	Shasta Union High	Redding, CA
105	7.3	Yuba City Unified	Yuba City, CA
112	7.4	Bishop Union Elementary	Bishop, CA
112	7.4	Fairfield Union Local SD	W Rushville, OH
112	7.4	Ganado Unified District	Ganado, AZ
112	7.4	Keller ISD	Keller, TX
112	7.4	Maricopa County Regional District	Phoenix, AZ
112	7.4	Santa Cruz Valley Unified District	Rio Rico, AZ
112	7.4	Tulare Joint Union High	Tulare, CA
119	7.5	Acalanes Union High	Lafayette, CA
119	7.5	Anderson Union High	Anderson, CA

This section ranks 120 school districts at both the "top" and "bottom" of each category for a total of 240 districts per category. The "top" list (descending order) appears first, followed by the "bottom" list (ascending order).

English Language Learner (ELL) Students

School districts ranked in *descending* order

Rank	Percent	District Name	City, State
1	99.5	Mentor Ex Vill SD	Mentor, OH
2	89.6	Gadsden Elementary District	San Luis, AZ
3	83.7	Earlimart Elementary	Earlimart, CA
4	79.9	Todd County SD 66-1	Mission, SD
5	77.8	Lower Yukon SD	Mountain Vlg, AK
6	76.3	Calexico Unified	Calexico, CA
7	73.6	Lamont Elementary	Lamont, CA
8	72.6	San Ysidro Elementary	San Ysidro, CA
9	72.2	Whiteriver Unified District	Whiteriver, AZ
10	72.1	Kayenta Unified District	Kayenta, AZ
11	71.3	Alisal Union Elementary	Salinas, CA
12	71.2	Lennox Elementary	Lennox, CA
13	71.0	Mendota Unified	Mendota, CA
14	69.9	Coachella Valley Unified	Thermal, CA
15	68.9	Arvin Union Elementary	Arvin, CA
16	68.5	Livingston Union Elementary	Livingston, CA
17	67.2	Ravenswood City Elementary	East Palo Alto, CA
18	67.1	San Juan SD	Blanding, UT
19	66.7	Toppenish SD 202	Toppenish, WA
20	66.4	Gadsden Independent Schools	Anthony, NM
20	66.4	Ganado Unified District	Ganado, AZ
22	66.4	Hamtramck Public Schools	Hamtramck, MI
23	65.4	Reef-Sunset Unified	Avenal, CA
24	65.2	Hatch Valley Public Schools	Hatch, NM
25	64.8	Somerton Elementary District	Somerton, AZ
26	64.5	Gonzales Unified	Gonzales, CA
27	64.1	Anaheim Elementary	Anaheim, CA
28	63.5	Santa Ana Unified	Santa Ana, CA
29	63.4	Parlier Unified	Parlier, CA
30	62.3	Bellevue Union Elementary	Santa Rosa, CA
31	61.6	Mountain View Elementary	El Monte, CA
32	61.3	West Las Vegas Public Schools	Las Vegas, NM
33	61.2	Murphy Elementary District	Phoenix, AZ
34	61.1	Aurora East Unit SD 131	Aurora, IL
35	60.5	Creighton Elementary District	Phoenix, AZ
36	60.1	Isaac Elementary District	Phoenix, AZ
37	60.1	Dalton City	Dalton, GA
38	59.7	Winton Elementary	Winton, CA
39	59.4	Cutler-Orosi Joint Unified	Orosi, CA
40	59.0	Lower Kuskokwim SD	Bethel, AK
41	58.9	Laredo ISD	Laredo, TX
42	58.7	East Holmes Local SD	Berlin, OH
43	58.4	Woodburn SD 103	Woodburn, OR
44	58.1	Wahluke SD 73	Mattawa, WA
45	58.0	Lindsay Unified	Lindsay, CA
46	58.0	Greenfield Union Elementary	Greenfield, CA
47	57.9	Golden Plains Unified	San Joaquin, CA
48	57.9	Soledad Unified	Soledad, CA
49	57.6	Chinle Unified District	Chinle, AZ
50	56.9	Delano Union Elementary	Delano, CA
51	55.6	King City Union Elementary	King City, CA
52	55.2	Alum Rock Union Elementary	San Jose, CA
53	55.2	Franklin-Mckinley Elementary	San Jose, CA
54	54.7	National Elementary	National City, CA
55	54.2	Santa Maria-Bonita Elementary	Santa Maria, CA
56	53.8	Cobre Consolidated Schools	Bayard, NM
57	53.7	Bering Strait SD	Unalakleet, AK
58	53.2	North Slope Borough SD	Barrow, AK
59	53.1	San Elizario ISD	San Elizario, TX
60	53.0	Central Consolidated Schools	Shiprock, NM
61	52.9	Compton Unified	Compton, CA
62	52.7	Phoenix Elementary District	Phoenix, AZ
63	52.7	Garden Grove Unified	Garden Grove, CA
64	52.7	Ontario-Montclair Elementary	Ontario, CA
65	52.5	Hidalgo ISD	Hidalgo, TX
66	52.4	Espanola Municipal Schools	Espanola, NM
67	52.3	Valley View ISD	Pharr, TX
68	52.2	Richland SD	Shafter, CA
69	52.1	Window Rock Unified District	Fort Defiance, AZ
70	51.6	Santa Paula Elementary	Santa Paula, CA
71	51.2	Donna ISD	Donna, TX
72	51.2	Macomb ISD	Clinton Twp, MI
73	51.0	Mount Pleasant Elementary	San Jose, CA
74	50.6	Lynwood Unified	Lynwood, CA
75	50.6	Redwood City Elementary	Redwood City, CA
76	50.4	Alhambra Elementary District	Phoenix, AZ
77	49.8	Roma ISD	Roma, TX
78	49.7	Magnolia Elementary	Anaheim, CA
79	49.6	Rio Grande City CISD	Rio Grande City, TX
80	49.6	Farmersville Unified	Farmersville, CA
81	49.4	Zuni Public Schools	Zuni, NM
82	49.3	Delano Joint Union High	Delano, CA
83	49.3	La Joya ISD	La Joya, TX
84	49.2	Fabens ISD	Fabens, TX
85	49.2	Cicero SD 99	Cicero, IL
86	49.1	Ocean View Elementary	Oxnard, CA
87	49.0	Wasco Union Elementary	Wasco, CA
88	47.9	Bernalillo Public Schools	Bernalillo, NM
89	47.7	Progreso ISD	Progreso, TX
90	47.3	Oxnard Elementary	Oxnard, CA
91	47.3	Delhi Unified	Delhi, CA
92	47.1	Brownsville ISD	Brownsville, TX
93	46.8	Pomona Unified	Pomona, CA
94	46.8	United ISD	Laredo, TX
95	46.7	El Centro Elementary	El Centro, CA
96	46.6	La Habra City Elementary	La Habra, CA
97	46.6	Rio Elementary	Oxnard, CA
98	46.5	Garvey Elementary	Rosemead, CA
99	46.4	Hawthorne Elementary	Hawthorne, CA
100	46.3	Pajaro Valley Unified School	Watsonville, CA
101	46.3	El Monte City Elementary	El Monte, CA
102	45.9	Holtville Unified	Holtville, CA
103	45.7	Montebello Unified	Montebello, CA
104	45.5	Salinas City Elementary	Salinas, CA
105	45.5	Santa Cruz Valley Unified District	Rio Rico, AZ
106	45.3	Weld County SD RE-8	Fort Lupton, CO
107	44.9	Alhambra City Elementary	Alhambra, CA
108	44.9	Storm Lake Community SD	Storm Lake, IA
109	44.8	Clint ISD	Clint, TX
110	44.4	Paramount Unified	Paramount, CA
111	44.3	Perris Elementary	Perris, CA
112	44.2	Hueneme Elementary	Port Hueneme, CA
113	43.8	Tuba City Unified District	Tuba City, AZ
114	43.8	San Rafael City Elementary	San Rafael, CA
115	43.7	Balsz Elementary District	Phoenix, AZ
116	43.4	Amphitheater Unified District	Tucson, AZ
117	43.4	Del Paso Heights Elementary	Sacramento, CA
118	43.3	Buena Park Elementary	Buena Park, CA
119	43.2	South Bay Union Elementary	Imperial Beach, CA
120	42.9	Los Angeles Unified	Los Angeles, CA

This section ranks 120 school districts at both the "top" and "bottom" of each category for a total of 240 districts per category. The "top" list (descending order) appears first, followed by the "bottom" list (ascending order).

English Language Learner (ELL) Students

School districts ranked in *ascending* order

Rank	Percent	District Name	City, State
1	0.0	Aberdeen SD	Aberdeen, MS
1	0.0	Aberdeen SD 06-1	Aberdeen, SD
1	0.0	Adams County-Ohio Valley Local SD	West Union, OH
1	0.0	Adams-Friendship Area	Friendship, WI
1	0.0	Adirondack CSD	Boonville, NY
1	0.0	Akron CSD	Akron, NY
1	0.0	Allen County	Scottsville, KY
1	0.0	Altmar-Parish-Williamstown CSD	Parish, NY
1	0.0	Amanda-Clearcreek Local SD	Amanda, OH
1	0.0	Amery	Amery, WI
1	0.0	Amherst Ex Vill SD	Amherst, OH
1	0.0	Anthony Wayne Local SD	Whitehouse, OH
1	0.0	Antigo	Antigo, WI
1	0.0	Antioch Community High SD 117	Lake Villa, IL
1	0.0	Apache Junction Unified District	Apache Junction, AZ
1	0.0	Arkadelphia SD	Arkadelphia, AR
1	0.0	Arkansas City	Arkansas City, KS
1	0.0	Arrowhead Uhs	Hartland, WI
1	0.0	Ashburnham-Westminster	Westminster, MA
1	0.0	Ashland	Ashland, WI
1	0.0	Ashwaubenon	Green Bay, WI
1	0.0	Atchison Public Schools	Atchison, KS
1	0.0	Atlantic Community SD	Atlantic, IA
1	0.0	Auburn	Auburn, MA
1	0.0	Augusta	Augusta, KS
1	0.0	Ball Chatham CUSD 5	Chatham, IL
1	0.0	Ballard County	Barlow, KY
1	0.0	Bamberg County SD 01	Bamberg, SC
1	0.0	Baraboo	Baraboo, WI
1	0.0	Barren County	Glasgow, KY
1	0.0	Basehor-Linwood	Basehor, KS
1	0.0	Bath CSD	Bath, NY
1	0.0	Bath County	Owingsv, KY
1	0.0	Bath Local SD	Lima, OH
1	0.0	Beaver Local SD	Lisbon, OH
1	0.0	Beaverton Rural Schools	Beaverton, MI
1	0.0	Belcourt 7	Belcourt, ND
1	0.0	Bell County	Pineville, KY
1	0.0	Bellaire Local SD	Bellaire, OH
1	0.0	Bellevue City SD	Bellevue, OH
1	0.0	Belvidere CUSD 100	Belvidere, IL
1	0.0	Bemidji	Bemidji, MN
1	0.0	Benton Carroll Salem Local SD	Oak Harbor, OH
1	0.0	Berlin Area	Berlin, WI
1	0.0	Berlin SD	Berlin, NH
1	0.0	Berrien County	Nashville, GA
1	0.0	Bethalto CUSD 8	Bethalto, IL
1	0.0	Bethel-Tate Local SD	Bethel, OH
1	0.0	Big Walnut Local SD	Galena, OH
1	0.0	Black River Falls	Black River Fls, WI
1	0.0	Black River Local SD	Sullivan, OH
1	0.0	Blackstone-Millville	Blackstone, MA
1	0.0	Blanchester Local SD	Blanchester, OH
1	0.0	Board of Ed of Garrett County	Oakland, MD
1	0.0	Bond County CUSD 2	Greenville, IL
1	0.0	Bonner Springs	Bonner Springs, KS
1	0.0	Boone County SD	Madison, WV
1	0.0	Boonville R-I	Boonville, MO
1	0.0	Bourne	Bourne, MA
1	0.0	Boyd County	Ashland, KY
1	0.0	Boyle County	Danville, KY
1	0.0	Bradley Bourbonnais CHSD 307	Bradley, IL
1	0.0	Brainerd	Brainerd, MN
1	0.0	Brandon Valley SD 49-2	Brandon, SD
1	0.0	Brantley County	Nahunta, GA
1	0.0	Braxton County SD	Sutton, WV
1	0.0	Breathitt County	Jackson, KY
1	0.0	Breckinridge County	Hardinsburg, KY
1	0.0	Bremen City	Bremen, GA
1	0.0	Brooke County SD	Wellsburg, WV
1	0.0	Brookfield Local SD	Brookfield, OH
1	0.0	Brookhaven SD	Brookhaven, MS
1	0.0	Brookings SD 05-1	Brookings, SD
1	0.0	Brookville Local SD	Brookville, OH
1	0.0	Brown Deer	Brown Deer, WI
1	0.0	Buckeye Local SD	Medina, OH
1	0.0	Buckeye Valley Local SD	Delaware, OH
1	0.0	Burlington	Burlington, MA
1	0.0	Burlington County Vocational	Westampton Twp, NJ
1	0.0	Butte County Joint District	Arco, ID
1	0.0	Butte HS	Butte, MT
1	0.0	Butts County	Jackson, GA
1	0.0	Byron	Byron, MN
1	0.0	Caldwell County	Princeton, KY
1	0.0	Calhoun County SD	Pittsboro, MS
1	0.0	Camden CSD	Camden, NY
1	0.0	Campbellsport	Campbellsport, WI
1	0.0	Canton Union SD 66	Canton, IL
1	0.0	Carmi-White County CUSD 5	Carmi, IL
1	0.0	Carrollton Ex Vill SD	Carrollton, OH
1	0.0	Carter County	Grayson, KY
1	0.0	Carterville CUSD 5	Carterville, IL
1	0.0	Carver	Carver, MA
1	0.0	Casa Grande Union High SD	Casa Grande, AZ
1	0.0	Casey County	Liberty, KY
1	0.0	Catahoula Parish School Board	Harrisonburg, LA
1	0.0	Catoosa	Catoosa, OK
1	0.0	Cedarburg	Cedarburg, WI
1	0.0	Celina City SD	Celina, OH
1	0.0	Centerville Community SD	Centerville, IA
1	0.0	Central Arizona Valley Inst of Tech	Coolidge, AZ
1	0.0	Central Berkshire	Dalton, MA
1	0.0	Central Clinton Community SD	De Witt, IA
1	0.0	Chagrin Falls Ex Vill SD	Chagrin Falls, OH
1	0.0	Champion Local SD	Warren, OH
1	0.0	Channahon SD 17	Channahon, IL
1	0.0	Chanute Public Schools	Chanute, KS
1	0.0	Charlton County	Folkston, GA
1	0.0	Chillicothe R-II	Chillicothe, MO
1	0.0	Chippewa Falls Area	Chippewa Falls, WI
1	0.0	Choctaw County SD	Butler, AL
1	0.0	Choctaw County SD	Ackerman, MS
1	0.0	Circle	Towanda, KS
1	0.0	Circleville City SD	Circleville, OH
1	0.0	Claiborne County SD	Port Gibson, MS
1	0.0	Clark-Shawnee Local SD	Springfield, OH
1	0.0	Clarke County SD	Grove Hill, AL
1	0.0	Clay Center	Clay Center, KS
1	0.0	Clay County	Manchester, KY
1	0.0	Clay County SD	Ashland, AL

This section ranks 120 school districts at both the "top" and "bottom" of each category for a total of 240 districts per category. The "top" list (descending order) appears first, followed by the "bottom" list (ascending order).

Migrant Students

School districts ranked in *descending* order

Rank	Percent	District Name	City, State
1	87.4	Robstown ISD	Robstown, TX
2	71.7	Lexington Public Schools	Lexington, NE
3	70.0	Firebaugh-Las Deltas Joint Unified	Firebaugh, CA
4	63.5	Wasco Union Elementary	Wasco, CA
5	56.8	Arvin Union Elementary	Arvin, CA
6	56.1	Gonzales Unified	Gonzales, CA
7	55.9	Golden Plains Unified	San Joaquin, CA
8	55.5	Mendota Unified	Mendota, CA
9	54.4	Alisal Union Elementary	Salinas, CA
10	54.0	King City Joint Union High	King City, CA
11	53.3	Reef-Sunset Unified	Avenal, CA
12	50.0	Salinas City Elementary	Salinas, CA
13	49.5	Richland SD	Shafter, CA
14	48.9	Lamont Elementary	Lamont, CA
15	48.5	Dumas ISD	Dumas, TX
16	47.4	Riverdale Joint Unified	Riverdale, CA
17	46.1	Delano Union Elementary	Delano, CA
18	45.7	Mcfarland Unified	Mcfarland, CA
19	44.3	Hereford ISD	Hereford, TX
20	44.0	Pajaro Valley Unified School	Watsonville, CA
21	42.9	Corcoran Joint Unified	Corcoran, CA
22	42.3	Storm Lake Community SD	Storm Lake, IA
23	41.7	Greenfield Union Elementary	Greenfield, CA
24	41.5	Mathis ISD	Mathis, TX
25	41.4	Parlier Unified	Parlier, CA
26	39.9	Hardee County SD	Wauchula, FL
27	39.6	King City Union Elementary	King City, CA
28	38.9	Soledad Unified	Soledad, CA
29	38.6	Dodge City	Dodge City, KS
30	38.4	Northwest Arctic SD	Kotzebue, AK
31	37.6	Raymondville ISD	Raymondville, TX
32	35.9	Bering Strait SD	Unalakleet, AK
33	35.9	Coalinga-Huron Joint Unified	Coalinga, CA
34	35.7	Lower Yukon SD	Mountain Vlg, AK
35	35.7	Hendry County SD	La Belle, FL
36	35.7	Lindsay Unified	Lindsay, CA
37	34.5	Woodlake Union Elementary	Woodlake, CA
38	34.4	North Monterey County Unified	Moss Landing, CA
39	34.0	Ontario SD 008	Ontario, OR
40	33.9	Salinas Union High	Salinas, CA
41	33.5	San Felipe-Del Rio CISD	Del Rio, TX
42	33.4	Rio Elementary	Oxnard, CA
43	33.2	Progreso ISD	Progreso, TX
44	32.7	Weslaco ISD	Weslaco, TX
45	32.5	Delano Joint Union High	Delano, CA
46	32.3	San Benito High	Hollister, CA
47	32.3	Norfolk Public Schools	Norfolk, NE
48	32.1	Rio Grande City CISD	Rio Grande City, TX
49	31.5	Denison Community SD	Denison, IA
50	31.1	Edcouch-Elsa ISD	Edcouch, TX
51	31.1	Farmersville Unified	Farmersville, CA
52	30.9	Kerman Unified	Kerman, CA
53	30.7	Fillmore Unified	Fillmore, CA
54	30.5	Santa Maria-Bonita Elementary	Santa Maria, CA
55	30.4	Linden Unified	Linden, CA
56	30.3	Escalon Unified	Escalon, CA
57	29.9	Donna ISD	Donna, TX
58	29.8	Woodburn SD 103	Woodburn, OR
59	29.5	Crete Public Schools	Crete, NE
60	29.3	Hollister SD	Hollister, CA
61	29.0	Patterson Joint Unified	Patterson, CA
62	28.6	Morrow SD 001	Lexington, OR
63	28.5	La Joya ISD	La Joya, TX
64	28.0	Hughson Unified	Hughson, CA
65	27.9	North Slope Borough SD	Barrow, AK
66	27.8	Dequeen SD	De Queen, AR
67	27.6	Ocean View Elementary	Oxnard, CA
68	27.4	Earlimart Elementary	Earlimart, CA
69	27.2	River Delta Joint Unified	Rio Vista, CA
70	27.2	Liberal	Liberal, KS
71	27.2	Riverbank Unified	Riverbank, CA
72	27.2	Holtville Unified	Holtville, CA
73	27.1	Lower Kuskokwim SD	Bethel, AK
74	26.8	Santa Paula Elementary	Santa Paula, CA
75	26.3	Lyford CISD	Lyford, TX
76	25.8	South Sioux City Community Schs	So Sioux City, NE
77	25.6	Crystal City ISD	Crystal City, TX
78	24.6	Santa Maria Joint Union High	Santa Maria, CA
79	24.1	Hueneme Elementary	Port Hueneme, CA
80	24.0	Coachella Valley Unified	Thermal, CA
81	23.4	Brawley Union High	Brawley, CA
82	23.4	Collier County SD	Naples, FL
83	23.4	Mount Pleasant ISD	Mt Pleasant, TX
84	23.4	Greenfield Union Elementary	Bakersfield, CA
85	23.0	Newman-Crows Landing Unified	Newman, CA
86	22.1	Lemoore Union Elementary	Lemoore, CA
87	21.8	Calexico Unified	Calexico, CA
88	21.6	Roma ISD	Roma, TX
89	21.6	Hood River County SD 1	Hood River, OR
90	21.4	Gustine Unified	Gustine, CA
91	21.2	Live Oak Unified	Live Oak, CA
92	20.9	Carpinteria Unified	Carpinteria, CA
93	20.8	Mercedes ISD	Mercedes, TX
94	20.8	Brawley Elementary	Brawley, CA
95	20.1	Jefferson County SD 509J	Madras, OR
96	19.7	Taft City Elementary	Taft, CA
97	19.5	Dos Palos Oro Loma Joint Unified	Dos Palos, CA
98	19.4	Winters Joint Unified	Winters, CA
99	19.4	Kelseyville Unified	Kelseyville, CA
100	19.3	Santa Paula Union High	Santa Paula, CA
101	19.1	Hanford Elementary	Hanford, CA
102	19.0	Ukiah Unified	Ukiah, CA
103	18.4	Perry Community SD	Perry, IA
104	18.2	Albertville City SD	Albertville, AL
105	18.0	Bakersfield City Elementary	Bakersfield, CA
106	17.7	Grand Island Public Schools	Grand Island, NE
107	17.5	Cloverdale Unified	Cloverdale, CA
108	17.5	Kodiak Island Borough SD	Kodiak, AK
109	17.4	Edinburg CISD	Edinburg, TX
110	17.4	Carrizo Springs CISD	Carrizo Springs, TX
111	17.3	Okeechobee County SD	Okeechobee, FL
112	17.3	Tulare City Elementary	Tulare, CA
113	17.3	Stockton City Unified	Stockton, CA
114	17.2	Eagle Pass ISD	Eagle Pass, TX
115	17.2	Great Bend	Great Bend, KS
116	17.2	Bonsall Union Elementary	Bonsall, CA
117	17.2	Uvalde CISD	Uvalde, TX
118	17.1	Gridley Unified	Gridley, CA
119	17.1	Dinuba Unified	Dinuba, CA
120	17.0	Hermiston SD 008	Hermiston, OR

This section ranks 120 school districts at both the "top" and "bottom" of each category for a total of 240 districts per category. The "top" list (descending order) appears first, followed by the "bottom" list (ascending order).

Migrant Students

School districts ranked in *ascending* order

Rank	Percent	District Name	City, State
1	0.0	Abbeville County SD	Abbeville, SC
1	0.0	Aberdeen SD	Aberdeen, MS
1	0.0	Abilene ISD	Abilene, TX
1	0.0	Abington	Abington, MA
1	0.0	Abington SD	Abington, PA
1	0.0	Academy 20	Colorado Spgs, CO
1	0.0	Acalanes Union High	Lafayette, CA
1	0.0	Acton	Acton, MA
1	0.0	Acton-Boxborough	Acton, MA
1	0.0	Adams-Cheshire	Cheshire, MA
1	0.0	Adelanto Elementary	Adelanto, CA
1	0.0	Affton 101	Saint Louis, MO
1	0.0	Agawam	Feeding Hills, MA
1	0.0	Alamo Heights ISD	San Antonio, TX
1	0.0	Alamogordo Public Schools	Alamogordo, NM
1	0.0	Albany	Albany, MN
1	0.0	Albany City Unified	Albany, CA
1	0.0	Albany County SD #1	Laramie, WY
1	0.0	Albert Gallatin Area SD	Uniontown, PA
1	0.0	Albert Lea	Albert Lea, MN
1	0.0	Albuquerque Public Schools	Albuquerque, NM
1	0.0	Alexander City City SD	Alexander City, AL
1	0.0	Alexander County Schools	Taylorsville, NC
1	0.0	Alexandria	Alexandria, MN
1	0.0	Alexandria City Public Schools	Alexandria, VA
1	0.0	Alhambra Elementary District	Phoenix, AZ
1	0.0	Alief ISD	Houston, TX
1	0.0	Allamakee Community SD	Waukon, IA
1	0.0	Alleghany County Public Schools	Covington, VA
1	0.0	Allendale County SD	Allendale, SC
1	0.0	Alpine Union Elementary	Alpine, CA
1	0.0	Alta Loma Elementary	Alta Loma, CA
1	0.0	Altoona Area SD	Altoona, PA
1	0.0	Amador County Unified	Jackson, CA
1	0.0	Ambridge Area SD	Ambridge, PA
1	0.0	Amelia County Public Schools	Amelia, VA
1	0.0	Amery	Amery, WI
1	0.0	Ames Community SD	Ames, IA
1	0.0	Amesbury	Amesbury, MA
1	0.0	Amherst County Public Schools	Amherst, VA
1	0.0	Amherst SD	Amherst, NH
1	0.0	Amory SD	Amory, MS
1	0.0	Amphitheater Unified District	Tucson, AZ
1	0.0	Andalusia City SD	Andalusia, AL
1	0.0	Anderson County SD 02	Honea Path, SC
1	0.0	Anderson County SD 03	Iva, SC
1	0.0	Anderson County SD 04	Pendleton, SC
1	0.0	Andover	Andover, KS
1	0.0	Ankeny Community SD	Ankeny, IA
1	0.0	Annandale	Annandale, MN
1	0.0	Anne Arundel County Pub Schls	Annapolis, MD
1	0.0	Anniston City SD	Anniston, AL
1	0.0	Annville-Cleona SD	Annville, PA
1	0.0	Anoka-Hennepin	Coon Rapids, MN
1	0.0	Anson County Schools	Wadesboro, NC
1	0.0	Ansonia SD	Ansonia, CT
1	0.0	Antigo	Antigo, WI
1	0.0	Antioch Unified	Antioch, CA
1	0.0	Apache Junction Unified District	Apache Junction, AZ
1	0.0	Apollo-Ridge SD	Spring Church, PA

Rank	Percent	District Name	City, State
1	0.0	Apple Valley Unified	Apple Valley, CA
1	0.0	Appleton Area	Appleton, WI
1	0.0	Appomattox County Public Schools	Appomattox, VA
1	0.0	Arab City SD	Arab, AL
1	0.0	Aransas County ISD	Rockport, TX
1	0.0	Aransas Pass ISD	Aransas Pass, TX
1	0.0	Archuleta County 50 Joint	Pagosa Springs, CO
1	0.0	Arkadelphia SD	Arkadelphia, AR
1	0.0	Arlington County Public Schools	Arlington, VA
1	0.0	Armstrong SD	Ford City, PA
1	0.0	Arrowhead Uhs	Hartland, WI
1	0.0	Asbury Park City	Asbury Park, NJ
1	0.0	Ascension Parish School Board	Donaldsonville, LA
1	0.0	Ashburnham-Westminster	Westminster, MA
1	0.0	Ashdown SD	Ashdown, AR
1	0.0	Asheville City Schools	Asheville, NC
1	0.0	Ashland	Ashland, MA
1	0.0	Ashland	Ashland, WI
1	0.0	Ashwaubenon	Green Bay, WI
1	0.0	Aspen 1	Aspen, CO
1	0.0	Astoria SD 001	Astoria, OR
1	0.0	Atchison Public Schools	Atchison, KS
1	0.0	Athol-Royalston	Athol, MA
1	0.0	Atlanta City	Atlanta, GA
1	0.0	Atlantic City	Atlantic City, NJ
1	0.0	Atlantic Community SD	Atlantic, IA
1	0.0	Attalla City SD	Attalla, AL
1	0.0	Auburn	Auburn, MA
1	0.0	Auburn City SD	Auburn, AL
1	0.0	Auburn Washburn	Topeka, KS
1	0.0	Audubon Boro	Audubon, NJ
1	0.0	Augusta	Augusta, KS
1	0.0	Austin	Austin, MN
1	0.0	Autauga County SD	Prattville, AL
1	0.0	Avery County Schools	Newland, NC
1	0.0	Avon SD	Avon, CT
1	0.0	Aztec Municipal Schools	Aztec, NM
1	0.0	Baker SD 05J	Baker City, OR
1	0.0	Bald Eagle Area SD	Wingate, PA
1	0.0	Baldwin County	Milledgeville, GA
1	0.0	Baldwin-Whitehall SD	Pittsburgh, PA
1	0.0	Balsz Elementary District	Phoenix, AZ
1	0.0	Baltimore County Public Schls	Towson, MD
1	0.0	Bamberg County SD 01	Bamberg, SC
1	0.0	Bandera ISD	Bandera, TX
1	0.0	Bangor Area SD	Bangor, PA
1	0.0	Banning Unified	Banning, CA
1	0.0	Baraboo	Baraboo, WI
1	0.0	Barbour County SD	Philippi, WV
1	0.0	Bardstown Independent	Bardstown, KY
1	0.0	Barnegat Twp	Barnegat, NJ
1	0.0	Barnwell County SD 45	Barnwell, SC
1	0.0	Barstow Unified	Barstow, CA
1	0.0	Bartow County	Cartersville, GA
1	0.0	Basehor-Linwood	Basehor, KS
1	0.0	Bayless	Saint Louis, MO
1	0.0	Bayonne City	Bayonne, NJ
1	0.0	Bear Valley Unified	Big Bear Lake, CA
1	0.0	Beaufort County SD	Beaufort, SC
1	0.0	Beaumont ISD	Beaumont, TX

This section ranks 120 school districts at both the "top" and "bottom" of each category for a total of 240 districts per category. The "top" list (descending order) appears first, followed by the "bottom" list (ascending order).

Students Eligible for Free Lunch Program

School districts ranked in *descending* order

Rank	Percent	District Name	City, State
1	99.5	National Elementary	National City, CA
2	99.4	Winton Elementary	Winton, CA
3	99.4	Los Nietos Elementary	Whittier, CA
4	98.8	Reef-Sunset Unified	Avenal, CA
5	97.6	Parlier Unified	Parlier, CA
6	96.0	Holmes County SD	Lexington, MS
7	95.0	Wilcox County SD	Camden, AL
8	94.3	Yazoo City Municipal SD	Yazoo City, MS
9	93.7	Coahoma County SD	Clarksdale, MS
10	93.4	Jefferson County SD	Fayette, MS
11	93.2	Delano Union Elementary	Delano, CA
12	93.2	West Harvey-Dixmoor PSD 147	Harvey, IL
13	93.0	Quitman County SD	Marks, MS
14	92.3	Roosevelt UFSD	Roosevelt, NY
15	91.9	Leflore County SD	Greenwood, MS
16	91.5	Humphreys County SD	Belzoni, MS
17	91.5	Hazlehurst City SD	Hazlehurst, MS
18	91.4	Claiborne County SD	Port Gibson, MS
19	90.9	Perry County SD	Marion, AL
20	90.9	Del Paso Heights Elementary	Sacramento, CA
21	90.5	Noxubee County SD	Macon, MS
22	89.2	Sumter County SD	Livingston, AL
23	88.8	Mendota Unified	Mendota, CA
24	88.8	Sunflower County SD	Indianola, MS
25	88.2	Canton Public SD	Canton, MS
26	87.9	Jefferson Davis County SD	Prentiss, MS
27	87.9	Tunica County SD	Tunica, MS
28	87.4	Golden Plains Unified	San Joaquin, CA
29	87.4	Wilkinson County SD	Woodville, MS
30	86.9	Indianola SD	Indianola, MS
31	86.1	Lowndes County SD	Hayneville, AL
32	85.9	Gadsden Independent Schools	Anthony, NM
33	85.8	Greenville Public Schools	Greenville, MS
34	85.5	East Carroll Parish School Board	Lake Providence, LA
35	85.4	North Panola Schools	Sardis, MS
36	85.3	Thermalito Union Elementary	Oroville, CA
37	84.4	Allendale County SD	Allendale, SC
38	84.3	Greene County SD	Eutaw, AL
39	83.9	Lee County SD	Marianna, AR
40	83.6	Lennox Elementary	Lennox, CA
41	83.1	Laurel SD	Laurel, MS
42	83.1	Richland SD	Shafter, CA
43	83.0	Earlimart Elementary	Earlimart, CA
44	83.0	Arvin Union Elementary	Arvin, CA
45	82.9	Soledad Unified	Soledad, CA
46	82.9	Bullock County SD	Union Springs, AL
47	82.4	Randolph County	Cuthbert, GA
48	82.1	Compton Unified	Compton, CA
49	81.9	Helena-West Helena SD	Helena, AR
50	81.7	Clint ISD	Clint, TX
51	81.1	Marengo County SD	Linden, AL
52	80.9	Robstown ISD	Robstown, TX
53	80.8	Aberdeen SD	Aberdeen, MS
54	80.5	Hattiesburg Public SD	Hattiesburg, MS
55	80.3	Greenwood Public SD	Greenwood, MS
56	80.3	South Pike SD	Magnolia, MS
57	80.1	San Diego County Office of Ed	San Diego, CA
58	80.0	Clarksdale Municipal SD	Clarksdale, MS
59	80.0	Hancock County	Sparta, GA
60	79.9	Belcourt 7	Belcourt, ND
61	79.9	Leslie County	Hyden, KY
62	79.8	Lamont Elementary	Lamont, CA
63	79.8	Hampton 2 County SD	Estill, SC
64	79.8	Natchez-Adams SD	Natchez, MS
65	79.7	Holly Springs SD	Holly Springs, MS
66	79.6	Muskegon Heights SD	Muskegon Hgts, MI
67	79.6	South San Antonio ISD	San Antonio, TX
68	79.2	Madison Parish School Board	Tallulah, LA
69	79.1	Union City	Union City, NJ
70	79.0	Anniston City SD	Anniston, AL
71	78.7	Orangeburg County SD 03	Holly Hill, SC
72	78.7	Knott County	Hindman, KY
73	78.6	Rio Grande City CISD	Rio Grande City, TX
74	78.6	Woodlake Union Elementary	Woodlake, CA
75	78.6	Mccreary County	Stearns, KY
76	78.6	Prairie-Hills Elem SD 144	Markham, IL
77	78.3	Selma City SD	Selma, AL
78	78.3	San Ysidro Elementary	San Ysidro, CA
79	78.2	Clay County	Manchester, KY
80	78.1	Taos Municipal Schools	Taos, NM
81	77.9	Magoffin County	Salyersville, KY
82	77.9	San Diego ISD	San Diego, TX
83	77.8	Middlesboro Independent	Middlesboro, KY
84	77.6	Knox County	Barbourvill, KY
85	77.5	Chicago Heights SD 170	Chicago Heights, IL
86	77.1	Bakersfield City Elementary	Bakersfield, CA
87	77.1	Harvey SD 152	Harvey, IL
88	77.1	Hamtramck Public Schools	Hamtramck, MI
89	77.0	Camden City	Camden, NJ
90	76.9	Bell County	Pineville, KY
91	76.8	Wapato SD 207	Wapato, WA
92	76.6	Hatch Valley Public Schools	Hatch, NM
93	76.4	Jackson Public SD	Jackson, MS
94	76.4	School City of East Chicago	East Chicago, IN
95	76.3	Whitley County	Williamsburg, KY
96	76.3	Lewis County	Vanceburg, KY
97	75.9	Woodburn SD 103	Woodburn, OR
98	75.9	Wasco Union Elementary	Wasco, CA
99	75.7	Brooks County ISD	Falfurrias, TX
100	75.7	Dooly County	Vienna, GA
101	75.6	Benton Harbor Area Schools	Benton Harbor, MI
102	75.4	Lower Yukon SD	Mountain Vlg, AK
103	75.4	Coachella Valley Unified	Thermal, CA
104	75.3	West Point SD	West Point, MS
105	75.3	Dollarway SD	Pine Bluff, AR
106	75.3	Mountain View Elementary	El Monte, CA
107	75.1	East Tallahatchie Consol SD	Charleston, MS
108	74.9	Lawrence County	Louisa, KY
109	74.9	Jefferson County	Louisville, GA
110	74.8	Breathitt County	Jackson, KY
111	74.5	Lee County SD	Bishopville, SC
112	74.4	Williamsburg County SD	Kingstree, SC
113	74.2	Western Line SD	Avon, MS
114	74.2	Canutillo ISD	El Paso, TX
115	74.2	Asbury Park City	Asbury Park, NJ
116	74.1	Conecuh County SD	Evergreen, AL
117	74.0	Iberville Parish School Board	Plaquemine, LA
118	73.9	Greene County	Greensboro, GA
119	73.8	Yazoo County SD	Yazoo City, MS
120	73.7	Todd County SD 66-1	Mission, SD

This section ranks 120 school districts at both the "top" and "bottom" of each category for a total of 240 districts per category. The "top" list (descending order) appears first, followed by the "bottom" list (ascending order).

Students Eligible for Free Lunch Program

School districts ranked in *ascending* order

Rank	Percent	District Name	City, State
1	0.0	Antioch Community High SD 117	Lake Villa, IL
1	0.0	Asheboro City Schools	Asheboro, NC
1	0.0	Aspen 1	Aspen, CO
1	0.0	Baldwin UFSD	Baldwin, NY
1	0.0	Beaufort County Schools	Washington, NC
1	0.0	Bremen Community HS District 228	Midlothian, IL
1	0.0	Briarcliff Manor UFSD	Briarcliff Manor, NY
1	0.0	Brunswick County Schools	Bolivia, NC
1	0.0	Burbank SD 111	Burbank, IL
1	0.0	Caldwell County Schools	Lenoir, NC
1	0.0	Caswell County Schools	Yanceyville, NC
1	0.0	Chapel Hill-Carrboro Schools	Chapel Hill, NC
1	0.0	Chatham County Schools	Pittsboro, NC
1	0.0	Cleveland County Schools	Shelby, NC
1	0.0	Clinton City Schools	Clinton, NC
1	0.0	Community CSD 93	Carol Stream, IL
1	0.0	Community High SD 94	West Chicago, IL
1	0.0	Consolidated High SD 230	Orland Park, IL
1	0.0	Croton-Harmon UFSD	Croton-On-Hud, NY
1	0.0	Deerfield SD 109	Deerfield, IL
1	0.0	Durham Public Schools	Durham, NC
1	0.0	Eastchester UFSD	Eastchester, NY
1	0.0	Edgemont UFSD	Scarsdale, NY
1	0.0	Fenton Community HSD 100	Bensenville, IL
1	0.0	Flossmoor SD 161	Chicago Heights, IL
1	0.0	Frankfort CCSD 157c	Frankfort, IL
1	0.0	Fremont SD 79	Mundelein, IL
1	0.0	Geneva Community Unit SD 304	Geneva, IL
1	0.0	Glen Ellyn CCSD 89	Glen Ellyn, IL
1	0.0	Glen Ellyn SD 41	Glen Ellyn, IL
1	0.0	Glen Ridge Boro	Glen Ridge, NJ
1	0.0	Grayslake Community High SD 127	Grayslake, IL
1	0.0	Gurnee SD 56	Gurnee, IL
1	0.0	Highland Park ISD	Dallas, TX
1	0.0	Hinsdale Twp HSD 86	Hinsdale, IL
1	0.0	Homer Community CSD 33C	Lockport, IL
1	0.0	Indian Prairie CUSD 204	Aurora, IL
1	0.0	Irvington UFSD	Irvington, NY
1	0.0	Kannapolis City Schools	Kannapolis, NC
1	0.0	Keeneyville SD 20	Hanover Park, IL
1	0.0	Kings Mountain District	Kings Mountain, NC
1	0.0	Kirby SD 140	Tinley Park, IL
1	0.0	Lake Forest Community HSD 115	Lake Forest, IL
1	0.0	Lake Forest SD 67	Lake Forest, IL
1	0.0	Lake Park Community HSD 108	Roselle, IL
1	0.0	Lansing SD 158	Lansing, IL
1	0.0	Lincoln County Schools	Lincolnton, NC
1	0.0	Lincolnshire-Prairieview SD 103	Lincolnshire, IL
1	0.0	Los Alamos Public Schools	Los Alamos, NM
1	0.0	Lyons Twp HSD 204	La Grange, IL
1	0.0	Maine Township HSD 207	Park Ridge, IL
1	0.0	Merrick UFSD	Merrick, NY
1	0.0	Mooresville City Schools	Mooresville, NC
1	0.0	Mountain Brook City SD	Mountain Brook, AL
1	0.0	Nash-Rocky Mount Schools	Nashville, NC
1	0.0	New Hyde Pk-Garden City Pk UFSD	New Hyde Park, NY
1	0.0	Niles Twp Community High SD 219	Skokie, IL
1	0.0	Northbrook SD 28	Northbrook, IL
1	0.0	Oak Lawn-Hometown SD 123	Oak Lawn, IL
1	0.0	Orland SD 135	Orland Park, IL
1	0.0	Ottawa Twp HSD 140	Ottawa, IL
1	0.0	Park Ridge CCSD 64	Park Ridge, IL
1	0.0	Pasquotank County Schools	Elizabeth City, NC
1	0.0	Pennsylvania Virtual CS	Norristown, PA
1	0.0	Perquimans County Schools	Hertford, NC
1	0.0	Piedmont City Unified	Piedmont, CA
1	0.0	Pleasantville UFSD	Pleasantville, NY
1	0.0	Prospect Heights SD 23	Prospect Hgts, IL
1	0.0	Queen Bee SD 16	Glendale Hgts, IL
1	0.0	Ramapo-Indian Hill Reg	Franklin Lakes, NJ
1	0.0	Randolph County Schools	Asheboro, NC
1	0.0	Richmond County Schools	Hamlet, NC
1	0.0	Robeson County Schools	Lumberton, NC
1	0.0	Rowan-Salisbury Schools	Salisbury, NC
1	0.0	Scarsdale UFSD	Scarsdale, NY
1	0.0	Schaumburg CCSD 54	Schaumburg, IL
1	0.0	Stanly County Schools	Albemarle, NC
1	0.0	Warren Twp High SD 121	Gurnee, IL
1	0.0	Washington County Schools	Plymouth, NC
1	0.0	Whiteville City Schools	Whiteville, NC
1	0.0	Wilmette SD 39	Wilmette, IL
1	0.0	Winnetka SD 36	Winnetka, IL
1	0.0	Yancey County Schools	Burnsville, NC
1	0.0	Yorkville Community Unit SD 115	Yorkville, IL
85	0.1	Cold Spring Harbor CSD	Cold Sprg Harbor, NY
85	0.1	Garden City UFSD	Garden City, NY
85	0.1	Lafayette Elementary	Lafayette, CA
85	0.1	Shoreham-Wading River CSD	Shoreham, NY
85	0.1	Verona Boro	Verona, NJ
90	0.2	Byram Hills CSD	Armonk, NY
90	0.2	Mount Lebanon SD	Pittsburgh, PA
90	0.2	Northern Valley Regional	Demarest, NJ
90	0.2	Riverside County Office of Ed	Riverside, CA
90	0.2	Twin Ridges Elementary	North San Juan, CA
90	0.2	Wyckoff Twp	Wyckoff, NJ
96	0.3	Caldwell-West Caldwell	West Caldwell, NJ
96	0.3	Holmdel Twp	Holmdel, NJ
96	0.3	Katonah-Lewisboro UFSD	South Salem, NY
96	0.3	Kinnelon Boro	Kinnelon, NJ
96	0.3	Orinda Union Elementary	Orinda, CA
96	0.3	Pascack Valley Regional	Montvale, NJ
96	0.3	Tenafly Boro	Tenafly, NJ
96	0.3	Watchung Hills Regional	Warren, NJ
96	0.3	West Morris Regional	Chester, NJ
105	0.4	Acalanes Union High	Lafayette, CA
105	0.4	Chappaqua CSD	Chappaqua, NY
105	0.4	La Canada Unified	La Canada, CA
105	0.4	Oakwood City SD	Dayton, OH
105	0.4	SD of The Chathams	Chatham, NJ
105	0.4	Syosset CSD	Syosset, NY
105	0.4	Upper Arlington City SD	Upper Arlington, OH
105	0.4	Warren Twp	Warren, NJ
113	0.5	Bernards Twp	Basking Ridge, NJ
113	0.5	East Williston UFSD	Old Westbury, NY
113	0.5	Indian Hill Ex Vill SD	Cincinnati, OH
113	0.5	Livingston Twp	Livingston, NJ
113	0.5	Los Gatos-Saratoga Joint Union High	Los Gatos, CA
113	0.5	New Providence Boro	New Providence, NJ
113	0.5	North Hunt-Voorhees Regional	Annandale, NJ
113	0.5	Saratoga Union Elementary	Saratoga, CA

This section ranks 120 school districts at both the "top" and "bottom" of each category for a total of 240 districts per category. The "top" list (descending order) appears first, followed by the "bottom" list (ascending order).

Students Eligible for Reduced-Price Lunch Program

School districts ranked in *descending* order

Rank	Percent	District Name	City, State
1	26.7	Twin Ridges Elementary	North San Juan, CA
2	24.6	Wheatland Elementary	Wheatland, CA
3	24.1	Santa Paula Elementary	Santa Paula, CA
4	23.0	Adair County	Columbia, KY
5	22.5	Gorman Elementary	Gorman, CA
6	22.2	Marion County	Lebanon, KY
7	21.2	Russell County	Jamestown, KY
8	21.0	Geary County Schools	Junction City, KS
9	20.7	Christian County	Hopkinsville, KY
10	20.5	Fleming County	Flemingsburg, KY
11	20.4	Rosemead Elementary	Rosemead, CA
12	20.3	Cheektowaga-Sloan UFSD	Sloan, NY
13	20.2	Washington County	Springfie, KY
14	20.2	Anderson Union High	Anderson, CA
15	20.1	Ocean View Elementary	Oxnard, CA
16	20.0	Clinton County	Albany, KY
17	20.0	Little Lake City Elementary	Santa Fe Spgs, CA
18	19.9	Jackson County	Mckee, KY
19	19.8	Anaheim Elementary	Anaheim, CA
20	19.6	Garrard County	Lancaster, KY
21	19.5	Passaic County Vocational	Wayne, NJ
22	19.5	Rockcastle County	Mount Verno, KY
23	19.3	Wayne County	Monticello, KY
24	19.2	Salinas City Elementary	Salinas, CA
25	19.1	Perris Elementary	Perris, CA
26	19.0	Dover Town	Dover, NJ
27	19.0	Downey Unified	Downey, CA
28	18.8	Hardin County	Elizabe, KY
29	18.8	Whittier City Elementary	Whittier, CA
30	18.8	Lincoln County	Stanford, KY
31	18.8	Alisal Union Elementary	Salinas, CA
32	18.8	Hillside Twp	Hillside, NJ
33	18.6	Santa Barbara Elementary	Santa Barbara, CA
34	18.6	Logan County	Russellville, KY
35	18.6	Burton Elementary	Porterville, CA
36	18.5	Harlan County	Harlan, KY
37	18.5	Pittsburg Unified	Pittsburg, CA
38	18.4	Whitley County	Williamsburg, KY
39	18.4	South Bay Union Elementary	Imperial Beach, CA
40	18.3	Lemon Grove Elementary	Lemon Grove, CA
41	18.3	Central Union Elementary	Lemoore, CA
42	18.1	Garfield City	Garfield, NJ
43	18.1	Casey County	Liberty, KY
44	18.1	Calloway County	Murray, KY
45	18.0	Indian River CSD	Philadelphia, NY
46	18.0	Letcher County	Whitesburg, KY
47	18.0	Mohave Valley Elementary District	Mohave Valley, AZ
48	17.9	Ohio County	Hartford, KY
49	17.8	Cobre Consolidated Schools	Bayard, NM
50	17.8	Jefferson Elementary	Daly City, CA
51	17.7	King City Union Elementary	King City, CA
52	17.6	Hardy County SD	Moorefield, WV
53	17.6	Emery SD	Huntington, UT
54	17.6	Azusa Unified	Azusa, CA
55	17.4	Trimble County	Bedford, KY
56	17.4	Meade County	Brandenburg, KY
57	17.4	Hart County	Munfordville, KY
58	17.3	Jay	Jay, OK
59	17.3	Todd County	Elkton, KY
60	17.3	Larue County	Hodgenville, KY
61	17.3	Lawndale Elementary	Lawndale, CA
62	17.3	Calexico Unified	Calexico, CA
63	17.2	Shamokin Area SD	Coal Township, PA
64	17.2	Greenfield Union Elementary	Greenfield, CA
65	17.2	Grayson County	Leitchfield, KY
66	17.1	Hemet Unified	Hemet, CA
67	17.0	Breckinridge County	Hardinsburg, KY
68	16.9	Perth Amboy City	Perth Amboy, NJ
69	16.9	Mclean County	Calhoun, KY
70	16.9	Bristow	Bristow, OK
71	16.9	Hacienda La Puente Unified	City of Industry, CA
72	16.8	Beaumont Unified	Beaumont, CA
73	16.8	Deer Park SD 414	Deer Park, WA
74	16.8	Vernon Parish School Board	Leesville, LA
75	16.8	West Covina Unified	West Covina, CA
76	16.7	Metcalfe County	Edmonton, KY
77	16.7	Hempstead UFSD	Hempstead, NY
78	16.7	Santa Rita Union Elementary	Salinas, CA
79	16.7	Brentwood UFSD	Brentwood, NY
80	16.6	Clinton	Clinton, OK
81	16.6	Lower Twp	Cape May, NJ
82	16.5	Henry County	New Castle, KY
83	16.5	Delano Joint Union High	Delano, CA
84	16.5	Cascade Union Elementary	Anderson, CA
85	16.5	Randolph County SD	Elkins, WV
86	16.4	Hueneme Elementary	Port Hueneme, CA
87	16.3	Live Oak Unified	Live Oak, CA
88	16.3	Lackawanna City SD	Lackawanna, NY
89	16.3	Bellevue Union Elementary	Santa Rosa, CA
90	16.2	Magnolia Elementary	Anaheim, CA
91	16.2	Killeen ISD	Killeen, TX
92	16.2	Trigg County	Cadiz, KY
93	16.2	North Sanpete SD	Mount Pleasant, UT
94	16.2	Cherokee County Schools	Murphy, NC
95	16.2	Euclid City SD	Euclid, OH
96	16.2	Knob Noster R-VIII	Knob Noster, MO
97	16.2	Pocahontas SD	Pocahontas, AR
98	16.1	Mount Pleasant Elementary	San Jose, CA
99	16.1	Silver Valley Unified	Yermo, CA
100	16.1	Millard SD	Delta, UT
101	16.1	Keansburg Boro	Keansburg, NJ
102	16.1	Central Islip UFSD	Central Islip, NY
103	16.0	Preston Joint District	Preston, ID
104	16.0	San Francisco Unified	San Francisco, CA
105	16.0	Lindenwold Boro	Lindenwold, NJ
106	16.0	Enterprise Elementary	Redding, CA
107	15.9	Monroe County	Tompkinsville, KY
108	15.9	Rabun County	Clayton, GA
109	15.9	Buena Park Elementary	Buena Park, CA
110	15.9	Waynesville R-VI	Waynesville, MO
111	15.9	Rio Elementary	Oxnard, CA
112	15.8	Staples-Motley	Staples, MN
113	15.8	Chula Vista Elementary	Chula Vista, CA
114	15.8	Somerset Independent	Somerset, KY
115	15.8	Santa Ana Unified	Santa Ana, CA
116	15.8	Livingston Union Elementary	Livingston, CA
117	15.8	Yorkshire-Pioneer CSD	Yorkshire, NY
118	15.8	Ruidoso Municipal Schools	Ruidoso, NM
119	15.8	Swain County Schools	Bryson City, NC
120	15.8	Prentiss County SD	Booneville, MS

This section ranks 120 school districts at both the "top" and "bottom" of each category for a total of 240 districts per category. The "top" list (descending order) appears first, followed by the "bottom" list (ascending order).

Students Eligible for Reduced-Price Lunch Program

School districts ranked in *ascending* order

Rank	Percent	District Name	City, State
1	0.0	Antioch Community High SD 117	Lake Villa, IL
1	0.0	Asheboro City Schools	Asheboro, NC
1	0.0	Baldwin UFSD	Baldwin, NY
1	0.0	Beaufort County Schools	Washington, NC
1	0.0	Belmont-Redwood Shores Elementary	Belmont, CA
1	0.0	Bremen Community HS District 228	Midlothian, IL
1	0.0	Brunswick County Schools	Bolivia, NC
1	0.0	Burbank SD 111	Burbank, IL
1	0.0	Byram Hills CSD	Armonk, NY
1	0.0	Caldwell County Schools	Lenoir, NC
1	0.0	Caswell County Schools	Yanceyville, NC
1	0.0	Chapel Hill-Carrboro Schools	Chapel Hill, NC
1	0.0	Chatham County Schools	Pittsboro, NC
1	0.0	Cleveland County Schools	Shelby, NC
1	0.0	Clinton City Schools	Clinton, NC
1	0.0	Clinton Twp	Annandale, NJ
1	0.0	Cold Spring Harbor CSD	Cold Sprg Harbor, NY
1	0.0	Community CSD 93	Carol Stream, IL
1	0.0	Community High SD 94	West Chicago, IL
1	0.0	Consolidated High SD 230	Orland Park, IL
1	0.0	Croton-Harmon UFSD	Croton-On-Hud, NY
1	0.0	Deerfield SD 109	Deerfield, IL
1	0.0	Delano Union Elementary	Delano, CA
1	0.0	Denville Twp	Denville, NJ
1	0.0	Department of Corrections SD 428	Springfield, IL
1	0.0	Durham Public Schools	Durham, NC
1	0.0	East Williston UFSD	Old Westbury, NY
1	0.0	Eastchester UFSD	Eastchester, NY
1	0.0	Edgemont UFSD	Scarsdale, NY
1	0.0	Fenton Community HSD 100	Bensenville, IL
1	0.0	Flossmoor SD 161	Chicago Heights, IL
1	0.0	Frankfort CCSD 157c	Frankfort, IL
1	0.0	Fremont SD 79	Mundelein, IL
1	0.0	Geneva Community Unit SD 304	Geneva, IL
1	0.0	Glen Ellyn CCSD 89	Glen Ellyn, IL
1	0.0	Glen Ellyn SD 41	Glen Ellyn, IL
1	0.0	Glen Ridge Boro	Glen Ridge, NJ
1	0.0	Grayslake Community High SD 127	Grayslake, IL
1	0.0	Gurnee SD 56	Gurnee, IL
1	0.0	Hastings-On-Hudson UFSD	Hastings-on-Hud, NY
1	0.0	Highland Park ISD	Dallas, TX
1	0.0	Hinsdale Twp HSD 86	Hinsdale, IL
1	0.0	Homer Community CSD 33C	Lockport, IL
1	0.0	Indian Prairie CUSD 204	Aurora, IL
1	0.0	Irvington UFSD	Irvington, NY
1	0.0	Kannapolis City Schools	Kannapolis, NC
1	0.0	Keeneyville SD 20	Hanover Park, IL
1	0.0	Kings Mountain District	Kings Mountain, NC
1	0.0	Kirby SD 140	Tinley Park, IL
1	0.0	Lafayette Elementary	Lafayette, CA
1	0.0	Lake Forest Community HSD 115	Lake Forest, IL
1	0.0	Lake Forest SD 67	Lake Forest, IL
1	0.0	Lake Park Community HSD 108	Roselle, IL
1	0.0	Lansing SD 158	Lansing, IL
1	0.0	Lincoln County Schools	Lincolnton, NC
1	0.0	Lincolnshire-Prairieview SD 103	Lincolnshire, IL
1	0.0	Los Alamos Public Schools	Los Alamos, NM
1	0.0	Los Gatos-Saratoga Joint Union High	Los Gatos, CA
1	0.0	Los Nietos Elementary	Whittier, CA
1	0.0	Lyons Twp HSD 204	La Grange, IL
1	0.0	Maine Township HSD 207	Park Ridge, IL
1	0.0	Merrick UFSD	Merrick, NY
1	0.0	Mooresville City Schools	Mooresville, NC
1	0.0	Moraga Elementary	Moraga, CA
1	0.0	Mountain Brook City SD	Mountain Brook, AL
1	0.0	Nash-Rocky Mount Schools	Nashville, NC
1	0.0	National Elementary	National City, CA
1	0.0	New Hyde Pk-Garden City Pk UFSD	New Hyde Park, NY
1	0.0	Niles Twp Community High SD 219	Skokie, IL
1	0.0	Northbrook SD 28	Northbrook, IL
1	0.0	Oak Lawn-Hometown SD 123	Oak Lawn, IL
1	0.0	Oakwood City SD	Dayton, OH
1	0.0	Orinda Union Elementary	Orinda, CA
1	0.0	Orland SD 135	Orland Park, IL
1	0.0	Ottawa Twp HSD 140	Ottawa, IL
1	0.0	Park Ridge CCSD 64	Park Ridge, IL
1	0.0	Parlier Unified	Parlier, CA
1	0.0	Pascack Valley Regional	Montvale, NJ
1	0.0	Pasquotank County Schools	Elizabeth City, NC
1	0.0	Pennsylvania Virtual CS	Norristown, PA
1	0.0	Perquimans County Schools	Hertford, NC
1	0.0	Piedmont City Unified	Piedmont, CA
1	0.0	Pleasantville UFSD	Pleasantville, NY
1	0.0	Prospect Heights SD 23	Prospect Hgts, IL
1	0.0	Queen Bee SD 16	Glendale Hgts, IL
1	0.0	Randolph County Schools	Asheboro, NC
1	0.0	Reef-Sunset Unified	Avenal, CA
1	0.0	Richmond County Schools	Hamlet, NC
1	0.0	Robeson County Schools	Lumberton, NC
1	0.0	Rowan-Salisbury Schools	Salisbury, NC
1	0.0	San Elizario ISD	San Elizario, TX
1	0.0	Scarsdale UFSD	Scarsdale, NY
1	0.0	Schaumburg CCSD 54	Schaumburg, IL
1	0.0	Shoreham-Wading River CSD	Shoreham, NY
1	0.0	Stanly County Schools	Albemarle, NC
1	0.0	Warren Twp	Warren, NJ
1	0.0	Warren Twp High SD 121	Gurnee, IL
1	0.0	Washington County Schools	Plymouth, NC
1	0.0	West Morris Regional	Chester, NJ
1	0.0	Whiteville City Schools	Whiteville, NC
1	0.0	Wilmette SD 39	Wilmette, IL
1	0.0	Winnetka SD 36	Winnetka, IL
1	0.0	Winton Elementary	Winton, CA
1	0.0	Yancey County Schools	Burnsville, NC
1	0.0	Yorkville Community Unit SD 115	Yorkville, IL
106	<0.1	Garden City UFSD	Garden City, NY
106	<0.1	Los Altos Elementary	Los Altos, CA
106	<0.1	Rye City SD	Rye, NY
106	<0.1	Wyckoff Twp	Wyckoff, NJ
110	0.1	Acalanes Union High	Lafayette, CA
110	0.1	Chagrin Falls Ex Vill SD	Chagrin Falls, OH
110	0.1	Millburn Twp	Millburn, NJ
110	0.1	Montville Twp	Montville, NJ
110	0.1	Naperville C U Dist 203	Naperville, IL
110	0.1	Orange County Office of Ed	Costa Mesa, CA
110	0.1	Riverside County Office of Ed	Riverside, CA
110	0.1	SD of The Chathams	Chatham, NJ
110	0.1	San Marino Unified	San Marino, CA
110	0.1	Saratoga Union Elementary	Saratoga, CA
110	0.1	Tenafly Boro	Tenafly, NJ

This section ranks 120 school districts at both the "top" and "bottom" of each category for a total of 240 districts per category. The "top" list (descending order) appears first, followed by the "bottom" list (ascending order).

Student/Teacher Ratio

School districts ranked in *descending* order

Rank	Ratio	District Name	City, State
1	197.1	Cedar Springs Public Schools	Cedar Springs, MI
2	177.4	Charlotte Public Schools	Charlotte, MI
3	171.1	Jenison Public Schools	Jenison, MI
4	158.4	Zeeland Public Schools	Zeeland, MI
5	148.0	Lansing Public SD	Lansing, MI
6	106.1	Meridian Public Schools	Sanford, MI
7	87.0	Peach Springs Unified District	Peach Springs, AZ
8	61.3	Galena City SD	Galena, AK
9	51.6	Ovid-Elsie Area Schools	Elsie, MI
10	49.4	Electronic Classroom of Tomorrow	Columbus, OH
11	44.8	Holt Public Schools	Holt, MI
12	42.3	Houghton Lake Community Schools	Houghton Lake, MI
13	42.2	Dundee Community Schools	Dundee, MI
14	40.7	Colorado River Union High SD	Fort Mojave, AZ
14	40.7	Indian River County SD	Vero Beach, FL
16	40.4	Pennsylvania Virtual CS	Norristown, PA
17	40.0	Tecumseh Public Schools	Tecumseh, MI
18	36.0	Gulf Shores Academy	Houston, TX
19	32.9	Waterford SD	Waterford, MI
20	32.5	Washtenaw ISD	Ann Arbor, MI
21	32.4	Department of Corrections SD 428	Springfield, IL
22	31.3	Butte County Joint District	Arco, ID
23	30.6	Detroit City SD	Detroit, MI
24	29.2	Fullerton Joint Union High	Fullerton, CA
25	28.9	Charter Oak Unified	Covina, CA
26	28.4	Westwood Unified	Westwood, CA
27	27.5	Santa Paula Union High	Santa Paula, CA
28	27.1	Montrose Community Schools	Montrose, MI
28	27.1	Oro Grande Elementary	Oro Grande, CA
30	26.9	Gorman Elementary	Gorman, CA
31	26.8	Maricopa County Regional District	Phoenix, AZ
32	26.3	Clintondale Community Schools	Clinton Twp, MI
33	25.9	Centinela Valley Union High	Lawndale, CA
33	25.9	Victor Valley Union High	Victorville, CA
35	25.8	Modesto City High	Modesto, CA
36	25.7	Gadsden Elementary District	San Luis, AZ
37	25.4	Beecher Community SD	Flint, MI
38	25.3	Antelope Valley Union High	Lancaster, CA
39	25.2	Huntington Beach Union High	Huntington Bch, CA
39	25.2	Lynwood Unified	Lynwood, CA
41	25.1	Val Verde Unified	Perris, CA
42	25.0	Whittier Union High	Whittier, CA
43	24.9	Central Point SD 006	Central Point, OR
43	24.9	King City Joint Union High	King City, CA
43	24.9	Santa Maria Joint Union High	Santa Maria, CA
46	24.7	Bethel SD 052	Eugene, OR
46	24.7	Julian Union Elementary	Julian, CA
48	24.6	William S Hart Union High	Santa Clarita, CA
49	24.5	Anaheim Union High	Anaheim, CA
49	24.5	El Monte Union High	El Monte, CA
49	24.5	Snowflake Unified District	Snowflake, AZ
52	24.4	Liberty Union High	Brentwood, CA
53	24.3	Oxnard Union High	Oxnard, CA
53	24.3	Tulare Joint Union High	Tulare, CA
55	24.2	Chaffey Joint Union High	Ontario, CA
55	24.2	Hanford Joint Union High	Hanford, CA
55	24.2	Nebo SD	Spanish Fork, UT
58	24.1	Julian Union High	Julian, CA
59	24.0	Alta Loma Elementary	Alta Loma, CA
60	23.9	Montebello Unified	Montebello, CA
60	23.9	Santa Cruz City High	Santa Cruz, CA
62	23.8	Alpine SD	American Fork, UT
62	23.8	Grossmont Union High	La Mesa, CA
62	23.8	Higley Unified District	Higley, AZ
65	23.7	Estacada SD 108	Estacada, OR
65	23.7	Jordan SD	Sandy, UT
67	23.6	Campbell Union High	San Jose, CA
68	23.5	Alhambra City High	Alhambra, CA
68	23.5	Eagle Point SD 009	Eagle Point, OR
70	23.4	Irvine Unified	Irvine, CA
70	23.4	Sonora Union High	Sonora, CA
72	23.3	Acton-Agua Dulce Unified	Acton, CA
72	23.3	Alisal Union Elementary	Salinas, CA
72	23.3	Delano Joint Union High	Delano, CA
72	23.3	Greene County Public Schools	Standardsville, VA
72	23.3	Linden Community Schools	Linden, MI
72	23.3	Oregon Trail SD 046	Sandy, OR
72	23.3	San Benito High	Hollister, CA
79	23.2	Amador County Unified	Jackson, CA
79	23.2	Medford SD 549	Medford, OR
79	23.2	Perris Union High	Perris, CA
79	23.2	Rim of The World Unified	Lake Arrowhead, CA
79	23.2	Riverside Unified	Riverside, CA
84	23.1	Jamul-Dulzura Union Elementary	Jamul, CA
84	23.1	Turlock Joint Union High	Turlock, CA
84	23.1	Yucaipa-Calimesa Joint Unified	Yucaipa, CA
87	23.0	Alvord Unified	Riverside, CA
87	23.0	Bonita Unified	San Dimas, CA
87	23.0	Compton Unified	Compton, CA
87	23.0	Greenville Public Schools	Greenville, MS
87	23.0	Kern Union High	Bakersfield, CA
87	23.0	Southern Kern Unified	Rosamond, CA
87	23.0	Ventura Unified	Ventura, CA
94	22.9	Glendora Unified	Glendora, CA
94	22.9	Los Alamitos Unified	Los Alamitos, CA
94	22.9	Merced Union High	Atwater, CA
94	22.9	Murrieta Valley Unified	Murrieta, CA
94	22.9	Ramona City Unified	Ramona, CA
94	22.9	Simi Valley Unified	Simi Valley, CA
100	22.8	Arcadia Unified	Arcadia, CA
100	22.8	Chino Valley Unified	Chino, CA
100	22.8	Downey Unified	Downey, CA
100	22.8	Garden Grove Unified	Garden Grove, CA
100	22.8	Juab SD	Nephi, UT
100	22.8	Livermore Valley Joint Unified	Livermore, CA
100	22.8	Parkrose SD 003	Portland, OR
100	22.8	South Pasadena Unified	South Pasadena, CA
100	22.8	Tooele SD	Tooele, UT
100	22.8	Victor Elementary	Victorville, CA
100	22.8	Washington SD	Saint George, UT
100	22.8	Weber SD	Ogden, UT
112	22.7	Capistrano Unified	San Juan Capis, CA
112	22.7	Davis SD	Farmington, UT
112	22.7	Eugene SD 04J	Eugene, OR
112	22.7	Huntington Beach City Elementary	Huntington Bch, CA
112	22.7	Lake Elsinore Unified	Lake Elsinore, CA
112	22.7	Lemoore Union High	Lemoore, CA
112	22.7	Saddleback Valley Unified	Mission Viejo, CA
112	22.7	Tri-Creek School Corp	Lowell, IN
120	22.6	Baldwin Park Unified	Baldwin Park, CA

This section ranks 120 school districts at both the "top" and "bottom" of each category for a total of 240 districts per category. The "top" list (descending order) appears first, followed by the "bottom" list (ascending order).

Student/Teacher Ratio

School districts ranked in *ascending* order

Rank	Ratio	District Name	City, State
1	3.2	Boces Eastern Suffolk (Suffolk I)	Patchogue, NY
2	3.6	Amphitheater Unified District	Tucson, AZ
2	3.6	Boces Nassau	Garden City, NY
4	4.4	Boces Monroe 1	Fairport, NY
5	7.2	Blackstone-Millville	Blackstone, MA
6	8.3	Dickenson County Public Schools	Clintwood, VA
7	8.4	Macomb ISD	Clinton Twp, MI
8	8.6	Middlesex County Vocational	E Brunswick, NJ
9	8.7	Bergen County Vocational	Paramus, NJ
9	8.7	Intermediate SD 287	Plymouth, MN
9	8.7	North Adams	North Adams, MA
12	8.9	Arlington County Public Schools	Arlington, VA
13	9.0	Alexandria City Public Schools	Alexandria, VA
13	9.0	Lee County Public Schools	Jonesville, VA
15	9.2	Santa Clara County Office of Ed	San Jose, CA
16	9.3	Belcourt 7	Belcourt, ND
16	9.3	Smyth County Public Schools	Marion, VA
16	9.3	Staunton City Public Schools	Staunton, VA
19	9.4	Area Coop Educational Services	North Haven, CT
19	9.4	Asbury Park City	Asbury Park, NJ
19	9.4	Carroll County Public Schools	Hillsville, VA
22	9.5	Easthampton	Easthampton, MA
23	9.6	Beachwood City SD	Beachwood, OH
23	9.6	Charlottesville City Pub Schools	Charlottesville, VA
23	9.6	Keansburg Boro	Keansburg, NJ
23	9.6	Pleasantville City	Pleasantville, NJ
27	9.7	Falls Church City Public Schools	Falls Church, VA
27	9.7	Harrisonburg City Public Schools	Harrisonburg, VA
29	9.8	Leonia Boro	Leonia, NJ
30	9.9	Goochland County Public Schools	Goochland, VA
30	9.9	Grayson County Public Schools	Independence, VA
30	9.9	Mansfield	Mansfield, MA
30	9.9	Rockbridge County Public Schools	Lexington, VA
34	10.0	Amherst	Amherst, MA
34	10.0	Dunkirk City SD	Dunkirk, NY
34	10.0	El Dorado	El Dorado, KS
34	10.0	Gloucester City	Gloucester City, NJ
34	10.0	Pittsfield	Pittsfield, MA
39	10.1	Montgomery County Public Schools	Christiansburg, VA
39	10.1	Passaic County Vocational	Wayne, NJ
39	10.1	State Voc-Tech Schools	Middletown, CT
42	10.2	Buchanan County Public Schools	Grundy, VA
42	10.2	Cambridge	Cambridge, MA
42	10.2	Halifax County Public Schools	Halifax, VA
42	10.2	Hoboken City	Hoboken, NJ
42	10.2	Long Branch City	Long Branch, NJ
42	10.2	Lunenburg County Public Schools	Victoria, VA
42	10.2	Roanoke City Public Schools	Roanoke, VA
42	10.2	San Bernardino County Supt.	San Bernardino, CA
42	10.2	Wise County Public Schools	Wise, VA
51	10.3	Augusta Dept of Public Schools	Augusta, ME
51	10.3	Belmont	Belmont, MA
51	10.3	Bering Strait SD	Unalakleet, AK
51	10.3	Jericho UFSD	Jericho, NY
51	10.3	Lancaster County Public Schools	Kilmarnock, VA
51	10.3	Mountain Lakes Boro	Mountain Lakes, NJ
51	10.3	Northampton County Public Schools	Machipongo, VA
51	10.3	Roanoke County Public Schools	Roanoke, VA
51	10.3	Winchester City Public Schools	Winchester, VA
60	10.4	Albemarle County Public Schools	Charlottesville, VA
60	10.4	Bristol City Public Schools	Bristol, VA
60	10.4	Essex County Public Schools	Tappahannock, VA
60	10.4	Hopewell City Public Schools	Hopewell, VA
60	10.4	MSAD 61 - Bridgton	Bridgton, ME
60	10.4	Madison County Public Schools	Madison, VA
60	10.4	Waltham	Waltham, MA
67	10.5	Brunswick County Public Schools	Lawrenceville, VA
67	10.5	Burlington City	Burlington, NJ
67	10.5	Clarke County Public Schools	Berryville, VA
67	10.5	Colonial Heights City Pub Schools	Colonial Hgts, VA
67	10.5	Nelson County Public Schools	Lovingston, VA
67	10.5	Ocean City	Ocean City, NJ
67	10.5	Oyster Bay-East Norwich CSD	Oyster Bay, NY
67	10.5	Phillipsburg Town	Phillipsburg, NJ
75	10.6	Holyoke	Holyoke, MA
75	10.6	Leavenworth	Leavenworth, KS
75	10.6	Martinsville City Public Schools	Martinsville, VA
75	10.6	Mohawk Trail	Shelburne Falls, MA
75	10.6	Salem	Salem, MA
75	10.6	Warren Twp	Warren, NJ
75	10.6	Williamsburg-James City Co Pub Schls	Williamsburg, VA
75	10.6	Woodbury City	Woodbury, NJ
83	10.7	Bourne	Bourne, MA
83	10.7	Cleveland Municipal SD	Cleveland, OH
83	10.7	Fresno County Office of Ed	Fresno, CA
83	10.7	Henry County Public Schools	Collinsville, VA
83	10.7	Lawrence UFSD	Lawrence, NY
83	10.7	Plattsburgh City SD	Plattsburgh, NY
83	10.7	Shenandoah County Public Schools	Woodstock, VA
83	10.7	Southampton UFSD	Southampton, NY
83	10.7	Todd County SD 66-1	Mission, SD
92	10.8	Amherst County Public Schools	Amherst, VA
92	10.8	Capitol Region Education Council	Hartford, CT
92	10.8	Danville City Public Schools	Danville, VA
92	10.8	Elizabeth City	Elizabeth, NJ
92	10.8	Fredericksburg City Public Schools	Fredericksburg, VA
92	10.8	Harrison CSD	Harrison, NY
92	10.8	Jamestown City SD	Jamestown, NY
92	10.8	North Shore CSD	Sea Cliff, NY
92	10.8	North Slope Borough SD	Barrow, AK
92	10.8	Orange County Public Schools	Orange, VA
92	10.8	Rockville Centre UFSD	Rockville Ctre, NY
92	10.8	Scott County Public Schools	Gate City, VA
92	10.8	Sherburne-Earlville CSD	Sherburne, NY
105	10.9	Agawam	Feeding Hills, MA
105	10.9	Alleghany County Public Schools	Covington, VA
105	10.9	Auburn School Department	Auburn, ME
105	10.9	Buckingham County Public Schools	Buckingham, VA
105	10.9	Great Neck UFSD	Great Neck, NY
105	10.9	King William County Public Schools	King William, VA
105	10.9	Llano ISD	Llano, TX
105	10.9	Mineola UFSD	Mineola, NY
105	10.9	Norfolk City Public Schools	Norfolk, VA
105	10.9	Powhatan County Public Schools	Powhatan, VA
105	10.9	Ramapo-Indian Hill Reg	Franklin Lakes, NJ
105	10.9	Watertown	Watertown, MA
105	10.9	Waterville Public Schools	Waterville, ME
118	11.0	Beekmantown CSD	Plattsburgh, NY
118	11.0	Carle Place UFSD	Carle Place, NY
118	11.0	Clay Center	Clay Center, KS

This section ranks 120 school districts at both the "top" and "bottom" of each category for a total of 240 districts per category. The "top" list (descending order) appears first, followed by the "bottom" list (ascending order).

Student/Librarian Ratio

School districts ranked in *descending* order

Rank	Ratio	District Name	City, State
1	50,502.5	Escondido Union Elementary	Escondido, CA
2	48,608.0	Capistrano Unified	San Juan Capis, CA
3	40,168.0	Fontana Unified	Fontana, CA
4	34,290.0	Etiwanda Elementary	Etiwanda, CA
5	32,643.3	Marysville Joint Unified	Marysville, CA
6	25,160.0	Orcutt Union Elementary	Orcutt, CA
7	24,068.0	Santa Maria-Bonita Elementary	Santa Maria, CA
8	23,226.0	Oak Grove Elementary	San Jose, CA
9	21,673.0	Simi Valley Unified	Simi Valley, CA
10	18,653.0	Cajon Valley Union Elementary	El Cajon, CA
11	15,902.5	Santa Ana Unified	Santa Ana, CA
12	15,660.0	Thermalito Union Elementary	Oroville, CA
13	14,960.0	Walled Lake Consolidated Schools	Walled Lake, MI
14	14,668.0	Huntington Beach Union High	Huntington Bch, CA
15	14,416.0	Alum Rock Union Elementary	San Jose, CA
16	13,910.0	San Marcos Unified	San Marcos, CA
17	13,867.0	Coachella Valley Unified	Thermal, CA
18	13,450.0	Panama Buena Vista Union Elementary	Bakersfield, CA
19	13,385.0	Norwalk-La Mirada Unified	Norwalk, CA
20	13,237.0	Upland Unified	Upland, CA
21	13,223.3	Amherst Ex Vill SD	Amherst, OH
22	13,068.0	Richmond City Public Schools	Richmond, VA
23	12,392.4	Antelope Valley Union High	Lancaster, CA
24	12,245.0	Waterford SD	Waterford, MI
25	12,202.0	Whittier Union High	Whittier, CA
26	11,715.0	Fairhaven	Fairhaven, MA
27	11,686.7	San Bernardino City Unified	San Bernardino, CA
28	11,441.0	Los Angeles County Office of Ed	Downey, CA
29	11,295.0	Fullerton Elementary	Fullerton, CA
30	11,223.0	Palos Verdes Peninsula Unified	Palos Verdes Est, CA
31	10,850.0	Compton Unified	Compton, CA
32	10,715.0	Santa Maria Joint Union High	Santa Maria, CA
33	10,497.0	Mountain View Elementary	El Monte, CA
34	10,494.3	Corona-Norco Unified	Norco, CA
35	10,445.0	Woodland Joint Unified	Woodland, CA
36	10,442.4	San Juan Unified	Carmichael, CA
37	10,134.0	Rio Linda Union Elementary	Rio Linda, CA
38	9,958.0	Penn-Harris-Madison Sch Corp	Mishawaka, IN
39	9,942.0	Arcadia Unified	Arcadia, CA
40	9,732.0	Lynwood Unified	Lynwood, CA
41	9,695.0	Indian Valley Local SD	Gnadenhutten, OH
42	9,660.0	Grass Valley Elementary	Grass Valley, CA
43	9,630.0	Gilroy Unified	Gilroy, CA
44	9,542.0	Pittsburg Unified	Pittsburg, CA
45	9,369.5	Rowland Unified	Rowland Heights, CA
46	9,259.0	Tustin Unified	Tustin, CA
47	9,242.0	Yucaipa-Calimesa Joint Unified	Yucaipa, CA
48	8,982.0	Dysart Unified District	El Mirage, AZ
49	8,891.5	Saddleback Valley Unified	Mission Viejo, CA
50	8,856.8	Pomona Unified	Pomona, CA
51	8,850.0	Liberty Hill ISD	Liberty Hill, TX
52	8,821.3	Placentia-Yorba Linda Unified	Placentia, CA
53	8,736.7	Fremont Unified	Fremont, CA
54	8,712.0	Beaumont Unified	Beaumont, CA
55	8,532.9	Saint Francis	Saint Francis, MN
56	8,467.7	Los Angeles Unified	Los Angeles, CA
57	8,427.5	Madera Unified	Madera, CA
58	8,271.0	Orange County Office of Ed	Costa Mesa, CA
59	8,229.0	Chino Valley Unified	Chino, CA
60	7,996.0	Glendora Unified	Glendora, CA
61	7,993.0	Redondo Beach Unified	Redondo Beach, CA
62	7,903.0	Alisal Union Elementary	Salinas, CA
63	7,717.0	Murrieta Valley Unified	Murrieta, CA
64	7,653.0	Natomas Unified	Sacramento, CA
65	7,401.0	Newark Unified	Newark, CA
66	7,389.0	Pleasant Valley School	Camarillo, CA
67	7,359.0	Covina-Valley Unified	Covina, CA
67	7,359.0	Ramona City Unified	Ramona, CA
69	7,332.7	Temecula Valley Unified	Temecula, CA
70	7,285.0	Conejo Valley Unified	Thousand Oaks, CA
71	7,183.3	Lemoore Union High	Lemoore, CA
72	7,111.3	Temple City Unified	Temple City, CA
73	7,045.3	Antioch Unified	Antioch, CA
74	7,017.3	Manteca Unified	Manteca, CA
75	6,998.8	Crane Elementary District	Yuma, AZ
76	6,876.0	Washington Unified	West Sacramento, CA
77	6,866.0	Claremont Unified	Claremont, CA
78	6,855.0	Ukiah Unified	Ukiah, CA
79	6,847.0	Wachusett	Jefferson, MA
80	6,816.0	Barstow Unified	Barstow, CA
81	6,671.0	Culver City Unified	Culver City, CA
82	6,603.7	Lodi Unified	Lodi, CA
83	6,493.3	Live Oak Elementary	Santa Cruz, CA
84	6,465.0	Manhattan Beach Unified	Manhattan Beach, CA
85	6,448.8	Indian Prairie CUSD 204	Aurora, IL
86	6,446.0	San Bernardino County Supt.	San Bernardino, CA
87	6,386.7	Weld County RE-1	Gilcrest, CO
88	6,320.0	Fountain Valley Elementary	Fountain Valley, CA
89	6,295.0	Desert Sands Unified	La Quinta, CA
90	6,240.5	Visalia Unified	Visalia, CA
91	6,240.0	Juab SD	Nephi, UT
92	6,219.0	Torrance Unified	Torrance, CA
93	6,217.0	Danville CCSD 118	Danville, IL
94	6,120.0	Three Rivers SD	Murphy, OR
95	6,109.0	North Monterey County Unified	Moss Landing, CA
96	6,047.0	Round Lake Area Schs - Dist 116	Round Lake, IL
97	6,040.0	Redmond SD 02J	Redmond, OR
98	5,958.0	Maywood-Melrose Park-Broadview-89	Melrose Park, IL
99	5,948.0	Selma Unified	Selma, CA
100	5,943.3	San Rafael City Elementary	San Rafael, CA
101	5,931.0	Sunnyvale Elementary	Sunnyvale, CA
102	5,913.7	Inglewood Unified	Inglewood, CA
103	5,871.3	Folsom-Cordova Unified	Folsom, CA
104	5,808.5	Lompoc Unified	Lompoc, CA
105	5,801.0	Northmont City SD	Englewood, OH
106	5,791.0	Atascadero Unified	Atascadero, CA
107	5,748.0	Shasta Union High	Redding, CA
108	5,650.0	Bear Valley Unified	Big Bear Lake, CA
109	5,636.2	Baldwin Park Unified	Baldwin Park, CA
110	5,620.5	Oceanside Unified	Oceanside, CA
111	5,567.0	Sierra Sands Unified	Ridgecrest, CA
112	5,551.0	Lincoln Way Community HSD 210	New Lenox, IL
113	5,507.0	Bethel SD 052	Eugene, OR
114	5,475.3	Sanger Unified	Sanger, CA
115	5,458.0	Lucia Mar Unified	Arroyo Grande, CA
116	5,436.7	Buna ISD	Buna, TX
117	5,372.0	Dekalb Community Unit SD 428	De Kalb, IL
118	5,357.2	Oakland Unified	Oakland, CA
119	5,337.3	Colton Joint Unified	Colton, CA
120	5,310.0	Dinuba Unified	Dinuba, CA

This section ranks 120 school districts at both the "top" and "bottom" of each category for a total of 240 districts per category. The "top" list (descending order) appears first, followed by the "bottom" list (ascending order).

Student/Librarian Ratio

School districts ranked in *ascending* order

Rank	Ratio	District Name	City, State
1	0.0	ABC Unified	Cerritos, CA
1	0.0	Acton-Agua Dulce Unified	Acton, CA
1	0.0	Addison SD 4	Addison, IL
1	0.0	Adelanto Elementary	Adelanto, CA
1	0.0	Alhambra City Elementary	Alhambra, CA
1	0.0	Alpine Union Elementary	Alpine, CA
1	0.0	Alta Loma Elementary	Alta Loma, CA
1	0.0	Amador County Unified	Jackson, CA
1	0.0	Anaheim Elementary	Anaheim, CA
1	0.0	Apple Valley Unified	Apple Valley, CA
1	0.0	Arvin Union Elementary	Arvin, CA
1	0.0	Auburn	Auburn, MA
1	0.0	Auburn Union Elementary	Auburn, CA
1	0.0	Azusa Unified	Azusa, CA
1	0.0	Banning Unified	Banning, CA
1	0.0	Bassett Unified	La Puente, CA
1	0.0	Beardsley Elementary	Bakersfield, CA
1	0.0	Belchertown	Belchertown, MA
1	0.0	Belleville SD 118	Belleville, IL
1	0.0	Bellevue Union Elementary	Santa Rosa, CA
1	0.0	Belmont-Redwood Shores Elementary	Belmont, CA
1	0.0	Benicia Unified	Benicia, CA
1	0.0	Bergen County Vocational	Paramus, NJ
1	0.0	Berkshire Hills	Stockbridge, MA
1	0.0	Berryessa Union Elementary	San Jose, CA
1	0.0	Berwyn South SD 100	Berwyn, IL
1	0.0	Bishop Union Elementary	Bishop, CA
1	0.0	Bonsall Union Elementary	Bonsall, CA
1	0.0	Brawley Elementary	Brawley, CA
1	0.0	Brawley Union High	Brawley, CA
1	0.0	Brea-Olinda Unified	Brea, CA
1	0.0	Brentwood Union Elementary	Brentwood, CA
1	0.0	Buena Park Elementary	Buena Park, CA
1	0.0	Bullard ISD	Bullard, TX
1	0.0	Burbank Unified	Burbank, CA
1	0.0	Burlington	Burlington, MA
1	0.0	Calaveras Unified	San Andreas, CA
1	0.0	Caldwell Parish School Board	Columbia, LA
1	0.0	Calexico Unified	Calexico, CA
1	0.0	Cambrian Elementary	San Jose, CA
1	0.0	Campbell Union Elementary	Campbell, CA
1	0.0	Carpinteria Unified	Carpinteria, CA
1	0.0	Cascade Union Elementary	Anderson, CA
1	0.0	Castaic Union Elementary	Valencia, CA
1	0.0	Centinela Valley Union High	Lawndale, CA
1	0.0	Central Union Elementary	Lemoore, CA
1	0.0	Centralia Elementary	Buena Park, CA
1	0.0	Channahon SD 17	Channahon, IL
1	0.0	Charter Oak Unified	Covina, CA
1	0.0	Chicago Heights SD 170	Chicago Heights, IL
1	0.0	Chowchilla Elementary	Chowchilla, CA
1	0.0	Cloverdale Unified	Cloverdale, CA
1	0.0	Coalinga-Huron Joint Unified	Coalinga, CA
1	0.0	Community CSD 168	Sauk Village, IL
1	0.0	Coronado Unified	Coronado, CA
1	0.0	Crookston	Crookston, MN
1	0.0	Cucamonga Elementary	Rcho Cucamong, CA
1	0.0	Cupertino Union School	Cupertino, CA
1	0.0	Cutler-Orosi Joint Unified	Orosi, CA
1	0.0	Cypress Elementary	Cypress, CA
1	0.0	Del Mar Union Elementary	Del Mar, CA
1	0.0	Del Norte County Unified	Crescent City, CA
1	0.0	Del Paso Heights Elementary	Sacramento, CA
1	0.0	Delano Joint Union High	Delano, CA
1	0.0	Delano Union Elementary	Delano, CA
1	0.0	Delta County 50(J)	Delta, CO
1	0.0	Department of Corrections SD 428	Springfield, IL
1	0.0	Dry Creek Joint Elementary	Roseville, CA
1	0.0	Du Quoin CUSD 300	Du Quoin, IL
1	0.0	Duarte Unified	Duarte, CA
1	0.0	Earlimart Elementary	Earlimart, CA
1	0.0	East Bridgewater	E Bridgewater, MA
1	0.0	East Lycoming SD	Hughesville, PA
1	0.0	East Whittier City Elementary	Whittier, CA
1	0.0	Easton	North Easton, MA
1	0.0	El Centro Elementary	El Centro, CA
1	0.0	El Monte City Elementary	El Monte, CA
1	0.0	El Rancho Unified	Pico Rivera, CA
1	0.0	Electronic Classroom of Tomorrow	Columbus, OH
1	0.0	Elma SD 68	Elma, WA
1	0.0	Encinitas Union Elementary	Encinitas, CA
1	0.0	Escalon Unified	Escalon, CA
1	0.0	Escondido Union High	Escondido, CA
1	0.0	Estacada SD 108	Estacada, OR
1	0.0	Eureka Union Elementary	Granite Bay, CA
1	0.0	Exeter Union Elementary	Exeter, CA
1	0.0	Fallbrook Union Elementary	Fallbrook, CA
1	0.0	Fallbrook Union High	Fallbrook, CA
1	0.0	Farmersville Unified	Farmersville, CA
1	0.0	Fillmore Unified	Fillmore, CA
1	0.0	Floyd County Public Schools	Floyd, VA
1	0.0	Forest Ridge SD 142	Oak Forest, IL
1	0.0	Frankfort CCSD 157c	Frankfort, IL
1	0.0	Fruitvale Elementary	Bakersfield, CA
1	0.0	Galt Joint Union Elementary	Galt, CA
1	0.0	Galt Joint Union High	Galt, CA
1	0.0	Glendale Unified	Glendale, CA
1	0.0	Golden Plains Unified	San Joaquin, CA
1	0.0	Goleta Union Elementary	Goleta, CA
1	0.0	Gorman Elementary	Gorman, CA
1	0.0	Greater Lowell Voc Tec	Tyngsborough, MA
1	0.0	Greater New Bedford	New Bedford, MA
1	0.0	Greeley 6	Greeley, CO
1	0.0	Greenfield Union Elementary	Bakersfield, CA
1	0.0	Gustine Unified	Gustine, CA
1	0.0	Hacienda La Puente Unified	City of Industry, CA
1	0.0	Hanford Elementary	Hanford, CA
1	0.0	Hawthorne Elementary	Hawthorne, CA
1	0.0	Healdsburg Unified	Healdsburg, CA
1	0.0	Hesperia Unified	Hesperia, CA
1	0.0	Hilmar Unified	Hilmar, CA
1	0.0	Hollister SD	Hollister, CA
1	0.0	Holtville Unified	Holtville, CA
1	0.0	Holyoke	Holyoke, MA
1	0.0	Homewood SD 153	Homewood, IL
1	0.0	Honors Academy	Dallas, TX
1	0.0	Hueneme Elementary	Port Hueneme, CA
1	0.0	Hughson Unified	Hughson, CA
1	0.0	Huntington Beach City Elementary	Huntington Bch, CA
1	0.0	Imperial Unified	Imperial, CA

This section ranks 120 school districts at both the "top" and "bottom" of each category for a total of 240 districts per category. The "top" list (descending order) appears first, followed by the "bottom" list (ascending order).

Student/Counselor Ratio

School districts ranked in *descending* order

Rank	Ratio	District Name	City, State
1	22,375.0	Anaheim Elementary	Anaheim, CA
2	20,120.0	Saugus Union Elementary	Santa Clarita, CA
3	17,616.0	Lansing Public SD	Lansing, MI
4	15,800.0	Fountain Valley Elementary	Fountain Valley, CA
5	14,953.3	Mountain View-Whisman Elementary	Mountain View, CA
6	14,668.0	Huntington Beach Union High	Huntington Bch, CA
7	12,704.4	Alhambra City Elementary	Alhambra, CA
8	11,856.7	Roseville City Elementary	Roseville, CA
9	11,442.0	Roosevelt Elementary District	Phoenix, AZ
10	11,431.7	Garvey Elementary	Rosemead, CA
11	9,572.0	Joliet Public SD 86	Joliet, IL
12	9,373.3	Encinitas Union Elementary	Encinitas, CA
13	9,270.0	Twin Ridges Elementary	North San Juan, CA
14	8,813.0	Redwood City Elementary	Redwood City, CA
15	8,220.0	Goleta Union Elementary	Goleta, CA
16	7,508.0	Palmdale Elementary	Palmdale, CA
17	7,106.0	Wheeling CCSD 21	Wheeling, IL
18	7,097.0	Delano Union Elementary	Delano, CA
19	6,537.5	Glendale Elementary District	Glendale, AZ
20	6,280.0	Hollister SD	Hollister, CA
21	6,146.8	Chula Vista Elementary	Chula Vista, CA
22	6,096.7	Moraga Elementary	Moraga, CA
23	6,076.0	Capistrano Unified	San Juan Capis, CA
24	5,648.0	Richland SD	Shafter, CA
25	5,248.5	Mountain View Elementary	El Monte, CA
26	5,195.0	Madison Elementary District	Phoenix, AZ
27	5,168.0	Ravenswood City Elementary	East Palo Alto, CA
28	4,866.0	Livingston Union Elementary	Livingston, CA
29	4,863.0	Zeeland Public Schools	Zeeland, MI
30	4,545.0	Ontario-Montclair Elementary	Ontario, CA
31	4,380.0	Fresno County Office of Ed	Fresno, CA
32	4,324.0	Hueneme Elementary	Port Hueneme, CA
33	4,248.6	Selma Unified	Selma, CA
34	4,243.0	Eureka Union Elementary	Granite Bay, CA
35	4,209.0	Electronic Classroom of Tomorrow	Columbus, OH
36	4,143.3	Savanna Elementary	Anaheim, CA
37	4,135.5	Orange County Office of Ed	Costa Mesa, CA
38	4,100.0	Julian Union Elementary	Julian, CA
39	4,088.0	Dolton SD 149	Calumet City, IL
40	4,032.0	Los Altos Elementary	Los Altos, CA
41	3,987.9	Antioch Unified	Antioch, CA
42	3,968.3	Cupertino Union School	Cupertino, CA
43	3,917.2	Marysville Joint Unified	Marysville, CA
44	3,909.0	CCSD 181	Hinsdale, IL
45	3,838.0	SD 45 Dupage County	Villa Park, IL
46	3,831.0	Addison SD 4	Addison, IL
47	3,814.0	Enterprise Elementary	Redding, CA
48	3,740.0	Walled Lake Consolidated Schools	Walled Lake, MI
49	3,577.0	Cary CCSD 26	Cary, IL
50	3,566.8	Fullerton Elementary	Fullerton, CA
51	3,516.0	Kildeer Countryside CCSD 96	Buffalo Grove, IL
52	3,494.5	Magnolia Elementary	Anaheim, CA
53	3,489.0	Cedar Springs Public Schools	Cedar Springs, MI
54	3,450.0	Newhall Elementary	Valencia, CA
55	3,439.0	Mountain View Elementary	Ontario, CA
56	3,378.0	San Diego County Office of Ed	San Diego, CA
57	3,362.5	Panama Buena Vista Union Elementary	Bakersfield, CA
58	3,216.7	Wiseburn Elementary	Hawthorne, CA
59	3,207.0	Deerfield SD 109	Deerfield, IL
60	3,176.3	Belmont-Redwood Shores Elementary	Belmont, CA
61	3,153.0	Laguna Salada Union Elementary	Pacifica, CA
62	3,147.3	Victor Elementary	Victorville, CA
63	3,096.0	Page Unified District	Page, AZ
64	3,048.0	King George County Public Schools	King George, VA
65	3,047.0	Fruitvale Elementary	Bakersfield, CA
66	3,015.8	Schaumburg CCSD 54	Schaumburg, IL
67	3,000.0	Maricopa County Regional District	Phoenix, AZ
68	2,995.0	Santa Rita Union Elementary	Salinas, CA
69	2,946.0	Waterford Unified	Waterford, CA
70	2,924.0	Keppel Union Elementary	Pearblossom, CA
71	2,912.1	Livermore Valley Joint Unified	Livermore, CA
72	2,900.0	Bonsall Union Elementary	Bonsall, CA
73	2,884.0	Kalamazoo Public SD	Kalamazoo, MI
74	2,862.7	Phoenix Elementary District	Phoenix, AZ
75	2,849.0	Mount Pleasant Elementary	San Jose, CA
76	2,807.0	Cambrian Elementary	San Jose, CA
77	2,774.0	Adelanto Elementary	Adelanto, CA
78	2,773.9	Community CSD 62	Des Plaines, IL
79	2,759.0	Fowler Elementary District	Phoenix, AZ
80	2,747.4	Prior Lake	Prior Lake, MN
81	2,739.3	Higley Unified District	Higley, AZ
82	2,731.0	Murphy Elementary District	Phoenix, AZ
83	2,685.3	Vail Unified District	Vail, AZ
84	2,654.0	Cutler-Orosi Joint Unified	Orosi, CA
85	2,652.0	Los Gatos Union Elementary	Los Gatos, CA
86	2,627.0	King City Union Elementary	King City, CA
87	2,620.3	Tulare City Elementary	Tulare, CA
88	2,618.3	Nippersink SD 2	Richmond, IL
89	2,613.0	Little Lake City Elementary	Santa Fe Spgs, CA
90	2,607.2	Duarte Unified	Duarte, CA
91	2,586.6	Palatine CCSD 15	Palatine, IL
92	2,494.3	Campbell Union Elementary	Campbell, CA
93	2,488.0	Delhi Unified	Delhi, CA
94	2,472.5	Cartwright Elementary District	Phoenix, AZ
95	2,469.9	Saddleback Valley Unified	Mission Viejo, CA
96	2,453.5	Tehachapi Unified	Tehachapi, CA
97	2,450.6	Washington Elementary District	Phoenix, AZ
98	2,428.0	Alpine Union Elementary	Alpine, CA
99	2,410.0	Hilmar Unified	Hilmar, CA
100	2,395.5	Jenison Public Schools	Jenison, MI
101	2,385.7	Walnut Creek Elementary	Walnut Creek, CA
102	2,380.0	Greenfield Union Elementary	Bakersfield, CA
103	2,376.0	Forrest County SD	Hattiesburg, MS
104	2,353.6	National Elementary	National City, CA
105	2,350.4	Kyrene Elementary District	Tempe, AZ
106	2,350.0	Los Nietos Elementary	Whittier, CA
107	2,318.5	Union Elementary	San Jose, CA
108	2,308.0	Newman-Crows Landing Unified	Newman, CA
109	2,296.0	Bensenville SD 2	Bensenville, IL
110	2,281.0	Mundelein Elem SD 75	Mundelein, IL
111	2,264.0	Dassel-Cokato	Cokato, MN
112	2,254.0	Lyons SD 103	Lyons, IL
113	2,244.6	Escondido Union Elementary	Escondido, CA
114	2,240.2	East Whittier City Elementary	Whittier, CA
115	2,215.0	Queen Bee SD 16	Glendale Hgts, IL
116	2,206.5	Moreland Elementary	San Jose, CA
117	2,204.8	Lawndale Elementary	Lawndale, CA
118	2,177.0	Oakley Union Elementary	Oakley, CA
118	2,177.0	Park Ridge CCSD 64	Park Ridge, IL
120	2,151.0	Millbrae Elementary	Millbrae, CA

This section ranks 120 school districts at both the "top" and "bottom" of each category for a total of 240 districts per category. The "top" list (descending order) appears first, followed by the "bottom" list (ascending order).

Student/Counselor Ratio

School districts ranked in *ascending* order

Rank	Ratio	District Name	City, State
1	0.0	Alisal Union Elementary	Salinas, CA
1	0.0	Alsip-Hazlgrn-Oaklawn SD 126	Alsip, IL
1	0.0	Alta Loma Elementary	Alta Loma, CA
1	0.0	Antioch CCSD 34	Antioch, IL
1	0.0	Aptakisic-Tripp CCSD 102	Buffalo Grove, IL
1	0.0	Arlington Heights SD 25	Arlington Hgts, IL
1	0.0	Arvin Union Elementary	Arvin, CA
1	0.0	Beach Park CCSD 3	Beach Park, IL
1	0.0	Beardsley Elementary	Bakersfield, CA
1	0.0	Belleville SD 118	Belleville, IL
1	0.0	Bellevue Union Elementary	Santa Rosa, CA
1	0.0	Bellwood SD 88	Bellwood, IL
1	0.0	Berwyn North SD 98	Berwyn, IL
1	0.0	Berwyn South SD 100	Berwyn, IL
1	0.0	Bourbonnais SD 53	Bourbonnais, IL
1	0.0	Bradley SD 61	Bradley, IL
1	0.0	Buena Park Elementary	Buena Park, CA
1	0.0	Burbank SD 111	Burbank, IL
1	0.0	Charter Oak Unified	Covina, CA
1	0.0	Chowchilla Elementary	Chowchilla, CA
1	0.0	Cicero SD 99	Cicero, IL
1	0.0	Community CSD 168	Sauk Village, IL
1	0.0	Community CSD 46	Grayslake, IL
1	0.0	Community CSD 59	Arlington Hgts, IL
1	0.0	Community CSD 93	Carol Stream, IL
1	0.0	Cook County SD 130	Blue Island, IL
1	0.0	Cottonwood-Oak Creek Elementary Dist	Cottonwood, AZ
1	0.0	Creighton Elementary District	Phoenix, AZ
1	0.0	Crystal Lake CCSD 47	Crystal Lake, IL
1	0.0	Cucamonga Elementary	Rcho Cucamong, CA
1	0.0	Cypress Elementary	Cypress, CA
1	0.0	Darien SD 61	Darien, IL
1	0.0	Del Mar Union Elementary	Del Mar, CA
1	0.0	Department of Corrections SD 428	Springfield, IL
1	0.0	Dolton SD 148	Riverdale, IL
1	0.0	Earlimart Elementary	Earlimart, CA
1	0.0	Eastside Union Elementary	Lancaster, CA
1	0.0	El Monte City Elementary	El Monte, CA
1	0.0	Elem SD 159	Matteson, IL
1	0.0	Elmont UFSD	Elmont, NY
1	0.0	Etiwanda Elementary	Etiwanda, CA
1	0.0	Evanston CCSD 65	Evanston, IL
1	0.0	Evergreen Elementary	San Jose, CA
1	0.0	Evergreen Park ESD 124	Evergreen Park, IL
1	0.0	Exeter Union Elementary	Exeter, CA
1	0.0	Floral Park-Bellerose UFSD	Floral Park, NY
1	0.0	Floyd County Public Schools	Floyd, VA
1	0.0	Frankfort CCSD 157c	Frankfort, IL
1	0.0	Franklin Square UFSD	Franklin Square, NY
1	0.0	Fremont SD 79	Mundelein, IL
1	0.0	Galt Joint Union Elementary	Galt, CA
1	0.0	Glenview CCSD 34	Glenview, IL
1	0.0	Gurnee SD 56	Gurnee, IL
1	0.0	Hanford Elementary	Hanford, CA
1	0.0	Harvey SD 152	Harvey, IL
1	0.0	Hawthorn CCSD 73	Vernon Hills, IL
1	0.0	Homewood SD 153	Homewood, IL
1	0.0	Huntington Beach City Elementary	Huntington Bch, CA
1	0.0	Indian Springs SD 109	Justice, IL
1	0.0	Intermediate SD 287	Plymouth, MN
1	0.0	Isle of Wight County Pub Schools	Isle Of Wight, VA
1	0.0	Jefferson Elementary	Daly City, CA
1	0.0	Jefferson Elementary	Tracy, CA
1	0.0	Julian Union High	Julian, CA
1	0.0	Keeneyville SD 20	Hanover Park, IL
1	0.0	Kerman Unified	Kerman, CA
1	0.0	Keyes Union Elementary	Keyes, CA
1	0.0	La Grange SD 102	La Grange Park, IL
1	0.0	La Habra City Elementary	La Habra, CA
1	0.0	Lake Villa CCSD 41	Lake Villa, IL
1	0.0	Lancaster Elementary	Lancaster, CA
1	0.0	Lansing SD 158	Lansing, IL
1	0.0	Lemon Grove Elementary	Lemon Grove, CA
1	0.0	Liberty Elementary District	Buckeye, AZ
1	0.0	Lincolnshire-Prairieview SD 103	Lincolnshire, IL
1	0.0	Little Egg Harbor Twp	Little Egg Hbr, NJ
1	0.0	Littleton Elementary District	Cashion, AZ
1	0.0	Loomis Union Elementary	Loomis, CA
1	0.0	Los Banos Unified	Los Banos, CA
1	0.0	Lowell Joint	Whittier, CA
1	0.0	Mannheim SD 83	Franklin Park, IL
1	0.0	Marquardt SD 15	Glendale Hgts, IL
1	0.0	Maywood-Melrose Park-Broadview-89	Melrose Park, IL
1	0.0	Mchenry CCSD 15	Mc Henry, IL
1	0.0	Menifee Union Elementary	Menifee, CA
1	0.0	Merrick UFSD	Merrick, NY
1	0.0	Midlothian SD 143	Midlothian, IL
1	0.0	Modesto City Elementary	Modesto, CA
1	0.0	Mohave Valley Elementary District	Mohave Valley, AZ
1	0.0	Mokena SD 159	Mokena, IL
1	0.0	Mount Diablo Unified	Concord, CA
1	0.0	Mount Prospect SD 57	Mount Prospect, IL
1	0.0	New Hyde Pk-Garden City Pk UFSD	New Hyde Park, NY
1	0.0	North Bellmore UFSD	Bellmore, NY
1	0.0	North Palos SD 117	Palos Hills, IL
1	0.0	O'Fallon CCSD 90	Ofallon, IL
1	0.0	Oak Lawn-Hometown SD 123	Oak Lawn, IL
1	0.0	Oak Park Elem SD 97	Oak Park, IL
1	0.0	Ocean View Elementary	Huntington Bch, CA
1	0.0	Old Adobe Union Elementary	Petaluma, CA
1	0.0	Orcutt Union Elementary	Orcutt, CA
1	0.0	Oro Grande Elementary	Oro Grande, CA
1	0.0	Oxnard Elementary	Oxnard, CA
1	0.0	Peach Springs Unified District	Peach Springs, AZ
1	0.0	Pembroke	Pembroke, MA
1	0.0	Pennsylvania Virtual CS	Norristown, PA
1	0.0	Perris Elementary	Perris, CA
1	0.0	Petaluma City Elementary	Petaluma, CA
1	0.0	Piner-Olivet Union Elementary	Santa Rosa, CA
1	0.0	Posen-Robbins El SD 143-5	Posen, IL
1	0.0	Prairie-Hills Elem SD 144	Markham, IL
1	0.0	Preble Shawnee Local SD	Camden, OH
1	0.0	Prospect Heights SD 23	Prospect Hgts, IL
1	0.0	Rantoul City SD 137	Rantoul, IL
1	0.0	Red Wing	Red Wing, MN
1	0.0	Ridgeland SD 122	Oak Lawn, IL
1	0.0	Rincon Valley Union Elementary	Santa Rosa, CA
1	0.0	Rio Elementary	Oxnard, CA
1	0.0	River Trails SD 26	Mount Prospect, IL
1	0.0	Riverside County Office of Ed	Riverside, CA

This section ranks 120 school districts at both the "top" and "bottom" of each category for a total of 240 districts per category. The "top" list (descending order) appears first, followed by the "bottom" list (ascending order).

Current Spending per Student in FY2001

School districts ranked in *descending* order

Rank	Dollars	District Name	City, State
1	44,947	San Diego County Office of Ed	San Diego, CA
2	39,805	Kern County Office of Ed	Bakersfield, CA
3	37,660	San Bernardino County Supt.	San Bernardino, CA
4	36,699	Riverside County Office of Ed	Riverside, CA
5	34,409	Santa Clara County Office of Ed	San Jose, CA
6	31,095	Los Angeles County Office of Ed	Downey, CA
7	28,881	Special SD - Saint Louis County	Town & Ctry, MO
8	26,743	Fresno County Office of Ed	Fresno, CA
9	26,729	San Joaquin County Office of Ed	Stockton, CA
10	23,317	Bergen County Vocational	Paramus, NJ
11	22,085	North Slope Borough SD	Barrow, AK
12	20,007	Hoboken City	Hoboken, NJ
13	19,485	Lawrence UFSD	Lawrence, NY
14	19,480	Manhasset UFSD	Manhasset, NY
15	19,318	Middlesex County Vocational	E Brunswick, NJ
16	18,881	Passaic County Vocational	Wayne, NJ
17	18,778	Greenburgh CSD	Hartsdale, NY
18	18,670	Jericho UFSD	Jericho, NY
19	18,380	Mineola UFSD	Mineola, NY
20	18,146	Oyster Bay-East Norwich CSD	Oyster Bay, NY
21	18,074	Southampton UFSD	Southampton, NY
22	18,072	North Shore CSD	Sea Cliff, NY
23	17,909	Trenton City	Trenton, NJ
24	17,893	Roslyn UFSD	Roslyn, NY
25	17,891	Great Neck UFSD	Great Neck, NY
26	17,509	Bering Strait SD	Unalakleet, AK
27	17,491	Asbury Park City	Asbury Park, NJ
28	17,417	Locust Valley CSD	Locust Valley, NY
29	17,286	Cambridge	Cambridge, MA
30	17,285	East Williston UFSD	Old Westbury, NY
31	17,180	Beachwood City SD	Beachwood, OH
32	17,004	Township High SD 113	Highland Park, IL
33	16,637	Camden County Vocational	Sicklerville, NJ
34	16,626	Bedford CSD	Mount Kisco, NY
35	16,621	Pascack Valley Regional	Montvale, NJ
36	16,387	Port Washington UFSD	Pt Washington, NY
37	16,240	Evanston Twp HSD 202	Evanston, IL
38	16,135	Lower Kuskokwim SD	Bethel, AK
39	16,073	Northwest Arctic SD	Kotzebue, AK
40	16,031	White Plains City SD	White Plains, NY
41	15,995	Nanuet UFSD	Nanuet, NY
42	15,868	Ramapo-Indian Hill Reg	Franklin Lakes, NJ
43	15,751	Carle Place UFSD	Carle Place, NY
44	15,718	New Brunswick City	New Brunswick, NJ
45	15,698	Long Beach City SD	Long Beach, NY
46	15,682	Central Islip UFSD	Central Islip, NY
47	15,667	East Hampton UFSD	East Hampton, NY
48	15,664	Huntington UFSD	Huntington Stn, NY
49	15,626	Wyandanch UFSD	Wyandanch, NY
50	15,371	Syosset CSD	Syosset, NY
51	15,274	East Ramapo CSD (Spring Valley)	Spring Valley, NY
52	15,241	Burlington County Vocational	Westampton Twp, NJ
53	15,109	Malverne UFSD	Malverne, NY
54	15,061	Uniondale UFSD	Uniondale, NY
55	15,047	Harrison CSD	Harrison, NY
56	15,040	Mount Pleasant CSD	Thornwood, NY
57	14,975	South Orangetown CSD	Blauvelt, NY
58	14,924	Englewood City	Englewood, NJ
59	14,896	Plainview-Old Bethpage CSD	Plainview, NY
60	14,878	Scarsdale UFSD	Scarsdale, NY
61	14,858	Orange County Office of Ed	Costa Mesa, CA
62	14,817	Gowanda CSD	Gowanda, NY
63	14,778	Morris Hills Regional	Rockaway, NJ
64	14,776	Putnam Valley CSD	Putnam Valley, NY
65	14,694	Newark City	Newark, NJ
66	14,630	Nyack UFSD	Nyack, NY
67	14,621	Briarcliff Manor UFSD	Briarcliff Manor, NY
67	14,621	South Country CSD	E Patchogue, NY
69	14,512	Hauppauge UFSD	Hauppauge, NY
69	14,512	Northern Valley Regional	Demarest, NJ
71	14,471	Katonah-Lewisboro UFSD	South Salem, NY
72	14,450	New Trier Twp HSD 203	Winnetka, IL
73	14,427	Morris SD	Morristown, NJ
74	14,402	Northfield Twp High SD 225	Glenview, IL
75	14,390	UFSD - Tarrytowns	Sleepy Hollow, NY
76	14,387	Hewlett-Woodmere UFSD	Woodmere, NY
77	14,357	Chappaqua CSD	Chappaqua, NY
78	14,333	Amityville UFSD	Amityville, NY
79	14,332	Croton-Harmon UFSD	Croton-On-Hud, NY
80	14,315	Hunterdon Central Reg	Flemington, NJ
81	14,310	Niles Twp Community High SD 219	Skokie, IL
82	14,294	Haverstraw-Stony Point CSD	Garnerville, NY
83	14,246	Hendrick Hudson CSD	Montrose, NY
84	14,198	Peekskill City SD	Peekskill, NY
85	14,187	Rockville Centre UFSD	Rockville Ctre, NY
86	14,177	Camden City	Camden, NJ
87	14,157	North Hunt-Voorhees Regional	Annandale, NJ
88	14,086	Irvington UFSD	Irvington, NY
89	14,068	Lake Forest Community HSD 115	Lake Forest, IL
90	14,037	Ramapo CSD (Suffern)	Hillburn, NY
91	14,013	Somers CSD	Lincolndale, NY
92	14,010	Onteora CSD	Boiceville, NY
93	13,977	Edgemont UFSD	Scarsdale, NY
94	13,915	Bethpage UFSD	Bethpage, NY
95	13,877	Mamaroneck UFSD	Mamaroneck, NY
96	13,868	Westhampton Beach UFSD	Westhampton Bch, NY
97	13,777	Orange City SD	Cleveland, OH
98	13,744	Passaic City	Passaic, NJ
99	13,737	Rye City SD	Rye, NY
100	13,726	Eastchester UFSD	Eastchester, NY
101	13,717	Teaneck Twp	Teaneck, NJ
102	13,715	West Hempstead UFSD	W Hempstead, NY
103	13,676	Westbury UFSD	Old Westbury, NY
104	13,654	Lower Merion SD	Ardmore, PA
105	13,649	Keansburg Boro	Keansburg, NJ
106	13,618	Herricks UFSD	New Hyde Park, NY
107	13,617	Maine Township HSD 207	Park Ridge, IL
108	13,609	West Morris Regional	Chester, NJ
109	13,595	Glen Cove City SD	Glen Cove, NY
110	13,578	Bay Shore UFSD	Bay Shore, NY
111	13,577	Hartford SD	Hartford, CT
112	13,564	Connetquot CSD	Bohemia, NY
113	13,557	Bayport-Blue Point UFSD	Bayport, NY
114	13,519	South Huntington UFSD	Huntington Stn, NY
115	13,505	Cold Spring Harbor CSD	Cold Sprg Harbor, NY
116	13,473	Essex County Voc-Tech	West Orange, NJ
117	13,470	Oak Park & River Forest Dist 200	Oak Park, IL
118	13,449	Hempstead UFSD	Hempstead, NY
119	13,423	Valley Stream Central HSD	Valley Stream, NY
120	13,407	Ossining UFSD	Ossining, NY

This section ranks 120 school districts at both the "top" and "bottom" of each category for a total of 240 districts per category. The "top" list (descending order) appears first, followed by the "bottom" list (ascending order).

Current Spending per Student in FY2001

School districts ranked in *ascending* order

Rank	Dollars	District Name	City, State
1	3,999	Globe Unified District	Globe, AZ
2	4,035	Bullhead City Elementary District	Bullhead City, AZ
3	4,084	Desoto County SD	Hernando, MS
4	4,093	Nogales Unified District	Nogales, AZ
4	4,093	Pearl River County SD	Carriere, MS
6	4,102	North Pike SD	Summit, MS
7	4,119	Alpine SD	American Fork, UT
7	4,119	Canton Public SD	Canton, MS
9	4,198	Will County SD 92	Lockport, IL
10	4,265	George County SD	Lucedale, MS
11	4,270	Tooele SD	Tooele, UT
12	4,290	Chino Valley Unified District	Chino Valley, AZ
13	4,308	Jordan SD	Sandy, UT
14	4,313	New Lenox SD 122	New Lenox, IL
15	4,363	Logan SD	Logan, UT
16	4,380	Colorado River Union High SD	Fort Mojave, AZ
17	4,389	Smith County SD	Carthage, TN
18	4,413	Weber SD	Ogden, UT
19	4,420	Mokena SD 159	Mokena, IL
20	4,421	Union County SD	New Albany, MS
21	4,447	Avondale Elementary District	Avondale, AZ
22	4,451	Granite SD	Salt Lake City, UT
23	4,452	Alhambra Elementary District	Phoenix, AZ
24	4,467	Washington SD	Saint George, UT
25	4,480	Nebo SD	Spanish Fork, UT
26	4,485	Box Elder SD	Brigham City, UT
27	4,489	West Point SD	West Point, MS
28	4,492	Juab SD	Nephi, UT
29	4,496	Scott County SD	Forest, MS
30	4,510	Marshall County SD	Holly Springs, MS
31	4,530	Cache SD	Logan, UT
32	4,531	Wylie ISD	Abilene, TX
33	4,536	Davis SD	Farmington, UT
34	4,551	Holmes County SD	Lexington, MS
34	4,551	Summit Hill SD 161	Frankfort, IL
36	4,554	Jackson County SD	Vancleave, MS
37	4,557	Preston Joint District	Preston, ID
38	4,560	Glendale Elementary District	Glendale, AZ
39	4,564	White County SD	Sparta, TN
40	4,569	Lewis County SD	Hohenwald, TN
41	4,571	Mcdonald County R-I	Anderson, MO
42	4,585	Chester County SD	Henderson, TN
43	4,594	Grenada SD	Grenada, MS
44	4,600	Fowler Elementary District	Phoenix, AZ
45	4,607	Kyrene Elementary District	Tempe, AZ
46	4,609	Santa Cruz Valley Unified District	Rio Rico, AZ
47	4,621	Rankin County SD	Brandon, MS
48	4,622	Lincoln County SD	Brookhaven, MS
49	4,624	Marana Unified District	Marana, AZ
50	4,634	Sequatchie County SD	Dunlap, TN
51	4,637	Festus R-VI	Festus, MO
52	4,642	Fort Leavenworth	Ft Leavenworth, KS
53	4,645	Pendergast Elementary District	Phoenix, AZ
54	4,646	Lake Havasu Unified District	Lk Havasu City, AZ
55	4,656	Prescott Unified District	Prescott, AZ
56	4,660	Mannford	Mannford, OK
57	4,661	Houston SD	Houston, MS
58	4,666	Grainger County SD	Rutledge, TN
58	4,666	Monroe County SD	Amory, MS
60	4,682	Morgan SD	Morgan, UT
61	4,686	Kuna Joint District	Kuna, ID
62	4,689	Murray SD	Murray, UT
63	4,690	Kearney R-I	Kearney, MO
64	4,697	Cartwright Elementary District	Phoenix, AZ
65	4,704	Hilldale	Muskogee, OK
66	4,706	Huntsville SD	Huntsville, AR
67	4,710	Nampa SD	Nampa, ID
68	4,717	Hinds County SD	Raymond, MS
68	4,717	Lakeland District	Rathdrum, ID
70	4,718	Owasso	Owasso, OK
71	4,720	Lowndes County SD	Columbus, MS
72	4,723	Macon County SD	Lafayette, TN
73	4,726	Itawamba County SD	Fulton, MS
73	4,726	Ocean Springs SD	Ocean Springs, MS
75	4,732	Jackson R-II	Jackson, MO
76	4,734	Augusta	Augusta, KS
76	4,734	Pontotoc County SD	Pontotoc, MS
78	4,739	Amphitheater Unified District	Tucson, AZ
79	4,740	Chandler Unified District	Chandler, AZ
80	4,745	South Tippah SD	Ripley, MS
81	4,751	Peoria Unified SD	Glendale, AZ
82	4,752	Gilbert Unified District	Gilbert, AZ
83	4,758	Liberty Elementary District	Buckeye, AZ
84	4,761	Bethel-Tate Local SD	Bethel, OH
85	4,767	Leake County SD	Carthage, MS
86	4,769	Piedmont	Piedmont, OK
87	4,774	Clarksdale Municipal SD	Clarksdale, MS
88	4,775	Robertson County SD	Springfield, TN
89	4,778	Lee County SD	Tupelo, MS
90	4,783	Deer Valley Unified District	Phoenix, AZ
90	4,783	Lamar County SD	Purvis, MS
90	4,783	Rio Rancho Public Schools	Rio Rancho, NM
90	4,783	Stewart County SD	Dover, TN
94	4,785	Troy R-III	Troy, MO
95	4,788	Bixby	Bixby, OK
96	4,789	Douglas Unified District	Douglas, AZ
97	4,790	Paradise Valley Unified District	Phoenix, AZ
98	4,793	Humphreys County SD	Belzoni, MS
99	4,795	Fruitland District	Fruitland, ID
100	4,796	Basehor-Linwood	Basehor, KS
101	4,805	Pontotoc City Schools	Pontotoc, MS
102	4,807	Indianola SD	Indianola, MS
103	4,811	Simpson County SD	Mendenhall, MS
104	4,820	Kinnikinnick CCSD 131	Roscoe, IL
105	4,825	Waldron SD	Waldron, AR
106	4,826	Fountain Hills Unified District	Fountain Hills, AZ
107	4,828	Bedford County SD	Shelbyville, TN
107	4,828	Gadsden Elementary District	San Luis, AZ
109	4,829	Mustang	Mustang, OK
110	4,837	Etiwanda Elementary	Etiwanda, CA
110	4,837	Gibson Special District	Dyer, TN
112	4,839	Smith County SD	Raleigh, MS
113	4,846	Lorena ISD	Lorena, TX
114	4,849	Wasatch SD	Heber City, UT
115	4,853	Community CSD 168	Sauk Village, IL
115	4,853	Dardanelle SD	Dardanelle, AR
117	4,855	Holly Springs SD	Holly Springs, MS
118	4,856	Meridian Joint District	Meridian, ID
118	4,856	Mohave Valley Elementary District	Mohave Valley, AZ
120	4,861	Madison County SD	Flora, MS

This section ranks 120 school districts at both the "top" and "bottom" of each category for a total of 240 districts per category. The "top" list (descending order) appears first, followed by the "bottom" list (ascending order).

Number of Diploma Recipients

School districts ranked in *descending* order

Rank	Number	District Name	City, State
1	37,915	New York City Public Schools	Brooklyn, NY
2	27,720	Los Angeles Unified	Los Angeles, CA
3	16,638	Dade County SD	Miami, FL
4	15,653	City of Chicago SD 299	Chicago, IL
5	11,654	Broward County SD	Fort Lauderdale, FL
6	10,452	Hawaii Department of Education	Honolulu, HI
7	10,450	Fairfax County Public Schools	Fairfax, VA
8	10,215	Clark County SD	Las Vegas, NV
9	8,559	Philadelphia City SD	Philadelphia, PA
10	8,282	Montgomery County Public Schls	Rockville, MD
11	7,968	Hillsborough County SD	Tampa, FL
12	7,945	Houston ISD	Houston, TX
13	7,687	Palm Beach County SD	West Palm Beach, FL
14	7,552	Prince Georges County Pub Schools	Upper Marlboro, MD
15	7,361	Orange County SD	Orlando, FL
16	6,859	Baltimore County Public Schls	Towson, MD
17	6,532	Dallas ISD	Dallas, TX
18	6,504	San Diego Unified	San Diego, CA
19	6,116	Gwinnett County	Lawrenceville, GA
20	5,741	Kern Union High	Bakersfield, CA
21	5,540	Detroit City SD	Detroit, MI
22	5,413	Pinellas County SD	Largo, FL
23	5,411	Wake County Schools	Raleigh, NC
24	5,334	Jefferson County R-1	Golden, CO
25	5,260	Duval County SD	Jacksonville, FL
26	5,231	Cobb County	Marietta, GA
27	5,087	Charlotte-Mecklenburg Schools	Charlotte, NC
28	4,932	Jefferson County	Louisville, KY
29	4,916	Jordan SD	Sandy, UT
30	4,768	Sweetwater Union High	Chula Vista, CA
31	4,708	Albuquerque Public Schools	Albuquerque, NM
32	4,664	Long Beach Unified	Long Beach, CA
33	4,524	Baltimore City Public Schools Sys	Baltimore, MD
34	4,467	East Side Union High	San Jose, CA
35	4,466	Anne Arundel County Pub Schls	Annapolis, MD
36	4,455	Virginia Beach City Public Schools	Virginia Beach, VA
37	4,387	Grossmont Union High	La Mesa, CA
38	4,191	Dekalb County	Decatur, GA
39	4,170	Granite SD	Salt Lake City, UT
40	4,014	Mesa Unified District	Mesa, AZ
41	3,938	Cypress-Fairbanks ISD	Houston, TX
42	3,933	Memphis City SD	Memphis, TN
43	3,928	Northside ISD	San Antonio, TX
44	3,912	Milwaukee	Milwaukee, WI
45	3,873	Chaffey Joint Union High	Ontario, CA
46	3,815	Polk County SD	Bartow, FL
47	3,765	Davis SD	Farmington, UT
48	3,721	Fresno Unified	Fresno, CA
49	3,705	Austin ISD	Austin, TX
50	3,688	Anaheim Union High	Anaheim, CA
51	3,630	Fort Bend ISD	Sugar Land, TX
52	3,578	Brevard County SD	Viera, FL
53	3,556	San Juan Unified	Carmichael, CA
54	3,534	Phoenix Union High SD	Phoenix, AZ
55	3,471	Orleans Parish School Board	New Orleans, LA
56	3,420	Seminole County SD	Sanford, FL
57	3,399	San Francisco Unified	San Francisco, CA
58	3,386	Volusia County SD	Deland, FL
59	3,360	Fulton County	Atlanta, GA
60	3,353	El Paso ISD	El Paso, TX
61	3,309	Tucson Unified District	Tucson, AZ
62	3,304	Guilford County Schools	Greensboro, NC
63	3,292	Chesterfield County Public Schools	Chesterfield, VA
64	3,222	Fort Worth ISD	Fort Worth, TX
65	3,208	North East ISD	San Antonio, TX
66	3,196	Prince William County Pub Schools	Manassas, VA
67	2,992	Antelope Valley Union High	Lancaster, CA
68	2,990	Howard County Pub Schls System	Ellicott City, MD
69	2,934	Greenville County SD	Greenville, SC
70	2,922	Cherry Creek 5	Greenwood Vlg, CO
71	2,905	Huntington Beach Union High	Huntington Bch, CA
72	2,894	District of Columbia Pub Schls	Washington, DC
73	2,875	Arlington ISD	Arlington, TX
74	2,854	Mobile County SD	Mobile, AL
75	2,851	Washoe County SD	Reno, NV
76	2,846	Lee County SD	Fort Myers, FL
77	2,842	Ysleta ISD	El Paso, TX
78	2,816	Boston	Boston, MA
79	2,815	East Baton Rouge Parish School Bd	Baton Rouge, LA
79	2,815	Modesto City High	Modesto, CA
79	2,815	Township High SD 214	Arlington Hgts, IL
82	2,809	Cumberland County Schools	Fayetteville, NC
83	2,795	Plano ISD	Plano, TX
84	2,738	Garden Grove Unified	Garden Grove, CA
85	2,728	Elk Grove Unified	Elk Grove, CA
86	2,727	San Antonio ISD	San Antonio, TX
87	2,726	Alpine SD	American Fork, UT
88	2,725	Township HSD 211	Palatine, IL
89	2,689	Garland ISD	Garland, TX
90	2,678	Tempe Union High SD	Tempe, AZ
91	2,670	Fullerton Joint Union High	Fullerton, CA
92	2,644	Capistrano Unified	San Juan Capis, CA
93	2,629	Seattle SD 1	Seattle, WA
94	2,612	Denver County 1	Denver, CO
95	2,609	Glendale Union High SD	Glendale, AZ
95	2,609	Nashville-Davidson County SD	Nashville, TN
97	2,600	Columbus City SD	Columbus, OH
98	2,592	Portland SD 1J	Portland, OR
99	2,553	Knox County SD	Knoxville, TN
100	2,550	Shelby County SD	Memphis, TN
101	2,529	Oxnard Union High	Oxnard, CA
102	2,505	Anchorage SD	Anchorage, AK
103	2,484	Santa Ana Unified	Santa Ana, CA
104	2,465	Frederick County Board of Ed	Frederick, MD
105	2,453	Pasco County SD	Land O' Lakes, FL
106	2,443	Cleveland Municipal SD	Cleveland, OH
107	2,425	Harford County Public Schools	Bel Air, MD
108	2,400	Henrico County Public Schools	Richmond, VA
109	2,393	William S Hart Union High	Santa Clarita, CA
110	2,372	Anoka-Hennepin	Coon Rapids, MN
111	2,320	Escambia County SD	Pensacola, FL
112	2,298	Chesapeake City Public Schools	Chesapeake, VA
113	2,278	Jefferson County SD	Birmingham, AL
114	2,271	Forsyth County Schools	Winston Salem, NC
115	2,270	Atlanta City	Atlanta, GA
116	2,267	Lewisville ISD	Flower Mound, TX
117	2,261	Jefferson Parish School Board	Harvey, LA
118	2,251	Riverside Unified	Riverside, CA
119	2,237	Sacramento City Unified	Sacramento, CA
120	2,230	Poway Unified	Poway, CA

This section ranks 120 school districts at both the "top" and "bottom" of each category for a total of 240 districts per category. The "top" list (descending order) appears first, followed by the "bottom" list (ascending order).

Number of Diploma Recipients

School districts ranked in *ascending* order

Rank	Number	District Name	City, State
1	0	Amsterdam City SD	Amsterdam, NY
1	0	Bonsall Union Elementary	Bonsall, CA
1	0	Central Arizona Valley Inst of Tech	Coolidge, AZ
1	0	Creighton Elementary District	Phoenix, AZ
1	0	Department of Corrections SD 428	Springfield, IL
1	0	East Valley Institute of Technology	Mesa, AZ
1	0	Escondido Union Elementary	Escondido, CA
1	0	Glendale Elementary District	Glendale, AZ
1	0	Hampton Bays UFSD	Hampton Bays, NY
1	0	Lawndale Elementary	Lawndale, CA
1	0	Lennox Elementary	Lennox, CA
1	0	Lindenwold Boro	Lindenwold, NJ
1	0	Litchfield SD	Hudson, NH
1	0	Madison Elementary District	Phoenix, AZ
1	0	Oak Park & River Forest Dist 200	Oak Park, IL
1	0	PDE Division of Data Services	Harrisburg, PA
1	0	Passaic City	Passaic, NJ
1	0	Pekin Public SD 108	Pekin, IL
1	0	Plumsted Twp	New Egypt, NJ
1	0	Public Schools of Petoskey	Petoskey, MI
1	0	Ravenswood City Elementary	East Palo Alto, CA
1	0	Red Bluff Union Elementary	Red Bluff, CA
1	0	San Bernardino County Supt.	San Bernardino, CA
1	0	Scotts Valley Unified	Scotts Valley, CA
1	0	Tempe Elementary District	Tempe, AZ
1	0	Wheatland Elementary	Wheatland, CA
27	1	Keyes Union Elementary	Keyes, CA
27	1	Mannheim SD 83	Franklin Park, IL
27	1	Watertown SD 14-4	Watertown, SD
30	3	Redding Elementary	Redding, CA
30	3	Redwood City Elementary	Redwood City, CA
32	4	Cheney SD 360	Cheney, WA
32	4	Windham School Department	Windham, ME
34	10	Riverside SD 416	Chattaroy, WA
35	11	Norwich SD	Norwich, CT
36	13	Lakeside Union Elementary	Lakeside, CA
37	18	Capitol Region Education Council	Hartford, CT
38	24	Area Coop Educational Services	North Haven, CT
39	28	Gorman Elementary	Gorman, CA
40	31	Electronic Classroom of Tomorrow	Columbus, OH
41	32	Waterford Unified	Waterford, CA
42	33	Julian Union Elementary	Julian, CA
42	33	Twin Ridges Elementary	North San Juan, CA
44	36	Butte County Joint District	Arco, ID
45	38	Virginia-New York District	Quantico, VA
46	45	Westwood Unified	Westwood, CA
47	46	Godfrey-Lee Public Schools	Wyoming, MI
48	47	Bering Strait SD	Unalakleet, AK
48	47	Peach Springs Unified District	Peach Springs, AZ
50	50	Lower Yukon SD	Mountain Vlg, AK
51	51	Jones County Schools	Trenton, NC
52	53	Atkinson County	Pearson, GA
52	53	East Tallahatchie Consol SD	Charleston, MS
52	53	Maywood-Melrose Park-Broadview-89	Melrose Park, IL
52	53	North Panola Schools	Sardis, MS
56	54	Terrell County	Dawson, GA
56	54	Todd County SD 66-1	Mission, SD
58	55	Bledsoe County SD	Pikeville, TN
58	55	Henderson County SD	Lexington, TN
58	55	Zuni Public Schools	Zuni, NM
61	56	Sunflower County SD	Indianola, MS
61	56	West Oso ISD	Corpus Christi, TX
63	57	Dooly County	Vienna, GA
63	57	Forrest County SD	Hattiesburg, MS
65	58	Conecuh County SD	Evergreen, AL
65	58	Forest Municipal SD	Forest, MS
65	58	Vail Unified District	Vail, AZ
68	62	Florence County SD 05	Johnsonville, SC
68	62	Hatch Valley Public Schools	Hatch, NM
70	63	Beecher Community SD	Flint, MI
70	63	Coahoma County SD	Clarksdale, MS
70	63	East Holmes Local SD	Berlin, OH
73	65	Bendle Public Schools	Burton, MI
73	65	Jefferson City	Jefferson, GA
73	65	Jefferson County SD	Monticello, FL
73	65	Quitman County SD	Marks, MS
73	65	Tunica County SD	Tunica, MS
73	65	Woodbridge SD	Greenwood, DE
79	66	Caldwell Parish School Board	Columbia, LA
79	66	Wyandanch UFSD	Wyandanch, NY
81	67	Dalhart ISD	Dalhart, TX
81	67	Westwood Community Schools	Dearborn Hgts, MI
83	68	Greene County SD	Eutaw, AL
83	68	Hampton 2 County SD	Estill, SC
83	68	Northwest Arctic SD	Kotzebue, AK
83	68	Sutherlin SD 130	Sutherlin, OR
87	69	Cleveland	Cleveland, OK
87	69	Heard County	Franklin, GA
87	69	Mcintosh County	Darien, GA
87	69	Tri County Area Schools	Howard City, MI
91	70	Hutto ISD	Hutto, TX
91	70	Michigan Center SD	Michigan Center, MI
91	70	North Pike SD	Summit, MS
91	70	Royal ISD	Brookshire, TX
95	71	Salamanca City SD	Salamanca, NY
96	72	Candler County	Metter, GA
96	72	Quaboag Regional	Warren, MA
96	72	Shaker Regional SD	Belmont, NH
96	72	Wahluke SD 73	Mattawa, WA
96	72	Wilkinson County SD	Woodville, MS
101	73	Coosa County SD	Rockford, AL
101	73	Croton-Harmon UFSD	Croton-On-Hud, NY
101	73	Mascoma Valley Reg SD	Enfield, NH
101	73	Muskegon Heights SD	Muskegon Hgts, MI
101	73	Pelham City	Pelham, GA
101	73	White Cloud Public Schools	White Cloud, MI
107	74	Cairo-Durham CSD	Cairo, NY
107	74	Hastings-On-Hudson UFSD	Hastings-on-Hud, NY
107	74	Humphreys County SD	Belzoni, MS
107	74	Jasper County	Monticello, GA
107	74	Newton County SD	Decatur, MS
107	74	Sto-Rox SD	Mckees Rocks, PA
107	74	Truth Or Consequences Schools	Truth or Conseq, NM
107	74	Wilkinsburg Borough SD	Wilkinsburg, PA
115	75	Calhoun County SD	Saint Matthews, SC
115	75	Eustace ISD	Eustace, TX
115	75	Long County	Ludowici, GA
115	75	North Newton School Corp	Morocco, IN
115	75	Red River Parish School Board	Coushatta, LA
120	76	Bacon County	Alma, GA

This section ranks 120 school districts at both the "top" and "bottom" of each category for a total of 240 districts per category. The "top" list (descending order) appears first, followed by the "bottom" list (ascending order).

High School Drop-out Rate

School districts ranked in *descending* order

Rank	Percent	District Name	City, State
1	53.5	Norwich SD	Norwich, CT
2	50.6	Maricopa County Regional District	Phoenix, AZ
3	44.1	Peach Springs Unified District	Peach Springs, AZ
4	33.3	Camden City	Camden, NJ
5	32.9	Youngstown City SD	Youngstown, OH
6	29.7	Todd County SD 66-1	Mission, SD
7	29.3	Whiteriver Unified District	Whiteriver, AZ
8	26.2	Dysart Unified District	El Mirage, AZ
9	26.1	New London SD	New London, CT
10	21.9	Atlanta City	Atlanta, GA
11	20.7	Excelsior Springs 40	Excelsior Spgs, MO
12	20.3	Grant Parish School Board	Colfax, LA
13	19.6	Cleveland Municipal SD	Cleveland, OH
14	19.2	Colorado River Union High SD	Fort Mojave, AZ
15	18.5	Lower Kuskokwim SD	Bethel, AK
16	18.3	Spalding County	Griffin, GA
17	18.1	Belcourt 7	Belcourt, ND
18	17.8	Canton City SD	Canton, OH
19	17.6	Seminole County	Donalsonville, GA
20	17.5	Tuba City Unified District	Tuba City, AZ
21	17.3	Honors Academy	Dallas, TX
22	17.0	Sunnyside Unified District	Tucson, AZ
23	16.8	City of Chicago SD 299	Chicago, IL
23	16.8	Page Unified District	Page, AZ
25	16.7	Parker Unified SD	Parker, AZ
26	16.6	Copiah County SD	Hazlehurst, MS
27	16.4	Pointe Coupee Parish School Board	New Roads, LA
28	16.0	New Brunswick City	New Brunswick, NJ
29	15.1	East Cleveland City SD	East Cleveland, OH
30	14.9	Santa Cruz Valley Unified District	Rio Rico, AZ
31	14.6	Intermediate SD 287	Plymouth, MN
31	14.6	Macon County	Oglethorpe, GA
33	14.3	North Panola Schools	Sardis, MS
34	14.2	Crisp County	Cordele, GA
34	14.2	Paterson City	Paterson, NJ
36	13.8	Northwest Arctic SD	Kotzebue, AK
37	13.7	Minneapolis	Minneapolis, MN
38	13.6	Coolidge Unified District	Coolidge, AZ
38	13.6	Higley Unified District	Higley, AZ
40	13.5	Breathitt County	Jackson, KY
41	13.4	Natchitoches Parish School Board	Natchitoches, LA
42	13.3	Clarke County	Athens, GA
42	13.3	Murray County	Chatsworth, GA
44	13.2	North Slope Borough SD	Barrow, AK
45	13.1	Thomaston-Upson County	Thomaston, GA
46	13.0	Brooks County	Quitman, GA
46	13.0	Reading SD	Reading, PA
46	13.0	Wilkinsburg Borough SD	Wilkinsburg, PA
49	12.9	Nampa SD	Nampa, ID
49	12.9	Texarkana SD	Texarkana, AR
51	12.8	Harrisburg City SD	Harrisburg, PA
52	12.7	Helena-West Helena SD	Helena, AR
53	12.6	Bibb County	Macon, GA
53	12.6	Jefferson County SD	Fayette, MS
53	12.6	Mcintosh County	Darien, GA
56	12.5	Baltimore City Public Schools Sys	Baltimore, MD
56	12.5	Lawrence	Lawrence, MA
56	12.5	Oklahoma City	Oklahoma City, OK
56	12.5	Phoenix Union High SD	Phoenix, AZ
60	12.4	Lima City SD	Lima, OH
61	12.3	Hazlehurst City SD	Hazlehurst, MS
61	12.3	Muscatine Community SD	Muscatine, IA
63	12.1	Dawson County	Dawsonville, GA
63	12.1	Greenwood Public SD	Greenwood, MS
65	12.0	Morehouse Parish School Board	Bastrop, LA
65	12.0	Randolph County	Cuthbert, GA
65	12.0	Red River Parish School Board	Coushatta, LA
68	11.9	Central Islip UFSD	Central Islip, NY
68	11.9	Madison Parish School Board	Tallulah, LA
68	11.9	Peoria SD 150	Peoria, IL
68	11.9	Portland SD 1J	Portland, OR
72	11.7	Franklin Parish School Board	Winnsboro, LA
73	11.6	Holbrook Unified District	Holbrook, AZ
74	11.5	Hartford SD	Hartford, CT
74	11.5	Jackson County	Jefferson, GA
76	11.4	Dougherty County	Albany, GA
76	11.4	Orleans Parish School Board	New Orleans, LA
76	11.4	Wickenburg Unified District	Wickenburg, AZ
79	11.3	Chatham County	Savannah, GA
79	11.3	Decatur SD 61	Decatur, IL
79	11.3	Hot Springs SD	Hot Springs, AR
79	11.3	Taylor County	Butler, GA
79	11.3	Warren County Schools	Warrenton, NC
84	11.2	Bridgeport SD	Bridgeport, CT
85	11.1	Marietta City	Marietta, GA
85	11.1	Valdosta City	Valdosta, GA
85	11.1	York City SD	York, PA
88	11.0	Assumption Parish School Board	Napoleonville, LA
88	11.0	Pawtucket SD	Pawtucket, RI
88	11.0	Phoenix-Talent SD 004	Phoenix, OR
88	11.0	Winslow Unified District	Winslow, AZ
92	10.9	Jefferson Parish School Board	Harvey, LA
92	10.9	Natrona County SD #1	Casper, WY
92	10.9	Pine Bluff SD	Pine Bluff, AR
92	10.9	Robeson County Schools	Lumberton, NC
92	10.9	Sumter County	Americus, GA
92	10.9	West Point SD	West Point, MS
98	10.8	Seminole	Seminole, OK
98	10.8	Tolleson Union High SD	Tolleson, AZ
98	10.8	West Carroll Parish School Board	Oak Grove, LA
101	10.7	Nashua SD	Nashua, NH
101	10.7	Payson Unified District	Payson, AZ
101	10.7	Wayne County	Jesup, GA
104	10.6	Blytheville SD	Blytheville, AR
104	10.6	Caddo Parish School Board	Shreveport, LA
104	10.6	Gordon County	Calhoun, GA
104	10.6	Hickory City Schools	Hickory, NC
108	10.5	Brantley County	Nahunta, GA
108	10.5	Chelsea	Chelsea, MA
108	10.5	Fairbanks North Star Boro SD	Fairbanks, AK
108	10.5	Humphreys County SD	Belzoni, MS
108	10.5	Madison County	Danielsville, GA
108	10.5	Milwaukee	Milwaukee, WI
108	10.5	Payette Joint District	Payette, ID
115	10.4	Burke County	Waynesboro, GA
115	10.4	Forrest City SD	Forrest City, AR
115	10.4	Hempstead UFSD	Hempstead, NY
115	10.4	Roxana Community Unit SD 1	Roxana, IL
119	10.3	Emanuel County	Swainsboro, GA
119	10.3	Park Rapids	Park Rapids, MN

This section ranks 120 school districts at both the "top" and "bottom" of each category for a total of 240 districts per category. The "top" list (descending order) appears first, followed by the "bottom" list (ascending order).

High School Drop-out Rate

School districts ranked in *ascending* order

Rank	Percent	District Name	City, State
1	0.0	Acton-Boxborough	Acton, MA
1	0.0	Agawam	Feeding Hills, MA
1	0.0	Ardsley UFSD	Ardsley, NY
1	0.0	Athens City Elementary SD	Athens, TN
1	0.0	Avon SD	Avon, CT
1	0.0	Bergen County Vocational	Paramus, NJ
1	0.0	Bernards Twp	Basking Ridge, NJ
1	0.0	Bound Brook Boro	Bound Brook, NJ
1	0.0	Butte County Joint District	Arco, ID
1	0.0	Byram Hills CSD	Armonk, NY
1	0.0	Campbell City SD	Campbell, OH
1	0.0	Canton SD	Collinsville, CT
1	0.0	Cape Elizabeth School Department	Cape Elizabeth, ME
1	0.0	East Williston UFSD	Old Westbury, NY
1	0.0	Eastchester UFSD	Eastchester, NY
1	0.0	Electronic Classroom of Tomorrow	Columbus, OH
1	0.0	Essex County Voc-Tech	West Orange, NJ
1	0.0	Euclid City SD	Euclid, OH
1	0.0	Evanston CCSD 65	Evanston, IL
1	0.0	Falmouth School Department	Falmouth, ME
1	0.0	Fayetteville-Manlius CSD	Manlius, NY
1	0.0	Fort Leavenworth	Ft Leavenworth, KS
1	0.0	Glen Ridge Boro	Glen Ridge, NJ
1	0.0	Greenburgh CSD	Hartsdale, NY
1	0.0	Gretna Public Schools	Gretna, NE
1	0.0	Hermantown	Duluth, MN
1	0.0	Hewlett-Woodmere UFSD	Woodmere, NY
1	0.0	Highland Park Boro	Highland Park, NJ
1	0.0	Kosciusko SD	Kosciusko, MS
1	0.0	Lakewood Twp	Lakewood, NJ
1	0.0	Lawrence Twp	Lawrenceville, NJ
1	0.0	Livingston Twp	Livingston, NJ
1	0.0	Locust Valley CSD	Locust Valley, NY
1	0.0	Lower Yukon SD	Mountain Vlg, AK
1	0.0	Lynbrook UFSD	Lynbrook, NY
1	0.0	Madison Boro	Madison, NJ
1	0.0	Mannheim SD 83	Franklin Park, IL
1	0.0	Middlesex Boro	Middlesex, NJ
1	0.0	Miller Place UFSD	Miller Place, NY
1	0.0	Minnewaska	Glenwood, MN
1	0.0	Montevideo	Montevideo, MN
1	0.0	New Canaan SD	New Canaan, CT
1	0.0	New Providence Boro	New Providence, NJ
1	0.0	Niagara Falls City SD	Niagara Falls, NY
1	0.0	North Chicago SD 187	North Chicago, IL
1	0.0	Pekin Public SD 108	Pekin, IL
1	0.0	Pelham UFSD	Pelham, NY
1	0.0	Perry Local SD	Perry, OH
1	0.0	Plainview-Old Bethpage CSD	Plainview, NY
1	0.0	Pleasantville UFSD	Pleasantville, NY
1	0.0	Plumsted Twp	New Egypt, NJ
1	0.0	Roslyn UFSD	Roslyn, NY
1	0.0	Three Village CSD	East Setauket, NY
1	0.0	Upper Saint Clair SD	Pittsburgh, PA
1	0.0	Warrensville Heights City SD	Warrensville Hgts, OH
1	0.0	Waverly SD 145	Waverly, NE
1	0.0	Webster City Community SD	Webster City, IA
1	0.0	Westhill CSD	Syracuse, NY
1	0.0	Weston	Weston, MA
1	0.0	Weston SD	Weston, CT
1	0.0	Westwood	Westwood, MA
1	0.0	Wyoming City SD	Wyoming, OH
63	0.1	Andover	Andover, MA
63	0.1	Burlington Twp	Burlington, NJ
63	0.1	Desoto County SD	Hernando, MS
63	0.1	Ellsworth Community	Ellsworth, WI
63	0.1	Franklin Public	Franklin, WI
63	0.1	Galena City SD	Galena, AK
63	0.1	Great Neck UFSD	Great Neck, NY
63	0.1	Harborfields CSD	Greenlawn, NY
63	0.1	Manhasset UFSD	Manhasset, NY
63	0.1	Menomonee Falls	Menomonee Fls, WI
63	0.1	Millburn Twp	Millburn, NJ
63	0.1	Mosinee	Mosinee, WI
63	0.1	Mountain Lakes Boro	Mountain Lakes, NJ
63	0.1	Northern Valley Regional	Demarest, NJ
63	0.1	Pascack Valley Regional	Montvale, NJ
63	0.1	Pequannock Twp	Pompton Plains, NJ
63	0.1	Pontotoc County SD	Pontotoc, MS
63	0.1	SD of The Chathams	Chatham, NJ
63	0.1	Seymour Community	Seymour, WI
63	0.1	Shaker Heights City SD	Shaker Heights, OH
63	0.1	Sparta Twp	Sparta, NJ
63	0.1	Tredyffrin-Easttown SD	Berwyn, PA
63	0.1	Wayland	Wayland, MA
63	0.1	Westfield Town	Westfield, NJ
87	0.2	Berlin Area	Berlin, WI
87	0.2	Byron	Byron, MN
87	0.2	Chardon Local SD	Chardon, OH
87	0.2	Cinnaminson Twp	Cinnaminson, NJ
87	0.2	Cold Spring Harbor CSD	Cold Sprg Harbor, NY
87	0.2	Cromwell SD	Cromwell, CT
87	0.2	Edgemont UFSD	Scarsdale, NY
87	0.2	Edina	Edina, MN
87	0.2	Elmbrook	Brookfield, WI
87	0.2	Glen Rock Boro	Glen Rock, NJ
87	0.2	Gorham-Middlesex CSD	Rushville, NY
87	0.2	Greater Lowell Voc Tec	Tyngsborough, MA
87	0.2	Hastings-On-Hudson UFSD	Hastings-on-Hud, NY
87	0.2	Herricks UFSD	New Hyde Park, NY
87	0.2	Hudson	Hudson, WI
87	0.2	Irvington UFSD	Irvington, NY
87	0.2	Kimberly Area	Kimberly, WI
87	0.2	King William County Public Schools	King William, VA
87	0.2	Kings Park CSD	Kings Park, NY
87	0.2	Levittown UFSD	Levittown, NY
87	0.2	Linn-Mar Community SD	Marion, IA
87	0.2	Lower Moreland Township SD	Huntingdon Vly, PA
87	0.2	Medfield	Medfield, MA
87	0.2	Metuchen Boro	Metuchen, NJ
87	0.2	Mitchell SD 17-2	Mitchell, SD
87	0.2	Monroe SD	Monroe, CT
87	0.2	Needham	Needham, MA
87	0.2	New Prague Area Schools	New Prague, MN
87	0.2	Ocean Twp	Oakhurst, NJ
87	0.2	Old Saybrook SD	Old Saybrook, CT
87	0.2	Pittsford CSD	Pittsford, NY
87	0.2	Pulaski Community	Pulaski, WI
87	0.2	Renwick	Andale, KS
87	0.2	Ridgefield Boro	Ridgefield, NJ

This section ranks 120 school districts at both the "top" and "bottom" of each category for a total of 240 districts per category. The "top" list (descending order) appears first, followed by the "bottom" list (ascending order).

A

C

D

E

F

G

H

I

J

K

L

M

N

Q

R

S

T

U

V

W

X

Y

Z

A

B

C

D

E

F

G

H

I

J

M

N

O

P

Q

R

S

T

U

V

W

Z

Working Americans 1880-1999 Volume IV: Their Children

This Fourth Volume in the highly successful *Working Americans 1880-1999* series focuses on American children, decade by decade from 1880 to 1999. This interesting and useful volume introduces the reader to three children in each decade, one from each of the Working, Middle and Upper classes. Like the first three volumes in the series, the individual profiles are created from interviews, diaries, statistical studies, biographies and news reports. Profiles cover a broad range of ethnic backgrounds, geographic area and lifestyles – everything from an orphan in Memphis in 1882, following the Yellow Fever epidemic of 1878 to an eleven-year-old nephew of a beer baron and owner of the New York Yankees in New York City in 1921. Chapters also contain important supplementary materials including News Features as well as information on everything from Schools to Parks, Infectious Diseases to Childhood Fears along with Entertainment, Family Life and much more to provide an informative overview of the lifestyles of children from each decade. This interesting account of what life was like for Children in the Working, Middle and Upper Classes will be a welcome addition to the reference collection of any high school, public or academic library.

600 pages; Hardcover ISBN 1-930956-35-5, $145.00

Working Americans 1880-2003 Volume V: Americans At War

Working Americans 1880-2003 Volume V: Americans At War is divided into 11 chapters, each covering a decade from 1880-2003 and examines the lives of Americans during the time of war, including declared conflicts, one-time military actions, protests, and preparations for war. Each decade includes several personal profiles, whether on the battlefield or on the homefront, that tell the stories of civilians, soldiers, and officers during the decade. The profiles examine: Life at Home; Life at Work; and Life in the Community. Each decade also includes an Economic Profile with statistical comparisons, a Historical Snapshot, News Profiles, local News Articles, and Illustrations that provide a solid historical background to the decade being examined. Profiles range widely not only geographically, but also emotionally, from that of a girl whose leg was torn off in a blast during WWI, to the boredom of being stationed in the Dakotas as the Indian Wars were drawing to a close. As in previous volumes of the *Working Americans* series, information is presented in narrative form, but hard facts and real-life situations back up each story. The basis of the profiles come from diaries, private print books, personal interviews, family histories, estate documents and magazine articles. For easy reference, *Working Americans 1880-2003 Volume V: Americans At War* includes an in-depth Subject Index. The *Working Americans* series has become an important reference for public libraries, academic libraries and high school libraries. This fifth volume will be a welcome addition to all of these types of reference collections.

600 pages; Hardcover ISBN 1-59237-024-1; $145.00
Five Volume Set (Volumes I-V), Hardcover ISBN 1-59237-034-9, $675.00

Weather America, A Thirty-Year Summary of Statistical Weather Data and Rankings

This valuable resource provides extensive climatological data for over 4,000 National and Cooperative Weather Stations throughout the United States. *Weather America* begins with a new Major Storms section that details major storm events of the nation and a National Rankings section that details rankings for several data elements, such as Maximum Temperature and Precipitation. The main body of *Weather America* is organized into 50 state sections. Each section provides a Data Table on each Weather Station, organized alphabetically, that provides statistics on Maximum and Minimum Temperatures, Precipitation, Snowfall, Extreme Temperatures, Foggy Days, Humidity and more. State sections contain two brand new features in this edition – a City Index and a narrative Description of the climatic conditions of the state. Each section also includes a revised Map of the State that includes not only weather stations, but cities and towns.

"Best Reference Book of the Year." –Library Journal

2,013 pages; Softcover ISBN 1-891482-29-7, $175.00

The Environmental Resource Handbook, 2004

The Environmental Resource Handbook, now in its second edition, is the most up-to-date and comprehensive source for Environmental Resources and Statistics. Section I: Resources provides detailed contact information for thousands of information sources, including Associations & Organizations, Awards & Honors, Conferences, Foundations & Grants, Environmental Health, Government Agencies, National Parks & Wildlife Refuges, Publications, Research Centers, Educational Programs, Green Product Catalogs, Consultants and much more. Section II: Statistics, provides statistics and rankings on hundreds of important topics, including Children's Environmental Index, Municipal Finances, Toxic Chemicals, Recycling, Climate, Air & Water Quality and more. This kind of up-to-date environmental data, all in one place, is not available anywhere else on the market place today. This vast compilation of resources and statistics is a must-have for all public and academic libraries as well as any organization with a primary focus on the environment.

"...the intrinsic value of the information make it worth consideration by libraries with environmental collections and environmentally concerned users." –Booklist

1,000 pages; Softcover ISBN 1-59237-030-6, $155.00 • Online Database $300.00

The American Tally, 2003/04 Statistics & Comparative Rankings for U.S. Cities with Populations over 10,000

This important statistical handbook compiles, all in one place, comparative statistics on all U.S. cities and towns with a 10,000+ population. *The American Tally* provides statistical details on over 4,000 cities and towns and profiles how they compare with one another in Population Characteristics, Education, Language & Immigration, Income & Employment and Housing. Each section begins with an alphabetical listing of cities by state, allowing for quick access to both the statistics and relative rankings of any city. Next, the highest and lowest cities are listed in each statistic. These important, informative lists provide quick reference to which cities are at both extremes of the spectrum for each statistic. Unlike any other reference, *The American Tally* provides quick, easy access to comparative statistics – a must-have for any reference collection.

"A solid library reference." -Bookwatch

500 pages; Softcover ISBN 1-930956-29-0, $125.00

The Asian Databook: Statistics for all US Counties & Cities with Over 10,000 Population

This is the first-ever resource that compiles statistics and rankings on the US Asian population. *The Asian Databook* presents over 20 statistical data points for each city and county, arranged alphabetically by state, then alphabetically by place name. Data reported for each place includes Population, Languages Spoken at Home, Foreign-Born, Educational Attainment, Income Figures, Poverty Status, Homeownership, Home Values & Rent, and more. Next, in the Rankings Section, the top 75 places are listed for each data element. These easy-to-access ranking tables allow the user to quickly determine trends and population characteristics. This kind of comparative data can not be found elsewhere, in print or on the web, in a format that's as easy-to-use or more concise. A useful resource for those searching for demographics data, career search and relocation information and also for market research. With data ranging from Ancestry to Education, *The Asian Databook* presents a useful compilation of information that will be a much-needed resource in the reference collection of any public or academic library along with the marketing collection of any company whose primary focus in on the Asian population.

1,000 pages; Softcover ISBN 1-59237-044-6 $150.00

The Hispanic Databook: Statistics for all US Counties & Cities with Over 10,000 Population

Previously published by Toucan Valley Publications, this second edition has been completely updated with figures from the latest census and has been broadly expanded to include dozens of new data elements and a brand new Rankings section. The Hispanic population in the United States has increased over 42% in the last 10 years and accounts for 12.5% of the total US population. For ease-of-use, *The Hispanic Databook* presents over 20 statistical data points for each city and county, arranged alphabetically by state, then alphabetically by place name. Data reported for each place includes Population, Languages Spoken at Home, Foreign-Born, Educational Attainment, Income Figures, Poverty Status, Homeownership, Home Values & Rent, and more. Next, in the Rankings Section, the top 75 places are listed for each data element. These easy-to-access ranking tables allow the user to quickly determine trends and population characteristics. This kind of comparative data can not be found elsewhere, in print or on the web, in a format that's as easy-to-use or more concise. A useful resource for those searching for demographics data, career search and relocation information and also for market research. With data ranging from Ancestry to Education, *The Hispanic Databook* presents a useful compilation of information that will be a much-needed resource in the reference collection of any public or academic library along with the marketing collection of any company whose primary focus in on the Hispanic population.

"This accurate, clearly presented volume of selected Hispanic demographics is recommended for large public libraries and research collections."-Library Journal

1,000 pages; Softcover ISBN 1-59237-008-X, $150.00

Ancestry in America: A Comparative Guide to Over 200 Ethnic Backgrounds

This brand new reference work pulls together thousands of comparative statistics on the Ethnic Backgrounds of all populated places in the United States with populations over 10,000. Section One, Statistics by Place, is made up of a list of over 200 ancestry and race categories arranged alphabetically by each of the 5,000 different places with populations over 10,000. This informative city-by-city section allows the user to quickly and easily explore the ethnic makeup of all major population bases in the United States. Section Two, Comparative Rankings, contains three tables for each ethnicity and race. In the first table, the top 150 populated places are ranked by population number for that particular ancestry group, regardless of population. In the second table, the top 150 populated places are ranked by the percent of the total population for that ancestry group. In the third table, those top 150 populated places with 10,000 population are ranked by population number for each ancestry group. These easy-to-navigate tables allow users to see ancestry population patterns and make city-by-city comparisons as well. Plus, as an added bonus with the purchase of *Ancestry in America*, a free companion CD-ROM is available that lists statistics and rankings for all of the 35,000 populated places in the United States. This brand new, information-packed resource will serve a wide-range or research requests for demographics, population characteristics, relocation information and much more. *Ancestry in America: A Comparative Guide to Over 200 Ethnic Backgrounds* will be an important acquisition to all reference collections.

"This compilation will serve a wide range of research requests ... it offers much more detail than other sources." –Booklist

1,500 pages; Softcover ISBN 1-59237-029-2, $225.00

To preview any of our Directories Risk-Free for 30 days, call (800) 562-2139 or fax to (518) 789-0556

Sedgwick Press
Health Directories

The Complete Learning Disabilities Directory, 2004/05

The Complete Learning Disabilities Directory is the most comprehensive database of Programs, Services, Curriculum Materials, Professional Meetings & Resources, Camps, Newsletters and Support Groups for teachers, students and families concerned with learning disabilities. This information-packed directory includes information about Associations & Organizations, Schools, Colleges & Testing Materials, Government Agencies, Legal Resources and much more. For quick, easy access to information, this directory contains four indexes: Entry Name Index, Subject Index and Geographic Index. With every passing year, the field of learning disabilities attracts more attention and the network of caring, committed and knowledgeable professionals grows every day. This directory is an invaluable research tool for these parents, students and professionals.

"Due to its wealth and depth of coverage, parents, teachers and others... should find this an invaluable resource." -Booklist

900 pages; Softcover ISBN 1-59237-049-7, $145.00 ◆ Online Database $195.00 ◆ Online Database & Directory Combo $280.00

The Complete Directory for People with Disabilities, 2005

A wealth of information, now in one comprehensive sourcebook. Completely updated for 2005, this edition contains more information than ever before, including thousands of new entries and enhancements to existing entries and thousands of additional web sites and e-mail addresses. This up-to-date directory is the most comprehensive resource available for people with disabilities, detailing Independent Living Centers, Rehabilitation Facilities, State & Federal Agencies, Associations, Support Groups, Periodicals & Books, Assistive Devices, Employment & Education Programs, Camps and Travel Groups. Each year, more libraries, schools, colleges, hospitals, rehabilitation centers and individuals add *The Complete Directory for People with Disabilities* to their collections, making sure that this information is readily available to the families, individuals and professionals who can benefit most from the amazing wealth of resources cataloged here.

"No other reference tool exists to meet the special needs of the disabled in one convenient resource for information." –Library Journal

1,200 pages; Softcover ISBN 1-59237-054-3, $165.00 ◆ Online Database $215.00 ◆ Online Database & Directory Combo $300.00

The Complete Directory for People with Chronic Illness, 2003/04

Thousands of hours of research have gone into this completely updated 2003/04 edition – several new chapters have been added along with thousands of new entries and enhancements to existing entries. Plus, each chronic illness chapter has been reviewed by an medical expert in the field. This widely-hailed directory is structured around the 90 most prevalent chronic illnesses – from Asthma to Cancer to Wilson's Disease – and provides a comprehensive overview of the support services and information resources available for people diagnosed with a chronic illness. Each chronic illness has its own chapter and contains a brief description in layman's language, followed by important resources for National & Local Organizations, State Agencies, Newsletters, Books & Periodicals, Libraries & Research Centers, Support Groups & Hotlines, Web Sites and much more. This directory is an important resource for health care professionals, the collections of hospital and health care libraries, as well as an invaluable tool for people with a chronic illness and their support network.

"A must purchase for all hospital and health care libraries and is strongly recommended for all public library reference departments." –ARBA

1,200 pages; Softcover ISBN 1-930956-83-5, $165.00 ◆ Online Database $215.00 ◆ Online Database & Directory Combo $300.00

The Complete Mental Health Directory, 2004

This is the most comprehensive resource covering the field of behavioral health, with critical information for both the layman and the mental health professional. For the layman, this directory offers understandable descriptions of 25 Mental Health Disorders as well as detailed information on Associations, Media, Support Groups and Mental Health Facilities. For the professional, *The Complete Mental Health Directory* offers critical and comprehensive information on Managed Care Organizations, Information Systems, Government Agencies and Provider Organizations. This comprehensive volume of needed information will be widely used in any reference collection.

"... the strength of this directory is that it consolidates widely dispersed information into a single volume." –Booklist

800 pages; Softcover ISBN 1-59237-046-2, $165.00 ◆ Online Database $215.00 ◆ Online & Directory Combo $300.00

To preview any of our Directories Risk-Free for 30 days, call (800) 562-2139 or fax to (518) 789-0556

The Complete Directory for Pediatric Disorders, 2004/05

This important directory provides parents and caregivers with information about Pediatric Conditions, Disorders, Diseases and Disabilities, including Blood Disorders, Bone & Spinal Disorders, Brain Defects & Abnormalities, Chromosomal Disorders, Congenital Heart Defects, Movement Disorders, Neuromuscular Disorders and Pediatric Tumors & Cancers. This carefully written directory offers: understandable Descriptions of 15 major bodily systems; Descriptions of more than 200 Disorders and a Resources Section, detailing National Agencies & Associations, State Associations, Online Services, Libraries & Resource Centers, Research Centers, Support Groups & Hotlines, Camps, Books and Periodicals. This resource will provide immediate access to information crucial to families and caregivers when coping with children's illnesses.

"Recommended for public and consumer health libraries." –Library Journal

1,200 pages; Softcover ISBN 1-59237-045-4, $165.00 ◆ Online Database $215.00 ◆ Online Database & Directory Combo $300.00

Older Americans Information Directory, 2004/05

Completely updated for 2004/05, this Fifth Edition has been completely revised and now contains 1,000 new listings, over 8,000 updates to existing listings and over 3,000 brand new e-mail addresses and web sites. You'll find important resources for Older Americans including National, Regional, State & Local Organizations, Government Agencies, Research Centers, Libraries & Information Centers, Legal Resources, Discount Travel Information, Continuing Education Programs, Disability Aids & Assistive Devices, Health, Print Media and Electronic Media. Three indexes: Entry Index, Subject Index and Geographic Index make it easy to find just the right source of information. This comprehensive guide to resources for Older Americans will be a welcome addition to any reference collection.

"Highly recommended for academic, public, health science and consumer libraries…" –Choice

1,200 pages; Softcover ISBN 1-59237-037-3, $165.00 ◆ Online Database $215.00 ◆ Online Database & Directory Combo $300.00

The Complete Directory for People with Rare Disorders, 2002/03

This outstanding reference is produced in conjunction with the National Organization for Rare Disorders to provide comprehensive and needed access to important information on over 1,000 rare disorders, including Cancers and Muscular, Genetic and Blood Disorders. An informative Disorder Description is provided for each of the 1,100 disorders (rare Cancers and Muscular, Genetic and Blood Disorders) followed by information on National and State Organizations dealing with a particular disorder, Umbrella Organizations that cover a wide range of disorders, the Publications that can be useful when researching a disorder and the Government Agencies to contact. Detailed and up-to-date listings contain mailing address, phone and fax numbers, web sites and e-mail addresses along with a description. For quick, easy access to information, this directory contains two indexes: Entry Name Index and Acronym/Keyword Index along with an informative Guide for Rare Disorder Advocates. The Complete Directory for People with Rare Disorders will be an invaluable tool for the thousands of families that have been struck with a rare or "orphan" disease, who feel that they have no place to turn and will be a much-used addition to the reference collection of any public or academic library.

"Quick access to information… public libraries and hospital patient libraries will find this a useful resource in directing users to support groups or agencies dealing with a rare disorder." –Booklist

726 pages; Softcover ISBN 1-891482-18-1, $165.00

The Directory of Drug & Alcohol Residential Rehabilitation Facilities, 2004

This brand new directory is the first-ever resource to bring together, all in one place, data on the thousands of drug and alcohol residential rehabilitation facilities in the United States. *The Directory of Drug & Alcohol Residential Rehabilitation Facilities* covers over 1,000 facilities, with detailed contact information for each one, including mailing address, phone and fax numbers, email addresses and web sites, mission statement, type of treatment programs, cost, average length of stay, numbers of residents and counselors, accreditation, insurance plans accepted, type of environment, religious affiliation, education components and much more. It also contains a helpful chapter on General Resources that provides contact information for Associations, Print & Electronic Media, Support Groups and Conferences. Multiple indexes allow the user to pinpoint the facilities that meet very specific criteria. This time-saving tool is what so many counselors, parents and medical professionals have been asking for. *The Directory of Drug & Alcohol Residential Rehabilitation Facilities* will be a helpful tool in locating the right source for treatment for a wide range of individuals. This comprehensive directory will be an important acquisition for all reference collections: public and academic libraries, case managers, social workers, state agencies and many more.

"This is an excellent, much needed directory that fills an important gap…" –Booklist

300 pages; Softcover ISBN 1-59237-031-4, $135.00

Grey House Publishing
Business Directories

Nations of the World, 2005 A Political, Economic and Business Handbook

This completely revised edition covers all the nations of the world in an easy-to-use, single volume. Each nation is profiled in a single chapter that includes Key Facts, Political & Economic Issues, a Country Profile and Business Information. In this fast-changing world, it is extremely important to make sure that the most up-to-date information is included in your reference collection. This 2005 edition is just the answer. Each of the 200+ country chapters have been carefully reviewed by a political expert to make sure that the text reflects the most current information on Politics, Travel Advisories, Economics and more. You'll find such vital information as a Country Map, Population Characteristics, Inflation, Agricultural Production, Foreign Debt, Political History, Foreign Policy, Regional Insecurity, Economics, Trade & Tourism, Historical Profile, Political Systems, Ethnicity, Languages, Media, Climate, Hotels, Chambers of Commerce, Banking, Travel Information and more. Five Regional Chapters follow the main text and include a Regional Map, an Introductory Article, Key Indicators and Currencies for the Region. New for 2004, an all-inclusive CD-ROM is available as a companion to the printed text. Noted for its sophisticated, up-to-date and reliable compilation of political, economic and business information, this brand new edition will be an important acquisition to any public, academic or special library reference collection.

"A useful addition to both general reference collections and business collections." –*RUSQ*

1,700 pages; Print Version Only Softcover ISBN 1-59237-051-9, $145.00 ◆ Print Version and CD-ROM $180.00

Sports Market Place Directory, 2005

For over 20 years, this comprehensive, up-to-date directory has offered direct access to the Who, What, When & Where of the Sports Industry. With over 20,000 updates and enhancements, the *Sports Market Place Directory* is the most detailed, comprehensive and current sports business reference source available. In 1,800 information-packed pages, *Sports Market Place Directory* profiles contact information and key executives for: Single Sport Organizations, Professional Leagues, Multi-Sport Organizations, Disabled Sports, High School & Youth Sports, Military Sports, Olympic Organizations, Media, Sponsors, Sponsorship & Marketing Event Agencies, Event & Meeting Calendars, Professional Services, College Sports, Manufacturers & Retailers, Facilities and much more. *The Sports Market Place Directory* provides organization's contact information with detailed descriptions including: Key Contacts, physical, mailing, email and web addresses plus phone and fax numbers. For over twenty years, *The Sports Market Place Directory* has assisted thousands of individuals in their pursuit of a career in the sports industry. Why not use "THE SOURCE" that top recruiters, headhunters and career placement centers use to find information on or about sports organizations and key hiring contacts.

1,800 pages; Softcover ISBN 1-59237-077-2, $225.00 ◆ CD-ROM $479.00

The Directory of Business Information Resources, 2005

With 100% verification, over 1,000 new listings and more than 12,000 updates, this 2005 edition of *The Directory of Business Information Resources* is the most up-to-date source for contacts in over 98 business areas – from advertising and agriculture to utilities and wholesalers. This carefully researched volume details: the Associations representing each industry; the Newsletters that keep members current; the Magazines and Journals - with their "Special Issues" - that are important to the trade, the Conventions that are "must attends," Databases, Directories and Industry Web Sites that provide access to must-have marketing resources. Includes contact names, phone & fax numbers, web sites and e-mail addresses. This one-volume resource is a gold mine of information and would be a welcome addition to any reference collection.

"This is a most useful and easy-to-use addition to any researcher's library." –*The Information Professionals Institute*

2,500 pages; Softcover ISBN 1-59237-050-0, $195.00 ◆ Online Database $495.00

The Grey House Performing Arts Directory, 2005

The Grey House Performing Arts Directory is the most comprehensive resource covering the Performing Arts. This important directory provides current information on over 8,500 Dance Companies, Instrumental Music Programs, Opera Companies, Choral Groups, Theater Companies, Performing Arts Series and Performing Arts Facilities. Plus, this edition now contains a brand new section on Artist Management Groups. In addition to mailing address, phone & fax numbers, e-mail addresses and web sites, dozens of other fields of available information include mission statement, key contacts, facilities, seating capacity, season, attendance and more. This directory also provides an important Information *The Grey House Performing Arts Directory* pulls together thousands of Performing Arts Organizations, Facilities and Information Resources into an easy-to-use source – this kind of comprehensiveness and extensive detail is not available in any resource on the market place today.

"Immensely useful and user-friendly … recommended for public, academic and certain special library reference collections." –*Booklist*

1,500 pages; Softcover ISBN 1-59237-023-3, $170.00 ◆ Online Database $335.00

To preview any of our Directories Risk-Free for 30 days, call (800) 562-2139 or fax to (518) 789-0556

The Directory of Venture Capital Firms, 2005

This edition has been extensively updated and broadly expanded to offer direct access to over 2,800 Domestic and International Venture Capital Firms, including address, phone & fax numbers, e-mail addresses and web sites for both primary and branch locations. Entries include details on the firm's Mission Statement, Industry Group Preferences, Geographic Preferences, Average and Minimum Investments and Investment Criteria. You'll also find details that are available nowhere else, including the Firm's Portfolio Companies and extensive information on each of the firm's Managing Partners, such as Education, Professional Background and Directorships held, along with the Partner's E-mail Address. *The Directory of Venture Capital Firms* offers five important indexes: Geographic Index, Executive Name Index, Portfolio Company Index, Industry Preference Index and College & University Index. With its comprehensive coverage and detailed, extensive information on each company, *The Directory of Venture Capital Firms* is an important addition to any finance collection.

"The sheer number of listings, the descriptive information provided and the outstanding indexing make this directory a better value than its principal competitor, Pratt's Guide to Venture Capital Sources. Recommended for business collections in large public, academic and business libraries." –Choice

1,300 pages; Softcover ISBN 1-59237-062-4, $450.00 ◆ Online Database (includes a free copy of the directory) $889.00

The Directory of Mail Order Catalogs, 2005

Published since 1981, this 2005 edition features 100% verification of data and is the premier source of information on the mail order catalog industry. Details over 12,000 consumer catalog companies with 44 different product chapters from Animals to Toys & Games. Contains detailed contact information including e-mail addresses and web sites along with important business details such as employee size, years in business, sales volume, catalog size, number of catalogs mailed and more. Four indexes provide quick access to information: Catalog & Company Name Index, Geographic Index, Product Index and Web Sites Index.

"This is a godsend for those looking for information." –Reference Book Review

1,700 pages; Softcover ISBN 1-59237-066-7 $250.00 ◆ Online Database (includes a free copy of the directory) $495.00

The Directory of Business to Business Catalogs, 2005

The completely updated 2005 *Directory of Business to Business Catalogs,* provides details on over 6,000 suppliers of everything from computers to laboratory supplies… office products to office design… marketing resources to safety equipment… landscaping to maintenance suppliers… building construction and much more. Detailed entries offer mailing address, phone & fax numbers, e-mail addresses, web sites, key contacts, sales volume, employee size, catalog printing information and more. Jut about every kind of product a business needs in its day-to-day operations is covered in this carefully-researched volume. Three indexes are provided for at-a-glance access to information: Catalog & Company Name Index, Geographic Index and Web Sites Index.

"An excellent choice for libraries… wishing to supplement their business supplier resources." –Booklist

800 pages; Softcover ISBN 1-59237-064-0, $165.00 ◆ Online Database (includes a free copy of the directory) $325.00

Thomas Food and Beverage Market Place, 2005

Thomas Food and Beverage Market Place is bigger and better than ever with thousands of new companies, thousands of updates to existing companies and two revised and enhanced product category indexes. This comprehensive directory profiles over 18,000 Food & Beverage Manufacturers, 12,000 Equipment & Supply Companies, 2,200 Transportation & Warehouse Companies, 2,000 Brokers & Wholesalers, 8,000 Importers & Exporters, 900 Industry Resources and hundreds of Mail Order Catalogs. Listings include detailed Contact Information, Sales Volumes, Key Contacts, Brand & Product Information, Packaging Details and much more. *Thomas Food and Beverage Market Place* is available as a three-volume printed set, a subscription-based Online Database via the Internet, on CD-ROM, as well as mailing lists and a licensable database.

"An essential purchase for those in the food industry but will also be useful in public libraries where needed. Much of the information will be difficult and time consuming to locate without this handy three-volume ready-reference source." –ARBA

8,500 pages, 3 Volume Set; Softcover ISBN 1-59237-058-6, $495.00 ◆ CD-ROM $695.00 ◆
CD-ROM & 3 Volume Set Combo $895.00 ◆ Online Database $695.00 ◆ Online Database & 3 Volume Set Combo, $895.00

The Grey House Safety & Security Directory, 2005

The Grey House Safety & Security Directory is the most comprehensive reference tool and buyer's guide for the safety and security industry. Arranged by safety topic, each chapter begins with OSHA regulations for the topic, followed by Training Articles written by top professionals in the field and Self-Inspection Checklists. Next, each topic contains Buyer's Guide sections that feature related products and services. Topics include Administration, Insurance, Loss Control & Consulting, Protective Equipment & Apparel, Noise & Vibration, Facilities Monitoring & Maintenance, Employee Health Maintenance & Ergonomics, Retail Food Services, Machine Guards, Process Guidelines & Tool Handling, Ordinary Materials Handling, Hazardous Materials Handling, Workplace Preparation & Maintenance, Electrical Lighting & Safety, Fire & Rescue and Security. The Buyer's Guide sections are carefully indexed within each topic area to ensure that you can find the supplies needed to meet OSHA's regulations. Six important indexes make finding information and product manufacturers quick and easy: Geographical Index of Manufacturers and Distributors, Company Profile Index, Brand Name Index, Product Index, Index of Web Sites and Index of Advertisers. This comprehensive, up-to-date reference will provide every tool necessary to make sure a business is in compliance with OSHA regulations and locate the products and services needed to meet those regulations.

"Presents industrial safety information for engineers, plant managers, risk managers, and construction site supervisors..." –Choice

1,500 pages, 2 Volume Set; Softcover ISBN 1-59237-067-5, $225.00

The Grey House Homeland Security Directory, 2005

This updated edition features the latest contact information for government and private organizations involved with Homeland Security along with the latest product information and provides detailed profiles of nearly 1,000 Federal & State Organizations & Agencies and over 3,000 Officials and Key Executives involved with Homeland Security. These listings are incredibly detailed and include Mailing Address, Phone & Fax Numbers, Email Addresses & Web Sites, a complete Description of the Agency and a complete list of the Officials and Key Executives associated with the Agency. Next, *The Grey House Homeland Security Directory* provides the go-to source for Homeland Security Products & Services. This section features over 2,000 Companies that provide Consulting, Products or Services. With this Buyer's Guide at their fingertips, users can locate suppliers of everything from Training Materials to Access Controls, from Perimeter Security to BioTerrorism Countermeasures and everything in between – complete with contact information and product descriptions. A handy Product Locator Index is provided to quickly and easily locate suppliers of a particular product. Lastly, an Information Resources Section provides immediate access to contact information for hundreds of Associations, Newsletters, Magazines, Trade Shows, Databases and Directories that focus on Homeland Security. This comprehensive, information-packed resource will be a welcome tool for any company or agency that is in need of Homeland Security information and will be a necessary acquisition for the reference collection of all public libraries and large school districts.

"Compiles this information in one place and is discerning in content. A useful purchase for public and academic libraries." –Booklist

800 pages; Softcover ISBN 1-59237-057-8, $195.00 ◆ Online Database (includes a free copy of the directory) $385.00

The Grey House Transportation Security Directory & Handbook, 2005

This brand new title is the only reference of its kind that brings together current data on Transportation Security. With information on everything from Regulatory Authorities to Security Equipment, this top-flight database brings together the relevant information necessary for creating and maintaining a security plan for a wide range of transportation facilities. With this current, comprehensive directory at the ready you'll have immediate access to: Regulatory Authorities & Legislation; Information Resources; Sample Security Plans & Checklists; Contact Data for Major Airports, Seaports, Railroads, Trucking Companies and Oil Pipelines; Security Service Providers; Recommended Equipment & Product Information and more. Using the *Grey House Transportation Security Directory & Handbook*, managers will be able to quickly and easily assess their current security plans; develop contacts to create and maintain new security procedures; and source the products and services necessary to adequately maintain a secure environment. This valuable resource is a must for all Security Managers at Airports, Seaports, Railroads, Trucking Companies and Oil Pipelines.

800 pages; Softcover ISBN 1-59237-075-6, $195

International Business and Trade Directories, 2003/04

Completely updated, the Third Edition of *International Business and Trade Directories* now contains more than 10,000 entries, over 2,000 more than the last edition, making this directory the most comprehensive resource of the worlds business and trade directories. Entries include content descriptions, price, publisher's name and address, web site and e-mail addresses, phone and fax numbers and editorial staff. Organized by industry group, and then by region, this resource puts over 10,000 industry-specific business and trade directories at the reader's fingertips. Three indexes are included for quick access to information: Geographic Index, Publisher Index and Title Index. Public, college and corporate libraries, as well as individuals and corporations seeking critical market information will want to add this directory to their marketing collection.

"Reasonably priced for a work of this type, this directory should appeal to larger academic, public and corporate libraries with an international focus." –Library Journal

1,800 pages; Softcover ISBN 1-930956-63-0, $225.00 ◆ Online Database (includes a free copy of the directory) $450.00

To preview any of our Directories Risk-Free for 30 days, call (800) 562-2139 or fax to (518) 789-0556

Sedgwick Press
Hospital & Health Plan Directories

The Directory of Hospital Personnel, 2005

The Directory of Hospital Personnel is the best resource you can have at your fingertips when researching or marketing a product or service to the hospital market. A "Who's Who" of the hospital universe, this directory puts you in touch with over 150,000 key decision-makers. With 100% verification of data you can rest assured that you will reach the right person with just one call. Every hospital in the U.S. is profiled, listed alphabetically by city within state. Plus, three easy-to-use, cross-referenced indexes put the facts at your fingertips faster and more easily than any other directory: Hospital Name Index, Bed Size Index and Personnel Index. *The Directory of Hospital Personnel* is the only complete source for key hospital decision-makers by name. Whether you want to define or restructure sales territories… locate hospitals with the purchasing power to accept your proposals… keep track of important contacts or colleagues… or find information on which insurance plans are accepted, *The Directory of Hospital Personnel* gives you the information you need – easily, efficiently, effectively and accurately.

"Recommended for college, university and medical libraries." -ARBA

2,500 pages; Softcover ISBN 1-59237-065-9 $275.00 ◆ Online Database $545.00 ◆ Online Database & Directory Combo, $650.00

The Directory of Health Care Group Purchasing Organizations, 2004

This comprehensive directory provides the important data you need to get in touch with over 800 Group Purchasing Organizations. By providing in-depth information on this growing market and its members, *The Directory of Health Care Group Purchasing Organizations* fills a major need for the most accurate and comprehensive information on over 800 GPOs – Mailing Address, Phone & Fax Numbers, E-mail Addresses, Key Contacts, Purchasing Agents, Group Descriptions, Membership Categorization, Standard Vendor Proposal Requirements, Membership Fees & Terms, Expanded Services, Total Member Beds & Outpatient Visits represented and more. With its comprehensive and detailed information on each purchasing organization, *The Directory of Health Care Group Purchasing Organizations* is the go-to source for anyone looking to target this market.

"The information is clearly arranged and easy to access…recommended for those needing this very specialized information." –ARBA

1,000 pages; Softcover ISBN 1-59237-036-5, $325.00 ◆ Online Database, $650.00 ◆ Online Database & Directory Combo, $750.00

The HMO/PPO Directory, 2005

The HMO/PPO Directory is a comprehensive source that provides detailed information about Health Maintenance Organizations and Preferred Provider Organizations nationwide. This comprehensive directory details more information about more managed health care organizations than ever before. Over 1,100 HMOs, PPOs and affiliated companies are listed, arranged alphabetically by state. Detailed listings include Key Contact Information, Prescription Drug Benefits, Enrollment, Geographical Areas served, Affiliated Physicians & Hospitals, Federal Qualifications, Status, Year Founded, Managed Care Partners, Employer References, Fees & Payment Information and more. Plus, five years of historical information is included related to Revenues, Net Income, Medical Loss Ratios, Membership Enrollment and Number of Patient Complaints. *The HMO/PPO Directory* provides the most comprehensive information on the most companies available on the market place today.

"Helpful to individuals requesting certain HMO/PPO issues such as co-payment costs, subscription costs and patient complaints. Individuals concerned (or those with questions) about their insurance may find this text to be of use to them." -ARBA

600 pages; Softcover ISBN 1-59237-057-8, $275.00 ◆ Online Database, $495.00 ◆ Online Database & Directory Combo, $600.00

The Directory of Independent Ambulatory Care Centers, 2002/03

This first edition of *The Directory of Independent Ambulatory Care Centers* provides access to detailed information that, before now, could only be found scattered in hundreds of different sources. This comprehensive and up-to-date directory pulls together a vast array of contact information for over 7,200 Ambulatory Surgery Centers, Ambulatory General and Urgent Care Clinics, and Diagnostic Imaging Centers that are not affiliated with a hospital or major medical center. Detailed listings include Mailing Address, Phone & Fax Numbers, E-mail and Web Site addresses, Contact Name and Phone Numbers of the Medical Director and other Key Executives and Purchasing Agents, Specialties & Services Offered, Year Founded, Numbers of Employees and Surgeons, Number of Operating Rooms, Number of Cases seen per year, Overnight Options, Contracted Services and much more. Listings are arranged by State, by Center Category and then alphabetically by Organization Name. *The Directory of Independent Ambulatory Care Centers* is a must-have resource for anyone marketing a product or service to this important industry and will be an invaluable tool for those searching for a local care center that will meet their specific needs.

"Among the numerous hospital directories, no other provides information on independent ambulatory centers. A handy, well-organized resource that would be useful in medical center libraries and public libraries." –Choice

986 pages; Softcover ISBN 1-930956-90-8, $185.00 ◆ Online Database, $365.00 ◆ Online Database & Directory Combo, $450.00

To preview any of our Directories Risk-Free for 30 days, call (800) 562-2139 or fax to (518) 789-0556